THE NEW
VELÁZQUEZ

Spanish and English

DICTIONARY

Part One *Spanish* to *English*

Part Two *English* to *Spanish*

THE NEW
VELÁZQUEZ

Spanish and English

DICTIONARY

Prepared by
Lexicon

by
Mariano Velazquez de la Cadena
Late Professor of Spanish, Columbia University

and

Edward Gray, A. B., M.D., F.R.M.S

and

Juan L Iribas, A. B., L. L. D.

Newly Revised by
Ida Navarro Hinojosa,
Manuel Blanco-González, M.A.

and

R.J. Nelson, Ph.D.

Velázquez Press

Velázquez Press   An imprint of Academic Learning Company, LLC

Visit www.VelazquezPress.com or www.AskVelazquez.com

Library of Congress Cataloging-in-Publication Data

Velázquez de la Cadena, Marlano, 1778-1860.
        [Pronouncing dictionary of the Spanish and English languages]
        New revised Velazquez Spanish and English dictionary/by Mariano Velázquez de la Cadena, and Edward Gray, and Juan L. Iribas; newly revised by Ida Navarro Hinojosa, Manuel Blanco-González, and R.J. Nelson; prepared by Lexicon.
                p. cm.
            Published in 1852 under the title: A pronouncing dictionary of the Spanish and English languages.
ISBN 1-59495-000-8
1. Spanish language Dictionaries—English. 2. English language Dictionaries—   Spanish.
I. Gray, Edward, 1849-1920. II. Iribas, Juan L. III. Navarro Hinojosa, Ida.
IV. Blanco-González, Manuel, 1932-   . V. Nelson, R. J. (Richard John).
VI. Lexicon Publications.
(Firm). VII. Title.
PC4640.V55 1999
463'.21—dc21

                                                    99-34721
                                                    CIP

Index

Preface

Humanity marches on at a rapidly advancing rhythm, and reference works intended to serve it, such as this dictionary, should keep in step with progress if they are to provide satisfactorily the information sought. That is why the *Velázquez Dictionary,* recognized throughout the world as the highest authority in bilingual Spanish-English dictionaries, needs to keep pace with all the new terms which the prodigious progress of our times is introducing in the fields of science, inventions and discoveries, as well as with those terms which constantly evolving customs and events introduce into both languages.

Thus the NEW REVISED VELÁZQUEZ DICTIONARY, without sacrificing any of the traditional characteristics which have made predecessor editions the pattern for dictionaries of this type, is without doubt the most modern and complete edition of the work ever published. Included in the main alphabetical word lists are thousands of new terms and idiomatic expressions of general use, replacing expressions no longer in common usage which consequently have no place in a book as eminently practical as this one.

This latest revision of the text has been exhaustive. The aim has been to have the *Velázquez Dictionary* respond more efficiently each day to the needs of those consulting it as a practical medium to solve their translation problems in the fields of business, of current events, of technology, of science in general, of literature, etc. At the same time particular attention has been paid to the terms and idioms commonly used in Spanish America and in the United States, since commercial and friendly relations between these two great regions of the modern world are daily becoming more frequent and important.

The equivalents of geographical names and adjectives which are not written identically in Spanish and English have been meticulously revised. The lists making up the present edition include all the changes which such names have undergone through recent historical events.

A similar study has been made of the lists of proper names appearing in the supplements of the book, as well as those of weights and measures. The list of abbreviations has been brought up-to-date so that it may also respond to the fundamentally practical nature of the book.

Through such innovations the usefulness of this dictionary has been tremendously enhanced, and its editors and publishers dare to hope that it may prove even more valuable than earlier editions to its users, whether they be students in process of learning a second tongue, scholars engaged in literary research in either or both languages, or professional and commercial translators—in fact anyone and everyone who has need of authoritative guidance over the difficult road of English-Spanish or Spanish-English translation.

A Synopsis of the

Spanish or Castilian Language.

THE PARTS OF SPEECH are: the *Article*, the *Noun* (substantive and adjective), the *Pronoun*, the *Verb*, the *Participle*, the *Adverb*, the *Preposition*, the *Conjunction*, and the *Interjection*.

THE ARTICLE

The article has the function of:

a) Pointing out the gender and the number of the grammatical elements before which it is placed, as it agrees with them in gender and number.

b) Pointing out the substantive character of these elements.

1. The articles are always placed before the noun, never behind. They admit another word between them and the name they determine.

- **Los** inquietos niños. - **El** ya famoso futbolista.

2. The masculine article el may indicate also the feminine when the word which determines starts by accented a.

-**El** agua, **el** alma, **el** hacha, **el** águila, **el** hambre, **el** ama.

There are also other exceptions:

- **El** turista, **el** problema, **el** esquema, **el** tema.

- **La** radio, **la** foto, **la** moto.

3. The article is used:

a) Before rivers, mountains and seas.

- **El** río Duero - **Los** Pirineos - **El** Mar Mediterráneo.

b) Before some countries:

- **La** Argentina, **El** Brasil, **El** Canadá, **La** China, **El** Ecuador, **Los** Estados Unidos.

Anyway, if there is any doubt, the article can be omitted.

- **La** China es un país enorme. - Voy a China.

c) Before the name of some regions and some cities:

- **La** Rioja, **La** Mancha, **La** Coruña, **La** Plata, **El** Cairo.

d) Before time expressions:

- Son **las** cinco. - Llegaré **el** sábado.

e) Before the parts of the body and garments:

- **El** niño tiene **la** cara sucia. - Se puso **el** abrigo.

f) With formulas of treatment, except before "Don".

- **El** señor Rodriguez. -**El** señor Presidente.
- **La** señorita Carmen.

g) With abstract nouns or used in a generative way.

- **La** belleza. - **Los** profesores. El mar.

h) With percentages:

- **El** diez por ciento. - **El** quince por ciento.

i) With titles:

- **El** conde de Montecristo - **El** Marqués de Villaverde

THE INDEFINITE ARTICLE OR INDETERMINATE

1. The indeterminate article is used preceding the substantive to which is refered.

- Es **un** genio. - Tenía **una** mirada profunda.
- Fue **una** reacción unánime.

2. The indeterminate article is used to emphasize.

- Era **un** valiente. - Sois **unos** cobardes. - Eres **un** idiota.

The indefinite article can be emphasized with the word **todo**.

- Era todo **un** valiente. - Es todo **un** héroe.

3. The feminine singular form **una** is transformed to **un** before the words which starts by accented **a** or **ha**, although these words are feminine.

- **un** alma. - **un** hacha. - **un** ala. - **un** aro. - **un** arco.

- Tengo **un** hambre feroz. - Hay **un** águila en el árbol.

Exceptions:

- Esta palabra tiene una hache. - Vimos **una** árabe.

The words which haven't got the accented **a**, don't change.

- **una** alumna. - **una** antena. - **una** alubia.

4. The indefinite article is sometimes used in an approximate sense:

- Había **unas** cien personas. - Tardaré **unas** dos horas.

5. Behind the impersonal "HAY" it is also used the indefinite article:

- Hay **un** árbol en la plaza. - En mi casa siempre hay **una** botella de vino.

However, with countless or plural things no article is used.

- Hay árboles - Hay café - Hay mucho tiempo.

6. The indefinite article is used to indicate that an object is included in a more general group or kind, at the same time it is individualized in that group.

- Eso es **un** castillo medieval. - Esto es **un** hotel de lujo.

7. It is used with some exlamations:

- ¡Hace **un** frío glacial! - ¡Hacía **un** calor tórrido!

- ¡Había **una** cantidad de gente terrible!

8. The indefinite article will be used before an abstract noun followed by a qualificative adjective.

- Había **una** quietud extraña. - Reinaba **un** caos terrible.

THE OMISSION OF THE ARTICLE

- Vendemos libros - Viajaron en avión

- Mi padre es profesor - Esa chica es artista.

In all these examples we want to specify that it's referred to a kind of objects or realities instead of an object or individual reality. So an article in not used.

1. The article is also omitted when a partitive sense is indicated, when the quantity is not specified.

- En las comidas bebemos agua.

- Yo no como pan.

If we want to specify we'll say:

- En las comidas bebo **un** poco de vino.

2. When we address to a person in a formal way:

- Buenos días, señor Presidente.

- Adiós, señor Pérez.

- Hasta el lunes, señor director.

3. The article is omitted with:

a) Names of people.

- Vi a Juan en el cine. - Estuvimos con Pedro en el parque.

b) With some words when verbs of movement are used (casa, caza, misa, palacio, paseo, presidio)

- Fue llevado a presidio. - Los domingos vamos a misa.

c) Before the names which indicate titles.

- Don Francisco. - Su Alteza Real Felipe.

d) With **medio** and **otro** the definite article can be used, but the indefinite cannot be used.

- Quiero **el** medio kilo de uva que le encargué.

- Prefiero **el** otro.

e) When an exact number in measures and distances is used.

- La aldea estaba a diez kilómetros.

- Tardarán tres horas en llegar.

f) With degrees (University).

- Mi hija estudia medicina.

g) Between the name of a king or pope and the number.

- Felipe IV Felipe Cuarto.

CONTRACTIONS

When "EL" goes after "A" or after "DE", both forms are contracted by "AL" or "DEL", respectively.

However, the contraction is not placed before proper names built with an article. (Although in spoken language this contraction exists).

- Ésta es una nueva edición de **El Quijote**.

- Ésta es la historia de **El Algarrobo**.

- Nos dirigimos a **El Ferrol**.

THE ARTICLE "LO"

The article "LO" never goes with substantives, because in Spanish neutral nouns don't exist. It normally goes with other elements with noun function:

a) It goes before adjectives, corresponding to them the singular masculine.

- Lo difícil es saber lo que va a hacer.

- Lo bueno es que tenemos mucho tiempo.

- Lo interesante sería llegar antes que ellos.

b) It is placed before adjectives, showing an intensity aspect. It must be noted that the substantive corresponds to the adjective.

- Ya sé **lo difícil** que es este problema.

- Comentaron **lo interesante** que fue la película.

c) With the same intensifying function it is placed before the adverbs.

- Verás **lo bien** que lo pasamos.

- Da pena **lo mal** que lo está pasando esa chica.

- Es increíble **lo temprano** que te levantas.

d) **Lo que** has a relative usage.

- Eso es **lo que** quería.

- **Lo que** me dices es mentira.

e) "Lo" is normally used when we refer to something wich is not specified.

- Es increíble **lo de** tu madre.

- **Lo del** otro día fue vergonzoso.

- **Lo de ese** chico no tiene sentido.

THE NOUN - GENDER

The **masculine** and the **feminine** are the only existing genres in Spanish.

La casa.

El profesor.

La canción.

El piano es grande.

La casa es pequeña.

La mesa es bonita.

Los libros son difíciles.

Las canciones son preciosas.

He vendido **el** coche.

---

1. Diferences in the gender.

a) The masculine and the femenine normally alternate **O/A**.

chico / chica, niño / niña, perro / perra, hijo / hija

b) Sometimes the masculine ends with the following consonants: **L, N, R, S, Z**.

chaval / chavala, patrón / patrona, pastor / pastora, francés / francesa, rapaz / rapaza.

c) There are also words in which the feminine is very different from the masculine.

padre / madre, hombre / mujer, toro / vaca, carnero / oveja, macho / hembra, caballo / yegua, yerno / nuera.

d) Some words are written the same in both genders.

El debutante / **La** debutante. **El** estudiante / **La** estudiante

El periodista / **La** periodista. **El** cantante / **La** cantante

El principiante / **La** principiante. **El** artista / **La** artista

However, some words change the meaning completely when the gender changes.

El cólera / **La** cólera. **El** cura / **La** cura. **El** radio / **La** radio

El orden / **La** orden. **El** corte / **La** corte. **El** guía / **La** guía

e) Some terminations are specific for the femenine:

Actor / Actriz. Emperador / Emperatriz. Poeta / Poetisa. Sacerdote / Sacerdotisa

Abad / Abadesa. Alcalde / Alcaldesa

f) Animals normally have one form; the sex is specified adding **macho** or **hembra**.

Elefante macho / Elefante hembra. Rana macho / Rana hembra. Araña macho / Araña hembra. Serpiente macho / Serpiente hembra.

2. The tipical masculine terminations are:

a) **aje, ambre, an, ma, o, or.**

Poema, fonema, hambre, sabotaje, color, cielo, pan.

Although there are a lot of exceptions: **la** moto, **la** radio, **la** mano, **la** foto.

Others are tipically feminine:

b) **a, dad, cia, ción, eza, nza, ncia, sión, tud, umbre.**

Mesa, casa, piedad, licencia, pronunciación, esperanza, presión, quietud, lumbre.

THE ADJECTIVE.

In Spanish the *Adjective* must agree with its noun, in *Gender* and *Number*; as, "un hombre *rico*" (a *rich* man), "**una mujer rica**" (a *rich* woman); "hombres ricos" (rich men), "**mujeres ricas**" (rich women).

PRONOUNS.

Personal Pronouns.

I, yo.	*We*, nosotros, nosotras.
Me, me.	*Us*, nos, nos.
Me, mí.	*Us*, nosotros, nosotras.
With me, conmigo.	*With us*, con nosotros, as.
You, tú.	*You*, vosotros, vosotras.
You, te,	*You*, os, os.
You, ti.	*You*, vosotros, vosotras.
With you, contigo.	*With you*, con vosotros, as.

You, in familiar polite style, is translated *usted* for both genders, and the verb agrees with it in the singular or plural, according to the sense. *Usted* and its plural are always written in abbreviation, thus: *V.* or *Vd.* for the first, and *Vds.* for the latter.

You, usted, (V.).	*You*, ustedes, (Vds.)
You a usted, le, la, se.	*You*, a Vds. los, las, se.

You, **a** V. le, se; **a** él, ella, sí.

With you, con Vds.

He or *it, él.*

Him or *it*, le, se; él, sí.

Him or *it*, le, se; él, sí

With him, it, con él, consigo.

She or *it*, ella.

Her or *it*, la, se; ella sí.

Her or *it*, le, se; ella sí.

With her, it, con ella, consigo.

You, **a** Vds. les, se; **a** ellos ellas, sí.

They, ellos.

Them, los, se; ellos, sí.

Them, les, se; ellos, sí.

With them, con ellos, consigo.

They, ellas

Them, las, se; ellas, sí.

Them, les, se; elles, sí.

With them, con ellas, consigo.

Mí, ti, sí, are always preceded by prepositions.

Me, te, se, le, los, la, las, les, are never placed after prepositions.

Possessive Adjectives.

My, mi, mis.   *His*, su, sus.   *Its*, su, sus.

Your, tu, tus.   *Her*, su, sus.   *Their*, su, sus.

Your, with reference to *Usted* or *Ustedes*, su, sus.

These adjectives agree in number with the noun that follows them; as, he sold *his horses* (él vendió *sus caballos*); they fulfilled *their* promise *(ellos cumpileron su promesa)*.

Possessive Pronouns.

Mine, mío, míos.   *His*, suyo, suyos.   *Its*, suyo, suyos.

   mía, mías.   suya, suyas.   suya, suyas.

Your, tuyo,.   *Hers*, suyo,   *Theirs*, suyo,

   tuyos   suyos.   suyos.suya,

   tuya, tuyas.   suya, suyas.   suyas.

Our, nuestro,   *Your*, vuestro,   *Your*, de Usted.

   nuestros.nuestra,   vuestros.   de Ustedes.

   nuestras.   vuestra, vuestras.

Your, with reference to *Usted,* is also translated suyo, suyos, suya, suyas, or su, sus . . . de. V. or Vds.

Relative and Interrogative Pronouns.

Who, which,   que, quien, quienes.

What, that,   que.

Which, what,   cual, cuales;

also,   el cual, los cuales, la cual, las cuales.

Whose,   cuyo, cuyos, cuya, cuyas;

also,   de quien, de cual, etc.

Demonstrative Pronouns

This, éste.   *These*, éstos.   *That*, aquél.

Those, aquéllos.

   « ésta. « estas. « aquélla. « aquéllas.

That, ése,   *Those*, ésos.   *This*, esto.

That, aquello.

   « ésa. « ésas. *That*, eso.

Indefinite Pronouns

One, uno.   *Such*, tal.

Each, cada.   *Something*, algo.

Nobody, { nadie,   *Nothing*, nada.

          ninguno.   *Each one*, cada cual.

                    Each other, uno y otro.

Somebody,

Anybody, } alguien.

VERBS

All Spanish verbs are classed into there conjugations. Verbs ending in *ar* belong to the first; those in *er*, to the second; and those in *ir*, to the third.

A TABLE

OF THE TERMINATIONS OF ALL THE REGULAR VERBS.

The numbers in the margin refer to the conjugation, those at the head of the columns, to the Persons.

Infinitive Mode.

1. Present, *ar*. Gerund, *ando*. Pastor Passive Part. *ado*.
2.   "   *er*.   "   *iendo*.   "   "   "   *ido*.
3.   "   *ir*.   "   *iendo*.   "   "   "   *ido*.

Indicative Mode

Present

1.	amo,	as,	a:	amos,	áis,	an.
2.	temo,	es,	e:	*emos,*	éis,	en.
3.	subo,	es,	e:	imos,	ís,	en.

Imperfect.

1.	amaba,	abas,	aba:	ábamos,	abais,	aban.
2.	temía.	ías,	ía;	íamos,	íais,	ían.
3.	subía,	ías,	ía:	íamos,	íais,	ían.

Preterite or Perfect.

1.	amé,	aste,	ó:	amos,	asteis,	aron.
2.	temí,	iste,	ió:	imos,	isteis,	ieron.
3.	subí,	iste,	ió:	imos,	isteis,	ieron.

Future.

1.	amaré,	arás,	ará:	aremos,	aréis,	arán.
2.	temeré,	erás,	erá:	eremos,	eréis,	erán.
3.	subiré,	irás,	irá:	iremos,	iréis,	irán.

Imperative Mode.

1.   ama,   e: emos,   ad,   en.
2.   teme,   a: amos,   ed,   an.
3.   sube,   a: amos,   id,   an.

Subjunctive Mode

Present.

1. ame,   es,   e: emos,   éis,   en.
2. tema,   as,   a: amos,   áis,   an.
3. suba,   as,   a: amos,   áis,   an.

Imperfect.—(First Termination.)

1. amara,   aras,   ara: áramos,   arais,   aran.
2. temiera,   ieras,   iera: iéramos,   ierais,   ieran.
3. subiera,   ieras,   iera: iéramos,   ierais,   ieran.

Conditional.

1. amaría,   arías,   aría: aríamos,   aríais,   arían.
2. temería,   erías,   ería: eríamos,   eríais,   erían
3. subiría,   irías,   iría: iríamos,   iríais,   irían

Imperfect.-(Second Termination.)

1. amase,   ases,   ase: asemos,   áseis,   asen.
2. temiese,   ieses,   iese: iésemos,   iéseis,   iesen.
3. subiese,   ieses,   iese: iésemos,   iéseis,   iesen.

COMPOUND TENSES.

These tenses are formed by placing after the verb *haber* (to have), the participle past of the verb that is conjugated; as (I *have* loved), "yo *he* armado."

CONJUGATION OF THE AUXILIARY VERBS.

Infinitive Mode.

Present.

Haber. Tener. *To have.*   Ser. Estar. *To be.*

Gerund.

Habiendo. Teniendo. *Having.*   Siendo. Estando. *Being.*

Past Participle.

Habido. Tenido. *Had.*   Sido. Estado. *Been.*

Indicative Mode.

Present.
I have I am

1. He.	Tengo.	Soy	Estoy
2. Has.	Tienes.	Eres.	Estás
3. Ha.	Tiene.	Es.	Está

1. Hemos.	Tenemos.	Somos.	Estamos.
2. Habéis.	Tenéis.	Sois.	Estáis.
3. Han.	Tienen.	Son.	Están.

Imperfect
I had.   *I was*

1. Había.	Tenía.	Era.	Estaba.
2. Habías.	Tenías.	Eras.	Estabas.
3. Había.	Tenía.	Era.	Estaba.
1. Habíamos.	Teníamos.	Éramos.	Estábamos.
2. Habíais.	Teníais.	Erais.	Estabais.
3. Habían	Tenían.	Eran.	Estaban.

Preterite
I had.   *I was*

1. Hube.	Tuve.	Fui.	Estuve.
2. Hubiste.	Tuviste.	Fuiste	Estuviste.
3. Hubo.	Tuvo.	Fue.	Estuvo.
1. Hubimos.	Tuvimos.	Fuimos.	Estuvimos.
2. Hubisteis.	Tuvisteis.	Fuisteis	Estuvisteis.
3. Hubieron	Tuvieron.	Fueron.	Estuvieron.

Future
I will have-   *I will be*

1. Habré.	Tendré.	Seré.	Estaré.
2. Habrás.	Tendrás.	Serás	Estarás.
3. Habrá.	Tendrá.	Será.	Estará.
1. Habremos.	Tendremos.	Seremos.	Estaremos.
2. Habréis.	Tendréis.	Seréis	Estaréis.
3. Habrán	Tendrán.	Serán.	Estarán.

Imperative Mode

Let me have.   *Let me be*

1.	Ten tú.	Sé.	Está.
2.	Tenga él.	Sea.	Esté.
3.	Tenga V.	Sea V.	Esté V.
1.	Tengamos.	Seamos.	Estemos.
2.	Tened.	Sed.	Estad.
3.	Tengan.	Sean.	Estén.
4.	Tengan Vds.	Sean Vds.	Estén Vds.

Subjuntive Mode

Present.
I may have.   *I may be.*

1. Haya.	Tenga.	Sea.	Esté.
2. Hayas.	Tengas.	Seas.	Estés.
3. Haya.	Tenga.	Sea.	Esté.
1. Hayamos.	Tengamos.	Seamos.	Estemos.
2. Hayáis.	Tengás.	Seáis.	Estéis.
3. Hayan	Tengan.	Sean.	Estén.

Imperfect-(First Termination.)

I would have.   I would be

1. Hubiera.	Tuviera.	Fuera.	Estuviera.
2. Hubieras.	Tuvieras.	Fueras.	Estuvieras.
3. Hubiera.	Tuviera.	Fuera.	Estuviera.
1. Hubiéramos.	Tuviéramos.	Fuéramos.	Estuviéramos.
2. Hubierais.	Tuvierais.	Fuerais.	Estuvierais.
3. Hubieran.	Tuvieran.	Fueran.	Estuvieran.

Conditional.

I would have.   I would be

1. Habría.	Tendría.	Sería.	Estaría.
2. Habrías.	Tendrías.	Serías.	Estarías.
3. Habría.	Tendría.	Sería.	Estaría.
1. Habríamos.	Tendríamos.	Seríamos.	Estaríamos.
2. Habríais.	Tendríais.	Seríais.	Estaríais.
3. Habrían.	Tendrían.	Serían.	Estarían.

Imperfect-(Second Termination.).

I should have.   I should be

1. Hubiese.	Tuviese.	Fuese.	Estuviese.
2. Hubieses.	Tuvieses.	Fueses.	Estuvieses.
3. Hubiese.	Tuviese.	Fuese.	Estuviese.
1. Hubiésemos.	Tuviésemos.	Fuésemos.	Estuviésemos.
2. Hubieseis.	Tuvieseis.	Fueseis.	Estuvieseis.
3. Hubiesen.	Tuviesen.	Fuesen.	Estuviesen.

Passive Verbs

Passive verbs are formed from active transitive verbs by adding their *participle past* to the auxiliary verb *ser* (to be), through all its changes, as in English, thus, from the active verb *amar* (to love), is formed the passive verb *ser amado* (to be loved).

The participle must agree in gender and number with the nominative it refers to; thus, he is loved (*él es amado*); she is loved (*ella es amada*); they are loved (*ellos, son amados*).

Pronominal or Reflexive Verbs.

A *pronominal* or *reflexive verb* is conjugated by prefixing the pronouns *me, te, se, V. se; nos, os, se, Vds. se* to the verb according to its person and number; as, he arms himself, *él se arma.*

In the infinitive and imperative modes the pronouns are placed after the verb, and in one word with it; the pronoun, therefore, must be suppressed, in order to find out the conjugation: thus, to approach; acercarse, (se) acercar, first conjugation.

Remarks On The Use Of The Subjunctive Mode.

Three are the terminations of the imperfect tense subjunctive mode; *ra, ría, se.*—The termination *ra,* or *se,* is used when the verb is governed by a conditional conjunction, and the verb that completes the sense of the phrase is placed in the termination *ría; If* he *had* money, he *would buy* the house, *si él tuviera dinero, compraría la casa:*—If the verb begins without a conditional conjunction, the termination *ría* may be used, placing the verb that completes the sense in the termination *se;* as, It would be proper that you should write to him, *sería bueno que V. le escribiese.*

Verbs signifying *command, wish, supplication,* etc., being in the present indicative, require the governed verb in the present subjunctive; and if they are in any of the past tenses of the indicative, the governed verb must he in the termination *ra* or *se,* of the subjunctive.

The Gerund.

The *gerund* is that part of the verb that terminates in *ando* in verbs of the first conjugation, and in *iendo* in those of the second and third, as *publicando* (publishing), from *publicar; prometiendo* (promising), from *prometer; asistiendo* (assisting), from asistir. It admits no change for gender or number.

It is translated by the English present participle, and conjugated with the verb *estar* (to be), as, Ana is reading, and Mary is playing on the piano (**Ana está leyendo, y María está tocando el piano**).

PARTICIPLE.

The passive or past participle terminates in *ado* in the first conjugation, and in *ido* in the second and third. It changes its termination according to the number and gender of the person it refers to; except when it follows immediately after the verb *haber,* in which case it does not admit of any change.

All passive participles that do not terminate in *ado* or *ido* are called irregular; such are the following from the verbs:

To open, **abrir, abierto.**   To die, **morir, muerto.**

To cover, **cubrir, cubierto.**   To resolve, **resolver,**

To say, **decir, dicho.**   **resuelto.**

To write, **escribir, escrito.**   To see, **ver, visto.**

To try, **freír, frito.**   To put, **poner, puesto.**

To do, **hacer, hecho.**   To turn, **volver, vuelto.**

To print, **imprimir, impreso.**

Their compounds have the same irregularity.

Verbs That Have Two Participles.

There are some verbs that have two passive participles, the one regular and the other irregular. They are eighty-three in number. Such are: To bless, *bendecir,* bendecido, *bendito;* to compel, *compeler,* compelido, *compulso,* to convert, convertir, convertido, *converso;* to awake, *despertar,* despertado, *despierto,* to elect, *elegir,* elegido, *electo;* to express, *expresar,* expresado, *expreso*; to fix, *fijar,* fijado, *fijo*; to satiate, hartar, hartado, *harto*; to include, *incluir,* incluido, *incluso*; to join, *juntar,* juntado, junto; to arrest, *prender,* prendido, *preso*; to provide, *proveer,* proveído, *provisto*; to *loosen, soltar,* soltado, *suelto*; to suspend, *suspender,* suspendido, *suspenso,* etc.

The *regular* participles of these verbs are used to form the compound tenses with *haber*; as, he has awaked early (**él ha despertado temprano**).

The irregular participles are used as verbal adjectives, and with the verbs ser, etc., and do not form compound tenses with *haber*; excepting *preso, prescrito, provisto, roto, injerto, proscrito,* and *supreso,* which have both uses; as, he is early awaked (**él está despierto temprano**); They have provided (**ellos han provisto or proveído**),

THE PLURAL

In Spanish the plural is formed adding s or es to the singular.

rosa	-	rosas.
edificio	-	edificios.
café	-	cafés.
piano	-	pianos.
mesa	-	mesas.
canción	-	canciones.
cárcel	-	cárceles.
árbol	-	árboles.
rubí	-	rubíes.
rey	-	reyes.

If we observe we'll see an s when the substantives finish with a non-accented vowel or with **é.**

But we add es to the substantives that finish with a consonant and with an accented vocal which is not **é. - Y** is considered a consonant in this case.

There are some exceptions: papá - papás, mamá - mamás, sofá - sofás, dominó - dominós.

1. The nouns which in singular finish with s, don't change in plural.

* el martes - los martes; el paraguas - los paraguas; el parabrisas - los parabrisas.

But there are some exceptions.

* interés - intereses, tos - toses.

The grave or esdrújulos substantives that finish with x or z don't have a plural.

* clímax, mantis, tórax, Pérez.

2. Other words only are used in plural:

alicates, tijeras, gafas, pantalones, tenazas, pinzas, nupcias, comestibles, víveres, tinieblas, esponsales, cosquillas, bragas, calzoncillos.

Changes in pronunciation and writing

a) Pronunciation:

El carácter - Los caracteres. El régimen - Los regímenes.

b) Writing:

The final **z** is changed to c in the plural form es.

capaz - capaces, capataz - capataces, rapaz - rapaces, voraz - voraces, lápiz - lápices.

Some words accented in the last sillable are:

canción - canciones, francés - franceses

varón - varones, balón - balones.

Sometimes the meaning of the word changes when it's put into plural.

* Está **bien** hecho. No tengo **bienes**

* Tiene una **esposa** francesa. Le pusieron las **esposas.**

The Personal Pronoun

The 1º and the 2º persons.

a) With the prepositions **según** and **entre** the forms **yo/tú** are used.

* **Según tú** eso no es verdad.

* **Entre tú y yo**, creo que se casará con él.

b) With the other prepositions we use the forms **mí/ti**:

* Este vaso es **para ti**.

* Están hablando **de mí**.

c) The preposition **con** originates the forms **conmigo** y **contigo**:

* Ven **conmigo** a Madrid.

* Ella no quiere ir **contigo**.

La 3ª persona.

It uses the forms subject, going before the following preposition:

* Tu madre está hablando **con él**.

* Esta carta es **para ella.**

The non-accented forms which correspond to the direct and indirect object, are placed before the verb.

* **Me** pidió que viniera.

* **Te** dije que fueras a la estación.

The forms **le, les** placed in front of **lo, la, los** or **las** acquire the form **se**.

* Yo **le** di dinero * Yo **se** lo di (**le** changes to **se**, and money changes to **lo**).

* Yo **le** compré los libros (a él). Yo **se** los compré (**le** changes to **se**, and the books c h a n g e to **los**).

* Yo **les** di pan - yo **se** lo di (**les** changes to **se**, and pan changes to **lo**).

* He entregado un paquete al cartero = **Le** (to the postman) he entregado un paquete = **Se** lo he entregado (**Le** changes to **se**, and packet changes to **lo**).

The form **se** will always go before when it is combined with **te** or **me**.

* **Se** me ocurre. * **Se** te advirtió.

LA LE LO

When only a pronoun-complement appears:

1. If the sentence is refered to objects, the forms **lo(s)** or **la(s)** are used for the masculine and feminine respectively:

   * Visitaron el museo **Lo** visitaron.
   * Vieron la foto **La** vieron.

With verbs of <u>adding, accumulation...</u> or their contraries, <u>add, put, to take away etc.,</u> the sentences are formed with the preposition A, and the pronoun will **LE(s).**

   * **A este coche le** falta velocidad.
   * **A este motor le** añadieron más potencia.
   * **A esta casa le** pusieron el tejado ayer.

2. If it is personal:

a) When it is an indirect complement, the form **le(s)** is always used.

   * Yo compré un libro a Pedro/María - Le compró un libro (to Pedro or to María).
   * Yo vendí el coche a los vecinos/las vecinas. - **Les** vendí el coche.

b) When it is a direct complement:

i) If it is feminine it is used the form **la(s).**

   * Juan vio a Luisa. - Juan **la** vio.
   * Enrique besó a su madre. - Enrique la besó.
   * Culparon a las mujeres del asesinato. - **Las** culparon.
   * Mató a la niña. - **La** matóo.

ii) If it is masculine **lo(s)** o **le(s)** can be used.

   * María vio a Pedro. - María **le/lo** vio.
   * Ella contempló al niñ. - Ella **le/lo** contempló
   * Ellos asesinaron al anciano. - Ellos **le/lo** asesinaron.
   * Pedro esperó a los niños. - Él **les/los** esperó.

iii) If the pronoun refers to usted(es), it is normally used the form **le(s).**

   * Tenía muchas ganas de conocer**le** (a usted).
   * Teníamos muchas ganas de conocer**les** (a ustedes).

GENERAL IRREGULARITIES OF SPANISH VERBS.

EUPHONIC CHANGES.

Verbs That Require A Change In Their Radical Letters.

1 Verbs ending in CAR change the **c** into **qu** when the first letter of the termination is E.

2. Verbs ending in CER change the c into z }

3. " CIR c " } When the first letter

4. " GER G " J } of the termination

5. " GIR G " J } is O *or* A

6. " QUIR QU " C }

7. " GUIR drop U " }

8. " GAR add U " } When the first letter of

9. " ZAR change z " c } the termination is E.

THE IRREGULAR VERBS.

Irregular verbs suffer some changes either in their radical letters or in the termination of the conjugations to which they belong, or in both cases. The total number of such verbs in the Spanish language is about eight hundred and seventy-six. Of these, however, four hundred and sixty-one are compound forms. But this apparently very long list may be reduced to six classes, as follows:

I. To the first class belong certain verbs like **acertar, ascender, sentir,** which have the vowel e in the penultimate syllable of the infinitive, and change this e when it bears the tonic accent, or is in the singular or the third person plural of the present tense (indicative, subjunctive, imperative), into **ie.** As a general rule, and with very rare exceptions, if in the kindred noun there is the diphthong *ie,* the verb is irregular of this class. Verbs of the third conjugation belonging to this class have the further peculiarity that the vowel *e* of the stem changes into *i* when unaccented and followed by a strong termination (that is, containing a strong vowel, viz., *a* or *o*), and in the preterite before a diphthong, To this class belong also the verbs **adquirir, concernir** (defective), **and discernir.**

II. To the second class belong certain verbs like, **mover**, and **dormir**, which have the vowel o in the penultimate syllable of the infinitive, and change this **o** into **u** when it bears the tonic accent or is in the singular and the third person plural of the present tense (indicative, subjunctive, and imperative). If the kindred noun has the diphthong *ue,* the verb generally belongs to this class. *Dormir* and *morir* (3d conj.) have *ue* in the same positions where *sentir* (class I) has *i.* The gerund in this class belongs uniformly to the *aorist* (or preterite) system.

III. To the third class belong verbs of the second and third conjugations ending in **cer** or **cir** preceded by a vowel, the irregularity consisting in their taking a **z** before the **c** when the terminations begin with *a* or *o*. This occurs in the first person singular of the present indicative, in all persons of the present subjunctive, and in those of the imperative which are formed from the subjunctive. About two hundred and eight verbs belong to this class, the forms in **ecer** being very numerous.

IV. This class is composed wholly of verbs of the third conjugation with the stem vowel **e** (like **pedir**), and change this **e** for **i** in the gerund in the third person (singular and plural) of the present indicative, the whole of the present subjunctive, and the imperative formed therefrom, the third persons of the past definite, and all those of the imperfect subjunctive.

NOTE: -The verbs which end in **eír** and **ñir,** like **reír, ceñir,** lose the i of their endings when it is not accented (gerund, third person past definite, and imperfect and future subjunctive), and thus is avoided the double sound of *i* which results; thus:

*Riendo, Rieron, Riera, Riese, etc.

V. To this class belong those verbs ending in **uir** in which both vowels are sounded, like **argüir** (excluding therefore those in *guir, quir*). Their irregularity consists in adding y to the stem when this is accented or followed by a strong vowel.

The preterite (florist) stem is regular, but the initial i of the diphthongal terminations *ie, io*, is changed to *y*, since it comes between two vowels. The gerund in this class belongs always to the *aorist* system.

VI. To this class are assigned all the remaining irregular verbs, among which there is, however, no common principle of classification. A portion of these have *florist* (preterite) systems resembling more or less closely the Latin, while the remainder are irregular in the strictest sense. These verbs are therefore given individually.

Examples:

1. *Acrecentar,* Acreciento, acrecientas, etc.: acreciente, acrecienta, etc.; acreciente, acrecientes, etc.

Attender, Atiendo, atiendes, etc.; atienda, atiende, etc.; atienda, atiendas, etc.

Asentir, Asiento, asientes, etc.; asienta, asiente, etc., asienta, asientas, etc.

Asintió, asintieron; asintiera; asintiese;

2. *Acordar* Acuerdo, acuerdas, etc.; acuerde, acuerda, etc.; acuerde, acuerdes, etc.

Mover Muevo, mueves, etc.; mueva, mueve, etc.; mueva, muevas, etc.

Dormir, Duermo, duermes, etc.; duerma, duerme, etc.; duerma, duermas, etc.

3. *Conocer* Conozco, conozca. *Obedecer,* obedezco, obedezca. *Lucir,* luzco, luzca.

Conducir Conduzco; conduzca, conduzcas, conduzcamos, etc.

Conduje, condujiste, condujo, V. condujo; condujimos, condujisteis, condujeron, VV. condujeron.—*Subj. Imperf. 1st term.* Condujera. etc.—*2d term.* Conduciría., etc.—*3d term.* Condujese, etc.—*Fut.* Condujere, etc.

4. *Poseer,* Poseyendo; poseyó, poseyera, etc.; poseyese, etc.; poseyere, etc.

Pedir, Pido, pides, etc.; pida, pide, etc.; pida, pidas, etc.

Pidió, pidieron, pidiera, etc. pidiese, etc.; pidiere, etc.

5. *Instruir,* Instruyendo, instruyo, instruyeron, instruyera, etc. instruyese, etc., instruyere, etc.

Instruyo, instruyes, etc.; instruya, instruye, etc.; instruya, instruyas, etc.

6. The auxiliary verbs *Ser, Estar, Haber; Tener; Dar, Caber,* etc., are given individually just below.

Verbs Whose Irregularity Is Confined To Them And Their Compounds.

N. B. The tenses not conjugated in the following verbs are regular. Thus in *Andar,* for instance, the present of the indicative mood is: 1 ando, 2 andas, 3 anda, etc. The imperfect tense: 1 *andaba,* 2 *andabas,* etc. The tenses or persons printed in *italics* are also regular.

ADQUIRIR, to *acquire*. C1. I.

Indic. Pres. 1 Adquiero, 2 adquieres, 3 él/Vd adquiere: 1 *adquirimos*, 2 *adquirís*, 3 ellos/Vds adquieren.

Imperative. 2 adquiere, 3 adquiera, adquiera Vd., 2 no adquieras: 1 *adquiramos*, 2 *adquirid.*, 2 *no adquiráis*.

Subj. Pres. 1 Adquiera, 2 adquieras,

3 él/Vd. adquiera: 1 *adquiramos*, 2 *adquiráis*, 3 ellos/Vds. adquieran.

ANDAR, *to walk*. C1. VI.

Indic. Preterit. 1 Anduve, 2 anduviste, 3 él/Vd. anduvo: 1 anduvimos, 2 anduvisteis, 3 ellos/Vds. anduvieron.

Subj. Imperf. 1st term. 1 Anduviera, 2 anduvieras, 3 él/Vd. anduviera: 1 anduviéramos, 2 anduvierais, 3 ellos/Vds. anduvieran.

Conditional. 1 *andaría* etc. 1 anduviese, 2 anduvieses, etc.

BENDECIR, *to bless*. C1. VI.

Is conjugated like *Decir,* except in the tenses and persons following, which are regular.

Past participle	Bendito
	Bendecido

Indic. Future. 1. Bendeciré, 2 bendecirás, 3 él/Vd. bendecirá: 1 bendeciremos, 2 bendeciréis, 3 ellos/Vds. bendecirán. —*Conditional*. 1 Bendeciría, 2 bendecirías, 3 él/Vd. bendeciría: 1 bendeciríamos, 2 bendeciríais, 3 ellos/Vds. bendecirían.—*Imperative*. 2 Bendice tú: 2 Bendecid.

CABER, *to be contained*. C1. VI.

Indic. Pres. 1 Quepo, 2 *cabes*, 3 él/Vd. *cabe*: 1 cabemos, 2 *cabéis*, 3 ellos/Vds. *caben*.–*Perf.* 1 Cupe, 2 cupiste, 3 cupo, Vd. cupo: 1 cupimos, 2 cupisteis, 3 cupieron, Vds. cupieron.

Fut. 1 Cabré, 2 cabrás, 3 él/Vd. cabrá: 1 cabremos, 2 cabréis, 3 ellos/Vds. cabrán.—*Imperative.* 2 *cabe,* 3 quepa él/Vd., 2 no quepas, 1 quepamos, 2 *cabed,* 3 quepan ellos/Vds., 2 no quepáis.

Subj. Pres. 1 Quepa, 2 quepas, 3 él/Vd. quepa: 1 quepamos, 2 quepáis, 3 ellos/Vds. quepan.—*Imperf. 1st term.* 1 Cupiera, 2 cupieras, 3 él/Vd. cupiera: 1 cupieramos, 2 cupierais, 3 ellos/Vds. cupieran.—*2d term.* 1 Cabría, 2 cabrías, 3 él/Vd. cabría: 1 cabríamos, 2 cabríais, 3 ellos/Vds. cabrían.—*3d term* 1 Cupiese, 2 cupieses, 3 cupiese, Vd. cupiese: 1 cupiésemos, 2 cupieseis, 3 cupiesen, Vds. cupiesen.

CAER, *to fall.* Cl. VI.

Gerund. Cayendo. *Past participle.* Caído.

Indic. Pres. 1 Caigo, 2 caes, 3 él/vd. cae: 1 *caemos,* 2 caéis, 3 ellos/Vds. caen.—*Prest.* 1 *Caí,* 2 *caíste,* 3 él/Vd. cayó: 1 *caímos,* 2 *caísteis,* 3 ellos/Vds. cayeron.

Imper. 2 cae. 3 *caiga* el, caiga él/Vd., 2 no caigas: 1 caigamos, 2 *caed,* 3 caigan ellos/Vds.. 2 no caigáis.—*Subj. Pres.* 1 Caiga, 2 caigas. 3 él/Vd caiga: 1 caigamos, 2 caigáis, 3 *ellos/Vds.* caigan.—*Imperf. 1st term.* 1 Cayera, 2 cayeras, 3 él/Vd cayera: 1 cayéramos, 2 cayerais, 3 ellos/Vds. cayeran.—*Conditional.* 1 *Caería,* etc., 1 *caeríamos,* etc.—*3d term.* 1 Cayese, 2 cayeses, 3 él/Vd cayese: 1. cayésemos, 2 cayeseis, 3 ellos/Vds. cayesen.—*Fut.* 1 Cayere, 2 cayeres, 3 cayere, él/Vd cayere: 1 cayéremos, 2 cayereis, 3 ellos/Vds. cayeren.

COCER, *to boil.* Cl. II.

Indic. Pres. 1 Cuezo, 2 cueces, 3 él/Vd cuece 1 cocemos, 2 *cocéis,* 3 ellos/Vds. cuecen.—*Subj. Pres.* 1 Cueza, 2 cuezas, 3 él/Vd cueza: 1 cozamos, 2 cozáis, 3 ellos/Vds. cuezan.—*Imper.* 2 cuece, 3 cueza él/Vd, 2 no cuezas: 1 cozamos, 2 *coced,* 3 cuezan ellos/Vds., 2 no cozáis.—*Subj. Pres.* 1. Cueza, 2 cuezas, etc.

DAR, *to give.* Cl. VI.

Indic. Pres. 1 Doy, 2 das, 3 *él/Vd da*: 1 *damos,* 2 *dáis,* 3 *ellos/Vds.* dan.—*Imperf.* 1 Daba, etc. 1 *Dábamos, etc.*—*Perf.* 1 Dí, 2 diste, 3 él/Vd dio: 1 dimos, 2 disteis, 3 ellos/Vds. dieron.

Fut. 1 Daré, etc. 1 *Daremos.*—*Imper.* 2 Da tú, etc. 1 *Demos,* etc.-*Subj. Pres.* 1 Dé, etc.: 1 *Demos,* etc.—*Imperf. 1st term.* 1 Diera, 2 dieras, 3 él/Vd diera: 1 diéramos, 2 dierais, 3 ellos/Vds. dieran.—*2d term.* 1 *Daría,* etc.: 1 *daríamos,* etc.-*3d term.* 1 Diese, 2 dieses, 3 él/Vd diese: 1 diésemos, 2 dieseis, 3 ellos/Vds. diesen.

DECIR, *to say.* Cl. VI.

Gerund, Diciendo. *Past participle.* Dicho.

Indic. Pres. 1 Digo, 2 dices, 3 él/Vd dice: 1 *decimos,* 2 *decís,* 3 ellos/Vds. dicen.—*Imperf.* 1 *Decía,* etc. —*Pret.* 1 Dije, 2 dijiste, 3 él/Vd dijo: 1 dijimos, 2 dijisteis, 3 ellos/Vds. dijeron.

Fut. 1 Diré, 2 dirás, 3 él/Vd dirá: 1 diremos, 2 diréis, 3 ellos/Vds. dirán.—*Imper.* 2 di tú, 3 diga él/Vd, 2 no digas :1 digamos, 2 *decid,* 3 digan ellos/Vds., 2 no digáis.-*Subj. Pres.* 1 diga, 2 digas, 3 él/Vd diga: 1 digamos, 2 digáis, 3 ellos/Vds. digan.—*Imperf. 1st term.* 1 dijera, 2 dijeras, 3 dijera, él/Vd dijera: 1 dijéramos, 2 dijerais, 3 ellos/Vds. dijeran.—*Conditional.* 1 diría, 2 dirías, 3 él/Vd diría: 1 diríamos, 2 diríais, 3 ellos/Vds. dirían.—*3d term.* 1 Dijese, 2 dijeses, 3 él/Vd dijese: 1 dijésemos, 2 dijeseis, 3 ellos/Vds. dijesen.

Contradecir, *to contradict;* Desdecirse, *to retract;* Predecir, *to predict.* These three verbs are conjugated like *decir,* except in the second person singular of the imperative, which is *contradice, predice, desdícete.*

DORMIR, *to sleep.* Cl. II.

Gerund. Durmiendo. *Past participle.* Dormido.

Indic. Pres. 1 Duermo, 2 duermes, 3 duerme: 1 *dormimos,* 2 *dormís,* 3 duermen.

Pret. 1 *Dormí,* 2 *dormis—te,* 3 durmió: 1 *dormimos,* 2 *dormisteis,* 3 durmieron.—*Imper.* 2 duerme, 3 duerma él/Vd., 2 no duermas: 1 durmamos, 2 *dormid,* 3 duerman *ellos/Vds.,* 2 no durmáis.—*Subj. Pres.* 1 Duerma, 2 duermas, 3 duerma: 1 durmamos, 2 durmáis, 3 duerman.—*Imperf. 1st term.* 1 Durmiera, 2 durmieras, 3 durmiera: 1 durmiéramos, 2 durmierais, 3 durmieran.—*Conditional.* 1 *Dormiría,* etc.—*3d term.* 1 Durmiese, 2 durmieses, 3 durmiese: 1 durmiésemos, 2 durmieseis, 3 durmiesen.

MORIR, *to die.* Cl. II.

Past participle. Muerto.

The rest is conjugated like *Dormir.*

ESTAR, *to be.* Cl. VI.

HABER, *to have.* Cl. VI.

As an auxiliary verb.

HABER, when signifying *there to be,* is conjugated only in the third person singular of each tense, whether the nominative be singular or plural; thus:

There to be, *Haber.* There being, *Habiendo.*

There is *hay* — There had been *había habido*
There are *hay* — There will have been *habrá*
There *was había* — *habido*
There were *hubo* — There may have been *haya*
There will be *habrá* — *habido*
Let there be *haya*
There may be *haya*
There has been *ha habido*
There have been *ha habido*

HACER, *to make*. C1. VI.

Gerund. Haciendo. *Past Participle*. Hecho.

Indic. Pres: 1 Hago, 2 *haces*, etc.—*Imperf*. 1. Hacía, etc.—*Pret*. 1 Hice, 2 hiciste, 3 hizo: 1 hicimos 2 hicisteis, 3 hicieron.—*Fut*. 1 Haré, 2 harás, 3 hará: 1 haremos, 2 haréis, 3 harán. —*Imper*. 2 haz, 3 haga: 1 hagamos, 2 *haced*, 3 hagan.—*Subj. Pres*. 1 Haga, 2 hagas, etc. —*Imperf. 1st term*. 1 Hiciera, 2 hicierais, 3 hiciera: 1 hiciéramos, 2 hicieras, 3 hicieran. —*Conditional*. 1 Haría, 2 harías, 3 haría: 1 haríamos, 2 haríais, 3 harían.—*2d term*. 1 Hiciese, 2 hicieses, 3 hiciese: 1 hiciésemos, 2 hicieseis, 3 hiciesen.

IR, *to go*. Cl. VI.

Gerund. Yendo. *Past participle*. Ido.

Indic. Pres. 1 Voy, 2 vas, 3 va: 1 vamos, 2 vais, 3 van.—*Imperf*. 1 Iba, 2 ibas, 3 iba: 1 Íbamos, 2 ibais, 3 iban.—*Pret*. 1 Fui, 2 fuiste, 3 fue: 1 fuimos, 2 fuisteis, 3 fueron.—*Fut*. 1 Iré, 2 irás, 3 iré: 1 iremos, 2 iréis, 3 irán.—*Imper*. 1 Vaya, 2 ve, 3 vaya: 1 vayamos, 2 *id*, 3 vayan.—*Subj. Pres*. 1 Vaya, 2 vayas, 3 vaya: 1 vayamos, 2 vayáis, 3 vayan. —*imperf. 1st. term*. 1 Fuera, 2 fueras, 3 fuera: 1 fuéramos, 2 fuerais, 3 fueran.—*Conditional*. 1 Iría, 2 irías, 3 iría: 1 iríamos, 2 iríais, 3 irían.—*2d term*. 1 Fuese, 2 fueses, 3 fuese: 1 fuésemos, 2 fueseis, 3 fuesen.

JUGAR, *to play*. C1. II.

Gerund. Jugando. *Past participle*. Jugado.

Indic. Pres. 1 juego, 2 juegas, 3 juega: 1 *jugamos, 2 jugáis*, 3 juegan.—*Imperf*. 1 *jugaba*, etc.—*Pret*. 1 jugué, 2 *jugaste*, etc.—*Fut*. 1 *jugaré*, etc.—*Imperf*. 2 juega, 3 juegue: 1 juguemos, 2 *jugad*, 3 jueguen.— *Subj. Pres*. 1 juegue, 2 juegues, 3 juegue: 1 juguemos, 2 juguéis, 3 jueguen.—*Imperf. 1st term*. 1 *jugara*, etc.—*Conditional*. 1 *jugaría*, etc.—*3d term*. 1 *jugase*, etc.—*Fut*. 1 *jugaré*, etc.

OIR, *to hear*. Cl. VI.

Gerund. Oyendo. *Past participle*. Oído.

Indic. Pres. 1 Oigo, 2 oyes, 3 oye: 1 oímos, 2 *oís*, 3 oyen.—*Imperf*. 1 *Oía*, etc.—*Pret*. 1 Oí, 2 oíste, 3 oyó: 1 *oímos, 3* oyeron.—*Fut*. 1 Oiré etc.—*Imper*. 2 oye, 3 oiga: 1 oigamos, 2 *oíd*, 3 oigan.—*Subj. Pres*. 1 Oiga, 2 oigas, 3 oiga: 1 oigamos, 2 oigáis, 3 oigan.—*Imperf. 1st term*. 1 Oyera, 2 oyeras, oyera: 1 oyéramos, 2 oyerais, 3 oyeran.—*Conditional*. 1 *Oiría*, etc.—*2d term*. 1 Oyese, 2 oyeses, 3 oyese: 1 oyésemos, 2 oyeseis, 3 oyesen.

OLER, *to smell*. C1. II.

Gerund. Oliendo. *Past participle*. Olido.

Indic. Pres. 1 Huelo, 2 hueles, 3 huele: 1 olemos, 2 *oléis*, 3 huelen.—*Imperf*. 1 *Olía*, etc.—*Pret*. 1 *Olí*. etc.—*Fut*. 1 *Oleré*, etc.—*Imper*. 2 huele, 3 huela: 1 *olamos*, 2 *oled*, 3 huelan.—*Subj. Pres*. 1 Huela, 2 huelas, 3 huela: 1 *olamos*, 2 *oláis*, 3 huelan.

—*Imperf. 1st term*. 1 Oliera, etc.—*Conditional*. 1 *Olería*, etc.—*2d term*. 1 *Oliese*, etc.

PODER, *to be able*. Cl. VI.

Gerund. Pudiendo. *Past participle*. Podido.

Indic. Pres. 1 Puedo, 2 puedes, 3 puede: 1 *podemos*, 2 *podéis*, 3 pueden.—*Imperf*. 1 Podía, etc.—*Pret*. 1 Pude, 2 pudiste, 3 pudo: 1 pudimos, 2 pudisteis, 3 pudieron.—*Fut*. 1 Podré, 2 podrás, 3 podrá: 1 podremos, 2 podréis, 3 podrán.—It has no *Imperative*.—*Subj. Pres*. 1 Pueda, 2 puedas, 3 pueda: 1 *podamos*, 2 *podáis*, 3 puedan.—*Imperf. 1st term*. 1 Pudiera, 2 pudieras, 3 pudiera: 1 pudiéramos, 2 pudierais, 3 pudieran.—*Conditional*. 1 Podría. 2 podrías, 3 podría. 1 podríamos, 2 podríais, 3 podrían.—*2d term*. 1 Pudiese, 2 pudieses, 3 pudiese: 1 pudiésemos, 2 pudieseis, 3 pudiesen.

PODRIR or PUDRIR, *to rot*. Cl. VI.

Gerund. Pudriendo. *Past Participle*. Podrido.

Indic. Pres. 1 Pudro, 2 pudres, 3 pudre: 1 *podrimos*, 2 *podrís*, 3 pudren.—*Imperf*. 1 *Pudría* or *podría*, etc.—*Pret*. 1 *Podrí*, 2 *podriste*, 3 pudrió: 1 *podrimos*, 2 *podristeis*, 3 pudrieron.—*Fut*. 1 *podriré*, etc.—*Imper*. 2 pudre, 3 pudra: 1 pudramos, 2 *podrid*, 3 pudran.—*Subj. Pres*. 1 Pudra, 2 pudras, 3 pudra, etc.—*Imperf. 1st term*. 1 pudriera, 2 pudrieras, 3 pudriera: 1 pudriéramos, 2 pudrierais, 3 pudrieran.—*Conditional*. 1 *pudriría, podriría*, etc.—*2d term*. 1 pudriese, 2 pudrieses, 3 pudriese: 1 pudriésemos, 2 pudrieseis, 3 pudriesen.

PONER, *to put*. Cl. VI.

Gerund. Poniendo. *Past participle*. Puesto.

Indic. Pres. 1 pongo, 2 *pones*, etc.—*Imperf*. 1 ponía, etc.—*Pret*. 1 puse, 2 pusiste, 3 puso: 1 pusimos, 2 pusisteis, 3 pusieron.—*Fut*. 1 pondré, 2 pondrás, 3 pondrá: 1 pondremos, 2 pondréis, 3 pondrán.—*Imper*. 2 pon, 3 ponga: 1 pongamos, 2 *poned*, 3 pongan.—*Subj. Pres*. 1 ponga, 2 pongas, 3 ponga: 1 pongamos, 2 pongáis 3 pongan.—*Imperf. 1st term*. 1 pusiera, 2 pusieras, *3* pusiera: 1 pusiéramos, 2 pusierais, 3 pusieran.—*Conditional*. 1 pondría, 2 pondrías, 3 pondría: 1 pondríamos, 2 pondríais, 3 pondrían.—*2d term*. 1 pusiese, 2 pusieses, 3 pusiese: 1 pusiésemos, 2 pusieseis, 3 pusiesen.

QUERER, *to want*. Cl. VI.

Gerund. Queriendo. *Past Participle*. Querido.

Indic. Pres. 1 quiero, 2 quieres, 3 quiere: 1 queremos, 2 *queréis*, 3 quieren.—*Imperf*. 1 *quería*, etc. —*Pret*. 1 quise, 2 quisiste, 3 quiso: 1 quisimos, 2 quisisteis, 3 quisieron.—*Fut*. 1. querré, 2 querrás, 3 querrá: 1 querremos, 2 querréis, 3 querrán.—*Subj. Pres*. 1 quiera, 2 quieras, 3 quiera: 1 *queramos, queráis*, 3 quieran.—*Inperf. 1st term*. 1 quisiera, 2 quisieras, 3 quisiera: 1 quisiéramos, 2 quisierais, 3 quisieran.—*Conditional*. 1. querría, 2 querrías, 3 querría: 1 querríamos, 2 querríais, 3 querrín.—*2d term*. 1 quisiese, 2 quisieses, 3 quisiese: 1 quisiésemos, 2 quisieseis. 3 quisiesen.

REÍR, *to laugh*. Cl. IV.

Gerund. Riendo. *Past participle*. Reído.

Indic. Pres. 1 río, 2 ríes, 3 ríe: 1 *reímos*, 2 *reís*, 3 ríen.—*Imperf.* 1 *Reía*, etc.—*Pret.* 1 *Reí.* 2 *reíste*, 3 rió: 1 *reímos*, 2 *reísteis*, 3 rieron.—*Fut.* 1 *reiré*, etc.—*Imper.* 2 ríe, 3 ría: 1 riamos, 2 *reíd.* 3 rían.—*Subj Pres.* 1 ría, 2 rías, 3 ría: 1 riamos. 2 riáis, 3 rían.—*Imperf. 1st* term. 1 riera, 2 rieras, 3 riera, etc.—*Conditional.* 1 reiría, etc.—*2d term* 1 riese, 2 rieses, 3 riese: 1 riésemos, 2 rieseis, 3 riesen, etc.

Freír, *to fry. Past participle*. Frito.

SABER, *to know*. C1. VI.

Gerund. Sabiendo. *Past participle*. Sabido.

Indic. *Pres.* 1 sé, 2 *sabes*, etc.—*Imperf.* 1 *sabía, etc.*—*Pret.* 1 supe, 2 supiste, 3 supo: 1 supimos, 2 supisteis, 3 supieron.—*Fut.* 1 sabré, 2 sabrás, 3 sabrá: 1 sabremos, 2 sabréis, 3 sabrán.—*Imper.* 2 *sabe*, 3 sepa: 1 sepamos, 2 *sabed*, 3 sepan.—*Subj. Pres.* 1 sepa, 2 sepas. 3 sepa: 1 sepamos, 2 sepáis, 3 sepan.—*Imperf. 1st term.* 1 supiera, 2 supieras, 3 supiera: 1 supiéramos, 2 supierais, 3 supieran.—*Conditional.* 1 sabría, 2 sabrías, 3 sabría: 1 sabríamos, 2 sabríais, 3 sabrían.—*2d term.* 1 supiese, 2 supieses, 3 supiese, etc.

SALIR, to go out. Cl. VI.

Gerund. Saliendo. *Past participle*. Salido.

Indic. Pres. 1 salgo, 2 sales, etc.—*Imperf. salía,* etc.—*Pret.* 1 *salí*, etc.—*Fut.* 1 saldré, 2 saldrás, 3 saldrá: 1 saldremos, 2 saldréis, 3 saldráan.—*Imper.* 2 sal, 3 salga: 1 salgamos, 2 *salid*, 3 salgan.—*Subj. Pres.* 1 salga, 2 salgas, 3 salga: 1 salgamos, 2 salgáis, 3 salgan.—*Imperf. 1st term.* 1 *saliera* etc.—*Conditional.* 1 saldría, 2 saldrías, 3 saldría: 1 saldríamos, 2 saldríais, 3 saldrían,—*3d term.* 1 saliese, etc.

SATISFACER, *to satisfy*. Cl. VI.

SATISFACER is a verb compounded of *satis* and *hacer*, and is conjugated like *hacer*, changing the *h* into *f*; thus, *satisfago, satisfizo*, etc., satisfacía, etc., *satisfice, satisficiste, satisfizo*, etc. Except the imperative, the second person singular of which is, *satisface*, or *satisfaz*.

TRAER, *to* bring. Cl. VI.

Gerund. Trayendo. *Past participle*. Traído.

Indic. Pres. 1 traigo, 2 *traes*, etc.—*Imperf.* 1 traía, etc.—*Pret.* 1 traje, 2. trajiste, 3 traje: 1 trajimos, 2 trajisteis, 3 trajeron.—*Fut.* 1 traeré, etc.—*Imper.* 2 *trae*, 3 traiga, traiga V., 2 no traigas: 1 traigamos, 2 *traed*, 3 traigan., 2 no traigais.—*Subj, Pres.* 1 traiga, 2 traigas, 3 traiga, etc.—*Imperf. 1st term.* 1 trajera, 2 trajeras. 3 trajera: 1 trajéramos, 2 trajerais,

3 trajeran.—*Conditional.* 1 *traería, etc.*—*2d term.* 1 trajese, 2 trajeses, 3 trajese, etc.—*Fut.* 1 trajere, 2 trajeres, 3 trajere: 1 trajéremos, 2 trajereis, 3 trajeron.

VALER, *to be worth*. Cl. VI.

I ndic. Pres. 1 valgo, 2 *vales*, etc.: 1 *valemos*, etc.—*Fut.* 1 valdré, 2 valdrás, 3 valdrá: 1 valdremos. 2 valdréis, 3 valdrán.—*Imper.* 2 *vale*, 3 valga, 2 no valgas, etc., 2 no valgáis.—*Subj. pres.* 1 valga, 2 valgas, 3 valga: 1 valgamos, 2 valgáis, 3 valgan.—*Imperf 1st term.* 1 *valiera, etc.*—*Conditional.* 1 valdría, 2 valdrías, 3 valdría: 1 valdríamos, 2 valdríais 3 valdrían.—*3d term.* 1 *valiese—*, 2 valieses etc.

VENIR, *to come*. Cl. VI.

Gerund. Viniendo. *Past participle*. Venido.

Indic. Pres. 1 vengo, 2 vienes, 3 viene, V. viene. 1 *venimos*, 2 *venís*, 3 vienen.—*Pret.* 1 vine, 2 *viniste*, 3 vino: 1 *vinimos*, 2 *vinisteis*, 3 vinieron.—*Fut.* 1 vendré, 2 vendrás, 3 vendrá: 1 vendremos, 2 vendréis, 3 vendrán.—*Imper.* 2 ven tú, 3 venga él, 2 no vengas: 1 vengamos, 2 *venid*, 3 vengan, 2 no vengais.—*Sub. Pres.* 1 venga, 2 vengas, 3 venga: 1 vengamos, 2 vengáis, 3 vengan.—*Imperf. 1st term.* 1 viniera, 2 vinieras, 3 viniera: 1 viniéramos, 2 vinierais, 3 vinieran.—*Conditional.* 1 vendría, 2 vendrías. 3 vendría, V. vendría: 1 vendríamos, 2 vendríais, 3 vendrían.—*2d term.* 1 viniese, 2 vinieses, 3 viniese V. viniese: 1 viniésemos, 2 vinieseis, 3 viniesen.

VER, *to see*. C1. VI.

Gerund. Viendo. *Past participle*. Visto.

Indic. Pres. 1 Veo, 2 *ves* 3 *ve*: 1 *vemos*, 2 *veis*, 3 *ven*—*Imperf.* 1 veía, 2 veías, 3 veía: 1 veíamos, 3 veíais, 3 veían.—*Pret.* 1 *Vi*, 2 viste, 3 vió: 1 *vimos*, 2 *visteis*, 3 vieron.—*Fut.* 1 veré, 2 verás, 3 verá, etc.—*Imper.* 2 ve tú, 3 vea él., 2 no veas: 1 veamos, 2 *ved*, 3 vean, 2 no veáis.—*Subj. Pres.* 1 vea, 2 veas, 3 vea, V. vea: 1 veamos, 2 veáis, 3 vean.—*Imperf. 1d term.* 1 *viera*, 2 *vieras*, etc.—*Conditional.* 1 *vería*, 2 *verías*, etc.—*2d term.* 1 *viese*, 2 *vieses*, etc.

Impersonal Verbs.

Impersonal verbs are those which are conjugated in the third person singular of each tense only, without expressing the nominative, as:

GRANIZAR, *to hail.*

-It hails *graniza* -It has hailed *ha granizado*

-It had hailed *había granizado*

-It hailed *granizaba, granizó*

-It will have hailed *habrá granizado*

-It will hail *granizará* -It may have hailed *quizá haya granizado*

-Let it hail *granice*

-It may hail *quizá granice*

-If it hailed, *granizara* -If it had hailed *hubiera granizado*

-If it would hail *granizaría* -It would have hailed *habría granizado*

The following are some of the impersonal verbs:

-To freeze *helar*, irr. -To lighten *relampaguear*

-To frost *escarchar* -To thunder *tronar, irr.*

-To thaw *deshelar* -To rain *llover*

-To drizzle *lloviznar* -To happen *suceder, acaecer, acontecer.*

-To snow *nevar* -To dawn *amanecer*

-To be cold *hacer frío* -To become night *anochecer*

Defective Verbs.

SOLER, *to accustom*. Cl. II.

This verb is used only in the two following tenses:

Indic. Pres. 1 suelo, 2 sueles, 3 suele, 2 Vd. suele: 1 *solemos*; 2 *soléis*, 3 suelen.—*Imperf.* 1 *solía*, 2 *solías*, 3 *solía*: 1 *solíamos*, 2 *solíais*, 3 *solían*.

PLACER, *to please*. Cl. III.

This verb is used only in the third person singular or plural, in the moods and tenses as follows: it is always accompanied by a personal pronoun in the objective case.

Indic. Pres. 1 *me* place, 2 *te* place, 3 *le* place, 2 *le* place a Vd.: 1 *nos* place, 2 *os* place, 3 *les* place. 2 *les* place a Vds.; *or* 1 me placen, 2 *te* placen, etc. —*Imperf.* 1 *me* placía, *or* placían, 2 *te* placía, *or* placían, etc.—*Pret.* 1 *me* plugo, 2 *te* plugo, etc.: 1 *me* pluguieron. 2 te pluguieron, etc.-*Subj. Pres.* 1 me plegue, etc.-*Imperf. 1st there.* me pluguiera, etc.-*2d term. Me* pluguiese. etc.

ROER, *to gnaw*. Cl. VI.

Indic. Pres. 1 roo, roigo, royo, 2 roes, 3 roe: 1 roemos, 2 roéis, 3 roen.—*Subj. Pres.* 1 roa, roiga, roya, 2 roes, roigas, royas, 3 roe, roiga, roya: 1 roamos, roigamos, royamos, 2 roáis, roigáis, royáis, 3 roan, roigan, royan.

Remark.—Corroer, to *corrode*, makes corroe, corroen, in the present indicative, and corroa, corroan, in the subjunctive.

A LIST OF ALL THE IRREGUALAR VERBS.

Obs. 1. The compound verbs are not inserted, when they have the same irregularity as the simple ones from which they are derived: as, *componer, contraponer*, etc., which are conjugated like *poner.*

For the convenience of the learner the strictness of this principle has been departed from in the two cases following: 1st. When the simple is no longer used by itself. To this list belong these nine: *cluir* (Cl. V), *cordar* (Cl. I), *ducir* (Cl. III), *manecer* (Cl. III), *stituir* (Cl. V), *tribuir* (Cl. V), *vertir* (Cl. I), *blandecer, bravecer* (Cl. III). 2d. Some compounds of *ad* (reduce to *a*) have been included, such as *asonar, atender,* and *asentir.*

On the other hand, compounds from nominal roots, as *enflaquecer, florecer*, have been inserted.

Obs. 2. The most general irregularities of the Spanish verbs consist in their taking *i, j, y*, or *ue,* or *i*, instead of *o*, or *e*. To find the infinitive mode of such verbs, separate the regular termination, and omit the letter or letters that do not belong to the radicals of such verbs: as in *comienzo, muestras, sintió, condujeron, trajeran, construyesen*, the terminations are *o, as, ió, eron, eran, esen.* The remaining letters are, *comienz, muestr, sint, conduj, tray, construy.* Add to these the regular terminations of the infinitive mode, and they will read *comienzar, muestrar, sintir, condujir, trajer, construyir.* Take off the *i, j*, and *y*, change *ue* into *o*, and the *i* into *e*; and a *c* before the termination to those in *ij* or *uj*; and they will be *comenzar, mostrar, sentir, conducir, traer, construir.*

Obs. 3. The irregular participles are set in italics after their verbs.

The verbs of the first column are conjugated like those of the second, which must be consulted in their respective places.

Cl.	
	Aferrar, I
Abastecer, III	Afluir, V
Aborrecer III	Aforar, II
Abrir, reg.	Agradecer, III
Abierto.	Alborecer, III
Abstenerse, VI	Alentar, I
(Abs)traer. VI	Aliquebrar, I
Abstracto and	Almorzar, II
Abstraído.	Amarillecer, III
Acaecer, III	Amoblar, II
Acertar, I	Amolar, II
Acollar, II	Andar, VI
Acontecer, III	Anochecer, III
Acordar, II	Apacentar, I
Acostar, II	Aparecer, III
Acrecentar, I	Apernar, I
Acrecer, III	Apetecer, III
(Ad)herir, I	Apostar, II
Adolecer, III	Apretar, I
Adormecer, III	Aprobar, II
Adquirir, I	Arrecirse, IV
Advertir, I	Arrendar, I
Aducir, III	Arrepentirse, I

Ascender, I
Asentar, I
Asentir, I
Aserrar, I
Asir, VI
Asolar, II
Asoldar, II
Asonar, II
Asosegar, I
Atender, I
Atento and
Atendido.
(A)tentar, I
Aterirse, I
Atestar, (rellenar) I
(A)traer, VI
Atravesar, I
Atribuir, V
(A)tronar, II
Avanecerse, III
(A)venir, VI
Aventar(se), I
Avergonzar, II
Azolar, II
Bendecir, VI
Bendito and
Bendecido.
Bienquerer, VI
Blanquecer, III
Caber, VI
Caer, VI
Calentar, I
Canecer, III
Carecer, III
Cegar, I
Ceñir, IV
Cerrar, I
Cimentar, I
Clarecer, III
Clocar, II
Cocer, II
Colar, II
Colgar, II
Comedirse, IV
Comenzar, Y
Competir, IV
Complacer, III

Concebir, IV
Concernir, I
Concertar, I
Concluir, V
Concluso and
Concluído.
Concordar, II
Condescender, I
Condolerse, II
Conducir, III
Conferir, I
Confesar, I
Confluir, V
Conocer, III
Conseguir, IV
Consentir, I
Consolar, II
Constituir, V
Construir, V
Contar, II
(Con)tener, VI
Contribuir, V
Controvertir, I
Convalecer, III
Convertir, I
Converso and
Convertido.
Corregir, IV
Correcto and
Corregido.
Costar II
Crecer III
Cubrir, reg.
Cubierto.
Dar, VI
Decentar, I
Decir, VI
Dicho.
Deducir, III
Defender, I
Deferir, I
Degollar, II
Demoler, II
Demostrar, II
Denegar, I
Denostar, II
Dentar, I
Derrengar, I

Derretir, IV
Derrocar, II
Derruir, V
Desbastecer, III
Desbravecer, III
Descaecer, III
Descender, I
Descollar, II
Descordar, II
Descornar, II
Describir, reg.
Descrito, or
descripto.
Desertar, I
Desflocar, II
Desherbar, I
Deshombre- ü III
cerse
Desleír, IV
Desmembrar, I
Desolar, II
Desollar, II
Desosar, II
Desovar, II
Despernar, I
Despertar, I
Despierto and
Despertado.
Desterrar, I
Destruir, V
Desvergon
zarse, II
Diferir, I
Digerir, I
Diluir, V
Discernir, I
Discordar, II
Disminuir, V
Disolver, II
Dispertar, I
Dispierto and
Dispertado.
Distribuir, V
Divertir, I
Cl.
Doler, II
Dormir, II
Educir, III

Elegir, IV
Electo and
Elegido.
Embarbecer, III
Embebecer(se), III
Embellecer, III
Embermejecer, III
Embestir, IV
Emblandecer, III
Embobecer, III
Embosquecer, III
Embravecer, III
Embrutecer, III
Emparentar, I
Empecer, III
Empederne- III
cerse
Empedernir, IV
Empedrar, I
Empellar, I
Empequeñecer, III
Empezar, I
Emplastecer, III
Emplumecer, III
Empobrecer, III
Empodrecer, III
Emporcar, II
Enaltecer, III
Enardecer, III
Encabellecerse, III
Encalvecer, III
Encallecer, III
Encandecer, III
Encarecer, III
Encender, I
Encentar I
Encerrar I
Enloquecer, III
Encomendar, I
Encontrar, II
Encorar II
Encordar, II
Encorecer, III
Encornar, II
Encovar, II
Encrudecer, III
Encruele- III
cer(se),

Encubertar, I	Entontecer III	Guarecer(se), III	Languidecer, III
Endentecer, III	Eutonpecer III	Guarnecer, III	Leer, IV
Endurecer, III	Entortar, II	Haber (see	Liquefacer, *V*. VI
Enfierecer(se), III	Entristecer, III	auxiliary VI	Lobreguecer, III
Enflaquecer, III	Entullecer, III	verbs),	Lucir, III
Enfranquecer, III	Entumecer III	Hacendar, I	Luir, V
Enfurecer, III	Envanecer III	Hacer, VI	Llover, II
Engorar, II	Envejecer, III	*Hecho.*	(Mal)decir, VI
Engrandecer, III	(En)verdecer III	Heder, I	*Maldito* and
Engreírse, IV	Envestir, IV	Helar, I	Maldecido.
Engrosar, II	Envilecer, III	Henchir, IV	Manifestar, I
Engrumecer- III	Erguir, I or IV	Hender, I	*Manifiesto* and
(se)	Errar, I	Heñir, IV	Manifestado.
Enloquecer, III	Escandecer, III	Herbar, I	(Man)tener, VI
Enmarecer, III	Escarmentar, I	Herbecer, III	Mecer, III
Enmarillecer- III	Escarnecer, III	Herir, I	Medir(se), IV
(se)	Esclarecer, III	Herrar, I	Melar, I
Enmelar, I	Escocer II	Hervir, I	Mentar, I
Enmendar, I	Escribir, reg.	Holgar II	Mentir, I
(En)mohecer, III	*Escrito.*	Hollar II	Merecer, III
Enmollecer III	Esforzar, II	Huir, V	Merendar, I
Enmudecer III	Establecer, III	Humedecer, III	Mohecer, III
Ennoblecer, III	*Estar* (see the	Imbuir, V	Moler, II
Ennudecer, III	auxiliary VI	Imprimir, reg.	Morder, II
Enorgullecer- III	verbs),	*Impreso.*	Morir, II
(se)	Estremecer(se), III	Incensar, I	*Muerto.*
Enrarecer. III	Estreñir, IV	Incluir, V	Mostrar, II
Enriquecer, III	Excluir, V	*Incluso* and	Mover, II
Enrobustecer, III	*Excluso* and	Incluído.	Nacer, III
Enrodar, II	Excluído.	Inducir, III	*Nato* and Nacido.
Enrojecer, III	Expedir, IV	Inferir, I	Negar, I
Enronquecer, III	Extender, I	Infernar, I	Negrecer, III
Enroñecer, III	*Extreso* and	Ingerir, I	Nevar, I
Enrudecer, III	Extendido.	*Ingerto* and	Obedecer, III
Enruinecerse, III	Fallecer, III	Ingerido.	Obscurecer, III
Ensalmorar II	Favorecer, III	Ingerir(se), I	Obstruir, V
Ensandecer III	Ferrar, I	Cl.	Ofrecer, III
Ensangrentar, I	Florecer, III	Inquirir, I	Oír, VI
Ensarnecer, III	Fluir, V	Instituir, V	Oler, II
Ensoberbecer, III	Follar, II	Instruir, V	Oponer, VI
Cl.	Fortalecer, III	Introducir, III	Oscurecer, III
Ensordecer, III	Forzar II	Invernar, I	Pacer, III
Entallecer, III	Fregar I	Invertir, I	Padecer, III
Entender, I	Freír, IV	*Inverso* and	Palidecer, III
Entenebrecer, III	*Frito*	Invertido.	Parecer(se), III
Enternecer(se), III	Frutecer, III	Investir, IV	Pedir, IV
Enterrar, I	Gemir, IV	Ir, irse, VI	Pensar, I
Entesar, I	Gobernar, I	Jugar, II	Perder, I

Perecer, III

Permanecer, III

Pertenecer, III

Pervertir, I

Pimpollecer, III

Placer (def.), III

Plastecer, III

Plegar, I

Poblar, II

Poder, VI

Podrecer, III

Podrir, VI

Poner, VI

Puesto.

Poseer, IV

Poseso and

Poseído.

Preferir, I

Prescribir, reg.

Prescripto.

Prevalecer, III

Probar, II

Producir, III

Proferir, I

Proscribir, reg.

Proscripto.

Prostituir, V

Proveer, IV

Provisto and

Proveído.

Quebrar, I

Querer, VI

Raer (def.), VI

Reblandecer, III

Recordar, II

Recostar, II

Recrudecer, III

Reducir, III

Referir, I

Regar, I

Regimentar, I

Regir IV

Regoldar, I

Reír, IV

Rejuvenecer, III

Relentecer, III

Remanecer, III

Remendar, I

Rendir, IV

Renovar, II

Reñir, IV

Repetir, IV

Requebrar, I

Requerir, I

Rescontrar, II

Resollar. II

Resplandecer, III

Restablecer, III

Restituir, V

Restregar, I

Retentar, I

Retoñecer, III

Retribuir, V

Revejecer, III

Reventar, I

Reverdecer, III

Revolcar, II

Robustecer, III

Rodar II

Roer (def.), VI

Rogar, II

Saber, VI

Salir VI

Salpimentar, I

Sarmentar, I

Satisfacer, V

Seducir, V

Segar, I

Seguir, IV

Sembrar, I

Sementar, I

Sentar(se), I

Sentir(se), I

Ser (see auxiliary verbs) VI

Serrar, I

Servir(se), IV

Sofreír, V. REIR IV

Sofrito

Solar, II

Soldar, II

Soler (ref.) II

Soltar, II

Suelto and Soltado.

Solver, II

Suelto

Sonar, II

Soñar, II

Sonreír, *V*. REÍR IV

Sosegar, I

Sugerir, I

Tallecer, III

Temblar I

Tender, I

Tener, VI

Tentar, I

Teñir, IV

Tinto and Teñido

Torcer, II

Tuerto and torcido

Tostar, II

Traducir, III

Traer, VI

Trascender, I

Trascordarse, II

Trasegar, I

Travesar, I

Trocar, II

Tronar, II

Tropezar, I

Tumefacerse, VI

Tumefacto.

Valer(se), VI

Venir, VI

Ventar, I

Ver, VI

Visto.

Verdecer, III

Vertir, I

Vestir, IV

Volar, II

Volcar, II

Volver, II

Vuelto.

Yacer, III

Zaherir, Y

THE REFLEXIVE PRONOUNS

Subject After a preposition Reflexive

yo conmigo me

tú contigo te

él consigo se

ella consigo se

ello ello se

nosotros, nosotros, nos

vosotros, vosotros, os

ellos, ellas ellos, ellas se

We talk about reflexive pronouns when the action of the verb is referred to the subject. The position of the reflexives is the same as those of the complements.

* **Me** he comprado un coche.

* La mujer **se** puso el sombrero.

* Los niños **se** compraron helados.

Placing of the reflexive pronoun:

a) With the INFINITIVE, the GERUND, and the afirmative IMPERATIVE they always go after and together.

* Cálla**te** y no hables.

* Lo mejor es callar**nos.**

* Estaban bañándo**se** en la playa.

b) With nos and os in the first person and the second person of the imperative plural, the verb loses its final **s** and **d** respectively before the pronouns.

* sentémos - sentémonos.

* sentad - sentaos.

If **me** or **te** come together with **se**, the last is always placed in the first place.

* Se **me** ha caído el libro.

* Se **te** ha roto el vestido.

2. It also expresses an idea of reciprocity:

* Mis padres **se** quieren. (each other)

* Ella y yo **nos** encontramos a la puerta del cine.

* Vosotros **os** odiáis.

3. The impersonal **se**:

* Se han hecho muchas averiguaciones.

* Se obtienen buenos resultados.

b) It is also called "the impersonal voice". **Se** + verb in the 3ª person in singular.

* Se cree que no vendrá.

* Se habla mucho de él.

* Se trabaja poco en esta empresa.

* Se espera que venga pronto.

PRONOUNS AND DEMONSTRATIVE ADJECTIVES

1. The demonstrative adjective accompanies the noun and agrees with the gender and the person (it has not accent).

* **Este** hombre. * **Esa** mujer. * **Esos** niños.

2. The demonstratives point out the relation of proximity between the object which is referred and the different participants of the dialogue.

It can be about the different kinds of proximity.

a) **Este, esta, esto, estos, estas** serve to express the proximity of the object which is referred.

* **Este** vaso que tengo en la mano.

* **Estos** periódicos que estoy leyendo.

b) Ese, esa, eso, esos, esas express a medium grade between proximity and distance according to the person who speaks.

* **Esa** revista que estás leyendo.

* **Esas** casas de enfrente.

c) **Aquel, aquella, aquello, aquellos, aquellas** indicate a certain distance according to the person who speaks.

* **Aquellos** árboles en la colina.

* **Aquellas** casas al otro lado del río.

3. There can be proximity or distance in the time:

* **Aquellas** vacaciones fueron más divertidas que **éstas.**

* **Aquel** año fue más seco que **éste.**

It can also be referred to the order of the sentence.

* Tuvieron dos hijos y una hija: **ésta** se casó, **aquéllos** trabajaron con su padre.

* Tenemos dos perros y un gato. **Éste** es muy independiente, **aquellos** son my cariñosos.

THE RELATIVE PRONOUN

The relative pronoun which:

Is invariable for masculine and feminine, singular and plural. It can be subject and direct complement.

Subject direct complement

Tengo un amigo **que** vive en París **que** no conoces todavía.

Jon tenía una hermana **que** estudiaba **que** tú no conocías.

Tengo un libro **que** es divertido **que** tú no has leído.

Vi una película **que** era aburrida **que** tú no has visto todavía.

Ella rompió un jarrón **que** era carísimo **que** yo todavía no había pagado.

Tengo un primo **que** vive en Nueva York **que** tú no has visto nunca.

The relative pronoun QUIEN/QUE as circumstantial complement (with preposition).

Persons Things

La chica **con la que** comparto la habitación es estudiante.

con quien

El chico **con el que** salgo es muy simpático.

con quien

La gente **para la que** trabajo es muy honrada.

para quien

El hombre **del que** te hablé está aquí.

de quien

Cosas

El edificio **en el que** vivimos es muy viejo.

La pluma **con la que** te escribo es un regalo tuyo.

La playa **desde la que** te mando la postal es muy bonita.

El examen **para el que** me estoy preparando es muy difícil.

El lugar **en el que** nos encontramos es maravilloso.

The antecedent

The antecedent is the word to which the relative is referred.

It can be:

A substantive:

* Ganó **el atleta que** estaba mejor preparado.

A pronoun:

* ¿ Y te preocupas por **ella, que** tanto daño te ha hecho?

An adjective:

* Es alto como un pino.

An adverb:

* Vete **ahora que** no hay nadie.

A whole sentence:

* **Era muy desdichada**, por lo **que** pensaba suicidarse.

SER

Present

Yo soy

Tú eres

Él /Ella / Usted es

Nos. somos

Vos. sois

Ellos /Ustedes son

a) In Spanish there is an obvious difference between the verbs **ser** and **estar.** Many students of the language find this difference dificult to see.

La mesa **es** redonda.

La habitación **es** grande.

Nuestra casa **es** vieja, pero **es** muy grande.

Estos chicos **son** muy simpáticos.

Mis zapatos **son** negros.

Pedro **es** alto, pero su hermana **es** baja.

If you see all these sentences, all of them show how the objects are. There is a description. A quality is pointed out.

---

b) The verb **ser** shows origin.

- Yo **soy** de España.

- Mi amigo **es** de Suiza.

- Este mármol **es** de Italia.

- Esa porcelana **es** de China.

c) When we talk about time we always use the verb **ser.**

- Hoy **es** lunes, 5 de marzo.

- Todavía **es** verano.

- ¿ Qué hora **es? Son** las dos.

- " ¡**Es** muy tarde!" " ¡No, todavía **es** pronto!

d) The verb **ser** always shows possession.

- Ese coche **es** de mi hermano.

- Esa **es** la casa de mi tío.

- Esos **son** los libros de mi amigo.

e) The professions and jobs are used with the verb **ser.**

- Mi padre **es** médico.

- Este hombre **es** carpintero.

- Nosotros **somos** estudiantes.

- Esos hombres **son** jugadores de fútbol.

ESTAR

Present

Yo estoy	Nos. estamos
Tú estás	Vos. estáis
Él / Ella / Usted esá	Ellos / Ustedes están

a) Situation and place.

Learn the following sentences:

Madrid **está** en el centro de España.

Los vasos **están** en la mesa.

El árbol **está** en el jardin.

Los niños **están** en el parque.

Tus zapatos **están** debajo de la cama.

All these sentences show a **situation or place** in which something or someone is. All of them answer the question **¿dónde? ¿Dónde está Madrid? ¿Dónde están los vasos?** etc.

---

b) Physical State

The verb **estar** denotes a physical state or a mind state.

Have a look at these examples.

-Mi madre **está** enfadada.

-Mi hermano siempre **está** alegre.

-La habitación **está** desordenada.

-La mesa **está** sucia.

-Pedro **está** enfermo.

-Hoy **estoy** muy nervioso.

All these sentences would answer the question **¿cómo está? ¿cómo se siente?**

c) Tense (estar a, estar en)

We normally use **estar a** with dates and days of the week. **Estar en** is also used with months and seasons.

- Todavía **estamos en** Febrero.

- **Estamos a** 5 de abril de 1999.

- Ya **estamos en** invierno.

- Hoy **estamos a** viernes, 10 de junio.

If the sentence is negative we put the negative but **not** before the verb.

- La taza **no está** en la mesa.

- Burdeos **no está** en España.

If the sentence is interrogative the order is changed subject-verb, verb-subject.

- Juanita está en el parque. - ¿Está Juanita en el parque?

THE ADJECTIVE

a) In Spanish the adjective is changeable; it agrees in gender and number with the noun.

- mesa **blanca**. - muro **pequeño**.

- puerta **pequeña**. - pasillo **largo**.

The adjective is normally placed after the substantive to which qualifies. It is called then qualifying adjective and it is used to describe the substantive.

- Es un hombre **alto**. - Es una mujer **alta**.

- Son unos hombres **altos**. - Son unas mujeres **altas**.

- Es un chico **listo**. - Es una chica **lista**.

b) However, the adjectives which don't describe but limit they are normally placed **before** the substantive. This category includes the ordinal numbers (once jugadores), quantity adjectives such as mucho, poco, demasiado, tanto, varios, cuanto, cada, demás, otro, tal; and the demonstrative and possessive adjectives.

- Esto es **demasiado** caro.

- Eso es **poco** educativo.

- Dame **otro** helado.

- **Cada** persona es un mundo.

c) The **predicative** adjectives change the substantive in an indirect way, so they go together by means of a verb.

- La casa es **grande**. - Ese libro parece **interesante**.

- Esos chicos son **listos**. - Esas chicas son **altas**.

d) A few adjectives don't change the gender, but they change the number.

- Ese chico es **inteligente**. - Esa chica es **inteligente**.

- Un hombre **hipócrita**. - Una mujer **hipócrita**.

- Esos chicos son **inteligentes**.

- Esos hombres son **hipócritas**.

Other similar adjectives are: grande, indígena, cosmopolita, probable, independiente, árabe, veloz, verde, azul, gris, peor, fenomenal, espectacular, etc.

To know if they are masculine or singular we must refer to the noun or to the article which goes with it.

- Un caballo veloz. - Una yegua veloz.

- Un lío fenomenal. - Una actuación fenomenal.

- El cielo gris. - La nube gris.

e) The following adjectives normally go before the noun: bueno, malo, joven, viejo, pequeño, hermoso, although this not a fixed rule. In general, if the adjective goes before the substantive, the emphasis goes in the substantive.

Some adjectives, when they go before, they apocopate in the singular masculine, it gets shorter (bueno - buen; malo - mal; alguno - algún; ninguno - ningún; primero - primer; tercero - tercer; cualquiera - cualquier).

- Un buen **libro**. - Una buena **revista**.

If the adjective is placed after the substantive is given more emphasis to the adjective.

- Un comienzo **bueno**. - Un libro **malo**.

Generally we give more emphasis with the word **muy**.

- Es un libro **muy bueno**. - Es una revista **muy mala**.

A Key to the Pronunciation as Represented in This Dictionary.

SPANISH ALPHABET.

Give to the vowel the sound that the syllable that follow it in *italics* has in English; and sound also, as in English, each of the syllables that represent said sound throughout all the dictionary.

VOWELS.

Pronounce a, *ah*; e, *ay*; i, *ee*; o, *oh*, u, *u* (in *bull*); y, *ee*.

The vowels have invariably the same sound, and must be fully and distinctly pronounced. The *u* is silent in the syllables *gue, gui, que, qui,* which are pronounced *gay, gee, kay, kee*: when the *u* is to be sounded, it is marked thus, *ü*, as in *argüir* (ar-goo-eer).

CONSONANTS.

b, bay.	f, *ai'fay,*	l, *ai'lay,*	ñ, *ai'nyay,*	s, *es'say,*	y griega *or* ye, *jay,*
c, *thay,*	g, *hay,* ll,	*ai'lyay,*	p, *pay,*	t, *tay,*	z, *thai tah.*
ch, *tchay,*	h, *ah'tchay,*	m, *ai'may,*	q, *coo,*	v, *vay,*	
d, *day,*	j, *hoe'tah,*	n, *ai'nay,*	r, *eráy, er'ray,*	x, *ay'kiss,*	

N. B. The *z* and the *c* (when the latter precedes *e* and *i*) are marked in this Dictionary to be pronounced as the English *th* in *thought*, which is the Castilian pronunciation. However, throughout Latin America they have the regular sound of *s*.

EXPLANATION OF THE ABBREVIATIONS.

a....................article.	Dim. ....Diminutive.	Myth. ....Mythology.
Acad. ....Academy.	Divin. ....Divinity.	n. ....neuter.
adv...................adverb.	Ec. ....Ecuador.	Naut. ....Nautical.
Aer. ....Aerial.	Elec. ....Electricity.	Neol. ....Neologism.
Agr. ....Agriculture.	Ent. ....Entomology.	Obs. ....Obsolete.
Am..........Ante Meridian.	Esp. ....Especially	Opt. ....Optics.
Amer ....America.	etc. ....etcetera.	Orn. ....Ormithology.
Anat................Anatomy.	f. ....feminine.	pa. ....present participle.
And...................Andes.	Fig. ....Figurative.	Per. ....Persia.
Andal..............Andalucía.	Geog. ....Geography.	Phil. ....Philosophy.
Ant...................Antique.	Geol................Geology.	Phy. ....Physics.
Arab....................Arab.	Geom...............Geometry.	pl.....................plural.
Arch. ....Architecture.	gr........................gram.	Poet. ....Poetry.
Argen. ....Argentina.	Gram. ....Grammar.	Pol. ....Poland.
Arith. ....Arithmetic.	Her. ....Heraldy.	poss. ....possessive.
Art......................Art.	imp.........imperfect; imperative	pp. ....past participle.
Astro. ....Astronomy.	impers. ....impersonal.	prep. ....preposition.
Aug. ....August.	Inc...................Inclusive.	Print. ....Printing.
aug. ....augmentative.	int. ....interrogative.	pron. ....pronoun.
Aut...................Automate.	Ir. ....Ireland.	Prov. ....Province; Provincial.
Biol. ....Biology.	irr. ....irregular.	Rhet. ....Rhetoric.
Bol. ....Bolivia.	LAm. ....Latin America.	sing. ....singular.
Bot. ....Botany.	Lat. ....Latin.	sup. ....superlative.
Calif................California.	Log. ....Logarithm.	Surg. ....Surgery.
CAm...........Central America.	lux. ....luxury.	Theol. ....Theology.
Carib...............Caribbean.	m. ....masculine.	Typ. ....Typography.
Cf. ....Confer.	Math. ....Mathematics.	Univ. ....Universe.
Col. ....Colombia.	Mech. ....Mechanic.	V. ....Verbe.
Coll................Colloquial.	Med. ....Medical.	va. ....verb active (transitive).
Com..............Commerce.	Met. ....Metaphorical.	Vet. ....Veterinary.
Comput............Computer.	Mex. ....Mexico.	vn. ....verb neuter.
conj................conjunction.	Mil. ....Military.	vr. ....verb reflexive.
Culin. ....Culinary.	Min. ....Minerology.	Vulg. ....Vulgarism.
Chem. ....Chemistry.	Miner. ....Mineral.	Zool. ....Zoology.
defect................defective.	Mus. ....Music.	

A

a [ah], First letter of the Spanish alphabet. It is pronounced as the **a** in **alarm**.

a, *prep.* **to, in, at**, according to, on, by, for, and of; as **voy a Madrid**, I am going to Madrid. **A la inglesa**, the English way. **A oriente**, to the east. **Jugar a los naipes**, to play cards. **A las ocho**, at eight o'clock. **Vino a pie**, he came on foot. **Quien a hierro mata a hierro muere**, he who lives by the sword, dies by the sword. **Dos a dos**, two by two. **¿A cómo sale el kilo? A diez pesos**, how much a kilo? Ten pesos. **Este vaso huele a vino**, this glass smells of wine. *V.* REAL. -A coalesces with the masculine article **el**, forming **al: Al rey**, to the king. **Al papa**, to the pope. This masculine article is also used before the infinitive form of verbs taken substantively: **Al amanecer**, at the break of day. **Al ir yo allá**, when I was going there. -A is equivalent to the limit or end of any place or time. **Pagaré a su debido tiempo**, I will pay in due course. **Desde aquí a San Juan**, from here to St. John. **Me llegaba el agua a la cintura**, the water was up to my waist. -A sometimes signifies the motive or reason: **A instancia de la ciudad**, at the request of the city. **¿A qué propósito?**, to what purpose? -It also serves to express distributive numbers: **A perdiz por barba**, a partridge a head. -Before the infinitive form, and at the beginning of a sentence, it sometimes has a conditional sense: **A decir verdad**, to tell the truth. -This preposition governs almost all parts of speech, whether nouns, adjectives, pronouns, or verbs: **A los hombres**, to men. **De mal en peor**, from bad to worse. **A mí, a ti, a vosotros**, to me, to you. **A jugar**, to play. **Vamos a pasear**, let's go for a walk. -It points out the person in whom the action of the verb terminates, and then is placed before the accusative or objective case, as **Amo a Pedro**, I love Peter. -A is still used in some phrases instead of **por, en, sin, para**, and **la**; and in obsolete writings for **con** and **de**. - In composition it serves to convert substantives and adjectives into verbs, as **abocar** from **boca, ablandar** from **blando**. Formerly it was prefixed to many words, as **abajar, amatar, etc.**; but being redundant, these words are now written **bajar, matar, etc.** -A is frequently used adverbially, as **A deshora**, unseasonably. **A diferencia de esto**, contrary to this. **A consecuencia de eso**, in consequence to that. **A decir verdad**, to tell the truth. **Al menos**, at least. **A sabiendas**, knowingly. **A veces**, sometimes. **A ojos vistas**, plainly, publicly; barefacedly. **A cuestas**, on the shoulders. **A escondidas**, privately, in a secret manner. **A prueba de bomba**, bomb-proof. -A denotes the number, price, rate, manner of action, instrument, height, depth, etc., as, **El gasto asciende a cien pesos**, the expense amounts to a hundred pesos. **Se hizo el seguro a tres por ciento**, the insurance was taken out at three per cent. **El azúcar se vende a tres pesos la libra**, sugar is sold at three pesos a pound. **Él se viste a la española**, he dresses after the Spanish fashion. **Pasaron el río con el agua a la cintura**, they crossed the river up to their waists in water. **No le llega el vestido a la rodilla**, her dress does not reach her knees. **A fe de hombre de bien**, on the faith of an honest man.

AA [ah-ah], contraction for *Aerolíneas Argentinas*.

aba [ah'-bah], *m.* 1. A woollen fabric, manufactured in the East. 2. Patriarch of Alexandria in older times.

ababa [ah-bah'-bah], *f.* Red poppy. *V.* AMAPOLA.

abacá [ah-bah-cah'], *m.* Abaca, Manila, hemp, inner fiber of a plant of the banana family, a native of the Philippine Islands.

abacería [ah-bah-thay-ree'-ah], *f.* A shop where oil, vinegar, etc., are sold. Grocery.

abacero, ra [ah-bah-thay'-ro, rah], *m. & f.* A retailer of provisions, oil, vinegar, etc. Grocer.

abacial [ah-bah-the-ahl'], *a.* Belonging to an abbot.

abaco [ah'-bah-co], *m.* 1. (*Arch.*) Abacus, highest moulding on the capital of a column. 2. Abacus, a calculating frame. 3. (*Miner.*) A washing-trough.

abad [ah-bahd'], *m.* 1. An abbot. 2. In some provinces the rector of a parish. Abbot having almost episcopal jurisdiction.

abada [ah-bah'-dah], *f.* The female rhinoceros.

abadejo [ah-bah-day'-ho], *m.* 1. A codfish, pollack, cod (bacalao). 2. Yellow crested wren (ave). 3. (*Ant.*) Spanish fly, cantharides (insecto).

abandengo, ga [ah-bah-den'-go, gah], *a.* Abbatial, belonging to an abbot. 2. *m.* Abbacy

abadesa [ah-bah-day'-sah], *f.* An abbess.

abadía [ah-bah-dee'-ah], *f.* 1. An abbey (convento). 2. Abbacy (rango). 3. Parsonage, vicarage (vicaría).

abadiado [ah-bah-de-ah'-do], *m.* (*Obs.*) Abbey-lands.

abadir [ah-bah-deer'], *m.* A stone from which ancient man made idols, and to which they attributed marvelous virtues.

abajadero [ah-bah-hah-de rho'], *m.* 1. Slope, incline.

abajamiento [ah-bah-hah-me-en'-to], *m.* (*Obs.*) 1. Dejection, casting down. 2. Abatement.

abajarse [ah-bah-har'-say], *vr.* To abase oneself, to be humbled.

abajeño, ña [ah-bah-hay'-nyo, nyah], *a.* (*Amer.*) A lowlander, coastal dweller. (*Mex.*) (costeño).

abajero [ah-bah-hay'ro], *m.* Cliff, precipice.

abajo [ah-bah'-ho], *adv.* Under, underneath, below. **Venirse abajo**, to fall, to tumble downstairs, (en casa). **¡Abajo el gobierno!**, down with the government! **Aquí abajo**, down here. **Cuesta abajo**, downhill. **Desde abajo**, from below. **El abajo firmante**, the undersigned. **Más abajo**, further down. **Río abajo**, downstream. - *prep.* below, under.

abalado, da [ah-bah-lah'-do, dah], *a.* (*Obs.*) Spongy, soft.

abalanzar [ah-bah-lan-thar'], *va.* 1. To balance. 2. To weigh, to compare. 3. To dart, to impel. -*vr.* 1. To rush on with impetuosity. **Se abalanzaron sobre el enemigo**, they rushed at the enemy 2. To venture. 3. To swoop. **El águila se abalanzó sobre el conejo**, the eagle swooped on the rabbit.

abalaustrado, da [ah-bah-lah-oos-trah'-do, dah], *a.* Balustered. *V.* BALAUSTRADO

abaldonar [ah-bal-d-nar'], *va.* (*Obs.*) 1. To debase, to revile, to undervalue, to reproach. 2 To abandon.

abalear [ah-bah-lay-ar'], *va.* To fan or winnow corn.

abalizar [ah-bah-le-thar'], *va.* (*Naut.*) To lay down buoys.

aballar [ah-bal-lyar'], *va.* (*Obs.*) 1. To strike down. 2. To carry off. 3. To move. 4. (*Ict.*) *V.* REBAJAR

aballestar [ah-bal-lyes-tar'], *m.* 1. A standard-bearer.

abalone [ah-bah-lo'-nay] *m.* A large Californian mollusk.

abalorio [ah-bah-lo'-re-o], *m. pl.* Bugle, glass bead. **No vale un abalorio**, it's worthless.

abaluartar [ah-bah-loo-ahr-tahr'] *va.* To fortify with bastions.

abanderado [ah-bahn-day-rah'-do] *m.* (*Mil.*) Standard-bearer. (*fig.*) Champion (defensor de una causa)

abanderizador, ra [ah-ban-day-re-thah- dor', rah], *m. & f.* A factious person; a ringleader, agitator.

abanderizar [ah-ban-day-re-thar'], *va.* To cabal; to stir up disturbances, to incite to revolution.

abandonado, da [ah-ban-do-nah'-do, dah], *a.* 1. Abandoned, helpless, forlorn, despondent. 2. Abandoned, profligate, graceless. -*pp.* of ABANDONAR.

abandonamiento [ah-ban-do-nah-me- en'-to], *m.* 1. The act of abandoning. 2. Lewdness, debauchery. 3. Forlornness.

abandonar [ah-ban-do-nar'], *va.* 1. To abandon, to leave, to desert, to fling up. **Abandonar la casa de los padres**, to leave home. **Abandonar a los hijos**, to abandon one's children. To forego, to fall from; to fail. 2. To give away, to relinquish. -*vr.* To despond, to despair; to flinch; to give oneself up to. **Abandonarse a la tentación**, to give way to temptation. **Abandonarse al alcohol**, to give oneself over to alcohol.

abandonismo [ah-ban-do-nes-mo] Defeatism.

abandono [ah-ban-do'-no], *m. V.* ABANDONAMIENTO. Abandon.

abanicar [ah-bah-ne-car'], *va.* To fan. *vr.* To fan oneself.

abanico [ah-bah-nee'-co], *m.* 1. A fan. 2. A spritsail. **En abanico**, fan-shaped, like a fan. 3. *(Mil.)* Defensive parapet of wood. 4. *(Naut.)* Derrick, sheers, a machine used for setting up and taking out masts; crane, outrigger, spritsail. 5. *(Phot.)* Screen. 6. *(Arch.)* Winding stairs; semicircular window. 7. *(Miner.)* Ventilator.

abaniquear [ah-bah-ne-kay-ahr] *va.* To fan (dar aire). *-vr.* To fan oneself (darse aire).

abaniquero [ah-bah-ne-kay'-ro], *m.* A fan-maker.

abanto [ah-bahn'-to], *m.* A bird of the vulture species.

abaratar [ah-bah-rah-tar'], *va.* To cheapen, to abate. *-vn.* To fall in price.

abarbetar [ah-bar-bay-tar'], *va. (Naut.)* To rack, to seize; to span, to lash, to jam, to mouse.

abarca [ah-bar'-cah], *f.* Sandal (worn by peasants).

abarcado, da [ah-bar-cah'-do, dah], *a.* Wearing peasant sandals on the feet. *-pp.* of ABARCAR. Embraced, contained.

abarcador, ra [ah-bar-cah-dor', rah], *m. & f.* 1. Embracer, clasper. 2. Monopolist.

abarcar [ah-bar-car'], *va.* 1. To clasp, to embrace, to take in (incluir). 2. To contain, to comprise (contener); to undertake many things at once. 3. To expand (extenderse a). 4. To monopolize goods, to corner (the market in), (monopolizar). **Este capítulo abarca un siglo**, this chapter covers one century. **Quien mucho abarca poco aprieta**, to bite off more than you can chew.

abarquillar [ah-bar-keel-lyar'], *va.* 1. To give a thing the form of a boat, also of a tube. 2. To warp. *vr.* To curl up, to roll up, (arrollarse).

abarrado, da [ah-bar-rah'-do, dah], *a. (Obs.)* Striped, clouded. *V.* BARRADO.

abarraganamiento [ah-bar-rah-gah-nah -me-en'-to]. *m. V.* AMANCEBAMIENTO.

abarraganarse [ah-bar-rah-gah-nar'-say], *vr.* To live in concubinage.

abarrajado, da [ah-bar-rah-hah'-do, dah], *a. (Amer.)* Libertine.

abarrajar [ah-bar-rrah-har], *vn.* To run away, to flee. 1. *-vr.* To fall flat on one's face. 2. To prostitute, to become corrupt (prostituirse).

abarrajo [ah-bah-rrah-ho] *m.* fall, stumble.

abarrancadero [ah-bar-ran-cah-day'-ro], *m.* 1. A deep, heavy road. 2. A precipice, rocky ledge. 3. *(Met.)* Difficult business.

abarrancamiento [ah-bar-ran-cah-me -en'-to], *m.* Act of making or falling into holes or pits; embarrassment.

abarrancar [ah-bar-ran-car'], *va.* To break up a road; to dig holes. *-vr.* 1. To fall into a pit. 2. To become embarrassed. 3. To get stopped up (atascarse).

abarrar [ah-bar-rar'], *va. (Obs.) V.* ACIBARRAR.

abarrisco [ah-bar-rees'-co], *adv. (Obs.)* Indiscriminately, promiscuously.

abarrotar [ah-bar-rotar'], *va.* 1. To put bars on (barrotes). 2. *(Naut.)* To stow the cargo (la carga). 3. To overstock, to cram, to overload (atestar). *(LAm.)* To buy up (acaparar). 4. To be over-plentiful (superabundar).

abarrote [ah-bar-ro'-tay], *m. (Naut.)* Fill-in package. *-pl. (Amer.)* 1. Groceries, provisions (artículos). 2. Grocery store (tienda). 3. Ironmongery (ferretería).

abarrotería [ah-bar-ro-tay-ree'-ah], *f. (Amer.)* Grocery store, general store.

abarrotero, ra [ah-bar-ro-tay'-ro, rah] *m. & f. (Amer.)* Grocer.

abastardarse [ah-bas-tar-dar'-say], *vr.* To degenerate, to vitiate.

abastecedor, ra [ah-bas-tay-thay-dor', rah], *m. & f.* A caterer, provider, purveyor, supplier. *(Amer.)* Butcher (carnicero). *a.* Providing, supplying.

abastecer [ah-bas-tay-therr'], *va.* 1. To provide necessities, to purvey. 2. To supply; **Abastecer un ejército de víveres**, to supply an army with provisions. (*Yo abastezco, abastezca*, from *Abastecer. V.* verbs in *ecer.*)

abastecido, da [ah-bas-tay-the'-do, dah] Supplied, provisioned. **Una ciudad bien abastecida**, a well-stocked city. 2. Stocked; **Un supermercado bien abastecido**, a well-stocked supermarket.

abastecimiento [ah-bas-tay-the-me-en'- to], *m.* 1. Provisioning, supplying (avituallamiento), the act and the effect of providing. 2. Provisions. 3. Supply; **abastecimiento de aguas**, the supply of water.

abastionar [ah-bas-te-o-nar'], *va.* To bastion, to construct bastions.

abasto [ah-bas'-to], *m.* 1. Provisioning, supplying (abastecimiento), the supply of a town with provisions, grist. 2. Abundance, great amount. Small embroideries. *(Amer.)* Slaughterhouse, abattoir. 3. *adv.* Copiously, abundantly.

abatanado, da [ah-bah-tah-nah'-do, dah] *a.* Fulled (paño).

abatanador [ah-bah-tah-nah-dor] *m.* Fuller.

abatanar [ah-bah-tah-nar'], *va.* To beat or full (el paño). 2. *(fig.)* To beat (golpear).

abatatar [ah-bah-tah-tahr] *va. (Amer.) (fam.)* To intimidate, to frighten (asustar).

abate [ah-bah'-tay], *m. (Rel.)* Father. **El abate Pierre**, Father Pierre.

abatí [ah-bah-te] *(Amer.)* Corn; drink distilled from corn (bebida).

abatidamente [ah-bah-tee-dah-men'-tay], *adv.* Dejectedly, heavily; basely.

abatidísimo [ah-bah-te-dee'-se-mo], *a. sup.* Very low-spirited, very dejected.

abatido, da [ah-bah-tee'-do, dah], *a.* 1. Downcast, dejected, spiritless, flat, low, faint, disheartened (desanimado). **Estaba muy abatido por la muerte de su esposa**, he was very depressed by the death of his wife. 2. Abject, mean, base. 3. Drooping. **Párpados abatidos**, drooping eyelids. *-pp.* of ABATIR.

abatimiento [ah-bah-te-me-en'-to], *m.* 1. Discouragement, lowness of spirits, heaviness, faintness, flatness. 2. Humbleness, obscure condition. Abatimiento del rumbo, *(Naut.)* The leeway of a ship.

abatir [ah-bah-teer'], *va.* 1. To throw down, to overthrow, to cut down, to flatten, to fall, to demolish (destruir). **Abatir un edificio**, demolish a building; to fell, to cut down (árbol); to take down (desmontar). **Abatí la tienda de campaña**, I took down the tent; to bring down, to shoot down (pájaro, avión). 2. To humble, to debase, to overwhelm, to lower, to discourage. 3. *(Mech.)* to depress, lower, *-vn.* To descend, to stoop. *-vr.* 1. To be disheartened, to be dismayed; to crouch. 2. *(Naut.)* To have leeway.

abayado [ah-bah-ya-do, da] *a. (Bot.)* Berry-shaped.

abdicación [ab-de-cah-the-on'], *f.* Abdication.

abdicar [ab-de-car'], *va.* 1. To abdicate. **Abdicar de algo**, to renounce something. **Abdicar en uno**, to abdicate in favor of somebody. 2. To revoke, to annul. **Abdicar la corona**, give up the crown.

abdomen [ab-doh'-men], *m.* Abdomen, belly.

abdominal [ab-doh-me-nahl'], *a.* Abdominal.

abducción [ab-dooc-the-on'], *f. (Anat.)* Abduction.

abductor [ab-dooc-tor'], *m. (Anat.)* Abductor, the muscles which draw back several members.

abecé [ab-bay-thay'], *m.* The alphabet. *(fig.)* Rudiments, basic elements.

abecedario [ah-bay-thay-dah'-re-o], *m.* 1. The alphabet. 2. A spelling-book. 3. A table of contents.

abedul [ah-bay-dool'], *m.* The common birch-tree. **Abedul plateado**, silver birch.

abeja [ah-bay'-hah], *f.* A bee. **Abeja reina**, queen-bee. **Abeja machiega**, breeding-bee. **Abeja albañila**, mason-bee. **Abeja obrera**, worker-bee. *(fig.)* Hard worker (hormiguita).

abejar [ah-bay-har'], *m.* A bee-hive. *V.* COLMENAR.

abejar [ah-bay-har'], *m.* **Uva abejar**, a grape of which bees are very fond.

abejarrón, abejorro [ah-bay-har-rone', or ah-bay-hor'-ro], *m.* 1. Bumblebee. *(Acad.)* 2. A large fly.

abejaruco, abejeruco [ah-bay-ha-roo'-co], [ah-bay-hay-roo'-co], *m.* 1. The bee-eater, a bird. 2. *(Met.)* A mean, despicable fellow.

abejera [ah-bay-hay'-rah], *f.* Apiary (colmenar).

abejero [ah-bay-hay'-ro], *m.* 1. A keeper of bee-hives. 2. *V.* ABEJARUCO.

abejica, illa, ita, juela [ah-bay-hee'-cah] *f. dim.* A little bee.

abejón [ah-bay-hone'], *m.* 1. A drone; a hornet; bumble-bee. **Jugar al abejón con uno**, *(coll.)* to make light of one, to mock him. 2. A rustic game of buzzing in and striking the ear. *(CAm.)* to whisper (cuchichear).

abejonazo [ah-bay-ho-nah'-tho], *m.* A large wild bee.

abejoncillo [ah-bay-hon-theel'-lyoh], *m.* dim. A small wild bee, a small drone.

abejonear [ah-bay-ho-nay-ahr'], *(And., Carib.)* 1. *vr. (fig.)* To whisper. 2. *va. (Carib.)* To mumble, to whisper (susurrar).

abejorro [ah-bay-hor'ro], *m. V.* ABEJARRÓN.

abejuno, na [ah-bay-hoo'-no, nah], *a.* Belonging to bees; bee.

abellacado, da [ah-bel-lyah-cah'-do, dah], *a.* Mean-spirited, accustomed to meanness. *-pp.* of ABELLACARSE.

abellacarse [ah-bel-lyah-car'say], *vr.* To become mean; to degrade oneself.

abellar [ah-bel-lyar'], *m. V.* ABEJAR.

abellotado [ah-bel-lyo-tah'-do], *a.* Made in the form of acorns.

abenuz [ah-bay-nooth'], *m. (Obs.)* The ebony-tree. *V.* ÉBANO.

aberengenado, da [ah-bay-ren-hay-nah' -do, dah], *a.* 1. Having the color or form of an eggplant, lilac. 2. Cut slantwise (carpintería).

aberración [ah-ber-rah-the-on'], *f.* 1. *(Astr.)* Aberration. **Es una aberración bañarse cinco veces al día**, it's crazy to have a bath five times a day. 2. *(Med.)* Hallucination, aberration. 3. *(Opt.)* Aberration, divergence of light-rays.

aberrante [ah-bay-rrahn-tay], *a.* Aberrant; (disparatado) crazy, ridiculous.

aberrar [ah-bay-rrahr'], *vn.* To be mistaken, to err.

aberrear [ah-bay-rrahr'], *vn.* To anger, to annoy.

aberrugado, da [ah-ber-roo-gah'-do, dah], *a.* Full of warts, warty.

abertura [ah-ber-too'-rah], *f.* 1. Aperture. 2. Outset, beginning. 3. An opening, chink, crevice, fissure, gap, loophole, a hole, a passage: *(Opt.)* stop. 4. Openness of mind; plain dealing. 5. A leak. 6. *(Mus.)* Overture.

abestiar [ah-bes-te-ar'], *va.* To stupefy.

abetal[ah-bay-tahl'], *m.* A spot covered with silver firs, fir wood.

abete [ah-bay'-tay], *m.* Hook for holding cloth while shearing it. *V.* ABETO.

abeterno [ab-ay-ter'-no] From all eternity.

abetinote, or **abietino** [ah-bay-te-no'-tay, ah-be-ay-te'-no], *m.* Resin which distills from the fir-tree. *V.* ACEITE.

abeto [ah-bay'-to], *m.* Fir, fir tree; the yew-leave fir. **Abeto blanco**, silver fir.

abetunado, da [ah-bay-too-nah'-do, dah], *a.* Resembling bitumen, bituminous; dark-skinned (persona).

abetunar [ah-bay-too-nar'], *va.* To bituminize; to do over with bitumen. To polish, to clean.

abiertamente [ah-be-er-tah-men'-tay], *adv.* Frankly, openly, fairly, plainly.

abierto, ta [ah-be-er'-to, tah], *a.* 1. Open, free, clear. 2. Sincere, candid, open-hearted, generous. 3. Full-blown. *-pp. irr.* of ABRIR. **La puerta está abierta**, the door is open. **Abierta de par en par**, wide open. **Dejar un grifo abierto**, to leave a tap running.

abigarrado, da [ah-be-gar-rah'-do, dah], *a.* Variegated, motley, of many colors, vivid, colorful. *-pp.* of ABIGARRAR.

abigarrar [ah-be-gar-rar'], *va.* To paint with a diversity of colors, without order or union; to fleck.

abigarramiento [ah-be-gah-rrah-me- ayn'-to], *m.* Variegation; many colors; motley coloring, vividness, colorfulness.

abigeato [ah-be-hay-ah'-to], *m. (Law.)* Theft of cattle. Rustling.

abigeo [ah-be-hay'-go], *m. (Law.)* A thief of cattle, rustler.

abigotado, da [ah-be-go-tah'-do, dah], *a.* A person wearing long mustaches.

abihares [ah-be-ah'-res], *m.* 1. Narcissus or daffodil. 2. A Precious stone of the color of the daffodil.

abiltar [a-beel-tar'], *vn.* To depress, to humiliate, to depreciate.

abinicio [ab-e-nee'-the-o] From the beginning.

abintestato [ab-in-tes-tah'-to], *m.* Process of a judge in cases where there is no will.

abiosa [ah-be-oh'-sah], *f.* The boa snake. The boa constrictor.

abiselar [ah-be-say-lar'], *va.* To bevel.

abisinio, a [ah-be-see'-ne-o, ah], *a.* Abyssinian.

abismado, da [ah-bis-mah'-do, dah], *a.* 1. Cast down, dejected, depressed. 2. Absorbed in profound meditation.

abismal [ah-bis-mahl'], *a.* Belonging to an abyss.

abismal [ah-bis-mahl'], *m.* Clasp nail, shingle nail.

abismar [ah-bis-mar'], *va.* To depress, to humble, to destroy. **Abismar a uno en la tristeza**, to plunge somebody into sadness. *-vr.* To be astonished, to be shocked or astounded.

abismo [ah-bees'-mo], *m.* 1. Abyss; gulf. 2. That which is immense, or incomprehensible. 3. Hell. **Desde los abismos de la Edad Media**, from the dark depths of the Middle Ages. **Estar al borde del abismo**, to be on the brink of ruin.

abitadura [ah-be-ta-doo'-rah], *f. (Naut.)* A turn of the cable around the bitts.

abitaque [ah-be-tah'-kay], *m.* A rafter or joist, the fourth part of a girder.

abitar [ah-be-tar'], *va.* To bitt (barcos).

abitas [ah-bee'-tas], *m. pl. (Naut.)* Bitts. **Abitas del molinete**, Carrickbitts.

abitones [ah-be-to-nes], *m. pl.* Topsail sheet, bitts.

abizcochado, da [ah-beth-co-chah'-do, dah], *a.* In the form of a biscuit. Spongy.

abjuración [ab-hoo-rah-the-on'], *f.* Abjuration, recantation.

abjurar [ab-hoo-rar'], *va.* To abjure, to recant upon oath. 2. *vn.* **Adjurar de**, to adjure.

ablación [ah-blah-the-on'], *f.* The removal of an organ or portion of the body by surgical means; ablation.

ablandador [ah-blahn-dah-dor'], *m.* **Ablandador de agua**, water-softener. Mollifier.

ablandabrevas [ah-blan-dah-bray-bahs], *m. & f.* A useless person, good-for-nothing.

ablandamiento [ah-blan-dah-me-en'-to], *m.* Softening.

ablandar [ah-blan-dar'], *va. & n.* 1. To soften, to mellow, to relent. 2. To loosen. 3. To assuage, to mitigate, to melt, to soothe. 4. To grow mild or temperate; to give. *-vr.* To soften, to soften up, to get soft (persona); to become less severe (frío).

ablande [ah-blan-day], *m. (LAm.)* Running-in.

ablano [ah-blah'-no], *m. (Prov. Astr.)* The hazel-tree.

ablativo [ah-blah-tee'-voh], *m.* Ablative. **Ablativo absoluto**, ablative absolute.

ablución [ah-bloo-the-on'], *f.* Ablution, (lavatorio).

abnegación [ab-nay-gah-the-on'], *f.* Abnegation, self-denial.

abnegadamente [ab-nay-gah-dah-men'-tay], *adv.* With abnegation.

abnegado [ab-nay-gah-do], *a.* Self-denying, self-sacrificing; unselfish.

abnegar [ab-nay-gar'], *va.* To renounce, to deny oneself anything. (*Yo abniego, abniegue,* from *Abnegar. V.* ACRECENTAR). *-vr.* To deny oneself, to go without, to act unselfishly.

abobado, da [ah-bo-bah'-do, dah], *a.* Stultified, simple, silly, **Mirar abobado,** to look bewildered. *-pp.* of ABOBAR.

abobamiento [ah-bo-bah-me-en'-to], *m.* Stupefaction, stupidity.

abobar [ah-bo-bar'], *va.* 1. To stupefy. 2. *V.* EMBOBAR. *-vr.* To grow stupid.

abocado [ah-bo-cah'-do], *a.* Mild, agreeable (vino). *-pp.* of ABOCAR.

abocamiento [ah-bo-cah-me-en'-to], *m.* A meeting, an interview.

abocar [ah-bo-car'], *va.* To take or catch with the mouth. **Abocar la artillería,** to bring the guns to bear. **Abocar un estrecho,** to enter the mouth of a channel or strait. *-vr.* To meet by agreement.

abocarse [ah-bo-cahr-say], *vr.* To approach (aproximarse). **Abocarse con uno,** to meet somebody, to have an interview with someone.

abocardado, da [ah-bo-car-dah'-do, dah], *a.* Wide-mouthed, like a trumpet.

abocardar [ah-bo-car-dar'], *va.* To countersink, to widen the mouth.

abocardo [ah-bo-car'-do], *m. (Miner.)* Countersinking drill.

abocastro [ah-bo-cahs-tro], *m. (And. Cono Sur)* Ugly devil.

abocetar [ah-bo-thay-tahr], *va.* Sketch.

abochornado, da [ah-bo-chor-nah'-do, dah], *a.* Out of countenance, flushed. *-pp.* of ABOCHORNAR. **Quedar abochornado,** to feel mortified.

abochornar [ah-bo-chor-nar'], *va.* 1. To swelter, to overheat. 2. To provoke by abusive language. *-vr.* To blush, to feel mortified.

abochornarse [ah-bo-chor-nahr-say], *vr.* To get flushed, to get overheated. *(Bot.)* to wilt. **Abochornarse de,** to feel ashamed at, to get embarrased about.

abocinado [ah-bo-the-nah'-do], *a.* Bent: applied to an elliptic arch, the two faces of which are nearly the same. *-pp.* of ABOCINAR.

abocinar [ah-bo-the-nar'], *vn. (Low.)* To fall upon the face. *va.* To raise, to broaden an arch upon one side. *vt.* To shape like a trumpet.

abocinarse [ah-bo-the-nahr-say], *vr.* To fall flat on one's face.

abodocarse [ah-bo-do-cahr-say], *vr. (CAm.)* To go lumpy (líquido); *(Mex.) (Med.)* To break out in boils.

abofado [ah-bo-fah-do], *a. (Carib. Mex.)* Swollen.

abofarse [ah-bo-fahr-say], *vr. (Mex.)* To stuff oneself (tragar).

abofellar [ah-bo-fel-lyar'], *vn.* To puff, to pant.

abofeteador, ra [ah-bo-fay-tay-ah-dor', rah], *m. & f.* One who slaps, one who insults.

abofetear [ah-bo-fay-tay-ar'], *va.* 1. To slap one's face. 2. To insult.

abogacía [ah-bo-gah-thee'-ah], *f.* Profession of a lawyer or advocate.

abogada [ah-bo-gah'-dah], *f.* 1. Mediatrix. 2. A counsellor's wife.

abogadear [ah-bo-gah-day-ar'], *vn.* To play the advocate: used in contempt.

abogaderas [ah-bo-gah-day-rahs], *f pl.* **Abogaderías.** 1. *(LAm.)* Specious (or false) arguments.

abogadillo [ah-bo-gah-deel'-lyo], *m. dim.* of ABOGADO. Ignorant or poor lawyer.

abogado [ah-bo-gah'-do] *m.* 1. Advocate, counsellor. 2. Mediator. 3. **Abogado criminalista,** criminal lawyer. **Abogado del diablo,** devil's advocate. **Abogado picapleito,** pettifogging lawyer. **Ejercer de abogado,** to practise law, be a lawyer. *-pp.* of ABOGAR.

abogar [ah-bo-gar'], *vn.* 1. To advocate, to plead the cause of another. 2. To intercede on behalf of another. (**Yo abogué,** from **Abogar,** *V.* verbs, in *gar.*)

abohetado, da [ah-bo-ay-tah'-do, dah], *a.* Inflated, swollen.

abolengo [ah-bo-len'-go], *m.* 1. Ancestry. 2. Inheritance coming from ancestors.

abolición [ah-bo-le-the-on'], *f.* Abolition, abrogation, extinction.

abolicionista [ah-bo-le-the-o-nees'-tah], *m.* Abolitionist.

abolir [ah-bo-leer'], *va.* To abolish, to annul, to revoke, to repeat.

abollado [ah-bol-lyah'-do], *a. & m. V.* ALECHUGADO. *-pp.* of ABOLLAR.

abolladura [ah-bo-lya-doo'-rah], *f.* 1. Inequality. 2. Embossed work, relief. 3. Bruise. 4. Dent.

abollar [ah-bo-lyar'], *va.* 1. To emboss. 2. To annoy with an unpleasant discourse. 3. To stun and confound. 4. To bruise. 5. To dent. 6. *(Mex.)* To blunt (filo).

abollarse [ah-bo-lyahr-say], *vr.* To get dented, to get bruised.

abollón [ah-bol-lyon'], *m. (Prov.)* A bud, in particular of the vine.

abollonar [ah-bol-lyo-nar'], *va.* To emboss. *-vn. (Prov.)* To bud, applied in particular to the vine.

abolorio [ah-bo-lo'-re-o], *m.* Ancestry. *V.* ABOLENGO.

abolsado, da [ah-bol-sah'-do, dah], *a.* Puckered, folded in the form of a purse.

abolsarse [ah-bol-sahr-say], *vr.* To form pockets, to be baggy.

abomaso [ah-bo-mah'-so], *m.* Abomasum, the fourth stomach of ruminating animals.

abombachado [ah-bom-bah-cha-do], *a.* Baggy (pantalón).

abombado [ah-.bom-baha-do], *a. (gen.)* Convex; domed. **Estar abombado** *(LAm. fig.),* to be bewildered (aturdido); to be silly (tonto); to be tight (or tipsy) (borracho). *(LAm.)* rotten (comida); **estar abombado,** to stink, to smell foul.

abombarse [ah-bom-bahr-say], *vr. (LAm.)* To rot, to decompose, to smell bad (pudrirse). To get tight; to get drunk. To go mad, lose one's head (enloquecer). To go soft (in the head) (atontarse).

abominablemente [ah-bo-me-nah-blay -men'-tay], *adv.* Abominably, detestably, execrably.

abominable [ah-bo-me-nah'-blay], *a.* Detestable, abominable, execrable, odious, heinous, cursed.

abominación [ah-bo-me-nah-the-on'], *f.* Abomination, detestation, execration, cursedness.

abominar [ah-bo-me-nar'], *va.* To detest, to abhor, to execrate, abominate.

abonable [ah-bo-nah-blay], *a.* Payable (pagadero). *(Agri.)* improvable.

abonado, da [ah-bo-nah'-do, dah], *m. & f.* A subscriber to a telephone company or any other thing. Holder of a season-ticket.

abonado, da [ah-bo-nah'-do, dah], *a.* 1. Creditable, rich. 2. Fit and disposed for anything: commonly understood in an ill sense. 3. Manured land. **Testigo abonado,** an irrefragable witness. *-pp.* of ABONAR.

abonamiento [ah-bo-nah-me-en'-to], *m. V.* ABONO. Bail, security.

abonanzar [ah-bo-nan-thar'], *vn.* To grow calm (tormentas). To clear up (tiempo).

abonar [ah-bo-nar'], *va.* 1. To bail, to insure. 2. To improve or ameliorate. 3. To make good an assertion. 4. To manure lands, to compost. 5. To give one credit; to allow. *(Com.)* To indemnify, to compensate. *-vr.* To subscribe to any work; to buy a season-ticket (for a theater, etc.); to pay in advance for anything. *-vn. V.* ABONANZAR.

abonaré [Ab-bo-na-ray'], *m.* Promissory note: a security for payment of a sum. *V.* PAGARÉ.

abonero [ah-bo-nay-ro], *m.* Street vendor, door-to-door salesman. *(Mex.)* (vendedor).

abono [ah-bo'-no], *m.* 1. Season ticket. 2. Part payment. **Pagar por abonos**, pay by instalments 3. Dung, manure. **Abono verde**, green manure. 4. Subscription (revista). 5. *(Mex.)* Receipt (recibo).

aboquillado [ah-bo-que-lyah-do], *a.* **Cigarrillo aboquillado**, tipped cigarette, filter-tipped.

abordable [ah-bor-dah'-blay], *a.* Accessible, of easy access, approachable, that can be tackled.

abordador [ah-bor-dah-dor'], *m.* 1. He that boards a ship. 2. An intruder, who accosts a person with an air of impudence.

abordaje [ah-bor-dah'-hay], *m. (Naut.)* Boarding (barco). Accosting, approach (en la calle).

abordar [ah-bor-dar'], *va.* 1. To board a ship, to fall aboard. 2. To run foul of a ship. 3. To put into a port. 4. *va. (Mex.) (Naut.)* To dock.

abordo [ah-bor'-do], *m.* 1. *(Met.)* Address, attack, shock or force in execution. 2. *(Obs.)* V. ABORDAJE.

aborigen [ah-bo-ree'-hen], *a.* Aboriginal, indigenous.

aborígenes [ah-bo-ree'-hay-nes], *m. pl.* Aborigines, the earliest inhabitants of a country.

aborrachado, da [ah-bor-rah-chah'-do, dah], *a.* 1. High-colored. 2. Inflamed, fiery, flushed.

aborrascarse [ah-bor-ras-car'-say], *vr.* To be tempestuous or stormy.

aborrecedor, ra [ah-bor-ray-thay-dor', rah], *m. & f.* A detester, a hater.

aborrecer [ah-bor-ray-therr'], *va.* 1. To hate, to abhor. 2. To relinquish, to desert: in the last sense it is chiefly applied to birds, which desert their eggs or young ones. 3. To spend money.

aborrecible [ah-bor-ray-thee'-blay], *a.* Hateful, detestable, loathsome, cursed, damned, forbidding.

aborreciblemente [ah-bor-ray-thee-blay -men'-tay], *adv.* With abhorrence, hatefully.

aborrecimiento [ah-bor-ray-thee-me-en'-to], *m.* Abhorrence, detestation, dislike, hate, grudge.

aborregado [ah-bo-rray-gah-do], *a.* **Cielo aborregado**, mackerel sky.

aborregarse [ah-bor-ray-gar' -say], *vr.* To be covered with light, fleecy clouds (firmamento).

aborrer, aborrescer [ah-bor-rerr', ah-bor-res-therr'], *va. (Obs.)* V. ABORRRECER. (Aborrezco. V. ABORRRECER.)

abortamiento [ah-bor-tah-me-en' -to], *m.* Abortion.

abortar [ah-bor-tar'], *va.* 1. To miscarry. **Hacerse abortar**, to abort. 2. To fail. 3. *(Med.)* To have a miscarriage (por accidente); To abort (con intención). **Hacer abortar a una mujer**, to procure an abortion for a woman.

abortista [ah-bor-tes-tah] 1. *m. & f.* 1. Abortionist (criminal). 2. (partidario) abortion campaigner, person seeking to legalize abortion. 2. *f.* Woman who has had an abortion.

abortivamente [ah-bor-tee' -vah-men' -tay], *adv.* Abortively, untimely.

abortivo, va [ah-bor-tee' -vo, vah], *a.* Abortive; producing abortion.

aborto [ah-bor' -to], *m.* 1. A miscarriage, abortion. 2. A monster. 3. A failure 4. Ugly man, ugly woman (persona).

abortón [ah-bor-tone'], *m.* 1. The abortion of a quadruped. 2. The skin of a lamb born before its time.

aborujar [ah-bo-roo-har'], *va.* To make parcels. *vr.* To be muffed or wrapped up.

abotagamiento [ah-bo-tah-gah-me-ayn-to], *m.* Swelling.

abotagarse [ah-bo-tah-gar'-say], *vr.* 1. To be swollen, to be inflated. 2. *(Met.)* To grow foolish, or stupid.

abotinado, da [ah-bo-te-nah' -do, dah], *a.* Made in the form of half-gaiters (bluchers), closing at the instep.

abotonador [ah-bo-to-nah-dor'], *m.* An instrument used for buttoning gaiters; button-hook.

abotonar [ah-bo-to-nar'], *va.* 1. To button, to fasten with buttons. 2. *(Naut.)* To lash, to rack, to seize. -*vn.* 1. To bud, to germinate. 2. To form a button: applied to eggs boiled with the white obtruding.

abovedado, da [ah-bo-vay-dah'-do, dah], *a.* Arched, vaulted. -*pp.* of ABOVEDAR.

abovedar [ah-bo-vay-dar'], *va.* To arch, to vault, to shape as a vault.

aboyado, da [ah-bo-yah'-do, dah], *a.* A farm rented, with the necessary stock of oxen for ploughing the ground. -*pp.* of ABOYAR.

aboyar [ah-bo-yar'], *va. (Naut.)* To lay down buoys, mark with buoys. *(Mex.)* To float (flotar).

abozalar [ah-bo-tha-lar'], *va.* To muzzle.

abra [ah'-brah], *f.* 1. Bay, haven; cover or creek. 2. A dale or valley. 3. A fissure in mountains; gorge.

abracadabra [ah-brah-cah-dah-brah], *f* Abracadabra.

abracadabrante [ah-brah-cah-da-brahn-tay], *a.* Spectacular (aparatoso); enchanting (atractivo), captivating; magic-seeming (mágico).

abracar [ah-brah-cahr], *va. (Mex.)* V. ABRAZAR.

abracijo [ah-brah-thee'-ho], *m. (coll.)* An embrace, a hug.

Abraham [ah-brah-ahm], *m.* Abraham.

abrahonar [ah-brah-o-nar'], *va. (coll.)* To hold one fast by the garment.

abrasadamente [ah-brah-sah-dah-men'-tay], *adv.* Ardently, eagerly.

abrasado [ah-brah-sah-do], *a.* Burnt, burnt up. **Estar abrasado**, to burn with shame. **Estar abrasado en cólera**, to be in a raging temper.

abrasador, ra [a-brah-sah-dor', rah], *a.* Very hot, burning, steaming. **Un sol abrasador**, a steaming, burning sun. **Una llama abrasadora**, an ardent flame.

abrasamiento [ah-brah-sah-me-en'-to], *m.* 1. The act of burning. 2. Inflammation. 3. The excess of passion. 4. Flagrancy.

abrasar [ah-brah-sar'], *va.* 1. To burn; to fire; to parch the ground. 2. To dissipate, to squander. 3. To provoke. -*vr.* To be agitated by any violent passion, to glow. **Abrasarse vivo**, to be burnt alive; to feel extremely hot. **Abrasarse en deseos**, to be aflame with desire.

abrasilado, da [ah-brah-se-lah'-do, dah], *a.* Of the color of Brazil-wood.

abrasión [ah-brah-se-on], *f.* Graze, abrasion.

abrasivo [ah-brah-se-vo], 1. *a.* Abrasive. 2. *m.* Abrasive.

abrazadera [ah-brah-thah-day'-rah], *f.* 1. Ferule, clasp. 2. A ring put around a thing as a band. 3. A cleat. 4. A piece of timber which fastens the plough-tail to the plough. 5. (Printing) A brace or bracket {.-*a.* V. SIERRA ABRAZADERA.

abrazador, ra [ah-brah-tha-dor'-rah], *m. & f.* 1. One that embraces.

abrazamiento [ah-brah-thah-me-en'-to], *m.* Embracing.

abrazar [ah-brah-thar', *va.* 1. To embrace, to hug, to caress; to clasp, to clip, to lock in, to fathom, to compress. 2. To surround. 3. To embrace the opinion of another; to go into. 4. To take one's charge. 5. To comprise.

abrazarse [ah-brah-thahr-say], *vr.* To embrace (each other).

abrazo [ah-brah'-tho], 1. *m.* A hug, an embrace. 2. **Un fuerte abrazo** (cartas), with best wishes, with kind regards, yours.

abreboca [ah-bray-bo-cah] *(LAm.)* 1. *a.* Absent-minded. 2. *m.* Appetizer.

abrecartas [ah-bray-cahr-tahs] *m.* Letter opener, paperknife.

abrego [ah'-bray-go], *m.* A south-west wind.

abrelatas [ah-bray-lah'-tahs], *m.* Can opener, tin-opener.

abrepuño [ah-bray-poo' -nyo] *m. (Bot.)* Milk-thistle. V. CARDO LECHERO.

abrevadero [ah-bray-vah-day' -ro], *m.* Watering-place for cattle.

abrevado [ah-bray-vah' -do], *a.* Softened in water (pieles). -*pp.* of ABREVAR.

abrevador [ah-bray-vah-dor'], *m.* 1. He who waters cattle. 2. Waterer. 3. Watering-place.

abrevar [ah-bray-var'], *va.* To water cattle, to give a drink to, to irrigate.

abrevarse [ah-bray-bahr-say], *vr.* 1. To drink, to quench its thirst (animal). 2. **Abrevarse en sangre**, to wallow in blood.

abreviación [ah-bray-vee-ah-the-on'], *f.* Abbreviation, abridgment, shortening, reduction.

abreviadamente [ah-bray-vee-ah-dah-men' -tay], *adv.* In few words, concisely.

abreviado [ah-bray-be-ah-do], *a.* Brief, short, shortened (breve). **Abreviador, ra** [ah-bray-vee-ah-dor', rah], *m. & f.* 1. An abridger one who abridges writings.

abreviar [ah-bray-vee-ar'], *va.* To abridge, to cut short.

abreviatura [ah-bray-vee-ah-too' -rah], *f.* 1. Abbreviation, contraction. 2. Shorthand. **En abreviatura**, in an abbreviated form, briefly; expeditiously.

abreviaturía [ah-bray-vee-ah-too-ree' -ah], *f.* Office of abreviator.

abribonarse [ah-bre-bo-nar' -say], *vr.* 1. To grow abject, to degenerate. 2. To act the scoundrel, to stroll about.

abridero [ah-bre-day' -ro], *m.* A sort of peach, which, when ripe, opens easily and drops the stone; freestone.

abridero, ra [ah-bre-day' -ro, rah], *a.* Of an aperitif nature; easily opened; freestone.

abridor [ah-bre-dor¡] *m.* 1. *(Bot.)* Nectarine, a species of the peach-tree. 2. Opener, the person who opens or unlocks. **Abridor de láminas**, an engraver. **Abridor en hueco**, a die or punch sinker. 3. Iron used for opening ruffs or plaits. 4. *(Agri.)* Grafting-knife. 5. **Abridor de guantes**, glove-stretcher. 6. **Abridor de heno**, hay-spreader, tedder. 7. **Abridor de latas**, can-opener.

abrigada [ah-bre-gah-dah], *f* Shelter, windbreak.

abrigadamente [ah-bre-gah-dah-men' -tay], *adv.* Warmly, well protected.

abrigadero [ah-bre-gah-day' -ro], *m.* Sheltered place. **Abrigadero de ladrones**, *(Mex.)* den of thieves.

abrigado [ah-bre-gah' -do], *m.* V. ABRIGADERO. *-pp.* of ABRIGAR.

abrigador [ah-bre-gah-dor], 1. *a. (And. Mex.)* Warm (que abriga). 2. Person who covers up for another.

abrigaña [ah-bre-gah'-nyah], *f. (Hort.)* Canvas screen, awning.

abrigaño [ah-bre-gah'-nyoh], *m.* A shelter for cattle.

abrigar [ah-bre-gar'], *va.* To shelter, to protect, to patronize; to over-shadow, to cover; to warm, to lodge. **Abríguese Vd. con ello**, *(coll.)* defend yourself with it.

abrigarse [ah-bre-gahr-say] *vr.* To take shelter, to cover up. **¡Abrígate bien!**, keep yourself warm!

abrigo [ah-bree' -go], *m.* 1. Coat, overcoat, topcoat, wrap. **Abrigo de pieles**, fur coat. 2. Shelter, protection, cover. 3. *(Naut.)* Harbor, haven.

abril [ah-breel'], *m.* April, the fourth month of the year. **Estar hecho un abril o parecer un abril**, to be young, florid, handsome. **Abril, aguas mil**, april showers bring May flowers. **Abril y Mayo, llaves de todo el año**, on the weather of these two months depends the goodness of the crops.

abrileño [ah-bre-lay-nyoh], *a.* Of Abril.

abrillantador [ah-brel-lyan-tah-dor'] *m.* Diamond-cutter; lapidary.

abrillantar [ah-brel-lyan-tar'], *va.* 1. To cut a diamond into angles; to make any precious stone sparkle by polishing it. 2. To impart brilliancy; to glaze, to polish.

abrimiento [ah-bre-me-en' -to], *m.* 1. The act of opening. 2. An opening.

abrir [ah-breer'], *va.* 1. To open, to begin, to inaugurate, to unlock. **Abrir una puerta con llave**, to unlock a door. **En un abrir y cerrar de ojos**, in the twinkling of an eye. 2. To remove obstacles. 3. To engrave. To expand, as flowers; to distend. **Abrir a chasco**, *(coll.)* To jest, to mock. **Abrir el día**, to dawn. **Abrir el ojo**, to be alert. **Abrir la mano**, to accept bribes; to be generous. **Abrir los ojos a uno**, to undeceive; to enlighten. *-vr.* 1. To be

open, to tear. 2. To extend itself. 3. To chink, to cleave, to yawn. 4. *(Met.)* To communicate, to disclose a secret. **Abrirse con alguno**, to disclose one's secret, or to unbosom and reveal it to a friend. **Abrirse o abrir una entrada al agua**, *(Naut.)* to spring a leak. 5. **Abrir registro** (barcos), to begin to take a cargo.

abrirse [ah-brer-say] *vr.* To open, to open out, to unfold, to spread out, to expand.

abrochador [ah-bro-chah-dor'], *m.* An instrument used by tailors to button on clothes; button-hook. V. ABOTONADOR.

abrochadura, *f.* **abrochamiento**, *m.* [ah-bro-chah-doo' -rah], [ah-bro-chah-me'en' -to]. The act of lacing or buttoning on.

abrochar [ah-bro-char'], *va.* To clasp, to buckle; to button on, to fasten with hooks and eyes, to do up. *(Mex.)* To tie up (atar).

abrocharse [ah-bro-chahr-say], *vr. (LAm.)* To struggle, to wrestle (luchar).

abrogable [ah-bro-gah' -blay], *a.* Repealable, abrogable.

abrogación [ah-bro-gah-the-on'], *f.* Abrogation, repeal, the act of repealing a law.

abrogar [ah-bro-gar'], *va.* To abrogate, to annul, to repeal. *(yo abrogué, from Abrogar. V. Verbs in gar.)*

abrojal [ah-bro-hal'], *m.* A place covered with thistles.

abrojo [ah-bro' -ho], *m.* 1. *(Bot.)* Caltrops. Thistle, thorn, prickle. 2. *(Mil.)* A thistle; a crowfoot. 3. Thistle fixed on a whip, and used by the flagellants to flog the shoulders. 4. A crab whose carapace has eight spines. *-pl.* Hidden rocks in the sea.

abromado, da [ah-bro-mah' -do], *a.* (nauto.) 1. Dark, hazy, foggy. 2. Worm-eaten. *-pp.* of ABROMARSE.

abromarse [ah-bro-mar' -say], *vr. (Naut.)* To be worm-eaten.

abroncar [ah-bron-car'], *va. (coll.)* To tease, to vex, to make angry, to make ashamed.

abroncarse [ah-bron-cahr-say], *vr.* To get angry.

abroquelado, da [ah-bro-kay-lah' -do, dah], *a. (Bot.)* Shield-shaped.

abroquelar [ah-bro-kay-lar'], *va. (Naut.)* To boxhaul. *vr.* 1. To cover oneself with a shield. 2. To use means of defence in support of one's character or opinion.

abroquelarse [ah-bro-kay-lahr-say], *vr.* **Abroquelarse con, abroquelarse de**, to shield oneself with, to defend oneself with.

abrótano [ah-bro' -tah-no], *m. (Bot.)* Southernwood, allied to wormwood.

abrumado, da [ah-broo-mah' -do, dah], *a.* Wary. *-pp.* of ABRUMAR.

abrumador [ah-broo-mah-dor], *a.* Crushing, burdensome, tiresome, overwhelming. **El trabajo es abrumador**, the work is killing.

abrumadoramente [ah-broo-mah-do-rah-mayn-tay], *a.* Crushingly, vastly, overwhelmingly.

abrumar [ah-broo-mar'], *va.* 1. To crush, to overwhelm, to oppress. 2. To cause great pain or trouble.

abrumarse [ah-broo-mahr-say], *vr.* To get foggy, to get misty.

abrupto, ta [ah-broop' -to, tah], *a.* Craggy, rugged, abrupt. **Pendiente**, steep.

abrutado, da [ah-broo-tah' -do, dah], *a.* Brutish, ungovernable in manners and habits.

absceso [abs-thay' -so], *m.* 1. An abscess; collection of pus. 2. A blemish.

abscisa [abs-thee' -sah], *f. (Geom.)* Abscisse.

abscisión [abs-the-se-on'], *f. (Med.)* 1. Ulcer. 2. Incision.

absenta [ahb-sayn-tah], *f.* Absinth (e).

absentista [ab-sen-tees' -tah], *a.* Absentee. *-m & f.* Absentee landowner.

abside [ab' -se-day], *m. & f.* 1. The central arch of a temple. 2. V. APSIDE.

absintio [ab-seen' -te-o], *m.* V. AJENJO.

absolución [ab-so-loo-the-on'], *f.* 1. The act of pardoning. 2. Absolution. 3. Acquittal.

absoluta [ab-so-loo'-tah], 1.*f.* Dogma, universal proposition. 2. Discharge. **Tomar la absoluta**, to take one's discharge.

absolutamente [ab-so-loo-tah-men'-tay], *adv.* Absolutely, without limits or restrictions, definitely. **Absolutamente nada**, nothing at all.

absolutismo [ah-so-loo-tees'-mo], *m.* Absolutism, unrestrained, despotism.

absolutista [ab-so-loo-tes-tah], 1. *a.* Absolutist, absolute. 2. *f.* Absolutist.

absolutizar [ab-so-loo-te-thahr], *va.* To pin down, be precise about.

absoluto, ta [ab-so-loo'-to, tah], *a.* 1. Absolute; unconditional, without condition or stipulation. 2. Imperious, domineering. 3. (en sentido negativo) **en absoluto**, nothing at all, by no means. **No sabía nada en absoluto de eso**, I knew nothing at all about it.

absolutorio, a [ab-so-loo-to'-re-o, ah], *a.* Absolutory, absolving, verdict of not guilty.

absolvederas [ab-sol-vay-day'-ras], *f. pl.* The facility of giving absolution.

absolver [ab-sol-verr'], *va.* 1. To absolve. 2. To acquit. (*Yo absuelvo, yo absuelva*, from *Absolver, V.* MOVER).

absorbencia [ab-sor-ben'-the-ah], *f.* The act of absorbing.

absorbente [ab-sor-ben'-tay], *m.* (*Med.*) Absorbent, demanding. -*pa.* of ABSORBER.

absorber [ab-sor-berr'], *va.* 1. To absorb, to imbibe. *V.* EMPAPAR. 2. (*Met.*) To attract, to charm. **Absorber la atención**, to captivate the attention. 3. To take up (energías).

absorberse [ab-sol-bayr-say], *vr.* **Absorberse en**, to become absorbed in, to become engrossed in.

absorbible [ab-sor-be-blay], *a.* Absorbable.

absorbido [ab-sor-bee'-do], *a.* (*Med.*) Absorbed. -*pp.* of ABORSBER.

absorción [ab-sor-the-on'], *va.* (*Med.*) Absorption.

absortar [ab-sor-tar'], *va.* (*Obs.*) To strike with amazement.

absorto, ta [ab-sor'-to, tah], *a.* Amazed, absorbed in thought. -*pp. irr.* of ABSORBER and of ABSORTAR.

abstemio, mia [abs-tay'-me-o, me-ah], *a.* Abstemious. teetotal. *s.* Teetotaler.

abstención [abs-ten-the-on'], *f.* Forbearance, self-denial, not participation.

abstencionismo [abs-tayn-the-o-nes-mo], *m.* Non-participation, refusal to take part.

abstencionista [abs-tayn-the-o-nes-tah], *f.* Non-participant, person who opts out.

abstenerse [abs-tay-ner-say], *vr.* To abstain, to forbear. **En la duda, abstente**, when in doubt, don't.

abstergente, abstersivo, va [abs-ter-hen'-tay, abs-ter-see'-vo, vah], *a.* Detergent, cleansing, abstergent.

absterger [abs-ter-herr'], *va.* To cleanse; to dispel purulent matter.

abstersión [abs-ter-se-on'], *f.* Abstersion, purification.

abstinencia [abs-te-nen'-the-ah], *f.* Forbearance, abstinence. **Día la abstinencia**, a day of abstinence, a fast-day. Abstinence, withdrawal (de drogas).

abstinente [abs-te-nen'-tay], *a.* Abstinent, abstemious.

abstracción [abs-trac-the-on'], *f.* 1. Abstraction, the act of abstracting and state of being abstracted. 2. Retirement from the world. 3. In art, pure abstraction, an abstract composition.

abstraccionismo [abs-trac-the-o-nee's-mo], *m.* Abstractionism.

abstractivo, va [abs-trac-tee'-vo, vah], *a.* Abstractive.

abstracto, ta [abs-trac'-to, tah], *a.* Abstract. -*pp. irr.* of ABSTRAER.

abstraer [abs-trah-err'], *va.* 1. To abstract, to separate ideas. 2. To pass over in silence. 3. To refrain from. 4. To differ in opinion. -*vr.* To withdraw the intellect from sensible objects, in order to employ it in contemplation.

abstraerse [abs-trah-ayr-say], *vr.* To be absorbed, to be lost in thought.

abstraído, da [abs-trah-ee'-do, dah], *a.* Retired. -*pp.* of ABSTRAER. (*Yo abstraigo, yo abstraje, yo abstraiga*, from *Abstraer. V.* TRAER)

abstruso, sa [abs-troo'-so, sah], *a.* Abstruse, difficult, recondite, absent-minded.

absuelto, ta [ab-soo-el'-to, tah], *a.* Free. -*pp. irr.* of ABSOLVER. (*Yo absuelvo, yo absuelva*, from *Absolver, V.* MOVER)

absurdamente [ab-soor-dah-mayn-tay], *adv.* Absurdly.

absurdidad [ab-soor-de-dahd], *f.* Absurdity.

absurdo, da [ab-soor'-do, dah], *a.* Nonsensical, absurd. **Es absurdo que…**, it's absurd that….

abubilla [ah-boo-beel'-lyah], *f.* (*Orn.*) The hoopoe, or hoopoo, a bird with a beautiful crest.

abucate [ah-boo-cah'-tay], *m.* The runner of a velvet loom.

abuchear [ah-boo-chay-ahr], *va.* To boo, hoot at. **Ser abucheado**, to be hissed at.

abucheo [ah-boo-chay-o], *m.* Booing, hooting.

abuela [ah-boo-ay'-la], *f.* Grandmother; (*fig.*) old woman, old lady. **No tiene abuela**, he's full of himself. **Éramos pocos y parió la abuela**, and that was the last straw.

abuelado [ah-boo-ay-lah-do], *adj* (*Cono Sur*) Spoiled by one's grandparents.

abuelita [ah-boo-ay-le-tah], *f.* Grandma, granny, grandmother.

abuelito [ah-boo-ay-le-to], *m.* Granddad, grandpa, grandfather.

abuelo [ah-boo-ay-lo], *m.* Grandfather, ancestor. (*fig.*) Old man, forbear. **Abuelos**, grandparents. **Está hecho un abuelo**, he looks like an old man.

abulia [ah-boo-le-ah], *f.* Lack of willpower, spinelessness, apathy.

abúlico [ah-boo-le-co], *a.* Lacking in willpower, weak-willed, spineless.

abultado, da [ah-bool-tah'do, dah], *a.* 1. Increased. 2. Bulky, massive, exaggerated. -*pp.* of ABULTAR.

abultamiento [ah-bool-tah-me-ayn-to], *m.* Bulkiness, (large) size, swelling, increase, exaggeration.

abultar [ah-bool-tar'], 1. *va.* To increase, to enlarge. -*vn.* To be bulky or large. 2. *vn.* To be bulky, to be big, to take up a lot of room.

abundamiento [ah-boon-tah-me-ayn-to], *m.* Abundance, plenty.

abundancia [ah-boon-dan'-the-ah], *f.* Abundance, fruitfulness, fertility, opulence, plenty. **Nadar en la abundancia**, to be rolling in money.

abundante [ah-boon-dahn'-tay], *a.* Abundant, plentiful. **Abundante en**, abounding in.

abundantemente [ah-boon-dan-tay-men'-tay], *adv.* Abundantly, plentifully, luxuriantly.

abundar [ah-boon-dar'], *vn.* To abound, to have plenty. (*Met.*) Followed by **en**, to hold identical opinions. **Abundar en dinero**, to be well supplied with money.

abuñuelar [ah-boo-nyoo-aylar'], *va.* To make something in the shape of a fritter.

aburar [ah-boo-rar'], *va.* (*Prov.*) To burn, to scorch.

aburelado, da [ah-boo-ray-lah'-do, dah], *a.* Of a dark red color.

aburguesado [ah-boor-gay-sah-do], *a.* **Un hombre aburguesado**, a man who has become burgeois, a man who has adopted middle-class ways.

aburguesamiento [ah-boor-gay-sah-me-ayn-to], *m.* Process of becoming bourgeois.

aburguesarse [ah-boor-gay-sar'-say], *vr.* To turn bourgeois, to become middle class.

aburrición [a-boor-ree-the-on'], *f. V.* ABURRIMIENTO.

aburridamente[ah-boor-re-dah-men'-tay], *adv.* Wearily, in a boring manner.

aburrido, da [ah-boor-ree'-do, dah], *a.* Boring, tedious, dull. Weary. -*pp.* of ABURRIR.

aburridón, [ah-boo-rre-don], *a. (And)* Rather boring.

aburrimiento [ah-boor-re-me-en'-to], *m.* Uneasiness of mind, despondency, tediousness; weariness, heaviness, tiresomeness, disquiet, sorrow.

aburrir [ah-boor-reer'], *va.* 1. To vex, to perplex, to weary; to be tedious, tired dull; to grow impatient; to bore. 2. To venture, to hazard. 3. To relinquish.

aburrirse [ah-boo-rrer-say], *vr.* To be bored, to get bored.

aburujado, da [ah-boo-roo-hah'-do, dah], *a.* 1. Pressed together. 2. Perplexed, entangled in difficulties. *-pp.* of ABURUJAR.

aburujonarse [ah-boo-roo-ho-nar'-say] *vr.* To clot, to curdle.

abusado- [ah-boo-sah-do], *(Mex.)* 1. *interj.* Look out!, careful! 2. *a.* Watchful, wary.

abusador [ah-boo-sah-dor], *a. (Cono Sur)* Abusive.

abusar [ah-boo-sar], *va.* To abuse or misapply a thing; to impose upon, to go too far, to exceed one's rights. **Abusar del tabaco,** to smoke too much.

abusión [ah-boo-se-on], *f.* Abuse, superstition.

abusivamente [ah-boo-se-vah-men'-tay], *adv.* Abusively, improperly.

abusivo, va [ah-boo-see'-vo, vah], *a.* Abusive, improper.

abuso [ah-boo'-so], *m.* Misusage, the abuse or ill use of a thing, imposition, demand, betrayal. **Abuso del tabaco,** excessive smoking. **Abuso de confianza,** betrayal of trust.

abusón- [ah-boo-son], *a.* Selfish (egoísta), big-headed (engreído).

abyección [ab-yee-the-on'], *f.* Abjection, abjectness, degradation.

abyecto, ta [ab-yee'-to, tah] *a.* Abyect, dejected, degradated.

A.C. *abr.* after Christ.

a/c. *abr.* a cuenta (on account).

acá [ah-cah'], *adv.* Here, hither, this way, this side. **Acá no se estila,** that's not the custom here. **Ven acá,** come along. **Acá y allá,** here and there. **Acá,** hey, (used in calling). **Está muy acá,** it's right here.

acabable [ah-cah-bah'-blay], *a.* What may be finished, achievable.

acabadamente [ah-cah-bah-dah-men'-tay], *adv.* 1. Perfectly. 2. Imperfectly, badly.

acabadero [ah-cah-bah-day-ro], *m. (Mex.)* the limit, the last straw.

acabado, da [ah-cah-bah'-do, dah], *a.* 1. Perfect, complete, faultless. 2. Old; ill-dressed; dejected. **Está muy acabado,** he's looking very old. *-pp.* of ACABAR.

acabador, ra [ah-cah-bah-dor', rah], *m. & f.* Finisher, completer.

acabalar [ah-cah-bah-lar'], *va.* To complete, to finish.

acaballadero [ah-cah-bal-lyah-day'-ro], *m.* The time and place when horses cover mares; stud farm.

acaballado, da [ah-cah-bal-lyah-do, dah], *a.* Like a horse. *-pp.* of ACABALLAR, Covered.

acaballar [ah-cah-bal-lyar'], *va.* To cover a mare.

acaballerado, da [ah-cah-bal-lyay-rah-do, dah], *a.* Gentleman-like. *-pp.* of ACABALLERAR.

acaballerar [ah-cah-bal-lyay-rar'], *va.* 1. To render genteel. 2. To make a person behave as a gentleman.

acabamiento [ah-cah-bah-me-en'-to], *m.* End, completion, death, consummation.

acabar [ah-cah-bar'], *va. & vn.* 1. To finish, to conclude, to complete, to make up; to compass; to archieve; to grow toward an end. **Acaba ya,** determine, resolve. 2. To harass. 3. To obtain. 4. To terminate in anything, as a sword which ends in a point. 6. To die; to consume; to extinguish; to fail, to destroy. **Esto acabará conmigo,** this will be the end of me. **Acabar con el negocio,** to make an end of the affair. **Acaba de salir,** it is just fresh from. *-vr.* To grow feeble. **La vela se está acabando,** the candle is flickering. **Es cosa de nunca acabarse,** it is an endless affair. **Acaba de llegar,** he has just arrived, **acabar de,** to have just. **Acabóse,** *(coll.)* No more to be said; that's the end of it.

acabarse [ah-cah-bahr-say], *vr.* To finish, to stop, to come to an end (terminar); to die (morir), to run out. **¡Se acabó!,** it's all over!.

acabestrillar [ah-cah-bes-trill-lyar'], *vn.* To stalk, or to fowl with a stalking-horse or ox that approaches the game and shelters the fowler.

acabildar [ah-cah-bil-dar'], *va.* To unite many persons by dint of persuasion to do something. 2. To put to vote.

acabóse [ah-cah-bo-say], *m.* The end, the limit. **La fiesta fue el acabóse,** it was the best party ever.

acachetear [ah-cah-chay-tay-ar'], *va.* To tap, to pat, to strike, to slap.

acachihuite [ah-cah-che-ooe-tay], *m. (Mex.)* Straw, hay (paja); straw basket (cesto).

acacia [ah-cah'-the-ah], *f.* 1. Acacia, a shrub of the thorn kind. 2. Acacia, the concentrated juice of acacia.

acacito [ah-cah-the-to], *adv. (LAm.)* V. Acá.

academia [ah-cah-day'-me-ah], *f.* 1. Academy; university; literary society, school. **Academia de baile,** dance school. **Academia de comercio,** business school. **Academia de conductores,** driving school. **Academia de idiomas,** language school. **Academia militar,** military academy. **Academia de música,** music school. In particular, the Spanish Academy, officially charged with the pureness of the language. It was founded in Madrid early in the eighteenth century. 2. A naked figure designed from nature.

académico [ah-cah-day'-me-co], *m.* An academician, member of an academy.

académico, ca [ah-cah-day'-me-co, cah], *a.* Academical, belonging to a university, etc.

acaecedero, ra [ah-cah-ay-thay-day'-ro, rah], *a.* Incidental.

acaecer [ah-cah-ay-therr'], *vn.* To happen, to come to pass, to take place.

acaecimiento [ah-cah-ay-the-me-en'-to], *m.* Event, incident, occurrence.

acahul [ah-cah-ool], *m. (Mex.)* Sunflower (girasol); tall grass (hierba).

acáis [Ah-cah-es], *mpl.* Peepers, eyes.

acal [ah-cahl'], *m.* Canoe used by Mexicans.

acalambrado, da [ah-cah-lam-brah'-do, dah], *a.* Cramped.

acalambrarse [ah-cah-lahm-brahr-say], *vr* To get cramped.

acalaminado [ah-cah-lah-me-nah-do], *a. (Cono Sur)* Rough, uneven, bumpy (camino).

acalefos [ah-ca-lay'-fos], *m. pl.* Acalephs, a group of radiates, inciuding jelly-fishes and hydroids.

acalenturarse [ah-cah-len-too-rar'-say], *vr.* To be feverish.

acalia [ah-cah'-leah], *f. V.* MALVAVISCO. Marsh-mallow.

acalicino, na [ah-cah-le-thee'-no, nah], *a.* Wanting a calyx.

acaloradamente [ah-cah-lo-rah-dah-men'-tay], *adv.* Warmly, with vehemency.

acalorado [ah-cah-lo-rah-do], *a.* Heated, hot; tired; *(fig.)* heated, excited (discusión). Agitated (agitado).

acaloramiento [ah-cah-lo-rah-me-en'-to], *m.* Ardor, heat; agitation.

acalorar [ah-cah-lo-rar'], *va.* 1. To warm. 2. To inflame, to overheat. 3. To urge on. 4. To forward, to promote. *-vr.* To grow warm in debate.

acalorarse [ah-cah-lo-rahr-say], *vr.* To get hot, to become overheated; *(fig.)* (persona) to get excited, get worked up, to get angry.

acaloro [ah-cah-lo-ro], *m.* Anger.

acalote [ah-cah-lo-tay], *m. (Mex.)* Channel.

acallamiento [ah-cah-lyah-me-ayn-to], *m.* Silencing, quietening; pacification.

acallar [ah-cal-lyar'], *va.* 1. To quiet, to silence, to hush. 2. To mitigate, to soften, to assuage.

acamado, da [ah-cah-mah'-do, dah], *a.* Laid flat. **Mieses acamadas,** crops laid by heavy storms.

acamar [ah-cah-mahr'], *va.* To beat down, to lay (cosecha).

acamastronarse [ah-cah-mas-tro-nahr-say], *vr.* To get crafty, to become artful.

acambrayado, da [ah-cam-brah-yah'-do, dah], *a.* Cambrie-like.

acampada [ah-cahm-pah-dah], *f.* Camp.

acampamento [ah-cam-pah-men'-to], *m.* *(Mil.)* Encampment, camp.

acampanado [ah-cahm-pah-nah-do], *a.* Bell-shaped.

acampar [ah-cam-par'], *va.* To encamp.

acampo [ah-cahm'-po], *m.* Portion of common given to graziers or herds for pasture, pasture.

acamuzado, da [ah-cah-moo-thah'-do, dah], *a.* Chamois-colored. *v.* AGAMUZADO.

acana [ah'-cah-nah], *f.* A hard reddish wood, which grows in the island of Cuba, used in ship-building.

acanalado, da [ah-cah-nah-lah'-do, dah], *a.* 1. What passes through a narrow passage or channel. 2. Striated, fluted. -*pp.* of ACANALAR.

acanalador [ah-cah-nah-lah-dor'], *m.* An instrument to cut grooves in timber; chamfering-plane, grooving-plane.

acanalados [ah-cah-nah-lah'-dos], *m. pl.* The ridge of a horse's back.

acanaladura [ah-cah-nah-lah-doo-rah], *f.* Groove, furrow; striation.

acanalar [ah-cah-nah-lar'], *va.* 1. To make a canal or channel. 2. To flute, to groove, to chamfer, to corrugate.

acanallado [ah-cah-nah-lah-do], *a.* Disreputable, low; worthless; degenerate.

acandilado, da [ah-can-de-lah'-do, dah], *a.* **Sombrero acandilado**, a hat cocked with sharp points.

acanelado, da [ah-cah-nay-lah'-do, dah], *a.* Of a cinnamon color.

acangrenarse [ah-can-gray-nar-say], *vr.* To mortify.

acanillado, da [ah-cah-nil-lyah'-do, dah], *a.* Ribbed, applied to any sort of cloth which forms furrows from the unevenness of its threads.

acantalear [ah-can-tah-lay-ar'], *vn. (coll.)* To hail large hail-stones.

acantarar [ah-can-tah-rar'], *va.* To measure by **cántaras** or four-gallon vessels.

acantilado, da [ah-can-te-lah'-do, dah], *a.* Bold, steep. **Costa acantilada**, accessible coast.

acantio [ah-cahn'-te-oh], *m. V.* TOBA

acanto [ah-cahn'-to], *m. (Bot.)* 1. Prickly thistle. 2. *(Arch.)* Acanthus leaf.

acantonamiento [ah-can-to-nah-me-en'-to], *m.* Cantonment.

acantonar [ah-can-to-nar'], *va.* To canton, to quarter troops, to billet.

acañaverear [ah-cah-nyah-vay-ray-ar'], *va.* To wound the flesh with sharp-pointed canes.

acañonear [ah-cah-nyo-nay-ar'], *va.* To cannonade.

acap [ah-cahp'], *m.* A Mexican wood suitable for cabinet-work.

acaparador [ah-cah-pah-rah-dor] 1. *a.* Acquisitive. **Tendencia acaparadora**, monopolizing tendency.

acaparamiento [aha-cah-pah-rah-me-ayn-to], *m.* Monopolizing; covering the market.

acaparar [ah-cah-pah-rar'], *va.* To monopolize, engross. **Ella acapara la atención**, she captures everyone's attention. *V.* ACOPIAR.

acaparrarse [ah-cah-par-rar'-say], *vr.* 1. To take refuge under another's cloak. 2. To resort to the protection of someone else: to take sides with.

acaparrosado, da [ah-cah-par-ro-sah'-do, dah], *a.* Of a copper color.

acapetate [ah-cah-pe-tah-tay], *m. (Mex.)* Straw mat.

acapillar [ah-cah-pe-lyahr], *va.* To grab.

acaponado, da [ah-cah-po-nah'-do, dah], *a.* Capon-like; eunuch.

acapullado [ah-cah-poo-lyah-do], *a.* In bud. (flores)

Acapulco [ah-cah-pool-co], *m.* Acapulco.

acapulqueño [ah-cah-pool-kay-nyo], *f.* From Acapulco.

acaracolado [ah-cah-rah-co-lah-do], *a.* Spiral, winding.

acaramelado [ah-cah-rah-may-lah-do], *a.* Toffee-flavored (sabor).

acaramelar [a-cah-rah-may-lar'], *va.* To reduce sugar to caramel.

acarar [ah-cah-rar'], *va. V.* CAREAR.

acardenalar [ah-car-day-nah-lar'], *va.* To make livid, to beat black and blue, to pinch, to bruise. *-vr.* To be covered with livid spots.

acardenalarse [ah-cahr-day-nah-lahr-say], *vr.* To get bruised.

acareamiento [ah-cah-ray-ah-me-en'-to], *m.* Comparing, confronting.

acariciador, ra [ah-cah-re-the-ah-dor', rah], *m. & f.* One who fondles and caresses.

acariciar [ah-ca-re-the-ahr'], *va.* To fondle, to caress, to hug.

acaricida [ah-cah-re-the-ah], *f. (Cono Sur)* Insecticide.

ácaro [ah'-ca-ro], *m.* Mite. **Ácaro de queso**, cheese-mite.

acarraladura [ah-cah-rrah-lah-doo-ra], *f. (And. Cono Sur)* Run, ladder (in stocking).

acarrarse [ah-car-rar'-say], *vr.* To shelter oneself from the heat of the sun: applied to sheep.

acarreadizo, za [ah-car-ray-ah-dee'-tho, thah], *a.* Portable.

acarreador, ra [ah-car-ray-ah-dor', rah], *m. & f.* A carrier; a porter.

acarrear [ah-car-ray-ar'], *va.* 1. To carry something in a cart or other carriage; to convey, to forward. 2. *(Met.)* To occasion, to cause. **Ello le acarreó muchos disgustos**, it brought him lots of trouble. 3. *vr.* To bring upon oneself.

acarreo [ah-car-ray'-oh], *m.* Carriage, the act of carrying, conveyance, cartage. *-pl.* Supplies. **Cosas de acarreo**, Goods forwarded.

acarreto [ah-cah-rray-to], *m. (Carb., Mex.) V.* ACARREO.

acartonado [ah-car-to-nah'-do], *a.* Resembling pasteboard, wizened.

acartonarse [ah-cahr-to-nahr-say], *vr.* To get like cardboard.

acaso [ah-cah'-so], *m.* Chance.

acaso [ah-cah'-so], *adv.* By chance, by accident; may be, maybe, perhaps. **¿Acaso?** How? how now? **Por si acaso**, just in case. **Por si acaso viene**, if by any chance he comes.

acastañado [ah-cahs-tah-nyah-do], *a.* Hazel (color).

acastillaje [ah-cas-til-lyah'-hay], *m. (Obs. Naut.)* The upper works of a ship.

acastorado, da [ah-cas-to-rah'-do, dah], *a.* Beavered; resembling the texture of beaver.

acatable [ah-cah-tha'-blay], *a.* Venerable.

acataléctico [ah-cah-tah-lec'-te-co], *a.* Verse which has the complete number of syllables; acatalectic.

acatamiento [ah-cah-tah-me-en'-to], *m.* 1. Esteem, veneration, respect, reverence, obeisance. 2. Acknowledgment. 3. Presence, view.

acatar [ah-cah-tar'], *va.* To respect, to revere, to venerate.

acatarrarse [ah-cah-tar-rar'-say], *vr.* To catch a cold.

acato [ah-cah-to], *m. V.* ACATAMIENTO.

acatólico [ah-cah-to-le-co], *a.* Non-catholic.

acaudalado, da [ah-cah-oo-dah-lah'-do, dah], *a.* Rich, wealthy, opulent, affluent, well-off. *-pp.* of ACAUDALAR.

acaudalar [ah-cah-oo-dah-lar'], *va.* 1. To hoard up riches. 2. To acquire a reputation.

acaudillador [ah-cah-oo-dil-lyah-dor'], *m.* Commander of troops.

acaudillar [ah-cah-oo-de-lyahr'], *va.* To lead, to command, to head.

acaule [ah-cah'-oo-lay], *a. (Bot.)* Acaulous: wanting a stem.

accedente [ac-thay-den'-tay], *va.* Acceding; he who accedes.

acceder [ac-thay-derr'], *vn.* To accede, to become accessory to a treaty or agreement concluded by others; to fall in or into an agreement. **Acceder a una base de datos**, to have access to a data base. **Acceder al trono**, to succeed to the throne.

accesibilidad [ac-thay-se-be-le-dahd], *f.* Accessibility.

accesible [ac-thay-see'-blay], *a.* 1. Accesible. 2. Attainable. 3. Of easy access, approachable.

accesión [ac-thay-se-on'], *f.* 1. Accession, the act of acceding. 2. Access or paroxysm of a fever.

accésit [ac-thay-set], *m.* Consolidation prize, second prize.

acceso [ac-thay'-so]. 1. Access. **Prohibido el acceso**, no admittance. **De fácil acceso**, of easy access. 2. Sexual intercourse. 3. Approach. **Acceso dirigido desde tierra**, Ground-control approach. 4. *(Med.)* Attack, fit (tos). **Acceso protegido** *(Comp.)*, protected access.

accesoria [ac-thay-so'-re-ah], *f.* 1. Outbuilding. 2. *(Andal.)* A room in the lower story of a house with the door opening to the street.

accesoriamente [ac-thay-so-re-ah-men'-tay], *adv.* Accessorily.

accesorio, a [ac-thay-so'-re-o, ah], *a.* Accessory, additional. **Obras accesorias**, *(Mil.)* The outworks of a fortress. **Accesorio del escritorio** *(Comp.)*, desk accessory.

accidentado, da [ac-the-den-tah'-do, dah], *a.* 1. Eventful (viaje); turbulent (history); troubled (vida); rough, rugged (terreno); broken (costa); 2. Hurt, injured (persona). *s.* Injured. **Llevaron a los accidentados al hospital**, the injured were taken to hospital. *-pp.* of ACCIDENTARSE.

accidental [ac-the-den-tahl'], *a.* Accidental, casual, fortuitous, contingent.

accidentalmente, accidentariamente [ac-the-den-tal-men'-tay, ac-the-den-tah-re-ah-men'-tay], *adv.* Accidentally, casually, fortuitously.

accidentarse [ac-the-den-tar'say], *vr.* To have an accident.

accidente [ac-the-den'-tay], *m.* 1. Accident, an unessential quality of something. 2. Chance, that which happens unforeseen, accident. 3. Privation of sensation. 4. Mode, integral part. 5. Accidental (música).

acción [ac-the-on'], *f.* 1. Action: feat. **Acción de gracias**, act of thanking, thanksgiving. 2. Faculty of doing something. 3. Lawsuit. 4. Gesticulation, gesture. 5. Battle. 6. Action, in the series of events represented in a fable, and the manner of representing them. 7. *(Art.)* Posture. 8. *(Com.)* Stock, capital in a company; share. 9. *(Poetic.)* The principal subject of a poem. *m.* Acción industrial (Com. e.g. de ferrocarril), Share (e.g. railway share).

accionamiento [ac-the-o-nah-me-en'-to], *m.* Drive, propulsion, operation.

accionar [ac-the-o-nar'], *vn.* to gesticulate. *-va.* 1. To sue, to bring suit. 2. To activate, to drive, to propel

accionista [ac-the-o-nees'-tah], *m.* Shareholder in a company's stock, actionary, stockholder.

acebadar [ah-thay-bah-dar'], *va.* V. ENCEBADAR.

acebedo [ah-thay-bay-do], *m.* A plantation of holly-trees.

acebo [ah-thay'-bo], *m. (Bot.)* Holly-tree.

acebolladura [ah-thay-bol-lyah-doo'-rah], *f.* Damage to a tree from splitting of the woody layers.

acebuchal [ah-thay-boo-chahl'], *m.* A plantation of wild olive-trees.

acebuche [ah-thay-boo'-chay], *m. (Bot.)* The wild olive-tree. Olea.

acebucheno, na [ah-thay-boo-chay'-no, nah], *a.* Belonging to the wild olive.

acebuchina [ah-thay-boo-chee'-nah], *f.* Fruit of the wild olive-tree.

acechador, ra [ah-thay-chah-dor', rah], *m. & f.* 1. A thief lying in ambush. 2. An intruder who pries into other people's affairs, watcher.

acechar [ah-thay-char'], *va.* 1. To waylay, to lie in ambush, to lurk, to spy on, to watch. 2. To pry into other people's affairs.

aceche [ah-thay'chay], *m.* V. CAPARROSA

acecho [ah-thay'-cho], *m.* The act of waylaying, or laying in ambush, spying, watching. **Al acecho, en acecho**, *a.* in wait, in ambush.

acechón, na [ah-thay-chone', nah], *m. & f. (coll.)* V. ACECHADOR. **Hacer la acechona**, to scrutinize, to inquire with care, to be inquisitive.

acecinar [ah-thay-the-nar'], *va.* To salt meat and dry it in the air or smoke. *-vr.* To grow old, dry, and withered.

acedar [ah-thay-dar'], *va.* 1. To sour, to make sour, to make bitter. 2. To displease, to vex.

acedera [ah-thay-day'-rah], *f. (Bot.)* Sorrel. **Acedera de Indias**, *(Bot.)* Indian sorrel.

acederilla [ah-thay-day-reel'-lyah], *f. (Bot.)* Wood-sorrel.

acedia [ah-thay-dee'-ah], *f.* 1. Acidity, sourness. 2. Squeamishness, roughness. 3. Asperity of address. 4. A flounder.

acedo, da [ah-thay'-do, dha], *a.* 1. Acid, sour. 2. Harsh, unpleasant.

acefalia [ah-thay-fah-lee'-ah], *f.* Deprivation of a head; headlessness.

acéfalo, la [ah-thay'-fah-lo, lah], *a.* Headless, acephalous.

aceitada [ah-thay-e-tha'-dah], *f. (coll.)* 1. Oil spilled. 2. Cake kneaded with oil.

aceitar [ah-thay-e-tar'], *va.* To oil, to rub with oil

aceite [ah-thay'-e-tay], *m.* (a)1. Oil; any unctuous liquor drawn from olives, almonds, nuts, fish, etc. 2. Resin which distils from the fir-tree. **Aceite de oliva**, olive oil. **Aceite de girasol**, sunflower oil. **Aceite de bergamota**, essence of bergamot. **Aceite de espliego**, spike oil, **aceite de trementina**, turpentine oil. **Aceite de pescado**, train oil. **Aceite de bacalao**, cod oil. **Aceite de linaza**, linseed oil. **Aceite de ricino**, castor oil. **Aceite de hígado de bacalao**, cod-liver oil. **Aceite de carbón, o aceite mineral**, coal-oil, petroleum. **Aceite lubricante**, *(Mech.)* Lube.

aceitera [ah-thay-e-tay'-rah], *f.* Oil jar, oil cruet, oil horn, **aceiteras**, vials for oil and vinegar.

aceitería [ah-thay-e-tay-ree'-ah], *f.* Oil-shop.

aceitero, ra [ah-thay-e-tay'-ro, rah], *m. & f.* 1. Oil merchant, oil-seller. 2. Any vessel for holding oil.

aceitoso, sa [ah-thay-e-toh'-so, sha], *a.* Oily, containing oil.

aceituna [ah-thay-e-too'-nah], *f.* Olive, the fruit of the olive-tree. **Aceituna rellena**, stuffed olive.

aceitunada [ah-thay-e-too-nah'-dah], *f.* The season for gathering olives.

aceitunado, da [ah-thay-e-too-nah'-do, dah], *a.* Of an olive color.

aceitunero [ah-thay-e-too-nay'-ro], *m.* A person who gathers, carries, or sells olives.

aceituno [ah-thay-e-too'-no], *m. (Bot.)* Olive-tree. V. OLIVO.

aceleración [ah-thay-lay-rah-the-on'], *f.* Acceleration, hastening.

acelerada [ah-thay-lay-rah-dah], *f.* Acceleration, speed-up.

aceleradamente [ah-thay-lay-rah-dah-men'-tay], *adv.* Speedily, swiftly, hastily.

acelerado [ah-thay-lay-rah-do], *a.* Jumpy, nervous (nervioso).

acelerador [ah-thay-lay-rah-dor'], *m.* Accelerator.

aceleramiento [ah-thay-lay-rah-me-en'-to], *m.* V. ACELERACIÓN

acelerar [ah-thay-lay-rar'], *va.* To accelerate, to hasten, to hurry, to forward, to expedite.

acelerarse [ah-thay-lay-rhar-say], *vr.* To hurry up, hasten.

aceleratriz [ah-thay-lay-rah-treeth'], *a.* Accelerative.

acelerómetro [ah-thay-lay-ro'-may-tro], *m. (Aer.)* Accelerometer.

acelerón [ah-thay-lay-ron], *m.* Sudden acceleration, leap forward.

acelga [ah-thel'-gah], *f. (Bot.)* Beet.

acémila [ah-thay'-me-la], *f.* 1. A mule, a beast of burden.

acemilar [ah-thay-me-lar'], *a.* Belonging to mules and muleteers.

acemilería [ah-thay-me-lay-ree'-ah], *f.* The stable or place where mules are kept.

acemilero, ra [ah-thay-me-lay'-ro, rah], *a.* Belonging to mules. -*m.* A muleteer.

acemita [ah-thay-mee'-tah], *f.* Bread made of fine bran. Graham bread.

acemite [ah-thay-mee'-tay], *m.* Fine bran, middlings.

acendrado, da [ah-then-drah'-do, dah], *a.* 1. Purified. 2. Refined. -*pp.* of ACENDRAR.

acendrar [ah-then-drar'], *va.* 1. To purify or refine metals. 2. To free from stain or blemish.

acensuar [ah-then-soo-ar'], *va.* To lease out for a certain rent; impose a tax.

acento [ah-then'-to], *m.* 1. Accent, a modulation of the voice. 2. Accent, a character placed over a syllable, to mark the modulation of the voice, to stress, emphasis. **Acento ortográfico**, written accent. **Acento agudo**, acute accent. **Confuerte acento Andaluz**, with a strong Andalusian accent. **Poner acento en algo**, to emphasize something.

acentor [ah-thayn-tor], *m.* Acentor común, hedgesparrow, dunnock.

acentuación [ah-then-too-ah-the-on'], *f.* Accent, accentuation.

acentuamiento [ah-thayn_too-ah-me-en-to], *m.* (*Cono Sur*) Accent, emphasis.

acentuar [ah-then-too-ar'], *va.* 1. To accent, to stress. 2. To put a written accent on. 3. (*Met.*) To accentuate, to stress.

acentuarse [ah-thayn-too-ahr-say], *vr.* To become more noticeable, be accentuated. **Se acentúa la tendencia a la baja en la Bolsa**, the slide on the Stock Exchange is accelerating.

aceña [ah-thay'-nyah], *f.* Water mill (for grinding flour).

aceñero [ah-thay-nyay-ro], *m.* Miller.

acepar [ah-thay-par'], *vn.* To take root, to become rooted.

acepción [ah-thep-the-on'], *f.* Meaning, acceptation. **Acepción de personas**, Partiality, prejudice.

acepilladora [ah-thay-pil-lyah-do'-rah], *f.* Planer, planing machine.

acepilladura [ah-thay-pil-lyah-doo'-rah, *f.* 1. The act of planing. 2. Timber shavings.

acepillar [ah-thay-pil-lyar'], *va.* 1. To plane. 2. To brush clothes. 3. To polish one's manners.

aceptabilidad [ah-thep-tah-be-le-dad'], *f.* Acceptability.

aceptable [ah-thep-tah'-blay], *a.* Worthy of acceptance, acceptable.

aceptablemente [ah-thep-tah'-blay-men'-tay], *adv.* Acceptably.

aceptación [ah-thep-tah-the-on'], *f.* 1. Acceptation. 2. Approbation. 3. Acceptance of a bill of exchange. **Aceptación de herencia**, acceptance of an inheritance. **Aceptación de personas**. V. ACEPCION.

aceptador, ra [ah-thep-tah-dor', rah], *m. & f.* Acceptor.

aceptante [ah-thep-tahn'-tay], *pa.* He who accepts.

aceptar [ah-thep-tar'], *va.* To accept. **Aceptar personas**, to favor particular persons. **Aceptar una letra**, to accept or to honor a bill. -*vr.* To be pleased.

acepto, ta [ah-thep'-to, tah], *a.* Acceptable, agreeable.

acequia [ah-thay'-ke-ah], *f.* Canal, trench, or drain. (*Arab.*)

acequiado, da [ah-thay-ke-ah'-do, dah], *a.* Intersected by canals. -*pp.* of ACEQUIAR.

acequiador [ah-thay-ke-ah-dor'], *m.* Canal-maker.

acequiar [ah-thay-ke-ar'], *va.* To construct canals or drains.

acequiero [ah-tahy-ke-ay'-ro], *m.* Person appointed to construct canals, a dike reeve.

acera [ah-thay'-rah], *f.* 1. Sidewalk, pavement. 2. The stones which form the face of a wall. **Ser de la cera de enfrente**, to be gay.

acerado, da [ah-thay-rah'-do, dah], *a.* 1. Steeled, made of steel. 2. Strong. -*pp.* of ACERAR.

acerar [ah-thay-rar'], *va.* 1. To steel, to point or edge with steel. 2. To impregnate liquors with steel. 3. To strengthen, to harden, to toughen.

acerarse [ah-thay-rahr-say], *vr.* To toughen.

acerbamente [ah-ther-bah-men'-tay], *adv.* Harshly, rudely.

acerbidad [ah-ther-be-dad'], *f.* 1. Acerbity, asperity. 2. Rigor, cruelty.

acerbo, ba [ah-ther'-bo, bah], *a.* 1. Rough to the taste, as unripe fruit. 2. Severe, cruel.

acerca [ah-ther'-cah], *prep.* About, relating to, bringing near. **Acerca de lo que hemos hablado**, in regard to what we have said.

acercar [ah-ther-car'], *va.* To approach, to place a person or thing close to another. -*vr.* To accost, to come near to, or up to.

acercarse [ah-thayr-cahr-say], *vr.* 1. To approach, to come near, draw near, to come close to. 2. To be reconciled (amantes). 3. **Acercarse a** (*Comp.*), to close in on.

ácere [ah-thay-ray], *m.* Maple.

acería [ah-thay-ree'-ah], *f.* Steel mill.

acerico, aceríllo [ah-thay-ree'-co, ah-thay-reel'-lyo], *m.* 1. Pin-cushion. 2. A small pillow.

acerino, na [ah-thay-ree'-no, nah], *a.* (*Poetic.*) Made of, or belonging to steel.

acerista [ah-thay-rees'-tah], *m.* Steel manufacturer.

acernadar [ah-ther-nah-dar'], *va.* To cover with ashes.

acero [ah-thay'-ro], *m.* 1. Steel. **Acero colado**, cast steel. **Acero inoxidable**, stainless steel. 2. Edged or pointed small arms. **Espada de buenos aceros**, sword of well-tempered steel. Aceros, (*fig.*) Spirit, courage. **Tener buenos aceros**, to have guts.

acerola [ah-thay-ro'-lah], *f.* Azarole, the fruit of the parsley-leaved hawthorn.

acerolo [ah-thay-ro'-lo], *m.* (*Bot.*) The parsley-leaved hawthorn.

acerrar [ah-ther-rar'], *va.* (*Low.*) To seize, to grasp.

acérrimamente [ah-ther'-re-mah-men-tay], *adv.* Strenuously.

acérrimo, ma [ah-ther'-re-mo, mah], *a. sup.* Very vigorous and strong.

acerrojar [ah-thay-rro-hahr], *va.* To lock, bolt.

acertadamente [ah-ther-tah-dah-men'-tay], *adv.* Opportunely, fitly.

acertado, da [ah-ther-tah'-do, dah], *a.* Fit, proper. **Su conducta fue acertada**, he conducted himself with propriety. **Me parece muy acertado**, that seems right to me. -*pp.* of ACERTAR.

acertante [ah-thayr-tahn-tay], 1. *a.* **Tarjeta acertante**, winning card. 2. *m. & f.* Solver, winner. **Hubo acertantes**, there were winners.

acertar [ah-ther-tar'], *va.* 1. To hit the mark. 2. To hit by chance; to meet or find, to succeed. **A ver si acertamos esta vez**, let's see if we can get it right this time. **No aciertas el modo de hacerlo**, you don't manage to find the proper way to do it. 3. To conjecture right. *vn.* 1. To happen unexpectedly, to be right, to hit the mark, to manage it. 2. To take root, as plants.

acertijo [ah-ther-tee'-ho], *m.* A riddle.

aceruelo [ah-thay-roo-ay'-lo], *m.* A sort of small pack-saddle used for riding.

acervo [Ah-ther'-vo], *m.* 1. A heap, common property. **Acervo Comunitario**, community. **Acervo Cultural**, cultural tradition. 2. The totality of titles, or of an inheritance.

acescencia [ah-thes-then'-the-ah], *f.* Acidosis.

acetato [ah-thay-tah'-to], *m.* Acetate.

acético, ca [ah-thay'-te-co, cah], *a.* Acetic; pertaining to vinegar.

acetificar [ah-thay-te-fe-car'], *va.* To acetify, convert into vinegar.

acetilénico [ah-thay-te-lay-ne-co], *a.* Acetylene.

acetileno [ah-thay-te-lay'-no], *m.* (*Chem.*) Acetylene.

acetímetro [ah-thay-tee'-may'-tro], *m.* Acetimeter.

acetona [ah-thay-to'-nah], *f.* Acetone; pyroacetic spirit.

acetosa [ah-thay-to'-sah], *f.* (*Bot.*) Sorrel. V. ACEDERA.

acetosilla [ah-thay-to-seel'-lyah], *f.* (*Bot.*) Wood-sorrel.

acetoso, sa [ah-thay-to'-so, sha], *a.* 1. Acetous. 2. *(Obs.)* Acid.

acezar [ah-thay-thahr], *vn.* To puff, to pant.

achacable [ah-chah-cah-blay], *a.* Attributable to.

achacar [ah-chah-car'], *va.* 1. To impute; to father. To put something down. **Achacar la culpa a uno**, to lay the blame on someone. 2. To frame an excuse.

achacarse [ah-chah-cahr-say], *vr.* To ascribe a thing or action to oneself.

achacosamente [ah-chah-co-sah-men'-tay], *adv.* Sickly.

achacoso, sa [ah-chah-co'-so, sah], *a.* Sickly, unhealthy.

achaflanar [ah-chah-flah-nar'], *va.* To lower one end of a table, plank, or board; to chamfer, bevel.

achahuistlarse [ah-chah-oo-es-tlahr-say], *vr.* To become depressed (entristecerse).

achampañado [ah-chahm-pah-nyah-do], *a.* Champagne-flavored.

achamparse [ah-chahm-pahr-say], *vr.* *(Cono Sur)* **Achamparse algo**, to keep something which does not belong to one.

achancharse [ah-chan-char'-say], *vr.* 1. (Peru) To become lazy like a hog. 2. *(Cono Sur)* To get fat (engordar). 3. To become embarrassed (encontrarse violento).

achantado [ah-chahn-tah-do], *a.* *(CAm.)* Bashful, shy.

achantar [ah-chahn-tahr], 1. *va.* To close. 2. *vn.* To be quiet, to shut up.

achantarse [ah-chahn-tahr-say], *vr.* 1. To hide away. 2. *(fig.)* To give in, comply. **Achantarse por las buenas**, to be easily intimidated.

achaparrado, da [ah-chah-par-rah'-do, dah], *a.* Of the size of a shrub. **Hombre achaparrado**, a short and lusty man.

achaparrarse [ah-chah-par-rahr'-say], *vr.* To grow stunded.

achapinarse [ah-chah-pe-nahr-say], *vr.* *(CAm.)* To adopt the local customs.

achaplinarse [a-cha-plee-nar'-say], *vr.* *(Coll. Ch.)* 1. To hesitate, turn back or change direction in a chaplinesque manner (after Charlie Chaplin). 2. To change plans suddenly.

achaque [ah-chah'-kay], *m.* 1. Habitual indisposition. 2. Monthly courses. 3. Excuse, pretext. **Con achaque de**, under the pretext of. 4. A failing. 5. *(Law.)* Mulet, penalty.

achaquiento, ta [ah-chah-kee-en'-to, tah], *a.* V. ACHACOSO.

achaquillo, ito [ah-chah-keel'-lyo, kee'-to], *m.* dim. A slight complaint.

achara [ah-chah-rah], *interj*: ¡Achara! *(CAm.)* What a pity! (lástima)

achares [ah-cah-rays], *m. pl.* Jealously; **dar achares a uno**, to make someone jealous.

achalorado [ah-chah-lo-rah-do], *a.* Patent leather.

acharolar [ah-chah-ro-lar'], *va.* To paint in imitation of varnish.

achatamiento [ah-chah-tah-me-ayn-to], *m.* 1. Flattening (allanamiento). 2. *(LAm.* Loss of morale (desmoralización). **Sufrieron un achatamiento**, they felt down.

achatar [ah-chah-tar'], *va.* To flatter.

achatarse [ah-chah-tahr-say], *vr.* 1. To get flat. 2. *(Cono Sur, Mex.)* To grow weak, decline (declinar). **Perder ánimo**, to lose heart; feel down. 3. *(Cono Sur, Mex.)* To be overcome with shame, be embarrassed (avergonzarse). 4. **Quedarse achatado**, *(Mex.)* to be put to shame.

achicado, da [ah-che-cah'-do, dah], *a.* Diminished. V. ANIÑADO, childish. *-pp.* of ACHICAR.

achicador, ra [ah-che-cah-dor', rah], *m. & f.* 1. Diminisher, reducer. 2. *(Naut.)* Scoop for baling boats. 3. He who bales a mine.

achicadura [ah-che-cah-doo'-rah], *f.* Diminution, reduction.

achicalado [ah-che-cah-lah-do], *a.* *(Mex.)* Sugared, honeyed.

achicalar [ah-che-cah-lahr], *va.* *(Mex.)* To cover in honey.

achicar [ah-che-car'], *va.* 1. To diminish, to lessen, to shorten, to take in. 2. To bale a boat or drain a mine. **Achicar un cabo**, to shorten a rope. **Achicar el agua del navío**, to free the ship. 3. *(fig.)* To humiliate; to intimidate. 4. To kill. 5. *(Carib.)* To fasten, hold down (sujetar).

achicarse [ah-che-cahr-say], *vr.* 1. To get smaller; to shrink. 2. *(fig.)* To humble, to eat humble pie. 3. *(LAm.)* To do oneself down, to belittle oneself (rebajarse).

achicharradero [ah-che-chah-rrah-day-ro], *m.* Place of oppressive heat.

achicharrante [ah-che-chah-rrahn-tay], *a.* Sweltering heat.

achicharrar [ah-che-char-rar'], *va.* To fry meat too much; to overheat, burn, scorch. **El sol achicharraba la ciudad**, the sun was roasting the city.

achicharrarse [ah-che-chah-rrahr-say], *vr.* To scorch, to get burnt.

achicharronar [ah-che-chah-rro-nahr], *va.* *(LAm.)* To flatten, crush.

achichiguar [ah-che-che-goo-ahr], *va.* *(Mex.)* *(fig.)* (Mimar), to cosset, spoil.

achichincle [ah-che-chen-clay], *m. & f.* *(Mex.)* Camp follower.

achiguado [ah-che-goo-ah-do], *a.* *(Mex.)* Spoiled.

achiguarse [ah-che-goo-ahr-say], *vr.* *(Cono Sur)* To grow a paunch.

achicopalado [ah-che-co-pah-lah-do], *a.* *(Mex.)* Down, depressed.

achichinque [ah-che-cheen'-kay], *m.* A miner whose business is to drain mines of water.

achicoria [ah-che-co'-re-ah], *f.* *(Bot.)* Succory, wild endive, chicory.

achilarse [ah-che-lahr-say], *vr.* *(Cono Sur)* To turn cowardly.

achimero [ah-che-may-ro], *m.* *(CAm.)* Peddler, hawker.

achimes [ah-che-mays], *mpl.* *(CAm.)* Cheap goods, trinkets.

achín [ah-chen], *m.* *(CAm.)* Peddler, hawker.

achinado [ah-che-nah-do], *a.* 1. *(Cono Sur)* **De aspecto indio**, with Indian features. 2. *(Carib.)* **De aspecto chino**, Chinese-like.

achinar [ah-che-nar'], *va.* *(coll.)* To intimidate, to terrify.

achinarse [ah-che-nahr-say], *vr.* *(Cono Sur)* To become coarse.

achinelado, da [ah-che-nay-lah'-do, dah], *a.* Slipper-shaped.

achique [ah-che-kay], *m.* Baling; pumping.

achiquillado [ah-che-ke-lyah-do], *a.* *(Mex.)* Childish.

achiquitar [ah-che-ke-tahr], *va.* *(LAm.)* To make smaller, to reduce in size.

achipolarse [ah-che-po-lahr-say], *vr.* *(Mex.)* To grow sad.

achirarse [ah-che-rahr-say], *vr.* **Nublarse**, to cloud over. **Oscurecerse**, to get dark.

achís [ah-ches], *interj* Atishoo!

achispado, da [ah-chis-pah'-do, dah], *a.* Tipsy.

achispar [ah-ches-pahr], *va.* *(LAm.)* To cheer up, to liven up.

achisparse [ah-chis-par'-say], *vr.* *(coll.)* To get tipsy.

acho, acha [ah-cho, cha], **suf.** de *n. y a.* ej: **hombracho**, hulking great brute, **vivaracho**.

achocar [ah-cho-car'], *va.* 1. To throw one against the wall. 2. To knock asunder. 3. *(coll.)* To hoard money.

achocharse [ah-cho-chahr-say], *yr.* To get doddery, begin to dodder.

achocolatado [ah-cho-co-lah-tah-do], *a.* 1. *(LAm.)* Like chocolate. 2. *(LAm.)* Dark brown (color), chocolate-colored, tan. 3. **Estar achocolatado** (borracho), to be drunk.

acholado [ah-cho-lah-do], *a.* *(LAm.)* 1. Racially mixed (mestizo), part-indian. 2. Cowed (acobardado); abashed (avergonzado).

acholar [ah-cho-lahr], *va.* *(LAm.)* To embarrass (avergonzar); to intimidate.

acholarse [ah-cho-lahr-say], *vr.* To have half-breed ways (adoptar).

acholo [ah-cho-lo], *m.* *(LAm.)* Embarrassment.

-achón, -achona [ah-chon, na], **suf** de *n. y a.* = **-acho; bonachón** etc.

achoramiento [ah-cho-rah-me-ayn-to], *m.* *(Cono Sur)* Threat.

achorizado, da [ah-cho-re-thah'-do, dah], *a.* Slashed; made into sausages.

achubascarse [ah-choo-bas-car'-say], *vr.* *(Naut.)* To get squally and showery, to become threatening, to cloud over.

achuchado [ah-choo-chah-do], *a.* **Estar achuchado** *(Cono Sur)* To have malaria (paludismo); To catch a chill (tener escalofríos); To be feverish (tener fiebre); *(fig.)* to be scared.

achuchar, achuchurrar [ah-choo-char', ah-choo-choor-rar'], *va. (coll.)* 1. To crush with a blow. 2. To shove, jostle (empujar); to harass, pester (acosar). 3. To urge on. **Achuchar un perro contra uno**, to set a dog on someone.

achucharse [ah-choo-char-say], *vr. (Cono Sur)* To catch malaria (paludismo); to catch a chill (acatarrarse); to get feverish (tener fiebre).

achuchón [ah-choo-chone'], *m.* 1. *(coll.)* A push, a squeeze. 2. **Tener un achuchón**, to fall ill; to have a relapse.

achucutado [ah-choo-coo-tah-do], *a. (LAm.)* Down (deprimido); overwhelmed (agobiado).

achucutarse [ah-choo-coo-tahr-say], *vr. (LAm.)* To be dismayed (estar afligido); to be down (deprimido); to wilt (marchitarse).

achucuyarse [ah-choo-coo-yahr-say], *vr. (CAm.)* V. ACUCHUTARSE.

achuicarse [ah-choo-e-cahr-say], *vr (Cono Sur)* To be embarrassed, to feel small (avergonzarse).

achulado, da [ah-choo-lah'-doo, dah], *a.* Waggish, frolicsome, cocky.

achumado [ah-choo-mah-do], *a. (LAm.)* Drunk.

achumarse [ah-choo-mahr-say], *vr. (LAm.)* To get drunk.

achunchar [ah-choon-chahr], *(LAm.) va.* 1. To shame, cause to blush (avergonzar). 2. To get scared (intimidar).

achuncharse [ah-choon-char-say], *vr.* To feel ashamed, blush (avergonzarse).

achuntar [ah-choon-chahr], *va. (Cono Sur)* To do properly, to get right, to do at the right time.

achuñuscar [ah-choo-nyoos-cahr], *va. (Cono Sur)* To squeeze.

achupalla [ah-choo-pah-lyah], *f. (LAm.)* Pineapple.

achura [ah-choo-rah], *f. (LAm.)* Offal.

achurar [ah-choo-rahr], 1. *va. (LAm.)* To gut (animal); to stab to death (persona), cut to pieces. 2. *vn. (LAm.)* To benefit from a share-out, to get something free.

achurrucarse [ah-choo-roo-cahr-say], *vr. (CAm.)* To wilt (marchitarse).

achurruscado [ah-choo-roos-cah-do], *a.* Rumpled, crumpled up.

achurruscar [ah-choo-rroos-cahr-say], *va.* To rumple, to crumple up.

aciago, ga [ah-the-ah'-go, gah], *a.* Unfortunate, melancholy, sad, fateful.

acial, aciar [ah-the-ahl', ah-the-ar'], *m.* Barnacle, twitch, an instrument put upon the nose of a horse to make him stand quiet.

aciano [ah-the-ah'-no], *m.* Corn-flower. V. ESTRELLAMAR.

acíbar [ah-thee'-bar], *m.* 1. The juice pressed from the aloes. 2. Aloes-plant. **Acíbar caballuno**, Horse aloes; Barbadoes aloes. *(Met.)* Harshness, bitterness, displeasure.

acibarar [ah-the-bah-rar'], *va.* 1. To put the juice of aloes into anything; to make bitter. 2. *(Met.)* To bitter, to cause displeasure.

acicalado [ah-the-cah-lah-do], *a.* Metal polished, bright and clean; smart, neat, spruce (persona).

acicalador, ra [ah-the-cah-lah-dor'-rah], *m. & f.* 1. A polisher, burnisher, furbisher. 2. A tool used for burnishing.

acicaladura, *f.* **acicalamiento,** *m.* [ah-the-cah-lah-doo'-rah, ah-the-cah-lah-me-en'-to]. The act and effect of burnishing.

acicalar [ah-the-cah-lar'], *vn.* To polish, to burnish. *-vr. (Met.)* To dress in style, to set oneself off to advantage; to prink.

acicalarse [ah-the-cah-lahr-say], *vr.* To smarten up, to get dressed up.

acicate [ah-the-cah'-tay], *m.* Long necked Moorish spur with a rowel at the end of it.

aciche [ah-thee'-chay], *m.* Tow-edged tool used by tilers for cutting and adjusting tiles.

acicula [ah-the-coo-lah], *f. (Bot.)* Needle.

acidez]ah-the-deth'], *f.* 1. *(Med.)* Acidosis. 2. Acidity.

acidia [ah-thee'-de-ah], *f. (Obs.)* V. PEREZA. Laziness, indolence, sloth.

acidificación [ah-the-de-fe-cah-the-on'}, *f. (Chem.)* Acidification.

acidificar [ah-the-de-fe-car'], *va.* To acidify.

acidificarse [ah-the-de-cahr-say], *vr.* To acidity.

acidímetro [ah-the-dee'-may-tro], *m.* Acidimeter.

acidismo [ah-the-dees'-mo], *m.* Acidosis.

ácido [ah'-the-do], *m. (Chem.)* Acid. **Ácido acético**, acetic acid. **Ácido deoxiribonucleico**, deoxyribonucleic acid. **Ácido nítrico**, nitric acid. **Ácido sulfúrico**, sulphuric acid.

ácido, da [ah'-the-do, dah], *a.* Acid, sour.

acidular [ah-the-doo-lar'], *va.* To acidulate, to make sour.

acídulo, la [ah-thee'-doo-lo, lah], *a. (Chem.)* Acidulous, disagreeable.

acierto [ah-the-er'-to], *m.* 1. The act and effect of hitting; a good hit. **Con acierto**, with effect. 2. Prudence, dexterity. 3. Chance, casualty. *(Yo acierto, yo acierte. V. ACERTAR)*

aciguatado, da [ah-the-goo-ah-tah'-do, dah], *a.* Jaundiced, silly, stupid. *-pp.* of ACIGUATARSE.

aciguatarse [ah-the-goo-ah-tahr-say], *vr. (Carib. Mex.)* To grow stupid; to go crazy, lose one's head.

acijado, da [ah-the-hah'-do, dah], *a.* Copperas-colored; of the color of acije.

acimboga [ah-thim-bo'-gah], *f.* The citron-tree. Citrus medica.

ación [ah-the-on'], *f.* Stirrup-leather.

acionero [ah-thi-o-nay'-ro], *m.* Maker of stirrup-leathers.

acipado, da [ah-the-pah'-do, dah], *a.* Well-milled; applied to broadcloth and other woollens.

acirate [ah-the-rah'-tay], *m.* Landmark which shows the limits and boundaries of fields.

actara [ah-the-tah'-rah], *f.* Thin wall, a partition wall; the rail of a bridge.

acitrón [ah-the-tron'], *m.* 1. Lemon dried and made into sweetmeat; candied lemon. 2. *(LAm.) (Bot.)* Bishop's weed, goutweed.

aclamación [ah-clah-mah-the-on'], *f.* Acclamation, the act of shouting with joy. **Elegir por aclamación**, to elect by acclamation.

aclamador, ra [ah-clah-mah-dor', rah], *m. & f.* Applauder.

aclamar [ah-clah-mar'], *va.* 1. To shout with joy, to applaud. **Aclamar a uno por jefe**, to claim somebody

aclamideo, a [ah-clah-mee'-day-o, ah], *a.* Having no floral envelopes; naked.

aclaración [ah-clah-rah-the-on'], 1. *f.* Illustration, explanation. 2. Rinse, rinsing (ropa).

aclarado [ah-clah-rah-do], *m.* Rinse.

aclarador, ra [ah-clah-rah-dor', rah], *a.* Explanatory, illustrative. *-m.* A kind of comb in looms for making silk fringes.

aclarar [ah-clah-rar'], *va.* 1. To rinse (ropa). 2. To clear from obscurity, to make bright. 3. To illustrate, to explain. **No me aclaro**, I can't work it out. 4. To widen, to clarify, to resolve. *-vn.* To clear into, to recover brightness.

aclaratorio [ah-clah-rah-to-reo], *a.* Explanatory, illuminating.

aclayos [ah-clah-yos], *mpl. (Mex.)* Eyes.

aclimatación [ah-cle-mah-tah-the-on'], *f.* Acclimation; acclimatization.

aclimatar [ah-cle-mah-tar'], *va.* To acclimatize, to habituate to a strange climate.

aclimatarse [ah-cle-mah-tahr-say], *vr.* To acclimatize oneself, to get acclimatized, acclimate (US). **Aclimatarse a algo**, to get used to something.

aclocado, da [ah-cloh-cah'-do, dah], *a.* Stretched at a fire, table, etc. *-pp.* of ACLOCARSE.

aclocarse [ah-cloh-car'say], *vr.* 1. To brood, to hatch eggs. 2. To stretch oneself on the ground, bench, etc.

acné [ac'-nay], *f.* Acne, a skin condition.

ACNUR [ac-noor], *m. abr.* de **Alto Comisario de las Naciones Unidas para los Refugiados** (United Nations High Commision for Refugees, UNHCR).

acobardar [ah-co-bar-dar'], *va.* To daunt, to intimidate, to terrify.

acobardarse [ah-co-bahr-dahr-say], *vr.* To be frightened, to get frightened; to flinch, to shrink back.

acobe [ah-co-bay], *m. (Carib.)* Iron.

acobrado [ahco-brah-do], *a.* Copper-colored, coppery.

acocear [ah-co-thay-ar'], *va.* To kick, to wince, to flinch. *(fig.)* **Maltratar**, to ill-treat, trample on. **Insultar**, to insult.

acocil [ah-co-thel], *m. (Mex.)* **Camarón**, freshwater shrimp.

acochambrar [ah-co-chahm-brar], *vt. (Mex.)* To make filthy.

acocharse [ah-co-char'-say], *vr.* To squat, to stoop down.

acochinar [ah-co-che-nar'], *va.* 1. To murder, to assassinate. 2. *(Met.)* To prevent or obstruct the regular course of a suit at law; to hush up. 3. To humble.

acocotar [ah-co-co-tar'], *va.* To kill by a blow upon the neck.

acocote [ah-co-coh'-tay], *m.* A long gourd pointed at both ends, used in Mexico for extracting the nectar of the maguey.

acodado [ah-co-dah-do], *a.* Bent, elbowed.

acodadura [ah-co-dah-doo'-rah], *f.* 1. The act of bending the elbow. 2. *(Agri.)* Layering.

acodalar [ah-co-dah-lar'], *va. (Arch.)* To put lintels or transoms in a wall to support a window or niche, to shore up, to prop up.

acodar [ah-co-dar], *va.* 1. *(Obs.)* To lean the elbow upon. 2. To lay cuttings of vines or other plants in the ground, that they may take root. 3. To square timber.

acoderarse [ah-co-day-rar'-say], *vr.* 1. To put a spring on a cable. 2. *(Naut.)* To bring the broadside to bear. 3. To lean on. **Acodarse en**, leaning on.

acodiciar [ah-co-de-the-ar'], *va. (Obs.)* To urge on; to urgently long for, covet, something. *-vr.* To be provoked, to be inflamed with passion.

acodiciarse [ah-co-de-the-ahr-say], *vr.* **Acodiciarse a**, to covet.

acodillar [ah-co-dil-lyar'], *va.* 1. To bend something to an elbow or angle. 2. To sink down under a burden. **Acodillarse con la carga**, *(Met.)* not to be able to fulfil one's engagements.

acodo [ah-co'-do], *m.* A shoot or knot of a layer; a scion.

acogedizo, za [ah-co-hay-dee'-tho, thah], *a.* Collected or gathered easily.

acogedor, ra [ah-co-hay-do', rah], *m. & f.* Harborer, protector. *a.* Welcoming, friendly, hospitable, warm.

acoger [ah-co-herr'], *va.* 1. To admit one into our house or company; to receive. 2. *(Met.)* To protect, to give asylum. *-vr.* 1. To take refuge, to resort to. 2. *(Obs.)* To embrace the opinion of another. 3. To make use of a pretext for dissimulation.

acogerse [ah-co-hayr-say], *vr.* To take refuge. **Acogerse a la ley**, to have recourse to the law.

acogible [ah-co-he-blay], *a. (Cono Sur)* Acceptable.

acogida [ah-co-hee'-dah], *f.* 1. Reception. 2. The concurrence of a multitude of things in the same place; confluence; asylum. **Dar acogida a una letra**. *(Com.)* to honor or protect a bill. **Reservar buena acogida a**, to meet prompt attention.

acogido [ah-co-hee'-do], *m.* 1. Collection of breeding mares given to the owner of the principal steed, to keep them at a certain price. 2. Temporary admission of flocks into pasture-ground. *-pp.* of ACOGER.

acogimiento [ah-co-he-me-en'-to], *m.* V. ACOGIDA.

acogollar [ah-co-gol-lyar'], *va.* To cover delicate plants with straw to provide shelter.

acogolladura [ah-co-gol-lyah-doo'-rah], *f.* Earthing up of plants.

acogombradura [ah-co-gom-brah-doo'-rah], *f.* Digging up of the ground about plants.

acogombrar [ah-co-gom-brar'], *va.* To dig up the ground about plants; to cover plants with earth.

acogotar [ah-co-go-tar'], *va.* To kill by a blow on the neck, to knock down. *(coll.)* To overcome a person.

acohombrar [ah-co-om-brahr], *va. (Agri.)* To earth up.

acojinar [ah-co-he-nahr], *va. (Tec.)* To cushion.

acojonador [ah-co-ho-nah-dhor], *a.* V. ACOJONANTE.

acojonar [ah-co-ho-nahr], *m. (Esp.)* 1. va 1. To put the wind up (atemorizar), intimidate. 2. To impress (impresionar); to amaze (asombrar), overwhelm.

acojonarse [ah-co-ho-nahr-say], *vr* To back down (acobardarse); To be amazed (asombrarse), be overwhelmed.

acojono [ah-co-ho-no], *m. (Esp.)* funk, fear.

acolada [ah-co-lah'-da], *f.* Accolade, a ceremony which consisted of an embrace and a touch with the flat of the sword on each shoulder of one who was receiving knighthood.

acolar [ah-co-lar'], *va. (Her.)* To arrange or unite two coats of arms under the same crown, shield, etc.

acolchado [ah-col-chah-do], *a.* Quilted, padded.

acolchar [ah-col-char'], *va.* To quilt, pad.

acólito [ah-co'-le-to], *m.* 1. Acolyte, assistant to a priest at mass. 2. An assistant.

acolladores [ah-col-lyah-do'-res], *m. pl. (Naut.)* Lanyards. **Acolladores de los obenques**, The lanyards of the shrouds.

acollarado, da [ah-col-lyah-rah'-do, dah], *a.* **Pájaros acollarados**, birds having about their necks a ring of feathers of a different color.

acollarar [ah-col-lyah-rar'], *va.* 1. To yoke or harness horses, oxen, etc. 2. To couple hounds. 3. *(Agri.)* To earth up. 4. *(Naut.)* To caulk.

acollerar [ah-co-lyahr], *va.* To gather, herd together.

acombar [ah-com-bar'], *va.* To bend, to crook.

acomedido [ah-co-may-te-do], *a. (LAm.)* Helpful, obliging (generoso); concerned, solicitous (solícito).

acomedirse [ah-co-may-der-say], *vr. (LAm.)* To offer to help. **Acomedirse a hacer algo**, to do something willingly.

acomendador [ah-co-men-dah-dor'], *m. (Obs.)* Protector, aider.

acometedor, ra [ah-co-may-tay-dor', rah], *m. & f.* An aggressor, energetic, enterprising.

acometer [ah-co-may-terr'], *va.* 1. To attack, to assault. 2. To undertake. 3. To tempt. **Acometerse mutuamente**, to jostle.

acometida, *f.* **acometimiento**, *m.* [ah-co-may-tee'-dah, ah-co-may-te-me-en'-to] Attack, assault. **Acometimiento de calentura**, a fit or access of fever.

acometividad [ah-co-may-te-be-dahd], *f.* 1. Energy, enterprise (energía). 2. Aggressiveness (agresividad).

acomodable [ah-co-mo-dah'-blay], *a.* Accommodable, suitable.

acomodación [ah-co-mo-dah-the-on'], *f.* Accommodation, adaptation.

acomodadamente [ah-co-mo-dah-dah-men'-tay], *adv.* Commodiously, suitably.

acomodado, da [ah-co-mo-dah'-do, dah], *a.* 1. Convenient, fit. 2. Rich, wealthy. 3. Fond of comfort. 4. Moderate. *pp.* of ACOMODAR.

acomodador, ra [ah-o-mo-dah-dor', rah], *m. & f.* 1. The person that accommodates; box-keeper in the theater. 2. Usher.

acomodamiento [ah-co-mo-dah-me-en'-to], *m.* Accommodation, the act an effect of accommodating, convenience.

acomodar [ah-co-mo-dar'], *va.* 1. To accommodate. 2. To put in a convenient place. 3. To reconcile; to compound. 4. To furnish. *-vn.* To fit, to suit. *-vr.* To condescend, to conform oneself, to comply.

acomodarse [ah-co-mo-dahr-say], *vr.* 1. To comply, conform. 2. To install, settle down. **¡Acomódese a su gusto!**, make yourself at home! 3. *(Cono Sur)* To fix oneself up (with a job) (colocarse), to pull strings; *(fig.)* to marry into money. 4. To reconcile oneself (acomodarse con); to come to an agreement.

acomodaticio, cia [ah-co-mo-dah-tee'-the-o, ah], *a.* 1. Accommodating, compliant. 2. *(Ant.)* Figurative, metaphorical.

acomodo [ah-co-mo'-do], *m.* 1. Employment, place, situation; lodgings. Agreement, understanding. 2. Post, job (puesto); *(LAm.)* soft (pluma), job. 3. *(LAm.)* bribe (soborno); *(Mex.)* deal (arreglo).

acompañado, da [ah-com-pah-nyah'-do, dah], *a.* 1. Accompanied. 2. Busy, frequented (lugar). 3. **Con falda acompañada**, with skirt to match, with a skirt of the same color. 4. **Estar acompañado**, *(Carib.)* to be drunk. 2. *m.* An asssistant judge, surgeon, physician, etc. -*pp.* of ACOMPAÑAR.

acompañador, ra [ah-com-pah-nyah-dor', rah], *m. & f.* 1. A chaperon, an attendant; companion. 2. *(Mus.)* Accompanyist.

acompañamiento [ah-com-pah-nyah-me-en'-to], *m.* 1. Attendance. 2. Retinue. 3. *(Mus.)* Accompaniment. 4. Supernumeraries at a theater. 5. *(Her.)* The ornament which is constantly placed at the side of the escutcheon. 6. Escort (persona).

acompañanta [ah-com-pah-nyan-tah], *f.* Female companion, chaperon. *(Mus.)* accompanist.

acompañante [ah-compah-nyan-tay], *m.* Companion, escort, *(Mus.)* accompanist.

acompañar [ah-com-pah-nyar'], *va.* 1. To accompany, to attend, to conduct, to follow, to lead along. **Prefiero que no me acompañen**, I prefer to go alone. **¿Quieres que te acompañe?**, do you want me to come with you? **Acompañar a uno a la puerta**, to see somebody to the door. 2. To join, or unite. 3. *(Mus.)* To sing or play in concert with others. 4. *(Mus.)* Accompany (a, con). 5. To enclose, attach (carta). 6. **Acompañar a uno en**, to join somebody in. 7. **Acompañar a la flaca**, *(Mex.)* to kick the bucket. -*vr.* To hold a consultation.

acompaño [ah-com-pah-nyo], *m. (CAm. Mex.)* Meeting, group, crowd.

acompasado, da [ah-com-pah-sah'-do, dah], *a.* 1. Measured by the metronome. 2. *(coll.)* Monotonous and slow in tone. 3. Of fixed, regular habits.

acompasar [ah-com-paha-sahr], *va.* 1. *(Mat.)* To measure with a metronome. *(Mus.)* To mark the rhythm of.

acomplejado [ah-com-play-hah-do], *a.* Full of complexes.

acomplejante [ah-com-play-hahn-tay], *a. (Cono Sur)* Inhibiting, embarrassing.

acomplejar [ah-com-play-hahr], *va.* To cause complexes in, to give a complex to.

acomplejarse [ah-com-play-hahr-say], *vr.* To get a complex.

acompletadores [ah-com-play-tah-do-rays], *mpl. (Mex.)* Beans.

acomplexionado, da [ah-com-plex-e-o-nah'-do, dah], *a.* Of a good or bad complexion or constitution.

acomunarse [ah-co-moo-nahr-say]. *vr.* To join forces.

Aconcagua [Ah-con-cah-goo-ah], *m.* **El monte Aconcagua**, *(Arg.)* (Mount) Aconcagua.

aconchabarse [ah-con-chah-bar'-say], *vr.* To gang up. *(coll.)* V. ACOMODARSE.

aconchado [ah-con-chah-do], *m. (Mex.)* Sponger, scrounger.

aconchar [ah-con-char'], *va.* 1. *(Naut.)* To fit out or repair a ship. 2. To drive ashore. 3. To put safety. 4. *(Mex.)* To tell off (reprender).

aconcharse [ah-con-chahr-say], *vr.* 1. *(Naut.)* To keel over; to run aground. 2. *(Cono Sur)* To settle, clarify (líquido). 3. **Vivir de otro**, to sponge, to live off somebody else.

aconcia [ah-con'-the-ah], *f. (Astr.)* Generic name of comets with a thick nebulosity and delicate tail.

acondicionado, da [ah-con-de-the'-o-nah'-do, dah], *a.* Of a good or bad condition. **Hombre bien o mal acondicionado**, a man of a good or bad disposition. **Géneros bien o mal acondicionados**, goods in a good or bad condition. -*pp.* of ACONDICIONAR.

acondicionador [ah-con-de-the-o-nah-dor], *m.* **Acondicionador de aire**, air conditioner.

acondicionamiento del aire [ah-con-de-the-o-nah-me-en'-to del ah'-e-ray], *m.* or **clima artificial** [clee'-mah ar-te-fe-the-ahl'], *m.* Air conditioning.

acondicionar [ah-con-de-the-o-nar'], *va.* 1. To prepare, to arrange, to dispose, to fit. 2. To affect. 3. To constitute. -*vr.* To acquire a determined quality or condition. **Acondicionar para uso invernal**, to winterize.

acongojado [ah-con-go-hah-do], *a.* Distressed, anguished.

acongojar [ah-con-go-har'], *va.* To vex, to oppress, to afflict.

acongojarse [ah-con-go-hahr-say], *vr.* To become distressed, to get upset. **¡No te acongojes!**, don't get upset.

acónito [ah-co'-ne-to], *m. (Bot.)* Aconite, wolf's bane.

aconsejable [ah-con-say-hah'-blay], *a.* Advisable, sensible, politic. **Nada aconsejable; poco aconsejable**, inadvisable.

aconsejado [ah-con-say-hah-do], *a.* Bien aconsejado, well advised.

aconsejador, ra [ah-con-say-hah-dor'-rah], *m. & f.* An adviser, counsellor.

aconsejar [ah-con-say-har'], *va.* To advise, to counsel. -*vr.* To take advice, to be advised.

aconsejarse [ah-con-say-hahr-say], *vr.* To seek advice, to take advice. **Aconsejarse con; aconsejarse de**, to consult.

aconsonantar [ah-con-so-nan-tar'], *va.* 1. To observe a complete rhyme at the end of each verse. 2. To use in prose rhymes suitable to poetry only.

acontecedero, ra [ah-con-tay-thay-day'-ro, rah], *a.* That which may happen.

acontecer [ah-con-tay-therr'], *v. impers.* To happen, to come about, to fare. **Acontecimiento** [ah-con-tay-the-me-en'-to], *m.* Event, incident, casualty, occurrence. **Fue realmente un acontecimiento**, it was an event of some importance.

acopado, da [ah-coh-pah'-do, dah], *a.* Having the form of a cup or vase. -*pp.* of ACOPAR.

acopar [ah-coh-par'], *vn.* To form a round head in the shape of a cup: applied to trees and plants.

acopiador [ah-co-pe-ah-dor'], *m. (Com.)* One who buys up goods to keep them off the market.

acopiamiento [ah-co-pe-ah-me-en'-to], *m.* The act and effect of gathering.

acopiar [ah-co-pe-ar'], *va.* To gather, to store up, to forestall.

acopio [ah-co'-pe-o], *m.* Gathering, storing. **Acopio usuario**, illicit or unfair buying up of goods; «rigging the market». **Hacer acopio**, to stock up, to lay in stocks.

acoplado, da [ah-co-plah'-do, dah], 1. *a.* Fitted, adjusted. 2. *m. (LAm.)* trailer. 3. *(Cono Sur)* hanger-on, sponger (parásito). -*pp.* of ACOPLAR.

acoplador [ah-co-plah-dor], *m.* **Acoplador acústico**, acoustic coupler.

acopladura [ah-co-plah-doo'-rah], *f. (Carp.)* Coupling, junction.

acoplamiento [ah-co-plah-me-ayn-to], *m. (Mech.)* Coupling, joint. *(Elec.)* Connection, hookup. **Acoplamiento en serie**, series connection. **Acoplamiento Universal**, universal joint.

acoplar [ah-co-plar'], *va.* 1. To accouple, to join. 2. To frame timber. 3. To settle differences. -*vr.* To make up matters, to be agreed.

acoplo [ah-co-plo], *m. (Elec.)* Feedback.

acoquinamiento [ah-co-ke-nah-me-ayn-to], *m.* Intimidation.

acoquinar [ah-co-ke-nahr], *va.* To scare, to intimidate, to cow.

acoquinarse [ah-ko-kee-nahr'-say], *vr.* To become terrified.

acorar [ah-ko-rar'], *va.* To grieve, to distress, to afflict, to upset.

acorazado, da [ah-ko-rah-thah'-do], *m.* Battleship, battlewagon.

acorazar [ah-ko-rah-thar'], *va.* To armor, to cover with armor plate. -*vr.* To steel oneself.

acorazonado, da [ah-co-rah-tho-nah'-do, dah] *a.* Heart-shaped.

acorchar [ah-cor-chahr], *va.* To cover with cork.

acorcharse [ah-cor-char'-say], *vr.* 1. To shrivel: applied to the fruits (from *corcho*, cork.) 2. To become torpid.

acordación [ah-cor-dah-the-on'], *f. (Obs.)* Remembrance.

acordada [ah-cor-dah'-dah], *f.* Resolution, decision.

acordadamente [ah-cor-dah-dah-men'-tay], *adv.* By common consent, jointly; with mature deliberation.

acordado, da [ah-cor-dah'-do, dah], *a.* 1. Agreed. 2. Done with mature deliberation. **Lo acordado**, decree of a tribunal enforcing the observance of prior proceedings. *-pp.* of ACORDAR.

acordar [ah-cor-dar'], *va.* 1. To resolve by common consent, to concert. 2. To remind. 3. To tune musical instruments; to dispose figures in a picture. *-vn.* To agree, to level. *-vr.* 1. (ponerse de acuerdo) to agree. To remember. **Si mal no recuerdo,** if my memory serves me right. **Acordarse de algo,** to remember something, to recollect. 2. To come to an agreement. **Te acordarás de mí,** you will remember me. **Acordarse o estar de acuerdo con uno,** to agree with one. (Yo acuerdo, yo acuerde. *V.* ACORDAR).

acorde [ah-cor'-day], *a.* 1. Conformable, correspondent. 2. Coinciding in opinion. *-m.* 1. Consonance.2. Harmony of sounds or colors.

acordelar [ah-cor-day-lar'], *va.* To measure with a cord; to draw a right line by a wall or street, in order to make it straight.

acordemente [ah-cor-day-men'-tay], *adv.* By common consent.

acordeón [ah-cor-day-on'], *m.* Accordion, musical instrument.

acordeonista [ah-cor-day-o-nes-tah], *f.* Accordionist.

acordeón-piano [ah-cor-day-on], *m.* Piano-accordion.

acordonado, da [ah-cor-do-nah'-do, dah], *a.*1. Surrounded, ribbed, cordoned off. 2. Made in the form of a cord. *-pp.* of ACORDONAR.

acordonamiento [ah-cor-do-nah-me-ayn-to], *m.* Ribbing, cordoning off; milling.

acordonar [ah-cor-do-nar'], *va.* 1. To make in the form of a cord or rope, to tie up. 2. To surround. 3. To mill (moneda). 4. *(LAm.)* To prepare (terreno).

acores [ah-co'-res], *m. pl. (Med.)* Achor, a species of herpes.

acornear [ah-cor-nay-ar'], *va.* To fight or strike with the horns, to butt.

acoro [ah'-cor-ro], *m. (Bot.)* Sweetsmelling lag, sweet cane, sweet grass.

acorralamiento [ah-co-rrah-lah-me-ayn-to], *m.* Enclosing, cornering, trapping.

acorralar [ah-cor-rah-lar'], *va.* 1. To shut up cattle or sheep in pens; to corral. 2. To intimidate. 3. To silence.

acorrer [ah-cor-rrer'], *va.* 1. To help. 2. To run to. 3. To shame.

acortamiento [ah-cor-tah-me-en'-to], *m.* 1. Shortening. 2. *(Astr.)* Difference in the distance from the center of the globe to the ecliptic and center of a planet in its orbit. 3. Restraint.

acortar [ah-cor-tar'], *va.* 1. To shorten, to lessen. 2. To obstruct. **Acortar la vela,** *(Naut.)* To shorten sail. *-vr.* 1. To shrivel, to be contracted. 2. To be bashful; to fall back.

acorullar [ah-cor-rro-lyar'], *va. (Naut.)* To bridle or hold up the cars.

acorvar [ah-cor-var'], *va.* To double, to bend. *V.* ENCORVAR.

acosador, ra [ah-co-sah-dor', rah], *m. & f.* A pursuer, persecutor.

acosamiento [ah-co-sah-me-en'-to], *m.* Persecution, molestation.

acosar [ah-co-sar'], *va.* 1. To pursue closely. 2. To vex, to molest, to harass. **Acosar a uno a preguntas,** to pester somebody with questions.

acosijar [ah-co-se-hahr], *va. (Mex.)* Acosar.

acoso [ah-co-so], *m.* Relentless pursuit; hounding, harassing; relentless questioning. **Acoso sexual,** sexual harassment.

acostado, da [ah-cos-tah'-do, dah], *a.* 1. Stretched, laid down. 2. *(Obs.)* Salaried. 3. *(Her.)* Accosted. *-pp.* of ACOSTAR.

acostamiento [ah-cos-tah-me-en'-to], *m.* 1. The act of stretching or laying down. 2. *(Obs.)* A certain pay, a salary.

acostar [ah-cos-tar'], *va.* To lay down, to put one in bed.

acostarse [ah-cos-tahr-say], *vr.* 1. To incline to one side; to lie down. To give birth. **Estar acostado,** to be lying down.

2. To approach. 3. *(Naut.)* To stand inshore. 4. *(Naut.)* To lie along; to have a list. **Acostarse con,** to sleep with.

acostumbradamente [ah-cos-toom-brah-dah-men'-tay], *adv.* Customarily, according to custom.

acostumbrado [ah-cos-toom-brah-do], *a.* Usual, customary, habitual.

acostumbrar [ah-cos-toom-brar'], *va.* To accustom, to use. **Acostumbrar a uno a hacer algo,** to accustom somebody to do something. *-vn.* To be accustomed, to habituate. **Los sábados acostumbra a ir al cine,** on Saturdays he usually goes to the movies.

acostumbrarse [ah-cos-toom-brahr-say], *vr.* 1. **Acostumbrarse a algo,** to accustom oneself to something, to get accustomed to something. 2. *(LAm.)* **No se acostumbra aquí,** it isn't usual here.

acotación [ah-co-tah-the-on'], *f.* 1. The act and the effect of setting bounds; limit. 2. Annotation or quotation in the margin.

acotado [ah-co-tah-do], *a.* Enclosed, fenced.

acotamiento [ah-co-tah-me-en'-to], *m.* Limitation.

acotar [ah-co-tar'], *va.* 1. To limit, to set bounds. **Acótome a Dios,** let God fix my end; used at sports to express confidence in the actual safety of the place. 2. To fix, to mark. 3. To quote, to make annotations in the margin. 4. To accept for a certain price. 5. To witness.

acotiledóneo, a [ah-co-te-lay-do'-nay-o, ah], *a.* Not provided with seed-leaves.

acotillo [ah-co-teel'-lyo], *m.* A large hammer used by smiths. Sledge-hammer.

acoyundar [ah-co-yoon-dar'], *va.* To yoke oxen to a load.

acr., *abr.* de **acreedor** (creditor, Cr.)

acracia [ah-crah-the-ah], *f.* Anarchy.

ácrata [ah-crah-tah], 1. *a.* Non-conformist, hippy, free-and-easy, unconventional, loose living. 2. *m. & f.* Non-conformist, hippy, drop out, unconventional.

acrático [ah-crah-te-co], *a. V.* ÁCRATA

acre [ah'-cray], *a.* 1. Sour, acrimonious, hot. 2. Mordant, keen. 3. Rough, rude.

acre [ah-cray], *m.* Acre (medida).

acrebite [ah-cray-bee'-tay], *m. & f.* Sulphur. *V.* ALCREBITE. *(Arab.).*

acrecencia, *f.* **acrecentamiento,** *m.* [ah-cray-then'-the-ah, ah cray-then-tah-me-en'-to], Increase, augmentation, growth.

acrecentador, ra [ah-cray-then-tah-dor', rah], *m. & f.* One that increases.

acrecentar, acrecer [ah-cray-then-tar', ah-cray-therr'], *va.* To increase. **Derecho de acrecer,** The right of accretion in cathedral chapters, where a distribution is made according to the present residence of the prebendaries. *(Yo acreciento, yo acreciente,* from *Acrecentar. V.* ACERTAR).

acrecentarse [ah-cray-thayn-tahr-say], *vr.* To increase, to grow.

acrecer [ah-cray-thayr], *va.* To increase.

acrecimiento [ah-cray-the-me-ayn-to], *m.* Increase, growth.

acreditación [ah-cray-de-tah-the-on], *f.* Accreditation.

acreditado, da [ah-cray-de-tah'-do, dah], *a.* Accredited, distinguished. Marca acreditada, reputable make. *-pp.* of ACREDITAR.

acreditar [ah-cray-de-tar'], *va.* 1. To assure, to affirm a thing for certain. 2. To credit, to procure credit. 3. To prove.

acreditarse [ah-cray-de-tahr-say], *vr.* To justify, to prove one's worth. **Acreditarse en,** to get a reputation in.

acreditivo [ah-cray-de-tah-te-bo], *a.* **Documentos acreditivos,** supporting documents.

acreedor [ah-cray-ay-dor'], *m.* 1. A creditor. **Acreedor hipotecario,** mortgagee. 2. *(Met.)* A meritorious person. 3. *a.* **Acreedor a,** worthy of.

acreedora [ah-cray-ay-do'-rah], *f.* Creditrix, creditress.

acreencia [ah-cray-en'-the-ah], *f. (Com.)* Claim, credit balance, debt.

acremente [ah-cray-men'tay], *adv.* Sourly, with acrimony.

acribadura [ah-cre-bah-doo'-rah], *f.* Sifting. *-pl.* Siftings, the remains of grain which has been sifted.

acribar [ah-cre-bar'], *va.* 1. To sift. 2. *(Met.)* To pierce like a sieve.

acribillado [ah-cre-be-lyah-do], *a.* Pitted, pockmarked, **Acribillado de**, filled with, **Acribillado de picaduras**, covered with stings.

acribillar [ah-cre-bil-lyar'], *va.* 1. To pierce like a sieve. 2. *(Met.)* To molest, to torment. **Acribillar a uno a preguntas**, to pester somebody with questions.

acridia [ah-cree'-de-ah], *f.* Acridia, a genus of locusts.

acridófago [ah-cre-do'-fah-go], *a.* Living on locusts.

acrílico, ca [ah-cree'-le-co, cah], *a.* Acrylic.

acriminación [ah-cre-me-nah-the-on'], *f.* Incrimination, the act of accusing or impeaching.

acriminador, ra [ah-cre-me-nah-dor', rah], *m. & f.* Accuser, informer.

acriminar [ah-cre-me-nar'], *va.* 1. To exaggerate a crime or fault. 2. To accuse, to impeach. 3. *(Law.)* To aggravate.

acrimonia [ah-cre-mo'-ne-ah], *f.* 1. Acrimony, sharpness, sourness. 2. *(Met.)* Asperity of expression, keenness, sharpness of temper. 3. *(Met.)* Vehemence in talking.

acrimonioso [ah-cre-mo-ne-o-so], *a.* Acrimonious.

acriollarse [ah-cre-o-lyah-say], *vr (LAm.)* To take on local habits (or the habits of the country).

acrisolado [ah-cre-so-lah-do], *a.* Pure; tried, tested; unquestionable. **El patriotismo más acrisolado**, the noblest kind of patriotism.

acrisolar [ah-cre-so-lar'], *va.* 1. To refine, to purify gold or other metals, to cleanse. 2. *(Met.)* To clear up a thing by means of witnesses.

acristalado [ah-cre-so-lah-do], *a.* Glazed.

acristalamiento [ah-cres-tah-lah-me-ayn-to], *m.* Glazing. **Los acristalamientos**, windows. **Doble acristalamiento**, double glazing.

acristianar [ah-cris-te-ah-nar'], *va. (coll.)* To baptize, to christen.

acritud [ah-cree-tood'], *f.* V. ACRIMONIA.

acrobacia [ah-cro-bah'-the-ah], *f.* Acrobatics; **Acrobacia aérea**, stunt flying.

acróbata [ah-cro'-ba-tah], *m. & f.* Rope-dancer, acrobat.

acrobático, ca [ah-cro-bah'-te-co, cah], *a.* Acrobatic.

acrobatismo [ah-cro-bah-tes-mo], *m.* Acrobatics.

acromático, ca [ah-cro-mah'-te-co, cah], *a. (Opt.)* Achromatic.

acromatismo [ah-cro-mah-tees'-mo], *m.* Achromatism, freedom from spherical aberration.

acromatizar [ah-cro-mah-tee-thar'], *va.* To render achromatic; to achromatize.

acrónicamente [ah-cro'-ne-cah-men'-tay], *adv. (Astr.)* Acronycally.

acrónico, ca [ah-cro'-ne-co, cah], *a.* Acronycal, applied to the rising of a star when the sun sets, or its setting when the sun rises.

acrópolis [ah-cro-po-les], *f.* Acropolis.

acróstico, ca [ah-cros'-te-co, cah], *a.* **Versos acrósticos**, acrostic verses.

acrotera, acroteria [ah-cro-tay-ra, ah-cro-tay'-re-a], *f.* 1. A small pedestal placed at the extremities of pediments, and serving also to support figures, etc. 2. The highest part of columns or buildings.

acroterio [ah-cro-tay'-re-o], *m.* The superior of the three parts of which the frontispiece of a building is composed.

acta [ahc'-tah], *f.* Act or record of proceedings. *-pl.* 1. The acts or records of communities, chapters, councils. Papers, file, etc. **Acta de defunción**, death certificate. **Acta constitutiva**, charter. **Acta de nacimiento**, birth certificate. *(Com.)* 2. **Actas de los santos**, the lives of the saints.

actimo [ac-tee'-mo], *m.* The twelfth part of a measure called **punto**; there are 1,728 actimos in a geometric foot.

actina [ac-tee'-nah], *m.* Actin.

actinia [ac-tee'-ne-ah], *f.* Actinia, sea anemone.

actínico [ac-te-ne-co], *a.* Actinic.

actinio [ac-te-ne-o], *m.* Actininium.

actitud [ac-te-tood'], 1. *f.* Attitude, position, posture. 2. *(fig.)* Attitude, position, outlook, policy. **La postura del gobierno**, the government's attitude. **Adoptar una actitud firme**, to take a firm stand.

activación [ac-te-va-the-on], *f.* Activation, expediting, speeding-up, stimulation.

activador [ac-te-vah-dor'], *m. (Chem.)* Activator.

activamente [ac-te-vah-men'-tay], *adv.* Actively.

activar [ac-te-var'], *va.* 1. To push, to make brisk, to hasten, 2. *(Comp.)* To switch on.

activas, *f. pl.* **activo**, *m.* [ac-tee'-vahs, ac-tee'-vo], *(Com.)* Assets, outstanding claims.

actividad [ac-te-ve-dad'], *f.* 1. Activity. 2. Quickness in performing; liveliness, nimbleness. **Estar en plena actividad**, to be in full swing.

activismo [ac-te-ves-mo], *m. (LAm.)* Political activity.

activista [ac-te-ves-tah], *m. & f.* Activist, political activist.

activo, va [ac-tee'-vo, vah], 1. *a.* Active, diligent, forward, fiery, lively, energetic. **Voz activa**, suffrage. 2. *m.* Assets. **Activo neto**, net worth. **Activo y pasivo**, assets and liabilities. 3. **Oficial en activo**, *(Mil.)* serving officer, to be on active service.

acto [ahc'-to], *m.* 1. Act or action. **Actos de los apóstoles**, acts (of the apostles) 2. Act of a play. 3. Thesis defended in universities. **Acto inaugural**, opening ceremony. 4. Carnal communication. **Actos** *(Obs.)* 1. *V.* AUTOS. 2. Document, papers.

actor [ac-tor'], *m.* 1. Performer, player, actor. 2. *(Obs.)* Author. 3. Plaintiff, claimant. 4. Proctor, attorney.

actora [ac-to'-rah], *f.* Plaintiff, she who seeks justice.

actriz [ac-treeth'], *f.* Actress. **Primera actriz**, leading lady.

actuación [ac-too-ah-the-on'], *f.* 1. Actuation, moving, acting. **Su actuación fue importante**, his role was an important one. 2. **Actuaciones** *(Jur.)* legal proceedings. 3. **Actuación pericial**, expert valuation.

actuado, da [ac-too-ah'-do, dah], *a.* 1. Actuated. 2. Skilled, experienced. *-pp.* of ACTUAR.

actual [ac-too-ahl'], *a.* Actual, present, fashionable. **El 6 del actual**, the 6th day of this month. **El rey actual**, the present king.

actualidad [ac-too-ah-le-dad'], *f.* 1. The actual or present state of things. **En la actualidad**, at present. 2. Present importance, current importance. **Ser de gran actualidad**, to be current. 3. **Actualidades**, current events.

actualización [ac-too-ah-le-thah-the-on], *f.* Modernization, bringing up to date; refresher course, course of retraining (curso); update, updating; discounting (contabilidad).

actualizador [ac-too-ah-le-thah-dor], *va.* Modernizing (influencia).

actualizado [ac-too-ah-le-thah-do], *a. (Comp.)* Refreshed.

actualizar [ac-too-ah-le-thar'], *va. (Prov.)* To realize. To modernize, bring up to date. To discount (contabilidad).

actualmente [ac-too-al-men'-tay], *adv.* At present, at the moment. **Actualmente está fuera**, he's away at the moment.

actuante [ac-too-an'-tay], *pa.* Defender of a thesis in colleges.

actuar [ac-too-ar'], *va.* 1. To work, to actuate, to operate. 2. *(Met.)* To consider, to weigh maturely. 3. To perform judicial acts. 4. To instruct; to support a thesis. *-vn.* to work, actuate, function; to act, perform (persona); **actuar de**, to act as. **Actúa de manera rara**, he's acting strangely.

actuarial [ac-too-ah-re-ahl], *a.* Actuarial.

actuario [ac-too-ah'-re-o], *m.* The clerk of a court of justice (who is always a notary public.)

acuache [ah-coo-ah-chay], *m. (Mex.)* Mate, pal.

acuadrillar [ah-coo-ah-dril-lyar'], *va.* To collect or head a band of armed men; to conduct a squadron of soldiers; to form or to head parties.

acuadrillarse [ah-coo-ah-dre-lyahr-say], *vr.* To band together, to gang up.

acuafortista [ah-coo-ah-for-tees'-tah, *m.* Etcher.

acuanauta [ah-coo-ah-nah'-oo-tah], *m.* Aquanaut.

acuaplano [ah-coo-ah-plah-no], *m.* Surfboarding.

acuarela [ah-coo-ah-ray-lah], *f.* Watercolor.

acuarelista [ah-coo-ah-ray-lees'-tah], *m.* Watercolorist.

acuarelístico, ca [ah-coo-ah-ray-lees'-te-co, cah], *a.* Watercolor.

acuario [ah-coo-ah-re-o], *m.* (Zodíaco) Aquarius.

acuartelado, da [ah-coo-ar-tay-lah'-do, dah], *a.* Divided into quarters. *-pp.* of ACUARTELAR.

acuartelamiento [ah-coo-ar-tay-lah-me-en'-to], *m.* 1. The act of quartering the troops. 2. Quarters.

acuartelar [ah-coo-ar-tay-lar'], *va.* To quarter troops. **Acuartelar las velas** (*Naut.*) To flat in the sails.

acuartelarse [ah-coo-ahr-tay-lahr-say], *vr.* To withdraw to barracks.

acuartillar [ah-coo-ar-til-lyar'], *vn.* To bend in the quarters under a heavy load; applied to beasts of burden.

acuático, ca [ah-coo-ah'-te-co, cah], *a.* V. ACUATIL.

acuátil [ah-coo-ah'teel], *a.* Aquatic, living or growing in water.

acuatinta [ah-coo-ah-ten-tah], *f.* Aquatint.

acuatizaje [ah-coo-ah-te-tha-hay], *m.* (*Aer.*) Touchdown (or landing) on the sea.

acuatizar [ah-coo-ah-te-thahr], *vn.* (*Aer.*) To come down on the water, to land on the sea.

acuchamado [ah-coo-chah-mah-do], *a.* (*Carib.*) Sad, depressed (triste).

acuchamarse [ah-coo-chah-mahr-say], *vr.* (*Carib.*) To get depressed.

acucharado, da [ah-coo-chah-rah'-do, dah], *a.* Spoon-like.

acuchillado, da [ah-coo-chee-lyah'-do, dah], *a.* 1. Slashed, stabbed. 2. (*Met.*) Experienced, skilful by long practice. 3. Slashed or cut in oblong pieces: applied to garments. *-pp.* of ACUCHILLAR.

acuchillador, ra [ah-coo-cheel-lyah-dor', rah], *m. & f.* 1. A quarrelsome person, a bully. 2. Gladiator.

acuchillar [ah-coo-cheel-lyar'], *va.* 1. To cut or hack, to give cuts with a knife. 2. (*Obs.*) To murder. 3. (*Tec.*) To plane down.

acuchillarse [ah-coo-che-lyahr-say], *vr.* To fight with knives or swords. **Se acuchillaron**, they fought with knives.

acuchucar [ah-coo-choo-cahr], *va.* (*Cono Sur*) To crush, to flatten; to crumple.

acucia [ah-coo-the-ah], *f.* Zeal, diligence, haste.

acuciadamente [ah-coo-the-ah-me-ayn-to], *a.* Diligently, keenly; hastily; longingly.

acuciador [ah-coo-the-ah-dor], *a.* **Acuciante** *a.* Pressing, urgent.

acuciar [ah-coo-the-ahr], *va.* To urge on, to goad, to prod (instar); to hasten (dar prisa); to harass (acosar); to mob.

acucioso, sa [ah-coo-the-o'-so, sah], *a.* Zealous, hasty, diligent.

acuclillado, da [ah-coo-cleel-lyah'-do, dah], *a.* Cowering, squatting (fr. *Cuclillas*).

acuclillarse [ah-coo-cleel-lyar'-say], *vr.* To crouch, squat.

acudimiento [ah-coo-de-me-en'-to], *m.* Aid, assistance.

acudir [ah-coo-deer'], *vn.* 1. To come (venir); to succour, to support; to run to, to repair to. **Asistir a la puerta**, to come to the door. 2. To produce; to be docile. 3. To have recourse. **A casa quemada acudir con el agua**, to come with the water when the house is burnt down. 4. To come to the rescue, to go to help (en auxilio).

acueducto [ah-coo-ay-dooc'-to], *m.* 1. Aqueduct. 2. Eustachian tube.

acueo, a [ah-coo-ay-oh, ah], *a.* Watery, aqueous.

acuerdado, da [ah-coo-er-dah'-do, dah], *a.* Constructed by line or rule.

acuerdo [ah-coo-er'-do], *m.* 1. Agreement, understanding 2. Body of the members of a tribunal assembled in the form of a court. 3. Opinion, advice. 4. Concurrence, accord. 5. Reflection, prudence. 6. Memory. 7. (*Art.*) Harmony of colors. **El acuerdo de dos colores**, the harmony of two colors. **De acuerdo**, Unanimously, by common consent. **Ponerse** or **estar de acuerdo**, To agree unanimously, to come to an understanding. (*Yo acuerdo, yo acuerde*, from *Acordar*. V. ACORDAR). (*Yo me acuerdo, yo me acuerde*, from *Acordarse*. V. ACORDAR).

acuicultura [ah-coo-e-cool-too-rah], *f.* Development of water resources, aquaculture.

acuidad [ah-coo-e-dahd], *f.* Acuity.

acuífero [ah-coo-e-fay-ro], *m.* Aquifer.

acuilmarse [ah-coo-el-mahr-say], *vr.* (*CAm.*) To get depressed; to cower, shrink away.

acuitadamente [ah-coo-e-tah-dah-mayn-tay], *a.* Sorrowfully, with regret.

acuitar [ah-coo-e-tar'], *va.* To afflict, to oppress.

acuitarse [ah-coo-e-tahr-say], *vr.* To grieve.

acular [ah-coo-lar'], *1. va.* (*coll.*) To force one into a corner; to oblige one to retreat. 2. *vn.* To back away.

aculebrinado, da [ah-coo-lay-bree-nah'-do, dah], *a.* Made in the form of a culverin: applied to a cannon which resembles a culverin.

acúleo, a [ah-coo'-lay-o, ah], *a.* Aculeate, possessing a string. *-m.* A section of hymenoptera. (*Bot.*) Aculeate, having prickles.

acullá [ah-cool-lyah'], *adv.* On the other side, yonder; opposite. **Aquí y acullá**, here and there.

acullicar [ah-coo-lyahr], *vn.* (*And. Cono Sur*) To chew coca (leaves).

aculturación [ah-cool-too-rah-the-on], *f.* Acculturation.

aculturar [ah-cool-too-rahr], *va.* To acculturate.

acúmetro [ah-coo'-may-tro], *m.* An acoumeter, a device for testing the hearing.

acumíneo, ea [ah-coo-me'-nay-o, ah], *a.* Acuminate, ending in a point.

acumuchar [ah-coo-moo-chahr], *va.* (*Cono Sur*) To pile up, to accumulate.

acumulación [ah-coo-moo-lah-the-on'], *f.* 1. Accumulation, gathering. 2. Act of filing records.

acumulador, ra [ah-coo-moo-lah-dor', rah], *a.* Accumulating *-m. & f.* Accumulator. *m.* Storage battery.

acumular [ah-coo-moo-lar'], *va.* 1. To accumulate, to heap together, to treasure up, to hoard, to lay up. **Acumular vapor**, to get steamed up. 2. To impute, to upbraid with a fault. 3. To file records.

acumularse [ah-coo-moo-lahr-say], *vr.* To accumulate, gather, collect.

acumulativamente [ah-coo-moo-lah-te-vah-men'-tay], *adv.* (*Law.*) 1. By way of prevention; by way of precaution. 2. Jointly, accumulatively.

acumulativo, va [ah-coo-moo-lah-te'-vo, vah], *a.* 1. Precautionary. 2. Accumulative.

acunar [ah-coo-nahr], *va.* To rock (to sleep).

acuñación [ah-coo-nyah-the-on'], *f.* Coining, milling.

acuñador, ra [ah-coo-nyah-dor, rah], *m. & f.* Coiner.

acuñar [ah-coo-nyar'], *va.* 1. To coin. 2. To wedge, or fasten with wedges. **Acuñar dinero**, (*Met.*) to hoard up money. **Hermano ayuda y cuñado acuña**, brothers and sisters-in-law are always at variance.

acuñarse [ah-coo-nyahr-say], *vr.* (*CAm.*) To hit, to sustain a blow.

acuosidad [ah-coo-o-se-dad'], *f.* Wateriness.

acuoso, sa [ah-coo-o'-so, sah], *a.* Watery, aqueous.

acupuntura [ah-coo-poon-too'-rah], *f.* Acupuncture, a surgical mode of counter-irritation by needle thrusts.

acurrado, da [ah-coo-rrah-do], *a.* 1. (*Mex.*) Handsome (guapo). 2. (*CAm.*) Squat, chubby (rechoncho).

acurrucarse [ah-coor-roo-car'-say], *vr.* To muffle oneself up, to squat, crouch; to huddle up (frío), to curl up.

acurrullar [ah-coor-rool-lyar'], *va.* (*Naut.*) To take down the sails of a galley.

acusable [ah-coo-sah'-blay], *a.* Accusable, indictable.

acusación [ah-coo-sah-the-on'], *f.* Accusation, impeachment, charge, expostulation. **Negar la acusación**, to deny the charge, to plead not guilty.

acusado, da [ah-coo-sah-do, dah], 1. *a.* 1. *(Jur.)* Accused. 2. Marked, pronounced (fuerte). 3. *m.* & *f* Accused, defendant.

acusador, ra [ah-coo-sah-dor', rah], *m.* & *f.* Accuser, informer.

acusar [ah-coo-sar'], *va.* 1. To accuse, to incriminate, to lay against, to indict. **Acusar a uno de haber hecho algo**, to accuse someone of having done something. 2. To acknowledge the receipt of. 3. To take charge of. 4. to show, reveal (revelar). **Su silencio acusa cierta cobardía**, his silence betrays a certain cowardice.

acusarse [ah-coo-sahr-say] *vr.* 1. To acknowledge sins to a confessor. **Acusarse de haber hecho algo**, to confess to having done it. 2. To become more marked, get stronger. **Esta tendencia se acusa cada vez más**, this tendency is becoming ever more marked, this tendency gets stronger all the time.

acusativo [ah-coo-sah-tee'-vo], *m.* Accusative, the fourth case in the declension of the Latin nouns.

acusatorio, ria [ah-coo-sah-to'-re-o, ah], *a.* Accusatory, belonging to an accusation.

acuse [ah-coo'-say], *m.* At cards, a certain number estimated to win so much. **Acuse de recibo**, acknowledgement of receipt.

acusetas [ah-coo-say-tahs], *m.* & *f.* *(And. Cono Sur)* Telltale, sneak.

acusica [ah-coo-se-cah] *m.* & *f.* Acusique, tell-tale, sneak.

acusón, na [ah-coo-son, na], *a.* Telltale, sneaking.

acústica [ah-coos'-te-cah], *f.* Acoustics, the doctrine or theory of sounds.

acústico, ca [ah-coos'-te-co, cah], *1. a.* Acoustic. 2. *m.* Hearing aid.

acutángulo [ah-coo-tahn'-goo-lo], *a.* *(Geom.)* Acute-angled.

ada [ah'-dah], *f.* 1. Small apple of the pippin kind. 2. A very poisonous snake. 3. *(Comp.)* Ada (Programming language).

adad [ah-dahd'], *m.* Name of the Creator among the Syrians; the dragon, a noted idol among the Philistines.

adagio [ah-dah'-he-o], *m.* 1. Proverb. 2. *(Mus.)* Adagio, a term used by musicians to mark a slow time. 3. A piece of music in adagio time.

adaguar [ah-dah-goo-ar'], *va.* *(Obs.)* V. ABREVAR.

adala [ah-dah'-lah], *f.* *(Naut.)* Pumpdeal.

adalid [ah-dah-leed'], *m.* A chief, a commander, a leader, a champion.

adamado, da [ah-dah-mah'-do, dah], *a.* Lady-like: applied to vulgar women.

adamantino, na [ah-dah-man-tee'-no, nah], *a.* Adamantine.

adamar [ah-dah-mar'], *va.* To love violently. -*vr.* To become as delicate in the face, or in manners, as a lady: to degenerate.

adamascado, da [ah-dah-mas-cah'-do, dah], *a.* Damask-like. -*pp.* of ADAMASCAR.

adamascar [ah-dah-mahs-cahr'], *va.* To damask.

adamita [ah-dah-mee'-tah], *m.* Adamite.

Adán [ah-dan'], *m.* 1. Adam. 2. Slovenly fellow (sucio); Lazy guy (vago); **estar hecho un Adán**, to go about in rags.

adaptabilidad [ah-dap-tah-be-le-dahd'], *f.* Adaptability, adjustment to environmental conditions.

adaptable [ah-dap-tah'-blay], *a.* Capable of being adapted.

adaptación [ah-dap-tah-the-on'], *f.* The act of fitting one thing to another accommodation, adaptation.

adaptadamente [ah-dap-tah-dah-men'-tay], *adv.* In a fit manner.

adaptador [ah-dap-tah-dor], *m.* *(Elec.)* Adapter.

adaptar [ah-dap-tar'], *va.* To adapt, to fit, to apply one thing to another, to fashion.

adaptarse [ah-dap-tahr-say], *vr.* To cohere, to adapt. **Saber adaptarse a las circunstancias**, to be able to cope.

adaraja [ah-dah-rah'-hah], *f.* *(Arch.)* Projecting stones left to continue a wall. Toothing.

adarce [ah-dar'-thay], *m.* 1. Salt froth of the sea dried on canes. 2. *pl.* Carbonate of lime which certain mineral waters deposit.

adarga [ah-dar'-gah], *f.* A shield of an oval form made of leather.

adargar [ah-dar-gar'], *va.* To shield.

adarguero [ah-dar-gay'-ro], *m.* *(Obs.)* One who used a shield.

adarguilla [ah-dar-geel'-lyah]; *f.* A small shield.

adarme [ah-dar'-may], *m.* 1. Half a drachm, the sixteenth part of an ounce. 2. Whit, jot. **Ni un adarme**, not a whit. **No me importa un adarme**, I couldn't care less.

adarvar [ah-dar-var'], *va.* *(Obs.)* To astonish, to astound.

adarve [ah-dar'-vay], *m.* The flat top of a wall.

adatar [ah-dah-tar'], *va.* To open an account; to credit. 2. To annotate, to comment.

adatoda [ah-dah-to'-dah], *f.* *(Bot.)* The willow-leaved Malabar nut-tree.

adaza [ah-dah'-thah], *f.* *(Bot.)* Common panic-grass. V. PANIZO.

A.de C. *m. abr.* de año de Cristo.

adecenamiento [ah-day-thay-nah-me-en'-to], *m.* Act of forming by ten and ten.

adecentar [ah-day-then-tar'], *va.* To render decent, to tidy up, clean up.

adecentarse [ah-day-thayn-tahr-say], *va.* To tidy oneself up.

adecuación [ah-day-coo-ah-the-on'], *f.* Fitness.

adecuadamente [ah-day-coo-ah-dah-men'-tay], *adv.* Fitly, properly, to the purpose.

adecuado, da [ah-day-coo-ah'-do, dah], *a.* Adequate, fit, competent. **Los documentos adecuados**, the appropriate documents. -*pp.* of ADECUAR.

adecuar [ah-day-coo-ar'], *va.* To fit, to accommodate.

adefesiero [Ah-day-fay-se-ay-ro], *a.* *(And. Cono Sur)* Comic, ridiculous (ridículo).

adefesio [ah-day-fay'-se-o], *m.* *(coll.)* Extravagance, folly; something not to the purpose. Ridiculous attire. **Ella está hecha un adefesio**, she looks a fright.

adefesioso [ah-day-fay-se-o-so], *a.* Nonsensical, ridiculous.

adehala [ah-day-ah'-lah], *f.* Gratuity, perquisite.

adehesado [ah-day-ay-sah'-do], *m.* Place converted into pasture. -*pp.* of ADEHESAR.

adehesamiento [ah-day-ay-sah-me-en'-to], *m.* Turning land to pasture, pasturage.

adehesar [ah-day-ay-sar'], *va.* To convert land into pasture.

A. de J.C. *abr.* de **antes de Cristo**, before Christ, B.C.

adela [ah-day-lah], *f.* *(CAm.)* Bittersweet.

adelaida [ah-day-lah-e-dah], *f.* *(Mex.)* Fuchsia.

adelantadamente [ah-day-lan-tah-dah-men-tay], *adv.* Beforehand.

adelantadillo [ah-day-lan-tah-deel'-lyo] *a.* *(Ant.)* Red wine made of the first ripe grapes.

adelantado [ah-day-lan-tah'-do], *m.* An appellation formerly given to the governor of a province.

adelantado, da [ah-day-lan-tah'-do, dah], *a.* 1. Anticipated, advanced, forehand, onward, bold, forward. 2. Early, when applied to fruit or plants. -*pp.* of ADELANTAR.

adelantador, ra [ah-day-lan-tah-dor', rah], *m.* & *f.* One that advances, extends, or amplifies.

adelantamiento [ah-day-lan-tah-me-en'-to], *m.* 1. Progress, improvement, increase; growth, furtherance; cultivation, good. 2. Anticipation. 3. The dignity of the governor formerly called **adelantado**, and the district of his jurisdiction.

adelantar [ah-day-lan-tar'], *va.* 1. To advance, to accelerate, to forward; to graduate; to grow, to keep on. **Adelantar los acontecimiento**, to anticipate events. 2. To anticipate, to pay beforehand. 3. *(Met.)* To improve. 4. *(Obs.)* To push forward. 5. To get ahead. **Estamos a punto de que se nos adelanten**, we are about to be overtaken. -*vr.* 1. To take the lead, to overrun, to come forward. 2. *(Met.)* To excel, to outdo.

adelantarse [ah-day-lahn-tahr-say], *vr.* 1. To go forward, to go ahead (tomar la delantera; to improve. to progress. 2. **Adelantarse a uno**, to get ahead of someone, to outstrip somebody, to pass someone. 3. **Adelantarse a algo**, to anticipate something. **Anticiparse a los deseos de uno**, to anticipate somebody's wishes.

adelante [ah-day-lahn'-tay], *adv.* 1. Farther off; higher up; forward, onward. **En adelante**, henceforth, in future, or for the future. **Quien adelante no mira, atrás se queda**, look before you leap, **adelante**, go on; or, I understand. 2. (cantidad) **De 100 ptas en adelante**, from 100 pesetas. up. 3. (tiempo) **De aquí en adelante; de hoy en adelante**, in the future.

adelanto [ah-day-lahn'-to], *m.* (*Com.*) Advance, progress. **Con los adelantos modernos**, with all the modern improvements. Advance payment.

adelfa [ah-del'-fah], *f.* (*Bot.*) Oleander. Rosebay.

adelfal [ah-del-fahl'], *m.* Plantation of rose-bay trees.

adelfilla [ah-del-feel'-lyah], *f.* The flowering osier, a shrub.

adelfo, fa [ah-del'-fo, fah], *a.* (*Bot.*) Adelphous, having stamens united by their filaments; chiefly used in composition.

adelgazado, da [ah-del-gah-tha'-do, dah], *a.* Made slender or thin. *-pp.* of ADELGAZAR.

adelgazador, ra [ah-del-gah-thah-dor', rah], *m. & f.* One that makes thin or slender.

adelgazamiento [ah-del-gah-tha-me-en'-to] *m.* Act of making slender.

adelgazante [ah-dayl-gah-than-tay], *a.* Slimming.

adelgazar [ah-dayl-gah-thar'], *va.* 1. To attenuate, to make thin (madera), to slender (persona). 2. To lessen. 3. To refine. 4. To taper (una punta). *Vr.* To get thin, to lose weight (persona), to slim. **He adelgazado mucho**, I have slimmed a lot.

adelgazarse [ah-dayl-gah-thahr-say], *vr.* To become slender, to slim.

adelógeno, na [ah-day-lo'-hay-no, nah], *a.* Adelogenous (rocas).

adema [ah-day'-mah], *f.* **ademe** [ah-day'-may], *m.* (*Miner.*) The timber with which the sides of mines are secured. Shore, strut.

ademador [ah-day-mah-dor'], *m.* (*Miner.*) A workman employed in lining the sides of mines with boards.

ademán [ah-day-mahn'], *m.* 1. A gesture, by which approbation or dislike is expressed; look, manner. 2. (*Art.*) Attitude. **En ademán**, in the attitude or posture of performing something.

ademar [ah-day-mar'], *va.* (*Miner.*) To secure the sides of mines with planks or timber; to shore.

además [ah-day-mahs'], *adv.* Moreover, likewise, further; short of this; besides. **Y además le pegó**, and he also beat her.

adementar [ah-day-men-tar'], *va.* To disturb the reason, to addle.

Adén [ah-dayn], *m.* Aden.

ADENA [ah-day-nah], *f.* (*Esp.*) *abr.* de **Asociación para la Defensa de la Naturaleza**.

adenitis [ah-day-nee'-tis], *f.* Adenitis, inflammation of a gland.

adenografía [ah-day-no-grah-fee'-ah], *f.* A treatise on the glands.

adenoideo [ah-day-no-e-do], *a.* Adenoidal.

adenología [ah-day-no-lo-hee'-ah], *f.* (*Anat.*) Description of the glands.

adenoso, sa [ah-day-no'-so, sah], *a.* Glandular.

adentellar [ah-den-tel-lyar'], *va.* To bite, to catch with the teeth. **Adentellar una pared**, To leave toothing-stones or bricks to continue a wall.

adentrarse [ah-dayn-trahr-say], *vr.* **Adentrarse en**, to go into; get into; get inside. **Adentrarse en la selva**, to go deep(er) into the forest.

adentro [ah-den'-tro], *adv.* Inside, within. **De botones adentro**, in my heart. **Ser muy de adentro**, to be intimate in a house. **Tierra adendro**, inland. **Mar adentro**, out to sea. **Reírse para sus adentros**, to laugh inwardly. *Interj.* **¡Adentro!** Come in!

adepto [ah-dep'-to], *m.* Adept, supporter, follower. *a.* In favor, supporting, who supports.

aderezado [ah-day-ray-thah-do], *a.* Favorable, suitable.

aderezar [ah-day-ray-thar'], *va.* 1. To dress, to adorn. 2. (*Obs.*) To prepare. 3. To clean, to repair. **Aderezar la comida**, to dress victuals.

aderezarse [ah-day-ray-thahr-say], *vr.* To dress up, to get ready.

aderezo [ah-day-ray'-tho], *m.* 1. Dressing and adorning; finery. 2. Gum, starch, and other ingredients, used to stiffen cloth with. **Aderezo de mesa**, a service for the table; applied to oil vinegar, and salt. **Aderezo de comida**, condiment. **Aderezo de diamantes**, a set of diamonds. **Aderezo de caballo**, trappings or caparisons of a saddle-horse. **Aderezo de casa**, furniture. **Aderezo de espada**, hilt, hook, and other appendages of a sword.

aderra [ah-der'-rah], *f.* A rope, made of rush, used for pressing the husks of grapes.

adestrado, da [ah-des-trah'-do, dah], *a.* 1. Broken in. 2. (*Her.*) On the dexter side of the escutcheon; it is also applied to the principal figure in an escutcheon, on the right of which is another. *-pp.* of ADESTRAR.

adestrador, ra [ah-des-trah-dor', rah] *m. & f.* 1. Teacher. 2. Censor, critic.

adestrar [ah-des-trar'], *va.* 1. To guide, to lead. 2. To teach. 3. To train. *-vr.* To exercise oneself.

adeudado, da [ah-day-oo-dah'-do, dah], *a.* 1. Indebted. 2. (*Obs.*) Obliged. *-pp.* of ADEUDAR.

adeudar [ah-day-oo-dar'], *va.* 1. To pay duty. 2. (*Com.*) To charge debit. 3. *vn.* To become related by marriage.

adeudarse [ah-day-oo-dahr-say], *vr.* To be indebted, to incur debt.

adeudo [ah-day-oo-do], *m.* Debit, indebtedness (deuda).

adeveras [ah-day-vay-rahs], (*LAm.*) **de adeveras = de veras**.

adherencia [ad-ay-ren'-the-ah], *f.* 1. Alliance, adherence to a sect or party. 2. Relationship, friendship. 3. Adhesion. *-pl.* (*Surg.*) Adhesions.

adherente [ad-ay-ren'-tay], *a.* Adherent. *-m.* Follower. *-pl.* Ingredientes.

adherido, da [ah-day-ree-do], *m & f.* Adherent, follower.

adherir [ad-ay-reer'], *vn.* To adhere to a sect or party; to espouse an opinion, to cleave to.

adherirse [ah-day-rer-say], *vr.* To hold. To glue.

adhesión [ah-ay-se-on'], *f.* Adhesion; cohesion, attachment.

adhesividad [ah-day-de-ve-dahd], *f.* Adhesiveness.

adhesivo, va [ad-ay-see'-vo, vah], *a.* Adhesive, capable of adhering. (**Yo adhiero, yo adhiera; él adhirió, él adhiriera, from Adherir.** *V.* ASENTIR).

adiado [ah-de-ah'-do]. *-pp.* ADIAR.

adiamantado, da [ah-de-ah-man-tah'-do, dah], *a.* Adamantine.

adiar [ah-de-ahr'], *va.* (*Obs.*) To appoint, to set a day.

adición [ah-de-the-on'], *f.* 1. Addition. 2. Remark or note put to accounts. **Adición de la herencia**, acceptance of an inheritance. 3. Addition, the first rule of arithmetic. 4. Advance (of salary).

adicionador, ra [ah-de-the-o-nah-dor', rah], *m. & f.* One that makes additions.

adicional [ah-de-the-o-nahl'], *a.* Supplementary.

adicionalmente [ah-de-the-o-nal-men'-tay], *adv.* Additionally.

adicionar [ah-de-the-o-nar'], *va.* To make additions, to add.

adictivo [ah-dec-te-vo], *a.* (*Cono Sur*) Addictive.

adicto, ta [ah-deec'-to, tah], *1. a.* Addicted, attached.

adicto, *m.* Addict.

adieso [ah-de-ay'-so], *adv.* (*Obs.*) At the moment, instantly.

adiestrado [ah-de-ays-trah-do], *a.* Trained.

adiestramiento [ah-de-ays-trah-me-ayn-to], *m.* Training; drilling; practice.

adiestrar [ah-de-es-trar'], *va. V.* ADESTRAR. (**Yo adiestro, yo adiestre**, from *Adestrar. V.* ACERTAR). To train, to teach, to coach; to drill; to guide, to lead.

adiestrarse [ah-de-ays-trahr-say], *vr.* To practise, to train.

adietar [ah-de-ay-tar'], *va.* To diet.

adifés [ah-de-fays] *a.* 1. With difficulty. 2. *(Carib.)* On purpose (a propósito), deliberately.

adinamia [ah-de-nah'-me-ah], *f.* Adynamia, debility, great weakness.

adinámico, ca [ah-de-nah'-me-co, cah], *a.* Adynamic, lacking force.

adinas [ah-dee'-nas], *f. pl. V.* ADIVAS.

adinerado, da [ah-de-nay-rah'-do, dah], *a.* Rich, wealthy.

adintelado, da [ah-din-tay-lah'-do, dah], *a.* Falling from an arch gradually into a straight line.

adiós [a-de-os'], *int.* Goodbye, bye-bye. **Ir a decir adiós a uno**, to go to say good-bye to somebody.

adiosito [ah-de-o-see-to], *int. (LAm.)* Bye-bye!, cheerio!

adipocira [ah-de-po-thee'-rah], *f.* Adipocere.

adiposidad [ah-de-po-see-dahd], *f. V.* ADIPOSIS

adiposo, sa [ah-de-po'-so, sah], *a. (Med.)* Fat, adipose, *V.* SEBOSO.

adir [ah-deer'], *va.* To accept, to receive an inheritance.

aditamento [ah-de-tah-men'-to], *m.* Addition.

aditivo [ah-de-te-vo], *m.* Additive.

adivina, *f. V.* ADIVINANZA.

adivinable [ah-de-ve-nah'-blay], *a.* Capable of conjecture, or foretelling.

adivinación [ah-de-ve-nah-the-on'], *f.* Divination, guessing, solving. **Adivinación de pensamientos**, thought-reading.

adivinador, ra [ah-de-ve-nah-dor', rah], *m. & f.* A diviner, a soothsayer.

adivinamiento [ah-de-ve-nah-me-en'-to], *m. V.* ADIVINACION.

adivinanza [ah-de-ve-nan'-thah], *f. (coll.)* 1. Prophesy, prediction. 2. Enigma, riddle, conundrum. 3. Guess. 4. *V.* ADIVINACION.

adivinar [ah-de-ve-nar'], *va.* 1. To foretell future events, to soothsay. 2. To conjecture, anticipate, or divine, to give a guess. **Adivina quién lo hizo**, it's anyone's guess who did it. 3. To unriddle an enigma or difficult problem; to find out.

adivino, na [ah-de-vee'-no, nah], *m. & f.* 1. Soothsayer. 2. Foreboder, fortuneteller.

a. abr. de **adjunto** (enclosed).

adjetivación [ad-hay-te-vah-the-on'], *f.* Act of uniting one thing to another.

adjetivar [ad-hay-te-var'], *va. (coll.)* To unite.

adjetivo [ad-hay-tee'-vo], *1. m. (Gram.)* Adjective. 2. *a.* Adjectival.

adjudicación [ad-hoo-de-cah-the-on'], *f.* Act of adjudging. *a.* **Pública subasta**, auction-sale; «knocking-down» at auction-**al mejor postor**, to the highest bidder.

adjudicar [ad-hoo-de-car'], *va.* To adjudge, to sell at auction. **Adjudicar algo a uno en 500 dólares**, to knock something down to someone for $ 500.

adjudicarse [ad-hoo-de-cahr-say], *vr.* To appropriate to oneself. **Adjudicarse el premio**, to win the prize.

adjudicativo, va [ad-hoo-de-cah-tee'-vo, vah], *a.* Adjudicating.

adjudicatario, ria [ad-hoo-de-cah-tah'-re-o, ah], *m. & f.* One to whom something is adjudged; grantee.

adjunta [ad-hoon'-tah], *f.* Letter enclosed in another.

adjuntar [ad-hoon-tahr], *va.* To append, attach, to enclose. **Adjuntamos factura**, we enclose our bill.

adjunto, ta [ad-hoo'-to, tah], *a.* 1. Joined, annexed, inclosed, Adjunct. 2. Assistant, profesor (persona).

adjurar [ad-hoo-rar'], *va. (Obs.)* to conjure, exorcise; supplicate.

adjutor, ra [ad-hoo-tor'-rah], *a. & n.* Adjuvant; helper.

adlátere [ad-lah-tay-ray], *m.* Companion; associate.

adminicular [ad-me-ne-coo-lar'], *va. (Law.)* To increase the power and efficacy of a thing by adding collateral aids.

adminículo [ad-me-nee'-coo-lo], *m.* Prop, support, aid, accessory.

administración [ad-me-nis-trah-the-on'], *1. f.* 1. Administration, managerement. 2. Office of an administrator. **En administración**, in trust: applied to places in which the occupant has no property. **Administración de Correos**, General Post Office. 3. Government administration. 4. Headquarters, central office.

administrador, ra [ad-me-nis-trah-dor', rah], *m. & f.* Administrator, management; steward, director, trustee. **Administrador de correos**, postmaster. **Administrador de fincas**, land agent. **Administrador de archivos de datos** *(Comp.)*, data file manager. **Administrador de bases de datos** *(Comp.)*, data base manager. **Administrador de operaciones informáticas** *(Comp.)*, computer operations manager. **Administrador de redes informáticas** *(Comp.)*, computer network manager. **Administrador de sistemas** *(Comp.)*, system manager.

administrar [ad-me-nis-trar'], *va.* 1. To administer, to govern. 2. To serve an office.

administrarse [ad-me-nes-trahr-say], *vr.* To manage one's own affairs, to organize one's life.

administrativo, va [ad-me-nis-trah-tee'-vo, vah], *a.* Administrative, the one who administers.

administratorio, ria [ad-me-nis-trah-to'-re-o, ah], *a. (Law.)* Belonging to an administration or administrator.

admirable [ad-me-rah'-blay], *a.* Admirable, excellent.

admirablemente [ad-me-rah-blay-men'-tay], *adv.* Admirably, marvelously.

admiración [ad-me-rah-the-on'], *f.* 1. Wonder; sudden surprise. **Esto llenó a todos de admiración**, this filled everyone with wonder. 2. Point of exclamation. ¡! 3. Prodigy. **Es una admiración**, it is a thing worthy of admiration.

admirador, ra [ad-me-rah-dor', rah], *m. & f.* Admirer.

admirar [ad-me-rar'], *va.* To cause admiration; to marvel, to contemplate. **Esto admiró a todos**, this astonished everyone.

admirarse [ad-me-rahr-say], *vr.* To be seized with admiration; to make a wonder, to be surprised.

admirativo, va [ad-me-rah-tee'-vo, vah], *a.* Admiring, wondering.

admisibilidad [ad-me-se-be-le-dahd], *f.* Admissibility.

admisible [ad-me-see'-blay], *a.* Admissible; acceptable, credible, legitimate. **Eso no es admisible**, that cannot be allowed.

admisión [ad-me-se-on'], *f.* Admission, acceptance.

admitir [ad-me-teer'], *va.* 1. To receive, to give entrance. **La sala admite 500 personas**, the hall holds 500 people. 2. To concede; to accept. **No admite otra explicación**, it allows no other explication. 3. To admit; to permit; to find. **Bien admitido**, well received. **El asunto no admite dilación**, the affair admits no delay.

admón *f. abr.* de **administración**.

admonición [ad-mo-ne-the-on'], *f.* Warning, counsel, advice.

admonitor [ad-mo-ne-tor'], *m.* Monitor, in some religious communities.

admonitorio [ad-mo-ne-to-reo], *a.* Señal, voz de warning.

ADN *abr.* de **ácido desoxirribonucleico**.

adnado, da [ad-nah'-do, dah], *m. & f.* Step-son, stepdaughter.

adnata [ad-nah'-tah], *f. (Anat.)* Adnata, the external white membrane of the eye.

adnato, ta [ad-nah'-to, tah], *a. (Bot.)* Adnate, adherent.

adobado, da [ah-do-bah'-do, dah], *a.* Marinated, pickled; curried, dressed, -*pp.* of ADOBAR.

adobado [ah-do-bah'-do], *m.* 1. Pickled pork. 2. Any sort of dressed meat.

adobador, ra [ah-do-bah-dor', rah], *m. & f.* Dresser, preparer.

adobamiento, *m.* A kind of stew.

adobar [ah-do-bar'], *va.* 1. To dress or make something up. 2. To pickle pork or other meat. 3. To cook. 4. To tan hides. 5. *(Obs.)* To contract, to stipulate.

adobasillas [ah-do-bah-seel'-lyas], *m.* One that makes or repairs straw bottoms for chairs.

adobe [ah-do'-bay], *m.* 1. Brick not yet burnt, baked in the sun. 2. *(Cono Sur)* Big foot, plate of meat. 3. **Descansar haciendo adobes** *(Mex.)* to moonlight, to do work on the side.

adobera [ah-do-bay'-rah], *f.* 1. Mould for making bricks. 2. *(Cono Sur, Mex.)* (queso) Brick-shaped cheese, (molde) cheese mould. 3. *(Cono Sur)* Big foot.

adobería [ah-do-bay'-re-ah], *f.* Brickyard. 2. *V.* TENERIA.

adobo [ah-do'-bo], *m.* 1. Repairing, mending. 2. Picklesauce. 3. Ingredients for dressing leather or cloth. 4. Pomade, cosmetic.

adocenado, da [ah-do-thay-nah'-do, dah], *a.* Common, ordinary, vulgar. *-pp.* of ADOCENAR.

adocenar [ah-do-thay-nar'], *va.* 1. To count or sell by dozens. 2. To despise.

adocenarse [ah-do-thay-nahr-say], *vr.* 1. To become commonplace. 2. To become mediocre; to remain stagnant.

adoctrinador [ah-doc-tre-nah-do], *a.* Indoctrinating, indoctrinatory.

adoctrinamiento [ah-doc-tre-nah-me-ayn-to], *m.* Indoctrination.

adoctrinar [ah-doc-tree-nar'], *va.* To instruct, to teach. *V.* DOCTRINAR.

adolecer [ah-do-lay-therr'], *vn.* 1. To be seized with illness. 2. To labor under disease or affliction. *-va. (Obs.)* To produce pain or disease.

adolescencia [ah-do-les-then'-the-ah], *f.* Adolescence.

adolescente [ah-do-les-then-tay], *a.* Adolescent, young. *-m. & f.* Adolescent, teenager. (**Yo adolezco,** from **Adolecer,** *V.* ABORRECER.)

Adolfo [ah-dol-pho], *m.* Adolphus, Adolph, Adolf.

adolorado, adolorido, *a. V.* DOLORIDO.

adomiciliarse [ah-do-me-the-le-ar'-say], *va. V.* DOMICILIARSE.

adonado, da [ah-do-nah'-do, dah], *a. (Obs.)* 1. Endowed by Nature; gifted. 2. Witty.

adonde [ah-don'-day], *adv.* Where, whither. **El lugar adonde voy,** the place I am going to. -Observ. In an interrogative sentence, *adonde* has a written accent: **¿adónde vas?,** where are you going?

adondequiera *adv.* Wherever, wheresoever (movimiento). **Adondequiera que vayas,** wherever you go.

adonis [ah-do'-nis], *m.* Adonis, handsome youth.

adopción [ah-dop-the-on'], *f.* 1. Adoption taking another woman's child for one's own. 2. **Madrileño de adopción,** a citizen of Madrid by adoption.

adoptable [ah-dop-tah'-blay], *a.* Adoptable, suitable for adopting.

adoptado, da [ah-dop-tah-do], *m. & f. (Mex.)* Adopted child.

adoptador, ra [ah-dop-tah-dor, rah], *m. & f.* Adopter.

adoptar [ah-dop-tar], *va.* 1. To adopt, to father. 2. To embrace an opinion. 3. *(Obs.)* To graft.

adoptivo, va [ah-dop-tee'-vo, vah], *a.* Adoptive.

adoquier, adoquiera [ah-do-ke-err', ah-do-ke-ay'-rah], *adv. (Obs.)* Where you please.

adoquín [ah-do-keen'], *m.* 1. Paving-stone, binding-stone of a pavement. 2. Fool, dope (tonto).

adoquinado [ah-do-ke-nah-do], *m.* Paving.

adoquinar [ah-do-ke-nar'], *va.* To pave.

ador [ah-dor'], *m.* The time for watering land, where the water is distributed.

adorable [ah-do-rah'-blay], *a.* Adorable, worshipful.

adoración [ah-do-rah-the-on'], *f.* Adoration, worship. **Una mirada llena de adoración,** an adoring look.

adorador, ra [ah-do-rah-dor'-rah], *m. & f.* One that adores, worshipper.

adorar [ah-do-rar'], *va.* 1. To adore, to reverence with religious worship, to idolatrize. 2. To love excessively.

adoratorio [ah-do-rah-to'-re-o], *m.* A name give by the Spaniards to the temples of idols in America; teocalli.

adormecedor, ra [ah-dor-may-thay-dor', rah], *a.* Soporiferous, soporific.

adormecer [ah-dor-may-therr'], *vr.* 1. To cause drowsiness or sleep; to lull asleep. 2. To calm, to lull.

adormecerse [ah-dor-may-thayr-say], *vr.* 1. To fall asleep. 2. To grow benumbed or torpid. 3. *(Met.)* To grow or persist in vice.

adormecido, da [ah-dor-may-thee'-do, dah], *a.* Mopish; sleepy, drowsy. *-pp.* of ADORMECER.

adormecimiento [ah-dor-may-the-me-en'-to], *m.* Drowsiness, slumber, sleepiness, numbness, mopishness. (**Yo adormezco,** from **Adormecer.** *V.* ABORRECER)

adormidera [ah-dor-me-day'-rah], *f. (Bot.)* Poppy, sleeping pill.

adormilarse [ah-dor-me-lahr-say], *vr.* To doze, to drowse.

adormir [ah-dor-meer'], *vn.* 1. To fall asleep. 2. *(Obs.)* To sound softly (said of a musical instrument).

adormitarse [ah-dor-me-tar'-say], *vr. V.* DORMITAR.

adornador, ra [a-dor-nah-dor', rah], *m. & f.* Adorner.

adornar [ah-dor-nar'], *va.* 1. To beautify, to embellish, to grace, to ornament. 2. To furnish: to garnish. 3. To accomplish; to adorn with talents.

adornista [ah-dor-nees'-tah], *f.* Decorator.

adorno [ah-dor'-no], *m.* 1. Adorning, accomplishment. 2. Ornament, finery, decoration, habiliment. 3. Garniture. 4. **Adorno de una casa,** Furniture.

adosado [ah-do-sah-do], 1. *a.* **Casa adosada,** Semidetached house.

adosar [ah-do-sahr'], *va.* 1. **Adosar algo a una pared,** to lean something against a wall. 2. *(LAm.)* To join firmly, to attach (juntar).

adquirido [ad-ke-re-do], *a.* **mal adquirido,** ill-gotten.

adquiridor, ra [ad-ke-re-dor', rah], *m. & f.* Acquirer. **A buen adquiridor buen expendedor,** after a gatherer comes a scatterer.

adquirir [ad-ke-reer'], *va.* To acquire, to obtain, to get. (**Yo adquiero, yo adquiera; él adquirió, él adquiriera.** *V.* ADQUIRIR.

adquisición [ad-ke-se-the-on'], *f.* 1. Acquisition; attainment; accomplishment. 2. Goods obtained by purchase or gift, not inherited. **Poder de adquisición,** Purchasing power.

adquisidor, ra [ad-ke-se-dor', rah], *m. & f.* Purchaser, acquirer.

adquisitivo, va [ad-ke-se-tee'-vo, vah], *a. (For.)* Acquisitive.

adquisitorio, ria [ad-ke-se-to'-re-o, re-ah], *a.* Purchasing, purchase.

adquisividad [ad-ke-se-ve-dahd], *f.* Acquisitiveness.

adra [ah'-drah], *f.* 1. Turn. 2. Section of town, neighborhood.

adral [ah-drahl], *m.* Rail, sideboard (carreta).

adragantina [ah-drah-gahn-tee'-nah], *f.* Tragacanthin.

adraganto [ah-drah-gahn'-to], *m.* Tragacanth.

adral [ah-drahl'], *m.* Sideboard (camión).

adrede, adredemente [ah-dray'-day, ah-dray-day-men'-tay], *adv.* Purposely, on purpose, knowingly.

adrenalina [ah-dray-nah-lee'-nah], *f.* Adrenaline, type of heart stimulant.

Adriano [ah-dre-ah-no], *m.* Hadrian.

Adriático, ca [ah-dree-ah'-te-co, cah], *a.* Adriatic.

adrizar [ah-dree-thar'], *va. (Naut.)* To right. **Adrizar un navío,** to right a ship.

adrolla [ah-drol'-lya], *f. (Obs.)* Deceit in trade.

adscribir [ads-cre-beer'], *va.* To appoint a person to a place or employment. **Estuvo adscrito al servicio de...,** he was attached to..., he was in the service of....

adscripción [ads-crip-the-on'], *f.* Nomination, appointment.

aduana [ah-doo-ah'-nah], *f.* A custom-house. **Pasar por todas las aduanas**, to undergo a close examination. **En la aduana**, *(Com.)* in bond.

aduanar [ah-doo-ah-nar'], *va.* 1. To enter goods at the custom-house. 2. To pay duty, to put in bond.

aduanero [ah-doo-ah-any'-ro], *m.* Custom-house officer, customs officer.

aduar [ah-doo-ar'], *m.* 1. Horde, a migratory crew. 2. Village of Arabs.

adúcar [ah-doo'-car], *m.* A coarse sort of silk stuff, silk refuse, ferret silk.

aducir [ah-doo-therr'], *va.* 1. To adduce, to cite. 2. To guide, to bring.

aductor [ah-dooc-tor'], *m. (Anat.)* Adductor (muscle).

aduendado, da [ah-doo-en-dah'-do, dah], *a.* Ghost-like, walking about like a ghost.

adueñarse [ah-doo-ay-nyar'-say], *vr.* To take possession of, to seize.

adufa [ah-doo'-fah], *f.* A half-door.

adufaso [ah-doo-fah'-so], *m.* Blow with a timbrel or tambourine.

adufe [ah-doo'-fay], *m.* Timbrel or tambourine. V. PANDERO.

adufero, ra [ah-doo-fay'-ro, rah], *m. & f.* Timbrel or tambourine player.

adujadas, adujas [ah-doo-hah'-das, ah-doo'-has], *f. pl. (Naut.)* Coil or a colled cable.

adujar [ah-doo-har'], *va. (Naut.)* To coil a cable.

adula [ah-doo'-lah], *f.* 1. *(Prov.)* A piece of ground for which there is no particular manner of irrigation.

adulación [ah-doo-lah-the-on'], *f.* Flattery, fawning, coaxing, cogging, soothing.

adulada [ah-doo-lah-dah], *f. (Mex.)* Flattery.

adulador, ra [ah-doo-lah-dor', rah], *m. & f.* Flatterer, fawner, soother.

adular [ah-doo-lar'], *va.* 1. To flatter, to soothe, to coax, to court, to compliment. 2. To fawn, to creep, to crouch.

adulate [ah-doo-lah-tay], *a, m. (LAm.).* ADULON

adulonería [ah-doo-lo-nay-re-ah], *f. (LAm.)* 1. Flattering, fawning. 2. Fawning nature, soapiness.

adulatorio, ria [ah-doo-lah-to'-re-o, ah], *a.* Flattering, honey-mouthed; parasitical.

adulear [ah-doo-lay-ar'], *vn.* To bawl, to cry out.

adulero [ah-doo-lay'-ro], *m.* Driver of horses or mules.

adulón, na [ah-doo-lone', nah], *m. & f. (coll. Amer.)* Flatterer.

adúltera [ah-dool'-tay-rah], *f.* Adulteress.

adulteración [ah-dool-tay-rah-the-on'], *f.* Adulteration, falsification (of goods, etc.)

adulterado, da [ah-dool-tay-rah'-do, dah], *a.* Sophisticated. *-pp.* of ADULTERAR.

adulterador, ra [ah-dool-tay-rah-dor', rah], *m. & f.* One who adulterates; falsifier.

adulterar [ah-dool-tay-rar'], *va.* To adulterate, to falsify. *-vn.* to commit adultery.

adulterinamente [ah-dool-tay-re-nah-men'-tay], *adv.* In an adulterous manner.

adulterino, na [ah-dool-tay-ree'-no, nah], *a.* 1. Adulterous; begotten in adultery. 2. Adulterated, falsified, forged.

adulterio [ah-dool'-tay-re-o], *m.* Adultery.

adúltero, ra [ah-dool'-tay-ro, rah], *m. & f.* Adulterer.

adultez [ah-dool-tayth], *f. (Cono Sur)* Adulthood.

adulto, ta [ah-dool'-to, tah], *a.* Adult, grown up.

adulzar [ah-dool-thar'], *va. (Obs.)* 1. To sweeten. 2. To soften. **Adulzar los metales**, To render metals more ductile.

adunación [ah-doo-nah-the-on'], *f. (Obs.)* The act of uniting, and the union itself.

adunar [ah-doo-nar'], *va.* To unite, to join; to unify.

adunco, ca [ah-doon'-co, cah], *a.* Aduncous, curved.

adustez [ah-doos-teth'], *f.* Disdain, aversion, asperity, austerity, severity.

adustamente [ah-doos-tha-men'-tay], *adv.* Austerely, severely.

adustión [ah-doos-te-on'], *f. (Med.)* Burning up or drying as by fire; cauterization.

adustivo, va [ah-doos-tee'-vo, vah], *a.* That which has the power of burning up.

adusto, ta [aah-doos'-to, tah], *a.* Gloomy, **austero**, intractable, sullen.

adútero [ah-doo'-tay-ro], *m. (Anat.)* The Fallopian tube.

advenedizo, za [ad-vay-nay-dee'-tho, thah], *a.* 1. Foreign. 2. Applied to a foreign immigrant.

advenimiento [ad-vay-ne-me-en'-to], *m.* Arrival; advents.

adventicio, cia [ad-ven-tee'-the-o, ah], *a.* 1. Adventitious; accidental. 2. *(Law.)* Acquired by industry or inheritance, independent of a paternal fortune.

adverar [ad-vay-rar'], *va. (Obs.)* To aver, affirm.

adverbial [ad-ver-be-ahl'], *a.* Belonging to an adverb.

adverbialmente [ad-ver-be-al-men'-tay], *adv.* Adverbially.

adverbio [ad-ver'-be-o], *m.* Adverb, one of the parts of speech.

adversamente [ad-ver-sah-men'-tay], *adv.* Adversely.

adversario [ad-ver-sah'-re-o], *m.* Opponent; antagonist, foe. *-pl.* Notes in a common-place book; a common-place book.

adversativo, va [ad-ver-sah-tee'-vo, vah], *a. (Gram.)* A particle which expresses some difference and opposition between that which precedes and follows.

adversidad [ad-ver-se-dad'], *f.* Calamity, misfortune, affliction, adversity.

adverso, sa [ad-ver'-so, sah], *a.* 1. Adverse, calamitous, afflictive. 2. Opposite, averse. 3. Favorless. 4. Facing, in front of.

advertencia [ad-ver-ten'-the-ah], *f.* 1. Attention to; regard to. 2. Advice. 3. Advertisement to the reader, remark. 4. Admonition, counsel.

advertidamente [ad-ver-te-dah-men'-tay], *adv.* Advisedly, deliberately.

advertido, da [ad-ver-tee'-do, dah], *a.* 1. Noticed. 2. Skillful, intelligent; acting with deliberation, sagacious, clever, prudent. *-pp.* of ADVERTIR.

advertimiento [ad-ver-te-me-en'-to], *m. V.* ADVERTENCIA.

advertir [ad-ver-teer'], *va.* 1. To take notice of, to observe. 2. To instruct, to advise, to give notice or warning. 3. To acquaint. 4. To mark, to note. **Se lo advierto a usted**, I warn you. **El señor Norton no dejó de advertir esta observación**, this remark was not lost upon Mr. Norton. *(Yo advierto, yo advierta; él advirtió, él advirtiera*; from **Advertir.** V. ASENTIR.)

Adviento [ad-ve-en'-to], *m.* Advent, the four weeks before Christmas.

advocación [ad-vo-cah-the-on'], *f.* 1. Appellation given to a church, chapel or altar, dedicated to the holy Virgin or a saint. 2. *(Obs.)* Profession of a lawyer. V. ABOGACION. Patronage, protection.

advocar [ad-vo-cahr'], *va. (LAm.)* To advocate.

advocatorio, ria [ad-vo-cah-to'-re-o, ah], *a.* **Carta advocatoria or convocatoria**, a letter of convocation calling an assembly.

adyacencia [ad-yah-thayn-the-ah], *f. (Cono Sur)* Nearness, proximity; (en las adyacencias) in the vicinity.

adyacente [ad-yah-then'-tay], *a.* Adjacent; contiguous.

adyuntivo, va [ad-yoon-tee'-vo, vah], *a.* Conjunctive; joining.

AECE *f. abr.* de **Asociación Española de Cooperación Europea.**

aechadero [ah-ay-chah-day'-ro], *m.* The place where grain is winnowed from the chaff; winnowing-floor.

aechador, ra [ah-ay-chah-dor', rah], *m. & f.* Winnower.

aechaduras [ah-ay-chah-doo'-ras], *f. pl.* The refuse of grain, chaff.

aechar [ah-ay-char'], *va.* To winnow, to sift grain from chaff.

aecho [ah-ay'-cho], *m.* Winnowing, cleansing.

aeración [ah-ay-rah'-the-on'], *f.* 1. Aeration, charging with gas. 2. Ventilation of air. *(Acad.).*

aéreo [ah-ay'-ray-o, ah], *a.* 1. Aerial. 2. *(Met.)* Airy, fantastic.

aerífero, a [ah-ay-ree'-fay-ro, rah], *a.* Air-conducting.

aeriforme [ah-ay-re-for'-may], *a. (Chem.)* Aeriform, gaseous.

aero [ah-ay-ro], *pref.* Aereo.

aerobic [ah-ay-ro-bek], *m.* **aeróbica,** *f.* Aerobics.

aeróbico [ah-ay-ro-be-co], *a.* Aerobic.

aerobismo [ah-ay-ro-bes-mo], *m. (Cono Sur)* Aerobics.

aerobús [ah-ay-ro-boos], *m. (Aer.)* Airbus.

aerocar [ah-ay-ro-cahr], *m.* Airbus.

aeroclub [ah-ay-ro-cloob] *m.* Airclub.

aerochati [ah-ay-ro-chah-te], *f.* Air hòstess.

aerodeslizador [ah-ay-ro-days-le-thah-dor], *m.* **aerodeslizante,** *m.* Hovercraft.

aerodinámica [ah-ay-ro-de-nah'-me-cah], *f.* Aerodynamics.

aerodinámico, ca [ah-ay-ro-de-nah'-me-co, cah], *a.* 1. Aerodynamic. 2. Streamlined.

aerodinamismo [ah-ay-ro-de-nah-mes-mo], *m.* Streamlining.

aerodinamizar [ah-ay-ro-de-nah-me-thahr], *va.* To streamline.

aeródromo [ah-ay-ro'-dro-mo], *m.* Airdrome.

aeroembolismo [ah-ay-ro-em-bo-lees'-mo], *m. (Med.)* Aeroembolism.

aeroenviar [ah-ay-ro-ayn-ve-ahr], *va.* To send by air.

aeroespacial [ah-ay-ro-ays-pa-the-ahl], *a.* Aerospace *(Aer.).*

aerofaro [ah-ay-ro-phah-ro], *m. (Aer.)* Beacon.

aerofoto [ah-ay-ro-pho-to], *f.* Aerial photograph.

aerofumigación [ah-ay-ro-foo-me-gah-the-on], *f.* Crop-dusting.

aerografía [ah-ay-ro-grah-fee'-ah], *f.* Aerography.

aerógrafo [ah-ay-ro'-grah-fo], *m.* Air brush.

aerograma [ah-ay-ro-grah'-mah], *m.* Wireless message.

aerolínea [ah-ay-ro-lee'-nay-ah], *f.* Airline.

aerolito [ah-ay-ro-lee'-to], *m.* Aerolite.

aerología [ah-ay-ro-lo-hee'-ah], *f.* Aerology.

aerolito [ah-ay-ro-lee'-to], *m.* Aerolite.

aerología [ah-ay-ro-lo-hee'-ah], *f.* Aerology.

aeromancia [ah-ay-ro-mahn'-the-ah], *f.* Aeromancy.

aeromedicina [ah-ay-ro-may-de-thee'-nah], *f.* Aeromedicine.

aerómetro [ah-ay-ro'-may-tro], *m. (Chem.)* Aerometer.

aeromodelismo [ah-ay-ro-mo-day-les-mo], *m.* Aeromodelling, making model aeroplanes.

aeromodelo [ah-ay-ro-mo-day-lo], *m.* Model aeroplane.

aeromotor [ah-ay-ro-mo-tor], *m.* Aero-engine.

aeromoza [ah-ay-ro-mo'-thah], *f.* Airline hostess, stewardess.

aeronauta [ah-ay-ro-nah'-oo-tah], *m.* Aeronaut.

aeronáutica [ah-ay-ro-nah'-oo-te-cah], *f.* Aeronautics.

aeronáutico, ca [ah-ay-ro-nah'-oo-te-co, cah], *a.* Aeronautical.

aeronaval [ah-ay-ro-nah-val], *a.* Air-sea; **base,** air-sea base.

aeronave [ah-ay-ro-nah'-vay], *f.* Airship.

aeronavegabilidad [ah-ay-ro-nah-vay-gah-be-le-dahd], *f.* Airworthiness.

aeronavegable [ah-ay-ro-nah-vay-gah-blay], *a.* Airworthy.

aeroplano [ah-ay-ro-plah'-no], *m.* Airplane. **Aeroplano de combate,** fighter plane.

aeroportuario [ah-ay-ro-por-too-ah-reo], *a.* Airport.

aeroposta [ah-ay-ro-pos-tah], *f. (LAm.)* Airmail.

aeropostal [ah-ay-ro-pos-tahl'], *a.* Airmail.

aeropuerto [ah-ay-ro-poo-err'-to], *m.* Airport. **Aeropuerto para helicópteros,** Heliport.

aerosol [ah-ay-ro-sol'], *m.* Aerosol.

aerospacio [ah-ay'ro-spah'-the-o], *m.* Aerospace.

aerostático, ca [ah-ay-ros-tah'-te-co, cah], *a.* Aerostatic.

aeróstato [ah-ay-ros-tah-to], *m.* Balloon, aerostat.

aerotermodinámica [ah-ay-ro-ter-mo-de-nah'-me-cah], *f.* Aerothermodynamics.

aeroterrestre [ah-ay-ro-tay-rrays-tray], *a.* Air-ground.

aerotransportado, da [ah-ay-ro-trans-por-tah'-do, dah], *f.* Airlifted, airborne.

aerovía [ah-ay-ro-vee'-ah], *f.* Airway.

AES *m. abr.* de **acuerdo económico social** (wages pact). **a/f** *abr.* de **a favor** (in favor).

afabilidad [ah-fah-be-le-dad'], *f.* Affability, graciousness, courteousness.

afable [ah-fah'-blay], *a.* Affable, complacent, kind; agreeable, familiar.

afablemente [ah-fah-blay-men'-tay], *adv.* Affably, good-naturedly.

afamado, da [ah-fah-mah'-do, dah], *a.* 1. Celebrated, noted. 2. *(Obs.)* Hungry.

afamar [ah-fah-mahr], *va.* To make famous.

afamarse [ah-fah-mahr-say], *vr.* To become famous, to make a reputation.

afán [ah-fahn'], *m.* 1. Anxiety, solicitude, eagerness, laboriousness in pursuit of worldly affairs. **El afán de,** the desire of. 2. *(Obs.)* Toil, fatigue.

afanadamente, afanosamente [ah-fa-nah-dah-men'-tay, ah-fah-no-sah-men'-tay], *adv.* Anxiously, laboriously.

afanador, ra [ah-fah-nah-dor', rah], *m. & f.* One eager for riches: painstaker.

afanar [ah-fah-nar'], *vn. & vr.* 1. To toil, to labor; to be over-solicitous. 2. *(Obs.)* To be engaged in corporeal labor. **Afanar, afanar y nunca medrar,** Much toil and little profit.

afanarse [ah-fah-nahr-say], *vr.* 1. To toil too much. *(coll.)* **Afanarse por nada,** to fidget. 2. To get angry (enfadarse).

afaneso [ah-fah-nay'-so], *m.* Arsenite of copper; Scheele's green.

afanoso, sa [ah-fah-no'-so, sah], *a.* Solicitous; laborious, painstaking.

afantasmado [ah-fahn-tahs-mah-do], *a.* Conceited.

afarolado [ah-fah-ro-lah-do], *a. (LAm.)* Excited, worked up.

afarolarse [ah-fah-ro-lahr-say], *vr. (LAm.)* To get excited, make a fuss, get worked up.

afasia [ah-fah'-see-a], *f.* Aphasia.

afásico [ah-fah-se-co], *a. (Med.)* Aphasic, suffering from aphasia.

afeador, ra [ah-fay-ah-dor, rah], *m. & f.* One that deforms or makes ugly.

afeamiento [ah-fay-ah-me-ayn-to], *m.* 1. Defacing, disfigurement (físicamente). 2. *(fig.)* Condemnation, censure.

afear [ah-fay-ar'], *va.* 1. To deform, to deface, to misshape. 2. *(Met.)* To decry, to censure, to condemn.

afeblecerse [ah-fay-blay-ther'-say], *vr.* To grow feeble, or delicate.

afección [ah-fec-the-on'], *f.* 1. Affection, inclination, fondness. **Afecciones del alma,** emotions. 2. Affection, the state of being affected by any cause or agent. 3. *(Phil.)* Quality, property. 4. Right of bestowing a benefice.

afeccionarse [ah-fayc-the-o-nahr-say], *vr.* **Afeccionarse a** *(Cono Sur)* To take a liking to, become fond of.

afectación [ah-fec-tah-the-on'], *f.* 1. Affectation, artificial appearance; daintiness, finicalness. 2. Presumption, pride.

afectadamente [ah-fec-tah-dah-men'-tay], *adv.* Affectedly, formally, hypocritically.

afectado, da [ah-fec-tah'-do, dah], *a.* 1. Affected, formal, conceited, finical, foppish. 2. *(Med.)* **Estar afectado del corazón,** to have heart trouble. *-pp.* of AFECTAR.

afectante [ah-fayc-tahn-tay], *a. (Cono Sur)* Disturbing, distressing.

afectar [ah-fec-tar'], *va.* 1. To make a show of something, to feign. 2. To affect, to act upon, to produce effect in any other thing; to affect, assume a manner. **Nos afecta gravemente,** it seriously affects us. 3. To unite benefices or livings. 4. *(Jur.)* To tie up, encumber. 5. *(LAm.)* To hurt, harm, damage (dañar). 6. *(LAm.)* To take on (forma), assume.

afectarse [ah-fayc-tahr-say], *vr.* To wound, to sadden.

afectísimo, ma [ah-fec-tee'-se-mo, mah], *a.* Yours sincerely, yours faithfully, yours truly (ending of a letter).

afectividad [ah-fayc-te-ve-dahd], *f.* Emotional nature, emotion; sensitivity.

afectivo, va [ah-fec-tee'-vo, vah], *a.* Affective, proceeding from affection.

afecto [ah-fec'-to], *m.* 1. Affection, love, kindness, fancy; concern. 2. Passion, sensation. 3. Pain, disease. 4. *(Art.)* Lively representation. **Afectos desordenados**, inordinate . desires. 5. *(Med.)* **Afecto de**, afflicted with. 6. *(Jur.)* subjected to, liable for.

afecto, ta [ah-fec'-to, tah], *a.* 1. Affectionate, loving. 2. Inclined. 3. Subject to some charge or obligation for lands, rents. 3. Dear. **Un amigo afecto**, a dear friend.

afectuosamente [ah-fayc-too-o-sah-mayn-tay], *adv.* Affectionately.

afectuosidad [ah-fec-too-o-se-dad'], *f.* Tenderness, benevolence, kindness. affection.

afectuoso, sa [ah-fec-too-o'-so, sah], *a.* Kind, gracious, loving, tender, affectionate.

afeitada [ah-fay-e-tah'-dah], *f.* Shave.

afeitadora [ah-fay-e-tah-do'-rah], *f.* Razor, shaver.

afeitar [ah-fay-e-tar'], *va.* 1. To shave. 2. To clip the box, walltrees, etc, in a garden. 3. To trim (crines, colas). 4. To make up (mujer). 5. To brush.

afeitarse [ah-fay-e-tahr-say], *vr.* 1. To shave, have a shave (hombre). 2. (Mujer) to make up, put one's make-up on.

afeite [ah-fay'-e-tay], *m.* Paint, rouge, cosmetic.

afelio [ah-fay'-le-o], *m.* *(Astr.)* Aphelion, that part of a planet's orbit which is most remote from the sun.

afelpado, da [ah-fel-pah'-do, dah], *a.* Shaggy, villous, like plush or velvet.

afelpar [ah-fel-par'], *va.* To make a nap, to shag or velvet.

afeminación [ah-fay-me-nah-the-on'], *f.* Effemination; emasculation.

afeminadamente [ah-fay-me-nah-dah-men'-tay], *adv.* Womanly.

afeminado, da [ah-fay-me-nah'-do, dah], *a.* Effeminate. - *pp.* of AFEMINAR.

afeminamiento [ah-fay-me-nah-me-en'-to], *m.* *V.* AFEMINACION.

afeminar [ah-fay-me-nar'], *va.* 1. To effeminate, to unman. 2. To debilitate, to enervate, to melt into weakness.

afeminarse [ah-fay-me-nahr-say]. *vr.* To become effeminate, feeble, lose courage.

aferente [ah-fay-ren'-tay], *a.* Afferent, conducting inward to a part or organ.

aféresis [ah-fay'-ray-sis], *f.* Apheresis, a figure in grammar that takes away a letter or syllable from the beginning of a word, as **Norabuena** for **Enhorabuena**.

aferrado, da [ah-fer-rah'-do, dah], *a.* Headstrong, obstinate; **seguir obstinado a**, to remain firm in. *-pp.* of AFERRAR.

aferramiento [ah-fer-rah-me-en'-to], *m.* 1. Grasping, grappling; seizing or binding. **Aferramiento de las velas**, *(Naut.)* The furling of the sails. 2. Headstrongness.

aferrar [ah-fer-rar'], *va.* 1. To grapple, to grasp, to seize. 2. *(Naut.)* To furl. 3. *(Naut.)* To moor.

aferrarse [ah-fay-rrahr-say], *vr.* 1. *(Naut.)* To grasp one another strongly. 2. *(Met.)* To persist obstinately in an opinion. **Aferrarse a una esperanza**, to clutch at a hope.

afestonado [ah-fays-to-nah-do] *a.* Festooned.

afgán, na [af-gahn', gah'-nah], *a.* Afghan, of Afghanistan.

Afganistán [af-gah-nes-tahn], *m.* Afghanistan.

afianzado, da [ah-fe-ahn-thah-do], *m. & f. (LAm.)* financé(e).

afianzamiento [ah-fe-an-thah-me-en'-to], *m.* 1. Security, guarantee, bail. 2. Prop, support.

afianzar [ah-fe-an-thar'], *va.* 1. To become bail or security, to guarantee. 2. To prop, to secure with stays, ropes, etc.: buttress. 3. To obligate, to make fast, to clinch.

afianzarse [ah-fe-ahn-thahr-say], *vr.* To steady oneself; to become strong, become established.

afición [ah-fe-the-on'], *f.* 1. Affection, inclination for a person or thing; mind. **Tener afición a**, to like. 2. Hobby, pastime. interest. **¿Qué aficiones tiene?**, what are his interests? 3. **La afición**, the experts; the fans, the supporters.

aficionado, da [ah-fe-the-o-nah'-do, dah], *a.* Fond of, enthusiastic about. **Es muy aficionado**, he's very keen. *m. & f.* 1. Fan, admirer, enthusiast. 2. Amateur. *-pp.* of AFICIONAR.

aficionar [ah-fe-the-o-nar'], *va.* To affect, to cause or inspire affection. **Aficionarse con exceso a**, to fancy, to give one's mind to.

aficionarse [ah-fe-the-o-nahr-say], *vr.* Aficionarse a algo, to get fond of something.

afidos [ah'-fe-dohs], *m. pl. (Ent.)* Aphids, aphidians.

afiche [ah-fe-chay], *m.* Poster (cartel): *(Cono Sur)* illustration, picture (dibujo).

aficávit [ah-fe-cah-vet], *m.* Affidavit, sworn statement.

áfido [ah-fe-do], *m.* Aphid.

afiebrado [ah-fe-ay-brah-do], *a.* Feverish.

afijo, ja [ah-fee'-ho, hah], *a. (Gram.)* Affix, united to the end of a word.

afiladera [ah-fe-lah-day'-rah], *f.* Whetstone.

afilado [ah-fe-lah'-do], *pp.* of AFILAR. *-a.* Sharp, keen.

afiladora [ah-fe-lah-do-rah], *f. (Cono Sur)* Flirt, coquette.

afiladura [ah-fe-lah-doo'-rah], *f.* Sharpening, whetting.

afilalápices [ah-fe-lah-lah-pe-thays], *m.* Pencil sharpener.

afilamiento [ah-fe-lah-me-en'-to], *m.* 1. The slenderness of the face or nose. 2. *V.* AFILADURA.

afilar [ah-fe-lar'], *va.* 1. To whet, to grind. 2. To render keen. **Afilar las uñas**, to make an extraordinary effort of genius or skill. 3. *(Cono Sur)* To court, to flirt with.

afilarse [ah-fe-lahr-say], *vr.* To grow thin and meagre.

afiliación [ah-fe-le-ah-the-on], *f.* Affiliation.

afiliado [ah-fe-le-ah'-do], *pp. & a.* Affiliated, adopted. **Los países afiliados**, the member countries.

afiliar [ah-fe-le-ar'], *va.* To adopt; to affiliate; to connect with a central body or society.

afiliarse [ah-fe-le-ahr-say], *vr.* To affiliate, to join.

afiligranado, da [ah-fe-le-grah-nah'-do, dah], *a.* 1. Resembling filigree. 2. *(Met.)* Applied to persons who are slender, and small-featured.

afilo, la [ah-fee'-lo, lah], *a. (Bot.)* Aphyllous, destitute of leaves.

afilón [ah-fe-lone'], *m.* 1. Whetstone. 2. An instrument made of steel for whetting any edged tool. 3. Leather strap, or strop (for razors, etc.)

afilorar [ah-fe-lo-rahr], *va. (Carib.)* To adorn.

afilosofado, da [ah-fe-lo-so-fah'-do, dah], *a.* 1. Eccentric. 2. Applied to the person who plays the philosopher.

afín [ah-feen'], *a.* Close by, contiguous, adjacent. *-m.* Relation by affinity.

afinación [ah-fe-nah-the-on'], *f.* 1. Completion; the act of finishing. 2. Refining. 3. Tuning of instruments.

afinadamente [ah-fe-nah-dah-men'-tay], *adv.* Completely, perfectly.

afinado, da [ah-fe-nah'-do, dah], *a.* Well-finished, perfect, complete. *-pp.* of AFINAR.

afinador, ra [ah-fe-nah-dor', rah], *m. & f.* 1. Finisher. 2. Key with which stringed instruments are tuned, as harp, piano, etc.

afinamiento [ah-fe-nah-me-en'-to], *m.* 1. *V.* AFINACION. 2. Refinement. *V.* FINURA.

afinar [ah-fe-nar'], *va.* 1. To complete, to polish. 2. To tune musical instruments. **Afinar los metales**, To refine metals. **Afinar la voz**, to tune the voice.

afinarse [ah-fe-nahr-say], *vr.* To become polished, civilized.

afincado [ah-fen-cah-do], *m. (Cono Sur)* Farmer.

afincarse [ah-fen-cahr-say], *vr.* To establish, to settle.

afincamiento [ah-fin-cah-me-en'-to], *m. (Obs.)* 1. Eagerness. 2. Anxiety polished, civilized.

afincar [ah-fin-car'], *va.* To buy up real estate; to acquire real property.

afine [ah-fee'-nay], *a.* Related, affinal.

afinidad [ah-fe-ne-dad'], *f.* 1. Affinity, relation by marriage. 2. *(Met.)* Analogy. 3. Relation to, connection with. 4. Friendship.

afirmación [ah-feer-mah-the-on'], *f.* Affirming, declaring; assertion.

afirmadamente [ah-feer-mah-dah-men'-tay], *adv.* Firmly.

afirmado [ah-fer-mah-do], *m. (Cono Sur)* Paving, paved surface (acera).

afirmador, ra [ah-feer-mah-dor', rah], *m. & f.* One who affirms.

afirmante [ah-feer-man'-tay], *pa.* The person who affirms.

afirmar [ah-feer-mar'], *va.* 1. To make fast, to secure, to clinch. 2. To affirm, to assure for certain; to contend. **Afirmar una carta**, at cards, to give one card a fixed value. *-vn.* To inhabit, to reside.

afirmarse [ah-fer-marh-say], *vr.* 1. To fix oneself in the saddle or stirrup. 2. To maintain firmly; to advance steadily.

afirmativa [ah-feer-mah-tee'-vah], *f. V.* AFIRMACION.

afirmativamente [ah-feer-mah-te-vah-men'-tay], *adv.* Affirmatively; positively. **Contestar afirmativamente**, to answer in the affirmative.

afirmativo, va [ah-fer-mah-tee'-vo, vah], *a.* Affirmative; opposed to negative.

afistolar [ah-fis-to-lar'], *va.* To render fistulous; applied to a wound.

aflautado [ah-flah-oo-tah-do], *a.* High, fluty (voz).

aflechada [ah-flay-chah'-dah], *a.* Arrow-shaped: used of leaves.

aflicción [ah-flic-the-on'], *f.* 1. Affliction, sorrow, grief, painfulness, mournfulness. 2. Heaviness, anguish of mind.

aflictivo, va [ah-flic-tee'-vo, vah], *a.* Afflictive, distressing; causing pain and grief. **Pena aflictiva**, Corporeal punishment.

aflicto, ta [ah-flic'-to, tah], *pp. irr.* of AFLIGIR.

afligente [ah-fle-hayn-tay], *a. (CAm. Mex.)* Distressing, upsetting.

afligidamente [ah-fle-he-dah-men'-tay], *adv.* Grievously.

afligido [ah-fle-he-do], *a.* Grieving, sorrowing, heartbroken. **Los afligidos padres**, the bereaved parents.

afligimiento [ah-fle-he-me-en'-to], *m. V.* AFLICCION.

afligir [ah-fle-heer'], *va.* To afflict, to put to pain, to grieve, to torment, to curse, to mortify.

afligirse [ah-fle-her-say], *vr.* To make one miserable, to lament, to languish, to repine. **No te aflijas**, don't grieve over it.

aflojadura [ah-flo-hah-doo'-rah], *f.* **aflojamiento** [ah-flo-hah-me-en'-to], *n.* 1. Relaxation, loosening or slackening. 2. Looseness. 3. Cooling.

aflojar [ah-flo-har'], *va.* 1. To loosen, to slacken, to relax, to let loose; to relent; to debilitate. 2. *(Pict.)* To soften the color in shading. 3. *(Naut.)* **Aflojar los obenques**. 4. To fork out (dinero). To ease the shrouds.

aflojarse [ah-flo-hahr-say], *vr.* 1. To grow weak; to abate. 2. To grow cool in fervor or zeal; to lose courage, to languish.

afloración [ah-flo-rah-the-on], *f.* Outcrop.

aflorado [ah-flo-rah'-do], *a. V.* FLOREADO.

afloramiento [ah-flo-rah-me-ayn-to], *m. V.* AFLORACION.

aflorar [ah-flo-rahr], *vn. (Geol.)* To crop out, To outcrop; to appear on the surface.

afluencia [ah-floo-en'-the-ah], *f.* 1. Plenty, abundance. 2. Fluency, volubility, crowd. **La afluencia de turistas**, the influx of tourists.

afluente [ah-floo-en'-tay], *a.* 1. Affluent, copious, abundant. 2. Loquacious. *-m.* Affluent, a tributary river.

afluir [ah-floo-eer'], *vn.* 1. To congregate, assemble. 2. To discharge into, or join another stream.

aflujo [ah-floo-ho] *m. (Med.)* Afflux, congestion.

aflús [ah-floos], *a. (LAm.)* Broke, skint.

afluxionarse [ah-flooc-se-o-nahr-say], *vr. (LAm.)* To catch a cold.

afma., afmo. *abr.* de **afectísima, afectísimo** (yours).

afocador, ra [ah-fo-cah-dor', rah], *a.* Focusing; as, **Cremallera afocadora**, Focusing-rack.

afocar [ah-fo-car'], *va.* To focus (optical instruments).

afoetear [ah-fo-ay-tay-ahr], *vt. (And. Carib.)* To whip, to beat.

afogarar [ah-fo-gah-rar'], *va.* 1. To scorch a sowed field through excessive heat. 2. To scorch a stew, by lack of juices or water. 3. *(Met.)* To be irritated or distressed.

afollado, da [ah-fol-lyah'-do, dah], *a.* Wearing large or wide trousers. *-pp.* of AFOLLAR.

afondar [ah-fon-dar'], *va.* 1. To put under water. 2. *(Naut.)* To sink. *-vn. (Naut.)* To founder.

afonía [ah-fo-nee'-ah], *f. (Med.)* Loss of voice, from disease of larynx, as distinguished from aphasia, loss of power to speak, due to brain-disease.

afónico, ca [ah-fo'-ne-co, cah], *a.* 1. Aphonic, not able to use or control the voice. 2. Silent; used of letters, as *h* in **hacer**.

afono [ah-fo-no] *V.* AFÓNICO.

aforado [ah-fo-rah'-do], *a.* Privileged person. *-pp.* of AFORAR.

aforador [ah-fo-rah-dor], *m.* Gauger, appraiser.

aforamiento [ah-fo-rah-me-en'-to], *m.* 1. Gauging. 2. Duty on foreign goods.

aforar [ah-fo-rar'], *va.* 1. To gauge, to measure vessels or quantities. 2. To examine goods for determining the duty. 3. To take to a court of justice. To give or take lands or tenements under the tenure of meliorating. 4. To give privileges. 5. To appraise.

aforisma [ah-fo-rees'-mah], *f.* A swelling in the arteries of beasts: aneurisin.

aforismo [ah-fo-rees'-mo], *m.* Aphorism, brief sentence, maxim.

aforístico, ca [ah-fo-rees'-te-co, cah], *a.* Aphoristica.

aforjudo [ah-for-hoo-do], *a. (Cono Sur)* Silly, stupid.

aforo [ah-fo'-ro], *m.* 1. Gauging, examination and appraisal of wine and other commodities for the duties; appraisement. 2. Capacity (teatro); **el teatro tiene un aforo de 2.000**, the theater has a capacity of 2,000, the theater can seat 2,000.

aforrador, ra [ah-for-rah-dor'-rah] *m. & f.* One who lines the inside of clothes.

aforrar [ah-for-rar'], *va.* 1. To line, to cover the inside of clothes; to face. **Aforrar una casa**, to ceil a house. 2. *(Naut.)* to sheathe. 4. *(Naut.)* **Aforrar un cabo**, to serve a cable.

aforrarse [ah-fo-rrahr-say], *vr.* 1. To wrap up warm (arropar). 2. To stuff (atiborrarse).

aforro [ah-for'-ro], *m.* 1. Lining. 2. *(Naut.)* Sheathing. 3. *(Naut.)* Waist of a ship.

afortunadamente [ah-for-too-nah-dah-men'-tay], *adv.* Luckily, fortunately.

afortunado, da [ah-for-too-nah'-do, dah], *a.* Fortunate, happy, lucky. **¡Qué afortunado eres!** How lucky you are! **Tiempo afortunado**, *(Obs.)* blowing weather. **Hombre afortunado en amores**, a man who is lucky in love. *-pp.* of AFORTUNAR.

afortunar [ah-for-too-nar'], *va.* To make happy.

afosarse [ah-fo-sar'-say], *vr. (Mil.)* To defend oneself by making a ditch.

afrailado [ah-frah-ee-lah-do], *a. (LAm.)* Churchy.

afrailar [ah-frah-e-lar'], *va. (Prov.)* To rim trees.

afrancesado, da [ah-fran-thay-sah'-do, dah], *a.* Frenchified, French-like. *-pp.* of AFRANCESAR.

afrancesamiento [ah-fran-thay-sah-me-ayn-to], *m.* Francophilism, pro-French feeling.

afrancesar [ah-fran-thay-sahr'], *va.* To Gallicize, to give a French termination to words.

afrancesarse [ah-fran-thay-sahr-say], *vr.* 1. To imitate the French. 2. To be naturalized in France.

afrechillo [ah-fray-che-lyo], *m. (Cono Sur) (Agri.)* Bran.

afrecho [ah-fray'-cho], *m. (Prov.)* Bran, the husks of grain ground.

afrenillar [ah-fray-nil-lyar'], *vn. (Naut.)* To bridle the oars.

afrenta [ah-fren'-tah], *f.* 1. Affront, dishonor, or reproach: outrage; an insult offered to the face; abuse. 2. Infamy resulting from the sentence passed upon a criminal. 3. Stigma.

afrentar [ah-fren-tar'], *va.* To affront; to insult to the face.

afrentarse [ah-fren-tahr-say], *vr.* To be affronted; to blush.

afrentosamente [ah-fren-to-sah-men'-tay], *adv.* Ignominiously; disgracefully.

afrentoso, sa [ah-fren-to'-so, sah], *a.* Ignominious; insulting.

afretar [ah-fray-tar'], *va.* To scrub and clean the bottom of a vessel.

África [ah-fre-cah], *f.* Africa; **África del Norte**, North Africa. **África del Sur**. South Africa.

africaans [ah-free-cah-ahns], *m.* Afrikaans.

africado [ah-fre-cah-do], *a.* (*Ling.*) Affricate.

africánder [ah-fre-cahn-dayr], *m.* Afrikander.

africanista [ah-fre-cah-nes-tah], *m. & f.* Person interested in Africa.

africanizar [ah-fre-cah-ne-thar'], *va.* To Africanize.

africano, na or **Afro** [ah-fre-cah'-no, nah], *a.* African.

Áfrico [ah'-fre-co], *m.* The south-west wind, V. ABREGO.

afrijolar [ah-fre-ho-lahr], *va.* To bother; to annoy.

afrisonado, da [ah-fre-so-nah'-do, dah], *a.* Resembling a Friesland draughthorse.

afro [ah-fro], *a.* Afro. **Peinado Afro**, afro hairstyle.

afroamericano, na [ah-fro-ah-may-re-cah'-no, nah], *a.* Afro-American.

afroasiático [ah-fro-ah-see-ah-te-co], *a.* Afro-Asian.

afrocubano, na [ah-fro-coo-bah'-no, nah], *a.* Afro-Cuban.

afrodisíaco [ah-fro-de-see'-ah-co], *a.* Aphrodisiac; exciting sexual appetite.

Afrodita [ah-fro-de-tah], *f.* Aphrodite.

afrontar [ah-fron-tar'], *va.* 1. To confront. 2. To reproach one with a crime to his face. -*vn.* To face.

afrutado [ah-froo-tah-do], 1. *a.* **Vino**, fruity. 2. *m.* Fruity flavor.

afta [af-tah], *f.* (*Med.*) sore.

aftoso, sa [af-to'-so, sah], *a.* Aphthous. **Fiebre aftosa**, (*Vet.*) Hoof-and-mouth disease.

afuera [ah-foo-ay'-ra], *adv.* 1. Abroad, out of the house, outward. 2. In public. 3. Besides, moreover. **¡Afuera! ¡Afuera!** Stand out of the way! clear the way!

afueras [ah-foo-ay'-ras], *f. pl.* Environs of a place.

afuereño [ah-foo-ay-ray-nyo], *a.* (*LAm.*) Foreign, strange.

afuerino, a [ah-foo-ay-re-no], *m. & f.* Itinerant worker.

afuetear [ah-foo-ay-tay-ahr], *va.* (*LAm.*) To whip, beat.

afufa [ah-foo'-fah], *f.* (*coll.*) Flight. **Estar sobre las afufas**, (*coll.*) preparing for flight; looking for «a soft place.»

afufar, afufarse [ah-foo-far', ah-foo-far'-say], *vn. & vr.* (*coll.*) To run away, to escape. **No pudo afufarlas**, he could not escape.

afufón [ah-foo-fon], *m.* Flight, escape.

afusilar [ah-foo-se-lahr], *va.* (*LAm.*) To shoot.

afusión [ah-foo-se-on'], *f.* Affusion, dashing on water.

afuste [ah-foos'-tay], *m.* A gun-carriage. **Afuste de mortero**. A mortar-bed.

afutrarse [ah-foo-trahr-say], *vr.* (*Cono Sur*) To dress up.

agabachado, da [ah-gah-bah-chah'-do, dah], *a.* Frenchified.

agachada [ah-gah-chah'-dah], *f.* (*coll.*) Stratagem, artifice.

agachadiza [ah-gah-chah-dee'-thah], *f.* (*Zool.*) A snipe. **Hacer la agachadiza.** (*coll.*) to stoop down, to conceal oneself.

agachar [ah-gah-chahr], *va.* To bend, to bow (cabeza).

agacharse [ah-gah-char'-say], *vr.* 1. To stoop, to squat, to crouch, to cower. **Agachar las orejas**, (*coll.*) To be humble; also, to be dejected, dispirited, chopfallen. 2. (*fig.*) to go into hiding, lie low. 3. (*LAm.*) (rendirse) to give in. 4. (*LAm.*) (prepararse) to get ready. 5. **Agacharse algo**, (*Mex.*) to keep quiet about something. 6. **Agacharse con algo** (*And. Mex.*) to make off with something.

agache [ah-gah-chay] *m.* (*And*) Fib, tale.

agachón [ah-gah-chon], *a.* (*LAm.*) Weakwilled, submissive.

agafar [ah-gah-fahr], *va.* To pinch.

agalbanado, da [ah-gal-bah-nah'-do, dah], *a.* Lazy. V. GALBANERO.

agalerar [ah-gah-lay-rar'], *va.* (*Naut.*) To tip an awning so as to shed rain.

agalla [ah-gal'-lyah], *f.* (*Bot.*) Gallnut. **Agalla de ciprés**, cypress gall. **Quedarse de la agalla**, or **colgado de la agalla**, to be deceived in his hopes. -*pl.* 1. Glands on the inside of the throat. 2. Fish gills. 3. Distemper of the glands under the cheeks or in the tensils. 4. Wind-galls of a horse. 5 Beaks of a shuttle. 6. The side of the head of birds corresponding to the temple. 7. Forced courage. **Es hombre de agallas**, he's got guts.

agallón [ah-gal-lyone'], *m.* A large gall-nut. **agallones**, *pl.* 1. Strings of large silver beads hollowed like gallnuts. 2. Wooden beads put to rosaries.

agalludo [ah-gal-lyoo-do], *a.* (*LAm.*) Daring, bold (atrevido).

agalluela [ah-gal-lyoo-ay'-lah], *f. dim.* A small gall-nut.

agamitar [ah-gah-me-tar'], *va.* To imitate the voice of a fawn.

agamo, ma [ah'-gah-mo, mah], *a.* Agamous, deprived of sexual organs: said of mollusks, and of such plants as fungi and algae.

agamuzado, da [ah-gah-moo-thah'-do, dah], *a.* Chamois-colored.

agangrenarse [ah-gan-gray-nar'-say], *vr.* To become gangrenous.

agapas [ah-gah'-pas], *f. pl.* Agapae, love-feast.

ágape [ah'-gah-pay], *m.* Banquet, testimonial dinner.

agarbado, da [ah-gar-bah'-do, dah], *a.* V. GARBOSO. -*pp.* of AGARBARSE.

agarbanzar [ah-gar-ban-thar'], *vn.* (*Prov.*) To bud.

agarbarse [ah-gar-bar'-say], *vr.* To hide away, to hide oneself.

agarbillar [ah-gar-beel-lyar'], *v.* AGAVILLAR.

agarbizonarse [ah-gar-be-tho-nar'say], *vr.* To make up into sheaves.

agareno, na [ah-gah-ray'-no, nah], *a.* A descendant of Agar; a Mohammedan.

agárico [ah-gah'-re-co], *m.* (*Bot.*) Agaric, a fungous excrescence on the trunks of larch-trees.

agarrada [ah-gar-rah-day'-ro], *f.* (*coll.*) Altercation, wordy quarrel.

agarradero, a [ah-gar-rah-day'-ro], *m.* 1. (*Naut.*) Anchoring-ground. 2. (*coll.*) Hold, haft.

agarrado, da [ah-gar-rah'-do, dah], *a.* Miserable, stingy, close-fisted. -*pp.* of AGARRAR.

agarrador, ra [ah-gar-rah-dor', rah], *m. & f.* 1. One that grasps or seizes. 2. Catch-pole, bailiff. 3. Holder, utensil to grasp plates when hot. 4. (*And. Cono Sur*) strong liquor.

agarrafar [ah-gar-rah-fahr], *va.* To grab hold of.

agarrama [ah-gar-rah'-mah], *f.* V. GARRAMA.

agarrar [ah-gar-rar'], *va.* 1. To grasp, to seize, to lay hold of, to compass. 2. To obtain, to come upon. 3. (*LAm.*) (coger) **Agarrar un autobús**, to catch a bus. 4. **Agarrarla**, to get plastered, get drunk. 5. (*Cono Sur*) **Agarrar el vuelo**, to take off. **Agarrar un resfriado**, to catch a cold. **Agarrar el brazo**, to take by the arm.

agarrarse [ah-gahr-rahr-say], *vr.* 1. To clinch, to grapple. **Agarrarse de un pelo**, to grasp at a hair to support an opinion or furnish an excuse. 2. To fight. **Se agarraron a puñetazos**, they fought it out with fists. 3. **Se le agarró la fiebre**, the fever took hold of him.

agarre [ah-gahr-ray], *m.* 1. (*LAm.*) hold. 2. Handle. 3. **Tener agarre**, to have pull.

agarrete [ah-gahr-ray-tay], *a.* (*And*) Mean, stingy.

agarro [ah-gar'-ro], *m.* Grasp.

agarrochador [ah-gar-ro-chah-dor'], *m.* Pricker, goader.

agarrochar, agarrochear [ah-gar-rochar', ah-gar-ro-chay-ar'], *va.* To prick with a pike or spear; to goad.

agarrón [ah-gahr-ron], *m.* (*LAm.*) Jerk, pull, tug (tirón).

agarroso [ah-gahr-ro-so], *a.* (*CAm.*) Sharp, acrid, bitter.

agarrotamiento [ah-gahr-ro-tah-me-ayn-to], *m.* Tightening; strangling.

agarrotar [ah-gar-ro-tar'], *va.* To compress bales with ropes and cords. **Esta corbata me agarrota**, this tie is strangling me.

agarrotarse [ah-gahr-ro-tahr-say], *vr.* (*Med.*) To stiffen, to become numb.

agasajado, a [ah-gah-sah-hah-do], *m. & f.* Chief guest, guest of honor.

agasajador, ra [ah-gah-sah-hah-dor', rah], *m. & f.* Officious, kind, obliging person.

agasajar [ah-gah-sah-har'], *va.* 1. To receive and treat kindly; to fondle. 2. (*coll.*) To regale.

agasajo [ah-gah-sah'-ho], *m.* 1. Graceful and affectionate reception. 2. Kindness. 3. A friendly present. 4. Refreshment or collation served up in the evening.

ágata [ah'-gah-tah], *f.* Agate, a precious stone.

agatas [ah-gah-tahs], *adv.* (*Cono Sur*) 1. With great difficulty. 2. Hardly, scarcely.

agauchado [ah-gah-oo-chah-do], *a.* (*Cono Sur*) Like a gaucho.

agaucharse [ah-gah-oo-chahr-say], *vr.* (*Cono Sur*) to imitate.

agavanzo [ah-gah-vahn'-tho], *m.* or **Agavanza** [ah-gah-vahn'-thah], *f.* (*Bot.*) Hip-tree, dog-rose, Rosa canina. V. ESCARAMUJO.

agave [ah-gah'-vay], *m.* V. PITA.

agavillar [ah-gah-veel-lyar'], . To bind or tie in sheaves.

agavillarse [ah-gah-ve-lyahr-say], *vr.* (*Met.*) To associate with, to form groups.

agazapar [ah-gah-thah-par], *va.* (*coll.*) To nab a person.

agazaparse [ah-gah-thah-pahr-say], *vr.* To nab a person. -*vr.* To hide oneself.

agencia [ah-hen'-the-ah], *f.* 1. Agency: ministration, commission. **Agencia de colocaciones**, employment agency. **Agencia de viajes**, travel agency. 2. Diligence, activity.

agenciar [ah-hen-the-ar'], *va.* To solicit.

agenciarse [ah-hen-the-ahr-say], *vr.* To manage, to get along. **Agenciarse algo**, to get hold of something.

agenciero [ah-hen-the-ay-ro], *m.* (*Cono Sur*) Lottery agent; representative.

agencioso, sa [ah-hen-the-oh'-so, sah], *a.* 1. Diligent, active. 2. Officious.

agenda [ah-hen'-dah], *f.* Note-book: memorandum.

agenesia [ah-hay-nay'-se-ah], *f.* (*Med.*) Impotence.

agente [ah-hen'-tay], *m.* 1. Agent, actor, minister. 2. Solicitor, attorney. **Agente de cambios**, bill broker. **Agente publicitario**, adman. **Agente inmobiliario**, estate agent. **Agente de policía**, policeman.

agerasia [ah-hay-rah'-se-ah], *f.* Old age free from indispositions.

agerato [ah-hay-rah'-to], *m.* (*Bot.*) Sweet milfoil or maudin.

agible [ah-hee'-blay], *a.* Feasible.

agigantado, da [ah-he-gan-tah'-do, dah], *a.* Gigantic; extraordinary, out of the general rules.

agigantar [ah-he-gan-tahr], 1. *va.* To enlarge, to increase greatly. 2. **Agigantar algo**, to make something seem huge.

agigantarse [ah-he-gan-tahr-say], *vr.* To become huge.

ágil [ah'-heel], *a.* Nimble, ready, fast, light, agile.

agilidad [ah-he-le-dad'], *f.* Agility, nimbleness, activity, lightness, liveliness, sprightliness.

agilipollarse [ah-he-le-po-lyahr-say], *vr.* 1. To become all confused, act like an idiot. 2. To get very stuck up (engreírse).

agilitar [ah-he-le-tar'], *va.* To render nimble, to make active.

agilitarse [ah-he-le-tahr-say], *vr.* To limber up.

agilización [ah-he-le-thah-the-on], *f.* Speeding-up.

agilizar [ah-he-le-thahr], *va.* To speed up.

agilizarse [ah-hge-le-thar-say], *vr.* To speed up.

ágilmente [ah'-hell-men-tay], *adv.* Nimbly, actively.

agio, agiotaje [ah'-he-oh, ah-he-o-tah'-hay], *m.* 1. Usury, high rate of interest on loans. 2. Premium on exchange of drafts, foreign money, etc.

agiógrafo [ah-he-oh'-grah-fo], *m.* Hagiographer, a holy writer.

agiógrafos [ah-he-oh'-grah-fos], *m. pl.* Hagiographa, holy writings, a name given to part of the books of Scripture.

agiotador [ah-he-oh-tah-dor'], *m.* Bill-broker, stock-broker.

agiotaje [ah-he-o-tah'-hay], *m.* Jobbing: «fing» in America.

agiotista [ah-he-oh-tees'-tah], *m.* Money-changer, bill-broker.

agitable [ah-he-tah'-blay], *a.* Agitable, capable of agitation.

agitación [ah-he-tah-the-on'], *f.* 1. Agitation, flurry, flutter, jactitation, fluctuation; fidget. 2. Fretting.

agitado [ah-he-tah-do], *a.* 1. Rough, choppy (agua); Jumpy (vuelo). 2. (*fig.*) agitated; upset, anxious (persona).

agitador, ra [ah-he-tah-dor', rah], *m. & f.* Fretter, agitator, shaker.

agitanado, da [ah-he-tah-nah'-do, dah], *a.* 1. Gipsy-like. 2. Bewitching.

agitar [ah-he-tar'], *va.* 1. To agitate, to ruffle, to fret, to irritate. 2. To stir, to discuss.

agitarse [ah-he-tahr-say], *vr.* To flutter, to palpitate.

aglomeración [ah-glo-may-rah-the-on'], *f.* Agglomeration, heaping up. **Aglomeración de tráfico**, traffic jam.

aglomerado [ah-glo-may-rah-do], *a.* Massed together, in a mass.

aglomerar [ah-glo-may-rar'], *va.* To heap upon, crowd together.

aglomerarse [ah-glo-may-rahr-say], *vr.* To agglomerate, form a mass.

aglutinación [ah-gloo-te-nah-the-on'], *f.* Agglutination.

aglutinante [ah-gloo-te-nan'-tay], *a.* Agglutinating. -*pa.* of AGLUTINAR. -*f.* (*Med.*) Sticking-plaster.

aglutinar [ah-gloo-te-nar'], *va.* To glue together, to agglutinate.

aglutinarse [ah-gloo-te-nahr-say], *vr.* To agglutinate; (*fig.*) to come together.

aglutinativo, va [ah-gloo-te-nah-tee'-vo, vah], *a.* agglutinative.

agnación [agnah-the-on'], *f.* (*Law.*) Relation by blood on the father's side.

agnado, da [agnah'-do, dah], *a.* (*Law.*) Related to a descendant of the same paternal line.C.f COGNADO, a relative on the mother's side.

agnaticio, cia [agnah-tee'-the-o, ah], *a.* Belonging to the *aguado*.

agnición [ag-ne-the-on'[, *f.* Recognition of a person on the stage.

agnocasto [ag-no-cahs'-to], *m.* (*Bot.*) Agnus castus or chaste-tree. V. SAUZGATILLO.

agnomento [ag-no-men'-to], *m.* (*Obs.*) V. COGNOMENTO and SOBRENOMBRE.

agnominación [agn-no-me-na-the-on'], *f.* (*Rhet.*) Paronomasia.

agnosticismo [agn-nos-te-thees'-mo], *m.* Agnosticism.

agnóstico, ca [ag-nos'-te-co, cah], *a. & m. & f.* Agnostic.

agobiador [ah-go-be-ah-dor], *a.* **agobiante**. Oppresive, unbearable.

agobiar [ah-go-be-ar'], *va.* 1. To bend the body down. 2. (*Met.*) To oppress, to grind. **Sentirse agobiado por**, to be overwhelmed by.

agobiarse [ah-go-be-ahr-say], *vr.* To bow, to couch. **Agobiarse con**, to be weighed down with.

agobio [ah-go-be-o], *m.* Burden, weight, oppression.

agolar [ah-go-lar'], *va.* (*Naut.*) To furl the sails. V. AMAINAR.

agolpamiento [ah-gol-pah-me-ayn-to], *m.* Throng, crush, rush, crowd.

agolparse [ah-gol-par'-say], *vr.* To crowd, to rush.
agonía [ah-go-nee'-ah], *f.* 1. Agony, the pangs of death. 2. Violent pain of body or mind. 3. An anxious or vehement desire.
agónico [ah-go-ne-co], *a.* Dying; *(fig.)* agonizing.
agonioso [ah-go-ne-o-so], *a. (LAm.)* Selfish; bothersome; **es tan agonioso**, he's such a pest.
agonista [ah-go-nees'-tah], *m. (Obs.)* A dying person.
agonizante [ah-go-ne-thahn'-tay], *pa.* 1. One that assists a dying person. 2. A monk of the order of St. Camillus. 3. A dying person. 4. In some universities, he who assists students in their examinations.
agonizar [ah-go-ne-thar'], *va.* 1. To be dying, to be moribund. 2. *(Obs.)* To desire anxiously. 3. *(Met.)* To annoy, to importune intolerably. **Estar agonizando**, To be in the agony of death.
agonizos [ah-go-ne-thos], *mpl (Mex.)* Worries, troubles.
agono [ah-go'-no], *a.* Without angles.
agora [ah-go'-rah], *adv. (Obs.)* AHORA.
agorar [ah-go-rar'], *va.* To divine to prognosticate.
agorería [ah-go-ray-ree'-ah], *f.* Divination.
agorero, ra [ah-go-ray'-ro, rah] *m. & f.* Diviner.
agorgojarse [ah-gor-go-har'-say], *vr.* To be destroyed by grabs; applied to corn.
agostadero [ah-gos-tah-day'-ro], *m.* Summer, pasture.
agostar [ah-gos-tar'], *va.* 1. To be parched. 2. *(Prov.)* To plough the land in August. *-vn.* To pasture cattle on stubbles in summer.
agostarse [ah-gos-tahr-say], *vr.* To dry up, shrivel; *(fig.)* to die.
agosteño [ah-gos-tay-nyo], *a.* August.
agostero [ah-gos-tay-ro], *m.* 1. A laborer in the harvest.
agostizo, za [ah-gos-tee'-tho, thah], *a.* A person born in August; a colt foaled in that month; weak.
agosto [ah-gos'-to], *m.* 1. August. 2. Harvest-time. 3. Harvest.
agotable [ah-go-tah'-baly], *a.* Exhaustible.
agotado [ah-go-tah-do], *a.* **Estar agotado**, to be exhausted, be worn out.
agotador [ah-go-tah-dor], *a.* Exhausting.
agotamiento [ah-go-tah-me-en'-to], *m.* Exhaustion.
agotar [ah-go-tar'], *va.* 1. To drain off waters. 2. *(Met.)* to beat out one's brains. 3. To run through a fortune; to misspend it. 4. To exhaust. **Agotar la paciencia**, To tire one's patience.
agotarse [ah-go-tahr-say], *vr.* to become exhausted; to be finished.
agracejo [ah-grah-thay'-ho], *m.* 1. A grape remaining small and failing to ripen. 2. *(Prov.)* An olive which falls before it is ripe. 3. A kind of shrub. V. MAROJO.
agraceño, ña [ah-grah-thay'-nyo, nyah], *a.* Resembling verjuice, tart, sour.
agracera [ah-grah-thay'-rah], *f.* Vessel to hold verjuice. *-a.* Applied to vines when their fruit never ripen.
agraciado, da [ah-grah-the-ah'-do, dah], *a.* Graceful, genteel, handsome. *-pp.* of AGRACIAR. *-m.* A grantee.
agraciar [ah-grah-the-ar'], *va.* 1. To adorn or embellish. 2. To grant a favor. 3. To communicate divine grace. 4. To give employment.
agracillo [ah-grah-theel'-lyo], *m.* V. AGRACEJO,
agradable [ah-grah-dah'-blay], *a.* 1. Agreeable, pleasing. 2. Merry, lovely, glad, gracious. 3. Luscious, grateful. **Ser agradable**, *(Com.)* To accommodate.
agradablemente [ah-grah-dah-blay-men'-tay], *adv.* Merrily, graciously.
agradar [ah-grah-dar'], *va.* To please, to gratify, to render acceptable; to humor, to like. **Esto no me agrada**, I don't like this. *vn.* To please; **su presencia siempre agrada**, it's always pleasant to have you with us.
agradarse [ah-grah-dahr-say], *vr.* To be pleased.
agradecer [ah-grah-day-therr'], *va.* 1. To acknowledge a favor, to show gratitude in any way. 2. To reward, to recompense. **Agradezco tu ayuda**, I am grateful for your help. **Se lo agradezco,** I am grateful to you.

agradecerse [ah-grah-day-thayr-say], *vr.* **¡Se agradece!**, much obliged! **Una copita de jerez siempre se agradece**, a glass of sherry is always welcome.
agradecidamente [ah-grah-day-the-dah-men'-tay], *adv.* Gratefully.
agradecido, da [ah-grah-day-thee'-do, dah], *a.* 1. Acknowledged. 2. Grateful, thankful. **Estamos muy agradecidos**, we are very grateful. *-pp.* of AGRADECER.
agradecimiento [ah-grah-day-the-me-en'-to], *m.* Gratefulness; act of acknowledging a favor conferred. (**Yo agradezco**, from **Agradecer**. V. ABORRECER).
agrado [ah-grah'-do], *m.* 1. Affability, agreeableness, the quality of pleasing, courteousness, grace; favorableness. 2. Comfortableness, gratefulness. 3. Pleasure, liking. **Esto no es de mi agrado**, that does not please me, I do not like that.
agramadera [ah-grah-mah-day'-rah], *f.* Brake, an instrument for dressing flax or hemp; scutcher.
agramar [ah-grah-mar'], *va.* To dress flax or hemp with a brake.
agramilar [ah-grah-me-lar'], *va.* To point and color a brick wall; to make even, adjust, the bricks.
agramiza [ah-grah-mee'-taht], *f.* 1. The stalk of hemp. 2. Refuse of dressed hemp.
agrandamiento [ah-gran-dah-me-en'-to], *m.* Enlargement.
agrandar [ah-gran-dar'], *va.* To increase, to greaten, to make larger.
agrandarse [ah-gran-dahr-say], *vr.* To get bigger.
agranijado [ah-grah-ne-hah-do], *a.* Pimply.
agranujado, da [ah-grah-noo-hah'-do, dah], *a.* 1. Filled or covered with grain. 2. Grain-shaped.
agrario, ria [ah-grah'-re-o, ah+, *a.* Agrarian, rustic. **Ley agraria**, agrarian law.
agrarismo [ah-grah-res-mo], *m. (Mex.)* Agrarian reform movement.
agrarista [ah-grah-res-tah], *m. & f. (Mex.)* Supporter (advocate) of land reform.
agravación [ah-grah-vah-the-on'], *f.* Aggravation.
agravador, ra [ah-grah-vah-dor' rah], *m. & f.* Oppressor.
agravamiento [ah-grah-vah-me-en'-to], *m.* The act of aggravating.
agravante [ah-grah-vahn'-tay], *a.* Aggravating, irritating, trying. **Circunstancia agravante**, (for.) Aggravating circumstance.
agravar [ah-gra-var'], *va.* 1. To oppres with taxes and public burdens; to aggrieve. 2. To render more intolerable. 3. To exaggerate, to complicate, to aggravate. 4. To ponder.
agravarse [ah-grah-vahr-say], *vr.* To worsen, get worse.
agravatorio, ria [ah-grah-vah-to'-re-o, ah], *a. (Law.)* Compulsory, aggravating.
agraviadamente [ah-grah-ve-ah-dah-men'-tay], *adv. (Obs.)* 1. Injuriously, insultingly. 2. Efficaciously, strongly.
agraviador, ra [ah-grah-ve-ah-dor', rah], *m. & f.* One that gives offence or injuries.
agraviar [ah-grah-ve-ar'], *va.* To wrong, to offend, to grieve, to harm.
agraviarse [ah-grah-ve-ahr-say], *vr.* To be aggrieved; to be piqued; to be offended.
agravio [ah-grah'-ve-o], *m.* 1. Offence, harm, grievance, mischief; insult; injury, affront. 2. *(Obs.)* Appeal.
agravión [ah-grah-ve-on], *a. (Cono Sur)* Touchy, quick to take offence.
agravioso [ah-gra-ve-o-so], *a.* Offensive, insulting.
agraz [ah-grath'], *m.* 1. Verjuice, the juice expressed from unripe grapes. 2. An unripe grape. 3. Displeasure, disgust. **En agraz**, *adv.* Unseasonably; unsuitably.
agrazar [ah-grah-thar'], *vn.* To have a sour taste. *-va.* To disgust, to vex.
agrazón [ah-grah-thone'], *m.* 1. Wild grape, grapes which do not ripen. 2. *(Bot.)* Gooseberry-bush. 3. Displeasure, resentment, disgust.
agredir [ah-gray-deer'], *va.* To assume the aggressive, assault, attack.

agregación [ah-gray-gah-the-on'], *f.* Aggregation, collecting into one mass.

agregado, da [ah-gray-gah'-do], *m.* 1. Aggregate. 2. Congregation. 3. An assistant, a supernumerary. 4. *(Tech.)* Concrete block (bloque). 5. **Agregada**, attaché. **Agregada cultural**, cultural attaché. 6. *(LAm.)* person newly added to a group.

agregar [ah-gray-gar'], *va.* 1. To aggregate, to collect and unite, to heap together. 2. To collate, to nominate.

agremiación [ah-gray-me-ah-theon'], *f.* 1. Unionization. 2. Labor union.

agremiar [ah-gray'-me-ar], *va. & vr.* To form a guild or society.

agremiarse [ah-gre-me-ahr-say], *vr.* To form a union.

agresión [ah-gray-se-on'], *f.* Aggression, attack, assault.

agresivamente [ah-gray-se-vah-men'-tay], *adv.* Aggressively.

agresividad [ah-gray-se-ve-dahd'], *f.* Aggressiveness.

agresivo, va [ah-gray-see'-vo, vah], *a.* Aggressive, provoking.

agresor, ra [ah-gray-sor', rah] *m. & f.* Aggressor, assaulter.

agreste [ah-gres'-tay], *a.* 1. Rustic, clownish, illiterate, churlish, homebred. 2. Wild.

agrete [ah-gray'-tay], *m.* Sourness with a mixture of sweet.

agriado [ah-gre-ah-do], *a. (Cono Sur)* 1. Sour, sharp. 2. *(fig.)* Sour, resentful (resentido).

agriamente [ah'-gre-ah-men-tay], *adv.* Sourly; with asperity or harshness.

agriar [ah-gre-ar'], *va.* 1. To make sour or tart. 2. *(Met.)* To make peevish, to irritate, to exasperate.

agriarse [ah-gre-ahr-say], *vr.* 1. To sour, turn acid. 2. *(fig.)* to get cross.

agrícola [ah-gree'-co-lah], *a. & n.* Agricultural; agriculturist.

agricultor [ah-gre-cool-tor'], *m.* Husbandman, farmer. 2. A writer upon agriculture.

agricultora [ah-gre-cool-to'-rah], *f.* The woman who tills the ground.

agricultura [ah-gre-cool-too'-rah], *f.* Agriculture, farming.

agricultural [ah-gre-cool-too-rahl'], *a. (LAm.)* Agricultural, farming.

agridulce [ah-gre-dool'-thay], *a.* Between sweet and sour, sub-sour.

agriera [ah-gre-ay-rah], *f. (LAm. Med.)* heartburn.

agrietado, da [ah-gre-ay-tah'-do, dah], *a.* Flawy, defective.

agrietar [ah-gre-ay-tahr], *va.* To crack, to crack open.

agrietarse [ah-gre-ay-tar'-say], *vr.* To be filled with cracks.

agrifolio [ah-gre-fo'-le-o], *m. (Bot.)* Holly-tree.

agrillado, da [ah-greel-lyah'-do, dah], *a.* Chained, put in irons. *-pp.* of AGRILLARSE.

agrillarse [ah-greel-lyar'-say], *vr.* V. GRILLARSE.

agrillo, lla [ah-greel'-lyo, lyah], *a. dim.* Sourish, tartish.

agrimensor, a [ah-gre-men-sor'], *m. & f.* Land surveyor.

agrimensura [ah-gre-men-soo'-rah], *f.* Art of surveying land.

agrimonia [ah-gre-mo'-ne-ah], *f. (Bot.)* Agrimony, liverwort, Agrimonia.

agringado [ah-gren-gah-do], *a. (LAm.)* Like (imitating) a foreigner.

agringarse [ah-gren-gahr-say], *vr.* To act like a foreigner.

agrio, ria [ah'-gre-o, ah], *a.* 1. Sour, acrid. 2. *(Met.)* Rough, applied to a road full of stones. 3. *(Met.)* Sharp, rude, unpleasant. **Una respuesta agria**, a smart reply. 4. Brittle, apt to break, unmalleable; applied to metals. 5. *(Art.)* Of bad taste in coloring or drawing.

agrio [ah'-gre-o], *m.* The acidity of some fruits, sour. **Agrios**, Sour fruit trees.

agrión [ah-gre-on'], *m. (Vet.)* Callosity in the joint of a horse's knee.

agripado [ah-gre-pah-do], *a. (LAm.)* **Estar agripado**, to have the flu.

agrisetado, da [àh-gre-say-tah'-do, dah], *a.* 1. Flowered like silks. 2. Gray-colored.

agriura [ah-gre-oo-rah], *f. (LAm.)* Sourness, tartness.

agro [ah-gro], *m.* Farming, agriculture.

agrobiología [ah-gro-be-o-lo-hee'-ah], *f.* Agrobiology.

agroindustria [ah-gro-en-doos-tre-ah], *f. (Cono Sur Econ.)* Agroindustry.

agronomía [ah-gro-no-mee'-ah], *f.* Theory of agriculture.

agronómico, ca [ah-gro-no'-me-co, cah], *a.* Agronomical.

agrónomo, ma [ah-gro'-no-mo, mah], *a.* Agronomous. *-m.* Agronomist.

agropecuario [ah-gro-pay-coo-ah-re-o], *a.* Farming, stockbreeding. **Política agropecuaria**, farming policy.

agrumarse [ah-groo-mar'-say], *vr.* To curdle, as in making cheese.

agrupación [ah-groo-pah-the-on], *f.* 1. Association, group. 2. Crowding, crowd.

agrupar [ah-groo-par'], *va.* To group, to cluster.

agruparse [ah-groo-pahr-say], *vr.* To form a group; to gather, to come together, to cluster.

agrura [ah-groo'-rah], *f.* 1. Acidity; acerbity. 2. *(Obs.)* A group of trees which yield fruit of sourish taste.

agua [ah'-goo-ah], *f.* 1. Water. 2. *(Chem.)* Liquor distilled from herbs, flowers, or fruit. 3. Lustre of diamonds. 4. *(Naut.)* Leak. **Agua de azahar**, orange-flower water. **Agua de olor**, scented water. **Agua rica**, a name given indifferently to all kinds of scented water in several provinces of Peru. **Agua llovediza**, rain-water. **Agua fuerte**, agua fortis. **Agua bendita**, holy water. **¡Agua va!** a notice to passers-by that water will be thrown. **Nunca digas de este agua no beberé**, don't be too sure. **Cambiar el agua al canario**, *(Esp.)* to take a leak. **Echarse al agua**, to dive in. **Estar con el agua al cuello**, to be over a barrel. **Agua viva**, running water. *-pl.* 1. Mineral waters in general. 2. Clouds in silk and other stuffs. 3. Urine. 4. Tide. **Aguas muertas**, neap-tides. **Aguas vivas**, spring tides. **Entre dos aguas**, between wind and water; in doubt, perplexed. **Agua abajo**, *adv.* down the stream. **Agua arriba**, *adv.* 1. Against the stream. 2. *(Met.)* With great difficulty. **Agua de Colonia**, Cologne-water. **Agua dulce**, fresh water. **Agua oxigenada**, hydrogen peroxide. **Agua potable**, drinking-water. **Agua del timón**, wake of a ship. **Agua de cepas**, *(coll.)* Wine. (Comparaciones), **como agua**, like water. **Venir como agua de mayo**, to be a godsend, be very welcome. **Aguas**, waters. **Aguas residuales**, sewage. **Aguas territoriales**, territorial waters.

aguacate, or **agualate** [ah-goo-ah-cah'-tay, or ah-goo-ah-lah'-tay], *m.* 1. (In Peru, **Palta**). A tree of this name and its fruit, resembling a large pear, miscalled alligator-pear. (From Mexican **ahuacatl**). The fruit of Persea gratissima. 2. Shaped as a pear. 3. *(CAm.)* Idiot, fool.

aguacatero [ah-goo-ah-kah-tay-ro], *m. (Mex.)* Avocado pear tree.

aguacero [ah-goo-ah-thay'-ro], *m.* A heavy shower of rain.

aguacibera [ah-goo-ah-the-bay'-rah], *f. (Prov.)* A piece of ground sowed when dry and afterward irrigated.

aguacil [àh-goo-ah-thell'], *m.* A constable. V. ALGUACIL. *(Cono Sur)* dragonfly.

aguachirle [ah-goo-ah-cheer'-lay], *f.* 1. Inferior wine. 2. Slipslop; any bad liquor.

aguacola [ah-goo-ah-co-lah], *f. (Mex.)* Fish glue.

aguachacha [ah-goo-ah-cha-cha], *f. (CAm.)* Weak, stagnant water.

aguachado [ah-goo-ah-cha-do], *a. (Cono Sur)* tame.

aguachento [ah-goo-ah-chayn-to], *a. (And. Cono Sur)* Watery, very juicy.

aguachinado [ah-goo-ah-che-nah-do], *a. (Carib.)* Watery (acuoso); Soft (blando).

aguachinarse [ah-goo-ah-che-nahr-say], *vr. (Mex. Agri.)* To be flooded.

aguachirle [ah-goo-ah-cher-lay], *f.* 1. Weak drink, nasty drink. 2. Trifle.

aguada [ah-goo-ah'-dah], *f.* 1. *(Naut.)* Water on board a ship. **Hacer aguada**, to water. 2. *(Art.)* Sketch, outline. 3. Flood, flooding.

aguadero [ah-goo-ah-day'-ro], *m.* 1. Watering-place for cattle. 2. *(Naut.)* watering-port for ships.

aguadija [ah-goo-ah-dee'-hah], *f.* Humor in pimples or sores.

aguado, da [ah-goo-ah'-do, dah], *a.* 1. Watered. 2. Abstemious, like a teetotaller. *-pp.* of AGUAR.

aguador, ra [ah-goo-ah-dor', rah], *m. & f.* 1. Water-carrier. 2. *(Mil.)* **Aguador del real**, Sutler. 3. Bucket of a water-wheel.

aguaducho [ah-goo-ah-doo'-cho], *m.* 1. Water-course. 2. Stall for selling water. 3. *(Prov.)* Place where earthen vessels with drinking water are kept.

agua dulce [ah'-goo-ah- dool'-thay], *f.* 1. Fresh water. 2. Sweet water.

aguafiestas [ah-goo-ah-fee-ess'-tahs], *m. & f.* Wet blanket, kill-joy.

aguafuerte [ah-goo-ah-foo-err'-tay], *m.* or *f.* Etching.

aguafuertista [ah-goo-ah-foo-err-tees'-tah], *m. & f.* Etcher.

aguagma [ah-goo-ah-go'-mah] *f.* Gum-water, used in the preparation of paints.

aguaitador, ra [ah-goo-ah-e-tah-dor', rah], *m. & f. (Obs.)* A spy.

aguaitar [ah-goo-ah-e-tar'], *va.* 1. *(Low.)* To discover by close examination. To spy on. 2. *(And. Carib.)* To wait for (esperar). 3. *(Cono Sur)* To look, to see (ver).

aguajaque [ah-goo-ah-hah'-kay], *m.* A sort of ammoniac gum.

aguajas [ah-goo-ah'-has], *f. pl.* Ulcers above the hoofs of a horse.

aguaje [ah-goo-ah'-hay], *m.* 1. A running spring. 2. *(Naut.)* A current in the sea, persistent or periodical; e.g. The Gulf Stream. 3. Place where ships go for water. 4. *(And. CAm.)* rainstorm. 5. *(CAm.)* Dressing-down (regañina).

aguajirado [ah-goo-ah-he-rah-do], *a. (Carib.)* Withdrawn, timid.

aguajirarse [ah-goo-ah-he-rahr-say], *vr. (Carib.)* To become countrified, acquire peasant's habits.

agualotal [ah-goo-ah-lo-tahl], *m. (CAm.)* Swamp, marsh.

aguamala [ah-goo-ah-mah-lah], *f. (And.)* Jellyfish.

aguamanil [ah-goo-ah-mah-neel'], *m.* 1. Water-jug. 2. A wash-stand.

aguamar [ah-goo-ah-mahr], *m.* Jellyfish.

aguamarina [ah-goo-ah-mah-ree'-nah], *f.* Aqua marina, a precious stone, pale green; a variety of bery.

aguamarse [ah-goo-ah-mahr-say], *vr. (And)* to get scared, be intimidated.

aguamelado, da [ah-goo-ah-may-lah'-do, dah], *a.* Washed or rubbed over with water and honey.

aguamiel [ah-goo-ah-me-el'], *f.* 1. Hydromel, honey and water, mead, metheglin. 2. The unfermented juice of the Mexican agave or **maguey**.

aguamuerta [ah-goo-ah-moo-ayr-tah], *f. (Cono Sur)* Jellyfish.

aguana [ah-goo-ah'-nah], *f.* A wood used in canoe-making in South America.

aguanafa [ah-goo-ah-nah'-fah], *f. (Prov.)* Orange-flower water.

aguanieve [ah-goo-ah-ne-ay'-vay], *f.* 1. Bird of the family of magpies. 2. Sleet, snow.

aguano [ah-goo-ah-no], *m. (And)* Mahogany.

aguanosidad [ah-goo-ah-no-se-dad'], *f.* Serous humors in the body.

aguanoso, sa [ah-goo-ah-no'-so, sah], *a.* Aqueous; extremely moist.

aguantable [ah-goo-ahn-tah-blay], *a.* Bearable, tolerable.

aguantaderas [ah-goo-ahn-tah-day-rahs], *f. & pl. (LAm.)* **Tener aguantaderas**, to be tolerant.

aguantadero [ah-goo-ahn-tah-day-ro], *m. (Cono Sur)* Hide-out.

aguantador [ah-goo-ahn-tah-dor], *a. (LAm.)* V. AGUANTÓN.

aguantar [ah-goo-an-tar'], *va.* 1. To sustain, to suffer, to bear, to endure; to abide. 2. To maintain. 3. *(Naut.)* To carry a stiff sail.

aguantarse [ah-goo-ahn-tahr-say], *vr.* 1. To restrain oneself, hold oneself, back, sit tight. 2. *(LAm.)* To keep one's mouth shut. **Tendrá que aguantarse**, he'll just have to put up with it.

aguante [ah-goo-ahn'-tay], *m.* 1. Fortitude, firmness; vigor in bearing labor and fatigue. 2. Patience. 3. *(Naut.)* **Navío de aguante**, a ship that carries a stiff sail.

aguantón [ah-goo-ahn-ton], 1. *a. (Carib. Mex.)* Long-suffering, extremely patient. 2. *m. (Carib.)* **Te darás un aguantón**, you'll have a long wait.

aguapié [ah-goo-ah-pe-ay], *m.* Weak wine, plonk.

aguañón [ah-goo-ah-nyon'], *m.* Constructor of hydraulic machines.

aguapa [ah-goo-ah'-ah], *f.* The white water-lily.

aguapié [ah-goo-ah-pe-ay'], *m.* Small wine. *V.* AGUACHIRLE.

aguar [ah-goo-ar'], *va.* 1. To mix water with wine, vinegar, or other liquor. 2. *(Met.)* To disturb or interrupt pleasure. 3. **aguarse** [ah-goo-ahr-say], *vr.* To be filled with water.

aguardada [ah-goo-ahr-dah-dah], *f.* Wait, waiting.

aguardadero [ah-goo-ahr-dah-day-ro], *m.* Hide (caza).

aguardar [ah-goo-ar-dar'], *va.* 1. To expect, to wait. 2. To grant time, e.g. to a debtor.

aguardentería [ah-goo-ar-den-tay-ree'-ah], *f.* Liquor-shop.

aguardentero, ra [ah-goo-ar-den-tay-ro, rah], *m. & f.* Retailer of liquors.

aguardentoso [ah-goo-ahr-den-to-so], *a.* Alcoholic.

aguardiente [ah-goo-ar-de-en'-tay], *m.* 1. Brandy. 2. Whisky. **Aguardiente de cabeza**, the first and strongest spirits drawn from the still.

aguardientoso [ah-goo-ahr-de-ayn-to-so], *a. (LAm.) V.* AGUARDENTOSO.

aguardo [ah-goo-ar'-do], *m.* Place where a sportsman waits to fire at the game.

aguarrás [ah-goo-ar-rahs'], *m.* Oil of turpentine.

aguarse [ah-goo-ar'-say], *vr.* 1. To be inundated. 2. To get stiff after much fatigue (caballos, mulas).

aguate [ah-goo-ah-tay], *m. (Mex.)* Prickle, thorn.

aguatero [ah-goo-ah-tay'-ro], *m.* Water carrier.

aguatocha [ah-goo-ah-to'-chah], *f.* Pump.

aguatocho [ah-goo-ah-to'-cho], *m. (Prov.)* Small quagmire.

aguatoso [ah-goo-ah-to-so], *a. (Mex.)* Prickle.

aguaturma [ah-goo-a-toor'-mah], *f. (Bot.)* Jerusalem artichoke.

aguavientos [ah-goo-ah-ve-en'-tos], *m. (Bot.)* Yellow sage-tree.

aguaviva [ah-goo-ah-ve-vah], *f. (Cono Sur)* Jellyfish.

aguayo [ah-goo-ah-yo], *m. (And)* Multicolored woolen cloth.

aguaza [ah-goo-ah'-thah], *f.* 1. Aqueous humor. 2. Juice extracted from trees by incision.

aguazal [ah-goo-ah-thahl'], *m.* Marsh, fen. *V.* PANTANO.

aguazar [ah-goo-ah-thahr], *va.* To flood, to waterlog.

aguazo [ah-goo-ah'-tho] (Pintura de). Painting drawn with gum-water of a dull, cloudy color.

aguazoso, sa [ah-goo-ah-tho'-so, sah], *a.* Aqueous.

agudamente [ah-goo-dah-men'-tay], *adv.* 1. Sharply, lively, keenly, 2. Ingeniously, finely; clearly.

agudeza [ah-goo-day'-thah], *f.* 1. Sharpness of instruments. 2. Acuteness, force of intellect, subtlety, fineness. 3. Witty saying, repartee. 4. Acidity of fruits and plants. 5. Smartness.

agudización [ah-goo-de-thah-the-on], *f.* Sharpening; worsening.

agudizar [ah-goo-de-thahr], *va.* To sharpen, to make more acute.

agudo, da [ah-goo'-do, dah], *a.* 1. Sharp-pointed, keen-edged; smart. 2. *(Met.)* Acute, witty. 3. Dangerous. 4. Brisk, ready, active. 5. *(Med.)* Acute, of rapid development.

agüé [ah-goo-ay], *interj. (CAm.)* hello!

agüela [ah-goo-ay'-lah], *m. & f. (Obs.)* Grandfather, grandmother.

agüero [ah-goo-ay'-ro], *m.* Augury, prognostication, omen. (*Yo agüero, yo agüere*, from *Agorar. V.* ACORDAR).

agüeitar [ah-goo-ay-tahr], *(LAm.) V.* AGUAITAR.

aguerrido, da [ah-ger-ree'-do, dah], *a.* Hardened, veteran. *-pp.* of AGUERRIR.

aguerrir [ah-ger-reer'], *va.* To accustom to war.

agüevar [ah-goo-ay-vahr] *va. (CAm. Mex.)* To put down, to shame.

agüevarse [ah-goo-ay-vahr-say], *vr.* To cower, to shrink.

aguijada [ah-ge-hah'-dah], *f.* 1. Spur, goad. 2. Stimulant, pungency.

aguijador, ra [ah-ge-hah-dor, rah], *m. & f.* One that goads or stimulates.

aguijadura [ah-ge-hah-doo'-rah], *f.* Spurring; the act of exciting.

aguijar [ah-ge-har'], *va.* 1. To prick, to spur, to goad. 2. To incite, to stimulate. *-vn.* To march fast.

aguijón [ah-ge-hone'], *m.* 1. Sting of a bee, wasp, etc. 2. Power of exciting motion or sensation. 3. Prick, spur, goad. **Dar o tirar coces contra el aguijón**, to kick against the spur or goad.

aguijonazo [ah-ge-ho-nah'-tho], *m.* Thrust with a goad.

aguijoncillo [ah-ge-hon-theel'-lyo], *m. dim.* Petty exciter.

aguijoneador, ra [ah-ge-ho-nay-ah-dor', rah], *m. & f.* One who pricks or goads.

aguijonear [ah-ge-ho-nay-ar'], *va.* 1. To thrust. *V.* AGUIJAR. 2. To incite.

águila [ah'-ge-lah], *f.* 1. Eagle. **Ve más que un águila**, he is more sharpsighted than an eagle. 2. A gold coin with an eagle of the reign of Charles *V.*

aguileño, ña [ah-ge-lay'-nyo, nyah], *a.* Aquiline; hooked, hawk-nosed.

aguilera [ah-ge-lay-rah], *f.* Eagle's nest, eyrie.

aguililla [ah-ge-leel'-lyah], *f. dim.* A little eagle, an eaglet. *V.* CABALLO AGUILILLA.

aguilón [ah-ge-lone'], *m.* 1. The boom of the instrument called a crane, used for lifting heavy weights. 2. *aug.* of AGUILA.

aguilucho [ah-ge-loo'-cho], *m.* 1. A young eagle. 2. Hobby.

aguinaldo [ah-ge-nahl'-do], *m.* New Year's gift, Christmas box.

aguisado [ah-gee-sah'-do], *a. & n. (Obs.)* Just, reasonable, prudent.

aguisar [ah-ge-sar'], *va. (Obs.)* 1. To dress, to arrange. 2. To cook or provide provisions.

agüita [ah-goo-ee'-tah], *f. dim.* A little rain or mist.

agüitado [ah-goo-ee-tah-do], *a. (Mex.)* depressed, down.

aguja [ah-goo'-hah], *f.* 1. Needle (de coser). 2. Spire (obelisco), steeple. 3. Needle-fish, horn-fish. 4. Needle-shell. 5. Hand (reloj). 6. Switch-rail (r. w.). 7. Spindle. 8. Pin (in typography and in artillery); a brad. 9. Graft. **Aguja de marear**, *(Naut.)* A mariner's compass. **Aguja de cámara**, *(Naut.)* a hanging compass. **Aguja capotera**, *(Naut.)* sailing needle. **Aguja de relinga**, *(Naut.)* boltrope-needle. **Aguja de hacer media**, knitting-needle. **Aguja de pastor**, *(Bot.)* shepherd's needle. **Aguja de mechar**, skewer. **Aguja imantada**, magnetic needle. **Aguja de gancho**, crochet hook. *pl.* 1. Ribs of the fore quarter of an animal. 2. Distemper of horses, affecting the legs, neck, and throat.

agujazo [ah-goo-hah'-tho], *m.* A prick with a needle.

agujerar [ah-goo-hay-rar'], *va.* To pierce. *V.* AGUJEREAR.

agujereado [ah-goo-hay-ray-ah-do], *a.* Full of holes, pierced with holes.

agujerear [ah-goo-hay-ray-ar'], *va.* To pierce, to bore, to make holes.

agujerico, illo, uelo [ah-goo-hay-ree'-co, reel'-lyo, oo-ay'-lo], *m. dim.* A small hole.

agujero [ah-goo-hay'-ro], *m.* 1. Hole in clothes, walls, etc. 2. Needle-maker, needle-seller. 3. *(Obs.)* Pin-case; needle-case. 4. *(Naut.)* Port, mouth of a river, or any opening in the coast. 5. A dug-out.

agujeta [ah-goo-hay'-tah], *f.* String or strap of leather. *-pl.* 1. Pains felt from fatigue. **Estar lleno de agujetas**, to be stiff all over.

agujetería [ah-goo-hay-tay-ree'-ah], *f.* Shop where leather straps, or girths, called **agujetas**, are made or sold.

agujetero, ra [ah-goo-hay-tay'-ro, rah], *m. & f.* Maker or seller of **agujetas** or laces.

agujón [ah-goo-hone'], *m. aug.* A large needle.

aguosidad [ah-goo-o-se-dad], *f.* Lymph, a transparent, colorless liquid in the human body.

aguoso, sa [ah-goo-o'-so, sah], *a.* Aqueous.

agur [ah-goor'], *adv. (coll.)* Adieu, farewell. Goodbye.

agusanado [ah-goo-sah-nah-do], *a.* Maggoty, wormy.

agusanarse [ah-goo-sah-nar'-say], *vr.* To be worm eaten, to be rotten.

Agustín [ah-goos-teen], *m.* Augustine.

agustiniano, na [ah-goos-te-ne-ah'-no, nah], *m. & f.* 1. *V.* AGUSTINO. 2. Belonging to the order of St. Augustine.

agustino, na [ah-goos-tee'-no, nah], *m. & f.* Monk or nun of the order of St. Augustine.

agutí [ah-goo-tee'], *m.* Agouti, a rodent of tropical America.

aguzadera [ah-goo-thah-day'-rah], *f.* Whetstone.

aguzadero [ah-goo-thah-day'-ro], *m.* Haunt of wild boars, where they whet their tusks.

aguzado, da [ah-goo-thah'-do, dah], *a.* Sharp, pointed, keen.

aguzadura [ah-goo-thah-doo'-rah], *f.* Whetting or sharpening a tool or weapon.

aguzamiento [ah-goo-thah-me-ayn-to], *m.* Sharpening.

aguzanieve [ah-goo-thah-ne-ay'-vay], *f.* Wagtail, a small bird.

aguzar [ah-goo-thar'], *va.* 1. To whet or sharpen. 2. *(Met.)* To stimulate, to excite. **Aguzar el ingenio**, to sharpen the wit. **Aguzar las orejas**, to cock up the ears, to listen quickly. **Aguzar la vista**, to sharpen the sight.

aguzonazo [ah-goo-tho-nah'-tho], *m. V.* HURGONZAO.

¡ah! [ah], *interj.* Ah! *V.* ¡AY!.

ahebrado, da [ah-ay-brah'-do, dah], *a.* Thread-like, fibrous.

ahechaduras [ah-ay-chah-doo-rahs], *f. & pl.* Chaff.

ahechar [ah-ay-chahr], *va.* To sift; to winnow.

ahelear [ah-ay-lay-ar'], *va.* To give gall to drink, to make bitter. *-vn.* To taste very bitter.

ahembrado, da [ah-em-brah'-do, dah], *a. (Obs.)* Effeminate. *V.* AFEMINADO.

aherrojamiento [ah-er-ro-hah-me-en'-to], *m.* Putting in irons.

aherrojar [ah-er-ro-har'], *va.* To chain, to put in irons.

aherrumbrarse [ah-er-room-brar'-say], *vr.* 1. To have the taste and color of iron or copper, to be ferruginous: applied especially to water which has percolated through an iron-bearing stratum. 2. To be full of scoria.

ahervorarse [ah-er-vo-rar'-say], *vr.* To be heated by fermentation: applied to piled-up grain.

ahí [ah-ee'], *adv.* There, in that place; over there; yonder. **De por ahí**, about that, indicating a common trifling thing. **Está por ahí**, it's around here. **¡Hasta ahí podíamos llegar!**, so it has come to this! **¡Ahí es nada!**, fancy that! **¡Ahí va!**, there it is! **Por ahí**, that way. **¡Vete por ahí!**, get away!

ahidalgado, da [ah-e-dal-gah'-do, dah], *a.* Gentlemanly.

ahijada [ah-e-hah'-dah], *f.* 1. Godchild, goddaughter. 2. *V.* AHIJADO. 3. A paddle-staff. *-pp.* of AHIJAR.

ahijado [ah-e-hah'-do], *m.* 1. Godchild. 2. Client, one protected or peculiarly favored.

ahijar [ah-e-har'], *va.* 1. To adopt. 2. (Among shepherds) To put every lamb with its dam. 3. *(Met.).* To impute. *-vn.* 2. To bring forth young: applied only to cattle. 2. To bud, to shoot out.

ahijuna [ah-e-hoo-nah], *interj. (Cono Sur)* Son of a bitch.

ahilado [ah-e-lah'-do], *a.* Withered (of plants and trees). *Cf.* AHILARSE. 4.

ahilar [ah-e-lahr] 1. *va.* To line up. 2. *vn.* To go in single file.

ahilarse [ah-e-lar'-say], *vr.* 1. to be faint for want of nourishment. 2. To grow sour, applied to leaven and bread. 3. To grow thin. 4. To be weak, applied to plants. *-vn.* To go single file. **Ahilarse el vino**, to turn ropy.

ahilo [ah-ee'-lo], *m.* Faintness, weakness for want of food.

ahincadamente [ah-en-cah-dah-mayn-tay], *adv.* hard, earnestly.

ahinco [ah-een'-co], *m.* Earnestness, eagerness, ardor.

ahitar [ah-e-tar'], *va.* To surfeit; to overload the stomach, to cloy, to satiate. ^*vr.* To be surfeited.

ahitera [ah-e-tay'-rah], *f. (coll.)* Violent or continued indigestion.

ahito, ta [ah-ee'-to, tah], *a.* 1. One that labors under an indigestion. 2. *(Met.)* Disgusted, tired of a person or thing. -*irr.* of AHITAR.

ahito [ah-ee'-to], *m.* Indigestion; surfeit; repletion.

AHN *abr.* de **Archivo Historico Nacional.**

¡aho! [ah-o] *int. (Obs.)* Hallo!

ahobachonado, da [ah-o-bah-cho-nah'-do, dah], *a. (coll.)* Dull, slovenly, lazy; cowardly.

ahocicar [ah-o-the-car'], *vn. (Naut.)* To pitch or plunge.

ahocinarse [ah-o-the-nar'-say], *vr.* To run precipitately (riachuelo).

ahogadero [ah-o-gah-day'-ro], *m.* 1. Hangman's rope. 2. Place difficult to breathe in. 3. Throat-band, a part of the head-stall of a bridle or halter.

ahogadizo, za [ah-o-gah-dee'-tho, thah], *a.* Harsh, unpalatable. **Carne ahogadiza,** Flesh of animals suffocated or drowned.

ahogado, da [ah-o-gah'-do, dah], *a.* Suffocated; close, unventilated. **Carnero ahogado,** Stewed mutton. **Dar mate ahogado,** to pin up the king at the game of chess. *(Met.)* To insist upon things being done without delay. **Estar ahogado or verse ahogado,** to be overwhelmed with business or trouble. -*pp.* of AHOGAR.

ahogador, ra [ah-o-gah-dor', rah], *m. & f.* One who suffocates another, hangman.

ahogamiento [ah-o-gah-me-en'-to], *m.* 1. Suffocation. 2. *V.* AHOGO. **Ahogamiento de la madre,** Hysterics, an hysteric fit.

ahogar [ah-o-gar'], *va.* 1. To choke, to throttle, to kill by stopping the breath, to smother. 2. To drown. 3. *(Met.)* To oppress. 4. *(Met.)* To quench, to extinguish. 5. To water plants to excess. 6. *(Naut.)* To founder. -*vr.* 1. To be suffocated. 2. To drown oneself, be drowned.

ahogo [ah-o'-go], *m.* Oppression, anguish, pain, severe affliction. (Fin) financial difficulty.

ahoguido [ah-o-gee'-do], *m. V.* AHOGUIO.

ahojar [ah-o-har'], *vn. (Prov.)* To eat the leaves of trees (ganado).

ahombrado, da [ah-om-brah-do, dah], *a. (coll.)* Masculine, applied to a woman. *V.* HOMBRUNO.

ahondar [ah-on-dar'], *va.* To sink. -*vn.* 1. To penetrate into a thing: to hollow out; to dip, as of the ground. 2. *(Met.)* To advance in the knowledge of things; to investigate. -*vr.* To go in more deeply.

ahonde [ah-on'-day], *m.* 1. Act and effect of sinking. 2. The depth to which a mine ought to reach in some countries of America to acquire title of ownership (7 varas).

ahora [ah-o'-rah], *adv.* Now, at present, **ahora mismo,** Just now. **Ahora mismo ha empezado la reunión,** the meeting began this moment. **Por ahora,** for the present. **Ahora bien,** well, granted, nevertheless. **Hasta ahora,** hitherto. **No puedo ir ahora,** I can't go just now. **Ahora o nunca,** it's now or never. **De ahora en adelante,** from now on. *conj.* Now, now then. **Lo hemos discutido, ahora, ¿qué hacemos?,** we've talked about it, now, what shall we do? **Ahora bien, si quieres te lo regalo,** I don't like it, but if you insist, I'll buy it for you.

ahorcado [ah-or-cah'-do], *m.* Hanged man. -*pp.* of AHORCAR.

ahorcadura [ah-or-cah-doo'-rah], *f.* The act of hanging.

ahorcajarse [ah-or-cah-har'-say], *vr.* To sit astride.

ahorcar [ah-or-car'], *va.* To kill by hanging. **Ahorcar los hábitos.** To abandon the ecclesiastical garb for another

profession. **Que me ahorquen si lo hago,** hang me if I do. -*vr.* To be vexed, to be very angry.

ahorita [ah-o-ree'-tah], *adv. (coll.)* Just now; this minute.

ahormar [ah-or-mar'], *va.* 1. To fit or adjust. 2. To wear clothes or shoes until they fit easy. 3. *(Met.)* To bring one to a sense of his duty.

ahornagarse [ah-or-nah-gar'-say], *vr.* To get scorched or burned: said of young leaves or shoots of plants.

ahornar [ah-or-nar'], *va.* To put in an oven. -*vr.* To be scorched or burnt in the oven without being backed inwardly: applied to bread.

ahorquillado, da [ah-or-kel-lyah'-do, dah], *a.* Forked. -*pp* of AHORQUILLAR.

ahorquillar [ah-or-keel-lyar'], *va.* To stay, to prop up with forks. -*vr.* To become forked.

ahorrado, da [ah-or-rah'-do, dah], *a.* Saved. -*pp.* of AHORRAR.

ahorrador, ra [ah-or-rah'-dor, rah], *m. & f.* Thrifty person.

ahorramiento [ah-or-rah-me-en'-to], *m.* Saving, enfranchisement.

ahorrar [ah-or-rar'], *va.* 1. To save, to economize, to spare. **Hemos ahorrado para irnos de vacaciones,** we have saved to go on vacation. 2. To enfranchise, to emancipate. 3. To shun labor, danger, or difficulties. -*vr.* **Ahorrarse molestias,** to save oneself troubles. **Ahorrarse trabajo, tiempo,** to save work, time.

ahorrativa [ah-or-rah-tee'-vah], *f. (coll.) V.* AHORRO.

ahorrativo, va [ah-or-rah-tee'-vo, vah], *a.* Frugal, thrifty, saving. **Andar or ir a la ahorrativa,** to go frugally to work.

ahorro [ah-or'-ro], *m.* 1. Parsimony, frugality, husbandry. 2. Saving, sparingness. **Banco de ahorros,** Savings-bank.

ahoyador [ah-o-yah-dor'], *m.* 1. *(Prov.)* One that makes holes for the pupose of planting. 2. *(Met.)* Gravedigger.

ahoyadura [ah-o-yah-doo'-rah], *f.* Making holes in the ground.

ahoyar [ah-o-yar'], *va.* To dig holes for trees.

ahuchador, ra [ah-o-chah-dor'-rah], *m. & f.* One who hoards; a miser.

ahuchar [ah-oo-char'], *va.* To hoard up.

ahuecamiento [ah-oo-ay-cah-me-en'-to], *m.* Excavation.

ahuecar [ah-oo-ay-car'], *va.* 1. To excavate, to scoop out. 2. To loosen a thing which was close pressed or matted. -*vr.* To grow haughty, proud, or elated.

ahuehué, or **ahuehuete** [ah-oo-ay-oo-ay'], *(Bot.)* Tree like a cypress.

ahuizote [ah-oo-e-tho-tay], *m. (CAm. Mex.)* 1. Bore, drag (persona). 2. Evil spell, curse (maleficio).

ahulado [ah-oo-lah-do], *m. (CAm. Mex.)* Oilskin; **ahulados,** rubber shoes.

ahumada [ah-oo-mah'-dah], *f.* 1. Signal given with smoke, from the coast, watch-towers, or high places. 2. Sea-fish.

ahumar [ah-oo-mar'], *va.* To smoke, to cure in smoke. -*vn.* To fume. -*vr.* To acquire a a burnt taste (comida).

ahur [ah-oor']. *V.* AGUR.

ahusado, da [ah-oo-sah'-do, dah] *a.* Spindle-shaped. -*pp.* of AHUSAR.

ahusar [ah-oo-sar'], *va.* To make slender as a spindle. -*vr.* To taper.

ahuyentador, ra [ah-oo-yen-tah-dor', rah], *m. & f.* A scarecrow.

ahuyentar [ah-oo-yen-tar'], *va.* 1. To drive away, to put to flight. **Ahuyentar los pájaros, o las moscas,** To scare away birds or flies. 2. *(Met.)* To overcome a passion; to banish care. -*vr.* To run away; *(Mex.)* to stay away.

AI *f. abr.* de **Amnistia Internacional,** Amnesty International.

AIH *abr.* de **Asociación Internacional de Hispanistas.**

aijada [ah-e-hah'-dah], *f.* Goad. *V.* AGUIJADA.

aína [ah-e-nah], *adv.* Speedily.

aindíado [ah-en-de-ah-do], *a. (LAm.)* Like Indians.

AINS *f. (Esp.) abr.* de **Administración Institucional Nacional de Sanidad.**

aiófilo, la [ah-e-ó-fe-lo, lah], *a.* Evergreen, whose leaves last more than a year.

airadamente [ah-e-rah-dah-men'-tay], *adv.* Angrily; in an angry manner, hastily.

airado, da [ah-e-rah'-do, dah], *a.* Angry, wrathful. *(Met.)* Furious, vexed.

airar [ah-e-rar'], *va.* To anger, to irritate. -*vr.* To grow angry.

airazo [ah-e-rah'-tho], *m. aug.* A violent gust of wind.

aire [ah'-e-ray], *m.* 1. Air. 2. Briskness, of the motion of a horse. 3. *(Met.)* Gracefulness of manners and gait; air, carriage, demeanor, sprightliness. 4. Aspect, countenance, look. 5. Musical composition. 6. Frivolity. 7. The veil which covers the chalice and paten in the Greek rite. **Aires naturales**, the native air. **Beber los aires** or **los vientos**, to desire anxiously. **Creerse del aire**, to be credulous. **Hablar al aire**, to talk idly. **¿Qué aires le traen a Vd. por acá?** what good wind brings you here? **Tomar el aire**, to take a walk. **En aire**, in a good mood. **De buen ó mal aire**, in a pleasing or peevish manner. **En el aire**, in a moment. *(fig.)* air, appearance; **darse aires**, to give oneself airs. **Darse aires de**, to boast of being. *(fig.)* resemblance; **aires de familia**, family likeness. **Darse un aire a**, to resemble. *(fig.)* elegance. *(Mus.)* tune, air. *(Med. Cono Sur)* stiff neck; paralysis.

aireación [ah-e-ray-ah-the-on], *f.* Ventilation.

airear [ah-e-ray-ar'], *va.* 1. To give air, to ventilate. 2. To aerate, charge with gas. -*vr.* 1. To take the air. 2. To cool oneself, to obstruct perspiration.

airecico, llo, to [ah-e-ray-thee'-co, thell'-lyo, thee'-to], *m. dim.* A gentle breeze.

aireo [ah-e-ray-o], *m.* Ventilation.

airón [ah-e-ron'], *m. aug.* 1. Violent gale. 2. Ornament of plumes; crest of hats or caps, or feminine headgear. 3. The crested heron, egret. 4. A deep Moorish well.

airosamente [ah-e-ro-sah-men'-tay], *adv.* Gracefully, lightly.

airosidad [ah-e-ro-se-dad'], *f.* Gracefulness, elegance, grace.

airoso, sa [ah-e-ro'-so, sah], *a.* 1. Airy, windy. 2. Graceful, genteel, lively. 3. Successful.

aislable [ah-is-lah'-blay], *a.* Insoluble; capable of being obtained pure.

aislación [ah-es-lah-the-on], *f.* Insulation; **aislación de sonido**, soundproofing.

aislacionismo [ah-is-lah-the-o-nees'-mo], *m.* Isolation, keeping aloof from other countries.

aislacionista [ah-is-lah-the-o-nees'-tah], *m. & f.* Isolationist, advocate of isolationism in international relations.

aisladamente âh-is-lah-dah-men'-tay], *adv.* Isolately; one by one.

aislado, da [ah-is-lah'-do, dah], *a.* Isolated, embarrassed. -*pp.* of AISLAR.

aislador, ra [ah-is-lah-dor', rah], *a.* Isolating, insulating.

aislamiento [ah-is-lah-me-en'-to], *m.* Isolation.

aislante [ah-is-lahn'-tay], *a.* Insulating. **Material aislante** or *aislador, (Elec.)* Insulating material.

aislar [ah-is-lar'], *va.* 1. To surround with water. 2. To insulate. -*vr.* To isolate; to live in isolation.

AITA *f. abr.* de **Asociación Internacional de Transporte Aéreo** (International Air Transport Association, IATA)

ajá [ah-hah'], *int.* Aha! Also ¡Ajajá!

ajada [ah-hah'-dah], *f.* A sauce made of bread steeped in water, garlic, and salt.

ajado, da [ah-hah'-do, dah], *a.* Garlicky. -*pp.* of AJAR.

ajamiento [ah-hah-me-en'-to], *m.* Disfiguration; deformity.

ajamonarse [ah-hah-mo-nahr-say], *vr.* To get plump.

ajar [ah-har'], *m.* Garlic-field.

ajar [ah-har'], *va.* 1. To spoil, to mar, to tarnish, to fade. 2. To abuse. **Ajar la vanidad a alguno**, to pull down one's pride. -*vr.* To get crumpled, get messed up.

ajardinar [ah-hahr-de-nahr'], *va.* To landscape.

ajay [ah-hah-e], *interj.* *(LAm:* risa) ha!

ajazo [ah-hah'-tho], *m.* A large head of garlic.

aje [ah'-hay], *m.* 1. A chronic complaint. 2. *(Bot.)* A tuber from the Antilles, like a yam, or sweet potato. 3. *(Met.)* Humiliation, disrespect.

ajea [ah-hay'-ah], *f.* A sort of brushwood used for firing in the environs of Toledo.

ajear [ah-hay-ar'], *va.* To cry like a partridge closely pursued.

ajedrea [ah-hay-dray-ah], *v.* *(Bot.)* savory.

ajedrecista [ah-hay-dray-thees'-tah], *m. & f.* Chess player.

ajedrez [ah-hay-dreth'], *m.* 1. Chess, a game. 2. *(Naut.)* Netting, grating.

ajedrezado, da [ah-hay-dray-thah'-do, dah], *a.* Checkered.

ajenabe [ah-hay-nah'-blay], *m.* *(Bot.)* Wild mustard.

ajenable [ah-hay-nah'-blay], *a.* Alienable.

ajengibre [ah-hen-hee'-bray], *m. V.* JENGIBRE.

ajenjo [ah-hen'-ho], *m.* 1. *(Bot.)* Wormwood. 2. Sagebrush.

ajeno, na [ah-hay-no, nah], *a.* 1. Another's. 2. Foreign, strange. 3. Abhorrent, contrary to, remote. 4. Ignorant. 5. *(Met.)* Improper. **Ajeno de verdad**, void of truth. **Estar ajeno de sí**, to be unselfish, without self-love. **Estar ajeno de una cosa**, not to have heard a rumor.

ajenuz [ah-hay-nooth'], *m.* *(Bot.)* Field fennnelflower.

ajeo [ah-hay-oh], *m. Perro de ajeo*, Setter-dog.

ajete [ah-hay'-tay], *m.* 1. Young or tender garlic. 2. Sauce made with garlic.

ajetreado [ah-hay-dray-ah-do], *a.* Busy, tiring (vida).

ajetrearse [ah-hay-tray-ar'-say], *vr.* To become bodily fatigued, to fidget.

ajetreo [ah-hay-tray-o], *m.* Bustle; fuss; drudgery.

ají [ah-hee'], *m.* 1. The red Indian dwarf pepper. *V.* CHILE. Capsicum. 2. A sort of sauce made in America of the ají-pepper.

ajiaceite [ah-he-ah-thay'-e-tay], *m.* Mixture of garlic and oil.

ajiaco [ah-he-ah'-co], *m.* 1. A dish made of boiled meat and vegetables. 2. A sort of sauce made with the *ají* for certain dishes in America.

ajibararse [ah-he-bah-rahr-say], *vr.* *(Carib.)* V. AGUAJIRARSE.

ajicola [ah-he-co'-lah], *f.* Glue made of cuttings of leather boiled with garlic.

ajigolones [ah-he-go-lo-nays], *m. & pl.* *(CAm. Mex.)* Troubles, difficulties.

ajilar [ah-he-lahr], *vn.* *(CAm. Mex.)* To set out for a place.

ajilimoje, or **ajilimójili** [ah-he-le-mo'-hay, ah-he-le-mo'-he-lee], *m.* Sauce of pepper and garlic.

ajillo [ah-heel'-lyo], *m.* Tender young garlic.

ajimez [ah-he-meth'], *m.* An arched window with a pillar in the centre to support it.

ajipuerro [ah-he-poo-er'-ro], *m.* Leek, *V.* PUERRO.

ajiseco [ah-he-say-co], *m.* *(And)* Mild red pepper.

ajises [ah-he-says], *m. & pl.* *(LAm.)* de ají.

ajizarse [ah-he-thahr-say], *vr.* *(Cono Sur)* To lose one's temper, to get mad.

ajo [aj'-ho], *m.* 1. *(Bot.)* Garlic. 2. Garlic-sauce for meat. 3. *(Met.)* Paint for ladies. 4. *(Met.)* Affair discussed by many. **Revolver el ajo** or **el ruido**, to stir up new disturbances. **Ajo blanco**, dish made of bruised garlic, bread, oil, an water. **Echar ajos y cebollas**, to insult one viley. **Se fué echando ajos y cebollas**, *(coll.)* he went off uttering oaths and imprecations. **En el ajo**, to be mixed in it.

ajoaceite [ah-ho-ah-thay-e-tay], *m.* Sauce of garlic and oil.

ajoarriero [ah-ho-ahr-re-ay-ro], *m.* Dish of cod with oil, garlic and peppers.

ajobar [ah-ho-bar'], *va.* *(coll.)* To carry upon one's back heavy loads.

ajobo [ah-ho'-bo], *m.* 1. *(Obs.)* Carrying heavy loads. 2. A heavy load.

ajofaina [ah-ho-fah'-e-nah], *f. V.* ALJOFAINA.

ajolio [ah-ho-le-o], *m.* *(Prov.)* Sauce made of oil and garlic.

ajolote [ah-ho-lo'-tay], *m.* An amphibian of the Lake of Mexico; the axolotl.

ajomate [ah-ho-mah'-tay], *m.* *(Bot.)* A delicate aquatic plant.

ajonjeo [ah-hon-hay-o], *m.* Ajonjo birdlime.

ajonjera [ah-hon-hay'-rah], *f.* **ajonjero** [ah-hon-hay'-ro], *m.* (*Bot.*) The low carline thistle, yielding ajonje.

ajonjolí, aljonjolí [ah-hon-ho-lee', al-hon-ho-lee'], *m.* (*Bot.*) Benne, sesame, an oily grain. Sesamum orientale.

ajoqueso [ah-ho-kay'-so], *m.* Dish made of garlic and cheese.

ajorca [ah-hor'-cah], *f.* Rings worn by the Moorish women about the wrists or ankles.

ajordar [ah-hor-dar'], *va.* (*Prov.*) To bawl, to cry out.

ajornalar [ah-hor-nah-lahr'], *va.* To employ by the day.

ajoto [ah-ho-to], *m.* (*Carib.*) rebuff.

ajuagas [ah-hoo-ah'-gas], *f. pl.* Malanders, a disease in horses; or ulcera over the hoofs. V. ESPARAVAN.

ajuar [ah-hoo-ar'], *m.* 1. Apparel and furniture which a bride brings to her husband. 2. Household furniture. **Ajuar de novia**, trousseau.

ajuarar [ah-hoo-ah-rahr*]*, *m.* To furnish.

ajudiado, da [ah-hoo-de-ah-do, dah], *a.* Jewish; Jew-like.

ajuiciado, da [ah-hoo-e-the-ah'-do, dah], *a.* Judicious, prudent. *-pp.* AJUICIAR.

ajuiciar [ah-hoo-e-the-ar'], *va.* To acquire judgment; to become prudent.

ajumado [ah-hoo-mah-do], 1. *a.* Tight. 2. *m.* drunk. *-vr.* To get tight.

ajuntarse [ah-hoon-tahr-say], *vr.* To live together.

ajurídico [ah-hoo-re-de-co], *a.* (*Cono Sur*) Illegal.

ajustadamente [ah-hoos-tah-dah-men'-tay], *adv.* Justly, rightly.

ajustado, da [ah-hoos-tah'-do, dah], *a.* Exact, right; stingy. **Es un hombre ajustado**, he is a man of strict morals. *-pp.* of AJUSTAR.

ajustador [ah-hoos-tah-dor'], *m.* 1. Close waistcoat, jacket. 2. Waist, jacket. 3. The person in a printing-office who arranges the form; justifier. 4. (*Mech.*) Adapter, coupler, adjusting tool.

ajustamiento [ah-hoos-tah-me-en'-to], *m.* 1. Agreement. 2. Settling of accounts. 3. Receipts.

ajustar [ah-hoos-tar'], *va.* 1. To regulate, to adjust, to accord, to compose, to guide, to measure, to justify type. 2. To concert, to make an agreement, to bargain. 3. To reconcile, to heal. 4. To examine accounts. 5. To settle a balance. 6. To press close, to oppress. 7. To fit; to fashion; to accommodate. *-vr.* 1. To settle matters. 2. To conform; to combine. **Ajustarse a las reglas**, to abide by the rules. 3. To approach. 4. To engage. **Ajustarse el cinturón**, to tighten the belt. **Ajustarse a razones**, to yield to reason.

ajuste [ah-hoos-tay], *m.* 1. Proportion of the constituent parts of a thing. 2. Agreement, contract, covenant, accommodation; engagement; settlement. *-pl.* Couplings.

ajusticiar [ah-hoos-te-the-ar'], *va.* To execute, to put to death.

ajustón [ah-hoos-ton], *m.* (*And*) Punishment (castigo); Ill-treatment (mal trato).

al [al], *art.* 1. Article formed by a syncope of the preposition *a* and the article *el*, and placed before nouns, etc.; e.g. **El juez debe castigar al delincuente**, the judge ought to punish the delinquent. 2. An Arabic article corresponding to the Spanish articles *el* and *la* in compound words; e.g. **Al árabe**, the Arab. 3. Used with the infinitive of various verbs; e.g. **Al amanecer**, at the dawn of day. **Traduce al inglés**, translate into English. **Dar la vuelta al mundo**, to go round the world.

al [al], *pron. indef.* (*Obs.*) Other, contrary, all other things. V. DEMÁS and OTRO. *Por al*, V. POR TANTO.

ala [ah'-lah], *f.* 1. Wing (ave, insecto, avión, edificio, ejército); aisle (iglesia). 2. Row or file. 3. (*Mil.*) Flank, wing (ejército). 4. Brim (sombrero). 5. Auricle (oreja). **Alas del corazón** (*Anat.*), auricles of the heart. 6. Fin of a fish. 7. Leaf of a hinge; of a door, of a table. **Ala de mesana**, (*Naut.*) a driver. *-pl.* (*Naut.*) upper studding-sails. **Alas de gavia**, main-top studding-sails. **Alas de velacho**, fore studding-sails. **Alas de sobremesana**, mizzen-top studding-sails. **Alas de proa**, head of the ship. **Alas**, protection. Boldness. **Cortar las** alas, to take one down a peg. (*Poetic.*) Velocity. (*Pol.*) **El ala izquierdo del partido**, the left wing of the party. (Frases) **ahuecar el ala**, to beat it. **Andar con el ala caída**, to be downcast.

alabado [ah-lah-bah'-do], *m.* 1. (*Cono Sur*) at dawn. 2. (*Mex.*) at nightfall.

alá [ah-lah'], *m.* Allah, an Arabic word for God.

alabado [ah-lah-bah'-do], *a.* Praised. **¡Alabado sea Dios!** God be praised! *LAm.* Down call. **Al alabado**, at dawn. *-pp.* of ALABAR.

alabador, ra [ah-lah-bah-dor', rah], *m. & f.* Applauder, commender.

alabacioso, sa [ah-lah-bah-the-oh'-so, sah], *a.* (*coll.*) Boastful, ostentatious.

alabamiento [ah-lah-bah-me-ayn-to], *m.* Praise.

alabancioso [ah-lah-ban-the-o-so], *a.* Boastful.

alabandina [ah-lah-ban-dee'-nah], *f.* 1. Manganese sulphide. 2. Alabandine, spinel ruby.

alabanza [ah-lah-bahn'-thah], *f.* Praise, commendation; glory. **Cantar las alabanzas a uno**, to sing someone's praises.

alabar [ah-lah-bar'], *va.* To praise, to extol, to glorify, to magnify, to commend, to cry up. *-vr.* To praise oneself.

alabarda [ah-lah-bar'-dah], *f.* 1. Halberd, a kind of battle-axe and pike at the end of a long staff. 2. (*Obs.*) Sergeant's place, from a halberd having formerly been borne by sergeants.

alabardazo [ah-lah-bar-dah'-tho], *m.* A blow with a halberd.

alabardero [ah-lah-bar-day'-ro], *m.* 1. Halberdier, armed with a halberd. 2. Claqueur, clapper, hired to applaud in a theatre. (*Recent.*)

alabastrado, da [ah-lah-bas-trah'-do, dah], *a.* Resembling alabaster.

alabastrina [ah-lah-bas-tree'-nah], *f.* A thin sheet of alabaster.

alabastrino, na [ah-lah-bas-tree'-no, nah], *a.* (*Poetic.*) 1. Made of alabaster. 2. Like alabaster.

alabastro [ah-lah-as'-tro], *m.* Alabaster.

álabe [ah'-lah-bay], *m.* 1. Drooping branch of an olive or other tree. 2. Bucket, flier of a water-wheel, float-board, which serves to set it in motion. 3. Mat used in carts. 4. Cam. 5. Tile of the caves.

alabear [ah-lah-bay-ahr], 1. *va.* To warp. 2. *vr.* To warp, to grow bent or crooked.

alabega [ah-lah-bay'-gah], *f.* (*Bot.*) Sweet basil. V. ALBAHACA.

alabeo [ah-lah-bay'-o], *m.* Warping, the state of being warped.

alabiado, da [ah-lah-be-ah'-do, dah], *a.* Lipped or ragged; applied to uneven coined money.

alacalufe [ah-lah-cah-loo-fay], *m. & f.* (*Cono Sur*) Indian inhabitant of Tierra del Fuego.

alacena [ah-lah-thay'-na], *f.* 1. Sideboard, buffet, a cupboard, small pantry in the wall. 2. (*Naut.*) Locker, a small box in the cabin and sides of a ship.

alaciar [ah-lah-the-ar'], *vn* V. ENLACIAR.

alacrán [ah-lah-crahn'], *m.* 1. A scorpion, a small poisonous animal. 2. Ring of the bit of a bridle. 3. Stop or hook fixed to the rocker of organbellows. 4. Chain or link of a sleevebutton. 5. Swivel.

alacranado, da [ah-lah-crah-nah'-do, dah], *a.* 1. Bit by a scorpion. 2. (*Met.*) Infected with some vice.

alacranear [ah-lah-crah-nay-ahr], *vn.* (*Cono Sur*) To gossip, to scandal monger.

alacraneo [ah-lah-crah-nay-o], *m.* (*Cono Sur*) Gossip, scandal.

alacranera [ah-lah-crah-nay'-rah], *f.* (*Bot.*) Mouse-ear, scorpion-grass.

alacridad [ah-lah-cre-dad'], *f.* Alacrity.

alada [ah-lah'-dah], *f.* Fluttering of the wings.

aladares [ah-lah-dah'-res], *m. pl.* Locks of hair over the temples; forelocks.

ALADI *f. abr.* de **Asociación Latinoamericana de Integración**.

aladierna [ah-lah-de-er'-nah], V. ALATERNO.

Aladino [ah-lah-de-no], *m.* Aladdin.

alado, da [ah-lah'-do, dah], *a.* Winged, feathered.

aladrada [ah-lah-drah'-dah], *f. (Prov.)* A furrow.

aladrar [ah-lah-drar'], *va. (Prov.)* To plough the ground.

aladro [ah-lah'-dro], *m.* 1. Plough. 2. Ploughed land.

aladroque [ah-lah-dro'-kay], *m. (Prov.)* An unsalted anchovy.

alafia [ah-lah'-fe-ah], *f. (coll.)* **Pedir alafia**, to implore mercy and pardon.

alafre [ah-lah-fray], *(Carib.)* 1. *a.* Wretched, miserable. 2. *m* Wretch.

alaga [ah'-lah-gah], *f.* A species of yellow wheat.

alagartado, da [ah-lah-gar-tah'-do, dah], *a.* Variegated; motley.

alaica [ah-lah'-ee-cah], *f.* Winged ant or emmet.

alajor [ah-lah-hor'], *m.* Ground-rent.

alajú [ah-lah-hoo'], *m.* Paste made of almonds, walnuts, honey, etc.

alama [ah-lah'-mah], *f. (Prov.)* Gold or silver cloth.

alamar [ah-lah-mar'], *m.* Loop of silken twist, or cord, used for buton-holes or trimming.

alambicado, da [ah-lam-be-cah-do, dah], *a.* 1. Distilled. 2. Euphuistic, pedantic (of diction). 3. *(Met.)* Given with a sparing hand. *-pp.* of ALAMBICAR.

alambicamiento [ah-lam-be-cah-me-en'-to], *m.* 1. Distillation. 2. Subtlety, euphuism of language.

alambicar [ah-lam-be-car'], *va.* 1. To distil. 2. To investigate closely. **Alambicar los sesos**, to cudgel one's wits. 3. To minimize, to reduce to a minimum.

alambique [ah-lam-bee'-kay], *m.* Alembic, still. **Por alambique**, sparingly, in a penurious manner.

alambiquería [ah-lam-be-kay-re-ah], *f. (Carib.)* Distillery.

alambiquero [ah-lam-be-ke-ro], *m. (Carib.)* Distiller.

alambor [ah-lam-bor'], *m. (Obs. Mil.)* Inside slope of a ditch. *V.* ESCARPA.

alambrada, do [ah-lam-brah-dah], *f.* Wire netting; Wire fence (cerca).

alambre [ah-lam'-bray], *m.* 1. Wire of any metal. 2. In olden times copper, or an alloy of copper; bronze. **alambre de latón**, brass wire. 3. Bells belonging to sheep, or to beasts of burden. 4. File for papers.

alambre de tierra [ah-lam'-bray day te-er'-rah], *m. (Elec.)* Ground wire.

alambrera [ah-lam-bray'-rah], *f.* 1. Wire netting. 2. *(Agri.)* Wire trellis. 3. Car basket (ferrocarril).

alambrista [ah-lam-bres-tah], *m. & f.* Tightrope walker.

alambrito [ah-lam-bre-to], *m. (LAm.)* Tall, thin person.

alameda [ah-lah-may'-dah], *f.* 1. A grove of poplar-trees. 2. Public walk, mall.

alamín [ah-lah-meen'], *m.* 1. *(Obs.)* Clerk of the market appointed to inspect weights and measures. 2. *(Prov.)* Architect, surveyor of buildings. 3. *(Prov.)* Farmer appointed to superinted irrigation or distribution of water.

alamirré [ah-lah-mir-ray'], *m.* Musical sign.

álamo [ah'-lah-mo], *m. (Bot.)* Poplar. **Álamo blanco**, white poplar. **Álamo temblón**, aspen-tree, trembling poplar-tree. **Álamo negro**, black poplar-tree.

alampar, *va.* **alamparse** [ah-lam-par'say], *vr. (coll.)* To long for, to crave.

alamud [ah-lah-mood'], *m.* A square bolt for a door.

alanceador [ah-lah-thay-ah-dor'], *m.* One who throws a lance, lancer.

alancear [ah-lan-thay-ar'], *va.* To dart, to spear.

alandrearse [ah-lan-dray-ar'-say], *vr.* To become dry, stiff, and blanched (gusanos de seda).

alanés [ah-lah-ness'], *m.* A kind of stag in New Mexico (Cervus alces).

alano [ah-lah'-no], *m.* Mastiff of a large kind.

alano, na [ah-lah'-no, nah], *a.* Belonging to the *Alans* or Vandals of the fifth century.

alanquía [ah-lan-kee'-ah], *f.* Cardass, waste-card used in silk-weaving.

alantoides [ah-lan-to'-e-des], *f. & a.* Allantois, the foetal urinary vesicle.

alanzada [ah-lan-thah'-dah], *f. (Obs.) V.* ARANZADA.

alanzar [ah-lan-thar'], *va.* To throw lances.

alaqueca [ah-lah-kay'-cah], *f.* Blood-stone.

alaqueques [ah-lah-kay'-kes], *m. pl. V.* ALAQUECA.

alar [ah-lar'], *va. (Naut.)* To haul (cuerda). Overhanging roof, eaves (tejado). *(LAm.)* acera, pavement. *V.* HALAR.

alara [ah-lah'-rah] *(Obs.)* An egg without a shell.

alárabe [ah-lah'-rah-bay], **alarbe** [ah-lar'-bay], *m.* 1. Arabian. 2. An unmannerly person.

alarde [ah-lar'-day], *m.* 1. Review of soldiers, muster, parade. 2. Ostentation, boasting, vanity. **Hacer alarde**, *(Met.)* To boast or brag of something. 3. Manifestation.

alardeado [ah-lahr-day-ah-do], *a.* Vaunted, much boasted-of.

alardear [ah-lar-day-ar'], *vn.* 1. To brag. 2. *(Obs.)* To review.

alardeo [ah-lahr-day-o], *m.* Boasting, bragging.

alargadera [ah-lar-gah-day'-rah], *f. (Chem.)* Nozzle, adapter; lengthening tube.

alargado [ah-lahr-gah-do], *a.* Long, extended.

alargador, ra [ah-lar-gah-dor', rah], *m. & f.* One who delays, or lengthens out a thing.

alargamiento [ah-lar-gah-me-en'-to], *m.* The act of lengthening out.

alargar [ah-lar-gar'], *va.* 1. To lengthen, to expand, to extend. 2. *(Met.)* To protract, to dwell upon. 3. To increase a marked number or quantity. 4. To reach or hand a thing to another. 5. To resign: yet in this sense *largar* is more used. 6. To send before; to hold out. **Alargar la conversación**, to spin out a conversation. **Alargar el salario**, to increase or augment the pay. **Alargar el cabo**, *(Naut.)* to pay out the cable. *-vr.* 1. To be prolonged. **Se alargan los días**, the days grow longer. 2. To launch; to withdraw from a place. 3. To expatiate or enlarge on an argument, to go beyond, to exceed. 4. *(Naut.)* To sheer off.

alarguez [ah-lar-geth'], *m. (Bot.)* Dogrose.

alargo [ah-lahr-go], *m. (Elec.)* Extension, lead.

alaria [ah-lah'-re-ah], *f.* A flat iron instrument used by potters to finish and polish their work; chisel.

alarida [ah-lah-ree'-dah], *f.* Hue and cry.

alarido [ah-lah-ree'-do], *m.* Outcry, shout, howl.

alarifazgo [ah-lah-re-fath'-go], *m.* Office of an architect and surveyor.

alarife [ah-lah-ree'-fay], *m.* Architect, builder.

alarijes [ah-lah-ree'-hes], *f. pl.* A large sort of grapes. *V.* ARIJE.

alarma [ah-lar'-mah], *m.* 1. *(Mil.)* Alarm. **Falsa alarma**, false alarm. **Alarma de incendios**, fire alarm. 2. Notice of any sudden danger.

alarmante [ah-lar-mahn'-tay], *a.* Alarming, dangerous.

alarmar [ah-lar-mar'], *va.* To alarm, to call to arms. *-vr.* To get alarmed, be alarmed; to get fright.

alarmismo [ah-lahr-mes-mo], *m.* Alarmism.

alarmista [ah-lar-mees'-tah], *m.* An alarmist.

alasálet]ah-lah-sah'-let], *m.* Sal ammoniac.

alastrar [ah-las-trar'], *va.* 1. To throw back the ears. *V.* AMUSGAR. 2. *(Naut.)* To ballast. **Alastrar un navío**, to ballast a ship. *-vr.* To squat close: applied to game.

alaterno [ah-lah-ter'-no], *m. (Bot.)* Mock-privet.

alatón [ah-lah-tone'], *m.* 1. *(Obs.)* Latten, brass. *V.* LATON. 2. *(Bot. Prov.)* The fruit of the lote-tree.

alatonero [ah-lah-to-nay'-ro], *m. (Bot. Prov.)* Nettle or lote-tree.

alatrón [ah-lah-trone'], *m.* Froth of saltpetre. Afronitro.

alavanco [ah-lah-vahn'-co], *m. V.* LAVANCO.

alazán, na [ah-lah-thahn', nah], *a.* Sorrel-colored.

alazo [ah-lah'-tho], *m.* A stroke with the wings.

alazor [ah-lah-thor'], *m. (Bot.)* Bastard saffron.

alba [ahl'-bah], *f.* 1. Dawn of day, day-spring. **Al rayar el alba**, at dawn. **Misa del alba**, early morning mass. 2. Alb, the white gown worn by priests.

albacea [al-bah-thay'-ah], *m.* Testamentary executor. *-f.* Executrix. *V.* TESTAMENTARIO.

albaceazgo [al-bah-thay-ahth'-go], *m.* Executorship.

albacora [al-bah-co'-rah], *f.* 1. Seafish much resembling a tunny, albicore. 2. An early fig of the largest kind. *V.* BREVA.

albada [al-bah'-dah], *f.* *(Prov.)* Matinade, music which young men in the country give their sweethearts at the break of day. *V.* ALBORADA. *(Mex.)* An attack at day break.

albahaca [al-bah-ah'-cah], *f.* *(Bot.)* Sweet basil. **Albahaca acuática**, a sort of winter thistle. **Albahaca salvaje or silvestre**, stone or wild thistle.

albahaquero [a-bah-ah-kay'-ro], *m.* 1. A flower-pot. 2. A vender of sweet basil.

albahaquilla (DE RIO) [al-ah-ah-keel'-lyah], *f.* *V.* PARIETARIA.

albaida [al-bah'-e-dah], *f.* *(Bot.)* The shrubby gypsophila.

albalá [al-bah-lah'], *m. & f.* 1. *(Obs.)* Royal letters patent. 2. A quittance given by the custom-house. **Albalá de guía**, a passport.

albanega [al-bah-nay'-gah], *f.* Net for catching partridges or rabbits.

albanés, esa [al-bah-ness', sah], *a.* Albanian.

Albania [ahl-bah-ne-ah], *f.* Albania.

albano [ahl-bah-no] *V.* ALBANÉS.

albañal, albañar [al-bah-nyah', al-bah-nyar'], *m.* Common sewer, gully-hole.

albañil [al-bah-nyeel'], *m.* Mason, bricklayer.

albañilería [al-bah-nye-lay-ree'-ah], *f.* Masonry.

albaquía [al-ban-kee'-ah], *f.* 1. *(Obs.)* Remnant. 2. In collecting titles, an odd portion which does not admit of division. *(Arab.)*

albar [al-bar'], *a.* White. This adjective is confined to a few botanical terms only.

albarán [al-bah'-rahn'], *m.* 1. Placard of apartments to let. 2. Delivery note, invoice (mercancías).

albarás [al-bah'-rahs'], *m. V.* ALBARAZO.

albarazada [al-bah-rah-thah'-dah], *f.* A marble-colored grape, common in Andalucía.

albarazado, da [al-bah-rah-thah'-do, dah], *a.* 1. Affected with white leprosy. 2. Pale, pallid.

albarazo [al-bah-rah'-tho], *m.* White leprosy.

albarca [al-bar'-cah], *f. V.* ABARCA.

albarcoquero [al-bar-co-kay'-ro], *m.* *(Prov.)* Apricot-tree.

albarda [al-bar'-dah], *f.* Pack-saddle. **Bestia de albarda**, beast of burden. **Albarda sobre albarda**, verbiage, useless repetition.

albardado, da [al-bar-dah'-do, dah], *a.* Applied to animals having a different colored skin at the loins. *-pp.* of ALBARDAR.

albardán [al-bar-dahn'], *m.* *(Obs.)* Jester, buffoon.

albardar [al-bar-dar'], *va.* 1. To put on a pack-saddle. 2. To cover fowls which are to be roasted with large slices of bacon. 3. *(Met.)* To put upon one, take advantage of another's patience. **No se deja poner la albarda**, Not to allow oneself to be maltreated.

albardear [ahl-bahr-de-ahr], *va.* *(CAm.)* To bother, vex.

albardela [al-bar-day'-lah], *f.* Small saddle.

albardería [al-bar-day-ree'-ah], *f.* 1. Place where packsaddles are made and sold. 2. The trade of a packsaddle maker.

albardero [al-bar-day'-ro], *m.* Pack saddle maker.

albardilla [al-bar-deel'-lyah], *f.* 1. Small packsaddle. 2. Coping of a wall. 3. Border of a garden-bed. 4. Small saddle made use of to tame colts. 5. Wood on the back of sheep or lambs. 6. Earth which sticks to a ploughshare. 7. Batter, with which hogs' tongues and feet are covered. *-pl.* Ridges of earth on the sides of deep foot-paths.

albardín [al-bar-deen'], *m.* *(Bot.)* Matweed.

albardón [al-bar-done'], *m.* Pannel, a pack-saddle.

albardoncillo [al-bar-don-theel'-lyo], *m. dim.* A small pack-saddle.

albarejo, albarigo [al-ah-ray'-ho, al-bah-ree'-go], *m.* *(Prov.)* A species of wheat. *V.* CANDEAL.

albarela [al-bah-ray'-lah], *f.* *(Bot.)* A species of edible fungus which grows upon the chestnut and polar.

albareque [ahl-bah-ray-kay], *m.* Sardine net.

albaricoque [al-bah-re-co'-kay], *m.* *(Bot.)* Apricot.

albaricoquero [al-bah-re-co-kay'-ro], *m.* Apricot-tree.

albarillo [al-bah-reel'-lyo], *m.* 1. A tune played on the guitar, for country dances. 2. A small kind of apricot.

albarino [al-bah-ree'-no], *m.* A white paint formerly used by women.

albarrada [al-bar-rah'-dah], *f.* 1. A dry wall, inclosure. 2. Ditch for defence in war.

albarradón [al-bar-rah-done'], *m.* A mound to hinder inundation.

albarrana [al-bar-rah'-nah], *f.* *(Bot.)* **Cebolla albarrana**, squill. **Torre albarrana**, a sort of watch-tower.

albarranilla [al-bar-rah-neel'-lya], *f.* A blue-flowered variety of onion.

albarraz [al-bar-rath'], *m.* *(Bot.)* 1. *V.* ALBARAZO. 2. Lousewort.

albatoza [al-bah-to'-thah], *f.* A small covered boat.

albatros [al-bah'-tros], *m.* The albatross.

albayaldado, da [al-bah-yal-dah'-do, dah], *a.* Covered with white-lead.

albayalde [al-bah-yahl'-day], *m.* White-lead, ceruse, lead carbonate.

albazano, na [al-bah-thah'-no, nah], *a.* Of a dark chestnut color.

albazo [al-bah'-tho], *m.* *(Obs.)* A military term implying an assault at day-break.

albeador [ahl-bay-ah-dor], *m.* *(Cono Sur)* Early riser.

albear [al-bay-ar'], *va.* To whiten. *V.* BLANQUEAR.

albedrío [al-bay-dree'-o], *m.* 1. Freedom of will. 2. Free will directed by caprice, and not by reason. **Libre albedrío**, liberty.

albéitar [al-bay'-e-tar], *m.* A farrier-veterinary surgeon.

albeitería [al-bay-e-tay-ree'-ah], *f.* Farriery; veterinary surgery.

albenda [al-ben'-dah], *f.* Hangings of white linen.

albendera [al-ben-day'-rah], *f.* 1. Woman who makes hangings. 2. A gadding idle woman.

albéntola [al-ben'-to-lah], *f.* A slight net, made of a very fine thread.

alberca [al-ber'-cah], *f.* 1. A pond or pool. 2. Reservoir, tank, mill-pond. 3. Vat (of tannery).

albercón [al-ber-cone'], *m. aug.* A large pool or pond.

albérchiga, or **Albérchigo** [al-ber'-che-gah, or al-ber'-che-go], *m. & f.* *(Bot.)* Peach, strictly a clingstone peach.

alberengena [al-bay-ren-hay'-nah], *f.* *(Bot.)* Eggplant. Solanum melongena. *V.* BERENGENA.

albergador, ra [a-ber-gah-dor', rah], *m. & f.* A hotel-keeper.

albergar [al-ber-gar'], *va.* 1. To lodge, to harbor. 2. To keep a lodging-house. *-vr.* To take a lodging.

albergue [al-ber'-gay], *m.* 1. Lodging or lodging-house. 2. Den for wild beasts. 3. Hospital for orphans. 4. Place, space, shelter. **Albergue para jóvenes**, youth hostel.

alberguería [al-ber-gay-ree'-ah], *f.* *(Obs.)* 1. Inn. 2. Hospital for poor travelers. *V.* POSADA.

alberguero [al-ber-gay'-ro], *m.* *(Obs.)* Innkeeper.

alberguista [ahl-bayr-ges-tah], *m. & f.* Youth-hosteller.

albericoque [al-bay-re-co'-kay], *V.* ALBARICOQUE.

albero [al-bay'-ro], *m.* 1. Whitish earth. 2. A cloth for cleaning plates and dishes.

alberquero [al-ber-kay'-ro], *m.* One who takes care of the pond where flax is steeped.

alberquilla [al-ber-keel'-lyah], *f. dim.* A little pool.

albicante [al-be-can'-tay], *a.* That which whitens or blanches.

albihar [al-be-ar'], *m.* *(Bot.)* Ox-eye. Buphthalmum.

albilla [al-beel'-lyah], *f.* **albillo** [al-beel'-lyo], *m.* An early white grape. Sweet water.

albillo [al-beel'-lyo], *a.* Applied to the wine of a white grape.

albin [al-been'], *m.* 1. Maltites or bloodstone, a sort of iron ore of a brown color. 2. Dark carmine pigment from this ore, used in fresco paintings.

albina [al-bee'-nah], *f.* A marshy piece of ground covered with nitre in the summer season.

albino, na [al-bee'-no, nah], *a.* 1. Albino. 2. *m.* A person having the skin and hair perfectly white, and the iris of the eye generally pink.

Albión [al-be-on'], *f.* Albion, the ancient name of England.

albis [ahl'-bis], *(Met.)* **Quedarse in albis**, to be frustrated in one's hopes, to be disappointed.

albitana [al-be-tah'-nah], *f.* 1. Fence used by gardeners to inclose plants. 2. *(Naut.)* An apron. **Albitana del codaste**, *(Naut.)* Inner post.

albo, ba [ahl'-bo, bah], *a.* Very white. *(Poetic.)*

alboaire [al-bo-ah'-ee-ray], *m.* Glazed tile work.

albogalla [al-bo-gahl'-lyah], *f.* A kind of gall-nut.

albogue [al-bo'-gay], *m.* 1. A pastoral flute much used in Biscay. 2. Martial music, played with two plates of brass resembling the *rotalum* of the ancients; a cymbal.

alboguero, ra [al-bo-gay'-ro, rah], *m. & f.* One who makes *albogues*, or pastoral flutes, or plays on them.

albohol [al-bo-ole'], *m. (Bot.)* A red poppy. *V.* AMAPOLA.

albóndiga [al-bon'-de-gah], *f.* A meatball, ball made of meat chopped fine with eggs and spice.

albondigón [ahl-bon-de-gon], *m.* Hamburger.

albondiguilla [al-bon-de-geel'-lyah], *f. dim.* A small ball of meat.

albor [al-bor'], *m. (Poetic.)* 1. Whiteness. 2. Dawn. **Los primeros albores del juicio**, the first dawnings of the mind.

alborada [al-bo-rah'-dah], *f.* 1. Twilight, the first dawn of day. 2. *(Mil.)* Action fought at the dawn of day. 3. Reveille, the first military call of the day. 4. Morning watch. *V.* ALBADA.

alborear [al-bo-ray-ar'], *vn.* To dawn.

alborga [al-bor'-gah], *f.* A sort of sandal made of mat-weed.

albornía [al-bor-nee'-ah], *f.* A large glazed jug.

alborno [al-bor'-no], *m. (Bot.)* Alburnum.

albornoz [al-bor-noth'], *m.* 1. Coarse woollen stuff, bathing wrap. 2. Cloak which forms part of the Moorish dress.

alboronía [al-bo-ro-nee'-ah], *f.* A dish made with eggplant, tomatoes, pumpkins, and pimento.

alboroque [al-bo-ro'-kay], *m.* Regalement given at the conclusion of a bargain: treat.

alborotadamente [al-bo-rotah-dah-men'-tay], *adv.* Noisily, confusedly.

alborotadizo, za [al-boro-tah-dee-tho', thah], *a. V.* ALBOROTADO.

alborotado, da [al-bo-rotah'-do, dah], *a.* Of a restless disposition, turbulent. *-pp.* of ALBOROTAR.

alborotador, ra [al-bo-ro-tah-dor', rah], *m. & f.* A violator of peace, rioter.

alborotapueblos [al-bo-ro-tah-poo-ay'-bos], *m.* 1. A mover of sedition. **alborotar** [al-bo-ro-tar'], *va.* To disturb, to vex, to excite, stir up. *-vr.* 1. To come over. 2. To fling out. 3. *(CAm.)* To become amorous (ponerse amoroso). 4. *(Cono Sur)* To rear up (caballos).

alboroto [al-bo-ro'-to], *m.* 1. Disturbance, tumult, riot, faction; convulsion. 2. Outcry, clatter, noisinness; fuss, hubbub.

alborotoso, sa [ahl-bo-ro-to-so], *(And. Carib.) a.* Troublesome, riotous.

alborozado [ahl-bo-ro-thah-do], *a.* Jubilant, overjoyed.

alborozador, ra [al-bo-ro-thah-dor', rah], *m. & f.* Promoter of mirth.

alborozar [al-bo-ro-thar'], *va.* To exhilarate, to promote mirth. *-vr.* To be overjoyed, rejoice.

alborozo [al-bo-ro'-tho], *m.* Merriment, exhilaration, gaiety.

albrán [al-brahn'], *m.* A duckling.

albricias [al-bree'-the-as], *f. pl.* Reward given for some good news. **Ganar las albricias**, to obtain a reward for some good news. *-int.* **¡Albricias, albricias!** Joy! Joy!

albudeca [al-boo-day'-cah], *f. (Bot.)* A watermelon. *V.* SANDIA.

albuérbola [al-boo-er'-bo-lah], *f.* Exhilaration, acclamation.

albufera [al-boo-fay'-rah], *f.* A large lake formed by the sea.

albugíneo, nea [al-boo-hee'-nay-o, nay-ah], *a.* Albugineous, entirely white, like the sclerotic. *(Anat.)* Albuminous.

albuginoso, sa [al-boo-he-no'-so, sah], *a. V.* ALBUGINEO.

albugo [al-boo'-go], *m.* Leucoma, a white opacity upon the cornea of the eye.

albuhera [al-boo-ay'-rah], *f.* A fresh-water lake. *V.* ALBUFERA.

álbum [ahl'-boom], *m.* Album. **Álbum de recortes**, scrapbook. **Álbum de sellos**, stamp album.

albumen [al-boo'-men], *m. (Bot.)* Albumen. Nourishing matter, not a part of the embryo, stored up in the seed.

albúmina [al-boo'-me-nah], *f. (Chem.)* Albumin, as represented in the white of an egg; a constituent of some animal fluids, and sparingly found likewise in some plants.

albuminoso, sa [al-boo-me-no'-so, sah], *a.* Albuminous.

albur [al-boor'], *m.* 1. Dace, a river fish. 2. A sort of game at cards. 3. Risk, contingency. **Correr un albur**, to venture, to chance.

albura [al-boo'-rah], *f.* 1. Whiteness. 2. *(Bot.) V.* ALBORNO. **Albura de huevo**, *(Obs.) V.* CLARA DE HUEVO.

alburear [ahl,-boo-ray-ahr], 1. *va. (CAm.)* To disturb, upset. 2. *vn.* To make money, get rich.

alburero [al-boo-ray'-ro], *m.* A player at the game *albures*.

albures [al-boo'-res], *m. pl.* A game at cards.

alburno [al-boor'-no], *m.* 1. *(Bot.) V.* ALBORNO.

alca [ahl'-cah], *f.* Razorbill, a bird.

alcabala [al-cah-bah'-lah], *f.* 1. Excise. **Alcabala del viento**, duty paid on goods sold by chance. **El caudal del fulano está en alcabala de viento**, he lives upon what he earns. 2. A net. *V.* JABEGA.

alcabalatorio [al-cah-bah-lah-to'-re-o] *m.* Book of rates of the *alcabala*.

alcabalero [al-cah-bah-lay'-ro], *m.* A tax-gathere; revenue officer.

alcabiaz [al-cah-be-ath'], *m.* Aviary, a large cage for birds. *V.* ALCAHAZ.

alcabor [al-cah-bor'], *m. (Prov.)* Flue of a chimney.

alcabuz [al-cah-booth'], *m. (Obs.) V.* ARCABUZ.

alcacel, alcacer [al-cah-thel', al-cah-therr'], *m.* Green barley.

alcachofa [al-cah-cho'-fah], *f.* 1. *(Bot.)* Artichoke. 2. Instrument serving to stop a flux of blood. 3. Fluted mallets used by ropemakers.

alcachofado, da [al-cah-cho-fah'-do, dah], *a.* Resembling an artichoke.

alcachofado [al-cah-cho-fah'-do], *m.* Dish of artichokes.

alcachofal [al-cah-cho-fahl'], *m.* Ground where artichokes grow.

alcachofera [al-cah-cho-fay'-rah], *f.* An artichoke-plant.

alcahaz [al-cah-ahth'], *m.* A large cage for birds.

alcahazada [al-cah-ah-thah'-dah], *f.* A number of birds in a cage.

alcahazar [al-cah-ah-thar'], *va.* To shut up birds in the **alcahazar**.

alcaheta [al-cah-ay'-tah], *f.* Alcahest, a supposed universal solvent.

alcahué [ahl,-cah-oo-ay], *m. V.* CACAHUETE.

alcahuete, ta [al-cah-oo-tay'-tay, tah], *m. & f.* Pimp, procurer, bawd, whoremonger, gossip.

alcahuetear [al-cah-oo-ay-tay-ar'], *va.* To bawd, to pander, to procure women.

alcahuetería [al-cah-oo-ay-tay-ree'-ah], *f.* 1. Bawdry. 2. Hiding persons who want concealment.

alcahuetillo, lla [al-cah-oo-ay-teel'-lyo, lyah], *m. & f. dim.* A little pimp.

alcahuetón, na, alcahuetazo, za [al-cah-oo-ay-tone', nah, al-cah-oo-ay-tah'-tho, thah], *m. & f. aug.* A great pander, a great bawd.

alcaicería [al-cah-e-thay-ree'-ah], *f.* Market-place for raw silk.

alcaide [al-cah'-e-day], *m.* 1. Governor of a castle or fort. 2. Jailer, warden.

alcaidesa [al-cah-e-day'-sah], *f.* Wife of a governor or jailer.

alcaidía [al-cah-e-dee'-ah], *f.* 1. Office of a governor, and district of his jurisdiction; wardenship. 2. Office of a jailer. 3. Ancient duty paid for the passage of cattle.

alcaldable [ahl-cahl-dah-blay], *m. & f.* Candidate for mayor.

alcaldada [al-cal-dah'-dah], *f.* 1. An inconsiderate action of an *alcalde* or petty judge. 2. *(coll.)* Any word said, or action performed, with an air of mock authority. 3. A preposterous act or deed that causes a great noise.

alcalde [al-cahl'-day], *m.* 1. Justice of the peace. 2. Mayor of a city, or chairman of a council (of town government). 3. He who leads off a country dance. **Tener al padre alcalde**. To enjoy the protection of a judge or other man in power. 4. Game at cards. **Alcalde de barrio**. Justice of the peace of a ward. **Alcalde de primera elección**, The senior judge. *De segunda elección*, The junior judge. The **alcalde** acts as the *mayor* of the city council.

alcaldear [al-cal-day-ar'], *vn. (coll.)* To play the alcalde.

alcaldesa [al-cal-day-sah], *f.* The wife of an alcalde.

alcaldía [al-cal-dee'-ah], *f.* Office and jurisdiction of an **alcalde**.

alcalescencia [al-cah-les-then'-the-ah], *f. (Chem.) V.* ALCALIZACION.

alcalescente [al-cah-les-then'-tay], *a. (Chem.)* Partaking of alkaline properties.

álcali [ahl'-cah-le], *m. (Chem.)* An alkali. **Álcali fijo**, fixed alkali.

alcalificable [al-cah-le-fe-cah'-baly], *a.* Changeable into an alkali.

alcalígeno, na [al-cah-lee'-hay-no, nah], *a.* Alkaligenous, producing alkali.

alcalímetro [al-cah-lee'-may-tro], *m.* Alkalimeter, an instrument for estimating percentage of fixed alkali.

alcalinidad [al-cah-le-ne-dad'], *f.* Alkalinity, state of being alkaline.

alcalino, na Alcalizado, da [al-cah-lee'-no, nah, al-cah-le-thah'-do, dah], *a.* Alkaline. *Alcalizado, da, pp.* of ALCALIZAR.

alcalización [al-cah-le-thah-the-on'], *f. (Chem.)* Alkalization.

alcalizar [al-cah-le-thar'], *va. (Chem.)* To render alkaline.

alcaloide [al-cah-lo'-e-day], *m.* Alkaloid, an organic base.

alcam [al-cahm'], *m. (Bot.)* Bitter apple.

alcamonias [al-cah-mo-nee'-as], *f. pl.* 1. Various aromatic seeds used in the kitchen, and other stimulants. 2. *m. V.* ALCAHUETE.

alcamonero [ahl-cah-mo-nay-ro], *a. (Carib.)* Interfering (entrometido).

alcaná [al-cah-nah'], *f.* 1. *(Obs.)* A place where shops are kept. 2. *(Bot.)* Alcanna, from which henna is obtained. Alkanet.

alcance [al-cahn'-thay], *m.* 1 Following and overtaking a person. 2. Balance of an account. 3. Arm's length. 4. Range of fire-arms. 5. Capacity, ability. 6. Fathom, compass. 7. The supplement of a newspaper; a postcript. 8. Portion of copy which a compositor takes for setting up. 9. Capacity, talent. **Ir a los alcances**, to be at one's heels. **No poderle dar alcance**, to be unable to get sight of one. **Estar al alcance de uno**, to be within one's reach. 10. **El alcance del problema**, the extent of the problem. 11. Adverse balance, deficit. 12. **Buzón de alcance**, late collection postbox. 13. *(CAm.)* Calumnies (calumnias).

alcancia [al-can-thee'-ah], *f.* 1. Money-box. 2. *(Mil.)* Inflamed combustible balls.

alcancil [al-can-thel], *m. (Cono Sur)* Procurer, pimp.

alcándara [al-can'-dah-rah], *f.* Perch of a falcon.

alcandía [al-can-dee'-ah], *f. (Bot.)* Turkey millet. *V.* ZAHINA.

alcandial [al-can-de-ahl'], *m.* Ground sown with millet.

alcandora [al-can-do-rah], *f.* Beacon.

alcanfeno [al-can-fay'-no], *m.* Camphene.

alcanfor [al-can-fore'], *m.* 1. Camphor. 2. *(LAm.)* Procurer, pimp (alcahuete).

alcanforada [al-can-fo-rah'-dah], *f.* Camphor-tree.

alcanforado, da [al-can-fo-rah-do, dah], *a.* Impregnated with camphor.

alcanforar [al-can-fo-rahr], 1. *va.* To camphorate. 2. *-vr. (And. CAm, Carib.)* To disappear.

alcanforero [al-can-fo-ray'-ro], *m.* The camphor-tree.

alcantarilla [al-can-tah-reel'-lyah], *f.* 1. Sewer. 2. Small bridge. 3. Drain. 4. Culvert. 5. *(Carib. Mex.)* Public fountain.

alcantarillado [al-can-tah-reel-lyay'-ro], *m.* Sewerage system, drains.

alcantarillar [al-can-tah-re-lyahr], *va.* To lay sewers in.

alcantarillero *m.* Sewer man.

alcanzable [al-can-thah'-blay], *a.* Attainable.

alcanzadizo, za [al-can-thah-dee'-tho, thah], *a.* Within reach, easily reached. **Hacerse el alcanzadizo**, *(Met.)* to affect ignorance.

alcanzado, da [al-can-thah'-do, dah], *a.* 1. Needy, hard up, broke. 2. *(And)* Tired (fatigado). *-pp.* of ALCANZAR.

alcanzadera [al-can-thah-dor'-rah], *f. (Vet.)* 1. A tumor or wound in the pastern of a horse. 2. Wound or contusion arising from a horse's cutting the fore hoof with the hind shoe.

alcanzamiento [al-can-thah-me-en'-to], *m. (Obs.) V.* ALCANCE.

alcanzar [al-can-thar'], *va.* 1. To catch up with. 2. To overtake, to come up, to reach, to carry far. 3. To reach a thing, to extend the hand to take it. 4. To acquire, to obtain, to possess power of obtaining a thing desired. 5. To comprehend. 6. To be creditor of a balance. 7. To know a long while. **La bala le alcanzó en el pecho**, the bullet hit him in his chest. *-vn.* 1. To share. 2. To suffice. 3. To reach: applied to a ball. 4. **Alcanzar en días**, to survive. *-vr.* To overreach. **Alcanzársele poco a alguno**, to prevail upon any one. **Alcanzar a ver**, to descry. **No alcanzar con mucho**, to fall short.

alcanzativo [al-can-thah-te-vo], *a. (CAm.)* Suspicious.

alcaparras, *f.* **alcaparro**, *m.* [al-cah-pahr'-rah, al-cah-pahr'-roh], *(Bot.)* 1. Caper-bush. Capparris. 2. Caper, the bud of the caper-bush.

alcaparrado, da [al-cah-par-rah'-do, dah], *a.* Dressed with capers.

alcaparral [al-cah-par-rahl'], *m.* Ground planted with caper-bushes.

alcaparrón [al-cah-par-rone], *m. aug.* A large caper.

alcarrosa [al-cah-par-ro'-sah], *f. V.* CAPARROSA.

alcarahueya [al-cah-rah-oo-ay'-yah], *f. (Bot.)* Caraway-seed.

alcaraván [al-cah-rah-vahn'], *m. (Orn.)* Bittern.

alcaravea [al-ah-rah-vay'-ah], *f. (Bot.) V.* ALCARAHUEYA.

alcarón [al-cah-rone'], *m.* Alcaron, a species of scorpion found in Africa.

alcarracero, ra [al-car-rah-thay'-ro, rah], *m. & f.* 1. A potter. 2. Shelf on which earthenware is placed.

alcarraza [al-car-rah'-thah], *f* Pitcher or jug unglazed and porous.

alcartaz [al-cartath'], *m. V.* CUCURUCHO.

alcatifa [al-cah-tee'-fah], *f.* 1. A sort of fine carpet. 2. Layer of earth put under bricks in paving. 3. Roof of a house.

alcatife [al-cah-tee'-fay], *m.* Silk. *V.* SEDA.

alcatraz [al-cah-trath'], *m.* 1. Pelican. *V.* CUCURUCHO.

alcaucil [al-cah-oo-theel'], *m.* 1. *(Prov.)* Wild artichoke. 2. *(Cono Sur)* Informer. *V.* ALCACHOFA.

alcaudón [ahl-cah-oo-don], *m.* Shrike, butcher-bird (ave).

alcayata [al-cah-yah'-tah], *f.* 1. A hook. 2. Scarp of a fortification. 3. A kind of knot often used on board ship. *V.* ESCARPIA.

alcayota [al-cah-yo-tah], *f.* Squash, vegetable marrow.

alcazaba [al-cah-tha-bah], *f.* Castle.

alcázar [al-cah'-thar], *m.* 1. Castle. 2. Fortress. 3. *(Naut.)* Quarter-deck.

alcazuz [al-cah-thooth'], *m.* V. REGALIZA and OROZUZ. Licorice.

alce [ahl'-thay], *m.* 1. *(Zool.)* Elk or moose. V. ANTA. 2. The «cut», at cards.

alcea [al-tahy'-ah], *f.* *(Bot.)* Marshmallow.

alcedón [al-thay-done'], *m.* A king-fisher. V. MARTIN PESCADOR.

alcino [al-thee'-no], *m.* *(Bot.)* Wild basil.

alcista [al-thees'-tah], *f.* *(coll.)* Bull. **Tendencia alcista**, upward tendency (bolsa). *a.* Rising.

alcoba [al-co'-bah], *f.* 1. Alcove. 2. Bedroom. 3. Case in which the tongue of a balance moves to regulate the weight.

alcobilla, alcobita [al-co-beel'-lyah, bee'-tah], *f. dim.* A small alcove.

alcohol [al-co-ole'], *m.* Alcohol, **alcohol etílico**, ethyl alcohol, grain alcohol. **Alcohol de granos**, grain alcohol. **Alcohol metílico**, wood alcohol. **Alcohol de quemar**, methylated spirit.

alcoholado, da [al-co-o-lah'-do, dah], *a.* Being of a darker color around the eyes than the rest of the body; applied to cattle. -*pp.* of ALCOHOLAR.

alcoholar [al-co-o-lar'], *va.* 1. To alcoholize. 2. To make up with kohl (pintarse). 3. To clear up with alcohol. 4. To tar (barcos) -*vn.* *(Obs.)* To pass in a tilt the adverse party of combatants.

alcoholemia [alco-o-lay-me-ah], *f.* Blood-level of alcohol.

alcoholera [al-co-o-lay'-rah], *f.* Vessel for antomony or alcohol.

alcoholero [al-co-o-lay-ro], *a.* Alcohol.

alcohólico, ca [al-co-o'-le-co, cah], *a.* Alcoholic, containing alcohol or spirits of wine.

alcoholímetro [al-co-o-lee'-may-tro], *m.* Alcoholimeter, alcoholometer.

alcoholismo [al-co-o-lees'-mo], *m.* Alcoholism, a diseased state caused by continued abuse of alcoholic beverages.

alcoholista [al-co-o-les-tah], *m. & f. (Cono Sur)* Drunk.

alcoholización [al-co-o-le-thah-the-on'], *f.* *(Chem.)* Alcoholization.

alcoholizado, da [al-co-le-thah'-do, dah], *a.* 1. Containing alcohol. 2. Affected by alcoholism.

alcoholizar [al-co-o-le-thar'], *va.* To alcoholize. -*vr.* **To drink heavily**, to become an alcoholic. V. ALCOHOLAR.

alcor [al-cor'], *m.* V. CERRO.

alcorán [al-co-rahn'], *m.* The Koran, the sacred book of the Mohammedans.

alcoranista [al-co-rah-nees'-tah], *m.* One who expounds the law of Mohammed.

alcornocal [al-cor-no-cahl'], *m.* Plantation of cork-trees.

alcornoque [al-cor-no'-kay], *m.* 1. *(Bot.)* Cork-tree. 2. *(Met.)* A person of rude, uncouth manners.

alcornoqueño, ña [al-cor-nokay'-nyo, nyah], *a.* Belonging to the cork-tree.

alcorque [al-cor'-kay], *m.* 1. *(Bot.)* Cork-tree. 2. *(Met.)* A person of rude, uncouth manners.

alcorza [al-cor'-thah], *f.* 1. A paste for sweetmeats. 2. A piece of sweetmeat. **Parece hecho de alcorza**, he looks as if he were made of sweetmeat.

alcorzar [al-cor-thar'], *va.* To cover with iced sugar.

alcotán [al-co-tahn'], *m.* Lanner, a bird of prey. Hobby.

alcotana [al-co-tah'-nah], *f.* Pickaxe, gurlet.

alcotancillo [al-co-tan-theel'-lyo], *m. dim.* A young lanner.

alcrebite [al-cray-bee'-tay], *m.* Sulphur. V. AZUFRE.

alcribis [al-cree'-bis], *m.* A small tube at the back of a forge through which runs the pipe of the bellows; twyer, tuyere.

alcubilla [al-coo-beel'-lyah], *f.* *(Prov.)* Reservoir of an aqueduct; basin, millpond.

alcucero, ra [al-coo-thay'-ro], *a.* Belonging to an oil-bottle.

alcucilla [al-coo-theel'-lyah], *f. dim.* A small oil-bottle or can.

alcuña [al-coo'-nyah], *f.* *(Obs.)* V. ALCURNIA.

alcurnia [al-coor'-ne-ah], *f.* Family, lineage, race.

alcurniado [al-koor-ne-ah-do], *a.* Aristocratic, noble.

alcuza [al-coo'-thah], *f.* Oil-bottle or cruet; oilcan, oiler (aceitera).

alcuzada [al-coo-thah'-dah], *f.* The oil contained in a full cruet.

alcuzcuz [al-cooth-cooth'], *m.* Flour, water, and honey, made into balls, and esteemed by the Moors.

alcuzón [al-coo-thone'], *m. aug.* A large oil-bottle.

aldaba [al-dah'-bah], *f.* 1. Knocker, hammer on the door, clapper; door-handle, latch. 2. A cross-bar to secure doors and windows. **Caballo de aldaba**, a steed, a horse for state or war. 3. **Tener buenas aldabas**, to have influence. 4. Tits (pechos).

aldabada [al-dah-bah-dah], *f.* Knock (en puerta).

aldabazo, aldabonazo [al-dah-bah'-tho, al-dah-bo-nah'-tho], *m.* Knocking.

aldabear [al-da-bay-ar'], *vn.* To rap or knock at the door.

aldabia [al-dah-bee'-ah], *f.* Beam horizontally placed on two walls, to which is a hanging partition.

aldabilla [al-dah-beel'-yah], *f. dim.* A small knocker.

aldabón [al-dah-bone'], *m.* 1. *(aug.)* A large knocker. 2. An iron handle of trunks.

aldabonazo [al-dah-bo-nah-tho], *m.* Bang, loud knock (puerta); *(fig.)* Knock, blow.

aldea [al-day'-ah], *f.* Small village, hamlet, a large farm.

aldeana [al-day-ah'-nah], *f.* Villager, country woman, lass.

aldeanismo [al-day-ah-nes-mo], *m.* Provincialism.

aldeano [al-day-ah'-no], *m.* Villager, a countryman.

aldebarán [al-day-bah-rahn'], *m.* *(Astr.)* Aldebaran or Bull's-Eye, a fixed star of first magnitude in the constellation of Taurus.

aldehida [al-day-ee'-dah], *f.* Aldehyde, a volatile, colorless fluid obtained by the oxidation of alcohol.

aldehuela, aldeilla [al-day-oo-ay'-lah, al-day-eel'-lyah], *f. dim.* A little village.

aldeorrio [al-day-or'-re-o], *m.* 1. A small, unpleasant village. 2. A town whose inhabitants are rude.

alderredor [al-dayr-ray-dor'], *adv.* V. ALREDEDOR.

aldiza [al-dee'-thah], *f.* A sort of small reed without knots.

aleación [ah-lay-ah-the-on'], *f.* The art of alloying metals; alloy, compound metal.

aleador [ah-lay-ah-dor'], *m.* Alloyer.

alear [ah-lay-ar'], *vn.* 1. To flutter. 2. *(Met.)* To move the arms quickly. 3. *(Met.)* To recover from sickness, to regain strength after fatigue. -*va.* To alloy.

aleatoriedad [ah-lay-ah-to-re-ay-dahd], *f.* Randomness.

aleatorio [ah-lay-ah-to-re-o], *a.* Accidental, fortuitous; uncertain.

aleatorizar [ah-lay-ah-to-re-thar'], *va.* To randomize.

alebrarse, alebrastrarse, alebrestarse [ah-lay-brar'-say, ah-lay-bras-trar'-say, ah-lay-brays-tar'-say], *vr.* 1. To squat close to the ground as hares do (agazaparse). 2. To cower.

alebestrarse [ah-lah-bays-trahr-say], *vr.* *(LAm.)* To become agitated.

alebronarse [ah-lay-bro-nar'-say], *vr.* To be dispirited.

aleccionador [ah-layc-the-o-nah-dor], *a.* Instructive, enlightening.

aleccionamiento [ah-layc-the-o-nah-me-ayn-to], *m.* Instruction, enlightenment; training.

aleccionar [ah-le-the-o-nar'], *va.* To teach, to instruct.

alece [ah-lay-thay], *m.* A ragout made of the livers of a large fish, called *mújo*, caught on the coast of Valencia.

alechado [ah-lay-chah-do], *a.* *(LAm.)* Milky, like milk.

alechigar [ah-lay-che-gar'], *va.* To soften. -*vr.* To turn milky.

alechugado, da [ah-lay-choo-gah'-do, dah], *a.* Curled like the leaf of lettuce. Fluted, plaited. -*pp.* of ALECHUGAR.

alechugar [ah-lay-choo-gar'], *va.* 1. To curl or contract like the leaf of lettuce. 2. To plait, to flute.

aleda [ah-lay'-dah], *f.* CERA ALEDA. Propolis, or bee-glue, used by bees in stopping cracks and cementing the comb to the hive.

aledaño [ah-lay-dah'-nyo], *m. & a.* Common boundary, border, limit.

alefanginas [ah-lay-fan-hee'-nas], *f. pl.* Purgative pills made of cinnamon, nutmeg, and the juice of aloes.

alefra [ah-lay-frah], *interj. (Carib.)* Touch wood!

alefris, alefruz [ah-lay-frees'], *m.* 1. Mortise, a hole cut into wood. 2. Rabbet.

alefrizar [ah-lay-fre-thar'], *va.* To rabbet.

alegación [ah-lay-gah-the-on'], *f.* Allegation; argument. **Alegación de inocencia**, *(Mex. Jur.)* Plea of not guilty.

alegador, ra [ah-lay-gah-dor], *a. (Cono Sur)* Argumentative.

alegal [ah-lay-gahl], *a. (Cono Sur Jur.)* Illegal.

alegar [ah-lay-gahr'], *va.* To allege, to affirm, to quote, to maintain, to adduce. *(LAm.)* (Disputar) To argue against, dispute.

alegata [ah-lay-gah-tah], *f. (LAm.)* Fight.

alegato [ah-lay-gah'-to], *m. (Law.)* Allegation, showing the ground of complaint by the plaintiff. Complaint, petition.

alegoría [ah-lay-go-ree'-ah], *f.* Allegory.

alegóricamente [ah-lay-go'-re-cah-men-tay], *adv.* Allegorically.

alegórico, ca [ah-lay-go'-re-co, cah], *a.* Allegorical, not literal.

alegorista [ah-lay-go-rees'-tah], *m.* Allegorist.

alegorizar]ah-lay-go-re-thar'], *va.* To turn into allegory.

alegrado, da [ah-lay-grah'-do, dah], *a.* Delighted. *-pp.* of ALEGRAR.

alegrador, ra [ah-lay-grah-dor', rah], *m. & f.* 1. *(Obs.)* One who produces merriment: a jester. 2. *(coll.)* Twisted slip of paper to shake the snuff of a candle. 3. *(Mech.)* Reamer, round broach; riming bit.

alegrar [ah-lay-grar'], *va.* 1. To make merry, to gladden, to comfort, to exhilarate. 2. *(Met.)* To enliven, to beautify. 3. *(Mech.)* To round, to make a bore; to ream, to widen. **Alegrar las luces**, to snuff the candles. *-vr.* 1. To rejoice, to congratulate, to exult. **Me alegro de saberlo**, I am glad to hear it. 2. To grow merry by drinking.

alegre [ah-lay'-gray], *a.* 1. Merry, joyful, content, light-hearted, full of gaiety, gleeful. 2. Lightsome, comic, ludicrous, facetious. 3. Gay, showy, fine: applied to inanimate things. **Un cielo alegre**, a clear, beautiful sky. 4. Brilliant, pleasing: applied to colors. 5. Lucky, fortunate, genial. 6. Bold, reckless (atrevido). 7. Fast, immoral (vida). 8. **Estar alegre**, to be merry, to be tight.

alegremente [ah-lay-gray-men'-tay], *adv.* 1. Merrily, gladly, gaily. 2. Facetiously, mirthfully, laughingly, good-humoredly.

alegría [ah-lay-gree'-ah], *f.* 1. Mirth, merriment, exhilaration, gaiety, glee, rejoicing. **Saltar de alegría**, to jump with joy. 2. Festivity. 3. Light-someness, 4. Ecstasy, pleasure. 5. *(Bot.)* Sesamum, oily grain. 6. Paste made of sesamum and honey. *-pl.* Rejoicings, public festivals.

alegrillo [ah-lay-greel'-lyo], *a.* Sprightly, gay.

alegro [ah-lay'-gro], *m.* 1. *(Mus.)* Allegro, a word denoting in music a sprightly motion. 2. A movement, or division of a sonata, in this time.

alegrón [ah-lay-grone'], *m. (coll.)* 1. Sudden, unexpected joy. 2. A flash.

alegrona [ah-lay-gro-nah], *f. (LAm.)* Prostitute.

alejado [ah-lay-hah-do], *a.* Distant, remote.

alejamiento [ah-lay-hah-me-en'-to], *m.* 1. Elongation, removal to a distance. 2. Distance. 3. Strangeness.

Alejandría [ah-lay-han-dre-ah], *n.* Alexandria.

alejandrino, na [ah-lay-han-dree'-no, nah], *a.* Alexandrine.

Alejandro [ah-lay-han-dro], *m.* Alexander.

alejar [ah-lay-har'], *va.* To remove to a greater distance, to separate. **Conviene alejar tales libros de los niños**, such books should be kept out of children's hands. *(fig.)* To cause a rift between, to separate, to estrange. *-vr.* To move away, to go away. **Alejémonos un poco más**, let's go a bit farther away.

alejijas [ah-lay-hee'-has], *f. pl.* Porridge made of barley, cleaned and roasted. **Tiene cara de alejijas**, he looks half-starved.

alelado [ah-lay-lah-do], *a.* Stupefied, bewildered.

alelamiento [ah-lay-lah-me-ayn-to], *m.* Bewilderment; stupidity.

alelar [ah-lay-lahr'], *va.* To stupefy.

alelarse [ah-lay-lar'-say], *vr.* To become stupid.

alelí [ah-lay-lee'], *m. (Bot.)* The winter gilliflower of various colors: also a general name for violets.

aleluya [ah-lay-loo'-yah], *f.* 1. Allelujah. 2. Joy, merriment. 3. Easter time. **Al aleluya nos veremos**, we'll meet again at Easter. 4. *(Bot.)* Woodsorrel (planta). V. ACEDERILLA. So called because it flowers at Easter. 6. *pl. (coll.)* Dull, poor verses.

alema [ah-lay'-mah], *f.* The allotted quantity of water for irrigating a piece of ground.

alemán, na [ah-lay-mahn'-mah'-nah], *a. & m.* 1. German. 2. German language.

Alemania [ah-lay-mah-ne-ah], *f.* Germany.

alemanisco, ca [ah-lay-mah-nees'-co, cah], *a.* Germanic: cloth made in Germany; huckaback; damask tablelinen.

alenguamiento [ah-len-goo-ah-me-en'-to], *m.* An agreement relative to pasture.

alenguar [ah-len-goo-ar'], *va.* To agree respecting sheepwalks or pasturage.

alentada [ah-len-tah'-dah], *f. (Obs.)* Interval between two respirations, a continued respiration; a full, deep breath.

alentadamente [ah-len-tah-dah-men'-tay], *adv.* Bravely, gallantly.

alentado, da [ah-len-tah'-do, dah], *a.* 1. Spirited, courageous, valiant. 2. *(Obs.)* Bold. *-pp.* of ALENTAR.

alentador, ra [ah-len-ta-dor', rah], *m. & f.* One who inspires courage. *-a.* Encouraging, animating.

alentar [ah-len-tar'], *vn.* To breathe. *(fig.)* To burn, to glow. *-va.* 1. To animate, to encourage, to comfort. **Alentar a uno a hacer algo**, to encourage somebody to do something. 2. *(And)* To clap (aplaudir). *-vr.* 1. To take heart, to cheer up. 2. *(Med.)* To get well. 3. *(And. CAm.)* To give birth (dar a luz).

aleonarse [ah-lay-o-nahr-say], *vr. (Cono Sur)* To get excited, to get worked up.

aleoyota [ah-lay-o-yo-tah], *f. (Cono Sur Bot.)* Pumpkin.

alepantado [ah-lay-pahn-tah-do], *a. (And)* Absent-minded.

alepín [ah-lay-peen'], *m.* A kind of bombasin, or bombazine.

alerce [ah-ler'-thay], *m. (Bot.)* Larch-tree.

alérgeno [ah-lehr-hay'-no], *m.* Allergen.

alergia [ah-lehr'-he-ah], *f.* Allergy.

alérgico, ca [ah-lehr'-hee-co, cah], *a.* Allergic.

alero [ah-lay'-ro], *m.* 1. The projecting part of a roof; eaves, gable-end, corona hood moulding, water-table. 2. Splashboard of a carriage. *-pl.* Snares for partridges.

alerón [ah-lay-rone'], *m.* Aileron (avión).

alerta [ah-ler'-tah], *f. (Mil.)* Watchword.

alerta, alertamente [ah-ler'-tah, ah-ler-tah-men'-tay], *adv.* Vigilantly, carefully. **Estar alerta**, to be on the watch. **Alerta a la buena guardia a proa**, *(Naut.)* lookout well there afore.

alertar [ah-ler-tar'], *va.* To render vigilant, to put one on his guard.

alerto, ta [ah-ler'-to, tah], *a.* Vigilant, alert, guarded.

alesna [ah-lays'-nah], *f. (Obs.)* Awl, a pointed instrument. V. LESNA.

alesnado, da [ah-les-nah'-do, dah], *a.* Awl-shaped, pointed like an awl.

aleta [ah-lay'-tah], *f.* 1. *(dim.)* A small wing. 2. Fin of fish. **Aletas**, *(Naut.)* Fashion pieces. 3. *(Arch.)* Aletta. 4. *(Mech.)* Leaf of a hinge, leaf of a pinion, teeth of a pinion. 5. *(Aer.)* Flap. **Aleta de la hélice**, 1. *(Aer.)* Propeller blade. 2. *(Naut.)* Screw blade.

aletada [ah-lay-tah'-dah], *f.* Motion of the wings.

aletargado, da [ah-lay-tar-gah'-do, dah], *a.* Lethargic. *-pp.* of ALETARGARSE.

aletargamiento [ah-lay-tahr-gah-me-ayn-to], *m.* Drowsiness, lethargy, numbness.

aletargar [ah-lay-tahr-gahr'], *va.* To make drowsy, to make lethargic.

aletargarse [ah-lay-tar-gar'-say], *vr.* To fall into a state of lethargy.

aletazo [ah-lay-tah'-tho], *m.* 1. Stroke of the wing, flapping. 2. *(Cono Sur) (fig.)* Slap (bofetada). 3. *(CAm.)* Robbery (hurto).

aleteado, da [ah-lay-tay-ah'-do, dah], *a.* Finlike, finned. *-pp.* of ALETEAR.

aletear [ah-lay-tay-ar'], *vn.* To flutter, to take short flights, to flit.

aleteo [ah-lay-tay'-o], *m.* 1. Clapping of the wings. 2. *(Med.)* Palpitation.

aletón [ah-lay-tone'], *m. aug.* A large wing.

aletría [ah-lay-tree'-ah], *m. (Prov.)* Vermicelli. *V.* FIDEOS.

aleudar [ah-lay-oo-dahr], *va.* To leaven, to ferment with yeast.

aleudarse [ah-lay-oo-dar'-say], *vr. (Obs.)* To become fermented, (fermentarse) (masa).

aleve [ah-lay'-vay], *a.* Treacherous, perfidious, guileful.

alevilla [ah-le-veel-lya], *a.* A moth like that of the silkworm, but differing in having the wings entirely white.

alevín [ah-lay-veen], *m.* Young fish, fry; *(fig.)* beginner, novice.

alevino [ah-lay-vee-no], *m. (LAm.)* Young fish, alevin, fry.

alevosa [ah-lay-vo'-sah], *f. (Vet.)* A tumor under the tongue of cows and horses. *V.* RANULA.

alevosamente [ah-lay-vo-sah-men'-tay], *adv.* Treacherously, guilefuly.

alevosía [ah-lay-vo-see'-ah], *f.* Perfidy, breach of trust.

alevoso, sa [ah-lay-vo'-so, sah], *a.* Treacherous. *m.* Traitor.

alexifármaco, ca [ah-lex-e-far'-mah-co, cah], *a. (Med.)* Antidotal, possessing the power of destroying or expelling poison.

alfa [ahl'-fah], *f.* Alpha, the first letter of the Greek alphabet. *(Met.)* The beginning.

alfábega [al-fah'-bay-gah], *f. V.* ALBAHACA.

alfabéticamente [al-fah-bay-te-cah-men-tay], *adv.* Alphabetically.

alfabético, ca [al-fah-bay'-te-co, cah], *a.* Alphabetical.

alfabetismo [al-fah-bay-tees-mo], *m.* Literacy.

alfabetista [al-fah-bay-tees'-tah], *m.* One that studies the alphabet and orthography.

alfabetización [al-fah-bay-te-thah-the-on], *f.* Teaching literacy.

alfabetizado [al-fah-bay-te-thah-do], *a.* Literate, that can write and read.

alfabetizador [al-fah-bay-te-thah-dor], *m. & f.* Literacy tutor.

alfabetizar [al-fah-bay-te-thahr], *va.* 1. To alphabetize. 2. **Alfabetizar a uno**, to teach someone to read and write.

alfabeto [al-fah-bay'-to], *m.* Alphabet.

alfadía [al-fah-dee'-ah], *f. (Obs.)* Bribe.

alfahar, alfaharero [al-fah-ar', al-fah-ah-ray'-ro], *V.* ALFAR, aLFARERO.

alfaharería [àl-fah-ah-ray-ree'-ah], *V.* ALFAR, aLFARERIA.

alfajía [al-fah-hee'-ah], *f.* Wood for windows and doors.

alfajor [al-fah-hor'], *m. V.* ALAJU.

alfalfa, *f.* **alfalfe**, *m.* [al-fahl'-fah, al-fahl'-fay]. *(Bot.)* Lucerne, alfalfa.

alfalfal, alfalfar [al-fal-fahl', al-fal-far'], *m.* A piece of ground sown with lucerne.

alfana [al-fah'-nah], *f.* A strong and spirited horse.

alfandoque [al-fan-do'-kay], *m.* A hollow cane shaken for a musical instrument. *(Ec.)* 2. *(CAm. Carib. Mex.)* A kind of sweet pastry (pasta). 3. *(Carib.)* Small honey cake.

alfaneque [al-fah-nay'-kay], *m.* 1. The white eagle. Falco albus. 2. Tent or booth.

alfanjazo [al-fan-hah'-tho], *m.* A wound with a cutlass.

alfanje [al-fahn'-hay], *m.* Hanger, cutlass.

alfanjete [al-fan-hay'-tay], *m. dim.* A small cutlass.

alfanjón [al-fan-hone'], *m. aug.* A large hanger or cutlass.

alfanjonazo [al-fan-ho-nah'-tho], *m.* A cut with a large hanger.

alfaque [al-fah'-kay], *m.* A shoal or bar.

alfaquí [al-fah-kee'], *m.* A doctor of, or wise in the law, among Moslems. *Cf.* FAKIR.

alfar [al-far'], *m.* 1. Pottery. 2. *V.* ARCILLA. *-a.* That raises the head too much: relating to horses.

alfar [al-far'], *vn.* To raise the forehead too much.

alfaraz [al-fah-rath'], *a.* Applied formerly to the horses on which the light cavalry of the Moors rode.

alfarda [al-far'-dah], *f.* 1. *(Prov.)* Duty paid for the irrigation of lands. 2. Thin beam.

alfardero [al-far-day'-ro], *m. (Prov.)* A collector of the duty for watering lands.

alfardilla [al-far-dell'-lyah], *f.* 1. Silk, now called galloon. 2. *(dim. Prov.)* A small duty for watering lands.

alfardón [al-far-done'], *m. (Prov.)* 1. Washer of a wheel. 2. Duty paid for watering lands.

alfarería [al-fah-ray-ree'-ah], *f.* 1. The art of a potter. 2. Pottery.

alfarero [al-fah-ray'-ro], *m.* Potter.

alfarje [al-far'-hay], *m.* 1. The lower stone of an oil-mill. 2. Ceiling of a room adorned with carved work. Wainscot.

alfarjía [al-far-hee'-ah], *f. V.* ALFAJIA.

alfayate [al-fah-yah'-tay], *m. (Obs.)* A tailor.

alféizar [al-fay'-e-thar], *m.* The aperture in a wall at the inside of a door or window; embrasure.

alfeñicado, da [al-fay-nye-cah'-do, dah], *a.* Weakly, delicate.

alfeñicar [al-fay-nye-car'], *va.* To ice with sugar.

alfeñicarse [al-fay-nye-car'-say], *vr. (coll.)* To affect peculiar delicacy.

alfeñique [al-fay-nyee'-kay], *m.* 1. A sugar-paste made with oil of sweet almonds. 2. *(Met.)* A person of a delicate constitution.

alferecía [al-fay-ray-thee'-ah], *f.* 1. Epilepsy, a nervous affection, in which the patient often falls. 2. *(Obs.)* An ensign's commission.

alférez [al-fay-reth], *m.* 1. Ensign. 2. **Alférez de navío**, ensign of the navy. 3. **Alférez real**, the chief ensign of the town.

alfil [al-feel'], *m.* Bishop in the game of chess.

alfiler [al-fe-lerr'], *m.* 1. A pin. 2. Jeweller's, broach. **Alfileres de gancho o de pelo**, hairpin. **Alfileres**, pin-money. **Con todos sus alfileres** *or* **de veinte y cinco alfileres**, in full dress, dressed in style. **No estar con todos sus alfileres**, not to be in good temper.

alflerar [al-fe-lay-rahr], *va.* To pin together.

alflerazo [al-fe-lay-rah'-tho], *m.* 1. Prick of a pin. 2. A large pin.

alflerera [al-fe-lay-ray'-rah], *f.* (Alfilería) the seed of some of the geranium family; form its shape.

alflerero [al-fe-lay-ray-ro],, *m.* A maker or seller of pins.

alfilerillo [al-fe-lay-re-lyo], *m. (And. Cono Sur)* 1. Fodder plant. 2. Cactus (pita).

alfilete, alfiletete [al-fe-lay'-tay, al-fe-lay-tay'-tay], *m.* Paste made of coarse wheat flour.

alfiletero [al-fe-lay-tay'-ro], *m.* Pincase, needle-case, pincushion.

alfolí [al-fo-lee'], *m.* 1. Granary. 2. Magazine of salt.

alfoliero, alfolinero [al-fo-le-ay'-ro, al-fo-le-nay'-ro], *m.* Keeper of a granary or magazine.

alfombra [al-fom'-brah], *f.* 1. Floor-carpet. 2. *(Poetic.)* Field adorned with flowers. 3. *(Med.)* Measles, an eruptive fever.

alfombrado [al-fom-brah-do], *m.* Carpeting.

alfombrar [al-fom-brar'], *va.* To cover with carpets.

alfombraza [al-fom-brah'-tha], *f. aug.* A large carpet.

alfombrero, ra [al-fom-bray-ro], *m. & f.* Carpet-maker.

alfombrilla [al-fom-breel'-lyah], *f.* 1. *(dim.)* A small carpet. 2. *(Med.)* Measles. 3. *V.* ALFOMBRA.

alfóncigo [al-fon'-the-go], *m.* 1. Pistachio, the fruit of the pistachio-tree. 2. Pistachio-tree.

alfonsearse [al-fon-say-ar'-say], *vr. (coll.)* To joke with each other, to ridicule each other.

alfonsí [al-fon-see'], *m. (Obs.)* V. ALFONSIN.

alfonsín, no, na [al-fon-seen', no, nah], *a.* Belonging to the Spanish kings called Alphonso.

alfonsina [al-fon-see'-nah], *f.* A solemn act held in the church of the Alphonsine college of Alcalá, where several questions. either theological or medical, are publicly discussed.

Alfonso [al-fon-so], *m.* Alphonso. **Alphonso el Sabio**, Alphonso The Wise.

alforfón [al-for-fon], *m.* Buckwheat.

alforja [al-for'-hah], *f.* 1. Saddle-bag, knapsack. **Hacerle a alguno la alforja**. to fill one's saddle-bag with provisions. 2. *(Cono Sur)* Go too far. **Para este viaje no se necesitan alforjas**, a fat lot of good that is.

alforjero [al-for-hay'-ro], *m.* 1. Maker or seller of saddle-bags. 2. One who carries the bag with provisions.

alforjilla, ita, uela [al-for-heel'-layh, hee'-tah, hoo-ay'-lah], *f. dim.* A small saddle-bag, a small wallet or knapsack.

alforjudo [al-for-hoo-do], *a. (Cono Sur)* Silly, stupid.

alforza [al-for'-thah], *f.* A plait in a skirt, a tuck. *(fig.)* Slash, scar.

alforzar [al-for-thahr], *va.* To plead, to tuck.

alfredo [al-fray-do], *m.* Alfred.

alfronito [al-fro-nee'-tro], *m.* V. ALATRON.

alga [ahl'-gah], *f. (Bot.)* Seaweed, alga; *pl. algae o algas.*

algadonera [al-gah-do-nay'-rha], *f. (Bot.)* Cudweed, graphalium.

algaida [al-gah'-e-dah], *f.* A ridge of shifting sand; sand-dune.

algaido, da [al-gah'-e-do, dah], *a. (Prov.)* Thatched, covered with straw. **Casas algaidas**, Thatched houses.

algalaba [al-gah-lah'-bah], *f. (Bot.)* White briony, wild hops.

algalia [al-gah'-le-ah], *f.* 1. Civet, a perfume. 2. Catheter, a hollow instrument used in surgery.

algaliar [al-gah-le-ar'], *va. (Obs.)* To perfume with civet.

algara [al-gah'-rah], *f.* 1. The thin integument which covers an egg, onion, etc. 2. *(Obs.)* A foraging party of cavalry.

algarabía [al-gah-rah-bee'-ah], *f.* 1. The Arabic language. 2. *(Met.)* Gabble, jargon. 3. *(Met.)* A confused noise of several people speaking or shouting at the same time. 4. *(Bot.)* Centaury, cornflower.

algarada [al-gah-rah'-dah], *f.* 1. A loud cry. 2. A sudden attack. 3. A sort of battering-ram of the ancients.

Algarbe [al-gahr-bay], *m.* **El algarbe**, the Algarve.

algarero, ra [al-gah-ray'-ro, rah], *a.* Prating, chattering, talkative. **La mujer algarera nunca hace larga tela**, a prating woman works but little.

algarero [al-gah-ray-ro], *m. (Obs.)* A horseman of the foraging party called **algara**.

algarrada [al-gar-rah'-dah], *f.* 1. Driving bulls into the pen for the bullfight. 2. *(Obs.)* Battering-ram.

algarroba [al-gar-ro'-bah], *f. (Bot.)* 1. Carob bean. 2. The honey-mesquite.

algarrobal [al-gar-ro-bahl'], *m.* Ground planted with carob-trees.

algarrobera, *f.* **algarrobo**, *m.* [al-gar-ro-bay'-rah, al-gar-ro'-bo], *(Bot.)* Carob-tree, or St. John's bread.

algazara [al-gah-thah'-rah], *f.* 1. Huzza. 2. The shout of a multitude.

algazul [al-gah-thool'], *m.* A seaweed, which when burned produces barilla, or impure soda.

algebra [ahl'-hay-brah], *f.* 1. Algebra, a branch of the higher mathematics. 2. *(Obs.)* Art of setting joints.

algebraico, ca [al-hay-brah'-e-co, cah], *a.* Algebraic.

algebrista [al-hay-brees'-tah], *m.* 1. Algebraist, a person that understands algebra. 2. *(Obs.)* One who understands setting dislocated members. Bone-setter.

algidez [al-he-deth'], *f. (Med.)* Icy coldness.

álgido, da [ahl'-he-do, dah], *a.* Icy.

algo [ahl'-go], *pron.* Somewhat, something, aught. **Habrá algo para ti**, there will be something for you. **Esto es algo nuevo**, this is something new. **Más vale algo que nada**, something is better than nothing. **Tener un algo**, to have a certain charm.

algo [ahl'-go], *pron.* Something. **Aquí hay algo raro**, there is something strange here. Anything (cualquier cosa). **Daría algo por verla**, I'd give anything to see her. **Algo así**, something like that. **Más vale algo que nada**, something is better than nothing. **Algo es algo**, something is better than nothing. **Quiero algo original**, I want something original. **¿Tienes algo para mí?**, have you got anything for me? **Por algo será**, there must be a reason. *adv.* Somewhat, rather, quite, a little. **La medida es algo escasa**, the measure is somewhat short. **Algo o nada**, all or nothing. **Ser algo tímido**, to be a little timid. **Ando algo escaso de dinero**, I'm somewhat short of money. *m.* Snack, something to eat. **Tomó algo antes de salir**, he had something to eat before going out.

algodón [al-go-done'], *m.* 1. Cotton. 2. *(Bot.)* The cottonplant. **Algodón de azúcar**, cotton plant. **Algodón dulce**, candy-floss. **Algodón en rama**, raw cotton. *Algodones, V.* CENDALES.

algodonado, da [al-go-do-nah'-do-dah], *a.* Filled with cotton.

algodonal [al-go-do-nahl'], *m.* A cotton-plantation.

algodonar [al-go-do-nar'], *va.* To cover or fill with cotton.

algodoncillo [al-go-don-thee-lyo], *m.* Milkweed.

algodonería [al-go-do-nay-ree'-ah], *f.* 1. Cotton-factory. 2. Cotton-trade.

algodonero [al-go-do-nay'-ro], *m.* The cotton-plant. 2. The cottonwood poplar.

algodonero, ra [al-go-do-nay'-ro, rah], *m. & f.* A cotton-broker.

algodonoso, sa [al-go-do-no'-so, sa], *a.* Cottony, covered with thick down; woolly, tasteless (fruta).

algol [al-gole'] *m.* Name of a variable star in the constellation Perseus.

algología [al-go-lo-hee'-ah], *f.* Algology, that branch of botany which treats of sea-weeds, marine or fresh-water.

algorín [al-go-reen'], *m. (Prov.)* A place in oil-mills for receiving the olives which are to be ground.

algoritmo [al-go-reet'-mo], *m.* Algorithm, an Arabic word signifying the science of numbers; arithmetic.

algoso, sa [al-go'-so, sah], *a.* Weedy, full of seaweeds.

alguacil [al-goo-ah-theel'], *m.* 1. Constable, a peace officer; a bum-bailiff. 2. The short-legged spider. 3. **Alguacil mayor**, high constable. **Alguacil de campo** or **del campo**, guard or watchman of corn-fields or vineyards.

alguacilazgo [ál-goo-ah-the-lath'-go], *m.* The place or office of an *alguacil.*

alguarín [al-goo-ah-reen'], *m. (Prov.)* 1. A small room, on the ground-floor in which anything is kept. 2. Bucket in which flour falls from the millstones.

alguaza [al-goo-ah'-thah], *f. (Prov.)* Hinge.

alguien [ahl'-gee-en], *pron.* Somebody, someone. **Si alguien viene**, if somebody comes. **Para alguien que conozca la materia**, for anyone who is familiar with the subject. **Alguien llama a la puerta**, somebody is knocking at the door. **¿Hay alguien en casa?**, is there anybody at home? **Si llama alguien...**, if anyone calls...

alguita [al-gees-tah], *f. (And)* Money.

alguito [al-gee-to], *(LAm.)* V. ALGO.

algún [al-goon'], *a.* Some, any (V. ALGUNO). **Algún pobre anciano**, some poor old man. **Algún tiempo**, some time. **En algún sitio**, somewhere. **Algún que otro libro**, the odd book.

alguno, na [al-goo'-nonah], *a.* Some, some or other, a, a certain. **¿Vino alguna niña?**, did a little girl come? **Quiero algunos libros**, I want some books. **¿Necesitáis alguna ayuda?**, do you need any help? **¿Ha venido alguno?**, has anyone come? **Alguna vez**, sometimes, now and then. *Pron.* **Alguno de ellos**, one of them. **Busco alguno que me ayude**, I'm looking for somebody to help me. **Alguna que otra**

vez, from time to time. **Algunas veces**, sometimes. **Sin prisa alguna**, without hurrying.

alhábega [al-ah'-bay-gah], *f. (Prov.) V.* ALBAHACA.

alhadida [al-ah-dee'-dah], *f.* 1. *(Chem.)* Burnt copper from which the saffron of copper is extracted. 2. *V.* MALAQUITA.

alhaja [al-ah'-hah], *f.* 1. Jewel, a thing of great value. 2. Showy furniture, gaudy ornament. **Él es una buena alhaja** (ironically), he is a good fellow: he is a good-for-nothing; beware of him. **Quien trabaja tiene alhaja**, he that labors spins gold.

alhajado [ah-lah-hah-do], *a. (LAm.)* Wealthy.

alhajar [al-ah-har'], *va.* 1. To adorn. 2. To furnish, to fit up.

alhajera [al-ha-hay-rah], *f. (Cono Sur)* Jewel box.

alhajuela [al-ah-hoo-ay-lay], *f. dim.* A little jewel.

alhamel [al-ah-mel'], *m. (Prov.)* 1. A beast of burden. 2. A porter. 3. Muleteer.

alhana [al-ah'-nah], *f.* Alhanna, Tripoli earth.

alhandal [al-an-dahl'], *m. (Pharm.)* Colocyth, bitter apple.

alharaca [al-ah-rah'-cah], *f.* Clamor, angry vociferation, complaint without sufficient reason.

alharaquiento, ta [al-ah-rah-ke-en'-to, ah], *a.* Noisy, clamorous, grumbling.

alhárgama, alharma [al-ar'-gah-mah, l-ar'-mah], *f. (Bot.)* Wild rue.

alhasa [al-ah'-sah], *f.* Hydroa, a vesicular disease of the skin.

alhehí [al-ay-lee']. *V.* ALELI.

alheña [al-ay'-nyah], *f.* 1. *(Bot.)* Privet. 2. Flower of privet; privet ground to powder. 3. *V.* AZUMBAR. 4. Laurentinus. 5. The blasting of corn. *V.* ROYA.

alheñar [al-ay-nyar'], *va.* To dye with the powder of privet. *-v.* To be mildewed: applied to corn. *V.* ARROYARSE.

alhoja [al-o'-hah], *f.* A small bird resembling a lark.

alholva [al-ol'-vah], *f. (Bot.)* Fenugreek.

alhóndiga [al-on'-de-gah], *f.* A public granary. *V.* POSITO.

alhondiguero [al-on-de-gay'-ro], *m.* The keeper of a public granary.

alhorma [al-or'-mah], *f.* Moorish camp, or royal tent.

alhorre [al-or'-ray], *m.* 1. The first dark discharge from an infant's bowels. 2. Eruption in the skin of infants.

alhoz [al-oth'], *m.* Limit or lot of land.

alhucema [al-oo-thay'-mah], *f. (Bot.)* Lavender. *(Andal.) V.* ESPLIEGO.

alhumajo [al-oo-mah'-ho], *m.* Name applied to leaves of the pine-tree.

aliabierto, ta [al-le-ah-be-er'-to, tah], *a.* Open-winged: applied to birds that have the wings expanded.

aliacán [ah-le-ah-cahn'], *m.* Jaundice. *V.* ICTERICIA.

aliacanado, da [ah-le-ah-cah-nah'-do, dah], *a.* Jaundiced.

aliáceo, a [ah-le-ah'-thay-o, ah], *a.* Alliaceous: like onions or garlic.

aliado, da [ah-le-ah'-do, dah], *a. & m.* 1. Ally. 2. Allied, confederate; leagued. 3. *(Cono Sur)* Toaste *-pp.* of ALIARSE.

aliaga [ah-le-ah'-gah], *f. (Bot.)* Furze, whin.

aliagar [ah-le-ah-gar'], *m.* Place covered with furze.

alianza [ah-le-ahn'-thah], *f.* 1. Alliance, league, coalition, confederacy, consocation. **Alianza Atlántica**, the Atlantic Alliance. 2. Agreement, convention, covenant. 3. An alliance contracted by marriage.

aliar [al-le-ahr'], 1. *va.* To ally, to bring into alliance. 2. *-vr.* To become allied.

aliara [ah-le-ah'-rah], *f.* A goblet made of a cow's horn.

aliaria [ah-le-ah'-re-ah], *f. (Bot.)* Garlic hedge-mustard.

aliarse [ah-le-ar'-say], *vr.* To be allied, leagued, or coalesced.

alias [ah-le-as], *adv. (Lat.)* 1. Otherwise. 2. By another name.

alible [ah-lee'-blay], *a.* Nutritive.

alica [ah-lee'-cah], *f. dim.* A small wing.

alica [ah-le-cah], *f.* Pottage made or corn, wheat, and pulse.

alicaído, da [ah-le-cah-ee'-do, dah], *a.* 1. Drooping. 2. Weak, extenuated. **Sombrero alicaído**, an uncocked hat.

alicántara [ah-le-cahn'-ta-rah], *f.* A kind of viper whose bite is said to be mortal.

alicante [ah-le-cahn'-tay], *m.* A poisonous snake. *V.* ALICANTARA.

alicantina [ah-le-can-tee'-nah], *f. (coll.)* Artifice, stratagem, cunning. **Tiene muchas alicantinas**, he is full of stratagems.

alicantino, na [ah-le-can-tee'-no, nah], *a.* Of Alicante.

alicatado [ah-le-cah-tah'-do], *m.* Work inlaid with Dutch tiles.

alicatar [ah-le-cah-tahr'], *va.* To cut, to shape (azulejo).

alicates [ah-le-cah'-tes], *m. pl.* Finepointed pincers; nippers.

Alicia [ah-le-the-ah], *f.* Alice; "Alicia en el país de las maravillas", "Alice in Wonderland".

aliciente [ah-le-the-en'-tay], *m.* Attraction, incitement, inducement.

alicón [ah-le-cone'], *m.* The name of the seventh heaven to which the angel Azrael carries the souls of the just [Mohammedan].

alicorarse [ah-le-co-rahr-say], *vr. (And)* To get boozed.

alicorear [ah-le-co-ray-ahr'], *va. (CAm.)* To decorate, adorn (adornar).

alicrejo [ah-le-cray-ho], *m. (CAm.)* Spider-like.

alicuanta [ah-lee-coo-ahn'-tah], *a.* **Parte alicuanta**, aliquant number, or odd part of a number.

alíuota [ah-lee'-coo-oh-tah], *a.* **Parte alícuota**, aliquot number, or even part of a number.

alicurco [ah-le-coor-co], *a. (Cono Sur)* Sly, cunning.

alidada [ah-le-dah'-dah], *f.* Geometrical ruler, sight vane, transom; alidade.

alidona [ah-le-do'-nah], *f.* 1. Stone in the intestines of a swallow. 2. Chalk.

alienación [ah-le-ay-nah-the-on'], *f.* Alienation (mente).

alienado, da [ah-le-nay-ah-do], *a.* Insane, mentally ill.

alienante [ah-le-nay-ahn-tay], *a.* Inhuman, dehumanizing.

alienar [ah-le-ay-nar'], *va. (Obs.) V.* ENAJENAR.

alienígena [ah-le-ay-ne-hay-nah], 1. *a.* Foreign; alien; extraterrestrial. 2. *m. & f.* Foreigner; alien.

alienista [ah-le-ay-nees'-tah], *m.* Alienist, specialist in treating disorders of the mind.

aliento [ah-le-en'-to], *m.* 1. Breath. 2. Vigor of mind, spirit, manfulness, courageousness. **Yo fuí allá de un aliento**, I went thither in a whiff, without drawing breath. **(Yo me aliento**, from Alentarse. *V.* ACERTAR.)

alier [ah-le-err'], *m. (Naut.)* 1. A rower. 2. Marine stationed on board a ship.

alifafe [ah-le-fah'-fay], *m.* 1. A callous tumor growing on a horse's hock. 2. *(coll.)* Chronic complaint.

alifar [ah-le-far'], *va. (Prov.)* To polish, to burnish.

alifara [ah-le-fah'-rah], *f. (Prov.)* Colation, luncheon.

alifero, ra [ah-lee'-fay-ro, rah], *a.* Aliferous, bearing wings.

aliforme [ah-le-for'-may], *a.* Aliform, wing-shaped.

aligación [ah-le-gah-the-on'], *f.* Alligation, tying together, **Regla de aligación**, rule of alligation, in arithmetic.

aligador [ah-le-gah-dor'], *m.* Alligator.

aligamiento [ah-le-gah-me-en'-to], *m.* Alligation, the act of binding together.

aligar [ah-le-gar'], *va.* 1. To tie, to unite. 2. *(Met.)* To oblige, to lie down.

aligeramiento [ah-le-hay-rah-me-en'-to], *m.* Alleviation; lightening.

aligerar [ah-le-hay-rar'], *va.* 1. To lighten. 2. *(Met.)* To alleviate, to ease. 3. To hasten. 4. To shorten. **Aligerar un caballo**, to make a horse move light and free. *-vr.* To get lighter. To put on lighter clothes.

aligero, ra [ah-lee'-hay-ro, rah], *a. (Poetic.)* Winged, quick, fast, fleet.

aligustre [ah-le-goos-tray], *m.* Privet (alheña).

alijador, ra [ah-le-hah-dor', dah], *m. & f.* 1. Smuggler. 2. *(Naut.)* One who lightens. **Lanchón alijador**, a lighter, used in unloading ships. 3. He who separates the seed from cotton wool.

alijar [ah-le'-har'], *va.* 1. *(Naut.)* To lighten, 2. To separate cotton from the seed by hand or with a gin. 3. To smuggle.

alijar [ah-le-har'], *m.* Waste, stony ground. To tile.

alijarar [ah-le-hah-rar'], *va.* To divide waste lands for cultivation.

alijarero [ah-le-hah-ray'-ro], *m.* One who takes waste lands to cultivate.

alijares [ah-le-hah'-res], *m. pl.* A royal pleasure resort of Granada.

alijariego, ga [ah-le-hah-re-ay'-go, gah], *a.* Relating to waste lands.

alijo [ah-lee'-ho], *m.* 1. *(Naut.)* Lightening of a ship. **Embarcación de alijo.** *(Naut.)* Lighter. 2. Alleviation. 3. Smuggled goods.

alilaya [ah-le-lah-yah], *f. (And. Carib)* excuse (excusa). 2. *m. & f.* Cunning person, sharp character.

alilla [ah-leel'-lyah], *f.* 1. *(dim.)* A small wing. 2. Fin of a fish.

alimaña [ah-le-mah'-nyah], *f.* Animal which destroys game, as the fox, etc.

alimañero [ah-le-mah-nyay-ro], *m.* Gamekeeper, vermin destroyer.

alimentación [ah-le-men-tah-the-on'], *f.* Act of nourishing. **El coste de la alimentación**, the cost of food. *(fig.)* Feed, supply; **bomba de alimentación**, feed pump. **Alimentación por arrastre** *(Comp.)* tractor feed. **Alimentación por fricción** *(Comp.)*, friction feed.

alimentador [ah-le-mayn-tah-dor], *m. (Tec.)* Feed, feeder. **Alimentador de hojas sueltas** *(Comp.)*, cut sheet feeder.

alimentar [ah-le-men-tar'], *va.* 1. To feed, to nourish, to nurse, to fatten. 2. To supply a person with the necessities of life. 3. *(Tec.)* To feed. **Alimentar una máquina de algo**, to feed something into a machine. *-vr.* To gorge, to feed.

alimentario, alimentista [ah-le-men-tah'-re-o, ah-le-men-tees'-tah], *m. & f.* One who enjoys a maintenance.

alimenticio, cia [ah-le-men-tee'-the-o, ah], *a.* Nutritious.

alimento [ah-le-men'-to], *m.* 1. Nourishment, food, nutriment. 2. *(Met.)* Encouragement, incentive. *-pl.* 1. Allowance given by the heir to his relatives; a pension, alimony, means of living.

alimentoso, sa [ah-le-men-to'-so, sah], *a.* Alimentary, nutritious.

alimón [ah-le-mon], *adv.* In collaboration.

alindado, da [ah-lin-dah-do, dah], *a.* Affectedly nice, or elegant. *-pp.* of ALINDAR.

alindar [ah-lin-dar'], *va.* 1. To mark limits. 2. To embellish, to adorn. **Alindar el ganado**, to drive the cattle to pasture as far as the limits extend. *V.* LINDAR.

alinde [ah-leen'-day], *m. (Obs.)* Quicksilver prepared for mirrors.

alinderar [ah-len-day-rahr], *va. (CAm. Cono Sur)* To mark out the boundaries of.

alineación [ah-le-nay-ah-the-on'], *m.* Laying out a line. **Estar fuera de alineación**, to be out of alignment.

alineado [ah-le-nay-do], *a.* **Está alineado con el partido**, he is in line with the party.

alineamiento [ah-le-nay-ah-me-ayn-to], *m.* Non-alignment.

alinear [ah-le-nay-ar'], *va.* To lay out by line. **Alinearse los soldados**, to fall in. *-vr.* To line up.

aliñador, ra [ah-le-nyah-dor', ah], *m. & f.* 1. One who embellishes. 2. *(Obs.)* Executor, administrator.

aliñar [ah-le-nyar'], *va.* 1. To arrange, to adorn. 2. To dress or cook victuals. 3. To season.

aliño [ah-lee'-nyo], *m.* 1. Dress, ornament, decoration, cleanliness. 2. Preparation for the performance of something. 3. *(Culin.)* Dressing, seasoning.

aliñoso, sa [ah-le-nyo'-so, sah], *a.* Dressed, decked out, decorated.

alioli [ah-le-o'-le], *m. (Prov.)* V. AJIACEITE.

alionar [ah-le-o-nahr], *va. (Cono Sur)* To stir up.

alionin [ah-le-o-neen'], *m.* The blue-feathered duck.

alipata [ah-le-pah'-tah], *m.* A tree of the Philippine Islands whose shade is harmful.

alipede [ah-lee'-pay-day], *a. (Poetic.)* One with winged feet, swift, nimble.

alipedo, da [ah-lee'-pay-do, dah], *a.* Cheiropterous, provided with a wing like membrane between the toes.

alípego [ah-le-pay-go], *m. (CAm.)* Extra, bonus.

aliquebrado, da [ah-le-kay-brah'-do, dah], *a.* 1. Broken-winged. 2. Dejected.

alisado [ah-le-sah-do], *a.* Smooth, polished.

alisador, ra [ah-le-sah-doo', rah], *m. & f.* 1. Polisher, planisher, smoothing-iron; silk stick. 2. An instrument used to make wax candles round and tapering.

alisadura [ah-le-sah-doo'-rah], *f.* Planing, smoothing, or polishing.

alisaduras [ah-le-sah-doo'-ras], *f. pl.* Shavings, cutting of any thing made smooth.

alisar [ah-le-sar'], *va.* To plane, to make smooth, to polish, to mangle.

alisar, *m.* **Aliseda**, *f.* [ah-le-sar', ah-le-say'-dah]. Plantation of alder-trees.

alisios [ah-lee'-se-os], *m. pl.* East winds, in particular those which blow in the tropics. Trade-winds.

alisma [ah-lees'-mah], *f. (Bot.)* Water-plantain.

aliso [ah-lee'-so], *m. (Bot.)* Alder-tree.

alistado, da [ah-lees-tah'-do, dah], *a.* 1. Enlisted, 2. Striped. *-pp.* of ALISTAR.

alistador [ah-lis-tah-dor'], *m.* 1. One who keeps accounts. 2. One who enlists.

alistamiento [ah-lis-tah-me-en'-to], *m.* Enrollment, conscription, levy.

alistar [ah-lis-tar'], *va.* 1. To enlist, to enrol, to recruit. 2. To get ready. 3. *-vr.* To enrol.

aliteración [ah-le-tay-rah-the-on'], *f. V.* PARONOMASIA.

aliterado [ah-le-tay-rah-do], *a.* Alliterative.

alitranca [ah-le-trahn-cah], *f. (And. Cono Sur)* Brake, braking device.

alitúrgico, ca [ah-le-toor'-he-co, cah], *a.* Said of days when there is no liturgy.

aliviadero [ah-le-ve-ah-day-ro], *m.* To overflow channel.

aliviador, ra [ah-le-ve-ah-dor', rah], *m. & f.* 1. An assistant. 2. A spindle that serves to raise or lower the running mill-stone. 3. Comforting.

alivianarse [ah-le-ve-ah-nahr-say], *vr. (Mex.)* To play it cool, to be cool.

aliviar [ah-le-ve-ar'], *va.* 1. To lighten, to help, to loose. 2. *(Met.)* To mitigate, grief, to relieve, to exonerate. 3. To hasten, to move with swiftness. 4. *-vr.* To become more bearable, to gain relief. **¡Que se alivie!**, get better soon!

alivio [ah-lee'-ve-o], *m.* 1. Alleviation, ease. 2. Mitigation of pain; comfort. 3. **De alivio**, awful; horrible.

alizace [ah-le-thah'-thay], *m.* A trench for the foundations of a building.

alizarina [ah-le-thah-ree'-nah], *f.* Alizarine.

aljaba [al-hah'-bah], *f.* 1. A quiver. 2. *(Cono Sur) (Bot.)* Fuchsia.

aljafana [al-hah-fah'-nah], *f. V.* ALJOFAINA.

aljama [ah-hah'-mah], *f.* An assembly of Moors or Jews. A synagogue.

aljamía [al-hah-mee'-ah], *f. (Obs.)* 1. Corrupted Arabic spoken by the Moors. 2. Moorish name of Spanish language. 3. *(Prov.)* Synagogue.

aljamiado [al-hah-me-ah-do], *a.* Text of Spanish written in Arabic characters.

aljarfa, *f.* **aljarfe**, *m.* [al-har'-fah, al-har'-fay], a tarred net with small meshes.

aljecero, ra [al-hay-thay'-ro, rah], *m. & f. (Prov.)* Plasterer.

aljevena [al-hay-vay'-na], *f. (Prov.)* V. ALJOFAINA.

aljez [al-heth'], *m.* Gypsum in its crude state.

aljezar [al-hay-thar'], *m.* Pit of gypsum. *V.* YESAR.

aljezón [al-hay-thone'], *m.* Gypsum, plaster of Paris. *V.* YESON.

aljibe [al-hee'-bay], *m.* A cistern, a reservoir of water. *(Mar.)* A tank-boat for supplying vessels with water.

aljibero [al-hee-bay'-ro], *m.* One who takes care of cisterns.

aljimierado [al-he-me-ay'-rah-do], *a.* Shaved, trimmed.

aljofaina [al-ho-fah'-e-nah], *f.* 1. An earthen jug. 2. A wash-bowl.

aljófar [al-ho'-far], *m.* 1. A misshapen pearl. 2. *(Met. Poet.)* Drops of water or dew.

aljofarado, da [al-ho-fah-rah'-do, dah], *a. (Poetic.)* Full of little drops or pearls. *-pp.* of ALJOFARAR.

aljofarar [al-ho-fah-rar'], *va.* 1. To adorn with pearls. 2. To imitate pearls.

aljofifa [al-ho-fee'-fah], *f.* A mop for floors.

aljofifar [al-ho-fe-far'], *va.* To rub with a cloth, to mop.

aljonje [al-hon'-jay], *m.* V. AJONJE.

aljonjera [al-hon-hay'-rah], *f.* V. AJONJERA.

aljonjero [al-hon-hay'-ro], *a.* V. AJONJERO.

aljonjoli [al-hon-ho-lee'], *m.* V. ALEGRIA.

aljor [al-hor'], *m.* Gypsum in its crude state.

aljorozar [al-ho-ro-thar'], *va.* To level, render smooth; to plaster.

aljorra [al-hor'-rah], *m. (Cuba.)* A very small insect which, carried by the wind, destroys plantations.

allá [al-lyah'], *adv.* 1. There, in that place; thither, or to that place; anciently, in other times. **Allá va con Dios**, *(Naut.)* about ship. **Allá arriba**, up there. **Allá mismo**, right there. **No sabe contar más allá de diez**, she can't count beyond 10. 2. **Allá en 1600**, back in 1600 (tiempo).

allacito [al-lyah-the-to] *adv. (LAm.)* V. ALLA.

allanador [al-lyah-nah-dor'], *m.* 1. Leveller. 2. Gold-beater's paper which contains the beaten gold-leaves. 3. Consent, agreement.

allanamiento [al-lyah-nah-me-en'-to], *m.* 1. Levelling, the act of making even. 2. Consent. 3. *(Met.)* Affability, suavity. 4. Removal (de obstáculos). 5. Pacification. 6. **Allanamiento de morada**, housebreaking.

allanar [al-lyah-nar'], *va.* 1. To level, to make even, to flatten, to reduce to a flat surface. 2. To remove or overcome difficulties. 3. To pacify, to subdue. **Allanar la casa**, to enter a house by force with a search-warrant. **Allanar el camino**, to pave the way for obtaining something. *-vr.* 2. To abide by a law or agreement, to acquiesce, to conform. 3. To fall to ruin.

allegadizo, da [al-lyay-gah-dee'-tho, thah], *a.* Collected without choice.

allegado, da [al-lyay-gah'-do, dah], *a.* Near, conjunct. **Según fuentes allegadas al ministro**, according to sources close to the minister. *-m.* Friend, ally. **Los más allegados y queridos**, those attached to…, those closest to..... *-pp.* of ALLEGAR.

allegador, ra [al-lyay-gah-dor', rah], *m. & f.* One who gathers or collects. **A padre allegador hijo expendedor**, after a gatherer comes a scatterer.

allegamiento [al-lyay-gah-me-en'-to], *m.* 1. Collecting, uniting. 2. Close friendship, union.

allegar [al-lyay-gar'], *va.* 1. To gather, to unite. 2. To draw near. 3. To solicit, to procure. *-vr.* To come near, to approach. **Allegarse a uno**, to go up to somebody. *(fig.)* **Allegarse a una opinión**, to adopt a view.

allende [al-lyen'-day], *adv. (Obs.)* On the other side. **Allende de** v. ÁDEMAS.

allí [al-lyee'], *adv.* 1. There, in that place. **Allí mismo**, in that very place. **De allí**. Thence, from that place. 2. At that moment.

allicito [ah-lye-the-to], *adv. (LAm.)* V. ALLI.

allo [ahl'-lyo], *m. (Amer.)* V. GUACAMAYO.

alloza [al-lyo'-thah], *f.* A green almond. V. ALMENDRUCO.

allozo [al-lyo'-tho], *m. (Bot.)* The wild almond-tree.

alludel [al-lyoo-del'], *m.* Earthen water-pipe. V. ALUDEL.

alma [ahl'-mah], *f.* 1. Soul, the spirit of man. 2. Human being. **No parece ni se ve un alma en la plaza**, there is not a soul in the market-place. 3. That which imparts spirit or vigor. **Un buen general es el alma de un ejército**, a good

general is the soul of an army. 4. The principal part of a thing. *(Mech.)* Attic ridge, scaffolding pole. *(Arm.)* Bore. Core (of rope, of a casting). **Vamos al alma del negocio**, let us come to the main point of the business. 5. *(Naut.)* Body of a mast. **En mi alma**, upon my soul. 6. Ghost. 7. The sounding-post in a fiddle, etc. **Alma mía, mi alma**, my dear, my love. **Alma de cántaro**, an ignorant, insignificant fellow. **El alma me da**, my heart tells me. **Dar el alma**, to expire. **Dar el alma al diablo**, to sacrifice everything to a caprice. **Alma de Dios**, he who is good-natured and simple. **Con el alma y la vida**, with all my heart. **Hablar al alma**, to speak plainly and fearlessly. **Írsele a uno el alma por** or **tras alguna cosa**, to be anxious. 8. (Comparaciones) **Estar como un alma perdida**, to be completely undecided. **Ir como alma que lleva el diablo**, to go like a bat out of hell. 9. *(And.)* Corpse (cadáver). 10. *(Bot.)* Pitch.

almacén [al-mah-then'], *m.* 1. Warehouse. 2. Magazine. 3. Naval arsenal or dock-yard. 4. *(Naut.)* **Almacén de agua**, a water-cask. 5. *(Naut.)* **Almacén de una bomba de agua**, the clamber of a pump.

almacenado, da [al-mah-thay-nah'-do, ah], *a.* Warehoused, stored, bonded.

almacenador [al-mah-thay-nah-dor'], *m.* Warehouseman.

almacenaje [al-mah-thay-nah'-hay], *m.* Warehouse rent, storage.

almacenamiento [al-mah-thay-nah-me-ayn-to], *m. (Comp.)* Storage. **Almacenamiento intermedio** *(Comp.)*, buffer.

almacenar [al-mah-thay-nar'], *va.* To lay up, to hoard; to warehouse. *(fig.)* To keep, to collect.

almacenero [al-mah-thay-nay-ro], *m.* Warehouse-keeper.

almacenista [al-mah-thay-nees'-tah], *m.* The person who sells goods in a warehouse.

almáciga [al-mah'-the-gah], *f.* 1. Mastic, a gum of the Pistacia lentiscus. 2. A nursery of trees or plants.

almacigado, da [al-mah-the-gah'-do], *a.* Composed of or perfumed with mastic.

almacigar [al-mah-the-gar'], *va.* To perfume anything with mastic.

almácigo [al-mah'-the-go], *m.* 1. Collection of plants for transplanting. 2. Mastic-tree. V. LENTISCO.

almaciguero, ra [al-mah-the-gay'-ro, rah], *a.* Relating to mastic.

almadana, ena, ina [al-mah-dah'-nah, day'-nah, de'-nah], *f.* A large hammer.

almadén [al-mah-den'], *m. (Obs.)* Mine or mineral.

almadía [al-mah-dee'-ah], *f.* 1. Canoe used in India. 2. Raft.

almadiado, da [al-mah-de-ah'-do, dah], *a. (Obs.)* Fainting.

almadiarse [al-mah-de-ahr-say], *vr.* To be sick.

almadiero [al-mah-de-ay'-ro], *m.* A raft-pilot.

almadraba [al-mah-drah'-bah], *f.* 1. Tunny-fishery. 2. Net used in the tunny-fishery. 3. *(Obs.)* Brickyard.

almadrabero [al-mah-drah-bay'-ro], *m.* 1. Tunny-fisher. 2. V. TEJERO.

almadraque [al-mah-drah'-kay], *m. (Obs.)* 1. A quilted cushion. 2. A mattress.

almadreña [al-mah-dray'-nyah], *f.* Wooden shoes or sabots. V. ZUECO.

almagacén [al-ma-gah-then'], *m. (Obs.)* Magazine. V. ALMACEN.

almaganeta [al-mah-gah-nay'-tah], *f.* V. ALMADANA or ALMADENA.

almagesto [al-mah-hays'-to], *m.* Almagesta, work on astronomy written by Ptolemy.

almagra [al-mah'-grah], *f.* V. ALMAGRE.

almagral [al-mah-grahl'], *m.* Place abounding in ochre.

almagrar [al-mah-grar'], *va.* 1. To color with red ochre. 2. *(Low.)* To draw blood in a quarrel.

almagre [al-mah'-gray], *m.* Red ochre, red earth, Indian red.

almaizal, almaizar [al-mah-e-thahl', al-mah-e-thar'], *m.* 1. A gauze veil worn by Moors. 2. A belt or sash worn by priests and sub-deacons.

almajar [al-mah-hah'-rah], *f. (Prov.) V.* ALMACIGA and SEMILLERO. A forcing-bed, hotbed.

almajara [al-mah-hah-rah], *f. (Agri.)* Hotbed, forcing frame.

almajo [al-mah'-ho], *m.* A fucus or other seaweed yielding barilla

almaleque [al-mah-lay'-kay], *f. (Obs.)* A long robe resembling a surtout, worn by Moors.

alma mater [ahl'-mah mah'-ter], *f.* Alma mater, one's university or college.

almanac, almanaque [al-mah-nak', al-mah-nah'-kay], *m.* almanac. **Hacer almanques**, *(Met.)* To muse, to be pensive. *(Arab.).*

almanaquero [al-mah-nah-kay-ro], *m.* A maker and vender of almanacs.

almancebe [al-man-thay'-bay], *m. (Obs.)* A fishing-boat used on the river Guadalquivir near Seville.

almandina [al-man-dee'-nah], *f. (Miner.)* The common red variety of garnet; almandine.

almanguena [al-man-gay'-nah], *f. V.* ALMAGRE.

almanta [al-mahn'-tah], *f.* 1. Space between the rows of vines and olive-trees. 2. Ridge between two furrows. **Poner a almanta**, to plant vines irregularly.

almarada [al-mah-rah'-dah], *f.* A triangular poniard. 2. Iron poker with wooden handle. Shoemaker's needle.

almarcha [al-mar'-cha], *f.* A town situated on marshy ground.

almariarse [al-mah-re-ahr-say], *vr. (CAm. Cono Sur)* To be sick. vomit.

alamario [al-mah'-re-o], *m. V.* ARMARIO.

almarjal [al-mar-hahl'], *m.* 1. Plantation of glasswort. 2. Marshy ground where cattle graze.

almarjo [al-mar'-ho], *m. (Bot.)* Glasswort.

almaro [al-mah'-ro], *m. (Bot.)* Common clary.

almarraes [al-mar-rah'-ess], *m. pl.* Instrument (cotton-gin) with which cotton is separated from the seed.

almarraja, almarraza [al-mar-rah'-hah, al-mar-rah'-thah], *f.* A glass vial with holes formerly used in sprinkling water.

almártaga, almártega, almártiga [al-mar'-tah-gah, al-mar'-tay-gah, al-mar'-tee-gah], *f.* 1. Litharge. 2. A sort of halter. 3. Massicot or lead made up with linseed-oil for painting.

almástiga [al-mahs'-te-gah], *f. V.* ALMACIGA. Mastic.

almastigado, da [al-mas-te-gah'-do, dah], *a.* Containing mastic.

almatrero [al-mah-tray'-ro], *m.* One fishing with shad-nets.

almatriche [al-mah-tree'-chay], *m.* A canal for irrigating land. *V.* REGUERA.

almazara [al-mah-thah'-rah], *f. (Prov.)* Oil-mill.

almazarero [al-mah-thah-ray'-ro], *m.* Oil-miller.

almazarrón [al-mah-thar-rone'], *m. V.* ALMAGRE.

almea [al-may'-ah], *f.* 1. A woman who improvises verses among the orientals. 2. The bark of the storax-tree. 3. *(Bot.)* The star-headed water-plantain.

almear [al-may-ar'], *m.* A stack of hay, corn, or straw.

almeja [al-may'-hah], *f.* Mussel, a shell-fish.

almejía [al-may-hee'-ah], *f.* A small cloak used by poor Moors.

almelga [al-mel'-gah], *f. (Agri.) V.* AMELGA.

almena [al-may'-anh], *f.* Each of the merlons of a battlement.

almenado [al-may-nah'-do], *m. V.* ALMENAJE

almenado, da [al-may-nah'-do, dah], *a.* Embattled. *-pp.* of ALMENAR.

almenaje [al-may-nah'-hay], *m.* A series of merlons around a rampart; battlement.

almenar [al-may-nar'], *va.* To crown a rampart or castle with merlons.

almenara [al-may-nah'-rah], *f.* 1. A beacon-light. 2. *(Prov.)* A channel which conveys back the overplus water in irrigation.

almenas [al-may-nahs], *f. & pl.* Battlements, crenellations.

almendra [al-men'-drah], *f.* 1. Kernel, the seed of pulpy fruits. 2. An almond. **Almendra amarga**, bitter almond. 3. (Among jewellers) A diamond of an almond-shape. 4. *(Prov.)* A cocoon which contains but one worm. **almendras de garapiña**, *or* **garapiñadas**, sugar almonds.

almendrada [al-men-drah'-dah], *f.* 1. Almond milk, an emulsion made of almonds and sugar. 2. *(Met.)* **Dar una almendrada**, to say something pleasing or pretty.

almendrado, da [al-men-drah'-do, dah], *a.* Almond-like. **De ojos almendrados**, almond-eyed.

almendrado [al-men-drah'-do], *m.* Macaroon, a kind of sweet biscuit.

almendral [al-men-drahl'], *m.* 1. A plantation of almondtrees. 2. *V.* ALMENDRO.

almendrera [al-men-dray'-rah], *f.* **almendrero** [al-men-dray'-ro], *m. V.* ALMENDRO.

almendrero, ra [al-men-dray'-ro, rah], *a.* **Plato almendrero**, a dish in which almonds are served.

almendrica, illa, ita [al-men-dree'-cah, eel'-layh, ee'-tah], *f. dim.* A small almond.

almendrilla [al-men-dreel'-lyah], *f.* A locksmith's file in the shape of an almond. **Almendrillas**, almondshaped diamond ear-rings.

almendrillo [al-mayn-dre-lyo], *m. (LAm.)* Almond tree.

almendro [al-men'-dro], *m.* Almond-tree.

almendrón [al-men-drone'], *m.* An American (cherry) tree and its fruit.

almendruco [al-men-droo'-co], *m.* A green almond.

almenilla [al-may-neel'-lyah], *f.* 1. *(dim.)* A small merlon. 2. Ancient fringe for dresses.

almería [al-may-re-ah], *f.* Almería.

almeriense [al-may-re-ayn-say], *a.* Of Almería.

almete [al-may'-tay], *m.* 1. A helmet. 2. A soldier wearing a helmet.

almez, almezo [al-meth', al-may'-tho], *m.* The lote-tree, or Indian nettle-tree, hackberry.

almeza [al-may'-thah], *f. (Bot.)* The fruit of the lote-tree.

almiar [al-me-ar'], *m.* Haystack.

almíbar [al-mee-bar'], *m.* Simple syrup. **Almíbares**. Preserved fruit.

almibarado, da [al-me-bah-rah'-do, dah], *a.* 1. *(Met.)* Soft, endearing, applied to word. 2. Effeminate. *-pp.* of ALMIBARAR.

almibarar [al-me-bah-rar'], *va.* 1. To preserve fruit in sugar. 2. *(Met.)* To conciliate with soft words.

almicantáradas [al-me-can-tah'-rah-das], *f. pl. (Astr.)* Circles parallel to the horizon imagined to pass through all the degrees of the meridian, and indicating the altitude and depression of the stars.

almidón [al-me-done'], *m.* Starch; amylum, fecula.

almidonado, da [al-me-do-nah'-do, dah], *a.* 1. Starched. 2. *(Met.)* Dressed with affected nicety; spruce. *-pp.* of ALMIDONAR.

almidonar [al-me-do-nar'], *va.* To starch. **Los prefiero sin almidonar**, I prefer them unstarched.

almijara [al-me-hah'-rah], *f.* Oil-tank (minas, ferrocarril).

almijarero [al-me-hah-ray'-ro], *m.* Porter in the mines of almadén.

almilla [al-meel'-lyah], *f.* 1. An under waistcoat. 2. A short military jacket. 3. Tenon. 4. Pork-chop.

almimbar [al-meem-bar'], *m.* The pulpit of a mosque.

alminar [al-me-nar'], *m.* Minaret, turret of a mosque.

almiranta [al-me-rahn'-tah], *f. (Naut.)* 1. The vice-admiral's ship, the flagship. 2. The admiral's lady.

almirantazgo [al-me-ran-tath'-go], *m. (Naut.)* 1. Board of admiralty. 2. Admiralty court. 3. Admiral's dues. 4. Duty of an admiral.

almirante [al-me-rahn'-tay], *m.* 1. Admiral, a commander of a fleet. **Vicealmirante**, Vice-admiral. 2. *(Prov.)* Swimming-master. 3. A beautiful shell, belonging to the species of rhomb-shells.

almirez [al-me-reth'], *m.* 1. A brass mortar, for kitchen use. 2. A wood engraver's tool of tempered steel.

almirón [al-me-rone'], *m.* Wild chicory.

almizclar [al-mith-clar'], *va.* To perfume with musk.

almizcle [al-mith'-clay], *m.* Musk.
almizcleña [al-mith-clay'-nyah], *f.* (*Bot.*) Musk, grape-hyacinth.
almizcleño, ña [al-mith-clay'-nyo, ah], *a.* Musky.
almizclera [al-mith-clay'-rah], *f.* Muskrat.
almizclero, ra [al-mith-clay'-ro, rah], *a.* V. ALMIZCLEÑO. The musk-deer which yields musk.
almizteca [al-mith-tay'-cah], *f.* (*Obs.*) V. ALMACIDA.
almo, ma [ahl'-mo, mah], *a.* (*Poetic.*) 1. Any source of support or maintenance; creating vivifying. 2. (*Poetic.*) Venerable, holy.
almocadén [al-mo-cah-den'], *m.* The commander of a troop of militia.
almocafrar [al-mo-cah-frar'], *va.* To make holes with a dibble.
almocafre [al-mo-cah-fray], *m.* A gardener's hoe, dibble.
almoceda [al-mo-thay-dah'], *f.* 1. Impost on water for irrigation. 2. Right of taking water for irrigation upon fixed days.
almocrate [al-mo-crha'-tay], *m.* Sal ammoniac.
almocri [al-mo-cree'], *m.* Reader of the Koran in a mosque.
almodí [al-mo-dee'], *m.* V. ALMUDI.
almodrote [al-mo-dro'-tay], *m.* 1. A sauce for the eggplant, composed of oil, garlic, cheese, etc. 2. Hodgepodge, a confused mixture of various ingredients.
almofar [al-mo-far'], *m.* A part of ancient armor reclining on the helmet.
almofía [al-mo-fee'-ah], *f.* V. ALJOFAINA.
almofré [al-mo-fray], *m.* (*LAm.*) Sleeping bag.
almogama [al-mo-gah'-mah], *f.* (*Naut.*) The stern-post of a ship. V. REDEL.
almogárabe, almogávar [al-mo-gah'-rah -bay, al-mo-gah'-var], *m.* An expert forager. **Almogávares,** a sort of light troops in the ancient militia of Spain chiefly employed to make frequent incursions into the Moorish dominions.
almohada [al-mo-ah'-dah], *f.* 1. Pillow or bolster, cushion, pillow-case. 2. (*Naut.*) A piece of timber on which the bowsprit rests. **Consultar con la almohada,** to think about something. **Almohada para arrodillarse,** a cushion to kneel upon.
almohadilla [al-mo-ah-deel'-lyah], *f.* 1. (*dim.*) A small bolster or pillow. 2. Working-case; sewing cushion; the pads of a harness. 3. Stone projecting out of a wall. 4. A callous excrescence on the backs of mules where the saddle is put.
almohadillado, da [al-mo-ah-deel-lyah'-do, dah], 1. *a.* In the form of a cushion. 2. *m.* Ashlar; dressed ashlar.
almohadón [al-mo-ah-done'], *m. aug.* A large cushion.
almohatre, almojatre [al-mo-ah'-tray, al-mo-hah'-tray], *m.* Sal ammoniac.
almohaza [al-mo-ah'-thah], *f.* Curry comb.
almohazado, da [al-mo-ah-thah'-do, dah], *a.* Curried. -*pp.* of ALMOHAZAR.
almohazador [al-mo-ah-thah-dor], *m.* A groom.
almohazar [al-mo-ah-thar'], *va.* To curry with a curry-comb.
almojaba [al-mo-hah'-bah], *f.* (*Obs.*) Smoked tunny-fish.
almojábana [al-mo-hah'-bah-nah], *f.* 1. Cake made of cheese and flour. 2. Hard sauce.
almojarifadgo, almojarifazgo [al-mo-hah-re-fad'-go, al-mo-hah-re-fath'-go], *m.* A duty on imports or exports.
almojarife [al-mo-ha-ree'-fay], *m.* 1. Tax-gatherer for the king. 2. Custom-house officer.
almojaya [al-mo-hah'-yah], *f.* Putlog, a cross-piece used in scaffolding.
almona [al-mo'-nah], *f.* 1. (*Prov.*) Soap manufactory. 2. (*Obs.*) Store-house. 3. Shad-fishery.
almóndiga, almondiguilla [al-mon'-de-gah, al-mon-de-geel'-lyah], *f. va.* ALBONDIGA an ALBONDIGUILLA
almoneda [al-mo-nay'-dah], *f.* An auction.
almonedear [al-mo-nay-day-ar'], *va.* To sell by auction.
almoradux [al-mo-rah-dooks'], *m.* 1. (*Bot.*) Sweet marjoram. 2. V. SANDALO.
almorávide [al-mo-rah-ve-day], *a.* Almoravid.

almorí, almurí [al-mo-ree', al-moo-ree'], *m.* A sweetmeat or cake.
almoronía [al-mo-ro-nee'-ah], *f.* V. ALBORONIA.
almorranas [al-mor-rah'-nas], *f. pl.* (*Med.*) Hemorrhoids or piles.
almorrefa [al-mor-ray'-fah], *f.* A mosaic floor; tiled floor.
almorta [al-mor-tah], *f.* (*Bot.*) Blue vetch.
almorzada [al-mor-thah'-dah], *f.* (*Prov.*) V. ALMUERZA.
almorzado, da [al-mor-thah'-do, dah], *a.* One who has breakfasted. -*pp.* of ALMORZAR.
almorzar [al-mor-tahr'], *va.* To have lunch.
almotacén [al-mo-tah-then'], *m.* 1. Inspector of weights and measures. 2. Clerk of the market.
almotazala [al-mo-tah-thah'-lah], *f.* (*Ant.*) Counterpane for a bed.
almozárabe [al-mo-thah'-rah-bay], *m.* A Christian who lived subject to the Moors.
almud [àl-mood'], *m.* A measure of grain and dry fruit, in some places the twelfth part of a *fanega,* and in some others half a *fanega.* **Almud de tierra,** (*Prov.*) about half an acre of ground.
almudada [al-moo-dah'-dah], *f.* A piece of ground which takes half a *fanega* of grain for sowing it.
almudí, almudín [al-moo-de', al-moo-deen'], *m.* 1. (*Prov.*) V. ALHONDIGA. 2. (*Prov.*) A measure containing six bushels.
almuecín [al-moo-ay-theen'], *m.* Muezzin.
almuédano [al-moo-ay'-dah-no], *m.* Muezzin, one who calls to prayer from the minaret.
almuérdago [al-moo-er'-dah-go], *m.* Bird-lime. V. MUERDAGO.
almuerza [al-moo-er'-thah], *f.* A double-handful. (**Yo almuerzo, yo almuerce,** from **Almorzar.** V. ACORDAR).
almuerzo [al-moo-er'-tho], *m.* 1. Breakfast, lunch. 2. Set of dishes, etc, for breakfast; breakfast cover.
alnado, da [al-nah'-do, dah], *m. & f.* A step-child. V. HIJASTRO.
aló [ah-lo], *interj.* (*LAm.*) Hullo?
alobadado, da [ah-lo-bah-dah'-do, dah], *a.* 1. Bit by a wolf. 2. Laboring under morbid swellings.
alobunadillo, lla [ah-lo-boo-nah-deel'-lyo, lyah], *a.* Resembling a wolf somewhat.
alobunadado, da [ah-lo-boo-nah'-do, dah], *a.* Resembling a wolf in color.
alocadamente [ah-lo-cah-dah-men'-tay], *adv.* Rashly, inconsiderately.
alocado, da [ah-lo-cah'-do, dah], *a.* 1. Half-witted, foolish. 2. Wild.
alocar [ah-lo-cahr'], *va.* To drive crazy. -*vr.* To go crazy.
alocución [ah-lo-coo-the-on'], *f.* 1. Allocution. 2. Address, speech, harangue. 3. Address of the Pope to the cardinals.
alodial [ah-lo-de-ahl'], *a.* (*Law.*) Allodial, free, exempt.
alodio [ah-lo'-de-o], *m.* Allodium, a possession not held by tenure of a superior lord.
áloe [ah'-lo-ay], *m.* 1. (*Bot.*) Aloes-tree. 2. Aloes.
aloético, ca [ah-lo-ay'-te-co, cah], *a.* Aloetic, any drug containing aloes.
aloina [ah-lo-ee'-nah], *f.* Aloin, active principle of aloes.
aloja [ah-lo'-hah], *f.* A beverage made of water, honey, and spice; metheglin. In South America, a fermented liquor from carob-beans.
alojado, a [ah-lo-hah-do], *m. & f.* (*LAm.*) Guest, lodger.
alojamiento [ah-lo-hah-me-en'-to], *m.* 1. Lodging. 2. (*Naut.*) Steerage.
alojar [ah-lo-har'], *va.* 1. To lodge, to let lodgings. 2. To dwell, to reside. -*vr.* To station troops, to put up at. **La bala se alojó en el pulmón,** the bullet lodged in the lung.
alojería [ah-lo-hay-ree'-ah], *f.* A place where metheglin is prepared and sold.
alojero [ah-lo-hay'-ro], *m.* 1. One who prepares or sells metheglin.

alomado, da [ah-lo-mah'-do, dah], *a.* Having a curved back: applied to horses. -*pp.* of ALOMAR.

alomar [ah-lo-mar'], *va.* 1. To distribute equally the load on a horse. 2. To cover with a seed-plough. -*vr.* To grow strong and vigorous.

alón [ah-lone'], *m.* The plucked wing of any bird.

alondra [ah-lon'-drah], 1. *f. (Orn.)* A lark (pájaro).

alongadero [ah-lon-gah-day'-ro], *a.* Dilatory. V. LARGA.

alongamiento [ah-lon-gah-me-en'-to], *m.* Delay.

alongar [ah-lon-gar'], *va.* To enlarge, to extend. -*vr.* To move away.

alónimo [ah-lo'-ne-mo], *m.* Allonymous, published under an assumed name.

alópata [ah-lo'-pah-tah], *m.* Allopath.

alopatía [ah-lo-pah-tee'-ah], *f.* Allopathy.

alopático, ca [ah-lo-pah'-te-co, cah], *a.* Allopathic.

alopecia [ah-lo-pay'-the-ah], *f. (Med.)* Alopecia, loss of the hair; baldness.

alopiado, da [ah-lo-pe-ah-do, dah], *a.* Composed of opium.

aloque [ah-l'o-kay], *a.* Applied to clear white wine, or a mixture of red and white.

aloquín [ah-lo-keen'], *m.* A stone wall of the inclosure where wax is bleached.

alosa [ah-lo'-sah], *f.* Shad.

alosna [ah-los'-nah], *f. (Bot. Prov.)* Wormwood.

alotar [ah-lo-tar'], *va. (Naut.)* V. ARRIZAR. **Alotar las anclas.** *(Naut.)* 1. To stow the anchors. 2. To sell fish by auction.

alpaca [al-pah'-cah], or **alpaga** [al-pah'-gah], *f.* 1. Alpaca and *Llama*, a ruminant of South America, esteemed for the fineness of its wool. 2. A fabric made from the wool of this animal. 3. An alloy of copper, zinc, and nickel, called white metal.

alpañata [al-pah-nyah'-tah], *f.* A piece of chamois-skin which potters use to smooth their work.

alpargata, *f.* **alpargate,** *m.* [al-pargah'-tah, al-par-gah'-tay], A sort of shoes or sandals made of hemp. **Compañía de la alpargata,** *(Prov.)* a set of ragamuffins.

alpargatado, da [al-par-gah-tah'-do, dah], *a.* Wearing hempen sandals. -*pp.* of ALPARGATAR.

alpargatar [al-par-gah-tar'], *va.* To make hempen sandals.

alpargatería [al-par-gah-tay-ree'-ah], *f.* A manufactory of hempen sandals, sandal shop.

alpargatero [al-par-gah-tay'-ro], *m.* A manufacturer of hempen sandals.

alpargatilla [al-par-gah-teel'-lyah], *f.* 1. *dim.* A small hempen sandal. 2. *(Met.)* A crafty, designing fellow.

alpechín [al-pay-cheen'], *m.* Water which oozes from a heap of olives.

alpende [al-pen'-day], *m.* Shed to keep mining implements in.

Alpes [al-pays], *m. & pl.* Alps.

alpestre, alpino, na [al-pes'-tray, al-pee'-no, nah], *a.* Alpine.

alpícola [al-pee'-co-lah], *a.* Growing in the Alps.

alpicoz [al-pe-coth'], *m. (Prov.)* V. ALFICOZ.

alpinismo [al-pe-nees'-mo], *m.* Alpinism, climbing the Alps.

alpinista [al-pe-nees'-tah], *m. & f.* Alpinist, climber.

alpino [al-pe-no], *a.* Alpine.

alpiste [al-pees'-tay], *m.* Canary-seed.

alpistela, alpistera [al-pis-tay'-lah, al-pis-tay'-rah], *f.* A cake made of flour, eggs, sesamum, and honey.

alpistero [al-pis-tay'-ro], *m.* A sieve for canary-seed.

alquequenje [al-kay-kane'-hay], *m.* Bardadoes winter-cherry, used as diuretic.

alquería [al-kay-ree'-ah], *f.* A farm-house, generally a farm with a house at a distance from neighbors.

alquermes [al-ker'-mes], *m.* 1. A compound cordial, of exciting character, in which the kermes is a principal ingredient. 2. A celebrated confection.

alquerque [al-ker'-kay], *m.* Place in oil-mills for laying the bruised olives.

alquez [al-keth'], *m.* A wine measure containing 12 cántaras.

alquibla [al-kee'-blah], *f.* The point towards the Mecca, where Mohammedans direct their eyes when praying.

alquicel, alquicer [al-ke-thel', al-ke-theer'], *m.* 1. Moorish garment resembling a cloak. 2. Covers for benches, tables, etc.

alquifol [al-ke-fol'], *m. (Miner.)* Alquifou, or potter's ore: lead ore.

alquiladizo, za [al-ke-lah-de-tho, thah], *a.* For rent, for hire, that can be rented.

alquilado, a [al-ke-lah-do, dah], *m. & f. (Carib.)* Tenant.

alquilamiento [al-ke-lah-me-en'-to], *m.* The act of hiring or letting.

alquilar [al-ke-lar'], *va.* To let, to hire, to rent, to fee. -*vr.* To serve for wages. **¡Se alquila!**, to let; for rent.

alquiler [al-ke-lerr'], *m.* 1. Wages or hire. 2. The act of hiring or letting. **Alquiler de una casa,** house-rent.

alquilón, na [al-ke-lone', nah] *a.* That which can be let or hired.

alquilona [al-ke-lo'-nah], *f.* A woman hired occasionally for odd work.

alquimia [al-kee'-me-ah], *f.* Alchemy.

alquímico, ca [al-kee'-me-co, cah], *a.* Relating to alchemy.

alquimila [al-ke-mee'-lah], *f. (Bot.)* Ladies' mantle. Alchemilla.

alquimista [al-ke-mees'-tah], *m.* Alchemist.

alquinal [al-ke-nahl'], *m.* A veil or head-dress for women.

alquitara [al-ke-tah'-rah], *f. V.* ALAMBIQUE.

alquitarar [al-ke-tah-rar'], *va.* To distil, to let fall in drops.

alquitira [al-ke-tee'-rah], *f.* Tragacanth, a gum.

alquitrán [al-ke-trahn'], *m.* 1. Tar or liquid pitch. 2. *(Naut.)* Stuff for paying a ship's bottom, composed of pitch, grease, resin, and oil: it is also used as a combustible matter. *(Met.)* **Es un alquitrán,** he is a passionate man.

alquitranado [al-ke-trah-nah'-do], *m. (Naut.)* Tarpaulin, a tarred hempen cloth. **Cabos alquitranados,** *(Naut.)* black or tarred cordage. **Alquitrado, da,** *pp.* of ALQUITRANAR.

alquitranar [al-ke-trah-nar'], *va.* To tar.

alrededor [al-ray-day-dor'], 1. *adv.* Around. **Todo alrededor,** all around. 2. *prep.* **Alrededor de,** around; about. **Mirar alrededor de sí,** to look about one. 3. *(fig.)* About, in the region of.

alrededores [al-ray-day-do'-res], *m. pl.* Environs.

alrota [al-ro'-tah], *f.* A very coarse sort of tow. V. ARLOTA.

alsacia [al-sah-thee-ah], *f.* Alsace.

alsaciano, na [al-sah-the-ah'-no, nah], *a.* Alsatian: of Alsace or Elsass.

alt. *abr.* de **altura.**

alta [ahl'-tah], *f.* 1. *(Mil.)* Orders to active duty. 2. Discharge (de un hospital). 3. New member. **Dar de alta,** to discharge, to release. **Darse de alta,** to join, to become a member. **Ser alta,** *(Mil.)* to go on active duty. **Alta densidad** (Inform), high density.

altabaque [al-tah-bah'-kay], *m.* Wicker basket.

altabaquillo [al-tah-bah-keel'-lyo], *m. (Bot.)* Field bindweed.

alta fidelidad [ahl'-tah fe-day-le-dadh'], *f.* High fidelity.

altaico, ca [al-tah'-e-co, cah], *a.* Altaic.

altamente [al-tah-men'-tay], *adv.* Highly, extremely, exceedingly.

altamía [al-tah-mee'-ah], *f. (Obs.)* A deep plate.

altamisa [al-tah-mee'-sah], *f. V:* ARTEMISA.

altanería [al-tah-nay-ree'-ah], *f.* 1. *(Lit. us.)* The towering flight of some birds. 2. Hawking.3. *(Met.)* Haughtiness, loftiness, contemptuousness.

altanero, ra [al-tah-nay'-ro, rah], *a.* 1. Soaring, towering. 2. *(Met.)* Haughty, arrogant, proud.

altar [al-tar'], *m.* 1. Altar, the table in Christian churches where the mass is celebrated. **Altar mayor,** high altar. **Llevar a una mujer al altar,** to lead a woman to the altar. 2. *(Astr.)* A southern constellation. 3. **Poner a una en un altar,** to put someone on a pedestal.

altarero [al-tah-ray'-ro], *m.* One who adorns altars for great festivals.

altaricón [al-tah-re-con], *a.* Big-built, large.

altavoz [al-tah-voth'], *m.* Loudspeaker. **Altavoz para sonidos agudos**, tweeter. **Altavoz para sonidos graves**, woofer.

altea [al-tay'-ah], *f. (Bot.)* Common mallow, marsh-mallow.

altear [al-tay-ar'], 1. *vn. (Naut.)* To rise above; said of a portion of a coast which rises beyond what adjoint it. 2. *va. (Cono Sur)* To order to stop.

al-tec *abr.* de **alta tecnología**, high technology.

alterabilidad [al-tay-rah-be-le-dahd'], *f.* Changeableness, mutability.

alterable [al-tay-rah-blay], *a.* That may be changed, alterable.

alteración [al-tay-rah-the-on'], *f.* 1. Alteration, mutation. 2. Unevenness of the pulse. **Alteración digestiva**, digestive upset. 3. Strong emotion of anger or other passion. 4. Disturbances, tumult, commotion. 5. Quarrel, dispute (disputa)

alterado, da [al-tay-rah'-do, dah], *a.* Alterative, agitated, disturbed; angry. **Caldo alterado**, medicated or alterative broth. *-pp.* of ALTERAR.

alterador, ra [al-tay-rah-dor, rah], *m. & f.* Alterer, one who alters.

alterante [al-tay-rahn'-tay], *pa. (Med.)* Alterative.

alterar [al-tay-rar], *va.* 1. To alter, to change. 2. To disturb, to stir up. **Alterar la moneda**, to raise or lower the value of coin. *-vr.* 1. To fling, alter, change. 2. To go bad, go off (comida). 3. To get upset, become agitated, become disturbed (enfadarse).

alterativo, va [al-tay-rah-tee'-vo, vah], *a.* Alterative.

altercación, *f.* **altercado**, *m.* [al-ter-cah-the-on', al-ter-cah'-do], a controversy; contest, strife, quarrel.

altercado [al-ter-cah'-do], *m.* Altercation, wrangle, quarrel.

altercador, ra [al-ter-cah-dor'-rah], *m. & f.* One who argues obstinately.

altercar [al-ter-car'], *va.* To contend, to dispute obstinately, to debate, to quarrel, to bicker, to expostulate.

alteridad [al-tay-re-dahd], *f.* Otherness.

alternación [al-ter-nah-the-on'], *f.* Alternation, reciprocate succession.

alternadamente [al-ter-nah-dah-men'-tay], *adv.* Alternately. V. ALTERNATIVAMENTE.

alternado [al-tayr-nah-do], *a.* Alternate.

alternador [al-tayr-nah-dor], *m. (Elec.)* Alternador.

alternancia [al-tayr-nahn-the-ah], *f.* Alternation; *(Pol.)* **Alternancia en el poder**, taking turns in office.

alternante [al-tayr-nan-tay], *a.* Alternating.

alternar [al-ter-nar'], *va.* 1. To alternate, to perform by turns, to change one for another. **Alternar a los mandos**, to take turns at the controls. 2. To mix, take part in the social round, socialize (participar). **Participar con un grupo**, to mix with a group. *-vn.* To succeed reciprocally. **Los gustos y los pesares alternan**, pleasures and sorrows alternate.

alternativa [al-ter-nah-tee'-vah], *f.* 1. Alternative, choice of two things. 2. The right of archbishops and bishops to dispose of prebends and benefices alternately with the Pope in their dioceses. 3. Alternation (Sucesión); shift work (trabajo). 4. Ceremony by which a novice becomes a fully-qualified bullfighter.

alternativamente [al-ter-nah-te-vah-men'-tay], *adv.* Alternatively.

alternativo, va [al-ter-nah-tee'-vo, vah], *a.* Alternate. *-m.* Rotation of crops.

alterne [al-tayr-nay], 1. *m.* Mixing, socializing. **Club de alterne**, singles club. 2. *f.* Hostess.

alterno, na [al-ter'-no, nah], *a. (Poetic.)* Alternate. *(Bot.)* Alternate.

alteza [al-tay'-thah], *f.* 1. Elevation sublimity. 2. Highness, a title given to the board of Castle, exchequer, etc. 3. *(Obs.)* Height.

altibajo [al-te-bah'-ho], *m.* 1. A downright blow in fencing. 2. *(Obs.)* A kind of lowered velvet. *-pl.* 1. Uneven ground. 2. *(Met.)* vicissitudes, the ups and downs in life.

altillo, lla [al-teel'-lyo, lyah], *a. dim.* Somewhat high.

altillo [al-teel'-lyo], *m. dim.* A hillock.

altilocuencia [al-te-lo-coo-en'-the-ah], *f.* Grandiloquence, high-sounding words.

altilocuente [al-te-lo-coo-en'-tay], *a. (Poetic.)* Pompous in language, grandiloquent.

altillo [al-te-lyo], *m.* 1. *(Geog.)* Small hill. 2. *(LAm.)* Attic (desván).

altimetría [al-te-may-tree'-ah], *f.* The art of taking or measuring altitudes or heights.

altímetro [al-tee'-may-tro], *m. (Naut., Aer.)* Altimeter.

altiplanicie [al-te-plah-nee'-the-ay], *f.* Highland.

altiplano [al-te-plah-no], *m.* High plateau; *(Geog. Bol.)* Altiplano.

altísimo, ma [al-tee'-se-mo, mah], *a. aug.* Extremely lofty.

altísimo [al-tee'-se-mo], *m.* The Most High, God.

altisonancia [al-te-so-nahn-the-ah], *f.* High-flown style; high-sounding nature.

altisonante, altísono, na [al-te-so-nahn'-tay, al-tee'-so-no, nah], *a.* highsounding.

altitonante [al-te-to-nahn'-tay], *a. (Poetic.)* Thundering.

altitud [al-te-tood'], *f. (Geog.)* V. ALTURA. Elevation or altitude above the level of the ocean. **Altitud absoluta**, *(Aer.)* absolute altitude.

altivamente [al-te-vah-men'-tay], *adv.* Highly, loftily, lordly.

altivarse [al-te-vahr-say], *vr.* To give oneself airs.

altivez [al-te-veth'], *f.* Haughtiness, arrogance, pride, lordliness.

altivo, va [al-tee'-vo, vah], *a.* 1. Haughty, proud, lofty, lordlike. 2. High, high-minded, consequential. 3. Overbearing.

alto, ta [ahl'-to, tah], *a.* 1. High, elevated; alto (cosa) **Es una montaña alta**, it is a high mountain. **Alta mar**, *(Naut.)* High seas. 2. Tall (persona). **Es un hombre alto**, he's a tall man. 3. *(Met.)* Arduous, difficult. 4. *(Met.)* Eminent. 5. Enormous. 6. Deep. 7. Late: applied to movable feasts. **Altas por abril son las pascuas**, Easter falls late in April.

alto [ahl'-to], *m.* 1. Height. 2. Story. **Casa de tres altos**, a house three stories high. 3. *(Naut.)* Depth or height of a ship. 4. High ground. 5. *(Mil.)* Halt; command to stop; and a place or time or fest. 6. *(Mus.)* Notes put over the bass. Contralto (voice). **Alto, or tenor violin**; viola. 7. **No hacer alto**, not to mind, not to observe. **Pasar por alto**, to overlook.

alto [ahl'-to], *int.* 1. **Alto ahí**, stop there. 2. **Alto de aquí**, move off.

alto [ahl'-to], *adv.* 1. Loud. 2. High. **De lo alto**, from above. 3. **Se me pasó por alto**, I forgot. 4. **Por alto**, by stealth; by particular favor. **Metió los géneros por alto**, he smuggled the goods.

altoparlante [al-to-par-lahn'-tay], *m.* Loudspeaker.

altorrelieve [al-to-ray-le-ay-vay], *m.* High relief.

altozanero [al-to-thah-nay-ro], *m. (And)* Porter.

altozano [al-to-thah'-no], *m.* 1. A height or hill. 2. *(And. Carib.)* Cathedral forecourt, church.

altramuz [al-trah-mooth'], *m. (Bot.)* Lupine, Lupinus. **Altramuces**, Lupines which are mixed with ivory beads, and used as black balls in giving votes in cathedral chapters, especially in Castle.

altruísmo [al-troo-ees'-mo], *m.* Altruism, unselfishness.

altura [al-too'-rah], *f.* 1. Height, loftiness. 2. One of the three dimensions of a solid body. 3. Summit of mountains. 4. Altitude, the elevation of the pole or of any of the heavenly bodies. *(Naut.)* the latitude. 5. *(Met.)* Exaltation of spirits. **Estar en grande altura**, to be raised to a high degree of dignity, favor, or fortune. **Alturas**, the heavens. **Dios de las alturas**, God, the Lord of the heavens. 6. *(fig.)* Sublimity, loftiness. **Ha sido un partido de gran altura**, it has been a match of real class.

ALU (Unidad Aritmética Lógica) [ah-loo],. *(Comp.)* ALU (Arithmetic Logical Unit). **ALU vectorial** *(Comp.)*, vectorial ALU.

aluar, or **tomar por la lúa**, *vn. (Naut.)* To bring under the lee.

alubia [ah loo' be ah], *f.* (Bot.) French bean. *V.* JUDIA.

aluciar [ah loo the ar'], *va.* To polish an article.

alucinación, *f.* **alucinamiento**, *m.* [ah loo the nab the on' ah loo the nah me en' to]. Hallucination.

alucinadamente [ah loo the nah dah men tay], *adv.* Erroneously.

alucinado [ah-loo-the-nah-do], *a.* Deluded, suffering hallucinations.

alucinador [ah-loo-the-nah-dor], *a.* Hallucination, delusion.

alucinante [ah-loo-the-nahn-tay], 1. *a. (Med.)* Hallucinatory. *(Esp. fig.)* Attractive, beguiling; mysterious. *(Esp.)* Absurd; fantastic (absurdo).

alucinar [ah loo the nar'], *va.* To deceive, to lend into error, to fascinate, to delude. -*vr.* To be hallucinated, be decluded.

alucinógeno [ah-loo-the-no-hay-no], *a.* Hallucinogenic (droga).

alucón [ah loo-cone'], *m.* The barn owl. Strix aluco.

alud [ah-lood'] *m.* Avalanche.

aluda [ah-loo'-dah], *f. (Ent.)* Winged ant or emmet. Formica.

aludel [ah-loo-del'], *m. (Chem.)* Subliming pots used in chemistry.

aludir [ah-loo-deer'], *vn.* To allude, to refer to.

aludo, da [ah-loo'-do, dah], *a.* Winged; large winged.

aluengar [ah-loo-en-gar'], *va. V.* ALONGAR.

aluego [ah-loo-ay-go], *adv.* Etc. *(LAm.)* = luego.

alueñe [ah-loo-ay'-nyay], *adv. (Obs.)* Far off.

alujado, *a. (CAm. Mex.)* Bright, shining.

alumbrado, da [ah-loom-brah'-do,-dah], *a.* 1. Aluminous, relating to Alum. **Alumbrado eléctrico**, electring lighting. 2. *(coll.)* Flustered with wine. -*pp.* of ALUMBRAR.

alumbrado [ah-loom-brah'-do], *m.* Illumination. **Alumbrado fluorescente**, fluorescent lighting. **Luz fluorescente**, fluorescent light.

alumbrador, ra [ah-loom-brah-dor', rah], *m. & f.* One who gives light, link boy.

alumbramiento [ah loom brah me en'-to], *m.* 1. The act of supplying with light. 2. *(Obs.)* Illusion, deceit, false appearance. 3. *(Met.)* Child birth. *V.* PARTO. **Alumbramiento bueno, or feliz**, a happy child birth.

alumbrar [ah loom brar'], *va.* 1. To light, to supply with light. 2. *(Obs.)* To restore sight to the blind. 3. To enlighten, to instruct, to adorn with knowledge. 4. Among dyers, to dip cloth into alum-water. 6. To dig about the roots of vines. 6. To bring forth. **Dios alumbre a Vd. con bien**, or **Dios dé a Vd. feliz parto**, God grant you a safe delivery. -*vr. (coll.)* To be intoxicated, to get drunk.

alumbre [ah loom' bray], *m.* Alum, a mineral salt. **Alumbre catino**, a kind of alkali drawn from the plant glass wort. **Alumbre de rasuras**, Salt of tartar. **Alumbre sucarino or zucarino**, alum and the white of an egg formed into a paste: alum-whey.

alumbrera [ah-loom-bray'-rahl, *f.* Alum mine. **Alumbrera artificial**, alum-works.

alúmina [ah-loo'-me-nah], *f. (Chem.)* Alumina or alumine.

aluminado, da [ah-loo-me-nah'-do, dah], *a. (Chem.)* Mixed with alum.

aluminio [ah-loo-mee'-ne-o], *m.* Aluminium or aluminum, one of the metallic elements.

aluminoso, sa [ah-loo-mi-no'-so, sah], *a.* Aluminous, consisting of alum.

alumnado [ah-loom-nah-do], *m.* Pupils (personas). *(Univ.)* Students.

alumno, na [ah-loom'-no, nahl, *m. & f.* Foster-child; disciple, pupil.

alunado, da [ah-loo-nah'-do, dah], *a.* 1. Insane, lunatic. 2. Spasmodic. 3. Spoiled, tainted.

alunarse [ah-loo-nahr-say], *vr. (CAm.)* To get saddlesore (horse).

alunita [ah-loo-nee'-tah], *f.* Alunite.

alunizaje [ah-loo-ne-thah' hay], *m.* Landing on the moon.

alunizar [ah-loo-ne-thar'], *vn.* To land on the moon.

alusión [ah-loo-se-on'], *f.* Allusion, reference.

alusivamente [ah-loo-se-vah-men'-tay,], *adv.* Allusively.

alusivo, va [ah-loo-see'-vo, vah], *a.* Allusive, hinting at.

alustrar [ah-loos-trar'], *va.* To give lustre to anything.

alutación [ah-loo-tah-the on'], *f. (Miner.)* Stratum of grains of gold, found in some mines.

aluvial [ah-loo-ve-ahl'], *a.* Alluvial.

aluvión [ah-loo-ve-on'], *f.* Alluvion, wash. *(fig.)* Flood. **Aluvión de improperios**, shower of insults.

alveario [al-vay-ah'-re-o], *m. (Anat.)* The inward cavity of the ear.

álveo [ahl'-vay-o], *m.* 1. Bed of a river. 2. Source of a river.

alveolar [al-vay-o-lar'], *a.* Alveolar, relating to the alveolus. **Alvéolo** [al vay' o lo], *m.* 1. Alveolus or socket of the teeth. 2. *(Bot.)* Alveolus, the cavity in which the seeds of plants are lodged.

alveolo [al-vay-o-lo], *m. (Anat.)* alveolus; socket.

alverja, alerjana [al ver' hah, al ver hah' nah], *f. (Bot.)* Common vetch or tare.

alverjas [al-ver'-hahs], *f. pl. (Bot.) (Sp. Amer.)* Peas.

alverjilla [al-vayr-he-lya], *f.* Sweet pea.

alvidriar [al-ve-dree-ar'], *va. (Prov.)* To glaze earthenware.

alvino, na [al-vee'-no, nah], *a. (Med.)* Alvine, relating to the bowels.

alvitana [al-ve-tah'-nah], *f.* A wind break (hedge or fence).

alza [ahl'-thah], *f.* 1. A piece of leather put round the last to make a shoe wider. 2. An instrument used in rope walks to hold up the rope yarn in the act of spinning it. 8. Advance in the price of anything. 4. *(Typ.)* Overlay, frisket sheet. **Alza y baja**, or **caída de los fondos públicos**, the rise and fall of public stocks.

alzacuello [al-thah-coo-ayl'-lyo], *m.* A black collar bound with linen, which clergymen wear.

alzada [al-thah'-dah], *f.* 1. Height, stature; of horses. 2. A town, village, etc. situated on an eminence. 3. Appeal. **Juez de alzadas**, a judge in appeal causes.

alzadamente [al-thah-dah-men'-tay], *adv.* Wholesale.

alzado [al thah' do], *m.* 1. A plan of a building which shows its front and elevation. 2. A fraudulent bankrupt. *(LAm.)* Vain, stuck-up (soberbio). 3. **Estar alzado**, *(Cono Sur)* to be on heat. **Alzados**, spare stores. **Alzado, da**, *pp.* of ALZAR. -*a.* Fraudulent.

alzadura [al-thah-doo'-rah], *f.* Elevation.

alzamiento [at-thah-me-en'-to], *m.* 1. The act of lifting or raising up. 2. Bidding a higher price at an auction. 3. *(Pol.)* Rising, revolt.

alzapaño [al-thah-pah'-nyo], *m.* A hook to hold up a curtain.

alzapié [al-thah-pe-ay'l, *m.* A foot stool.

alzaprima [al-thah-pree'-mah], *f.* 1. A lever. 2. *(Naut.)* Heaver. 3. *(Mech.)* Fulcrum. **Dar alzaprima**, *(Met.)* to deceive, to ruin by artifice.

alzaprimar [al-thah-pre-mar'], *va.* 1. To raise by means of a lever. 2. *(Naut.)* To move with handspikes. 3. To incite, spur on.

alzapuertas [al-thah-poo-er'-tas], *m.* A player who acts only the part of dumb servant.

alzar [al-thar'], ra. 1. To raise, to lift up, to heave, to erect, to construct. 2. To repeal a decree of excommunication; to recall from banishment. 3. To carry off. 4. To hide, to lock up. 5. To deal cards; to gather up and arrange in order the printed sheets for the binder. 6. To elevate the host, in mass. 7. *(Naut.)* To heave. **Alzar cabeza**, to recover from a calamity or disease. **Alzar de codo or el codo**, to drink much wine or liquor. **Alzar de obra**, to cease working. **Alzar de eras**, to finish the harvesting of grain in the farm-yards. **Alzar figura**, to assume an air of importance. **Alzar el dedo**, to raise the forefinger in asseveration or affirmation of anything. **Alzar**

la casa, to quit a house, to move out of it. **Alzar velas**, *(Naut.)* to set the sails. *(Met.)* To move off. *-vr.* 1. To rise in rebellion. 2. To rise from kneeling. 3. To make a fraudulent bankrupt. 4. To appeal. **Alzarse con el dinero**, to run away with the money. **Alzarse a mayores**, to be petulant. **Alzarse con algo**. 5. *(And.)* To get drunk (emborracharse). 6. *(LAm.)* To run away (animal). *V.* APROPIARSE.

alzatirantes [al-thah-te-rahn'-tes], *m. pl.* Straps attached to the harness of a horse to suspend the traces.

alzaválvulas [al-thah-val-voo-lahs], *m.* Invar *(Mech.)* tappet.

alzo [al-tho], *m. (CAm.)* Theft.

A.M. *abr.* de **amplitud.**

a.m. *(LAm.) abr.* de **ante meridiem.**

ama [ah'-mah], *f.* 1. A mistress of the house. **El ama de casa**, the lady or mistress of the house. **Ama de llaves** or **de gobierno**, house-keeper. **Ama de leche**, wet-nurse. 2. Foster mother (de niño).

amabilidad [ah-mah-be-le-dahd'], *f.* Amiability, affability, loveliness. **Tuvo la amabilidad de**, he was good enough to.

amable [ah-mah'-blay], *a.* Amiable, pleasing, lovely. **Muy amable**, thanks very much. **Si es tan amable**, if you would be so kind.

amablemente [ah-mah-blay-men'-tay], *adv.* Amiably, lovely.

amacena [ah-mah-thay'-nah], *f. (Bot.)* A damson plum.

amaceno, na [ah-mah-thay'-no, nah], *a.* Damascene.

amachambrarse [ah-mah-cham-brahr-say], *vr. (Cono Sur)* etc. *V.* AMACHINARSE.

amacharse [ah-mah-chahr-say], *vr. (LAm.)* To dig one's heels in, to refuse to be moved.

amachinarse [ah-mah-che-nahr-say], *vr. (LAm.)* To live with somebody.

amacho [ah-mah-cho], *a. (CAm. Cono Sur)* Strong, vigorous (fuerte).

amacollarse [ah-mah-col-lyar'-say], *vr.* To throw out shoots.

amacrático, ca [ah-ma-crah'-te-co, cah], *a.* Amacratic, said of a photographic lens which brings all the chemical rays to one focus.

amadamado, da [ah-mah-dah-mah'-do, dah], *a.* Effeminate, womanish, frivolous.

amado, da [ah-mah-do, dah], *a.* Dear, beloved.

amador, ra [ah-mah-dor', rah], *m. & f.* A lover, a sweetheart, suitor.

amadriada [ah-mah-dree'-ah-dah], *f.* Hamadryad, a wood nymph.

amadrigar [ah-mah-dre-gar'], *va.* To receive well, especially one not deserving. *-vr.* 1. To burrow. 2. *(Met.)* to live retired, to decline all intercourse with the world.

amadrinar [ah-mah-dre-nar'], *va.* 1. To couple, to yoke together. 2. *(Naut.)* To join one thing to another. 3. To act as godmother or bridesmaid.

amadroñado, da [ah-mah-dro-nyah'-do, dah], *a.* Resembling **madroños**, the fruit of the madroño-tree. **Rosario amadroñado**, rosary, the beads of which resemble madroños.

amaestrado, da [ah-mah-es-trah'-do, dah], *a.* 1. Taught, tutored. **Caballo amaestrado**, horse completely broken in. 2. *(Obs.)* rightfully contrived. *-pp.* of AMAESTRAR.

amaestradura [ah-mah-es-trah-doo'-rah], *f.* 1. Artifice, cunning. 2. Awning before a window.

amaestramiento [ah-mah-ays-trah-me-ayn'-to], *m.* Training; drill.

amaestrar [ah-mah-es-trar'], *va.* To instruct, to break in, to lead.

amagar [ah-mah-gar'], *va.* 1. To be in a threatening attitude. 2. To threaten. 3. To have some symptoms of a disease. 4. *(Met.)* To manifest a desire. *-vr. (Prov.)* To couch, to stoop.

amago [ah-mah'-go], *m.* Bitter stuff found in some beecells. *(Met.)* Nausea, loathing. Threat (amenaza). Sign, symptom. **Amago tormentoso**, outbreak of bad weather.

amainar [ah-mah-e-nar'], *va.* 1. *(Naut.)* To lower the sails. 2. To relax. *-vr.* To abate, to moderate (ira, viento etc.).

amaine [ah-mah-e-nay], *m.* Shortening, moderation, lessening.

amaitinar [ah-mah-e-te-nar'], *va.* To observe attentively, to watch closely.

amaizado [ah-mah-e-tha-do], *a. (And)* Rich.

amajadar [ah-mah-hah-dar'], *vn.* 1. To seek shelter in a sheep-fold. 2. To secure sheep.

amalaya [ah-mah-lah-lya], *interj. (LAm.) V.* OJALA.

amalayar [ah-mah-lah-yahr], *va. (And.* CAm, *Mex.)* To covet, to long for.

amalecita [ah-mah-lay-thee'-tah], *m.* Amalekite.

amalgama [ah-mal-gah'-mah], *f.* Amalgam.

amalgamación [ah-mal-gah-mah-the-on'], *f.* Amalgamation.

amalgamar [ah-mal-gah-mar'], *va.* To amalgamate, to unite metals with quicksilver.

amalo, la [ah-mah'-lo, lah], *a.* One of the most noted families of the Goths.

amamantar [ah-mah-man-tar'], *va.* To nurse, to suckle.

amamblucea [ah-man-bloo-tahy-ah], *f.* A sort of cotton stuff.

amancebado, da [ah-man-tahy-bah'-do, dah], *a.* Attached, excessively devoted. *-pp.* of AMANCEBARSE.

amancebamiento [ah-man-thay-bah-me-en'-to], *m.* Concubinage.

amancebarse [ah-man-thay-bar'-say], *vr.* To live in concubinage.

amancillar [ah-man-theel-lyar'], *va.* 1. To stain, to pollute. 2. To offend, to injure. 3. *(Met.)* to tarnish one's reputation.

amanecer [ah-mah-nay-therr'], *vn.* 1. To dawn. 2. To arrive at break of day. **Al amanecer**, at the break of day. 3. *(Met.)* To begin to appear, or to show itself. 4. *(LAm.)* **Amaneció bailando**, he danced all night. 5. *(LAm.)* **¿Como amaneció?,** how are you?

amanecida [ah-mah-nay-the-dah], *f.* Dawn, daybreak.

amanerado, da [ah-mah-nay-rah'-do, dah], *a.* Applied to painters, mannerists, and to their works.

amaneramiento [ah-mah-nay-rah-me-ayn-to], *m.* Affectation; mannerism.

amanerarse [ah-mah-nay-rar'-say], *vr.* To adopt a mannerism, or affectation in style. Used of artists or writers.

amanezca [ah-mah-nayth-cah], *f. (Carib. Mex.)* Dawn; breakfast (desayuno).

amanezquera [ah-mah-nayz-kay-rah], *f. (Carib. Mex.)* Early morning, daybreak.

amanojar [ah-mah-no-har'], *va.* To gather by handfuls.

amansa [ah-mahn-sah], *f. (Cono Sur)* Taming; breaking in.

amansado [ah-mahn-sah-do], *a.* Tame.

amansador, ra [ah-man-sah-dor', rah], *m. & f.* 1. Tamer, subduer. 2. Soother, appeaser.

amansamiento [ah-man-sah-me-en'-to], *m.* The act of taming.

amansar [ah-man-sar'], *va.* 1. To tame to domesticate, to subdue. 2. *(Met.)* To soften, to pacify. *-vr.* To calm down (persona).

amanse [ah-mahn-say], *m. (And. Mex.)* Taming.

amantar [ah-man-tar'], *va. (coll.)* To cover with any loose garment.

amante [ah-mahn'-tay], *pa. & n.* Loving, lover, sweetheart, fond. *-pl. (Naut.)* ropes which form part of the running rigging of a ship.

amantillar [ah-man-teel-lyar'], *va. (Naut.)* To top the lifts, to hoist one end of the yard-arms higher than the other.

amantillo [ah-man-teel'-lyo], *m. (Naut.)* Lift.

amanuense [ah-mah-noo-en'-say], *m.* Amanuensis, clerk.

amañado [ah-mah-nya-do], *a.* 1. Skilful, clever. 2. Fake, faked (falso).

amañar [ah-mah-nyar'], *va.* To do a thing cleverly. To fake, to alter, tamper with. *-vr.* 1. To accustom oneself to do things with skill, to be handy. 2. *(Carib.)* To tell lies. **Amañarse con**, to get along with.

amaño [ah-mah'-nyo], *m.* Way or means of doing a thing, expertness, cleverness. **Tener amaño**, to have an aptitud for. *-pl.* 1. Tools or implements. 2. *(Met.)* Intrigue or machinations.

amapola ah-mah-po'-lah], *f. (Bot.)* Poppy. Papaver. **Amapola morada**, corn poppy, corn rose.

amar [ah-mar'], *va.* 1. To love, to like, to fancy. 2. *(Met.)* To have a tendency to: applied to inanimate things.

amaraje [ah-mah-rah-hay], *m. (Aer.)* Landing (on the sea); splashdown, touchdown.

amaracino [ah-mah-rah-thee'-no], *a.* **Ungüento amaracino**, a sort of ointment made of marjoram.

amáraco [ah-mah'-rah-co], Marjoram. V. MEJORANA.

amaranto [ah-mah-rahn'-to], *m. (Bot.)* Amaranth, flowering bush.

amarar [ah-mah-rahr], *vn. (Aer.)* To land (on the sea), to come down, to splash down.

amarchantarse [ah-mahr-chan-tahr-say], *vr.* Amarchantarse en *(LAm.)* To become a customer of.

amargado, da [ah-mar-gah'-do, dah], *a.* Embittered. *-pp.* of AMARGAR.

amargaleja [ah-mar-gah-lay'-hah], *f.* The bitter or wild plum. V. ENDRINA.

amargamente [ah-mar-gah-men'-tay], *adv.* Bitterly.

amargar [ah-mar-gar'], *va.* 1. To make bitter. 2. *(Met.)* To exasperate, to offend. *-vn.* To be bitter or acrid; to taste bitter. *-vr.* To get bitter.

amargo, ga [ah-mar'-go, gah], *a.* 1. Bitter, having a hot, acrid taste. 2. Painful. 3. *(Cono Sur)* Cowardly.

amargo [ah-mar'-go], *m.* 1. V. AMARGOR. 2. Sweetmeat made of bitter almonds. *-pl.* Bitters.

amargón [ah-mar-gone'], *m. (Bot.)* Dandelion.

amargor [ah-mar-gor'], *m.* 1. Bitterness. 2. Sorrow, vexation.

amargosamente [ah-mar-go-sah-men'-tay], *V.* AMARGAMENTE.

amargoso, sa [ah-mar-go'-so, sah], *a.* Bitter. V. AMARGO.

amarguillo, lla [ah-mar-geel'-lyo, lyah], *a. dim.* Somewhat bitter. It is also used as a substantive.

amargura [ah-mar-goo'-rah], *f.* Bitterness, acerbity, sorrow.

amaricado, da [ah-mah-re-cah'-do, dah], *a. (coll.)* Effeminate.

amarilis [ah-mah-ree'-lis], *f.* Amaryllis.

amarilla [ah-mah-reel-lyah], *f.* 1. Gold coin, especially the ounce. 2. A vat. 3. A liver disease of woolly flocks.

amarillazo, za [ah-mah-reel-lyah'-tho, thah], *a.* Of a pale yellow color.

amarillear [ah-mah-reel-lyay-ar'], *vn.* 1. To incline to yellow. 2. To be yellowish (tirar a amarillo). 3. To pale (palidecer).

amarillecer [ah-mah-reel-lyay-thayr], *vn.* To turn yellow.

amarillejo, ja [ah-mah-reel-lyay-ho, hah], *a. dim.* Yellowish.

amarillento, ta [ah-mah-reel-lyen'-to, tah], *a.* Inclining to yellow golden.

amarillez [ah-mah-reel-lyeth'], *f.* The yellow color of the body.

amarillismo [ah-mah-reel-lyes-mo], *m.* Sensationalist; paleness, sallowness.

amarillito, ta [ah-mah-reel-lyee'-to, tah], *a. dim.* V. AMARILLEJO.

amarillo, lla [ah-mah-reel'-lyo, lyah], *a.* 1. Yellow; gold color. 2. Gutter (prensa sensacionalista). 3. **Sindicato amarillo**, trade union which is in league with the bosses.

amarillo [ah-mah-reel'-lyo], *m.* 1. Jaundice. 2. A disease of the silkworm.

amarilloso [ah-mah-reel-lyo-so], *a. (Cono Sur)* Yellowish.

amarinar [ah-mah-re-nar'], *va.* V. MARINAR.

amariposado, da [ah-mah-re-po-sah'-do, dah], *a.* 1. *(Bot.)* Papilionaceous, applied to flowers. 2. Butterfly-like. 3. Effeminate.

amaro [ah-mah'-ro], *m. (Bot.)* Common clary.

amarra [ah-mar'-rah], *f.* 1. A cable. 2. A martingale. **Amarra**, *(Naut.)* A word of command, corresponding to the English belay, lash, or fasten. **Amarras fijas**, moorings. **Amarras de popa**, stern-fasts. **Amarras de proa**, bow-fasts. **Amarras de través**, fasts amidships. **Tener buenas amarras**, *(Met.)* to have powerful friends or interest.

amarradera [ah-mahr-rah-day-rahs], *f. (And)* mooring (para barcos); *(Mex.)* Rope, line (cuerda).

amarradero [ah-mar-rah-day'-ro], *m.* 1. A post to which anything is made fast. 2. *(Naut.)* A berth, the place where a ship is moored.

amarrado [ah-mahr-rah-do], *a. (LAm.)* Mean, stingy.

amarradura [ah-mahr-rah-doo-rah], *f.* Mooring.

amarraje [ah-mahr-rah-hay], *m.* Mooring charges.

amarrar [ah-mar-rar'], *va.* To tie, to fasten, to lash. **Amarrar un cabo de labor**, to belay a running rope. **Amarrar un bajel entre viento y marea**, to moor a vessel between wind and tide. **Amarrar un bajel con codera sobre el cable**, to moor a ship with a spring on the cable. **Amarrar con reguera**, to moor by the stern. *-vr. (And.* CAm) To get drunk.

amarrazones [ah-mar-rah-tho'-nes], *pl. (Naut.)* Ground-tackle.

amarre [ah-mahr-ray], *m.* Fastening, tying; mooring.

amarrete [ah-mahr-ray-tay], *(LAm.)* 1. *a.* Mean, stingy.

amarrido, da [ah-mar-ree'-do, dah], *a.* Dejected, gloomy, melancholy.

amarro [ah-mahr-ro], *m. (And)* Knotted string, knotted rope (cuerda).

amarrocar [ah-mahr-ro-cahr], *va. (Cono Sur)* To scrimp and save.

amarroso [ah-mahr-ro-so], *a. (CAm.)* Acrid, sharp (fruta).

amartelado [ah-mahr-tay-lah-do], *a.* Lovesick; **andar amartelado con**, to be in love with.

amartelamiento [ah-mahr-tay-lah-mee-ayn-to), *m.* Lovesickness, infatuation.

amartelar [ah-mar-tay-lar'], *va.* 1. To court, to make love to a lady. 2. To love most devotedly.

amartillar [ah-mar-teel-lyar'], *va.* 1. To hammer, to knock in. 2. To cock a gun or pistol.

amasadera [ah-mah-sah-day-rah], *f.* A kneading-trough.

amasado [ah-mah-sah-do], *a. (Carib.)* Doughy (sustancia). Plump (persona).

amasador, ra [ah-mah-sah-dor', rah], *m. & f.* Kneader.

amasadura [ah-mah-sah-doo'-rah], *f.* Act of kneading.

amasamiento [ah-mah-sah-me-en'-to], *m.* 1. The act of uniting or joining. 2. V. AMASADURA.

amasandería [ah-mah-sahn-day-re-ah], *f. (And. Cono Sur)* Bakery, baker's shop.

amasandero, ra [ah-mah-sahn-day-ro], *m. & f. (And. Cono Sur)* Bakery worker.

amasar [ah-mah-sar'], *va.* 1. To kned. 2. To mould. 3. *(Met.)* To arrange matters well for the attainment of some purpose. 4. *(fig.)* To cook up, concoct. 5. To pile up, accumulate.

amasiato [ah-mah-se-ah'-to], *m. (Sp. Amer.)* Concubinage.

amasigado [ah-mah-se-gah-do], *a. (And)* Dark, swarthy.

amasijar [ah-mah-se-hahr], *va. (Cono Sur)* To do in (matar).

amasijo [ah-mah-see'-ho], *m.* 1. Dough. 2. The act of kneading, or the preparation for it. 3. A quantity of mortar or plaster. 4. *(Met.)* A medley. 5. A task. 6. A plotting agreement. 7. The place where the dough for bread is made.

amasio [ah-mah-se-o], *m. & f. (CAm. Mex.)* Lover, mistress (mujer).

amate [ah-mah'-tay], *m. (Mex.)* A fig-tree, the milky juice of which is used as a resolvent.

amateur [ah-mah-tayr], 1. *a.* Amateur.

amateurismo [ah-mah-te-oo-res-mo], *m.* Amateurism.

amatista [ah-mah-tees'-tah], *f. (Miner.)* Amethyst, a precious stone of purplish violet color.

amatorio, ría [ah-mah-to'-re-o, ah], *a.* Amatory.

amarufis [ah-mah-roo'-fis], *m.* A kind of Indian linen.

amaurosis [ah-mah-oo-ro'-sis], *f.* blindness from disease of the optic nerve.

amaurótico, ca [ah-mah-oo-ro'-te-co, cah], *a.* Amaurotic, affected by amaurosis.

amauta [ah-mah-oo-tah], *m.* (And Hist.) Inca elder.

amayorado [ah-mah-yo-rah-do], *a. (And)* Precious, forward (niño).

amayorazgado, da [ah-mah-yo-rath-gah'-do, dah], *a.* Entailed.

amazacotado [ah-mah-thah-co-tah-do], *a.* Heavy, clumsy, awkward; shapeless, formless.

amazona [ah-mah-tho'-nah], *f.* 1. An amazon; a masculine woman. 2. A large parrot of Brazil. 3. A long riding-skirt or habit.

Amazonas [ah-mah-tho-nahs], *m*: **el río Amazones**, the Amazon.

amazónico, ca [ah-mah-tho'-ne-co, cah], *a.* Amazonian.

ambages [am-bah'-hes], *m. pl.* 1. *(Obs.)* circuit. 2. *(Met.)* Circumlocution or multiplicity of words used to describe or explain a thing.

ambagioso [am-bah-he-o-so], *a.* Involved, circuitous, roundabout.

ámbar [ahm'-bar], *m.* Amber. Succinum. **ambar gris**, ambergris. **Es un ámbar**, it is excellent, it is very sweet: applied to liquors.

ambareado [am-bah-ray-ah-do], *a. (And)* Chestnut, auburn (pelo).

ambarilla [am-bah-reel'-lyah], *f. (Bot.)* Amber-seed or musk-seed.

ambarina [am-bah-ree'-nah], *f. V.* ALGALIA.

ambarino, na [am-bah-ree'-no, nah], *a.* Relating to amber.

ambición [am-be-the-on'], *f.* 1. Ambition, a desire of preferment or honour. 2. Covetousness.

ambicionar [am-be-the-o-nar'], *va.* To pursue with anxious desire, to covet. **Ambicionar ser algo**, to have an ambition to be somebody.

ambiciosamente [am-be-the-oh-sah-men'-tay], *adv.* Ambitiously; highly.

ambicioso, sa [am-be-the-oh'-so, sah], *a.* 1. Ambitious, aspiring. 2. covetous. 3. High-minded.

ambidextro, tra [am-be-decs'-tro, trah], *a.* Ambidextrous.

ambientación [am-be-ayn-tah-the-on], *f.* 1. Orientation. 2. Sound-effects (cine).

ambientado [am-be-ayn-tah-do], *a. (LAm.)* Air-conditioned; **Estar ambientado**, to be settled in (persona).

ambientador, ra [am-be-ayn-tah-dor], *m. & f.* Dresser (TV.)

ambiental [a-be-en-tahl'], *a.* Environmental. **Música ambiental**, piped music.

ambientalismo [am-be-ayn-tah-les-mo], *m.* Environmentalism.

ambientalista [am-be-ayn-tah-les-tah], *a.* Environmentalist.

ambientar [am-be-en-tar'], *va.* 1. To provide with a suitable environment. **Ambienta el escenario con bailes folklóricos**, he enlivens the scene with folk dances. 2. To set; **la novela está ambientada en una sociedad de…**, the novel is set in a society of…. 3. To orientate, direct. *-vr.* To orientate oneself, get a sense of direction.

ambiente [am-be-en'-tay], *m.* Environment. *(fig.)* Atmosphere; climate; environment. **No me gusta el ambiente**, I don't like the atmosphere. **Se crió un ambiente de violencia**, he grew up in an atmosphere of violence. *(And)* Room; **ambiente artificial**, air-conditioning.

ambigú [am-be-goo'], *m.* Ambigu, a French word signifying a meal, usually served in the evening at entertainments or receptions, and composed of cold and warm dishes, set all at once on the table.

ambiguamente [am-be-goo-ah-men'-tay], *adv.* Ambiguously.

ambigüedad [am-be-goo-ay-dahd'], *f.* Ambiguity, doubt, uncertainty, double meaning.

ambiguo, gua [am-be'-goo-o, ah], *a.* Ambiguous, doubtful.

ambilado [am-be-lah-do], *a. (Carib.)* **Estar ambilado**, to be left open-mouthed.

ámbito [am'-be-to], *m.* Circuit, circumference, compass. **Dentro del ámbito**, within the limits of; **en el ámbito nacional**, on a nationwide basis.

ambivalencia [am-be-va-layn-the-ah], *f.* Ambivalence.

ambivalente [am-be-vah-layn-tay], *a.* Ambivalent.

ambivertido [am-be-ver-tee'-do], *m.* Ambivert.

ambladura [am-blah-doo-rah], *f.* **A paso de ambladura**, at an amble.

amblar [am-blar'], *va. (Obs.)* To amble: to pace.

ambleo [am-blay-o], *m.* A short, thick wax-candle.

ambligonio [am-ble-go'-neo], *m.* Obtuse-angled. *V.* TRIANGULO.

ambliopía [am-ble-o-pee'-ah], *f.* Weakness of sight, without any opacity of the cornea.

ambo [ahm'-bo], *m.* Combination of two numbers in the lottery. *(Cono Sur)* two-piece suit.

ambón [am-bone'], *m.* A pulpit on each side of the high altar.

ambos, bas [ahm-bos, bas], *a.* Both. **Ambos or Ambas a dos**, both, or both together.

ambrosía [am-bro-see'-ah], *f.* 1. Ambrosia. 2. *(fig.)* Any delicious viand or liquor. 3. *(Bot.)* Ragweed.

ambucía [am-boo-thee-ah], *f. (Cono Sur)* greed, greediness.

ambuciento [am-boo-thee-ayn-to], *a. (Cono Sur)* greedy; voracious.

ambulancia [am-boo-lahn'-the-ah], *f.* Ambulance, a field hospital; also the conveyance.

ambulante [am-boo-lahn'-tay], *a.* Ambulatory, walking; roving; itinerant; traveling, etc.

ambulativo, va [am-boo-lah'-tee'-vo, vah], *a.* Of a roving turn (personas).

ambulatorio, a [am-boo-lah-to'-re-o, ah], *a.* Ambulatory, used for walking or progressing. *(Zool.).* State-health-service hospital.

ameba [ah-may-bah], *f.* Amoeba.

amebeo, bea [ah-may-bay'-o, ah], *a.* Amebean, a kind of dialogue in verse.

amedrentador, ra [ah-may-dren-tah-dor', rah], *m. & f.* Threatener, discourager, -a. Terrifying, frightening.

amedrentar [ah-may-dren-tar'], *va.* to frighten, to deter, to discourage, to fear; to intimidate;: vulgarly, to cow. *-vr.* To get scared.

amejoramiento [ah-may-ho-rah-me-ayn-to], *m. (LAm.) V.* MEJORAMIENTO.

amejorar [ah-may-ho-rahr], *va. (LAm.) V.* MEJORAR.

amelcocharse [ah-mayl-co-char-say], *vr. (Carib.)* To fall in love; *(Mex.)* To harden.

amelga [ah-mel'-gah], *f.* A ridge between two furrows thrown up by the plough.

amelgado [ah-mel-gah'-do], *m. (Prov.)* A little hillock to mark the boundaries of a field. **Amelgado, da**, *pp.* of AMELGAR.

amelgar [ah-mel-gar'], *va.* 1. To open furrows. 2. *(Prov.)* To throw up earth to mark boundaries.

amelo [a-may'-lo], *m. (Bot.)* Golden star-wort.

amelonado, da [ah-may-lo-nah'-do, dah], *a.* Shaped liked a melon.

amén [ah-men'], *m.* Amen, so be it. **Voto de amén**, a partial vote, given without the least previous discussion or inquiry. **Sacristán de amén**, one who blindly adheres to the opinion of another. **amén de**, *(coll.)* besides: except; over and above.

amenaza [ah-may-nah'-thah], *f.* A threat, a menace.

amenazador, ra [ah-may-nah-thah-dor', rah], *m. & f.* One who threatens. *-a.* Threatening.

amenazante [ah-may-nah-thahn'-tay], *pa.* Minacious, threatening.

amenazar [ah-may-nah-thar'], *va.* To threaten, to menace. **Amenazar a uno a muerte**, to threaten somebody with death. **Una especie amenazada de extinción**, a species threatened with extinction. *-vn.* To threaten; to loom.

amencia [ah-men'-the-ah], *f.* (Ant. and Amer.) Dementia; insanity.

amenguar [ah-men-goo-ar'], *va.* 1. To diminish. 2. To defame.

amenidad [ah-may-ne-dahd'] *f.* 1. Amenity, agreeableness. 2. *(Met.)* A pleasant strain of language.

amenizar [ah-may-nee-thar'], *va.* 1. To render pleasant or agreeable. 2. *(Met.)* To adorn a speech with pleasing sentiments.

ameno, na [ah-may'-no, nah], *a.* 1. Pleasant, delicious. 2. Delightful, elegant: applied to the language of a work. 3. Pleasant, readable (libro). **Prefiero una lectura más amena**, I prefer lighter reading.

amentáceo, cea [ah-men-tah'-tahy-o, ah], *a. (Bot.)* Amentaceous, resembling a thong.

amento [ah-men'-to], *m. (Bot.)* Ament, amentum, eatkin.

ameos. *V.* AMI.

amerar [ah-may-rar'], *va.* To mix wine or liquor with water. *-vr.* To soak or enter gradually, as water.

amerengado, da [ah-may-ren-gah'-do, dah], *a.* 1. Like, or having, meringue. 2. *(coll.)* Nice, prudish.

América [ah-may-re-cah], *f.* America (depending on context, may mean the whole continent, the United States, or Latin America); **América Central**, Central America. **América del Norte**, North America. **América del Sur**, South America. **Hacerse las Américas**, to make a fortune.

americana [ah-may-re-cah'-nah], *f.* Sackcoat, jacket.

americanada [ah-may-re-cah-nah-dah], *f.* Typically American thing (to do).

americanismo [ah-may-re-cah-nees'-mo], *m.* 1. Americanism, feeling for Spanish-American culture. 2. Spanish-American expression.

americanista [ah-may-re-cah-nes-tah], *m. & f.* Americanist, specialist in indigenous American culture; specialist in American culture; specialist in American literature.

americanización [ah-may-re-cah-ne-thah-the-on'], *f.* Americanization.

americanizar [ah-may-re-cah-ne-thar'], *va.* To Americanize, to make Spanish-American, to make North American. *-vr.* To be Americanized.

americano, na [ah-may-ree-cah'-no, nah], *a. & m. & f.* American.

americio [ah-may-ree-thee-o], *m.* (Quim.) Americium.

amerindio, a [ah-may-reen-dee-o], *a., m. & f.* American, American Indian.

ameritado [ah-may-ree-tah-do], *a. (LAm.)* Worthy.

ameritar [ah-may-ree-tahr], *va. (LAm.)* To win credit, do well.

amerizaje [ah-may-ree-thah-hay], *m.* Landing (on the sea); splashdown.

amerizar [ah-may-ree-thahr], *vn. (Aer.)* To land (on the sea).

amestizado [ah-mays-tee-thah-do], *a.* Like a half-breed.

ametalado, da [ah-may-tah-lah'-do, dah], *a.* Having the color of brass.

ametista, *f.* **ametisto**, *m.* [ah-may-tees'-tah, ah-me-tees'-to], *V.* AMATISTA.

ametrallador [ah-may-trahl-lyah-dor], *m.* Machine gunner.

ametralladora [ah-may-trahl-lyah-do'-rah], *f.* Machine gun.

ametrallar [ah-may-trahl-lyar'], *va.* To machine gun.

amia [ah'-me-ah], *f.* Lamia, the white shark.

amianto, m. amianta, *f.* [ah-me-ahn'-to, ah-me-ahn'-tah]. *(Miner.)* Amiarchus a filamentous fossil: asbestos.

amiba [ah-mee'-bah], *f.* Amoeba, a rhizopod; a type of the simplest animal life.

amiento [ah-mee-ayn'-to], *m.* A leather strap, with which a helmet is tied on.

amiga [ah-mee'-gah], *f.* 1. *(Prov.)* A school for girls. Friend; lover (amante); girlfriend (de chico). 2. *(Obs.)* V. BARRAGANA. Mistress.

amigable [ah-me-gah'-blay], *a.* 1. Friendly. 2. *(Met.)* Fit, suitable.

amigablemente [ah-me-gah'-baly-men'-tay], *adv.* Amicably.

amigacho [ah-me-gah-cho], *m.* Mate, buddy (esp. US), bachelor friend.

amigarse [ah-me-gahr-say], *vr.* To get friendly; to set up house together (amantes).

amigazo [ah-me-gah-tho], *m. (Cono Sur)* pal, buddy (esp. US).

amígdala [ah-meeg'-dah-lah], *f.* A tonsil.

amigdalitis [ah-meeg-dah-lee'-tis], *f. (Med.)* Tonsilitis.

amigo, ga [ah-mee'-go, gah'], *m. & f.* 1. A friend: comrade. 2. Lover. **Un amigo íntimo**, a familiar, an intimate. **Es amigo de ganar la vida**, he is fond of gain; he is eager to do any thing to procure a livelihood. **Amiga del alma**, intimate friend. **Amigo por correspondencia**, penfriend.

amigo, ga [ah-mee'-go, gah], *a. V.* AMISTOSO an AMIGABLE.

amigote [ah-me-go'-tay], *m. aug. (coll.)* A great friend, an intimate. *(Cono Sur)* sidekick, crony.

amiguero [ah-me-gay-ro], *a. (LAm.)* Friendly.

amiguete [ah-me-gay-tay], *m.* Buddy, mate; influential friend.

amiguismo [ah-me-gees-mo], *m.* Old buddy (esp. US); *(Cono Sur)* sidekick.

amiguita [ah-me-gee-tah], *f.* Girlfriend; lover.

amiguito [ah-me-gee-to], *m.* boyfriend; lover.

amiláceo [ah-me-lah'-thay-o], *a.* Amylaceous, starchy.

amilanamiento [ah-me-lah-nah-me-en'-to], *m.* Spiritlessness.

amilanar [ah-me-lah-nar'] *va.* To frighten, to terrify, to crush. *-vr.* To flag, to get scared.

amillaramiento [ah-meel-lyah-rah-me-en'-to], *m.* Assessment of a tax.

amillarar [ah-meel-layh-rar'], *va.* To assess a tax.

amillonado, da [ah-meel-lyo-nah'-do, dah], *a.* 1. Liable to pay a tax called millones, which is levied on wine, vinegar, etc. 2. Very rich *-m.* A millionaire.

aminoácido [ah-mee-no-ah'-thee-do], *m.* Amino acid.

aminorar [ah-me-no-rar'], *va.* To lessen, to enfeeble.

amir [ah-meer'], *m.* Ameer, one of the Mohammedan nobility of Afghanistan and Seinde.

amistad [ah-mis-tahd'], *f.* 1. Amity, friendship; commerce. 2. A connection founded upon a carnal intercourse. 3. Gallantry. 4. Civility, favor. 5. *(Obs.)* inclination, desire. **hacer las amistades**, to make up. **Invitar a las amistades**, to invite one's friends.

amistar [ah-mis-tar'], *va. & vr.* To reconcile, to bring together, make friends (hacer amigos). To bring about a reconciliation. *-vr.* To become friends, establish a friendship.

amistosamente [ah-mis-to-sah-men'-tay], *adv.* In a friendly manner, familiarly.

amistoso, sa [ah-mis-toh'-so, sah], *a.* Friendly, amicable, cordial.

amito [ah-mee'-to], *m.* Amice, a square piece of linen with a cross in the middle, which forms the undermost part of a priest's garment when he officiates at the mass.

amnesia [am-nay'-se-ah], *f.* Amnesia; loss of memory.

amnios [ahm'-ne-os], *f.* Amnion, a foetal envelope.

amnistia [am-nis-tee'-ah], *f.* An amnesty.

amnistiar [am-nis-te-ar'], *va.* To grant a pardon, to amnesty, *-vr.* To receive amnesty.

amo [ah'-mo], *m.* 1. Master of a house. 2. Proprietor. 3. Foster-father. 4. Overseer. 5. *(Vulg.)* Good-man. 6. Lord. **Amo de casa**, a householder. *V.* AMA. **Amo de buque**, a shipowner.

amoblado [ah-mo-blah-do], 1. *a.* Furnished. 2. *m. (CAm.)* Furniture.

amoblar [ah-mo-blar'], *va.* To furnish. *V.* MOBLAR = AMUEBLAR.

amodita [ah-mo-dee'-tah], *f.* A sort of horned serpent. *V.* ALICANTE.

amodorrado, da [ah-mo-dor-rah'-do, dah], *a.* Heavy with sleep. *-pp.* of AMODORRARSE.

amodorramiento [ah-mo-dor-rah-me-ayn-to], *m.* Sleepiness, drowsiness.

amodorrarse [ah-mo-dor-rar'-say], *vr.* To be drowsy, to grow heavy with sleep.

amodorrido, da [ah-mo-dor-ree'-do, dah], *a. V.* AMODORRADO.

amogotado, da [ah-mo-go-tah'-do, dah], *a.* Steep with a flat crown: applied to a mountain descried at sea.

amochecerse [ah-mo-chay-therr'-say], *vr.* To grow mouldy or rusty. *V.* ENMOHECERSE.

amohinar [ah-mo-e-nar'], *va.* To irritate. *-vr.* To get annoyed.

amohosado [ah-mo-o-sah-do], *a. (Cono Sur)* Rusty.

amojonador [ah-mo-ho-nah-dor'], *m.* One who sets landmarks.

amojonamiento [ah-mo-ho-nah-me-en'-to], *m.* The act of setting landmarks.

amojonar [ah-mo-ho-nar'], *va.* To set landmarks, to mark roads.

amojosado [ah-mo-ho-sah-do], *a. (Cono Sur)* Rusty.

amoladera [ah-mo-lah-day'-rah], *f.* Whetstone, grindstone.

amolado [ah-mo-lah'-do], *a.* 1. *(Cono Sur)* Bothered, irritated (fastidiado). 2. *(And. Mex.)* Offended (ofendido).

amolador [ah-mo-lah-dor'], *m.* 1. Grinder, whetter. 2. *(coll.)* Unskillful couchman. 3. An unskillful artist.

amoladura [an-mo-lah-doo'-rah], *f.* The act of whetting or grinding. **Amoladruas,** the small sand which falls from the whetstone at the time of whetting.

amolar [ah-mo-lar'], *va.* To whet, grind, or sharpen an edged tool by attrition. To upset, to annoy, to pester, to damage, ruin. *-vr. (Cono Sur, Mex.)* To get cross (enfadarse).

amoldador, ra [ah-mol-dah-dor, rah], *m. & f.* A moulder: one who moulds.

amoldar [ahmol-dar'], *va.* 1. To cast in a mould, to fashion, to figure. **Amoldar las agujas,** to polish needles. 2. *(Met.)* To adjust according to reason, to bring one to his duty. 3. *(Obs.)* To brand or mark cattle. *-vr.* To adapt oneself.

amole [ah-mo'-lay], *m.* Soap-root. *(Mex.)* Chlorogalum.

amollar [ah-mol-lyar'], *va.* 1. *(Naut.)* To ease off. 2. To play an inferior card to a winning one.

amolletado, da [ah-mol-lyay-tah'-do, dah], *a.* Having the shape of a loaf of bread.

amomo [ah-mo'-mo], *m. (Bot.)* Grain of paradise.

amonarse [ah-mo-nahr-say], *vr.* To get tight.

amondongado, da [ah-mon-don-gah'-do, dah], *a. (coll.)* Sallow, coarse, stout. **Mujer amondongada,** a coarsefeatured stout woman.

amonedación [ah-mo-nay-dah-the-on], *f.* Coining, minting.

amonedar [ah-mo-nay-dar'], *va.* To coin.

amonestación [ah-mo-nes-tah-the-on'], *f.* 1. Advice, admonition, warning. 2. Publication of marriage banns. **Correr las amonestaciones,** to publish the banns of marriage.

amonestador, ra [ah-mo-nes-tah-dor'-rah], *m. & f.* A monitor, an admonisher.

amonestar [ah-mo-nes-tar'], *va.* 1. To advise, to admonish; to correct. 2. To publish banns of marriage, or of ordination.

amoniacal [ah-mo-ne-ah-cahl'], *a.* Ammoniacal.

amoníaco [ah-mo-nee'-ah-co], *m.* 1. Ammonia, NH3. 2. Ammoniac, a gumresin.

amonio [ah-mo'-ne-o], *m. (Chem.)* Ammonium.

amonita [ah-mo-nee'-tah], *f.* 1. Ammonite, a fossil mollusk. 2. *m.* Ammonite, tribe.

amontarse [ah-mon-tar'-say], *vr.* To flee or take to the mountains.

amontillado [ah-mon-teel-lyah-do], *m.* (pale dry sherry).

amontonador, ra [ah-mon-to-nah-dor', rah], *m. & f.* Heaper, accumulator.

amontonadamente [ah-mon-to-nah-dah-mayn-tay], *adv.* In heaps.

amontonado [ah-mon-to-naah-do], *a.* heaped, piled up; **Viven amontonados,** they live on top of each other.

amontonamiento [ah-mon-to-nah-me-en'-to], *m.* The act of heaping, accumulating, hoarding, gathering; lodgment.

amontonar [ah-mon-to-nar'], *va.* 1. To heap or throw things together without order or choice; to accumulate, to gather, to hoard, to lay up. **Vive amontonando fichas,** he's been collecting data in large quantities. 2. *(Pict.)* To group a crowd of figures in a painting. *-vr. (coll.)* To fly into a passion; to grow angry or vexed, and not listen to reason, to pile up, to accumulate. To go up in smoke. *(And)* To revert to scrub

(terreno). **La gente se amontonó en la salida,** people crowded into the exit.

amor [ah-mor'], *m.* 1. Tenderness, affection, love, fancy. 2. The object of love. 3. A word of endearment, **amor mío or mis amores,** my love. **Por amor de Dios,** for God's sake. **Amor de hortelano,** *(Bot.)* goose-grass. **Al amor de la lumbre,** close to the fire. **Amor propio,** self-love; conceitedness. *-m. & f. pl.* 1. gallantry. 2. Amours. **De mil amores,** *adv.* with all my heart.

amoral [ah-mo-ral'], *a.* Amoral, without a sense of moral responsibility.

amoralidad [ah-mo-rah-le-dahd], *f.* Amorality.

amoratado, da [ah-mo-rah-tah'-do, dah], *a.* Livid, purple, purplish. **Ojo amoratado,** black eye.

amoratarse [ah-mo-rah-tahr-say], *vr. (LAm.)* To turn purple.

amorcillo [ah-mor-theel'-lyo], *m. dim.* Slight love, kindness.

amordazar [ah-mor-dah-thar'], *va.* 1. To gag. *(Naut.)* to fasten with bitts. 2. *(Met.)* To deprive of the liberty of speaking or writing.

amores, or **Amores mil** [ah-mo'-res], *m. (Bot.)* Red valerian.

amorfo, fa [ah-mor'-fo, fah], *a.* Amorphous, without definite shape.

amorgado, da [ah-mor-gah'-do, dah], *a.* Stupefied from eating the husks of pressed olives.

amoricones [ah-mo-re-co'-nes], *m. pl. (coll.)* Looks, gestures, and actions, expressive of love and fondness.

amorío [ah-mo-ree'-o], *m. (coll.)* Friendship, love affair, romance. *V.* ENAMORAMIENTO.

amoriscado, da [ah-mo-ris-cah'-do, dah], *a.* Resembling the Moors.

amormado, da [ah-mor-mah'-do, dah], *a.* Applied to horses having the glanders.

amorochado [ah-mo-ro-chah-do], *a. (LAm.) V.* MOROCHO.

amorosamente [ah-mo-ro-sah-men'-tay], *adv.* Lovingly.

amoroso, sa [ah-mo-ro'-so, sah], *a.* 1. Affectionate, kind, loving. **En tono amoroso,** in an affectionate tone. 2. Pleasing. 3. Gentle, mild, serene. **La tarde está amorosa,** it is a charming evening. 4. Tractable, easy.

amorrar [ah-mor-rar'], *vn. (coll.)* 1. To hold down the head; to muse. 2. To remain silent with downcast looks. 3. *(Naut.)* To pitch.

amortajar [ah-mor-tah-har'], *va.* To shroud a corpse.

amortecer [ah-mor-tay-therr'], *va. V.* AMORTIGUAR. *-vr.* To faint, to be in a swoon.

amortecimiento [ah-mor-tay-the-me-en'-to], *m.* Swoon, fainting. **(Yo me amortezco,** from **Amortecerse.** *V.* ABORRECER)

amortiguación, *f.* **amortiguamiento,** *m.* [ah-mor-te-goo-ah-the-on', ah-mor-te-goo-ah-me-en'-to] 1. Deadening, absorption. 2. Softening, toning down.

amortiguador, ra [ah-mor-te-goo-ah-dor', rah], *a.* Cushioning, absorbing. *-m.* Bumper. **Amortiguador de golpes,** Shock absorber. **Amortiguador de luz,** Dimmer. **Amortiguador de sonido,** Muffler, silencer.

amortiguamiento [ah-mor-te-goo-ah-me-ayn-to], *m.* Deadening; muffling, cushioning.

amortiguar [ah-mor-te-goo-ar'], *va.* 1. To cushion, to deaden, to absorb. 2. To tone down, to lessen, 3. To soften. *-vr. (Cono Sur) (Bot.)* To wither.

amortizable [ah-mor-te-thah'-blay], *a.* Amortizable.

amortización [ah-mor-te-thah-the-on'], *f.* Amortization, paying off.

amortizar [ah-mor-te-thar'], *va.* 1. To amortize, to pay back. 2. To write off, to depreciate. 3. To recuperate, to regain. *-vn.* To depreciate, to decrease in value.

amoscar [ah-mos-car'], *va.* To flap flies. *-vr.* 1. To shake off the flies. 2. To become irritated.

amosquilado, da [ah-mos-ke-lah'-do, dah], *a.* Applied to cattle when tormented with flies.

amostachado [ah-mos-tah-cha'-do], *a.* Wearing mustaches.

amostazar [ah-mostah-thar'], *va. (coll.)* To exasperate, to provoke. *-vr.* to fly into a violent passion; to be vexed.

amotinadamente [ah-mo-te-nah-dah-men'-tay], *adv.* Mutinouly.

amotinado, da [ah-mo-te-nah'-do, dah], *a.* Mutinous, rebellious. *-pp.* of AMOTINAR.

amotinador, ra [ah-mo-te-nah-dor', rah], *m. &f.* Mutineer.

amotinamiento [ah-mo-te-nah-me-en'-to], *m.* The act of stirring up a sedition: mutiny.

amotinar [ah-mo-te-nar'], *va.* 1. To excite rebellion. 2. *(Met.)* To disorder the mind. *-vr.* To rise against authority.

amover [ah-mo-verr'], *va.* To remove, to dismiss from employment.

amovibilidad [ah-mo-ve-be-le-dahd'], *f.* The possibility of being removed, or revoked.

amovible [ah-mo-vee'-blay], *a.* Removable: a term applied to ecclesiastical livings.

ampac [am-pahk'], *m. (Bot.)* Champak, a tree of the East Indies, possessing an odor like styrax.

ampara [am-pah'-rah], *f.* 1. *(Law.)* Seizure of chattels or movable property. 2. *(Obs.)* V. AMPARO.

amparada [am-pah-rah'-dah], V. MINA.

amparador, ra [am-pah-rah-dor', rah], *m.* Protector; shelter.

amparar [am-pah-rar'], *va.* 1. To shelter, to protect, to help, to support, to assist. **Amparar a los pobres**, to help the poor. 2. *(Law. Prov.)* To make a seizure of chattels or movable property; to sequestrate. **Amparar en la posesión**, *(Law.)* to maintain in possession. *-vr.* 1. To claim or enjoy protection. 2. To preserve; to recover. 3. To avail oneself of. **Ampararse de**, to seek the protection of.

amparo [am-pah'-ro], *m.* 1. Favor, aid, protection, sanction, support, countenance. 2. Guardship, refuge, asylum. 3. *(Obs.)* Brenstwork, parapet.

ampáyar [am-pah-yahr], *m. (LAm.)* Referee, umpire.

ampe [am-pay], *interj. (And)* please!

ampelita [am-pay-lee'-tah], *f.* Cannelcoal.

ampelografía [am-pay-lo-grah-fee'-ah], *f. (Agri.)* Ampelography, a description of the wine.

amperaje [am-pay-rah'-hay], *m. (Elec.)* Amperage.

amperímetro [am-pay-ree'-may-tro], *m. (Elec.)* Ammeter.

amperio [am-pay-re-o], *m.* Ampère, amp.

amplectivo, va [am-plec-tee'-vo, vah], *a.* Amplective, embracing other organs (of plants.).

ampliable [am-ple-ah-blay], *a.* Expandable *(Comp.)*.

ampliación [am-ple-ah-teh-on'], *f.* enlargement; the act of enlarging.

ampliado [am-ple-ah-do], *m.* (LAm Pol) General meeting.

ampliador, ra [am-ple-ah-dor', rah], *m. & f.* Amplifier.

ampliamente [am-ple-ah-men'-tay], *adv.* Largely, copiously, fully.

ampliar [am-ple-ar'], *va.* To amplify, to enlarge.

ampliativo, va [am-ple-ah-tee'-vo, vah], *a.* Amplifying, having the power of enlarging.

amplificación [am-ple-fe-cah-the-on'], *f.* 1. Enlargement. 2. *(Rhet.)* Amplification.

amplificador [am-ple-fe-cah-dor'], *m.* Amplifier, loudspeaker.

amplificar [am-ple-fe-car'], *va.* 1. To amplify, to enlarge, to extend. 2. To use the figure of speech termed **amplification.**

amplio, ia [ahm'-ple-o, ah], *a.* Ample, extensive; large; handsome; absolute.

amplitud [am-ple-tood'], *f.* 1. Extend, greatness, largeness. 2. *(Naut.)* **Amplitud magnética**, magnetic amplitude. 3. *(Astr.)* Amplitude, an arch of the horizon intercepted between the true east and west point thereof, and the centre of the sun or star at their rising or setting. 4. Absoluteness.

amplo, la [ahm'-plo, plah], *(Obs.)* V. AMPLIO.

ampo [am-po], *m.* Whiteness. **Blanco como el ampo de la nieve**, white as the driven snow. V. LAMPO.

ampolla [am-pol'-lyah], *f.* 1. A blister on the skin. 2. Avial, a cruet. 3. A small bubble of water.

ampollar [am-pol-lyar'], *va.* 1. To blister. 2. To make hollow, to excavate. *-vr.* To rise in bubbles by the force of the wind.

ampolleta [am-pol-lyay'-tah], *f. dim.* 1. A small vial: a cruet. 2. An hourglass. 3. *(Naut.)* Watch-glass.

ampón [am-pon], *a.* Bulky.

amprar [am-prar'], *vn. (Prov.)* To borrow.

ampulosamente [am-poo-lo-sah-mayn-tay], *adv.* bombastically, pompously.

ampulosidad [am-poo-lo-see-dahd], *f.* bombast.

ampuloso, sa [am-poo-lo'-so, sah], *a.* Pompous, bombastic.

amputación [am-poo-tah-the-on'], *f.* Amputation.

amputar [am-poo-tar'], *va.* To amputate, or to cut off a limb.

amuchachado, da [ah-moo-chah-chah'-do, dah], *a.* Boyish, childish.

amuchar [ah-moo-chahr], *va. (And. Cono Sur)* To increase.

amuchigar [ah-moo-chee-goo-ar'], *vn. (Obs.)* To augment, to multiply.

amueblado [ah-moo-ay-blah-do], *a & f.* Furnished, hotel.

amueblar [ah-moo-ay-blar'], *va.* To furnish. **(Yo amueblo, amueble**, *etc.*, from **Amoblar**. *v.* ACORDAR.

amuermar [ah-moo-ayr-mahr], *va.* To bore. *-vr.* To feel sleepy. To vegetate, rot.

amugamiento [ah-moo-gah-me-en'-to], *m.* V. AMOJONAMIENTO.

amugronador, ra [ah-moo-gro-nah-dor', rah], *m. & f.* One who trains vine-shoots.

amugronar [ah-moo-gro-nar'], *va.* To lay the shoot of a vine under the earth in order that it may take root.

amuinar [ah-moo-e-nahr] *(Mex.)* 1. *va.* To annoy, irritate. 2. *-vr.* To get cross.

amujerado, da [ah-moo-hay-rah'-do, dah], *a.* Effeminate.

amujeramiento [ah-moo-hay-rah-me-en'-to], *m.* V. AFEMINACION.

amularse [ah-moo-lar'-say], *vr.* To become sterile (yeguas). *(Mex.)* To get stubborn (persona).

amulatado, da [ah-moo-lah-tah'-do, dah], *a.* Of a tawny complexion, resembling a mulatto.

amuleto [ah-moo-lay'-to], *m.* An amulet.

amunicionar [ah-moo-ne-the-o-nar'], *va.* To supply with ammunition.

amuñecado, da [ah-moo-nyay-cah'-do, dah], *a.* Puppet-like.

amura [ah-moo'-rah], *f.* 1. *(Naut.)* Tack of a sail. **Amura mayor, amura de trinquete**, the foretack. 2. *(Naut.)* A word of command. **Amura a babor**, aboard board tacks. **Amura a estribor**, aboard starboard-tacks. **Cambiar la amura**, to stand on the other tack.

amuradas [ah-moo-rah'-das], *f. pl. (Naut.)* The range of planks between the water-ways and the lower edge of the gun-ports of a ship of war.

amurallado [ah-moo-rahl-lyah-do], *a.* Walled city.

amurallar [ah-moo-rahl-lyar'], *va.* To wall. V. MURAR.

amurar [ah-moo-rar'], *va. (Naut.)* To haul the tack aboard.

amurcar [ah-moor-car'], *va.* To gore with the horns.

amurco [ah-moor'-co], *m.* Blow or stroke with the horns.

amurillar [ah-moo-reel-lyar'], *va. (Agri.)* To earth up.

amurrarse [ah-moor-rhar-say], *vr. (LAm.)* To get depressed, become sad.

amurriarse [ah-moo-rre-ahr-say], *vr. (Esp.)* To become sad.

amurruñarse [ah-moor-roo-nyahr-say] *vr. (Carib.)* To cuddle up.

amusco [ah-moos'-co], *a.* Brown.

amusgar [ah-moos-gar'], *va.* 1. To throw back the ears (caballos). **Amusgar las orejas**, *(Met. Obs.)* To listen. 2. To contract the eyes to see better. *-vr. (CAm.)* To feel ashamed.

Ana [ah'-nah], *f.* 1. An ell. 2. A kind of fox in the Indies. 3. An abbreviation used by medical men to signify equal parts. 4. Ann(e).

anabaina [ah-nah-bah'-e-nah], *f. (Bot.)* Euphorbiaceous plant of Brazil.

anabatista, anabaptista [ah-nah-bah-tees'-tah, ah-nah-bap-tees'-tah], *m.* Anabaptist.

anabás [ah-nah-bahs'], *m.* The climbing-fish. Anabas.

anabeno, na [ah-nah-bay'-no, nah], *a. (Zool.)* Tree-climbing.

anabólico [ah-nah-bo-le-co], *a.* Anabolic.

anacalifa [ah-nah-cah-lee'-fah], *m.* A poisonous animal of Madagascar.

anacalo, la [ah-nah-cah'-lo, lah], *m. & f. (Obs.)* A baker's servant.

anacarado, da [ah-nah-cah-rah'-do, dah], *a.* Of a pearly white color.

anacardel [ah-nah-car-del'], *m.* A kind of Madagascar serpent.

anacardina [ah-nah-car-dee'-nah], *f.* Confection made of anacardium or cashew-nut.

anacardio [ah-nah-car'-de-o], *m. (Bot.)* Cashew-tree.

anacatártico, ca [ah-nah-cah-tar'-te-co, cah], *a. & m. (Med.)* Emetic.

anaco [ah-nah'-co], *m.* Dress of Indian women in Peru and Bolivia; in Ecuador their hair-dressing.

anaconda [ah-nah-con'-dah], *f. (Zool.)* Anaconda.

anacoreta [ah-nah-co-ray-tah], *m.* An anchorite, a hermit.

anacorético, ca [ah-nah-co-ray'-te-co, cah], *a.* Anchoretical, belonging to a recluse.

anacosta [ah-nah-cos'-tah], *f.* A sort of woollen stuff.

anacreóntico, ca [ah-nah-cray-on'-te-co, cah], *a.* Anacreontic.

anacronía [ah-nah-cro-ne-ah], *f.* Timelessness.

anacrónico [ah-nah-cro-ne-co], *a.* Anachronistic, anachronic.

anacronismo [ah-nah-cro-nees'-mo], *m.* Anachronism, an error in computing time.

ánade [ah'-nah-day], *m. & f.* Duck.

anadear [ah-nah-day-ar'], *vn.* To waddle.

anadeja [ah-nah-day'-hah], *f. dim.* A duckling.

anadeo [ah-nah-day-o], *m.* Waddle, waddling.

anadeón [ah-nah-day-on], *m.* Duckling.

anadino, na [ah-nah-dee'-no, nah], *m. & f.* A young duck.

anadón [ah-nah-done'], *m.* Mallard.

anadoncillo [ah-nah-don-theel'-lyo], *m. dim.* A grown duckling.

anaerobio [ah-nah-ay-ro-be-o], *a.* Anaerobic.

anafalla, or **anafaya** [ah-nah-fahl'-lyah], *f.* A kind of thick corded silk.

anafe, or **anafre** [ah-nah'-fay], *m.* A portable furnace or stove.

anáfora [ah-nah'-fo-rah], *f.* Anaphora, a figure in rhetoric when several periods of a speech are begun with the same word.

anafrodisia [ah-nah-fro-dee'-se-ah], *f.* Anaphrodisia, loss of sexual appetite.

anáglifo [ah-nah'-glee-fo], *m.* Vase, vessel, or other work adorned with sculpture in basso relievo.

anagoge, *m.* **anagogía,** *f.* [ah-nah-go'-hay, ah-nah-go-hee'-ah]. Anagogices, the mystic sense of the Holy Scriptures.

anagógicamente [ah-nah-go'-he-cah-men-tay], *adv.* In an anagogical manner.

anagógico, ca [ah-nah-go'-he-co, cah], *a.* Anagogical.

anagrama [ah-nah-grah'-mah], *f.* An anagram, a transposition of the letters of a name.

anal, [ah-nahl], *a.* Anal, relating to the anus.

analcohólico [ah-nahl-co-le-co], *a.* Non-alcoholic, soft (bebida).

analéptico, ca [ah-nah-lep'-te-co, cah], *a. (Med.)* Analeptic, restorative, comforting.

analepsia [ah-nah-lep'-se-ah], *f. (Med.)* Analepsis.

anales [ah-nah'-les], *m. pl.* Annals or historical accounts related in order.

analfabeta [ah-nahl-fah-bay'-tah], *m. & f.* Illiterate person. *-a.* Illiterate, ignorant.

analfabetismo [ah-nahl-fah-bay-tees'-mo], *m.* Illiteracy.

analfabeto, ta [ah-nahl-fah-bay-to], *a.* illiterate.

analgesia [ah-nahl-hay-se-ah], *f.* Analgesia.

analgésico, ca [ah-nal-hay'-se-co, cah], *m. & a.* Analgesic.

análisis [ah-nah'-le-sis], *m. & f.* 1. Analysis. 2. *(Gram.)* Parsing. 3. *(Math.)* Algebraic solution. **Análisis de mercados,** marketing research, market research.

analista [ah-nah-lees'-tah], *m.* Annalist. **Analista de sistema,** systems analyst *(Comp.).* **Analista programador** *(Comp.),* programmer analyst.

analíticamente [ah-nah-lee'-te-cah-men-tay], *adv.* Analytically.

analítico, ca [ah-nah-lee'-te-co, cah], *a.* Analytical, method of resolving something into first principles.

analizable [ah-nah-le-thah'-blay], *a.* Capable of analysis, analyzable.

analizador [ah-nah-le-thah-dor'], *m.* Analyzer. **Analizador de instrucciones** *(Comp.),* instruction analyser.

analizar [ah-nah-le-thar'], *va.* To analyze.

análogamente [ah-nah'-lo-gah-men-tay], *V.* ANALOGICAMENTE.

analogía [ah-nah-lo-hee'-ah], *f.* 1. Analogy, resemblance or relation which things bear to each other. 2. A part of grammar.

analógicamente [ah-nah-lo'-he-cah-men-tay], *adv.* Analogically.

analógico, ca, análogo, ga [ah-nah-lo'-he-co, cah, ah-nah'-lo-go, ah], *a.* Analogous.

analogismo [ah-nah-lo-hees'-mo], *m.* Analogism, an argument form the cause to the effect.

analogizar [ah-nah-lo-he-thar'], *va. (Lit. us.)* To explain by way of analogy.

análogo, ga [ah-nah'-lo-go, gah], *a.* Analogous, similar.

anama [ah-nah'-mah], *m.* A longicorn beetle of Java.

anamnesia [ah-nam-nay'-se-ah], *f.* Mnemonics, the art of remembering or acquiring memory.

anamorfosis [ah-nah-mor-fo'-sis], *f.* A deformed image drawn upon a curved or plane surface in such a way that when viewed from some particular point it appears perfectly regular and well-proportioned.

anana [ah-nah'-nah], *f.* or **Ananas** *(Bot.)* Ananas, pineapple. This is the European name; in America it is called *piña.*

anapelo [ah-nah-pay'-lo], *m. (Bot.)* Wolf's bane.

anaplastia [ah-nah-plas'-te-ah], *f.* Anaplasty, plastic surgery.

anaquel [ah-nah-kel'], *m.* Shelf or board on which any thing may be placed.

anaquelería [ah-nah-kay-lay-ree'-ah], *f.* Shelving, case of shelves.

anaranjado, da [ah-nah-ran-hah'-do, dah], *a.* Orange-colored.

anarca [ah-nahr-cah] *V.* ANARQUISTA.

anarcosindicalismo [ah-nahr-co-sen-de-cah-les-mo], *m.* Anarcho-syndicalism.

anarcosindicalista [ah-nahr-co-sen-de-cah-les-tah], *a. & m. & f.* Anarcho-syndical.

anarquía [ah-nar-kee'-ah], *f.* Anarchy.

anárquico, ca [ah-nar'-ke-co, cah], *a.* Anarchical, confused, without rule.

anarquismo [ah-nar-kes-mo], *m.* Anarchism.

anarquista [ah-nar-kees'-tah], *m.* Anarchist: enemy of organized government.

anarquizante [ah-nahr-ke-than-tay], *a.* Anarchic.

anarquizar [ah-nahr-ke-thahr], *va.* To produce anarchy in.

anasarca [ah-nah-sar'-cah], *f. (Med.)* Anasarca, general dropsy of the connective tissue.

anascote [ah-nas-co'-tay], *m.* A kind of woollen stuff like serge.

anastasia [ah-nas-tah'-se-ah], *f. V.* ARTEMISA.

anastomosis [ah-nas-to-mo'-sis], *f. (Anat.)* Anastomosis, the inosculation of blood-vessels. *(Bot.)* Junction of branches which should be separate.

anástrofe [ah-nahs'-tro-fay], *m. (Rhet.)* Anastrophe, an inversion of words.

anata [ah-nah'-tah], *f.* Annates, the first fruits or emoluments which a benefice or employ produces. **Media anata.** The annats of the half year.

anatema [ah-nah-tay'-mah], *m. & f.* 1. Anathema, excommunication. 2. *(Obs.)* A person anathematized or excommunicated.

anatematismo [ah-nah-tay-mah-tees'-mo], *m.* V. EXCOMUNION.

anatematizar [ah-nah-tay-mah-te-thar'], *va.* 1. To anathematize, to excommunicate. 2. To curse.

anatista [ah-nah-tees'-tah], *m.* Officer for the half-year annates.

anatomía [ah-nah-to-mee'-ah], *f.* 1. Anatomy. 2. *(Pict.)* Skeleton by which painters and sculptors study the structure of the human frame.

anatómicamente [ah-nah-to'-me-cah-men-tay], *adv.* Anatomically.

anatómico, ca [ah-nah-to'-me-co, cah], *a.* Anatomical.

anatomista [ah-nah-to-mees'-tah], *m.* Anatomist.

anatomizar [ah-nah-to-me-thar'], *va.* 1. To anatomize or dissect. 2. *(Pict.)* To draw, with the utmost exactness, the bones and muscles in statues and figures.

anca [ahn'-cah], *f.* The croup of a horse, haunch. **A ancas or a las ancas**, Behind. **A ancas or a las ancas de fulano**, with the assistance of somebody. *(fig.)* **No sufre ancas**, he can't take a joke.

ancado [ah-cah'-do], *m. (Vet.)* A distemper, consisting in a painful contraction of the muscles.

ancestral [an-thays-trahl], *a.* Ancestral; *(fig.)* Ancient.

ancestro [an-thays-tro], *m. (LAm.)* 1. Ancestor. 2. Ancestry.

ancharguantes [an-chah-goo-ahn'-tes], *m.* A glove-stretcher.

anchamente [an-chah-men'-tay], *adv.* Widely, largely.

ancharia [an-chah'-re-ah], *f. (Obs.)* Among merchants and traders, the width of cloth.

ancheta [an-chay'-tah], *f.* 1. Venture. 2. Gain, profit; *(Mex.)* Bargain; profitable deal. 3. *(And Cono Sur)* Prattle, babble (panadería). 4. *(Carib.)* Joke.

anchicorto, ta [an-che-cor'-to, tah], *a.* That which is wider than it is long.

ancho, cha [ahn'-cho, chah], *a.* 1. Broad, large. **Ponerse muy ancho**, *(Met.)* to look big; to be elated with pride. **Vida ancha**, a loose life. **Recorrer un país a lo ancho y a lo largo**, to cross and recross a country. 2. *(fig.)* Liberal, broad-minded; fast (vida); **ancho de conciencia**, not overscrupulous. **Quedarse tan ancho**, to go on as if nothing had happened. 3. **Estar a sus anchas**, to be at one's ease, to be comfortable.

ancho, anchor [ahn'-cho, an-chor'], *m.* V. ANCHURA.

anchoa, anchova [an-cho'-ah, an-cho'-vah], *f.* Anchovy.

anchoas [an-cho'-ahs], *f. pl. (Mex.)* Pin curls (in hair curling).

anchoveta [an-cho-vay-tah], *f. (And.)* Anchory (for fishermeal).

anchuelo, la [an-choo-ay'-lo, lah], *a. dim.* Somewhat wide.

anchura [an-choo'-rah], *f.* 1. Width, largeness, extensiveness; latitude. 2. Laxity. **A mis anchuras**, or **a sus anchuras**, at large, at full liberty. **Vivo a mis anchuras**, I live just as I choose.

anchuroso, sa [an-choo-ro'-so, sah], *a.* Large, spacious, extensive, broad.

anchusa [an-choo'-sah], *f. (Bot.)* Alkanet. Anchusa.

ancianar [ah-the-ah-nar'], *vn. (Poetic.)* V. ENVEJECER.

ancianidad [an-the-ah-ne-dahd'], *f.* 1. Old age. 2. Antiquity.

anciano, na [an-the-ah'-no, nah], *a.* Old, elderly.

ancilar [an-the-lahr'], *a.* Ancillary.

ancla [an'-clah], *f.* Anchor. **Echar ancla**, to cast anchor, to anchor. **Levar ancla**, to weigh anchor. **Zafar el ancla para dar fondo**, to clear the anchor for coming to. **El ancla viene al bajel**, the anchor comes home. **El ancla ha soltado el fondo**, the anchor is a-trip. **Pescar un ancla**, to drag for an archor. **Alotar las anclas**, to stow the anchors. **Arganeo de ancla**, an anchoring. **Caña del ancla**, the shank of the anchor. **Cepa del ancla**, the anchor-stock. **Cruz del ancla**, the crown of the anchor. **Orejas del ancla**, the flukes of the anchor. **Uñas del ancla**, the anchor arms. **Pico del ancla**, the bill of the anchor. **Al ancla or anclado**, at anchor. **Ancla de**

esperanza, sheet-anchor. **Ancla del ajuste** or *de* uso, the best bower-anchor. **Ancla sencilla** or the leva, the small bower-anchor. **Ancla del creciente**, the flood-anchor. **Ancla del menguante**, the ebb-anchor. **Ancla de la mar hacia fuera**, sea-anchor. **Ancla de la tierra or playa**, shore-anchor. **Anclas de servidumbre**. bower-anchors.

ancladero [an-clah-day'-ro], *m. (Naut.)* Anchorage, anchoring-place.

anclaje [an-clah'-hay], *m.* 1. The act of casting anchor. 2. Anchoring-ground. **Derecho de anclaje**, anchorage.

anclar [an-clar'], *vn.* To anchor.

anclote [an-clo'-tay], *m.* Stream-anchor, grapple, kedge.

anclotillo [an-clo-teel'-lyo], *m.* Kedge anchor.

ancón, *m.* **anconada**, *f.* [an-cone', ah-co-nah'-dah]. An open road, a bay. *(And. Mex.)* Corner.

áncora [ahn'-co-rah], V. ANCLA.

ancoraje [an-co-rah'-hay], *m.* V. ANCLAJE.

ancorar [an-co-rar'], V. ANCLAR.

ancorca [an-cor'-cah], *f.* A yellow ochre.

ancorel [an-co-rel'], *m.* A large stone used by fishermen to secure their nets.

ancorería [an-co-ray-ree'-ah], *f.* Anchor-forge.

ancorero [an-co-ray'-ro], *m.* Anchor-smith.

ancusa [an-coo'-sah], *f. (Bot.)* V. ANCHUSA. **Ancusa oficinal**, common alkanet. **Lengua de buey**.

¡anda! [an-dar'], *int.* Well, never mind. **¡Anda!** Get off the way. **¡Anda, hijo!** Come along, child!

andada [an-dah'-dah], *f.* 1. Track, trail, pathway. 2. A thin, hard-baked cake. **Andadas**, the traces of game on the ground. **Volver a las andadas**, to relapse back into some vice or bad habit.

andaderas [an-dah-day'-ras], *f. pl.* Gocarts, baby-walker.

andadero, ra [an-dah-day'-ro, rah], *a.* Of easy access: applied to the ground.

andado [an-dah'-do], *m.* Stepchild. V. ALNADO.

andado, da [an-dah'-do, dah], *a.* 1. Beaten: applied to a path. 2. Worse for use, threadbare. 3. Customary. *-pp.* of ANDAR.

andador, ra [an-dah-dor', rah], *m. & f.* 1. A good walker. **Es andador**, he's a good walker. 2. Messenger of a court. 3. Wanderer (andarín). 5. Alley or small walk in a garden (senda). 6. *(Mex.)* Prostitute, streetwalker.

andadura [an-dah-doo'-rah], *f.* 1. Gait; pacing. 2. Amble. 3. Advance; **comenzar nuevas andaduras**, to start again.

andalia [an-dah'-le-ah], *f. (Obs.)* Sandal. V. SANDALIA.

andalón [an-dah-lon], *a. (Mex.)* Well-paced, long-striding (caballo).

andaluz, za [an-da-looth', thah], *a.* Andalusian.

andaluzada [an-dah-loo-thah'-dah], *f.* 1. Bullying, boasting, rodomontade. 2. Exaggeration.

andamiada [an-dah-me-ah'-dah], *f.* Scaffolding.

andamiaje [an-dah-me-ah'-hay], *m.* Scaffolding.

andamio [an-dah'-me-o], *m.* 1. Scaffold. 2. *(Obs.)* Platform of a rampart. 3. *(Naut.)* Gang Board.

andana [an-dah'-nah], *f.* 1. Row, line. 2. *(Naut.)* **Andana de los cañones de un costado**, a tier of guns. 3. *(Naut.)* **Andana de rizos**, the reefs in the sails of ships. 4. **Andana de cuartos**, a suite of apartments. 5. A tier. **Llamarse andana**, not to fulfil a promise.

andanada [an-dah-nah'-dah], *f.* 1. Barrage. 2. Broadside. 3. Tirade, severe reprimand. **Andanada verbal**, verbal broadside. 4. Layer, row (de ladrillos etc.).

andaniño [an-dah-nee'-nyo], *m.* A kind of go-cart in which children learn to walk. V. POLLERA.

andante [an-dahn'-tay], *m. (Mus.)* Andante.

andantesco, ca [an-dan-tes'-co, cah], *a.* Belonging to knighthood, or knight-errants.

andantino [an-dan-tee'-no], *m. (Mus.)* Andantino.

andanza [an-dahn'-thah], *f. (Obs.)* Occurrence, event, fortune. **Buena or mala andanza**, good or bad fortune.

andar [an-dar'], *va.* 1. To walk, to come, or to move along. 2. To act, to behave, to transact. 3. To elapse. 4. To act:

applied to machine. 5. To be. **Andar en cuerpo,** to go out without a coat. **Andar por decir** or **por hacer una cosa,** to be determined to say or do a thing. **Andar a caza de gangas,** to waste one's time in fruitless pursuits. **Andar en carnes or en cueros,** to go stark naked. **Andar de Ceca en Meca,** to be roving and wandering about. **Todo se andará,** everything will be looked into. **Es preciso andar con el tiempo,** it is necessary to conform to the times. **Andar en dares y tomares** or **en dimes y diretes,** to dispute and quarrel. **Andar a sombra de tejado,** to hide, to skulk. **Andar a trompis.** to come to blows. **Andar en buena vela.** (*Naut.*) To keep the sails full. **Andar todo,** (*Naut.*) to put up the helm. **A mejor andar,** at best, at most. **A peor andar,** at worst. **A más andar,** in full speed. **Andar el mundo al revés,** to reverse the order of nature, to do something contrary to the manner it ought to be. **No andar en contemplaciones,** not to spare a person; to have recourse to hard measures. **El poco andar del barco,** (*Naut.*) the slow way of the vessel. **Andando el tiempo,** in the lapse of time. **Anden y ténganse,** fast and loose. **Andar de nones,** to be idle. **Andar con mosca,** to fly into a passion. **Mal me andarán las manos,** if nothing prevents me, I will do it. **Andar a derechas,** to act honestly. **Andársele a uno la cabeza,** to have vertigo, to become dizzy. **Andarse en flores,** to decline entering into a debate.

andar [an-dahr] *m.* To walk.

andaraje [an-dah-rah'-hay], *m.* The wheel of a well.

andaribel [an-dah-re-bel'], *m.* (*Naut.*) A light rope improvised to lower or lift some object; a gantline.

andarica [an-dah-re-cah], *f.* Crab (*Prov.*).

andariego, ga [an-da-re-ay'-go, gah], *a.* Restless, of a roving disposition.

andarilla [an-dah-rel-lya], *f.* (*And. Mus.*) Type of flute.

andarín [an-dah-reen'], *m.* (*coll.*) A fast walker. **Andarines,** an Italian paste.

andario [an-dah-ree'-o], *m.* (*Orn.*) The white wagtail.

andarivel [an-dah-re-vayl], *m.* 1. (*Tec.*) Cableway, cable ferry; (*Cono Sur*) Rope, barrier. 2. (*And*) Adornments, trinkets (adornos).

andas [ahn'-das], *f. pl.* 1. A frame on which a person or most commonly an image is carried; a stretcher. 2. A bier with shafts, to be carried on men's shoulders.

ándele [an-day-lay], *interj.* (*Mex.*) Come on! (¡siga!); See what I mean! (¡ya ves!).

andén [an-den'], *m.* 1. A shelf. V. ANAQUEL. 2. A path for the horse round the draw-well or in a mill. 3. The sidewalk by a road or on a dock. 4. The platform of a railway station.

andero [an-day'-ro], *m.* One who carries the shafts of a bier on his shoulders.

Andes [an-days], *m. & pl.* Andes.

andilú [an-de-loo'], *m.* A burnishing stick used by shoemakers.

andinismo [an-de-nes-mo], *m.* (*LAm.*) Mountaineering, mountain climbing; **hacer andinismo,** to go mountaineering.

andinista [an-de-nes-tah], *m. & f.* (*LAm.*) Mountaineer, climber.

andino [an-de-no], *a.* Andean, of the Andes.

andito [an'-de-to], *m.* A gallery which surrounds the whole or a part of a building.

andoba [an-do-bah], *m.* Guy, bloke.

andola [an-do'-lah], *f.* An meaningless jocular expletive.

andolina, andorina, andarina [an-do-lee'-nah, an-do-ree'-nah, an-dah-ree'-nah], *f.* **Swallow.** V. GOLONDRINA.

andón [an-don], *a.* (*LAm.*) V. ANDADOR.

andonear [an-do-nay-ahr], *va.* (*Carib.*) To amble (persona).

andorga [an-dor'-gah], *f.* (*coll.*) Belly. **Llenar la andorga,** To eat much.

andorina [an-do-ree'-nah], *f.* (*Naut.*) A truss, swallow.

Andorra [an-dor'-rah], *f.* Andorra.

andorrear [an-dor-ray-ar'], *vn.* To go about.

andorrera [an-dor-ray'-rah], *f.* Street-walker.

andorrero [an-dor-ray'-ro], *m.* A person of a roving disposition; tramp.

andosco, ca [an-dos'-co, cah], *a.* Two years old; applied to sheep.

andrajo [an-drah'-ho], *m.* 1. Rag, tatter. **Estar hecho un andrajo,** to be in rags. 2. (*Met.*) A despicable person. **Hacer andrajos,** to tear to rags.

andrajosamente [an-drah-ho-sah-men'-tay], *adv.* Raggedly.

andrajoso, sa [an-drah-ho'-so, sah], *a.* Ragged, dressed in tatters.

andriana [an-dree-ah'-nah], *f.* A kind of gown formerly worn by women.

andrina [an-dree'-nah], *f.* A sloe. V. ENDRINA.

andrino [an-dree'-no], *m.* (*Bot.*) Sloetree, blackthorn.

andrógeno [an-dro'-hay-no], *m.* Androgen.

andrógino [an-dro'-he-no], *m.* Hermaphrodite, androgynus, androgyne.

androide [an-dro-e-day], *m.* Android.

andrómina [an-dro'-me-nah], *f.* (*coll.*) Trick, fraud, artifice.

androsemo [an-dro-say'-mo], *m.* (*Bot.*) Parkleaves. V. TODABUENA.

androtomia [an-dro-to-mee'-ah], *f.* Dissection of human bodies.

andularios [an-doo-lah'-re-os], *m. pl.* (*coll.*) A long and wide gown.

andullo [an-dool'-lyo], *m.* A long. rolled leaf of tobacco (*Cuban*).

andurriales [an-door-re-ah'-les], *m. pl.* By-roads, retired places.

aneaje [ah-nay-ah'-hay], *m.* Alnage, ell measure.

anear [ah-nay-ar'], *va.* 1. To measure by ells. 2. (*Prov. Sant.*) To rock in a cradle.

aneblar [ah-nay-blar'], *va.* To cloud, to darken, to obscure. - *vr.* To get misty, get cloudy.

anécdota [ah-nee'-do-tah], *f.* Anecdote.

anecdotario [ah-nayc-do-tah-re-o], *m.* Collection of stories.

anecdótico [ah-nayc-do-te-co], *a.* Anecdotal; **contenido anecdótico,** story content.

anega [ah-nay-gah], *f.* (*Cono Sur*) V. FANEGA.

anegación [ah-nay-gah-the-on'], *f.* Overflowing, inundation.

anegadizo, za [ah-nay-gah-dee'-tho, thah], *a.* Liable to be overflowed.

anegado, da [ah-nay-gah'-do, dah], *a.* Overflowed. **Navío anegado,** (*Naut.*) A water-logged ship. *-pp.* of ANEGAR.

anegadizo [ah-nay-gah-de-tho], *a.* Subject to flooding, frequently flooded (tierra).

anegamiento [ah-nay-gah-me-en'-to], *m.* (*Obs.*) V. ANEGACION.

anegar [ah-nay-gar'], *va.* To inundate, to submerge. (*fig.*) Destroy. *-vr.* To be inundated. **Anegarse en llanto,** to dissolve into tears.

anegociado, da [ah-nay-go-the-ah'-do, dah], *a.* (*Obs.*) Overwhelmed with business.

anejo, ja [ah-nay'-ho, hah], *a.* Annexed, joined. V. ANEXO, XA.

anejo [ah-nay'-ho], *m.* A benefice or church depending on another as its principal or head.

anélido [ah-nay'-le-do], *m.* (*Zool.*) Annelid, a many-jointed worm.

anemia [ah-nay'-me-ah], *f.* (*Med.*) Anaemia, diminution of red corpuscles in the blood.

anémico, ca [ah-nay'-me-co, cah], *a.* Anaemic, affected with anaemia.

anemografía [ah-nay-mo-grah-fee'-ah], *f.* Anemography, the description of the winds.

anemometría [ah-nay-mo-may-tree'-ah], *f.* Anemometry, measuring the force of the winds.

anemómetro [ah-nay-mo'-may-tro], *m.* Anemometer, an instrument to measure the force of the wind.

anémona or **Anémone** [ah-nay'-mo-nay], *f.* (*Bot.*) Anemone or windflower. Anemone.

anemoscopio [ah-nay-mos-co'-pe-o], *m.* Anemoscope, a machine to show the changes of the wind.

anepígrafo, fa [ah-nay-pee'-grah-fo, fah], *a.* Without title or inscription. *V.* MEDALLA.

anequín (A), or **de anequín** [ah-nay-keen'], *adv.* So much a head: applied to the shearing of sheep.

aneroide [ah-nay-ro'-e-day], *a. & m.* Aneroid, without fluid; barometer in clock-form.

anestesia [ah-nes-tay'-se-ah], *f.* Anaesthesia.

anestesiar [ah-nes-tay-se-ar'], *va.* To anaesthetize.

anestésico, ca [ah-nes-tay'-se-co, cah], *a.* Anesthetic, producing insensibility. *-m.* Anesthetic.

anestesista [ah-nays-tay-ses-tah], *f. & m.* Anaesthetic.

aneurisma [ah-nay-oo-rees'-mah], *m. & f. (Med.)* Aneurism, a disease of the arteries and of the heart.

anexar [ah-nees-sar'], *va.* To annex, to join, to unite.

anexidades [ah-nees-se-dah'-des], *f. .* Annexes, belongings.

anexión [ah-nees-se-on'], *f.* Annexion, union; annexation.

anexionar [ah-nec-se-o-nahr'], *va.* To annex.

anexionista [an-nec-se-o-nees'-tah], *m.* Annexationist.

anexo, xa [ah-nec-so, sah], *a. m. (Arquit.)* Annexe, outbuilding. *V.* ANEJO, JA.

anfeta [an-fay-tah], *f. V.* ANFETAMINAS.

anfetaminas [an--fay-tah-me-nahs], *f. & pl.* Amphetamines.

anfibio, bia [an-fee'-be-o, ah], *a.* Amphibious.

anfibología [an-fe-bo-lo-hee'-ah], *f.* Amphibology, words or sentences of a double or doubtful meaning.

anfibológicamente [an-fe-bo-lo'-he-cah-men-tay], *adv.* Amphibologically.

anfibológico, ca [an-fe-bo-lo'-he-co, cah], *a.* Amphibological, doubtful.

anfisbena, anfisibena [an-fis-bay'-nah, an-fe-se-bay'-nah], *f.* Amphisb+na, an amphibious serpent of America.

anfiscios [an-fees'-the-os], *m. pl.* Amphiscii, people of the torrid zone, whose shadows at different times fall north and south.

anfiteatro [an-fe-tay-ah'-tro], *m.* Amphitheater, arena. *(Theat.)* Dress circle.

anfitrión [an-fe-tre-on'], *m. (Met.)* Host, he who does the honors at the table before invited company.

anfitriota [an-fe-tree-o-tah], *f.* Hostess.

anfitrite [an-fe-tree'-tay], *f.* Amphitrite. *(Poet. and Zool.)*

ánfora [ahn'-fo-rah], *f.* 1. Amphora, ancient vase. 2. *(pl.)* Jars or cruets of silver to preserve consecrated oils. 3. Ancient name of the sign Aquarius. 4. The lower valve of certain fruits which opens on ripening. 5. Ancient Greek and Roman measure for liquids equivalent to about eight gallons.

anfractuosidad [an-frac-too-o-se-dahd'], *f.* Crookedness. *-f. pl. (Ant.)* Anfractuosities, convolutions of the brain or cerebrum.

anfractuoso, sa [an-frac-too-oh'-so, sah], *a.* Anfractuous, sinuous, unequal, rough, uneven.

angaria [an-gah'-re-ah], *f.* 1. Ancient servitude. 2. Forced delay in the sailing of a ship, for employ in public service.

angarillas [an-gah-reel'-lyas], *f. pl.* 1. Handbarrow. 2. Panniers. 3. Cruet stands. *V.* AGUADERAR.

angarillón [an-gah-reel-lyon'], *m.* A large wicker basket; a large handbarrow.

angaripola [an-gah-re-po'-lah], *f.* Calico. **Angaripolas,** Gaudy ornaments on clothes.

ángaro [ahn'-gah-ro], *m.* Fire or smoke, used as a signal.

angarrio [an-gahr-re-o], *a. (And. Carib.)* Terribly thin.

angas [an-gahs], **por angas o por mangas,** like it or not *(And.).*

ángel [ahn'-hel], *m.* 1. Angel, a spiritual being. 2. A sort of fish resembling a ray. **Manga de ángel,** sleeve of a coat ruffled or plaited. **Ángel custodio,** or **de la guarda,** guardian angel. **Ángel de guarda,** protector. **Ángel patudo,** nickname of a person rather malicious.

Ángeles [an-hay-lays], *m. & pl.* Los Angeles.

angélica [an-hay'-le-cah], *f. (Bot.)* Garden angelica. Angelica archangelica. **Angélica carlina,** *(Bot.)* Carline thistles. **Angélica palustre,** Wild angelica.

angelical, angélico, ca [an-hay-le-cal', an-hay'-le-co, cah], *a.* Angelical or angelic, heaven born.

angelicalmente [an-hay-le-cal-me-tay], *adv.* Angelically.

angelico, ito [an-hay-lee'-co, an-hay-lee'-to], *m. dim.* A little angel.

angelino, na [an-hay-le-no, nah], *a.* Of Los Angeles. Los Angelinos, the people of Los Angeles.

angelito [an-hay-le-to], *m.* Little angel; *(LAm.)* Dead child; *(Cono Sur)* Don't play the innocent!; **¡no seas angelito!** *(Cono Sur)* Don't be silly!

angelón, angelonazo [an-hay-lone', an-hay-lo-nah'-tho], *m. aug.* Great angel. **Angelón de retablo,** nickname given to a person, commonly a child, disproportionately corpulent.

angelopolitano, na [an-hay-lo-po-le-tah-no, nah], *m. & f. (Mex.)* Of Puebla.

angelote [an-hay-lo'-tay], *m. aug.* 1. A large figure of an angel placed on altars. 2. A fat, good-natured child.

Ángelus [ahn'-hay-loos], *m.* The angelus, a midday prayer in the Roman Catholic Church.

angeo [an-hay'-o], *m.* A coarse sort of linen: upholsterer's canvas.

angina [an-hee'-nah], *f.* Tonsilitis, sore throat. **Angina de pecho,** angina Pectoris.

angiografía [an-he-o-grah-fee'-ah], *f.* Angiography, a description of vessels in the human body.

angiología [an-he-o-lo-he'-ah], *f.* Angiology, the doctrine of the vessels of the human body.

angiosperma [an-he-os-per'-mah], *a. (Bot.)* Angiospermous.

anglicanismo [an-gle-cah-nees'-mo], *m.* Anglicanism, the church religion in England.

anglicano, na [an-gle-cah'-no, nah], *a.* Anglican, belonging to England. **La Iglesia Anglicana,** the Anglican Church.

anglicismo [an-gle-thees'-mo], *m.* Anglicism.

anglicista [an-gle-thes-tah], 1. *a.* **Tendencia anglicista,** anglicising tendency. 2. *m. & f.* Anglicist.

angliparla [an-gle-pahr-lah], *f.* Spanglish *(hum.).*

anglo, gla [ahn'-glo, ah], *a.* Anglian, English-speaking. *-m. & f.* English-map.

angloamericano, na [an-glo-ah-may-re-cah'-no, nah], *a.* Anglo-american.

anglófobo [an-glo-fo-bo], 1. *a.* Anglophobe, anglophobic. 2. Anglophobe.

anglófono [an-glo-fo-no], *a, m& f.* English-speaking.

anglohablante, angloparlante [an-glo-ah-blahn-tay], *a., m. & f.* English-speaking.

anglomanía [an-glo-mah-nee'-ah], *f.* Anglomania, excessive enthusiasm for the English people and their belongings.

anglómano [an-glo'-mah-no], *m.* Anglomaniac, servile imitator of the English.

anglosajón, na [an-glo-sah-hone', nah], *a. & m.* Anglo-Saxon.

angora [an-go'-rah], *a.* The Angora cat or goat: long-haired creatures.

angorina [an-go-re-nah], *f.* Artificial angora.

angostamente [an-gos-tah-men'-tay], *adv.* Narrowly.

angostar [an-gos-tar'], *va.* To narrow, to contract. *-vr.* To narrow, to get narrow.

angosto, ta [an-gos'-to, tah], *a.* Narrow, close. **Venir angosto,** to fall short of one's expectations, ambition, or merit.

angostura [an-gos-too'-rah], *f.* 1. Narrowness. 2. A narrow pass.

angra [ahn'-grah], *f.* A small bay, a cove.

anguarina [an-goo-ah-ree'-nah], *f.* A loose coat hanging down to the knees.

anguila [an-gee'-lah], *f. (Zool.)* Eel. **Anguila de cabo,** *(Naut.)* a port rope with which the sailors were flogged on board the galleys. **Anguilas**, ways on which a ship slides when launching.

anguilazo [an-ge-lah'-tho], *m.* A stroke with a port-rope.

anguilero, ra [an-ge-lay'-ro, rah], *m. & f.* Basket or pannier for eels.

anguina [an-gee'-nah], *f. (Vet.)* The vein of the groins.

angula [an-goo'-lah], *f.* The brood of eels, elver, baby eel.

angulado, da [an-goo-lah'-do, dah], *a.* Having angles.

angular [an-goo-lar'], *a.* Angular. **Piedra angular**, the corner-stone.

angularmente [an-goo-lar-men'-tay], *adv.* With angles; in the form of an angle.

angulema [an-goo-lay'-mah], *f.* A sort of coarse linen manufactured at Angouleme of hemp or tow. -*pl. (coll.)* V. ZALAMERIAS.

ángulo [ahn'-goo-lo], *m.* Angle, corner; nook. **ángulo óptico**, the visual angle. **Ángulos de un picadero**, the corners of a riding-house. **ángulo recto**, right angle. **En ángulo**, at an angle. **Formar ángulo con**, to be at an angle to.

anguloso, sa [an-goo-lo'-so, sah], *a.* Angular, cornered.

angurria [an-goor-re-ah], *f. (And. Cono Sur)* Voracious hunger, greed, meanness, stinginess.

angurrimiento [an-goor-re-me-ayn-to], *a. (And. Cono Sur)* Greedy, mean.

angustia [an-goos'-te-ah], *f.* Anguish, affliction, pang; heartache, heaviness.

angustiadamente [an-goos-te-ah-dah-men'-tay], *adv.* Painfully.

angustiado, da [an-goos-te-ah'-do, dah], *a.* 1. Painful. 2. *(Met.)* Narrow-minded, miserable. -*pp.* of ANGUSTIAR.

angustiar [an-goos-te-ar'], *va.* To cause anguish, to afflict. -*vr.* To be distressed, to grieve.

angustiosamente [an-goos-te-o-sah-mayn-tay], *a.* In an anguished tone.

angustioso [an-goos-te-o-so], *a.* 1. Distressed, anguished; anxious. 2. Distressing, agonizing; heartbreaking.

angustura [an-goos-too'-rah], *f. (Bot.)* Angustura bark.

anha [ah-nah], *interj. (Cono Sur)* V. ANJA.

anhelación [an-ay-lah-the-on'], *f.* 1. Panting, difficulty of breathing. 2. *(fig.)* Longing, yearning.

anhelante [an-ay-lahn'-tay], *a.* Eager, avid, keenly desirous.

anhelar [an-ay-lar'], *vn.* 1. To breathe with difficulty. 2. To desire anxiously, to long, to covet. 3. To gape, to gasp. **Anhelar honores**, to aspire at honors.

anhélito [an-ay'-le-to], *m.* Difficult respiration.

anhelo [an-ay'-lo], *m.* A vehement desire; anxiousness, eagerness. **Anhelo de superación**, urge to do better.

anheloso, sa [an-ay-lo'-so, sah], *a.* Anxious, desirous. *(Med.)* Gasping, panting.

anhídrico, ca [an-ee'-dre-co, cah], *a. V.* ANHIDRO.

anhidrita [an-e-dree'-tah], *f.* Anhydrite, a rock, the base of which is sulphate of lime.

anhidro, dra [an-ee'-dro, drah], *a.* Anhydrous, lacking water.

anhinga [an-een'-gah], *f. (Orn.)* An aquatic bird of prey in Brazil, called the darter.

ani [ah-nee'], *m.* A pretty creeping bird indigenous to South America.

anidar [ah-ne-dar'], *vn.* 1. To nestle, to make a nest. 2. *(Met.)* To dwell, to reside. 3. To cherish, to shelter. **andar anidando**, to prepare for lying in.

anieblar [an-ne-ay-blar'], *va.* To darken, to obscure, to mystify.

aniego [an-ne-ay-go], *m. (And. Cono Sur), m. (Mex.)* Flood.

anilina [ah-ne-lee'-nah], *f. (Chem.)* Aniline.

anilla [ah-ne-lyah], *f.* Curtain ring (de cortina); small ring (anillito); cigar band (de puro).

anillado, da [ah-neel-lyah'-do, dah], *a.* Annulated, ringed. -*pl.* Annelids, worms whose bodies are a series of ringed segments.

anillar [ah-neel-lyar'], *va.* To form rings circles in work; used by cutlers.

anillejo, anillete [ah-neel-lyay'-ho, ah-neel-lyay'-tay], *m. dim.* A small ring.

anillo [ah-neel'-lyo], *m.* 1. A finger ring; circlet. **Anillo de compromiso**, engagement ring. 2. *(Naut.)* Hank or grommet. **Venir como anillo al dedo**, to come in the very nick of time. 3. *(Arch.)* Astragal.

ánima [ah'-ne-mah], *f.* 1. Soul. *V.* ALMA. 2. *(Mech.)* The bore of a gun. **Ánimas**, ringing of bells at sunset, in the old days. **A las ánimas me volví a casa**, at sunset I returned home.

animable [ah-ne-mah'-blay], *a.* Susceptible of animation.

animación [ah-ne-mah-the-on'], *f.* Animation, liveliness. **Campaña de animación social**, campaign of social awakening. **Había poca animación**, there wasn't much life about it.

animadamente [ah-ne-mah-dah-mayn-tay], *adv.* In lively fashion, gaily; animatedly.

animado, da [ah-ne-mah'-do, dah], *a.* Manful, lively, gay; bustling, busy, animated; merry, in high spirits. -*pp.* of ANIMAR.

animador, ra [ah-ne-mah-dor', rah], *m. & f.* 1. One who animates or cheers. 2. Entertainer (cabaret); compère (presentador); hostess (presentadora).

animadversión [ah-ne-mad-ver-se-on'], *f.* Animadversion, remark, stricture.

animal [ah-ne-mal'], *m.* 1. Animal. 2. Animal; used in contempt. **El animal de Juan**, that beast of John.

animal [ah-ne-mah'], *a.* Animal, relating to an animal.

animalada [ah-ne-mah-lah-dah], *f.* 1. *(LAm.)* group of animals. 2. *(fig.)* Foolishness, stupidity (cualidad). **Hacer una animalada**, to do something silly.

animalaje [ah-ne-mah-lah-hay], *m. (Cono Sur)* Animals; herd of animals.

animalejo [ah-ne-mah-lay-ho], *m.* Odd-looking creature.

animalidad [ah-ne-mah-le-dahd], *f.* Animality; sensuality.

animalización [ah-ne-mah-le-thah-the-on'], *f.* Animalization; effect of making an animal.

animalizar [ah-ne-mah-le-thar'], *va.* To animalize. -*vr.* To grow brutish.

animalazo [ah-ne-mah-lah'-tho], *m. aug.* A large or big animal.

animalejo, ico, illo [ah-ne-mah-lay'-ho, lee'-co, leel'-lyo], *m. dim.* A small animal, animalcule.

animalón, animalote [ah-ne-mah-lone', ah-ne-mah-lo'-tay], *m. aug.* A large or big animal.

animalucho [ah-ne-mah-loo'-cho], *m.* An ugly, hideous animal.

animar [ah-ne-mar'], *va.* 1. To animate, to enliven, to comfort, to revive. **Animar a uno a hacer algo**, to encourage somebody to do something. 2. To incite, to excite. 3. To give power or vigor to inanimate things. -*vr.* To become more lively; to brighten up. **A ver si se animan**, we'll wait and see if they do anything about it. **No me animo a hacerlo, I** can't bring myself to do it.

anime, or **Goma Anime** [ah-nee'-may], *1. f.* A resin resembling myrrh. 2. *m. (Carib.)* Polyethylene.

animero [ah-ne-may'-ro], *m.* One who used to ask for charity for the souls in purgatory.

anímico [ah-ne-me-co], *a.* Mental, of mind; **Estado anímico**, state of mind.

anímita [ah-ne-me-tah], *f. (Cono Sur)* Roadside shrine.

ánimo [ah'-ne-mo], *m.* 1. Spirit. **Apaciguar los ánimos**, to calm people down. 2. Courage, valor, fortitude, manfulness; hardiness. **Dar ánimos a**, to encourage. 3. Mind, intention, meaning, will. **Con ánimos de**, with the intention of. **Tener ánimos para algo**, to be in the mood for something. 4. Thought, attention. **Hacer buen ánimo**, to bear up under adversities. -*int.* Come on!

animosamente [ah-ne-mo-sah-men'-tay], *adv.* In a spirited manner, courageously.

animosidad [ah-ne-mo-se-dahd'], *f.* Animosity, valor, courage; boldness.

animoso, sa [ah-ne-mo'-so, sah], *a.* Brave, spirited, courageous, gallant.

aniñadamente [ah-nee-nyah-dah-men'-tay], *adv.* In a childish, puerile manner.

aniñado, da [ah-nee-nyah'-do, dah], *a.* 1. Childish. 2. *(Cono Sur)* Spirited, lively. 3. *(Cono Sur)* Handsome (guapo).

aniñarse [ah-nee-nyar'-say], *vr.* To grow childish.

aniquilable [ah-ne-ke-lah-blay], *a.* Annihilable, destructible.

aniquilación [ah-ne-ke-lah-the-on'], *f.* Annihilation, extinction.

aniquilador, ra [ah-ne-ke-lah-dor'-rah], *m. & f.* A destroyer.

aniquilar [ah-ne-ke-lar'], *va.* To annihilate, to destroy, to overthow, *-vr.* To decline, to decay; to humble; to consume.

anís [ah-nees'], *m. (Bot.)* Anise. **Anises**, anise-seeds preserved in sugar. **Llegar a los anises**, to come the day after the feast. **Estar hecho un anis**, to be elegantly dressed.

anisado, da [ah-ne-sah'-do, dah], *a.* Applied to spirits tinctured with anise. *-pp* of ANISAR.

anisar [ah-ne-sar'], *va.* To tincture with anise.

aniseros [ah-ne-say-ros], *m. & pl. (And.)* **Entregar los aniseros**, to kick the bucket.

anisete [ah-ne-say'-tay], *m.* Anisette.

anisófilo, la [ah-ne-so'-fe-lo, lah], *a.* Anisophyllous, having unequal leaves.

anisol [ah-ne-sole'], *m.* A liquid substance isomeric with creasote.

anisómero, ra [ah-ne-so'-may-ro, rah], *a.* An isomeric, composed of unequal parts.

anivelar [ah-ne-vay-lahr], *va. V.* NIVELAR.

aniversario, ria [ah-ne-ver-sah'-re-o, ah], *a.* Annual, yearly.

aniversario [ah-ne-ver-sah'-re-o], *m.* 1. Anniversary. **Aniversario de boda,** wedding anniversary.

¡anjá! [an-hah'], *int.* (Cuba) Well! bravo!

anjeo [an-hay-o], *m.* Anjou.

Ankara [an-kah-rah], *f.* Ankara.

ano [ah'-no], *m.* The anus.

anoche [ah-no'-chay], *adv.* Last night.

anochecedor, ra [ah-no-chay-thay-dor], *m. & f.* Late bird, person who keeps late hours.

anochecer [ah-no-chay-therr'], *vn.* To grow dark. **Anochecerle a uno en alguna parte**, to be benighted somewhere. **Al anochecer**, at nightfall, *-vr. (Poetic.)* to grow dark. **Yo amanecí en Veracruz, y anochecí en Acapulco,** I was in Vera0cruz at dawn, and in Acapulco at dusk.

anochecida [ah-no-chay-thee'-dah], *f.* Dusk, nightfall.

anodinar [ah-no-de-nar'], *va.* To administer anodyne medicines.

anodino, na [ah-no-dee'-no, nah], *a. (Med.)* Anodyne, allaying pain.

anodizar [ah-no-de-thar'], *va.* To anodize.

ánodo [ah'-no-do], *m. (Elec.)* Anode.

anomalía [ah-no-mah-lee'-ah], *f.* 1. Anomaly, deviation from rules. 2. *(Astr.)* Distance of a planet at its aphelion.

anómalo, la [ah-no'-mah-lo, lah], *a. (Gram.)* Anomalous.

anón [ah-none'], *m. (Bot.)* The custard apple-tree. Annona.

anona [ah-no'-nah], *f.* 1. Annona or custard-apple. In some parts it is called guanara. 2. Store of provisions. *V.* CHIRIMOYA.

anonadación [ah-no-nah-dah-the-on'], *f.* **Anonadamiento**, *m.* 1. Annihilation. 2. Self-contempt.

anonadar [ah-no-nah-dar'], *va.* 1. To annihilate. 2. *(Met.)* To diminish or lessen in a considerable degree. *-vr.* To humble oneself to a low degree.

anónimamente [ah-no'-ne-mah-men-tay], *ad.* Anonymously.

anonimato [ah-no-ne-mah-to], *m.* Anonimity. **Mantenerse en el anonimato**, to remain anonymous.

anónimo, ma [ah-no'-ne-mo, mah], *a.* Anonymous; nameless. **Guardar el anónimo**, to preserve one's anonymity. Anonymous person, unknown person.

anorac [ah-no-rak], *m. V.* ANORAK.

anorexia [ah-no-ree'-se-ah], *f. (Med.)* Anorexia, loss of appetite.

anormal [ah-nor-mahl'], *a.* Abnormal; irregular, unusual. Mentally handicapped.

anormalidad [ah-nor-mah-le-dahd], *f.* Abnormality; irregularity; unusual nature.

anormalmente [ah-nor-mal-mayn-tay], *adv.* Abnormality.

anotación [ah-no-tah-the-on'], *f.* Annotation, note, notation.

anotador, ra [ah-no-tah-dor', rah], *m. & f.* 1. Commentator. 2. *m. (LAm.)* Scorecard.

anotar [ah-no-tar'], *va.* To write notes, to comment.

anoxia [ah-noe'-ce-ah], *f. (Med.)* Anoxia.

anquera [an-kay'-rah], *f. (Mex.)* A round covering for the hind quarter of a horse; semi-lunar tail-piece of a saddle.

anqueta [ah-kay'-tah], **Estar de media anqueta**. to be incommodiously seated.

anquiboyuno, na [an-ke-bo-yoo'-no, nah], *a.* Having a croup like an ox; applied to horses and mules.

anquilosado [an-ke-lo-sah-do], *a. (fig.)* Stagnant; paralyzed.

anquilosamiento [an-ke-lo-sah-me-ayn-to], *m. (fig.)* Stagnation; paralysis.

anquilosar [an-ke-lo-sahr], 1. *va.* To paralyze. 2. *vn. (Aut. Mec.)* To seize up. 3. *-vr.* To decline; to become eroded.

anquilosis [an-ke-lo'-sis], *f. (Anat.)* Anchylosis, a stiff joint.

anquilostoma [an-ke-los-to-mah], *m.* Hookworm.

anquiseco, ca [an-ke-say'-co, cah], *a.* Lean crouped.

ansa [ahn'-sah], *f.* Commercial bond among the free cities of Germany.

ánsar [ahn'-sar], *m.* A goose. **Ánsar macho**, gander.

ansarería [an-sah-ray-ree'-ah], *f.* The place where geese are reared.

ansarero [ah-sah-ray'-ro], *m.* A gooseherd.

ansarino, na [an-sah-ree'-no, nah], *a. (Poetic.)* Belonging to geese.

ansi [an-see'], *(Obs.) V.* Así.

ansia [ahn'-see-ah], *f.* Anxiety anguish, eagerness, ardent desire; longing, hankering; greediness.

ansiadamente [an-se-ah-dah-men'-tay], *adv.* Anxiously, earnestly.

ansiado [an-se-ah-do], *a.* Longed-for; **el momento tan ansiado**, the moment which we had so much longed for.

ansiar [an-se-ar'], *va.* To desire anxiously, to long, to hanker. **Ansiar por uno**, to be madly in love with somebody.

ansiedad [an-se-ay-dahd'], *f.* A state of anxiety. *V.* ANSIA.

ansina [an-see'-nah], *(Obs.) V.* Así.

ansiosamente [an-se-o-sah-men'-tay], *adv.* Anxiously, earnestly, ardently, eagerly, fervently; heartily.

ansiolítico [an-se-o-le-te-co], *a.* Sedative, tranquillizer.

ansioso, sa [an-se-oh'-so, sah], *a.* 1. Anxious, eager, greedy; hot. **Esperamos ansiosos**, we waited anxiously. 2. Attended with great uneasiness.

anta [ahn'-tah], *f.* An elk. *-pl. (Arch.)* Antes, pillars of a building.

antaceo [an-tah'-thay-o], *m. (Zool.)* A large fish of the family of sturgeons.

antagallas [an-tah-gahl'-lyas], *f. pl. (Naut.)* Spritsail, reef-bands.

antagónico, ca [an-tah-go'-ne-co, cah], *a.* Antagonistic; in opposition.

antagonismo [an-tah-go-nees'-mo], *m.* Antagonism, antipathy.

antagonista [ah-tah-go-nees'-tah], *m.* 1. Antagonist, an opponent; competitor. 2. Opposer, foe, foeman.

antana [an-tah'-nah], **Llamarse antana**, to contradict, to retract.

antañazo [an-tah-nyah'-tho], *adv.* A long time since.

antaño [an-tah'-nyo], *adv.* 1. Last year. **En los nidos de antaño no hay pájaros hogaño,** time must be seized by the forelock. *(Lit.)* There are no birds in last year's nest. 2. Long ago.

antañón [an-ta-nye-on], *a.* Ancient, very old.

antañoso [an-tah-nyo-so], *a. (LAm.)* Ancient, very old.

antara [an-tah-rah], *f.* *(And.)* Pan pipes.

antártico, ca [an-tar'-te-co, cah], *a.* Antarctic.

Antártida [an-tahr-te-dah], *f.* Antartica.

ante [ahn'-tay], *m.* 1. Buckskin, a dressed buck or buffalo skin. 2. An elk. **Piel de ante**, suede. **Guantes de ante**, suede gloves.

ante [ahn'-tay], *prep.* Before. **Ante mí**, before me, in my presence. **Ante todas cosas or ante todo**, before all things, above all.

ante [an-tay], *pref.* Ante.

anteado, da [an-tay-ah'-do, dah], *a.* Buff-colored, of a paleyellow color.

anteanoche [an-tay-ah-no'-chay], *adv.* The night before last.

anteanteanoche [an-tay-an-tay-ah-no'-chay], *adv.* Three nights ago.

anteanteayer [an-tay-an-tay-ah-yerr'], *adv.* Three days ago.

anteantier [an-tay-an-te-err'], *adv.* *(Obs.)* V. ANTEANTEAYER.

anteayer [an-tay-ah-yerr'], *adv.* The day before yesterday.

antebrazo [an-tay-brah'-tho], *m.* The fore-arm.

antecama [an-tay-cah'-mah], *f.* A carpet laid in front of a bed.

antecámara [an-tay-cah'-mah-rah], *f.* 1. Antechamber. 2. Lobby; hall. 3. *(Naut.)* The steerage.

antecamarilla [an-tay-cah-mah-reel'-lyah], *f.* A room leading to the king's antechamber.

antecapilla [an-tay-cah-peel'-lyah], *f.* The porch.

antecedente [an-tay-thay-den'-tay], *m.* Antecedent, previous, preceding. **Visto lo antecedente,** in view of the foregoing. **Antecedentes**; record, history, background; **¿cuáles son sus antecedentes?,** what's his history? **Antecedentes delictivos,** criminal record. **Tener buenos antecedentes,** to have a good record.

antecedentemente [an-tay-thay-den-tay-men'-tay], *adv.* Antecedently, previously, beforehand.

anteceder [an-tay-thay-derr'], *va.* To precede, to forege.

antecesor, ra [an-tay-thay-sor', rah], *m. & f.* Predecessor, forefather. **Antecesores,** ancestors.

antechinos [an-tay-chee'-nos], *m. pl.* *(Arch.)* Fluted mouldings.

anteco, a [an-tay'-co, cah], *a.* Antoeci, or inhabitants of the same meridian.

antecoger [an-tay-co-herr'], *va.* 1. To bring any person or thing before one. 2. To gather in fruit before the due time.

antecolumna [an-tay-co-loom'-nah]; *f.* *(Arch.)* A column of a portico.

antecomedor [an-tay-co-may-dor], *m.* *(LAm.)* Room adjoining the dining room.

antecocina [an-tay-co-the-nah], *f.* Scullery.

antecoro [an-tay-co'-ro], *m.* The entrance which leads to the choir.

Antecristo [an-tay-crees'-to], *m.* Antichrist.

antedata [an-tay-dah'-tah], *f.* Antedate.

antedatar [an-tay-dah-tar'], *va.* To antedate.

antedecir [an-tay-day-theer'], *va.* To predict. to foretell.

antedicho, cha [an-tay-dee'-cho, chah], *a.* Foresaid.

ante diem [an-tay-dee'-em]. *(Lat.)* The preceding day.

antediluviano, na [an-tay-de-loo-ve-ah'-no, nah], *a.* Antediluvian.

antefechar [an-tay-fay-char'], *va.* To anticipate the date of. *V.* ANTEDATAR.

antefirma [an-tay-feer'-mah], *f.* The style of address which is put before the signature in any communication.

anteiglesia [an-tay-e-glay'-se-ah], *f.* *(Obs.)* The porch of a church.

antejuela [an-tay-hoo-ay-lah], *f.* *(CAm.)* V. LENTEJUELA.

antelación [an-tay-lah-the-on'], *f.* Precedence in order of time. **Con mucha antelación,** long in advance.

antelina [an-tay-le-nah], *f.* Suede, artificial buckskin.

antellevar [an-tay-lyay-vahr'], *va.* *(Mex. Aut.)* To run down.

antellevón [an-tay-lyay-von'], *m.* *(Mex. Aut.)* Accident.

antemano [an-tay-mah'-no], *adv.* **De antemano,** beforehand.

antememoria [an-tay-may-mo-re-ah], *(Comp.)* Cache memory. **Antememoria de Video** *(Comp.)*, Video buffer.

antemeridiano, na [an-tay-may-re-de-ah'-no, nah], *a.* In the forenoon.

antemural [an-tay-moo-ral'], *m.* 1. A fort, rock, or mountain, which serves for the defence of a fortress. 2. *(Met.)* A safeguard.

antemuralla [an-tay-moo-rahl'-lyah], *f.* or **Antemuro** [an-te-moo'-ro], *m.* V. ANTEMURAL.

antena [an-tay'-nah], *f.* 1. (Radio) Aerial. 2. Antenna or feeler of insects. *(fig.)* **Tener antena para**, to have a feeling for. 3. *(Naut.)* Lateen yard.

antenallas [an-tay-nahl'-lyas], *f. pl.* Pincers.

antenatal [an-tay-nah-tahl], *a.* Antenatal, prenatal.

antenoche [an-tay-no'-chay], *adv.* 1. The night before last. 2. *(Obs.)* Before nightfall.

antenombre [an-tay-nom'-bray], *m.* Title (Sir, Saint, etc., en inglés; (Don, San, etc. en español).

anténula [an-tay'-noo-lah], *f.* Antennule: applied to the smaller pair of antennas or feelers of crustacea.

antenupcial [an-te-noop-the-ahl'], *a.* Antenuptial, before marriage.

anteojera [an-tay-o-hay'-rah], *f.* 1. Spectacle-case. 2. Eye-flap.

anteojero [an-tay-o-hay'-ro], *m.* Spectacle-maker.

anteojo [an-tay-o'-ho], *m.* A spy-glass; an eye-glass. **Anteojo de larga vista,** a telescope. **Anteojo de puño,** or **de teatro,** opera-glass. *-pl.* 1. Spectacles. **Anteojos de camino,** goggles. 2. Pieces of felt or leather put before the eyes of vicious horses.

antepagar [an-tay-pah-gar'], *va.* To pay beforehand.

antepasado, da [an-tay-pah-sah'-do, dah], *a.* Passed, elapsed, previous, before last. *m.* Ancestor.

antepasados [an-tay-pah-sah'-dos], *m. pl.* Ancestors, predecessors.

antepecho [an-tay-pay'-cho], *m.* 1. Balcony, bridge-rail; sill of a window. 2. Breastwork, parapet, battlement. 3. Footstep of a coach. 4. Harness for the breast of a draught-horse; poitrel. 5. Breast roller of a loom. 6. The part of a ribbon frame or loom, which passes from the right to the left, to the point in which the weaver's strap is placed. **Antepechos,** *(Naut.)* The iron horse of the head.

antepenúltimo, ma [an-tay-pay-nool'-te-mo, mah], *a.* Antepenult, last but two.

anteponer [an-tay-po-nerr'], *va.* 1. To prefer. 2. *(Obs.)* To place before. (**Yo antepongo,** from **Anteponer.** V. PONER). *-vr.* To be in front.

anteportada [an-te-por-tah'-dah], *f.* A fly-leaf bearing the title only of a book.

anteportal, or **antepórtico** [an-tay-por'-te-co], *m.* Vestibule or porch.

anteprotecto [an-tay-pro-tayc-to], *m.* Preliminary sketch, preliminary plan.

antepuerta [an-tay-poo-er'-tah], *f.* 1. A curtain placed before a door. 2. Anteport.

antepuerto *m.* *(Naut.)* Anteport.

antepuesto [an-tay-poo-ays-to], *a.* Preceding, coming before.

antequino [an-tay-kee'-no], *m.* *(Arch.)* V. ESGUCIO.

antera [an-tay'-rah], *f.* *(Bot.)* Anther, the part of the stamen which contains the pollen of flowers.

anterior [an-tay-re-or'], *a.* Anterior, former. **Cada uno es mejor que el anterior,** each one is better than the last. **Se había olvidado de todo lo anterior,** he had forgotten all that had happened previously. Front, fore. **En la parte anterior del coche,** on the front part of the car.

anterioridad [an-tay-re-o-re-dahd'], *f.* Priority (prioridad); preference; anteriority (tiempo). **Con anterioridad,** previously.

anteriormente [an-tay-re-or-men'-tay], *adv.* Previously, before.

anteroversión [an-tay-ro-ver-se-on'], *f. (Med.)* Anteversion of an organ.

antes [ahn'-tes], *adv.* 1. Before. **Tres días antes**, three days before. **Antes que llegues**, before you arrive. 2. Beforehand, in advance (con antelación). **Su hijo había ido anteriormente a preparar la entrevista**, his son had gone beforehand to prepare the meeting. **La última bocacalle antes de los semáforos**, the last turning before the traffic lights. **Antes que nada**, above all. **Mucho antes**, a long time before. **Lo antes posible, cuanto antes**, as soon as possible. *conj.* On the contrary (más bien). **No temo la muerte, antes la deseo**, I don't fear death, on the contrary, I long for it. *a.* Before, previous. **La semana antes**, the week before, the previous week.

antesacristía [an-tay-sah-cris-tee'-ah], *f.* An apartment which leads to the sacristy.

antesala [an-tay-sah'-lah], *f.* Antechamber. **Hacer antesala**, to attend in an antechamber.

antesalazo [an-tay-sah-lah-tho], *m. (Mex.)* Long wait.

antestatura [an-tes-tah-too'-rah], *f. (Mil.)* A small intrenchment of palisadoes and sandbags.

antetemplo [an-tay-tem'-plo], *m.* Portico.

anteúltimo [an-tay-ool-te-mo], *a. (Cono Sur)* Penultimate.

antever [an-tay-verr'], *va.* To foresee. (**Yo anteveo**, from **Antever**. *V.* VER.)

antevíspera [an-tay-vees'-pay-rah], *f.* The day before yesterday.

anti [ahn'-te], *pref.* Anti [indicating «against» or «opposite»].

antiácido, da [an-te-ah'-the-do, dah], *a.* Antacid.

antiadherente [an-te-ah-day-rayn-tay], *a.* Non-stick.

antiaéreo, rea [an-te-ah-ay'-ray-o, ray-ah], *a.* Antiaircraft.

antiafrodisíaco, ca [an-te-ah-fro-de-se-ah'-co, cah], *a.* Anaphrodisiac.

antialcohólico, ca [an-te-al-co-o-le-co], *a.* Teetotal. *m. & f.* Teetotaller.

antialcoholismo [an-te-al-co-o-lees'-mo], *m.* Antialcoholism.

antiamericano [an-te-ah-may-re-cah-no], *a.* Anti-American.

antiartrítico, ca [an-te-ar-tree'-te-co, cah], *a.* Arthritis-combatting.

antiatómico [an-te-ah-to-me-co], *a.* **Refugio antiatómico**, nuclear fallout shelter.

antibalas [an-te-bah-lahs], *a.* Bullet proof.

antibelicista [an-te-bay-le-thees-tah], *a. m. & f.* Anti-war; pacifist.

antibiótico, ca [an-te-be-o'-te-co, cah], *a. & m.* Antibiotic.

anticanceroso, sa [an-te-can-the-ro'-so, sah], *a.* Cancer-fighting.

anticarro [an-te-car'-ro], *a.* Antitank.

anticatarral [an-te-ca-tar-rahl'], *a.* Cold-fighting, cold-curing.

anticiclón [an-te-the-clon'], *m.* Anticyclone.

anticiclonal [an-te-the-clo-nahl'], *a.* Anticiclonic.

anticipación [an-te-the-pah-the-on'], *f.* 1. Anticipation. 2. Expectation. **Hacer algo con anticipación**, to do something well beforehand. **Reservar con anticipación**, to book in advance.

anticipada [an-te-the-pah'-dah], *f.* Catching one's opponent off guard.

anticipadamente [an-te-the-pah-da-men'-tay], *adv.* In advance, with plenty of time.

anticipado [an-te-the-pah-do], *a.* Future, prospective; in advance.

anticipar [an-te-the-par'], *va.* 1. To anticipate. 2. To move up (a date), to move up the date of. **Anticiparon las vacaciones**, they took their holiday early. *-vr.* 1. To get ahead. 2. To come early, to occur early. **Anticiparse a hacer algo**, to do something ahead of time.

anticipo [an-te-thee'-po], *m.* 1. Anticipation. 2. Advance payment. **Esto es sólo un anticipo**, this is just a foretaste.

anticlerical [an-te-clay-re-cahl'], *a.* Anticlerical.

anticlericalismo [an-te-clay-re-cah-lees-mo], *m.* Anticlericalism.

anticlinal [an-te-cle-nal], *m. (LAm.)* Watershed.

anticoagulante [an-te-co-a-goo-lahn'-tay], *m. & a.* Anticoagulant.

anticoba [an-te-co-bah], *f.* Brutal frankness.

anticolonialismo [an-te-co-lo-ne-a-lees'-mo], *m.* Anticolonialism.

anticomunismo [an-te-co-moo-nees'-mo], *m.* Anticommunism.

anticomunista [an-te-co-moo-nees'-tah], *m.* com. Anticommunist.

anticoncepcional [an-te-con-thep-the-o-nahl'], *m. & a.* Contraceptive, birth control.

anticoncepcionismo [an-te-con-thep-the-o-nees'-mo], *m.* Birth control, use of contraceptives.

anticonceptivo [an-te-con-thep-te-vo], *a.* Birth control, family-planning. **Métodos anticonceptivos**, birth control methods.

anticonformismo [an-te-con-for-mees'-mo], *m.* Nonconformity.

anticogelante [an-te-con-hay-lahn'-tay], *m. & a.* Antifreeze.

anticonstitucional [an-te-cons-te-too-the-o-nahl'], *a.* Unconstitutional.

anticontaminante [an-te-con-tah-me-nahn-tay], *a. (Cono Sur)* Anti-pollution.

anticorrosivo [an-te-cor-ro-se-vo], *a.* Anticorrosive, antirust.

anticonstitucional [an-te-cons-te-too-the-o-nahl], *a.* Unconstitutional.

anticresis [an-te-cray'-sis], *f.* A contract between debtor and creditor by which the former yields to the latter the fruits of a farm until the debt is paid.

anticresista [an-te-cre-sees'-tah], *m.* The creditor in anticresis.

anticristiano, na [an-te-cris-te-ah'-no, nah], *a. & m. & f.* Antichristian.

anticrítico [an-te-cree'-te-co], *m.* Anticritic, an opponent to a critic.

anticristo [an-te-crees-to], *m.* Antichrist.

anticuado, da [an-te-coo-ah'-do, dah], *a.* Antiquated; obsolete, out of use (machine). Old fashioned (person). Out-of-date (película). *-pp.* of ANTICUAR.

anticuar [an-te-coo-ar'], *va.* To antiquate, to outdate.

anticuario [an-te-coo-ah'-re-o], *m.* Antiquary, antiquarian.

anticuarse [an-te-coo-ahr-say], *vr.* To become antiquated, to get out of date.

anticucho [an-te-coo-cho], *m. (And. Culin.)* Kebab.

anticuerpo [an-te-coo-err'-po], *m. (Chem.)* Antibody.

antidemocrático, ca [an-te-day-mo-crah'-te-co, cah], *a.* Nondemocratic.

antideportividad [an-te-por-te-ve-dahd], *f.* Unsporting attitude.

antideportivo [an-te-day-por-te-vo], *a.* Unsporting.

antidepresivo [an-te-day-pray-se-vo], *a.m.* Antidepressant, antidepressing.

antideslizante [an-te-des-le-thahn'-tay], *a.* Nonskid.

antideslumbrante [an-te-days-loom-brahn-tay], *a.* Antidazzle.

antidetonante [an-te-day-to-nahn'-tay], *a.* Antiknock.

antidiabético, ca [an-te-de-ah-bay'-te-co, cah], *a.* To control diabetes.

antidisturbios [an-te-des-toor-be-os], *a.:* **Policía antidisturbios**, riot police.

antídoto [an-tee'-do-to], *m.* 1. Antidote, counterpoison. 2. *(Met.)* A preventive or preservative against vice or error.

antidroga [an-te-dro-gah], *a.* **Brigada antidroga**, drug squad.

antidumping [an-te-doom-pin], *a.* **Medidas antidumping**, antidumping measures.

antieconómico [an-te-ay-co-no-me-co], *a.* Uneconomic; wasteful.

antiemético, ca [an-te-ay-may'-te-co, cah], *a. (Med.)* Antemetic.

antiepiléptico, ca [an-te-ay-pe-lep'-te-co, cah], *a. (Med.)* Antiepileptic.

antiescorbútico, ca [an-te-es-cor-boo'-te-co, cah], *a. (Med.)* Antiscorbutic.

antier [an-te-err'], *adv. (coll.)* The day before yesterday; a contraction of **antes de ayer**.

antiespamódico, ca [an-te-es-pas-mo'-de-co, cah], *a. (Med.)* Antispasmodic.

antifanático, ca [an-te-fah-nah'-te-co, cah], *a.* Antifanatic.

antifascismo [an-te-fahs-thes-mo], *m.* Antifascism.

antifascista [an-te-fahs-thes-tah], *a. m. & f.* Antifascist.

antifatiga [an-te-fah-te-gah], *a.* **Píldora antifatiga,** antifatigue pill.

antifaz [an-te-fath'], *m.* A veil which covers the face. A mask.

antifebril [an-te-fay-breel'], *a. (Med.)* Antifebrile.

antifeminismo [an-te-fay-me-nes-mo], *m.* Antifeminism.

antifeminista [an-te-fay-me-nes-tah], *a. m. & f.* Antifeminist.

antiflogístico, ca [an-te-flo-hees'-te-co, cah], *a. & m. (Med.)* Antiphlogistic. **antífona** [an-tee'-fo-nah], *f.* Antiphony, an anthem.

antifonal, antifonario [an-te-fo-nahl', an-te-fo-nah'-re-o], *m.* Antiphonal, a book of anthems.

antifrasis [an-tee'-frah-sis], *f.* Antiphrasis.

antifricción [an-te-free-the-on'] *f.* Antifriction alloy.

antifriccional [an-te-frac-the-o-nahl], *a.* Antifriction

antifrís [an-te-fres], *m. (LAm.)* Antifreeze.

antigás [an-te-gahs], *a.* **Careta antigás,** gasmask.

antígeno [an-tee'-hay-no], *m.* Antigen.

antigolpes [an-te-gol-pay], *a.* Shockproof.

antígona [an-te-go-nah], *f.* Antigone.

antigravedad [an-te-grah-vay-dhad'], *f.* Weightlessness.

antigripal [an-te-gre-pahl], *a.* **Vacuna antigripal,** flu vaccine.

antigualla [an-te-goo-ahl'-lyah], *f.* 1. A monument of antiquity; antique. 2. Antiquity. 3. Ancient custom out of use.

antiguamente [an-te-goo-ah-men'-tay], *adv.* Anciently, formerly.

antiguar [an-te-goo-ar'], *vn.* To obtain seniority, as member of a tribunal, college, etc. *-va. (Obs.)* 1. To make obsolete. 2. To abolish the ancient use of a thing.

antigüedad [an-te-goo-ay-dahd'], *f.* 1. Antiquity, oldness. 2. Ancient times, the days of yore. **La fábrica tiene una antigüedad de 200 años,** the factory is 200 years old. 3. The ancients. 4. Antique.

antiguerra [an-te-gay-rrah], *a.* Anti-war.

antiguo, gua [an-tee'-goo-o, goo-ah], *a.* Antique, stricken in years, old; having long held an employment or place. **Un antiguo alumno mío,** an old pupil of mine.

antiguo [an-tee'-goo-o], *m.* 1. An antique of Greece or Rome. 2. An aged member of a college or community; senior of a college. **Antiguos,** The ancients; the illustrious men of antiquity.

antihelmíntico, ca [an-te-el-meen'-te-co, cah], *a. (Med.)* Anthelminthic.

antihéroe [an-te-ay-ro-ay], *m.* Antihero.

antihigiénico, ca [an-te-he-ay'-ne-co, cah], *a.* Unsanitary, unhygienic.

antihistamina [an-tees-tah-me'-nah], *f.* Antihistamine.

antihistamínico [an-te-es-tah-me-ne-co], *a. m.* Antihistamine.

antiflacionista [an-te-en-flah-the-o-nes-tah], *a.* Anti-inflationary.

antilogaritmo [an-te-lo-gah-reet'-mo], *m.* Antilogarithm.

antilogía [an-te-lo-hee'-ah], *f.* An apparent contradiction between two sentences or passages of an author.

antilógico, ca [an-te-lo'-he-co, cah], *a.* Illogical, contrary to logic.

antílope [an-tee'-lo-pay], *m.* Antelope.

antillanismo [an-te-lyah-nes-mo], *m.* Word or phrase peculiar to the Antilles.

antillano, na [an-teel-lyah'-no, nah], *a.* Native or relating to the Antilles.

antillas [an-te-lyahs], *f. & pl.* Antilles, West Indian, of the Antilles.

antimacasar [an-te-mah-cah-sahr], *m.* Antimacasar.

antimateria [an-te-mah-tay'-re-ah], *f.* Antimatter.

antimisil [an-te-me-seel], *a.* Antimissile: **misil antimisil,** antimissile missile.

antimonárquico, ca [an-te-mo-nar'-ke-co, cah], *a.* Antimonarchic, antimonarchical.

antimonial [an-te-mo-ne-ahl'], *a.* Antimonial, belonging to antimony.

antimonio [an-te-mo'-ne-o], *m.* Antimony.

antimonopolio [an-te-mo-no-po'-le-o], *a.* Antitrust, antimonopoly.

antinacional [an-te-nah-the-o-nahl'], *a.* Against one's national interests.

antinatural [an-te-nah-too-rahl'], *a.* Unnatural.

antineutrón [an-te-ne-oo-tron'], *m.* Antineutron.

antimoral [an-te-mo-rahl'], *a.* Contrary to morality.

antinomía [an-te-no'-me-ah], *f. (Law.)* A conflict between laws or parts of a law.

antioquía [an-te-o-ke-ah], *f.* Antioch.

antioxidante [an-te-oc-se-dahn-tay], *a.* Antirust.

antipalúdico [an-te-pah-loo-de-co], *a.* Antimalarial.

antipapa [an-te-pah'-pah], *m.* Antipope, a pope who is not canonically elected.

antipapado [an-te-pah-pah'-do], *m.* The unlawful dignity of antipope.

antipapal [an-te-pah-pahl'], *a.* Antipapal.

antipara [an-te-pah'-rah], *f.* 1. A screen, or anything which serves as a screen.

antiparabólico [an-te-pah-rah-bo-le-co], *a. (Carib.)* Wild.

antiparásito, antiparasitario [an-te-pah-rah'-se-to, an-te-pah-rah-se-tah'-re-o], *a.* Preventing or reducing static or interference. *-m.* Static suppressor, interference filter.

antiparras [an-te-pahr'-ras], *f. pl. (coll.)* Specs, glasses.

antipartícula [an-te-par-tee'-coo-lah], *f.* Antiparticle.

antipatía [an-te-pah-tee'-ah], *f.* Antipathy.

antipático, ca [an-te-pah'-te-co, cah], *a.* Having a natural aversion for anything. Disagreeable, unpleasant. **Es un tipo antipático,** he's a disagreeable sort.

antipatizar [an-te-pah-te-thar'], *vn. (Amer.)* To dislike, to have a feeling against.

antipatriótico [an-te-pah-tre-o-te-co], *a.* Unpatriotic.

antiperístasis [an-te-pay-rees'-tah-sis], *f.* Antiperistasis, the action of two contrary qualities.

antiperistáltico, ca [an-te-pay-ris-tahl'-te-co, cah], *a.* Antiperistaltic, a reverse movement of the intestines; also, quieting the natural peristalsis.

antiperras [an-te-pay-rrahs], *f. & pl. (And.)* Half-moon glasses.

antípodas [an-tee'-po-das], *m. pl.* 1. Antipodes. 2. *(Met.)* Persons of contrary dispositions, sentiments or manners.

antipolilla [an-te-po-le-lyah], *a.* Mothproof.

antiprotón [an-te-pro-ton'], *m.* Antiproton.

antiproyectil [an-te-pro-yayc-teel], *a.* Antimissile.

antipútrido, da [an-te-poo'-tre-do, dah], *a.* Antiseptic.

antiquísimo, ma [an-te-kee'-se-mo, mah], *a. sup.* Very ancient.

antiquista [an-te-kes-tah], *(Mex.) a & m.* Antiquarian.

antirrábico [an-ter-rah-be-co], *a.* **Vacuna antirrábica,** antirabies vaccine.

antirradar [an-teer-rah-dar'], *a.* Antiradar.

antirreligioso, sa [an-te-ray-le-he-oh'-so, sah], *a.* Antireligious.

antirresbaladizo [an-ter-res-ba-lah-de-tho], *a. (Aut.)* Non-skid.

antirrevolucionario, ria [an-tee-ray-vo-loo-the-onah'-re-o, ah], *a.* Antirevolutionary.

antirrino [an-te-rre-no], *m.* Antirrhinum.

antirrobo [an-te-rro-bo], *a.* **Sistema antirrobo,** anti-theft system.

antisemita [an-te-say-mee'-tah], *a.* Anti-Semitic. -*m. & f.* Anti-Semite.

antisemítico, ca [an-te-say-mee'-te-co, cah], *a.* Anti-Semitic.

antisemitismo [an-te-say-me-tees'-mo], *m.* Anti-Semitism.

antiséptico, ca [an-te-sep'-te-co, cah], *a.* Antiseptic, counteracting existing sepsis, and thus contrasted with aseptic.

antisifilítico, ca [ah-te-se-fe-lee'-te-co, cah], *a.* Antisyphilitic.

antisociable [an-te-so-the-ah'-blay], *a.* Antisocial.

antisocial [an-te-so-the-ahl'], *a.* Antisocial.

antisodural [an-te-so-doo-rahl], *(LAm.) a & m.* Deodorant.

antisubmarino, na [an-te-soob-mah-ree'-no, nah], *a.* Antisubmarine.

antisuero [an-te-soo-ay'-ro], *m.* Antiserum.

antitanque [an-te-tahn-ke], *a.* Antitank.

antiterrorista [an-te-tayr-ro-res-tah], *a.* **Medidas antiterroristas**, measures against terrorism.

antítesis [an-tee'-tay-sis], *f.* 1. *(Gram.)* Antithesis. 2. *(Rhet.)* A contrast or opposition in the words of a discourse.

antitético, ca [an-te-tay'-te-co, cah], *a.* Antithetical.

antitipo [an-te-tee'-po], *m.* Antitype, figure, image, symbol.

antitoxina [an-te-toc-see'-nah], *f.* Antitoxin.

antivirus [an-te-vee'-roos], *m.* Antivirus.

antiviviseccionista [an-te-ve-ve-sayc-the-o-nes-tah], *m. & f.* Antivivisectionist.

Antofagasta [an-to-fo-gahs-tah], *f.* Antofagasta.

antofagastino [an-to-fah-gahs-te-no], *(Cono Sur). a.* Of Antofagasta.

antófago, ga [an-to'-fah-go, gah], *a.* Living on flowers.

antojadizo, za [an-to-ha-dee'-tho, thah], *a.* Capricious, whimsical, fickle.

antojado, da [an-to-hah'-do, dah], *a.* Anxious, longing. -*pp.* of ANTOJARSE.

antojarse [an-to-har'-say], *vr.* To long, to desire earnestly. **Antojársele a uno alguna cosa**, to desire or judge without reflection. **No se le antoja ir**, he doesn't feel like going.

antojera [an-to-hay'-rah], *f.* 1. A spectacle-case. 2. An eye-flap for horses; blinder, blinker.

antojitos [an-to-he-tos], *m. & pl. (Cono Sur)* Sweets, candy.

antojo [an-to'-ho], *m.* 1. Whim; a vehement desire, a longing, a hankering; fancy. **Hacer a su antojo**, to do as one pleases. **Tener antojos**, to have cravings. 2. A surmise.

antología [an-to-lo-hee'-ah], *f.* Anthology.

antológica [an-to-lo-he-cah], *f.* (Arte) Selective exhibition.

antológico [an-to-lo-he-co], *a.* **Exposición antológica**, selective exhibition (arte).

antónimo [an-to'-ne-mo], *m.* Antonym.

antonomasia [an-to-no-mah'-se-ah], *f. (Rhet.)* antonomasia, a figure by which a title is put for a proper name; as, The Orator, for Cicero.

antor [an-tor'], *m. (Law. Prov.)* Vendor of stolen goods, bought in good faith.

antorcha [an-tor'-chah], *f.* 1. Torch, flambeau, taper. 2. A cresset.

antorchero [an-tor-chay'-ro], *m. (Obs.)* A candlestick for tapers, etc.

antoría [an-to-ree'-ah], *f.* 1. *(Law. Prov.)* The action of discovering the first seller of stolen goods. 2. Right of reclaiming against the seller of stolen goods.

antracita [an-trah-thee'-tah], *f.* Anthracit coal; hard coal.

antrax [ahn-trahx], *m. (Med.)* Carbuncle; also anthrax or splenic fever.

antro [ahn'-tro], *m.* 1. *(Poetic.)* Cavern, den, grotto. 2. *(Med.)* Antrum, a cavity in bone.

antropofagia [an-tro-po-fah-hee'-ah], *f.* Anthropophagy.

antropófago [an-tro-po'-fah-go], *m.* A cannibal. -*pl.* Anthropophagi. In English it has no singular.

antropografía [an-tro-po-grah-fee'-ah], *f.* Anthropography, descriptive anatomy of man.

antropoide [an-tro-poy'-day], *m. & f.* Anthropoid.

antropoideo [an-tro-poy'-day-oh], *a.* Anthropoid. **Mono antropoideo**, anthropoid, ape.

antropología [an-tro-po-lo-hee'-ah], *f.* Anthropology, the science of the human structure.

antropológico, ca [an-tro-po-lo'-he-co, cah], *a.* Anthropological.

antropólogo [an-tro-po'-lo-go], *m.* Anthropologist.

antropomorfismo [an-tro-po-mor-fees'-mo], *m.* The attribution to God of a human body.

antropomorfo, fa [an-tro-po-mor'-fo, fah], *a.* Anthropomorphous, said of apes.

antroposofía [an-tro-po-so-fee'-ah], *f.* Anthroposophy, the knowledge of the nature of man.

antruejar [an-troo-ay-har'], *va. (Prov.)* To wet with water, or play some trick.

antruejo [an-troo-ay'-ho], *m.* The three days of the carnival.

antruido [an-troo-ee'-do], *m. (Obs.)* V. ANTRUEJO.

antucá [an-too-cah], *m. (Cono Sur)* Sunshade, parasol.

antuviada [an-too-ve-ah-dah], *f.* Sudden blow, bump.

antuvión [an-too-ve-on'], *m. (coll.)* A sudden, unexpected stroke or attack. **De antuvión**, unexpectedly. **Fulano vino de antuvión**, so and so came unexpectedly.

anual [ah-noo-ahl'], *a.* Annual. **Plantas anuales**, *(Bot.)* annual plants.

anualidad [ah-noo-ah-le-dahd'], *f.* 1. State or quality of being annual. 2. Pensions paid by the state. 3. Annuity. *(Com.)*

anualmente [ah-noo-al-men'-tay], *adv.* Annually.

anuario [ah-noo-ah'-re-o], *m.* A year book of information. **Anuario telefónico**, telephone directory.

anúbada [ah-noo'-bah-dah], *f.* 1. *(Obs.)* An ancient tax paid in Spain. 2. A call to arms.

anubarrado, da [ah-noo-bar-rah'-do, dah], *a.* Clouded.

anubarse [ah-noo-bar'-say], *vr.* To vanish.

anubladamente [ah-noo-blah-dah-men'-tay], *adv.* Mistily.

anublado, da [ah-noo-blah'-do, dah], *a.* 1. Overcast, clouded, dim, mistful. 2. (Speaking of colors), somewhat more obscure than the rest. -*pp.* of ANUBLAR.

anublar [ah-noo-blar'], *va.* 1. To cloud, to darken the light of the sun. 2. To overcast. 3. *(Met.)* To cloud or obscure merit. -*vr.* 1. To be blasted, withered, or mildewed: applied to corn and plants. 2. *(Met.)* To miscarry, to be disconcerted: speaking of plans.

anudar [ah-noo-dar'], *va.* 1. To knot. 2. To join, to unite. -*vn.* To wither, to fade, to pine away. **Anudarse la voz**, *(Met.)* to throb from passion or grief; not to be able to speak.

anuencia [ah-noo-en'-the-ah], *f.* Compliance, consent.

anuente [ah-noo-en'-tay], *a.* Condescending, courteous.

anulable [ah-noo-lah'-blay], *a.* That which can be annulled.

anulación [ah-noo-lah-the-on'], *f.* 1. Cessation, abrogation. 2. Abscission.

anulador, ra [ah-noo-lah-dor', rah], *m. & f.* A repealer.

anular [ah-noo-lar'], *va.* 1. To annul, to make void, to frustrate. 2. To cancel, rescind. *(For.)* To irritate. -*vr.* To lose one's identity; to renounce to everything.

anular [ah-noo-lar'], *a.* Annular, ring-shaped. **Dedo anular**, the ring-finger, or fourth finger.

anulativo, va [ah-noo-lah-tee'vo, vah], *a.* Having the power of making void.

anuloso, sa [ah-noo-lo'-so, sah], annular, composed of many rings.

anunciación [ah-noon-the-ah-the-on'], *f.* Annunciation; the angel's salutation to the blessed Virgin.

anunciada [ah-noon-the-ah'-dah], *f.* 1. An order of monks. 2. A religious order for women. 3. An order of knights, instituted by Amadeus VI., Duke of Savoy.

anunciador, ra [ah-noo-the-ah-dor', rah], *m. & f.* Announcer, one who announces.

anunciante [ah-noon-the-ahn'-tay], *m. & f. (Com.)* Advertiser.

anunciar [ah-noon-the-ar'], *va.* 1. To announce, to proclaim, to declare. **No nos anuncia nada nuevo**, it augurs ill for us. 2. To advertise, to publicize. 3. To forbode, to portend. -*vr.* **El festival se anuncia animado**, the festival loois like it'll be lively.

anuncio [ah-noon'-the-o], *m.* 1. Omen, forerunner. 2. Advertisement. **Anuncios económicos, anuncios por palabras**, classified advertisements, small advertisements. 3. *(Com.)* Statement, advice.

anuo, ua [ah'-noo-o, ah], *a. V.* ANUAL.

anúteba [ah-noo'-tay-bah], *f.* 1. *V.* ANUBADA. 2. Call to war.

anverso [ah-verr'-so], *m.* Obverse: applied to the head side in coins and medals.

anvir [ahn'-veer], *m.* (South Amer.) A red liquor expressed from the fermented leaves of tobacco.

anzolero [an-tho-lay'-ro], *m.* (Prov.) One whose trade it is to make fish-hooks.

anzuelo [an-thoo-ay-lo], *m.* 1. Fish-hook. 2. *(Met.)* Allurement, incitement. 3. A kind of fritters made in the shape of a hook. **Caer en el anzuelo**, to be tricked or defrauded. **Roer el anzuelo**, to escape a danger. **Tragar el anzuelo**, to swallow the bait.

aña [ah'-nyah], *f.* Hyena.

añada [ah-nyah'-dah], *f.* 1. The good or bad season in a year. 2. Piece of arable land.

añadido [ah-nyah-dee'-do], *m.* False hair.

añadidura [ah-nyah-de-doo'-rah], *f.* Addition, extra, thing added. **Dar algo de añadidura**, to give something extra.

añadimiento [ah-nyah-de-me-en'-to], *m.* Addition. **Añadidura a los pesos en la venta de cosas**, over-weight allowed in the sale of goods.

añadir [ah-nyah-deer'], *va.* 1. To add. 2. To exaggerate.

añafea [ah-nyah-fay'-ah], *f.* **Papel de añafea**, brown paper.

añafil [ah-nyah-feel'], *m.* A musical pipe used by the Moors.

añafilero [ah-nyah-fe-lay'-ro], *m.* A player on the *añafil*.

añagaza [ah-nyah-gah'-thah], *f.* 1. A call, lure, or decoy, for catching birds. 2. *(Met.)* Allurement, enticement to mischief.

añal [ah-nyahl'], *a.* Annual. **Cordero añal**, a yearling lamb.

añal [ah-nyahl'], *m.* 1. An annual offering on the tomb of a person deceased. 2. *(Obs.)* Anniversary.

añalejo [ah-nyah-lay'-ho], *m.* An ecclesiastical almanac, pointing out the regulations of the divine service.

añangá [ah-nyahn-gah], *m.* (Cono Sur) The devil.

añañay [ah-nyah-nyah-e], *interj.* (Cono Sur) Great.

añapar [ah-nyah-pahr], *va.* (LAm.) to smash to bits.

añascar [ah -nyas-car'], *va.* 1. *(Col.)* To collect by degrees small things of little value. 2. *(Obs.)* To entangle.

añaz [ah-nyath], *m.* *(And.)* Shrunk.

añeja [ah-nyay-hah], *f.* (Carib.) Old lady.

añejar [ah-nyay-har'], *va.* To make old. *-vr.* To grow old, to become stale.

añejo, ja àh-nyay'-ho. hah], *a.* Old, stale, musty.

añicos [ah-nyee'-cos], *m. pl.* Bits or small pieces of something. **Hacer añicos**, to break into small bits. **Hacerse añicos**, to take too much exercise, to overheat oneself.

añil [ah-nyell'], *m.* 1. *(Bot.)* The indigo plant. 2. Indigo, a mass extracted from the indigo plant: the best quality is called **añil flor**, or **tisate; añil** the middling sort, (sobresaliente); and the common kind, (corte).

añilar [ah-nye-lar'], *va.* To treat the clothes with bluing, in laundry-work.

añinero [ah-ny-nay'-ro], *m.* A dealer in lambskins.

añinos [ah-nyee'-nos], *m. pl.* The fleecy skins of yearling lambs.

año [ah'-nyo], *m.* Year. **Año bisiesto**, leap-year. **Tener diez años**, to be ten years old. **El año de gracia**, the year of our Lord. **Año luz**, light year. **¡Feliz Año Nuevo!** Happy New Year! **Hace años**, years ago. **No pasan los años para él**, he doesn't seem to get any older. **Una vez al año**, once a year. **Estar de buen año**, to be in good health.

añojal [ah-nyo-hahl'], *m.* Fallow land.

añojo, ja [ah-nyo'-ho, hah], *m. & f.* A yearling calf.

año luz [ah'-nyo-looth], *m.* (Astr.) Light year.

añorante [ah-nyo-rahn-tay], *a.* Yearning, longing; nostalgic; affectionate.

añoranza [ah-nyo-rahn-tha], *f.* Longing, yearning, sense of loss.

añorar [ah-nyo-rahr], 1. *va.* To long for, yearn for, pine for. 2. *vn.* To yearn, pine, grieve.

añoso, sa [ah-nyo'-so, sah], *a.* Very old, ancient.

añublado, da [ah-nyoo-blah'-do, dah], *a.* Blindfolded. *-pp.* of AÑUBLAR.

añublar, se [ah-nyoo-blahr], *V.* ANUBLAR.

añublo [ah-nyoo'-blo], *m.* Mildew. *V.* TIZON.

añudador, ra [ah-nyoo-dah-dor, rah], *m. & f.* One who knots or ties.

añudar [ah-nyoo-dar'], *va.* 1. *v.* ANUDAR. 2. To make fast, to unite, to tie close. **Añudar los labios**, to impose silence.

aojado, da [ah-o-hah'-do, dah], *a.* Bewitched. *-pp.* of OJAR.

aojador, ra [ah-o-hah-dor', rah], *m. & f.* A conjurer.

aojadura [ah-o-hah-doo'-rah], *f.* **Aojamiento** [ah-o-hah-me-en'-to], *m.* Witchcraft, fascination.

aojar [ah-o-har'], *va.* To fascinate, to charm to bewitch.

aojo [ah-o-ho], *m.* Evil eye, hoodoo.

aoristo [ah-o-res-to], *m.* (Ling.) Aorist.

aorta [ah-or'-tah], *f.* (Anat.) Aorta, the great artery.

aorteurismo [ah-or-tay-oo-rees'-mo], *m.* Aneurism of the aorta.

aórtico, ca [ah-or'-te-co, cah], *a.* Aortic: relating to the aorta.

aovado, da [ah-o-vah'-do, dah], *a.* Oviform, in the shape of an egg. *-pp.* of AOVAR.

aovar [ah-o-var'], *va.* To lay eggs.

aovillarse [ah-o-veel-lyar'-say], *vr.* To grow or be contracted into the shape of a clew.

a.p. *abr.* de **apartado de correos** (Post Office Box, P.O.B.).

APA *abr.* de **Asociación de Padres de Alumnos** (Parent-Teacher Association).

apa [ah-pah], *interj.* (Mex.) Good God! Cheer up!, get up!

apabilar [ah-pah-be-lar'], *va.* To prepare the wick of a waxcandle for being lighted. *-vr.* 1. *(Obs.)* To die away (luz). 2. *(Met.)* To sink under the hand of death.

apabullante [ah-pah-boo-lyahn-tay], *a.* Shattering, crushing.

apabullar [ah-pah-bool-lyar'], *va.* Coll.) to flatten, squeeze, crush.

apacentadero [ah-pah-then-tah-day'-ro], *m.* Pasture; feeding-place for cattle.

apacentador [ah-pah-then-tah-dor'], *m.* A herdsman.

apacentamiento [ah-pah-then-ta-me-en'-to], *m.* 1. The act of tending grazing cattle. 2. Pasturage.

apacentar [ah-pah-then-tar'], *va.* 1. To tend grazing cattle. 2. To graze, to feed cattle. 3. *(Met.)*. To teach, to instruct spiritually. 4. *(Met.)* to inflame the passions. *-vr.* 1. *(Agri.)* To graze, feed. 2. *(fig.)* To feed. (*Yo apaciento, yo apaciente*, from *Apacentar. V.* ACERTAR)

apacibilidad [ah-pah-the-be-le-dahd'], *f.* Affability, mildness of manners, meekness of temper.

apacible [ah-pah-thee'-blay[, *a.* 1. Affable, meek, gentle, inoffensive. 2. Placid, still, quiet. 3. Pleasant, calm. moderate. **Tiempo apacible**, *(Naut.)* moderate weather. **Semblante apacible**, a serene countenance. **Sitio apacible**, a pleasant place.

apaciblemente [ah-pah-the-blay-men'-tay], *adv.* Mildly, gently, agreeably.

apaciguador, ra [ah-pah-the-goo-ah-dor', rah], *m. & f.* Pacificator, peace-maker.

apaciguamiento [ah-pa-the-goo-ah-me-en'-to], *m.* Pacification.

apaciguar [ah-pah-the-goo-ar'], *va.* To appease, to pacify, to calm, to compose. *-vn.* (Naut.) To grow moderate (viento, mar). *-vr.* To calm down, quieten down.

apache [ah-pah'-chay], *m.* Apache (Indian); *(Esp. Fig.)* Apache, street ruffian, thug.

apacheta [ah-pah-chay-tah], *f.* (Amer.) A heap of stones on hills. *(Met.)* **Hacer la apacheta**, to accomplish the most difficult part of a task. **Hacer su apacheta**, to have made a fortune: to make one's «pile».

apachico [ah-pah-che-co], *m.* (*LAm.*) Bundle.

apachurrar [ah-pah-choor-rar'], *va.* (*Amer.*) To crush, to squeeze, to flatten. **Morir a apachurrones**, To be squeezed to death. *V.* DESPACHURRAR.

apadrinador, ra [ah-pah-dre-nah-dor', rah], *m. & f.* 1. Patron, defender, protector. 2. Second, in a duel.

apadrinamiento [ah-pah-dre-nah-me-ayn-to], *m.* Sponsorship; patronage.

apadrinar [ah-pah-dre-nar'], *va.* 1. To support, to favor, to patronize, to protect. 2. To sponsor. 3. To serve as godfather. 4. To act as second in a duel.

apadronarse [ah-pah-dro-nahr-say], *vr.* To register (as a resident).

apagadizo [ah-pah-gah-de-tho], *a.* Slow to burn, difficult to ignite.

apagado, da [ah-pah-gah'-do, dah], *a.* Humble-minded, submissive, pusillanimous. *-pp.* of APAGAR.

apagador [ah-pah-gah-dor'], *m.* 1. One who extinguishes. 2. Damper, extinguisher, a hollow cone. 3. A small bit of cloth to deaden the echo of the strings; damper.

apagaincendios [ah-pah-gah-in-then'-de-os], *m.* A fireengine.

apagamiento [ah-pah-gah-me-en'-to], *m.* The act of quenching.

apagapenoles [ah-pah-gah-pay-no'-les], *m. pl.* (*Naut.*) Leech-ropes, leech-lines.

apagar [ah-pah-gar'], *va.* 1. To quench (sed), to extinguish, to put out (fire). 2. (*Met.*) To efface, to destroy. 3. (*Art.*) To glaring colors which are too bright or garling. 4. To switch off, to turn off (luz). 5. (*Mech.*) To dead, deaden. **Apagar la cal**, to slake lime. **Apagar la sed**, to quench the thirst. **Apagar la voz**, to put a mute on the bridge of stringed musical instruments for the pupose of softening the sound. **Apagarse la lumbre, la luz o el fuego**, to go out.

apagavelas [ah-pah-gah-vay-lahs], *m.* Canddle snuffer.

apagógico, ca [ah-pah-go'-he-co, cah], *a.* Apagogical, that shows the absurdity which arises from denying a thing.

apagón [ah-pah-gone'], *a.* (*Mex.*) Blackout.

apagoso [ah-pah-go-so], *a.* (*LAm.*) *V.* APAGADIZO.

apainelado, da [ah-pah-e-nay-lah'-do, dah], *a.* (*Arch.*) In imitation of half an ellipsis (arcos).

apaisado, da [ah-pah-e-sah'-do, dah], *a.* Resembling a landscape: applied to a painting broader than it is high. Squat, flattened.

apajarado [ah-pah-hah-rah-do], *a.* (*Cono Sur*) Daft, scatterbrained.

apalabrar [ah-pah-lah-brahr], *va.* To agree to; **estar apalabrado**, to be committed, have given one's word. *-vr.* To come to a verbal agreement.

apalabrear [ah-pah-lah-bray-ahr], (*LAm.*) *V.* APALABRAR.

Apalaches [ah-pah-lah-chays], *m. & pl.* **Montes Apalaches**, Appalachians.

apalambrar [ah-pah-lam-brar'], *va.* (*Obs.*) To set on fire. **Apalambrarse de sed**, to be parched with thirst.

apalancamiento [ah-pah-lahn-cah-me-ayn-to], *m.* Leverage.

apalancar [ah-pah-lan-car'], *va.* To move with a lever. (*fig.*) To support; (*Cono Sur*) **apalancar a uno**, to wangle a job for somebody. *-vn.* To hide; to settle down.

apalé [ah-pah-lay], *interj.* (*Mex.*) Goodness me!, look out!, watch it!.

apaleada [ah-pah-lay-ah-dah], *f.* (*Cono Sur, Mex.*) (*Agri.*) Winnowing.

apaleador, ra [ah-pah-lay-ah-dor' rah], *m. & f.* One who uses cudgels, cudgeller.

apaleamiento [ah-pah-lay-ah-me-en'-to], *m.* Drubbing; beating.

apalear [ah-pah-lay-ar'], *va.* 1. To cane, to drub, to cudgel, to maul. 2. To beat out the dust, to horsewhip. 3. To move grain to prevent its being spoiled. **Apalear el dinero**, to heap up money with shovels, to be excessively rich.

apaleo [ah-pah-lay'-o], *m.* Act of moving or shovelling grain.

apalmada [ah-pal-mah'-dah], *a.* (her.) Palm of the hand stretched out in a coat of arms.

apallar [ah-pah-lyahr], *va.* (*LAm.*) To harvest.

apamparse [ah-pahm-pahr-say], *vr.* (*Cono Sur*) to become bewildered, to lose one's grip.

apanado [ah-pah-nah-do], 1. *a.* (*LAm.*) Breaded, cooked in breadcrumbs. 2. *m.* (*And*) Beating.

apanaje [ah-pah-nah'-hay], *m.* Appanage, yearly income.

apanalado, da [ah-pah-nah-lah'-do, dah], *a.* Like honeycomb; deeply pitted.

apanar [ah-pah-nahr], *va.* (*LAm. Culin.*) To cover in breadcrumbs.

apancle [ah-pahn-clay], *m.* (*Mex.*) Irrigation ditch.

apancora [ah-pan-co'-rah], *f.* The seahedgehog: echinus.

apandar [ah-pan-dar'], *va.* (coll.) To pilfer, to steal.

apandillar [ah-pan-deel-lyar], *va.* To form a league, a party, or a faction. *vr.* To be united to form a party or a faction: it is taken generally in a bad sense.

apandorgarse [ah-pan-dor-gar'-say], *vr.* To grow fat (used of women).

apanicar [ah-pah-ne-cahr], *va.* (*Cono Sur*) To cause panic.

apani(a)guarse [ah-pah-ne-ah-goo-ahr-say], *vr.* (*And. Carib.*) To gang up.

apanojado, da [ah-pah-no-hah'-do, dah], *a.* (*Bot.*) Paniculate, bearded like seeds.

apantallado [ah-pahn-tah-lyah-do], *a.* (*Mex.*) Impressed, overwhelmed; crushed; **quedar apantallado**, to be left open-mouthed.

apantallar [ah-pahn-tah-lyahr], *va.* (*Mex.*) To impress; to fill with wonder.

apantanar [ah-pan-tah-nar'], *va.* 1. To fill a piece of ground with water; to make a pool of water.

apantuflado, da [ah-pan-too-flah'-do, dah], *a.* Wearing slippers.

apañado, da [ah-pah-nyah-do, dah], *a.* 1. Resembling woollen cloth in body. (coll.) 2. Suitable, fit (for), apposite. 3. Dexterous, skillful. *-pp.* of APAÑAR

apañador, ra [ah-pah-nyah-dor', rah], *m. & f.* 1. One who grasps or seizes. 2. A pilferer.

apañadura [ah-pah-nyah-doo'-rah], *f.* The act of seizing, snatching, or grasping away.

apañamiento [ah-pah-nyah-me-en'-to], *m.* V. APAÑO.

apañar [ah-pah-nyar'], *va.* 1. To grasp or seize. 2. (*Met.*) To carry away. 3. To pilfer. 4. To dress, to clothe. 5. To patch, to mend. *-vr.* (coll.) To submit to, to reconcile oneself to a thing. To be skillful, to be clever, to manage, to get along without help, to find a way. **Apañaos como podáis**, manage as best you can. (*Cono Sur*) **apañarse algo**, to get one's hands on something.

apaño [ah-pah'-nyo], *m.* 1. The act of seizing or grasping. 2. Cleverness or ability to do a thing. 3. (*Prov.*) A patch or other way of mending a thing. **Esto no tiene apaño**, there's no answer to this one.

apañuscar [ah-pah-nyoos-car'], *va.* (coll.) To rumple, to crush.

apapachar [ah-pah-pah-chahr], *va.* (*Carib.*) To cuddle.

apapagayado, da [ah-pah-pah-gah-yah'-do, dah], *a.* Parrotlike; very often applied to the nose.

aparador [ah-pah-rah-dor'], *m.* 1. Sideboard; dresser. 2. Side-table in churches for the service of the altar. 3. Workshop of an artisan. 4. Plate rack. **Estar de aparador**, (coll.) to be decked out or dressed in style.

aparadorista [ah-pah-rah-do-res-tah], *m. & f.* (*Mex.*) Window dresser.

aparadura [ah-pah-rah-doo'-rah], *f.* (*Naut.*) Garboard, garboard plank, garboard strake.

aparar [ah-pah-rar'], *va.* 1. To stretch out the hands or skirts for catching any thing. 2. To heap the earth round plants. 3. Among shoemakers, to close the quarters of a shoe. 4. To dress with an adze, dub. **Aparar un navío**, (*Naut.*) to dub a ship.

aparasolado, da [ah-pah-rah-so-lah'-do, dah], *a.* *(Bot.)* Umbelliferous.

aparatarse [ah-pah-rah-tahr-say], *vr.* *(And. Cono Sur)* **Se aparata**, it's brewing up for a storm.

aparato [ah-pah-rah'-to], *m.* 1. Apparatus, preparation, disposition. **Aparato auditivo**, hearing aid. **Aparato fotográfico**, camera. **Aparato de fax**, facsimile machine (fax). **"Aparato de datos preparado" (DSR)** *(Comp.)*, "data set ready" (DSR). 2. Pomp, ostentation, show. 3. Circumstance or token which precedes or accompanies something. 4. Appliance, engine, machine. 5. Collection of instruments for a surgical operation.

aparatosamente [ah-pah-rah-to-sah-mayn-tay], *adv.* Showily, ostentatiously; pretentiously.

aparatosidad [ah-pah-rah-to-see-dahd], *f.* Showiness. ostentation; pretentiousness.

aparatoso, sa [ah-pah-rah-to'-so, sah], *a.* *(Ant.)* Pompous, showy, ushered in with great preparations.

aparcadero [ah-par-cah-day-ro], *m.* Parking lot.

aparcamiento [ah-par-ca-me-en'-to], *m.* 1. Parking. 2. Parking lot. **Aparcamiento subterráneo**, underground parking.

aparcar [ah-par-car'], *va.* To park.

aparcería [ah-par-thay-ree'-ah], *f.* Partnership.

aparcero [ah-par-thay'-ro], *m.* 1. Partner in a farm. 2. An associate in general.

aparear [ah-pah-ray-ar'], *va.* To match, to mate, to suit one thing to another. *-vr.* To be coupled in pairs.

aparecer [ah-pah-ray-therr'], *vn. & vr.* To appear unexpectedly, to go forth, to come up. **Apareció borracho**, he turned up drunk. **No ha aparecido ese libro**, that book still hasn't turned up.

aparecido [ah-pah-ray-thee'-do], *m.* Ghost. **Aparecido**, *da, pp.* of APARECER.

aparecimiento [ah-pah-ray-the-me-en'-to], *m.* An apparition, appearing.

aparejado, da [ah-pah-ray-hah'-do, dah], *a.* Prepared, fit, ready. *-pp.* of APAREJAR.

aparejador, ra [ah-pah-ray-hah-dor', rah], *m. & f.* 1. One who prepares or gets ready. 2. Overseer of a building. 3. *(Naut.)* Rigger.

aparejar [ah-pah-ray-har'], *va.* 1. To get ready. 2. To saddle or harness horses. 3. *(Naut.)* To rig a ship, to furnish. 4. To prepare the work which is to be painted or gilded. 5. To prepare the timber and stones for a building. *-vr.* To get ready, to equip.

aparejo [ah-pah-ray'-ho], *m.* 1. Preparation, disposition. 2. Harness, gear. 3. *(Pict.)* Sizing of a piece of linen or board. 4. *(Naut.)* Tackle and rigging on a ship, furniture. **Aparejo de amante y estrella**, runner and tackle. **Aparejo de amura**, tacktackle. **Aparejo de bolinear**, bowline tackle. **Aparejo de combés**, luff-tackle. **Aparejo de estrelleras de combés**, winding-tackle. **Aparejo de estrique**, garnet, a tackle where with goods are hoisted in and out of the hold. **Aparejo de peñol**, yard-tackle. **Aparejo de pescante**, fish-tackle. **Aparejo de polea**, burton, a small tackle used in hoisting things in and out of a ship. **Aparejo real**, main-tackle. **Aparejo de virador**, Top-tackle. **Aparejo de rolín**, rolling-tackle. **Aparejo del tercio de las vergas mayores**, quarter-tackle. 5. Pack-saddle. *V.* ALBARDA. *-pl.* 1: The apparatus, tools, or instruments necessary for a trade. 2. *(Art.)* The materials necessary for priming, burnishing, and gilding.

aparejuelo [ah-pah-ray-hoo-ay'-lo], *m. dim.* A small apparatus. **Aparejuelos**, *(Naut.)* Small-tackle. **aparejuelos de portas**, port-tackle.

aparencial [ah-pah-ren-the-ahl], *a.* Apparent.

aparentado, da [ah-pah-ren-tah'-do-do], *a. (Obs.)* Related, allied, *-pp.* of APARENTAR.

aparentar [ah-pah-ren-tar'], *va.* To affect, to pretend, to make a false show. **El rico aparenta pobreza y el vicioso virtud**, the rich man affects poverty, and the vicious virtue. *-vn.* To show off.

aparente [ah-pah-ren'-tay], *a.* 1. Apparent, not real, flashy. 2. Convenient, seasonable, fit, suited. 3. Conspicuous, evident.

aparentemente [ah-pah-ren-tay-men'-tay], *adv.* Apparently, outwardly.

aparición [ah-pah-re-the-on'], *f.* Apparition, act of appearing. **Un libro de próxima aparición**, a book soon to be published.

apariencia [ah-pah-re-en'-the-ah], *f.* 1. Appearance, outside. **Las apariencias engañan**, appearances are deceptive. 2. Face, likeness, resemblance. 3. Vestige. 4. Pageant. 5. *(Obs.)* Probability, conjecture. **Caballo de apariencia**, a stately horse. *-pl.* 1. Phenomena discovered by astonomical observations. 2. Decorations of the stage.

aparrado, da [ah-par-rah'-do, dah], *a.* Crooked, or like vines, shrubby: applied to trees and plants.

aparragado [ah-pah-rrah-gah-do], *(Cono Sur)* *a. m.* Dwarfish.

aparragarse [ah-pah-rrah-gahr-say], *vr.* 1. *(CAm.)* To roll up, to curl up. 2. *(Cono Sur)* To squad, to crouch down. 3. *(CAm. Cono Sur, Mex.)* To remain stunted, to stay small. 4. *(CAm. Cono Sur)* To shrink, to grow small.

aparroquiado, da [ah-par-ro-ke-ah'-do, dah], *a.* Belonging to a parish, parishioner. *-pp.* of APARROQUIAR.

aparroquiar [ah-par-ro-ke-ar'], *va.* To bring or attract customers.

apartación [ah-par-tah-the-on'], *f.* *(Chem.)* Separation of some one or more of the component parts of a body.

apartadamente, *adv.* Privately, apart.

apartadero [ah-par-tah-day'-ro], *m.* 1. Parting-place, crossroads, cross way, side-track, siding, railroad switch; shunting. 2. A turn-out; widened space, in canals. 3. A sorting-room for wool or other materials.

apartadijo [ah-par-tah-dee'-ho], *m.* A small part, share or portion. **Hacer apartadijos**, to divide a whole into shares.

apartadizo [ah-par-tah-dee'-tho], *m.* A small room, separated or taken from another apartment.

apartado, da [ah-par-tah'-do, dah], *a.* 1. Separated. 2. Distant, retired. 3. Distinct, different. *-pp.* of APARTAR.

apartado [ah-par-tah'-do], *m.* 1. Post-office box. 2. A room separate from the rest of the house. 3. A smelting house. 4. (Metal) Extraction.

apartador, ra [ah-par-tah-dor', rah], *m. & f.* 1. One who divides or separates. 2. A sorter in paper-mills. **Apartador de ganado**, one who steals sheep or cattle. **Apartador de metales**, smelter, one who smelts ores.

apartamiento [ah-par-tah-me-en'-to], *m.* 1. Apartment. **Apartamiento amueblado**, furnished apartment. 2. Separation, withdrawal.

apartar [ah-par-tar'], *va.* 1. To part, to separate, to divide. 2. To dissuade one. **Apartar a uno de un propósito**, to dissuade somebody from an intention. 3. To remove a thing. **Apartó el plato con la mano**, he pushed his plate aside. 4. To sort letters. *-vr.* 1. To withdraw from a place, to hold off. **Apartarse de un camino**, to turn off a road. 2. To be divorced. 3. To desist from a claim, action, or plea. 4. *va. & vr.* **Apartar**, or **apartarse del derecho**, to cancel any claim or right.

aparte [ah-par'-tay], *m.* 1. Break in a line, space marking a paragraph. 2. *(Theat.)* An aside. 3. Apart, aside; separately; **eso aparte**, we shall to consider that separately. 3. *prep.* **Aparte de**, apart from that.

apartidismo [ah-par-te-des-mo], *m.* Non-political nature, non-party character.

apartidista [ah-par-te-des-tah], *a.* Apolitical.

aparvar [ah-par-var'], *va.* 1. To arrange the corn for being thrashed. 2. To heap, to throw together.

apasionadamente [ah-pah-se-o-nah-dah-men'-tay], *adv.* Passionately, intensely, fervently.

apasionado, da [ah-pah-se-o-nah'-do, dah], *a.* 1. Passionate. 2. Affected with pain. 3. Devoted to a person or thing. *-pp.* of APASIONAR. *-m.* Admirer.

apasionamiento [ah-pah-se-o-nah-mee-en'-to], *m.* Passion, intense emotion, vehemence.

apasionante [ah-pah-se-o-nahn'-tay], *a.* Exciting. **Una novela apasionante**, a thrilling, exciting novel.

apasionar [ah-pah-se-o-nar'], *va.* To inspire a passion. **Me apasionan las gambas**, I adore prawns. **Es una lectura que apasiona**, it's stirring stuff to read. *-vr.* To be taken with a person or thing to excess **Apasionarse de**, to dote upon.

apaste [ah-pas-tay], *m.* Apaxte *(CAm.)* Clay to pot.

apasturar [ah-pas-too-rar'], *va.* to pasture, to forage.

apatía [ah-pah-tee'-ah], *f.* Apathy.

apático, ca [ah-pah'-te-co, cah], *a.* Apathetic, indifferent.

apátrida [ah-pah-tre-dah], *a. m. & f.* Stateless, unpatriotic.

apatronarse [ah-pah-tro-nahr-say], *vr. (And. Cono Sur)* To find a protector in somebody; to seek a domestic post with somebody.

apatusco [ah-pah-toos'-co], *m.* 1. *(coll.)* Ornament, dress. 2. A thing done with precipitation and confusion.

apazote [ah-pah-tho'-tay], *m. (Mex. Epasote) (Bot.)* American basil.

apdo. *abr.* de **Apartado de correos** (post office box).

apea [ah-pay'-ah], *f.* A roe with which the fore feet of horses are fettered.

apeadero [ah-pay-ah-day'-ro], *m.* An alighting-place, halt (ferrocarriles). **La línea cuenta con 10 estaciones y dos apeaderos**, the line has 10 stations and 2 halts. Horse block (apoyo). Small flat (casa).

apeador [ah-pay-ah-dor'], *m.* A land surveyor.

apeamiento [ah-pay-ah-me-en'-to], *m. V.* APEO.

apear [ah-pay-ar'], *va.* 1. To alight from a horse, or carriage. 2. To measure lands, tenements, or buildings; to set landmarks. 3. To block or scotch a wheel. 4. To prop a building. 5. *(Arch.)* To take a thing down from its place; to prop, stay, or shore a building, while alterations are in progress. 6. *(Met.)* To dissuade. 7. *(Met.)* To remove difficulties. **Apear el río**, to wade or ford a river. **Apear una caballería**, to shackle a horse or mule. 8. **Apear a uno de su opinión**, to make somebody give up his view, to persuade somebody that his opinion is wrong. 9. **Apear el tratamiento a uno**, to drop somebody's title, address somebody without formality. 9. To dismiss, to sack. 10. *(And.)* To kill. *-vr.* 1. To alight. **Apearse por la cola or por las orejas**, to give some absurd answer. 2. To get out, to dismount. 3. **Apearse de algo**, to get rid of something.

apechugar [ah-pay-choo-gar'], *va.* 1. To push with the breast. 2. *(Met.)* To undertake a thing with spirit and boldness, without consideration. *-vr.* **Apechugarse algo,** *(CAm.)* To snatch something.

apedazar [ah-pay-dah-thar'], *va.* 1. To patch, to mend, to repair. 2. *V.* DESPEDAZAR.

apedernalado, da [ah-pay-der-anh-lah'-do, dah], *a.* Flinty.

apedrar [ah-pay-drar'], *va. (Obs.) V.* APEDREAR.

apedreadero [ah-pay-dray-ah-day'-ro], *m.* A place where boys assemble to throw stones at each other.

apedreado, da [ah-pay-dray-ah'-do, dah], *a.* 1. Stoned, pelted. 2. **Cara apedreada**, a face pitted with the small pox. *-pp.* of APEDREAR.

apedreador [ah-pay-dray-ah-dor'], *m.* One who throws stones.

apedreamiento [ah-pay-dray-ah-me-en'-to], *m.* Lapidation.

apedrear [ah-pay-dray-ar'], *va.* To stone; to kill with stones. *-vn.* 1. To hail. 2. *(Met.)* To talk in a rude manner. *-vr.* To be injured by hail.

apedreo [ah-pay-dray'-o], *m.* A stoning. *(Met.)* Hail; damage by hail.

apegadamente [ah-pay-gah-dah-men'-tay], *adv.* Studiously, devotedly.

apegado [ah-pay-gah-do], *a.* Apegado a, attached to.

apegamiento [ah-pay-gah-me-en'-to], *m. (Obs.)* 1. Adhesion. 2. *V.* APEGO.

apegarse [ah-pay-gar'-say], *vr.* 1. To abide by. 2. To become attached (to).

apego [ah-pay'-go], *m.* Attachment, fondness.

apelable [ah-pay-lah'-blay], *a.* Appealable, subject to appeal.

apelación [ah-pay-lah-the-on'], *f.* Appeal from an inferior to a superior court. **Médico de apelación**, consultant doctor. **Recurso de apelación**, appeal. **Tribunal de apelación**, court of appeal. **Sin apelación**, hopeless. **No haber or no tener apelación**, to be despaired.

apelado, da [ah-pay-lah'-do, dah], *a.* Of the same coat or color: applied to mules or horses. *-pp.* of APELAR.

apelambrar [ah-pay-lam-brar'], *va.* To steep skins or hides in vats filled with lime-water.

apelante [ah-pay-lahn'-tay], *pa.* Appellant.

apelar [ah-pay-lar'], *vn.* 1. To appeal, to transfer a cause from an inferior to a superior court. **Apelar a**, to resort to, to recourse to. 2. To have recourse to, to seek remedy. 3. To be of the same color. **Apelar una sentencia**, to appeal against a sentence. **Apelar el enfermo**, to escape from the jaws of death in a fit of sickness.

apelativo [ah-pay-lah-tee'-vo], *a. (Gram.)* Appellative. **Nombre apelativo**, an appellative name.

apeldar [ah-pel-dar'], *vn. (coll.)* To flee, to set off, to run away, used generally with *las. va.* **Apeldarlas**, to beat it.

apelde [ah-pel'-day], *m. (coll.)* 1. Flight, escape. 2. The first ringing of a bell before daybreak in convents.

apellar [ah-pel-lyar'], *va.* To dress leather; to prepare for receiving any color.

apellidado, da [ah-pel-lye-dah'-do, dah], *a* Named. *-pp.* of APELLIDAR.

apellidamiento [ah-pel-lye-dah-me-en'-to], *m.* The act of giving a name.

apellidar [ah-pel-lye-dar'], *va.* 1. To call one by his name. 2. To proclaim, to raise shouts. 3. *(Obs.)* To convene; to assemble troops.

apellido [ah-pel-lyee'-do], *m.* 1. Surname. 2. A peculiar name given to things. 3. A nickname; epithet. 4. *(Obs.)* The assembling of troops.

apelmazado [ah-payl-mah-thah-do], *a.* Compact, compressed, solid.

apelmazar [ah-pel-mah-thar'], *va.* 1. To compress, to render less spongy. 2. *(Amer.)* To be lazy, sluggish.

apelotonar [ah-pay-lo-to-nar'], *va. & r.* 1. To form balls, to mass. 2. To crowd together.

apellidar [ah-pay-lye-dahr], *va.* To name, to surname, to call. *vr.* To be called. **¿Cómo se apellida usted?**, what's your family name?

apellido [ah-pay-lye-do], *m.* Name; surname, family name.

apenado [ah-pay-nah-do], *a. (LAm.)* Ashamed, embarrassed.

apenar [ah-pay-nar'], *va. & vr.* 1. To grieve. 2. To become embarrassed. **Apenarse por algo**, to grieve about something.

apenas [ah-pay'-nas], *adv.* 1. Scarcely, hardly; with a deal of trouble. **Apenas si pude levantarme**, I could hardly get up. 2. No sooner than, as soon as. **Apenas hube llegado cuando....**, no sooner had I arrived than...

apencar [ah-pen-car'], *vn* To accept with repugnance.

apendectomía [ah-pen-dayc-to-me-ah], *f.* Appendectomy.

apendejarse [ah-pen-day-hahr-say], *vr. (Carib.)* To get silly.

apéndice [ah-pen'-de-thay], *m.* Appendix, supplement.

apendicitis [ah-pen-de-thee'-tis], *f. (Med.)* Appendicitis.

Apenino, na [ah-pay-nee'-no, nah], *a.* Apennine.

apenitas [ah-pay-ne-tahs], *adv. (And. Cono Sur) V.* APENAS.

apensionado [ah-pen-se-o-nah-do], *a. (And. Cono Sur, Mex.)* Depressed, sad; grieved.

apensionar [ah-pen-se-o-nahr], *(And. Cono Sur, Mex.)* To sadden, to grieve. *-vr.* To become sad.

apeñuscarse [ah-pay-nyoos-car-say], *vr.* *(Cono Sur)* To crowd together.

apeo [ah-pay'-o], *m.* 1. Survey, mensuration of lands or buildings. 2. Props, stays, etc., put under the upper parts of a building, while the lower are repaired.

apeonar [ah-pay-o-nar'], *va.* To walk or run swiftly: used of birds.

apeorar [ah-pay-o-rahr], *vn.* To get worse.

apepsia [ah-pep'-se-ah], *f.* *(Med.)* Apepsy, indigestion.

aperado [ah-pay-rah-do], *a.* *(Cono Sur)* Well-equipped.

aperador [ah-pay-rah-dor'], *m.* 1. A farmer. 2. A wheelwright.

aperar [ah-pay-rár'], *va.* To carry on the trade of a wheelwright, -*vr.* **Aperarse de algo**, *(Cono Sur)* To equip oneself.

apercibimiento [ah-per-the-be-me-en'-to], *m.* 1. The act of providing or getting ready. 2. Arrangement. 3. Order, advice, warning. 4. Summons.

apercibir [ah-per-the-beer'], *va.* 1. To provide, to get ready. 2. To warm, to advise. 3. *(Law.)* To summon. **(Yo apercibo, yo apercibí**, from **Apercibir**, *V.* PEDIR). 4. *(LAm.)* To notice. -*vr.* To prepare oneself, To get ready.

aperción [ah-per-the-on'], *f.* Act of opening. *V.* ABERTURA.

apercollar [ah-per-col-lyar'], *va.* 1. *(coll.)* To seize one by the collar. 2. *(Met.)* To snatch away (arrebatar). 3. *(coll.)* To assassinate (asesinar).

aperchar [ah-payr-chahr], *va.* *(CAm. Cono Sur)* To pile up, to stack up.

aperdigado, da [ah-per-de-gah'-do, dah], *a.* 1. Broiled, toasted. 2. Condemned and burned by the Inquisition. -*pp.* of APERDIGAR.

aperdigar [ah-per-de-gar'], *va.* *V.* PERDIGAR.

apergaminado, da [ah-per-gah-me-nah'-do, dah], *a.* Dry and yellow like parchment.

apergaminarse [ah-payr-gah-me-nahr-say], *vr.* To get like parchment; to dry up, to get yellow and wrinkled.

apergollar [ah-payr-go-lyahr], *va.* *(LAm.)* To grab by the throat.

aperital [ah-pay-re-tahl], *m.* *(Cono Sur)* *V.* APERITIVO.

aperitivo, va [ah-pay-re-tee'-vo, vah], *a.* 1. Aperitive. 2. Appetizer (bebida).

apero [ah-pay'-ro], *m.* 1. The implements used on a farm. 2. The tools necessary for a trade. 3. Gear (utensilio).

aperreado, da [ah-per-ray-ah'-do, dah], *a.* Harassed. **Andar aperreado**, to be harassed or fatigued. -*pp.* of APERREAR.

aperredor, ra [ah-per-ray-ah-dor', rah], *m. & f.* *(coll.)* One that is importunate, an intruder.

aperrear [ah-per-ray-ar'], *va.* To throw one to the dogs. -*vr.* To toil and beat about; to overwork oneself.

aperreo [ah-pay-rray-o], *m.* Harassment, worry; toil, overwork. *(LAm.)* Nuisance.

apersogar [ah-payr-so-gahr], *va.* To tether, tie up. *(Carib.)* To string together.

apersonado [ah-payr-so-nah-do], *a.* **Bien apersonado**, presentable, nice looking.

apersonarse [ah-per-so-nar'-say], *vr.* 1. *(Law.)* *V.* COMPADECER. 2. *(Obs.)* To appear genteel.

apertura [ah-per-too'-rah], *f.* *V.* ABERTURA. The calling to order of assemblies. corporations. etc.

aperturismo [ah-payr-too-res-mo], *m.* Liberalization; relaxation, loosening-up.

aperturista [ah-payr-too-res-tah], *a.* Liberalizing.

apesadumbrado, da [ah-pay-sah-doom-brah'-do, dah], *a.* Anxious, vexed, mournful. -*pp.* of APESADUMBRAR.

apesadumbrar [ah-pay-sah-doom-brar'], *va.* To vex, to cause affliction. -*vr.* To grieve.

apesaradamente [ah-pay-sah-rah-dah-men'-tay], *adv.* Mournfully, grievously.

apesarar [ah-pay-sah-rar'], *va.* *V.* APESADUMBRAR.

apescollar [ah-pays-co-lyahr], *va.* *(Cono Sur)* To seize by the neck.

apesgamiento [ah-pes-gah-me-en'-to], *m.* The act of sinking under a burden.

apesgar [ah-pes-gar'], *va.* To overload, to sink under a load. -*vr.* To grow dull; to be aggrieved.

apestado, da [ah-pes-tah'-do, dah], *a.* 1. Pestered, annoyed. 2. Full. **Estar apestado de alguna cosa**, to have plenty of a thing, even to loathing and satiety. **La plaza está apestada de verduras**, the market-place is full of greens. -*pp.* of APESTAR.

apestar [ah-pes-tar'], *va.* 1. To infect with the plague. 2. To cause an offensive smell. In this sense it is commonly used as a neuter verb in the third person; e.g. **aquí apesta**, there is here an offensive smell. 3. *(Met.)* To corrupt, to turn putrid. 4. To pester, to cause displeasure, to nauseate. **Fulano me apesta con su afectación**, he sickens me with his affectation. -*vr* *(Med.)* To catch the plague. *(LAm. Bot.)* To be blighted. *(And.)* To catch a cold.

apestillar [ah-pays-te-lyahr], *va.* 1. *(Cono Sur)* To catch, to grab, to hold of. 2. To tell off.

apestoso, sa [ah-pes-to'-so, sah], *a.* Foul-smelling, sickening, nauseating.

apétalo, la [ah-pay-tah-lo, ah], *a.* *(Bot.)* Apetalous, without flower-leaves.

apetecedor, ra [ah-pay'-tah-lo, lah], *m. & f.* One who longs for a thing.

apetecer [ah-pay-tay-therr'], *va.* To long for a thing, to crave. **Me apetece un helado**, I feel like an ice-cream.

apetecible [ah-pay-tay-thee'-blay], *a.* Desirable, worthy of being wished for.

apetencia [ah-pay-ten'-the-ah], *f.* 1. Appetite, hunger. 2. Natural desire of something. **(Yo apetezco**, from **apetecer**, *V.* ABORRECER).

apetite [ah-pay-tee'-tay], *vn.* Sauce. *m.* Appetizer; *(fig.)* incentive.

apetitivo, va [ah-pay-te-tee'-vo, vah], *a.* Appetitive, having a strong wish or urge.

apetito [ah-pay-tee'-to], *m.* 1. Appetite, the natural desire for food. 2. Hunger. 3. Desire, liking, willingness

apetitoso, sa [ah-pay-te-to'-so, sah], *a.* 1. Pleasing to the taste, tempting the appetite. 2. *(Obs.)* Pursuing sensual pleasures.

apezuñar [ah-pay-thoo-nyar'], *vn.* To tread firm on the hoof. **API** *m. & f.* Abr de **Agente de la propiedad immobiliaria** (Real estate agent).

apí [ah-pe'], *m. & f.* A non- alcoholic maize drink. *(And. Cono Sur)* **El vaso se hizo apí**, the glass was smashed to pieces.

apiadar [ah-pe-ah-dahr'], *va.* To move to pity.

apiadarse [ah-pe-ah-dar'-say], *vr.* To pity, to treat with compassion.

apiado [ah-pe-ah-do], *m.* *(Cono Sur)* Celery liquor.

apiaradero [ah-pe-ah-ra-day-ro], *m.* A shepherd's account of the number of sheep which compose his flock.

apiario, ria [ah-pe-ah'-re-o, ah], *a.* Resembling or relating to the honey-bee.

apicarado, da [ah-pe-cah-rah'-do, dah], *a.* Roguish, knavish, impudent.

apicararse [ah-pe-cah-rar'-say], *vr.* To acquire the manners of a rogue.

ápice [ah'-pe-thay], *m.* 1. Apex, summit, utmost height. 2. The upper part of a thing. 3. *(Met.)* The most intricate or most arduous point of a question. **Ápices**, anthers of flowers. **Estar en los ápices**, to have a complete and minute knowledge of a thing.

apichicarse [ah-pe-che-car-say], *vr.* *(Cono Sur)* To squat, to crouch.

apiculado, da [ah-pe-coo-lah'-do, dah], *a.* Apiculate; sharp-pointed

apículo [ah-pee'-coo-lo], *m.* A small, keen point.

apicultor, ra [ah-pe-cool-tor'], *m. & f.* Beekeeper, apiculture.

apicultura [ah-pe-cool-too'-rah], *f.* Apiculture, raising of bees.

apilador [ah-pe-lah-dor'], *m.* One who piles the wool up at the sheep-shearing time.

apilar [ah-pe-lar'], *va.* To heap up, to put one thing upon another.

apilonar [ah-pe-lo-nahr'], *va. (LAm.) V.* APILAR.

apimplado [ah-pem-plah-do], *a. (LAm.)* Tight, tipsy.

apimpollarse [ah-pim-pol-lyar'-say], *vr.* To germinate.

apiñado, da [ah-pe-nyah-do'-dah], *a.* Pyramidal, pineshaped. Crowded, packed, congested. -*pp.* of APIÑAR.

apiñadura [ah-pe-nyah-doo'-rah], *f.* Crowding, congestion.

apiñamiento [ah-pe-nyah-me-en'-to], *m.* The act of pressing together.

apiñar [ah-pe-nyar'], *va.* To press together, to join, to unite. -*vr.* To clog, to crowd. **La multitud se apiñaba alrededor de él**, the crowd pressed round him.

apio [ah'-pe-o], *m. (Bot.)* Celery. **Apio montano or levístico**, *(Bot.)* Common lovage. **Apio de risa**, *(Bot.)* Crow-foot.

apiolar [ah-pe-o-lar'], *va.* 1. To gyve a hawk. 2. To tie game together by the leg. 3. *(Met. Coll.)* To seize, to apprehend. 4. *(coll.)* To kill, to murder.

apio-nabo [ah-pe-o-nah-bo], *m.* Celeriac.

apiparse [ah-pe-pahr-say], *vr.* To stuff oneself.

apir(i) [ah-pe-re], *m. (LAm.)* Mineworker.

apirético, ca [ah-pe-ray'-te-co, cah], *a.* Apyretic, free from the access of fever.

apirularse [ah-pe-roo-lahr-say], *vr. (Cono Sur)* To get dressed up to the nines.

apisonadora [ah-pe-so-nah-do'-rah], *f.* Steam roller.

apisonar [ah-pe-so-nar', *va.* 1. To roll. 2. To tamp, to drive down.

apitiquarse [ah-pe-te-car-say], *vr. (Cono Sur)* To get depressed.

apitonamiento [ah-pe-to-nah-me-en'-to], *m.* 1. Putting forth the tenderlings. 2. Passion, anger.

apitonar [ah-pe-to-nar'], *vn.* 1. To put forth the tenderlings; applied to horned animals. 2. To bud, to germ. -*va.* To pick as chickens in the eggshell. -*vr.* To treat with abusive language. To get into a huff.

apizarrado, da [ah-pe-thar-rah'-do, dah], *a.* Slate-colored.

APL *(Comp.)* APL (A Programming Language).

aplacable [ah-plah-cah'-blay], *a.* Placable, easy to be appeased, meek, gentle.

aplacación [ah-plah-cah-the-on'], *f.*

aplacamiento [ah-plah-cah-me-en'-to], *m.* Appeasableness. -*m.* Stay of execution.

aplacador, ra [ah-plah-cah-dor', rah], *m. & f.* One who appeases.

aplacar [ah-plah-car'], *va.* To appease, to pacify, to mitigate.

aplacer [ah-plah-therr'], *va.* To please. *V.* AGRADAR.

aplacerado, da [ah-plah-thay-rah'-do, dah], *a.* 1. *(Naut.)* Level and not very deep: said of the bottom of the sea. 2. *(Amer.)* Open, cleared of trees. **Sitio aplacerado**, a clearing.

aplacible [ah-plah-thee'-blay], *a.* Pleasant.

aplaciente [ah-plah-the-en'-tay], *pa.* Appeasive.

aplanacalles [ah-plah-nah-cah-lyays], *m. (LAm.)* Idler, layabout.

aplanadera [ah-plah-nah-day'-rah], *f.* 1. A roller for levelling the ground. 2. Beetle, rammer.

aplanador [ah-plah-nah-dor'], *m.* 1. A leveller. 2. *(Mech.)* Battledoor, brusher, riveter; ingot hammer; cylinder roller. 3. *(Typ.)* Planer, planishing mallet.

aplanamiento [ah-plah-nah-me-en'-to], *m.* Levelling, the act of making level.

aplanar [ah-plah-nar'], *va.* 1. To level, to make even, to flatten (terreno). 2. To terrify, or astonish by some unexpected novelty. -*vr.* 1. To tumble down (edificio). 2. To lose animation or vigor (persona).

aplanático, ca [ah-plah-nah'-te-co, cah], *a.* Aplanatic, free of spherical aberration.

aplanchado [ah-plan-chah'-do], *m.* 1. Linen which is to be, or has been ironed. 2. Act of smoothing or ironing linen.

aplanchadora [ah-plan-chah-do'-rah], *f.* A woman whose trade is to iron linen.

aplanchar [ah-plan-char'], *va.* To iron linen.

aplantillar [ah-plan-teel-lyar'], *va.* To adjust or fit stones, timber, or boards, according to the model.

aplastado, da [ah-plas-tah'-do, dah], *a.* Caked; dispirited. -*pp.* of APLASTAR.

aplastante [ah-plas-tahn-tay], *a.* Overwhelming, crushing.

aplastar [ah-plas-tar'], *va.* 1. To cake, to flatten, or crush a thing, to smash. 2. To confound an opponent. -*vr.* To become flat. **Se aplastó contra la pared**, he fattened himself against the wall. 3. *(Arquit.)* To collapse. 4. *(Cono Sur)* To get discouraged. 5. *(Cono Sur)* To be drained (exhausto).

aplatanado [ah-plah-tah-nah-do], *a.* **Está aplatanado**, *(Carib.)* he has gone native. *(fig.)* Lumpish, lacking all ambition.

aplatanarse [ah-plah-tah-nahr'-say], *vr.* To become lethargic, sink into lethargy.

aplatarse [ah-plah-tahr'-say], *vr. (Carib.)* To get rich.

aplaudir [ah-plah-oo-deer'], *va.* To applaud, to extol with shouts. *vr.* To boast of, to be elated by.

aplauso [ah-plah'-oo-so], *m.* Applause, approbation, praise.

aplayar [ah-plah-yar'], *vr.* To overflow the banks.

aplazamiento [ah-plah-thah-me-en'-to], *m.* 1. Convocation, citation. 2. Deferring, postponement.

aplazar [ah-plah-thar'], *va.* 1. To convene. 2. To invest. 3. To concert, to regulate, to summon. 4. To defer, to adjourn (asunto); to treat something later. To postpone. **Se ha aplazado decisión por tiempo indefinido**, the decision has been postponed indefinitely.

aplebeyado [ah-play-bay-lyah-do], *a.* Coarse, coarsened.

aplebeyar [ah-play-bay-yar'], *va. (Obs.)* To render vile or servile. to degrade, to coarsen. -*vr.* To become coarse.

aplegar [ah-play-gar'], *va. (Prov.)* To join, to unite.

aplicabilidad [ah-plah-cah-be-le-dahd], *f.* Applicability.

aplicable [ah-ple-cah'-blay], *a.* Applicable.

aplicación [ah-ple-cah-the-on'], *f.* 1. Application. 2. Assiduity, laboriousness, close study. **Aplicación de bienes or hacienda**, the act of adjudging estates or other property. **Aplicaciones de gestión**, management applications.

aplicado, da [ah-ple-cah'-do, dah], *a.* 1. Studious, intent on a thing. 2. Industrious, laborious, painful. -*pp.* of APLICAR.

aplicar [ah-ple-car'], *va.* 1. To apply, to put one thing to another; to clap. 2. *(Met.)* to consider a subject under discussion. 3. *(Met.)* To attribute or impute. 4. *(Law.)* To adjudge. -*vr.* 1. To study or devote oneself to a thing. 2. To earn a living.

aplique [ah-ple-kay], *m.* Wall lamp, *(Theat.)* Piece of stage decor.

aplomado, da [ah-plo-mah'-do, dah], *a.* 1. Of the color of lead. 2. Leaden. 3. *(Met.)* Heavy, dull, lazy. 4. Self-confident. -*pp.* of APLOMAR.

aplomar [ah-plo-mar'], *va. (Obs.)* To overload, to crush. -*vn.* To use a plummet and line to see if a wall has been perpendicularly raised. -*vr.* To tumble, to fall to the ground: applied to buildings. *(fig.)* To gain confidence. *(Cono Sur)* To get embarrassed.

aplomo [ah-plo'-mo], *m.* 1. Tact, prudence, management, self-possession. 2. Plumb-line, plummet. 3. *(Mus.)* Exactness in time. 4. Due proportion among the figures of a picture. -*a.* Plumb, perpendicular. *V. (á)* PLOMO.

apnea [ap-nay'-ah], *f.* Apnea, temporary inability to breathe.

apoca [ah'-po-cah], *f. (Law. Prov.)* Receipt, acquittance, discharge.

apocado, da [ah-po-cah'-do, dah], *a.* 1. Pusillanimous, mean-spirited, cowardly. 2. Narrow-hoofed. 3. Of mean, low extraction. -*pp.* of APOCAR.

apocador, ra [ah-po-cah-dor', rah], *m. & f.* One who lessens or diminishes.

apocalipsi, apocalipsis [ah-po-cah-leep'-se, sis], *m.* Apocalypse, the Relation of St. John.

apocalíptico, ca [ah-po-cah-lep'-te-co, cah], *a.* Apocalyptical.

apocamiento [ah-po-cah-me-en'-to], *m.* Abjectness of mind, meanness of spirit, littleness.

apocar [ah-po-car'], *va.* 1. To lessen. 2. *(Met.)* To cramp, to contract. *-vr.* To humble oneself, to undervalue oneself.

apócema, apócima [ah-po'-thay-mah, ah-po'-the-mah], *f. (Med.)* Apozem, a decoction.

apocopar [ah-po-co-par'], *va.* To take away the last letter or syllable of a word. To apocopate.

apócope [ah-po'-co-pay], *f. (Poetic.)* A figure, where the last letter or syllable of a word is taken away.

apócrifamente [ah-po'-cre-fah-men-tay], *adv.* Apocryphally, uncertainly, on a false foundation.

apócrifo, fa [ah-po'-cre-fo, fah], *a.* Apocryphal, fabulous, of doubtful authority.

apocrisiario [ah-po-cre-se-ah'-re-o], *m.* A Greek ambassador.

apochongarse [ah-po-chon-gahr-say], *vr. (Cono Sur)* To get scared.

apodador [ah-po-dah-dor'], *m.* A wag, one who ridicules or scoffs.

apodar [ah-po-dar'], *va.* To give nicknames, to ridicule.

apodencado, da [ah-po-den-cah'-do, dah], *a.* Pointer-like.

apoderado, da [ah-po-day-rah'-do, dah], *a.* 1. Empowered, authorized. 2. *(Obs.)* Powerful. *-pp.* of APODERAR.

apoderado [ah-po-day-rah'-do], *m.* Proxy, attorney, agent.

apoderar [ah-po-day-rar'], *va.* To empower; to grant a power of attorney. *-vr.* To possess oneself of a thing. 2. *(Obs.)* To become powerful or strong.

apodíctico, ca [ah-po-deec'-te-co, cah], *a.* Apodictical, demonstrative.

apodo [ah-po'-do], *m.* A nickname.

ápodo, da [ah'-po-do, dah], *a. (Zool.)* Apodous, without feet.

apódosis [ah-po'-do-sis], *f.* Apodosis, the conclusion of a conditional sentence; correlative to protasis.

apófise, apófisis [ah-po'-fe-say, ah-po'-fe-sis], *f. (Med.)* The prominent part of some bones, the same as process.

apoflegmático, ca [ah-po-fleg-mah'-te-co, cah], *a.* Apophlegmatic, drawing away phlegm.

apogeo [ah-po-hay'-o], *m.* 1. *(Astr.)* Apogee. 2. Culmination, apex. **En todo su apogeo**, in all its glory, at is peak.

apógrafo [ah-po'-grah-fo], *m.* Apograph, transcript, or copy of some book or writing.

apolillado, da [ah-po-leel-lyah'-do, dah], *a.* Moth-eaten, worm-eaten. *-pp.* of APOLILLAR.

apolilladura [ah-po-leel-layh-doo'-rah], *a.* A hole eaten by moths in clothes and other things made of wool.

apolillar [ah-po-lee'-lyar], *va.* To gnaw or eat clothes, or other things. *(Cono Sur)* **Estar apolillado**, to be snoozing. *-vr.* To be moth-eaten.

apolinar, apolíneo, nea [ah-po-le-nar', ah-po-lee'-nay-o, ah], *a. (Poetic.)* Belonging to Apollo.

apolinarista [ah-po-le-nah-rees'-tah], *m.* Apollinarian, name given to the followers of a sect of Christians in the fourth century.

apolismar [ah-po-les-mah], *va. (LAm.)* To ruin, destroy. *-vr. (LAm.)* To grow weak, weaken.

apolítico [ah-po-le'-te-co], *a.* Apolitical, non-political.

apoliyar [ah-po-le-yahr], *va. V.* APOLILLAR.

Apolo [ah-po-lo], *m.* Apollo.

apologético, ca [ah-po-lo-hay'-te-co, cah], *a.* 1. Apologetic, excusatory. 2. Belonging to an apologue or fable. 3. Applied to the writers of apologues.

apología [ah-po-lo-hee'-ah], *f.* Apology, defence, excuse. **Una apología del terrorismo**, a statement in support of terrorism.

apológico, ca [ah-po-lo'-he-co, cah], *a.* That which relates to an apologue.

apologista [ah-po-lo-hees'-tah], *m.* An apologist.

apólogo [ah-po'-l-go], *m.* Apologue, a fable or story, to convey moral truth.

apoltronado [ah-pol-tro-nah-do], *a.* Lazy.

apoltronarse [ah-pol-tro-nar'-say], *vr.* To grow lazy, to loiter.

apolvillarse [ah-pol-ve-lyahr-say], *vr. (Cono Sur Agri.)* To be blighted.

apomazar [ah-po-mah-thar'], *va.* 1. To glaze printed linens with pumice-stone for the purpose of painting on them. 2. To burnish a surface with pumice-stone.

apomeli [ah-po-may'-le], *f.* A decoction prepared of honeycomb disolved in vinegar and water.

aponeurosis [ah-po-nay-oo-ro'-sis], *f.* Aponeurosis, fascia.

aponeurótico, ca [ah-po-nay-oo-ro'-te-co, cah], *a.* Aponeurotic, fascia-like.

apoplejía [ah-po-play-hee'-ah], *f.* Apoplexy.

apoplético, ca [ah-po-play'-te-co, cah], *a.* Apoplectic.

apoquinar [ah-po-ke-nahr], *va.* To fork out, to pay up.

aporcadura [ah-por-cah-doo'-rah], *f.* The act of raising earth around plants; earthing up.

aporcar [ah-por-car'], *va.* To cover garden-plants with earth for the purpose of whitening them and making them tender; to hill.

aporisma [ah-po-rees'-mah], *m.* Ecchymosis, an extravasation of blood between the flesh and skin.

aporismarse [ah-po-ris-mar'-say], *vr.* To become an ecchymosis.

aporracear [ah-por-rah-thay-ar'], *va. (Prov.)* To pommel, to give repeated blows.

aporrar [ah-por-rar'], *vn. (coll.)* To stand mute, to get stuck for words. *-vr. (coll.)* To become a bore.

aporreado, da [ah-por-ray-ah'-do, dah] *a.* 1. Cudgelled. 2. Dragged along. *-pp.* of APORREAR.

aporreamiento [ah-por-ray-ah-me-en'-to], *m.* The act of beating or pommelling.

aporreante [ah-por-ray-ahn'-tay], *pa. (coll.)* Cudgeller, applied to bad fencers.

aporrear [ah-por-ray-ar'], *va.* 1. To beat or cudgel, to knock, to maul. **Aporrear el piano**, to thumb the piano. 2. *(fig.)* To bother, pester. 4. To bang away at, to thump. *-vr*, To slave away, slog. To study with intense application.

aporreo [ah-por-ray'-o], *m.* The act of beating, pommelling, or cudgelling.

aporrillarse [ah-por-reel-lyar'-say], *vr.* to get swellings in the joints; a term applied to horses.

aporrillo [ah-por-reel'-lyo], *adv. (coll.)* Plentifully.

aportación [ah-por-tah-the-on'], *f.* Contribution.

aportadero [ah-por-tah-day'-ro], *m.* A place where a ship or person may stop.

aportar [ah-por-tar'], *vn.* 1. To make a port, to arrive at a port. 2. To reach an unexpected place when one is benighted. 3. *-va.* To bring, contribute, to bring forward.

aporte [ah-por-tay], *m.* Contribution.

aportellado [ah-por-tel-lyah'-do], *m. (Obs.)* Formerly an officer of justice, a member of the council of large towns, that administered justice to the people of the neighboring villages.

aportillar [ah-por-teel-lyar'], *va.* 1. To make a breach in a rampart. 2. To break down, to break open. *-vr.* To tumble down, to fall into ruins.

aposentador, ra [ah-po-sen-tah-dor', rah], *m. & f.* 1. One who lets lodgings. 2. Usher in a theater (acomodador).

aposentamiento [ah-po-sen-tah-me-en'-to], *m.* The act of lodging or affording a temporary habitation.

aposentar [ag-po-sen-tar'], *va.* To lodge. *-vr.* To take a lodging; to tarry at night.

aposentillo [ah-po-sen-teel'-lyo], *m. dim.* A small room, a bedroom.

aposento [ah-po-sen'-to], *m.* 1. A room or apartment. 2. A temporary habitation; an inn. 3. A box or seat in the theater.

aposesionar [ah-po-say-se-o-nar'], *va.* To give possession. - *vr.* To take possession; to possess oneself of a thing.

aposición [ah-po-se-the-on'], *f. (Gram.)* Apposition a grammatical term.

aposiopesis [ah-po-se-o-pay'-sis], *f. (Rhet.)* A figure of speech, in which the speaker breaks off suddenly, as if unable or unwilling to declare his mind.

apósito [ah-po'-se-to], *m.* Any external medicinal application.

apospelo [ah-pos-pay'-lo], *adv. (Obs.)* 1. Against the grain. 2. Contrary to the natural order.

aposta, apostadamente [ah-pos'-tah, ah-pos-tah-dah-men'-tay], *adv.* Designedly, on purpose. V. ADREDE.

apostadero [ah-pos-tah-day'-ro], *m.* 1. A place where soldiers or other persons are stationed. 2. *(Naut.)* A naval station.

apostador, ra [ah-po-tah-dor'], *m. & f.* Better, one that wagers or bets.

apostal [ah-pos-tahl'], *m. (Prov.)* A convenient fishing-place in a river.

apostáleos [ah-pos-tah'-lay-os], *m. pl. (Naut.)* Thick planks for gun platforms.

apostar [ah-pos-tar'], *va.* 1 To bet, to hold a wager, to lay a bet. 2. To place relays. 3. To post soldiers or other persons in a place. **Apostarlas or apostárselas**, to contend, to defy. -*vr.* To emulate, to rival, to stand in competition. **Apostar carreras**, to run races.

apostasia [ah-pos-tah-see'-ah], *f.* 1. Apostasy. 2. *(Bot.)* A plant of the orchid family.

apostasis [ah-pos-tah'-sis], *f. (Med.)* 1. A purulent deposit at a distance from the seat of inflammation; metastatic abscess. 2. A splinter of bone.

apóstata [ah-pos'-tah-tah], *m.* Apostate; forsaker, fugitive.

apostatar [h-pos-tah-tar'], *vn.* To apostatize, to fall away.

apostema [ah-pos-tay'-mah], *f.* An aposteme, abscess.

apostemación [ag-pos-tay-mah-the-on'], *f. (Med.)* Forming an abscess, apostemation.

apostemar [ah-pos-tay-mar'], *va.* To form an abscess. -*vr.* To get an abscess; to be troubled with a purulent humor.

apostemero [ah-pos-tay-may'-ro], *m.* Bistoury, an instrument for opening abscesses.

apostemilla [ah-pos-tay-meel'-lyah], *f.dim.* 1. A small abscess or pimple. 2. Gum-boil.

apostemoso, sa [ah-pos-tay-mo'-so, sah], *a.* Relating to abscesses.

apostilla [ah-pos-teel'-lyah], *f.* A marginal note put to a book or writing; annotation, remark; gloss.

apostillar [ah-pos-teel'-lyar], *va.* To put marginal notes to a book or writing. -*vr.* To break out in pimples or pustules.

apóstol [ah-pos'-tol], *m.* Apostle, missionary. **Apóstoles**, *(Naut.)* Hawsepieces.

apostolado [ah-pos-to-lah'-do], *m.* 1. Apostleship. 2. The congregation of the apostles. 3. The images or pictures of the twelve apostles.

apostólicamente [ah-pos-to'-le-cah-men-tay], *adv.* Apostolically.

apostólico, ca [ah-pos-to'-le-co, cah], *a.* 1. Apostolical. 2. Apostolic; that which belongs to the Pope, or derives from him apostolical authority.

apóstolos [ah-pos'-to-los], *m. pl. (Law. Obs.)* Dimissory apostolical letters.

apostrofar [ah-pos-tro-far'], *va.* To apostrophize, to address one by apostrophe; to insult.

apóstrofe [ah-pos'-tro-fay], *f. (Rhet.)* Apostrophe; insult, reprimand.

apóstrofo [ah-pos'-tro-fo], *m.* Apostrophe, a typographical sign.

apostura [ah-pos-too'-rah], *f.* 1. Gentleness, neatness in person. 2. Good order and disposition of things; high breeding.

apoteca [ah-po-tay'-cah], *f. V.* BOTICA.

apotecario [ah-o-tay-cah'-re-o], *m. (Prov.) V.* BOTICARIO.

apotegma [ah-po-teg'-mah], *m.* Apothegm; maxim.

apoteósico [ah-po-tay-o'-se-co], *a. (fig.)* Huge, tremendous.

apoteosis [ah-po-tay-oh'-sis], *f.* Apotheosis, deification.

apotome [ah-po-to'-may], *m.* (Alg.) The remainder or difference of two incommensurable qualities.

apotrerar [ah-po-tray-rar'], *va.* To turn horses out to pasture.

apotrosis [ah-po-tro'-sis], *f. (Surg.)* 1. A fracture of the skull, with splinters. 2. Extraction of a splinter of bone.

apoyabrazos [ah-po-yah-brah-thos], *m.* Armrest.

apoyadero [ah-po-yah-day-ro], *m.* Prop, support.

apoyador [ah-po-yah-dor], *m.* Support, bracket.

apoyadura [ah-po-yah-doo'-rah], *f.* A flow of the milk when nurses give the bottle to babies.

apoyar [ah-po-yar'], *va.* 1. To favor, to protect, to patronize, to countenance, to further. 2. To bear upon the bit; spoken of horses which hang down their heads. **Apoyar las espuelas**, to spur. 3. To confirm, to prove, to corroborate, to hold up; to ground, to found. **Apoya esta sentencia con un texto de la Escritura**, he confirms this sentence by a text of Scripture. **Apoyar una proposición or propuesta**, to second a motion. -*vn.* To rest on; to lie. **La columna apoya sobre el pedestal**, the column rests on the pedestal. -*vr.* To lean upon a person or thing. **Apoyarse en los estribos**, to bear upon the stirrups. To rest on, be supported by. **Apoyarse contra una pared**, to lean against a wall.

apoyatura [ah-po-yah-too'-rah], *f. (Mus.)* Appoggiatura, leaning or leading note, used to prepare the ear for, or guide it to, the note it precedes.

apoyo [ah-po'-yo], *m.* 1. Prop, stay, support, fulcrum. 2. *(Met.)* Protection, patronage, help, countenance, muniment, maintenance.

apozarse [ah-po-thahr-say], *va. (And. Cono Sur)* To form a pool.

apreciable [ah-pray-teh-ah'-blay], *a.* 1. Valuable, respectable, worthy of esteem, creditable. **Los apreciables esposos**, the esteemed couple. 2. That which can fetch a price; marketable. **Una cantidad apreciable**, an appreciable quantity.

apreciación [ah-pray-teh-ah-the-on'], *f.* Estimation, valuation, appreciation. **Según nuestra apreciación**, according to our estimation.

apreciadamente [ah-pray-the-ah-dah-men'-tay], *adv.* In a valuable, respectable manner.

apreciador, ra [ah-pray-the-ah-dor', rah], *m. & f.* Estimator, appraiser, a person appointed to set a price upon a thing.

apreciar [ah-pray-the-ar'], *va.* 1. To appreciate, to appraise, to estimate, to value. 2. *(fig.)* To esteem, value. **Aprecia mucho a los niños**, she's very fond of children. 3. *(Art., mus.* etc.) To appreciate. 4. To see, notice, observe. 4. *(LAm.)* To add value to enhance, improve. 5. *(LAm.)* To be grateful for, appreciate; **lo aprecio mucho**, I much appreciate it.

apreciativo, va [ah-pray-the-ah-tee'-vo, vah], *a.* Relating to the value set upon a thing. **Una mirada apreciativa**, an appraising look.

aprecio [ah-pray'-the-o], *m.* 1. Appraisement, appreciation, the value set upon a thing; account. **No hacer aprecio de algo**, to pay no attention to something. 2. Esteem, approbation, regard. **Tener a uno en gran aprecio**, to hold somebody in high regard.

aprehender [ah-pray-en-derr'], *va.* 1. To apprehend, to seize. 2. To fancy, to conceive, to form an idea of a thing. **Aprehender la posesión**, to take possession. **Aprehender los bienes**, to seize or distrain goods.

aprehensible [ah-prayn-se-blay], *a.* Understandable, conceivable; **una idea difícilmente aprehensible**, an idea which is difficult to pin down.

aprehensión [ah-pray-en-se-on'], *f.* 1. The act of seizing, apprehending, or taking up a criminal. 2. Apprehension, perception, acuteness; a ready and witty saying. 3. Apprehension, fear. 4. Misapprehension.

aprehensivo, va [ah-pray-en-see'-vo, vah], *a.* Apprehensive, quick to understand, fearful; sensitive; perceptive.

aprehensor, ra [ah-pray-en-sor', rah], *m. & f.* One who apprehends.

aprehensorio, ria [ah-pray-en-so'-re-o, rah], *m. & f.* Apprehending, seizing.

apremiador, ra [ah-pray-me-ah-dor', rah], *m. & f.* Compeller, one who compels to do a thing.

apremiante [ah-pray-me-ahn'-tay], *a.* Urgent, pressing. -*pa.* of APREMIAR.

apremiar [ah-pray-me-ar'], *va.* 1. To press, to urge. 2. To compel, to oblige by a judicial order. **Apremiar a uno a hacer algo**, to press somebody to do something. 3. To hurry. 4. To oppress, to harass. 5. -*vn.* To press, to be urgent. **El tiempo apremia**, time presses.

apremio [ah-pray'-me-o], *m.* 1. Pressure, constriction; constrain, force, urgency. **Por apremio de tiempo**, because time is pressing. **Por apremio de trabajo**, because of pressure of work. 2. Judicial compulsion.

aprendedor, ra [ah-pren-day-dor', rah], *a.* Learning; apt to learn.

aprender [ah-pren-der'], *va.* 1. To learn; to acquire knowledge. 2. To retain in the memory. **Aprender a hacer algo**, to learn to do something.

aprendiz, za [ah-pren-deeth', thah], *m. & f.* Apprentice or prentice; learner. **Aprendiz de todo, oficial de nada**, Jack of all trades. **Estar de aprendiz con uno**, to be apprenticed to somebody.

aprendizaje [ah-pren-de-tha'-hay], *m.* 1. Apprenticeship. 2. (*Comp.*) Training.

aprensador [ah-pren-sah-dor'], *m.* A presser or calenderer.

aprensar [ah-pren-sar'], *va.* 1. To dress cloth in a press, to calender. 2. To vex, to crush, to oppress. 3. (*Naut.*) To stow wool, cotton, etc., on board a ship.

aprensión [ah-pren-se-on'], *f.* 1. Apprehension. 2. False concept, and unfounded fear. 3. Mistrust, suspicion; particularly of one believing himself sick.

aprensivo, va [ah-pren-see'-vo, vah], *a.* Apprehensive, hypochondriac, fearful of being ill; squeamish.

apresador, ra [ah-pray-sah-dor', rah], *m. & f.* 1. Privateer, cruiser. 2. Captor.

apresamiento [ah-pray-sah-me-en'-to], *m.* Capture; clutch, hold.

apresar [ah-pray-sar'], *va.* 1. To seize, to grasp. 2. (*Naut.*) To take or capture an enemy's ship.

aprestado [ah-prays-tah-do], *a.* Ready; **estar aprestado para**, to be ready to.

aprestar [ah-pres-tar'], *va.* 1. To prepare, to make ready. 2. -*vr.* To prepare, get ready. **Aprestarse para**, to get ready to.

apresto [ah-press'-to], *m.* Preparation (preparación). Sizing (acción).

apresuración [ah-pray-soo-rah-the-on'], *f.* Acceleration, the act of quickening motion, or making haste.

apresuradamente [ah-pray-soo-rah-dah-men'-tay], *adv.* Hastily, quickly.

apresurado, da [ah-pray-soo-rah'-do, dah], *a.* 1. Brief, hasty. 2. Acting with precipitation. -*pp.* of APRESURAR.

apresuramiento [ah-pray-soo-rah-meen'-to], *m.* Eagerness, readiness to act, forwardness. V. APRESURACIÓN.

apresurar [ah-pray-soo-rar'], *va.* To accelerate, to hasten, to hurry, to cut off delay, to rush. -*vr.* To accelerate, to hurry, make haste. **Me apresuré a sugerir que…**, I hastened to suggest that…

apretadamente [ah-pray-tah-dah-men'-tay], *adv.* Tightly, closely; nearly; close, fast.

apretadera [ah-pray-tah-day'-rah], *f.* A strap (correa).

apretadero [ah-pray-tah-day'-ro], *m.* Truss or bandage by which ruptures are restrained from relapsing. V. BRAGUERO.

apretadillo, lla [ah-pray-tah-deel'-lyo, lyah], *a.dim.* Somewhat constrained, rather hard put to it. **Apretadillo está el enfermo**, The patient is in great danger.

apretadizo, za [ah-pray-tah-dee'-tho, thah], *a.* Easily compressible.

apretado, da [ah-pray-tah'-do, dah], *a.* 1. Mean, miserable, narrow-minded, illiberal; close, close-fisted; costive. 2. Hard, difficult, dangerous. **Estar apretado de dinero**, to be short of money. **En un caso apretado**, it's a tricky business. -*pp.* of APRETAR.

apretador [ah-pray-tah-dor'], *m.* 1. One who presses or beats down. 2. A sort of doublet without sleeves. 3. A sort of corset for chidren. 4. A broad bandage put upon infants. 5. A net for tying up the hair. 6. An instrument which serves for tightening; a rammer.

apretadura [ah-pray-tah-doo'-rah], *f.* Compression.

apretamiento [ah-pray-tah-me-en'-o], *m.* 1. Crowd, great concourse of people. 2. Conflict. 3. (*Obs.*) Avarice, closeness; contractedness.

apretar [ah-pray-tar'], *va.* 1. To compress, to tighten, to press down, to crowd, to constrict, to contract, to hug. **Apretar a uno entre los brazos**, to hug somebody in one's arms. **Apretar a uno contra la pared**, to pin somebody against the wall. 2. To constrain, to clutch. 3. To distress, to afflict with calamities. 4. To act with more vigor than usual. 5. To urge earnestly. 6. To darken that part of a painting which is too bright and glaring. **Apretar de soletas**, to run away. **Apretar con uno**, To attack a person. **Apretar la mano**, to correct with a heavy hand, to punish severely. 7. To get worse; **cuando el calor aprieta**, when the heat becomes oppresive.

apretón [ah-pray-tone'], *m.* 1. Pressure. **Apretón financiero**, financial squeeze. 2. Struggle, conflict. 3. A short but rapid race. 4. The act of throwing a thicker shade on one part of a piece of painting. 5. Press, crush, jam; **el apretón en el metro**, the crush in the subway.

apretujar [ah-pray-too-har'], *va.* (*coll.*) To squeeze, to crowd in a crowd of persons. **Estar apretujado entre dos personas**, to be crushed between two people.

apretujón [ah-pray-too-hon], *m.* 1. Hard squeeze; big hug. 2. Press, crush, jam.

apretura [ah-pray-too'-rah], *f.* 1. A crowd, a multitude crowding. 2. Distress, conflict, anguish. 3. A narrow, confined place; narrowness.

apriesa [ah-pre-ay'-sah], *adv.* In haste, in a hurry.

aprieto [ah-pre-ay'-to], *m.* Difficulty, pinch, pressure, stress. **Estar en un aprieto**, To be in a jam, to be in a tight position, under stress.

apriorismo [ah-pre-o-res-mo], *m.* Tendency to resolve matters hastily.

apriorístico [ah-pre-o-res-te-co], *a.* 1. A priori, deductive (deductivo). 2. Hasty, premature (precipitado).

aprisa [ah-pree'-sah], *adv.* Swiftly, promptly; fast; in a hurry.

aprisar [ah-pre-sar'], *va.* (*Obs.*) To hasten, to hurry, to push forward.

apriscadero [ah-pris-cah-day'-ro], *m.* (*Obs.*) V. APRISCO.

apriscar [ah-pris-car'], *va.* To carry to the sheep-fold, to a sure spot.

aprisco [ah-prees'-co], *m.* Sheep-fold.

aprisionar [ah-pre-se-o-nar'], *va.* 1. To confine, to imprison. 2. To bind, to subject.

aproar [ah-pro-ar'], *vn.* (*Naut.*) To turn the head of a ship toward any part; to trim by the head.

aprobación [ah-pro-bah-the-on'], *f.* Approbation, concurrence; consent, liking; run. **Dar su aprobación**, to give one's consent, approve.

aprobado, da [ah-pro-bah'-do, dah], *a.* 1. Approved. 2. Passed (in an examination). -*m.* Passing mark.

aprobador, ra [ah-pro-bah-dor', rah], *m. & f.* Approver, one who approves.

aprobante [ah-pro-bahn'-tay], *pa.* 1. Approver. 2. One who proves the qualifications of a person for being a member of some corporations.

aprobar [ah-pro-bar'], *va.* To approve; to like, to be pleased with; to find. -*vn.* (*Univ.*) To pass. **Aprobé en francés**, I passed in French.

aprobatorio, ria [ah-pro-bah-to'-re-o, re-ah], *a.* Approbative, approving. **Una mirada aprobatoria**, an approving look.

aproches [ah-pro'-ches], *m.pl.* (*Mil.*) approaches, the several works made by besiegers for advancing and getting nearer to a fortress. **Contraaproches**, Counter-approaches. **Las trincheras se llaman líneas de aproches**, the trenches are called lines of approach.

aprón [ah-prone'], *m.* (*Zool.*) A small fresh-water fish resembling a gudgeon.

aprontamiento [ah-pron-tah-me-ayn-to], *m.* Quick delivery, rapid service.

aprontar [ah-pron-tar'], *va.* To prepare hastily, to get ready with despatch.

apronte [ah-pron-tay], *m.* (*Cono Sur*) 1. Heat, preliminary race. 2. **Aprontes**, preparations; **irse en los aprontes**, to waste one's energy on unnecessary preliminaries.

apronto [ah-pron'-to], *m.* A speedy preparation.

apropiación [ah-pro-pe-ah-the-on'], *f.* Appropriation, assumption, the act of appropriating or assuming a thing. **Apropiación ilícita**, illegal seizure, misappropriation.

apropiadamente [ah-pro-pe-ah-dah-men'-tay], *adv.* Conveniently, fitly, properly.

apropiado, da [ah-pro pe-ah'-do, dah], *a.* Appropriate, fit; official. -*pp.* of APROPIAR.

aprópiador [ah-pro-pe-ah-dor'], *m.* Appropriator.

apropiar [ah-pro-pe-ar'], *va.* 1. To appropriate, to assume. 2. To bring to a resemblance. 3. To accommodate, to apply. -*vr.* To appropriate any thing to oneself, to encroach. **Apropiarse de algo**, to appropriate something.

apropincuación [ah-pro-pin-coo-ah-the-on'], *f.* Approach.

aprovechable [ah-proh-vay-chah'-blay], *a.* Profitable, useful, or serviceable.

aprovechadamente [ah-pro-vay-chah-dah-mayn-tay], *adv.* Profitably.

aprovechado, da [ah-pro-vay-chah-do, dah], *a.* 1. Improved; taken advantage of. 2. Sparing, parsimonious. 3. Hard working, diligent. 4. Thrifty, economical. 4. Well spent (tiempo). -*pp.* of APROVECHAR.

aprovechamiento [ah-pro-vay-chah-me-en'-to], *m.* 1. Profit, utility, advantage. 2. Progress made in an art or science; growth. 3. Lands, commons, houses, etc., belonging to a town or city. *V.* PROPIOS.

aprovechar [ah-pro-bay-char'], *vn.* To make progress, to become useful, to come forward, to get forward. **Eso aprovecha poco**, that is of little use. **No aprovechar para nada**, to be completely useless. -*va.* 1. To profit by a thing, to employ it usefully. 2. (*Obs.*) To protect, to favor. 3. (*Obs.*) To meliorate. -*vr.* To avail oneself of a thing.

aprovechón [ah-pro-vay-chon'], *a.* Opportunistic, having an eye to the main chance.

aprovisionamiento [ah-pro-ve-se-o-nah-me-ayn-to], *m.* Supply, supplying.

aprovisionar [ah-pro-ve-se-o-nahr'], *va.* To supply.

aproximación [ah-proc-se-mah-the-on'], *f.* Approximation, closeness, nearness, approach.

aproximadamente [ah-proc-se-mah-dah-men'-tay], *adv.* Nearly, about.

aproximado [ah-proc-se-mah'-do], *a.* Approximate.

aproximar [ah-proc-se-mar'], *va.* To approximate, to approach, to bring near, to bring up. -*vr.* To come near, come closer, approach; **el tren se aproxima a su destino**, the train was nearing its destination.

aproximativo, va [ah-proc-se-mah-tee'-vo, vah], *a.* Approximate, rough (aproximado).

apside [ahp'-se-day], *m.* (*Astr.*) The extremities of the major axis of the orbit of a star. Mostly used in plural.

aptamente [ap-tah-men'-tay], *adv.* Conveniently, fitly, commodiously, expediently.

aptero, ra [ahp'-tay-ro, rah], *a.* (*Ent.*) Apterous: applied to insects.

aptitud [ap-te-tood'], *f.* 1. Aptitude or fitness for an employment; ability. **Demostrar tener aptitudes**, to show ability. **Carece de aptitud**, he hasn't got the talent. 2. Expediency; aptness.

apto, ta [ahp'-to, tah], *a.* Apt, fit; competent, clever, congruous; good, convenient. **Ser apto para aprender**, to be quick to learn. **No es apto para conducir**, he's not fit to drive.

apto [ap'-to], *abr.* de **apartamento**.

apuesta [ah-poo-ess'-tah], *f.* A bet, a wager. **Apuestas mutuas**, pari-mutuel.

apuesto, ta [ah-poo-ess'-to, tah], *a.* 1. Elegant, smart (elegante), handsome, good-looking (guapo). 2. (*Obs.*) Opportune, fit. (**Yo apuesto, yo apueste**, from **Apostar. V.** ACORDAR.)

apulgarar [ah-pool-gah-rar'], *va.* To force with the thumb. -*vr.* (*coll.*) To contract black spots (ropa blanca).

apunarse [ah-poo-nahr'-say], *vr.* (*And. Cono Sur*) To get mountain sickness.

apunchar [ah-poon-char'], *va.* Among comb-makers, to cut out the teeth of a comb.

apuntación [ah-poon-tah-the-on'], *f.* 1. Annotation, the act of noting down; memorial 2. The act of marking musical notes with exactness.

apuntado, da [ah-poon-tah'-do, dah], *a.* 1. Pointed, marked. 2. **El cañón está apuntado muy bajo**, the gun dips. -*pp.* of APUNTAR.

apuntador [ah-poon-tah-dor'], *m.* 1. Observer, one who notes or marks. 2. (*Naut.*) Gunner, who points the guns. **Apuntador de comedias**, a prompter to the players. **Apuntador electrónico**, teleprompter. 3. (*Mex. Dep.*) Scorer.

apuntalamiento [ah-poon-tah-lah-me-en'-to], *m.* Propping, pinning. **Apuntalamiento por la base**, Underpinning.

apuntalar [ah-poon-tah-lar'], *va.* 1. To prop, to support with props. 2. (*Naut.*) To shore a vessel. 3. -*vr.* To have a snack.

apuntamiento [ah-poon-tah-me-en'-to], *m.* 1. Remark. 2. Abstract, summary, a judicial report.

apuntar [ah-poon-tar'], *va.* 1. To aim; to level, to make after. **Apuntar a un blanco**, to aim at a target. 2. To point out, to mark, to hint. 3. To put down in writing; to note. 4. To touch lightly upon a point. 5. To fix or fasten provisionally a board or any other thing; (sew) to stitch. 6. To begin to appear or show itself. **Apunta el día**, the day peeps or begins to appear. 7. To sharpen edged tools. 8. To prompt or help actors by suggesting the word to them. 9. To offer. **Apuntar y no dar**, to promise readily and not perform. 10. (*LAm.*) To bet (apostar). -*vn.* To begin to show, appear. -*vr.* 1. To begin to turn; applied to wine. 2. (*Low.*) To be half-seas over, or half-drunk. **Apuntar los vegetales**, to grow up. 3. To get tight (emborracharse). 4. To sign on, to sign up. 5. To agree. 5. **¿Te apuntas a un café?**, how about a coffee?

apunte [ah-poon'-tay], *m.* 1. *V.* APUNTAMIENTO. 2. Annotation, memorandum. (Engin.) Rough sketch. **Sacar apuntes**, to take notes. 3. The words suggested by a prompter on the stage; in the act of prompting. 4. Stake in some games. **Apunte de cambios**, exchange-list. 5. (*Cono Sur*) Note of debts; **llevar el apunte**, to respond to somebody's advances. 6. (*LAm.*) Bet (apuesta).

apuntillar [ah-poon-te-lyahr'], *va.* 1. To finish off (toro). 2. (*fig.*) To round off.

apuñadar [ah-poo-nyah-dar], *va.* (*Prov.*) To strike with the fist.

apuñadura [ah-poo-nyah-doo-rah], *f.* Knob, handle.

apuñalado, da [ah-poo-nyah-lah'-do, dah], *a.* Shaped like a dagger.

apuñalar [ah-poo-nyah-lar'], *va.* To thrust with a dagger. (*fig.*) **Apuñalar a uno por la espalda**, to stab somebody in the back. **Apuñalar a uno con la mirada**, to look daggers at somebody.

apuñar [ah-poo-nyar'], *va.* (*Obs.*) To seize with the fist.

apuñear [ah-poo-nyay-ar'], *va. (coll.)* To strike with the fist.

apuracabos [ah-poo-rah-cah-bos], *m.* A candle-safe; save-all.

apuración [ah-poo-rah-the-on'], *f.* 1. *(Obs.)* Investigation. 2. *V.* APURO. Trouble, misfortune.

apuradamente [ah-poo-rah-dah-men'-tay], *adv.* 1. In the nick of time. 2. Punctually, exactly. 3. *(Obs.)* Radically.

apuradero [ah-poo-rah-day'-ro], *m. (Obs.)* Inquiry, disquisition which ascertains the true nature of a thing.

apurado, da [ah-poo-rah'-do, dah], *a.* 1. Rushed, in a hurry. 2. Needy. **Estar apurado**, 1. To be in a hurry. 2. To be in need (of money). 3. Exhausted (agotado). 4. Precise, exact.

apurador [ah-poo-rah-dor'], *m.* 1. A refiner, purifier. 2. One who spends or consumes. 3. *(Prov.)* One who gleans and picks up olives left by the first reapers.

apuramiento [ah-poo-rah-me-en'-to], *m.* Research, inquiry, verification.

apurar [ah-poo-rar'], *va.* 1. To purify. 2. To clear up, to verify, to investigate minutely, to know a thing radically. 3. To consume, to drain, to exhaust. **Apurar a uno**, to tease and perplex one, to press. 4. To hurry, to press, urge on. *-vr.* 1. To grieve, to be aflicted. 2. To exert oneself. **Verse apurado**, to be hard up; to be put to. **¡Apure Vd. que es tarde!** Hurry! it is late. 3. To make an effort, go hard at it. **Apurarse por hacer algo**, to strive to do something.

apurativo [ah-poo-rah-tee'-vo], *a.* Detersive.

apuro [ah-poo'-ro], *m.* 1. Want. 2. Anguish, pain, affliction. 3. Exigency; gripe. 4. Want, financial need. **Pasar apuros**, to suffer hardships; **verse en apuros**, to be in trouble. 5. *(LAm.)* Haste, hurry.

apurón [ah-poo-ron'], *m. (LAm.)* Great haste; *(Cono Sur)* **Andar a los apurones**, to do things in a rush.

apurruñar [ah-poo-roo-nyahr], *va. (Carib.)* To maltreat, handle roughly.

aquejar [ah-kay-har'], *va.* 1. To complain, to lament, to grieve. 2. To fatigue, to afflict. **¿Qué le aqueja?**, what's up with him? 3. *(Obs.)* To stimulate, to incite. 4. *(Obs.)* To pin up closely.

aquél, aquélla, llo [ah-kel', ah-kel'-lyah, ah-kel'-lyo], *pron. dem.* That one;. It denotes persons or objects at a distance from both the speaker and the person addressed. **Éste es más barato que aquél**, this one is cheaper than that one. **Aquéllos, aquéllas**. Those. **Éstos son más grandes que aquéllos**, these are bigger than those.

aquel, aquella, llo [ah-kel, ah-kel-lyah, ah-kel-lyo] *a. dem.* That (*pl.* those). **Aquel hombre**, that man. **Aquella casa**, that house. **Aquellos años**, those years. **Aquellas chicas**, those girls.

aquelarre [ah-kel-lar'-ray], *m.* Witches' Sabbath. Also applied to any motley and noisy meeting.

aquende [ah-ken'-day], *adv.* Hither, here.

aqueno [ah-kay'-no], *m.* Akene, a single, hard pericarp.

aquerenciado [ah-ke-rayn-the-ah-do], *a. (Cono Sur. Mex.)* In love, loving.

aquerenciarse [ah-kay-ren-the-ar'-say], *vr.* To be fond of a place: applied to cattle.

aqueridarse [ah-ke-re-dahr-say], *vr. (Carib.)*. To set up house together, move in together.

aquese, sa, so [ah-kay'-say, sah,so], *pron. dem.* That. **Aquesos, aquesas**, Those. This pronoun is used mainly in speaking of persons or things not very distant. Hardly used except in poetry.

aqueste, ta, to [ah-kess'-tay, tah, to], *pron. dem.* This, that.

aquí [ah-kee'], *adv.* 1. Here, in this place. 2. To this place. 3. Now, at present. 4. Then, on that occasion. **De aquí en adelante**, Henceforth. **De aquí para allí**, to and fro, up and down. **De aquí**, from this, hence. **De aquí en adelante**, henceforth, henceforward. **Aquí alrededor**, hereabouts. **Aquí dentro**, herein, hereinto. **Fuera de aquí**, out of here. **Hasta aquí**, hitherto. **Aquí abajo**, down here. **Aquí está**, here it is. **¡Aquí fue Troya!**, that was when it started. **Aquí yace**, here lies. **Hasta aquí**, as far as here. **Por aquí y por allí**, here and there.

aquiescencia [ah-ke-es-then'-the-ah], *f. (Law.)* Aquiescence, consent.

aquiesciente [ah-ke-ays-the-ayn-tay], *f.* Acquiescence.

aquietar [ah-ke-ay-tar'], *va.* 1. To quiet, to lull, to pacify; to hush; to allay. *-vr.* To grow calm, to be quiet.

aquila-alba [ah'-ke-lah-ahl'-bah], *f.* Corrosive sublimate mixed with fresh mercury.

aquilatar [ah-ke-lah-tar'], *va.* 1. To assay gold and silver. 2. To examine closely, to find out the truth of a thing. 3. *-vr. (Cono Sur)* To improve.

aquilea [ah-ke-lay'-ah], *f. (Bot.)* Milfoil, yarrow.

Aquiles [ah-ke'-lays], *m.* Achilles.

aquileña [ah-ke-lay'-nyah], *f. (Bot.)* Columbine.

aquilífero [ah-ke-lee'-fay-rao], *m.* Among the Romans, the standard-bearer, he who carried the Roman eagle.

aquilino, na [ah-ke-lee'-no, nah], *a.* Aquiline, hooked: applied commonly to the nose. *V.* AGUILEÑO.

aquilón [ah-ke-lone'], *m.* 1. Due north wind. 2. The north point.

aquilonal, aquilonar [ah-ke-lo-nahl', ah-ke-lo-nar'], *a.* Northern, northerly. **Tempo aquilonal**, *(Met.)* the winter season.

aquillado, da [ah-keel-lyah'-do, dah], Keel-shaped.

aquísito [ah-ke'-se-to], *adv. (LAm.)* = aquí.

aquistar [ah-kes-tahr'], *va.* To win, gain, acquire.

Aquitania [ah-ke-tah-ne-ah], *f.* Aquitaine.

A.R. *abr.* de **Alteza Real** (Royal Highness, R. H.)

ara [ah'-rah], *f.* 1. An altar. 2. The consecrated stone, on which a consecrated linen cover is laid during the celebration of the mass. 3. Among plumbers, a cistern-head. 4. *m. (LAm.)* Parrot.

árabe, arábigo [ah'-rah-bay, ah-rah'-be-go], 1. *m.* The Arabic language; Arabic. 2. *m. & f. (Mex.)* Hawker, street vendor. 3. *m. (Ling.)* Arabic.

arabesco [ah-rah-bess'-co], *m. (Pict.)* Arabesque, whimsical ornaments of foliage in painting; moresque-work.

arabias [ah-rah'-be-as], *f. pl.* Arabias, a kind of linen so called.

arábico, ca or **go, ga** [ah-rah-be-co, cah], *a.* Arabian. **Estar en arábico**, to be incomprehensible.

arabismo [ah-rah-bees'-mo], *m.* Arabism: idiom of the Arabic language transferred to some other.

arabista [ah-rah-bes'-tah], *m. & f.* Arabist.

arabizar [ah-rah-be-thar'], *va.* To Arabicize, to Arabize.

arable [ah-rah'-blay], *a. (LAm.)* Arable.

aracacha [ah-rah-cah'-chah], *f.* An umbelliferous plant of Colombia, having an edible farinaceous root, cultivated in large quantities.

arácnido, da [ah-rahc'-ne-do, dah], *a. (Zool.)* Arachnid, a class of arthropods; relating to the arachnoids.

aracnoides [ah-rac-no'-e-des], *f.* The archnoid membrane of the brain and spinal cord.

arada [ah-rah'-dah], *f. (Agri.)* 1. Ploughed ground, husbandry. 2. *V.* ARADURA. 3. Work in the fields.

arado [ah-rah'-do], *m.* A plough.

arador [ah-rah-dor'], *m.* 1. A ploughman. 2. A sarcoptic mite that causes itch or scabies. 3. Harvest-mite, or harvest-bug; Leptus.

aradro [ah-rah'-dro], *m. (Prov.)* V. ARADO.

aradura [ah-rah-doo'-rah], *f.* 1. The act or practice of ploughing. 2. *(Prov.)* Quantity of land which a yoke of oxen can conveniently plough in the course of a day.

araguato [ah-rah-goo-ah-to], 1. *a. (Carib.)* Dark, tawny-colored. 2. *m. (And. Carib. Mex.)* Howler monkey.

arambel [ah-ram-bel'], *m. (Obs.)* 1. Drapery, furniture of a room or bed. 2. *(Met.)* Rag, or piece hanging from cloths.

arambre [ah-ran'-bray], *m. (Obs.)* V. ALAMBRE.

aramía [ah-rah-mee'-ah], *f. (Prov.)* A piece of ploughed ground fit for sowing.

arana [ah-rah'-nah], *f. (Obs.)* Imposition, trick, deception.

araná [ah-rah-nah'], *m. (Carib.)* Straw hat.

aranata [ah-rah-nah'-tah], *f.* An animal of the shape and size of a dog, a native of America.

arancel [ah-ran-thel'], *m.* 1. The regulations by which the rate and price of bread and other things are fixed. 2. The tariff of duties, fees, taxes, etc., of the custom-house, courts, etc.; the book of rates.

arancelario, ria [ah-ran-thay-lah'-re-o, re-ah], *a.* Pertaining or referring to the tariff. **Protección arancelaria**, tariff protection.

arándano [ah-rahn'-dah-no], *m.* Cranberry. **Arándano azul**, Blueberry.

arandela [ah-ran-day'-lah], *f.* 1. The pan of the socket of a candlestick. 2. A guard around the staff of a lance. 3. Navebox of a gun-carriage. *(Mech.)* Washer, axleguard; rivetplate, collar-plate. 4. *(Naut.)* Halfports, square boards with a hole in the middle, to which a piece of canvas is nailed, to keep the water out when the cannon is in the port-hole. 5. A tin trough or funnel put around trees, with water, to prevent ants from climbing up. 6. A candelabrum, of glass, to be set upon a table.

arandillo [ah-ran-del-lyo] *m.* Marsh warbler (pájaro)

aranero, ra [ah-rah-nay'-ro, rah], *a.* Deceptive, tricky.

araniego [ah-rah-ne-ay'-go], *a.* Taken in a net, which is called *arañuelo*: applied to a young hawk.

aranzada [ah-ran-thah'-dah], *f.* A measure of land.

araña [ah-rah'-nyah], *f.* 1. *(Ent.)* Spider. 2. *(Zool.)* Common weaver, seaspider. 3. Chandelier, girandole, sconce. *(Bot.)* Crow foot. **Es una araña**, He is an industrious man. 4. *(Prov.) V.* ARREBATIÑA.

arañador, ra [ah-rah-nyah-dor', rah], *m. & f.* Scratcher, one who scratches.

arañamiento [ah-rah-nya-me-en'-to], *m.* The act of scratching.

arañar [ah-rah-nyar'], *va.* 1. To scratch, to claw, to scrabble. 2. To scrape, to gather by penurious diligence. **Arañar riquezas**, to gather riches with great eagerness. **Arañarse con los codos**, to rejoice in other people's misfortunes. **Arañar la cubierta**, to make great exertions; to get clear of danger.

arañazo [ah-rah-nayh-tho], *m. aug.* A long, deep scratch.

arañero, ra [ah-rah-nyay'-ro, rah], *a. V.* ZAHAREÑO.

araño [ah-rah'-nyo], *m.* A scratch, any slight wound; nipping.

arañón [ah-rah-nyon'], *m. (Pov.)* Sloe, the fruit of the backthorn.

arañuela [ah-rah-nyoo-ay'-lah], *f.dim.* 1. A small spider. 2. *V.* ARAÑUELO. 3. A plant.

arañuelo [ah-rah-nyoo-ay'-lo], *m.* 1. A small species of spider; grub or larva, web-spinning, which destroys plants. 2. *V.* CAPARILLA. 3. Foldnet, a very slight net for catching birds.

arao [ah-rah'-o], *m.* Guillemot.

arar [ah-rahr'], *va.* To plough; to till, to cultivate.

arapende [ah-rah-pen'-day], *m.* Ancient measure of 120 square feet.

arar [ah-rar'], *va.* 1. To plough, to labor. 2. *(Poetic.)* To run or pass through the surface of a liquid. **Arar con el ancla**, *(Naut.)* to drag the anchor. **No me lo harán creer cuántos aran y cavan**, no man shall ever make me believe it.

arar [ah-rar'], *m.* An African coniferous tree; its wood was employed in constructing the cathedrals of Seville and Córdoba.

arate [ah-rah-tay], *m.* Blood.

araucano, na [ah-rah-oo-cah'-no], *a. m. & f.* Araucanian.

araucaria [ah-rah-oo-cah'-re-ah], *f.* Araucaria, a tall conifer, of pine family, native of South America.

arbellón [ar-bel-lyone'], *m. (Prov.)* Gutter for drawing off the water from roads. *V.* ARBOLLON.

arbelo [ar-bay'-lo], *m. (Geom.)* A curvilinear figure composed of three segments of a circle and three acute angles.

arbitrable [r-be-trah'-blay], *a.* Arbitrable, depending upon the will.

arbitración [ar-be-trah-the-on'], *f.* Arbitration.

arbitrador [ar-be-trah-dor'], *m.* Arbitrator, umpire, referee.

arbitradora [ar-be-trah-do'-rah], *f.* Arbitress, a female arbitrator.

arbitraje, arbitramento, arbitramiento [ar-be-trah'-hay, ar-be-trah-men'-to, ar-be-trah-me-en'-to], *m.* Arbitration, the award of an arbitrator; arbitrament. **Arbitraje de bus**, bus arbitration.

arbitral [ar-be-trahl], *a.* Arbitral; of a referee. **Una decisión arbitral**, a referee's ruling. *V.* ARBITRATORIO.

arbitrar [ar-be-trar'], *va.* 1. To adjudge, to award. 2. To judge after one's own feelings and sentiments. 3. To contrive means and expedients. 1. *-vn.* To arbitrate; *(Dep.)* To umpire, referee; **arbitrar en una disputa**, to arbitrate in a dispute. 2. To act freely, to judge freely. *-vr.* To get along, to manage.

arbitrariamente [ar-be-trah-re-ah-men'-tay], *adv.* Arbitrarily, in an arbitrary manner; without control.

arbitrariedad [ar-be-trah-re-ay-dahd'], *f.* Arbitrariness.

arbitrario, ria, arbitrativo, va [ar-be-trah'-re-o, ah, ar-be-trah-tee'-vo, vah], *a.* 1. Arbitrary, that which depends upon the will; absolute. 2. *(For.)* Relating to arbitrators.

arbitratorio, ria [ar-be-trah-to'-re-o, ah], *a.* That which belongs or relates to arbitrators.

arbitrio [ar-bee'-tre-o], *m.* 1. Free and uncontrolled will and pleasure; mercy. 2. Means, expedient. 3. Arbitration, bond, compromise. 4. **Arbitrio de juez**, the discretionary power of a judge in cases not clearly decided by law. 5. **Arbitrios**, duty or taxes imposed on provisions exposed for sale. **Propios y arbitrios**, ways and means. **No hay arbitrio**, there is no change.

arbitrista [ar-be-trees'-tah], *m.* Schemer, projector, contriver.

árbitro [ar'-be-tro], *m.* 1. Arbitrator. 2. Umpire.

árbol [ar'-bol], *m.* 1. *(Bot.)* A tree. 2. *(Naut.)* Mast. *V.* PALO. 3. In some machines, the upright post which serves to give them a circular motion. *(Mech.)* Arbor, upright shaft; wheel spindle. 4. A drill. 5. Body of a shirt without sleeves. 6. Crown post, upright post, around which winding stairs turn. **Árbol de amor**, *(Bot.)* Judastree. **Árbol de clavo**, clovetree. **Árbol de fuego**, a wooden frame of fireworks. **Árbol del paraíso or árbol paraíso**, flowering-ash. **Árbol del pan**, bread-fruit-tree. **Árbol marino**, a radiate much ressembling the star-fish, but larger. **Árbol pagano**, a wild or uncultivated tree. **De árbol caído todos hacen leña**, overthrown pride inspires only contempt.

arbolado, da [ar-bo-lah'-do, dah], *a.* 1. Wooded, woodland; planted with trees. **Región arbolada**, wooded area. 2. Masted. **Arbolado en la hoya**, Masted hoy-fashion. *-pp.* of ARBOLAR. *-m.* Woodland.

arboladura [ar-bo-lah-doo'-rah], *f. (Naut.)* A general name for masts, yards, and all sorts of round timber. **Maestre de arboladura**, a master mast-maker.

arbolar [ar-bo-lar'], *va.* To hoist, to set upright. **Arbolar el navío**, *(Naut.)* To mast a ship. *-vr.* Arbolarse, to rear on the hind feet: applied to horses.

arbolario [ar-bo-lah'-re-o], *m.* 1. *V.* HERBOLARIO. 2. Madcap.

árbol de levas [ar'-bol day lay'-vash], *f.* Camshaft.

arbolecico, arbolecillo, arbolico, arbolito, arborcillo [ar-bo-lay-thee'-co, etc.], *m. dim.* Arboret, a small tree.

arboleda [ar-bo-lay'-dah], *f.* Grove, plantation of trees.

arboledo [ar-bo-lay'-do], *m.* Woodland.

arbolejo [ar-bo-lay'-ho], *m. dim.* A small tree.

arbolete [ar-bo-lay'-tay], *m.* Branch of a tree put on the ground, to which bird-catchers fasten their lime-twigs.

arbolillo [ar-bo-leel'-lyo], *m.* Side of a blast-furnace.

arbolista [ar-bo-lees'-tah], *m.* A dresser or planter of trees, arborist.

arbollón [ar-bol-lyone'], *m.* Flood-gate, sluice, conduit, channel.

arbóreo, rea [ar-bo'-ray-o, ah], *a.* Relating or belonging to trees.

arborescencia [ar-bo-res-then'-the-ah], *f.* Arborescence, tree-like growth or formation.

arborescente [ar-bo-res-then'-tay], *a.* Arborescent, having the form of a tree.

arboricultor [ar-bo-re-cool-tor'], *m. & f.* Forester.

arboricultura [ar-bo-re-cool-too'-rah], *f.* Arboriculture, cultivation of trees.

arborización [ar-bo-re-thah-the-on'], *f.* Replanting (of trees).

arborizado, da [ar-bo-re-thah'-do, dah], *a.* Arborescent, resembling trees and foliage: applied to dendrites or stones having the appearance of foliage.

arborizar [ar-bo-re-thahr'], *vn.* To plant trees, replant trees.

arbotante [ar-bo-tahn'-tay], *m.* Arch of stone or brick raised against a wall to support a vault. **Arbotante de pie de campana**, *(Naut.)* bell-crank, the place where the ship's bell is hung.

arbusto [ar-boos'-to], *m.* Shrub.

arbustillo [ar-boos-tell'-lyo], *m. dim.* Arbuscle, a small shrub.

arca [ar'-cah], *f.* 1. A chest. **Arcas**, Coffer, iron chest for money. **Hacer arcas**, to open the coffers or treasury chest. 2. In glass-houses, the tempering oven, in which glassware, just blown, is put to cool. 3. *(Met.)* A reserved person. **Arca de Noé**, *(Met.)* lumber-chest. **Arca de fuego**, *(Naut.)* fire-chest, a small box, filled with combustibles, used to annoy an enemy that attempted to board a ship. **Ser arca cerrada**, to be yet unknown (personas, cosas). **Sangrar a uno de la vena del arca**, to drain one of his money. **Arca de agua**, reservoir, cistern. **Arcas**, cavities of the body under the ribs.

arcabucear [ar-cah-boo-thay-ar'], *va.* 1. To shoot with the crossbow. 2. To shoot a criminal by way of punishment.

arcabucería [ar-cah-boo-thay-ree'-ah], *f.* 1. A troop of archers. 2. A number of cross-bows. 3. Manufactory of bows and arrows.

arcabucero [ar-cah-boo-thay'-ro], *m.* 1. Archer. 2. Gunsmith. 3. Manufacturer of bows and arrows.

arcabuco [ar-cah-boo'-co], *m. (Amer.)* A caggy spot full of brambles.

arcabuz [ar-cah-booth'], *m.* Arquebuse, a fire-arm, a hand-gun.

arcabuzazo [ar-cah-boo-thah'-tho], *m.* A shot from a gun and the wound it causes.

arcacil [ar-cah-theel'], *m. (Bot.)* A wild artichoke.

arcada [ar-cah'-dah], *f.* 1. Violent motion of the stomach, which excites vomiting. 2. Arcade or row of arches.

arcade [ar'-cah-day], *a.* Arcadian, belonging to the Roman academy of polite literature called *Arcades.*

arcadia [ar-cah-de-ah], *f.* Arcady.

arcadio, dia [ar-cah'-de-o, ah], *a.* Arcadian.

arcádico [ar-cah'-de-co], *a.* Arcadian.

arcaduz [ar-cah-dooth'], *m.* 1. Conduit or pipe for the conveyance of water. 2. Bucket for raising water out of a draw-well. 3. *(Met.)* Channel for enforcing a claim, obtaining a place, etc. **Llevar una cosa por sus arcaduces**, to conduct an affair through its proper channel.

arcaduzar [ar-cah-doo-thar'], *va. (Obs.)* To convey water through conduits.

arcáico, ca [ar-cah'-e-co, cah], *a.* Archaic, ancient.

arcaismo [ar-cah-ees'-mo], *m.* Archaism, the mixture of ancient or antiquated words with modern language.

arcaizante [ar-cah-e-than'-tay], *a.* Archaic.

arcaizar [ar-cah-e-thar'], *vr.* To use archaisms.

arcam [ar-cahm'], *m.* A very venomous serpent, spotted black and white, which is found in Turkestan.

arcángel [ar-cahn'-hel], *m.* Archangel.

arcangelical [ar-cahn-hay-le-cahl'], *a.* Archangelical.

arcanidad [ar-cah-ne-dahd'], *f. (Obs.)* A profound secret of great moment.

arcano [ar-cah'-no], *m.* Arcanum, a secret which is carefully kept. -*a.* Secret, recondite, reserved.

arcar [ar-car'], *va.* To beat the wool with a bow of one or two cords.

arcaza [ar-cah'-thah], *f. aug.* A large chest.

arcazón [ar-cah-thone'], *m.* 1. Arbuscle. 2. Osier, water-willow. 3. Willow-plot.

arce [ar'-thay], *m. (Bot.)* Maple-tree. Acer.

arcedianato [ar-thay-de-ah-nah'-to], *m.* Archdeaconship; archdeaconry.

arcediano [ar-thay-de-ah'-no], *m.* Archdeacon.

arcedo [ar-thay'-do], *m.* Maple-grove.

arcén [ar-then'], *m.* 1. *(Ant.)* Border, brim, edge. 2. *(Prov.)* Stone laid round the brim of a well.

arcilla [ar-theel'-lyah], *f.* Argil, white pure earth, alumina, clay. **Arcilla cocida**, baked clay.

arcilloso, sa [ar-theel-lyo'-so, sah], *a.* Clayey, argillaceous.

arciprestadgo, arciprestazgo [ar-the-pres-tad'-go, ar-the-pres-tath'-go], *m.* The dignity of an archpriest.

arcipreste [ar-the-pres'-tay], *m.* Archprelate, archpriest, the first or chief presbyter.

arco [ar'-co], *m.* 1. Arc, a segment of a circle. 2. Arch, arc, a part of a circle not more than the half. 3. Arch of a building, bridge, and other works. 4. Bow for throwing arrows. 5. Fiddle-bow. 6. Hoop, anything circular with which something else is bound, particularly casks and barrels. 7. *(Naut.)* Bow of a ship. **Arco Iris**, rainbow.

arcón [ar-cone'], *m. aug.* 1. A large chest, bin, bunker. 2. A great arch or arc.

arcontado [ar-con-tah'-do], *m.* Archonship.

arconte [ar-con'-tay], *m.* Archon, a magistrate of Athens.

árctico, ca [arc'-te-co, cah], *a. V.* ÁRTICO.

archera [ar-chay'-rah], *f.* Archeress.

archero [ar-chay'-ro], *m.* Archer.

archi Arch-. a prefix from the Greek, meaning pre-eminent. **Un niño archimalo**, a terribly naughty child.

archicofradía [ar-che-co-frah-dee'-ah], *f.* A privileged brotherhood or confraternity.

archiconocido [ar-che-co-no-the'-do], *a.* Extremely well-known.

archidiácono [ar-che-de-ah'-co-no], *m. V.* ARCEDIANO.

archidiócesis [ar-che-de-o'-thay-sees], *f.* Archdiocese.

archiducado [ar-che-doo-cah'-do], *m.* 1. Archdukedom, archduchy, the territory belonging to an archduke. 2. The dignity or an archduke.

archiducal [ar-che-doo-cahl'], *a.* Archducal, that which belongs or relates to an archduke or archduchy.

archiduque [ar-che-doo'-kay], *m.* Archduke.

archiduquesa [ar-che-doo-kay'-sah], *f.* Archduchess.

archienemigo [ar-che-ay-nay-me-go], *m.* Arch-enemy.

archilaúd [ar-che-lah-ood'], *m.* A musical instrument shaped and stringed as a lute, but of a larger size.

archimandrita [ar-che-man-dree'-tah], *m.* Name in the orient, of the abbot of a monastery.

archimillonario, ria [ar-che-meel-lyo-nah'-re-o, ah], *a.* Multimillionaire.

archipámpano [ar-che-pahm'-pah-no], *m. (coll.)* A word used to express an imaginary dignity or authority.

archipiélago [ar-che-pe-ay'-lah-go], *m.* Archipelago, a part of the sea crowded with islands.

archisabido [ar-che-sah-be-do], *a.* Extremely well-known; **Un hecho archisabido**, a perfectly well-known fact.

architonto [ar-che-ton-to], *a. m. & f.* Utterly silly.

architriclino [ar-che-tre-clee'-no], *m.* (Antiquities) He who ordered and directed banquets.

archivado [ar-che-vah-do], *a. (LAm.)* Out-of-date, old-fashioned.

archivador, ra [ar-che-vah-dor], *m. f.* Filing cabinet.

archivar [ar-che-var'], *va.* 1. To deposit a thing or writing in an archive. 2. To hide away (esconder). 3. *(LAm.)* To take away of circulation. 4. *(Cono Sur Mex.)* To jail.

archivero, archivista [ar-che-vay'-ro, ar-che-vees'-tah], *m.* Keeper of the records.

archivo [ar-chee'-vo], *m.* 1. Archives, the place where public records are kept. **Archivo Nacional**, Public Record Office. 2. *(Met.)* A person who is intrusted with the most profound secrets, a confidant. 3. *(Cono Sur. Mex.)* Jail. **Archivo de tarjetas** *(Comp.)*, card file. **Archivos integrados** *(Comp.)*, integrated filestore.

arda [ar'-dah], *f.* Squirrel. *V.* ARDILLA.

ardalear [ar-dah-lay-ar'], *va.* To make thin or clear. *V.* RALEAR.

ardasa, ardases [ar-dah'-sas, ar-dah-ses], *f. pl.* The coarser sort of Persian silk.

ardasinas, ardazinas [ar-dah-see'-nas, ar-dah-thee'-nas], *f. pl.* The finer sort of Persian silk.

ardea [ar-day'-ah], *f.* Bittern. *V.* ALCARAVAN.

ardedor [ar-day-dor'], *m.* A species of serpent. *a.* (Carib. Mex.) Quick burning, easy to light.

ardentía [ar-den-tee'-ah], *f.* 1. Heat. 2. *(Naut.)* Phosphoric sparkling of the sea when it is agitated.

ardeola [ar-day-o'-lah], *f.* A small kind of heron.

arder [ar-derr'], *vn.* 1. To burn, to blaze, to glow. 2. To be agitated by the passions of love, hatred, anger, etc., to heat, to kindle. **Arderse en pleitos**, to be entangled in law-suits. **Arder de amor**, to burn with love. 3. To ferment. *-vr.* To burn away.

ardero, ra [ar-day'-ro, rah], *a.* Squirrel-hunter: applied to dogs.

ardid [ar-deed'], *m.* Stratagem, artifice, cunning.

ardido, da [ar-dee'-do, dah], *a.* 1. Heated: applied to grain, olives, tobacco, etc. 2. *(Obs.)* Bold, intrepid, valiant. 3. *(LAm.)* Cross, angry. *-pp* of ARDER.

ardiente [ar-de-en'-tay], *pa.* and *a.* 1. Ardent, flagrant, burning. **Calentura ardiente**, a burning fever. 2. Passionate, active, mettlesome, hot, fervent, fiery, fearless; feverish.

ardientemente [ar-de-en-tay-men'-tay], *adv.* Ardently, flagrantly, fervidly; fearlessly.

ardiloso [ar-de-lo'-so], *a.* (And. Cono Sur) Crafty, wily.

ardilla [ar-dee'-lyah], *f.* 1. Squirrel. 2. *(Mech.)* Granulating machine. 3. *(LAm.)* Clever businessman; businesswoman. *a.* Sharp, clever.

ardimiento [ar-de-me-en'-to], *m.* 1. *(Obs.)* Conflagration. 2. *(Met.)* Valor, intrepidity, undaunted courage.

ardínculo [ar-deen'-coo-lo], *m.* *(Vet.)* An inflamed swelling or ulcer on the back of animals.

ardita [ar-dee'-tah], *f.* A squirrel. *V.* ARDILLA.

ardite [ar-dee'-tay], *m.* An ancient coin of little value, formerly current in Spain. **No vale un ardite**, it is not worth a dime.

ardor [ar-dor'], *m.* 1. Great heat, hotness, flagrancy. 2. *(Met.)* Valor, vivacity, spirit, vigor, mettle. 3. Fieriness, fervency. 4. Life.

ardoroso, sa [ar-do-ro'-so, sah], *a.* Fiery, restless: applied to a horse. Hot, burning. **En lo más ardoroso del estío**, in the hottest part of the summer.

arduamente [ar-doo-ah-men'-tay], *adv.* Arduously, in a difficult, arduous manner.

arduidad [ar-doo-e-dahd'], *f.* Arduousness.

arduo, dua [ar'-doo-o, ah], *a.* Arduous, difficult; high.

área [ar'-ray-ah], *f.* 1. Area, the surface contained between any lines or boundaries. **Área de servicios**, service area. 2. Area of a building. 3. Halo, a bright circle which surrounds the sun, moon, or stars. 4. A square decametre: equivalent to about 143 square varas. **Área de la hoja de trabajo** *(Comp.)*, worksheet area. **Área de la ventana** *(Comp.)*, window area.

areca [ah-ray'-cah], *f.* A palm-tree of the Philippine Islands, used in building huts.

arefacción [ah-ray-fac-the-on'], *f.* Dryness, extenuation.

arel [ah-rel'], *m.* A kind of large sieve used to sift the corn.

arelar [ah-ray-lar'], *va.* To sift the corn with the kind of sieve called *arel.*

arena [ah-ray'-nah], *f.* 1. Sand, grit. **Arenas movedizas**, quicksands, shifting sands. 2. Arena, place where wrestlers and gladiators fought. **Sembrar en arena**, to labor in vain. **Arena hoya**, pit-sand. **Arenas**, gravel formed in the kidneys.

arenáceo, ea [ah-ray-nah'-thay-o, ah], *a.* Arenaceous, gravelly.

arenal [ah-ray-nahl'], *m.* A sandy ground, a sandy beach.

arenalejo, arenalillo [ah-ray-nah-lay'-ho, ah-ray-nahleel'-lyo], *m. dim.* 1. A small sandy piece of ground. 2. Small, fine sand.

arenar [ah-ray-nar'], *va.* To cover with sand; to fill with sand.

arenaria [ah-ray-nah'-re-ah], *f.* *(Orn.)* Sandpiper.

arencar [ah-ren-car'], *va.* To salt and dry sardines, etc., like herrings.

arencón [ah-ren-cone'], *m. aug.* of ARENQUE.

arenero [ah-ray-nay'-ro], *m.* One who deals in sand; sand-box.

arenga [ah-ren'-gah], *f.* Harangue, speech, oration, address. *(Cono Sur)* Argument.

arengador [ah-ren-gah-dor'], *m.* A speech-maker.

arengar [ah-ren-gar'], *vn.* To harangue, to deliver a speech or oration; to hold forth.

arenguear [ah-ren-gay-ahr], *vn.* *(Cono Sur)* To argue, quarrel.

arenícola [ah-ray-nee'-co-lah], *f.* *(Zool.)* An annelid, used by fishermen for bait; lugworm, or lobworm.

arenilla [ah-ray-neel'-yah], *f.* 1. Moulding sand, sand. 2. Powder to dry writing. *-pl.* In gunpowder-mills, saltpetre refined, and reduced to grains as small as sand. *(Med.)* Stones, gravel.

arenisca [ah-ray-nees'-cah], *f.* *(Miner.)* Sandstone.

arenisco, ca, arenoso, sa [ah-ray-nees'-co, cah, ah-ray-no'-so, sah], *a.* Sandly, abounding with sand; gravelly, gritty.

arenque [ah-ren'-kay], *m.* Herring. **Arenque ahumado**, smoked herring.

aréola [ah-ray'-oh-lah], *f.* 1. *(Anat.)* Areola, circle around the nipple. 2. The reddened area around a pustule.

areómetro [ah-ray-o'-may-tro], *m.* Areometer, an instrument for measuring the density and gravity of spirituous liquors.

areopagita [ah-ray-o-pah-hee'-tah], *m.* Areopagite, judge of the supreme court of judicature in Athens.

areópago [ah-ray-o'-pah-go], *m.* Areopagus, the supreme court of judicature in Athens.

areóstilo [ah-ray-os'-te-lo], *m.* Aræostyle, the distance from column to column of eight or more modules.

areotectónica [ah-ray-o-tec-to'-ne-cah], *f.* Areotectonics, a part of the science of fortification.

arepa [ah-ray'-pah], *f.* *(Amer.)* A griddle-cake made of soaked corn ground into a paste or dough. *V.* TORTILLA.

arepero [ah-ray-pay-ro], *m.* *(Carib.)* Poor wretch.

arequipa [ah-ray-ke-pah], *f.* *(And.)* Rice pudding. Arequipa.

arequipeño, ña [ah-ray-ke-pay'-nyo, nya], *a.* Of Arequipa.

aresta [ah-res'-tah], *f.* *(Obs.)* 1. Coarse tow. 2. *V.* ESPINA.

arestín [ah-res-teen'], *m.* *(Vet.)* Frush, a disease in the heel of horses.

arestinado, da [ah-res-te-nah'-do, dah], *a.* Afflicted with the disease called the frush.

arete [ah-ray'-tay], *m.* *V.* ZARCILLO, PENDIENTE. Eardrop.

arfada [ar-fah'-dah], *f.* *(Naut.)* The pitching of a ship.

arfar [ar-far'], *va.* *(Naut.)* To pitch: applied to a ship.

arfil [ar-feel'], *m.* *V.* ALFIL.

argadijo, argadillo [ar-gah-dee'-ho, ar-gah-deel'-lyo], *m.* 1. Reel, bobbin, winder. *V.* DEVANADERA. 2. *(Met.)* A blustering, noisy, restless person. 3. *(Prov.)* Large basket made of twigs of osier.

argado [ar-gah'-do], *m.* Prank, trick, artifice.

argal [ar-gahl'], *m.* Argol, crude tartar.

argalia [ar-gah'-le-ah], *f.* *V.* ALGALIA.

argallera [ar-gal-lyay'-rah], *f.* A saw for cutting grooves; forkstaff plane, reed-plane.

argamandel [ar-gah-man-del'], *m.* Rag, tatter.

argamandijo [ar-gah-man-dee'-ho], *m*. 1. *(coll.)* Collection of trifling implements used in trade or business. **Dueño or señor del argamandijo**, powerful lord and master. 2. Set of tools.

argamasa [ar-gah-mah'-sah], *f*. Mortar, a cement for building.

argamasar [ar-gah-mah-sar'], *va*. 1. To make mortar. 2. To cement with mortar.

argamasón [ar-gah-mah-sone'], *m*. A large piece of mortar found among the ruins of a building.

argamula [ar-gah-moo'-lah], *f*. *(Bot. Prov.)* V. AMELO.

argana, *f*. **argano**, *m*. [ar'-gah-nah]. A machine resembling a crane, for raising stones and other weighty things. **Arganas**, 1. Baskets or wicker vessels in which things are carried on a horse. 2. Large nets in which forage is carried.

arganel [ar-gah-nel'], *m*. A small brass ring used in the composition of an astrolabe.

arganeo [ar-gah'-nay-o], *m*. *(Naut.)* Anchor-ring, a large ring in the anchor to which the cable is fastened.

Argel [ar-hek], Algiers.

argel [ar-hel'], *a*. 1. Horse whose right hind foot only is white. 2. *(Met.)* Unlucky, unfortunate.

argelino, na [ar-hay-lee'-no, nah], *a*. Algerine; of Algiers.

argema, argemón [ar-hay'-mah, ar-hay-mone'], *m*. *(Med.)* Argema or argemon, a small white ulcer of the globe of the eye.

argémone [ar-hay-mo-nay], *f*. *(Bot.)* Prickly or horned poppy. Argemone mexicana.

argén [ar-hen'], *m*. *(Her.)* White or silver color, argent.

argentado, da [ar-hen-tah'-do, dah], *a*. Silver plated, silvered (bañado en plata). 2. Silvery (color de plata). -*pp*. of ARGENTAR.

argentador [ar-hen-tah-dor'], *m*. One who silvers or covers superficially with silver.

argentar [ar-hen-tar'], *va*. 1. To plate or cover with silver. 2. To give a silver color (platear).

argénteo [ar-hayn'-tay-o], *a*. 1. *(Tec.)* Silver-plated. 2. *(Poetic)* Silver, silvery.

argentería [ar-he-tay-ree'-ah], *f*. 1. Embroidery in gold or silver. 2. *(Met.)* An expression more brilliant than solid.

argentífero, ra [ar-hen-tee'-fay-ro, rah], *a*. Argentiferous; silver-bearing.

argentifodina [ar-hen-te-fo-dee'-nah], *f*. Silver-mine.

Argentina [ar-hen-tee'-nah], *f*. Argentina. *(Bot.)* Satin cinquefoil.

argentino, na [ar-hen-tee'-no, nah], *a*. 1. Of silver, or like it; argentine. 2. *(Geog.)* Belonging to the River la Plata: Argentine Republic, southern-most country of South America.

argento [ar-hen'-to], *m*. 1. *(Poetic.)* Silver. 2. **Argento vivo sublimado**, Sublimate. V. SOLIMAN.

argilla [ar-heel'-lyah], *f*. V. ARCILLA.

argiritas [ar-he-ree'-tas], *m. pl*. Marcasites, which are found in silver-mines; white pyrites.

argo [ar'-go], *m*. The ship of Jason and the Argonauts. Argon.

argolla [ar-gol'-lyah], *f*. 1. Large iron ring; buckle, ring, collar; a staple. **Argollas de cureña**, draught-hooks of a gun-carriage. **Argollas de amarra**, lashing-rings. 2. Carcan, iron collar (castigo público). 3. *(LAm.)* Engagement ring. 4. Serviette ring. 5. Collar (adorno).

argollar [ar-go-lyahr'], *va*. *(And.)* To ring (cerdo); *(Mex.)* To hitch to a ring; **argollar a uno** *(Mex.)* To have a hold over somebody. -*vr*. *(And.)* To get engaged.

argolleta, ica, ita [ar-gol-lyay'-tah], *f. dim*. A small staple; a small iron ring.

argollón [ar-gol-lyone'], *m. aug*. A very large iron ring; a large staple.

argoma [ar'-go-mah], *f*. *(Bot.)* V. ALIAGA. Furze. V. AULAGA.

argomal [ar-go-mahl'], *m*. Ground covered with furze.

argomón [ar-go-mone'], *m. aug*. Large prickly broom.

Argón [ar-gon'], *m*. Argon.

argonauta [ar-go-nah'-oo-tah], *m*. 1. Argonaut, 2. *(Zool.)* The paper nautilus (molusco). 4. A group of diurnal butterflies.

Argos [ar'-gos], *m*. *(Myth.)* Argus, fabled to have a hundred eyes; watchful person. **Ser un argos** *or* **estar hecho un argos**, to be very vigilant, to be very solicitous.

argot [ar-got'], *m. pl*. Argots, slang.

argótico [ar-go'-te-co], *a*. Slang.

argoudán [ar-go-oo-dahn'], *m*. A kind of cotton, manufactured in India.

arguajaque [ar-goo-ah-hah'-kay], *m*. Gum-ammoniac.

argucia [ar-goo'-the-ah], *f*. Subtilty, which degenerates into sophistry.

argüe [ar'-goo-ay], *m*. 1. Machine for moving large weights; windlass, crane; whim. 2. Machine for drawing fine gold wire.

argüellarse [ar-goo-ayl-layr'-say], *vr*. *(Prov.)* To be emaciated; to be in bad health: applied to children.

argüello [ar-goo-el'-lyo], *m*. Faintness, want of health.

argüende [ar-goo-ayn'-day], *m*. *(LAm.)* Argument.

argueñas [ar-gay'-nyas], *f. pl*. V. ANGARILLAS.

arguerita [ar-gay-ree'-tah], *f*. *(Miner.)* Argyrite, or argentite.

argüir [ar-goo-eer'], *vn*. To argue, to dispute, to oppose. -*va*. To give signs, to make a show of something. **Argüirle a uno su conciencia**, to be pricked by one's conscience. To reproach, to accuse. **Me argüían con vehemencia**, they vehemently reproached me.

arguma [ar'-goo-mah], *f*. V. ALIAGA.

argumentación [ar-goo-men-tah-the-on'], *f*. Argumentation.

argumentador, ra [ar-goo-men-tah-dor', rah], *m. & f*. Arguer, a reasoner, a disputant.

argumentar [ar-goo-men-tar'], *vn*. To argue, to dispute; to conclude.

argumentativo, va [ar-goo-men-tah-tee'-vo, vah], *a*. Argumentative.

argumentillo [ar-goo-men-teel'-lyo], *m. dim*. A slight argument, an unreasonable objection.

argumento [ar-goo-men'-to], *m*. 1. Argument, a reason alleged for or against a thing. 2. Argument, the subject of a discourse or writing. 3. The person who argues or disputes (universidades). 4. Argument, summary of the points treated on in a work, or in a book or chapter of a poem. **Argumento de la obra**, summary of the plot. 5. Indication, sign, token.

arguyente [ar-goo-yen'-tay], *pa*. Arguer; opponent.

aria [ah'-re-ah], *f*. *(Mus.)* 1. Tune or air for a single voice. 2. Verses to be set to music.

aribar [ah-re-bar'], *va*. To reel yarn into skeins.

aribo [ah-ree'-bo], *m*. Reel for making skeins.

Arica [ah-re-cah], *f*. Arica.

aricar [ah-re-car'], *va*. To plough across the ground sown with corn (arar); to clear it of weeds. V. ARREJACAR.

aridecer [ah-re-day-thayr'], 1. *va*. To dry up. 2. *vn. & vr*. To dry up, become arid.

aridez [ah-re-deth'], *f*. Drought.

árido, da [ah'-re-do, dah], *a*. 1. Dry, wanting moisture. 2. *(Met.)* Dry, barren, jejune (conversación). **Terreno árido**, arid land.

Aries [ah'-re-es], *m*. Aries or ram, one of the signs of the zodiac.

arieta [ah-re-ay'-tah], *f. dim*. Arietta, a short air, song, or tune.

ariete [ah-re-ay'-tay], *m*. Battering ram (máquina de guerra). Center forward (fútbol).

arietino, na [ah-re-ay-tee'-no, nah], *a*. Resembling the head of a ram.

arigua [ah-re-goo-ah], *f*. *(Carib.)* Wild bee.

arigue [ah-ree'-gay], *m*. A Philippine timber.

arije [ah-ree'-hay], *m*. V. UVA ARIJE.

arijo, ja [ah-ree'-ho, hah], *a*. Light, easily tilled: applied to soil.

arillo [ah-reel'-lyo], *m. dim.* 1. A small hoop. 2. Ear-ring. -*pl.* Hoops for ear-rings.

arimez [ah-re-meth'], *m.* Part of a building which juts or stands out.

arindajo [ah-rin-dah'-ho], *m. (Orn.)* Jay. Corvus glandarius.

ario, ia [ah'-re-o, ah], *a.* Aryan, a primitive people and language of Central Asia.

arisaro [ah-re-sah'-ro] *m. (Bot.)* Wake-robin.

ariscar [ah-res-cahr'], *va. (CAm. Carib, Mex.)* To pacify, control (animal).

arisco, ca [ah-rees'-co, cah], *a.* 1. Fierce, rude, wild, untractable, stubborn (animales). 2. *(Met.)* Harsh, unpolished, churlish, shy (personas).

arismética [ah-ris-may'-te-cah], *f. (Obs.)* Arithmetic. V. ARITMETICA.

arismético [ah-ris-may'-te-co], *a. (Obs.)* V. ARITMETICO.

arisnegro, arisprieto [ah-ris-nay'-gro, ah-ris-pre-ay'-to], *a.* **Trigo arisnegro or arisprieto,** species of wheat with a blackish beard.

arisquillo, lla [ah-ris-keel'-lyo, lyah], *a. dim.* of ARISCO.

arista [ah-rees'-tah], *f.* 1. Beard or awn of cereal grains; chaff. 2. Edge of a rough piece of timber in naval architecture. 3. Cant, edge, groin, rib, arris. -*pl. (Mil.)* Salient angles.

aristado, da [ah-ris-tah'-do, dah], *a.* Awned, bearded.

aristarco [ah-ris-tar'-co], *m.* A severe censurer of another's writings.

aristino [ah-ris-tee'-no], *m.* V. ARESTIN.

aristocracia [ah-ris-to-crah'-the-ah], *f.* An aristocracy.

aristócrata [ah-ris-to'-rah-tah], *m.* Aristocrat, a favorer of aristocracy.

aristocrático, ca [ah-ris-to-crah'-te-co, cah], *a.* Aristocratical.

Aristófanes [ah-res-to'-fah-nays], *m.* Aristophanes.

aristoloquia [ah-ris-to-lo'-ke-ah], *f. (Bot.)* Birthwort.

aristón [ah-res-ton'], *m. (Mus.)* Mechanical organ.

aristoso, sa [ah-ris-to'-so, sah], *a.* 1. Having many beards on the ear (grano).

Aristóteles [ah-res-to'-tay-lays], *m.* Aristotle.

aristotélico, ca [ah-ris-to-tay'-le-co, cah], *a.* Aristotelian, belonging to the doctrine of Aristotle.

aritmancia [ah-rit-mahn'-the-ah], *f.* Arithmancy, foretelling future events by numbers.

aritmética [ah-rit-may'-te-cah], *f.* Arithmetic.

aritméticamente [ah-rit-may'-te-cah-men-tay], *adv.* Arithmetically, in an arithmetical manner.

aritmético [ah-rit-may'-te-co], *m.* Arithmetician, accountant.

aritmético, ca [ah-rit-may'-te-co, cah], *a.* Arithmetical.

aritmo [ah-reet'-mo], *a.* Arrhythmic, irregular (pulso).

arlequín [ar-lay-keen'], *m.* Harlequin, a buffoon who plays tricks to amuse the populace. Neapolitan ice cream.

arlequinada [ar-lay-ke-nah'-dah], *f.* A harlequin's trick, or joke; a clownish action.

arlequinesco [ar-lay-ke-nays-co], *a. (fig.)* Grotesque, ridiculous.

Arlés [ar-lays], *f.* Arles.

arlo [ar'-lo], *m. (Bot.)* Barberry or piperidge bush.

arlota [ar-lo'-tah], *f.* Tow of flax or hemp.

arlote [ar-lo'-tay], *m. (Obs.)* Vagabond, idler.

arma [ar'-mah], *f.* 1. Weapon, instrument of offence, arm. **Armas portátiles,** small arms. **Arma de caballería,** cavalry arm. **Armas nucleares,** nuclear weapons. **Arma arrojadiza,** missile, projectile. **Arma blanca,** steel, cold steel. **Arma de fuego,** firearm. **Arma homicida,** murder weapon. **De armas tomar,** formidable (temible). **Descansar las armas,** to order arms. **Licencia de armas,** firearm licence. **Llegar a las armas,** to take up arms. **Medir las armas,** to cross swords. **Presentar armas,** to present arms. **Rendir las armas,** to surrender one's arms. **Tomar las armas,** to take up arms. **Velar las armas,** to carry out the vigil of arms. **Volver el arma contra alguien,** to turn the tables on someone. 2. -*pl.* 1. Troops, armies. 2. Armorial ensigns, coat of arms. 3. **Armas de agua,** *(Mex.)* skins attached to the pommel of the saddle to protect the thighs and legs from rain. **Armas y dineros buenas manos quieren,** arms and money ought to be put into wise hands. **Hombre de armas,** a military man. **Maestro de armas,** fencing-master. **Pasar por las armas,** to be shot as a criminal. **Rendir las armas,** to lay down the arms. **No dejar las armas de la mano,** not to lay down the arms. **Estar sobre las armas,** to be under arms, and ready for action. **Un hecho de armas,** an achievement, exploit. 3. *(Met.)* Means, power, reason. **Hacerse a las armas,** to inure oneself to do or perform something.

armada [ar-mah'-dah], *f.* Navy; fleet, squadron, armada. **Armada de barlovento,** *(Naut.)* fleet stationed to the windward. *(Cono Sur)* Noose, lasso (lazo).

armadera [ar-mah-day'-rah], *f. (Naut.)* The principal timbers of a ship.

armadía [ar-mah-dee'-ah], *f.* Raft, a frame or float made by pieces of timber.

armadijo [ar-mah-dee'-ho], *m.* Trap or snare for catching game.

armadillo [ar-mah-deel'-lyo], *m.* Armadillo, a small fourfooted animal, covered with hard scales like armor.

armado, da [ar-mah'-do, dah], *a.* 1. Armed (en armas). **Armado hasta los dientes,** armed to the teeth. 2. Loaded. **La pistola está armada,** the gun is loaded. 3. Gold or silver placed on other metal. 4. *(Mech.)* Assembled, mounted (montado), set. -*pp.* of ARMAR.

armado [ar-mah'-do], *m.* A man armed with a coat of mail.

armador [ar-mah-dor'], *m.* 1. One who fits out privateers. 2. Privateer, cruiser. 3. One who recruits sailors for the whale and cod fishery. 4. Outfitter, shipowner. 5. *(Mech.)* Framer, adjuster, fitter. 6. Jacket.

armadura [ar-mah-doo'-rah], *f.* 1. Armor. 2. The union of the integral parts of a thing; framework 3. *(Mech.)* Setting, fitting; truss; armature *(Elec.)* 4. Skeleton. 5. Frame of a roof. **Armadura del tejado,** The shell of a building. **Armadura de una mesa,** the frame of a table.

armaduría [ar-mah-doo-re'-ah], *f. (LAm.)* Car assembly plant.

armagedón [ar-mah-gay-don'], *m.* Armageddon.

armajara [ar-mah-hah'-rah], *f. (Prov.)* A plot of ground well dug and dunged for rearing garden plants.

armamentista [ar-mah-mayn-tes'-tah], *a.* Arms; carrera armamentista, arms race.

armamento [ar-mah-men'-to], *m.* Armament, warlike preparation.

armandijo [ar-man-dee'-ho], *m. (Obs.)* V. ARMADIJO.

armar [ar-mar'], *va.* 1. To arm, to furnish with arms; to man. 2. To furnish, to fit up. 3. To square with one's opinion. 4. To arm or to plate with anything that may add strength. 5. To set a snare. 6. To place one thing above another. 7. To set up a person in business. 8. *(Mech.)* To adjust, set, mount; truss, put together. **Armar la cuenta,** to make up an account. **Armarla,** to cheat at cards. **Armarla con queso,** to decoy. **Armar navío or bajel,** to fit out a ship. **Armar pleito or ruido,** to stir up disturbances; to kick up a dust. **Armar un lazo,** to lay a snare. **Armar una cama,** to set up a bed-sted. **Armar una casa,** to frame the timber-work of the roof of a house. **Armar caballero,** to knight. -*vr.* 1. To prepare oneself for war. **Armarse de paciencia,** to prepare oneself to suffer. 2. To prepare, to get ready. 3. *(CAm. Carib, Mex.)* To become obstinate. 4. *(LAm.)* To be lucky. 5. **¡Te vas a armar!** *(Cono Sur)*, forget it!

armario [ar-mah'-re-o], *m.* Wardrobe (ropa), cupboard (cocina), cabinet, commode. **Armario botiquín,** first-aid chest. **Armario empotrado,** built-in wardrobe, fitted wardrobe.

armatoste [ar-mah-tos'-tay], *m.* 1. Hulk, monstrosity (cosa grande y fea). 2. A trap, a snare. V. ARMADIJO. 3. A great brute (persona corpulenta).

armazón [ar-mah-thone'], *f.* 1. Framework, skeleton, frame. 2. Hulk of a ship. -*m.* 3. Skeleton, of the animal body. **No tener más que la armazón,** to be skin and bones.

armelina [ar-may-lee'-nah], *f.* Ermine skin.

armella [ar-mayl'-lyah], *f.* Staple or ring made of iron or other metal; box staple, bushing, screw-eyes. **Armellas,** *(Naut.)* Pieces of iron doubled in shape of a **U.**

armelluela [ar-mayl-lyoo-ay'-lah], *f. dim.* A small staple or ring.

armenio, nia [ar-may'-ne-o, ne-ah], *a.* Armenian, relating to Armenia.

armería [ar-may-ree'-ah], *f.* 1. Armory, arsenal. 2. *(Obs.)* Trade of an armorer or gunsmith. 3. Heraldry.

armero [ar-may'-ro], *m.* 1. Armorer or gunsmith. 2. Keeper of arms or armor. 3. *(Mil.)* A rack or stand for fire-arms.

armígero, ra [ar-mee'-hay-ro, rah], *a. (Poetic.)* Warlike.

armilar [ar-me-lar'], *a.* **Esfera armilar,** armillary sphere.

armilla [ar-meel'-lyah], *f.* Principal part of the base of a column.

armiño [ar-mee'-nyo], *m.* 1. Ermine, a small animal furnishing a valuable fur. *a.* 2. The fur of the ermine. **Armiños** *(Her.)* Figures of a white field interspersed with black spots.

armipotente [ar-me-po-ten'-tay], *a. (Poetic.)* Mighty in war.

armisticio [ar-mis-tee'-the-o], *m.* Armistice, suspension of hostilities.

armoisín [ar-mo-e-seen'], *m.* A thin silk or taffeta.

armón [ar-mone'], *m.* The fore carriage of a piece of artillery.

armonía [ar-mo-nee'-ah], *f.* 1. Harmony, just proportion or concord of sound; harmoniousness, number. 2. Concord or correspondence of one thing with another. **Hacer or causar armonía,** to excite admiration, to produce novelty. 3. Friendship. **Correr con armonía,** to live in peace.

armónica [ar-mo'-ne-cah], *f.* Harmonica, mouth organ.

armónicamente [ar-mo'-ne-cah-mayn'-tay], *adv.* Harmoniously; harmonically.

armónico, ca [ar-mo'-ne-co, cah], *a.* Harmonical, adapted to each other, musical, rhythmical.

armonio [ar-mo'-ne-o], *m.* Harmonium, or reed organ. Strictly, the harmonium has force-bellows and the cabinet organ suction-bellows.

armoniosamente [ar-mo-ne-osah-men'-tay], *adv.* Harmoniously.

armonioso, sa [ar-mo-ne-o'-so, sah], *a.* 1. Harmonious, sonorous, pleasing to the ear; consonous. 3. *(Met.)* Adapted to each other, having the parts proportioned to each other.

armonista [ar-mo-nees'-tah], *f.* Harmonist.

armonizable [ar-mo-ne-tha'-blay], *a. (fig.)* That can be reconciled.

armonización [ar-mo-ne-thah-the-on'], *f.* Harmonization; *(fig.)* Reconciliation; co-ordination. **Ley de cordinación,** coordinating law.

armonizador [ar-mo-ne-thah-dor'], *a.* **Ley armonizadora;** *V.* ARMONIZACIÓN.

armonizar [ar-mo-ne-thar'], *va.* To harmonize, to put in harmony: to produce harmony. *-vn.* To harmonize; *(fig.)* To harmonize, to blend with, to be in keeping with; **armonizar con,** to blend with, to tone in with (colores).

armuelle [ar-moo-el'-lyay], *m. (Bot.)* Orach. Atriplex.

arna [ar'-nah], *f. (Prov.)* Bee-hive.

arnacho [ar-nah'-cho], *m.* 1. *(Bot.)* Rest harrow. 2. Wild amaranth. 3. Orach.

arnaco [ar-nah'-co], *m. (And.)* Useless object, piece of lumber.

arnero [ar-nay-ro], *m. (LAm.)* Sieve.

arnés [ar-ness'], *m.* 1. Harness, coat of mail or steel network for defence; armor. 2. Store-room for the accoutrements of cavalry. **Arneses,** necessary tools, utensils, furniture used in a house, trade or kitchen. **Arnés de caballo,** gear, trapping, and furniture of a horse.

árnica [ar'-ne-cah], *f.* Arnica, a medicinal plant.

arnilla [ar-neel'-lyah], *f. dim. (Prov.)* A small bee-hive.

aro [ah'-ro], *m.* 1. Hoop of wood, iron, or other metals, iron staple; hoop poles. 2. *(Bot.) V.* YARO. **Meterle a uno por el aro or arillo,** to decoy somebody. 3. *(LAm.)* **Pasar a uno por el aro,** to play tricks on somebody.

aroca [ah-ro'-cah], *f.* A sort of linen.

aroma [ah-ro'-mah], *m.* Aroma, perfume, fragance. **El aroma del café,** the aroma of coffee. *f.* Flower of the aromatic myrrh-tree. *-m.* 1. *(Chem.)* The odorant principle, the volatile spirit of plants. 2. A general name given to all balsams, woods, and herbs of strong fragrance.

aromaticidad [ah-ro-mah-te-the-dahd'], *f.* An aromatic or fragrant quality, perfume.

aromático, ca [ah-ro-mah'-te-co, cah], *a.* Aromatic, fragrant.

aromatización [ah-ro-mah-te-thah-the-on'], *f.* Aromatization, the act of scenting with aromatics.

aromatizador [ah-ro-mah-te-thah-dor'], *m.* Aromatizer, spray.

aromatizar [ah-ro-mah-te-thar'], *va.* To aromatize, to perfume.

aromo [ah-ro'-mo], *m. (Bot.)* The aromatic myrrh-tree.

aroza [ah-ro'-thah], *m.* Foreman in iron-works or forges.

arpa [ar'-pah] *f.* 1. Harp, lyre. **Tocar el arpa,** to be a thief. 2. *(Astr.)* Harp, a constellation.

arpado [ar-pah'-do], *a.* Serrated, toothed. *-pp.* of ARPAR.

arpador [ar-pah-dor'], *m. (Obs.)* Harp player.

arpadura [ar-pah-doo'-rah], *f. V.* ARAÑO.

arpar [ar-par'], *va.* 1. To tear clothes to pieces, to rend to tatters. 2. To claw, to tear with nails or claws. 3. *(LAm.)* To pinch, nick.

arpegio [ar-pay'-he-o], *m. (Mus.)* Arpeggio.

arpella [ar-payl'-lyah], *f. (Orn.)* Harpy.

arpeo [ar-pay'-o], *m. (Naut.)* Grappling iron.

arpero [ar-pay'-ro], *m. & f. (Mex.)* Thief, burglar (ladrón).

arpía [ar-pee'-ah], *f.* 1. *(Poetic.)* Harpy, a bird of prey represented by poets. 2. Harpy, a ravenous woman; an ugly, scolding shrew.

arpicordio [ar-pe-cor'-de-o], *m.* Harpsichord.

arpillar [ar-pe-lyahr'], *va. (CAm.)* To pile up.

arpillera [ar-peel-lyay'-rah], *f.* Sackcloth, coarse linen made of tow, packcloth.

arpir [ar-peer'], *m. (And. Cono Sur)* Mineworker.

arpista [ar-pees'-tah], *m.* 1. Harper, player on the harp by profession, harpist. 2. *(Cono Sur)* Thief (ladrón).

arpón [ar-pone'], *m.* 1. Harpoon, a harping-iron. 2. *(Naut.)* Fish-gig.

arponado, da [ar-po-nah'-do, dah], *a.* Harpooned, like a harpoon.

arponar [ar-po-nahr'], *va,* To harpoon; to gaff.

arponear [ar-po-nay-ar'], *va.* To throw the harpoon.

arponero [ar-po-nay'-ro], *m.* Harpooner, he who throws the harpoon.

arqueada [ar-kay-ah'-dah], *f.* Stroke with the fiddle-bow, whereby sounds are produced from the strings of a musical instrument. **Dar arqueadas,** *(coll.)* to show symptoms of nausea.

arqueador [ar-kay-ah-dor'], *m.* 1. Ship-gauger, an officer whose job is to measure the dimensions of ships. 2. One who forms arches. 3. Woolbeater.

arqueaje [ar-kay-ah'-hay], *m.* The gauging of a ship.

arqueamiento [ar-kay-ah-me-en'-to], *m. V.* ARQUEO.

arquear [ar-kay-ar'], *va.* 1. To arch, to form in the shape of an arch. 2. Among clothiers, to beat the dust out of the wool. 3. *(Naut.)* To gauge or measure the dimensions of ships. **Arquear las cejas,** to arch the eyebrows; to frown. **Arquear para vomitar,** to retch. 4. *(LAm.)* To check. *-vr.* To arch, to bend.

arqueo [ar-kay'-o], *m.* 1. The act of bending anything into the form of an arch. 2. *(Naut.)* The tonnage or burden of a ship. *V.* ARQUEAJE. 3. Verification of money and papers in a safe *(Com.).*

arqueolítico [ar-ke-o-le'-te-co], *a.* Stone-Age.

arqueología [ar-kay-o-lo-hee'-ah], *f.* Archaeology, a discourse on antiquity.

arqueológico [ar-ke-o-lo'-he-co], *a.* Archaeological.

arqueólogo [ar-kay-o'-lo-go], *m.* Archaeologist.

arquería [ar-kay-ree'-ah], *f.* 1. Series of arches. 2. *(Mex.)* Aqueduct.

arquero [ar-kay'-ro], *m.* 1. One whose trade is to make bows for arrows. 2. Treasurer, cashier. 3. Bowman, archer.

arqueta [ar-kay'-tah], *f. dim.* A little chest, a small trunk.

arquetipo [ar-kay-tee'-po], *m.* Archetype.

arquetón [ar-kay-tone'], *m. aug.* A large trunk.

arquetoncillo [ar-kay-ton-theel'-lyo], *m. dim.* A trunk or chest of a middling size.

arquibanco [ar-kay-bahn'-co], *m.* A bench or seat with drawers.

arquiepiscopal [ar-ke-ay-pis-co-pahl'], *a.* Archiepiscopal. *V.* ARZOBISPAL.

arquifilósofo [ar-ke-fe-lo'-so-fo], *m.* Archphilosopher.

arquilla, ita [ar-keel'-lyah, kke'-tah], *f. dim.* A little chest.

arquillo [ar-keel'-lyo], *m. dim.* A small arch or bow.

arquimesa [ar-ke-may'-sah], *f. (Prov.)* Scrutoire, a case of drawers for writing, with a desk, escritoire.

Arquímides [ar-ke'-may-days], *m.* Archimedes.

arquimesa [ar-ke-may-sah], *f.* Desk, escritoire.

arquisinagogo [ar-ke-se-nah-go'-go], *m.* Principal in the synagogue.

arquitecto [ar-ke-tec'-to], *m.* An architect. **Arquitecto de sistemas de datos** *(Comp.)*, data systems architect.

arquitectónico, ca [ar-ke-tec-to'-ne-co, cah], *a.* Architectonic, architectural.

arquitectura [ar-ke-tee-too'-rah], *f.* Architecture. **Arquitectura de jardines**, landscape gardening, landscaping.

arquitrabe [ar-ke-trah'-bay], *m.* Architrave, that part of a column which lies immediately upon the capital, and is the lowest member of the entableture.

arrabal [ar-rah-bal'], *m.* Suburb. *pl.* **Arrabales**, suburbs or outskirts of a large town.

arrabalero, ra [ah-rah-bah-lay'-ro, rah], *a.* 1. Belonging to the outskirts; illbred, churlish. 2. Coarse in dress or manners.

arrabio [ar-rah'-be-o], *m.* Cast iron.

arraca [ar-rah'-cah], *f. (Naut.)* Traveler, an iron traveler.

arracacha, cho [ar-rah-cah'-cha], *f. & m. (And.)* Idiocy, silliness.

arracada [ar-rah-cah'-dah], *f.* Earring.

arracimado, da [ar-rah-the-mah'-do, dah], *a.* Clustered. *-pp.* of ARRICIMARSE. Botryoid, botryoidal.

arracimarse [ar-rah-the-mar'-say], *vr.* To cluster, or to be clustered together like a bunch of grapes.

arraclán [ar-rah-clahn'], *m. V.* ALISO. Alder-tree.

arráez [ar-rah'-eth], *m.* Captain or master of a Moorish ship. Used also in the Philippine Archipelago.

arraigadamente [ar-rah-e-gah'-dah-mayn-tay], *adv.* Firmly, securely.

arraigadas [ar-rah-e-gah'-das], *f. pl. (Naut.)* Futtock-shrouds.

arraigado, da [ar-rah-e-gah'-do, dah], *a.* 1. Possessed of landed property, real estate. Well-rooted, deep-rooted. 2. Fixed, inveterate, speaking of evils.

arraigar [ar-rah-e-gar'], *vn.* 1. To root. 2. To give security in land. 3. *-va. (LAm. Jur.)* To put somebody under a restriction. *-vr.* 1. To establish oneself in a place. 2. To be of long continuance, as a custom, habit, etc. **La costumbre se arraigó en él**, the habit grew on him.

arraigo [ar-rah'-e-go], *m.* 1. Landed property. **Es hombre de arraigo**, he is a man of considerable landed property. 2. Rooting; **de fácil arraigo**, easily-rooted. 3. *(fig.)* Settling, establishment. 4. *(fig.)* Hold, influence; **Tener arraigos**, to have influence.

arralar [ar-rah'-lar¡], *vn.* To thin out (árboles). *V.* RALEAR.

arramblar [ar-ram-blar'], *va.* 1. To cover with sand and gravel (arroyos, torrentes). 2. To sweep away, to drag along. *-vn.* **Arramblar con**, to make off with (robar).

arranca-clavos [ar-rahn'-cah-clah'-vos], *m.* Nail-puller.

arrancada [ar-ran-cah'-dah], *f. (coll.)* Sudden departure, violent sally.

arrancadera [ar-ran-cah-day'-rah], *f.* Large bell worn by those animals which guide the rest of the flocks.

arrancadero [ar-ran-cah-day'-ro], *m.* 1. *(Prov.)* The thickest part of the barrel of a gun. 2. Starting-point, course, or route.

arrancado, da [ar-ran-cah'-do, dah], *a.* 1. *(coll.)* Poor, penniless. 2. *(Naut.)* **Boga arrancada**, with long strokes of the oars. 3. Uprooted (plantas, árboles) *-pp.* of ARRANCAR.

arrancador, ra [ah-ran-cah-dor', rah], *m. & f.* An extirpator, a destroyer. *(Aut.)* Starter.

arrancadura [ar-ran-cah-doo'-rah], *f. (Obs.)* **Arrancamiento** [ar-ran-cah-me-en'-to], *m.* Extirpation, the act of pulling up by the roots.

arrancapinos [ar-ran-cah-pee'-nos], *m.* Nickname for little persons.

arrancar [ar-ran-car'], *va.* 1. To pull up by the roots, to extirpate. **Una historia que arranca lágrimas**, a story to make one cry. 2. To force out, to wrest. **Le arrancó el bolso**, he snatched her handbag. 3. To pull out a nail, to draw out a tooth. 4. To carry off with violence. 5. To force up phlegm, bile, etc. 6. To start and pursue one's course. 7. To begin an arch or vault. 8. *(Naut.)* To get afloat, or set sail. **Arrancar de raíz**, to root out or up. **Arrancar la espada**, to unsheath the sword. **Arrancársele a uno el alma**, to die broken-hearted. *-vr. (And. Carib. Mex.)* To peg out, to kick the bucket; **arrancarse con los tarros**, *(Cono Sur)* to run off with the profits.

arrancasiega [ar-ran-cah-se-ay'-gah], *f.* 1. Poor corn, half mowed and half pulled up. 2. *(Prov.)* A quarrel or dispute, with injurious language.

arranciarse [ar-ran-the-ar'-say], *vr.* To grow rancid.

arranchar [ar-rahn-chahr'], *vt.* 1. To brace (velas). 2. To skirt, to sail close to (costa). 3. *(And.)* To snatch away. *-vr.* 1. To mess together. 2. *(Carib. Mex.)* To settle in, to make oneself comfortable.

arrancón [ar-rahn-con'], *m. (Mex.) V.* ARRANCADA.

arranque [ar-rahn'-kay], *m.* 1. Extirpation, act of pulling up by the roots. 2. Wrench. 3. Flight of the imagination, sudden, unexpected gesture. 4. Violent fit, impetuousness. 5. Initiative, daring. **Arranque del caballo**, sudden start of the horse. **Arranque automático**, self-starter. **Un hombre de mucho arranque**, a man of daring, a man of an enterprising nature. 6. *(Arquit.)* Starting point. 7. *(LAm.)* **Estar en el arranque**, to be completely broke. 8. *(fig.)* Sally, witty remark. 9. *(Comp.)* Starting up.

arranquera [ar-rahn-kay-rah], *f. V.* ARRANQUE.

arrapar [ar-rah-par'], *va.* To snatch away, to carry off. *V.* ARREBATAR.

arrapiezo, arrapo [ar-rah-pe-ay'-tho, ar-rah'-po], *m.* 1. Tatter or rag hanging from old clothes. 2. *(Met.)* A mean, worthless, despicable person.

arras [ar'-ras], *f. pl.* 1. Thirteen pieces of money, which the bridegroom gives to the bride, as a pledge, in the act of marriage. 2. Dowry. 3. Earnest-money, handsel. **Arras de la bodega**, *(Naut.)* Wings of the hold.

arrasado [ar-rah-sah'-do], *m.* A silk stuff, satin face; satin.

arrasador [ar-rah-sah-dor'], *a. V.* ARROLLADOR.

arrasadura [ar-rah-sah-doo'-rah], *f. V.* RASADURA.

arrasamiento [ar-rah-sah-me-en'-to], *m.* Demolition of a fortress or fortified place.

arrasar [ar-rah-sar'], *va.* 1. To level, to make even, to smooth the surface of a thing. 2. To destroy, to raze, to demolish. 3. To obliterate. **Arrasar un bajel**, *(Naut.)* to cut down a vesel, to cut away part of her dead works. *-vn. & vr.* 1. To clear up, to grow fine (tiempo). 2. To fill with tears (ojos). **Arrasarse los ojos de lágrimas**, to weep bitterly.

arrastracueros [ar-rahs-trah-coo-ay'-ros], *m. (Carib.)* Crook; rascal, rogue.

arrastradamente [ar-ras-trah-dah-men'-tay], *adv.* 1. Imperfectly. 2. Painfully, wretchedly.

arrastraderas [ar-ras-trah-day'-ras], *f. pl. (Naut.)* Lower studding-sails.

arrastradero [ar-ras-trah-day'-ro], *m. (Naut.)* 1. A place on the seacoast, gently sloping toward the sea, where ships are careened; a careening-place. 2. Road by which logs are dragged. 3. Spot whence dead bulls are taken off.

arrastradizo [ar-rahs-trah-de'-tho], *a.* Dangling, trailing.

arrastrado, da [ar-ras-trah'-do, dah], *a.* 1. Dragged along. 2. Rascally, knavish. 3. Living in abject poverty. *-f. (coll.)* A fallen woman, prostitute. **Andar arrastrado**, to live in the utmost misery and distress. *-pp.* of ARRASTRAR.

arrastramiento [ar-ras-trah-me-en'-to], *m.* The act of dragging along the ground.

arrastrante [ar-ras-trahn'-tay], *m.* Claimant of a degree in colleges.

arrastrar [ar-ras-trar'], *va. & vn.* 1. To creep, to crawl. 2. To drag along the ground. 3. To bring one over to our opinion. 4. To lead a trump at cards. **Arrastrar la causa, el pleito, los autos**, etc., to move a lawsuit into another court. **Hacer alguna cosa arrastrando**, to do a thing against one's will, to do it ill. 5. To carry away; **No te dejes arrastrar por esa idea**, don't get carried away by that idea. 6. **Arrastrar a uno a hacer algo**, to lead somebody to do something. *-vr.* To crawl, creep; **Se arrastró hasta la puerta**, he dragged himself to the door. 2. To drag, to trail along the ground, to hang down. 3. To drag (tiempo). 4. To grovel, to fawn, to creep.

arrastre [ar-ras'-tray], *m.* 1. The act of leading a trump at cards. 2. The act of dragging; haulage, drayage. **Flota de arrastre**, trawling fleet. **Arrastre por correa**, belt-drive. 3. Slope of the wall of a shaft. 4. *(Amer.)* A mill where silver ores are pulverized. 5. *(Carib.)* Influence, pull. 6. *(Taur.)* Dragging away of the dead bull. 7. **Arrastre de dientes**, tractor. **Arrastre de papel por tracción**, tractor feed.

arrate [ar-rah'-tay], *m.* A pound of sixteen ounces.

arrayán [ar-rah-yahn'], *m. (Bot.)* Myrtle.

arrayanal [ar-rah-yah-nahl'], *m.* Plantation of myrtles.

arre [ar'-ray], Gee, get up; a word used by drivers to horses, mules, etc. **¡Arre aborrico!** Go on, ass!

¡Arre allá! Be off with you!

arreada [ar-ray-ah'-dah], *f. (Amer.)* 1. Act of herding the grazing flock. 2. Conscription for military service.

arreado [ar-ray-ah'-do], *a. (And. Cono Sur, Mex.)* Sluggish, ponderous.

arreador [ar-ray-ah-dor'], *m.* Muleteer.

arrear [ar-ray-ar'], *va.* 1. To drive horses, mules, etc. 2. To harness (caballo). 3. *(CAm. Cono Sur, Mex.)* To steal, rustle (ganado). *-vn.* To hurry along, get moving; *(fig.)* get away! *-vr. (Obs.)* To be a muleteer.

arrebañador, ra [ar-ray-bah-nyah-dor', rah], *m. & f.* Gleaner, gatherer.

arrebañadura [ar-ray-bah-nyah-doo'-rah], *f.* The act of gleaning, picking up, or scraping together.

arrebañar [ar-ray-bah-nyar'], *va.* To glean, to gather, to scrap together.

arrebatadamente [ar-ray-bah-tah-dah-men'-tay], *adv.* Precipitately, headlong.

arrebatadizo [ar-ray-bah-tah-dee'-tho], *a.* Excitable, hot-tempered.

arrebatado, da [ar-ray-bah-tah'-do, dah], *a.* 1. Rapid, violent. 2. Precipitate, rash, inconsiderate, impetuous. **Muerte arrebatada**, a sudden death. **Hombre arrebatado**, a rash, inconsiderate man. *-pp.* of ARREBATAR.

arrebatador, ra [ar-ray-bah-tah-dor', rah], *m. & f.* One who snatches away, or takes a thing by violence.

arrebatamiento [ar-ray-bah-tah-me-en'-to], *m.* 1. The act of carrying away by violence or precipitation. 2. Fury, rage, extreme passion. 3. Rapture, ecstasy, fit.

arrebatar [ar-ray-bah-tar'], *va.* 1. To carry off, to take away by violence. 2. To snatch and seize things with precipitation. **Le arrebató el revólver**, he snatched the pistol from him. 3. To attract attention, notice, etc. 4. *(fig.)* To move deeply, to stir; to captivate, enrapture. 5. *(Agri.)* To parch. *-vr.* 1. To be led away by passion. **Arrebatarse de cólera**, to be overcome with anger. 2. To be gathered earlier than usual on account of hot weather (cosecha). 3. To get roasted or scorched. **Arrebatarse el caballo**, said of a horse which is overheated.

arrebatiña [ar-ray-bah-tee'-nyah], *f.* The act of carrying off a thing precipitately out of a crowd.

arrebato [ar-ray-bah'-to], *m.* Surprise, a sudden and unexpected attack upon an enemy; paroxysm, start. **Arrebato de cólera**, sudden burst of passion.

arrebiatarse [ar-ray-be-ah-tahr'-say], *vr. (CAm.)* To join up; *(Mex.)* To follow the crowd.

arrebol [ar-ray-bole'], *m.* 1. The red glow in the sky. 2. Rouge, red paint for ladies. **El sol poniente tiene arreboles magníficos**, the sun sets off a magnificent red glow at sunset.

arrebolada [ar-ray-bo-lah-dah] *f.* Red clouds (at sunrise or sunset).

arrebolar [ar-ray-bo-lar'], *va.* To paint red, to redden, to give a red glow. *-vr* To rouge or to lay on rouge. *(Carib.)* To dress up.

arrebolera [ar-ray-bo-lay'-rah], *f.* 1. *(Prov.)* A woman who sells rouge. 2. Alkanet, a plant of which vegetable rouge is made. 3. A small pot or saucer with red paint. 4. *(Bot.)* Marvel of Peru.

arrebozar [ah-rray-bo-thar'], *va.* To cover; to conceal. *(Culin.)* To cover, to coat. *-vr.* To cover one's face; to muffle up.

arrebozo [ar-ray-bo'-tho], *m.* V. REBOZO.

arrebujadamente [ar-ray-boo-hah-dah-men'-tay], *adv.* Confusedly, with disorder.

arrebujar [ar-ray-boo-har'], *va.* To gather up without order; to throw together with confusion, to huddle. *-vr.* To cover and roll oneself in the bed-clothes.

arrecafe [ar-ray-cah'-fay], *m.* Cardoon.

arrechada [ah-rray-chah-dah], *f. (CAm. Mex.)* V. ARRECHERA.

arrechar [ah-rray-char'], *vn.* 1. *(CAm.)* To show energy, to begin to make an effort. 2. *(CAm. Mex.)* To feel randy. *-vr. (CAm. Mex.)* To get angry.

arrechera [ah-rray-chay-rah], *f.* 1. *(Cono Sur)* Heat, mating urge; *(Mex.)* Randiness, lust. 2. *(Mex.)* Whim, fancy.

arrecho [ah-rray-cho], 1. *a. (CAm. Mex.)* Vigorous, energetic. 2. *(CAm.)* Randy, lecherous; **estar arrecho**, to be on heat; to be in the mood (persona). 3. *(CAm. Mex.)* In heat. 4. *(CAm.)* **Es un arrecho**, he's a bloody nuisance.

arrechucho [ar-ray-choo'-cho], 1. A fit of anger. 2. Sudden and passing indisposition.

arreciar [ar-ray-the-ar'], *vn.* To become intensified. **Arreció la lluvia**, it rained harder. To get worse. *-vr. (Med.)* To get stronger.

arrecife [ar-ray-thee'-fay], *m.* 1. Causeway, a road paved with stone; mole. 2. *(Naut.)* A reef, ridge of hiden rocks lying close under the surface of the water.

arrecil [ar-ray-theel'], *m. (Prov.)* A sudden flood.

arrecirse [ar-ray-theer'-say], *vr.* To be benumbed with excessive cold, to grow stiff with cold.

arredilar [ar-ray-de-lar'], *va.* To put into the sheep-fold.

arredo [ah-rray'-do], *adv. (CAm. Mex.)* **¡Arredo vaya!**, get lost!

arredomado, da [ar-ray-do-mah'-do, dah], *a.* V. REDOMADO.

arredondar, arredondear [ar-ray-don-dar', ar-ray-don-day-ar'], *va. (Obs.)* To round. V. REDONDEAR.

arredramiento [ar-ray-drah-me-en'-to], *m.* The act of removing to a greater distance.

arredrar [ar-ray-drar'], *va.* 1. To remove to a greater distance. 2. To terrify, to cause dread. *-vr.* V. ATEMORIZARSE.

arregazado, da [ar-ray-gah-thah'-do, dah], *a.* Having the point turned up. **Nariz arregazada** *or* **arremangada,** a cocked nose. *-pp.* of ARREGAZAR.

arregazar [ar-ray-gah-thar'], *va.* To truss, to tuck up the skirts of clothes.

arregionado, da [ah-rre-he-o-nah'-do], *a.* *(And. Mex.)* Illtempered, sharp; impulsive, cross.

arreglada [ah-rray-glah'-dah], *f.* *(Cono Sur)* **Arreglada de bigotes,** dirty deal, shady business.

arregladamente [ar-ray-glah'-dah-men-tay], *adv.* Regularly.

arreglado, da [ar-ray-glah'-do, dah], *a.* Regular, moderate. *-pp.* of ARREGLAR.

arreglador [ar-ray-gla-dor'], *m.* *(Com.)* Surveyor, valuer (of averages).

arreglamiento [ar-ray-glah-me-en'-to], *m.* *(Obs.)* Regulation, instruction in writing.

arreglar [ar-ray-glar'], *va.* 1. To regulate, to reduce to order, to guide, to moderate. 2. To compound; to frame. *(Com.)* To arrange, to settle; to adjust. **Yo lo arreglaré,** I'll see to it. 3. To adjust the administration of provinces, and enact laws for them. 4. To tidy up, to smarten up, to do. **Voy a que me arreglen el pelo,** I'm going to have my hair done. *-vr.* 1. To conform to law. 2. To come to terms; **por fin se arreglaron,** eventually they reached an agreement. 3. **Arreglarse el pelo,** to have one's hair done. 4. To work out, to solve. **Ya es hora de arreglarse,** it's time to get ready.

arreglo [ar-ray'-glo], *m.* 1. Rule, order. **Vivir con arreglos,** to live an orderly life. 2. *(Com.)* Arrangement, settlement. **Con arreglo,** conformably, according to. 3. Agreement, understanding. **Llegar a un arreglo,** to reach a settlement. 4. Trim (pelo).

arregostarse [ar-ray-gos-tar'-say], *vr.* To relish or have a taste for a thing, to be attached to it.

arregosto [ah-rray-gos'-to], *m.* Fancy, taste.

arrejaca [ar-ray-hah'-cah], *f.* *V.* ARREJAQUE.

arrejacar [ar-ray-hah-car'], *va.* To plough across a piece of ground, to clear of weeds.

arrejaco [ar-ray-hah'-co], *m.* *(Orn.)* Swift, martin. *V.* VENCEJO.

arrejada [ar-ray-hah'-dah], *m.* Fork with three prongs bent at the point.

arrejarse [ah-rray-hahr'-say], *vr.* *(Cono Sur.)* To take a risk.

arrejuntarse [ah-rray-hoon-tahr'-say], *vr.* To move in together.

arrel, arrelde [ar-rel', ar-rel'-day], *m.* 1. Weight of four pounds. 2. A bird of a very small size.

arrellanarse [ar-rel-lyah-nar'-say], *vr.* 1. To sit at ease; to incline one's seat for greater ease. 2. *(Met.)* To make oneself comfortable. 3. To be satisfied with one's employment.

arremangado, da [ar-ray-man-gah'-do, dah], *a.* Lifted upward. **Ojos arremangados,** uplifted eyes. *-pp.* of ARRREMANGAR.

arremangar [ar-ray-man-gar'], *va.* To tuck up the sleeves or petticoats. *-vr.* To be fully resolved. To roll up one's sleeves. To take a firm line (actitud).

arremango [ar-ray-mahn'-go], *m.* The act of tucking up the clothes.

arrematar [ah-rray-mah-tahr'], *va.* To finish, to complete.

arremedador, ra [ar-ray-may-dah-dor', rah], *m. & f. (Obs.)* A mimic, a ludicrous imitator.

arremetedor [ar-ray-may-tay-dor'], *m.* Assailant, aggressor.

arremeter [ar-ray-may-ter'], *va.* 1. To assail, to attack with impetuosity, to make at. 2. To seize briskly. 3. To shock or offend the sight. *-vn.* 1. To rush forth, to attack. **Arremeter a uno,** to rush at somebody. 2. *(fig.)* To offend good taste, to shock the eye.

arremetida [ar-ray-may-tee'-dah], *f.* 1. Attack, assault, invasion. 2. Start of horses from a barrier or other place.

arremolinado, da [ar-ray-mo-le-nah'-do, dah], *a.* Whirled, turned round; (trigo) blown down by a storm.

arremolinar [ar-ray-mo-le-nar'], *va. & vr.* 1. To eddy, to form eddies. 2. To gather together, to form a crowd.

arrempujar [ar-rem-poo-har'], *va.* *V.* REMPUJAR.

arremueco [ar-ray-moo-ay'-co], *vn.* 1. A Caress. 2. A movement of the lips expressive of contempt or scorn. *V.* ARRUMACO.

arrendable [ar-ren-dah'-blay], *a.* Rentable; farmable, tenantable.

arrendación [ar-ren-dah-the-on'], *f.* The act of renting, or taking at a certain rent.

arrendadero [ar-ren-dah-day'-ro], *m.* An iron ring fastened to the manager, to which horses are tied.

arrendado, da [ar-ren-dah'-do, dah], *a.* Obedient to the reins, applied to horses. *-pp.* of ARRENDAR.

arrendador [ar-ren-dah-dor'], *m.* 1. Landlord lessor, hirer, tenant, lessee, holder; farmer; copyholder. 2. *V.* ARRENDADERO. **Arrendador de plomo,** a very tiresome person.

arrendadorcillo [ar-ren-dah-dor-theel'-lyo], *m. dim.* A petty tenant.

arrendajo [ar-ren-dah'-ho], *m.* 1. *(Orn.)* The mocking-bird. 2. Mimic, buffoon.

arrendamiento [ar-ren-dah-me-en'-to], *m.* 1. The act of renting, letting, or hiring to a tenant; lease. 2. The house or lease-rent. 3. Contract, agreement.

arrendante [ar-ren-dahn'-tay], *m.* A tenant.

arrendar [ar-ren-dar'], *va.* 1. To rent (alquilar), to hold by paying rent, for rent, to lease, to hire. 2. To bridle a horse. 3. To tie a horse by the reins of a bridle. 4. To mimic, to imitate as a buffoon, to ridicule by a burlesque imitation. 5. To thin out plants. **Arrendar tierras,** to lease land. **No le arriendo la ganancia,** I wouldn't like to be in his shoes.

arrendatario, ria [ar-ren-dah-tah'-re-o, ah], *m. & f.* 1. One who rents, a lessor. 2. Lessee. 3. Farmer.

arrendero [ah-rrayn-day'ro], *m.* *(Cono Sur. Mex.)* *V.* ARRENDATARIO.

arrentado, da [ar-ren-tah'-do, dah], *a.* Enjoying a considerable income from landed property.

arreo [ar-ray'-o], *m.* Dress, ornament, decoration. *-pl.* 1. Appendages. 2. Trappings of a horse.

arreo [ar-ray'-o], *adv. (coll.)* Successively, uninterruptedly. **Llevar arreo,** to carry something on one's shoulders.

arrepápalo [ar-ray-pah'-pah-lo], *m.* A sort of fritters or buns.

arrepentida [ar-ray-pen-tee'-dah], *f.* A woman of previous evil life who repents and shuts herself within a convent.

arrepentidamente [ah-rray-payn-te'-dah-mayn-tay], *adv.* Regretfully, repentantly.

arrepentido, da [ar-ray-pen-tee'-do, dah], *a.* Repentant. *-pp.* of ARREPENTIRSE.

arrepentimiento [ar-ray-pen-te-me-en'-to], *m.* 1. Repentance, penitence, contriteness, compunction; conversion. 2. Emendation in composition and drawing (pintura).

arrepentirse [ar-ray-pen-teer'-say], *vr.* To repent, to express sorrow for having said or done something. **(Yo me arrepiento, yo me arrepienta; él se arrepintió, él se arrepintiera;** from **Arrepentirse.** *V.* ASENTIR).

arrepistar [ar-ray-pis-tar'], *va.* To grind or pound rags into a fine pulp (papeleras, fábricas de papel).

arrepisto [ar-ray-pees'-to], *m.* The act of grinding or pounding rags.

arrepticio, cia [ar-rep-tee'-the-o, ah], *a.* Possessed or influenced by the devil.

arrequesonarse [ar-ray-kay-so-nar'se], *vr.* To be curded or coagulated; to curdle.

arrequife [ar-ray-kee'-fay], *m.* Singeing-iron for burning or taking off the down which remains on cotton goods.

arrequín [ah-rray-ken'], *m.* 1. *(LAm.)* Helper, assistant. 2. *(LAm.) (Agri.)* Leading animal.

arrequives [ar-ray-kee'-ves], *vn. pl.* 1. Ornaments, adornments. 2. Circumstances of a case. 3. Requisites.

arrestado, da [ar-res-tah'-do, dah], *a.* Intrepid, bold, audacious. *-pp.* of ARRESTAR.

arrestar [ar-res-tar'], *va.* To arrest, to confine, to imprison. **Arrestar en el cuartel**, to confine to barracks. *-vr.* To be bold and enterprising, to engage with spirit in an enterprise or undertaking.

arresto [ar-res'-to], *m.* 1. Spirit, boldness in undertaking an enterprise. 2. Detention. *(Mil.)* Prison, arrest. **Estar bajo arresto**, to be under arrest.

arretín [ar-ray-teen'], *m.* V. FILIPICHIN.

arretranca [ar-ray-trahn'-cah], *f.* A broad crupper for mules.

arrevesado [ar-ray-vay-sah'-do], *a.* Queer, odd.

arrezafe [ar-ray-thah'-fay], *m.* A place full of thistles, brushwood, and brambles.

arria [ar'-re-ah], *f.* Drove of beasts.

arriada [ar-re-ah'-dah], *f. (Prov.)* Swell of waters, flood, overflowing.

arriado [ah-rre-ah'-do], *a. (LAm.)* V. ARREADO.

arrianismo [ar-re-ah-nees'-mo], *m.* Arianism.

arriano, na [ar-re-ah'-no, anh], *a.* Arian (hereje), adherent to the teachings of Arius.

arriar [ar-re-ar'], *va. (Naut.)* 1. To lower, to strike. **Arriar la bandera**, to strike the colors. **Arriar las vergas y los masteleros**, to strike the yards and top-masts. **Arriar un cabo**, to pay out the cable. **Arriar la gávia**, to let go the maintop-sail. 2. *vr.* To destroy by floods or a sudden fall of rain. **¡Arría!** Let go!

arriata [ar-re-ah'-tah], *f.* V. ARRIATE.

arriate [ar-re-ah'-tay], *m.* 1. A border in gardens where herbs, flowers, etc., are planted. 2. Trellis around beds or walks in a garden. 3. Causeway, a paved road.

arriaz, arrial [ar-re-ath'-, ar-re-ahl'], *m.* Hilt-bar of a sword.

arriba [ar-ree'-bah], *adv.* 1. Above, over, up, high, overhead, upstairs (en casa). 2. *(Naut.)* Aloft. 3. In writings, previously mentioned. **Lo escrito arriba**, what has been said above. 4. *(Met.)* A high post or station with respect to others. 5. In the hands of the king. **Está decretado de arriba**, it is decreed by high authority. **Arriba dicho**, above mentioned. **De arriba, abajo**, from top to bottom. **Arriba de seis varas**, *(coll.)* above six yards. **Ir aguas arriba**, *(Naut.)* to work up the river. **De arriba**, from heaven.

arribada [ar-re-bah'-dah], *m.* 1. Arrival. 2. Spot where a ship may approach.

arribaje [ah-rre-bah'-hay], *m. (Naut.)* Arrival, entry into harbor.

arribar [ar-re-bar'], *vn. (Naut.)* 1. To put into a harbor in distress. 2. To arrive by land at a stopping-place. 3. To fall off to leeward; to bear away. 4. *(Met.)* To recover from a disease or calamity; to convalesce. 5. *(coll.)* To accomplish one's desire. **Arribar todo**, to bear away before the wind. **Arribar a escote larga**, to bear away large. **Arribar sobre un bajel**, to bear down upon a ship.

arribazón [ah-rre-bah-thon'], *f.* Coastal abundance of fish, off-shore shoal.

arribeño [ah-rre-bay'-nyo], *m. & f. (LAm.)* Highlander, inlander. *(Cono Sur)* Stranger.

arribista [ah-rre-bes'-tah], *m. & f.* Go-getter, arriviste, social climber.

arribo [ar-ree'-bo], *m.* Arrival.

arricete [ar-re-thay'-tay], *m.* Shoal, sand-bank.

arricisces [ar-re-thee'-ses], *m. pl.* The saddle-straps to which the girths are fastened.

arriendo [ar-reen'-do], *m.* Ablocation, lease, rental. V. ARRENDAMIENTO. (**Yo arriendo, yo arriende**, from **arrendar**. V. ACERTAR).

arriería [ar-re-ay-ree'-ah], *f.* The calling of a driver of mules.

arrierico, illo, ito [ar-re-ay-ree'-co, eel'-yo, ee'-to], *m. dim.* One who carries on mule-driving in a petty way.

arriero [ar-re-ay'-ro], *m.* Muleteer, he who used to drive mules, carrying goods from one place to another.

arriesgadamente [ar-re-es-gah-dah-men'-tay], *adv.* Dangerously, hazardously.

arriesgado, da [ar-re-es-gah'-do, dah], *a.* 1. Perilous, dangerous, hazardous. 2. Dangerous to be dealt with; daring. **Hombre arriesgado**, a dangerous man. *-pp.* of ARRIESGAR.

arriesgar [ar-re-es-gar'], *va.* To risk, to hazard, to expose to danger, to jeopard. *-vr.* To be exposed to danger; to dare. **Arriesgarse a hacer algo**, to dare to do something.

arrimadero [ar-re-mah-day'-ro], *m.* Scaffold, a stage; a stick or support to lean upon.

arrimadillo [ar-re-mah-deel'-lyo], *m.* A mat or wainscot upon a wall.

arrimadizo [ar-re-mah-dee'-tho], *a. & m.* 1. That which is designed to be applied to any thing. 2. *(Met.)* Parasite, sponger, one who meanly hangs upon another for subsistence. 3. *(Obs.)* Support, prop.

arrimado, da [ar-re-mah'-do, dah], *pp.* of ARRIMAR. **Tener arrimado or arrimados**, To be possessed by evil spirits.

arrimador [ar-re-mah-dor'], *m.* The back-log in a fire-place.

arrimadura [ar-re-mah-doo'-rah], *f.* The act of approaching.

arrimar [ar-re-mar'], *va.* 1. To approach, to draw near, to join one thing to another. **Lo arrimamos a la ventana**, we put it against the window. 2. *(Naut.)* To stow the cargo, to trim the hold. 3. To lay a thing aside, to put by; to reject. **El plan quedó arrimado**, the plan was shelved. 4. To lay down a command. 5. To displace, to dismiss. 6. **Arrimar el clavo**, to prick a horse at the time of shoeing him. **Arrimar el clavo a uno**, *(Met.)* to impose, to deceive. 7. *(Cono Sur)* **Arrimar la culpa a uno**, to lay the blame on somebody. *-vr.* 1. To lean upon a thing. 2. To join others for the purpose of forming a body with them. 3. *(Met.)* To come to the knowledge of a thing. **Arrimarse al punto de la dificultad**, to come to the point. **Arrimarse al parecer de otro**, to espouse another's opinion. 4. *(LAm.)* To sponge.

arrime [ar-ree'-may], *m.* In the game of bowls, the mark for the balls to arrive at.

arrimo [ah-ree'-mo], *m.* 1. The act of joining one thing to another. 2. Staff, stick, crutch. 3. *(Met.)* Protection or support of a powerful person; help. 4. Among builders, an insulated wall which has no weight to support; idle wall.

arrimón [ar-re-mone'], *m. (Hacer el) (coll.)* 1. To stagger along a wall, supported by it, in a state of intoxication. 2. **Estar de arrimón**, To stand watch over somebody.

arrinconado, da [ar-rin-co-nah'-do, dah], *a.* Out of favor, retired from the world, abandoned. *-pp.* of ARRINCONAR.

arrinconar [ar-rin-co-nar'], *va.* 1. To put a thing in a corner; to lay aside, to reject. 2. *(Met.)* To remove one from a trust, to withdraw one's favor or protection. *-vr.* To retire from the world.

arriñonado [ah-rre-nyo-nah'-do], *a.* Kidney-shaped; **estar arriñonado**, to be knackered.

arriscadamente [ar-ris-cah-dah-men'-tay], *adv.* Boldly, audaciously.

arriscado, da [ar-ris-cah'-do, dah], *a.* 1. Forward, bold, audacious, impudent. 2. Brisk, easy, free. **Caballo arriscado**, a high-mettled horse. 3. Broken or craggy ground. *-pp.* of ARRISCARSE.

arriscador [ar-ris-cah-dor'], *m. (Prov.)* A gleaner of olives.

arriscamiento [ah-rres-cah-me-ayn'-to], *m.* Boldness, resolution.

arriscar [ar-ris-car'], *va.* **To risk.** *-vr.* 1. To hold up one's head; to be proud, haughty, or arrogant. 2. To plunge over a cliff (rebaño ovejas). *(Acad.)* **Quien no arrisca, no aprisca**, nothing ventured, nothing gained.

arriscar [ah-rres-cahr'], 1. *va. (And. Cono Sur, Mex.)* To turn up (doblarse). 2. *vn.* To draw oneself up, to straighten up. 3. *-vr.* To get conceited. To dress up to the nines.

arriscocho [ah-rres-co'-cho], *a. (And.)* Restless; turbulent.

arristranco [ar-ris-trahn'-co], *m.* (Cuba) Useless furniture; lumber.

arrivista [ah-rre-ves'-tah], *V.* ARRIBISTA.

arrizar [ar-re-thar'], *va. (Naut.)* 1. To reef. 2. To stow the boat on deck. **Arrizar el ancla**, to stow the anchor. **Arrizar la**

artillería, to house the guns. 3. On board the galleys, to tie or lash one down.

arroba [ar-ro'-bah], *f.* 1. Spanish weight of twenty-five pounds; a quarter = 11.5 kilos. 2. A Spanish measure, containing thirty-two pints.; about four gallons. **Por arrobas**, wholesale. **Echar por arrobas**, *(Met.)* to exaggerate, to make hyperbolical amplifications.

arrobadizo, za [ar-ro-bah-dee'-tho, thah], *a. (coll.)* Feigning ecstasy and rapture.

arrobado [ar-ro-bah'-do], *pp.* of ARROBAR. *Por arrobado, (Obs.)* By wholesale.

arrobador, ra [ar-ro-bah-bor', rah], *a.* Enchanting, delightful, ecstatic.

arrobamiento [ar-ro-bah-me-en'-to], *m.* 1. Ecstatic rapture, or elevation of the mind to God. 2. Amazement, astonishment, high admiration. 3. Ecstasy, ravishment.

arrobar [ar-ro-bar'], *va. (Obs.)* To weigh or measure by arrobas. To entrance, enchant. -*vr.* To be in a state or rapturous amazement, to be out of one's senses.

arrobero, ra [ar-ro-bay'-ro, rah], *m. & f. (Prov.)* 1. About an *arroba* or quarter in weight. 2. Baker for a community.

arrobita [ar-ro-bee'-tah], *f. dim.* The weight of an *arroba* in a small compass.

arrobo [ar-ro'-bo], *m. V.* ARROBAMIENTO and EXTASIS.

arrocabe [ar-ro-cah'-bay], *m.* A wooden frieze.

arrocero [ar-ro-thay'-ro], *m.* A grower of or dealer in rice.

arrochelarse [ar-ro-chay-lahr'-say], *vr. (And.)* To take a liking to a place; to refuse to go out; to balk, to shy.

arrocinado, da [ar-ro-the-nah'-do, dah], *a.* 1. Dull, stupid, like a worn-out horse or *rocín.* 2. Hack-like (caballos). -*pp.* of ARROCINARSE.

arrocinar [ar-ro-the'-nar], *va.* To reduce, to brutish habits, to brutify. -*vr.* To become dull and stupid.

arrodajarse [ar-ro-dah-har'-say], *vr. (Costa Rica)* To sit upon the ground.

arrodelado, da [ar-ro-day-lah'-do, dah], *pp.* of ARRODELARSE. Bearing a target, shield, or buckler.

arrodelarse [ar-ro-day-lar'-say], *vr.* To be armed with a shield or buckler.

arrodeo [ar-ro-day'-o], *m. V.* RODEO.

arrodilladura [ar-ro-deel-lyah-doo'-rah], *f.* Arrodillamiento [ar-ro-deel-lyah-me-en'-to], *m.* The act of kneeling or bending the knee.

arrodillar [ar-ro-deel-lyar'], *vn.* To bend the knee down to the ground. -*vr.* To kneel to the ground.

arrodrigar, arrodrigonar [ar-ro-dre-gar', ar-ro-dre-go-nar'], *va. (Prov.)* To prop vines.

arrogación [ar-ro-gah-the-on'], *f.* 1. Arrogation, the act of claiming in a proud manner. 2. Adoption of a child which has no father or is independent of him.

arrogador [ar-ro-gah-dor'], *m.* One who claims in a proud manner.

arrogancia [ar-ro-gahn'-the-ah], *a.* 1. Arrogance, haughtiness, loftiness, conceit; confidence. 2. Stately carriage of a high-mettled horse.

arrogante [ar-ro-gahn'-tay], *a.* 1. Highminded, spirited. 2. Arrogant, haughty, proud, assuming; magisterial, masterly.

arrogantemente [ar-ro-ga-tay-men'-tay], *adv.* Arrogantly, haughtily, forwardly; highly; magisterially.

arrogar [ar-ro-gar'], *va.* 1. *(Law.)* To adopt. 2. To arrogate, to claim in a proud manner. -*vr.* To appropriate to oneself, to claim unjustly.

arrojadamente [ar-ro-hah-dah-men'-tay], *adv.* Audaciously, boldly.

arrojadillo [ar-ro-hah-deel'-lyo], *m. (Obs.)* Handkerchief, or other piece of silk or linen, which women used formerly to tie around the head to keep warm.

arrojadizo, za [ar-ro-hah-dee'-tho, thah], *a.* 1. That which can be easily cast, thrown, or darted; missile. 2. *(Obs.)* Spirited, bold, courageous.

arrojado, da [ar-ro-hah'-do, dah], *a.* 1. Rash, inconsiderate, forward, foolhardy, hasty, dashing. 2. Bold, intrepid, fearless. -*pp.* of ARROJAR.

arrojador [ar-ro-hah-dor'], *m.* A thrower, a flinger.

arrojallamas [ar-ro-hah-lyah'-mahs], *m. & pl.* Flamethrower.

arrojar [ar-ro-har'], *va.* 1. To dart, to launch, or to fling something, to hurl, to jerk, to dash, to belch out (lava), to drop (bombas), to give out (rayos). **Arrojar una piedra**, to throw a stone. **El volcán está arrojando lava**, the volcano is belching out lava. **Arrojar rayos**, to give off rays. 2. To shed a fragrance, to emit light. **Este estudio arroja alguna luz sobre el tema**, this study throws some light on the subject. 3. To shoot, to sprout, to grow up (plantas). 4. *(Naut.)* To drive or cast on rocks or shoals (viento). 5. To make red hot, as an oven. 6. To turn away or dismiss in an angry manner. -*vr.* 1. To launch, to throw oneself forward with impetuosity. **Arrojarse al agua**, to jump into the water. 2. *(Met.)* To venture upon an enterprise in an inconsiderate manner.

arroje [ar-ro'-hay], *m.* 1. The left side of the stage of a theater. 2. The person who throws himself from this spot, with a rope fastened, to raise the curtain.

arrojo [ar-ro'-ho], *m.* Boldness, intrepidity, fearlessness. **Arrojo al agua**, or **a la mar**, jettison, jetsam.

arrollado [ar-ro-lyah'-do], *m. (Cono Sur) (Culin.)* Rolled pork.

arrollador [ar-rol-lyah-dor'], *m.* 1. Roller, a kind of cylinder used for moving weighty things. 2. *(fig.)* Sweeping, overwhelming, crushing. **Por una mayoría arrolladora**, by an overwhelming majority. 3. *(Obs.) V.* ARRULLADOR.

arrollamiento [ar-roh-lyah-me-en'-to], *m.* 1. Winding, coiling. 2. Sweeping, carrying of.

arrollar [ar-rol-lyar'], *va.* 1. To roll up, to roll any thing round, to wrap or twist round. 2. To carry off, to sweep away (tormentas, torrente). To expel. 3. *(Met.)* To defeat, to rout an enemy. 4. *(Met.)* To confound an opponent. 5. **Arrollar a un niño**, *(Prov.)* to dandle a child. 6. *(Obs.)* To lull to rest.

arromadizarse [ar-ro-mah-de-thar'-say], *vr.* To catch cold.

arromanzar [ar-ro-man-thar'], *va. (Obs.)* To translate into the common or vernacular Spanish language.

arromar [ar-ro-mar'], *va.* To blunt, to dull the edge or point.

arromper [ar-rom-perr'], *va. (Obs.)* To break up the ground for sowing.

arrompido [ar-rom-pee'-do], *m.* A piece of ground newly froken.

arronzar [ar-ron-thar'], *va. (Naut.)* To haul a hawser, without the aid of the capstan, windlass, or tackle.

arropado, da [ar-ro-pah'-do, dah], *a.* Mixed with must (vino). -*pp.* of ARROPAR.

arropamiento [ar-ro-pah-me-en'-to], *m.* The act of clothing or dressing.

arropar [ar-ro-par'], *va.* 1. To cover the body with clothes, to dress. **Arrópate que sudas**, cover yourself, as you sweat: ironically addressed to a person who has done little and affects to be fatigued. 2. **Arropar el vino**, To mix wine, to give it a body. 3. **Arropar las viñas**, to cover the roots of vines with dung and earth. -*vr.* To wrap oneself up.

arrope [ar-ro'-pay], *m.* 1. Must or new wine boiled until it is as dense as a sirup. 2. A kind of decoction made in imitation of boiled honey. **Arrope de moras**, mulberry sirup.

arropea [ar-ro-pay'-ah], *f.* Irons, fetters; shackles for horses.

arropera [ar-ro-pay'-rah], *f.* Vessels for holding boiled must, sirup, etc.

arropia [ar-ro-pee'-ah], *f. (Prov.)* Cake made of flour, honey, and spice. *V.* MELCOCHA.

arropiero [ar-ro-pe-ay'-ro], *m. (Prov.)* Maker or seller of sweet cakes.

arrorró [ar-ro-rro'], *m. (LAm.)* Lullaby.

arrostrado [ah-rros-trah'-do], *a.* **Bien arrostrado**, nice-looking.

arrostrar [ar-ros-trar'], *va.* 1. To set about or perform a thing in a cheerful manner. 2. **Arrostrar los peligros, los trabajos, la muerte**, to encounter dangers, fatigues, death. -*vr.* To close with the enemy, to fight him face to face.

arroyada, *f.* **arroyadero**, *m.* [ar-ro-yah'-dah, ar-ro-yah-day'-ro], 1. The valley through which a rivulet runs. 2. The channel of a rivulet.

arroyar [ar-ro-yar'], *va.* To flood sown ground; to form gutters from heavy rain. -*vr.* To be affected with rust (trigo, grano).

arroyato [ar-ro-yah'-to], *m.* (*Obs.*) V. ARROYO.

arroyico, arroyuelo [ar-ro-yee'-co, ar-ro-yoo-ay'-lo], *m. dim.* A little river, a small brook, a rivulet.

arroyo [ar-ro'-yo], *m.* 1. Rivulet, a small river, current. 2. The watercourse of a street; (*Mex.*) **Estar en el arroyo**, to be on one's uppers; **poner a uno en el arroyo**, to turn somebody out of the house.

arroyuelo [ar-ro-yoo-ay'-lo], *m.* Small stream, brook.

arroz [ar-roth'], *m.* Rice. **Arroz blanco**, boiled rice. **Arroz a la cubana**, rice with banana and fried egg. **Arroz integral**, brown rice. *a.* (*coll.*) **Arroz gallo muerto**, a grand dinner, a banquet.

arrozal [ar-ro-thal'], *m.* Field sown with rice.

arrozar [ar-ro-thar'] *va.* To ice a liquid, to freeze it a little.

arruar [ar-roo-ar'], *vn.* To grunt like a wild boar when it sniffs pursuers.

arrufado, da [ar-roo-fah'-do, dah], *pp.* of ARRUFAR. Sheered, curved. **Navío muy arrufado**, (*Naut.*) moonsheered ship.

arrufadura [ar-roo-fah-doo'-rah], *f.* (*Naut.*) Sheer of a ship.

arrufar [ar-roo-far'], *va.* (*Naut.*) To incurvate, to form the sheer of a ship. -*vr.* To snarl, to show teeth (perro), to get angry.

arrufianado, da [ar-roo-fe-ah-nah'-do, dah], *a.* Ruffianly, impudent.

arrufo [ar-roo'-fo], *m.* V. ARRUFADURA.

arruga [ar-roo'-gah], *f.* 1. Wrinkle, corrugation. 2. Rumple, or rude plait in clothes, fold, crease. 3. (*And.*) Trick, swindle.

arrugación, *f.* **arrugamiento**, *m.* [ar-roo-gah-the-on', ar-roo-gah-me-en'-to], Corrugation, the act and effect of wrinkling.

arrugado [ar-roo-gah'-do], *a.* Wrinkled, lined (cara); creased (papel); rucked up, crumpled (vestido).

arrugar [ar-roo-gar'], *va.* 1. To wrinkle, to contract into wrinkles, to corrugate, to constrict, to crumple, to cockle. 2. To rumple, to fold, to gather, to crease, to pleat. **Arrugar la frente**, to knit the brow, to frown. -*vr.* To wrinkle, to get wrinkled, to crease, to get creased.

arrugia [ah-roo'-hee-ah], *f.* (*Obs. Miner.*) A hole dug in the ground to discover gold.

arrugón [ar-roo-gone'], *m.* Prominent decoration of carved work.

arrugue [ar-roo'-gay], *m.* (*Carib.*) V. ARRUGA.

arruinado [ar-roo-e-nah'-do], *a.* 1. Ruined. 2. (*Cono Sur. Mex.*) Sickly, stunted; (*Cono Sur*) wretched, down and out (miserable).

arruinador, ra [ar-roo-e-nah-dor', rah], *m. & f.* Ruiner, demolisher, a destroyer.

arruinamiento [ar-roo-en-nah-me-en'-to], *m.* Ruin, destruction, ruinousness.

arruinar [ar-roo-e-nar'], *va.* 1. To throw down, to demolish, to lay level. 2. To ruin, to confound, to crack; to crush. 3. (*Met.*) To destroy, to cause great mischief. -*vr.* To be ruined, to fall down.

arrullador, ra [ar-rool-lyah-dor', rah], *m. & f.* 1. A person who lulls babies to rest. 2. Flatterer, cajoler.

arrullar [ar-rool-lyar'], *va.* 1. To lull babes. 2. To court, to coo and bill. -*vr.* To bill and coo, to whisper endearments.

arrullo [ar-rool'-lyo], *m.* 1. The cooing and billing of doves. 2. Lullaby.

arrumaco [ar-roo-mah'-co], *m.* Caress, the act of endearment, profession of friendship.

arrumaje [ar-roo-mah'-hay], *m.* (*Naut.*) Stowage of a ship's cargo.

arrumar [ar-roo-mar'], *va.* (*Naut.*) To stow the cargo.

arrumazón [ar-roo-mah-thone'], *f.* 1. (*Naut.*) The act and effect of stowing. 2. Horizon overcast with clouds.

arrumbadas [ar-room-bah'-das], *f. pl.* (*Naut.*) Wales of a rowgalley.

arrumbador, ra [ar-room-bah-dor', rah], *m. & f.* 1. One who heaps or piles. 2. (*Naut.*) Steersman.

arrumbamiento [ar-room-bah-me-en'-to], *m.* The direction of a thing as it moves, with respect to another.

arrumbar [ar-room-bar'], *va.* 1. (*Prov.*) To put something away in a lumber-room. 2. (*Met.*) To refute one in conversation. 3. To decant wine, to pour it off gently. -*vr.* (*Naut.*) To resume and steer the proper course. 2. To be seasick. 3. (*And. Cono Sur*) To rust; to turn sour.

arruncharse [ar-roon-chahr'-say], *vr.* (*And.*) To curl up, to roll up.

arrunflarse [ar-roon-flar'-say], *vr.* To have a flush of cards of the same suit.

arrurruz [ar-roo-rooth'], *m.* Arrowroot.

arrutanado [ar-roo-tah-nah'-do], *a.* (*And.*) Plump.

arsenal [ar-say-nahl'], *m.* 1. Shipyard, dockyard, navy-yard. 2. Arsenal (armas).

arsenalera [ar-say-nah-lay'-rah], *f.* (*Cono Sur*) (*Med.*) Surgeon's assistant.

arseniato [ar-say-ne-ah'-to], *m.* (*Chem.*) Arseniate.

arsenical [ar-say-ne-cahl'], *a.* (*Chem.*) Arsenical, relating to arsenic.

arsénico [ar-say'-ne-co], *m.* (*Chem.*) Arsenic, a mineral substance, which facilitates the fusion of metals, and is a violent poison; ratsbane.

arsenioso [ar-say-ne-o'-so], *a.* Arsenious.

arsenito [ar-say-nee'-to], *m.* Arsenite.

arsolla [ar-sol'-lyah], *f.* V. ARZOLLA.

arta [ar'-tah], *f.* V. PLANTAIN *a.* Plantain, **arta de agua**. V. ZARAGATONA.

artal [ar-tahl'], *m.* A kind of pie.

artalete [ar-tah-lay'-tay], *m.* A sort of tart.

artanica, artanita [ar-tah-nee'-cah, ar-tah-nee'tah], *f.* (*Bot.*) Sow-bread.

arte [ar'-tay], *m. & f.* 1. Art. **Una obra de arte**, a work of art. **El arte culinario**, the art of cooking. 2. Art, the power of doing something not taught by nature and instinct. 3. Caution, skill, craft, cunning. 4. Artifice, machine. 5. Everything done by human industry. **No tener arte ni parte en alguna cosa**. to have neither art nor part in a thing, to have nothing to do with the business. **Arte tormentaria**, art of artillery or military enginery. **Artes**, *f. pl.* Intrigues, improper means. **Artes mecánicas**, mechanical arts, occupations, or handicrafts. **Artes liberales**, liberal arts. **Las bellas artes**, the fine arts. **Buen arte**, gracefulness of manners and gait. **Mal arte**, awkwardness of manners and gait. **Por amor al arte**, for the love of it. *pl.* **Artes**. The word *arte* is always feminine in plural. **Las artes gráficas**, the graphic arts.

artecillo, lla [ar-tay-theel'-lyo, lyah], *m. & f. dim.* Petty art or trade.

artefacto [ar-tay-fac'-to], *m.* 1. Device, contrivance. 2. Artifact. **Artefacto sideral**, space artifact.

artejo [ar-tay'-ho], *m.* Joint or knuckle of the fingers.

artemisa, artemisia [ar-tay-mee'-sah, ar-tay-mee'-se-ah], *f.* (*Bot.*) Mugwort, feverfew.

artena [ar-tay'-nah], *f.* An aquatic fowl of the size of a goose.

arteramente [ar-tay-rah-men'-tay], *adv.* Craftily, fraudulently.

arteria [ar-tay'-re-ah], *f.* (*Anat.*) Artery (vena). **Arterias de la madera**, veins formed in wood and timber by the various ramifications of the fibres. **Áspera arteria or traquiartería**, the wind-pipe.

artería [ar-tay-ree'-ah], *f.* Artifice, stratagem, cunning; sagacity.

arterial [ar-tay-re-ahl'], *a.* Arterial, belonging to the arteries.

arteriola [ar-tay-re-oh'-lah], *f. dim.* Small artery; arteriole.

arteriosclerosis [ar-tay-re-os-clay-ro'-sis], *f.* Arteriosclerosis, hardening of the arteries.

arterioso, sa [ar-tay-re-o'-so, sah], *a.* V. ARTERIAL.

arteriotomía [ar-tay-re-o-to-mee'-ah], *f.* (*Anat.*) Arteriotomy, the letting blood from an artery.

artero, ra [ar-tay'-ro, rah], *a.* Dexterous, cunning, artful.

artesa [ar-tay'-sah], *f.* 1. Trough in which dough of bread is worked. 2. Canoe. **Artesa de panaderos**, wooden bowl.

artesanal [ar-tay-sah-nahl'], *a.* Craft; **industria artesanal**, craft industry.

artesanía [ar-tay-sah-ne-ah'], *f.* Craftsmanship; handicraft, skill; **objeto de artesanía**, hand-made article.

artesano [ar-tay-sah'-no], *m.* Artisan, mechanic, artificer, handicraftsman.

artesiano, na [ar-tay-se-ah'-no, nah], *a.* Artesian. **Pozo artesiano**, artesian well.

artesilla [ar-tay-seel'-lyah], *f.* 1. (*dim.*) A small trough. 2. A sort of festive exercise on horseback. 3. A trough for water at a draw-well.

artesón [ar-tay-sone'], *m.* 1. A round kitchen trough for dishes, plates, etc. 2. Ceiling carved in the shape of a trough; ornamented vaulting; panelled ceilling. **Artesón de lavar**, washtub.

artesonado, da [ar-tay-so-nah'-do, dah], *a.* Panelling, trelliswork: applied to ceillings.

artesonar [ar-tay-so-nahr'], *va.* To coffer, to stucco, to mould.

artesoncillo [ar-tay-son-theel'-lyo], *m. dim.* A small trough.

artesuela [ar-tay-soo-ay'-lah], *f.* dim A small kneading-trough.

artético, ca [ar-tay-te-co, cah], *a.* 1. Afflicted with arthritis. 2. Arthritis.

ártico, ca [ar'-te-co, cah], *a.* (*Astr.*) Arctic, northern.

articulación [ar-te-coo-lah-the-on'], *f.* 1. Articulation, a joint. 2. Articulation, distinct pronunciation of words and syllables. **Articulación universal**, (*Mech.*) universal joint.

articuladamente [ar-te-coo-lah-dah-men'-tay], *adv.* Distinctly, articulately.

articulado, da [ar-te-coo-lah'-do, dah], *a.* Articulate, provided with a joint. (*Zool.*) Articulate, belonging to that large division of the animal kingdom, the articulate.

articular [ar-te-coo-lar'], *va.* 1. To articulate, to pronounce words clearly and distinctly. 2. To form the interrogatories which are put to witnesses examined in the course of law proceedings. 3. (*Poetic.*) To accent. 4. (*And. Cono Sur*) To tell off, to dress down. -*vn.* (*Cono Sur*) To quarrel.

articular, articulario, ria [ar-te-coo-lar', ar-te-coo-lah'-re-o, ah], *a.* Articular, belonging to the joints.

articulista [ar-te-coo-lees'-tah], *m. & f.* Newspaper or magazine feature writer.

artículo [ar-tee'-coo-lo], *m.* 1. Article, section; a word or term separately defined in a dictionary. **Artículos alimenticios**, food stuffs. 2. Plea put in before a court of justice. 3. Article, essay, in a periodical. **Un artículo de periódico**, a newspaper article. 4. (*Gram.*) Article, part of speech. **Artículo definido, indefinido**, definite, indefinite articles. 5. Clause, condition, stipulation. 6. (*Bot.*) Geniculation. 7. (*Anat.*) Joint of movable bones. **Varios artículos**, (*coll.*) sundry articles, things, knick-knacks. **Formar artículo**, to start an incidental question in the course of a lawsuit. **Artículo de la muerte**, point of death. 8. (*Comp.*) Item; **Artículo del equipo**, item of equipment.

artífice [ar-tee'-fe-thay], *m.* 1. Artificer, artisan, craftsman. 2. Inventor, contriver, maker.

artificial [ar-te-fe-the-ahl'], *a.* Artificial, made by art. **Fuegos artificiales**, fire works.

artificialidad [ar-te-fe-the-ah-le-dahd'], *f.* Artificiality.

artificializar [ar-te-fe-the-ah-le-thar], *va.* To make artificial.

artificialmente [ar-te-fe-the-al-men'-tay], *adv.* Artificially.

artificiero [ar-te-fe-the-ay'-ro], *m.* Explosives expert, bomb-disposal officer.

artificio [ar-te-fee'-the-o], *m.* 1. Art with which a thing is performed, workmanship, craft. 2. (*Met.*) Artifice, cunning, trick, guilefulness, contrivance, finesse, craft, fraud. 3. Machine which facilitates the exercise of some art.

artificiosamente [ar-te-fe-the-o-sah-men'-tay], *adv.* 1. Artificially. 2. Artful, craftily, fraudulently.

artificioso, sa [ar-te-fe-the-o'-so, sah], *a.* 1. Skilful, ingenious. 2. Artful, crafty, cunning, fraudulent.

artiga [ar-tee'-gah], *f.* Land newly broken up.

artigar [ar-te-ar'][, *va.* To break and level land before cultivation.

artillar [ar-teel-lyar'], *va.* To mount cannon.

artillería [ar-teel-lyah-ree'-dah], *f.* 1. Gunnery. 2. Artillery, cannon, piece or ordenance. 3. The division of the army assigned to this service. **Parque de artillería**, park of artillery. **Tren de artillería**, train of artillery. **Poner** *or* **asestar toda la artillería**, (*Met.*) to set all engines at work for obtaining something, to leave no stone unturned. **Artillería pesada**, heavy artillery. **Artillería antiaérea**, antiaircraft guns.

artillero [ar-teel-lyay'-ro], *m.* Gunner (aviones, barcos); artilleryman.

artimaña [ar-te-mah'-nyah], *f.* 1. Trap, snare, gin. 2. Device, stratagem, artifice, counterfeit, cunning.

artimón [ar-te-mone'], *m.* (*Naut.*) Mizzen-mast; sail of a galley.

artina [ar-tee'-nah], *f.* (*Prov.*) The fruit of the box-thorn.

artista [ar-tees'-tah], *m.* 1. Artist (pintor, escultor); artisan, tradesman, craftsmaster. **Artista de teatro**, artist, actor; actress (actriz). 2. He who studies logic, physics, or metaphysics.

artísticamente, *adv.* Artistically.

artístico, ca [ar-tees'-te-co, cah], *a.* Artistic, belonging to art.

artolas [ar-to'-las], *f. pl.* Pannier; a pack-saddle for two persons.

artólitos [ar-to'-le-tos], *m.* A concave stone of the nature of a sponge.

artos [ar'-tos], *m.* 1. Various species of thistles. 2. (*Prov.*) The box thorn. *V.* CAMBRONERA.

artrítico, ca [ar-tree'-te-co, cah], *a.* Arthritic, arthritical.

artritis [ar-tree'-tees], *f.* (*Med.*) Arthritis.

artrópodo [ar-tro'-po-do], *m. & a.* (*Zool.*) Arthropod.

artuña [ar-too'-nyah], *f.* A ewe whose lamb has perished.

Arturo [ar-too'-ro], *m.* 1. (*Astr.*) Arcturus, a fixed star of the first magnitude in the constellation Bootes. 2. Proper name, Arthur.

arugas [ar-oo'-gas], *f.* (*Bot.*) *V.* MATRICARIA. Feverfew.

aruñar [ah-roo'-nyar], *va. V.* ARAÑAR.

aruñazo [ah-roo'-nyah'-tho], *m.* A large scratch. *V.* ARAÑAZO.

aruño [ah-roo'-nyo], *m. V.* ARAÑO.

aruñón [ah-roo-nyon'], *m.* 1. A scratcher. 2. Pickpocket.

arúspice [ah-roos'-pe-thay], *m.* Augurer, soothsayer.

aruspicina [ah-roos-pe-thee'-nah], *f.* Aruspicy, divining from the intestines of animals.

arveja [ar-vay'-hah], *f.* (*Bot.*) Vetch, tare.

arvejal, arvejar [ar-vay-hahl', ar-vay-har'], *m.* Field sown with vetches.

arvejo [ar-vay'-ho], *m.* (*Bot.*) Bastard chick-pea, or Spanish pea.

arvejón [ar-vay-hone'], *m.* (*Bot.*) Chickling-vetch.

arvejona [ar-vay-ho'-nah], *f.* (*Prov.*) 1. *V.* ARVEJA. 2. *V.* ALGARROBA.

arvela [ar-vay-lah], *f.* A blue-feathered bird, the kingfisher.

arvense [ar-ven'-say], *a.* (*Bot.*) A term applied to all plants which grow in sown fields.

arza [ar'-thah], *f.* (*Naut.*) Fall of a tackle.

arzobispado [ar-tho-bis-pah'-do], *ml.* Archbishopric (dignidad, territorio). Archiepiscopate (dignidad, duración).

arzobispal [ar-tho-bis-pahl'], *a.* Archiepiscopal.

arzobispo [ar-tho-bees'-po], *m.* Archbishop.

arzolla [ar-thol'-lyah], *f.* (*Prov.*) *V.* ALMENDRUCO. 1. Lesser brudock, 2. Milk thistle.

arzón [ar-thone'], *m.* Fore and hind bow of a saddle, saddle-tree.

as [ahs], *m.* 1. Ace. 2. Roman copper coin.

asa [ah'-sah], *f.* 1. Handle, haft. 2. Vault made in the form of the handle of a basket. 3. **Asa dulce**, Gum benzoin, asa dulcis. 4. **Asafétida**, asafoetida, a gum resin. **Amigo del asa or ser muy del asa**, To afford or borrow a pretence. **En asas**, having the hands on the hips. **En asas**, a kimbo.

asacar [ah-sah-car'], *va.* 1. To impute, defame, vilify. 2. To invent, newly apply.

asadero, ra [ah-sah-day'-ro, rah], *a.* That which is fit for roasting. *-m. (Mex.)* A small, flat cheese made of the richest of the milk and by beating the curd while making it.

asado, da [ah-sah'-do, dah], *a.* Roasted; dressed. **Asado a la parrilla,** broiled; grilled. 2. *(LAm.)* Cross, angry. 3. *(Carib.)* To be broke. *-pp.* of ASAR.

asador [ah-sah-dor'], *m.* 1. A spit. 2. Jack, an engine which turns the spit. **Parece que come asadores,** he walks as stiffly as if he had swallowed a spit. 3. **Asador de bomba,** *(Naut.)* the pump-hook.

asadorazo [ah-sah-do-rah'-tho], *m.* Blow with a spit.

asadorcillo [ah-sah-dor-theel'-lyo], *m. dim.* Small spit.

asadura [ah-sah-doo'-rah], *f.* 1. Entrails of an animal, chitterlings. **Asadura de puerco,** hastet or harslet. 2. Laziness. **Tiene asaduras,** he's terribly lazy. 3. Stolid person.

asaeteador [ah-sah-ay-tay-ah-dor'], *m.* Archer, bow-man.

asaetear [ah-sah-ay-tay-ar'], *va.* To attack, wound, or kill with arrows.

asaetinado, da [ah-sah-ay-te-nah'-do, dah], *a.* Like satin (ropa).

asafétida [ah-sah-fay'-te-dah], *f.* Asafoetida, a gum resin, of fetid odor.

asainetado, da [ah-sah-e-nay-tah'-do, dah], *a.* That which ought to be serious, but seems farcical.

asalariado, da [ah-sah-lah-re-ah'-do, dah], *a.* Paid; wage-earning.

asalariar [ah-sah-lah-re-ar'], *va.* To give a fixed salary or pay.

asalmonado, da [ah-sal-mo-nah'-do, dah], *a. V.* SALMONADO.

asaltabancos [ah-sal-tah-ban'-cos], *m. & f.* Bank robber.

asaltador [ah-sal-tah-dor'], *m.* 1. Assailant, assaulter. 2. Highwayman.

asaltar [ah-sal-tar'], *va.* 1. To form an assault, to storm a place. **Le asaltaron 4 bandidos,** he was held up by 4 bandits. 2. To assail, to surprise, to fall upon. 3. To occur suddenly. **Le asaltó una idea,** he was struck by an idea.

asalto [ah-sahl'-to], *m.* 1. Assault against a place. 2. Assault, the act of offering violence to a person. 3. *(Met.)* A sudden gust of passion.

asamblea [ah-sam-blay'-ah], *f.* 1. Assembly, meeting (reunión), congress (congreso), junta, congregation, convention, gathering. 2. In the order of Malta, a tribunal established in every grand priory of the order. 3. A beat of the drum directing the soldiers to join their companies, or to assemble in the alarmplace.

asambleario, ria [ah-sam-blay-ah'-re-o], *m. & f.* Member of an assembly.

asapán [ah-sah-pahn'], *m. (Mex.)* Flying squirrel.

asar [ah-sar'], *va.* 1. To roast. **Asar al horno,** to bake. 2. *(fig.)* to pester, plague. 3. To shoot, gun down. *-vr.* To be excessively hot. **Me aso de calor,** I'm roasting.

asáraca, asarabácara, [ah-sah'-rah-cah], [ah-sah-rah-bah'-cah-rah] *f. (Bot.)* Wild ginger or nard, common asarabacca.

asarero [ah-sah-ray'-ro], *m. (Bot.) V.* ENDRINO.

asargado, da [ah-sar-gah'-do, dah], *a.* Serge-like, made in imitation of serge; twilled.

asarina [ah-sah-ree'-nah], *f. (Bot.)* Bastard asarum.

asaro [ah-sah'-ro], *m. V.* ASARABACAR *a.*

asascuarse [ah-sahs-coo-ahr'-say], *vr. (Mex.)* To roll up into a ball.

asativo, va [ah-sah-tee'-vo, vah], *a. (Pharm.)* Dressed or boiled in its own juice, without any other fluid.

asaz [ah-sath'], *adv. (Obs. Poet.)* Enough, abundantly.

asbestino, na [as-bes-tee'-no, nah], *a.* Belonging to asbestos.

asbesto [as-bes'-to], *m.* 1. Asbestos, a mineral, incombustible. 2. A sort of incombustible cloth made of the filaments of asbestos.

ascalonia [as-cah-lo'-ne-ah], *f.* A seed onion.

ascárides [as-cah'-re-des], *f. pl.* Ascarides, thread-worms in the rectum.

ascendencia [as-then-den'-the-ah], *f.* A line of ancestors, as parents, grandparents, etc.; family-tree; origin, original.

ascendente [as-then-den'-tay], *m.* 1. An ascendant. 2. Horoscope, the configuration of the planets at the hour of birth. *-pa.* Ascending.

ascender [as-then-derr'], *vn.* 1. To ascend, to mount, to climb. 2. To be promoted. **Fue ascendido a teniente,** he was promoted to lieutenant. 3. **Ascender a,** *(Com.)* to amount to.

ascendiente [as-then-de-en'-tay], *m. & f.* 1. An ancestor, forefather. 2. *m.* Ascendency, influence, power.

ascensión [as-then-se-on'], *f.* 1. Ascension, the act of mounting or ascending. 2. Feast of the ascension of Christ. 3. Exaltation to the papal throne. 4. Rising point of the equator.

ascensional [as-then-se-o-nahl'], *a. (Astr.)* Ascensional, that which belongs to the ascension of the planets, right or oblique.

ascesionista [as-thayn'-se-o-nest], *m. & f.* Balloonist

ascenso [as-then'-so], *m.* Promotion.

ascensor [as-then-sor'], *m.* Elevator, lift, hoist.

ascensorista [as-thayn-so-res-tah], *m. & f.* Elevator operator, lift attendant.

ascesis [as-thay'-ses], *f.* Asceticism.

asceta [as-thay'-tah], *m.* Ascetic, hermit.

asceticismo [as-thay-te-thees-mo], *m.* Asceticism.

ascético, ca [as-thay'-te-co, cah], *a.* Ascetic, employed wholly in exercises of devotion and mortification.

ascetismo, *m. V.* ASCETICISMO.

ascidio [as-thee'-de-o], *m. (Zool.)* An ascidian.

ascios [as'-the-os], *m. pl.* Ascii, people of the torrid zone, who, at certain times of the year, have no shadow at noon.

asciro [as-thee'ro], *m. (Bot.)* St. John's wort. St. Andrew's cross.

ascitis [as-thee'-tis], *f.* Ascites, dropsy of the abdominal cavity.

ascítico, ca [as-thee'-te-co, cah], *a.* Belonging to the ascites, ascitic.

asclepiada [as-clay-pe-ah'-dah], *f. (Bot.)* Swallow-wort.

asclepias [as-clay'-pe-as], *f.* Asclepias, milkweed or silkweed; type genus of the Asclepiadae.

asco [ahs'-co], *m.* Nausea, loathsomeness, quality of raising disgust. **Es un asco,** it is a mean, despicable thing. **Hacer ascos,** to excite loathsomeness, to turn the stomach. **Coger asco a algo,** to get sick of something. **Me dan asco las aceitunas,** I loathe olives.

ascua [ahs'-coo-ah], *f.* Red-hot coal. **Estar como ascua de oro,** to be shining bright. **Arrimar el ascua a sus sardina,** to look after number one. *V.* BRASA. *pl.* **Ascuas. Estar en ascuas,** to be very uneasy; to be upon thorns. **Estar hecho un ascua or echar ascuas,** to be flushed in the face by agitation or anger. **Tener a uno sobre ascuas,** to keep somebody on tenterhooks.

aseadamente [ah-say-ah-dah-men'-tay], *adv.* Cleanly, elegantly, neatly.

aseado, da [ah-say-ah'-do, dah], *a.* Clean, elegant, neatly finished. *-pp.* of ASEAR.

asear [ah-say-ar'], *va.* To wash (lavar), to clean (limpiar), to decorate (adornar), to tidy up (arreglar), to set off, to adorn, to embellish; to polish. *-vr.* To tidy oneself up (lavarse).

asechador [ah-say-chah-dor'], *m.* Insnarer, waylayer; plotter.

asechamiento [ah-say-chah-me-en'-to], *m.* **Asechanza** [ah-say-chahn'-thah], *f.* 1. Waylaying. 2. Artifice, trick, stratagem; plot, intrigue.

asechar [ah-say-char'], *va.* To waylay, to watch insidiously, to lie in wait, to lie in ambush.

asechoso, sa [ah-say-cho'-so, sah], *a. (Obs.)* Inclined to insidious artifices, intriguing.

asedado, da [ah-say-dah'-do, dah], *a.* Silky, that which resembles silk in softness and smoothness. *-pp.* of ASEDAR.

asedar [ah-say-dar'], *va. (Prov.)* To work flax and hemp so as to make it feel like silk (suavizar). To hackle (el cáñamo).

asediador, ra [as-say-de-ah-dor', rah], *m. & f.* Besieger, one who besieges or blockades.

asediar [ah-say-de-ar'], *va.* 1. To besiege, to lay siege to a strong place or fortress; to blockade. 2. *(fig.)* To bother, to pester.

asedio [ah-say'-de-o], *m.* A siege, a blockade.

aseglararse [ah-say-glah-rar'-say], *vr.* To secularize oneself, or to make oneself worldly (sacerdotes, clérigos).

asegún [ah-say-goon'], *adv. prep. (LAm.)* V. SEGÚN.

asegundar [ah-say-goon-dar'], *va.* To repeat with little or no intermission of time.

asegurable [ah-say-goo-rah'-blay], *a.* Insurable.

aseguración [ah-say-goo-rah-the-on'], *f.* 1. *(Obs.)* Security, safety. 2. Insurance.

asegurado, da [ah-say-goo-rah'-do, dah], *a.* 1. Assured, guaranteed. 2. Decided, fixed; anchored. *-m.* The insured.

asegurador, ra [ah-say-goo-rah-dor'], *m. & f.* Insurer, underwriter.

aseguradora [ah-say-goo-rah-do'-rah], *f.* Insurance company.

aseguramiento [ah-say-goo-rah-me-en'-to], *m.* 1. The act of securing; security, safe conduct. 2. Insurance.

asegurar [ah-say-goo-rar'], *va.* 1. To secure, to insure; to fasten, to fix firm. 2. To preserve, to shelter from danger. 3. To bail, to give security. 4. To state, to assert. **Se lo aseguro**, I assure you. 5. *(Com.)* To insure against the dangers of the seas of fire, or other risk. 6. To secure, by mortgage, the fulfilment of an obligation. *-vr.* To escape danger. To be certain of a thing. **Asegurar las velas**, to secure the sails. **Asegurarse de la altura**, to ascertain the degree of latitude in which we find ourselves. **Asegurar la bandera**, to salute the flag when raising it.

aseidad [ah-say-e-dahd'], *f.* Self-existence, an attribute of God.

aselarse [ah-say-lar'-say], *vr. (Prov.)* To make ready for passing the night (aves).

asemejar [ah-say-may-har'], *va.* To assimilate, to bring to a likeness or resemblance, to favor. *-vr.* To resemble, to be like another person or thing.

asendereado, da [ah-sen-day-ray-ah'-do, dah], *a.* Beaten, frequented (caminos, carreteras). *-pp.* of ASENDEREAR. Deserted, afflicted.

asenderear [ah-sen-day-ray-ar'], *va.* 1. To persecute, to pursue with vengeance and enmity. 2. To open a path.

asengladura [ah-sen-glah-doo'-rah], *f. (Naut.)* A day's run, the way a ship makes in twenty-four hours. *V.* SINGLADURA.

asenso [ah-sen'-so], *m.* Assent, consent, aquiescence, credence, credit.

asentada [ah-sen-tah'-dah], *f.* A stone ranged in its proper place. **De una asentada**, at once, at one sitting. **A asentadas**, *V.* A ASENTADILLAR.

asentaderas [ah-sen-tah-day'-ras], *f. pl. (coll.)* Buttocks, behind, bottom. *V.* NALGAS.

asentadillas (A) [ah-sen-tah-deel'-lyas], *adv.* Sitting on horseback, like a woman, with both legs on one side.

asentado, da [ah-sen-tah'-do, dah], *a. (Obs.)* 1. Seated, planted, situated (situado). 2. Clear, serene. **El hombre asentado ni capaz tendido, ni camisón curado**, idleness is the mother of vice. *-pp.* of ASENTAR.

asentador [ah-sen-tah-dor'], *m.* 1. *(Obs.)* A stone-mason, a stone-cutter. 2. Razor-strop. 3. Grinding slip; turning chisel.

asentadura [ah-sen-tah-doo'-rah], *f.*

asentamiento [ah-sen-tah-me-en'-to], *m.* 1. *(Law.)* Possession of goods given by a judge to the claimant or plaintiff for non-appearance of the defendant. 2. Establishment, settlement, residence. 3. *(Obs.)* Session. 4. *(Obs.)* Site.

asentar [ah-sen-tar'], *va.* 1. To place on a chair, or set; to cause to sit down. **Asentar el rancho**, to stop in any place or station to eat, to sleep, or to rest. 2. To suppose, to take for granted. 3. To affirm, to assure. 4. To adjust, to make an agreement. 5. To note, to take down in writing, to register. **Asentar al crédito de**, to place to one's credit. 6. To fix a thing in any particular place, to form, to adjust. 7. *(Law.)* To put a claimant or plaintiff in possession of the goods claimed for non-appearance of the respondent or defendant. 8. To assess. **Asentar bien su baza**, to establish one's character or credit. **Asentar casa**, to set up house for oneself. **Asentar con maestro**, to bind an aprentice to a master. **Asentar plaza**, to enlist in the army. *-vn.* 1. To fit (ropa). 2. To sit down. 3. To settle, to establish a residence (establecerse). *-vr.* 1. To subside (licores). 2. To perch or settle after flying (pájaros). 3. *(Arch.)* To sink, to give way under weight; to settle.

asentimiento [ah-sen-te-me-en'-to], *m.* Assent. *V.* ASENSO.

asentir [ah-sen-teer'], *vn.* To coincide in opinion with another; to acquiesce, to concede, to yield. **Asentir a la verdad de algo**, to recognize the truth of something.

asentista [ah-sen-tees'-tah], *m.* A contractor, one who contracts to supply the navy or army with provisions, ammunition, etc. **Asentista de construcción**, *(Naut.)* contractor for shipbuilding.

aseñorado [ah-say-nyo-rah-do], *a.* Lordly; dressed like a gentleman.

aseo [ah-say'-o], *m.* Cleanliness (limpieza), neatness (pulcritud). Bathroom, toilet (retrete, servicios). **Aseo personal**, personal toilet.

aséptico [ah-sayp'-te-co], *a.* Aseptic; germ-free.

asequible [ah-say-kee'-blay], *a.* Attainable, obtainable, that which may be acquired.

aserción [ah-ser-the-on'], *f.* Assertion, affirmation.

aserradero [ah-ser-rah-day'-ro], *m.* 1. A saw-pit. 2. Horse or wooden machine on which timber or other things are sawed.

aserradizo, za [ah-ser-rah-dee'-tho, thah], *a.* Proper to be sawed.

aserrado, da [ah-ser-rah'-do, dah], *a.* Serrate, serrated, dented, like a saw (plantas). *-pp.* of ASERRAR.

aserrador [ah-ser-rah-dor'], *m.* Sawer or sawyer.

aserradura [ah-ser-rah-doo'-rah], *f.* Sawing, the act of cutting timber with the saw; saw-cut, kerf. **Aserraduras**, Saw-dust.

aserrar [ah-ser-rar'], *va.* 1. To saw, to cut with a saw, to cut down. 2. *(Met. and coll.)* To saw, to play the violin badly. **Aserrar piedras en un molino**, to saw stones in a sawmill.

aserrido [ah-ser-ree'-do], *m.* Noisy, rasping respiration in diseases of the chest.

aserrín [ah-ser-reen'], *m.* Saw-dust.

asserruchar [ah-sayr-roo-chahr'], *va.* *(LAm.)* V. ASSERRAR.

asertivo, va [ah-ser-tee'-vo, vah], *a.* Assertive. *V.* AFIRMATIVO.

aserto[ah-ser'-to], *m. V.* ASERCION.

asertorio [ah-ser-to'-re-o], *a. V.* JURAMENTO. Affirmatory.

asesar [ah-say-sar'], *vn.* To become prudent, to acquire discretion.

asesina [ah-say-se'-nah], *f.* Murderess.

asesinado, da [ah-say-se-nah'-do,-dah], *m. & f.* Murder victim, murdered person.

asesinar [ah-say-se-nar'], *va.* 1. To assassinate, to kill treacherously. 2. To betray the confidence of another, to be guilty of a breach of trust.

asesinato [ah-say-se-nah'-to], *m.* 1. Assassination, murder. 2. Treachery, deceit, fraud.

asesino [ah-say-see'-no], *m.* 1. Assassin, murderer, cut-throat. 2. Impostor, cheat, one who practises fraud, and betrays the confidence of another. 3. Small spot of black silk which ladies put near the corner of the eye.

asesor, ra [ah-say-sor'-rah], *m. & f.* 1. A counseller, adviser, conciliator. **Asesor de imagen**, public-relations adviser. 2. Assessor. **Asesor jurídico**, legal adviser.

asesoramiento [ah-say-so-rah-me-ayn-to], *m.* Advice.

asesorar [ah-say-so-rahr'], *va.* To advise, to give legal advice to.

asesorarse [ah-say-so-rar'-say], *vr.* To take the assistance of counsel.

asesorato [ah-say-so-rah-to], *m. (LAm.)* 1. Advising. 2. Consultant's office.

asesoría [ah-say-so-ree'-ah], *f.* 1. Consultant's office (oficina). 2. Consultant's fee, (estipendio, honorarios).

asestador [ah-ses-tah-dor'], *m.* Gunner, who points the cannon.

asestadura [ah-ses-tah-doo'-rah], *f.* Aim, pointing cannon, or taking aim.

asestar [ah-ses-tar'], *va.* 1. To aim, to point, to level, to make after. **Asestar una puñalada a uno**, to stab somebody. 2. *(Met.)* To try to do some mischief to others.

aseveración [ah-say-vay-rah-the-on'], *f.* Asseveration, solemn affirmation.

aseveradamente [ah-say-vay-rah-dah-men'-tay], *adv. V.* AFIRMATIVAMENTE.

aseverar [ah-say-vay-rar'], *va.* To asseverate; to affirm with great solemnity, as upon oath.

asexuado [ah-sayc-soo-ah-do], *a.* Sexless.

asexual [ah-sec-soo-ahl'], *a.* Asexual.

asfaltado [as-fahl-tah'-do], 1. *a.* Asphalt, asphalted. **Caretera asfaltada**, asphalted road. 2. *m.* Asphalting.

asfaltar [as-fal-tar'], *va.* To apply or cover with asphalt, to asphalt.

asfáltico, ca [as-fahl'-te-co, cah], *a.* Of asphaltum; bituminous.

asfalto [as-fahl'-to], *m.* Asphaltum, a kind of bitumen.

asfíctico, ca [as-fic'-te-co, cah], *a.* Asphyxial, or asphyctic.

asfixia [as-fic'-se-ah], *f. (Med.)* Asphyxia, a disease.

asfixiador [as-fic-se-ah-do'], *a.* Suffocating.

asfixiante [as-fic-se-ahn'-tay], *a.* Asphyxiating. **Calor asfixiante**, suffocating heat.

asfixiar [as-fic-se-ar'], *va.* 1. To asphyxiate, suffocate. 2. **Estar asfixiado**, to be broke (dinero). *-vr.* To be asphyxiated, suffocated.

asfódelo [as-fo'-day-lo], *m.* Asphodel, day-lily. *V.* GAMON.

así [ah-see'], *adv.* 1. So, thus, in this manner. 2. Therefore, so that, also, equally. **Así bien**, as well, as much so, equally. **Así que**, so that, therefore. **Es así, o no es así**, thus it is, or it is not so. **Así fuera yo santo, como fulano es docto**, if I were as sure of being a saint, as he is learned. 3. Followed immediately by *como*, is equivalent to, in the same manner or proportion, as, **así como la modestia atrae, así se huye la disolución**, in the same proportion that modesty attracts, dissoluteness deters. But when the particle *como* is in the second part of the sentence, **así** is equal to so much. **Así, así**, So, so; middling. **Así que llegó la noticia**, as soon as the news arrived. **Así como así**, or **Así que así**, any way; it matters not. **Así que asá** or **asado**, any way; it makes no difference. **Así me estoy**, it is all the same to me. **Como así**, even so, just so, how so. **Así como así**, by all means. **Iremos así llueva a cántaros**, we'll go even if it pours down. **¿Cómo así?**, how's that? **Así sea**, let it be so.

Asia [ah'-se-ah], Asia.

asiano, na *a.* Asian.

asiático, ca [ah-se-ah'-te-co, cah], *a.* Asiatic.

asidero [ah-se-day'-ro], *m.* 1. Handle. 2. *(Met.)* Occasion, pretext. **Asideros**, *(Naut.)* Ropes with which vessels are hauled along the shore. 3. *(Cono Sur)* Basis, support.

asido, da [ah-see'-do, dah], *pp.* of ASIR. Seized, grasped, laid hold of. *a.* Fastened, tied, attached. **Fulano está asido a su propia opinión**, he is wedded to his own opinion. *(Yo asgo, tú ases; yo asga, from* ASIR*).*

asiduamente [ah-se'-doo-ah-mayn-tay], *adv.* Assiduously; frequently, regularly.

asiduidad [ah-se-doo-e-dahd'], *f.* Assiduity, assiduousness.

asiduo, dua [ah-see'-doo-o, ah], *a.* Assiduous, laborious. **Parroquiano asiduo**, regular customer. **Era un asiduo del café**, he was a regular customer of the coffee-shop.

asiento [ah-se-en'-to], *m.* 1. Chair. **Asiento trasero**, rear seat. 2. Seat in a tribunal or court of justice. 3. Spot on which a town or building is or was standing; site. 4. Solidity of a building resulting from the reciprocal pressure of the materials upon each other: settling. 5. Bottom of a vessel. 6. Sediment of liquors. 7. Treaty. 8. Contract for supplying an army, town, etc., with provisions, etc. 9. Entry, the act of registering or setting down in writing. 10. Judgment, prudence, discretion. 11. District of the mines in South America. 12. List, roll. 13. Sort of pearls, flat on one side and round on the other. 14. Surfeit, fit of indigestion. 15. The state and order which things ought to take. **Hombre de asiento**, a prudent man. **Asientos de popa**, *(Naut.)* stern seats in the cabin. **Asiento de molino**, bed or lowest stone in a mill. **Dar** or **tomar asiento en las cosas**, to let things take a regular course. (**Yo asiento, yo asienta**, from **Asentir**. *V.* ASENTIR). (*Yo asiento, yo asiente, from* **Asentar**. *V.* ACERTAR).

asignable [ah-sig-nah'-blay], *a.* Assignable.

asignación [ah-sig-nah-the-on'], *f.* 1. Assignation. 2. Distribution, partition. 3. Destination. **Asignación de bus**, bus allocation.

asignado [ah-sig-nah'-do], *m.* Assignat: paper money issued by France in 1790. *-pp.* of ASIGNAR.

asignar [ah-sig-nar], *va.* To assign, to mark out, to determine, to ascribe, to attribute.

asignatario, ria [ah-seg-nah-ta'-re-o], *f. (LAm.)* Heir, legatee.

asignatura [ah-sig-nah-too'-rah], *f.* Subject (disciplina). **Aprobé cinco asignaturas y suspendí una**, I passed five subjects and failed one.

asigunas [ah-se-goo'-nahs], *f. & pl.* **Según asigunas** *(Carib.)*, it all depends.

asilado, da [ah-se-lah-do, dah], *m. & f.* Inmate, refugee.

asilar [ah-se-lahr'], *va.* To take in, to give shelter. Put into a home. *-vr.* To take refuge, to seek political asylum. To enter a home.

asilo [ah-see'-lo], *m.* 1. Asylum, sanctuary, place of shelter and refuge. **Derecho de asilo**, right of sanctuary. 2. Harborage. 3. *(Met.)* Protection, support, favor. 4. *(Ent.)* Asilus, a genus of large and voracious diptera; represented by the bee-killer and robber-fly.

asilla [ah-seel'-lyah], *f. dim.* 1. A small handle. 2. A slight pretext. *-pl.* 1. The collar-bones of the breast. 2. Small hooks or keys employed in the different parts of an organ.

asimesmo [ah-se-mes'-mo], *adv. (Obs.) V.* ASIMISMO.

asimetría [ah-se-may-tree'-ah], *f.* Lack of symmetry, asymmetry.

asimétrico, ca [ah-se-may'-tre-co, cah], *a.* Asymmetrical, out of proportion.

asimiento [ah-se-me-en'-to], *m.* 1. Grasp, the act of seizing or grasping. 2. Attachment, affection.

asimilable [ah-se-me-lah'-blay], *a.* Assimilable; capable of assimilation.

asimilación [ah-se-me-lah-the-on'], *f.* Assimilation.

asimilar [ah-se-me-lar'], *vn.* To resemble, to be like. *-va.* To assimilate; to convert into living tissue.

asimilativo, va [ah-se-me-lah-tee'-vo, vah], *a.* Assimilating, having the power of rendering one thing like another.

asimismo [ah-se-mees'-mo], *adv.* Exactly so, in the same manner, likewise (del mismo modo).

asimplado, da [ah-sim-plah'-do, dah], *a.* Like a simpleton, or silly person.

asín, asina [ah-seen', ah-see'-nah], *adv. (Low.) V.* ASI.

asinarias [ah-se-nah'-re-as], *f. pl.* Birds, in Brazil, which are very ugly, and whose voice resembles the braying of an ass.

asindeton [ah-seen'-day-tone], *m.* Asyndeton, a figure of speech in which conjunctions are supressed to give liveliness to the style.

asinino, na [ah-se-nee'-no, nah], *a.* Asinine, ass-like.

asíntota [ah-seen'-to-tah], *f. (Geom.)* Asymptote.

asir [ah-seer'], *va. & vn.* 1. To grasp or seize with the hand, to lay hold of. 2. To hold, to gripe, to come upon. 3. To strike or take root. -*vr.* To dispute, to contend, to rival. **Asirse de alguna cosa**, to avail oneself of an opportunity to do or say something.

asiriano, na or **asirio, ria** [ah-se-re-ah'-no, nah, ah-see'-re-o, ah], *a.* Assyrian.

asisia [as-see'-se-ah], *f. (Law. Arab.)* 1. Part of law proceedings containing the depositions of witnesses. 2. Court of assizes.

asisito [as-see-se-to], *adv. (And. etc.) V.* ASÍ.

asísmico [ah-ses'-me-co], *a. (LAm.)* **Construcción asísmica**, earthquake-resistant building.

asisón [ah-se-sone'], *m. (Prov.)* Bird belonging to the family of *francolins.*

asistencia [ah-sis-ten'-the-ah], *f.* 1. Actual presence. 2. Reward gained by personal attendance. 3. Assistance, favor, aid, help, comfort, furtherance. **La asistencia es obligatoria**, assistance is compulsory. **Asistencias**, allowance made to any one for his maintenance and support; alimony. **Se alquila un cuarto amueblado, con asistencia o sin ella**, to rent a furnished room, with or without board. **Hónreme Vd. con su asistencia**, please, honor me with your company (presencia).

asistencia social [ah-sis-ten'-the-ah, so-thee-ahl'], *f.* Social work, social service.

asistenta [ah-sis-ten'-tah], *f.* 1. Charwoman, charlady, daily help (criada no permanente). Assistant (convento). Chambermaid (en un palacio). **Asistenta social**, welfare worker.

asistente [ah-sis-ten'-ta], *p a. & m.* 1. Assistant, helper, helpmate. 2. The chief officer of justice in Seville. 3. The soldier who attends an officer as a servant, an orderly.

asistido, da [ah-ses-te'-do, dah], *a. m. & f.* **Asistido por ordenador**, computer assisted.

asistir [ah-sis-teer'], *vn.* 1. To be present, to assist, to attend (clase). 2. To live in a house, or frequent it much. -*va.* 1. To accompany one in the execution of some public act. **No asistió a la clase**, he did not attend the class. 2. To minister, to further, to countenance. 3. To serve or act provisionally in the room of another. 4. To attend a sick person. **El médico que le asiste**, the doctor who attends him.

asma [ahs'-mah], *f.* Asthma.

asmático, ca [as-mah'-te-co, cah], *a.* Asthmatic, troubled with asthma.

asna [ahs'-nah], *f.* A she-ass, jenny. **Asnas**, rafters of a house.

asnacho [as-nah'-cho], *m. (Bot.) V.* GATUÑA.

asnada [as-nah'-dah], *f.* A foolish action.

asnado [as-nah'-do], *m.* Large piece of timber with which the sides and shafts in mines are secured.

asnal [as-nahl'], *a.* 1. Asinine. 2. Brutal.

asnales [as-nah'-les], *m. pl.* Stockings larger and stronger than the common sort.

asnalmente [as-nal-men'-tay], *adv.* 1. Foolishly. 2. Mounted on an ass.

asnallo [as-nahl'-lyo], *m. (Bot.) V.* GATUÑA.

asnaucho, cha [as-nah'-oo-cho], *m.* A sort of very sharp pepper of South America.

asnazo [as-nah'-tho], *m. aug.* 1. A large jackass. 2. *(Met.)* A brutish, ignorant fellow.

asnear [as-nay-ahr'], *vn. (LAm.)* To act the fool.

asnería [as-nay-ree'-ah], *f. (coll.)* Stud of asses. *V.* ASNADA.

asnerizo, asnero [as-nay-ree'-tho, as-nay'-ro], *m. (Obs.)* Asskeeper.

asnico, ca [as-nee'-co, cah], *m. & f.* 1. *(dim.)* A little ass. 2. *(Prov.)* Irons at the end of a fire-grate in which the spit turns.

asnilla [as-neel'-lyah], *f.* Stanchion or prop which supports a ruinous building.

asnillo, lla [as-neel'-lyo, layh], *m. & f. dim.* A little ass. *Asnillo*, field-cricket.

asnino, na [as-nee'-no, nah], *a. (coll.)* resembling an ass.

asno [ahs'-no], *m.* 1. An ass. 2. *(Met.)* A dull, stupid, heavy fellow. **Asno de muchos, lobos le comen**, everybody's business is nobody's business. **Cada asno con su tamaño**, birds of a feather flock together. **No se hizo la miel para la boca del asno**, it is not for asses to lick honey, we should not throw pearls before swine.

asobinarse [ah-so-be-nar'-say], *vr.* To fall down with a burden (bestias de carga).

asocarronado, da [ah-so-car-ro-nah'-do, dah], *a.* Crafty, cunning, waggish.

asociación, *f.* **asociamiento,** *m.* [ah-so-the-ah-the-on', ah-so-the-ah-me-en'-to], association; fellowship, copartnership; knot. Union.

asociado [ah-so-the-ah'-do], *m.* Associate; comrade. *(Com.)* Partner. -*pp.* of ASOCIAR.

asociar [ah-so-the-ar'], *va.* To associate, to unite with another as a confederate, to conjoin. -*vr.* To accompany, to consociate, to consort, to herd. **Asociarse con uno**, to team up with somebody.

asocio [ah-so'-the-o], *m. (LAm.)* **En asocio**, in association.

asolación, asoladura [ah-so-lah-the-on', ah-so-lah-doo'-rah], *f.* Desolation, devastation.

asolador, ra [ah-so-lah-dor', rah], *m. & f.* A destroyer, desolater.

asolamiento [ah-so-lah-me-en'-to], *m.* Depopulation, destruction, havoc.

asolanar [ah-so-lah-nar'], *va.* To parch or dry up (vientos).

asolapar [ah-so-lah-par'], *V.* SOLAPAR.

asolar [ah-so-lar'], *va.* To level with the ground, to destroy, to waste, to harrow, to pillage, to devastate. -*vr.* To settle and get clear (licores).

asoldar, or **asoldadar** [ah-sol-dar'], *va.* To hire (mercenarios).

asoleado, da [ah-so-lay-ah'-do, dah], *a.* 1. Sunny. 2. Suntanned. Stupid (persona).

asolear [ah-so-lay-ar'], *va.* To sun, to expose to the sun. -*vr.* To be sunburnt. *(Cono Sur, Mex.)* To get sunstroke. *(CAm.)* To get stupid.

asoleo [ah-so'-lay-o], *m. (Mex.)* Sunstroke.

asolvamiento [ah-sol-vah-me-en'-to], *m.* Stoppage, the act of stopping.

asolvarse [ah-sol-var'-say], *vr.* To be stopped (tuberías, canales). *V.* AZOLVAR.

asomado, da [ah-so-mah'-do, dah], *a.* Fuddled. -*pp.* of ASOMAR.

asomadero [ah-so-mah-day'-ro], *m. (And.)* Viewing point.

asomar [ah-so-mar'], *vn.* 1. To begin to appear, to become visible. **Asoma el día**, the day begins to peep. 2. *(Naut.)* To loom. -*va.* To show a thing, to make it appear. **Asomé la cabeza a la ventana**, I poked my head out of the window. -*vr.* To be flustered with wine. To show, appear. Show up. **Ella estaba asomada a la ventana**, she was leaning out of the window.

asombradizo, za [ah-som-brah-dee'-tho, thah], *a.* Fearful, timid, easily frightened.

asombrador, ra [ah-som-brah-dor', rah], *m. & f.* Terrifier, one who frightens. Amazing.

asombramiento [ah-som-bra-me-en'-to], *m. V.* ASOMBRO.

asombrar [ah-som-brar'], *va.* 1. To shade, to darken, to obscure, to overshadow. 2. To frighten, to terrify. 3. To astonish, to cause admiration. **No deja de asombrarme**, it never ceases to amaze me. -*vr.* To take fright. To be astonished. **Asombrarse de saber algo**, to be surprised to learn something.

asombro [ah-som'-bro], *m.* 1. Dread, fear, terror. 2. Amazement, astonishment, high admiration.

asombrosamente [ah-som-bro-sah-men'-tay], *adv.* Amazingly, wonderfully, marvellously.

asombroso, sa [ah-som-bro'so, sah], *a.* Wonderful, astonishing, marvellous.

asomo [ah-so'-mo], *m.* 1. Mark, token, sign. 2. Supposition, conjecture, surmise. **Ni por asomo**, not in the least, by no means.

asonada [ah-so-nah'-dah], *f.* Tumultuous hostility.

asonancia [ah-so-nahn'-the-ah], *f.* 1. Assonance, consonance. A peculiar kind of rhyme, in which the last accented vowel and those which follow it in one word correspond in sound with the vowels of another word, while the consonants differ: as *cálamo* and *plátano*. 2. Harmony or connection of one thing with another.

asonantar [ah-so-nan-tar'], *va. (Poetic.)* To mix assonant with consonant, verses in Spanish poetry, which is inadmissible in modern verse.

asonante [ah-so-nahn'-tay], *a.* Assonant, last word in a Spanish verse whose vowels are the same, beginning with that in which the accent is, as those of the other word, with which it must accord.

asonar [ah-so-nar'], *vn.* 1. To be assonant, to accord. 2. To unite in riots and tumultuous assemblies.

asordar [ah-sor-dar'], *va.* To deafen with noise.

asorocharse [ah-so-ro-chahr-say], *vr. (And. Cono Sur)* To get mountain sickness.

asosegar, *va.* **Asosegarse**, *vr. V.* SOSEGAR.

asotanar [ah-so-tah-nar'], *va.* To vault, to make vaults or arched cellars.

aspa [ahs'-pah], *f.* 1. A cross. A reel, a turning frame. 3. Wings of a wind-mill. 4. Cross stud, diagonal stays. *(Naut.)* Cross gore, bentinck shrouds. Knitting-bar. **Aspa de cuenta**, a clock-reel. **Aspa de San Andrés**, colored cross on the yellow cloaks of penitents by the Inquisition.

aspadera [as-pah-day'-rah], *f. (Mech.)* A reel.

aspado, da [as-pah'-do, dah], *a.* 1. Having the arms extended in the form of a cross, by way of penance or mortification. 2. *(Met.)* Having one's arms confined, and their movements obstructed by tight clothes. *-pp.* of ASPAR.

aspador [as-pah-dor'], *m.* A reel.

aspador, ra [as-pah-dor', rah], *m. & f.* Reeler, one who reels yarn, thread, or silk.

aspalato [as-pah-lah'-to], *m. (Bot.)* Rosewood, aspalathus.

aspalto [as-pahl'-to], *m.* 1. Asphalt. 2. *V.* ESPALTO.

aspamentero [as-pah-mayn-tay'-ro], *a. (Cono Sur. Mex.) V.* ASPAVENTERO.

aspar [as-par'], *va.* 1. To reel, to gather yarn off the spindle, and form it into skeins. 2. To crucify. 3. *(Met.)* To vex or mortify. **Asparse a gritos**, to hoot, to cry out with vehemence. *-vr.* To writhe. *(fig.)* To do one's utmost.

aspaventero, ra [as-pah-vayn-tay'-ro, rah], *a. m. & f.* Excitable, emotional; fussy.

aspaviento [as-pah-ve-en'-to], *m.* 1. Exaggerated dread, fear, consternation. 2. Astonishment, admiration, expressed in confused and indistinct words. **Aspavientos**, boasts, brags, bravadoes.

aspecto [as-pec'-to], *m.* 1. Sight, appearance; **un hombre de aspecto feroz**, a man with a fierce look, appearance. 2. Look, aspect, countenance. 3. *(Arch.)* Situation or position of a building with reference to the cardinal points; outlook. 4. *(Astr.)* Relative position of stars and planets. **A primer aspecto** or **al primer aspecto**, at first sight. **Tener buen o mal aspecto**, to have a good or bad aspect; to be in a good or bad state.

ásperamente [ash'-pay-rah-men-tay], *adv.* Rudely, in a harsh manner, grumly, crabbedly, abruptly, obdurately, gruffly.

asperear [as-pay-ray-ar'], *vn.* To be rough and acrid to the taste. *-va. (Obs.)* To exasperate, to irritate.

asperete [as-pay-ray'-tay], *m. V.* ASPERILLO.

aspereza, asperidad [as-pay-ray'-thah, as-pay-re-dahd'], *f.* 1. Asperity; acerbity, acrimony, gall, keenness. **Contestar con aspereza**, to answer with asperity. 2. Roughness, ruggedness, inequality or unevenness of the ground, craggedness, gruffness. 3. Austerity, sourness, gruffness, harshness of temper, snappishness, moroseness.

asperges [ahs-per-hess]. Sprinkling. **Quedarse asperges**, To be disappointed in one's expectations; not to understand a thing.

asperiego, ga [as-pay-re-ay'-go, gah], *a.* Applied to a sour apple of the pippin kind.

asperilla [as-pay-reel'-lyo], *m.* The sourish taste of unripe fruit and other things.

asperillo, lla [as-pay-reel'-lyo, lyah], *a. dim.* Tart, sourish.

asperjar [as-per-har'], *va.* To sprinkle.

áspero, ra [ahs'-pay-ro, rah], *a.* 1. Rough, rugged, cragged, grained, knotty; horrid. 2. *(Met.)* Harsh and unpleasing to the taste or ear; acerb; hard; crabbed. 3. *(Met.)* Severe, rigid, austere, gruff, crusty. **Áspera arteria**. *V.* TRAQUIARTERIA.

asperón [as-pay-rone'], *m.* Grindstone; flag-stone; holystone.

aspérrimo, ma [as-per'-re-mo, mah], *a.* Sup. of ASPERO.

aspersión [as-per-se-on'], *f.* Aspersion, the act of sprinkling. *(Agri.)* Spray; **riego por aspersión**, watering by spray.

aspersorio [as-per-so'-re-o], *m.* Water-sprinkler; instrument with which holy water is sprinkled in the church.

áspid, áspide [ahs'-pid, ahs',pe-day], *m.* Asp, aspic, a small kind of serpent.

aspidistra [as-pe-des-trah], *f.* Aspidistra.

aspillera [as-pel-lyay'-rah], *f.* Loop-hole, embrasure, crenel.

aspiración [as-pe-rah-the-on'], *f.* 1. Aspiration. 2. Inspiration, the act of drawing in the breath. 3. Aspiration, pronunciation of a vowel with full breath. 4. *(Mus.)* A short pause which gives only time to breathe.

aspirada, do [as-pe-rah'-dah], *a & f.* Aspirate.

aspirador [as-pe-rah-dor'], 1. *a.* Suction; **bomba aspirador**, suction pump. 2. *m.* **Aspirador de polvo**, vacuum cleaner.

aspiradora [as-pe-rah-do'-rah], *f.* Vacuum cleaner.

aspirante [as-pe-rahn'-tay], *pa.* 1. Aspirant, neophyte. **Aspirante de marina**, naval cadet. 2. **Bomba aspirante**, suction pump.

aspirar [as-pe-rar'], *va.* 1. To inspire the air, to draw in the breath. 2. To aspire, to covet. 3. To pronounce a vowel with full breath. *-vn.* **Aspirar a algo**, to aspire to something. **El que no sepa eso que no aspire a aprobar**, whoever doesn't know that can have no hope of passing.

aspiratorio, ria [as-pe-ra-to'-re-o, ah], *a.* Proper to inspiration, or what produces it.

aspirina [as-pe-ree'-nah], *f.* Aspirin.

aspisera [as-pe-say'-rah], *f. V.* ALPISTERA.

aspudo [as-poo'-doh], *a. (Cono Sur)* Big-horned.

asquear [as-kay-ar'], *va.* To nauseate, to sicken, to turn the stomach. **Me asquean las ratas**, I loathe rats. *-vr.* To be nauseated, feel disgusted.

asquerosamente [as-kay-ro-sah-men'-tay], *adv.* Nastily, nauseously, foully, filthily.

asquerosidad [as-kay-ro-se-dahd'], *f.* Nastiness, filthiness, fulsomeness. Obscenity.

asqueroso, sa [as-kay-ro'-so, sah], *a.* 1. Nasty, filthy, nauseous, impure. 2. Loathsome, fastidious, disgusting, squeamish, fulsome. **Una comida asquerosa**, a revolting meal. **Tienes unas manos asquerosas**, your hands are filthy. 3. Dirty, squalid. 4. Disgusting (conductas). 5. Vile, loathesome (muy malo).

asquia [ahs'-ke-ah], *f. (Zool.)* A kind of grayling or umber, a delicate freshwater fish.

asquiento [as-ke-ayn'-to], *a.* 1. *(And.)* Fussy. 2. *V.* ASQUEROSO.

asta [ahs'-tah], *f.* 1. Lance. 2. Part of the deer's head which bears the antlers; horn. 3. Handle of a pencil, brush. 4. *(Naut.)* Staff or light pole erected in different parts of the ship, on which the colors are displayed. 5. *(Mas.)* Binder, curb-stone. Shank of a tool; shaft, spindle. **Asta de bandera de popa**, ensign-staff. **Asta de bandera de proa**, jack-staff. **Asta de tope**, flag-staff. **Asta de bomba**, pump-spear. **Astas**, horns of animals, as bulls, etc. **Darse de las astas**, to snap and carp at cach other.

astabandera [as-tah-bahn-day'-rah], *f. (LAm.)* Flagstaff, flagpole.

ástaco [ahs'-tah-co], *m.* Lobster, crayfish, or crawfish.

astado, astero [as-tah'-do, as-tay-ro], *m.* Roman pikeman or lancer.

astático, ca [as-tah'-te-co, cah], *a.* Astatic, in equilibrium.

astear [as-tay-ahr'], *va. (Cono Sur)* To gore.

astenia [as-tay-ne-ah], *f.* Asthenia, physical debility.

asténico, ca [as-tay'-ne-co, cah], *a. (Med.)* Asthenic.

aster [as-ter'], *m. (Bot.)* Starwort.

asteria [as-tay'-re-ah], *f.* 1. Star-stone, a kind of precious stone. 2. Cat's eye, a sort of false opal.

asterisco [as-tay-rees'-co], *m.* 1. An asterisk, a mark in printing. **Señalar con un asterisco**, to asterisk. 2. *(Bot.)* Oxeye.

asteroide [as-tay-ro'-e-day], *m.* Asteroid, a telescopie planet, of a group between Mars and Jupiter.

astigmático [as-teg-mah'-te-co], *a.* Astigmatic.

astigmatismo [as-tig-mah-tees'-mo], *m. (Med.)* Astigmatism.

astil [as-teel'], *m.* 1. Handle of an axe, hatchet, etc. 2. Shaft of an arrow. 3. Beam of a balance. 4. *(Obs.)* Anything which serves to support another.

astilejos [as-te-lay'-hos], *m. pl. V.* ASTILLEJOS.

astilico [as-te-lee'-co], *m. dim.* A small handle.

astilla [as-teel'-lyah], *f.* 1. Chip of wood, splinter of timber. **Hacer algo astillas**, to smash something into little pieces. 2. *(Obs.)* Reed or comb of a loom. 3. **Astilla muerta de un bajel**, *(Naut.)* the dead rising of the floor-timbers of a ship. **De tal palo, tal astilla**, or **astilla del mismo palo**, a chip of the same block. **Sacar astilla**, to profit by a thing.

astillar [as-teel-lyar'], *va.* To chip, to splinter. *-vr.* To splinter, to shatter.

astillazo [as-teel-lyah'-tho], *m.* 1. Crack, the noise produced by a splinter being torn from a block. 2. *(Met.)* The damage which results from an enteprise to those who have not been its principal authors and promoters.

astillejos [as-teel-lyay'-hos], *m. pl. (Astr.)* Castor and Pollux, two brilliant stars.

astillero [as-teel-lyay'-ro], *m.* 1. Rack on which lances, spears, pikes, etc., are placed. 2. Shipwright's yard, dockyard. **Poner en astillero**, *(Met.)* to place one in an honorable post.

astracán [as-trah-kahn'], *m.* Karakul.

astracanada [as-trah-cah-nah-dah], *f.* Silly thing; piece of buffoonery.

astrágalo [as-trah'-gah-lo], *m.* 1. *(Arch.)* Astragal, an ornament at the tops and bottoms of columns. 2. *(Mil.)* A kind of ring or moulding on a piece of ordenance. 3. *(Bot.)* Milkvetc. 4. *(Anat.)* Astragalus, the anklebone, articulating with the tibia. 5. Round moulding; beads.

astral [as-trahl'], *a.* Astral, that which belongs to the stars.

astrancia [as-trahn'-the-ah], *f. (Bot.)* Master-wort.

astreñir [as-tray-nyr'], *V.* ASTRINGIR.

astricción, astringencia [as-tric-the-on', as-trin-hen'-the-ah], *f.* Astriction, compression.

astrictivo, va [as-tric-tee'-vo, vah], *a.* Astrictive, styptic.

astricto, ta [as-treec'-to, tah], *a.* 1. Contracted, compressed. 2. Determined, resolved. *-pp. irr.* of ASTRINGIR.

astrífero, ra [as-tree'-fay-ro, rah], *(Poetic.)* Starry, full of stars.

astrilla [as-tre'-lyah], *f. (Cono Sur) V.* ASTILLA.

astringencia [as-trin-hen'-the-ah], *f.* Astringency, constriction.

astringente [as-trin-hen'-tay], *a.* Astringent.

astringir [as-trin-heer'], *a.* To astringe, to contract, to compress; *(Med.)* To bind.

astro [ahs'-tro], *m.* 1. Luminous body of the heavens, such as the sun, moon and stars. 2. Illustrious persons of uncommon merit.

astrobiología [as-tro-be-o-lo-hee'-ah], *f.* Astrobiology.

astrofísica [as-tro-fee'-se-cah], *f.* Astrophysics.

astrofísico, ca [as-tro-fe'-se-co], *m. & f.* Astrophysicist.

astrografía [as-tro-grah-fee'-ah], *f.* Astrography, the science of describing the stars.

astroite [as-tro'-e-tay], *m.* Astroite, a radiated fossil.

astrolabio [as-tro-lah'-be-o], *m.* Astrolabe, an instrument chiefly used for taking the altitude of stars at sea, now disused. Sextant.

astrología [as-tro-lo-hee'-ah], *f.* Astrology.

astrológico, ca, astrólogo, ga [as-tro-lo'-he-co, cah, as-tro'-lo-go, gah], *a.* Astrological, that which belongs to astrology.

astrólogo [as-tro'-lo-go], *m.* Astrologer.

astronauta [as-tro-nah'-oo-tah], *m. & f.* Astronaut.

astronáutica [as-tro-nah'-oo-te-cah], *f.* Astronautics, space travel.

astronave [as-tro-nah'-vay], *f.* Spaceship.

astronavegación [as-tro-nah-vay-gah-the-on'], *f.* Astronavigation.

astronomía [as-tro-no-mee'-ah], *f.* Astronomy.

astronómicamente [as-tro-no'-me-cah-men-tay], *adv.* Astronomically.

astronómico, ca [as-tro-no'-me-co, cah], *a.* Astronomical, that which belongs to astronomy.

astrónomo, ma [as-tro'-no-mo], *m. & f.* Astronomer.

astroso [as-tro'-so], *a.* 1. Ill-fated, unfortunate. 2. Contemptible. 3. Dirty; untidy.

astucia [as-too'-the-ah], *f.* Cunning, craft, finesse, slyness. **Actuar con astucia**, to act cunningly.

asturión [as-too-re-on'], *m.* 1. A pony, a small horse. 2. *(Zool.) V.* SOLLO.

astutamente [as-too-tah-men'-tay], *adv.* Cunningly, craftily, feigningly, jesuitically.

astuto, ta [as-too'-to, tah], *a.* Astute, cunning, sly, crafty, fraudulent.

asueto [ah-soo-ay'-to], *m.* Holiday for schoolboy and students, vacation. **Día de asueto**, day off.

asumir [ah-soo-meer'], *va.* 1. To take to, or for oneself, or take for granted; assume. 2. To raise by election or acclamation to certain dignities. *-vr. V.* ARROGARSE.

asunceño, ña [ah-soon-thay'-nyo], *(Cono Sur) a. m. & f.* From Asunción.

Asunción [ah-soon-the-on'], *f.* 1. Assumption. 2. Elevation to a higher dignity. 3. Ascent of the Holy Virgin to heaven. 4. Assumption, the thing supposed, a postulate.

asunto [ah-soon'-to], *m.* Subject, the matter or thing treated upon; affair, business. **El asunto está concluido**, the matter is closed. **Asunto de honor**, affair of honor. 2. Study, attention. 3. *(Cono Sur)* **¿ A asunto de qué lo hiciste?**, why did you do it? *-pl.* **Asuntos**, effects, business, stock.

asurar [ah-soo-rahr], *va.* (Culin. etc.) To burn; to burn up.

asuramiento [ah-soo-rah-me-en'-to], *m.* The act of burning, and the state of being burnt: applied only to ragouts, and to the corn before it is reaped.

asurarse [ah-soo-rar'-say], *vr.* 1. To be burnt in the pot or pan (carne). 2. To be parched with drought.

asurcano, na [ah-soor-cah'-no, nah], *a.* Neighboring: said of lands which adjoin, and their tillers.

asurcar [ah-soor-car'], *va.* To furrow sown land, in order to kill the weeds. *V.* SURCAR.

asuso [ah-soo'-so], *adv. (Obs.)* Upward, above.

asustadizo, za [ah-soos-tah-dee'-tho, thah], *a.* Applied to a person easily frightened.

asustar [ah-soos-tar'], *va.* To frighten, to terrify. *-vr.* To be frightened. **Asustarse de o por algo**, to be frightened at something, get alarmed about something. **¡No te asustes!**, don't be alarmed.

asusto [ah-soos-to], *m. (And.) V.* SUSTO.

A. T. *abr. de* **Antiguo Testamento** (Old Testament).

atabaca [ah-tah-bah'-cah], *f. (Bot.)* Groundsel. *V.* OLIVARDA.

atabacado, da [ah-tah-bah-cah'-do, dah], *a.* Having the color of tobacco.

atabal [ah-tah-bahl'], *m.* 1. Kettledrum. 2. *V.* ATABALERO.

atabalear [ah-tah-bah-lay-ar'], *vn.* To imitate the noise of kettledrums (caballos).

atabalejo, atabalete, atabalillo [ah-tah-bah-lay'-ho, etc.], *m. dim.* A small kettle-drum.

atabalero [ah-tah-bah-lay'-ro], *m.* Kettle-drummer.

atabanado, da [ah-tah-bah-nah'-do, dah], *a.* Spotted white (caballos).

atabardillado, da [ah-tah-bar-deel-lyah'-do, dah], *a.* Applied to diseases of the nature of spotted fevers.

atable [ah-tah'-bay], *m.* A small vent or air-hole left in water-pipes.

atabernado, da [ah-tah-ber-nah'-do, dah], *a.* Retailed in taverns (licores).

atabillar [ah-tah-beel-lyar'], *va.* To fold a piece of cloth so that the selvages are open to view on both sides.

atabladera [ah-tah-blah-day'-rah], *f.* A kind of roller or levelling board to level land sown with corn.

atablar [ah-tah-blar'], *va.* To level land sown with corn by means of a levelling board.

atacable [ah-tah-cah'-blay], *a.* Attackable, assailable.

atacadera [ah-tah-cah-day'-rah], *f.* Rammer used in splitting stones with gunpowder.

atacado, da [ah-tah-cah'-do, dah], *a.* 1. *(Met.)* Irresolute, inconstant, undecided. 2. *(Met.)* Close, miserable, narrow-minded. **Calzas atacas**, breeches formerly worn in Spain. **Hombre de calzas atacadas**, a strict and rigid observer of old customs. *-pp.* of ATACAR.

atacador [ah-tah-cah-dor'], *m.* 1. Aggressor, he that invades or attacks. 2. Ramrod or rammer for a gun.

atacadura, *f.* **atacamiento,** *m.* [ah-tah-cah-doo'-rah, ah-tah-cah-me-en'-to], Stricture, act and effect of tightening.

atacamita [ah-tah-cah-mee'-tah], *f.* *(Miner.)* Native oxychloride of copper.

atacante [ah-tah-chan'-tay], *m. & f.* Attacker, assailant.

atacar [ah-tah-car'], *va.* 1. To attack, to assault, to fall upon, to come upon. 2. To pin down an argument. **Atacar a un adversario**, to attack an adversary. To overcome (sueño). To corrode (ácido). To tackle (una dificultad, un problema). To begin, to start. **Atacaron el Everest**, they started to climb Everest. *-vr.* *(LAm.)* To scoff, stuff oneself.

atachar [ah-tah-chahr'], *va.* *(Mex. Elec.)* To plug in.

ataché [ah-tah-shay'], *m.* *(CAm. Carib.)* Paper clip.

atacir [ah-tah-theer'], *m.* *(Astrol.)* A division of the celestial arch into twelve parts by circles which pass through points north and south of the horizon.

atacola [ah-tah-co'-lah], *f.* A strap for a horse's tail.

ataderas [ah-tah-day'-rahs], *f. & pl.* Garters.

atadero [ah-tah-day'-ro], *m.* 1. Cord or rope, with which something may be tied. 2. The place where a thing is tied. **No tener atadero**, to have neither head nor tail: applied to a discourse without meaning, and to the person uttering it.

atadijo, ito [ah-tah-dee'-ho, dee'-to], *m. dim. (coll.)* An illshaped little bundle or parcel.

atadito, ita [ah-tah-dee'-to, tah], *a. dim.* Somewhat cramped or contracted: a little bundle.

atado [ah-tah'-do], *m.* Bundle, parcel. **Atado de cebollas**, a string of onions. Atado de cigarrillos, *(Cono Sur)* Packet of cigarettes.

atado, da [ah-tah'-do, dah], *a.* Pusillanimous, easily embarrassed, good for nothing. *-pp.* of ATAR.

atador, ra [ah-tah-dor'], *m. & f.* 1. The person who ties. 2. Binder. The person who binds sheaves of corn. 3. The sting of a child's bonnet or cap.

atadura [ah-tah-doo'-rah], *f.* 1. Alligation, the act of tying together. 2. Tie, fastening. 3. *(Met.)* Union, connection. **Atadura de galeotes y presos**, a number of prisoners tied together, to be conducted to the galleys.

atafagar [ah-tah-fah-gar'], *va.* 1. To stupefy, to deprive of the use of the senses, especially by strong odors, good or bad. 2. *(Met.)* To tease, to molest by incessant importunity.

atafetanado, da [ah-tah-fay-tah-nah'-do, dah], *a.* Taffeta-like, resembling taffeta.

ataguía [ah-tah-gee'-ah], *f.* Cofferdam.

ataharre [ah-tah-ar'-ray], *m.* The broad crupper of a pack-saddle.

atahona [ah-tah-o'-nah], *f. V.* TAHONA. A mill turned by horse-power.

atahorma [ah-tah-or'-mah], *f. (Orn.)* Osprey, a kind of sea-eagle.

ataifor, ataiforico [ah-tah-e-for', ah-tah-e-fo-ree'-co], *m.* 1. Soup plate or deep dish. 2. A round table formerly used by the Moors.

atairar [ah-tah-e-rar'], *va.* To cut mouldings in the panels and frames of doors and windows.

ataire [ah-tah'-e-ray], *m.* Moulding in the panels and frames of doors and windows.

atajadero [ah-tah-hah-day'-ro], *m.* A sluice-gate.

atajadizo [ah-tah-hah-dee'-tho], *m.* Partition of boards, linen, etc., by which a place or ground is divided into separate parts. **Atajadizo de la caja de agua**, *(Naut.)* the manger-board.

atajador [ah-tah-hah-dor'], *m.* 1. One that intercepts or stops a passage, or obstructs the progress of another. 2. *(Mil.)* Scout. 3. **Atajador de ganado**, a sheep-thief. 4. *(Miner.)* The lad who unloads the work-horses.

atajar [ah-tah-har'], *vn.* To go the shortest way; or cut off part of the road. *-va.* 1. To overtake flying beasts or men, by cutting off part of the road, and thus getting before them. 2. To divide or separate by partitions. 3. To intercept, stop, or obstruct the course of a thing. **Este mal hay que atajarlo**, we must put an end to this evil. 4. To mark with lines, in a play or writing, the parts to be omitted in acting or in reading. 5. **Atajar ganado**, to steal sheep. 6. **Atajar la tierra**, to reconnoitre the ground. *-vr.* To be confounded with shame, dread, or reverential fear. **Hay que atajar la delincuencia juvenil**, juvenile delinquency must be checked. **Atajar un incendio**, to stop a fire. **Atajar una enfermedad**, to check an illness.

atajasolaces [ah-tah-hah-so-lah'-thes], *m.* A disturber of a pleasant reunion.

atajea, atajía [ah-tah-hay'-ah, ah-tah-hee'-ah], *f. V.* ATARJEA.

atajo [ah-tah'-ho], *m.* 1. Cut by which a road or path is shortened; short cut. 2. Ward or guard made by a weapon in fencing. 3. *(Obs.)* Agreement, expedient, means taken to conclude any difference or dispute. 4. Net with frame. **No hay atajo sin trabajo**, no gains without pains. **Salir al atajo**, to interrupt another's speech, and anticipate in a few words what he was going to say in many. **Tirar por el atajo**, to take the easy way out.

atalajar [ah-tah-lah-har'], *va. (Obs.)* To stun, to stupefy. *-vn.* To agree, to accord; to be pleased.

atalaje [ah-tah-lah'-hay], *m. V.* ATELAJE.

atalaya [ah-tah-lah'-yah], *f.* 1. Watchtower, which overlooks the adjacent country and sea-coast. 2. Height, from where a considerable part of country may be seen. 3. *m.* Guard, placed in a watchtower to keep a watchful eye over the adjacent country and sea-coast.

atalayador, ra [ah-tah-lah-yah-dor', rah], *m. & f.* 1. Guard or sentry stationed in a watchtower. 2. *(Met.)* Observer, investigator.

atalayar [ah-tah-lah-yar'], *va.* 1. To overlook and observe the country and seacoast form a watchtower. 2. To spy or pry into the actions of others.

atamiento [ah-tah-me-en'-to], *m.* 1. *(coll.)* Pusillanimity, meanness of spirit, want of courage. 2. Embarrassment, perplexity.

atanasia [ah-tah-nah'-se-ah], *f.* 1. *(Bot.)* Costmary or alecost. 2. *(Print.)* A size of type named English (14-point).

atanor [ah-tah-nor'], *m.* *(Prov.)* A siphon or tube for conveying water.

atanquía [ah-tan-kee'-ah], *f.* 1. Depilatory, a sort of ointment, to take away hair; mixture of orpiment and lime. 2. Refuse of silk which cannot be spun. 3. *V.* CADARZO.

atañer [ah-tah-nyerr'], *v. imp.* To belong, to appertain. To concern, to have to do; **En lo que atañe a eso**, with regard to that. **Eso no te atañe**, that is not your business.

atapuzar [ah-tah-poo-thar'], (Carib.) 1. va. To fill, to stop up. 2. vr. To stuff oneself.

ataque [ah-tah'-kay], m. 1. Attack, onset. **Ataque fingido**, sham attack. 2. Fit of apoplexy. 3. Fit of anger. 4. (Mil.) Attack. **Ataque aéreo o incursión aérea**, air raid, air attack. 5. (Med.) Stroke. **Ataque cardíaco**, heart attack.

ataquiza [ah-tah-kee'-thah], f. The act of layering or laying a branch of a vine in the ground to take root.

ataquizar [ah-tah-ke-thar'], va. To layer or lay a branch of a vine in the ground to take root.

atar [ah-tar'], va. 1. To tie, to bind, to fasten, to knit; to lace. 2. (Met.) To deprive of motion, to stop. **Atar bien su dedo**, to take care of oneself, to be attentive to one's own interest. **Al atar de los trapos**, at the close of the accounts. **Loco de atar**, as mad as a hatter. **Atar cabos**, to put two and two together. **Este trabajo me ata mucho**, this work ties me down a lot. **Atar corto a uno**, to keep a tight rein over someone. **Atar de pies y manos**, to tie hand and foot. -vr. 1. To be embarrassed or perplexed, to be at a loss how to extricate oneself from some difficulties. **Atarse en una dificultad**, to get tied in a difficulty. 2. To confine oneself to some certain subject or matter. **Atarse a la letra**, to stick to the letter of the text. **Atarse las manos**, to tie oneself down by promise.

ataracea [ah-tah-rah-thay'-ah], f. Marquetry, checker, checker-work; inlaid work, veneer work.

ataracear [ah-tah-rah-thay-ar¡], va. To checker, to inlay or variegate.

atarantado, da [ah-tah-ran-tah'-do, dah], a. 1. Bitten by a tarantula. 2. Stunned, stupefied, dazed (aturdido). 3. Restless (bullicioso). 4. Frightened, terrified (espantado). 5. (Met.) Surprised, astonished, amazed.

atarantar [ah-tah-rahn-tahr'], va. To stun (aturdir), to daze; **quedó atarantado**, he was stunned. (fig.) To stun, to dumbfound. -vr. To be stunned. 2. (And.) To hurry, to dash. 3. (Mex.) To stuff oneself. 4. (CAm. Mex.) To get drunk.

ataranza [ah-tah-rahn'-tah], f. Dockyard.

atarazana [ah-tah-rah-thah'-na], f. 1. (Obs.) Arsenal, a public dockyard. 2. Shed in rope-walks, for the spinners to work under cover. 3. (Prov.) Cellar, where wine is kept in casks.

atarazar [ah-tah-rah-thar'], va. To bite or wound with the teeth.

atardecer [ah-tahr-day-thayr'], 1. vn. To get dark; **atardecía**, it was getting dark. 2. m. Late afternoon; dusk, evening.

atareado, da [ah-tah-ray-ah'-do, dah], a. Busied, occupied; intent. **Andar muy atareado**, to be very busy. -pp. of ATAREAR.

atarear [ah-tah-ray-ar'], va. To task, to impose a task, to exercise. -vr. To overdo oneself, to labor or work with great application. **Atarearse a hacer algo**, to be busy doing something.

atarjea [ah-tar-hay'-ah], f. 1. A small vault over the pipes of an aqueduct, to prevent them from being damaged. 2. A small sewer or drain.

atarquinar [ah-tar-ke-nar'], va. To bemire, to cover with mire. -vr. To be bemired, to be covered with mire.

atarraga [ah-tar-rah'-gah], f. (Bot.) V. OLIVARDA.

atarragar [ah-tar-rah-gar'], va. To fit a shoe to a horse's foot. -vr. (Carib. Mex.) To stuff oneself, to overeat.

atarrajar [ah-tar-rah-har'], va. To form the thread of a screw. V. ATERRAJAR.

atarraya [ah-tar-rah'-yah], f. A castnet.

atarugado, da [ah-tah-rro-gah'-do, dah], a. (coll.) Abashed, ashamed. -pp. of ATARUGAR.

atarugar [ah-tah-roo-gar'], va. 1. To fasten or secure with wedges. 2. (Mech.) To plug, to bung; to cram. 3. (Met.) To silence and confound a person. -vr. 1. To swallow the wrong way, choke. 2. (fig.) To get confused, be in a daze. 3. To stuff oneself, to overeat.

atasajado, da [ah-tah-sah-hah'-do, dah], a. (coll.) Stretched across a horse. -pp. of ATASAJAR.

atasajar [ah-tah-sah-har'], va. To cut meat into small pieces, and dry it in the sun.

atascadero, atascamiento [ah-tas-cah-day'-ro, ah-tas-cah-me-en'-to], m. 1. Bog, mire, mudhole 2. (Met.) Obstruction, impediment (estorbo).

atascar [ah-tas-car'], va. 1. (Naut.) To stop a leak, to plug (agujero). 2. (Met.) To obstruct, to block [up], to choke, to clog (tubería) -vr. 1. To stick in a deep miry place. 2. To get stopped up: applied to drains, etc. 3. (Met.) To stop short in a discourse, unable to proceed.

atasco [ah-tahs'-co], m. 1. Barrier, obstruction, blockage (cosa que atasca). 2. Bogging down (de un coche). 3. Traffic jam (tráfico). 4. Jamming, sticking (mecanismo). 5. Stumbling block (obstáculo). 6. Muddle, tangle (discurso).

ataúd [ah-tah-ood'], m. 1. Casket in which dead bodies are put into the ground, coffin. 2. (Obs.) A measure for corn.

ataudado, da [ah-tah-oo-dah'-do, dah], a. Made in the shape of a coffin.

ataujía [ah-tah-oo-hee'-ah], f. Damaskeening, the art of adorning metals with inlaid work.

ataujiado, da [ah-tah-oo-he-ah'-do, dah], a. Damaskeened.

ataviado, da [ah-tah-ve-ah'-do, dah], a. Ornamented, ornated. -pp. of ATAVIAR.

ataviar [ah-tah-ve-ar'], va. To dress out, to trim, to adorn, to embellish, to accoutre. (LAm.) To adapt, to adjust. -vr. To dress up, to get oneself up.

atavío [ah-tah-vee'-o], m. The dress and ornament of a person, accoutrement, finery, gear.

atavismo [ah-tah-vees'-mo], m. Atavism, resemblance to ancestor; the tendency of hybrids to revert to the original type.

ataxia [ah-tac'-se-ah], f. 1. (Med.) Ataxia, ataxy. 2. A graminaceous plant of Java.

atáxico, ca [ah-tac'-se-co, cah], a. Ataxic, in disordered movement.

ate [ah'-tay], f. (Bot.) A rochidaccous plant, resembling habenaria. (CAm. Mex.) (Culin.) Jelly.

atediante [ah-tay-de-ayn'-tay], a. Boring, wearisome.

atediar [ah-tay-de-ar'], va. To disgust or displease, to consider with disgust. -vr. To be vexed, to be tired.

ateísmo [ah-tay-ees'-mo], m. Atheism; denial of God.

ateísta [ah-tay-ees'-tah], m. Atheist; infidel, unbeliever.

atejonarse [ah-tay-ho-nahr'-say], vr. (Mex.) 1. To curl up into a ball. 2. To become sharp.

atelaje V. ATALAJE. Also a team.

atembado [ah-taym-bah'-do], a. (And.) Silly, stupid; lacking in will-power.

atemorizar [ah-tay-mo-re-thar'], va. To terrify, to strike with terror, to daunt. -vr. To get scared.

atempa [ah-tem'-pah], f. (Asturian) Pasture in plains and open fields.

atempar [ah-taym-pahr'], vn. (CAm.) To wait, to hang around.

atemperación [ah-tem-pay-rah-the-on'], f. The act and effect of tempering.

atemperar [ah-tem-pay-rar'], va. 1. To temper, to form metals to a proper degree of hardness. 2. To soften, to mollify, to assuage; to cool. 3. To accommodate, to modify. **Atemperar los gastos a los ingresos**, to balance outgoings with income.

atemporado, da [ah-tem-po-rah'-do, dah], a. (Obs.) Alternate, serving by turns. Moderate, temperate.

atemporal [ah-taym-po-rahl'], a. Timeless.

atemporalidad [ah-taym-po-rah-le-dahd'], f. Timelessness.

atenacear, atenazar [ah-tay-na-thay-ar', ah-tay-na-thar'], va. To tear off flesh with pincers.

Atenas [ah-tay-nahs], Athens.

atenazar [ah-tay-nah-thahr'], va. (fig.) 1. To torment, to beset; **El miedo me atenazaba**, I was gripped by fear. 2. To tear [the flesh] with red hot pincers (suplicio).

atención [ah-ten-the-on'], f. 1. Attention, the act of being attentive; heed, heedfulness, mindfulness. **¡Atención a los**

pies!, mind your feet! 2. Civility, kindness, complaisance, courteousness, observance, courtesy, politeness (cortesía). 3. In the wool-trade, a contract of sale, whereby the price is not determined. **En atención**, attending; in consideration. **Hacer un trabajo con mucha atención**, to do a job with great care. -*pl.* Affairs, business, occupation. **Atenciones**, affairs.

atencioso [ah-tayn-the-o'-so], *a.* (*LAm.*) *V.* ATENTO.

atender [ah-ten-derr'], *va.* 1. To attend or be attentive, to mind, or to fix the mind upon a subject. 2. To heed, to hearken. 3. To expect, to wait or stay for, to look at. 4. To meet an emergency with succour or money. 5. To look after. **Atiende a esta gente**, look after these people. 6. To comply with; **atender a un cliente**, to serve a customer. 7. To meet one's obligations; **atender el teléfono**, to mind the telephone. 8. (*LAm.*) To attend, to be present at. -*vn.* To attend to, to pay attention to. **Atender a un caso urgente**, to see about an urgent matter.

atendible [ah-ten-dee'-blay], *a.* Meriting attention.

ateneo [ah-teay-nay'-o], *m.* Atheneum, in its various significations. Cultural association.

ateneo, a *a.* (*Poetic.*) or **ateniense** [ah-tay-ne-en'-say], athenian.

atener [ah-tay-nerr'], *vn.* (*Obs.*) 1. To walk at the same pace with another. 2. To guard, to observe. -*vr.* 1. To stick or adhere to one for greater security. **Atenerse a alguna cosa**, to abide. 2. To rely on. **No saber a qué atenerse**, not to know what to expect. **Atenerse a las consecuencias**, to bear the consequences in mind.

ateniense [ah-tay-ne-ayn'-say], *a. m. & f.* Athenian.

atentación [ah-ten-tah-the-on'], *f.* (*Law.*) procedure contrary to the order and form prescribed by the laws.

atentadamente [ah-ten-tah-dah-men'-tay], *adv.* 1. Attentively (con atención). Courteously, politely. *V.* ATENTAMENTE.

atentado, da [ah-ten-tah'-do, dah], *a.* 1. Discreet, prudent, moderate. 2. Done without noise, and with great circumspection. -*pp.* of ATENTAR.

atentado [ah-ten-tah'-do], *m.* 1. (*Law.*) Proceeding of a judge not warranted by the law. 2. Excess, transgression. Illegal act, offense; outrage, crime; assault, attack. **Atentado terrorista**, terrorist outrage.

atentamente [ah-ten-tah-men'-tay], *adv.* 1. Attentively, with attention, mindfully. 2. Civilly, politely, obligingly, observingly. **Suyo atentamente**, yours sincerely (cartas).

atentar [ah-ten-tar'], *va.* 1. To attempt, to commit a crime. 2. To try with great circumspection. -*vn.* **Atentar contra**, to commit an outrage against. -*vr.* (*Obs.*) To proceed with the utmost circumspection in the execution of an enterprise.

atentatorio, ria [ah-ten-tah-to'-re-o, ah], *a.* (*Law.*) Contrary to the order and form prescribed by the laws. Illegal, criminal.

atento, ta [ah-ten'-to, tah], *a.* 1. Attentive, bent upon a thing, listful, helpful; observing; mindful. **Estar atento a los peligros**, to be mindful of the dangers. 2. Polite, civil, courteous, mannerly, compliant, complaisant, considerate; notable. **Ser atento con uno**, to be kind to somebody. -*pp. irr.* of ATENDER, *adv.* **Atento**, in consideration.

atenuación [ah-tay-noo-ah-the-on'], *f.* 1. Attenuation, the act of making thin or slender. 2. Maceration. 3. The rhetorical figure litotes.

atenuante [ah-tay-noo-ahn'-tay], *a.* Attenuating, palliative. Extenuating (circumstancias), lessening fault.

atenuar [ah-tay-noo-ar'], *va.* To attenuate, to render thin and slender; to diminish, to lessen, to macerate, to mince. -*vr.* To weaken.

ateo [ah-tay'-o], *m.* Atheist. *V.* ATEISTA.

ateperetarse [ah-tay-pay-ray-tahr'-say], *vr.* (*CAm. Mex.*) To get confused.

atepocate [ah-tay-po-cah'-tay], *m.* (*Mex.*) Frog spawn.

atercianado, da [ah-ter-the-ah-nah'-do, dah], *a.* Afflicted with a tertian or intermittent fever.

aterciopelado, da [ah-ter-the-o-pay-lah'-do, dah], *a.* Velvet-like, resembling velvet.

aterido, da [ah-tay-ree'-do, dah], *a.* Stiff with cold. -*pp.* of ATERIRSE.

aterimiento [ah-tay-re-me-en'-to], *m.* Act of growing stiff with cold.

aterino [ah-tay-ree'-no], *m.* Atherine, a sand-smelt, about 0.15 meter in length, and which presents the rare distinction of being translucent.

aterirse [ah-tay-reer'-say], *vr.* To grow stiff with cold.

aternerao, da [ah-ter-nay-rah'-do, dah], *a.* Calf-like.

ateroma [ah-tay-ro'-mah], *f.* Atheroma, fatty degeneration of an artery.

aterrada [ah-tay-rrah-dah], *f.* (*Naut.*) Landfall.

aterrador, ra [ah-ter-rah-dor', rah], *a.* Frightful, terrible, dreadful.

aterrajar [ah-ter-rah-har'], *va.* To cut the thread of a screw; to tap with the die.

aterraje [ah-tayr-rah'-hay], *m.* (*Aer.*) Landing; (*Naut.*) Landfall.

aterramiento [ah-ter-rah-me-en'-to], *m.* 1. Ruin, destruction. 2. Terror, communication of fear. 3. (*Naut.*) A landing-place.

aterrar [ah-ter-rar'], *va.* 1. To destroy, to pull or strike down; to prostrate. 2. To terrify, to appal, to cause terror or dismay. -*vr.* (*Naut.*) To stand inshore, to keep the land on board.

aterrizaje [ah-ter-re-thah'-hay], *m.* (*Aer.*) Landing. **Aterrizaje forzoso**, emergency landing.

aterrizar [ah-ter-re-thar'], *vn.* (*Aer.*) To land.

aterronar [ah-ter-ro-nar'], *va.* To clod, to gather into concretions, to coagulate. -*vr.* To get lumpy; to cake, harden.

aterrorizar [ah-ter-ro-re-thar'], *va.* To frighten, to terrify.

atesador [ah-tay-sah-dor'], *m.* (*Mech.*) Stretcher, line-tightener, tensor, take-up. Brace-pin.

atesar [ah-tay-sar'], *va.* 1. To brace, or stiffen a thing. 2. (*Naut.*) To haultaut.

atesorador [ah-tay-so-rah-dor'], *m.* A hoarder.

atesorar [ah-tay-so-rar'], *va.* 1. To treasure or hoard up riches, to lay in, to lay up. 2. To possess many amiable qualities.

atestación [ah-tes-tah-the-on'], *f.* Attestation, testimony, evidence.

atestado, da [ah-tes-tah'-do, dah], *a.* 1. Attested, witnessed. -*pp.* of ATESTAR.

atestado [ah-tays-tah'-do], *a.* Packed, cram-full; **atestado de**, packed with.

atestados [ah-tes-tah'-dos], *m. pl.* Certificates, testimonials.

atestadura [ah-tes-tah-doo'-rah], *f.* 1. The act of cramming or stuffing. 2. Must, poured into pipes and butts, to supply the leakage.

atestamiento [ah-tes-tah-me-en'-to], *m.* The act of cramming, stuffing or filling.

atestar [ah-tes-tar], *va.* 1. To cram, to stuff; to overstock, to clog. 2. To stuff, to crowd. 3. To fill up pipes or butts of wine. 4. To attest, to witness. **Una palabra no atestada**, an unattested word. 5. (*Prov.*) *V.* ATRACAR.

atestiguación, *f.* **atestiguamiento**, *m.* [ah-tes-te-goo-ah-the-on', ah-tes-te-goo-ah-me-en'-to]. Deposition upon oath.

atestiguar [ah-tes-te-goo-ar'], *va.* To depose, to witness, to attest, to affirm as a witness, to give evidence. **Atestiguar con alguno**, to cite or summon one as a witness.

atesto [ah-tes'-to], *m.* Certificate, paper. (*Com.*)

atetado, da [ah-tay-tah'-do, dah], *a.* Mammillated, mammiform. -*pp.* of ATETAR.

atetar [ah-tay-tar'], *va.* To suckle, to nurse.

atetillar [ah-tay-teel-lyar'], *va.* To dig a trench around the roots of trees.

atezado, da [ah-taay-thah'-do, dah], *a.* Black, tanned. *-pp.* of ATEZAR.

atezamiento [ah-tay-thah-me-en'-to], *m.* The act and effect of blackening.

atezar [ah-tay-thar'], *va.* To blacken, to make black, to tan. *-vr.* To grow black, to get tanned.

atiborrado [ah-te-bor-rah'-do], *a.* **Atiborrado de**, full of.

atiborrar [ah-te-bor-rar'], *va.* 1. To stuff or pack up close with locks of wool, tow, etc. **Atiborrar a un niño de dulces**, to stuff a child with sweets. 2. To cram with victuals. *-vr.* To stuff oneself.

aticismo [ah-te-thees'-mo], *m.* 1. Atticism, elegance and grace in language. 2. Nice, witty, and polite joke.

ático, ca [ah'-te-co, cah], *a.* 1. Attic, elegant, poignant: applied to wit and humor. 2. Superior to objection or confutation. **Testigo ático**, an irrefragable witness. *-m.* Upper part of a building, attic.

aticurga [ah-te-coor'-gah], *f.* Base of an attic column. (*Yo atiendo*, from *Atender. V.* ATENDER.) (*Yo atierro, yo atierre*, from *Aterrar. V.* ACERTAR.) (*Yo atiento*, from *Atentar. V.* ACERTAR.)

atierre [ah-te-err'-ray], *m.* Attle, heap of waste ore.

atiesar [ah-te-ay-sar'], *va.* To make hard or stiff. *-vr.* To get stiff, to stiffen.

atifle [ah-tee'-flay], *m.* An instrument in the shape of a trevet, which potters place between earthen vessels to prevent them from sticking to each other in the kiln or oven.

atigrado [ah-te-grah'-do], 1. *a.* Striped, marked like a tiger. 2. *m.* Tabby.

atigronarse [ah-te-gro-nahr'-say], *vr.* (*Carib.*) To get strong.

Atila [ah-te'-lah], *m.* Attila.

atildado, da [ah-teel-dah'-do, dah], *a.* Elegant, neat, fastidious. **Atildado caballero**, perfect gentleman.

atildadura [ah-teel-dah-doo'-rah], *f.* 1. Dress, attire, ornament. 2. Culture of the mind, good breeding. 3. Punctuation.

atildar [ah-teel-dar'], *va.* 1. To put a dash or stroke over a letter. 2. To censure the speeches and actions of others. 3. To deck, to dress, to adorn. *-vr.* To spruce oneself up.

atilincar [ah-te-len-cahr'], (*CAm.*) To tighten, to stretch.

atillo [ah-teel'-lyo], *m.* Bundle. *V.* HATILLO. **Hacer atillo**, To pack up.

atinadamente [ah-te-nah-dah-men'-tay], *adv.* 1. Cautiously, judiciously, prudently. 2. Pertinently, appositely, to the purpose. 3. Considerately, consideringly.

atinado [ah-te-nah'-do], *a.* Accurate, correct, wise, sensible, judicious; **unas observaciones atinadas**, some pertinent remarks.

atinar [ah-te-nr'], *vn.* 1. To hit the mark, to reach the point. 2. To hit upon a thing by conjecture, to guess. **Él siempre atina**, he always gets it right. 3. To find out. 4. **Atinar al blanco**, to hit the target. 5. **Atinar a hacer algo**, to succeed in doing something. *-va.* To hit upon, find.

atincar [ah-teen'-car], *m.* Tincal: when refined, it is the borax of commerce.

atinconar [ah-tin-co-nar'], *va.* To secure temporarily the walls of an excavation.

atingencia [ah-ten-hayn'-the-ah], *f.* (*LAm.*) 1. Connection, bearing. 2. Obligation. 3. Qualification.

atingido [ah-ten-he'-do], *a.* (*And.* Cono Sur.) 1. Depressed, down-in-the-mouth; feeble, weak; timid. 2. (*And.*) Penniless.

atingir [ah-ten-gerr'], *va.* 1. (*LAm.*) To concern, to bear on, to relate to. 2. (*And.*) To oppress.

atiparse [ah-te-pahr'-say], *vr.* To eat one's fill.

atípico [ah-te'-pe-co], *a.* Atypical, untypical, exceptional.

atiplado [ah-te-plah'-do], *a.* Treble, high-pitched (voz).

atiplar [ah-te-plar'], *va.* To raise the sound of a musical instrument. *-vr.* To grow very sharp or acute (instrumento, voz).

atipujarse [ah-te-poo-hahr'-say], *vr.* (*CAm. Mex.*) To stuff oneself.

atirantar [ah-te-ran-tar'], *va.* (*Arch.*) To fix collar-beams in a building. To tighten, tauten; to stretch; **estar atirantado entre dos decisiones**, to be torn between two decisions. *-vr.* (*Mex.*) To peg out.

atisba [ah-tis'-bah], *m.* (*And.*) Watchman, look-out; spy.

atisbadero [ah-tis-bah-day'-ro], *m.* Peephole.

atisbador, ra [ah-tis-bah-dor', rah], *m. & f.* A person who pries into the business and actions of others.

atisbadura [ah-tis-bah-doo'-rah], *f.* The act of prying into the business and actions of others.

atisbar [ah-tis-bar'], *va.* 1. To scrutinize, to pry, to examine closely. 2. **Atisbar a uno a través de una grieta**, to peep at somebody through a crack. To watch, to waylay.

atisbo [ah-tis'-bo], *m.* 1. Spying; watching; look, peep. 2. (*fig.*) Inkling, slight sign.

atisuado, da [ah-te-soo-ah'-do, dah], *a.* Tissue-like. *-i. e.* like *tisú*, a silk stuff interwoven with gold and silver, presenting a flower pattern.

atizadero [ah-te-thah-day'-ro], *m.* 1. Pocker. 2. (*fig.*) Spark, stimulus.

atizador, ra [ah-te-thah-dor', rah], *m. & f.* 1. One who stirs up or incites others. 2. Poker, an instrument to stir the fire. 3. In oil-mills, the person who puts the olives under the mill-stone. 4. In glasshouses, he who supplies the furnace with wood or coals; feeder.

atizar [ah-te-thar'], *va.* 1. To stir the fire with a poker. 2. (*Met.*) To stir up or rouse and incite the passions. **Atizar la lámpara or el candil**, to raise the lamp wick, and fill it with oil. **Atizar la lámpara**, (*coll.*) to fill the glasses. **Pedro ¿por qué atiza? Por gozar de la ceniza**, Why does Peter sow? Because he expects to reap. 3. To give; **se atizó el vaso**, he knocked back a glassful. *-vn.* ¡**Atiza!**, gosh! *-vr.* To smoke pot.

atizonar [ah-te-tho-nar'], *va.* To join bricks and stones close together, and fill up the chinks in a wall with mortar and brickbats. *-vr.* To be smutted: applied to grain.

atlante [at-lahn'-tay], *v.* He who bears the weight of government, in allusion to Atlas. **Atlantes**, (*Arch.*) Figures or half-figures of men, sometimes used instead of columns; atlantes or telamones. Cf. CARIATIDES.

Atlántico [at-lahn'-te-co], *a.* Atlantic.

Atlántida [at-lahn'-te-dah], *f.* Atlantis.

atlantista [at-lahn-tes'-tah], 1. *a.* Relating to the Atlantic Alliance. 2. *m. & f.* Supporter of the Atlantic Alliance.

Atlas [at'-las], *m.* 1. Atlas, a range of mountains, a collection of maps. 2. (*Naut.*) Atlas, the name of the first cervical vertebra. 3. (*Com.*) A kind of rich satin, manufactured in the East Indies.

atleta [at-lay'-tah], *m.* Athlete, wrestler, gymnast.

atlético, ca [at-lay'-te-ci, cah], *a.* Athletic, belonging to gymnastics; robust.

atletismo [at-lay-tis'-mo], *m.* Athletics.

atmósfera [ar-mos'-fay-rah], *f.* 1. Atmosphere, the air. 2. The space over which the influence of anything extends, or is exerted. 3. Measure of force founded upon the pressure exerted by the atmosphere.

atmosférico, ca [at-mos-fay'-re-co, cah], *a.* Atmospherical.

atoaje [ah-to-ah'-hay], *m.* Towage, warping.

atoar [ah-to-ar'], *va.* (*Naut.*) to tow a vessel with the help of a rope.

atoc [ah-toc'], *m.* (*And.*) Fox.

atocar [ah-to-cahr'], *va.* (*LAm.*) *V.* TOCAR.

atocinado, da [ah-to-the-nah'-do, dah], *a.* (*Low.*) Corpulent, fut, fleshy. *-pp.* of ATOCINAR.

atocinar [ah-to-the-nar'], *va.* 1. To cup up a pig, to make bacon. 2. (*Met.*) To assassinate or murder. *-vr.* 1. (*coll.*) To sell with anger and rage, to be exasperated. 2. To be violently enamoured.

atocle [ah-to'-clay], *m.* (*Mex.*) Sandy soil rich in humus.

atocha [ah-to'-chah], *f.* (*Bot.*) Tough feather-grass, bass-weed, esparto.

atochal, atochar [ah-to-chahl', ah-to-char'], *m.* A field where bass-weed grows.

atochamiento [ah-to-chah-me-ayn-to], *m. (Cono Sur)* Traffic jam.

atochar [ah-to-chahr'], *m. V.* ATOCHAL.

atochón [ah-to-chone'], *m. (Bot.)* Name of the tender panicle of the tough feather-grass.

atolada [ah-to-lah'-dah], *m. (CAm.)* Party.

atole [ah-to'-lay], or **Atol**, *m. (Mex. and Cuba)* A gruel made by boiling Indian corn, or maize, pounded to flour, in water, and also in milk. In Peru called mazamorra.

atoleada [ah-to-lay-ah'-dah], *f. (CAm.)* Party.

atolería [ah-to-lay-re'-ah], *f. (LAm.)* Stall where atol is sold.

atolón [ah-to-lone'], *m.* Atoll, a coral island.

atolondrado [ah-tolon-drah'-do, dah], *a.* Harebrained, thoughtless, mad-brain, giddy, careless, heedless; harum-scarum. *-pp.* of ATOLONDRAR.

atolondramiento [ah-to-lon-drah-me-en'-to], *m.* Stupefaction, the act and effect of stupefying, consternation.

atolondrar [ah-to-lon-drar'], *va.* To stun, to stupefy, to confound, to render stupid. *-vr.* To be stupefied, to grow dull or stupid.

atolladero [ah-tol-lyah-day'-ro], *m.* 1. A deep miry place. 2. *(Met.)* Obstacle, impediment, obstruction. **Estar en un atolladero**, to be in a jam.

atollar [ah-tol-lyar'], *vn.* To fall into the mire, to stick in the mud. *-vr. (Met.)* To be involved in great difficulties.

atomía [ah-to-me'-ah], *f. (LAm.)* 1. Evil deed, savage act. 2. **Decir atomías**, to shoot one's mouth off.

atómico, ca [ah-to'-me-co, cah] *a.* Atomic. **Bomba atómica**, atomic bomb. **Era o edad atómica**, atomic age.

atomismo [ah-to-mees'-mo], *m.* Atomism, the atomical philosophy.

atomista [ah-to-mees'-tah], *m.* Atomist, one who holds the atomical philosophy, or the system of atoms.

atomístico, ca [ah-to-mees'-te-co, cah], *a.* Atomical, consisting of atoms.

atomizar [ah-to-me-thahr'], *va.* To atomize; to spray.

átomo [ah'-to-mo], *m.* 1. Atom, corpuscle, ace, mote. 2. Anything extremely small. **No exceder en un átomo**, to stick closely to one's orders and instructions. **Reparar en un átomo**, to remark the minutest actions. **atómos**, minute parts seen by a solar ray in any place.

atonal [ah-to-nahl'], *a.* Atonal.

atondar [ah-ton-dar'], *va.* To spur a horse.

atónito, ta [ah-to'-ne-to, tah], *a.* Astonished, amazed. **Me miró atónito**, he looked at me in amazement.

átono, na [ah'-to-no, nah], *a.* Unaccented; used of a syllable in prosody, atonic.

atontadamente [ah-ton-tah-dah-men'-tay], *adv.* Foolishly, stupidly.

atontado, da [ah-ton-tah'-do, dah], *a.* Mopish, foolish, stupid. *-pp.* of ATONTAR.

atontamiento [ah-ton-tah-me-en'-to], *m.* Stupefaction, the act of stupefying, and state of being stupefied.

atontar [ah-ton-tar'], *va.* To stun, to stupefy, to flatten, to confound. *-vr.* To be stupid, to grow stupid.

atontolinar [ah-ton-to-le-nhar'], *va.* To daze; to stun; **quedar atontolinado**, to be in a daze.

atora [ah-to'-rah], *f.* Law of Moses.

atorafo [ah-to-fo-rah'-do], *a. (Carib.)* Anxious.

atorar [ah-to-rahr'], *va.* To stop up, to choke, to obstruct. *(Carib. Mex.)* To block, impede. *-vr.* To choke, to swallow the wrong way; *(Mex.)* To get tongue-tied.

atorarse [ah-to-rar'-say], *vr.* 1. To stick in the mire. 2. To fit closely the bore of a cannon: applied to a ball. 3. To choke, to suffocate.

atormentadamente [ah-tor-men-tah-dah-men'-tay], *adv.* Anxiously, tormentingly.

atormentado, da [ah-tor-men-tah'-do, dah], *a.* Painful, full of pain, beset with affliction. *-pp.* of ATORMENTAR.

atormentador, ra [ah-tor-men-tah-dor', rah], *m. & f.* Tormentor.

atormentar [ah-tor-men-tar'], *va.* 1. To torment, to give pain. 2. *(Met.)* To cause affliction, pain, or vexation. 3. To rack or torment by the rack. *-vr.* To torment oneself.

atornillar, [ah-tor-neel-lyar'], *va.* To screw, to fasten with screws. *(LAm.)* To pester, harass.

atoro [ah-to'-ro], *m. (LAm.)* Destruction; *(fig.)* Tight spot, difficulty.

atorozonarse [ah-to-ro-tho-nar'-say], *vr.* To suffer gripes or colic, to be griped (caballos).

atorozarse [ah-to-ro-thar'-say], *vr. (CAm.)* To choke, to swallow the wrong way.

atorrante [ah-tor-rahn'-tay], *m. (Arg.)* Vagabond, idler, tramp.

atorrantear [ah-tor-rahn-tay-ahr'], *vn. (Cono Sur)* To live like a tramp, to be on the bum.

atortolado [ah-tor-to-lah'-do], *a.* **Están atortolados**, they are like two turtle-doves.

atortolar [ah-tor-to-lar'], *va. (coll.)* To confound, to intimidate. *-vr.* To be frightened or intimidated, like a turtle-dove.

atortorar [ah-tor-to-rar'], *va. (coll.)* To confound, to intimidate. *-vr.* To be frightened or intimidated, like a turtle-dove.

atortorar [ah-tor-to-rar'], *va. (Naut.)* to frap a ship, to strengthen the hull with ropes tied round it.

atortujar [ah-tor-too-har'], *va. (coll.)* To squeeze, to make flat. *-vr. (CAm.)* To be shattered.

atorunado [ah-to-roo-nah'-do], *a. (Cono Sur)* Stocky, bull-necked.

atosigador [ah-to-se-gah-dor'], *a.* 1. Poisonous. 2. *(fig.)* Pestering, harassing, harrying (que apremia).

atosigamiento [ah-to-se-gah-me-en'-to], *m.* The act of poisoning, and state of being poisoned.

atosigar [ah-to-se-gar'], *va.* 1. To poison. 2. *(Met.)* To harass, to oppress.

atoxicar [ah-too-se-car'], *va.* To poison.

atóxico, ca [ah-toc'-se-co, cah], *a.* Non-poisonous.

atrabancar [ah-trah-ban-car'], *va.* To huddle, to perform a thing in a hurry, and carelessly. *-vr.* To be in a fix, to get into a jam.

atrabanco [ah-trah-bahn'-co], *m.* The act of huddling, or doing a thing hurriedly.

atrabiliario [ah-trah-be-la'-re-o], *a.* Bad-tempered, difficult, moody.

atrabilis [ah-trah-bee'-lis], *f.* The state of being atrabilious; black bile. *(fig.)* Bad temper.

atracable [ah-trah-cah'-blay], *a.* Approachable.

atracadero [ah-trah-cah-day'-ro], *m. (Naut.)* A landing-place for small vessels.

atracado [ah-trah-cah'-do], *a. (CAm.)* Mean, stingy.

atracador [ah-trah-cah-dor'], *m.* Hold-up man, bandit.

atracar [ah-trah-car'], *va.* 1. *(Naut.)* To overtake another ship; to approach land; to come alongside. 2. To cram with food and drink, to glut, to pamper. 3. To hold up, to attack. *-vn. (Naut.)* To tie up, to moor, to bring alongside. *-vr.* 1. To be stuffed with eating and drinking, to fill. 2. *(Naut.)* **Atracarse al costado**, To come alongside of a ship.

atracción [ah-trac-the-on'], *f.* Attraction, the act or power of attracting. Appeal, charm. **Atracción sexual**, sexual attraction.

atraco [ah-trah'-co], *m.* Hold-up, robbery; hijack; **atraco a mano armada**, armed robbery.

atracón [ah-trah-cone'], *m.* Over-eating; gluttony.

atractivamente [ah-trac-tee'-vah-mayn-tay], *adv.* Attractively.

atractivo, va [ah-trac-tee'-vo, vah], *a.* 1. Attractive, having the power of attracting, magnetic, magnetical. 2. Engaging.

atractivo [ah-trac-tee'-vo], *m.* Charm, something fit to gain the affections; grace; cooing.

atractriz [ah-trac-treeth'], *a.* Powerful to attract.

atraer [ah-trah-err'], *va.* 1. To attract, to draw to something; to lead. **Dejarse atraer por**, to allow oneself to be drawn towards. 2. To allure, to lure, to invite, to make another submit to one's will and opinion, to conciliate. -*vr.* *(Obs.)* V. JUNTARSE and EXTENDERSE.

atrafagado, da [ah-trah-fah-gah'-do, dah], *a.* 1. Much occupied; laborious. -*pp.* of ATRAFAGAR. 2. Fidgety.

atrafagar [ah-trah-fah-gar'], *vn.* To toil, to exhaust oneself with fatigue. -*vr.* To fidget.

atragantarse [ah-trah-gan-tar'-say], *vr.* 1. To stick in the throat or windpipe. **Se me atragantó una miga**, a crumb went the wrong way. 2. *(Met.)* To be out short in conversation. 3. **Pepe se me ha atragantado**, *(fig.)* Pepe sticks in my throat.

atrague [ah-trah'-gay], *m.* **¡Que atrague!**, what an idiot!

atraible [ah-trah-ee'-blay], *a.* Attractable, subject to attraction.

atraidorado, da [ah-trah-e-do-rah'-do, dah], *a.* Treacherous, faithless, perfidious. (*Yo atraigo*, from *Atraer.* V. TRAER).

atraillar [ah-trah-eel-lyar'], *va.* 1. To leash, to bind with a string. 2. To follow game guided by a dog in leash.

atraimiento [ah-trah-e-me-en'-to], *m.* *(Obs.)* The act of attracting, and state of being attracted.

atramento [ah-trah-men'-to], *m.* Black color.

atramentoso, sa [ah-tra-men-to'-so, sah], *a.* *(Obs.)* That which has the power of dyeing black.

atramparse [ah-tram-par'-say], *vr.* 1. To be caught in a snare. 2. To be choked, to be stopped or blocked up. 3. To be involved in difficulties.

atramuz [ah-trah-mooth'], *m.* *(Bot.)* Lupine. V. ALTRAMUZ.

atrancar [ah-tran-car'], *va.* 1. To bar a door. 2. Coll.) To step out, to take long steps. 3. *(Met. Coll.)* To read hurriedly. -*vr.* 1. To get stuck, to get bogged down. 2. *(Cono Sur) (Med.)* To get constipated. 3. *(Mex.)* To dig one's heels in.

atranco [ah-trahn'-co], *m.* 1. Mudhole. 2. Jam, difficulty, embarrassment.

atrapa-moscas [ah-trah'-pa-mos'-cas], *f.* *(Bot.)* The Venus's fly-trap.

atrapar [ah-trah-par'], *va.* 1. To catch, to trap, to lay hold of one who is running away. 2. To impose upon, to deceive.

atrás [ah-trahs'], *adv.* 1. Backward, toward the back. **Estar atrás**, to be behind. 2. Past, in time past. **Hacerse atrás**, to fall back. **Quedarse atrás**, to remain behind. **Volverse atrás**, *(Met.)* to retract, to unsay. **Hacia atrás**, *(coll.)* far from that, quite the contrary. **En las filas de atrás**, in the back rows. **Marcha atrás**, reverse. **Quedarse atrás**, to fall behind. **Echarse para atrás**, to change one's mind.

atrasado, da [ah-trah-sah'-do, dah], *pp.* of ATRASAR. 1. **Atrasado de medios**, short of means. **Atrasado de noticias**, *(coll.)* behind the times. **Estar atrasado en pagos**, to be behind in payments, to be in arrears. 2. Backward; underdeveloped; slow, backward. 3. *(Cono Sur)* ill. *m.* **Es un atrasado**, he's behind the times. **Un número atrasado**, a back number (revista). **Un atrasado mental**, a mentally retarded person.

atrasados [ah-trah-sah'-dos], *m. pl.* Arrears, sums remaining unpaid though due.

atrasar [ah-trah-sar'], *va.* 1. To put back, to set back; to retard, to slow down. **Atrasar un reloj**, to put a clock back. 2. To postpone the execution or performance of something. *vr.* 1. To remain behind. 2. To be in debt.

atraso [ah-trah'-so], *m.* 1. Backwardness, lateness, delay. **El tren lleva atraso**, the train is late. 2. Loss of fortune or wealth. 3. Arrears of money.

atravesado, da [ah-trah-vay-sah'-do, dah], *a.* 1. Squint-eyed, looking obliquely. 2. Oblique. 3. Cross-grained, perverse, troublesome. 4. Mongrel, of a mixed or cross breed. 5. Lying across. **Hay un árbol atravesado**, There is a tree lying across. -*pp.* of ATRAVESAR.

atravesador [ah-trah-vay-sah-dor'], *m.* Disturber, a violator of peace.

atravesaño [ah-trah-vay-sah'-nyo], *m.* Cross-timber, timber which crosses from one side to another. **Atravesaño firme de colchar**, *(Naut.)* a cross-piece for belaying ropes. **Atravesaños de los propaos**, Cross-pieces of the breast-work. **Atravesaños de las latas**, Carlines or carlings, two pieces of timber lying fore and aft from one beam to another, directly over the keel.

atravesar [ah-trah-vay-sar'], *va.* 1. To lay, or put across (árbol, viga). 2. To run through with a sword, to pass through the body. **Atravesar a uno con una espada**, to run somebody through with a sword. 3. To cross, to cross over, to pass over, to get or go over, to go through, to overpass. 4. *(Low.)* to bewitch by a spell or charm. 5. To bet, to stake at a wager. 6. To lay a trump on a card which has been played. 7. *(Naut.)* to lie to. **Atravesar el corazón**, *(Met.)* To move to compassion. **Atravear los géneros**, to buy goods by wholesale in order to sell them by retail. **Atravesar todo el país**, to overrun or traverse the whole country. **No atravesar los umbrales**, not to darken one's door. -*vr.* 1. To be obstructed by something thrown in the way. 2. To interfere in other people's business or conversation. **Atravesarse en una conversación**, to butt into a conversation. 3. To have a dispute. 4. *(Naut.)* to cross the course of another vessel under her head or stern. (**Yo atravieso, yo atraviese**, from **Atravesar**. V. ACERTAR).

atrayente [ah-tra-yen'-tay], *a.* Attractive.

atrazar [ah-tra-thar'], *va.* To practise artifices, to scheme.

atrechar [ah-tray-chahr'], *vn.* *(Carib.)* To take a short cut.

atrecho [ah-tray'-cho], *m.* *(Carib.)* A short cut.

atreguado, da [ah-tray-goo-ah'-do, dah], *a.* Rash, foolish, precipitate, or deranged.

atreguar [ah-tray-goo-ahr'], *va.* To grant a truce to. -*vr.* To agree to a truce.

atrenzo [ah-trayn'-tho], *m.* *(LAm.)* Trouble, difficulty; **estar en un atrenzo**, to be in trouble.

atresia [ah-tray'-se-ah], *f.* Closure or absence of a natural passage or channel of the body; atresia.

atresnalar [ah-tres-nah-lar'], *va.* *(Prov.)* To collect sheaves of corn into heaps.

atreverse [ah-tray-verr'-say], *vr.* 1. To dare, to venture. **No me atrevo, no me atrevería**, I wouldn't dare. **Atreverse a hacer algo**, to dare to do something. 2. To be insolent or disrespectful. 3. To manage. **¿Te atreves con un pastel?** Can you manage a cake?

atrevidamente [ah-tray-ve-dah-men'-tay], *adv.* Audaciously, daringly, boldly, confidently.

atrevidillo, lla [ah-tray-ve-deel'-lyo, lyah], *a. dim.* Somewhat audacious.

atrevidísimo, ma [ah-tray-ve-dee'-se-mo, mah], *a. sup.* Most audacious.

atrevido, da [ah-tray-vee'-do, dah], *a.* 1. Bold, audacious, daring, fearless, high-spirited, hardy. 2. Forward, free, confident, insolent. -*pp.* of ATREVERSE.

atrevido [ah-tray-vee'-do], *m.* A muscle on the shoulderblade.

atrevimiento [ah-tray-ve-me-en'-to], *m.* 1. Boldness, audaciousness, daringness. 2. Confidence, face, front.

atrevismo [ah-tray-ves'-mo], *m.* Ostentatious daring.

atrezzo [ah-tray'-tho], *m.* *(Theat.)* Properties.

atriaquero [ah-tre-ah-kay'-ro], *m.* A manufacturer and retailer of treacle.

atribución [ah-tre-boo-the-on'], *f.* 1. The act of attributing something to another. 2. Attribute.

atribuible [ah-tre-boo-e'-blay], *a.* Attributable. **Obras atribuibles a Góngora**, works which are attributed to Góngora.

atribuir [ah-tre-boo-eer'], *va.* To attribute, to ascribe as a quality, to impute as to a cause, to count, to charge to. **Las funciones atribuidas a mi cargo**, the powers conferred on me by my post. -*vr.* To assume, to arrogate to oneself.

atribulación [ah-tre-boo-lah-the-on'], *f.* affliction, suffering, tribulation.

atribulado [ah-tre-boo-lah-do], 1. *a.* Afflicted, suffering. 2. *m.* **Los atribulados**, the afflicted.

atribular [ah-tre-boo-lar'], *va.* To vex, to afflict. -*vr.* To be vexed, to suffer tribulation.

atributar [ah-tre-boo-tar'], *va. (Obs.)* to impose tribute.

atributivo, va [ah-tre-boo-tee'-vo, vah], *a.* Attributive.

atributo [ah-tre-boo'-to], *m.* Attribute, the thing attributed to another; a quality adherent. (*Yo atribuyo, atribuya; atribuyó, atribuyeron*, from *Atribuir. V.* INSTRUIR).

atricapilla [ah-tre-cah-peel'-lyah], *f. (Orn.)* The Epicurean warbler.

atriceses [ah-tre-tahy'-ses], *m. pl.* The staples or iron rings to which the stirrup-straps are fastened.

atrición [ah-tre-the-on'], *f.* 1. Contrition, grief for sin arising from the fear of punishment. 2. *(Vet.)* Contraction of the principal nerve in a horse's fore leg. 3. Attrition, the wearing away of anything by rubbing, or friction.

atril [ah-treel'], *m.* 1. Reading-desk; stand for the missal. 2. A music-stand, or holder.

atrincar [ah-treen-cahr'], *va. (LAm.)* To tie up tightly. -*vr.* (*Mex.*) To be stubborn, dig one's heels in.

atrincheramiento [ah-trin-chay-rah-me-en'-to], *m.* Entrenchment, lodgment, mound. **Atrincheramientos de abordaje**, *(Naut.)* Close quarters, breast-works on board of merchant ships, from behind which the crew defend themselves when boarded by an enemy.

atrincherar [ah-trin-chay-rar'], *va.* To entrench, to fortify with a trench, to mound. -*vr.* To cover oneself from the enemy by means of trenches. **Están muy fuertemente atrincherados**, *(fig.)* They are very strongly entrenched.

atrio [ah'-tre-o], *m.* 1. Porch, a roof supported by pillars between the principal door of a palace and the staircase. 2. Portico, a covered walk before a church-door. 3. An interior, uncovered courtyard.

atrípedo, da [ah-tree'-pay-do, dah], *a. (Zool.)* Black-footed.

atrirrostro, tra [ah-trir-ros'-tro, trah], *a.* Black-beaked (pájaros).

atrito, ta [ah-tree'-to, tah], *a.* Contrite through fear.

atrochar [ah-tro-char'], *vn.* To go by cross paths; to make a short cut.

atrocidad [ah-tro-the-dahd'], *f.* 1. Atrocity or atrociousness, flagitiousness, foulness, outrage, grievousness; enormous wickedness. 2. Excess. **Es una atrocidad lo que come o lo que trabaja**, he eats or works to excess. 3. Silly remark; **decir atrocidades**, to say silly things.

atrofia [ah-tro'-fe-ah], *f.* Atrophy, a gradual wasting of the body.

atrofiar [ah-tro-fe-ahr'], *f.* Atrophy. *vr.* To waste away, to atrophy.

atrojarse [ah-tro-har'-say], *vr. (Mex. Coll.)* To be stumped, to find no way out of a difficulty.

atrompetado, da [ah-trom-pay-tah'-do, dah] *a.* Trumpetlike, having the shape of a trumpet. **Tiene narices atrompetadas**, his nostrils are as wide as the mouth of a trumpet.

atronadamente [ah-tro-nah-dah-men'-tay], *adv.* Precipitately, without prudence or reflection.

atronado [ah-tro-nah'-do], *m.* Blunderer, wild. -*a.* Acting in a precipitate, imprudent manner. -*pp.* of ATRONAR.

atronador, ra [ah-tro-nah-dor, rah], *m. & f.* Thunderer, one who makes a thundering noise.

atronadura [ah-tro-nah-doo'-rah], *f.* 1. Crack or split in wood, from periphery inward, following the medullary rays. 2. *V.* ALCANZADURA.

atronamiento [ah-tro-nah-me-en'-to], *m.* 1. The act of thundering. 2. Stupefaction caused by a blow. 3. Crepance or ulcer in the feet or legs of horses.

atronar [ah-tro-nar'], *va.* 1. To make a great noise in imitation of thunder. 2. To stun, to stupefy. 3. To stop the ears of horses, to prevent their fright at noises. -*vr.* 1. To be thunder-struck. 2. To die from effect of a thunder-storm, said of chickens in the egg and of silkworms in the cocoon.

atronerar [ah-tro-nay-rar'], *va.* To make embrasure in a wall.

atropado, da [ah-tro-pah'-do, dah], *a.* Grouped, clumped (árboles, plantas). -*pp.* of ATROPAR.

atropar [ah-tro-par'], *va.* To assemble in groups without order, to conglomerate, to clutter.

atropelladamente [ah-tro-pel-lyah-dah-men'-tay], *adv.* Tumultuously, confusedly, helter-skelter.

atropellado, da [ah-tro-pel-lyah'-do, dah], *a.* Hasty, precipitate, speaking or acting in a hasty, precipitate manner. -*pp.* of ATROPELLAR.

atropellador, ra [ah-tro-pel-lyah-dor', rah], *m. & f.* 1. Trampler, one who overturns or tramples underfoot. 2. Transgressor, violator. 3. Lout, hooligan.

atropellamiento [ah-tro-pel-lyah-me-en'-to], *m.* Trampling underfoot; confusedness.

atropellaplatos [ah-tro-pel-lyah-plah'-tos], *f.* Clumsy servant; clumsy sort.

atropellar [ah-tro-pel-lyar'], *va.* 1. To run over, to tread underfoot. 2. **Atropellar las leyes**, to act in defiance of the law. 3. To insult with abusive language. 4. To hurry, to confuse. **Atropellar al caballo**, to overwork a horse. 5. *(LAm.)* To make love to; to seduce, dishonor. -*vn. (fig.)* To disregard; **atropellar por todo**, not to respect anything. -*vr.* To hurry oneself too much.

atropello [ah-tro-payl'-lyo], *m.* 1. Upset, act of upsetting. 2. Abuse, insult, outrage. **Los atropellos del dictador**, the dictator's crimes.

atropina [ah-tro-pee'-nah], *f.* Atropine, an alkaloid extracted from (Atropa) belladonna: highly poisonous.

atropos [ah-tro'-pos], *f.* 1. One of the three Fates. 2. A species of African viper. 3. *m.* The death's-head moth.

atroz [ah-troth'], *a.* 1. Atrocious, enormous, heinous, fiendlike. 2. Cruel, dreadful, outrageous. 3. Huge, vast, immense. **Estatura atroz**, enormous stature.

atrozar [ah-tro-thar'], *va. (Naut.)* To truss a yard to the mast.

atrozmente [ah-troth'-men-tay], *adv.* 1. Atrociously, heinously. 2. Excessively, to excess. **Trabajar atrozmente**, to work to excess.

atruhanado, da [ah-troo-ah-nah'-do, dah], *a.* Scurrilous, acting the buffoon, using low jests. (*Yo atrueno, yo atruene*, from *Atronar. V.* ACORDAR).

A.T.S. *m. & f. abr.* de **ayudante técnico sanitario** (nursing assistant).

atta., atto. *abr.* de **atenta, atento** (in courtesy formula in letters).

attaché [ah-tah-shay'], *m.* Attaché case:

attrezzo [ah-tray'-tho], *m. (Theat.)* Properties.

atuendo [ah-too-enn'-do], *m.* Attire, garb. 2. Pomp, ostentation.

atufado [ah-too-fah'-do], *a. (Cono Sur)* Angry, mad. *(CAm. Carib.)* Proud, vain, stuck-up.

atufamiento [ah-too-fah-me-ayn'-to], *m. (fig.)* Irritation, vexation.

atufar [ah-too-far'], *va.* To vex, to plague; to inhale noxious vapors. To irritate. -*vr.* 1. To be on the fret (licores fermentados). 2. To be angry. 3. *(CAm. Carib.)* To be proud.

atufo [ah-too'-fo], *m.* Vexation, irritation.

atulipanado [ah-too-le-pah-nah-do], *a.* Tulip-shaped.

atún [ah-toon'], *m.* 1. Tunny, tunnyfish, tuna, tuna fish. **Pedazo de atún**, an ignorant, stupid fellow. **Por atún y ver al duque**, to kill two birds with one stone. 2. A shrub of the Moluccas.

atunara [ah-too-nah'-rah], *f.* A place where tunny-fishes are caught.

atunera [ah-too-nay'-rah], *f.* A fishing-hook used in the tunny-fishery.

atunero [ah-too-nay'-ro], *m.* A fisherman engaged in the tunny fishery; a fishmonger who deals in tunny-fish.

aturar [ah-too-rar'], *va.* 1. To endure; to bear toil. 2. To work with judgement or prudence. 3. To stop or close tightly, hermetically.

aturdidamente [ah-toor-dee'-dah-men-tay], *adv.* 1. Thought-lessly, recklessly. 2. In a bewildered way.

aturdido, da [ah-toor-dee'-do, dah], *a.* Hare-brained, madbrain, giddy, wild, stupid. *-pp.* of ATURDIR.

aturdidura [ah-toor-de-doo'-rah], *f. (Cono Sur)* Stunned, dazed condition; bewilderement, confusion.

aturdimiento [ah-toor-de-me-en'-to], *m.* Perturbation of mind; dullness, drowsiness, consternation.

aturdir [ah-toor-deer'], *va.* 1. To perturb or perturbate, to confuse, to stun. 2. To stupefy with wonder or admiration. **La noticia nos aturdió**, the news stunned us. *-vr.* To be out of one's wits; to be perturbed or stupefied.

aturrullado [ah-too-roo-lyah'-do], *a.* Bewildered, perplexed; flustered.

aturrullar [ah-too-roo-lyar'], 1. *va.* To bewilder, perplex; to fluster. *-vr.* To get bewildered; to get flustered; **no te aturrulles cuando surja una dificultad**, don't get flustered when something awkward comes up.

aturullar [ah-toor-rool-lyar'], *va. (coll.)* To confound, to reduce to silence. Cf. TURULATO.

atusador [ah-too-sah-dor'], *m.* 1. Hair-dresser. 2. One who trims plants in a garden.

atusar [ah-too-sar'], *va.* 1. To cut hair even, to comb it smooth and even. 2. To trim the plants in a garden. *-vr.* To dress oneself with too much care.

atutía [ah-too-tee'-ah], *f.* Tutty, a sublimate of calamine collected in a furnace; crude zinc oxide.

auca [ah'-oo-cah], *f.* A goose. *V.* OCA.

audacia [ah-oo-dah'-teh-ah], *f.* Audacity, boldness.

audaz [ah-oo-dath'], *a.* Bold, audacious, fearless.

audazmente [ah-oo-dath'-men-tay], *adv.* Boldly, audaciously.

audibilidad [ah-oo-de-be-le-dahd'], *f.* Audibility.

audible [ah-oo-dee'-blay], *a.* Audible, that may be heard.

audición [ah-oo-de-the-on'], *f.* Audition, hearing. 2. *(Theat. etc).* Audition; **dar audición a uno**, to audition somebody. 3. *(Mus.)* Concert. 4. *(LAm.)* Audit.

audiencia [ah-oo-de-en'-the-ah], *f.* 1. Audience, a hearing given by men in power to those who have something to propose or represent. 2. Audience-chamber. 3. A court of oyer and terminer. 4. Law-officers appointed to institute some judicial inquiry. 5. **Audiencia pública**, public hearing. 6. **Audiencia pretorial en Indias**, a court of judicature in the West Indies.

audífono [ah-oo-dee'-fo-no], *m.* 1. Earphone, hearing aid. 2. Telephone receiver.

audiófilo, la [ah-oo-de-o'-fe-lo, lah], *m. & f.* Audiophile.

audiofrecuencia [ah-oo-de-o-fray-coo-en'-the-ah], *f.* Audiofrequency.

audiología [ah-o -de-o-lo-hee'-ah], *f.* Audiology.

audiómetro [ah-oo-de-o'-may-tro], *m.* Audiometer.

audión [ah-oo-de-on'], *m.* Audion, (used in long distance telephone calls and radio communication).

audioteleconferencia [ah-oo-de-o-tay-lay-con-fay-ren-the-ah], *f. (Comp.)* Audio teleconferencing

audiovisual [ah-oo-de-o-ve-soo-ahl'], *a.* Audio-visual.

auditar [ah-oo-de-tahr'], *va.* To audit.

auditivo, va [ah-oo-de-tee'-vo, vah], *a.* 1. Auditive, auditory, having the power of hearing. 2. Invested with the right of giving an audience.

audito [ah-oo-de'-to], *m.* Audit, auditing.

auditor [ah-oo-de-tor'], *m.* 1. Auditor, a hearer. 2. A judge advocate. **Auditor de la nunciatura**, a delegate of the Nuncio, appointed to hear and decide appeal causes respecting complaints against bishops. **Auditor de Rota**, one of the twelve prelates who compose the Rota at Rome, a court which inquires into and decides appeal causes in ecclesistical matters. **Auditor de proceso electrónico de datos** *(Comp.)*, Electronic data processing auditor (o EDP auditor).

auditoría [ah-oo-de-to-ree'-ah], *f.* The place and office of an *auditor.*

auditorio [ah-oo-de-to'-re-o], *m.* Auditory, an audience; congregation.

auditorio, ría [ah-oo-de-to'-re-o, ah], *a.* Auditory, *V.* AUDITIVO.

auge [ah'-oo-hay], *m.* 1. Meridian, the highest point of glory, power, dignity or fortune. 2. *(Astr.)* Apogee of a planet or star.

augur [ah-oo-goor'], *m.* Augur, augurer, person who pretends to predict future events by the flight of birds.

auguración [ah-oo-goo-rah-the-on'], *f.* Auguration, the act or prognosticating by the flight of birds.

augurar [ah-oo-goo-rahr'], *va.* To augur, to foresee, to foretell, to predict (predecir).

augurual [ah-oo-goo-rahl'], *a.* Augurial, belonging to augury.

augurio [ah-oo-goo'-re-o], *m.* Augury; omen, portent; prediction; **consultar los augurios**, to take the auguries. *V.* AGÜERO.

augustal [ah-goos-tahl'], *a.* Augustan.

Augusto, ta [ah-oo-goos'-to, tah], *a.* August, magnificent, majestic. *-m.* title of the Roman emperors after Octavious Cesar.

aula [ah'-oo-lah], *f.* 1. Hall where lectures are given. 2. The court or palace of a sovereign.

aulaga [ah-oo-lah'-gah], *f.* Furze, gorse.

aulario [ah-oo-lah'-re-o], *m. (Univ.)* Lecture room building, block of lecture rooms.

áulico [ah'-oo-le-co], 1. *a.* Court, palace. 2. *m.* Courtier.

aullador, ra [ah-ool-lyah-dor', rah], *m. & f.* Howler.

aullar [ah-ool-lyar'], *vn.* To howl, to yell, to cry: applied to wolves and dogs.

aullido, aúllo [ah-ool-lyee'-do, ah-ool'-lyo], *m.* Howl, the cry of a wolf or dog; a cry of horror or distress.

aumentación [ah-oo-men-tah-the-on'], *f.* 1. Augmentation, increase. 2. *(Rhet.)* Climax.

aumentado, da [ah-oo-men-tah-do, dah], *a.* Increased, augmented, onward. *-pp.* of AUMENTAR.

aumentador, ra [ah-oo-men-tah-dor', rah], *m. & f.* Enlarger, amplifying.

aumentar [ah-oo-men-tar'], *va.* To augment, to increase, to enlarge. **Aumento de población**, population increase. **Aumento de precio**, rise in price. **En aumento**, to increase. *-vr.* To gather, to grow larger.

aumentativo, va [ah-oo-men-tah-tee'-vo, vah], *a.* Increasing, enlarging.

aumento [ah-oo-men'-to], *m.* 1. Augmentation, increase, enlargement. 2. Access, accession; growth. **Aumento**, Promotion, advancement.

aun [ah-oon'], *adv.* 1. Even, nevertheless. **Te daría 100 dólares, y aun 200**, I'd give 100 dollars, even 200. **El libro es bueno aun con esas faltas**, the book is good even with those faults. 2. **Aun cuando**, even though.

aún [ah-oon'] *adv.* Still, yet. *V.* TODAVÍA and TAMBIÉN. **No ha llegado aún**, he hasn't arrived yet. **Aún está aquí**, he's still here.

aunar [ah-oo-nar'], *va.* 1. To unite, to assemble. 2. To incorporate, to mix. *-vr.* To be united or confederated for one end.

aunque [ah-oon-kay'], *adv.* Though, although, even if. **Aunque llueva vendremos**, we'll come even if it rains. **Es guapa aunque algo bajita**, she's pretty although rather short.

aúpa [ah-oo'-pah], *(coll.)* Up, up: a word used to animate children to get up. *-a.* **Una función de aúpa**, a slap-up do. **Una paliza de aúpa**, a thrashing and a half.

aupar [ah-oo-pahr'], *va.* To help up, get up (persona); *(fig.)* To boost, praise up; **aupar a uno al poder**, to raise somebody to power.

aura [ah'-oo-rah], *f.* 1. A vulture of Mexico and Cuba. 2. *(Poetic.)* A gentle breeze. **Aura popular**, *(Met.)* Popularity. 3. Aura, a peculiar premonitory symptom of epilepsy, a feeling as of a breath of air rising from below to the trunk and head.

auranciáceo [ah-oo-ran-the-ah'-thay-o], *a. (Bot.)* Citrus, citrous.

áureo, rea [ah'-oo-ray-o, ah], *a.* Golden, gilt, gold.

aureolar, auréola [ah-oo-ray-o'-lah], *f* Aureola, a circle of rays of light emblematic of glory.

aurícula [ah-oo-ree'-coo-lah], *f.* 1. Auricle, one of the two upper cavities of the heart. 2. *(Bot.)* The bear's-ear. 3. Auricle, the external ear.

auricular [ah-oo-re-coo-lar'], *a.* 1. Auricular, within the sense or reach of hearing. 2. Auricularis (dedo meñique).

auricular, *m.* 1. Headphone. 2. Earpiece or telephone receiver. **Auricular de casco**, headset.

aurífero, ra [ah-oo-ree'-fay-ro, rah], *a. (Poetic.)* Auriferous, containing or producing gold.

auriga [ah-oo-ree'-gah], *m.* 1. *(Poetic.)* A coachman. 2. *(Astr.)* Charioteer or Wagoner, one of the Northern constellations.

aurora [ah-oo-ro'-rah], *f.* 1. Dawn. 2. *(Poetic.)* The first appearance of a thing. 3. A beverage, simond-milk and cinnamon-water. 4. *(Naut.)* The morning watch-gun. 5. **Aurora boreal**, aurora borealis, or northern lights.

auscultación [ah-oos-cool-tah-the-on'], *f.* Sounding, auscultation.

auscultar [ah-oos-cool-tar'], *va.* To auscultate, to listen with ear or stethoscope as a means of diagnosis.

ausencia [ah-oo-sen'-the-ah], *f.* Absence. **Servir ausencias y enfermedades**, to perform the functions of absent or sick persons. **Tener alguno buenas o malas ausencia**, to be ill or well spoken of in one's absence. **En ausencia del gato se divierten los ratones**, when the cat's away the mice will play.

ausentarse [ah-oo-sen-tar'-say], *vr.* To absent oneself.

ausente [ah-oo-sen'-tay], *a.* Absent, distant. **Estar ausente de**, to be absent from.

auspiciado [ah-oos-pe-the-ah'-do], *a. (LAm.)* Sponsored, backed.

auspiciar [ah-oos-pe-the-ar'], *va.* To promote, sponsor, foster.

auspicio [ah-oos-pee'-the-o], *m.* 1. Auspice, or presage drawn from birds. 2. *(Met.)* Prediction of future events. 3. Protection, favor, patronage. **Bajo los auspicios de Vd.**, under your protection or your guidance.

austeramente [ah-oos-tay-rah-men'-tay], *adv.* Austerely, frowningly.

austeridad [ah-oos-tay-re-dahd'], *f.* Austerity, severity, rigor. **Austeridad económica**, economic austerity.

austero, ra [ah-oos-tay'-ro, rah], *a.* 1. Harsh, astringent to the taste. 2. Retired, mortified, and penitent. 3. Severe, rigid, harsh, austere.

austral, austrino, na [ah-oos-trahl', ah-oos-tree'-no, nah], *a.* Austral, southern.

Australia [ah-oos-trah-le-ah] Australia.

australiano, na [ah-oos-trah-le-an'-no, nah], *a. & m. & f.* Australian.

austriaco, ca [ah-oos-tre-ah'-co, cah], *a.* Austrian; of Austria.

austro [ah'-oos-tro], *m.* South wind; Notus.

autarquía [ah-oo-tar-kee'-ah], *f.* 1. Autarchy. Self government. 2. Autarky.

autazo [ah-oo-tah'-tho], *m. (LAm.)* Theft of a car.

auténtica [ah-oo-ten'-te-cah], *f.* Certificate, certification; authorized copy.

autenticación [ah-oo-ten-te-cah-the-on'], *f.* Authentication.

auténticamente [ah-oo-ten'-te-cah-men'-tay], *adv.* Authentically.

autenticar [ah-oo-ten-te-car'], *va.* To authenticate, to attest.

autenticidad [ah-oo-ten-te-the-dahd'], *f.* Authenticity.

auténtico, ca [ah-oo-ten'-te-co, cah], *a.* Authentic, genuine, veritable, indisputable, official. **Es un auténtico campeón**, he's a real champion. **Días de auténtico calor**, days of real heat.

autentificar [ah-ten-te-fe-cahr'], *va.* To authenticate.

autería [ah-oo-tay-re'-ah], *f. (Cono Sur)* Evil omen, bad sign; witchcraft.

autero, ra [ah-tay'-ro], *m. & f. (LAm.)* Car thief.

autero, ra [ah-oo-tay'-ro], *m. & f. (Cono Sur)* Pessimistic, defeatist; jins, person who brings bad luck.

autillo [ah-oo-teel'-lyo], *m.* 1. *(dim.)* A particular act of decree of the Inquisition. 2. *(Orn.)* The barn-owl.

autismo [ah-oo-tes'-mo], *m.* Autism.

autista [ah-oo-tes'-tah], *a.* Autistic.

auto [ah'-oo-to], *m.* 1. A judicial decree or sentence. 2. A writ, warrant. 3. An edict, ordinance. **Auto de Fe**, the sentence given by the Inquisition. 4. *(Obs.)* Act, action. **Auto definitivo**, definitive act, which has the force of a sentence. **Auto sacramental**, an allegorical or dramatical piece of poetry on some religious subject, repreented as a play. **Autos**, the pleadings and proceedings in a lawsuit. **Estar en autor or en los autos**, to know a thing profoundly. **Auto acordado**, a sentence or decision of a supreme court, to be observed as a precedent.

auto [ah'-oo-to], *m.* Auto, automobile, car.

autoabastecerse [ah-oo-to-ah-bas-tay-thayr'-say], *vr.* To supply oneself.

autoacusación [ah-oo-to-ah-coo-sah-the-on'], *f.* Self-accusation.

autoacusarse [ah-oo-to-ah-coo-sahr'-say], *vr.* To accuse oneself.

autoadhesivo [ah-oo-to-ah-day-se'-vo], *a.* Self-adhesive; self-sealing.

autoadulación [ah-oo-to-ah-doo-lah-the-on'], *f.* Self-pray.

autoaislarse [ah-oo-to-ah-es-lahr'-say], *vr.* To isolate oneself.

autoalimentación [ah-oo-to-ah-le-mayn-tah-the-on'], *f.* **Autoalimentación de hojas**, automatic paper feed.

autoanálisis [ah-oo-to-ah-nah'-le-ses], *m.* Self-analysis.

autoayuda [ah-to-ah-yoo'-dah], *f.* Self-help.

autobiografía [ah-oo-to-be-o-gra-fee'-ah], *f.* Autobiography.

autobiográfico, ca [ah-oo-to-be-o-grah'-fe-co, cah], *a.* Autobiographical.

autobombearse [ah-oo-to-bom-bay-ahr-say], *vr.* To blow one's own trumpet, to shoot a line.

autobombo [ah-oo-to-bom'-bo], *m.* Self-praise.

autobús [ah-oo-to-boos'], *m.* Bus, motorbus. **Autobús de dos pisos**, double-decker bus.

autocamión [ah-oo-to-cah-me-on'], *m.* Motor truck.

autocar [ah-oo-to-car'], *m.* Coach, bus.

autocaravana [ah-oo-to-cah-rah-vah'-nah], *f.* Camper, camping vehicle.

autocarril [ah-oo-to-car-reel'], *m. (LAm.)* Railway car.

autocensura [ah-oo-to-thayn-soo-rah], *f.* Self-censorship.

autocine [ah-oo-to-the'-nay], *m.* Drive-in cinema.

autoclave [ah-oo-to-clah'-vay], *f.* Autoclave, sterilizer.

autoconfesado [ah-oo-to-con-fay-sah'-do], *a.* Self-confessed.

autoconfesarse [ah-oo-to-con-fay-sahr'-say], *vr.* To confess oneself.

autoconfesión [ah-oo-to-con-fay-se-on'], *f.* Self-confession.

autoconfianza [ah-oo-to-con-fe-ahn'-thah], *f.* Self-confidence.

autoconservación [ah-oo-to-con-ser-vah-the-on'], *f.* Self-preservation.

autoconvencerse [ah-oo-to-con-vayn-thayr'-say], *vr.* To convince oneself.

autocracia [ah-oo-to-crah'-the-ah], *f.* Autocracy, absolute sovereignty.

autócrata [ah-oo-to'-crah-tah], *m.* Autocrat.

autocrático, ca [ah-oo-to-crah'-te-co, cah], *a.* Autocratical.

autocremarse [ah-oo-to-cray-mahr'-say], *vr.* To set fire to oneself, to burn oneself.

autocrítica [ah-oo-to-cre'-te-cah], *f.* Self-criticism, self examination.

autocrítico [ah-oo-to-cre'-te-co], *a.* Self-critical.

autóctono, na [ah-oo-toc'-to-no, nah], *a.* Autochthonous, native of the country.

auto-choque [ah-oo-to-cho'-ke], *m.* Bumper car.
autodefensa [ah-to-day-fen'-sah], *f.* Self-defence.
autodegradación [ah-oo-to-day-grah-dah-the-on'], *f.* Self-abasement.
autodenominarse [ah-oo-to-day-no-me-nahr'-say], *vr.* To call oneself.
autodestructivo [ah-oo-to-days-trooc-te'-vo], *a.* Self-destructive.
autodestruirse [ah-oo-to-days-troo-eer'-say], *a.* To self-destruct.
autodeterminación [ah-oo-to-day-tayr-me-nah-the-on'], *f.* Self-determination.
autodidacta [ah-to-de-dac'-tah], *a. m. & f.* V. AUTODIDACTO.
autodidacto [ah-oo-to-de-dac'-to], 1. *a.* Self-educated, self-taught. 2. *m. & f.* Autodidact.
autodisciplina [ah-oo-to-dis-the-plee'-na], *f.* Self-discipline.
autodominio [ah-oo-to-do-me'-ne-o], *m.* Self-control.
autoengaño [ah-oo-to-ayn-gah'-nyo], *m.* Self-deception.
autoescuela [ah-oo-to-es-coo-ay'-lah], *f.* Driving school.
autoexpresión [ah-oo-to-ex-pray-se-on'], *f.* Self-expression.
autofinanciarse [ah-oo-to-fe-nahn-the-ahr'-say], *vr.* To finance oneself.
autógena [ah-oo-to'-hay-nah], *f.* Welding.
autogiro [ah-oo-to-hee'-ro], *m.* Autogiro.
autogobernarse [ah-oo-to-go-bayr-nahr'-say], *vr.* To govern itself.
autogobierno [ah-oo-to-go-be-ayr-no], *m.* Self-government.
autogol [ah-oo-to-gol'], *m.* Own goal.
autografía [ah-oo-to-grah-fee'-ah], *f.* The art of copying a writing or drawing by lithography.
autográfico, ca [ah-oo-to-grah'-fe-co, cah], *a.* Autographical.
autógrafo [ah-oo-toh'-grah-fo], *m.* Autograph.
autohotel [ah-oo-to-o-tel'], *m.* Motel.
autoimpuesto [ah-oo-to-em-poo-ays'-tao], *a.* Self-imposed.
autoinducción [ah-oo-to-in-dooc-the-on'], *f.* (Elec.) Self-induction.
autoinducido [ah-oo-to-en-doo-the'-do], *a.* Self-induced.
autoinflamación [ah-oo-to-en-flah-mah-the-on'], *f.* Spontaneous combustion.
autoinfligido [ah-oo-to-en-fle-he'-do], *a.* Self-inflicted.
autointoxicación [ah-oo-to-in-toc-se-cah-the-on'], *f.* Autointoxication, poisoning from toxic substances in the body.
autolesionarse [ah-oo-to-lay-se-o-nahr'-say], *vr.* To inflict injury on oneself.
autolimpiable [ah-oo-to-leem-pe-ah'-blay], *a.* Self-cleaning.
autollamarse [ah-oo-tol-lyah-mahr'-say], *vr.* To call oneself.
automación [ah-oo-to-mah-the-on'], *f.* Automation.
automarginado, da [ah-oo-to-mahr-he-nah-do], *a. m. & f.* Drop-out.
automarginarse [ah-oo-to-mahr-he-nahr'-say], *vr.* To drop out, to stay away from, to keep clear of.
autómata [ah-oo-toh'-mah-tah], *m.* 1. A machine containing in itself the power of motion. 2. Automaton, a machine imitating the actions of living animals.
automáticamente [ah-to-mah-te-cah-mayn-tay], *adv.* Automatically.
automático, ca [ah-oo-to-mah'-te-co, cah], *a.* Automatic.
automastismo [ah-oo-to-mah-tees'-mo], *m.* Automatism.
automatización [ah-oo-to-mah-tee-tha-the-on'], *f.* Automation. **Automatización de la oficina** (Comp.), office automation.
automatizar [ah-oo-to-mah-tee-thar'], *va.* To automate.
automedicarse [ah-oo-to-may-de-cahr'-say], *vr.* To treat oneself.
automedonte [ah-oo-to-may-don'-tay], *m.* (LAm.) Busdriver; driver.
automercado [ah-oo-to-mayr-cah'-do], *m.* (Carib.) Supermarket.
automoción [ah-oo-to-mo-the-on'], *f.* **La industria de la automoción**, the car industry.

automotor, ra [ah-oo-to-mo-tor', rah], *a.* Self-propelling.
automotriz [ah-oo-to-mo-treeth'], *a.* Automotive.
automóvil [ah-oo-to-mo'-veel], *m.* Automobile, car. **Automóvil acorazado**, armored car. **Automóvil de plaza**, taxi, taxicab. **Automóvil de segunda mano**, used car, second-hand car. **Automóvil de turismo**, touring car.
automovilismo [ah-oo-to-mo-ve-lees'-mo], *m.* Motoring; **automovilismo deportivo**, motor racing.
automovilista [ah-oo-to-mo-ve-lees'-tah], *m. & f.* Motorist, automobile rider.
automovilístico [ah-oo-to-mo-ve-lees'-te-co], *a.* Car; **accidente automovilístico**, car accident.
automutilación [ah-oo-to-moo-te-lah-the-on'], *f.* Self-mutilation.
automutilarse [ah-oo-to-moo-te-lahr'-say], *vr.* To mutilate oneself.
autonomía [ah-oo-to-no-mee'-ah], *f.* Autonomy, the condition of self-government, independence. 2. (Náut, Aer.) Range; **un avión de gran autonomía**, a long-range aircraft.
autonómico [ah-oo-to-no'-me-co], *a.* Relating to autonomy; **elecciones autonómicas**, elections for the autonomous regions.
autónomo, ma [ah-oo-to'-no-mo, mah], *a.* Autonomous, independent, free.
autopatrulla [ah-oo-to-pah-troo'-lyah], *m.* (Mex.) Patrol car.
autopegado [ah-oo-to-pay-gah-do], *a.* Self-sealing (sobre).
autopiano [ah-oo-to-pe-ah'-no], *m.* Player piano.
autopista [ah-oo-to-pees'-tah], *f.* Highway, freeway. **Autopista de acceso limitado**, freeway.
autoplastia [ah-oo-to-plahs'-te-ah], *f.* Anaplasty, plastic surgery.
autopolinización [ah-oo-to-po-le-ne-thah-the-on'], *f.* Self-pollination.
autoproclamado [ah-oo-to-pro-cla-mah-do], *a.* Self-proclaimed.
autoprofesor [ah-oo-to-pro-fay-sor'], *m.* Teaching machine.
autopropulsado [ah-oo-to-pro-pool-sah'-do], *a.* Self-propelled.
autopropulsión [ah-oo-to-pro-pool-se-on'], *f.* Self-propulsion.
autoprotegerse [ah-oo-to-pro-tay-her'-say], *vr.* To protect oneself.
autopsia [ah-oo-top'-se-ah], *f.* Autopsy.
autopublicidad [ah-oo-to-poo-ble-the-dahd'], *f.* Self-advertisement.
autor [ah-oo-tor'], *m.* 1. Author, maker, composer. 2. Writer, one that composes a literary work. 3. Manager of a theater. 4. (Law.) Plaintiff or claimant. **Autor de nota**, a celebrated writer. 5. Speaking of watches, the maker. 6. The cause of anything. **Ser autor de**, to author.
autora [ah-oo-to'-rah], *f.* Authoress.
autoría [ah-oo-to-re'-ah], *f.* Authorship.
autoridad [ah-oo-to-ree-dahd'], *f.* 1. Authority or power derived from a public station, merit, or birth; credit. **Las autoridades**, the authorities. 2. Ostentation, display of grandeur. 3. Authority, words cited from a book or writing.
autoritario, ria [ah-oo-to-re-tah'-re-oh, ah], *m. & f. a.* Authoritarian.
autoritarismo [ah-oo-to-re-tah-res'-mo], *m.* Authoritarianism.
autoritativo, va [ah-oo-to-re-tah-tee'-vo, vah], *a.* Arrogant, assuming.
autorización [ah-oo-to-re-tha-the-on'], *f.* Authorization, permission, licence.
autorizadamente [ah-oo-to-re-thah-dah-men'-tay], *adv.* Authoritatively.
autorizado, da [ah-oo-to-re-thah'-do, dah, *a.* Respectable, commendable. -*pp.* of AUTORIZAR.
autorizador [ah-oo-to-re-thah-dor'], *m.* He who authorizes.
autorizar [ah-oo-to-re-thar'], *va.* 1. To authorize, to give power or authority to. **Autorizar a uno para**, to authorize somebody to. 2. To legalize, 3. To exalt.
autorradio [ah-oo-tor-rah'-de-o], *f.* Car radio.

autorretrato [ah-oo-to-ray-trah'-to], *m.* Self-portrait.

autorzuelo [ah-oo-tor-thoo-ay-lo], *m.* Scribbler, hack, pen-pusher.

autoservicio [ah-oo-to-ser-vee'-the-o], *m.* Self-service.

autosostenerse [ah-oo-to-sos-tay-nayr'-say], *vr.* To pay one's own way, to be self-supporting.

auto-stop [ah-oo-to-stop'], *m.* Hitch-hiking. **Hacer autostop**, to hitch-hike.

autostopismo [ah-oo-to-ays-to-pes'-mo], *m.* Hitch-hiking.

autostopista [ah-oo-to-ays-to-pes'-tah], *m. & f.* Hitch-hiker.

autosuficiencia [ah-oo-to-soo-fe-the-en'-the-ah], *f.* Self-sufficiency.

autosuficiente [ ], *a.* Self-sufficient.

autosugestión [ah-oo-to-soo-hes-te-on'], *f.* Autosuggestion, self-suggestion.

autotitularse [ah-oo-to-tee-too-lahr'-say], *vr.* To title oneself.

autoventa [ah-oo-to-vayn'-tah], *atr.* **vendedor autoventa**, traveling salesman.

autovía [ah-oo-to-ve'-ah], *f.* Main road.

autovivienda [ah-oo-to-ve-ve-ayn'-dah], *f.* Caravan, trailer.

auvernia [ah-oo-ver'-ne-ah], *f.* Auvergne.

auxiliador, ra [ah-ook-se-le-ah-dor', rah], *m. & f.* Auxiliary, assistant.

auxiliar [ah-ook-se-le-ar'], *va.* 1. To aid, to help, to assist. 2. To attend a dying person.

auxiliar [ah-ook-se-le-ar'], *a.* Auxiliar, auxiliatory, helping, assistant. **Tropas auxiliares**, auxiliary troops. **Obispo auxiliar**, an assistant bishop. **Verbo auxiliar**, an auxiliary verb.

auxiliatorio, ria [ah-ook-se-le-ah-to'-re-o, ah], *a. (Law.)* Auxiliary.

auxilio [ah-ook-se'-lyo], *m.* Aid, help, assistance. **Auxilio social**, social work.

av. *abr.* de **Avenida** (avenue, av, ave.).

a/v. *(Com.) abr.* de **a vista** (at sight).

avacado, da [ah-vah-cah'-do, dah], *a.* Cow-like, resembling a cow: applied to a big-bellied horse.

avada [ah-vah'-dah], *m. (Carib.)* Queer.

avadarse [ah-vah-dar'-say], *vr.* 1. To become fordable. 2. *(Obs.)* to subside: applied to passion.

avahar [ah-vah-ar'], *va.* 1. To warm with the breath, or with steam and vapor. 2. To wither (plantas). *-vr.* To steam, to give off steam.

aval [ah-vahl'], *m.* Security, guarantee, indorsement (letras, cheques).

avalancha [ah-vah-lahn'-chah], *f.* Avalanche. *V.* ALUD.

avalar [ah-vah-lar'], *v. imp. (Prov.)* (The earth) trembles. *-va. (Com.)* To guarantee; *(fig.)* To support.

avalentado, da [ah-vah-len-tah'-do, dah], *a.* Bragging, boasting.

avalizar [ah-vah-le-thar'], *va.* To mark the dangerous spots in a channel with buoys.

avalo [ah-vah'-lo], *m. (Prov.)* 1. A slight movement. 2. An earthquake.

avalorar [ah-vah-lo-ar'], *va.* 1. To estimate, to value. 2. *(Met.)* To inspirit, to animate.

avaluación [ah-vah-loo-ah-the-on'], *f.* Valuation, rate, assessment.

avaluar [ah-vah-loo-ar'], *va.* To value, to appraise, to estimate.

avalúo [ah-vah-loo'-oh], *m.* Valuating, official appraisement.

avallar [ah-vah-lyar'], *va.* To inclose a piece of ground with pales or hedges.

avambrazo [ah-vam-brah'-tho], *m.* Piece of ancient armor that served to cover the forearm.

avampiés [ah-vam-pe-ess'], *m. (Obs.)* Instep of boots, or spatterdashes.

avancarga [ah-van-car'-gah]: **cañon de avancarga**; muzzle loader.

avance [ah-van'-thay], *m.* 1. *(Mil.)* Advance, attack, assault. 2. Among merchants, an account of goods received and sold. 3. A balance in one's favor. 4. *(Elec.)* Lead; *(Med.)* feed. 5. *(Cine)* Trailer; preview. **avance informativo**, advanced news, update. 6. *(CAm.)* Theft, looting.

avandicho [ah-van-dee'-cho], *(Obs.) V.* SOBREDICHO. Aforesaid.

avantal [ah-van-tahl'], *m. (Obs.)* Apron. *V.* DELANTAL.

avantalillo [ah-van-tah-leel'-lyo], *m. dim. (Obs.)* A small apron.

avante [ah-van'-tay], *adv.* 1. *(Naut.)* Ahead. **Hala avante**, pull ahead. 2. *(Obs.) V.* ADELANTE.

avantrén [ah-van-tren'], *m.* Limbers of a gun-carriage.

avanzada [ah-van-thah'-dah], *f. (Mil.)* Quitpost, reconnoitring body.

avanzado, da [ah-van-thah'-do, dah], *a.* Advanced; onward. **Avanzado de edad**, or **de edad avanzada**, advanced in years, stricken in years. *-pp.* of AVANZAR.

avanzar [ah-van-thar'], *vn.* 1. To advance, to attack, to engage, to come on. 2. To have a balance in one's favor. *-va.* 1. To advance, to push forward. 2. *(Carib.)* To vomit, to throw up. *-vr.* To advance, to move on, to push on. **No avanzo nada**, I'm not making any headway. **Avanzar a velocidad máxima** *(Comp.)*, to hurtle.

avanzo [ah-van'-tho], *m.* 1. Among merchants an account of goods received and sold. 2. A balance in one's favor.

avaramente [ah-vah-rah-men'-tay], *adv.* Avariciously, in a covetous manner, miserably.

avaricia [ah-vah-ree'-the-ah], *f.* Avarice, cupidity, covetousness.

avariciar [ah-va-ree-the-ar'], *va. & vn. (Obs.)* To covet, to desire anxiously.

avariciosamente [ah-vah-re-the-o-sah-men'-tay], *adv.* Greedily, covetously.

avaricioso, sa [ah-vah-re-the-o'-so, sah], *a.* 1. *V.* AVARIENTO. 2. Anxious to eat or drink.

avariento, ta [ah-vah-re-en'-to, tah], *a.* Avaricious, covetous, miserly, miserable, close, narrow.

avariosis [ah-v-ah-re-o'-sees], *f. (LAm.)* Syphillis.

avaro, ra [ah-vah'-ro, rah], *a.* Miserably, mean; **ser avaro de alabanzas**, to be sparing in one's praise, to be mean with one's praises. *V.* AVARIENTO.

avasallador [ah-vah-sah-lyah-dor'], *a.* Overwhelming; domineering.

avasallamiento [ah-vah-sah-lyah-me-ayn-to], *m.* Subjugation.

avasallar [ah-vah-sal-lyar'], *va.* To subdue, to subject, to enslave, to mancipate. *-vr.* To become subject, to become a vassal.

avatar [ah-vah-tahr'], *m.* Avatar, change, transformation; incarnation.

avda. *abr.* de **Avenida** (Avenue, av., ave.).

ave [ah'-vay], *f.* 1. Bird, a general name for the feathered kind. 2. Fowl. **Ave de rapiña**, a bird of prey. **Ave brava or silvestre**, a wild bird. **Ave fría**, lapwing, a kind of plover. Vanellus. **Todas las aves son sus pares**, birds of a feather flock together. **Es un ave**, he is very swift, active. **Ave nocturna**, *(Met.)* one who rambles about in the night-time. **Ave zonza**, a lazy, half-foolish person. **Ave de mal agüero**, bird of ill omen. **Ave de paso**, migratory bird, rolling stone (personas). **Ave zancuda**, Wader.

avecinar [ah-vay-the-nar'], *va.* 1. *(Obs.)* To bring near. 2. *V.* AVECINAR. *-vr.* To come near, to approach.

avencidamiento [ah-vay-thin-dah-me-en'-to], *m.* 1. Acquisiton of the rights of a citizen or freeman. 2. The act of residing in a place invested with the rights of a citizen.

avecindar [ah-vay-thin-dar'], *va.* To admit to the privilege of a denizen, to enrol in the number of the citizens of a place. *-vr.* 1. To acquire the rights and priviledges of a denizen or citizen. 2. To approach, to join.

avechucho [ah-vay-choo'-cho], *m.* 1. An ugly bird. 2. *(Orn.)* Sparrowhawk. 2. *(Met.)* Ragamuffin, a paltry mean fellow.

avechuco [ah-vay-choo'-co], *m.* Ugly bird (pájaro). Ragamuffin, pest (persona).

avefría [ah-vay-fre'-ah], *f.* Lapwing.

avejentado, da [ah-vay-hen-tah'-do, dah], *a.* Appearing old without being really so, oldish. *-pp.* of AVEJENTAR.

avejentar [ah-vay-hen-tar'], *va. & vr.* To look old, to appear older than one really is.

avejigar [ah-vay-he-gar'], *va.* To produce pimples or small blisters. *-vr.* To blister.

avelar [ah-vay-lar'], *vn. (Naut.)* To set sail.

avellana [ah-vel-lyah'-nah], *f.* Filbert, hazelnut. **Avellana índica** or **de la India**, or **nuez ungüentaria**, myrobalan, or Indian nut, used only in perfumes.

avellanado, da [ah-vel-lyah-nah'-do, dah], *a.* Nut-brown, of the color of nuts. *-pp.* of AVELLANARSE.

avellanador [ah-vel-lyah-na-dor'], *m.* Countersink bit, rose-bit; rimer.

avellanal [ah-vayl-lyah-nah'], *m.* Hazel wood, hazel plantation.

avellanar [ah-vel-lyah-nar'], *m.* 1. A plantation of hazels or nut-trees. 2. *-va. (Tec.)* To countersink.

avellanarse [ah-vel-lyah-nar'-say], *vr.* To shrivel, to grow as dry as a nut.

avellanedo [ah-vay-lyah-nah'-do], *m.* Hazel wood, hazel plantation.

avellanera [ah-vel-lyah-nay'-rah], *f. V.* AVELLANO.

avellanero, ra [ah-vel-lyah-nay'-ro, rah], *m. & f.* A dealer in nuts and filberts.

avellanica [ah-vael-lyah-nee'-cah], *f. dim.* A small filbert.

avellano [ah-vel-lyah'-no], *m. (Bot.)* The common hazel-nut tree. Filbert-tree.

Avemaría [ah-vay-mah-ree'-ah], *f.* Ave Mary, the angel's salutation of the holy Virgin. **Al avemaría**, at the fall of night. **Es un avemaría**, in an instant. **Saber una cosa como el avemaría**, to know by heart, thoroughly. **¡Ave María!** Exclamation denoting surprise. **¡Ave María purísima!** God bless you!. **Un Avemaría**, a Hail Mary.

avena [ah-vay'-nah], *f. (Bot.)* 1. Oats. Avena, L. **Avena blanca**, Cultivated white oat. **Avena sativa alba. Avena negra**, cultivated black oat. **Avena sativa negra. Avena desnuda**, naked oat. (Avena nuda). **Avena estéril, cugua** or **cula**, bearded oat-grass. Avena esterilis. **Avena estrigosa, or afreitas** of the Gallicians, bristle-pointed oat. **Avena** estrigosa. **Avena pubescente**, downy oat-grass. Avena pubescens. **Avena flavescente**, narrow-leaved oat-grass. Avena pratensis. **Avena alpina**, great alpine oat-grass. Avena alpina. **Avena flavescente**, yellow oat-grass. Avena flavescens. **Avena loca** or **silvestre**, wild oat. **Avena común**, French oat. **Avena oriental**, tartarian oat. Avena orientalis. **Avena geórgica**, potato oat. 2. *(Poetic.)* A pastoral pipe, made of the stalks of corn, and used by shepherds.

avenáceo, cea [ah-vay-nah'-thay-o, ah], *a.* Oat-like.

avenado, da [ah-vay-nah'-do, dah], *a.* 1. *(Obs.)* Belonging or relating to oats. 2. Lunatic, liable to fits of madness, with lucid intervals. *-pp.* of AVENAR.

avenal [ah-vay-nahl'], *m.* A field sown with oats.

avenamiento [ah-vay-nah-me-en'-to], *m.* The act of draining off water.

avenar [ah-vay-nar'], *va.* To drain or draw off water.

avenate [ah-vay-nah'-tay], *m.* Water-gruel, oatmeal-gruel.

avenenar [ah-vay-nay-nar'], *va.* To poison. *V.* ENVENENAR.

avenencia [ah-vay-nen'-the-ah], *f.* 1. Agreement, compact, bargain. 2. Conformity, union, concord. **Más vale mala avenencia, que buena sentencia**, a bad compromise is better than a good lawsuit.

avenenteza, aveninteza [ah-vay-nen-tay'-thah, ah-vay-nin-tay'-thah], *f. (Obs.)* Occassion, opportunity. *(Yo avengo, yo avine*, from *Avenir. V.* VENIR). (*Yo me avengo, yo me avine*, from *Avenirse, V.* VENIR).

aveníceo, cea [ah-vay-nee'-tahy-o, ah], *a.* Oaten, belonging to or made of oats.

avenida [ah-vay-nee'-dah], *f.* 1. Avenue (calle). 2. Flood, inundation, freshet. 3. *(Met.)* A concurrence of several things. 4. Agreement, concord. **Avenidas**, 1. Avenues or roads meeting in a certain place. 2. *(Naut.)* Freshes.

avenido, da [ah-vay-nee'-do, dah], *a.* Agreed. **Bien or mal avenidos**, Living on good or bad terms. *-pp.* of AVENIR.

avenidor, ra [ah-vay-ne-dor'-rah], *m. & f. (Lit. us.)* Mediator, one that interferes between two parties to reconcile them.

avenimiento [ah-vay-ne-me-en'-to], *m.* Convention.

avenir [ah-vay-neer'], *va.* To reconcile parties at variance. *-vr.* 1. To settle differences on friendly terms. **No se avienen**, they don't get on. 2. To join, to unite, to consent; be in harmony with. 3. To compound, to compromise.

aventadero [ah-ven-tah-day'-ro], *m. (Prov.)* A winnowing-place.

aventado, da [ah-ven-tah'-do, dah], *a.* **Escotas aventadas**, flowing sheets. *(CAm. Mex.)* Brave, daring. *-pp.* of AVENTAR.

aventador [ah-ven-tah-dor'], *m.* 1. Fanner, blower, blowing fan, ventilator. *(Arch.)* Scutcher. (Gas) Bat-wing. 2. Winnover, one who separates chaff from grain. 3. A wooden fork with three or four prongs, used for winnowing corn. 4. A fan used for blowing the fire.

aventadora [ah-vayn-tah-do'-rah], *f.* Winnowing machine.

aventadura [ah-ven-tah-doo'-rah], *f.* Wind-gall, a disease of horses, **aventadura de estopa**, *(Naut.)* A leak.

aventaja [ah-ven-tah'-hah], *f.* 1. Advantage, profit. 2. *(Law. Prov.)* Part of the personal estate or chattels of a person deceased, which his or her surviving consort takes before a division of the furniture is made.

aventajadamente [ah-ven-tah-hah-dah-men'-tay], *adv.* 1. Advantageously, conveniently, opportunely. 2. *(Prov.)* Exceedingly, well.

aventajado, da [ah-ven-tah-hah'-do, dah], *a.* 1. Advantageous, profitable, convenient. 2. Beautiful, excellent. 3. Having additional pay (soldados). *-pp.* of AVENTAJAR.

aventajar [ah-ven-tah-har'], *va.* 1. To acquire or enjoy advantages. 2. To ameliorate, to improve. 3. To surpass, to excel, to cut out. *-vr.* To exceed, to excel.

aventar [ah-ven-tar'], *va.* 1. To move the air, to fan, to air. 2. To toss something in the wind, such as corn, to winnow it. 3. To expel, to drive away. 4. *(Naut.)* To work out the oakum (barcos). *-vr.* 1. To be inflated or puffed up. 2. To escape, to run away. 3. *(Prov.)* To be tainted (carne). 4. To beat it (largarse). 5. *(Mex.)* To decide. 5. *(LAm.)* To throw oneself, to take risks.

aventino [ah-ven-tee'-no], *m.* Aventine, one of the seven hills of Rome.

aventón [ah-vayn-ton], *m. (Mex.)* Throw; lift; **pedir aventón**, to hitch a lift.

aventura [ah-ven-too'-rah], *f.* 1. Adventure, event, incident. 2. Casualty, contingency, chance. 3. Adventure, an enterprise in which something must be left to hazard. 4. Hazar, risk. 5. Duty formerly paid to lords of the manor.

aventurado, da [ah-ven-too-rah'-do, dah], *a.* **Bienaventurado**, fortunate. **Malaventurado**, unfortunate. *-pp.* of AVENTURAR.

aventurar [ah-en-too-rar'], *va.* To venture, to hazard, to risk, to endanger, to jump. *-vr.* To dare, take risks, take a chance.

aventurera [ah-vayn-too-ray'-rah], *f.* Adventuress.

aventurero [ah-ven-too-ray'-ro, rah], *a.* 1. Voluntary; undisciplined (reclutas, soldados). 2. Applied to a person who voluntarily goes to market to sell any articles. 3. *V.* ADVENEDIZO.

averamia [ah-vay-rah'-me-ah], *f.* A kind of duck.

averar [ah-vay-rar'], *va.* To aver, to certify, or affirm.

avergonzado, da [ah-ver-gon-thah'-do, dah], *a.* Ashamed, embarrassed, abashed.

avergonzar [ah-ver-gon-thar'], *va.* To shame, to abash, to confound, or to make ashamed, to put to the blush, to put out of countenance. *-vr.* To shame, or be ashamed, to blush for. **Avergonzarse por**, to be ashamed about. (*Yo avergüenzo,* *yo avergüence*, from *Avergonzar. V.* ACORDAR). (*Yo me avergüenzo, yo me avergüence*, from *Avergonzarse. V.* ACORDAR).

avería [ah-vay-ree'-ah], *f.* 1. Breakdown (coche). **Tuvieron una avería**, they had a breakdown. 2. Damage (mercancías). 3. Average. **Avería gruesa**, general average. **Avería particular**, particular average. **Avería ordinaria**, usual average. 4. In the India trade, a certain duty laid on merchants and merchandise. 5. A collection of birds; an aviary. **Hacer una avería**, to suffer an average. 6. (*Cono Sur*) Dangerous criminal, thug.

averiado, da [ah-vay-re-ah'-do, dah], *a.* Averaged, damaged. **Los faros están averiados**, the lights have failed. -*pp.* of AVERIARSE.

averiar [ah-vay-re-ahr'], *va.* To damage, spoil; (*Mech.*) To cause a breakdown.

averiarse [ah-vay-re-ar'-sa], *vr.* To make average, to sustain damage, to be damaged.

averiguable [ah-vay-re-goo-ah'-blay], *a.* Investigable, what may be verified or ascertained.

averiguación [ah-vay-re-goo-ah-the-on'], *f.* Investigation. **Averiguación judicial**, a judicial inquiry, an inquest.

averiguadamente [ah-vay-re-goo-ah-dah-men'-tay], *adv.* Certainly, surely.

averiguado [ah-vay-re-goo-dah'-do], *a.* Certain, established. **Es un hecho averiguado**, it is an established fact.

averiguador, ra [ah-vay-re-goo-ah-dor', rah], *m. & f.* A scarcher or examiner.

averiguar [ah-vay-re-goo-ar'], *va.* To inquire, to investigate, to find out. **Averiguarse con alguno**, to bring one to reason. **Averíguelo Vargas**, it is difficult to investigate. -*vn.* (*CAm. Mex.*) To quarrel, fight. -*vr.* **Averiguarse con uno**, to tie somebody down; to get along with somebody.

averiguata [ah-vay-re-goo-ah'-tah], *f.* (*Mex.*) Argument, fight.

averigüetas [ah-vay-re-goo-ay'-tahs], *m. & f.* Snooper, busybody.

averío [ah-vay-ree'-o], *m.* 1. (*Prov.*) Beast of burden. 2. Flock of birds. 3. Aviary.

averrugado, da [ah-ver-roo-gah'-do, dah], *a.* Having many pimples in the face. Warty.

averrugarse [ah-ver-roo-gar'-say], *vr.* (*Med.*) To show pimples or warts (piel).

aversión [ah-ver-se-on'], *f.* 1. Aversion, opposition, dislike. 2. Malevolence, abhorrence, loathing. 3. Fear, apprehension.

averso, sa [ah-ver'-so, sah], *a.* Averse, hostile; perverse.

avertir [ah-ver-teer'], *va. V.* APARTAR.

avestruz [ah-ves-trooth'], *m.* 1. (*Orn.*) Ostrich. 2. (*LAm.*) Idiot.

avetado, da [ah-vay-tah'-do, dah], *a.* Veined, scamed (minerales, madera).

avetarda, *f. V.* AVUTARDA.

avetoro [ah-vay-to'-ro], *m.* Bittern.

avezado [ah-vay-thah'-do], *a.* Accustomed; inured, experienced. **Los avezados en estos menesteres**, those experienced in such activities.

avezar [ah-vay-thar'], *va.* 1. To accustom, to habituate. 2. To train the hawk. -*vr.* To get used; to become accustomed. *V.* ACOSTUMBRAR.

aviación [ah-ve-ah-the-on'], *f.* Aviation, flying. **Aviación comercial**, commercial aviation or flying.

aviado [ah-ve-ah-do], *m.* (*Amer.*) One supplied with money and other articles to work a silver-mine. **Dejar a uno aviado**, to leave somebody in the lurch.

aviador [ah-ve-ah-dor'], *m.* 1. Aviator, flyer. 2. Supplier, provider. 3. (*And.* Carib, *Cono Sur*) (*Com.*) Mining speculator; moneylender.

aviadora [ah-ve-ah-do'-rah], *f.* Aviator, pilot.

aviar [ah-ve-ar'], *va.* 1. To provide articles for a journey. 2. To accoutre. To furnish one what is lacking for some object, especially money. 3. To hasten the execution of a thing. 4. **Aviar a uno**, to hurry somebody up. 5. (*LAm.*) (*Agri.*) To

castrate. -*vr.* To get ready, to prepare oneself. **Aviarse para hacer algo**, to get ready to do something.

aviatorio [ah-ve-ah-to-re-o], *a.* (*LAm.*) **Accidente aviatorio**, air crash, plane crash.

aviciar [ah-ve-the-ar'], *va.* 1. (*Obs.*) To render vicious. 2. To give a luxuriant bloom and verdure to plants and trees.

avícola [ah-ve'-co-lah], *a.* Chicken, poultry; **granja avícola**, chicken farm.

avicultor, ra [ah-ve-cool-tor'], *m. & f.* Chicken farmer, poultry farmer; bird fancier.

avicultura [ah-ve-cool-too'-rah], *f.* Aviculture, rearing of birds.

ávidamente [ah'-ve-dah-mayn-tay], *adv.* Avidly, eagerly; greedily.

avidez [ah-ve-deth'], *f.* Covetousness, greediness, avidity.

ávido, da [ah'-ve-do, dah]; *a.* (*Poetic.*) Greedy, covetous; open-mouthed.

aviejarse [ah-ve-ay-har'-say], *vr.* To grow old. *V.* AVEJENTARSE.

aviento [ah-ve-en'-to], *m.* A winnowing fork with two or three prongs *V.* BIELDO. (*Yo aviento, yo aviente*, from *Aventar. V.* ACERTAR). (*Yo me aviento, yo me aviente*, from *Aventarse. V.* ACERTAR).

aviesamente [ah-ve-ay-sah-men'-tay], *adv.* Sinistrously, perversely.

avieso, sa [ah-ve-ay'-so, sah], *a.* 1. Fortuitous, irregular. 2. (*Met.*) Mischievous, perverse. 3. *m.* Abortion.

avigorar [ah-ve-go-rar'], *va.* To invigorate; to revive.

avilanado, da [ah-ve-lah-nah'-do, dah], *a.* (*Bot.*) Villous, downy (simiente de plantas). (*Zool.*) Hairy, feathery (insectos).

avilantarse [ah-ve-lan-tahr'-say], *vr.* To be insolent.

avilantez, avilanteza [ah-ve-lan-teth', ah-ve-lan-tay'-thah], *f.* Forwardness, boldness, audaciousness; shamelessness.

avillanado, da [ah-veel-lyah-nah'-do, dah], *a.* Having the manners of a peasant, clownish, mean. -*pp.* of AVILLANAR.

avillanar [ah-veel-lyah-nar'], *va.* To villanize, to debase. -*vr.* To grow mean or abject, to degenerate.

avinado, da [ah-ve-nah'-do, dah], *a.* Wine-colored; bibulous, hard-drinking (personas).

avinagrado, da [ah-ve-nah-grah'-do, dah], *a.* (*Met.*) Harsh of temper, crabbed, peevish. Sour, acid. -*pp.* of AVINAGRAR.

avinagrar [ah-ve-nah-grar'], *va.* To render sour, to make acid. -*vr.* To turn sour.

avío [ah-vee'-o], *m.* 1. Preparation, provision. 2. (*Amer.*) Money and other articles advanced for working silver-mines. 3. **Hacer su avío**, to make one's pile. 4. **¡Al avío!**, get cracking!, get on with it! -*pl.* **Avíos de pescar**, fishing-tackle; the trimmings and other necessary articles for anything.

avión [ah-ve-on'], *m.* Airplane, aeroplane, plane. **Avión de bombardeo**, bomber. **Avión de reacción**, jet. **Avión de turbohélice**, turboprop. **Avión de turborreacción**, turbojet. **Avión supersónico**, supersonic plane. **Por avión**, By plane, by air mail. 2. (*Orn.*) Martin. 3. **Hacer el avión a uno**, to do somebody down, to cause harm to somebody.

avionazo [ah-ve-o-nah'-tho], *m.* Plane crash, accident to an aircraft.

avionero [ah-ve-o-nay'-ro], *m.* (*And. Cono Sur*) Airman, aircraftsman.

avioneta [ah-ve-o-nay'-tah], *f.* Light aircraft.

avisadamente [ah-ve-sah-dah-men'-tay], *adv.* Prudently.

avisado, da [ah-ve-sah'-do, dah], *a.* 1. Prudent, cautious. 2. Expert, sagacious, skilful, clever, clear-sighted. **Mal avisado**, Il-advised, injudicious. -*pp.* of AVISAR.

avisador [ah-ve-sah-dor'], *m.* Adviser; admonisher. (*Cine., Theat.*) Program seller.

avisar [ah-ve-sar'], *va.* 1. To inform, to give notice, to acquaint. **Avisar a uno con una semana de anticipación**, to let somebody know a week in advance, give somebody a week's notice. 2. To advise, to counsel, to admonish. **Avisar**

con tiempo, avisar anticipadamente, to warn or to give warning.

aviso [ah-vee'-so], *m.* 1. Information, intelligence, notice, legal notice in the newspapers. 2. Prudence, care, attention; counsel. **Estar or andar sobre aviso**, to be on one's guard. 3. *(Naut.)* Advice-boat, a light vessel sent with despatches.

avispa [ah-vees'-pah], *f.* Wasp.

avispado, da [ah-vis-pah'-do, dah], *a.* Lively, brisk, vigorous. *(LAm.)* Jumpy, nervous. *-pp.* of AVISPAR.

avispar [ah-vis-par'], *va.* 1. to spur, to drive with the spur. 2. To investigate, to observe closely. *-vr.* To fret, to be peevish.

avispero [ah-vis-pay'-ro], *m.* 1. Nest made by wasps. 2. Cavities in which wasps lodge their eggs. 3. *(Med.)* Carbuncle: so named for the numerous perforations resembling the cells of a wasp-nest.

avispón [ah-vis-pone], *m.* Hornet, a large wasp.

avistar [ah-vis-tar'], *va.* To descry at a distance, to see far off. *-vr.* To have an interview, to transact business.

avitar [ah-ve-tar'], *va. (Naut.)* To bitt the cable.

avitelado [ah-ve-tay-lah'-do], *a.* Vellum-like.

avituallamiento [ah-ve-too-ah-lyah-me-ayn'-to], *m.* Victualling, provisioning, supplying.

avituallar [ah-ve-too-al-lyar'], *va. (Mil.)* To victual, to supply with provisions.

avivadamente [ah-ve-vah-dah-men'-tay], *adv.* In a lively manner, briskly.

avivado [ah-ve-vah'-do], *a. (Cono Sur)* Forewarned, alerted.

avivador, ra [ah-ve-vah-dor', rah], *m. & f.* 1. Enlivener; hastener. 2. Rabbet-plane; panel-plane. 3. *(Prov.)* Paper full of pin-holes laid over the eggs of silk-worms, that the young worms may creep through it. 4. *(Arch.)* Groin between mouldings; quirk.

avivar [ah-ve-var'], *va.* 1. To quicken, to enliven, to encourage, to hasten, **avivar el paso**, to hasten one's step. 2. To heat, to inflame. 3. To vivify the eggs of silk-worms; to revive. 4. To heighten colors. 5. *(Carp.)* To rabbet. *-vr.* To revive, to cheer up, to grow gay. **Avivar el ojo**, to be watchful.

avizor [ah-ve-thor'], *a.* **Estar ojo avizor**, to be on the alert.

avizorar [ah-ve-tho-rar'], *va.* To watch with attention, to spy, to search narrowly.

avo [ah'-vo], *m.* 1. One of the fractional parts into which a whole number is divided. Used as a suffix; as, *dozavo*, twelfth. 2. A tree from which Indians make paper.

avocable [ah-vo-cah'-blay], *a.* Transferable to a superior court.

avocación, *f.* **avocamiento**, *m.* [ah-vo-cah-the-on', ah-vo-cah-me-en'-to], *(Law.)* The act of removing a lawsuit to a superior court.

avocado [ah-vo-cah'-do], *m.* The fruit of Persea gratissima, «alligator-pear». *V.* AGUACATE.

avocar [ah-vo-car'], *va. (Law.)* To remove a lawsuit to a superior court.

avocastro [ah-vo-cas'-tro], *m. (Cono Sur) V.* AVOCASTRO.

avoceta [ah-vo-thay'-tay], *f.* Avocet, a wading bird.

avogalla [ah-vo-gahl'-lyah], *f.* Gall-nut.

avolcanado, da [ah-vole-cah-nah'-do, dah], *a.* Volcanic.

avora [ah-vo'-rah], *f.* A kind of medicinal palm.

avorazado [ah-vo-rah-thah'-do], *a. (Mex.)* Greedy, grasping.

avucasta [ah-voo-dahs'-tah], *f.* Widgeon, a kind of wild duck.

avucastro [an-voo-cahs'-tro], *m.* Troubler or importunate person.

avugés *V.* AVUGUES.

avugo [ah-voo'-go], *m.* The fruit of the avuguero.

avuguero [ah-voo-gay'-ro], *m. (Bot.)* A kind of pear-tree.

avugués [ah-voo-gays'], *m. (Bot.) V.* GAYURA.

avulsión [ah-vool-se-on'], *f. (Surg.)* A forcible separation, tearing away.

avutarda [ah-voo-tar'-dah], *f.* Bustard, a wild turkey.

avutardado, da [ah-voo-tar-dah'-do, dah], *a.* Bustard-like.

axial [ac-see-ahl'], *a.* Axial.

axil [ac-seel'], *a. (Bot.)* Axial, relating to the axis. *(Zool.)* Axillary, relating to the base of the wing, or to the thoracic limb of some animals. *-m.* The axil of a plant.

axila [ac-see'-lah], *f.* 1. *(Anat.)* Axilla, armpit. 2. *(Bot.)* Axilla, upper end and inside of the base of leaves or branches.

axilar [ac-se-lar'], *a.* 1. Axillar, axillary, belonging to the armpit. 2. *(Bot.)* Axillary.

axioma [ac-se-oh'-mah], *m.* Axiom, maxim.

axiomático, ca [ac-se-o-mah'-te-co, cah], *a.* Axiomatic, selfevident.

axiómetro [ac-se-o'-may-tro], *m. (Naut.)* An instrument which marks the movements of the helm.

axis [ac'-sis], *m. (Anat.)* The second vertebra of the neck. 2. *(Zool.)* Indian deer.

¡ay! [i, or ah'-e], *int.* Alas! an exclamation of pain or grief. **¡Ay de mi!** Alas, poor me! Woe is me!. 2. Oh!, goodness! 3. Moan, groan; cry. **Un ay desgarrador**, a heartrending cry. *-m. V.* QUEJIDO and GEMIDO.

aya [ah'-yah], *f.* Governess, instructress. *V.* AYO.

ayanque [ah-yahn'-kay], *m. (Naut.)* The main halliard.

ayate [ah-yah'-tay], *m.* A kind of fabric manufactured of the thread of the agave, or *pita*.

ayatola [ah-yah-to-lah'], *m.* Ayatollah.

ayax [ah'-yacs], *m.* Ayax.

aye aye [ah'-yay-ah'-yay], *m. (Zool.)* The aye-aye, a nocturnal lemur of Madagascar.

ayer [ah-yerr'], *adv.* 1. Yesterday. **Ayer por la mañana**, yesterday morning. 2. Lately, not long ago, **De ayer acá**, from yesterday to this moment. 3. *m.* Yesterday, past; **el ayer madrileño**, Madrid in the past.

ayllu [ah-ee-lyoo'], *m. (And.) (Hist. Famil.)* Family, tribe, community.

aymará [ah-ee-mah'-rah], *(And.)* 1. *m. & f.* Aymara Indian. 2. *m. (Ling.)* Aymara, language of the Aymara Indians.

ayo [ah'-yo], *m.* Tutor or governor; a teacher.

ayocote [ah-yo-co'-tay], *(Mex.)* A kidney-bean larger than the common sort.

ayocuantoto [ah-yo-coo-an-to'-to], *m.* A mountain bird of Mexico.

ayote [ah-yo-tay], *m. (Mex.)* Small pumpkin; *(CAm.)* pumpkin, squash.

ayotoste [ah-yo-tos'-tay], *m.* Armadillo.

ayto. *abr.* de **Ayuntamiento**.

ayuda [ah-yoo'-dah], *f.* 1. Help, aid, assistance, comfort; support, succour, friendship. **Ayuda de parroquia**, chapel of ease. 2. An injection, enema, or clyster. 3. Syringe. 4. *(Naut.)* Preventer-rope. **Ayuda de costa**, a gratification paid over and above a salary, a gratuity. *-m.* 1. Deputy or assistant of one of the high officers at court. **Ayuda de cámara**, a valet-de-chambre, valet. **Ayuda de cámara del rey**, groom of the bed-chamber. 2. Helper, a supernumerary servant. **Dios y ayuda**, this cannot be done but with the assistance of God. **Ayuda de oratorio**, clergyman in an oratory who performs the office of sacristan. **Ayuda de cocinero**, *(Naut.)* the cook's shifter. **Ayuda de dispensero**, *(Naut.)* the steward's mate. **Ayuda de virador**, *(Naut.)* a false preventer. **Prestar ayuda**, to give help. **Ayuda estatal**, state aid.

ayudado [ah-yoo-dah'-do], *m. (Taur.)* Two-handed pass with the cape (toros).

ayudador, ra [ah-yoo-dah-dor', rah], *m. & f.* Assistant, helper; a shepherd's assistant.

ayudante [ah-yoo-dahn'-tay], *m.* 1. *(Mil.)* Adjutant; aide-de-camp. 2. **Ayudante de cirujano**, a surgeon's assistant. 3. **Ayudante de dirección** *(Theat. etc.)*, production assistant.

ayudantía [ah-yoo-dahn-te'-ah], *f.* Assistantship; adjutancy; *(Tec.)* post of technician.

ayudar [ah-yoo-dar'], *va.* To aid, to help, to favor, to assist. **Ayudar a misa**, to serve the priest at mass. *-vr.* To adopt proper measures to obtain success.

ayudista [ah-yoo-des'-tah], *m. & f. (Cono Sur)* Supporter.

ayuga [ah-yoo'-gah], *f. (Bot.)* Groundpine. *V.* PINILLO.

ayunador, ra [ah-yoo-nah-dor', rah], *m. & f.* Faster, one who fasts.

ayunar [ah-yoo-nar'], *vn.* To fast; to keep the canonical fast. **Ayunar al traspaso**, to fast from holy Thursday to the following Saturday. **Ayunar después de harto**, to fast after a good repast.

ayunas (En) [ah-yoo'-nas], *adv.* 1. Fasting. 2. Without knowledge. **Quedar en ayunas**, to be ignorant of an affair. 3. **Salir en ayunas**, to go out without any breakfast.

ayuno, [ah-yoo'-no], *m.* Fast, abstinence.

ayuno, na [ah-yoo'-no, nah], *a.* 1. Fasting, abstaining from food. **Estoy ayuno**, I have not yet broken my fast. 2. Abstaining from certain pleasures. 3. Ignorant of a subject of conversation.

ayunque [ah-yoon'-kay], *m.* Anvil. *V.* YUNQUE.

ayuntable [ah-yoon-tah'-blay], *a.* Capable of being joined.

ayuntador, ra [ah-yoon-tah-dor, rah], *m. & f.* One who unites, joins, or assembles.

ayuntamiento [ah-yoon-tah-me-en'-to], *m.* 1. City, town council (institucín). City hall, Town hall (edificio). Meeting (reunión). **Ayuntamiento carnal**, sexual intercourse.

ayuntar [ah-yoon-tar'], *va.* 1. *(Naut.)* To splice. 2. *(Agri.)* To yoke. *(Obs.) V* JUNTAR and AÑADIR.

ayustar [ah-yoos-tar'], *va. (Naut.)* To bend, two ends of a cable or rope, to splice. **Ayustar con costura**, to bend with a splice.

ayuste [ah-yoos'-tay], *m. (Naut.)* Bending or splicing whereby two ends of a rope or cable are joined; scarf, scarfing.

ayuya [ah-yoo'-yah], *f. (Cono Sur)* Flat roll, scone.

azabachado, da [ah-thah-bah-chah'-do, dah], *a.* Jetty, black as jet.

azabache [ah-thah-bah'-chay], *m. (Miner.)* Jet, a black shining mineral. *pl.* **Azabaches**, trinkets of jet.

azábara [ah-thah'-bah-rah], *f. (Bot.)* Common aloe.

azacán [ah-thah-can'], *m. (Obs.)* 1. Water-carrier. 2. *V.* ODRE. **Estar or andar hecho un azacán**, To be very busy.

azacanarse [ah-thah-cah-nahr'-say], *vr.* To drudge, slave away.

azacaya [ah-thah-cah'-yah], *f. (Prov.)* Conduit of water, a water-pipe.

azache [ah-thah'-chay], *a.* Of an inferior quality (seda).

azada [ah-thah'-dah], *f. (Agri.)* Spade, hoe.

azadada [ah-thah-dah'-dah], *f.* Blow with a spade.

azadica, ill, ita [ah-thah-dee'-cah, deel'-lyah, dee'-tah], *f. dim.* A small spade.

azadón [ah-thah-done'], *m.* Pickaxe, mattock, hoe. **Azadón de peto**. hand-spike, or lever armed with a kind of chisel.

azadonada [ah-thah-do-nay'-dah], *f.* Blow with a pickaxe. **A la primera azadonada déis en el agua**, to detect straightway that one is not worthy of the consideration in which he is held. **A la primera azadonada ¿queréis sacar agua?**, do you expect to accomplish a difficult task without effort? **A tres azadonadas sacar agua**. *(Met.)* To obtain easily the object of one's wishes.

azadonar [ah-thah-do-nar'], *va.* To dig with a spade or pickaxe.

azadonazo [ah-thah-do-nah'-tho], *m.* Stroke with a mattock.

azadoncillo [ah-thah-don-thee;'-lyo], *m. dim.* A small pickaxe.

azadonero [ah-thah-do-nay'-ro], *m.* 1. Digger, one that opens the ground with a spade. 2. *(Mil. Obs.)* Pioneer.

azafata [ah-thah-fah'-tah], *f.* 1. Airline hostess, stewardess. 2. Queen's maid of the wardrobe.

azafate [ah-thah-fah'-tay], *m.* A low, flat-bottomed basket; a kind of waiter, a tray.

azafrán [ah-thah-frahn'], *m. (Bot.)* Saffron. **Azafrán bastaror** *o* **azafrán romí or romín**, *(Bot.)* bastard saffron, dyers' saffron. **Azarán del timón** *(Naut.)* after-piece of the rudder. **Azafrán del tajamar**, *(Naut.)* forepiece of the cut-water. **azafrán de Venus**, *(Chem.)* crocus Veneris, the caix or

oxide of metals of a saffron color. **Azafrán de Marte**, crocus powder; copperas calcined to a reddish or purple color, for polishing *(Arab.)*.

azafranado, da [ah-thah-frah-nah'-do, dah], *a.* Saffron-like, croceous. *-pp.* of AZAFRANAR.

azafranal [ah-thah-frah-nahl'], *m.* A plantation of saffron.

azafranar [ah-thah-frah-nar'], *va.* To tinge or dye with saffron.

azafranero [ah-thah-frah-nay'-ro], *m.* Dealer in saffron.

azagador [ah-thah-gah-dor'], *m.* The path for cattle.

azagaya [ah-thah-gah'-yah], *f.* Javelin, a spear or half-pike.

azagayada [ah-thah-gah-yah'-dah], *f.* Cast of a javelin.

azahar [ah-thah-ar'], *m.* Orange or lemon flower. **Agua de azahar**, orange-flower water. **Azahar bravo**, arrow-leaved blue lupine. **azainadamente** [ah-thah-e-nah-dah-men'-tay], *adv.* Perfidiously, viciously.

azalá [ah-thah-lah'], *m* Prayer, among the Mohammedans.

azalea [ah-thah-lay'-ah], *f.* Azalea.

azalón [ah-thah-lone'], *m. (Orn.)* A small bird.

azamboa [ah-tham-bo'-ah], *f. (Bot.)* The fruit of the zamboatree; a kind of sweet quince; citron. *V.* ZAMBOA.

azamboo, or azamboero [ah-tham-bo'-o, ah-tham-bo-ay'-ro], *m. (Bot.)* The zamboa-tree; citron.

azanca [ah-trahn'-cah], *f. (Miner.)* Subterranean spring.

azándar [ah-thahn'-dar], *m. (Prov.) V.* SANDALO.

azanoria [ah-thah-no'-re-ah], *f. (Bot.)* Carrot. *V.* ZANAHORIA.

azanoriate [ah-thah-no-re-ah'-tay], *m. (Prov.)* 1. Preserved carrots. 2. *(Prov.)* Fulsome, affected compliments.

azar [ah-thar'], *m.* 1. Unforeseen disaster, an unexpected accident, disappointment. 2. Unfortunate card or throw a dice. 3. Obstruction, impediment. 4. Hazard. **Los azares de la vida**, life's ups and downs.

azarado, da [ah-thah-rah'-do, dah], *a. & pp.* of AZARAR. Confused, rattled; used especially of a player. A term much used in billiards.

azarar [ah-thah-rar'], *va.* To confuse, to bewilder, to rattle. - *vr.* To get rattled in a game. **Azararse una bola**, said of a ball which loses its direction or effect by striking against a pocket.

azarbe [ah-thar'-bay], *m. (Prov.)* Trench or drain for irrigation waters.

azarbeta [ah-thar-bay'0-tah], *dim.* Azarbe, small trench for irrigating.

azarcón [ah-thar-cone'], *m.* 1. Minium, red lead. 2. Orange color. 3. Earthen pot.

azarear [ah-thah-ray-ahr'], *va.* Azarearse, *vr. V.* AZORARSE.

azaría [ah-tha-ree'-ah], *f.* A kind of coral.

azarja [ah-thar'-hah], *f.* Instrument for winding raw silk.

azarnefe [ah-thar-nay'-fay], *m.* Orpiment. *V.* OROPIMENTE.

azarolla [ah-thah-rol'-lyah], *f. (Bot. Prov.)* The fruit of the true service-tree. *V.* ACEROLA.

azarollo [ah-thah-rol'-lyo], *(Bot. Prov.)* True service-tree.

azarosamente [ah-thah-ro-sah-men'-tay], *adv.* Unfortunately.

azaroso, sa [ah-thah-ro'-so, sah], *a.* Unlucky, unfortunate, ominous, risky.

azaya [ah-thah'-yah], *f.* 1. Instrument used for reeling silk. 2. *(Prov. Gal.) V.* CANTUESO. French lavender.

azazel [ah-thah'-thel], *m.* 1. In Islam, the angel nearest to Allah. 2. The scape-goat of the Mosaic dispensation.

azcón, m. azonca, f. [ath-cone' ath-co'-nah], *(Obs.)* A dart.

azer [ah-ther'], *m.* 1. Name of the fire adored by the Magi. 2. A title of Zoroaster.

azimo, ma [ah'-the-mo, mah], *a.* Azymous, unleavened.

azimut [ah-themoot'], *m. (Astr.)* Azimuth.

azimutal [ah-the-moo-tahl'], *a.* Azymous, unleavened.

azimut [ah-the-moot'], *m. (Astr.)* Azimuth.

azimutal [ah-the-moo-tahl'], *a.* Relating to the azimuth.

aznacho, aznallo [ath-nah'-cho, ath-nahl'-lyo], *m. (Bot.)* 1. Scotch fir. 2. A species of the three-toothed rest-harrow.

azce [ah'-th-ay], *m. (Chem.)* Azote or nitrogen.

-azo, -aza sufijo de *n.* 1. **Librazo**, big book (aumentativo). 2. **Exitazo**, huge success. 3. **Actorazo**, top-flight actor. 3. **Cornetazo**, bugle call. 4. **Dar un frenazo**, to brake hard.

azocar [ ], *va. (Carib.)* To pack tightly.

azofaifa [ah-tho-fah'-e-fah], *f. V.* AZUFAIFA.

azófar [ah-tho'-far], *m.* Brass, latten. *V.* LATON.

azogadamente [ah-tho-gah-dah-men'-tay], *adv.* In a quick and restless manner.

azogado, da [ah-tho-gah'-do, dah], *a. (Amer.)* Restless, in perpetual movement; trembling.

azogamiento [ah-tho-gah-me-en'-to], *m.* 1. The act of overlaying with quicksilver. 2. Slaking lime. 3. State of restlessness.

azogar [ah-tho-gar'], *va.* To overlay with quicksilver, to coat a mirror. **Azogar la cal**, to slake lime. *-vr.* 1. To suffer from mercurialism. 2. To be in a state of agitation.

azogue [ah-tho'-gay], *m.* 1. *(Miner.)* Mercury, quicksilver. **Es un azogue**, he is as restless as quicksilver. **Azogues**, ships which carry quicksilver. 2. A market-place.

azoguejo [ah-tho-gay'-ho], *m.* A market-place.

azoguería [ah-tho-gay-ree'-ah], *f. (Amer.)* The place where quicksilver is incorporated with metals; amalgamating works.

azoguero [ah-tho-gay'-ro], *m.* 1. Dealer in quicksilver. 2. *(Amer.)* A workman who incorporates quicksilver, etc., with pounded silver ore, to extract the silver.

azoico, ca [ah-tho'-e-co, cah], *a.* 1. Nitric. 2. *(Geol.)* Azoic, antedatin life. **Era azoica**, azoic era.

azolar [ah-tho-lar'], *va.* To model timber.

azolvar [ah-thol-var'], *va.* To obstruct water-conduits.

azolve [ah-thol'-vay], *m. (Mex.)* Sediment, deposit.

azolvo [ah-thol'-vo], *m.* The blocking of pumps or water-pipes.

azomar [ah-tho-mar'], *va. (Obs.)* To incite animals to fight.

azonzado [ah-thon-tha'-do], *a. (Cono Sur)* Silly, stupid.

azor [ah-thor'], *m. (Orn.)* Goshawk.

azora [ah-tho-rah], *f. (LAm.) V.* AZORAMIENTO.

azorado [ah-tho-rah'-do], *a.* **Navío azorado**, a ship which sails heavily on account of her cargo being badly stowed. Alarmed, upset. Embarrassed, flustered. *-pp.* of AZORAR.

azoramiento [ah-tho-rah-me-en'-to], *m.* Trepidation, confusion, alarm, embarrassment.

azorar [ah-tho-rar'], *va.* 1. To terrify; to confound. 2. To incite, to irritate. *-vr.* To be restless, to get upset, alarmed.

Azores [ah-tho'-rays], *f. & pl.* Azores.

azoro [ah-tho'-ro], *m.* 1. *(LAm.)* Azoramiento. 2. *(CAm.)* Ghost.

azorrado, da [ah-thor-rah'-do, dah], *a.* Drowsy, sleepy. *-pp.* of AZORRARSE. *(Naut.)* Water-logged.

azorramiento [ah-thor-rah-me-en'-to], *m.* Heaviness of the head.

azorrarse [ah-thor-rar'-say], *vr.* To be drowsy from heaviness.

azorrillarse [ah-thor-ree-lyar'-say], *vr. (Mex.)* To hide away, keep out of sight.

azotacalles [ah-tho-tah-cahl'-lyes], *m.* Street-lounger, idler.

azotado [ah-tho-tah'-do], *m.* 1. A criminal publicly whipped. 2. He who lashes himself by way of mortification. *-pp.* of AZOTAR.

azotador, ra [ah-tho-tha-dor', rah], *m. & f.* Whipper, one who inflicts lashes with a whip.

azotaina, azotina [ah-tho-tah'-e-nah, ah-tho-tee'-nah], *f. (coll.)* A drubbing, a sound flogging, beating.

azotalengua [ah-tho-ta-len'-goo-ah], *f. (Bot.)* Goose-grass, cleavers.

azotar [ah-tho-tar'], *va.* 1. To whip, to lash, to horsewhip, to flagellate. **Azotar las calles**, to lounge about the streets. 2. *(Met.)* **Azotar el aire**, to act to no purpose. 3. *(Naut.)* **Azotar con paleta**, to inflict the punishment called *cobbing* on board English ships. 4. *(Naut.)* **Azotar la ampolleta**, to flog the glass, when the steersman turns it before the sand has entirely run out. *-vr. (Mex.)* To put on airs.

azotazo [ah-tho-tah'-tho], *m. aug.* A severe lash or blow on the breech.

azote [ah-tho-tay], *m.* 1. Whip. 2. Lash given with a whip. 3. *(Met.)* Calamity, affliction. 4. The person who is the cause of a calamity. **Pena de azotes**, a public shipping. **Mano de azotes**, or **vuelta de azotes**, the number of lashes a criminal is to receive.

azotea [ah-tho-tay'-ah], *f.* The flat roof of a house, a platform. 2. **Estar mal de la azotea**, to be round the bend.

azotera [ah-tho-tay-rah], *f. (LAm.)* Beating, thrashing.

azótico [ah-tho'-te-co], *a.* **Gas azótico**, *(Chem.)* azotic gas.

azre [ath'-ray], *m. (Bot.)* Maple-tree.

azteca [ath-tay'-cah], *a. & m.* Aztec; belonging to the race, dynasty, or language of ancient Mexico.

azúa [ah-thoo'-ah], *f.* Beverage prepared by the Indians from Indian corn.

azúcar [ah-thoo'-car], *m.* Sugar. **Azúcar de pilón**, loafsugar. **Azúcar de lustre**, double loaves, fine powdered sugar. **Azúcar mascabado**, unclarified sugar. **Azúcar quebrado**, brown sugar. **Azúcar prieto** or **negro**, coarse brown sugar. **Azúcar piedra** or **cande**. sugar-candy. **Azúcar terciado** or **moreno**, brown sugar. **Azúcar pardo**, clayed sugar. **Azúcar de plomo**, calcined sugar of lead. **Azúcar y canela**, sorrel-gray: a color peculiar to horses.

azucarado, da [ah-thoo-car-rah'-do, dah], *a.* 1. Sugared. 2. Sugary, having the taste of sugar. 3. Sugar coated. 4. *(Met.)* Affable, pleasing. **Palabras azucaradas**, soothing, artful words *-pp.* of AZUCARAR.

azucarado [ah-thoo-car-rah'-do], *mm.* A kind of paint for ladies.

azucarar [ah-thoo-ca-rar'], *va.* 1. To sugar, to sweeten; to soften. 2. To ice with sugar, to coat with sugar.

azucarería [ah-thoo-cah-ray-re'-ah], *f.* Sugar refinery; *(Carib., Mex.)* Sugar shop.

azucarero [ah-thoo-ca-ray'-ro], *m.* 1. Sugar-dish, sugarbowl. 2. *(Prov.)* Confectioner.

azucarillo [ah-thoo-ca-reel'-lyo], *m.* Sweetmeat of flour, sugar, and rosewater.

azucena [ah-thoo-thay'-nah], *f. (Bot.)* White lily. **Azucena amarilla**, yellow amaryllis. **Azucena anteada**, Coppercolored day-lily. **Azucena pajiza**, yellow day-lily. **Azucenas**, the military order of the lily, founded by Kind Ferdinand of Aragón.

azud [ah-thood'], *f.* A dam with a sluice or flood-gate.

azuda [ah-thoo'-dah], *f.* Persian wheel to raise water for irrigation. *cf.* NORIA.

azuela [ah-thoo-ay'-lah], *f.* Adze, a carpenter's tool; howell, a cooper's tool. **Azuela de construcción**, a ship-wright's adze. **Azuela curva**, a hollow adze.

azufaifa [ah-thoo-fah'-e-fah], *f.* Jujube or jujubes, the fruit of the jujube-tree.

azufaifo, azufeifo [ah-thoo-fah'-e-fo, ah-thoo-fay'-e-fo], *m.* Jujube-tree.

azufrado, da [ah-thoo-frah'-do, dah], *a.* 1. Whitened or fumigated with sulphur. 2. Sulphureous. 3. Greenish yellow. *-pp.* of AZUFRAR.

azufrador [ah-thoo-frah-dor'], *m.* 1. Machine for drying linen. 2. Instrument for sulphuring vines.

azufrar [ah-thoo-frar'], *va.* To bleach, to fumigate with sulphur.

azufre [ah-thoo'-fray], *m.* Sulphur, brimstone. **Azufre vivo**, native sulphur.

azufrón [ah-thoo-frone'], *m.* Pyrites in powder.

azufroso, sa [ah-thoo-fro'-so, sah], *a.* Sulphureous.

azul [ah-thool'], *a.* Blue. **Azul celeste**, sky-blue. **Azul oscuro**, dark blue. **Azul de Prusia**, Prussian blue. **Azul subido**, bright blue. **Azul turquí** or **turquizado**, Turkish or deep blue; indigo, sixth color of the spectrum. **Azul de esmalte**, smalt. **Azul verdemar** or **de costras**, sea-blue. **Darse un verde con dos azules**, to be highly entertained.

azul [ah-thool'], *m.* Lapis lazuli; a mineral.

azulado, da [ah-thoo-lah'-do, dah], *pp.* of AZULAR. Azulado claro, azure, azured; bluish.

azulaque [ah-thoo-lah'-kay], *m. V.* ZULAQUE.

azular [ah-thoo-lar'], *va.* To dye or color blue.

azulear [ah-thoo-lay-ar'], *vn.* To have a bluish cast.

azulejado, da [ah-thoo-lay-hah'-do, dah], *a. (Prov.)* Covered with bluish tiles.

azulejar [ah-thoo-lay-hahr'], *va.* To tile.

azulejeria [ah-thoo-lay-hay-re'-ah], *f.* Tiling. Tile industry.

azulejillo [ah-thoo-lay-heel'-lyo], *m.* Little bluebird.

azulejo [ah-thoo-lay'-ho], *m.* 1. Glazed tile painted with various colors, or plain white. 2. *(Bot.)* Blue-bottle, cornflower. -a. Applied in Spain to several kinds of wheat. 3. *(Orn.)* The blue jay.

azulenco, ca [ah-thoo-len'-co, cah], *a. V.* AZULADO.

azulete [ah-thoo-lay'-tay], *m.* Blue color given to stockings and other garments.

azulino, na [ah-thoo-lee'-no, nah], *a.* Bluish.

azuloso [ah-thoo-lo'-so], *a. (LAm.)* Bluish.

azumagarse [ah-thoo-mah-gahr'-say], *vr. (Cono Sur)* To rust, get rusty.

azumar [ah-thoo-mar'], *va.* To dye the hair.

azumbrado, da [ah-thoom-brah'-do, dah], *a.* Measured by *azumbres.*

azumbre [ah-thoom'-bray], *f.* A measure of liquids, containing about half an English gallon.

azur [ah-thoor'], *a. (Her.)* Azure.

azurita [ah-thoo-ree'-tah], *f.* 1. Blue variety of copper carbonate, azurite. 2. Double phosphate aluminium and magnesium.

azurumbado [ah-thoo-room-bah'-do], *a. (CAm.)* Silly, stupid; drunk (borracho).

azutero [ah-thoo-tay'-ro], *m.* Sluice-master, he who has the care of dams, Sluices, etc.

azuzador, ra [ah-thoo-thah-dor', rah], *m. & f.* Instigator.

azuzar [ah-thoo-thar'], *va.* 1. To halloo, to set on dogs. 2. To irritate, to provoke.

azuzón [ah-thoo-thone'], *m.* Instigator, provoker of quarrels.

B

b [bay]. The second letter of the Spanish alphabet: it is pronounced in Spanish as in English.

baba [bah'-bah], *f.* Drivel, slaver, spittle, saliva, slobber; *(Bio.)* mucus; secretion. **Echar baba**, to drool, to slobber. **Se le cae la baba**, *(fig.)* he's thrilled to bits.

bababuí [bah-bah-boo-ee'], *m.* The mocking-bird *V.* ARRENDAJO.

babadero, babador [bah-bah-day'-ro, bah-bah-dor'], *m.* Bib, chin-cloth.

babasfrías [bah-bah-fre'-ahs], *m. (And. Méx.)* Fool.

babaza [bah-bah'-thah], *f.* 1. Frothy fluid from the mouth. Slime, mucus. 2. Aloe. 3. A viscous worm of the snail kind. Slug.

babazorro [bah-bah-thor'-ro], *m. (Prov.)* Clown, an illbred man.

babear [bah-bay-ar'], *vn.* 1. To drivel, to slaver. 2. *(Met. and coll.)* To be smitten with; to court, to woo. -vr. *(Cono Sur)* To feel flattered, to grow with satisfaction.

Babel [bah-bayl'], *m.* Babel. **Torre de Babel**, tower of Babel.

babel [bah-bayl'], *m.* of bedlam; confusion, mess.

babeo [bah-bay'-o], *m.* The act of drivelling or slavering.

babera [bah-bay'-ra], *f.* 1. Fore part of the helmet which covers the cheeks, mouth, and chin. 2. A silly fellow. 3. A bib.

babero [bah-bay'-ro], *m.* Bib. *V.* BABADOR.

baberol [bah-bay-role'], *m. V.* BABERA, as part of the helmet.

babia [bah'-bee-ah], *f.* **Estar en babia**, to be absent in mind, heedless, or inattentive.

babieca [bah-be-ay'-cah], *m.* **Es un babieca**, he is an ignorant, stupid fellow; an idiot.

babilla [bah-beel'-lyah], *f.* Thin skin about the flank of a horse.

Babilonia [bah-be-lo'-ne-h], *f.* **Es una babilonia**, there is such a crowd, it is all uproar and confusion. Babylon.

babilónico, ca, or **onio, nia** [bah-be-lo'-ne-co, cah, ne-o, ne-ah], *a.* Babylonian.

babilla [bah-bee'-lyah], *f. (Vet.)* Stifle.

babismo [bah-bees'-mo], *m.* Babism, Persian religious doctrine.

bable [bah'-blay], *m.* The Asturian dialect.

babor [bah-bor'], *m. (Naut.)* Port, the left-hand side of a ship, looking forward. **A babor del timón**, a-port the helm. **A babor todo**, head a-port. **De babor a estribor**, athwart ship.

babosa [bah-bo'-sah], *f.* 1. A slug. 2. Aloe. 3. An old onion transplanted. 4. A young onion.

babosada [bah-bo-sah'-dah], *f. (LAm.)* Stupid things; dead loss, useless thing. *(CAm. Méx.)* Stupid comment.

babosear [bah-bo-say-ar'], *va.* 1. To drivel, to slaver. 2. *(fig.)* To drool over; *(CAm.)* Insult; *(Mex.)* To manhandle; *(CAm. Méx.)* To take for a fool. **Muchos han baboseado este problema** *(Mex.)*, many have taken a superficial look at this problem. -vn. To drool.

baboseo [bah-bo-say'-o], *a.* Drooling, slobbering; slimy. *(fig.)* Infatuation, drooling.

babosilla [bah-bo-seel'-lyah], *f. dim.* Slug.

babosillo, illa; uelo, uela [bah-bo-seel'-lyo, lyah, oo-ay'-lo, lah], *a. dim.* Somewhat drivelling or slavering.

baboso, sa [bah-bo'-so, sah], *m. & f.* Idiot, simpleton. -a. Idiotic. *a.* Drooling, slobbering; slimy. *(fig.)* Sloppy (sobre mujeres). Foolishly sentimental; fawning, snivelling; dirty.

babucha [bah-boo'-chah], *f.* A kind of slipper. *(Carib.)* Child's bodice; *(LAm.)* Loose blouse, smock. **Babuchas** *(Carib.)* Rompers; *(Mex.)* High-heeled boot. **Llevar algo a babuchas** *(Cono Sur)*, to carry something on one's back.

babuino [bah-boo-e'-no], *m.* Baboon.

babuyal [bah-boo-yahl'], *m. (Carib.)* Witch, sorcerer.

baby [bah'-be], *m. & f.* 1. *(LAm.)* baby; *(Aut.)* Small car, mini. **Baby crece**, babygrow. **Baby fútbol**, table football. 2. Bib (babero).

baca [bah'-cah], *f.* 1. Berry. **Baca de laurel**, bay-berry. 2. Breach in a dike or dam. 3. *(Jew.)* A kind of pearl. 4. Leather cover of a car or stage-coach.-m. & f. pl. Quick tune on the guitar.

bacal [bah-cahl'], *m. (Mex.) (Agri.)* Corncob.

bacalada [bah-cah-lah'-dah], *f.* Sweetener, bribe.

bacalao [bah-cah-lah'-o], *m.* 1. Codfish. **Aceite de hígado de bacalao**, cod-liver oil. **Bacalao a la vizcaína**, Codfish stew made with olive oil, tomatoes, olives, capers, etc. 2. **¡Te conozco bacalao!**, I've rumbled you! 3. *(Cono Sur)* Miser. 4. *(Esp.)* Cunt (vajina).

bacán [bah-can'], *m. (Cono Sur)* Wealthy man; sugar daddy; playboy, dundy.

bacanal [bah-cah'-nah], *a.* Bacchanalian.

bacanalear [bah-cah-nah-lay-ahr'], *va. (CAm.)* To have a wild time.

bacanales [bah-cah-nah'-les], *f. pl.* Bacchanals, feasts of Bacchus.

bacane [bah-cah'-nay], *m. (Carib.) (Aut.)* Driving license, driver's licence (GB).

bacanería [bah-cah-nay-re'-ah], *f. (Cono Sur)* Sharp dressing, nattiness; vulgar, display.

bacante [bah-cahn'-tay], *f.* 1. Bacchante, bacchant, priestess of Bacchus. 2. Bacchante, a lewd drinking person.

bácara, bacaris [bah'-ca-rah, bah'-ca-ris], *f.* *(Bot.)* Great flea-bane. Baccharis.

bacelador [bah-thay-lah-dor'], *m.* *(Carib.)* Con man.

bacelar [bah-thay-lar'], *m.* Land newly planted with vines. *-va. (Carib.)* To con, to trick.

bacenica [bah-the-ne'-cah], *f. (LAm.)* V. BACINICA.

bacera [ba-thay'-rah], *f. (Coll.)* Obstruction in the milt, a swelling of the belly, in cattle.

bacía [ba-thee'-ah], *f.* 1. A metal basin; wash-pot. 2. Barber's basin; shaving-dish.

báciga [bah'-the-gah], *f.* A game played with three cards.

bacilar [bah-the-lahr'], *a.* Bacillary.

bacilarse [bah-the-lahr'-say], *vr. (And.)* To have a good time.

bacilo [bah-thee'-lo], *m.* Bacillus, a rodshaped bacterium.

bacilón [bah-thee-lon'], 1. *a.* Brilliant, great. 2. *m. (And.)* Fun, good time.

bacín [bah-theen'], *m.* 1. A large and very high vase, or basin, which serves as a close-stool. 2. A despicable man.

bacina [bah-thee'-nah], *f.* 1. *(Coll.)* Poor-box. 2. V. BACIA. 3. A small basin which serves as a close-stool.

bacinada [bah-tbe-nah'-dah], *f.* Filth thrown from a close-stool.

bacinejo [bah-the-nay'-ho], *m. dim.* A small close-stool.

bacineta [bah-the-nay'-tah], *f.* **Bacineta de arma de fuego**, the pan of a gun-lock.

bacinete [bah-the-nay'-tay], *m.* A head-piece formerly worn by soldiers, in the form of a helmet, basinet (de armadura).

bacinica [bah-the-nee'-cah], *f.* 1. A small earthen close-stool for children. 2. Chamber-pot.

bacinilla [bah-the-neel'-lyah], *f.* 1. A chamber-pot.

bacitracina [bah-the-trah-thee'-nah], *f. (Med.)* Bacitracin.

background [bac-go'-oon], *m. (Cono Sur)* Background.

baco [bah'-co], *m.* Bacchus. Wine.

bacon [bah-con'], *m.* Bacon.

bacteria [bac-tay'-re-ah], *f.* Bacteria, germ.

bacteriano [bac-tay-re-ah'-no], *a.* Bacterial.

bactericida [bac-tay-re-thee'-dah], *m.* Bactericide, bacteria killer.

bactérico [bac-tay'-re-co], *a.* Bacterial.

bacteriología [bac-tay-re-o-lo-ge'-ah], *f.* Bacteriology.

bacteriólogo, ga [bac-tay-re-o'-lo-go, gah], *m. & f.* Bacteriologist.

báculo [bah'-coo-lo], *m.* 1. Walking-stick, a staff. **Báculo de Jacob**, Jacob's staff, a mathematical instrument which serves to measure heights and distances. **Báculo de peregrino**, pilgrims staff. **Báculo pastoral**, bishop's crosier. 2. *(Met.)* Support, relief, consolation.

bacha [bah'-chah], *f. (Carib.)* Spree, merry outing.

bachata [bah-chah'-tah], *f. (Carib.)* Party, good time.

bachatear [bah-chah-tay-ahr'], *vn. (Carib.)* To go on a spree, to go out for a good time.

bachatero [bah-chah-tay'-ro], *m. (Carib.)* Reveller, carouser.

bache [bah'-chay], *m.* 1. A deep hole in a road. 2. A place where sheep are put to sweat, previous to their being shorn. V. SUDADERO. 3. Stick of a hatter for beating felt. 4. Economic depression. **Salir del bache**, to get out of the rut.

bachicha [bah-che'-chah], *m.* 1. *(Cono Sur)* Dago, wop. 2. Leftovers (restos); Cigarette end, cigar stub; dregs (de bebida). 3. *(Mex.) (Fin.)* Nest egg, secret hoard.

bachiche [bah-chee'-chay], *m. (And.)* V. BACHICHA.

bachiller [bah-cheel-lyerr'], *m.* 1. Bachelor, one who has obtained the first degree in sciences and liberal arts. 2. Babbler, prater.

bachiller [bah-cheel-lyerr'], *a.* Garrulous, loquacious.

bachillera [bah-cheel-lyay'-rah], *a.* Forward, loquacious woman.

bachillerato [bah.cheel-lyay-rah'-to], *m.* Bachelorship, the degree and function of a bachelor. **Bachillerato commercial**, certificate in business studies. **Bachillerato elemental**, lower examination.

bachillerear [bah-cheel-lyay-ray-ar'], *vn.* To babble, to prattle, to talk a lot.

bachillerejo [bah-cheel-lyay-ray'-ho], *m. dim.* A talkative little fellow.

bachillería [bah-cheel-lyay-ree'-ah], *f.* Babbling, prattling.

bada [bah'-dah], *f.* V. ABADA.

badajada [bah-dah-hah'-dah], *f.* 1. A stroke of the clapper against the bell. 2. Idle talk.

badajazo [bah-dah-bah'-tho], *m. aug.* A large clapper.

badajear [bah-dah-hay-ar'], *vn. (Obs.)* 1. To talk nonsense. 2. To swing to and fro.

badajo [bah-dah'-ho], *m.* 1. Clapper of a bell. 2. An idle talker.

badajuelo [bah-dah-hoo-ay'-lo], *m. dim.* A small clapper.

badal [bah-dahl'], *m.* 1. Muzzle. **Echar un badal a la boca**, to stop one's mouth. 2. *(Prov.)* Shoulder and ribs of butcher's meat. 3. *(Surg.)* Instrument for opening the mouth.

badana [bah-dah'-nah], *f.* A dressed sheep-skin. **Zurrar la badana**, to dress a sheep-skin; to give one a flogging.

badaza [bah-dah-tha], *f. (Carib.)* Strap (para pasajeros de pie).

badazas [bah-dah'-thas], *f. pl. (Naut.)* Keys of the bonnets, ropes with which the bonnets are laced to the sails. V. BARJULETA.

badea [bah-day'-ah], *f.* 1. Pompion or pumpkin. 2. *(Met.)* A dull, insipid being.

badén [bah-den'], *m.* 1. Channel made by a sudden fall of water. 2. Catchwater, conduit.

badiana [bah-de-ah'-nah], *f. (Bot.)* Indian aniseed, badiana.

badil, m. badila, *f.* [bah-deel', bah-dee'-lah]. Fire-shovel.

badilejo [bah-de-lay'-ho], *m. (And.)* Trowel (de constructor).

badina [bah-dee'-nah], *f. (Obs.)* Pool of water in the roads.

bádminton [bahd'-meen-ton], *m.* Badminton.

badomía [bah-do-mee'-ah], *f.* Nonsense, absurdity.

badulacada [bah-doo-lah-cah'-dah], *f. (Peru.)* V. CALAVERADA.

badulaque [bah-doo-lah'-kay], *m.* 1. Ragout of stewedlivers. 2. A stupid person. 3. A person not to be relied on.

badulaquear [bah-doo-lah-kay-ahr'], *vn.* To be an idiot, act like an idiot. 2. *(Cono Sur)* To be a rogue, to be dishonest, to act like a rogue.

bafetas [bah-fay'-tas], *f. pl.* Fabric, of white cotton from India.

baf(f)le [bah'-flay], *m. (Elec.)* Speaker, loudspeaker.

baga [bah'-gah], *f.* 1 *(Prov.)* A rope or cord with which the loads of beasts of burden are fastened. 2. A little head of flax with its seeds.

bagaje [bah-gah'-hay], *m.* 1. Beast of burden. 2. Baggage, the furniture of an army and the beasts of burden on which it is carried.

bagajero [bah-gah-hay'-ro], *m.* Driver, he who conducted the beasts which carried military baggage.

bagar [bah-gar'], *vn.* To yield the seed: applied to flax.

bagasa [bah-gah'-sah], *f.* A prostitute.

bagatela [bah-gah-tay'-lah], *f.* Begatelle, trifle. **Son bagaletas**, those are trivialities.

bagayo [bah-gah'-yo], *m. (Cono Sur)* 1. Bundle, tramp's bundle; heavy (carga), loot. 2. *(fig.)* Useless lump, berk, old bag (mujer fea).

bagazo [bah-gah'-tho], *m.* 1. *(Prov.)* The remains of sugarcane, grapes, olives, palms, etc., which have been pressed. 2. *(fig.)* Dead loss. 3. *(Carib.)* Down-and-out.

bagre [bah'-gray], *m.* 1. Catfish. 2. *m. & f. (LAm.)* Unpleasant person, sly sort; ugly mug. Old bag (mujer). 3. *(Cono Sur)* **Pica el bagre**, I'm starving. *-a.* 1. *(And.)* Vulgar, coarse, loud. 2. *(CAm.)* Clever, sharp.

bagrero [bah-gray'-ro], *a. (And.)* Fond of ugly women.

bagual [bah-goo-ahl'], 1. *a. (And. Cono Sur)* 1. Wild, untamed. 2. Rough, loutish, rude. 3. *m. (And. Cono Sur)* Wild horse. **Ganar los aguales**, *(Cono Sur) (Hist.)* to escape.

bagualada [bah-goo-ah-lah'-dah], *f. (Cono Sur)* 1. Herd of wild horses. 2. *(fig.)* Stupid thing (to do).

bagualón [bah-goo-ah-lon'], *a. (Cono Sur)* Half-tamed.

baguío [bah-gee'-o], *m.* A hurricane in the Philippine Islands.

¡bah! *int.* Bah! That's nothing!

Bahama [bah-ah'-mah], *f. & pl.* **Las Bahamas**, the Bahamas.

baharí [bah-ah-ree'], *m. (Orn.)* Sparrow-hawk.

bahía [bah-ee'-ah], *f.* 1. Bay, an arm of the sea. 2. **Bahía**, a city of Brazil.

baho [bah'-o], *m. (CAm.) (Culin.)* Dish of meat and yucca.

bahorrina [bah-or-ree'-nah], *f.* 1. Collection of filthy things. 2. Rabble.

bahuno, na [bah-oo'-no, nah], *a.* Base, vile. *V.* BAJUNO.

baila [bah'-e-lah], *f.* 1. *(Obs.) V.* BAILE. 2. *(Zool.)* Seatrout. **Ser dueño de la baila**, *(Prov.)* to be the principal of any business.

bailable [bah-e-lah'-blay], *a.* Danceable.-*m.* A pantomime with dancing. Ballet.

bailada [bah-e-lah'-dah], *f. (LAm.)* Dance, dancing.

bailadero [bah-e-lah-day'-ro], *m.* Dance hall, dance floor.

bailador, ra [bah-e-lah-dor', rah], *m. & f.* 1. Dancer. 2. *(Low.)* Thief.

bailaor(a) [bah-e-lah-or', rah], *m. & f.* Flamenco dancer.

bailar [bah-e-lar'], *vn.* 1. To dance. 2. To move by a short, brisk gallop (caballos). **Bailar el agua adelante**, to dance attendance. **Bailar sin son**, to dance without music; to be too eager for performing anything to require a stimulus. 3. *(fig.)* **Bailar al son que tocan**, to toe the line. **Le bailaban los ojos de alegría**, her eyes sparkled with happiness. **Le bailaron la casa**, *(LAm.)* they cheated her out of her house.

bailarín, na [bah-e-lah-reen', nah], *m. & f.* 1. Dancer, caperer. 2. A fiery, high-mettled dancer.

baile [bah'-e-lay], *m.* 1. Dance. 2. Ball, rout. 3. *(Prov.)* Bailiff, a judge or justice. **Baile de disfraces, o trajes**, fancy ball. **Baile de San Vito**, St. Vitus's dance, chorea.

bailecito(s) [bah-e-lay-the'-tos], *m. & pl. (LAm.)* Folk dance.

bailete [bah-e-lay'-tay], *m.* A short dance introduced into some dramatic works.

bailía, *f.* **bailiazgo**, *m.* [bah-e-lee'-ah, bah-e-le-ahth'-go]. 1. District of the jurisdiction of a *baile* or bailiff. 2. District of commandery in the order of the Knights of Malta.

bailiaje [bah-e-le-ah'-hay], *m.* A commandery or dignity in the order of Malta.

bailío [bah-e-lee'-o], *m.* The knight commander of the order of Malta.

bailón [bah-e-lon'], *a.* Fond of dancing.

bailongo [bah-e-lon'-go], *m. (LAm.)* Local dance.

bailotear [bah-e-lo-tay-ar'], *vn.* To skip and jump in dancing; to dance without grace.

bailoteo [bah-e-lo-tay'-o], *m.* A mean ball.

baivel [bah-e-vel'], *m.* In masonry and joinery, bevel, a kind of square, one leg of which is frequently crooked.

bajá [bah-hah'], *m.* Pasha, bashaw, a Turkish title.

baja [bah'-hah'], *f.* 1. Fall or diminution of price. **Una baja de 5 por ciento**, a fall of 5%. 2. *(Obs.)* A dance. 3. *(Mil.)* Ticket of admission in a hospital. 4. *(Mil.)* List of casualties in a muster-roll. Places vacant in a company, or regiment. 5. Blackball, adverse vote. **Dar de baja**, to make a return of the casualties which have happened in a military corps. 6. Casualty. **Las bajas son grandes**, the casualties are heavy. 7. **Dar de baja a un empleado**, to give notice to an employee.

bajada [bah- hah'-dah], *f.* 1. Descent, the road or path by which a person descends. 2. Inclination of an arch

bajado, da [bah-hah'-do, dah], *a.* Descended, fallen down, lowered. **Bajado del cielo**, dropped from heaven, uncommonly excellent; unexpected. *-pp.* of BAJAR.

bajalato [bah-hah-lah'-to], *m.* The dignity and office of a pasha, and the territory belonging thereto.

bajamar [bah-hah-mar'], *f.* Low water, low tide.

bajamente [bah-hah-men'-tay], *adv.* Basely, meanly, abjectly, lowly.

bajante [bah-hahn'-tay], *m.* Drainpipe.

bajar [bah-har'], *vn.* 1. To descend, to come down, to fall. **La venta nunca ha bajado de mil**, sales have never been less than a thousand. 2. To lower, to lessen. *-va.* 1. To lower, to hang down, to let down. **Bajar el equipaje al taxi**, to take the luggage down to the taxi. 2. To reduce the price in selling. 3. To lessen the value of a thing; to narrow. 4. To humble, to bring down. 5. *(Carib.)* To pay up, to cough up. 6. *(And.)* To do in (matar). *-vr.* To crouch, to grovel, to lessen. **Bajar de punto**, to decay, to decline. **Bajar el punto**, to temper. **Bajar la cerviz**, to humble oneself. **Le bajaré los bríos**, I will pull down his courage. **Bajar los humos**, to become more humane. **Bajar los ojos**, to be ashamed. **Bajar la cabeza**, to obey without objection. **Bajar la tierra**, *(Naut.)* to lay the land. **Bajar por un río** *(Naut.)* to drop down a river. **Bajar las velas**, *(Naut.)* to lower the sails. To get off, to get out (vehículo). *(Comp.)* Downloading

bajareque [bah-hah-ray'-kay], *m.* 1. *(LAm.)* Mud wall; *(Carib.)* Hovel, shack. 2. *(CAm.)* Drizzle (llovizna).

bajativo [bah-hah-tee'-vo], *a. (Cono Sur)* Digestive.

bajel [bah-hel'], *m.* Vessel: a general name for water-craft. **Bajel desaparejado**, a ship laid up in ordinary. **Bajel boyante**, a light ship. **Bajel de bajo bordo**, a low-built ship. **Bajel marinero**, a good sea-boat. **Bajel velero**, a swift sailor.

bajelero [bah-hay-lay'-ro], *m.* Owner or master of a vessel.

bajero, ra [bah-hay'-ro, rah], *a. (Prov.)* That which is under. **Sábana bajera**, the under sheet. 1. Lower ground floor, basement. 2. *(And. CAm, Carib.)* Lower leaves of the tobacco plant; rough tobacco. 3. *(And. Cono Sur, Carib.) (fig.)* Insignificant person.

bajete [bah-hay'-tay], *m. dim.* 1. A person of low stature. 2. *(Mus.)* Voice between a tenor and a bass, barytone.

bajetón [bah-hay-ton'], *a. (And.)* Short, small.

bajeza [bah-hay'-thah], *f.* 1. Meanness, fawning, paltriness. 2. A mean act. 3. Abjectness, littleness. 4. Lowliness, lowness, mechanicalness. 5. *(Obs.)* A low, deep place. **Bajeza de ánimo**, weakness of mind, lowness of spirits. **Bajeza de nacimiento**, meanness of birth.

bajini(s) [bah-hee'-nee], *adv.* **Por lo bajini**, very quietly.

bajío [bah-hee'-o], *m.* 1. A shoal, sandbank, shallow, or flat. 2. Decline of fortune or favor. 3. *(Mex.)* Fertile plateau of northern Mexico.

bajista [bah-hees'-tah], *m.* 1. *(Com.)* Bear, a broker who speculates upon the fall of prices or stocks. 2. A doublebass viol, and one who plays it. Bass guitar player.

bajo, ja [bah'-ho, hah], *a.* 1. Low. 2. Abject, despicable, faint. 3. Common, ordinary; mechanical, humble. 4. Dull, faint (colores). 5. Mean, coarse, vulgar (lenguaje). 6. Bent downward. **Bajo de ley**, Of a base quality (metales). **Con los ojos bajos**, with downcast eyes.

bajo [bah'-ho], *adv.* 1. Under, underneath, below. *V.* ABAJO and DEBAJO. 2. Low, with depression of the voice. 3. Low, in a state of subjection. 4. In a humble, submissive manner. **Por lo bajo**, cautiously, in a prudent manner. **Bajo mano**, Underhand secretly.

bajo [bah'-ho], *m.* 1. Bass, the lowest part in music. **Bajo profundo**, basso profundo. 2. Player on the bassviol or bassoon. 3. Low situation or place. **Bajo relieve**, *(Sculp.)* Bassrelief. **Cuarto bajo**, Ground-floor. *-pl.* 1. Underpetticoats of women. 2. Hoofs or feet of horses.

bajoca [bah-ho'-cah], *f. (Prov.)* 1. Green kidney-beans. 2. A dead silk worm.

bajón [bah-hone'], *m.* 1. Bassoon. 2. A player on the bassoon. 3. Decline, fall. *(Fin.)* 4. Sharp fall in price; slump. 5. Slump in moral. **Dar un bajón**, to fall away sharply.

bajoncillo [bah-hon-theel'-lyo], *m.* Counter-bass.

bajonista [bah-ho-ness'-tah], *m.* Bassoon player.

bajorrelieve [bah-hor-ray-le-ay'-vay], *m.* Bas-relief.

bajovientre [bah-ho-ve-en'-tray], *m.* Hypogastrium.

bajuno, na [bah-hoo'-no, nah], *a.* Vile, low, contemptible (personas).

bajura [bah-hoo'-rah], *f.* 1. *a.* Lowness; shortness, smallness, small size. 2. *(Carib.) (Geog.)* Lowland. 3. **Pesca de bajura**, inshore fishing, coastal fishing.

bakelita [bah-kay-lee-tah], *f. V.* BAQUELITA.

bala [bah'-lah], *f.* 1. Bullet, shot. **Bala de metralla**, grapeshot. **Bala expansiva**, dumdum bullet. **Como una bala**, quick as a flash. 2. Bale (de papel, mercancías). 3. Small ball of wax to play tricks at carnival time. 4. *(Com.)* Bale. **Bala de algodón**, bale of cotton. 5. **Bala de entintar** *(Typ.)* inkball, inking ball.

balaca [bah-lah'-cah], *f. (LAm.)* Boast, piece of boasting, brag; *(And)* Show, pomp.

balacada [bah-lah-cah'-dah], *f. (Cono Sur) V.* BALACA.

balacear [bah-lah-thay-ar'], *va. (Mex.)* To shoot haphazardly, to shoot at random.

balacera [bah-lah-thay'-rah], *f. (Mex.)* Haphazard shooting, shooting at random.

balada [bah-lah'-dah], *f.* Ballad, a song.

baladí [bah-lah-dee'], *a.* Mean, despicable, worthless, trivial.

balador, ra [bah-lah-dor', rah], *m. & f.* Bleating animal.

baladrar [bah-lah-drar'], *vn.* To cry out, to shout.

baladre [bah-lah'-dray], *m. (Bot.)* Rose bay.

baladrero [bah-lah-dray'-ro], *a.* Loud, noisy.

baladro [bah-lah'-dro], *m.* Scream, howl; shout.

baladrón [bah-lah-drone'], *m.* Boaster bragger, bully.

baladronada [ba-lah-dro-nah'-dah], *f.* 1. Boast, brag, fanfaronade, bravado. 2. Rodomontade.

baladronear [bah-lah-dro-nay-ar'], *vn.* To boast, to brag, to hector.

balagar [bah-lah-gar'], *m. (Prov.)* Long straw or hay preserved for winter fodder.

bálago [bah'-lah-go], *m.* 1. *V.* BALAGAR. 2 Hayrick 3. Thick spume of soap, of which wash-balls are made. **Sacudir or menear a uno el bálago**, to give a sound srubbing.

balaguero [bah-lah-gay'-ro], *m.* Rick of straw.

balahú [bah-lah-oo'], *m.* A schooner.

balaj [bah-lah'], *m.* Balas or spinel ruby.

balance [bah-lahn'-thay], *m.* 1. Fluctuation, vibration. 2. Libration, swinging, see-saw. 3. Equilibrium or equipoise of a rider on horseback. 4. Balance of accounts, balancesheet. **Balance de situación**, balance sheet. 5. *(Obs.)* Doubt. 6. Rolling of a ship. **Balance de comercio**, balance of trade.

balanceado [bah-lahn-thay-ah'-do], *m.* Swing.

balancear [bah-lan-thay-ar'], *va. & vn.* 1. To balance, to vibrate; to librate, to poise, to hold in equipoise. 2. *(Met.)* To waver, to be unsettled. 3. To weigh, to examine. 4. To settle accounts.

balanceo [bah-lan-thay'-o], *m.* Oscillation, rocking motion.

balancero, *m. V.* BALANZARIO.

balancín [bah-lan-theen'], *m.* 1. Splinter-bar of a carriage, swing-bar of a cart. Singletree, whiffletree. *(Mech.)* Walking-beam, balance-beam. 2. Iron beam for striking coins and medals; minting mill. 3. Poy, a rope-dancer's pole. 4. *(Amer.)* A sort of gig drawn by three horses abreast. **Balancines** *(Naut.)* lifts, ropes serving to raise or lower the yards. **Balancines de la brújula**, *(Naut.)* brass rings by which the compass is suspended in the binnacle.

balandra [bah-lahn'-drah], *f. (Naut.)* 1. Bilander, a small vessel carrying but one mast. 2. Sloop.

balandrán [bah-lahn'-drah], *m.* A loose surtout worn by priests, cassock.

balandrista [bah-lahn-drees'-tah], *m. & f.* Yachtman, yachtswoman; sailing enthusiast.

balandro [bah-lahn'-dro], *m.* Yacht; *(Carib.)* Fishing vessel.

balano [bah-lahn'-tay], *m.* 1. Balanus, the glans penis. 2. Barnacle.

balante [bah-lahn'-tay], *pa. (Poet.)* Bleating.

balanza [bah-laan'-thah], *f.* 1. Scale. **Balanza de presión**, precision balance. 2. Balance, a pair of scales. 3. A kind of fishing-net. 4. *(Met.)* Comparative estimate, judgment. **Fiel de balanza de la romana**, needle of the balance. **Fiel de balanza**, (in the mints) the weigh-master. **Andar en balanza**, *(Met.)* to be in danger of losing one's property or place. 5. Gallows, in cant.

balanzar [bah-lan-thar'], *va. (Obs.) V.* BALANCEAR.

balanzario [bah-lan-thah'-re-o], *m.* Balancer, he who weighs and adjusts the coins in the mint.

balanzón [bah-lan-thone'], *m.* Copper pan used by silversmiths.

balaou [bah-lah'-o-oo], *m. (Zool.)* A kind of sprat.

balaquear [bah-lah-kay-ahr'], *vn.* To boast.

balar [bah-lar'], *vn.* To bleat. **Andar balando por alguna cosa**, to be gaping after something.

Balasor [bah-lah-sor'], *m.* Balassor.

balastar [bali-las-tar'], *va.* To ballast a railroad track.

balaste [bah-lahs'-tay], *m.* Ballast, a layer of gravel between the ties.

balasto [bah-lahs'-to], *m.* Ballast. Sleeper *(Ferro.)*.

balastro [bah-lahs'-to], *m. V.* BALASTO.

balate [bah-lah'-tay], *m.* 1. A boundary mark (heap of stones, etc.). 2. Border of a trench.

balaustrada, balaustrería [bah-lah-oos-trah'-dah, oos-tray-ree'-ah], *f.* Balustrade.

balaustrado, da [bah-lah-oos-trah'-do, dah], **Balaustral**, *a.* Balustered.

balaustre [bah-lah-oois'-tray], *m.* Baluster. **Balaustres de navío**, *(Naut.)* Balusters or head-rails of a ship.

balay [bah-lah'-ee], *m. (LAm.)* Wicker basket.

balazo [bah-lah'-tho], *m.* A shot; wound from a ball.

balboa [bal-bo-ah], *m.* Balboa, monetary unit of Panama.

balbucear [bal-boo-thay-ar'], *m.* To speak and pronounce indistinctly like little children; to stutter, to stammer.

balbucencia [hal-boo-then'-the-ah], *f.* Stuttering speech.

balbuceo [bal-boo-thay'-o], *m.* Stammering, stuttering.

balbuciente [bal-boo-the-en'-tay], *a.* Stammering, stuttering.

balbucir [bal-boo-theer'], *vn.* To lisp.

Balcanes [bahl-cah'-nays], *m. & pl.* The Balkans. **La Península de los Balcanes**, the Balkan Peninsula.

balcánico [bahl-cah'-nee-co], *a.* Balkan.

balcanización [bahl-cah-nee-thah-thee-on'], *f.* Balkanization.

balcarrias [bahl-cah'-rree-ahs], *f. & pl.* **Balcarrotas** *(And.)* Sideburns.

balcón [bal-cone'], *m.* Balcony; (mirador).

balconada [bahl-co-nah'-dah], *f.* Row of balconies.

balconaje [bal-co-nah'-hay], *m.* **balconería**, *f.* Range of balconies.

balconazo [bai-co-nah'-tho], *m. aug.* A large balcony.

balconcillo [bal-con-theel'-lyo], *m. dim.* A small balcony.

balconeador(a) [bahl-co-nay-ah-dor'], *m. & f.* Onlooker, observer.

balconear [bahl-co-nay-ahr'], 1. *va. (Cono Sur)* To watch closely. 2. *(CAm.)* To talk at the window.

balconero [bahl-co-nay'-ro], *m.* Cat burglar.

balda [bahl'-dah], *f.* Trifle, a thing of little value. **A la balda**, living in a heedless, imprudent manner. Shelf.

baldada [bahl-dah'-dah], *f. (Cono Sur)* Bucketful.

baldado [bahl-dah'-do], 1. *a.* Crippled, disabled. **Estar baldado**, to be knackered. 2. *m. f.* Cripple, disabled person.

baldaquín [bahl-dah-keen'], *m.* **baldaquino**, canopy, daldachin.

baldar [bal-dar], *va.* 1. To cripple. 2. *(Prov.)* To break a set of books, or other things. 3. To trump or win a trick in a game at cards. 4. To obstruct, or hinder.

balde [bahl'-day], *m.* Bucket, used on board ships.

balde (De), *adv.* (Gratis) free of cost. **En balde**, in vain, to no purpose.

baldear [bal-day-ar'], *vn. (Naut.)* To throw water on the deck and sides of a ship for the purpose of cleaning them.

baldeo [bal-day'-o], *m. (Naut.)* Washing the decks with bucketfuls of water.

baldés [bal-dess'], *m.* A piece of soft dressed skin for gloves, etc.

baldío, día [bal-dee'-o, ah], *a.* 1. Untilled, uncultivated (tierras). 2. Unappropriate. **Los baldíos**, the lay-land, the commons; waste or waste land. 3. *(Ibs.)* Idle, lazy. **Hombre baldío**, vagrant, vagabond.

baldón [bal-done'], *m.* Affront, reproach, insult, contumely.

baldonar, baldonear [Bal-do-nar', bal-do-nay-ar'], *va.* To insult with abusive language, to reproach, to stigmatize.

baldosa [bal-do'-sah], *f.* 1. A fine square tile. 2. Flat pavingstones.

baldosado [bahl-do-sah'do], *m.* Tiled floor, tiling; paving.

baldosar [bahl-do-sahr'], *va.* To tile; to pave.

balduque [bal-doo'-kay], *m.* Narrow red tape, for tying papers.

balear [bah-lay-ahr'], 1. *va. (LAm.)* To shoot, to shoot dead. 2. To cheat. -*vr. (LAm.)* To exchange shots.

baleárico, ca [bah-le-ah'-re-co, cah], **baleario, ia** [bah-le-ah'-re-o, ah], *a.* Balearic.

baleo [bah-lay'-o], *m.* 1. *(LAm.)* Shooting. 2. *(Mex.)* Fan.

balero [bah-lay'-ro], *m.* A ball-mould.

baleta [bah-lay'-tah], *f. dim.* A small bale of goods.

balí [ba-lee'], *m.* 1. A learned language of the Indo-Chinese. 2. One of the five Indian commandments, that of offering food to every animated being.

balido [bah-lee'-do], *m.* Bleating, bleat.

balija [bah-lee'-hah], *f.* 1. Portmanteau. 2. Mail, the postman's bag. 3. Post.

balijero [bah-le-hay'-ro], *m.* A post or post-boy who carries letters out of the post-road.

balijilla [bah-le-heel'-lyah], *f. dim.* A small bag.

balijón [bah-lee'-hone], *m. aug.* A large portmanteau.

balín [bah-leen'], *m.* Small bullet, pellet.

balinera [bah-lee-nay'-rah], *f. (And.)* Ball-bearing.

balines [bah-lee'-nes], *m. pl. (Amer.)* Mould-shot, buckshot.

balista [bah-lees'-tah], *f.* Ballista, engine used in ancient warfare for hurling heavy stones.

balística [bah-lees'-te-cah], *f.* Ballistics, science that deals with the impact, path, and velocity of projectiles.

balístico, ca [bah-lees'-te-co, cah], *a.* Ballistic. **Proyectil balístico**, ballistic missile.

balita [bah-lee'-tah], *f.* 1. Small bullet, pellet. 2. *(Cono Sur)* Marble.

baliza [bah-lee'-tha], *f. (Naut.)* Buoy, marker; *(Aer.)* Beacon, marker.

balizaje [bah-lee-thah'hay], *m.* **Balizaje de pista**, runway lighting.

ballena [bahl-lyay'-nah], *f.* 1. Whale (mamífero). 2. Trainoil. 3. Bone (de cuello). 4. *(Astr.)* One of the northern constellations. 5. **Parece una ballena**, she's as fat as a whale.

ballenato [bahl-lyay-nah'-to], *m.* Cub, the young of a whale.

ballener [bahl-lyay-ner'], *m. (Obs.)* A vessel in the shape of a whale.

ballenera [bahl-lyay-nay'-rah], *f.* Whaler, whaling ship.

ballenero [bahl-lyay-nay'-ro], 1. *a.* Whaling. **Industria ballenera**, whaling industry. 2. *m.* Whaler (persona). 3. Whaling ship.

ballesta [bal-lyes'-tah], *f.* Shot from a cross-bow, **A tiro de ballesta**, *(Met.)* at a great distance.

ballestazo [bal-lyes-tah-tho'], *m.* Blow given by or received from a cross-bow.

ballesteador [bal-lyes-tay-ah-dor'], *m.* Cross-bowman.

ballestear [bal-lyes-tay-ar'], *va.* To shoot with a cross-bow.

ballestera [bal-lyes-tay'-rah], *f.* Loopholes through which crossbows were discharged.

ballestería [bal-lyes-tay-ree'-ah], *f.* 1. Archery, the art of an archer. 2. Number of crossbows, or persons armed with crossbows. 3. Place where crossbows are kept, or arbalists quartered.

ballestero [bal-lyes-tay'-ro], *m.* 1. Archer, crossbowman. 2. Crossbow maker. 3. King's archer or armorer. **Ballestero**

de maza, mace-bearer. **Ballesteros de corte**, the King's porters and the portes of the privy council were formerly so called.

ballestilla [bal-lyes-teel'-lyah], *f.* 1. *(Dim.)* Small crossbow. 2. *(Obs.)* The instrument for bleeding cattle, at present called *a fleam.* 3. Cross-staff, an instrument for measuring heights, 4. *(Naut.)* Fore-staff, an instrument used for measuring the altitude of the sun, stars, etc.

ballestón [bal-lyes-tone'], *m. aug.* Large cross-bow, arbalet.

ballestrinque [bal-lyes-treen'-kay], *m. (Naut.)* Clove-hitch, by which one rope is fastened to another.

ballet [bah-lay'], *m.* Ballet.

ballico [bal-lyee'-co], *m. (Bot.)* Red or perennial darnal, rye-grass.

ballueca [bal-lyoo-ay'-cah], *f. (Bot. Prov.)* Wild oats.

balneario, *m.* Spa, bathing beach (con playa), bathing resort.

balneario, ria [bal-nay-ah'-re-o, ah], *a.* Of or pertaining to baths and bathing.

balompédico [bah-lon-pay'-dee-co], *a.* Football.

balompié [bah-lom-pe-ay'], *m.* Soccer.

balón [bah-lon'], *m.* 1. Soccer ball. 2. Glass ball. 3. Balloon. 4. Bale. **Balón medicinal**, Medicine ball. 5. *(And. Cono Sur)* Drum, canister.

baloncestista [bah-lon-thays-tees'-tah], *m. & f.* Basketball player.

baloncestístico [bah-lon-thays-tees'-tee-co], *a.* Basketball.

baloncesto [bah-lon-thes'-to], *m.* Basketball.

balonmanear [bah-lon-mah-nay-ahr'], *vn.* To handle, to handle the ball.

balonmano [bah-lon-mah'-no], *m.* Handball.

balonvolea [bah-lon-vo-lay'-ah], *m.* Volleyball.

balota [bah-lo'-tah], *f.* Ballot, a little ball used in voting.

balotada [bah-lo-tah'-dah], *f.* Balotade, leap of a horse, in which he shows the shoes of his hinder feet.

balotaje [bah-lo-tah-hay], *m. (Mex.)* Balloting, voting; continuing of votes.

balotar [bah-lo-tar'], *vn.* To ballot, to choose by ballot.

balsa [bahl'-sah], *f.* 1. Pool, lake. 2. *(Naut.)* Raft of float for conveying persons across a river. 3. *(Prov.)* Half a butt of wine. 4. In oil-mills, the room where the oil is kept. **Estar como una balsa de aceite**, to be as quiet as a pool of oil; spoken of a place or country, or of the sea.

balsadera [bahl-sah-day-rah], *f.* **Balsadero** *m.* Ferry (station).

balsámico, ca [bal-sah'-me-co, cah], *a.* Balsamic, balsamical, balmy.

balsamina [bal-sah-mee'-nah], *f. (Bot.)* Balsam-apple.

balsamita mayor [bal-sah-mee'-tah mah-yor']. *(Bot.)* V. ATANASIA. **Balsamita menor**, *(Bot.)* Maudlin, annual costmary, tansy.

bálsamo [bahl'-sah-mo], *m.* 1. Balsam balm. **Bálsamo de María**, gum of the calaba-tree. **Bálsamo de copaiba**, copaiba balsam. **Es un bálsamo**, it is a balsam (licores). 2. *(Med.)* The purest part of the blood. *(fig.)* Balm, comfort.

balsar [bal-sar'], *m.* A marshy piece of ground with brambles.

balsear [bal-say-ar'], *va.* To cross rivers on rafts.

balsero [bal-ay'-ro], *m.* Ferry-man.

balsón [bahl-son'], *m. (Mex.)* Swamp, bog; stagnant pool. *a. (And.)* Fat, flabby.

balsopeto [bal-so-pay'-to], *m. (Coll.)* 1. A large pouch carried near the breast. 2. Bosom, the inside of the breast.

balsoso [bahl-so'-so], *a. (And.)* Soft, spongy.

Baltasar [bal-tah-sar'], *m.* Belshazzar, the last King of Babylon.

Báltico [bahl'-te-co], *m.* The Baltic Sea.

bálteo [bahl'-tay-o], *m.* Officer's belt.

baluarte [bah-loo-ar'-tay], *m.* 1. *(Fort.)* Bastion, formerly bulwark, a mass of earth raised in the angles of a polygon. 2. *(Met.)* Bulwark, defence, support.

balumba [bah-loom'-bah], *f.* Bulk or quantity of things heaped together.

balumbo, balume [bah-loom'-bo, bah-loo'-may], *m.* A heap of things which take up a lot of room.

balumoso [bah-loo-mo'-so], *m. (And. Cam. Méx.)* Bulky.

baluquero [bah-loo-kay'-ro], *m. (Fin.)* Forger.

balurdo [bah-loor'-do], 1. *a. (LAm.)* Flashy. 2. *m. (Cono Sur)* Crooked deal.

balzo [bahl'-tho], *m. (Naut.)* A bend.

bamba [bam'-bah], *m. & f.* 1. *(Carib.)* Negro, negress. 2. *(And.) (Bot.)* Bole, swelling. Fat, flabbiness.

bambalear, babanear [bam-bah-lay-ahr], *vn.* V. BAMBOLEAR.

bambalina [bam-bah-lee'-nah], *f.* The upper part of the scenes in theaters.

bambalúa [bam-bah-loo'-ah], *m. (LAm.)* Clumsy fellow, lout.

bambarria [bam-bar'-re-ah], *m.* 1. *(Low.)* A fool, an idiot. 2. An accidental but successful stroke at billiards

bambochada bam-bo-chah'-dah], *f.* **bamboche** [bam-bo'-chay], *m.* A landscape representing banquets or drunken feasts, with grotesque figures. **Es un bamboche**, or **parece un bamboche**; applied to a thick, short person with a red, bloated face.

bambolear, bambonear [bam-bo-lay-ar', bam-bo-nay-ar'], *vn.* To reel, to stagger, to totter. -*vr.* To swing, sway; to sway, roll, ree.

bamboleo, bamboneo [bam-bo-lay'-o, bam-bo-nay'-o], *m.* Reeling, staggering.

bambolla [bam-bol'-lyah], *f.* Ostentation, boast, vain show, froth.

bambollero [bam-bol-laye'-ro], *a.* Showy, flashy; sham, bogus.

bambú, or **bambuc** [bam-boo' or bam-book], *m.* Bamboo, the largest of the grass family.

bambuco [bam-boo'-co], *m.* Popular musical rhythm of Colombia.

bambudal [bam-boo-dahl], *m. (And.)* Bamboo grove.

ban [ban], *m.* A sort of fine Chinese muslin.

banal [bah-nahl], *a.* Banal, trivial, ordinary.

banalidad [bah-nah'-lee-tee], *f.* 1. Banality, triviality, ordinariness. 2. Banality, trivial thing. **Intercambiar banalidades con uno**, to exchange trivialities with somebody.

banana, *f.* V. PLÁTANO.

bananal [bah-nah-nahl'], *m. (LAm.)* Banana plantation.

bananero [bah-nah-nay'-ro], 1. *a. (LAm.)* Banana. **Compañía bananera**, banana company. 2. *m.* Banana plantation. Banana tree.

banano, *m. (Bot.)* V. PLÁTANO.

banas [bah'-nahs], *f. & pl. (Mex.)* Banns.

banasta [bah-nahs'-tah], *f.* A large basket made of twigs or laths. **Meterse en banasta**; to meddle with things which do not concern one.

banastero [bah-nas-tay'-ro], *m.* 1. Basket-maker or dealer. 2. *(Low.)* Jailer.

banasto [bah-nahs'-to], *m.* A large round basket.

banca [bahn'-cah], *f.* 1. Bench. 2. Banking. **Horas de banca**, banking hours. 3. Bank (juegos). **Hacer saltar la banca**, to break the bank. 4. *(Cono Sur)* Pull, influence. **Tener banca**, to have pull.

bancada [ban-cah'-dah], *f.* A sort of bench on which to spread cloth to be measured.

bancal [ban-cahl'], *m.* 1. An oblong plot of ground for raising, roots, and fruit-trees. 2. Terrace in a garden. 3. Cover placed over a bench by way of ornament.

bancar [ban-cahr'], *va. (Cono Sur)* To pay for. *(fig.)* To put up with (aguantar). -*vr.* **Bancarse algo a uno**, to put up with something/somebody.

bancaria, [bahn-cah'-ree-ah] *f.* V. FIANZA, BANCARIA.

bancario, ria [ban-cah'-re-o, ah], *a.* Bank, banking, **Cuenta bancaria**, bank account.

bancarrota [ban-car-ro'-tah], *f.* Bankruptcy, failure.

bancaza [ban-cah'-thah], *f.* **Bancazo** [ban-cah'-tho], *m. aug.* A large form or bench. *m. (Mex.)* Bank robbery.

banco [bahn'-co], *m.* 1. Form or bench without a back. 2. A strong bench for the use of carpenters. **Banco de acepillar**, a planing-bench. 3. A thwart, or bench for rowers. 4. A bank, a place where money is kept. 5. Company of persons concerned in managing a joint stock of money. 6. The cheeks of the bit of a bridle. 7. A pedestal on which any piece of architecture is raised. **Banco de ahorros**, savings-bank. **Banco de arena**, sand-bank. **Banco de hielo**, field of ice. **Banco de río**, sand-bank in a river. **Banco pinjado**, ancient warlike machine for battering. **Pasar Banco**, to flog the sailors on board a galley. **Razón de pie de banco**, an absurd reason, a groundless motive. **Banco de la paciencia**, *(Naut.)* bench on the quarter-deck. **Banco de piedra**, a vein or stratum of a single kind of stone.

banco de sangre [bahn'-co day sahn'-gray], *m.* Bloodbank.

banda [bahn'-dah] *f.* 1. Sash formerly worn by military officers when on duty. 2. Ribbon worn by the knights of the military orders. 3. Band or body of troops. 4. Scarf. 5. Party of persons; crew; military band; brass band; 6. Covey, a number of birds together. V. BANDADA. 7. Bank, border, edge: side of a ship. 8. Felloe, of wheel. 9. Cushion (billiards). **La banda del norte**, the north side. **La banda izquierda del río**, the left bank of the river. **A la banda**, *(Naut.)* heeled or hove down. **En banda**, *(Naut.)* amain. **Arriar en banda**, to let go amain. **Caer or estar en banda**, to be amain. **Dar a la banda**, to heel. **Bandas del tajamar**, *(Naut.)* the cheeks of the head. **No ir or tirar a ninguna banda**, not to make any odds. **De banda a banda**, from party to party, from one side to another. 10. **Coger a uno por banda**, to make somebody do the dirty work.

bandada [ban-dah'-dah], *f.* Covey: flock of birds.

bandarria [ban-dar'-re-ah], *f. (Naut.)* An iron maul.

bandazo [bahn-dah'-tho], *m.* Heavy fall; *(Naut.)* Heavy roll (de un barco). *(LAm.)* Air pocket, sudden drop.

bandear [ban-day-ar'], 1. *va. (Obs.)* To traverse, to pass, to cross from one side to another; to band. 2. *(CAm.)* To pursue, to chase. 3. *(CAm.)* To wound severely, to hurt. -*vn.* To conduct oneself with prudence, to shift for oneself. **Saber bandeárselas**, to know how to look for himself. -*vr.* To move to and fro; *(Mex.)* To move to the other side of a boat. 2. *(Cono Sur)* To change parties. 3. *(Mex.)* To vacillate; to go one way and then another. 4. To manage, to get organized.

bandeja [ban-day'-hah], *f.* Tray, kind of metallic waiter. *(fig.)* **Servir algo a uno en bandeja**, to hand something to somebody on a plate.

bandera [ban-day'-rah], *f.* 1. Banner, standard. 2. Flag, ensign, a pair of colors of a regiment of infantry. 3. Infantry. 4. Flag or colors which distinguish the ships of the different nations. **Bandera de popa**, *(Naut.)* the ensign. **Bandera de proa** *(Naut.)*, the jack. **Bandera blanca or de paz**, the flag of truce. **Vuelo de la bandera**, the flag of the ensign. **Arriar la bandera**, to strike the colors **Salir con banderas desplegadas**, to get off with flying colors. **Asegurar la bandera**, to fire a cannon-shot with ball at the time of hoisting the colors. **Dar la bandera**, *(Met.)* to submit to the superior talents or merits of another. **Levantar banderas**, *(Met.)* to put oneself at the head of a party. **De banderas**, terrific, marvellous.

bandereta [ban-day-ray'-tah], *f. dim.* Banneret, bannerol, a small flag. **Baderetas**, *(Mil.)* Camp-colors.

bandería [bahn-day-ree'-ahs], *f.* Faction; *(fig.)* Bias, partiality.

baderica, illa [ban-day-raree'-cah, eel'-lyah], *dim.* Banneret, a small flag.

banderilla [ban-day-reel'-lyah], *f.* 1. A small dart with a banderole, thrust into the nape of a bull. **Poner a uno una banderilla**, *(Met.)* to taunt, to ridicule to revile, to vex. 2. *(LAm.)* Swindle. 3. *(Culin.)* Savory appetizer (tapa en bar).

banderillear [ban-day-reel'-lyay-ar'], *va.* To put *banderillas* on bulls.

banderillero [ban-day-reel-lyay'-ro], *m.* He who sticks *banderrillas* in a bull's nape.

banderín

banderín [ban-day-reen'], *m.* 1. Camp colors. 2. Flag, railway signal. 3. Recruiting post.

banderita [bahn-day-ree'-tah], *f.* Little flag; flag sold for charity.

banderizar, *va. V.* ABANDERIZAR.

banderizo, za [ban-day-ree'-tho, thah], *a.* Factious, given to party.

banderola [ban-day-ro'-lah], *f.* 1. Banderol, camp colors. 2. Carabine belt. 3. Streamer, a pennant.

bandidaje [bahn-dee-dah-hay], *m.* Banditry.

bandido [ban-dee'-do], *m.* 1. Bandit, highwayman, outlaw, freebooter. 2. Fugitive pursued with judicial advertisements.

bandín [ban-deen'], *m. (Naut.)* Seat in a row-galley.

bandita [ban-dee'-tah], *f. dim.* A small band.

bando [bahn'-do], *m.* 1. Proclamation. A public declaration by government. 2. Edict or law solemnly published by superior authority. 3. Faction, party. **Echar bando**, to proclaim an edict. **Pasarse al otro bando**, to go over to the other side.

bandola, *f.* **bandolín**, *m.* [ban-do'-lah]. 1. Mandolin, a small musical instrument resembling a lute. 2. *(Naut.)* Jury-mast. 3. *(And.)* Bullfighter's cape. 4. *(Carib.)* Knotted whip.

bandolera [ban-do-lay'-rah], *f.* 1. Bandoleer, carabine belt, cross belt. 2. Woman bandit.

bandolerismo [bahn-do-lay-rees'-mo], *m.* Brigandage, banditry.

bandolero [ban-do-lay'-ro], *m.* Highwayman (bandido), robber.

bandolina [ban-do-lee'-nah], *f.* Bandoline, viscous substance used as a hair fixative.

bandoneón [ban-do-lay-on'], *m. (LAm.)* Large accordion.

bandujo [ban-doo'-ho], *m. (Obs.)* Large sausage.

bandullo [ban-dool'-lyo], *m. (Vulg.)* Belly; the bowels.

bandurria [ban-door'-re-ah], *f.* Bandurria, a musical instrument resembling a fiddle.

bangaña [ban-gah'-nyah], *f.* Bangaño *m. (LAm.)* Calabash, gourd; vessel made from a gourd.

Bangladesh [ban-glah-desh'], *m.* Bangladesh.

banjo [bahn'-ho], *m. (Mus.)* Banjo.

bánova [bah'-no-vah], *f. (Prov.)* Bedquilt, bed-cover.

banquear [ban-kay-ahr'], *va. (And.)* To level, flatten out.

banqueo [ban-kay'-o], *m.* Terraces, terracing.

banquera [ban-kay'-rah], *f. (Prov.)* 1. Small open beehive. 2. Frame, on which bee-hives are placed in a beehouse.

banquero, ra [ban-kay'-ro], **m, f.** Banker, exchanger. *V.* CAMBISTA.

banqueta [ban-kay'-tah], *f.* 1. A stool with three legs. 2. *(Mil.)* Banquette or footbank behind the parapet. 3. A sidewalk. **Banquetas de cureña**, *(Naut.)* Gun-carriage beds. **Banquetas de calafate**, *(Naut.)* calking-stools.

banquetazo [ban-kay-tah'-tho], *m.* Spread, blow out.

banquete [ban-kay'-tay], *m.* 1. Banquet, a splendid repast. **Banquete casero**, family feast. 2. Stool.

banquetear [ban-kay-tay-ar'], *vn.* To banquet, to feast.

banquillo [ban-keel'-lyo], *m. dim.* A little stool, bench. **Banquillo de los acusados**, prisoner's seat.

banquisa [ban-kee'-sah], *f.* Ice field, ice floe.

banquito [ban-kee'-to], *m. dim.* (from BANCO). A stool, footstool.

bantam [ban'-tam] *f.* Bantam. *(LAm.) (fig.)* Small restless person.

bantú [ban-too'], 1. *a.* Bantu. 2. *m.* Bantu.

banyo [ban'-yo], *m. (LAm.)* Banjo.

banzo [bahn'-tho], *m.* Check or side of an embroidering or quilting-frame.

bañada [bah-nyah'dah], *f. (LAm.)* Bath, dip, swim.

bañadera [ba-nyah-day'-rah], *f.* 1. Bathtub, bath. 2. Tub, vat. 3. *(Naut.)* Skeet, a narrow oblong ladle or scoop for wetting the sails, decks, and sides of a ship, or for bailing a boat.

bañadero [ba-nyah-day'-ro], *m.* Puddle, in which wild beasts wallow; bathing-place.

bañado [bah-nyah'-do], *m. (And. Cono Sur)* Swamp, marshland; flash, rain pool.

bañador, ra [ba-nyah-dor', rah], *m. & f.* Swimmer, bather (que se baña). 2. Swimming suit, swimsuit, bathing costume, bathing suit (de hombre y mujer), bathing trunks (de hombre).

bañar [ban-nyar'], *va.* 1. To bathe, to wash in water. 2. To water, to irrigate. **El río baña las murallas de la ciudad**, the river washes the walls of the town. 3. To candy biscuits, plums, etc., with sugar. 4. *(Art.)* To wash over a painting, with a second coat of transparent colors. 5. To overlay with something shining or pellucid. **Loza bañada or vidriada**, glazed earthenware. **Bañarse en agua de rosas**, to bathe in rose-water, to be highly pleased. 6. To extend or enlarge.

bañata [bah-nyah'-tah], *m. (Esp.)* Swimsuit, bathing costume.

bañera [bah-nyay'-rah], *f.* Bathtub.

bañero [bah-nyay'-ro], *m.* 1. Owner of baths. 2. Bath-keeper or attendant.

bañil [bah-nyeel'], *m.* A pool in which deer bathe.

bañista [bah-nyees'-tah], *m.* He who bathes in or drinks mineral waters.

baño [bah'-nyo], *m.* 1. Bath. **Tomar un baño**, to bath. 2. Bathing. 3. Bath, bathtub. **Cuarto de baño**, bathroom. **Baño de María**, cooking in a double boiler. 4. Coat of paint put over another. 5. Basting (in cooking).

bañuelo [bah-nyoo-ay'-lo], *m. dim.* A little bath.

bao [bah'-oh], *m. (Naut.)* Beam, the main cross timber. **Baos de las cubiertas altas**, the beams of the upper deck. **Bao maestro**, the midship beam. **Baos del saltillo de proa**, the collar beams. **Baos de los palos**, trestle-trees. **Baos y crucetas de los palos**, cross and trestle trees.

baobal [bah-o-bahl'], *m. (Bot.)* Baobab; a great tree of Africa. (Native name).

baptismo, *m. (Obs.) V.* BAUTISMO.

baptista [bap-tees'-tah], *m. & f.* Baptist. **La iglesia Baptista**, the Baptist church.

baptisterio [bap-tis-tay'-re-o], *m.* Baptistery.

baque [bah'-kay], *m.* 1. The blow which a body gives in falling. 2. A water-trough in glasshouses.

baqueano [bah-kay-ah'-no], *m.* etc. *V.* Baquiano.

baquelita [bah-kay-lee'-tah], *f.* Bakelite. (A trade mark for a synthetic resin.)

baqueriza [bah-kay-ree'-thah], *f.* Stable, place to keep cow in winter.

baqueta [bah-kay'-tah], *f.* 1. Ramrod, gunstick. 2. Switch used in a riding-house, in breaking in young horses. **Mandar a baqueta, a la baqueta**, to command imperiously. **Tratar a baqueta**, to treat a person in a haughty manner. -*pl.* 1. Drumsticks. 2. Gantlet, gantlope, a military punishment. 3. *(Arch.)* Beads, reeds, a semicylindric moulding. 4. Rods of hollywood, used in beating wool.

baquetazo [bah-kay-tah'-tho], *m.* 1. Violent fall, great blow given by the body when falling. 2. A blow with the ramrod. **Tropecé y di un baquetazo**, I tripped and fell violently. 3. **Tratar a uno a baquetazo limpio**, to treat somebody harshly.

baqueteado, da [bah-kay-tay'-ah-do, dah], *a.* Inured, habituated. -*pp.* of BAQUETEAR.

baquetear [bah-kay-tay-ar'], *va.* 1. *(Obs.)* To inflict the punishment of the gantlet. 2. To annoy, vex. 3. To make someone toil heavily. **Baquetear la lana**, to beat wool.

baqueteo [bah-kay-tay'-o], *m.* Beating of wool. Annoyance, bother.

baquetón [bah-kay-tone'], *m.* Gunworm, wiper, cleaningrod. *V.* SACATRAPOS.

baquetilla [bah-kay-teel'-lyah], *f. dim.* A little rod.

baquetudo [bah-kay-too'-do], *a. (Carib.)* Sluggish, slow.

baquía [bah-kee'-ah], *f.* 1. *(LAm.)* Intimate knowledge of a region, local expertise. 2. *(And. Cono Sur)* Expertise, dexterity, skill.

baquiano [bah-kee-ah'-no], *a. (LAm.)* 1. Familiar with a region. 2. *(And. Cono Sur)* Expert, skillful. **Para hacerse**

baquiano hay que perderse alguna vez, one learns the hard way. -*m.* (*LAm.*) Pathfinder, guide; local expert.

báquico, ca [bah'-ke-co, cah], *a.* Bacchanal, relating, to Bacchus. Drunken.

baquio [bah'-ke-o], *m.* (*Poet.*) A metrical foot consisting of a short and two long syllables.

baquira [bah-kee'-rah], *f.* (*Amer.*) A wild hog; peccary.

bar [bar], *m.* 1. Bar (taberna); café; snack bar. 2. Bar (unidad de presión atmosférica).

baracutey [bah-ra-coo-tay'-e], *a.* (*Amer. Cuba*) Morose, sad, retired, fond of solitude.

baradero [bah-rah-day'-ro], *m.* (*Naut.*) Skeed or skid. **Baradero de baja mar**, a muddy place in which vessels stick at low water.

baradura [bah-rah-doo'-rah], *f.* (*Naut.*) The grounding of a vessel.

baraha [ba-rah'ah], *f.* A burlesque song of Indians.

barahunda, *f.* V. BARAÚNDA. Uproar, hubbub, racket, din.

baraja [bah-rah'-hah], *f.* 1. A complete pack of cards. 2. (*Obs.*) A quarrel. **Meterse en barajas**, to seek a quarrel.

barajador, ra [ba-rah-ha-dor', rah], *m. & f.* One who shuffles or jumbles together.

barajadura [bah-rah-hah-doo'-rah], *f.* 1. Shuffling of cards. 2. Dispute, difference.

barajar [bah-rah-har'], *va.* 1. To shuffle the cards. 2. (*Met.*) To jumble things or persons together. **Barajar un negocio**, to entangle or confuse an affair. **Barajarle a alguno una pretensión**, to frustrate one's pretensions. **Barajar una proposición**, to reject a proposal. -*vn.* (*Obs.*) To wrangle, to contend. -*vr.* 1. (*Cono Sur*) To fight. 2. To get mixed up. 3. **Se baraja la posibilidad de que…**, they are juggling the possibility that…

barajo [bah-rah'-ho], 1. *interj.* (*LAm.*) V. CARAJO. 2. (*And.*) Pretext, excuse; loophole.

barajuste [bah-rah-hoos'-tay], *m.* (*Carib.*) Stampede, rush.

baranda [bah-rahn'-dah], *f.* Railing, handrail, banister (escalera). **Barandas de los corredores de popa de un navío**, sternrails. **Echar de baranda**, (*Met.*) to exaggerate something, to boast. -*m.* Boss, chief.

barandado, daje [bah-ran-dah'-do, dah'-hay], *m.* Balustrade.

barandal [bah-ran-dahl'], *m.* 1. The upper and under-piece of a balustrade, in which the balusters are fixed. 2. A balustrade or railing.

barandilla [bah-ran-deel'-lyah], *f. dim.* A small balustrade, a small railing.

barangay [bah-ran-gah'-e], *m.* 1. An Indian vessel, worked with oars. 2. Each group of forty-five or fifty families of Indians, into which a Philipine village is divided.

barata [bah-rah'-tah], *f.* 1. (*Coll.*) Barter, exchange. 2. Low price of things exposed for sale. V. BARATURA. **A la barata**, confusedly, disorderly. **Mala barata**, (*Obs.*) profusion, prodigality. -*f.* (*Cono Sur*) Cockroach.

baratador [bah-rah-tah-dor'], *m.* 1. Barterer. 2. Impostor, deceiver.

baratar [bah-rah-tar'], *va.* 1. To barter, to traffic by exchanging commodities. 2. To make fraudulent barters, to deceive. 3. To give or receive a thing under its just value.

baratear [bah-rah-tay-ar'], *vn.* To sell under price, at a loss.

baratería [bah-rah-tay-ree'-ah], *f.* 1. Barratry. 2. Fraud, deception.

baratero [bah-rah-tay'-ro], *m.* 1. He who obtains money from fortunate gamesters. 2. One who provokes quarrels.

baratez [bah-rah-tayth'], *f.* (*Carib.*), **baratía** *f.* (*And.*) Cheapness.

baratijas [bah-rah-tee'-has], *f. pl.* Trifles, toys. Cheap novelty, inexpensive articles.

baratillero [bah-rah-teel-lyay'-ro], *m.* 1. A peddler. 2. A seller of second-hand goods or articles.

baratillo [bah-rah-teel'-lyo], *m.* 1. A place where new and second-hand furniture, clothing, jewellery, etc., are sold cheap. 2. A heap of trifling articles.

baratista [bah-rah-tees'-tah], *m.* Barterer, trafficker.

barato, ta [bah-rah'-to, tah], *a.* 1. Cheap, inexpensive, bought or sold for a low price. **De barato**, gratuitously. 2. (*Met.*) Easy.

barato [bah-rah'-to], *m.* Money given by the winners at a gaming-table to the bystanders. **Hacer barato**, to sell under value in order to get rid of goods, to sell things under cost price. **Dar de barato**, (*Met.*) to grant for argument's sake, to grant readily, without objection. **Lo barato es caro**, the cheapest goods are dearest. **Ni juega, ni da barato**, to act with indifference, without taking part with a faction. -*adv.* Cheaply.

baratón [bah-rah-ton'], *a.* (*And. CAm, Méx.*) 1. Weak, feeble (argumento). 2. Bargain.

báratro [bah'-rah-tro], *m.* (*Poet.*) Hell, abyss.

baratura [bah-rah-too'-rah], *f.* Cheapness, little value set upon things.

baraúnda [bah-rah-oon'-dah], *f.* Noise, hurly-burly, confusion, din, fluttering.

barauste, *m.* (*Obs.*) V. BALAUSTRE.

barba [bar'-bah], *f.* 1. Chin. 2. Beard, the hair which grows on the chin. 3. The first swarm of bees which leaves the hive. **Barba cabruna**, (*Bot.*) yellow goat's-beard. **Barba de Aarón**, (*Bot.*) green dragon arum. **Barba de cabra or cabrón**, goat's-beard. **Amarrado a barba de gato**, (*Naut.*) moored by the head. **Temblar la barba**, to shake with fear. **Barba a barba**, face to face. **A barba regada**, in great plenty. **Barba cabosa**, noble, earnest fellow. **A la barba, en la barba**, to his face, in his presence. **Por barba**, a head, apiece. **A polla por barba**, every man his bird. -*m.* 1. Actor who acts the part of old men. 2. *pl.* The portion of rays opposite to the tail of a comet; the head. 3. (*Bot.*) Slender roots of trees or plants; fibres. **Barbas enredadas**, a full hawse. **Barbas de ballena**, whale bone. **Barbas de gallo**, wattle. **Barbas honradas**, A respectable or honorable man. **Cuales barbas, tales tobajas**, treat every one with due respect. **De tal barba, tal escama**. we must expect people to act in accordance with their condition and education. **Decir a uno en sus barbas alguna cosa**, to tell a man a thing to his face. **Echarlo a las barbas**, to reproach a man with something. **Hacer la barba**, 1. To shave, to take off beard. 2. To suck up to somebody. **Mentir por la barba**, to tell a barefaced lie. **Pelarse las barbas**, to fly into a violent passion. **Subirse a las barbas**, to fly in one's face. **Tener buenas barbas**, to have a graceful mien: applied to a fine woman. **Echar a la buena barba**, to induce one to pay for what he and his companions have eaten and drunk. **Andar, estar**, or **traer la barba sobre el hombro**. to wear one's face on one's shoulder, to be alert, to live watchful and careful. **Tener pocas barbas**, to be young or inexperienced. **Hacerse la barba**, to shave oneself. **Hacer la barba a alguno**, (*Amer.*) to flatter, to cajole.

barbacana [bar-bah-cah'-nah], *f.* 1.(*Mil.*) Barbican, an advanced work defending a castle or fortress, or loopholes in a fortification to fire missiles through. 2. A low wall around a church-yard.

barbacoa [bar-ba-co'-ah], *f.* (*Amer.*) 1. Barbecue, meat roasted in a pit in the earth. 2. A framework suspended from forked sticks. 3. (*And.*) Loft (desván). 4. (*And.*) Tap dance.

barbada [bar-bah'-dah], *f.* 1. Lower part of the lower jaw of a horse (where the bridle-curb rests). 2. Curb or iron chain, made fast to the upper part of the bridle, and running under the beard of the horse. 3. Dab, a small flat fish, related to the codfishes. **Agua de la Barbada**, Barbadoes water, a liquor distilled from sugar-cane.

barbadillo, illa [bar-bah-deel'-lyo, lyah], *a. dim.* 1. Having little beard. 2. Having slender filaments (plantas).

barbado, da [bar-bah'-do, dah], *a.* 1. Bearded. 2. Barbed, barbated. -*pp.* of BARBAR.

barbado [bar-bah'-do], *m.* 1. Full grown man. 2. Vine or tree transplanted. 3. Shoots issuing from the roots of trees.

Barbados [bar-bah'-dos], *m.* Barbados.

barbaja [bar-bah'-hah], *f. (Bot.)* Cut leaved viper's grass. *-pl.* *(Agri.)* The first roots of the plants.

barbar [bar-bar'], *vn.* 1. To get a beard. 2. Among beemasters, to rear or keep bees. 3. To begin to strike root (plantas).

Bárbara [bar'-ba-rali], *f.* **Santabárbara**, *(Naut.)* Powder-room or magazine on board a warship.

bárbaramente [bar'-ba-rah-men-tay], *adv.* 1. Barbarously, savagely. 2. Rudely, without culture.

barbárico, ca [bar-bah'-re-co, cah], *a.* Barbarous, barbarian.

barbaridad [bar-bah-re-dahd'], *f.* 1. Barbarity, barbarism, cruelty. **Es capaz de hacer cualquier barbaridad**, he's capable of doing something terrible. 2. Rashness, temerity. 3. Rudeness, want of culture. 4. Barbarous expression or action. 4. *(fig.)* **¡Que barbaridad!**, how awful! 5. A huge amount, loads, tons. **Había una barbaridad de gente**, there were an awful lot of people. 6. **Una barbaridad**, a lot; lots. **Me quiere una barbaridad**, he's terribly fond of me.

barbarie [bar-bah'-re-ay], *f.* 1. Barbarousness, incivility of manners; rusticity. 2. Cruelty.

barbarismo [bar-boh-reea'-mo], *m.* 1. Barbarism, impurity of language; use of words foreign to the language in which they are employed. 2. *(Poet.)* Crowd of barbarians. 3. Barbarousness. *V.* BARBARIE.

barbarizar [bar-bah-re-thar'], *va.* To barbarize, to make barbarous, wild, or cruel.

bárbaro, ra [bar'-bah-ro, rah], *a.* 1. Barbarous, barbarian, fierce, cruel, heathenish, murderous. 2. Rash, bold, daring. 3. Rude, ignorant, unpolished. 4. Tremendous, terrific, smashing; **¡Que bárbaro!**, How marvellous! **Es un tío bárbaro**, he's a great guy. *Adv.* Marvellous; terrifically. **Lo pasamos bárbaro**, we had a tremendous time, *m. (fig.)* Rough sort, uncouth person. **Conduce como un bárbaro**, he drives like a madman.

barbarote [bar-bah-ro'-tay], *m. aug.* A great savage or barbarian.

barbasco [bar-bahs'-co], *m.* A poison from Jacquinia armillaris, an ever-green bush.

barbato, ta [bar-bah'-to, tah], *a.* Bearded: applied to a comet.

barbaza [bar-bah'-thah], *f. aug.* A long beard.

barbear [bar-bay-ar'], *vn.* 1. To reach with the beard or lips. 2. To reach one thing almost to the height of another. *-va.* 1. *(LAm.)* To shave. 2. *(CAm. Méx.)* To fawn on, suck up to. 3. *(LAm.)* To throw, fell. 4. To see, spot. 5. *(CAm.)* To tell off.

barbechar [bar-bay-char'], *va.* To prepare ground for sowing; to fallow.

barbechazón [bar-bay-chah-thone'], *f.* Among, farmers, the fallowing-time.

barbechera [bar-bay-chay'-rah], *f.* 1. Series of successive ploughings. 2. Fallowing season. 3. Act and effect of ploughing or fallowing.

barbecho [bar-bay'-cho], *m.* 1. First ploughing of the ground. 2. Fallow, ground ploughed in order to be sown. **Como en un barbecho or por un barbecho**, with too much confidence or assurance.

barbel [bar-bel'], *m.* A small barbo; barbel, a river fish.

barbélula [bar-bay-loo-lah], *f.* Spiny involucre of certain flowers.

barbera [bar-bay'-rah], *f.* 1. Chin-piece of a helmet.

barbería [bar-bay-ree'-ah], *f.* 1. Trade of a barber. 2. Barber's shop.

barbero [bar-bay'-ro], *m.* 1. Barber. 2. *(Zool.)* Mutton-fish. 3. Barber, hairdresser. 4. *(CAm. Méx.)* Flattered. 5. *a. (CAm. Méx.)* Groveling, cuddly, affectionate (niño).

barbeta [bar-bay'-tah], *f.* 1. *(Naut.)* Rackline, gasket. 2. *(Naut.)* Ring-rope, a rope occasionally tied to the ingbolts of the deck. **Batería a barbeta**, barbet-battery, having neither embrasures nor merlons. 4. *(Cono Sur)* Fool.

barbetear [bar-bay-tay-ahr'], *va. (Mex.)* To throw, to fell, to throw to the ground.

barbiblanco, ca [bar-be-blahn'-co, cah], *a.* Having a beard gray or white with age.

barbica, ita [bar-bee'-cah, ee'-tah], *f. dim.* A small beard.

barbicacho [bar-be-cah'-cho], *m. (Prov.)* Ribbon or band tied under the chin; guard ribbon.

barbicano, na [bar-be-cah'-no, nah], *a.* Graybeard, having a gray beard.

barbiespeso, sa [bar-be-es-pay'-so, sah], *a.* One who has a thick beard.

barbihecho, cha [bar-be-ay'-cho, chah], *a.* Freshly shaved.

barbijo [bar-be'-ho], *m.* 1. *(And. Cono Sur)* Chinstrap; *(And. Carib. Cono Sur)* Headscarf. 2. *(And. Cono Sur)* Scar.

barbilampiño, ña [bar-be-larn-pee'-nyo,_nyah], *a.* Having a thin beard, or none. Inexperience. *m. (fig.)* Novice, greenhorn.

barbilindo, da [bar-be-leen'-do, dah], *a.* Well-shaved and trimmed; effeminate and pretty,

barbilucio, cia [bar-be-loo'-the-o, ah], *a.* Smooth-faced, pretty, genteel.

barbilla [bar-beel'-lyah], *f.* 1. Point of the chin. 2. Morbid tumor under the tongue of horses and cattle. 3. *(Dim.)* Small beard.

barbillera [bar-beel-lyay'-rah], *f.* 1. Tuft of tow, put between the staves of a cask or vat to prevent it from leaking. 2. Bandage put under the chin of a dead person.

barbinegro, gra [bar-be-nay'-gro, grah], *a.* Black-bearded.

barbiponiente [bar-be-po-ne-en'-tay], *a.* 1. *(Coll.)* Having the beard growing; applied to a boy or lad. 2. *(Met.)* Beginning to learn an art or profession.

barbiquejo [bar-be-kay'-ho], *m.* 1. Handkerchief, which females in some parts of America muffle the chin with, or put round their heads and tie under the chin. 2. A guard-ribbon for a hat. 3. *(Naut.)* Bobstay. 4. Curb-chain.

barbiquí or **barbiquejo** [bar-be-kee'-bar, be-kay'-ho], *m.* A brace and bit.

barbirrubio, bia [bar-be-roo'-be-o, ah], *a.* Having a black and white beard.

barbital [bar-be-tahl], *m. (Chem.)* Barbital.

barbiteñido, da [bar-be-tay-nyee'-do, dah], *a.* Having a dyed beard.

barbiturato [bar-be-too-rah'-to], *m. V.* BARBITURICO.

barbitúrico [bar-be-too'-ree-co], *m. (Chem.)* Barbiturate.

barbo [bar'-bo], *m. (Zool.)* Barbel, a river fish.

barbón [bar-bone'], *m.* 1. An old man of a grave and austere aspect. 2. A man with a thick, strong beard. 3. A lay brother of the Carthusian order.

barboquejo [bar-bo-kay'-ho], *m.* 1. Chin-strap. 2. Bandage put under the chin of a dead person.

barbotar [bar-bo-tar'], *vn.* To mumble, to mutter.

barbote [bar-bo'-tay], *m.* Fore part of a helmet. *V.* BABERA.

barbotear [bar-bo-tay-ahr'], *vti.* Mutter, mumble.

barboteo [bar-bo-tay'-o], *m.* Mutter, muttering, mumbling.

barbudo, da [bar-boo'-do, dah], *a.* Having a long beard.

barbudo [bar-boo'-do], *m.* Vine transplanted with the roots.

barbulla [bar-bool'-lyah], *f.* Loud, confused noise, made by people talking all at the same time. Clamor.

barbullar [bar-bool-lyar'], *vn.* To talk loud and fast, with disorder and confusion.

barbullón, na [bar-bool-lyone', nah], *a.* Talking loud, fast, and confusedly.

barca [bar'-cah], *f. (Naut.)* Boat, barge, bark, barkentine. **Barca chata para pasar gente**, a ferry-boat. **Barca longa**, fishing-boat. **Conduce bien su barca**, he steers his course well.

barcada [bar-cah'-dah], *f.* 1. Passage across a river in a ferryboat. 2. A boat full of persons or goods. **Barcada de lastre**, a boat-load of ballast.

barcaje [bar-cah'-hay], *m.* 1. Ferriage. 2. Ferry, passageboat for carrying goods or persons. Toll.

barcal [bar-cahl'], *m. (Prov. Gal.)* A wooden vessel in which a caldron is put.

barcarola [bar-cah-ro'-lah], *f.* Barcarole, the song of an Italian boatman or gondolier.

barcaza [bar-cah'-thah], *f.* A privilege conceded in some ports of loading and unloading.

barcazo [bar-cah'-tho], *m.* A large barge.

Barcelona [bar-thay-lo-nah], Barcelona.

barceo [bar-thay'-o], *m.* Dry bass or sedge for making mats, ropes, etc.

barcia [bar'-thee-ah], *f.* Chaff.

barcina [bar-thee'-nah], *f. (Prov.)* 1. Net for carrying straw. 2. Large truss of straw.

barcinar [bar-thee-nar'], *va. (Prov.)* To load a cart or wagon with heaves of corn.

barcino, na [bar-thee'-no, nah], *a.* Ruddy, approaching to redness.

barco [bar'-co], *m.* Boat, ship, barge. A word comprising every floating craft, of whatever size, strength, or use. **Barco aguador**, a watering boat. **Barco chato**, A flat-bottomed boat. **Barco de pasajeros**, passenger-boat.

barcolongo, barcoluengo [bar-co-lon'-go, bar-co-loo-en'-go], *m.* An oblong boat with a round bow.

barco-madre [bar'-co-mah'-dray], *m, pl.* **Barcos madre**, mother ship.

barcón, barcote [bar-cone', bar-co'-tay], *m. aug.* A large boat.

barchilón, na [ ], *m. & f.* Nurse, hospital aide; quack doctor, quack surgeon.

barda [bar'-dah], *f.* 1. Bard, ancient armor of horses. 2. Straw, brush-wood, etc., laid on fences, etc., to preserve them. **Aún hay sol en bardas**, there are still hopes of attaining it.

bardado, da [bar-dah'-do, dah], *a.* Barbed, caparisoned with defensive armor (caballos).

bárdago [bar'-dah-go], *m. (Naut.)* Pendant; luff-tackle-rope.

bardaguera [bar-dah-gy'-rah], *f.* Chaste-tree; a willow.

bardal [bar-dahl'], *m.* Mud wall, covered at the top with straw or brush. **Saltabardales**, a nickname given to mischievous boys.

bardana [bar-dah'-nah], *f.* Common burdock, or cockle burr. Bardana menor, *(Bot.)* Lesser burdock.

bardanza [bar-dahn'-thah], *f.* **Andar de bardanza**, to go here and there.

bardar [bar-dar'], *va.* To cover the tops of fences or walls with straw or brushwood.

bardilla [bar-deel'-lyah], *f. dim.* Small brushwood.

bardiota [bar-de-o'-tah], *a. & m.* Soldier of the Byzantine court.

bardo [bar'-do], *m.* Bard, poet.

bardoma [bar-do'-mah], *f. (Prov.)* Filth, mud.

bardomera [bar-do-may'-rah], *f. (Prov.)* Weeds or small wood carried off by currents.

baremo [bah-ray'-mo], *m.* Table; ready-reckoner; *(fig.)* Scale, schedule; yardstick, gauge, criterion.

bareo [bah-ray'-o], *m.* **Ir de bareo**, to go drinking, to go around the bars.

barfol [bar-fol'], *m.* A coarse stuff, from the coast of Gambia.

barga [bar'-gah], *f.* 1. The steepest part of a declivity. 2. *(Obs.)* Hut covered with straw or thatched.

barganal [bar'-gah-nahl], *m.* A fence of wooden stakes.

bárgano [bar'-gah-no], *m.* A stake, six or seven feet high, of split wood.

barí, or baril [bah-ree' or bah-reel'], *a. (Andal.)* Excellent.

bariga [bah-ree'-gah], *f.* A sort of silk from India.

barillero [bah-reel-lyah'-ro], *m. (Mex.)* Hawker, street vendor.

barillo [bah-reel'-lyo], *m.* An inferior sort of silk from the East Indies.

barimetría [bah-re-may-tree'-ah], *f.* A treatise on the measure and weight of bodies.

bario [bah'-re-o], *m. (Chem.)* Barium.

baripto [bah-reep'-to], *m.* A precious stone of a blackish color.

barita [bah-ree'-tah], *f. (Chem.)* Baryta, or barytes.

baritel [bah-re-tel'], *m.* A hoisting winch, or whim, used in mines.

barítico, ca [bah-ree'-te-co, cah], *a. (Chem.)* Barytic, belonging to baryta.

baritina [bah-re-tee'-nah], *f.* Barium sulphate, heavy spar.

barítono [bah-ree'-to-no], *m. (Mus.)* Voice of a low pitch, between a tenor and a bass; baritone.

barjuleta [bar-hoo-lay'-tah], *f.* Knapsack, haversack, tool-bag. **Ladroncillo de agujeta, después sube a barjuleta**, a young filcher becomes an old robber.

barloar [bar-lo-ar'], *vn. (Naut.)* To grapple for the purpose of boarding. *V.* ABARLOAR.

barloas [bar-lo'-as], *f. pl. (Naut.)* Relieving tackles, or relieving tackle pendants.

barloventear [bar-lo-ven-tay-ar'], *m. (Naut.)* To ply to windward, to about. 2. *(Met.)* To rove about.

barlovento [Bar-lo-ven'-to], *m. (Naut.)* Weather-gage, the point whence the wind blows. **Costa de barlovento**, the weather shore. **Costado de barlovento**, the weather side. **Ganar el barlovento**, to get to windward.

barman [bar'-man], *m. pl.* **Barmans, bármanes, barmen**. Barman, bartender.

barnabita [bar-nah-bee'-ah], *m.* Member of the religious community of St. Paul.

barnacle [bar-nah'-clay], *m.* Barnacle, a kind of shell-fish.

barniz [bar-neeth'], *m.* 1. Varnish; japan, lacquer, gloss. **Dar de barniz a**, to varnish. 2. Paint or colors laid on the face. 3. Gum of the juniper-tree. 4. Printer's ink.

barnizado [bar-nee-thah'-do], *m.* Varnish, varnishing.

barnizar [bar-ne-thar'], *va.* To varnish, to gloss, to lacquer.

barométrico, ca [bah-ro-may'-tre-co, cah], *a.* Barometrical.

barómetro [bah-ro'-may-tro], *m.* Barometer, weather-glass.

barón [bah-rone'], *m.* Baron, a degree of nobility. **Barones del timón**, *(Naut.)* Rudder pendants and chains. *(Carib.)* Pal, buddy.

baronesa [bah-ro-nay'-sah], *f.* Baroness, a baron's lady.

baronía [bah-ro-nee'-ah], *f.* 1. Barony, honor or lordship which gives title to a baron. 2. Baronage, the dignity of a baron, and the land which gives his title.

baronial [bah-ro-nee'-ah], *a.* Baronial.

barosánemo [bah-ro-sah'-nay-mo], *m.* Aerometer, an instrument for measuring the air.

barquear [bar-kay-ar'], *vn.* To cross in a boat.

barquero [bar-kay'-ro], *m.* Bargeman, waterman, boatman, ferryman.

barqueta [bar-kay'-tah], *f. dim.* A small boat.

barquía [bar-kee'-ah], *f.* Skiff, rowing boat.

barquichuelo [bar-ke-choo-ay'-lo], *m. dim.* Small bark or boat.

barquilla [bar-keel'-lyah], *f.* 1. *(Dim.)* A little boat. 2. **Barquilla de la corredera**, *(Naut.)* the log, a triangular piece of wood which serves to measure the ship's way. 3. Thin boat-formed of conical pastry cake. 4. *(Carib.)* Icecream cone.

barquillero [bar-keel-lyay'-ro], *m.* 1. One who makes or sells rolled cakes, and the iron mould for making them. 2. Waffle-iron.

barquillo [bar-keel'-lyo], *m.* 1. Cock-boat, a small boat used on rivers and near a sea-coast. 2. Cot or cott, a little boat. 3. Paste made to close letters. 4. A thin pastry cake rolled up in the form of a tube or cone. 5. A mould with holes, used by wax-chandlers.

barquín [bar-keen'], *m.* **barquinera** [bar-ke-nay'-rah], *f.* Large bellows for iron-works or furnaces.

barquinazo [bar-ke-nah'-tho], *m. (Coll.)* The blow which a body gives in falling

barquinero [bar-ke-nay'-ro], *m.* Bellows-maker.

barquino [bar-kee'-no], *m.* Wine-bag. *V.* ODRE.

barra [bar'-rah], *f.* 1. Iron crow or lever. 2. Bar or ingot of gold, silver, etc. 3. Bar, rock, or sand-bank at the mouth of a harbor. 4. List or gross-spun thread in cloth. 5. A mould for small (wax) candles. 6. *(Mech.)* Lever, rod, cross-bar, chasebar. 7. The shaft of a carriage. 8. *(Her.)* The third part of a shield. 9. *(Naut.)* Spar. 10. *(Mus.)* Bar, or measure. 11. Bar, or railing in a court-room. **Estirar la barra** *(Met.)* to make the utmost exertions for attaining some purpose. **Tirar la barra** *(Met.)* to increase the price. **De barra a barra**, from one point to another. **Barras**, among pack-saddle makers, the arched trees of a pack-saddle. **Barras de cabrestante y molinete,** *(Naut.)* the bars of the capstan and windlass. **Barras de escotilla,** *(Naut.)* bars of the hatches. **Barras de portas,** *(Naut.)* gun-port bars. **Estar en barras,** *(Met.)* to be on the point of settling an affair. **Sin daño de barras,** *(Met.)* without injury or danger. **A barras derechas,** fairly. 12. *(LAm.)* Public, members of the public; *(Cono Sur)* Spectators, audience. 13. *(Carib. Cono Sur, Méx.)* River mouth, estuary.

Barrabás [bar-rah-bahs'], *m.* Barrabas. **Ser un Barrabás,** to be wicked.

barrabasada [bar-rah-bah-sah'-dah], *f.* *(Coll.)* Trick, plot, intrigue; a bold action.

barraca [bar-rah'-cah], *f.* 1. Barrack for soldiers; a cabin, a hut. 2. *(And.)* Booth, stall. **Barraca del tiro al blanco,** shooting gallery. 3. *(LAm.)* Large store shed. 4. **Creerse algo a la barraca,** to believe something implicitly.

barrachel [bar-rah-chel'], *m.* *(Obs.)* Head-constable, the principal *alguacil.*

barraco [bar-rah'-co], *m.* *(Prov.)* 1. A boar. 2. Spume thrown up by must when in a state of fermentation. 3. An ancient kind of ship guns. 4. *(Prov.)* Snag, a tooth which grows over another.

barracón [bar-rah-cone'], *m.* 1. Big hut; *(Carib.)* Farmworkers' living quarter.

barracuda [bar-ra-coo'-dah], *f.* A Californian food fish.

barrado, da [bar-rah'-do, dah], *a.* 1. Among clothiers, corded or ribbed; striped. 2. *(Her.)* Barred. *-pp.* of BARRAR.

barragán [bar-rah-gahn'], *m.* 1. *(Obs.)* Companion. 2. Barracan, a strong kind of camlet.

barragana [bar-rah-gah'-nah], *f.* *(Obs.)* Concubine.

barraganería [bar-rah-gah-nay-ree'-ah], *f.* Concubinage.

barraganía [bar-rah-gah-nee'-ah], *f.* *(Obs.)* V. AMANCEBAMIENTO.

barraganete [bar-rah-gah-nay'-tay], *m.* *(Naut.)* Top-timber, timber-head, futtock.

barrajes [bar-rah'-hays], *m. & pl.* *(And.)* Shanty town.

barral [bar-rahl'], *m.* A large bottle containing an *arroba* or twenty-five pints.

barranca, *f.* **barrancal,** *m.* [bar-rahn'-cah, bar-ran-cahl']. 1. A deep break or hole made by heavy falls of rain. 2. Ravine. 3. A precipice.

barranco [bar-rahn'-co], *m.* 1. V. BARRANCA. 2. Dell, a narrow valley. 3. *(Met.)* Great difficulty which obstructs the attainment of a purpose.

barrancoso, sa [bar-ran-co'-so, sah], *a.* Broken, uneven, full of breaks and holes.

barranquera [bar-ran-kay'-rah], *f.* 1. V. BARRANCA. 2. Obstruction, embarrassment.

barraque [bar-rah'-kay], V. TRAQUE BARRAQUE.

barraquear [bar-rah-kay-ar'], *vn.* To grunt like a bear.

barraquilla [bar-rah-keel'-lyah], *f. dim* A little hut.

barraquillo [bar-rah-keel'-lyo], *m.* A short light field-piece.

barraquismo [bar-rah-kees'-mo], *m.* Phenomenon of shanty towns, shanty town problem.

barrar [bar-rar'], *va.* 1. To daub, to smear, to paint coarsely. 2. To bar, to barricade.

barrate [bar-rah'-tay], *m.* A little joist.

barreal [bar-ray-ahl'], *m.* *(Cono Sur)* Heavy clay land; *(CAm.)* Bog (pantano).

barrear [bar-ray-ar'], *va.* 1. To bar, to barricade, to fortify with timbers, stakes, etc. 2. *(Prov.)* To cancel a writing. 3. To secure or fasten a thing with a bar of iron. *-vn.* To graze a knight's armor without piercing it: applied to a lance. *-vr.* 1.

V. ATRINCHERARSE. 2. *(Prov.)* To wallow, to roll in mire: applied to wild boars.

barreda [bar-ray'-dah], *f.* V. BARRERA.

barredera [bar-ray-day'-rah], *f.* Street sweeper; *(Aut.)* Street cleaning vehicle. **Barrera de alfombras,** carpet sweeper.

barrederas [bar-ray-day'-ras], *f. pl.* *(Naut.)* Studding-sails.

barredero [bar-ray-day'-ro], *m.* Mop; generally, the mop used for wiping an oven where bread is baked.

barredero, ra [bar-ray-day'-ro, rah], *a.* Sweeping along anything met with. **Red barredera,** drag-net.

barredura [bar-ray-doo'-rah], *f.* Act of sweeping. *-pl.* 1. Sweeping. 2. Remains, residue, that which is left.

barreminas [bar-ray-me'-nahs], *m.* Minesweeper.

barrena [bar-ray'-nah], *f.* 1. Boring bit, auger. **Barrena grande,** auger borer. **Barrena pequeña,** gimlet. **Barrena de gusano,** wimble. 2. A rock-drill for blasting. **Barrena de diminución,** a taper auger. **Barrena de guía,** a centerbit.

barrenado, da [bar-ray-nah'-do, dah], *a.* *(Met.)* **Barrenado de cascos,** crack brained, crazy. *-pp.* of BARRENAR.

barrenador [bar-ray-nah-dor'], *m.* *(Naut.)* Auger or borer.

barrenar [bar-ray-nar'], *va.* 1. To bore, to pierce, to make holes, to drill. **Barrenar un navío,** *(Naut.)* to scuttle or sink a ship. **Barrenar una roca or mina,** to blast a rock or a mine. 2. *(Met.)* To defeat one's intentions, to frustrate one's designs.

barrendero, ra [bar-ren-day'-ro, rah], *m. & f.* Sweeper, dustman.

barrenero [bar-ray-nay'-ro], *m.* Driller, borer.

barrenillo [bar-ray-neel'-lyo], *m.* 1. An insect which gnaws through the bark and attacks the sap-wood. 2. A disease produced by it in elms and other trees. 3. Borer. 4. *(Carib.)* Foolish; *(Cono Sur. Méx.)* Constant worry.

barreno [bar-ray'-no], *m.* 1. A large borer or auger. 2. Hole made with a borer, auger, or gimlet; blast-hole. 3. *(Met.)* Vanity, ostentation. **Dar barreno,** *(Naut.)* to bore and sink a ship. 4. *(Cono Sur. Méx.)* Constant worry.

barreño [bar-ray'-nyo], *m.* 1. Earthen pan. 2. A tub. 3. Washing-up basin.

barrer [bar-rerr'], *va.* 1. To sweep. 2. *(Met.)* To carry off the whole of what there was in a place. **Barrer un navío de popa a proa,** *(Naut.)* To rake a ship fore and aft. **Al barrer,** on an average. *(Com.).* 3. *(fig.)* To sweep aside; to sweep clean. **Los candidatos del partido barrieron a sus adversarios,** the party's candidates swept aside their rivals. *-vn.* 1. **Comprar algo al barrer,** *(Cono Sur)* To buy something in a job lot. 2. **Barrer hacia dentro,** to look after number one. *-vr.* 1. *(Mex.)* To shy, to start. 2. *(Mex.)* To grovel.

barrera [bar-ray'-rah], *f.* 1. Clay-pit. 2. Barrier, circular paling within which bullfights are performed. 3. Mound or heap of earth from which saltpetre is extracted. 4. Cupboard with shelves where crockery is kept. 5. Barricade, barrier, parapet. 6. Barrier, a bar to mark the limits of a place. 7. Tollgate, barrier, turnpike. **Barrera antiaérea,** flak. **Barrera sónica,** sonic barrier. **Salir a barrera,** *(Met.)* to expose oneself to public censure.

barrero [bar-ray'-ro], *m.* 1. Potter. 2. *(Prov.)* Height, eminence, a high ridge of hills. 3. Clay-pit

barreta [bar-ray'-tah], *f.* 1. *(Dim.)* Small bar. 2. Lining of a shoe. 3. Helmet, casque. **Barretas,** pieces of iron which hold the bows of a saddle together.

barretear [bar-my-tay-ar'], *va.* 1. To fasten a thing with bars. 2. To line the inside of a shoe.

barretero [bar-ray-tay'-ro], *m.* In mining, one who works with a crow, wedge, or pick.

barretina [bar-ray-tee'-nah], *f.* Catalan cap.

barretón [bar-ray-tone'], *m. aug.* Large bar.

barriada [bar-re-ah'-dah], *f.* Suburb, district or precinct of a city: applied frequently to a part of a suburb.

barrial [bar-re-ahl'], *m.* V. LODAZAL. A muddy spot.

barrica [bar-ree'-cah], *f.* A cask containing sixty gallons.

barricada [bar-re-cah'-dah], *f.* Barricade, a collection of barrels or beams to form a cover like a parapet.

barrida [bar-ree'-dah], *f. (LAm.)* 1. Sweep, sweeping; sweep raid. 2. Landslide.

barrido [bar-ree'-do], *m.* 1. Sweep, the act of sweeping. *-pp.* of BARRER. 2. **Barrido de televisión o barrido de trama** *(Comp.)*, raster scan.

barriga [bar-ree'-gah], *f.* 1. Abdomen, belly, stomach. 2. Pregnancy, state of being pregnant. 3. Middle part of a vessel where it swells out into a larger capacity. 4. *V.* COMBA. **Estar, hallarse, con la barriga a la boca**, to be near confinement. **Tener la barriga a la boca**, *(Coll.)* to be big with child. **Volverse la albarda a la barriga**, to be frustrated in one's wishes and expectations.

barrigón, na [bar-re-gone'], *a.m.f. aug.* Potbelly, a big belly.

barrigudo, da [bar-re-goo'-do, dah], *a.* Big-bellied, pot-bellied.

barriguera [bar-re-gay'-rah], *f.* Girth (de caballos).

barriguilla [bar-re-geel'-lyah], *f. dim,* A little belly.

barril [bar-reel'], *m.* 1. Barrel. **Cerveza de barril**, draft beer. 2. Jug. 3. *(Naut.)* Water-cask. 4. *(LAm.)* Hexagonal kite.

barilame, *m.* **barrilería**, *f.* [bar-re-lah'-may, bar-re-lay-ree'-ah]. A number of barrels collected in one place; stock of casks.

barrilejo [bar-re-lay'-rah], *m. dim.* Rundlet, a small barrel.

barrilería [bar-re-lay-ree'-ah], *f.* 1. Barrel store. 2. Cooper's shop. 3. *(Art.)* Cooperage.

barrilero [bar-re-lay'-ro], *m.* One who makes barrels, cooper.

barrilete [bar-re-lay'-tay], *m.* 1. Holdfast, dog, clamp. 2. *(Naut.)* Mouse. 3. *(Zool.)* A crab covered with prickles. **Barrilete de estay**, the mouse of a stay. **Barrilete de remo**, the mouse of an oar. **Barrilete de virador**, the mouse of a voyol. **Barrilete de banco**, hold-fast, a tool used by joiners, to keep their stuff steady. 4. *(Dim.)* Keg. 5. *(Prov.)* Kite. 6. Chamber. *-f. (Cono Sur)* Restless woman.

barrilico, illo, ito [bar-re-lee'-co, eel'-lyo, ee'-to], *m. dim.* Keg, rundlet, a small barrel, firkin.

barrilla [bar-reel'-lyah], 1. *(Dim.)* A little bar. 2. A rod. 3. *(Bot.)* Saltwort, glass-wort, an herb. **Barrilla fina**, cultivated saltwort. **Barrilla borde**, prickly saltwort. **Barrilla salicor**, long fleshy-leaved saltwort. **Barrilla carambillo** or **caramillo**, small-leaved salt-wort. **Barrilla escobilla**, tamarisk-leaved salt-wort. 4. Impure soda, called in commerce barilla, a mineral alkali extracted from plants belonging to the genus Salicornia. **Barrilla de Alicante**, *(Com.)* Spanish or Alicante soda.

barrillar [bar-reel-lyar'], *m.* Barillapits, where the plants, from which the barilla is extracted, are burnt, and collected at the bottom in a stony mass. Called *rocheta;* it is the barilla ashes of commerce.

barrillo [bar-reel'-lyo], *m.* Blackhead, pimple.

barrio [bar'-re-o], *m.* 1. One of the districts or wards into which a large town or city is divided. **Barrio chino**, *(Esp.)* Red-light district. *(fig.)* **Irse al otro barrio**, to snuff it. 2. Suburb. **Andar de barrio or vestido de barrio**, to wear a plain, simple dress.

barriobajero [ ], *a.* Slum; *(fig.)* Vulgar, coarse, common.

barriquita [bar-re-kee'-tah], *f.* A cask. **Barrita** [bar-ree'-tah], *f. dim.* 1. A small bar. 2. A small keg.

barrisco [bar-rees'-co], *adv.* Jumbled together, in confusion; indiscriminately.

barritar [bar-re-tahr'], *vn.* To trumpet (elefante).

barrito [bar-ree'to], *m.* Trumpeting.

barrizal [bar-ree-thahl'], *m.* Clay-pit, a place full of clay and mud.

barro [bar'-ro], *m.* Clay, mud. 2. Earthenware. 3. Drinking-vessel of different shapes and colors, made of sweet-scented clay; sugar-clay. 4. Lock of wool put into the comb. **Dar or tener barro a mano**, to have money or the necessary means to do a thing. *-pl* 1. Red pustules or pimples in the faces of young persons. 2. Fleshy tumors growing on the skin of horses or mules.

barrocho, *m. V.* BIRLOCHO.

barroco [bar-ro'-co], 1. *a.* Baroque. 2. *m.* Baroque; baroque period.

barroquismo [bar-ro-kees'-mo], *m.* Baroque (stilo); baroque taste.

barroso, sa [bar-ro'-so, sah], *a.* 1. Muddy, full of mire. **Camino barroso**, muddy road. 2. Pimpled, full of pimplescalled *barros.* 3.-Reddish (bueyes).

barrote [bar-ro'-tay], *m.* 1. Iron bar with which tables are made fast. 2. Ledge of timber laid across other timbers. **Barrotes**, *(Naut.)* battens, scantlings, or ledges of stuff, which serve many purposes on board ship. **Barrotes de las escotillas**, battens of the hatches.

barrotines [bar-ro-tee'-nes], *m. pl.* **Barrotines de los baos**, *(Naut.)* carlings or carlines. **Barrotines o baos de la toldilla** *(Naut.)*, carling knees, or the beams of the stern.

barrueco [bar-roo-ay'-co], *m.* Pear of irregular form.

barrumbada [bar-room-bah'-dah], *f.* 1. *(Coll.)* Great and ostentatious expense. 2. Boastful saying.

barruntador, ra [bar-roon-tah-dor', rah], *m. & f.* Conjecturer, one who guesses by signs and tokens.

barruntamiento [bar-roon-tah-me-en'-to], *m.* The act of conjecturing or guessing by signs and tokens.

barruntar [bar-roon-tar'], *va.* To foresee or conjecture (by signs or tokens); to guess, to have a presentiment. **Barruntar algo**, to sense something.

barrunte [bar-roon'-tay], *m.* Sign, indication. *V.* NOTICIA.

barrunto [bar-roon'-to], *m.* Conjecture, the act of conjecturing. *(Carib. Méx.)* North wind which brings rain.

bartola [bar-to'-lah], *f. (Coll.)* Belly. **A la bartola**, on the back, in lazy fashion, careless.

bartolear [bar-to-lay-ahr'], *vn. (Cono Sur)* To be lazy, to take it easy.

bartolillo [bar-to-leel'-lyo], *m.* A little meat pie, in triangular form.

bártulos [bar'-too-los], *m. pl. (Coll.)* Tools, affairs or business. **Liar los bártulos**, to pack up one's belongings.

baruca [bah-roo'-cah], *f.* Artífice, cunning, deceit.

barullento [bah-rool-lyayn'-do], *a. (Cono Sur)* Noisy, rowdy.

barullo [bah-rool'-lyo], *m.* 1. Confusion, disorder, tumult. 2. **A barullo**, in abundance.

barzón [bar-thone'], *m.* 1. *(Prov.)* Idle walk. 2. The strap with which oxen are yoked to the plough-beam.

barzonear [bar-tho-nay-ar'], *vn. (Prov.)* To loiter about without a certain design. To wander about.

basa [bah'sah], *f.* 1. Basis or pedestal of a column or statue, base. 2. *(Met.)* Basis or foundation of a thing.

basácula [bah-sah'-coo-lah], *f.* Locker of the thumb-plate in a stocking frame.

basáltico, ca [bah-sahl'-te-co], *a.* Basaltic, of basalt.

basalto [bah-salil'-to], *m.* Basalt, basaltes, a kind of stone.

basamento [bah-sah-men'-to], *m. (Arch.)* Basement, base and pedestal.

basar [bah-sar'], *va.* 1. To fix, to establish; to secure upon a base. 2. To rest upon, to set up a theory. 3. To start from a fixed base-line. *-vr.* 1. **Basarse en**, to be based on, to rest on. 2. *(fig.)* To base oneself on, to rely on.

basca [bahs'-cah], *f.* 1. Squeamishness, inclination to vomit, nausea. **Dar bascas a uno**, to make somebody feel sick. 2. *(fig.)* Fit of rage, tantrum. 3. Group, set of people. **Toda la basca**, all of them, every one of them.

bascosidad [bas-co-se-dahd'], *f* Uncleanliness, nastiness, filth.

bascoso [bas-co'-so], *a.* 1. Squeamish, easily upset. 2. *(And.)* Nauseating, sickening; obscene.

báscula [bahs'-coo-lah], *f.* 1. Lever, pole, staff. 2. Platform-scale.

basculable [bas-coo-lah'-blay], *a. (Aut.)* Directional, with swinging beam.

basculante [bas-coo-lahn'-tay], *m.* Dump truck, tip-up lorry.

báscula-puente [bas'-coo-lah-poo-ayn'-tay], *f.* Weighbridge.

bascular [bas-coo-lahr'], *vn.* To tilt, to tip up; to seesaw; to rock to and fro; to swing.

base [bah'-say], *f.* 1. Base, basis; ground, foot, footing; groundwork. 2. Chief or ground color, the principal color used in dyeing any stuff. **Base de distinción**, focus of glasses convex on both sides. 3. Baseline in surveying. 4. *(Mus.)* Bass or base. 5. *(Chem.)* In any combination, the most electro-positive element. 6. *(fig.)* Basis, foundation. **A base de**, on the basis of. **En base a que…**, in view of the fact that… 7. *(Inform. Mat.)* **Base de datos**, database. **Base de misiles**, missile base. 8. **Bases**, conditions; rules. *-a.* Basic, base. **Color base**, basic color.

baseballista [bah-say-bahl-lyees'tah], *m. f.* Baseball player.

basebolero, ra [bah-say-bo-lay'-ro], *a. m. & f.* Baseball, baseball player.

basic [bah-seek], *(Comp.)* Basic (Beginner's All-purpose Symbolic Instruction Code).

básico [bah'-see-co], *a.* Basic.

Basilea [bah-see-lay'-ah], *f.* Bastle, Basel, Bâle.

basílica [bah-see'-le-cah], *f.* 1. Royal or imperial palace. 2. Public hall where courts of justice hold their sittings. 3. *(Anat.)* Basilica. 4. Basilica, large and magnificent church.

basilicón [bah-see-le-cone'], *m. (Med.)* Basilicon, an ointment, resin salve.

basilio, lia [bah-see'-le-o, ah], *a.* Basilian, monk or nun of the order of St. Basil.

basilisco [bah-see-lees'-co], *m.* 1. Basilisk, cockatrice, a fabulous kind of serpent. 2. Basilisk, an ancient piece of artillery. **Estar hecho un basilisco**, to get angry.

basketbol [bas-ket-bol'], *m.* Basketball.

basquear [bas-kay-ar'], *vn.* To be squeamish, or inclined to vomit.

básquet [bas'-ket], *m.*, **básquetbol** *m.* *(CAm. Méx.)* Basketball.

basquetbolero, ra [bas-ket-bo-lay'-ro], *a. m. & f.* Basketball player.

basquetbolista [bas-ket-bo-lees'-tee-co], *m. & f. (LAm.)* Basketball player.

basquetbolístico [bas-ket-bo-lees'-tee-co], *a. (LAm.)* Basketball.

basquilla [bas-keel'-lyah], *f.* Disease in sheep.

baisquiña [bas-kee'-nyah], *f.* Upper petticoat that Spanish women used to wear.

basta [baha'-tah], *adv.* Enough; halt, stop.

basta [bahs'-tah], *f.* Stitch made by tailors to keep clothes even when basting. **Bastas.** Stitches put into a mattress at certain distances to form a quilt.

bastaje [bas-tah'-hay], *m.* Porter, carrier.

bastante [bas-tahn'-tay], *adv.* 1. Sufficient, enough, competent. 2. Not a little. 3. *(LAm.)* Too much, more than enough. **Estoy bastante cansado**, I'm really tired. **Bastante bueno**, fairly good.

bastar [bas-tar'], *vn.* To suffice, to be proportioned to something, to be enough. **¡Basta ya!**, that's quite enough. **Eso me basta**, that's enough for me. *-vr.* **Bastarse a sí mismo**, to be self-sufficient.

bastarda [bas-tar'-dah], *f.* 1. Bastard file. 2. Piece of ordnance. 3. *(Naut.)* Bastard, a lateen main-sail. 4. *(Print.)* Italic, a type, 5. *a.* A packsadle.

bastardear [bas-tar-day-ar'], *vn.* 1. To degenerate, to fall from its kind (animales, plantas). 2. *(Met.)* To fall from the virtues of our ancestors, or the nobleness of our birth. 3. To bastardize, or to bastard.

bastardelo [bas-tar-day'-lo], *m. (Prov.)* Draft-book of a notary, which contains the minutes or first drafts of acts, deeds, instruments, etc.; blotter. *V.* MINUTARIO.

bastardía [bas-tar-dee'-ah], *f.* Bastardy, state of being born out of wedlock. 2. *(Met.)* Speech or action unbecoming the birth or character of a gentleman; meanness.

bastardilla [bas-tar-deel'-lyah], *f.* 1. *(Obs.)* A kind of flute. 2. *(Print.)* Italic, a type.

bastardo, da [Bas-tar'-do, dah], *a.* Bastard, spurious, degenerating from its kind and original qualities. 2. Bastard, illegitimate. 3. Bastard, a type having a face smaller or larger than proper for its body.

bastardo [bas-tar'-do], *m.* 1. Bastard, a son born out of wedlock. 2. Boa, a short, thick-bodied, and very poisonous snake. **Bastardo de un racamento**, *(Naut.)* Parrel rope.

baste [bahs'-tay], *m. (Prov.)* V. BASTO.

bastear [bas-tay-ar'], *va.* To baste, to stitch loosely, to sew slightly.

bastero [bas-tay'-ro], *m.* One who makes or retails packsaddles. *-ro, -ra, m. f. (Mex.)* Pickpocket.

bastes [bas-tayth'], *m. & pl. (Esp.)* Dabs, fingers.

bastez [bas-tayth'], *f.* Coarseness, vulgarity.

bastida [bas-tee'-dah], *f.* An ancient warlike engine for covering approaches.

bastidor [bas-tee-dor'], *m.* 1. Frame for stretching linen, silk, etc., which is to be painted, embroidered, or quilted. 2. Frame, sash, panel. 3. A frame through which passes the shaft of a screw propeller. 4. Linen stretched in frames: applied to the painted linen used on the sides of the stage to represent the scene. 5. *(Phot.)* Carrier, for films; place-holder. **Bastidores**, *(Naut.)* Frames for canvas bulkheads, provisional cabins, and other temporary compartments. **Bastidos or bastidores**, (on the stage) Scenery.

bastillar [bas-teel'-lyar'], *f.* Hem, the edge of cloth doubled and sewed.

bastillar [bas-teel-lyar'], *va.* To hem.

bastimentar [bas-te-men-tar'], *va.* To victual, to supply with provisions.

bastimento [bas-te-men'-to], *m.* 1. Supply of provisions for a city or army. 2. Building, structure 3. Thread with which a mattress is quilted. 4. *(Naut.)* Vessel. **Bastimentos**, first fruits, in the military order of *Santiago* or St. James.

bastión [bas-te-on'], *m.* Bastion. V. BALUARTE.

basto [bahs'-to], *m.* 1. Packsaddle for beasts of burden. 2. Pad. 3. Ace of clubs in several games of cards. **Bastos**, clubs, one of the four suits at cards.

basto, ta [bahs'-to, tah], *a.* 1. Coarse, rude, unpolished, unhewn, clumsy, gross, rugged; cyclopean; linsey-woolsey. 2. Home-spun, clownish. 3. Rude, uncouth.

bastón [bas-tone'], *m.* 1. Cane or stick with a head or knob to lean upon; gad. 2. Truncheon, a staff of command. 3. *(Met.)* Military command. **Empuñar el bastón**, to take command. 4. Among silk-weavers, the roller of a silk-frame which contains the stuff. 5. Carrot of snuff, weighing about three pounds. 6. *(Arch.)* Fluted moulding. **Dar bastón**, to stir must with a stick, to prevent its being ropy. **Bastones**, *(Her.)* Bars in a shield.

bastonada [bas-to-nah'-dah], *f.* **bastonazo** [bas-to-nah'-tho], *m.* Bastinado, stroke or blow given with a stick or cane.

bastoncillo [bas-ton-theel'-lyo], *m.* 1. *(Dim.)* Small cane or stick. 2. Narrow lace for trimming clothes.

bastonear [bas-to-nay-ar'], *va.* To stir must with a stick to prevent its becoming ropy.

bastonera [bas-to-nay'-rah], *f.* Umbrella stand.

bastonero [bas-to-nay'-ro], *m.* 1. Canemaker or seller. 2. Marshal or manager of a ball, steward of a feast. 3. Assistant jail-keeper. 4. *(Carib.)* Scoundrel, tough.

bastón-taburete [bas-tone'-tah-boo-ray-tay], *m.* Shooting stick.

basura [bah-soo'-rah], *f.* 1. Trash, garbage, sweepings, filth swept away, rubbish. 2. Dung, manure, ordure, excrement used to manure the ground; off-scouring. **Basura radioactiva**, radioactive waste. 3. *(fig.)* Trash, rubbish. **La novela es una basura**, the novel is rubbish.

basural [bah-soo'-rah], *m. (LAm.)* Rubbish dump.

basurear [bah-soo-ray-ar'], *va. (Cono Sur)* **Basurear a uno**, to push somebody along; to humiliate somebody; to be rude to somebody.

basurero [bah-soo-ray'-ro], *m.* 1. Dustman, he who carries dung to the field. 2. Dust-pan. 3. Dung-yard, dung-hill.

basuriento [bah-soo-ree-ayn'-to], *a.* (*And. Cono Sur*) Dirty, full of rubbish.

bata [bah'-tah], *f.* 1. Dressing-gown, wrapper, a loose gown. 2. Refuse of silk. 3. A lady's dress with a train. Laboratory coat. 4. Mother.

bata [bah'-tah], *m.* An Asiatic of minor age in the Philippine Islands.

batacazo [bah-tah-cah'-tho], *m.* Violent contusion from a fall. (*fig.*) Stroke of luck, fluke.

bataclán [bah-tah-clan'], *m.* (*LAm.*) Burlesque show, striptease show.

bataclana [bah-tah-clah'-nah], *f.* (*LAm.*) Striptease girl, stripper.

batahola [bah-tah-oh'-lah], *f* Hurley-burley, bustle, clamor, clutter, hubbub.

bataholear [bah-tah-o-lay-ar'], *vn.* To brawl, to be mischievous, to play pranks.

batalla [bah-tahl'-lyah], *f.* 1. Battle, the contest, conflict, or engagement of one army with another; fight, combat. 2. Center of an army, in contradistinction to the van and rear. 3. Fencing with foils. 4. (*Met.*) Struggle or agitation of the mind. **Batalla campal**, pitched battle. 5 (*Art.*) Battle-piece, a painting which represents a battle, 6. Joust, tournament. **Campo de batalla**, field of batttle. **Cuerpo de batalla de una escuadra**, the center division of a fleet. **En batalla**, (*Mil.*) with an extended front.

batallador, ra [bah-tal-lyah-dor', rah], *m. & f.* 1. Battler, combatant; warrior. 2. Fencer with foils.

batallar [bah-tal-lyar'], *vn.* 1. To battle, to fight, to be engaged in battle. 2. To fence with foils. 3. (*Met.*) To contend, to argue, to dispute.

batallita [bah-tahl-lyee'-tah], *f.* **Contar batallitas**, to shoot a line.

batallón [bah-tal-yone'], *m.* 1. Battalion, a division of infantry. 2. (*Cono Sur*) Dry cleaner's. 3. (*And.*) Thickness.

batán [bah-tahn']; *m.* Fulling-mill where cloth is fulled, or cleaned from oil and grease. **Batanes**, a boyish game of striking the soles of the feet, hands, etc.

batanar [bah-tah-nar'], *va.* To full cloth.

batanear [bah-tah-nay-ar'], *va.* (*Coll.*) To bang or beat, to handle roughly. **Batanero** [bah-tah-nay'-ro], *m.* Fuller, a clothier.

batanga [bah-tahn'-gah], *f.* An outrigger of bamboo applied to boats in the Philippine Islands.

bataola [bah-tah-o'-lah], *f. V.* BATAHOLA.

batata [bah-tah'-tah], *f* 1. (*Bot.*) Spanish potato, or sweet potato of Malaga, yam. 2. (*And. Carib.*) Calf. 3. (*Cono Sur*) Bashfulness, embarrassment. 4. (*Cono Sur*) Car. -*a.* 1. (*Cono Sur*) Bashful, shy. 2. (*Carib. Cono Sur*) Simple. 3. (*Carib.*) Chubby, plump.

batatar [bah-tah-tar'], *m.* (*LAm.*) Sweet potato field.

batatazo [bah-tah-tah'-tho], *m.* (*LAm.*) *V.* BATACAZO.

bátavo, va [bah'-tah-vo, vah], *a.* 1. Batavian, relating to ancient Batavia, or the Netherlands; now Holland. 2. Of Batavia, in Java.

batayola [bah-tah-yo'-lah], *f.* (*Naut.*) Rail. **Batayolas de los empalletados**, (*Naut.*) Quarter-netting rails. **Batayolas de las cofas**, (*Naut.*) Top-rails. **Batayolas del pasamano**, (*Naut.*) Gangway rails.

bate [bah'-tay], *m.* (*LAm.*) (baseball) Bat. (*CAm. Carib.*) **Estar al bate de algo**, to be in charge of something.

batea [bah-tay'-ah], *f.* 1. Painted tray or hamper of Japanned wood which comes from the East Indies. 2. Trough for bathing hands and feet. 3. Boat made in the form of a trough, punt. 4. Flat car.

bateador, ra [bah-tay-ah-dor', rah], *m. & f.* 1. (*Sports*) Batter, hitter. 2. (*Mech.*) Tamper.-*f.* Power tamper.

batear [bah-tay-ar'], *va. & vn.* (*Sports*) 1. To bat, to hit. 2. (*Mech.*) To tamp.

batei [bah-tay'-e], *m.* (*Cuba*) 1. A grass-plot. 2. *V.* BATEY.

batel [bah-tel'], *m.* Small vessel.

batelero [bah-tay-lay'-ro], *m.* Boatman.

batelón [bah-tay-lone'], *m.* (*And.*) Canoe.

bateo [bah-tay'-o], *m. V.* BAUTIZO.

batería [bah-tay-ree'-ah], *f.* 1. Battery, a number of pieces of ordnance arranged to play upon the enemy; also, the work in which they are placed. **Batería a barbeta**, a barbet battery. **Batería enterrada**, a sunk battery. **Batería a rebote**, a ricochet battery. **Batería cruzante**, cross battery. **Batería de cocina**, kitchen furniture. 2. (*Naut.*) Tier or range of guns on one side of a ship. **Batería entera de una banda**, (*Naut.*) a broadside. **Navío de batería florada**, (*Naut.*) a ship which carries her ports at a proper height out of the water. 3. Battery, the act and effect of battering. 4. (*Met.*) Anything which makes a strong impression on the mind. 5. (*And.*) Round of drinks. 6. (*LAm.*) Hit, stroke. 7. (*Mex.*) **Dar batería**, to keep at it. **Dar batería a**, to make trouble for. -*m. & f.* Drummer.

baterista [bah-tay-rees'-tah], *m. & f.* (*LAm.*) Drummer.

batero, ra [bah-tay'-ro, rah], *m. & f.* Mantua-maker, one whose trade is to make gowns.

batey [bah-tay'], *m.* 1. Machinery and appurtenances for sugar-making. 2. Premises surrounding a sugar mill in the West Indies. 3. (*Carib.*) Clearing in front of a country house, forecourt.

batiborrillo [bah-te-bor-reel'-ly], *m.* BATIBURRILLO.

batiburrillo [bah-te-boor-reel'-lyo], *m.* Hotchpotch.

baticola [bah-te-co'-lah], *f.* Crupper, (*And.*) Loincloth; (*Cono Sur*) Nappy.

batida [bah-tee'-dah], *f.* 1. A hunting party for chasing wild animals; battue. 2. Noise made by huntsmen to cheer the hounds and rouse the game. 3. (*Cono Sur*) Raid.

batidera [bah-te-day'-rah], *f.* 1. Beater, an instrument used by plasterers and bricklayers for beating and mixing mortar. 2. An instrument used by glass-makers for stirring the sand and ashes in melting-pots. 3. Batlet. 4. Batting arm, scutcher. 5. Flap of a churn. 6. Small instrument for cutting honey-combs from the hives.

batidero [bah-te-day'-ro], *m.* 1. Collision, the clashing of one thing against another. 2. Uneven ground, which renders the motion of carriages unpleasant. **Guardar los batideros**, to drive carefully on broken road. **Guardar batideros**, (*Met.*) to guard against inconveniences. 3. (*Naut.*) washboard. **Batidero de una vela**, foot-tabling of a sail. **Batidero de proa**, war-board of the cut-water.

batido, da [bah-tee'-do, dah], *a.* 1. Changeable; shot, chatoyant (seda). 2. Beaten, as roads.-*pp.* of BATIR.

batido [bah-tee'-do], *m.* Batter of flour and water for making the host, wafers, or cookies.

batidor [bah-te-dor'], *m.* 1. Scout, one who is sent to explore the condition of the enemy, and the condition of the roads. 2. Ranger, one who rouses the game in the forest. 3. One of the life-guards, who rides before a royal coach 4. An out-rider. 5. Leather beater. 6. Stirring-rod. 7. (*Naut.*) Strengthening line. **Batidor de oro o plata**, a gold or silver beater. 8. (*CAm. Méx.*) Wooden bowl, mixing bowl. 9. Wide-toothed comb.

batidora [bah-tee-do'-rah], *f.* (*Culin.*) Beater, whisk, mixer; (*Tec.*) Beater; **batidora eléctrica**, electric mixer.

batiente [bah-te-en'-tay], *m.* 1. Jamb or post of a door. 2. Leaf of a folding-door. 3. Port-sill. 4. Hammer of a pianoforte. 5. Spot where the sea beats against the shore or a dike. **Batiente de la bandera**, (*Naut.*) Fly of an ensign. **Batiente de un dique**, apron of a dock.-*pa.* of BATIR.

batifondo [bah-tee-fone'-do], *m.* (*Cono Sur*) Uproar, din.

batifulla [bah-te-fool'-lya], *m.* (*Prov.*) *V.* BATIHOJA.

batihoja [bah-te-o'-hah], *m.* 1. Gold-beater. 2. Artisan who works iron and other metals into sheets. 3. Warp of cloth which crosses the woof.

batimiento [bah-te-me-en'-to], *m.* (*Obs.*) 1. The act and effect of beating. 2. The thing beaten.

batín [bah-teen'], *m.* A morning gown.

batintín [bah-tin-teen'], *m.* A gong used on Chinese junks.

bationdeo [bah-te-on-day'-o], *m.* The fluttering of a banner, or curtain, caused by the wind.

batiportar [bah-te-por-tar'], *va. (Naut.)* To house a gun on board a ship, to secure it by tackles and breechings.

batiportes [bah-te-por'-tes], *m. pl* Portsills.

batir [bah-teer'], *va.* 1. To beat, to dash, to strike two bodies together. 2. To clash, to clout, to clap. 3. To demolish, to raze, to throw down. 4. To move in a violent manner. 5. In paper-mills, to fit and adjust the reams of paper already made up. 6. To strike or fall on without injury: spoken of the sun or wind. **El cierzo bate a Madrid**, the north wind blows on Madrid. **Batir banderas**, to salute with the colors, *(Naut.)* to strike the colors. **Batir el campo**, *(Mil.)* to reconnoitre the enemy's camp. **Batir moneda**, to coin money. **Batir las olas**, to ply the seas. **Batir las cataratas** *or* **nubes de los ojos**, to crouch. **Batir hoja**, to foliate, or to beat metals into leaves or plates. 7. *(And.)* To rinse (ropa). 8. *(Cono Sur)* To inform. *-vn.* 1. To lose courage, to decline in health or strength. 2. *(Med.)* To beat violently. *-V.* ABATIRSE. 1. *(Met.)* **Batirse el cobre**, to toil hard for useful purposes. 2. To fight, to have a fight.

batíscafo [bah-tees'-cah-fo], *m.* Bathyscaphe.

batista [bah-tees'-tah], *f.* Batiste, the finest cambric or lawn.

bato [bah'-to], *m.* 1. A rustic, simpleton. 2. Father.

batojar [bah-to-har'], *va. (Prov.)* To beat down the fruit of a tree.

batología [bah-to-to-hee'-ah], *f.* Needless repetition.

batonista [bah-to-nees'-tah], *f.* Drum majorette.

batracios [bah-trah'-the-ose], *m. pl.* Batrachians, aquatic amphibians like the frog.

batucar [bah-too-car'], *va.* To beat liquors and other things; to mix things by agitation.

batuque [bah-too'-kay], *m. (Cono Sur)* Rumpus, racket.

batuquear [bah-too-kay-ar'], *va. (CAm.)* To pester, annoy.

baturrillo [bah-toor-reel'-lyo], *m.* 1. Hodge-podge, hotchpotch, mash, salmagundi, a miscellany, potpourri. 2. *(Met.)* Mixture of unconnected and incongruous ideas.

batusino, -na [bah-too-se'-no], *m. & f.* Idiot, fool.

batuta [bah-too'-tah], *f. (It.)* A conductor's wand; baton. **Llevar la batuta**, to be the boss.

baudio [bah-oo-de-o], *(Comp.)* Baud.

baúl [bah-ool'], *m.* 1. Trunk, a chest for clothes. 2. Belly. **Llenar el baúl**, *(Low.)* To fill the paunch. 3. *(Aut.)* Boot, trunk.

bauprés [bah-oo-press'], *m. (Naut.)* Bowsprit. **Botalón del bauprés**, the bowsprit boom.

bausa [bah'-oo-sah], *f. (And. Méx.)* Laziness, idleness.

bausán, na [bah-oo-sahn', nah], *m. & f.* 1. Manikin, effigy; image or likeness. 2. Fool, idiot. 3. *(Naut.)* Bowsprit. 4. Down, downy hair.

bausano [bah-oo-sah'-no], *m. (CAm.)* Idler, lazy person.

bauseador [bah-oo-say-ah-dor'], *m. (And.)* Idler, lazy person.

bautismal [bah-oo-tees-mahl'], *a.* Baptismal.

bautismo [bah-oo-tees'-mo], *m.* 1. Baptism. 2. *(Naut.)* Ducking.

bautista [bah-oo-tees'-tah], *m.* **El bautista, San Juan, St.** John the Baptist. *-a.* **Iglesia Bautista**, Baptist church.

bautisterio [bah-oo-tis-tay'-re-o], *m.* Baptistery.

bautizante [bah-oo-te-thahn'-tay], *pa.* Baptizing, christening.

bautizar [bah-oo-te-thar'], *va.* 1. To baptize, to christen. 2. *(Naut.)* To duck seamen in those seas where they have not been before. **Bautizar un bajel**, to give a name to a ship. **Bautizar el vino**, to add water to the wine. **Bautizo** [bah-oo-tee'-tho], *m.* 1. Baptism, christening. 2. Christening party.

bauxita [bah-ook-xe'-tah], *f.* Bauxite, a mineral.

bávaro, ra [bah'-vah-ro, rah], *a.* Bavarian.

baya [bah'-yah], *f.* 1. Berry. Any small fruit with seeds or stones. *V.* VAINA. 2. *(Prov.)* Pole used to separate horses in a stable.

bayajá [bah-yah-hah'], *m. (Carib.)* Headscarf.

bayal [bah-yahl], *a.* Not steeped or soaked: applied to flax.

bayal [ba -yahl'], *m.* Lever used in raising: mill-stones.

báyer [bah'-yah], *f. (Cono Sur)* Dope, pot.

bayeta [bah-yay'-tah], *f.* Baize, a sort of flannel. 2. Blanket in typography. **Bayeta de alconcher**, colchester baize. **Bayeta fajuela**, lancashire baize. **Bayeta miniquina**, long baize. **Bayeta del sur** or **de cien hilos**, white list baize. **Bayeta fina**, swanskin. **Arrastrar bayetas**, to claim a degree in superior colleges, the claimants being obliged to visit the college in wide loose gowns, with a train of baize. **Arrastrar bayetas**, *(Met.)* to enforce a claim with care and assiduity. 3. Diaper. *-pl.* 1. Pall, the covering of the dead. 2. In paper-mills, felts used in the manufacture of paper.

bayetón [bah-yay-tone'], *m.* 1. Coating. **Bayetón moteado**, spotted coating. **Bayetón de nubes**, clouded coating. **Bayetón rayado**, striped coating. **Bayetón común**, coarse baize. 2. *(And.)* Long poncho.

bayo, ya [bah'-yo, yah], *a.* Bay, inclining to a chestnut color: spoken of a horse.*-m.* Brown butterfly used in angling.

bayoco [bah-yo'-co], *m.* 1. Copper coin current in Rome and other parts of Italy. 2. *(Prov.)* Unripe or withered fig.

bayón [bah-yone'], *m.* Sack of matting for baling.

bayoneta [bah-yo-nay'-tah], *f.* Bayonet. **Bayoneta calada**, A fixed bayonet.

bayonetazo [bah-yo-nay-tah'-tho], *m.* Thrust with a bayonet.

bayonetear [bah-yo-nay-tay-ar'], *va. (LAm.)* To bayonet.

bayoya [bah-yo'-yah], *m. (Carib.)* Row, uproar. **Es un bayoya aquí**, it's pandemonium here.

bayunca [bah-yoon'cah], *f.* Tippling house; tavern. *(Coll.)* *(Naut.).*

bayunco [bah-yoon'-co], 1. *a. (CAm.)* Silly, stupid; shy; crude, vulgar. 2. *m.* **Bayunca** *f. (CAm.)* Uncouth peasant.

baza [bah'-thah], *f.* 1. Trick at cards. **No dejar meter baza**, not to allow anyone to put in a single word. **Tener bien asentada su baza**, to have one's character well established. 2. *(Naut.)* Oozy ground. 3. **Meter baza**, to butt in. **No deja meter baza a nadie**, not to let somebody get a word in edgeways. **Tiene sentada la baza de discreto**, he has a reputation for good sense. *(fig.)*

bazar [bah-thar'], *m.* Bazaar, market-place, second-hand shop. *(Cono Sur)* Ironmonger's.

bazo [bah'-tho], *m.* Spleen or milt.

bazo, za [bah'-tho, thah], *a.* Brown inclining to yellow. **Pan bazo**, brown bread.

bazofia [bah-tho'-fe-a], *f.* 1. Offal, waste meat. 2. Refuse, thing of no value, remnants. 3. Hogwash.

bazuca [bah-thoo-cah], *f.* Bazooka.

bazucar [bah-thoo-car'], *va.* 1. To stir liquids by shaking. 2. To dash.

bazuqueo [bah-thoo-kay'-o], *m.* The act of stirring liquids by shaking; jumble.

be [bay'], *m.* Baa, the cry of sheep.*-f.* The name of the second letter, B.

be [bay'], *m.* Baa.

bearnés, esa [bay-ar-ness', nay'-sah], *a.* Of Berne, in Switzerland, Bernese.

beata [bay-ah'-tah], *f.* 1. Woman who wears a religious habit, and is engaged in works of charity. 2. Female hypocrite.

beatería [bay-ah-tay-ree'-ah], *f.* Act of affected piety, bigotry.

beaterio [bay-ah-tay'-re-o], *m.* House inhabited by pious women.

beatico, ca [bay-ah-tee'-co, cah], *m. & dim.* Hypocrite.

beatificación [bay-ah-te-fe-cah-the-on'], *f.* Beatification.

beatificamente [bay-ah-tee'-fe-cah-men-tay], *adv.* Beatifically.

beatificar [bay-ah-te-fe-car'], *va.* 1. To beatify. 2. To render a thing respectable.

beatífico, ca [bay-ah-tee'-fe-co, cah], *a. (Theol.)* Beatific, beatifical.

beatilla [bay-ah-teel'-lyah], *f.* A sort of fine linen.

beatísimo, ma [bay-ah-tee'-se-mo, mah], *a. sup.* **Beatísimo padre**, Most holy father: applied to the Pope:

beatitud [bay-ah-te-tood'], *f*. 1. Beatitude, blessedness. 2. Holiness, a title given to the Pope.

beatnik [beat'-neek], *m, pl.* **beatniks.** Beatnik.

beato, ta [bay-ah'-to, tah], *a*. 1: Happy, blessed; beatified. 2. Wearing a religious habit without being a member of a religious community. 3. Devout.

beaton, ta [bay-ah' -to, tah], *m. & f*. 1. A pious person abstaining from public diversions. 2. One who lives in pious retirement, and wears a religious dress.

beatón, na [bay-ah-tone', nah], *m*. Hypocrite, bigot.

bebé [bay-bay'], *m. & f*. Baby.

bebecina [bay-bay-thee'-nah], *f.(And.)* Drunkenness.

bebedero [bay-bay-day'-ro], *m*. Drinking vessel for birds and domestic animals; drawer of a bird-cage. 2. A drinking trough for beasts. 3. Place where birds drink. 4. Gate hole, jet. **Bebederos,** strips of cloth used by tailors for lining clothes, facing.

bebedero, ra, bebedizo, za [bay-bay-day'-ro, rah, bay-bay-dee'-tho, thah], *a*. Potable, drinkable. Given to drink.

bebedizo [bay-bay-dee'-tho], *m*. 1. Philter or love potion. 2. A physical potion, a drench.

bebedo, da [bay'-bay-do, dah], *a. (Prov.)* Drunk, intoxicated.

bebedor, ra [bay-bay-dor', rah], *m. & f*. Tippler, toper. Hard drinking.

bebendurria [bay-bayn-door'-ree-ah], *f*. 1. *(Cono Sur)* Drinking party. 2. *(And. Méx.)* Drunkenness.

bebé-probeta [bay-bay'-pro-bay-tah], *m. & f*. Test-tube baby.

beber [bay-berr'], *va*. 1. To drink. 2. To pledge, to toast. **Beber a la salud de alguno,** to drink to another's health. **Sin comerlo ni beberlo,** to suffer an injury without having had any part in the cause or motive of it. **Beber de codos,** to drink at leisure and luxuriously. **Beber las palabras, los acentos, los semblantes, las acciones a otro,** to listen with the greatest care, to swallow or adopt the speech, accent, features, and actions of another. **Beber los pensamientos a alguno,** to anticipate one's thoughts. **Beber los vientos,** to solicit with much eagerness. **Le quisiera beber la sangre,** I would drink his heart's blood. **Beber como una cuba,** to drink as a fish. **Beber en las fuentes,** to obtain information at headquarters, or first hand. **Beber el pilón,** to believe current rumors. **Beber los sesos,** to bewitch. **Beber fresco,** to be tranquil.

beberaje [bay-bay-rah'-hay], *m. (Cono Sur)* Drink.

beberrón [bay-ber-rone'], *m. (Lit. us.)* Tippler, malt-worm, low drunkard.

bebestible [bay-bays-tee'-blay], *a*. 1. *(LAm.)* Drinkable. 2. *m.pl.* **Bebestibles,** drinks.

bebezón [bay-bay-thone'], *f*. 1. *(Carib.)* Drink, booze. 2. *(Carib)* Drunkenness; drinking spree.

bebible [bay-bee'-blay], *a*. Drinkable. **No bebible,** undrinkable.

bebida [bay-bee'-dah], *f*. 1. Drink, beverage, potion. **Bebida alcohólica,** alcoholic drink. 2. *(Prov.)* The time allowed to workmen to drink and refresh themselves in the interval of labor. 3. *(Cono Sur)* Bib.

bebido, da [bay-bee'-do, dah], *pp. of* BEBER.-*a*. Applied to an intoxicated person. **Bien bebido,** drunk.-*m. & f*. 1. Drench or physical potion for brutes. 2. *(Obs.)* V. BEBIDA.

bebistrajo [bay-bis-trah'-ho], *m. (Coll.)* An irregular and extravagant mixture of drinks.

beca [bay'-cah], *f*. 1. Grant, scholarship. 2. Part of a collegian's dress worn over the gown. 3. Fellowship, pension, an establishment in a college. 4. Fellow or member of a college, who shares the revenue. 5. Tippet worn formerly by the dignitaries of the church. **Beca de merced,** scholarship. **Becas,** strips of velvet, satin, etc., with which cloaks are faced.

becada [bay-cah'-dah], *f. (Orn.)* Wood-cock. V. CHOCHA.

becado [bay-cah-do], *a*. 1. *a*. Who holds scholarship; who holds an award. **Está aquí becado,** *(LAm.)* He's here on a grant. 2. *m.* **Becada** *f*. Scholarship holder; award holder.

becafigo [bay-cah-fee'-go], *m. (Orn.)* Fig-pecker, epicurean warbler. Motacilla ficedula, *Becafigo raro, (Orn.)* Great redpole, or red-headed linnet. V. PAPAFIGO.

becardón [bay-car-done'], *m. (Prov.)* Snipe. V. AGACHADIZA.

becar [bay-car'], *va*. To award scholarship.

becario, ria [bay-cah'-ree-o], *m. & f*. Scholarship holder; award holder.

becerra [bay-the'-rah], *f*. 1. *(Bot.)* Snap-dragon. V. ANTIRRINO MAYOR, 2. Earth and stones swept down by mountain floods.

becerrada [bay-thayr-rah'-dah], *f. (Taur.)* Fight with young bulls.

becerril [be-ther-reel'], *a*. Bovine calf.

becerrillo, illa, ito, ita [bay-ther-ree'-lyo, lyah, ee'-to, ee'-tah], *m. & f. dim.* 1. Cal 2. Tanned and dressed calf-skin.

becerro, ra [be-ther'-ro, rah], *m. & f*. 1. A yearling calf, 2. Calf- skin tanned and dressed. **Becerros barnizados,** varnished calf-skins. **Becerros charolados,** patent leather calf-skins. 3. Registers in which are entered the privileges and appurtenances of cathedral churches and convents. 4. Manuscript bound in calf-skin, and found in the archives of Simancas, containing an account of the origin and titles of the Spanish nobility. **Becerro marino,** A sea-calf, the seal.

becoquín [bay-co-keen'], *m*. Cap tied under the chin.

becuadrado [bay-coo-ah-drah'-do], *m*. The first property in plain song, or Gregorian mode.

becuadro [bay-coo-ah'-dro], *m. (Mus.)* A natural; the sign.

bedel [bay-del'], *m*. 1. Beadle, an officer in universities, whose business it is to inspect the conduct of the students. 2. Warden. 3. Apparitor of a court of justice.

bedelía [bay-day-lee-'ah], *f*. Beadleship, wardenship.

bedelio [bay-day'-le-o], *m*. Bedellium, an aromatic gum.

bedoya [bay-do'-yah], *m. (And.)* Idiot.

beduino, na [bay-doo-ee'-no, nah], *a*. 1. Bedouin, Arab of the desert. 2. Harsh, uncivil.

befa [bay'-fah], *f*. 1. Derision, jeer, scoff, mock, taunt.

befabemí [bay-fah-bay-mee'], *m*. A musical sign.

befar [bay-far'], *va*. 1. To mock, to scoff, to ridicule, to jeer, to laugh at. 2. To move the lips, and endeavor to catch the chain of the bit (caballos).

befo, fa [bay'-fo, fah], *a*. 1. Blubber-lipped. 2. Bandy-legged.

befo [bay'-fo], *m*. 1. Lip of a horse or other animal. 2. A person with thick skin projecting under lip and bandy legs.

begardo, da [bay-gar'-do, dah], *m. & f*. Beggardus, heretic of the 18th century.

begonia [bay-go'-ne-ah], *f. (Bot.)* Begonia.

beguino, na [bay-gee'-no, nah], *m. & f*. Beguin, heretic of the 14th century.

behetria [bay-ay-tree'-ah], *f*. 1. A town whose inhabitants were free from subjection to any lord. 2. Confusion, disorder. **Lugar de behetría,** a place where perfect equality prevails.

beige [baysh'], *a*. Beige.

béisbol [base'-ball], *m*. Baseball.

bejín [bay-heen'], *m*. 1. *(Bot.)* Puff, common puff-ball, fuzz-ball. 2. Whining, peevish child. 3. One who is angry over trifles.

bejinero [bay-he-nay'-ro], *m. (Prov.)* One who separates the lees or watery sediment from the oil.

bejucal [bay-hoo-cabl'], *m*. A place where reeds grow.

bejuco [bay-hoo'-co], *m*. 1. Thin or pliable reed or cane growing in India. 2. Filaments growing on some trees in America.

bejuquear [bay-hoo-kay-ar'], *va. (LAm.)* To beat, to thrash.

bejuquillo [bay-hoo-keel'-lyo], *m*. 1. A small gold chain of Chinese manufacture. 2. Root of a Brazilian plant called ipecacuanha. 3. A rattan.

belcho [bel'-cho], *m. (Bot.)* Great ephedra, or horsetail-tree.

beldad [ble-dahd'], *f*. Beauty: applied only to the beauty of women. **Una beldad,** fair, a beauty, elliptically for a fair woman.

beldar [bel-dahd'], *va*. To winnow (with a fork).

belduque [bel-doo'-kay], *m.* A large heavy knife *(Mex.)*.

beledín [bay-lay-deen'], *m.* Sort of cotton stuff.

belemnita [bay-lem-nee'-tah], *f.* Belemnites, arrow-head or finger-stone.

Belén [bay-len'], *m.* 1. Birth. 2. Confusion, bedlam. 3. Nativity scene.

beleño [bay-lay'-nyo], *m.* 1. *(Bot.)* Henbane. **Beleño negro,** Common henbane. 2. Poison.

belérico [bay-lay'-re-co], *m.(Bot.)* The fruit and the tree of a kind of myrobalan. *V.* MIRABOLANOS.

belfo, fa [bel'-fo, fah], *a.* Blob-lipped, or blubber-lipped. **Diente belfo,** snag tooth, a tooth which projects.

belfo [bel'-fo] *m.* Thick underlip of a horse.

belga [bel'-gah], *m. & f.* Belgian, a native of Belgium.

Bélgica [bel'-he-cah], Belgium.

belicista [bay-lee-thees'-tah], 1. *a.* Warmongering, militarism.

bélico, ca [bay'-le-co-, cah], *a.* Warlike, martial, military.

belicoso, sa [bay-le-co'-so, sah], *a.* 1. Warlike, martial, military, belligerent, belligerous, 2. Quarrelsome, irascible, easily irritated.

belicosidad [bay-le-co-se-dahd'], *f.* Warlike state.

belicoso [bay-lee-co'-se], *a.* Warlike; bellicose, aggressive; militant.

beligerancia [bay-lee-hay-rahn-the-ah], *f.* Belligerency; militancy, warlike spirit.

beligerante [bay-le-hay-rahn'-tay], *a.* Belligerent, militant, warlike.

belígero, ra [bay-lee'-hay-ro, rah], *a.* *(Poet.)* Warlike, belligerent.

belitre [bay-lee'-tray], *a.* *(Coll.)* Low, mean, vile, vulgar; roguish. *(And. CAm.)* Shrewd child; restless child.

bellacada [bel-lyah-cah'-dah], *f.* 1. A nest of rogues, a set of villains. 2. *(Low.)* Knavery, roguery.

bellacamente [bel-lyah-cah-men'-tay] *adv.* Knavishly, roguishly.

bellaco, ca [bel-lyah'-co, cah], *a.* 1. Artful, sly. 2. Cunning, roguish, deceitful.

bellaco [bel-lyah'-co], *m.* Rogue, a villain, a swindler, a knave.

bellacón, na, bellaconazo, za [bel-lyah-cone', nah], *m. & f.* *aug* Great knave, an arrant rogue.

bellacuelo [bel-lyah-coo-ay'-lo], *m. dim.* Artful, cunning little fellow.

belladama, belladona [bel-lyah-dah'-mah], *f.* 1. *(Bot.)* Deadly nightshade, belladonna, dwale. 2. *(Zool.)* A butterfly whose caterpillar lives in thistles.

bellamente [bel-lyah-men'-tay], *adv.* Prettily, gracefully, fairly.

bellaquear [bel-lyah-kay-ar'], *vn.* To cheat, to swindle, to play knavish; roguish tricks. 2. *(fig.)* To be stubborn.

bellaquería [bel-lyah-kay-ree'-ah], *f.* Knavery, roguery, the act of swindling or deceiving; cunning, counterfeit.

belleza [bel-lyay'-thah], *f.* 1. Beauty fair, fairness, handsomeness, flourish. **Las bellezas de Mallorca,** the beauties of Majorca. 2. Decoration or ornament for the front of buildings. **Decir bellezas,** to say things wittily, or with grace.

bello, lla [bel'-lyo, lyah], *a.* Beautiful handsome, fair, fine; perfect. **Bella pedrería,** fine jewels. **Bello principio,** an excellent beginning. **Por su bella cara no se le concederá,** it will not be granted for his pretty face's sake, or without a good reason.

bellorio, ia [bel-lyo'-re-o, ah], *a.* Mouse-colored (caballos).

bellorita [bel-lyo-ree'-tah], *f.* *(Bot.)* Primrose, cowslip. **Bellorita primaveral,** common cowslip.

bellota [bel-lyo'-tah], *f.* 1. Acorn. 2. Balsam or perfume box, in the shape of an acorn. **Bellota marina,** centre shell, a shell in the shape of an acorn.

bellote [bel-lyo'-tay], *m.* Large round headed nail.

bellotear [bel-lyo-tay-ar'], *vn.* To feed upon acorns (cerdos).

bellotera [bel-lyo-tay'-rah], *f.* Season for gathering acorns, and feeding swine with them.

bellotero, ra [bel-lyo-tay'-ro, rah], *m. & f.* One who gathers or sells acorns.

bellotero [bel-lyo-tay'-ro], *m.* *(Obs.)* A tree which bears acorns.

bellotica, illa, ita [bel-lyo-tee'-cah, eel'-lyah, ee'-tah],*f.dim.* Small acorn.

belorta [bay-lor'-tah], *f.* The ring or screw with which the plough is fastened to the beam.

Beltrán [bel-trahn'], *m.* *(Pro. n.)* Bertram. **Quien bien quiere a Beltrán bien quiere a su can,** love me, love my dog.

belvedere [bel-vay-day'-ray], *m.* Arbor, belvedere.

bemol [bay-mole'], *m.* *(Mus.)* A flat; the sign. **Esto tiene muchos bemoles,** this is a tough one.

bemolado [bay-mo-lah'-do], *a.* Flat (ted), lowered a semitone.

bemolar [bay-mo-lar'], *va.* To flat.

ben, behén [ben', bay-en'], *m.* Fruit of the size of a filbert which yields a precious oil.

benarriza [bay-nar-ree'-thah], *f.* A savory bird of the family of ortolans.

benceno [ben-thay'-no], *m.* Benzene.

bencina [ben-thee'-nah], *f.* Benzine, a light hydrocarbon fluid.

bendecir [ben-day-theer'], *va.* 1. To devote to the service of the church; to consecrate. **Bendecir la bandera,** to consecrate the colors. 2. To bless, to praise, to exalt. **Dios te bendiga,** God bless you.

bendición [ben-de-the-on'], *f.* 1. Benediction. **Bendición de la mesa,** grace. 2. The marriage ceremony. **Echar la bendición,** to give one's blessing to somebody. **Es una bendición,** it is a blessing, it's a godsend. **Toca que es una bendición,** he plays marvellously. **Nos echaron las benediciones,** the knot has been tied (matrimonio). **(Yo bendigo, yo bendiga, from Bendecir.)**

bendito, ta [ben-dee'-to, tah], *a.* 1. Sainted, blessed. 2. Simple, silly. **Es un bendito,** he is a simpleton. **El bendito,** a prayer which begins with this word. 3. Happy, lucky, 4. **¡Benditos los ojos que te ven¡,** lucky eyes to be looking at you. -*m.* 1. Saint. 2. *(fig.)* Simple soul, good soul. **Es un bendito,** he's a good kind person. 3. *(Cono Sur)* Player. 4. *(Cono Sur)* Native hut (cabaña). -*pp. err.* of BENDECIR

benedicta [bay-nay-deec'-tah], *f.* Benedict. An electuary.

benedictino, na [bay-nay-dic-tee'-no, nah], *a.* Benedictine, of the order of St. Benet.

benefactor [bay-nay-fac-tor'], *m.* *(Ant. and Amer.)* Benefactor. -*a.* Salutary; beneficient. *V.* BIENHECHOR.

beneficencia [bay-nay-fe-the-ah-the-ah], *f.* 1. Beneficence, kindness, well-doing. 2. Charity; charitable organization.

beneficiación [bay-nay-fe-the-ah-the-on'], *f.* Benefaction.

beneficiado [bay-nay-fe-the-ah'-do], *m.* The incumbent of a benefice which is neither a curacy nor prebend; curate, beneficiary.

beneficiador, ra [bay-nay-fe-the-ah-dor', rah], *m. & f.* 1. Benefactor. 2. Improver. 3. A careful administrator.

beneficial [bay-nay-fe-the-ahl'], *a.* Relating to benefices or ecclesiastical livings.

beneficiar [bay-nay-fe-the-ar'], *va.* 1. To benefit. 2. To cultivate the ground. 3. To work and improve mines; to submit ores, etc., to metallurgical processes. 4. *(Prov.)* To confer an ecclesiastical benefice. 5. To purchase a place or employ. **Beneficiar los efectos, libranzas y otros créditos,** to resign and make over effects, credits, and other claims. -*vn.* To be of benefit. -*vr.* To benefit, profit. **Beneficiarse de,** to benefit from, to take advantage of.

beneficiario, ria [bay-nay-fe-the-ah'-re-o], *m.f.* Beneficiary.

beneficiencia [bay-nay-fe-then'-thee-ah], *f.(Mex.)* Welfare.

beneficio [bay-nay-fee'-the-o], *m.* 1. Benefit, favor, kindness, benefaction. **A beneficio de,** for the benefit of. **En beneficio propio,** to one's own advantage. 2. The proceeds of a public entertainment given in favor of some person or charity. 3. Right belonging to one either by law or charter. 4. Labor and culture: applied to the ground, trees, mines. 5. Utility, profit. **Beneficio bruto,** gross profit. **Beneficio neto,** net profit. 6. Benefice, ecclesiastical living. **Beneficio curado,** benefice to which a curacy is annexed. 7. Purchase of public places, employs, or commissions in the army. 8. Act of resigning and making over credits and demands for sums not equal to their amount. **Beneficio de inventario**, benefit of inventory, the effect of which pay debts to a larger amount than that of the inheritance. **No tener oficio ni beneficio**, to have neither profession nor property (vagabundos). 9. *(LAm.)* Slaughter, slaughtering (matanza). 10. *(LAm.)* Slaughterhouse (matadero).

benefio marginal [bay-nay-fee'-the-o mar-he-nahl'], *m. (Com.)* Fringe benefit.

beneficioso, sa [bay-nay-fe-the-o'-so, sah], *a.* Beneficial, advantageous, profitable.

benéfico, ca [bay-nay'.-fe-co, cah], *a.* 1. Beneficent, kind, charitable. 2. Charitable (trabajo, organismo etc.). **Obra benéfica**, charity.

benemérito, ta [bay-nay-may'-re-to, tah], *a.* 1. Meritorious, deserving of reward, worthy. **Benemérito de la patria**, well-deserving of the country. 2. **El benemérito hispanista**, the distinguished hispanist.

beneplácito [bay-nay-plah'-the-to], *m.* Goodwill, approbation, permission, consent.

benevolencia [bay-nay-vo-len'-the-ah], *f.* Benevolence, goodwill, kindness, humanity, good-nature, courteousness.

benevolente [bay-nay-bo-len'-tay], *a.* Benevolent, kind, kindly; genial. **Benevolente con**, well-disposed towards, kind to.

benévolo, la [bay-nay'-vo-lo, lah], *a.* Benevolent, kind, gentle, courteous, favorable, good, kind-hearted, good-natured, gracious.

bengala [ben-gah'-lah], *f* 1. Bengal, a sort of thin slight stuff. 2. Cane from which walking-sticks are made.

bengalí [ben-gah-lee'], *m.* 1. Native of Bengal or belonging to it. 2. Language of the Bengalese people, Bengalee.

benignamente [be-nig-nah-men'-tay], *adv.* Kindly, benevolently, mercifully, favorably, graciously, humanely, clemently.

benignidad [bay-nig-ne-dahd'], *f.* 1. Benignity, graciousness, mercifulness, kindness, piety, courtesy, lenity. 2. Mildness of the air or weather.

benigno, na [bay-neeg'-no, nah], *a.* 1. Benign (tumor), merciful, gracious, pious, clement, humane. 2. Kind, courteous, favorable. 3. Mild (clima), temperate, gentle.

benito, ta [bay-nee'-to, tah], *m. & f. & a.* Benedictine friar or nun.

benjamín [ben-hah-meen'], *m.* Baby of the family, youngest child; favorite child.

benjuí [ben-hoo-ee'], *m.* Benzoin or benjamín, a gum-resin.

benzina [ben-thee'-nah], *f. (Cono Sur)* V. BENCINA.

beodo, da [bay-o'-do, dah], *a.* Drunk.

beorí [bay-o-ree'], *m.* American tapir.

beque [bay'-kayl, *m. (Naut.)* 1. Head of the ship. 2. Privies for sailors in the head gratings. *-a. (CAm.)* Stammering.

bequebo [bay'-kay'-bo], *m. (Orn.)* Woodpecker.

berám [bay-rahm'], *f.* Coarse cotton stuff brought from the East Indies.

berberecho [ber-bay-ray'-cho], *m.* Cockle.

berberí, isco. or **bereber** [ber-bay-ree', rees'-co, bay-ray-berr'], *a.* Belonging to Barbary, Berber.

berberís [ber-bay-rees'], *m. (Bot.)* Barberry, berberry, piperidge-bush.

berbí [ber-bee'], *m.* A sort of woollens.

berbiquí [ber-be-kee'], *m.* A carpenter's brace. Wimble.

bercería [ber-thay-ree'-ah], *f.* Green-market, where vegetables are sold.

bercero, ra [ber-thay'-ro, rah], *m. & f.* Greengrocer.

berdel [ber-dayl'], *m.* Mackerel.

bereber, beréber [bay-ray-ber'], *a. m. & f.* Berber.

berenjena [bay-ren-hay'-nah], *f. (Bot.)* Aubergine, eggplant. 2. *(Carib.)* Nuisance, bother (fastidio).

berenjenado, da [bay-ren-hay-nah'-do, dah], *a. (Obs.)* Having the color of an egg-plant.

berenjenal [bay-ren-hay-nahl'], *m.* A bed of eggplants. **Meterse en un berenjenal**, to involve oneself in difficulties.

bergamota [ber-gah-mo'-tah], *f.* 1. Bergamot, a sort of pear. 2. Bergamot, snuff scented with the essence of bergamot.

bergamote, bergamoto [ber-gah-mo'-tay1, *m. (Bot.)* Bergamot-tree.

bergante [ber-gan'-tay], *m.* Brazenfaced villain, a ruffian, rascal.

bergantín [ber-gan-teen'], *m. (Naut.)* Brig or brigantine, a two-masted vessel with square sail.

bergantinejo [ber-gan-te-nay'-ho], *m. dim.* Small brig.

bergantón, na [ber-gan-tone', nah], *m. & f. aug.* Brazenfaced, impudent person.

bergantonazo [ber-gan-to-nah'-tho], *m. aug* Most impudent ruffian.

berilo [bay-ree'-lo], *m.* Beryl, a precious stone.

berkelio [ber-kay'-lee-o], *m.* Berkelium.

berlín [ber-leen'], *m.* 1. Berlin. 2. *(Cono Sur) (Culin.)* Doughnut, donut.

berlina [ber-lee'-nah], *f.* Landau or berlin, an open carriage.

berlinés, sa [ber-lee-nays', sah], *a.* Of Berlin, berliner.

berlinga [ber-leen'-gah], *f.* 1. *(Prove.)* Pole driven into the ground, at the top of which is fastened a rope, carried to another pole, which serves to hang clothes upon to be dried. 2. *(Naut.)* Round timber of six inches in diameter.

bermejar, bermejecer [ber-may-hay-ar', ber-may-hay-herr'], *vn.* To be of a reddish color.

bermejizo, za [ber-may-hee'-tho, thah], *a.* Reddish.

bermejo, ja [ber-may'-ho, hah], *a.* Of a bright reddish color; *(Carib. Mex.)* Light brown (vaca). 2. *(Carib.)* Matchless, unsurpassed (único).

bermejón, na [ber-may-hone, nah], *a.* 1. Reddish. 2. *V.* BERMEJO. 3. *(Obs.) V.* BERMELLÓN.

bermejuela [ber-may-hoo-ay'-lah], *f.* 1. *(Zool.)* Red gurnard, a small river fish. 2. *(Bot.)* Heather.

bermejuelo, la [ber-may-hoo-ay'-lo, lah], *a. dim.* A little reddish.

bermejura [ber-may-hoo'-rah], *f.* Reddishness, ruddy color.

bermellón, bermillón [ber-mel-lyone'], *m.* Vermilion.

Bermudas [ber-moo'-dahs], *m. & pl.* Bermuda shorts.

bermudiana [ber-moo-de-ah'-nah], *f. (Bot.)* Grass-flower, blue-eyed grass.

Berna [ber'-nah], *f.* Berne.

bernardina [ber-nar-dee'-nah], *f. (Coll.)* Fanfaronade, false boast, lie.

bernardo, da [ber-nar'-do, dah], *m. & f. & a.* Bernardine monk or nun.

bernegal [ber-nay-gahl'], *m.* Bowl, a vessel to hold liquids.

bernés, sa [ber-ness', sah], *a.* Bernese, relating to Berne.

bernia [ber'-ne-ah], *f.* 1. Rug, a coarse woollen cloth, of which coverlets are made. 2. Cloak made of rug. 3. *(Coll.)* A bore.

bernicla [ber-nee'-clah], *f.* Barnacle, a bird like a goose.

berra [ber'-rah], *f. (Bot.)* The strong, watercress plant.

berraza [ber-rah'-thah], *f.* Waterparsnip. **Berraza común** or **nodiflora**, procumbent water parsnip.

berrear [ber-ray-ar'], *vn.* 1. To cry like a calf, to bellow; to howl (niño); *(Mus.)* to bawl; to screech. 2. *(fig.)* To fly off the handle. *-va.* To squeal.

berrenchín [ber-ren-cheen'], *m.* 1. Foaming, grunting, and blowing of a wild boar. 2. Cry of wayward-children.

berrendearse [ber-ren-day-ar'-say], *vr.* 1. *(Prove.)* To grow yellow: applied to wheat nearly ripe. 2. To be stained or tinged with two colors.

berrendo, da [ber-ren'-do, dah], *a.* 1. Stained or tinged with two colors. 2. Ripe wheat which gets a yellow color. 3. *(Prov.)* Applied to a silkworm which has duskish brown color.

berrido [ber-ree'-do], *m.* The bellowing of a calf or other animal, howl (niño); *(Mus.)* Bawl, bawling; screech.

berrín [ber-reen'], *m.* Person in a violent passion. *V.* BEJIN.

berrinche [ber-reen'-chay], *m.* 1. Anger, passion, great petulance (niños); sulkiness. **Coger un berrinche**, to fly into a rage. 2. *(LAm.)* Pong, stink (hedor).

berrizal [ber-re-thahl'], *m.* Place full of watercresses.

berro [ber'-ro], *m. (Bot.)* Watercress, common watercress, fen-cress; *(Carib.)* Rage, anger (enojo).

berrocal [ber-ro-cahl'], *m.* A craggy or rocky place.

berroqueña [ber-ro-kay'-nyah], *a.* **Piedra berroqueña**, coarse-grained granitic stone.

berrueco [ber-roo-ay'-co], *m.* 1. Rock. 2. Pin, a small horny induration of the membranes of the eye.

berrusa [ber-roo'-sah], *f.* Sort of stuff manufactured at Lyons.

Berta [bayr'-tah], *f.* 1. Bertha, proper name. 2. A kind of cape called bertha.

berza [bayr'-thah], *f. (Bot.)* Cabbage. Brassica. **Berza or col común**, savoy cabbage. **Berza colinabo**, *V.* COLINABO. **Berza coliflor**, *V.* COLIFLOR. **Berza bróculi**, *V.* BRÓCULI. **Berza rizada or bretón**, *V.* BRETÓN. **Berza lombarda**, Red cabbage. **Berza repollo**, *V.* REPOLLO. **Berza de perro**, *(Bot.)* wild mercury dog's cabagge.

berzal [ber'-thahl], *m. (Esp.)* Cabbage patch.

berzaza [ber-thah'-thah], *f. aug.* A large head of cabbage.

besamel [bay-sah-mayl'], *f. (Culin.)* White sauce, bechamel sauce.

besana [bay-sah'-nah], *f.* First furrow opened in the ground with a plough.

besar [bay-sar'], *va.* 1. To kiss. 2. To touch closely, applied to inanimate things. **A besar**, *(Naut.)* Home, or block on block. **Llegar y besar el santo**, no sooner said than done. **Besar la mano** or **los pies**, old expressions of courtesy and respect. *-vr.* 1. To strike heads or faces together accidentally. 2. To kiss, to kiss one another.

besico, sillo, sito [bay-see'-co, seel'-lyo, see'-to], *m. dim.* A little kiss. **Besicos de monja**, *(Bot.) V.* FAROLILLOS.

beso [bay'-so], *m.* 1. Kiss. **Beso de tornillo**, French kiss. **Echar un beso**, to blow a kiss. 2. Violent collision of persons or things. 3. Among bakers, kissing-crust, where one loaf-touches another. **Dar un beso al jarro**, *(Low.)* to toss about the pot, to drink freely.

bestezuela [bes-tay-thoo-ay'-lah], *f. dim.* A little beast.

bestia [bes'-te-ah], *f.* 1. Beast, a quadruped. **Bestia de carga**, beast of burden. **Bestia de tiro**, draught animal. **Bestia de silla**, a saddle mule. **Gran bestia**, an elk, an animal of the stag kind. 2. *(Met.)* Dunce, idiot, ill-bred fellow. **¡No seas bestia!**, don't be an idiot! 3. Creature, an animal not human. 4. **¡Est's hecho un bestia!**, you are great! (admirativo). *-a.* Stupid. **Juan es muy bestia**, John is a bit stupid. **El muy bestia**, the great idiot.

bestiaje, bestiame [bes-te-ah'-hay, beste-ah'-may], *m.* An assembly of beasts of burden.

bestial [bes-te-ahl'], *a.* 1. Bestial, brutal. 2. Terrific (estupendo); tremendous, marvellous; smashing.

bestialidad [bes-te-ah-le-dahd'], *f.* 1. Beast-like nature, bestiality. 2. *(fig.)* Stupidity (estupidez); silly thing (disparate). 3. **Una bestialidad de gente**, lots and lots of people. *V.* BRUTALIDAD.

bestialmente [bes-te-al-men'-tay], *adv.* Bestially, brutally, marvellously. **Lo pasamos bestialmente**, we had a super time.

bestiaza [bes-te-ah'-thah], *m. aug.* 1. A great beast. 2. An idiot.

bestiecica, illa, ita, bestiezuela [bes-te-ay-thee'-cah, eel'-yah, ee'-tah, bes-te-ay-thoo-ay'-lah], *f. dim.* 1. A little beast. 2. An ignorant person.

béstola [bes'-to-lah], *f.* Paddle, or paddle-staff, for cleaning the coulter of the plough.

best-seller [best-say'-layr], *m. pl.* Best-sellers, best seller.

besucar [bay-soo-car'], *va.* To give many kisses, kiss repeatedly. *V.* BESUQUEAR.

besucón [bay-soo-cone'], *m. (Low.)* Hearty kiss, smack. *-a.* Fond of kissing.

besugada [bay-soo-gah'-dah], *f.* A luncheon or dinner of sea breams.

besugo [bay-soo'-go]. *m. (Zool..)* 1. Sea bream, or red gilthead. 2. **Ojo de besugo**, squint-eyed. 2. **Ya te veo, besugo**, 4. *(Met.)* I can anticipate your design. 5. Idiot (idiota).

besuguera [bay-soo-gay'-rah], *f.* 1. A pan for dressing besugos or breams.

besuguero [bay-soo-gay'-ro], *m.* 1. Fishmonger who sells breams. 2. *(Prov.)* Fishing-tackle for catching breams.

besuguete [bay-soo-gay'-tay], *m. (Zool.)* Red sea-bream.

besuquear [bay-soo-kay-ar'], *va.* To cover with kisses, keep on kissing. *-vr.* To kiss (each other) a lot; to pet.

besuqueo [bay-soo-kay'-o], *m.* Hearty and repeated kisses.

beta [bay'-tah], *f. (Prov.)* 1. A bit or line of thread (cuerda). 2. Beta, the second letter of the Greek alphabet. **Rayos beta**, beta rays. **Betas**, *(Naut.)* pieces of cordage, all sorts of tackle.

betabel [bay-tah-bell'], *m. (Mex.)* Sugar beet.

betarraga, betarrata [bay-tar-rah'-gah, bay-tai,-rah'-tah], *f. (Bot.) V.* REMOLACHA. Beet.

betarraga [bay-tar-rah'-gah], *f. (LAm.)*, **betarrata** *f.* Beet, beetroot.

betatrón [bay-tah-tron'], *m.* Betatron.

betel [bay-tel'], *m.* Betel, an Indian shrub.

Bética [bay'-te-cah]. *f.* Ancient name of the province now *Andalucía*.

bético, ca [bay'-te-co, cah], *a.* Andalusian.

betlemita [bet-lay-mee'-tah], *m.* Bethlemite, a friar of a religious order established in America.

betón [be-tone'], *m.* Hydratilic cement.

betónica [bay-to'-ne-cah], *f. (Bot.)* Betony. Betonica.

betum, betume, betumen [bay-toon', bay-too'-may, bay-too'-men], *m. V.* BETÚN.

betún [bay-toon'], *m.* 1. Bitumen. 2. Cement made chiefly of lime and oil. 3. Shoe-blacking, shoe polish. **Dar de betún a**, to polish. 4. *(Naut.)* Substance with which the masts and bottoms of ships are treated. **Betún de colmena**, Coarse wax, found at the entrance of a bee-hive. **Betún judaico**, *V.* ASFALTO.

betunar [bay-too-nar'], *va.* To pay or cover a thing with pitch, tar, resin, etc.

beuna [bay-oo'-nah], *f. (Prov.)* A gold-colored wine, made of a grape of the same name.

beut [bay-oot'], *m.* A kind of sea-fish.

bevatrón [bay-vah-trone'], *m. (Phy.)* Bevatron.

bey [bay'-e], *m.* Bey, a Turkish governor.

bezante [bay-thahn'-tay], *m. (Her.)* Round figure on a shield.

bezo [bay'-tho], *m.* 1. Blubber-lip, a thick lip.

bezoar [bay-tho-ar'], *m.* Bezoar, a calculous concretion found in the intestines of certain ruminant animals, and once considered antidotal to poison.

bezo'rico, ca [bay-tho-ah'-re-co, cah], *a.* 1. Bezoaric. 2. An ancient preparation of the oxide of antimony.

bezón [bay-thone'], *m. (Obs.)* Battering-ram.

bezote [bay-tho'-tay], *m.* A ring, which the Indians wear in their upper lip.

bezudo, da [bay-thoo'-do, dah], *a.* Blubber-lipped or blob-lipped.

bi [be], *pref.* bi.

biambonas [be-am-bo'-nas], *f. pl.* A stuff made in China, of bark.

biangular [be-an-goo-lar'], *a.* Biangulated, biangulous.

bianual [be-ah-noo-al'], *a. m. (Bot.)* Biennial.

biasa [be-ah'-sah], *f.* A kind of coarse silk, from the Levant.

biazas [be-ah'-thas], *f. pl.* Saddle-bags. *V.* BIZAZA.

biberón [be-bay-rone'], *m.* A baby-bottle for infants.

Biblia [be'-ble-ah], *f.* 1. Bible. **La Santa Biblia**, the Holy Bible. 2. **Saber la biblia**, to know everything.

bíblico, ca [be'-ble-co, cah], *a.* Biblical.

bibliobús [be-ble-o-boos'], *m.* Traveling library, library van.

bibliofilia [be-ble-o-fe'-lee-ah], *f.* Bibliophily, love of books.

bibliófilo, a [be-ble-o'-fe-lo], *m. & f.* Booklover, bookworm, bibliophile.

bibliografía, [be-ble-o-grah-fee'-ah], *f.* Bibliography.

bibliográfico, ca [be-ble-o-grah'-fe-co, **cah**], *a.* Bibliographical, bibliographic.

bibliógrafo, fa [be-ble-o'-grah-fo], *m. & f.* Bibliographer.

bibliomanía [be-ble-o-mah-nee'-ah], *f.* Bibliomania.

bibliómano, na [be-ble-o'-mah-no, nah], *m. & f.* Bibliomaniac.

biblioteca [be-ble-o-tay'-cah], *f.* 1. Library. **Biblioteca pública**, public library. **Biblioteca de consulta**, reference library. Catalog, catalogue, collection of authors. 2. Bookcase, bookshelves (estante).

bibliotecario, ria [be-ble-o-tay-cah'-re-o], *m. & f.* Librarian, bibliothecary. **Bibliotecario de sistemas** *(Comp.),* systems librarian.

bibliotecnia, bibliotecnología, biblioteconomía [be-ble-o-tayc'-ne-ah], *f.* Librarianship.

bica [be-cah], *f.* 1. A sea-fish resembling a bream. 2. An unleavened cake of corn.

bicameral [be-cah'-may-rahl], *a. (Pol.)* Two-chambered, bicameral.

bicameralismo [be-cah-may-rah-lees'-mo], *m.* System of two-chamber government.

bicapsular [be-cap-soo-lar'], *a. (Bot.)* Bicapsular.

bicarbonato [be-car-bo-nah'-to], *m.* Bicarbonate. **Bicarbonato sódico, bicarbonato de sosa** bicarbonate of soda; *(culin.)* Baking soda.

bicentenario [be-then-tay-nah'-re-o], *m.* Bicentenary.

biceps [be-theps'], *m. (Anat.)* A muscle of two heads or points of origin.

bicerra [be-ther'-rah], *f.* A kind of wild or mountain goat.

bici [be'-the], *f.* Bike.

bicicleta [be-the-clay'-tah], *f.* Bicycle, cycle. **Bicicleta estática**, exercise bicycle. **Andar en bici**, to cycle.

bicloruro [be-clo-roo'-ro], *m. (Chem.)* Bichloride.

bicoca [be-co'-cah], *f.* 1. Sentrybox. 2. Thing of little esteem or value; trifle. 3. Bargain (ganga); plumb job. 4. *(And. Cono Sur)* Priest's skull cap. 4. *(And. Cono Sur)* snap of the fingers (capirotazo); slap, smack (golpe).

bicolor [be-co-lor'], *a.* Of two colors, *(Aut.)* Two-tone.

bicóncavo, va [be-con'-cah-vo, vah], *a.* Biconcave.

biconvexo, a [be-con-vec'-so, sah], *a.* Double convex.

bicoquete [be-co-kay'-tay], *m.* A bonnet or head dress formerly worn.

bicoquín [be-co-keen'], *m.* Cap. *V.* BECOQUÍN and BIRRETE.

bicorpóreo, rea [be-cor-po'-ray-o, ah], *a.* Bicorporal.

bicos [bee'-cos], *m. pl.* Small gold points or lace, formerly put on velvet bonnets.

bicromato [be-cro-mah'-to], *m.* Bichromate or dichromate.

bicuadrática [be-coo-ah-drah'-te-cah], *a. (Alg.)* Biquadrate, biquadratic.

bicúspide [be-coos'-pe-day], *a.* Bicuspid.

bicha [bee-chah], *f.1. (Naut.)* Trailboard. 2. *(Arch.)* Caryatid in form of a savage. 3. *(Ant.)* Strumpet, bitch. 4. Snake (serpiente); *(fig.)* Bogy. **Mentar la bicha**, to bring up an unpleasant subject. 5. *(CAm.)* Child, little girl. 6. *(And.)* Large cooking pot. 7. *(Obs.)* V. BICHO.

biche [be'-chay], 1. *a. (Cono Sur)* Weak (debil); of an unhealthy color; *(And.)* stunted, immature (no desarrollado); *(Mex.)* Soppy, empty-headed (foto). 2. *m. (And.)* Large cooking pot.

bicherío [be-chay-ree'-o], *m. (LAm.)* Insects, bugs, creepy-crawlies.

bichero [be-chay'-ro], *m. (Naut.)* Boathook. **Asta de bichero**, the shaft of boat-hook. **Gancho de bichero**, the hook of a boat-hook.

bicho [bee'-cho], *m.* 1. A general name for small grubs or insects; bug, creepy crawly; *(Carib, Cono Sur)* Maggot, brub (gusano); *(And.)* Snake (serpiente); *(LAm.)* Odd-looking creature (animal extraño). 2. *(Met.)* A little fellow of a ridiculous figure and appearance. **Mal bicho**, a mischievous urchin. 3. *(Taur.)* Bull. 4. Odd-looking person,

queer fish (persona), **bicho raro**, weirdo. **Mal bicho**, rogue, villain. 5. Brat (niño); *(Mil.)* Squaddle, recruit (niño); *(CAm.)* Child, little boy. 6. *(LAm.)* **De puro bicho**, out of sheer pig-headedness. **Matar el bicho**, to have a drink. 7. *(Carib.)* Thingummy (fulano). *-pl.* Vermin. (Hindu.)

BID *m.* abr de **Banco Internacional de Desarrollo.**

bidé, bidel, bidet, bidets [be-day'], *m.pl.* Bidet.

bidente [be-den'-tay], *m.1. (Poet.)* Two-pronged spade. 2. Sheep. 3. *(Bot.)* A sort of hemp called waterhamp.

bidmensional [be-de-men-see-o-nal'], *a.* Two-dimensional, bidimentional.

bidireccional [be-de-rayc-the-o-nal'], *a. In* Duplex, bidirectional.

bidón [be-done'], *m.* Drum; can, tin.

biela [be-ay'-lah], *f.* 1. Brace-strut. 2. Axle-tree, connecting-rod.

bielda [be-el'-dah], *f.* Pitchfork with six or seven prongs, and a rack used in gathering and loading straw.

bieldar [be-el-dar'], *va.* To winnow corn by means of a wooden fork with two or three prongs.

bieldo, bielgo [be-el'-do, be-el'-go], *m.* Winnowing-fork.

bien [be-en], *m.* 1. Supreme goodness. 2. Object of esteem or love. 3. Good, utility, benefit. **El bien de la comunidad**, the public welfare. **Hombre de bien;** honest man. **En bien de**, for the good of. **Hacer bien**, to do good. **Bienes**, property, fortune, riches, land. **Bienes de fortuna**, worldly goods. **Bienes de consumo**, consumer goods. **Bienes de equipo**, capital goods. **Bienes inmuebles**, landed property. **Bienes públicos**, government property. **Bienes de la tierra**, produce. 4. **Mi bien**, my dear.

bien [be-en], *adv.* 1. Well, right, properly. **Ha vivido bien**, he has lived uprightly. **Contestar bien**, to answer right. **No veo muy bien, I** can't see all that well. **De bien en mejor**, better and better. **Ya est' bien de quejas**, we've had enough complaints. 2. Happily, prosperously. **El enfermo va bien**, the patient is doing well. 3. Willingly, readily. 4. Heartily. **Comió bien**, he dined heartily. **Caminó bien**, he walked at a great rate. After a negative, it means, as soon as. **No bien la vio**, as soon as (just as) he saw her. It is used sometimes as a distributive conjunction: **bien ... bien** ...; whether ... or. 5. Well, well: it is all well: often used in an ironical sense. 6. As well as, in the same manner as. 7. **Bien que**, although. 8. **Bien si**, but if. 9. **Ahora bien**, now this being so. **Bien está** very well. 10. **Más bien**, rather. **Más bien bajo**, rather short. **Si bien me acuerdo**, to the best of my recollection. **Hay bien de eso**, there is plenty of that. **Un coche bien caro**, a very expensive car. **¿Y bien, y qué tenemos con eso?** Well, and what of that? Joined to adjectives or adverbs it is equivalent to **very**, as **bien rico**, very rich; and to verbs, *much*, as. **El bebió bien**, he drank much. **Tener a bien**, to be kind enough.

bienal [be-ay-nahl'], *a.* Biennial.

bienamado, da [be-en-ah-mah'-do, dah], *a.* Dearly, beloved.

bienandante [be-en-an-dahn'-tay]. *a.* Happy, successful, prosperous.

bienandanza [be-en-an-dahn'-thah], *f.* Felicity, prosperity, success.

bienaventuradamente [be-en-ah-ven-too-rah-dah-men'-tay], *adv.* Fortunately, happily.

bienaventurado, da [be-en-ah-ven-too-rah'-do, dah], *a.* 1. Blessed; happy. 2. Fortunate, successful, felicitous. 3. Simple; silly harmless.

bienaventuranza [be-en-ah-ven-too-rahn'-thah], *f.* 1. *(Ecl.)* Blessedness; bliss (eternal). **Las bienaventuranzas**, the beatitudes. 2. Happiness (felicidad); well-being, prosperity (bienestar).

bienestar [be-en-es-tar'], *m.* Well-being, welfare, comfort.

bienfortunado, da [be-en-for-too-nah'-do, dah]. *a.* Fortunate, successful.

bienhablado, da [be-en-ha-blah'-do, dah], *a.* Well and civilly spoken.

bienhadado, da [be-en-ah-dah'-do, dah], *a.* Lucky, fortunate, happy.

bienhecho, cha [be-en-ay'-cho, chah], *a.* Well shaped, well-performed.

bienhechor, ra [be-en-ay-char', rah], *m. & .f.* Benefactor.

bienintencionado [be-en-een-ten-the-o-nah'-do], *a.* Well-meaning.

bienio [be-ay'-ne-o], *m.* Term or space of two years.

bienquerencia [be-en-kay-ren'-the-ah], *f.* Goodwill. *V.* BIENQUERER as noun.

bienquerer [be-en-kay-rerr'], *va.* To wish the good of another, to esteem.

bienquerer [be-en-kay-rerr'], *m.* Esteem, attachment.

bienquistar [be-en-kees-tar'], *va.* To reconcile, to bring together. *-vr.* To become reconciled. **Bienquistarse con uno**, to gain somebody's esteem.

bienquisto, ta [be-en-kees'-to, tah], *a.* Generally esteemed and respected. *-pp.* of BIENQUISTAR.

bienvenida [be-en-vay-nee'-dah], *f.* WELCOME.

bienvenido, da [be-en-vay-nee'-do, dah], *a.* Welcome; greeting (saludo). **Dar la bienvenida a uno**, to welcome somebody, make somebody welcome.

bienventuranza [be-en-ah-ven-too-rahn-thah], *f.* 1. Beatitude. 2. Prosperity, human felicity. **Bienaventuranzas**, the eight beatitudes mentioned in the Scriptures.

bienvivir [be-en-vee-veer'], *vn.* To live in comfort; to live decently, lead a decent life.

bies [be-ays'], *m.* *(Cos.)* **Al bies**, cut on the cross.

bifásico [be-fah'-see-co], *a.* *(Elec.)* Two-phase.

bifocal [be-fo-cahl'], *a.* Bifocal. **Lentes bifocales**, bifocals, bifocal glasses.

biforme [be-for'-may], *a.* *(Poet.)* Biformed, biform.

bifronte [be-fron'-tay], *a.* *(Poet.)* Double-fronted or double-faced.

biftec [beef-tayc'], *m.* Steak, beefsteak.

bifurcación [be-foor-cah-the-on'], *f.* Branch, bifurcation, junction.

bifurcado, da [be-foor-cah'-do, dah], *a.* Forked, branched, bifurcated.

bifurcarse [be-foor-car'-say], *vr* To branch off, as a river or railway, to fork, to bifurcate.

bigamia [be-gah'-me-ah], *f.* 1. Bigamy. 2. *(Law.)* Bigamy, second marriage.

bígamo, ma [bee'-gah-mo], *m. & f.* 1. Bigamist. 2. *(Law.)* Person who has married a widow or widower 3. *(Law.)* A widower or widow who has married again.

bigardear [be-gar-day-ar'], *vn.* To live licentiously; to wander without an object.

bigardía [be-gar-dee'-ah], *f.* Jest, fiction, dissimulation.

bigardo [be-gar'-do], *m.* 1. An opprobrious appellation given to a friar of loose morals and irregular conduct; a lubber. 1. *a.* Lazy, idle; licentious. 2. *m.* Idler (vago); libertine (libertino).

bigarrado, da [be-gar-rah'-do, dah], *a.* V. ABIGARRADO.

bigarro [be-gar'-ro], *m.* *(Prov.)* A large sea-snail.

bignonia [be-no'-ne-ah], *f.* *(Bot.)* Trumpet-flower.

bigorneta [be-gor-nay-tah], *f. dim.* A small anvil.

bigornia [be-gor'-ne-ah], *f.* Anvil.

bigotazo [be-go-tah'-tho], *m. aug.* Large mustache.

bigote [be-go'-tay], *m.* 1. Mustachio, mustache; whiskers (de gato etc.). **De bigote**, terrific, marvellous. 2. Block. *(Typ.)* Dash rule. **Hombre de bigote**, *(Met.)* A man of spirit and vigor. *(Cono Sur)* **chuparse los bigotes**, to lick one's lips.

bigotera [be-go-tay'-rah], *f.* 1. Leather cover for mustache, mustache protector. 2. *(Obs.)* Ornament of ribbons worn by women on the breast 3. Folding seat put in the front of a chariot. 4. Bow compass **Pegar una bigotera**. To play one a trick. **Bigoteras**, Face, mien. **Tener buenas bigoteras**, *(Coll.)* To have a pleasing face, or graceful mien (mujeres).

bigotería [be-go-tay-ree'-ah], *f.* Bigotry.

bigotudo [be-go-too'-do] *a.* Having a large mustache, full-whiskered.

bigudí [be-goo-dee'], *m.* Hair-curler.

bikini [be-kee'-nee], *m.* Bikini.

bilánder [be-lahn'-der], *m.* *(Naut.)* Bilander, a small merchant vessel.

bilateral [be-lah-tay'-rahl], *a.* Bilateral.

biliario, ria [be-le-ah'-re-o, ah], *a.* Biliary.

biliar [be-le-ar'], *a.* Bile, gall.

bilingüe [e-leen'-goo-ay], *a.* Bilingual. Double-tongued, deceitful.

bilingüismo [be-leen-goo-ees'-mo], *m.* Bilingualism.

bilioso, sa [be-le-oh'-so, sah], *a.* 1. *(gen.)* Bilious. 2. *(fig.)* Bilious, peevish (irritable).

bilis [bee'-lis], *f.* 1. *(Anat.)* Bile. 2. *(fig.)* Bile, spleen (cólera). **Se le exalta la bilis**, he gets very cross.

billa [beel'-lyah], *f.* In billiards; the pocketing of a ball after it has struck another.

billalda, or **billarda** [beel-larh'-dah], *f.* A kind of children's play.

billar [beel-lyar'], *m.* 1. Billiards (juego). **Billar americano**, pool. **Billar ruso**, snooker. **Billar automático**, pin table. 2. Billard room (sala).

billete [beel-lyeh'-tay], 1. *(Esp.)* Ticket *(ferro..)* **Billete de abono**, season ticket. **Billete de ida y vuelta**, return ticket. **Billete sencillo**, single ticket. **Pagar el billete**, to pay one's fare. **Sacar un billete**, to get a ticket. 2. *(Fin.)* Banknote; note, bill. **Billete de banco**, banknote. 3. Note, short letter (carta).

billetera, *ro* [beel-lay-tay'-rah], *f. & m.* Wallet, pocketbook.

billetero, ra [beel-lyeh-tay'-ro, rah] *m. & f.* Vendor of lottery tickets. *-f.* Billfold.

billón [beel-lyee-on'], *m.* **Un billón**, a trillion (GB billion).

billonario, ria [beel-lyo-nah'-re-o, ah], *m. & f.* Billionaire:

billonésimo, ma [beel-lyo-nay'-se-mo, mah], *m. & f. & a.* Billionth, one of a billion equal parts.

bilocarse [be-lo-car'-say], *vr.* To be in two different places at the same time.

bilongo [be-lon'-go], *m.* *(Carib.)* Evil influence, evil eye. **Echar bilongo en**, to put the evil eye on. **Tener bilongo**, to bristle with difficulties.

bilorta [be-lor'-tah], *m.* 1. Ring made of a twisted yellow twig. 2. Flying report 3. *(Naut.)* Burr, a kind of iron ring used for various purposes on board ships. 4. A sport among country people, resembling cricket.

bimano, na [be-mah'-no, nah], *m. & f. & a.* Bimanous: said only of mankind.

bimba [beem'-bah], *f. (Mex.)* 1. Drunkenness (embriaguez); drinking spree (juerga). 2. Top hat, topper. 3. Wallet.

bimbollo [beem-bol'-lyo], *m.* *(Mex.)* Bun.

bimensual [be-men-soo-al'], *a.* Twice-monthly.

bimensuario, ria [be-men-soo-ah'-ree-o], *a. m.* Twice-monthly, publication appearing twice-monthly.

bimestral [be-mes-trahl'], *a.* Bimonthly, once in two months. **Publicación bimestral**, bimonthly, bimonthly publication.

bimestre [be-mes'-tray], *a.* Of two months' duration. *-m.* Two months' leave of absence or furlough.

bimotor [be-mo-tor'], *m.* Two-engine plane.

binadera, dor [be-nah-day'-rah], *m. & f.* Weeding hoe.

binar [be-nar'], *va.* To dig or plough ground the second time.

binario, ria [be-nah-re-o], *a.* Binary; of two elements or units.

bincha [been'-chah], *f.* *(And. Cono Sur)* Hairband.

bingo [been'-go], *m.* Bingo (juego); bingo hall (sala).

binocular [be-no'-coo-lar], *a.* Binocular.

binóculo [be-no'-coo-lo], *m.* Binocle, a dioptric telescope; marine or field glasses.

binomial, binominal [be-no-me-ahl', be-no-me-nahl] *a.* Binomial. **Sistema binomial**, *(Math.)* Binomial system.

binomio [be-no'-me-o], *m.* 1. Binominal. 2. **El binomio pueblo**, *(fig.)* the people-army relationship.

binza [been'-thah], *f.* Pellicle, lining of the shell of an egg; any thin membrane.

bio .....*pref.* bio....

biodegradable [be-o-day-grah-dah'-blay], *a.* Biodegradable.

biodegradar [be-o-day-grah-dar'], 1. *va.* To biodegrade. 2. *-vr.* To biodegrade.

biodinámica [be-o-de-nah'-me-cah], *f.* Biodynamics, the doctrine of vital force or energy.

bioecología [be-o-ay-co-lo-hee'-ah], *f.* Bioecology.

biofísica [be-fee'-see-cah], *f.* Biophysics.

biofísico, ca [be-o-fee-se-co, cah], *a.* Biophysical.

biografía [be-o-grah-fee'-ah], *f.* Biography, life.

biográfico, ca [be-o-grah'-fe-co, cah], *a.* Biographical.

biógrafo [be-o'-grah-fo], *m.* Biographer. *(Cono Sur)* Cinema.

biología [bi-o-lo-hee'-ah], *f.* Biology. **Biología molecular**, molecular biology.

biológico, ca [be-o-lo'-he-co, cah] *a.* Biological.

biólogo, ga [be-o'-lo-go], *m& f.* Biologist.

biomasa [be-o-mah'-sah], *f.* Biomass.

biombo [be-om'-bo], *m.* Folding screen (Chinese word).

biometría [be-o-may-tree'-ah], *f.* Biometry, biometrics.

biónica [be-o'-ne-cah], *f. (Biol.)* Bionics.

biónico [be-o'-ne-co], *a.* Bionic.

biopsia [be-op'-see-ah], *f.* Biopsy.

bioquímica [be-o-kee'-me-cah], *f.* Biochemistry

bioquímico, ca [be-o-kee'-me-co, cah] *a.* Biochemical. *-m.* Biochemist. *-f.* Biochemistry.

biosfera [be-os-fay'-rah], *f.* Biosphere.

biotecnología [be-o-tayc-no-lo-hee'-ah], *f.* Biotechnology.

biótico [be-o'-tee-co], *a.* Biotic.

biotina [be-o-tee'-nah], *f.* Biotin.

bióxido [be-ok'-se-do], *m. (Chem.)* Dioxide. **Bióxido (or dióxido) de carbons**, carbon dioxide.

bipartido, da [bee-par-tee'-do, dah], *a. (Poet.)* Bipartite.

bipartidismo [be-par-tee-dees'-mo], *m.* Two-party system.

bipedal [be-pay-dahl'], *a.* Bipedal.

bipede, or bípedo [bee'-pay-day, do], *a.* Biped.

bipétalo, la [be-pay'-tah-lo, lah] *a. (Bot.)* Bipetalous.

biplano [be-plah'-no], *m.* Biplane.

biplaza [be-plah'-thah], *m. (Aer.)* Two-seater.

biricu [be-re-coo'], *vn.* Sword-belt.

birimbao [be-rim-bah'-o], *m. (Mus.)* A Jew's harp. (imitative word.)

birla, *f. (Prov.)* **birlo**, *vn.* [bee-lah, lo] Bowl for playing.

birlador [beer-lah-dor'], *m.* 1. One who knocks down with one blow; used in the game of nine-pins. 2. Pilferer.

birlar [beer-lar'], *va.* 1. At the game of nine-pins, to throw a bowl a second time from the same place. 2. To knock down with one blow, to kill with one shot. 3. To snatch away an employment which another was aiming at. 4. To rob, to pilfer. **Juan le birló la novia**, John pinched his girl. **Le birlaron el empleo**, he was done out of the job.

birlibirloque [beer-le-beer-lo'-kay], *m.* **Por arte de birlibirloque**, *(Coll.)* To do something by occult and extraordinary means.

birlocha [beer-lo'-chah], *f.* 1. Paper kite. 2. *(Mex.) (Aut.)* Old banger, old crock.

birlocho [beer-lo'-cho], *m.* High open carriage.

birlón [beer-lone'], *m. (Prov.)* Large middle pin in the game of nine-pins.

birlonga [beer-lon'-gah], *f.* Mode of playing in the game at cards called *ombre*. **A la birlonga**, in a negligent, careless manner.

Birmania [beer-mah'-nee-ah], *f.* Burma.

birmano, na [beer-mah'-no, nah], *a. m. & f.* Burmese.

birreactor [ber-ray-ac-tor'], *m. & f.* Twin-jet (plane).

birreme [beer-ray'-may], *a.* Two-oared (barco); bireme.

birreta [beer-ray'-tah], *f.* Cardinal's red cap.

birrete [beer-ray'-tay], *m.* Mortarboard, professional cap.

birria [ber'-ree-ah], f. 1. *(Esp.)* Monstrosity, ugly old thing (cosa fea); wretched piece of work (obra); trash (basura); useless object (cosa inútil). **La novela es una birria**, the novel is trash. **Entre tanta birria**, among so much trash. 2. *(Cono Sur. Méx.)* Tasteless drink; *(Mex.)* Stew (guiso). 3.

(And.) Set idea, mania; obstinacy (obsesión). 4. *(LAm.)* **Jugar de birria**, to play heartedly. 5. *(CAm.)* Beer (cerveza).

bis [bees], a Latin word meaning twice; used in composition.

bisabuela [be-sah-boo-ay'-lah], *f.* Great-grandmother.

bisabuelo [be-sah-boo-ay'-lo], *m.* Great-grandfather.

bisagra [be-sah'-grah], *f.* 1. Hinge. 2. Piece of boxwood, with which shoemakers polish soles of shoes. **Bisagras y pernos**, hooks and hinges. **Bisagras de la portería**, *(Naut.)* port hinges.

bisanuo, nua [be-sah'-noo-o, ah], *a. (Bot.)* Bisannual.

bisar [be-sar'], 1. *va.* To give an encore, to repeat. 2. *(Cono Sur)* To encore, demand as an encore. *-vn.* To give an encore.

bisbisar [bis-be-sar'], *va.* To mutter, to mumble; *(Cono Sur)* to whisper (susurrar).

bisbiseo [bis-be-say'-o], *m.* Mutter, muttering, mumbling.

bisecar [be-say-car'], *va.* To bisect.

bisección [be-sec-the-on'], *f.* Bisection.

bisector, triz [be-sec-tor', treeth], *a. (Geom.)* Bisecting.

bisel [be-sel'], *m.* The bevel, bevel edge, chamfer. *(Coop.)* Sloping tool.

biselado [be-say-lah-do], *a.* Bevel, bevelled.

biselar [be-say-lar'], *va.* To bevel.

bisemanal [be-say-mah-nah], *a.* Semiweekly, twice a week.

bisemanario [be-say-mah-nah'-re-o], *m.* Semiweekly publication.

bisexual [be-sec-soo-ahl'], *a.* Bisexual.

bisexualidad [be-sec-soo-ah-lee-dahd'], *f.* Bisexuality.

bisiesto [be-se-es'-to], *a.* Bissextile; leap year (año).

bisílabo, ba [be-see'-lah-bo, bah], *a.* Consisting of two syllables.

bismuto [bis-moo'-to], *m.* Bismuth.

bisnieto, ta [bis-ne-ay'-to, tah], *m. & f. V.* BIZNIETO.

bisojo, ja [be-so'-ho, hah], *a.* Squint-eyed, cross eyed.

bisonte [be-son'-tay], *m.* Bison, buffalo.

bisoñada [be-so-nyah'-dah], *f.* Naïve remark, naïve thing to do.

bisoñé [be-so-nyay'], *m.* Wig, toupee.

bisoñería [be-so-nyay-ree'-ah], *f.* A rash and inconsiderate speech or action.

bisoñez [be-so-nyayth'], *f.* Inexperience; rawness.

bisoño, ña [be-so'-nyo, nyah], *a.* 1. Raw, undisciplined: applied to recruits or new-levied soldiers. 2. Novice, tyro. 3. Horse not yet broken.

bispón [bis-pone'], *m.* Roll of oil-cloth, a yard in length, used by sword cutlers.

bistec, bisté, bisteck, bisteque [bees-tec'], *m.* Beefsteak, steak. 2. Tongue (lengua). **Achatar el bisté**, to shut one's trap.

bisturí [bee-too-ree'], *m.* Scalpel, surgeon's knife.

bisulco, ca [be-sool'-co, cah], *a.* Bisulcate, cloven-footed.

bisulfato [be-sool-fah'-to], *m. (Chem.)* Bisulfate.

bisulfito [be-sool-fee'-to], *m. (Chem.)* Bisulfite.

bisunto, to [be-soon'-to, tah], *a. (Obs.)* Dirty or greasy.

bisutería [be-soo-tay-ree'-ah], *f.* Imitation jewelery, trinkets.

bit [beet'], *m. pl. (Comp.)* Bit. **Bit de inicio**, start bit. **Bit de parada**, stop bit. **Bit de control**, check bit. **Bit de ejecución**, running bit. **Bit de orden inferior**, low order bit. **Bit de orden superior**, high order bit. **Bit de paridad par**, even parity bit.

bitácora [be-tah'-co-rah], *f. (Naut.)* Binnacle. **Lámpara de la bitácora**, binnacle-lamp.

bitadura [be-tah-doo'-rah], *f. (Naut.)* Cable-bitt, a turn of the cable round the bitts. **Bitadura entera de cable**, weather-bitt of a cable. **Tomar la bitadura con el cable**, to bitt the cable.

bitas [bee'-tas], *f. pl. (Naut.)* Bitts, large pieces of timber placed abaft the manager, to belay the cable, when the ship rides at anchor. **Forro de las bitas**, lining of the bits. **Contrabitas**, standards of the bitts. **Bita de molinete**, knight-head of the windlass.

bitensional [be-ten-see-o-nahl'], *a. (Elec.)* Equipped to work at two different voltages.

bitones [be-to'-nes], *m. pl. (Naut.)* Pins of the capstan.

bitoque [be-to'-kay], *m. (Prov.)* Bung, the wooden stopple of a cask. **Tener ojos de bitoque**, *(Cold.)* to squint.

bitor [be-tor'], *m. (Orm.)* Rail, a bird called the king of the quails.

bitumen [be-too'-men], *m. V.* BETÚN.

bituminoso, sa [be-too-me-no'-so, sah], *a.* Bituminous.

bivalvo, va [be-vahl'-vo, vah], *a. (Conch.)* Bivalve, bivalvular.

biverio [be-vay'-re-o], *m.* 1. *V.* BÍBARO 2. *V.* VIVERO.

bivio [be-vee-o], *m. (LAm.)* Road junction.

biza [bee'-thah], *f. (Zool.)* Fish belonging to the family of tunnies. *V.* BONITO.

Bizancio [be-than'-the-o], *n.* Byzantium.

bizantino [be-than-te'-no], *a.* 1. Byzantine. 2. *(fig.)* Decadent (decadente). 3. *(fig.)* Idle, pointless (discusión). *-m.* (Bizantina) *f.* Byzantine.

bizarramente [be-thar-rah-men'-tay], *adv.* Courageously (generosamente), gallantly (valientemente), with spirit.

bizarrear [be-thar-ray-ar'], *vn.* To act in a spirited and gallant manner.

bizarría [be-thar-ree'-ah], *f.* 1. Gallantry, valor, fortitude; mettle. 2. Liberality, generosity, splendor, gentility.

bizarro, rra [be-thah'-ro, rah], *a.* 1. Gallant, brave, high-spirited (valiente). 2. Generous, liberal, high-minded.

bizaza [be-thah'-thah], *f.* Saddlebag.

bizbirindo [beeth-be-reen-do], *a. (Mex.)* Lively, bright.

bizcacha [bith-cah'-chah], *f.* An animal with a long tail in Peru, the flesh of which resembles that of a rabbit.

bizcar [bith-car'], *vn.* To squint, to be cross-eyed. *-va.* To wink (ojo).

bizco, ca [beeth'-co, cah], *a.* Cross-eyed, squinting, cross-eyed look. **Dejar a uno bizco**, to impress somebody strongly. **Ponerse bizco**, to squint, to look cross-eyed. *-adv.* **Mirar bizco**, to squint, to look cross-eyed. *V.* BISOJO.

bizcochada [bith-co-chah'-dah], *f.* Soup made of cookies boiled in milk with sugar and cinnamon.

bizcochar [bith-co-char'], *va.* To make or bake cookies. To bake bread a second time.

bizcochero [bith-co-chay'-ro] *m.* 1. Cookies-cask. 2. One who makes or sells cookies.

bizcocho [bith-co'-cho], *m.* 1. *(Naut.)* Cookie, hard tack. **Embarcarse con poco bizcocho**, to set out unprepared. 2. Sponge, sponge cake; sponge finger; paste made of fine flour eggs and sugar. 3. Whiting made of the plaster of old walls.

bizcochuelo [bith-co-choo-ay'-lo], *m.* 1. Dim. of BIZCOCHO. 2. *(Amer.)* Sponge-cake.

bizma [beeth'-mah], *f.* Cataplasm, poultice.

bizmar [bith-mar'], *va.* To poultice, to apply a cataplasm.

bizna [beeth'-nah], *f.* Zest, membrane which quarters the kernel of a walnut.

biznaga [bith-nah'-gah], *f.* 1. *(Bot.)* Carrot-like ammi, the sprigs of which are used as toothpicks. Ammi visnaga. 2. *(Coll. and Amer.)* A useless, worthless thing.

biznieta [bith-ne-ay'-tah], *f.* Great-granddaughter.

biznieto [bith-ne-ay'-to], *m.* Great-grandson.

bizquear [bith-kay-ar'], *vn.* To squint.

bizquera [bith-kay'-rah], *f. (And.)* Squint.

blanca [blahn'-cah], *f.* 1. Copper coin of the value of half a maravedí; mite. **No tener blanca or estar sin blanca**, to be broke. 2. *(Orn.)* Magpie. 3. **Blanca morfea**, *(Vet.)* alphosis, a white scurf, tetter, or ring-worm. 4. White woman (mujer). 5. *(Mus.)* Minim. 6. Cocaine (cocaína); heroin (heroína).

blanca-espina [blahn'-cah-es-pee'-nah], *f.* Hawthorn, white thorn.

blancal [blan-cahl'], *a. & m.* White wheat.

blancazo, za [blan-cah'-tho, thah], *a.* 1. *(aug.)* Very white. 2. *(Coll.) V.* BLANQUECINO.

blanco, ca [blahn'-co, cah], *a.* 1. White, blank: hoar, hoary; fair. **La raza blanca**, the white race. **Más blanco que la nieve**, as white as snow. 2. Honored, respected (personas).

3. *(Naut.)* Untarred. 4. Blank (página). 5. Blank (verso). 6. Cowardly (cobarde). 7. **Estar blanco**, to have a clean record.

blanco [blahn'-co], *m.* 1. White star, or any other remarkable white spot in horses. 2. Target, blank, mark to shoot at. **Dar en el blanco**, to hit the mark. 3. Blank left in writing. **Con dos páginas en blanco**, with two blank pages. **Cheque en blanco**, blank cheque. **Botar en blanco**, to return a blank voting paper. 4. *(Met.)* Aim; object of our desire. 5. First white sheet pulled at a printing-press, after the form is got ready. 6. Interlude: speaking of plays. 7. Interval (intervalo). 8. White page. 9. *(Her.)* Argent. 10. Mixture of whiting, lime, etc., to size or lay the first coat for painting. **Blanco de estuco**, stucco whiting, made of lime and pounded marble. **Blanco de ballena**, Spermaceti. **Blanco de España**, Spanish white. **Blanco de perla**, pearl white. **Tela or ropa blanca**, linen. **Armas blancas**, side-arms. **De punta en blanco**, point-blank. **Dejar en blanco alguna cosa**, to pass over a thing in silence. **Quedarse en blanco**, to be frustrated in one's expectations, to be left in the lurch.

blancor [blan-cor'], *m.* **blancura** [bland-coo'-rah], *f.* Whiteness, freedom from color, hoariness. **Blancura del ojo**, *(Vet.)* A white spot or film on the eye.

blancuzco [blan-cooth'-co], *a.* Whitish.

blandamente [blahn'-dah-men-tay], *adv.* Softly, mildly, gently, sweetly, smoothly.

blandeador, ra [blan-day-ah-dor', rah] *m. & f.* Softener.

blandear [blan-day-ar'], *va.* 1. To soften, to render mild. 2. To make one change his opinion. 3. To brandish, to flourish. *-vn.* 1. To slacken, to yield, to be softened, 2. To tread tenderly. 3. **Blandear con otro**, to fall in with another's opinion. *-vr.* To be unsteady, to move from one place to another; to give way. **Blandearse con uno**, to humor somebody.

blandengue [blan-den'-gay], *m.* 1. A soldier, armed with a lance, who defended the limits of the province of Buenos Aires. 2. Soft sort, softie. *-a.* Soft, weak.

blandeo [blan-day'-o], *m.* The good or bad quality of the soil of forests and pasture-lands.

blandicia [blan-dee'-the-ah], *f.* Flattery, adulation.

blandiente [blan-de-en'-tay], *a.* Having a tremulous motion from one side to another.

blandillo, illa [blan-deel'-lyo, -yah], *a. dim.* Somewhat soft.

blandimiento [blan-de-me-en'-to], *m.* Adulation, flattery.

blandir [blan-deer'], *va.* 1. To brandish a sword, pike, lance, etc. 2. To hurtle, to whirl round. 3. To flatter. *-vr.* To quiver, to move tremulously from one side to another.

blando, da [blahn'-do, dah], *a.* 1. Soft pliant, smooth to the touch; cottony; milky; flabby liquid. **Blando al tacto**, soft to the touch. 2. Lithe. 3. *(Met.)* Soft, mild, bland, gentle, grateful, pleasing. **Blando de corazón**, sentimental, tender-hearted. 4. Mild, moderate (tiempo). 5. Soft, effeminate, delicate, not bearing fatigue or labor. 6 Tractable, good-natured, kindly; fair. 7. Tender-mouthed (caballos). **Blando de boca**, tender-mouthed. 8. *(Met.)* Indiscreet, talkative. 9. *(Met.)* Soft. 10 *(Met.)* Fond of women, apt to fall in love. **Hombre blando**, a gentle, mild man.

blandón [blan-done'], *m.* 1. Wax taper with one wick. 2. A large church candlestick, in which wax tapers or flambeaux are placed. 3. Light of the stars.

blandocillo [blan-don-theel'-lyo], *m. dim.* A small candlestick for wax tapers.

blanducho, cha, blandujo, ja [blan-doo'-cho, chah, blan-doo'-ho, hah], *a. (Low.)* Flabby, loose, soft, not firm; flabby, slack (carne).

blandujo [ban-doo'-ho], *a.* Softish.

blandura [blan-doo'-rah], *f.* 1. Softness, litheness. 2. Daintiness, delicacy. 3. *(Met.)* Gentleness of temper, sweetness of address; favor, lenity 4. Lenitive or emollient application 5. Soft, endearing language; blandishing. 6. White paint, used by women. 7. Mild temperature of the air.

blandurilla [blan-doo-reel'-yah], *f.* A sort of fine soft pomatum.

blanduzco [blan-dooth'-co], *a.* Softish.

blanqueación [blan-kay-ah-the-on'], *f.* Blanching, the act of blanching metal before it is coined.

blanqueador, ra [blan-kay-ah-dor', rah], *m. & f.* Blancher, whitener, bleacher.

blanqueadura [blan-kay-ah-doo'-rah], *f.* Whitening, bleaching.

blanqueamiento [blan-kay-ah-me-en'-to], *m. (Obs.)* V. BLANQUEADURA.

blanquear [blan-kay-ar'], *va.* 1. To bleach, to whiten, to blanch, to fleece, to clear. 2. To whitewash (tela). 3. To give coarse wax to bees in winter. **Blanquear cera**, To bleach wax; to launder (dinero). 4. *(Carib.)* To kill (matar); to beat (ganar). *vn.* To go white (volverse blanco): to show white (mostrarse blanco).

blanquecedor [blan-kay-thay-dor'], *m.* An officer employed in the mint to blanch, clean, and polish the coin.

blanquecer [blan-kay-therr'], *va.* To blanch coin, to give gold, silver, and other metals their due colors. V. BLANQUEAR.

blanquecimiento [blan-kay-the-me-en'-to], *m. (Obs.)* V. BLANQUEACIÓN.

blanquecino, na [blan-kay-thee'-no, nah], *a.* Whitish, hoary.

blanqueo [blan-kay'-o], *m.* 1. Whitening, making white or bleaching. 2. Whitewash. **El blanqueo del lienzo** the bleaching of linen.

blanquería [blan-kay-ree'-ah], *f.* 1. Bleaching-place, bleach-field.

blanquero [blan-kay'-ro], *m. (Prov.)* Tanner.

blanqueta [blan-kay'-tay], *f. (Obs.)* Coarse blanket.

blanquete [blan-kay'-tay], *m.* White wash.

blanquilla [blan-keel'-lyah], *f.* 1. Doit, a very small coin. 2. Sort of long yellowish plum. 3. White grape. 4. Blanket, a kind of pear.

blanquillo, lla [blan-keel'-lyo, lya], *a. dim.* Whitish, somewhat white. *-m.* A Californian fish.

blanquimiento [blan-ke-me-en'-to], *m.* Water mixed with salt of tartar and other things, to bleach wax, linen, etc.

blanquinegro [blan-kee-ne'-gro], *a.* White-and-black.

blanquita [blan-kee'tah], *f. (Carib.)* Cocaine.

blanquizal, or **blanquizar** [blan-ke-thahl'], *m. (Agri.)* Whitish clay, pipeclay. V. GREDAL.

blanquizco, ca [blan-keeth'-co, cah], *a.* Whitish.

blao [blah'-o], *a. (Her.)* Azure, faint blue.

blasfemador, ra [blas-fay-mah-dor', rah], *m. & f.* Blasphemer.

blasfemar [blas-fay-mar'], *vn.* 1. To blaspheme. 2. To course, to make use of imprecations.

blasfematorio, ria [blas-fay-mah-to'-re-o, ah], *a.* Blasphemous.

blasfemia [blas-fay'-me-ah], *f.* 1. Blasphemy. 2. Blaspheming. **Decir blasfemias**, to blaspheme.

blasfemo, ma [blas-fay'-mo, mah], *a.* Blasphemous. *-m. & f.* Blasphemer.

blasón [blah-sone'], *m.* 1. Heraldry, blazon, blazonry, drawing or explaining coats of arms. 2. Figures and devices which compose coats of arms or armorial ensigns. 3. Honor, glory. **Hacer blasón**, to blazon, to boast, to bray.

blasonador, ra [blah-so-nah-dor', rah] *m. & f.* Boaster, bragger.

blasonante [blah-so-nahn'-tay], *pa.* Vainglorious; boaster.

blasonar [blah-so-nar']. *va.* 1. To blazon, to draw or explain armorial ensigns. 2. To make a pompous display of one's own merits. **Blasonar del arnés**, to boast of achievements never performed.

blavo, va [blah'-vo, vah], *a.* Yellowish gray and reddish color.

blázer [blah'-thayr], *m.* Blazer.

bledo [blay'-do], *m. (Bot.)* Wild amaranth. **No me importa un bledo**, I don't care a straw. **No vale un bledo**, it is not worth a cent.

blefaritis [blay-fah-ree'-tis], Blepharitis, inflammation of the borders of the eyelids.

blenda [blen'dah], *f. (Miner.)* Blende.

bleno, blino [blay'no, blee'no], *(Zool.)* Hake, blenny.

blenorragia [blay-nor-rah'-heah], *f. (Med.)* Blennorrhagia, a disease.

blindado, da [blin-dah'-do, dah], *a. & m.* Iron-clad, armored; an armored war-vessel; armored-plated; *(Mech.)* Shielded, protected, encased. **Puertas blindadas**, reinforced doors.

blindaje [blin-dah'-hay], *m.* 1. *(Mil.)* Blind, a covering made by the besiegers of a strong place, to protect themselves from the enemy's fire. 2. Armor-plate; *(Tec.)* Shield, protective plating, casing.

blindar [blin-dar'], *va.* To apply plates of armor; to armor; *(Tec.)* to shield.

bloc [bloc'], *m, pl.* Pad, writing pad; calendar pad; notebook; *(Escol.)* Exercise book. **Block de dibujos**, sketching pad. **Block de notas**, pad for notes; (reporter's) notebook.

blocaje [blo-kah-hay], *m. (Dep.)* Tackle; stop; *(Mil.)* Blockade.

blocar [blo-kay-ar'], *va. (Dep.)* To tackle (jugador); to stop (balón), to trap, to catch.

blofear [blo-fay-ar'], *(LAm.) vn.* To boast, to brag.

blonda [blon'-dah], *f.* Broad lace made. of silk, blond lace. **Escofieta de blonda**, Headdress made of silk lace.

blondina [blon-dee'-nah], *f.* Narrow silk lace, narrow blonde lace.

blondo, da [blon'-do, dah], *a.* Flaxen, flaxy, light, having a fair complexion or flaxen hair. 2. *(LAm.)* Soft, smooth, silken (liso); *(CAm.)* Lank; *(Cono Sur. Méx.)* Curly (rizado).

bloque [blo'-kay], *m.* 1. Block (of stone). **Bloque de casas**, block of houses. **Bloque de hormigón**, block of concrete. 2. *(Mech.)* Cylinder block. **En bloque**, *(fig.)* As a whole, without distinction. 3. *(Pol.)* Bloc, group. **El bloque comunista**, the communist bloc. 4. **Bloque de datos** *(Comp.),* data block.

bloquear [blo-kay-ar'], *va.* 1. *(Mil.)* To form a blockade, to obstruct; *(Dep.)* To tackle (jugador); to stop (pelota); *(Rad.)* To jam. **Bloquear una ley en el congreso**, to block a bill in the congress. **Los manifestantes bloquearon las calles**, the demonstrators blocked the streets. **Bloquear un puerto**, *(Naut.)* To blockade a port. 2. *(Mech.)* To block, jam. **El mecanismo está bloqueado**, the mechanism is jammed, the mechanism is stuck. 3. To cut off (aislar). **La inundación bloqueó el pueblo**, the flood cut off the village. 4. *(Aut.)* To brake, to pull up; to lock (volante). 5. *(Com.) (Fin.)* To freeze, block. **fondos bloqueados**, frozen assets. *-vr.* **Boquearse de** *(fig.),* to shut oneself off from, to shield oneself from.

bloqueo [blo-kay-o] *m.* 1. *(Mil.)* Blockade. **Burlar el bloqueo**, to run the blockade. 2. *(Com.) (Fin.)* Freezing, blocking; squeeze. **Bloqueo de fondos**, freezing of assets. 3. **Bloqueo mental**, mental, block.

bluff [bloof'], *m.* Bluff.

blusa [bloo'-sah], *f.* A blouse.

blusón [bloo-sone'], *m.* Smock; *(Mil.)* Jacket.

B.° *m.* 1. *(Fin.)* abr. de **banco** *(Bank.)* 2. *(Com.)* abr. de **beneficiario** (beneficiary).

boa [bo'-ah], *f.* 1. Boa, a large serpent. 2. Boa, tippet.

boaleje [bo-ah-lah'-hay], *m. (Prov.)* Pasturage of black cattle.

boato [bo-ah'-to], *m.* 1. Ostentation, pompous show. 2. Shout of acclamation.

bob [bob], *m.* Bobsleigh.

bobada [bo-bah-'dah], *f.* Silly thing, stupid thing. **Esto es una bobada**, this is nonsense. **Decir bobadas**, to say silly things, talk nonsense. V. BERÍA.

bobalías [bo-bah-lee'-as], *m. (Coll.)* A very stupid fellow, a dolt.

bobalicón, bobazo [bo-bah-le-cone', bo-bah'-tho], *m.* 1. *(aug.)* Great blockhead. 2. Stupid: used commonly in jest, particularly with children.

bobamente [bo-bah-men'-tay], *adv.* 1. Without trouble or care. 2. Foolishly, stupidly. **Está comiendo su renta bobamente**, he spends his income in a foolish manner.

bobarrón, na [bo-bar-rone', nah], *a. (Coll.)* Slightly foolish, a little stupid.

bobatel [bo-bah-tel'], *m. (Coll.)* V. BOBO.

bobático, ca [bo-bah'-te-co, cah], *a.* Silly, foolish, stupid.

bobazo, za [bo-bah'-tho, thah], *a. aug.* Very foolish: often used as an endearing expression.

bobear [bo-bay-ar'] *va.* 1. To act or talk in a foolish and stupid manner. 2. To dally, to fribble. 3. To waste one's time in trifles, to loiter about.

bobería [bo-bay-ree'-ah], *f.* Foolish speech or action; foolery, folly, foolishness. *-l.* Idle conceits.

bóbilis [bo'-be-lis], *adv.* **De bóbilis bóbilis**, *(Coll.)* Without pain or merit; without effort; free; for nothing.

bobillo, illa, ito, its [bo-bee'-lyo, lyah, ce'-to, ce'-tah], *m. & a; f. dim.* A little dolt or fool.

bobillo [bo-bee'-lyo], *m.* 1. Big-bellied jug with one handle. 2. Modesty piece, a frill or lace formerly worn by women around the tucker.

bobina [bo-bee'-nah], *f.* Bobbin, a large sort of spool used in ribbon looms and electrical machines; reel (de cinta); *(Aut. Elec.)* Coil. **Bobina de encendido**, ignition coil.

bobinado [bo-be-nah'-do], *m. (Elec.)* Winding.

bobinadora [bo-be-nah-do'-rah], *f.* Winder, winding machine.

bobinar [bo-be-nar'], *va.* To wind.

bobísimamente [bo-bee'-see-mah-men-tay], *adv.* Most foolishly.

bobo, ba [bo'-bo, bah], *m. & f* 1. Dunce, dolt, fool, mooncalf, silly, stupid; *(Theat.)* clown, funny man. **A los bobos se les aparece la madre de Dios**, fortune favors fools. **Entre bobos anda el juego**, they are well matched. 2. One who is easily cheated. 3. Sort of ruff formerly worn by women. 4. Stage buffoon. 5. *(Orn.)* Booby. **A bobas**, foolishly. *-a.* Ample, large.

bobón, na [bo-bone', nah], *m. & f. aug.* Big dolt, great fool.

boboncillo, lla [bo-bon-theel'-lyo, lyah], *m. & f. dim.* A little dolt.

bobote [bo-bo'-tay], *m. aug.* Great idiot or simpleton.

bobsleigh [bob'-es-lay-e], *m.* Bobsleigh.

boca [bo'-cah], *f.* 1. Mouth. 2. Entrance, opening, hole, nozzle. 3. Muzzle, the mouth of anything: vulgarly, chops. 4. Chops, the mouth of man, in contempt. 5. Bunghole. 6. Pincers with which cray-fish hold something. 7. Thin or cutting part of edge tools. 8. Taste, flavor, relish; one who eats. **Instrumento de boca**, wind-instrument. 9. *(Zool.)* Shrimp. **Boca de escorpión**, caluminator. **Boca de estómago**, pit of the stomach. **Boca de un arma de fuego**, the muzzle of a fire arm. **Boca de lobo**, wolf's mouth. 10. *(Met.)* Dark dungeon. 11. *(Naut.),* mast-hole, lubbers' hole. **Boca de la escotilla**, hatchway. **Boca de río o de puerto**, mouth of a river or of a harbor. **Andar de boca en boca**, to be the talk of the town. **Cerrar or tapar a uno la boca**, to stop one's mouth. **Coserse la boca**, to shut one's mouth. **Boca de oro**, mellifluous tongue. **A boca de jarro**, 1. A hearty draught, drinking without glass or measure. 12. Very near. **Decir alguna cosa con la boca chica**, to offer a thing for mere ceremony's sake. **Andar con la boca abierta**, to go gaping about. **Irse de boca**, to speak much without reflection. **No decir esta boca es mía**, to keep a profound silence. **No tener boca para negar or decir no**, not dare to say no. **Tener buena o mala boca**, to talk well or ill of others. **A boca de invierno**, about the beginning of winter. **Boca arriba**, reversed, upside down, on one's back. **Boca abajo**, face downward. **Boca a boca**, *adv.* by word of mouth. **Boca con boca**, face to face. **A boca llena**, perspicuously, openly. **A pedir de boca**, according to one's desire. **De boca**, verbally; not really; used of boasting or threatening. **Andar en boca de la gente**, to be talked about. **Se me hace la boca agua**, my mouth is watering. **Meter a uno en la boca del lobo**, to put somebody on the spot. **Por la boca muerde el pez**, silence is gold. *-m* Screw, warder.

bocacalle [bo-cah-cahl'-lyay], *f.* Entry, end or opening of a street.

bocacaz [bo-cah-cath'], *m.* Opening left in the weir or dam of a river, sluice, or flood-gate.

bocací, bocacín [bo-cah-thee', bo-cah. theen'], *m.* Fine glazed buckram; crimson calico.

bocada [bo-cah-dah], *f.* A mouthful.

bocadear [bo-cah-day-ar'], *va.* To divide into bits or morsels; to cut up for eating.

bocadico, illo, ito [bo-cah-dee'-co, eel'-lyo, ee'-to], *m. dim.* Small bit or morsel.

bocadillo [bo-cah-dee'-lyo], *m.* 1. Sandwich (emparedado); snack, bite to eat. **Un bocadillo de queso**, a cheese sandwich. 2. Thin, middling sort of linen. 3. Narrow ribbon or lace, tape, gimp.

bocado [bo-cah'-do], *m.* 1. Morsel, a mouthful of food. **Bocado exquisito**, titbit. 2. Gobbet, a mouthful, as much as can be swallowed at once. 3. Modicum, small portion. 4. Bite, a wound made with the teeth. 5. Part of a thing torn off with the teeth or pincers. 6. Poison given in eatables. 7. Bit of a bridle. 8. *(Art.)* Wad of a large cannon. 9. *(Naut.)* The hold of a ship. **Bocado sin hueso**, profitable employment without labor; a sinecure. **Con el bocado en la boca**, immediately after dinner or supper. **Contarle a uno los bocados**, to watch how another eats. **No tener para un bocado**, to be in extreme distress, to be completely broke. 10 Bit, bridle (freno). 11. *(And.)* Poison (veneno). *-pl.* 1. Slices of quinces, apples, pumpkins, etc., made up into conserves. 2. *(Naut.)* Wads of great guns, hawseplugs. **A bocados or bocaditos**, by piecemeals.

bocaina [bo-cah'-ee-nah], *f. (Naut.)* The mouth of a bar.

bocajarro [bo-cah-hah'-rro], *adv. (Mil.)* **A bocajarro**, at close range, point blank. **Decir algo a bocajarro**, to say something straight out.

bocal [bo-cahl'], *m.* 1. Pitcher. 2. Mouth-piece of a wind instrument 3. *(Naut.)* The narrows of a harbor.

bocamanga [bo-cah-mahn'-gah], *f.* 1. That part of a sléeve which is closest to the wrist, cuff, wristband (puño). 2. *(Mex.)* Hole for the head (agujero) (in a cape).

bocamina [bo-cah-me'-nah], *f.* Pithead, mine entrance.

bocana [bo-cah'-nah], *f.* (River) mouth.

bocanada [bo-cah-nah'-dah], *f.* 1. A mouthful of liquor. 2. Whiff, puff of smoke. **Bocanada de gente**, mob, a rout. **Bocanada de viento**, sudden blast of wind. **Echar bocanadas**, to boast of one's valor, noble birth, etc. **Echar bocanadas de sangre**, 1. To throw up mouthfuls of blood. 2. To vaunt of noble blood.

bocarán [bo-cah-rahn'], *m.* Fine sort of buckram.

bocarón [bo-cah-rone'], *m.* Wind chest of an organ; wind trunk.

bocarte [bo-car-tay], *m.* 1. Ore-crusher, stamp, stamp mill. 2. Small sardine.

bocata [bo-cah'-tah], *m. V.* BOCADILLO.

bocateja [bo-cah-tay'-hah], *f.* The last tile of each line on a tiling.

bocatijera [bo-ca-te-hay'-rah], *f.* Socket for the pole of a carriage.

bocaza [bo-cah'-thah], *f. aug. (Coll.)* A large, wide mouth.

bocel [bothel'], *m.* 1. Astragal; a fluted moulding, torus. 2. Fluting-plane, an instrument for fluting mouldings.

bocelar [bo-thay-lar'], *va.* To make fluted mouldings.

bocelete [bo-they-lay'-tay], *m. dim.* Small moulding-plane.

bocelón [bo-thay-lone'], *m. aug.* Large moulding-plane.

boceras [bo-thay'-rahs], *m. & f.* Idiot, fool; bigmouth.

boceto [bo-thay'-to], *m.* A sketch, delineation, cartoon.

bocezar [bo-thay-thar'], *va. (Vet.)* To move lips from one side to another, as horses and other animals do when they eat.

bocín [bo-theen'], *m.* 1. Round piece of bass mat put about the nave of a cart, as a cap of defence. 2. The iron, nozzle. 3. Hub of wheel.

bocina [bo-thee'-nah], *f.* 1. Large trumpet, bugle-horn. **Bocina de cazador**, a huntsman's horn. 2. Hearing trumpet. 3. Automobile horn. 4. *(Cono Sur)* Informer (soplón). 5. *(LAm.)* Ear-trumpet (trompetilla).

bocinada [bo-the-nah'-dah], *f.* Empty boast, rant.

bocinar [bo-the-nar'], *va.* To sound the trumpet, bugle-horn, or huntsman's horn.

bocinazo [bo-the-nah'-tho], *m. (Aut.)* Hoot, toot, blast (of the horn). **Dar el bocinazo**, to grass.

bocinero [bo-the-nay'-ro], *m. & f.* Trumpet or, horn-blower.

bocio [bo'-the-o], *m. (Med.)* Goitre.

bocón [bo-cone'], *m.* 1. *(aug.)* A wide-mouthed person. 2. Braggart, a talkative boaster. 3. *(Carib. Cono Sur)* loud-mouthed; backbiting (chismoso), gossipy; *(Mex.)* Indiscreet.

bocoy [bo-co'-e], *m.* Hogshead.-*pl.* **Bocoyes abatidos**, shooks of hogsheads.

bocudo, da [bo-coo'-do, dah], *a.* Large. mouthed.

bocha [bo'-chah], *f.* 1. Bowl, a wooden ball for playing at bowls. 2. *(Prov.)* Fold or double in clothes. **Juego de las bochas**, the game of bowls.

bochar [bo-char'], *va.* 1. To throw a ball so that it hits another, in the game of bowls. 2. *(Carib. Méx.)* To rebuff, reject. 3. *(Cono Sur)* to fail, to flunk.

bochazo [bo-chah'-tho], *m.* Stroke of one bowl against another.

boche [bo'-chay], *m.* 1. Cherry-pit or chuck-hole. V. BOTE. 2. *(Cono Sur)* Husks, chaff. 3. *(Carib.)* Telling off, dressing down. 4. *(Carib.)* Snub, slight. **Dar boche a uno**, to snub somebody. 5. *(And. Cono Sur)* uproar, din. 6. *(Carib.)* Muddle, mess.

bochinche [bo-cheen'-chay], *m.* 1. Uproar, disorder, tumult 2. *(Sp. Amer.)* Mess, quarrel, gossip. 3. *(And. Carib.)* Piece of gossip. 4. *(Mex.)* Rave up; wild party. 5. *(Mex.)* Seedy bar, dive; local stores. 6. *(Carib.)* Muddle, mess.

bochista [bo-chees'-tah], *m.* A good bowler or player at bowling.

bochorno [bo-chor'-no], *m.* 1. Hot, sultry weather, scorching heat. 2. Blush, flushing, the color of cheeks raised by shame or passion. 3. *(fig.)* Embarrassment, flush, shame; stigma (tacha), dishonor.

bochornoso, sa [bo-chor-no'so, sah], *a.* 1. Shameful, reproachful, causing shame or confusion. **Es un espectáculo bochornoso**, it's a degrading spectacle. 2. Sultry. 3. *(Met.)* Sultry, oppressive; thundery; stuffy.

boda [bo'-dah], *f.* Marriage, nuptials, match, the feast by which it is solemnized, a wedding. **Bodas de diamante**, diamond wedding. **Bodas de oro**, golden-wedding. **Bodas de plata**; silver wedding.

bode [bo'-day], *m.* A he-goat.

bodega [bo-day'-gah], *f.* 1. Wine-vault, a cellar. 2. Abundant vintage or yield of wine. 3. Storeroom, warehouse, magazine. 4. A grocery. 5. *(Naut.)* Hold of a ship. **Bodega de popa**, after-hold. **Bodega de proa**, fore-hold.

bodegón [bo-day-gone'], *m.* 1. Eating-house, or cook's shop. 2. Sign of a cook's shop or eating-house. **¿En qué bodegón hemos comido juntos?** where have we ever eaten together? A rebuke for too much familiarity.

bodegoncillo [bo-day-gon-theel'-lyo], *m. dim.* Low chophouse.

bodegonear [bo-day-go-nay-ar'], *va.* To run from one tippling house to another, to frequent mean eating-houses.

bodegonero, ra [bo-day-go-nay'-ro, rah], *m. & f.* One who keeps a low chophouse or tippling-house.

bodegonista [bo-day-go-nees'-tah], *m. & f.* Still life painter.

bodeguero, ra [bo-day-gay'-ro, rah], *m. & f.* 1. Butler, one who has the care of a cellar. 2. *(Cuba)* Grocer. 3. *(Carib.)* Coarse, common. 2. Wine producer (productor); *(Com.)* owner of wine cellar.

bodeguilla [bo-day-geel'-lyah], *f. dim.* Small cellar or vault.

bodián [bo-de-ahn'], *m.* Sea-fish, resembling a tench.

bodigo [bo-dee'-go], *m.* A small loaf made of the finest flour and presented as an offering in the church.

bodijo [bo-dee'-ho], *m. (Coll.)* Unequal match, a hedge-marriage, performed with little ceremony or solemnity.

bodocal [bo-do-cahl'], *a. (Prov.)* Applied to a kind of black grapes.

bodocazo [bo-do-cah'-tho], *m.* Stroke of a pellet shot from a cross-bow.

bodollo [bo-dol'-lyo], *m. (Prov.)* Pruning-knife, pruning-hook.

bodoque [bo-do'-kay], *m.* 1. Pellet, a small ball of clay shot from a crossbow. 2. Dunce, idiot. **Hacer bodoques**, *(Coll.)* To be reduced to dust, to be dead. 3. *(Mex.)* Badly-made thing. 4. *(CAm. Méx.)* Lump, swelling; lump, ball (bolita).

bodoquera [bo-do-kay'-rah], *f.* 1. Mould in which pellets are formed. 2. Cradle, or that part of the stock of a cross-bow where the pellet is put. 3. Strings with which the cord of a cross-bow is tied.

bodoquero, ra [bo-do-kay'-ro, rah], *a. (Amer.)* Contraband, smuggling.

bodoquillo [bo-do-keel'-lyo], *m. dim.* Small pellet or bullet of clay.

bodrio [bo'-dre-o], *m.* 1. Soup, broken meat, and garden-stuff, given to the poor at the doors of convents. 2. A hash poorly prepared, a medley of broken meat. 3. Piece of trash. **Un bodrio de sitio**, an awful place.

B.O.E. *m. (Esp.)* abr de **Boletín Oficial del Estado.**

boezuelo [bo-ay-thoo-ay'-lo], *m.* Stalking-ox, which serves to screen fowlers engaged in the pursuit of birds.

bofada [bo-fah'-dah], *f.* Ragout or fricassee made of the livers and lungs of animals.

bofe [bo'-fay], *m.* Lung, lights. **Echar el bofe or los bofes**, to strain one's lungs; to labor very closely; to be very anxious.

bofeta [bo-fay'-tah], *f.* **bofetán** [bo-fay. tahn'], *m.* A sort of thin, stiff linen.

bofetada [bo-fay-tah'-dah], *f.* Slap, buffet, box, a blow on the face with the hand. **Dar una bofetada, to hit somebody.** *(Met.)* To treat with the utmost contempt.

bofetón [bo-fay-tone'], *m.* 1. A cuff or violent blow with the hand upon the face. 2. Stage decorations representing folding-doors.

bofetoncillo [bo-fay-ton-theel'-lyo], *m. dim.* A slight box or slap, on the face.

bofía [bo'-fee-ah], 1. *f.* **La bofía**, the cops. 2. *m.* Cop, copper.

bofordo [bo-for'-do], *m. (Obs.)* A short lance or spear. V. BOHORDO.

boga [bo'-gah], *f.* 1. *(Zool.)* Ox-eyed cackerel, mendole. 2. Act of rowing. 3. *(Naut.)* Rower, one who rows: in this sense it is masculine. 4. *(Prov.)* Small knife in the shape of a poinard. 5. Vogue, fashion. V. VOGA. **Boga arrancada**, *(Naut.)* All hands rowing together with all their strength. **Boga larga**, a long stroke. **Dar la boga**, to give the stroke. **Estar en boga alguna cosa**, to be fashionable; to be commonly used.

bogada [bo-gah'-dah], *f.* 1. Rowing stroke. 2. Bucking of clothes with lye.

bogador, ra [bo-gah-dor'], *m. & f.* Rower, oarsman, oarswoman.

bogar [bo-gar'], *vn.* To row. **Bogar a cuarteles**, to row by divisions. **Bogar a sotavento**, to row to leeward. **(Yo bogué**, from *Bogar.* V. verbs in *gar.*)

bogavante [bo-gah-vahn'-tay], *m.* 1. *(Naut.)* Strokesman of a row galley. 2. Lobster of a large size.

Bogotá [bo-go-tah'], *m.* Bogotá.

bogotano, na [bo-go-tah'-no, nah], *a.* Of Bogotá

bohemiano, na, or **bohemo, ma** [bo-ay-me-ah'-no, nah, bo-ay'-mo, mah], *a.* A Bohemian.

bohémico, ca [bo-ay'-me-co], *a.* Belonging to Bohemia or its people.

bohemio, mia [bo-ay'-me-o, ah], *a.* Bohemian, unconventional. *m. & f.* Bohemian, unconventional person.

bohena, boheña [bo-ay'-nah, bo-ay'-'nyah], *f.* 1. V. BOFES. 2. Pork sausages.

bohío [bo-ee'-o], *m.* Indian hut, a humble hut in the West Indies.

bohordo [bo-or'-do], *m.* 1. Blade of flag, a water-plant. 2. Wands, the hollow end of which is filled with sand, which tilters threw at each other in tournaments. 3. (*Bot.*) A scape: flower-peduncle.

boicot [bo-e-cot'], *m. pl.* **Boicots**, boycott.

boicotear [bo-e-co-tay-ahr'], *va.* To boycott.

boicoteo [bo-e-co-tay'-o], *m.* Boycott.

boíl [bo-eel'], *m.* Ox-stall, a stand for oxen. *V.* BOYERA.

boina [bo'-e-nah], *f.* Flat, round woollen cap; beret.

boite [bo'-e-tay], *m.* Discotheque, night club, ballroom.

boj [boh], *m.* 1. Box-tree, boxwood. 2. A boxwood tool, on which shoemakers close their work.

bojar [bo-har'], or **bojear**, *va.* 1. (*Naut.*) To sail round an island or cape and measure its circumference. 2. To scrape off the rough integuments; stains, and moisture of leather. -*vn.* To measure around, to contain.

bojedal [bo-hay-dahl'], *m.* Plantation of box-trees.

bojeta [bo-hay'-tah], *f.* (*Ichth. Prov.*) A kind of herring.

bol [bole], *m.* 1. Bowl. *V.* PONCHERA. 2. Bolo, by apocope. 3. Armenian bole, a red earth, used chiefly by gilders.

bola [bo'lah], *f.* 1 Ball, globe; marble, bolus. **Bola de billar**, billiard ball. **Bola de cristal**, crystal ball. **Bola de nieve**, snow ball. **Bola del mundo**, globe. 2. Game of throwing bullets or bowls. 3. (*Coll.*) Lie, falsehood, humbug, hoax, fib. 4. (*Naut.*) Truck, acorn; a round piece of wood at the end of the ensign staffs and vanes. 5. Blacking for shoes. 6. Basin of the glassgrinder. **Escurrir la bola**, to take French leave, to run away. **No da pie con bola**, he's always wrong. **Bola de jabón**, wash-ball. **Juego de bolas**, bowling-green, bowling-ground; playing marbles. 7. (*Carib.*) **Cambiar la bola**, to change one's mind. (*Cono Sur*) **Dar bola;** take notice. (*LAm.*) **Hacerse bolas**, to get oneself tied up in knots. 8. Slam, grand slam (naipes). 9. Fib, tale (cuento). 10. (*Mex.*) **Una bola de gente**, a crowd of people.

bolada [bo-lah'-dah], *f.* 1. Throw or cast of a ball or bowl. 2. (*Cono Sur*) **bolada de aficionado**, intervention. 3. (*LAm.*) Piece of luck (suerte). 2. (*LAm.*) Fib, lie; (*Mex.*) Joke, witty, comment (chiste). 4. (*Cono Sur*) Titbit, treat (golosina).

bolado [bo-lah'-do], *m.* (*Prov.*) 1. Cake of clarined sugar used in Spain to sweeten water for drinking. 2. (*CAm. Cono Sur, Méx.*) Deal; (*Mex.*) Love affair, flirtation (amorío). 3. (*CAm.*) Clever stroke (billar). 4. (*LAm.*) **¡Hazme un bolado!**, do me a favor!

bolantín [bo-lan-teen'], *m.* Fine sort of packthread.

bolarménico [bo-lar-may'-ne-co], *m. V.* BOL.

bolazo [bo-lah'-tho], *m.* 1. Violent blow with a bowl. 2. (*Cono Sur*) silly remark, piece of nonsense (disparate); false news; fib, lie; mistake, error. **Mandarse un bolazo**, to put one's foot in it. 3. (*LAm.*) **¡Hazme un bolazo!**, do me a favor!

bolchaca, *f.* **bolchaco**, *m.* [bol-chah'-cah, co]. (*Prov.*) Pocket; purse.

bolchevique [bol-chay-vee'kay], *m. & f. & a.* Bolshevik.

bolchevismo [bol-chay-vees'-mo], *m.* Bolshevism.

bolea [bo-lay'-ah], *f.* (*Dep.*) Volley.

boleadoras [bo-lay-ah-do'-rahs], *f. pl.* (*Cono Sur*) Lasso with balls.

bolear [bo-lay-ar'], *vn.* 1. To play billiards for mere amusement. 2. To throw wooden or iron balls for a wager. 3. (*Prov.*) To boast; to lie extravagantly.-*va.* 1. To dart, to launch. 2. (*LAm.*) To hunt (cazar); to catch with (atrapar bolas). 3. (*LAm.*) To reject, blackball (candidato); to sack, fire (obrero). -*vr.* 1. (*Cono Sur*) to rear and fall on its back (caballo); (*Aut.*) to overturn. 2. (*Cono Sur*) To get confused, to get bewildered.

boleo [bo-lay'-o], *m.* The road or place where balls are thrown.

bolera [bo-lay'-rah], *f.* Bowling alley.

bolero [bo-lay'-ro], *m.* 1. Bolero, a Spanish dance and musical rhythm. 2. Bolero, a lady's garment. 3. (*Mex.*) Bootblack. 4. (*CAm. Méx.*) Top hat (chistera). *a.* 1. Truant. 2. Fibbing, lying.

boleta [bo-lay'-tah], *f.* 1. Ticket giving the right of admission to a place. 2. Billet or ticket which directs soldiers where they are to lodge. 3. Voucher or warrant for receiving money or other things 4. (*Prov.*) Small paper with tobacco, sold at chandlers' shops. 4. (*Cono Sur*) **Hacer la bola a uno**, to murder somebody, to knock off somebody.

boletar [bo-lay-ar'], *va.* (*Prov.*) To roll up tobacco in small bits of paper for the purpose of selling them.

boletería [bo-lay-tay-ree'-ah], *f.* (*Amer.*) 1. Box office, ticket office. 2. Gate, takings (recaudación).

boletero [bo-le-tay'-ro], *m.* Ticket agent.

boletín [bo-lay-teen'], *m.* 1. Warrant given for the payment of money. 2. Ticket for the quartering of soldiers. 3. Ticket granting free admittance at a theater or other place of amusement. **Boletín de inscripción**, registration form. 4. Bulletin of news: official military or medical notice. **Boletín facultativo**, medical report. 5. (*Com.*) List, statement. **Boletín de precios**, price list. **Boletín de prensa**, press release.

boleto [bo-lay'-to], *m.* 1. Ticket. **Boleto de ida y vuelta** or **boleto redondo**, Roundtrip ticket. 2. Coupon (quiniela). **Boleto de apuestas**, betting slip.

bolichada [bo-le-chah'-dah], *f.* At one throw, at once. **De una bolichada**, by chance.

boliche [bo-lee'-chay], *m.* 1. Jack, a small bell which serves as a mark for bowl-players: block. 2. All the small fish caught at once in a drag-net near the shore, and the dragnet with which they are caught. **Juego de boliche**, pigeon-holes, a game played on a concave table with a ball; troll-madam. **Boliches**, (*Naut.*) Fore-top bowlines, and top-gallant bowlines. 3. A furnace for lead-smelting. 4. The toy called cup and ball. (*And. Cono Sur*) Small grocery shop (tienda); (*Cono Sur*) cheap snack bar; (*And.*) Low-class bakery; (*Cono Sur*) gambling den (garita). 5. (*LAm.*) Bolivian.

bolichero, ra [bo-le-chay'-ro, rah], *m. & f.* One who keeps a pigeon-hole; small shopkeeper.

bólido [bo'-le-do], *m.* 1. Meteorite, shooting-star. 2. (*Aut.*) Racing car, hot rod; (*hum.*) Car. **iba como un bólido**, he was really shifting.

bolígrafo [bo-lee'-grah-fo], *m.* Ballpoint pen.

bolillo [bo-leel'-lyo], *m.* 1. Dim. of BOLO. 2. Jack, a small ball. 3. Bobbin, a small pin of box or bone used in making bone-lace. 4. Mould or frame on which the cuffs of linen or gauze, worn on the sleeves of counsellors of state, are starched and made up. 5. Bone joined to skull of horses. 6. (*LAm.*) (*Mus.*) Drumstick. 7. (*Mex.*) (*Culin.*) Bread roll. *pl.* 1. Paste-nuts, small balls made of sweet paste.

bolín [bo-leen'], *m.* Jack, a small ball which serves as a mark for bowl-players. **De bolín, de bolán**, (*Coll.*) At random, inconsiderately, rashly, thoughtlessly.

bolina [bo-lee'-nah], *f.* 1. (*Coll.*) Noise and clamor of a scuffle or dispute. 2. (*Naut.*) Bowline, a rope fastened to the leech or edge of a square-sail, to make it stand close to the wind. 3. A kind of punishment on shipboard like baqueta, or the gantlet. **Bolina de barlovento**, weather bowline. **Bolina de sotavento o de revés**, lee bowline. **Bolina de trinquete**, forebowline. **Dar un salto a la bolina**, to ease or check the bowline. **Navegar de bolina**, to sail with bowlines hauled. **Ir a la bolina**, to sail with a side wind. **Navío buen bolinador**, a good player, a ship which makes great progress against the wind. **Echar de bolina**, (*Met.*) to make fanfaronades, or idle boasts.

bolinear [bo-le-nay-ar'], *va.* To haul up the bowline in light winds.

bolinete [bo-le-nay'-tay], *m.* (*Naut.*) A movable capstan on deck, in which the whipstaff moves.

bolisa [bo-lee'-sah], *f.* (*Prov.*) Embers, hot cinders.

bolita [bo-le'-tah], *f.* 1. Small ball; pellet; (*Cono Sur*) marble (canica). 2. (*Cono Sur*) ballot paper.

bolívar [bo-le'-vahr], *m.* Bolivar (Venezuelan unit of currency). **No verle la cara a Bolívar**, to be broke.

Bolivia [bo-le'-ve-ah], *f.* Bolivia.

boliviano, na [bo-le-ve-ah'-no], *a. m. & f.* Bolivian.

bolla [bol'-lyah], *f.* 1. Duty on woollens and silks retailed for home consumption formerly levied in Catalonia. 2. In South America, great richness of an ore.

bollar [bol-lyar'], *va.* 1. To put a leaden seal on clothes to indicate their place of manufacture. 2. To emboss, to raise figures.

bollería [bol-lyay-re'-ah], *f.* Baker's, bakery, pastry shop.

bollero, ra [bol-lyay-ro, rah], *m. & f.* Pastry-cook, seller of sweet cakes.

bollo [bol'-lyo], *m.* 1. Small loaf or roll made of fine flour. 2. Small cookie or cake made of sugar, flour, milk, and eggs. 3. Bruise made in metal or any similar matter. 4. Morbid swelling. 5. **Bollos**, ancient headdress of women, consisting of large buckles. 6. In Peru, bars of silver extracted from the ore by means of fire or quicksilver. **Bollos de relieve**, embossed or raised work. 7. *(fig.)* Confusion; mix-up. **meter a uno en el bollo**, to get somebody in trouble. 8. *(CAm. Cono Sur)* punch (puñetazo). 9. *(And.)* **Bollos**, troubles. 10. *(CAm. Carib.)* Cunt (vagina).

bollón [bol-yone'], *m.* 1. Brass-headed nail used in coaches and furniture. 2. *(Prov.)* Button which shoots from a plant, especially from a vine-stock. 3. Button earring.

bollonado, da [bol-lyo-nah'-do, dah], *a.* 1. Adorned with brass-headed nails. 2 Furnished with shoots, buds, or buttons.

bolo [bo'-lo], *m.* 1. One of the ninepins set up to be knocked down by a bowler. 2. *(Prov.)* Round or oblong cushion on which women make lace. 3. Large piece of timber, in which the shafts and rests of a winding staircase are fitted. 4. Idiot, stupid. 5. Bolus, a very large pill. 6. The game of ninepins or tenpins. 7. A large knife, like a machete, used in the Philippines. **Es un bolo**, he is an idiot, an ignorant, stupid fellow. **Juego de bolos**, a game of nine-pins. *(And.)* **Andar en bolos**, to be naked. *(Carib.)* **Ir en bolos**, to run off. **Echar a rodar los bolos**, *(fig.)* to create a disturbance. 8. *(Med.)* Large pill. 9. *(Carib. Méx.)* One-peso coin; (Ven.) one-bolívar coin. 10. Slam (cartas). 11. *(Mex.)* Christening present (regalo).

bolo [bo'-lo], *a. (CAm.)* Drunk, plastered (borracho).

bolonio [bo-lo'-ne-o], *m.* An ignorant rattle-brained fellow.

bolsa [bol'-sah], *f.* 1. Purse. 2. Pursenet made of silk or worsted, with strings to draw the mouth together. 3. Money. 4. Exchange, the place where merchants meet to negotiate their affairs. **Bolsa de trabajo**, labor exchange. **Precio en la bolsa**, price on the stock exchange. V. LONJA. 5. Pouch or net used by sportsmen to put game in. 6. Bag in which public papers and despatches are carried by ministers and secretaries of state. 7. Bag for the hair. 8. Bag lined with furs or skins to keep the feet warm. 9. In a gold-mine, the vein which contains the purest gold: a pocket. 10. *(Med.)* A morbid swelling full of matter. 11. *(Anat.)* Scrotum. **Bolsa de pastor**, *(Bot.)* shepherd's-purse. **Bolsa rota**, spendthrift. **Tener or llevar bien cerrada la bolsa**, to have the purse well lined; to have money. **Bolsa de agua caliente**, hot-water bottle. **Bolsa de compra**, shopping bag. **Bolsa de herramientas**, toolbag. **Bolsa de patatas fritas**, packet of potato chips. **Bolsa de té**, tea bag. 12. *(Cos.)* Bag. **Hacer bolsa**, to bag. 13. *(Mil.)* Pocket.

bolsear [bol-say-ar'], *vn. (Prov.)* To purse up, to pucker: applied to clothes, hangings, and other things.

bolsería [bol-say-ree'-ah], *f.* Manufacture of purses, and the place where they are sold.

bolsero [bol-say-ro], *m.* 1. *(Obs.)* Cashier, treasurer 2. Manufacturer of purses, one who makes purses.

bolsico [bol-see'-co], *m.* Pocket.

bolsillo [bol-see'-lyo], *m.* 1. Purse. 2. Pocket. 3. Money. 4. *Dim.* of BOLSO. **Guardar algo en el bolsillo**, to put something in one's pocket. **Meterse a uno en el bolsillo**, to win somebody over. **Rascarse el bolsillo**, to pay up, to fork out. 5. **De bolsillo**, pocket *(atr.)*, Pocket size. **Edición de bolsillo**, pocket edition.

bolsín [bol-seen'], *m.* Gathering of brokers out of the stock exchange and the hours observed there.

bolsista [bol-sees'-tah], *m.* Stookbroker, speculator.

bolso [bol'-so], *m.* Purse of money, a money-bag. **Bolso de mano, bolso de mujer**, handbag, purse. **Bolso de viaje**, traveling bag.

bolsón [bol-sone'], *m.* 1. *Aug.* of BOLSO Large purse. 2. Large bar of iron put in vaults or arches to secure the building. 3. In oilmills, large plank or board with which the oil-reservoir is lined. 4. Stone on which an arch or vault is sprung. 5. *(Mex.)* Lagoon (lago). 6. *(And.)* Fool. -*a.* 1. *(And.)* Silly, foolish. 2. *(Carib. Méx.)* Lazy (perezoso).

bomba [bom'bah], *f.* 1. Pump, pumping engine. 2. Bomb; shell, bomb shell. 3. Lamp chimney. 4. Earthen jar for skimming oil from water. ¡**Bomba!** your attention, please. **Bomba atómica**, atomic bomb. **Bomba de alimentación**, feed pump. **Bomba de apagar incendios**, fire engine. **Bomba de cadena** or **de rosario**, chain pump. **Bomba de circulación**, circulating pump. **Bomba de cobalto**, cobalt pump. **Bomba de compresión, de impelente**, force pump. **Bomba de fragmentación**, fragmentation pump. **Bomba de fuego** or **de vaho**, steam engine. **Bomba de guimbalete**, *(Naut.)* common pump. **Bomba de hidrógeno**, hydrogen bomb. **Bomba de mano**, hand pump. **Bomba de proa**, head pump. **Bomba de profundidad**, depth charge. **Bomba de vacío**, vacuum pump. **Bomba de vapor**, steam engine. **Bomba incendiaria**, incendiary bomb. **Bomba inyectora**, injection pump. **Bomba or manga marina**, water spout. **Bomba neutrona**, neutron bomb. **Cargar la bomba**, to prime the pump. **Estar a prueba de bomba**, to be bomb-proof. **La bomba está atascada**, the pump is clogged. 5. *(fig.)* surprise; bombshell, surprising item of news; great success. **Es la bomba del año**, it's the surprise of the year. 6. Shade; glass, globe (de lámpara). 7. *(And.)* Soap bubble. 8. *(Carib.)* Big drum (tambor). 9. *(And. Carib.)* Balloon (globo); *(Carib. Cono Sur)* Round kite. 10. *(Carib. Méx.)* Top hat. 11. *(And. CAm, Cono Sur)* drinking spree; drunkenness (embriaguez). 12. *(LAm.)* False rumor; lie; *(Carib..)* Piece of news. 13. *(Carib. Cono Sur)* gas station. 14. *(Comp.)* "**Bomba lógica**", "logic bomb". -*a.* 1. Sensational. **Noticia bomba**, shattering piece of news. 2. *(And.)* **Estar bomba**, to be clapped out. -*adv.* **Pasarlo bomba**, to have a grand time.

bombacho [bom-bah'-chos], 1. *a. (LAm.)* Baggy, loose-fitting. 2. *m. (Mex.)* Baggy trousers.

bombardear [bom-bar-day-ar'], *va.* To bombard, to discharge bombs; to shell.

bombardeo [bom-bar-day'-o], *m.* Bombardment, bombing, **bombardeo aéreo**, air raid, air bombing. **Bombardeo en picado**, dive bombing.

bombardero [bom-bar-day'-ro], *m.* 1. Bomber (plane). 2. Bombardier. -*a.* Bombing.

bombardino [bom-bar-dee'-no], *m.* Saxhorn.

bombasí [bom-bah'-see'], *m.* Bombazine, dimity, fustian.

bombazo [bom-bah'-tho], *m.* Report of a bursting bomb.

bombear [bom-bay-ar'], *va.* To shell. 1. 2. To pump (líquido). 3. *(Cos.)* To pad. 4. *(fig.)* To praise up, inflate the reputation of. 5. *(Cono Sur)* To sabotage, wreck; *(Univ.)* to fail, flunk. 6. *(And.) (Hist.)* To spy on; to reconnoitre. 7. *(CAm.)* To steal. -*vn.* 1. *(CAm. Méx.)* To screw, to fuck (copularse). 2. *(Carib.)* To get drunk (emborracharse). -*vr. (Arquit.)* To camber; to wrap, to bulge. V. BOMBARDEAR.

bombeo [bom-bay'-o], *m.* 1. Pumping (bomba). 2. *(Arquit.)* Camber; warping, bulging; crown (of the road).

bombero [bom-bay'-ro], *m.* 1. Fireman. **Cuerpo de bomberos**, fire brigade. 2. Howitzer.

bombilla [bom-beel'-lyah], *f.* 1. *(Amer.)* A small silver or gold perforated tube for drinking Mate. 2. *(Elec.)* Light bulb. **Bombilla de flash**, flash bulb. 3. *(Mex.)* Ladle (cuchara).

bombillo [bom-beel'-lyo], *m.* 1. Lamp chimney. 2. Water-closet trap. 3. Small pump. 4. Tube to draw off liquids. 5. *(Carib. And. CAm.)* light bulb.

bombín [bom-been'], *m.* 1. Bowler hat (sombrero). 2. *(Cono Sur)* pump, bicycle pump.

bombo [bom'-bo], *m.* 1. Large drum. **Hacer algo a bombo y platillos**, to make a great song and dance about something. **Tengo la cabeza hecha un platillo**, I've got a splitting headache. 2. Player on bass drum. 3. *(Naut.)* Barge or lighter. 4. Ballyhoo, excessive praise. **Darse el bombo mutuo**, to indulge in mutual backslapping. 5. *(Carib.)* Bowler hat (sombrero). 6. *(Cono Sur)* **irse al bombo**, to come to grief, to blow it. *(Cono Sur)* **mandar a uno al bombo**, to knock somebody off. 7. **Estar con bombo**, to be in the family way. *a.* 1. Astonished. 2. *(Cuba and Amer.)* Tepid. 3. *(Mex.)* Bad, off (carne).

bombón [bom-bon'], *m,* 1. Chocolate. 2. Beauty, gem (objeto); peach (chica), smasher. 3. Gift (chollo).

bombona [bom-bo'-nah], *f.* Carboy. **Bombona** (de gas), canister, cylinder.

bombonaje [bom-bo-nah'-hay], *m.* A screw-pine (sombreros de paja).

bombonera [bom-bo-nay'-rah], *f.* Sweet box (caja para dulces); sweet can (lata para dulces). 2. Cosy little place (lugar).

bombonería [bom-bo-nay-re'-ah], *f.* Sweetshop, confectioner's (shop).

bonachón, na [bo-nah-chone', nah], *m. & f. & a.* Good-natured, easy person.

bonaerense [bo-nah-ay-ren-say], *m. & f.* Native or resident of Buenos Aires, Argentina.

bonancible [bo-nan-thee-blay], *a.* Moderate, calm, fair, serene: applied to the weather at sea.

bonanza [bo-nahn'-thah], *f.* 1. Fair weather at sea. **ir en bonanza**, *(Naut.)* to sail with fair wind and weather. 2. Prosperity, success. **ir en bonanza**, *(Met.)* To go on prosperously, to do well.

bonaso [bo-nah'-so], *m.* Bonasus, a kind of buffalo.

bonazo, za [bo-nah-tho, thah], *a. (Coll.)* Good-natured, kind.

bondad [bon-dahd'], *f.* 1. Goodness, either moral or physical; excellence, healthfulness. 2. Goodness, kindness, good-will, graciousness, clemency; frankness, courtesy, suavity, or madness of temper. **Tener la bondad de**, to be so kind as to. **Tenga la bondad de no fumar**, please do not smoke. 3. Liberality.

bondadoso, sa [bon-dah-do'-so, sah], *a.* Kind, generous, beautiful V. BENÉVOLO.

bonetas [bo-nay'-tas], *f. pl. (Naut.)* Bonnets, pieces of canvas laced to the sails to make more way in light winds.

bonete [bo-nay'-tay], *m.* 1. Bonnet or cap used by clergymen, collegians, and doctors or professors of the universities. 2. Secular clergyman who wears a bonnet, in contradistinction to a monk who wears a hood or cowl. 3. Bonnet, a kind of outworks of a fortress. **Tirarse los bonetes**, to pull caps. **Bravo or gran bonete A** great dunce. 4. *(Obs.)* Widemouthed vial for conserves. 5. Second stomach, reticulum, of ruminants. 6. *(CAm. Méx.)* Not on your life!, no way. **A tente bonete**, insistently.

bonetería [bo-nay-tay-ree'-ah], *f.* Shop where bonnets are made or sold.

bonetero, ra [bo-nay-tay'-ro, rah], *m. & f.* 1. Bonnet maker. 2. *(Bot.)* Prickwood, gatheridge, or common spindletree.

bonetillo [bo-nay-teel'-lyo], *m.* 1. *(Dim.)* Small cap or bonnet. 2. Ornament in the shape of a bonnet, which women wear over their headdress.

boniato (BUNIATO or MONIATO) [bo-ne-ah'-to], *m.* A sweet potato.

bonico, ca [bo-nee'-co, cah], *a.* Pretty good, passable. **Andar a las bonicas**, *(Met.)* To take things easily, to do them at ease, not to burden oneself with business. **Jugar a las bonicas**, to play at ball by passing it from one hand into another.

bonificación [bo-ne-fe-cah-the-on'], *f. (Com.)* Allowance, discount, bonus; allowance of points.

bonificar [bo-ne-fe-car'], *va.* 1. *(Obs.)* To credit, to place to one's credit. 2. To meliorate, to improve. *-vr.* To improve.

bonijo [bo-nee'-ho], *m.* The pit of the olive after having been crushed in the mill.

bonillo, illa [bo-neel'-lyo, lyah], *a. dim.* 1. Somewhat handsome. 2. Somewhat great, or big.

bonísimo, ma [be-nee'-se-mo, mah], *a. sup.* of BUENO.

bonitamente [bo-ne-tah-men'-tay], *adv.* Nicely, neatly, craftily. *(Coll.)* V. BONICAMENTE.

bonito [bo-nee'-to], *m.* Sea-fish, resembling a tuna. (Pacific Ocean) Striped tuna.

bonito, ta [bo-nee'-to, tah], *a.* 1. Dim of BUENO. Pretty good, passable. Nice-looking; handsome. **Bonito como un sol**, as pretty as a picture. **Una bonita cantidad**, a nice tidy sum. 2 Affecting elegance and neatness. 3 Pretty. 4. Graceful, minion. 5. Soft, effeminate. 6. *(Cono Sur)* Well, nicely. **Ella canta bonito**, she sings nicely. **Se te ve bonito**, it looks good on you.

bono [bo'-no], *m. (Com.)* Bond, certificate. **Bono alimenticio**, food stamp. **Bono del estado**, government bond.

bono-bus [bo-no-boos'], *m, pl. (Esp.)* Bus pass.

bonzo [bon'-tho], *m.* Bonze, a priest of Buddha in China, Japan, and other heathen nations.

boñiga [bo-nyee'-gah], *f.* Cow-dung, horse dung.

boom [boom], *m.* Boom. **Dar boom a un problema**, to exaggerate a problem.

boomerang [boo-may-rahn'], *m, pl.* **Boomerangs**, boomerang.

bootes [bo-o'-tes], *m.* Bootes, a northern constellation.

boqueada [bo-kay-ah'-dah], *f.* Act of opening the mouth, a gasp. **A la primera boqueada**, immediately, without delay. **La última boqueada**, the last gasp.

boquear [bo-kay-ar'], *vn.* 1. To gape, to gasp, to open the mouth wide. 2 To breathe one's last, to expire. 3. *(Met.)* To end to terminate. *-va.* To pronounce, to utter a word or expression.

boquera [bo-kay'-rah], *f.* 1. Sluice made in a canal for irrigating lands 2. *(Prov.)* Opening made in inclosures to let in cattle. 3. Lip sore, mouth ulcer. 4. Ulcer in the mouth of beasts. *-m.* Screw, warder.

boquerón [bo-kay-rone'], *m.* 1. Wide opening, a large hole. 2. *(Zool.)* Anchovy. 3. *(Naut.)* Mouth of a channel between shallow bottoms.

boquete [bo-kay'-tay], *m.* Gap, narrow entrance.

boquiabierto, ta [bo-ke-ah-be-err'-to, tah], *a. (Coll.)* Gaping, having the mouth open; walking about gaping. **Estar boquiabierto**, to stand open-mouthed.

boquiancho, cha [bo-ke-ahn'-cho, chah], *a.* Wide-mouthed.

boquiangosto, ta [bo-ke-an-gos'-to, tah], *a.* Narrow-mouthed.

boquiconejuno na [bo-ke-co-nay-hoo'-no, nah], *a.* Rabbit-mouthed; harelipped (caballos).

boquiduro, ra [bo-ke-doo'-ro, rah], *a.* Hard-mouthed (caballos).

boquifresco, ca [bo-ke-fres'-co, cah], *a.* Fresh-mouthed; applied to horses which have a soft salivous mouth; outspoken; cheeky.

boquifruncido, da [bo-ke-froon-thee' do, dah], *a.* Having the mouth contracted.

boquihendido, da [bo-ke-en-dee'-do, dah], *a.* Large-mouthed, flewed.

boquihundido, da [bo-ke-oon-dee'-do, dah], *a.* Having the mouth sunk in, from age or toothlessness.

boquilla [bo-keel'-lyah], *f.* 1. *(Dim.)* Little mouth. 2. Opening of breeches at the knees. 3. Opening in a canal for irrigating lands. 4. Chisel for mortising. 5. Mouth-piece of a musical wind instrument. 6. Cigar holder. 7. *(Mas.)* Verge, course. 8. *(Mech.)* Bushing, bush. 9. Bomb-hole. 10. *(Cos.)* Trouser bottom. **Boquilla de filtro**, filter tip. **Hablar de boquilla**, to talk out of the side of one's mouth. 11. *(And.)* Rumor, piece of gossip. 12. **Promesa de boquilla**, insincere promise.

boquín [bo-keen'], *m.* Coarse sort of balize.

boquirroto, ta [bo-keer-ro'-to, tah], *a.* Loquacious, garrulous.

boquirrubio, bia [bo-keer-roo'-be-o, ah], *a.* Simple, artless, easily imposed upon. 2. Talkative (gárrulo); indiscreet, loose-tongued.

boquita [bo-kee'-tah], *f. dim.* Small mouth.

borácico, ca [bo-rah'-the-co, cah], *a.* Boracic. V. BÓRICO.

borato [bo-rah'-to], *m.* Borate.

bórax [bo'-rax], *m.* Borax; sodium biborate.

borbollar, borbollonear [bor-bol-lyar'], *vn.* To bubble out, to stream or to gush out, to flash.

borbollón, borbotón [bor-bol-lyone', bor-bo-tone'], *m.* 1. Bubbling, gushing up of water in large bubbles, flash 2. *(Met.)* Flow of language hastily and incorrectly uttered. **A borbollones**, in a bubbling or impetuous manner, in hurry and confusion. **Hirviendo a borbollones** or **a borbotones**, boiling hot.

borbónico, ca [bor-bo'-ne-co, cah], *a.* Bourbon.

borborigno [bor-bo-reeg'-mo], *m.* Rumbling in the bowels.

borbotar [bor-bo-tar'], *vn.* To gush out with violence; to boil over, to bubble (burbujas).

borceguí [bor-thay-gee'], *m.* 1. Buskin, a kind of half-boot. 2. Laced shoes.

borceguinería [bor-thay-gee-nay-ree'-ah], *f.* A shop where buskins are made or sold.

borceguinero, ra [bor-thay-gee-nay'-ro, rah], *m. & f.* Maker or retailer of buskins.

borcellar [bor-thel-lyar'], *m. (Prov.)* Brim of a vessel.

borda [bor'-dah], *f.* 1. *(Prov.)* Hut, cottage. 2. *(Naut.)* Gunwale of a ship. **Motor fuera de borda**, outboard motor. **Echar algo por la borda**, to throw something overboard. 3. *(Naut.)* Mainsail (vela).

bordada [bor-dah'-dah], *f. (Naut.)* Board, tack. **Dar una bordada**, to tack, to make a tack.

bordadillo[bor-dah-deel'-lyo], *m.* Double-flowered, taffeta.

bordado [bor-dah'-do], *m.* Embroidery. **Bordado de pasado**, plain embroidery, without light or shade.-*pp* of BORDAR.

bordador, ra [bor-dah-dor', rah], *m. & f.* Embroiderer.

bordadura [bor-dah-doo'-rah], *f.* 1. Embroidery; variegated needlework.

bordage [bor-dah'-hay], *m. (Naut.)* Side planks of a ship.

bordar [bor-dar'], *va.* 1. To embroider. 2. To perform a thing according to art. **Baila que lo borda**, he dances charmingly. **Bordar a tambor**, to tambour, to embroider with a tambour needle.

borde [bor'-day], *m.* 1. Border, the outer edge. 2. Margin, the edge of a thing; verge, fringe. **Borde de la acera**, kerb. **Borde del camino, de la carretera**, roadside, verge. 3. Ledge, a rising or projecting ridge. 4. Hem of a garment. 5. Brim of a vessel. 6. Bastard child. 7. Shoot or bud of a vine. 8. Board the side of a ship. **A borde**, On the brink; on the eve. 9. *(fig.)* **Estar al borde de una crisis nerviosa**, to be on the verge of a nervous breakdown. **Estar en el mismo borde del desastre**, to be on the very brink of disaster. -*a.* Wild, savage, uncultivated: applied to trees not ingrafted or cultivated. -*a.* 1. Anti-social; difficult, bad tempered (persona). 2. Illegitimate (niño). 3. *(Bot.)* Wild.

bordear [bor-day-ar'], *vn.* 1. *(Naut.)* To ply to windward. 2. To skirt, to go along (seguir el borde de). 3. To border on; to flank; *(fig.)* To verge on. 4. *(Cono Sur)* **Bordear un asunto**, to skirt round (avoid) a subject. 5. *(Cono Sur)* to border, line. **Los árboles bordean el camino**, trees line the road.

bordo [bor'-do], *m.* 1. Border, the outer edge. 2. Ship or vessel. **Fue a bordo**, *(Naut.)* He was aboard ship. 3. Board the side of a ship. **Bordo con bordo**, board and board, side by side: when two ships are close to each other. **Bordo sobre bordo**, hank for hank: when two ships tack together, and ply to windward. **Bordo a la mar**, to stand off. 4. *(Naut.)*

Board, tack. **Bordo corto**, a short board. **Bordo largo**, a long board. **Buen bordo**, a good board. **Dar bordos**, *(Naut.)* 1. To tack. 2. *(Met.)* To go frequently to and fro. 5. *(Cono Sur)* raised furrow; *(CAm.)* Peak, summit.

bordón [bor-done'], *m.* 1. Jacob's staff, a pilgrim's staff. 2. Bass-string. 3. Bass of an organ. 4. Repetition of words in a discourse. 5. Refrain of a song. 6. *(Met.)* Staff, guide, or support of another. 7. **Bordones**, *(Naut.)* Shores, outriggers. 8. *(And. CAm.)* Youngest son.

bordoneado, da [bor-do-nay-ah'-do, dah], *a. (Her.)* Pommelled.-*pp.* of BORDONEAR.

bordonear [bor-do-nay-ar']; *vn.* 1. To try the ground with a staff or stick. 2. To strike with a staff or cudgel. 3. To rove or wander about, to avoid labor. 4. To play well on the thorough bass. 5. *(Aer.)* To buzz.

bordonería [bor-do-nay-ree'-ah], *f.* Vicious habit of wandering idly about, on pretence of devotion.

bordonero, ra [bor-do-nay'-ro, rah], *m. & f.* Vagrant, vagabond, tramp.

bordura [bor-doo'-rah], *f. (Her.)* V. BORDADURA.

Boreal [bo-ray-ahl'], *a.* Boreal, northern **Boreas** [bo'-ray-as], *m.* Boreas, the north wind.

Borgoña [bor-go'-nyah], *f.* Burgundy wine. Burgundy, the district.

borgoñota [bor-go-nyo'-tah], *f.* Sort of ancient helmet. **A la borgoñota**, in the Burgundy fashion.

bórico, ca [bo-re-co, cah], *a.* Boric.

borinqueño, ña [bo-ren-kay'-nyo, nyah], *a. & m. & f.* Puerto Rican.

borla [bor'-lah]. *f.* 1. Tassel, bunch of silk, gold, or silver lace. 2. Tuft, lock, flaunt. 3. In universities, doctor's bonnet decorated with a tassel. 4. Doctorship. 5. Powder staff (de empolvarse).

borlilla [bor-leel'-lyah], *f.* Anther.

borlón [bor-lone'], *m.* 1. *(aug.)* Large tassel. 2. Napped stuff, made of thread and cotton yarn.

borne [bor'-nay], *m.* 1. The end of a lance. 2. Kind of oak tree. 3. *(Elec.)* Terminal.

borneadero [bor-nay-ah-day'-ro], *m. (Naut.)* Berth of a ship at anchor, swinging berth.

borneadizo, za [bor-nay-ah-dee'-tho, thah], *a.* Pliant, flexible.

bornear [bor-nay-ar'], *va.* 1. To bend, turn, or twist. 2. *(Arch.)* To model and cut pillars all round. **Bornear la verdad**, to comment, to explain or expound. **Bornear las palabras**, to turn words into different senses. 3. *(Mex.)* To spin, turn (pelota). -*vn.* 1. To edge, to sidle. 2. To warp, to turn. **El navío bornea**, *(Naut.)* The ship swings or turns round her anchor. -*vr.* To warp, bulge.

borneo [bor-nay'-o], *m.* 1. Act of turning or winding a thing. 2. *(Naut.)* Swinging round the anchor. 3. Twisting, bending (torcer).

bornera [bor-nay'-rah], *a.* Applied to a blackish sort of millstone.

bornero, ra [bor-nay'-ro, rah], *a.* Ground by a black millstone: applied to wheat.

borní [bor-nee'], *m. (Orn.)* Lanner, a kind of falcon.

boro [bo'-ro], *m.* Boron, one of the chemical elements.

borona [bo-ro'-nah], *f.* 1. A sort of grain resembling Indian corn. 2. Bread made from this grain. 3. *(LAm.)* Crumb (migaja).

boronía [bo-ro-nee'-ah], *f.* Dish made of chopped apples, pumpkins, and green peppers. V. ALBORONÍA.

borra [bor'-rah], *f.* 1. Yearling ewe. 2. The thickest part of the wool. 3. Goat's hair. 4. Nap on the cloth; floss, burl. 5. Tax on sheep. 6. Lees sediment, waste. 7. Refined borax. **Borra de castor**, beaver's hair. **Borra de lana**, flock wool, waste wool. **Borra de seda**, floss silk, waste silk. 8. Empty talk (charla insustancial); trash, basura.

borracha [bor-rah'-chah], *f. (Coll.)* Leather bag or bottle for wine.

borrachear [bor-rah-chay-ar'], *vn.* To be drunk often.

borrachera, borrachería [bor-rah-chay'-rah, bor-rah-chay-ree'-ah], *f*. 1. Drunkenness, hard-drinking. **Quitarse la borrachera**, to sober up, get rid of one's hangover. 2. Revelry; drunken feast, wassail. 3. *(Met.)* Madness, great folly.

borrachero [bor-rah-chay'-ro], *m*. A shrub of South America: the seed ingested causes delirium.

borrachez [bor-rah-cheth'], *f*. 1. Intoxication, drunkenness. 2. Perturbation of the judgment or reason.

borrachín [bor-rah-cheen'], *m*. Drunkard, sot, toper.

borracho, cha [bor-rah'-cho, chah], *a*. 1. Drunk, intoxicated. **Estar más borracho que una cuba**, to be as drunk as a Lord. 2. *(Met.)* Inflamed by passion. 3. Applied to cookie baked with wine. 4. Applied to fruits and flowers of a violet color. 5. *(Esp.)* **Es un negocio borracho**, it's a real money-spinner, it's money for old rope.

borrachón, borrachonazo [bor-rah-chone', bor-rah-cho-nah'-tho], *m. aug*. Great drunkard, a tippler.

borrachuela [bor-rah-choo-ay'-lah], *f*. *(Bot.)* Ray-grass: its seeds, mixed with breadcorn, intoxicate.

borrador [bor-rah-dor'], *m*. 1. Rough draft of a writing in which corrections are made. 2. Waste-book of merchants, blotter. 3. Eraser (para borrar).

borraja [bor-rah'-hah], *f*. *(Bot.)* Borage.

borrajear [bor-rah-hay-ar'], *vn*. To scribble, to write carelessly on any subject.

borrajo [bor-rah'-ho], *m*. *(Prov.)* V. RESCOLDO.

borrar [bor-rar'], *va*. 1. To cross out, to strike out. 2. To blot with ink, to efface. 3. To blur, to erase, to rub out, obliterate. 4. To cause to vanish. 5. *(Met.)* To cloud, to darken, to obscure. **Borrar la plaza**, to abolish a place or employ. 6. To eliminate, dispose of. **Eliminar a uno de una lista**, to cross somebody off a list. *-vr*. To resign (from a club, etc.). *(Comp.)* To wipe out.

borrasca [bor-rahs'-cah], *f*. 1. Storm, tempest, violent squall of wind. 2. Barren rock. **Dar o caer en borrasca**, in the mines, a mine that yields nothing, unprofitable. 3. *(Met.)* Hazard, danger, obstraction. 4. Orgy, spree.

borrascoso, sa [bor-ras-co'-so, sah], *a*. Stormy, boisterous, gusty, tempestuous.

borregada [bor-ray-gah'-data], *f*. Large flock of sheep or lambs.

borrego, ga [bor-ray'-go, gah], *m. & f.* 1. Lamb not yet a year old. 2. *(Met.)* Simpleton, a soft, ignorant fellow. **No hay tales borregos**, *(Coll.)* there is no evidence of its truth, there is not such a thing. 3. *(Carib.)* Con, hoax (trampa); *(Mex.)* Lie, tall story (mentira). *-m.pl.* Fleecy clouds (nubes); white horses, foamy crests of waves.

borreguero [bor-ray-gay'-ro], *m*. Shepherd who tends lambs.

borreguito [bor-ray-gee'-to], *m. dim.* Little lamb.

borrén [bor-ren'], *m*. A saddlecloth; saddle; bolster, straw cushion.

borriba [bor-ree'-bah], *f*. Engine for raising water.

borrica [bor-ree'-cah], *f*. 1. A she-ass. 2. Stupid woman. V. BORRICO.

borricada [bor-re-cah'-dah], *f*. 1. Drove of asses. 2. Procession on asses. 3. *(Met.)* Silly or foolish word or action.

borrico [bor-ree'-co], *m*. 1. Ass, donkey. 2. Fool. 3. Trestle-horse of carpenters. **Es un borrico**, he can bear great labor and fatigue.

borricón, borricote [bor-re-cone', bor-re-có-tay], *m*. 1. *(aug.)* Large jackass. 2. *(Met.)* Plodder, dull, heavy, and laborious man. 3. Among sawyers, horse, a frame on which timber is sawed.

borrilla [bor-reel'-lyah], *f*. 1. The downy matter enveloping fruits. 2. Shearing or flue cut from clothes.

borriqueña, ña [bor-re-kay'-nyo, nyah], *a*. Asinine.

borriquero [bor-re-kay'-ro], *m*. One who keeps or tends asses.

borriquete de proa [bor-re-kay'-tay], *m*. *(Naut.)* Fore-topmast.

borriquillo, illa; ito, ita [bor-re-keel'-lyo, lyah, bor-re-kee'-to, tah], *m. & f dim.* a little ass.

borriquillos [bor-re-keel'-lyos], *m. pl.* Cross-bars of a table-frame.

borro [bor'-ro], *m*. 1. Wether not two years old. 2. *(Coll.)* Dolt, of slow understanding. 3. Duty laid on sheep.

borrón [bor-rone'], *m*. 1. Blot of ink on paper, blur. 2. Rough draft of a writing. 3. First sketch of a painting. **Estos borrones**, these humble jottings. 4. Blemish which tarnishes or defaces. 5. Stigma, slur. **Hacer borrón y cuenta nueva**, to wipe the slate clean (and start again).

borronear [bor-ro-nay-ar'], *va*. 1. To sketch. 2. To waste paper by scribbling on it.

borroso, sa [bor-ro'-so, sah], *a*. 1. Full of dregs and lees: turbid, thick, muddy. 2. Done in a bungling manner. **Letra borrosa**, letter badly written, and full of blots and corrections.

borroso [bor-ro'-so], *m*. *(Prov.)* Bungler, a petty mechanic.

borrufalla [bor-roo-fahl'-yah], *f*. *(Coll. Prov.)* Bombast, a pompous show of empty sounds or words.

borujo [bo-roo'-ho], *m*. Lump, pressed mass, packed mass. V. ORUJO.

borujón [bo-roo-hone'], *m*. Knob, protuberance; *(Med.)* Bump, lump.

borusca [bo-roos'-cah], *f*. Withered leaf. V. SEROJA.

bosar [bo-sar'], *va*. 1. To run over, to overflow. 2. To vomit. 3. *(Met.)* To utter lofty words.

boscaje [bos-cah'-hay], *m*. 1. Boscage, cluster of trees, grove. 2. *(Pict.)* Boscage, landscape.

boscoso [bos-co'-so], *a*. Wooded.

bósforo [bos'-fo-ro], *m*. Bosphorus, channel by which two seas communicate.

bosque [bos'-kay], *m*. Wood, tract of land planted with trees and brushwood: forest, grove; any woody place.

bosquecillo [bos-kay-theel'-lyo], *m. dim.* Small wood, a coppice, a knoll covered with trees.

bosquejar [bos-kay-har'], *va*. 1. To make a sketch of a painting. 2. To design or project a work without finishing it. 3. To explain a thought or idea in a rather obscure manner 4. To make a rough model of a figure; or *basso-relievo*, in clay, plaster, or any soft substance.

bosquejo [bos-kay'-ho], *m*. 1. Sketch of a painting. 2. Any unfinished work. 3. Unfinished writing or composition. **Estar en bosquejo**, to be in an unfinished state.

bosquete [bos-kay'-tay], *m*. An artificial grove, small wood.

bosquimano [bos-ke-mah'-no], *m*. Bosquimano, African bushman.

bosta [bos'-tah], *f*. Dung, droppings; manure.

bostar [bos-tar'], *m*. Ox-stall, or stand for oxen.

bostezar [bos-tay-thar'], *vn*. To yawn, to gape, to oscitate.

bostezo [bos-tay'-tho], *m*. Yawn, yawning, oscitation.

bota [bo'-tah], *f*. 1. Small leather wine-bag. 2. Butt or pipe, to contain wine or other liquids. 3. Boot. **Botas de campaña**, top boots. **Botas de esquí**, ski boots. **Botas de goma**, gumboots. **Botas de fútbol**, football boots. 4. *(Naut.)* Water-cask. **Bota fuerte;** jackboot, a wide, strong boot. **Morir con las botas puestas**, to die in harness. **Ponerse las botas**, to strike it rich (enriquecerse), to get a lot of something. **Cotes de botas**, Bootlegs.

botadero [bo-tah-day'-ro], *m*. *(And. Méx.)* Ford; *(LAm.)* Rubbish dump (vertedero).

botado [bo-tah'-do], *a*. 1. Cheeky (descarado). 2. *(CAm.)* Spendthrift (gastador). 3. *(And.)* Resigned, ready for anything. 4. *(CAm.)* Dirt cheap. 5. *(CAm. Méx.)* Blind drunk (borracho). *m*. **Botada** *f. (LAm.)* Abandoned child, foundling.

botador [bo-tah-dor'], *m*. 1. Driver, one who drives. 2. Punch, an instrument for driving out nails. 3. Nail set. 4. Crow's bill or pelican, used by dentists to draw teeth. 5. *(Naut.)* Starting-pole used to shove off a boat from the shore, boathook. 6. *(Mech.)* Furnace-bar, fire-iron; bolt-driver. 7. *(Med.)* Retractor. 8. *(LAm.)* Spendthrift.

botadura [bo-tah-doo'-rah], *f. (Naut.)* Launching. *(LAm.)* V. BOTADA.

botafuego [bo-tah-foo-ay'-go], *m.* 1. Linstock, a staff with a match at the end of it, used by gunners in firing cannons. 2. An irritable, quick-tempered person.

botagueña [bo-tah-gay'-nyah], *f.* Sausage made of pigs' haslets.

botal [bo-tahl'], *a.* 1. *(Anat.)* **Agujero botal or de botal,** foramen ovale, formerly called botale foramen, an opening between the two auricles of the heart of the foetus. 2. *(Arch.)* Arched buttress.

botalón [bo-tah-lone'], *m. (Naut.)* Boom, a pole used in setting up studding or stay-sails. **Botalón de foque,** Jibboom. **Botalones,** fire-booms.

botana [bo-tah'-nah], *f.* 1. Plug or stopple used to stop up the holes made on the leather bags to carry wine. 2. *(Coll.)* Cataplasm or plaster put on a wound 3. *(Low.)* Scar remaining after a wound is healed.

botánica [bo-tah'-ne-cah], *f.* Botany, the science treating of plants.

botánico, ca [bo-tah'-ne-co, cah], *a.* Botanic, botanical.

botánico, botanista [bo-tah'-ne-co, bo-tah-nees'-tah], *m.* Botanist.

botanoancia [bo-tah-no-mahn'-the-ah], *f.* Botanomancy, superstitious divination by herbs.

botantes [bo-tahn'-tes], *m. pl. (Naut.)* Shores, outriggers.

botar [bo-tar'], *va.* 1. To cast, to throw, to fling, to launch. 2. To bound, to rebound. 3. To squander, to misspend. **Le botaron de su trabajo,** they sacked him from his job. 4. *(Naut.)* To shift the helm. **Botar al agua alguna embarcación,** *(Naut.)* to launch a ship. **Botar en vela,** to fill the sails. 5. *(LAm.)* To lose. -*vn.* 1. To bounce (pelota); *(Aut.)* To bump, to bounce, jolt; to buck, to rear (caballo). **Está que bota,** he's hopping mad. 2. **Botar a babor** *(Naut.),* to put over to port. 3. *vr. (Cono Sur)* to change jobs.

botaratada [bo-tah-ra-tah'-dah], *f.* A blustering, thoughtless action; wild thing.

botarate [bo-ta-rah'-tay], *m.* 1. *(Coil.)* Madcap, thoughtless, blustering person. 2. *(LAm.)* Spendthrift.

botarel [bo-tah-rel], *m. (Arch.)* Buttress, a mass of stone which supports the spring of arches or valuts; abutment, spur, counter pillar.

botarga [bo-tar'-gah], *f.* 1. Sort of wide breeches formerly worn, gaskins. 2. Motley dress of a harlequin. 3. Harlequin, buffoon. 4. Kind of large sausages. 5. *(Prov.)* V. DOMINGILLO.

botavante [bo-tah-vahn'-tay], *m. (Naut.)* Pike used by seamen to defend themselves against an enemy who attempted to board.

botavara [bo-tah-vah'-rah], *f. (Naut.)* 1. A small boom or pole which crosses the sail of a boat in a diagonal direction, gaff, sprit. 2. Boat-hook. **Botavara de cangreja,** gaffsail boom.

bote [bo'-tay], *m.* 1. Thrust with a pike, lance, or spear. 2. Rebound or bound of a ball on the ground. **De bote y boleo,** instantly. **Dar un bote,** to jump. **Darse el bote;** to beat it. 3. Gallipot, a small glazed earthen vessel. 4. Canister, a tin vessel for tea, coffee, etc. **Bote de tabaco,** snuff canister. **Bote de basura** *(Mex.),* dustbin. **Bote de humo,** smoke bomb. **Estar en el bote,** it's in the bag. 5. *(Naut.)* Boat. **Bote de pasaje,** ferryboat. **Bote de remos,** rowing boat. **Bote patrullero,** patrol boat. **Bote salvavidas,** lifeboat. **Bote de pescar,** fishingboat. **Estar de bote en bote,** to be full of people. **De bote y voleo,** instantly. -*pl.* 1. In places where wool is washed, heaps of wool piled separately. 2. Frolicsome bounds of a horse.

botecico, illo, ito [bo-tay-thee'-co, eel'-yo, ee'-to], *m. dim.* 1. Small canister. 2. Skiff.

botella [bo-tel'-lyah], *f.* 1. Bottle, flask; also the liquor contained in a bottle. **Hemos bebido tres botellas,** we drank three bottles. **Cerveza de botella,** bottled beer. 2. *(Carib.)* Sinecure, soft job (in government.).

botellazo [bo-tayl-lye-ah'-tho], *m.* A blow with a bottle.

botellero [bo-tayl-lay'-ro], *m.* Wine rack.

botellín [bo-tay-lyeen'], *m.* Small bottle, half bottle.

botellón [botel-lyone'], *m.* A demijohn.

botepronto [bo-tay-pron'-to], *m. (Dep.)* Half-volley.

botequín [bo-tay-keen'], *m. (Naut.)* Cog, a small boat.

botero [bo-tay'-ro], *m.* 1. One who makes leather bags and bottles for wine. 2. Boatman, wherryman.

botica [bo-tee'-cah], *f.* 1. Apothecary's shop; pharmacy, drugstore. 2. Potion given to a sick person. 3. Shop in general. 4. Furnished house or lodging.

boticario [bo-te-cah'-re-o], *m.* Pharmacist, druggist, apothecary.

botiguero [bo-te-cay'ro], *m. (Prov.)* Shopkeeper.

botija [bo-tee'-hah], *f.* 1. Earthen jug. **Botija para aceite,** an oil-jar. 2. Fat person. **Estar como una botija,** to be as fat as a sow. **Poner a uno como botija verde** *(LAm.),* to call somebody every name under the sun. 3. *(CAm. Carib.)* Buried treasure. -*m. & f. (Cono Sur)* baby, child.

botijero [bo-te-har'-ro], *m.* One who makes or sells jars.

botijo [bo-tee'-ho], *m.* 1. An earthen jar. 2. *(Met.)* A plump little child.

botijón [bo-te-hone'], *m.* 1. *(aug.)* A large earthen jar. 2. A plump little child. -*a. (Mex.)* Potbellied.

botillería [bo-teel-lyay-ree'ah], *f.* 1. Ice-house, where iced creams, jellies, etc., are prepared or sold. 2. *(Naut.)* Steward's room and stores. 3. Ancient war tax.

botillero [bo-teel-lyar'-ro], *m.* 1. One who prepares or sells iced liquids and jellies. 2. *(Mex.)* Shoemaker, cobbler.

botillo [bo-teel'-lyo], *m. dim.* A small wine-bag, a leather bottle.

botín [bo-teen'], *m.* 1. Buskin, a half-boot formerly worn by stage-players. 2. Spatterdash; leggings. 3. Booty taken by soldiers; excoriation. 4. *(Naut.)* Lashing.

botina [bo-tee'-nah], *f.* A gaiter, high shoe.

botinero [bo-te-nar'-ro], *m.* 1. A soldier who takes care of and sells the booty. 2. One who makes and sells gaiters.

botinico, illo, ito [bo-te-nee'-co, eel'-lyo, ee'-to], *m. dim.* A little gaiter or spatterdash.

botiquería [bo-te-kar-ree'-ah], *f.* Perfumer's shop.

botiquín [bo-te-keen'], *m.* 1. First aid kit. 2. Medicine chest (in a bathroom, etc.) 3. *(Carib.)* Drinks; cupboard.

boto, ta [bo'-to, tah], *a.* 1. Blunt, round at the point. 2. *(Met.)* Dull of understanding.

botón [bo-one'], *m.* 1. Sprout, bud, or gem put forth by vines and trees in the spring. 2. Button, of wood or bone. **Botón de metal dorado or plateado,** a gilt or plated button. 3. *(Fen.)* Tip of a foil. 4. Button or knob of doors or windows. **Botón de cerradura,** the button of a lock. **Botón de contacto,** push-button. **Botón de arranque,** starter, starting switch. 5. Annulet of balusters, and also of keys, serving for ornament 6. Piece of wood which fastens a fowling-net. 7. Crank-pin. 8. Dowel. 9. Handle, knob (cerraduras). **Botón de fuego,** cautery in the form of a button. **Botón de oro,** *(Bot.)* Creeping double flowered crow-foot. **Botón del ratón** *(Comp.),* mouse button.

botonadura [bo-to-nah-doo', rah], *f.* Set of buttons for a suit of clothes.

botonar [bo-to-nahr'], *(LAm.)* 1. *va.* To button. 2. *vn.* To bud, sprout.

botonazo [bo-to-nah'-tho], *m. (Fen.)* Thrust given with a foil.

botoncito [bo-ton-thee'-to], *m. dim.* A small button.

botonería [bo-to-nay-ree'-ah], *f* Button-maker's shop.

botonero, ra [bo-to-nay'-ro, rah], *m. & f.* Button-maker; button-seller.

botones [bo-to'-nees], *m. pl.* Bellboy.

bototo [bo-to'-to], *m.* Gourd or calabash to carry water. *(Amer.)*

botulismo [bo-too-lees'-mo], *m.* Botulism.

bou [bo'-oo], *m.* A joint casting of a net by two boats, which separate and bring up the haul.

boutique [boo-teek'], *f.* Boutique.

bóveda [bo'-vay-dah], *f.* 1. Arch or vault. 2. Vault, cave or cavern, a subterraneous habitation. **Bóveda de cañón,** barrel vault. 3. Vault for the dead in churches. **Bóveda de jardín,** Bower.

bovedar [bo-vey-dar'], *va. (Obs.)* To vault or cover with arches. *V.* ABOVEDAR.

bovedilla [bo-vay-deel'lyah], *f.* A small vault in the roof of a house. **Bovedillas,** *(Naut.)* Counters, arched part of a ship's poop. **Subirse a las bovedillas,** *(Met.)* To be nettled, to be in a passion; to go up the wall.

bovino, na [bo-vee'-no, nah], *a.* Belonging to cattle.

box [box]. *m.* **boxes** *pl.* Stall (de caballo); pit (en carreras de coches); *(CAm. Carib.)* Post office box. *(LAm.)* Boxing.

boxeador [boc-say-ah-dor], *m.* Boxer.

boxear [boc-say-ar'] *vn.* To box.

boxeo [boc-say'-o], *m.* Boxing.

boxer [boc'-sayr], *m.* Boxer (dog).

boxeril [boc-say-reel'], *a. (Cono Sur)*, **boxítisco** *a.* Boxing.

boya [bo-yah], *f.* 1. *(Naut.)* Float for a net or submerged rope; beacon, buoy. 2. Butcher. 3. Hangman, executioner. **Boya de barril,** nun-buoy. **Boya cónica,** canbuoy. **Boya de palo,** wooden buoy. **Boya de cable,** cable-buoy. **Echar afuera la boya a la mar,** to stream the buoy.

boyada [bo-yah'-dah], *f.* Drove of oxen.

boya [bo-yahl'], *a.* Relating to cattle: applied generally to pasture-grounds where cattle are kept.

boyante [bo-yahn'-tay], *pa.* Buoyant, floating. *-a.* 1. *(Naut.)* Light, sailing well (barcos). 2. *(Met.)* Fortunate, successful.

boyar [bo-yar'], *m. (Naut.)* To buoy, to be afloat (barcos).

boyazo [bo-yah'-tho], *m. aug.* 1. Large ox. 2. *(CAm. Cono Sur)* Punch.

boyé [bo-yay'], *m. (Cono Sur)* Snake.

boyera, boyeriza [bo-yay'-rah, bo-yay-ree'-thah], *f.* Ox-stall, ox-house, cowhouse, a stand for oxen.

boyero [bo-yay'-ro], *m.* Oxherd, cattle shed, oxdriver, cowherd.

boyezuelo [bo-yay-thoo-ay'-lo], *m. dim.* A young or small ox.

boyuno, na [bo-yoo'-no, nah], *a.* Belonging to cattle; bovine.

boza [bo-thah], *f. (Naut.)* One end of a rope made fast in a bolt-ring, till the other brings the tackle to its place. **Bozas,** *(Naut.)* Stoppers, short ends of cables used to suspend or keep something in its place. **Bozas de la uña del ancla,** shank-painter. **Bozas de cable or cubiertas,** cable-stoppers. **Bozas de combate or de las vergas,** the stoppers of the yards. **Bozas de los obenques,** the stoppers of the shrouds.

bozal [bo-thahl'], *m.* 1. Muzzle worn by horses, dogs, and calves. 2. A temporary headstall for a horse.

bozal [bo-thal'], *a.* 1. Novice, inexperienced in trade or business. 2. Stupid, foolish. 3. Wild, not broken in (caballos).

bozo [bo'-tho], *m.* 1. Down, which precedes the beard. 2. Head-stall of a horse. 3. Mouth, lips.

brabante [brah-bahn'-tay], *m.* Brabant or Flemish linen.

brabera [brah-bay'-rah], *f.* Airhole, ventilator.

bracamonte [Brah-cah-mon'-tay], *m. (And.)* Ghost.

braceada [brah-thay-ah-dah], *f.* Violent extension of the arms.

braceaje [brah-thay-ah'-hay], *m.* 1. Coinage, the art and act of coining money. 2. Act of beating the metal for coining in the mint. 3. *(Naut.)* Bracing of the yards. Depth of water 4. Brewing.

bracear [brah-thay-ar'], *vn.* To move or swing the arms. *-va.* 1. *(Naut.)* To brace. **Bracear las vergas,** to brace the yards. 2. To measure by fathoms. 3. To brew.

bracero [brah-thay'-ro], *m.* 1. Day-laborer. 2. A strong-armed man.

bracete [brah-thay'-tsy], *adv.* **De bracete,** arm in arm.

bracillo [brah-theel'-lyo], *m.* Branch of the mouth-bit of a horse's bridle.

Bracmán [brac-mahn'], *m.* Brahmin, a Hindu priest.

braco, ca [brah'-co, cah], *a.* 1. Pointing or setting: applied to a pointer. 2. Broken-nosed, flat-nosed. *-m. & f.* A pointer-dog.

bráctea [brahc'-tay-ah], *f. (Bot.)* Bract.

bractéola [brahc-tay'-o-lah], *f.* Bractlet.

bredipepsia [brah-de-pep'-se-ah], *f.* Bradypepsia, slow digestion.

brafonera [brah-fo-nay'-rah], *f.* 1. Piece of ancient armor for the arm. 2. In clothes, a roller which girded the upper part of the arms; a plaited sleeve.

braga [brah'-gah], *f. (Prov.)* 1. Child's diaper. 2. **Bragas,** gaskins, a kind of wide breeches; breeches in general; hose. 3. *(Mil.)* Breeching, lashing-rope. **Calzarse las bragas;** to wear the pants (mujeres). **Coger a uno en bragas,** to catch somebody with his pants down.

bragada [brah-gah'-dah], *f.* 1. The flat of the thigh in beasts. 2. Elbow, throat. **Bragada de una curva,** *(Naut.)* the throat of a knee. **Madera de bragada,** compass-timber.

bragado, da [brah-gah'-do, dah], *a.* 1. Having the flanks of a different color from the rest of the body (animales). 2. *(Met.)* Ill-disposed, of depraved sentiments. 3. Energetic, tough; wicked, vicious.

bragadura [brah-gah-doo'-rah], *f.* 1. Part of the human body where it begins to fork, crotch. 2. Fork of a pair of breeches. 3. Flat of the thigh in beasts, from the flank to the trough.

bragazas [brah-gah-thas], *f. pl.* 1. *(aug.)* Wide breeches. 2. *m. (Met.)* A person easily persuaded or ruled: generally applied to a hen-pecked husband.

braguero [brah-gay'-ro], *m.* 1. Truss, bandage for a rupture, brace. 2. **Braguero de cañón,** *(Naut.)* breeching of a gun, with which it is lashed to the ship's side. **Braguero de una vela,** bunt of a sail. 3. Piece put into clothes to make them stronger.

bragueta [brah-gay'-tah], *f.* Pants fly. **Estar como bragueta de fraile,** *(Cono Sur)* to be very solemn. **Ser hombre de bragueta,** to be a real man.

braguetazo [brah-gay-tah'-tho], *m. aug.* **Dar braguetazo,** *(Coll.)* to marry a rich woman.

braguetero [brah-gay-tay'-ro], *a.* 1. Lecherous, randy (lascivo). 2. *(LAm.)* Who marries for money. *m.* Lecher, womanizer.

braguillas [brah-geel'-lyas], *m.* 1. Boy wearing long pants for the first time. 2. *(Coll.)* Brat, little whippersnapper.

braguita(s) [brah-gee'-tahs], *f.* Panties.

Brahma [brah'mah], *f.* Brahma, a deity of the Hindus.

brahmán, or **brahmín** = BRACMAN.

brahminismo [brah-me-nees'-mo], *m.* Brahminism, the religious system of the Brahmins.

brahón [brah-on'], *m.* A fold which, in ancient apparel, surrounded the upper part, of the arm.

brama [brah'-mah], *f.* Rut, the season of copulation of deer and other wild animals.

bramadera [brah-mah-day'-rah], *f.* 1. Rattle. 2. Call or horn used by shepherds to rally and conduct the flock. 3. Horn used by keepers of vineyards and olive plantations, to frighten away cattle.

bramadero [brah-mah-day'-ro], *m.* 1. Rutting-place of deer and other wild animals. 2. *(LAm.)* Tethering, post.

bramador, ra [brah-mah-dor', rah], *m. & f.* 1. Roarer, brawler, a noisy person. 2. *(Poet.)* Inanimate things, emitting a sound like roaring or groaning

bramante [brah-mahn'-tay], *m.* 1. Packthread, a strong thread made of hemp. 2. Bramant or brabant, a linen so called. **Bramante blanco,** white bramant. **Bramante crudo,** unbleached bramant. 3. Roaring. 4. Twine, string.

bramar [brah-mar'], *vn.* 1. To roar, to groan, to bellow. 2. *(Met.)* To roar, to storm, to bluster, to be boisterous (viento, mar). 3. *(Met.)* To fret, to be in a passion, to be sorely vexed, to cry.

bramido [brah-mee'-do], *m.* 1. Cry uttered by wild beasts. 2. Clamor of persons enraged. 3. Tempestuous roaring of the elements.

bramil [brah-meel'], *m.* Chalk-line used by sawyers to mark the place where timbers are to be cut.

bramín [brah-meen'], *m. V.* BRACMÁN.

bramo [brah'-mo], *m.* Shout, cry. *(Slang.)*

bramona [brah-mo'-nah], *f.* **Soltar la bramona,** to break out into injurious expressions, to use foul language: chiefly applied to gamblers.

branca [brahn'-cah], *f.* 1. Gland of the throat. 2. Point. *Brancas,* Claws, talons, etc.

brancada [bran-cah'-dah], *f.* Dragnet or sweep net, used at the mouth of rivers or in arms of the sea.

brancaursina [bran-cah-oor-see'-nah], *f. (Bot.)* Bear's breech, brank-ursine.

branchas [brahn'-chas], *f. pl.* Gills of a fish.

brandales [bran-dah'-les], *m. pl. (Naut.)* Backstays. **Brandales del mastelero de gavia,** the maintop backstays. **Brandales volantes,** shifting backstays.

brandís [bran-dees'], *m.* Great coat used formerly. **Brandises,** collars of ladies' nightgowns.

brando [brahn'-do], *m.* Tune adapted to a dance.

brano [brah'no], *m. V.* ESTAMENTO.

branquia [brahn'-kee-ab], *f.* The gill of a fish or other aquatic creature.

branquiado, da [bran-ke-ah'do, dah], *a.* Gillbreathing, branchiate.

branquial [bran-keahl'], *a.* Branchial, relating to gills.

branquifero, ra [bran-kee'-fay-ro, rah], *a.* Gillbearing

branza [brahn'-thah], *f.* Staple or ring to which the chains of galley slaves were fastened.

braña [brah'-nyah], *f. (Prov.)* 1. Summer pasture. 2. Dung, withered leaves, and other remains of fodder, found on summer pasture grounds.

braquial [brah-ke-ahl'], *a.* Brachial, belonging to the arm.

braquiceros [brah-ke-thay'-ros], *m. pl.* The brachycera, a suborder of the diptera, having short antennae.

braquigrafía [brah-ke-grah-fee'-ah], *f.* Brachygraphy, the art of writing in short-hand.

braguigrafo [brah-kee'-grah-fo], *m.* Brachygrapher, a shorthand writer.

braquillo, lla [brah-keel'-lyo, lyah], *m. & f. dim.* Small pointer.

braquiocefálico [brah-ke-o-thay-fah'-le-co], *a.* Brachycephalic, in relation with the arm and the head.

brasa [brah'-sah], *f.* Live coal; burning wood that has ceased to flame; redhot coal or wood. **Estar hecho a la brasa,** grilled. **Ir, correr or pasar como gato por brasas,** to run as light as a cat on burning coals. **Estar hecho unas brasas,** to be all in a blaze; redfaced.

braserito [brah-say-ree'-to], *m. dim.* A small pan to hold coals; a chafing-dish.

brasero [brah-say'-ro], *m.* 1. Brazier, a pan to hold coals. 2. Firepan. 3. Place where criminals were burnt. 4. Hearth, fireplace. *(Mex.)*

Brasil [brah-seel'], *m.* 1. *(Bot.)* Braziletto. 2. Brazilwood, used by dyers. 3. Rouge, a red paint used by ladies. 4. Brazil.

brasilado, da [brah-se-lah'-do, dah], *a.* Of a red or Brazilwood color; ruddy.

brasileño, ña [brah-se-lay'-nyo, nyah], *a.* Brazilian.

brasilete [bra-se-lay'-tay], *m.* Jamaica-wood, braziletto, an inferior sort of Brazilwood.

brasilina [bra-se-lee'nah], *f.* Brazilin, a red coloring matter from Brazilwood.

brasmología [bras-molo-he-ah'], *f.* The science which treats of the flux and reflux of the sea.

braulis [bra-hoo'-lis], *f.* Cloth or stuff, with white and blue stripes, which comes from the coast of Barbary.

brava [brah'-vah], *f.* 1. *(Naut.)* Heavy swell of the sea. 2. *(Mex.)* Row, fight (disputa). 3. **A la brava tendrás que ir,** you'll have to go whether you like it or not. 4. *(Carib.)* **Dar una brava a,** to intimidate.

bravada [brah-vah'-dah], *f. V.* BRAVATA.

bravamente [bra-vah-men'-tay], *adv.* 1. Bravely, gallantly. 2. Cruelly, inhumanly, barbarously. 3. Finely, extremely well. 4. Plentifully, copiously. **Hemos comido bravamente,** we have made a hearty dinner.

bravata [brah-vah'-tah], *f.* Bravado, boast, or brag, braggardism, an arrogant menace, impudent sally, intended to frighten and intimidate.

bravato, ta [brah-vah'-to, tah], *a.* Boasting, impudent.

braveador, ra [brah-vay-ah-dor', rah], *m. & f.* Bully, hector.

bravear [brah-vay-ar'], *vn.* 1. To bully, to hector, to menace in an arrogant manner. 2. To applaud, shout bravo.

bravera [brah-vay'-rah], *f.* Vent or chimney of ovens, wind. *V.* SUSPIRALES. 1. Bravery, valor. 2. Vigor. 3. Ferocity. 4. Fury of the elements.

bravero [brah-vay'-ro], *(Carib.)* 1. *a.* Bullying. 2. *m.* Bully.

braveza [brah-vay'-tha], *f.* 1. Ferocity, savageness; *(met.)* Fury, violence. 2. Bravery.

bravillo, illa [brah-veel'-lyo, lyah], *a. dim.* Rather wild, not yet tamed.

bravío, vía [brah-vee'-o, ah], *a.* 1. Ferocious, savage, wild, untamed. 2. Wild, propagated by nature, not cultivated (plantas). 3. Coarse, unpolished (modales).

bravío [brah-vee'-o], *m.* Fierceness or savageness of wild beasts.

bravo, va [brah'-vo, vah], *a.* 1. Brave, valiant, strenuous, manful, hardy, fearless. 2. Bullying, hectoring. 3. Savage, wild, fierce (animales). 4. *(Met.)* Severe, untractable. 5. *(Met.)* Rude, unpolished, uncivilized, angry. **Ponerse bravo con uno,** to get angry with somebody. 6. Sumptuous, expensive. 7. Excellent, fine. **Brava cosa,** Very fine indeed! **Mar bravo,** swollen sea. **¡Bravo!** *int.* Bravo!. 8. *(LAm.)* Hot, strong (picante). -*m.* Thug.

bravonel [brah-vo-nel'], *m. (Obs.)* Brave, a hector.

bravosidad [brah-vo-se-dahd'], *f. (Obs.) V.* GALLARDIA.

bravucón, na [bra-voo-cone', nah], *a.* Boastful, braggart.

bravuconada [bra-voo-co-nah'-dah], *f.* 1. Bluster (cualidad), boastfulness. 2. Boast (acto); boasting, bragging.

bravura [brah-voo'-rah], *f.* 1. Ferocity, fierceness (animales). 2. Courage, manliness (personas). 3. Bravado, boast, brag.

braza [brah'-thah], *f.* 1. Fathom, a measure of six feet. 2. *(Naut.)* Brace which is tied to the yards. **Brazas,** *(Naut.)* Braces, ropes belonging to the yards of a ship. **Afirmar las brazas de barlovento,** to secure the weatherbraces. 3. **Braza de pecho,** breast stroke. **Braza de mariposa,** butterfly stroke (natación).

brazada [brah-thah'-dah], *f.* 1. Movement of the arms out and up. 2. Armful. **Brazada de pecho,** crawl stroke (natación). 3. Stroke (remo). 4. *(LAm.) (Naut.)* Fathom.

brazado [brah-thah'-do], *m.* An armful. **Un brazado de leña,** an armful of firewood. **Un brazado de heno,** a truss of hay.

brazaje [brah-thah'-hay], *m.* 1. *(Naut.)* Number of fathoms, depth of water. 2. *V.* BRACEAJE.

brazal [brah-thahl'], *m.* 1. Brachial muscle. 2. Bracer, ancient piece of armor for the arms. 3. Bracelet. 4. *(Prov.)* Ditch or channel from a river or canal, to irrigate lands. 5. Bracer, a wooden instrument for playing balloons. 6. *(Naut.)* Rail. **Brazales de proa,** headrails. **Brazal de medio de proa,** the middle rail of the prow.

brazalete [brah-thah-lay'-tay], *m. (Vul.* BRACELETE) 1. Armlet, bracelet. *V.* MANILLA, PULSERA. 2. Bracelet, ancient iron piece of armor. **Brazaletes,** *(Naut.)* Brace pendants.

brazazo [brah-thah'-tho], *m. aug.* Large or long arm.

brazo [brah-tho], *m.* 1. Arm, anatomically from the shoulder to the elbow. By extension, arm of a lever, of a balance beam; each half of a yard. etc. 2. The correlative limb in some of the inferior creatures. 3. *(Met.)* Bough of a tree. 4. *(Met.)* Valor, strength, power. 6. Each end of a beam or balance. **Brazo de dirección,** steering arm. **Brazo de gitano** *(Culin.),* Swiss roll. **Ir del brazo** *(LAm.),* to walk arm-in-arm. **Mover algo a brazo,** to move something by hand. **Brazo de**

una trompeta, branch of a trumpet. **Brazo de silla,** arm of a chair. **Con los brazos abiertos,** with open arms, cheerfully. **Cruzados los brazos,** with the arms folded, idle. **Ser el brazo derecho de alguno,** to be one's right hand, or confidant. 7. **Brazos** *(fig.)* Hands, workers (trabajadores).

brazolas [brah-tho'-las], *f. pl. (Naut.)* Coamings of the hatch-ways.

brazuelo [brah-thoo-ay'-lo], *m.* 1. *(Dim.)* Small arm. 2. Shoulder or forethigh of beasts. 3. Branch of the mouthbit of a bridle for a horse or mule.

brea [bray'-ah], *f.* 1. Pitch. 2. Tar, artificial bitumen composed of pitch, resin, and grease. 3. Coarse canvas for wrapping up wares, sackcloth.

brear [bray-ar'], *f. va.* 1. To pitch. 2. To tar, to vex, to plague, to thwart. 3. *(Met.)* To cast a joke upon one. 4. To abuse, to ill-treat. **Brear a uno a golpes,** to beat somebody up.

brebaje [bray-bah'hay], *m.* 1. Beverage, a drink made up of different ingredients harsh to the taste, medicine. 2. *(Naut.)* Grog.

breca [bray'-cah], *f.* Bleak or bray, a river fish. *V.* ALBUR.

brecina [bray-the'-nah], *f. (Bot.)* Heath.

brécol, *m.* **brecolera,** *f.* [bray-col, bray-colay'-rah]. *(Bot.)* Broccoli *V.* BRÓCULI.

brecha [bray'-chah], *f.* 1. Breach made in the ramparts of a fortress. 2. Opening made in a wall or building. **Abrir brecha en una muralla,** to breach a wall. 3. *(Met.)* Impression made upon the mind. 4. Ball of pebbles. **Batir en brecha,** 1. To batter a breach in a fortification. 2. *(Met.)* To persecute someone, and cause his destruction. 6. Wound. 7. **Estar en la brecha,** to be in the thick of things. **Seguir en la brecha,** to go on with one's work, keep at it.

brecho [bray'-cho], *m. V.* ESCARO.

bredo [bray'-do], *m. (Bot.) V.* BLEDO.

brega [bray'-gah], *f.* 1. Strife, contest, affray. 2. *(Met.)* Pun, jest, or trick played upon one. **Dar brega,** to play a trick. 3. *vn.* Struggle, fight (luchar).

bregar [bray-gar'], *vn.* 1. To contend, to struggle. 2. *(Met.)* To struggle with troubles, difficulties, and dangers. 3. To quarrel, to scrap (reñir). 4. To slog away, to toil hard (trabajar). **Tendremos que hacerlo bregando,** we shall have to do it by sheer hard work. *-va.* To work up dough with a rolling-pin. (**Yo bregué,** from **Bregar.** *V.* verbs in *gar.*)

breguetear [bray-gay-tay-ahr'], *vn. (And.)* To argue.

brejetero [bray-hay-tay'-ro], *a. (Carib.)* Trouble-making, mischief-making. **bren** [brayn], *m.* Bran. *V.* SALVADO.

brenca [bren'-cah], *f.* 1. *(Bot. Obs.)* Maidenhair. Veneris, *V.* CULANTRILLO. 2. Sluicepost, one of the posts of a water or floodgate. 3. Filament, one of the three cristated anthers of saffron.

breña [bray'-nyah], *f.* Craggy, broken ground.

breñal, breñar [bray-nyahl', bray-nyar'], *m.* Place where the ground is craggy and broken, and full of briers and brambles.

breñoso, sa [bray -nyo'-so, sah], *a.* Craggy and brambled (terreno).

breque [bray'-kay], *m.* 1. Small river fish. 2. *(LAm.) (Hist.)* Break (vehículo). 3. *(And. Cono Sur)* Luggage van, baggage car. 4. *(LAm.) (Mech.)* Brake. *V.* BRECA. **Ojos de breque,** weak or bloodshot eyes.

brequear [bray-kay-ahr'], *(LAm.)* To brake.

brequero [bray-kay'-ro], *m. (And. CAm, Méx.)* Brakeman.

bresca [bres'-cah], *f. (Prov.)* Honey comb.

brescadillo [bres-cah-deel'-lyo], *m.* A small tube made of gold or silver.

brescado [bres-cah'-do], *m.* Embroidered with **brescadillo.**

bretador [bray-tah-dor'], *m.* Call, whistle, or pipe to call birds.

Bretaña [bray-tah'-nyah], *f.* Brittany.

brete [bray'-tay], *m.* 1. Fetters, shackles, irons for the feet. 2. Indigence; perplexity, difficulties. **Estar en un brete,** to be hard put to. 3. Kind of food in India. 4. *(Carib.)* Screw, lay.

breton [bray-tone'], *m.* 1. *(Bot.)* Bore-core, kale. 2. A native of Brittany.

breva [bray'-vah], *f.* 1. The early fruit of a variety of the common figtree. 2. Early large acorn. **Más blando que una breva,** more pliant than a glove; brought to reason. 3. Pure cigar, rather flat. 4. *(Coll.)* Any valuable thing or position easily obtained. **¡No caerá esa breva!,** *(Esp.)* No such luck! **Poner a uno como una breva,** to beat somebody black and blue.

breval [bray-vahl'], *m. (Prov. Bot.)* Early figtree.

breve [bray'-vay], *m.* 1. Apostolic brief, granted by the Pope or his legates. 2. Card of invitation, ticket, memorandum in a pocketbook. 3. *f.* Breve, the longest note in music, seldom used.

breve [bray'-vay], *a.* Brief, short, concise, laconic, compact, compendious, close. **En breve,** shortly, in a little time.

brevecico, illo, ito [bray-vay-thee'-co, eel'-lyo, ee'to], *a. dim.* Somewhat short or concise.

brevedad [bray-vay-dahd'], *f.* Brevity, briefness, shortness, conciseness, compendiousness. **Con la mayor brevedad,** as soon as possible. **Llamado por brevedad,** call for short.

brevemente [bray-vay-men',-tay], *adv.* Briefly, concisely.

brevería [bray-vay-ree'-ah], *f. (Typ.)* Note, short news item.

brevete [bray-vay'-tay], *m.* Note, memorandum; *(LAm.)* Driving licence. *V.* MEMBRETE.

breviario [bray-ve-ah'-re-o], *m.* 1. Breviary, which contains the daily service of the church of Rome. 2. Brevier, a small size of type between minion and bourgeois: of eight points. 3. Memorandum book. 4. Abridgment, epitome.

brezal [bray-thahl'], *m.* Heath, place planted with heaths.

brezar [bray-thar'], *va.* To rock, to lull (cuna).

brezo [bray'-tho], *m. (Bot.)* Heath, heather.

briaga [bre-ah'-gah], *f.* 1. Rope made of bass-weed, tied round the shaft or beam of a winepress. 2. *(Mex.)* Drunkenness.

briago [bre-ah-go], *a. (Mex.)* Drunk.

brial [bre-ahl'], *m.* 1. Rich silken skirt, formerly worn by ladies.

briba [bree'-bah], *f.* Truantship, idleness, neglect of business or duty. **A la briba,** in an idle and negligent manner.

bribia [bree'-be-ah], *f.* A beggar's tale to move compassion. **Echar la bribia,** to go begging.

bribón, na [bre-bone', nah], *m. & f. & a.* Vagrant, impostor; a knave, a scoundrel, rascal, lazy, idle (vago).

bribonada [bre-bo-nah'-dah], *f.* Knavery, petty villainy, mischievous trick or practice, beggar's trick, mean cunning.

bribonazo [bre-bo-nah'-tho], *m. aug.* Great cheat, impudent impostor.

briboncillo [bre-bon-theel' -lyo], *m. dim.* Little gull, young impostor.

bribonear [bre-bo-nay-ar'], *vn.* To rove and loiter about; to lead a vagabond's life.

bribonería [bre-bo-nay-ree'-ah], *f.* Life of a vagrant or vagabond, a beggar's trade.

bribonesco [bre-bo-nays'-co], *a.* Rascally, knavish.

bribonzuelo [bre-bon-thoo-ay'-lo], *m. dim. V.* BRIBONCILLO.

bricho [bree'-cho], *m.* Spangle, used in embroidery.

bricolage [bre-co-lah'-hay], *m.* Do-it-yourself.

bricolagista [bre-co-lah-hes'-tah], *m. & f.* Do-it-yourself expert.

bricolaje [bre-co-lah'-hay], *m. V.* BRICOLAGE.

brida [bree'-dah], *f.* 1. Bridle of a horse. 2. The reins of a bridle. **Ir a toda brida,** to go at top speed. **Tener a uno a brida corta,** to keep somebody on a tight rein. 3. Horsemanship; the art of managing a horse by means of a bridle. 4. *(Met.)* Curb, restraint, check. **A bridas,** riding a bur-saddle with long stirrups. 5. Rail-coupling, fish-plate 6. Flange. 7. Clamp, staple (watch-making).

bridar [bre-dar'], *va.* 1. To put a bridle to a horse, to bridle. 2. To curb, to check, to restrain.

bridge [breach], *m.* Bridge (cartas).

bridón [bre-done'], *m.* 1. Horseman riding a bur-saddle with long stirrups. 2. Horse accoutred with a bur-saddle and long stirrups. 3. Small bridle used instead of a larger one.

brigada [bre-gah'-dah], *f.* 1. Brigade, a certain number of battalions or squadrons. 2. A certain number of soldiers in some military bodies. 3. A certain number of beasts of burden to carry the baggage and provisions of an army. 4. Squad, gang (de obreros). 5. Squad (de policía, etc.). **Brigada antidisturbios**, riot squad. **Brigada antidrogas**, drug squad. **Brigada de bomberos**, bomb-disposal unit. **Brigada sanitaria**, sanation department. -*m. (Mil.)* Staff-sergeant, sergeant-mayor; warrant officer.

brigadier [bre-gah-de-err'], *m.* 1. Brigadier or general of brigade. 2. **Brigadier en la real armada**, officer of the navy, who commands a division of a fleet.

brigán [bre-gahn'], *m. (CAm. Carib.)(Hist.)* Brigand, bandit.

brigandaje [bre-gahn-dah'-hay], *m. (Carib.) (Hist.)* Brigandage, banditry.

brigola [bre-go'-lah], *f.* Ram, ancient machine for battering walls.

brillador, ra [bree'-lyah-dor', rah], *a.* Brilliant, sparkling, radiant.

brilladura [breel-lyah-doo'-rah], *f. (Obs.)* V. BRILLO.

brillante [breel-lyahn'-tay], *a.* 1. Brilliant, bright, shining, sparkling, radiant, glossy. 2. Resplendent, golden, lustrous, light, lucid. 3. Glittering, gaudy, gorgeous, gay, grand. 4. *(fig.)* Brilliant.

brillante [breel-lyahn'-tay], *m.* Brilliant, a diamond cut in triangular faces.

brillantemente [breel-lyan-tay-men'-tay], *adv.* Brilliantly, brightly, resplendently, splendidly.

brillantez [breel-lyan-teth'], *f.* 1. Brilliance, brightness (color); splendor. 2. *(fig.)* Brilliance. V. BRILLO.

brillantina [bril-lyan-tee'-nah], *f.* Brilliantine, hair oil.

brillar [breel-lyar'], *vn.* 1. To shine, to emit rays of light, to sparkle, to glisten, to glister, to glitter, to gleam. 2. To flare. 3. To glare, to glance. 4. *(Met.)* To outshine in talents, abilities, or merits. 4. *(fig.)* To shine; to be outstanding. **Brillar por su ausencia**, to be conspicuous by one's absence.

brillazón [breel-lyah-thone'], *f. (Cono Sur)* mirage.

brillo [breel'-lyo], *m.* 1. Brilliancy, brilliantness, brightness, luminousness 2. Lustre, splendor, glitter. **Sacar brillo a**, to polish, to shine. 3. Resplendence, resplendency, shining.

brilloso [brel-lye-o'-so], *a. (And. Carib. Cono Sur)* V. BRILLANTE.

brin [breen'], *m. 1. (Prov.)* Fragments of the stamens of saffron. 2. Sailcloth. **Brin ancho**, wide Russia sheeting. **Brin angosto**, raven duck.

brincador, ra [brin-cah-dor', rah], *m. & f.* Leaper, jumper.

brincar [brin-car'], *vn.* 1. To leap, to jump, to frisk. 2. To skip, to gambol, to hop, to bounce. 3. *(Met.)* To step over others in point of promotion. 4. *(Met.)* To omit something on purpose and pass to another. 5. *(Met.)* To fling, to flounder, to flounce, to fret, to fly into a passion. **Está que brinca**, he is in a great passion.

brincia [breen'-the-ah], *f.* Peel of an onion

brinco [breen'-co], *m.* 1. Leap, jump, frisk, hop, jerk, bounce, bound. **De un brinco**, in one bound. **De un brinco** *(LAm.)*, On the spot. **Dar brincos**, to hop, jump. **¿Para que son tantos brincos estando el suelo parejo?**, *(CAm. Méx.)* What's all the fuss about? 2. Small jewel fastened to a spring, formerly worn by ladies in their headdress.

brindar [brin-dar'], *vn.* 1. To drink one's health, to toast. **¡Brindemos por la unidad!**, let's drink to unity! 2. To offer cheerfully to invite. 3. To allure, to entice. *(Ger.)* -*va.* 1. To offer, present, afford. **Brindar a uno con algo**, to offer something to somebody. **Le brinda la ocasión**, it offers him the opportunity. 2. *(Taur.)* To dedicate. 3. **Brindar a uno a hacer algo**, to invite somebody to do something.

brindis [breen'-dis], *m.* Health or the act of drinking to the health of another; a toast. 2. *(And. Carib.)* Official reception; cocktail party.

bringabala [brin-gah-bah'-lah], *f. (Naut.)* Brake or handle of a pump. V. GUIMBALETE.

bringas [breen'-gas], *f.pl.* 1. The osiers which cross the ribs of baskets. 2. The fleshy part of lean meat.

brinquillo, brinquiño [brin-keel'-lyo, kee'-nyo], *m.* 1. Gewgaw, a small trinket. 2. Sweetmeat which comes from Portugal. **Estar or ir hecho un brinquiño**, to be as spruce and trim as a game-cock.

brinza [breen'-thah], *f.* 1 Blade, slip. 2. Sprig, shoot.

brío [bree'-o], *m.* 1. Strength, force, vigor, manliness. 2. *(Met.)* Spirit, resolution, courage, valor. **Es un hombre de bríos**, he is a man of spirit, he is a man of mettle. **Bajar los bríos a alguno**, to pull down one's spirits, to humble.

briol [bre-ol'], *m. (Naut.)* Buntline, line fastened to sails to draw them up to the yards.

briolín [bre-o-leen'], *m. (Naut.)* Slabline, fastened to the footrope of the mainsail and foresail, to draw them up a little.

brión [bre-on'], *m.* Bryum, wall-moss.

brionia [bre-oh'-ne-ah], *f. (Bot.)* Briony.

briosamente [bre-ho-sah-men'-tay], *adv.* Spiritedly, courageously, mettlesomely, vigorously, lively.

brioso, sa [bre-o'-so, sah], *a.* Vigorous, spirited, high-minded, mettlesome, courageous, lively.

briqueta [bre-kay-tah], *f.* Briquette.

brisa [bree'-sah], *f.* 1. Breeze from the northeast. 2. **Brisa carabinera**, a violent gale. 3. *(Prov.)* Skin of pressed grapes. V. ORUJO.

brisca [bress-cah], *f.* A game at cards.

briscado, da [bris-cah'-do, dah], *a.* Mixed with silk: applied to gold and silver twist. -*pp.* of BRISCAR.

briscar [bris-car'], *va.* To embroider with gold or silver twist mixed with silk.

brisera, ro [bre-say'-rah], *f.m. & f. (LAm.)* Windshield (for a lamp, etc.).

brisita [bre-se'-tah], *f.* **Tener una brisita**, to be hungry, to have an empty stomach.

británica [bre-tah'-ne-cah], *f. (Bos.)* Great water-dock.

británico, ca [bre-tah'-ne-co, cah], *a.* British, *m. & f.* Britisher.

britano, na [ ], *a. m. & f. (Hist.)* British, Briton.

brizar [bre-thar'], *va. (Obs.)* To rock the cradle.

brizna [breeth'-nah], *f.* 1. Fragment, splinter, chip. **No me queda ni una brizna**, I haven't a scrap left. 2. Nervure or filament in the pod of a bean *(Acad.)*. 3. *(Carib.)* Drizzle (llovizna).

briznar [breth-nahr'], *vn. (Carib.)* To drizzle.

briznoso, sa [brith-no'-so, sah], *a.* Full of fragments or scraps.

brizo [bree'-tho], *m.* 1. Cradle which is rocked. 2. A species of sea-urchin.

broa [bro'-ah], *f. 1. (Naut.)* A cove of shallow depth and dangerous. 2. Mouth of a river.

broca [bro'-cah], *f.* 1. Reel for twist, silk, or thread. 2. Drill for boring holes in iron. 3. Shoemaker's tack. 4. Button.

brocadel, brocatel [bro-cah-del', tel'], *m.* Brocade, a silk stuff.

brocadillo [bro-cah-deel'-lyo], *m.* Brocade with gold or silver flowers.

brocado [bro-cah'-do], *m.* Brocade; gold or silver brocade.

brocado, da [bro-cah'-do, dah], *a.* Embroidered, like brocade.

brocadura [bro-cah-doo-rah], *f.* Bite of a bear.

brocal [bro-cahl'], *m.* 1. Curbstone of a well. 2. Metal ring of the scabbard of a sword. **Brocal de bota**, mouthpiece of a leathern wine-bottle.

brocamantón [bro-cah-man-tone'], *m.* Crochet of diamonds worn by ladies.

brocatel [bro-cah-tel'], *m.* 1. Stuff made of hemp and silk. 2. Spanish marble with white veins.

brocato [bro-cah'-to], *m. (Prov.)* BROCADO.

brócula [bro'-coo-lah], *f.* Drill for piercing metals.

bróculi [bro'-coo-le], *m.* Broccoli, a sort of cabbage.

brocha [bro'-chah], *f.* 1. Painter's brush. **Brocha de afeitar**, shaving brush. **De brocha gorda**, poorly done (pintores, decoradores). 2. Cogged dice used by gamblers. 3. *(Cono Sur)* Skewer, spit. 4. *(CAm.)* Creep (zalamero). -*a.* *(CAm.)* meddling; creeping; servile. **Hacerse brocha** *(CAm.),* to play the fool.

brochada [bro-chah'-dah], *f.* Each stroke of the brush made in painting;

brochado da [bro-chah'-do, dah], *a.* Relating to brocade.

brochadura [bro-chah-doo'-rah], *f.* Set of hooks and eyes.

broche [bro'-chay], *m.* Clasps; hooks and eyes; locket; hasp; brooch; *(LAm.)* Cufflink; *(And. Carib. Cono Sur)* paper clip (sujetapapeles); *(Cono Sur)* **broche para la ropa**, clothes peg.

brocheta [bro-chay'-tah], *f.* Skewer.

brochón [bro-chone'], *m.* 1. *(aug.)* Large brush. 2. Whitewash-brush. -*a. (Carib.)* Flattering.

brochura [bro-choo'-rah], *f.* The act of putting a book in boards.

bróder [bro'-dayr], *m. (CAm.)* Lad, fellow.

brodio [bro'-de-o], *m.* 1. *V.* BODRIO. 2. A mixture of things put together without order. 3. Hotchpotch.

broker [bro'-kayr], *m. (Cono Sur)* lad, fellow.

brollero [brol-lyay'-ro], *a.* *(Carib.)* Trouble-making, mischief-making.

broma [bro'-mah], *f.* 1. Joke, jest. **Broma pesada**, practical joke. **Dar broma**, to tease, to indulge in jokes applied to anyone present. **No es ninguna broma**, this is serious. **Fue una broma nada más**, it was just a joke. **No está para bromas**, he's in no mood for jokes. **La broma me costó cara**, the affair cost me dearly. **Lo decía en bromas**, I was only joking. **En bromas**, in fun. **Ni en bromas**, never. 2. Clatter, confused noise. 3. Rubbish mixed with mortar formerly used to fill up chinks of foundations of walls. 4. *(Carib. Cono Sur)* disappointment, annoyance (molestía). 5. *(Zool.)* Shipworm.

bromado, da [bro-mah'-do, dah], *a.* Worm-eaten: applied to the bottom of a ship. -*pp.* of BROMAR.

bromar [bro-mar'], *va.* To gnaw, like the shipworm called woodborer.

bromato [bro-mah'-to], *m.* Bromate.

bromazo [bro-mah'-tho], *m.* Unpleasant joke, stupid practical joke.

brómico [bro'-me-co], *a.* Bromic.

bromear [bro-may-ar'], *vn.* To droll, to jest. **Estaban bromeando**, they were ragging each other, they were pulling each other's leg. **Creía que bromeaba**, I thought he was joking.

bromista [bro-mees'-tah], *m.* A droll, comical, merry fellow, joker, leg-pulling. **Lo ha hecho algún bromista,** some joker did this. -*a.* Fond of joking, full of fun. **Es muy bromista**, he's full of jokes, he's a great one for jokes.

bromo [bro'-mo], *m.* 1. *(Bot.)* Brome grass. 2. Bromine, one of the elements.

bromuro [bro-moo'-ro], *m.* Bromide.

bronca [bron'-cah], *f.* 1. Row, scrap, set-to (follón). **Armar una bronca**, to kick up a row; make a great fuss. **Se armó una tremenda bronca**, there was an almighty row. 2. Ticking off (reprimenda). **Nos echó una bronca fenomenal**, he gave us a severe ticking-off. 3. *(Cono Sur)* anger, fury. -*a.* Boring, tedious.

broncamente [bron-ca-men'-tay], *adv.* Peevishly, morosely, crustily, rudely, roughly.

bronce [bron'-thay], *m.* 1. Bronze, brass. **Bronze dorado**, ormolu. **Bronze de cañon**, gunmetal. 2. *(Poet.)* Trumpet. 3. Anything strong and hard. **Ser un bronce**, to be indefatigable. **Ser de bronce or tener un corazón de bronce**, to have a heart as hard as steel. *(Per.).* 4. Copper coin (moneda).

bronceado [bron-thay-ah'-o], *m.* 1. Brassiness; the act and effect of bronzing. 2. Tan, suntan (de piel).

bronceado, da [bron-thay-ah'-do, dah], *a.* Brass-paved, brazen. *pp.* of BRONCEAR.

bronceador [bron-thay-ah-dor'], *m.* Suntan lotion.

bronceadura [bron-thay-ah-doo'-rah], *f. V.* BRONCEADO.

broncear [bron-thay-ar'], *va.* 1. To bronze, to give a bronze or brass color. 2. To adorn with pieces of brass, latten, or gilt copper. -*vr.* To brown, to get a suntan.

broncería [bron-thay-ree'-ah], *f.* 1. Collection of things made of bronze. 2. *(Cono Sur)* ironmonger's (shop), ironmongery.

broncista [bron-thees'-tah], *m.* A worker in bronze.

bronco, ca [bron'-co, cah], *a.* 1. Rough, coarse, unpolished. 2. Crusty, sturdy, morose, crabbed. 3. Rude, unmannerly, clownish, hard, abrupt. 4. Hoarse (voz). 5. Applied to musical instruments of a harsh sound.

bronconeumonía [bron-co-nay-oo-mo-nee'-ah], *f. (Med.)* Bronchopneumonia.

broncotomía [bron-co-to-mee'-ah], *f. (Surg.)* Bronchotomy.

broncha [bron'-chah], *f.* 1. Kind of poniard. 2. Jewel. 3. Plasterer's washing-brush.

bronquedad [bron-kay-dahd'], *f.* 1. Harshness, roughness of sound. 2. Rudeness of manners. 3. Unmalleability (metales). 4. *V.* ASPEREZA.

bronquial [bron-ke-ahl'], *a. (Anat.)* Bronchial, belonging to the throat.

bronquina [bron-kee'-nah], *f. (Coll.)* Dispute, contention, quarrel.

bronquinoso [bron-ke-o'-so], *a. (Carib.)* Quarrelsome, brawling.

bronquio, *m.* **Bronquia**, *f.* [bron'-ke-o, ah]. Bronchia.

bronquitis [bron-kee'-tis], *f.* Bronchitis.

brontología [bron-to-lo'-he-ah], *f.* The study of storms and their causes.

broquel [bro-kel'], *m.* 1. Shield; buckler of wood, iron, etc. 2. *(Met.)* Support, protection. **Raja broqueles**, bully, bragger, boaster.

broquelarse [bro-kay-lar'-say], *vr.* To shield oneself.

broquelero [bro-kay-lay'-ro], *m.* 1. One who makes shields or bucklers. 2. He that wears shields or bucklers. 3. Wrangler, disputer.

broquelillo [bro-kay-leel'-lyo], *m.* 1. *(Dim.)* Small shield. 2. Small earrings worn by women.

broquero [bro-kay'-ro], *m. (Mex.)* Brace.

broqueta [bro-kay'-tah], *f.* Skewer. *V.* BROCHETA.

brota [bro'-tah], *f.* Bud, shoot. *V.* BROTE.

brotadura [bro-tah-doo'-rah], *f.* Budding, the act of shooting forth buds and germs.

brótano [bro'-tah-no], *m. (Bot.)* Southern-wood. *V.* ABRÓTANO.

brotar [bro-tar'], *vn.* 1. To bud, to germinate, to put forth shoots or germs: to come out. 2. To gush, to flow or rush out. 3. *(Med.)* To issue, to break out, to appear (granos, diviesos). 4. To appear, spring up. **Han brotado las manifestaciones**, demonstrations have ocurred. **Como princesa brotada de un cuento de hadas**, like a princess out of a fairy tale. -*va.* To bring forth (tierra); to sprout (planta); *(fig.)* To sprout; to pur out.

brote, broto [bro'-tay, bro'-to], *m.* 1. Germ of vines, bud of trees. 2. *(Prov.)* Fragment, crumb, chip. 3. *(Med.)* To break out, appearance; rash, pimples (erupción cutánea). **Un brote de sarampión**, an outbreak of measles. 4. *(fig.)* Outbreak, rash (ola). 5. *(fig.)* Origin; earliest beginnings, first manifestation (comienzo).

brotón [bro-tone'], *m.* 1. Large clasp for a kind of wide coat called *sayo* 2. Shoot, tender-twig. 3. Sprout of cabbage.

broza [bro'-thah], *f.* 1. Dead leaves, bark of trees, and other rubbish. 2. Thicket, brushwood, on mountains. 8. Useless stuff spoken or written, a hotchpotch. 4. Printer's brush to brush off the ink from types. **Gente de toda broza**, people without trade or employment. **Servir de toda broza**, to do all sorts of work.

brozar [bro-thar'], *va.* Among printers, to brush the types.

brozoso, sa [bro-tho'-so, sah], *a.* Full of rubbish.

brucero [broo-thay'-ro], *m.* Brush-maker.

bruces [broo'-thes], *adv.* **A bruce's** or **de bruces**; with the face to the ground. **Caer** *or* **dar de bruces**, to fall headlong to the ground.

brugo [broo'-go], *m. (Prov.)* A sort of vine-grub, plantlouse.

bruja [broo'-ha], *f.* 1. Witch, hag, sorceress. **Parece una bruja**, she looks like a witch. 2. Hag, old witch, shrew. 3. *(Carib. Cono Sur)* spook, ghost (fantasma); whore (prostituta). -*a. (Mex. coll.)* Broke; out of funds.

brujear [broo-hay-ar'], *vn.* 1. To practise witchcraft 2. To rove about in the night-time. -*va. (Carib.) (fig.)* To stalk, to pursue.

brujería [broo-hay-ree'-ah], *f.* Witchcraft, hagship. 2. *(Carib.)* Poverty.

brujidor [broo-he-dor'], *m.* Glaziers' nippers used in paring glass.

brujidura [broo-he-doo'-rah], *f.* Bewitching, casting spells.

brujir [broo-heer'], *va.* To pare off the corners and edges of panes of glass.

brujo [broo'-ho], *m.* Sorcerer, conjurer, wizard, warlock, a male witch, *(LAm.)* Medicine man.

brújula [broo'-hoo-lah], *f.* 1. *(Naut.)* Sea-compass. **Brújula de bolsillo**, pocket compass. **Perder la brújula**, to lose one's bearings. 2. Sight, a small hole which serves as a direction to point a gun. **Mirar por brújula**, *(Met.)* To pry into other people's affairs.

brujulear [broo-hoo-lay-ar'], *va.* 1. At cards, to examine the cards for the purpose of knowing one's hand. 2. *(Met.)* To discover by conjectures the nature and issue of an event. -*vn.* 1. To manage, get along, keep going. 2. *(And. Carib.)* To go on the booze, to go on a bender.

brujuleo [broo-hoo-lay'-o], *m.* 1. Act of examining the cards held at a game, 2. Scrutation, close examination. 3. Guess, conjecture.

brulote [broo-lo'-tay], *m.* 1. *(Naut.)* Fire-ship, a vessel loaded with combustible matters. 2. Warlike machine of the ancients for throwing darts or fire-arrows. 3. *(And. Cono Sur)* obscene remark (comentario); *(Cono Sur)* Obscene letter (escrito).

bruma [broo'-mah], *f.* 1. Winter season. 2. Mist rising from the sea. 3. Haziness.

brumador, ra [broo-mah-dor', rah], *m. & f. V.* ABRUMADOR.

brumal [broo-mahl'], *a.* Brumal, belonging to winter.

brumamiento [broo-mah-me-en'-to], *m.* Weariness, lassitude.

brumar [broo-mar'], *va. V.* ABRUMAR.

brumazón [broo-mah-thone'], *m.* Thick fog or mist at sea.

brumo [broo'-mo], *m.* The whitest and finest wax, which wax-chandlers use to polish tapers and wax-candles.

brumoso, sa [broo-mo'-so, sah], *a.* Foggy, misty.

brunela [broo-nay'-lah], *f. (Bot.)* Common selfheal or heal-all.

bruneta [broo-nay'-tah], *f.* 1. Sort of black cloth. 2. Unwrought silver.

brunete [broo-nay-tay], *m.* Coarse black cloth.

bruno, na [broo'-no, nah], *a.* Of a brown-dark; color; almost black.

bruno [broo'-no], *m. (Prov.)* 1. A little black plum. 2. Plum-tree.

bruñido [broo-nyee'-do], *m.* Polish, burnish. **Bruñido de zapato**, shoeshine. -*pp.* of BRUÑIR

bruñidor, ra [broo-nye-dor', rah], *m. & f.* Burnisher, polisher.

bruñidor [broo-nye-dor], *m.* 1. Burnisher, an instrument used in burnishing. 2. Tool of boxwood, used in finishing leather breeches.

bruñimiento [broo-nye-me-en, to], *m.* 1. Act of polishing or burnishing. 2. Polish, the effect of burnishing or polishing.

bruñir [broo-nyeer'], *va.* 1. To burnish, to polish. 2. To put on rouge. 3. *(CAm.)* To harass, to pester. -*vr.* To make oneself up.

brusca [broos'-cah], *f.* 1. *(Naut.)* Bevel, sweep, or rounding of masts, yards, etc., on board a ship. 2. Brush wood, small wood.

bruscamente [broos-cah-men'-tay], *adv.* Abruptly, peevishly.

bruscate [broos-cah'-tay], *m.* A sort of hash made of milt, lambs' livers, chopped up with eggs, and stewed in a pan with almond-milk, herbs, and spice.

brusco [broos'-co], *m.* 1. *(Bot.)* Kneeholly, butcher's-broom or prickly pettigree. 2. Trifling remains of little value; as, loose grapes dropping at the vintage; fruit blown from the tree, etc. 3. Refuse of wool at shearing-time.

brusco, ca [broos'-co, cah], *a.* Rude, peevish, forward; sudden (ataque); Sharp (de temperatura); sudden, marked, violent (cambio).

brusela [broo-say'-lah], *f.* 1. *(Bot.)* Lesser periwinkle. 2. **Bruselas**, pincers used by silversmiths.

Bruselas [broo-say'-lahs], *f.* Brussels.

brusquedad [broos-kay-dahd], *f.* Brusqueness, rudeness, suddenness, sharpness. **Hablar con brusquedad**, to speak sharply.

brutal [broo-tahl], *a.* 1. Brutal, brutish, churlish, currish, savage, ferocious. 2. Terrific, tremendous (estupendo) 3. *(CAm.)* Incredible, extraordinary (asombroso). 4. *(LAm.)* Great, brilliant (estupendo). *m. V.* BRUTO.

brutalidad [broo-tah-le-dahd'], *f.* 1. Brutality, savageness, brutishness. 2. Brutal action. 3. Clownishness, hoggishness. 4. Stupidity. 5. **Me gusta una brutalidad**, I like it tremendously.

brutalizar [broo-tah-lee-thar'], *va.* To brutalize, to treat brutally; to rape (mujer). -*vr.* To become brutalized.

brutalmente [broo-tahl-men'-tay], *adv.* Brutally, currishly, churlishly, brutishly.

brutesco, ca [broo-tes'-co, cah], *a.* Grotesque.

brutez [broo-teth'], *f. V.* BRUTALIDAD.

bruteza [broo-tay'-thah], *f.* 1. Roughness, want of polish (piedras). 2. Brutality. 3. Coarseness, roughness.

bruto [broo'-to], *m.* 1. Brute. 2. *(Met.)* An ignorant, rude, and immoral person.

bruto, ta [broo'-to, tah], *a.* 1. Coarse, unpolished, in a rough state. **Diamante en bruto**, a rough diamond. **Madera en bruto**, rough timber. 2. Stupid. **Más bruto que un adoquín**, as dumb as an ox. **Pepe es muy bruto**, Joe is pretty rough. 3. Gross. **Peso bruto**, gross weight. 4. Brute, brutish; bestial (brutal). 5. *(Carib.)* **Pegar a uno en bruto**, to beat somebody mercilessly. 6. *(Cono Sur)* Poor-quality, inferior. 7. **Estar bruto**, to be randy. 8. *(LAm.)* Silly, foolish. -*m.* Brute, beast.

bruza [broo'-thah], 1. Round brush for cleaning horses and mules. **Bruzas**, brushes (fábricas textiles). **De bruzas**, *(Obs.) V.* DE BRUCES.

Bs.As. *abr.* de **Buenos Aires** (B.A.).

Bta, Bto *a. abr.* de **Beata, Beato** (Beatus, Blessed, B.)

búa [boo'-ah], *f.* Pustule, a pimple containing pus.

buaro, buarillo [boo-ah'-ro, boo-ah-reel'-lyo], *m.* Buzzard, a bird of prey.

buba [boo'-bah], *f.* Pustule, small tumor. **Bubas**, buboes.

búbalo [boo'-bah-lo], *m. (Obs.)* BÚFALO.

bubático, ca [boo-bah'-te-co, cah], *a.* Having buboes or glandular tumors.

bubilla [boo-beel'-lyah], *f. dim.* Small pustule, a pimple.

bubón [boo-bone'], *m.* Morbid tumor, full of matter.

bubónico, ca [boo-bo'-ne-co, cah], *a.* Bubonic. **Peste bubónica**, bubonic plague.

buboso, sa [boo-bo'-so, sah], *a.* Afflicted with pustules or buboes.

bubute [boo-boo-tay], *m. (Carib.)* Beetle.

bucal [boo-cal'], *a.* Oral, of the mouth. **Por vía bucal**, through the mouth.

bucanero [boo-cah-nay'-ro], *m.* Buccaneer.

bucarán [boo-ca-rahn'], *m. (Prov.)* Fine glazed buckram.

bucare [boo-cah'-ray), *m.* A tree in Venezuela planted to shield plants of coffee and cocoa from the sun.

bucarito [boo-ca-ree'-to], *m. dim.* Small earthen vessel of odoriferous earth.

búcaro [boo'-ca-ro], *m.* Vessel made of an odoriferous earth of the same name.

buccino [book-thee'-no], *m.* Buccinum, whelk, a gasteropod mollusk.

buceador, ra [boo-thay-ah-dor'], *m. & f.* Diver, underwater swimmer, skin-diver.

bucear [boo-thay-ar'], *vn.* 1. To dive, to go underwater in search of anything; to skin-dive; to work as a diver. 2. *(fig.)* To delve, to explore, to look below the surface.

bucéfalo [boo-thay'-fah-lo], *m.* 1. Bucephalus, horse of Alexander. 2. *(Met.)* A stupid, dull man.

buceo [boo-thay'-o], *m.* Diving, the act of going underwater in search of anything.

bucero [boo-thay'-ro], *a.* Black-nosed (perro rastreador).

bucle [boo'-clay], *m.* 1. Ringlet, curl, hair crisped and curled. 2. *(fig.)* Curve, bend, loop; *(Comp.)* Loop.

buco [boo'-co], *m.* 1. *(Naut.)* Ship, vessel. 2. Buck, a male goat. 3. Opening, aperture.

bucólica [boo-co'-le-cah], *f.* 1. Bucolic, a bucolical poem; Pastoral or rural poetry. 2. *(Coll.)* Food.

bucólico, ca [boo-co'-le-co, cah], *a.* Bucolic, bucolical, relating to pastoral poetry.

bucha [boo'-chah], *f.* Large chest or box. *V.* HUCHA. **Bucha pescadera,** *(Naut.)* Buss, a vessel employed in the herring-fishery.

buchaca [boo-chah'-cah], *f.* *(CAm. Carib. Méx.)* Bag; saddlebag (de caballo); pocket (billar).

buchada [boo-chah'-dah], *f.* Mouthful of liquid. *V.* BOCANADA.

buchante [boo-chahn'-tay], *m.* Shot.

buche [boo'-chay], *m.* 1. Craw or crop, of birds and fowls. 2. Maw or stomach of quadrupeds. 3. Mouthful of a fluid. 4. Young sucking ass, foal. 5. Purse, wrinkle, or pucker in clothes. **Hacer buche,** to be baggy, wrinkle up. 6. Breast, the place where secrets are pretended to be kept. 7. *(Coll.)* Human stomach. **Ha llenado bien el buche,** *(Coll.)* He has stuffed his belly well. **Hacer el buche,** *(Low.)* to eat. **Hacer el buche a otro,** to make one dine heartily. 8. *(Carib.)* Idiot, fool. 9. *(And.)* Top hat. 10. *(LAm.)* *(Med.)* Goitre, thyroid; mumps (paperas).

buché [boo-chay'], *m.* *(CAm.)* Rustic, peasant.

buchear [boo-chay-ar'], *va.* To jest, to mock.

buchecillo [boo-chay-theel'-lyo], *m. dim.* Little craw.

buchete [boo-chay'-tay], *m.* Cheek puffed with wind.

buchinche [boo-cheen'-chay], *m.* *(Carib.)* Hovel; pokey little shop (tienda).

Buda [boo'-dah], *m.* Buddha, founder of Buddhism.

búdico, ca [boo'-de-co, cah], *a.* Buddhic, Buddhistic.

budín [boo-deen'], *m.* Pudding; cake (pastel); trifle (postre). **Budín de pescado,** fish pie. **Esa chica es un budín,** that girl's a smasher.

budión [boo-de-on'], *m.* *(Zool.)* Peacock fish.

budismo [boo-dees'-mo], *m.* Buddhism, the religion of the followers of Buddha.

budista [boo-dees'-tah], *m. & f.* Buddhist adherent of Buddhism.

buen [boo-en'], *a.* Apócope de **bueno.** Used only before a masculine noun. **Buen hombre,** good man, and before a substantive feminine beginning with accented *a,* as **buen alma,** a good soul.

buenamente [boo-ay-nah-men'-tay], *adv.* 1. Freely, spontaneously, conveniently. 2. Easily, commodiously, without much exertion.

buenamoza [boo-ay-nah-mo'-tha'], *f. (And.)* Jaundice.

buenaventura [boo-ay-nah-ven-too'-rah], *f.* 1. Fortune, good luck. 2. Prediction of fortune-tellers. **Decir la buenaventura a uno,** to tell somebody's fortune.

buenazo [boo-ay-nah'-tho], *a.* Kindly, good-natured; long-suffering. 2. *m.* Good-natured person; ser un buenazo, to be kind-hearted, be easily imposed upon.

bueno, na [boo-ay'-no, nah], *a.* 1. Good, nice. **El bueno del cura,** *(Coll.)* the good curate. **La buena gente,** good people, decent people. **Lo bueno es que,** the best thing about it is that. 2. Simple, fair, plain, without cunning or craft. 3. Fit or proper for something. **En el momento bueno,** at the right moment. **Ser bueno para,** to be suitable for. **Bueno de comer,** good to eat. 4. Sociable, agreeable, pleasant, loving, gracious. **Tener buen día en buena compañía,** to spend a pleasant day in agreeable company. 5. Great, strong, violent. **Buena calentura,** a strong fever. **No estar bueno de la cabeza,** to be weak in the head. 6. Sound, healthy. 7. Useful, serviceable. 8. Strange, wonderful, notable. **Buenos días,** good morning, good-day: a familiar salute. **Buenas noches,** good-night. **Buenas tardes,** good afternoon or evening. **Las bellas artes y las buenas letras,** the fine arts and belles-lettres. **A buenas,** willingly. 9. **¿Adónde bueno?,** where are you off to? **¿De dónde bueno?,** ¿where do you come from? 10. *(Cono Sur)* **Estar en la buena,** to be in a good mood.

bueno [boo-ay'-no], *adv.* Enough, sufficiently. **Bueno** or **bueno está,** enough, no more.

buenón [boo-ay-non'], *a.* Nice-looking, good-looking.

buenparecer [boo-en-pah-ray-therr'], *m.* *(Coll.)* Pleasing aspect.

buenpasar [boo-en-pah-sar'], *m.* *(Prov.)* Independent situation, comfortable subsistence.

bueña [boo-ay'-nyah], *f.* *V.* MORCILLA.

buera [boo-ay'-rah], *f.* *(Prov.)* Pustule or pimple near the mouth.

buey [boo-ay'-e], *m.* 1. Ox, bullock. 2. **Buey marino,** sea-calf. 3. **Buey de cazo,** stalking-ox. **A paso de buey,** at a snail's gallop. **Buey de agua,** body of water issuing from a conduit or spring. *-pl.* Oxen. 4. *(LAm.)* *(fig.)* Cuckold (cornudo). 5. *(Carib.)* *(fig.)* Big sum of money. 6. *(fig.)* *(And. Cono Sur)* **Buey corneta,** busybody, nose-poker (entrometido). *(Carib.)* **Buey muerto,** bargain. **Como bueyes,** enormous bedbugs. **Es un buey para el trabajo,** he's a tremendous worker. **Cuando vuelen los bueyes,** when pigs learn to fly.

bueyazo [boo-ay-yah'-tho], *m. aug.* Big ox.

bueyecillo, bueyezuelo [boo-ay-yay-theel'-lyo, thoo-ay'-lo], *m. dim.* Little ox.

bueyuno, na [boo-ay-yoo'-no, nah], *a.* Pertaining to cattle, bovine.

bufa [boo'-fah] *a.* *(Carib. Méx.)* Tight, drunk. 2. *f.* Joke, piece of clowning. 3. *(Carib. Méx.)* Drunkenness (embriaguez).

bufado, da [boo-fah'-do, dah], *a.* Bursting with a noise, blown: applied to glass drops blown extremely thin. *-pp.* of BUFAR.

bufalino, na [boo-fah-lee'-no, nah], *a.* Belonging to buffaloes.

búfalo [boo'-fah-lo], *m.* 1. Buffalo (animal). 2. Emery stick, buff-stick.

bufanda [boo-fahn'-dah], 1. Muffler, comforter.

bufar [boo-far'], *vn.* 1. To puff and blow with anger, to swell with indignation or pride. 2. To snort.

bufarrón [boo-fahr-ron'], *m.* *(Cono Sur)* pederast, child molester.

bufé [boo-fay'], *m.* *V.* BUFET.

bufeo [boo-fay'-o], *m.* *(CAm. Carib. Méx.)* Tunny (atún); dolphin (delfín).

bufet [boo-fayt'], *m. pl.* **bufets.** 1. Sideboard (mueble). 2. Buffet, supper. 3. Dining-room.

bufete [boo-fay'-tay], *m.* 1. Desk or writing-table. 2. An office designed for writing documents, as of a lawyer or notary. 3. Bureau, sideboard.

bufetillo [boo-fay-teel'-lyo], *m. dim.* Small desk or writing table.

bufí [boo-fee'], *m.* *(Prov.)* Kind of watered camlet.

bufido [boo-fee'-do], *m.* 1. Blowing of an animal, snorting of a horse. 2. Huff, swell of sudden anger or arrogance; expression of anger and passion.

bufo [boo'-fo], *m.* 1. Harlequin or buffoon on the stage, funny man. 2. *(Cono Sur)* Queer (homosexual).

bufo, fa [boo'-fo, fah], *a.* 1 **Ópera bufa,** comic opera. 2. *(Carib.)* Spongy.

bufón [boo-fone'], *m.* 1. Buffoon, harlequin, merry-andrew, mimic, masquerader. 2. Scoffer, jester, humorist.

bufón, na [boo-fone', nah], *a.* Funny, comical.

bufonada [boo-fo-nah-dah], *f.* 1. Buffoonery, a low jest, waggery, scurrility. 2. Jesting, mimicry pleasantry. Raillery, sarcastic taunt, ridicule; repartee.

bufonazo [boo-fo-nah'-tho], *m. aug.* Great buffoon.

bufoncillo [boo-fon-theel'-lyo], *m. dim.* Little merry-andrew.

bufonear [boo-fo-nay-ar'], *vn.* V. BUFONEARSE.

bufonearse [boo-fo-nayar'-say], *vr.* To jest, to turn into ridicule.

bufonería [boo-fo-nay-ree'-ah], *f.* V. BUFONADA.

bufonesco [boo-fo-nays'-co], *a.* Funny, comical; clownish.

bufos [boo'-fos], *m. pl.* Ancient headdress of women.

buga [boo'-gah], *m.* Car.

bugaceta, bugaleta [boo-gahthay'-tah, lay'tah], *f. (Naut.)* A small vessel.

bugalla [boo-gahl'-lyah], *f.* Gallnut growing on oak leaves.

bugle [boo'-glay], *m.* Bugle.

buglosa [boo-glo'-sah], *f. (Bot.)* Alkanet; bugloss, oxtongue.

bugui-bugui [boo'-ge-boo'-ge], *m.* Boogie-woogie.

buharda [boo-ar'-dah], *f.* 1. Window in the roof, garret-window, dormer-window. 2. Skylight, a window placed horizontally in the ceiling of a room. 3. Garret, a room on the highest floor of a house

buhardilla [boo-ar-deel'-lyah], *f. dim.* Small garret.

buharro [boo-ar'-ro], *m. (Orn.)* Eagleowl.

buhedera [boo-ay-day'-rah], *f.* Embrasure, loophole. V. TRONERA.

buhedo [boo-ay'do], *m.* Marl, a kind of calcareous earth.

búho [boo'-o], *m.* Owl. **Es un búho,** he is an unsocial man, he shuns all intercourse with others.

buhonería [boo-o-nay-ree'-ah], *f.* 1. Peddler's box, in which his wares are carried and sold. 2. Peddlery, the hardware or other small commodities carried in the peddler's box. 3. Peddling, hawking (acto).

buhonero [boo-o-nay'ro], *m.* Peddler or hawker.

buído da [boo-ee'do, dah], *a. (Met.)* 1. Thin, lean, slender. 2. Sharp-pointed (armas blancas).

buir [boo-eer'], *va.* To polish, to burnish.

buitre [boo-ee'-tray], *m.* 1. Vulture. 2. Go-getter (ambicioso).

buitrear [boo-ee-tray-ar'], *va.* 1. *(LAm.)* To kill. 2. *(And. Cono Sur)* to throw up, vomit. *-vn. (And. Cono Sur)* To be sick.

buitrera [boo-ee-tray'rah], *f.* Place where fowlers put carrion to catch vultures. **Estar ya para buitrera,** spoken of a beast so lean as to be fit food for vultures.

buitrero [boo-ee-tray'-ro], *m.* Vulturefowler; one who feeds vultures.

buitrero, ra [boo-e-tray'-ro, rah], *a.* Vulturine, belonging to a vulture.

buitrón [boo-'e-trone'], *m.* 1. Osier basket to catch fish. 2. Partridge net. 3. Furnace where silver ores are smelted. 4. Snare for game.

buja [boo'-hah], *f.* Chuck (relojería).

bujano [boo'-hah-no], *m.* V. TARANTELA.

bujarra [boo-hahr'-rah], *m.* **Bujarrón.** *m.* Queer.

bujarrón [boo-hahr'-rone'], *m. (Vul.)* V. SODOMITA.

buje [boo'-hay], *m.* Axlebox, bushbox, iron ring; pillow of a shaft.

bujeda, *f.* **bujedal, bujedo,** *m.* [boo-hay'-dah, dahl', do]. Plantation of boxtrees.

bujería [boo-hay-ree'-ah], *f.* Gewgaw, bauble, toy, knickknack.

bujero [boo-hay'-ro], *m.* Hole.

bujeta [boo-hay'-tah], *f.* 1. Box made of boxwood. 2. Perfume box. 3. Box of any kind of wood.

bujeto [boo-hay'-to], *m.* Burnisher, a polishing stick used by shoemakers.

bujía [boo-hee'-ah], *f.* 1. Wax candle. 2. Candlestick for wax candle. 3. Spark plug. 4. Candle, candlepower.

bujiería [boo-he-ay-ree'-ah], *f.* Office at court where wax-candles are kept, and given out for the use of the palace.

bujo [boo'-ho], *m.* Wooden frame on which painters fix their canvas.

bul [boo'l], *m.* Arse.

bula [boo'-lah], *f.* 1. Bull, an instrument despatched from the papal chancery, and sealed with lead. **Echar las bulas a uno,** *(Met.)* to impose a burden or troublesome duty. **No poder con la bula,** to have no strength left for anything. 2. Bubble on water.

bulario [boo-lah'-reo], *m.* Collection of papal bulls.

bulbo [bool'-bo], *m. (Bot.)* Bulb. **Bulbo costaño,** *(Bot.)* Great earthnut, pignut.

bulboso, sa [bool-bo'-so, sah], *a.* Bulbous.

bule [boo-lay], *m. (Mex.) (Bot.)* Gourd; water pitcher (jarro). **Llenarse hasta los bules,** to stuff oneself.

bulero [boo-lay'ro], *m.* One charged with distributing bulls of crusades, and collecting the alms contributed for them.

buleto [boo-lay'-to], *m.* Brief or apostolic letter granted by the Pope, or by his legate or nuncio.

bulevar [boo-lay-var], *m.* Boulevard.

Bulgaria [bool-gah'-ree-ah], *f.* Bulgaria.

búlgaro, ra [bool'-gah-ro, rah], *a.* Bulgarian; native of or belonging to Bulgaria.

bulimia [boo-lee'-me-ah], *f. (Med.),* Bulimy or bulimia, voracious appetite.

bulímico, ca [boo-lee'-me-co, cah], *a.* Bulimic, relating to voracious appetite.

bulín [boo-leen'], *m. (Cono Sur)* 1. Bachelor flat (de soltero). 2. Room (especie de burdel).

bulla [bool'-lyah], *f.* 1. Noise, any sound made by one or more persons. **Armar bulla,** to make a row. 2. Clatter, shout, or loud cry. 3. Crowd, mob. **Meterlo a bulla,** to carry off the matter with a joke. 4. Crowd, mob. 5. *(Carib.)* **Ser el hombre de la bulla,** to be the man of the moment.

bullaje [bool-lyah'-hay], *m.* Crowd, a multitude confusedly pressed together.

bullanga [bool-lyahn'-gah], *f.* Tumult, riot.

bullanguero, ra [bool-lyan-gay'-ro, rah], *m. & f.* Rioter, a seditious, turbulent person.

bullar [bool-lyar'], *va.* To cut the wild boar's throat while the dogs hold him.

bullaranga [bool-lya-rahn'-gah], *f. (LAm.)* Noise, row; riot (disturbio).

bullarengue [bool-lyah-rayn'-gay], *m.* Bottom (mujer).

bulldozer [bool-do'-thayr], *m. pl.* **Bulldozers,** bulldozer.

bullebulle [bool-lyay-bool'lyay], *m. (Coll.)* Busybody, bustler, a person of lively and restless disposition, vulgarly smart.

bullero [bool-lyay'ro], *a. (LAm.)* V. BULLICIOSO.

bullicio [bool-lyee'-the-o], *m.* 1. Bustle, noise, and clamor raised by a crowd. 2. Tumult, uproar, sedition heat.

bulliciosamente [bool-lye-the-oh-sah-men'-tay], *adv.* In a noisy, tumultuous manner, mutinously.

bullicioso, sa [bool-lye-the-oh'-so, sah], *a.* 1. Lively, restless, noisy, clamorous, busy. 2. Seditious, turbulent. 3. *(Poet.),* Boisterous (mar).

bullidor, ra [bool-lye-dor', rah], *a.* BULLICIOSO.

bullir [bool-lyeer'], *m.* 1. To boil, as water and other liquids. 2. *(Met.)* To bustle, to be lively or restless, to fluster. 3. *(Met.)* To be industrious and active in business. *-va.* To move a thing from place to place; to stir; to manage a business. **No bulló pie ni mano,** he did not lift a finger. *-vn.* 1. To boil (hervir); to bubble, bubble up. **El agua bullía ligeramente,** the water rippled slightly. 2. To swarm; to teem; (bullir de) *(fig.)*, To teem with, swarm with. **Bullía de indignación**, he was seething with indignation. *-vr.* To move, to stir, to budge.

bullón [bool-lyone'], *m.* 1. Kind of knife. 2. Dye bubbling up in a boiler. 3. A metallic ornament for large books. 4. Bouillon, a clear meat broth; particularly used in bacteriology. 5. Puff, in sewing.

bulo [boo'-lo], *m.* Hoax, false report.

bulón [boo-lon'], *m.* Bolt; spring pin.

bultito [bool-tee'-to], *m. dim.* Little lump or tumor.

bulto [bool'-to], *m.* 1. Bulk, any thing which appears bulky. **De gran bulto**, bulky. **De mucho bulto**, heavy. **De poco bulto**, small. **Agumentos de bulto**, arguments of substance. **Hacer bulto**, to swell the number. 2. Protuberance, tumor, swelling; massiness. 3. Bust, image of the human head and neck. 4. Pillowcase. **A bulto**, indistinctly, confusedly. **Comprar las cosas a bulto**, to buy wholesale, or by the lump. 5. *(Com.)* Package, parcel. 6. Shape, form (forma). **Estimación a bulto**, rough estimate. **Buscar el bulto a uno**, to provoke. **Calcular a bulto**, to calculate roughly. **Escurrir el bulto**, to dodge, duck out of it. 7. *(Mil.)* Squaddie, recruit.

bululú [boo-loo-loo'], *m.* 1. Strolling comedian, who formerly represented all the characters in a farce, by changing his voice. 2. *(Carib.)* Excitement, agitation.

bumerán, bumerang [boo-may-rahn'], *m.* Boomerang.

bunga [boon-gah], *f. (Carib.)* Lie.

bungalow [boon'-gah-lo], *m. pl.* **bungalows**, bungalow.

bungo [boon'-go], *m.* A Nicaraguan flatboat.

buniato [boo-neah'-to], *m. V.* BONIATO.

bunio [boo'-ne-o], *m.* Sort of earthnut or pignut.

bunjo [boon'-ho], *m.* **Hacer bunjo** *(Carib.)* To hit the jacket.

búnker [boon'-kayr], *m. pl.* **Bunkers.** 1. Bunker (golf, fortificación). 2. *(Pol.)* Reactionary clique, reactionary core.

buñolada [boo-nyo-lah'-dah], *f.* A large plate of buns.

buñolería [boo-nyo-lay-ree'-ah], *f.* A bunshop; place where fritters are made and sold.

buñolero, ra [boo-nyo-lay'-ro, rah], *m. & f* One that makes or sells buns.

buñuelo [boo-nyoo-ay'lo], *m.* 1. Fritter made of flour and eggs, and fried in oil; pancake. 2. *(Coll.)* Anything poorly done or spoiled; a failure.

B.U.P. [boop], *m. (Esp.) (Escol.)* abr. de **Bachillerato Unificado y Polivalente** (secondary school education, 14-17 age group, and leaving certificate).

bupréstidos [boo-pres'-te-dos], *m. pl.* Buprestidans, a family of beetles, destructive of wood in their larval state.

buque [boo'-kay], *m.* 1. Ship, vessel, boat. 2. Hull of a ship. **Buque de guerra**, war vessel. **Buque de vela**, sailboat. **Buque de abastecimiento**, supply ship. **Buque de carga**, freighter. **Buque hospital**, hospital ship. **Buque mercante**, merchant-man, merchant-ship. **Buque de pasajeros**, passenger ship. **Buque de vapor**, steamer. 3. Capacity, tonnage. 4. Hull (casco).

buqué [boo-kay'], *m.* Bouquet (of wine).

buquinista [boo-ke-nees'-tah], *m.* A collector of old books.

buraco [boo-rah'-co], *m. (Cono Sur)* hole.

burata [boo-rah'-tah], *f. (Carib.)* Cash, dough.

burato [boo-ran'-to], *m.* 1. Canton crape. 2. Cyprus, sort of woollen stuff much worn for mourning, and by clergymen. 3. Transparent veil of light silk, worn by women.

burbá [boor-bah], *f.* African coin of small value.

burbalur [boor-ba-loor'], *m.* Whale of a large kind.

burbuja [boor-boo'-hah], *f.* Bubble; bleb.

burbujeante [boor-boo-hay-ahn'-tay], *a.* Bubbly, fizzy; bubbling.

burbujear [boor-boo-hay-ar'], *vn.* To bubble.

burbujeo [boor-boo-hay'-o], *m.* bubbling.

burbujita [boor-boo-hee'-tah], *f. dim.* Small bubble.

burcho [boor'-cho], *m. (Naut.)* Large sloop or barge.

burda [boor'-dah], *f.* Door.

burdas [boor'-das], *f. pl. (Naut.)* Backstays.

burdégano [boor-day'-gah-no], *m.* Hinny, offspring of a stallion and a she-ass; mule.

burdel [boor-del'], *m.* Brothel, brothel-house. *-a.* Libidinous

burdelero, ra [boor-day-lay'-ro, rah], *m. & f. V.* ALCAHUE.

Burdeos [boor-day'-os], *m.* 1. Bordeaux. 2. Claret, Bordeaux (vino). *a.* Maroon, dark red.

burdinalla [boor-de-nahl'-lyah], *f. (Naut.)* Sprit-topsail stay.

burdo, da [boor'-do, dah], *a.* Coarse, common, ordinary.

burear [boo-ray-ar'], *(And.)* 1. **va.** To con, to trick. 2. **vn.** To go out on the town.

burel [boo-rel'], *m.* 1. *(Her.)* Bar, the ninth part of a shield. 2. *(Naut.)* Fid, marline-spike.

bureles [boo-ray'-les], *m. pl. (Naut.)* Pointed wooden rollers. **Bureles de hierro para engarzar motones,** splicing-fids. *V.* PASADOR.

burengue [boo-ren'-gay], *m. (Prov.)* Mulatto slave.

bureo [boo-ray'-o], *m.* 1. Court of justice, in which matters are tried relative to persons of the king's household. 2. Entertainment, amusement, diversion. **Entrar en bureo**, to meet for the purpose of inquiring into or discussing a subject. **Ir de bureo**, to have a good time. 3. Stroll (paseo).

bureta [boo-ray'-tah], *f.* Burette, drop measurer.

burga [boor'-gah], *f. (Prov.)* Hot spring of mineral waters used for bathing.

burgés. [boor-ges'], *m.* Native or inhabitant of a village.

burgo [boor'-go], *m.* Borough.

burgomaestre [boor-go-mah-es-tray], *m.* Burgomaster, magistrate of a Dutch or German city.

burgués, sa [boor-gess'-sah], *a.* Burgess; a citizen of a town of the middle class.

burguesía [boor-gay-see'-ah], *f.* Burgessship; yeomanry; middle-class. **Alta burguesía**, upper middle class.

burí [boo-ree'], *m.* A palm growing in the Philippine Islands; the pith yields sago.

buriel [boo-re-el'], *a.* Reddish, dark red.

buriel [boo-re-el'], *m.* 1. Kersey, a coarse cloth. 2. Ropewalk, manufactory for cordage.

buril [boo-reel'], *m.* Burin, tool of an engraver. **Buril de punta**, sharp-pointed burin. **Buril chaple redondo,** curved burin.

burilada [boo-re-lah'-dah], *f.* 1. Line or stroke of a burin. 2. Silver taken by an assayer to be tested.

buriladura [boo-re-lah-doo'-rah]. *f.* Act of engraving with a graver or burin.

burilar [boo-re-lar'], *va.* To engrave with a burin or graver.

burjaca [boor-hah'-cah], *f.* Leather bag carried by pilgrims or beggars.

burla [boor'lah], *f.* 1. Scoff, flout, mock mockery, fling, abuse, derision, sneer. 2. Jest, run, trick. 3. Jeer, jeering, flirt, gibe. 4. Hoax, low trick. **Burla pesada**, biting jest, bad trick. **Burlas**, falsities uttered in a jocular style. **Burlas aparte**, setting jokes aside. **Hablar de burlas**, to speak in jest. **Decir algunas cosas entre burlas y veras**, to say something between joke and earnest. **De burlas**, in jest. **Fue una broma cruel**, it was a cruel sort of joke. **Gastar bromas a uno**, to make fun of somebody.

burladero [boor-lah-day'-ro], *m.* A narrow doorway in the bullring, for protection of the fighter; *(Taur.)* Refuge, shelter.

burlador, ra [boor-lah-or', rah], *m. & f.* 1. Wag, jester, scoffer, mocker, jeerer. 2. Libertine, seducer. *(Acad.)* 3. Conjurer's cup, a vessel so contrived that the liquor runs out through hidden holes when it is put to the lips. 4. Concealed squirt, which throws out water on those who come near.

burlar [boor-lar'], *va.* 1. To ridicule, to mock, to scoff, to laugh, to burlesque. 2. To hoax, to gibe, to fetch over, to flout, to abuse, to play tricks, to deceive. 3. To destroy one's hopes. *-vr.* 1. To jest, to laugh at. 2. To fleer, to gibe, to flout. **Yo no me burlo**, I'm not joking. 3. **Burlarse de**, to mock, to ridicule.

burlería [boor-lay-ree'-ah], *f.* 1. Fun, pun, artifice; drolling. 2. Romantic tale. 3. Deceit, illusion. 4. Derision, reproach.

burlescamente [boor-les-ca-men'-tay], *adv.* Comically, ludicrously.

burlesco, ca [boor-les'-co, cah], *a.* Joker, jocular, ludicrous, comic, mock, funny.

burlesco [boor-les'-co], *m.* Burlesquer, wag, jester, scoffer; mimic.

burleta, illa, ita [boor-lay'-tah, eel-lyah, ee'-tah], *f. dim.* Little trick, fun, or joke.

burlete [boor-lay'-tay], *m.* Weather-strip; kersey.

burlisto [boor-lees'-to], *a. (Cono Sur, CAm, Méx.) V.* BURLON.

burlón, na [boor-lone', nah], *m. & f.* Great wag, jester, or scoffer.

buro [boo'-ro], *m. (Prov.)* Chalk, marl.

buró [boo-roh'], *m.* Bureau; a chest of drawers, with or without conveniences for writing.

burocracia [boo-ro-crah'-the-ah], *f.* Bureaucracy.

burócrata [boo-ro'-crah-tah], *m. & f.* Civil servant, administrative official, official of the public service.

burocrático [boo-ro-crah'-te-co]. *a.* Bureaucratic; civil service.

burra [boor'-rah], *f.* 1. A she-ass. **Caer de su burra**, to fall from one's hobbyhorse, to become sensible of one's errors. 2. A dirty, ignorant, and unteachable woman. *Cf.* BURRO, 2d def. *(Acad.)* 3. A laborious woman of much patience.

burrada [boor-rah'-dah], *f.* 1. Drove of asses. 2. Stupid or foolish action or saying. **Decir burradas**, to talk nonsense, to say silly things. 3. A play contrary to rule in the game of *burro.* 4. **Una burrada de cosas**, a whole heap of things, heaps of things. 5. *adv,* **Me gusta una burrada**, I like it a lot.

burrajo [boor-rah'-ho], *m.* Dry stable-dung to heat ovens. - *a. (Mex.)* Vulgar, rude.

burrazo, za [boor-rah'-tho, thah], *m. & f. aug.* Large or big ass.

burrear [boor-ray-ahr'], *va.* To rip off (robar); to con (engañar).

burrero [boor-ray'-ro], *m.* 1. Ass-keeper, who sells asses' milk for medicine. 2. Jackass-keeper. 3. *(CAm.)* A large herd of donkeys. 4. *(Carib.)* Coarse (malhablado). *-a. (Cono Sur)* horse loving; racegoing.

burricie [boor-re'-the-ay], *f.* Stupidity.

burrillo [boor-reel'-lyo], *m. (Coll.) V.* AÑALEJO.

burrito [boor-ree'-to], *m. dim.* A little ass.

burro [boor'-ro], *m.* 1. Ass, jument. 2. Ass, a stupid, ignorant being. **Burro cargado de letras**, pumpous ass. 3. Jack or horse on which sawyer saw boards or timber. 4. Wheel which puts the machine in motion that twists and reels silk. 5. A game at cards. 6. Windlass, in mining. **Caer de su burro**, to fall from one's hobbyhorse. **Es un burro en el trabajo**, he works and drudges like an ass. **Poner a uno a caer de un burro**, to beat somebody black and blue. **No ver tres en un burro**, to be as blind as a bat. **Ver burros negros** *(Cono Sur);* to see stars. 7. *(LAm.)* Step ladder. 8. *(And. Carib.)* Swing (columpio). *-a.* 1. Stupid. **El muy burro**, the great oaf. 2. **Estar burro**, to feel hot. **Poner burro a uno**, to make somebody feel hot (cachondo).

burrucho [boor-roo'-cho], *m.* Young or little ass.

burrumazo [boor-roo-mah'-tho], *m. (Carib.)* Blow, thump.

burrumbada [boor-room-bah'-dah], *f. V.* BARRUMBADA.

bursátil [boor-sah'-teel], *a.* Stock-exchange.

bursitis [boor-see'-tes], *f.* Bursitis.

burujaca [boo-roo-hah'-dah], *f. (LAm.)* Saddlebag.

burujo [boo-roo'-ho], *m.* 1. Dregs of pressed olives or grapes. 2. Lump of pressed wood or other matter. 3. Parcel, package.

burujón, burullón [boo-roo-hone', boo-rool-lyone',], *m.* 1. *(aug.)* Large knob or lump. 2. Protuberance in the head caused by a stroke.

burujoncillo [boo-roo-hon-theel'-lyo], *m. dim.* Little knob or protuberance.

burundanga [boo-roon-dahn-gah], *f. (Carib.)* 1. Worthless object; piece of junk. **De burundanga**, worthless. 2. Mess, mix-up (lío).

burusca [boo-roos-cah], *f. (CAm.)* Kindling.

bus [boos], *m.* 1. Bus, long-distance bus. 2. *(Comp.)* **Bus asíncrono**, asynchronous bus. **Bus Camac**, Camac bus. **Bus de control**, control bus. **Bus de datos**, data bus. **Bus de dirección**, address bus. **Bus EISA**, EISA bus. **Bus IBM PC**, IBM PC bus. **Bus múltiple**, multiple bus. **Bus PC / AT**, PC / AT bus. **Bus principal**, primary bus. **Bus privado**, private bus. **Bus S-100**, S-100 bus. **Bus SBI**, SBI bus. **Bus síncrono**, synchronous bus. **Bus VME**, VME bus.

busa [boo'-sah], *f.* **Tener busa** *(Esp.),* To feel hungry.

busaca [boo-sah'-cah], *f. (And. Carib.)* Saddlebag; *(Carib.)* Satchel.

busardas [boo-sar'-das], *f pl. (Naut.)* Breast-hooks, compass-timbers, which serve to strengthen the stem.

busardo [boo-sar'-do], *m.* Buzzard, bird of prey.

busca [boos'-cah], *f.* 1. Search, the act of searching. 2. Pursuit. 3. Terrier or other dog which starts or springs game. 4. Troop of huntsmen, drivers, and terriers, that overrun a forest to rouse game.

buscabulla [boos-cah-bool'-lyah], *m. (Carib. Méx.)* Brawler, troublemaker.

buscabullas [boos-cah-bool'-lyahs], *a. (Mex.)* Troublemaker.

buscada [boos-cah'-dah], *f.* Search, research; inquiry, the act of searching.

buscador, ra [boos-cah-dor', rah], *m. & f.* Searcher, investigator. *-m.* Viewfinder (cámara, máquina fotográfica).

buscamiento [boos-cah-me-en'-to], *m. (Obs.)* Search, research, inquiry.

buscaniguas [boos-cah-ne'-goo-as], *m. (And. CAm.)* Squib, cracker.

buscapié [boos-cah-pe-ay'], *m. (Met.)* Hint, feeler.

buscapiés [boos-cah-pe-ess'.], *m.* Squib running about between people's feet, serpent (pirotécnia).

buscar [boos-car'], *va.* 1. To seek, to search, to endeavor to find out. 2. To look, to look after, to look for, or to look out; to hunt or hunt after. **Buscar por todos lados**, to hunt up and down. **Buscar tres pies al gato**, to pick a quarrel. **Quien busca halla**, he that seeks will find. **Ven a buscarme a la oficina**, come and find me in the office. **Nadie nos buscará aquí**, nobody will look for us here. **El terrorista más buscado**, the most wanted terrorist. 3. *(LAm.)* To ask for (pedir). 4. *(Mex.)* To provoke (riña). 5. *(LAm.)* Perks, extras. *-vr.* To bring upon oneself. 2. **Se busca piso** *(Esp.),* apartment wanted. 3. To manage, to get along; to be looking for trouble (buscar camorra). 4. **Buscarlas**, to fend for oneself.

buscarruidos [boos-car-roo-ee'-dos], *m.* Restless, quarrelsome fellow.

buscas [boos'-cas], *f. pl. (Carib. Mex. And.)* Perks, profits on the side.

buscavidas [boos-cah-vee'-das], *m.* 1. A person prying into the actions of others. 2. One diligent in finding subsistence for himself and his family. 3. Hustler (ambicioso); snooper (entrometido).

busco [boos'-co], *m.* Track of an animal.

buscón, na [boos-cone', nah], *m. & f.* 1. Searcher. 2. Cheat, pilferer, filcher, petty robber. 3. Whore.

busilis [boo-see'-lis], *m. (Coll.)* The point in question where the difficulty lies; a mystery, riddle. **Dar en el busilis,** to hit the mark.

buso [boo'-so], *m. (Obs.)* Hole. *V.* AGUJERO. *(Yo busqué,* from *Buscar. V.* verbs in *car.)*

búsqueda [boos'-kay-dah], *f.* Search, investigation. **Búsqueda de un modelo** *(Comp.),* search and pattern matching. *V.* BUSCADA.

buten [boo'-tayn], **De buten**, terrific, tremendous.

busto [boos'-to], *m.* 1 Bust. 2. *(Obs.)* Tomb.

bustrófedon [boos-tro'-fay-done], *m.* Method of writing continuously from left to right, and vice versa. It receives its name from the trail of oxen ploughing.

butaca [boo-tah'-cah], *f.* 1. Armchair, easychair. 2. Seat in a theater.

butifarra [boo-te-far'-rah], *f.* 1. Sort of sausage made in Catalonia. 2. Gaskins, long wide breeches.

butiondo [boo-te-on'-do], *a.* Fetid, goatish, lustful.

butiráceo, cea [boo-te-rah'-thay-o, ah], *a.* Butyraceous, of a consistency like butter.

butírico, ca [boo-tee'-re-co, cah], *a.* Butyric, an acid found in butter, which gives it its odour.

butorio [boo-to'-re-o], *m.* (*Orn.*) Bittern.

butrino [boo-tree'-no], *m.* Fowling-net for catching birds.

butrón [boo-tro-ne'], *m.* Net for birds. Burglary. *V.* BUITRÓN.

butronero [boo-tro-nay-ro], *m.* Burglar.

butuco [boo-too'-co], *m.* A thick stumpy plantain.

buya [boo'-yah], *m. V.* CASTOR.

buyador [boo-yah-dor'], *m.* (*Prov.*) Brazier. *V.* LATONERO.

buyo [boo'-yo], *m. 1.* (*Prov.*) Hut shepherd's cottage. 2. Boa constrictor. 3. A compound of bonga-fruit, betel-leaves, and lime, for chewing.

buzamiento [boo-thah-me-ayn'-to], *m.* (*Geol.*) Dip.

búzano [boo'-thah-no], *m.* (*Obs.*) 1. Diver. 2. Kind of culverin.

buzar [boo-thar'], *va.* To dip downward, as a geological stratum.

buzardas [boo-thar'-das], *f. pl.* (*Naut.*) Breast-hooks, forehooks.

buzo [boo'-tho], *m.* 1. Diver, one that goes underwater in search of things dropped into the sea or rivers. 2. An ancient kind of ship.

buzón [boo-thone], *m.* *1.* (*Arch.*) Conduit, canal. 2. (*Prov.*) Hole through which letters are thrown into the post-office, letterbox, dropbox. **Cerrar el buzón**, to keep one's trap shut. **Echar una carta al buzón**, to post a letter. **Vender un buzón a uno**, (*Cono Sur*) to sell somebody a dummy. 3. Lid or cover of cisterns, ponds, jars; etc. 4. In foundries, hooks to take off the lids of melting pots. 5. Sluice of a watercourse at a mill. 6. Ancient kind of battering-ram.

buzonero [boo-tho-nay'-ro], *m.* (*LAm.*) Postal employee.

buzonora [boo-tho-nay'-rah], *f.* A drain or gutter in a courtyard.

byte [bah'-eets], *m.* (*Comp.*) Byte. **Bytes por pulgada**, bytes per inch.

C

c [thay], is the third letter of the alphabet, and before *e* and *i* has generally the sound of the English *th* in *thick;* before *a, o, u, l,* and *r,* it sounds like *k.* **C** 1. *abr.* de **Centígrado** (Centigrade, C). 2. *abr.* de **Compañía** (Company, Co). 3. (*Inform.*) C (Portable assembly language).

C/ *abr.* de **Calle** (Street, st.).

c/ *abr.* de **cuenta** (account, a/c.) 2. *abr.* de **capítulo** (*Chapter.*).

¡ca! [cah], *int.* (*coll.*) Oh, no! No, indeed! *V.* ¡QUIÁ!

C.A. *abr.* de **corriente alterna**, (altering current, A.C.).

cabal [cah-bahl'], *a.* 1. Just, exact (pesos, medidas). 2. Perfect, complete, accomplished, faultless, consummate; clever. 3. Falling to one's share or dividend. **Por su cabal**, With all his might, most earnestly. **Por sus cabales**, exactly, perfectly, to the very point; according to rule and order: for its just price, according to what it is worth. **Estar en sus cabales**, to be in one's right mind.

cábala [cah'-bah-lah], *f.* 1. Cabala, mystical knowledge of the celestial bodies. 2. Secret science of the Hebrew rabbis. 3. Cabal, intrigue, plot, conspiracy. 4. Confederation or confederacy; (junta).

cabalgada [cah-bal-gah'-dah], *f.* 1. Foray. 2. Cavalcade, a procession on horseback. 3. Booty or spoils taken by an incursion into an enemy's country.

cabalgadero [cah-bal-gah-day'-ro], *m.* Mounting block.

cabalgador [cah-bal-gah-dor'], *m.* 1. Rider. 2. Horseman who goes in procession. 3. Horse-block.

cabalgadura [cah-bal-gah-doo'-rah], *f.* A beast of burden, mount, horse.

cabalgar [cah-bal-gar'], *vn.* 1. To parade on horseback, to go in a cavalcade. 2. To get on horseback, to mount on horseback. *-va.* 1. To cover a mare (semental). 2. **Cabalgar la artillería**, to mount cannon on their carriages. 3. Harness.

cabalgata [cah-bal-gah'-tah], *f.* Cavalcade, procession. **Cabalgata de los Reyes Magos**, the procession of the Three Wise Men.

cabalista [cah-bah-lees'-tah], *m.* Cabalist, one skilled in the traditions of the Hebrews. 2. Schemer, intriguer.

cabalístico, ca [cah-bah-lees'-te-co, cah], *a.* Cabalistic; (*fig.*) Occult, mysterious.

cabalmente [cah-bal-men'-tay], *adv.* Exactly, completely, perfectly, fairly.

caballa [cah-bahl'-lyah], *f.* Horsemackerel.

caballada [cah-bal-lyah'-dah], *f.* 1. (*Lit. us.*) Stud of horses or mares. 2. A number of horses. 3. (*Prov.*) Any game performed by horsemen at public festivals. 4. Gaffe, blunder (animalada). **Has hecho una caballada**, that was a stupid thing to do.

caballaje [cah-bal-lyah'-hay], *m.* 1. Place where mares and she-asses are covered by stallions or jackasses. 2. Money paid for that service. 3. Horsepower.

caballar [cah-bal-lyar'], *m.* Mackerel.

caballar [cah-bal-lyar'], *a.* Belonging to or resembling horses, equine.

caballazo [cah-bahl-lya-tho], *m.* (*LAm.*) Collision between two horsemen, accident involving a horse.

caballejo [cah-bal-lyar'-ho], *m.* *1* (*dim.*) Little horse, nag. 2. Wooden frame for shoeing unruly horses.

caballerango [cah-bahl-lyay-rahn'-go], *m.* (*Mex.*) Groom.

caballerato [cah-bal-lya-rah'-to], *m.* 1. Right of laymen to enjoy ecclesiastical benefices by virtue of the Pope's dispensation. 2. The benefice enjoyed by virtue of the said dispensation. 3. Privilege of a gentleman or esquire.

caballerescamente [cah-bal'-lya-res-cah-men'-tay], *adv.* Knightly, cavalierly, gentlemanly.

caballeresco, ca [cah-bal-lyar-res'-co, cah], *a.* 1. Knightly, befitting a knight; adventurous. **Literatura caballeresca**, chivalresque literature, books of chivalry. 2. Chivalrous. 3. Belonging to or having the appearance of a gentleman.

caballerete [cah-bal-lyay-ray'-tay], *m. dim.* Spruce young gentleman.

caballerete [cah-bahl-lyay-ray'-tay], *m.* Dandy, fop, dude.

caballería [cah-bal-lyay-ree'-ah], *f.* 1. A riding beast. **Caballería de carga**, beast of burden; **caballería menor**, ass. 2. Cavalry horse or horsetroops. **Caballería ligera**, light horse, light cavalry. 3. Art of managing and mounting a horse. 4. Chivalry, the order of knights, and particularly military order. **Caballería andante**, knight-errantry. 5. Knighthood; martialism, nobleness of mind. 6. Assembly of knights of military orders. 7. Chivalry, the institution and profession of knights 8. Body of nobility of a province or place. 9. Service rendered by knights and nobles. 10. Share of spoils given to a knight, according to his rank and merit. 11. A tract of land about thirty-three and one third acres, U. S. measure. 12. Preeminence and privileges of knights. **Libros de caballería**, books of knight errantry. **Andarse en caballerías**, (*Met.*) to make a fulsome show of superfluous compliments.

caballericero [cah-bahl-lyay-re-thay'-ro], *m.* (*CAm. Carib.*) Groom.

caballerito [cah-bal-lyay-ree'-to], *m. dim.* A young gentleman.

caballeriza [cah-bal-lyay-ree' -thah], *f.* 1. Stable. 2. Number of horses, mules, etc., standing in a stable. 3. Stud of horses. 4. The staff of grooms, coachmen, etc., in any establishment.

caballerizo [cah-bal-lyay-ree-tho], *m.* Head groom of a stable. **Caballerizo del rey,** equerry to the king. **Caballerizo mayor del rey,** master of the king's horse.

caballero [cah-bal-lyay'-ro], *m.* 1 Knight. 2. Cavalier, knight. 3. A nobleman. 4. A gentleman. **Cosas indignas de un caballero,** things unworthy of a gentleman. **Es un mal caballero,** he's no gentleman. 5. A rider. 6. Horseman, soldier on horseback. 7. Cavalier, a sort of fortification. 8. *(Orn.)* Redlegged horseman, gambet. 9. **Caballero andante,** knight errant. **Armar a uno caballero,** to knight, to make one a knight. **Caballero de industria,** a defrauder, a knave. **Meterse a caballero,** to assume the character of a gentleman or knight. **Ir caballero** or **caballera,** to go on horseback.

caballero, ra [cah-bal-lyay'-ro, rah], *a.* Applied to a person who goes on horseback. **Ir caballero en burro,** *(Coll.)* to ride on an ass.

caballerosamente [cah-ba'I-lyay-ro-sah-men'-tay], *adv.* 1. Generously, nobly, in a gentlemanlike manner. 2. Knightly.

caballerosidad [cah-bal-lyay-ro-se-dahd'], *f.* Gentlemanliness, behavior of a gentleman. **Caballerosidad deportiva,** good sportsmanship.

caballeroso, sa [cah-bal-lyay-ro'-so, sah] *a.* 1. Noble, generous, genteel. 2. Gentlemanlike.

caballerote [cah-bal-lyay-ro'tay], *m.* 1. A gentleman of an ancient family, and of an unblemished character. 2. *(Coll.)* Graceless, unpolished gentleman.

caballeta [cah-bal-lyay'-tah], *f.* Field cricket.

caballete [cah-bal-lyay'-tay], *m.* 1. *(Aruit.)* Ridge of a house forming an acute angle **(de techo);** bolster, ridge-piece, hip; carpenter's horse, trestle-horse, bench, *(Tec.)* Trestle. 2. Horse, an instrument of torture. 3. Brake, for dressing hemp and flax. 4. Ridge between furrows, raised by a ploughshare. 5. Cover over the funnel of a chimney in a pyramidal form. 6. Bridge (of the nose). 7. Gallows of a printing-press. 8. *(Arte)* easel. 9. *(Aer.)* Gantry tower. **Caballete de aserrar,** sawyer's trestle or horse. **Caballete de pintor,** painter's easel.

caballico, ito [cah-bal-lyee'-co, ee'to], *m.* 1. *(dim.)* Little horse, pony. 2. Hobby or hobby-horse, a rocking-horse; a stick or cane on which children ride.

caballista [cah-bah-lyees'-tah], *m.* Horse-man, expert in horses.

caballito [cah-bahl-lee-to], *m.* Small horse, pony. **Caballito de niño,** hobby-horse. **Caballito del diablo,** dragonfly. **Caballito de mar,** sea horse.

caballitos [cah-bal-lyee'-tos], *m. pl.* 1. Small horses. 2. Merry-go-round, carrousel.

caballo [cah-bahl-lyo], *m.* 1. Horse. **Caballo padre,** a stallion, stone horse. **Caballo de montar** or **silla,** saddle horse. **Caballo de carga,** packhorse. **Caballo castrado** or **capado,** gelding. **Caballo de coche,** coachhorse. **Caballo de guerra,** charger. **Caballo de caza,** hunter. **Caballo de carrera** or **corredor,** racer, racehorse. **Caballo desorejado,** cropped horse. **Caballo de alquiler,** hack, hackney. **Caballo de tiro,** draught-horse. **Caballo de vaivén,** rocking horse. **Las cosas andan a caballo** *(Cono Sur),* the price of things is sky-high. **Pararle el caballo a uno,** *(Mex.)* to be stupid; **caballo bayo dorado,** bright bay horse. **Caballo moro,** piebald horse. **Caballo pardo,** gray horse. **Caballo desbocado,** runaway horse. **Caballo de buena boca,** *(Met.)* A person who accommodates himself readily to circumstances. **Caballo de palo,** 1. *(Coll.)* Any vessel fit for sea. 2. *(Vulg.)* Rack for criminals. 3. (Tannery) Tanner's beam. **Caballo marino.** 2. Pipefish, seahorse. 3. Figure on horseback, equivalent to the queen, at cards. 4. Trestle, bench on which planks or boards are laid for masons and plasterers to work on. 5. Knight in the game of chess. **A caballo,** on horseback. **Caballos,** horses, cavalry, mounted soldiers. 6. Bubo, tumor in the groin. *V.* POTRO. 7. Thread which ravels others. 8. Barren rook in a vein (mining). **Huir a uña de caballo,** to have a

hairbreadth escape; to extricate oneself from difficulty by prudence and energy. **Echarle a uno el caballo de cara,** *(Coll.)* to upbraid roughly. **A caballo regalado no le mires el diente,** you must not look a gift horse in the mouth. **Una dosis de caballo,** a huge dose, a massive dose. 9. *(Mech.)* **Caballo de vapor,** a dynamic unit which represents the force necessary to raise seventy-five kilograms one meter in one second. **Caballo de fuerza,** horsepower. **Un motor de 18 caballos,** an 18 horsepower engine. **Caballo de Troya,** *(Inform.)* "Trojan Horse".

caballón [cah-bal-lyone'], *m.* 1. *(aug.)* Large, clumsy horse. 2. Ridge of ploughed land between two furrows.

caballuelo [cah-bal-lyoo-ay'-lo], *m. dim.* Little horse.

caballuno, na [cah-bal-lyoo'-no, nah], *a.* Belonging to a horse.

cabanga [cah-bahn-gah], *f.* *(CAm.)* Homesickness (nostalgia). **Estar de nostalgia,** to be homesick.

cabaña [cah-bah'-nya], *f.* 1. Shepherd's hut, cottage, cot, cabin. **Cabaña de madera,** log cabin. 2. Hole, hovel, mean habitation. 3. Flock of ewes or breeding sheep. 4. Drove of asses for carrying grain. 5. *(Prov.)* Weekly allowance of bread, oil vinegar, and salt, for shepherds. 6. Balk, a line drawn on a billiard table, limiting the players. 7. Landscape representing a shepherd's cottage, with fowls, and other domestic animals. 8. Cabana.

cabañal [cah-bah-nyahl'], *a.* Applied to the road for flocks of traveling sheep and droves of cattle.

cabañería [cah-bah-nyay-ree'-ah], *f.* Rations for a week, of bread, oil, vinegar, and salt, allowed to shepherds.

cabañero, ra [cah-bah-nyay'-ro, rah], *a.* Belonging to the drove of mules and asses which go with a flock of traveling sheep. *-m.* Herdsman.

cabañil [cah-bah-nyeel'], *a.* Applied to the mules which go with the flocks of traveling sheep *m.* Herd or keeper of mules and asses, kept for carrying corn.

cabañuela [cah-bah-nyoo-ay'-lah], *f. dim.* Small hut or cottage.

cabañuelas [cah-bah-nyoo-ay'-lahs], *f. pl.* *(LAm.)* Weather predictions; *(And.)* First summer rains; *(Mex.)* First twelve days of January (used to predict the weather).

cabaré [cah-bah-ray'], *m.* Cabaret.

cabaret [cah-bah-ret'], *m.* Cabaret, night club, floor show. **Cabaret de desnudo,** nude show, striptease show, strip club.

cabaretera [cah-bah-ray-tay'-rah], *f.* Cabaret dancer, cabaret entertainer; night club hostess, showgirl.

cabas [cah-bahs], *m.* Schoolbag, satchel.

cabaza [cab-bah'-thah], *f.* *(Obs.)* Large or wide cloak with hood and sleeves.

cabe [cah'-bay], *m.* 1. Stroke given by balls, in the game of *argolla,* whereby the player gains a point. **Dar un cabe al bolsillo, a la hacienda,** *etc. (Met.)* to give a shake to one's purse, to hurt one in his business, fortune, etc. **Dar un cabe a,** to harm. 2. Header.

cabeceada [cah-bay-thay-ah'-dah], *f.* *(LAm.)* Nod, shake of the head.

cabecear [cah-bay-thay-ar'], *vn.* 1. To nod with sleep, to hang the head on one side. 2. To shake the head in disapprobation (negando). 3. To raise or lower head (caballos). 4. To incline to one side, to hang over (peso, carga), 5. *(Naut.)* To pitch. 6. *(Aut.)* To lurch: used of carriages. *-va.* 1. In writing, to give letters the necessary thick stroke or loop. 2. Among bookbinders, to put the headband to a book. 3. To garnish cloth with edgings of tape or lace. 4. To cauterize a vein. 5. To head new wine, by adding some old wine to give it strength. 5. To head (balón).

cabeceo [cah-bay-thay'-o], *m.* Nod of the head (negativa); toss of the head (de caballo). 2. *(Naut.)* Pitching; *(Aut.)* Lurch, lurching, shifting; slipping.

cabecequia [cah-bay-thay'-ke-ah], *m.* *(Prov.)* Inspector of sluices, guardian of watercourses.

cabecera [cah-bay-thay'-rah], *f.* 1. The beginning or principal part of something. 2. Head or headboard of a bed; also a

C-D

railing at the head of a bed to prevent pillows from falling. 3. Seat of honor. 4. Headwaters, source of a river. **Cabecera (de río),** headwaters. 5. Capital of a province, district, or nation. 6. A fortified point of a bridge. 7. Headpiece or vignette at the beginning of a chapter. 8. Each extremity of the back of a book. 9. A pillow or bolster of a bed. 10. The summit of a hill or ridge. 11. **Cabecera del cartel,** *(Theat.)* top of the bill. **Médico de cabecera,** family doctor.

cabecero [cah-bay-thay'-ro], *m.* 1. Lintel, the upper part of a doorframe. 2. *(Obs.)* Head of a branch of a noble family. 3. Compress.

cabeciancho, cha [cah-bay-the-ahn'-cho, chah], *a.* Broad or flat headed (clavos).

cabeciduro [cah-bay-the-doo'-ro], *a. (And. Cono Sur)* Stubborn, pigheaded.

cabecil [cah-bay-theel'], *m.* A pad of cloth which women place on their head for carrying a pail or anything heavy.

cabecilla [cah-bay-theel'-lyah], *m.* 1. Wrongheaded person, full of levity, indiscretion, and whims. 2. Leader of rebels. 3. Ringleader.

cabellazo [cah-bel-lyah'-tho], *m. aug.* Large bush of hair.

cabellera [cah-bel-lyay'-rah], *f.* 1. Long hair spead over shoulders; (**soltarse las melenas**), to act or speak in a forthright way. 2. False hair. 3. Tail of a comet. Any other body which presents a tuftlike appearance, as the branches of willows, etc.

cabello [cah-bayl'-lyo], *m.* Hair of the head. **Cabello de Venus,** *(Bot.)* maidenhair. **Estar pendiente de un cabello,** to hang by a thread. **Estar en cabello,** to have one's hair down. -*pl.* 1. Large sinews in mutton. 2. Fibres of plants; the silk of corn. **Cabellos de ángel,** conserve of fruit cut into small threads. **Estar colgado de los cabellos,** to be in anxious expectation of the issue of a critical affair. **Tomar la ocasión por los cabellos,** to take time by the forelock, *(Met.)* O profit by the occasion. **Traer alguna cosa por los cabellos,** *(Met.)* to appropriate a phrase, an authority, or a quotation, to a thing which has no relation with it. **Arrancarse los cabellos,** to pull or tear one's hair. **Arrastrar a uno por los cabellos,** to drag one away by the hair.

cabelludo, da [cah-bel-lyoo'-do, dah], *a.* Hairy, **Cuero cabelludo,** scalp.

caber [cah-berr'], *vn.* 1. To be able or capable to contain, or to be contained; to fit. 2. To have room, place, or right of admission. **No cabe el libro,** the book won't go in. **Caben 3 más,** there's room for three more. **En este depósito caben 20 litros,** this tank holds 20 litres. **Eso no cabe por esta puerta,** that won't go through this door. 3. To be entitled to a thing. 4. To fall to one's share. **No caber de gozo,** to be overjoyed. **No caber de pies,** to have no room to stand. **No caber en el mundo,** to be elated with excessive pride, to be puffed up with vanity. **No caber en sí,** to be full of one's own merits; to be very uneasy. **Todo cabe,** it is all possible; it may well be so. **No cabe más,** nothing more to be desired: applied to something that has arrived at its ultimate point. **No cabe en él hacerlo,** it is not in him to do it. **Todo cabe en ese chico,** that lad is capable of any mischief. -*va.* To contain, to comprise, to include.

cabero [cah-bay'-ro], *m. (Prov.)* Maker of handles for tools.

cabestraje [cah-bes-trah-hay], *m.* 1. Halter, and other headtackling for beasts. 2. Money paid to a driver for conducting cattle to market.

cabestrante [cah-bes-trahn'-tay], *m.* V CABRESTANTE.

cabestrar [cah-bes-trar'], *va.* To halter, to bind with a halter. -*vn.* To fowl with a stalking-ox.

cabestrear [cah-bes-tray-ar'], *vn.* To follow one willingly who leads by a halter or collar (animales).

cabestrería [cah-bes-tray-ree'-ah], *f.* Shop where halters and collars are made and sold.

cabestrero [cah-bes-tray'-ro], *m.* One who makes or retails halters and collars.

cabestrero, ra [cah-bes-tray'-ro, rah], *a. (Prov.)* Being so tame as to be led by a halter.

cabestrillo [cah-bes-treel'-lyo], *m.* 1. Sling suspended from the neck, in which a sore arm or hand is carried. Kind of hoop which keeps the cheeks of a saw tight. **Con el brazo en cabestrillo,** with one's arm in a sling 3. Gold or silver chain. **Buey de** *cabestrillo,* stalking-ox.

cabestro [cah-bes'-tro], *m.* 1. Halter. 2. Bellox, a tame bullock that leads the rest of a drove of black cattle. **Traer a alguno de cabestro,** to lead one by the nose. 3. *(Obs.)* Chain. *V.* CABESTRILLO. 4. Cuckold (cornudo).

cabeza [cah-bay'-thah], *f.* 1. Head. 2. Part of the head which comprehends the cranium and forehead. **Cabeza de chorlito,** scatterbrain. 3. Head, the whole person, and more generally the person as exposed to any danger or penalty. 4. Head, chief, principal person; leader. 5. Head, understanding, faculties of the mind, judgment, talents. 6. Beginning of a thing, e. g. of a book. 7. End or extremity of a thing, e. g. of a beam or bridge. 8. Head, the top of many things, as the head of a nail, of a pin, etc. **Cabeza sonora,** recording head. 9. Head, the upper part of many things. 10. The principal town of a province, district, etc. 11. Head of cattle. **Cabeza menor,** head of sheep, goats etc. 12. *(Naut.)* Head of a ship. 13. Diameter of a column. 14. **Cabeza de autos** or **proceso,** head of a process. **Cabeza de ajos,** bulb of garlic. **Cabeza de moro,** moorshead. **Cabeza de turco,** scapegoat. **Cabeza de perro,** *V.* ANTIRRINO MAYOR and BECERRA. **Cabezas,** principal parts of a vessel, an equestrian game. **Cabeza torcida,** wrongheaded fellow. **Cabeza hueca,** addled head. **Cabeza redonda,** *(Met.)* blockhead. **Dar de cabeza,** to fall into misfortunes, to decline in one's fortune, power, or authority. **Hablar de cabeza,** to speak without ground or foundation. **Levanter** or **alzar cabeza,** to take courage, to retrieve one's health or fortune. **No levantar** or **no alzar cabeza,** to continue to be ill, or unfortunate in business. **Andar de cabeza,** to be snowed under. **Meterse de cabeza en algo,** to plunge into something. **Calentarse la cabeza,** to get tired out. **Se me fue la cabeza,** I felt giddy. **Está que no levanta cabeza,** she's totally engrossed in her work. **Mover la cabeza afirmativamente,** to nod (one's head). **Sentar la cabeza,** to settle down. **Volver la cabeza,** to look round. **No tener pies ni cabeza alguna cosa,** to not make sense. **Otorgar de cabeza,** to give a nod of approbation. **Perder la cabeza,** to lose one's senses, to be at a loss how to act. **Sacar de su cabeza alguna cosa,** to strike out a thing. **No tener a quien volver la cabeza,** to have neither money nor friends. **Ser** or **tener mala cabeza,** to be a man of bad principles: to be weakminded, without judgment or reflection. **Volvérsele la cabeza a alguno,** to lose one's senses. **De cabeza,** 1. From memory. 2. Headlong. **Caer con la cabeza abajo** or **caer de cabeza,** to fall headlong. **Pagar a tanto por cabeza,** to pay so much a piece or so much a head. -*m. & f.* Head; chief, leader (persona). **Cabeza de familia,** head of the household. **Cabeza de lista,** person at the head of the list.

cabezada [cah-bay-thah'-dah], *f.* 1. Headshake, stroke or butt given with the head, or received upon it. 2. Halter collar. 3. Headstall of a bridle. 4. Pitching of a ship. **Dar cabezadas,** to pitch. 5. Among bookbinders, headband of a book. 6. Instep of a boot. 7. The part of a piece of ground more elevated than the rest. 8. Nod, of one asleep with the head unsupported. **Dar cabezadas** to nod, to fall asleep. **Darse de cabezadas,** to screw one's wits in the investigation of a thing without success.

cabezal [cah-bay-thahl'], *m.* 1. Headpiece in a powdermill. 2. Small square pillow. 3. Compress of folded linen used by surgeons. 4. Long round bolster which crosses a bed. 5. Post of a door. **Cabezales de coche,** standards of the fore and hind parts of a coach, to which the braces are fastened. 6. Mattress or piece of cloth on which peasants sleep on benches or stones at the fire. 7. Title page of a book.

cabezazo [cah-bay-tha-tho], *m.* Butt; header.

cabezo [cah-bay'-tho], *m.* 1. Summit of a hill. 2. Shirt-collar.

cabezón [cah-bay-thone'], *m.* 1. Register of the taxes paid to government, and of the names of the contributors 2. Collar of a shirt. 3. Opening of a garment for the head to pass through 4. Cavesson or noseband, used in breaking in a horse. **Llevar por los cabezones**, to drag along by the collar. **Entra por la manga, y sale por el cabezón**, applied to favorites who assume authority and dominion, and originating in the ancient ceremony of adoption, by passing the person through the wide sleeve of a shift.

cabezorro [cah-bay-thor'-ro], *m. aug. (Coll.)* Large disproportioned head.

cabezota [cah-bay-thoh'-tah], *m. aug.* 1. Bigheaded. 2. Clubheaded, having a thick head.

cabezudo [cah-bay-thoo'-do], *m. (Zool.)* Chub, mullet. *V.* MÚJOL. *(Acad.)*

cabezudo, da [cah-bay-thoo'-do, dah], *a.* 1. *(fig.)* Big head. 2. *(fig.)* pigheaded. 3. Heady (vino). 4. Headstrong, obstinate, morose, stubborn.

cabezuela [cah-bay-thoo-ay'-lah], *f.* 1. *(dim.)* Small head. 2. Blockhead, dolt, simpleton. 3. Coarse flour. 4. Rosebud, from which rosewater is distilled. 5. Little glass tube in a velvet loom. 6. *(Bot.)* Eryngo. 7. *(Bot.)* Ragwort-leaved centaury.

cabezuelo [cah-bay-thoo-ay'-lo], *m. dim.* Little head or top of something.

cabida [cah-bee'-dah], *f.* 1. Content, space, or capacity of something. *(Coll.)* **Eso no tiene cabida**, that cannot be permitted or allowed. **Dar cabida a**, to make room for. **Tener cabida**, to have room for. 2. *(fig.)* Tener cabida en uno, to have influence with somebody.

cabido [cah-bee'-do], *m.* Knight of the order of Malta, who has the right to claim a commandery. **-Cabido, da**, *pp.* of CABER.

cabildada [cah-beel-dah'-dah], *f. (Coll.)* Hasty, ill-grounded proceeding of a chapter or other body.

cabildeo [cah-beelday'o], *m.* Lobbying, intriguings.

cabildero, ra [cah-beel-day'-ro], *a. m. & f. (Obs.)* Belonging to a chapter. 2. Lobbyist; member of a pressure group.

cabildo [cah-beel'-do], *m.* 1. Chapter of a cathedral or collegiate church. 2. Meeting of a chapter, and the place where the meeting is held. 3. *(Prov.)* The corporation of a town.

cabilla [cah-beel'-lyah], *f. (Naut.)* 1. Dowell, round iron bar for securing the knees of a vessel. 2. Treenail, belaying-pin. **2. Dar cabilla a**, to fuck, to screw.

cabillo [cah-beel'-lyo], *m.* 1. *(Bot.)* Flowerstalk. 2. *(dim.)* Small end of a rope.

cabimiento [cah-be-me-en'to], *m.* 1. Right of claiming a commandery in the order of Malta. 2. *V.* CABIDA.

cabina [cah-bee'-nah], *f.* 1. Cabin. 2. Cockpit (of a plane). 3. Booth, encasing. **Cabina a presión**, pressurized cabin. **Cabina cerrada transparente**, *(Aer.)* Canopy. **Cabina telefónica**, telephone booth. **Cabina del conductor**, driver's cap.

cabinera [cah-bee-nay-rah], *f. (And.)* Air hostess, stewardess.

cabío [cah-bee'-o], *m.* 1. Lintel of a door. 2. A kind of rafter used in building.

cabito [cah-bee'-to], *m. dim.* The small end of a candle. *V.* CABO, CABILLO; *cabitos, pl.* Small lines, ends of lines.

cabizbajo, ja [cah-bith-bah'-ho, hah], *a.* 1. Down in the mouth, crestfallen. 2. Thoughtful, pensive, melancholy. 3. *(Bot.)* Drooping.

cabiztuerto, ta [cah-bith-too-er'-to, tah], *m. & f.* Hypocritical, sly.

cabla [cah-blah], *f. (LAm.)* Trick.

cable [cah'-blay], *m.* 1. Cable; rope, hawser. **Cable sencillo** or **de leva**, small bower cable. **Cable de alambre**, wire cable. **Cable submarino**, submarine cable. **Cable telegrafico**, telegraphic cable. **Echar un cable a uno**, to give somebody a helping hand. 2. Cable's length, a measure of 120 fathoms.

cablear [cah-blay-ar'], *va.* To cable.

cablegrafiar [cah-blay-grah-fee-ar'], *vn.* To cable.

cablegráfico, ca [cah-blay-grah'-fe-co, cah], *a.* By cable; **dirección cablegráfico**, cable address; **mensaje cablegráfico**, cable message.

cablegrama [cah-blay-grah-mah], *m.* A cablegram, message sent by cable. **cablero** [cah-blay'-ro], *m.* Cable ship (barco).

cablista [cah-blees'-tah], *a. (LAm.)* Sly, cunning.

cabo [cah'-bo], *m.* 1. Extreme, extremity; end of a thing; tip. 2. Cape, headland, or promontory, foreland. 3. Handle, haft, hold. 4. The extremity of a thing remaining after the principal part has been consumed or destroyed. **Cabo de vela**, candle-end. **Cabo suelto**, loose end. **No dejar ningún cabo suelto**, to leave no loose ends. 5. Lowest card in the game called *revesino*. 6. *(Prov.)* Paragraph, article, head. 7. Chief, head, commander. 8. *(Naut.)* Any of the cords employed on a ship. 9. Thread. 10. Complement, perfection, completion. 11. At the custom-house a parcel or package smaller than a bale. 12. Place, position, site. **13.** End; termination, conclusion (de periodo, proceso). **Al cabo de 3 meses**, at the end of 3 months. **Estar al cabo de la calle**, *(fig.)* to know what's going on; **llevar a cabo**, to carry out, to execute. 14. *(Geog.)* Cape, point; **Cabo de Buena Esperanza**, cape of Good Hope. **Islas de Cabo Verde**, Cape Verde Island. -*pl.* 1. The tail and mane of horses. 2. Loose pieces of apparel, as stockings, shoes, hat, etc. 3. Divisions of a discourse. **Cabo de año**, the religious offices performed on the anniversary of a person's death. **Cabo de barras, chiselled dollar of Mexico.** Last payment or balance of an account. **Cabo de escuadra**, corporal. **Cabo de presa**, prizemaster. **Coger todos los cabos**, *(Met.)* To weigh all the circumstances of a case. **Atar cabos**, to collect and examine together various circumstances bearing on a case. **Cabos blancos**, *(Naut.)* Untarred cordage. **Car cabo**, *(Naut.)* To throw out a rope for another to take hold of. **Al cabo**, at last. **De cabo a rabo**, from head to tail. **Estar al cabo de algún negocio**, to be thoroughly acquainted with the nature of an affair. **No tener cabo ni cuenta una cosa**, to have neither head nor tail (negocios). **Por ningún cabo**, by no means.

cabotaje [cah-bo-tah'-hay] *m. (Naut.)* 1. Coasting trade. 2. Pilotage.

cabra [cah'-brah], *f.* 1. Goat. Capra. 2. Engine formerly used to throw stones. 3. **Cabra montés**, wild goat. **Estar como una cabra**, to be crazy. **La cabra siempre tira al monte**, what is bred in the bone will come out in the flesh: a man's acts show what he is. 4. *(And. Carib.)* Trick, swindle (trampa); loaded dice (dado). 5. Light carriage (carro). 6. *(Cono Sur)* little girl. -*pl.* 1. Red marks on the legs caused by fire. 2. Small white clouds floating in the air. **Piel de cabra**, goatskin.

cabrahigal, cabrahigar [cah-bra-he-gahl', cah-bra-he-gar'], *m.* Grove or plantation of wild fig-trees.

cabrahigar [cah-brah-e-gar'], *va.* To improve a fig-tree; that is, to string up some male figs, and hang them on the branches of the female fig-tree, to make it produce better fruit.

cabrahigo [cah-brah-ee'-go], *m.* The male wild fig-tree, or its fruit which does not ripen.

cabreante [cag-bray-ahn'-tay], *a.* Infuriating.

cabrear [cah-bay-ar'], *va.* To infuriate, make livid. -*vr.* 1. To get furious, to get livid (enojarse). 2. To get suspicious. 3. *(Cono Sur)* to get bored.

cabreía [cah-bray-ee'-ah], *f.* Wooden machine for throwing stones.

cabreo [cab-bray-'o], *m.* 1. *(Prov.)* Register, especially of the privileges and charters of cathedral churches. 2. Fury, anger; fit of bad temper. **Coger un cabreo**, to get angry.

cabrería [cah-bray-ree'-ah], *f.* 1. Herd of goats. 2. The place where goat's milk is sold.

cabreriza [cah-bray-ree'-thah], *f.* A hut for goatherds, goat shed.

cabrerizo [cah-bray-ree'-tho], *m. V.* CABRERO. -*a.* Goatish.

cabrero, ra [cah-bray'-ro, rah], *m. & f.* 1. Goatherd. 2. *(Cono Sur)* bad-tempered.

cabrestante [cah-bres-tahn'-tay], *m. (Naut.)* Capstan.

cabria [cah'-bre-ah], *f.* 1. Axle-tree. 2. *(Naut.)* Sheers, a machine used for setting up and taking out masts. 3. Crane, wheel and *(atr.)* winch, windlass, hoist.

cabrial [cah-bre-ahl'], *m. (Obs.)* Beam. *V.* VIGA.

cabrilla [cah-breel'-lyah], *f.* 1. *(dim.)* Little goat. 2. *(Zool.)* Prawn. -*pl.* 1. *(Astr.)* Pleiades, a constellation. 2. Stones thrown obliquely on the water, called duck and drake. 3. Marks on the legs, produced by being continually too near the fire. 4. *(Naut.)* White caps on the water.

cabrilleo [cah-breel-lyay'-o], *m.* The lapping of the waves when the sea is not high.

cabrillo [cah-breel'-lyo], *m.* Cheese from goat's milk.

cabrina [cah'-bree'-nah], *f.* Goatskin.

cabrio [cah'-bree-o], *m.* Rafter, beam, or other timber, used in building.

cabrío [cah'-bree-o], *a.* Belonging to goats, goatish. **Ganado cabrío**, goats.

cabriol [cah-bree'-ol], *m.* Rafter. *V.* CABRÍO.

cabriola [cah-bre-oh'-lah], *f.* 1. Caper movement made in dancing, gamble; hop, skip, prance. **Hacer cabriolas**, to caper about. 2. Nimble leap, hop, or jump, gambol, skip. **Dar cabriolas**, to leap for joy. 3. *(Carib.)* Prank, piece of mischief.

cabriolar, cabriolear [cah-bre-o-lar', cah-bre-o-lay-ar'], *vn.* To caper or cut capers, to jump, to curvet, to frisk.

cabriolé [cah-bre-o-lay'], *m.* 1. Kind of cloak used by ladies. 2. Narrow riding-coat without sleeves. 3. **Cabriolet**, a kind of open carriage.

cabriolear [cah-bree-o-lay-ar'], *vn. V.* CABRIOLAR.

cabrión [cah-bre-on'], *m.* 1. Block or wedge for checking the wheel of a carriage. 2. *(Naut.)* Quoin, wedge for fastening the wheels of cannon to the decks in a gale.

cabrita [cah-bree'-tah], *f.* 1. *(dim.)* Little she-kid up to one year of age. 2. Kidskin dressed. 3. Ancient engine for cast stones.

cabritada [cah-bre-tah'-dah], *f.* Dirty trick.

cabritero [cah-bre-tay'-ro], *m.* 1. Dealer in kids. 2. One who dresses or sells kidskins.

cabritilla [cah-bre-teel'l-yah], *f.* A dressed lamb or kidskin.

cabritillo [cah-bre-teel'-lyo], *m. dim.* Kid.

cabrito [cah-bree'-to], *m.* 1. Kid, kidling, up to one year of age. 2. Cuckold (cornudo); client (de prostituta). 3. *(Cono Sur)* Popcorn.

cabro [cah'-bro], *m.* 1. *(LAm.) (Zool.)* He-goat, billy goat. 2. *(Cono Sur)* small child; boy; lover, sweetheart; guy (sujeto).

cabrón [cah-brone'], *m.* 1. Buck, he-goat. 2. One who consents to the adultery of his wife. 3. **El muy cabrón le robó el coche**, the bastard stole his car (insulto). 4. *(LAm.)* Brothel keeper; *(And. Cono Sur)* pimp; *(CAm. Cono Sur)* traitor.

cabronada [cah-bro-nah'-dah], *f.* 1. *(Low.)* Infamous action which a man permits against his own honor. 2. Dirty trick. **Hacer una cabronada a uno**, to play a dirty trick on somebody. 3. Tough job, (faena).

cabronazo [cah-bro-nah'-tho], *m. aug.* 1. One who prostitutes his own wife. 2. Rotter, villain.

cabroncillo, cito, zuelo [cah-bron-theel-yo, thee'-to, thooay'-lo], *m.* 1. *(dim.)* Easy husband. 2. Fetid herb resembling the Celtic spikenard.

cabronismo [cah-bro-nees'-mo], *m.* Cuckoldism by consent; the state of a husband who consents to the adultery of his wife.

cabruno, na [cah-broo'-no, nah], *a.* Goatish; goatlike.

cabu [cah'-boo], *m. (Prov.)* Barren ground.

cabujón [cah-boo-lah], *m.* Rough, unpolished ruby.

cabula [cah-boo-lah], *f.* 1. *(And. Cono Sur)* amulet (amuleto). 2. *(Cono Sur)* cabal, intrigue (intriga). 3. *(And. Carib. CAm.)* Trick, stratagem.

cabulear [cah-boo-lay-ar'], *vn. (And. CAm. Carib.)* To scheme (intrigar).

cabulero [cah-boo-lay'-ro], *(And. CAm. Carib.)* 1. *a.* Tricky, cunning, scheme. 2. *m.* Trickster, schemer.

cabuya [cah-boo'-yah], *f.* 1. *(Bot.)* Common American agave, a sort of sedge or grass, of which cords are made. 2. *(Prov.)* Cord or rope made of the aloes-plant. 3. Sisal hemp. **Dar cabuya**, to tie. **Ponerse en la abuya**, to grasp the trend of a topic. **Verse a uno las cabuyas**, to see what somebody is up to, to see through somebody's scheme.

cabuyero [cah-boo-yay'-ro], *m. (Amer.)* Ship chandler.

cabuyería [cah-boo-yay-ree'-ah], *f. (Amer.)* Ship chandlery.

caca [cah'-cah], *f.* 1. Excrements, cack, muck (excremento, suciedad). **Eso es una caca**, that's junk, trash. **Tira eso, es una caca**, throw that away, it's dirty.

cacaguatal [cah-cah-goo-ah-tahl'], *m. (CAm.)* Cocoa field.

cacahual, cacaotal [cah-cah-oo-ahl', cah-cah-oh-tahl'], *m.* Plantation of chocolate-trees.

cacahuate, cacahuete [cah-cah-oo-ah'-tay, cah-cah-oo-ay'-tay], *m. (Bot.) V.* MANÍ. The peanut, or earthnut; called also goober and pindar.

cacalote [cah-cah-lo'-tay], *m.* 1. A sweet paste made in Cuba from corn toasted without being ground. 2. *(Prov.)* A very absurd blunder.

cacao [cah-cah'-o], *m.* 1. *(Bot.)* Smooth-leaved chocolate nut-tree. 2. Cocoa, the fruit of the chocolate-tree. **Manteca de cacao**, cocoa-butter, or butter of cacao. 3. **Ser gran cacao**, to have influence. **Tener un cacao en la cabeza**, to be all mixed up. **No vale un cacao** *(LAm.)*, to be worthless, to be insignificant.

cacaotal [cah-caho-tahr], *m.* A cacao orchard, cacao plantation.

cacaraña [cah-cah-rah'-nyah], *f.* Pit; the mark made by smallpox.

cacarañado, da [cah-cah-rah-nyah'-do, dah] *m. & f. & a.* Pitted by smallpox.

cacarañar [cah-cah-rah-nyar'], *va. (Mex.)* To scratch, to pinch; to pit, to scar, to pockmark.

cacareador, ra [cah-cah-ray-ah-dor', rah], *m. & f.* 1. Cackler. 2. Cock that crows, a hen that cackles. 3. Cackler, boaster, braggart.

cacarear [cah-cah-ray-ar'], *vn.* 1. To crow, to cackle. 2. To exaggerate one's own actions, to brag, to boast. **Ese triunfo tan cacareado**, that triumph that was so much talked of. 3. To humbug.

cacareo [cah-cah-ray'-o], *m.* 1. Crowing of a cock, cackling of a hen. 2. Boast, brag, humbug.

cacarico [cah-cah-ree'-co], *a. (CAm.)* Numb.

cacarizo [cah-cah-ree'-tho], *a. (Mex.)* Pitted, pockmarked.

cacaste [cah-cahs'-tlay], *m.* A box or crate to carry fruit.

cacastle [cah-cahs'-tlay], *m. (CAm. Mex.)* Skeleton; large wicker basket (canasta); wicker carrying frame (armazón).

cacatoes, or **cacatue** [cah-cah-to'es, or cah-cah-too'-ay], *m. (Zool.)* Cockatoo, a bird of the parrot family.

cacatúa [cah-cah-too'-ah], *f.* 1. Cockatoo. 2. Old bat, old cow (bruja).

cacaxtle [cah-cax'-tlay], *m. (CAm. Mex.)* Skeleton; frame.

cacera [cah-thay'-rah], *f.* 1. Canal, channel, or conduit of water, employed in watering lands. 2. Sort of pignuts.

cacería [cah-thay-ree'-ah], *f.* 1. Hunting or fowling party. **Cacería de brujas**, witch-hunt. **Cacería de zorros**, fox hunt. **Organizar una cacería**, to organize a hunt. 2. *(Art.)* Landscape representing field sports. 3. Bag, total of animals (animales cazados).

cacerilla [cah-thay-reel'-lyah], *f. dim.* Small drain or canal.

cacerina [cah-thay-ree'-nah], *f.* Cartridge-box or pouch for carrying powder and ball.

cacerola [cah-thay-ro'-lah], *f.* Stewpan, saucepan.

caceta [cah-thay'-tah], *f. dim.* Small pan used by apothecaries.

cacha [cah'-chah], *f.* 1. Handle of a razor. **Hasta las cachas**, full to the brim. 2. *(Prov.)* Tardiness, inactivity. 3. *(And.)* Horn. 4. *(And.)* metal spur attached to the leg of a fighting cock (de gallo). 5. *(And.)* Large chest (arca). 6. **Cachas**, bottom (culo); legs (piernas). 7. *(Mex.)* **Estar a medias cachas**, to be tipsy (locuciones); *(CAm.)* **Hacer cachas**, to try hard. 8. *(LAm.)* Cheek (cachete). 9. *(CAm.)* Crooked deal (negocio). 10. *(CAm.)* Opportunity.

cachaciento [cah-chah-the-ayn'-do], *a.* *(CAm. Cono Sur)* V. CACHAZUDO.

cachaco [cah-chah'-co], *m.* 1. *(And. Carib.)* Fop, dandy. 2. *(And.)* Copper (policía). 3. *(Carib.)* Busybody, noseyparker (entrometido).

cachada [cah-chah'-dah], *f.* 1. Stroke of one top against another, when boys play at tops. 2. *(LAm.)* *(Taur.)* Butt, thrust; goring. 3. *(Cono Sur)* Joke, leg-pull.

cachador [cah-chah-dor'], *(Cono Sur)* 1. *a.* Fond of practical jokes. 2. *m.* Practical joker.

cachafaz [cah-cha-fath'], *a.* *(LAm.)* Rascally (pillo); crafty (taimado); cheeky (fresco).

cachalote [cah-chah-loh'-tay], *m.* The sperm whale. V. MARSOPLA.

cachancha [cah-chan'-cha], *f.* *(Carib.)* Patience. **Estar de cachancha con uno**, to grease up to somebody.

cachaña [cah-cha'-nya], *f.* *(Cono Sur)* 1. Small parrot. 2. Hoax, leg-pull (broma). 3. Arrogance (arrogancia). 4. Stupidity (estupidez). 5. Rush, scramble (arrebatiña).

cachañar [cah-cha-nyar'], **va.** *(Cono Sur)* V. CACHAR. **Cachañar a uno**, to pull somebody's leg.

cachapa [cah-chah'-pa], *f.* Cornbread with sugar, used in Venezuela.

cachar [cah-char'], *va.* 1. *(Prov.)* To break in pieces. 2. To divide a plank in two lengthwise by a saw or axe. 3. *(And. CAm.)* To butt, gore. 4. *(And. CAm. Cono Sur)* to scoff at, deride, ridicule (ridiculizar). 5. *(And. Cono Sur)* To screw. 6. *(Mex.)* To search (registrar).

cachar [cah-char'], *va.* 1. *(Cono Sur)* to catch (autobús). 2. *(CAm.)* To get, obtain (obtener); *(CAm. Cono Sur)* to steal (robar). 3. *(Cono Sur, Mex.)* To surprise, to catch in the act. 4. *(Cono Sur)* To penetrate. 5. *(And. CAm. Carib.)* To catch (pelota).

cacharado [cah-chah-rah'-do], *m.* Kind of linen.

cacharpas [cah-char'-pas], *f. pl.* *(LAm.)* Useless objects, lumber, junk; odds and ends.

cacharpaya [cah-char-pah'-ya], *f.* *(And. Cono Sur)* sendoff, farewell party; *(Cono Sur)* farewell; minor festivity.

cacharpearse [cah-chahr-pay-ar'-say], *vr.* *(LAm.)* To dress up.

cacharra [cah-chahr'-rah], *f.* Rod, pistol.

cacharrear [cah-chahr-ray-ar'], *va.* *(Cam, Carib.)* To throw into jail.

cacharrería [cah-chahr-ray-ree'-ah], *f.* 1. Crockery shop. 2. Crockery pots (cacharros). 3. *(And.)* Ironmongery.

cacharro [cah-char'-ro], *m.* 1. Coarse earthen pot; also a piece of it. 2. *(Met.)* Any useless, worthless thing. 3. Piece of pottery, postsherd. 4. *(CAm. Carib.)* Jail (cárcel). 5. Rod, pistol.

cachas [cáh-chas], *a.* **Estar cachas**, to be tough, to be well set-up. **Está cachas**, he's buff.

cachativa [cah-chah-tee-vah], *f.* **Tener cachativa** *(Cono Sur),* to be quick on the uptake.

cachaza [cah-chah'-thah], *f.* *(Con.)* 1. Inactivity, tardiness: forbearance. 2. *(Amer.)* Rum. 3. First froth on canejuice when boiled to make sugar.

cachazo [cah-chah-tho], *m.* *(LAm.)* Butt, thrust (golpe); goring (herida).

cachazudamente, [cah-chah-thoo-dah-mayn'-tay] *adv.* Calmly.

cachazudo, da [cah-chah-thoo'-do, dah], *a.* Cool, calm, phlegmatic, tranquil.

caché [cah-chay'], *m.* Cachet.

cachear [cah-chay-ar'], *va.* 1. *(LAm.)* *(Taur.)* To butt, gore. 2. *(LAm.)* To punch, slap. 3. To frisk (registrar), search (for weapons).

cachejo [cah-chay-ho], *m.* *(Esp.)* **Un cachejo de pan**, a little bit of bread.

cachemarín [cah-chay'-mah-reen'], *m.* A small two-masted craft used in Brittany and on the northern Spanish coast.

cachemir [cah-chay-meer'], *m.* Cashmere, a fine, soft, costly fabric.

cachemira [cah-che-mee'-rah], *f.* V. CACHEMIR.

cacheo [cah-chay-o], *m.* Searching, frisking (for weapons).

cachera [cah-chay'-rah], *f.* Coarse shagged cloth or baize.

cachería [cah-chay-ree-ah], *f.* 1. *(And. CAm.)* Small business, sideline. 2. *(Cono Sur)* bad taste; slovenliness (desaseo).

cachero [cah-chay'-ro], *a.* 1. *(CAm. Carib.)* Lying, deceitful. 2. *(CAm.)* Hard-working (trabajador). -*m.* *(LAm.)* Sodomite.

cachet [cah-chayt'], *m.* 1. Cachet (sello distintivo); character, temperament. 2. Appearance money, fee (de artista).

cachetada [cah-chay-tah'-dah], *f.* *(LAm.)* Slap, box on the ear; beating (paliza).

cachetas [cah-chay'-tas], *f.pl.* Teeth or wards in a lock.

cachetazo [cah-chay-tah'-tho], *m.* 1. *(LAm.)* Slap, punch (bofetada); *(fig.)* Snub. 2. *(LAm.)* Swig, slug (trago). 3. **¡Hazme un cachetazo!** *(CAm. Carib.)* Do me a favor.

cachete [cah-chay'-tay], *m.* 1. Cheek. 2. Fist, a blow given with the hand clenched. 3. A cuff on the ear. **Cachetes de un navío**, *(Naut.)* Bow of a ship.

cacheteada [cah-chay-tay-ah'-dah], *f.* *(Cono Sur)* Slap, box on the ear.

cachetear [cah-chay-tay-ar'], 1. *vr.* *(And. Cono Sur)* To slap on the face. 2. *vn.* *(Cono Sur)* to eat well.

cachetero [cah-chay-tay'-ro], *m.* Short and broad knife.

cachetina [cah-chay-tee'-nah], *f.* A hand to hand fight.

cachetón, ona [cah-chay-tone', nah], *a.* 1. Fatcheeked. 2. *(Mex.)* Impudent, barefaced (descarado); *(Cono Sur)* proud, haughty (orgulloso). 3. *(CAm.)* Attractive, congenial (atractivo).

cachetudo, da [cah-chay-too'-do, dah], *a.* Plumpcheeked, fleshy.

cachicamo [cah-che-cah'-mo], *m.* An armadillo. South American name.

cachicán [cah-che-cahn'], *m.* Overseer of a farm.

cachicuerno, na [cah-che-coo-er'-no, nah], *a.* Having a handle or haft of horn.

cachidiablo [cah-che-de-ah'-blo], *m.* 1. Hobgoblin. 2. Disguised in a devil's mask. 3. Having an odd and extravagant appearance.

cachifa [cah-che'-fah], *f.* *(CAm. Carib.)* Girl, kid.

cachifo [cah-che'-fo], *m.* *(And. CAm. Carib.)* Lad, kid; young boy.

cachifollar [cah-che-fol-lyar'], *va.* 1. To puff or blow with the cheeks. 2. *(Prov.)* To play a trick.

cachigordete, eta, ito, ita [cah-che-gor-day'-tay, tah, dee'-to, tah], *a.* Squat, thick, and plump.

cachilla [cah-cheel'-lyah], *f.* *(Cono Sur)* jalop(p)y, old banger.

cachillada [cah-cheem'-bah], *f.* *(Coll.)* Litter, young brought forth by an animal.

cachimba [cah-cheem'-bah], *f.* 1. *(Cuba)* A smoking-pipe. 2. *(LAm.)* Empty cartridge (cartucho). 3. *(Carib.)* Tart, slut (puta). 4. **Fregar la cachimba**, to get on somebody's nerves. -*a.* Fantastic, terrific.

cachimbazo [cah-cheem-bah'-tho], *m.* *(CAm.)* 1. Thump, blow (golpe). 2. Shot, slug (trago).

cachimbo [cah-cheem'-bo], *m.* 1. A ladle with a long handle. (para hacer azúcar) 2. *(LAm.)* Pipe. 3. *(Carib.)* Small sugar mill. 3. *(Carib.)* Poor man (pobre). 4. Freshman. 4. *(CAm.)* Pile, heap (montón). 5. *(And.)* Soldier, squaddy.

cachimbón [cah-cheem-bon'], *a.* *(CAm.)* Smart, sharp.

cachipolla [cah-che-pol'-lyah], *f.* Dayfly, or mayfly: of very brief life, hence the name. One of the Ephemerids.

cachiporra, *f.* **cachiporro**, *m.* [cah-che-por'-rah]. 1. A stick with a big knob used by country people; a cudgel. 2. A fruit-eating bat. 3. An Indian club.

cachiporra [cah-che-por'-rah], *int.* A vulgar exclamation. -*f.* Truncheon; club, big stick, cosh. 2. *(Cono Sur)* braggart.

cachiporrazo [cah-chee-por-rah'-tho], *m.* Blow with a truncheon (etc.).

cachiporrear [cah-chee-por-ray-ar'], 1. *va. (Mus.)* To bash, pound. 2. *vr. (Cono Sur)* to brag, boast.

cachiporro [cah-che-por'-roh], *m. (Prov. Coll.)* Chubface.

cachirulo [cah-che-roo'-lo], *m.* 1. Earthen, glass, or tin pot for preserving brandy or other liquors. 2. Bow or rosette worn on the head by women toward the end of the 18th century. 3. *(Mex.)* Lining of cloth or chamois placed in the seat and legs of trousers for riding.

cachirulo [cah-che-roo'-lo], *m.* Small three-masted vessel.

cachito [cah-chee'-to], *m.* 1. *(And.)* Dice game; dice cup (cubito). 2. *(LAm.)* **Espera un cachito**, just a minute, hang on.

cachivache [çah-che-vah'-chay], *m.* 1. Broken crockery, or other old trumpery, laid up in a corner. 2. *(Met.)* A despicable, useless, worthless fellow. 3. **Cachivaches**, pots, pants, kitchen utensils.

cacho [cah'-cho], *m.* 1. Slice, piece (fruta, pan). 2. Small horn. 3. Game of chance at cards. 4. *(Zool.)* Red surmullet. 5. *(And. Cono Sur)* dice, set of dice (dados); **Jugar al cacho**, to play dice. 6. *(Cono Sur)* Bunch of bananas (plátanos). 7. *(Cono Sur)* unsaleable goods. 8. *(LAm.)* Funny story, joke (chiste); prank (broma), practical joke. 9. *(Carib.)* Joint (marijuana). 10. *(Carib.)* Prick (pene) 11. **Echar cacho a uno** *(And.),* to do better than someone. **Estar fuera de cacho**, to be safe. **Raspar el cacho a uno** *(Cono Sur),* to tell somebody off.

cacho, cha [cah'-cho, chah], *a.* Bent, crooked, inflected. *V.* GACHO.

cachó [cah-cho'], *m.* Chub (pez de río); surmullet (de mar).

cacholas [cah-cho'-las], *f. pl. (Naut.)* Cheeks of the masts.

cachón [cah'-chone], *m.* 1. A breaker, wave. *V.* CACHONES. 2. A fall of water.

cachondear [cah-chon-day-ar'], *(CAm. Mex.)* 1. *vn.* To pet (acariciar); to snog (besarse). 2. *vr.* To take things as a joke. **Cachondearse de uno**, to take the mickey out of somebody; to make fun of somebody; *(LAm.)* To get turned on (calentarse sexualmente).

cachondeo [cah-chon-day'-o], *m.* 1. Joking; teasing; nagging; messing about (guasa). **Estar de cachondeo**, to be in a joking mood. **Tomar algo a cachondeo**, to take something as a joke, to live it up, have a good time. 2. Trouble, disturbance (jaleo). Farce. mess (farsa); poor show. **¡Esto es un cachondeo!**, what a mess!

cachondez [cah-chon-deth'], *f.* 1. *(Coll.)* Sexual appetite. 2. Heat, rut, readiness to mate.

cachondo, da [cah-chone'-do, dah], *a.* Ruled by sexual appetite; in heat (hembra). **Cachondas,** Slashed trousers formerly worn. **Estar cachondo,** to feel randy, be in the mood. **Cachondo mental,** crazy but likable.

cachones [cah-cho'-nes], *m. pl.* Breakers, waves broken by the shore, rocks, or sandbanks.

cachopo [cah-cho'-po], *m.* 1. *(Naut.)* Gulf of the sea between rocks. 2. *(Prov.)* Dry trunk or stump of a tree.

cachorrenas [cah-chor-ray'-nas], *f. pl. (Prov.)* Sort of soap, made of oil, orange, bread, and salt.

cachorrillo, ito [cah-chor-reel'-lyo, ree'-to], *m. dim.* 1. A little cub or whelp. 2. A young man (despectivo). 3. A little pistol.

cachorro, ra [cah-chor'-ro, rah], *m. & f.* 1. Grown whelp or puppy. 2. Cub, the young of a beast. 3. Pocket pistol. 4. A lizard.

cachucha [cah-choo'-chah], *f.* 1. A wellknown Spanish dance in triple measure. 2. Man's cloth or fur cap. 3. A little boat used in rivers and ports of America. 4. *(And.)* Nick, prison.

cachucho [cah-choo'-cho], *m.* 1. Oil measure, containing the sixth part of a pound. 2. *(Obs.)* Cartridge. 3. *(Prov.)* Clumsy earthen pot. 4. Place for each arrow in a quiver. 5. Sea bream (pez). 6. Pin box (alfiletero). 7. *(And.)* Daily bread. **Ganarse el cachucho,** to make a living.

cachudo [cah-choo'-do], *a.* 1. *(And. Mex.)* Horned, with horns (con cuernos). 2. *(And.)* Wealthy (rico). 3. *(Cono Sur)* Suspicious, distrustful (receloso); cunning (taimado). 4.

(Mex.) Long-faced, miserable (triste). -*m.* **El cachudo, the devil**, the horned one.

cachuela [cah-choo-ay'-lah], *f.* 1. Fricassee made of the livers and lights of rabbits. 2. *(And.)* Rapids (remolinos).

cachuelo [cah-choo-ay'-lo], *m. (Zool.)* Small river fish resembling an anchovy.

cachulera [cah-choo-lay'-rah], *f. (Prov.).* Cavern or hiding place.

cachumbo [cah-choom'bo], *m.* Kind of hard cocoa-wood.

cachunde [cah-choon'-day], *f.* Paste made of musk and other aromatics, which the Chinese carry in their mouth to strengthen the stomach.

cachupín [cah-choo-peen'], *m.* A Spaniard who settles in Mexico or South America. *V.* GACHUPÍN. (*Port. cachopo,* child.).

cachureo [cah-choor-ray'-o], *m. (Conor Sur)* Bric-à-brac.

cachuzo [cah-choo'-do], *a. (Cono Sur)* Worn-out, old.

cacicada [cah-the-cah'-dah], *f.* Despotic act, high-handed; abuse of authority.

cacicazgo [cah-the-cath'-go]' *m.* The dignity of a chief or cacique and his territory.

cacillo, ito [cah-theel'-lyo, ee'-to], *m. dim.* Small saucepan.

cacimba [cah-theem-bah], *f.* 1. *(And. Carib. Cono Sur)* Well (pozo); *(Carib.)* Hollow of tree where rainwater is collected; *(And.)* Outdoor privy. 2. *(Carib. Mex.)* Hovel, slum (casucha).

cacique [cah-thee'-kay], *m.* 1. Cacique, a prince or nobleman among the Indians 2. Any leading inhabitant of a small town or village, party boss, local boss; *(fig.)* Petty tyrant, despot; *(Cono Sur)* person who lives idly in luxury (vago). 2. *(And. CAm. Mex.)* Oriole (ave).

caciquismo [cah-the-kees'-mo], *m. (Pol.)* (system of) dominance by the local boss; petty tyranny, despotism.

cacle [cah'-clay], *m. (Mex.)* A kind of sandals worn by friars, indians, and soldiers.

caco [cah'-co], *m.* 1. Pickpocket, burglar. 2. A coward.

cacófago, ga [cah-co'-fah-go, gah], *a.* Cacophagous, having a depraved appetite.

cacofonía [cah-co-fo-nee'-ah], *f.* Cacophony, a harsh or unharmonious sound.

cacofónico [cah-co'-fo-no], *a.* Cacophonous.

cacografía [cah-co-grah-fee'-ah], *f.* Bad spelling.

cacomite [cah-co-mee'-tay], *m.* A Mexican plant which produces handsome flowers.

cacoquimia [cah-co-kee'-meah], *f.* Abnormal metabolism.

cacoquímico, ca [cah-co-kee'-me-co. cah], *a.* Suffering from or related to abnormal metabolism.

cacoquimio [cah-co-kee'-me-o], *m.* Suffering from melancholy.

cácteo, ea [cahc'-tay-o, ah], *a.* Cactaceous, relating to cacti.

cacto [cahc'-to], *m.* The cactus.

cacumen [cah-coo'-men], *m.* 1. The top, the height. 2. Insight, understanding; comprehension.

cada [cah'-dah], *pron.* Every, everyone, each. **Cada uno** or **cada cual**, every one, each. **Cada vez**, every time. **Cada día**, every day. **A cada palabra**, at every word. **Dar a cada uno**, to give to every one. **Cada vez que**, every time that. **Cada y cuando**, whenever, as soon as. **Cada cierto tiempo**, every so often.

cadalso [cah-dahl'-so], *m.* 1. Scaffold raised for the execution of malefactors. 2. Temporary gallery or stage, erected for shows or spectators. 3. Fortification or bulwark made of wood.

cadañal, cadañego, ga, cadañero, ra [cah-dah-nyahl', cah-dah-nyay'-go, gah, cah-dah-nyay'-ro, rah], *a.* Annual. **Mujer cadañera**, a woman who bears every year.

cadarzo [cah-dar'-tho], *m.* Coarse, entangled silk, which cannot be spun with a wheel

cadáver [cah-dah'-ver], *m.* Corpse, corse, cadaver. **Cadáver en el armario**, *(fig.)* skeleton in the cupboard. **¡Sobre mi cadáver!**, over my dead body! **Ingresó cadáver**, he was dead on arrival (at the hospital).

cadavérico, ca [cah-dah-vay'-re-co, cah], *a.* Cadaverous; death-like; ghastly, deathly.

caddie [cah'-dee], *n.* (Golf) caddle.

cadejo [cah-day'-ho], *m.* 1. Entangled skin of thread. 2. Entangled hair. 3. Threads put together to make tassels.

cadena [cah-day'-nah], *f.* 1. Chain. **Cadenas antideslizantes**, tire chains. 2. (*Met.*) Tie caused by passion or obligation. 3. Mortice, a hole cut into wood. 4. (*Met.*) Series of events. 5. Chain, link, any series linked together. 6. Number of malefactors chained together to be conducted to the galleys: punishment next after the death penalty. **Cadena perpetua**, life imprisonment. 7. Bar of iron with which a way is strengthened. 8. Frame of wood put round the hearth of a kitchen. 9. Treadle of a ribbon, weaver's loom. 10. Turning handle which moves a wheel. 11. **Cadena alimenticia**, food chain. **Cadena de hoteles**, chain of hotels. **Reacción en cadena**, chain reaction. 12. (*Jur.*) Chain-gang.

cadencia [cah-den'-the-ah], *f.* 1. Cadence, fall of the voice. 2. Cadence, number, measure, flow of verses or periods. 3. In dancing, the correspondence of the motion of the body with the music. **Hablar en cadencia**, to affect the harmonious flow of rhythm when speaking in prose.

cadencioso, sa [cah-den-the-o'-so, sah], *a.* Belonging to a cadence, numerous.

cadeneta [cah-day-nay'-tah], *f.* 1. Lace or needlework wrought in form of a chain; chain-stitch. 2. Work put upon the heads of books for security of the sewing.

cadenilla, ita [cah-day-neel'-lyah, ee'-tah], *f. dim.* Small chain. **Cadenilla y media cadenilla**, pearls distinguished by their size.

cadente [cah-den'-tay], *a.* 1. Decaying, declining, going to ruin. 2. Having a correct modulation in delivering prose or verse.

cadera [cah-day'-rah], *f.* Hip, the joint of the thigh.

caderamen [cah-day-rah'-men], *m.* Hips (de mujer).

cadereta [cah-day-ray'-tah], *f.* (*Mus.*) A kind of small organ, manipulated by a second keyboard, that imitates the great organ which contains it; echo organ.

caderillas [cah-day-reel'-lyas], *f. pl.* 1. Hoops worn by ladies to distend the skirts over the hips. 2. Bustle.

cadetada [cah-day-tah'-dah], *f.* Thoughtless action, irresponsible act.

cadete [cah-day'-tay], *m.* 1. Cadet, a volunteer in the army who serves in expectation of a commission. 2. A young man in a military school.

cadí [cah-dee'], *m.* Cadi, a magistrate among the Turks and Moors.

cadí [cah-dee'], *m.* (Golf) Caddie.

cadillar [cah-deel-lyar'], *m.* Place abounding with bur-parsley.

cadillero, ra [cah-dee-lyay'-ro, rah], *a.* (*Bot.*) Applied to plants bearing fruit covered with hooked bristles or prickles.

cadillo [cah-deel'-lyo], *m.* (*Bot.*) Bur-parsley.

cadmía [cad-mee'-ah], *f.* Calamine. V. CALAMINA. Tutty, impure oxide of zinc, collected from a furnace or a crucible.

cadmio [cahd'-me-o], *m.* Cadmium, a metal, in color like tin, associated with zinc.

cado [cah'-do], *m.* (*Prov.*) Ferret-hole. V. HURONERA.

cadoce [cah-do'-thay], *m.* (*Zool. Prov.*) Gudgeon.

caducamente [cah-doo-cah-men'-tey], *adv.* In a weak, doting manner.

caducante [cah-doo-cahn'-tay], *pa.* Doting, one who dotes.

caducar [cah-doo-car'], *vn.* 1. To dote, to have the intellect impaired by age. 2. To be worn out by service, to fall into disuse, to become superannuated. **El abono ha caducado**, the season ticket has expired. 3. To deteriorate.

caduceo [cah-doo-thay'-o], *m.* 1. Caduceus or caduce, the wand with which Mercury is depicted. 2. Herald's staff among the ancient Greeks.

caducidad [cah-doo-the-dahd'], *f.* (*Law.*) Caducity, decrepitude, the state or quality of being worn out by age or labor; lapsed, expiry. **Fecha de caducidad** (alimentos), sell-by date.

caduco, ca [cab-doo'-co, cah], *a.* 1. Worn out or broken with fatigue, senile, enfeebled by age, decrepit. 2. Perishable, frail. *3.* (*Bot.*) Deciduous. 4. Fleeting, perishable. 5. (*Com. Jur.*) Lapsed, expired, invalid. **Quedar caduco**, to lapse.

caduquez [cah-doo-keth'], *f.* Caducity, senility, last stage of life.

C.A.E., Abbreviation of **Cóbrese al entregar,** C.O.D., cash on delivery.

caedizo, za [cah-ay-dee'-tho, thah], *a.* 1. Ready to fall, being of short duration, or little consistence. **Hacer caediza una cosa**, to let a thing fall on purpose. **Peras caedizas**, pears dropping from the tree. 2. (*Bot.*) Deciduous.

caedura [cah-ay-doo'-rah], *f.* Among weavers, the loose threads dropping from the loom when weaving.

caer [cah-err'], *vn.* 1. To fall to the ground, to tumble down: to lighten. **El edificio se está cayendo**, the building is falling down. **Cayó un rayo en la torre**, the tower was struck by lighting. 2. To lose one's situation, fortune, or influence. 3. To fall into an error or danger. 4. (*Met.*) To deviate from the right road, or to take the wrong one. 5. (*Met.*) To fall due: as instalments or payments of debts. 6. To fall, to decrease, to decline, to come into any state of weakness, misery, etc. 7. To fall to one's lot. 8. To fall, to befall, to happen to, to come to pass. 9. To die. 10. (*Mil.*) To fall, to yield, to surrender. 11. To decline, to approach the end. **La luz cae**, the light declines. **El día cae**, the day is drawing to a close. 12. To be situated. **Caer a esta parte**, to be situated on this side. **Las ventanas caen al río**, the windows overlook the river; **caer a la mar**, (*Naut.*) To fall overboard. **Caer de espaldas,** to fall backward. **Caer en la cuenta**, to bethink oneself, to see the point, to correct one's habits. **No caer en las cosas**, not to comprehend a thing. **Caerse de sueño**, to fall asleep. **Caer bien alguna cosa**, to fit, to suit, to become. **Este color cae bien con este otro**, this color is well matched with the other. **Caer en cama**, to become sick. **Caer en alguna cosa**, to remember or obtain knowledge of a thing. **Caer en gracia**, to please, to be agreeable. **Caer la balanza**, to be partial. **Caerse a pedazos**, to be very fatigued, or very foolish. **Caerse de ánimo**, to be dejected. **Caerse de risa**, to shake with laughter. **Al caer de la hoja**, at the fall of the leaf, about the end of fall. **Dejar caer alguna cosa en la conversación**, to drop something, in the course of conversation. **Caer en ello**, to understand or comprehend a thing. **Estar a la que cae**, to be alert. **Ya caigo en ello**, now I have it. **Estar al caer**, to be arriving. **Caérsele a uno la cara de vergüenza**, to blush deeply with shame. 13. To fall, to lie, to be located. **Cae en el segundo tomo**, it comes in the second volume. 14. (*Com. fin.*) To fall due. 15. **Caer a** (herencia), to fall to, to come to. 15. **No me cae bien** (impresión), I don't like him at all. 16. **Caer mal a** (comida), to disagree with. 17. (*Cono Sur*) To come by, to visit, to drop in. **Suele caer por aquí**, he often comes here.

caerse [cah-er'-say], *vr.* 1. All the meanings of the active form. 2. To be, afflicted, to be overwhelmed, to be disconsolate. **Dejarse caer**, to allow oneself to be down-hearted. **Caerse de su peso**, to be very true, or manifest.

cafa [cah'-fah], *f.* Cotton stuff of various colors and kinds.

café [cah-fay'], *m.* 1. Coffee tree. 2. Coffee, beverage prepared from the coffee bean. **Café americano**, large black coffee. **Café cortado**, coffee with a dash of milk. **Café soluble**, instant coffee. **Café molido**, ground coffee. **Café tostado**, roasted coffee. 3. **Estar de mal café**, to be in a bad mood.

café, *m.* Cafe, restaurant, coffee-house.

cafecito [cah-fay-thee'-to], *m.* (*LAm.*) Black coffee.

cafeína [cah-fay-ee'-nah], *f.* Caffein, an alkaloid extracted from coffee.

cafetal [cah-fay-tahl'], *m.* Plantation of coffee-trees.

cafetalero [cah-fay-tah-lay'-ro], *(LAm.)* 1. *a.* Coffee, coffee-growing. **Industria cafetalera**, coffee-growing industry. 2. *m.* **Cafetalera** *f.* Coffee grower.

cafetalista [cah-fay-tah-lees'-tah], *m. & f. (LAm.)* Coffee grower.

cafetán, caftán [cah-fay-tahn'], *m.* Caftan, embroidered garment worn by the chief Turkish or Persian officers.

cafetear [cah-fay-tay-ar'], *va. (Cono Sur)* to tick off, to tell off.

cafetera [cah-fay-tay'-rah], *f.* 1. Coffee-pot. **Cafetera automática**, electric ketle. **Cafetera filtradora**, percolator. 2. *(Aut.)* Old car, old crock. 3. Coffee-service.

cafetería [cah-fay-tay-ree'-ah], *f.* 1. Café, coffee-house. 2. Buffet, refreshment room (ferrocarril); *(And. Carib, Cono Sur)* coffee retailer.

cafetero [cah-fay-tay'-ro], *m.* 1. One who makes or sells coffee. 2. *(Bot.)* Coffee-tree. **Cafetero árabe**, Arabian coffee-tree. **Cafetero occidental** or **americano**, Jamaica or western coffee-tree.

cafetín [cah-fay-teen'], *m.* Low-class bar, small café.

cafeto [cah-fay-to], *m.* The coffee-tree.

cafetucho [cah-fay-too'-cho], *m.* Seedy little café.

caficultor [cah-fee-cool-tor'], *m. & f. (CAm.)* Coffee grower.

caficultura [cah-fee-cool-too'-rah], *f. (CAm.)* Coffee growing.

cafiche [cah-fee'-chay], *m.* Pimp.

cafila [cah'-fe-lah], *m.* 1. Multitude of people, animals, or other things. 2. Caravan. 3. Single file, one after another.

cafiolo [cah-fee-o'-lo], *m. (Cono Sur)* Pimp, ponce.

cafishear [cah-fee-shay-ar'], *vn. (Cono Sur)* to live off somebody else.

cafisho [cah-fee'-sho], *m. (Cono Sur)* Pimp, ponce.

cafre [cah'-fray], *a.* 1. Savage, inhuman. 2. Belonging or relating to the Caffres. 3. *(Prov.)* Clownish, rude, uncivil.

caftán [caf-tahn'], *m.* Caftan, kaftan.

cafúa [cah-foo-ah], *f. (Arg. Coll.)* Jail, arrest. **Ir a la cafúa**, to go to jail, to be arrested.

cagada [cah-gah'-dah], *f. (Coll.)* 1. Excrement. 2. Ridiculous action: unfortunate issue.

cagadero [cah-gah-day'-ro], *m.* Latrine.

cagadillo [cah-gah-deel'-lyo], *m. dim. (Low.)* A sorry little fellow.

cagado [cab-gah'-do], *a. (Low.)* A mean-spirited, chicken-hearted fellow, yellow, funky. *pp.* of CAGAR.

cagafierro [cah-gah-fe-er'-ro], *m.* Scoria, dross of iron.

cagajón [cah-gah-hone'], *m,* 1. Horsedung. 2. The dung of mules or asses.

cagalar [cah-gah-lar'], *m.* V. TRIPA. *(Anat.)* Caecum.

cagalera [cah-gah-lay-rah], *f.* Looseness of the body, diarrhoea.

cagamelos [cah-gah-may'-los], *m.* Kind of mushroom.

cagar [cah-gar'], *va.* 1. To defecate. 2. *(Low.)* To stain, or defile a thing. 3. To shit, to crap. 4. To dirty, to soil (ropa). 5. *(fig.)* To cock up, to fuck up. **¡La cagamos!**, we blew it! *-vn.* To shift, to have a shift. *-vr.* **¡Me cago en la mar!**, well, I'm damned!, **¡me cago en el gobierno!**, to hell with the government! ...**y se caga la perra**... *(Esp.)*, and you never saw anything like it.

cagarrache [cah-gar-rah'-chay], *m.* 1. One who washes the olives in an oilmill. 2. Bird of the family of starlings.

cagarria [cah-gar-re-ah], *f.* Kind of mushroom, called St. George's agaric.

cagarruta [cah-gar-roo'-tah], *f.* Dung of sheep, goats, and mice.

cagatinta [cah-gah-teen'-tah], *m.* 1. Pettifogger. 2. A nickname given in contempt to attorneys' clerks. 3. *(And.)* Miser.

cagón, na [cah-gone', nah], *m. & f.* 1. Person afflicted with diarrhoea. 2. Cowardly, timorous person.

cagueta [cah-gay-tah], *m. & f.* Coward.

caguitis [cah-gee'-tis], *f.* Fear. **Le entra caguitis**, he gets the wind up.

cahiz [cah-eeth'], *m.* Nominal measure, commonly of twelve fanegas, or about twelve English bushels.

cahizada [cah-e-thah'-dah], *f.* Tract of land which requires about one *cahiz* of grain in order to be properly sown.

cahué [cah-oo-ay'], *m.* Turkish name of coffee and a café.

cahuín [cah-boo-een'], *m. (Cono Sur)* 1. Drunkenness, drunken spree. 2. Rowdy gathering. 3. *(Cono Sur)* mess, cock up (lío).

caída [cah-ee'-dah], *f.* 1. Fall, falling; tumble. 2. Fall, the effect of falling. 3. Fall, downfall; lapse. 4. Fall, diminution, declination, declension. 5. Fall, declivity, descent. 6. Anything which hangs down, as a curtain or tapestry. 7. Fall, the violence suffered in falling. 8. *(Geol.)* A landslip. 9. An interior gallery in houses of Manila, with views upon the courtyard. (See CAER, 12th accept.) 10. *(Vulg.)* The earnings of a harlot. 11. Failure. **La caída del gobierno**, the fall of the government. **La caída del imperio**, the collapse of the empire. **La caída de los dientes**, the falling-out of the teeth. **Sufrir una caída**, to have a fall. **Caída de una vela**, depth or drop of a sail. **Caída de agua**, waterfall. **Caída incontrolada**, free fall. **Ir o andar de capa caída**, *(Met.)* To decline in fortune and credit. **A la caída de la tarde**, at nightfall. **A la caída del sol**, at sunset. 12. **Caída radiactiva**, radioactive fallout. *-pl.* 1. That part of a headdress which hangs loose. 2. Coarse wool cut off the skirts of fleece. 3. *(Tec.)* Low-grade wool. 4. Witty remarks. **¡Qué caídas tiene!**, isn't he witty!

caído, da [cah-ee'-do, dah], *a.* 1. Languid: downfallen. **Estar de sueño caído**, to be dead tired. 2. *(fig.)* Crestfallen, dejected. 3. **Caído de color**, pale. *-m* 1. **Los caídos**, the fallen. **Monumento a los caídos**, war memorial. 2. *(Mex.)* Backhander (soborno), graft. *-pp.* of CAER.

caídos [cah-ee'-dos], *m. pl* 1. Rents or annual payments become due and not paid. 2. Arrears of taxes. 3. Sloping lines to show the proper slant in writing. *(Yo caigo, yo caiga; yo caí, él cayó; yo cayera, from Caer. V. CAER.)*

caifán [cah-ee-fahn'], *m. (Mex.)* Pimp, ponce.

caigo [cah'-ee-go], etc. V. CAER.

caimacán [cah-ee-mah-can'], *m. (And.)* Important person, big shot; star, expert.

caimán [cah-e-mahn'], *m.* 1. Cayman, alligator, an American crocodile. 2. A cunning man. 3. *(LAm.)* Twister, swindler (estafador). 3. *(Mex.) (Mech.)* Chain wrench. 4. *(And.)* Lazy fellow (gandul).

caimanear [cah-ee-mah-nay-ar'], *(LAm.).* 1. *va.* To swindle, cheat. 2. *vn.* To hunt alligators.

caimiento [cah-e-me-en'-to], *m.* 1. Lowness of spirits; languidness, want of bodily strength. 2. Fall, the act of falling.

Caín [cah-een'], *m.* Cain. **Pasar las de Caín**, to have a ghastly time.

caique [cah-ee'-kay], *m. (Naut.)* Caic, a kind of skiff or small boat.

cairel [cah-e-rel'], *m.* 1. False hair or wig worn by women to embellish their head-dress. 2. Furbelow, a kind of flounce with which women's dresses are trimmed. 3. Silk threads to which wig-makers fasten the hair of wigs.

cairelado, da [cah-e-ray-lah'-do, dah], *a.* Adorned with flounces. *-pp.* of CAIRELAR.

cairelar [cah-e-ray-lar'], *va.* To adorn with flounces.

cairelear [cah-e-ray-lay-ar'], *va.* To trim, fringe.

Cairo [cah'-e-ro], *m.* **El Cairo**, Cairo.

caita [cah-e'-tah], 1. *a. (Cono Sur)* Wild, untamed; unsociable, withdrawn (huraño). 2. *m. (Cono Sur)* Migratory agricultural worker.

caite [cah-e'-tay], *m. (CAm.)* Rough rubber-soled sandal.

caitearse [cah-e-tay-ar'-say], *vr.* **Caitearselas**, *(CAm.)* To run away.

caja [cah'-hah], *f.* 1. Box, case. 2. Coffin. V. ATAÚD. 3. Chest in which money is kept; cash-box or safe. *(Com.)* Cash, funds; cashier's office. 4. A sheath. 5. Drum. 6. Printer's case. 7. Room in post-office where letters are sorted. 8. Portable writing-desk. 9. The well or cavity in which a staircase is raised. 10. Wooden case of an organ. **Caja alta, caja baja,** *(Typ.)* upper case, lower case. **Caja de polvo,** snuffbox. **Caja de brasero,** a wooden case where the brasier is placed in the room. **Caja de coche,** body of a coach. **Caja de balas,** shotlocker. **Caja de bombas,** *(Naut.)* Pump-well of a ship. **Caja de cartuchos,** *(Mil.)* cartridge-box. **Libro de caja,** among merchants, cash-book. **Estar en caja,** to equilibrate, to be in equipoise. **Caja de música,** music box. **Caja de herramientas,** toolbox. **Caja del tambor, del tímpano,** *(Anat.)* Eardrum. **Caja de seguridad,** safe-deposit. **Caja de engranajes,** gear-box. **Caja de empalmes,** junction box. 11. *(Com. Fin.)* Cash-box, safe-deposit box (de caudales). **Caja de compensación,** equalization fund. **Hacer caja,** to make up the accounts for the day. **Ingresar en caja,** to pay in. 12. *(Cono Sur)* Riverted (lecho seco de río).

Caja de Ahorros [cah'-hah day ah-or'-ros], *f.* Savings Bank.

caja de cambios [cah'-hah day cam'-be-os], *f.* Transmission, gear box.

caja de caudales [cah'-hah day cah-oo-dah'-les], *f.* Strong box.

caja fuerte [cah'-hah foo-err'-tay], *f.* Safe, vault.

caja registradora [cah'-hah ray-hes-trah-do'-rah], *f.* Cash register.

cajear [cah-hay-ar'], *va. (CAm.)* To beat up.

cajero [cah-hay'-ro], *m.* 1. Cashier. **Cajero automático,** cash-dispenser. 2. Boxmaker.

cajeta [cah-hay'-tah], *f.* 1. Snuffbox. 2. *(Prov.)* Poorbox. **Cajetas,** *(Naut.)* Caburns. 3. *(Mex.)* Box of jelly. 4. *(And. CAm.)* Lip (de animal). 5. *(CAm. Mex.)*

cajete [cah-hay'-tay], *m. (Mex.)* 1. A flat bowl of unburnished clay, in which the *pulque* (the juice of the century plant or maguey) is sold to people. 2. Toilet, loo. 3. Bottom; arse (culo).

cajetilla [cah-hay-teel'-lyah], *f.*

cajetín [cah-hay-teen'], *m. dim.* 1. Very small box. 2. *(Typ.)* Fount-case, letter-case. 3. Spindle-case.

cajista [cah-hees-tah], *m.* Compositor (in printing).

cajo [cah'-ho], *m.* Among bookbinders, groove for the pasteboards in which *(Aer.)* are bound.

cajón [cah-hone'], *m.* 1. Box or chest for goods. 2. Chest of drawers; drawer under a table; locker; moneydrawer. 3. Mould for casting the pipes of an organ. 4. Space between the shelves of a bookcase. 5. Tub in which wet cloth is laid. 6. Wooden shed for selling provisions; *(Mex.)* Dry-goods store. 7. Crib, caisson. **Ser de cajón,** or **una cosa de cajón,** to be a matter of course, or a common thing. **Ser un cajón de sastre,** *(Met.)* 1. To have one's brain full of confused ideas. 2. To know a great many things. **Cajones de cámara,** *(Naut.)* Lockers in the cabins of ships. 8. Stall, booth. **Cajón de ropa** *(Mex.),* Draper's (shop), dry-goods store. 9. *(Tec.)* **Cajón hidráulico, cajón de suspensión,** caisson. 10. *(CAm. Cono Sur)* Ravine.

cajonada [cah-ho-nah'-dah], *f. (Naut.)* Lockers.

cajoncito [cah-hon-thee'-to], *m. dim.* 1. A small box, chest, or drawer. 2. Compartments or pigeon-holes.

cajonera [cah-ho-nay'-rah], *f.* A box in which flowers or shrubbery are grown; a wood and glass frame for hothouses.

cajonería [cah-ho-nay-ree'-ah], *f.* Chest of drawers.

cajuela [cah-hoo-ay'-lah], *f. (Mex.) (Aut.)* Boot, trunk.

cal [cahl], *f.* Lime. **Cal viva,** quick or unslaked lime. **Pared de cal y canto,** a wall of rough stone and mortar. **Ser de cal y canto,** *(Met.)* to be as strong as if built with lime and stone. **Dar una de cal y otra de arena,** to apply a policy of the carrot and the stick.

cala [cah'-lah], *f.* 1. *(Naut.)* Creek, a small bay. 2. Small piece cut out of a melon or other fruit to try its flavor. 3. Hole made in a wall to try its thickness. 4. *(Med.)* Suppository. **Hacer cala y cata,** to examine a thing to ascertain its quantity and quality.

calabacear [cah-lah-bah-thay-ar'], *va. (Univ.)* To fail, plough; to jilt.

calabacera [cah-lah-bah-thay'-rah], *f. (Bot.)* Pumpkin or gourd-plant. V. CALABAZA.

calabacero [cah-lah-bah-thay'-ro], *m.* Retailer of pumpkins.

calabacica, illa, ita [cah-lah-bah-thee'-cah, eel'-lyah, ee'-tah], *f. dim.* Small pumpkin.

calabacilla [cah-lah-bah-theel'-lyah], *f.* 1. Core, piece of wood in the shape of a gourd, around which a tassel of silk or worsted is formed. 2. Earring made of pearls in the shape of a gourd.

calabacín [cah-lah-bah-theen'], *m.* 1. A small, young, tender pumpkin. 2. *(Coll.)* Doll, a silly person.

calabacinate [cah-lah-bah-the-nah'-tay], *m.* Fried pumpkins.

calabacino [cah-lah-bah-thee'-no], *m.* Dry gourd or pumpkin scooped out, in which wine is carried; a calabash.

calabacita [cah-lah-bah-thee'-tah], *f. (Esp.)* Courgette.

calabaza [cah-lah-bah'-thah], *f.* 1. *(Bot.)* The fruit of the pumpkin or gourd. **Calabaza anaranjada,** orange-fruited gourd. **Calabaza verruguera** or **verrugosa,** warted gourd. 2. Calabash. 3. Small button joining the ring of a key. **Dar calabazas,** 1. to reprove, to censure. 2. To give a denial; to give the mitten: applied to a woman who rejects a proposal of marriage. **Llevar calabazas,** to be dismissed, to be sent away. **Salir calabazas,** to be plucked, to fail in an examination. 4. *(fig.)* Dolt (idiota). 5. Bonce, head (cabeza).

calabazada [cah-lah-bah-thah-dah], *f.* 1. Knock one's against something. **Darse de calabazadas,** *(Met.)* To labor in vain to ascertain something. 2. Liquor drunk from a calabash.

calabazar [cah-lah-bah-thar'], *m.* Piece of ground planted with pumpkins.

calabazate [cah-lah-bah-thah'-tay], *m.* 1. Preserved pumpkin candied with sugar. 2. Piece of a pumpkin steeped in honey or must. 3. Knock of the head against a wall.

calabazazo [cah-lah-bah-thah'-tho], *m.* Bump on the head.

calabazo [cah-lah-bah-tha'-tho], *m.* Prison; prison cell; *(Hist.)* Dungeon; glasshouse.

calabazón [cah-lah-bah-thone'], *m. aug.* Large winter pumpkin.

calabobos [cah-lah-bo'-bos], *m.* Small, gentle, continued rain; drizzle.

calabozo [cah-lah-bo'-tho], *m.* 1. Dungeon, cell, calaboose: generally applied to such as are below ground. 2. *(Prov.)* Pruning-hook or knife.

calabriada [cah-lah-bre-ah'-dah], *f.* 1. A mixture of different things. 2. A mixture of white and red wine.

calabrote [cah-lah-bro'-tay], *m. (Naut.)* Stream cable, cablerope.

calache [cah-lah'-chay], *m. (CAm.)* Thing. **Reúne tus calaches,** get your things.

calada [cah-lah'-dah], *f.* 1. Rapid flight of birds of prey. 2. Introduction. 3. Narrow, craggy road. 4. Reprimand. **Dar una calada,** to reprimand. 5. Soaking (mojada). 6. Lowering (de red). 7. Puff (cigarrillo).

caladero [cah-lah-day-ro], *m.* Fishing-grounds.

caladio [cah-lah'-de-o], *m. (Bot.)* Caladium, an ornamental-leaved plant.

calado [cah-lah-do], *m.* 1. Open work in metal, stone, wood, or linen; fretwork. 2. *(Naut.)* Draught, the depth of water which a vessel draws; **calados,** lace; **calado, da,** *pp.* of CALAR. *-a.* **Estar calado** (hasta los huesos), to be soaked.

calador [cah-lah-dor'], *m.* 1. Perforator, borer. 2. *(Naut.)* Caulking-iron. 3. A surgeon's probe.

caladre [cah-lah'-dray], *f.* A bird of the family of larks.

calafate, calafateador [cah-lah-fah' tay, cah-lah-fah-tay-ah-dor'], *m.* Caulker.

calafateadura [cah-lah-fah-tay-ah-doo'-rah], *f.* Caulking.

calafatear, calafetear [cah-lah-fah-tay-ar'], *va. (Naut.)* To caulk.

calafateo [cah-lah-fah-tay'-o], *m.* Caulking.

calafatería [cah-lah-fah-tay-ree'-ah], *f.* The act of caulking.

calafetín [cah-lah-fay-teen'], *m.* Caulker's boy or mate.

calafraga [cah-lah-frah'-gah], *f. (Bot.)* Saxifrage.

calagozo [cah-lah-go'-tho], *m.* Bill or hedging-hook.

calaguala [cah-lah-goo-ah'-lah], *f. (Bot.)* A medicinal fern.

calaguasca [cah-lah-goo-ah'-sah], *f. (LAm.)* Rum.

calaje [cah-lah'-hay], *m. (Prov.)* Chest, trunk, or coffer.

calaluz [cah-lah-looth'], *m. (Naut.)* Kind of East Indian vessel.

calamaco [cah-lah-mah-co], *m.* Calamanco, woollen material. **Calamacos, floreados**, flowered calamancoes. **Calamacos lisos**, plain calamancoes. **Calamacos rayados**, striped calamancoes.

calamar [cah-lah-mar'], *m.* Squid, or sea-sleeve: a variety of cuttle-fish which has the power of emitting an inky fluid. It contains an internal horny plate shaped much like a quillpen, and which gives rise to its name.

calambrazo [cah-lam-brah'-tho], *m.* Attack of cramp, spasm.

calambre [cah-lam'-bray], *m.* Spasm, cramp.

calambuco [cah-lam-boo'-co], *m. (Bot.)* Calaba-tree.

calambuco, ca [cah-lam-boo'-co, cah], *a. (Cuba)* Pharisaical, hypocritical.

calambur [cah-lam-boor'], *m. (LAm.)* Pun.

calamento, *m.* **calaminta**, *f.* [cah-lah-men'-to, meen'-tah]. *(Bot.)* Mountain balm or calamint.

calamidad [cah-lah-me-dahd'], *f.* Misfortune, calamity, misery, grievousness, mishap, oppression. **Es una calamidad**, it's a great pity (suceso); it's a nuisance (persona). **Estar hecho una calamidad**, to be in a very bad way.

calamina, or **piedra calaminar** [cah- lah-mee'-nah], *f.* Calamine, zinc ore, a hydrous silicate of zinc. The carbonate, once known as calamine, is now called smithsonite.

calaminado [cah-lah-me-nah-do], *a. (LAm.)* Firm, bumpy, uneven.

calamís [cah-lah-mees'], *m.* V. CÁLAMO AROMÁTICO.

calamita [cah-lah-mee'-tah], *f.* 1. Loadstone. 2. V. CALAMITE. 3. A fossil, equisetaceous plant of coal formations.

calamite [cah-lah-mee'-tay], *m.* Kind of small green frog. The little green tree-frog.

calamitosamente [cah-lah-me-to-sah- men'-tay], *adv.* Unfortunately, disastrously.

calamitoso, sa [can-lah-me-to'-so, sah], *a.* Calamitous, unfortunate, wretched.

cálamo [cah'-lah-mo], *m.* 1. *(Bot.)* Sweet-flag. **Cálamo aromático**, calamus, sweet cane, sweet flag. 2. Pen; **empuñar el cálamo**, to take up one's pen. **Menear el cálamo**, to wield a pen. 3. Sort of flute.

calamocano [cah.-lah-mo-cah'-no], *a.* **Estar** or **ir calamocano**, to be somewhat fuddled (ancianos).

calamoco [cah-lah-mo'-co], *m.* Icicle.

calamón [cah-lah-mone'], *m.* 1. *(Orn.)* Purple water hen or gallinule. 2. Round-headed nail. 3. Stay which supports the beam of an oil-mill.

calamorra [cah-lah-mor'-rah], *f. (Coll.)* The head.

calamorrada [cah-lah-mor-rah'-dah], *f.* Butt of horned cattle.

calandraco [cah-lahn-drah-co], *a. (And. Cono Sur)* Annoying (fastidioso), tedious; scatterbrained (casquivano).

calandrajo [cah-lan-drah'-ho], *m.* 1. Rag hanging from a garment. 2. Ragamuffin.

calandria [cah-lahn'-dre-ah], *f.* 1. *(Orn.)* Bunting, calendra lark. 2. Calender, a clothier's press, beetle mill, rolling-press. 3. A genus of rhyncophorous beetles. 4. Mangle.

calaña [cah-lah'-nyah], *f.* 1. Pattern, sample. 2. Character, quality. **Es hombre de buena** or **mala calaña**, he is a good- or ill-natured man. **Es una cosa de mala calaña**, it is a bad thing.

cálao [cah'-lah-o], *m. (Orn.)* Hornbill.

calapatillo [cah-lah-pah-teel'-lyo], *m.* A weevil, or its grub, very destructive to grains, nuts, and roots.

calar [cah-lar'], *va.* 1. To penetrate, to pierce, to perforate, to plug. 2. *(Met.)* To discover a design, to comprehend the meaning or cause of a thing. 3. To put, to

place. 4. To imitate net or lace work in linen or cotton. 5. *(Mech.)* To wedge. **Calar el timón**, *(Naut.)* to hang the rudder; 6. *(Tec.)* To do fretwork on (metal); to do openwork. 7. To size up; to see through *(fig.)* (penetrar). **A éstos los tengo muy calados**, I've got them thoroughly weighed up. 8. To lower, to let down (puente); to lower (vela). 9. To crush, to flatten, to sit on; *(fig.)* To humiliate. 10. *(Naut.)* To draw. **El buque cala 12 metros**, the ship draws 12 meters, the ship has a draught of 12 meters. -*vn.* 1. To sink in, soak in; to lead (zapato). 2. *(fig.)* **Calar en**, to go deeply into. **Hay que calar más hondo**, this must be investigated further. -*vr.* 1. To enter, to introduce oneself; to insinuate oneself into. 2. To be wet through, to soak, to imbibe. 3. To stoop, to dart down on prey. **Calarse el sombrero**, to stick one's hat down; to put one's hat on firmly.

calar [cah-lar'], *a.* Calcareous.

calatear [cah-lah-tay-ar'], 1. *va. (And. Cono Sur)* To undress, to strip. 2. *vr.* To get undressed, to strip off.

calato [cah-lah-to], *a. (And.)* Naked, bare; *(fig.)* Penniless, broke.

calatraveño, ña, or **calatravo** [cah-lah-trah-vay'-nyo, nyah, or cah-lah-trah'-vo], *a.* Pertaining to Calatrava.

calavera [cah-lah-vay'-rah], *f.* 1. Skull. 2. *(Met.)* A wild, hotbrained fellow. 3. *(Ent.)* Death's-head moth. 4. *(Mex.) (Aut.)* Rear light. -*m.* Gay dog (juerguista); madcap (loculeo); rotter (canalla).

calaverada [cah-lah-vay-rah'-dah], *f.* Ridiculous, foolish, or ill-judged action.

calaverear [cah-lah-'vay-ray-ar], *vn.* To live it up; to have one's fling.

calaverilla, ita [cah-lah-vay-reel'-lyah, ee'-tah], *f. dim.* 1. Little skull. 2. *m. (Met.)* Little crazy fellow.

calbote [cal-bo'-tay], *m. (Prov.)* Bread made from acorns or chestnuts.

calca [cal'-cah], *f. (And.) (Agri.)* Barn, granary. 2. *(LAm.)* copy (copia).

calcado [cal-cah'-do], *m.* A counter-drawing, tracing.

calcamar [cal-cah-mar'], *m.* Sea-fowl on the coast of Brazil.

calcañal, calcañar [cal-cah-nyahl', cal-cah-nyar], *m.* Heel, heel bone, to be stupid.

calcaño [cal-cah'-nyo], *m.* Heel of the foot.

calcáneo [cal-cah'-nay-o], *m. (Anat.)* Calcaneum, the largest bone in the tarsus, which forms the heel.

calcañuelo [cal-cah-nyoo-ay'-lo], *m.* A disease of bees.

calcar [cal-car'], *va.* 1. To counterdraw, or to copy a design by means of pressure, to trace. 2. *(Prov.)* To trample on.

calcáreo, rea [ca-cah'-ray-o, ah], *a.* Calcareous.

calce [cahl-thay], *m.* 1. The tyre of a wheel. 2. A piece of iron or steel added to the coulter of a plough, when it is worn. 3. A wedge. 4. Wheel-shoe, a form of brake. 5. *(Naut.)* Top. 6. A cup, a chalice. 7. Small canal for irrigation. 8. *(CAm. Carib. Mex.)* Foot, lower margin (of a document). **Firmar el calce**, to sign at the foot of the page.

calcedonia [cal-thay-do'-ne-ah], *f.* Chalcedony, a precious stone.

calcés [cal-thess'], *m. (Naut.)* Masthead.

calceta [cal-thay'-tah], *f.* 1. Understocking, generally of thread. 2. *(Met.)* Fetters worn by criminals.

calcetería [cal-thay-ree'-ah], *f.* 1. Hosiery (oficio). 2. Hosier's (shop).

calcetero, ra [cal-thay-tay'-ro, rah], *m. & f.* 1. One who makes, mends, or sells thread stockings. 2. Knitter of stockings.

calcetilla, calcilla [cal-thay-teel'-lyah, cal-theel-lyah], *f. dim.* Small stocking, sock.

calcetín [cal-thay-teen'], *m.* V. CALCETILLA. Halfhose, sock.

calcetón [cal-thay-tone'], *m. aug.* Large stocking worn under boots.

calciditos [cal'-the-dee'-tose], *m. pl.* Chalcididae, a family of hymenopterous insects, many parasitic, and useful to the husbandman.

calcificar [cal-the-fe-car'], *va.* To calcify.

calcificarse [cal-the-fe-car'-say], *vr.* To calcify, to turn into calcium.

calcina [cal-thee'-nah], *f.* Mortar, concrete.

calcinación [cal-the-nah-the-on'], *f. (Chem.),* Calcination.

calcinar [cal-the-nar'], *va.* 1. To calcine; to burn, to reduce to ashes. **Las ruinas calcinadas del edificio**, the blackened ruins of the building. 2. To bother, annoy (fastidiar). *-vr.* To calcine.

calcinatorio [cal-the-nah-to'-re-o], *a.* **Vaso calcinatorio**, calcinatory.

calcio [cahl'-the-o], *m.* Calcium, a metallic element, widely distributed in limestone, gypsum, etc.

calco [cahl'-co], *m.* A counter-drawing copied by means of pressure: a drawing made from another by means of a transparent paper; a tracing.

calcografía [cal-co-grah-fee'-ah], *f.* 1. Chalcography, art of engraving. 2. Shop where engravings are sold and the place where they are engraved.

calcógrafo [cal-co'-grah-fo], *m.* Engraver.

calcomanía [cal-co-mah-nee'-ah], *f.* Decalcomania, a process of transfering prints from paper and making them adhere to porcelain, etc.

calcopirita [cal-co-pe-ree'-tah], *f.* Copper pyrites, chalcopyrite, native copper sulphide.

calculable [cal-coo-lah'-blay], *a.* Calculable.

calculación [cal-coo-lah-the-on'], *f.* Computation, calculation.

calculador, ra [cal-coo-lah-dor', rah], *m. & f.* 1. Calculator. **Calculador electrónico**, electronic calculator. **Calculadora**, adding machine. 2. *(LAm.)* Selfish, mercenary (egoísta).

calcular [cal-coo-lar'], *va.* To calculate, to reckon.

calculista [cal-coo-lees'-tah], *m.* Schemer

cálculo [cahl'-coo-lo], *m.* 1. Calculation, computation, the result of an arithmetical operation; estimate, count, account. 2. *(Med.)* Calculus, gravel, stone. 3. Small stone used by the ancients in arithmetical operations. **Cálculo diferencial**, *(Math.)* Differential calculus. **Cálculo integral**, integral calculus. **Según mis calculos**, according to my calculations.

calculoso, sa [cal-coo-lo-so, sah], *a.* Calculose, calculous.

Calcuta [Cal-coo'-tah], *f.* Calcutta.

calcha [cal'-cha], *f.* 1. *(Cono Sur)* clothing (ropa), bedding (de cama); harness (arreos). 2. *(Cono Sur)* fetlock; fringe.

calchona [cal-cho-nah], *f. (Cono Sur)* ghost, bogey (fantasma); *(fig.)* Hag (bruja).

calchudo [cal-choo'-do], *a. (Cono Sur)* shrewd, cunning.

calda [cahl'-dah], *f.* 1. Warmth, heat. 2. Act of warming or heating. **Caldas**, natural hot mineral-water baths.

caldaria [cal-dah'-re-ah], *f.* **Ley caldaria**, water ordeal.

caldeamiento [cal-day-ah-me-ayn'-to], *m.* Warming, heating.

caldear [cal-day-ar'], *va.* 1. To weld iron, and render it fit to be forged. 2. To warm, to heat. **Estar caldeado**, to be very hot. *-vr.* to get very hot, to get overheated.

caldeo [cal-day-o], *m.* Chaldaic, warming, heating; *(Tec.)* Welding.

caldera [cal-day'-rah], *f.* Caldron, boiler, sugar-kettle. **Caldera de Pedro Botero**, *(Coll.)* Davy Jones's locker; devil's boiler, hell. **Caldera de vapor**, steamboiler.

calderada [cal-day-rah'-dah], *f. A* caldronful, a capperful.

calderería [cal-day-ray-ree'ah], *f.* 1. Brazier's shop. 2. Trade of a brazier.

calderero [cal-day ray'-ro], *m.* 1. Brazier, coppersmith, blacksmith. 2. Tinker. 3. Among wool-washers, one charged with keeping the fire burning under the boiler.

caldereta [cal-day-ray'-tah], *f.* 1. *(dim.)* Small caldron, a kettle, a pot. **Caldereta de agua bendita**, holy-water pot. 2. Kettleful. **Caldereta de pescado guisado**, kettleful of stewed fish. 3. *(Mex.)* Chocolate-pot. 4. Stew of meat.

calderico, ica, illo, illa [cal-day-ree'-co, cah, eel'-lyo, lyah], *m. & f. dim.* A small kettle.

calderilla [cal-day-reel'-lyah], *f.* 1. Holywater pot. 2. Any copper coin. 3. The lowermost part of a well, in the shape of a caldron.

caldero [cal-day-ro], *m.* 1. A caldron or boiler in the form of a bucket, a copper. 2. **Caldero de brea**, *(Naut.)* pitch-kettle.

calderón [cal-day-ron'], *m.* 1. Copper, large caldron or kettle. 2. Mark of a thousand. 3. *(Print.)* Paragraph. 4. *(Mus.)* Sign denoting a suspension of the instruments.

calderuela [cal-day-roo-ay'-lah], *f.* 1. *(dim.)* Small kettle. 2. Small pot or dark-lantern, used by sportsmen to drive partridges into the net.

caldillo, caldito [cal-deel'-lyo, cal-dee'-to], *m.* 1. Sauce of a ragout or fricassee. 2. Light broth.

caldo [cahl'-do], *m.* Broth, beef-tea, bouillon. **Caldo de carne**, consommé. **Cambiar el caldo a las aceitunas**, to have a leak; **Dar un caldo a uno;** *(Cono Sur)* to torture somebody. **Poner a uno a caldo**, to give somebody a bashing. **Caldos**, wine, oil, and all spirituous liquors which are transported by sea. **Los caldos jerezanos**, the wines of Jerez, sherries. 3. Fag, gasper (cigarrillo). 4. *(Mex.)* Sugar cane juice.

caldosito [cal-do-see'-to], *a. (Coll.)* Not too thick.

caldoso, sa [cal-do'-so, sah], *a.* Having plenty of broth, thin. *-a.* Watery, weak.

calducho [cal-doo'-cho], *m.* 1. *(Coll.)* Broth ill-seasoned and without substance, hog-wash. 2. *(Cono Sur)* day off.

cale [cah'-lay], *m.* Slap, smack.

calé [cah-lay'], 1. *a.* Gipsy. 2. *m. f.* Gipsy.

calecico [cah-lay-thee'-co], *m. dim.* Small chalice.

Caledonia [cah-lay-do'-ne-ah], *f.* Caledonia, ancient name of Scotland.

caledonio, ia [cah-le-do'-ne-o, ah], *a.* Caledonian, Scotsman, Scottish, Scots.

calefaciente [cah-lay-fah-the-en'-tay], *a. (Med.)* Heating.

calefacción [cah-lay-fac-the-on'], *f.* Calefaction, heating. **Calefacción central**, central heating.

calefactorio [cah-lay-fac-to'-re-o], *m.* Stove or place in convents designed for warming.

calefán [cah-lay-fan'], *m. (Cono Sur)* Water heater.

calefón [cah-lay-fon'], *m. (Cono Sur)* Hot water heater.

caleidoscopio [cah-lay-e-dos-co'-pee-o], *m.* Kaleidoscope.

calencas [cah-len'-cas], *f.* Kind of East India calico.

calenda [cah-len'-dah], *f.* The part of the martyrology which treats of the acts of the saints of the day. **Calendas**, calends, first day of every month; **a las calendas griegas**, i. e. never, because the Greeks had no calends; **a** or **en estas calendas**, at that time.

calendar [cah-len-dar'], *va.* To date, to programme.

calendario [cah-len-dah'-re-o], *m.* 1. Almanac, calendar. **Calendario de pared**, wall calendar. 2. Date. **Hacer calendarios**, *(Met.)* To make almanacs; to muse, to be thoughtful. **Calendario de Flora**, floral calendar, a table of the time of flowering of plants. **Calendario electrónico**, *(Inform.)* electronic calendar.

caléndula [cah-len'-doo-lah], *f. (Bot.)* Marigold.

calentador [cah-len-tah-dor'], *m.* Heater. **Calentador de agua**, water-heater. **Calentador eléctrico**, electric fire. **Calentador a gas**, gas heater. **Calentador de inmersión**, immersion heater.

calentamiento [cah-len-ta-me-en'-to], *m.* 1. Calefaction, warming, heating 2. Disease incidental to horses. 3. Warm-up (deporte).

calentar [cah-len-tar'], *va.* 1. To warm, to heat; to glow, to make warm. 2. To roll and heat a ball in one's hand before it is played. 3. *(Met.)* To urge, to press forward, to despatch speedily. **Calentar a alguno las orejas**, to chide or reprove one severely. **No calentar el asiento**, to retain office for but a short time. 4. **Calentar al rojo**, to make red-hot. 5. To arouse (excitar). *-vr.* 1. To be in heat (animales). 2. To mowburn, to ferment and heat in the mow (grano, trigo). 3. To grow hot, to dispute warmly, to be hurried by the ardor of debate. **Calentársele a uno la boca**, to speak incoherently from excessive ardor.

calentón [cah-len-tone'], *m.* **Darse un calentón**, *(Coll.)* To take a bit of a warming; to feel randy (sexy). -a. Sexy, randy.

calentura [cah-len-too'-rah], *f.* 1. A fever. **Estar con calentura**, to be feverish, have a temperature. 2. Warmth, gentle heat. *3. (Cono Sur)* tuberculosis. 4. *(And. Cono Sur)* Randiness, sexual excitement. 5. *(And.)* Fit of rage, tantrum (rabieta). 6. **Calentura de pollo**, *(Mex.)* Imaginary illness.

calenturiento ta, [cah-len-too-re-en'-to, tah], *a.* 1. Feverish; fever-sick. 2. *(Cono Sur)* comsumptive, tubercular. 3. Dirty, prurient (mente indecente). 4. Rash, impulsive (exaltado). **Las mentes calenturientas**, the hotheads.

calenturilla [cah-len-too-reel'-lyah], *f. dim.* Slight fever.

calenturón [cah-len-too-rone'], *m. aug.* Violent fever.

calanturoso, sa [cah-len-too-ro'-so, sah], *a.* Feverish. *V.* CALENTURIENTO.

calepino [cah-lay-pee'-no], *m. (Coll.)* Vocabulary, dictionary (de latín).

calera [cah-lay-rah], *f.* Lime-kiln; lime-pit.

calería [cah-lay-ree'-ah], *f.* House, place, or street, where lime is burnt and sold.

calero, ra [cah-lay-ro, rah], *a.* Calcareous.

calero [cah-lay'-ro], *m.* Lime-burner, lime-maker, or seller.

calés [cah-lays'], *m. & pl.* Bread, money.

calesa [cah-lay'-sah], *f.* Calash, a Spanish chaise.

calesera [cah-lay-say'-rah], *f.* 1. Type of bolero jacket. 2. Andalusian song.

calesero [cah-lay-say'-ro], *m.* Driver of a calash.

calesín [cah-lay-seen'], *m.* Single-horse chaise, a gig.

calesita [cah-lay-see'-tah], *f. (And. Cono Sur)* merry-go-round, carousel.

caleta [cah-lay'-tah], *f.* 1. *(Naut.)* Cove, creek, fleet, a small bay or inlet. 2. *(And.) (Naut.)* Coasting vessel, coaster. 3. *(And.)* Hiding-place (escondite).

caletero [cah-lay'-ro], *m.* 1. *(Carib.)* Docker, port worker (estibador). 2. *(LAm.) (Ferro.)* Milk-train. 3. *(Carib.)* Shop assistant.

caletre [cah-lay'-tray], *m.* 1. *(Coll.)* Understanding, judgment, discernment. **No le cabe en el caletre**, he can't get it into his thick head. 2. In abusive language, the head.

cali [cah'-le], *m. (Chem.) V.* ÁLCALI.

calibeado, da [cah-le-bay-ah' do, dah], *a. (Med.)* 1. Chalybean, relating to steel. 2. Chalybeate, impregnated with iron.

calibración [cah-le-brah-the-on'], *f.* Calibration.

calibrador [cah-le-brah-dor'], *m.* Gauge, caliper, calipers.

calibrar [cah-le-brar'], *va.* To examine the calibre of a ball or fire-arm; to gauge, to size.

calibre [cah-lee'-bray], *m.* 1. Calibre. 2. Diameter of a column. 3. *(Met.)* Calibre, sort, kind. **Ser de buen o mal calibre**, to be of a good or bad quality. 4. *(Cono Sur)* **Palabras de grueso calibre**, crude language; swearing.

calicanto [cah-le-cahn'-to], *m.* 1. *(Bot.)* Allspice. 2. *(Carib. Cono Sur)* stone wall; jetty (muelle).

calicata [cah-le-cah'-tah], *f. (Min.)* A trial-pit; the test of a piece of ground by auger, or tools, or mere inspection.

cálice [cah'-le-thay], *m. (Obs.) V.* CÁLIZ.

calicinal [cah-le-the-nahl'], *a.* Relating to a calyx, calycine, or calycinal.

caliche [cah-lee'-chay], *m.* 1. Pebble or small piece of limestone accidentally introduced into a brick or tile at the time of its being burnt. 2. A crust of lime which flakes from a wall. 3. *(Peru and Chile)* Native saltpeter, or crude sodium nitrate.

calicó [cah-le-co'], *m.* Calico.

calicud, calicut [cah-le-cood', cah-le-coot'], *f.* Silk stuff from India.

calidad [cah-le-dahd'], *f.* 1. Quality; condition, character; kind or particular nature. **De calidad**, of quality. **De mala calidad**, of bad quality. 2. Importance or consequence of a thing. 3. Nobility, quality, condition, rank, fashion. 4. Condition, stipulation, requisite. **Calidades**, conditions in playing a game. **En calidad de**, in the capacity of. 5. Stipulation, term (contrato). **A calidad de que...**, provided that.

calidez [cah-le-deth'], *f. V.* ENCENDIMIENTO.

cálido, da [cah'-le-do, dah], *a.* 1. Hot (clima, país), Piquant, calid. 2. Crafty, artful.

calidoscópio o caleidoscopio [cah-lee-dos-co'-pe-o], *a.* Kaleidoscopic. *m.* Kaleidoscope.

calientacamas [cah-lee-ayn-tah-cah'-mas], *m.* Electric blanket.

calientapiernas [cah-lee-ayn-tah-pe-ayr'-nas], *m.* Legwarmer.

calientapiés [cah-lee-ayn-tah-pe-ays'], *m.* Hot-water bottle; foot warmer.

calientaplatos [cah-lee-ayn-tah-pla'-tos], *m.* Hotplate.

caliente [cah-le-en'-tay], *a.* 1. Warm, hot; scalding. 2. Warm, fiery, feverish, vehement. **Tener la sangre caliente**, *(Met.)* To face dangers with great spirit. **En caliente**, Piping hot, on the spot, immediately, instantaneously. **Caliente de cascos**, hot-headed. **Estar caliente**, to be in heat (animales); to feel randy. *(Yo caliento, yo caliente, from Calentar. V.* ACERTAR.

calieta [cah-le-ay'-tah], *f.* Kind of mushroom.

califa [cah-lee'-fah], *m.* Caliph, successor: a title assumed by the successors of Mohammed.

califato [cah-le-fah'-to], *m.* Caliphate, the dignity of caliph.

calificación [cah-le-fe-cah-the-on'], *f.* 1. Qualification. 2. Judgment, censure. 3. Proof 4. Habilitation. 5. Grade, mark (escuela). **Calificación de sobresaliente**, first-class mark.

calificado, da [cah-le-fe-cah'-do, dah], *a.* 1. Qualified, authorized, competent. 2. Well-known, eminent (conocido); undisputed; proven, manifest. 3. *(Mex.) (Jur.)* Qualified, conditional. *-pp.* of CALIFICAR.

calificador [cah-le-fe-cah-dor'], *m.* 1. One who is qualified to spy and do something. 2.**Calificador del Santo Oficio**, officer of the Inquisition, appointed to examine books and writings.

calificar [cah-le-fe-car'], *va.* 1. To qualify. 2. To authorize, to empower. 3. To certify, to attest. 4. To illustrate, to ennoble. 5. To assess; to rate; to grade, to mark (examen). 6. **Calificar a uno**, to distinguish somebody, to give somebody his standing (reputación). 7.**Calificar a uno de tonto**, to call somebody silly, to describe somebody as silly, to label somebody silly. *-vr.* To prove one's noble birth and descent according to law. 2. *(LAm.)* To register as a voter.

calificativo [cah-le-fe-cah-te-vo], *a.* Qualifying.

California [cah-le-for'-nee-ah], *f.* California.

california [cah-le-for'-nee-ah], *f. (Cono Sur)* Horse-race (carrera). 2. *(Cono Sur) (Tec.)* Wire-stretcher.

californiano, na [cah-le-for-ne-ah'-no, nah], *a. & m. & f.* Californian, from California.

californio, ia [cah-le-for'-ne-o, ah], *a.* Native of California.

caliga [cah-lee'gah], *f.* A kind of half-boots worn by Roman soldiers.

calígine [cah-lee'-he-nay], *f.* Mist, obscurity, darkness.

caliginoso, sa [cah-le-he-no'-so, sah], *a.* 1. Caliginous, dark, dim. 2. Intricate, obscure, difficult to be understood.

caligrafía [cah-le-grah-fee'-ah], *f.* Caligraphy, elegant penmanship.

caligráfico [cah-le-grah'-fee-co], *a.* Calligraphic.

calígrafo [cah-lee'-grah-fo], *m.* One who writes a beautiful hand: a penman.

calilla [cah-leel'-lyah], *f. dim.* 1. A small suppository. 2. *(CAm. Mex.)* Bore, nuisance. 3. Hoax (engaño); boring (joke).

calima [cah-lee'-mah], *f.* 1. *V.* CALINA. 2. A rosary of corks employed in seafishing.

calimaco [cah-le-mah'-co], *m. (Prov.) V.* CALAMACO.

calimocho [cah-le-mo'-cho], *m.* Drink of mixed Coca-cola and wine.

calín [cah-leen'], *m.* A metallic composition resembling lead.

calina [cah-lee'-nah], *f.* Thick vapor, resembling a mist or fog.

calinda [cah-leen'-dah], *f. (Cuba)* A popular dance of the creoles.

calino, na [cah-lee'-no, nah], *a.* Chalky, or containing chalk.

calinoso [cah-lee-no'-so], *a.* Hazy, misty.

calio [cah'-le-o], *m.* Kalium or potassium, a metallic element.

calíope [cah-lee'-o-pay], *f.* Calliope, muse of epic poetry.

calípedes [cah-lee'-pay-des], *m.* A slow-paced animal.

calipso [cah-leep'-so], *m.* 1. *(Bot.)* Calypso. 2. *(Mus.)* Calypso, musical rhythm from Trinidad.

caliqueño [cah-le-kay'-nyo], *m.* Prick. **Echar un caliqueño**, to have a screw.

calis [cah'-lis], *f.* 1. *(Bot.)* Alkanet or orchanet.

calisaya [cah-le-sah'-yah], *f. (Bot.)* Calisaya, a highly prized variety of cinchona bark, indigenous to Peru.

calistenia [cah-lees-tay-ne-ah], *f.* Cal(l)isthenics.

calisténica [cah-lees-tay'-ne-cah], *f.* Calisthenics, gymnastics.

calixto [cah-leex'-to], *m. (Astr. and Poet.)* The constellation of the Great Bear.

cáliz [cah-leeth], *m.* 1. Chalice, a communion cup. 2. Bitter cup of grief and affliction. 3. *(Bot.)* Calyx of a flower. **Cáliz de amargura, cáliz de dolor**, cup of sorrow.

caliza [cah-lee'-thah], *f.* Calcium carbonate in its various forms, whether limestone, marble, gypsum, or other.

calizo, za [cah-lee'-tho, thah], *a.* Calcareous, limy: calc (spar).

callada [cal-lyah'-dah], *f.* 1. Dish of tripe. 2. Silence: employed only in certain phrases. **A las calladas** or **de callada**, without noise, privately, on the quiet. **Dar la callada por respuesta**, to answer by silence.

calladamente [cal-lyah-dah-men'-tay], *adv.* Silently, tacitly, secretly, privately, in a reserved manner.

calladaris [cal-lyah-dah'-ris], *f.* A kind of cotton stuff.

callado, da [cal-lyah'-do], *a.* 1. Silent, reserved, noiseless. 2. Discreet. **Todo estaba muy callado**, everything was very quiet. **Tener algo callado**, to keep quiet about something. **Pagar para tener callado a uno**, to pay to keep somebody quiet. **Nunca te quedas callado**, you always have an answer for everything. *-pp.* of *CALLAR.*

callamiento [cal-lyah-me-en'-to], *m. (Obs.)* Imposing or keeping silence.

callampa [cahl-lyam-bah], *f. (Cono Sur) (Bot.)* Mushroom; umbrella; **callampas**, big ears.

callana [cahl-lyah'-nah], *f. (LAm, Cono Sur)* Flat earthenware pan; *(Cono Sur)* pocket watch.

callandico, ito [cal-lyah-dee'-co, to], *adv.* In a low voice; silently; without noise, slyly, softly.

callar [cal-lyar'], *vn.* 1. To keep silence, to be silent. 2. To omit speaking of a thing, to pass it over in silence, to conceal, to hush. 3. To cease singing: said of birds. 4. To dissemble. 5. *(Poet.)* To abate, to become moderate, to grow calm (viento, mar). **Callar el pico**, to hold one's tongue, to pretend not to have heard or seen anything of the matter in question. **Mátalas callando**, by crafty silence he obtains his ends. **Quien calla otorga**, silence implies consent. *-vr.* To be silent, to be quiet, to remain silent. **¡Calla! ¡cállate!**, shut up!, be quiet, **Hacer callar a uno**, to make somebody be quiet. **Sería mejor callarse**, it would be best to say nothing. **Callar como un muerto**, to shut up like a clam.

calle [cahl'-lyay], *f.* 1. Street, paved way. 2. Lane, a narrow way between hedges. 3. Lane, a passage between men standing on each side 4. *(Coll.)* Gullet. 5. (Kant) Liberty. 6. Pretext, excuse, means for evading a promise. **Calle de árboles**, alley or walk in a garden. **Calle mayor**, main street. **Calle sin salida**, dead-end street. **Alborotar la calle**, to cause an uproar in the street. **Dejar a uno en la calle**, to strip one of his all, also to turn one out of doors. **Echar algún secreto en la calle**, to proclaim a secret in the streets. **Hacer calle**,

a) to make way, to clear the passage. b) *(Met.)* to overcome difficulties. **Pasear** or **rondar la calle**, to court a woman, flirt on the street. **Pasear las calles**, to loiter about. **Quedar en la calle**, to be in the utmost distress. **Calles públicas**, the public streets. **Calle abajo**, down the street. **Calle de dirección única**, one-way street. **Calle peatonal**, pedestrian precinct. **Hacer la calle**, to be on the streets (prostituta). **Llevarse a uno de calle**, to bowl somebody over. **Poner a uno de patitas en la calle**, to kick somebody out. *-int.* 1. Strange! Wonderful! You don't say so! 2. Make way!

callear [cal-lyay-ar'], *va.* To clear the walks in a vineyard of loose branches.

calleja [cal-lyay'-hah], *f. V.* CALLEJUELA.

callejear [cal-lyay-hay-ar'], *vn.* To walk or loiter about the streets, to gad, to ramble.

callejero, ra [cal-lyay-hay'-ro, rah], *a.* 1. Applied to a loiterer; a gadder. 2. Street. **Accidente callejero**, street accident. **Disturbios callejeros**, trouble in the streets. **Perro callejero**, stray dog. *-m.* Street directory.

callejo, calleyo [cal-lyay'-ho, cal-lyay'-yo], *m. (Prov.)* Pit into which game falls when pursued.

callejón [cal-lyay-hone'], *m.* 1. Narrow lane. 2. Narrow pass between mountains. **Callejón sin salida**, 1. Blind alley. 2. Impasse, predicament. **Gente de callejón**, *(And.)* Low-class people.

callejoncillo [cal-lyay-hon-theel'-lyo], *m. dim.* A little narrow passage.

callejuela [cal-lyay-hoo-ay'-lah], *f.* 1. Lane or narrow passage. 2. *(Met.)* Shift, subterfuge, evasion. **Dar pan y callejuela**, to help one in his flight.

callemandra [cal-lyay-mahn'-drah], *f.* Kind of woollen stuff.

callialto, ta [cal-lye-ahl'-to, tah], *a.* Having swelling welts or borders (herraduras).

callicida [cahl-lye-the'-dah], *m.* Corn cure.

callista [cal-lyees'-tah], *m. & f.* A corn-doctor, chiropodist.

callizo [cal-lyee'-tho], *m. (Prov.) V.* CALLEJÓN and CALLEJUELA.

callo [cahl-lyo'], *m.* 1. Corn, a callous substance on the feet. 2. Wen. **Criar callos**, to become inured, become hardened. **Pisar los callos a uno**, to tread on somebody's toes. 3. *(Esp.) (Culin.)* **Callos**, tripe. **Callos al ajo**, tripe with garlic. 4. Old bat, old cow; ugly woman. 5. **Dar el callo**, *(Esp.)* to work hard.

callón [cal-lyone'], *m.* 1. *(aug.)* Big corn or wen. 2. Among shoemakers, rubber, a whetstone for smoothing the blades of awls.

callosidad [cal-lyo-se-dahd'], *f.* Callosity, callus.

calloso, sa [cal-lyo'-so, sah], *a.* Callous: corny, corneous horny.

calma [cahl'-mah], *f.* 1. *(Naut.)* A calm. **Estar en calma**, to be calm. 2. Calmness, tranquility, composure. 3. Suspension of business, cessation of pain. **Estar en calma**, to be steady (mercado). **En calma**, *(Naut.)* Smooth sea. **Calma muerta** or **chicha**, *(Naut.)* Dead calm. 4. Slowness in speaking or doing *(Coll.)* **Hacer algo con calma**, to do something calmly. **Perder la calma**, to get ruffled, to lose one's composure.

calmadamente [cal-mah-dah-men'-tay], *adv.* Quietly, calmly.

calmado, da [cal-mah'-do, dah], *a.* Quiet, calm. *-pp.* of CALMAR.

calmante [cal-mahn'-tay], *m. (Med.)* Anodyne; sedative; tranquillizer. *pa. & m. & f.* 1. Mitigating, mitigant. 2. *(Med.)* Narcotic, anodyne, sedative.

calmar [cal-mar'], *va.* 1. To calm, to quiet, to compose, to pacify, to still, to hush. 2. To alleviate, to allay, to lay, to mitigate, to lull, to moderate, to soothe, to soften. *-vn.* To fall calm, to be becalmed. *-vr. (Met.)* To be pacified, to calm down oneself; to improve (tiempo), to settle down; **¡Cálmate!**, calm down!

calmazo [cal-mah-tho], *m.* Dead calm.

calmécac [cal-may-cahc'], *m. (Mex.) (Hit.)* Aztec school for priests.

calmia [cahl'-me-ah], *f.* Kalmia, a genus of shrubs of the heath family.

calmo, ma [cahl'-mo, mah], *a.* 1. Uncultivated, untilled; without trees or shrubbery (tierras). 2. Slow, steady, measured.

calmoso, sa [cal-mo'-so, sah], *a.* 1. Calm. 2. *(Met.)* Tranquil, soothing. 3. Slow, tardy.

caló [cah-lo'], *m.* 1. Gipsy language. 2. Cant.

calocar [cah-lo-car'], *m.* Kind of white earth or clay.

calocha [cah-lo'-chah, *f.* 1. Clog or wooden shoe. 2. Overshoe, galosh.

calofillo, lla [cah-lo-feel'-lyo, lyah], *a.* Having handsome leaves.

calofriado, da [cah-lo-fre-ah'-do, dah], *a.* Chilly, shivering with cold. *-pp.* of CALOFRIARSE.

calofriarse, calosfriarse [cah-lo-fre-ar'-say], *vr.* To be chilly, to shudder or shiver with cold; to be feverish or with shiverings. *V.* ESCALOFRIARSE.

calofrío, calosfrío [cah-lo-free'-o], *m.* Shiver, shudder, cold sweat.

caloma [cah-lo'-mah], *f. (Naut.)* Singing out of sailors when they haul a rope.

calomel or **calomelanos** [cah-lo-may-lah'-nos], *m. pl. (Med.)* Calomel.

calón [cah-lone'], *m.* 1. Rod for spreading nets. 2. Perch for measuring the depth in shallow water.

calóptero, ra [cah-lop'-tay-ro, rah], *a.* Which has beautiful wings.

calor [cah-lor'], *m.* 1. Heat; hotness, calidity; glow. 2. Burning, blazing. 3. *(Met.)* Warmth, ardor, fervor, fieriness (sentimientos, acciones). 4. Brunt of an action or engagement. 5. Favor, kind reception. **Dar calor a la empresa**, to encourage an undertaking. **Dar calor**, among tanners, to raise the color of a hide by heating it. **Un calor agradable**, a pleasant warmth. **Un calor excesivo**, an excessive heat. **Entrar en calor**, to get warm. **Hace mucho calor**, it's very hot.

caloría [cah-lo-ree'-ah], *f.* Calorie.

calórico, ca [cah-lo'-re-co, cah], *a.* Caloric.

calorífero, ra [cah-lo-ree'-fe-ro, rah], *a.* Heat-producing. *-m.* Furnace, heater. **Calorífero de aire caliente**, hot-air heater.

calorífico, ca [cah-lo-ree'-fe-co, cah], *a.* Heat-producing, calorific.

calorifugar [cah-lo-ree-foo-gar'], *va.* To lag (caldera, tubo).

calorífugo, ga [cah-lo-ree'-foo-go, gah], *a.* 1. Heat-resistant. 2. Incombustible.

calorímetro [cah-lo-ree'-may-tro], *m.* Calorimeter.

caloroso, sa [cah-lo-ro'-so, sah], *a. V.* CALUROSO.

calorro, rra [cah-lor'-ro], *a. m. & f.* Gipsy.

calostro [cah-los'-tro], *m.* Colostrum.

calote [cah-lo-tay], *m. (Cono Sur)* Con, swindle. **Dar calote**, to skip payments, leave without paying.

calotear [cah-lo-tay-ar'], *va. (Sp. Amer.)* To con, to swindle.

caloyo [cah-lo'-yo], *m.* Newborn lamb or kid.

calpense [cal-pen'-say], *a.* From Gibraltar, Gibraltarian.

calpul [cal-pool'], *m. (Sp. Amer.)* Gathering, get-together.

calseco, ca [cal-say'-co, cah], *a.* Cured with lime.

calta [cahl-tah], *f.* Marsh marigold.

caluga [cah-loo'-gah], *f. (Cono Sur)* Toffee.

caluma [cah-loo'-mah], *f. (And.)* Mountain pass (in the Andes).

calumbrecerse [ca-loom-bray-therr'-say], *vr.* To grow mouldy.

calumnia [cah-loom'-ne-ah], *f.* Calumny, false charge, slander. **Afiazar de calumnia**, *(Law.)* Applied to an accuser giving security to subject himself to legal penalties if he cannot prove his allegations.

calumniador, ra [cah-loom-ne-ah-dor', rah], *m. & f.* Calumniator, a slanderer.

calumniar [cah-loom-ne-ar'], *va.* To calumniate, to slander, to accuse falsely.

calumniosamente [cah-loom-ne-o'-sah-men'-tay], *adv.* Calumniously, slanderously.

calumnioso, sa [cah-loom-ne-o'-so, sah], *a.* Calumnious, slanderous.

calurosamente, *adv.* Warmly, ardently, hotly.

caluroso, sa [cah-loo-ro-so, sah], *a.* 1. Warm, hot, hearty, enthusiastic. 2. Heating.

calva [cahl'-vah], *f.* 1. Bald crown of the head, bald pate, bare spot, worn place.

calvar [cal-var'], *va.* 1. To impose upon one, to deceive.

Calvario [cal-vah'-re-o], *m.* 1. *(Met. Coll.)* Debts, tally, score. **Pasar un Calvario**, to suffer agonies. 2. A charnel-house. 3. Calvary, hill or elevation on which are crosses representing the stations at Mount Calvary.

calvatrueno [cal-vah-troo-ay'-no], *m.* 1. Baldness of the whole head. 2. *(Met.)* A wild person.

calvaza [cal-vah'-thah], *f. aug.* Large bald pate.

calvero, calvijar, calvitar [cal-vay'-ro, cal-ve-har', tar'], *m.* 1. Barren ground among fruitful lands. 2. Chalkpit, marlpit.

calvez, calvicie [cal-veth', cal-vee'-the-ay], *f.* Baldness. **Calvicie precoz**, premature baldness.

calvinismo [cal-ve-nees'-mo], *m.* Calvinism.

calvinista [cal-ve-nees'-tah], *m. f.* Calvinist.

calvo, va [cahl'-vo, vah], *a.* 1. Bald, without hair. **Quedarse calvo**, to go bald. 2. Barren, uncultivated (terreno). **Tierra calva**, barren soil.

calza [cahl'-thah], *f.* 1. Long, loose breeches, trousers. 2. Hose, stockings. **Medias calzas**, short stockings, reaching only to the knees. **Estar en calzas prietas**, to be in a fix. 3. *(LAm.)* Filling (de diente).

calzada [cal-thah'-dah], *f.* 1. Causeway, a paved highway. 2. The high road. 3. Gravel-walk. 4. Avenue.

calzadera [cal-thah-day'-rah], *f.* 1. Hempen cord for fastening the *albarcas,* a coarse kind of leather shoes. 2. Net twine.

calzadillo, ito [cal-thah-deel'-lyo, dee'-to], *m. dim.* Small shoe.

calzado, da [cal-thah'-do, dah], *a.* Calceated, shod, wearing shoes. **Calzado de**, shod with: **Conviene ir calzado**, it's better to wear shoes. *-pp.* of CALZAR.

calzado [cal-thah'-do], *m.* 1. Footwear of all kinds. 2. Horse with four white feet. 3. All articles serving to cover the legs and feet. **Tráeme el calzado**, bring me my stockings, garters, and shoes.

calzador [cal-thah-dor'], *m.* 1. Shoeing leather, a piece of leather used to draw up the hind quarters of tigh shoes. 2. Shoe-horn, a piece of horn used for the same purpose as the shoeing-leather. **Entrar con calzador**, *(Met.)* To find great difficulties in entering a place.

calzadura [cal-thah-doo'-rah], *f.* 1. Act of putting on the shoes. 2. Felloe of a cart-wheel.

calzar [cal-thar'], *va.* 1. To put on shoes. 2. To strengthen with iron or wood. 3. To scot or scotch a wheel. 4. To carry a ball of a determined size (armas de fuego). 5. To wedge, chock, key. 6. *(Typ.)* To overlay, to raise, underlay. 7. *(LAm.)* To fill (diente). 8. To pit, to put an iron tip on. **Calzar las herramientas**, to put a steel edge to iron tools. **Calzar los guantes**, to put on gloves. **Calzaba zapatos verdes**, she was wearing green shoes. **¿Qué numero calza Vd?**, what size do you take? **El primero que llega se calza**, first come first served. **Me ayudó a ponerme las botas**, he helped me to put my boots on. *-vn.* **Calza bien**, he wears good shoes. *-vr.* 1. **Calzarse los zapatos**, to put on one's shoes. **¿Qué zapatos calzaba?**, what shoes was he wearing? 2. **Calzarse un empleo**, to get a job. **Calzarse a uno**, to keep somebody under one's thumb.

calzatrepas [cal-thah-tray'-pas], *f.* Snare, trap.

calzo [cahl'-tho], *m. V.* CALCE. 1. *(Typ.)* Frisket-sheet, overlay. 2. Block, brake-shoe (ferrocarril). 3. *(Mech.)* Wedge, quoin. 4. Shoe of a felloe. 5. *(Naut.)* Skid, chock, bed, shoe.

calzón [cal-thone'], *m.* 1. Ombre, a game of cards. 2. Breeches, small clothes, hose: commonly used in the plural.

3. *(Mex.)* A disease of the sugar-cane from lack of irrigation. **Calzones marineros**, pants worn by sailors. **Calzones de baño**, bathing suit. **Amarrarse los calzones**, *(LAm.)* to get stuck in. **Ponerse los calzones**, *(fig.)* To wear the pants (mujer). **Tener muchos calzones**, *(Mex.)* to be tough. **Calzones de vinilo**, plastic pants (de plástico). - *pl.* *(Naut.)* Goose-wings: applied to sails when furled in a peculiar manner.

calzonarias [cal-tho-nah'-re-ahs], *f. pl. (Sp. Amer.)* Suspenders.

calzonario [cal-tho-nah'-re-o], *m. (LAm.)* Pants, underwear.

calzonazos [cal-tho-nah'-thos], *m.* 1. *(Coll.)* Mollycoddle, jellyfish. 2. Stupid fellow (tonto); weak-willed fellow (débil); henpecked husband (marido).

calzoncillos [cal-thon-theel'-lyos], *m. pl.* Shorts, drawers, pants, underpants, slips.

calzoneras [cal-tho-nay'-ras], *f. pl. (Mex.)* Pants open down both sides and the openings closed by buttons.

calzoneta [cal-tho-nay'-tah], *f. (CAm. Mex.)* Swimming suit (traje de baño).

calzonudo [cal-tho-noo-do], *a. (And. CAm. Cono Sur)* Stupid, weak-willed (débil); timid; *(Mex.)* energetic; bold, brave.

cama [cah'-mah], *f.* 1. Bed, couch, a place of repose. **Cama con ruedas**, a truck-bed. 2. Bed hangings and furniture. 3. Seat or cause of wild animals. 4. Floor or body of a cart. 5. *V.* CAMADA. 6. Litter, the straw laid under animals or on plants. 7. Slice of meat put upon another, to be both dressed together. 8. The axle of a wheel. 9. Branch of a bridle to which the reins are fastened; the cheek. 10. Piece of cloth cut slopewise, to be joined to another to make a round cloak. 11. Layer of dung and earth for raising plants; a garden-bed. 12. *(Mech.)* CAm. cog, catch, tooth. 13. Bed plate, base. 14. *(Geol.)* Layer, stratum. **Hacer cama**, to keep one's bed, to be confined to one's bed on account of sickness. **Hacer la cama**, to make the bed. **Caer en cama**, to fall sick. **Cama elástica**, trampoline. **Camas gemelas**, twin beds. **Cama de matrimonio**, double bed. **Cama plegable**, folding bed. **Cama redonda**, group sex. **Cama turca**, divan bed.

camachuelo [cah-may-choo-ay-lo], *m.* Bullfinch.

camada [cah-mah'-dah], *f.* 1. Brood of young animals, a litter. 2 Layer (of eggs, etc.). **Camada de ladrones**, den of thieves, nest of rogues.

camafeo [cah-mah-fay'-o], *m.* Cameo, a gem on which figures are engraved in basso-relieve.

camagua [cah-mah'-goo-ah], *f. (CAm.)* Ripening corn; *(Mex.)* Unriped corn.

camal [cah-mahl'], *m.* 1. Hempen halter. 2. Camail, a piece of chain mail attached to a basinet. 3. Slalughterhouse (matadero).

camaleón [cah-mah-lay-on'], *m.* 1. Chameleon. **Camaleón negro**, *(Bot.)* Corymbed carline thistle; *(Mex.)* The horned toad, properly lizard, of the U.S Phrynosoma. 2. A flatterer who changes his language according to the presumed tastes of the person addressed.

camaleónico [cah-mah-lay-o'-ne-co], *a.* Chameleon-like.

camaleopardo [cah-mah-lay-o-par'-do], *m.* Cameleopard, giraffe.

camalote [cah-mah-lay-o'-tay], *m.* Camalote (planta acuática).

camamila, camomila [cah-mah-mee'-lah, cah-mo-mee'-lah], *f. (Bot.)* Camomile. *V.* MANZANILLA.

camanance [cah-mah-nahn'-thay], *m. (CAm.)* Dimple.

camanchaca [cah-mahn-chah'-cah], *f. (Cono Sur)* thick fog, pea-soup.

camándula [cah-mahn'-doo-lah], *f.* Chaplet or rosary of one or three decades. **Tener muchas camándulas**, *(Coll.)* To make use of many tricks and artifices, to shuffle.

camandulear [cah-mahn-doo-lay-ar'], *vn.* To be a hypocrite, be falsely devout; *(LAm.)* to intrigue, scheme; to bumble (vacilar), avoid taking decisions.

camandulense [cah-man-doo-len'-say], *a.* Belonging to the religious order of Camandula or reformed Benedictines.

camandulería [cah-man-doo-lay-ree'-ah], *f.* Hypocrisy, insincerity, dissimulation.

camandulero, ra [cah-man-doo-lay'-ro, rah], *a. & n.* Full of tricks and artifices, dissembling, hypocritical; *(LAm.)* Intriguing (enredador); scheming; fawning (zalamero).

cámara [ca'-mah-rah], *f.* 1. Hall or main room of a house. 2. Granary, mow, a store-house of threshed corn. 3. Stool, evacuation by stool, laxity, laxness. 4. *V.* CILLA. 5. *(Naut.)* Cabin of a ship. 6. **Cámara alta**, *(Naut.)* Roundhouse of a ship. 7. Chamber in a mine. 8. Chamber of great guns and other fire-arms. 9. Bed-chamber. 10. Residence of the king and court. **Cámara del rey**, 1. Room in which the king holds a levee for gentlemen of the bedchamber, etc. 2. Exchequer. 11. The legislative body of foreign nations. 12. A photographic camera. **Cámara plegadiza**, a folding camera. **Cámara de mano**, a hand camera. **Cámara estereoscópica**, steroscopic camera. **Pie de la cámara** (oscura), camera-stand. **Cámara de bolsillo**, pocket-camera. **Cámara con frente de quita y pon**, removable front camera. **Cámara baja o de los comunes**, the House of Commons. **Cámara nupcial**, bridal suite. **Música de cámara**, chamber music. **Médico de cámara**, royal doctor. **Cámara de comercio**, chamber of commerce; **Cámara de los Lores**, House of Lords. **Cámara de gas**, gas-room. **Cámara de aire**; tire, inner tube. **Cámara de cine**, movie-camera. **Cámara de televisión**, television camera. -*m.* Cameraman.

camarada [cah-mah-rah'-dah], *m.* 1. Comrade, partner, companion, mate, buddy, fellow; crony, chum. -*f.* 2. Society or company of people united; assembly. 3. **Camaradas de rancho**, messmates. **Camaradas de navío**, shipmates.

camaradería [cah-mah-rah-day-ree'-ah], *f.* Comradeship, fellowship.

camaraje [cah-mah-rah-hay], *m.* Granary, rent for a granary.

camaranchón [cah-mah-ran-chone'], *m.* 1. Garret. 2. Retired place, recess.

camarera [cah-mah-ray'-rah], *f.* Waitress, stewardess (azafata).

camarero [cah-mah-ray'-ro], *m.* 1. Waiter. 2. Steward (aviones); (camarero principal), head waiter.

camareta [cah-mah-ray'-tah], *f. dim. (Naut.)* Small cabin, deck-cabin, midshipmen's cabin.

camarico [cah-mah-re'-co], *m. (Cono Sur)* 1. Favorite place. 2. Love affair (amor).

camariento, ta [cah-mah-re-en'-to, tah], *a.* Troubled with diarrhoea.

camarilla [cah-mah-reel'-lyah], *f.* 1. *(dim.)* Small room. 2. The coterie of private advisers of the king. 3. *(Pol.)* Pressure group.

camarín [cah-mah-reen'], *m.* 1. Place behind an altar where the images are dressed, and the ornaments destined for that purpose are kept. 2. Closet. 3. A dressing-room in a theatre. 4. *(Naut.)* Cabin. 5. Elevator car (de ascensor).

camariña [cah-mah-ree'-nyah], *f.* Copse, short wood, a low shrub.

camarógrafo [cah-mah-roh'-grah-fo], *m.* Camera man.

camarón [cah-mah-rone'], *m.* 1. Shrimp; prawn. 2. *(CAm.)* Tip, gratuity. 3. *(And.)* Turncoat (traidor); **hacer camarón**, to change sides. 4. *(CAm.)* Casual word (trabajo). 5. *(Cono Sur)* Bunk (bed).

camaronear [cah-mah-ro-nay-ar'], *vn.* 1. *(Mex.)* To go shrimping (pescar camarones). 2. *(And.) (Pol.)* To change sides.

camaronero [cah-mah-ro-nay'-ro], *m.* Shrimper.

camarote [cah-mah-ro'-tay], *m. (Naut.)* Room on board a ship, a berth.

camarotero [cah-mah-ro-tay'-ro], *m. (LAm.)* Steward, cabin servant.

camaruta [cah-mah-roo'-tah], *f.* Bar girl.

camastro [cah-mahs'-tro], *m.* Poor, miserable bed.

camastrón [cah-mas-trone'], *m.* Sly, artful, cunning fellow. 2. *(CAm.)* Large bed.

camastronazo [cah-mas-tro-nah'-tho], *m. aug.* Great impostor, hypocrite or dissembler.

camastronería [cah-mas-tro-nay-ree'-ah], *f.* Cunning, artifice.

camatones [cah-mah-to'-nes'], *m. pl. (Naut.)* Iron fastenings of the shrouds.

camayo(c) [cah-mah'-yo], *m. (And.)* Foreman, overseer (finca).

cambado [cam-bah'-do], *a. (And. Cono Sur, Carib.)* Bow-legged.

cambalache [cam-bah-lah'-chay], *m.* 1. *(Coll.)* Barter. 2. Swap, exchange. 3. *(LAm.)* Second-hand shop.

cambalachear [cam-bah-lah'-chay-ar'], *va.* To barter, to swap, to exchange.

cambalachero [cam-bah-lah-chay'-ro], *m.* Barterer.

cambaleo [cam-bah-lay'-o], *m.* An ancient company of comedians consisting of five men and a woman; the latter sang.

cambalés [cam-bah-less'], *a.* Relating to a *cambaleo.*

cambar [cam-bar'], *va. (Carib. Cono Sur) V.* COMBAR.

cámbaro [cahm'-bah-ro], *m.* The crabfish. *V.* CANGREJO. *(Acad.).*

cambas [cahm'-bas], *f. pl.* Pieces put into a cloak, or other round garment, to make it hang round.

cambayas [cam-bah'-yas], *f. pl.* Kind of cotton stuff.

cambiable [cam-be-ah'-blay], *a.* Fit to be bartered or exchanged.

cambiadiscos [cam-be-aha-dees-cos], *m.,* Record-changer.

cambiadizo [cam-be-ah-tho], *a.* Changeable.

cambiador [cam-be-ah-dor'], *m.* 1. One who barters. 2. Money changer, money-broker. 3. *(Mex.)* Switchman (ferrocarril).

cambial [cam-be-ahl'], *m.* Bill of exchange.

cambiamano [cam-be-ah-mah'-no], *f.* A railroad switch.

cambiante [cam-be-ahn'-tay], *a.* 1. Bartering, exchanging. **Cambiante de letras**, a banker, exchanger. 2. *(Pey.)* Fickle, temperamental.

cambiante, *m.* Fabrics changeable in color according to the manner in which the light is reflected.

cambiar [cam-be-ar'], *va.* 1. To barter, to commute, to exchange one thing for another. 2. To change, to alter. **Cambiar de mano**, to change from the one side to the other (caballos). 3. To give or take money on bills, to negotiate bills and exchange them for money. 4. To transfer, to make over, to remove. **Cambiar las velas**, *(Naut.)* to shift the sails. 5. To carry on the business of a banker. **Cambiar dólares por pesos**, to change dollars for pesos. **Cambiar saludos**, to exchange greetings. **¿Lo cambiamos a otro lado?**, shall we move it somewhere else? *-vn.* To change, to alter. **Cambiar a un nuevo sistema**, to change to a new system. **No ha cambiado nada**, nothing has changed. **Está muy cambiado**, he's changed a lot. *-vr.* 1. To be translated or transferred, to change, to change round. 2. **Cambiarse en**, to change into.

cambiario [cam-be-ah'-re-o], *a. (Fin.)* Exchange. **Liberización cambiario a**, freeing of exchange controls.

cambiavía [cam-be-ah-vee'-ah], *m. (Carib. Mex.) (Ferro.)* 1. Switch man (persona). 2. Switch, points.

cambiazo [cam-be-ah'-tho], *m. (Com.)* Switch (dishonest). **Dar el cambiazo**, to switch the goods.

cámbija [cahm'-be-hah], *f.* Reservoir, basin of water.

cambio [cahm'-be-o], *m.* 1. Barter, commutation. 2. Giving or taking of bills of exchange. 3. Rise and fall of the course of exchange. 4. Public or private bank. 5. Alteration, change; flux. 6. Compensation. 7. *(Vet.)* A tumor contained in the small veins of an animal. 8. Return of a favor, recompense. **Libre cambio**, free trade. **Cambio manual**, note of hand. **Dar o tomar a cambio**, to lend or borrow money on interest. **Cambio por letras**, trade in bills of exchange. **Ha habido muchos cambios**, there have been many changes. **Cambio de domicilio**, change of address. **Cambio de guardia**, changing of the guard. **Cambio de velocidades**, *(Aut.)* Gear change. **Cambio radical**, turning point. **Cambio de vía**, *(Ferro.)* Points. **¿Tienes cambio?**, have you got any change? **A las primera de cambio**, *(fig.)* at the very start. **Cambio de frecuencia**, *(Inform.)* frequency shift, keying.

cambista [cam-bees'-tah], *m.* Banker, trader in money, broker, cambist; goldsmith.

cambiunte [cam-be-oon'-tay], *m.* 1. Changeable silk stuff. 2. A kind of camlet.

cambogio [cam-bo'-he-o], *m.* The tree which yields gamboge; garcinia. **Camboya** [Cam-bo'-yah], *f. (Hist.)* Cambodia.

camboyano, na [cam-bo-yah-no], *a. m. & f. (Hist.)* Cambodian.

cambrón [cam-brone'], *m. (Bot.)* Common buckthorn.

cambrona [cam-bro'-nah], *f. (Cono Sur)* Tough cotton cloth.

cambronal [cam-bro-nahl'], *m.* Thicket of briers, brambles, and thorns.

cambronera [cam-bro-nay'-rah], *f. (Bot.)* Boxthorn, a genus of plants. **Cambronera europea** or **común**, European boxthorn. **Cambronera africana**, African boxthorn. **Cambronera berberisca**, willow-leaved boxthorn.

cambucho [cam-boo'-cho], *m. (Cono Sur)* paper cone (cono); straw basket for waste paper or dirty clothes; straw cover (envase); miserable little room (cuartucho).

cambuj [cam-booh'], *m.* 1. Child's cap tied close to its head to keep it straight. 2. Mask, veil.

cambujo, ja [cam-boo'-ho, hah], *a.* An Indian mestizo; offspring of an Indian woman and a negro, or of a negress and an Indian; dark (persona), black (animal).

cambullón [cam-bool-lyone'], *m. (Peru)* Imposition, swindle.

cambur [cam-boor'], *m.* 1. *(Carib.)* Banana (plátano). 2. Government post, soft job, cushy number; windfall (dinero).

cambuto [cam-boo'-to], *a. (And.)* Small, squat; chubby.

cambuy [cam-boo'-e], *m.* American myrtle-tree.

camedrio [cah-may'-dre-o], *m. (Bot.)* Wall germander.

camedris [cah-may'-dris], *m. (Bot.)* Germander, speedwell, wild germander. **Camedris de agua**, water germander.

camelar [cah-may-lar'], *va.* 1. To court, to woo. 2. *(Coll.)* To seduce, to deceive by flattering. 3. *(Mex.)* To look into.

camelea [cah-may-lay'-ah], *f. (Bot.)* Widow-wail, a shrub.

camelete [cah-may-lay'-tay], *m. (Obs.)* Kind of great gun.

cameleuca [cah-may-lay'-oo-cah], *f. (Bot.)* Colt's-foot.

camelia [cah-may'-le-ah], *f.* Camellia, an Asiatic genus of small shrubs.

camelista [ ], *m. & f.* Flatterer, creep.

camella [cah-mayl'-lyah], *f.* 1. She-camel. 2. Ridge in ploughed land. 3. A milk-pail. 4. Yoke.

camellar [cah-mayl-lyar'], *vn. (Carib.)* To work (hard).

camellear [cah-mayl-lay-ar'], *vn.* To push drugs, to be a pusher.

camellejo [cah-mel-lyay'-ho], *m. dim.* Small camel.

camelleo [cah-mahl-lay-o], *m.* Drug-pushing.

camellería [cah-mel-lyay-ree'-ah], *f.* 1. Stable or stand for camels. 2. Employment of a camel-driver.

camellero [cah-mel-lyay'-ro], *m.* Keeper or driver of camels.

camello [cah-mayl'-lyo], *m.* 1. Camel. 2. Ancient cannon. 3. Engine for setting ships afloat in shoal water. 4. Drug pusher. *V.* GIRAFA.

camellón [cah-mel-lyone'], *m.* 1. Ridge turned up by the plough or espade. 2. *(Prov.)* Long wooden drinking-trough for cattle. 3. Carpenter's horse. 4. Bed of flowers. 5. *(Prov.)* Camlet. **Camellones listados**, camleteens.

camelo [cah-may'-lo], *m.* 1. Gallant, wooer. 2. *(Coll.)* A joke, jest. **Dar camelo a uno**, to make fun of somebody. **Me huele a camelo**, it smells fishy.

camelote [cah-may-lo'-tay], *m.* Camlet.

camelotillos, camelloncillos [cah-may-lo-teel'-lyos, cah-may-lyon-theel'-lyos], *m.* Light or thin camlets.

camemoro [cah-may-mo'-ro], *m. (Bot.)* Cloud berry bramble.

camepitios [cah-may-pee'-te-os], *m. (Bot.)* Common ground pine.

camerino [cah-may-re'-no], *m. (Theat.)* Dressing room; *(Mex.)* roomette (ferrocarril).

camero [cah-may'-ro], *m.* 1. Upholsterer. 2. One who lets beds for rent.

camero [cah-may'-ro], *a.* Belonging to a bed or mattress

camerododendro [cah-may-ro-do-den'-dro], *m. (Bot.)* Rusty-leaved rhododendron.

Camerún [cah-may-roon'], *m.* Cameroon.

camilla [cah-meel'-lyah], *f.* 1. *(dim.)* Small bed, pallet, or cot; litter, stretcher. **Camilla baja**, low frame, on which cloth-shearers put their work.

camillero, ra [cah-mel-lay'-ro], *m. & f.* Stretcher-bearer.

camilucho [cah-me-loo'-cho], *m. (Cono Sur, Mex.)* Indian day laborer.

caminada [cah-me-nah'-dah], *f.* V. JORNADA.

caminador [cah-me-nah-dor'], *m.* Good walker.

caminante [cah-me-nahn'-tay], *m.f.* Traveler, walker.

caminar [cah-me-nar'], *vn.* 1. To travel, to walk, to go, to march. 2. To move along (ríos, objetos). **Caminar con pies de plomo,** *(Met.)* to act with prudence. **Caminar derecho,** *(Met.)* to act uprightly. **Venir caminando,** *(LAm.)* to come on foot. **Caminar derecho**, to behave properly. 3. *(LAm.) (Mech.)* To work.

caminata [cah-me-nah'-tah], *f. (Coll.)* 1. Long walk for exercise. 2. Excursion, jaunt.

caminera [cah-me-nay'-rah], *f. (And.)* Flask containing liquor carried by travelers.

caminero [cah-me-nay'-ro], 1. *a.* Road; V. PEON. 2. *m. (LAm.)* Road builder.

caminito [cah-me-ne'-to], *m.* **Caminito de rosas.** *(fig.)* Primrose path.

camino [cah-mee'-no], *m.* 1. Path, beaten road; high road. 2. Journey. 3. Turn of a boat or cart, for removing goods from place to place. 4. Gate, way, passage, road. 5. *(Met.)* Profession, station, calling. 6. *(Met.)* Way, manner or method of doing a thing. 7. *(Min.)* Drift, gait. 8. *(Naut.)* Ship's way rate of sailing. **Camino cubierto,** *(Mil.)* Covert-way. **Camino carretero**, road for carriages and wagons. **Camino de Santiago.** *(Astr.)* Galaxy, the Milky Way; **ir fuera de camino** *(Met.)* to be put out of one's latitude, to act contrary to reason. **Procurar el camino**, to clear the way. **Salir al camino**, 1. to go to meet a person. 2. *(Met.)* to go on the highway to rob. **De camino**, in one's way, going along. **Ful a Los Angeles y de camino hice una visita,** I went to Los Angeles, and on my way there I paid a visit. **Echarse al camino**, to take to the roads, to become a highway robber. **Ponerse en camino**, set out, start off. **Camino vecinal**, country road. **El camino a seguir**, the road. **Vamos camino de la muerte**, death awaits us all. **Después de tres horas de camino**, after traveling for three hours. **Es mucho camino**, it's a long way. **Ir por el buen camino**, *(fig.)* to be on the right track. **Traer a uno por buen camino**, *(fig.)* to put somebody on the right way. **Todos los caminos van a Roma**, all roads lead to Rome.

camino de acceso [cah-mee'-no day ac-thay'-so], *m.* Access road.

camión [cah-me-on'], *m.* Truck; lorry; van. **Camión de basura**, trash truck. **Camión de bomberos**, fire engine. **Camión cisterna**, tanker. **Camión de reparto**, delivery truck. **Camión de riego**, water cart.

camionaje [cah-me-o-nah'-hay], *m.* Haulage, cartage.

camionero [cah-me-o-nay'-ro], *m.* Truck-driver, teamster.

camioneta [cah-me-o-nay'-tah], *f.* 1. Station wagon. 2. Small truck.

camionista [cah-me-o-nees'-tah], *m.* V. CAMIONERO.

camión-tanque [cah-me-on'tan-kay], *m. pl.* **Camiones-tanque,** *(Aut.),* tanker.

camisa [cah-mee'-sah], *f.* 1. Shirt. 2. Shift, chemise, the undergarment of women. 3. Alb or surplice, worn by priests and deacons. 4. Thin skin of almonds and other fruit. 5. Slough of a serpent. 6. *(Mil.)* Chemise, side of a rampart toward the field. 7. Stock of counters used at a game of cards. 8. Catamenia. 9. Rough casting or plastering of a wall before it is whitewashed. 10. Jacket, case, casing, in steam-engines (motores). 11. Internal lining of a furnace (hornos). **Camisa de una vela,** *(Naut.)* the body of a sail. **Meterse en camisa de once varas**, to interfere in other people's affairs; to undertake very difficult or dangerous business, or above one's power or means. **Vender hasta la camisa**, to sell all to the last shirt. **No llegarle a uno la camisa al cuerpo**, to be frightened, to be anxious. **Dejar a uno sin camisa**, to leave somebody destitute. **Camisa de dormir**, night gown. **Camisa de gas**, gas mantle. **Camisa de agua**, water jacket.

camisería [cah-me-say-ree'-ah], *f.* Shirt-store.

camisero [cah-me-say'-ro], *m.* Shirt-maker.

camiseta [cah-me-say'-tah], *f.* 1. Undershirt. V. ELASTICA. 2. *(Obs.)* Short shirt or shift with wide sleeves. 3. Chemisette.

camisilla [cah-me-seel'-lyah], *f. (Carib. Cono Sur)* V. CAMISETA.

camisola [cah-me-so'-lah], *f.* 1. Ruffled shirt. 2. Dicky. **Camisola de fuerza**, a strait-jacket.

camisolín [cah-me-so-leen'], *m.* Shirt-front, tucker, wimple.

camisón [cah-me-sone'], *m.* 1. *(aug.)* Long and wide shirt. 2. Frock worn by laborers and workmen. 3. *(Amer.)* Gown, a woman's upper garment. 4. *(Cuba and Puerto Rico)* Chemise. 5. Nightdress.

camisote [cah-me-so'-tay], *m.* Ancient armor.

camita [cah-mee'-tah], *f. dim.* Small bed, pallet, or cot.

camita [cah-me-tah], *a.* Hamitic.

camomila [cah-mo-me'-lah], *f.* Camomile.

camón [cah-mone'], *m.* Frame of laths, which serves to form an arch. **Camón de vidrios**, partition made by a glass frame. -*pl.* 1. Felloes of cartwheels, shod with evergreen oak instead of iron. 2. Incurvated pieces of timber in the wheels of corn-mills.

camoncillo [cah-mon-theel'-lyol], *m.* State stool in a drawing-room; cricket richly garnished.

camorra [cah-mor'-rah], *f. (Coll.)* Quarrel, dispute. **Armar camorra**, to kick up a row. **Buscar camorra**, to go looking for trouble.

camorrear [cah-mor-ray-ar'], *vn. (Coll.)* To dispute often.

camorrero [cah-mor-ray'-ro], *m.* V. CAMORRISTA.

camorrista [cah-mor-rees'-tah], *com. (Coll.)* Noisy, quarrelsome person, hooligan.

camote [cah-mo'-tay], *m. (Bot.)* A variety of sweet potato. 2. *(CAm. Cono Sur) (Med.)* Dump, swelling. 3. *(Cono Sur)* large stone. 3. *(Cono Sur)* bore, tedious person (persona). 4. *(CAm.)* Calf of the leg. 5. *(CAm.)* Nuisance, bother (molestia). 6. *(LAm.)* Love; crush (amor). **Tener camote con uno**, to have a crush on somebody. 7. *(And. Cono Sur)* Lover, sweetheart. 8. *(Cono Sur)* fib (mentirilla). 9. *(And. Cono Sur)* fool (tonto).

camotear [cah-mo-tay-ar'], *va.* 1. *(Cono Sur)* To rob, to fleece. 2. *(CAm.)* To annoy. -*vn. (CAm.)* To be trying, to cause trouble.

campa [cam-pah], 1. *a.* Tierra campa, treeless land. 2. *f.* Open land.

campal [cam-pahl'], *a.* Belonging to the field and encampments. **Batalla campal;** pitched battle.

campamentista [cam-pah-mayn-tees'-tah], *m. & f.* Camper.

campamento [cam-pah-men'-to], *m.* Encampment, camp. **Campamento para prisioneros**, prison camp. **Campamento de verano**, summer camp.

campana [cam-pah'-nah], *f.* 1. Bell. 2. Bell glass, receiver; anything which has the shape of a bell. 3. *(Met.)* Parish church, parish. 4. Bottom of a well made in the form of a bell. 5. In woollen factories, iron hoop, serving to keep the yarn from the bottom of the dyeing copper. 6. *(Arch.)* Drum, corbel. 7. *(LAm.)* Thieves' look out. **Hacer de campana**, to keep watch, to be on the lookout. **Campana de vidrio**, a bell-shaped glass vessel. **Campana de chimenea**, mantel, the funnel of a chimney when made in the form of a bell. **A toque de campana**, at the sound of the bell. **Oír campanas y no saber dónde**, to have heard of a fact, but not to be well informed of its true nature and complexion. **No haber oído campanas**, not to be informed of the most common things. **Echar las campanas al vuelo**, to peal the bells. **Campana de bucear**, diving bell.

campanada [cam-pah-nah'-dah], *f.* Sound produced by the clapper striking against the bell. **Dar campanada**, *(Met.)* to cause scandal, to make a noise.

campanario [cam-pah-nah'-re-o], *m.* 1. Belfry, bell tower. 2. *(Coll.)* Noddle, head. 3. Rack in velvet-looms.

campanazo [cam-pah-nah'-tho], *m.* 1. *V.* CAMPANADA. 2. *(And.)* Warning.

campaneado [cam-pah-nay-ah'-do], *a.* *(fig.)* Much talked of.

campanear [cam-pah-nay-ar'], *va.* 1. To ring the bell frequently. 2. To divulge, to noise about. 3. *(LAm.)* To keep watch (ladrón).

campanela [cam-pah-nay'-lah], *f.* Sudden motion of the feet in dancing.

campaneo [Cam-pah-nay'o], *m.* 1. Bell ringing, chime. 2. *V.* CONTONEO,

campanero [cam-pah-nay-ro], *m.* 1. Bell-founder. 2. Bellman.

campaneo [cam-pah-nay'-tah], *f. dim.* Small bell.

campaniforme [cam-pa-ne-for'- may], *a.* *(Bot.)* Campaniform, bell-shapped. *V.* CAMPANUDO.

campanil [cam-pah-neel'], *m.* 1. Small belfry. -*a.* 2. **Metal campanil**, bell-metal.

campanilla [cam-pah-neel'-lyah], *f.* 1. *(dim.)* Small bell, hand-bell. 2. Small bubble. 3. *(Anat.)* Uvula. 4. Little tassel for ladies' gowns. 5. *(Naut.)* Cabin-bell. 6. *(Bot.)* Bell flower. 7. **Campanillas de otoño** *(Bot.)* Fall snowflake, garden daffodil. **De campanillas** or **de muchas campanillas**, of importance or consideration.

campanillazo [cam-pah-neel-lyah'-tho], *m.* 1. Violent ringing of a bell. 2. Signal given with a bell.

campanillear [cam-pah-neel-lyay'-ar'], *va.* To ring a small bell often.

campanilleo [cam-pah-neel-lyay'-o], *m.* Ringing, tinkling.

campanillero [cam-pah-neel-lyay'-ro], *m.* Bellman, public crier.

campanino [cam-pah-nee'-lyay'-ro], *a.* Applied to a kind of marble.

campanólogo, ga [cam-pah-no'-lo-go], *m. & f.* Campanologist, bell-ringer.

campante [cam-pahn'-tay], *pa.* 1. Excelling, surpassing. 2. Buoyant, triumphant, cheerful. 3. Intrepid, robust. **Siguió tan campante**, he went on cheerfully. **Allí estaba tan campante**, there he was as large as life.

campanudo, da [cam-pah-noo'-do, dah], *a.* 1. Wide, puffed up, bell-shaped (ropa). 2. *(Bot.)*

campánula [cam-pah'-noo-lah], *f. (Bot.)* Bell-flower, campanula.

campanulado, da [cam-pah-noo-lah' do, dah], *a. (Bot.)* Campanulate, bell-shaped.

campaña [cam-pah'-nyah], *f.* 1. Campaign, level country. 2. Campaign of an army. **Campaña naval**, *(Naut.)* Cruise. 3. *(Agri.)* Season. **Hacer campaña**, to campaign. **Hacer campaña en contra de**, to campaign against. **Hacer campaña a favor**, to campaign for.

campañola [cam-pah-nyo'-lah], *f.* Water rat.

campar [cam-par'], *vn.* 1. To encamp, to be encamped. 2. To excel in abilities, arts, and sciences. **Campar con su estrella**, to be fortunate or successful.

campeador [cam-pay-ah-dor'], *m.* 1. Combater, warrior. 2. A surname applied particularly to the Cid, Rodrigo Diaz de Vivar.

campear [cam-pay-ar'], *vn.* 1. To be in the field; to go out to pasture. 2. To frisk about (animales). **Campear de sol a sombra**, to be at work from morning to night. 3. To be eminent; to excel. 4. **Ir campeando**, to carry on. 5. *(LAm.)* To camp, to go camping. 6. *(And.)* To make one's way through. 7. *(And.)* To bluster. **Campea por sus respetos**, he acts as if he were lord of the manor.

campechanería [campay-chah-nay-ree'-ah], *f. (LAm.)*, **Campechanía** *f.*, Frankness, opennes; heartiness, cheerfulness.

campechno, na [cam-pay-chah'-no, nah], *a.* 1. Frank, hearty, ready for amusement. 2. *(Mex, Carib.)* Cocktail.

campeche [cam-pay'-chay], *m.* Campeachy-wood, log-wood.

campeón [cam-pay-on'], *m.* 1. Champion, combatant. 2. Champion, a judicial combatant, either in his own case or another's.

campeonato [cam-pay-o-nay'-to], *m.* Championship. **De campeonato**, *(fig.)* absolute, out-and-out; huge.

campero, ra [cam-pay'-ro, rah], *a.* 1. Exposed to the weather in the open field. 2. *(Mex.)* Having a gait like gentle trotting, pacing. 2. *(LAm.)* Knowledgeable about the countryside; expert in farming matters.

campero [cam-pay'-ro], *m.* 1. Friar who superintends a farm. 2. One who inspects another's lands and fields. 3. Pig brought up in the fields.

camperuso [cam-pay-roo'-so], *(Carib.) a.* 1. Rural, rustic. 2. Reserved, stand-offish. -*m. f.* Peasant.

campesino, na, campestre [cam-pay-see'-no, nah, cam-pes'-tray], *a.* Rural, campestral, rustic. -*m. & f.* A countryman, countrywoman.

campillo [cam-peel'-lyo], *m.dim.* Small field.

camping [cam'-peen], *m. pl.* 1. Campings, camping. **Hacer camping**, to go camping. 2. Camping site (sitio).

campiña [cam-pee'-nyah], *f.* Flat tract of arable land, field, campaign.

campirano [cam-pee-rah'-no], *m.* *(LAm.)* 1. Peasant (campesino); rustic, country bumpkin. 2. *(Agri.)* Expert in farming matters; guide, pathfinder; skilled horseman; stock-breeding expert (ganadero).

campista [cam-pees'-tah], *m. & f.* Camper. *a.* 1. *(CAm. Carib.)* Rural, country. 2. *(LAm.) V.* CAMPERO. -*m. (CAm.)* Herdsman.

campisto [cam-pees'-to], *a. (CAm.)* Rural, country. -*m* 1. *(CAm.)* Peasant. 2. *(CAm.) (Agri.)* Amateur vet.

campo [cahm'-po], *m.* 1. Country. 2. Any tract of flat and even country. 3. Field, space, range of things. 4. Crops, trees, plantations. 5. Ground of silks and other stuffs. 6. Camp. 7. Ground on which an army is drawn up. 8. Ground of a painting. 9. **Campo santo**, burial-ground, cemetery. **Campo abierto**, plain, open country. **Campo de batalla**, battlefield. **Hacerse al campo**, to retreat, to flee from danger. **Dejar el campo abierto, libre**, to decline an undertaking where there are competitors. **Hombre de campo** or **del campo**, one who leads a country life. **Ir campo a través**, to take a short cut. **El campo está espléndido**, the countryside looks lovely. **Campo de aterrizaje**, landing field. **Campo de deportes**, sports ground. **Campo de fútbol**, football ground. **Campo de golf**, golf course. **Campo de minas**, minefield. **Campo de tiro**, firing range. **Levantar el campo**, *(Mil.)* to retire from the field. **Se le hizo el campo orégano**, *(Cono Sur)* it all turned out nicely for him. **No hay campo**, there's no room. **Hay campo para más**, there's scope for more. **Campo de concentración**, Concentration camp.

camposantero [cam-po-sahn-tay'-ro], *m.* Cemetery official.

campusano [cam-poo-sah'-no], *m.* Campus. -*m. (CAm.)* Peasant.

camuesa [cah-moo-ay'-sah], *f.* Pippin, an apple. **Camuesa blanca**, white pippin.

camueso [cah-moo-ay'-so], *m.* 1. *(Bot.)* Pippin tree. 2. Simpleton, fool.

camuflado [cah-moo-flah'-do], *a.* Camouflaged.

camuflaje [cah-moo-flah'-hay], *m.* Camouflage.

camuflar [cah-moo-flar'], *va. (fig.)* To camouflage.

camuza [cah-moo-thah], *f.* Chamois goat. *V.* GAMUZA.

camuzón [cah-moo-thone'], *m. aug.* Large chamois-skin.

can [cahn], *m.* 1. *(Ant.)* Dog. 2. *(Arch.)* Bracket, shoulder, modillion, corbel. 3. *(Poet.)* Dog-star. 4. Ace in dice. 5. Trigger of guns, etc. 6. Ancient piece of ordnance. **Can rostro**, Pointer or setting-dog. **Can de busca**, terrier. **Can que mata al lobo**, wolfdog.

cana [cah'-nah], *f.* 1. Long measure, containing about two ells. 2. Gray or white hair. **Peinar canas**, to grow old. **Tener**

canas, to be old, to have white hair. **Echar una cana al aire**, to paint the town red, to have a good time, to go on a spree.
cana [cah'-nah], *f. (LAm.)* Jail; prison cell. 2. *(LAm.)* Police. **Caer en cana**, to land in jail. *-m.* Policeman (persona).
canaballa [cah-nah-bahl'-lyah], *f. (Naut.)* Fishing-boat.
canabis [cah-nah-bees'], *m.* Cannabis.
canaca [cah-nah'-cah], *m. & f. (And. Cono Sur)* chink; Chinese. 2. *(Cono Sur)* brothel keeper (dueño).
Canadá [Cah-nah-dah'], *m.* **El Canadá**, Canada.
canadiense [cah-nah-de-en'-say], *a.* Canadian.
canal [cah-nahl], *f.* 1. Channel, canal. Any of the paths by which the waters and vapors circulate in the bosom of the earth. 2. Drinking-trough for cattle. 3. Gutter, eaves-trough, pantile. 4. Duct or tube by which secretions of the body are conducted. 5. Comb of the loom, among weavers. 6. A domestic animal killed and dressed; particularly the hog. 7. Hemp which has been once hackled. 8. Front edge of a book. 9. Crease, slot (metales). **Canal de Panamá**, Panama Canal. **Canal de riego**, irrigation channel. **Canal de la Mancha**, English Channel. **Canal digestivo**, digestive tract, alimentary canal. *-m.* 10. Canal, an artificial waterway. 11. Channel, a strait between islands or continents. 12. Channel, navigable entrance to a harbor. 13. Channel, bed of a river. 14. Bed of a hot-press. 15. Pole of copper. **En canal**, from top to bottom. **Canal de desagüe**, *(And.)* Sewer. **Canal de humo**, *(Mex.)* Flue. **Canal inclinado**, chute. **Canal de entrada/salida**, input/output channel.
canalado, da [cah-nah-lah'-do'-dah], *a V.* ACANALADO.
canaleja [cah-nah-lay'-hah], *f.* 1. *(dim.)* Small drinking-trough for cattle. 2. In corn-mills, small channel to convey grain from the hopper to the millstones; mill-spout. 3. A priest's hat shaped like a trough.
canalera [cah-nah-lay'-rah], *f. (Prov.)* Gutter.
canaleta [cah-nah-lay'-tah], *f. (Cono Sur)* pipe, conduit; roof gutter.
canalete [cah-nah-lay'-tay], *m.* Paddle, a small oar.
canalita [cah-nah-lee'-tah], *f. dim.* Small channel or canal.
canalización [cah-nah-lee-tha-the-on'], *f.* 1. Canalization, chanelling. 2. *(Tec.)* Piping; *(Elec.)* Wiring; mains (de gas); *(LAm.)* Sewerage system, drainage (de cloacas).
canalizar [cah-nah-le-thar'], *va.* To channel, to canalize, provide an outlet.
canalizo [cah-nah-lee'-tho], *m.* Narrow channel between two islands or sand-banks.
canalón [cah-nah-lon'], *m.* 1. *(Arch.)* Gutter, guttering; spout; drainpipe. 2. Shovel hat (sombrero). 3. **Canalones** *(Culin.)*, Cannelloni.
canalla [cah-nahl'-lyah], *f.* Mob, rabble, multitude, populace, canaille. 2. Pack of hounds.
canallada [cah-nahl-lyah-dah], *f.* **canallería** *f. (LAm.)* Dirty trick, mean thing (to do), despicable act; nasty remark.
canallesco [cah-nahl-lyays'-co], *a.* Mean, rotten, despicable. **Diversión canallesca**, low form of amusement.
canalluza [cah-nal-lyoo'-thah], *f.* Roguery, vagrancy.
canalón [cah-nah-lone'], *m.* Large gutter or spout, eaves-trough, leader, waterway, rain-conductor.
canameño [cah-nah-may'-nyo], *m.* A traveling hammock. *(Cent. Amer.)*
canana [cah-nah'-nah], *f.* 1. A kind of cartridge-belt. 2. Fricassee of chicken. 3. *(LAm.) (Med.)* Goitre. 4. *(Carib.)* Mean trick, low prank.
canapé [cah-nah-pay'], *m.* 1. Couch or seat with a mattress, to sit or lie on. 2. Settee. 3. Lounge. 4. *(Culin.)* Canapé.
canario [cah-nah'-re-o], *m.* 1. Canarybird. 2. A native of the Canary Islands. 3. *(Naut.)* Barge used in the Canary Islands. 4. *(LAm.)* Yellow (amarillo).
canasta [cah-nahs'-tah], *f.* 1. Basket, hamper. **Canasta para los papeles**, wastepaper basket. 2. Canasta, card game.
canastero, ra [cah-nas-tay'-ro, rah], *m. & f.* Basket-maker.
canastilla [cah-nas-teel'-lyah], *f.* 1. *(dim.)* Small basket. **Canastilla de costura**, sewing basket. 2. An infant's basket; wardrobe for a baby. 3. A bride's trousseau.

canastillo [cah-nas-teel'-lyo], *m.* 1. Wicker tray; pannier. 2. Small basket. 3. Maund, a hand-basket.
canasto, canastro [cah-nahs'-to, cah-nahs'-tro], *m.* 1. Large basket. 2. **¡Canastos!** *int.* Denoting surprise or annoyance. 3. *(And.)* Servant.
cáncamo [cahn'-cah-mo], *m.* 1. *(Naut.)* Bolt-ring, to which the breeches and tackle of guns are fixed. **Cáncamos de argolla**, ring-bolts. **Cáncamos de gancho**, hook-bolts. **Cáncamos de ojo**, eye-bolts. 2. Blending of gums resembling myrrh.
cancamurria [cahn-cah-moor'-ree-ah], *f.* Blues, gloom.
cancamusa [can-cah-moo'-sah], *f.* Trick to deceive. **Ya le entiendo la cancamusa**, I am aware of the device.
cancán [cahn-cahn'], *m.* Cancan, a French dance.
cáncana [cahn'-cah-nah], *f.* Cricket, a kind of stool. 2. *(And.)* Thin person.
cancanco [cahn-cah'-no], *m. (Carib.) (Aut.)* Breakdown.
cancanear [cahn-cah-nay-ar'], *vn.* 1. To loiter, loaf about. 2. *(Cono Sur)* to dance the cancan. 3. *(And. CAm. Cono Sur)* to express oneself with difficulty, to stammer; to read haltingly.
cancaneo [cahn-cah-nay'-o], *m. (And. CAm. Mex.)* Faltering (al leer); stammering (tartamudeo).
cancanilla [can-cah-neel'-lyah], *f.* 1. Thing to play a trick with. 2. Deception, fraud.
cáncano [cahn'-cah-no], *m. (Coll.)* Louse. **Andar como cáncano loco**, to go round in circles.
cancel [can-thel'], *m.* 1. Wooden screen at the doors of churches and halls. 2. Glass-case in chapel behind which the king stands. 3. Limits or extent of a thing. 4. Windproof door, storm door.
cancela [can-thay'-lah], *f.* A grating or screen of open ironwork between the porch and the yard.
cancelación, canceladura [can-thay-lah-the-on', can-thay-lah-doo'-rah], *f.* Cancellation, expunging, obliteration, closing up.
cancelar [can-thay-lar'], *va.* To cancel or annul a writing. **Cancelar de la memoria**, *(Met.)* To efface from the memory.
cancelaría, cancelería [can-thay-lah-ree'-ah, lay-ree'-ah], *f.* Papal chancery, the court at Rome, whence apostolic grants and licenses are expedited.
cancelario [can-thay-lah'-re-o], *m.* Chancellor in universities who grants degrees.
cancellería [can-thel-lyay-ree'-ah], *f.* Chancery.
cáncer [cahn'-ther], *m.* 1. Cancer, virulent ulcer. 2. Cancer, one of the signs of the zodiac.
cancerado [cahn-thay-rah'-do], *a.* Cancerous; *(fig.)* Corrupt.
cancerarse [can-thay-rar'-say], *vr.* 1. To be afflicted with a cancer. 2. To cancerate or become a cancer.
cancerbero [can-ther-bay'-ro], *m.* 1. Cerberus, the three-headed dog which guarded the gate of the nether world. 2. *(Met.)* A severe and incorruptible guard. 3. A worthless gatekeeper.
cancerígeno, na [can-thay-ree'-hay-no, nah], *a.* Carcinogenic, cancerogenic.
cancerólogo, ga [cahn-thay-ro'-lo-go], *m. & f.* Cancer specialist.
canceroso, sa [can-thay-ro'-so, sah], *a.* Cancerous.
cancha [cahn'-chah], *f.* 1. Field, ball park, court. **Cancha de tenis**, tennis court. **Cancha de pelota**, pelota court. **Estar en su cancha**, *(Cono Sur)* to be in one's element. **En la cancha se ven los pingos**, *(LAm.)* Deeds speak louder than words. 2. Toasted corn. 3. *(Peru)* Popcorn.
canchar [cahn-chay-ar'], *va. (And. Cono Sur)* to toast.
canche [cahn'-chay], *a.* 1. *(CAm.)* Blonde (rubio). 2. *(And.)* Poorly seasoned, tasteless.
canchero, ra [cahn-chay-ro], *m. & f.* 1. Experienced person. 2. *(LAm.)* Groundsman, groundswoman (cuidador); experienced player. 3. *(Cono Sur)* layabout, loafer (vago).
canchilagua [can-chah-lah'-goo-ah], *f. (Bot.)* A medicinal herb growing in Peru.
canchón [cahn-chon'], *m. (And.)* Enclosed field.

cancilla [can-theel'-lyah], *f.* (*Prov.*) Wicker-door or wicker-gate.

canciller [can-theel-lyerr'], *m.* Chancellor.

cancilleresco, ca [can-theel-lyay-res'-co, cah], *a.* 1. Belonging to the writing characters used in chancery business. 2. (*Admin.*) Chancellery.

cancillería [can-theel-lyay-ree'-ah], *f.* (*Obs.*) V. CHANCILLERÍA.

canción [can-the-on'], *f.* 1. Song, verses set to music. **Canción de cuna**, lullaby, cradle song. 2. Poem of one or more stanzas, a lay. **Volver a la misma canción**, to return to the old tune, to repeat the old story. **Volvemos a la misma canción**, here we go again.

cancioncica, illa, ita [can-the-on-thee'-cah, eel'-lyah, ee'-tah], *f. dim.* Canzonet, a little song.

cancionero [can-the-o-nay'-ro], *m.* 1. Song-book. 2. Songwriter.

cancionista [can-the-o-nees'-tah], *m.* Author or singer of songs.

canco [cahn'-co], *m.* (*Chile*) 1. Earthen pot. 2. Flower pot. 3. Big hip. 4. (*Bol.*) Buttocks, hips.

cancriforme [can-cre-for'-may], *a.* Cancriform, having the shape of a crab.

cancrinita [can-cre-nee'-tah], *f.* Cancrinite, a variously colored silicate, which crystallizes in the hexagonal system.

cancro [cahn'-cro], *m.* V. CÁNCER.

cancrófago, ga [can-cro'-fah-go, gah], *a.* Crab-eating.

cancroideo, ea [can-cro-e-day'-o, ah], *a.* Cancroid, resembling cancer.

candado [can-dah'-do], *m.* 1. Padlock. 2. Pendant, earring. **Echar** or **poner candado a los labios**, (*Met.*) To keep a secret, to be silent. 3. (*And.*) Beard.

candanga [can-dahn'-gah], *m.* El candanga, the devil.

candar [can-dar'], *va.* To lock, to shut.

cándara [cahn'-dah-rah], *f.* (*Prov.*) Frame of laths for sifting sand, earth, and gravel.

cande [cahn'-day], *a.* Sugar-candy. V. AZÚCAR.

candeal [can-day-ahl'], *a.* **Trigo candeal**, white wheat, summer wheat. **Pan candeal**, bread made of the white wheat.

candeda [can-day'-dah], *f.* Blossom of the walnut-tree.

candela [can-day'-lah], *f.* 1. Candle. 2. Flower or blossom of the chestnut-tree. 3. Candlestick. 4. Inclination of the balance-needle to the thing weighed. 5. (*Prov.*) Light, fire. **Arrimarse a la candela**, (*Prov.*) To draw near the fire. **Acabarse la candela**, (*Met.*) To be near one's end. **Estar con la candela en la mano**, to be dying. **Dar candela**, to be a nuisance. **Echar candela** to sparkle (ojos). **Prender candela**, to set fire.

candelabro [can-day-lah'-bro], *m.* Candlestick. V. CANDELERO.

candelada [can-day-lah'-dah], *f.* (*Prov.*) Sudden blaze from straw or brushwood. V. HOGUERA.

candelaria [can-day-lah'-re-ah], *f.* 1. Candlemas. 2. (*Bot.*) Mullein. V. GORDOLOBO.

candelejón [can-day-lay-hone'], *a.* (*So. Amer.*) Candid, simple-minded, dumb.

candelerazo [can-day-lay-rah'-tho], *m.* 1. (*aug.*) Large candlestick. 2. Stroke or blow given with a candlestick

candelería [can-day-lay-ree'-ah], *f.* Tallow and wax chandler's shop. V. VELERÍA.

candelero [can-day-lay'-ro], *m.* 1. Candlestick. **Candelero con muchos brazos**, chandelier. 2. (*Obs.*) Wax or tallow chandler. 3. Lamp. 4. Fishing-torch. **Estar en candelero**, (*Met.*) To be high in office, to hold an exalted station. **Candeleros**, (*Naut.*) Stanchions or crotches, pieces of timber which support the waist-trees. **Candeleros de trincheras y parapetos**, quarter-netting stanchions. **Tema en candelero**, hot subject. **Poner en candelero a uno**, to give somebody a high post. **Poner algo en candelero**, to bring something into the limelight.

candeletón [can-day-lay-tone'], *m.* Large stanchion.

candelilla [can-day-leel'-lyah], *f.* 1. (*Surg.*) Bougie, catheter. 2. Blossom of poplars and other trees. Catkin, ament. **Hacer la candelilla**, to stand on the hands and head, as boys do in play. **Le hacen candelillas los ojos**, (*Coll.*) He is half-seas over, or his eyes sparkle with the fumes of wine. 3. Small candle. 4. (*Carib. Cono Sur*) hem, border.

candelizas [can-day-lee'-thas], *f. pl.* (*Naut.*) Brails, small ropes reeved through a block. **Candelizas de barlovento**, weather-braces. **Candelizas de sotavento**, lee-braces.

candelizo [cahn-day-lee'-tho], *m.* Icicle.

candelo [cahn-day'-lo], *a.* (*And.*) Reddish-blonde.

candencia [can-den'-the-ah], *f.* Incandescence, white heat.

candente [can-den'-tay], *a.* 1. Incandescent, red-hot, tending to a white heat. 2. (*fig.*) Burning (cuestión).

candi [cahn'-de], *a.* **Azúcar candi**, sugar-candy, rock-candy.

candial [can-de-ahl'], *a.* V. CANDEAL.

cándidamente [cahn'-de-dah-men-tay], *adv.* Candidly.

candidato, ta [can-de-dah'-to], *a.m. & f.* 1. Candidate; applicant for. 2. (*Cono Sur*) sucker.

candidatura [can-de-dah-too'-rah], *f.* 1. Candidacy; candidature; soliciting votes. 2. A list of those who aspire to some elective position.

candidez [can-de-deth'], *f.* 1. Whiteness. 2. Candor, sincerity, purity of mind. 3. Candidness, ingenuousness. 4. Simplicity.

cándido, da [cahn'-de-do, dah], *a.* 1. White, snowy, gray, pale. 2. Candid, guileless. 3. Simple.

candil [can-deel'], *m.* 1. A kitchen or stable lamp. 2. Lamp with oil, etc. 3. Cock of a hat. 4. Long irregular fold in petticoats. 5. Fishing-torch. V. CANDELERO. 6. (*Mex.*) A chandelier. **Puede arder en un candil**, it would burn in a lamp (vino generoso, personas brillantes); it is used ironically in the last sense. 7. Top of a stag's horn. **Baile de candil**, a ball held by the light of a poor lamp. **Dar candil a uno**, (*fig.*) to be very strong.

candileja [can-de-lay'-hah], *f.* 1. Inner part of a kitchen lamp. 2. The foot-lights of a theater. 3. (*Bot.*) Willows, deadly carrot.

candilejera [can-de-lay-hay'-rah], *f.* (*Bot.*) Spanish birth wort.

candilejo [can-de-lay'-ho], *m. dim.* 1. Small kitchen lamp. 2. (*Bot.*) V. LUCÉRNULA.

candilera [can-de-lay'-rah], *f.* (*Bot.*) Lamp-wick.

candilón [can-de-lone'], *m. aug.* Large open lamp.

candinga [cahn-deen'-dah], *f.* 1. (*Cono Sur*) impertinence, insistence. **El candinga**, (*Mex.*) the devil.

candiota [can-de-o'-tah], *f.* 1. Barrel or keg for carrying wine in vintage time. 2. Large earthen jar, the inside of which is pitched, wherein wine is fermented. 3. An inhabitant of the island of Candia.

candiotera [can-de-o-tay'-rah], *f.* A wine-cellar: storage place of casks, tuns.

candiotero [cahn-dee-o-tay'-ro], *m.* Cooper.

candonga [can-don'-gah], *f.* 1. Mean, servile civility, intended to deceive. 2. Merry, playful trick. 3. Old mule unfit for service. 4. An old, ugly woman. 5. (*Col.*) Earring.

candongo, ga [can-don'-go, gah], *a.* 1. A cunning, fawning person. 2. Smooth oily (zalamero); sly (taimado), crafty; lazy. 2. *m.* Creep, toady, flatterer; sly sort; shirker, idler, lazy blighter.

candonguear [can-don-gay-ar'], *va.* (*Coll.*) To jeer, to sneer, to turn into ridicule.

candonguero, ra [can-don-gay'-ro, rah], *a.* (*Coll.*) The one who is mischievous or plays bad tricks. V. CANDONGO.

candor [can-dor'], *m.* 1. (*Obs.*) Supreme whiteness. 2. (*Met.*) Candor, purity of mind, ingenuousness fairness, frankness, openness.

candoroso, sa [can-do-ro'-so, sah], *a.* Ingenuous, frank, honest, straightforward.

canear [cah-nay-ar'], *va.* To bash, to hit (con vara).

caneca [cah-nay'-cah], *f.* 1. Glazed liquor bottle made of clay. 2. (*Arg.*) Wooden tub. 3. (*Cuba*) Hot-water bottle made of earthenware. 4. (*Cuba*) Liquid measure of 19 liters.

caneco [cah-nay'-co], *a. (And.)* Tipsy.

canecillo [cah-nay-theel'-lyo], *m. (Arch.)* Corbel, modillion, truss, cantilever; console.

canela [cah-nay'-lah], *f.* 1. *(Bot.)* Cinnamon. **Agua de canela**, cinnamon-water. 2. *(fig.)* Lovely thing, exquisite object. **Es canela fina**, she's wonderful. 3. *Interj.* Good gracious!

canelado, da [cah-nay-lah'-do, dah], *a. V.* ACANELADO.

canelero [cah-nay-lay'-ro], *m.* Cinnamon tree.

canelo [cah-nay-'lo], *m.* 1. *(Bot.)* Cinnamon-tree or cinnamon laurel. 2. *m.* Cinnamon-colored.

canelón [cah-nay-lone'], *m.* 1. Gutter. *V.* CANALÓN. 2. Sweetmeat. 3. Icicle. 4. *(Bot.)* A kind of bastard cinnamon, commonly called **Canelón de Santa Fe. Canelones**, end of a cat of nine-tails, thicker and more twisted than the rest. 5. *(CAm.)* Corkscrew curl.

canesú [cah-nay-soo'], *m.* 1. A bodice. 2. Upper part of a shirt for either sex. 3. *(Cos.)* Yoke.

caney [cah-nay'-e], *m.* 1. A logcabin. 2. Bight; riverbend.

canez [cah-neth'], *f.* Hair hoary or gray with age; old age. *(Yo canezco, yo canezca,* from *Canecer. V.* CONOCER).

canfín [cahn-feen'], *m. (CAm. Carib.)* Petrol, gasoline.

canforero [can-fo-ray'-ro], *m.* The camphor-tree.

canga [cahn'-gah], *f.* Cangue, a heavy wooden collar or yoke, worn around the neck by convicts in China as a punishment.

cangalla [can-gahl'-lyah], 1. *(Salv.)* Tattered shred of clothing. 2. *(Col.) m.* or *f.* Thinned-out animal or person. 3. *(Arg. & Peru)* A coward. 4. *(Bol.)* Packsaddle. 5. *(Arg. & Chile)* Mineral wastings.

cangallar [can-gahl-lyar'], *va. (Arg. & Chile)* To ransack metal in the mines.

cangilón [can-he-lone'], *m.* 1. Earthen jar or pitcher. 2. Oblong earthen jar fastened to the rope of a draw-well, or to a wheel for lifting water. 3. Metal tankard for wine or water. 4. *(LAm.)* Cart track.

cangreja [can-gray'-hah], *a.* **Vela cangreja**, *(Naut.)* boom sail, brig-sail, or gaffsail.

cangrejal [can-gray'-hahl'], *m. (Amer.)* A spot frequented by crabs.

cangrejo [can-gray'-ho], *m.* 1. *(Zool.)* Craw-fish, crab. 2. Truckle-cart. 3. Trolley. **Andar como el cangrejo**, to go backward. 4. *(Naut.)* Gaff. 5. *(And.)* Idiot, crafty person. 6. *(LAm.)* Mystery, enigma.

cangrejuelo [can-gray-hoo-ay'-lo], *m. dim.* Small crawfish.

cangrena [can-gray'-nah], *f.* Gangrene, mortification. *V.* GANGRENA.

cangrenarse [can-gray-nar'-say], *vr.* To be afflicted with gangrene or mortification. *V.* GANGRENARE.

cangrenoso, sa [can-gray-no'-so, sah], *a.* Gangrenous, mortified.

cangri [cahn'-gree], *m.* 1. Nick (cárcel), prison. 2. Church.

cangro [cahn'-gro], *m. (And. CAm. Mex.)* Cancer.

canguelo [cahn-goo-ay'-lo], *m.* Canguis *m.* Funk.

canguro [cahn-goo'-ro], *m.* 1. *(Zool.)* Kangaroo. 2. Baby-sitter. **Hacer de canguro**, to baby-sit. 3. Light jacket, light coat.

cania [cah'-ne-ah], *f. (Bot.)* Small nettle.

caníbal [ca-nee'-bal], *m.* Cannibal, a man-eater.

canibalismo [cah-nee-bah-lees'-mo], *m.* Cannibalism; *(fig.)* fierceness, savageness.

canicas [cah-nee'-cahs], *f. pl.* Marbles.

caniche [cah-nee-chay], *m.* Poodle.

canicie [ca-nee'-the-ay], *f.* Whiteness of the hair.

canícula [ca-nee'-coo-lah], *f.* 1. *(Astr.)* Dog-star. 2. *V.* CANICULARES. **Entra la canícula**, the hot days begin. **Canícula marina**, *(Zool.)* lesser spotted dog-fish.

canicular [ca-ne-coo-lar'], *a.* 1. Canicular belonging to the dog-star. 2. **Calores caniculares**, midsummer heat.

caniculares [ca-ne-coo-lah'-res], *m. pl.* Dog-days.

canido [ca-nee'-do], *m.* Kind of parrot found in the West Indies.

canijo, ja [ca-nee'-ho, hah], *a. & m. & f.* Weak, infirm, sickly. **Es un canijo**, he is a weak, puny being.

canilla [ca-nee'-lyah_, *f.* 1. A long bone of either extremity. **Canilla de la pierna**, shin-bone. **Canilla del brazo**, arm-bone. 2. Any of the principal bones of the wing of a fowl 3. Stopcock, faucet, spigot. 4. Reel, bobbin, spool; quill put into a shuttle on which the woof is wound. 5. Unevenness or inequality of the wool in point of thickness or color. **Irse como una canilla**; to let the tongue run like the clapper of a mill. 6. Rib (paño). 7. *(Carib.)* Cowardice. 8. *(Mex.)* **Tener canilla**, to have great physical strengh.

canillado, da [ca-neel-lyah'-do, dah], *a. V.* ACANILLADO.

canillento [cah-neel-lyayn'-to], *a. (And.)* Long-legged.

canillera [ca-nee'-lyay'-rah], *f.* 1. Ancient armor for the shin-bone. 2. Woman who distributes thread to be wound on spools. 3. *(LAm.)* Fear; cowardice.

canillero [ca-neel-lyay'-ro], *m.* 1. Hole in a cask or vat to draw off its contents. 2. Weaver's quill-winder.

canillita [cah-neel-lyee'-tah], *m. (Arg.)* A newsboy; a newsvendor.

canillón [cah-neel-lyone'], *a. (LAm.),* **Canilludo** *a. (LAm.)* Long-legged.

canina [ca-nee-nah], *f.* Excrement of dogs.

caninamente [ca-ne-nah-men'-tay], *adv.* In a passionate, snarling manner; like a dog.

canino, na [ca-nee'-no, nah], *a.* Canine. **Hambre canina**, canine appetite, inordinate hunger. **Dientes caninos**, eye-teeth or canine-teeth. **Músculo canino**, canine muscle, which serves to elevate the upper lip.

canje [cahn'-hay], *m.* Exchange, used in speaking of prisoners, ratified treaties, or the credentials of diplomats.

canjear [can-hay-ar'], *va.* To exchange prisoners of war, treaties, or credentials, to change over, to interchange; to cash in.

cano, na [cah'-no, nah], *a.* 1. Hoary, hoar, frosty, gray-headed. 2. *(Met.)* Deliberate, prudent, judicious.

canoa [ca-no'-ah], *f.* 1. Canoe, a boat used by the Indians. **Canoa automóvil**, motor boat. 2. *(LAm.)* Conduit; pipe; feeding trough (comedero); chicken coop (de gallinas); dovecot (de palomas).

canódromo [cah-no'-dro-mo], *m.* Dog track.

canoero [ca-no-ay'-ro], *m.* One who conducts a canoe.

canoi [ca-no'-e], *m. (Amer.)* Basket used by Indians on a fishing party.

canoita [ca-no-ee'-tah], *m. dim.* Small canoe.

canon [cah'-non], *m.* 1. Canon, the decision of an ecclesiastical council relative to the doctrines or discipline of the church. 2. Catalogue of the books which compose the Holy Scriptures. 3. *(Law.)* Fee paid in acknowledgment of superiority in a higher lord. **Canon de tránsito**, *(Aut.)* Toll. **Como mandan los cánones**, as the rules require, in accordance with sound principles. 4. Catalogue, list. 5. *(Print.)* Canon, a large sort of type. **Cánones**, canons or canonical law. 6. *(Mus.)* Canon. A composition in which the music sung by one part, after a short rest, sung by another part, note for note.

canonesa [ca-no-nay'-sah], *f.* Canoness, a woman who lives in a religious house and observes its rules, without having taken the vows of a monastic life.

canonical [ca-no-ne-cahl'], *a.* Canonical, relating to canons, *(fig.)* Easy.

canónicamente [ca-no'-ne-cah-men-tay], *adv.* Canonically.

canonicato [ca-no-ne-cah'-to], *m.* Canonry; sinecure, cushy job. *V.* CANONJÍA.

canónico, ca [ca-no'-ne-co, cah], *a.* 1. Canonical canonic. **Iglesia o casa canónica**, house or monastery of regular canons. 2. Canonical; applied to the books which compose the Holy Scriptures.

canónigo [ca-no'-ne-go], *m.* Canon or prebendary.

canonista [ca-no-nees'-tah], *m.* Canonist, a professor or student of the canon law.

canonizable [ca-no-ne-thah'-blay], *a* Worthy of canonization.

canonización [ca-no-ne-thah-the-on'], *f.* Canonization, consecration.

canonizar [ca-no-ne-thar'], *va.* 1. To canonize, to consecrate, to declare one a saint. 2. *(Met.)* To applaud or praise a thing. 3. *(Met.)* To prove a thing good.

canonjía [ca-non-hee'-ah], *f.* Canonry canonship, prebend or benefice of a canon: canonicate.

canoro, ra [ca-no'-ro, rah], *a.* 1. Canorous, melodious, musical. 2. Shrill, loud.

canoso, sa [ca-no'-so, sah], *a.* 1. Hoary, hoar, frosty, gray-headed. 2. Old.

canotaje [cah-no-tah'-hay], *m.* Boating.

canotier [cah-no-te-ayr'], *m.* **canotié** *m.* Straw hat, boater.

cansadamente [can-sah-dah-men'-tay], *adv.* 1. Importunely, troublesomely. 2. Wearily, in a tired way.

cansado, da [can-sah'-do, dah], *a.* 1. Weary, wearied, exhausted, tired. 2. Tedious, tiresome, troublesome. **Una vista cansada**, an impaired eyesight. **Con voz cansada**, in a weary voice. **Estoy cansado de hacerlo**, I'm tired of doing it. 3. Performed with pain or fatigue. *-pp.* of CANSAR. *-vr.* To tire, to get tired, to grow weary, to get bored. **Cansarse de hacer algo**, to get tired of doing something.

cansado [can-sah'-do], *m.* Bore.

cansancio [can-sahn'-the-o], *m.* Weariness, lassitude, fatigue.

cansar [can-sar'], *va.* 1. To weary, to tire, to fatigue, to overcome. 2. To harass, to molest, to bore. 3. To exhaust land. *-vr.* To tire oneself, to be fatigued, to grow weary.

cansera [can-say'-rah_, *f.* Fatigue, weariness.

casinamente [cahn-see-nah-mayn'-tay], *adv.* Wearily; lifeless.

cansino, na [can-see'-no, nah], *a.* Worn by work (animales).

cantable [can-tah'-blay], *a.* 1. Tunable, harmonious, musical. 2. Pathetic, affecting.

Cantábrico, ca [can-tah'-bre-co, cah], **cántabro, bra** [cahn'-tah-bro, brah], *a.* 1. Cantabrian, of Cantabria 2. Name given to the part of the Atlantic Ocean which washes the northern coast of Spain.

cantada [can-tah'-dah], *f.* Cantata, a musical composition.

cantadera [cahn-tah-day'-rah], *f. (LAm.)* Loud singing, prolonged singing.

cantador, ra [can-tah-dor'], *m. & f. V.* CANTOR.

cantal [cahn-tahl'], *m.* 1. Boulder (piedra); stone block. 2. Stony ground.

cantaleta [can-ta-lay'-tah], *f.* 1. Charivari, a confused noise of voices or instruments. 2. Pun, jest, joke, humbug. **Dar cantaleta**, to deride, to laugh at, to turn into ridicule.

cantaloup [can-tah-loop'], *m.* Cantaloup or cantaloupe.

cantante [can-tahn'-tay], *m. & f.* A singer, especially one who sings for a livelihood.

cantaor, ora [cahn-tah-or'], *m. & f. V.* CANTADOR, RA. (De cante flamenco).

cantar [can-tar'], *m. (Coll.)* Song set to music. **Cantares**, canticles or Song of Solomon. **Cantares de gesta**, old metrical romances.

cantar [can-tar'], *va.* 1. To sing. 2. To recite in a poetical manner. 3. *(Met. Coll.)* To creak, to make a harsh, grinding noise. 4. *(Coll.)* To divulge a secret 5. At cards, to announce the trump. **Cantar a libro abierto**, to sing off-hand. **Cantar de plano**, to make a plain and full confession. **Cantar la victoria**, *(Met.)* To triumph. **Cantar misa**, to say the first mass. **Ése es otro cantar**, that is another kind of speech. **¿Lo digo cantado o rezado ?** how would you have me say it? **Al fin se canta la gloria**, do not triumph till all is over, don't whistle before you are out of the woods. **Cantar las claras**, to speak out. **Cantar a dos voces**, to sing a duet.

cántara [cahn'-ta-rah_, *f.* 1. Large, narrow-mouthed pitcher. *V.* CÁNTARO 2. Wine measure containing about thirty-two pints.

cantarcico, illo, ito [can-tar-thee'-co, theel'-lyo, thee'-to], *m. dim.* Little song.

cantarera [can-ta-ray'-rah], *f.* Shelf for jars, pitchers, etc.

cantarería [cahn-tah-ray-ree'-ah], *f.* 1. Pottery shop, earthenware shop. 2. Pottery (shop).

cantarero, ra [can-ta-ray'-ro, rah], *m. & f.* A dealer in earthen jars, pitchers, pans, etc.

cantárida [can-tah'-re-dah], *f.* 1. Cantharis, Spanish-fly, the blistering fly. 2. Blistering plaster made with the blistering fly. 3. Blister, the vesicle raised on the skin by the blistering plaster.

cantarillo [can-ta-reel'-lyo], *m.* 1. *(dim.)* Small jar or pitcher. 2. *(Bot.)* Oval-leaved androsace. **Cantarillo que muchas veces va a la fuente, o deja el asa o la frente**, the pitcher which goes often to the well gets broken in the end.

cantarín [can-ta-reen'], *m. (Coll.)* One who sings constantly.

cantarina [can-ta-ree'-nah], *f.* A woman who sings on the stage.

cántaro [cahn'-ta-ro], *m.* 1. Large, narrow-mouthed pitcher, and the liquid contained in it. 2. Wine measure of different sizes. **Llover a cántaros**, to rain by bucketfuls, to pour, to rain cats and dogs.

cantata [cahn-tah'-tah], *f.* Cantata.

cantazo [can-tah'-tho], *m.* Wound given by flinging a stone.

cante [cahn'-tay], *m.* **Cante flamenco, conte jondo**, Andalusian gipsy singing.

cantegriles [cahn-tay-gree-lays], *m. pl. (Cono Sur)* Shantytown.

canteles [can-tay'-les], *m. pl. (Naut.)* Ends of old ropes put under casks to keep them steady.

cantera [can-tay'-rah], *f.* 1. Quarry where stones are dug. **Cantera de arena**, sandpit. **Cantera de piedra**, stone quarry. 2. *(Met.)* Talents or genius.

canterear [can-tay-ray-ar'], *va.* To hang up flitches of bacon, that the brine may run off.

cantería [can-tay-ree'-ah], *f.* 1. Art of hewing stone, the trade of a stone-cutter. 2. Building made of hewn stone 3. Quarry. 4. Parcel of hewn stone.

cantero [can-tay'-ro], *m.* 1. Stone-cutter. 2. The extremity of a hard substance which can be easily separated from the rest. **Cantero de pan**, crust of bread. 3. *(Cono Sur)* bed, plot (sembradío). 4. *(Mex. And.)* Plot of sugar.

canterón [can-tay-rone'], *m. (Prov.)* Large tract of land.

canticio [can-tee'-the-o], *m. (Coll.)* Constant or frequent singing.

cántico [cahn'-te-co], *m.* Canticle. **Cántico de los cánticos**, the Song of Solomon.

cantidad [can-te-dahd'], *f.* 1. Quantity. 2. Measure, number, time used in pronouncing a syllable. 3. Quantity, large portion of a thing. **Por una cantidad alzada**, for a sum of money agreed upon. **Hacer buena alguna cantidad**, to pay a sum of money due. **En cantidad**, in quantity. **Tengo una cantidad de cosas que hacer**, I've got lots of things to do. **Este coche mola cantidad**, that car is really nice; **esto está degenerando cantidad**, this is really going down hill.

cantiga [can-tee'-gah], *f. (Obs.) V.* CANTAR. A poetical composition divided into strophes; after each follows a refrain.

cantil [can-teel'], *m.* Steep rock; shelf; ledge, coastal shelf (de costa); cliff (risco).

cantilagua [can-te-lah'-goo-ah], *f. (Prov.)* Purging flax.

cantilena [can-te-lay'-nah], *f.* Ballad, song, chant. *V.* CANTINELA.

cantillo [can-teel'-lyo], *m. dim.* A little stone.

cantimarones [can-te-mah-ro'-nes], *m. pl. (Naut.)* Kind of boats.

cantimplora [can-tim-plo'-rah], *f.* 1. Siphon, a crooked tube or pipe. 2. Vessel for cooling liquors; liquor-case.

cantina [can-tee'nah], *f.* 1. Saloon, tavern, bar, barroom. 2. Cellar for wine. 3. Canteen, shop where liquors and provisions are sold in barracks or military camps. 4. Canteen (used to carry water on a journey or march).

cantinela [can-te-nay'-lah], *f.* 1. Ballad. 2. Irksome repetition of a subject. **¿Ahora se viene con esa cantinela?**, does he come again with that old story?

cantinero [can-te-nay'-ro], *m.* 1. Bartender. 2. Keeper of a tavern or saloon.

cantinflear [cahn-teen-flay-ar'], *vn. (Coll.)* 1. To speak in a silly and nonsensical manner, without meaning (after Cantinflas). 2. To babble. To act like Cantinflas (Mex. comedic actor).

cantinflismo [cahn-teen-flees'-mo], *m. (Mex.)* Babble, empty chatter.

cantiña [can-tee'-nyah], *f.* A song in Galicia and Asturias.

cantió [cahn-tee-o], *m. (Carib.)* Folksong, popular song.

cantiral [cahn-tee-rahl'], *m.* Stony ground, stony place.

cantizal [can-te-thahl'], *m.* Stony ground, place full of stones.

canto [cahn'-to], *m.* 1. Singing. 2. A short poem, of heroic type. 3. Canto, a division of a long poem. 4. A chant or canticle. **Al canto del gallo**, at midnight. **El canto de los pájaros**, the singing of the birds. 5. End, edge, or border. 6. Extremity, point. 7. The crust (of a loaf). 8. Thickness of any thing; back of a knife. 9. The front edge of a book. 10. Dimension less than square. **Al canto**, by the side of. **De canto**, on edge. **El ladrillo está de canto y no de plano**, the brick stands on edge, and not flatwise. **Ni un canto de uña**, absolutely nothing. **Faltó el canto de un duro**, he had a close shave.

canto, *m.* 1. A stone, pebble. 2. Game of throwing the stone (duck on a rock). 3. Quarry-stone, block, dressed ashlar.

cantón [can-tone'], *m.* 1. Corner. 2 *(Her.)* Part of an escutcheon. 3. Canton, region, tract of land, district. 4. *(LAm.) (Cost.)* Cotton (material).

cantonada [can-to-nah'-dah], *f. (Prov.)* Corner. **Dar cantonada**, to laugh at a person on turning a corner; to disappoint a person by not taking notice of what he says or does.

cantonal [can-to-nahl'], *a.* Cantonal, relating to the canton or district.

cantonar [can-to-nar'], *va. V.* ACANTONAR.

cantonear [cahn-to-nay-ar'], *vn.* To loaf around.

cantonease [can-to-nay-ar'-say], *vr. V.* CONTORNEARSE.

cantoneo [can-to-nay'-o], *m. V.* CONTONEO.

cantonera [can-to-nay'-rah], *f.* 1. Plate nailed to the corners of a chest, etc., to strengthen it. 2. Corner cabinet (rinconera). 3. Angle-iron, corner bracket. 4. Wench, a woman of the town.

cantonero, ra [can-to-nay'-ro, rah], *a. (Obs.)* Standing idle at the corner of a street.

cantor, ra [can-tor', rah], *m. & f.* 1. Singer; minstrel. 2. One who composes hymns or psalms. 3. Small singing-bird.

cantorcillo [can-tor-theel'-lyo], *m. dim.* Petty, worthless singer.

cantoría [can-to-ree'-ah], *f.* Musical canto; singing.

cantorral [can-tor-rahl'], *m.* Stony ground, place full of stones.

cantueso [can-too-ay'-so], *m. (Bot.)* French lavender, spike.

cantuja [cahn-too'-hah], *f. (And.)* Slang.

cantúo [cahn-too'-o], *a.* **Una mujer cantúa**, a woman with a smashing figure.

canturía [can-too-ree'-ah], *f.* 1. Vocal music. 2. Musical composition. 3. Method of performing musical compositions. **Esta composición tiene buena canturía**, this piece of music may be easily sung.

canturrear, canturriar [can-toor-ray-ar', re-ar'], *vn.* To hum, to sing in a low voice.

canturreo [can-too-ray'-o], *m.* Humming, crooning, soft singing; chanting; droning.

cantusar [can-too-sar'], *va. V.* ENGATUSAR.

canudo, da [ca-noo'-do, dah], *a.* Hoary, gray; ancient.

canula [cah'-noo-lah], *f. (Med.)* Canula, a metal tube for withdrawing fluids; often fitted with a trocar.

canutazo [cah-noo-tah'-tho], *m.* Telephone call.

canutero [cah-noo-tay'-ro], *m. (LAm.)* Barrel (of pen).

canutillo [cah-noo-teel'-lyo], *m. V.* CANUTILLO.

canuto [cah-noo'-to], *a.* 1. Super, smashing. 2. **Pasarlas canutas**, to have a rough time of it. *-m.* 1. Small tube, small container. 2. *(Bot.)* Internode. 3. Tell-tale (persona). 4. Joint (porro). 5. Telephone.

canzonetista [cahn-tho-nay-tees'-tah], *f.* Vocalist, crooner.

caña [cah'-nyah], *f.* 1. Cane, reed. Arundo. 2. Stem, stalk. **La caña del trigo**, stem of corn 3. Walking-stick. **Caña común**, cultivated reed. **Caña dulce** or **de azúcar, or cañamiel**, common sugar-cane. 4. *V.* CANILLA for a bone. 5. Subterraneous passage in the mines of Almadén. 6. Shaft of a column or pillar. 7. Marrow. 8. Tournament 9. *(Naut.)* Helm. 10. Lever drill, ratchet drill. 11. Glass-blower's pipe. 12. *(Carp.)* Shank. 13. Reed of wind instruments. **Caña del timón**, *(Naut.)* tiller. **Caña de pescar**, fishing-rod. **Hubo toros y cañas**, *(Met.)* there was the devil to pay. **Caña de cerveza**, glass of beer. **¡Dos cañas!**, two beers please.

cañada [cah-nyah'-dah], *f.* 1. Glen or dale between mountains; glade. 2. **Cañada real**, sheep-walk for the flocks passing from the mountainous and colder parts of Spain to the flat and warmer parts. 3. *(Prov.)* Measure of wine. 4. *(Amer.)* Rivulet, brook.

cañadicas, cañaditas [cah-nyah-dee'-cass, dee'-tas], *f. pl. (Prov.)* Small measures for wine.

cañadón [cah-nyah-done'], *m. (Cono Sur)* Low-lying part of a field.

cañafístula [cah-nyah-fees'-too-lah], *f.* Cassia fistula, the fruit of the purging cassia.

cañafístulo [can-nyah-fees'-too-lo], *m. (Bot.)* Purging cassia-tree.

cañaheja, cañaherla [ca-nyah-ay'-hah, cah-nyah-err'-lah], *f. (Bot.)* Common fennel-giant, or gigantic fennel.

cañahuate [cah-nyah-oo-ah'-tay], *m.* A species of lignum-vitae which grows in Colombia.

cañal [cah-nyahl'], *m.* 1. Weir or wear for fishing, made of canes or reeds. 2. Plantation of canes or reeds. 3. Small sluice or channel, for catching fish. 4. Conduit of water.

cañaliega [cah-nyah-le-ay'-gah], *f.* Wear or weir for fishing.

cáñama [cah'-nyah-mah], *f.* Assessment of taxes, paid by a village or other place. **Casa cáñama**, house exempt from taxes. **Cogedor de cáñama**, tax gatherer.

cañamar [cah-nyah-mar'], *m.* Hempfield.

cañamazo [cah-nyah-mah'-tho], *m.* 1. Tow of hemp. 2. Coarse canvas made of hemp-tow. 3. Painted or checkered stuff for table-carpets, made of hemp.

cañamelar [cah-nyah-may-lar'], *m.* Plantation of sugar-cane. Cane-field.

cañameño, ña [cah-nyah-may'-nyo, nyah], *a.* Hempen, made of hemp.

cañamero [cah-nyah-may'-ro], *a.* Hemp.

cañamiel [cah-nyah-me-el'], *f. (Bot.)* Sugar-cane. *V.* CAÑADULCE.

cañamiz [cah-nyah-meeth'], *m.* Kind of Indian vessel.

cañmiza [cah-nyah-mee'-thah], *f.* Stalk of hemp; bullen, bun. *V.* AGRAMIZA.

cáñamo [cah'-nyah-mo], *m.* 1. *(Bot.)* Hemp. **Cáñamo silvestre**, bastard hemp. 2. Cloth made of hemp. 3. *(Poet.)* Slings, rigging, and other things made of hemp. **Cáñamo en rama**, undressed hemp.

cañamón [cah-nyah-mone'], *m.* Hempseed.

cañar [cah-nyar'], *m.* 1. Plantation of canes or reeds. 2. Weir for catching fish.

cañareja [cah-nyah-ray'-hah], *f. V.* CAÑAHEJA.

cañariego, ga [cah-nyah-re-ay'-go, gah], *a.* **Pellejos cañariegos**, skins of sheep which die on the road.

cañarroya [cah-nyar-ro'-yah], *f. (Bot.)* Pellitory, wall-wort.

cañavera [cah-nyah-vay'-rah], *f. (Bot.)* Common reed-grass.

cañaveral [cah-nyah-vay-rahl'], *m.* Plantation of canes or reeds. **Recorrer los cañaverales**, to go from house to house, to get something.

cañaverero [cah-nyah-vay-ray-ro], *m.* Retailer of canes or reeds.

cañvete [cah-nyah-vay'-tay], *m.* The knife with which shepherds slaughter their animals.

cañazo [cah-nyah'-tho], *m.* 1. Hostile blow with a cane. **Dar cañazo**, *(Met.)* To confound one by a rude communication. 2. Rum. *(Peru).*

cañear [cah-nyay-ar'], *vn.* To drink, to carouse.

cañeo [cah-nyay'-o], *m.* Drinking, carousal.

cañengo [cah-nyayn'-go], *a.* **cañengue** *a. (And. Carib.)* Weak, sickly; skinny.

cañería [cah-nyay-ree'-ah], *f.* 1. Aqueduct, a water-pipe. 2. Water-main, gas-main. **Cañería maestra**, (gas) main. 3. *(Naut.)* Bilge-holes.

cañero [cah-nyay'-ro], *m.* 1. Conduit-maker, director of waterworks. 2. *(Prov.)* Angler.

cañero [cah-nyay'-ro], *a.* 1. *(LAm.)* Sugar-cane. **Machete cañero**, sugar-cane knife. 2. *(And. Carib.)* Lying (mentiroso); buffler, boaster.

cañete [cah-nyay'-tay], *m.* Small pipe.

cañilavado, da [cah-nye-la-vah'-do, dah], *a.* Small-limbed (caballos, mulas).

cañilla, ita [cah-nyeel'-lyah, ee'-tah], *f. dim.* Small cane or reed.

cañillera [cah-nyeel-lyay'-rah], *f.* Ancient armor for the shin-bone.

cañivete [cah-nye-vey'-tay], *m.* Small knife, penknife.

cañita [cah-nyee'-tah], *f. (And.)* (Drinking) straw.

cañiza [cah-nyee'-thah], *f.* Coarse linen.

cañizal, cañizar [cah-nye-thahl', thar'], *m. V.* CAÑAVERAL.

cañizo [cah-nyee'-tho], *m.* 1. Hurdle, a frame for rearing silkworms 2. Hurdle, used by hatters for shearing hats. 3. *(Naut.)* Flake.

caño [cah'-nyo], *m.* 1. Tube, pipe, or cylinder, of wood, glass, or metal. 2. Common sewer, gutter. 3. Spring; spout or conduit for spring-water. 4. Cellar or other place for cooling water. 5. Mine. 6. Subterranean passage. 7. *(Prov.)* Warren or burrow. *V.* VIVAR. **Caños** or **cañones del órgano**, tubes or pipes of an organ. 8. The channel which forms at the entrance to seaports.

cañocazo [cah-nyo-cah'-tho], *m.* Coarse flax.

cañón [cah-nyone'], *m.* 1. Cylindrical tube or pipe. 2. In glass-houses, tube or pipe for blowing glass. 3. Quill. 4. Down, or soft feathers. 5. Hollow folds in clothes. 6. Part of the beard next to the root. 7. Cannon, gun. **Escopeta de dos cañones**, doubled-barrelled gun. **Cañón rayado**, rifled barrel. 8. *(Min.)* Gallery. 9. *(Mech.)* Socket. 10. Gorge, ravine, canyon. 11. Quill pen (de pluma). 12. *(And.) (Bot.)* Trunk. 13. *(And. Mex.)* Mountain path. *V.* CAÑADA. **A boca de cañón**, at the mouth of a cannon. **Canón reforzado**, a re-enforced cannon. **Cañón de agua**, water cannon. **Cañón antiaéreo**, anti-aircraft gun. **Cañón de campaña**, field gun. 14. One of the four spindles of the bar of a velvetloom. *-a.* Fabulous, marvelous. **¡La función estaba cañón!**, the show was great! **Una noticia cañón**, a stunning piece of news.

cañonazo [cah-nyo-nah'-tho], *m.* 1. *(aug.)* Large piece of ordnance. 2. Cannon-shot. **Cañonazo de advertencia**, *(Naut.)* warning shot. 3. Report of a gun or shot.

cañoncico, illo, ito [cah-nyon-thee'-co, eel'-lyo, ee'-to], *m. dim.* Small cannon: small tube or pipe.

cañonear [cah-nyo-nay-ar'], *va.* To cannonade, to shell, to bombard. *-vr.* To cannonade each other; to exchange guns.

cañoneo [cah-nyo-nay'-o], *m.* Cannonade, shell fire.

cañonera [cah-nyo-nay'-rah], *f.* 1. Embrasure for cannon. 2. Large tent. 3. *V.* PISTOLERA. 4. *(Naut.)* A gunboat.

cañonería [cah-nyo-nay-ree'-ah], *f.* The pipes of an organ collectively.

cañonero, ra [cah-nyo-nay'-ro, rah], *a. (Naut.)* Mounting cannon; a gun boat.

cañota [cah-nyo'-tah], *f. (Bot.)* Panicled sorghum. **Cañota suave**, yellow-seeded soft grass.

cañucela [cah-nyoo-thay'-lah], *f.* A slender cane or reed.

cañuela [cah-nyoo-ay'-lah], *f. (Bot.)* Fescue grass, a genus of grasses. **Cañuela ovina** or **ovejuna**, sheep's fescue grass. **Cañuela durilla**, hard fescue grass.

cañusero [cah-nyoo-say'-ro], *m. (And.)* Owner of sugar-cane plantation.

cañutazo [cah-nyoo-tah'-tho], *m. (Low.)* Information, private accusation, suggestion, whisper, tale. **Fue con el cañutazo**, he went to carry his tale.

cañutería [cah-nyoo-tay-ree'-ah], *f.* 1. *V.* CAÑONERÍA. 2. Gold or silver twist for embroidery.

cañutero [cah-nuo-tay'-ro], *m.* Pincushion.

cañutillo [cah-nyoo-teel'-lyo], *m.* 1. *(dim.)* Small tube or pipe. 2. Bugle, small glass ornamental tubes stitched to the tassels and flounces of women's gowns. **Cañutillo de hilo de oro o de plata para bordar**, quill of gold or silver twist for embroidery. 3. A mode of grafting. *(Acad.)*

cañuto [cah-nyoo'-to], *m.* 1. Part of a cane, from knot to knot, internode. 2. Pipe made of wood or metal. 3. *(Prov.)* Pincase. 4. Blast, gust. *V.* SOPLO. 5. Informer, tale-bearer. *V.* SOPLÓN. 6. **Cañutos helados**, *(Mex.)* Small ice-cream cylinders. 7. *V.* CANUTO.

caoba, caobana [cah-o'-bah, cah-o-bah'-nah], *f. (Bot.)* Mahogany-tree.

caolín [cah-o-leen'], *m.* Kaolin, chinaclay.

caos [cah'-os], *m.* 1. Chaos. 2. Confusion.

caótico, ca [cah-o'-te-co, cah], *a.* Chaotic; in disorder and confusion.

caoup [cah-o-oop'], *m. (Bot.)* Caoup, an American tree with fruit like an orange.

cap [cap], *abr.* de **capítulo** *(Chapter.)*.

capa [cah'-pah], *f.* 1. Cloak. 2. Mantle. 3. Layer, strata, lamina. 4. Coat or hair of a horse. 5. Cover, anything laid over another. 6. *(Met.)* Cloak, pretence or pretext, mask, cover. 7. Hider, harborer. 8. Property, fortune. *V.* CAUDAL. 9. An American rodent; the spotted cavy. *V.* PACA. 10. Among bell-founders, the third mould used in casting bells. 11. Coat of paint. 12. Bed, stratum, vein, seam, ledge. 13. *(Mas.)* Bed, course. 14. Wrapper for tobacco. **Capa del cielo**, *(Met.)* canopy of heaven. **Capa pluvial**, a pluvial or choircope, worn by prelates in processions. **Capa y sombrero**, *(Naut.)* hat-money, allowance per ton to the captain on his cargo; **ponerse a la capa**, *(Naut.)* to lie to. **Andar** or **ir de capa caída**, to be down in the mouth, crestfallen. **Echar la capa al toro**, *(Met.)* to expose oneself to danger. **Estar o estarse a la capa**, *(Met.)* to have a good or sharp lookout. **Sacar bien su capa**, *(Met.)* to disengage oneself from difficulties; (capa rota), *(fig.)* secret emissary. **Capa torera**, bullfighter's cape. **Hacer de su capa un sayo**, to do what one likes with one's own things, act freely. **Comedia de capa y espada**, cloak-and-dagger play. **Primera capa**, undercoat. **Capas sociales**, social layers. **Madera de tres capas**, three-ply wood.

capá [cah-pah'], *m.* Capá, a tree which grows in Cuba and Porto Rico; often used in building vessels.

capaburro [cah-pah-boor'-ro], *m. (LAm.)* Piranha.

capacete [cah-pah-chay'-tay], *m.* Helmet, casque.

capacha [cah-pah'-chah], *f.* 1. Frail, hamper. *V.* CAPACHO. 2. Frail, a basket made of rushed 3. *(Coll.)* The religious order of St. John of God. 4. *(And. Cono Sur)* jail. *(Cono Sur)* **Caer en la capacha**, to fall into the trap.

capacheca [cah-pah-chay-cah], *f. (And. Cono Sur)* Street-vendor's barrow.

capacho [cah-pah'-cho], *m.* 1. Frail, hamper, large basket. 2. **Capacho de albañil**, bricklayer's hod. 3. In oilmills, the bass, or willow frail through which oil is filtered. 4. Mendicant hospitaller, who collects charity for the sick. 5. *(Orn.)* Common owl, barn owl. 6. *(And. Cono Sur)* Old hat.

capacidad [cah-pah-che-dad'], *f.* 1. Capacity, capability. **Capacidad de compra**, purchasing power. **Capacidad de arrastre**, drawing power (de orador etc.). **Capacidad de carga**, carrying capacity. 2. Extent, extensiveness of a place. **Una sala con capacidad para 900**, a hall with room for 900. **Un avión con capacidad para 20 plazas**, a 20-seater plane 3. Opportunity or means of executing a thing. 4. *(Naut.)* Bulk or burden of a ship. 5. *(Met.)* Talent, genius, mental ability. **Tener capacidad para**, to have an aptitude for. **No tiene capacidad para los negocios**, he has no business sense. 6. *(LAm.)* Able person (persona hábil).

capacitación [cah-pah-the-tah-the-one'], *f.* Capacitation (jurado); Training, education.

capacitado [cah-pah-the-tah'-do], *a.* Qualified. **Estar capacitado para**, to be qualified to.

capacitar [cah-pah-the-tar'], *va.* 1. **Capacitar a uno para algo**, to fit somebody for something; to train (educate) somebody for something. 2. *(And. Cono Sur, Mex.)* **Capacitar a uno para hacer algo**, to empower somebody to do something. *-vr.* **Capacitarse para algo**, to fit oneself for something.

capador [cah-pah-dor'], *m.* 1. One whose business is to geld or castrate. 2. A kind of whistle employed by those whose business is to geld.

capadura [cah-pah-doo'-rah], *f.* 1. Castration. 2. Scar which remains after castration. 3. Leaf of tobacco of the second cutting; used for filling.

capar [cah-par'], *va.* 1. To geld, to castrate. 2. *(Met. Low.)* To castrate, to take away a part; to curtail, to diminish one's authority, income, etc. 3. *(And. Carib.)* To start on (comida). 4. *(Carib. Mex.)* To cut back, to prune.

caparazón [cah-pah-ra-thone'], *m.* 1. Carcass of a fowl. 2. Caparison, a sort of cover over the saddle of a horse. 3. Cover of a coach, or other things made of oilcloth. 4. *(Prov.)* Frail made of grass, in which horses feed when out of the stable. 5. *(Zool.)* Shell.

caparra [cah-par'-rah], *f.* 1. Sheeplouse. *V.* GARRAPATA. 2. Earnest money given to confirm a bargain. 3. *V.* ALCAPARRA.

caparrón [cah-par-rone'], *m.* *(Obs.)* Bud of a vine or tree.

caparrós [cah-par-ros'], *m.* *(Prov.)* *V.* CAPARROSA.

caparrosa [cah-par-ro'-sah], *f.* Copperas, or vitriol, ferrous sulphate. **Caparrosa azul**, blue vitriol, copper sulphate. **Caparrosa blanca**, white vitriol, zinc sulphate. **Caparrosa verde**, green vitriol, copperas.

capataz [cah-pah-tath'], *m.* 1. Overseer, superintendent. 2. One charged with receiving the marked metal to be coined in the mint. 3. Steward who superintends a farm. 4. Warden of a company or guild. 5. Conductor. 6. Foreman.

capaz [cah-path'], *a.* 1. Capacious, capable, able to hold other things. 2. Capacious, ample, spacious, roomy, wide. **Capaz para**, with a capacity of. **Coche capaz para 4 personas**, a car with room for 4 people. 3. *(Met.)* Fit, apt, suitable, competent. **Ser capaz de algo**, to be capable of something. **Es capaz de cualquier tontería**, he is able of any stupidity. **Capaz de funcionar**, operational. **Ser capaz para un trabajo**, to be qualified for a job. 4. *(Met.)* Learned, ingenious, capable, clever. **Hacerse capaz de alguna cosa**, *(Met.)* To render oneself master of a thing. 5. *(LAm.)* **Es capaz que venga**, he'll probably come. *-adv.* *(LAm.)* **¿Vendrá?...capaz que sí**, will he come?

capaza [cah-pah'-thah], *f.* *(Prov.)* *V.* CAPACHO.

capazmente [cah-path-men'-tay], *adv.* Capaciously, amply.

capazo [cah-pah'-tho], *m.* 1. Large frail or basket made of rushes.

capazón [cah-pah-thone'], *m.* *aug.* Very large frail made of brass.

capción [cap-the-on'], *f.* *(Obs.)* *V.* CAPTURA.

capciosamente [cap-the-o-sah-men'-tay], *adv.* Insidiously, captiously, artfully, cunningly.

capcioso, sa [cap-the-o'-so, sah], *a.* Captious, insidious, artful, cunning, faultfinding, wily, deceitful.

capea [cah-pay'-ah], *f.* Bullfighting with young bulls.

capeador [cah-pay-ah-dor'], *m.* 1. A bull-fighter who challenges the bull with his cloak. 2. Cloak-stealer.

capear [cah-pay-ar'], *va.* 1. To strip or rob one of a cloak in an inhabited place. 2. *(Naut.)* To try or lay to. 3. To challenge a bull with one's cloak. 4. To dodge (esquivar). 5. *(Naut.)* *(fig.)* To ride out, weather (temporal). *-vn.* *(Naut.)* To ride out the storm.

capeja [cah-pay'-hah], *f.* *(dim.* of depreciation) A poor or mean cape.

capel [cab-pel'], *m.* *(Prov.)* Cocoon or ball of a silkworm.

capela [cah-pay'-lah], *f.* *(Astr.)* Capella, the brightest star in Auriga.

capelina [cah-pay-lee'-nah], *f.* Capelline, a bandage especially fitted to the head.

capelo [cah-pay'-lo], *m.* 1. Dues received in ancient times by bishops from their clergy. 2. Hat. *V.* SOMBRERO. 3. Cardinal's hat. 4. Dignity of a cardinal, cardinalate.

capellán [cah-pel-lyahn'], *m.* 1. Chaplain, a clergyman who has obtained a chaplaincy: *V.* CAPELLANÍA. 2. Chaplain, a clergyman that officiates in domestic worship. **Capellán de navío**, chaplain of the navy. **Capellán de altar**, the priest who chants the mass. **Capellán de honor**, the king's private champlain. **Capellán mayor de los ejércitos**, the vicar-general of the army.

capellar [cah-pel-lyar'], *m.* A kind of Moorish cloak.

capellina [cah-pel-lyee'-nah], *f.* 1. Head piece of a helmet or casque. 2. Hood worn by country people. 3. Trooper armed with a helmet.

capeo [cah-pay'-o], *m.* Act of challenging a bull with a cloak.

caperuceta, illa [cah-pay-roo-thay'-tah, theel'-lyah], *f. dim.* Small hood.

Caperucita Roja [cah-pay-roo-the'-tah ro-hah], *f.* Red Ridding Hood.

caperuza [cah-pay-roo'-thah], *f.* Hood or cap ending in a point, holster-cap. **Caperuza de chimenea**, covering of the top of a chimney. **Caperuza de palo**, hood of a mast-head when the ship is unrigged.

caperuzón [cah-pay-roo-thone'], *m. aug.* Large hood.

capeta [cah-pay'-tah], *f.* A short cape not reaching below the knee, and without collar.

capialzado [cah-pe-al-thah'-do], *a.* *(Arch.)* Applied to an arch, widening outward; arched cap-piece, back arch.

capi [cah'-pe], *f.* *(And. Cono Sur)* White cornflour (harina); corn; vaina unripe pod.

capia [cah'-pe-ah], *f.* *(And. Cono Sur)* White cornflour (harina); corn.

capiango [cah-pee-ahn'-go], *m.* *(Cono Sur)* Clever thief.

capibara [cah-pe-bah'-rah], *m.* Capybara, a large South American rodent, about three and a half feet long.

capichola [cah-pe-cho'-lah], *f.* Ribbed silk stuff.

capicúa [cah-pee-coo'-ah], *m.* Reversible number, symmetrical number; palindrome.

capidengue [cah-pe-den'-gay], *m.* Small cloak worn by ladies.

capiello [cah-pe-ayl'-lyo], *m.* *(Prov.)* *V.* CAPILLO.

capigorra [cah-pe-gor'-rah], *m.* Idler.

capigorrón [cah-pe-gor-rone'], *m.* 1. *(Coll.)* Vagabond; a parasite. 2. *(Prov.)* Student who has taken the minor orders.

capil [cah-peel'], *m.* *(Prov.)* Little cap or hood.

capiláceo, cea [cah-pe-lah'-thay-o, ah], *a.* *(Bot.)* Capillaceous, hair-like.

capilar [cah-pe-lar'], *a.* Capillary; slender as hair. *-m.* A capillary blood vessel; capillaries intervene between arteries and veins.

capilaridad [cah-pe-lah-re-dahd'], *f.* Capillarity, capillary attraction.

capilla [cah-peel'-lyah], *f.* 1. Hood. 2. Cowl of a monk or friar. 3. Chapel. 4. Chapel, a small church. 5. The priests and others employed in chapel service. 6. Chapter or assembly of collegians. 7. Among printers, the proof-sheet. 8. Portable chapel for military corps. **Caja de capilla**, *(Naut.)* Chest for chapel ornaments. **Estar en capilla**, a) to prepare for death: spoken of criminals, b) *(Coll.)* to await with impatience the issue of an affair. 10. Group of supporters, following; informal club (peña).

capillada [call-peel-lyah'-dah], *f.* A hoodful of something.

capilleja, ita [cah-peel-lyay'-hah, lyee'-tah], *f. dim.* Small chapel.

capillejo [cah-peel'-lyay'-ho], *m.* 1. (*dim.*) Small hood. 2. Skein of sewing-silk.

capiller, capillero [cah-peel-lyerr', cah-peel-lyay'-ro], *m.* Clerk or sexton of a chapel; a churchwarden.

capilleta [cah-pee'-lyay'-tah], *f.* 1. (*dim. Obs.*) Small chapel. 2. Hood used by the knights of Calatrava.

capillo [cah-peel'-lyo], *m.* 1. Child's cap. 2. Hood of a hawk. 3. Bud of a rose. 4. Lining under the toepiece of a shoe. 5. Cap of distaff. *V.* ROCADERO. 9. Net for catching rabbits. 6. Colander through which wax is strained. 7. Cocoon of the silkworm. *V.* CAPULLO. 8. The covering or cloth which covered the offering of bread which used to be presented to the church. 9. The prepuce. 10. A kind of hood and cape worn by women.

capilludo, da [cah-peel-lyoo'-do, dah], *a.* Resembling the hood or cowl of a monk.

capirotada [cah-pe-ro-tah'-dah], *f.* Sort of American paste made of herbs, eggs, etc.

capirotazo [cah-pe-ro-tah'-tho], *m.* A blow on the nose with the finger; a flip.

capirote [cah-pe-ro'-tay], *m.* 1. Hood, ancient cover for the head. **Tonto de capirote**, blockhead, ignorant fool. 4. **Capirote de colmena**, cover of a bee-hive when full of honey. 5. (*Culin.*) Cloth strainer (for coffee etc.). *V.* PAPIROTE.

capirotero [cah-pe-ro-tay'-ro], *a.* Accustomed to wearing a hood: applied to a hawk.

capirucho [cah-pe-roo'-cho], *m.* (*Coll.*) *V.* CAPIROTE.

capiruchu [cah-pe-roo'-choo], *m.* (*CAm.*) Child's toy consisting of wooden cup and ball.

capisayo [cah-pe-sah'-yo], *m.* 1. Garment which serves both as a cloak and riding-coat. 2. A vesture proper to bishops.

capiscol [cah-pis-col'], *m.* The precentor: sub-chanter.

capiscolía [cah-pis-co-lee'-ah], *f.* Office and dignity of a preceptor.

capistrato, to [cah-pis-trah'-to, tah], *a.* Capistrate, epithet applied to animals whose snout appears to have a muzzle or halter.

capistrato, *m.* A squirrel of Carolina.

capistro [cah-pees'-tro], *m.* 1. Capistrum, a bandage for the head. 2. Tonic spasm of the muscles of the lower jaw. 3. (*Zool.*) Capister, the part of a bird's head about the base of the bill.

capitación [cah-pe-tah-the-on'], *f.* Poll tax, capitation.

capital [cah-pe-tahl'], *m.* 1. Sum of money put at interest. 2. Capital stock of a merchant or trading company. 3. (*Mil.*) Line drawn from the angle of a polygon to the point of the bastion and the middle of the gorge. 4. A capital letter; upper case of printers. **Capital de explotación**, working capital. **Capital físico**, (*Cono Sur*) capital assets. -*f.* Capital city (ciudad) of a country. **Capital de provincia**, provincial capital. **En Méjico capital**, in the city of Mexico.

capital [cah-pe-tahl'], *a.* 1. Capital, relating to the head. 2. Principal, leading; capital, essential. **Enemigo capital**, mortal enemy. **Error capital**, capital error. **Pecados capitales**, deadly sins. **Pena capital**, capital punishment.

capitalidad [cah-pe-tah-le-dahd'], *f.* The state of being capital, whether city or thing.

capitalino [cah-pe-tah-lee'-no], (*LAm.*) 1. *a.* Of capital. 2. *m. f.* Native of the capital; **los capitalinos**, the people of the capital. 3. City slicker.

capitalismo [cah-pe-tah-lees'-mo], *m.* Capitalism.

capitalista, [cah-pe-tah-lees'-tah], *com.* Capitalist.

capitalización [cah-pe-tah-le-thah-the-on'], *f.* Capitalization, conversion of property into money.

capitalizar [cah-pe-tah-le-thar'], *va.* To capitalize, convert into capital; to put a value on; to add overdue dividends to the capital stock, in order to obtain increased interest.

capitalmente [cah-pe-tal-men'-tay], *adv.* Capitally, mortally.

capitán [cah-pe-tahn'], *m.* 1. Captain, a military officer. 2. (*Obs.*) Commander-in-chief of an army. 3. Ringleader of a band of robbers. 4. Leader. 5. The commander of a ship of war or merchant vessel. **Capitán a guerra**, the mayor or chief magistrate of a place, invested with military power. **Capitán de fragata**, the commander of a frigate, with the rank of lieutenant-colonel. **Capitán de navío**, the commander of a man-of-war, with the rank of colonel. **Capitán general de ejército**, field-marshal. **Capitán general de provincia**, the commander-in-chief of a military district. **Capitán de puerto**, (*Naut.*) Port-captain. **Capitán del puerto**, (*Naut.*), harbor-master, water-bailiff. 6. In the wool trade, the overseer, who superintends the washing of wool.

capitana [cah-pe-tah'-nah], *f.* 1. Admiral's ship. 2. A captain's wife.

capitanear [cah-pe-tah-nay-ar'], *va.* 1. To have the command in chief of an army. 2. To head a troop of people.

capitanía [cah-pe-tah-nee'-ah], *f.* 1. Captainship, captaincy. 2. Company of officers and soldiers commanded by a captain. 3. A tax paid to the port captain by ships anchored in the harbor. 4. Military government of a province. 5. Chief authority, power, command.

capitel [cah-pe-tel'], *m.* 1. Spire over the dome of a church. 2. (*Arch.*) Capital of a column or pilaster. 3. Lid of a refining-furnance.

capitolino, na [cah-pe-to-lee'-no, nah], *a.* Belonging to the capitol.

capitolio [cah-pe-to'-le-o], *m.* 1. Capitol, a temple of Jupiter in Rome. 2. The Capitol, legislative building in Rome. 3. Any lofty or majestic public building.

capitón [cah-pe-tone'], *m.* (*Zool.*) Pollard, chub.

capitoné [cah-pe-to-nay'], *m.* 1. Removal van, furniture van. 2. (*Cono Sur*) Quilt, quilted blanket.

capitonear [cah-pe-to-nay-ar'], *va.* (*Cono Sur*) To quilt.

capitoso, sa [cah-pe-to'-so, sah], *a.* Obstinate, capricious, whimsical.

capitoste [cah-pe-tos'-tay], *m.* Chief, boss; petty tyrant.

capítula [cah-pee'-too-lah], *f.* Part of the prayers read at divine service.

capitulación [cah-pe-too-lah-the-on'], *f.* 1. Capitulation, stipulation, agreement. **Capitulación de matrimonio**, articles of marriage. 2. (*Mil.*) Capitulation, surrender of a place.

capitulante [cah-pe-too-lahn'-tay], *pa.* Capitulator.

capitular [cah-pe-too-lar'], *m.* Capitular, member of a chapter.

capitular [cah-pe-too-lar'], *a.* Capitulary, belonging to a chapter. **Sala capitular**, chapter house.

capitular [cah-pe-too-lar'], *va.* 1. To conclude an agreement, to draw up the articles of a contract; to compound. 2. (*Mil.*) To capitulate, to settle the terms of surrender. 3. (*Law.*) To impeach. -*vn.* 1. To sing prayers at divine service. 2. To come to terms, to make an agreement. 2. To capitulate, to surrender.

capitulario [cah-pe-too-lah'-re-o], *m.* Book of prayers for divine service.

capitularmente [cah-pe-too-lar-men'-tay], *adv.* Capitulary, according to the rules of a chapter.

capitulear [cah-pe-too-lay-ar'], *vn.* (*Add. Cono Sur*) To lobby.

capituleo [cah-pe-too-lay'-o], *m.* (*And. Cono Sur.*) (*Parl.*) Lobbying.

capitulero [cah-pe-too-lay'-ro], *m. & a.* Capitular.

capítulo [cah-pee'-too-lo], *m.* 1. (*Prov.*) Chapter of a cathedral. 2. A meeting of the prelates of religious orders, and the place where they meet. 3. Meeting of a secular community or corporation. **Llamar a uno a capítulo**, to take somebody to task. 4. Chapter of a book or other writing. 5. Charge preferred for neglect of duty. 6. **Capítulos matrimoniales**, articles of marriage. 7. A public reproof for some fault. (*Acad.*) **Ganar o perder capítulo**, (*Met.*) to carry or lose one's point.

capnomancia [cap-no-mahn'-the-ah], *f.* Capnomancy, divination by the flying of smoke.

capnomante [cap-no-mahn'-tay], *m.* Fortune-teller by smoke.

capo [cah'-po], *(Cono Sur)* 1. *a.* Great, fabulous. 2. *m.* Boss, bigwig (persona de influencia).

capó [cah'-po'], *m. (Aut.)* Bonnet, hood; *(Aer.)* Cowling.

capoc [cah-poc'], *m.* **capoca**, *f.* A sort of cotton so short and fine that it can not be spun; used for mattresses.

capolado [cah-po-lah'-do], *m. (Prov.)* 1. Minced meat. V. PICADILLO. 2. Act of cutting or tearing into ends and bits. **-Capolado, da**, *pp.* of CAPOLAR.

capolar [cah-po-lar'], *va. (Prov.)* 1. To mince or chop meat. 2. To behead, to decapitate.

capón [cah-pone'], *m.* 1. Eunuch. 2. Gelding. 3. Capon (pollo). 4. *(Coll.)* Rap with the knuckles on the head. 5. *(Prov.)* A bundle of brush-wood. 6. *(Naut.)* Anchor-stopper at the cat-head. 7. Sheep (carnero).

capón [cah-pone'], *a.* Castrated.

capona [cah-po'-nah], *f.* Shoulder-knot. **Capona** or **charretera capona**, an epaulet without fringe.

caponado, da [cah-po-nah'-do, dah], *a.* Tied together, as branches of vines. *-pp.* of CAPONAR.

caponar [cah-po-nar'], *va.* 1. *(Prov.)* To tie the branches of vines. 2. To cut, to curtail, to diminish.

caponera [cah-po-nay'-rah], *f.* 1. Coop, inclosure to fatten poultry. 2. *(Met. Coll.)* Place where one lives well at other people's expense. *(Met. and Coll.)* A Jail. 3. *(Mil.)* Caponier, a passage under a dry moat to the outworks. **Estar metido en caponera**, to be locked up in jail. 4. V. YEGUA CAPONERA 5. Stew-pan for oressing fowls.

capoquero [cah-po-kay'-ro], *m. (Bot.)* Capoc-tree.

caporal [cah-po-rah'], *m.* 1. Chief, ringleader. 2. *(Obs.)* Corporal 3. *(Mex.)* Keeper of horned cattle. 4. *(Cant.)* A cock.

capot [cah-pot'], *m. (Aut.)* V. CAPÓ.

capota [cah-po'-tah], *f.* 1. Car top. 2. Cape without a hood. 3. A light bonnet.

capotar [cah-po-tar'], *vn. (Aut.)* To turn over, to turn turtle; to somersault.

capote [cah-po'-tay], *m.* 1. Sort of cloak with sleeves to keep off rain. 2. A short cloak, without hood, of bright color, used by bullfighters. 3.. *(Met.)* Austere, angry look or mien. 4. *(Coll.)* Thick cloud or mist over a mountain. 5. In games at cards, capot, when one player wins all the tricks. **Dar capote**, 1. To leave a guest without dinner, for coming late. 2. To win all the tricks at cards. **A mi capote**, in my opinion. **Dije para mi capote**, I said in my sleeve. **Capote de monte**, poncho. **Car un capote a**, *(Mex.)* to give up one's job. **Decir para su capote**, to say to oneself.

capotear [cah-po-tay-ar'], *va.* 1. To trick a bull with a capote; to hold a cloak before oneself for him to spring at. 2. To wheedle, bamboozle. 3. To evade cleverly difficulties and promises.

capotera [cah-po-tay'-rah], *f.* 1. *(CAm.)* Clothes peg. 2. *(Cono Sur)* beating. 3. *(CAm.)* Tarpaulin (lona).

capotudo, da [cah-po-too'-do, dah], *a.* Frowning. V. CEÑUDO.

capra-capela [cah'-pra-cah-pay-lah], *f.* Cobra, a very venomous snake of tropical Asia.

capricho [cah-pree'-cho], *m.* 1. Caprice, whim, fancy, mood, humor, conceit. 2. *(Mus.)* Irregular but pleasing composition. 3. *(Art.)* Invention or design of a painting. **Hombre de capricho**, queer, whimsical fellow. **Capricho extravagante**, a crotchet or odd fancy, a capricious prank. **Por puro capricho**, just to please oneself. **Es un capricho nada más**, it's just a passing whim.

caprichosamente [cah-pre-cho-sah-men'-tay], *adv.* Fantastically, fancifully, humorously, moodily, whimsically.

caprichoso, sa [cah-pre-cho'-so, sah], *a.* 1. Capricious, whimsical, obstinate. 2. Fanciful.

caprichudo, da [cah-pre-choo'-do, dah], *a.* Obstinate, stubborn, capricious.

capricornio [cah-pre-cor'-ne-o], *m.* 1. Capricorn, a sign of the zodiac. 2. *(Zool.)* A Capricorn beetle, one of the longhorned cerambycids.

caprimulga [cah-pre-mool'-gah], *f.* Goat-sucker, a kind of owl.

caprino, na [cah-pree'-no, nah], *a. (Poet.)* Goatish. V. CABRUNO.

cápsula [cap'-soo-lah], *f.* 1. *(Bot.)* Capsule, a seed-vessel in plants. 2. *(Anat.)* Capsule, a sac enveloping a joint or other region of the body. 3. *(Chem.)* Capsule, a vessel for the evaporation of liquids. 4. The cap or top of a bottle. 5. *(Mil.)* Cartridge. **Cápsula de emergencia** *(Aer.),* escape capsule. **Cápsula espacial**, space capsule. **Cápsula fulminate**, detonator, percussion cap.

capsular [cap-soo-lar'], *a.* Capsular, capsulary. **En forma capsular**, in capsule form.

captador [cap-tah-dor'], *m. (Tec.)* Sensor.

captafaros [cap-tah-fah'-ros], *m.* **Placa de captafaros**, reflector.

captar [cap-tar'], *va.* 1. To captivate, to win, to capture. 2. To grasp, to get, to catch. 3. To collect; to dam, to harness (aguas). 4. To tune in to; to pick up, to receive (emisora).

captividad [ca-te-ve-dahd'], *f.* V. CAUTIVIDAD,

captura [cap-too'-rah], *f. (Law.)* Capture, seizure.

capturar [cap-too-rar'], *va.* To capture; to seize; to arrest.

capuana [cah-poo-ah'-nah], *f.* A whipping.

capucha [cah-poo-chah], *f.* 1. *(Print.)* Circumflex (^), an accent. 2. Hood of a woman's cloak. 3. Cowl or hood of a friar.

capuchina [cah-poo-chee'-nah], *f.* 1. Capuchin nun. 2. *(Bot.)* Great Indian cress. **Capuchinas**, *(Naut.)* crotches and knees. 3. A small lamp of metal with extinguisher in the form of a hood. 4. Confection of egg yolk. *(Acad.)*

capuchino [cah-poo-chee'-no], *a.* 1. Capuchin monk. 2. *(LAm.)* Capuccino (coffee).

capuchino, na [cah-poo-chee'-no, nah], *a.* Relating to Capuchin friars or nuns. **Chupa capuchina**, waistcoat.

capucho [cah-poo'-cho], *m.* Cowl or hood.

capuchón [cah-poo-chone'], *m.* 1. *aug.* of CAPUCHO. 2. A lady's cloak with hood, especially one worn at night. 3. **Capuchón de válvula** *(Aut.),* valve cap.

capujar [cah-poo-har'], *va. (Cono Sur)* To catch in the air (atrapar); to snatch (arrebatar); to say what somebody else was about to say.

capulí [cah-poo-lee'], *(Mex.)* **Capulín** [cah poo-leen'], *m. (Bot.)* An American fruit resembling a cherry.

capullada [cah-pool-lyah'-dah], *f.* Silly thing, piece of nonsense.

capullito [cah-pool-lyee'-to], *m. dim.* Small pod of a silkworm.

capullo [cah-pool-lyo], *m.* 1. Cocoon of a silkworm. 2. Flax knetted at the end; *(Com.)* a bunch of boiled flax. 3. Germ or bud of flowers. 4. Coarse stuff or spun silk. **Seda de capullos**, ferret-silk, grogram yarn. 5. Cup of an acorn. 6. Burr of a chestnut. 7. *(Anat.)* Prepuce.

capumpeba [cah-poom-pay'-bah], *f. (Bot.)* A Brazil plant.

capuz [cah-pooth'], *m.* 1. The act of ducking a person. V. CHAPUZ. 2. Old-fashioned cloak.

capuzar [cah-poo-thar'], *va.* **Capuzar un bajel**, *(Naut.)* to sink a ship by the head. V. CHAPUZAR.

caquéctico, ca [cah-kayc'-te-co, cah], *a.* Cachectical, cachectic, affected by cachexia.

caquexia [cah-kayc'-se-ah], *f. (Med.)* Cachexia, a condition of general bad health, especially from a specific morbid process, such as cancer or tuberculosis.

caqui or **kaki** [cah'-ke], *a.* Khaki. **Marcar el caqui**, to finish military service.

caqui [cah'-ke], *m. (Cono Sur)* date plum; *(fig.)* Red.

caquimia [cah-kee'-me-ah], *f.* An imperfect metallic substance.

caquino [cah-ke'-no], *m.* **Reírse a caquinos**, *(Mex.)* To laugh uproariously, cackle.

car, *f. (Naut.)* Extreme end of the mizzen-yard and mizzen.

cara [cah'-rah], *f.* 1. Face, visage, countenance. **Me recibió con buena cara**, he received me with a cheerful countenance.

Ella me mostró mala cara, I was received by her with a frown. 2. Head (de una moneda). 3. Presence of a person. 4. Face, front, surface, facing, side. 5. Boldness, nerve (valor). **Cara de acelga**, pale sallow face. **Cara de pocos amigos**, churlish look. **A cara descubierta**, openly, plainly. **Andar con la cara descubierta**, to act openly; to proceed with frankness, and without evasion or reserve. **Dar a alguno con las puertas en la cara**, to shut the door in one's face. **Jugar a cara o cruz**, to toss up a coin. **Dar en cara**, *(Met.)* to reproach, to upbraid. **Dar el sol de cara**, to have the sun in one's face. **Decírselo en su cara**, *(Met.)* to tell one to his face. **Hacer cara**, to face an enemy. **Hombre de dos caras**, double dealer, an insidious, artful fellow. **La cara se lo dice**, his face betrays him. **Lavar la cara a alguno**, *(Met.)* to flatter, to please with blandishments. **Lavar la cara a alguna cosa**, to brush up, to clean; e. g. a painting, house or coach. **No tener cara para hacer o decir alguna cosa**, not to have the face or courage to do or say a thing. **Saltar a la cara**, to answer reproof or admonition, etc., angrily. **Sacar cara por otro**, to sustain or defend another. **No volver la cara atrás**, *(Met.)* to pursue with spirit and perseverance; not to flinch. **Salir a la cara el contento, la enfermedad, la vergüenza**, satisfaction, infirmity, shame, expressed in the face. **Cara a cara**, face to face. **De cara**, opposite, over against, regarding in front. **El bien o el mal, a la cara sale**, the face is the mirror of the soul. **Cruzar la cara**, to give a blow or a cut with a whip on the face. **Echar a la cara**, to throw in one's face; to tell one his faults; also to remind of some benefit done. **Nos veremos las caras**, we will meet again (amenaza). **Cara adelante**, facing forwards. **Cara al norte**, facing north. **Cara al futuro**, with an eye to the future. **Tener cara de**, to look like. **Poner al mal tiempo buena cara**, to put a brave face on. **Cara de vinagre**, sour expression. **Tener más cara que…**, to have more nerve than…

caraba [cah-ra'-bah], *f.* **Esto es la caraba**; it's the absolute tops; it's the last straw, the limit.

carabao [cah-rah-bah'-o], *m.* Philippine buffalo.

cárabe [cah'-ra-bay], *m.* Amber.

carabela [cah-ra-bay'-lah], *f.* 1. *(Naut.)* Caravel, a threemasted vessel 2. *(Prov.)* Large basket or tray for provisions.

carabelón [cah-ra-bay-lone'], *m.* *(Naut.)* Brig or brigantine.

carabina [cah-ra-bee'-nah], *f.* 1. Rifle. 2. Carbine or carabine. **Carabina rayada**, rifle carabine. **Es lo mismo que la carabina de Ambrosio**, it is not worth a straw. 3. Chaperon. **Hacer de carabina, ir de carabina**, to go as chaperon; to play gooseberry.

carabinazo [cah-ra-be-nah'-tho], *m.* Report of a carbine, effect of a carbine-shot.

carabinero [cah-ra-be-nay'-ro], *m.* 1. Carabineer, rifleman. 2. *(Obs.)* Light horse attached to cavalry. 3. *(Zool.)* Prawn.

cárabo [cah'-ra-bo], *m.* 1. *(Zool.)* Sort of crab or cockle. 2. *(Orn.)* Large horned owl. V. AUTILLO. 3. Kind of setterdog. 4. A ground beetle: a carabid; it is insectivorous.

carabú [cah-ra-boo'], *m.* A handsome tree of India.

Caracas [cah-rah'-cahs], *n.* Caracas.

caracoa [cah-ra-co'-ah], *f.* Small row-barge used in the Philippine Islands.

caracol [cah-ra-col'], *m.* 1. Fusee of an early watch or clock. 2. Snail. **Caracol marino**, periwinkle. **Caracol comestible**, edible snail. 3. **Escalera de caracol**, winding or spiral staircase. **Subir en caracol**, to spiral up (humo). 4. Caracole, the prancing of a horse. 5. A wide though short nightdress, used by women in Mexico. 6. Cochlea, of the ear. **Hacer caracoles**, *(Met.)* To caracole. **No importa un caracol**, it does not matter, it is not worth a rush. 7. **¡Caracoles!**, good heavens! (sorpresa). 8. Curl (de pelo).

caracola [cah-ra-co'-lah], *f.* 1. *(Prov.)* A small snail with a whitish shell. 2. A conch-shell used as a horn.

caracolear [cah-ra-co-lay-ar'], *vn.* To caracole.

caracolejo [cah-ra-co-lay'-ho], *m. dim.* Small snail, snail shell.

caracoleo [cah-ra-co-lay'-o], *m.* The act of caracoling.

caracolero, ra [cah-ra-co-lay'-ro, rah], *m. & f.* One who gathers snails.

caracoles!, [cah-ra-co'-les], *int.* V. CARAMBA.

caracoli [cah-ra-co'-lee], *m.* *(Min.)* Metallic composition resembling pinchbeck.

caracolilla [cah-ra-co-leel'-lyah], *f. dim.* Small snail shell.

caracolillo [cah-ra-co-leel'-lyo], *m.* 1. *(dim.)* Small snail. 2. *(Bot.)* Snail-flowered kidney bean. 3. Purple colored thread. **Caracolillos**, shell-work wrought on the edgings of clothes, for ornament. 4. A prized variety of coffee, smaller than the ordinary sort. 5. A much veined kind of mahogany.

caracolito [cah-ra-co-lee'-to], *m. dim.* Small snail.

caracón [cah-ra-cone'], *m.* *(Obs.)* Small vessel.

carácter [cah-rahc'-ter], *m.* 1. A written sign. 2. Character, condition, mark. **De medio carácter**, of an ill-defined nature. **De carácter totalmente distinto**, of quite a different kind. 3. Character, consequence, note, adventitious quality impressed by a post of office. 4. Character, handwriting. 5. Character, type, any letter used in writing or printing. 6. Character, personal qualities, particular constitution of mind, humor, manners. **Una persona de carácter**, a person with character. **De carácter duro**, hard-natured. **No tiene carácter**, he lacks firmness. 7. Temper, nature, genius. 8. Spiritual stamp impressed upon the soul by the sacraments of baptism and confirmation. Mark put upon sheep; brand. 9. Character, loftiness of soul, firmness, energy. 10. Style of speaking or writing. 11. **Caracters de imprenta**, printing types. **Carácter elite / pica**, *(Inform.)* elite / pica-sized character.

característica [cah-rahc-tay-rees-te-cah], *f.* 1. Characteristic; trait, quality. 2. *(Theat.)* Character actress. 3. *(Inform.)* **Característica de recálculo**, recalculation feature.

característicamente [cah-rac-tay-rees'-te-cah-men-tay], *adv.* Characteristically.

característico, ca [cah-rac-tay-rees'-te-co, cah], *a.* 1. Characteristic, typical. 2. *m.* *(Theat.)* Character actor.

caracterizado, da [cah-rac-tay-re-thah'-do, dah], *a.* Characterized. **Es hombre muy caracterizado**, he is a man conspicuous either for his qualities or for the posts he fills, typical. *-pp.* of CARACTERIZAR.

caracterizar [cah-rac-tay-re-thar'], *va.* 1. To characterize, to distinguish by peculiar qualities. **Le caracterizaron de sabio**, he was classed among wise men. 2. to confer a distinguished employment, dignity, or office. 3. To mark, to point out. 4. *(Theat.)* To play with great effect. *-vr.* *(Theat.)* To make up, to dress for the part.

caracú [cah-rah-coo'], *m.* *(LAm.)* Bone marrow.

caracumbé [cah-rah-coom-bay'], *m.* Popular Afro-Latin dance.

caracha [cah-rah'-chah], *f.* or **Carache** [ca-rah'-chay], *m.* Itch, manage, scab.

carachento [cah-rah-chayn'-to], 1. *a.* **Carachoso** *a.* *(LAm.)* Mangy, scabby.

caracho [cah-rah'-cho], 1. *a.* Violet-colored. 2. *interj.* Good heavens!

caradelante [cah-ra-day-lahn'-tay], *adv.* 1. *(Obs.)* V. EN ADELANTE. 2. *(Prov.)* Forward.

carado, da [cah-rah'-do, dah], *a.* Faced. This adjective is always joined to the adverbs *bien* or *mal* -e.g. **Biencarado**, pretty-faced; **malcarado**, ill-faced.

caradura [cah-rah-doo'-rah], 1. *m. & f.* Rotter, cad, shameless person; you swine! 2. *V.* CARA.

caraguata [cah-ra-goo-ah'-tah], *f.* A kind of hemp in Paraguay from a plant of the same name.

caraja [cah-rah'-hah], *f.* A certain sail used by fishermen at Vera Cruz. **Tener la caraja**, to look absolutely knackered.

carajear [cah-rah-hay-ar'], *va.* *(Cono Sur)* to insult, to swear at.

carajiento [cah-rah-he-ayn'-to], *a.* *(And.)* Foul-mouthed.

carajillo [cah-rah-hel'-lyo], *m.* Coffee with a dash of brandy.

carajito [cah-rah-he'-to], *m.* *(LAm.)* Kid, small child.

carajo [cah-rah-ho], *m.* 1. prick. 2. **De carajo,** tremendous, awful. **Ese conductor del carajo,** that shit of a driver. **En el quinto carajo,** miles away. **No entiende un carajo,** he doesn't know a damned thing about it. **Me importa un carajo,** I don't give a damn. **Irse al carajo,** to fail, to go down the drain. **Mandar a uno al carajo,** to tell somebody to go to hell.

caramallera [cah-ra-mal-lyay'-rah], *f.* A rack, a toothed bar. *Cf.* CREMALLERA.

caramanchel [cah-ra-man-chel'], *m.* A covering like a shed over the hatchways ships, fixed or movable.

caramanchón [cah-ra-man-chone'], *m.* Garret. *V.* CAMARANCHÓN.

¡caramba! [cah-rahm'-bah], *int.* (*Coll.*) Goodness me! (asombro, sorpresa); damn it! (enfado). **¡Caramba con él!,** to hell with him!

carámbano [cah-rahm'-bah-no], *m.* Icicle, a shoot of ice.

carambillo [cah-ram-beel'-lyo], *m.* (*Bot.*) Saltwort, a source of barilla.

carambola [cah-ram-bo'-lah], *f.* 1. Cannon, the impact, in billiards, of the cue-ball against two other balls in succession. 2. Device or trick to cheat or deceive. **Lo hizo por carambola,** he accomplished it by mere chance, through luck, etc.

carambolear [cah-ram-bo-lay-ar'], *va.* To play the *carambola;* to carom.

carambolero [cah-ram-bo-lay'-ro], *m.* Player at *carambola.*

carambú [cah-ram-boo'], *m.* (*Bot.*) Willow herb, tall jussiena.

caramel [cah-ra-mel], *m.* (*Zool.*) Kind of pilchard or sardine.

caramelear [cah-rah-may-lay-ar'], *va.* (*And.*) To con, to deceive; to suck up to (engatusar).

caramelización [cah-ra-may-le-thah-the-one'], *f.* The reduction of sugar to candy by heat.

caramelo [cah-ra-may'-lo], *m.* Lozenge made of sugar and other ingredients; sugar-candy.

caramente [cah-ra-men'-tay], *adv.* 1. Dearly. 2. Exceedingly, highly. 3. (*Law.*) Rigorously.

caramillar [cah-ra-meel'-lyar'], *vn.* (*Obs.*) To play on the flageolet, a small flute.

caramilleras [cah-ra-meel-lyay'-ras], *f. pl.* (*Prov.*) Pot-hooks.

caramillo [cah-ra-meel'-lyo], *m.* 1. Flageolet, a small flute. 2. (*Bot.*) *V.* BARRILLA. 3. Confused heap of things. 4. Deceit, fraudulent trick. 5. A piece of gossip. **Armar un caramillo,** to cause disturbances. 6. (*Bot.*) A wild shrub of the rose kind.

caramilloso [cah-rah-mel-lyo'-so], *a.* Fussy.

cáramo [cah'-ra-mo], *m.* Wine.

caramuyo [cah-ra-moo'-yo], *m.* Kind of sea-snail.

caramuzal [cah-ra-moo-thahl'], *m.* Transport vessel used by the Moors.

caranchear [cah-rahn-chay-ar'], *va.* (*Cono Sur*) To irritate, to annoy.

carancho [cah-rahn'-cho], *m.* (*And.*) Owl; (*Cono Sur*) vulture (buitre).

caranga [cah-rahn'-gah], *f.* (*And. CAm.*), **Carango** *m.* (*LAm.*) Louse.

carángano [cah-rahn'-gah-no], *m.* 1. (*Sp. Amer.*) Louse. 2. (*Col.*) Native musical instrument.

carangue [cah-rahn'-gay], *m.* **Caranga** [cah-rahn'-gah], *f.* (*Amer.*) Kind of flat-fish in the West Indies.

carantamaula [cah-ran-ta-mah'-oo-lah], *f.* (*Coll.*) 1. Hideous mask or visor. 2. (*Met.*) Ugly, hard-featured person.

carantoña [cah-ran-to'-nyah], *f.* 1. Hideous mask or visor. 2. Old coarse woman, who paints and dresses in style. 3. Ugly mug. *-pl.* Caresses, soft words and acts of endearment to wheedle or coax a person. **Hacer carantoñas a uno,** to make faces at somebody (muecas).

carantoñera [cah-ran-to-nyay'-rah], *f.* Coquette.

carantoñero [cah-ran-to-nyay'-ro], *m.* Flatterer, wheedler, cajoler.

caraña [cab-rah'-nyah], *f.* Kind of resinous American gum.

caraos [cah-rah'-os], *m.* (*Obs.*) Act of drinking a full bumper to one's health.

carapa [cah-rah'-pah], *f.* Oil of an American nut, which is said to cure the gout.

carapacho [cah-ra-pah'-cho], *m.* Carapace, shell (tortugas, crustáceos). **Meterse en un carapacho,** to go into one's shell.

caraqueño, ña [cah-ra-kay'-nyo, nyah], *a.* Of or relating to Caracas.

caráspita [cah-rahs'-pe-tah], *Excl.* (*Cono Sur*) damn!

carátula [cah-rah'-too-lah], *f.* 1. Mask of pasteboard. 2. A wire cover for the face to defend it from bees, mosquitoes, etc. 3. The title-page of a book. 4. (*Met.*) The stage, the theater. 5. (*CAm. Mex.*) Face, dial (de reloj). 6. Sleeve (de disco).

caratulero [cah-ra-too-lay'-ro], *m.* One who makes or sells masks.

cárava [cah'-ra-vah], *f.* (*Obs.*) Meeting of country people on festive occasions. **Quien no va a Cárava no sabe nada,** he who would know what is going on must mix in the world.

caravana [cah-ra-vah'-nah], *f.* 1. (*Naut.*) Sea-campaign performed by the Knights of Malta. 2. Caravan, a company of traders, pilgrims, and the like; a camel-train in the desert. **Hacer** or **correr caravanas,** (*Met.*) To take a variety of steps for obtaining some end. **Caravana de automóviles,** autocade, motorcade. (*Pers. caruán.*) 3. Group, band; crowd of trippers (excursionistas). 4. (*Aut.*) Stream of cars; jam, tailback. 5. (*Carib.*) Bird tramp (trampa). 6. (*LAm.*) Long earrings.

caravanera [cah-ra-vah-nay'-rah], *f.* Caravansary.

caravanero [cah-ra-vah-nay'-ro], *m.* 1. Leader of a caravan. 2. (*Prov.*) A wild fellow.

caray [cah-rah'-e], *m.* 1. Tortoise-shell. *V.* CAREY. 2. (*Amer.*) *int.* An exclamation denoting surprise or impatience, equivalent to *caramba;* good heavens!; well I am blowed!

caraza [cah-rah'-thah], *f. aug.* Broad large face.

carbohidrato [cah-bo-e-drah'-to], *m.* Carbohydrate.

carbol [car-bole'], *m.* A certain Turkish vessel.

carbólico [car-bo'-le-co], *a.* Carbolic.

carbón [car-bone'], *m.* 1. Coal. 2. Charcoal. 3. Black pencil. **Carbón animal,** animal charcoal. **Carbón de leña** or **carbón vegetal,** charcoal. **Papel carbón,** carbon paper. **Al carbón,** charcoal grilled. 4. (*Elec.*) Carbon. 5. (*Agri.*) Smut.

carbonada [car-bo-nah'-dah], *f.* 1. Load of coal (para horno). 2. A native meat stew. 3. Kind of pancake. 4. Grilled meat ball.

carbonadilla [car-bo-nah-deel'-lyah], *f. dim.* Small *carbonada.*

carbonario [car-bo-nah'-re-o], *m.* An individual of a secret society formed to destroy absolutism. (*Acad.*)

carbonatado, da [car-bo-nah-tah'-do, dah], *a.* Carbonated.

carbonato [car-bo-nah'-to], *m.* (*Chem.*) Carbonate. **Carbonato de calcio,** calcium carbonate. **Carbonato sódico,** sodium carbonate.

carboncillo [car-bon-theel'-lyo], *m.* 1. (*dim.*) Small coal. 2. Black crayon. 3. (*Aut.*) Carbon deposit.

carbonear [car-bo-nay-ar'], *va.* 1. To reduce to charcoal by the action of fire. 2. (*Cono Sur*) to push, to egg on.

carbonera [car-bo-nay'-rah], *f.* 1. Place where charcoal is made 2. Coalhouse, coalhole, or coal-cellar. 3. Coal-pit, colliery, coal-mine.

carbonería [car-bo-nay-ree'-ah], *f.* Coal-yard; coal-shed; coal-mine.

carbonero [car-bo-nay'-ro], *m.* 1. Charcoal-maker. 2. Collier, coal-man, coal-miner. 3. Coal-merchant, collier. 4. (*Naut.*) Coal-ship, collier. **Barco carbonero,** collier. **Estación carbonera,** coaling station.

carbónico, ca [car-bo'-ne-co, cah], *a.* 1. (*Chem.*) Carbonic. 2. *m.* (*Cono Sur*) **Papel carbónico,** carbon paper.

carbonífero [car-bo-nee'-fay-ro], *a.* Carboniferous. **Industria carbonífera,** coal industry.

carbonilla [car-bo-neel'-lyah], *f.* 1. (*Min.*) Small coat, coaldust; cinder. 2. (*Aut.*) Carbon, carbon deposit. 3. (*LAm.*) Charcoal.

carbonización [car-bo-ne-thah-the-on'], *f.* Carbonization.

carbonizado, da [car-bo-ne-thah'-do, dah], *a.* Carbonated. -*pp.* of CARBONIZAR.

carbonizar [car-bo-ne-thar'], *va.* 1. To combine carbon with another body. 2. To char. **Quedar cabornizado,** to be charred; (*Elec.*) To be electrocuted; to be burnt down (edificio). -*vr.* (*Quim.*) To carbonize.

carbono [car-bo'-no], *m.* (*Chem.*) Carbon.

carbonoso [car-bo-no'-so], *a.* Carbonaceous.

carborundo [car-bo-roon'-do], *m.* Carborundum.

carbuncal [car-boon-cahl'], *a.* Resembling a carbuncle.

carbunclo, carbunco [car-boon'-clo], *m.* 1. Carbuncle, a precious stone, 2. Red pustule or pimple. V. CARBÚNCULO.

carbuncoso, sa [car-boon-co'-so, sah], *a.* Of the nature of a carbuncle.

carbúnculo [car-boon'-coo-lo], *m.* V. RUBÍ.

carburador [car-boo-rah-dor'], *m.* Carburettor.

carburante [car-boo-rahn'-tay], *m.* Fuel.

carburar [car-boo-rahr'], *vn.* 1. To go, to work (funcionar). 2. To think over (pensar).

carbureto [car-boo-ray'-to], or **carburo** [car-boo'-ro], *m.* (*Chem.*) Carburet, or carbide.

carca [car'-cah], *a.* Square; narrow-minded, having a closed mind; ancient; dead-beat. -*m. & f.* 1. Square; narrow-minded person; old fogey; reactionary; (*And.*) Muck, filth.

carcacha [car-cah'-chah], *f.* (*Mex.*) (*Aut.*) Old crock, old banger.

carcaj [car-cah'], *m.* Quiver (para flechas); (*LAm.*) Rifle case, pistol holster. V. CARCAX.

carcajada [car-ca-hah-dah], *f.* Loud laughter, hearty laughter, cachinnation. **Hubo carcajadas,** there was loud laughter. **Reírse a carcajadas,** to laugh heartily.

carcajear [car-cah-hay-ar'], *vn.* **carcajearse** *vr.* To roar with laughter, to have a good laugh.

carcajú [car-ca-hoo'], *m.* The glutton, wolverine, a ravenous carnivorous animal.

carcamal [car-ca-mahl'], *m.* 1. Nickname of old people, especially of old women. 2. Old crock (vejestorio). **Es un carcamal;** he's a wreck.

carcamán [car-ca-mahn'], *m.* 1. Tub, a heavy, big, unseaworthy vessel; (*And. Carib.*) Old crock, wreck. 2. Carcamana *f.* 3. (*Carib.*) Low-class person; (*And. Carib.*) Poor immigrant. 4. (*Cono Sur*) reactionary.

cárcamo [car'-ca-mo], *m.* (*Amer.*) Riffle, a cleated trough.

carcancha [car-chahn'-chah], *f.* (*Mex.*) Bus.

carcañal, carcañar [car-ca-nyal', car-ca nyar'], *m.* Heel-bone, calcaneum. V. CALCAÑAR.

carcaño [car-cah'-nyo], *m.* Heel of the foot.

carcápuli [car-cah'-poo-le], *m.* 1. (*Bot.*) Indian yellow orange of Java and Malabar. 2. (*Bot.*) The large carcapulla-tree in America, which produces a fruit resembling a cherry.

carcasa [car-cah'-sah], *f.* (*Aut.*) Chassis, grid; carcass (deneumático); (*Tec.*) Casing.

cárcava [car'-ca-vah], *f.* (*Obs.*) 1. Inclosure, mound, hedge, ditch. 2 Pit or grave for the dead. 3. Gully made by torrents of water.

carcavera [car-ca-vay'-rah], *f.* A bad woman; a witch.

cárcavo [car'-ca-vo], *m.* 1. The cavity of the abdomen 2. The hollow in which a water-wheel turns. 3. The footprint of an animal

carcavón [car-ca-vone'], *m.* Large and deep ditch.

carcavuezo [car-cah-voo-ay'-tho], *m.* A deep pit.

carcax [car-cahx'], *m.* 1. Quiver. 2. Ribbon with a case at the end, in which the cross is borne in a procession. 3. (*Amer.*) A leather case in which a rifle is carried at the saddle-bow. 4. Ornament of the ankle worn by the Moors. V. AJORCA.

carcayú [car-cah-yoo'], *m.* Wolverine.

cárcel [car-thel], *f.* 1. Prison, goal, jail. **Salir de la cárcel,** to come out of prison. 2. Among carpenters, a wooden clamp

to keep glued. 4. Cheek of a printing-press. **Cárceles,** among weavers, cog-reeds of a loom.

carcelaje, carcerje [car-thay-lah-hay, car-thay-rah'-hay], *m.* Prison-fees, jailer's fees, paid on leaving.

carcelario [car-thay-lah'-re-o], *a.* Prison.

carcelería [car-they-lay-ree'-ah], *f.* 1. Imprisonment. 2. Bail given for the appearance of a prisoner.

carcelero [car-thay-lay'-ro], *m.* Jailkeeper, jailer. **Fiador carcelero,** one who is bail, or surety for a prisoner.

carcinogénico [car-the-no-hay'-ne-co], *a.* Carcinogenic.

carcinógeno [car-the-no'-hay-no], *m.* (*Med.*) Carcinogen.

carcinoma [car-the-no'-mah], *f.* Carcinoma, cancer.

carcinomatoso [car-the-no-mah-to'-so], *a.* Carcinomatous, cancerous.

carcoa [car-co'-ah], *f.* Row-barge used in India.

cárcola [car'-co-lah], *f.* Treadle of a loom.

carcoma [car-co'-mah], *f.* 1. Woodborer, the larva of various beetles which burrow in wood. 2. Dust made by the wood-borer. 3. (*Met.*) Grief, anxious concern. 4. (*Met.*) One who runs by degrees through his whole fortune.

carcomer [car-co-merr'], *va.* 1. To gnaw, to corrode (carcoma). 2. To consume a thing by degrees. 3. (*Met.*) To gradually impair health, virtue, etc. -*vr.* 1. To decay, to decline in health, virtue, etc. 2. To get worm-eaten.

carcomido, da [car-co-mee'-do, dah], *a.* 1. Worm-eaten, consumed. 2. (*Met.*) Decayed, declined, impaired. -*pp.* of CARCOMER.

carcoso [car-co'-so], *a.* (*And.*) Dirty, mucky.

carda [car'-dah], *f.* 1. Teasel, for raising the nap on cloth. 2. Card, with which wool is combed. 3. Hatter's jack. 4. (*Met.*) Severe reprimand or censure. **Dar una carda a uno,** to rap somebody over the knuckles. 5. (*Naut.*) Small vessel built like a galley.

cardador [car-dah-dor'], *m.* Carder, comber.

cardadura [car-dah-doo'-rah], *f.* Carding, combing wool.

cardamomo [car-dah-mo'-mo], *m.* (*Bot.*) Cardamom, a medicinal seed.

cardán [car-dahn'], *m.* 1. (*Mech.*) Universal joint. 2. (*Cono Sur*) (*Aut.*) Propellor shaft; (*LAm.*) (*Aut.*) Axle.

cardar [car-dar'], *va.* 1. To card or comb wool. 2. To raise the nap on cloth with a teasel. **Cardarle a uno la lana,** (*Met.*) To win a large sum at play. **Cardarle a alguno la lana,** (*Met.*) To reprimand severely.

cardelina [car-day-lee'-nah], *f.* (*Orn.*) Goldfinch, thistlefinch. V. JILGUERO.

cardenal [car-day-nahl'], *m.* 1. Cardinal. 2. (*Orn.*) Virginian nightingale, cardinal grosbeak. 3. Discoloration from a lash or blow; lividity, burise, mark. V. EQUIMOSIS.

cardenalato [car-day-na-lah'-to], *m.* Cardinalate, cardinalship.

cardenalicio, cia [car-day-na-lee'-the-o, ah] *a.* Belonging to a cardinal.

cardencha [car-den'-chah], *f.* 1. (*Bot.*) Teasel, a genus of plants. **Cardencha cardadora,** manured or fuller's teasel. **Cardencha silvestre,** wild teasel. **Cardencha laciniada,** laciniated teasel. **Cardencha pelosa,** small teasel, shepherd's staff. 2. Card or comb, for carding or combing of wool.

cardenchal [car-den-chahl'], *m.* Place where teasels grow.

cardenillo [car-day-neel'-lyo], *m.* 1. Verdigris. 2. (*Painting*) Verditer, a green paint made of verdigris; Paris green.

cárdeno, na [car'-day-no, nah], *a.* Livid, of a dark purple color.

cardería [car-day-ree'-ah], *f.* Cardery, the workshop where combs or cards are made.

cardero [car-day'-ro], *m.* Card-maker.

cardíaca [car-dee'-ah-cah], *f.* (*Bot.*) Common motherwort.

cardíaco, ca [car-dee'-ah-co, cah], *a.* (*Med.*) 1. Cardiac (enfermedades del corazón). 2. Cardiac, cardiacal, cordial, having the quality of invigorating (medicinas).

cardial [car-de-ahl'], *a.* Cardiacal, cardiac.

cardialgía [car-de-al-hee'-ah], *f.* (*Med.*) Cardialgia, heartburn.

cardias [car'-de-as], *m.* The upper or cardiac orifice of the stomach.

cardillo [car-deel'-lyo], *m.* 1. *(Bot.)* Golden thistle. **Cardillo español,** *(Bot.)* perennial golden thistle or star-thistle. **Cardillo manchado,** annual golden thistle. 2. *(Mex.)* V. VISO. 3. Thistle-down.

cardinal [car-de-nahl'], *a.* Cardinal, principal, fundamental. **Vientos cardinales,** winds from the four cardinal points. **Virtudes cardinales,** cardinal virtues. **Números cardinales,** cardinal numbers.

cardiógrafo [car-de-o'-grah-fo], *m.* Cardiograph.

cardiograma [car-de-o-grah'-mah], *m.* Cardiogram.

cardiología [car-de-o-lo-hee'-ah], *f* Cardiology.

cardiológico [car-de-o-lo'-he-co], *a.* Cardiological.

cardiólogo, ga [car-de-o'-lo-go], *m. & f.* Cardiologist, heart specialist.

cardiovascular [car-de-o-vas-coo-lar'], *a.* Cardiovascular.

carditis [car-dee'-tis], *f.* Inflammation of the muscular tissue of the heart.

cardizal [car-de-thahl'], *m.* Land covered with thistles.

cardo [car'-do], *m. (Bot.)* Thistle, a genus of plants. **Cardo silvestre** or **borriqueño;** *(Bot.)* Spear-plume thistle. **Cardo de comer,** cardon artichoke. **Cardo alcachofero,** garden artichoke. **Cardo santo,** blessed thistle, centaury, holy thistle, carduus benedictus. **Cardo de burro** or **crespo,** curled thistle. **Cardo lechero** or **cardo mariano,** milk thistle. **Más áspero que un cardo,** rougher than a thistle (personas).

cardón [car-done'], *m.* 1. *(Bot.)* V. CARDENCHA. **Cardón de cochinilla,** cochineal, fig cactus. **Cardón lechal** or **lechar,** V. CARDILLO DE COMER. **Cardón cabezudo,** turk's-cap cactus. 2. The act and effect of carding.

cardoncillo [car-don-theel'-lyo], *m. (Bot.)* Mountain carthamus.

carducha [car-doo'-chah], *f.* Large comb for wool.

cardume, cardumen [car-doo'-may, car-doo'-men], *m.* 1. Shoal of fishes. 2. *(And. Cono Sur)* great number, mass. **Un cardumen de gente,** a lot of people.

carduza [car-doo'-thah], *f. (Obs.)* V. CARDA.

carduzador [car-doo-thah-dor'], *m.* Carder. V. CARDADOR.

carduzal [car-doo-thahl'], *m.* V. CARDIZAL.

carduzar [car-doo-thar'], *va.* 1. To card or comb wool. 2. To shear cloth.

careador [cah-ray-ah-dor'], *a.* **Perro careador,** a shepherd-dog, watchdog. V. CAREAR.

carear [cah-ray-ar'], *va.* 1. *(Law.)* To confront criminals. 2. To compare. 3. To tend a drove of cattle or flock of sheep. *-vn.* To come face to face. *-vr.* To assemble or meet for business, to come face to face.

carecer [car-ray-therr'], *vn.* 1. To want, to be in need, to lack. **Carece de talento,** he lacks talent. **No carecemos de dinero,** we don't lack money. **Eso carece de sentido,** that doesn't make sense. 2. *(Cono Sur)* **Carece hacerlo,** it is necessary to do it.

carel [car-rayl'], *m.* Side, edge.

carena [cah-ray'-nah], *f. (Naut.)* 1. Careening or repairing of a ship. **Carena mayor,** thorough repair. 2. *(Poet.)* Ship. 3. *(Obs.)* Forty days' penance on bread and water. **Dar carena,** *(Met.)* to blame, to find fault with, to reprimand; to bunter, to joke.

carenaje [cah-ray-nah'-hay], *m.* V. CARENERO.

carenar [cah-ray-nar'], *va.* To careen a ship, to pay a ship's bottom. **Aparejo de carenar,** careening gear.

carencia [cah-ren'-the-ah], *f.* Want, need, lack.

carencial [cah-rayn-the-al'], *a.* **Estado carencial,** state of want. **Mal carencial,** deficiency disease.

carenero [cah-ray-nay'-ro], *m.* Careening-place.

carente [cah-rayn-tay], *a.* **Carente de,** lacking, devoid of.

carentón [cah-rayn-tone'], *a. (Cono Sur)* large-faced.

careo [cah-ray'-o], *m.* 1. *(Law.)* confrontation, the act of bringing criminals or witnesses face to face. 2. Comparison. 3. *(Fort.)* Front of a bastion or fortress.

carero, ra [cah-ray'-ro, rah], *a. (Coll.)* Selling things dear.

carestía [cah-res-tee'-ah], *f.* 1. Scarcity, want. 2. Famine, famishment; jejuneness. 3. Dearness, or high price originating from scarcity. **Carestía de la vida,** period of shortage.

careta [cah-ray'-tah], *f.* 1. Mask made of pasteboard. 2. Wire cover of the face worn by bee-keepers. 3. V. JUDÍA. 4. *(Med.)* Breathing apparatus, respirator. **Careta antigás,** gasmask. **Careta de esgrima,** fencing mask.

careto, ta [cah-ray'-to, tah], *a.* 1. Having the forehead marked with a white spot or stripe (caballos). 2. Ugly.

carey [cah-ray'-e], *m.* Tortoise-shell. *(Malay, carah.).*

careza [cah-ray'-thah], *f.* V. CARESTÍA. *(Yo carezco, yo carezca,* from *Carecer.* V. CONOCER.)

carga [car'-gah], *f.* 1. Load, burden, freight, lading. 2. Cargo, the lading of a ship. 3. Charge of a cannon or other firearm, and the nozzle of the flask which measures the powder of such charge. **Carga muerta,** over-loading, dead load. 4. Old corn measure, containing four *fanegas* or bushels. 5. Medical preparation for curing sprains and inflammation in horses and mules, composed of flour, whites of eggs, ashes, and Armenian bole, all beaten up with the blood of the sane animal. 6. Impost, duty toll, tax. **Carga fiscal,** tax burden. **Carga de pago,** payload 7. *(Met.)* Burden of the mind, heaviness. 8. Load, weight, hindrance, pressure, cumbrance, or encumbrance. **Bestia de carga,** a beast of burden; a mule or sumpter-horse. 9. *(Obs.)* Discharge of firearms. 10. Charge, an attack upon the enemy, responsibility. **Echar la carga a otro,** *(Met.)* to throw the blame upon another. **Llevar la carga,** to be the one responsible. **Carga de familia,** dependent relative. **Carga personal,** personal commitments. **Llevar los soldados a la carga,** *(Mil.)* to lead soldiers to the charge. **Volver a la carga sobre el enemigo,** to return to the charge; **navío de carga,** *(Naut.)* Ship of burden, a merchant ship. **Andén de carga,** loading platform. **Permitido carga y descarga,** loading and unloading. **A cargas,** abundantly, in great plenty. **A cargas le vienen los regalos,** he receives loads of presents. **Carga útil,** *(Aer.)* Payload.

cargada [car-gah'-dah], *f.* 1. *(Cono Sur)* unpleasant practical joke. 2. *(Mex.)* V. CARGA. 3. **Ir a la cargada,** *(Mex.)* To jump on the bandwagon.

cargadera [car-gah-day'-rah], *f. (Naut.)*, Down-hauls, brails. **Cargaderas de las gavias,** topsail brails. **Aparejo de cargadera de recamento,** down-haul tackle.

cargadero [car-gah-day'-ro], *m.* 1. Place where goods are loaded or unloaded. 2. *(Arquit.)* Lintel.

cargadilla [car-gah-deel'-lyah], *f. (Coll.)* Increase of a debt newly contracted.

cargado, da [car-gah'-do, dah], *a.* 1. Loaded, full, fraught. **Cargado de espaldas,** round-shouldered, stooping. **Estar cargado de vino,** to be top-heavy, or half-seas over. **Un árbol cargado de fruto,** a tree laden with fruit. **Tener los ojos cargados de sueño,** to have eyes heavy with sleep. 2. *(Elec.)* Live; charged. 3. Strong (café). 4. Overcast (cielo). *-pp.* of CARGAR.

cargador [cah-gar-tor'], *m.* 1. Loader, he who loads; porter. 2. Rammer, ramrod. **Cargador de acumuladores, cargador de baterías,** battery charger. 3. He that loads great guns. 4. A large pitchfork for straw. 5. *(Arch.)* A post put in a doorway or window. 6. Magazine (recámara). *-pl.* 1. *(Naut.)* Tackles. V. PALANQUINES. 2. Plates of copper or pallets used in gilding.

cargadora [car-gah-do'-rah], *f. (And. Carib.)* Nursemaid.

cargamento [car-gah-men'-to], *m.* 1. *(Naut.)* Cargo. **Cargamento de retorno,** return cargo. 2. Loading.

cargante [car-gahn'-tay], *a.* Demanding (persona), fussy; annoying, troublesome; tiring (niño); irksome (tarea).

cargar [car-gar'], *va. &* vn. 1. To load, to burden, to freight; to carry a load (hombres, animales). 2. To charge, to attack the enemy. 3. To ship goods for foreign markets. 4. To load or charge a gun. 5. To overload or overburden, to clog; to lay in an abundant stock. 6. To charge in account, to book. 7. To impose or lay taxes. 8. To impute, to impeach. 9. To incline with the whole body towards a point or place. 10. To rest, to recline for support. 11. To take a charge, a duty, or any trust. 12. To crowd. 13. In cards, in some games, to take a card by playing one higher. **Cargar con,** to carry, take. **Cargar sobre,** to be responsible for another's deficiencies. *(Gram.)* For one letter or syllable to have more value in prosody than another. **Cargar arriba una vela,** *(Naut.)* to clew up a sail. **Cargar sobre uno,** to importune, tease, or molest. **Cargar a uno de deudas,** to encumber somebody with debts. 14. *(LAm.)* To carry, to have use; to wear. **Cargar anteojos,** to wear glasses. **¿Cargas dinero?,** have you got any money on? 15. To bore, to annoy. **Esto me carga,** this annoys me. 16. To fall (acento). 17. **Cargar en,** to lean on. *-vr.* 1. To recline, to rest, or to lean against anything. **El viento se ha cargado al norte,** the wind has veered to the north. 2. To charge one's own account with the sums received. 3. To maintain, to support, or take a new duty upon oneself. **Cargarse de algo,** to be full of something. **Cargarse de hijos,** to overburden oneself with children. **El árbol se carga de manzanas,** the tree produces apples in abundance. 4. **¡Algún día me lo cargaré!,** I'll get him one day. 5. **Cargarse algo,** to break something. **Cargar energía,** *(Inform.)* to eat an energizer.

cargareme [car-ga-ray-may], *m.* Receipt, voucher. *(Cargaré,* future, and *me,* pronoun.)

cargazón [car-ga-thone'], *f.* 1. Cargo of a ship. 2. **Cargazón de cabeza,** heaviness of the head. 3. **Cargazón de tiempo,** cloudy, thick weather. 3. *(Med.)* Heaviness (estómago). 4. Abundance.

cargo [car'-go], *m.* 1. Burden, loading. 2. *(Prov.)* Load of stones which weighs forty *arrobas.* 3. A number of baskets piled one on the other and put in the oil-press. 4. A load of pressed grapes. 5. Wood measure, about a cubic yard. 6. Total amount of what has been received, in a general account. 7. *(Met.)* Employment, dignity, office, honor, ministry. **Desempeñar un cargo,** to fill an office. **Jurar el cargo,** to take the oath of office. 8. Charge, keeping, care. 9. *(Met.)* Obligation to perform something. 10. *(Met.)* Command or direction of a thing 11. Fault or deficiency in the performance of one's duty. 12. Charge, accusation. *(Law.)* Count. **Cargo de conciencia,** remorse, sense of guilt. **Hacer cargo a alguno de una cosa,** to charge one with a fault, to hold him responsible; to accuse, to impeach. **Apenas si pude hacerme cargo de ello,** I could scarcely grasp what was going on. 13. A merchant ship that carries goods from one port to another. 1. To take into consideration; to reflect. 2. To make oneself acquainted with a thing. **Hacerse uno cargo de algo,** to take upon oneself. **Ser en cargo,** to be debtor.

cargosear [car-go-say-ar'], *va. (And. Cono Sur)* To pester, to keep on at.

cargoso, sa [car-go'-so, sah], *a.* 1. Heavy. 2. Bothersome, annoying.

cargue [car'-gay], *m.* 1. Loading a vessel 2. License to load.

carguero, ra [car-gay'-ro, ra], *a.* 1. He who bears a burden, cargo boat, transport plane. **Carguero militar,** air-force transport. 2. *f. (And. Carib.)* Nursemaid.

carguica, illa, ita [car-gee'-cah, eel'-lyah, ee-tah], *f. dim.* Small, or light load.

carguío [car-gee-o], *m.* 1. Cargo of merchandise. 2. A load.

cari [cah'-re], *m.* Caraway-seed.

carí [cah-ree'], *m. (Amer. Bot.)* Black berry-bush.

cari [cah-re']*a. (Cono Sur)* Gray.

caria [cah'-re-ah], *f. (Arch.)* 1. The shaft (or fust) of a column. 2. V. CARIES.

cariacedo, da [cah-re-ah-thay'-do, dah], *a.* Having a sour-looking countenance.

cariacontecido, da [cah-re-ah-con-tay-thee'-do, dah], *a.* Sad, mournful; expressive of grief.

cariacuchillado, da [cah-re-ah-coo-cheel-lyah'-do, dah], *a.* Having the face marked with cuts or gashes.

cariado, da. [cah-re-ah'-do, dah], *a.* Carious, rotten. *-pp.* of CARIARSE.

cariadura [cah-re-ah-doo-rah], *f. (Med.)* Caries, decay.

cariaguileño, ña [cah-re-ah-gee-lay'-nyo, nyah], *a. (Coll.)* Long-faced, with an aquiline or hooked nose.

carialegre [cah-re-ah-lay'-gray], *a.* Smiling, cheerful.

cariampollado, da [cah-re-am-pol-lyah'-do, dah], *a.* Round-faced, plump cheeked.

cariancho, cha [cah-re-ahn'-cho, chah], *a.* Broad-faced, chubby, chub-faced, bull-faced.

cariar [cah-re-ar'], *va.* To cause to decay.

cariarse [cah-re-ar'-sayh], *vr. (Med.)* To grow carious (huesos).

cariarú [cah-re-ah-roo'], *m.* A liana of the Antilles yielding a crimson dye.

cariátide [cah-re-ah'-te-day], *f. (Arch.)* Caryatides, columns or pilasters under the figure of women.

Caribe [cah-ree'-bay], *m.* Carib. *-pl.* Caribs, Indians of the Antilles. *a.* Caribbean. **Mar Caribe,** Caribbean Sea.

caribeño [cah-re-bay'-nyo], *V.* CARIBE.

caribito [cah-re-bee'-to], *m.* A river fish of the bream species.

caribobo, ba [cah-re-bo'-bo, bah], Having a stupid look.

caribú [cah-re-boo'], *m.* Caribou.

carica [cah-ree'-cah], *f. (Prov.)* Sort of kidney beans.

caricato [cah-re-cah'-to], *m. (Cono Sur. Mex.) V.* CARICATURA.

caricatura [cah-re-cah-too'-rah], *f.* 1. Caricature. 2. Cartoon. **Caricatura animada,** animated cartoon film.

caricaturar [cah-re-cah-too-rar'], *va.* To caricature.

caricaturesco, ca [cah-re-cah-too-res'-co, cah], *a.* Caricaturist, caricatural; belonging to caricature.

caricaturista [cah-re-cah-too-rees'-tah], *m.* Caricaturist.

caricaturizar [cah-re-cah-too-ree'-sahr], *va.* To caricature.

caricia [cah-ree'-the-ah], *f.* Caress, act of endearment, endearing expression.

cariciosamente [cah-re-the-o-sah-men'-tay], *adv.* In a fondling or endearing manner.

caricioso, sa [cah-re-the-o'-so, sah], *a.* Fondling, endearing, caressing.

caricuerdo, da [cah-re-coo-err'-do, dah], *a.* Having a serene or composed mien.

caridad [cah-re-dahd'], *f.* 1. Charity, charitableness, kindness, good-will, benevolence. 2. Alms. **La caridad empieza por nosotros mismos,** charity begins at home. **Hacer caridad a uno,** to give alms to somebody.

caridoliente [cah-re-do-le-en'-tay], *a.* Having a mournful countenance.

caries [cah'-re-es], *f.* Caries or cariosity, ulceration of bone.

cariescrito [cah-re-es-cree'-to], *a.* Corrugated, shrivelled.

carifruncido, da [cah-re-froon-thee'-do, dah], *a.* Having a face contracted into wrinkles.

carigordo, da [cah-re-gor'-do, dah], *a.* Full-faced.

carijusto, ta [cah-re-hoos'-to, tah], *a.* Dissembling; hypocritical.

carilampiño [cah-re-lam-pe'-nyo], *a.* Clean-shaven; smooth-faced beardless.

carilargo, ga [cah-re-lar'-go, gah], *a.* Long-faced.

carilla, [cah-reel'-lyah], *f.* 1. *(dim.)* Little or small face. 2. Mask used by bee-keepers. V. CARETA.

carilleno, na [cah-reel-lyay'-no, nah], *a. (Coll.)* Plump-faced.

carillero, ra [cah-rel-lyay'-ro], *a.* Round-faced.

carillo, lla [cah-reel'-lyo, lyah], *a. dim.* Dear, high-priced.

carillón [cah-rel-lyone'], *m.* Carillon.

carilucio, cia [cah-re-loo'-the-o, ah], *a.* Having a shining or glossy face.

carimbo [cah-reem'-bo], *m. (LAm.)* Branding iron.

carina [cah-ree'-nah], *f.* 1. *(Arch.)* Building raised by the Romans in form of a ship. 2. *(Bot.)* The two power petals of papilionaceous flowers; the keel, carina.

carinegro, gra [cah-re-nay'-gro, grah], *a.* Of a swarthy complexion.

carininfo [cah-re-neen'-fo], *a.* Having a womanish face (hombres).

cariño [cah-ree'-nyo], *m.* 1. Love, fondness, tenderness, affection, kindness; concern. **Por el cariño que le tengo,**

because I am fond of him. **Tomar cariño a,** to take a liking to. 2. Soft or endearing expression. 3. *(Obs.)* Anxious desire of a thing. 4. *(LAm.)* Caress, stroke; gift (regalo). **Hacerle cariños a uno,** to caress somebody.

cariñosamente [cah-re-nyo-sah-men'-tay], *adv.* Fondly, affectionately; kindly; good-naturedly.

cariñoso, sa [cah-re-nyo'-so, sah], *a.* 1. Affectionate, endearing, lovely, benevolent, kind, good, good-natured, natural. 2. Anxious, desirous, longing.

carioca [cah-re-o'-cah], *a.* Of Rio de Janeiro.

cariocar [cah-re-o-car'], *m.* *(Bot.)* A remarkable tree of tropical America, which yields an oil which replaces butter in Guiana.

cariofíleo, ea [cah-re-o-fee'-lay-o, ah], *a.* Caryophyllaceous; like a pink or carnation in structure or habits.

cariofilo [cah-re-o-fee-lo], *m.* 1. The garden pink. 2. The clove.

carioso, sa [cah-re-o'-so, sah], *a.* Carious, liable to corruption.

cariota [cah-re-oh'-tah], *f.* *(Bot.)* Wild carrot.

caripando, da [cah-re-pahn'-do, dah], *a.* *(Prov.)* Idiot-like, stupid-faced.

cariparejo, ja [cah-re-pa-ray'-ho, hah], *a.* & *m.* & *f.* *(Low.)* Resembling, having a similar face; likeness.

carirraído, da [cah-rir-rah-ee'-do, dah], *a.* *(Coll.)* Brazen-faced, impudent.

carirredondo, da [cah-rir-ray-don'-do, dah], *a.* Round-faced.

caris [cah'-ris], *m.* Kind of ragout or fricassee.

carisellado [cah-re-sayl-lyah'-do], *m.* *(And.)* Toss of a coin. **Echar un carisellado,** to toss a coin.

carisma [cah-rees'-mah], *m.* *(Divin.)* Divine gift or favor.

carismático [cah-res-mah'-te-co], *a.* Charismatic.

carita [cah-ree'-tah], *f. dim.* Little or small face.

caritativamente [cah-re-tah-te-vah-men'-tay], *adv.* Charitably.

caritativo, va [cah-re-tah-tee'-vo, vah], *a.* Charitable, hospitable.

cariucho [cah-re-oo'-cho], *m.* An Indian national dish of Ecuador.

cariz [cah-reeth'], *m.* 1. The face of the sky; the aspect of the atmosphere or of the horizon, or of a business. 2. *(fig.)* Outlook. **Poner mal cariz,** to scowl. **En vista del cariz que toman las cosas,** in view of the way things are going.

carlán [car-lahn'], *m.* *(Prov.)* He who owns the duties and jurisdiction of a district.

carlanca [car-lahn'-cah], *f.* 1. A mastiff's collar. **Tener muchas carlancas,** to be very cunning or crafty. 2. *(CAm. Cono Sur)* bore, pest, drag (persona); boredom, tedium (aburrimiento). 3. **Carlancas,** tricks, cunning.

carlancón [car-lan-cone'], *m.* *(Met. Coll.)* Person very subtle and crafty.

carlear [car-lay-ar'], *vn.* To pant. *V.* JADEAR.

carlina [car-lee'-nah], *f.* *(Bot.)* Carline thistle.

carlinga [car-leen'-gah], *f.* 1. *(Naut.)* Step of a mast. 2. Pilot's cabin.

Carlomagno [car-lo-mahg'-no], *m.* Charlemagne.

carlovingio, gia [car-lo-veen'-he-o, he-ah], *a.* Carlovingian, relating to Charlemagne.

carmañola [car-ma-nyo-lah], *f.* 1. A French republican song, composed in 1792. 2. A kind of jacket with narrow neck and short skirt, much used in the time of the revolution.

carmel [car-mel'], *m.* *(Bot.)* Ribwort, plantain, rib-grass.

carmelita [car-may-lee'-tah], *m.* & *f.* 1. Carmelite. 2. *f.* Flower of the great Indian cress.

carmelitano, na [car-may-le-tah'-no, nah], *a.* Belonging to the Carmelite order.

Carmen [car'-men], *m.* 1. *(Prov.)* Country-house and garden. 2. Carmelite order. 3. Verse. 4. Woman' name.

carmenador [car-may-nah-dor'], *m.* Teaser, one who scratches cloth to raise the nap.

carmenadura [car-may-nah-doo'-rah], *f.* Act of teasing or scratching cloth, to raise the nap.

carmenar [car-may-nar'], *va.* 1. To prick or card wool. 2. To scratch cloth for the purpose of raising the nap. 3. To pull out the hair of the head. **Carmenar el pelo a uno,** to pull somebody's hair. *V.* REPELAR. 4. To win another's money at play.

carmes [car'-mes], *m.* Kermes, the cochineal insect.

carmesí [car-may-see'], *m.* Cochineal powder.

carmesí [car-may-see'], *m.* & *a.* Crimson, bright red, somewhat darkened with blue; purple.

carmín [car-meen'], *m.* 1. Carmine, the coloring matter of cochineal. **Carmín bajo,** pale rose color; lipstick. 2. *(Bot.)* Pokeweed; phytolacca.

carminar [car-me-nar'], *va.* To expel wind.

carminativo [car-me-nah-tee'-vo], *m.* Carminative, relieving wind.

carmíneo [car-me'-nay-o], *a.* Carmine, crimson.

carnada [car-nah'-dah], *f.* Bait.

carnaje [car-nah'-hay], *m.* 1. Salt beef. 2. Carnage, slaughter.

carnal [car-nahl'], *a.* 1. Carnal, fleshy. 2. Sensual, carnal, fleshly, lustful, lecherous. 3. *(Met.)* Worldly, outward: opposed to spiritual. 4. United by kindred. **Hermano carnal,** full brother. **Primo carnal,** first cousin.

carnal, *m.* Time of the year in which meat may be eaten: opposed to Lent and other fast-days.

carnalidad [car-nah-le-dahd'], *f.* Carnality, lustfulness.

carnalmente [car-nal-men'-tay], *adv.* Carnally, sensually.

carnaval [car-nah-val'], *m.* Carnival, the feast held before Shrovetide. *V.* CARNESTOLENDAS.

carnavalero [car-nah-vah-lay'-ro], *a.* Carnival.

carnaza [car-nah'-thah], *f.* 1. Fleshy part of a hide or skin. 2. *(Coll.)* Meal consisting of an abundance of meat.

carne [car'-nay], *f.* 1. Flesh. 2. Meat or flesh-meat, for food, in contradistinction to fish. 3. The pulp of fruit. 4. A boyish game with a hollow bone. **Carne de membrillo,** pulp of quinces, boiled, cooled, and preserved. **Carne de gallina,** gooseflesh, goose pimples. **Carne asada en horno,** baked meat. **Carne asada en parrillas,** broiled meat. **Carne fiambre,** cold meat. **Color de carne,** flesh color. **Caldo de carne,** meat broth. **Poner toda la carne en el asador,** *(Met.)* to hazard one's all. **Ser uña y carne,** *(Met.)* to be hand and glove, to be intimate or familiar. **Entrado en carnes,** *(LAm.)* plump, overweight. **En carne viva,** on the raw. **Se me abrieron las las carnes, I** was terrified. **Ser de carne y hueso,** to be only human. **Carne de cerdo,** pork. **Carne congelada,** frozen meat. **Carne molida,** *(LAm.)* Mince. **Carne picada,** mince. **Carne de ternera,** veal. **Carne de vaca,** beef.

carné [car-nay'], *m.* *V.* CARNET.

carneada [car-nay-ah'-dah], *f.* *(Cono Sur)* slaughter (de animales); slaughter, massacre (masacre).

carnear [car-nay-ar'], *va.* 1. *(Cono Sur)* to slaughter (animal); *(fig.)* To murder, to butcher. 2. *(Cono Sur)* To cheat, to swindle.

carnecería, carnescería [car-nay-thay-ree'-ah, car-nes-thay-ree'-ah], *f.* *V.* CARNICERIA.

carnecilla [car-nay-theel'-lyah], *f.* Small excrescence in some part of the body; caruncle.

carnerada [car-nay-rah'-dah], *f.* Flock of sheep.

carneraje [car-nay-rah'-hay], *m.* Tax or duty on sheep.

carnerario [car-nay-rah'-re-o], *m.* *(Prov.)* Charnel-house.

carnereamiento [car-nay-ray-ah-me-en'-to], *m.* Poundage, penalty for the trespass of sheep.

carnerear [car-nay-ray-ar'], *va.* To fine the proprietor of sheep for damage done. *-vn.* *(Cono Sur)* To blackleg, to be a strikebreaker.

carnerero [car-nay-ray'-ro], *m.* Shepherd. *V.* PASTOR,

carneril [car-nay-reel'], *m.* Sheep-walk, pasture for sheep.

carnero [car-nay'-ro], *m.* 1. Sheep, mutton. 2. Mutton, the flesh of sheep dressed for food. 3. *(Prov.)* Sheepskin dressed or tanned. 4. Family vault, burying-place; charnel-house. 5. Larder. **Carnero manso para guía,** bellwether. **Carnero marino,** *(Zool.)* white shark. **Carnero de la sierra,** *(LAm.)*

Llama, alpaca, vicuña. **No hay tales carneros,** there's no such thing. 6. *(Cono Sur)* Weak-willed person (débil); blackleg, strikebreaker.

carneruno, na [car-nay-roo'-no, nah], *a.* Resembling or belonging to sheep.

carnestolendas [car-nes-to-len'-das], *f. pl.* Three carnival days before Shrovetide or Ash-Wednesday.

carnet [car-net'], *m.* 1. Notebook. 2. Account book. 3. Dance program. 4. Identification card. **Carnet de conducir,** driving licence. **Carnet de identidad,** identity card. **Carnet sindical,** union card.

carnicería [car-ne-thay-ree'-ah], *f.* 1. Meat-market, meat shop. 2. Slaughterhouse; butcher's (shop). 3. Carnage, havoc, slaughter. **Hacer carnicería,** 1. To cut away a great quantity of flesh. 2. To wound in many places. **Carnicería en las carreteras,** *(fig.)* Carnage on the roads.

carnicero [car-ne-thay'-ro], *m.* Butcher.

carnicero, ra [car-ne-thay'-ro, rah], *a.* 1. Carnivorous (animales). 2. Bloodthirsty, sanguinary. 3. Applied to pasture-grounds for cattle. 4. *(Coll.)* Applied to a person who eats much meat. 5. Belonging to shambles. **Libra carnicera,** pound for butcher's meat, which varies from twenty-four to thirty-six ounces.

cárnico [ ], *a.* Meat. **Industria cárnica,** meat industry.

carnicol [car-ne-cole'], *m.* Hoof of cloven-footed animals. *V.* TABA.

carnificación [car-ne-fe-ca-the-on'], *f.* Carnification, a morbid change of a tissue to the consistency of flesh, as in hepatization of the lungs.

carnificarse [car-ne-fe-car'-say], *vr.* To carnify, to breed flesh.

carnitas [car-nee'-tas], *f. pl. (Mex.)* Barbecue pork.

carnívoro, ra [car-nee'-vo-ro, rah], *a.* Carnivorous, flesh-eating; meat-eating.

carniza [car-nee-thah'], *f. (Low.)* 1. Refuse of meat. 2. Cats' or dogs' meat.

carnosidad [car-no-se-dahd'], *f.* 1. Carnosity, proud flesh, growing on a wound, or a fleshy excrescence of any part of the body. 2. Fatness, abundance of flesh and blood. 3. Fleshiness.

carnoso, sa [car-no'-so, sah], *a.* 1. Fleshy, carnous, carneous. 2. Full of marrow; pulpous (fruta). 3. Papescent, containing pap.

carnudo, da [car-noo'-do, dah], *a. V.* CARNOSO.

carnuza [car-noo'-thah], *f.* Abundance of meat, producing loathing.

caro, ra [cah'-ro', rah], *a.* 1. Dear, high-priced, costly. 2. Dear, beloved, affectionate. **Las cosas que nos son tan caras,** the things which are so dear to us. 3. Dear, expensive. **Lo barato es caro,** cheap things are dearest. **Un coche carísimo,** a terribly expensive car.

caro [cah'-ro], *adv.* Dearly, at a high price, at too great a price. **Le costó muy caro,** it cost him dear. **Éso sale bastante caro,** that comes rather expensive.

carobo [ca-ro'-bo], *m.* 1. Weight of the twenty-fourth part of a grain. 2. Kind of Turkish vessel.

caroca [ca-ro'-cah], *f. (Coll.)* Caress, endearing action or expression made with a selfish purpose, commonly used in the plural; flattery (exaggerated); soft soap (jabón).

carocha [ca-ro'-chah], *f.* 1. White glutinous secretion (probably from the appendicular glands) of the queen bee, in which she lays her eggs; this with the egg in each cell. 2. *(Mex.)* Old banger, old crock.

carochar [ca-ro-char'], *va.* To hatch eggs (colmenas).

caroleno [cah-ro-lay'-no], *m. (Mex.)* Back slang.

Carolina [ca-ro-le'-nah], *f. (Geog.)* **Carolina del Norte,** North Carolina; **Carolina del Sur,** South Carolina.

carolingio [cah-ro-leen'-ge-o], *a.* Carolingian.

caromomia [ca-ro-mo'-me-ah], *f.* The dry flesh of a mummy.

carón [ca-rone'], *a. (LAm.)* Broad-faced.

carona [ca-ro'-nah], *f.* 1. Padding of the saddle, which touches the animal's back. 2. Part of the animal's back on which the saddle lies. **Esquilar la carona,** to shear the back of a mule; **andar con las caronas ladeadas,** *(Cono Sur)* to have problems. 3. *(Cono Sur)* Bed.

caronada [ca-ro-nah'-dah], *f.* Carronade, an absolete naval gun of short barrel and large bore.

caroñoso. sa [ca-ro-nyo'-so, sah], *a.* Old, galled, and cast off (bestias de carga).

caroquero, ra [ca-ro-kay'-ro, rah], *m. & f.* Wheedler, flatterer; caressing.

carosiera [ca-ro-se-ay-rah], *f.* 1. *(Bot.)* Species of the palm-tree. 2. Date, the fruit of that species of the palm.

carota [cah-ro'-tah], *a.* 1. Barefaced, brazen. 2. *m. & f.* Rotter; shameless person.

carotas [ca-ro'-tas], *f. pl.* Rolls of tobacco ground to powder.

carótida [ca-ro'-te-dah], *f. (Prov.)* The carotid artery.

carozo [ca-ro'-tho], *m.* 1. *(Prov.)* Core of a pomegranate, or other fruit. 2. Cob of corn.

carpa [car'-pah], *f.* 1. *(Zoöl.)* Carp, a fresh-water fish. 2. Part of a bunch of grapes which is torn off. 3. *(Peru)* A tent of canvas or cloth.

carpanel [car-pa-nel'], *m. (Arch.)* Arch in a semi-elliptic form.

carpanta [car-pahn'-tah], *f.* Ravenous hunger.

carpe [car'-pay], *m. (Bot.)* Common horn-beam tree, witch-hazel.

carpedal [car-par-dahl'], *m.* Plantation of common horn-beam trees.

carpelo [car-pay'-lo], *m.* Carpel.

carpeta [car-pay'-tah], *f.* 1. Table-cover, covering of a table. 2. Portfolio, portable writing-desk. **Carpeta de información,** information folder. **Cerrar la carpeta,** to close the file. 3. Label, or indorsement, upon a bundle of papers; a wrapper.

carpetazo [car-pay-tah'-tho], *m.* A blow or stroke with a *carpeta.* **Dar carpetazo a,** to shelve, to put on one side.

carpetovetónico [car-pay-to-vay-to'-ne-co], *a.* Terribly Spanish, Spanish to the core.

carpidor, ra [car-pe-dor'], *m. & f. (LAm.)* Weeding hoe.

carpintear [car-pin-tay-ar'], *vn.* To do carpenter's work.

carpintería [car-pin-tay-ree'-ah], *f.* 1. Carpentry. 2. Carpenter's shop.

carpintero [car-pin-tay'-ro], *m.* 1. Carpenter, joiner. **Carpintero de prieto** or **de carretas,** cartwright, wheelwright. **Carpintero de ribera** or **de navío,** ship carpenter, shipwright. **Mestro carpintero de remos,** master oar-maker. **Segundo carpintero,** carpenter's mate. **2. Pájaro carpintero,** *(Orn.)* Woodpecker. **Carpintero real,** ivory-billed woodpecker.

carpión [car-pe-on'], *m.* Large carp resembling a trout.

carpir [car-peer'], *vn.* To tear, to scrape, to scratch, to scold. *-vn. (LAm.)* To weed, to hoe.

carpo [car'-po], *m. (Anat.)* Carpus, wrist.

carpobálsamo [car-po-bahl'-sah-mo], *m.* Carpobalsamum, fruit of the tree which yields the balm of Gilead.

carpófago [car-po'-fah-go], *m.* One who lives on fruit.

carqueja, or **carqueija** [car-kay'-hah, car-kay'-e-hah], *f. (Bot.) V.* CARQUESA, for a plant.

carquesa, carquesia [car-kay'-sah, car- kay'-se-ah], *f.* In glass-houses, the annealing furnace.

carquexia [car-kek'-se-ah], *f.* A species of broom-plant.

carraca [car-rah'-cah], *f.* 1. Carrack, large and slow-sailing cargo ship. 2. Rattle (instrumento). 3. A rachet brace. 4. Old crock (coche).

carraco, ca [car-rah'-co, cah], *a.* Old, withered, decrepit.

carracón [car-rah-cone'], *m.* 1. Large cargo ship. 2. *(aug.)* Large rattle. 3. Animal worn out with age and fatigue.

carrada [cahr-rah'-dah], *f. (Cono Sur) V.* CARRETADA.

carral [car-rahl'], *m.* Barrel, butt, vat, pipe for transporting wine in carts and wagons.

carraleja [car-rah-lay'-hah], *f.* 1. Black beetle with yellow stripes; the oil-beetle, meloe. 2. Spanish blistering beetle. *(Acad.)*

carralero [car-rah-lay'-ro], *m.* Cooper.

carranclán [car-ran-clahn'], *m.* Gingham.

carranque [car-rahn'-kay], *m.* A Peruvian bird resembling a crane.

carrasca [car-rahs'-cah], *f. (Bot.)* V. CARRASCO; **ser de carrasca,** V. AÚPA.

carrascal [car-ras-cahl'], *m.* Plantation of evergreen oaks.

carrasco [car-rahs'-co], *m. (Bot.)* Ever green oak. V. COSCOJA.

carrascoloso [cahr-ras-co-lo'-so], *a. (LAm.)* Grumpy, touchy, irritable.

carrascon [car-ras-cone], *m. (Bot.)* Large evergreen oak.

carraspada [car-ras-pah'-dah], *f.* Negus, a beverage made of red wine, honey, and spice.

carraspante [car-ras-pahn'-tay], *a. (Prov.)* Harsh, acrid, strong.

carraspear [car-ras-pay-ar'], *vn.* To be hoarse, to have a frog in one's throat.

carraspeo [car-ras-pay'-o], *m.* Sore throat.

carraspera [car-ras-pay'-rah], *f.* 1. Hoarseness. 2. Sore throat, attended with hoarseness.

carraspique [car-ras-pee'-kay], *m. (Bot.)* Candytuft.

carrasposo [car-ras-po'-so], *a.* 1. Hoarse, having a sore throat. 2. *(LAm.)* Rough, harsh.

carrasqueño, ña [car-ras-kay'-nyo, nyah], *a.* 1. Harsh, sharp, biting. 2. Rough, rude, sullen. 3. Belonging to the evergreen oak 4. *(Prov.)* Strong, nervous.

carrasquilla [car-ras-keel'-lyah], *f. (Bot. Prov.)* A species of the genus Rhamnus; a buckthorn.

carrear, carrejar [car-ray-ar', car-ray-har'], *va. (Obs.)* V. ACARREAR.

carrera [car-ray'-rah], *f.* 1. Race (deportes), course. **Carrera ciclista,** cycling. **Carrera de caballos,** horse racing. **Carrera pedestre,** footrace. **Carrera de sacos,** sack race. **Carrera de fondo,** long-distance race. 2. Run (béisbol, cricket). 2. The course of the stars. 3. Career (estudios). 4. High-road, from one town to another. 5. In Madrid, a broad and long street, as, **la carrera de San Francisco,** St. Francis street. 6. Alley, a walk in a garden; an avenue leading to a house, planted with trees. 7. Row of things, ranged in a line. 8. Range of iron teeth in combing-cards. 9. Line made by dividing and separating the hair. 10. Girder, in a floor. 11. Stitch in a stocking which has broken or fallen. 12. Course and duration of life. 13. Profession of arms or letters. 14. Course, method of life, train of actions. 15. Course, conduct, manner of proceeding, mode of action. V. CARRERILLA. **Carrera de Indias,** trade from Spain to South America. **No poder hacer carrera con alguno,** not to be able to bring one to reason. **A carrera abierta,** at full speed. **De carrera,** without thinking, rashly. **Carrera de armamentos,** arms race. **Carrera de relevos,** relay race. **Carrera de vallas,** hurdles. **Tomar carrera,** to back up in order to get a running start. **No poder hacer carrera con,** not to be able to do a thing with, not to make any headway with. **Dar carrera libre a,** to give free rein to. **Hacer el trabajo a la carrera,** to race through one's work. **Carrera de despegue,** take-off run. **Carrera por carretera,** road race. **Carrera de coches,** car race. **Carrera de medio fondo,** middle-distance race. **Carrera de maratón,** marathon. **Carrera ascendente,** upstroke. **Diplomático de carrera,** career diplomat. **No hago carrera con este niño,** I can't make any headway with this child. **No tiene carrera,** he has no profession.

carrerilla, ta [car-ray-reel'-lyah, ree'-tah], *f.* 1. *(dim.)* Small race or course. 2. Rapid motion in a Spanish dance. 3. *(Mus.)* Rise or fall of an octave. 4. Non-stop, continually. **Lo dijo de carrerilla,** he reeled it off.

carrerista [car-ray-rees'-tah], *m. & f.* 1. Fond of racing. 2. Racing cyclist. 3. *f.* Street walker.

carrero [car-ray'-ro], *m.* Carter, cart driver.

carreta [car-ray'-tah], *f.* 1. Long narrow cart, wagon. **Carreta de mano,** V. CARRETILLA. **Tener la carreta llena,** *(Carib.)* to be weighted down by problems. 2. **Carreta cubierta,** gallery of a siege, or the covered passage to the walls of a fortress.

carretada [car-ray-tah'-dah], *f.* 1. Cartful, cart-load. 2. Great quantity. **A carretadas,** *(Coll.)* copiously, in abundance.

carretaje [car-ray-tah'-hay], *m.* Cartage, haulage.

carrete [car-ray'-tay], *m.* 1. Spool, bobbin, reel. 2. Small reel for winding silk or gold and silver twist. 3. Reel of a fishing-rod. 4. *(Elec.)* Bobbin, wire coil. **Carrete de encendido,** induction coil. **Dar carrete a uno,** to keep somebody guessing.

carretear [car-ray-tay-ar'], *va.* 1. To cart, to convey in a cart. 2. To drive a cart. -*vr.* To draw unevenly (bueyes, mulos).

carretel [car-ray-tel'], *m.* 1. Spool, reel, bobbin. 2. *(Prov.)* A fishing-reel, line-reel. 3. *(Naut.)* Log-reel. 4. Spun-yarn winch. 5. Ropewalk reel. 6. **Carretel de carpintero,** carpenter's marking-line.

carretela [car-ray-tay'-lah], *f.* Caleche, calash, a four-wheeled carriage on springs.

carretera [car-ray-tay'-rah], *f.* Highway, road. **Por carretera,** by road. **Carretera nacional,** Arterial highway. **Carretera secundaria,** secondary road. **Carretera de circunvalación,** bypass. **Red de carreteras,** road network. **Mapa de carreteras,** road map.

carretería [car-ray-tay-ree'-ah], *f.* 1. Number of carts. 2. Trade of a carman. 3. Cartwright's yard; wheel wright's shop.

carretero [car-ray-tay'-ro], *m.* 1. Cartwright 2. Carman carrier, carter. **Voz de carretero,** harsh, loud, and unpleasant voice; **jurar como un carretero,** to swear like a tropper. 3. *(Astr.)* Wagoner, a northern constellation. -*a.* **Camino carretero,** vehicular road.

carretil [car-ray-teel'], *a.* Suitable for carts.

carretilla [car-ray-teel'-lyah], *f.* 1. Wheelbarrow. 2. Hand truck. 3. Hand cart. 4. Walker (for babies). 5. Firecracker. 6. Cake decorator. **Carretilla elevadora,** fork-lift truck. **Saber de carretilla una cosa,** to know something perfectly. 7. *(And.)* Lot, series. 8. *(Cono Sur)* jaw, jawbone (quijada).

carretón [car-ray-tone'], *m.* 1. Small cart, in the shape of an open chest, wagon. 2. Go-cart. 3. *(Obs.)* Gun-carriage. 4. **Carretón de lámpara,** pulley for raising or lowering lamps. 5. In Toledo, stage for religious plays. 6. Truck, dray, van.

carretoncillo [car-ray-ton-theel'-lyo], *m. dim.* Small go-cart for children.

carretonero [car-ray-to-nay'-ro], *m.* Driver of the *carretón;* drayman, truckman.

carricoche [car-re-co'-chay], *m.* 1. Cart with a box like a coach. 2. *(Prov.)* Old-fashioned coach, wagonette. 3. *(Prov.)* Muck-cart, dungcart.

carricuba [car-re-coo'-bah], *f.* Water cart.

carricureña [car-re-coo-ray'-nyah], *f. (Mil.)* Carriage of a light field-piece.

carriego [car-re-ay'-go], *m.* 1. Osier basket used for fishing. 2. Large rough basket used in bleaching flaxyarn.

carriel [car-re-ayl'], *m. (And. CAm.)* Leather case.

carril [car-reel'], *m.* 1. Rut, cart-way, cart-rut. 2. Narrow road where one cart only can pass at a time. 3. Furrow opened by the plough. 4. A rail of a railway. **Carril de autobús,** bus lane.

carrilada [cah-re-lah'-dah], *f.* Rut, the track of a cart or coach.

carrilano [car-re-lah'-no], *m. (Cono Sur)* 1. Robber, hold up man. 2. Railwayman (ferroviario).

carrilera [car-re-lay'-rah], *f.* 1. Rut, track (rodera). 2. *(Carib.) (Ferro.)* Siding.

carrilero [car-re-lay'-ro], *m. (And.) (Ferro.)* Railwayman; *(Cono Sur)* con man (embaucador).

carrillada [car-reel-lyah'-dah], *f.* Oily or medullar substance of a hog's cheek. **Carrilladas de vaca o carnero,** *(Prov.)* Cow or sheep's head without the tongue.

carrillar [car-reel'-lyar], *va. (Naut.)* To hoist light things out of the hold with a tackle.

carrillera [car-reel-lyay'-rah], *f.* 1. The jaw. 2. Each of two straps, covered with metal scales used to fasten a soldier's helmet; chin-strap.

carrillo [car-reel'-lyo], *m.* 1. *(dim.)* Small cart. 2. Cheek, the fleshy part of the face. 3. *(Naut.)* Tackle for hoisting light things. **Comer a dos carrillos,** to eat greedily. 4. *(Tec.)* Pulley. 5. Trolley, pushcart (mesa para servir).

carrilludo, da [car-reel-lyoo'-do, dah], *a.* Plump or round checked.

carrindanga [car-reen-dahn'-ga], *f. (Cono Sur)* old crock, old banger.

carriola [car-re-o-lah], *f.* 1. Trundle-bed. 2. Small chariot; curricle.

carrito [car-ree'-to], *m.* 1. Trolley, shopping cart (de supermercado); tea trolley, serving trolley. 2. *(Carib.)* Taxi.

carrizal [car-re-thahl'], *m.* Land which is full of reed-grass.

carrizo [car-ree'-tho], *m.* 1. *(Bot.)* Common reed-grass. 2. *(And. Mex.)* **Carrizos,** thin legs; *(And.)* **Hacer carrizos,** to cross one's legs. 3. *(Carib.)* **No nos ayudan en un carrizo,** they do nothing at all to help us. 4. *(And. CAm. Carib.),* V. CARAMBA.

carro [car'-ro], *m.* 1. Cart, a carriage with two wheels, chariot, cart. **Varas del carro,** shafts of a cart. **Toldo del carro,** tilt, the cloth thrown over the hoops of a cart. 2. A railway car. 3. The running gear of a carriage without the body. 4. *(Astr.)* The Greater Bear, a northern constellation. **Carro menor,** the Lesser Bear. **Carro de oro,** Brussels camlet, fine camlet. 5. *(Naut.)* Manufactory for cables and other ship cordage. 6. Measure for wood; a cartload. **Medio carro de leña,** a cord of wood. **Un carro de problemas,** *(fig.)* a whole load of problems. 7. The bed of a printing-press. **Carro de combate,** tank. **Carro fúnebre,** hearse. **Aguantar carros y carretas,** to put up with anything. **Apearse del carro,** to back down.

carrocería [car-ro-thay-re'-ah], *f.* 1. Coachbuilder's (taller); carriage repair shop. 2. *(Aut.)* Body work, coachwork.

carrocero [car-ro-thay'-ro], *m.* Coachbuilder, carriage builder.

carrocilla [car-ro-theel'-lyah], *f. dim.* Small coach.

carrocín [car-ro-theen'], *m.* Chaise, curricle.

carrocha [car-ro'-chah], *f.* Seminal substance in bees and other insects. Eggs.

carrochar [car-ro-char'], *vn.* To lay eggs, to shed the seminal substance (abejas, insectos).

carrofuerte [car-ro-foo-er'-tay], *m.* A strong cart or truck for transporting artillery or heavy weights.

carromatero [car-ro-mah-tay'-ro], *m.* Carter, charioteer, carman.

carromato [car-ro-mah'-to], *m.* A long, narrow cart with two wheels and tilt, for transporting goods, etc.

carroña [car-ro'-nyah], *f.* Carrion, putrid flesh.

carroñar [car-ro-nyar'], *va.* To infect sheep with the scab.

carroñero [car-ro-nyay'-ro]. Rotten, vile, foul. **Animal carroñero,** animal which feeds on carrion.

carroño, ña [car-ro'-nyo, nyah], *a.* Putrefied, putrid, rotten.

carroza [car-ro'-thah], *f.* 1. Large coach; superb state coach. **Carroza fúnebre,** hearse. 2. *(Naut.)* Awning over a boat, or part of a ship. 3. *(Naut.)* Kind of cabin on the quarter-deck of a ship. *-m.* 1. Old geezer (viejo); old boy; square (carca); old reactionary. 2. Gay, queer, old queen (homesexual). *-a.* Archaic, passé; square.

carruaje [ca-roo-ah'-hay], *m.* All sorts of vehicles for transporting persons or goods.

carruajero [ca-roo-ah-hay'-ro], *m.* Carrier, carter, wagoner.

carruco [car-roo- co], *m.* Small cart used in mountainous parts.

carrujado, da [car-roo-hah'-do, dah], *a.* Corrugated, wrinkled. V. ENCARRUJADO.

carrujo [car-roo'-ho], *m. (LAm.)* Joint, reefer.

carrusel [car-roo-sayl'], *m.* Merry-go-round, roundabout.

carry-all [car-ree-ol'], *m. (Cono Sur)* estate car, station wagon.

carta [car'-tah], *f.* 1. Letter; *(Com.)* Favor. 2. Royal ordinance. 3. Map, chart. 4. Card for playing. 5. A written constitution, charter. 6. *(Obs.)* Writing-paper. **Carta blanca,** letter or commission with a blank for the name to be inserted at pleasure; full powers given to one. **Carta abierta,** *(Obs.)* open order,

addressed to all persons. **Carta certificada,** a registered letter. **Carta cuenta,** bill or account of sale. **Carta credencial** or **de creencia,** credentials. **Carta de crédito,** letter of credit. **Carta de dote,** articles of marriage. **Carta de encomienda,** letter of safe conduct. **Carta de espera** or **moratoria,** letter of respite given to a debtor. **Carta de guía,** passport; **carta de naturaleza,** letters of naturalization. **Carta de pago,** acquittance, receipt, discharge in full. **Carta de portes,** booking ticket. **Carta de presentación,** letter of introduction. **Carta de seguridad,** safeguard, protection. **Carta de sanidad,** bill of health. **Carta de venta,** bill of sale. **Carta devuelta,** a deadletter. **Carta pastoral,** pastoral letter. **Carta receptoria,** warrant, voucher, **Perder con buenas cartas,** *(Met.)* To fail although protected or deserving. **Traer** or **venir con malas cartas,** *(Met.)* to attempt to enforce an illgrounded claim. **Carta de pésame,** letter of condolence. **Carta postal,** *(LAm.)* Post-card. **Carta urgente,** special delivery letter. **Echar una carta al correo,** to post a letter. **Carta Magna,** Magna carta. **Carta verde,** green card. **Carta marítima,** chart. **Carta meteorológica,** weather map. **Echar las cartas,** to tell somebody's fortune. **Poner las cartas sobre la mesa,** to put one's cards on the table. **Tomar cartas en el asunto,** to intervene in a matter.

carta aérea [car'-tah ah-ay'-ray-ah], *f.* Airletter.

carta-bomba [car-tah-bom'-bah], *f. pl.* Letter-bomb.

cartabón [car-tah-bone'], *m.* 1. A carpenter's square, rule, an instrument to measure and form angles. **Echar el cartabón,** *(Met.)* to adopt measures for attaining one's end. **Cartabón de cola,** small square piece of glue. 2. Shoemaker's slide, size-stick. 3. Quadrant, a gunner's square, or instrument for elevating and pointing guns.

cartaginense [car-tah-he-nen'-say], *a.* Carthaginian: of Carthage.

cartaginés [car-tah-ge-nays'], *a.* Carthaginian.

Cartago [car-tah'-go], *f.* Carthage.

cártama [car'-tah-mah], *f. (Bot.)* Officinal carthamus. V. ALAZOR.

cártamo [car'-tah-mo], *m. (Bot.)* 1. A generical name of plants. 2. V. CÁRTAMA. Safflower.

cartapacio [car-tah-pah'-the-o], *m.* 1. Memorandum-book. 2. A student's note-book. 3. Satchel.

cartapartida [car-tah-par-tee'-dah], *f.* Charter-party. **Cartapartida bajo forma,** memorandum of charter-party.

cartapel [car-tah-pel'], *m.* 1. Memorandum filled with useless matter. 2. Edict, ordinance.

cartazo [car-tah'-tho], *m. (Coll.)* Letter or paper containing a severe rebuke.

cartear [car-tay-ar'], *vn.* To play low cards, in order to try how the game stands. *-va.* 1. *(Naut.)* To steer by the sea-chart. 2. To turn over the leaves of a book. *-vr.* To correspond by letter. **Se cartearon durante 2 años,** they wrote to each other for 2 years.

cartel [car-tel'], *m.* 1. Placard, handbill, poster. **Torero de cartel,** star bullfighter. **Se prohibe fijar carteles,** post no bills. 2. Cartel, a written agreement made by belligerent powers relative to the exchange of prisoners. 3. *(Obs.)* Challenge sent in writing. 4. *(Naut.)* Cartel-ship or flag of truce. 5. A fishing-net which spreads eighty fathoms.

cartela [car-tay'-lah], *f.* 1. Slip of paper, piece of wood, or other materials on which a memorandum is made. 2. Console, bracket, or stay on which carved work rests. 3. Iron stay, which supports a balcony.

cartelear [car-tay-lay-ar,], *va.* To publish libels.

cartelera [car-tay-lay'-rah], *f.* Billboard; notice (tablón); list of plays, theater section. **Mantenerse en la cartelera,** to be on. **Se mantuvo en la cartelera durante 3 años,** it ran for 3 years.

catelero [car-tay-lay'-ro], *m.* Billsticker, billposter.

cartelón [car-tay-lone'], *m. aug.* 1. Long edict. 2. Show-bill.

carteo [car-tay'-o], *m.* Frequent intercourse by letters.

carter [car'-ter], *m.* Crank case (of an auto).

cartera [car-tay'-rah], *f.* 1. Wallet. 2. Portfolio, briefcase. 3. Lettercase, letter-box. 4. Portfolio, the office of a cabinet minister. **Cartera de bolsillo,** wallet. **Cartera de herramientas,** saddlebag. **Cartera de pedidos,** order-book. **Proyecto en cartera,** plane in the pipeline. **Ministro sin cartera,** minister without portfolio. 5. *(Fin.)* Portfolio, holdings. **Efectos en cartera,** holdings, stocks.

carterero [car-tay-ray'-ro], *m. (Cono Sur)* pickpocket; bag-snatcher.

carteriana [car-tay-re-ah'-nah], *f.* Sort of silk.

carterista [car-tay-rees'-tah], *m.* Pickpocket.

carterita [car-tay-ree'-tah], *f.* **Carterita de fósforos,** book of matches.

cartero [car-tay'-o], *m.* Letter-carrier, postman.

carteta [car-tay'-tah], *f.* A game at cards. *V.* PAPAR.

cartibanas [car-te-bah'-nas], *f. pl.* Pieces of paper glued to the leaves of a book to facilitate the binding; fly-sheets.

cartica, ita [car-tee'-cah, ee'-tah], *f. dim.* Small letter or note.

cartilaginoso, sa [car-te-lah-he-no'-so, sah], *a.* Cartilaginous, gristly.

cartílago [car-tee'-lah-go], *m. (Anat.)* 1. A cartilage, gristle. 2. Parchment. *V.* TERNILLA.

cartilla [car-teel'-lyah], *f.* 1. *(dim.)* Small or short letter or note. 2. The first book of children, horn-book. 3. Certificate of a clergyman duly ordained. **Leerle a uno la cartilla,** *(Met.)* to give one a lecture. **No saber la cartilla,** *(Met.)* to be extremely ignorant. 4. *V.* AÑALEJO. 5. Savings bank book; deposit book. **Cartilla de ahorros,** savings bank book. **Cartilla de racionamiento,** ration book. **Cartilla de seguro,** social security card.

cartografía [car-to-grah-fee'-ah], *f.* Chartography, the art of map-drawing.

cartográfico, ca [car-to-grah'-fe-co, cah], *a.* Chartographic, relative to the drawing of maps.

cartógrafo [car-to'-grah-fo], *m.* Chartographer, a drawer of maps.

cartomancia [car-to-man'-the-ah], *f.* Fortune-telling.

cartón [car-tone'], *m.* 1. Pasteboard, binders' board. **Cartón de bingo,** bingo card. **Cartón de encuadernar,** millboard. **Cartón piedra,** papier mâché. 2. Kind of iron ornament, imitating the leaves of plants. 3. Cartoon, a painting or drawing on strong paper. **Parece de cartón,** he is as stiff as a poker. 4. Artist's cartoon.

cartoné [car-to-nay'], *m. (Typ.)* En cartoné, in boards.

cartonera [car-to-nay'-rah], *f.* A papermaking wasp, a social wasp. So called from the appearance of its cells. *-pl.* Pasteboard cases for filing papers.

cartonero [car-to-nay'-ro], *m.* One whose business is to make pasteboard.

cartuchera [car-too-chay'-rah], *f.* Cartridge-box, pouch, belt.

cartucho [car-too'-cho], *m.* 1. Cartouch, a cartridge, a charge of powder contained in paper. **Cartucho de fusil,** musket-cartridge. **Cartucho de fogeo,** blank cartridge. **Luchar hasta quemar el último cartucho,** to fight on the last ditch. 2. Small target. *V.* TARJETA.

cartuja [car-too'-hah], *f.* Carthusian order.

cartujano, na [car-too-hah'-no, nah], *a.* Carthusian.

cartujo [car-too'-ho], *m.* 1. Carthusian monk. 2. Kind of skin first used by Carthusian monks.

cartulaje [car-too-lah'-hay], *m.* Pack of cards.

cartulario [car-too-lah'-re-o], *m.* 1. Archives or registry. 2. The archivist. 3. Coucher, a register book in monasteries.

cartulina [car-too-lee'-nah], *f.* Bristol-board, cardboard. **Cartulina común,** Mill-board. **Cartulina en hojas,** sheet card.

carúncula [cah-roon'-coo-lah], *f.* 1. Caruncle. 2. Crustaceous excrescence on an ulcer or wound. **Carúncula lagrimal,** the lachrymal caruncle, a reddish elevation at the inner angle of the eye.

carunculado, da [cah-roon-coo-lah'-do, dah], *a.* Carunculated (pájaros).

carunculoso, sa [ca-roon-coo-lo'-so, sah], *a.* Relating to or like a caruncle.

carura [cah-roo-rah], *f.* 1. *(And. CAm. Cono Sur)* high price, dearness. 2. *(And. CAm. Cono Sur)* expensive thing. **En esta tienda sólo hay caruras,** everything in this shop is dear.

carvallo [car-vahl'-lyo], *m. (Bot.)* Common British oak.

carvi [car'-ve], *m.* 1. *(Bot.)* Common caraway. 2. Caraway, seed.

casa [cah'-sah], *f.* 1. House, edifice, dwelling. 2. Home, our own house, the private dwelling. 3. House, household, the family residing in a house. 4. Line or branch of a family. 5. Checkers, or squares, of a chess or draught-board. 6. Firm, business house. **Casa de campo,** country house. **Casa de socorro,** a receiving or emergency hospital. **Casa de locos,** 1. Mad-house. 2. *(Met.)* Noisy or riotous house. **Casa de posada, casa de huéspedes** or **casa de pupilos,** lodging-house, or lodging and boarding-house. **Casa pública,** brothel, bawdy-house. **Casa de sanidad,** office of the board of health. **Guardar la casa,** to stay at home. **Hacer su casa** *(Met.),* to raise or aggrandize one's own family. **No tener casa ni hogar,** to have neither house nor home. **Poner casa,** to establish house, to begin housekeeping. **Ponerle a uno casa,** to furnish a house for another. **Ser muy de casa,** to be very intimate in a house, to be on familiar terms. **Casa del Señor, de Dios** or **de oración,** church or temple. **Casa Santa,** Church of the Holy Sepulchre at Jerusalen. **Casa de alquiler,** block of flats. **Casa de baños,** public baths. **Casas baratas,** low-costing housing. **Casa de citas,** brothel. **Casa consistorial,** city hall. **Casa de correos,** post office. **Casa cuna,** nursery. **Casa de maternidad,** maternity hospital. **Un complejo como una casa,** a massive complex. **Casa y comida,** board and lodging. **Casa paterna,** parent's house. **Es una casa alegre,** it's a happy home. **Ir a casa,** go home. **Estar en casa,** to be at home. **Zapatos de andar por casa,** shoes for wearing around the house. **Ser de la casa,** to be like one of the family. **Echar la casa por la ventana,** to go to enormous expense. **Empezar la casa por el tejado,** to put the cart before the horse. **Cada uno manda en su casa,** one's home is one's castle. **Sentirse como en casa,** to feel at home. **Casa bancaria,** banking house. **Casa editorial,** publishing house; **Casa Blanca,** White House. **Casa real,** royal house.

casabe [cah-sah'-bay], *m. (LAm.)* Cassava.

casablanca [cah-sah-blahn'-cah], *f.* Casablanca.

casaca [ca-sah'-cah], *f.* 1. Coat, upper garment of a man; dress-coat; **casaca de mujer,** a woman's jacket. **Cambiar de casaca,** to turn one's coat. 2. The marriage contract.

casación [cah-sah-the-on'], *f. (Law.)* Cassation, abrogation, the act of annulling or repealing a law or reversing a judicial sentence.

casacón [cah-sah-cone'], *m.* 1. Greatcoat, worn over other clothes. 2. Cassock.

casada [cah-sah'-dah], *f.* 1. *(Prov.)* Ancient family mansion. 2. Married woman.

casadero, ra [cah-sah-day'-ro, rah], *a.* Marriageable, fit for marriage.

casado [cah-sah'-do], *m.* 1. Imposition (imprenta). 2. Married. **Los casados,** married men. **Los recién casados,** the newlyweds. *a.* Married. **Bien casado,** happily married. **Casado y arrepentido,** marry in haste and repent at leisure. **Estar casado,** to be married.

casador [cah-sah-dor'], *m.* One who annuls or repeals.

casal [cah-sahl'], *m.* 1. Countryhouse of an ancient family. 2. *(Cono Sur)* Married couple.

casalero [cah-sah-lay'-ro], *m.* One who resides in his country-house.

casalicio [cah-sah-lee'-the-o], *m.* House, edifice.

casamata [cah-sah-mah'-tah], *f. (Mil.)* Casemate.

casamentero, ra [cah-sah-men-tay'-ro, rah], *m. & f.* Match or marriage-maker.

casamiento [cah-sah-me-en'-to], *m.* 1. Marriage, marriage contract; matrimony; match. **Casamiento de conveniencia,** marriage of convenience. **Casamiento a la fuerza,** forced marriage. 2. In games, betting money on a card. 3. A wife's fortune.

casampolga [cah-sahm-pol'-gah], *f.* *(CAm.)* *(Zool.)* Black widow spider.

casamuro [cah-sah-moo'-ro], *m.* *(Mil.)* Single wall without a terreplein.

casapuerta [cah-sah-poo-err'-tah], *f.* Porch; entrance of a house.

casaquilla [cah-sah-keel'-lyah], *f.* Kind of short and loose jacket, worn over other clothes.

casar [cah-sar'], *m.* 1. Hamlet, a small village. 2. *(Prov.)* Country-house for laborers to sleep in.

casar, *va.* 1. To marry, to join a man and woman in marriage or in wedlock (sacerdotes). 2. To marry, to dispose of in marriage; to couple, to unite in marriage. 3. *(Met.)* To sort things so as to match one another, to mate, to suit or proportion one thing to another. 4. To repeal, to abrogate, to annul. 5. *(Paint.)* To blend. 6. *(Typ.)* To impose. **Antes de que te cases mira lo que haces,** look before you leap. *-vr.* To marry, to take a wife or husband, to get married. **Ana se casó con Pedro,** Anne married Peter. **¿Cuándo te vas a casar?,** when are you getting married? **Volver a casarse en segunda nupcias,** to marry again.

casatienda [cah-sah-te-en'-dah], *f.* Tradesman's shop.

casave [cah-sah'-vay], *m.* Cassava, tapioca. Also CASABE and CAZABE.

casazo [cah-sah'-tho], *m. (Coll.aug.)* Great event.

casca [cahs'-cah], *f.* 1. Skins of grapes after the wine has been pressed out. 2. *(Prov.)* Bad wine or liquor. 3. Bark for tanning leather. 4. Kind of sweetbread.

cascabel [cas-cah-bel'], *m.* 1. Hawksbell, bell used for hawks, cats, or dogs, and also for beasts of burden. 2. Knob at the end of the breech of a cannon, cascabel. 3. Rattlesnake. **Echar a uno el cascabel,** *(Met.)* to throw off a burden and lay it on another. **Echar** or **soltar el cascabel,** *(Met.)* to drop a hint in conversation, to see how it takes. **Ser un cascabel,** *(Met.)* to be a crazy or rattle-brained fellow.

cascabela [cas-cah-bay'-lah], *f. (LAm.)* Rattlesnake.

cascabelada [cas-cah-bay-lah'-dah], *f.* 1. Jingling with small bells. 2. Inconsiderate speech or action. 3. Noisy feast.

cascabelear [cas-cah-bay-lay-ar'], *va.* To feed one with vain hopes, to induce one to act on visionary expectations. *-vn.* 1. To act with levity, or little forecast and prudence. 2. *(LAm.)* To jingle, to tinkle (tintinear). 3. *(Cono Sur)* to moan, to grumble (refunfuñar).

cascabeleo [cas-cah-bay-lay'-o], *m.* Jingle, jingling, tinkling.

cascabelero, ra [cas-cah-bay-lay'-ro, rah], *a.* Light-witted, scatterbrained.

cascabelillo [cas-cah-bay-leel'-lyo], *m. dim.* Small black plum.

cascabillo [cas-cah-beel'-lyo], *m.* 1. Hawk's bell. *V.* CASCABEL. 2. Chaff of wheat or other grain. 3. Husk of an acorn.

cascaciruelas [cas-cah-the-roo-ay'-las], *m.* Mean, despicable fellow.

cascada [cas-cah'-dah,], *f.* Cascade, water-fall. **Cascadas,** small plaits or folds in the drapery of paintings.

cascado, da [cas-cah'-do, dah], *a.* Broken, burst, decayed, infirm; crazy. **Vidrio cascado,** *(Met.)* singer who has lost his voice. **Estar muy cascado,** to be in a precarious state of health. *-pp.* of CASCAR.

cascadura [cas-cah-doo'-rah], *f.* Act of bursting or breaking asunder.

cascajal [cas-cah-hahl'], 1. Place full of gravel and pebbles. 2. Place in which the husks of grapes are thrown.

cascajar [cas-cah'-har], *m.* Place full of gravel and pebbles.

cascajo [cas-cah'-ho], *m.* 1. Pebble. 2. Fragments of broken vessels. 3. Rubbish. 4. *(Lit. us.)* Old and useless furniture. 5. Pod or silique; shell of a nut. 6. *(Met.)* Copper coin. 7. Bit of a bridle. **Estar hecho un cascajo,** to be very old and infirm.

cascajoso, sa [cas-cah-ho'-so, sah], *a.* Gravelly.

cascallo [cas-cahl'-lyo], *m.* Brazilian name of a diamond-field.

cascamajar [cas-cah-ma-har'], *va. (Prov.)* To break, bruise, or pound a thing slightly.

cascamiento [cas-cah-me-en'-to], *m.* Act of breaking or bruising.

cascanueces [cas-cah-noo-ay'-thes], *m.* Nut-cracker.

cascar [cas-car'], *va.* 1. To crack burst, or break into pieces. 2. To crunch. 3. To lick, to beat, or strike. 4. *(Prov.)* To talk much. 5. To shatter, to undermine. 6. To belt, to smack (pegar). 7. **Cascarla,** to kick the bucket. *-vr.* 1. To be broken open. 2. To crack up; to break (salud). *-vn.* To talk too much.

cáscara [cahs'-ca-rah], *f.* 1. Rind, peel, hull, or husk of various fruits, etc. **Cáscara de limón,** lemmon peel. **Patatas cocidas con cáscara,** potatoes in their jackets. 2. Bark of trees. **Cáscara sagrada,** dried bark of à tree which is used as a laxative. 3. *(CAm.)* **Tener cáscara,** to have a cheek, to be shameless.

¡cáscaras! [cahs'-ca-ras], *int.* Oh! exclamation expressive of astonishment or admiration.

cascarazo [cas-cah-rah'-zo], *m.* 1. *(And. Carib.)* Punch; lash. 2. *(Carib.)* Swig, slug.

cascarear [cas-cah-ray-ar'], *va. (And. CAm.)* To belt, smack. *- vn. (Mex.)* To scrape a living.

cascarilla, cascarita [cas-cah-reel'-lyah, ree'-tah], *f.* 1. *(dim.)* Small thin bark. 2. Peruvian bark, Jesuit's bark. 3. Cascarilla bark. 4. *(And. Cono Sur)* *(Med.)* Medicinal herb; dried cacao husks (used as tea). *-a. (Carib. Cono Sur)* touchy, quick-tempered.

cascarillero [cas-cah-reel-lyay'-ro], *m.* A gatherer of Peruvian bark.

cascarrillo [cas-car-reel'-lyo], *m.* The cinchona shrub.

cascaroja [cas-car-ro'-hah], *f.* Woodborer, shipworm, ship-piercer. *V.* BROMA.

cascarón [cas-cah-rone'], *m.* 1. Egg-shell of a fowl or bird. 2. *(Arch.)* Arch or vault which contains the fourth part of a sphere; calotte. 3. Niche where the sacrament is placed for adoration in Roman Catholic churches.

cascarrabias [cas-car-rah'-be-as], *com.* A testy, irritable person.

cascarrabieta [cas-car-rah-be-ay'-tah], *a. V.* CASCAR-RABIAS.

cacarrabio, ia [cas-car-rah'-be-o, ah], *a.* Grumbling, testy, irritable.

cascarria [cas-car'-ree-ah], *f. (Cono Sur)* filth, muck; sheep droppings (ovejas).

cascarriento [cas-car-re-ayn'-to], *a. (Cono Sur)* filthy, mucky.

cascarrón, na [cas-car-rone', nah], *a. (Coll.)* Rough, harsh, rude. **Vino cascarrón,** wine of a rough flavor. **Voz cascarrona,** harsh, unpleasant tone of voice.

cascarudo, da [cas-ca-roo'-do, dah], *a.* Hully, having a thick rind or shell.

cascaruleta [cas-ca-roo-lay'-tah], *f. (Coll.)* Noise made by the teeth in consequence of patting under the chin.

casco [cahs'-co], *m.* 1. Skull, cranium, the bone which incloses the brain. 2. Potsherd, fragments of an earthen vessel. 3. Quarter of an orange, lemon, or pomegranate. 4. Coat or tegument of an onion. 5. Helmet, casque, or head-piece of ancient armor. 6. *(Prov.)* Cask, pipe, vat, or other wooden vessel in which wine is preserved. 7. **Casco de un navío,** *(Naut.)* Hull or hulk, of a ship. 8. Crown of a hat. 9. Printer's inking-ball. 10. Sheep-skin stripped of the wool. 11. Hoof of a horse. 12. **Casco** or **tapa de un barril,** the head of a cask. 13. **Casco de una silla de montar,** the tree of a saddle. **Cascos,** heads of sheep or bullocks without the tongues and brains. **Tener los cascos a la jineta,** *(Met.)* to be on the high horse. **Tener malos cascos,** *(Met.)* to be crazy or hare-brained. **Romperse los cascos,** to rack one's brain. **Ligero de cascos,** scatterbrained, frivolous. 14. Inner part, central area (de ciudad); **Casco comercial,** business quarter. **El casco antiguo de la ciudad,** the old part of the city. 15. *(LAm.)* Empty building.

cascolote [cas-co-lo'-tay], *m. (Mex.)* Thick bark of oaks, etc.; a fragment of thick bark.

cascorros [cas-cor'-ros], *m. & pl. (Mex.)* Shoes.

cascorvo, va [cas-cor'-vo, vah], *a. (Mex.)* Bowlegged.

cascote [cas-co'-tay], *m.* Rubbish, rubble, ruins of buildings, fragments of matter used in building.

cascotería [cas-co-tay-ree'-ah], *f.* Wall or work made of rubbish.

cascudo, da [cas-coo'-do, dah], *a.* Large-hoofed (animales).

cascundear [ ], *va. (CAm.)* To beat, to thrash.

caseación [cah-say-ah-the-on'], *f.* Coagulation of milk to form cheese.

caseína [cah-say-ee'-nah], *f.* Casein, the albuminous proximate principle of milk.

cáseo [cah'-say-o], 1. *a.* Cheesy. 2. *m.* Curd.

caseoso, sa [cah-say-o'-so, sah], *a.* Caseous, cheesy.

casera [cah-say'-rah], *f. (Prov.)* House-keeper, a woman servant that has the care of a single man. V. CASERO.

caseramente [cah-say-rah-men'-tay], *adv.* Homely, in a plain manner.

casería [cah-say-ree'-ah], *f.* 1. Isolated farm house. 2. Economical household management. 3. *(Sp. Amer.)* Clientele, customers.

caserío [cah-say-ree'-o], *m.* 1. A series of houses; village or very small town. 2. Country house, farmhouse.

caserna [cah-serr'-nah], *f. (Mil.)* Casern, a bomb-proof vault below a rampart; barracks.

casero, ra [cah-say'-ro, rah], *m. & f.* Landlord or steward of a house.

casero, ra [cah-say'-ro, rah], *a.* 1. Domestic, homely, in a family way. 2. Home-bred. **Familia,** house-keeping. **Baile casero,** family-dance. **Mujer casera,** A good housewife. **Remedio casero,** domestic medicine. **Pan casero,** household bread. 3. *(LAm.)* Customer, client.

caserón [cah-say-rone'], *m. aug.* 1. A large house. 2. A large house, ill-proportioned and without order.

caseta [cah-say'-tah], *f. dim.* Small house, hut, cottage, stall, booth; pavillion; changing-room (de piscina); bathing hut (de playa). **Caseta de perro,** kennel, doghouse. **Caseta del timón,** *(Naut.)* Wheelhouse.

casetera [cah-say-tay'-rah], *f. (LAm.)* Cassette deck.

caset(t)e [cah-say'-tay], 1. *m.* Cassette. 2. *f.* Cassette-player.

cash [cash], *m. pl.* Cash-and-carry store.

casi [cah'-se], *adv.* Almost, nearly, somewhat, more or less; just. **Casi casi,** very nearly. **Está casi acabado,** it's almost finished. **Casi nada,** next to nothing. **Casi nunca,** almost never.

casia [cah'-se-ah], *f. (Bot.)* Bastard cinnamon, cassia.

casica, illa, ita [cah-see'-cah, eel'-lyah, ee'-tah], *f. dim.* Small house, cabin.

casilla [cah-seel'-lyah], *f.* 1. Ticket office. 2. Booth, cockpit, cubbyhole. **Casilla de correos** or **Casilla postal,** post-office box. 3. *(Aut. Ferro.)* Cab. 4. *(And.)* Laboratory.

casillas [cah-seel'-lyas], *f.pl.* 1. Pigeon-holes: ruled columns in accounts, books or papers. 2. Points or houses of a backgammon table. 3. Square or checkers of a chess or draftboard. **Sacarle a uno de sus casillas,** *(Met.)* to molest, tease, or harass. **Salir de sus casillas,** to deviate from one's accustomed mode, especially through anger.

casillero [cah-seel-lyay'-ro], *m.* A desk fitted with pigeon-holes. -*pl.* V. CASILLAS.

casillo [cah-seel'-lyo], *m.* 1. *(dim.)* Trifling or slight cause. 2. A momentous affair, matter of consequence.

casimba [cah-seem-bah], *f. (LAm.)* V. CACIMBA.

casimbas [cah-seem'-bas], *f. pl. (Naut.)* Buckets for baling the water made by a ship, which the pumps are unable to discharge.

casimiro [cah-se-mee'-ro], *m.* Cashmere, kerseymere. **Casimir doble,** double-twilled kerseymere. **Casimir sencillo,** single-twilled kerseymere.

casimiro [cah-see-me'-ro], *a. (LAm.)* Cross-eyed.

casimodo [cah-se-mo'-do], *m.* V. CUASIMODO.

casinista [cah-see-nes'-tah], *m.* Clubman, member of a casino.

casino [cah-see'-no], *m.* 1. Casino, a room or building used as a public resort, for dancing, social, or club meetings, etc. 2. A club.

Casiopea [cah-se-o-pay-ah], *f.* Cassiopeia, the name of a northern constellation.

casís [cah-sees'], *f. (Bot.)* The blackcurrant.-*m. (Zool.)* A mollusk of the Mediterranean and the Indian Ocean.

casita [cah-see'-tah], *f.* Small house; cottage (de campo).

casiterita [cah-se-tay-ree'-tah], *f.* Cassiterite, oxide of tin; its chief ore.

caso [cah'-so], *m.* 1. Event, case, occurrence. 2. Case, contingency, hap, casualty, unexpected accident. 3. Occasion, opportunity. 4. Case stated to lawyers, physicians, etc. 5. *(Gram.)* Case. **Caso de conciencia,** case of conscience. 6. Peculiar figure of written characters. **En ese caso,** in that case. **En todo caso,** in any case. **Estar o no estar en el caso,** to comprehend or not comprehend something. **Hacer caso de una persona,** to esteem or respect a person. **Hacer caso de una cosa,** to take notice. **Ser o no ser al caso,** to be or not to be to the purpose. **Vamos al caso,** let us come to the point. **No estoy en el caso,** I do not understand the matter. **Dado el caso** or **demos el caso,** supposing that. **Caso negado,** proposition admitted only to be refuted. **Caso de que venga,** in case he should come. **En el mejor de los casos,** at best. **En último caso,** as a last resort. **Ponte en mi caso,** put yourself in my position. **Venir al caso,** to be relevant. **Verse en el caso de,** to be compelled to. **Maldito el caso que me hace,** a fat lot of notice he takes of me. **Hacer caso omiso de,** to ignore.

casona [cah-so'-nah], *f.* Large house.

casoar [cah-so-ar'], **casobar** [cah-so-bar'], *m.* The cassowary.

casorio [cah-so'-re-o], *m.* 1. *(Coll.)* Inconsiderate marriage. 2. A wedding.

caspa [cahs'-path], *f.* Dandruff, scurf.

Caspio, ia [cahs'-pe-o, ah], *a.* Caspian.

¡cáspita! [cahs'-pe-tah], *int.* Wonderful!

caspitoso [cas-pe-to'-so], *a.* 1. Full of dandruff, scurfy. 2. *(fig.)* Shoddy, tawdry.

casposo, sa [cas-po'-so, sah], *a.* Full of dandruff, lentiginous.

casquería [cas-kay-ree'-ah], *f.* Tripe and offal shop.

casquero, ra [cas-kay'-ro], *m. & f.* Seller of tripe and offal.

casquetazo [cas-kay-tah'-tho], *m.* Blow given with the head.

casquete [cas-kay'-tay], *m.* 1. Helmet, casque; skull-cap, cap. **Casquete de hielo,** icecap. **Casquete polar,** polar cap. 2. Scull, wig, scratch. 3. Helmet shell. 4. Cataplasm to take the scurf off the heads of children. 5. **Echar un casquete,** to have a screw.

casquiblando, da [cas-ke-blahn'-do, dah], *a.* Soft-hoofed (caballos).

casquiderramado, da [cas-ke-der-rah-mah'-do, dah], *a.* Wide-hoofed (caballos).

casquijo [cas-kee'-ho], *m.* Gravel; ballast material.

casquilla [cas-keel'-lyah], *f.* Cell of the queen bee.

casquillo [cas-keel'-lyo], *m.* 1. *(dim.)* Small steel helm. 2. Tip, cap, ferule, socket. 3. An iron arrow-head.

casquilucio, cia [cas-ke-loo'-the-o, ah], *a.* Gay, frolicsome.

casquimuleño, ña [cas-ke-moo-lay'-nyo, nyah], *a.* Narrow-hoofed like mules (caballos).

casquinona [cas-ke-no'-nah], *f. (And.)* Beer bottle; beer (cerveza).

casquivano, na [cas-ke-vah'-no, nah], *a.* Impudent, inconsiderate, acting with levity; foolishly conceited.

cassette [cah-sayt'], V. CASET(T)E.

casta [cahs'-tah], *f.* 1. Caste, race, generation, lineage, particular breed, clan; offspring, kindred. 2. Kind or quality of a thing. **Hacer casta,** to get a particular breed of horses or other animals. **De casta,** of quality. **Carecer de casta,** to lack breeding.

castalia [cas-tah'-le-ah], *f.* Castalia, a fountain of Mount Parnassus, and the nymph whose name it received.

castamente [cas-tah-men'-tay], *adv.* Chastely, purely.

castaña [cas-tah'-nyah], *f.* 1. (*Bot.*) Chestnut. 2. Bottle, jug, or jar, in the shape of a chestnut. 3. Club of hair; chignon. 4. An abandoned mine. **Castaña pilonga** or **apilada,** dried chestnut. **Sacar las castañas del fuego,** to pull somebody's chestnuts out of the fire for him. 5. **Coger una castaña,** to get drunk. 6. Bash, bow (golpe).

castañal, castañar [cas-ta-nyahl', cas-ta-nyar'], *m.* Grove or plantation of chestnut-trees.

castañazo [cas-ta-nyah'-tho], *m.* 1. Blow from a chestnut. 2. (*Cono Sur*) punch, thump.

castañedo [cas-ta-nyay'-do], *m.* (*Prov.*) Chestnut-grove or plantation.

castañera [cas-ta-nyay'-rah], *f.* (*Prov.*) Country abounding with chestnut-trees.

castañero, ra [cas-ta-nyay'-ro, rah], *m. & f.* Dealer in chestnuts.

castañeta [cas-ta-nyay'-tah], *f.* 1. Snapping of the fingers 2. Castanet. V. CASTAÑUELA.

castañetazo [cas-ta-nyay-tah'-tho], *m.* 1. Blow with a castanet. 2. Sound of a chestnut bursting in the fire. 3. Cracking of the joints.

castañeteado [cas-ta-nyay-tay-ah-do], *m.* Sound of castanets. -*pp.* of CASTAÑETEAR.

castañetear [cas-ta-nyay-tay-ar'], *vn.* 1. To rattle the castanets. 2. To crackle, to clack (rodillas). 3. To cry (perdices). -*va.* 1. To snap (dedos). 2. To play on the castanets.

castañeteo [cas-tah-nyay-tay'-o], *m.* 1. Snap(ping); click(ing); clatter(ing); chatter(ing); rattling; crack(ing) (huesos). 2. (*Mus.*) Sound of the castanets.

castaño [cas-tah'-nyo], *m.* (*Bot.*) Common chestnut-tree. **Castaño de Indias,** horse-chestnut-tree. **Esto pasa de castaño oscuro,** this is really too much, this is beyond a joke.

castaño, ña [cas-tah'-nyo, nyah], *a.* Hazel.

castañuela [cas-ta-nyoo-ay'-lah], *f.* Castanet. **Estar como unas castañuelas,** to be very gay.

castañuelo, la [cas-ta-nyoo-ay'-lo, lah] *a. dim.* Of a light chestnut color (caballos).

castellanía [cas-tel-lyah-nee'-ah], *f.* Castellany, district belonging to a castle. **castellanizar** [cas-tel-lyah-nethar'], *ra.* To adapt a foreign word for use in Spanish: to castilianize.

castellano [cas-teil-lyah'-no], *m.* 1. Ancient Spanish coin. 2. Fiftieth part of a mark of gold. 3. Spanish language. 4. (*Obs.*) Castellan, the governor or warden of a castle.

castellano, na [cas-tel-lyah'-no, nah], *a.* 1. Castilian. 2. Applied to a mule got by a jackass and a mare. 3. (*Prov.*) Applied to the foremost mule in a cart or wagon.

castellar [cas-tel'-lyar'], *m.* 1. (*Obs.*) Place fortified with a castle. 2. (*Bot.*) St. John's wort, tutsan, park-leaves.

casticidad [cas-te-the-dahd'], *f.* 1. (*Ling.*) Purity, correctness. 2. Traditional character; thoroughbred charter, true-born nature; authenticity, genuineness.

casticismo [cas-te-thees'-mo], *m.* 1. (*Ling.*) Purity, correctness. 2. Love of tradition, traditionalism.

casticista [cas-te-thes,tah], *m. & f.* Purist.

castidad [cas-te-dahd'], *f.* Chastity, purity, honor.

castigación [cas-te-gah-the-on'], *f.* 1. Castigation. 2. Correction of errors of the press.

castigadera [cas-te-gah-day'-rah], *f.* 1. Rope with which a bell is tied to a mule, or other beast of burden. 2. Small cord with which the ring of a stirrup is tied to the girth.

castigador, ra [cas-te-gah-dor', rah], *m. & f.* 1. A punisher or chastiser, castigator. 2. (*Obs.*) One that reproaches. 3. Seducer, libertine.

castigar [Cas-te-gar'], *va.* 1. To chastise, to punish, to castigate. 2. To afflict to put to pain, to grieve. **Castigar mucho a un caballo,** to ride a horse hard. 3. To advise, to inform. 4. (*Met.*) To correct proof-sheets or writings. 5. To reduce (gastos). 6. (*Mex.*) (*Mech.*) To tighten up. -*vr.* To mend.

castigo [cas-tee'-go], *m.* 1. Chastisement, punishment, correction, penalty. 2. Censure, animadversion, reproach. 3. Example, instruction. 4. Alteration or correction made in a work. **Castigo de Dios,** God's judgment. **Castigo de la miseria,** miser, skinflint.

Castilla [cas-teel'-lyah], *f.* Castile. **Castilla la Nueva,** New Castile. **Castilla la Vieja,** Old Castile.

castillejo [cas-teel'-lay'-ho], *m.* 1. (*dim.*) A small castle. 2. Go-cart. 3. (*Arquit.*) Scaffolding.

castillería [cas-teel-lyay-ree'-ah], *f.* 1. Toll paid on passing through a district which belongs to a castle. 2. Government of a castle.

castillo [cas-teel'-lyo], *m.* 1. Castle, fort. 2. The mounting of a velvetloom. 3. Cell of the queen-bee. 4. **Castillo de proa,** (*Naut.*) Forecastle. **Hacer castillos en el aire,** (*Met.*) to build castles in the air or in Spain. **Castillo de fuego,** firework set piece. **Castillo de naipes,** house of cards.

castilluelo [cas-teel-lyoo-ay'-lo], *m. dim.* Castlet, a small castle.

castizo, za [cas-tee'-tho, thah], *a.* 1. Of a noble descent, of a good breed, pure-blooded. **Caballo castizo,** blood-horse. **Estilo castizo,** a chaste, pure style.

casto, ta [cahs'-to, tah], *a.* 1. Pure, chaste, honest, modest, continent, cold, clean. 2. Perfect. 3. Pure (estilo).

castor [cas-tor'], *m.* 1. Castor, a beaver, an amphibious quadruped. Castor. 2. Beaver, a heavy cloth, of smooth surface, made for overcoats. 3. (*Mex.*) Fine red baize. 2. The two brightest stars in the constellation Gemini.

castorcillo [cas-tor-theel'-lyo], *m.* Kind of rough serge like cloth.

castoreño [cas-to-ray'-nyo], *m.* Beaver (hat); picador's hat.

castra [cahs'-trah], *f.* Act of pruning trees or plants.

castración [cas-trah-the-on'], *f.* 1. Castration, gelding, spaying. 2. (*Agri.*) Extraction of honeycombs.

castradera [cas-trah-day'-rah], *f.* Iron instrument with which honey is taken from a hive.

castrado [cas-trah'-do], *m.* A eunuch. -*a.* Castrated.

castrador [cas-trah-dor'], *m.* One that gelds or castrates.

castradura [cas-trah-doo'-rah], *f.* 1. Castration. 2. Scar which remains after an animal has been castrated.

castrametación [cas-trah-may-tah-the-on'], *f.* Castrametation, encamping.

castrapuercas [cas-trah-poo-err'-cas], *m.* Sow-gelder's whistle.

castrar [cas-trar'], *va.* 1. To geld, to castrate, to spay. 2. To cut away the proud flesh about a wound. 3. To prune trees or plants. 4. **Castrar las colmenas,** to cut the honey-combs from bee-hives.

castrazón [cas-trah-thone'], *f.* 1. Act of cutting honey-combs out of hives. 2. Castrating or gelding season.

castrense [cas-tren'-say], *a.* Belonging to the military profession. **Las glorias castrenses,** military glories.

castro [cahs'-tro], *m.* 1. Place where an army is encamped. 2. (*Prov.*) Ruins of ancient fortified places. 3. Game played by boys. 4. Act of taking honey-combs out of hives.

castrón [cas-trone'], *m.* Castrated goat; a gelded animal.

casual [cah-soo-ahl'], *a.* Casual, accidental, contingent, fortuitous, occasional, circumstantial. **Desinencia casual,** case ending.

casualidad [cah-soo-ah-le-dahd'], *f.* Casualty, hazard, contingency, occasion, coincidence, accident; **por casualidad,** by chance. **Me encontraba allí por casualidad,** I happened to be there. **Un día entró por casualidad,** one day he dropped in. **Dio la casualidad que,** it happened that.

casualmente [cah-soo-al-men'-tay], *adv.* Casually, accidentally, contingently, haply. **Le vi ayer casualmente,** I happened to see him yesterday.

casuca [cah-soo'-chah], *f.* Hovel, shack; slum.

casucha [cah-soo'-chah], *f.* (*Coll.*) Miserable hut or cottage, crib.

casucho [cah-soo'-cho], *m.* V. CASUCHA.

casuel [cah-soo-el'], *m.* *(Orn.)* Cassowary, emeu.

casuísta [cah-soo-ees'-tah], *m.* Casuist.

casuístico, ca [cah-soo-ees'-te-co, cah], *a.* Casuistical.

casulla [cah-sool'-lyah], *f.* Chasuble, vestment worn by priests.

casullero [cah-sool-lyay'-ro], *m.* One who makes chasubles and other vestments for priests.

casus belli [cah'-soos, bayl'-lee], *(Lat.)* Cause for war (lenguaje diplomático).

cata [cat'-tah], *f.* 1. Act of trying a thing by the taste. **Dar a cata,** to give upon trial. 2. Plummet for measuring heights. 3. *(LAm.)* *(Min.)* Trial excavation, test bore. 4. *(And. Cono Sur, Mex.)* Parrot.

cata [cah'-tah], *adv.* *(Coll.)* Mark, beware. *(Imp.* of CATAR.)

catabolismo [cah-tah-bo-lees'mo], *m.* *(Biol.)* Catabolism.

catabre [cah-tah'-bray], *m.* 1. *(Naut.)* Sheep-shank. 2. *(And. Carib.)* Gourd; basket.

catacaldos [cah-tah-cahl-dos], *m.* 1. Taster of wine, liquors, soup, etc. 2. Rolling stone; quitter; person who starts things but gives up easily (persona inconstante).

cataclismo [cah-tah-clees'-mo], *m.* Cataclysm, deluge, inundation: a convulsion of nature.

catacumbas [cah-tah-coom'-bas], *f. pl.* Catacombs.

catacústica [cah-tah-coos'-te-cah], *f.* Catacoustics.

catadióptrico, ca [cah-tah-de-op'-tre-co-cah], *a.* Catadioptric, relating to light reflected and refracted.

catador, ra [cah-tah-dor'], *m. f.* Taster, blender, sampler.

catadura [cah-tah-doo'-rah], *f.* 1. Trying by the taste, tasting. 2. *(Coll.)* Gesture, face, countenance. 3. Mode of guarding or inspecting criminals.

catafalco [cah-tah-fahl'-co], *m.* A temporary cenotaph to celebrate funeral rites, catafalque.

catafotos [cah-tah-fo'-tos], *m. pl.* *(Aut.)* Cat's eyes.

catajarría [cah-tah-hahr-re'-ah], *f.* *(Carib.)* String, series.

catalán, na [cah-tah-lahn', lah'-nah], *a.* Catalonian.

catalejo [cah-tah-lay'-ho], *m.* Telescope,

cataléctico [cah-tah-layc'-te-co], *a.* *(Poet.)* Catalectic.

catalepsia [cah-tah-lep'-se-ah], *f.* Catalepsy, trance.

cataléptico, ca [ ], *a. m. & f.* Cataleptic.

catalicón [cah-tah-le-cone'], *m.* Catholicon, universal medicine.

catálisis [cah-tah'-le-sis], *f.* *(Chem.)* Catalysis.

catalizador [cah-tah-le-thah-dor'], *m.* *(Chem.)* Catalyst.

catalizar [cah-tah-le-thar'], *va.* To catalyse.

catalogación [cah-tah-lo-gah-the-one'], *f.* Cataloguing.

catalogar [cah-tah-lo-gar'], *va.* To catalog, to list, to catalogue.

catálogo [cah-tah'-lo-go], *m.* Catalog, catalogue, roll, file, matricula.

catalpa [cah-tahl'-pah], *f.* The catalpa, a genus of American and East Indian flowering trees, bearing long, cylindrical pods.

catalufa [cah-tah-loo'-fah], *f.* Kind of floor carpet.

catamarán [cah-tah-mah-rahn'], *m.* Catamaran.

catamiento [cah-tah-me-en'-to], *m.* Observation, inspection.

catamito [cah-tah-mee'-to], *m.* Catamite. V. SODOMITA.

catán [cah-tahn'], *m.* Indian sabre or cutlass.

catanance, catananque [ch-tah-nahn'-thay, kay], *f.* *(Bot.)* Lion's-foot. **Catanance azul,** blue catananche.

cataplasma [cah-tah-plahs'-mah], *f.* Poultice. **Cataplasma de mostaza,** mustard plaster.

cataplines [cah-tah-ple-nays], *m. pl.* Balls.

cataplum [cah-tah-ploom'], *interj.* Bang!, crash!

catapucia menor [cah-tah-poo'-the-ah may-nor'], *f.* *(Bot.)* Lesser or caper spurge. **Catapucia mayor,** castor-oil plant.

catapulta [cah-tah-pool'-tah], *f.* Catapult, an ancient war machine for throwing stones.

catapultar [cah-tah-pool-tar'], *va.* To catapult.

catapún [cah-tah-poon'], *a.* **Una cosa del año catapún,** an antiquated thing. **Películas del año catapún.** very old films.

catar [cah-tar'], *va.* 1. To taste, to try by the taste. 2. To view, to inspect, to inquire, to investigate, to examine. 3. To judge,

to form an opinion. 4. To esteem, to respect. 5. To bear in mind. 6. To cut the combs out of bee-hives; **¡cátale!,** just look at him!

catarata [cah-ta-rah'-tah], *f.* 1. Cataract, opacity of the crystalline lens of the eye. 2. Cataract, waterfall, cascade. **Extraer las cataratas,** to remove or extract cataracts. **Tener cataratas,** *(Met.)* not to understand clearly. **Cataratas del Niágara,** Niagara falls.

catarral [cah-tar-rahl'], *a.* Catarrhal.

catarribera [cah-tar-re-bay'-rah], *m.* 1. Man-servant appointed to follow the hawk on horseback, and bring it down with its prey. 2. *(Joc.)* Lawyer appointed to examine into the proceedings of magistrates charged with the administration of justice.

catarriento, ta [cah-tar-re-en'-to, tah], *a.* V. CATARROSO.

catarro [cah-tar'-ro], *m.* Catarrh. **Catarro epidémico,** influenza. **Catarro crónico del pecho,** chest trouble.

catarroso, sa [cah-tar-ro'-so, sah], *a.* 1. Catarrhal. 2. Subject to or troubled with a cold.

catarsis [cah-tar'-sees], *f.* Catharsis.

catártico, ca [cah-tar'-te-co, cah], *a.* Cathartic, purging.

catasalsas [cah-tah-sal'-sahs], *m.* V. CATACALDOS.

catastro [cah-tahs'-tro], *m.* 1. A tax-list of the real property in every district of a country. 2. The office of this tax-list.

catástrofe [cah-tahs'-tro-fay], *f.* 1. Catastrophe. 2. Catastrophe, dénouement.

catastrófico [cah-tas-tro'-fe-co], *a.* Catastrophic.

catastrofismo [cah-tas-tro-fes'-mo], *m.* Alarmism; doomwatching.

catastrofista [cah-tas-tro-fes'-tah], *m. & f.* Alarmist, doomwatcher.

catatán [cah-tah-tahn'], *m.* *(Chile)* Punishment.

catatar [cah-tah-tar'], *va.* *(And.)* To ill-treat.

catauro [cah-tah'-oo-ro], *m.* *(Carib.)* Basket.

cataviento [cah-tah-ve-en'-to], *m.* *(Naut.)* Dogvane. Weathercock.

catavino [cah-tah-vee'-no], *m.* 1. Small jug or cup used to taste wine. 2. *(Prov.)* Small hole at the top of large wine-vessels for tasting the wine. *-pl.* Tipplers who run from tavern to tavern to drink.

catavinos [cah-ta-vee'-nos], *m.* A winetaster, expert sampler. V. CATACALDOS.

cate [cah'-tay], *m.* 1. A weight, common in the Philippine Islands, equivalent to 1 lb. 6 oz. Spanish, or gm. 632.60. 2. Punch, bash (golpe). **Dar cate a uno,** to plough somebody. 3. *m.f.* Teacher.

catear [cah-tay-ar'], *va.* 1. To inquire after, to investigate, to discover. 2. *(Min.)* To prospect. 3. *(Univ.)* To plough, to fail (candidato). 3. *(Cono, Sur, Mex.)* To make test borings in, to explore. 4. *(Mex.)* To search, to make a search.

catecismo [cah-tay-thees'-mo], *m.* Catechism.

catecú [cah-tay-coo'], *m.* Catechu, an astringent extracted from East Indian plants, particularly from an acacia. V. CATO.

catecúmeno, na [cah-tay-coo'-may-no, nah] *m. & f.* Catechumen.

cátedra [cah'-tay-drah], *f.* 1. Seat or chair of a professor. 2. Professorship, office and functions of a professor or teacher; **Pedro regentó la cátedra tantos años,** Peter filled the professor's chair so many years. **Libertad de cátedra,** freedom to teach. **Explicar una cátedra,** to hold a chair. 3. See, the seat of pontifical or episcopal power. 4. Subject (asignatura). 5. Lecture room. 6. Group of students, class. 7. *(Carib.)* Wonder, marvel. **Es cátedra,** it's marvellous.

catedral [cah-tay-drahl'], *a. & f.* Cathedral.

catedralicio [cah-tray-lah-le'-the-o], *a.* Cathedral.

catedrático [cah-tay-drah'-te-co], *m.* 1. Professor in a university, or any other literary establishment. 2. Contribution formerly paid by the inferior clergy to bishops and prelates.

catedrilla [cah-tay-dreel'-lyah], *f.* 1. *(dim.)* Small or poor professor's chair. 2. In some universities, the less important professorship.

categoría [cah-tay-go-ree'-ah], *f.* 1. Predicament or category. 2. Character of a person. **Ser hombre de categoría,** to be a man of estimable qualities and talents; a man of rank. **De categoría,** important. **Hombre de cierta categoría,** he is a man of some standing. **De baja categoría,** of low quality.

categóricamente [cah-tay-co'-re-cah-men'-tay], *adv.* Categorically.

categórico, ca [cah-tay-go'-re-co, cah], *a.* Categorical, categoric.

catenaria [cah-tay-nah'-re-ah], *f.* (*Elec.*) (*Ferro.*) Overhead power cable.

catequesis [cah-tay-kay'-sis], *f.* A brief and simple explanation of a doctrine.

catequismo [cah-tay-kees'-mo], *m.* 1. Catechizing, instruction in religious doctrine. 2. (*Obs.*) *V.* CATECISMO.

catequista [cah-tay-kees'-tah], *m.* Catechizer.

catequístico, ca [cah-tay-kees'-te-co, cah], *a.* Catechetical, catechetic, catechistical.

catequizante [cah-tay-ke-thahn-tay], *pa.* Catechiser, catechist.

catequizar [cah-tay-ke-thar'], *va.* 1. To catechise, to instruct in the Christian faith. 2. (*Met.*) To persuade.

caterva [cah-terr'-vah], *f.* A great number, a swarm, a throng, a crowd; the vulgar.

catete [cah-tay'-tay], *m.* (*Chile Coll.*) The devil.

caéter [cah-tay'-ter], *m.* Catheter, a tube of metal, rubber, or woven material for surgical uses; as for drawing off urine, or for introducing air into the middle ear.

cateterismo [cah-tay-tay-rees'-mo], *m.* Catheterism, employment of the catheter.

cateterizar [cah-tay-tay-re-thar,], *va.* To catheterize, to use a catheter remedially.

cateto [cah-tay'-to], *m.* 1. (*Arch.*) Cathetus, perpendicular line which intersects the volute by passing through its centre. 2. *pl.* The sides which form the right angle of a right angled triangle. 3. Peasant, country bumpkin.

catimbao [cah-teem-bah'-o], *m.* 1. Clown. 2. (*Chile*) Someone ridiculously garbed. 3. (*Peru*) Short and stout person.

catinga [cah-teen'-gah], *f.* (*Sp. Amer.*) 1. Bad odor exuded by some plants and animals. 2. Name which sailors give to soldiers.

catingoso [cah-ten-go'-so], *a.* (*And. Cono Sur*), **catingudo** *a.* (*And. Cono Sur*) skinting, foul-smelling.

catisumba(da) [cah-te-soom'-bah, dah], *f.* (*CAm.*) Lot, great number. **Una catisumba de,** lots of.

catire [cah-tee'-ray], *m. & f.* (*Sp. Amer.*) Blond mulatto.

catita [cah-tee'-tah], *f.* (*Arg. Bol.*) Type of parrot.

catite [cah-tee'-tay], *m.* Loaf of the best refined sugar.

catitear [cah-te-tay-ar'], *vn.* (*Cono Sur*) to dodder, to shake (with old age).

cato [cah'-to], *m.* Japan earth, an extract obtained by the decoction of vegetable substance in water. *V.* CATECU.

catoche [cah-to'-chay], *m.* (*Mex.*) Bad humor.

catódico, ca [cah-to'-de-co, cah], *a.* (*Phy. & Chem.*) Cathodic.

cátodo [cah'-to-do], *m.* (*Phy. & Chem.*) Cathode.

católicamente [cah-to'-le-cah-men-tay], *adv.* In a catholic manner.

catolicidad [cah-to-le-the-dahd], *f.* Catholicity.

catolicismo [cah-to-le-thees'-mo], *m.* 1. Catholicism. 2. Catholicism, the orthodox faith of the Catholic church.

católico, ca [cah-to'-le-co, cah], *a.* 1. Catholic 2. General or universal. 3. True, infallible. **El rey católico,** his catholic majesty. **No estar muy católico,** not to be in good health, not to be very well.

católico [cah-to-le-co'], *m.* 1. Catholic, a Roman Catholic. 2. (*Chem.*) Chemical furnace.

catolicón [cah-to-le-cone'], *m.* Catholicon, a panacea.

catón [cah-tone'], *m.* 1. A very wise man or one who affects wisdom. 2. A reading-book for children. **Eso está en el catón,** that is absolutely elementary. 3. (*Met.*) A severe censor.

catoniano, na [cah-to-ne-ah'-no, nah], *a.* Catonian, relating to Cato.

catóptrica [cah-top'-tre-cah], *f.* Catoptrics, the science of reflected light.

catóptrico, ca [cah-top'-tre-co, cah], *a.* Catoptrical.

catorce [cah-tor'-thay], *a.* Fourteen.

catorcena [cah-tor-thay'-nah], *f.* The conjunction of fourteen units.

catorceno, na [cah-tor-thay'-no, nah], *a.* Fourteenth. *V.* PAÑO.

catorrazo [cah-tor-rah'-tho], *m.* (*Mex.*), **Catarro** *m.* (*Mex.*) Punch, blow.

catorzavo, va [cah-tor-thah'-vo, vah]. One of the fourteen parts of a unit, fourteenth.

catre [cah'-tray], *m.* 1. Small bedstead. **Catre de mar,** hammock or cot. **Catre de tijera,** camp bed. (*fig.*) **Cambiar el catre,** to change the subject. 2. **Catre de balsa,** *Cono Sur)* raft (barquito).

catrecillo [cah-tray-thel-lyo], *m.* Camp stool, folding seat.

catrera [cah-tray-rah], *f.* (*Cono Sur*) Bunk, bed.

catricofre [cah-tre-co'-fray], *m.* Press-bed which shuts up; a folding-bed, bed-lounge.

catrín [cah-treen'], *m.* (*CAm. Mex.*) Toff, dude.

caucarse [cah-oo-car'-say], *vr.* (*Cono Sur*) To grow old (persona); to go stale (comida).

caucáseo, ea [cah-oo-cah'-say-o, ah], **Caucásico, ca,** *a.* Caucasian.

Cáucaso [cah'-oo-cah-so], *m.* Caucasus.

cauce [cah'-oo-thay], *m.* 1. The bed of a river. 2. Trench. irrigation ditch, for conveying water to fields, gardens, etc.

caución [cah-oo-the-on'], *f.* 1. Security or pledge given for the performance of an agreement; gage, guarantee. 2. (*Law.*) Bailbond. **Caución juratoria,** oath taken by a person having no bail to return to prison. 3. Caution, warning, foresight, prevention.

caucionar [cah-oo-the-o-nar'], *va.* (*Law.*) To guard against an evil or loss; to bail, to prevent.

cauchal [cah-oo-chah'], *m.* Rubber plantation.

cauchar [cah-oo-char'], 1. *m.* (*And.*) Rubber plantation. 2. *vn.* (*And.*) To tap (trees for rubber).

cauchero, ra [cah-oo-chay'-ro, rah], *a.* Pertaining to rubber. -*m.* Rubber worker. -*f.* Rubber plant.

caucho [cah'-oo-cho], *m.* 1. Rubber. **Árbol del caucho,** rubber plant. **Caucho sintético,** synthetic rubber. **Caucho esponjoso,** foam rubber. 2. (*LAm.*) Raincoat, mac; (*And.*) Waterproof blanket.

cauchutado [cah-oo-choo-tah'-do], *a.* Rubberize.

caudal [cah-oo-dahl'], *m.* 1. Property, fortune, wealth, means, fund: especially in money. 2. Capital or principal sum, stock. 3. (*Met.*) Plenty, abundance. **Hacer caudal de alguna cosa,** to hold a thing in high esteem.

caudal [cah-oo-dahl'], *a.* (*Zool.*) Caudal, relating to the tail. **Águila caudal,** the red-tailed eagle.

caudalejo [cah-oo-dah-lay-ho], *m. dim.* Middling fortune.

caudaloso, sa [cah-oo-dah-lo'-so, sah], *a.* 1. Carrying much water (ríos). 2. Rich, wealthy (personas).

caudatario [cah-oo-dah-tah'-re-o], *m.* Clergyman who carries the train of an officiating bishop's robe.

caudato, ta [cah-oo-dah'-to, tah], *a.* 1. Having a tail (cometa). 2. Bearded, hairy.

caudatrémula [cah-oo-dah-tray'-moo-lah], *f.* (*Orn.*) The wagtail.

caudillaje [cah-oo-de-lyah'-hay], *m.* 1. Leadership. **Bajo el caudillaje de,** under the leadership of. 2. (*LAm.*) Tyranny, rule by political bosses.

caudillo [cah-oo-deel'-ly], *m.* 1. Commander of an armed troop. 2. Chief, leader, or director of a company.

caudón [cah-oo-done'], *m.* A bird of prey, a kind of falcon. *V.* PEGA REBORDA.

caula [cah'-oo-lah], *f.* (*CAm. Cono Sur*) Plot, intrigue.

caulícolo [cah-oo-lee'-co-lo], *m.* (*Arch.*) Ornament of the capital of columns.

cauri [cah'-oo-re], *m.* Cowrie.

causa [cah'-oo-sah], *f.* 1. Cause; occasion. 2. Consideration, motive of action, motive or reason of doing a thing. 3. Causality. 4. Cause, side, or party, affair in which one takes an interest. 5. Lawsuit, trial 6. Criminal cause or information. **Causa pública,** public good. **A causa de,** considering, on account of. **Veamos cuál es la causa de esto,** let us see what is the reason for this. **Causa primera,** first cause. **Por mi causa,** for my sake. **Fuera de causa,** irrelevant.

causa [cah'-oo-sah], *f. (Cono Sur)* snack, light meal; picnic lunch. 2. *(And.)* Potato salad.

causador, ra [cah-oo-sah-dor', rah], *m. & f.* Occasioner, causer.

causal [cah-oo-sahl'], *a.* Causal, ground on which something is done.

causalidad [cah-oo-sah-le-dahd'], *f.* Causality.

causante [cah-oo-sha'-ta,], *pa. & m.* Occasioner, causer. 2. *(Law.)* The person from whom a right is derived; constituent, principal. *-a.* Causing, originating. **El coche causante del accidente,** the car which caused the accident.

causar [cah-oo-sar'], *va.* 1. To cause, to produce, to generate, to create, to gender, to make. 2. To sue, to enter an action. 3. To occasion, to originate. **Causar risa a uno,** to make somebody laugh.

causear [cah-oo-s-ay-ar'], *vn. (Cono Sur)* to have a snack; to have a picnic.

causídico [cah-oo-see-de-co], *m.* Advocate, counsellor.

causídico, ca [cah-oo-see'-de-co, cah], *a. (Law.)* Relative to causes or litigation.

castor [cas-tor'], *m.* 1. Castor, a beaver, an amphibious quadruped.

cáustico, ca [cah'-oos-te-co, cah], *a.* 1. Caustic, caustical. 2. Applied to a ray of reflected light which unites with others in one point.

cautamente [cah-oo-tah-men'-tay], *adv.* Cautiously, warily, carefully.

cautchuc [cah-oot-chooc'], **Cauchuco** [cah-oo-choo'-co], *m.* Caoutchouc, the tree and the gum. **Cautchuc vulcanizado,** vulcanized rubber.

cautela [cah-oo-tay'-lah], *f.* 1. Caution, prudence, foresight, prevention, precaution and reserve. 2. Heed, heedfulness, guard. 3. Artfulness, craft, cunning. **Tener cautela de,** to take the precaution of.

cautelar [cah-oo-tay-lar'], *va.* To take the necessary precaution, to proceed with prudence. *-vr.* To be on one's guard.

cautelosamente [cah-oo-tay-lo-sah-men'-tay], *adv.* Cautiously, warily, guardedly.

cauteloso, sa [cah-oo-tay-lo'-so, sah], *a.* Cautious, heedful, cunning, crafty.

cauterio [cah-oo-tay'-ree-o], *m.* 1. *(Med.)* Cautery. **Cauterio actual,** actual cautery, burning with hot iron. **Cauterio potencial,** potential cautery procured by chemicals. 2. *(fig.)* Remedy.

cauterización [cah-oo-tay-re-thah-the-on'], *f.* Cauterization, cauterizing.

cauterizador [cah-oo-tay-re-thah-dor'], *m.* He who cauterizes.

cauterizar [cah-oo-tay-re-thar'], *va.* 1. To cauterize. 2. To correct or reproach with severity.

cautín [cah-oo-teen'], *m.* A soldering-iron.

cautivante [cah-oo-te-vahn'-tay], *a.* Captivating.

cautivar [cah-oo-te-var'], *va.* 1. To make prisoners of war. 2. To imprison. 3. *(Met.)* To captivate, to charm, to subdue.

cautiverio, *m.* **cautividad,** *f.* [cah-oo-te-vay'-re-o, cah-oo-te-ve-dahd']. 1. Captivity. 2. Confinement.

cautivo, va [cah-oo-tee'-vo, vah], *m. &. f.* Captive among infidels. 2. Captive, one charmed by beauty.

cauto, ta [cah'-oo-to, tah], *a.* Cautious, wary.

cava [cah'-vah], *f.* 1. Digging and earthing of vines. 2. Cellar where wine and water are kept. 3. Ditch. 4. *(Prov.)* Subterraneous vault. 5. *(Carib.)* Closed truck, lorry. *-m.* Sparkling wine.

cavacote [cah-vah-co'-tay], *m.* Mound of earth made with the hoe to serve as a mark or temporary boundary.

cavadiza [cah-vah-dee'-thah], *a.* Dug out of a pit (arena).

cavado, da [cah-vah'-do, dah], *a.* Hollow, concave. *-pp.* of CAVAR.

cavador [cah-vah-dor'], *m.* 1. Digger, excavator. **Cavador de greda,** chalk-cutter. **Cavador de oro,** gold digger. 2. Grave-digger.

cavadura [cah-vah-doo'-rah], *f.* Digging, excavation.

cavallillo [cah-val-lyeel'-lyo], *m.* Water-furrow between ridges.

caván [cah-vahn'], *m.* A measure used in the Philippine Islands equivalent to seventy-five liters.

cavar [cah-var'], *va.* 1. To dig, to excavate. 2. To paw (caballos). *-vn.* 1. To penetrate far into a thing. 2. To penetrate, to think intensely or profoundly.

cavatina [cah-vah-tee'-nah], *f.* Cavatina, a melody of a more simple form than the aria; a song without a second part.

cavazón [cah-vah-thone'], *f.* Digging, excavation.

caverna [cah-verr'-nah], *f.* 1. Cavern, cave. 2. Hollow inside or depth of wounds; cavity resulting from tuberculous ulceration or from an abscess.

cavernícola [cah-vayr-ne'-co-lah], 1. *a.* Cave dwelling. **Hombre cavernícola,** caveman. 2. Reactionary. *-m. & f.* Cave dweller, caveman, troglodyte. 3. Reactionary, backwoodsman.

cavernilla [cah-ver-neel'-lyah], *f. dim.* small cavern.

cavernoso, sa [cah-ver-no'-so, sah], *a.* 1. Cavernous, caverned. **Cuerpo cavernoso,** *(Anat.)* Corpus cavernosum. 2. Resounding, deep, hollow (sonido).

caveto [cah-vay'-to], *m. (Arch.)* Flute, fluting, groove, hollow moulding.

caví [cah-vee'], *m.* A Peruvian root, called *oca.*

cavia [cah'-ve-ah], *f.* Circular excavation at the foot of a tree to collect water.

cavial, or **caviar** [cah-ve-ahl', cah-ve-ar'], *m.* Caviar, the roe of the sturgeon pressed and salted.

cavidad [cah-ve-dahd'], *f.* Cavity, excavation, space.

cavidos [cah-vee'-dos], *m.* Portuguese measure of length.

cavilación [cah-ve-lah-the-on'], *f.* 1. Cavilling, deep thought, rumination. 2. Suspicion, apprehension.

cavilar [cah-ve-lar'], *va.* 1. To cavil, find fault. 2. To find subtle excuses to escape from a difficulty.

cavilosear [ ], *vn. (Carib.)* To harbor illusions; *(Carib.)* To vacillate, to hesitate; *(CAm.)* To gossip.

cavilosamente [cah-ve-lo-sah-me'-tay], *adv.* Cavillously.

cavilosidad [cah-ve-lo-se-dahd'], *f.* Captiousness; cavillingness.

caviloso, sa [cah-ve-lo'-so, sah], *a.* 1. Captious, cavillous. 2. *(CAm.)* Gossipy, backbiting. 3. *(And.)* Quarrelsome, touchy; fussy (agresivo).

cavilla [cah-veel'-lyah], *f.* 1. *(Bot.)* Sea-holly. 2. *(Naut.)* Treenail. *V.* CABILLA.

cavillador [cah-veel-lyah-dor'], *m. (Naut.)* Treenail maker.

cavillar [cah-veel-lyar'], *va. (Naut.)* To use treenails. **Cavillar un bajel,** to drive treenails into a ship.

cavo, va [cah'-vo, vah], *a.* 1. Concave. 2. Having only twenty-nine days (meses).

cayadilla [cah-yah-deel'-lyah], *f. dim.* Small shepherd's hook.

cayado [cah-yah'-do], *m.* 1. Shepherd's hook, crook. 2. Crozier of a bishop. 3. Walking-staff.

cayán [cah-yahn'], *m.* 1. *V.* TAPANCO. 2. A covering of matting put on certain Philippine boats to protect the person within.

cayanto [cah-yahn'-to], *m.* A kind of stuff.

cayelac [cah-yay-lahc'], *m.* Sweet-scented wood of Siam.

cayeput [cah-yay-poot'], *m.* Cajeput-oil.

cayo [cah'-yoh], *m.* A rock, shoal or islet in the sea; key.

cayote [cah-yo'-tay], *m. (Bot.) V.* CIDRACAYOTE.

cayou [cah-yo'-oo], *m.* Cashew-nut.

cayubro [cah-yoo'-bro], *a. (And.)* Reddish-blonde, red-haired.

cayuca [cah-yoo'-cah], *f. (Carib.)* Head, bean.

cayuco [cah-yoo'-co], *m.* (*Naut.*) Small fishing-boat used in Venezuela.

caz [cath], *m.* Canal, trench, or ditch, near rivers for irrigation; mill-race, conduit.

caza [cah'-thah], *f.* 1. Chase, hunting, fowling, field-sports. 2. Game. 3. (*Naut.*) Chase, pursuit of a vessel at sea. 4. Thin linen resembling gauze. **Caza mayor,** hunting wild-boars, stags, wolves, etc. **Caza menor,** shooting or fowling; chasing hares, rabbits partridges, etc. **Andar a caza,** to hunt. **Andar a caza de alguna cosa,** (*Met.*) to go in pursuit of a thing. **Andar a caza de gangas,** to spend one's time uselessly. **Dar caza,** (*Naut.*) to give chase to a vessel. **Espantar la caza,** (*Met.*) to injure one's claim by an untimely application. **Caballo de caza,** hunter, hunting horse. **Trompa de caza,** hunting horn. **Partida de caza,** hunting party. **Caza del tesoro,** treasure hunt. **Caza de patos,** duck shooting.

caza [cah'-thah], *m.* (*Aer.*) Fighter plane, pursuit plane.

cazabe [cah-thah'-bay], *m.* (*Sp. Am.*). Cassava bread.

caza-bombardeo [cah-tha bom-bahr-day'-o], *m.* Fighter-bomber.

cazaclavos [cah-thah-clah'-vos], *m.* Nail puller.

cazadero [cah-thah-day'-ro], *m.* Hunting ground.

cazador [cah-tha-dor'], *m.* 1. Hunt, hunter, chaser, huntsman, sportsman. 2. Anímal which gives chase to another. 3. (*Naut.*) Vessel which gives chase to another. 4. (*Met.*) One who prevails upon another, and brings him over to his party. **Cazador de pieles,** trapper. **Cazador de cabezas,** head-hunter.

cazadora [cah-tha-do'-rah], *f.* 1. Huntress. 2. Windcheater, hunting jacket, jerkin (prenda). **Cazadora de piel,** leather jacket.

cazadotes [cah-tha-do'-tays], *m.* Fortune-hunter.

cazafortunas [cah-tha-for-too'-nas], *f.* Fortune hunter, gold digger.

cazagenios [cah-thah-hay'-ne-os], *m.* Talent scout, talent spotter.

cazamoscas [cah-tha-mos'-cas], *m.* (*Orn.*) Flycatcher, a bird.

cazar [cah-thar'], *va.* 1. To chase, to hunt, to fowl, to sport, to course. 2. (*Met.*) To gain a difficult point by dexterity and skill. 3. (*Met.*) To gain one's friendship by caresses and deceitful tricks. 4. (*Naut.*) To give chase to a ship. 5. **Cazar una vela,** (*Naut.*) to tally a sail, to haul the sheet aft. **Cazar moscas,** (*Met.*) to waste one's time in idle amusements. **Le cacé por fin en la tienda,** I eventually ran him down in the shop.

cazasubmarinos [cah-tha-soob-mah-re'-nos], *m.* Submarine chaser.

cazatalentos [cah-tha-tah-layn'-tos], *m.* Talent scout, talent spotter.

cazatorpederos [cah-thah-tor-pay-day'-ros], *m.* Torpedo-boat destroyer.

cazcalear [cath-cah-lay-ar'], *vn.* 1. (*Coll.*) To go from one place to another affecting diligence. 2. To fidget.

cazcarria [cath-car'-re-ah], *f.* Splashings of dirt on clothes: used commonly in the plural.

cazcarriento [cath-thahr-re-ayn'-to], *a.* Splashed with mud, mud-stained.

cazo [cah'-tho], *m.* 1. Copper saucepan with an iron handle. 2. Copper or iron ladle for taking water out of a large earthen vessel. 3. Large kettle or boiler. 4. Back part of a knife-blade.

cazoleja, eta [cah-tho-ley'-hah, tah], *f.* 1. (*dim.*) Small saucepan. 2. Pan of a musket-lock.

cazolero [cah-tho-lay'-ro], *m.* (*Coll.*) Mean person who does women's work in the kitchen; milksop.

cazolero, ra [cah-tho-lay'-ro, rah], *a.* Applied to a person too officious. *V.* COMINERO.

cazoleta [cah-tho-lay'-tah], *f.* 1. Pan of a musket-lock. 2. Boss or defence of a shield. 3. Hand-guard or languet of a sword. 4. Kind of perfume. 5. *V.* CAZOLEJA.

cazolilla [cah-tho-leel'-lyah], *f. dim.* small earthen pan.

cazolón [cah-tho-lone'], *m. aug.* Large earthen pot or stew-pan.

cazón [cah-thone'], *m.* 1. (*Zool.*) Dogfish or small shark. 2. (*Obs.*) Brown sugar.

cazonal [cah-tho-nahl'], *m.* (*Prov.*) Fishing-tackle for the shark-fishery.

cazonete [cah-tho-nay'-tay], *m.* (*Naut.*) Toggle, a pin used to fasten a portrope.

cazú [cah-thoo'], *m.* An edible African fruit resembling cacao.

cazudo, da [cah-thoo'-do, dah], *a.* Having a thick back (cuchillos).

cazuela [cah-thoo-ay-lah], *f.* 1. An earthen pan to dress meat in, stewing-pan, crock. 2. Meat dressed in an earthen pan, the gallery of playhouses in Spain reserved for women. 4. **Cazuela mojí** or **mojil,** (*Prov.*) Tart made of cheese, bread, apples, and honey. 5. Earthen pans for baking pies. *V.* TARTERA.

cazumbrar [cah-thoom-brar'], *va.* To join staves together with hempen cords.

cazumbre [cah-thoom'-bray], *m.* Hempen cord with which the staves of wine-casks are joined and tightened.

cazembrón [cah-thoom-brone'], *m.* Cooper.

cazurro, ra [cah-thoor'-ro, rah], *a.* 1. (*Coll.*) Taciturn, sulky, sullen. 2. (*Obs.*) Making use of low language. 3. Thick-headed.

cazuz [cah-thooth'], *m.* (*Bot.*) Ivy.

c/c abr de **cuenta corriente** (current account).

C.D. *m.* 1. *abr.* de **Cuerpo Diplomático** (Diplomatic Corps). 2. *abr.* de **Club Deportivo** (sports club).

c/d 1. *abr.* **de en casa de** (care of). 2. (*Cono Sur*) *abr.* de **descuento** (discount).

CDR *m.* (*Cuba*) **Comité de Defensa de la Revolución.**

CD ROM. CD ROM (Compact Disc Read Only Memory).

CDS *m.* 1. (*Esp.*) *abr.* de **Centro Democrático y Social.** 2. (*Nicaragua*) *abr.* de **Comité de defensa Sandinista.**

CDU *f. abr.* de **Clasificación Decimal Universal** (Dewey decimal system).

CE *m. abr.* de **Consejo Europeo** (Council of Europe).

Ce [thay], 1. *f.* Name of the third letter of the alphabet. 2. *int.* Hark, here, come hither. **Ce por be,** or **ce por ce,** minutely, circumstantially; **por ce o por be,** in one way or another.

cea [thay'-ah], *f.* Thigh-bone. *V.* CÍA.

ceanoto [thay-ah-no'-to], *m.* Ceanothus, a genus of American and Oceanic shrubs of the buckthorn family; Jersey tea, redroot, etc.

ceática [thay-ah'-te-cah], *f.* (*Med.*) Sciatica, a disease.

ceático, ca [thay-ah'-te-co, cah], *a.* (*Med.*) Sciatical, *V.* CIÁTICO.

ceba [thay'-bah], *f.* 1. The fattening of fowls or other domestic animals. 2. (*LAm.*) Charge priming. 3. Stoking (de horno).

cebada [thay-bah'-dah], *f.* (*Bot.*) Barley. **Cebada común,** spring barley. **Cebada común blanca,** a variety of the spring barley with white seeds. **Cebada negra,** black barley. **Cebada perlada,** pearl barley.

cebadal [thay-bah-dahl'], *m.* Field sown with barley.

cebadar [thay-bah-dar'], *va.* To feed barley to horses.

cebadazo, za [thay-bah-dah'-tho, thah], *a.* Belonging to barley.

cebadera [thay-bah-day'-rah], *f.* 1. Kind of bag in which feed is given in the field to working cattle. 2. (*Naut.*) Spritsail.

cebadería [thay-bah-day-ree'-ah], *f.* Barley-market.

cebadero [thay-bah-day'-ro], *m.* 1. Place where game or fowls are fed. 2. One whose business is to breed and feed hawks. 3. Mule which on a journey carries barley for the rest. 4. Bell-mule which takes the lead. 5. Painting which represents domestic fowls in the act of feeding. 6. Entrance of a tilekiln. 7. Dealer in barley.

cebadilla [thay-bah-deel'-lyah], *f.* 1. (*Bot.*) Indian caustic barley or cevadilla. 2. (*Bot.*) Sneezewort. 3. (*Bot. Prov.*) Prickly oxeye. 4. Hellebore powdered and used as snuff.

cebado [thay-bah'-do], *a.* Fattened (un animal). Very fat. Fatted (becerro en la Biblia). **-Cebado, da,** *pp.* of CEBAR.

cebador [thay-bah-dor'], *m.* 1. One who fattens fowls or other animals. 2. Priming-horn, powder-horn. 3. *(Cono Sur) (Aut.)* Choke.

cebadura [thay-bah-doo'-rah], *f.* 1. Act of feeding or fattening fowls or other domestic animals. 2. Priming, stoking.

cebar [thay-bar,], *va. & vn.* 1. To feed ammals, to stuff; to cram. 2. To fatten fowls and other domestic animals. 3. *(Met.)* To keep up a fire. 4. To grapple, or to lay fast hold on one thing. 5. *(Met.)* To excite and cherish a passion or desire. 6. To prime a gun. 7. To let off a rocket or squib. 8. **Cebar un anzuelo,** to bait a fish-hook. *-vr.* 1. To be firmly bent upon a thing. 2. *(CAm. Mex.)* To fail to go off (tiro, fuegos artificiales); *(fig.)* to go wrong. 3. **Cebarse en,** to vent one's fury on, to prey upon. 4. **Cebarse en un estudio,** to devote oneself to study. 5. **Cebarse en la sangre,** to gloat over the blood (shed).

cebato [thay-bah'-to], *m.* A climbing plant of Arabia.

cebellina [thay-bel-lyee'-nah], *f.* 1. Sable. 2. Sable, the skin of the sable.

cebica [thay-bee'-cah], *f. V.* CIBICA.

cebiche [thay-bee'-chay], *m. (And.)* Marinaded fish.

cebo [thay'-bo], *m.* 1. Food given to animals; fodder. 2. Fattening of fowls and other animals. 3. Bait for wolves and birds of prey. 4. *(Met.)* That which excites or foments a passion. 5. Kind of monkey. *V.* CEFO. 6. Cart-grease. **Cebo de pescar,** bait for fishing. 7. Priming of guns. **Cebo or ceba fulminante,** percussion-cap.

cebolla [thay-bol'-lyah], *f.* 1. *(Bot.)* Onion. 2. The bulb of the onion. 3. Any kind of bulbous root. 4. The round part of a lamp into which oil is put. **Cebolla albarrana,** *(Bot.)* Squill. **Cebolla ascalonia,** *(Bot.)* Shallot garlic or ascalonian garlic.

cebollado [cay-bol-lye-ah'-do], *a. (LAm.)* Cooked with onions.

cebollana [thay-bol-lyah'-nah], *f. (Bot.)* Three-toothed globularia, chive.

cebollar [thay-bol-lyar'], *m.* Plot of ground sown with onions.

cebollero, ra [thay-bol-lyay'-ro, rah], *m. & f.* Dealer in onions.

cebolleta [thay-bol-lyay'-tah], *f. dim.* A tender onion.

cebollino [thay-bol-lyee'-no], *m.* 1. A young onion fit to be transplanted. 2. The onion's seeds. 3. *(Bot.)* Chive or cive; a plant allied to the leek and the onion.

cebollón [thay-bol-lyone'], *m. aug.* 1. A large onion. 2. *(Cono Sur)* old bachelor.

cebollona [thay-bol-lyo'-nah], *f. (Cono Sur)* old maid, spinster.

cebolludo, da [thay-bol-lyoo'-do, dah], *a.* 1. Among gardeners, applied to any plant with a big bulb. 2. *(Coll.)* Ill-shaped (personas).

cebón [thay-bone'], *m.* A fat bullock or hog. **Cebones de Galicia,** stall-fed bullocks.

ceboncillo [thay-bon-theel'-lyo], *m. dim.* Fatling, a young animal fed for slaughter, particularly a pig.

ceboruco [thay-bo-roo'-co], *m.* 1. *(Carib.)* Reef. 2. *(Mex.)* Rough rocky place (terreno quebrado). 3. *(Carib.)* Brush, scrub *(land.)*

cebra [thay'-brah], *f.* 1. Zebra, a kind of ass whose body is marked with dark bands. 2. (Cebras), zebra crossing.

cebratana [thay-brah-tah'-nah], *f.* 1. A long wooden tube or pipe. *V.* CERBATANA. 2. *(Art.)* Piece of ordnance resembling a culverin.

cebruno, na [thay-broo'-no, nah], *a.* Having the color of deer or hares.

cebú [thay-boo'], *m.* Zebu.

ceburro [thay-boor'-ro], *a. V.* MIJO CEBURRO and CANDEAL. **CECA***f. (Esp.) (Hist.) abr.* de **Comunidad Europea del Carbón y del Acero,** (European Coal and Steel Community, ECSC).

ceca [thay'-cah], *f.* 1. A mint for the coining of money. 2. *m.* Name of the mosque which the Arabs had in Cordova, the most venerated after Mecca. **Andar de ceca en meca,** to rove, to wander about, hither and thither.

ceceo [thay-thay'-o], *m.* 1. Lisping, lisp. 2. Act of calling someone by the word *ce-ce,* which corresponds to *I say.*

ceceoso, sa [thay-thay-o'-so, sah], *m. & f.* Lisper. *-a.* Lisping.

cecial [thay-the-ahl'], *m.* Hake or similar fish cured and dried in the air.

cecias [thay'-the-as], *m.* North-west wind.

cecina [thay-thee'-nah], *f.* Hung beef, smoked meat, dry meat. **Echar en cecina,** to salt and dry meat.

cecinar [thay-the-nar'], *va.* To make hung beef. *V.* ACECINAR.

ceda [thay'-dah], *f. .V.* ZEDA. *-m.* **Ceda el paso,** *(Aut.)* Priority, right of way.

cedacería [thay-dah-thay-ree'-ah], *f.* Shop where sieves or cribs are made or sold.

cedacero [thay-dah-thay'-ro], *m.* One who makes or sells sieves, cribs, etc.

cedacillo, ito [thay-dah-theel'-lyo, ee'-to], *m. dim.* A small sieve. **Cedacito nuevo tres días en estaca,** a new broom sweeps clean.

cedazo [thay-dah'-tho], *m.* Hair sieve or strainer; tamis, flour-sieve, bolting-cloth.

cedazuelo [thay-dah-thoo-ay'-lo], *m. dim.* A small hair sieve or strainer.

ceder [thay-derr'], *va.* To grant, to cede, to resign, to yield, to deliver up, to make over, to give up. *-vn.* 1. To yield or yield to, to submit, to comply, to give out, to give over, to give way, to come in, to go back. *(Mech.)* To sag, slacken. **No ceden fácilmente a las innovaciones,** they do not give in easily to innovations. **No cede a nadie en experiencia,** he is inferior to none in experience. 2. To happen, to turn out ill or well. 3. To abate, to grow less.

cedilla [thay-deel'-lyah], *f.* Cedilla, a mark formerly placed under a **c** to show that it sounded like **z** (ç). *V.* ZEDILLA.

cediza [thay-dee'-thah], *a.* Tainted (carne).

cedizo [thay-de'-tho], *a.* High, tainted.

cedoaria [thay-do-ah'-re-ah], *f.* Zedoary, a medicinal root.

cedras [thay'-dra], *f. pl.* Saddle-bags of skin, in which shepherds carry bread and other provisions.

cedría [thay-dree'-ah], *f.* Cedria, cedrium, a resin distilled from the cedar.

cédride, cedrio [thay'-dree-day, thay'-dre-o], *m.* Fruit of the cedar-tree.

cedrino, na [thay-dree'-no, nah], *a.* Cedrine, cedarn.

cedro [thay'-dro], *m. (Bot.)* 1. Cedar. **Cedro de América,** Barbadoes bastard cedar. **Cedro del Líbano,** cedar of Lebanon. 2. *(Prov.)* Spanish juniper.

cédula [thay'-doo-lah], *f.* 1. Document. 2. Order, bill, degree. 3. I.O.U. (reconocimiento de deuda). 4. Lot. 5. Schedule; warrant, share, scrip. **Cédula de aduana,** a permit. **Cédula de abono,** order to remit a tax in a town or a province. **Cédula de cambio,** bill of exchange. **Cédula de diligencias,** a warrant which was issued by the Council of the Chamber, commissioning a judge to make some investigation. **Cédula personal** or **de vecindad,** an official document declaring the name, occupation, domicile, etc., of each citizen, and to serve for identification. **Car cédula de vida,** to show bravery by sparing the life of one who is in his opponent's power. **Cédula de inválidos,** warrant for the reception of invalids. **Echar cédulas,** to draw or cast lots.

cedulaje [thay-doo-lah'-hay], *m.* Fees or dues paid for the expedition of decrees or grants.

cedulilla, ita [thay-doo-leel-layh, ee'-tah], *f. dim.* A small slip of paper.

cedulón [thay-doo-lone'], *m. aug.* A large bill, long edict, a large libellous bill or paper. **Poner cedulones,** to post up bills, edicts, or libels.

CE *f. abr.* de **Comunidad Europea,** (European Community, EC).

cefalagia [thay-fah-lahl'-he-ah], *f. (Med.)* Cephalalgia, headache.

cefalea [thay-fah-lay'-ah], *f.* Violent headache, generally onesided, like migraine.

cefálico, ca [thay-fah'-le-co, cah], *a.* Cephalic, belonging to the head; cephalic (vein).

céfalo [thay-fah-lo], *m.* (*Zool.*) Mullet, a kind of perch.

cefalina [thay-fah-lee'-nah], *f.* The root of the tongue.

cefalópodo [thay-fah-lo'-po-do], *m.* Cephalopod, the highest class of mollusks.

cefalotomía [thay-fah-lo-to-mee'-ah], *f.* Cephalotomy, the act of opening or dividing the head of the foetus, to facilitate delivery.

cefeo [thay-fay'-o], *m.* Cepheus, a constellation of the northern hemisphere, near Cassiopeia and Draco.

céfiro [thay'-fe-ro], *m.* Zephyr.

cefo [thay'-fo], *m.* A large African monkey.

cegador [thay-gah-dor'], *a.* Blinding. **Brillo cegador**, blinding glare.

cegajo [thay-gah'-ho], *m.* A he-goat, two years old.

cegajoso, sa [thay-gah-ho'-so, sah], *a.* Bleary-eyed.

cegar [thay-gar'], *vn.* To grow blind. *-va.* 1. To blind, to make blind. 2. (*Met.*) To deprive of good sense, reason, or judgement. 3. To shut a door or window. **Cegar los conductos, los pasos o caminos**, to stop up channels, passages, or roads. **Le ciega la pasión**, he is blinded by passion. *-vr.* (*fig.*) To become blinded.

cegarra [thay-gar'-rah], *a. Coll.* for CEGATO.

cegarrita [thay-gar-ree'-tah], *m.* (*Coll.*) One who contracts the eye to see at a distance.

cegato, ta [thay-gah'-to, tah], *a.* (*Coll.*) Short-sighted.

cegatoso, sa [thay-gah-to'-so, sah], *a. V.* CEGAJOSO.

ceguecillo, ceguezuelo [thay-gay-theel'-lyo, thay-gay-thoo-ay'-lo], *m. dim.* Little blind fellow.

ceguedad [thay-gay-dahd'], *f.* 1. Blindness, cecity. 2. (*Met.*) Blindness, ignorance, intellectual darkness.

ceguera [thay-gay'-rah], *f.* 1. Disorder in the eye. 2. Absolute blindness.

cegueríes [thay-gay-ree'-es], *m.* Kind of marten or the fur of this animal.

ceguiñuela [thay-gee-nyoo-ay'-lah], *f.* (*Naut.*) Whip-staff of the helm. *V.* PINZOTE.

ceiba [thay'-e-bah], *f.* 1. (*Bot.*) Five-leaved silk-cotton tree. 2. By the seashore, sea-moss, alga.

Ceilán [thay-e-lahn'], *m.* (*Hist.*) Ceylon.

ceilanés, esa [thay-e-lahn-days'], *a. m. & f.* Ceylones(*Geog.*) [thay'-hah], *f.* 1. Eye-brow. 2. Edging of clothes; projecting part, as in the binding of books. 3. In stringed instruments, bridge on which the cords rest. 4. Summit of a mountain. 5. Circle of clouds round a hill; cloud-cap. 6. (*Arch.*) Weather-moulding, rim. 7. (*Naut.*) An opening in a cloudy horizon; **dar entre ceja y ceja**, (*Met.*) To tell one to his face unpleasant truths. **Tomar a uno entre cejas**, to take a dislike to anyone. **Quemarse las cejas**, (*Met.*) to study with intense application. **Fruncir las cejas**, to knit one's brows.

cejadero [thay-hah-day'-ro], *m.* Traces of a harness.

cejar [thay-har'], *vn.* 1. To retrograde, to go backward. 2. (*Met.*) To slacken, to relax. **Sin cejar**, unflinchingly, undaunted. **No cejar en sus esfuerzos**, to keep (*Aer.*)'s efforts.

cejijunto, ta [thay-he-hoon'-to, tah], *a.* Having eyebrows which meet.

cejo [thay'-ho], *m.* 1. Thick fog which rises from rivers. 2. A cord tied around a bundle of esparto-grass, made of the same. 3. Frown, a look of displeasure.

cejudo, da [thay-hoo'-do, dah], *a.* Having heavy and long eyebrows.

cejuela [thay-hoo-ay'-lah], *f. dim.* A small eyebrow.

celada [thay-lah'-dah], *f.* 1. Helm, helmet. **Celada borgoñona**, burgundy helmet. 2. Ambuscade, ambush, lurch. 3. Artful trick. 4. Part of the key of the crossbow. 5. Horse soldier formerly armed with a crossbow. 6. (*Naut.*) Decoy or stratagem used by a small ship of war to bring an inferior vessel within gunshot. **Caer en la celada**, to fall into the trap.

celadilla [thay-lah-deel'-lyah], *f. dim.* Small helmet.

celador, ra [thay-lah-dor', rah], *m. & f.* 1. Curator. 2. Monitor in schools. 3. Warden.

celaje [thay-lah'-hay], *m.* 1. Color of the clouds 2. Small cloud moving before the wind, scud. 3. Painting which represents the rays of the sun breaking through clouds. 4. Presage, prognostic. 5. Skylight; upper part of a window; the sky of a picture. **Celajes**, light swiftly moving clouds, scud.

celán [thay-lahn'], *m.* A kind of herring.

celar [thay-lar'], *vn. &* va. 1. To fulfill the duties of an office with care. 2. To keep a watchful eye on. 3. To cover, to conceal. 4. *V.* RECELAR. (To conceal.) 5. To engrave; to cut in wood. (To grave).

celda [thel'-dah], *f.* 1. Cell in a convent. 2. Cell in beehives. 3. (*Naut. Obs.*) Small cabin. 4. (*Obs.*) Small room. **Celda de castigo**, solitary confinement cell. 5. (*Inform.*) **Celda actual**, current cell. **Celda de almacenamiento de datos**, memory cell, storage cell. **Celda de memoria**, memory cell, storage cell.

celdilla [thel-deel'-lyah], *f..* (*Bot.*) Cell, the part of a pericarp or capsule in which seeds are lodged.

cele [thay-lay], *a.* (*CAm.*) Light green; unripe (inmaduro).

celebérrimo, ma [thay-lay-ber'-re-mo, mah], *a. sup.* Most celebrated.

celebración [thay-lay-brah-the-on'], *f.* 1. Celebration, solemn performance. 2. Celebration, praise, applause, acclamation.

celebrador, ra [thay-lay-brah-dor', rah], *m. & f.* Applauder, praiser, celebrator.

celebrante [thay-lay-brahn'-tay], *m.* 1. Celebrator. 2. A priest celebrating the mass.

celebrar [thay-lay-brar'], *va.* 1. To celebrate, to perform in a solemn manner. **Celebrar misa**, to say mass. 2. To hold, take place. **Celebrar un contrato**, to draw up a contract; **celebrar una reunión**, to hold a meeting. 3. To celebrate, to praise, to applaud, to commend. **Lo celebro mucho por él**, I'm very happy for his sake. 4. (*Carib.*) To fall in love. *-vr.* To fall, to occur, to be celebrated, to take place.

célebre [thay'-lay-bray], *a.* 1. Celebrated, famous, renowned, noted. 2. (*Met. Coll.*) Gay, facetious, agreeable in conversation.

célebremente [thay'-lay-bray-men-tay], *adv.* Facetiously, merrily.

celebridad [thay-lay-bre-dahd'], *f.* 1. Celebrity. 2. Renown, fame. 3. Pomp, magnificence, or ostentation, with which a feast or event is celebrated. 4. Public demonstration to commemorate some event.

celebrillo [thay-lay-breel'-lyo], *m. dim.* Small brains.

celebro [thay-lay'-bro], *m.* 1. Skull. 2. Brain. *V.* CEREBRO. 3. (*Met.*) Fancy imagination. 4. Prudence.

celemín [thay-lay-meen'], *m.* 1. Dry measure, the 12th part of a *fanega*, about an English peck. 2. The quantity of grain contained in a **celemín.**

celeminero [thay-lay-me-nay'-ro], *m.* (*Obs.*) Hostler who measures grain in inns.

celeque [thay-lay'-kay], *a.* (*CAm.*) Green, unripe.

celerado, celerario [thay-lay-rah'-do. thay-lay-rah'-re-o], *a. V.* MALVADO.

célere [thay'-lay-ray], *a.* Quick, rapid. *-m.* One of the select three hundred knights of ancient Roman nobility.

celeridad [thay-lay-re-dahd'], *f.* Celerity, velocity. **Con celeridad**, quickly.

celerímetro [thay-lay-ree'-may-tro], *m.* Speedometer.

celeste [thay-les'-tay], *a.* 1. Celestial. 2. Heavenly. 3. Sky-blue.

celestial [thay-les-te-ahl'], *a.* 1. Celestial, heavenly. 2. (*Met.*) Perfect, agreeable, delightful, excellent. 3. Silly.

celestialmente [thay-les-te-al-men'-tay], *adv.* Celestially, heavenly; perfectly.

celestina [thay-lays-te'-nah], *f.* Bawd, procuress; madam (burdel).

celestinazo [thay-lays-te-nah'-tho], *m.* Pimping, procuring.

celfo [thel'-fo], *m. V.* CEFO.

celíaco, ca [thay-lee'-ah-co, cah], *a. (Med.)* 1. Coeliac, relating to the coeliac passion. 2. Applied to a person afflicted with the coeliac passion.

celibato [thay-le-bah'-to], *m.* 1. Celibacy. 2. A bachelor. a single man.

célibe [thay'-le-bay], *m. f.* Single, unmarried.

célico, ca [thay'-le-co, cah], *a.* Celestial, heavenly.

celidonia [thay-le-do'-ne-ah], *f.* 1. *(Bot.)* Common celandine, swallowwort, tether-wort. 2. Swallow-stone, a small stone with several impressions.

celindrate [thay-lin-drah'-tay], *m.* Ragout made with coriander-seed.

celita [thay-lee'-tah], *f.* A fish caught in the Straits of Gibraltar.

celo [thay'-lo], *m.* 1. Zeal, ardor, devotion. 2. Heat, rut. 3. Religious zeal, fervor. **Caer en celo,** to come into rut. *-pl.* 1. Jealousy. **Dar celos,** to give grounds for jealousy. **Tener celos de uno,** to be jealous of somebody. 2. Suspicious. **Dar celos,** to excite suspicions.

celofán [thay-lo-fahn'], *m.* Cellophane.

celosamente [thay-lo-sah-men-tay], *adv.* 1. Zealously; eagerly; fervently. 2. *(fig.)* Suspiciously, distrustfully.

celosía [thay-lo-see'-ah], *f.* Lattice of a window, Venetian blind.

celoso, sa [thay-lo'-so, sah], *a.* 1. Jealous. 2. Light and swift-sailing (pequeños barcos). 3. Crank, unsteady, top-heavy: spoken of vessels and boats. 4. *(LAm.) (Mec.)* Highly sensitive; *(And.)* Unsteady, easily upset; *(LAm.)* Delicate (arma). **Este es un fusil celoso,** this gun is quite liable to go off.

celotipia [thay-lo-tee'-pe-ah], *f.* Jealousy.

celsitud [thel-see-tood'], *f.* 1. Elevation, grandeur. 2. Highness, a title now expressed by *Alteza.*

celta [thel'-tah], *com.* Celt, Celtic. *-m.* The Celtic language.

celtibérico, ca [thel-te-bay'-re-co, cah], *a.* Celtiberian.

céltico ca [thel'-te-co, cah], *a.* Celtic.

celtista [thel-tees'-tah], *com.* Celtist, one who cultivates Celtic language and literature.

célula [thay'-loo-lah], *f. (Med.)* Cellule. **Célula nerviosa,** nerve cell. **Célula sanguínea,** blood cell.

celular [thay-loo-lar'], or **celulario, ia** [thay-loo-lah'-re-o, ah], *a.* 1. *(Med.)* Cellular. 2. A system of isolation among those imprisoned for grave crimes. 3. Cell, V. COCHE.

celulilla [thay-loo-leel'-lyah], *f. dim.* A very small cell or cavity.

celulitis [thay-loo-le'-tes], *f.* Cellulitis.

celuloide [thay-loo-lo'-e-day], *m.* Celluloid.

celulosa [thay-loo-lo'-sah], *f.* Cellulose, woody fibre.

celuloso, sa [thay-loo-lo'-so, sah], *a.* Cellulose, containing cells.

cellenco, ca [thel-lyen'-co, cah], *a. (Coll.)* Decrepit.

cellisca [thel-lyees'-cah], *f.* V. VENTISCA. Fine rain or snow, sleet, driven by a heavy wind.

cellisquear [thel-lyees-kay-ar'], *vn.* To sleet, to be squally with fine snow or rain.

cembellina [them-bel-lyee'-nah], *f.* Hartshorn.

cementación [thay-men-tah-the-on'], *f.* Cementation.

cementar [thay-men-tar'], *va.* To cement. V. CIMENTAR.

cementerio [thay-men-tay'-re-o], *m.* Cemetery, churchyard, graveyard; **cementerio de coches,** used car dump.

cemento [thay-men'-to], *m.* 1. Cement, concrete. **Cemento armado,** reinforced concrete. 2. *(Anat.)* Cement (de dientes).

cemita [thay-me'-tah], *f. (LAm.)* White bread roll.

cena [they'-nah], *f.* 1. Dinner, supper. 2. Scene, stage. **Jueves Santo** or **de la Cena,** Maundy Thursday, Thursday before Good Friday. **La Última Cena,** The Last Supper.

cenáculo [thay-nah'-coo-lo], *m.* The dining-hall in which our Lord celebrated The Last Supper with his disciples.

cenacho [thay-nah'-cho], *m.* Basket or hamper for fruit and greens.

cenadero [thay-nah-day'-ro], *m.* 1. A place for supping. 2. Summerhouse in a garden.

cenador [thay-nah-dor'], *m.* 1. One fond of suppers, or who eats in excess. 2. Summer-house in a garden, an arbor, bower.

cenaduría [they-nah-doo-ree'-ah], *f. (Mex.)* Eating house, restaurant.

cenagal [thay-nah-gahl'.], *m.* Quagmire. **Meterse en un cenagal,** *(Met.)* To be involved in an unpleasant, arduous affair. **Salir de un cenagal,** to get rid of an unpleasant affair.

cenagoso, sa [thay-nah-go'-so, sah], *a.* Muddy, miry, marshy.

cena-homenaje [they-nah-o-may-nah'-hay], *f. pl.* **Cenas homenajes,** formal dinner. **Ofrecer una cena-homenaje,** to hold a dinner for somebody.

cenar [thay-nar'], *va.* To dine, to have dinner or supper. **Invitar a uno a cenar,** to invite someone to dinner. **Quedarse sin cenar,** to go without dinner or supper. *-vn.* To have one's supper; **vengo cenado,** I've had dinner.

cenata [thay-nah'-tah], *f. (Col.)* Merry banquet or dinner.

cenceño, ña [then-thay-nyo, nyah], *a.* Lean, thin, slender. 2. Pure, simple. **Pan cenceño,** unleavened bread.

cencerra [then-ther'-rah], *f.* 1. Bell worn by the leading mule. V. CENCERRO. 2. Clack of a mill which strikes the hopper and promotes the running of the corn. 3. The meat between the throttle and ribs of a saddle of mutton.

cencerrada [then-ther-rah'-dah], *f.* 1. Noise with bells and horns at the door of an old bridegroom or widower, the night of his marriage; charivari, din.

cencerrear [then-ther-ray-ar'], *vn.* 1. To jangle continually (mulas, caballos). 2. To clack. 3. To play on an untuned guitar. 4. To make a dreadful noise, as by windows and doors shaken by the wind.

cencerreo [then-ther-ray'-o], *m.* 1. Noise made by mule or horse bells. 2. Dreadful noise.

cencerril [then-ther-reel'], *a.* Resembling the noise of horse-bells.

cencerrilla, illo [then-ther-reel'-lyah, eel'-lyo], *f. & m. dim.* A small wether, horse, or mule bell.

cencerro [then-ther'-ro], *m.* 1. Bell worn by the leading wether, or mule. 2. Ill-tuned guitar. 3. *(Orn.)* Woodcrow. **No quiero perro con cencerro,** I do not want a dog with a bell; that is, I do not like to engage in a business that is more troublesome than profitable. **A cencerros tapados,** privately, stealthily. **Estar como un cencerro,** to be crazy.

cencerrón [then-ther-rone'], *m.* A small bunch of grapes which remains after the vintage.

cencerruno, na [then-ther-roo'-no, nah], *a.* V. CENCERRIL.

cencido, da [then-thee'-do, dah], *a.* Untilled, uncultivated (tierra).

cencro [theen'-cro], *m.* A serpent of Brazil.

cendal [theen-dahl], *m.* 1. Light thin stuff made of silk or thread. 2. Furbelow, flounce or trimming of gowns, etc. 3. *(Poet.)* Garter.

cendea [then-day'-ah], *f. (Prov.)* In Navarre, meeting of the inhabitants of several villages to deliberate on public business.

cendolilla [then-do-leel'-lyah], *f.* A forward girl acting with little judgment.

cendra [then'-drah], *f.* 1. Paste used to clean silver. 2. Cupel. **Ser una cendra,** *(Met.)* to be lively as a cricket.

cendrar [then-drar'], *va.* V. ACENDRAR.

cenefa [thay-nay'-fah], *f.* 1. Frame of a picture. 2. Border or list of any kind of stuff. 3. Valance, fringes and drapery of a bed. 4. Trimming. 5. Middle piece of a priest's garment, called chasuble. 6. *(Poet.)* Bank of a river or lake, the brim of a ond. 7. **Cenefa de un toldo,** *(Naut.)* center of an awning. *(Arab.).*

cení [thay-nee'], *m.* A kind of fine brass or bronze.

cenicero [thay-ne-thay'-ro], *m.* Ashtray.

Cenicienta [they-ne-thay'-ayn'-tah], *f.* Cinderella. **La Cenicienta de la casa,** I'm always the one left out.

ceniciento, ta [thay-ne-the-en'-to, tah], *a.* Ash-colored, cinereous. *-m.* Scullion.

cenit [thay-neet'], *m. (Astr.)* Zenith; vertex.

cenital [thay-ne-tahl'], *a.* Vertical, relating to the zenith.

ceniza [thay-nee'-thah], *f.* 1. Ashes, cinders. 2. Coarse ashes, which remain in the strainer when the lye is made. *V.* CERNADA. 3. Ashes, the remains of the dead. **Cenizas de estaño;** putty. **Día de ceniza** or **Miércoles de ceniza,** ash-Wednesday. **Hacerse ceniza** or **cenizas alguna cosa,** *(Met.)* to be reduced to nothing, to come to nothing. **Reducir algo a cenizas,** to reduce something to ashes.

cenizal [thay-ne-thahl'], *m.* Heap of ashes.

cenizo [thay-nee'-tho], *m.* 1. *(Bot.)* White goosefoot. 2. *(Coll.)* Jinx, bearer of ill luck. **Es un avión cenizo,** it's a plane with a jinx on it. **Entrar el cenizo en casa,** to have a spell of bad luck. *-a.* 1. Ashen, ash-colored. 2. Ill-omened; alarming.

cenizo, za [thay-nee'-tho, thah], *a. V.* CENICIENTO.

cenizoso, sa [thay-nee-tho'-so, sah], *a.* Covered with ashes, cineritious.

cenobio [thay-no'-be-o], *m.* Cenobium. *V.* MONASTERIO.

cenobita [thay-no-bee'-tah], *m.* Cenobite, a monk.

cenobítico, ca [thay-no-bee'-te-co, cah], *a.* Cenobitical.

cenotafio [thay-no-tah'-fe-o], *m.* Cenotaph, a monument.

cenote [thay-no'-tay], *m.* Deposit of water, generally at a great depth in the center of a cavern.

censal [then-sahl'], *m. & f. & a. (Prov.) V.* CENSO and CENSUAL.

censalista [then-sah-lees'-tah], *m. (Prov.) V.* CENSUALISTA.

censar [thayn-sar'], *va. (Cono Sur)* to take a census (población).

censatario, censero [then-sah-tah'-re-o, then-say'-ro], *m.* One who pays an annuity out of his estate to another person.

censista [thayn-thes'-tah], *m. & f.* Census official, census taker.

censo [then'-so], *m.* 1. An agreement by which a person acquires the right of receiving an annual pension. 2. Quitrent. 3. Census, censual roll or book, where all the inhabitants of a kingdom or of a state are enumerated. **Censo electoral,** electoral roll. 4. Poll-tax, formerly in use among the Romans. 5. **Censo al quitar or reservativo,** a quit-rent or annuity which can be paid at once by a certain sum. **Censo de por vida,** annuity for one or more lives. 6. **Ser un censo,** to be a constant drain.

censontli, censontle [then-son'-tlee, then-son'-tlay], *m. (Mex.)* The Mexican mocking-bird. *Cf.* SINSONTE.

censor [then-sor'], *m.f.* 1. Censor, an officer appointed to examine new books and publications, to see if they contain something contrary to religion and good manners. 2. Critic, reviewer of literary compositions. 3. Censorious person. 4. *(Com. fin.)* **Censora de cuentas,** auditor. **Censor jurado de cuentas,** chartered accountant.

censual [then-soo-ahl'], *a.* 1. Pertaining to a quit-rent, annuity, or any other annual rent paid for the possession of land. 2. Pertaining to interest on money invested. 3. *(Pol.)* Relating to the electoral roll.

censualista [then-soo-ah-lees'-tah], *m.* 1. A person in whose favor an annuity has been imposed, and who has the right to enjoy it until his death. 2. A copyholder.

censualmente [then-soo-al-men'-tay], *adv.* With a right to enjoy an annuity.

censuario [then-soo-ah'-re-o], *m. V.* CENSUALISTA.

censura [then-soo'-rah], *f.* 1. A critical review of literary productions. 2. Censure, blame, reproach, reprimand, reprehension, objurgation. 3. Reproach without foundation, gossiping. 4. Censure, a spiritual punishment inflicted by an ecclesiastical judge; fulmination or denunciation of censure. 5. Register, list. 6. Censorship. **Someter a la censura,** to censor. 7. *(Com. fin.)* **Cesura de cuentas,** auditing.

censurable [then-soo-rah'-blay], *a.* Censurable, reprehensible.

censurador [then-soo-rah-dor'], *m.* Censurer, fault-finder.

censurante [then-soo-rahn'-tay], *pa.* Censurer, censuring.

censurar [then-soo-rar'], *va.* 1. To review, to criticise, to judge. 2. To censure, to blame, to find fault with, to expose. 3. To accuse, to note, to reprehend. 4. To record, to enter into a list or register. 5. To correct, to reprove.

censurista [thayn-soo-res'-tah], 1. *a.* Censorious. 2. *m. & f.* Critic, faultfinder.

centaura, centaurea [then-tah'-oo-rah], *f. (Bot.)* Centaury. **Centaurea mayor,** great centaury. **Centaurea menor,** common erythraea.

centauro [theen-tah'-oo-ro], *m.* 1. Centaur. 2. *(Astr.)* Centaur, a southern constellation.

centavo [then-tah'-vo], *m.* The hundredth part of something; a cent, as the hundredth of a dollar.

centella [then-tayl'-lyah], *f.* 1. Lightning. 2. Flash of a flint struck with steel; flake of fire. 3. Remaining spark of passion or discord. **Ser vivo como una centella** or **ser una centella,** to be all life and spirit.

centellante [then-tel-lyahn'-tay], *pa.* Sparkling, flashing.

centellar, centellear [then-tel-lyar', then-tel-lyar-ar'], *vn.* To sparkle, to throw out sparks.

centellenate [thayn-tayl-lyay-ahn'-tay], *a.* 1. Sparkling, gleaming, glinting *(Aer.)(fig.)* Sparkling.

centelleo [then-tel-lyay'-o], *m.* Sparkle, scintillation, glinting, flashing.

centellón [then-tel-lyone'], *m. aug.* A large spark or flash.

centena [then-tay'-nah], *f.* 1. Hundred. 2. Centenary, the number of a hundred. 3. Stubble of rye.

centenadas [then-tay-nah'-das]' *adv.* **A centenadas** or **a centenares,** by hundreds.

centenal [then-tay-nahl'], *m.* 1. Field sown with rye. 2. Centenary, the number of a hundred.

centenar [then-tay-nar'], *m.* 1. A hundred. 2. Field sown with rye. *V.* CENTENARIO.

centenario, ria [then-tay-nah'-re-o, ah], *a.* 1. Centenary, secular, happening but once in a century. 2. *m.* Centennial, feast celebrated every hundred years.

centenazo, za [then-tay-nah'-tho, thah], *a.* Belonging to rye. **Paja centenaza,** rye-straw.

centeno [then-tay'-no], *m. (Bot.)* Common rye.

centeno, na [then-tay'-no, nah], *a.* A numerai adjective which signifies hundred.

centenoso, sa [then-tay-no'-so, sah], *a.* Mixed with rye.

contésimal [thayn-tay'-se-mahl], *a.* Centesimal.

centésimo, ma [then-tay'-se-mo, mah], *a.* Centesimal, hundredth.

centi [then-te]. A prefix from the Latin, signifying the one one-hundredth.

centiárea [then-te-ah'ray-ah], *f.* Centiare, the one one-hundredth of an acre, square measure.

centígrado, da [then-tee'-grah-do, dah], *a.* Centigrade, a scale divided into one hundred degrees.

centigramo [then-te-grah'-mo], *m.* Centigramme, 0.01 gramme, about one-sixth of a grain.

centilitro [then-te-lee'-tro], *m.* Centilitre.

centiloquio [then-te-lo'-ke-o], *m.* A work divided into a hundred parts or chapters.

centímano, na [then-tee'-may-tro], *a. (Poet.)* Having a hundred hands.

centímetro [then-tee'-may-tro], *m.* Centimeter: 0.01 meter.

céntimo, [then'-te-mo], *m.* Cent.

céntimo, ma [then'-te-mo, mah], *a.* The one-hundredth. **No tiene un céntimo,** he hasn't got a penny. **No vale un céntimo,** it's worthless.

centinela [then-te-nay'-lah], *com.* 1. *(Mil.)* Sentry or sentinel. 2. *(Met.)* One who pries into another's actions. **Centinela a caballo,** vedette, a sentinel on horseback. **Hacer centinela** or **estar de centinela,** to stand sentry, to be on guard.

centinodia [then-te-no'-de-ah], *f. (Bot.)* Knotgrass, persicaria.

centiplicado, da [then-te-ple-cah'-do, dah], *a.* Centuple, a hundred-fold.

centiplicar [then-te-ple-car'], *va. V.* CENTUPLICAR.

centollo, centolla [then-to'-lah, then-tol-lyah], *f.* Spider crab.

centón [then-tone'], *m.* 1. Crazy quilt. 2. Cento, a literary composition.

centrado; da [then-trah'-do, dah], *a.* Centered, balanced, **Una persona bien centrada,** a well balanced person.

central [then-trahl'], *f.* Main office (compañía telefónica). **Central telefónica,** telephone exchange, telephone office. **Central de correos,** main post office. **Central azucarera,** sugar mill. **Central nuclear,** nuclear power station. **Central de bombeo,** pumping station.

central, centrical [then-trahl', then-tre-cahl'], *a.* Central, centric.

centralidad [then-trah-le-dhad'], *f.* Centrality.

centralismo [thayn-trah-les'-mo], *m.* Centralism.

centralita [then-trah-lee'-tah], *f.* Telephone exchange.

centralización [then-trah-le-tha-the-on'], *f.* Centralization.

centralizar [then-trah-le-thar'], *va.* To centralize. *-vr.* To be centralized.

centralmente [then-tral-men'-tay], *adv.* Centrally.

centrar [thayn-trar'], *va.* 1. To center; to concentrate (esfuerzos). 2. To concentrate (fuego), *(fot.)* To focus on. *-vr.* **Centrarse en,** to center on, to be centered on. 2. To settle in (en un empleo).

céntrico, ca [then'-tre-co, cah], *a.* Focal. **Punto céntrico,** object, end of one's views. *V.* CENTRO. **Es muy céntrico,** it's very central; it's very convenient. **Un restaurante céntrico,** a restaurant in the center of town.

centrífugo, ga [then-tree'-foo-go, gah], *a.* Centrifugal.

centrifugar [thayn-tre-foo-gar'], *va.* To centrifuge; to spin (colada).

centrífugo [thayn-tre'-foo-go], *a.* Centrifugal.

centrípeto, ta [then-tree'-pay-to, tah], *a.* Centripetal.

centro [then'-tro], *m.* 1. Center (medio), middle, root, origin. **El centro del círculo,** the center of the circle. **El centro de la ciudad,** the city center. 2. Height and depth of a thing. 3 *(Met.)* The principal object of desire and exertion 4. *(Bot.)* Disk of flowers. 5. A short dress of flannel which Indian women and half-breeds use in Ecuador. **Estar en el centro de la batalla,** to be in the center of the action. **El mando es el centro a que aspira la ambición,** command is the point to which ambition aspires. **Centro de salud,** health center. **Centro social,** community center. **Centro de gravedad,** center of gravity. **Centro docente,** teaching institution. 6. *(Dep.)* Center. **Centro del campo,** midfield. **Delantero centro,** center-forward. **Medio centro,** half-back.

Centroamérica [then-tro-ah-may'-re-cah], *f.* Central America.

centroamericano, na [tehn-tro-ah-may-re-cah'-no], *a. m. & f.* Central American.

centro comercial [then'-tro-co-mer-the-ahl'], *m.* Shopping center.

centrocampista [then-tro-cahm-pes'-tah], *m. & f. (Dep.)* Midfield player.

centrocampo [then-tro-cahm-po], *m. (Dep.)* Midfield.

Centroeuropa [then-tro-e-oo-ro'-pah], *f.* Central Europe.

centuplicar [then-too-ple-car'], *va.* To centuplicate, increase enormously.

céntuplo, pla [then'-too-plo, plah], *a.* Centuple, hundredfold.

centuria [tehn-too'-re-ah], *f.* 1. Century. 2. Among the Romans, one hundred soldiers, commanded by a centurion.

centurión [then-too-re-on'], *m.* Centurion.

centurionazgo [then-too-re-o-nath'-go], *m.* The office of a centurion.

cenutrio [the-noo'-trio], *m.* Twit, twerp.

cenzalino, na [then-tha-lee'-no, nah], *a.* Pertaining to a *cénzalo.*

cénzalo [then'-tha-lo], *m.* Mosquito.

ceñido, da [thay-nyee'-do, dah], *a.* 1. Moderate in pleasure or expense. **Ceñido al tema,** keeping close to the point. **Ceñido y corto,** brief and to the point. 2. Ringed (abejas, insectos). 3. Tight, close-fitting, clinging. *-pp.* of CENIR.

ceñidor [thay-nye-dor'], *m.* Belt, girdle, girdle-belt, sash.

ceñidura [thay-nye-doo'-rah], *f.* The act of girding.

ceñir [thay-nyeer'], *va.* 1. To gird, to surround, to circle, to girdle. **La muralla ciñe la ciudad,** the wall surrounds the city. 2. To environ, to hem in. 3. *(Met.)* To reduce, to abbreviate, to contract. 4. To fasten round one's waist. **Ceñir espada,** to wear a sword. **El vestido ciñe bien el cuerpo,** the dress fits well. 5. *(fig.)* To shorten, to cut down. *-vr.* 1. To reduce one's expenses, to tighten one's belt. **Ceñirse a un tema,** to limit oneself to a subject. 2. To put something on. **Ceñirse la corona,** to take the crown.

ceño [thay'-nyo], *m.* 1. Frown, a supercilious look. **Arrugar el ceño,** to frown. **Mirar con ceño,** to frown, to scowl at. 2. Ring or ferrule. 3. *(Vet.)* Circle round the upper part of a horse's hoof. 4. *(Poet.)* A gloomy aspect, as of the sea, clouds, etc.

ceñoso, sa [thay-nyo-so, sah], *a.* 1. Hoof surrounded with rings. 2. *V.* CEÑUDO.

ceñudo, da [thay-nyoo'-do, dah], *a.* Frowning, supercilious; grim; gruff, sour of aspect.

cepa [thay'-pah], *f.* 1. The stump of a tree. 2. Stock of a vine 3. *(Met.)* Stock or origin of a family. **De buena cepa,** of good stock. 4. *(Met.)* Bud or root of the horns and tails of animals. 5. Root of the wool. 6. Foundation of columns, pilasters, or arches. 7. *(Mex.)* Pit, trench (hoyo).

cepeda [thay-pay'-dah], or **cepedera** [thay-pay-day'-rah], *f.* A spot where heath abounds.

cepejón [thay-pay-hone'], *m.* The largest part of a branch torn from the trunk.

cepillado [they-peel-lyah'-do], *m.* Brush. **Se elimina con un suave ceñido,** it goes away with a gentle brush.

cepilladuras [thay-peel-lyah-doo'-ras], *f. pl.* Shavings.

cepillar [thay-peel-lyar'], *va.* 1. To brush (trajes); to plane (carpintería). 2. To plane. *V.* ACEPILLAR. 3. To rip off (robar). 4. To win (ganar). 5. To bump off (matar). 6. To spank (pegar azotes). *-vr.* 1. **Cepillarse a uno,** to bump somebody off. 2. **Cepillarse algo,** to rip something off. 3. **Cepillarse a una,** to screw somebody.

cepillo [thay-peel'-lyo], *m.* 1. Plane, carpenter's tool. 2. Brush for clothes. 3. Poor-box; corban. **Cepillo de dientes,** toothbrush, **cepillo para las uñas,** nailbrush. **Cepillo para el suelo,** scrubbing brush. 4. *(Tec.)* Plane. 5. *(LAm.)* Flatterer, creep (adulador).

cepillón [thay-peel-lyone'], *a.* Soapy. *-m.* cepillona *f.* Creep.

cepita [thay-pee'-tah], *f. dim.* A small stock of a vine.

cepo [thay'-po], *m.* 1. Block on which an anvil is put. 2. Stocks, for punishment; on board of ships they are called *bilboes.* 3. Reel on which silk is wound. 4. Trap for wolves or other animals. 5. Charity, box in churches and public places. 6. *V.* CEFO. 7. The stocks with which a gun is made fast in the carriage. 8. Clamp, joining-press; horse (herreros). **Cepo del ancla,** *(Naut.)* anchor-stock. **Cepo de molinete,** *(Naut.)* Knight head of the windlass. **Cepos,** notched cleats or timbers fixed across other timbers to strengthen or secure them where they are pierced; anchor-stocks.

cepón [thay-pone'], *m. aug.* The large trunk of a tree or vine-stock.

ceporro [thay-por'-ro], *m.* 1. An old vine pulled up by the roots. 2. Twit (idiota).

cequiaje [thay-ke-ah'-hay], *m.* Annual contribution paid for irrigation rights by the towns of a community.

cequión [they-ke-one'], *m. (Cono Sur)* Large irrigation channel.

cera [thay'-rah], *f.* 1. Candle (vela), wax. 2. Tapers and candles of wax. **Cera virgen,** virgin wax. **Cera de dorar,** gold-size. **Cera de los oídos,** ear-wax. **Ceras,** the cells of wax and honey formed by bees. **Cera para suelos,** floor polish.

ceráceo, ea [thay-rah'-thay-o, ah], *a.* Of the consistency of wax.

ceración [thay-rah-the-on'], *f.* Ceration, preparation of a metal for fusion.

cerachates [thay-rah-chah'-tes], *f. pl.* Wax-stones, a yellow agate.

cerafolio [thay-rah-f'-le-o], *m. (Bot.)* Common chervil. *V.* PERIFOLLO.

cerámica [thay-rah'-me-cah], *f.* The ceramic art; ceramics, art of making pottery.

cerámico, ca [thay-rah'-me-co, cah], *a.* Ceramic, relating to pottery.

ceramista [they-rah-mes'-tah], *m. & f.* Potter.

cerapez [thay-rah-peth'], *f.* Cerate, a plaster of wax and pitch.

cerasina [thay-rah-see'-nah], *f.* Cerasin, the insoluble part of cherry, peach, and similar gums.

cerasta, *f.* **ceraste, cerastes,** *m.* [thay-rahs'-tah, thay-rahs'-tay, thay-rahs'-tes]. Horned, serpent.

cerato [thay-rah'-to], *m.* (*Pharm.*) Cerate.

ceratófilo, ceratófilon [thay-rah-to'-fe-lo, thay-rah-to'-felone], *m.* (*Bot.*) Hornwort, or pondweed.

ceraunia, or **ceraunita** [thay-rah'-oo-ne-ah, thay-rah-oonee'-tah], *f.* Ancient name of jasper or flint, oriental jade.

cerbatana [ther-bah-tah'-nah], *f.* 1. Blowpipe, popgun, peashooter, acoustic trumpet for the deaf. 3. Ancient culverin of small calibre.

cerca [therr'-cah], *f.* 1. Inclosure, hedge, or wall which surrounds a garden, park, or corn-field; fence. 2. Yard. *-m. pl.* **Los cercas,** among painters, objects in the foreground of a painting.

cerca [therr'-cah], *adv.* Near, at hand, not far off, close by, preceding the noun or pronoun to which it refers, it demands the preposition *de.* **Estar cerca de,** to be near. 1. **Aquí cerca, cerca de aquí,** just by. 2. **Cerca de,** close, near. **Hay cerca de 8 toneladas,** there are about 8 tons. 3. **Tocar de cerca,** 1. (*Met.*) To be nearly allied to, or near akin. 2. To be concerned in, to be interested.

cercado [ther-cah'-do], *m.* 1. A garden or field enclosed with a fence (valla); an enclosure (terreno cercado), a lock, a close or small enclosed field.

cercado, da, *pp.* of. CERCAR. 2. (*And.*) Communal lands. 3. (*And.*) (*Hist.*) State capital and surrounding towns.

cercador [ther-cah-dor'], *m.* 1. Hedger, one who encloses. 2. An iron graver marking-iron.

cercadura [ther-cah-doo'-rah], *f.* Enclosure, wall, fence.

cercamiento [ther-cah-me-en'-to], *m.* Act of enclosing.

cercanamente [ther-cah-nah-men'-tay], *adv.* Nearby, close by (a poca distancia); nearly.

cercanía [ther-ca-nee'-ah], *f.* 1. Proximity, neighborhood, vicinity, closeness. 2. **Cercanías,** outskirts, outer suburbs. **Tren de cercanías,** suburban train.

cercano, na [ther-cah'-no, nah], *a.* Near, close by, neighboring, adjoining.

Cercano Oriente, Near East.

cercar [ther-car'], *va.* 1. To inclose, to environ, to hem, to circle, to compass, to gird, to wall in (rodear con una cerca). 2. To fence, to secure by an inclosure; to surround with a hedge or wall, to pale. 3. (*Mil.*) To siege a town, to block up a fortress. 4. To crowd about a person. 5. To bring or put near. **Cercado de desdichas y trabajos,** involved in troubles and distress.

cercén [ther-then'], *adv.* **A cercén,** at the root. **Cercén a cercén,** from end to end, completely. **Cortar un brazo a cercén,** to cut an arm off completely.

cercenadamente [ther-thay-nah-dah-men'-tay], *adv.* In a clipping manner, with retrenchment.

cercenadera [ther-thay-nah-day'-rah], *f.* Clipping-knife used by wax-chandlers.

cercenador [ther-thay-nah-dor'], *m.* Clipper.

cercenadura [ther-thay-nah-doo'-rah], *f.* Clipping, retrenchment. *-pl.* Cuttings.

cercenar [ther-thay-nar'], *ra.* 1. To pare, to retrench, to clip. 2. To lop off the ends or extremities. 3. To lessen (gastos). 4. To curtail, to cut away; to abridge.

cercera [ther-thay'-rah], *f.* Air-tube of a vault to extract the foul air.

cerceta [ther-thay'-tah], *f.* 1. (*Orn.*) Widgeon, garganey, a species of duck. 2. Among sportsmen, the first pearl which grows about the bur of a deer's horn: an antler.

cercillo [ther-theel'-lyo], *m.* 1. Earring. V. ZARCILLO. 2. Tendril of a vine. V. TIJERETA. 3. Hoop.

cercio, cerción [therr'-the-o, ther-the-on'], *m.* An Indian mocking-bird.

cerciorar [ther-the-o-rar'], *va.* To assure, to ascertain, to affirm.

cerco [therr'-co], *m.* 1. Hoop or ring. 2. (*Mil.*) Blockade of a place. 3. Circular motion. 4. Circle, a private assembly. 5. Frame or case of a door or window. **En cerco,** round about. **Poner cerco a una plaza,** to block up a place. **Levantar el cerco,** to raise a blockade. **Echar cerco,** to surround game with dogs. **Cerco de puerta o ventana,** the frame of a door or window. **Hacer un cerco,** to strike a circle.

cercón [thayr-kone'], *adv.* (*LAm.*) Rather close.

cercopiteco [ther-co-pe-tay'-co], *m.* Cercopithecus, a kind of long-tailed monkey.

cercha [therr'-chah], *f.* A wooden rule for measuring convex or concave objects.

cerchar [ther-char'], *va.* V. ACODAR.

cerchón [ther-chone'], *m.* V. CIMBRIA.

cerda [therr'-dah], *f.* 1. Strong hair in a horse's tail or mane; a bristle. 2. (*Prov.*) Corn just cut and formed into sheaves. 3. (*Prov.*) Bundle of flax broken but not yet hackled. 4. Sow. **Cerda de puerco,** hog's bristle. 5. Slut, whore.

cerdada [thayr-dah'-dah], *f.* Dirty trick; nasty thing.

cerdamen [ther-dah'-men], *m.* Handful of bristles.

cerdana [ther-dah'-nah], *f.* Kind of dance in Catalonia.

cerdazo [ther-dah'-tho], *m.* 1. (*aug.*) A large hog or pig. 2. Hair sieve. V. CEDAZO.

cerdear [ther-day-ar'], *vn.* 1. To be weak in the forequarter (animales). 2. To emit a harsh and inharmonious sound (instrumentos de cuerda). 3. To decline a request or demand by subterfuges and evasions. 4. (*Mus.*) To scratch, to rasp, to grate; (*Mech.*) To work badly. 2. To hedge, to jib, to hold back. 3. To play a dirty trick.

Cerdeña [ther-day'-nyah], *f.* Sardinia.

cerdillo [ther-deel'-lyo], *m. dim.* A small hog or pig.

cerdito, ta [ther-dee'-to], *f. & m.* Piglet.

cerdo [therr'-do], *m.* 1. Hog or pig. **Cerdo salvaje,** wild pig. 2. **Cerdo marino,** porpoise. 3. (*Culin.*) Pork. 4. (*fig.*) Dirty person, slovenly fellow. *-a.* 1. Dirty, filthy. 2. Rotten.

cerdoso [ther-do'-so], *m.* Bristly.

cereal [thay-ray-ahl'], *a.* Cereal, relating to the food-producing grasses. *-m. pl.* Cereals.

cerebelo [thay-ray-bay'-lo], *m.* (*Anat.*) Cerebellum, the hind-brain.

cerebral [thay-ray-brahl'], *a.* Cerebral, brain; calculating.

cerebro [thay-ray'-bro], *m.* 1. Cerebrum, the front brain. 2. The entire brain. 3. Intelligence. **Cerebro eléctronico,** electronic brain. **Estrujar el cerebro,** to rack one's brains.

cerecilla [thay-ray-theel'-lyah], *f. dim.* V. GUINDILLA.

cerecita [chay-ray-thee'-tah], *f. dim.* A small cherry.

ceremonia [thay-ray-mo'-ne-ah], *f.* 1. Ceremony, outward rite, external form of religion. 2. Ceremony, formality, forms of civility. 3. Ceremony, outward form of state. 4. Course, empty form, an affected compliment paid to a person. **Lo hace de pura ceremonia,** he does it out of mere ceremony. **De ceremonia,** with all ceremony or pomp. **Reunirse de ceremonia,** formal meeting, ceremonial meeting.

ceremonial [thay-ray-mo-ne-ahl'], *m.* A book of ceremonies for public occasions.

ceremonial [thay-ray-mo-ne-ahl'], *a.* Ceremonial, ceremonious.

ceremonialmente [thay-ray-mo-ne-all-men'-tay], *adv.* V. CEREMONIOSAMENTE.

ceremoniáticamente [thay-ray-mo-ne-ah'-te-cah-men-tay], *adv.* Ceremoniously.

ceremoniático, ca [thay-ray-mo-ne-ah'-te-co, cah], *a.* Ceremonious.

ceremoniosamente [thay-ray-mo-ne-o-sah-men'-tay], *adv.* Ceremoniously; formally; stiffly, with an excess of politeness.

ceremonioso, sa [thay-ray-mo-ne-o'-so, sah], *a.* Ceremonious, polite, formal, complimental.

céreo [thay'-ray-o], *m. (Bot.)* Torchthistle. *-a.* Wax, waxen.

cereolita [thay-ray-o-lee'-tah], *f.* A soft, waxy-looking lava.

cerería [thay-ray-ree'-ah], *f.* 1. Wax-chandler's shop.

cerero [thay-ray'-ro], *m.* 1. Waxchandler. 2. *(Prov.)* An idle person, a vagrant.

cereza [thay-ray'-thah], *f.* Cherry. **Cereza silvestre,** wild cherry.

cerezal [thay-ray-thahl'], *m.* Plantation of cherry-trees; cherry orchard.

cerezo [thay-ray'-tho], *m. (Bot.)* Cherry-tree, cherry-wood.

ceribón, ceribones [thay-re-bone', bo'-ness], *m.* Act of an insolvent debtor surrendering his estate to his creditors. **Hacer ceribones,** To make submissive and affected compliments.

cérico, ca [thay'-re-co, cah], *a.* Ceric, relating to cerium.

ceriflor [thay-re-flor'], *f. (Bot.)* Honey-wort, honey-flower Cerinthe. *V.* CERINTO.

cerilla [thay-reel'-lyah], *f.* 1. Thin wax tapers rolled up in different forms. 2. Ball of wax and other ingredients used formerly by women as a kind of paint. 3. Wax-tablet. 4. Wax of the ear. 6. A wax-match.

cerillo [thay-reel'-lyo], *m. (Mex.)* Match.

cerina [thay-ree'-nah], *f.* A variety of wax (or waxlike material) extracted from the cork-tree.

cerinto [thay-reen'-to], *m. (Bot.)* Wax-flower, honey-wort, a plant of the borage family.

cerio, cererio [thay'-re-o, thay-ray'-re-o], *m. (Chem.)* Cerium or cererium Cerio, an annual solanaceous plant of Cochin China.

cerita [thay-ree'-tah], *f.* Cerite, a resinous brown silicate of cerium found in copper mines.

cermeña [ther-may'-nyah], *f.* A small early pear called the muscadine.

cermeño [ther-may'-nyo], *m. (Bot.)* Muscadine pear-tree.

cernada [ther-nah'-dah], *f.* 1. Coarse ashes which remain in the strainer after the lye is put on. 2. Size laid on canvas to prepare it for painting. 3. Plaster of ashes and other ingredients used by farriers in the cure of horses.

cernadero [ther-nah-day'-ro], *m.* 1. Coarse linen which serves as a strainer for the lye to buck clothes with 2. Thread and silk skeins for making ribbon. 3. Apron worn sifting flour. 4. Place for sifting flour.

cernedor [ther-nay-dor'], *m.* Sieve.

cerneja [ther-nay'-hah], *f.* Fetlock of a horse growing behind the pastern joints.

cernejudo, da [ther-nay-hoo'-do, dah], *a.* Having large fetlocks.

cerner [ther-nerr'], *va.* 1. To sift, to bolt. 2. *(fig.)* To scan, to watch. *-vn.* 1. To bud and blossom. 2. To drizzle, to fall in small drops. *-vr.* 1. To waggle, to wiggle, to move from side to side. 2. To soar (pájaros). 3. To hover (subir); to circle (helicóptero); to hang over.

cernícalo [ther-nee'-cah-lo], *m.* 1. *(Orn.)* Kestrel, sparrowhawk, windhover. 2. A person of scanty abilities. **Coger** or **pillar un cernícalo,** to be fuddled, to be tight, to be drunk.

cernidillo [ther-ne-deel'-lyo], *m.* 1. Thick mist or small rain; mizzle, drizzle. 2. A short and waddling gait.

cernido [ther-nee'-do], *m.* 1. Sifting. 2. The flour sifted. **Cernido, da,** *pp.* of CERNER.

cernidor [ther-nee-dor'], *m.* Sieve.

cernidura [ther-ne-doo'-rah], *f.* Sifting.

cernir [ther-neer'], *va.* 1. *V.* CERNER. 2. To examine, to purify.

cero [thay'-ro], *m.* 1. Zero, cipher, an arithmetical symbol, nothing, nought. **Ser un cero,** to be a mere cipher. **Por 3 goles a cero,** by three goals to nill. **Estamos a 40 a 0,** the game stands at 40-love. **Yo en eso estoy cero, I**'m not good at that. **Tendremos que partir nuevamente de cero,** *(fig.)* we shall have to start from scratch again. 2. Police car.

ceroferario [thay-ro-fay-rah'-re-o], *m.* The acolyte who carries the *cirial* or large candle-stick.

cerografía [thay-ro-grah-fee'-ah], *f.* Cerography, the art or process of engraving or writing on wax.

cerollo, lla [thay-rol'-lyo, lyah], *a.* Reaped when green and soft (grano).

cerón [thay-rone'], *m.* Dregs of pressed wax formed into a cake.

ceroso [thay-ro'-so], *a.* Waxen, waxy, waxlike.

cerote [thay-ro'-tay], *m.* 1. Shoemaker's wax, shoeblacking. 2. *(Coll.)* Panic, fear. 3. Cerate, a plaster. 4. *(CAm. Mex.)* Piece of human excrement, stool. **Estar hecho un cerote,** to be covered in dirt.

cerotear [thay-ro-tay-ar'], *va.* To wax (hilo).

ceroto [thay-ro'-to], *m.* A soft cerate of oil and wax.

ceroya [thay-ro'-yah], *f.* Crops of corn which begin to grow yellow.

cerquillo [ther-keel'-lyo], *m.* 1. *(dim.)* A small circle or hoop. 2. The seam or welt of a shoe. 3. The ring of hair or tonsure on the head; fringe (fleco).

cerquita [ther-kee'-tah], *f. dim.* Small inclosure.

cerquita [ther-kee'-tah], *adv.* At a small distance, nigh or near in point of time or place. **Aquí cerquita,** just by.

cerrada [ther-rah'-dah], *f.* 1. The strongest part of a hide or skin which covers the backbone of an animal. 2. *(Obs.)* Shutting or locking up of a thing. **Hacer cerrada,** to commit a gross fault or palpable mistake.

cerradero [ther-rah-day'-ro], *m.* 1. Staple which receives the bolt of a lock. 2. Any hole made to receive the bolt of a lock. 3. *(Obs.)* Purse-strings.

cerradero, ra [ther-rah-day'-ro, rah], *m. & f. & a.* Applied to the place locked, and to the thing with which it is locked, locking, fastening. **Echar la cerradera,** to lend a deaf ear, to refuse. **Caja cerradera,** box that can be locked.

cerradizo, za [ther-rah-dee'-tho, thah], *a.* That which may be locked or fastened.

cerrado [ther-rah'-do], *m. V.* CERCADO.

cerrado, da [ther-rah'-do, dah], *a.* 1. Close, reserved, dissembling. 2. Secret, concealed. 3. Obstinate, inflexible. **A ojos cerrados,** without examination. **A puerta cerrada,** privately, secretly. **Cerrado por obras,** closed for repair. **Aquí huele a cerrado,** it smells stuffy in here. 4. Obscure, incomprehensible. 5. Sharp, tight (curva). 6. Thick, full. 7. Reserved, quiet, uncommunicative; secretive. **Cerrado de mollera,** dense, dim (poco inteligente). 8. Typical, all-too-typical. 9. With a broad accent, marked, strong (persona); **habló con cerrado acento,** he spoke with a strong accent. *-pp.* of CERRAR.

cerrador [ther-rah-dor'] *m.* 1. Shutter, one that shuts. 2. Porter or doorkeeper. 3. Tie, fastening. 4. Bond, obligation.

cerradura [ther-rah-doo'-rah], *f.* 1. Closure, the act of shutting or lockiny up. 2. Lock. **Cerradura de golpe** or **de muelle,** springlock. **Cerradura de combinación,** combination lock. **Cerradura de seguridad,** safety lock. 3. Park or piece of ground surrounded with an inclosure.

cerradurilla, ita [ther-rah-doo-reel'-lyah, ee'-tah], *f. dim.* A small lock.

cerraja [ther-rah'-hah], *f.* 1. Lock of a door. 2. *(Bot.)* Common sow thistle. **Todo es agua de cerrajas,** it is all good for nothing, or it is nothing but empty words.

cerrajear [ther-rah-hay-ar'], *vn.* To carry on the trade of a locksmith.

cerrajería [ther-rah-hay-ree'-ah], *f.* 1. Trade of a locksmith. 2. Locksmith's shop or forge.

cerrajero [ther-rah-hay'-ro], *m.* Locksmith.

cerramiento [ther-rah-me-en-to], *m.* 1. Closure, occlusion, the act of shutting or locking up. 2. Costiveness. 3. Inclosure. 4. The finishing of the roof of a building. 5. Partition walls of a house. 6. *(For.)* Conclusion of an argument; inference.

cerrar [ther-rar], *va. & vn.* 1. To close, to shut, to occlude, to foreclose, to shut up the inlets or outlets of a place, to obstruct a passage. 2. To fit a door or window in its frame or case. 3. To lock, to fasten with a bolt or latch. 4. To include, to contain. 5. To fence or inclose a piece of ground. 6. *(Met.)*

To terminate or finish a thing. 7. To stop up, to obstruct. 8. To prohibit, to forbid, to interdict. 9. To engage the enemy. **Cerrar la carta,** to fold a letter. **Cerrar algo con llave,** to lock something. **Han cerrado la frontera,** they've closed the border. 10. To turn off (grifo, agua, gas). 11. To bring up the rear. **Cerrar la marcha,** to come last, to bring up the rear. **La carretera está cerrada por la nieve,** the road is blocked by snow. **Cerrar la cuenta,** to close an account. **Cerrar la boca,** *(Met.)* to be silent. **Cerrar la mollera,** *(Met.)* to begin to get sense. **Cerrar la puerta,** *(Met.)* to give a flat denial. **Cerrar a alguno la puerta para que no entre,** to lock one out, to shut out. **Cerrar los ojos,** 1. To die. 2. To sleep. 3. *(Met.)* Blindly, to submit to another's opinion. **Al cerrar del día,** at the close of day, at nightfall. -*vn.* **Esta puerta cierra bien,** this door closes tightly. **Cerramos a las 9,** we close at 9. **Dejar una puerta sin cerrar,** to leave a door open. -*vr.* 1. To remain firm in one's opinion. 2. To be shut or locked up. 3. To grow cloudy and overcast. 4. To close up (tropas). **Cerrarse todas las puertas,** to be completely destitute.

cerraurgal [ther-rah-oor-gahl'], *m.* Water conduit.

cerrazón [ther-rah-thone'], *f.* 1. Fog preceding a storm. 2. Ignorant stubbornness, intolerance, etc.

cerrejón [ther-ray-hone'], *m.* Hillock.

cerrero, ra [ther-ray'-ro, rah], *a.* 1. Running wild. **Caballo cerrero,** an unbroken horse. 2. Haughty, lofty. 3. *(And. Carib.)* Unsweetened; bitter; ordinary; simple.

cerreta [ther-ray'-tah], *f. (Naut.)* Spar, rough tree. V. PERCHA.

cerril [ther-reel'], *a.* 1. Mountainous, rough, uneven (terreno). 2. Wild, untamed (ganado). **Puente cerril,** a small narrow bridge for cattle. 3. *(Met.)* Rude, unpolished, unmannerly.

cerrilismo [thayr-re-les'-mo], *m.* Roughness, uncouthness; obstinacy; small-mindedness.

cerrilla [ther-reel'-lyah], *f.* A die for milling coins.

cerrillar [ther-reel'-lyr], *va.* To mill coined metal, or to mark it at the edge.

cerrillo [ther-reel'-lyo], *m. dim.* A little eminence. **Cerrillos,** the dies for milling coined metal.

cerrión [ther-re-on'], *m.* 1. Icicle. 2. Fresh cheese.

cerro [therr'-ro], *m.* 1. Hill or high land. 2. Neck of an animal 3. Backbone, or the ridge it forms. 4. Flax or hemp which is hackled and cleaned. 5. Lot, heap. **Un cerro de,** a heap of. **Cerro enriscado,** a steep and inaccessible mountain. **En cerro,** nakedly, barely. **Como por los cerros de Úbeda,** *(Coll.)* his mind is far away.

cerrojazo [thayr-ro-hah'-tho], *m.* Slamming. **Dar cerrojazo,** to slam the bolt; to end unexpectedly; to close unexpectedly. **Dar cerrojazo a uno,** to slam the door in somebody's face.

cerrojillo [ther-ro-heel'-lyo], *m.* 1. *(Orn.)* A wagtail warbler. 2. *(dim.)* A small bolt.

cerrojo [ther-ro'-ho], *m.* Bolt, latch. **Táctica de cerrojo,** defensive play, negative play. **Echar el cerrojo,** to bolt the door.

cerrotino [ther-ro-tee'-no], *m.* Carded hemp.

cerruma [ther-roo'-mah], *f.* Weak or defective quarter in horses.

certamen [ther-tah'-men], *m.* 1. Duel; battle. 2. Literary controversy, disputation; competition. **Certamen de belleza,** beauty contest.

certeramente [ther-tay-rah-men-tay], *adv.* Accurately, unerringly.

certero, ra [ther-tay'-ro, rah], *m. & f.* 1. Sharpshooter. -*a.* 2. An excellent shot, well-aimed. 3. Accurate, sure, certain. 4. Well-informed.

certeza [ther-tay'-thah], *f.* Certainty, certitude. **Tener la certeza de que...,** to know for certain that..

certidumbre [ther-te-doom'-bray], *f.* 1. V. CERTEZA. 2. Security, obligation to fulfil a thing.

certificación [ther-te-fe-cah-the-on'], *f.* 1. Certificate, attesting the truth of a fact or event. 2. Return of a writ. 3. Certainty, security.

certificado [ther-te-fe-cah'-do], *m.* Certificate. **Certificado de actitud,** testimonial. **Certificado de ciudadanía,** naturalization papers. **Certificado médico,** medical certificate. **Certificado de vacuna,** vaccination certificate. *V.* CERTIFICACIÓN. -**Certificado, da,** *pp.* of CERTIFICAR.

certificador, ra [ther-te-fe-cah-dor', rah], *m. & f.* Certifier.

certificar [ther-te-fe-car'], *va.* 1. To assure, to affirm, to certify. **Certificar la carta,** in the post-office, to assure that a letter will reach its destination; to register a letter. 2. To prove by a public instrument.

certificativo, va, or **certificatorio, ria** [ther-te-fe-cah-tee'-vo, vah, ther-te-fe cah-to'-re-o, ah], *a.* That which certifies or serves to certify.

certísimo [ther-tee'-se-mo], *a. sup.* of CIERTO; most certain.

certiud [ther-tee-tood'], *f.* Certainty, certitude.

cerúleo, lea [thay-roo'-lay-o, ah], *a.* Cerulean, skyblue.

cerumen [thay-roo'-men], *m.* Earwax, cerumen.

ceruminoso, sa [thay-roo-me-no'-so, sah], *a.* Ceruminous, producing cerumen.

cerusa [thay-roo'-sah], *f.* Ceruse, whitelead.

cerval [ther-vahl'], *a.* Belonging to a deer. **Miedo cerval,** great fear.

cervantesco, ca [ther-van-tes'-co, cah], **Cervántico** [ther-vahn'-te-co], *a.* In the style of Cervantes.

cervantino [thayr-vahn-te'-no], *a.* Cervantine; relating to Cervantes. **Estilo cervantino,** Cervantine style. **Estudios cervantinos,** Cervantes studies.

cervantista [ther-van-tees'-tah], *a.* Admiring Cervantes, specialist in Cervantes

cervático, illo [ther-vah-tee'-co, eel'-lyo], *m. dim.* A small deer.

cervato [ther-vah'-to], *m.* A fawn.

cervecería [ther-vay-thay-ree'-ah], *f.* 1. Brewery. 2. Alehouse.

cervecero [ther-vay-thay'-ro], *m.* 1. Brewer. 2. Beer-seller. *a.* **La industria cervezera,** the brewing industry.

cerveda [ther-vay'-dah], *f.* Extremity of the ribs of pork.

cerveza [ther-vay'-thah], *f.* Beer or ale, malt liquor. **Cerveza de barril,** draught beer, beer on draught. **Cerveza de botella,** bottled beer. **Cerveza clara,** light beer. **Cerveza negra,** brown beer. **Cerveza de sifón,** draught beer.

cervicabra [ther-ve-cah'-brah], *f.* Gazelle.

cervical [ther-ve-cahl'], *a. (Anat.)* Cervical.

cervigudo, da [ther-ve-goo'-do, dah], *a.* 1. High or thick-necked. 2. Obstinate, stubborn.

cerviguillo [ther-ve-geel'-lyo], *m.* Nape of the neck.

cervino, na [ther-vee'-no, nah], *a.* Resembling a deer.

cerviolas [ther-ve-oh'-las], *f. pl. (Naut.)* Catheads. *V.* SERVIOLAS.

cerviz [ther-veeth'], *f.* Cervix, nape of the neck. **Ser de dura cerviz,** to be incorrigible. **Doblar** or **bajar la cerviz,** *(Met.)* to humble oneself. **Levantar la cerviz,** *(Met.)* to be elated, to grow proud.

cervuno, na [ther-voo'-no, nah], *a.* 1. Resembling or belonging to a deer. 2. Of the color of a deer.

CES *m. (Esp.) abr.* de **Consejo Económico y Social.**

cesacio or **Cesación a Divinis,** [thay-sah'-the-o or thay-sa-the-on'ah de-vee'nis], *f. (Lat.)* Suspension from religious functions.

cesación, *f.* **cesamiento,** *m.* [thay-sah-the-on', they-sah-me-en'-to]. Cessation, ceasing, pause.

cesante [thay-sahn'-tay], *m.* A public officer dismissed for economical or political reasons, but left in some cases with a portion of his salary until he obtains a new position; a retired official. -*pa.* Ceasing.

cesante [thay-sahn'-tay], *a.* Jobless, dismissed from a position.

cesantía [thay-san-tee'-ah], *f.* 1. The state of being a *cesante,* and the salary he receives. 2. Retirement pension, redundancy compensation.

cesar [thay-sar'], *vn.* 1. To cease, to give over, to forbear. 2. To leave or leave off, to desist. **Cesar de hacer algo,** to stop doing something. **No cesa de hablar,** she never stops talking.

Sin cesar, ceaselessly. -*va.* 1. To cease, to stop; to stop, to suspend. 2. To sack, to fire, to remove from office; **le cesaron en el trabajo,** they sacked him from his work.

César [they'-sar], *m.* Caesar (emperador).

cesárea, rea [thay-sah'-ray-o, ah], *a.* Imperial. **Operacion cesárea,** *(Surg.)* Cesarean operation.

cesariano, na [thay-sah-re-ah'-no, nah], *a.* Relating to Julius Caesar.

cesariense [thay-sah-re-en'-say], *a.* Pertaining to Caesar.

cese [thay'-say], *m.* 1. Cease: a mark put up against the names of persons who receive payment from the public treasury, that their pay should cease. **Dar el cese a uno,** to retire somebody. 2. Cessation; suspension, stoppage. **Cese de alarma,** all-clear signal. **Cese de fuego,** cease fire. **Cese de pagos,** suspension of payments.

cesible [thay-see'-blay], *a. (Law.)* That which may be ceded.

cesión [thay-se-on'], *f.* Cession, or tranfer of goods or estates made in one's favor; resignation, concession. **Cesión de bienes,** surrender of the estate of an insolvent debtor into the hands of his creditors.

cesionario, cesonario, ria [thay-se-onah'-re-o, thay-so-nah'-re-o, ah], *m. & f.* Cessionary, one in whose favor a tranfer is made, granted, assign.

cesionista [thay-se-o-nees'-tah], *m.* Transferer, assigner.

césped, céspede [thes'-ped, thes'-pay-day], *m.* 1. Lawn, grass. **Cortar el césped,** to mow the lawn. 2. Pitch (para juegos). Green (boachas). Sod, turf (trozo de tierra con hierba).

cespedera [thes-pay-day'-rah], *f.* Field where green sods are cut.

cesta [thes'-tah], *f.* Basket, pannier. **Cesta de la compra,** shopping basket. **Cesta de costura,** sewing basket. **Cesta para papeles,** wastepaper basket. **Llevar la cesta,** to go along as chaperon.

cestada [thes-tah'-dah], *f.* A basketful.

cestería [thes-tay-ree'-ah], *f.* Place where baskets are made or sold.

cestero, ra [thes-tay'-ro], *m. & f.* Basket maker or seller.

cestica, illa, ita [thes-tee'-cah, eel'-lyah, ee'tah], *f. dim.* A small basket, handbasket.

cestico, illo, ito [thestee'-co, eel'-lyo, ee'-to], *m. dim.* A little basket.

cesto [thes'-to], *m.* A handbasket, hutch. **Estar hecho un cesto,** to be overcome by sleep or liquor. **Cesto de la colada,** clothes basket. **Cesto para papeles,** wastepaper basket.

cestón [thes-tone'], *m.* 1. A large pannier or basket. 2. *(Mil.)* Gabion. -*pl.* Corbeils.

cestonada [thes-to-nah'-dah], *f.* Range of gabions.

cesura [thay-soo'-rah], *f.* Caesura, a figure or pause in poetry.

cetáceo, cea [thay-tah'-thay-o, ah], *a.* Cetaceous, of the whale kind.

cetárea, cetaría [ ], *f.* Shellfish farm.

cetís [thay-tees'], *m.* An old Galician coin.

cetorrino [thay-tor-re'-no], *m.* Basking shark.

cetre [thay'-tray], *m.* A small brass or copper bucket. V. ACETRE.

cetrería [thay-tray-ree'-ah], *f.* 1. Falconry. 2. Hawking; fowling with falcons.

cetrero [thay-tray'-ro], *m.* 1. Verger. 2. Falconer, sportsman.

cetrífero [thay-tree'-ro], *m. (Poet.)* One who bears a sceptre.

cetrino, na [thay-tree'-no, nah], *a.* 1. Citrine, lemon-colored, greenish-yellow. 2. *(Met.)* Jaundiced, melancholy. 3. Belonging to citron.

cetro [thay'-tro], *m.* 1. Sceptre. 2. *(Met.)* Reign of a prince. **Empuñar el cetro,** to ascend the throne. 3. Verge carried by chaplains on solemn occasions. 4. Wand or staff borne by the deputies of confraternities.

chabacana [chah-bah-cah'-nah], *f.* An insipid kind of plum.

chabacanada [chah-bah-ca-nah'-dah], *f.* A very vulgar expression or observation.

chabacanamente [chah-bah-ca-nah-men'-tay], *adv.* In a bungling manner.

chabacanear [chah-bah-cah-nay-ar'], *vn. (LAm.)* To say coarse things.

chabacanería [chah-bah-ca-nay-ree'-ah], *f.* 1. Want of cleanliness and elegance. 2. Vulgarity, bad taste; commonness. 3. Coarse thing, vulgar remark.

chabacano, na [chah-bah-cah'-no, nah], *a.* Coarse, unpolished, ill-finished. -*m. (Mex.)* A kind of apricot.

chabán [chah-bahn'], *m.* A month corresponding to May among the ancient orientals.

chabeta [chah-bay'-tah], *f.* 1. Forelock key. 2. *(Coll.)* Judgment, reason. **Perder la chabeta,** *(Met.)* to lose one's senses, to run crazy. 3. *(Cuba)* A kind of knife used by cigar-makers.

chabola [chah-bo'-lah], *f.* Shack, shanty. **Chabolas** *(LAm.),* Shanty town.

chabolismo [cha-bo-les'mo], *m.* Shanty towns.

chabolista [cha-bo-les'-tah], *m. & f.* Shanty town dweller.

chabón [chah-bone'], *a.* Daft, stupid. -*f.* Twit.

chaborra [chah-bor'-rah], *f. (Coll. Prov.)* A young lass, fifteen to twenty years old.

chaborreta [chah-bor-ray'-tah], *f. dim. (Coll. Prov.)* A very young lass.

chaca [chah'-cah], *f.* **Estar en chaca,** *(Carib.)* to be flat broke.

chacal [chah-cahl'], *m.* Jackal.

chacalín, na [chah-cah-leen'], *m. f.* 1. *(CAm.)* Kid, child. 2. Shrimp (camarón).

chacanear [chah-cah-nay-ar'], *va.* 1. *(Cono Sur)* To spur violently. 2. *(Cono Sur)* To pester, to annoy. 3. *(And.)* To use daily.

chacaneo [chah-cah-nay'-o], *m.* **Para el chacaneo,** *(And.)* For daily use.

chácara [chah'-ca-rah], *f.* 1. *(S. Amer.)* A small plantation. V. CHACRA. 2. *(And. CAm. Cono Sur)* Sore, ulcer. 3. *(And. CAm. Carib.)* Large leather bag.

chacarería [chah-cah-ray-ree'-ah], *f.* 1. *(LAm.) (Agri.)* Market gardens, truck farms. 2. *(And. Cono Sur)* horticulture, market gardening, truck farming.

chacarero [chah-cah-ray'-ro], *m.* 1. *(LAm.)* Farmer, grower; market gardener, truck farmer. 2. *(Cono Sur)* Sandwich.

chacina [chah-thee'-nah], *f. (Prov.)* Pork seasoned with spice for sausages and balls.

chacinería [chah-thee-nay-ree'-ah], *f.* Pork butcher's.

chacó [chah-co'], *m.* A high military cap, shako.

chacolí [chah-co-lee'], *m.* A light white wine made in the Basque Country.

chacolotear [chah-co-lo-tay-ar'], *vn.* To clatter (caballos).

chacoloteo [chah-co-lo-tay'-o], *m.* The clapping of a loose horseshoe.

chaconá [cha-con-nah'], *m.* **chaconada** [cha-co-nah'-dah], *f.* Jaconet, a soft cotton cloth for summer dresses.

chacota [chah-co'-tah], *f.* Noisy mirth. **Echar a chacota alguna cosa,** to carry a thing off with a joke. **Hacer chacota de alguna cosa,** to turn a thing into ridicule.

chacotear [chah-co-tay-ar'], *vn.* To indulge in noisy mirth, to scoff, to have fun. -*vr.* **Chacotearse de algo,** to make fun of something.

chacotero, ra [chah-co-tay'-ro, rah], *a.* Waggish, ludicrous, acting the merry-andrew. *m.* fond of a laugh.

chacra [chah'-crah], *f. (Amer.)* An Indian rustic habitation, plantation, or farm.

chacuaco [chah-coo-ah'-co], *m.* 1. *(Mex.)* A small furnace for melting metals. 2. *(CAm.)* Roughly-made cigar. -*a. (Coll.)* Rustic, boorish, clownish.

chacual [chah-coo-ahl'], *m. (Mex.)* A gourd-cup.

chacha [chah'-chah], *f.* Familiar abbreviation of *muchacha,* maid, nurse maid. Girly." V. CHACHO.

chachacaste [chah-chah-cas'-tay], *m. (CAm.)* Liquor, brandy.

chachal [chah-chahl'], *m.* 1. *(Peru)* Graphite, plumbago. 2. *(CAm.)* Charm necklace.

chachalaca [chah-cha-lah'-cah], *f. (Mex.)* A grouse, a bird which cries continually while flying; *(Met.)* A chatterer.

chachar [chah-char'], *va. (And.)* To chew (coca).

cháchara [chah'-cha-rah], *f.* 1. *(Coll.)* Chitchat, idle talk, garrulity. **Todo eso no es más que cháchara,** that is all mere chitchat. 2. *(And.)* Joke. 3. *(Cono Sur. Mex.)* **Cháchara,** things, bits and pieces.

chacharadas [chah-chah-rah'-das], *f. pl. (Cono Sur)* Useless ornaments; trinkets.

chacharear [chah-cha-ray-ar'], *vn. (Coll.)* To prate. *-va. (Mex.)* To deal in, to sell.

chacharera [chah-cha-ray'-rah], *f. & a.* Forward, talkative woman.

chacharería [chah-cha-ray-ree'-ah], *f. (Prov.)* Verbosity, verbiage, garrulity.

chacharero, chacharón [chah-chah-ray'-ro, chah-cha-rone'], *m. & : a.* 1. Prater, gabbler. 2. Chattering, garrulous. *-m.* Chatterbox (parlanchín). 3. *(Mex.)* Rag-and-bone man.

chache [chah'-chay], *m.* Oneself, me, the speaker. **El perjudicado es el chache,** I'll be the one to suffer.

chachi [chah'-che], *V.* CHANCHI.

chacho [chah'-cho], *m.* Boy, kid, lad (muchacho). Girl, lass (muchacha). **¡Ven aquí, chacho!,** come here, lad!

Chad [chad], *m.* Chad.

chafa [chah'-fah], *a. (Mex.)* Useless.

chafadura [chah-fah-doo'-rah], *f.* 1. Act of matting velvet. 2. Rumpling; soiling clothes.

chafaldetes [chah-fal-day'-tes], *m. (Naut.)* Clew lines.

chafaldita [chah-fa-dee'-tes], *f.* Joke, fun, repartee.

chafalla [chah-fahl'-lyah], *f. (Prov.)* A tattered suit of clothes.

chafallar [chah-fal-lyar'], *va.* To botch, to mend in a clumsy manner.

chafallo [chah-fahl'-lyo], *m.* Coarse patch, place mended in a botching and clumsy manner.

chafallón, na [chah-fal-lyone', nah], *m. & f.* A botcher.

chafalonía [chah-fa-lo-nee'-ah], *f.* 1. *(Amer. Peru)* Old plate, or broken articles of silver for remelting. 2. *(And.)* Worn-out gold jewellery.

chafalote [chah-fah-lo'-tay], *a. (Cono Sur)* common, vulgar. *-m. V.* CHAFAROTE. 3. *(LAm.)* Prick (pene).

chafar [chah-far'], *va.* 1. To make velvet or plush lose its lustre by pressing or crushing the pile. 2. To crease, to rumple, to soil clothing. 3. *(Met.)* To cut one short in his discourse. **Quedó chafado,** he was speechless. 4. To mess up, to make a hash of. **Le chafaron el negocio,** they messed up the deal for him. 5. *(Cono Sur)* To hoax, to deceive.

chafarote [chah-fa-ro'-tay], *m.* 1. A short, broad Turkish sword. 2. *(CAm.)* Cop.

chafarrinada [chah-far-re-nah'-dah], *f.* 1. Blot or stain in clothes or other things. 2. *(Met.)* Spot in reputation and character.

chafarrinar [chah-far-re-nar'], *va.* To blot, to stain.

chafarrinón [chah-far-re-none'], *m.* Blot, stain. **Echar un chafarrinón,** *(Met.)* To disgrace one's family by a mean or dishonorable action.

chafir(r)o [chah-fe'-ro], *m. (CAm. Mex.)* Knife.

chaflán [chah-flahn'], *m.* 1. Bevel, obtuse angle, chamfer. 2. Corner house. 3. *(Aut.)* Street corner.

chaflanar [chah-fla-nar'], *va.* To form a bevel, to cut a slope.

chagila [chah-hee'-lah], *f. (Amer.)* A slender reed which serves as a weapon among Indians of Ecuador.

chagra [chah'-grah], *m.* 1. Farm (chacra). 2. Peasant.

chagua [chah'-goo-ah], *f. (And.)* Gang; system of gang labor.

chaguar [chah-goo-ar'], *va. (Cono Sur)* To milk (vaca); to wring out (ropa).

chaguar [chah-goo-ar'], *m. (And.)* Agave fiber, hemp; rope of agave fiber.

chagüe [chah'-goo-ay], *m. (CAm.)* Swamp, bog.

chagüite [chah-goo-e'-tay], *vn. (CAm. Mex.)* Swamp; flooded field; banana plantation.

chagüitear [chah-goo-e-tay-ar'], *vn. (CAm. Mex.)* To chatter, to natter.

chai [chah'-e], *f.* Bird, dame.

chai(ne) [chah-e'-nay], *m. (And. CAm.)* Shoeshine.

chainear [chah-e-nay-ar'], *va. (CAm.)* To shine, to polish.

chair [chah-ear'], *m.* The inner side of a skin, among tanners.

chaira [chah'-e-rah], *f.* 1. A shoemaker's steel knife for sharpening. 2. Sharpener (para afilar).

chairar [chah-e-rahr'], *va. (Cono Sur)* To sharpen.

chal [chahl], *m.* Shawl. **Chal angosto,** long scarf.

chala [chah'-lah], *f.* 1. Leaf of corn, serving as fodder, chiefly while green. 2. *(And. Cono Sur)* money, dough. 3. *(Cono Sur)* sandal.

chalado, da [chah-lah'-do, dah], *a.* Dotty, round the bend; crazy, mad. **¡Estás chalado!,** you're mad! **Estar chalado por Jane, jazz,** to be crazy about Jane, jazz.

chaladura [chah-lah-doo'-rah], *f.* Crankiness.

chalán, na [chah-lahn', nah], *m. & f.* 1. Hawker, huckster. 2. Jockey, a dealer in horses.

chalana [chah-lah'-nah], *f.* A scow, lighter; square boat.

chalanear [chah-lah-nay-ar'], *va.*

chalaneo [chah-lah-nay-o], *m.* Hard bargaining, horse trading; trickery, deception.

chalanería [chah-lah-nay-ree'-ah], *f.* Artifice and cunning used by dealers in buying and selling.

chalaquear [chah-lah-kay-ar'], *(CAm.)* 1. *vn.* To chatter away, to rabbit on. 2. *va.* To trick, to con.

chalar [chah-lar'], *va.* To drive crazy, to drive round the bend. *-vr.* To go crazy, to go off one's rocker. **Chalarse por,** to be crazy about.

chalaza [chah-lah'-thah], *f.* 1. Chalaza, one of the ligaments uniting the yolk of an egg to the ends; treadle. 2. *(Med.)* Chalazion, a sebaceous tumor of the eyelid, resembling a stye.

chalcosina [chal-co-see'-nah], *f.* Modern name of copper pyrites; chalcopyrite.

chalchigüite, chalchihuite [chal-che-goo-ee'-tay], *m. (Amer.)* Stone of the color and fineness of the emerald. *(Mex.)* Jade.

chale [chah'-lay], *m. & f. (Mex.)* Chink.

chalé [chah-lay'], *m. V.* CHALET.

chaleco [chah-lay'-co], *m.* A waistcoat, vest. **Chaleco anti-balas,** bulletproof, vest. **Chaleco salvavidas,** life jacket.

chalecón [chah-lay-cone'], 1. *a. (Mex.)* Tricky, deceitful. 2. *m.* Conman.

chalequear [chah-lay-kay-ar'], *va. (Cono Sur. Mex.)* Trick.

chalet [chah-layt'], *m. pl*

chalí [chah-lee'], *m. (Com.)* 1. Mohair: a fabric of goat's hair, which is sometimes mixed with silk. 2. Challis, shalli; delaine.

chalina [chah-lee'-nah], *f.* Cravat, scarf.

chalón, chalún [chah-lone', chah-loon'], *m.* Shaloon, a kind of woollen stuff.

chalona [chah-lo'-nah], *f. (Peru)* Mutton cured on ice without salt.

chalupa [chah-loo'-pah], *f.* 1. *(Naut.)* Shallop, launch, a small light vessel, a longboat. 2. *(Mex.)* A canoe for one or two persons. *(Mex.) (Culin.)* Stuffed tortilla.

chalupa [chah-loo'-pah], 1. *a.* Crazy. **Volver chalupa a uno,** to drive somebody crazy. 2. *m.* Madman, crackpot.

chalupero [chah-loo-pay'-ro], *m.* A boatman, canoeman.

chamaca [chah-mah'-cah], *f. (Mex.)* Girl; girlfriend, sweetheart.

chamaco [chah-mah'-co], *m. (Mex.)* Boy, lad; boyfriend.

chamada [chah-mah'-dah], *f.* Chips, splinters of wood, to quicken a fire.

chamagoso, sa [chah-ma-go'-so, sah], *a. (Mex.)* 1. Greasy, filthy. 2. Ill-performed. 3. Vulgar (cosas).

chamaleón [chah-ma-le-on'], *m. V.* CAMALEÓN.

chamano [chah-mah'-no], *m.* A shrub of the Andes.

chamar [chah-mar'], To smoke.

chámara [chah'-mah-ra], *f.* Kindling, brushwood; brush fire, blaze.

chamarasca [chah-ma-rahs'-cah], *f.* 1. A brisk fire, made of brushwood. 2. *(Bot.)* Annual costmary.

chamaraz [chah-ma-rath'], *m. (Bot.)* Water-germander.

chamarilero, chamarillero [chah-ma-re-lay'-ro, chah-ma-reel-lyay'-ro], *m.* 1. Broker who deals in old pictures and furniture. 2. Gambler.

chamarillón [chah-ma-reel-lyone'], *m.* A bad player at cards.

chamariz [chah-ma-reeth'], *m. (Orn. Prov.)* Blue titmouse.

chamarón [chah-ma-rone'], *m. (Orn.)* Long-tailed titmouse.

chamarra [chah-mar'-rah], *f.* 1. Lumber jacket, mackinaw. 2. *(CAm. Carib.)* Blanket, poncho. 3. *(CAm.)* Con, swindle (engaño).

chamarrear [chah-mahr-ray-ar'], *va. (CAm.)* To con, to swindle.

chamarrero [chah-mahr-ray'-ro], *m. (Carib.)* Quack doctor.

chamarreta [chah-mar-ray'-tah], *f.* A short loose jacket with sleeves.

chamarro [chah-mahr'-ro], *m. (CAm. Cono Sur, Mex.)* Coarse woollen blanket; poncho, wollen cap.

chamba [cham'-bah], *f.* 1. *(And.)* Turf, sod. 2. *(And.)* Pond, pool (charca); *(And.)* Ditch (zanja). 3. *(CAm. Mex.)* Work; business; occupation. 4. *(Mex.)* Wages, pay (sueldos); low pay; soft job. 5. *(Carib. Mex.)* Dough, bread.

chamba [chahm'-bah], *f.* Fluke, lucky break. **Por chamba,** by a fluke.

chambeador [cham-bay-ah-dor'], *(Mex.) a & m.f.* Hard-working

chambear [cham-bay-ar'], *(Mex.) va.* To exchange, to swap, to barter. *-vn.* To work; to slave (inútilmente).

chambelán [cham-be-lahn'], *m.* Chamberlain.

chambergo, ga [cham-ber'-go, gah], *a.* Slouched, uncocked (sombrero); coat worn by the regiment of *Chamberga,* and ever since a round uncocked hat has retained that name.

chambero [cham-bay'-ro], *m. (Mex.)* Draughtsman.

chambira [cham-bee'-rah], *f.* A forest palm.

chambón, na [cham-bone', nah], 1. *a.* Awkward, unhandy (person); botcher, lucky. 2. *m. f.* Fluky player, lucky player. **Hacer algo a la chambona,** *(And.) (fig.)* To do something in a rush.

chambonada [cham-bo-nah'-dah], *f.* A blunder, piece or stupidity; at billiards, a fluke.

chambonear [cham-bo-nay-ar'], *vn. (LAm.)* To have a stroke of luck, to win by a fluke.

chamborote [cham-bo-ray'-tay], *a. (And. CAm.)* Long-nosed.

chambra [cham'-brah], *f.* Morning-jacket, a short white blouse used by women over the chemise.

chambra [cham'-brah], *f.* 1. *(Carib.)* Din, hubbub. 2. *(Carib.)* Broad knife.

chambrana [cham-brah'-nah], *f.* 1. Doorcase, jamb-dressing. 2. *(And. Carib.)* Row, uproar, brawl.

chambre [cham'-bray], *m. (CAm.)* Tittle-tattle, gossip.

chambroso [cham-bro'-so], *a. (CAm.)* Gossipy.

chamburgo [cham-boor'-go], *m. (And.)* Pool, stagnant water.

chamelicos [chah-may-lee'-cos], *m. pl. (And. Cono Sur)* lumber, junk, old clothes; *(And.)* Old clothes.

chamelote [chah-may-lo'-tay], *m.* Camlet. **Chamelote de aguas,** clouded camlet. **Chamelote de flores,** flowered camlet.

chamelotina [chah-may-lo-tee'-nah], *f.* Kind of coarse camlet.

chamicera [chah-me-thay'-rah], *f.* A piece of forest where the wood has been scorched by fire.

chamicero, ra [chah-me-thay'-ro, rah], *a.* Belonging to scorched wood.

chamiza [chah-mee'-thah], *f.* Kind of wild cane or reed; chemise.

chamizal [chah-mee-thahl'], *m.* A thicket.

chamizo [chah-mee'-tho], *m.* 1. A piece of wood half burnt. 2. Thatched hut; shack, slum. 3. Den, joint.

chamo, ma [chah'-mo], *m. & f. (LAm.)* Kid, child.

chamorra [chah-mor'-ah], *f.* A shaved or shorn head.

chamorrada [chah-mor-rah'-dah], *f. (Low.)* Butt given with a shorn head.

chamorrar [chah-mor-rar'], *va.* To cut the hair with shears.

chamorro, ra [chah-mor'-ro, rah], 1. *a.* Shorn, bald, shorn. 2. *m.* **Chamorro de cerdo,** *(Mex.)* leg of pork.

champa [cham-pah], *f. (LAm.)* Sod, turf; ball of earth. 2. Mop of hair (greña). 3. *(fig.)* Tangled mass. 4. *(CAm. Mex.)* Roughly-built hut.

champán [cham-pahn'], *m.* 1. Kind of vessel in South America of seventy or eighty tons. 2. Champagne.

champaña [cham-pah'-nyah], *m.* Champagne.

champañazo [cham-pah-nyah'-tho], *m. (Cono Sur)* Champagne party.

champiñón [cham-pee-nyone'], *m.* Mushroom.

champiñones [cham-pe-nyo'-ness], *m. pl.* Edible mushrooms.

champú [cham-poo'], *m.* Shampoo. **Champú anticaspa,** anti-dandruff shampoo.

champudo [cham-poo'-do], *a. (LAm.)* Dishevelled, messy; long-haired (persona).

champurrado [cham-poor-rah'-do], *m. (Coll.)* 1. Jargon. 2. *(Prov.)* A mixture of different liquors. 3. *(Mex.)* Chocolate made in *atole* instead of water. **-Champurrado, da,** *pp.* of CHAMPURRAR.

champurrar [cham-poor-rar'], *va. (Coll.)* 1. To mix liquors. 2. *(Met.)* To speak with a mixture of words of different languages.

champurreado [cahm-poor-ray-ar'], *m.* 1. *(Cono Sur) (Culin.)* Hastily-prepared dish; *(fig.)* Hash, botch. 2. *V.* CHAMPURRADO.

chamuchina [chah-moo-chee'-nah], *f. (Peru)* Populace, rabble.

chamullar [chah-mool-lyar'], *va. vn.* To speak, to talk. **Yo también chamullo el caló,** I can talk slang too. **Chamullaban en Árabe,** they were jabbering away in Arabic.

chamuscado, da [chah-moos-cah-do, dah], *a.* 1. Tipsy, flustered with wine; tinged, inclined, addicted to vice. 2. Smitten, scorched, burnt with a passion. *(Met.)* Contaminated, tainted. *-pp.* of CHAMUSCAR.

chamuscar [chah-moos-car'], *va.* 1. To singe or scorch; to sear. 2. *(Mex.)* To sell cheap. *-vr.* To get scorched, singed.

chamusco [chah-moos'-co], *m. V.* CHAMUSQUINA.

chamuscón [chah-moos-cone'], *m. aug.* A large singe or scorch.

chamusquina [chah-moos-kee'-nah], *f.* 1. Scorching or singeing. 2. *(Met.)* Scolding, wrangling, high words. **Oler a chamusquina,** *(Met.)* to come from hot words to hard blows. 3. *(And CAm.)* Bunch of kids.

chan [chan], *m. (CAm.)* Local guide.

chanada [chah-nah'-dah], *f.* Trick, joke, deceit.

chanar [chah-nar'], *va.* To understand.

chanate [chah-nah'-tay], *m. (Mex.)* A blackbird.

chanca [chan'-cah], *f.* 1. *(And. Cono Sur)* Grinding, crushing. 2. *(And. Cono Sur)* Beating (paliza).

chancaca [chan-cah'-cah], *f.* 1. **Azúcar de chancaca,** the refuse of the sugar in the boiler; raw sugar. 2. *(CAm.) (Culin.)* Maize cake, wheat cake.

chancadora [chan-cah-do'-rah], *f. (LAm.)* Grinder, crusher.

chancal [chan-cahl'], *m.* The moraine of a glacier.

chancar [chan-car'], *va.* 1. *(LAm.)* To grind, to crush (moler); to beat; to beat up; to ill-treat (maltratar). 2. *(And. Cono Sur)* To botch, to bungle.

chance [chan'-thay], *m. (LAm.)* 1. Chance (oportunidad). **Dale chance,** let him have a go. 2. Good luck (suerte).

chancear [chan-thay-ar'], *vn.* To jest, to joke. *-vr.* To jest, to joke, to fool.

chancero, ra [chan-thay'-ro, rah], *a.* Jocose, sportful, merry; fond of a joke.

chancha [chan'-chah], *f.* 1. *(LAm.) (Zool.)* Sow. 2. *(Cono Sur)* Small wooden cart (carro); bike. 3. *(And.)* Mouth. **Hacer la chancha,** to play truant.

chánchamo [chan'-cha-mo], *m. (Mex.) (Culin.)* Tamale.

cháncharras máncharras [chahn´-char-ras mahn´-char-ras], *f. pl. (Low.)* **No andemos en cháncharras máncharras,** let us not beat about the bush, or use subterfuges and evasions.

chanchería [chan-chay-ree'-ah], *f. (LAm.)* Pork-butcher's shop.

chanchero [chan-chay'-ro], *m. (LAm.)* Pork butcher.

chanchi [chan'-che], 1. *a.* Marvelous, smashing, jolly good; dishy (chica), smashing. **¡Estás chanchí!, I** think you are marvelous. *-adv.* Marvelously, jolly well. **Me fue chanchi, I** had a smashing time.

chancho [chan'-cho], *a.* *(LAm.)* Dirty, filthy. *-m.* 1. *(LAm.)* Pig, hog; pork (carne). **Chancho salvaje,** wild boar. 2. *(LAm.)* Blocked piece. 3. *(Cono Sur) V.* CHANCADORA. 4. *(LAm.) (fig.)* **Son como chanchos,** they're as thick as thieves. **Quedar como chancho,** to come off badly.

chanchono [chan-cho'-no], *m.* Lie.

chanchullear [chan-chool-lyay-ar'], *va.* 1. To be guilty of crooked or underhand actions; to do vile things. 2. *(Coll.)* To smuggle.

chanchullero [chan-chool-lyay'-ro], *a.* Crooked, bent. *-m.* Crook, twister.

chanchullo [chan-chool'-lyo], *m.* Unlawful conduct to attain an end, and especially to get gain. Sharp practice, vile trick. *(Amer.)* Contraband.

chancica, illa [chan-thee'-cah, eel'-lyah], *f. dim.* A little fun or jest.

chanciller [chan-theel-lyerr'], *m.* *(Ant.) V.* CANCILLER, chancellor.

chancilleresco, ca [chan-theel-lyay-res'-co, cah], *a.* Belonging to the court of chancery.

chancillería [chan-theel-lyay-ree'-ah], *f.* 1. Chancery. 2. Chancellorship. 3. The right and fees of a chancellor.

chancita [chan-thee'-tah], *f. dim.* A little fun.

chancla [chan'-clah], *f.* 1. An old shoe with worn-down heel. 2. *V.* CHANCLETA.

chancleta [chan-clay'-tah], *f.* 1. Slipper. *V.* CHINELA. **Andar en chancleta,** to go slipshod. 2. *(LAm.)* Baby girl. 3. *(Carib.) (Aut.)* Accelerator. *-mf.* Muggings, charlie.

chancletear [chan-clay-tay-ar'], *vn.* To go slipshod.

chancletero [chan-clay-tay'-ro], *a. (And. Carib.)* **Chancletudo** *a.* 1. Common, low-class. 2. Scruffy.

chanclo [chahn'-clo], *m.* 1. Patten worn under the shoes by women. 2. Strong leather clog worn over shoes to guard against moisture and dirt. 3. Clog, galosh, overshoe.

chancón, cona [chan-cone'], *m. & f. (And.)* Swot.

chancro [chan'-cro], *m.* Chancre.

chandal [chan'-dal], *m.* Tracksuit.

chanelar [cha-nay-lar'], *va.* To catch on to, to twig.

chanfaina [chan-fah'-e-nah], *f.* 1. Ragout of livers and lights. 2. A trifling, worthless thing.

chanfle [chan'-flay], *m. (Cono Sur)* Bobby, cop.

chanflón, na [chan-flone', nah], *m. & f.* Bungler. *-a.* Bungling; made in a bungling manner.

changa [chahn'-gah], *f.* 1. *(Cuba)* Jest, joke, diversion. 2. Odd job, occasional job.

changador [chan-gah-dor'], *m. (S. Amer.)* Porter, carrier of burdens.

changamé [chan-gah-may'], *m. (Orn.)* A thrush of Panama.

changango [chan-gan'-go], *m. (Cono Sur)* Small guitar.

changarro [chan-gar'-ro], *m.* 1. *(Agri.)* A small cowbell. 2. *(Aut.)* Old car, jalopy. 3. *m. (Mex.)* Small shop.

changarse [chan-gar'-say], *vr.* To break down, to go wrong.

chango [chan'-go] *a.* 1. *(Mex.)* Quick, sharp; alert. 2. *(Carib. Mex.)* Mischievous, playful. 3. *(Carib.)* Silly, brainless (tonto); affected. 4. *(Cono Sur)* Annoying (molesto). 5. **La gente está changosa,** *(Mex.)* There are a lot of people. *-m.* **Changa** *f.* 1. *(Mex.)* Small monkey. 2. *(Cono Sur. Mex.)* Child; young servant. 3. *(Mex.)* Cunt (vagina).

changote [chan-go'-tay], *m.* An oblong bar of iron.

changuear [chan-gay-ar'], *vn.* To be jocose with others.

changüí [chan-goo-ee'], *m.* 1. *(Vulg.)* Jest, trick. 2. *(Cuba)* A dance.

changurro [chan-goor'-ro], *m.* Crab.

chanquete [chan-kay'-tay], *m.* White bait.

chanta [chan'-tah], *m. & f. (Cono Sur)* Loudmouth (fanfarrón); fraud.

chantado [chan-tah'-do], *m. (Prov. Gal.)* Wall or fence of slate in upright rows.

chantaje [chan-tah'-hay], *m.* Blackmail.

chantajismo [chan-tah-hees'-mo], *m.* Blackmailing.

chantajista [chan-tah-hees'-tah], *m. & f.* Blackmailer.

chantar [chan-tar'], *va.* 1. **Chantar a alguno una cosa,** to brave a person to his face. 2. To put on (vestido). 3. To thrust, to stick. 4. *(And. Cono Sur)* to throw, to chuck. 5. *(And. Cono Sur)* To put, to throw. **Chantar a uno en la calle,** to throw somebody out. 6. *(And. Cono Sur)* To give, to deal. 7. *(Cono Sur)* to leave in the lurch (abandonar).

chantre [chahn'-tray], *m.* Precentor, a dignified canon of a cathedral church. **chantría** [chan-tree'-ah], *f.* Precentorship.

chanza [chahn'-thah], *f.* Joke, jest, fun. **Chanza pesada, a** sarcastic taunt, a bad trick. **Hablar de chanza,** to joke, to jest, to speak in jest.

chanzoneta [chan-tho-nay'-tah], *f.* 1. Joke, jest. 2. A little merry song, a ballad.

chanzonetero [chan-tho-nay-tay'-ro], *m.* Writer of ballads, a petty poet.

chañaca [chan-nyah-cah], *f. (Cono Sur)* 1. *(Med.)* Itch, rash. 2. *(fig.)* Bad reputation.

chao [chah'-o], *m.* Chow.

chao [chah'-o], *excl. (Cono Sur)* bye-bye!, so long!.

chapa [chah'-pah], *f.* 1. Plate, sheet (of metal). Bodywork (coche). **Chapa acanalada, chapa ondulada,** corrugated iron. 2. A kind of rosy shot on the check. 3. Rouge used by ladies. 4. A small bit of leather laid by shoemakers under the last stitches to prevent the binding from giving way. 5. **Chapas de freno,** the two bosses on each side of the bit of a bridle. 6. Transom and trunnion plates in gun carriages; judgment, good sense. **Chapas de caoba,** mahogany veneers. **Hombre de chapa,** a man of judgment, abilities, and merit. **Chapa de matricula,** licence plate. **Estar sin placa,** to be broke.

chapado [chah-pah'-do], *a.* 1. Covered with sheet metal (adornos, muebles). **Chapado de roble,** with an oak veneer. **Chapado de oro,** gold-plated.

chapaleo [chah-pah-lay'-o], *m. vn.* 1. Splash(ing); lap(ping). 2. Clatter(ing).

chapaleta [chah-pah-lay'-tah], *f. (Naut.)* A valve of strong leather put at the bottom of a ship's pump, which serves as a sucker.

chapapote [chah-pah-po'-tay], *m.* A tar from Cuba and Santo Domingo.

chapar [chah-par'], *va.* 1. To plate, to coat, to cover; to tile (pared). 2. To throw out, to come out with (observación). 3. To learn, to memorize. 4. To shut, to close. 5. To spy on. 6. *(And.)* To catch (atrapar); to catch up with, to overtake; to seize, to grasp; to kiss.

chaparra [cah-par'-rah], *f.* 1. Species of oak. *V.* CHAPARRO. 2. A coach with a low roof. 3. *(Amer.)* Bramblebush.

chaparrada [chah-par-rah'-dah], *f. V.* CHAPARRÓN.

chaparral [chah-par-rahl'], *m.* 1. Plantation of evergreen oaks. 2. *(Amer.)* Thick bramble-bushes entangled with thorny shrubs in clumps.

chaparrear [chah-pahr-ray-ar'], *vn.* To spur in torrents.

chaparreras [chah-par-ray'-ras], *f. pl.* Leather leggings for horseback riders.

chaparro [chah-par'-ro], *m. (Bot.)* Evergreen oak tree. *-a.* Squat, short and chubby. *-m. f. (fig.)* Short chubby person; *(Mex.)* Child, kid.

chaparrón [chah-par-rone'], *m.* A violent shower of rain.

chapatal [chah-pa-tahl'], *m.* A mire; muddy place. *V.* LODAZAL.

chape [chah'-pay], *m. (And. Cono Sur)* trees, pigtail.

chapear [chah-pay-ar'], *va.* 1. To adorn with metal plates. 2. *(LAm.) (Agri.)* To weed. 3. **Chapear a uno,** *(Carib.)* to cut somebody's throat. *-vn. V.* CHACOLOTEAR.

chapeleta [chah-pah-lay'-tah], *f.* Flap valve, clack valve (válvula).

chapelete [chah-pay-lay'-tay], *m. (Prov.)* An ancient cover for the head.

chapeo [chah-pay'-o], *m. (Coll.)* Hat.

chapería [chah-pay-ree'-ah], *f.* Ornament of metal plates.

chapero [chah-pay'-ro], *m.* Queer (homosexual); male prostitute.

chaperón [chah-pay-rone'], *m.* Ancient hood or cowl.

chapeta [chah-pay'-tah], *f.* 1. A small metal plate. 2. Red spot on the cheek. 3. A stud for shirts or other articles.

chapetón [chah-pay-tone'], *m.* (*Amer.*) A wheel of silver to adorn a riding harness.

chapetón, na [chah-pay-tone', nah], *a.* A European lately arrived in America *V.* POLIZÓN.

chapetonada [chah-pay-to-nah'-dah], *f.* 1. A disease incident to Europeans in America, before they become accustomed to the climate. 2. (*And. Cono Sur*) awkwardness, clumsiness. 3. (*Carib.*) Sudden downpour.

chapín [chah-peen'], *m.* 1. Clog with a cork sole, worn by women. **Chapín de la reina,** tax formerly levied in Spain on the occasion of the king's marriage. **Poner en chapines** (a una hija), to marry off a daughter. **Ponerse en chapines,** to raise oneself above one's conditions. 2. (*CAm.*) (*Hum.*) Guatemalan.

chapinada [chah-pe-nah'-dah], *f.* (*CAm.*) (*Hum.*) Action typical of a Guatemalan, dirty trick.

chapinería [chah-pe-nay-ree'-ah], *f.* Shop where clogs and pattens are made and sold, and the art of making them.

chapinero [chah-pe-nay'-ro], *m.* Clog maker or seller.

chapinito [chah-pe-nee'-to], *m. dim.* A small clog.

chapiri [chah-pe'-re], *m.* Titfer, hat.

chápiro [chah'-pe-ro], *m.* A word of annoyance or menace used only in the phrases: **¡Por vida del chápiro (verde)! ¡Voto al chápiro!** about equal to "By Jupiter!"

chapisca [chah-pes'-cah], *f.* (*CAm.*) Corn harvest.

chapista [chah-pes'-tah], *m.* Tinsmith; (*Aut.*) Car-body worker, panel-beater.

chapistería [chah-pes-tay-ree'-ah], *f.* Car-body works, panel-beating shop.

chapita [chah-pe'-tah], *f.* (*And.*) Cop.

chapitel [chah-pe-tel'], *m.* 1. The upper part of a pillar rising in a pyramidal form. 2. A small movable brass plate over the compass. 3. *V.* CAPITEL.

chaple [chah'-play], *m.* Graver, the tool used in engraving.

chapo [chah'-po], *m.* 1. A short, stout person. (*Mex.*) 2. Corn porridge.

chapodar [chah-po-dar'], *va.* 1. To lop off the branches of trees and vines. 2. (*fig.*) To cut down, to reduce.

chapola [chah-po'-lah], *f.* (*And.*) Butterfly.

chapón [chah-pone'], *m.* A great blot of ink.

chapona [chah-po'-nah], *f. V.* CHAMBRA.

chapo(po)te [chah-po'-tay], *m.* (*Carib. CAm. Mex.*) Pitch, tar (pez); asphalt.

chapotear [chah-po-tay-ar'], *va.* To wet with a sponge or wet cloth. *-vn.* To paddle in the water; to dabble.

chapoteo [chah-po-tay'-o], *m.* 1. Sponging; moistening (limpieza con esponja). 2. Splashing; paddling; dabbling.

chapucear [chah-poo-thay-ar'], *va.* 1. To botch, to bungle, to cobble, to fumble, to clout. 2. (*Mex.*) To swindle (estafar).

chapuceramente [chah-poo-thay-rah-men'-tay], *adv.* Fumblingly, clumsily, bunglingly.

chapucería [chah-poo-thay-ree'-ah], *f.* A clumsy, bungling work.

chapucero [chah-poo-thay'-ro], *m.* 1. Blacksmith, who makes nails, trivets, shovels, etc.; nailer. 2. Bungler, botcher.

chapucero, ra [chah-poo-thay'-ro, rah], *a.* Rough, unpolished, clumsy, bungling, rude.

chapulín [chah-poo-leen'], *m.* 1. (*Prov. Mex.*) A grasshopper, locust. 2. Trickster. 3. Child, kid.

chapupa [chah-poo'-pah], *f.* **Me salió de pura chapupa,** (*CAm.*) it was pure luck, it was a sheer fluke.

chapuro [chah-poo'-ro], *m.* (*CAm.*) Asphalt.

chapurrado [chah-poor-rah'-do], *m.* (*Coll.*) Jargon, broken language.

chapurr(e)ar [chah-poor-rar'], *va.* (*Coll.*) To speak gibberish. **Chapurrea el Italiano,** he speaks broken Italian. *V.* CHAMPURRAR.

chapuz [chah-pooth'], *m.* 1. The act of ducking one. 2. A clumsy performance. **Chapuces,** (*Naut.*) Mast spars.

chapuza [chah-poo'-thah], *f.* 1. Botched job, shoddy piece of work, mess; odd job (trabajillo), spare time job; small job about the house. 2. (*Mex.*) Trick, swindle.

chapuzar [chah-poo-thar'], *va.* 1. To duck. 2. To paddle with the oars. *-vn. & vr.* To dive; to draggle, to duck.

chapuzón [chah-poo'-thone'], *m.* 1. Dip, swim; ducking. **Darse un chapuzón,** to go for a dip. 2. Splashdown (de cápsula). 3. (*LAm.*) Cloudburst, downpour.

chaqué [chah-kay'], *m.* Morning coat.

chaquet [chah'-kayt], *m. pl.* **Chaqueta.** *V.* CHAQUE.

chaqueta [chah-kay'-tah], *f.* 1. Jacket. **Chaqueta de cuero,** leather jacket. 2. (*fig.*) Cambiar la chaqueta, *V.* CHAQUETEAR. 3. **Volarse la chaqueta,** (*CAm.*) to toss off.

chaquetar [chah-kay-tar'], *vn.* (*Mex.*), **Chaquetear** *vn.* To change sides, to be a turncoat, to turn traitor; to go back on one's word.

chaquete [chah-kay'-tay], *m.* Game resembling backgammon.

chaquetero, ra [chah-kay-tay'-ro], *m. & f.* Turncoat. **Es una chaquetera,** she is always changing sides.

chaquetón [chah-kay-tone'], *m.* Long jacket, reefer, shooting jacket; three-quarter coat.

chaquira [chah-kee'-rah], *f.* Seedglass beads of all colors. (*Peru*)

charada [chah-rah'-dah], *f.* Charade, enigma.

charadrio [chah-rah'-dre-o], *m.* (*Orn.*) Common roller. *V.* GÁLGULO.

charalado [chah-rah-loo'-do], *a.* (*Mex.*) Thin.

charamusca [chah-ra-moos'-cah], *f.* 1. (*Mex.*) Twisted candy. 2. (*Peru*) *V.* CHAMARASCA. 3. (*Carib.*) Noise, row.

charamusquero [chah-ra-moos-kay'-ro], *m.* (*Mex.*) A seller of twisted candy.

charanchas [cha-rahn'-chas], *f. pl.* (*Naut.*) Battens used as supporters on board a ship.

charanga [chah-rahn'-gah], *f.* A military band of wind instruments only, fanfare, informal dance.

charango [chah-rahn'-go], *m.* (*And. Cono Sur*) A small five-stringed guitar.

charanguero, ra [chah-ran-gay'-ro, rah], *a.* 1. Clumsy, unpolished, artless (chapucero). 2. Applied to a bungler or bad workman.

charanguero [chah-ran-gay'-ro], *m.* (*Prov.*) 1. Peddler, hawker. 2. A kind of ship for the coast trade. 3. (*Coll.*) A lucky person.

charape [chah-rah'-pay], *m.* (*Mex.*) Type of pulque.

charca [char'-cah], *f.* Pool of water collected to make it congeal into ice.

charcanas [char-cah'-nas], *f.* Stuff of silk and cotton.

charco [char'-co], *m.* Pool of standing water; small lake. **Pasar el charco,** to cross the seas.

charcón [char-cone'], *a.* (*And. Cono Sur*) Thin, skinny.

charcoso, sa [char-co'-so, sah], *a.* (*Prov.*) Fenny, moorish, watery.

charcutería [char-coo-tay-ree'-ah], *f.* 1. Cooked pork products. 2. Pork butcher's, delicatessen (tienda).

charchina [char-che'-nah], *f.* (*LAm.*) Old crock, old banger.

charla [char'-lah], *f.* 1. (*Orn.*) Bohemian chatterer, silk-tail. 2. Idle chitchat or prattle, garrulity, gossip, loquaciousness. **Charla literaria,** literary talk. **Es de charla común,** it's common knowledge. **Echar una charla,** to have a chat.

charlado [char-lah'-do], *m.* **Echar un charlado,** to have a chat.

charlador, ra [char-lah-dor', rah], *m. & f.* Gabbler, prater, a chattering fellow, a garrulous person, a chatterer.

charladuría [char-lah-doo-ree'-ah], *f.* Garrulity, gossip.

charlante [char-lahn'-tay], *m. & ; pa.* Gabbler, chatterer.

charlantín [char-lan-teen'], *m.* (*Coll.*) A mean prattler or gossip.

charlar [char-lar'], *vn.* To prattle, to babble, to chatter, to prate, to gabble, to gossip, to jabber, to clack, to chat.

charlatán, na [char-lah-tahn', nah], *m. & f.* 1. Prater, babbler, idle talker, gabbler. 2. Charlatan, a quack, a mountebank. *a.* Empirical.

charlatanear [char-lah-tah-nay-ar'], *vn.* To chatter away, to babble on. *V.* CHARLAR.

charlatanería [char-lah-tah-nay-ree'-ah], *f.* Garrulity, verbosity; quackery, charlatanism.

charlatanismo [char-lah-tah-nees'-mo], *m.* Charlatanry, quackery, empiricism, verbosity.

charleta [char-lay'-tah], *m. & f. (Cono Sur)* Chatterbox; gossip.

Charlot [Char-lot'], *m.* Charlie Chaplin.

charlotear [char-lo-tay-ar'], *vn.* To chatter, to talk a lot.

charmilla [char-meel'-lyah], *f. (Bot.)* Common hornbeam-tree.

charneca [char-nay'-cah], *f. (Bot.)* Mastic-tree, pistachia-tree. *V.* LENTISCO.

charnecal [char-nay-cahl], *m.* Plantation of mastic-trees.

charnel [char-nel'], *m.* 1. Two *maravedís*. 2. Small change.

charnela [char-nay'-lah], *f.* Hinge (bisagra); hinge-joint knuckle.

charneta [char-nay'-tah], *f.* Iron plate.

charol [chah-rol'], *m.* 1. Varnish (barniz). 2. Patent leather (cuero barnizado). Tray (bandeja). **Darse charol,** to boast, to blow one's trumpet, to brag.

charola [chah-ro'-lah], *f.* 1. *(LAm.)* Tray. 2. **Charolas,** *(CAm.)* Eyes.

charolado [chah-ro-lah-do], *a.* Polished, shiny.

charolar [chah-ro-lar'], *va.* To varnish.

charolista [chah-ro-lees'-tah], *m.* Gilder, varnisher, or japanner.

charpa [char'-pah], *f.* 1. Leather belt with compartments for pistols and poniards. 2. Sling for a broken arm. 3. *(Naut.)* Sling.

charpar [char-par'], *va.* To scarf, to lap one thing over another.

charque, or **charquí** [char'-kay, char-kee'], *m.* Meat dried in the sun; jerked beef. *V.* TASAJO.

charquear [char-kay-ar'], *va.* 1. To jerk beef; to dry it in the air. 2. To carve up, to slash, to wound severely.

charquecillo [char-kay-thel-lyo], *m. (And.) (Culin.)* Dried Salted fish.

charqueo [char-kay'-o], *m.* Act of cleaning holywater fonts.

charqui [char'-ke], *m. (LAm.)* Dried beef, jerked meat; *(Cono Sur)* dried fruit, dried vegetables. **Hacer charqui a uno,** *(fig.) V.* CHAQUEAR.

charquicán [char-ke-cahn'], *m.* Sauce prepared with charquí.

charquillo [char-kee'-lyo], *m. dim.* A small pool or puddle.

charra [chahr'-rah], *f.* 1. *(fig.)* Peasant woman, coarse woman. 2. *(CAm.)* Broad-brimmed hat. 3. *(And.)* Itch, pimple. 4. *(CAm.)* Prick, tool.

charrada [char-rah'-dah], *f.* 1. Speech or action of a clown. 2. A dance. 3. *(Coll.)* Tawdriness, tinsel, finery. 4. Flashy ornament, vulgar adornment; tastelessly decorated object. 5. Coarse thing, piece of bad breeding.

charral [chahr-rahl'], *m. (CAm.)* Scrub, scrubland.

charramente [char-rah-men'-tay], *adv.,* Clownishly, tastelessly, ostentatiously fine.

charrán [char-rahn'], *a.* Rascally, knavish.

charrán [chahr-rahn'], *m. (Orn.)* Tern.

charranada [chahr-rah-nah'-dah], *f.* Dirty trick.

charranear [char-rah-nay-ar'], *vn.* To play the knave, the rascal.

charranería [char-rah-nay-ree'-ah], *f.* Rascality, knavery.

charrar [chahr-rar'], *vn.* To talk, to burble; to blab.

charrasca [chahr-ras'-cah], *f.* Trailing sword; *(And. Cono Sur, Mex.)* Knife, razor.

charrasquear [chahr-ras-kay-ar'], *va.* 1. *(Mex.)* To knife, to stab (apuñalar). 2. *(And. CAm. Carib.)* To strum (rasguear).

charrería [chahr-ray-ree'-ah], *f. (Mex.)* Horsemanship.

charretera [char-ray-tay'-rah], *f.* 1. Strip of cloth, silk, etc., placed on the lower part of pants to fasten them with a buckle. 2. The buckle with which the strips are fastened. 3. Epaulet. **Charretera mocha,** shoulder-knot.

charro, ra [char'-ro, rah], *m. &f.* 1. A coarse, ill-bred person. 2. A tawdry, showy person. 3. A name given to the peasants of the province of Salamanca in Spain. 4. Mexican. 5. *(Mex.)* Picturesque, quaint; traditional. 6. Rustic, boor, coarse, individual; flashy sort, overdressed individual. 7. *(Mex.)* Horseman, cowboy; typical Mexican. 8. *(Mex.)* Wide-brimmed hat. 9. *(Mex.)(Pol.)* Corrupt union boss.

charro, ra [char'-ro-rah], *a.* Gaudy, tawdry.

chárter [char'-tayr], *atrib.* **Vuelo chárter,** charter flight.

chas [chas], *m.* A low word, denoting the noise made by the cracking of wood or tearing of linen.

chasca [chahs'-cah], *f. (Amer.)* Disordered hair.

chascar [chas-car'], *vn.* To crackle, sputter: said of wood which sends off little pieces from a fire. *-va.* 1. To click (lengua etc.); to snap (dedos); to crack (látigo); to crunch (grava). 2. To gobble (comida), to gulp down.

chascarrillo [chas-car-reel'-lyo], *m.* Spicy anecdote, gossipy story.

chasco [chahs'-co], *m.* 1. Fun, joke, a trick, a sham. 2. Foil, frustration, disappointment. 3. Lash, the thong or point of the whip. **Dar un chasco,** to play a trick. **Dar chasco,** to disappoint. **Llevarse chasco,** to be disappointed.

chascón [chas-cone'], *a. (And. Cono Sur)* 1. Dishevelled, matted, entangled (pelo). 2. Slow, clumsy (torpe).

chasí [chah-see'], *m.* A photographic plateholder.

chasis [chah'-sis], *m.* Chassis (of a vehicle). **Quedarse en el chasis,** to be terribly thin.

chasque [chas'-kay], *m. (LAm.) V.* CHASQUI.

chasquear [chas-kay-ar'], *va.* To crack with a whip or lash. - *vn.* 1. To crack as timber at the approach of dry weather: to snap; to crepitate. 2. To fool, to play a waggish trick. 3. To disappoint, to fail, to fall short; to cheat.

chasqui [chahs'-kee], *m. (Peru)* Postboy, or messenger on foot.

chasquido [chas-kee'-do], *m.* 1. Crack of a whip or lash. 2. Crack, the noise made by timber when it breaks or splits.

chasquista [chas-kees'-tah], *m. (Low.)* A person fond of playing tricks; a sycophant.

chata [chah'-tah], *f.* 1. *(Naut.)* A flatbottomed boat. **Chata alijadora,** lighter. **Chata de arbolar,** sheerhulk. **Chata de carenar,** careening-hulk. 2. *(Cono Sur) (Aut.)* Lorry, truck.

chatarra [chah-tahr'-rah], *f.* Scrap, iron, junk; coppers (dinero), small change; medals. **Vender para chatarra,** to sell for scrap.

chatarrero [chah-tar-ray'-ro], *m.* Junkman, dealer, scrap merchant.

chate [chah'-tay], *m. (Bot.)* Roundleaved Egyptian or hairy cucumber.

chatear [chah-tay-ar'], *vn.* To go drinking, to have a few drinks.

chateo [chah-tay'-o], *m.* Drinking expedition.

chatí [chah-te'], *f.* Girl, bird; **¡oye chatí!,** hey beautiful!.

chato, ta [chah'-to, tah], *a.* 1. Flat, flattish: flatnosed. **Embarcación chata,** a flatbottomed vessel. 2. **¡Oye chata!,** hey, beautiful! 3. *(Carib. Cono Sur)* mean, wretched. 4. *(LAm.)* **Dejar chato a uno,** to crush somebody (anonadar); to embarrass somebody; *(Mex.)* To swindle somebody (estafar). *-m.* Wine glass. **Tomarse unos chatos,** to have a few drinks.

chatón [chah-tone'], *m.* 1. Bezel, the bevelled part of a ring in which a diamond is set. 2. Kind of coarse diamond. 3. Ornamental nail or button. 4. *pl.* Knobs which fasten one thing to another.

chatre [chah'-tray], *a.* 1. (Ecuador) Richly decked out. 2. *(And. Cono Sur)* smartly-dressed. **Está hecho un chatre,** he's looking very smart.

chatungo [chah-toon'-go], *a. V.* CHATO.

chau [chah'-oo], *interj. (Cono Sur)* So long!

chaucha [chah'-oo-chah], a. 1. *(And. Cono Sur)* early; unripe (inmaduro), not fully grown; premature (nacimiento). 2. *(Cono Sur)* poor-quality; insipid, tasteless; characterless; in poor taste. -*f.* 1. Early potato, small potato; *(And. Cono Sur)* string bean; *(And.)* Food. **Pelar la chaucha,** to brandish one's knife. 2. *(And. Cono Sur)* 20-cent coin. 3. *(Cono Sur)* **Chauchas;** peanuts.

chauchau [chah'-oo-chah'-oo], *m. (And. Cono Sur)* Grub, chow.

chauchera [chah-oo-chay'-rah], *f. (And. Cono Sur)* Purse, pocket-book.

chauchero [chah-oo-chah'-ro], *m. (Cono Sur)* Errand boy; odd-jobman; poorly-paid worker.

chaúl [chah-ool'], *m.* A kind of blue silk material manufactured in China.

chauvinismo [chah-oo-ve-nees'-mo], *m.* Chauvinism.

chauvinista [chah-oo-ve-nees'-tah], *a. & m. & f.* Chauvinist.

chava [chah'-vah], *f. (CAm. Mex.)* Lass, girl.

chaval [chah-vahl'], *a.* Among the common people, young. **Estar hecho un chaval,** to feel very young again.

chavala [chah-vah'-lah], *f.* Girl, kid. **Mi chavala,** my bird; my girlfriend.

chavalo [chah-vah'-lo], *m. (CAm.)* Street urchin; boy.

chavalongo [chah-vah-lon'-go], *m. (Cono Sur)* fever; sunstroke; drowsiness (modorra).

chavea [chah-vay'-ah], *m. & f.* Kid, youngster.

chaveta [chah-vay'-tah], *f.* Bolt, cotter pin. **Perder la chaveta,** to lose one's head, to become rattled.

chavetear [chah-vay-tay-ar'], *va. (And. Carib.)* To knife.

chavo [chah'-vo], *m.* **1. No tener un chavo,** to be stone-broke. 2. Kid, boy. 3. *(CAm. Mex.)* Guy.

chayote [chah-yo'-tay], *m. (Mex.)* Mexican fruit. *V.* CHIOTE.

chayotera [chah-yo-tay'-rah], *f.* Chayote (plant).

chaza [chah'-thah], *f.* 1. Point where the ball is driven back, or where it stops, in a game at balls. 2. *(Naut.)* Berth on board a ship. **Hacer chaza,** to walk on the hind feet (caballos).

chazador [chah-thah-dor'], *m.* A person employed to stop the ball and mark the game.

chazar [chah-thar'], *va.* 1. To stop the ball before it reaches the winning point. 2. To mark the point whence the ball was driven back.

che [chay], *interj.* Oh Dear!; *(Cono Sur)* hey!, hi!; *(CAm.)* Who cares!

checa [chay'-cah], *f.* 1. Secret police. 2. Secret police headquarters.

cheche [chay'-chay], *m. (Carib.)* bully, braggart.

chechear [chay-chay-ar'], *va. (Cono Sur) V.* VOSEAR.

chécheres [chay'-chay-rays], *m. pl. (And. CAm.)* Things, gear; junk.

chechón [chay-chaone'], *a. (Mex.)* Spolit, pampered.

checo, ca [chay'-co], *a. m. & f.* Czech.

checoslovaco, ca [chah-cos-lo-vah'-co-cah], *a.* Czechoslovakian. -*m. & f.* Czechoslovak.

Checoslovaquia [chay-cos-lo-vah'-ke-ah], Czechoslovakia.

chelear [chay-lay-ar'], *va. (CAm.)* To whiten, to whitewash.

chele [chay'-lay], *a. (CAm.)* Fair, blond.

cheli [chay'-le], *m.* Guy; boyfriend; **ven cheli acá,** come here, man.

chelín [chay-leen'], *m.* Shilling, an old English coin.

chelista [chay-les'-tah], *m. & f.* Cellist.

chelo [chay'-lo], *a. (Mex.)* Fair, blond(e).

chenil [chay-neel'], *m.* Chenille.

chepa [chay'-pah], *f.* A hump, hunch.

cheque [chay'-kay], *m.* Check, cheque. **Cheque de caja,** cashier's check. **Cheque en blanco,** blank check. **Cheque al portador,** bearer check. **Cheque de viaje,** traveler's check.

chequear [chay-kay-ar'], *va.* To check (cuenta, documento); to check (persona); to register, to check in; *(Mex.) (Aut.)* To service.

chequeo [chay-kay'-o], *m. (LAm.)* Check; checking up; *(Med.)* Check-up; *(Aut.)* Service.

chequera [chay-kay'-rah], *f. (LAm.)* Check book.

cherife [chay-reef'], *m. (LAm.)* Sheriff.

cherna [cherr'-nah], *f. (Zool. Prov.)* Ruffle, a fish resembling a salmon.

chero [chay'-ro], *m. (CAm.)* Pal, mate; buddy.

cheruto [chay-roo'-to], *m.* Cheroot.

cherva [cherr'-vah], *(Bot.)* The castoroil plant.

cheurón [chay-oor-rone'], *m. (Her.)* Chevron, a representation of two rafters of a house in heraldry.

chévere [chay-vay'-re], *a. (And. Carib. Mex.)* Smashing, super. -*m. (Carib.)* Bully, bragart.

chevronado, da [chay-vro-nah'-do, dah], *a. (Her.)* Chevroned, coat of arms charged with chevrons.

chía [chee'-ah], *f.* 1. A short black mantle, formerly worn in mournings. 2. Cowl of fine cloth, formerly worn by the nobility for distinction. 3. A white medicinal earth. 4. *(Bot.)* Limeleaved sage.

chiar [che-ar'], *vn.* To chirp (pájaros). *V.* PIAR.

chibcha [cheeb'-chah], *m.* A dweller of the elevated territory about Bogotá.

chibola [che-bo'-lah], *f. (CAm.)* 1. Fizzy drink, pop. 2. **Chibolo,** marble.

chibolo [che-bo'-lo], *m. (And. CAm.)* Bump, swelling; wen.

chibón [che-bone'], *m.* 1. A young cock-linnet. 2. Sort of gum from America.

chic [cheec], *a. m.* Chic, smart, elegant, elegance; composure.

chica [chee'-cah], *f.* 1. Girl (muchacha). **Es una linda chica,** *(Coll.)* she is a pretty girl. 2. Maid, servant.

chicada [che-cah'-dah], *f.* Herd of sickly kids.

chicalote [che-cah-lo'-tay], *m.* Mexican argemone.

chicana [che-cah'-nah], *f. (LAm.)* Chicanery.

chicanear [che-cah-nay-ar'], *vn.* To use trickery, to be cunning. -*va.* To trick, to take in.

chicanería [che-cah-nay-re'-ah], *f. (LAm.)* Chicanery.

chicanero [che-cah-nay'-ro], *a.* 1. *(LAm.)* Tricky, crafty. 2. *(And.)* Mean (tacaño).

chicano, na [che-cah'-no, nah], *a.* (Of) Mexican American. -*m. & f.* Mexican American, Chicano.

chicar [che-car'], *vn. (And.)* To booze, to drink.

chicarrón [che-cahr-rone'], *a.* Strapping, sturdy. -*m. f.* Strapping lad; sturdy lass.

chicato [che-cah'-to], *a. (Cono Sur)* short-sighted.

chicha [chee'-chah], *f.* 1. Meat: used only with children. **De chicha y nabo,** Insignificant. 2. Beverage made of pineapple rinds, sugar, or molasses. **Tener pocas chichas,** to be very lean or weak. 3. *(And. CAm.)* **Estar de chichas,** to be in a bad mood. 4. *(And.)* Thick-soled shoe. *a. (Naut.)* **Calma chicha,** dead calm.

chícharo [chee'-chah-ro], *f. (Bot.)* Pea.

chicharra [che-char'-rah], *f.* 1. Cicada (cigarra). 2. A talkative woman. **Hablar como una cicada,** to be a real chatterbox. 3. Kazoo, a child's plaything making a harsh, grating noise. **Cantar la chicharra,** *(Coll.)* to be scorching hot. 4. Bell, buzzer. 5. Reefer.

chicharrear [che-char-ray-ar'], *vn.* To creak, to chirp.

chicharrero [che-char-ray'-ro], *m.* 1. A hot place or climate. 2. One who makes or sells kazoos.

chicharro [che-char'-ro], *m.* 1. A young tunnyfish. 2. Horsemackerel.

chicharrón [che-char-rone'], *m.* 1. Crackles, morsel of fried lard left in the pan. **Estar hecho un chicharrón,** to be burnt to a cinder, to be as red as a lobster (persona). 2. *(fig.)* Sunburnt person. 3. *(Carib.)* Flatterer (adulador).

chiche [chee'-chay], *m.* 1. *(Amer. Prov.)* A kind of sauce. 2. *(LAm.)* Precious thing, delightful object; fancy jewel (joya); trinket; small boy (juguete); clever person; well-dressed person (pulcro); elegant place, nice room. -*a. -adv. (CAm.)* Easy, simple, easily. **Está chiche,** it's a cinch. -*f. (Mex.)* Nursemaid.

chichear [che-chay-ar'], *va & vn.* To hiss.

chicheo [che-chay'-o], *m.* Hissing a speaker.

chichera [che-chay'-rah], *f. (CAm.)* Jail, clink.

chichería [che-chay-ree'-ah], f. Tavern where *chicha* is sold.

chichi [che-che], 1. m. Cunt. -f. (Mex.) 1. Teat (teta). 2. Nursemaid (niñera).

chichicaste [che-che-cas'-tay], m. (CAm.) (Bot.) Nettle; (Med.) Nettle rash.

chichigua [che-chee'-goo-ah], f. 1. (Mex. vulg.) Wet nurse. 2. (Carib.) Kite. 3. (Mex.) Tame animal; nursing animal. 4. (Mex.) Pimp.

chichimeco, ca [che-che-may'-co, cah], a. Of Chichimec.

chichisbeador [che-chis-bay-ah-dor'], m. Gallant, wooer.

chichisbear [che-chis-bay-ar'], va. To woo, to court.

chicho [che'-cho], m. 1. Curl, ringlet. 2. Curler, roller.

chichón [che-chone'], m. 1. Bump, on the head. 2. Bruise. V. ABOLLADURA.

chichón [che-chone'], a. 1. (Cono Sur) Merry, jovial. 2. (CAm.) Easy, straightforward. **Está chichón,** it's a cinch, a piece of cake.

chichoncillo, cito [che-chon-theel'-lyo, thee'-to], m. dim. Small lump.

chichonear [che-cho-nay-ar'], vn. (Cono Sur) To joke.

chichonera [che-cho-nay_-rah], f. Tumblingcap, helmet.

chichota [che-cho'-tah], f. **Sin faltar chichota,** it wants not an iota; it is all complete.

chichus [che'-chus], m. (CAm.) Flea.

chicle [chee'-clay], m. (Bot.) (Chicle), chewing gum.

chiclear [che-clay-ar'], vn. (CAm. Mex.) 1. To extract gum. 2. To chew gum (mascar).

chico, ca [chee'-co, cah], m. & f. 1. Boy, girl. **Es un buen chico,** (Coll.) he is a good boy. **Es una chica guapa,** she is a pretty girl. 2. Son, boy (hijo). 3. Daughter, girl (hija)

chico, ca [chee'-co, cah], a. Little, small. **Los chicos de la oficina,** the fellows at the office. **Es un buen chico,** he's a good lad. **Chicos de la calle,** street urchins. **Como chico con zapatos nuevos,** as happy as a lark. -a. Small-size, tiny. **Dejar chico a uno,** to put somebody in the shade.

chicolear [che-co-lay-ar'], va. To joke or jest in gallantry. -vn. 1. To flirt, to murmur sweet nothings, to say nice things. 2. To amuse oneself, to have a good time. -vr. (And.) To amuse oneself.

chicoleo [che-co-lay'-o], m. 1. (Coll.) Joke, jest in gallantry. 2. Compliment, flirtatious remark. **Decir chicoleos,** to say nice things. 3. Flirting (acto). **Estar de chicoleo,** to be in a flirtatious mood. 4. (And.) Childish thing. **No andemos con chicoleos,** let's be serious.

chicolero [che-co-lay'-ro], a. Flirtatious.

chicoria [che-co'-re-ah], f. V. ACHICORIA.

chicorrotico, ca [che-cor-ro-tee'-co, cah], a. dim. Very little or small (niños).

chicorrotín [che-cor-ro-teen'], a. Very small (niños).

chicotazo [che-co-tah'-tho], m. (LAm.) Lash, swipe.

chicote, ta [che-co'-tay, tah], m. & f. 1. (Coll.) A fat strong boy or girl. 2. (Naut.) End of a rope or cable. 3. (Coll.) End of a cigar partly smoked.

chicotear [che-co-tay-ar'], va. (LAm.) To whip, to lash (azotar); (LAm.) To beat up (pegar); (And.) To kill. -vn. (LAm.) To lash about (cola).

chicozapote [che-co-thah-po'-tay], m. A delicious American fruit. V. ZAPOTE.

chifa [chee'-fah], (And.) f. Chinese restaurant. -a. Chinky, Chinese.

chifla [chee'-flah], f. 1. Whistle. 2. With bookbinders, a paring-knife. 3. Hissing in a theater or public meeting.

chiflacayote [che-flah-cah-yo'-tay], m. A large kind of pumpkin in America.

chifladera [che-flah-day'-rah], f. 1. Whistle. 2. (CAm. Mex.) Crazy idea.

chiflado [che-flah'-do], a. Daft, barmy, cranky, crackpot. **Estar chiflado con, estar chiflado por,** to be crazy about. -m. f. Crank, crackpot.

chifladura [che-flah-doo'-rah], f. 1. Whistling. 2. (Coll.) Craziness. 3. Crazy idea, whim, fad, mania. **Su chifladura es el ajedrez,** he is crazy about chess. **Ese amor no es más que una chifladura,** what he calls love is just a foolish infatuation.

chiflar [che-flar'], va. 1. To pare, to skive (cuero). 2. To hiss, to whistle at, to boo. 3. To drink, to knock back, to gulp (beber). 4. To captivate; to drive crazy. **Me chifla ese conjunto,** I rave about that group. **Me chiflan los helados,** I just adore ice cream. **Esa chica le chifla,** he's crazy about that girl. -vn. 1. To whistle. 2. To mock, to jest. 3. To tipple, to drink to excess. -vr. 1. (Coll.) To run mad, to be crazy. 2. **Chiflárselas** (CAm.) To peg out, to kick the bucket.

chiflato [che-flah-to], m. V. SILBATO.

chifle [chee'-flay], m. 1. Whistle. 2. Call, an instrument used to decoy birds. 3. (Naut.) Priming-horn used by the gunners of the navy. 4. (Naut.) Tide. **Aguas chifles,** neaptide.

chiflete [che-flay'-tay], m. V. CHIFLA.

chiflido [che-flee'-do], m. Whistling, shrill sound.

chiflo [che-flo], m. V. CHIFLA.

chiflón [che-flone'], m. 1. Draft, draught (current of air). 2. (CAm. Carib, Cono Sur) rapids, violent current; (CAm.) Waterfall; (Mex.) Flume, race; (Mex.) Nozzle (tobera).

chihuahuense [che-hooa-hoo'en-say], (Mex.) m. & f. Of Chihuahua.

chilaba [che-lah'-bah], f. Jellabah.

chilacayote [che-lah-cah-yo'-tay], m. (Bot.) American or bottle gourd.

chilanco [che-lahn'-coh], m. Pool or well of water remaining in a river when it has lost its current through drought.

chilango, ga [che-lahn'-go], (Mex.) m. & f. Of Mexico city.

chilar [che-lar'], m. A spot planted with Chile peppers.

chile [chee'-lay], f. (Bot.) American red pepper. **Chile ancho,** dried-up pepper in a broad shape. **Chile relleno,** (Mex.) Green pepper stuffed with minced meat, coated with eggs, and fried.

Chile [chee'-lay], m. Chile.

chilear [che-lay-ar'], vn. (CAm.) To tell jokes.

chileno, na, chileño, ña [che-lay'-nyo, nya], a. Chilean; of Chile.

chilera [che-lay'-rah], f. (Naut.) Rowlock hole.

chilicote [che-le-co'-tay], m. (And. Cono Sur) Cricket.

chilindrina [che-lin-dree'-nah], f. 1. (Coll.) Trifle, a thing of little value. **Meterse en chilindrinas,** to meddle in unimportant, but ticklish business. 2. Joke, fun, witticism.

chilindrinero, ra [che-lin-dre-nay'-ro, rah], a. Meddling in trifles.

chilindrón [che-lin-drone'], m. 1. Game at cards for four persons. 2. (Low.) Cut in the head. 3. **Al chilindrón,** cooked with tomatoes and peppers.

chilla [cheel'-lyah], f. 1. Call for foxes, hares, or rabbits. 2. (Mex.) 1. (Theat.) Gallery. 2. Poverty. **Estar en la chilla,** to be flat broke. 3. Decoy, call (caza).

chillado [cheel-lyah'-do], m. (Prov.) Roof of shingles or thin boards. **-Chillado, da,** pp. of CHILLAR.

chillador, ra [cheel-lyah-dor', rah], m. & f. Person who shrieks or screams; a thing that creaks.

chillante [cheel-lyahn'-tay], pa. Screaming, shrieking, screeching.

chillar [cheel-lyar'], vn. 1. To scream, to shriek. 2. To crackle, to creak. 3. To imitate the notes of birds. 4. To hiss: applied to things frying in a pan. **Chillar a uno,** to yell at somebody, to be loud. 5. To scream, to be loud (colores). 6. (LAm.) To shout, to protest. **No chillar** (Carib. Cono Sur), to keep one's mouth shut, not to say a word. **El cochino chilló,** (Carib. Mex.) They let the cat out of the bag. 7. (LAm.) To sob (llorar). -vr. 1. (LAm.) To complain, to protest. 2. (And. Carib. Mex.) To get cross; to take offence. 3. (CAm.) To get embarrassed (sofocarse).

chilleras [cheel-lyay'-ras], f. pl. (Naut.) Shotlockers for balls.

chillería [chel-lay-ree'-ah], f. Row, hubbub.

chillido [cheel-lyee'-do], *m.* 1. Squeak or shriek; a shrill, disagreeable sound. 2. Bawling of a woman or child. **Dar un chillido,** to utter a scream.

chillo [cheel'-lyo], *m.* 1. Call. V. CHILLA. 2. *(CAm.)* Debt. 3. *(Carib.)* Rabble, mob (muchedumbre). 4. Anger; loud protest.

chillón [cheel-lyone'], *m.* 1. *(Coll.)* Bawler, screamer, shrieker. 2 *(Prov.)* Common crier. 3. Nail, tack. **Chillón real,** spike used to fasten large timbers or planks. **Clavo chillón,** tack or small nail.

chillón, na [cheel-lyone', nah], *a.* Applied to showy or tawdry colors.

chilote [che-lo'-tay], *m. (Mex.)* V. JILOTE.

chilposo [chel-po'-so], *a. (Cono Sur)* Ragged, tattered.

chiltipiquín, chiltepín [cheel-te-pe-keen', cheel-tay-peen'], *m. (Mex.)* A red pepper, the size of a caper, and very pungent.

chimal [che-mahl'], *m. (Mex.)* Dishevelled hair, mop of hair.

chimar [che-mahr'], *va.* 1. *(CAm.)* To scratch. 2. *(CAm. Mex.)* To annoy, to bother (molestar). 3. *(CAm.)* To fuck, to screw.

chimate [che-mah'-tay], *m.* V. CHANCACA.

chimba [chem'-bah], *f.* 1. *(And. Cono Sur)* opposite bank (orilla); *(Cono Sur)* poor quarter (barrio); *(And.)* Ford (vado). 2. *(And.)* Pigtail.

chimbar [chem-bar'], *va. (And.)* To ford (río).

chimbero [cehm-bay'-ro], *a. (Cono Sur)* Slum (de chimba; coarse, rough (grosero).

chimbo [chem'-bo], *a.* 1. *(And. Carib.)* Worn-out, wasted, old. 2. *(And.)* Bad (cheque). *-m. (And.)* Piece of meat.

chimenea [che-may-nay'-ah], *f.* 1. Chimney. 2. *(Met. Coll.)* Head. 3. Hearth, fireplace. **Se le subió el humo a la chimenea,** the vapor has mounted to his head (borracho).

chimiscolear [che-mes-co-lay-ar'], *vn. (Mex.)* To gossip; to poke one's nose in (curiosear).

chimiscolero, ra [che-mes-co-lay'-ro], *m. & f. (Mex.)* Gossip.

chimpancé [chim-pan-thay'], *m.* Chimpanzee.

chimpín [chem-peen'], *m. (And.)* Brandy, liquor.

chimpipe [chim-pee'-pay], *m.* (Nicaragua) Turkey.

chimuelo [che-moo-ay'-lo], *a. (LAm.)* Toothless.

China [chee'nah], **f.** China.

china [chee'-nah], *f.* 1. Pebble, a small stone. 2. Chinaroot, a medicinal root. 3. Porcelain, china, chinaware. 4. China silk or cotton stuff. **Media china,** cloth coarser than that from China. 5. Boyish game of shutting hands, and guessing which contains the pebble. **Le tocó la china,** he had bad luck. 6. *(LAm.)* Woman (Indian); *(And. Cono Sur)* Nursemaid; *(And. Cono Sur)* servant girl; *(LAm.)* Mistress, concubine.

chinaca [che-nah'-cah], *f.* **La chinaca** *(Mex.),* the plebs, the proles.

chinado [che-nah'-do], *a.* Crazy.

chinaloa [che-nah-lo'-ah], *f. (Mex.)* Heroin, smack.

chinampa [che-nahm'-pah], *f.* A small garden tract in lakes near the city of Mexico; anciently a floating garden.

chinampero [che-nam-pay'-ro], *m.* The tiller of a *chinampa.*

chinar [che-nar'], *vn.* To carve up, to slash. *(Obs.)* V. RECHINAR.

chinarro [che-nar'-ro], *m.* A large pebble.

chinateado [che-nah-tay-ah'-do], *m.* Stratum or layer of pebbles.

chinazo [che-nah'-tho], *m.* 1. *(aug.)* A large pebble. 2. Blow with a pebble. **le tocó el chinazo,** he had bad luck.

chincate [chin-cah'-tay], *m. (Amer.)* The last brown sugar which comes from the caldrons.

chinchada [chin-chah'-dah], *f. (Cono Sur)* Tug-of-war.

chinchal [chin-chahl'], *m. (Carib.)* Tobacco stall; small shop.

chinchar [chin-char'], *va.* To pester, to bother, to annoy; to upset. **Me chincha tener que,** it upsets me to have to. *-vr.* To get cross, to get upset. **¡Para que te chinches!,** so there!

chincharrazo [chin-char-rah'-tho], *m. (Coll.)* Thrust or cut with a sword. V. CINTARAZO.

chincharrero [chin-char-ray'-ro], *m.* Place swarming with bugs.

chinche [cheen'-chay], *f.* 1. Bedbug. **Caer como chinches,** to die like flies. 2. Thumbtack. 3. *(Cono Sur)* Pique, irritation (rabieta). *-m. & f. (fig.)* Nuisance; annoying person, pest, bore; *(And. CAm.)* Naughty child.

chinchero [chin-chay'-ro], *m.* Bugtrap made of twigs.

chincheta [chin-chay'-tah], *f.* Drawing pin, thumbtack.

chinchilla [chin-cheel'-lyah], *f.* Chinchilla, a small quadruped in Peru, well known for its fur.

chinchín [chin-cheen'], *m.* 1. *(Cuba)* Drizzling rain, mizzle. 2. Street music, tinny music. 3. *(CAm.)* Baby's rattle.

chincho [cheen-cho], *m. (Naut.)* A small plumb-line used by constructors of curved timbers.

chinchón [chin-chone'], *m.* Bump. V. CHICHÓN.

chinchona [chin-cho'nah], *f.* Quinine.

chinchorreo [chin-chor-ray'-o], *m. (Prov.)* Tiresome importunity or solicitation.

chinchorrería [chin-chor-ray-ree'-ah], *f.* 1. Lying jest. 2. *(Coll.)* Mischievous tale. 3. Fussiness; critical nature, disrespectful manner. V. CHISME.

chinchorrero, ra [chin-chor-ray'-ro, rah], *m. & f.* 1. A gossip. 2. V. CHINCHARRERO.

chinchorro [chin-chor'-ro], *m.* 1. Fishingboat used in America. 2. Kind of fishing-net. 3. A hammock used by Indians, suspended from trees. 4. The smallest rowboat on board a ship.

chinchoso, sa [chin-cho'-so, sah], *a.* 1. Peevish, fastidious, tiresome. 2. Full of bugs (chinches). 3. Tiresome, annoying (pesado). 3. *(And. Carib.)* Touchy, irritable (quisquilloso).

chinchudo [chin-choo'-do], *a.* **Estar chinchudo,** *(Cono Sur)* to be in a huff.

chindar [chin-dar'], *va.* To chuck out.

chinear [che-nay-ar'], *va. (CAm.)* To carry in one's arms (niño); to care for. *-vn. (Cono Sur)* To have an affair with a half-breed girl.

chinel [che-nayl'], *m.* Guard.

chinela [che-nay'-lah], *f.* 1. Slipper. 2. Kind of pattens or clogs worn by women in dirty weather.

chinero [che-nay'-ro], *m.* A china-closet, or cupboard.

chinero [che-nay'-ro], *a. (And. Cono Sur)* fond of the (half-breed) girls.

chinesco, ca [che-nes'-co, cah], *a.* Chinese; relating to China.

chinetero [che-nay-tay'-ro], *a. (Cono Sur)* V. CHINERO.

chinflaina [chin-flah'-e-nah], *f.* Felt of a silk hat.

chinga [chin'-gah], *f.* 1. *(CAm. Carib.)* Fag end; cigar stub; *(fig.)* Drop, small amount. **Una chinga de agua,** a drop of water. 2. *(Carib.)* Drunkenness.

chingada [chin-gah'-dah], *f. (CAm. Mex.)* Fuck (acto sexual), screw; bloody nuisance (molestia).

chingana [chin-gah'-nah], *f. (Peru, Bol.)* 1. A small dramshop, where low people resort to dance and to get drunk; a "dive." 2. A tunnel, underground gallery.

chinganear [chin-gah-nay-ar'], *vn. (And. Cono Sur)* to go on the town, to live it up.

chinganero [chin-gah-ray'-ro], *(And. Cono Sur) a.* Fond of living it up, wildly social. *-m.* **chinganera,** the owner of a chingana.

chingar [chin-gar'], *va.* 1. To drink a lot. 2. *(CAm.)* To dock (animal); to cut off the tail. 3. *(LAm.)* To fuck, to screw. **Hijo de la chingada,** bastard. 4. *(Cono Sur)* to aim badly, to miss with (tiro). 5. *(Carib.)* To carry on one's shoulder. *-vn.* 1. To drink too much. 2. *(LAm.)* To fuck, to screw. 3. *(CAm.)* To joke. *-vr.* 1. To get intoxicated. 2. *(LAm.)* To fail, to fall through, to come to nothing. **La fiesta se chingó,** the party was a failure.

chingo [chin'-go], *a.* 1. *(CAm.)* Short (vestido); blunt (cuchillo); docked (animal). 2. *(And. Carib.)* Small (chico). 3. *(Cam, Carib.)* Snub-nosed (persona); flat, snub (nariz). **Estar chingo por algo,** *(Carib.)* To be crazy about. *-m.* 1. *(And.)* Colt (potro). 2. *(And. CAm.)* Small boat. 3. **Chingos,** *(CAm.)* Underclothes. 4. **Un chingo de,** *(Mex.)* Lots of; loads of.

chingue [chin'-gay], *a. (Cono Sur)* Stinking, repulsive. *-m. (Cono Sur)* skunk.

chinguear [chin-gay-ar'], *va. (CAm.)* V. CHINGAR.

chinguirito [chin-ge-ree'-to], *m.* (*Mex. and Cuba*) 1. Rum from less of sugar. 2. Draught, swallow. 3. Rough liquor.

chinilla, ita [che-neel'-lyah, ee'-tah], *f. dim.* A small pebble.

chinita [che-nee'-tah], *f.* 1. (*Amer.*) V. NIÑA. 2. Small stone, pebble. **Poner chinas a uno,** (*fig.*) to make trouble for somebody.

chinito, ta [che-nee'-to], *m. & f.* 1. (*Cono Sur*) servant. 2. (*LAm.*) Dear, dearest (en oración directa). 3. (*And. Carib. Cono Sur*) Indian boy, indian girl.

chino, na [chee'-no, nah], *a.* Chinese. **¿Somos chinos?,** do you think me a simpleton? **Ni que hablara en chino,** don't you understand?

chino, *m.* Chinese.

chino [che'-no], *a.* 1. (*CAm.*) Bald, hairless. 2. (*Mex.*) Curly, kinky (pelo); Curly-haired. 3. (*CAm. Carib.*) Angry, furious. 4. (*LAm.*) Young. -*m.* 1. (*LAm.*) Half-breed (mestizo); (*Cono Sur, Carib.*) Indian; offspring of Indian and Negress; (*Carib.*) Offpring of mulatto and Negress; (*And. Carib. Cono Sur*) servant; street urchin (golfo). **Quedarse como un chino,** (*Carib, Cono Sur*) to come off badly. **Trabajar como un chino,** (*Carib. Cono Sur*) to work like a slave. 2. (*And. CAm.*) Pig. 3. Chins, curls. 4. (*CAm. Carib.*) Anger. **Le salió el chino,** he got angry.

chinoidina [che-no-e-dee'-nah], *f.* Quinoidine, an alkaloid from cinchona bark.

chinorri [che-nor'-re], *f.* Bird, chick.

chip [chip], *m. pl.* Chips. **Chip de silicio,** silicon chip. **Chip informático con conjunto de instrucciones reducidas (RISC),** reduced instruction set computer (RISC) chip.

chipa [chee'-pah], *f.* (*Amer.*) 1. Wooden basket in which Indians carry fruits. 2. Strap of leather.

chipe [chee'-pay], *a.* (*CAm.*) 1. Weak, sickly. 2. Whining (llorón), snivelling, -*m. & f.* (*And. CAm. Mex.*) Baby of the family.

chipé(n) [che-pay'], *a.* Super, smashing. -*adv.* Marvellously, really well. **Comer de chipé(n),** to have a super meal. -*f.* **La chipé(n),** the truth.

chipear [chee-pay-ar'], *va.* (*CAm.*) To bother, to pester. -*vn.* (*And. CAm.*) To moan, to whine (quejarse).

chipichipi [che-pe-chee'-pe], *m.* (*Mex.*) Mist, drizzle, mizzle.

chipichusca [che-pe-choos'-cah], *f.* Whore.

chipión [che-pe-one'], *m.* (*CAm.*) Telling off.

chipirón [che-pe-rone], *m.* Small cuttlefish.

chipotear [che-po-tay-ar'], *va.* (*CAm.*) To slap.

Chipre [che-pray], *f.* Cyprus.

chiprino, na [che-pree'-no, nah], *a.* (*Poet.*) Proper to or proceeding from Cyprus.

chipriota [che-pre-o'-tah], *a. m. & f.* Native of Cyprus.

chiqueadores [che-kay-ah-do'-res], *m. pl.* Ring of tortoise-shell formerly used in Mexico as a feminine ornament.

chiquear [che-kay-ar'], *va.* (*Carib. Mex.*) To spoil, to indulge; to flatter, to suck up to (dar coba). -*vr.* 1. (*Mex.*) To be spoiled (mimarse). 2. (*CAm.*) To swagger along.

chiqueo [che-kay'-o], *m.* 1. (*Carib. Mex.*) Flattery, toadying. 2. (*CAm.*) Swagger (contoneo).

chiquero [che-kay'-ro], *m.* 1. Pigsty. 2. (*Prov.*) Hut for goats and kids. 3. (*Prov.*) Place where bulls are shut up in bull-feasts.

chiquichaque [che-ke-chah'-kay], *m.* 1. (*Coll.*) awer, sawyer. 2. Noise made by things rubbing against each other.

chiquichuite [che-ke-choo-ee'-tay], *m.* (*Mex.*) A willow basket.

chiquilicuatro [che-ke-le-coo-ah'-tro], *m.* Dabber, meddler. V. CHISGARABÍS.

chiquilín [che-ke-leen'], *m.* (*CAm. Cono Sur, Mex.*) Tiny tot, small boy.

chiquillada [che-keeh-lyah'-dah], *f.* A childish speech or action.

chiquillería [che-keel-lyay-ree'-ah], *f.* A great number of small children.

chiquillo, illa [che-keel'-lyo], *m. & f. dim.* A small child.

chiquirritico, ica, illo, illa, ito, ita [che-keer-re-tee'-co, ee'-cah], *a. dim.* Very small, very little.

chiquirritín, chiquitín [che-keer-re-teen', che-ke-teen'], *m.* (*Coll.*) A small boy.

chiquitico, ca, chiquitillo, lla [che-ke-tee'-co, cah, che-ke-teel'-lyo, lyah], *a. dim.* Very small or little.

chiquitear [che-kee-tay-ar'], *vn.* 1. To play like a child. 2. To tipple (beber).

chiquito, ta [che-kee'-to, tah], *a. dim.* Little, small. **Hacerse chiquito,** (*Met.*) To dissemble or to conceal one's knowledge or power.

chiquitura [che-kee-too'-rah], *f.* 1. (*CAm.*) Small thing; insignificant detail. 2. (*CAm.*) V. CHIQUILLADA.

chira [che-rah], *f.* 1. (*And.*) Rag, tatter. 2. (*CAm.*) Wound, sore (llaga).

chirajos [che-rah'-hos], *m. pl.* 1. (*CAm.*) Lumber, junk (trastos). 2. (*And.*) Rasgs, tatters (andrajos).

chiribitas [che-re-bee'-tas], *f. pl.* 1. (*Coll.*) Particles which wander in the interior of the eyes and obscure the sight; spark (chispa). **Echar chiribitas, estar que echa chiribitas,** to be furious, to blow one's top. **Le hacían chiribitas los ojos,** her eyes sparkled. 2. (*Bot.*) Daisy.

chiribitil [che-re-be-teel'], *m.* 1. Den, garret, cubbyhole. 2. A small room or chamber.

chirigaita [che-re-gah'-e-tah], *f.* (*Prov.*) Kind of gourd.

chirigota [che-ree-go'-tah], *f.* Joke; fun. **Hacer de uno una chirigota,** to poke fun at somebody.

chirigotero [che-ra-go-tay'-ro], *a.* Full of jokes, facetious.

chirimbolo [che-rem-bo'-lo], *m.* Thingummyjig; strange object, odd-looking implement. **Chirimbolos,** things, gear, equipment; lumber (trastos), junk; (*Culin.*) Kitchen things.

chirimía [che-re-mee'-ah], *f.* Oboe, a musical, wind instrument. -*m.* Oboe-player.

chirimiri [che-re-me'-re], *m.* Drizzle.

chirimoya [che-re-mo'-yah], *f.* Most delicious American fruit.

chirimoyo [che-re-mo'-yo], *m.* The tree which yields the *chirimoya.*

chirinada [che-re-nah'-dah], *f.* 1. (*Cono Sur*) failure, disaster. 2. V. CHIRINOLA.

chiringuito [che-ren-ge'-to], *m.* Small shop, stall; open air restaurant, open air drinks stall; bar; night club.

chirinola [che-re-no'-lah], *f.* 1. Game played by boys. 2. Trifle, a thing of little importance or value. **Estar de chirinola,** to be in good spirits. 3. Fight, scrap; heated discussion; lengthy conversation, lively talk. **Pasar la tarde de chirinola,** to spend the afternoon deep in conversation.

chiripa [che—ree'-pah], *f.* (*Coll.*) Fortunate chance; windfall, good bargain, in billiards, a lucky stroke; a scratch, a fluke. **Por chiripa,** by chance.

chiripá [che-re-pah'], *m.* (*And. Cono Sur*) kind of blanket worn as trousers. **Gente de chiripá,** country people, peasants.

chiripear [che-re-pay-ar'], *va.* 1. To make a lucky hit; to procure a windfall. 2. To make a scratch or fluke at billiards.

chiripero [che-re-pay'-ro], *m.* A lucky person by chance.

chirís [che-rees'], *m. & f.* (*CAm.*) Kid, child.

chirivía [che-re-vee'-ah], *f.* 1. (*Bot.*) Parsnip. 2. (*Orn.*) Wagtail. V. AGUZANIEVE.

chirivisco [che-re-ves'-co], *m.* (*CAm.*) Firewood, kindling.

chirla [cheer'-lah], *f.* Mussel. V. ALMEJA.

chirlador, ra [chir-lah-dor', rah], *m. & f.* A clamorous prattler, a talkative person.

chirlar [chir-lar'], *vn.* To prattle, to talk much and loud.

chirle [cheer'-lay], *m.* 1. The dung of sheep and goats. 2. A wild grape. 3. Watery, wishy-washy (sopa). 4. Flat, dull, wishy-washy.

chirlo [cheer'-lo], *m.* A large wound in the face, and the scar it leaves when cured.

chirola [chee-ro'-lah], *f. (CAm. Carib.)*, **chirona** *f.* Jug, jail. **Estar en chirola,** to be in the jug.

chiros [che'-ros], *m. pl. (And.)* Rags, tatters.

chiroso [che-ro-so], *a. (And. CAm.)* Ragged, tattered.

chirota [che-ro'-tah], *f. (CAm.)* Tough woman.

chirote [che-ro'-tay], *a. (And.)* Daft.

chirriado [chir-re-ah'-do], *m. V.* CHIRRIDO. *-a. (And.)* Witty (gracioso). **-Chirriado, da,** *pp.* of CHIRRIAR.

chirriador, ra [chir-re-ah-dor', rah], *a.* 1. Hissing (en la sartén). 2. Creaking (puerta). 3. Chirper.

chirriar [chir-re-ar'], *vn.* 1. To hiss (en la sartén). 2. To creak (puerta). 3. To crepitate; to creep. 4. To chirp, or to chirk. 5. To sing out of tune or time. 6. *(And.)* To shiver with cold. 7. *(And.)* To go on a spree.

chirrichote [chir-re-cho'-tay], *m. (Prov.)* A presumptuous man.

chirrido [chir-ree'-o], *m.* Chirping of birds; crick; chattering, shrill, sound; screech(ing); squeal(ling).

chirrío [chir-ree'-o], *m.* The creaking noise made by carts and wagons; crick; crepitation.

chirrión [chir-re-on'], *m.* 1. Tumbrel, a strong muck or dung cart; one-horse cart. 2. A whiphandle and lash. 3. Scraping on a violin by one who cannot play lightly. 4. *(CAm.)* String, line (sarta). 5. *(CAm.)* Chat, conversation.

chirrionar [cher-re-o-nar'], *va. (And. Mex.)* To whip, to lash.

chirrionero [chir-re-o-nay'-ro], *m.* Scavenger, dungcart driver.

chirrisco [cher-res'-co], *a.* 1. *(CAm. Carib.)* Very small, tiny. 2. *(Mex.)* Flirtatious. **Viejo chirrisco,** dirty old man.

chirumbela [che-room-bay'-lah], *f. V.* CHURUMBELA.

chirumen [che-roo'-men], *m.* Judgment. *V.* CALETRE.

chirusa [che-roo'-sah], *f. (Cono Sur)* girl, kid; poor woman.

chis [chis], *interj.* Hey!, psst! (pidiendo silencio); *(LAm.)* Ugh! (asco).

chischás [chis-chahs'], *m. (Coll.)* Clashing of swords or other sidearms.

chiscón [chis-cone'], *m.* Shack, hovel, slum.

chischís [chis-chees'], *m. (And. CAm. Carib.)* Drizzle.

chisgarabís [chis-gah-ra-bees'], *m.* A dabbler, an insignificant, noisy fellow, who meddles and interferes in everything.

chisguete [chis-gay'-tay], *m. (Coll.)* A small draft of wine; a small spout of any liquid.

chisguetear [chis-gay-te-ar'], *va.* To drink a small draught.

chisme [chees'-may], *m.* 1. Gossip, misreport, misrepresentation; any account maliciously false; a tale or story intended to excite discord and quarrels. **No me vengas con esos chismes,** don't bring those tales to me 2. Variety of lumber of little value; thing, whatnot. **Dame el chisme ese,** give me that whatsit, please. 3. *(Tec.)* Gadget, contrivance, jigger.

chismear [chis-may-ar'], *va.* To tattle, to carry tales, to misrepresent, to misreport, to tell tales.

chismería [chis-may-ree'ah], *f.* **chismerío** *m. (Cono Sur, Carib.)* Gossip, tittle-tattle, scandal.

chismero, ra [chis-may'-ro, ah], **chismoso, sa** [chis-mo'-so, sah], *a.* Tattling, tale-bearing, propagating injurious rumors.

chismorrear [chis-mor-ray-ar'], *vn. V.* CHISMEAR.

chismorreo [chis-mor-ray'-o], *m. V.* CHISMEAR.

chispa [chis'-pah], *f.* 1. Spark (centella); *(fig.)* Sparkle, gleam. **Echar chispas,** *(fig.)* To be hopping mad. 2. Drop (gota de Illuvia). **Caen chispas,** there are a few drops falling. 3. *(fig.)* Bit, tiny amount. **Ni chispa,** not the least bit. **Eso no tiene ni chispa de gracia,** that's not in the least bit funny. **Si tuviera una chispa de inteligencia,** if he had an atom of intelligence. 4. *(fig.)* Sparkle, wit; life (ingenio). **El cuento tiene chispa,** the story has some wit. **Dar chispas,** to show oneself to be bright. **Tener mucha chispa,** to be a lively sort. 5. Drunkenness. **Coger una chispa,** to get tight. 6. *(And.)* Rumor. 7. *(And.)* Gun, weapon, *-a.* 1. *(Mex.)* Funny, amusing. 2. **Estar chispa,** to be tight. *-m.* Electrician.

chisparse [chis-par'-say], *vr.* 1. *(Amer.)* To become intoxicated, to get drunk. 2. *(CAm. Mex.)* To run away (huir).

¡chispas! [chees'-pas], *int.* Fire and tow! Blazes!

chispazo [chis-pah'-tho], *m.* 1. Spark. **Me saltó un chispazo a la cara,** a spark flew into my face. 2. *(Met.)* Tale or story mischievously circulated.

chispeante [chis-pay-ahn'-tay], *a. (fig.)* Sparkling, scintillating.

chispear [chis-pay-ar'], *vn.* 1. To sparkle, to emit sparks. 2. To rain gently or in small drops. 3. *(And.)* To gossip, to spread scandal. *-vr. (Carib. Cono Sur)* to get drunk.

chispeo [chis-pay'-o], *m.* Sparkle, brilliancy.

chispero [chis-pay'-ro], *m.* 1. Smith who makes kitchen utensils. 2. *(And. Carib.)* Gossiping, scandal-mongering. 3. *(CAm.)* Lighter; *(Aut.)* Sparkling plug.

chispero, ra [chis-pay'-ro, rah], *a.* Emitting a number of sparks.

chispita [chis-pee'-tah], *f.* **Una chispita de vino,** a drop of wine.

chispo [chees'-po], *m.* 1 *(Coll.)* Tipsy. 2. *V.* CHISGUETE.

chisporrotear [chis-por-ro-tay-ar'], *vn. (Coll.)* To hiss and crackle, as burning oil or tallow mixed with water; to sputter.

chisporroteo [chis-por-ro-tay'-o], *m. (Coll.)* Sibilation, hissing, crackling.

chisposo, sa [chis-po'-so, sah], *a.* Sparkling, emitting sparks.

chisquero [chis-kay-ro], *m.* Pocket lighter.

chist [chist], **interj** *V.* CHIS.

chistar [chis-tar'], *vn.* To mumble, to mutter. **No chistó palabra,** he did not open his lips.

chiste [chees'-tay], *m.* 1. A fine witty saying 2. Facetiousness. 3. Fun, joke, jest. **Dar en el chiste,** to hit the nail on the head. **Chiste pesado,** scurvy trick. **No veo el chiste,** I don't get it. **Tomar algo a chiste,** to take something as a joke.

chistera [chis-tay'-rah], *f.* 1. Angler's basket, narrow basket for fish. 2. *(Coll.)* Top hat, topper (sombrero de copa).

chistosamente [chis-to-sah-men-tay], *adv.* Facetiously, wittily, merrily, gaily.

chistoso, sa [chis-to'-so, sah], *a.* Gay, cheerful, lively, facetious, humorous; funny.

chistu [chis-too], *m.* Flute (Basque).

chistulari [chis-too-lah'-re], *m.* (Basque) Flute player.

chita [chee'-tah], *f.* 1. The anklebone in sheep and bullocks. 2. Game with this bone. **No vale una chita,** it is not worth a rush. **Dar en la chita,** *(Met.)* to hit the nail on the head. **A la chita callando,** secretly, very quietly, by stealth. 3. *(Mex.)* Net bag; money; small savings, nest egg.

chite [chee'tay], *m.* Kind of cotton stuff, chintzes; India calico.

chiticalla [che-te-cal'-lyah], *m. (Coll.)* One who keeps silence.

chiticallar [chetecal-lyar'], *vn. (Coll.)* To keep silence. **Ir** or **andar chiticallando,** to go on one's tiptoes, not to make a noise.

chito [chee'-to], *m.* A piece of wood, bone, or other substance, on which the money is put in the game of *chita*. **Irse a chitos,** *(Coll.)* to lead a debauched life.

¡chito, chitón ! [chee'-to, che-tone'], *int.* Hush! not a word! hist! silence! mum!

chiva [chee'-vah], *f.* 1. Kid, a female goat. 2. *(LAm.)* Goatee (barba). 3. *(And. CAm.)* Bus; car. 4. *(CAm.)* Blanket, bedcover. 5. *(Carib. Cono Sur)* Naughty little girl; *(CAm. Cono Sur)* mannish woman; *(And. Carib, Cono Sur)* immoral woman. 6. *(CAm. Cono Sur)* Fib, tall story. 7. *(Carib.)* Grass, informer (delator). *-a. (CAm.) (excl.)* Look out!

chival [che-vahl'], *m. (Obs.)* Herd of goats.

chivalete [che-vah-lay'-tay], *m.* Chest of drawers with a desk for writing. *V.* ESCRITORIO.

chivar [che-var'], *(LAm.) (Prov.)* *va.* To annoy, to upset (molestar), to swindle. *-vr.* 1. To get annoyed. 2. To tell, to split. **Chivarse de algo al maestro,** to tell the teacher, to split to the teacher.

chivata [che-vah'-tah], *f.* 1. (*Prov.*) Shepherd's club or staff. 2. Torch.

chivatazo [che-vah-tah-tho], *m.* Tip-off. **Dar chivatazo,** to inform, to give a tip-off.

chivatear [che-vah-tay-ar'], *vn.* To split (soplar); to inform, to squel; to blow the gaff. 2. (*And. Cono Sur*) To shout, to make a hullabaloo; to jump about; to indulge in horseplay (retozar). 3. (*Carib.*) To create a big impression. -*vr.* (*Carib.*) To get scared.

chivato [che-vah'-to], *m.*

chivera [che-vay'-rah], *f.* (*And. CAm.*) Goatee (beard).

chivero [che-vay'-ro], *m.* 1. (*Amer.*) The puma, American lion. 2. (*And.*) Bus-driver. 3. (*And.*) Brawler (matón). 4. (*Carib.*) Intriguer.

chivetero, chivital [che-vay-tay'-ro, che-ve-tahl'], *m.* Fold for kids.

chivo [chee-vo], *m.* 1. Kid, he-goat. 2. (*Prov.*) Pit, a place for the lees of oil. 3. (*CAm.*) Dice; game of dice. 4. (*Carib.*) Fraud (estafa); plot, intrigue (intriga); smuggling; illegal trading; contraband (géneros). 5. (*And. CAm. Carib, Cono Sur*) fit of anger. 6. (*Mex.*) Day's wages (jornal); advance (anticipo); back-hander (soborno). 7. (*Carib.*) Punch, blow (golpe). 8. (*And. CAm.*) Naughty boy. 9. (*CAm.*) Guatemalan. 10. (*CAm.*) Pimp (chulo). -*a.* (*CAm.*) Guatemalan.

chivón [che-vone'], (*Carib.*) 1. *a.* Annoying, irritating. 2. *m.* **Chivona** *f.* Bore.

¡cho! [cho], *int.* A word used by the drivers of mules or horses to make them stop: whoa!

choca [cho'-cah], *f.* 1. Part of the game given to a hawk. 2. Stick or paddle used by soapboilers.

chocallo [cho-cahl'-lyo], *m.* (*Obs.*) *V.* ZARCILLO.

chocante [cho-cahn'-tay], *a.* 1. Starling, striking (sorprendente); odd, strange; note-worthy. **Es chocante que...,** it is odd that..... 2. Shocking, scandalous. 3. (*LAm.*) Tiresome, tedious, annoying; cheeky (fresco), impertinent.

chocantería [cho-cahn-tay-ree'-ah], *f.* (*LAm.*) 1. Impertinence. 2. Coarse joke (chiste).

chocar [chocar'], *vn.* 1. To strike, to knock, to dash against one another. **Chocar con,** to collide with. **El buque**

chocarrear [cho-car-ray-ar'], *vn.* To joke, to jest, to act the buffoon.

chocarrería [cho-car-ray-ree'-ah], *f.* 1. Buffoonery, low jests, scurrilous mirth. 2. Deceiving, cheating at play. *V.* FULLERÍA.

chocarrero [cho-car-ray'-ro], *m.* 1. Buffoon, low jester, merry-andrew, mimic. 2. (*Obs.*) Cheat, or sharper at at play. 3. Vulgar. *V.* FULLERO.

chocarrero, ra [cho-car-ray'-ro, rah], *a.* Practising indecent raillery; scurrilous, buffoonlike.

chocarresco, ca [cho-car-res'-co, cah], *a.* (*Obs.*) *V.* CHOCARRERO.

chocha, chochaperdiz [cho'-chah, cho-chah-per-deeth'], *f.* (*Orn.*) Woodcock.

chochada [cho-chah'-dah], *f.* 1. Cunt (vagina). 2. (*CAm.*) Triviality. **Chochas,** bits and pieces.

chochear [cho-chay-ar'], *vn.* 1. To dodder, to be doddery, to be senile; to be in one's dotage. 2. (*fig.*) To be soft, to go all sentimental.

chochera, chochez [cho-chay'-rah, cho-cheth'], *f.* 1. Dotage, the speech and action of a dotard. 2. Silly thing. 3. (*And. Cono Sur*) favorite, pet. **Tener chochera por una,** to dote on somebody.

chochín [cho-cheen'], *m.* 1. Wren. 2. Bird; girl-friend.

chochita [cho-che'-tah], *f.* Wren.

chocho, cha [cho'-cho, chah], *a.* 1. Doting, having the intellect impaired by age. 2. Doddering, doddery, senile. 3. (*Cono Sur*) happy. 4. (*CAm.*) Nicaraguan.

chocho [cho'-cho], *m.* 1. (*Bot.*) Lupine *V.* ALTRAMUZ. 2. A sweetmeat or confection. **Chochos,** all sorts of sweetmeats given to children; dainties. 3. Drug addict. 4. (*CAm.*) Nicaraguan. 5. (*CAm.*) *Excl.* No kidding!, Really!. 6. (*Anat.*) Cunt.

chochoca [cho-cho-cah], *f.* (*CAm.*) Nut, head.

chocholear [cho-cho-lay-ar'], *va.* (*And.*) To spoil, to pamper.

chocilla [cho-theel'-lyah], *f. dim.* A small hut, a low cottage.

choclar [cho-clar'], *vn.* 1. In the Spanish game of *argolla,* to drive the ball out by the rings. 2. To bolt into a room.

choclo [cho'-clo], *m.* 1. *V.* CHANCLO. 2. (*Amer.*) Green ear of corn in a state fit for eating. 3. (*Cono Sur*) **choclos,** children's arms; children's legs. 4. (*And.*) (*fig.*) **Un choclo de,** a group of 5. (*Cono Sur*) difficulty, trouble.

choco [cho'-co], *m.* (*Prov.*) 1. The small cuttlefish. 2. Hiding place (children) *V.* JIBIA.

choco [cho'-co], *a.* (*And. Cono Sur*) Dark red; chocolate-colored; swarthy dark (moreno). 2. (*CAm. Cono Sur, Mex.*) One-armed (manco); one-legged (cojo); one-eyed (tuerto); -*m.* 1. (*Cono Sur*) stump. 2. (*And.*) Top hat. 3. (*Mex.*) Cunt, fanny.

chocolate [cho-colah'tay], *m.* 1. Chocolate. 2. Chocolate the liquor made by a solution of chocolate in water, milk, or *atole.* 3. (*LAm.*) Blood. **Dar a uno agua de su propio chocolate,** to give somebody a taste of his own medicine. 4. Hash, pot. **Darle al chocolate,** to be hooked on drugs.

~~**chocolatera** [cho-co-lah-tay'rah], *f.* Chocolate pot.~~

chocolatería [cho-co-lah-tay-ree'-ah], *f.* Shop where only chocolate is sold; chocolate factory. ·

chocolatero [cho-colah-tay'-ro], *m.* 1. One who grinds or makes chocolate. 2. The seller of chocolate. 3. (*Mex.*) A stiff north wind, but not tempestuous like that of winter. -*a.* Fond of chocolate.

chocolatina [cho-co-lah-te'-nah], *f.* Chocolate.

chocolear [cho-co-lay-ar'], (*And.*) -*va.* To dock, to cut off the tail of. -*vn.* To get depressed.

chode [cho'-day], *m.* (*Prov.*) Paste of milk, eggs, sugar and flour.

chofer [chofer'], *m.* Chauffeur, automobile driver, motorist.

chofero [cho-fay'-ro], *m. V.* CHOFISTA.

chofes [cho'-fess], *m. pl.* Lungs. *V.* BOFES.

chofeta [cho-fay'-tah], *f.* Chafing-dish, firepan; a portable grate for coals.

chofista [chofees'tah], *m.* One who lives upon livers and lights.

cholada [cho-lah'-dah], *f.* (*And.*) Action typical of a cholo.

cholería [cho-lay-ree'-ah], *f.* (*And.*), **cholerío** *m.* (*And.*), Group of cholos.

cholga [chol-gah], *f.* (*LAm.*) Mussel, clam.

cholla [chol'-lyah], *f.* 1. (*Coll.*) Skull. 2. (*Met.*) Faculty, powers of the mind, judgment. **No tiene cholla,** he has not the brains of a sparrow; he is bird-brained. 3. (*CAm.*) Wound, sore. 4. (*And. CAm.*) Laziness, slowness.

chollo [chol'-lyo], *m.* 1. (*Com.*) Bargain, snip. **Es un chollo,** it's a doddle. 2. Love affair.

cholludo [chol-loo'-do], *a.* (*And. CAm.*) Lazy, slow.

cholo, la [cho'-lo, lah], *a.* (*Amer.*) 1. Halfbreed of European and Indian parentage. 2. Familiar diminutive in kindly tone, equivalent to son, deary. 3. (*Cono Sur*) coward.

chongo [chon'-go], *m.* 1. (*Cono Sur*) blunt knife, worn-out knife. 2. (*Carib.*) Old horse. 3. Chongos (*CAm. Mex.*) Pigtails, tresses (trenzas); bun (moño).

chonta [chon-tah], *f.* A kind of palmtree, the wood of which is harder than ebony. *Cf.* CHORITA.

chontal [chon-tahl'], *m.* 1. A grove of chonta-trees. 2. (*Mex.* and *CAm.*) An Indian with no training, uncivilized; coarse, rough.

chop [chop], *m.* (*LAm.*) Tankard, mug.

chopa [cho'-pah], *f.* 1. (*Zool.*) Kind of seabream. 2. (*Naut.*) Topgallant poop, or poop royal. 3. Jacket.

chopazo, chope [cho-pah'-tho], *m.* (*Cono Sur*) punch, bash.

chopera [cho-pay'-rah], *f.* Poplar grove.

chopo [cho'-po], *m.* 1. (*Bot.*) Black poplar-tree. 2. Gun. **Cargar con el chopo,** (*fig.*) To join up, to do one's military service.

choque [cho'-kay], *m.* 1. Shock, clash, dash, collision. 2. Congress, encounter. 3. (*Mil.*) Skirmish, a slight engagement. 4. Difference, dispute, contest; jar. **Entrar choque,** to clash. 5. *(Naut.)* Chock, fur. **Choques de entremises,** *(Naut.)* Faying-chocks. 6. Crash, collision. **Choque de frente,** head-on collision. 7. *(Med.)* Shock.

choquear [cho-kay-ar'], *va.* To beat the soda-ash with the paddle in order to secure soap in fine pieces.

choquecilla [cho-kay-theel'-lyah], *f. V.* CHOQUEZUELA.

choqueo [cho-kay'-o], *m.* The act of beating the soapashes.

chorar [cho-rar'], *va.* To burgle (casa); to rip off (objeto).

chorba [chor'-bah], *f.* Bird, girlfriend.

chorba [chor'-bo], *m.* 1. Boyfriend, guy, bloke (tío). 2. Pimp.

chorca [chor'-cah], *f. (Prov.)* Pit or hole dug in the ground. *V.* HOYO.

chorcha [chor'-chah], *f.* 1. *(Mex.)* Noisy party. **Una chorcha de amigos,** a group of friends. 2. *(CAm.)* Crest, comb. 3. *(CAm.) (Med.)* Goitre. 4. *(CAm.)* Clit, clitoris. *V.* CHOCHA.

chorchero [chor-chay'-ro], *a. (Mex.)* Party-loving.

chorchi [chor'-che], *m.* Soldier.

chorear [cho-ray-ar'], *vn. (Cono Sur)* To grumble, to complain. -*va.* 1. **Me chorea,** it gets up my nose. 2. To pinch (robar).

choreo [cho-ray'-o], *m. (Cono Sur)* Grouse, complaint.

chori [cho'-re], *m.* 1. Knife. 2. Thief.

choricear [cho-re-thay-ar'], *va.* To rip off, to lift.

choricería [cho-re-thay-ree'-ah], *f. V.* SALCHICHERÍA.

choricero [cho-re-thay'-ro], *m.* 1. Sausage maker or seller. 2. Crook.

chorillo [cho-reel'-lyo], *m. (Peru)* Mill for coarse fabrics without fulling-stocks.

chorita [cho-ree'-tah], *m. (Amer.)* A palm-tree, the wood of which is black, solid, and heavier than ebony. *V.* CHONTA.

chorizar [cho-re-thar'], *va.* To nick, to rip off.

chorizo [cho-ree'-tho], *m.* 1. Pork sausage. 2. Balancing pole (circo). 3. *(Anat.)* Prick. 4. *(And. Cono Sur)* rump steak. 5. *(And. Cono Sur) (Arquit.)* Mixture of clay and straw used in plastering. 6. Thug, lout (matón). 7. *(And.)* Idiot. 8. *(Carib.)* Mulatto.

chorlito [chor-lee'to], *m.* 1. *(Orn.)* Curlew or gray plover. 2. *(Orn.)* Red shank. **Cabeza de chorlito,** hare-brained, frivolous.

chorlo [chor'-lo], *m.* 1. Schorl, tourmaline, especially the black variety. 2. *(And. CAm. Carib.)* Great-grand-grandchild.

choro [cho'-ro], *m.* 1. Thief, burglar. 2. *(And. Cono Sur) (Zool.)* Mussel.

chorote [cho-ro'-tay], *m.* A certain chocolate which the poor people of Venezuela take.

chorra [chor-rah], *f.* 1. Luck, jam. **¡Qué chorra tiene!,** look at that for jam! 2. *(Cono Sur)* underworld slang. 3. *(Anat.)* Prick. 4. *adv.* By chance.

chorreado, da [chor-ray-ah'-do, dah], *a.* Applied to a kind of satin. -*pp.* of CHORREAR.

chorreadura [chor-ray-ah-doo'-rah], *f.* Dripping, dropping, welling.

chorrear [chor-ray-ar'], *va.* 1. To fall or drop front a spout, to outpour, to gush, to drip. 2. *(Met.)* To come successively, or one by one. 3. To tick off (regañar). 4. *(And.)* To soak (mojar). -*vn.* 1. To gush, to spout. **Chorrear de sudor,** to run with sweat. **La ropa chorrear todavía,** his clothes are still wringing wet. 2. *(Fit.)* To trickle. **Chorrean todavía las solicitudes,** the applications are still trickling in. -*vr.* **Chorrearse algo,** to pinch something.

chorreo [chor-ray'-o], *m.* 1. The act and effect of dropping, dripping. 2. *(fig.)* Constant drain (de fuentes) 3. Ticking off (reprimenda). 4. **Chorreo mental,** nonsense.

chorrera [chor-ray'-rah], *f.* 1. Spout or place whence liquids drop. 2. Mark left by water or other liquids 3. Ornament formerly appended to crosses or badges of military orders. 4. Frill of a shirt. 5. *(LAm.) (fig.)* String, stream, lot. **Una chorrera de,** a whole string of, a lot of. 6. *(Carib.)* Ticking off. 7. *V.* JAMON.

chorrero [chor-ray'-ro], *a.* Jammy, lucky.

chorretada [chor-ray-tah'-dah], *f. (Coll.)* Water or other liquid rushing from a spout.

chorrillo [chor-reel'-lyo], *m.* 1. *(dim.)* A small spout of water or any other liquid. 2. The continual coming in and out going of money. **Irse por el chorrillo,** *(Met.)* to drive with the current, to conform to custom.

chorrito [chor-ree'-to], *m. dim.* A small spout of water or any other liquid.

chorro [chor'-ro], *m.* 1. Water or any other liquid, issuing from a spout or other narrow place, gush. **Beber a chorro,** to drink a jet of wine (from a wineskin). **Salir a chorros,** to gush forth. 2. A jet of water. 3. A strong and coarse sound emitted by the mouth. **Un chorro de palabras,** a stream of words. **Hablar a chorros,** to talk nineteen to the dozen. 4. Hole made in the ground for playing with nuts. **Soltar el chorro,** *(Met.)* to burst out into laughter. **A chorros,** abundantly, copiously. 5. Strand (látigo). 6. *(CAm.)* Tap (grifo) 7. *(Cono Sur)* thief, pickpocket. 8. *(Carib.)* Ticking off (ladrón).

chorro de arena [chor'-ro day ah-ray'-nah], *m.* Sandblast.

chorrón [chor-rone'], *m.* Hackled or dressed hemp.

chortal [chor-tahl'], *m.* Fountain or spring at the surface of the ground.

chota [cho'-tah], *f.* 1. A sucking kid. 2. Heifer calf. -*m. & f.* Hanger-on; creep, toady.

chotacabras [cho-tah-cah'-bras], *f. (Orn.)* Goatsucker, churnowl.

chotar [cho-tar'], *va. (Obs.)* To suck. *V.* MAMAR.

chote [cho'-tay], *m. V.* CHAYOTE.

chotear [cho-tay-ar'], *va.* 1. To tease. 2. To spoil, to pamper (mimar). 3. *(CAm.)* To shadow, to tail (sospechoso). -*vr.* 1. To joke, to take things as a joke. 2. To cough, to inform.

choteo [cho-tay'-o], *m.* Raillery, badinage, teasing.

chotis [cho'-tees], *m.* 1. Scottische. 2. Traditional dance of Madrid. 3. **Ser más agarrado que un chotis,** to be tight-fisted.

choto [cho'-to], *m.* 1. A sucking kid. 2. A calf. 3. Stupid old git.

choto [cho'-to], *a.* 1. *(CAm.)* Abundant, plentiful. **Estar choto de,** to be full of.

chotuno, na [cho-too'-no, nah], *a.* 1. Sucking (cabritas). 2. Poor, starved (corderos). 3. Goatish. **Oler a chotuna,** to stink like a goat.

chova [cho'-vah], *f. (Orn.)* Jay, chough.

chovinismo [cho-ve-nees'-mo], *m.* etc. *V.* CHAUVINISMO.

choya [cho'-yah], *f. (Orn.)* Jackdaw, crow. *V.* CORNEJA.

choz [choth], *m. (Coll.)* Sound of a blow or stroke. **Esta especie me ha dado choz,** *(Coll.)* I was struck with amazement at this affair.

choza [cho'-thah], *f.* Hut, cottage, hovel.

chozna [choth'-nah], *f.* Great-granddaughter.

chozno [choth'-no], *m.* Great-grandchild.

chozo [cho'-tho], *m.* A small hut; hovel.

chozuela [cho-thoo-ay'-lah], *f. dim.* A small hut or cottage.

chrisma, christma, christmas [chris'-mas], *f. m. pl.* Christmas card.

chual [choo-ahl'], *m.* A wild plant of California; a pigweed or goosefoot.

chualar [choo-ah-lar'], *m.* A spot abounding in chual plants.

chubarba [choo-bar'-bah], *f. (Bot.)* Stonecrop.

chubasco [choo-bahs'-co], *m. (Naut.)* Squall, a violent gust of wind and rain.

chubascoso, sa [choo-bas-co'-so, sah], *a.* Squally, gusty, stormy.

chubasquero [choo-bas-kay'-ro], *m.* 1. Oilskin; light raincoat (gabardina). 2. French letter.

chuca [choo'-cah], *f.* The concave part of a ball used by boys in play.

chucán [choo-cahn'], *a. (CAm.)* Buffoonish (bufón); coarse (grosero), rude.

chucallo [choo-cahl'-lyo], *m. (Obs.) V.* ZARCILLO.

chúcaro [choo'-cah-ro], *a. (LAm.)* Wild, untamed (animal); shy (persona).

chucear [choo-thay-ar'], *va. (LAm.)* To prick, to goad.

chucero [choo-thay'-ro], *m. (Mil.)* Pikeman.

chucha [choo'-chah], *f.* 1. A female dog, bitch. 2. **¡Chucha!** exclamation to restrain her.

chucha [choo'-chah], *f.* 1. Opossum. 2. *(And.)* Body odour. 3. *(And. Cono Sur)* Cunt.

chuchada [choo-chah'-dah], *f. (CAm.)* Trick, swindle.

chuchear [choo-chay-ar'], *va.* To fowl with calls, gins, and nets.-*vn.* To whisper. *V.* CUCHICHEAR.

chuchería [choo-chay-ree'-ah], *f.* 1. Gewgaw, bauble, a pretty trifle, a toy. 2. Tidbit which is nice, but not expensive. 3. Mode of fowling with calls, gins, and nets.

chuchero [choo-chay'-ro], *m.* Birdcatcher.

chucho [choo'-cho], *m.* 1. *(Orn.)* Longeared owl. 2. A dog. 3. **¡Chucho!** exclamation used to call a dog. 3. Sweetheart. 4. *(Carib.)* Switch; siding. 5. *(Carib.)* Rawhide whip (látigo). 6. *(Cono Sur)* jail. 7. *(LAm.)* Shakes, shivers. **Entrarle a uno el chucho,** to get the jitters. 8. *(CAm.)* Spiv (ostentoso). 9. *(LAm.)* Reefer; joint. 10. *(And. CAm. Mex.) (Culin.)* Tamale. -*a.* 1. *(And.)* Soft, watery (fruta); wrinkled (persona). 2. *(CAm.)* Mean (tacaño). 3. *(Mex.)* Gossipy.

chuchumeco [choo-choo-may'-co], *m.* 1. A sorry, contemptible little fellow. 2. Mean person (tacaño). 3. *(Cono Sur)* sickly person. 4. *(And. Carib.)* Toff, dude. 5. *(Carib.)* Idiot.

chuchupate [choo-choo-pah'-tay], *m.* A plant of the umbelliferae, indigenous to the Pacific coast.

chueca [choo-ay'-cah], *f.* 1. Pan or hollow of the joints of bones. 2. A small ball with which country people play at crickets. 3. *(Coll.)* Fun, trick. *V.* CHASCO. A soap-maker's paddle. 4. *(Bot.)* Stump.

chuecazo [choo-ay-cah'-tho], *m.* Stroke given to a ball.

chueco [choo-ay'-co], *a.* 1. *(LAm.)* Knock-kneed; *(And. Cono Sur)* pigeon-toed (patituerto); *(And.)* Lame (cojo); *(Mex.)* One-armed (manco); one-legged; *(CAm. Carib. Mex.)* Crooked, twisted, bent (torcido); bent, crooked (corrupto); left-handed (zurdo). **Un negocio chueco,** a crooked deal.

chufa [choo'-fah], *f.* 1. *(Bot.)* The edible cyperus; a sedge, the root of which is used as a substitute for coffee. 2. *(Obs.)* Rodomontade, an empty boast. **Echar chufas,** to hector, to act the bully.

chufeta [choo-fay'-tah], *f.* 1. Jest, joke. 2. *(Prov.)* Small pan used to hold live coals.

chufla [choo-flah], *f.* Joke, merry quip. **Tomar algo a chufla,** to take something as a joke.

chuflarse [choo-flar'-say], *vr.* To joke, to make jokes; to take things as a joke.

chufleta [choo-flay'-tah], *f.* Taunt, jeer, gibe, fling, scoff.

chufletear [choo-flay-tayar'], *vn.* To sneer, to taunt, to show contempt, to joke.

chufletero, ra [choo-flay-tay'-ro, rah], *a.* Taunting, sneering.

chula [choo'-lah], *f.* 1. Woman from the back streets, low-class woman. 2. Loud wench, flashy female; brassy girl (charra). 3. *(LAm.)* girlfriend.

chulada [choo-lah'-dah], *f.* 1. Droll speech or action, pleasant conversation. 3. Indecorous action of persons of bad breeding or low condition. 3. contemptuous word or action.

chulear [choo-layar'], *va..* To jest, to joke. 2. To sneer, to taunt, to ridicule. -*vr.* **Chulearse de,** to take the mickey out of.

chulería [choo-lay-ree'-ah], *f.* 1. A pleasing manner of acting and speaking, vulgarity, natural charm. 2. *V.* CHULADA.

chulesco [choo-lays'-co], *a. V.* CHULO.

chuleta [choo-lay'-tah], *f.* 1. Chop, cutlet. 2. *(Cos.)* Insert, piece let in. 3. Punch, bash (golpe). 4. *(Univ.)* Crib, trot; (TV) Autocue, teleprompter. 5. Side whiskers, sideboards (patillas). 6. Toff (persona). 7. Divot (golf).

chulillo [choo-leel-lyo], *m. (And.)* Tradesman's assistant.

chulo, la [choo'-lo, lah], *m. & f.* 1. Punster, jester, merry-andrew. 2. An artful, sly, and deceitful person. 3. A funny person. 4. Butcher's mate or assistant. 5. Bullfighter's assistant. 6. *V.* PÍCARO. A playful term of endearment. 7. Smart, attractive (aspecto). 8. Proud, jaunty, swaggering. **Con el sombrero a lo chulo,** with his hat at a rakish angle. **Iba muy chulo,** he walked with a swagger. 9. Brilliant, super. 10. Villain, rascal. **Chulo de putas,** pimp, pander.

chulla [chool'-lyah], *f. (Prov.)* Slice of bacon.

chumacera [choo-mah-thay'-rah], *f.* 1. *(Mech.)* Bearing, journal bearing; cushion. 2. *(Naut.)* Rowlock, a strip of wood put on the gunwale of a boat to prevent the oars from wearing it.

chumarse [choo-mar'-say], *vr. (And.)* To get drunk.

chumbar [choom-bar'], *va.* 1. *(Cono Sur)* To attack, to go for (perro). 2. *(And.)* To shoot (fusilar). 3. To swaddle (bebé).

chumbo or higo chumbo [choom-bo], *m.* 1. Indian fig, pricky pear. 2. *(Cono Sur)* shot, pellet.

chumeco [choo-may'-co], *m. (CAm.)* Apprentice.

chuminada [choo-me-nah'-dah], *f.* 1. Silly thing, piece of nonsense. 2. Petty detail.

chumpipe [choom-pee'-pay], *m. (Costa Rica and Nicaragua)* Turkey.

chuncaca [choon-cah'-cah], *f. (Amer.)* Cane sirup boiled, but unclarified, of which coarse sugar is made. *V.* CHANCACA.

chuncho [choon'-cho], *(And.)* 1. *a.* Savage; uncivilized; bashful, shy. 2. *m. f.* Savage, bashful, shy.

chunga [choon'gah], *f.* Jest, joke. **Estar de chunga,** to be merry or in good humor.

chungo [choon-go], *a.* Bad, rotten; nasty (desagradable); ugly; dicey (dudoso), dodgy; dud (falso, billete).

chungón, gona [choon-gone'], *m. & f.* Joker.

chunguear [choon-gay-ar'], *vn. (Coll.)* To be merry, to be in good humor. -*vr.* To gag, to crack jokes; to be in a merry mood; to banter. **Chunguearse de uno,** to have a bit of fun with somebody.

chunguero, ra [choon-gay-ro, rah], *a* Diverting, amusing, humorous, fun-loving.

chunopa [choo-no'-pah], *f. (Peru) V.* YUCA.

chuño, chano [choo'-nyo, choo'-no], *m. (Peru)* Dried potatoes cured on ice, for making vegetable soup.

chupa [choo'-pah], *f.* 1. Waistcoat; jacket (*fr.* Aljuba). 2. Drunkenness. 3. *(CAm.)* Bag.

chupa [choo'-pah], *f.* **Poner a uno como una chupa de dómine,** to give somebody a tremendous ticking off.

chupachupa [choo-pah-choo'-pah], *m. & f.* Sucker.

chupada [choo-pah'-dah], *f.* Suck; pull, puff; chupadas; sucking. **Dar chupadas a la pipa,** to puff away at one's pipe.

chupadero, ra [choo-pah-day'-ro, rah], *a.* Sucking, sucker, drawing out milk or other liquids with the lips; absorbent.

chupado, da [choo-pah'-do, dah], *a.* 1. *(Coll.)* lean, emaciated. 2. Tight (falda). 3. **Estar chupado,** *(LAm.)* to be drunk. 4. **Está chupado,** it's dead easy. -*pp.* of CHUPAR. -*m. (Cono Sur)* Missing person.

chupador, ra [choo-pah-dor', rah], *m. & f.* 1. Sucker, one who sucks or draws out with the lips. **Chupador de niños,** a sucking-bottle; a child's coral. 2. *(Amer.)* Tippler, one who gets intoxicated often, drunkard.

chupadura [choo-pah-doo'-rah], *f.* Sucking, suction, the act and effect of sucking.

chupaflores, chupamiel, chupamirtos, chuparomeros, [choo-pah-flo'-res, choo-pah-me-el', choo-pah-mir'-tos, choo-pah-ro may'-ros], *m. & f. (Orn.)* Humming-birds.

chupalandero [choo-pah-lan-day'-ro], *m. (Prov.)* A kind of snail that lives on trees and plants.

chupalla [choo-pahl'-lyah], *f. (Cono Sur. Mex.)* Straw hat.

chupamangas [choo-pah-mahn'-gas], *m. (And. Cono Sur),* **chupamedias,** creep, bootlicker.

chupar [choo-par'], *va.* 1. To suck. 2. To imbibe moisture (vegetales). 3. *(Met. Coll.)* To sponge, to hang upon others for subsistence; to fool. **Chuparse los dedos,** to eat with much pleasure, to be overjoyed. **Chupar la sangre,** *(Met.)* to suck one's blood, to stick to him like a leech, living at his expense. 4. *(LAm.)* To smoke. 5. To drink, to knock back. 6. *(fig.)* To milk, to sap. **Le chupan el dinero,** they are milking him of his money. **El trabajo le chupa la salud,** his work is undermining his health. 7. To put up with (aguantar). -vn. 1. To suck. 2. To booze (beber). 3. (LAm.) To smoke. -vr. 1. **¡Chúpate ésa!,** put that in your pipe and smoke it. 2. **Chuparse el dedo,** to suck one's finger; V. DEDO. 3. **Chuparse un insulto,** (LAm.) To put up with an insult. 4. (Med.) To waste away, to decline.

chupatintas [choo-pah-teen'-tas], m. Penpusher; petty clerk; minor bureaucrat; today, creep.

chupativo, va [choo-pah-tee'-vo, vah], a. Of a sucking nature.

chupe [choo'-pay], m. A stew prepared with potatoes, eggs, cheese, etc.

chupeno, na [choo-pay'-no, nah], a. Attractive, delightful.

chupeta, illa, ita [choo-pay'-tah, eel'-lyah, ee'tah], f. dim. A short jacket or waistcoat.

chupete [choo-pay'-tay], m. 1. **Ser alguna cosa de chupete,** to possess great delicacy and good taste. 2. Dummy, pacifier. 3. Teat (de biberón); (LAm.) Lollipop (pirulí). 4. (LAm.) Suck (chupada). 5. V. RECHUPETE.

chupetada [choo-pay-tah'-dah], f V. CHUPADURA.

chupetear [choo-pay-tay-ar'], va. To suck gently; to suck over and over.

chupeteo [choo-pay-tay'-o], m. Gentle sucking.

chupi, chupinudo [choo'-pe], a. Super, brilliant.

chupilote [choo-pe-lo'-tay], m. (Amer.) A vulture.

chupinazo [choo-pe-nah-tho], m. 1. Loud bang. 2. (Dep.) Hard kick, fierce shot.

chupo [choo-po], m. 1. (LAm.) (Med.) Boil. 2. (And.) Baby's bottle.

chupón [choo-pone'], m. 1. Sucker, a young twig. 2. The act of sucking. V. Doublet. V CHUPETÍN. 3. Lollipop, sucking sweet (dulce). **Chupón de caramelo,** toffee apple. 4. (LAm.) Dummy, pacifier; baby's bottle. 5. (And. Carib.) Puff, pull (de pipa etc.). 6. (And.) (Med.) Boil. 7. (Mex.) Teat (biberón).

chupón, na [choo-pon', nah], a. (Coll.) One who cunningly deprives another of his money.

chuquelas [choo-kay'-las], m. A cotton cloth of India.

churdón [choor-done'], m. Raspberry jam.

churi [choo'-re], m. Chiv, knife.

churo [choo'-ro], a. (And. Cono Sur) handsome, attractive.

churo [choo'-ro], m. 1. (And.) (Mus.) Coiled wind instrument. 2. (And.) Spiral staircase. 3. (And.) Curl (rizo). 4. (And.) Jail.

churra [choor'-rah], f. The little pintailed grouse. -a. One year old heifer.

churrasco [choor-rahs'-co], m. (Amer.) Piece of meat broiled over coals.

churrascón [choor-ras-cone'], m. Act and effect of scorching.

churrasquear [choor-ras-kay-ar'], vn. (Cono Sur) To eat steak.

churre [choor'-ray], m. 1. (Coll.) Thick dirty grease. 2. Bloke, guy.

churrería [choor-ray-re'-ah], f. Fritter stall.

churrero, ra [choo-ray'-ro], a. m. & f. 1. Lucky, jammy. 2. Fritter seller.

churrete [choo-ray'-tay], m. Grease spot, dirty mark.

churretear [choo-ray-tay-ar'], va. (LAm.) To spot, to stain.

churretoso, sa [choo-ray-to'-so, sah], a. (Prov.) Gushing, spouting (líquidos).

churriento, ta [choor-re-en'-to, tah], a. 1. Greasy. 2. (LAm.) (Med.) Loose.

churillero, ra [choor-reel-lyay'-ro, rah], m. & f. (Obs.) Tattler, prattler, gossip.

churro, ra [choor'-ro, rah], a. Applied to sheep that have coarse wool, and to their wool. m. 1. A sort of fritter. 2. Botch, mess. **El dibujo ha salido un churro,** the sketch came out all wrong. 3. Fluke (chiripa). 4. (Anat.) Prick. 5. **Juan es un churro,** (And. Cono Sur) Juan is a dish. 6. (Mex.) Bad film.

churrullero, ra [choor-rool-lyay'-ro, rah], m. & f. Tattler, prattler, gossip.

churrupear [choor-roo-pay-ar'], vn. To sip, to drink by small draughts.

churrús [choor-roos'], m. Kind of silk stuff interwoven with a little gold and silver.

churruscar [choor-roos-kay-ar'], va. To burn, to scorch.

churruscarse [choo-roos-car'-say], vr. To be scorched, as bread, etc.

churrusco [choor-roos'-co], m. Bread too toasted or scorched. -a. (And. CAm.) Kinky, curly.

churruscón [choor-roos-cone'], m. V. CHURRASCÓN.

churumbela [choo-room-bay'-lah], f. Flageolet, wind instrument resembling an oboe; shawm.

churumen, m. V. CHIRUMEN.

churumo [choo-roo'-mo], m. Juice or substance of a thing. **Hay poco churumo,** there is little cash, little judgment.

chus ni mus [choos ne moos]. (Coll.) **No decir chus ni mus,** not to say a word.

chuscada [choos-cah'-dah], f. Pleasantry, drollery, buffoonery, fun, joke.

chusco, ca [choos'-co, cah], a. Pleasant, droll, merry.

chusma [choos'-mah], f. 1. The crew and slaves of a row-galley. 2. Rabble, mob.

chuspa [choos'-pah], f. (Amer.) A pouch of skin used among the country folk of the La Plata to carry maté, coca, money, and suchlike things.

chusquero [choos-kay'-ro], m. (Mil.) Ranker.

chut [choot], m. 1. (Dep.) Shot (at goal). 2. Shot (droga).

chuta [choo'-tah], f. V. CHUT. 2. excl. (Cono Sur) Good God! Good heavens!

chutar [choo-tar'], vn. 1. To shoot (at goal). 2. **Está que chuta,** he's hopping mad. 3. To go well. **Esto va que chuta,** it's going fine. -vr. To give oneself a shot (of drugs).

chute [choo'-tay], m. V. CHUT. -a. (Cono Sur) Spruce, natty.

chuza [choo'-thah], f. (Mex.) A stroke in the game of pigeon-holes knocking all at once with one ball.

chuzar [choo-thar'], va. (And.) To prick; to sting, to hurt.

chuzazo [choo-thah'-tho], m. 1. A large pike. 2. The blow or stroke given with it.

chuzo [choo'-tho], m. 1. Pike. 2. (Naut.) Boarding-pike. **Chuzos,** abundance of rain, snow, or hail. **A chuzos,** abundantly, impetuously. **Llover a chuzos,** to rain pitchforks, or bucketfuls. **Echar chuzos,** to brag.

chuzón, na, [choo-thone', nah], m. & ; f. 1. A crafty, artful person. 2. Wag punster, jester.

C.I. m. abr. de **Coeficiente de inteligencia** (intelligence quotient).

cía [thee'-ah], f. Hipbone, huckle bone.

Cía, abr. de **Compañia** (Company, Co.).

ciaboga [the-ah-bo'-gah], f. (Naut.) The act of putting a row-galley about with the oars. **Hacer ciaboga,** to turn the boat (treineras)

ciánido [the-ah'-ne-do], m. Cyanide, a compound of cyanogen.

ciano [the-ah'-no], m. (Bot.) The bluebottle.

cianógeno [the-ah-no'-hay-no], m. Cyanogen, a colorless, poisonous, liquefiable gas.

cianosis [the-ah-no'-sis], f. Cyanosis, a livid hue resulting from insufficient oxygenation of the blood.

cianotipia [the-ah-no-tee'-pe-ah], f. Blueprint. **Copiar a la cianotipia,** to blueprint.

cianuro [the-ah-noo'-ro], m. Cyanide, a compound of cyanogen.

ciar [the-ar'], va. 1. (Naut.) To hold water, to back a row-galley, to stop with oars. 2. To retrograde. 3. (Met.) To slacken in the pursuit of an affair.

ciática. [the-ah'-te-cah], f. Sciatica, or hip-gout.

ciático, ca [the-ah'-te-co, cah], a. Sciatic, sciatical.

ciato [the-ah'-to], m. (Bot.) A tree-fern of tropical regions.

cibario, ria [the-bah'-re-o, ah], a. Cibarious, relating to food.

cibera [the-bay'-rah], f. 1. Quantity of wheat put at once in the hopper. 2. All seeds or grains fit for animal food. 3. Coarse remains of grain and fruit, husks, etc. 4. Every operation which engages the powers of imagination and fancy. 5. (Prov.) Hopper in a cornmill.

cibernética [the-behr-nay'-te-cah], *f.* *(Med. & Elec.)* Cybernetics.

cibica. [the-bee'-cah], *f.* Clout, the iron plate nailed to an axle-tree, to prevent friction.

cibicón [the-be-cone'], *m.* A large kind of clout.

cíbolo, la [thee'-bo-lo, lah], *m. & f.* The Mexican bull, with horns turned backward; apparently the bison.

cibrú [the-broo'], *m.* Peruvian name of the cedar-tree.

cicaba [the-cah'-bah], *f.* A nocturnal bird of prey.

cicatear [the-cah-tay-ar'], *vn. (Coll.)* To be sordidly parsimonious.

cicatería [the-cah-tay-ree'-ah], *f.* Niggardliness, parsimony.

cicatero, ra [the-cah-tay'-ro, rah], *a.* Niggardly, sordid, parsimonious, mean.

cicateruelo [the-cah-tay-roo-ay'-lo], *m. dim.* An avaricious or niggardly little fellow, a little miser.

cicatricera [the-cah-tre-thay'-rah], *f.* A woman who used to follow troops and care for wounds.

cicatriz [the-cah-treeth'], *f.* 1. Cicatrice or cicatrix, a scar. 2. Gash, mark of a wound. 3. *(Met.)* Impression remaining on the mind.

cicatrización [the-cah-tre-thah-the-on'], *f.* Cicatrization.

cicatrizal [the-cah-tre-thahl'], *a.* Belonging to a cicatrice or scar.

cicatrizar [the-cah-tre-thar'], *va.* To cicatrize, to heal a wound. -*vr.* To heal.

cícero [thee'-thay-ro], *m. (Typ.)* Pica.

Cicerón [thee-thay-rone'] *m.* Cicero.

cicerone [the-thay-ro'-nay], *m.* A guide.

cicindela [the-thin-day'-lah], *f. (Zool.)* 1. A carabid beetle, tiger-beetle; the name is sometimes carelessly used for a firefly. 2. *(Obs.)* Glow-worm.

ción [the-the-on'], *m. (Prov.)* An intermittent fever.

cíclada [thee'-clah-dah], *f.* Kind of dress formerly worn by ladies.

ciclamor [the-clah-mor'], *m.* The sycamore, buttonwood, plane-tree.

ciclán [the-clahn'], *m.* 1. Ridgel. 2. A cryptorchid (or cryptorchis), an individual whose testicles have not descended into the scrotum (hombres, animales). 3. *(Met.)* Single, having no companion.

ciclatón [the-clah-tone'], *m.* A tunic once used by women.

cíclico, ca [thee'-cle-co, cah], *a.* Cyclical, belonging to a cycle.

ciclismo [the-clees'-mo], *m.* Bicycling, cycling; cycle racing.

ciclista [the-clees'-tah], *m. & f.* Cyclist.

ciclo [thee'-clo], *m.* 1. Cycle, a round of time. 2. *(Univ.)* Year, course. **Ciclo vital,** life-cycle. **Ciclo de reloj,** clock cycle. **Ciclo instrucción-decodificación-carga,** *(Inform.)* instruction-decoding-loading cycle

ciclo-cross [thee-clo-cros'], *m.* Cycle-cross.

ciclodiatomía [the-clo-de-ah-to-mee'-ah], *f. (Mil.)* Calculation of the direction of a projectile.

cicloidal [the-clo'-e-dal], *a.* Cycloidal.

cicloide [the-clo'-e-day], *f. (Math.)* Cycloid.

ciclómetro [the-clo'-may-tro], *m.* Cyclometer.

ciclomotor [the-clo-mo-tor'], *m.* Motorbike, autocycle.

ciclón [the-clon'], *m.* 1. Cyclone. 2. Hurricane.

ciclonal, ciclónico, ca [the-clo-nahl', the-clo'-ne-co, cah], *a.* Cyclonic, cyclonical.

cíclope [thee'-clo-pay], *m.* Cyclops.

ciclópeo, ea [the-clo'-pay-o, ah], *a.* Cyclopean, gigantic.

ciclorama [the-clo-rah'-mah], *m.* Cyclorama, pictorial representation.

ciclotrón [the-clo-trone'], *m.* Cyclotron.

cicuta [the-coo'-tah], *f.* 1. *(Bot.)* Hemlock. **Cicuta acuática,** *(Bot.)* waterhemlock. **Cicuta virosa, cicuta de España,** Spanish hemlock. 2. Pipe or flute made of reed, a flageolet.

Cid [theed], *m.* 1. Chief, commander. 2. Surname of the Spanish hero, Rodrigo Díaz de Vivar.

C.I.D. *m. abr.* de **Centro Internacional para el Desarrollo.**

cidra [thee'-drah], *f.* 1. Citron. 2. Conserve of citrons.

cidracayote [the-drah-cah-yo'-tay], *f. (Bot.)* The American gourd.

cidrada [the-drah'-dah], *f.* A conserve made of citrons.

cidral [the-drahl'], *m.* Plantation of citron-trees.

cidria [thee'-dreah], *f.* V. CEDRIA.

cidro [thee'-dro], *m. (Bot.)* Citron-tree.

cidronela [the-dro-nay'-lah], *f. (Bot.)* Common balm.

ciegamente [the-ay-gah-men'-tay], *adv.* Blindly.

ciego, ga [the-ay'-go, gah], *a.* 1. Blind. 2. *(Met.)* Swayed by violent passion. **Ciego de ira,** blind with passion. 3. Choked or shut up (corredor). **A ciegas** 1. Blindly, in the dark. 2. Thoughtlessly, carelessly. **Quedar ciego,** to go blind. **Más ciego que un topo,** as blind as a bat. **Ciego para,** blind to. **Con una fe ciega,** with a blind faith.

ciego, *m.* 1. *(Anat.)* Caecum or blind gut. 2. Large black-pudding. V. MORCÓN. *(Yo ciego, yo ciegue,* from *Cegar.* V. ACERTAR.)

cielo [the-ay'-lo], *m.* 1. The sky, firmament, heaven(s). 2. Heaven, the habitation of God and pure souls departed. 3. Heaven, the supreme power, the sovereign of heaven. 4. Climate; atmosphere. **Éste es un cielo benigno,** this is a mild climate. 5. Roof, ceiling. 6. Glory, felicity; paradise. **Cielo raso,** flat roof or ceiling. **El cielo de la cama,** tester or cover of a bed. **Bajado del cielo,** prodigious, excellent, complete. **Cerrarse el cielo,** to cover over with clouds. **Dormir a cielo raso,** to sleep in the open air. **Estar hecho un cielo,** to be splendid, to be most brilliant. **Tomar el cielo con las manos,** *(Met.)* to be transported with joy, grief, or passion. **Venirse el cielo abajo,** the sky falling, i. e. to rain heavily. **Ver el cielo abierto,** to find an unforeseen opportunity. **Se le juntaron el cielo con la tierra,** *(LAm.)* he lost his nerve. **Poner a uno en el cielo,** to praise somebody to the over-optimistic.

cielo máximo [the-ay'-lo-mahc'-se-mo], *m. (Aer.)* Ceiling.

ciempiés, *m.* V. CIENTOPIES.

cien [the-en'], *a.* One hundred; used before nouns instead of *ciento.* **Cien hombres,** a hundred men. **Cien mujeres,** a hundred women. **Cien mil,** a hundred thousand. **Me pone a cien,** it drives me up the wall. 10 por cien, ten per cent. **Lo apoyo cien por cien,** I support it a hundred per cent.

ciénaga [the-ay'-nah-gah], *f.* Marsh moor, a miry place. V. CENEGAL.

ciencia [the-en'-the-ah], *f.* 1. Science. 2. Knowledge, certainty. **A ciencia y paciencia,** by one's knowledge and permission. **Ciencias exactas,** mathematics. **Apostar or hacer alguna cosa a ciencia cierta,** to bet, or to do any thing with certainty, knowingly. **Ciencias naturales,** natural sciences. **Ciencias ocultas,** occult sciences.

ciencia-ficción [the-ayn-the-ah feec-the-aone'], *f.* Science fiction.

cienmilésimo, ma [the-en-me-lay'-se-mo, mah], *a.* The hundred thousandth.

cienmilmillonésimo, ma [the-en-mil-mil-lyo-nay'-se-mo, mah], *a.* The hundred thousand milionth.

cienmillonésimo, ma, *a.* The hundred millionth.

cieno [the-ay'-no], *m.* Mud, mire, a marshy ground.

cienoso [the-ay-no'-so], *a.* Muddy, miry; slimy.

cientemente [the-en-tay-men'-tay], *adv.* In a knowing, sure, and prudent manner.

científicamente [the-en-tee'-fe-cah-men-tay], *adv.* Scientifically.

científico, ca [the-en-tee'-fe-co, cah], *m. & f.* Scientific.

cientista [the-ayn-tes'-tah], *m. & f. (LAm.)* Scientist.

ciento [the-en'-to], *a.* One hundred. V. CIEN.

ciento [the-en'-to], *m.* 1. A hundred. **Un ciento de huevos,** a hundred eggs. 2. A hundredweight. **Por ciento,** per cent. **Diez por ciento,** ten per cent. **Un tanto por ciento,** a percentage. **Estar al ciento por ciento,** to be in top form. **Por cientos,** in hundreds. **Había ciento y la madre,** there were far too many.

cientopiés [the-en-to-pe-ess'], *m.* Wood-louse, milleped, sowbug.

cierna [the-err'-nah], *f.* The staminate blossom of vines; corn, and some other plants.

cierne [the-err'-ney], *m.* **En cierne**, in blossom. **Estar en cierne**, to be in its infancy. *(Yo cierno, yo cierne,* from *Cerner. V. ATENDER.)*

cierre [the-err'-ray], *m.* 1. Closing, shutting, locking. 2. Lock, clasp. **Cierre automático,** zipper. **Cierre de cremallera,** zipper. **Cierre hidráulico,** water seal. **Echar el cierre,** to shut.

cierro [the-err'-ro], *m.* 1. Inclosure. *(Yo cierro, yo cierre,* from *Cerrar.).* 2. *(Cono Sur)* Wall; envelope.

ciertamente [the-er-tah-men'-tay], *adv.* Certainly, forsooth, surely.

cierto, ta [the-err'-to, tah], *a.* 1. Certain, doubtless, evident, constant. 2. Used in an indeterminate sense: **cierto lugar,** a certain place. **Me dan por cierto que,** I have been credibly informed that. **Por cierto,** for certain, for sure. **Es cierto que**…, it is certain that… **Lo cierto es que**…, the thing is that… **Estar cierto de,** to be sure of. **Estar en lo cierto,** to be right. **Por cierto**…, by the way… *-adv. V.* CIERTAMENTE.

cierva [the-err'-vah], *f.* Hind, the female stag, or red deer.

ciervo [the-err'-vo], *m.* Deer, hart, stag.

ciervo volante [the-err'-vo vo-lahn'-tay], *m.* Stagbeetle.

cierzo [the-err'-tho], *m.* A cold northerly wind. **Tener ventana al cierzo,** *(Met.)* To be haughty, lofty, elated with pride.

cifac, cifaque [the-fahe', the-fah'-kay], *m. (Obs. Anat.)* The peritoneum.

cifra [thee'-frah], *f.* 1. Cipher, the symbol 0.2. Cipher, a secret or occult manner of writing. 3. Cipher, monogram engraved on seals or stamped upon stationery, etc. 4. Contraction, abbreviation. 5. Any arithmetical mark. 6. Music written with numbers. **Cifra arábiga,** Arabic numeral. **Escribirlo en cifras y palabras,** to write it down in figures and words. **Cifra global,** lump sum. **La cifra de este año es elevada,** the quantity this year is large. **La cifra de los muertos,** the number of dead.

cifradamente [the-frah-dah-mayn'-tay], *adv.* I. In codee. 2. In brief, in a shortened form.

cifrado [the-frah'-do], *a.* Coded, in code.

cifrar [the-frar'], *va.* 1. To cipher or write in ciphers. 2. To abridge a discourse. 3. To inclose. **Una duración cifrada en miles de años,** a duration reckoned in thousands of years.

cigala [the-gah'-lah], *f.* Norway lobster.

cigarra [the-gar'-rah], *f.* Balmcricket, cicada, harvestfly.

cigarrera [the-gar-ray'-rah], *f.* Cigar-case.

cigarrero [the-gar-ray'-ro], *m.* Cigar maker; cigar-seller.

cigarrillo [the-gar-reel'-lyo], *m.* Cigarette.

cigarrista [the-gar-rees'-tah], *m.* Person who smokes many cigars.

cigarro [the-gar'-ro], *m.* Cigar, cigarette.

cigarrón [the-gar-rone'], *m.* 1. *(aug.)* A large cigar. 2. A large balm-cricket.

cigatera [the-gah-tay'-rah], *f. (Low.)* Prostitute.

cigoñino [the-go-nyee'-no], *m. (Orn.)* A young stork.

cigoñuela [the-go-nyoo-ay'-lah], *f. (Orn.)* A small bird resembling a stork.

cigoto [the-go'-to], *m. (Biol.)* Zygote.

ciguatera [the-goo-ah-tay'-rah], *f. (Amer.)* Kind of jaundice, from eating fish diseased with an affection like jaundice.

ciguato, ta [the-goo-ah'-to, tah], *a. V.* ACIGUATADO.

cigüente [the-goo-en'-tay], *a.* Applied to a kind of white grape.

cigüeña [the-goo-ay'xs-nyah], *f.* 1. *(Orn.)* White stork, a bird of passage; crane. 2. Crank of a bell to which a cord is fastened to ring it. 3. **Cigüeña de piedra de amolar,** the iron winch of a grindstone. 4. **Cigüeña de cordelería,** *(Naut.)* A laying hook or winch.

cigüeñal [the-goo-ay-nyahl'], *m. (Mech.)* Crankshaft.

cigüeño [the-goo-ay'-nyo], *m.* A male stork.

cigüeñuela [the-goo-ay-nyoo-ay'-lah], *f. dim.* Small crank of a bell.

cigüeñuelo de la Caña del Timón [the-goo-ay-nyco-ay'-lo]. *(Naut.)* The gooseneck of the tiller.

cija [thee'-hah], *f.* 1. *(Prov.)* Dungeon. 2. *(Obs.)* Granary. 3. Sheep shed.

cilampa [the-lam'-pah], *f. (CAm.)* Drizzle.

cilampear [the-lam-pay-ar'], *vn. (CAm.)* To drizzle.

cilanco [the-lahn'-co], *m.* A deep pool in bends, or slack water, of rivers.

cilantro [the-lahn'-tro], *m. (Bot.)* Coriander. *V.* CULANTRO.

ciliado, da [the-le-ah'-do, dah], *a.* Ciliated, provided with cilia.

ciliar [the-le-ar'], *a.* Ciliary, belonging to the eyelids.

cilicio [the-lee'-the-o], *m.* 1. Haircloth, very rough and prickly. 2. A cilicium or hair covering for the body, worn as penance. 3. Girdle of bristles or netted wire, with points, worn in mortification of the flesh. 4. *(Mil. Obs.)* Haircloth laid on a wall to preserve it.

cilífero, ra [the-lee'-fay-ro, rah], *a. V.* CILIADO.

ciliforme [the-le-for'-may], *a.* Like an eyelash in form; ciliform.

cilindrada [the-leen-drah'-dah], *f.* Cylinder capacity.

cilindradora [the-leen-drah-do'-rah], *f.* Steamroller, road roller.

cilindrar [the-leen-drar'], *va.* To roll, to roll flat.

cilíndrico, ca [the-leen'-dre-co, cah], *a.* Cylindric or cylindrical.

cilindrín [the-leen-dreen'], *m.* Fag, cigarette.

cilindro [the-leen'-dro], *m.* Cylinder; a roller. **Cilindro de escarchar,** silversmiths' rolls. **Cilindro compresor, cilindro de caminos,** steamroller, road roller. **Cilindro de datos,** *(Inform.)* data cylinder.

cilla [theel'-lyah], *f.* Granary for tithes and other grain.

cillerero [theel-lyay-ray'-ro], *m.* In some religious houses, the cellarist or butler.

cilleriza [theel-lyay-ree'-thah], *f.* A nun who directs the domestic affairs of the convent.

cillerizo [theel-lyay-ree'-tho], *m.* Keeper of a granary.

cillero [theel-lyay'-ro], *m.* 1. Keeper of a granary or storehouse for tithes. 2. Granary. 3. Vault, cellar, storeroom.

cima [thee'-mah], *f.* 1. Summit of a mountain or hill. 2. Top of trees. 3. Heart and tender sprouts of cardoons. 4. End or extremity of a thing. 5. Acme. **Por cima,** at the uppermost part, at the very top. **Dar cima,** to conclude happily.

cimacio [the-mah'-the-o], *m. (Arch.)* Cymatium, ogee, ogive, moulding which is half convex and half concave. **Cimacio del pedestal,** cornice of a pedestal.

cimar [the-mar'], *va.* To clip the tops of dry things, as plants, hedges.

cimarrón, na [the-mar-rone', nah], *a. (Amer.)* Wild, unruly (hombres, animales). *-m. & f.* A runaway slave, maroon. *-m. (Cono Sur)* Unsweetened maté.

cimba [theem'-bah], *f.* 1. *(And.)* Plaited rope of hard leather. 2. *(And.)* Pigtail. 3. *(And.)* Rope ladder (escala).

cimbalaria [thim-bah-lah'-re-ah], *f.* Ivywort, a plant which grows on old walls.

cimbalillo [thim-bah-leel'-lyo], *m. dim.* A small bell.

címbalo [theem'-bah-lo], *m.* 1. Cymbal. 2. A small bell.

cimbanillo [thim-bah-neel'-lyo], *m. V.* CIMBALILLO.

címbara [theem'-bah-rah], *f. (Prov.)* A large sickle, used to cut shrubs and plants.

cimbel [thim-bel'], *m.* 1. Decoy-pigeon. 2. Rope with which decoy-pigeons are made fast. 3. Prick (pene).

cimborio, cimborrio [thim-bo'-re-o, thim-bor'-re-o], *m.* Cupola. *V.* CÚPULA.

cimbornales [thim-bor-nah'-les], *m. pl. (Naut.)* Scupperholes. *V.* IMBORNALES.

cimbra [theem'-brah], *f.* 1. A wooden frame for constructing an arch. 2. **Cimbra de una tabla,** *(Naut.)* the bending of a board.

cimbrar, cimbrear [thim-brar', thim-bray-ar'], *va.* To brandish a rod or wand. **Cimbrar a alguno,** to give one a drubbing. **Cimbrar a uno,** to clout somebody. *-vr.* 1. To bend, to vibrate. 2. To walk gracefully.

cimbreño, ña [thim-bray'-nyo, nyah], *a.* Pliant, flexible (vara, caña).

cimbreo [thim-bray'-o], *m.* Crookedness, curvature, bending or moulding of a plank, shaking.

cimbria [theem'-bre-ah], *f. V.* CIMBRA.

cimbrón [theem-brone'], *m. (And. CAm. Cono Sur)* shudder; *(And.)* Sharp pain; *(Cono Sur. Mex.)* Blow with the flat of a sword; *(LAm.)* Crack (de lazo etc.); jerk, yang (tirón).

cimbronada [theem-bro-nah-dah], *f. (And. Cono Sur) V.* CIMBRON; *(Carib.)* Earthquake (terremoto).

cimbronazo [thim-bro-nah'-tho], *m.* Stroke given with a foil. *V.* CINTARAZO.

cimentación [the-mayn-tah-the-one'], *f.* 1. Foundation. 2. Laying of foundations.

cimentado [the-men-tah'-do], *m.* Refinement of gold. **Cimentado, da,** *pp.* Of CIMENTAR.

cimentador [the-men-tah-dor'], *m.* He who lays the foundation of a thing.

cimentar [the-men-tar'], *va.* 1. To lay the foundation of a building, to found, to ground. 2. *(Met.)* To establish the fundamental principles of religion, morals, and science. 3. To refine metals.

cimentera [the-men-tay'-rah], *f.* The art of laying the foundation of a building.

cimento [the-men'-to], *m.* Cement. *V.* CEMENTO.

cimera [the-may'-rah], *f.* Crest of a helmet, or coat of arms.

cimerio, ria [the-may-re-o, ah], *a.* Cimmerian; of a tribe which dwelt on the shores of the sea of Azov.

cimero, ra [the-may'-ro, rah], *a.* Placed at the height of some elevated spot.

cimiento [the-me-en'-to], *m.* 1. Foundation of a building. 2. *(Met.)* Basis, origin. **Abrir los cimientos,** to make the trenches for laying foundations. *(Yo cimiento, yo cimiente, from Cimentar. V.* ACRECENTAR.)

cimillo [the-meel'-lyo], *m.* Decoy-pigeon.

cimitarra [the-me-tar'-rah], *f.* Scimitar, falchion.

cimófana [the-mo'-fah-nah], *f.* Cymofane, the oriental cat's eye: a variety of chrysoberyl.

cimorra [the-mor'-rah], *f. (Vet.)* Glanders, a disease in horses.

cinabrio [the-nah'-bre-o], *m.* 1. Kind of gum, distilled from a tree in Africa. 2. Cinnabar. 3. Vermilion or artificial cinnabar.

cinamómino [the-nah-mo'-me-no], *m. (Med.)* An aromatic ointment, the chief ingredient of which is taken from the bead-tree.

cinamomo [the-nah-mo'-mo], *m. (Bot.)* The bead-tree.

cinc [think], *m. (Acad.)* Zinc, a metallic element.

cincel [thin-thel'], *m.* Chisel.

cincelado [thin-thay-lah'-do], *m.* Chiselling; engraving.

cincelador [thin-thay-lah-dor'], *m.* Engraver, sculptor, stone-cutter.

cincelar [thin-thay-lar'], *va.* To chisel, to engrave, to emboss.

cincelito [hin-thay-lee'-to], *m. dim.* Small chisel.

cinco [theen'-co], *m. & a.* Five. **Decir cuántas son cinco,** to threaten with reproof or punishment. **Él te dirá cuántas son cinco,** *(Met.)* he will oblige you to do it in spite of you. **No sabe cuántas son cinco,** *(Coll.)* he is a fool. **¡Vengan esos cinco!,** ¡shake it! *-m.* 1. *(And. CAm. Carib.)* 5-stringed guitar. 2. *(Mex.)* Bottom, backside. 3. *(CAm. Mex.)* 5-peso piece (moneda).

cincoañal [thin-co-ah-nyahl'], *a.* Five years old (animales).

cincoenrama [theen-co-en-rah'-mah], *f. (Bot.)* Common cinquefoil.

cincografía [thin-co-grah-fee'-ah], *f.* Zincography, a process of etching printing plates upon zinc.

cincomesino, na [thin-co-may-see'-no, nah], *a.* Five months old.

cincuenta [thin-coo-en-tah'], *m. & a.* Fifty, fiftieth.

cincuentavo [thin-coo-en-tah'-vo], *a.* The one-fiftieth part.

cincuentañero, a [thin-coo-ayn-tah-nyay'-ro, ah], *m.* Man, woman of about fifty.

cincuentavo [thin-coo-ayn-tah'-vo], *a.m.* Fiftieth.

cincuentén [thin-coo-en-ten'], *m.* A piece of wood, fifty palms in length (50 x 3 x 2).

cincuenteno, na [thin-coo-en-tay'-no, nah], *a.* Fiftieth.

cincuentón, na [thin-coo-en-tone', nah], *a.* Fifty years old.

cincha [theen'-chah], *f.* 1. Girth, cingle, cinch. **Ir rompiendo cinchas,** to drive on full speed. 2. *(Cos.)* Webbing (para sillas). 3. **Tener cincha;** *(And.)* To have a strain of Negro blood.

cinchada [thin-chah'-dah], *f. (Cono Sur. Mex.)* Tug-of-war.

cinchadura [thin-chah-doo'-rah], *f.* The act of girting.

cinchar [thin-char'], *va.* To girt, to bind with a girth.

cinchera [thin-chay'-rah], *f.* 1. Girthplace, the spot where the girth is put on a mule or horse. 2. Vein which horses or mules have in the place where they are girted. 3. Disorder incident to horses and mules, which affects the place where they are girted.

cincho [theen'-cho], *m.* 1. Belt or girdle used by laborers to keep their bodies warm. 2. The tire of a wheel. 3. Vessel of bassweed, in which cheese is moulded and pressed. 4. Disorder in the hoofs of horses. *V.* CEÑO.

cinchón [thin-chone'], *m. aug.* A broad girdle.

cinchona [thin-cho'-nah], *f. (LAm.)* Quinine bark.

cinchuela [thin-choo-ay'-lah], *f.* 1. *(dim.)* A small girth. 2. A narrow ribbon.

cine [thee'-nay], *m.* Motion pictures, movies; cinema. **Hacer cine,** to make films. **Cine mudo,** silent films. **Ir al cine,** to go to the cinema.

cineasta [the-nay-as'-tah], *m. & f.* Film fan, movie fan; film buff (experto); film critic (crítico); film maker, director.

cine-club [the-nay-cloob'], *m. pl.* Cine club, film society.

cinefilia [the-ney-fe'-le-ah], *f.* Love of the cinema.

cinéfilo, la [the-nay'-fe-lo], *m. & f.* Film fan, movie fan.

cinegética [the-nay-hay'-te-cah], *f.* Hunting, the chase.

cinegético [the-nay-hay'-te-co], *a.* Hunting, of the chase.

cinema [the-nay'-mah], *m.* Cinema, moving pictures, movies.

cinemateca [the-nay-mah-tay'-cah], *f.* Film library.

cinemática [the-nay-mah'-te-cah], *f.* Cinematics, the study of motion as limited only by space.

cinemático [the-nay-mah'-te-co], *a.* Cinematic.

cinematografía [the-nay-ma-to-grah-fe'-ah], *f.* Films, film-making, cinematography.

cinematografiar [the-nay-mah-to-grah-fe-ar'], *va.* To film.

cinematográfico, ca [the-nay-mah-to-grah'-fe-co, cah], *a.* Cinematographic.

cinematógrafo [the-nay-mah-to'-grah-fo], *m.* Motion pictures, movies, cinema.

cineración [the-nay-rah-the-on'], *V.* INCINERACIÓN.

cinerama [the-nay-rah-mah], *m.* Cinerama.

cinerario, ia [the-nay-rah'-re-o-ah], *a.* 1. *V.* CINÉREO. Ashy. 2. Cinerary.

cinéreo [the-nay'-ray-o], *a.* Ashy; ash-grey, ashem.

cinescopio [the-nes-co'-pe-o], *m.* Kinescope.

cineteca [the-nay-tay'-cah], *f. (LAm.)* Film archive.

cinético, ca [the-nay'-te-co, cah], *a.* Kinetic, pertaining to motion. **Energía cinética,** Kinetic energy.

cíngaro, ra [theen'-gah-ro, rah], *m. & f.* Gipsy. *V.* GITANO.

cinguería [then-gay-re'-ah], *f. (Cono Sur)* Sheet metalwork; sheet metal-shop.

cinguero [then-gay'-ro], *m. (Cono Sur)* Sheet metalworker.

cíngulo [theen'-goo-lo], *m.* 1. Girdle or band with which a priest's alb is tied up. 2. Cordon, band, a wreath. 3. A military badge. 4. Ring or list at the top and bottom of a column.

cínicamente [the'-ne-cah-mayn-tay], *adv.* 1. Cynically. 2. Brazenly, shamelessly, impudently.

cínico, ca [thee'-ne-co, cah], *a.* Cynic, cynical; satirical.

cínico [hee'-ne-co], *m.* Cynic, a philosopher of the sect of Diogenes.

cínife [thee'-ne-fay], *m.* The longshanked buzzing gnat.

cinismo [the-nees'-mo], *m.* 1. Cynicism, the philosophy of the Cynics. 2. Shamelessness in defending or practicing blamable actions or doctrines.

cinnámico, ca [thin-nah'-me-co, cah], *a.* Cinnamic; derived from cinnamon.

cinocéfalo [the-no-thay'-fah-lo], *m.* 1. Kind of monkey or baboon. 2. The name of the inhabitants of a fantastic country, who had dogs' heads.

cinosura [the-no-soo'-rah], *f.* 1. Cynosure, the constellation of the Lesser Bear, which contains the polar star. 2. An object strongly challenging attention.

cinta [theen'-tah], *f.* 1. Ribbon, tape. **Cinta de seda,** silk ribbon. **Cinta aisladora,** *(CAm. Mex.)* insulating tape. **Cinta de freno,** brake lining. **Cinta para máquina de escribir,** typewriter ribbon. **Cinta del cartucho,** *(Inform.)* cartridge ribbon. Cinta **magnética,** magnetic tape. 2. A strong net used in the tunny-fishery. 3. The lowest part of the pastern of a horse. 4. **Cinta para cinchas,** girth-web. 5. **Cintas de navío,** *(Naut.)* Wales. 6. *(Obs.)* Girdle. *V.* CINTO. 7. First course of floor-tiles. 8. *(LAm.)* Tin, can. 9. *(Mex.)* Shoelaces. 10. Kerb; tile skirting (de habitación).

cintadero [thin-tah-day'-ro], *m.* Part of a crossbow to which the string is fastened.

cintagorda [thin-tah-gor'-dah], *f.* Coarse hempen net for the tunny-fishery.

cintajos, cintarajos [thin-tah'-hos, thin-tah-rah'-hos], *m. pl.* 1. Knot or bunch of tumbled ribbons. 2. **Tawdry ornaments** in female dress.

cintar [thin-tar'], *va. (Prov.)* To adorn with ribbons.

cintarazo [thin-tah-rah'-tho], *m.* 1. Stroke or blow with the flat part of a broadsword. 2. Chastisement of a horse with the stirrup-leather.

cinta transportadora [theen'-tah trans-por-tah-dor'-rah], *f.* *(Mech.)* Conveyor belt.

cinteado, da [thin-tay-ah'-do, dah], *a.* Adorned with ribbons.

cintero [thin-tay'-ro], *m.* 1. One who weaves or sells ribbons. 2. Harness-maker. 3. Belt, girdle. 4. *(Prov.)* Truss. 5. Rope with a running knot thrown on a bull's head.

cintilla [thin-teel'-lyah], *f. dim.* 1. Small ribbon. 2. Narrow tape.

cintillo [thin-teel'-lyo], *m.* 1. Hat. band. 2. Ring set with precious stones.

cinto [theen'-to], *m.* .Belt, girdle. *V.* CINTURA and CÍNGULO.

cintrel [thin-trel'], *m. (Arch.)* Rule or line placed in the center of a dome to adjust the ranges of brick or stone.

cintura [thin-too'-rah], *f.* 1. The waist. **Cintura de avispa,** wasp waist. 2. Small girdle for the waist. **Meter en cintura,** *(Met.)* To keep one in a state of subjection. 3. Narrow part of a chimney. *V.* CANAL.

cinturero [thin-too-ray'-ro], *m. (Prov.)* Girdler.

cinturica, illa, ita [thin-too-ree'-cah, eel'-lyah, ee'-tah], *f. dim.* 1. A small girdle. 2. Small or delicate waist.

cinturón [thin-too-rone'], *m.* 1. Belt. 2. Sash. **Cinturón salvavidas,** life-belt. **Cinturón de seguridad,** safety belt. 3. *(fig.)* Belt, zone. **El cinturón industrial de Buenos Aires,** Buenos Aires industrial belt.

cipayo [the-pah'-yo], *m.* Sepoy, a native of India, serving in the British troops.

cipero [the-pay'-ro], *m. (Bot.)* Cyperus or sedge.

cipo [thee'-po], *m.* Cippus, a short stone pilar used as a burial monument, as a boundary mark or as a signpost or milestone.

cipote [the-po'-tay], *a.* 1. *(And. Carib.)* Stupid, thick. 2. *(CAm.)* Plump, chubby. *-m.* 1. *(CAm. Carib.)* Lad, youngster; urchin. 2. *(CAm.)* Indian club. 3. Chump, blockhead (idiota). 4. *(And.)* **Cipote de chica,** smashing girl.

cipotear [the-po-tay-ar'], *va.* To screw.

ciprés [the-press'], *m. (Bot.)* Cypress tree.

cipresal [the-pray-sahl'], *m.* Grove or plantation of cypress trees.

cipresino, na [the-pray-see'-no, nah], *a.* Resembling or belonging to cypress.

ciprino, na [the-pree'-no, nah], *a.* Relating to or made of cypress wood.

ciprio, ia [thee'-pre-o, ah], *a.* Cyprian; of the island of Cyprus.

ciquiricata [the-ke-re-cah'-tah], *f. (Coll.)* Caress, act of endearment; flattery.

circasiano, na [theer-cah-se-ah'-no, nah], *a.* Circassian.

circense [theer-then'-say], *a.* Circensial or circensian, relating to the exhibitions in the amphitheaters of Rome; circus, of the circus.

circo [theer'-co], *m.* 1. Circus, amphitheater. 2. *(Orn.)* The moorbuzzard.

circón [theer-cone'], *m. (Acad.)* Zircon, a zirconium silicate, of various colors' transparent to opaque.

circonio [theer-co-ne-o], *m.* Zirconium, an earthy metallic element, of no practical application, derived from zircon.

circuir [theer-co-eer'], *va.* To surround, to compass, to encircle.

circuito [theer-coo-ee'-to], *m.* 1. Circuit, circle, extent. 2. Circumference. 3. *(Elec.)* Circuit. **Corto circuito,** short circuit. 4. Radio hookup. **En circuito cerrado,** closed-circuit. 5. *(Inform.)* **Circuito aritmético MSI, MSI** arithmetic circuit. **Circuito basculante,** flip-flop. **Circuito combinacional,** combinatory, combinatorial, combinational circuit. **Circuito de Integración a Muy Gran Escala,** Very Large Scale Integration Circuit. **Circuito de Integración a Pequeña Escala,** Small Scale Integration Circuit. **Circuito de Integración a Gran Escala,** Large Scale Integration Circuit. **Circuito de Integración a Media Escala,** Medium Scale Integration circuit. **Circuito en caja QUIP,** Quad Inline Package circuit. **Circuito multiplexor MSI, MSI** multiplexer circuit. **Circuito secuencial,** sequential circuit. **Circuito SSI,** SSI circuit.

circulación [theer-coo-lah-the-on'], *f.* 1. Circulation, currency. **Circulación sanguínea,** circulation of the blood. **Estar fuera de circulación,** to be out of circulation. **Poner algo en circulación,** to issue something. 2. Traffic, movement of traffic. **La circulación es por la derecha,** they drive on the right. **Calle de gran circulación,** busy street. **Circulación única,** *(Mex.)* One way traffic.

circulante [theer-coo-lahn'-tay], *pa. & a.* Circulatory, circling, circulating.

circular [theer-coo-lar'], *a.* Circular, circulatory circling. **Carta circular,** a circular letter.

circular [theer-coo-lar'], *vn.* 1. To circulate, to surround, to travel round, to go from hand to hand. **Hacer circular una carta,** to circulate a letter. 2. To move about, to walk around (personas). **Hacer circular a la gente,** to move people along. 3. To drive. **Circular por la izquierda,** to drive on the left. 4. To run (transporte). **No circula los domingos,** it does not run on Sundays.

circularmente [theer-coo-lar-men'-tay], *adv.* Circularly.

círculo [theer'-coo-lo], *m.* 1. Circle. **Círculo máximo,** great circle. **Círculo polar antártico,** Antartic Circle. 2. Orb, circlet; compass. 3. A superstitious ring or circle. 4. District. 5. Figure of speech, wherein a sentence begins and ends with the same words. 6. Circle, club. 7. *(fig.)* Scope, compass, extent.

circumambiente [theer-coom-am-been'-tay], *a.* Circumambient, surrounding.

circumcirca [theer-coom-theer'-cah], *adv. (Coll. Lat.)* About, thereabout; almost.

circumpolar [theer-coom-po-lar'], *a.* Circumpolar, near the pole.

circun... *pref.* circum...

circuncidante [theer-coon-the-dahn'-tay], *m. & pa.* Circumciser.

circuncidar [theer-coon-the-dar'], *va.* 1. To circumcise. 2. *(Met. Coll.)* To diminish, to curtail or modify.

circuncisión [theer-coon-the-se-on'], *f.* 1. Circumcisión. 2. A religious festival celebrated on the 1st of January, or New Year's day.

circunciso, sa [theer-coon-thee'-so, sah], *pp. irr.* of CIRCUNCIDAR. Circumcised.

circundante [ther-coon-dahn'-tay], *a.* Surrounding.

circundar [theer-coon-dar'], *va.* To surround, to circle, to compass.

circunferencia [theer-coon-fay-ren'-the-ah], *f.* Circumference.

circunferencial [theer-coon-fay-ren-the-ahl'], *a.* Circumferential, circular, surrounding.

circunferencialmente [theer-coon-fay-ren-the-al-men'-tay], *adv.* In a circular manner.

circunflejo, ja [theer-coon-flay'-ho, hah], *a.* **Acento circunflejo,** circumflex accent (^), composed of the acute and grave.

circunlocución [theer-coon-lo-coo-the-on'], *f.* Circunlocution, periphrasis, roundabout expression.

circunloquio [theer-coon-lo'-ke-o], *m.* Circumlocution, circle.

circunnavegación [theer-coon-nah-ve-gah-the-on'], *f.* Circumnavigation.

circunnavegar [theer-coon-nah-ve-gar'], *va.* To circumnavigate, sail round the world.

circunscribir [theer-coons-cre-beer'], *va.* To circumscribe, to inclose. *-vr. (fig.)* To limit oneself.

circunscripción [theer-coons-crip-the-on'], *f.* Circumscription, division.

circunscriptivo, va [theer-coons-crip-tee'-vo, vah], *a.* Circumscriptive, inclosing superficies.

circunspección [theer-coons-pec-the-on'], *f.* Circumspection, prudence, watchfulness, general attention.

circunspectamente [theer-coons-pec-tah-men'-tay], *adv.* Circumspectly.

circunspecto, ta [theer-coons-pec'-to, tah], *a.* Circumspect, cautious, considerate, judicious, grave.

circunstancia [theer-coons-tahn'-the-ah], *f.* 1. Circumstance. **Refirió el caso con todas sus circunstancias,** he gave a full and minute account of the case. 2. Incident, event. 3. Condition, state of affairs. **En las circunstancias presentes,** in the actual state of things. **En las circunstancias,** in the circumstances. **Las circunstancias cambian los casos,** circumstances alter cases.

circunstanciadamente [theer-coons-tan-the-ah-dah-men'-tay], *adv.* Circumstantially, minutely.

circunstanciado, da [theer-coons-tan-the-ah'-do, dah], *a.* 1. According to circumstances. 2. Circumstantial, minute. *-pp.* of CIRCUNSTANCIAR.

circunstancial [theer-coons-tahn-the-ahl'], *a.* 1. Circumstantial. 2. Emergency; incidental. **Mi estancia en Lima era circunstancial, I** just happened to be in Lima.

circunstante [theer-coons-tahn'-tay], *a.* circumstant, surrounding.

circunstantes [theer-coons-tahn'-tes], *m. pl.* By standers, persons present.

circunvalación [theer-coon-vah-lah-the-on'], *f.* Circumvallation, the act of surrounding a place.

circunvalar [theer-coon-vah-lar'], *va.* 1. To surround, to encircle. 2. *(Mil.)* To circumvallate, to surround with trenches.

circunvecino, na [theer-coon-vay-thee'-no, nah], *a.* Neighboring, adjacent, contiguous.

circunvención [theer-coon-ven-the-on'], *f.* Circumvention, overreaching, deceit.

circunvenir [theer-coon-vay-neer'], *va.* To circumvent, to overreach.

circunvolución [theer-coon-vo-loo-the-on'], *f.* Circumvolution.

circunyacente [theer-coon-yah-then'-tar], *a.* Circumjacent, lying near.

cirial [the-re-ahl'], *m.* Church candlestick (candelero). Processional candlestick (en procesiones)

cirílico [the-re'-le-co], *a.m.* Cyrillic.

cirineo [the-re-nay'-o], *m. (Coll.)* Mate, assistant.

cirio [thee'-re-o], *m.* A thick and long wax-candle; **cirio pascual,** paschal candle.

cirquero, ra [theer-kay'-ro], *m. & f. (Mex.)* Circus performer, acrobat; circus impresario.

cirro [theer'-ro], *m.* 1. *(Med.)* Schirrus. 2. Tuft of mane hanging over a horse's face

cirrosis [theer-ro'-sis], *f.* Cirrhosis, a morbid deposit of connective tissue in an organ, especially the liver, resulting in contraction and impaired function.

cirroso, sa [theer-ro'-so, sah], *a.* 1. Scirrhous. 2. Fibrous. **Raíces cirrosas,** fibrous roots.

ciruela [the-roo-ay'-lah], *f.* Plum, prune. **Ciruela pasa,** a dried plum; a prune. **Ciruela verdal,** a green gage.

ciruelar [the-roo-ay-lar'], *m.* A large plantation of plumtrees.

ciruelica, illa, ita [the-roo-ay-lee'-cah], *f. dim.* A small plum.

ciruelico, illo, ito [the-roo-ay-lee'-co], *m. dim.* A dwarf plumtree.

ciruelo [the-roo-ay'-lo], *m.* 1. *(Bot.)* Plum-tree. 2. Dolt, idiot.

cirugía [the-roo-hee'-ah], *f.* Surgery. **Cirugía dental,** dental surgery. **Cirugía plástica,** plastic surgery, anaplasty.

cirujano [the-roo-hah'-no], *a.* Surgeon. **Cirujano dentista,** dental surgeon.

cis. A Latin prefix meaning on this side of, toward Rome.

cisalpino, no [this-al-pee'-no'-nah], *a.* Cisalpine, on this side of the Alps: between the Alps and Rome.

cisca [thees'-cah], *f. (Prov.)* Reed for roofing huts and cottages. *V.* CARRIZO.

ciscar [this-car'], *va.* 1. *(Coll.)* To besmear, to make dirty. 2. *(Carib. Mex.)* To shame, to put down. 3. *(Carib, Mex.)* To provoke, to needle. *-vr.* **Ciscarse de miedo,** to dirty oneself from fear, to soil oneself; to do one's business. **Los que ciscan en las teorías,** those who thumb their noses at theories.

cisco [thees'-co], *m.* 1. Coaldust, broken coal. **Hacer algo cisco,** to tear something to bits. **Estar hecho cisco,** to be a wreck. 2. Row, shindy. **Armar un cisco,** to kick up a row, to make trouble. 3. *(Mex.)* Fear, fright.

ciscón [thees-cone'], *a. (Carib. Mex.)* Touchy.

cisión [the-se-on'], *f.* Incision. *V.* CISURA or INCISION.

cisma [thees'-mah], *m.* 1. Schism. 2. Disturbance in a community.

cismático, ca [this-mah'-te-co, cah], *a.* 1. Schismatic. 2. Applied to the author of disturbances in a community.

cismontano, na [this-mon-tah'-no, nah], *a.* Living on this side of the mountains.

cisne [thees'-nay], *m.* 1. *(Orn.)* Swan. 2. Cygnus, the Swan, constellation in the northern hemisphere. 3. *(Met.)* A good poet or musician. 4. *(Low.)* Prostitute. 5. *(Cono Sur)* Powder puff (borla).

cisquero [thees-kay'-ro], *m.* A small linen bag with coaldust, used by painters and draftsmen.

ciste [thees'-tay], *m.* Cyst, bladder. *V.* QUISTE.

cistel, cister [this-tel', this-terr'], *m.* Cistercian order of St. Bernard.

cisterciense [this-ter-the-en'-say], *a.* Cistercian.

cisterna [this-terr'-nah], *f.* 1. Cistern. 2. Reservoir, an inclosed fountain.

cístico [thee's'-te-co], *a. (Surg.)* Cystic.

cistitis [this-tee'-tis], *f.* Cystitis, inflammation of the bladder.

cisto [thees'-to], *m. (Bot.)* Cistus.

cistotomía [this-to-to-mee'-ah], *f. (Surg.)* Cystotomy.

cistótomo [this-to'-to-mo], *m.* Cystotome; now called lithotome.

cisura [the-soo'-rah], *f.* Incisure, incision.

cita [thee'-tah], *f.* 1. Appointment, engagement, a meeting appointed; rendez-vous. **Acudir a una cita,** to keep an appointment; turn up for an appointment. **se dieron una cita para las 8,** they agreed to meet at 8. **Faltar a una cita,** to miss an appointment. 2. Citation, quotation of a passage of a book.

citable [the-tah'-blay], *a.* Worthy of being cited, quoted.

citación [the-tah-the-on'], *f.* 1. Citation, quotation. 2. Summons, judicial notice. **Citación judicial,** summons. **Citación a licitadores,** invitation to bidders.

citado [the-tah'-do], *a.* Afore mentioned. **En el país citado,** in the afore mentioned country; in this country.

citador, ra [the-tah-dor', rah], *m. & f.* Citer.

citano, na [the-tah'-no, nah], *m. & f. (Coll.)* V. ZUTANO.

citar [the-tar'], *va.* 1. To make a business appointment. **Le cité para las 8,** I arranged to meet her at 8.2. To convoke, to convene, to cite. 3. To quote, to cite. 4. To cite, to summon before a judge; to give judicial notice. **Dijo que se da por citado,** he declared that he was duly summoned. 5. *(Taur.)* To incite, to provoke, to stir up. *-vr.* **Citarse con uno,** to arrange to meet somebody. **Citémonos delante del estadio,** let's meet outside the stadium.

cítara [thee'-ta-rah], *f.* 1. Cithara or cithern, a musical instrument; a guitar strung with wire, zither. 2. Body of troops covering the flanks of those advancing to the charge.

citara [the-tah'-rah], *f.* Partition-wall of the thickness of a brick.

citarista [the-ta-rees'-tah], *m. & f.* 1. A player of the cithern. 2. A maker or seller of citherns.

citarístico, ca [the-ta-rees'-te-co, cah], *a. (Poet.)* Belonging to poetry, adapted to the cithara.

citarizar [the-ta-re-thar'], *vn.* To play the cithara.

citatorio, ria [the-ta-to'-re-o, ah], *a. (Law.)* Citatory: applied to a summons.

citerior [the-tay-re-or'], *a.* Hither, nearer, toward this part. **España citerior,** the higher or northeastern part of Spain.

cítola [thee'-to-lah], *f.* 1. In cornmills, clack or clapper, a piece of wood which strikes the hopper and promotes the running of the corn. 2. V. CÍTARA. **La cítola es por demás, cuando el molinero es sordo,**

citología [the-to-lo-hee'-ah], *f.* Cytology.

citote [the-to'-tay], *m. (Coll.)* Summons, a judicial citation.

citramontano, na [the-trah-mon-tah'-no, nah], *a.* On this side of the mountains.

citrato [the-trah'-to], *m. (Chem.)* Citrate.

cítrico [thee'-tre-co], *a. (Chem.)* Citric.

citrícola [the-tre'-co-lah], *a.* Citrus.

cítrino, na [the-tree'-no, nah], *a. (Obs.)* Lemon-colored. V. CETRINO.

citrón [the-trone'], *m.* Lemon.

ciudad [the-oo-dahd'], *f.* 1. City, town. **Ciudad del Cabo,** Cape Town. **Ciudad del Vaticano,** Vatican City. **Es el mejor café de la ciudad,** it's the best café in town. 2. Corporation, civic body.

ciudadanía [the-oo-dah-dah-nee'-ah], *f.* Citizenship. **Ciudadanía de honor,** freedom of a city.

ciudadano, na [the-oo-da-dah'-no, nah], *a.* 1. City, relating to a city. 2. Civil, relating to any man, as member of a community. 3. Citizen-like.

ciudadano, *m.* 1. Citizen, freeman. 2. Inhabitant of a city. 3. A degree of nobility inferior to that of *caballero,* and superior to the condition of a tradesman.

ciudadela [the-oo-da-day'-lah], *f.* 1. *(Mil.)* Citadel, a small fortress. 2. *(LAm.)* Tenement block (casa pobre).

ciudad-estado [ ], *f. pl.* **Ciudades-estado,** city-state.

civeta [the-vay'-tah], *f.* Civet-cat. V. *Gato de algalia.*

civeto [the-vay'-to], *m.* Civet, the perfume.

cívico, ca [thee'-ve-co, cah], *a.* Civic. V. DOMÉSTICO.

civil [the-veel'], *a.* 1. Civil, relating to the community. 2. Civil, relating to man, as a member of a community. 3. Civil, polite, courteous, gentleman-like. 4. Civil, not military or ecclesiastical. **Derechos civiles,** civil rights. 5. Of low rank or extraction. 6. In law, civil, not criminal. **Población civil,** civilian population. *-m.* 1. Civil guard. 2. Civilian.

civilidad [the-ve-le-dahd'], *f.* 1. Civility, politeness, urbanity, good manners (cortesía).

civilista [the-ve-lees'-tah], *m.* 1. An attorney skilled in the civil law, especially the Roman law. 2. *(Amer.)* Partisan of civil government, opponent of militarism.

civilización [the-ve-le-thah-the-on'], *f.*

civilizador, ra [the-ve-le-thah-dor', rah], *a.* Civilizing.

civilizar [the-ve-le-thar'], *va.* To civilize. *-vr.* To become civilized.

civilmente [the-veel-men'-tay], *adv.* 1. Civilly, courteously, politely. 2. According to the common law.

civismo [the-vees'-mo], *m.* Patriotism, zeal for one's country.

cizalla [the-thahl'-lyah], *f.* Fragments or filings of gold, silver, or other metal clippings. *-pl.* **Cizallas,** Cutting-pliers, or strong shears for clipping metal or wire.

cizallar [the-thahl-lyah], *va.* To use cutting pliers, or shears, in cutting wire or metal.

cizaña [the-thah'-nyah], *f. (Acad.)* 1. *(Bot.)* Darnel. 2. Discord. **Sembrar cizaña,** to sow discord. V. ZIZAñA.

cizañar [the-thah-nyahr'], *va.* To sow discord among.

cizañero, ra [the-thah-nyay'-ro], *m. & f.* Troublemaker, mischief-maker.

cl. *abr.* de **centilitro** (centiliter, cl.).

clac [clahc'], *m.* 1. A clapping of the hands. 2. A hat of tall crown provided with springs for shutting close; opera-hat.

clacote [clah-co'-tay], *m. (Mex.)* Pimple, pustule.

claitonia [clah-e-to'-ne-ah], *f. (Bot.)* Claytonia.

clamar [clah-mar'], *va.* 1. To call. V. LLAMAR. 2. To cry out in a mournful tone. 3. *(Met.)* To show a want of something (sustancias inanimadas). **La tierra clama por agua,** the ground wants water. *-vn.* To cry out, to clamor. **Clamar contra,** to cry out against. **Clamar por,** to clamor for. **Esto clama al cielo,** this cries out to heaven.

clámide [clah'-me-day], *f.* A short cape, the chlamys of the Greeks.

clamor [clah-mor'], *m.* 1. Clamor, outcry, scream, shriek, cry. 2. Sound of passing bells. 3. The public voice.

clamorear [clah-mo-ray-ar'], *va.* To clamor, to implore assistance. *-vn.* To toll the passing bell.

clamoreo [clah-mo-ray'-o], *m.* 1. Knell, clamor(ing), shouting. 2. *(fig.)* Sustained outcry, vociferous protests. **Clamoreo de protesta,** vigorous protests.

clamorosamente [clah-mo-ro-sah-men'-tay], *adv.* Clamorously.

clamoroso, sa [clah-mo-ro'-so, sah], *a.* 1. Clamorous, loud, noisy. 2. *(fig.)* Resounding, enormous (éxito). V. VOCINGLERO.

clamoso, sa [clah-mo'-so, sah], *a.* That which calls out, or solicits.

clan [clan], *m.* Clan; faction, group.

clandestinamente [clan-des-te-nah-men'-tay], *adv.* Clandestinely, secretly.

clandestinidad [clan-des-te-ne-dahd'], *f.* Clandestinity, privacy, or secrecy. **en la clandestinidad,** in secrecy. **Movimiento en la clandestinidad,** *(Pol.)* in secrecy. **Pasar a la clandestinidad,** to go into hiding.

clandestino, na [clan-des-tee'-no, nah], *a.* Clandestine, secret, private.

clanga [clahn'-gah], *f.* V. PLANGA.

clangor [clan-gor'], *m. (Poet.)* The sound of a trumpet.

claque [clah'-kay], *f. (Theat.)* Claque, paid applauders.

claqué [clah-kay'], *m.* Tap-dancing.

claqueta [clah-kay'-tah], *f.* Clapperboard.

clara [clah'-rah], *f. (Coll.)* A short interval of fair weather on a rainy day. **Me aproveché de una clara para salir,** I availed myself of a fair moment to go out. **Clara de huevo,** white of an egg. **Claras,** pieces of cloth ill-woven, through which the light can be seen. **A las claras,** clearly, evidently.

clarabela [clah-ra-bay'-lah], *f.* Clarabella, an organstop of open wood pipes, soft and sweet.

claraboya [clah-ra-bo'-yah], *f.* Skylight, bull's-eye, window; dormer-window.

claramente [clah-ra-men'-tay], *adv.* Clearly, openly, manifestly, conspicuously, obviously, fairly.

clarea [clah-ray'-ah], *f.* White wine with cinnamon, sugar and spices added.

clarear [clah-ray-ar'], *vn.* To dawn, to grow light. *va.* 1. To brighten; to light up. 2. *(fig.)* To clarify, to make clear. 3. *(Mex.)* To go right through, to penetrate (atravesar). *-vr.* 1.

To be transparent, translucent. 2. *(Met.)* To be cleared up by conjectures or surmises.

clarecer [clah-ray-therr'], *vn.* To dawn, to grow light.

clareo [clah-ray'-o], *m.* **Darse un clareo,** to take a stroll (pasear).

clarete [clah-ray'-tay], *m.* Claret. *-a.* **Vino clarete,** claret wine.

claridad [clah-re-dahd'], *f.* 1. Clarity, brightness, splendor, light. 2. Clearness, distinctness, freedom from obscurity and confusion. 3. That which is said resolutely, to upbraid. **Lo explicó todo con claridad,** he explained it all very clearly. 4. Glory of the blessed. 5. *(Met.)* Celebrity, fame.

claridoso [clah-re-do'-so], *a.* *(CAm. Mex.)* Blunt, plain-spoken.

clarificación [clah-re-fe-cah-the-on'], *f.* Clarification, refining.

clarificar [clah-re-fe-car'], *va.* 1. To brighten, to illuminate. 2. To clarify, to purify, to refine.

clarificativo, va [clah-re-fe-cah-tee'-vo, vah], *a.* Purificative or purificatory.

clarimentos [clah-re-men'-tose], *m. pl.* The lights in a picture.

clarín [clah-reen'], *m.* 1. Trumpet, bugle (insturmento). 2. In organs, a trumpet or clarion stop. *-V.* CLARÓN. 3. Trumpeter. 4. Kind of batiste (tela).

clarinada [clah-re-nah'-dah], *f.* 1. Trumpet-call. 2. *(Met. and Coll.)* Extravagant answer.

clarinado, da [clah-re-nah'-do, dah], *a.* *(Her.)* Applied to animals with bells in their harness.

clarinazo [clah-re-nah-tho], *m. (fig.)* Trumpet call.

clarinero [clah-re-nay'-ro], *m.* Trumpeter.

clarinete [clah-re-nay'-tay], *m.* 1 Clarinet. 2. Player on the clarinet; clarinetist.

clarinetista [clah-re-nay-tees'-tah], *m.* Clarinetist, player upon the clarinet.

clarión [clah-re-on'], *m.* Crayon.

clarisa [clah-ree'-sah], *f.* Clare, a nun of the order of St. Clara.

clarísimo, ma [clah-ree'-se-mo, mah], *a.* Super, of *Claro,* most illustrious.

clarividencia [clah-re-ve-dayn'-the-ah], *f.* 1. Clairvoyance. 2. *(fig.)* Far-sightedness (previsión); discernment (discernimiento); intuition.

clarividente [clah-re-ve-dayn'-tay], *a.* Far-sighted, far-seeing; discerning, *-m. & f.* Clairvoyant.

claro, ra [clah'-ro, rah], *a.* 1. Clear, bright, transparent, lightsome. 2. Clear, transparent, pellucid, crystalline, fine, limpid. 3. Clear, thin, rare, not dense. 4. Clear, thin, not close. 5. Clear, free from clouds, serene, fair. 6. Light, not deeply tinged. **Azul claro,** light blue. 7. Clear, perspicuous, intelligible, not obscure. 8. Clear, obvious, explicit, evident, manifest, indisputable, apparent. **Es una verdad clara,** it is an undeniable truth. **Tan claro como la luz del día,** as plain as a day. **Más claro que el sol,** as clear as day light. 9. Open, frank, ingenuous. 10. Celebrated, illustrious. 11. *(Met.)* Sagacious, quick of thought.

claro [clah'-ro], *m.* 1. A kind of skylight. 2. Break in a discourse or writing; spacing in printing. 3. Rays of light falling on a painting. 4. Opening or space between the columns of a building or other things. 5. *(Naut.)* A clear spot in the sky. **Poner o sacar en claro** *(Met.)* to place a point in its true light, to explain, to expound, or interpret. **Pasar la noche de claro en claro,** to have not a wink of sleep all night. **De claro en claro,** evidently, manifestly. **Por lo claro,** clearly, manifestly, conspicuously. 6. Opening (abertura); gap, break, space (brecha, espacio); opening (en bosque); gap (en tráfico); bald patch (en pecho). 7. *(Arquit.)* Light, window; skylight. 8. *(Carib.)* *(Culin.)* Guava jelly. 9. *(Carib.)* Sugar-cane brandy. 10. **Clara de huevo,** eggwhite.

claro, *adv. V.* CLARAMENTE.

¡claro! [clah'-ro], *interj.* Of course! naturally. **¡Claro que sí!** yes, definitely, of course.

clarol [clah-rol'], *m.* Inlaid work (muebles).

clarón [clah-rone'], *m.* Clarion, a register of the organ.

claroscuro [clah-ros-coo'-ro], *m.* Monochrome, a painting in one color.

clarucho, cha [clah-roo'-cho, chah], *a.* Too watery, too liquid.

clase [clah'-say], *f.* 1. Class or rank of the people, order of persons. 2. Division of schoolboys. 3. Classis, kind, generical class, a set of beings or things. **Con toda clase de,** with all kinds of. **De otra clase,** of another sort. **De primera clase,** first class. 4. Class, species, family. 5. *(Com.)* Sort, description, quality. **Navío de primera clase,** a first class ship. **Primera clase,** first class. **Clase intermedia,** *(Naut.)* cabin class. 6. *(Escol.)* Class; lecture. **Clase de geografía,** geography class; geography lesson. **Clase nocturna,** evening class. **Dar clases,** to teach. **Faltar a clase,** to miss class. 7. *(Escol.)* Classroom. 8. *(Pol.)* Class. **Clase alta,** upper class. **Clase obrera,** working class. **Las clases pudientes,** the well-to-do classes.

clase acomodada [clah'-say ah-co-mo-dah'-dah], *f.* Well-to-do class, people of wealth.

clase media [clah'-say may'-de-ah], *f.* Middle class.

clásicamente [clah-se-cah-mem'-tay], *adv.* Classically.

clasicismo [clah-se-thees'-mo], *m.* Classic style; classicism.

clásico, ca [clah'-se-co, cah], *a.* 1. Classical, classic. 2. Principal, remarkable, of the first order or rank. **Error clásico,** a gross error. **Autores clásicos,** classics. **Le dio el clásico saludo,** he gave him the time-honored salute.

clasificable [clah-se-fe-cah'-blay], *a.* Classifiable.

clasificación [clah-se-fe-cah-the-one'], *f.* Classification; sorting (Correos); *(Naut.)* Rating. **Clasificación nacional del disco,** top twenty, record hit parade.

clasificador [clah-se-fe-cah-dor'], *m.* 1. Classifier (persona). 2. Filing cabinet (mueble). **Clasificador de cartas,** letter file.

clasificar [clah-se-fe-car'], *va.* To clasify, to arrange, to class. *-vr.* 1. *(Dep.)* To win a place; to occupy a position; **Meca se clasificó después de la Ceca,** Meca came after Ceca. 2. *(Dep.)* To qualify. **No se clasificó el equipo para la final,** the team did not qualify for the final.

clasismo [clah-sees'-mo], *m.* Class, feelings; class-consciousness; class structure.

clasista [clah-sees'-tah], *a.* *(Pol.)* Class; class-conscious; snobbish.

claudia [clah'-oo-de-ah], *f.* Greengage.

claudicación [clah-oo-de-cah-the-on'], *f.* Claudication, halting or limping.

claudicante [clah-oo-de-cahn'-tay], *a. & pa.* Claudicant, claudicating halting, limping.

claudicar [clah-oo-de-car'], *vn.* 1. To claudicate, to halt or limp. 2. *(Met.)* To proceed in a bungling manner, without rule or order.

Claudio [clah'-oo-de-o], *m.* Claudius.

clauquillar [clah-oo-keel-lyar'], *va.* *(Obs. Prov.)* To put the customhouse seal on bales of goods.

claustral [clah-oos-trahl'], *a.* 1. Claustral. 2. Claustral (monjes). *-m. & f.* *(Univ.)* Member of the Senate.

claustrico, illo, ito [clah-oos-tree'-co, eel'-lyo, ee'-to], *m. dim.* Small cloister.

claustro [clah'-oos-tro], *m.* 1. Cloister, piazza, or gallery around the court of a convent. 2. Assembly or meeting of the principal members of a university. 3. Womb. 4. *(Obs.)* Room, chamber.

claustrofobia [clah-oos-tro-fo'-be-ah], *f.* Claustrophobia.

claustrofóbico [clah-oos-tro-fo'-fe-co], *a.* Claustrophobic.

cláusula [clah'-oo-soo-lah], *f.* 1. Period, clause of a discourse. 2. Clause, condition, an article or particular stipulation.

clausular [clah-oo-soo-lar'], *va.* To close a period; to terminate a speech.

clausulilla [clah-oo-soo-leel'-lyah], *f. dim.* A little clause.

clausura [clah-oo-soo'-rah], *f.* 1. Cloister, the inner recess of a convent. **Convento de clausura,** enclosed convent. 2. Clausure, confinement, retirement. **Guardar clausura** or **vivir en clausura,** to lead a monastic or retired life.

clausurar [clah-oo-soo-rar'], *va.* 1. To close, to bring to a close; to adjourn, to close. 2. *(LAm.)* To close (casa).

clava [clah'-vah], *f.* 1. Club. 2. (*Naut.*) Scupper.

clavada [clah-vah'-dah], *f.* **Pegar una clavada a uno,** to rip somebody off, overcharge somebody.

clavado [clah-vah'-do], *m.* (*Mex.*) Fancy dive. **Echarse un clavado,** to dive.

clavado, da [clah-vah'-do, dah], *a.* 1. Exact, precise. **El reloj está clavado a las cinco,** it is just five by the clock. **Venir clavada una cosa a otra,** to fit exactly. 2. Nailed, armed or furnished with nails. 3. Relating to a club, especially to that of Hercules. 4. Just right, exactly fitting (vestido). 5. **Dejar a uno clavado,** to leave somebody speechless. 6. **Está clavado a su padre,** (*LAm.*) he's the spitting image of his father. -*pp.* of CLAVAR.

clavador [clah-vah-dor'], *m.* Nail-driver.

clavadura [clah-vah-doo'-rah], *f.* Nailing, driving a nail to the quick in horse-shoeing.

clavar [clah-var'], *va.* 1. To nail; to fasten with nails; to fasten in, to force in. 2. To stick, to prick, to gore; to introduce a pointed thing into another. **Se clavó un alfiler,** he pricked himself with a pin. **Me clavé una espina,** I pricked myself with a thorn. **Clavar los ojos** or **la vista,** to stare, to look with fixed eyes. 3. To cheat, to deceive. **Me clavaron 50 dólares,** they stung me for 50 dollars. 4. To set in gold or silver. 5. (*Mil.*) To ground. -*vr.* 1. To penetrate, to go in. 2. **Clavarse una astilla en el dedo,** to get a splinter in one's finger. 3. (*fig.*) To be mistaken. 4. **Clavársela,** to get drunk. 5. **Clavarse algo,** (*Mex.*) To pocket something.

clavaria [clah-vah'-re-ah], *f. V.* LLAVERA.

clavario [clah-vah'-re-o], *m.* 1. Treasurer, cashier. 2. A dignitary of the military order of Montesa.

clavazón [clah-va-thone'], *f.* 1. Set of nails. 2. (*Naut.*) Assortment of the different nails used in the construction of ships.

clave [clah'-vay], *f.* 1. Code, key. **El telegrama está en clave,** the telegram is in code. 2. (*Mus.*) Key, clef. **Clave de sol,** treble clef. 3. (*Arch.*) Keystone of an arch. 4. Harpsichord. -*m.* (*Mus.*) Harpsichord.

clavecín [clah-vay-theen'], *m.* Spinet.

clavel [clah-vel'], *m.* Carnation. **No tener un clavel,** to be broke.

clavelina [clah-vay-lee'-nah], *f.* (*Bot.*) 1. The plant which bears the common pink. 2. Mignonette.

clavelón [clah-vay-lone'], *m.* (*Bot. aug.*) Marigold; African marigold.

clavellina [clah-vel-lyee'-nah], *f.* 1. (*Bot.*) The pink, carnation.

claveque [clah-vay'-kay], *m.* Rock crystal.

clavera [clah-vay'-rah], *f.* 1. Mould for nail-heads. 2. Hole through which a nail is fastened. 3. Nail-hole in a horse-shoe. 4. (*Prov. Ext.*) Boundary where landmarks are set up.

claveria [clah-vay-ree'-ah], *f.* Office and dignity of the key-bearer in the military orders of Calatrava and Alcántara.

clavero, ra [clah-vay'-ro, rah], *m. & f.* 1. Keeper of the keys, treasurer, cashier. 2. (*Bot.*) Aromatic clove-tree. 3. Key-bearer, the knight of the orders of Calatrava and Alcantara, who takes care of the castle, convent, and archives.

clavete [clah-vay'-tay], *m. dim.* Tack, a small nail.

claveteado [clah-vay-tay-ah'-do], *m.* Studs, studding.

clavetear [clah-vay-tay-ar'], *va.* 1. To nail, to garnish with brass or other nails. 2. To point or tag a lace. 3. (*fig.*) To clinch, to close, to wind up (trato).

clavicémbalo [clah-ve-them'-bah-lo], *m.* Harpsichord.

clavicordio [clah-ve-cor'-de-o], *m.* Harpsichord, manichord.

clavícula [clah-vee'-coo-lah], *f.* (*Anat.*) Clavicle, the collarbone.

clavidista [clah-ve-dees'-tah], *m. & f.* (*Mex.*) (*Dep.*) Diver.

clavija [clah-vee'-hah], *f.* Pin, peg, or tack of wood or iron, thrust into a hole for rolling or winding something around. 2. A peg for hanging something on. 3. Peg of a stringed instrument. **Clavija maestra,** the fore axle-tree pintle. **Apretar a uno las clavijas.** (*Met.*) to push home an argument.

clavijera [clah-ve-hay'-rah], *f.* (*Prov.*) Opening in mud walls to let in the water.

clavijero [clah-ve-hay'-ro], *m.* 1. Bridge of a harpsichord. 2. Rack or perch for clothing or hats.

clavillo, ito [clah-vee'-lyo, ee'-to], *m. dim.* A small nail. **Clavillo de hebilla,** Rivet of a buckle. **Clavillos,** cloves.

claviórgano [clah-ve-or'-gah-no], *m.* An organized harpsichord, composed of strings and pipes, like an organ.

clavo [clah'-vo], *m.* 1. Nail, an iron spike. **Clavo de herradura,** hobnail. **Clavo plateado,** tinned nail, a nail dipped in lead or solder. 2. Corn, a hard and painful excrescence on the feet. 3. Spot in the eye. 4. Lint for wounds or sores; a tent. (*Surg.*) 5. **Clavo** or **clavo de especia,** clove, a valuable spice. 6. (*Naut.*) Rudder of a ship. 7. (*Met.*) Severe grief or pain. 8. Tumor between the hair and the hoof of a horse. 9. (*Prov.*) Headache. *V.* JAQUECA. 10. **Clavos romanos,** (*Amer.*) Curtain knobs. **Clavo,** in the mines of Mexico, a bunch of rich ore. **Arrimar el clavo,** in horseshoeing, to strike the quick and make the horse limp. **Dar en el clavo,** (*Met.*) to hit the mark, to succeed in a doubtful matter. **Agarrarse a un clavo ardiendo,** to clutch. **Estar como un clavo,** to be terribly thin. **Llegar como un clavo,** to arrive on the dot. **Remachar el clavo,** (*fig.*) to make matters worse. 11. (*CAm. Mex.*) Problem, snag. 12. (*And. Cono Sur*) unpleasant thing; nasty situation; unsaleable article.

clavulina [clah-voo-lee'-nah], *f.* A microscopic shell.

claxon [klak'-son], *s.* (*Mex.*) Auto horn. **Tocar el claxon,** to sound one's horn, to hoot.

claxonar [clak-so-nar'], *vn.* To sound one's horn, to hoot.

claxonazo [clak-so-nah'-tho], *m.* (*Aut.*) Hoot, toot (on the horn).

clemátide [clay-mah'-te-day], *f.* (*Bot.*) Traveler's-joy, virgin's-bower, or the upright lady's-bower, clematis.

clemencia [clay-men'-the-ah], *f.* Clemency, mercy, forbearance.

clemente [clay-men'-tay], *a.* Clement, merciful.

clementemente [clay-men-tay-men'-tay], *adv.* Mercifully, clemently.

clementina [clay-men-tee'-nah], *f.* 1. The canons of Pope Clement V, contained in the collection called *Clementinas,* published by Pope John XXII. 2. Tangerine.

clementisimo, ma [clay-men-tee'-se-mo, mah], *a. sup.* of CLEMENTE.

Cleopatra [Clay-o-pah-trah], *f.* Cleopatra.

clepsidra [Clep-see'-drah], *f.* Clepsydra, waterclock, an hourglass.

cleptomanía [clep-to-mah-nee'-ah], *f.* Kleptomania.

cleptómano, na [clep-to'-mah-no, nah], *m. & f. & a.* Kleptomaniac.

clerecía [clay-ray-thee'-ah], *f.* 1. Clergy. 2. The body of clergymen who attend with surplices at religious festivals.

clergyman [clayr-he-man], *a.* Clergyman (clérigo protestante). **Traje clergyman,** clergyman's suit.

clerical [clay-re-cahl'], *a.* Clerical.

clericalismo [clay-re-cah-lees'-mo], *m.* Clericalism.

clericalmente [clay-re-cal-men'-tay], *adv.* In a clerical manner.

clericato [clay-re-cah'-to], *m.* State and dignity of a clergy-man. **Clericato de cámara,** some distinguished offices in the palace of the Pope.

clericatura [clay-re-cah-too'-rah], *f.* State of a clergyman.

clericó [clay-re-co'], *m.* (*Cono Sur*) Mulled wine.

clérigo [clay'-re-go], *m.* A clergyman, a cleric, a clerk. **Clérigo de misa,** a presbyter.

clero [clay'-ro], *m.* Clergy. **Clero secular,** secular clergy, who do not make the three solemn vows of poverty, obedience, and chastity. **Clero regular,** regular clergy who profess a monastic life, and make the above vows.

clerofobia [clay-ro-fo'-be-ah], *f.* Anticlericalism.

clerófobo [clay-ro'-fo-bo], *a.* Anticlerical.

cliché [cle-chay'], *m.* 1. (*Typ.*) Cliché, stereotype plate. 2. (*Liter.*) Cliché; *V.* CLISE.

cliente [cle-en'-tay], *m. & f. com.* 1. Client, a person under the protection and tutorage of another. 2. Customer, patient.

clientela [cle-en-tay'-lah], *f.* 1. A body of clients or dependents; a following; clientele. 2. Protection or patronage. 3. Clientship, condition of a client.

cliéntulo, la [cle-en'-too-lo, lah], *m. & f. (Obs.) V.* CLIENTE.

clima [clee'-mah], *m.* Climate, clime. **Clima artificial** or **acondicionamiento del aire,** air conditioning. **Clima cálido,** warm climate. **Clima templado,** temperate climate.

climatérico, [cle-mah-tay'-re-co, cah], *a.* Climatic, climatical. **Estar climatérico,** *(Coll.)* to be ill-humored.

climático [cle-mah'-te-co], *a.* Climatic.

climatización [cle-mah-te-thah-the-one'], *f.* Air-conditioning.

climatizado [cle-mah-te-thah'-do], *a.* Air-conditioned.

climatizador [cle-mah-te-thah-dor'], *m.* Air-conditioner.

climatología [cle-mah-to-lo-hee'-ah], *f.* Climatology, that part of meteorology which deals with climate.

climatológico, ca [cle-mah-to-lo'-he-co, cah], *a.* Climatological, relating to climate.

clímax [clee'-max], *m.* Climax, a rhetorical figure.

clin [cleen], *f. (Coll.) V.* CRIN. The part of a horse's neck from which the mane grows. **Tenerse a las clines,** *(Met.)* to make every effort not to decline in rank or fortune.

clínica [clee'-ne-cah], *f.* Clinic.

clínico, ca [clee'-ne-co, cah], *a.* Clinical. **Termómetro clínico,** clinical thermometer.

clínico, *m.* 1. *(Med.)* Clinician, physician. 2. The medical student who attends clinical lectures in hospitals.

clinométrico, ca [cle-no-may'-tre-co, cah], *a.* Clinometric, pertaining to the clinometer.

clinómetro [cle-no'-may-tro], *m.* Clinometer, generic name of the instruments used for measuring the inclination of any line or plane to the horizontal.

clip [clip], *m.pl.* **Clips;** paper clip; clip (para pelo); pant clip (de pantalón); clip (joya); *(LAm.)* Earing.

cliper [cle'-payr], *m. (Naut.)* Clipper (barco, avión).

clisado [cle-sah'-do], *m.* Stereotyping the act and effect.

clisar [cle-sar'], *va.* To stereotype, to make a cliché or stereotype plate.

clisé [cle-say'], *m.* 1. The matrix for a stereotype plate. 2. A stereotype plate.

cliso [clee'-so], *m.* 1. *(Med.)* Medicament obtained by the vapors of nitre burned with other substances. 2. *(Chem.)* Product of the distillation of antimony, nitre, and sulphur previously mixed.

clisos [cle-sos], *m. pl.* Peepers, eyes.

clistel, clister [clis-tel', clis-tayr'], *m.* Clyster, an injection into the rectum. *V.* AYUDA.

clítoris [clee'-to-ris], *m.* Clitoris, a small erectile organ at the summit of the vulva.

clivoso, sa [cle-vo'-so, sah], *a. (Poet.)* Declivous, gradually descending.

clo clo, *m.* Clucking of a hen when she is hatching or calling her chickens.

cloaca [clo-ah'-cah], *f.* Sewer, drain (alcantarilla).

cloacal [clo-ah-cahl'], *a.* Lavatorial (chiste, etc.).

clocar [clo-car'], *va.* To cluck. *V.* CLOQUEAR.

cloche [clo'-chay], *m. (CAm. Carib.) (Aut.)* Clutch.

clon [clone], *m.* Clone.

clonación, clonaje [clo-nah-the-on'], *f. m.* Cloning.

clonar [clo-nar'], *va.* To clone.

cloque [clo'-kay], *m.* 1. *(Naut.)* Grapnel, a grappling-iron. *V.* COCLE. 2. Harpoon.

cloquear [clo-kay-ar'], *vn.* 1. To cluck, to chuck to make a noise like a hen. -*va.* 2. To angle.

cloqueo [clo-kay'-o], *m.* Cluck, chuck, the voice of a hen.

cloquera [clo-kay'-rah], *f.* The state of hatching in fowls.

cloquero [clo-kay'-ro], *m.* A person who manages the harpoon in the catching of tunas.

cloral [clo-rahl'], *m.* Chloral.

cloramfenicol [clo-ram-fay-ne-col'], *m. (Med.)* Chloramphenicol.

cloremia [clo-ray'-me-ah], *f. (Med.)* Chloremia.

clorhidrato [clor-e-drah'-to], *m.* Hydrochlorate, clorhydrate.

clorhídrico [clor-ee'-dre-co], *m.* Clorhydric, hydrochloric.

clórico [clo'-re-co], *a.* Chloric, pertaining to or obtained from chlorine.

clorinar [clo-re-nar'], *va.* To chlorinate.

clorinda [clo-ren-dah], *f. (Cono Sur)* Bleach.

cloris [clo'-ris], *f. (Orn.)* Greenfinch.

cloro [clo'-ro], *m.* Chlorine, a yellowish green pungent gas; an element allied to iodine and bromine.

clorofila [clo-ro-fee'-lah], *f.* Chlorophyll, green coloring matter in plants.

cloroformar [clo-ro-for-mar'], *va.* To chloroform.

cloroformización [clo-ro-for-me-thah-the-on'], *f.* Chloroformization, anaesthesia by chloroform.

cloroformizar [clo-ro-for-me-thar'], *va.* To anaesthetize by chloroform; to chloroform.

cloroformo [clo-ro-for'-mo], *m.* Chloroform.

cloromicetina [clo-ro-me-thay-tee'-nah], *f. (Med.)* Chloromycetin.

clorosis [clo-ro'-sis], *f. (Med.)* Chlorosis, greensickness.

clorótico, ca [clo-ro'-te-co, cah], *a.* Chlorotic, affected by chlorosis.

cloruro [clo-roo'-ro], *m.* Chloride, a compound of chlorine.

closet [clo'-set], *m. (LAm.)* Built-in cupboard, wardrobe (armario).

clown [clo'-oon], *m. pl.* **Clowns,** clown.

club [cloob], *m.* Club, an association of persons. **Club campestre,** country club. **Club nocturno,** night club.

clueca [cloo-ay'-cah], *f.* Clucking and hatching (gallinas).

clueco, ca [cloo-ay'-co, cah], *a.* 1. *(Coll.)* Decrepit, worn out with age. 2. Broody (gallina). 3. *(Cono Sur)* Sickly, weak. 3. *(Carib.)* Stuck-up (engreído).

cm abr. de **centímetro** (centimeter, cm).

CN *f. abr.* de **Carretera Nacional.**

coa [co'-ah], *f.* 1. Hoe.

coacción [co-ac-the-on'], *f.* Coercion, compulsion.

coaccionar [co-ac-the-o-nar'], *va.* To coerce, to compel, to put great pressure on.

coacervar [co-ah-ther-var'], *va.* To heap together.

coactivo, va [co-ac-tee'-vo, vah], *a.* Coactive, coercive; compulsive.

coacusar [co-ah-coo-sar'], *va. (For.)* To accuse jointly with another or others.

coadjutor [co-ad-hoo-tor'], *m.* 1. Coadjutor, assistant. 2. Coadjutor, a person elected or appointed to a prebend without enjoying the benefit thereof until the death of the incumbent. **Obispo coadjutor,** assistant bishop.

coadjutora [co-ad-hoo-to'-rah], *f.* Coadjutrix.

coadjutoría [co-ad-hoo-to-ree'-ah], *f.* 1. Coadjuvancy, help, assistance. 2. Right of survivorship of a coadjutor. 3. Office or dignity of a coadjutor.

coadjuvar [co-ad-hoo-var'], *va.* To help, to assist; to help in, to contribute to.

coadministrator [co-ad-me-nis-trah-dor'], *m.* One who governs a díocese by virtue of a bull, or by appointment of a bishop.

coadunación [co-ah-doo-nah-the-on'], *f.* Coadunation, the conjunction of different substances into one mass.

coadunamiento [co-ah-doo-nah-me-en'-to], *m. V.* COADUNACIÓN.

coadunar [Co-ad-doo-nar'], *va.* To jumble things together.

coadyudador [co-ad-yoo-dah-dor'], *m. V.* COADYUVADOR.

coadyutor [co-ad-yoo-tor'], *m. V.* COADJUTOR.

coadyutorio, ria [co-ad-yoo-to'-re-o, ah], *a.* That which assists.

coadyuvador [co-ad-yoo-vah-dor'], *m.* Fellowhelper, assistant.

coadyuvante [coad-yoo-vahn'-tay], *a. & pa.* Coadjutant, helper, assistant.

coadyuvar [co-ad-yoo-var'], *va.* To help, to assist.

coagulable [co-ah-goo-lah'-blay], *a.* Coagulable.

coagulación [co-ah-goo-la-the-on'], *f.* Coagulation; clotting.

coagulador, ra [co-ah-goo-lah-dor', rah], *a.* Causing coagulation; coagulatory, coagulative.

coagulante [co-ah-goo-lahn'-tay], *pa.* Coagulant, that which coagulates.

coagular [co-ah-goo-lar'], *va.* To coagulate, to curd. *-vr.* To coagulate, to condense, to become concrete, to clod, to curdle.

coagulativo, va [co-ah-goo-lah-tee'-vo, vah], *a.* Coagulative.

coágulo [co-ah'-goo-lo], *m.* 1. Coagulum, coagulated blood. 2. Coagulation, the body formed by coagulation. 3. Coagulator, that which causes coagulation.

coalabar [co-ah-lah-bar'], *va.* To join in praising.

coalescencia [co-ah-les-then'-the-ah], *f.* Coalescence, union of parts.

coalición [co-ah-le-the-on'], *f.* Coalition, confederacy.

coalla [co-ahl'-lya], *f. (Orn.)* Woodcock. *V.* CHOCHA and CODORNIZ.

coamante [co-ah-mahn'-tay], *a.* A partner or companion in loving.

coarmador [co-ar-mah-dor'], *m.* Part owner of a vessel.

coarrendador [co-ar-ren-dah-dor'], *m.* A joint partner in renting something.

coartación [co-ar-tah-the-on'], *f. (Law.)* Obligating to be ordained within a certain time to enjoy a benefice.

coartada [co-ar-tah'-dah], *f.* Alibi. **Probar la coartada,** to prove an alibi.

coartar [co-ar-tar'], *va.* To limit, to restrain, to restrict.

coatí [co-ah-tee'], *m. (Zool.)* Coati raccoon.

coautor, ra [co-ah-oo-tor', rah], *m. &. f.* Coauthor, joint author.

coaxial [co-ac-se-al'], *a. (Mech.)* Coaxial.

coba [co'-bah], *f. (Coll.)* Ingenious fib. 2. Flattery. **Dar coba,** to flatter, to softsoap.

cobaltífero, ra [co-bal-tee'-fay-ro, arh], *a.* Cobalt-bearing, cobaltiferous.

cobalto [co-bahl'-to], *m.* Cobalt, a grayish semi-metal.

cobanillo [co-bah-neel'-lyo], *m.* A small basket used by vintners during the vintage.

cobarde [co-bar'-day], *a.* Coward, cowardly, timid, fearful, fainthearted.

cobardear [co-bar-day-ar], *vn.* To be a coward, to be timid or fearful.

cobardemente [co-bar-day-men'-tay], *adv.* Cowardly.

cobardía [co-bar-dee'-ah], *f.* Cowardice, dastardy, dastardness, abjectness.

cobardón [co-bar-done'], *m.* Shameful coward, great coward.

cobayismo [co-bah-ees'-mo], *m.* Use of animals in medical experiments.

cobayo [co-bah'-yo], *m.* The guinea pig, a familiar rodent.

cobea [co-bay'-ah], *f.* Coboea, a climbing plant, having purple bell-shaped flowers; it is a garden plant native of Mexico.

cobertera [co-ber-tey'-rah], *f.* 1. Cover, Pot-lid. 2. *(Met.)* Bawd, procuress. 3. *(Prov. Tol.)* White waterlily. *V.* NENÚFAR. **Coberteras,** the two middle feathers of a hawk's tail.

cobertizo [co-ber-tee'-tho], *m.* 1. A small roof jutting out from the wall, to shelter people from the rain. 2. A covered passage. **Cobertizo para automóvil,** carport.

cobertor [co-ber-tor'], *m.* Coverlet, quilt, cloth, counterpane.

cobertura [co-ber-too'-rah], *f.* 1. Cover, covering, coverlet. 2. **Cobertura de seguro,** insurance cover.

cobija [co-bee'-hah], *f.* 1. A gutter tile. 2. A small cloak for women. 3. Fire screen. 4. *(Arquit.)* Coping tile. 5. Bedclothes. **Pegársele a uno las cobijas,** to oversleep.

cobijador, ra [co-be-hah-dor'], *a.* Covering, protective.

cobijadura [co-be-hah-doo'-rah], *f.* The act of covering.

cobijamiento, cobijo [co-be-hah-me-en'-to, co-bee'-ho], *m.* 1. The act of covering. 2. Lodging.

cobijar [co-be-har'], *va.* 1. To cover, to overspread, to shelter.
Quien a buen árbol se arrima, buena sombra le cobija,

(Prov.) he who gets under a good tree, has a good shelter. 2. To protect, to lodge. *-vr.* To take shelter.

cobijo [co-be-ho], *m.* 1. *(Lit.)* Shelter, lodging. 2. *(fig.)* Cover.

cobil [co-beel'], *m.* Corner, angle.

cobista [co-bees'-tah], *a.* Soapy, smarmy. *-m.* Soapy individual.

cobo [co'-bo], *m. (Carib.)* 1. *(Zool.)* Sea snail. 2. Unsociable person, shy person. **Ser un cobo,** to be shy.

cobol [co'-bol], *(Inform.)* Cobol (Common Business-Oriented Language)

cobra [co'-brah], *f.* 1. *(Zool.)* Cobra. 2. Rope for yoking oxen. 3. Retrieving (in hunting).

cobrable [co-brah'-blay], *a.* Retrievable. 2. Chargeable (dinero).

cobradero, ra [co-brah-da'-ro, rah], *a.* That which may be recovered or collected.

cobrado, da [co-brah'-do, dah], *a. & pp.* of COBRAR. 1. Recovered, received. 2. Complete, undaunted.

cobrador [co-brah-dor'], *m.* 1. Receiver or collector of rents and other money. 2. Conductor, collector.

cobradora [co-brah-do'-rah], *f.* Conductress.

cobramiento [co-brah-me-en'-to], *m.* 1. Recovery, restoration. 2. Utility, profit, emolument.

cobranza [co-brahn'-thah], *f.* 1. Recovery or collection of money. 2. Act of fetching game which is killed or wounded.

cobrar [co-brar'], *va.* 1. To recover, to collect, or receive what is due. 2. To recover what is lost. 3. To fetch game that is wounded or killed. 4. To gain affection or esteem. **Cobrar ánimo** or **corazón,** to take courage. **Cobrar fuerzas,** to gather strength. **El accidente se cobró la vida de 50 personas,** the accident took the lives of 50 people. 5. To charge (precio). **Cobran 200 dólares por componerlo,** they charge 200 dollars to repair it. **Me han cobrado demasiado,** they've charged me too much. To collect, to receive. **Fue a la oficina a cobrar el sueldo,** he went to the office to get his wages. **Cuenta por cobrar,** unpaid bill. *-vn* 1. *(Fin.)* To draw one's pay, to get one's wages; to collect one's salary. **Cobra los viernes,** he gets paid on Fridays. **Vino el lechero a cobrar,** the milkman came for his money. 2. **Cobrar al número llamado,** to reverse the charges. *-vr.* 1. To recover, to return to oneself. 2. To gain celebrity or fame. **Contra reembolso,** C. O. D., collect on delivery. 3. **Cobrar de una pérdida,** to make up for a loss.

cobratorio, ia [co-bra-to'-re-o, ah], *a.* Pertaining to the collection of money; collectible.

cobre [co'-bray], *m.* 1. Copper, a red-colored metal. 2. Kitchen furniture. 3. *(Obs.)* String of onions or garlic. 4. **Batir el cobre,** *(Met.)* to pursue with spirit and vigor. 5. *(LAm.)* Cent, small copper coin. 6. *(LAm.)* **Enseñar el cobre,** to show one's true colors.

cobreado [co-bray-ah'-do], *a.* Copperplated.

cobrero [co-bray'-ro], *m.* Coppersmith.

cobrizo, za [co-bree'-tho, thah], *a.* Coppery, cupreous, copperish.

cobro [co'-bro], *m.* 1. Collection, payment (deudas). **Cargo por cobro,** collection charge. **Deuda de cobro difícil,** debt that is hard to collect. **Cobro a la entrega,** collect on delivery. 2. Safe place. **Poner algo en cobro,** to put something in a safe place. **Ponerse en cobro,** to take refuge. *V.* COBRANZA.

coca [co'-cah], *f.* 1. Coca (arbusto). The dried leaves of a South American shrub (Erythroxylon coca) of the flax family, chewed by the natives as a stimulant, yields cocaine, a local anaesthetic. 2. Indian berry. 3. A bugbear; figure of a serpent borne at the festival of Corpus Christi. 4. *(Naut.)* A sort of small vessel 5. Two puffs of hair of women put back from forehead and fastened behind the ears. 6. A rap with the knuckles on the head. 7. Nut, head. 8. Cake, loaf.

cocacolo, la [cah-cah-co'-lo], *m. & f. (And.)* Frivolous teenager, idle young person.

cocacho [co-cah'-cho], *m. (And. Cono Sur)* Tap on the head.

cocada [co-cah'-dah], *f.* 1. Type of coconut jam (dulce). 2. Lump of coca for chewing. 3. Nougat (turrón).

cocador, ra [co-cah-dor', rah], *a.* Wheedling, coaxing, flattering.

cocaína [co-cah-ee'-nah], *f.* Cocaine, the alkaloid and active principle of the coca-plant, remarkable for its anaesthetic power locally.

cocainomanía [co-cah-e-no-mah-ne'-ah], *f.* Addiction to cocaine.

cocainómano, na [co-cah-e-no'-mah-no], *m. & f.* Cocaine addict.

cocal [co-cahl'], *m.* 1. *(Ven.)* V. COCOTAL. 2. *(Peru)* The cocoa-tree and the spot where it abounds.

cocar [co-car'], *va.* 1. To make grimaces or wry faces. 2. *(Met. Coll.)* To coax, to gain by wheedling and flattering.

cocarar [co-ca-rar'], *va.* To gather the leaves of the plant called coca.

cocción [coc-the-on'], *f.* 1. Coction. 2. *(Tec.)* Baking, firing.

coce [co'-thay], *f. (fibs.)* A kick. V. Coz.

coceador, ra [co-thay-ah-dor', rah], *m. & f.* Kicker.

coceadura [co-thar-ah-doo'-rah], *f.* **Coceamiento,** *m.* Kicking.

cocear [co-thay-ar'], *va.* 1. To kick, to fling out. V. ACOCEAR. 2. *(Met.)* To repugn, to resist. 3. *(Obs.)* To trample, to tread under foot.

cocedero, ra [co-thay-day'-ro, rah], *a.* Easily boiled.

cocedero, *m.* Place where bread is kneaded or baked, or where anything is boiled.

cocedor [co-thay-dor'], *m.* A person whose business it is to boil must and new wine.

cócedra [co'-thay-drah], *f.* Featherbed. V. CÓLCEDRA.

cocedura [co-thay-doo'-rah], *f.* The act of boiling.

cocer [co-therr'], *va.* 1. To boil, to dress victuals. 2. To bake bricks, tiles, or earthenware. 3. To digest.-*vn.* 1. To boil: to ferment. 2. To seethe, ferment, without fire, as wine. -*vr.* To suffer intense and continued pain.

cocido, da [co-thee'-do, dah], *a. & pp.* Of COCER. 1. Boiled, baked. **Carne bien cocida,** meat well done. 2. *(Met.)* Skilled, experienced. **Estar cocido en alguna cosa,** to understand business well. 3. **Estar cocido,** to be plastered, to be drunk.

cocido [co-thee'-do], *m.* V. OLLA.

cociente [co-the-en'-tay], *m. (Math.)* Quotient. **Cociente intelectual,** intelligence quotient, I.Q.

cocimiento [co-the-me-en-to], *m.* 1. Coction, decoction. 2. *(Med.)* Decoction. 3. With dyers, a bath or mordant preparatory to dyeing. 4. A quick, lively sensation. V. ESCOZOR.

cocina [co-thee'-nah], *f.* 1. Kitchen. 2. Cookery, the art of cooking. 3. Range, stove. **Cocina económica,** stove, cooking range. **Libro de cocina,** cookbook. **Utensilios de cocina,** cooking utensils. **Cocina eléctrica,** electric cooker.

cocinar [co-the-nar'], *va.* 1. To cook or dress victuals. 2. *(Met.)* To meddle in other people's affairs. -*vn.* 1. To cook, to do the cooking. 2. *(fig.)* To meddle.

cocinera [co-the-nay'-rah], *f.* Cook, cookmaid, kitchenmaid.

cocinería [co-the-nay-ree'-ah], *f. (Chile & Peru)* Cheap restaurant.

cocinero [co-the-nay'-ro], *m.* Cook. **Haber sido cocinero antes que fraile,** a guarantee of success in one who directs a thing from having practised it himself.

cocinilla [co-the-neel'-lyah], *f.* 1. Chafing dish, cooker. 2. Small kitchen.

cocinita [co-the-nee'-tah], *f.* Small kitchen.

cocker [co'-kayr], *m.* Cocker spaniel, cocker (perro).

cocle [co'-clay], *m. (Naut.)* Grapnel, a grappling-iron.

cóclea [co'-clay-ah], *f.* 1. An ancient machine for raising water. 2. An endless screw. 3. The inner cavity of the ear.

coclear [co-clay-ar'], *va.* To harpoon. -*vn.* To cluck or hatch. V. CLOQUEAR.

coclearia [co-clay-ah'-re-ah], *f. (Bot.)* Common scurvygrass.

coco 1 [co'-co], *m.* 1. *(Bot.)* Coconut-tree (árbol); Indian palm-tree. 2. Coconut, coconut (fruto). 3. Chocolate-cup made of the coconut. 4. *(LAm.)* Cup made from a coconut palm (vasija). 5. Noodle, brain. **Me estoy comiendo el coco,** I am trying to think. 6. Derby, bowler (sombrero). 7. *(And. Cono Sur)* percale. 8. **Cortarse el pelo a coco, (And.)** To have one's head shaved. 9. **Cocos,** Diamonds (Naipes). -*a.* 1. *(Carib.)* Hard, strong. 2. Obstinate.

coco 2 *m.* 1. Worm or grub bred in seeds and fruit. 2. Coccus; scale insect. 3. Coccus, a bacterium of spherical form.

coco 3 *m.* 1. Boogie-man for frightening children, phantasm. **Ser un coco,** or **parecer un coco,** to be an ugly-looking person.

coco 4 *m.* (from COCA, 1st *art.*). Cocos, India berries from which rosaries are made.

coco 5 *m.* Gesture, grimace, a flattering gesture; **hacer cocos,** *(Met.)* To flatter, wheedle, gain one's affections. *(Coll.)* To make signs of affections, to flirt.

cocobolo [Co-co-bo'-lo], *m. (Bot.)* A species of coconut-tree, much used by cabinet-makers.

cococha [co-co'-chah], *f.* Barbel (de bacalao).

cocodrilo [co-co-dree'-lo], *m.* Crocodile.

cocoí [co-co-ee'], *m.* A crested heron, of the size of a stork.

cocoliche [co-co-le-chay], *m. (Cono Sur)* pidgin Spanish; Italian.

cocoliste [co-co-lees'-tay], *m.* In New Spain or Mexico, an epidemic fever.

cócona [co'-co-nah], *f. (Carib.)* Tip.

coconote [co-co-no'-tay], *m. (Mex.)* Child, chubby child; squat person.

cócora [co'-co-rah], *com.* An impertinent and annoying person.

cocoroco [co-co-ro'-co], *a. (Cono Sur)* Vain, stuck-up; insolent, cheeky.

cocoso, sa [co-co'-so, sah], *a.* Worm-eaten, gnawed by grubs.

cocota [co-co'-tah], *f.* V. COGOTERA.

cocotal [co-co-tahl'], *m.* A clump of coconut-trees.

cocote [co-co'-tay], *m. (Prov.)* Occiput. V. COGOTE.

cocotero [co-co-tay'-ro], *m. (Bot.)* Cocoa-tree. V. COCO1.

cóctel [cok-tell'], *m.* 1. Cocktail. 2. Cocktail party. **Ofrecer un cóctel en honor de uno,** to hold a cocktail party in somebody's honor.

coctelera [cok-tay-lay'-rah], *f.* Cocktail shaker.

cocuyo [co-coo'-yo], or **cocuyo,** *m.* The fire-fly or fire-beetle of the West Indies, about an inch and a half long.

cocha [co'-chah], *f.* In mines, a small reservoir of water.

cochambre [co-chahm'-bray], *m.* A greasy, dirty, stinking thing.

cochambrería [co-cham-bray-ree'-ah], *f. (Coll.)* Heap of filthy things.

cochambroso, sa [co-cham-bro'-so, sah], *a. (Coll.)* Nasty, filthy, stinking.

cocharro [co-char'-ro], *m.* A wooden dish, cup, or platter.

cocharse [co-char'-say], *vr.* To hasten, to accelerate.

cochastro [co-chahs'-tro], *m.* A little sucking wild boar.

coche 1 [co'-chay], *m.* 1. Coach carriage. 2. Car, motorcar, automobile. **Coche de alquiler,** car for hire. **Coche de línea,** long-distance bus. **Ir en coche,** to go by car. **Coche patrulla,** patrol car. **Coche de bomberos,** fire engine. 3. Coach, carriage. 4. *(Mex.)* Taxi, cab.

coche 2 [co'-chay], *m. (CAm. Mex.)* Pig, hog; pork. **Coche de monte,** wild pig.

cochear [co-chay-ar'], *vn.* To drive a coach.

coche-bomba [co'-chay bom'-bah], *m.* Car bomb.

coche-cama [co'-chay-cah-mah], *m.* Sleeping car.

cochecillo [co-chay-thee'-lyo], *m.* Small carriage, child's carriage, baby buggy.

cochecito [co-chay-thel'-lyo], *m.* Baby carriage. **Cochecito de niño,** go-cart.

coche-correo [co-chay cor-ray'-o], *m.* Mail van.

coche-cuba [co-chay-coo-bah], *m.* Tank lorry, water wagon.

cochera [co-chay'-rah], *f.* 1. Carriage. 2. Garage (para coches). Coach house (para carruajes). Depot. **Cochera de autobuses,** bus depot.

cocherada [cho-ray-dah'-dah], *f. (Mex.)* Coarse expression.

coche-restaurante [co-chay res-tah-oo-rahn'-tay], *m.* Dining car, restaurant car.

cocheril [co-chay-reel'], *a.* (*Coll.*) Relating to coachmen.

cocherillo [co-chay-reel'-lyo], *m. dim.* A little coachman.

cochero [co-chay'-ro], *m.* 1. Coachman. 2. Coachmaker. 3. Wagoner, a northern constellation.

cochero, ra [co-chay'-ro, rah], *a.* (*Prov.*) Easily boiled.

cocherón [co-chay-rone'], *m.* (*aug.*) 1. Large coach-house. 2. Engine-house; roundhouse.

cochevira [co-chay-vee'-rah], *f.* Lard.

cochevís [co-chay-vees'], *m.* The crested shorelark.

coche-vivienda [co-chay ve-ve-ayn'-dah], *m.* Caravan, trailer.

cochifrito [co-che-free'-to], *m.* Fricassee of lamb, mutton, etc.

cochigato [co-che-gah'-to], *m.* A bird of Mexico, having the head and neck black, with a red collar and green belly; the bill seven inches long.

cochina [co-chee'-nah], *f.* Sow.

cochinada [co-che-nah'-dah], *f.* 1. Herd of swine. 2. Hoggishness; any mean, dirty action. **Eso fue una cochinada,** that was a beastly thing to do. **Hacer una cochinada a uno,** to play a dirty trick on somebody.

cochinamente [co-che-nah-men'-tay], *adv.* 1. Foully, hoggishly, filthily, nastily. 2. Meanly, basely.

cochinata [co-che-nah'-tah], *f.* (*Naut.*) Rider, a piece of timber to strengthen a vessel.

cochinería [co-che-nay-ree'-ah], *f.* 1. Dirtiness, foulness, filthiness, nastiness. 2. Meanness, niggardliness.

cochinero, ra [co-che-nay'-ro, rah], *a.* Use of fruits poor in quality, given to hogs.

cochinilla [co-che-neel'-lyah], *f.* 1. Woodlouse, a small insect. 2. Cochineal, an insect of commercial value. 3. (*Carib. Mex.*) Trivial, unimportant.

cochinillo, illa [co-che-neel'-lyo, lyah], *m. & f. dim.* A little pig. **Cochinillo,** *m.* An animal in Brazil resembling a pig. **Cochinillo de Indias,** guinea pig.

cochino, na [co-chee'-no, nah], *a.* Dirty, nasty, filthy. **Esta vida cochina,** this wretched life.

cochino [co-chee'-no], *m.* Pig. *V.* PUERCO.

cochio, ia, cochizo, za [co-chee'-o, ah, co-chee'-tho, thah], *a.* Easily boiled.

cochiquera [co-che-kay'-rah], *f.* Hog-sty, pigsty.

cochite hervite [co-chee'-tay er-vee'-tay]. (*Coll.*) Helter-skelter: applied to something done hastily.

cochitril [co-che-treel'], *m.* (*Coll.*) 1. A pigsty. 2. A filthy room, quarters.

cocho, cha [co'-cho, chah], *a.* 1. *V.* COCIDO. 2. Old, past. *-m.f.* Old man; old woman.

cochón, ona [co-chone'], *m. & f.* Poof (hombre); dyke.

cochoso [co-cho'-so], *a.* (*And.*) Filthy.

cochura [co-choo'-rah], *f.* 1. Act of boiling. 2. Dough for a batch of bread.

cod. *m. abr.* de **código** (code).

coda [co'-dah], *f.* (*Prov.*) 1. Tail. *V.* COLA. 2. Burden of a song or other piece of music.

codadura [co-dah-doo'-rah], *f.* Part of an old vine laid on the ground, from which young buds shoot forth.

codal [co-dahl], *m.* 1. Piece of ancient armor for the elbow. 2. A short and thick wax-candle, of the size of the elbow. 3. Shoot issuing from a vine. 4. Frame of a handsaw. **Codales,** a carpenter's square. 5. Prop, shore, stay strut, staybolt.

codal [co-dahl'], *a.* Cubital, containing only the length of a cubit. **Palo codal,** a stick of the length of a cubit, hung round the neck as a penance.

codaste [co-dahs'-tay], *m.* (*Naut.*) Sternpost.

codazo [co-dah'-tho], *m.* 1. Blow with the elbow: a hunch. 2. (*Mex.*) Tip-off (consejo).

codear [co-day-ar'], *vn.* 1. To elbow. **Codearse con,** to rub elbows with. 2. (*And. Cono Sur*) To live off somebody (vivir de gorra). *-va.* 1. To elbow, to nudge, to jostle. 2. (*And. Cono Sur*) **Codear a uno,** to keep on at somebody,

pester somebody. *-vr.* **Codearse con,** to hobnob with, to rub shoulders with.

codecillar, codicilar [co-day-theel-lyar', co-de-the-lar'], *vn.* To make a codicil.

codeína [co-day-ee'-nah], *f.* Codeine, an alkaloid obtained from opium.

codena [co-day'-nah], *f.* Body or thickness required in cloth.

codeo [co-day'-o], *m.* (*And.*) Sponging; pesterings (insistencia).

codera [co-day'-rah], *f.* 1. Itch or scabbiness on the elbow. 2. A piece reinforcing the elbows of jackets. **Codera en un cable,** (*Naut.*) A spring on a cable.

codesera [co-de-say'-rah], *f.* A spot grown over with hairy cytisus.

codeso [co-day'-so], *m.* (*Bot.*) Hairy cytisus. **Codeso de los Alpes,** laburnum, ebony of the Alps.

códice [co'-de-thay], *m.* Old manuscript, dealing with remarkable points of antiquity; codex.

codicia [co-dee'-the-ah], *f.* 1. Covetousness, cupidity. 2. (*Obs.*) Sensual appetite, lust. 3. (*Met.*) Greediness, an ardent desire of good things. **La codicia rompe el saco,** covet all, lose all.

codiciable [co-de-the-ah'-blay], *a.* Covetable.

codiciado [co-de-the-ah'-do], *a.* Widely desired; much in demand; sought-after, coveted.

codiciador [co-de-the-ah-dor,], *m.* Coveter.

codiciante [co-de-the-ahn'-tay], *pa.* Coveting.

codiciar [co-de-the-ar'], *va.* To covet.

codicilar [co-de-the-lar'], *a.* Pertaining to a codicil.

codicilo [co-de-thee'-lo], *m.* Codicil, a supplement to a last will.

codiciosamente [co-de-the-o-sah-men'-tay], *adv.* Covetously, greedily.

codiciosito, ita [co-de-the-o-see'-to, tah], *a. dim.* Somewhat covetous.

codicioso, sa [co-de-the-o'-so, sah], *a.* 1. Greedy, covetous, avericious 2. (*Met. Coll.*) Diligent, laborious, assiduous.

codificaión [co-de-fe-cah-the-one'], *f.* 1. Codification. 2. (*Inform.*) Encryption.

codificar [co-de-fe-car'], *va.* To codify laws; reduce to a code.

código [co'-de-go], *m.* Code (of laws). **Código de comercio,** mercantile law. **Código de señales,** signal code. **Codigo de circulación,** highway code. **Código de leyes,** law code. **Código territorial,** area code. **Mensaje en código,** message in code. **Código ASCII,** (*Inform.*) American Standard Code for Information Interchange. **Código de control de la impresora,** (*Inform.*) printer control code. **Código EBCDIC,** (*Inform.*) Extended Binary Coded Decimal Interchange Code. **Código reutilizable,** (*Inform.*) reusable code. **Código de corrección de errores,** error-correcting code.

codillera [co-deel-lyay'-rah], *f.* (*Vet.*) Tumor on the knee of horses.

codillo [co-deel'-lyo], *m.* 1. Knee of horses and other quadrupeds. 2. Angle. 3. Codille. 4. That part of a branch of a tree which joins the trunk. 5. **Codillo de una curva,** (*Naut.*) breech of a knee 6. Stirrup of a saddle. **Jugársela a uno de codillo,** (*Met.*) to trick or outwit a person. **Codillos,** file used by silversmiths. **Tirar a uno al codillo,** to endeavor to destroy one; doing him all possible damage.

codo [co'-do], *m.* 1. Elbow. 2. Cubit, a measure of length equal to the distance from the elbow to the end of the middle finger. **Alzar de codo** or **el codo,** to drink too much wine. **Comerse los codos de hambre,** to be starved with hunger. **Dar de codo,** to elbow, to push with the elbow, to treat with contempt. **Hablar por los codos,** to chatter, to prattle. **Levantar de codo, empinar el codo,** to booze; to drink. **Morderse el codo,** (*Cono Sur. Mex.*) to restrain oneself, to bite one's lip. **Trabajar codo con codo,** to work side by side.

codón [co-done'], *m.* A leather cover of a horse's tail.

codoña [co-do'-nyah], *f.* Quince.

codoñero [co-do-nyay'-ro], *m.* Quince-tree.

codorniz [co-dor-neeth'], *f. (Orn.)* Quail.

coecual [co-ay-coo-ahl'], *a. (Div.)* Coequal.

coeducación [co-ay-doo-cah-the-on'], *f.* Coeducation.

coeducacional [co-ay-doo-cah-the-o-nahl'], *a.* Coeducational.

coeficiente [co-ay-fe-the-en'-tay], *a.* Coefficient. **Coeficiente de inteligencia,** intelligence quotient.

coepíscopo [co-ay-pees'-co-po], *m.* Contemporary bishop.

coercer [co-er-therr'], *va.* To coerce, to check, to restrain.

coercibilidad [co-er-the-be-le-dahd'], *f.* Coercibility: liability to restraint.

coercible [co-er-thee'-blay], *a.* Coercible; subject to check.

coerción [co-er-the-on'], *f.* Coercion, restraint, check.

coercitivo, va [co-er-the-tee'-vo, vah], *a.* Coercive, restraining.

coesencial [co-ay-sen-the-ahl'], *a.* Coessential, consubstantial.

coetáneo, nea [co-ay-tah'-nay-o, ah], *a.* Coetaneous, contemporary.

coevo, va [co-ay'-vo, vah], *a.* Coeval.

coexistencia [co-ek-sis-ten'-the-ah], *f.* Coexistence.

coexistente [co-ek-sis-ten'-tay], *pa.* Coexistent.

coexistir [co-ek-sis-teer'], *vn.* To coexist.

coextenderse [co-ex-ten-der'-say], *vr.* To coextend.

cofa [co'-fa], *f. (Naut.)* Top. **Cofa mayor,** main top.

cofia [co'-fe-ah], *f.* 1. A net of silk or thread worn on the head; a kind of cowl, head-dress, headgear, coif. 2. An iron case in which the die is fastened for coining.

cofiezuela [co-fe-ay-thoo'-lah], *f. dim.* A small net.

cofín [co-feen'], *m.* A small basket for fruit.

cofina [co-fee'-nah], *f.* Cofino, *m. V.* COFÍN.

cofrade, da [co-fraih-day, dah], *m. & f.* Confrier, a member of any confraternity or brotherhood.

cofradía [co-frah-dee'-ah], *f.* 1. Confraternity, brotherhood, or sisterhood. 2. Association of persons for any purpose.

cofre [co'-fray], *m.* 1. Trunk for clothes. 2. Fish found in the West Indies. 3. *(Mil.)* Coffer, a hollow lodgement across a dry moat. 4. *(Print.)* Coffin of a printing press.

cofrecico, illo, ito [co-fray-thee-co], *m. dim.* A small trunk.

cofrero [co-fray'-ro], *m.* Trunk-maker or seller of trunks.

cofundador, ra [co-foon-dah-dor', rah], *m. & f.* Cofounder, a joint founder.

cogedera [co-hay-day'-rah], *f.* A sort of beehive used to gather a swarm which has quit the stock.

cogedero, ra [co-hay-day'-ro, rah], *m. & f.* Collector, gatherer. *-a.* Ripe; ready to be picked (fruto).

cogedizo, za [co-hay-dee'-thoh, thah], *a.* That which can be easily collected or gathered.

cogedor [co-hay-dor'], *m.* 1. Collector, gatherer. 2. Dustbox or dustpan. 3. *(Obs.)* Tax-gatherer. 4. Among velvet-weavers, a box in which the woven velvet is put.

cogedura [co-hay-doo'-rah], *f.* Act of gathering or collecting.

coger [co-herr'], *va.* 1. To take, to catch, to grasp, to seize with the hand, to get, to lay hold of, to come upon. 2. To imbibe, to soak. **La tierra no ha cogido bastante agua,** the earth has not drawn in sufficient water. 3. To gather the produce of the ground. 4. To have room to hold. **Esta cámara coge mil fanegas de trigo,** this granary holds a thousand bushels of wheat. 5. To occupy, to take up. **Cogió la alfombra toda la sala,** the carpet covered the whole room. 6. To find, to procure. **Me cogió descuidado,** he took me unawares. **Procuré cogerle de buen humor,** I endeavored to see him when in a good mood. 7. To surprise, to attack unexpectedly. **La tempestad me cogió por sorpresa,** the storm overtook me unexpectedly. **Coger en mentira,** to catch in a lie. 8. To intercept, to obstruct. **Coger la calle,** to flee, to escape. **Coger a deseo,** to obtain one's wishes. **Coger una mona,** to be intoxicated. 9. To take, to pinch (robar). **En la aduana le cogieron una radio,** they found a radio on him at customs. **Me coge siempre las cerillas,** he always takes my matches. 10. To catch

(persona); to arrest; to take prisoner. **Coger un buen marido,** to catch oneself a good husband. **La guerra nos cogió en Francia,** the war caught us in France. **Coger a uno detrás de la puerta,** to catch somebody at a disadvantage. 11. To take, to accept. **Cogió la noticia sin interés,** he received the news without interest. 12. To catch (enfermedad, resfriado). **El niño cogió sarampión,** the child got measles. **Los perros cogen pulgas,** dogs get fleas. 13. To get, to understand, to pick up (radio); to learn. **Con esta radio cogemos Praga:** with his set we can get Prague. 14. To take down. **Le cogieron el discurso taquigráficamente,** they took his speech down in shorthand. To take, to catch, to go by. **Vamos a coger el tren,** let's take the train. *-vn.* 1. *(Bot.)* To take, to strike. 2. To fit, to go, to have room (caber). **Aquí no coge,** it doesn't fit in here. 3. **Cogió y se fue,** he just upped and left. 4. *(LAm.)* To fuck, to screw. *-vr.* 1. To catch. **Cgerse los dedos en la puerta,** to catch one's fingers in the door. 2. **Cogerse algo,** to steal something. 3. *(Carib.)* **Cogerse con uno,** to get on with somebody.

cogestión [co-hays-te-on'], *f.* Co-partnership (en industria, etc.).

cogida [co-hee'-dah], *f.* 1. The gathering or harvesting of fruits. 2. The yield of fruits. 3. The act of the bull's catching the bullfighter.

cogido, da [co-hee'-dah], *a.* Joined, untied. *-m.* Fold, accidental or designed, made in women's clothing, curtains, etc.

cogienda [co-he-ayn'-dah], *f.* 1. *(And. Carib.) V.* COGIDA. 2. *(Mil.)* Forced enlistment. 3. *(Mex.)* Fucking, screwing (acto sexual).

cogimiento [co-he-me-en'-to], *m.* Gathering, collecting, or catching.

cogitabundo, da [co-he-tah-boon'-do, dah], *a.* Pensive, throughful, musing.

cogitación [co-he-tah-the-on'], *f.* Reflection, meditation, cogitation.

cogitar [co-he-tar'], *va.* To reflect, to meditate, to muse.

cogitativo, va [co-he-tah-tee'-vo, vah], *a.* Cogitative, given to meditation.

cognación [cog-nah-the on'], *f.* Cognation, kindred.

cognado, da [cog-nah'-do, dah], *a.* Cognate, related by consanguinity.

cognaticio, ia [cog-nah-tee'-the-o, ah], *a.* Order of succession of the collateral relatives by the female line, through lack of male succession.

cognición [cog-ne-the-on'], *f. V.* CONOCIMIENTO.

cognitivo [cog-ne-te'-vo], *a.* Cognitive.

cognomento [cog-no-men'-to], *m.* Cognomination, surname.

cognoscible [cog-nos-thee'-blay], *a.* Cognoscible, that may be known.

cognoscitivo, va [cog-nos-the-tee'-vo, vah], *a.* Cognitive, having the power of knowing.

cogollico, ito [co-gol-yee'-co, ee'-to], *m. dim.* A small heart or flower of garden plants, such as cabbage, etc.

cogollo [co-gol'-lyo], *m.* 1. Heart of garden plants, such as lettuce, cabbage, etc. 2. Shoot of a plant. 3. Top, summit. **Cogollos,** ornaments of the friezes of Corinthian capitals. 4. *(fig.)* Best part, cream. **El cogollo de la sociedad,** the cream of society. 5. *(fig.)* Centre, core, nucleus, 6. *(Carib.)* Straw hat.

cogolmar [co-gol-mar'], *va.* To fill up a vessel. *V.* COLMAR.

cogombradura [co-gom-brah-doo'-rah], *f. (Obs.)* Digging and earthing about plants.

cogombro [co-gom'-bro], *m. V.* COHOMBRO.

cogorza [co-gor'-thah], *f.* **Pescar una cogorza,** to get very drunk.

cogotazo [co-go-tah'-tho], *m.* Blow on the back of the neck; rabbit punch (boxeo).

cogote [co-go'-tay], *m.* 1. Occiput, hind part of the head. 2. Crest at the back of the helmet. **Coger a uno por el cogote,** to take somebody by the scruff of the neck. **Estar hasta el cogote,** *(Carib.)* to have had it up to here.

cogotera [co-go-tay'-rah], *f.* The hair combed down on the neck.

cogotudo [co-go-too'-do], *a. (And. Cono Sur)* Well-heeled, filthy rich; *(Carib.)* Powerful in politics. *-m. (LAm.)* Self-made man.

cogucho [co-goo'-cho], *m.* The most inferior sort of sugar.

cogujada [co-goo-hah'-dah], *f. (Orn.)* Crested lark.

cogujón [co-goo-hone'], *m.* Corner of a mattress or bolster.

cogujonero, ra [co-goo-ho-nay'-ro, rah], *a.* Pointed, as the corners of mattresses or bolsters.

cogulla [co-gool'-lyah], *f.* Cowl, monk's hood or habit.

cogullada [co-gool-lyah'-dah], *f. V.* PAPADA DE PUERCO.

cohabitación [co-ah-be-tah-the-on'], *f.* Cohabitation, living together as man and wife, whether lawfully or illicitly.

cohabitar [co-ah-be-tar'], *vn.* To cohabit, to accustom, to live together.

cohecha [co-ay'-chah], *f. (Agri.)* Cultivating the land the last time before sowing the crop.

cohechador [co-ay-chah-dor'], *m.* 1. Bribed, suborner. 2. Bribed judge.

cohechamiento [co-ay-chah-me-en'-to], *m. V.* COHECHO.

cohechar [co-ay-char'], *va.* 1. To bribe, to gain by bribes, to suborn, to hire, to daub, to fee. 2. To force, to oblige. 3. *(Agri.)* To plough the ground the last time before it is sown.

cohechazón [co-ay-chah-thone'], *f. (Prov.)* 1. Act of breaking up the ground for cultivation. 2. The last ploughing of the ground before it is sown.

cohecho [co-ay'-cho], *m.* 1. Bribery. 2. *(Agri.)* Season for ploughing the ground.

cohén [co-en'], *m. & f.* 1. Soothsayer. 2. Procurer, pimp.

coheredera [co-ay-ray-day'-rah], *f.* Co-heiress, joint-heiress.

coheredero [co-ay-ray-day'-ro], *m.* Co-heir, fellow heir, joint-heir.

coherencia [co-ay-ren'-the-ah], *f.* 1. Co-herence, the relation of one thing to another; connection. 2. Adhesion of molecules.

coherente [co-ay-rent-tay], *a.* Coherent, consistent, cohesive.

coherentemente [co-ay-ren-tay-men'-tay], *adv.* Cohesively.

cohermano [co-er-mah'-no], *m.* First cousin. *V.* PRIMO.

cohesión [co-ay-se-on'], *f.* Cohesion.

cohesionar [co-ay-se-o-nar'], *va.* To unite.

cohesivo [co-ay-se'-vo], *a.* Cohesive.

cohete [co-ay'-tay], *m.* 1. Sky-rocket; fire-cracker. 2. Fuse. **Cohete de ignición múltiple,** *(Aer.)* multistage rocket. **Cohete de señales,** flare. **Cohete impulsor,** *(Aer.)* Booster rocket. **Cohete espacial de combustible sólido,** solid-fueled space rocket. 3. *(CAm. Mex.)* Pistol. 4. *(Mex.)* Blasting fuse (mecha). 5. **Al cohete,** *(And. Cono Sur)* without rhyme or reason. *-a. (Mex. CAm.)* Drunk, tight.

cohetería [co-hay-tay-ree'-ah], *f.* Rocketry.

cohetero [co-hay-tay'-ro], *m.* Rocketeer.

cohibición [co-e-be-the-on'], *f.* Prohibition, restraint.

cohibido [co-e-be-do], *a.* Restrained, restricted; full of inhibitions (de temperamento); shy, timid. **Sentirse cohibido,** to feel shy.

cohibir [co-e-beer'], *va.* To cohibit, to prohibit, to restrain. *-vr.* 1. To restrain oneself. 2. To fell inhibited; to get uneasy, to become shy.

cohobar [co-o-bar'], *va.* To redistil, cohobate. (Early chemistry.)

cohombral [co-om-brahl'], *m.* Cucumberbed.

cohombrillo [co-om-breel'-lyo], *m. dim.* Gherkin. **Cohombrillo amargo,** the bitter cucumber, squirting cucumber.

cohombro [co-om'-bro], *m.* 1. Cucumber, or snake cucumber. **Cohombro marino,** or **de mar,** sea-cucumber, a holothurian. 2. A fritter made of the same mass as used for buns, and after being fried cut into pieces like a cucumber.

cohonder [co-on-derr'], *va.* To corrupt, to vilify.

cohondimiento [co-on-de-me-en'-to], *m.* Corruption, reproach, infamy.

cohonestar [co-o-nes-tar'], *va.* 1. To give an honest or decent appearance to an action. 2. To blend, to harmonize.

cohorte [co-or'-tay], *f.* Cohort, a body of Roman infantry, numbering usually five hundred.

COI *m. abr.* de **Comité Olímpico Internacional** (International Olympic Committee, IOC).

coi, or **Coy,** *pl.* **Coyes** [co'-e], *m. (Naut.)* Hammock.

coima [co'-e-mah], *f.* 1. Perquisite received by the keeper of a gaming-table. 2. *(Low.)* A prostitute.

coime, coimero [co'-e-may, co-e-may'-ro], *m.* 1. Keeper of a gaming table. 2. Pimp, ponce (chulo). 3. *(And.)* Waiter.

coimero [co-e-may'-ro], *a. (And. Cono Sur)* Easily bribed, bribable, bent.

coincidencia [co-in-the-den'-the-ah], *f.* 1. Coincidence; concurrence. 2. Agreement. **En coincidencia con,** in agreement with.

coincidente [co-in-the-den'-tay], *pa.* Coincident, concurrent, consistent.

coincidir [co-in-the-deer'], *vn.* 1. To fall upon or meet in the same point, to fall in. **Todos coinciden en que…,** everybody agrees that… 2. To concur, to coincide.

coindicación [co-in-de-cah-the-on'], *f. (Med.)* Coindication.

coindicante [co-in-de-cahn'-tay], *m. & a. (Med.)* Coindicant.

coinquinarse [co-in-ke-nar'-say], *vr.* To be stained. *V.* MANCHARSE.

cointeresado, da [co-in-tay-ray-sah-do, dah], *a.* Jointly interested.

coitivo, va [co-e-tee'-vo, vah], *a.* Relating to the act of generation or coition.

coito [co'-e-to], *m.* Coitus, coition, carnal copulation,

coja [co'-hah], *f.* 1. Back of the knee; popliteal space. 2. A lewd woman.

cojear [co-hay-ar'], *vn.* 1. To limp, to halt, to hobble. 2. To deviate from virtue. **Cojear del mismo pie,** to have the same defect or passion. **Saber de qué pie cojea,** to know a person's weak points.

cojera, cojez [co-hay'-rah, co-heth'], *f.* Lameness, halt, hobble, limp.

cojijoso, sa [co-he-ho'-so, sah], *a.* Peevish, irritable.

cojín [co-heen'], *m.* Cushion; soft pad placed on a saddle. **Cojines de bote,** *(Naut.)* Boat cushions.

cojincillo [co-hin-thee'-lyo], *m. dim.* Small cushion or pillow.

cojinete [co-he-nay'-tay], *m.* 1. Small cushion, pad. 2. *(Mech.)* **Coginete de bolas,** roller bearing. 3. *(Ferro. etc.)* Chair. 3. *(And. Carib. Mex.)* Saddlebags.

cojinillos [co-he-nel-lyos], *m. pl. (CAm. Mex.)* Saddlebags.

cojitranco, ca [co-he-trahn'-co, cah], *a.* Applied as a nickname to evil-disposed lame persons.

cojo, ja [co'-ho, hah], *n. & a.* 1. Cripple, halter. 2. Lame, cripple, halt (personas, sillas, mesas). **No ser cojo ni manco,** to have all the necessary requisites to do something: to be very intelligent and skilled in the matter at hand. 4. *(fig.)* Lame, weak, shaky. **El verso queda cojo,** the line is defective. **La frase está coja,** the sentence is incomplete.

cojón [co-hone'], *m.* 1. *(Low.)* Testicle. *V.* TESTÍCULO. **Una película de cojones,** a tremendous film. **Me lo paso por los cojones,** I just laugh at it. 2. *(fig.)* Guts. **Es un tío con cojones,** he's got guts. **Hace falta tener cojones,** you've got to have guts. 3. *adv.* **Hace un frío de cojones,** it's terribly cold. **Me importa un cojón,** I don't give a damn.

cojonudamente [co-ho-noo-dah-mayn'-tay], *adv.* Marvelously, splendidly.

cojonudo [co-ho-noo'-do], *a.* 1. Strong; brave; full of guts. 2. Huge, colossal; very important. 3. Marvelous, splendid; smashing bird. **Un tío cojonudo,** a great guy. 4. Very funny, highly amusing.

cojudo, da [co-hoo'-do, dah], *a.* Entire, not gelt, or castrated.

cojuelo, ela [co-hoo-ay'-lo, lah], *a. dim.* A small cripple.

cok [coke], *m.* Coke, retorted coal.

cokera [co-kay'-rah], *f.* A hod for coke.

col [cole], *f.* Species of cabbage with large leaves and short stalk. **Entre col y col, lechuga,** variety is pleasing. **Coles de Bruselas,** sprouts. **Col roja,** red cabbage.

cola [co'-lah], *f.* 1. Tail (animales, aviones). 2. Train (vestido). **La cola del traje de la novia,** the train of the wedding dress. 3. Tail (chaqué, cometa). 4. In music, the prolonged sound of the voice at the end of a song. **A la cola,** backwards, behind. **Cola de caballo,** *(Bot.)* horsetail. **Cola de rata,** rattail file. **Estar en la cola de clase,** to be at the bottom of the class. **Venir a la cola,** to come last. **Vagón de cola,** last truck. 5. Line. **Hacer cola,** to form a line. 6. *(fig.)* Consequences. **Traer cola,** to have serious consequences. **Menea la cola el can, no por ti, sino por el pan,** the dog wags his tail, not for the love of you but for what you will give him.

Cola, *f.* 1. Glue. **Cola fuerte,** strong glue made of oxhides. **Cola de pescado,** isinglass; **eso no pega ni con cola,** that has nothing whatsoever to do with it. 2. *(And.)* Fizzy drink.

cola [co-lah], *f.* Coke, Coca-Cola.

colaboración [co-lah-bo-rah-the-on'], *f.* Collaboration, working together.

colaboracionismo [co-la-bo-rah-the-o-nees'-mo], *m.* Collaboration.

colaboracionista [co-lah-bo-rah-the-o-nees'-tah], *m. & f.* (Political) Collaborator.

colaborador, ra [co-lah-bo-rah-dor', rah], *m. & f.* 1. Collaborator, associate 2. Contributor (periódico). **Colaboradores de un libro,** joint authors of a book.

colaborar [co-lah-bo-rar'], *va.* To collaborate; to help, to assist. **Colaborar con uno en un trabajo,** to callaborate with somebody on a piece of work.

colación [co-lah-the-on'], *f.* 1. Collation, comparing of one thing with another. 2. Collation, act of bestowing an ecclesiastical benefice, or conferring degrees in universities. 3. Conference or conversation between the monks on spiritual affairs. 4. Collation, a slight repast. 5. Potation, the act of drinking. 6. Sweetmeats given to servants on Christmas eve. 7. Precinct or district of a parish. **Sacar a colación,** to make mention of a person or thing. **Traer a colacion,** to produce proofs or reasons to support a cause; to introduce, in conversation, something irrelevant.

colacionar [co-lah-the-o-nar'], *va.* 1. To collate one thing of the same kind with another, to compare. 2. To collate, to place in an ecclesiastical benefice.

colada [co-lah'-dah], *f.* 1. Washing (ropa). **Tender la colada,** to hang out the washing. 2. The linen thus bucked. 3. An open ground. 4. Road for cattle over a common.

coladera [co-lah-day'-rah], *f.* 1. Strainer, colander. 2. Sieve or scarce used by wax-chandlers.

coladero [co-lah-day'-ro], *m.* 1. Colander, a sieve through which liquors are poured, a strainer. 2. A narrow passage. 3. Bucking of clothes.

colado [co-lah'-do], *a.* 1. Metal cast (molde). 2. **Aire colado,** draught. 3. **Estar colado,** to be in love. *-m. f.* Intruder; uninvited guest, gate-crasher.

colador [co-lah-dor'], *m.* 1. Colander. V. COLADERO. 2. Collator, one who confers ecclesiastical benefices. 3. In printing-offices, a leach-tub for making lye.

coladora [co-lah-do'-rah], *f.* A woman who bucks.

coladura [co-lah-doo'-rah], *f.* 1. Straining, filtration. 2. **Coladuras,** dregs or bees of clarified wax. 3. Absurdity, piece of nonsense.

colaire [co-lah'-e-ray], *m.* *(Prov.)* Place through which a current of air passes.

colambre, *f.* V. CORAMBRE.

colanilla [co-lah-neel'-lyah], *f.* A small bolt.

colaña [co-lah'-nyah], *f.* Joist about twenty palms long and six inches broad.

colapez, colapiscis [co-lah-peth', co-la-pees'-thees], *f.* Isinglass. V. COLA DE PESCADO.

colapsar [co-lahp-sar'], *va.* 1. To overthrow, cause to collapse. 2. *(Aut.)* To jam, to block; to disrupt. *-vn.* To collapse, to go to pieces.

colapso [co-lap'-so], *m.* *(Med.)* Collapse, prostration, destruction. **Colapso nervioso,** nervous breakdown.

colar [co-lar'], *va. & vn.* 1. To strain. to filter. 2. To bleach clothing after washing. 3. To collate or confer ecclesiastical benefices. 4. To obtain some difficult matter. 5. *(Coll.)* To spread false news as certain facts; to pass counterfeit money. 6. To pass through a strait place. **Colar algo por un sitio,** to slip something through a place. **Colar unos géneros por la aduana,** to slip goods through the customs. 7. To drink wine. *-vr.* 1. To strain or to be filtered. 2. To steal into a place, to creep in by stealth. 3. To be displeased with a jest. 4. To jump the queue. **La moto se cuela por entre la circulación,** the motorcycle slips through the traffic. **Se ha colado algún indeseable,** some undesirable has slipped in.

colateral [co-lah-tay-rahl'], *a.* 1. Collateral. 2. Standing equal in relation to some ancestor.

colativo, va [co-lah-tee'-vo, vah], *a.* 1.

colca [col'-cah], *f.* *(And.)* Barn, granary (troje); storeroom (almacén); attic store.

colcha [col'-chah], *f.* 1. Coverlet, counterpane. 2. *(Naut.)* V. COLCHADURA.

colchadura [col-chah-doo'-rah], *f.* 1. Quilting. 2. *(Naut.)* Laying or twisting ropes.

colchar [col-char'], *va.* 1. To quilt. V. ACOLCHAR. 2. **Colchar cabos,** *(Naut.)* To lay or twist ropes. **Carro de colchar,** a rope-maker's sledge.

colchero [col-chay'-ro], *m.* Quiltmaker.

cólchico [col'-che-co], *m.* *(Bot.)* Colchicum, meadow saffron. V. CÓLQUICO.

colchón [col-chone'], *m.* Mattress. **Colchón de pluma,** feather-bed. **Colchón de aire** airbed. **Colchón de muelles,** spring mattress. **Servir de colchón a,** *(fig.)* to act as a buffer for.

colchoncico, illo, ito [col-chon-thee'-co], *m. dim.* A small mattress.

colchonero, ra [col-cho-nay'-ro, rah], *m. & f.* Mattress-maker, feather-bed-maker.

colchoneta [col-cho-nay'-tah], *f.* Mat.

colcótar [col-co'-tar], *m.* *(Chem.)* Colcothar, crocus, rouge.

colcrén [col-crayn'], *m.* Cold cream.

cole [co'-lay], *m.* V. COLEGIO.

coleada [co-lay-ah'-dah], *f.* Wag or motion of the tail of fishes or other animals.

coleadura [co-lay-ah-doo'-rah], *f.* 1. Wagging of the tail. 2. Wriggling, a ridiculous motion of women in walking.

colear [co-lay-ar'], *vn.* 1. To wag the tail (as dogs). 2. To wriggle or move in walking. **Todavía colea,** it's still pending (referring to a business not yet settled). *-va.* *(Sp. Amer.)* 1. To annoy, to nag. 2. To pursue (a person). 3. In bullfights, to take the bull by the tail, and while running, to overturn him. *-vr.* *(Carib.)* 1. *(Aut.)* To skid (sin control). 2. To arrive unexpectedly (huésped).

colección [co-lec-the-on'], *f.* Collection, an assemblage of things, collation, knot, compilement. **Es de colección,** it's a collector's item.

coleccionador, ra [co-lec-the-o-nah-dor'], *m. & f.* Collector.

coleccionar [co-lec-the-o-nar,], *va. vn.* To collect. **Coleccionar sellos de correo,** to collect postage stamps.

coleccionista [co-lec-the-o-nees'-tah], *m. & f.* Collector.

colecitas de Bruselas [co-lay-thee'-tahs day broo-say'-lahs], *f. pl.* *(Bot.)* Brussel sprouts.

colecta [co-lec'-tah], *f.* 1. Distribution of a tax levied on a town 2. Collect, a prayer of the mass. 3. Collection of voluntary offerings for pious uses. 4. Assemblage of the faithful in churches for the celebration of divine service.

colectación [co-lec-tah-the-on'], *f.* Levy, the act of collecting rents, taxes, or other dues. V. RECAUDACIÓN.

colectar [co-lec-tar'], *va.* To collect taxes. V. RECAUDAR.

colecticio, cia [co-lec-tee'-the-o, ah], *a.* Collectitious, applied to troops without discipline.

colectivamente [co-lec-te-vah-men'-tay], *adv.* Collectively.

colectivero [co-lec-te-vay'-ro], *m.* *(Cono Sur)* bus driver.

colectividad [co-lec-te-ve-dahd'], *f.* Community.

colectivismo [c-lec-te-vees'-mo], *m.* Collectivism.

colectivización [co-lec-te-ve-thah-the-on'], *f.* Collectivization.

colectivizar [co-lec-te-ve-thar'], *va.* To collectivize.

colectivo, va [co-lec-tee'-vo, vah], *a.* Collective. **Contrato colectivo,** closed shop (laboral), -*m.* 1. *(Pol.)* Collective. 2. *(And. Cono Sur)* bus, minibus; *(And.)* Taxi.

colector [co-lec-tor'], *m.* 1. Collector, gatherer. 2. Tax or rent-gatherer. 3. Collector of the contributions for religious services. 4. *(Mech.)* Sump, trap, container; sewer (albañil).

colecturía [co-lec-too-ree'-ah], *f.* 1. Collectorship. 2. Office of the collector.

colega [co-lay'-gah], *m.* Colleague; chum, mate, pal.

colegatario, ria [co-lay-gah-tah'-re-o, ah], *m. & f.* Collegatary, colegatee.

colegiado, da [co-lay-he-ah'-do], *a. m. & f.* Collegiate, a member of a college or corporation, etc.

colegial [co-lay-ge-ah'], *m.* Collegian, collegiate, a member of a college, schoolboy; inexperienced person.

colegial [co-lay-he-ahl'], *a.* Collegial, relating to a college. **Iglesia colegial,** a collegiate church composed of dignitaries and canons, who celebrate divine service.

colegiala [co-lay-he-ah'-lah], *f.* A woman who is a member of a college; schoolgirl.

colegialmente [co-lay-he-al-men'-tay], *adv.* In a collegial manner.

colegiarse [co-lay-he-ar'-say], *vr.* To unite in a college those of the same profession or class.

colegiata [co-lay-he-ah'-tah], *f.* A collegiate church.

colegiatura [co-lay-he-ah-too'-rah], *f.* Fellowship or establishment in a college.

colegio [co-lay'-he-o], *m.* 1. College, school. **Colegio de internos,** boarding school. **Colegio de pago,** fee-paying school. 2. College, the house in which collegians reside. 3. A seminary of education for young ladies. 4. College, a society of men of the same profession. **Colegio de abogados,** bar association. **Colegio electoral.** electoral college.

colegir [co-lay-heer'], *va.* 1. To collect or gather things which are scattered. 2. To collect, to deduce, to infer.

colegislador, ra [co-lay-his-lah-dor', rah], *a.* Colegislative (body).

coleo [co-lay'-o], *m. (Coll.)* V. COLEADURA.

coleóptero, ra [co-lay-op'-tay-ro, rah], *a.* Coleopterous, belonging to the division of insects named coleoptera. -*m. pl.* The coleoptera.

cólera [co'-lay-rah], *f.* 1. Choler, bile. 2. Choler, anger, fury, rage, passion. **Montar en cólera,** to be angry, to be in a passion. **Descargar la cólera en,** to vent one's anger on. -*m.* 3. **Cólera asiática,** Asiatic cholera.

colera [co-lay'-rah], *f.* Ornament for the tail of a horse.

coléricamente [co-lay'-re-cah-men-tay], *adv.* Fumingly, passionately.

colérico, ca [co-lay'-re-co, cah], *a.* 1. Choleric. 2. Passionate, hasty; hotheaded.

coleriforme [co-lay-re-for'-may], *a.* Choleriform.

colerina [co-lay-ree'-nah], *f.* Cholerine, a diarrhoea, sometimes premonitory of cholera.

colesterina [o-les-tay-ree'-nah], *f.* Cholesterol.

colesterol [co-les-tay-role'], *m.* Cholesterol.

coleta [co-lay'-tah], *f.* 1. Pigtail. **Gente de coleta,** bullfighters. **Cortarse la coleta,** to quit the ring, give up bullfighting, 2. *(Coll.)* A short addition to a discourse or writing; postscript. 3. *(Bot.)* Nineleaved coronilla. 4. Nankin, or nankeen.

coletáneo, nea [co-lay-tah'-nay-o, ah], *a. (Obs.)* V. COLACTÁNEO.

coletazo [co-lay-tah'-tho], *m.* 1. Lash, blow with the tail. 2. Sway, swaying movement (de vehículo). **Dar coletazos,** to sway about. 3. *(fig.)* Sting with the tail; unexpected after-effect.

coletero [co-lay-tay'-ro], *m.* One who makes buff doublets and breeches.

coletilla [co-lay-teel'-lyah], *f. dim.* Filler phrase or cliched phrase added at the end of sentences.

coletillo [co-lay-teel'-lyo], *m. dim.* A small doublet of buff or other skins.

coleto [co-lay'-to], *m.* 1. Buff doublet or jacket. 2. *(Coll.)* Body of a man; interior of a person. **Dije para mi coleto, I** said to myself. **Echarse al coleto,** *(Coll.)* to read from cover to cover (libro). **Echarse algo al coleto,** to eat or drink something.

colgadero [col-gah-day'-ro], *m.* Hook to hang things upon.

colgadero, ra [col-gah-day'-ro, rah], *a.* Fit to be hung up.

colgadizo [col-gah-dee'-tho], *m.* 1. Shed, a temporary covering from the weather. 2. Flat roof.

colgadizo, za [col-gah-dee'-tho, thah], *a.* Pendent, suspended.

colgado, da [col-gah'-do, dah], *a.* 1. Suspended. **Dejar a alguno colgado** or **quedarse alguno colgado,** to frustrate one's hopes or desires. **2. Estar colgado,** to have withdrawal pains (drogas). **Quedar colgado,** to get hooked (drogas). -*pp.* of COLGAR.

colgador [col-gah-dor'], *m.* Peel-hanger (imprenta). Hook (gancho). Coat hanger (percha).

colgadura [col-gah-doo'-rah], *f.* Tapestry, hanging or drapery. **Colgadura de cama,** bed furniture. **Colgaduras de papel pintado,** paper hangings.

colgajo [col-gah'-ho], *m.* 1. Tatter or rag hanging from clothes. 2. **Colgajo de uvas,** bunch of grapes hung up to be preserved. -3. *pl.* The fleshy tissues left in some amputations to form the stump.

colgante [col-gahn'-tay], *pa.* Hanging, pending, clinging, **Colgantes,** earrings, trinkets; *(Carib. Cono Sur)* watch chain; *(Arquit.)* Festoon; **colgantes,** fringe.

colgar [col-gar'], *va.* 1. To hang up, to suspend in the air, to flag, to flow, to hover. 2. To adorn with tapestry or hangings. 3. To hang or kill by hanging. -*vn.* 1. To hang from, to be suspended. 2. To be in a state of dependence. **Colgar los habitos,** to doff the cassock. **Ella está siempre colgada de la ventana,** she is always fixed at the window. **Colgar los libros,** to abandon one's studies.

colia [co'-le-ah], *f.* **colias** [co'-le-as], *m.* A small fish resembling a pilchard.

coliblanca [co-le-blahn'-cah], *f. (Zool.)* An eagle of South America.

coliblanco, ca [co-le-blahn'-co, cah], *a.* White-tailed.

colibre, colibrí [co-lee'-bray, co-le-bree'], *m. (Orn.)* Colibri, a beautiful American humming-bird, especially one with a curved beak.

cólica [co'-le-cah], *f.* Colic.

colicano, na [co-le-cah'-no, nah], *a.* Having gray hair in the tail (caballos).

cólico or **dolor cólico** [co'-le-co], *m.* 1. Colic, a condition caused by acute spasmodic abdominal pain. 2. *(Cono Sur)* **energía cólico,** wind power.

colicorto ta [co-le-cor'-to, tah], *a.* Short-tailed.

colicuación [co-le-coo-ah-the-on'], *f.* Colliquation, the act of melting or dissolving.

colicuante [co-le-coo-ahn'-tay], *pa.* Colliquant, colliquative.

colicuar [co-le-coo-ar'], *va.* To colliquate, to melt, to dissolve.-*vr.* To colliquate, to become liquid.

colicuativo, va [co-le-coo-ah-tee'-vo, vah], *a.* Colliquative.

colicuecer [co-le-coo-ay-therr'], *va.* To fuse or melt.

coliculoso, sa [co-le-coo-lo'-so, sah], *a. (Bot.)* Presenting knobs, rounded prominences in a small space.

colidir [co-le-deer'], *va. (Obs.)* To collide, to dash or knock together.

colifato [co-le-fah'-to], *(Cono Sur)* 1. *a.* Nuts. 2. *m.* Madman, nutcase.

colifero, ra [co-lee'-fay-ro, rah], *a. (Bot.)* Cauliferous: said of the ovary of plants when it has a neck.

coliflor [co-le-flor'], *f. (Bot.)* Cauliflower. -*pl.* Cauliflower excrescences, venereal warts.

coligación [co-le-gah-the-on'], *f.* 1. Colligation, the binding of things together. 2. Connection of one thing with another. 3. Union, alliance.

coligado, da [co-le-gah'-do; dah], *m. & f.* Leaguer, covenanter. *-a.* A greed and associated for some purpose. *-pp.* of COLIGARSE.

coligadura [co-le-gah-doo'-rah], *f.* Combining or connecting of one thing with another.

coligamiento [co-le-gah-me-en'-to], *m. V.* COLIGACIÓN,

coligancia [co-le-gahn'-the-ah], *f.* Connection, relation, correspondence of one thing with another.

coligarse [co-le-gar'-say], *vr.* To colligate, to colleague, to unite; to join together. *(Yo colijo, yo colija; él colijió, from* Colegir. *V.* PEDIR.).

colilla [co-leel'-lyah], *f.* 1. *(dim.)* A small tail. 2. Train of a gown. 3. Stub of a cigar or cigarette. **Ser una colilla,** to be past it, to be all washed up.

colimba [co-leem'-bah], *(Cono Sur)* 1. *m.* Conscript. 2. *f.* Military service; **hacer la colimba,** to do military service.

colimbo [co-leem'-bo], *m.* Diver.

colimense, colimeño, *m. & f. V.* COLIMOTE.

colimote [co-le-mo'-tay], *m. & f.* Of Colima province.

colín [co-leen'], *m. (Carib.)* Machete, cane knife.

colina [co-lee'-nah], *f.* 1. Hill, hillock, hummock. 2. Seed of cabbage. 3. *V.* COLINO.

colinabo [co-le-nah'-bo], *m. (Bot.)* Turnip.

colindante [co-lin-dahn'-tay], *a.* Contiguous, adjacent.

colindar [co-lin-dar'], *vn.* To be contiguous, to be adjacent.

colino [co-lee'-no], *m.* Small cabbage not transplanted.

colinsia [co-leen'-se-ah], *f.* Collinsia, a garden plant of the figwort family, native of California.

colirio [co-lee'-re-o], *m.* Collyrium, a wash for the eyes.

colirrojo [cor-ro'-ho], *m.* Redstart.

colís [co-lees'], *m. (And.)* Machete, cane knife.

colisa [co-lee'-sah], *f.* A swivel gun.

coliseo [co-le-say'-o], *m.* Theater, opera-house, playhouse, Coliseum.

colisión [co-le-se-on'], *f.* 1. Collision, crush, clash. 2. A gall, fretting, chafing. 3. Opposition, clash of ideas.

colisionar [co-le-se-o-nar'], *vn.* To collide. **Colisionar con,** to collide with.

colista [co-lees'tah], 1. *m.* Bottom club (liga). 2. *m. & f.* Person who stands in line.

colitea [co-le-tay'-ah], *f. (Bot.)* Judas tree.

colitigante [co-le-te-gahn'-tay], *m.* One who carries on a lawsuit with another.

colitis [co-le'-tes], *f.* Colitis.

colla [col-lyah], *f.* 1. Collet, a piece of ancient armor for the neck. 2. Continuous squalls preceding the monsoons, at times followed by a hurricane. 3. Channel of an auger. 4. Last oakum placed in a seam.

collado [col-lyah'-do], *m.* Hill, fell, a small eminence.

collage [col-lya'-hay], *m.* Collage (arte).

collar [col-lyar'], *m.* 1. Necklace. 2. Chain or cord from which hang certain insignia of honor. 3. Collar, collet. 4. **Collar de un estay,** *(Naut.)* collar of a stay. 5. *(Mech.)* Collar, ring. 6. **Collar de fuerza,** strangle-hold.

collarcito [col-lyar-thee'-to], *m. dim.* A small necklace, string of beads, or chain.

collarín [col-lyah-reen'], *m.* 1. A black collar, edged with white, worn by the Roman Catholic clergy. *V.* ALZACUELLO. 2. Collar of a coat. 3. Surgical collar.

collarino [col-lyah-ree'-no], *m. (Arch.)* Ring or list at the top and bottom of the shaft of a column; a half round, torus. *V.* ASTRÁGALO.

collazo [col-lyah'-tho], *m.* Ploughman who tills the ground for a master, for which he gets some small tenement or ground to till for himself. **Collazos,** poles on which barill-plants are carried to the pit to be burnt.

colleja [col-lyay'-hah], *f.* 1. *(Bot.)* Lamb's-lettuce, or corn-salad. **Collejas,** slender nerves found in a sheep's neck. 2. Dandelion.

collera [col-lyay'-rah], *f.* 1. Collar, breastharness of leather stuffed with hay or straw for draught cattle. 2. Horse collar. 3. Chain gang. 4. Pair (de animales). 5. *(Arg.)* Cufflinks.

collerón [col-lyay-rone'], *m.* Harness collar, hame.

colleta [col-lyay'-tah], *f. (Bot. Prov.)* A small kind of cabbage.

collín [col-lyeen'], *m. (CAm.)* Cane Knife.

collón [col-lyone'], *m. (Coll.)* Coward, a poltroon, mean fellow.

collonada [col-lyo-nah'-dah], *f.* Cowardliness.

collonería [col-lyo-nay-ree'-ah], *f.* 1. Cowardice. 2. *(Coll. Vul.)* Nonsense.

colmadamente [col-mah-dah-men-tay], *adv.* Abundantly, plentifully.

colmado, da [col-mah'-do, dah], *a.* Filled, heaped. **Una cucharada colmada,** one heaped spoonful. **Una tarde colada de incidentes,** an afternoon full of incidents. *-pp.* of COLMAR. *-m.* Cheap seafood restaurant.

colmar [col-mar'], *va.* 1. To heap up to fill to the brim. 2. To fulfil, to make up. *V.* LLENAR. 3. *(Met.)* To confer great favors. **Colmar a uno de honores,** to shower honors upon somebody. **Colmar a uno de alabanzas,** to heap praises on somebody. **Colmar a uno de favores,** to lavish favors on somebody.

colmataje [col-ma-tah'-hay], *m.* A heaping up, brimming.

colmena [col-may'-nah], *f.* Beehive. **Tener la casa como una colmena,** to have one's house well stocked with provisions.

colmenar [col-may-nar'], *m.* Apiary.

colmenero, ra [col-may-nay'-ro], *m.f.* Bee-keeper, bee-master. **Oso colmenero,** a bear who eats the honey of bee-hives.

colmenilla [col-may-neel'-lyah], *f.* Morel or moril, a kind of mushroom.

colmillada [col-meel-lyah'-dah], *f.* An injury made by an eye tooth.

colmillazo [col-meel-lyah'-tho], *m.* 1. *(aug.)* A large eye tooth. 2. A wound made by an eye tooth or fang.

colmillo [col-meel'-lyo], *m.* 1. Eye tooth, canine-tooth. 2. Fang, the long tusk of a boar or other animal. **Mostrar los colmillos,** *(Met.)* to show spirit and resolution. **Tener colmillos,** *(Mex.)* to be long in the tooth. **Tener el colmillo torcido,** to be an old fox.

colmilludo, da [col-meel-lyoo'-do, dah], *a.* 1. Having eye teeth fangs, or tusks (personas, animales). 2. Sagacious, quick-sighted, not easily imposed upon.

colmo [col'-mo], *m.* 1. Heap, that which rises above the brim of a measure of grain, flour, etc. 2. Complement, finishing, completion, crown. 3. Over-measure, full; height. **Ella llegó al colmo de sus deseos,** she attained the summit of her wishes. **El colmo de la elegancia,** the height of elegance. **El colmo de lo absurdo,** the height of absurdity. **Para colmo de desgracias,** to make matters worse. **Sería el colmo si…,** it would be the last straw if…

colmo, ma [col'-mo, mah], *a. V.* COLMADO.

colo [co'-lo], *m.* A coleopterous, tetramerous, curculionid insect of South America.

colobo [co-lo'-bo], *m.* 1. A kind of linen tunic worn by Egyptian monks. 2. *(Zool.)* Colobus, an African monkey, having the thumb absent or rudimentary.

coloboma [co-lo-bo'-mah], *m.* Coloboma, defect of substance; specifically, of the iris of the eye.

colocación [co-lo-cah-the-on'], *f.* 1. Employment, place, office. **No encuentro colocación,** I can't find a job. 2. Arrangement of the parts of a building, speech, etc., collocation, location. 3. Position, situation.

colocado [co-lo-cah'-do], *a.* **Apostar para colocado,** to back (a horse) for a place; **estar colocado,** to be high (on drugs).

colocar [co-lo-car'], *va.* 1. To arrange, to put in due place or order, to place. **Colocar la quilla de un buque,** to lay down a ship. **Colocar un satélite en órbita,** to put a satellite in orbit. 2. To place, to put in any place, rank, condition, or office, to provide one with a place or employment. 3. To collocate, to locate to lay. 4. **Colocar una responsabilidad a uno,** to saddle somebody with a responsibility. 5. To nick, to arrest. -*vr.* 1. To place oneself, to station oneself; *(Dep.)* to get a place. **El equipo se ha colocado en quinto lugar,** the team has climbed to fifth position. 2. To get a job.

colocasia [co-lo-cah'-se-ah], *f. (Bot.)* The Egyptian bean, a plant with thick, tuberous rootstocks, large leaves, and rose-colored blossoms.

colocho [co-lo'-cho], *(CAm.)* 1. *a.* Curly-haired. 2. *m. pl.* Curls (rizos); wood shavings.

colocutor, ra [co-lo-coo-tor', rah], *m. & f.* He who holds coloquial intercourse with another; collocutor.

colodión [co-lo-de-on'], *m.* Collodion.

colodra [co-lo'-drah], *f.* 1. Milkpail, a kit; a pailful. 2. A wooden can with which wine is measured and retailed. 3. A wooden can with a handle, used for drinking. 4. A horn with a cork bottom, used as a tumbler. **Ser una colodra,** *(Coll.)* to be a toper or tippler. 5. *(Prov. Sant.)* A wooden case tied about the waist, in which the mower carries a whetstone.

colodrazgo [co-lo-drath'-go], *m.* Tax or excise on wine sold in small quantities.

colodrillo [co-lo-dreel'-lyo], *m.* Occiput, hind part of the head.

colodro [co-lo'-dro], *m.* 1. A wooden shoe. 2. *(Prov.)* Wine measure.

colofón [co-lo-fone'], *m.* Colophon, an inscription or device put at the end of a book, giving the printer''s name and date and place of printing.

colofonia [co-lo-fo-nee-ah], *f.* Colophony, a kind of resin.

colofonita [co-lo-fo-nee'-tah], *f.* A garnet of a light-green or rosy-red color, the least fusible of all garnets.

coloide [co-lo'-e-day], *m.* Colloid.

Colombia [co-lom'-be-ah], *f.* Colombia.

colombiano, na [co-lom-be-ah'-no, nah], *a.* Columbian, of Colombia.

colombicultura [co-lom-bee-cool-too'-rah], *f.* Pigeon-breeding.

colombino, na [co-lom-bee'-no, nah], *a.* Pertaining to Columbus or his family.

colombofilia [co-lom-bo-fee'-lee-ah], *f.* Pigeon-fancying.

colombófilo, la [co-lom-bo'-fe-lo], *m. & f.* Pigeon-fancier.

colombroño [co-lom-bro'-nyo], *m.* Namesake. *V.* TOCAYO.

colon [co'-lone], *m.* 1. Colon (:) (dos puntos). Semicolon (;) (punto y coma). 2. Colon, the largest of the intestines. 3. *(Gram.)* Principal part or member of a period.

colón [co-lone'], *m.* Colon (unit of currency of Costa Rica and El Salvador).

colonche [co-lone'-chay], *m.* An intoxicating drink made in Mexico from the sap of the red prickly pear (catus) and sugar.

colonia [co-lo'-ne-ah], *f.* 1. Colony. **Colonia escolar,** summer camp for school-children. **Colonia obrera,** working-class. **Colonia penal,** penal settlement. **Colonia veraniega,** holiday camp. 2. Colony, a plantation. 3. *(Mex.)* Each subdivision in which cities are divided. **Colonia residencial,** residential district.

colonia [co-lo'-ne-ah], *f.* Eau-de-Cologne.

coloniaje [co-lo-ne-ah'-hay], *m. (LAm.)* Colonial period; system of colonial government; slavery, slave status.

colonial [co-lo-ne-ahl'], *a.* Colonial.

colonialismo [co-lo-ne-ah-lees'-mo], *m.* Colonialism.

colonialista [co-lo-ne-ah-lees'-tah], *a. & m. & f.* Colonialist.

colonización [co-lo-ne-thah-the-on'], *f.* Colonization, the making of a colony.

colonizador, ra [co-lo-ne-tha-dor'], *m. & f.* Colonist, colonizer. -*a.* Colonizing.

colonizar [co-lo-ne-thar'], *va.* To colonize, form a settlement.

colono [co-lo'-no], *m.* 1. Colonist, planter. 2. Laborer, who cultivates a piece of ground and lives on it. 3. A farmer.

coloqueta [co-lo-kay'-tah], *f.* 1. Arrest. 2. Police sweep (redada).

coloquial [co-lo-ke-al'], *a.* Colloquial, familiar.

coloquio [co-lo'-ke-o], *m.* Discussion, colloquy, chat, conversation, talk.

color [co-lor'], *m.* 1: Color, hue, dye. 2. Rouge. 3. *(Met.)* Color, pretext, pretence, false show or appearance. 4. Color, the tint of the painter. -*pl.* 1. Color, the freshness or appearance of blood in the face. 2. *(Pict.)* Color, or mixture of paint. **Color lleno** or **cargado,** a deep color. **Color vivo,** a bright color. **Mudar de colores,** *(Met.)* to change color. **Sacarle los colores a una persona,** *(Met.)* to make a person blush. **Gente de color,** colored people. **Zapatos de color,** brown shoes. **Color muerto,** dull color. **Verlo todo color de rosa,** to see everything through rose-colored spectacles. 5. **Colores,** colors. **Los colores nacionales,** the national colors.

coloración [co-lo-rah-the-on'], *f.* 1. Coloring, coloration. 2. Blush. **Coloración protectora,** protective coloring, mimetism.

coloradamente [co-lo-rah-dah-men'-tay], *adv.* Speciously, under a pretext.

colorado, da [co-lo-rah'-do, dah], *a.* 1. Ruddy, florid, red. 2. Indelicate, smutty (historias, frases). 3. Colored, specious. **Ponerse colorado,** to blush with shame. **Poner a alguno colorado,** to put one to the blush. -*pp.* of COLORAR. -*m.* 1. Bread, money. 2. *(Carib.)* Scarlet fever. 3. **Los Colorados,** Uruguayan political party.

coloradote [co-lo-rah-do'-tay], *a.* Red-faced, ruddy.

coloramiento [co-lo-rah-me-en'-to], *m. V.* ENCENDIMIENTO.

colorante [co-lo-rahn'tay], *m.* Dye, coloring, -*a.* Dyeing, coloring. **Materia colorante,** dyeing matter, coloring substance.

colorar [co-lo.rar'], *va.* 1. To dye, to color. 2. To make plausible. *vn.* To blush with shame. -*vr.* To be ashamed.

colorativo, va [co-lo-rah-tee'-vo, vah], *a.* Colorific, tingeing.

colorear [co-lo-ray-ar'], *va.* To color, to make plausible, to palliate, to excuse. -*vn.* To redden, to grow red.

colorete [co-lo-ray'-tay], *m.* Rouge.

colorido [co-lo-ree'-do], *m.* 1. Coloring or color. 2. Pretext, pretence.

colorido, da [co-lo-ree'-do, dah], *a.* Colorate. -*pp.* of COLORIR.

colorín [co-lo-reen'], *m.* 1. *(Orn.)* Linnet. 2. Bright, vivid color. **Gustar de colorines,** to like showy colors. **Colorín, colorado, este cuento se ha acabado,** traditional ending of children's stories. 3. *(Orn.)* Goldfinch. 4. *(Med.)* Measles. 5. Magazine of love stories.

colorir [co-lo-reer'], *va.* 1. To color, to mark with some hue or dye. 2. *V.* COLOREAR.

colorista [co-lo-rees'-tah], *m.* Colorist.

colosal [co-lo-sahl'], *a.* Colossal, giant, huge.

coloso [co-lo'-so], *m.* 1. Colossus, a statue of enormous magnitude. 2. *(Cono Sur)* Trailer.

colpa [col'-pah], *f.* A whitish sort of copperas, a flux.

colpez [col-peth'], *f.* Isinglass; fish glue.

cólquico [cole''-ke-co], *m.* Colchicum meadow saffron; used in medicine as a remedy for gout.

coludir [co-loo-deer'], *va.* 1. To collude. 2. To collide.

columbio [co-loom'-be-o], *m. (Min.)* Columbium, a metal.

columbino, na [co-loom-bee'-no, nah], *a.* Dovelike, innocent, candid.

columbo [co-loom'-bo], *m.* Columbo root. Radix cocculi palmati.

columbrar [co-loom-brar'], *va.* 1. To discern at a distance, to see far off. 2. *(Met.)* To pursue or trace a thing by conjectures.

columelar [co-loo-may-lar'], *m.* Incisor. *V.* CORTADORES.

columna [co-loom'-nah], *f.* 1. Column, a round pillar. **Columna ática, compuesta, corintia, dórica, jónica,** etc. Attic Composite, Corinthian, Doric, Ionic, etc., column. 2. Column of air. 3. **Columna fosfórica,** lighthouse, built on a rock. **Columna hueca,** a hollow column, in which is a spiral staircase. 4. *(Met.)* Supporter or maintainer, **La justicia, la paz y la religión son las columnas del estado,** justice, peace, and religion are the supporters of the state. 5. Column, a long file of troops. 6. Column, part of a page. 7. *(Anat.)* **Columna vertebral,** spine.

columnario, ria [co-loom-nah'-re-o, ah], *a.* Columnar: applied to the money coined in Spanish America, with the impressions of two columns. -*m. & f. (Obs.) V.* COLUMNATA.

columnata [co-loom-nah'-tah], *f.* Colonnade.

columnista [co-loom-nees'-tah], *m. & f.* Columnist.

columpiar [co-loom-pe-ar'], *va.* To swing.-*vr.* 1. To swing, to fly forward or backward on a rope. 2. *(Met.)* To waddle, to shake in walking from side to side.

columpio [co-loom'-pe-o], *m.* A swing. **Columpio basculante,** seesaw.

colurión [co-loo-re-on'], *m. (Orn.)* Lesser butcher-bird, flusher.

coluro [co-loo'-ro], *m. (Astr.)* Colure, one of the two great circles of the celestial sphere which pass from the pole through the equinoxes and solstices respectively.

colusión [co-loo-se-on'], *f.* 1. Collusion, deceitful agreement. 2. Shock, collision.

colusoriamente [co-loo-so-re-ah-men'-tay], *adv.* Collusively, fraudulently.

colusorio, ria [co-loo-so'-re-o, ah], *a.* Collusory, collusive.

colza [cole'-thah], *f.* Colza, summer rape, a variety of turnip.

colzal [col-thahl'], *f.* Colewort seed.

coma [co'-mah], *f.* 1. Comma (,). 2. Each of the parts into which a tone divided. 3. **Sin faltar una coma,** or **sin faltar punto ni coma,** without a title being wanting in the account or narrative.

coma [co'-mah], *m.* Coma, profound insensibility.

comadre [co-mah'-dray], *f.* 1. Midwife (partera). 2. The name by which the godfather and godmother address the mother of their godson or daughter, and by which she also always addresses the godmother. 3. *(Coll.)* A gossip. **Un grupo de comadres,** a group of gossips. 4. Pansy (maricón). 5. Neighbor (vecina).

comadrear [co-mah-dray-ar'], *vn.* To gossip, to tattle.

comadreja [co-mah-dray'-hah], *f.* Weasel. **Comadreja marina,** weaselblenny.

comadreo [co-mah-dray'-o], *m.* **comadrería** [co-mah-dray-ree'-ah], *f.* Gossip, gossiping, chattering.

comadrero, ra [co-mah-dray'-ro, rah], *a.* Gossiping from house to house.

comadrón [co-mah-drone'], *m.* Man-midwife, accoucheur.

comadrona [co-mah-dro'-nah], *f.* Midwife.

comal [co-mahl'], *m. (Mex.)* A flat earthen ware pan for cooking corn cake.

comalía, comalición [co-mah-lee'-ah, co-man-le-the-on'], *f.* An epizootic disease, not contagious, among the wool-bearing animals, characterized by (chronic) dropsy.

comandado, da, *a. (Mil.)* Officered. -*pp.* of COMANDAR.

comandamiento [co-man-dah-me-en'-to], *m. (Obs.) V.* MANDO and MANDAMIENTO.

comandancia [co-man-dahn'-the-ah], *f.* 1. Command, the office of a commander. 2. The province or district of a commander. **Comandancia militar,** a military command. **Comandancia general de Marina,** the High Court of Admiralty. 3. Commander's headquarter.

comandanta [co-mahn-dah'-tah], *f.* 1. *(Mil.)* Major (woman); *(Hist.)* Mayor's wife. 2. *(Naut.)* Flagship.

comandante [co-man-dahn'-tay], *m.* Commander, a chief, a commandant, a leader. **Commandante en Jefe,** commander-in-Chief.

comandar [co-man-dar'], *va.* 1. To command, to govern. 2. *(Obs.)* To commend, to recommend.

comandita [co-man-dee'-tah], *f.* A silent partnership.

comanditario [co-man-de-tah'-re-o], *m.* A sleeping partner.

comando [co-mahn'-do], *m.* 1. Command. 2. *(Mil.)* Commando. **Comando suicida,** suicide squad.

comarca [co-mar'-cah], *f.* 1. Territory, district. 2. Border, boundary, limit.

comarcal [co-mar-cahl'], *a.* Local, regional.

comarcano, na [co-mar-cah'-no, nah], *a.* Neighboring, near, bordering upon.

comarcar [co-mar-car'], *va.* To plant trees in a straight line, so as to form paths. -*vn.* To border, to confine upon; to be on the borders.

comato ta [co-mah'-to, tah], *a.* **Cometa comato,** hairy or comate comet.

comatoso, sa [co-ma-to'-so, sah], *a.* Comatose, in a profound stupor.

comaya [co-mah'-yah], *f.* 1. A large basket, a pannier. 2. *(Orn.)* The white owl, or barn owl. *V.* ZUMAYA.

comba [com'-bah], *f.* 1. Curvature or inflexion of timber when warped, or iron when bent; a curve, a bend; convexity. 2. The game of jumping or skipping rope. 3. The skipping rope itself. **Hacer combas,** to bend and twist the body from one side to the other. 4. **No pierde comba,** he doesn't miss a trick.

combadura [com-bah-doo'-rah], *f.* Curvature, convexity, warping, bending.

combar [com-bar'], *va.* To bend, to curve. -*vr.* To warp, to become crooked, to jut.

combate [com-bah'-tay], *m.* 1. Combat, conflict, engagement, fray, fight. **Combate naval,** naval battle. **Estar fuera de combate,** to be out of action. 2. Agitation of the mind.

combatidor [com-bah-te-dor'], *m.* Combatant, champion.

combatiente [com-bah-te-en'-tay], *m. pa.* Combatant, fighter.

combatir [com-bah-teer'], *va. & vn.* 1. To combat, to fight. 2. To contend, to contest, to meet or meet with. 3. To attack, to invade. 4. To contradict, conflict with. 5. *(Met.)* To agitate the mind, to rouse the passions. **Combatir a la retreta,** *(Naut.)* To keep up a running fight.

combatividad [com-ba-te-ve-dahd'], *f.* *(Phren.)* Combativeness; agressiveness.

combativo [com-bah-te-vo], *a.* Full of fight, spirited; aggressive, combative.

combazo [com-bah-tho], *m. (Cono Sur)* punch.

combeneficiado [com-bay-nay-fe-the-ah-do], *m.* Prebendary of the same church as another.

combés [com-bess'], *m. (Naut.)* Waist of a ship.

combi [com'-be], *f.* 1. Fiddle (ardid), wangle. 2. Slip (prenda).

combinable [com-be-nah'-blay], *a.* Combinable.

combinación [com-be-nah-the-on'], *f.* 1. Combination. 2. Aggregate of several words which begin with the same syllable. 3. Concurrence. 4. *(Chem.)* A compound; cocktail (bebida). 5. Arrangement, set-up, scheme; plan (proyecto). 6. *(Ferro. etc.)* Connection. **Hacer combinación con,** to connect with.

combinado [com-be-nah'-do], *m.* Cocktail.

combinar [com-be-ner'], *va.* 1. To combine, to join, to unite, to connect. 2. To compare. -*vr.* To combine; to get together, to join together.

combinatorio, ria [com-be-nah-to'-re-o, ah], *a.* Combining, uniting.

combo, ba [com'-bo, bah], *a.* Bent, crooked, warped.

combo [com'-bo], *m.* 1. Stand or frame for casks. 2. *(LAm.)* Sledge-hammer (martillo). 3. *(And. Cono Sur)* slap; punch (puñetazo).

combustibilidad [com-boos-te-be-le-dahd'], *f.* Combustibility.

combustible [com-boos-tee'-blay], *a.* Combustible.

combustible [com-boos-tee'-blay], *m.* 1. Combustible, a combustible material. 2. Fuel. **Combustible de alta potencia,** exotic fuel.

combustion [com-boos-te-on'], *f.* Combustion, burning.

comebolas [co-may-bo'-lahs], *m. (Carib.)* Simple soul, gullible individual.

comedero [co-may-day'-ro], *m.* 1. Dining-room. 2. A feeding trough for fowls and other animals. 3. *(Carib.)* Brothel (prostíbulo). 4. *(And.)* Haunt, hang-out (sitio favorito).

comedero, ra [co-may-day'-ro, rah], *a.* Eatable, edible.

comedia [co-may'-de-ah], *f.* Comedy. **Es una comedia,** it is a complete farce: applied to ridiculous speeches or actions. **Comedia de enredo,** that whose merit consists principally in the ingenuity and complexity of the plot. **Hacer la comedia,** to make believe, to pretend.

comedianta [co-may-de-ahn'-tah], *f. V.* ACTRIZ. Comedienne.

comediante [co-may-de-ahn'-tay], *m.* Player; actor, comedian. **Comediante de la lengua,** strolling player; hypocrite, fraud.

comediar [co-may-de-ar'], *va.* 1. To divide into equal shares. 2. To regulate, to direct.

comédico, ca [co-may'-de-co, cah], *a.* Comical. *V.* CÓMICO.

comedidamente [co-may-de-dah-men'-tay], *adv.* Gently, courteously, moderately.

comedido, da [co-may-dee'-do, dah], *a.* 1. Civil, polite, gentle, courteous. 2. Kind, obsequious, obliging.-*pp.* of COMEDIRSE.

comedimiento [co-may-de-me-en'-to], *m.* 1. Civility, politeness, urbanity, moderation. 2. Kindness, obsequiousness.

comedio [co-may'-de-o], *m.* 1. Middle of a kingdom or place. 2. Intermediate time between epochs.

comediógrafo, fa [co-may-de-o'-grah-fo], *m. & f.* Playwright.

comedión [co-may-de-on'], *m.* A poor or long and tedious comedy.

comedirse [co-may-deer'-say], *vr.* 1. To govern oneself, to regulate one's conduct, to be civil, obliging, kind. 2. *(LAm.)* **Comedirse a,** to offer to.

comedón [co-may-done'], *m.* Blackhead.

comedor, ra [co-may-dor', rah], *m. & f.* 1. Eater (personas). 2. *m.* Dining-room.

comefuego [co-may foo-ay'-go], *m.* Fire-eater (circo).

comegente [co-may-hayn-tay], *m. (And. Carib.)* Glutton.

comején [co-may-hen'], *m.* 1. Kind of termite or white ant, very destructive to houses and their contents in tropical America. 2. A sort of woodborer which pierces pipe-staves. 3. *(And.)* Nagging worry (preocupación). 4. *(And.)* Glutton.

comelina [co-may-lee'-nah], *f. (Bot.)* Commelina, a large genus of herbs of the spiderwort family.

comelitona [co-may-le-to'-nah], *f. (Mex.) V.* COMILONA.

comelón [co-may-lone'], *a. (LAm.) V.* COMILON.

comendable [co-men-dah'-blay], *a.* Commendable. *V.* RECOMENDABLE.

comendador [co-men-dah-dor'], *m.* 1. Knight commander of a military order. 2. Prelate or prefect of religious houses.

comendadora [co-men-dah-do'-rah], *f.* The superior of a nunnery of a military order, and also of other nunneries.

comendamiento [co-men-dah-me-en'-to], *m. V.* ENCOMIENDA and MANDAMIENTO.

comendar [co-men-dar'], *va. V.* RECOMENDAR.

comendatario [co-men-dah-tah'-re-o], *m.* Commendator, commendatory, a secular clergyman who enjoys a benefice belonging to a military order.

comendatorio, ria [co-men-dah-to'-re-o, ah], *a.* Relating to letters of introduction or recommendation.

comensal [co-men-sahl'], *com.* Commensal, one that eats at the same table. *V.* CONMENSAL. -*m. & f.* 1. Fellow guest. **Habrá 13 comensales,** there will be 13 to dinner. **Me lo dijo mi comensal,** the man sitting next to me at dinner told me so.

comensalía [co-men-sah-lee'-ah], *f.* Fellowship of house and table.

comentador, ra [co-men-tah-dor', rah], *m. & f.* 1. Commentator, expositor, annotator, expounder, glosser. 2. Inventor of falsehoods.

comentar [co-mentar'], *va.* To comment, to explain, to expound, to gloss.

comentario [co-men-tah'-re-o], *m.* 1. A commentary. 2. Commentary, an historical work written in a familiar manner. 3.

Comment, remark, observation. **Y ahora sin más comentario…,** and now without further comment… **4. Comentarios,** gossip, talk. **Dar lugar a comentarios,** to cause gossip.

comentarista [co-men-tah-rees'-tah], *m. & f.* Commentator. **Comentarista deportivo,** sports commentator.

comento [co-men'-to], *m.* Comment, exposition, or explanation of some writing or circumstance.

comenzar [co-men-thar'], *va.vn.* To commence, to start, to begin (empezar). **Comenzar a hacer algo,** to begin to do something. **Comenzar por,** to begin with.

comer [co-merr'], *va.* 1. To eat, to chew or swallow something, to feed. 2. To dine. 3. *(Coll.)* To be in possession of an income. **Él se come diez mil dólares de renta,** he spends ten thousand dollars a year. 4. To run through a fortune. 5. To have an itching all over one's body. 6. *vr.* To suppress some letter or syllable in the pronunciation of words. **Se lo comió todo,** he ate it all up. **Se come las palabras,** he mumbles. **Tiene muchos nombres y se come el García,** she has lots of names and drops the García. 7. *(Met.)* To corrode, to consume. 8. **Comerse una dama;** to take a queen in the game of chess. **Comerse un peón,** to take a pawn in the same game. **Comerse de risa,** to refrain from laughing. **Comerse unos a otros** *(Met.),* to be constantly at drawn daggers. **Comerse a uno con los ojos,** to look daggers at any one. **¿En qué bodegón hemos comido juntos ?** where have we eaten together? (a rebuke for undue familiarity). **Tener que comer,** to have a competency to live upon. **Ganar de comer,** to earn a livelihood. 9. *(fig.)* **Le come la envidia,** she is eaten up with envy. -*vn.* 1. To eat; (comer de), to eat, to partake. **Comer como una vaca,** to eat like a horse. 2. *(fig.)* **El mismo que come y viste,** the very same. **Este pescado es de buen comer,** this fish is good eating. **No tienen qué comer,** they don't have enough to live on.

comer [co-merr'], *m. (Obs.) V.* COMIDA.

comerciable [co-mer-the-ah'-blay], *a.* Commercial, trading, **Barrio comercial,** business quarter. **Centro comercial,** business center.

comercial [co-mer-the-ahl'], *a.* Commercial, trading. **Barrio comercial,** business quarter. **Centro comercial,** business center.

comercialización [co-mer-the-ah-le-tha-the-on'], *f.* 1. Commercialization. 2. Marketing.

comercializar [co-mer-the-ah-le-thar'], *va.* 1. To commercialize. 2. To market.

comercialmente [co-mer-te-al-men'-tay], *adv.* Commercially.

comerciante [co-mer-the-ahn'-tay], *m. pa.* Trader, merchant, trafficker.

comerciar [co-mer-the-ar'], *va. f.* To trade, to traffic. 2. *(Met.)* To commerce, to have intercourse with (personas, lugares).

comercio [co-merr'-the-o], *m.* 1. Trade, commerce, traffic; mart. **Comercio de,** trade in. **El comercio español,** Spanish trade. **Comercio exterior,** foreign trade. **Comercio de exportación,** export trade. 2. Communication, intercourse. 3. An unlawful connection between the sexes. 4. Body or company of merchants. 5. The most frequented place in large towns. 6. A kind of card game.

comestible [co-mes-tee'-blay], *a.* Eatable, edible. **Comestibles,** *m. pl.* Provisions, groceries. **Tienda de comestibles,** grocery store.

cometa [co-may'-tah], *m.* 1. Comet. **Cometa comado or crinito,** hairy comet. -*f.* 2. Kite, a plaything for boys. 3. Kind of card game in which the nine of diamonds is called **cometa.** 4. *(Her.)* Allegorical figure in form of a star. 5. *(Zool.)* A longicorn beetle of Brazil.

cometario, ia [co-may-tah'-re-o, ah], *a.* Relating to comets, cometary.

cometedor [co-may-tay-dor'], *m.* 1. Offender, a criminal. 2. Assaulter. *V.* ACOMETEDOR.

cometer [co-may-terr'], *va.* 1. To commit, to charge, to entrust. 2. To undertake, to attempt. 3. To attack, to assault. 4. To commit some criminal act or error. 5. *(Gram.)* To use tropes and figures. 6. *(Com.)* To order. -*vr.* 1. To expose oneself.

2. To take something to one's charge. 3 To commit oneself, to make a mistake (equivocación).

cometido [co-may-tee'-do], *m.* Commission, charge, trust.

cometografía [co-may-to-grah'-fee-ah], *f.* Cometography.

comezón [co-may-thone'], *f.* 1. Itch or itching. **Siento comezón en el brazo,** my arm itches. 2. *(Met.)* The anxiety or trouble of mind produced by a longing desire.

comible [co-me'-blay], *a.* Edible, fit to eat.

cómicamente [co'-me-cah-men-tay], *adv.* Comically.

comic [co'-meec], *m.* **comics** *pl.* Comic.

cómica [co'-me-cah], *f.* Actress; comedian (comediante).

comicastro [co-me-cahs-tro], *m.* Ham, third-rate actor (actor).

comicial [co-me-the-ahl'], *a.* Pertaining to the Roman comitia; comitial.

comicidad [co-me-the-dahd'], *f.* Humor, comedy, comicalness.

comicios [co-mee'-the-ose], *m. pl.* 1. Comitia, Roman assembly. 2. Government elections, voting.

cómico, ca [co'-me-co, cah], *a.* 1. Comic, comical, relating to the stage. 2. Comic, comical, ludicrous, funny, mock.

cómico, *m.* **cómica.** *f.* [co'-me-co, cah] 1. Player, actor, comedian. *V.* COMEDIANTE. 2. *(Obs.)* Comedian, a writer of comedies.

comida [co-mee'-dah], *f.* 1. Eating, food, dressed victuals. 2. Dinner; fare, feed. 3. The board. **Comida y alojamiento,** board and lodging. **Hacer una buena comida,** to make a good meal. **Comida rápida,** fast food. **Bendecir la comida,** to say grace.

comidilla [co-me-deel'-lyah], *f.* 1. *(dim.)* A slight repast. 2. Peculiar pleasure afforded by something which strikes our fancy. 3. **Ser la comidilla de la ciudad,** to be the talk of the town.

comido, da [co-mee'-do, dah], *a.* Satiate, full to satiety. **Comido por servido,** meat for work signifying the small value of any employ. *-pp.* of COMER. *(Yo me comido, él se comidió,* from *Comedirse. V.* PEDIR.)

comience [co-me-ayn'-thay], *m. (And.) V.* COMIENZO.

comienzo [co-me-en'-tho], *m.* Origin, beginning, initiation. **Al comienzo,** from the beginning. **En los comienzos de este siglo,** at the beginning of this century. *(Yo comienzo, yo comience,* from *Comenzar. V.* ACERTAR.)

comilitón [co-me-le-tone'], *m.* Parasite, sponger. *V.* CON-MILITÓN.

comilitona, comilona [co-me-le-to'-nah, co-me-lo'-nah], *f. (Coll.)* A splendid and plentiful repast.

comilón, na [co-me-lone', nah], *m. & f.* A great eater, a glutton.

comilla [co-meel'-lyah], *f. dim.* fr. COMA. *-pl.* Quotation marks (" "). Also guiding marks (,,).

cominillo [co-me-neel'-lyo], *m.* Darnel. *V.* JOYO.

comino [co-mee'-no], *m. (Bot.)* Cumin plant, cuminseed. **Cominos,** cuminseed. **No vale** or **no monta un comino,** it is not worth tuppence. **No se me da un comino.** *(Coll.)* It's not worth a damn. **No me importa un comino,** I don't care two hoots.

comisar [co-me-sar'], *va.* To confiscate (confiscar), to declare a thing confiscated; to sequestrate (secuestrar), to attach.

comisaría [co-me-sah-ree'-ah], *f.* **comisariato,** *m.* Commissaryship, commissariat, police station; sheriff's office.

comisario [co-me-sah'-re-o], *m.* Commissary, delegate, deputy, manager; **comisario de entradas,** in some hospitals, the person charged with taking an account of the patients who enter. **Comisario de cuartel** or **de barrio,** justice of the peace of a ward. **Comisario de policía,** police super-intendent.

comiscar [co-mes-car'], *va.* To nibble from time to time.

comisión [co-me-se-on'], *f.* 1. Trust, commission, warrant by which a trust is held. 2. Mandate, charge, precept, or commission sent or transmitted; ministration, ministry. 3. Commission, perpetration, act of committing a crime. **Pecado de comisión,** a sin of commission. 4. Commission,

committee. **Comisión de preparativos y disposiciones,** committee of arrangements. **Comisiones obreras,** worker's unions. **Comisión permanente,** standing committee. 5. Commission (pago). **Comisión sobre las ventas,** sales commission.

comisionado, da [co-me-se-o-nah'-do, dah], *a. & pp.* of COMISIONAR. 1. Commissional or commissionary. 2. Commissioned, deputed, empowered, *-m. & f.* 1. Commissioner. 2. *(Com.)* Agent, proxy.

comisionar [co-me-se-o-nar'], *va.* To commission, to depute, to empower, to appoint.

comisionista [co-me-se-o-nees'-tah], *m.* 1. Commissioner. 2. Commission merchant. 3. Commission agent.

comiso [co-mee'-so], *m.* 1. *(Law.)* Confiscation of prohibited goods, and the goods when confiscated. 2. *(Com.)* Seizure, attachment.

comisorio, ria [co-me-so-re-o, ah], *a.* Obligatory for a time or valid for a fixed day.

comisquear [co-mes-kay-ar'], *va. V.* COMISCAR.

comistión [co-mis-te-on'], *f. V.* CONMISTIÓN.

comistrajo [co-mis-trah'-ho], *m. (Coll.)* Hodgepodge, a medley of eatables.

comisura [co-me-soo'-rah], *f.* 1. *(Anat.)* Commissure, suture. **Comisura de los labios,** corner of the mouth. 2. Corner, angle.

comital [co-me-tahl'], *a. V.* CONDAL.

cómite [co'-me-tay], *m.* Count. *V.* CONDE.

comité [co-me-tay'], *m.* Committee; **Comité de No Intervención,** Non Intervention Committee.

comitente [co-me-ten'-tay], *pa.* Constituent.

comitiva [co-me-tee'-vah], *f.* Suite, retinue, followers.

cómitre [co'-me-tray], *m. (Naut.)* 1. Boatswain on board a galley. 2. A sea-captain under orders of the admiral of the fleet.

comiza [co-mee'-thah], *f. (Zool.)* A kind of barbel.

como [co'-mo], *adv.* 1. How, in what manner, to what degree. **¿Cómo estamos de cosecha?** how is the harvest? **2. As,** in a sense of comparison, e. g. **Es tan fuerte como un león,** he is as strong as a lion. 3. Why? 4. In such a manner. **Hago como tú haces,** I do as you do. 5. In what manner. **Diga Vd. cómo hemos llegado,** please, say in what condition we arrived. 6. If. **Como sea todo así…,** if it is all like this… 7. Like, in the same manner, in the same manner as. 8. So that. 9. Used in a causal sense it precedes *que.* 10. Used with the subjunctive it is equivalent to the gerund of the same verb. **Dar como** or **dar un como,** *(Coll.)* to play a trick, to joke. **Como quiera que sea,** however, at any rate. **Como quiera,** however, notwithstanding, nevertheless, yet: used with the negative *no.* **Como quiera que,** notwithstanding that, although, yet, howsoever. **Como** used interrogatively or as an exclamation receives the accent: **¡Cómo! ¿Cómo son?,** what are they like? **¿Cómo es de alto?,** how tall is it? **No veo cómo,** I don't see how. *-conj.* 1. As, since. **Como no tenía dinero,** as I had no money. **Como que…,** because…. **Hacía como que no nos veía,** he pretended not to see us.

cómoda [co'-mo-dah], *f.* A chest of drawers, bureau.

comodable [co-mo-dah'-blay], *a.* That which can be lent or borrowed.

cómodamente [co'-mo-dah-men-tay], *adv.* Conveniently, commodiously, comfortably.

comodante [co-mo-dahn'-tay], *m. (For.)* One who lends gratuitously for a limited time.

comodatario [co-mo-dah-tah'-re-o], *m. (Law.)* 1. Borrower. 2. Pawnbroker.

comodato [co-mo-dah'-to], *m. (Law.)* Loan; a contract of loan and restitution at a stipulated time.

comodidad [co-mo-de-dahd'], *f.* 1. Comfort, convenience, accommodation. **Pensar en su propia comodidad,** to consider one's own convenience. **Venga a su comodidad,** come at your convenience. 2. Convenience, ease, or cause of ease freedom from want. 3. Leisure: opportunity. 4. Profit, interest, advantage. **5. Comodidades,** comforts, amenities, pleasant things.

comodín [co-mo-deen'], *m.* 1. *(Coll.)* Something of general utility; in cards, to make a suit. 2. *(Mec. etc.)* Useful gadget. 3. Pretext, excuse, standby. 4. *(Ling.)* Catch-all, useful vague word, all-purpose word. a. *(And. Carib. Mex.)* V. COMODON.

cómodo [co'-mo-do], *m.* Utility, profit, convenience.

cómodo, da [co'-mo-do, dah], *a.* Convenient, commodious, suitable, comfortable. **Así estarás cómodo,** you'll be comfortable this way. **Ponerse cómodo,** to make oneself comfortable.

comodón [co-mo-done'], *a.* Comfort-loving (regalón); easygoing (pasivo); spoiled, spoilt. **Es muy comodón,** he'll do anything for a quiet life.

comodonería [co-mo-do-nay-re'-ah], *f.* Love of comfort; liking for a quiet life.

comodoro [co-mo-do'-ro], *m.* Commodore.

comoquiera [co-mo-ke-ay'-rah], *conj.* *(Liter.)* 1. **Comoquiera que…,** since…, in view of the fact that. 2. **Comoquiera que sea eso,** however that may be, in whatever way that may be.

comorar [co-mo-rar'], *vn.* To cohabit, to live together.

compa [com'-pah], *m.* *(CAm.)* 1. *(Pol.)* Comrade. 2. Pal (amigo).

compacidad [com-pah-the-dahd'], *f.* Compactness.

compactación [com-pac-tah-the-on'], *f.* Compacting, compression.

compactar [com-pac-tar'], *va.* To compact, to press together.

compacto, ta [com-pac'-to, tah], *a.* Compact, close, dense.

compadecer [com-pah-day-thayr'], *va.* To pity, to be sorry for.

compadecerse [com-pah-day-therr-say], *vr.* 1. To pity, to be compassionate; in this sense it is now very often used in an active sense, as **compadezco a Vd.,** I pity you, I feel for you, I commiserate your distress. 2. To agree with each other. *(Yo me compadezco, yo me compadezca, from Compadecerse. V.* CONOCER.*)*.

compadrada [com-pah-drah'-dah], *f.* *(Cono Sur)* Cheek, insolence.

compadrar [com-pah-drar'], *vn.* To become a godfather or mother, to contract a spiritual affinity.

compadrazgo [com-pah-drath'-go], *m.* 1. In canon law, a spiritual affinity or connection contracted by a godfather with the parents of a child for which he stands sponsor. 2. *(LAm.)* Close friendship.

compadre [com-pah'-drary], *m.* 1. Godfather, the word by which the godfather and godmother address the father of their godson or daughter, and by which the father and mother address him. 2. Protector, benefactor. 3. Friend. 4. *(Cono Sur)* Braggart; show-off (engreído); bully (matón).

compadrear [com-pah-dray-ar'], *vn.* 1. To be pals (ser amigos). 2. *(Cono Sur)* to brag, to show off (presumir); to give threatening looks (amenazar).

compadrería [com-pah-dray-ree'-ah], *f.* Friendly intercourse between godfathers, friends, or companions.

compadrito [com-pah-dre'-to], *m.* *(LAm.)* V. COMPADRE.

compage [com-pah'-hay], *f.* Compages, a system of many parts united.

compaginación [com-pah-he-nah-theon'], *f.* Compagination, union, structure.

compaginador [com-pah-he-nah-dor'], *m.* One who joins, unites, or couples.

compaginar [com-pah-he-nar'], *va.* To join, to unite, to couple, to compact, to compaginate. -*vr.* To agree, to tally. **Compaginarse con,** to agree with. **No se compagina esa conducta con su cáracter,** such conduct does not fit in with his character.

companage [com-pah-nah'-hay], *m.* A cold lunch; bread, cheese, raisins, etc.

compaña [com-pah'-nyah], *f.* 1. Out-house, office. 2. Company of soldiers. 3. Family. 4. Company.

compañería [com-pah-nyay-ree'-ah], *f.* V. MANCEBÍA.

compañerismo [com-pah-nyay-rees'-mo], *m.* Harmony, good- fellowship; team spirit.

compañero, ra [com-pah-nyay'-ro, rah], *m. & f.* 1. Companion, friend, consort, an equal, a match, a compère, a mate, one with whom a person frequently converses; fellow. **Compañero de viaje,** fellow traveler. **Compañero de juego,** playmate. 2. **Compañero de cuarto,** roommate; chum, a roommate in the universities. 3. Comrade, colleague, fellowmember, condisciple. **Compañero de armas,** comrade-in-arms. **Compañero de trabajo,** workmate. 4. Partner, associate, coadjutor. 5. Follower, one who shares the lot and fortune of another. 6. One thing suited to another. **Dos clacetines que no son compañeros,** two socks which do not match. **¿Dónde está el compañero de éste?,** where is the one that goes with this?

compañía [com-pah-nyee'-ah], *f.* 1. Company or society of persons, an assembly or meeting together, fellowship. 2. Partnership, fellowship; copartnership, company. **Hacer compañía a uno,** to keep somebody company. **Andar en malas compañías,** to keep bad company. 3. Company, troop, a body of soldiers. 4. Company, a number of players. 5. Company, conversation of a companion. 6. Family confederacy. **Compañía de Jesús,** Order of Jesuits, founded by Ignatius de Loyola.

compaño, compañón [Com-pah-nyo], *m.* V. COMPAÑERO.

compañón [com-pah-nyone'], *m.* Testicle. V. TESTÍCULO.

comparable [com-pah-rah'-blay], *a.* Comparable.

comparación [com-pah-rah-the-on'], *f.* 1. Comparison, conference. **En comparación con,** in comparison with. **No tiene comparación,** it is beyond compare. 2. Compare; collation, conferring.

comparado [com-pah-rah'-do], *a.* 1. **Comparado con,** compared with, in comparison. 2. Comparative (estudio).

comparador [com-pah-rah-dor'], *m.* An instrument serving to show the smallest difference in the length of two rules; comparing-rule.

comparanza [com-pah-rahn'-thah], *f.* *(Coll.)* V. COMPARACIÓN.

comparar [com-pah-rar'], *va.* To compare, to estimate, to confront, to confer, to collate.

comparativamente [com-pah-rah-te vah-men'-tay], *adv.* Comparatively.

comparativo, va [com-pah-rah-tee'-vo, vah], *a.* 1. Comparative. 2. Comparative, a degree of comparison in grammar.

comparecencia [com-pah-ray-then'-theah], *f.* Appearance before a judge.

comparecer [com-pah-ray-therr'], *vn.* To appear before a judge.

compareciente [com-pah-ray-the-en'-tay], *pa.* of COMPARECER.

comparendo [com-pah-ren'-do], *m.* Summons, citation, admonition to appear. *(Yo comparezco, yo comparezca, from Comparecer.)*

comparición [com-pah-re-the-on'], *f.* *(Law.)* Appearance.

comparsa [com-par'-sah], *f.* 1. Retinue of characters represented on the stage. 2. A party composed of persons masked and costumed as students, Moors, soldiers, etc. -*m. & f.* *(Theat.)* Extra, supernumerary; *(Carib.)* Dance team.

comparsería [com-par-say-re'-ah], *f.* *(Theat.)* Extras, supernumeraries.

comparte [com-par'-tay], *m. & f.* *(Law.)* Joint party or accomplice in a civil or criminal cause.

compartimiento [com-par-te-me-en'-to], *m.* 1. Compartment, the division of a whole into proportionate parts. 2. Inclosure, department. **Compartimiento interior de un navío,** accommodations on board a ship. **Compartimiento de cargo,** hold.

compartir [com-par-teer'], *va.* 1. To compart or divide into equal parts. 2. *(Art.)* To arrange or dispose the different parts of a painting. -*vn.* To divide, to share. **No comparto ese criterio,** I do not share that view.

compás [com-pahs'], *m.* 1. Pair of compasses, a mathematical instrument. *V.* PANTÓMETRA. **Compás de relojero,** clockmaker's compass. 2. A territory and district assigned to a monastery. 3. Power of the voice to express the notes of music. 4. Measure, time in music. **A compás,** in right musical time. **Al compás de la música,** in time to the music. **Entraron a los compases de un vals,** they came in to the strains of a waltz. 5. Motion of the hand of a conductor of an orchestra. 6. Measure, the space upon the staff between two bars. 7. Size, compass. 8. *(Met.)* Rule of life, principle to be governed by, pattern. 9. **Compás de muelle,** springs compass, springs of metal to raise or lower a coachroof. 10. **Compás de mar,** mariner's compass. *V.* BRÚJULA and BITACÓRA. 11. **Compás mixto,** *(Fenc.)* Mixed movement, partly direct and partly curved; a feint.

compasadamente [com-pah-sah-da.-men'-tay], *adv.* By rule and measure.

compasado [com-paah-sah'-do], *a.* Measured, moderate.

compasar [com-pah-sar'], *va.* 1. To measure with a rule and compass. 2. *(Met.)* To regulate things so that there may be neither too much nor too little. 3. *(Mus.)* To divide a musical composition into equal parts. 4. To adjust (tiempo).

compasible [com-pah-see'-blay], *a.* 1. Lamentable, deserving pity. 2. Compassionate.

compasillo [com-pah-seel'-lyo], *m.* Quick musical time.

compasión [com-pah-se-on'], *f.* Compassion, pity, commiseration, mercifulness; **tener compasión de,** to feel sorry for; **¡por compasión!,** for pity's sake!

compasivamente [com-pah-se-vah-mayn'-tay], *adv.* Compassionately; pityingly; sympathetically.

compasivo, iva [com-pah-see'-vo, vah], *a.* Compassionate, merciful, tender-hearted, humane.

compaternidad [com-pah-ter-ne-dahd'], *f.* *V.* COMPADRAZGO.

compatibilidad [com-pah-te-be-le-dahd'], *f.* Compatibility, consistency, conjuncture.

compatibilizar [com-tah-be-le-thar'], *va.* To harmonize, to bring into line, to make compatible.

compatible [com-pah-tee'-blay], *a.* Compatible, suitable to, fit for, consistent with.

compatricio [com-pah-tree'-the-o], or **compatriota** [com-pah-tre-o'-tah], *com.* Countryman or countrywoman, compatriot, fellow-citizen.

compatronato [com-pah-tro-nah'-to], *m.* Common right of patronage, the right of conferring a benefice in common with another.

compatrono, na [com-pah-tro'-no, nah], *m. & f.* Fellow-patron or patroness, joint-patron.

compeler, compelir [com-pay-lerr', coin-pay-leer'], *va.* 1 To compel, to constrain. 2. To extort.

compendiador [com-pen-de-ah-dor'], *m.* Epitomizer, abridger.

compendiar [com-pen-de-ar'], *va.* To eptiomize, to shorten, to abridge, to extract, to contract; to cut short.

compendio [com-pen'-de-o], *m.* Compendium, eptiome, abridgment, summary, compend, abstract.

compendiosamente [com-pen-de-o-sah-men'-tay], *adv.* Briefly, compendiously, in a concise manner.

compendioso, sa [com-pen-de-o'-so, sah], *a.* Brief, abridged, compendious, laconic or laconical, compact.

compendizar [com-pen-de-thar'], *va.* *V.* COMPENDIAR.

compenetración [com-pay-nay-trah-the-on'], *f.* Mutual understanding, fellow feeling, natural sympathy; mutual influence.

compenetrarse [com-pay-nay-trar'-say], *vr.* 1. *(Quim. etc.)* To interpenetrate, to fuse. 2. *(fig.)* To share each other's feelings; to undergo mutual influence; to enter into the spirit of.

compensable [com-pen-sah-blay], *a.* Compensable.

compensación [com-pen-sah-the-on], *f.* 1. Compensation, recompense. 2. Handicap (en deportes). 3. *(Com.)* Clearing; **bolsa** or **banco de compensación,** clearing house.

compensador [com-pen-sah-dor'], *m.* Compensator, a mechanical device of two or more metals to counteract the effect of variations of temperature.

compensar [com-pen-sar'], *va. & vn.* 1. To compensate, to counterbalance, to countervail. 2. To make amends, to make up. **Los malos años se compensan con los buenos,** good years make amends for bad ones. 3. To enjoy an equivalent for any loss or injury, to compensate. **Le compensaron con 100 dólares por los cristales rotos,** they gave him 100 dollars' compensation for the broken windows.

compensatorio [com-pen-sah-to'-re-o], *a.* Compensatory.

competencia [com-pay-ten'-the-ah], *f.* 1. Competition, rivalry, contest, contention. **Competencia desleal,** unfair competition. **En competencia con,** in competition with. 2. Competence, cognizance, the power or competency of a court or judge. 3. Incumbency. 4. Aptitude, fitness. **A competencia,** contentiously, contestingly. 5. Domain, field, province. **Y otras cosas de su competencia,** and other things which concern him. **No es de mi competencia,** that is not my responsibility.

competente [com-pay-ten'-tay], *a.* Competent, sufficient, fit for, consistent with, applicable to; adequate. **Esto se elevará al ministerio competente,** this will be sent to the appropriate ministry. **De fuente competente,** from a reliable source.

competentemente [com-pay-ten-tay-men'-tay], *adv.* Competently, appropriately.

competer [com-pay-terr'], *vn.* To be one's due, to have a fair claim to something.

competición [com-pay-te-the-on'], *f.* Competition, rivalry, *V.* COMPETENCIA.

competidor, ra [com-pay-te-dor', rah], *m. & f.* Competitor, rival, opponent, contender; competitrix.

competir [com-pay-teer'], *vn.* 1. To vie, to contest, to contend, to strive. 2. To stand in competition, to rival, to cope. 3. To be on a level or par with another, to rival, to vie with. **Los dos cuadros compiten en belleza,** the two pictures vie with each other in beauty.

competitividad [com-pay-te-te-ve-dahd'], *f.* Competitiveness.

competitivo [com-pay-te-te'-vo], *a.* Competitive.

compilación [com-pe-lah-the-on'], *f.* 1. Compilation. 2. Compilement.

compilador, ra [com-pe-lah-dor', rah], *m. & f.* Compiler, compilator, collector.

compilar [com-pe-lar'], *va.* To compile.

compincharse [com-peen-chahr'-say], *vr.* To band together, to team up.

compinche [com-peen'-chay], *m.* *(Coll.)* Bosom friend, comrade, confidant, crony. *(Yo compito, yo compita, from Competir, V. PEDIR.)*

complacedero, ra [com-plah-thay-day'-ro, rah], *a.* *V.* COMPLACIENTE.

complacencia [com-plah-then'-the-ah], *f.* Pleasure, satisfaction, gratification; complacency, compliance, condescendence. **Lo hizo con complacencia,** he did it gladly.

complacer [com-plah-therr'], *va.* To please, to humor, to content. **Nos complace que sea así,** we are glad it is so. *-vr.* To be pleased with or take delight in a thing. **El Banco se complace en comunicar a su clientela que…,** the Bank is glad to tell its clients that…

complacido [com-plah-the-do], *a.* Pleased, satisfied. **Me miró complacido,** she gave me a grateful look.

complaciente [com-plah-the-en'-tay], *pa.* Pleasing, one who pleases.

complañir [com-plah-nyeer'], *vn.* *(Obs.)* To weep, to be compassionate. *(Yo complazco, yo complazca, from Complacer. V. CONOCER.)*

complejidad [com-play-he-dahd'], *f.* Complexity.

complejo, ja [com-play'-ho, hah], *a.* Complex. *V.* COMPLEXO.

complementario, ia [com-play-men-tah'-re-o, ah], *a.* Complementary, serving to complete.

complemento [com-play-men'-to], *m.* 1. Complement, perfection, accomplishment, completion; accomplishment. 2. *(Ling.)* Complement, object; complemento directo, direct object. 3. Essential part, natural concomitant. **El vino es un complemento de la buena comida,** wine is an essential complement to good food. 4. *(Aut.)* Accessories. 5. *(Mil.)* **Offical de complemento,** reserve officer.

completa [com-play'-tah], *f. (Carib.) (Culin.)* Full meal.

completamente [com-play-tah-men'-tay], *adv.* Completely, perfectly, finally.

completar [com-play-tar'], *va.* To complete, to perfect, to finish, to accomplish, to crown, to consummate, to make up.

completas [com-play'-tas], *f. pl.* Compline, the last of the canonical hours or evening prayers.

completivamente, *adv.* V. COMPLETIVO.

completivo, va [com-play-tee'-vo, vah], *a.* Completive, absolute.

completo, ta [com-play'-to, tah], *a.* Complete, perfect, finished: concluded; full, absolute, all-out. **Por completo,** completely, totally. **Fue un completo fracaso,** it was a complete failure.

complexión [com-plek-se-on'], *f.* Constitution, temperament of the body, habit, nature.

complexionado, da [com-plek-se-o-nah'-do, dah], *a.* Constituted. **Bien o mal complexionado,** of a good or bad constitution.

complexional [com-plek-se-o-nahl,], *a.* Constitutional, temperamental.

complexo [com-plek'-so], *m.* Complex.

complexo [com-plek'-so], *a.* 1. Arduous, difficult, complicated. 2. Complex, not simple; of several parts. 3. *(Anat.)* Applied to one of the muscles of the head.

complicatión [com-ple-cah-the-on'], *f.* Complication, complex, complexure; **una persona sin complicación,** an uncomplicated person.

complicadamente, *adv.* V. COMPLICADO.

complicado, da, *a.* Complicated, complex. *-pp.* of COMPLICAR.

complicar [com-ple-car'], *va.* To complicate, to jumble things together, *-vr.* 1. To get complicated. 2. **Complicarse en un asunto,** to get involved in a matter.

cómplice [com'-ple-thay], *com.* Accomplice, cooperator, associate, complice, abetter, accessory.

complicidad [com-ple-the-dahd'], *f.* Accessoriness, complicity.

compló [com-plo'], *m.* V. COMPLOT.

complot [com-plot'], *m.* Plot, conspiracy, a joint agreement to commit crime.

complutense [com-ploo-ten'-say], *a. & n.* Native of or belonging to Alcalá de Henares.

componedor, ra [com-po-nay-dor', rah], *m. m. & . f.* Composer, writer, author 2. Arbitrator.

componenda [com-po-nen'-dah], *f.* 1. Compromise (acuerdo); settlement (provisional), arrangement (temporalmente). 2. Shady deal.

componente, *pa.* [com-po-nayn'-tay], *a.* Component. *-m.* *(Quim. etc.)* Component; ingredient (de bebida etc.). **Componentes lógicos,** software *(Inform.).* **Un viento de componente norte,** a northerly wind.

componer [com-po-nerr'], *va.* 1. To compose, to compound. 2. To construct. 3. To sum up. 4. To frame, to devise, to invent. 5. To mend, to repair, to heal, to restore. 6. To strengthen, to fortify, to restore. 7. To furnish, to fit up, to garnish. 8. To compose, to reconcile, to accommodate, to adjust, to settle, to compose differences. 9. To ward off a danger. 10. To compose, to calm, to quiet. 11. *(Mus.)* To note, to set down the notes of a tune, to form a tune. 12. To compose or compile a boo. 13. To compose or write verses. **El compone muy bien,** he writes very good verses. 14. *(Print.)* To compose types. *-vr.* 1. To deck oneself with clothes. 2. **Componerse de,** to consist of. **Se compone de seis partes,** it consists of 6 parts. 3. **Componerse con uno,**

to come to terms with somebody. 4. **Componérselas,** to manage, to get along. 5. *(LAm.) (Med.)* To recover, to get better. **Las cosas se compondrán,** everything will be all right.

componibe [com-po-nee'-blay], *a.* Compoundable, accommodable, mendable,

comporta [com-por'-tah], *f. (Prov.)* A large basket in which grapes are carried during the vintage.

comportable [com-por-tah'-blay], *a.* Supportable, tolerable.

comportamiento [com-por-tah-me-en'-to], *m. (Prov.)* Behavior, conduct.

comportar [com-por-tar'], *va.* 1. To carry or bring together. 2. To suffer, to tolerate. 3. To involve, to carry with it. **Ello no comporta obligación alguna,** it carries no obligation. *-vr.* To comport, to behave or conduct oneself. **Comportarse como es debido,** to behave properly.

comporte [com-por'-tay], *m.* 1. V. SUFRIMIENTO. 2. Proceeding, conduct. 3. Air, manner.

comportilla [com-por-teel'-lyah], *f. dim.* A small basket:

composición [com-po-se-the-on'], *f.* 1. Composition, the act of composing something, composure, making up. 2. Composition of a difference, adjustment, agreement, compact. 3. A literary, scientific, or musical work. 4. *(Print.)* Arrangement of types. 5. Calm, modest, or sedate appearance.

compositivo, va [com-po-se-tee'-vo, vah], *a.* Compositive, synthetic; used of a preposition or particle forming a compound word.

compositor, ra [com-po-se-tor'], *m. & f.* 1. Composer of musical compositions. 2. *(Print.)* Compositor. 3. *(Cono Sur)* Quack doctor, bone-settler.

compostura [com-pos-too'-rah], *f.* 1. Composition, composure. 2. Mending or repairing. **Estar en compostura,** to be undergoing repairs. 3. Cleanliness, neatness of dress. 4. Composition of a difference, composure, accommodation, adjustment, agreement, compact. **Perder la compostura,** to lose one's composure. 5. Modesty, circumspection, sedateness, composure. 6. A mixture with which something is adulterated.

compota [com-po'-tah], *f.* Preserves, sweetmeats, compote. **Compota de manzanas,** stewed apples.

compotera [com-po-tay'-rah], *f.* Vessel in which jams are served up for the table.

compra [com'-prah], *f.* 1. Purchase. **Compra al contado,** cash purchase; **compra a plazos,** hire purchase. 2. Collection of necessaries bought for daily use, shopping. **Hacer las compras,** to do the shopping.

comprable [com-prah'-blay], *a.* Purchasable.

comprador, ra [com-prah-dor'-rah], *m.&.f.* 1. Buyer, purchaser. 2. Caterer.

comprante [com-prahn'-tay], *pa.* Buyer, purchaser.

comprar [com-prar'], *va.* 1. To buy, to purchase, to shop; to acquire. **Comprar al contado,** to pay cash for. **Comprar a plazos,** to buy on installments. 2. *(fig.)* To buy off, to bribe; to win over.

compraventa [com-prah-ven'-tah], *f.* Buying and selling. V. CONTRATODECOMPRAVENTA.

comprendedor, ra [com-pren-day-dor', rah], *m. & f.* One who comprehends or understands.

comprender [com-pren-derr'], *va.* 1. To embrace, to encircle, to comprehend. 2. To comprise, to include, to contain. **Servicio no comprendido,** service not included. **Todo comprendido,** everything included. 3. To comprehend, to understand, to conceive, to know. **No comprendo cómo,** I don't see how. **Comprendo su actitud,** I understand his attitude. **Hacerse comprender,** to make oneself understood.

comprensibilidad [com-pren-se-be-le-dahd'], *f.* Comprehensibleness, comprehensibility.

compresible [com-pren-see'-blay], *a.* Comprehensible, conceivable.

comprensiblemente, *adv.* Comprehensibly.

comprensión [com-pren-se-on'], *f.* 1. Comprehension, comprisal, conceiving, conception. 2. Comprehensiveness. 3. Act of comprising or containing. 4. Understanding; sympathy, tolerance, kindness.

comprensivo, va [com-pren-see'-vo, vah], *a.* 1. Comprehensive, having the power to comprehend. 2. Comprehensive, having the quality of comprising much.

comprensor, ra [com-pren-sor', rah], *m. & f.* 1. *(Theol.)* The blessed, one who enjoys the presence of God in the heavenly mansions. 2. One that understands, attains, or embraces a thing.

compresa [com-pray'-sah], *f.* Compress, folded linen put under a bandage. **Compresa higiénica,** sanitary towel.

compresibilidad [com-pray-se-be-le-dahd'], *f.* Compressibility.

compresible [com-pray-see'-blay], *a.* Compressible.

compresión [com-pray-se-on'], *f.* 1. Compression, pressing together, compressure. 2. *(Gram.)* V. SINÉRESIS.

compresivamente [com-pray-se-vah-men'-tay], *adv.* Compressibly, contractedly.

compresivo, va [com-pray-see'-vo, vah], *a.* Compressive, compressing or reducing to a smaller compass.

compresor [com-pray-sor'], *m.* Compressor.

comprimible [com-pre-mee'-blay], *a.* 1. Compressible. 2. Repressible.

comprimido [com-pre-me'-do], *a.* Compressed. *-m.* Tablet, pill. **Comprimido para dormir,** sleeping pill.

comprimir [com-pre-meer'], *va.* 1. To compress; to constrain; to condense. 2. To repress, to restrain, to keep in awe. *-vr.* 1. To subdue one's passion. **Tuve que comprimirme para no reír,** I had to keep myself from laughing.

comprobable [com-pro-bah'-blay], *a.* Verifiable, capable of being checked. **Un alegato fácilmente,** an allegation which is easy to check.

comprobación [com-pro-bah-the-on'], *f.* 1. Comprobation, attestation. 2. Comparison, verification of printer's proof corrections. **En comprobación de ello,** in proof whereof, as proof of what I stay. **De difícil comprobación,** hard to check. **Comprobación de paridad par,** *(Inform.)* even parity check.

comprobador [com-pro-bah-dor'], *m.* Tester.

comprobante [com-pro-bahn'-tay], *pa.* 1. Proving, one who proves. 2. Voucher, schedule, document. **Documento comprobante,** supporting document.

comprobar [com-pro-bar'], *va.* 1. To verify, to confirm by comparison. 2. To comprobate; to compare. 3. To prove, to give evidence.

comprofesor [com-pro-fay-sor'], *m.* Colleague.

comprometedor, ra [com-pro-may-tay-dor', rah], *m. & f.* Compromiser, one who compromises. *-a.* Compromising.

comprometer [com-pro-may-terr'], *va.* 1. To compromise. **Aquellas cartas le comprometieron,** those letters compromised him. 2. To engage, to bind by an appointment or contract; to render one accountable or answerable. 3. To expose, to put in danger. **Comprometer la reputación,** to risk one's reputation. 4. To agree formally. 4. **Comprometer a uno a algo,** to hold somebody to something. *-vr.* 1. To comprise oneself, to get involved. 2. To undertake, to promise to. **Se compromete a todo,** he'll say yes to anything.

comprometido, da [com-pro-may-tee'-do, dah], *a.* 1. Obligated, obliged. 2. Engaged to be married. *-m. & f.* Fiancé, fiancée.

comprometimiento [com-pro-may-te-me-en'-to], *m.* Compromise, a compact or adjustment.

compromisario, ria [com-pro-me-sah'-re-o], *m.f.* Arbitrator, umpire, compromiser, referee.

compromiso [com-pro-mee'-so], *m.* 1. Compromise. 2. Arbitration bond. 3. Difficulty, embarrassment. **Estar en un fuerte compromiso,** to be in real difficulty. **Poner a uno en un compromiso,** to place somebody in an embarrassing situation. 4. An obligation contracted. **Poner en compromiso,** to compromise, to render doubtful. **Libre de compromiso,** without

obligation. **Atender sus compromisos,** to meet one's obligations. **Tener muchos compromisos,** to have many commitments. 5. Agreement. **Compromiso matrimonial,** engagement. **Compromiso verbal,** verbal agreement.

compropietario, in [com-pro-pe-ay-tah'-re-o, ah], *m. & f. & a.* Joint owner, owning jointly with another, or others. *V.* COPROPIETARIO.

comprotector [com-pro-tec-tor'], *m.* A joint protector.

compuerta [com-poo-err'-tah], *f.* 1. Hatch or halfdoor. 2. Lock or sluice, floodgate. **Compuerta de marea,** *(Naut.)* tidegate, tiderace.

compuestamente [com-poo-es-tah-nen'-tay], *adv.* Regularly, orderly.

compuesto [com-poo-es'-to], *m.* Compound, commixture, composition. **Compuesto químico,** chemical compound.

compuesto, ta [com-poo-es'-to, tah], *a. & pp.* of COMPONER. Composed, compound, complex, made up; fresh, repaired. **Orden compuesto,** the composite order in architecture. **Flores compuestas,** composite flowers; the family of Compositae. **Estar compuesto de,** to be composed of.

compulsa [com-pool'-sah], *f.* 1. *(Law.)* An authentic or attested copy of some instrument or writing. 2. To collate, to compare.

compulsar [com-pool-sar'], *va.* 1. *(Obs.)* To compel, to force. 2. *(Law.)* To make an authentic copy or transcript. 3. To compare, to collate.

compulsión [com-pool-se-on'], *f.* 1. Compulsion, forcing. 2. Compulsion,

compulsivo, va [com-pool-see'-vo, vah], *a.* Compulsive, compulsory.

compulso, sa [com-pool'-so, sah], *pp.irr.* of COMPELER.

compulsorio, ria [com-pool-so'-re-o, ah], *a.* 1. Compulsory, compulsatory. 2. Ordering an authentic copy to be made: applied to the decree of a judge or magistrate.

compunción [com-poon-the-on'], *f.* Compunction, repentance, contrition.

compungido, da [com-poon-hee'-do, dah], *a.* Compunctious, sorry. *-pp.* of COMPUNGIR.

compungir [com-poon-heer'], *va.* To make remorseful, to arouse feelings of contrition in.

compungirse [com-poon-heer'-say], *vr.* To feel compunction, to be pierced with remorse.

compungivo, va [com-poon-hee'-vo, vah], *a.* Compunctive, pricking, stinging.

compurgación [com-poor-gah-the-on'], *f.* Compurgation.

compurgador [com-poor-gah-dor'], *m.* Compurgator.

compurgar [com-poor-gar'], *va.* To prove one's veracity or innocence by the oath of another.

computable [com-poo-tah'-blay], *a.* Computable.

computación [com-poo-tah-the-on'], *f.* Computation, manner of calculating time.

computador, ra [com-poo-tah-dor', rah], *m. & f.* 1. One who computes (persona). Computer (aparato). **Computadora digital,** *(Mech.)* digital computer.

computar [com-poo-tar'], *va.* To compute, to estimate by years or ages.

computerización [com-poo-tay-re-thah-the-on'], *f.* Computerization.

computerizar [com-poo-tay-re-thar'], *va.* To computerize.

computista [com-poo-tees'-tah], *m.* Computist, computer, user.

cómputo [com'-poo-to], *m.* Computation, calculation account. **Según nuestros cómputos,** according to our calculations.

comulación [co-moo-lah-the-on'], *f.* Cumulation. *V.* ACUMULACIÓN.

comulgar [co-mool-gar'], *va.* To administer the holy Eucharist. *-vn.* To communicate or to receive the sacrament.

comulgatorio [co-mool-gah-to'-re-o], *m.* Communion altar.

común [co-moon'], *a.* 1. Common. **Los intereses comúnes,** common interests. **A no tiene nada de común con B,** A has nothing in common with B. 2. Common, usual, general, customary, ordinary, familiar, generally received. **Es costumbre muy común,** it is a very widespread custom. 3. Common, much used, frequent, current, habitual. 4. Vulgar, mean, low. **Por lo común,** in general, generally.

común [co-moon'], *m.* 1. Community, public. 2. *V.* SECRETA. **En común,** conjointly, collectively; **por lo común,** commonly, frequently. 3. Toilet. 4. **Los Comunes,** the Commons (Britain).

comuna [co-moo'-nah], *f.* 1. *(Prov.)* The principal canal of irrigation. 2. Commune (comunidad). 3. *(LAm.)* Municipality, city council.

comunal [co-moo-nahl'], *m.* Commonalty, common people. *-a.* Common, commonable.

comunalmente [co-moo-nahl'-men-tay], *adv.* Communally; as a community.

comunaleza [co-moo-nah-lay'-thah], *f.* 1. Mediocrity. 2. Communication, intercourse. 3. Common.

comunero, ra [co-moo-nay'-ro, rah], *a.* 1. Popular, common, and pleasing to the people. 2. Commoner, one of the common people, as distinguished from the nobility.

comunero *m.* 1. A joint holder of a tenure of lands. 2. An individual of the party that upheld Spanish liberty against the encroachments of Charles *V.*

comunicabilidad [co-moo-ne-cah-be-le-dahd'], *f.* Communicability.

comunicable [co-moo-ne-cah'-blay], *a.* 1. Communicable. 2. Sociable, affable.

comunicación [co-moo-ne-cah-the-on], *f.* 1. Communication. **Las comunicaciones están rotas,** communications are broken. **No hemos tenido más comunicación con él,** we have had no further contact with him. **Comunicaciones interactivas remotas** *(Inform.),* remote interactive communications. 2. Communication, intercourse, converse. 3. Junction or union of one thing with an other. 4. Message; report. 5. *(Liter.)* Rhetorical question. 6. **No hay comunicación entre los dos pueblos,** *(Mex.)* there's no way of getting from one town to the other.

comunicado [co-moo-ne-cah'-do], *m.* An article of a personal nature sent to a periodical for publication.

comunicante [co-moo-ne-cahn'-tay], *pa.* Communicating; a communicant; letter writer.

comunicar [co-moo-ne-car'], *va.* 1. To communicate, to impart, to extend, to discover or make known. **Nos comunicó su miedo,** he affected us with his fear. 2. To communicate with another either by word or writing. 3. To consult or confer upon a subject. 4. To communicate, to take the Lord's Supper. 5. To connect, to join, to open a way between. **Cuartos comunicados,** connecting rooms. *-vr.* To be joined, united, or contiguous to each other. **Comunicarse entre sí,** to interchange sentiments or ideas. *-vn.* 1. To send a report. **Comunican desde Lisboa que...,** it is reported from Lisbon that... 2. *(Telec.)* **Estar comunicando,** to be engaged. 3. *(Arch.)* **Comunicarse con,** to connect with.

comunicativo, va [co-moo-ne-cah-tee'-vo, vah], *a.* Communicative, liberal, not reserved.

comunidad [co-moo-ne-dahd'], *f.* 1. Commonness. 2. Commonalty, the common people. 3. Community, corporation, guild, society. **De comunidad,** conjointly, collectively; **Comunidad Europea,** European Community. **Comunidad Británica de Naciones,** British Commonwealth. **Comunidad de vecinos,** residents' association. 4. The cities of Castile, which at the beginning of the reign of Charles V rose against his government, in support of Spanish liberty.

comunión [co-moo-ne-on'], *f.* 1. Communion, fellowship, common possession. 2. Familiar intercourse. 3. Communion, the act of receiving the blessed sacrament. 4. Congregation of persons who profess the same religious faith.

comunismo [co-moo-nees-mo], *m.* Communism, the doctrine of the community of property.

comunista [co-moo-nees'-tah], *m. & f.* Communist, an advocate of communism.

comunistoide [co-moo-nees-toy'-day], *m.* Fellow traveler, communist sympathizer.

comunitario [co-moo-ne-tah-re-o], *a.* 1. Community. 2. Member of the European Community. *-m.* Member nation of the EC.

comúnmente [co-moon-men'-tay], *adv.* 1. Commonly, customarily, usually, generally, 2. Frequently, often.

comuña [co-moo'-nyah], *f.* 1. Mixed grain; as wheat and rye, maslin, or meslin. **Comuñas,** seeds. *V.* CAMUÑAS.

con [cone], *prep.* 1. With, by. **Atado con cuerda,** tied with string. **Con su ayuda,** with his help. 2. Although. **Con tal que** or **con que,** so that, provided that, on condition that. **Yo lo haré, con tal que,** etc., I will do it, provided that, etc. 3. **Con que,** then, so then. **Con que Vd. ha hecho esto,** you have done this, then. **Con todo** or **con todo eso,** nevertheless, notwithstanding. **Con que vámonos,** well, then, let us go. **Con que, adiós, señoras,** then goodbye, ladies. **Con que sí, con que no,** Shillyshally. **Con tantas dificultades, no se descorazonó,** in spite of all the difficulties he was not discouraged. **Amable con todos,** kind to everybody. **Con decirle que no voy,** when I tell you I'm not going.

con que, *m. (Coll.)* Condition, stipulation, circumstance.

conato [co-nah'-to], *m.* 1. Conatus, endeavor, effort, exertion. 2. *(Law.)* Crime attempted but not executed. **Conato de hurto,** attempt at robbery.

conaviero [co-nah-ve-ay'-ro], *m.* Copartner, or part owner in a ship.

concadenar [con-cah-day-nar'], *va. (Met.)* To concatenate; to chain or link together.

concambio [con-cahm'-be-o], *m.* Exchange. *V.* CAMBIO.

concanónigo [con-ca-no'-ne-go], *m.* A fellow canon.

concatedralidad [con-cah-tay-drah-le.-dahd'], *f.* Union of two cathedral churches.

concatenación [con-cah-tay-nah-the-on'], *f.* Concatenation, linking. **Concatenación de circunstancias,** chain of circumstances.

concatenar [con-cah-tay-nar'], *va.* To link together, to concatenate.

concausa [con-cah'-oo-sah], *f.* A joint cause, a shared cause.

cóncava, concavidad [con'-cah-vah], *f.* Concavity, hollowness, hollow.

cóncavo, va [con'-cah-vo, vah], *a.* Concave, hollow.

cóncavo [con'-cah-vo], *m.* Concavity. *V.* CONCAVIDAD.

concebible [con-thay-bee'-blay], *a. V.* COMPRENSIBLE. **No es concebible que..,** it is unthinkable that.

concebimiento [con-thay-be-me-en'-to], *m.* Conception.

concebir [con-thay-beer'], *va. & vn.* 1. To conceive, to become pregnant. 2. To conceive, to imagine, to have an idea of. 3. To conceive, to comprehend, to think to understand; to look on. **La cláusula está concebida en estos términos,** the clause is expressed in these terms. **Concebir esperanzas,** to nourish hopes. **No concibo que...,** I cannot understand how...

concedente [con-thay-den'-tay], *pa.* Conceding, one who concedes.

conceder [con-thay-derr'], *va.* 1. To give, to grant, to bestow a boon or gift. 2. To concede, to allow, to grant. to admit.

concedido, da [con-thay-dee'-do, dah], *a. & pp.* of CONCEDER-ER. Conceded, granted. **Dado y no concedido,** admitted but not agreed.

concejal, la [con-thay-hal'], *m. & f.* Member of a council or board.

concejal [con-thay-hal'], *a.* Relating to public boards or councils.

concejalía [con-thay-hah-le'-ah], *f.* Post of town councillor; seat on the city council.

concejil [con-thay-heel'], *m.* 1. An alderman, or member of a corporation. 2. *(Prov.)* Foundling, a child found without parent or owner.

concejil, *a.* Common, public, belonging to the public.

concejo [con-thay'-ho], *m.* 1. The civic body of a small town or village, and the house where its members hold their meetings. 2. District composed of several parishes with one common jurisdiction. 3. Foundling. **Concejo abierto,** a meeting of the inhabitants of a small town or village presided over by the *alcalde,* deliberate upon public affairs.

concelebrar [con-thay-lay-brar'], *va.* To celebrate jointly, together.

concento [con-then'-to], *m.* 1. Concord, a concert of voices, harmony. 2. Meter, verse, cadence.

concentración [con-then-trah-the-on'], *f.* 1. Concentration. 2. Gathering, meeting, rally. 3. *(LAm.) (Com.)* Merger.

concentrado, da [con-then-trah'-do, dah], *a.* Concentrated, tending to the center. *-pp.* of CONCENTRAR.

concentrar [con-then-trar'], *va.* To concentrate. *V.* RECONCENTRAR. *-vr.* 1. *(Mil.)* To gather together. 2. **Concentrarse a,** to concentrate on. **El interés se concentra en esta lucha,** the interest is centered on this fight.

concéntrico, ca [con-then'-tre-co, cah], *a.* Concentric, concentrical.

concepción [con-thep-the-on'], *f.* 1. Conception, the act of conceiving. 2. Conception, idea, comprehension, conceit, image in the mind, fancy.

conceptáculo [con-thep-tah'-coo-lo], *m.* 1. Conceptacle, a cavity containing the spores of cryptogamous plants. 2. Fruit, follicle.

conceptear [con-thep-tay-ar'], *vn.* To give smart repartees, to abound in witty sayings.

conceptible [con-thep-tee'-blay], *a.* Conceivable, that may be imagined.

conceptillo [con-thep-teel'-lyo], *m. dim.* A witty trifle, an attempt at wit.

conceptista [con-thep-tees'-tah], *m.* 1. A wit. 2. A man of genius, a man of fancy. 3. A humorist. 4. Punster.

concepto [con-thep'-to], *m.* 1. Conceit, thought, idea, conception. **Un concepto grandioso,** a bold conception. **Formarse un concepto de algo,** to get an idea of something. 2. Foetus. *V.* FETO. 3. Sentiment, striking, thought, flash of wit, pun, 4. Judgment, opinion. 5. Estimation, favorable opinion. 6. Heading, section. **Bajo todos los conceptos,** from every point of view. **Por dicho concepto,** for this reason. **Se le pagó esa cantidad por concepto de derechos,** he was paid that amount as royalties. 7. *(Inform.)* **Concepto de Von Neumann,** Von Neumann concept.

conceptual [con-cep-too-ahl'], *a.* Conceptual.

conceptualismo [con-thep-too-ah-lees'-mo], *m.* A philosophical system, designed to reconcile nominalism and realism, dating from 12th century.

conceptualizar [con-thep-too-ah-le-thar'], *va.* To conceptualize.

conceptuar [con-thep-too-ar'], *va.* To conceive, judge, think or be of opinion. **Conceptúo que debe hacerse esto,** I am of opinion that this should be done. **Conceptuar a uno de,** to regard somebody as.

conceptuosamente [con-thep-too-o-sah-men'-tay], *adv.* Ingeniously wittily.

conceptuoso, sa [con-thep-too-o'-so, sah], *a.* Witty, conceited.

concernencia [con-ther-nen'-the-ah], *f.* Concernment, relation, influence.

concerniente [con-ther-ne-en'-tay], *pa.* Concerning. **Por lo concerniente,** concerning.

concernir [con-ther-neer'], *v. imp.* To regard, to concern, to belong or appertain to. *V.* ATAÑER.

concertación [con-ther-tah-the-on'], *f.* Harmonizing; coordination; reconciliation.

concertadamente, *adv.* 1. Regularly, orderly, methodically. 2. By agreement.

concertado [con-ther-tah-do], 1. *a.* Methodical, systematic. 2. *m.f.* Contract worker.

concertador [con-ther-tah-dor'], *m.* Regulator, adjuster, expediter.

concertante [con-ther-tahn'-tay], *a. (Mus.)* Concerted, arrangement for two or more voices or instruments.

concertar [con-ther-tar'], *va.* 1. To concert, to settle by mutual communication, to adjust, to harmonize. **Concertar a varias personas para que...,** to get several people. 2. To settle the price of things. 3. To bargain, to convenant, to conclude an agreement. **Concertar una venta en 20 dólares,** to agree to sell something for 20 dollars. 4. To tune musical instruments. 5. To compare, to estimate the relative qualities of things. 6. To beat about the bush, to start or rouse the game. *-vn.* To agree, to accord, to suit one another. *-vr.* 1. To dress or deck oneself. 2. To go hand in hand; to concert, to contrive, to form or design.

concertina [con-ther-te'-nah], *f.* Concertina (instrumento).

concertino, na [con-ther-te'-no], *m. & f.* First violin, leader (de la orquesta); concertmaster.

concertista, [con-ther-tis'-tah], *m. & f.* Soloist, solo performer.

concesión [con-thay-se-on'], *f.* Concession, grant, granting or yielding acknowledgment.

concesionario [con-thay-se-o-nah'-re-o], *m.* 1. *(Law.)* Grantee. 2. Concessionary, one to whom a special privilege is granted.

concesivo [con-the-se'-vo], *a.* Concessive.

concha [con'-chah], *f.* 1. Shell. 2. Oyster. 3. Tortoise-shell. 4. An ancient copper coin, worth about three farthings, or eight maravedis. **Concha de nácar,** mother-of-pearl shell. 5. *(Arch.)* Volute, any ornament in the form of a shell, conch. 6. The external ear. 7. Shell of a dagger or cutlass. 8. The shell-shaped covering of the spike of Indian corn. 9. **Concha de cabrestante,** *(Naut.)* socket of the capstan. **Tener muchas conchas,** *(Met.)* to be very reserved, artful, cunning. 10. Flake, chip (porcelana). 11. Prompt, box (teatro.). 12. *(And. Carib.)* Nerve, cheek (descaro). **¡Qué concha la tuya!,** you've got a nerve! 13. *(And.)* Sloth, sluggishness (pereza). 14. *(Carib.)* Cartridge case (cartucho). 15. **Concha de su madre,** *(Cono Sur)* son of a bitch, bastard.

conchabado, da [con-chah-bah'-do], *m. & f. (LAm.)* Servant.

conchabanza [con-chah-bahn'-thah], *f.* 1. The manner of making oneself easy and comfortable. 2. *(Coll.)* The act of meeting or collecting in unlawful assemblies. 3. Plotting, conspiracy.

conchabar [con-chah-bar'], *va.* 1. To join, to unite. 2. To mix inferior wool with the superior or middling quality instead of separating it into three kinds at shearing-time. 3. *(LAm.)* To hire, to engage, to employ (criado). 4. *(LAm.)* To barter (trocar). *-vr.* 1. To unite, to join or unite for some evil purpose; to plot, to conspire. 2. *(LAm.)* To hire oneself out, to get a job (como criado).

conchabo [con-chah-bah-do], *m.* 1. *(LAm.)* Hiring, engagement (contractación). **Oficina de conchabo,** employment agency for domestics. 2. *(Cono Sur)* bater(ing).

conchado, da [con-chah'-do, dah], *a.* Scaly, crustaceous, shelly.

conchal [con-chahl'], *a. V.* SEDA CONCHAL.

cónchale [con'-chah-lay], *interj. (Carib.)* Well!, goodness!

conchil [con-cheel'], *m.* Rockshell. Murex, the mollusk which yielded the purple of the ancients. *Cf.* PÚRPURA.

conchilla, ita [con-cheel'-lyah, chee-tah], *f. dim.* A small shell.

conchite [con-chee'-tay], *f.* Conchite, a sort of petrified shell.

conchito [con-che'-to], *m. (And. Cono Sur)* youngest child, baby of the family.

concho [con'-cho], *m. (Carib.)* 1. Taxi. 2. *(CAm.) a.* Crude, vulgar. 3. *m.* Peasant; rustic. 4. Dregs, sediment; residue; left-overs (drogas). **Hasta el concho,** to the very end. 5. *(And. Cono Sur). (Anat.) V.* COÑO.

conchología [con-cho-lo-hee'-ah], *f.* Conchology.

conchudo, da [con-choo'-do, dah], *a.* 1. Scaly, crustaceous, ostraceous. 2. Cunning, crafty, close, reserved. *-m.* **Conchuda,** *f.* 1. *(And. Mex.)* Shameless person, cheeky bastard. 2. *(LAm.)* Stubborn person.

conchuela [con-choo-ay'-lah], *f. dim. V.* CONCHILLA.

concibimiento [con-the-be-me-en'-to], *m.* 1. Conceit, thought, idea, conception. 2. Act of conceiving.

conciencia [con-the-en'-the-ah], *f.* 1. Conscience. **Conciencia doble,** double personality. **Tener mala conciencia,** to have a bad conscience. 2. Scrupulosity, conscientiousness. 3. Consciousness, knowledge of one's personality. **Tener plena conciencia de,** to be fully aware of. **Tomar conciencia de que,** to become aware that. **Hacer conciencia de alguna cosa,** to be scrupulous about a thing. **A conciencia,** conscientiously. **En conciencia,** in earnest, in truth.

concienciación [con-the-ayn-the-ah-the-on'], f. Arousal, awakening.

concienciar [con-the-ayn-the-ar'], *va.* To arouse, to awaken, to make aware. *-vr.* To be aroused, to become aware of.

concienzudamente [con-the-ayn-thoo-dah-men'-tay], *adv.* Conscientiously, painstakingly, thoroughly.

concienzudo, da [con-the-en-thoo'-do, dah], *a.* Conscientious, scrupulous, exactly just: applied generally to a person too scrupulous.

concierto [con-the-err'-to], *m.* 1. The good order and arrangement of things. 2. Concert, communication of designs: bargain, agreement, or contract between two or three persons. **Quedar de concierto a cerca de,** to be in agreement with regard to. 3. Accommodation. 4. Act of beating the wood with hounds to start the game. 5. Concert, an assembly of musicians performing a musical composition. 6. Concert, a piece of music composed for a concert. **De concierto,** according to agreement, by common consent. *(Yo concierto, yo concierto from Concertar. V.* ACERTAR.)

conciliable [con-the-le-ah'-blay], *a.* Reconcilable, capable of conciliation.

conciliábulo [con-the-le-ah'-boo-lo], *m.* Secret meeting (reunión); unlawful assembly; confabulation (entrevista).

conciliación [con-the-le-ah-the-on'], *f.* 1. Conciliation. 2. Resemblance or affinity which different things bear to each other. 3. Act of obtaining esteem, friendship, or favor.

conciliador, ra [con-the-le-ah-dor', rah], *m. & f.* Conciliator, peacemaker, reconciler. *-a.* Conciliatory.

conciliar [con-the-le-ar'], *va.* 1. To conciliate or compose differences. 2. To conciliate, to gain, to win the affection or esteem of others; to reconcile. 3. To accord, to reconcile two or more doctrines or propositions seemingly contraries. **Conciliar el sueño,** to induce sleep. **Conciliar las amistades,** to make friends.

conciliar [con-the-le-ar'], *a.* Conciliar, relating to councils.

conciliar [con-the-le-ar'], *m.* Member of a council.

conciliativo, va [con-the-le-ah-tee'-vo, vah], *a.* Conciliatory.

conciliatorio [con-the-le-ah-to'-re-o], *a.* Conciliatory.

concilio [con-thee'-le-o], *m.* 1. Council. 2. Council, an assembly of bishops to deliberate upon points of religion. 3. Collection of decrees of a council. **Hacer** or **tener concilio,** *(Coll.)* to keep or hold unlawful meetings.

concinidad [con-the-ne-dahd'], *f.* Harmony, just proportion of sound.

concino, na [con-the'-no, nah], *a.* Harmonious, agreeable to number and harmony.

concisamente [con-the-sah-men'-tay], *adv.* Concisely, briefly, shortly laconically.

concisión [con-the-se-on'], *f.* Conciseness, brevity, terseness.

conciso, sa [con-thee'-so, sah], *a.* Concise, brief, short, laconic.

concitación [con-the-tah-the-on'], *f.* Incitation, the act of stirring up.

concitador [co-the-tah-dor'], *m.* Instigator, troublemaker.

concitar [con-the-tar'], *va.* To excite; to stir up commotions, to incite.

concitativo, va [con-the-tah-tee'-vo, vah], *a.* Inciting; stirring up commotions.

conciudadano [con-the-oo-da-dah'-no], *m.* Fellow citizen, townsman, countryman.

conclave [con-clah'-vay], *or* **cónclave,** *m.* 1. Conclave, place in which the cardinals meet to elect a pope. 2. Conclave, the meeting held for that purpose by the cardinals. 3. Conclave, a close meeting or assembly.

conclavista [con-clah-vees'-tah], *m.* Conclavist, a domestic of a cardinal.

concluir [con-cloo-eer'], *va.* 1. To conclude, to end, to terminate, to finish, to close, to complete, to make up. 2. To complete a thing suddenly. 3. To convince with reason, to make evident. 4. To decide finally, to determine. 5. To infer, to deduce. 6. To close judicial proceedings; to submit to a final decision. 7. *(Fenc.)* To disarm an adversary by laying hold of the hilt of his sword. *-vn.* To end, to conclude, to finish. **Concluir de,** to finish; **todo ha concluido,** it's all over. *-vr.* To end, to conclude.

conclusión [con-cloo-se-on'], *f.* 1. Conclusion. 2. Conclusion, end, close or closure, date, issue. 3. *(Fenc.)* Act of laying hold of the hilt of an adversary's sword. 4. The conclusion of the proceedings in a suit of law. 5. Conclusion, consequence. 6. Thesis controverted and defended in schools. **En conclusión,** finally.

conclusivo, va [con-cloo-see'-vo, vah], *a.* Conclusional, conclusive, final.

concluso, sa [con-cloo'-so, sah], *a.* 1. Concluded, closed, terminated. 2. *(Obs.)* Inclosed, contained. *-pp. irr.* of CONCLUIR.

concluyente [con-cloo-yen'-tay], *pa.* Concluding; conclusive.

concluyentemente [con-cloo-yen-tay-men'-tay], *adv.* Conclusively. *(Yo concluyo, yo concluyera. el concluyó, from Concluir. V.* INSTRUIR.)

concofrade [con-co-frah'-day], *m.* He who belongs to the same brotherhood as another.

concoidal [con-co-e-dahl'], *a. V.* CONCOIDEO.

concoide [con-co'-e-day], *f. (Math.)* Conchoid.

concoideo, a [con-co-e-day'-o, ah], *a.* Conchoidal, resembling a shell.

concolega [con-co-lay'-gah], *m.* Fellow-collegian.

concolón [con-co-lone'], *m. (LAm.) (Culin.)* Scrapings.

concomerse [con-co-merr'-say], *vr.* To shrug the shoulders.

concomimiento, concomio [con-co-me-me-en'-to, con-co'-me-o], *m.* Shrugging of the shoulders.

concomitancia [con-co-me-tahn'-the-ah], *f.* 1. Concomitance, existence together with some other thing. 2. Circumstantial evidence.

concomitante [con-co-me-tahn'-tay], *pa.* 1. Concomitant, concurrent, accompanying. 2. Accessory.

concomitar [con-co-me-tar'], *va.* To concomitate, to attend, to accompany.

concomete [con-co-nay'-tay], *m. (Mex.)* Child, little one.

concordable [con-cor-dah'-blay], *a.* Concordant, conformable, agreeable, accommodable, consistent with.

concordación [con-cor-dah-the-on'], *f.* Coordination, combination, conformation.

concordador [con-cor-dah-dor'], *m.* Conciliator, peacemaker.

concordancia [con-cor-dahn'-the-ah], *f.* 1. Concordance, concord, agreement between persons and things. 2. Harmony, concord of sounds. 3. A concordance of Scripture texts or words. 4. Grammatical concord.

concordante [con-cor-dahn'-tay], *pa.* Concordant, agreeing.

concordar [con-cor-dar'], *va.* 1. To accord, to regulate, to make one thing agree with another; to compromise. *-vn.* 1. To accord, to agree, to comport, to concord. 2. To be congenial, be in accord. **La copia concuerda con su original,** the copy agrees with the original. **Esto no**

concuerda con los hechos, this does not square with the facts.

concordato [con-cor-dah'-to], *m.* Concordat, a convenant made by a state or government with the Pope upon ecclesiastical matters.

concorde [con-cor'-day], *a.* Concordant, agreeable, agreeing. **Poner a dos personas concordes,** to bring about agreement between two people.

concordemente [con-cor-day-men'-tay], *adv.* With one accord.

concordia [con-cor'-de-ah], *f.* 1. Concord, conformity, union, harmony. 2. Agreement between persons engaged in a lawsuit. **De concordia,** jointly, by common consent.

concorpóreo, rea [con-cor-po'-ray-o, ah], *a.* Concorporeal, of the same body.

concreción [con-cray-the-on'], *f.* Concretion.

concrecionar [cone-cray-the-o-nar'], *vn.* To form concretions.

concrescencia [con-cres-then'-the-ah], *f. (Phys.)* Concrescence, growing by the union of separate particles.

concretamente [con-cray-tah-men'-tay], *adv.* Concretely, specifically; exactly. **Se refirió concretamente a dos,** he referred specifically to two. **No es concretamente una fiesta,** it's not exactly a party.

concretar [con-cray-tar'], *va.* To combine, to unite, to concrete. **Concreta sus esperanzas a ganar el premio,** he is concentrating all his hopes on winning the prize. **Vamos a concretar los puntos esenciales,** let sum up the essential points. *-vr.* to be reduced to speaking or treating of one subject only.

concreto, ta [con-cray-to', tah], *a.* 1. Concrete, in logic, not abstracted: applied to a subject. 2. Concrete, formed by concretion: in this last sense it is used as a substantive. **En este caso concreto,** in this particular instance. **No me dijo ninguna hora concreta,** he didn't tell me any definite time. **En concreto había 7,** there were 7 to be exact. *-m.* 1. Concretion. 2. *(LAm.)* Concrete (hormigón).

concubina [con-coo-bee'-nah], *f.* Concubine, mistress.

concubinario [con-coo-be-nah'-re-o], *m.* One who keeps a mistress.

concubinato [con-coo-be-nah'-to], *m.* Concubinage.

concúbito [con-coo'-be-to], *m.* Coition, copulation. *(Yo concuerdo, yo concuerde,* from *Concordar.* V. ACORDAR.)

conculcación [con-cool-cah-the-on'], *f.* Trampling.

conculcar [con-cool-car'], *va.* 1. To trample under foot. 2. To mock, despise, break to pieces, heap abuse upon. 3. To infringe.

concuñado, da [con-coo-nyah'-do, dah], *m. & f.* Brother or sister-in-law; a term confined to persons who are married to two brothers or sisters.

concupiscencia [con-coo-pis-then'-the-ah], *f.* 1. Concupiscence, lust, cupidity. 2. Avarice, Inordinate desire.

concupiscente [con-coo-pis-then'-tay], *a.* 1. Greedy (avaro), acquisitive, 2. Lews (lujurioso), lustful, concupiscent.

concupiscible [con-coo-pis-thee'-blay], *a.* Concupiscible; impressing desire.

concurrencia [con-coor-ren'-the-ah], *f.* 1. Convention or assembly of persons. **Había una numerosa concurrencia,** there was a big attendance. 2. Concurrence, coincidence. 3. Conspiracy, tendency of many causes to one event.

concurrente [con-coor-ren'-tay], *pa.* Concurrent, coincident. **Concurrente cantidad,** the quantity necessary to make up the deficiency of a determinate sum. *-m.* 1. Person present, person attending. **Concurrente al cine,** cinema goer. **Los concurrentes,** those present. 2. Competition.

concurrido [con-coor-re'-do], *a.* Crowded (lugar); much frequented; busy, crowded; popular, well-attended; full (of people).

concurrir [con-coor-reer'], *vn.* 1. To concur, to meet in one point, time, or place. **Concurrir a un baile,** to go to a dance. 2. To concur, to contribute, to coincide, to conspire, to agree with or to agree together, to assist. **Concurrir a la derrota,** to contribute to the defeat. **Concurrir al éxito de una empresa,** to contribute to the success of an enterprise. **Concurrir con una empresa,** to cooperate in an undertaking. 3. To be found. **Concurren de ella muchas buenas cualidades,** she has many good qualities. 4. To compete. **Concurir a un mercado,** to compete in a market.

concursado, da [con-coor-sah'-do], *m. & f.* Insolvent debtor, bankrupt.

concursante [con-coor-sahn'-tay], *m. & f.* Competitor, contestant, participant.

concursar [con-coor-sar'], *va.* 1. To lay an injunction on the goods and chattels of an insolvent debtor. 2. To compete in, to compete for. **Va a concursar a la vacante,** he is going to compete for the vacancy. *-vn.* To compete, to participate.

concurso [con-coor'-so], *m.* 1. Concourse or confluence of persons or things; crowd, congregation, assembly. 2. Aid, assistance. **Con el concurso de,** with the help of. 3. Contest, competition. **Concurso de belleza,** beauty contest. **Concurso hípico,** horse show. **Concurso radiofónico,** radio quiz. **Concurso literario,** literary competition. 4. Proceedings against an insolvent debtor.

concusión [con-coo-se-on'], *f.* Concussion, shaking, the act of shaking. **Concusión violenta,** extortion.

concusionario, ia [con-coo-se-o-nah'-re-o. ah], *a.* Concussive, shaking, extortioner.

condado [con-dah'-do], *m.* 1. Earldom, county. 2. Dignity of a count or earl. 3. County, a political division.

condal [con-dahl'], *a.* Relating to the dignity of an earl or count.

conde [con'-day], *m.* 1. Earl, count. 2. *(Prov.)* Overseer. 3. Head or chief of the gypsies, appointed by election.

condecoración [con-day-co-rah-the-on'], *f.* Decoration, embellishing or decorating.

condecorar [con-day-co-rar'], *va.* To ornament, to adorn, to embellish, to honor, to reward.

condena [con-day'-nah], *f.* 1. The clerk of the court's attestation of the sentence of a condemned criminal. 2. Sentence. **Condena de reclusión perpetua,** life sentence. **Cumplir una condena,** to serve a sentence.

condenable [con-day-nah'-blay], *a.* Condemnable, blamable, culpable, damnable.

condenación [con-day-nah-the-on'], *f.* 1. Condemnation, sentence to punishment. 2. Punishment. **Es una condenación,** *(Coll.)* It is unbearable, intolerable. 3. *(Met.)* Eternal damnation.

condenadamente [con-day-nah-dah-men'-tay], *adv.* **Una mujer condenadamente lista,** a darned clever woman. **Es un trabajo condenadamente duro,** it's darned hard work.

condenado, da [con-day-nah'-do, dah], *m. & f.* One condemned to eternal punishment. **El condenado a muerte,** the condemned man. **El condenado de mi tío,** that ruddy uncle of mine.

condenado, da [con-day-nah'-do, dah], *a. & pp.* 1. of CONDENAR. Condemned, damned, sentenced. **Ser** or **salir condenado en costas,** to be sentenced to pay the costs of a suit at law. **Puerta condenada,** a door boarded up and no longer used. **Aquel condenado teléfono,** that ruddy telephone. 2. Naughty, mischievous (niño). 3. *(Ecl.)* Dammed soul.

condenador, ra [con-day-nah-dor', rah], *m. & f.* Condemner, blamer, censurer.

condenar [con-day-nar'], *va.* 1. To condemn, to pronounce judgment, to sentence. **Condenar a uno a una multa,** to sentence somebody to pay a fine. **Le condenaron por ladrón,** they found him guilty or robbery. 2. To damn. 3. To condemn, to censure, to blame. 4. To refute a doctrine or opinion, to disapprove. **Condenar una puerta, una ventana** or **un pasadizo,** to stop or shut a door, window, or passage, to nail or wall up a door, etc. 5. To vex, to annoy (fastidiar). -vr. 1. To condemn oneself, to acknowledge one's fault. 2. To incur eternal punishment in a future state. 3. To be dammed.

condenatorio, ria [con-day-nah-to'-re-o, ah], a. Condemnatory, damnatory.

condensabilidad [con-den-sah-be-le-dahd'], f. The quality of being condensable.

condensable [con-den-sah'-blay], a. Condensable.

condensación [con-den-sah-the-on'], f. Condensation, compression.

condensado, da [con-den-sah'-do, dah], a. Condensed. **Leche condensada,** condensed milk.

condensador, ra [con-den-sah-dor', rah], m. & f. Condenser.

condensamiento [con-den-sah-me-en'-to], m. V. CONDENSACIÓN.

condensante [con-den-sahn'-tay], pa. Condensing.

condensar [con-den-sar'], va. To thicken, to condense. -vr. To be condensed, to gather.

condensativo, va [con-den-sah-tee'-vo, vah], a. Condensative.

condensidad [con-den-se-dahd'], f. Condensity, condensation.

condesa [con-de'-sah], f. Countess, the wife of a count or the heiress to an earldom.

condescendencia [con-des-then-den'-the-ah], f. Condescendence, condescension, condescending, compliance, complacency, flexibility.

condescender [con-des-then-derr'], vn. To condescend, to yield, to submit, to comply; **condescender a algo,** to consent to something. **Condescender en,** to agree to.

condescendiente [con-des-then-de-en'-tay], a. & pa. Complacent, compliant, acquiescent.

condescendientemente, adv. Condescendingly. (Yo condesciendo, yo condescienda, from Condescender. V. ATENDER.)

condesita [con-day-see'-tah], f. dim. A little or young, countess.

condesito [con-day-see'-to], m. dim. A little earl, a little count.

condestable [con-des-tah'-blay], m. 1. Constable, a lord high constable. **2 Condestable de arsenales,** (Naut.) Gunner of a dockyard. **Segundo condestable,** gunner's mate. 3. (Naut.) Sergeant of marine artillery.

condestablía [con-des-tah-blee'-ah], f. Constableship.

condición [con-de-the-on'], f. 1. Condition, quality. 2. Condition, state, footing, habit. 3. Condition, natural quality of the mind, natural temper or constitution. 4. Quality, rank, or class in society; fashion, especially implying nobility. 5. Condition, clause, stipulation. **Tener mala condición** or **tener condición,** to be of a peevish or irritable disposition; bad tempered. **Tener** or **poner en condición,** to hazard, to expose to danger. **De condición** or **con condición,** so as, on the condition that. **Persona de condición,** person of rank. **La condición humana,** the human condition. **De excelentes cualidades,** of splendid qualities. **Condiciones de trabajo,** working conditions. **Las condiciones del contrato,** the terms of the contract. **Ayuda sin condiciones,** help with no strings attached.

condicionado, da [con-de-the-o-nah'-do, dah], a. 1. Conditioned; well or bad conditioned. 2. V. CONDICIONAL. -pp. of CONDICIONAR.

condicional [con-de-the-o-nahl'], a. Conditional, not absolute.

condicionalmente [con-de-the-o-nal-men'-tay], adv. Conditionally, hypothetically.

condicionante [con-de-the-o-nahn'-tay], m. Determining factor, determinant.

condicionar [con-de-the-o-nar'], vn. To agree, to accord, to condition. -vr. To be of the same nature, condition, or temper.

condicionaza [con-de-the-o-nah'-thah], f. aug. A violent disposition or temper.

condicioncilla, ita [con-de-the-on-theel'-lyah, ee'-tah], f. dim. 1. A hasty or passionate disposition or temper. 2. A small clause, or stipulation.

condignamente [con-dig-nah-men'-tay], adv. Condignly, deservedly.

condigno, na [con-deeg'-no, nah], a. Condign, suitable, deserved, merited.

cóndilo [cone'-de-lo], m. (Anat.) Condyle.

condimentar [con-de-men-tar'], va. To dress or season victuals.

condimento [con-de-men'-to], m. Condiment, seasoning, sauce.

condiscípulo, la [con-dis-thee'-poo-lo], m.f. Condisciple, school-fellow, fellow-scholar or fellow-student.

condistinguir [con-dis-tin-geer'], va. To distinguish, to make a distinction.

condolecerse, condolerse [con-do-lay-therr'-say, con-do-lerr'-say], vr. To condole, to be sorry for, to sympathize with.

condolencia [con-do-layn'-the-ah], f. Condolence, sympathy.

condominio [con-do-mee'-ne-o], m. 1. Joint ownership. 2. Condominium.

condómino [con-do'-me-no], m. A joint owner.

condón [con-done'], m. Condom, preservative, sheath.

condonación [con-do-nah-the-on'], f. Remission, pardoning, forgiving.

condonar [con-do-nar'], va. To pardon, to forgive.

cóndor [con'-dor], m. (Orn.) Condor.

condrila [con-dree'-lah], f. (Bot.) Common gum-succory. Chondrilla juncea.

condrín [con-dreen'], m. A weight for precious metals in the Philippines = 0.3768 gramme.

condritis [con-dree'-tis], f. Inflammation of cartilage, chondritis.

condrografía [con-dro-grah-fee'-ah], f. A description of cartilages.

conducción [con-dooc-the-on'], f. 1. Conveyance. 2. Carriage, the act of carrying. 3. The act of conveying or conducting. 4. Leading, guiding, conduct. 5. Reward for conducting. **Conducción a la derecha,** right-handed drive. **Conducción de agua,** water pipe. **Conducción principal de agua,** water main.

conducencia [con-doo-then'-the-ah], f. The conducing to or promoting any end, conducement.

conducente [con-doo-then'-tay], a. & pa. Conducive, conducent, conducible; official.

conducidor [con-doo-the-dor'], m. Conductor, leader.

conducir [con-doo-theer'], va. & vn. 1. To drive (coches), to convey, to carry, or conduct a thing from one place to another. 2. To conduct, to guide or direct to a place, to show the way, to lead (un ejército). 3. To direct, to manage, to conduct or adjust any affair or business. **Los cables conducen la electricidad,** the cables carry the electricity; **me condujeron por un pasillo,** they led me along a passage. 4. vn. To conduce, to contribute, to favor, to be fitted for. -vr. To behave, to act, to conduct oneself.

conducta [con-dooc'-tah], f. 1. Conduct, management, course, manner of proceeding. 2. Conduct, behavior, comportment, conversation. 3. Life, conduct. 4. Number of mules or horses carrying money from one place to another. 5. Government, command, direction. 6. Party of recruits conducted to the regiment.

conductibilidad [con-dooc-te-be-le-dahd'], f. Conductibility.

conductible [con-dooc-tee'-blay], a. Conveyable, conductible.

conductividad [con-dooc-te-ve-dahd'], f. Conductivity (electricidad).

conductivo, va [con-duc-tee'-vo, vah], a. Having the power of conveying or transporting.

conducto [con-dooc'-to], m. 1. Conduit, sewer, drain, sink. **Conducto alimenticio,** alimentary canal. **Conducto de humo,** flue. 2. Channel, mediation. **Por conducto de, vía,** through. **Salvo conducto,** Safe-conduct.

conductor [con-dooc-tor'], m. 1. Conductor, leader, usher, conduct, guide, conveyer. **Conductor de embajadores,** one whose business is to introduce ambassadors. 2. **Conductor eléctrico,** electric rod. 3. *(Aut.)* Driver, motorist. **Aprendiz de conductor,** learner-driver. 4. *(LAm.) (Mus.)* Conductor. **Conductor de autobuses,** bus driver.

conductora [con-dooc-to'-rah], *f.* 1. Conductress, directress. 2. Woman driver (coches). *(Yo me conduelo, yo me conduela,* from *Condoler. V.* MOVER.)

condueño [con-doo-ay'-nyo], *m. (Com.)* Joint owner.

condumio [con-doo'-me-o], *m.* 1. *(Coll.)* Meat dressed to be eaten with bread. 2. Plenty of food.

conduplicación [con-doo-ple-cah-the-on], *f.* The rhetorical figure of reduplication; the repetition of the last word of the clause just preceding.

condutal [con-doo-tahl'], *m.* Spout to carry off the rainwater from the houses. *V.* CANAL. *(Yo conduzco, yo conduzca; él condujo, el condujera;* from *Conducir. V.* CONDUCIR.

conectado [co-nec-tah'-do], *a.* Connected. **Estar conectado,** to be on; to be live.

conectar [co-nec-tar'], *va.* 1. *(Mech.)* To connect, to couple up. **Conectar un aparato a tierra,** to earth a piece of apparatus. **Conectar a uno con otra persona,** to put somebody in touch with somebody else. **Yo les puedo conectar, I** can put you in touch. *-vn.* **Conectar con,** to communicate with. **Ellos conectan bien,** they get on well. **Ahora conectamos con Londres,** now we're going over to London. *-vr.* To make a connection.

conectículo [co-nec-tee'-coo-lo], *m. (Bot.)* Connective, elastic ring or ferns.

conectivo [co-nec-te'-vo], *a.* Connective.

conector [co-nec-tor'], *m.* Connector.

coneina [co-nay-ee'-nah], *f.* Conein, coneia, an alkaloid obtained from hemlock.

coneja [co-nay'-hah], *f. V.* CONEJO.

conejal [co-nay-hahl'], *m.* 1. Rabbit warren. *V.* CONEJERA. 2. *(Met.)* Suburb inhabited by the common people.

conejar [co-nay-har'], *m.* Rabbit warren.

conejera [co-nay-hay'-rah], *f.* 1. Warren for breeding rabbits. 2. *(Met.)* Brothel. 3. *(Met.)* Den or cavern inhabited by poor people.

conejero [co-nay-hay'-ro], *m.* Warrener, the keeper of a rabbit warren.

conejero [co-nay-hay'-ro, rah], *a.* That which hunts rabbits (perros).

conejito [co-nay-hee'-to], *m. dim.* A little rabbit.

conejo [co-nay'-ho], *a.* **Alambre conejo,** Rabbit wire, copper wire.

conejo, ja [co-nay'-ho, hah], *m. & f.* 1. Rabbit. **Es una coneja,** *(Met.)* She breeds like a rabbit. 2. *(CAm.)* Detective; (andar de conejo), *(LAm.)* To be undercover (policía). 3. *(Mil.)* Recruit, squaddle.

conejuna [co-nay-hoo'-nah], *f.* Rabbit down or fur.

conejuno, na [co-nay-hoo'-no, ah], *a.* Relating to the rabbit kind.

cóneo, a [co'-nay-o, ah], *a.* Like a cone; conical.

conexidades [co-nek-se-dah'-des], *f.pl.* Rights annexed to the principal.

conexión [co-nek-se-on'], *f.* 1. Connection, conjunction, union, conjucture, cohesion, closeness, coherence. 2. *(fig.)* Relationship.

conexionarse [co-nec-se-o-nar'-say], *vr.* To get in touch; to make connections.

conexivo, va [co-nek-see'-vo, vah], *a.* Connective.

conexo, xa [co-nek'-so, sah], *a.* Connected, united.

confabulación [con-fah-boo-lah-the-on'], *f.* 1. Confabulation, easy conversation, chat. 2. Leaguing, conspiracy, collusion.

confabulador, ra [con-fah-boo-lah-dor', rah], *m. & f.* A story-teller, gossip; schemer.

confabular [con-fah-boo-lar'], *vn.* 1. To confabulate, to talk easily together, to chat. 2. To tell stories. 3. *vr.* To league, to enter into conspiracy.

confalón [con-fah-lone'], *m.* Gonfalon, standard, an ensign.

confalonier [con-fah-lo-ne-err'], **Confaloniero,** *m.* Gonfalonier, chief standardbearer.

confección [con-fec-the-on'], *f.* Confection, making, construction. **Confección de vestidos,** dressmaking. **Traje de confección,** ready-to-wear suit. **Es una confección Pérez,** it's a Pérez creation.

confeccionado [con-fec-the-o-nah'-do], *a.* Ready-made, ready-to-wear.

confeccionador, ra [con-fec-the-o-nah-dor', rah], *m. & f.* Confectioner.

confeccionar [con-fec-the-o-nar'], *va.* 1. To make, to prepare, to put together, to complete. 2. To confect.

confecciones, *(Sp. Amer.)* Readymade dresses.

confederación [con-fay-day-rah-the-on'], *f.* 1. Confederacy, league, union, confederation, federation, coalition. 2. Agreement or mutual treaty between monarchs or republics.

confederado, da [con-fay-day-rah'-do, dah], *a. & m. & f.* Confederate, allied, conjoint, federate, covenanter, federal, consociate, *-pp.* of CONFEDERAR.

confederar [con-fay-day-rar'], *va.* To confederate. to join in a league. *-vr.* To confederate, to conjoin, to league.

conferencia [con-fay-ren'-the-ah], *f.* 1. Conference, meeting, conversation, collocution; congress. **Conferencia de desarme,** disarmament conference. **Conferencia de prensa,** press conference. 2. Daily lecture studied by students in universities. **Dar una conferencia,** to give a lecture. 3. Telephone call. **Conferencia de cobro invertido,** reversed-charge call. **Conferencia de persona a persona,** personal call.

conferenciante [con-fay-ren-the-ahn-tay], *m. & f.* Lecturer, speaker.

conferenciar [con-fay-ren-the-ar'], *va.* To confer; to hold a conference.

conferencista [con-fay-ren-thees'-tah], *m. & f.* Lecturer, orator, speaker.

conferir [con-fay-reer'], *va.* 1. To confer, to compare, to estimate the relative qualities of things. 2. To confer, to deliberate, to commune. 3. To give, to bestow, to confer; **conferir un beneficio,** to confer a benefice.

conferva [con-ferr'-vah], *f. (Bot.)* Conferva, a filamentous freshwater alga.

confesa [con-fay'-sah], *f. V.* CONFESO.

confesado, da [con-fay-sah'-do, dah], *a. & pp.* of CONFESAR, Confessed. *-n. (Coll.)* Penitent, one under the spiritual direction of a confessor.

confesante [con-fay-sahn'-tay], *pa.* He who confesses by word or writing before a judge, penitent.

confesar [con-fay-sar'], *va.* 1. To manifest or assert one's opinion. 2. To confess, to acknowledge, to own, to avow, to grant. 3. To confess, to hear or receive confessions. 4. To confess to the priest. **Confesar sin tormento,** to confess, to acknowledge or avow a fault, a crime, etc., freely and readily. *-vr.* To confess, or make confession; to shrive. **Confesarse de sus pecados,** to confess one's sins.

confesión [con-fay-se-on'], *f.* 1. Confession, acknowledgment. 2. Confession to a priest. **Hijo** or **hija de confesión,** a person who has a certain constant confessor. 3. Declaration of a criminal either denying or confessing the charges against him.

confesional [con-fay-se-o-nahl'], *a.* 1. Confessional. **Secreto confesional,** secrecy of confession. 2. Confessional, denominational.

confesionario [con-fay-se-o-nah'-re-o], *m.* 1. Treatise which lays down rules for confessing or hearing confessions, confessional box. 2. Confessional.

confeso, sa [con-fay'-so, sah], *m. & f.* Jewish proselyte. 2. A lay brother; a nun who was before a widow.

confeso, sa [con-fay'-so, sah], *a. (Law.)* Confessed; applied to the person who has acknowledged a crime. *pp. irr.* Of CONFESAR.

confesonario [con-fay-so-nah'-re-o], *m.* Confessional.

confesor [con-fay-sor'], *m.* 1. Confessor, a priest of the Roman church authorized to hear confession of sins and to grant absolution. 2. A title given to holy men by the Roman Catholic church; as, **San Juan Crisóstomo, Doctor, Obispo y Confessor,** St. John Crysostom, B. C. D.

confeti, [con-fay'-te], *m.* Confetti.

confiabilidad [con-fe-a-be-le-dahd'], *f.* Reliability, trustworthiness.

confiable [con-fe-ah'-blay], *a.* Trusty.

confiadamente [con-fe-ah-dah-men', tay], *adv.* Confidently, trustingly, hopefully.

confiado, da [con-fe-ah'-do, dah], *a.* Confident, secure, unsuspicious, trusting; presumptuous, arrogant, forward.

confiador [con-fe-ah-dor'], *m.* 1. A joint surety, a fellow-bondsman. 2. He who confides or expects.

confianza [con-fe-ahn'-thah], *f.* 1. Confidence, trust, reliance, firm belief. **Persona de toda confianza,** reliable person. **Puesto de confianza,** responsible post. **Poner su confianza en,** to put one's trust in. 2. Confidence, honest boldness, firmness of opinion. **Con toda confianza,** with complete confidence. **Estar lleno de confianza,** to be full of confidence. 3. Confidence, presumptuousness, forwardness, assurance. **En confianza,** privately, secretly, confidentially. 4. Confidences; familiarities. **Se toma demasiadas confianzas,** he is too familiar, he's too fresh. 5. Intimacy, familiarity. **Amigo de confianza,** close friend. **Reunión de confianza,** intimate gathering. **Tener confianza con uno,** to be on close terms with somebody.

confianzudo [con-fe-ahn-thoo'-do], *a.* 1. Overfamiliar, fresh. 2. *(LAm.)* Meddlesome (entrometido).

confiar [con-fe-ar'], *va. & vn.* 1. To confide, to trust in. 2. To confide, to credit, to commit to the care of another. 3. To hope; to feed with hope. **Confiar algo en uno,** to entrust something to somebody. **Confiar el éxito de algo,** to feel confident about the success of something. *-vr.* 1. **Confiarse a algo,** to entrust oneself to something. 2. **Confiarse a uno,** *(fig.)* To open one's heart to somebody.

confidencia [con-fe-den'-the-ah], *f.* 1. Confidence. V. CONFIANZA. 2. Secret information.

confidencial [con-fe-den-the-ahl'], *a.* Confidential.

confidencialidad [con-fe-den-the-a-le-dahd'], *f.* Confidentiality, confidential nature.

confidencialmente [con-fe-den-the-al-men'-tay], *adv.* Confidentially.

confidente [con-fe-den'-tay], *m.* 1. Confident, intimate, neighbor, counsellor, 2. A spy.

confidente [con-fe-den'-tay], *a.* True, faithful, trusty.

confidentemente [con-fe-den-tay-men'-tay], *adv.* 1. Confidently, fiducially. 2. Faithfully. *(Yo confiero, yo confiera; él confirió, él confiriera;* from *Conferir.* V. ASENTIR.) *(Yo confieso, yo confiese,* from *Confesar.* V. ACERTAR.)

configuración [con-fe-goo-rah-the-on'], *f.* Configuration. **La configuración del futuro,** the shape of things to come.

configurado, da [con-fe-goo-rah'-do, dah], *a.* Configurated. *-pp.* of CONFIGURAR.

configurar [con-fe-goo-rar'], *va.* To configure, to arrange the parts of something; to configurate: also used reciprocally.

confin [con-feen'], *m.* Limit, boundary, confine, border.

confín, confinante [con-feen', con-fe-nahn'-tay], *a.* Bordering upon, conterminous. **-Confinante,** *pa.* of CONFINAR.

confinar [con-fe-nar'], *va. & vn.* 1. To banish, to exile. 2. To confine, to imprison or immure. 3. To confine, to border upon, to abut. *-vr.* To shut oneself away.

confirmación [con-feer-mah-the-on'], *f.* 1. Confirmation, corroboration, attestation. 2. Evidence; additional proof. 3. Confirmation, a sacrament of the Catholic church.

confirmadamente [con-feer-mah-dah-men'-tay], *adv.* Firmly, unalterably.

confirmador, ra [con-feer-mah-dor', rah], *m. & f.* Confirmator, attester, confirmer.

confirmante [con-feer-mahn'-tay], *pa.* Confirmer.

confirmar [con-fer-mar'], *va.* 1. To confirm, to corroborate, to fortify. 2. To strengthen or support a person or thing. 3. To confirm, to admit to the full privileges of a Christian by the solemn imposition of hands. **La excepción confirma la regla,** the exception proves the rule.

confirmativamente [con-feer-mah-te-vah-men'-tay], *adv.* Confirmingly.

confirmatorio, ria [con-feer-mah-to'-re-o, ah], *a.* Confirmatory, confirmative.

confiscable [con-fis-cah'-blay], *a.* Confiscable, forfeitable.

confiscación [con-fis-cah-the-on'], *f.* Confiscation, forfeiture.

confiscado, da [con-fis-cah'-do, dah], *a. & pp.* of CONFISCAR. Confiscate, confiscated.

confiscar [con-fis-car'], *va.* To confiscate, to transfer private property to the public use.

confiscado [con-fes-cah'-do], *a.* *(CAm.)* Mischievous, naughty.

confitado [con-fe-tah'-do], *a.* **Fruta confitada,** crystallised fruit.

confitar [con-fe-tar'], *va.* 1. To confect, to candy with melted sugar. 2. To make up into sweetmeats. 3. *(Met.)* To dulcify, to sweeten.

confite [con-fee'-tay], *m.* Sweet, candy, sugarplum. **Confites.** 1. Dainties, sugarplum.

confitera [con-fe-tay'-rah], *f.* Candy dish, bonbon dish. V. CONFITERO.

confitería [con-fe-tay-ree'-ah], *f.* 1. A confectioner's shop. 2. Confectionery, sweets, candies.

confitero, ra [con-fe-tay'-ro, rah], *m. & f.* 1. Confectioner. 2. Tray in which sweetmeats are served up.

confitillo [con-fe-teel'-lyo], *m.* 1. Decoration on coverlets. 2. *(dim.)* Small comfit; a sugar-coated sweet containing a nut or seed.

confitón [con-fe-tone'], *m. (aug.)* A large comfit.

confitura [con-fe-too'-rah], *f.* Confiture, comfit, confection, sweetmeats.

conflación [con-flah-the-on'], *f.* Fusion, melting metals, smelting.

conflagración [con-flah-grah-thee-on'], *f.* 1. Conflagration. 2. A sudden and violent perturbation of towns and nations.

conflátil [con-flah'-teel], *a.* Fusible.

conflictividad [con-fleec-te-ve-dahd'], *f.* 1. Tensions and disputes; strains; potentiality for conflict. 2. Controversial nature.

conflictivo [con-fleec-te'-vo], *a.* Troubled (sociedad), filled with conflict; unstable (sistema); controversial. **La edad conflictiva,** the age of conflict. **Zona conflictiva,** area of conflict.

conflicto [con-fleec'-to], *m.* 1. Conflict, struggle, a violent combat or contest. 2. *(Met.)* Struggle, agony, pang.

confluencia [con-floo-en'-the-ah], *f.* Confluence, conflux, flux.

confluente [con-floo-en'-tay], *pa.* Confluent.

confluir [con-floo-eer'], *vn.* 1. To join or meet (ríos, corrientes). 2. *(Met.)* To meet or assemble in one place (muchedumbre).

conformación [con-for-ma-the-on'], *f.* Conformation, shape, form.

conformado [con-for-mah-do], *a.* 1. **Bien conformado,** well-made, well-shaped. 2. Patient, resigned, long-suffering.

conformar [con-for-mar'], *va.* To conform, to adjust, to fit. *-vn.* 1. To suit, to fit, to conform, to cohere, to level. 2. To comply with, to agree in opinion. *-vr.* To yield, to submit, to accommodate. **Se conforma con cualquier cosa,** he agrees to anything. **No me conformo con hacerlo así, I** do not agree to doing it that way.

conforme [con-for'-may], *a.* 1. Conformable, correspondent, suitable, congruent, consonant, convenient, accordant. 2. Consistent, similar. 3. Compliant, resigned. **Conforme a,**

consistent with, agreeable to. **Son muy conforme en todo,** they are very similar in every respect. **Un premio conforme a sus méritos,** a prize consistent with his merits. **Estar conformes,** to agree. **Estamos conformes en que**..., we agree that... **No se quedó conforme con la propina,** he was not satisfied with the tip. *-prep.* **Conforme a,** in conformity with. **Lo hicieron conforme a sus instrucciones,** they acted according to their instructions.

conforme [con-for'-may], *adv.* 1. In proportion, or according to proportion. **Conforme lo iban sacando,** as they were taking it out. 2. Agreeably, according to, *-m.* Agreement. **Dar el conforme,** to agree.

conformemente [con-for-may-men'-tay], *adv.* Conformably, unanimously.

conformidad [con-for-me-dahd'], *f.* 1. Similitude, resemblance, likeness, conformity. 2. Agreement, consistence, consonance, congruence. 3. Union, concord, concordance. 4. Symmetry. 5. A close attachment of one person to another. 6. Submission, acquiescence, patience, resignation. **De conformidad,** by common consent; together, in company. **En conformidad,** agreeably, suitably, according to. **Dar su conformidad,** to consent.

conformismo [con-for-mes'-mo], *m.* Conformism.

conformista [con-for-mees'-tah], *m.f.* Conformist.

confort [con-fort'], *m. pl.* **Conforts** 1. Comfort. 2. *(Cono Sur)* Toilet paper.

confortable [con-for-tah'-blay], *a.* Comfortable. *-m.* Sofa.

confortablemente [con-for-tah-blay-men'-tay], *adv.* Comfortably.

confortación [con-for-tah-the-on'], *f.* Comfort, consolation.

confortador, ra [con-for-tah-dor', rah], *m. & f.* Comforter.

confortante [con-for-tahn'-tay], *pa.* Comforting, soothing. *-m.* Calmative, a soothing remedy; stomachic, relating to food. *-pl.* Mitts.

confortar [con-for-tar'], *pa.* 1. To comfort, to corroborate, to strengthen, to enliven, to invigorate. 2. To console.

confortativo, va [con-for-tah-tee'-vo, vah], *a.* Comfortable, corroborative, cordial; it is frequently used as a substantive. *-m.* 1. Comfort, consolation; encouragement. 2. *(Med.)* Tonic, restorative.

confracción [con-frac-the-on'], *f.* Fraction, breaking.

confraguación [con-frah-goo-ah-the-on'], *f.* The act of mixing, uniting, or incorporating metals with each other.

confraternidad [con-frah-ter-ne-dahd'], *f.* Confraternity, brotherhood.

confraternizar [con-frah-ter-ne-thar'], *vn.* To fraternize.

confrontación [con-fron-tah-the-on'], *f.* 1. Confrontation. 2. Comparing one thing with another. 3. *(Met.)* Sympathy, natural conformity.

confrontante [con-fron-tahn'-tay], *pa.* Confronting, confronter.

confrontar [con-fron-tar'], *va.* 1. To confer, to collate, to confront. 2. To compare one thing with another. *-vn.* 1. To agree in sentiments and opinion. 2. To border upon. *-vr.* **Confrontarse con,** to confront, to face.

confundible [con-foon-de'-blay], *a.* **Fácilmente confundible,** easily mistaken, confused.

confundir [con-foon-deer'], *va.* 1. To confound, to jumble. 2. To confound, to perplex, to confuse, to darken, to throw into disorder. **Confundimos el camino,** we mistook our way. **Ha confundido todos los sellos,** he has mixed up all the stamps. 3. To confute by argument **Confundir a uno con atenciones,** to overwhelm somebody with kindness. 4. To abase, humiliate. *-vr.* 1. To be bewildered, perplexed, or confounded. **Usted se ha confundido de número,** you have the wrong number. 2. To be ashamed and humbled by the knowledge of one's own character. 3. To mix, to blend. **Se confundió con la multitud,** he became lost in the crowd.

confusamente [con-foo-sah-men'-tay], *adv.* Confusedly, mingledly, helterskelter.

confusion [con-foo-se-on'], *f.* 1. Confusion, tumult, disorder, misrule. 2. Confusion, perplexity, perturbation of mind. 3. Confusedness, indistinct combination, obscurity. 4. Humiliation, debasement of mind. 5. Shame, ignominy, reproach. **Echar la confusión a alguno,** *(Law. Obs.)* To imprecate or curse someone.

confusional [con-foo-se-o-nahl'], *a.* **Estado confusional,** confused state, state of confusion.

confusionismo [con-foo-se-o-nes'-mo], *f.* Confusion; uncertainty; confused state. **Sembrar el confusionismo y el desconcierto,** to spread alarm and despondency.

confuso, sa [con-foo'-so, sah], *a.* 1. Confused, mixed, confounded, jumbled together. 2. Obscure, doubtful, indistinct. 3. Fearful, timorous. 4. Perplexed. **En confuso,** confusedly, obscurely, indistinctly.

confutación [con-foo-tah-the-on'], *f.* Confutation, disproof.

confutar [con-foo-tar'], *va.* To confute, to disprove, to falsify, to convict.

conga [con'-gah], *f. (LAm.) (Mus.)* To confute.

congal [con-gahl'], *m. (Mex.)* Brothel.

congelación [con-hay-lah-the-on'], *f.* Freezing, congealing. **Congelación rápida,** deep freezing. **Congelación de salarios,** wage freeze.

congelado [con-hay-lah'-do], *a.* 1. Frozen, chilled (carne). 2. *(Med.)* Frostbitten. 3. *(Fin. etc.)* Frozen, blocked.

congelador [con-hay-lah-dor], *m.* or **congeladora** [con-hay-lah-do'-rah], *f.* Freezer, deepfreeze. **Almacenar en congeladora,** to deepfreeze.

congelar [con-hay-lar'], *va.* 1. To freeze, to congeal. **Congelar alimentos,** to freeze food. 2. *(Med.)* To freeze, affect with frostbite. 3. *(Fin. etc.)* To freeze, to block; to suspend, to freeze. *-vr.* 1. To freeze, to be very cold. 2. *(Med.)* To get frostbitten.

congelativo, va [con-hay-lah-tee'-vo, vah], *a.* Having the power of congealing.

congénere [con-hay'-nay-ray], **congenérico, ca** [con-hay-nay'-re-co, cah], *a.* Congeneric, of like kind.

congenial [con-hay-ne-ahl'], *a.* Congenial, analogous.

congeniar [con-hay-ne-ar'], *vn.* To be congenial, to sympathize. **Congeniamos con los dos hermanos,** we hit it off with the two brothers.

congenital [con-hay-ne-tahl'], *a. (LAm.)* Congenital.

congénito [con-hay'-ne-to], *a.* Congenital, connate.

congerie [con-hay'-re-ay], *f.* Congeries, heap, mass.

congestión [con-hes-te-on'], *f.* Congestion.

congestionado [con-hays-te-o-nah'-do], *a.* 1. Congested. 2. *(Med.)* Congested, chesty; flushed (cara).

congestionamiento [con-hays-te-o-nah-me-ayn'-to], *m.* *(Aut.)* Traffic jam.

congestionar [con-hes-te-oh-nar'], *vn. & vr.* To congest, become congested.

congio [con'-he-o], *m.* Ancient Roman liquid measure: gallon.

conglobación [con-glo-bah-the-on'], *f.*

conglobar [con-glo-bar'], *va.* To conglobate; to heap together.

conglomeración [con-glo-may-rah-the-on'], *f.* Conglomeration, heterogeneous mixture.

conglomerado, da [con-glo-may-rah'-do, dah], *a.* Conglomerate. *-pp.* of CONGLOMERAR.

conglomerar [con-glo-may-rar'], *va.* To conglomerate. *-vr.* to conglomerate.

congloriar [con-glo-re-ar'], *va.* To fill or cover with glory.

conglutinación [con-gloo-te-nah-the-on'], *f.* Conglutination, glutination; gluing together.

conglutinado, da [con-gloo-te-nah'-do, dah], *a.* Conglutinate. *-pp.* of CONGLUTINAR.

conglutinar [con-gloo-te-nar'], *va.* To conglutinate, to cement, to reunite. *-vr.* To conglutinate.

conglutinativo, va [con-gloo-te-nah-tee'-vo, vah], **Conglutinoso, sa,** *a.* Viscous, glutinous.

Congo [con'-go], *m.* The Congo.

congoja [con-go'-hah], *f.* Anguish, dismay, anxiety of mind.

congojar [con-go-har'], *va.* To oppress, to afflict. *V.* ACONGOJAR.

congojosamente [con-go-ho-sah-men'-tay], *adv.* Anxiously, painfully.

congojoso, sa [con-go-ho'-so, sah], *a.* 1. Afflictive, painful, tormenting, distressing. 2. Afflicted.

congola [con-go-lah], *f. (And.)* Pipe.

congoleño, ña [con-go-lay'-nyo, nyah], *a.* Relating to or native of the Congo region, in Africa.

congolés [con-go-lays'], *V.* CONGOLEÑO.

congosto [con-gos'-to], *m.* Narrow pass, canyon.

congraciador, ra [con-grah-the-ah-dor', rah], *m. & f.* Flatterer, fawner, wheedler, congratulator.

congraciamiento [con-grah-the-ah-me-en'-to], *m.* Flattery, false praise, mean obsequiousness.

congraciante [con-grah-the-ahn'-tay], *a.* Ingratiating.

congraciar [con-grah-the-ar'], *va.* To ingratiate, to flatter, to win over. *-vr.* To get into one's good graces.

congratulación [con-grah-too-lah-the-on'], *f.* Congratulation.

congratular [con-grah-too-lar'], *va.* To congratulate, to compliment upon any happy event, to greet. *-vr.* To congratulate, to be pleased. **De eso nos congratulamos,** we congratulate ourselves on that.

congratulatorio, ria [con-grah-too-lah-to'-reo, ah], *a.* Congratulatory, congratulant.

congregación [con-gray-gah-the-on'], *f.* 1. Congregation, a meeting or assembly. 2. Fraternity, brotherhood. 3. Congregation, an assembly met to worship God. 4. In some religious orders, union of many monasteries under the direction of a superior general. **Congregación de los fieles,** the catholic or universal church.

congregacionalismo [con-gray-gah-the-o-nah-lees'-mo], *m.* Congregationalism.

congregacionalista [con-gray-gah-the-o-nah-lees'-tah], *com.* Congregationalist.

congregante, ta [con-gray-gahn'-tay, tah], *m. & f.* Member of a congregation, fraternity, or brotherhood.

congregar [con-gray-gar'], *va.*

congresal [con-gray-sahl'], *m. & f. V.* CONGRESISTA.

congresista [con-gray-sees'-tah], *m. & f.* Delegate, member of a congress.

congreso [con-gray'-so], *m.* 1. Congress. 2. Consistory, convention, any solemn assembly or congress. 3. Congress, a meeting of commissioners to settle terms of peace between powers at war. 4. Congress, carnal union of man and women.

congresual [con-gray-soo-ahl'], *a.* **Reunión congresual,** meeting of parliament.

congrio [con'-gre-o], *m. (Zool.)* Conger-eel, or sea-eel.

congrua [con'-groo-ah], *f.* A stipend paid to someone who is to be ordained a priest.

congruamente [con-groo-ah-men'-tay], *adv.* Conveniently, becomingly.

congruencia [con-groo-en'-the-ah], *f.* Convenience, fitness, congruence.

congruente [con-groo-en'-tay], *a.* Congruent, agreeing, corresponding.

congruentemente [con-groo-en-tay-men'-tay], *adv.* Suitably, congruously.

congruidad [con-groo-e-dahd'], *f. V.* CONGRUENCIA.

congruismo [con-groo-ees'-mo], *m.* Congruism, a religious doctrine which explains the efficacy of grace by its appropriateness.

congruista [con-groo-ees'-tah], *m.* A supporter of the foregoing theory.

congruo, ua [con'-groo-o, ah], *a.* Congruous, apt, fit, suitable.

conicidad [co-ne-the-dahd'], *f.* Conicity, the figure which the tire of a wheel presents in machines and railroad carriages.

cónico, ca [co'-ne-co, cah], *a.* Conical or conic.

conífero, ra [co-nee'-fay-ro, rah], *a. (Bot.)* Coniferous (plantas, árboles).

coniza [co-nee'-thah], *f. (Bot.)* Great fleabane. *V.* ZARAGATONA.

conjetura [con-hay-too'-rah], *f.* Conjecture, surmise, guess. **Por conjetura,** by guess-work.

conjeturable [con-hay-too-rah'-blay], *a.* Conjecturable.

conjeturador, ra [con-hay-too-rah-dor', rah], *m. & f.* Conjecturer, guesser.

conjetural [con-hay-too-rahl'], *a.* Conjectural.

conjeturalmente [con-hay-too-ral-men'-tay], *adv.* Conjecturally, guessingly.

conjeturar [con-hay-too-rar'], *va.* To conjecture, to guess.

conjuez [con-hoo-eth'], *m.* A judge jointly with another upon the same matter.

conjugación [con-hoo-gah-the-on'], *f.* 1. Conjugation, the form of inflecting verbs. 2. The act of comparing one thing with another.

conjugado, da [con-hoo-gah'-do, dah], *a. & pp.* of CONJUGAR. Conjugated, inflected; compared. **Nervios conjugados,** *(Anat.)* Conjugate nerves, those which discharge analogous functions or serve for the same sensation.

conjugar [con-hoo-gar'], *va.* 1. To conjugate or inflect verbs. 2. To compare, to bring together. **La obra conjuga cualidades y defectos,** the work has both qualities and defects. **Es difícil conjugar los deseos de los dos,** it is difficult to fit their wishes together. *-vr.* 1. *(Ling.)* To be conjugated. 2. To fit together, to blend.

conjunción [con-hoon-the-on'], *f.* 1. Conjunction, union, association, league, conjugation, copulation, the act of coupling or joining together; consolidation. 2. Conjunction, a part of speech. 3. *(Astr.)* Conjunction of two planets in the same degree of the zodiac.

conjuntamente [con-hoon'-tah-men-tay], *adv.* Conjunctly, jointly.

conjuntero, ra [con-hoon-tay'-ro], *m. & f.* Member of a musical group.

conjuntiva [con-hoon-tee'-vah], *f.* Conjunctiva, the mucous membrane of the eye.

conjuntivitis [con-hoon-te-vee'-tis], *f. (Med.)* Conjunctivitis.

conjuntivo, va [con-hoon-tee'-vo, vah], *a.* Conjunctive, copulative, connexive.

conjuntivo [con-hoon-tee'-vo], *m.* The conjunctive mood of a verb. *V.* SUBJUNTIVO.

conjunto, ta [con-hoon'-to, tah], *a.* 1. Conjunct, united, connected, conjunctive, contiguous. 2. Allied by kindred or friendship. 3. Mixed or incorporated with another thing.

conjunto [con-hoon'-to], *m.* 1. The whole, aggregate, entirety. **En conjunto,** as a whole. **Vista de conjunto,** all-embracing view. 2. *(Cos.)* Ensemble; costume. 3. *(Mus.)* Ensemble (de cámara); group (de pop); team. 4. *(Theat.)* Chorus. 5. *(Mech.)* Unit, assembly.

conjuntura [con-hoon-too'-rah], *f. V.* COYUNTURA and CONJUNCIÓN.

conjura [con-hoo'-rah], *f. V.* CONJURACIóN.

conjuración [con-hoo-rah-the-on'], *f.* 1. Conspiracy, conjuration, plot, complot, machination. 2. Conjuration, the form or act of summoning another in some sacred name. 3. *V.* CONJURO.

conjurado, da [con-hoo-rah'-do, dah], *m. & f.* Conspirator; leaguer, covenanter. *-pp.* of CONJURAR.

conjurador [con-hoo-rah-dor'], *m.* 1. Conjurer, enchanter, impostor 2. Exorcist. 3. Conspirator.

conjuramentar [con-hoo-rah-men-tar'], *va.* 1. To bind by an oath. 2. To take an oath to another. *-vr.* To bind oneself by an oath. *V.* JURAMENTARSE.

conjurante [con-hoo-rahn'-tay], *pa.* Conjuring, conspiring.

conjurar [con-hoo-rar'], *vn.* To conjure, to conspire, to plot, to hatch or concert treason. 2. To conspire. 3. To join in a conspiracy formed by others. 4. To swear or take an oath improperly with others. *-va.* 1. To exorcise. 2. To conjure, to summon in a sacred name. 3. To entreat, to implore, to ask anything in a solemn manner. 4. To avert, ward off, a mischief or danger.

conjuro [con-hoo'-ro], *m.* 1. Conjuration, exorcism. **Al conjuro de sus palabras,** under the magical effect of his words. 2. Incantation.

conllevador [con-lyay-vah-dor'], *va.* Helper, assistant.

conllevar [con-lyay-var'], *va.* 1. To aid or assist another in his labors; to bear with anyone. 2. To convey, to carry, to imply, to involve, to bring with it, to bring in its wake.

conmaterial [con-mah-tay-re-ahl'], *a.* (Rare) Of the same material.

conmemoración [con-may-mo-rah-theon'], *f.* 1. Remembrance of a person or thing. 2. Commemoration, public celebration. 3. **Conmemoración de los difuntos,** anniversary celebrated by the Roman Catholic church in memory of the deceased, Nov. 2; Allsouls' day.

conmemorar [con-may-mo-rar'], *va.* To commemorate by public acts.

conmemorativo, va [con-may-mo-rah-tee'-vo, vah], *a.* Commemorative. **Un sello conmemorativo,** a commemorative stamp.

conmensal [con-men-sahl'], *m.* Commensal, mate, messmate, one who lives and boards with another at his expense.

conmensalía [con-men-sah-lee'-ah], *f.* Commensality.

conmensurabilidad [con-men-soo-rah-be-le-dahd'], *f.* Commensurability.

conmensurable [con-men-soo-rah'-blay], *a.* Commensurable.

conmesuración [con-men-soo-rah-the-on'], *f.* Commensuration.

conmensurar [con-men-soo-rar'], *va.* To commensurate.

conmensurativo, va [con-men-soo-rah-tee'-vo, vah], *a.* Commensurable.

conmigo [con-mee'-go], *pron. pers.* With me, with myself.

conmilitón [con-me-le-tone'], *m.* Comrade, a fellow soldier.

conminación [con-me-nah-the-on'], *f.* Commination, a threat.

conminar [con-me-nar'], *va.* To threaten or denounce punishment to a criminal in order to make him declare the truth.

conminatorio, ria [con-me-nah-to'-re-o, ah], *a.* Comminatory, denunciatory, threatening.

conminuta [con-me-noo'-tah], *a.* Comminuted. *V.* FRACTURA.

conmiseración [con-me-say-rah-the-on'], *f.* Commiseration, pity, compassion.

conmistión, conmistura [con-mis-te-on'], *f.* Mixture.

conmisto, ta, or **conmixto, ta** [con-mees'-to, tah], *a.* Mixed, mingled, incorporated.

conmoción [con-mo-the-on'], *f.* 1. Commotion of the mind or body. 2. Excitement, stirring up; flurry, fretting. 3. Commontion, tumult, disturbance, convulsion. **Una conmoción social,** a social upheaval. **Producir una conmoción desagradable a uno,** to give somebody a nasty shock.

conmocionado [con-mo-te-o-nah'-do], *a. (Med.)* Shocked, concussed.

conmocionar [con-mo-the-o-nar'], *va.* 1. To move, to affect deeply. 2. *(Med.)* To put into shock.

conmonitorio [con-mo-ne-to'-re-o], *m.* 1. A written narration of an event. 2. Order from a superior to an inferior judge, reminding him of his duty.

conmovedor [con-mo-vay-dor'], *-a.* Touching, moving; poignant.

conmover [con-mo-verr'], *va.* 1. To move, to touch, to disturb, to affect (persona). 2. To shake, to disturb (edificio). *-vr.* 1. To shake, to be shaken. 2. *(fig.)* To be moved.

conmovimiento [con-mo-ve-me-en'-to], *m. V.* CONMOCIÓN. *(Yo conmuevo, yo conmueva,* from *Conmover. V.* MOVER.).

conmuta [con-moo'-tah], *f. (And. Cono Sur)* Change, alteration.

conmutabilidad [con-moo-tah-be-le-dahd'], *f.* Commutability.

conmutable [con-moo-tah'-bay], *a.* Commutable.

conmutación [con-moo-tah-the-on'], *f.* Commutation, exchange.

conmutador [con-moo-tah-dor'], *m.* Electric switch, telegraph key, cutout, commutator.

conmutar [con-moo-tar'], *va.* To commute, to change, to barter.

conmutativo, va [con-moo-tah-tee'-vo, vah], *a.* Commutative.

connato, ta [con-nah'-to, tah], *a.* 1. *(Med.)* Connate, congenital, innate. 2. *(Bot.)* Connate, conjoined.

connatural [con-nah-too-rahl'], *a.* Connatural, inborn.

connaturalización [con-nah-too-rah-le-thah-the-on'], *f.* Naturalization, investing aliens with the privileges of native subjects.

connaturalizar [con-nah-too-rah-le-thar'], *va.* To naturalize, to invest with the privileges of native subjects. *-vr.* To accustom oneself to labor, climate, or food; to inure.

connaturalmente [con-nah-too-ral-men'-tay], *adv.* Connaturally.

connexidad [con-nek-se-dahd,], *f. V.* CONEXIDAD.

connivencia [con-ne-ven'-the-ah], *f.* 1. Connivance. 2. Action of confabulating.

connotación [con-no-tah-the-on'], *f.* 1. Connotation. 2. A distant relation.

connotado [con-no-tah'-do], *m.* Relationship, kindred. *Connotado, da pp.* of CONNOTAR. *-a.* Notable, famous.

connotar [con-no-tar'], *va.* To connote, to connotate, to imply.

connotativo, va [con-no-tah-tee'-vo, vah], *a. (Gram.)* Connotative or connotive, applied to nouns which signify the quality of the object designated by the primitive noun, or the office of the subject from which it is derived, as *aquilino, caballar, bacanal, lírico,* etc.

connovicio, cia [con-no-vee'-the-o, ah], *m. & f.* A fellow-novice.

connubial [con-noo-be-ahl'], *a.* Connubial, matrimonial, conjugal.

connubio [con-noo'-be-o], *m. (Poet.)* Matrimony, marriage, wedlock.

connumerar [con-noo-may-rar'], *va.* To enumerate; to include in a number.

cono [co'-no], *m.* 1. *(Geom.)* Cone. 2. *(Zool.)* Genus of mollusks which has the spiral of the shell flattened. 3. *(Bot.)* Cone, the fruit of the pine family. 4. **El Cono Sur** = Argentina, Chile, Uruguay.

conocedor, ra [co-no-thay-dor', rah], *m. & f.* 1. Connoissuer, expert. 2. Judge or critic in matters of taste. **Es buen conocedor de ganado,** he's a good judge of cattle.

conocencia [co-no-then'-the-ah], *f. (LAm.)* Girlfriend, sweetheart.

conocer [co-no-therr'], *va.* 1. To know, to be acquainted with. 2. To possess a clear or distinct idea of a person's physiognomy, or the figure of a thing, to feel. 3. To perceive, to comprehend. 4. To experience, to observe. 5. To conjecture, to surmise. 6. To know carnally. 7. To acknowledge a crime, or debt. **Conocer de una causa or pleito,** to try a cause (jueces). **Conocer a uno de vista,** to know somebody by sight. **Conozco las dificultades,** I know the difficulties. **Vengo a conocer Portugal,** I have come to get to know Portugal. **Dar a conocer,** to introduce. **Conocer a uno por su modo de andar,** to know somebody by his walk. **No me conoce de nada,** he doesn't know me from Adam. *-vr.* 1. To know one another. **Se conocieron en un baile,** they met at a dance. 2. To appreciate one's own good or bad qualities. *-vn.* **Conocer de,** to know about. 2. **Conocer de una causa,** *(Jur.)* To try a case.

conocible [co-no-thee'-blay], *a.* Cognoscible, knowable.

conocidamente [co-no-the-dah-men'-tay], *adv.* Knowingly, evidently, confessedly.

conocido, da [co-no-thee'-do, dah], 1. *m. & f.* Acquaintance. 2. *a.* Person of family or distinction. *-pp.* of CONOCER.

conocimiento [co-no-the-me-en'-to], *m.* 1. Knowledge, understanding, skill. **Hablar con conocimiento de causa,** to know what one is talking about. **Ha llegado a mi conocimiento que...**, it has come to my attention that... **Mis pocos conocimientos de filosofía,** my small knowledge of philosophy. **Conocimientos avanzados,** expert knowledge. 2. Acquaintance, the person with whom we are acquainted. 3. Acquaintance, a slight or initial knowledge, a sort of friendship. 4. Cognizance, judicial notice. 5. *(Com.)* Bill of lading. 6. A note of identification, relative to business matters. 7. *(Amer.)* A check for baggage. 8. *(Med.)* Consciousness. **Estar sin conocimiento,** to be unconcious. *-pl.* Accomplishments, science. **Venir en conocimiento,** to remember or recollect a thing distinctly, to comprehend a thing clearly after thinking of it.

conoidal [co-no-e-dahl'], *a.* Conoidal, conoidical.

conoide [co-no'-e-day], *f.* Conoid.

conopial, conopio [co-no-pe-ahl', co-no-pe-o], *m. (Arch.)* Ogee arch *(Yo conozco, yo conozca,* from *Conocer. V.* ABORRECER.).

conque [con-kay'], *m. (Coll.)* Condition, quality.

conquiforme [con-ke-for'-may], *a.* Conchiform, shaped line onehalf of a bivalve shell.

conquista [con-kees'-tah], *f.* 1. Conquest, subjection. 2. Conquest, acquisition by victory; the thing gained. 3. Act of winning another's affections.

conquistador [con-kees-tah-dor'], *m.* 1. Conqueror. 2. Wolf, lady-killer. *-a.* Conquering.

conquistadora [con-kees-tah-do'-rah], *f.* Conqueress.

conquistar [con-kees-tar'], *va.* 1. To conquer, to overcome, to subdue. 2. To acquire, to win another person's affections.

conrear [con-ray-ar'], *va.* 1. In manufactories, to grease wool. 2. To hoe the soil. *V.* BINAR.

conregnante [con-reg-nahn'-tay], *a.* Reigning with another.

conreinar [con-ray-e-nar'], *vn.* To reign with another.

consabido, da [con-sah-bee'-do, dah], *a.* Already known; alluded to, in question: applied to persons or things already treated of. *-pp.* of CONSABER.

consabidor, ra [con-sah-be-dor', rah], *m. & f.* One who possesses knowledge jointly with others.

consagración [con-sah-grah-the-on'], *f.* Consecration.

consagrado, da [con-sah-grah-do, dah], *a. & pp.* of CONSAGRAR. 1. Consecrate, consecrated, sacred, devoted. 2. *(fig.)* Time-honored, hallowed, ritual, traditional. **Actor consagrado,** an established actor.

consagrante [con-sah-grahn'-tay], *m. & pa.* Consecrator.

consagrar [con-sa-grar'], *va.* 1. To consecrate, to hallow, to make sacred. 2. Among the Romans, to deify their emperors. 3. To consecrate, to devote, to dedicate. 4. To erect a monument. 5. To confirm. **Este triunfo le consagra como un cirujano excepcional,** this success confirms him as a really exceptional surgeon. *-vr.* To devote oneself.

consanguíneo, nea [con-san-gee'-nay-o, ah], *a.* Consanguineous, cognate, kindred.

consanguinidad [con-san-gee-ne-dahd'], *f.* Consanguinity.

consciencia, *f.* Consciousness; awareness. *V.* CONCIENCIA.

consciente [cons-the-en'-tay], *a.* 1. Conscious, in possession of one's faculties. **Ser consciente de,** to be conscious of. 2. *(Med.)* **Estar consciente,** to be conscious. 3. *(Jur.)* Fully responsible for one's actions. *-m.* Conscious, conscious mind.

conscientemente [cons-the-ayn-tay-men'-tay], *adv.* Consciously.

conscripción [cons-crip-the-on'], *f.* Conscription.

conscripto [cons-creep'-to], *m.* Conscript, taken by lot, or compulsorily enrolled to serve in the army or navy. *a.* Conscript (senadores romanos).

consectario [con-sec-tah'-re-o], *m.* Consectary, corollary.

consectario [con-sec-tah'-re-o], *a.* Consectary, consequent.

consecución [con-say-coo-the-on'], *f.* Attainment of a benefice. employment, or other desirable object, obtaining, acquisition. **De difícil consecución,** hard to

obtain. **Para la consecución de estos objetos,** for the attainment of these aims.

consecuencia [con-say-coo-en'-the-ah], *f.* 1. Consequence, conclusion, inference. **Por consecuencia,** therefore. 2. Result or effect of a cause, issue. **En consecuencia de eso,** as a result of that. **Aceptar las consecuencias,** to take the consequences. 3. Consistence, firmness, coherence. **Guardar consecuencia,** to be consistent. 4. Consequence, importance, moment, concern, matter; consideration, note. **De consecuencia,** of importance. **Ser de consecuencia,** to be important. **Ser de consecuencia,** to be very important. **En consecuencia,** consequently, therefore, in consequence of.

consecuente [con-say-coo-en'-tay], *m.* 1. Consequent, consequence. 2. Effect. 3. Important. **No demasiado consecuente,** not very important.

consecuente, [con-say-coo-ayn'-tay], *a.* 1. Consequent, following by rational deduction. 2. Following, as the effect of a cause. 3. Consistent, coherent. **Ser consecuente en sus operaciones,** to act with consistency.

consecuentemente [con-say-coo-en-tay-men'-tay], *adv.* 1. Consequently. 2. By consequence, necessarily, inevitably.

consecutivamente [con-say-coo-te-vah-men'-tay], *adv.* Consecutively.

consecutivo, va [con-say-coo-tee'-vo, vah], *a.* Consecutive, consequential.

conseguible [con-say-gee'-blay], *a.* Obtainable, attainable.

conseguimiento [con-say-gee-me-en'-to], *m.* Attainment, obtainment. *V.* CONSECUCIÓN.

conseguir [con-say-geer'], *va.* To attain, to get, to gain, to obtain, to succeed. **Conseguir que uno haga algo,** to manage to make somebody do something. **Lo consigue como mi abuela,** he has as much chance of getting it as the man in the moon.

conseja [con-say'-hah], *f.* A fable, tale, story, legend.

consejera [con-say-hay'-rah], *f.* Counsellor's wife; woman who gives advice.

consejería [con-say-hay-ree'-ah], *f.* Council, commission.

consejero, ra [con-say-hay'-ro], *m. & f.* 1. Counsellor, member of a council. 2. Counsellor, adviser. 3. Anything which may give warning. 4. **Consejero de estado,** a counsellor of state.

consejo [con-say'-ho], *m.* 1. Counsel, advice, opinion. **Agradezco el consejo,** I am grateful for your advice. **Pedir consejo a uno,** to ask somebody for advice. 2. Council, an assembly of magistrates. 3. Councilhouse. **Consejo directivo,** board of directors. **Consejo de ministros,** cabinet. **Consejo de guerra,** court-martial. **Consejo de disciplina,** disciplinary board.

consejuela [con-say-hoo-ay'-lah], *f. dim.* A little tale or story.

conseminado, da [con-say-me-nah'-do, dah], *a. (Agri.)* Sown with different kinds of grain.

consenciente [con-sen-the-en'-tay], *pa.* Consenting, conniver.

consenso [con-sen'-so], *m.* A general assent, agreement of opinion: consensus.

consensual [con-sen-soo-ahl'], *a.* Agreed. **Unión consensual,** common-law marriage.

consensuar [con-sen-soo-ar'], *va.* To agree on, to reach an agreement on, to reach a consensus on.

consentido [con-sen-tee'-do], *a.* 1. Applied to a spoiled child. 2. Applied to a cuckold by his own consent. **- consentido, da,** *pp.* of CONSENTIR.

consentidor, ra [con-sen-te-dor', rah], *m. & f.* Complier, conniver.

consentimiento [con-sen-te-me-en'-to], *m.* 1. Consent, connivance, compliance, acquiescence, concurrence, consenting, acknowledgment. 2. *(Med.)* Consent.

consentir [con-sen-teer'], *va.* 1. To consent, to agree. **Aquí no se consiente hablar,** they don't let you speak. 2. To comply, to acquiesce, to accede, to condescend, to admit. **La plata-**

forma no consiente más peso, the platform will not bear any more weight. 3. To believe for certain, to rely, to depend. 4. To coddle, spoil, overindulge children or servants. *(Acad.).* *-vn.* To agree, to consent, to say yes; to give in. **Consentir en hacer algo,** to agree to. *-vr.* To break, to give; to split, to crack.

conserje [con-serr'-hay], *m.* Keeper or warden of a royal palace, castle, or public building. *(Cf.* Concierge.)

conserjería [con-ser-hay-ree'-ah], *f.* 1. Wardenship of a royal palace or castle. 2. Warden's dwelling.

conserva [con-serr'-vah], *f.* 1. Conserve, preserve. **Conservas alimenticias,** canned foods. **Conservas de carne,** canned meat. **En conservas,** preserved. 2. Pickles. 3. Fleet of merchant men under convoy of a ship of war. **Ir** or **navegar de conserva,** to sail under convoy, to navigate in company with other ships. *-pl.* Tinned, canned food.

conservación [con-ser-vah-the-on'], *f.* 1. Conservation, preservation. 2. Maintenance, upkeep. **Conservación del suelo,** soil conservation. **Conservación de la naturaleza,** nature conservation. **Instinto de conservación.** instinct of self-preservation.

conservacionismo [con-ser-vah-the-o-nes'-mo], *m.* Conservationist; conservation; conservation movement.

conservacionista [con-ser-vah-the-o-nes-tah], *a. m. & f.* Conservationist.

conservador [con-ser-vah-do,], *m.* Conservator, preserver.

conservadora [con-ser-vah-do'-rah], *f.* 1. Conservatrix. 2. Curator, keeper (de museo).

conservadurismo [con-ser-vah-doo-res'-mo], *m. (Pol. etc.)* Conservatism.

conservante [con-ser-vahn'-tay], *pa.* Conserving, conserver, preservative.

conservar [con-ser-var'], *va.* 1. To conserve, to maintain, to preserve, to keep, to hold. 2. To guard, to observe, to continue. 3. To preserve or pickle fruit. **Conservo varias cartas suyas,** I have a few letters of his. **Conserva todavía la señal,** he still has the mark. *-vr.* 1. To survive, to remain; to be retained, to be kept. 2. To keep (persona); to take good care of; **conservar con salud,** to keep well.

conservatismo [con-ser-vah-tes'-mo], *m.* Conservatism.

conservativo, va [con-ser-vah-tee'-vo, vah], *a.* Conservative, preservative.

conservativos [con-ser-vah-tee'-vos], *m. pl.* Glasses with preservative lenses.

conservatoría [con-ser-vah-to-ree'-ah], *f.* 1. Place and office of a *Juez conservador,* who is responsible for preserving and defending the rights and privileges of a community. 2. Indult or apostolical letters granted to communities, by virtue of which they choose their own judges conservators; **conservatorías,** letters patent granted by conservatory judges in favor of those under their jurisdiction.

conservatorio [con-ser-vah-to'-re-o], *m.* 1. Conservatory, a place for instruction in the fine arts. 2. *(Cono Sur)* Greenhouse. 3. *(Cono Sur)* private school.

conservatorio, ria [con-ser-vah-to'-re-o, ah], *a.* Conservatory, having a preservative quality.

conservero, ra [con-ser-vay'-ro, rah], *m. & f.* Conserver, a preparer of conserves.

considerable [con-se-day-rah'-blay], *a.* 1. Considerable. 2. Great, large, plentiful.

considerablemente [con-se-day-rah.-blay-men'-tay], *adv.* Considerably.

consideración [con-se-day-rah-the-on'], *f.* 1. Consideration, regard, notice, sake, account. **Hablar sin consideración,** to speak disrespectfully. **Tratar a uno sin consideración,** to treat somebody without consideration. 2. Consideration; reflection, contemplation, meditation. 3. Consideration, importance, claim to notice, worthiness of regard. **Una casa de cierta consideración,** a sizeable house. **Una herida de consideración,** a serious wound. 4. Urbanity, respect. **Ser de consideración,** to be of great importance. **En**

consideración, considering, in consideration, in proportion.

consideradamente [con-se-day-rah-dah-men'-tay], *adv.* Considerately, calmly.

considerado [con-se-day-rah'-do], *a.* Prudent, considerate. **-Considerado, da.** *pp.* of CONSIDERAR.

considerador, ra [con-se-day-rah-dor', rah], *m. & f.* Considerer, considerator, a person of prudence or reflection.

considerando [con-se-day-rahn'-do], *m. (Jur.)* Word with which each item in a judgement begins; point, item, statement.

considerante [con-se-day-rahn'-tay], *pa.* Considering.

considerar [con-se-day-rar'], *va.* 1. To consider, meditate. 2. To treat with urbanity, respect, consideration. 3. To take into account. **Considera que...,** bear in mind that... **Bien considerado, es razonable,** on reflection, that is reasonable. **Lo considero imposible,** I consider it impossible. **Considerar poco a,** to scorn, to despise.

consigna [con-seeg'-nah], *f.* 1. *(Mil.)* Watchword, countersign, order, instruction. **Consignas de un vuelo,** operating instructions for a flight. 2. *(Ferro. etc.)* Cloakroom, left-luggage office, check-room.

consignación [con-sig-nah-the-on'], *f.* 1. Consignation. 2. Sum of money destined to serve for a certain time some peculiar purpose. 3. Consignment, cargo of goods.

consignador, ra [con-sig-nah-dor'], *m. & f.* Consignor, one who consigns goods or merchandise to a foreign correspondent.

consignar [con-sig-nar'], *va.* 1. To consign, assign, or make over the rent of a house or any other sum for the payment of a debt. 2. To consign, to yield, to entrust, to lay to. 3. To lay by, to deposit. 4. To deliver. 5. To consign goods or merchandise to a foreign correspondent, to be sold on behalf of the consigner. 6. To sign with the mark of a cross. 7. *(CAm. Mex.) (Jur.)* To remand, to hold for trial. **Olvidé consignar mi nombre,** I forgot to write my name in, I forgot to state my name. **El hecho no quedó consignado en ningún libro,** the fact was not recorded in any book.

consignatario, ria [con-sig-nah-tah'-re-o], *m. & f.* 1. Trustee, who receives money in trust for another. 2. Mortgagee who possesses and enjoys the lands or tenements mortgaged, until the debt be paid out of the proceeds. 3. Consignee, a merchant or factor to whom a ship or cargo, or merely part of the latter, is consigned.

consigo [con-see'-go], *pro.pers.* With oneself, with himself, herself, themselves, yourself, or yourselves. **Consigo mismo,** alone, by oneself. **(Yo consigo, yo consigo, from Conseguir.** V. PEDIR.)

consiguiente [con-se-gee-en'-tay], *m. (Log.)* Consequence, result.

consiguiente [con-se-gee-en'-tay], *a.* Consequent, consecutive, consequential. **De consiguiente, por consiguiente,** or **por el consiguiente, consequently,** by consequence, pursuantly.

consiguientemente [con-se-ge-en-tay-men'-tay], *adv.* Consequently.

consiliario [con-se-le-ah'-re-o], *m.* Counsellor or assistant to the heads of colleges, convents, etc. V. CONSEJERO.

consintiente [con-sin-te-en'-tay], *pa.* Consenting, agreeing.

consistencia [con-sis-ten'-the-ah], *f.* 1. Consistence, or consistency, degree of density or rarity. 2. Consistency, stability, duration; coherence, conformity. 3. Consistency, firmness, solidity, intellectual strength.

consistente [con-sis-ten'-tay], *a.* 1. Consistent, firm, solid. 2. **Consistente en,** consisting of.

consistir [con-sis-teer'], *vn.* 1. To consist, to subsist, to continue fixed; to lie. 2. To consist, to be comprised, to be contained. 3. To consist, to be composed. **Consistir en,** to be due to, to be accounted for by. **No consiste en eso la dificultad,** the difficulty does not lie in that. **Swatractivo consiste en su naturalidad,** her charm lies in her naturalness.

consistorial [con-sis-to-re-ahl'], *a.* 1. Consistorial, belonging or relating to an ecclesiastical court. 2. **Casa consistorial,** or **casas consistoriales,** senatehouse, guildhall, townhouses or townhalls, courthouse.

consistorio [con-sis-to'-re-o], *m. (Ecl.)* Consistory; *(Pol.)* Town council; town hall (edificio).

consocio [con-so'-the-o], *m.* Partner, companion, fellow-partner.

consol [con-sol'], *m. (Peru)* = CONSOLA.

consola [con-so'-lah], *f.* Console, bracket-shelf.

consolable [con-so-lah'-blay], *a.* Consolable, relievable, comfortable.

consolación [con-so-lah-the-on'], *f.* Consolation, comfort.

consolado, da [con-so-lah'-do, dah], *a.* Consoled, comforted. *pp.* of CONSOLAR.

consolador, ra [con-so-lah-dor', rah], *m. & f.* 1. Consolator, comforter. 2. *m.* Comforter, a name of sthe Holy Spirit.

consolador, ra [con-so-lah-dor', rah], *a.* Consolatory, comfortable.

consolante [con-so-lahn'-tay], *pa.* Comforting, consoling, comfortable.

consolar [con-so-lar'], *va.* To console, to comfort, to cheer. **Me consuela de no haber ido,** it consoles me for not having gone. *-vr.* To console oneself; to find consolation, to take comfort.

consolativo, va [con-so-lah-tee'-vo, vah], **consolatorio, ria,** *a.* consolatory, comfortable.

consoldamiento, *m. (Obs.) V.* CONSOLIDACIÓN.

consólida [con-so'-le-dah], *f. (Bot.) V.* CONSUELDA. **Consólida real,** larkspur.

consolidación [con-so-le-dah-the-on'], *f.* Consolidation.

consolidado, da [con-so-le-dah'-do, dah], *a.* Consolidated. *-pl.* Consolidated annuities, consols, government securities.

consolidar [con-so-le-dar'], *va.* To consolidate, to compact, to close, to harden, to strengthen. *-vr.* 1. To consolidate, to grow firm, hard, or solid. 2. *(Law.)* To unite the interest with the principal.

consolidativo, va [con-so-le-dah-tee'-vo, vah], *a.* Consolidant, consolidative.

consommé [con-so-may'], *m.* Consommé, beef broth.

consonancia [con-so-nahn'-the-ah], *f.* 1. Consonance, harmony, accord of sound. 2. Consistency, congruence, consent. 3. *(Met.)* Conformity.

consonante [con-so-nahn'-tay], *m.* 1. Rhyme, a word, the last syllable or syllables of which, from the vowel where the accent is, corresponds with that of another. 2. *(Mus.)* A consonous or corresponding sound. 3. *f. (Gram.)* A consonant.

consonante [con-so-nahn'-tay], *a.* Consonant, agreeable, consistent, concordant, conformable. **Letras consonantes,** the consonants.

consonantemente [con-so-nan-tay-men'-tay], *adv.* Consonantly, agreeably.

consonántico [con-so-nahn'-te-co], *a.* Consonantal.

consonar [con-so-nar'], *vn.* 1. To make a body sound; to play on musical instruments. 2. To rhyme. 3. *(Met.)* To agree, to resemble.

cónsones [con'-so-nes], *m. pl. (Mus.)* Concordant sounds.

cónsono, na [con'-so-no, nah], *a.* Consonous, harmonious, consonant.

consorcio [con-sor'-the-o], *m.* 1. Consortium, partnership, society. 2. Friendly intercourse, mutual affection.

consorte [con-sor'-tay], *com.* 1. Consort, companion, partner; mate. 2. Consort, a person joined in marriage with another. **Príncipe consorte,** prince consort. 3. One who enters or defends an action jointly with another.

conspicuamente [con-pe-coo-ah-men'-tay], *adv.* Conspicuously.

conspicuo, cua [con-pee'-coo-o, ah], *a.* 1. Conspicuous, obvious, observable. 2. Conspicuous, eminent, famous, distinguished.

conspiración [con-pe-rah-the-on'], *f.* Conspiracy, plot, complot, conjuration, conspiration: an agreement of men to do anything evil or unlawful.

conspirado [con-pe-rah'-do], *m. V.* CONSPIRADOR. **-Conspirado, da,** *pp.* of CONSPIRAR.

conspirador, ra [con-pe-rah-dor'], *m.f.* Conspirator, one who plots, traitor.

conspirante [con-pe-rahn'-tay], *pa.* Conspiring. **Fuerzas conspirantes,** conspiring powers, co-operating mechanical powers which concur in producing the same effect.

conspirar [con-pe-rar'], *va.* To implore the assistance or solicit the favor of another.*-vn.* 1. To conspire, to concert a crime, to plot. 2. To conspire, to agree, to cooperate, to combine.

conspirativo [con-pe-rah-te'-vo], *a.* Conspiratorial.

constancia [con-tahn'-the-ah], *f.* 1. Constancy, steadiness, immutability. 2. Certainty; proof, evidence. **No hay constancia de ello,** there is no certainty of it. **Dejar constancia de algo,** to place something on record. **Para que quede constancia de la fecha,** in order to give proof of the date. 3. *(LAm.)* Documentary proof, written evidence. **Dar constancia,** to give proof.

constante [con-tahn'-tay], *a.* 1. Constant, firm, unalterable, immutable. 2. Loyal, constant. 3. Manifest, apparent, clear. 4. *m. & f.* One who is constant. *-pa.* Composed of, consisting in. 5. *(Inform.)* **Constante numérica,** numeric constant.

constantemente [con-tan-tay-men'-tay], *adv.* 1. Constantly, firmly, unalterably. 2. Evidently, undoubtedly.

Constantino [con-tahn-te'-no], *m.* Constantine.

constantinopolitano, na [con-tan-te-no-po-le-tah'-no, nah], *a.* Of Constantinople.

constar [con-tar'], *v. imp.* 1. To be clear, evident, certain. **Consta en autos** or **de autos,** it appears from the judicial proceedings. **Consta que…,** it is clear that. **Conste que yo no lo aprobé,** let it be clearly understood that I did not approve it. **Que conste que lo hice por ti,** believe me, I did it for your own good. 2. To be composed of, to consist in. 3. Of verses, to have the measure and accent corresponding to their class. 4. To exist in recorded form, to be on record. **No consta en el catálogo,** it is not listed in the catalog.

constatable [con-tah-tah-blay], *a.* Observable, evident. **Es constatable que…,** it can be observed that…

constatación [con-tah-tah-te-on'], *f.* Confirmation, verification.

constatar [con-tah-tar'], *va.* To confirm, to verify, to check, to show.

constelación [con-tay-lah-the-on'], *f.* 1. Constellation, a cluster of fixed stars. 2. Climate, temperature of the air.

constelado [con-tay-lah-do], *a.* Starry, full of stars.

consternación [con-ter-nah-the-on'], *f.* Consternation, perturbation of mind, amazement, horror, distress.

consternado [con-ter-nah-do], *a.* **Estar consternado,** to be dismayed

consternar [con-ter-nar'], *va.* To terrify, to strike with horror or amazement, to confound. *-vr.* To be dismayed, to be shattered; to be aghast.

constipación [con-te-pah-the-on'], *f.* 1. Cold (resfriado). 2. Constipation (estreñimiento).

constipado [con-te-pah'-do], *m.* Cold (resfriado). -**Constipado, da,** *pp.* of CONSTIPAR; **coger un constipado,** to catch a cold.

constipar [con-te-par'], *va.* To cause a cold, to obstruct the perspiration.*-vr.* 1. To catch cold. 2. To be costive.

constipativo, va [con-te-pah-tee'-vo, vah], *a.* Constrictive.

constitución [con-te-too-the-on'], *f.* 1. Constitution. 2. Constitution, corporeal frame, temper of body with respect to health or disease, habit of the body. 3. Constitution, established form of government; system of laws and customs. 4. Constitution, particular law or established usage. 5. Any of the by-laws by which a body or corporation is governed.

constitucional [cons-te-too-the-o-nahl'], *m.* Constitution-alist, constitutionist. *a.* Constitutional.

constitucionalidad [cons-te-too-the-o-nah-le-dahd'], *f.* Constitutionality.

constitucionalismo [cons-te-too-the-o-nah-lees'-mo], *m.* Constitutionalism, love of the constitution of a country.

constitucionalmente, *adv.* Constitutionally.

constituir [cons-te-too-eer'], *va.* 1. To constitute, to produce. **Eso no constituye estorbo,** that isn't an obstacle. 2. To erect, to establish, to make; to create. **Lo constituyen 12 miembros,** it consists of 12 members. **Constituir una nación en república,** to make a country into a republic. **Constituir a uno en árbitro,** to set somebody up as an arbiter. 3. To appoint, to depute. 4. **Constituir la dote,** to pay off a woman's portion, either by installments or in one sum. 6. **Constituirse en obligación de alguna cosa,** to bind oneself to perform anything. -*vr.* 1. **Constituirse en juez,** to set oneself up as a judge. 2. **Constituirse en un lugar,** to present oneself at a place.

constitutivo, va [cons-te-too-tee'-vo, vah], *a.* Constitutive, essential, productive, formal, hypostatical. -*m. & f.* Constituent.

constituto [cons-te-too'-to], *m.* A legal fiction of alienation and transference.

constituyente [cons-te-too-yen'-tay], *m.* 1. Constituent. 2. V. COMITENTE. -*a.* Constituent, that which makes a thing what it is *pa.* of CONSTITUIR.

constreñidamente [cons-tre-nye-dah-men'-tay], *adv.* Compulsively.

constreñimiento [cons-tray-nyee-me-en'-to], *m.* Constraint or compulsion.

constreñir [cons-tray-nyeer'], *va.* 1. To constrain, to compel, to force, to constrict. **Constreñir a uno a hacer algo,** to compel somebody to do something. 2. *(Med.)* To bind or make costive (comida).

constricción [cons-tric-the-on'], *f.* Constriction, contraction.

constrictivo, va [cons-tric-tee'-vo, vah], *a.* Binding, astringent, or constringent.

constrictor [cons-tric-tor'], *m. & a.* Constrictor.

constringente [cons-trin-hen'-tay], *a. & pa.* Constringent: constrictor.

constriñir, *va. (Obs.)* V. CONSTREÑIR. *(Yo constriño, yo constriña; él constriñó, constriñera;* from *Constreñir.* V. PEDIR.)

Construcción [cons-trooc-the-on'], *f.* 1. Construction. **Construcción de carreteras,** road building. 2. Construction, the putting of words together. 3. Construction, arranging terms in their proper order; the sense or the meaning. 4. Interpretation, version, translation. 5. Shipbuilding, naval architecture. **Construcción de buques,** shipbuilding.

constructivamente [cons-trooc-te-vah-men-tay], *adv.* Constructively.

constructivo [cons-trooc-te-vo], *a.* Constructive.

constructor, ra [cons-trooc-tor', rah], *a.* Building, constructing. **Ingeniero constructor,** constructing engineer. -*m.* Constructor. **Constructor de caminos,** road builder.

constructora [cons-trooc-to-rah], *f.* Construction company.

construir [cons-troo-eer'], *va.* 1. To form, to build, to construct, to fabricate, to frame. 2. To construe, to range words in their natural order. 3. To translate literally. -*vr. (Ling.)* **Este verbo se construye con subjuntivo,** this verb goes into the subjunctive.

constuprador [cons-too-prah-dor'], *m.* A debaucher, a defiler, a corruptor.

constuprar [cons-too-prar'], *va.* To defile, to corrupt.

consubstanciación [con-soobs-tan-the-ah-the-on'], *f.* 1. The mingling of one thing with another. 2. Consubstantiation, the doctrine of the Lutherans upon the Eucharist.

consubstanciador [con-soobs-tan-the-ah-dor'], *a.* Epithet applied by the Catholics to the Lutherans, who hold the doctrine of consubstantiation.

consubstancial, [con-soobs-tahn-the-ahl'], *a.* Consubstantial: applied to the Holy Trinity; of one and the same substance.

consubstancialilad [con-soobs-tan-the-ah-le-dahd'], *f.* Consubstantiality.

consuegrar [con-soo-ay-grar'], *vn.* To become joint fathers or mothers-in-law.

consuegro, gra [con-soo-ay'-gro, grah], *m. & f.* Father-in-law or mother-in-law of one's child.

consuelda [con-soo-el'-dah], *f. (Bot.)* Comfrey. **Consuelda media,** common bugle, bugleweed.

consuelo [con-soo-ay'-lo], *m.* 1. Consolation, comfort, relief, comfortableness. 2. Joy, merriment. 3. Charity. 4. *(Coll.)* **Sin consuelo,** out of rule or measure. **Premio de consuelo,** consolation prize. *(Yo consuelo, yo consuele,* from *Consolar.* V. ACORDAR.) *(Yo consueno, yo consuene,* from *Consonar.* V. ACORDAR.)

consueta [con-soo-ay'-tah], *m. &. f.* 1. *(Prov.)* Stage prompter. 2. *(Prov.)* Directory, which contains the order for divine service. **Consuelas,** short prayers used on certain days in divine service.

consuetudinario, ria [con-soo-ay-too-de-nah'-re-o, ah], *a.* 1. Customary, generally practised. 2. *(Theol.)* In the habit of sinning. 3. **Derecho consuetudinario,** common law.

cónsul [cone'-sool], *m.* 1. Consul, the chief magistrate in ancient Rome. 2. Member of the tribunal of commerce. 3. Consul, an officer commissioned in foreign countries to protect the commerce of his country.

consulado [con-soo-lah'-do], *m.* 1. Consulate. 2. Term of office as consul. 3. Tribunal of commerce, appointed to try and decide causes which concern navigation and trade. 4. Office of consul and territory of same.

consulaje [con-soo-lah'-hay], *m.* Fees paid to consuls by all merchant vessels.

consular [con-soo-lar'], *a.* Consular. **Varón consular,** one who has been consul.

consulta [con-sool'-tah], *f.* 1. A question proposed, or a proposal made in writing. 2. Consultation, conference, meeting for deliberation. 3. Report made and advice given to the king in council. 4. Advice to the king by the supreme tribunals and officers of state, with regard to persons proposed to fill public employments. 5. *(Med.)* Consulting room. **Consulta externa,** out-patients department. 6. *(Med.)* Examination. **Horas de consulta,** surgery hours. **El doctor no pasa consulta a domicilio,** the doctor does not make home visits.

consultable [con-sool-tah'-blay], *a.* Worthy or necessary to be deliberated upon.

consultación [con-sool-tah-the-on'], *f.* Consultation, conference, meeting.

consultante [con-sool-tahn'-tay], *pa.* Consulting, consulter. **Ministro consultante,** minister who lays before the king the opinion of his council.

consultar [con-sool-tar'], *va.* 1. To consult, to ask or take another's advice. **Consultar a un médico,** to consult a doctor. 2. To advise, to give advice. 3. To consult, to deliberate, to take counsel together. **Consultar con la almohada,** to take into mature consideration: literally, to consult the pillow. 4. To consult (libro); to look up.

consultivo, va [con-sool-tee'-vo, vah], *a.* 1. Consultative. 2. Applied to matters which the councils and tribunals are obliged to lay before the king, accompanied with their advice.

consultor, ra [con-sool-tor', rah], *m. & f.* 1. Consultor, adviser, counsel. 2. *(Inform.)* Consultant. **Consultor del centro de información,** information center consultant

consultoría [con-sool-to-re'-ah], *f.* Consultancy.

consultorio [con-sool-to'-ryo], *m.* 1. Consulting office. 2. Doctor's office.

consumación [con-soo-mah-the-on'], *f.* 1. Consummation, perfection, end, finishing, accomplishment. 2. Destruction, suppression. **Consumación de los siglos,** consummation, the end of the present system of things.

consumadamente [con-soo-mah-dah-men-tay], *adv.* Perfectly, completely, consummately.

consumado, da [con-soo-mah'-do, dah], *a.* Consummate, complete, perfect, accomplished, exquisite. *-pp.* of CONSUMAR. *-m.* 1. Loot, swag (cosas robadas). 2. Hash (droga).

consumador, ra [con-soo-mah-dor', rah], *m. & f.* Finisher, one who consummates, perfects, or finishes.

consumar [con-soo-mar'], *va.* 1. To consummate, to finish, to perfect, to complete. 2. *(And. CAm.)* To submerge.

consumativo, va [con-soo-mah-tee'-vo, vah], *a.* Consummate, that which consummates or completes (sacramentos).

consumible [con-soo-mee'-blay], *a.* Consumable.

consumición [con-soo-me-the-on'], *f.* *(Com.)* V. CONSUMO. **Consumición mínima,** minimum charge. **Pager la consumición,** to pay for what one has had.

consumido, da [con-soo-mee'-do, dah], *a.* 1. Lean, meagre, exhausted, spent. 2. Easily afflicted. *-pp.* of CONSUMIR.

consumidor, ra [con-soo-me-dor', rah], *m. & f.* Consumer, destroyer. **Consumidor de drogas,** drug-taker. **Productos al consumidor,** consumer products.

consumimiento [con-soo-me-me-en'-to], *m.* Consumption.

consumir [con-soo-meer], *va.* 1. To consume, to destroy, to waste, to exhaust; to lick up: to obliterate; to melt. **Le consumen los celos,** he is eaten up with jealously. **Ese deseo le consume,** that desire is burning him up. **Me consume su terquedad,** his obstinacy is getting on my nerves. 2. In the sacrifice of the mass, to swallow the elements of bread and wine in the Eucharist. *-vr.* 1. To be spent, to be exausted. **Se ha consumido la vela,** the candle is finished. 2. To fret, to be uneasy, to be vexed. **Consumirse de envidia,** to be eaten up with jealously. **Consumirse de rabia,** to fume with rage. 3. To wear away, to waste away, to languish, to consume, to linger, to fail.

consumismo [con-soo-mes'-mo], *m.* Consumerism (tendencia); consumer society.

consumista [con-soo-mes'-tah], *a.* **El sector consumista,** the consumer section. *-m. & f.* Consumer.

consumo [con-soo'-mo], *m.* The consumption of provisions and merchandise. **Consumo de drogas,** drug-taking. **Sociedad de consumo,** consumer society. 2. A tax upon the traffic in provisions and other merchandise.

consunción [con-soon-the-on'], *f.* 1. Consumption, waste. 2. Consumption, the state of wasting. 3. *(Mod.)* Consumption.

consuno (De) [con-soo'-no], *adv.* V. JUNTAMENTE.

consuntivo, va [con-soon-tee'-vo, vah], *a.* Consumptive.

consurrección [con-soor-rec-the-on'], *f.* Revival, revivification.

consustanciación [con-soos-tan-the-ah.-the-on'], *f.* V. CONSUBSTANCIACIÓN.

consustancial [con-soos-tahn-the-ahl'], *a.* Consubstantial. **Ser consustancial con,** to be inseparable from.

contabilidad [con-tah-be-le-dahd'], *f.* Accounting, bookkeeping, the art of keeping accounts.

contabilizar [con-tah-be-le-thar'], *va.* To enter in the accounts.

contable [con-tah'-blay], *a.* Countable, *-m. & f.* Accountant, book-keeper.

contactar [**con-tac-tar'**], *va. vn.* To contact, to get in touch.

contacto [con-tac'-to], *m.* 1. Contact, touch, union. **Estar en contacto con,** to be in touch with. **Ponerse en contacto con,** to get in touch with. **Lo hizo el municipio en contacto con el gobierno,** the city did it in collaboration with the government. 2. Means by which a contagious or epidemic disease is communicated to the healthy. 3. A soft iron guard for bar-magnets. 4. Intersection of two lines. 5. Switch, contact breaker.

contadero, ra [con-tah-day'-ro, rah], *a.* Countable, numerable, that which may be numbered.

contadero, [con-tah-day-ro], *m.* A narrow passage where sheep or cattle are counted. **Salir** or **entrar por contadero,** to go in or out through a narrow passage.

contado, da [con-tah'-do, dah], *a.* 1. Scarce, rare, uncommon, infrequent. **De contado,** instantly, immediately; in hand. **Al contado,** with ready money, for cash. 2. Designed, marked, or pointed out. **En contadas ocasiones,** on rare ocasions. **Contadas veces,** seldom. *-pp.* of CONTAR. *-m.* 1. Naturally, of course. 2. *(And.)* Installment (plazo).

contador, ra [con-tah-dor', rah], *m. &;f.* 1. Computer, reckoner, one skilled in accounts, accountant. 2. Numberer, numerator. 3. Counter, tell-tale a device attached to a machine for counting its strokes or revolutions, a meter for gas or water. **Contador de gas,** gas meter. **Contador de revoluciones,** tachometer. 4. Counter, the table on which money is told in a shop. 5. Desk. 6. An auditor. 7. Counting-house. 8. Counter, a false piece of money used for marking the game. **Contador de marina,** purser in the navy. **Contador en serie,** *(Inform.)* serial counter.

contador Geiger [con-tah-dor', gay'-ger], *m.* Geiger counter.

contaduría [con-tah-doo-ree'-ah], *f.* 1. Accountant's or auditor's office at the exchequer. 2. Auditorship, place and employment of a public auditor of receipts.

contagiar [con-tah-he-ar'], *va.* 1. To infect, to communicate disease, to hurt by contagion. 2. *(Met.)* To corrupt one's morals by a bad example, to pervert. *-vr.* 1. *(Med.)* To be contagious. **El mal ejemplo se contagia,** a bad example is contagious. **La anarquía se contagia a otros,** anarchy spreads to others.

contagio [con-tah'-he-o], *a.* 1. Contagion. 2. *(Met.)* Contagion, corruption of morals.

contagión [con-tah-he-on'], *f.* 1. The progressive malignity of a disease, as cancer. 2. *(Met.)* Propagation of vice and evil habits. 3. *V.* CONTAGIO.

contagioso, sa [con-tah-he-o'-so, sah], *a.* 1. Contagious, malign, infectious. 2. *(Met.)* Infectious (doctrinas peligrosas, malos ejemplos). 3. *(Coll. Mex.)* Odd, particular.

contáiner [con-tah'-e-nayr], *m.* Container.

contal de cuentas [con-tahl'-day-coo-en'-tas], *m.* A string of beads for counting or reckoning.

contaminación [con-tah-me-nah-the-on'], *f.* Contamination, pollution, defilement; stain, blot. **Contaminación de aire,** air pollution. 2. *(fig.)* Taint, corrupting.

contaminado, da [con-tah-me-nah'-do, dah], *a. & pp.* of CONTAMINAR. Contaminated, corrupted, polluted.

contaminante [con-tah-me-nahn'-tay], *m.* Pollutant.

contaminar [con-tah-me-nar'], *va.* 1. To contaminate, to defile or pollute. 2. To infect by contagion. 3. To corrupt, to vitiate or destroy the integrity of a text or original. 4. *(Met.)* To profane, to violate anything sacred. *-vr.* To be contaminated.

contante [con-tahn-tay], *a.* That can be counted. **Dinero contante y sonante,** ready cash.

contar [con-tar'], *va.* 1. To count, to reckon, to number, to enumerate, to relate, to mention. **Contar con los dedos,** to count on one's fingers. **Le cuento entre mis amigos,** I reckon him among my friends. **Sin contar,** not counting. 2. To calculate, to compute. 3. To book, to place to account. 4. To class, to range according to some stated method of distribution. 5. To consider, to look upon. 6. To depend, to rely. **Contar con la amistad de uno,** to rely upon one's friendship. **Mire a queén se lo cuenta,** an expressions signifying that he who hears knows more than he who relates the particulars of an event. *-vn.* 1. *(Math.)* To count, to count up. **Hay que contar mucho para llegar con la paga al final del mes,** we have to go carefully in order to get to the end of the month. 2. *(fig.)* To count, to matter. **Unas pocas equivocaciones no cuentan,** a few errors don't matter. 3. To rely on. **Contar con,** to rely on. **Cuenta conmigo,** trust me. **Contaban por segura su**

ayuda, they were relying absolutely on his help. *-vr.* 1. To be counted. **Se le cuenta entre los más famosos,** he is reckoned among the most famous. 2. To be told. **Cuéntese que…,** it is said that… **Cuenta y no acaba de hablar,** he never stops talking.

contemperante [con-tem-pay-rahn'-tay], *pa.* Tempering; moderator.

contemperar [con-tem-pay-rar'], *va.* To temper, to moderate. *V.* ATEMPERAR.

contemplación [con-tem-plah-the-on'], *f.* 1. Contemplation, meditation. 2. Holy meditation, a holy exercise of the soul. 3. Compliance, complaisance. **No andarse con contemplaciones,** not to stand on ceremony. **No tiene contemplaciones en eso,** he makes no compromises with that sort of things. **Sin contemplaciones, without ceremony, without any explanation.**

contemplador [con-tem-plah-dor'], *m.* Contemplator. *V.* CONTEMPLATIVO.

contemplar [con-tem-plar'], *va.* 1. To contemplate, to consider with conntinued attention, to study. 2. To view, to behold, to look upon. 3. To contemplate, to meditate, to muse. 4. To assent, to condescend, to yield a point. *-vn.* To meditate.

contemplativamente [con-tem-plah-te-vah-men'-tay], *adv.* Attentively, thoughtfully.

contemplativo, va [con-tem-plah-tee'-vo, vah], *a.* Contemplative, studious, meditative. **Vida contemplativa,** a life spent in contemplation and study.

contemplativo [con-tem-plah-tee'-vo], *m.* 1. Contemplator; one employed in contemplation and study. 2 A pious devotee.

contemporáneamente, *adv.* At the same time, contemporaneously.

contemporaneidad [con-tem-po-nay-e-dahd'], *f.* Contemporariness.

contemporáneo, nea [con-tem-po-rah'-nay-o, ah], *a.* Contemporary, coetaneous, coeval.

contemporización [con-tem-po-re-thah-the-on'], *f.* Temporizing, compliance.

contemporizador [con-tem-po-re-tha-dor'], *a.* Excesively compliant; temporizing; lacking firm principles. *-m. f.* Timeserver, compromiser; person who lacks firm principles.

contemporizar [con-tem-po-re-thar'], *vn.* To temporize, to comply with the will and opinion of another.

contención [con-ten-the-on'], *f.* 1. Contention, emulation. 2. Contest, dispute, strife, fighting.

contenciosamente, *adv.* Contentiously, contestingly.

contencioso, sa [con-ten-the-o'-so, sah], *a.* 1. Contentious, concertative, contradictious, quarrelsome, disputatious. 2. Being the object of strife or dispute; contestable. 3. Quarrelsome, litigious.

contendedor [con-ten-day-dor'], *m. V.* CONTENDOR.

contender [con-ten-derr'], *vn.* 1. To contend, to strive, to struggle, to contest, to conflict, to debate, to litigate. 2. *(Met.)* To argue, to discuss, to expostulate.

contendiente [con-ten-de-en'-tay], *pa.* Disputant, litigant.

contendor [con-ten-dor'], *m.* Contender, antagonist, opponent.

contendedor, ra [con-tay-nay-dor', rah], *m. & f.* Holder; a tenant, container.

contenencia [con-tay-nen'-the-ah], *f.* 1. Suspension in the flight of birds, especially birds of prey. 2. *(For.)* A demurrer; a written denial of the cause of action.

contener [con-tay-nerr'], *va.* 1. To contain, as a vessel: to comprise, as a writing; to comprehend. 2. To refrain, to curb, to restrain, to coerce. 3. To repress, to check the motion or progress of a time g. *vr.* 1. To keep one's temper, to refrain, to hold. 2. To contain, **Él no puede contenerse,** he has no command of himself. *(Yo contengo, yo contuve,* from *Contener. V.* TENER.

contenido, da [con-tay-nee'-do, dah], *a.* Moderate, prudent, temperate, modest. 2. Contained, suppressed. **Risa contenida,** contained laughter. *-pp.* of CONTENER.

contenido [con-tay-nee'-do], *m.* Contents, context.

conteniente [con-tay-ne-en'-tay], *pa.* Containing, comprising.

contenta [con-ten'-tah], *f.* 1. Endorsement. *V.* ENDOSO. 2. Reception or present which satisfies anyone. 3. Certificate of good conduct, given by the magistrate of a place to the commander of troops which have been quartered there; also, a similar certificate, given by the commanding officer to the magistrate.

contentadizo, za [con-ten-tah-dee'-tho, thah], *a.* **Bien contentadizo,** easily contented; **mal contentadizo,** hard to please.

contentamente [con-ten-tah-men'-tay], *adv.* Contentedly.

contentamiento [con-ten-tah-me-en'-to], *m.* Contentment, joy, satisfaction, content.

contentar [con-ten-tar'], *va.* 1. To content, to satisfy, to gratify, to please, to fill. 2. To indorse. *V.* ENDOSAR. *-vr.* To be contented, pleased, or satisfied. **Ser de buen o mal contentar,** to be easily pleased, or difficult to be pleased.

contentible [con-ten-tee'-blay], *a.* Contemptible.

contentivo, va [con-ten-tee'-vo, vah], *a.* Containing, comprising.

contento, ta [con-ten'-to-tah], *a.* 1. Glad, pleased, full of joy, mirthful. **Estar contento con,** to be satisfied with. **Están contentos con el coche,** they are pleased with the car. **Viven muy contentos,** they live very happily. 2. Contented, satisfied, content. 3. Moderate, temperate, prudent.

contento con-ten'-to], *m.* 1. Contentment, joy, satisfaction, content, mirth. **No caber en sí de contento,** to be overjoyed. 2. Receipt, discharge.

conteo [con-tay'-o], *m.* Countdown (deporte). Used also in rocket launchings.

contera [con-tay'-rah], *f.* 1. Chape, a piece of brass, tin, or silver, put at the end of a cane, stick, or scabbard. 2. Button of the cascabel of a gun. 3. *(Poet.)* Prelude of a song, or other musical composition. **Por contera,** ultimately, finally.

contérmino, na [con-terr'-me-no, nah], *a.* Contiguous, bordering upon.

conterráneo, nea [con-ter-rah'-nay-o, ah], *m. & f.* Countryman, countrywoman.

contertuliano, na [con-ter-too-le-ah'-no, nah], *or* **contertulio,** *a.* Belonging to the same social circle; of the same set.

contesta [con-tays'-tah], *f. (LAm.)* Answer.

contestable [con-tes-tah'-blay], *a.* Contestable, disputable, controvertible.

contestación [con-tes-tah-the-on'], *f.* 1. Answer, reply, 2. Contestation, the act of contesting: debate, strife. 3. Altercation, disputation, contention. **Contestación a la demanda,** *(Jur.)* Defence plea. **Mala contestación,** sharp report.

contestador [con-tays-tah-dor'], *a.* Cheeky, saucy. *-m.* **Contestador automatico,** answering machine.

contestar [con-tes-tar'], *va.* 1. To confirm the deposition of another. 2. to prove, to attest. 3. To answer, to reply. **Contestar una pregunata,** to answer a question. **Contestar una carta,** to reply to a letter. *-m.* To agree, to accord. *-vn.* 1. *(Mex.)* To chat, to talk. 2. *(Pol.)* To protest.

contestatario [con-tes-tah-tah'-re-o], *a.* Rebellious; nonconformist, anti-establishment. *-m. f.* Rebel; nonconformist.

conteste [con-tes'-tay], *a.* Confirming the evidence of another, making the same deposition as another witness.

contesto [con-tays-tao], *m. (And, Cono Sur, Mex.)* Answer, reply.

contexto [con-tex'-to], *m.* 1. Intertexture, diversification of things mingled or interwoven. 2. Context of a discourse.

contextura [con-tex-too'-rah], *f.* 1. Contexture. 2. Context, the general series of a discourse. 3. *(Met.)* Frame and structure of the human body.

conticinio [con-te-thee'-ne-o], *m.* Dead of night.

contienda [con-te-en'-dah], *f.* 1. Contest, dispute, debate, expostulation. 2. Conflict, contention, clashing, fray, jarring. (*Yo contiendo, yo contienda,* from *Contender. V.* ENTENDER.)

contigo [con-tee'-go], *pron. pers.* With you.

contiguamente, *adv.* Contiguously, closely.

contigüidad [con-te-goo-e-dad'], *f.* Contiguity, closeness.

contiguo, gua [con-te'-goo-o, ah], *a.* Contiguous, close.

continencia [con-te-nen'-the-ah], *f.* 1. Continence, self-command. 2. Continence, abstinence from carnal pleasures. 3. Continence, moderation in lawful pleasures. 4. The act of containing. **Continencia de la causa,** (*Law.*) Unity which should exist in every judgment or sentence.

continental [con-te-nen-tahl'], *a.* Continental.

continente [con-te-nan'-tay], *m.* 1. Continent, that which contains something. 2. Countenance, air, mien, gait. 3. Continent, a large extent of land; mainland.

continente [con-te-nen'-tay], *a.* Continent, chaste, abstinent, moderate in pleasures. **En continente,** (*Obs.*) Immediately.

continentemente [con-te-nen-tay-men'-tay], *adv.* Moderately, abstemiously, chastely.

contingencia [con-tin-hen'-the-ah], *f.* Contingence or contingency, possibility, risk.

contingentación [con-tin-hen-tah-the-on'], *f.* Quota system.

contingentar [con-tin-hen-tar'], *va.* To make subject to quotas; to fix quotas for.

contingente [con-tin-hen'-tay], *a.* Contingent, fortuitous, accidental.

contingente [con-tin-hen'-tay], *m.* Contingent, a proportion that falls to any person upon a division.

contingentemente [con-tin-hen-tay-men'-tay] *adv.* Casually, accidentally, contingently.

continuación [con-te-noo-ah-the-on'], *f.* 1. Continuation, protraction, an uninterrupted succession, lengthening. 2. Continuity, connection uninterrupted. 3. Continuance, stay. **Según lo expuesto a continuación,** as set below.

continuadamente [con-te-noo-ah-dah-men'-tay], *adv.* Continually.

continuador [con-te-noo-ah-dor'], *m.* Continuer, continuator.

continuamente [con-te-noo-ah-men'-tay], *adv.* Continually.

continuar [con-te-noo-ar'], *va. & vn.* 1. To continue, to remain in the same state, to hold. **La puerta continúa cerrada,** the door is still shut. 2. To continue, to last, to endure. **Continuaba en Noruega,** he was still in Norway. **Continuar consalud,** to keep in good health. 3. To continue, to pursue, to protract, to carry on.

continuativo, va [con-te-noo-ah-tee'-vo, vah], *a.* Denoting continuation: said of a conjunction; continuative.

continuidad [con-te-noo-e-dahd'], *f.* Continuity, cohesion, continuance.

continuismo [con-te-noo-ees'-mo], *m.* Politics of continuity; wish for everything to go on as before.

continuo, nua [con-tee'-noo-o, ah], *a.* 1. Continuous, joined together without intervening space; continual. 2. Constant, lasting. **Sus continuas quejas,** his continual complaints. 3. Assiduous, persevering; perennial.

continuo, *m.* 1. A whole, composed of united parts. **Continuo** or **de continuo,** *adv.* Continually, constantly.

contómetro [con-to'-may-tro], *m.* Comptometer, calculating machine.

contonearse [con-to-nay-ar'-say], *vr.* To walk with an affected air or manner, to waggle.

contoneo [con-to-nay'-o], *m.* An affected gait or manner of walking.

contorcerse [con-tor-therr'-say], *vr.* To distort, twist, or writhe one's body.

contorción [con-tor-the-on'], *f. V.* RETORCIMIENTO and CONTORSIÓN.

contornado [con-tor-nah'-do], *a.* (*Her.*) Applied to the heads of animals, turned toward the sinister side of the shield. **-Contornado, da,** *pp.* of CONTORNAR.

contornar, contornear [con-tor-nar', con-tor-nay-ar'], *va.* 1. To trace the contour or outline of a figure. 2. To form according to a proposed model or design.

contorneo [con-tor-nay'-o], *m. V.* RODEO.

contorno [con-tor'-no], *m.* 1. Environs or vicinity of a place. **Caracas y sus contornos,** Caracas and its environs. **En estos contornos,** in these parts. 2. Contour, outline. 3. Every line in a spiral or volute. **En contorno,** round about. 4. Measurement round, distance round. **El contorno de cintura es de 26 pulgadas,** her waist measurement is 26 inches.

contorsión [con-tor-se-on'], *f.* 1. Contortion, twist, wry motion. 2. A grotesque gesture.

contorsionarse [con-tor-se-o-nar'-say], *vr.* To contort oneself.

contorsionista [con-tor-se-o-nes'-tah], *m. & f.* Contorsionist.

contra [cohn' trah], *prep.* Against, in opposition to, counter, contrary to, opposite to. **En contra,** against or in opposition to another thing. **Ni a favor ni en contra,** neither pro nor con. *-adv.* Against. **Puntos en contra,** points against. **Votar en contra,** to vote against. **Opinar en contra,** to disagree. *-m.* 1. Opposite sense. 2. (*Mus.*) The pedal organ; the pipes forming the lowest bass, more common in plural. 3. Trouble, inconvenience. 4. **Hacer la contra,** to be consistently obtrusive. 5. (*LAm.*) (*Med.*) Antidote. 6. (Bridge) double. *-f.* 1. Difficulty, inconvenience. 2. Counter, in fencing, a parry in which one foil follows another in a small circle.

contraabertura [con-trah-ah-ber-too'-rah], *f.* (*Med.*) Counter-opening.

contraábside [con-trah-ahb'-se-day'], *m. & f.* Western apse or apsis.

contraaletas [con-trah-ah-lay'-tas], *f. pl.* (*Naut.*) Counter-fashion pieces, the outermost timbers of the stern of the ship on both sides.

contraalmirante or **contralmirante** [con-trah-al-me-rahn'-tay], *m.* Rear admiral.

contraamantillas [con-trah-ah-man-teel'-lyas], *f. pl.* (*Naut.*) Preventer-braces which serve to succour the main or foreyard of a ship.

contraamura [con-trah-ah-moo'-rah], *f.* (*Naut.*) Preventert-ack, which serves to support the tacks.

contraaproches [con-trah-ah-pro'-chess], *m. pl.* Counter-approaches made by the besieged against the besiegers.

contraarmiños [con-trah-ar-mee'-nyos], *m. pl.* (*Her.*) Contrary to ermine, i. e. black field and white spots.

contraatacar [con-trah-ah-tah-car'], *va. vn.* To counter-attack.

contraataques [con-trah-ah-tah'-kes], *m. pl.* Counter attacks made by the besieged.

contrabajo [con-trah-bah'-ho], *m.* 1. Counterbass, the deepest of all musical sounds. 2. Bass, or baseviol; double bass.

contrabalancear [con-trah-bah-lan-thay-ar'], *va.* To counter-balance, to counterpoise.

contrabalanza [con-trah-bah-lahn'-thah], *f. V.* CONTRAPESO and CONTRAPOSICIÓN.

contrabanda [con-trah-bahn'-dah], *f.* (*Her.*) 1. A band divided into two of different metals, one of them colored. 2. The piece which crosses the shield in a sense contrary to the bend.

contrabandear [con-trah-bahn-day-ar'], *vn.* To smuggle.

contrabandista [con-trah-ban-dees'-tah], *m.* Smuggler, contrabandist.

contrabando [con-trah-bahn'-do], *m.* 1. A prohibited commodity. **Géneros de contrabando,** smuggled prohibited article. 2. Contraband trade, smuggling. **Contrabando de armas,** gun-runner. 3. (*Met.*) Any unlawful action. **Ir** or **venir de contrabando,** to go or come by stealth.

contrabarrado da [con-trah-bar-rah'-do, dah], *a. (Her.)* A shield counterbarred.

contrabasa, *f. (Arch.) V.* PEDESTAL.

contrabatería [con-trah-bah-tay-ree'-ah], *f.* Counterbattery.

contrabatir [con-trah-bah-teer'], *va.* To fire upon the enemy's batteries.

contrabitas [con-trah-bee'-tas], *f. pl. (Naut.)* Standards of the bitts.

contrabolina [con-tra-bo-lee'-nah], *f. (Naut.)* Preventer bowline.

contrabovedilla [con-trah-bo-vay-deel'-lyah], *f. (Naut.)* Second counter, upper counter.

contrabracear [con-trah-brah-thay-ar'], *va. (Naut.)* To counterbrace.

contrabranque [con-trah-brahn'-kay], *m. (Naut.)* Stemson, a strong piece of timber intended to re-enforce the stem.

contrabraza [con-trah-brah'-thah], *f. (Naut.)* Preventer-brace.

contrabrazola [con-trah-brah-tho'-lah], *f. (Naut.)* Head ledge.

contracalcar [con-trah-cal-car'], *va.* To print a drawing backward, in order to obtain another in the same position as the original.

contracambiada [con-trah-cam-be-ah'-dah], *f.* Changing of the forefoot by a horse.

contracambio [con-trah-cahm'-be-o], *m.*

contracanal [con-trah-cah-nahl'], *m.* Channel or conduit leading from another; counterchannel.

contracarril [con-trah-car-reel'], *m.* Checkrail, guardrail, safety-rail, wingrail.

contracción [con-trac-the-on'], *f.* 1. Contraction, shrinking, shriveling, contractedness, constriction; corrugation. 2. Contraction, the state of being contracted. 3. Abbreviation, abridgment.

contracebadera [con-trah-thay-bah-day'-rah], *f. (Naut.)* Sprit topsail.

contracédula [con-trah-thay'-doo-lah], *f.* A decree which reverses or annuls another of an anterior date.

contracepción [con-trah-thep-the-on'], *f.* Contraception.

contraceptivo [con-trah-thep-tee'-vo], *m.* Contraceptive. **Contraceptivo bucal,** oral contraceptive.

contrachapado [con-trah-chah-pah'-do], *a.* **Madera contrachapado,** *V.* PLYWOOD.

contracifra [con-trah-thee'-frah], *f.* Countercipher, the key to a secret manner of writing.

contraclave [con-trah-clah'-vay], *f. (Arch.)* The voussoir next to the keystone.

contracodaste interior [con-trah-co-dahs'-tay in-tay-re-or'], *m. (Naut.)* The inner sternpost. **Contracodaste exterior,** *(Naut.)* The back of the sternpost.

contracorriente [con-trah-cor-re-en'-tay], *f. (Naut.)* Counter-current, stop-water.

contracosta [con-trah-cos'-tah], *f.* Coast opposite to another.

contráctil [con-trahc'-teel], *a.* 1. Contractile. 2. Contractible.

contractilidad [con-trac-te-le-dahd'], *f.* Contractility, contractibility.

contractual [con-trac-too-ahl'], *a.* Contractual.

contractura [con-trac-too'-rah], *f. (Med.)* Contracture, rigidity of muscles in a state of flexion, from whatever cause.

contracuerdas [con-trah-coo-err'-das], *f. pl. (Naut.)* The outward deckplanks or platforms.

contradancista [con-trah-dan-thees'-tah], *m. & f.* A person very fond of dancing country dances.

contradanza [con-trah-dahn'-thah], *f.* Square dance, country dance.

contradecir [con-trah-day-theer'], *va.* To contradict, to gainsay.

contradicción [con-trah-dic-the-on'], *f.* 1. Contradiction, controversy. 2. Control, controlment. 3. Clashing, oppugnancy, hostile resistance. 4. Contradiction, inconsistency with itself; incongruity in words or thoughts. 5. Contradic-

tion, opposition, gainsaying. **Espíritu de contradicción,** contradictory temper. **Contradicción de términos,** contradiction in terms.

contradicho, cha, [con-trah-de'-cho], *pp. irr.* of CONTRA-DECIR.

contradictor, ra [con-trah-dic-tor', rah], *m. & f.* Contradictor, gainsayer.

contradictoria [con-trah-dic-to'-re-ah], *f. (Log.)* Contradictory.

contradictoriamente, *adv.* Contradictorily, inconsistenly.

contradictorio, ria [con-tra-dic-to'-re-o, ah], *a.* Contradictory. (*Yo contradigo, yo contradije, yo contradiga,* from *Contradecir. V.* DECIR.)

contradique [con-trah-dee'-kay], *m.* Counterdike, a second dike.

contradriza [con-trah-dree'-thah], *f. (Naut.)* Second halliard.

contraeje [con-trah-ay'-hay], *m.* A countershaft.

contraemboscada [con-trah-em-bos-cah'-dah], *f.* Counterambuscade.

contraemergente [con-trah-ay-mer.-hen'-tay], *a. (Her.)* Countersalient.

contraempuje [con-trah-em-poo-hay], *m.* Counter-thrust.

contraempuñadura [con-trah-em-poo-nyay-doo'-rah], *f. (Naut.)* Preventer earring.

contraendosar [con-trah-en-do-sar'], *va.* To reindorse, indorse back.

contraer [con-trah-err'], *va. & vn.* 1. To contract, to knit, to furl, to shrink, to join, to unite. 2. To bring two parties together, to make a bargain. 3. To procure, to incur, to get. *-vr.* 1. To contract, to shrink up, as nerves, etc., to crumple. 2. To reduce a discourse to an idea or phrase. **Contraer deudas,** to run into debt. **Contraer enfermedad,** to contract a disease. **Contraer matrimonio,** to marry. **Contrae su teoría a ciertos puntos,** he limits his theory to certain points.

contraescarpa [con-trah-es-car'-pah], *f. (Mil.)* Counterscarp.

contraescota [con-trah-es-co'-tah], *f. (Naut.)* Preventer-sheet.

contraescotín [con-trah-es-co-teen'], *m. (Naut.)* Preventer topsail sheet.

contraescritura [con-trah-es-cre-too'-rah], *f.* Counterdeed, instrument granted to protest against what had been previously given.

contraesmaltar [con-trah-es-mal-tar'], *va.* To enamel the back part.

contraespaldera [con-trah-es-pal-day'-rah] *f.* A kind of hedge or fence of trees in front of a hedge; a second espalier.

contraespionaje [con-trah-es-pe-o-nah'-hay], *m.* Counterintelligence, counterespionage.

contraestay del mayor, or **del trinquete** [con-trah-es-tah'-e del mah-yor', or del treen-kay'-tay], *m. (Naut.)* Preventer stay of the main or foremast.

contrafajado, da [con-trah-fah-hah'-do, dah], *a. (Her.)* A shield having faces opposed in metal or color.

contrafallar [con-trah-fal-lyar'], *va.* At cards, to trump after another, to overtrump.

contrafaz [con-trah-fath'], *f.* The reverse of every face.

contrafianza [con-trah-fe-ahn'-thah], *f.* Indemnity bond.

contrafigura [con-trah-fe-goo'-rah], *f.* A person or dummy which imitates a personage in the theater.

contrafilo [con-trah-fee'-lo], *m.* Back edge (near the point).

contrafirma [con-trah-feer'-mah], *f. (Law. Prov.)* Inhibition of an anterior decree.

contrafirmante [con-trah-feer-mahn'-tay], *pa. (Law. Prov.)* The party who obtains an inhibition or injunction.

contrafirmar [con-trah-feer-mar'], *va. (Law Prov.)* To obtain a countermanding decree or inhibition.

contraflorado, da [con-trah-flo-rah'-do, dah], *a. (Her.)* Having flowers opposed in color and metal.

contrafoque [con-trah-fo'-kay], *m. (Naut.)* The foretop staysail; also the jib or flying-jib of a smack.

contraforjar [con-trah-for-har'], *va.* To hammer alike on the flat and on edge.

contrafoso [con-trah-fo'-so], *m.* The outer ditch of a fortress.

contrafractura [con-trah-frac-too'-rah], *f.* A fracture made by counter-stroke or contre-coup.

contrafuero [con-trah-foo-ay'-ro], *m.* Infringement or violation of a charter or privilege.

contrafuerte [con-trah-foo-err'-tay], *m.* 1. Counterfort, a fort constructed in opposition to another. 2. Abutment, buttress, spur, a pillar of masonry serving to prop and support a wall. 3. Strap of leather to secure the girths on a saddle-tree. 4. Stiffener of a shoe.

contragambito [con-trah-gahm-be'-to], *m.* Counter-gambit.

contragolpe [con-trah-gole'-pay], *m. (Med.)* A counter-stroke (contrecoup), lesion produced in a part other than that which received the blow.

contraguardia [con-trah-goo-ar'-de-ah], *f.* Counterguard, a work erected to cover a bastion or ravelin.

contraguía [con-trah-gee'ah], *f.* In a pair of draught animals, the mule which goes forward, to the left.

contraguiñada [con-trah-gee-nyah'-dah], *f. (Naut.)* Counteryaw, a movement of the tiller to correct the course of a ship.

contrahacedor, ra [con-trah-ah-thay-dor', rah], *m. & f.* Imitator, counterfeiter.

contrahacer [con-trah-ah-ther'], *va.* 1. To counterfeit. 2. To falsify, to forge. 3. To imitate, to copy. 4. To pirate the works of an author. 5. To mimic.

contrahacimiento [con-trah-ah-the-me-en'-to], *m. (Obs.)* Counterfeit. *(Yo contrahago, yo contrahaga, from Contrahacer. V. HACER.)*

contrahaz [con-trah-ath'], *m.* The wrong side of cloth and some other things.

contrahecho, cha [con-trah-ay' -cho, chah], *a.* 1. Humpbacked, deformed. 2. Counterfeit, counterfeited, fictitious. *-pp.* of CONTRAHACER.

contrahechura [con-trah-ay-choo'-rah], *f.* Counterfeit; forgery, fake; pirated edition, spurious edition.

contrahierba [con-trah-e-err'-bah], *f.* 1. *(Bot.)* Dorstenia contrayerba, a South American medicinal plant. 2. Antidote.

contrahilera [con-trah-e-lay'-rah], *f.* A second line formed to defend another.

Contrahojas de las ventanas [con-trah-o'-has day las ven-tah'-nas], *f. pl. (Naut.)* Deadlights of the cabin.

contrahoradar [con-trah-o-rah-dar'], *va.* To bore on the opposite side. *(Yo contraigo, yo contraiga from Contraer. V. TRAER.)*

contraído [con-trah-e'-do], *a.* 1. Contracted, shrunken, wasted. 2. *(And.)* Diligent, industrious.

contraindicación [con-trah-in-de-cah-the-on'], *f. (Med.)* Contraindication.

contraindicante *m. (Med.)* Contra-indicant.

contraindicar [con-trah-in-de-car'], *va. (Med.)* To contraindicate.

contrainteligencia [con-trah-en-te-le-hen'-the-ah], *f.* Counter-intelligence.

contralizo [con-trah-lee'-tho], *m.* A rod of wood to move the threads in a loom; a back leash.

contralor [con-trah-lor'], *m.* Comptroller, inspector.

contraloría [con-trah-lo-ree'-ah], *f.* Comptrollership.

contralto [con-trahl'-to], *m.* Contralto, countertenor, middle voice between the treble and tenor.

contraluz [con-trah-looth'], *f.* 1. View against the light. 2. Backlight. 3. Bad light. **A contraluz,** against the light, into the sun.

contramaestre [con-trah-mah-es'-tray], *m.* 1. *(Naut.)* Boatswain. 2. Overseer of a manufactory. 3. **Contramaestre de construcción,** the foreman of a dockyard.

contramalla, contramalladura [con-trah-mahl'-lyah, con-trah-mahl-lyah-doo'-rah], *f.* A double net for catching fish.

contramallar [con-trah-mal-lyar'], *va.* To make nets with double meshes.

contramandar [con-trah-man-dar'], *va.* To countermand.

contramangas [con-trah-mahn'-gas], *f. pl.* Oversleeves.

contramaniobra [con-trah-mah-ne-o'-brah], *f.* Counter-maneuver, a sudden change of tactics.

contramano [con-trah-mah'-no], *adv.* **A contramano,** in the wrong direction, the wrong way.

contramarca [con-trah-mar'-cah], *f.* 1. Countermark, a particular or additional mark. 2. A duty to be paid on goods which have no custom house mark. 3. A mark added to a medal or other piece of coined metal long after it has been struck, by which the curious know the several changes in value. 4. **Cartas** or **patentes de contramarca,** letters of marque.

contramarcar [con-trah-mar-car'], *va.* To countermark, to put a second or additional mark on bale goods, etc.

contramarco [con-trah-mar'-co], *m.* Counterframe of a glass window.

contramarcha [con-trah-mar'-cha], *f.* 1. Countermarch, retrocession. 2. Part of a weaver's loom. V. VIADERA. 3. *(Mil. and Naut.)* Evolution, by means of which a body of troops or division of ships change their front.

contramarchar [con-trah-mar-char'], *vn.* To countermarch.

contramarea [con-trah-mah-ray'-ah], *f. (Naut.)* Countertide, or springtide.

contramatar [con-trah-mah-tar'], *va.* **Contramatar a uno,** *(LAm.)* To hang somebody against the wall. *-vr. (LAm.)* To crash into something.

contramedida [con-trah-may-de'-dah], *f.* Counter-measure.

contramesana [con-trah-may-sah'-nah], *f. (Naut.)* Mizzenmast.

contramina [con-trah-mee'-nah], *f.* 1. Countermine, a mine intended to seek out and destroy the enemy's mines. 2. A subterraneous communication between two or more mines of metals or minerals.

contraminar [con-tra-me-nar'], *va.* 1. To countermine. 2. To counterwork, to defeat by secret measures.

contramolde [con-trah-mole'-day], *m.* 1. Countermould: an enveloping mould. 2. A kind of pasteboard on which is moulded, in relief or depression, what it is desired to represent.

contramotivo [con-trah-mo-tee'-vo], *m. (Mus.)* A motive or subject opposed to another; countersubject.

contramuelle [con-trah-moo-ayl'-lyay], *m. (Mech.)* A duplicate spring.

contramuralla [con-trah-moo-rahl'-lyah], *f. (Mil.)* Countermure, a low rampart.

contramuro [con-trah-moo'-ro], *m.* 1. Countermure.

contranatural [con-trah-nah-too-rahl'], *a.* Counternatural, contranatural, unnatural.

contraofensiva [con-trah-o-fen-see'-vah] *f.* Counteroffensive.

contraoferta [con-trah-o-fer'-tah], *f.* Counter-offer.

contraorden [con-trah-or'-den], *f.* Countermand; counter or revoking order.

contraordenar, *va.* V. CONTRAMANDAR

contrapares [con-trah-pah'-es], *m. pl. (Arch.)* Counter rafters in a building.

contraparte [con-trah-par'-tay], *f.* 1. Counterpart. 2. A duplicate copy of a deed.

contrapartida [con-trah-par-tee'-dah], *f.* 1. In book-keeping, corrective entry. 2. *(fig.)* Compensation; counterweight. **Pero como contrapartida añade que…,** but in contrast she adds that… **Como contrapartida de,** as compensation for.

contrapás [con-trah-pahs'], *m.* Kind of dance or step in dancing.

contrapasamiento [con-trah-pah-sah-me-en'-to], *m.* The act and effect of passing to the opposite side or party.

contrapasar [con-trah-pah-sar'], *vn.* To join the opposite party.

contrapaso [con-trah-pah'-so], *m.* 1. A backstep in walking or dancing. 2. Counterpace, contrary measure to any scheme. 3. *(Mus.)* Counternote.

contrapelear [con-trah-pay-lay-ar'], *vn. (Obs.)* To defend oneself in an engagement.

contrapelo (a) [con-trah-pay'-lo], *adv.* Against the grain; the wrong way. **Todo lo hace a contrapelo,** he does everything the wrong way around. **Acariciar un gato a contrapelo,** to stroke a cat the wrong way.

contrapesar [con-trah-pay-sar'], *va.* 1. To counterpoise, to counterbalance, to counterweigh 2. To countervail, to be equivalent to. 3. To act with equal power against any person or cause.

contrapeso [con-trah-pay'-so], *m.* 1. Counterpoise, equiponderance, counterbalance, countervail. 2. A rope dancer's pole. 3. *(Met.)* Equipollence, equivalence of power. 4. Counterpoise in a velvet-loom 5. An addition of inferior quality thrown to complete the weight of meat, fish, etc.

contrapeste [con-trah-pes'-tay], *m.* Remedy against pestilence.

contrapié [con-trah-pe-ay'], *m.* 1. The loss by a dog of the scent or the trail of what it was following. 2. Stratagem, trick.

contrapilastra [con-trah-pe-lahs'-trah], *f.* 1. *(Arch.)* Counterpilaster 2. Moulding on the joints of doors or shutters, to keep out the wind.

contraponedor [con-trah-po-nay-dor'], *m.* He who compares one thing with another.

contraponer [con-trah-po-nerr'], *va.* To compare, to oppose. **Contraponer A a B,** to set up A against B. **A esta idea ellos contraponen su teoría de que**…, against this idea they set up their theory that…

contraportada [cocn-trah-por-tah-dah], *f.* Inside cover (de libro).

contraposición [con-trah-po-se-the-on'], *f.* 1. Contraposition, the placing over against. 2. Counterview, contrast, a position in which two dissimilar things illustrate each other. 3. An act by which the execution of a sentence is barred.

contrapresión [con-trah-pray-se-on'], *f.* Counterpressure, back pressure.

contraprincipio [con-trah-prin-thee'-pe-o], *m.* Assertion contrary to a principle known as such.

contraproducente [con-trah-pro-doo-then'-tay], *a.* Self-defeating, counterproductive, defeating its own purpose. **Tener un resultado contraproducente,** to have a boomerang effect.

contrapromesa [con-trah-pro-may'-sah], *f.* 1. Declaration annulling a thing promised. 2. Conflict of one promise with another.

contraproposición [con-trah-pro-po-se-the-on'], *f.* Counterproposition.

contrapropuesta [con-trah-pro-poo-ays'-tah], *f.* Counterproposal.

contraprueba [con-trah-proo-ay'-bah], *f.* Counterproof, a second impression of a print taken off by printers; counterdrawing.

contrapuerta [con-trah-poo-err'-tah], *f.* 1. Storm door. 2. Inner large door of a house.

contrapuesto, ta [con-trah-poo-es'-to, tah], *a. & pp.* of CONTRAPONER. Compared.

contrapunta [con-trah-poon'-tah], *f.* Cutting part of the edge of a sabre's blade.

contrapuntante [con-trah-poon-tahn'-tay], *m.* He who sings in counterpoint.

contrapuntear [con-trah-poon-tay-ar'], *va.* 1. *(Mus.)* To sing in counterpoint. 2. To compare. 3. To taunt, to revile. -*vr.* To treat one another with abusive language, to wrangle, to dispute.

contrapunteo [con-trah-poon-tay'-o], *m. (And. Carib, Cono Sur)* argument, quarrel; *(And. Cono Sur)* improvised verse duel.

contrapuntista [con-trah-poon-tees'-tah], *m.* Contrapuntist, one skilled in counterpoint.

contrapunto [con-trah-poon'-to], *m.* 1. *(Mus.)* Counterpoint, harmony. 2. *(Lit.)* Counterpoint.

contrapunzón [con-trah-poon-thone'], *m.* 1. Puncheon for driving in a nail. 2. Counterpunch, an instrument wich

serves to open others. 3. The gunsmith's countermark on guns, to prevent their being exchanged for others, or purloined.

contraquerella [con-trah-kay-rayl'-lyah], *f.* A cross-complaint.

contraquilla [con-trah-keel'-lyah], *f. (Naut.)* False keel. *V.* ZAPATADELAQUILLA.

contrariamente [con-trah-re-ah-men-tay], *adv.* Contrarily, contrariously. **Contrariamente a lo que habíamos pensado,** contrary, to what we had thought.

contraiar[con-trah-re-ar'], *va.* To contradict, to oppose, to counteract, to counterwork; to vex.

contraiedad [con-trah-re-ay-dahd'], *f.* 1. Contrariety, repugnance, opposition, contradiction. 2. Vexation, annoyance. **Producir a uno contrariedad,** to upset somebody.

contrario [con-trah'-re-o], *m.* 1. Opponent, antagonist. 2. Competitor, rival. 3. Impediment, obstacle, obstruction.

contrario, ria [con-trah'-re-o, ah], *a.* 1. Contrary, repugnant, opposite, contradictory, contrarious. **En sentido contrario,** the other way. **Se ha interpretado en sentido contrario,** it has been interpreted in the opposite sense. 2. Contrary, adverse, abhorrent, cross. 3. Harmful, mischievous. **Tiempo contrario,** *(Naut.)* Foul weather. **Echar al contrario,** to cross the breed. **Al contrario** or **por el contrario,** on the contrary. **En contrario,** against, in opposition to. **Llevar la contraria,** to contradict, to oppose. **Contrario a los intereses del país,** contrary to the nation's interests. **Al contrario de lo que habíamos pensado,** against what we had thought. **Todo lo contrario,** quite the reverse.

contrarracamento [con-trar-rah-cah-men'-to], *m. (Naut.)* Preventerparrel.

contrarrampante [con-trar-ram-pahn'-tay], *a. (Her.)* Rampant, and face to face.

contrarreclamación [con-trar-ray-clah-mah-the-on'], *f.* Counterclaim.

contrarreforma [con-trar-re-for'-mah], *f.* Counter-Reformation.

contrarregistro [con-trar-ray-hess'-tro], *m.* Control, a register or account kept to be compared with any other.

contrarreguera [con-trar-ray-gay-rah], *f.* A lateral drain, to prevent mischief to the tilled land, and to aid in even distribution of irrigation.

contrarreparo [con-trar-ray-pah'-ro], *m. (Mil.)* Counterguard, or counterdefence.

contrarréplica [con-trar-ray'-ple-cah], *f.* Rejoinder, reply to an answer: it is sometimes also rebutter, or an answer to a rejoinder.

contrarrestar [con-trar-res-tar'], *va.* 1. To strike back a ball, to counterbuff. 2. To resist, to oppose, to check, to countercheck, to counterwork.

contrarresto [con-trar-res'-to], *m.* 1. A player who is to strike back the ball. 2. Check, opposition, contradiction.

contrarrevolución [con-trar-ray-vo-loo-the-on'], *f.* Counterrevolution.

contrarrevolucionario ria [con-trar-ray-vo-loo-the-o-nah'-re-o, ah], *m. & f. & a.* 1. Counterrevolucionist. 2. Belonging to a counterrevolution.

contrarroa, contrarroda [con-trar-ro'-ah, con-trar-ro'-dah], *f. (Naut.)* Stemson.

contrarronda [con-trar-ron'-dah], *f.* 1. *(Mil.)* Counterround, which follows the first round for greater safety's sake, to visit the different posts. 2. Round made by officers to inspect the posts, guards, and sentinels.

contrarrotura [con-trar-ro-too'-rah], *f. (Vet.)* Plaster or poultice applied to fractures or wounds by veterinarians.

contras [cone'-trass], *m. pl. (Mus.)* The bass pipes of a large organ. *V.* CONTRA.

contrasalida [con-trah-sah-lee'-dah], *f.* Countersally; resistance of besiegers to a sally.

contrasalva [con-trah-sahl'-vah], *f. (Mil.)* Countersalute.

contrasellar [con-trah-sayl-lyar'], *va.* To counterseal, to seal with others.

contrasentido [con-trah-sen-tee'-do], *m.* 1. Countersense, opposed meaning. 2. A deduction opposed to the logical antecedents. **Aquí hay un contrasentido**, there is a contradiction here. **Es un contrasentido que él actúe así**, it doesn't make sense for him to act like that.

contraseña [con-trah-say'-nyah], *f. L* Countersign or countermark. 2. *(Mil.)* Watchword. 3. Password.

contrasol [con-trah-sole'], *m.* Sunshade, a tub in greenhouses to protect certain plants likely to be injured by full sunlight.

contrastable [con-tras-tah'-blay], *a.* Contrastable, capable of contrast.

contrastante [con-tras-tahn'-tay], *pa.* Contrasting.

contrastar [con-tras-tar'], *va.* 1. To contrast, to place in opposition: to oppose. 2. To resist, to contradict. 3. To assay metals. 4. To examine measures and weights. 5. *(Naut.)* To endure misfortunes, or contrary winds, and resist them mechanically. -*vn.* 1. To contrast, to form a contrast (hacer contraste). 2. **Contrastar con, contrastar contra**, to resist, to face up.

contraste [con-trahs'-tay], *m.* 1. Assayer of the mint. 2. Assayer's office where gold and silver are tried and marked. 3. Assayer of weights and measures. 4. *(Prov.)* A public office where raw silk is weighed. 5. Counterview contrast, a position in which two dissimilar things illustrate each other. **Hacer contrastar con**, to contrast with. 6. Opposition and strife between persons and things. 7. Contrast, opposition and dissimilitude of figures. 8. *(Nat.)* Sudden change of the wind, by which it becomes foul or contrary.

contrata [con-trah'-tah], *f.* 1. Contract, a deed in which the terms of a contract, bargain, or agreement are set forth. 2. Territory, district.

contratación [con-trah-tah-the-on'], *f.* 1. Trade, commerce, traffic, enterprise, undertaking, business transaction. 2. Contract (contrato), hiring. **Contrato temporal**, temporary contract. 3. Engagement, taking-on.

contratante [con-trah-tahn'-say], *pa.* Contracting; contractor, one of the parties to a contract.

contratar [con-trah-tar'], *va.* 1. To trade, to traffic. 2. To contract or bargain. 3. To contract, to stipulate, to covenant. -*vr.* To sign on. **Contratarse para hacer algo**, to contract to do something.

contratela [con-trah-tay'-lah], *f.* Second inclosure of canvas, within which game is enveloped or wild boars are fought.

contratiempo [con-trah-te-em'-po], *m.* Disappointment, misfortune, calamity, trouble, frustration.

contratista [con-trah-tees'-tah], *m.f.* Contractor, lessee, patentee, conventionist, covenanter. **Contratista de obras**, building contractor.

contrato [con-trah'-to], *m.* 1. Contract, convention, or mutual agreement, pact; stipulation, covenant. 2. Contract, a deed in which the terms of a contract or bargain are set forth. **Entrar en contrato**, to make a covenant. **Contrato temporal o indefinido**, definite or indefinite contract. **Contrato aleatorio**, aleatory contract. **Contrato de compraventa**, a contract of bargain and sale.

contratrancaniles [con-trah-tran-ca-nee'-les], *m. pl. (Naut.)* Inner waterways, serving to carry off the water by the scupers.

contratreta [con-trah-tray'-tah], *f.* Counterplot.

contratrinchera [con-trah-trin-chay'-rah], *f. (Mil.)* Countertrench, an intrenchment made by the besieged against the besiegers.

contratuerca [con-trah-too-ayr-cah], *f.* Locknut.

contravalación [con-trah-vah-la-the-on'], *f.* *(Mil.)* Contravallation.

contravalar [con-trah-vah-lar'], *va.* To form a line of contravallation.

contravalor [con-trah-vah-lor'], *m.* Countervalue, equivalent. *(Com.)*

contravención [con-trah-ven-the-on'], *f.* Contravention, violation of a law.

contraveneno [con-trah-vay-nay'-no], *m.* 1. Counterpoison, antidote. 2. *(Met.)* Precaution taken to avoid some infamy or mischief.

contravenir [con-trah-vay-neer'], *va.* 1. To contravene, to transgress a command, to violate a law. 2. To oppose, to obstruct, to baffle, to countermine.

contraventana [con-trah-ven-tah'-nah], *f.* 1. Storm window. 2. Outside window shutter.

contraventor, ra [con-trah-ven-tor', rah], *m. & f.* 1. Transgressor, offender. 2. Contravener, he who opposes another.

contravidriera [con-trah-ve-dre-ay'-rah], *f.* A second glass window, to keep off cold or heat.

contravirar [con-trah-ve-rar'], *va.* To turn in the opposite direction.

contray [con-trah'-e], *m.* Sort of fine cloth.

contrayente [con-trah-yen'-tay], *pa.* Contracting (matrimonios).

contrayugo [con-trah-yoo'-go], *m. (Naut.)* Inner transom.

contrecho, cha [con-tray'-cho, chah], *a.* Crippled, maimed.

contrete [con-tray'-tay], *m.* 1. *(Naut.)* Breastshore. 2. Crochet, angle iron, stay. 3. Gusset.

contribución [con-tre-boo-the-on'], *f.* 1 Contribution. **Poner a contribución**, to make use of. 2. Contribution, tax. **Única contribución**, income tax. **Contribución directa**, direct tax. **Exento de contribuciones**, free of tax.

contribuidor, ra [con-tre-boo-e-dor', rah], *m. & f.* Contributor.

contribuir [con-tre-boo-eer'], *va.* 1. To contribute, to pay one's share of a tax. 2. To contribute, to give to some common stock. **Contribuir con una cantidad**, to contribute with a sum. **Contribuir al éxito de algo**, to contribute to the success of something. 3. To contribute, to bear a part in some common design.

contribulado, da [con-tre-boo-lah'-do, dah], *a.* Grieved, afflicted.

contributario [con-tre-boo-tah'-re-o], *m.* Contributor, taxpayer.

contribuyente [con-tre-boo-yen'-tay], *pa.* Contributing; contributor; cooperative, contributory.

contrición [con-tre-the-on'], *f.* Contrition, penitence, compunction.

contrincante [con-trin-cahn'-tay], *m.* Competitor, rival, opponent.

contristar [con-trees-tar'], *va.* To afflict, to sadden. -*vr.* To grow sad, to grieve.

contrito, ta [con-tree'-to, tah], *a.* Contrite, compunctious, penitent.

control [con-trol], *m.* Control, check, regulation. **Control remoto**, remote control. **Control de natalidad**, birth control. **Control de precios**, price control. **Perder el control**, to lose control. **Control de la circulación**, traffic control. **Control de sí mismo**, self-control. **Control nuclear**, nuclear inspection.

controlador, ra [con-tro-laah-dor'], *m. & f.* Controller; *(LAm.) (Ferro.)* Inspector, ticket-collector. **Controlador de estacionamiento**, traffic warden. Driver *(Comput.).* **Controlador de pantalla**, monitor controller. **Controlador del dispositivo**, device controller. **Controlador de la impresora**, printer driver. **Controlador del ratón**, mouse driver.

controlar [con-tro-lar'], *va.* 1. To control, to regulate. 2. To restrain to hold in check. 3. To monitor to verify; to check.

controversia [con-tro-verr'-se-ah], *f.* Controversy, debate.

controversial [con-trah-ver-se-ah], *a.* Controversial.

controversista [con-tro-ver-sees'-tah], *m.* Controversialist, disputant, controverter.

controvertible [con-tro-ver-tee'-blay], *a.* Controvertible, disputable, litigious.

controvertido [con-trah-ver-tee'-do], *a.* Controversial.

controvertir [con-tro-ver-teer'], *va.* To controvert, to dispute a thing in writing. 2. To discuss, to argue against. -*vn.* To argue. (*Yo controvierto, yo controvierta; él controvirtió, él controvirtiera; from Controvertir. V. ASENTIR.*)

contubernal [con-too-ber-nahl'], *m.* Chamberfellow, companion in the same apartment.

contubernio [con-too-berr'-ne-o], *m.* 1. Cohabitation, inhabiting the same place with another. 2. Concubinage, living with a woman not married.

contumacia [con-too-mah'-the-ah], *f.* 1. Obstinacy; perverseness, stubborness. 2. (*Law.*) Contumacy, a wilful contempt and disobedience to any lawful summons or judicial order, nonappearance; contempt of court; default.

contumaz [con-too-math'], *a.* 1. Obstinate, stubborn. perverse. 2. Contumacious, disobedient. 3. (*Med.*) Disease-carrying, germ-laden.

contumazmente, *adv.* Contumaciously, obstinately.

contumelia [con-too-may'-le-ah], *f.* Contumely, reproach, contumeliousness, abuse.

contumeliosamente, *adv.* Contumeliously, reproachfully.

contumelioso, sa [con-too-may-le-o'-so, sah], *a.* Contumelious, reproachful, sarcastic.

contumerioso [con-too-may-re-o-so], *a.* (*CAm.*) Finicky, fussy.

contundencia [con-toon-den'-the-ah], *f.* Forecefulness, power, conclusive nature; crushing nature; strictness, severity; toughness; aggressive nature.

contundente [con-toon-den'-tay], *pa.* 1. Producing a contusion (armas); (instrumento contundente), blunt instrument. 2. (*fig.*) Forceful, convincing, powerful (argumento); conclusive (prueba); forceful (tono); crushing (derrota); strict, severe.

contundir [con-toon-deer'], *va.* To contuse, to contund; to bruise; to cause a contusion.

conturbación [con-toor-bah-the-on'], *f.* Perturbation, uneasiness of mind.

conturbado, da [con-toor-bah'-do, dah], *a.* Turbulent, troublesome.-*pp.* of CONTURBAR.

conturbador [con-toor-bah-dor'], *m.* Perturber, disturber.

conturbamiento [con-toor-bah-me-en'-to], *m.* Perturbation, disquietude.

conturbar [con-toor-bar'], *va.* To perturb, to disquiet, to disturb. -*vr.* To be troubled, to be dismayed, to become perturbed.

conturbativo, va [con-toor-bah-tee'-vo, vah], *a.* That which perturbs or disquiets.

contusión [con-too-se-on'], *f.* Contusion, bruise.

contusionar [con-too-se-o-nar'], *va.* To bruise; to hurt, to damage.

contuso, sa [con-too'-so, sah], *a.* Bruised. -*pp irr.* of CONTUNDIR.

contutor [con-too-tor'], *m.* Assistant tutor, fellow-tutor.

conuco, or **cunuco** [co-noo'-co, coo-noo'-co], *m.* 1. (*Amer.*) A very small farm or plantation, often given by masters to their slaves to cultivate for themselves. 2. Cornfield.

conuquero [co-noo-kay'-ro], *m.* (*And. Carib.*) Smallholder, farmer.

conusco, *pron. pers.* (*Obs.*) With us.

conusfusorio [co-noos-foo-so'-re-o], *m.* A metallic crucible, shaped like an inverted cone, used in smelting.

convalaria [con-vah-lah'-re-ah], *f.* Lily of the valley.

convalariado, da, convalárico, ca, *a.* Resembling the lily of the valley.

convalecencia [con-vah-lay-then'-the-ah], *f.* Convalescence, recovery from disease. **Casa de convalecencia** or only **convalecencia**, a hospital for convalescent patients.

convalecer [con-vah-lay-therr'], *vn.* 1. To recover from sickness. 2. (*Met.*) To recover lost prosperity and power.

convaleciente [con-vah-lay-the-en'-tay], *pa.* Convalescent.

convalidación [con-vah-le-dah-the-on'], *f.* Acceptance, recognition; validation; ratification, confirmation.

convalidar [con-vah-le-dar'], *va.* To accept, to recognize; to validate; to ratify, to confirm (documento).

convección [con-vec-the-on'], *f.* Convection.

convecino, na [con-vay-thee'-no, nah], *a.* Neighboring, conterminous.

convelerse [con-vay-lerr'-say], *vr.* To twitch, to be contracted: applied to muscular fibers, membranes, blood-vessels, etc.

convencedor, ra [con-ven-thay-dor', rah], *m. & f.* One who demonstrates and convinces.

convencer [con-ven-therr'], *va.* To convince, to convict, to demonstrate. **Convencer a uno de que algo es mejor**, to convince somebody something is better. **No me convence del todo**, I'm not fully convinced. -*vn.* To convince. **El argumento no convence**, the argument does not convince. -*vr.* To be assured, to become convinced ¡**Convéncete!**, believe me!

convencible [con-ven-thee'-blay], *a.* Convincible, convictible.

convencido, da [con-ven-thee'-do, dah], *a.* Convict. -*pp.* of CONVENCER.

convencimiento [con-ven-the-me-en'-to], *m.* Conviction, confutation. **Llegar al convencimiento de**, to become convinced of. **Tener el convencimiento de que…**, to be convinced that…

convención [con-ven-the-on'], *f.* 1. Convention, contract, agreement, pact, composition. 2. Convenience, convening.

convencional [con-ven-the-o-nahl'], *a.* Conventional, conventionary.

convencionalismo [con-ven-the-o-nah-les'-mo], *m.* Conventionalism.

convencionalmente, [con-ven-the-o-nahl'-men-tay] *adv.* Conventionally.

convencionero [con-ven-the-o-nay-ro], *a.* (*And. Mex.*) Comfort-loving, self-indulgent.

convenible [con-vay-nee'-blay], *a.* 1. Docile, tractable, compliant, obsequious. 2. Convenient. 3. Of a moderate or reasonable price.

convenido, da, *a. & pp.* of CONVENIR. Settled by consent, agreed, done.

conveniencia [con-vay-ne-en'-the-ah], *f.* 1. Conformity, congruity, consistence. 2. Utility, profit, advantage, comfort. **A la primera conveniencia**, at one's earliest opportunity. 3. Agreement, convention, adjustment. 4. Service, a servant's place in a house or family. 5. Convenience, ease or cause of ease, commodiousness, accommodation, commodity. **Es amigo de conveniencia**, he loves his ease or comfort. 6. Convenience, fitness, expedience. **Conveniencias**, 1. Emoluments, perquisites. 2. Income, property.

conveniente [con-vay-ne-en'-tay], *a.* 1. Useful, profitable, advantageous, good. **Sería conveniente que..**, it would be a good thing if… 2. Accordant, conformable. 3. Fit, suitable, agreeable. **Nada conveniente**, unsuitable. 4. Convenient, expedient, correspondent, opportune. 5. Commodious, timely. 6. Decent.

convenientemente, [con-vay-ne-en-tay-men'-tay], *adv.* Conveniently, fitly, suitably, expediently.

convenio [con-vay'-ne-o], *m.* 1. Convention, contract, agreement, pact, concert, consent. **Convenio colectivo**, collective bargain. **Convenio salarial**, wages agreement. 2. Contrivance. 3. Plot.

convenir [con-vay-neer'], *vn.* 1. To agree, to be of the same opinion to coincide to cohere, to consist, to compromise. **Convenir en hacer algo**, to agree to do something. 2. To agree, to fit, to harmonize, to comport, to suit. **Si le conviene**, if it suits you. **No me conviene**, it's not in my interest. **Lo que más le conviene es un reposo completo**, the best thing for him is complete rest. 3. To correspond, to belong to. 4. To assemble, to convene. 5. To cohabit carnally. 6. To litigate. -*v. imp.* To suit, to be to the purpose. -*vr.* To compound, to agree, to close, to suit one's interests. **Convenir**

en, to close upon, to close with, to settle. **Conviene saber**, that is, to wit.

conventazo [con-ven-tah'-tho], *m. aug.* A large convent or monastery.

conventículo [con-ven-tee'-coo-lo], *m.* Conventicle, a secret assembly or meeting for some unlawful purpose.

conventillero [con-ven-tel-lyay'-ro], *(And. Cono Sur)* 1. *a.* Gossipy. 2. *m, f.* Sandalmonger, gossip, telltale.

conventillo [con-ven-tel'-lyo], *m. (And. Cono Sur)* Tenement, inner city slum.

convento [con-ven'-to], *m.* 1. Convent of monks or nuns, monastery, nunnery. 2. Community of religious men or women.

conventual [con-ven-too-ahl'], *a.* Conventual, monastic.

conventual [con-ven-too-ahl'], *m.* 1. Conventual, a monk, one that lives in a convent. 2. Franciscan friar possessing estates or property.

conventualidad [con-ven-too-ah-le-dahd'], *f.* 1. The state of living together as religious persons in a convent or monastery. 2. Assignment of a monk to a determined convent.

conventualmente *adv.* Monastically, reclusely.

convergencia [con-ver-hen'-the-ah], *f.* 1. Convergence. 2. *(fig.)* Common tendency, common direction; concurrence. **Convergencia de izquierdas**, grouping of left-wing forces.

convergente [con-ver-hen'-say], *a.* Convergent, converging.

convergentemente [con-ver-hen-tay-men'-tay], *adv.* **Convergentemente con**, together with, jointly with.

converger [con-ver-herr'], *vn.* V. CONVERGIR *(Acad.)* 1. To converge. 2. *(fig.)* To have a common tendency, to tend in the same direction; to concur, to be in accord. **Sus esfuerzos convergen a un fin común**, their efforts have a common purpose.

convergir [con-ver-heer'], *vn.* 1. To converge. 2. To agree in opinions.

conversa [con-ver'-sah], *f.* 1. *(Geom.)* Converse. 2. *(LAm.)* Talk, chat; smooth talk.

conversable [con-ver-sah'-blay], *a.* 1. Conversable, sociable. 2. *(Theology)* Communicable.

conversación [con-ver-sah-the-on'], *f.* 1. Conversation, easy talk, chat, converse, conference, communication, colloquy. **Cambiar de conversación**, to change the subject. **Tratar conversación con uno**, to get into conversation with somebody. 2. Conversation, commerce, intercourse, society, company. 3. *(Obs.)* Room, bedroom. 4. Criminal intercourse. 5. Club, an assembly. V. TERTULIA.

conversacional [con-ver-sah-the-o-nahl'], *a.* Conversational; colloquial (estilo).

conversador [con-ver-sah-dor'], 1. *a. (LAm.)* Talkative, chatty. 2. *m. (LAm.)* Smooth talker (zalamero).

conversar [con-ver-sar'], *vn.* 1. To converse, to have a chat, to discourse familiarly, to commune, to talk together. 2. To live together in the company of others. 3. *(Mil.)* To change front, wheel.

conversata [con-ver-sah'-tah], *f. (Cono Sur)* Talk, chat.

conversión [con-ver-se-on'], *f.* 1. Conversion. 2. Conversion, change from one state to another. 3. *(Rhet).* Apostrphe. 4. *(Mil.)* Wheel, wheeling. **Cuarto de conversión**, quarterwheeling. **Conversión paralelo-serie**, *(Inform.)* parallel-to-serial conversion.

conversivo, va [con-ver-see'-vo, vah], *a.* Having the power of converting or changing one thing into another.

converso [con-verr'-so], *m.* 1. Convert, a person converted from one religion or opinion to another. 2. Lay brother, a man admitted for the service of a religious house without being ordained. *-a.* Converted.

conversón [con-ver-sone'], *(And.)* 1. *a.* Talkative, gossiping. 2. *m. f.* Talkative person.

conversor [con-ver-sor'], *m. (Rad.)* Converter.

convertibilidad [con-ver-te-be-le-dahd'], *f.* Convertibility, capability of being exchanged.

convertible [con-ver-tee'-blay], *a.* 1. Convertible. 2. Movable, transferable, *-m.* Convertible (automobile).

convertido, da [con-ver-tee'-do, dah], *a. & pp.* of CONVERTIR. Converted, changed, transformed.

convertidor [con-ver-te-dor'], *m.* Converter, transformer.

convertir [con-ver-teer'], *va.* 1. To convert, to change into another substance, to permute. 2. To convert, to change from one religion or opinion to another. **Convertir a uno al catolicismo**, to convert somebody to Catholicism. 3. To convert, to turn from a bad to a good life. 4. To apply things to a use for which they were not intended. 5. To convert, to direct, to appropriate. **Todo lo convierte en substancia**, *(Met.)* He minds nothing, nothing makes the least impression upon him; he wants nothing but real facts. *-vr.* To be converted, to undergo a change either in religion or life.

convexidad [con-vek-se-dahd'], *f.* Convexity.

convexo, xa [con-vek'-so, sah], *a.* Convex, convexed.

convicción [con-vic-the-on'], *f.* Conviction, convincement.

convicto, ta [con-veec'-to, tah], *pp. irr.* of CONVENCER. Convicted, guilty.

convidada [con-ve-dah'-dah], *f.* An invitation to drink; a treat. **Dar una convidada**, to buy around.

convidante [con-ve-dahn'-tay], *m. & f.* One who invites, host.

convidado, da [con-ve-dah'-do, dah], *a. & pp.* of CONVIDAR. Invited, it is often used as a substantive for a guest, or a person invited to a dinner, party, etc.

convidador, ra [con-ve-dah-dor', rah], *m. & f.* Inviter.

convidar [con-ve-dar'], *va.* 1. To invite, to bid, to ask or call to anything pleasing, to treat. **Convidar a uno a hacer algo**, to invite somebody to do something. **Convidar a uno a una cerveza**, to buy somebody a beer. 2. To treat someone to something. 3. *(Met.)* To allure, to invite, to persuade. **El ambiente convida a la meditación**, the setting invites one to indulge in meditation. *-vr.* To offer one's services spontaneously.

convincente [con-vin-then'-tay], *a.* Convincing, convincible.

convincentemente, *adv.* Convincingly, convictively.

convite [con-vee'-tay], *m.* 1. Invitation. 2. Feast to which persons are invited.

convivencia [con-ve-ven'-the-ah], *f.* Living together, life together; good fellowship, socializing.

conviviente [con-ve-ve-en'-tay], *a.* Living together. *-m. & f.* *(LAm.)* Live-in lover.

convivir [con-ve-ver'], *vn.* To live together; to share the same life; *(Pol.)* To coexist; *(fig.)* To exist side by side.

convocación [con-vo-ca-the-on'], *f.* Convocation, calling.

convocadero, ra [con-vo-cah-day'-ro, rah], *a.* That is to be convened or convoked.

convocador, ra [con-vo-cah-dor', rah], *m. & f.* Convener, convoker.

convocar [con-vo-car'], *va.* 1. To convene, to convoke, to call together, to congregate. 2. To shout in triumph or exultation. *-vn.* Convocar a, to call for.

convocatoria [con-vo-cah-to'-re-ah], *f.* Letter of convocation, an edict.

convocatrio, ria [con-vo-cah-to'-re-o, ah], *a.* That which convokes.

convoluto, ta [con-vo-loo'-to, tah], *a.* Convolute, wrapped around itself.

convolvuláceo, cea [con-vol-voo-lah'-thay-o, ah], *a.* Convolvulaceous, of the convolvulus family.

convólvulo [con-vol'-voo-lo], *m.* 1. *(Bot.)* Convolvulus, bindweed. 2. A small worm which destroys the vines and wraps itself in their leaves. 3. A vinefretter.

convoy [con-vo'-e], *m.* 1. Convoy, conduct, an escort or guard. 2. The things conveyed with an escort or convoy. 3. *(Coll.)* Retinue, suite. 4. A railway train. 5. *(Carib.)* Salad (ensalada).

convoyante [con-vo-yahn'-tay], *pa.* Convoying.

convoyar [con-vo-yar'], *va.* 1. To convoy, to escort, or guard. 2. *(Cono Sur)* to back, to sponsor (financiar). *-vr. (Carib.)* To connive together, to plot.

convulsar [con-vool-sar'], *vn. (Vet.)* To feel an involuntary contraction of the nerves.-*vr.* To be convulsed.

convulsión [con-vool-se-on'], *f.* Convulsion.

convulsionar [con-vool-se-o-nar'], *va. (Med.)* To produce convulsions in; *(fig.)* To convulse, to cause an upheaval in.

convulsivamente [con-vool-se-vah-men'-tay], *adv.* Convulsively.

convulsivo, va [con-vool-see'-vo, vah], *a.* Convulsive, disturbed.

convulso, sa [con-vool'-so, sah], *a.* Convulsed.

convusco [con-voos'-co], *pron. pers.* With you.

conyúdice [con-yoo'-de-thay], *m. (Obs.) V.* CONJUEZ.

conyugal [con-yoo-gahl'], *a.* Conjugal, connubial, married.

conyugalmente, *adv.* Conjugally, matrimonially.

cónyuge [con'-yoo-hay], *m. & f.* Spouse; partner; husband, wife.

cónyuges [con'-yoo-hess], *m. pl.* A married couple, husband and wife.

conyunto, ta [con-yoon'-to, tah], *a.* CONJUNTO.

coña [co'-nyah], *f.* 1. Humor, humorous tone, joking way. **Estar de coña**, to be in a joking mood. **Tomar algo a coña**, to take something as a joke. 2. Annoyance, bind.

coñac [co-nyac'], *m.* Cognac.

coñazo [co-nyah'-tho], *m.* 1. Pain (persona, cosa). 2. **Dar el coñazo**, to be a real pain.

coñe [co'-nyay], *excl. V.* COÑO.

coñearse [co-nyay-ar'-say], *vr.* To speak in a joking way, to adopt a humorous tone. **Coñearse de**, to make fun of.

coñete [co-nyay'-tay], *a. (And. Cono Sur)* stingy, tighfisted.

coño [co'-nyo], *m.* 1. *(Anat.)* Cunt. 2. *excl.* Hell!, damn!, damn it all!; well I'm damned! (sorpresa). **¡Esto hay que celebrarlo, coño!**, we jolly well must celebrate this! 3. *adv.* **¿Qué coño haces aquí?**, what in hell's name are you up to? 4. **¡Qué libro ni qué coño!**, what a goddamned book! **Viven en el quinto coño**, they live way out. 5. *(Cono Sur. Mex.)* pejorative term applied to Spaniards.

cooperación [co-o-pay-rah-the-on'], *f.* Cooperation, conspiracy, coefficiency.

cooperador, ra [co-o-pay-rah-dor', rah], *m. & f.* Cooperator.

cooperante [co-o-pay-rahn'-tay], *pa. & a.* Cooperating, cooperator, cooperative, coactive, contributive.

cooperar [co-o-pay-rar'], *va.* To cooperate, to labor jointly with another, to concur. **Cooperar a un mismo fin**, to work for a common aim. **Cooperar en**, to collaborate in. **Los factores que cooperaron al fracaso**, the factors which together led to failure.

cooperario [co-o-pay-rah'-re-o], *m. V.* COOPERADOR.

cooperativa [co-o-pay-rah-te'-vah], *f.* Cooperative, mutual association. **Cooperativa agrícola**, agricultural cooperative.

cooperativamente, *adv.* Coefficiently.

cooperativista [co-o-pay-rah-te-ves'-tah], *m. & f.* Member of a cooperative.

cooperativo, va [co-o-pay-rah-tee'-vo, vah], *a.* Cooperative.

coopositor [co-o-po-se-tor'], *m.* He who is a candidate with another for a prebend, professorship, etc., which is obtained by a public trial of skill; competitor, rival.

coordenada [co-or-day-nah'-dah], *f. (Math.)* Coordinate.

coordinación [co-or-de-nah-the-on'], *f.* Coordination; classification; collateralness.

coordinadamente [co-or-day-na-dah-men'-tay] *adv.* Coordinately.

coordinado, da [co-or-de-nah'-do, dah], *a.* Coordinate.-*pp.* of COORDINAR.

coordinador, ra [co-or-de-nah-dor'], *m. & f.* Coordinator.

coordinadora [co-or-de-nah-dor'], *f.* Coordinating, committee.

coordinar [co-or-de-nar'], *va.* To coordinate, to arrange, to adjust, to class, to classify.

copa [co'-pah], *f.* 1. Cup, a small drinking vessel; goblet, wineglass. **Copa Mundial**, World Cup. **Llevar una copa de más**, to have one over the eight. 2. Meeting of the branches of a tree, a bower. 3. Crown of a hat. 4. Brazier, firepan. 5. Gill liquid measure, the fourth part of a pint; teacupful. 6. Each of the cards with a heart. 7. *(fig.)* **Copa de la amargura**, cup of sorrow. **Apurar la copa**, to know the utmost depths of suffering. -*pl.* 1. Hearts, one of the four suits at cards. 2. Bosses of a bridle.

copado, da [co-pah'-do, dah], *a.* Tufted, copped.-*pp.* of COPAR.

copaiba [co-pah'-e-bah], *f.* 1. *(Bot.)* The copaiba-tree, from which the copaiba gum or balsam distils. 2. Balsam copaiba.

copal [co-pahl'], *m.* Copal, a transparent resin.

copaljocol [co-pal-ho-cohl'], *m. (Bot.)* Tree in New Spain resembling a cherrytree.

copar [co-par'], *va.* 1. In monte, to put on a card a sum equal to what there is in the bank. 2. *(Met. and Coll.)* To possess oneself of many persons and things united; to corner. **Quedar copado en un trabajo**, to get bogged down in a place of work. 3. *(Mil.)* To surprise, cut off the retreat of a military force, making it prisoner. 4. *(Mex.)* To monopolize.

coparticipación [co-par-te-the-pah-the-on'], *f.* Joint participation.

copartícipe [co-par-tee'-the-pay], *com.* Participant, copartner, collaborator.

copaza [co-pah'-thah], *f. aug.* A large cup or glass with a foot.

copazo [co-pah'-tho], *m. aug.* A large fleece of wool. 2. Large snowflake.

copear [co-pay-ar'], *vn.* 1. To booze, to tipple; to go on a drinking spree. 2. *(Com.)* To sell wine by the glass.

copela [co-pay'-lah], *f.* Cupel or coppel, a vessel used in assaying precious metals.

copelación [co-pay-lah-the-on'], *f.* Cupellation, the act of refining metals.

copelar [co-pay-ar'], *va.* To refine or purify metals.

copeo [co-pay-o], *m.* **Ir de copeo**, to go drinking.

copera [co-pay'-rah], *f.* Cupboard: closet for glassware.

coperillo [co-pay-reel'-lyo], *m. dim.* A little cupbearer or attendant at a feast to serve wine.

Copérnico [co-per'-ne-co], *m.* Copernicus.

copero [co-pay'-ro], *m.* Cupbearer, one who serves drink at a feast.

copeta [co-pay'-tah], *f. dim.* A small cup or drinking-vessel.

copete [co-pay'-tay], *m.* 1. A crest, a tuft, aigret, toupee. **Estar hasta el copete**, *(Carib. Mex.)* To be fed up to the back teeth. 2. Forelock of a horse. 3. Crownwork of a looking-glass frame, made in the shape of a shell. 4. Top of the shoe which rises over the buckle. 5. Top, summit. 6. The projecting top or cop of sherbets or ice cream. **Hombre de copete**, a man of respectability and character. **Tener copete** or **mucho copete**, to assume an air of authority, to be lofty, supercilious, and haughty. **Asir la ocasión por el copete**, *(Prov.)* To profit by the opportunity.

copetín [co-pay-teen'], *m. (Arg.)* A before dinner drink; aperitif; liquor glass.

copetón [co-pay-tone'], *a.* 1. *(LAm.) V.* COPETUDO. 2. *(And.)* **Estar copetón**, to be tight.

copetudo, da [co-pay-too-do, dah], *a.* 1. Copped, rising to a top or head. 2. High, lofty, supercilious, on account of one's noble descent.

copey [co-pay'-e], *m.* 1. American tree, of excellent wood for engraving. 2. A bitumen found in Ecuador, and employed in repairing ships.

copia [co'-pe-ah], *f.* 1. Copiousness, plenty, abundance, fulness; fertility. 2. Copy, transcript; counterpart. 3. Portrait from an original design; copy of a picture. 4. Rate or valuation of tithe. 5. *(Gram.)* List of nouns and verbs, and the cases they govern. **Sacar una copia de**, to make a copy of. **Copia en limpio**, fair copy. **Copia carbónica**, *(Cono Sur)* carbon copy. 6. *(Inform.)* **Copia impresa**, hard copy.

copiador [co-pe-ah-dor'], *m.* Copyist, copier, transcriber.

Copiador or **libro copiador**. among merchants, book in which letters are copied, a copybook.

copiante [co-pe-ahn'-tay], *m.* Copyist, copier, an imitator.

copiar [co-pe-ar'], *va.* 1. To copy, to transcribe, to exemplify. 2. To imitate, to draw after life. 3. To write on the same subject with another, and nearly in the same manner. 4. *(Poet.)* To describe, to depict. **Copiar del natural**, to copy from life; among artists, to design from the naked body.

copilador [co-pe-lah-dor'], *m.* Compiler, collector. *V.* COMPILADOR.

copilar [co-pe-lar'], *va.* To compile; to collect. *V.* COMPILAR.

copilla [co-pee'-lyah], *f.* 1. *dim.* of COPA. 2. Cigar-lighter.

copiloto [co-pe-lo'-to], *m. & f. (Aut.)* Co-driver; *(Aer.)* Co-pilot.

copín [co-peen'], *m.* In Asturias, a Spanish measure, equal to half a *celemín*, or the twelfth part of a quintal or *fanega*.

copina [co-pee'-nah], *f. (Mex.)* A skin taken off whole.

copinar [co-pe-nar'], *va.* To remove an entire skin.

copiosamente [co-pe-o-sah-men'-tay], *adv.* Copiously, abundantly, plentifully, largely.

copioso, sa [co-pe-o'-so, sah], *a.* Copious, abundant, full, fruitful, plentiful, fluent, large.

copista [co-pees'-tah], *m.* 1. Copyist, transcriber. 2. A copying-machine.

copita [co-pee'-tah], *f. dim.* A small cup or drinking vessel. **Tomarse unas copitas**, to have a drink or two.

copito [co-pee'-to], *m. dim.* A small fleece or flake.

copla [co'-plah], *f.* 1. A certain number of consonant verses, a couplet; a stanza of four lines, of eight or eleven syllables, the second and fourth lines rhyming; by extension, short rhymes. 2. A sarcastic hint or remark, a lampoon. 3. *(Prov.)* Ballad. **Echar coplas de repente**, to talk nonsense. **Andar en coplas**, to be on everyone's lips. **Echar coplas a uno**, to speak ill of someone.

copleador [co-play-ah-dor'], *m. (Obs.)* Poetaster, rhymer.

coplear [co-play-ar'], *vn.* To versify, to make couplets.

coplero [co-play'-ro], *m.* 1. Poetaster, petty poet. 2. Ballad-seller.

coplica, illa, ita [co-plee'-cah, eel'-lyah, ee'-tah], *f. dim.* A little couplet.

coplista [co-plees'-tah], *m. V.* COPLERO.

coplón [co-plone'], *m. aug.* Low, vile poetry: generally used in the plural number, **coplones**.

copo [co'-po], *m.* 1. A small bundle of cotton, hemp, flax, or silk, put on the distaff to be spun. **Copo de algodón**, cotton ball. **Copos de avena**, oatmeal, rolled oats. 2. Snow flake. 3. Thick part of a fishing-net. 4. *(Prov.)* Odor of the flower of the aromatic myrrh-tree. 5. *(And. Carib.)* Tree-top (de árbol). 6. *(Cono Sur)* Piled-up clouds.

copón [co-pone'], *m.* 1. *(aug.)* A large cup or drinking vessel. 2. Ciborium, a large cup used in Catholic churches. 3. *(Naut.)* A small cable for weighing the anchor. **Y todo el copón**, and all the rest. **Un susto del copón**, a tremendous fright.

coposo, sa [co-po'-so, sah], *a. V.* COPADO.

copra [co'-prah], *f.* Copra, dried coconut meat.

coproducción [co-pro-dooc-the-one'], *f.* Joint production.

copropietario, ia [co-pro-pe-ay-tah'-re-o, ah], *a.* Jointly owning, coproprietor.

cóptico, ca [cop'-te-co, cah], *a.* Coptic, ancient Egyptian, or from that stock.

copto [cop'-to], *m.* Coptic, the language of the Copts.

copucha [co-poo'-chah], *f. (Cono Sur)* lie, fib (mentira); gossip (chismes).

copuchar [co-poo-chahr'], *vn. (Cono Sur)* To lie, to fib; to gossip.

copudo, da [co-poo'-do, dah], *a.* Tufted, bushy, thick-topped.

cópula [co'-poo-lah], *f.* 1. The joining or coupling two things together. 2. Copulation, carnal union. 3. *(Arch.) V.* CÚPULA. 4. *(Log.)* Copula, the word which unites the predicate with the subject.

copular [co-poo-lar'], *va.* To connect, to join, or unite. *-vr.* To copulate, to come together.

copulativamente [co-poo-lah-te-vah-men'-tay], *adv.* Jointly.

copulativo, va [co-poo-lah-tee'-vo, vah], *a.* 1. *(Gram.)* Copulative. 2. Joining or uniting together.

coque [co'-kay], *m.* Coke.

coqueluche [co-kay-loo'-chay], *f.* Whooping cough.

coqueta [co-kay'-tah], *f.* 1. *(Prov.)* Feruling or blow with a ferule on the hand by school teachers. 2. *(Prov.)* A small loaf. 3. Coquette, flirt.

coquetear [co-kay-tay-arr'], *vn.* To coquet, to flirt.

coqueteo [co-kay-tay'-o], *m.* 1. Flirtatiousness, flightiness, coquetry; flirtatious disposition; *(fig.)* affection. 2. Flirtation.

coquetería [co-kay-tay-ree'-ah], *f.* Coquetry, flirtation.

coqueto, coquetón [co-key-tone'] [ ], *m.* A male flirt, ladykiller. *-a.* Smart, natty (vestido).

coquilla [co-keel'-lyah], *f. (Cono Sur)* shell.

coquillo [co-keel'-lyo], *m.* 1. Vinefretter, an insect which destroys vines. *V.* CONVÓLVULO. 2. Jean, a twilled fabric.

coquina [co-kee'-nah], *f.* 1. *(Prov.)* Shellfish in general. 2. Cockle.

coquinero [co-ke-nay'-ro], *m. (Prov.)* Fishmonger, one who deals in shellfish.

coquito [co-kee'-to], *m.* 1. *(dim.)* A small coconut. 2. Grimace to amuse children. **Hacer coquitos**, to make faces. 5. A turtle dove of Mexico, having a song like the cuckoo's.

cor [cor], *m..* 1. *V.* CORAZÓN. 2. *V.* CORO. **De cor**, By heart.

coráceo, cea [co-rah'-thay-o, ah], *a. V.* CORIÁCEO.

coracero [co-rah-thay'-ro], *m.* 1. Cuirassier. 2. *(Coll.)* A poor cigar.

coracha [co-rah'-chah], *f.* A leather bag.

corachín [co-rah-cheen'], *m. dim.* A little leather bag.

coracilla [co-rah-theel'-lyah], *f. dim.* A small coat of mail.

coracina [co-rah-thee'-nah], *f.* A small breast-plate, anciently worn by soldiers.

corada, coradela [co-rah'-dah, co-rah-day'-lah], *f. V.* ASADURA.

coraje [co-rah'-hay], *m.* 1. Courage, bravery, fortitude, mettle. 2. Anger, passion. 3. **Eso me da tanto coraje**, *(Met.)* That puts me in such a rage.

corajina [co-rah-he'-nah], *f.* Fit of temper, explosion of rage.

corajudo, da [co-rah-hoo'-do, dah], *a.* 1. Angry, passionate, easily irritated. 2. Spirited; tough; bold; *(Cono Sur)* brave.

coral [co-rahl'], *m.* 1. Coral, a marine calcareous production. **Corales**, strings of corals. 2. The polyp which produces the substance known as coral; these polyps are mostly anthozoan or hydroid. 3. *(Naut.)* A large knee which fastens the sternpost to the keel.

coral [co-rahl'], *a.* Choral, belonging to the choir.

coralero [co-rah-lay'-ro], *m.* A worker or dealer in corals.

coralífero, ra [co-rah-lee'-fay-ro, rah], *a.* Coralbearing.

coralillo [co-rah-leel'-lyo], *m.* The coral-colored snake, extraordinarily venomous.

coralina [co-rah-lee'-nah], *f.* 1. Sea-coralline or white worm-seed. 2. *(Naut.)* coral fishing-boat. 3. Every sea animal resembling coral.

coralino, na [co-rah-lee'-no, nah], *a.* Coralline.

corambre [co-rahm'-bray], *f.* All hides and skins of animals, dressed or undressed; pelts.

corambrero [co-ram-bray'-ro], *m.* Dealer in hides and skins.

coramvobis [co-ram-vo'-bis], *m. (Coll.)* A corpulent person, strutting about with affected gravity.

Corán [co-rahn'], *m.* Koran, the sacred book of the Mohammedans. *V.* ALCORÁN.

corana [co-rah'-nah], *f. (And. Cono Sur) (Hist.)* Sickle.

coránico [co-rah'-ne-có], *a.* Koranic.

corascora [co-ras-co'-rah], *f. (Naut.)* Corascora, a coasting vessel in India.

coraza [co-rah'-thah], *f.* 1. Cuirass, an ancient breast-plate. 2. **Coraza** or **caballo coraza**, cuirassier. 3. A plate of armor, iron or steel, for men-of-war. 4. Shell or carapace of a turtle, or other defensive armor of some reptiles.

coraznada [co-rath-nah'-dah], *f.* 1. Pith of a pine-tree. 2. Fricassee of the hearts of animals.

corazón [co-rah-thone'], *m.* 1. Heart, core. 2. Heart, benevolence, affection. 3. Heart, spirit, courage. 4. Will, mind. 5. Heart, the middle or center of anything. 6. In a loom, cam. 7. Pith of a tree. 8. **Corazón de un cabo,** *(Naut.)* Heartstrand. **Llevar** or **tener el corazón en las manos,** to be sincere and candid; to wear one's heart on one's sleeve. **De corazón,** *adv.* 1. Heartily, sincerely. 2. From memory. **Clavarle (a uno) en el corazón,** to cause or to suffer great affliction. **Estar enfermo del corazón,** to have heart trouble. **Revista del corazón,** magazine of love stories. **Encoger a uno el corazón,** to fill somebody with fear. **No tener corazón,** to have no heart.

corazonada [co-rah-tho-nah'-dah], *f.* 1. Courage, an impulse of the heart to encounter dangers. 2. Presentiment, foreboding. 3. Entrails.

corazonazo [co-rah-tho-nah'-tho], *m. aug.* A great heart.

corazoncico, illo, ito [co-rah-thon-thee'-co], *m. dim.* A little heart, a pitiful or faint-hearted person.

corazoncillo [co-rah-thon-theel'-lyo], *m. (Bot.)* Perforated St. John's wort.

corbachada [cor-bah-chah'-dah], *f.* A stroke or lash given with a *corbacho.*

corbacho [cor-bah'-cho], *m.* The tendon or aponeurosis of an ox or a bull, with which the boatswain of a galley punished the convicts.

corbás [cor-bahs'], *f. pl. (Falc.)* The four largest feathers of a hawk.

corbata [cor-bah'-tah], *f.* 1. Tie, cravat, a neckcloth, neck handkerchief. 2. A sash or ribbon ornamented with gold or silver fringe tied to banners. 3. Ribbon, insignias of an order. -*m.* Magistrate not brought up to the law; also a layman who has neither studied the civil nor canon law.

corbatín [cor-bah-teen'], *m.* 1. Cravat. *V.* CORBATA. 2. Stock, a close neckchoth.

corbato [cor-bah'-to], *m.* Cooler, a vat filled with water in which the worm of a still is placed to cool.

corbatón [cor-bah-tone'], *m. (Naut.)* A small knee used in different parts of a ship.

corbe [cor'-bay], *m.* An ancient measure for baskets.

corbeta [cor-bay'-tah], *f.* 1. Corvette, a light vessel with three masts and squaresails. 2. **Corbeta de guerra,** a sloop of war.

corca [cor'-cah], *f.* Woodworm.

Córcega [cor'-the-gah], *f.* Corsica.

corcel [cor-thel'], *m.* A steady horse, a charger.

corcesca [cor-thes'-cah], *f.* Ancient pike or spear.

corcha [cor'-chah], *f. V.* CORCHO and CORCHERA.

corche [cor'-chay], *m.* A sort of sandal or shoe, open at the top, and tied with latchets.

corchea [cor-chay'-ah], *f. (Mus.)* Crochet, half a minim.

corchear [cor-chay-ar'], *va.* Among curriers, to grain leather with a cork.

corchera [cor-chay'-rah], *f.* Vessel of pitched cork or staves, in which a bottle or flask is put with ice or snow, to cool liquor.

corchero [cor-chay'-ro], *a.* Cork. **Industria corchera,** cork industry.

corcheta [cor-chay'-tah], *f.* Eye of a hook or clasp.

corchete [cor-chay'-tay], *m.* 1. Clasp, a hook and eye: commonly used in the plural. **Corchetes,** hooks and eyes. 2. Locket, a small lock; crotch. 3. *(Coll.)* An arresting officer. 4. An iron instrument for flattening tin plates. 5. Brace used to connect lines in writing or printing. 6. Benchhook of a carpenter's bench.

corchetear [cor-chay-ar'], *va. (Cono Sur)* to staple.

corchetera [cor-chay-tay'-rah], *f. (Cono Sur)* stapler.

corcho [cor'-cho], *m.* 1. Cork, the bark of the corktree. 2. Icevessel. *V.* CORCHERA. 3. Beehive. *V.* COLMENA. 4. Cork, the stopple of a bottle, flask, or jar. 5. Box made of cork, for carrying estables. 6. Corkboard, put before beds and tables to serve as a shelter. **Sacar el corcho,** to draw the cork. **Cor-cho virgen,** virgin cork. -*pl.* 1. Clogs, a sort of pattens used by women to keep their shoes clean and dry. 2. *(Mil.)* Tampion or tompion, a plug placed in a gun's muzzle when the gun is not in use.

córcholis [cor'-cho-les], *excl.* Good lord!, dear me!

corchoro [cor-cho'-ro], *m. (Bot.)* Corohorus, a genus of plants.

corchoso, sa [Cor-cho'-so, sah], *a.* Like cork in appearance or condition.

corcillo, illa [cor-theel'-lyo, lyah], *m. & f. dim.* A small deer or little fawn.

corcino [cor-thee'-no], *m.* A small deer.

corcor [cor-cor'], *m. (CAm. Carib.)* Gurgle. **Beber corcor,** to swig, to knock it back.

corcova [cor-co'-vah], *f.* 1. Hump, a crooked back, hunch. 2. Convexity, protuberance, curvature, gibbosity. 3. *(And. Cono Sur)* all night party (fiesta).

corcovado, da [cor-co-vah'-do, dah], *a.* Hump-backed, gibbous, crooked. -*pp.* of CORCOVAR.

corcovar [cor-co-var'], *va. (Obs.)* To crook.

corcovear [cor-co-vay-ar'], *vn.* 1. To curvet, to cut capers. 2. *(And. Carib, Cono Sur)* to grumble, to grouse. 3. *(Mex.)* to be frightened.

corcoveta [cor-co-vay'-tah], *com.* A crookbacked person.

corcovilla, ita [cor-co-veel'-lyah], *f. dim.* Little hump or crooked back.

corcovo [cor-co'-vo], *m.* 1. Spring, or curvest, made by a horse on the point of leaping. 2. A wrong step, unfair proceeding.

córculo [cor'-coo-lo], *m.* Heartshell, an aquatic insect.

corcusido, da [cor-coo-see'-do, dah], *a.* Clumsily mended or sewed on. -*pp.* of CORCUSIR.

corcusir [cor-coo-seer'], *va. (Coll.)* To darn holes in cloth or stuff, to patch.

corda [cor'-dah], *f.* **Estar el navío a la corda,** *(Naut.)* To be closehauled, or lying to (barco).

cordada [cor-dah'-dah], *f.* Team, roped team (alpinismo).

cordaje [cor-dah'-hay], *m. (Naut.)* Cordage, all sorts of rope used in the rigging of ships; strings (raqueta).

cordal [cor-dahl'], *m.* Double tooth. **Cordales,** grinders.

cordato, ta [cor-dah'-to, tah], *a.* Wise, prudent, discreet, judicious, considerate.

cordel [cor-del'], *m.* 1. Cord, a rope of several strands. 2. *(Naut.)* A thin rope or line used on board a ship; a line. **Cordel alquitranado,** a tarred line. **Cordel blanco,** an untarred line. **Cordel de corredera,** logline. **Mozo de cordel,** porter, one who carries burdens for hire. **Apretar los cordeles,** to oblige one to say or do a thing by violence. **Echar el cordel,** 1. To mark with a line or cord. 2. *(Met.)* To administer justice impartially. 3. *(Met.)* To draw lines in order to consider the manner of executing a thing. **Estar a cordel,** to be in a right line.

cordelado, da [cor-day-lah'-do, dah], *a.* Twisted for ribbons or garters: applied to silk.

cordelazo [cor-day-lah'-tho], *m.* Stroke or lash with a rope.

cordelejo [cor-day-lay'-ho], *m.* 1. *(dim.)* A small rope. 2. Fun, jest joke. 3. **Dar cordelejo,** *(Met.)* To pump out a secret artfully.

cordelería [cor-day-lay-ree'-ah], *f.* 1. Cordage, all sorts of ropes. 2. Ropewalk. 3. *(Naut.)* Rigging.

cordelero [cor-day-lay'-ro], *m.* Rope-maker, cordmaker.

cordelito [cor-day-lee'-to], *m. dim.* A small rope, cord, or line.

cordellate [cor-del-lyah'-tay], *m.* Grogram, a sort of stuff.

cordera [cor-day'-rah], *f.* 1. Ewe lamb. 2. Meek, gentle, or mild woman.

cordería [cor-day-ree'-ah], *f.* 1. Cordage, cords, ropes. 2. Place where cordage is kept.

corderica, illo, ito [cor-day-ree'-cah], *f. dim.* Little lamb.

corderico, illo, ito [cor-day-ree'-co], *m. dim.* A young or little lamb.

corderillo [cor-day-reel'-lyo], *m.* Lambskin dressed with the fleece.

corderina [cor-day-ree'-nah], *f.* Lambskin.

corderino, na [cor-day-ree'-no, nah], *a.* Of the lamb kind, belonging to lambs.

cordero [cor-day'-ro], *m.* 1. Lamb. 2. A dressed lambskin. 3. Meek, gentle, or mild man. **Cordero lechal**, houselamb. **Cordero asado**, roast lamb. **Cordero de Dios**, Lamb of God.

corderuna [cor-day-roo'-nah], *f.* Lambskin.

cordeta [cor-day'-tah], *f. (Prov.)* A small rope made of the platted strands of bassweed.

cordezuela [cor-day-thoo-ay'-lah], *f. dim.* A small rope.

cordíaco, ca [cor-dee'-ah-co, cah], *a. V.* CARDÍACO.

cordial [cor-de-ahl'] *a.* 1. Cordial, affectionate, sincere. 2. Cordial, invigorating reviving.

cordial [cor-de-ahl'], *m.* Cordial, a strengthening medicine.

cordialidad [cor-de-ah-le-dahd'], *f.* Cordiality, intimacy.

cordialmente [cor-de-ahl-men'-tay], *adv.* Cordially, sincerely, affectionately, heartily.

cordila [cor-dee'-lah], *f.* Spawn of a tunnyfish

cordilo [cor-dee'-lo], *m.* An amphibious animal resembling a crocodile.

cordilla [cor-deel'-lyah], *f.* Guts of sheep, given to cats to eat.

cordillera [cor-deel-lyay'-rah], *f.* Chain or ridge of mountains. In particular, the Andes.

cordillerano [cor-del-lay-rah'-no], *a. (Cono Sur)* Andean.

cordita [cor-dee'-tah], *f.* Cordite.

Córdoba [cor'-do-bah], *f.* 1. Standard monetary unit of Nicaragua. 2. Cordova (city).

cordobán [cor-do-bahn'], *m.* Cordovan, cordwain, morocco or Spanish leather, tanned goatskin.

cordobana [cor-do-bah'-nah], *f.* Nakedness, nudity. **Andar a la cordobana**, to go stark naked.

cordobés, sa [cor-do-bess', bay'-sah], *f.* Native of or belonging to Cordova.

cordojo [cor-do'-ho], *m. (Obs.)* Anguish, anxiety, affliction.

cordón [cor-done'], *m.* 1. Cord or string made of silk, Wool, hemp, etc. 2. Twisted or platted lace. 3. Cord or girdle with which monks tie up their habits. 4. A military cordon, formed by line of troops to prevent any communication. **Cordón sanitario**, sanitary cordon. 5. *(Naut.)* Strand of a cable or rope. **Cabo de tres o cuatro cordones**, a three or four stranded rope or cable. 6. *(Mil.)* Cordon, a row of stones jutting out between the rampart and the basis of the parapet, where the wall begins to be perpendicular. 7. *(Arch.) V.* BOCEL. 8. The milled edge of coined metal. 9. *(Anat.)* Cord. **Cordón umbilical**, umbilical cord. 10. *(Cono Sur)* kerb. 11. *(And. Carib, Cono Sur)* **Cordón de cerros**, chain of hills. 12. *(And. Carib.)* Liquor, brandy. 13. *(Cono Sur)* **Cordón detonante**, fuse. *-pl.* 1. Silver or gold cords from the right shoulder to the breast, worn by the cadets and other military men. 2. Harness cords of a velvetloom.

cordonazo [cor-do-nah'-tho], *m.* 1. Stroke with a cord or rope. 2. *(aug.)* Large cord.

cordoncico, illo, ito [cor-don-thee'-co], *m. dim.* A small cord or line.

cordoncillo [cor-don-theel'-lyo], *m.* 1. A twisted cord, round lace, lacing, braid. 2. Milling round the edge of coin.

cordonería [cor-do-nay-ree'-ah], *f.* 1. All the work of twisters or lacemakers in general. 2. A lacemaker's shop.

cordonero, ra [cor-do-nay'-ro, rah], *m. & f.* 1. Lacemaker, lace-man, or woman. 2. Ropemaker.

cordura [cor-doo'-rah], *f.* Prudence, practical wisdom; judgment. **Hacer cordura**, To act in a prudent manner.

Corea [Co-ray'-ah], *f.* Korea; **Corea del Norte**, North Korea; **Corea del Sur**; South Korea.

corea [co-ray'-ah], *f.* 1. Dance, accompanied with a chorus. 2. Chorea, St. Vitus's dance. 3. Corea *(Geog.)*.

coreano, na, [co-ray-ah'-no], *m. & f.* Korean.

corear [co-ray-ar'], *va.* To sing or play in a chorus. **Música coreada**, chorus music.-*vn.* To speak all together; *(Mus.)* To sing all together, to join in.

corecico [co-ray-thee'-co], *m. dim.* of CUERO, Small hide or skin.

corecillo [co-ray-theel'-lyo], *m.* A roasted sucking pig.

coreo [co-ray'-o], *m.* 1. A foot in Latin verse. 2. Connected harmony of a chorus.

coreografía [co-ray-o-gra-fee'-ah], *f.* 1. The part of dancing. 2. Choreography, the art of arranging dances and ballets.

Coreográfico [co-ray-o-gra'-fe-co], *a.* Choreographic.

coreógrafo, fa [co-ray-o'-gra-fo], *m. & f.* Choreographer.

corezuelo [co-ray-thoo-ay'-lo], *m.* 1. *(Prov.)*

corisáceo, cea [co-re-ah'-thay-o, ah], *a.* Coriaceous, leathery.

coriambico, ca [co-re-ahm'-be-co, cah], *a.* Applied to Latin verses written with coriambics.

coriambo [co-re-ahm'-bo], *m.* Coriambic, a foot of prosody; a troche and an iambus combined.

coriana [co-re-ah'-nah], *f. (And.)* Blanket.

coriandro [co-re-ahn'-dro], *m.(Bot)* Coriander, or common coriander.

coribante [co-re-bahn'-tay], *m.* Corybantes, priests of Cybele.

coribantismo [co-re-ban-tees'-mo], *m.* A kind of frenzy accompanied by many contorsions.

coríceo [co-ree'-thay-o], *m.* A hall for playing ball in ancient gymnasiums.

córida [co'-re-dah], *f.* 1. A substance which the Arabs use against small pox. 2. Cowry, a kind of shell used for money by some African tribes.3.*(Bot.)* A perennial plant of the cowslip family.

corifeo [co-re-fay'-oh], *m.* 1. Coryphaeus, the leader of the ancient dramatic chorus. 2. Coryphaeus, leader of a sect or party.

corillo [co-reel'-lyo], *m. dim.* A small choir, an organ loft.

corimbífero [co-rim-bee'-fay-ro], *a.(Bot.)* Corymbiferous, bearing fruit or berries in clusters.

corimbo [co-reem'-bo], *m. (Bot.)* Corymb, a flower cluster of indeterminate florescence.

corindón [co-rin-done'], *m.* Corundum, the hardest known substance, next to the diamond.

corintio, tia [co-reen'-te-o, ah], *a.* 1. Native of or belonging to Corinth. 2. Corinthian (arquitectura).

corinto [co-ren'-to], *a. m.* Maroon, purplish.

corion [co'-re-on], *m. (Anat.)* Chorion, the exterior membrane that envelopes the foetus.

corisanto [co-re-sahn'-to], *m. (Bot.)* Perennial orchidaceous plant cultivated in European botanical gardens, native of Chili and California.

corista [co-rees'-tah], *com.* Chorist or chorister; *(Mus.)* Member of the chorus.

coristerión [co-ris-tay-re-on'], *m.* An organ secreting the glutinous material with which insects fasten their eggs to one another.

corito [co-ree'-to-], *a.* 1. Timid, pusillanimous. 2. Naked. -*m.* A workman who treads grapes in the winepress.

coriza [co-ree'-thah], *f.* 1. A kind of shoe of undressed leather, laced from the toe to the instep, worn by common people in some parts of Spain. 2. Coryza, a copious running from the nose. *V.* ROMADIZO.

corladura [cor-lah-doo'-rah], *f.* Goldvarnish.

corlar, corlear [cor-lar'-cor-lay-ar'], *va.* To put on goldvarnish.

corma [cor'-mah], *f.* 1. The stocks. 2. *(Met.)* Trouble, uneasiness.

cormorán [cor-mo-rán'], *m.* Cormorant, a waterfowl.

cornac, or **cornaca** [cor-nah'-cah], *m.* A keeper of domesticated elephants: native name.

cornada [cor-nah'-dah], *f.* 1. Thrust with a bull's or cow's horn. 2. Thrust with a foil in a cunning manner, with the vulgar.

cornadillo [cor-nah-deel'-lyo], *m.* A small piece of money of little value. **Emplear su cornadillo,** to attain one's end by low means.

cornadura [cor-nah-doo'-rah], *f.* Horns; antlers (de ciervo).

cornal [cor-nahl'], *m.* A strap or thong with which oxen are tied to the yoke by the horns.

cornalina [cor-nah-lee'-nah], *f.* Cornelian, a red variety of chalcedony.

cornamenta [cor-nah-men'-tah], *f.* Horns of any animal; antlers (de ciervo); cuckold's horns (de marido). **Poner la cornamenta a uno,** to cuckold somebody.

cornamusa [cor-nah-moo'-sah], *f.* 1. Cornemuse, a wind instrument; a sort of long trumpet (metal). 2. *(Naut.)* A belaying cleat. **Cornamusas de los palos,**

cornas [cor'-nas], *f. pl. (Naut.)* Backstays. V. BRANDALES.

cornatillo [cor-nah-teel'-lyo], *m.* A kind of olive.

córnea [cor'-nay-ah], *f.* 1. Cornea, the transparent part of the eye: applied also, in Spanish, to the sclerotic or white of the eye. 2. A stone like jasper.

corneador, ra [cor-nay-ah-dor', rah], *m. & f.* A horned animal, which butts or plays with the horns.

corneal [cor-nay-ahl'], *a.* Corneal.

conear [cor-nay-ar'], *va.* To butt or play with the horns. V. ACORNEAR.

cornecico, illo, ito [cor-nay-thee'-co], *m. dim.* Cornicle, a small horn.

corneja [cor-nay'-hah], *f. (Orn.)* Crow, fetlock, dow.

cornejal [cor-nay-hahl'], *m.* A collection of dogwood-trees.

cornejalejo [cor-nay-hah-lay'-ho], *m.* A kind of pod in which some seed or fruit is contained.

cornejo [cor-nay'-ho], *m. (Bot.)* Hound-tree or cornel-tree, dogwood.

cornelina [cor-nay-lee'-nah], or **cornerina,** *f.* V. CORNALINA.

córneo, ea [cor'-nay-o, ah], *a.* Horny, corny, callous.

córner [cor'-nayr], *m. pl.* **córnes** [cor'-nays], Corner, corner kick.

cornerina [cor-nay-re'-nah], *f.* Cornelian, carnelian.

cornero [cor-nay'-ro], *m.* **Cornero de pan,** *(Prov.)* Crust of bread.

corneta [cor-nay'-tah], *f.* 1. A wind instrument in the shape of a horn; **corneta acústica,** ear trumpet. 2. A French horn. 3. A postillion's horn; hunting-horn. 4. Cornet, an ensign of horse who carries the standard. 5. Troop of horse. 6. *(Naut.)* Broad pennant; a rear admiral's flag. 7. Horn used by swineherds to call their hogs. -*m. & f.* Burgler; cornet player.

cornete [cor-nay'-tay], *m. dim.* A small musical horn, or buglehorn. -*pl.* 1. *(Anat.)* Small bony plates of the nasal fossae. 2. A surgical instrument.

cornetear [cor-nay-tay-ar'], *vn. (Carib.) (Aut.)* To sound the horn.

cornetín [cor-nay-teen'], *m.* 1. *dim.* of CORNETA. 2. Cornet, a brass instrument of the trumpet family, now provided with three valves.

corneto [cor-nay'-to], *a. (CAm.)* Bow-legged.

cornezuelo [cor-nay-thoo-ay'-lo], *m.* 1. Ergot of rye. 2. An instrument for bleeding horses. 3. *(Bot.)* V. CORNICABRA.

cornflaques [con'-flayks], *m. pl.* cornflakes.

corniabierto, ta [cor-ne-ah-be-err'-to, tah], *a.* Having widespread horns.

cornial [cor-ne-ahl'], *a.* In the shape of a horn.

corniapretado, da [cor-ne-ah-pray-tah'-do, dah], *a.* Having close set horns.

cornicabra [cor-ne-cah'-brah], *f.* 1. *(Bot.)* Turpentine-tree, pistachia-tree, of which the *Orihuela* snuff-boxes are made in Spain. 2. A sort of olives.

corniculata [cor-ne-coo-lah'-tah], *a.* Horned, as the new moon.

cornículo [cor-nee'-coo-lo], *m.* Old name for the antenna of insects.

corniforme [cor-ne-for'-may], *a.* In the shape of horns.

cornigacho, cha [cor-ne-gah'-cho, chah], *a.* Having the horns turned slightly downward.

cornígero, ra [cor-nee'-hay-ro, rah], *a. (Poet.)* Horned.

cornija [cor-nee'-hah], *f. (Arch.)* Cornice, a horizontal moulding.

cornijal [cor-ne-hahl'], *m.* Angle or corner of a building.

cornijamento, cornijamiento [cor-ne-hah-men'-to], *m.* *(Arch.* V. CORNIJÓN.

cornijÓn [cor-ne-hone'], *m (Arch.).* The third of the three principal pieces on the tops of columns, consisting of the architrave, frieze, and cornice; the entablature.

cornil [cor-neel'], *m.* V. CORNAL.

corniola [cor-ne-o'-lah], *f.* V. CORNALINA.

cornisa [cor-nee'-sah], *f. (Arch.)* Cornice.

cornisamento, cornisamiento [cor-nee-sah-men'-to], *m.* V. CORNIJÓN.

cornisica, illa, ita [cor-ne-see'-cah], *f. dim.* Small cornice.

corniveleto, ta [cor-ne-vay-lay'-to, tah], *a.* Having horns turned strongly upward.

corno [cor'-no], *m.* 1. *(Bot.)* Cornel-tree. V. CORNEJO. 2. Corno, English horn, a reed instrument resembling the oboe, pitched onefifth lower.

cornucopia [cor-noo-co'-pe-ah], *f.* 1. Cornucopia, the horn of plenty. 2. Sconce, a branched candlestick. 3. A pierglass.

cornudico, illo, ito [cor-noo-dee'-coh], *m. dim.* A little cuckold.

cornudo, da [cor-noo'-do, dah], *a.* Horned.-*m.* Cuckold.

cornúpeta [cor-noo'-pay-tah], *a.* Attacking with the horns. *(Acad.)*

coro [co'-ro], *m.* 1. Choir, a part of a church where the service is sung. 2. Choir, chorus, an assembly or band of singers; also a quartette of voices, or even a trío. **La chica del coro,** a girl from the chorus. 3. Choir, the singers in divine worship. 4. Chorus of a song. **Cantar a coros,** to sing alternately. 5. Memory. **Decir** or **tomar de coro,** to say or get by heart. 6. Chorus of a Greek tragedy. 7. Dance. 8. *(Poet.)* Summer solstitial wind. 9. Choir of angels. **Hablar a coros,** to speak alternately. 10. A dry measure of the Hebrews, about six bushels.

corocha [co-ro'-chah], *f.* 1. *(Prov.)* Vinefretter or vinegrub, an insect destructive to vines. 2. Coat.

corografía [co-ro-grah-fee'-ah], *f.* Chorography, the art of describing particular regions.

corográcamente, *adv.* Chorographically.

corográfico, ca [co-ro-grah'-fe-co, cah], *a.* Chorographical.

Corógrafo [co-ro'-grah-fo], *m.* Chorographer.

coroidea [co-ro-e-day'-ah], *f.* The choroid coat of the eye.

corola [co-ro'-lah], *f. (Bot.)* Corolla, the envelope of a flower next to the stamens and pistils; usually colored.

corolario [co-ro-lah'-re-o], *m.* Corollary, inference, deduction.

corona [co-ro'-nah], *f.* 1. Crown, the emblem of royalty. **Ceñirse la corona,** to take the crown. 2. Coronet, an inferior crown worn by the nobility. 3. Crown, the top of the head. 4. A clerical tonsure. 5. An old Spanish gold and silver coin. 6. Crown, an English silver coin. 7. Crown, regal power, royalty. 8. Kingdom, monarchy. 9. Crown, reward, distinction. 10. Crown, honor, splendor, ornament, decoration. 11. Aureola with which saints are crowned. 12. Rosary of seven decades offered to the Holy Virgin. 13. End of a work. 14. Corona, a luminous halo about the sun, seen in total eclipses. **Corona de espinas,** crown of thorns. 15. Crown, completion, reward. 16. *(Naut.)* Pendant; a rope used for various purposes. **Coronas de palos,** maintackle pendants. 17. *(Bot.)* Appendices of a corolla, resembling a crown; the persistent, dry limb of the calyx of a flower. 18. Glory, triumph. **Corona de rosas,** chaplet of roses. 19 *(Mil.)* Crownwork. 20. *(Arch.)* Corona, a large flat member of the cornice, which crowns the entablature. 21. *(Her.)* The ornament painted in the upper part of a coat of arms, and which denotes the rank of nobility or distinction of the family to which it belongs. **Corona de fraile,** *(Bot.)* Three-toothed globularia. V. CABOLLANA. **Corona de rey,** *(Bot.)* Common melilot trefoil.

coronación [co-ro-nah-the-on'], *f.* 1. Coronation. 2. The end of any work. 3. *(Arch.) V.* CORONAMIENTO. 4. Queening (ajedrez).

coronado [co-ro-nah'-do], *m.* A Roman Catholic clergyman who received the tonsure. **-Coronado, da,** *pp.* of CORONAR.

coronador, ra [co-ro-nah-dor', rah], *m. & f.* 1. Crowner. 2. Finisher.

coronal [co-ro-nahl'], *m. & f. & a. (Anat.)* 1. Frontal bone. 2. Belonging to the frontal bone.

coronamiento [co-ro-nah-me-en'-to], *m.* 1. Ornament placed on the top of a building. 2. *(Obs.)* Coronation. 3. *(Naut.)* Taffrail.

coronar [co-ro-nar'], *va.* 1. To crown, to invest with the crown. **Coronar a uno rey,** to crown somebody king. 2. *(Met.)* To crown, to complete, to perfect, to finish. **Coronar algo con éxito,** to crown something with success. 3. *(Met.)* To decorate the top of a building. 4. To fill a glass up to the brim. 5. To queen (ajedrez). 6. *(And. Carib, Cono Sur)* to cuckold, to make a cuckold of.

coronaria [co-ro-nah'-re-ah], *a.* 1 *(Anat.)* Coronary. 2. Applied to the crownwheel of a watch.

coronario, ria [co-ro-nah'-re-o, ah], *a.* 1. Coronary, relating to a crown. 2. *(Bot.)* Coronary. 3. Extremely refined (oro).

corondel [co-ron-del], *m.* (Printing) Column-rule; reglet.

coronel [co-ro-nel'], *m.* 1. Colonel. **Coronel de aviación,** group captain, colonel. 2. *(Her.)* Crown.-*pl.* In paper-mills, the worked little sticks which there are to sustain the mould.

coronela [co-ro-nay'-lah], *f.* Colonel's wife; colonel.

coronela [co-ro-nay'-lah], *a.* Applied to the company, flag, etc., supposed to belong to the colonel of a regiment.

coronelía [co-ro-nay-lee'-ah], *f.* Colonelship. *V.* REGIMIENTO.

coronilla [co-ro-neel'-lyah], *f.* 1. Crown, top of the head, coxcomb. 2. Among bellfounders, the car by which a bell is suspended. 3. A genus of plants. **Coronilla** or **coronilla de rey**, *(Bot.)* nine-leaved coronilla. **Coronilla de fraile**, *(Bot.)* the French daisy. 4. In Castile, the kingdoms of Aragon, Valentia, Catalonia, and Majorca, which composed the ancient kingdom of Aragon. **Andar de coronilla,** to slog away. **Dar de coronilla,** to bump one's head. **Estar hasta la coronilla,** to be utterly fed up.

coroto [co-ro'-to], *m. (And. CAm. Carib.)* Gourd, vessel (vasija).

corotos [co-ro'-tos], *m. pl. (Sp. Amer. Coll.)* Belongings, things.

corozo [co-ro'-tho], *m. (Bot.)* A species of high palm-tree in Africa and America.

corpacho, corpanchón, corpazo [cor-pan-chone', cor-pah'-tho], *m. aug.* A very big body or carcass. **Corpanchón de ave,** carcass of a fowl.

corpecico, illo, ito, corpezuelo [cor-pay-thee'-co], *m. dim.* A little or small body, or carcass.

corpezuelo [cor-pay-thoo-ay'-lo], *m.* An under waiscoat without sleeves or skirts.

corpiño [cor-pee'-nyo], *m.* Waist, bodice. *V* JUSTILLO.

corporación [cor-po-rah-the-on'], *f.* Corporation, guild; community.

corporal [cor-po-rahl'], *a.* Corporal, belonging to the body. **Castigo corporal,** corporal punishment.

corporal [cor-po-rahl'], *m.* Corporal, altar linen on which the communion bread and wine are put to be consecrated.

corporalidad [cor-po-rah-le-dahd'], *f.* 1. Corporality, the quality of being embodied. 2. Any corporeal substance.

corporalmente [cor-po-rahl-men'-tay], *adv.* Corporally, bodily.

corporativismo [cor-po-rah-te-ves'-mo], *m.* Corporate nature; corporate spirit.

corporativo [cor-po-rah-te'-vo], *a.* Corporate.

corporeidad [cor-po-ray-e-dahd'], *f.* Corporeal nature.

corpóreo, rea [cor-por'-ray-o, ah], *a.* Corporeal, corporeous.

corps [corps], *m.* Corps, a French term, implying body. **Los guardias de corps,** the lifeguards.

corpudo da [cor-poo'-do, dah], *a.* Corpulent, bulky.

corpulencia [cor-poo-len'-the-ah], *f.* Corpulence, corpulency. **Cayó con toda su corpulencia,** he fell with his full weight.

corpulento, ta [cor-poo-len'-to, tah], *a.* Corpulent, fleshy, fat.

corpus [cor'-poos], *m.* Corpus Christi day, or the procession held on that day in Roman Catholic countries.

corpuscular [car-poos-coo-lar], *a.* Corpuscular.

corpusculista [cor-poos-coo-lees'-tah], *m.* Atomist.

corpúsculo [cor-poos'-coo-lo], *m.* Corpuscle, atom, molecule.

corral [cor-rahl'], *m.* 1. Yard, inclosure; a poultry-yard (aves). 2. Court, open space before a house. 3. Fishpond. 4. Playhouse. 5. Blank left by students in writing lectures. **Aves de corral,** poultry. 6. Square formed by a body of foot. **Corral de madera,** timber yard. **Corral de ganado, corral del concejo,** pound. *(Naut.)* Place where cattle are kept on board a ship. **Hacer corrales,** *(Met.)* to loiter about in school or business hours. **Corral de vecindad,** tenement.

corralera [cor-rah-lay'-rah], *f.* 1. A brazenfaced impudent woman.

corralero [cor-rah-lay'-ro], *m.* Keeper of a dungyard.

corralillo, ito [cor-rah-leel'-lyo], *m. dim.* A small yard.

corraliza [cor-rah-lee'-thah], *f.* Yard, court.

corralón [cor-rah-lone'], *m. aug.* A large yard.

correa [cor-ray'-ah], *f.* 1. Leather strap or thong. 2. Leash. 3. Among saddlers, strap which fastens the holsters to the saddle. 4. Flexibility or extension of anything. 5. Leather belting, belt (cinturón), for machinery. **Besar la correa,** *(Met.)* to be obliged to humble oneself to another. **Tener correa,** to bear wit or raillery without irritation. **Correa de seguridad,** safety belt. **correaje** [cor-ray-ah'-hay], *m.* Heap of leather straps or thongs.

correal [cor-ray-al'], *m.* Dressed deerskin. **Coser correal,** or **labrar de correal,** to sew with small leather thongs instead of thread.

correar [cor-ray-ar'], *va.* To draw out wool and prepare it for use.

correazo [cor-ray-ah'-tho], *m.* Blow with a leather strap or thong.

correcalles [cor-ray-cahl'-lyes], *m.* Idler, lounger.

corrección [cor-rec-the-on'], *f.* 1. Correction, reprehension, lecture. 2. Correction, amendment, alteration to a better state. 3. Correction, that which is substituted in the place of anything wrong, emendation; **corrección de pruebas,** *(Typ.)* Proofreading, proof-correction.

correccional [cor-rec-the-o-nahl'], *a.* Correctional, corrective, reformatory.

correcorre [cor-re-cor-re], *m. (Carib.)* Headlong rush, stampede.

correctamente [cor-rec'-tah-men-tay], *adv.* 1. Correctly; accurately. 2. Regularly. 3. Politely; properly, fittingly.

correctivo, va [cor-rec-tee'-vo, vah], *a.* Corrective.

correctivo [cor-rec-te'-vo], *m.* 1. Corrective, that which has the power of altering or correcting. 2. *(Med.)* Corrective, a medicine which abates the force of another.

correcto, ta [cor-rec'-to, tah], *a.* 1. Exact, correct, conformable to the rules. 2. Regular, well-formed (rasgos). 3. Correct; courteous, polite, well-mannered (persona). -*pp. irr.* of CORREGIR.

corrector, ra [cor-rec-tor'], *m. & f.* 1. Corrector, amender. 2. Corrector of the press, proofreader. 3. *m.* Superior, or abbot, in the convent of St. Francis de Paula. 4. *(Inform.)* **Corrector gramatical,** grammar checker. **Corrector ortográfico,** spell checker.

corredentor, ra [cor-ray-den-tor', rah], *m. & f.* One who redeems from captivity, jointly with another.

corredera [cor-ray-day'-rah], *f.* 1. Race-ground. 2. A small wicket or backdoor. 3. Runner or upper grinding stone in a cornmill. 4. Street. 5. *(Coll.)* Pimp, procuress.

6. *(Naut.)* Log or logline. 7. In glasshouses, roller, a metal cylinder for rolling plate grass. 8. Cockroach. *V.* CUCARACHA. 9. A slide-valve. 10. *(Typ.)* Track, slide, rail. **Puerta corredera**, sliding door. 11. *(Mech.)* Tongue, rail, guide, runner. 12. *(Mint.)* A milling-machine. 13. *(Astr.)* A thread which crosses the field of a lens and serves to measure the apparent diameter of a star.

corredizo, za [cor-ray-dee'-tho, thah], *a.* Easy to be untied, like a running knot.

corredor, ra [cor-ray-dor', rah], *m. & f.* 1. Runner. **Corredor automovilista**, racing driver. **Corredor de fondo**, long-distance runner. 2. Racehorse. 3. Corridor, a gallery. 4. *(Mil.)* Corridor, covertway, lying round a fortress. 5. *(Mil.)* Scout. 6. Forerunner. 7. Broker, one who does business for another. 8. A certain net, upon some coasts, which drags at the surface of the water, and is drawn into an oared boat. 9. *-f.* A name given to certain wandering, non-web-weaving spiders. **Corredor de popa**, *(Naut.)* balcony, or stern gallery of a ship. **Corredor de Bolsa**, stockbroker.

corredorcillo [co-ray-dor-theel'-lyo], *m. dim.* A small corridor.

corredura [cor-ray-doo'-rah], *f.* 1. Liquor which flows over the brim of a vessel with which liquids are measured. 2. Incursions into enemy's country.

correduría [cor-ray-doo-ree'-ah], *f.* 1. Brokerage. 2. *(Coll.)* Fine, penalty.

correería [cor-ray-ay-ree'-ah], *f.* Trade of a strapmaker.

correero [cor-ray-ay'-ro], *m.* Strap-maker.

corregencia [cor-ray-hen'-the-ah], *f.* Co-regency.

corregente [cor-ray-hen'-tay], *m.* Co-regent.

corregibilidad [cor-ray-he-be-le-dahd'], *f.* Correctibleness, susceptibility to being corrected.

corregible [cor-ray-hee'-blay], *a.* Corrigible, docile.

corregidor [cor-ray-he-dor'], *m.* 1. Corrector, one who punishes and corrects. 2. Corregidor, a Spanish magistrate in old days; a mayor of a town.

corregidora [cor-ray-he-do'-rah], *f.* Chief magistrate.

corregimiento [cor-ray-he-me-en'-to], *m.* The place, office, and district of a *corregidor*.

corregir [cor-ray-heer'], *va.* 1. To correct, to amend, to mend, to take away faults. 2. To correct, to remark faults, to reprehend, to admonish. 3. To correct, to temper, to mitigate, to make less active. 4. To adorn, to embellish. *-vr.* To mend; to mend one's way. **Corregirse su terquedad**, to stop being obstinate.

corregnate [cor-reg-nahn'-tay], *a.* Reigning with another.

corregüela, or **correhüela** [cor-ray-goo-ay'-lah], *f.* 1. *(dim.)* A small strap or thong. 2. Game among boys with a stick and small strap. 3. *(Bot.)* Bindweed.

correinante [cor-ray-e-nahn'-tay], *a.* *(Acad.)* *V.* CORREGNANTE.

correlación [cor-ray-lah-the-on'], *f.* Correlations analogy.

correlacionar [cor-ray-lah-the-o-nar'], *va.* To corretale.

correlativamente [cor-re-lah-te-vah-men'-tay], *adv.* Correlatively.

correlativo, va [cor-ray-lah-tee'-vo, vah], *a.* Correlative.

correligionario, ia [cor-ray-le-he-o-nah'-re-o, ah], *a.* 1. Of the same religion with another, fellow-believer. 2. Of the same politics.

correlón [cor-ray-lone'], *a.* 1. *(LAm.)* Fast, good at running. 2. *(CAm. Mex.)* Cowardly.

correncia [cor-ren-the-ah], *f.* *(Coll.)* Looseness, diarrhoea.

correndilla [cor-ren-deel'-lyah], *f.* *(Coll.)* Incursion. *V.* CORRERÍA.

correntada [cor-ren-tah'-dah], *f.* *(Cono Sur)* Rapids, strong current.

correntía [cor-ren-tee'-ah], *f.* 1. *(Prov.)* An artificial irrigation of stubble ground, to make the stalks rot, and convert them into manure. 2. *V.* CORRENCIA.

correntiar [cor-ren-te-ar'], *va.* *(Prov.)* To irrigate stubble ground.

correntío, tía [cor-ren-teo'-o, ah], *a.* 1. Current, running. 2. Light, free, unembarrassed.

correntón, na [cor-ren-tone', nah], *a.* 1. Gay, fond of company, pleasant; cheerful. 2. Taking a great deal of snuff. 3. A clever fellow. 4. Busy, active (activo). *-m.* *(And. Carib.)* Strong current.

correntoso [cor-ren-to'-so], *a.* *(LAm.)* Fast-flowing, rapid (río); in flood, in spate; torrential (agua).

correo [cor-ray'-o], *m.* 1. Post, mail. 2. Post office. **Correo aéreo**, air mail. **Correo marítime**, mail via steamer. **Correo ordinario**, regular mail. **Casilla** or **apartado de correos**, post office box. **Correo de primera clase**, first-class mail. **Echar al correo**, to post. **Por correo**, by post. **Correo electrónico**, *(Inform.)* electronic mailbox. **Correo**, mailing.

correón [cor-ray-on'], *m. aug.* A large leather strap for holding up the body of ancient coaches.

correosidad [cor-ray-o-se-dahd'], *f.* Toughness, leatheriness; flexibility.

correoso, sa [cor-ray-o'-so, sah], *a.* Ductile, flexible, easily bent.

correr [cor-rerr'], *va. & vn.* 1. To run, to move at a quick pace. 2. To run, to flow, or to stream (líquidos). 3. To blow (viento). 4. To run, to pass away: as time and life. 5. To hasten to put anything in execution. 6. To solicit one's protection. 7. *(Met.)* To take the proper course, to pass through the proper channel (negocios). 8. To snatch away. 9. *(Coll.)* To persecute. 10. To extend, to expand. 11. To put one to the blush. 12. To arrive: said of the time fixed for payments. 13. To receive or admit a thing. 14. To flourish, to prevail for the time. 15. To tend, to guard, to take care of anything. 16. To be said, to be related. 17. Preceded by *con*, to charge oneself with a matter. 18. To travel. 19. To pursue a course. 20. To file right or left. 21. To have relations with, acquaintance with someone: used with *bueno* or *malo*. 22. To be smooth, fluent in style. **Correr los mares**, *(Naut.)* to follow the sea, to lead a mariner's life. **Correr en el mismo rumbo**, to stand onward in the same course. **Correr viento en popa**, to sail before the wind. **Correr la cortina**, to draw the curtain; to discover anything; to conceal, to quash. **Correr a rienda suelta**, 1. To ride full speed. 2. *(Met.)* To give a loose rein to one's passions. **Corre la voz**, it is reported, it is said, the story goes. **Correr la voz**, to pass the word, to be divulged. **Correr mal tiempo**, the times are evil. **A más correr, a todo correr**, as swiftly as possible. **Correrse**, to be ashamed or confused; to run away. **A todo correr**, happen what may. **El que no corre, vuela**, he who is observant while pretending indifference. **Quien más corre, menos vuela**, the more haste, the less speed. **Corre la flecha**, the arrow flies (said when Indian tribes agree to make war upon a common enemy). **Correr el velo**, to discover a secret; to take off the mask. **Correr la palabra**, *(Mil.)* to give the word. **Ha corrido medio mundo**, he has been round half the world. **Correr a uno**, *(CAm. Carib. Mex.)* To throw somebody out. **Echar a correr**, to start to run. **Dejar correr las cosas**, to let things run on. **Dejar correr la sangre**, to let the blood flow. **Su sueldo correrá desde el primer día del mes**, his salary will be payable from the first of the month. **Correr con los gastos**, to pay the expenses. **Esto correr por tu cuenta**, *(fig.)* that's your problem. **Correrse una juerga**, *V.* JUERGA.

correría [cor-ray-ree'-ah], *f.* 1. A hostile incursion, a foray. 2. Leather strap.

correspondencia [cor-res-pon-den'-the-ah], *f.* 1. Correspondence relation. 2. Correspondence, commerce, intercourse. **Correspondencia particular, private** correspondence. **Curso por correspondencia**, correspondence course. **Estar en correspondencia con uno**, to be in correspondence with somebody. 3. Correspondence, friendship, interchange of offices or civilities. 4. Proportion, symmetry, congruity. 5. Consentaneousness, consent, agreement. **Mis ofertas no tuvieron correspondencia**, my offers met with no response. **Yo esperaba más correspondencia**, I had expected a greater response. **corresponder** [cor-res-pon-derr'], *va. & vn.* 1. To return a favor, to make a suitable return. 2. To correspond, to answer, to fit, to suit, to belong, to, to regard. **Ese libro no corresponde aquí**, that book doesn't belong here. **La llave corresponde a esa cerradura**, the key fits this lock. **Corresponder dignamente a**, to make a fitting reply to. **Ella le correspondió con una corbata**, she gave him a tie in return. 3. To agree. 4. To fall to the lot of. **Le dieron lo que le correspondía**, they gave him his share. 5. To concern; to rest with, to devolve upon. **Me corresponde hacerlo**, it is my job to do it. **Me corresponde jugar a mí**, it's my turn to play. -*vr.* 1. To correspond, to keep up commerce by alternate letters. 2. To respect or esteem each other. **A todos aquéllos a quienes corresponda**, *(Met.)* to all whom it may concern.

correspondiente [cor-res-pon-de-en'-tay], *a.* Correspondent, conformable, agreeable, suitable.

correspondiente [cor-res-pon-de-en'-tay], *m.* V. CORRESPONSAL.

corresponsal, *m.* 1. Correspondent, one with whom intelligence is kept up by messages or letters. 2. One who deals with another that resides in a different place. **Corresponsal de guerra**, war correspondent.

corretaje [cor-ray-tah'-hay], *m.* 1. Brokerage, money paid to a broker for making sales or purchases. 2. *(Coll.)* Money paid to a pimp or procurer.

corretear [cor-ray-tay-ar'], *va.* 1. To walk the streets, to rove, to ramble, to go up and down, to jaunt, to gad, to flirt. 2. *(CAm.)* To scare off (ahuyentar). 3. *(Cono Sur)* to sell on behalf of. 4. *(Cono Sur)* to hurry along (trabajo). -*vn.* 1. To run about. 2. To loiter, to hang about the streets (vagar).

correteo [cor-ray-tay'-o], *m.* **Andar en correteos**, *(CAm.)* to rush about.

corretero [cor-ray'-tay-ro], *m.* Gadder.

corretora [cor-ray-to'-rah], *f.* In some convents, the nun who directs the choir.

correvedile, correveidile [cor-ray-vey-dee'-lay], *m.* *(Coll.)* 1. Talebearer, mischiefmaker. 2. Procurer, pimp, go between.

correverás [cor-ray-vay-rahs'], *m.* 1. A child's toy, representing a coach or a living figure, and moved by a spring. 2. Something offered to a child to induce it to take medicine, or comply with its parents' wishes. *(Acad.)*

corricorriendo [cor-re-cor-re-en'-do], *adv. (Coll.)* In haste, at full speed.

corrida [cor-ree'-dah], *f.* 1. Course, race, career. 2. Incursion. 3. **Corrida de toros**, bullfighting. 4. Flow of any liquid. **De corrida**, at full speed, swiftly, in haste, 5. *(Carib, Cono Sur)* party, rave-up. 6. *(Cono Sur)* row, line, file. 7. *(Mex.)* Run, journey. 8. *(Geol.)* Outcrop.

corridamente [cor-re-dah-men'-tay], *adv.* Currently, easily, plainly.

corridita [cor-re-dee-tah], *f. dim.* A small course.

corrido [cor-ree'-do], *m.* 1. Romance, a merry song, accompanied with a guitar, in the *fandango* style. **Corridos**, Rents due and not paid. V. CAIDOS. 2. *(And.)* Fugitive from justice.

corrido, da [cor-ree'-do, dah], *a.* 1. Expert, experienced, artful. **Es una mujer corrida**, she's a woman who has been around. 2. Abashed, ashamed.-*pp.* of CORRER. 3. **Tresnoches corridas**, three nights running. 4. *(Arch. etc.)* Continuous. 5. Fluent, confident (estilo). **Decir algo decorrido**, to rattle something off. 6. Excellent, splendid (fiesta). 7. Cursive (escritura).

corriente [cor-re-en'-tay], *f.* 1. Course of rivers. **Corriente del Golfo**, Gulf Stream. **Corriente submarina**, undercurrent. 2. Current, a running stream. 3. Current, course, progression. 4. *(Elec.)* Current. **Corriente alterna**, alternating current. **Corriente directa**, direct current. **Corriente de aire**, draft or draught, current of air. 5. Course, tendency; drift. **Dejarse llevar de la corriente**, to drift along. **Las corrientes modernas del arte**, modern trends in art.

corriente [cor-re-en'-tay], *pa.* Runner, running.

corriente [cor-re-en'-tay], *a.* 1. Current, plain, easy. 2. Current, generally received, uncontradicted. 3. Current, common, general. **Aquí es corriente ver eso**, it's common to see that here. **Es una chica corriente**, she's an ordinary sort of girl. 4. Current, what is now passing; the present month or year; instant. **El año corriente**, the current year. 5. Fluent (estilo). 6. Current, running. **Moneda corriente**, current coin. 7. Marketable, merchantable. **Géneros de consumo corriente**, staple commodities. **Ir corriente en los pagos**, to be up to date in one's payments.

corrientemente [cor-re-ayn-tay-men'-tay], *adv.* Currently.

corrillero, ra [cor-reel-lyay'-ro], *m.f.* Braggadocio, idle person, person with time to gossip.

corrillo [cor-reel'-lyo], *m.* A circle of persons standing to talk of the news of the day, or to censure the conduct of others.

corrimiento [cor-re-me-en'-to], *m.* 1. *(Met.)* Shame, bashfulness. 2. An acrid humor. 3. Concourse, act of assembling. 4. Act of running; course or flow of waters. **Corrimiento de tierras**, landslide. V. CORRERÍA. 5. *(Med.)* Discharge; *(Carib, Cono Sur)* rheumatism; *(And.)* Tooth abscess.

corrincho [cor-reen'-cho], *m.* Meeting of low, vulgar people.

corrivación [cor-re-vah-the-on'], *f.* A diversion of brooks, and storing their water in a reservoir.

corro [cor'-ro], *m.* 1. Circle, ring formed by people who meet to talk or see a show. **Hacer corro**, to clear the way, to make room. 2. Sort of dance. 3. Small area, part, piece; *(Agri.)* Plot, small field, patch.

corroboración [cor-ro-bo-rah-the-on'], *f.* Corroboration.

corroborante [cor-ro-bo-rahntay], *m. & pa.* Corroborative, corroborant.

corroborar [cor-ro-bo-rar'], *va.* 1. To corroborate, to strengthen, to fortify, to confirm. 2. *(Met.)* To give new force to an argument or opinion.

corroborativo, va [cor-ro-bo-rah-tee'-vo, vah], *a.* V. CORROBORANTE.

corrobra [cor-ro'-brah], *f.* Treat or entertainment given at the conclusion of a bargain or contract. V. ALBOROQUE.

corroer [cor-ro-err'], *va.* To corrode, to eat away by degrees. **Le corroen los celos**, he is eaten up with jealously. -*vr.* To corrode, to become corroded.

corrompedor, ra [cor-rom-pay-dor', rah], *m. & f.* Corrupter.

corromper [cor-rom-perr'], *va.* 1. To corrupt, to vitiate, to mar, to turn from a sound to a putrescent state, to mortify. 2. To seduce a woman. 3. To corrupt, to bribe, to suborn. -*vn.* To stink, to emit an offensive smell.-*vr.* 1. To corrupt, to rot, to become putrid. 2. *(fig.)* To become corrupted, to become perverted.

corrompidamente [cor-rom-pe-dah-men'-tay], *adv.* Corruptly, viciously.

corrompido, da. *a.* Corrupt, spoiled, unsound. -*pp.* of CORROMPER.

corrompimiento [cor-rom-pe-me-en'-to], *m.* 1. Corruption, depravation, depravity. 2. Bribery. V. CORRUPCIÓN.

corroncha [cor-ron'-chah], *f. (And. CAm.)* Crust, scale.

corroncho [cor-ron'-cho], *a.* 1. *(Carib.)* Slow, sluggish. 2. *(fig.)* Corrupted, corrupt; depraved, degenerate.

corronchoso [cor-ron-cho'-so], *a. (And. CAm. Carib.)* Rough, coarse; crusty, scaly (escamoso).

corrongo [cor-ron'-go], *a. (CAm. Carib.)* First-rate, splendid; charming (encantador), attractive.

corrosca [cor-ros'-cah], *f. (Col.)* Wide straw hat tor the sun.

corrosible [cor-ro-see'-blay], *a.* Corrosible.

corrosión [cor-ro-se-on'], *f.* Corrosion, exulceration.

corrosivo, va [cor-ro-see'-vo, vah], *a.* Corrosive, acrid, corrodent, acrimonious.

corroyente [cor-ro-yen'-tay], *pa.* Corroding, corrodent.

corroyera [cor-ro-yay'-rah], *f.* A kind of sumac which is employed in tanning.

corrugación [cor-roo-gah-the-on'], *f.* Corrugation, contraction into wrinkles.

corrugador [cor-roo-gah-dor'], *m.* Corrugater, a small muscle of the face which wrinkles the skin.

corrugar [cor-roo-gar'], *va. V.* ARRUGAR.

corrulla [cor-rool'-lyah], *f. (Naut.)* Room under deck in a row galley.

corrupción [cor-roop-the-on'], *f.* 1. Corruption, putrefaction, corruptness, corrupting. 2. Corruption, pollution, filth. 3. A spurious alteration in a book or writing. 4. Looseness of the bowels. 5. Destruction. 6. Corruption, depravity, depravation or perversion of manners or principles. **En el gobierno existe mucha corrupción**, there is a lot of corruption in the government. 7. Complete disorganization of any substance.

corruptamente [cor-roop'-tah-men-tay], *adv.* Corruptly, viciously.

corruptela [cor-roop-tay'-lah], *f.* 1. Corruption, depravation, corruptness. 2. *(Law.)* Bad habit or practice contrary to law; abuse.

corruptibilidad [cor-roop-te-be-dahd'], *f.* Corruptibility, corruptibleness.

corruptible [cor-roop-tee'-blay], *a.* 1. Corruptible (persona). 2. Perishable (alimentos).

corruptivo, va [cor-roop-tee'-vo, vah], *a.* Corruptive.

corrupto, ta [cor-roop'-to, tah], *pp. irr.* Of CORROMPER, and *a.* Corrupted, corrupt; defiled, perverse.

corruptor [cor-roop-tor'], *m.* Corrupter, misleader, one who taints or vitiates. *-a.* Corrupting.

corrusco [cor-roos'-co], *m. (Coll.)* Offal, broken bread. *V.* MENDRUGO.

corsa [cor'-sah], *f. (Naut. Obs.)* A coasting voyage, a cruise.

corsario [cor-sah'-re-o], *m.* Corsair, privateer, pirate.

corsario, ria [cor-sah'-re-o, ah], *a.* Cruising: applied to a privateer or letter or marque, authorized to cruise against the enemy.

corsé [cor-say'], *m.* Corset, stays for women.

corsear [cor-say-ar'], *va.* To cruise against the enemy.

corsetera [cor-say-tay'-rah], *f.* A woman who makes or sells corsets.

corsí [cor-see'], *m.* The second of the thrones of God, according to Mohammedan belief, from which he is to judge men at the last day.

corsia [cor'-se-ah], *f.* Passage between the sails in a row-galley.

corso [cor'-so], *m. (Naut.)* Cruise, cruising, privateering.

corso [cor'-so], *a. m. & f.* Corsican.

corta [cor'-tah], *f.* Felling of wood, said also of reeds.

cortaalambres [cor-tah-a-lam'-brays], *m.* Wire cutters.

cortabolsas [cor-tah-bol'-sas], *m.* Pick-pocket, filcher, petty robber.

cortacésped [cor-tah-thes'-ped], *m.* Lawnmower.

cortacircuitos [cor-tah-theer-coo-ee'-tose], *m. (Elec.)* Circuit breaker.

cortacorriente [cor-tah-cor-re-ayn'-tay], *m.* Switch.

cortacutícula [ ], *f.* Cuticle scissors.

cortada [cor-tah'-dah], *f.* 1. *(LAm.)* Cut, slash; trench (zanja); short cut (atajo). 2. Slice (de pan).

cortadera [cor-tah-day'-rah], *f.* 1. Chisel for cutting hot iron. 2. Knife or instrument used by beekeepers to cut out the honey-combs.

cortadero, ra [cor-tah-day'-ro, rah], *a.* Cutting readily; easily cut.

cortadillo [cor-tah-deel'-lyo], *m.* 1. A small drinking glass, a tumbler. 2. A. liquid measure, about a gill, the quantity which the glass will hold. 3. The block of iron which, with others, forms grapeshot. 4. A clipped piece of money. **Echar cortadillos**. 1. To speak in an affected manner. 2. To drink wine. 5. Lump of sugar. 6. Affair (ligue).

cortado [cor-tah'-o], *m.* 1. Caper; a leap or jump in dancing. 2. Coffee with a little milk.

cortado, da [cor-tah'-do, dah], *a.* 1. Adapted, proportioned, accommodated, fit exact. 2. Sculptured. 3. *(Her.)* Parted in the middle. 4. Confounded. 5. Short, interrupted (estilo de escritura). 6. **Estar cortado,** *(Cono Sur)* to be broke. **7. Tener el cuerpo cortado,** *(Mex.)* to feel off color. *-pp.* of CORTAR. **Quedarse cortado** or **cortarse**, to be out of countenance.

cortador, ra [cor-tah-dor', rah], *m. & f.* 1. Cutter, one who cuts. 2. That which cuts. *-a.* **Cortadora de césped**, lawnmower.

cortador [cor-tah-dor'], *m.* 1. Butcher. *V.* CARNICERO. 2. Slicing-machine, cutter. 3. *(Tel.)* Interrupter. 4. *(Zool.)* Scissorbill. *-pl.* Incisor teeth.

cortadora [cor-tah-do'-rah], *f.* Cutting board in a velvet loom.

cortadura [cor-tah-doo'-rah], *f.* 1. Cut, the action of a sharp instrument. 2. Cut, the separation of continuity by a sharp instrument; cutting, abscission. 3. Incision, cut, a wound made by cutting. 4. Fissure, or scissure 5. *(Mil.)* Parapet with embrasures and merlons, made in a breach to prevent the enemy from taking possession of it. 6. *(Mil.)* Work raised in narrow passes to defend them. **Cortaduras**, 1. Shreds of cloth, cuttings of paper, parings. 2. Figures cut in paper.

cortafrío [cor-tah-free'-o], *m.* A cold chisel; chisel for cutting cold iron.

cortafuego [cor-tah-foo-ay'-go], *m.* Fire-break, fire lane.

cortahierro [cor-tah-e-err'-ro], *m. V.* CORTAFRÍO.

cortahuevos [cor-tah-oo-ay'-vos], *m.* Egg-slicer.

cortahumedades [cor-tah-oo-may-dah'-days], *m*: Damp course.

cortalápiz [cor-tah-lah'-peeth], *m.* Pencil-sharpener.

cortamalla [cor-tah-mahl'-lyah], *f. (Agri.)* Alternate pruning of vineshoots when they are close.

cortamechas [cor-tah-may'-chas], *m.* A cuttingboard or table.

cortamente, *adv.* Sparingly, frugally, scantily.

cortamiento [cor-tah-me-en'-to], *m. (Obs.)* The act of cutting or amputating.

cortán [cor-tahn'], *m.* 1. *(Prov.)* Measure for grain, containing about a peck. 2. Oil measure, containing 8 lbs. 5 oz.

cortante [cor-tahn'-tay], *m.* Cutter, butcher.

cortante [cor-tahn'-tay], *pa.* Cutting, edged, sharp.

cortapapel [cor-tah-pa-pel], *m.* Papercutter, paperknife.

cortapicos y callares [cor-tah-pee'-cos ee cal-lyah'-res]. 1. *(Coll.)* Keep quiet! No more questions! (usado con niños). 2. *-m.* Earwig.

cortapiés [cor-tah-pe-ess'], *m. (Coll.)* Thrust made at the legs in fencing.

cortapisa [cor-tah-pee'-sah], *f.* 1. Obstacle, hindrance, impediment. **Sin cortapisas**, without strings attached. 2. Elegance and grace in speaking. 3. Condition or restriction with which a thing is given.

cortaplumas [cr-tah-ploo'-mas], *m.* 1. Penknife. 2. Earwig.

cortapuros [cor-tah-poo'-ros], *m.* Cigar cutter.

cortar [cor-tar'], *va.* 1. To cut, to cut off, to cut out, to curtail. 2. To cut, to disjoin, to separate, to hew, to chop. **Cortar por la mitad**, to cut down the middle. 3. *(Mil.)* To cut off part of the enemy's army. 4. To cut, to divide packs of cards in card-playing. 5. To interrupt the course of things. 6. To cut or interrupt a conversation, to cut short. 7. To cut, to form by cutting. 8. To abridge a speech or discourse. 9. To take a short cut, shorten the way. 10. To suspend, to restrain, to keep back. **Cortar el agua**, 1. To cut off the water. 2. *(Met.)* To navigate or sail through water. 11. To arbitrate or decide. 12. To cut figures in paper. 13. *(Naut.)* To cut away a mast or cable. **Cortar la corriente**, *(Elec.)* to break contact. **Cortar la lengua**, to speak a language with propriety and elegance. **Aire que corta**, a cutting, piercing, or nipping wind. **Cortar a alguno**, *(Met.)* to put one to the blush. *-vn.* 1. To cut. **Este cuchillo no corta**, this knife doesn't cut. 2. To cut (cartas). 3. **Cortar con el pasado**, to break with the past. 4. **¡Corta!**, get away! *-vr.* 1. To be daunted, ashamed, or confounded, to stop short, not to know what to say. 2. To open out the folds or wrinkles in cloth. 3. To separate, as the serous part of milk from the butter. 4. Of geometrical figures, to cross, intersect. 5. To interpose one's forces, dividing those of the enemy. 6. To add to a liquid another to subdue its properties. 7. *(Vet.)*

To injure the forefeet with the shoes, in walking. 8. **Cortarse el pelo**, to have one's hair cut. 9. *(Cono Sur)* to be out of breath (caballo). 10. *(And. Carib. Mex.) (Med.)* To shiver, to get the shivers. 11. *(Cono Sur)* to die.

cortaúñas [cor-tah-oo'-nyas], *m*. Nail clippers.

cortavapor [cor-tah-vah-por'], *m*. Cut off of a steam-engine.

cortavidrios [cor-tah-ve'-dre-os], *m*. Glass cutter.

corte [cor'-tay], *m*. 1. Edge of a sword, knife, or any other cutting instrument. 2. Exsection, abscission, the act of cutting. **Corte de pelo**, haircut. 3. Cut, the effect of a cutting instrument. 4. Felling of trees. 5. Mediation or reconciliation of persons at variance. 6. Measure, expedient, or step taken in an affair. 7. Notch, hack, a hollow cut in something, the stuff necessary for a garment. **Corte de chaleco**,' a vest pattern. **Un corte de vestido**, the stuff required for a full dress. 8. The surface which all the edges of the leaves of a book form. **Con cortes dorados**, with gilt edges. 9. (Mining) A shaft made in searching for a vein of mineral. 10. *(Arch.)* A sectional view of a building. *(Acad.)* 11. Resolutions which states adopt when they cannot satisfy overdue obligations. *(Acad.)* 12. Closing an account by a debtor without the assent of the creditor *(fr. Cortar)*. 13. *(Elec. etc.)* Cut, failure. **Corte de corriente**, power cut. **Hay corte de agua**, the water has been cut off. 14. Start, surprise. 15. Snub, rebuff (desaire). 16. Sharp answer (réplica).

corte [cor'-tay], *f*. 1. Court, the town or place where the sovereign resides. 2. Court, persons who compose the retinue of a monarch. 3. Levee. 4. **Corte Suprema**, Supreme court. 5. Retinue, suite. 6. Yard, court. 7. Court, courtship, art of pleasing, civility. **Hacer la corte**, 1. To court, to endeavor to please. 2. To attend the levees of the sovereign or of men in power, to pay court. 8. Stable for cattle; sheepfold. 9. *(Obs.)* District of five leagues round the court. *-pl.* **Cortes**, the senate and congress of deputies of Spain.

cortecica, illa, ita [cor-tay-thee'-cah], *f. dim*. A small crust, peel, or bark.

cortedad [cor-tay-dahd'], *f*. 1. Smallness, littleness, minuteness. 2. Dulness, stupidity, want of intellect or instruction. 3. Pusillanimity, timidity, diffidence. **Cortedad de medios**, poverty, indigence, want of means.

cortejador [cor-tay-hah-dor'], *m*. Wooer.

cortejante [cor-tay-hahn'-tay], *pa*. Courting; courtier, he who makes love, gallant.

cortejar [cor-tay-har'], *va*. 1. To accompany, to assist another. 2. To court, to pay homage. 3. To make love; **cortejar una dama**, to pay one's addresses to a lady. **Cortejar a alguno**, *(Coll.)* To stand treat.

cortejo [cor-tay'-ho], *m*. 1. Court, homage paid to another, courtship. 2. Gift, present, gratification. 3. Gallant, beau, lover, sweetheart. 4. Lady courted or sued for love; paramour. 5. Procession; solemn gathering. **Cortejo fúnebre**, funeral procession.

cortés [cor-tess'], *a*. Courteous, gentle, mild, civil, complaisant, complacent, gracious, courtly, mannerly, genteel, polite.

cortesanamente [cor-tay-sah-nah-men'-tay], *adv*. Courteously, politely.

cortesanazo, za [cor-tay-sa-nah'-tho, thah], *a. aug*. Awkwardly or fulsomely civil.

cortesanía [cor-tay-sa-nee'-ah], *f*. Courtesy, civility, politeness, complaisance, good manners.

cortesano, na [cor-tay-sah'-no, nah], *a*. 1. Courtlike. 2. *V.* CORTÉS. 3. Courteous, gentle, mild, obliging; courtly. **Cortesana or dama cortesana**, courtesan.

cortesano [cor-tay-sah'-no], *m*. Courtier.

cortesía [cor-tay-see'-ah], *f*. 1. Courtesy, an act of civility and respect, obeisance, courteousness; good manners. **Visita de cortesía**, formal visit. 2. Compliment, an expression of civility; a title of courtesy. 3. Gift, present, gratifications. 4. Days of grace allowed by custom for the payment of a bill of exchange, after it becomes due. 5. Mercy, favor. **Título or tratamiento de cortesía**, a title or appellation of honor, not

of right, but by courtesy. **Hacer una cortesía**, to drop a courtesy.

cortésmente [cor-tays-men'-tay], *adv*. Courteously, civilly, genteelly, politely, obligingly.

corte transversal [cor'-tay trans-ver-sahl'], *m*. Cross section.

corteza [cor-tay'-thah], *f*. 1. Bark of a tree. 2. Peel, skin, or rind of many things. **Añadir una corteza de limón**, to add a bit of lemon peel. 3. Crust of bread pies, etc. 4. A wild fowl of the family of widgeons. 5. *(Met.)* Outward appearance of things. 6. *(Met.)* Rusticity, want of politeness, crustiness.

cortezón [cor-tay-thone'], *m. aug*. Thick bark, rind, crust, or peel.

cortezoncito [cor-tay-thon-thee'-to], *m. dim*. Thin bark, rind, crust, or peel.

cortezudo, da [cor-tay-thoo'-do, dah], *a*. 1. Corticose, barky; having a strong rough bark. 2. Rustic, unmannerly, unpolished.

cortezuela [cor-tay-thoo-ay'-lah], *f. dim. V.* CORTENZOCITO.

cortical [cor-te-cahl'], *a*. Cortical.

cortijada [cor-te-hah'-dah], *f*. A collection of houses put up by the laborers or owners of a grange.

cortijo [cor-tee'-ho], *m*. Farmhouse, grange, manse.

cortil [cor-teel'], *m. V.* CORRAL.

cortina [cor-tee'-nah], *f*. 1. Curtain, shade, screen, portiere. 2. *(Mil.)* Curtain, part of a wall or rampart which lies between two bastions. 3. Any veil or covering. **Cortina de hierro**, iron curtain. **Cortina de humo**, smoke screen. **Correr la cortina**, *(fig.)* to draw a veil over something. **Descorrer la cortina**, *(fig.)* To draw back the veil.

cortinado [cor-tee-nah'-do], *m. (Cono Sur)* curtains.

cortinaje [cor-te-nah'-hay], *m*. Set of curtains for a house.

cortinal [cor-te-nahl'], *m*. A piece of ground near a village or farmhouse, which is generally sown every year.

cortinilla [cor-te-neel'-lyah], *f*. Screen, shade, portiere, thin curtain.

cortinón [cor-te-none'], *m. aug*. A large curtain to keep out the air.

cortiña [cor-te'-nyah], *f*. A plot of vegetables and cereals.

cortisona [cor-te-so'-nah], *f. (Med.)* Cortisone.

corto, ta [cor'-to, tah], *a*. 1. Short, not long, scanty, narrow, curt. **El vestido le ha quedado corto**, the dress has got too short for her. **El niño va todavía de corto**, the child is still wearing short trousers. 2. Small, little. 3. Short, not of long duration. 4. *(Met.)* Dull, stupid, weak of intellect. 5. *(Met.)* Timid, pusillanimous, fearful. **Quedarse corto**, to say less than one should say. 6. *(Met.)* Short of words, concise. 7. Imperfect, defective. **Corto de vista**, short-sighted. **Corto de oído**, hard of hearing. **Corto de manos**, slow at work, unhandy, not handy, not dexterous. **Pongamos 50 dólares y me quedo corto**, let's say 50 dollars and that's an underestimate. **Se quedó corta en la comida**, she did not provide enough food. *-m*. Short (cine).

cortocircuito [cor-to-theer-coo-e'-to], *m*. Short-circuit, shift circuit. **Poner en cortocircuito**, to short-circuit.

cortometraje [cor-to-may-trah'-hay], *m*. Short (cine).

cortón [cor-tone'], *m*. Worm, ringworm which destroys plants in gardens.

cortón [cor-tone'], *a*. 1. Bashful, timid. 2. **Es muy cortón**, *(CAm.)* He's always interrupting.

cortopunzante [cor-to-poon-than'-tay], *a. (Cono Sur)* sharp.

corulla [co-rool'-lyah], *f*. In galleys, place for the stoppers of cables.

coruscante, corusco, ca [co-roo-cahn-tay, co-roos'-co, cah], *a. (Poet.)* Coruscant, glittering by flashes, brilliant.

corva [cor'-vah], *f*. 1. Ham, a part of the leg. 2. Curb, a disease in horses' knees.

corvadura [cor-vah-doo'-rah], *f*. 1. Curvature, crookedness, inflexion; gibbousness. 2. *(Arch.)* Bend of an arch or vault.

corval [cor-vahl'], *a*. Of an oblong shape: applied to olives.

corvato [cor-vah'-to], *m*. A young crow or rook.

corvaza [cor-vah'-thah], *f*. Curb, a disease in horses' knees.

corvecito [cor-vey-thee'-to], *m. dim.* A young little crow or rook.

corvejón [cor-vay-hone'], *m.* 1. Hough, the joint of the hind leg of beasts. 2. Spur of a cock.

corvejos [cor-vay'-hose], *m. pl* An articulation of six bones joined by ligaments with which animals make movements of flexion and extension.

corveta [cor-vey'-tah], *f.* Curvet, corvetto, leap or bound of a horse.

corvetear [cor-vey-tay-ar'], *vn.* To curvet, to bound, to leap.

corvídeo, ea [cor-vee'-day-o, ah], *a.* Like or belonging to a crow.

córvidos [cor'-ve-dose], *m. pl. (Zool.)* The family of crows, jays, etc.; corvidae.

corvillo [cor-veel'-lyo], *m.* 1. Bill, a kind of hatchet with a hooked point. 2. **Corvillo de podón**, pruning-knife. 3. **Corvillo de zapatero**, a shoemaker's paring-knife. 4. A small sickle to cut thread and form velvet in velvet looms. **Miércoles corvillo**, Ash Wednesday.

corvina [cor-vee'-nah], *f.* 1. A kind of conger or sea-eel in the Mediterranean. 2. White sea bass of California.

corvino, na [cor-vee'-no, nah], *a.* Rook-like, belonging to a rook.

corvo, va [cor'-vo, vah], *a.* 1. Bent, crooked arched. 2. Stingy, mean.

corvo [cor'-vo], *m.* 1. *(Zool. Prov.)* Crawfish, a kind of seafish. 2. Pot-hook.

corza [cor'-thah], *f.* Doe.

corzo, za [cor'-tho, thah], *m. & f.* Roe deer, fallow deer.

corzuelo [cor-thoo-ay'-lo], *m.* Wheat left in the husks by the thrashers.

cosa [co'-sah], *f.* 1. Thing, substance, that which has being or existence; **cosa de entidad**, an important thing. **Cosa de risa** or **cosa ridícula**, laughing-stock. **Cosa de ver**, a thing worth seeing. **No hay tal cosa o no es así**, no such thing. **Alguna cosa**, something. **No me queda otra cosa**, I have no alternative. **Es poca cosa**, it's not important. **Tal como están las cosas**, as things stand. **Decir cuatro cosas a uno**, to give somebody a piece of one's mind. 2. **Es cosa de nunca acabar**, there's no end to it. **Es cosa distinta**, that's another matter. **Es cosa fácil**, it's easy. **Cosa rara**, strange thing. **Las cosas de palacio van despacio**, *(fig.)* it all takes time. 3. Affair, business. **Ésa es cosa tuya**, that's your affair. 4. **Cosas**, odd ideas. **¡Tienes unas cosas!**, what dreadful things you say! 5. *(LAm.) (conj.)* **No le digas nada, como que no se ofenda**, don't say anything to him, that way he won't get offended.

cosa de, *adv.* About, little more or less. **Cosa de media legua**, half a league, more or less.

cosaco, ca [co-sah'-co, cah], *a.* 1. Cossack. 2. *(Cono Sur)* mounted policeman.

cosar [co-sar'], *m. (Com.)* Kind of cotton stuff made in India.

cosario [co-sah'-re-o], *m.* 1. Privateer, corsair, pirate, cruiser. 2. Carrier, one who carries goods. 3. Huntsman by profession.

cosario, ria [co-sah'-re-o, ah], *a.* 1. Belonging or relating to privateers or corsairs. 2. Beaten, frequented (carreteras).

coscacho [cos-ca-cho], *m. (And. Cono Sur)* Rap on the head.

coscarana [cos-ca-rah'-nah], *f. (Prov.)* Cracknel, a crisp cake.

coscarse [cos-car'-say], *vr.* To catch on. *(Coll:)* V. CONCOMERSE.

coscoja [cos-co'-hah], *f.* 1. *(Bot.)* Kermes or scarlet-oak. 2. Dry leaves of the kermes oak. 3. Ring or knob on the crossbit of a bridle.

coscojal, coscojar [cos-co-hahl', cos-co-har'], *m.* Plantation of kermes or scarlet oaks.

coscojo [cos-co'-ho], *m.* Scarlet or kermes grain, after the worn or insect has left it. **Coscojos**, bits of iron composing the chain fastened to the mouthpiece of a horse's bridle.

coscolino [cos-co-le'-no], *a.* 1. *(Mex.)* Peevish, touchy; naughty (niño). 2. Of loose morals (moralmente).

coscón, na [cos-cone', nah], *a.* Crafty, sly.

coscorrón [cos-cor-rone'], *m.* 1. Contusion, a blow or bruise on the head 2. Bruise in a loaf. 3. *(fig.)* Set-back, disappointment, knock.

coscorronera [cos-cor-ro-nay'-rah], *f.* A kind of bonnet put upon children to avoid blows upon the head. *V.* CHICHONERA.

coscurro [cos-coor'-ro], *m.* Flat loaf.

cosecante [co-say-cahn'-tay], *m. (Geom.)* Cosecant.

cosecha [co-say'-chah], *f.* 1. Harvest, harvest time. 2. Harvest, the corn ripened and gathered. 3. The season of reaping and gathering olives, etc. 4. The act of gathering the harvest. **Cosecha de vino**, vintage. 5. *(Met.)* Collection of immaterial things, as virtues, vices, etc. **De su cosecha**, of one's own invention.

cosechadora [co-say-chah-do'-rah], *f.* Combine-harvester.

cosechar [co-say-char'], *va.* 1. *(Prov.)* To crop, to reap, to gather the corn at harvest time, cultivate, grow. **Aquí no cosechan sino patatas**, the only thing they grow here is potatoes. 2. *(fig.)* To reap, to reap the reward of. **No cosechó sino disgustos**, all he got was troubles.

cosechero, ra [co-say-chay'-ro], *m. &f.* The person who has corn, olives, etc., of his own to reap and gather: commonly used to designate the proprietor of the produce.

cosechón [co-say-chone'], *m.* Bumper crop.

cosederos de los tablones, *m. pl. (Naut.)* Plank seams.

cosedora [co-say-do'-rah], *f.* Seamstress, stitcher.

conselete [co-say-lay'-tay], *a.* 1. Corselet, ancient coat of armor. 2. A light corselet. 3. Pikeman, anciently armed with a corselet. 4. The thorax of insects.

coseno [co-say'-no], *m. (Geom.)* Cosine. **Coseno verso**, the coversed sine. **coser** [co-serr'], *va.* 1. To sew. 2. To join and unite things. **Coser a puñaladas**, *(Coll.)* to stab or give wounds with a pointed weapon. **Coser y cantar**, to offer no difficulties; or, more fully. **Ya no queda más que coser y cantar**, what remains to be done is a trifle. **Coserse la boca**, not to speak a word.

cosera [co-say'-rah], *f. (Prov.)* Piece of ground which can be irrigated at once.

cosetada [co-say-tah'-dah], *f.* Race, a violent course.

cosiaca [co-se-ah'-cah], *f. (LAm.)* Small thing, trifle.

cosible [co-say'-blay], *a. (Obs.)* That which may be sewed.

cosido [co-see'-do], *m.* 1. Clothing collectively, and needle work. 2. Action of sewing. **Cosido de cama**, quilt and blankets of a bed stitched together to prevent their separation. **-Cosido da**, *pp.* of COSER, Devoted to, wedded to.

cosiduras [co-see-doo'-ras], *f. pl. (Naut.)* Lashings, ends of ropes used in ships to secure movable things.

cosignatario, ria [co-seg-nah-tah'-re-o], *m. & f.* Cosignatory.

cosijoso [co-se-ho'-so], *a.* 1. *(CAm. Mex.)* Bothersome (molesto). 2. *(CAm. Mex.)* Peevish, irritable.

cosita [co-see'-tah], *f. dim.* A small thing, a trifle.

cosmético [cos-may'-te-co], *m.* Cosmetic.

cósmico, ca [cos'-me-co, cah], *a.* 1. Cosmic, belonging to the universe. 2. A rising or setting star, which coincides with the rising of the sun.

cosmocracia [cos-mo-crah'-the-ah], *f.* Cosmocracy, a system of universal monarchy.

cosmócrate [cos-mo'-crah-tah], *a.* Cosmocratic, aspiring to universal monarchy.

cosmocrático, ca [cos-mo-crah'-te-co, cah], *a.* Cosmocratic, relating to cosmocracy.

cosmódromo [cos-mo'-dro-mo], *m.* Space station.

cosmogonía [cos-mo-go-nee'-ah], *f.* Cosmogony.

cosmografía [cos-mo-grah-fee'-ah], *f.* Cosmography.

cosmográfico, ca [cos-mo-grah'-fe-co, cah], *a.* Cosmographical.

cosmógrafo, fa [cos-mo'-grah-fo], *m. & f.* Cosmographer.

cosmología [cos-mo-lo-hee'-ah], *f.* Cosmology.

cosmonauta [cos-mo-nah'-oo-tah], *m. & f.* Astronaut, spaceman, cosmonaut (astronauta).

cosmopolita [cos-mo-po-lee'-tah], *com.* Cosmopolite.

cosmorama [cos-mo-rah'-mah], *a.* Cosmorama.

cosmos [cose'-mose], *m.* The universe, cosmos.

cosmotrón [cos-mo-trone'], *m.* Cosmotron.

cosmovisión [cos-mo-ve-se-on'], *f.* World view.

coso [co'-so], *m.* 1. *(Prov.)* Place or square for bullfights or other public entertainments. 2. Worm which lodges in the trunks of some fruit-trees. 3. V. COSA.

cospe [cose'-pay], *m.* Chipping with an adze or hatchet.

cospel [cos-pel'], *m.* Coin blank, in the mint.

cospillo [cos-peel'-lyo], *m.* Lees of the olive, after expression.

cosquillar [cos-ke-lyar'], *va.* To tickle.

cosquillas [cos-keel'-lyas], *f. pl.* Tickling, titillation. **Hacer cosquillas alguna cosa**, *(Met.)* to be tickled by anything; to excite desire, curiosity, or suspicion. **No sufrir cosquillas**, *(Met.)* to understand or suffer no jokes. **Tener malas cosquillas**, *(Met.)* to be easily offended, to be ill-tempered. **Siento cosquillas en el pie**, my foot tickles. **Tener cosquillas**, to be ticklish.

cosquillear [cos-keel-lyay-ar'], *va.* To tickle.

cosquilleo [cos-keel-lyay'-o], *m.* Sensation of tickling.

cosquilloso, sa [cos-keel-lyo'-so, sah], *a.* 1. Ticklish. 2. Susceptible, easily offended.

costa [cos'-tah], *f.* 1. Cost, the price paid for a thing. 2. Cost, charge, expense. 3. Expensiveness. 4. Expense or charges of a lawsuit: in this sense it is almost always used in the plural. **Condenar en costas**, to sentence a party to pay the costs of a suit. 5. *(Met.)* Labor, expense, fatigue. **A costa de**, at the expense of. **A toda costa**, at all hazards, at all events. 6. Coast; the shore. **Dar a la costa**, or **en la costa**, to get on shore. **Arrimado a la costa**, close inshore.

costado [cos-tah'-do], *m.* 1. Side, the lateral part of animals. 2. V. LADO. 3. *(Mil.)* Flank. 4. *(Obs.)* Hind or back part. 5. Side of a ship. **Presentar el costado a un enemigo**, to bring the broadside to bear upon an enemy's ship. **Costados**, race, lineage, succession of ancestors. **Español por los 4 costados**, Spanish on both sides of the family. **Es un gandul por los 4 costados**, he's an absolute idler. **costados**, he's an absolute idler.

costal [cos-tahl'], *m.* 1. Sack or large bag. **Estar hecho un costal de huesos**, to be all skin and bones. 2. Rammer, to beat down the earth of a mud wall or rampart.

costal [cos-tahl'], *a.* Costal, belonging to the ribs.

costalada [cos-tah-lah'-dah], *f.* A fall flat on the ground.

costalazo [cos-tah-lah'-tho], *m.* Blow with a sack. **Dar un costalazo**, to fall flat on the ground like a sack; to fail.

costalero [cos-tah-lay'-ro], *m.* *(Prov.)* Porter, who carries goods.

costalito [cos-tah-lee'-to], *m. dim.* A small sack.

costanera [cos-tah-nay'-rah], *f.* 1. Side, flank. 2. Slope (cuesta). 3. *(Cono Sur)* jetty; paved area beside the sea. 4. *(Carib.)* Firm ground (alrededor de un pantano).

costaneras [cos-tah-nay'-ras], *f. pl.* In building, rafters.

costanero, ra [cos-tah-nay'-ro, rah], *a.* 1. Belonging to a coast. 2. Declivous, inclining downward. **Buque** or **bajel costanero**, coaster, a vessel employed in the coasting trade. **Navegación costanera**, coasting navigation.

costanilla [cos-tah-neel'-lyah], *f. dim.* Gentle declivity, side of a small hill; a steep street.

costar [cos-tar'], *vn.* 1. To cost, to be bought for, to be had at a price. **Me cuesta tanto**, it's such an effort. 2. To suffer detriment or loss. **Cuesta poco**, it's easy. **Le ha costado caro**, it has cost him dear. **Es un trabajo que cuesta unos minutos**, it's a job which takes a few minutes. **Me cuesta hablar alemán**, I find it difficult to speak German.

Costa Rica [cos-tah-ree'-cah], *f.* Costa Rica.

costarricense [cos-tar-re-then'-say], or **costarriqueño, ña** [cos-tar-re-kay'-nyo, nyah], *a.* Costa Rican, of Costa Rica.

coste [cos'-tay], *m.* cost, expense, price paid for a thing. **Coste humano**, *(fig.)* human cost.

costeable [cos-tay-ah'-blay], *a.* Financially feasible.

costear [cos-tay-ar'], *va.* 1. To pay the cost of. **Costea los estudios a su sobrino**, he is paying for his nephew's education. 2. To skirt. 3. *(Naut.)* To sail along the coast of. -*vr.* 1. To pay its own way, to cover the costs involved.

costeño [cos-tay'-nyo], *a.* 1. **Barco costeño**, a small boat wed only in the coasting trade. 2. *m. & f.* Coastal.

costera [cos-tay'-rah], *f.* 1. Side of a bale of goods. 2. A fisherman's basket. 3. Each of the two parts of the mould into which tubes of lead or tin empty. 4. Time of fishing for surmullets. 5. Outside quire of a ream of paper. 6. Sea coast.

costero [cos-tay'-ro], *m.* First plank cut from a pinetree.

costero, ra [cos-tay'-ro, rah], *a.* 1. Outward; **papel costero**, outside quires. 2. Oblique: applied to a cannonshot or a declivity. 3. Coastal.

costezuela [cos-tay-thoo-ay'-lah], *f. dim.* Slight declivity or coast.

costífero, ra [cos-tee'-fay-ro, rah], *a.* *(Zool.)* Ribbed longitudinally.

costilla [cos-teel'-lyah], *f.* 1. Rib. 2. Stave, the board of a barrel. 3. A piece of timber which serves to strengthen joists. 4. The rib of a cupola, springer. 5. *(Met. Coll.)* Property, support, wealth. 6. *(Coll.)* Rib (esposa). 7. *(Bot.)* A thick nervure or rib of a leaf. 8. Chop (carne). **Costilla de cerdo**, pork chop. -*pl.* 1. Shoulders, back. **Todo carga sobre mis costillas**, I get all the burdens, everything is put on my back. 2. *(Agri.)* Wooden strips to which horses are tied in ploughing. 3. *(Mech.)* Cramp irons, chimney ties for securing chimney flues. **Medirle a uno las costillas**, to cudgel him.

costillaje, costillar [cos-teel-lyah'-hay cos-teel-lyar'], *m.* 1. The whole of the ribs, and their place in the body. 2. The ribs in a flitch of bacon. 3. *(Naut.)* The timbers or frame of a ship.

costilludo, da [cos-teel-lyoo'-do, dah], *a.* *(Coll.)* 1. Broad shouldered. 2. Clownish, unmannerly.

costípedo, da [cos-tee'-pay-do, dah], *a.* Said of birds which are perfectly balanced upon their legs.

costo [cos'-to], *m.* 1. Cost, price. **Costo efectivo**, actual cost. 2. Charges, expense. **Costo de expedición**, shipping charges. 3. Labor, fatigue. **Hacerse el costo de hacer algo**. *(Cono Sur)* to take the trouble to do something. 4. *(Bot.)* Costus arabicus, or sweet and bitter ostus. 5. Costus root. 6. Drugs, dope (drogas).

costosamente [ ], *adv.* Costly, at a high price, expensively; extravagantly.

costoso, sa [cos-to'-so, sah], *a.* 1. Costly, dear, expensive. 2. *(Met.)* Dear, difficult to be obtained. 3. Dear, sad, grievous.

costra [cos'-trah], *f.* 1. Crust. 2. Crust, scab. 3. Broken biscuit given to the people on board of galleys. 4. An encrusted part of a wick.

costrada [cos-trah'-dah], *f.* Seedcake, candied with melted sugar, beaten eggs, and grated bread.

costribar [cos-tre-bar'], *va..* To indurate, to harden; to make strong.

costringir [cos-trin-heer'], *va.* To constrain, to compel.

costroso, sa [cos-tro'-so, sah], *a.* Crusty, covered with a crust.

costumbre [cos-toom'-bray], *f.* 1. Custom, habit, haunt, habitude, familiarity. **Las costumbres de esta provincia**, the customs of this province. **He perdido la costumbre**, I have got out of the habit. 2. Custom, a law which has obtained force by usage. 3. Custom, the common way of acting, fashion, established manner. **Persona de buenas costumbres**, respectable person. 4. Periodical indisposition of women, catamenia, courses. **Costumbres**, customs, the characteristic manners and habits of a nation or a person.

costumbrismo [cos-toom-bres'-mo], *m.* Literary genre of customs and manners.

costumbrista [cos-toom-bres'-tah], *a.* Customs and manners (novela etc.). -*m. & f.* Writer of customs and manners.

costura [cos-too'-rah], *f.* 1. Seam. **Sin costuras**, seamless. **Sentar las costuras**, to press the seams. 2. Needlework, especially upon white goods: sheets, shirts, etc. **Alta costura**, haute couture. **La costura Italiana**, Italian fashion. 3. *(Naut.)*

Splicing of a rope. *(Carp.)* A joint between two pieces of wood. **Costuras de los tablones de un navío,** *(Naut.)* the seams of the planks of a ship. **Costuras abiertas,** seams of a ship from which the oakum has been washed out.

costurar [cos-too-rar'], *va. vn. (LAm.) V.* COSER.

costurera [cos-too-ray'-rah], *f.* Seamstress, dressmaker.

costurero [cos-too-ray'-ro], *m.* 1. A lady's workbox. 2. *(Obs.),* Tailor.

costurón [cos-too-rone'], *m.* 1. Seam, a coarse suture which joins two edges. 2. A large scar.

cota [co'-tah], *f.* 1. Coat of mail. 2. Coat of arms, formerly worn by the kings at arms. 3. *(Topog.)* A number indicating the height of a point above the sea or some other level. **Misil de baja cota,** low-flying missile. 4. Quota, a share assigned to each. 5. The back and callous part of a boar's hide.

cotana [co-tah'-nah], *f.* Mortise, mortise hole.

cotangente [co-tan-hen'-tay], *f. (Geom.)* Cotangent.

cotanza [co-tahn'-than], *f.* Sort of linen, medium fineness.

cotar [co-tar'], *va. V.* ACOTAR.

cotarrera [co-tar-ray'-rah], *f. (Coll.)* A gadding woman.

cotarro [co-tar'-ro], *m.* 1. Charity hut for the reception of beggars. **Andar de cotarro en cotarro,** to wander about. **Alborotar el cotarro,** to cause disturbance. 2. *(Cono Sur)* mate, pal.

cote [co'-tay], *m. (Naut.)* Half hitch, knot. **Dos cotes,** clovehitch.

coteja [co-tay'-hah], *f. (And. CAm.)* Equal, match.

cotejar [co-tay-har'], *va.* 1. To compare one thing with another, to confront, to confer. 2. *(And. Carib.)* To arrange.

cotejo [co-tay'-ho], *m.* 1. Comparison, collation, parallel. 2. *(Dep.)* Match, game, *-a. (LAm.)* Similar, same.

cotelé [co-tay-lay'], *m. (Cono Sur)* Corduroy.

cotense [co-ten'-say], *m. (Mex.)* Coarse brown linen wrapper.

cotí [co-tee'], *m.* 1. Sort of linen. 2. Ticking used for mattresses.

cotidianamente [co-te-de-ah-nah-men'-tay], *adv.* Daily.

cotidiano, na [co-te-de-ah'-no, nah], *a.* Daily, each day; quotidian.

cotiledón [co-te-lay-done'], *m.* 1. *(Bot.)* Cotyledon, seedleaf. 2. *(Anat.)* Cotyledon, a lobule of the placenta.

cotiledonado, da, or **cotiledóneo, ea** [co-te-lay-do-nah'-do, dah, co-te-lay-do'-nay-o, ah], *a.* Cotyledonous.

cotiliforme [co-te-le-for'-may], *a. (Bot.)* Cotyliform, having a wide cylindrical tube and straight limb.

cotilo [co-tee'-lo], *m. (Antiq.)* Cotyle, a cup-like cavity.

cotilóidea [co-te-loi'-day-ah], *f.* The cotyloid cavity which receives the head of the thighbone.

cotilóideo, ea [co-te-loi'-day-o, ah], *a.* Cotyloid, cup-like.

cotilla [co-teel'-lyah], *f.* 1. Stays, corsets. **Varillas de cotilla,** whalebones. *-m. & f.* Busybody, gossip.

cotillear [co-teel-lyay-ar'], *vn.* To gossip.

cotilleo [co-teel-lay'-o], *m.* Gossip(ing).

cotillero [co-teel-lyay'-ro], *m.* 1. Staymaker. 2. *V.* COTILLA.

cotillo [co-teel'-lyo], *m.* The peen of a hammer: end opposite to flat surface; claw of hammer.

cotillón [co-teel-lyone'], *m.* A dance, generally a waltz, at the end of a society ball.

cotín [co-teen'], *m.* 1. A back stroke given in the air to a ball. 2. Bedticking.

cotiza [co-tee'-thah], *f.* 1. *(Her.)* Band of a shield, fret. 2. *(Mech.)* Each of the grooves for the warp of the silk fabric called lustering. 3. *(And. Carib.)* Sandal.

cotizable [co-te-thah'-blay], *a.* Quotable, valued at.

cotización [co-te-thah-the-on'], *f. (Com.)* Quotation; price-current, price-list. **Cotización de apertura,** opening price. **Cotización de cierre,** closing price.

cotizado, da [co-te-thah'-do, dah], *a.* 1. *(Her.)* Banded, having bands. 2. In demand, popular, sought-after. 3. *(fig.)* Valued, esteemed.

cotizante [co-te-thahn'-tay], *m. & f.* Contributor.

cotizar [co-te-thar'], *va.* 1. To quote prices; to cry out the current prices in the exchange. 2. To fix (cuota); to pay (suscripción). 3. *(Carib. Cono Sur)*

coto [co'-to], *m.* 1. Inclosure of pasture-grounds. **Coto de caza,** game preserve. 2. Landmark. 3. *(Prov.)* Territory, district. 4. Combination among merchants not to sell goods under a certain rate. 5. Measure of a handbreadth. 6. *(Prov.)* Fine. 7. Chub, a small freshwater fish. 8. Rate or price of a thing. 9. *(Amer.)* A morbid swelling in the throat, goitre. *V.* PAPERA. 10. Boundary stone; *(fig.)* Limit. **Poner coto a,** to put a stop to.

cotobelo [co-to-bay'-lo], *m.* Opening in the branch of a bridle.

cotón [cotone'], *m.* 1. Printed cotton. 2. *(LAm.)* Shirt (camisa); *(Mex.)* Blouse.

cotona [co-toh'-nah], *f.* 1. *(Mex.)* Chamois jacket. 2. *(LAm.)* Strongly-made shirt. 3. *(Carib.)* Child's nightdress.

cotonada [co-to-nah'-dah], *f.* Sort of cotton cloth, striped and flowered; calico, prints.

cotoncillo [co-ton-theel'-lyo], *m.* Button of a maulstick or painters staff.

cotonete [co-to-nay'-tay], *m. (Mex.) (Med. etc.)* Cotton bud.

cotonía [co-to-nee'-ah], *f.* Dimity, fine fustian.

cotorina [co-to-re'-nah], *f. (Mex.)* Jerkin.

cotorra [co-tor'-rah], *f.* 1. *(Orn.)* A parrot of the smallest kind. 2. *(Orn.)* Magpie. 3. *(Met.)* A loquacious woman. 4. *(Mex.)* Chamber-pot (orinal). 5. *(Mex.)* Whore (puta).

cotorrear [co-tor-ray-ar'], *vn.* To chatter, to gabble.

cotorreo [co-tor-ray'-o], *m.* 1. Chattering, gossiping. 2. *(Mex.)* fun, good time.

cotorrera [co-tor-ray'-rah], *f.* 1. A hen parrot. 2. *(Met.)* A prattling woman.

cotorrería [co-tor-ray-ree'-rah], *f. (Coll.)* Loquacity: speaking of women.

cotorro [co-tor'-to], *a. (Mex.)* Chatty, talkative; loud, noisy (alborotado).

cototo [co-to'-to], *m. (Cono Sur)* Bump, bruise (on the head).

cotrai [co-trah-e'], *m.* Sort of linen.

cotral [co-trahl'], *m.* An old worn-out ox, set to graze.

cotudo, da [co-too'-do, dah], *a.* 1. Hairy, cottony. 2. *(LAm.) (Med.)* Suffering from goitre. 3. *(And.)* Stupid.

cotufa [co-too'-fah], *f.* 1. *(Bot.)* Jerusalem artichoke. 2. Tidbits, delicate food. **Pedir cotufas en el golfo,** to require impossibilities. 3. **Cotufas,** *(LAm.)* Popcorn.

cotufero, ra [co-too-fay'-ro, rah], *a.* Producing tidbits or delicate food.

cotunio [co-too'-ne-o], *m.* A transparent and viscous fluid which fills the cavities of the internal ear.

cotunnio, cotunnito [co-toon'-ne-o, nee'-to], *m.* Cotunnite, a lead chloride found in volcanic craters.

coturno [co-toor'-no], *m.* Cothurnus, buskin, a kind of high boot worn by the ancient actors of tragedy. **Calzar el coturno,** *(Met.)* to make use of pompous language in poetry.

coutelina [co-oo-tay-lee'-nah], *f.* A blue or white cotton cloth imported from India.

covacha [co-vah'-chah], *f.* 1. A small cave or hollow underground; a grot or grotto. 2. *(And. Carib, Cono Sur)* lumber room (trastera). 3. *(CAm. Carib.)* Hut. 4. *(And.)* Vegetable stall. 5. *(Carib.)* Kennel (perrera).

covachuela [co-vah-choo-ay'-lah], *f.* 1. *(dim.)* A small cave or grot. 2. *(Coll.)* Office of secretary of state.

covachuelista, or **covachuelo** [co-vah-choo-ay-lees'-tah], *m. (Coll.)* Clerk in one of the offices of the secretaries of state.

covadera [co-vah-day'-rah], *f. (And. Cono Sur)* Guano deposit.

covanillo [co-vah-neel'lyo], *m. dim.* Basket with a wide mouth, used for gathering grapes.

covin [co-veen'], *m. (Cono Sur)* popcorn.

coxalgia [coc-sahl'-he-ah], *f.* Hip-joint disease, coxalgia.

coxcojilla, ita [cox-co-heel'-lyah, hee'-tah], *f.* A children's play; hopscotch.

coxcoj (a), or **coxcojita (a)** [ah cox-coh, or ah cocs-co-hee'-tah], *adv.* Lamely, haltingly, limpingly.

coxis [coc'-sees], *m.* The coccyx.

coy [co'-e], *m.(Naut.)* Hammock, cot, a sailor's bed. **Afuera coys**, all hammocks up.

coya [co'-yah], *f.(Peru)* The queen, wife, and sister of the inca.

coyote [co-yo'-tay], *a.* 1. (*Amer.*) Native, of the country; domestic. **Cidra coyote, indio coyote.** 2. *(Mex.)* Astute person; guide of illegal immigrants; *(Com. Fin.)* Speculator, dealer in shares; middleman (intermediario). 3. *(Mex.)* Youngest child (hijo). *-m.(Mex.)* A kind of wolf; coyote.

coyotear [co-yo-tay-ar'], *vn.* (*CAm. Mex.*) 1. To be smart, to be clever. 2. *(Com. Fin.)* To deal in shares.

coyoteo [co-yoh-tay'-oh], *m.* *(Mex. Coll.)* Lobbying.

coyunda [co-yoon'-dah], *f.* 1. A trap or cord with which oxen are tied to the yoke. 2. *(Met.)* Dominion, power. 3. Matrimonial union.

coyundado, da [co-yoon-dah'-do, dah], *a.* Tied to the yoke with a strap or cord.

coyundilla [co-yoon-deel'lyah], *f. dim.* A small strap or cord.

coyuntura [co-yoon-too'-rah], *f.* 1. Joint, articulation. 2. Occasion, conjuncture, juncture; a critical point of time, a seasonable opportunity. **La coyuntura política**, the political situation. **Esperar una coyuntura favorable**, to await a favorable moment.

coyuntural [co-yoon-too-ral'], *a.* Relating to the moment. **Datos coyunturales**, relevant data. **Medidas coyunturales**, immediately relevant measures.

coz [coth], *f.* 1. Kicking with the hind leg (caballos, mulas). **Dar cozes**, to kick. 2. Kick or blow with the foot. 3. Recoil of a gun 4. Flowing back of a flood. 5. *V.* CULATA. 6. The back of a pistol from the guard to the end of the tip 7. *(Coll.)* Churlishness, unprovoked brusqueness. **A coces**, by dint of kicking. **Tirar coces contra el aguijón**, to kick against the pricks, to spurn at superiority. 8. Insult, rude remark. **Tratar a uno a coces**, to be rude to somebody.

C.P.A. *f. abr.* de **Caja Postal de Ahorros** (Post Office Savings Bank).

CNP *m. (Esp.) abr.* de **Cuerpo de la Policía Nacional**.

cra [crah], *m.* Caw of the crow.

crabrón [crah-brone'], *m.* Hornet.

crac 1 [crac], *m.* 1. *(Com. fin.)* Failure, crash; bankruptcy. **Crac financiero**, financial crash. 2. *(fig.)* Crack-up.

crac 2 [crac], *interj.* Snap! **Hizo ¡crac! y se abrió**, it went crack! and it opened up.

crac 3 [crac], *m. & f. (LAm.)* Star player, star performer; best horse.

crambo [crahm'-bo], *m.* Name formerly common to all cabbages and kales.

crameria [crah-may-re-ah], *f.* Krameria, rhatany, a medicinal plant of the polygala family indigenous to Peru. It is astringent.

crampón [cram-one'], *m.* Crampon.

cran [crahn], *m. (Typ.)* Nick, one of the grooves cast upon the front of the shank of a type to aid the compositor in rightly placing it.

craneano, na [crah-nay-ah'no, nah], *a.* Cranial, relating to the skull.

cráneo [crah'nay-o], *m.* The skull; cranium. **Ir de cráneo con uno**, to be on bad terms with somebody.

craneología [crah-nay-olo-he'-ah], *f.* Craniology, phrenology.

crápula [crah'-poo-lah], *f.* Inebriation, intoxication, crapulence.

crapuloso, sa [crah-poo-lo'-so, sah], *a.* 1. Drunken; gluttonous, surfeited. 2. Dissolute, dissipated.

craquear [cra-kay'ar'], *va.* To crack.

craqueo [cra-kay'-o], *m. (Quim.)* Cracking.

crasamente [cra-sah-men'-tay], *adv.* Grossly, rudely.

crascitar [cras-the-tar'], *vn.* To crow, to croak.

crasiento, ta, *a.* Greasy. *V.* GRASIENTO.

crasino [crah-see'-no], *m. (Orn.) V.* Hoco.

crasitud [crah-se-tood'], *f.* 1. Fatness, corpulency, crassitude, obesity. 2. Ignorance, stupidity, dullness.

craso, sa [crah'-so, sah], *a.* 1. Fat, greasy, oily, unctuous. 2. Thick, gross, crass. **Ignorancia crasa**, gross ignorance. **Error craso**, gross error. 3. *(And. Cono Sur)* coarse (grosero).

cráter [crah'tayr], *m.* Crater of a volcano.

crátera [crah'tayrah], *f.* Krater or crater, amphora, type of Grecian urn.

cratícula [crah-tee'-coo-lah], *f.* A small wicket or window, through which nuns receive the communion.

crawl [crol], *m.* Crawl.

crayón [crah-yone'], *m.* Crayon, chalk.

craza [crah'-thah], *f.* A receptacle for melted metal.

crea [cray'-ah], *f.* Linen.

creable [crayah'blay], *a.* Creative, creatable.

creación [cray-ah-the-on'], *f.* Creation.

creado, da [crey-ah'do, dah], *a.* Created, begotten, made. *-pp.* of CREAR.

creador [cray-ah-dor'], *m.* The Creator, God. *-a.* Creative.

crear [cray-ar'], *va.* 1. To create, to make, to cause to exist. 2. *(Met.)* To institute, to establish; to compose, produce literary or artistic works of relative merit. 3. To nourish, to support.

creatividad [cray-ah-te-ve-dahd'], *f.* Creativity.

creativo [cray-ah-te'-vo], *a.* Creative.

crébol [cray'-bol], *m.* Hollytree. *V.* ACEBO.

crece [cray'-thay], *m, f. (Cono Sur) V.* CRECIDA.

crecedero, ra [cray-thay-day'-ro, rah], *a.* Able to grow, that which can grow.

crecepelos [cray-thay-pay'-los], *m.* Hair restorer.

crecer [cray-therr'], *vn.* 1. To grow, to increase. **Dejar crecer la barba**, to grow a beard. 2. To grow or increase in stature. 3. To become larger. 4. To grow, to swell: a sea term. 5. To augment the extrinsic value of money. *-vr.* 1. *(Cos.)* **Se crece un punto**, increase by one stitch. 2. To grow bolder, to acquire greater confidence; to get conceited, to have an exaggerated sense of one's importance.

creces [cray'thes], *f. pl.* 1. Augmentation, increase; excess, in some things. **Para los niños se hace ropa con creces**, children's clothes are made to be let out. 2. The additional quantity of corn paid by a farmer to a public granary, besides what he borrowed from it.

crecida [cray-thee'-dah], *f.* Freshet, swollen state of rivers in consequence of heavy fulls of rain. *V.* AVENIDA.

crecidamente [cray-the-dah-men'-tay], *adv.* Plentifully, copiously, abundantly.

crecidito, ta [cray-the-dee'-to, tah], *a. dim.* Somewhat increased or grown.

crecido, da [cray-thee'-do, dah], *a.* 1. Grown, increased. **Ya eres crecido para eso**, you're too big for that now. 2. Grave, important. 3. Large, great. *-pp.* of CRECER. 4. **Estar crecido**, to be in flood. 5. *(fig.)* Vain, conceited.

crecidos [craythee'-dos], *m pl.* Widening stitches with knitting needles, to enlarge the width of a stocking.

creciente [cray-the-en'tay], *pa.* 1. Growing, increasing, crescent. 2. Susceptible of increase. 3. *(Her.)* A halfmoon with points upward.

creciente [cray-the-ayn'-tay], *f.* 1. Swell, freshet of waters. 2. *(Prov.)* Leaven. 3. Crescent, the moon in her state of increase.

crecimiento [cray-the-me-en'-to], *m.* 1. Increase or increment, growing, growth. **Crecimiento de la marejada**, *(Naut.)* Swell of the sea. 2. Increase of the value of money.

credencia [cray-den'-the-ah], *f.* 1. Sideboard of an altar, on which all the necessaries are placed for celebrating high mass. 2. Credentials.

credencial [cray-den-the-ahl'], *f.* Credential, that which gives a title to credit, accreditation. **Credenciales** or **cartas credenciales**, credentials or credential letters. *-a.* Accrediting; *V.* CARTA.

credibilidad [cray-de-be-le-dahd'], *f.* Credibility.

crediticio [cray-de-te'-the-o], *a. (Fin.)* Credit.

crédito [cray'-de-to], *m.* 1. Acquiescence, assent. 2. Credit, a sum of money due to any one. **Abrir un crédito a,** to open a credit for. 3. Credence, credit, belief, faith. **Dar crédito a,** to believe. 4. Reputation, character, name. 5. Credit, trust, confidence, esteem, authority. **Persona de crédito,** reliable person. 6. Note, bill, order for payment. **Créditos activos,** assets. **Créditos pasivos,** liabilities.

credo [cray'-do], *m.* Creed, articles of faith. **Cada credo,** every moment. **En un credo,** in a trice, in a moment.

credulidad [cray-doo-le-dahd'], *f.* 1. Credulity. 2. *V.* CREENCIA.

crédulo, la [cray'-doo-lo, lah], *a.* Credulous.

creedero, ra [crayay-day'ro, rah], *a.* Credible. **Tener buenas creederas,** to be easy of belief, to swallow the bait.

creedor, ra [cray-ay-dor', rah], *a.* Credulous

creencia [cray-en'the-ah], *f.* 1. Credence, belief, credit. 2. Credence, belief of the truths of religion, creed, persuasion. 3. *V.*MENSAJE and SALVA.

creer [cray-err'], *va.* 1. To believe, to give faith and credit to a thing. **Creo que sí,** I think so **¡Ya lo creo!,** I should think so! 2. To believe, to have a firm persuasion of the revealed truths of religion. 3. To credit, to receive a thing as probable. **Ver y creer,** to believe only what we see. 4. To think, to deem, to consider. **No le creo tan culpable, I** don't think him so much to blame. **Lo creo de mi deber, I** consider it my duty. *-vn.* **Creer en,** to believe in. *-vr.* 1. To believe oneself, to consider oneself. **Se cree muy astuto,** he thinks he's pretty clever. **¿Qué se ha creído?,** who does he think he is? 2. **No me lo creo, I** don't believe it. **Se cree todo lo que le dicen,** he swallows everything he's told. **Hace falta que yo me lo crea,** I still have to be convinced.

crehuela [cray-oo-ay'-lah], *f.* Sort of linen, osnaburgs.

creíble [cray-e'blay], *a.* Credible, likely.

creíblemente [cray-e'-blay-men-tay], *adv.* Credibly.

creído [cray-e'-do], *a.* 1. *(LAm.)* Gullible, trusting. 2. *(And. Cono Sur)* Vain, conceited.

crema [cray'-mah], *f.* 1. Cream of milk (nata). **Crema batida,** whipped cream. **Un coche color crema,** a cream-colored. 2. Custard. 3. Diaeresis. 4. Cream, the select of society. **La crema de la sociedad,** the cream of society. 5. Cream, cosmetic of creamy consistency. **Crema de afeitar,** shaving cream. **Crema dental,** toothpaste. **Crema hidratante,** moisturizing cream. 6. **Crema para el calzado,** shoe polish.

cremación [cray-mah-the-on'], *f.* 1. Cremation, the act of burning. 2. Incineration of dead bodies.

cremallera [cray-mahl-lyay'-rah], *f.* 1. *(Mech.)* Rack. 2. Zipper. 3. Cog railway.

cremar [cray-mar'], *va.* To cremate.

crematística [cray-mah-tees'-te-cah], *f.* Science of acquiring and preserving wealth.

crematístico [cray-mah-tes'-te-co], *a.* Financial, economic.

cremató logo [cray-mah-to'-lo-go], *m.* Political economist.

crematología [cray-mah-tolo-he'-ah], *f.* Political economy.

crematológico, ca [cray-mah-to-lo'-he-co, cah], *a.* Economical, relating to political economy.

crematorio [cray-mah-to'-re-o], *a.* **Horno crematorio.** *-m.* Crematorium; incinerator.

cremonés, sa [cray-mo-ness', sah], *a.* Relating to Cremona.

crémor [cray'-mor], *m.* **Crémor** or **crémor tártaro,** cream of tartar.

cremoso [cray-mo'-so], *a.* Creamy.

crencha [cren'-chah], *f.* The parting of the hair into two equal parts; each of these parts.

creosota, creosoto [cray-o-so'tah, to], *f. & m.* Creosote.

crep [crayp], *m.* **Crepa** *f. (LAm.)* Pancake, crêpe.

crepar [cray-par'], *vn. (Cono Sur)* To peg out, to kick the bucket.

crepitación [cray-pe-tah-the-on'], *f.* 1. Crepitation, crackling. 2. Crepitus of fractures.

crepitante [cray-pe-tahn'-tay], Crackling, crepitant.

crepitar [cray-pe-tar'], *vn.* To crackle, crepitate.

crepuscular [cray-poos-coo-lar'], *a.* Crepuscular; **luz crepuscular,** twilight.

crepúsculo [cray-poos'-coo-lo], *m.* Crepuscle, twilight, dawn.

cresa [cray'-sah], *f.* Flyblow, the egg of a fly; maggot.

crescendo [crays-then'-do], *m.* Crescendo.

Creso [cray'-so], *m.* Croesus.

crespar [cres-par'], *va.* To curl the hair. *-vr.* To grow angry, to be displeased.

crespilla [cres-peel'-lyah], *f.* An agaric. *V.* CAGARRIA.

crespina [cres-pee'-nah], *f.* Net used by women for holding up their hair.

crespino [cres-pee'-no], *m. (Bot.)* The barberry tree.

crespo, pa [cres'-po, pah], *a.* 1. Crisp, curled, crispy. 2. *(Bot.)* Crisp-leaved. 3. *(Met.)* Obscure and bombastic (estilo). 4. *(Amer.)* A curl. 5. *(Met.)* Angry, displeased, vexed. *-m.* Hair, head of hair.

crespón [cres-pone'], *m.* Crape. **Crespón de Cantón,** Canton crape.

cresta [cres'tah], *f.* 1. Comb, cock's comb. 2. Crest of birds. 3. Crest of a helmet. 4. Crest or summit of lofty mountains. 5. Cramp iron supporting the runner. *(Mil.)* **Alzar** or **levantar la cresta,** *(Met.)* To be elated with pride. 6. Wig, toupée (peluca).

crestado, da [cres-tah-do, dah], *a.* Crested.

crestería [crays-tay-re'-ah], *f. (Arch.)* Crenellations, battlements.

crestomatía [cres-to-mah-tee'-ah], *f.* Chrestomathy, a selection of pieces from various authors arranged for study.

crestón [cres-tone'], *m.* 1. Crest of a helmet in which the feathers are placed. 2. *(Min.)* An outcropping of a vein, ore.

creta [cray'-tah], *f.* Chalk.

Creta [cray'-tah], *f.* Crete.

cretáceo, cea [cray-tah'-theo, ah], *a.* Cretaceous, chalky.

cretense, or **crético, ca** [cray-ten'-say, cray'te-co, cah], *a.* Cretan, belonging to Crete.

crético [cray'-te-co], *m.* A verse of three syllables, the first and third long, the second short.

cretinismo [crey-te-nees'-mo], *m.* Cretinism, a kind of idiocy, with deformity.

cretino, na [cray-tee'-no, nah], *a.* A cretin, one affected with cretinism.

cretona [cray-to'-nah], *f.* Sort of linen, cretonne.

cretoso [cray-to'-so], *a.* Chalky.

creyente [cray-yen'-tay], *pa.* Believing, he who believes.

crezneja [creth-nay'-hah], *f.* Streak of bleached bassweed.

CRI *f. abr.* de **Cruz Roja Internacional** (International Red Cross).

cría [cree'-ah], *f.* 1. Brood of animals. **Cría de ganado,** cattle breeding. **Cría de peces,** fish farming. **Hembra de cría,** breeding female. 2. Suckling. 3. *(Coll.)* Child reared by a nurse. 4. A concise and pathetic narrative.

criada [cre-ah'-dah], *f.* 1. Female servant, maid or maidservant, hand-maid. **Criada de menaje,** housemaid. **Criada por horas,** hourly-paid woman. **Criada para todo,** maid of all work. 2. Wash bat, with which washer-women used to beat clothes.

criadero [cre-ah-day'-ro], *m.* 1. Plantation of young trees taken from the nursery. 2. Place for breeding animals. 3. Cocoon-bed.

criadero, ra [cre-ah-day'-ro, rah], *a.* Fruitful, prolific.

criadilla [cre-ah-deel'-lyah], *f.* 1. Testicle of an animal. 2. A small loaf. 3. *(dim.)* A little worthless servant-maid. 4. *(Bot.)* Truffle, a kind of mushroom.

criado [creah'do], *m.* Servant, menial, groom. **Criado capitulado,** a person who, wishing to go to a colony, engages to serve it a certain time in payment for his passage.

criado, da [cre-ah'-do, dah], *a.* Educated, instructed, bred. *-pp.* of CRIAR.

criador, ra [cre-ah-dor', rah], *m. & f.* 1. One who rears and trains domestic animals and fowls; a breeder. 2. The Creator.

criadora [cre-ah-do'-rah], *a.* Fruitful, fecund (tierra).

criamiento [cre-ah-me-en'-to], *m.* Renovation and preservation of something.

criandera [cre-an-day'-rah], *f. (Amer.)* Wet nurse.

crianza [cre-ahn'-thah], *f.* 1. Creation, act of creating. 2. Lactation. 3. Breeding, manners, education, nursery. **Dar crianza**, to breed, to educate, to bring up. **Mala crianza**, bad breeding. **Sin crianza**, ill-bred.

criar [crear'], *va.* 1. To create, to give existence, to feed. **Criar a los pechos**, to breast-feed, to nurse. 2. To breed, to procreate, to produce. **Esta tierra no produce hierba**, this land does not grow grass. **Está criando pelo**, he's getting some hair. 3. To rear, to bring up from infancy. 4. To nurse, to suckle, to foster, to nourish. 5. To rear or fatten fowls and other animals. 6. To breed, to educate, to instruct. 7. To institute a new office or employment. *V.* CREAR. **Criar carnes**, to grow fat and lusty.*-vn.* To have young, to produce.*-vr.* To grow. **Secriaron juntos**, they were brought up together. **Criarse en buena cuna**, to be born with a silver spoon in one's mouth.

criatura [cre-ah-too'rah], *f.* 1. Creature. 2. A newborn child, a baby. 3. An unborn child, a foetus. 4. Creature, a person who owes his rise or fortune to another. **Es una criatura**, he is but an infant, or like an infant. **Tengo lástima de la pobre criatura**, I pity the poor thing.

criba [cree'-bah], *f.* 1. Cribble, sieve, crib, riddle, screen. 2. *(fig.)* Sifting, selection; screening. **Hacer una criba**, *(fig.)* to sort out the sheep from the goats.

cribador, ra [cre-bah-dor', rah], *m. & f.* Sifter.

cribadura [cre-bah-doo'-rah], *f.* Sifting.

cribar [cre-bar'], *va.* 1. To sift with a sieve, to screen. 2. *(fig.)* To sift, to select; to screen.

cribo [cree'-bo], *m. V.* CRIBA.

cric [creek], *m.* Jackscrew, lifting-jack. *V.* GATO.

crica [cree'-cah], *f.* 1. Fissure. 2. *(Med.)* The female pudenda.

Crimea [cree-may'-ah], *f.* Crimea.

crimen [cree'-men], *m.* 1. Crime, offence, guilt. **Crimen de guerra**, war crime. 2. *(Theol.)* A mortal sin. **Sala del crimen**, a criminal tribunal.

criminal [creme-nahl'], *a.* 1. Criminal, guilty of a crime. 2. Criminal, not civil. 3. Censorious.

criminalidad [cre-me-nah-le-dahd'], *f.* 1. Criminality, guiltiness. 2. Crime rate (índice).

criminalista [cre-me-nah-lees'-tah], *m.* 1. An author who has written on criminal matters. 2. A criminal lawyer.

criminalística [cre-me-nah-les'-te-cah], *f.* Criminology; study of the criminal.

criminalmente [cre-me-nal-men'-tay], *adv.* Criminally, guiltily.

criminar [cre-me-nar'], *va.* To accuse, to incriminate.

criminología [cre-me-no-lo-hee'-ah], *f.* Criminology.

criminólogo, ga [cre-me-no'-lo-go], *m. & f.* Criminologist.

criminoso, sa [cre-me-no'so, sah], *m. & f.* Delinquent, criminal. *a.* Criminal.

crimno [creem'-no], *m.* Sort of coarse flour generally used in making a certain kind of fritters.

crin [creen], *f.* 1. Mane, horse hair. 2. A loom, specially constructed for weaving horse hair.

crinado, da, crinito, ta [cre-nah'do, dah, cre-nee'-to, tah], *a.* Crinite, maned, having long hair. **Cometa crinito**, a long-bearded comet.

crinífero, ra [cre-nee'-fay-ro, rah], *a.* Mane-bearing; having a mane.

crinóideo [cre-no-i'-day-o], *m. (Geol.)* A crinoid.

crinolina [cre-no-lee'-nah], *f.* 1. Crinoline a coarse fabric. 2. Crinoline, a hoop-skirt.

crinudo [cre-noo'-do], *a. (LAm.)* Long-maned (caballo).

criogenía [cre-o-hay-nee'-ah], *f.* Cryogenics.

criógeno, na [cre-o'-hay-no, nah], *a.* Cryogenic. *-m.* Cryogen.

criollismo [cre-ol-lyees'-mo], *m. (Amer.)* 1. Feature of the New World culture. 2. Inclination for the New World culture.

crío [cre'-o], *m.* Kid, child; brat.

criollaje [cre-ol-lyah'-hay], *m. (LAm.)* Creoles; peasantry.

criollo, lla [cre-ol'-lyo, lyah], *a. & n.* 1. Creole, one born in America or the West Indies, of European parents. 2. The Negro born in America, as opposed to one brought from Africa. *-a.* Indigenous, national.

crioterapia [cre-o-tay-rah'-pe-ah], *f.* Crymotherapy.

cripta [creep'-tah], *f.* Crypt.

cripto…*pref.* crypt…

criptógamo, ma [crip-to'gah-mo, mah], *a. (Bot.)* Cryptoga-mous, of concealed fertilization.

criptografía [crip-to-grah-fee'-ah], *f.* Cryptography, the art of writing secret characters.

criptográfico [crip-to-grah'-fe-co], *a.* Cryptographic.

criptógrafo, fa [crip-to'-grah-fo], *m. & f.* Cryptographer.

criptograma [crip-to-gra'-mah], *m.* Cryptogram.

criptología [crip-to-lo-hee'-ah], *f.* Cryptology, enigmatical language.

cris [crees], *m.* A dagger of a wavy blade used in the Philippines and Malay peninsula.

crisálida [cre-sah'-le-dah], *f. (Ent.)* Pupa, the chrysalis of a caterpillar.

crisalidar [cre-sah-le-dar'], *vn.* To pupate.

crisantemo [cre-san-tay'-mo], *m. (Bot.)* Chrysanthemum, a genus of plants.

crisis [cree'-sis], *f.* 1. Crisis, the point in which a disease kills or changes for the better. 2. Judgment, criterion. 3. The decisive moment. **Crisis económica**, economic crisis. **Llegar a la crisis**, to reach crisis point.

crisma [crees'-mah], *m.* 1. Chrism, oil mixed with balsam and consecrated by bishops, used in baptism, confirmation, and the consecration of bishops. 2. *(Coll.)* As synonym of head; in this sense it is feminine. **Romper la crisma**, to break (bruise) the head. 3. Christmas card.

crismar [cris-mar'], *va.* 1. To perform the rite of confirmation. 2. *(Coll.)* To break one's skull.

crismera [cris-may'-rah], *f.* Vial or urn, commonly of silver, in which the chrism or consecrated oil is preserved.

crisoberilo [cre-so-bay-ree'-lo], *m.* Chrysoberyl, a precious stone.

crisol [cre-sole'], *m.* 1. Crucible for melting metals, croslet or crosslet. 2. Cruset, a goldsmiths melting pot.

crisolada [cre-so-lah'-dah], *f.* Crucible full of metal; a charge.

crisólito [cre-so'-le-to], *m.* Chrysolite, a precious stone.

crisopeya [cre-so-pay'-yah], *f.* Alchemy, the transmutation of metals.

crispación, [cris-pah-the-one'], *f. (fig.)* Tension, nervousness; increase of tension; outrageous nature. **Una escena de absoluta crispación**, an utterly shattering scene.

crispamiento [cris-pah-me-en'-to], *m.* Contraction, twitching. *V.* CRISPATURA.

crispante [cris-pahn'-tay], *a.* Infuriating; outrageous; shattering.

crispar [cris-par'], *va.* 1. To cause muscles to contract convulsively; to twitch or contract convulsively. **Con el rostro crispado por la ira**, with his face contorted with anger. 2. **Crispar a uno**, to annoy somebody intensely. *-vr.* To twitch, to contract (músculo).

crispatura [cris-pah-too'-rah], *f. (Med.)* Crispation, a spasmodic contraction of the muscles.

crispetas [cris-pay'-tahs], *f. pl. (And.)* Popcorn.

crispir [cris-peer'], *va.* To spatter with a hard brush, to imitate granite, porphyry, or grained stone.

crista [crees'-tah], *f. (Her.)* Crest, the ornament of a helmet.

cristal [cris-tahl'], *m.* 1. Glass, crystal. 2. *(Chem.)* Crystal or crystals, salts congealed in the manner of crystal. 3. Crystal, the best and clearest glass manufactured in glasshouses, flint-glass. **Cristal ahumado**, smoked glass. 4. Looking-glass. **Cristal de aumento**, lens. 5. *(Poet.)* Water. 6. **Cristal tártaro**, cream of tartar. 7. Fine shining woollen stuff. **Cristal de roca**, rock crystal, transparent quartz. **Cristal cilindrado**, plate glass.

cristalera [cris-tah-lay'-rah], *f.* China closet.

cristalería [cris-tah-lay-ree'-ah], *f.* 1. Glassware. 2. Repository of glass-ware.

cristalero [cris-tah-lay'-ro], *m. (Cono Sur)* glass cabinet.

cristalino, na [cris-tah-lee'-no, nah], *a.* 1. Crystalline, crystal, transparent, glassy, pellucid, bright. 2. *(Anat.)* Crystalline lens of the eye.

cristalizable [cris-tah-lethah'-blay], *a.* Crystallizable.

cristalización [cris-tah-le-thah-the-on'], *f.* Crystallization.

cristalizador [cris-tah-de-thah-dor'], *m. (Chem.)* A vessel in which crystals are made.

cristalizar [cris-tah-le-thar'], *va.* To crystallize, to cause to congeal in crystals. *-vr.* To crystallize, to coagulate or concrete into crystals.

cristalografía [cris-tah-lo-grah-fee'-ah], *f.* Crystallography.

cristel [cris-tel'], *m.* Clyster. *V.* CLISTER.

cristianamente [cris-te-ah-nah-men'-tay], *adv.* Christianly. **Morir cristianamente**, to die as a Christian.

cristianar [cris-te-ah-nar'], *va. (Coll.)* To baptize, to christen.

cristiandad [cris-te-an-dahd'], *f.* 1. Christianity, the body of professing Christians. 2. Christendom. 3. Observance of the law of Christ.

cristianismo [cris-te-ah-nees'-mo], *m.* 1. Christianity. 2. The body of Christians. 3. Christening. *V.* BAUTIZO.

cristianización [cris-te-ah-ne-thah-the-on'], *f.* Christianization.

cristianizar [cris-te-ah-ne-thar'], *va.* To Christianize.

cristiano. na [cris-te-ah'-no, nah], *a.* 1. Christian. 2. Watered wine. 3. *(LAm.)* Simple minded.

cristiano, na [cris-te-ah'-no, nah], *m. & f.* 1. A Christian. 2. The Spanish language, opposed to Arabic or other foreign tongues; *(Acad.)* **A ley de cristiano**, upon the word of a Christian. **Hablar en cristiano**, to speak straightforwardly. *-m.* Person. soul. **Eso lo sabe cualquier cristiano**, any idiot knows that. **Eso no hay cristiano que lo entienda**, that is beyond anyone's comprehension.

Cristo [crees'-to], *m.* 1. Christ, Messiah, our blessed Savior. 2. Image of Christ crucified. **Ni por un Cristo**, by no means, not for the world. **El año 41 antes de Cristo**, 41 BC. **Donde Cristo perdió la gorra**, at the back of beyond. **Eso no lo sabe ni Cristo**, nobody knows that. **Todo Cristo**, every mortal soul.

Cristobal [cris-to'-bal], *m.* Christopher.

Cristus [crees'-toos], *m.* 1. Cross printed at the beginning of the alphabet. 2. The alphabet; crisscross row *(Obs.)*. **No saber el Cristus**, to be very ignorant. **Estar en el Cristus**, *(Met.)* to be the ABC of something.

crisuela [cre-soo-ay'-lah], *f.* The dripping-pan of a lamp.

criterio [cre-tay'-re-o], *m.* 1. Criterion, a standard by which a judgment can be formed. **Lo dejo a su criterio**, I leave it to your discretion. **Tiene buen criterio**, his taste is admirable. 2. Judgment, discernment. 3. View, opinion. **En mi criterio**, in my opinion. **Cambiar de criterio**, to change one's mind. 4. Viewpoint, attitude, approach. **Depende del criterio de cada uno**, it depends on the individual viewpoint.

crítica [cree'-te-cah], *f.* 1. Criticism. 2. Critique, critic, critical examination of any writing or publication. **Crítica literaria**, literary criticism. 3. Censure. 4. Refutation.

criticable [cre-te-cah'-blay], *a. V.* CENSURABLE.

criticador, ra [cre-te-cah-dor'], *m. & f.* Critic, censurer.

criticar [cre-te-car'], *va.* 1. To criticize. 2. To criticise, to judge.

criticastro, tra [cre-te-cahs'-tro], *m. & f.* Would be critic.

crítico [cree'-te-co], *m.* 1. Critic, criticizer. 2. *(Coll.)* An affected refiner of style and language. 3. Critic, a censurer, a man apt to find fault.

crítico, ca [cree'-te-co, cah], *a.* 1. Critical, critic, decisive. 2. Hypercritical, nicely judicious. 3. *(Med.)* Critical, producing a crisis in a disease.

criticón, ona [cre-te-cone', nah], *a.* Eager to criticize, fault-finding. *-m. & f.* Would be critic, fault-finder.

critiquear [cre-te-kay-ar'], *va.* To criticize, to play the critic, to censure.

critiquizar [cre-te-ke-thar'], *va. (Coll.)* To criticize, to censure, to find fault.

crizneja [crith-nay'-hah], *f.* Trace or rope of hair or osiers.

Croacia [co-ah'-the-ah], *f.* Croatia.

croar [cro-ar'], *vn.* To croak like a frog.

croata [cro-ah'-tah], *a.* Croatian.

crocante [cro-cahn'-tay], *m.* Brittle. **Crocante de cacahuate o maní**, peanut brittle.

croché [cro-chay'], *m. (Cos.)* Crochet. **Hacer croché**, to crochet.

crochet [cro-chayt'], *m.* 1. *(Cos.) V.* CROCHÉ. 2. Hook (boxeo).

crocino, na [cro-thee'-no, nah], *a.* Of crocus, saffron.

crocitar [cro-the-tar'], *vn.* To crow, to caw.

crocodilo [cro-co-dee'-lo], *m.* Crocodile. *V.* COCODRILO.

crol [crol], *m.* Crawl (natación).

cromado [cro-mah'-do], *a.* Chromiun-plated. *-m.* Chromium plating, chrome.

cromático, ca [cro-mah'-te-co, cah], *a.* 1. *(Mus.)* Chromatic, proceeding by semitones. 2. *(Opt.)* Chromatic, showing prismatic colors; uncorrected.

cromatismo [cro-mah-tees'-mo], *m.* Chromatic aberration.

cromato [cro-mah'-to], *m.* Chromate, a salt of chromic acid.

crómico, ca [cro'-me-co, cah], *a.* Chromic, belonging to chromium.

cromo [cro'-mo], *m.* 1. Chromium, a metallic element; discovered in 1797. 2. Chromo: a chromolithograph.

cromolitografía [cro-mo-le-to-grah-fee'-ah], *f.* 1. Chromolithograph, a print in colors. 2. The art of printing in colors; chromolithography.

cromolitográfico, ca [cro-mo-le-to-grah'-fe-co, cah], *a.* Chromolithographic, printed in colors.

cromoso, sa [cro-mo'-so, sah], *a.* Relating to chromium; chrome, chromous.

cromosoma [cro-mo-so'-mah], *m. (Biol.)* Chromosome.

crómula [cro'-moo-lah], *f.* The green coloring-matter of leaves, chlorophyll.

cromurgia [cro-moor'-he-ah], *f.* Treatise on coloring-matters industriously applied.

cromúrgico, ca [cro-moor'-he-co, cah], *a.* Relating to dyes or coloring-matters.

crónica [cro'-ne-cah], *f.* Chronicle, a register of events. **Crónica literaria**, literary page. **Crónica de sociedad**, society column.

crónico, ca [cro'-ne-co, cah], *a.* Chronic, applied to diseases.

cronicón [cro-ne-cone'], *m.* Chronicle, a succinct account of events.

cronista [cro-nees'-tah], *m.* Chronicler, annalist. **Cronista de radio**, radio commentator.

crono [cro'-no], *m. V.* CRONOMETRO.

cronografía [cro-no-grah-fee'-ah], *f.* Chronography, the science of time.

cronografista [cro-no-grah-fes'-tah], *m. & f. (Cono Sur)* Timekeeper.

cronógrafo [cro-no'-gra-fo], *m.* Chronograph.

cronograma [cro-no-grah-mah], *f.* Chronogram, an inscription including the date of any action.

cronología [cro-no-lo-hee'-ah], *f.* Chronology.

cronológicamente [cro-no-lo'-he-cah-men-tay], *adv.* Chronologically.

cronológico, ca [cro-no-lo'-he-co, cah], *a.* Chronological, chronologic.

cronologista, cronólogo [cro-no-lo-hees'-tah, crono'logo], *m.* Chronologist, chronologer.

cronometrador, ra [cro-no-may-trah-dor'], *m. & f.* Timekeeper.

cronometraje [cro-no-may-trah'-hay], *m.* Timing.

cronometrar [cro-no-may-trar'], *va.* To time.

cronometría [cro-no-may-tree'-ah], *f.* Chronometry, measurement of time.

cronométrico, ca [cro-no-may'-tree-co, cah], *a.* Chronometic, chronometrical.

cronometrista [cro-no-may-trees'-tah], *m.* Chronometer-maker.

cronómetro [cro-no'-may-tro], *m.* 1. Chronometer. 2. Stopwatch.

croque [cro'-kay], *m.* Hook or crook, used in the tunny-fishery.

croquet [cro-kayt], *m.* Croquet.

croqueta [cro-kay'-tah], *f.* A croquette.

croquis [cro'-kees], *m.* 1. A light sketch, of some ground or military position. 2. Any sketch, rough draft.

croscitar [cros-the-tar'], *vn.* V. CRASCITAR.

cross [cros], *m.* Cross-country race; cross-country running.

crotafal [cro-tah-fahl'], *a.* (*Anat.*) Crotaphite: applied to the elementary bony pieces of the head.

crotáfico, ca [cro-tah'-fe-co, cah], *a.* Relative to the temples or temporal region; crotaphic

crótalo [cro'-tah-lo], *m.* 1. Castanet. 2. The rattlesnake (Crotalus).

crotalogía [cro-tah-lo-hee'-ah], *f.* The art of playing the castanets.

croto [cro-to], *m.* (*Cono Sur*) Bum, layabout.

crotón [crotone'], *m.* A great genus of the spurge family.

CRT. (*Inform.*) CRT (cathode ray tube).

cruasán [croo-ah-sahn'], *m.* Croissant.

cruce [croo'-thay], *m.* 1. Crossing. 2. Crossroads. **Cruce de carreteras,** crossroads. **Cruce giratorio,** roundabout. **Cruce de peatones,** pedestrian crossing. 3. (*Telec.*) Crossing of lines. **Hay un cruce en las líneas,** the wires are crossed. 4. (*Ling.*) Cross, mutual interference.

crucera [croo-thay'-rah], *f.* Withers of a horse. **Cruceras,** the two large pins which fasten the body of a cart or wagon to the axle-tree; bolling pine.

crucería [croo-thay-ree'-ah], *f.* Gothic architecture.

crucero [croo-thay'-ro], *m.* 1. Crossvault of a church under the dome. 2. Crossbearer, one who carries the cross before the archbishop in a procession. 3. Piece of timber which lies across the rafters in a building 4. A crossing of two streets or roads; a railway crossing. 5. (*Print.*) Crossbar of a chase. 6. (*Naut.*) Cruising station. 7. (*Naut.*) Cruiser. **Crucero de paseo,** pleasure cruise. 8. (*Astr.*) Cross, a southern constellation.

cruceta [croo-thay'-tah], *f.* Crosspiece, headstick.

crucial [croo-the-ahl'], *a.* Crucial, making the shape of a cross.

cruciata [croo-the-ah'-tah], *f.* (*Bot.*) Crosswort, vallantia.

cruciferario [croo-the-fay-rah'-reo], *m.* Crossbearer.

crucífero [croo-thee'-fay-ro], *m.* 1. Crossbearer. 2. Crouched, cruched, or crutched friar, a friar of the order of the Holy Cross.

crucífero, ra [croo-thee'-ro] *a.* 1. Cruciferous or crucigerous, bearing a cross. 2. (*Bot.*) Having petals in the form of a cross.

crucíferas [croo-the-fay-rahs] *f. pl.* The cruciferae, mustard family.

crucificado, da [croo-the-fe-cah'-do, dah], *pp.* of CRUCIFICAR. Crucified; **el Crucificado,** Jesus Christ.

crucificar [croo-the-fe-car'], *va.* 1. To crucify. 2. To molest, to vex, to torment.

crucifijo [croo-the-fee'-ho], *m.* Crucifix.

crucifixión [croo-the-fik-se-on'], *f.* Crucifixion.

cruciforme [croo-the-for'-may], *a.* Cruciform.

crucígero, ra [croo-thee'-hay-ro, rah], *a.* Carrying or bearing the sign of the cross.

crucigrama [croo-the-grah'-mah], *m.* Crossword puzzle.

crucillo [croo-theel'lyo], *m.* Push-pin, a play.

cruda [croo'-dah], *f.* (*LAm.*) Hangover.

crudamente [croo-dah-men'-tay], *adv.* Rudely, crudely.

crudeza [croo-day'-thah], *f.* 1. Crudity, crudeness, unripeness. 2. (*Met.*) Rudeness, severity, cruelty. 3. (*Coll.*) Vapor, vain boasting. **Crudezas del estómago,** the crudities or indigestions of the stomach.

crudo [croo'-do], *m.* 1. Packing or wrapping cloth. 2. (*Mex.*) Hangover. 3. Crude (petróleo).

crudo, da [croo'-do, dah], *a.* 1. Raw, crude. 2. (*Prov.*) Green, unripe (fruta). 3. Rude, cruel, pitiless, grievous. 4. Crude, unfinished, immature. 5. Crude, hard of digestion. 6. A blustering, hectoring person. 7. (*Med.*) Unripe, not mature (tumores). **Tiempo crudo,** bleak, raw weather.

cruel [croo-el'], *a.* 1. Cruel, hard-hearted. 2. (*Met.*) Intolerable, insufferable; **un frío cruel,** an intense cold. **Dolores crueles,** severe pains. 3. Hard, oppressive. 4. (*Met.*) Bloody, violent, murderous, merciless, fierce, fiendlike.

crueldad [croo-el-dahd'], *f.* 1. Cruelty, inhumanity, savageness, mercilessness, ferociousness. 2. Hardness, oppression, acerbity. 3. Cruelty, a barbarous action, outrage.

cruelmente [croo-el-men'-tay], *adv.* Cruelly, mercilessly.

cruentamente [croo-en-tah-men'-tay], *adv.* Bloodily, with effusion of blood.

cruento, ta [croo-en'-to, tah], *a.* Bloody, cruel, inhuman.

crufia [croo'-fe-ah], *f.* Sign by which obscure passages are marked in literary works, in form of a semicircle with a point in the middle.

crujía [croo-hee'-ah], *f.* 1. (*Naut.*) The midship gangway of a galley. 2. A large open hall or passage in a building. **La crujía de un hospital,** the great hall of a hospital, with beds on each side; the aisle of a ward. 3. Passage with rails on each side, from the choir to the high altar in cathedral churches; **pasar crujía.** 1. To run the gantlet. 2. (*Met.*) To suffer great fatigue and misery.

crujido [croo-hee'-do], *m.* Crack, noise made by wood, creak, clash, crackling.

crujidor [croo-he-dor'], *m.* A glass trimmer.

crujiente [croo-he-ayn'-tay], *a.* Rustling; creaking; crunchy; grinding; cracking.

crujir [croo-heer'], *vn.* 1. To crackle, to rustle. 2. To grind (one's teeth). **Hacer crujir los nudillos,** to crack one's knuckles.

crúor [croo-or'], *m.* 1. Cruor, a blood clot, gore, congealed blood. 2. The coloring-matter of the blood; also the blood-globules.

cruórico, ca [croo-o'-re-co, cah], *a.* Bloody.

crup [croop], *m.* Croup, membranous or true croup.

crupal [croo-pahl'], *a.* Croupal, croupous, belonging to croup. (*Acad.*).

crupier [croo-pe-ayr'], *m.* Croupier.

crural [croo-rahl'], *a.* Crural, belonging to the leg.

crustáceo, cea [croos-tah'-thay-o, ah], *a.* Crustaceous, shelly, having jointed shells or carapaces.

cruz [crooth], *f.* 1. Cross. 2. Cross, a line drawn through another. 3. The sign of the cross, the ensign of the Christian religion. 4. Cross, the badge of some military order. 5. Cross, trial of patience, anything that thwarts; toil, trouble, vexation. 6. Withers, the upper juncture of the shoulder bone in beasts. 7. Dagger, in printing; obelisk. **Cruz y botón.** (*Naut.*) Frapping, the crossing and drawing together the several parts of a tackle. **Cruz Roja,** Red Cross; **en cruz,** cross-shaped. **Firmar con una cruz,** to make one's mark. **Con los brazos en cruz,** with arms crossed.

cruza [croo'-tha], *f.* (*Cono Sur*) 1. (*Agri.*) Second ploughing. 2. (*Biol.*) Cross, crossing.

cruzada [croo-thah'-dah], *f.* 1. Crusade. 2. Tribunal of the crusade. 3. Indulgences granted to those who support the crusade.

cruzado [croo-thah'-do], *m.* 1. Cruzado, an old Spanish coin of gold, silver, or brass. 2. Crusado, a Portuguese coin of gold or silver. 3. Crusader, a soldier enlisted under the banners of the crusade. 4. Knight who wears the badge of some military order. 5. Manner of playing on the guitar. 6. Figure in dancing.

cruzado, da [croo-thah'-do, dah], *a.* 1. Crucial, transverse, twilled. **Estarse con los brazos cruzados**, To be idle.-*pp.* of CRUZAR. 2. (*Cos.*) Double-breasted. 3. (*Zool.*) Crossbred, hybrid. 4. (*And.*) Hopping mad, furious.

cruzador, ra [croo-thah-dor', rah], *a.* Crossing from one side to another. -*m. & f.* (*Mex.*) Shoplifter.

cruzamen de una vela [croo-thah'-men day oo'-nah vay'-lah], *m.* (*Naut.*) Square or width of a sail.

cruzamiento [croo-thah-me-ayn'-to], *m.* 1. (*Biol.*) Crossing. 2. (*Ferro.*) Crossover.

cruzar [croo-thar'], *va.* 1. To cross, to lay one body across another. **Cruzar un palo sobre otro**, to place a stick across another. 2. To cross a street or road. **Cruzar el lago a nado**, to swim across the lake. 3. (*Naut.*) To cruise. 4. To cross the breed. 5. To twill. **Cruzar la cara a alguno**, to cut and hack one's face. -*vr.* 1. To be knighted, to obtain the cross or badge of a military order. 2. To cross and trip, as horses do when they are weak in their pasterns and quarters; **Cruzarse con uno**, (*And. Cono Sur*) to fight somebody. **Cruzarse con uno en la calle**, to pass somebody in the street.

CSD *m. abr.* de **Consejo Superior de Deportes**.

c.s.f. *abr.* de **coste, seguro y flete** (cost, insurance and freight).

CSN *m.* (*Esp.*) *abr.* de **Consejo de Seguridad Nuclear** (nuclear safety council).

CSP *m. abr.* de **Cuerpo Superior de Policía**.

cta. *abr.* **de cuenta** (account, a/c).

cta. cto. *abr.* de **Carta de crédito** (letter of credit, L.C.).

cte. *abr.* de **corriente, de los corrientes** (of the present months, instant, inst.).

c/u *abr.* **de cada uno** (each, ea.).

Cu [coo], *m.* Name which the ancient historians give to the Mexican temples.

cuacar [coo-ah-car'], *va.* (*And. Carib, Cono Sur*) **no me cueca**, I don't want to.

cuácara [coo-ah'-cah-rah], *f.* (*And.*) Frock, coat; (*Cono Sur*) workman's blouse

cuaco [coo-ah'-co], *m.* 1. (*Carib. Mex.*) Nag (caballo). 2. Bag snatcher (bolsista).

cuaderna [coo-ah-derr'-nah], *f.* 1. (*Prov.*) The fourth part of something, especially of bread and of money. 2. (*Naut.*) Frame, the timber work which forms the ribs of a ship. 3. Double fours, in the game of backgammon. **Cuaderna maestra**, (*Naut.*) Midship frame. **Cuaderna del cuerpo popes**, (*Naut.*) Stern frame. **Cuadernas a escuadra**, (*Naut.*) Square timbers.

cuadernal [coo-ah-der-nahl'], *m.* (*Naut.*) Block, a piece of wood with sheaves and pulleys, on which the running rigging is reeved. **Cuadernales de carenar**, (*Naut.*) Careening gears.

cuadernalete [coo-ah-der-nah-lay'-tay], *m.* (*Naut.*) Short and double block.

cuadernillo [coo-ah-der-neel'-lyo], *m.* 1. Five sheets of paper placed within each other. 2. Clerical directory, containing the daily order of divine service.

cuadernillo, ito, *m. dim.* Small parcel of paper stitched together.

cuaderno [coo-ah-derr'-no], *m.* 1. Parcel of paper stitched together. 2. Small memorandum book. 3. In printing-offices, four printed sheets placed within each other. **Cuaderno de bitácora**, (*Naut.*) Logbook.

cuadra [coo-ah'-drah], *f.* 1. Hall, saloon; drawing-room. 2. Stable, a house for beasts. 3. (*Amer.*) A block of houses. 4. (*Naut.*) Quarter of a ship. 5. (*Mil.*) Hut. 6. Hall, large room. 7. Ward (hospital). 8. (*And. Cono Sur*) 125.50 meters (medida).

cuadrada [coo-ah-drah-dah], *f.* (*Mus.*) Breve.

cuadrado, da [coo-ah-drah'do, dah], *a.* 1. Square, quadrate. 2. Perfect, without defect. 3. With squares. 4. Broad, square-shouldered (persona). 5. (*Carib. Cono Sur*) coarse, rude. 6. (*And.*) Elegant, graceful. -*pp.* of CUADRAR.

cuadrado [coo-ah-drah-do], *m.* 1. Square, quadrate. 2. Clock, the flowers or inverted work in stockings. 3. Gusset of a shirt sleeve. 4. Die. V. TROQUEL. 5. (*Print.*) Quadrat, quad. **De cuadrado**, in front, opposite, face to face; squared.

cuadragenario, ria [coo-ah-drah-hay-nah'-reo, ah], *a.* Forty years old, of forty years.

cuadragésima [coo-ah-drah-hay'-se-mah], *f.* Lent. V. CUARESMA.

cuadragesimal [coo-ah-drah-hay-se-mahl'] *a.* 1. Quadragesimal. 2. Lenten, used in Lent.

cuadragésimo, ma [coo-ah-drah-hay'-se-mo, mah], *a.* Fortieth.

cuadral [coo-ah-drahl'], *m.* (*Arch.*) Piece of timber which crosses two others diagonally.

cuadrangular [coo-ah-dran-goo-lar'], *a.* Quadrangular,

cuadrángulo [coo-ah-drahn'-goo-lo], *m. & a.* Quadrangle, a surface with four angles.

cuadrantal [coo-ah-dran-tahl'], *a.* (*Math.*) Quadrantal.

cuadrante [coo-ah-drahn'-tay], *m.* 1. Quadrant, the fourth part of a circle. 2. Quadrant, a mathematical instrument for taking the latitude. 3. Dial plate of a sundial; dial of a clock or a watch. 4. A square board put up in churches, pointing out the order of masses to be celebrated. 5. The fourth part of an inheritance. 6. The smallest coin current in a country. **Hasta el último cuadrante**, to the last farthing.

cuadrar [cooahdrar'], *va. & vn.* 1. To square, to form into a square. 2. To square, to reduce to a square. 3. To square timbers. 4. (*Arith.*) To multiply a number by itself. 5. (*Pict.*) V. CUADRICULAR. 6. To square, to fit, to suit, to correspond. **Si le cuadra**, if it suits you. 7. To regulate, to adjust. 8. To please, to accommodate. -*vr.* 1. To square up, to square one's shoulders, to stand to attention. 2. (*fig.*) To dig one's heels in; to refuse to budge. 3. **Cuadrarse con uno**, to become very solemn towards somebody. 4. (*Carib.*) To make one's pile (enriquecerse). 5. (*Carib.*) To come out on top (tener éxito).

cuadrática [coo-ah-drah'-te-cah], *f.* Quadratic (equation); containing the square of a quantity.

cuadratín [coo-ah-drah-teen'], *m.* (*Typ.*) Quadrat (commonly abreviated to quad); quotation, piece of type metal used to fill up blanks.

cuadratura [coo-ah-drah-too,-rah], *f.* 1. Quadrature. 2. First and last quarter of the moon. 3. Pantograph, an instrument for copying designs. 4 (Watch) The dial train work; interior works of a watch.

cuadrete [coo-ah-dray'-tay], *m. dim.* A small square.

cuadricenal [coo-ah-dre-thay-nahl'], *a.* Done every forty years.

cuadrícula [coo-ah-dree'-coo-lah], *f.* A series of squares, uniform in size used by painters and sculptors to plot their studies in due proportion.

cuadricular [coo-ah-dre-coo-lar'], *va.* (*Pict.*) To copy a drawing with the pantograph; to copy by means of squares. -*a.* Ruled in squares (papel), divided into squares.

cuadrienal [coo-ah-dre-ay-nahl'], *a.* Quadrennial, comprising four years.

cuadrienio [coo-ah-dre-ay'-neo], *m.* Time and space of four years.

cuadriforme [coo-ah-dre-for'-may], *a.* Fourfaced.

cuadriga [coo-ah-dree'-gah], *f.* Carriage drawn by four horses.

cuadril [coo-ah-dreel'], *m.* Haunch-bone in beasts.

cuadrilátero, ra [coo-ah-dre-lah'-tay-ro, rah], *a.* Quadrilateral.

cuadriliteral [coo-ah-dre-le-tay-rahl'], *a.* Consisting of four letters

cuadrilongo [coo-ah-dre-lon'-go], *m.* 1. Rectangle; rightangled parallelogram. 2. Formation of a corps of infantry into an oblong form.

cuadrilongo, ga [coo-ah-dre-lon'-go, gah], *a.* Having the shape or form of a rectangle.

cuadrilla [coo-ah-dreel'-lyah], *f.* 1. Meeting of four or more persons, for some particular purpose. 2. Gang, crew, herd, troop. 3. Bullfighter's team. **Cuadrilla de demolición**, demolition squad. **Cuadrilla de noche**, night shift.

cuadrillazo [coo-ah-dreel-lah-tho], *m.* (*And. Cono Sur*) Gang attack.

cuadrillero [coo-ah-dreel-lyay'-ro], *m.* 1. Group leader; chief; gang leader. 2. The commander of an armed band.

cuadrillo [coo-ah-dreel'-lyo], *m.* 1. (*dim.*) A small square. 2. A kind of dart formerly used by the Moors.

cuadrimestre [coo-ah-dre-mes'-tray], *m.* Space of four months.

cuadringentésimo, ma [coo-ah-din-hen-tay'-se-mo, mah], *a.* One four-hundredth.

cuadrinomio [coo-ah-dre-no'-me-o], *m.* (*Alg.*) Quadrinomial.

cuadripartido [coo-ah-dre-par-tee'-do], *a.* Quadripartite, divided in four.

cuádriple [coo-ah'-dre-play], *a.* V. CUÁDRUPLE.

cuadriplicado, da [coo-ah-dre-ple-cah'-do, dah], *a.* Quadrupled.

cuadrisílabo, ba [coo-ah-dre-see'-lah-bo, bah], *a.* Quadrisyllable.

cuadrito [coo-ah-dre'-to], *m.* (*Culin. etc.*) Cube. **Cortar en cuadrito**, to dice.

cuadrivio [coo-ah-dree'-ve-o], *m.* 1. Quadrivium, place where four roads meet. 2. Anything which may be undertaken four different ways.

cuadríyugo [coo-ah-dree'-yoo-go], *m.* Cart with four horses.

cuadro, dra [coo-ah'-dro, drah], *a.* V. CUADRADO.

cuadro [coo-ah'-dro], *m.* 1. Square, figure having four equal sides and four angles. **En cuadro**, squared, in a square form. 2. Picture, painting. **Dos cuadros de Velázquez**, two Velazquez' paintings. 3. A square bed of earth in a garden. 4. Picture frame, frame of a window. 5. (*Mil.*) Square body of troops. **Formar el cuadro**, to close ranks. 6. (*Print.*) Platen, part of a printing press which makes the impression. 7. Scene, a division of an act of a play or of a poem. (*Acad.*). **Fue un cuadro desgarrador**, it was a heart-breaking scene. 8. (*Arch. Téc.*) Frame. **Cuadro de bicicleta**, bicycle frame. 9. Description, picture. **Cuadro de costumbres**, description of customs. 10. (*Elec.*) Panel. **Cuadro de conexión manual**, switchboard. **Cuadro de instrumentos**, instrument panel. 11. (*And.*) Blackboard (pizarra). 12. (*Cono Sur*) slaughterhouse (matadero). 13. Cadre, staff, establishment of officials (personas).

cuadrumano, na [coo-ah-droo-mah'-no, nah], *a.* Quadrumanous; fourhanded. -*m. pl.* The quadrumana.

cuadrupedal [coo-ah-droo-pay-dahl'], *a.* Quadrupedal, fourfooted (animales).

cuadrupedante [coo-ahdroo-paydahn'-tay], *a.* (*Poet.*) Quadrupedant.

cuadrúpede, cuadrúpedo, da [coo-ah-droo'-pay-day], *a.* Quadruped, having four feet.

cuádruple [coo-ah'-droo-play], *a.* Quadruple, composed of four parts, four-fold.

cuadruplicación [coo-ah-droo-ple-cah-the-on'], *f.* Quadruplicating.

cuadruplicado [coo-ah-droo-ple-cah'-do], *a.* Quadruplicate. **Por cuadruplicado**, in quadruplicate.

cuadruplicar [coo-ah-droo-ple-car'], *va.* To quadruplicate. -*vr.* To quadruple.

cuádruplo, pla [coo-ah'-droo-plo, plah], *a.* Quadruple, fourfold, quadripartite; **al cuádruplo**, quadruply.

cuaga [coo-ah'-gah], *m.* Quagga, a South African animal of the horse tribe.

cuaja [coo-ah'-hah], *f.* 1. The act of fructifying a tree or plant. 2. In some countries the mire collected after the sun has dried a pond.

cuajada [coo-ah-hah'-dah], *f.* Curd of the milk separated from the whey.

cuajadillo [coo-ah-hah-deel'-lyo], *m.* Sort of silk gauze with flowers.

cuajado [coo-ah-hah'-do], *m.* A dish made of meat, herbs, or fruits, with eggs and sugar, dressed in a pan. -*a.* 1. Immobile, paralyzed with astonishment. (*Acad.*) 2. Curdled, set, coagulated. 3. (*fig.*) **Cuajado de**, full of. **Un texto cuajado de problemas**, a text bristling with problems. **Una corona cuajada de joyas**, a crown covered with jewels. 4. **Estar cuajado**, To fall asleep. 5. **Quedarse cuajado**, (*fig.*) To fall asleep. -**Cuajado, da**, *pp.* of CUAJAR.

cuajaleche [coo-ah-hah-lay, chay], *f.* 1. (*Bot.*) Lady's bedstraw, yellow goosegrass, cheese rennet. 2. Cheese rennet.

cuajamiento [coo-ah-hah-meen'-to], *m.* Coagulation.

cuajar [coo-ah-har'], *m.* Rennet bag, maw or stomach of a calf or sucking animal, the crop of a fowl; the fourth stomach, abomasum, of a ruminant animal.

cuajar [coo-ah-har'], *va.* 1. To coagulate, to concrete, to curd. 2. To ornament or decorate with too many ornaments. **Cuajó el tablero de cifras**, he covered the board with figures. 3. **Cuajar con azúcar**, to ice with sugar. -*vn.* (*Coll.*) 1. To succeed, to have the desired effect. 2. To please, to like, to choose. 3. (*fig.*) To become set, to become firm, to become established; to jell, to take shape; to come off, to work. **El noviazgo no cuajó**, the engagement did not work. -*vr.* 1. To coagulate, to run into concretions, to curdle. 2. (*fig.*) **Coagularse de**, (*fig.*) To fill with, to fill up with; to become crowded with. 3. (*fig.*) To go fast asleep.

cuajarón [coo-ah-hah-rone'], *m.* Grume, clot, gore.

cuajo [coo-ah'-ho], *m.* 1. A lacteal substance found in the stomach of animals before they feed. 2. Rennet, a liquor made by steeping the stomach of a calf in hot water, and used to coagulate milk for curds and cheese. 3. Concretion, coagulation. **Tener buen cuajo**, to be too dull and patient. **Arrancar de cuajo**, to eradicate, to tear up by the roots. **Hierba del cuajo**, cheese rennet. 4. (*Mex.*) Chat; chatter. 5. (*Mex.*) Fib (mentira). 6. (*Mex.*) Pipe dream (proyecto). 7. (*Mex.*) Playtime (en escuela).

cuakerismo, or **cuaquerismo** [coo-ah-kay-rees'-mo], *m.* Quakerism.

cuákero, ra, or **cuáquero, ra** [coo-ah'-kay-ro, rah], *m. & f.* A Quaker.

cual [coo-ahl'], *pron.* 1. Which; he who. **Cada cual**, each one, everyone. V. EL QUE. **¿Cuál de los dos quiere usted?**, which of the two will you have? **¿Cuál es el que dices?**, which one are you talking about? **Ignora cuál será el resultado**, he does not know what the result will be. 2. Same, like, such. V. CUALQUIERA. 3. One, other, partly. *Cual o cual*, V. TAL CUAL. **El cual**, which. **Ése es el policía el cual me puso una multa**, that's the policeman who gave me a fine. -*adv.* As. V. COMO. **Cual el padre tal el hijo**, like father like son. **Cual llega el día tras la noche**, just as day follows night. -*int.* How then.

cualesquiera [coo-ah-les-ke-ay'-rah], *pl.* of CUALQUIERA, *q. v.*

cualidad [coo-ha-le-dahd'], *f.* Quality. V. CALIDAD. **Tiene buenas cualidades**, he has good qualities.

cualificado [coo-ah-le-fe-cah'-do], *a.* 1. Skilled, qualified. **Obrero no cualificado**, unskilled worker. 2. **Estar cualificado para**, to be entitled to.

cualitativamente [coo-ah-le-tah-te-vah-men'-tay], *adv.* Qualitatively.

cualitativo, va [coo-ah-le-tah-tee'-vo, vah], *a.* Qualitative. **Análisis cualitativo**, qualitative analysis.

cualquier [coo-al-ke-err'], *a.* Any. **Cualquier hombre de los de aquí**, any man from these parts. **En cualquier sitio donde los busques**, in whatever place you look for it. 2. **Hay cualquier cantidad**, *(LAm.)* There's a large quantity, there's any amount. 3. Any. **Ella no es una mujer cualquiera**, she's not just any woman.

cualquiera [coo-al-ke-ay'-rah], *pron..* 1. Anyone, someone, either one or the other, whichever, whoever. **Te lo diría cualquiera**, anyone would tell you the same. **Cualquiera puede hacer eso**, anybody can do that. 2. **Cualquiera que sea**, whoever he is. 3. **Es un cualquiera**, he's a nobody. 4. **Una cualquiera**, a whore.

cuan [coo-ahn'], *adv.* How, as. *V.* CUANTO.

cuando [coo-ahn'-do], *adv.* 1. When, pointing out a certain time. 2. In case that; if. 3. Though, although; even. **Incluso cuando no hubiera más razón**, even if there were no other reasons. 4. Sometimes, at times. **De cuando en cuando**, from time to time; now and then. **Cuando más** or **cuando mucho**, at most, at best. **Cuando menos**, at least. **Cuando quiera**, when you please, whenever. **¿Hasta cuándo?**, when shall I see you again? literally, until when? **Cuando no sea así**, even if it is not so. **Eso fue cuando la guerra**, that was during the war. **Cuando niño**, as a child.

cuantía [coo-an-te-ar'], *f.* 1. Quantity, amount. **De mayor cuantía**, first-rate. **De poca cuantía**, second-rate. *V.* CANTIDAD. 2. Rank, distinction. **Hombre de gran cuantía**, a man of high rank.

cuantiar [coo-an-te-ar'], *va.* To estimate or appraise possessions; to fix a price.

cuántico [coo-ahn'-te-co], *a.* **Teoría cuántica**, quantum theory.

cuantidad [coo-an-te-dahd'], *f.* Quantity; a word especially used by mathematicians. *V.* CANTIDAD.

cuantificación [coo-ahn-te-fe-cah-the-on'], *f.* Quantifying.

cuantificar [coo-ahn-te-fe-car'], *va.* To quantify.

cuantimás. *(Obs.) V.* CUANTO MÁS.

cuantiosamente [coo-ahn-te-o'-sah-men-tey], *adv.* Copiously.

cuantioso, sa [coo-an-te-o'-so, sah], *a.* Numerous, copious, rich.

cuantitativamente [coo-ahn-te-tah-te'-vah-men-tay], *adv.* Quantitatively.

cuantitativo, va [coo-an-te-tah-tee'-vo, vah], *a.* Quantitative, estimable, according to quantity. *(Chem.)* **Análisis cuantitativo**, quantitative analysis.

cuanto, ta [coo-ahn'-to, tah], *a.* 1. Containing quantity or relating to it, susceptible of quantity. **Daremos cuantos créditos se precisen**, we will give all the credits that may be necessary. **Unos cuantos libros**, a few books. 2. **¿Cuánto?** how much? **¿Cuánto has gastado?**, how much have you spent? **¿Cuánto durará esto?**, how long will this last? **¿Cuántos?**, how many? 3. As many as, as much as, the more; correlative of *tanto*. **Cuanto uno es más pobre, se le debe socorrer más**, the poorer a person is the more should he be supported. **Cuanto usted quiera**, as much as you like. 4. All, whatever. 5. Excessive, great in some way. (Note. *-Cuanto*, signifying "how much." receives an accent, thus: **cuánto. ¡Cuánta sabiduría!**, how much wisdom! *-adv.* Respecting, whilst. **Cuanto antes**, immediately, as soon as possible. **Cuanto más**, moreover, the more as. **En cuanto a**, with regard to, as to, in the meantime. **Cuanto quiera**, although. **Por cuanto**, inasmuch as. **En cuanto lo supe me fui**, as soon as I heard it I left. **Cuanto más difícil parezca**, the more difficult it may seem.

cuaquerismo [coo-ah-kay-res'-mo], *m.* Quakerism.

cuáquero, ra [cooah'kayro, rah], *m. & f. & a.* Quaker.

cuarango [coo-ah-rahn'-go], *m.* The vulgar name of the *Cinchona* or Peruvian bark tree.

cuarenta [coo-ah-ren'-tah], *a. & m.* Forty. **Cantar a uno las cuarenta**, to tell someone a few home truths.

cuarentañera [coo-ah-ren-tay'-nyah], *f.* Woman of about forty.

cuarentañero [coo-ah-ren-tay'-nyah], *m.* Man of about forty.

cuarentavo, va [coo-ah-ren-tah'-vo, vah], *a.* Fortieth.

cuarentena [coo-ah-ren-tay'-nah], *f.* 1. Space of forty days, months, or years; the fortieth part. 2. Lent, the forty days of fast prescribed by the Church. 3. *(Met.)* Suspension of assent to anything. 4. The number 40 in general. 5. *(Naut.)* Quarantine, the time when a ship, suspected of infection, is obliged to abstain from intercourse with the inhabitants of a country. **Hacer cuarentena**, *(Naut.)* To perform quarantine.

cuarentón, na [coo-ah-ren-tone', nah], *a. & m & f.* Person forty years old.

cuaresma [coo-ah-res'-mah], *f.* 1. Lent, the forty days' fast prescribed by the Church. 2. Collection of Lent sermons.'

cuaresmal [coo-ah-res-mahl'], *a.* Lenten.

cuarta [coo-ar'-tah], *f.* 1. Fourth, fourth part; a quarter. 2. Quadrant, fourth part of a circle. 3. *(Naut.)* Quarter point of the compass. 4. Sequence of four cards in the game of piquet. 6. *(Fen.)* Quart, or carte. 7. Palm, a handbreadth. 8. Quart, a liquid measure. 9. *(Mil.)* Quarter of a company of soldiers. 10. *(Mus.)* A fourth. 11. A piece of timber square in section. 12. *(Prov.)* A guide mule. 13. *(Hex.)* A sort of whip. 14. *(Cono Sur)* Extra pair of oxen. 15. **Andar de la cuarta al pértigo**, *(Conso Sur)*, **vivir a la cuarta**, *(Conso Sur. Mex.)* to be on the bread line.

cuartago [coo-ar-tah'-go], *m.* Nag, pony, hack.

cuartal [coo-ar-tahl'], *m.* 1. Kind of bread weighing the fourth part of a loaf. 2. Quarter, dry measure, fourth part of a fanega.

cuartán [coo-ar-tahn'], *m. (Prov.)* A grain measure, equal to 18 litres and 8 centilitres.

cuartanal [coo-ar-tah-nahl'], *a.* Intermittent.

cuartanario, ria [coo-ar-tah-nah'-reo, ah], *a.* Laboring under a quartan.

cuartar [coo-ar-tar'], *va.* To plough the ground the fourth time.

cuartazo [coo-ar-tah'-tho], *m. aug.* A large room; a large quarter. **Cuartazos**, a coarse, corpulent person; a stroke with a whip.

cuartear [coo-ar-tay-ar'], *va.* 1. To quarter, to divide into four parts. 2. To bid a fourth more at public sales. 3. To make a fourth person at a game. 4. To zigzag up steep places. 5. *(Naut.)* **Cuartear la aguja**, to box the compass. 6. *(Carib. Mex.)* To whip, to beat (azotar). *-vn.* 1. To make a fourth (naipes). 2. *(Taur.)* To dodge, to step aside. *vr.* 1. To split into pieces. 2. *(Taur.)* To dodge, to step aside. 3. *(Mex.)* To go back to one's word.

cuartel [coo-ar-tell'], *m.* 1. Quarter, the fourth part of a garden or other thing. 2. Quarter, district, ward of a city. 3. Quarter, the place where soldiers are lodged and stationed. 4. Dwelling, habitation, home. 5. Quarter, remission of life granted by hostile troops. 6. *V.* CUARTETO. 7. *(Naut.)* Hatch, the lid of a hatchway. **Cuartel de la salud**, a safe place free from hazard and danger. **Cuartel de bomberos**, fire station. **Estar de cuartel**, to be on half-pay. **Guerra sin cuartel**, war without mercy. **Dar cuartel, a**, to support, to encourage.

cuartelada, cuartelazo [coo-ar-tay-lah'-dah], *f. m.* Military uprising, mutiny, coup.

cuartelar [coo-ar-tay-lar'], *va. (Her.)* To quarter.

cuartelero [coo-ar-tay-lay'-ro], *m. (Mil.)* Soldier in each company appointed to keep the apartments clean.

cuartera [coo-ar-tay'-rah], *f.* A dry measure in Catalonia, containing about fifteen pecks.

cuartería [coo-ar-tay-re'-ah], *f. (Carib. Cono Sur)* Bunkhouse (en un rancho).

cuartero, ra [coo-ar-tay'-ro, rah], *a. (Prov.)* Applied to those who collect the rents of the grain of farms, which pay the fourth part to the landlords.

cuarterola [coo-ar-tay-ro'-lah], *f.* Quarter cask of liquors or fluids.

cuarterón [coo-ar-tay-rone'], *m.* 1. Quartern, quarter, the fourth part of a whole; quarter of a pound. 2. Upper part of windows which may be opened and shut. **Cuarterones**, squares of wainscot in a door or window shutter. 3. *(LAm.)* Quadroon.

cuarterón, na, [coo-ar-tay-rone' *a.* *(Amer.)* Applied to a child begotten of a creole and a native of Spain; quadroon.

cuarteta [coo-ar-tay'-tah], *f.* *(Poet.)* Quatrain, a metrical composition of four lines.

cuartete, cuarteto [coo-ar-tay'-tay, coo-ar-tay-to], *m.* 1. *(Poet.)* Quatrain, a stanza of four verses. 2. *(Mus.)* Quartet.

cuartilla [coo-ar-teel'-lyah], *f.* 1. Fourth part of an *arroba*, or sixteenth part of a quintal. 2. Fourth part of a sheet of paper. 3. Pastern of horses.

cuartillo [coo-ar-teel'lyo], *m.* 1. Pint, the fourth part of a bottle in liquids. 2. The fourth part of a peck in grain. 3. Fourth part of a real. **Ir de cuartillo**, to share the profits or losses in any business.

cuartilludo, da [coo-ar-teel-lyoo'-do, dah], *a.* Applied to a horse with long pasterns.

cuartito [coo-ar-tee'-to], *m. dim.* A small room.

cuarto [coo-ar'-to], *m.* 1. Fourth part, quadrant, quarter. **Cuarto creciente**, first quarter. **Tardó tres cuartos de hora**, he took three-quarters of an hour. 2. Habitation, dwelling, room, apartment. **Cuarto de baño**, bathroom. **Cuarto de juego**, playroom. **Cuarto de los niños**, nursery. *V.* APOSENTO; **cuarto bajo**, room on the ground floor. 3. Copper coin worth four *maravedís*. 4. Series of paternal or maternal ancestors. 5. Crack in horses' hoofs. 6. Quarter of clothes, quarter of animals or of criminals whose body is quartered and exposed in public places. **De tres al cuarto**, of little moment. **Poner cuarto**, to take lodgings; to furnish apartments. **Cuarto principal**, first floor. **No tener un cuarto**, not to be worth a cent; **cuartos**, 1. Cash, money. 2. Well proportioned members of an animal's body. **Por 5 cuartos**, for a song. **Estar sin un cuarto**, to be broke.

cuarto, ta [coo-ar'-to, tah], *a.* Fourth, the ordinal of four.

cuartogénito, ta [coo-ar-to-hay'-ne-to, tah], *a.* The fourth born child.

cuartón [coo-ar-tone'], *m.* 1. Quarter, a large joist or girder, a beam sixteen feet long. 2. *(Prov.)* Measure of wine and vinegar.

cuartucho [coo-ar-too'-cho], *m.* Hovel; poky little room.

cuarzo [coo-ar'-tho], *m.* Quartz, a crystallized silicious stone. **Cuarzo citrino**, occidental topaz.

cuarzoso, sa [coo-ar-tho'-so, sah], *a.* Quartzose.

cuás [coo-ahs'], *m, (Mex.)* Bosom pal.

cuásar [coo-ah'-sahr], *m.* Quasar.

cuasi [coo-ah'-se], *adv.* Almost. *V.* CASI and COMO.

cuasicontrato [coo-ah-se-con-trah'-to], *m.* *(Law.)* Quasi-contract; a contract though not formal, yet effectual. *Cuasidelito, (Law.)* Quasi-crime or delict.

cuasimodo [coo-ah-semo'-do], *m.* First Sunday after Easter.

cuate [coo-ah'tay], *m.* *(Mex.)* V. GEMELO. **Eso no tiene cuate,** *(Coll.)* that has no match.

cuaterna [coo-ah-terr'-nah], *f.* 1. Union of four things. 2. *V.* CUADERNA. 3. Lesson for four.

cuaternario, ria [coo-ah-ter-nah'-re-o, ah], *a.* Quaternary.

cuaternidad [coo-ah-tar-ne-dahd'], *f.* Quaternity, quaternary.

cuaternión [coo-ah-ter-ne-on'], *m.* Union of four things, of four sheets in printing.

cuatralbo [coo-ah-trahl'-bo], *a.* Having four white feet (animales). *m.* Commander of four galleys.

cuatre(re)ar [coo-ah-tray-ar'], *va.* *(Cono Sur)* To rustle (ganado), to steal. *-vn.* *(Cono Sur)* To act treacherously.

cuatrero [coo-ah-tray'-ro], *m.* Thief who steals horses, sheep, or other beasts. *-a.* Trecherous, disloyal.

cuatridial, cuatridiano [coo-ah-tre-de-ahl'], *a.* Lasting four days.

cuatrienal [coo-ah-tre-ah-nahl'], *a.* Four-year.

cuatrienio [coo-ah-tre-ay'-ne-o], *m.* V. CUADRIENIO.

cuatrillizos, zas [coo-ah-trel-lye'-thos], *m, f.* & *pl.* Quadruplets.

cuatrimestre [coo-ah-tre-mes'-tray], *a.* Lasting four months. *-m.* The space of four months.

cuatrimotor [coo-ah-tre-mo-tor'], *a.* Four-engined. *-m.* Fourengined plane.

cuatrinca [coo-ah-treen'-cah], *f.* 1. Union of four persons or things. 2. Four cards of the same print in the game of *báciga*.

cuatrisílabo, ba, [coo-ah-tre-se'-lah-bo], *a.* *V.* CUADRISÍLABO.

cuatro [coo-ah'tro], *a.* 1. Four, twice two. 2. *V.* CUARTO. **Más de cuatro,** *(fig.)* quite a few. **Sólo había cuatro muebles**, there were only a few pieces of furniture. **Cayeron cuatro gotas**, a few drops fell.

cuatro, *m.* 1. Character or figure 4. 2. One who votes for four absent persons. 3. Musical composition sung by four voices. 4. Card with four marks. 5. *f.* Four o'clock. **Más de cuatro**, a great number of persons.

cuatrocientos, tas [coo-ah-tro-theen'-tos, tas], *a.* Four hundred.

cuatrodial [coo-ah-tro-de-ahl'], *a.* That which is of four days

cuatrodoblar [coo-ah-tro-do-blar'], *va.* To quadruple.

cuatropear [coo-ah-tro-pay-ar'], *vn.* To run on all fours.

cuba [coo'-bah], *f.* 1. Cask for wine or oil. 2. *(Met.)* Toper, drunkard. **Estar hecho una cuba**, to be as drunk as a skunk. 3. Tub. **Cuba para el agua de lluvia**, rainwater butt.

Cuba [coo'-bah], *f.* Cuba.

cubaje [coo-bah'-hay], *m.* *(LAm.)* Volume, contents.

cuba-libre [coo'-bah le'-bray], *m. pl.* **cubas-libres**, drink of rum and Coca Cola.

cubanismo [coo-bah-nes'-mo], *m.* Cubanism, word peculiar to Cuba.

cubano, na [coo-bah'-no, nah], *a.* Cuban.

cubar [coo-bar'], *va.* To cube, to raise to the third power.

cubata [coo-bah-tah], *m.* V. CUBA LIBRE.

cubaza [coo-bah'-thah], *f. aug.* A large pipe, a hogshead.

cubeba [coo-bay'-bah], *f.* *(Bot.)* Cubeb or cubebs, the berries of the Piper.

cubero [coo-bay'-ro], *m.* A cooper.

cubertería [coo-ber-tay-re'-ah], *f.* Cutlery.

cubertura [coo-ber-too'-rah], *f.* Cover, Covering. *V.* COBERTURA.

cubeta [coo-bay'-tah], *f.* 1. A small barrel or cask. 2. Tub, pail. 3. Back, vat of brewers. 4. Beck, or trough of dyers. **Cubeta** or **bidón donde se come**, *(Naut.)* mess bucket. **Cubeta para alquitrán**, *(Naut.)* tar bucket.

cubetilla, ita [coo-bay-teel'-lyah], *f. dim.* A small bucket.

cubeto [coo-bay'-to], *m.* A small barrel.

cúbica [coo'-be-cah], *f.* A woollen stuff finer than serge.

cubicación [coo-be-cah-the-on'], *f.* 1. Measurement of edifices. 2. Act of cubing.

cubicaje [coo-be-cah'-hay], *m.* *(Aut.)* Cylinder capacity.

cúbicamente [coo'-be-cah-men-tay], *adv.* Cubically.

cubicar [coo-be-car'], *va.* 1. To cube, to raise to the third power. 2. To determine the volume of.

cubichete [coo-be-chay'-tay], *m.* *(Naut.)* Waterboards or weatherboards, on the upper part of a ship's side, to keep off a rough sea.

cúbico, ca [coo'-be-co, ca], *a.* Cubical, cubic, cubiform.

cubiculario [coo-be-coo-lah'-re-o], *m.* Groom of the bedchamber, valet-de-chambre.

cubículo [coo-be'-coo-lo], *m.* Cubicle.

cubierta [coo-be-err'-tah], *f.* 1. Cover, covering, covert. **Cubierta de cama**, coverlet. **Cubierta de lona**, tarpaulin, canvas. **Cubierta flexible o de plástico corrugado** *(Inform.)*, flexible or rugged plastic-coated cover. 2. *(Met.)* Pretext or pretence. 3. *(Naut.)* Deck of a ship. **Cubierta primera** or **principal**, the lower or gundeck. **Segunda cubierta**, the middle deck. **Cubierta arqueada**, a cambering deck.

Cubierta de vuelo, flight deck. **Cubierta de paseo**, promenade deck. 4. Cover of a letter, envelope. 5. Casing, coat, facing: roofing. 6. Hood of a carriage.

cubiertamente [coo-be-ayr-tah-men'-tay], *adv.* Privately, secretly.

cubierto [coo-be-err'-to], *m.* 1. Cover, part of a table service, consisting of a plate, fork, spoon, knife, and napkin, for every one who sits down to table. **Cubiertos**, cutlery. 2. Roof of a house, or any other covering from the inclemency of the weather; covert, coverture, cover. 3. Allowance of a soldier billeted in a house. 4. Course, a number of dishes set at once on a table. 5. A metal at a fixed price. **Cubiertos de 80 pesos**, 80-peso meal. *(Acad.)* **Ponerse a cubierto**, to shelter oneself from an apprehended danger. *-pp. irr.* of CUBRIR; 1. Covered; overcast. 2. **La vacante está ya cubierta**, the place has already been filled.

cubil [coo-beel'], *m.* 1. Lair or couch of wild beasts. 2. *(Prov.)* Hogsty.

cubilar [coo-be-lar'], *vn.* To take shelter. *V.* MAJADEAR.

cubilete [coo-be-lay'-tay], *m.* 1. A copper pan for baking pies and other pastry, and the pie or pastry made on it; used also by jugglers. 2. *(Ant.)* Tumbler, goblet, a drinking-cup. 3. A cup made of a medicinal wood, such as quassia. 4. Cup (en juegos); dice box (de dados). 5. *(LAm.)* Intrigue. 6. *(LAm.)* Top hat (chistera); bowler hat (hongo).

cubiletear [coo-be-lay-tay-ar'], *vn.* 1. To shake the dice box. 2. *(fig.)* To intrigue, to scheme.

cubiletero [coo-be-lay-tay'-ro], *m.* 1. Pastemould. 2. A large mug. *-m. & f.* Conjurer.

cubilote [coo-be-lo'-tay], *m.* Cupola smelting furnace, smelting-pot.

cubillo [coo-beel'-lyo], *m.* 1. Spanish-fly, blister-beetle. 2. A piece of table-service for keeping water cool. 3. A small box near the stage. 4. *(Naut.)* A socket for the flagpole. **Cubillos**, the ladles or receptacles of a millwheel.

cubismo [coo-bees'-mo], *m.* Cubism.

cubista [coo-bes'-tah], *a.* Cubist. *-m. & f.* Cubist.

cubital [coo-be-tahl'], *a.* Cubital, the length of a cubit.

cúbito [coo'-be-to], *m. (Anat.)* Ulna, the largest bone of the forearm.

cubito [coo-be'-to], *m.* 1. Bucket, beach pail (de niño). 2. **Cubito de hielo**, ice cube.

cubo [coo'-bo], *m.* 1. Cube, a solid body of six equal sides. 2. A wooden pail with an iron handle, bucket. **Cubo de la basura**, trash can. 3. Millpond. 4. Barrel of a watch or clock. 5. *(Mil.)* A small tower formerly raised on old walls. 6. Cube, product of the multiplication of a square number by its root. 7. Nave or hub of a wheel. 8. Bayonet socket. 9. Among masons, a hodful of mixed mortar. 10. *(Com.)* Tongue way, socket, shaft-case.

cuboide [coo-bo'-e-day], *m.* 1. Cuboid bone of the tarsus. 2. Rhomboid, little differing from a cube.

cubreasientos [coo-bray-ah-se-en'-tose], *m.* Seatcover.

cubrebocas [coo-bray-bo'-cas], *m. (Med.)* Mask.

cubrecama [coo-bray-cah'-mah], *f.* Bedspread, coverlet.

cubrellanta [coo-bray-lyahn'-tah], *m.* Tire covering, tire casing.

cubremesa [coo-bray-may'-sah], *f. (LAm.)* Table cover.

cubreobjetos [coo-bray-ob-hay'-tos], *m*

cubrepán [coo-bray-pahn'], *m.* Sort of fire-shovel, used by shepherds.

cubriente [coo-bre-en'-tay], *pa.* Covering, hiding.

cubrimiento [coo-bre-me-en'-to], *m.* 1. Covering, act of covering. 2. Roofing.

cubrir [coo-breer'], *va.* 1. To cover, to lay, to spread one thing over another. **Lo cubrieron las aguas**, the waters closed over it. **El agua casi me cubría**, the water almost covered me. 2. To face, or cover with additional superficies. 3. *(Met.)* To cover, to screen, to consent, to palliate. **Cubrir a uno de improperios**, to shower insults on somebody. **Cubrir a uno de atenciones**, to overwhelm somebody

with kindness. 4. To cover, to disguise, to dissemble, to cloak. **Cubre su tristeza con una falsa alegría**, she covers up her sadness with a false cheerfulness. 5. To cover or protect a post, to prevent its being attacked by the enemy. **Cubrir su retirada**, to cover one's retreat. 6. To roof a building. 7. To cover, to copulate; to fecundate (animales, plantas). 8. **Cubrir la mesa**, to lay the table. **Cubrir la cuenta**, to balance an account. 9. To cover, to travel. *-vr.* 1. To take measures to insure oneself against loss. **Cubrirse contra un riesgo**, to cover oneself against a risk. 2. To put a place in a state of defence. 3. To be covered, to put on one's hat. 4. To become overcast.

cuca [coo'-cah], *f.* 1. A kind of root-tubercle of a sedge, used in place of coffee. *V.* CHUFA. 2. A Peruvian plant. *V.* COCA. 3. Sort of caterpillar. *V.* Cuco. 4. **Cuca y matacán**, sort of card game. **Mala cuca**, *(Coll.)* A wicked person. **Cuca de aquí**, *(Coll.)* Begone! 5. Sweets. 6. *(CAm.)* Cunt (vagina).

cucambé [coo-cam'-bay], *m. (And.)* Hide-and-seek.

cucamonas [coo-ca-mo'-nas], *f. pl.* Sweet nothings (palabras); caresses (caricias); fondling (magreo). **Ella me hizo cucamonas**, she gave me a come-hither look. *(Coll.)* *V.* CARANTOñAS.

cucaña [coo-cah'-nyah], *f.* 1. A public amusement, climbing a greased pole. 2. Anything acquired with little trouble, and at other people's expense. 3. Soft job; bargain; easy thing.

cucañero, ra [coo-ca-nyay'-ro], *m. & f.* Parasite, one who lives at other people's expense.

cucar [coo-car'], *va.* 1. To wink. 2. To deride, to mock. 3. *(LAm.)* To urge on, to incite.

cucaracha [coo-ca-rah'-chah], *f.* 1. Cockroach. 2. Hazelcolored snuff. 3. Scare-crow. 4. *(Mex.) (Aut.)* Old crock. *-m.* Priest.

cucarachera [coo-ca-rah-chay'-rah], *f. (Vulg.)* Luck, good fortune. **Hallarse buena cucarachera**, to be lucky or fortunate.

cucarachero [coo-ca-rah-chay'-ro], *m. (And. Carib.)* Parasite, hanger-on; *(And.)* Flatterer, creep (adulador).

cuceranita [coo-thay-rah-nee'-tah], *f. (Min.)* A certain silicate of aluminium.

cuchar [coo-char'], *f.* 1. Tax or duty on grain. 2. *(Prov.)* Spoon. 3. Ancient corn measure, the twelfth part of a *celemín* or peck. **Cuchar herrera**, iron spoon.

cuchara [coo-chah'-rah], *f.* 1. Spoon. **Cuchara de café**, coffee spoon. **Cuchara de sopa**, soup spoon. **Despacharse con la cuchara grande**, *(LAm.)*, to give oneself a big helping. 2. An iron ladle, for taking water out of a large earthen jar. 3. *(Mas.)* A trowel. **Cuchara para brea**, *(Naut.)* pitchladle. **Cuchara para sacar el agua de los barcos**, *(Naut.)* scoop for baling boats. **Cucharas**, ladleboards of a waterwheel in an overshot mill. 4. *(LAm.)* Flat trowel. **Albañil de cuchara**, skilled bricklayer. 5. *(CAm. Carib, Cono Sur)* Pout. **Hacer cuchara**, to pout. 6. *(Mex.)* Pickpoket (carterista). **cucharada** [coo-chah-rah'-dah], *f.* Spoonful, ladleful. **Meter su cucharada**, to meddle in other people's conversation, to have a linger in the pie.

cucharadita [coo-chah-rah-dee'-tah], *f.* Teaspoonful.

cucharal [coo-chah-rahl], *m.* Bag in which shepherds preserve their spoons.

cucharazo [coo-chah-rah'-tho], *m.* Stroke or blow with a spoon.

cucharear [coo-chah-ray-ar'], *va. (Culin.)* To spoon out, to ladle out; *(Agri.)* To pitch.

cuchareta [coo-chah-ray'-tah], *f. dim.* 1. A small spoon. 2. A variety of wheat. 3. Inflammation of the liver in sheep. *(Acad.)*

cucharetear [coo-chah-ray-tay-ar'], *vn. (Coll.)* 1. To stir with a spoon. 2. *(Met.)* To busy oneself with other people's affairs.

cucharetero [coo-chah-ray-tay'-ro], *m.* 1. Maker or retailer of wooden spoons. 2. List or linen, nailed to a board, with small intersices to hold spoons. 3. Fringe sewed to under petticoats.

cucharilla [coo-chah-reel'-lyah], *f.* 1. Liver disease in swine. *(Acad.)* 2. *(Surg.)* A scoop. 3. Small spoon, teaspoon.

cucharita [coo-chah-ree'-tah], *f.* Tea-spoon.

cucharón [coo-chah-rone'], *m.* 1. Ladle for the kitchen, a soup-spoon for the table. 2. *(aug.)* A large spoon, dipper; scoop, bucket. **Tener el cucharón por el mango**, to be the boss.

cucharro [coo-char'-ro], *m.* 1. *(Naut.)* Harping. **Tablones de cucharros**, *(Naut.)* serving-planks. 2. *(Agri.)* A vessel made from a gourd used for watering plants by hand.

cuche [coo'-chay], *m.* *(CAm.)* Pig.

cuchichear [coo-che-chay-ar'], *vn.* To whisper.

cuchicheo [coo-che-chay'o], *m.* Whisper, whispering.

cuchichero, ra [coo-che-chay'-ro', rah], *m. & f. (Coll.)* Whisperer.

cuchichiar [coo-che-che-ar'], *vn.* 1. To call like a partridge. 2. To whisper.

cuchilla [coo-cheel'-lyah], *f.* 1. A large kitchen-knife; a chopping-knife. 2. Sort of ancient poniard. 3. *(Poet.)* Sword. **Cuchilla de afeitar**, razor blade. 4. *(Geog.)* Ridge, crest; *(LAm.)* Line of low hills; *(Carib.)* Mountain top.

cuchillada [coo-cheel-lyah'-dah], *f.* 1. Cut or clash with a knife or other cutting instrument. 2. Gash, a deep wound. 3. Slash, a cut in cloth, formerly made to let the lining open to view: it was commonly used in the plural. 4. *-pl.* Wrangles, quarrels. 5. Galley-stick, sidestick. 6. Truss, girder.

cuchillar [coo-cheel-lyar'], *a.* Belonging or relating to a knife.

cuchillazo [coo-chel-lah-tho], *m. (LAm.)* V. CUCHILLADA.

cuchillejo [coo-cheel-lyay'-ho], *m.* 1. *(dim.)* A small knife; a paring-knife (herreros). 2. *(Bot.)* Cockleweed.

cuchillera [coo-cheel-lyay'-rah], *f.* Knife-case or scabbard.

cuchillería [coo-cheel-lyayree'-ah], *f.* Cutler's shop, and the place or street where there are many cutlers' shops; cutlery.

cuchillero [coo-cheel-lyay'-ro], *m.* Cutler. *-a.(LAm.)* Quarrelsome.

cuchillo [coo-cheel'-lyo], *m.* 1. Knife of one blade, with a handle. 2. Gore, a triangular piece of cloth sewed into a garment. 3. *(Met.)* Right of governing and putting the laws in execution. 4. A beam, girder. 5. *(Naut.)* Every plank cut on the bevel. 6. A cut, crevice, fissure. 7. Every triangular sail, leg-of-mutton sail. 8. *(Arch.)* Upright, support. 9. Fang, tusk (de jabalí etc.). **Cuchillo de monte**, a hunter's cutlass. **Pasar a cuchillo**, to put to the sword. **Cuchillo de hoja automática**, switch-blade. **Cuchillo de postres**, fruit knife. **Cuchillo mantequillero**, butter knife.

cuchillón [coo-cheel-lyone'], *m. aug.* A large or big knife.

cuchipanda [coo-che-pahn'-dah], *f.* A cheerful dinner shared by several persons.

cuchitril [coo-chee-treel'], *m.* A narrow hole or corner; a very small room; a hut.

cucho [coo'-cho], *m.* 1. *(CAm.)*, hunchback; *(Mex.)* limbless (manco). 2. *(Cono Sur)* Puss. 3. *(And.)* V. CUCHILTRIL.

cuchuche [coo-choo'-chay], *m.* **Ir de cuchuche**, *(CAm.)* To ride piggyback.

cuchuchear [coo-choo-chay-ar'], *vn. (Coll.)* 1. To whisper, to speak with a low voice. 2. *(Met.)* To carry tales.

cuchufleta [coo-choo-flay'-tah], *f.* 1. Joke, jest, fun. 2. *(Mex.)* Trinket (baratija).

cuchuflí [coo-choo-fle'], *m. (Carib.)* Uncomfortable place; cell.

cuchugos [coo-choo'-cho], *m. & pl. (And. Carib.)* Saddlebags.

cuchumbo [coo-choom'-co], *m. (CAm.)* Funnel (embudo); bucket, pail; dice box (de dados); game of dice.

cucioso, sa [coo-the-oh'-so, sah], *a.* Diligent. V. SOLÍCITO.

cucita [coo-thee'-tah], *f.* Lapdog.

cuclear [coo-clay-ar'], *m.* To sing like the cuckoo.

cuclillas (En) [coo-cleel'-lyas], *adv.* In a cowering manner. **Sentarse en cuclillas**, to squat, to sit cowering, to sit close to the ground.

cuclillo [coo-cleel'-lyo], *m.* 1. *(Orn.)* Cuckoo. 2. *(Met.)* Cuckold.

cuco [coo'-co], *m.* 1. Sort of caterpillar. 2. Person of a swarthy complexion. 3. Sort of game at cards. 4. Cuckoo. 5. A gambler. **Reloj de cuco**, cuckoo clock. 6. *(Mex.)* **Hacer cuco a uno**, to poke fun at somebody. 7. *(And. Cono Sur)* bogeyman (fantasma).

cuco, ca [coo'-co, cah], *a. (Coll.)* Cunning, crafty, astute, shrewd.

cucú [coo-coo'], *m.* Word imitative of the cuckoo's note.

cucuche [coo-coo'-chay], *(CAm.)* **Ir de cucuche**, to ride astride.

cucufato [coo-coo-fah'-to], *m. (And. Cono Sur)* Hypocrite; prude (mojigato); nut (loco).

cucuiza [coo-coo-ee'-thah], *f. (Amer.)* Thread of the agave.

cuculí [coo-coo-le'], *m. (And. Cono Sur)* Wood pigeon.

cuculla [coo-cool'-lyah], *f.* Cowl, a kind of hood formerly worn by men and women.

cucuma [coo-coo'-mah], *f.* Kind of bread made in Colombia from a root like yucca.

cucumeráceo, cea [coo-coo-may-rah'-thay-o, ah], *a.* Cucumberlike.

cucúrbita [coo-coor'-be-tah], *f.* 1. A retort, for distilling. 2. Scientific name of the gourd.

cucurbitáceo, cea [coo-coor-be-tah'-thay-o, ah], *a. (Bot.)* Cucurbitaceous.

cucurucho [coo-coo-roo'-cho], *m.* 1. A paper cone, used by grocers; cornucopia. 2. *(Ecl.)* Hooded garment; pointed hat. 3. *(And. CAm. Carib.)* Top, summit, apex. 4. *(Carib.)* Hovel, shack (cuchitril).

cudria [coo'-dre-ah], *f.* A flat woven bassrope.

cueca [coo-ay'-cah], *f. (Cono Sur)* Handkerchief dance.

cuelga [coo-el'-gah], *f.* 1. Cluster of granes or other fruit hung up for use. **Cuelga** or **ristra de cebollas**, bunch of onions. 2. A birthday present. 3. *(And. Cono Sur) (Geog.)* Fall.

cuelgacapas [coo-el-gah-cah'-pas], *m.* A cloak-hanger. *(Yo cuelgo, yo cuelgue*, from *Colgar.* V. ACORDAR.)

cuelgue [coo-ayl'-gay], *m.* **Llevar un cuelgue**, to be broke; to be all at sea (confuso); to need a fix (drogas).

cuelmo [coo-el'-mo], *m.* Candlewood, a piece of pine, or other seasoned wood, which burns like a torch. V. TEA.

cuellicorto, ta [coo-el-lye-cor'-to, tah], *a.* Shortnecked.

cuellierguido, da [coo-el-lyee-er-gee'-do, dah], *a.* 1. Stiffnecked. 2. Elated with pride.

cuellilargo, ga [coo-el-lyee-lar'-go, gah], *a.* Longnecked.

cuello [coo-el'-lyo], *m.* 1. The neck. **Cuello de botella**, *(fig.)* Bottleneck. 2. *(Met.)* Neck of a vessel, the narrow part near its mouth. 3. Collar of a priest's garment. 4. Small end of a waxcandle. 5. A large plaited neckcloth, formerly worn. 6. Collar-band of a cloak, coat, shirt, etc. **Cuello alto**, high collar. **De cuello blanco**, white-collar. 7. Collar of a beam in oilmills. **Levantar el cuello**, *(Met.)* to be in a state of prosperity.

cuenca [coo-on'-cah], *f.* 1. A wooden bowl. 2. Socket of the eye. 3. The basin of a river. 4. Deep valley surrounded by mountains.

cuenco [coo-en'-co], *m.* 1. An earthen bowl. 2. *(Prov.)* Hod.

cuenda [coo-en'-dah], *f.* 1. End of packthread, which divides and keeps together a skein of silk or thread. 2. End of a skein of silk or thread.

cuenta [coo-en'-tah], *f.* 1. Computation, calculation. 2. Account, count, reckoning. 3. Account, narrative. 4. Obligation, care, duty. 5. One of the beads of a rosary. 6. Answerableness; reason, satisfaction. 7. Consideration, merit, importance. *(interj.)* **¡Cuenta!** take care! **Cuenta corriente**, *(Com.)* Current account; *(Com.)* **Cuenta de venta**, account sales. **A buena cuenta** or **a cuenta**, on account, in part payment. **A esa cuenta**, at that rate. **Dar cuenta de su persona**, to answer, or give a justificatory account of what has been intrusted to any one. **Dar cuenta**, to answer, to give account. **Dar cuenta de algo**, *(Coll.)* to waste or destroy something. **Estar fuera de cuenta**, to have completed the full term of pregnancy. **Tomar en cuenta**, to take into account. **Tomar por su cuenta**, to take care of. **En resumidas cuentas**, in short. **Perder la cuenta**, to lose track (count). **Cuenta de la vieja**, counting on one's fingers. **Contar al revés**, countdown. **Cuenta de ahorros**, savings account. **Abrir una cuenta**, to open an account. **La cuenta del sastre**, the tailor's bill. **Cuenta de gastos**, expense account. **Echar las cuentas**, to reckon up. **Llevar la cuenta de**, to keep an account of. **Vivir a cuenta de**, to live at the expense of. **Ajustar cuentas**, to settle up. **Tener cuentas pendientes con uno**, to have a matter to settle with somebody. **Rendir cuentas de uno**, to report to somebody. **De cuenta y riesgo de uno**, at one's own risk. **Por mi cuenta**, in my opinion. **No querer cuentas con uno**, to want nothing to do with somebody. **No tiene cuenta**, there is no point in. **Por la cuenta que le tiene**, because it is to his benefit.

cuenta correntista [coo-ayn-tah-cor-ren-tes'-tah], *m. & f.* Depositor.

cuenta corriente [coo-en'-tah cor-reen'-tay], *f.* 1. Charge account. 2. Checking account.

cuentagotas [coo-en-tah-go'-tahs], *m.* Dropper, medicine dropper.

cuentahilos [coo-en-tah-ee'-los], *m.* Thread counter, a kind of microscope for counting the threads in a fabric.

cuenta inversa [coo-en-tah in-ver'-sah], *f. (Aer.)* Countdown.

cuentakilómetros [coo-en-tah-ke-lo'-may-tros], *m.* A milometer; speedmeter.

cuentapasos [coo-en-tah-pah'-sos], *m.* Odometer, an instrument for measuring distances.

cuentarrevoluciones [co-en-tahr-re-vo-loo-the-o-nays], *m.* Tachometer.

cuentear [coo-en-tay-ar'], *va. (And.)* To court (pretender); to compliment. *-vn. (CAm.)* To gossip.

cuenterete [coo-en-tay-ray'-tay], *m. (CAm.)* Piece of gossip; tall story, tale.

cuentero, ra, [coo-en-tay'-ro], *m. & f. & a. V.* CUENTISTA.

cuentista [coo-en-tees'-tah], *m.* Tale-bearer, informer, misrepresenter.

cuento [coo-en'-to], *m.* 1. Relation of an event, tale, story. 2. Fable, fictitious story for children. **Cuento de viejas**, old women's stories, idle story. 3. Variance, disagreement between friends. **Andar en cuentos**, to be at loggerheads; to carry tales, to breed quarrels. 4. Articulation of the wing. 5. Account, number. **A cuento**, to the purpose, seasonably, opportunely. **Ése es el cuento**, there is the rub, that is the difficulty. **Dejarse de cuentos**, or **quitarse de cuentos**, to come to the point. **En cuento de**, in place of, instead of. **Poner en cuentos**, to expose, to risk. **Ser mucho cuento**, to be excessive, exaggerated. **Cuento de hadas**, fairy tale. **Es un cuento largo**, it's a long story. **Eso no viene a cuento**, that's off the point. **Sin cuento**, countless. **Tener más cuento que siete viejas**, to be given to fibbing. **Han tenido no se qué cuentos entre ellos**, they've had some upset among themselves. **Tiene mucho cuento**, he makes a lot of fuss.

cuento 2 [coo-en'-to], *m.* 1. The butt-end of a pike, spear, or like weapon. 2. Prop, shore, support. (*Yo cuento, yo cuente*, from *Contar. V.* ACORDAR.)

cuera [coo-ay'-rah], *f.* 1. A leather jacket. 2. *(LAm.)* Hide (piel); strap (correa). 3. **Cueras**, *(CAm.)* Leggings. 4. *(And. Carib. CAm.)* Flogging (paliza).

cuerazo [coo-ay-rah'-tho], *m. (LAm.)* Lashing.

cuerda [coo-err'-dah], *f.* 1. Cord, rope, halter, string, (fishing) line. 2. A string for musical instruments, catgut or wire. 3. Compass, number of notes which a voice reaches; the four fundamental voices *(Acad.)* 4. *(Geom.)* Chord, a right line which joins the two ends of an arc. 5. Match for firing a gun. 6. Chain of a watch or clock. 7. *(Anat.)* Tendon. **Aflojar la cuerda**, to ease up. **Bajo cuerda**, underhandedly. **Cuerdas vocales**, vocal cords. **Dar cuerda a**, 1. To wind. 2. *(Coll.)* to give free rein to. **De cuerda automática**, selfwinding. **Tocar la cuerda sensible**, to get through to. **Cuerda floja**, tightrope. **Cuerda de tendedero**, clothesline.

Bailar en la cuerda floja, to keep in with both parties. **Dar cuerda al reloj**, to wind up one's watch. **Tienen cuerda para rato**, they've something to keep them going.

cuerdamente [coo-ayr-dah-men'-tay], *adv.* Prudently, advisedly, deliberately.

cuerdo, da [coo-err'-do, dah], *a.* 1. Prudent, discreet, sensible, judicious. 2. In his senses, not mad.

cuereada [coo-ay-ray-ah'-dah], *f. (LAm.)* Beating, tanning.

cuerear [coo-ay-ray-ar'], *va.* 1. *(LAm.)* To skin, to flay. 2. *(LAm.)* To whip (persona). 3. **Cuerear a uno**, *(Carib. Cono Sur)* to tear a strip off somebody.

cuerezuelo [coo-ay-ray-thoo-ay'-lo], *m.* A sucking pig. *V.* COREZUELO.

cuerito [coo-ay-re'-to], **De cuerita**, *adv. (LAm.)* From end to end.

cueriza [coo-ay-re-tha], *f. (LAm.)* Beating, tanning.

cuerna [coo-err'-nah], *f.* 1. A horn vessel, not which cows or goats are milked. 2. Stag's or deer's horn. 3. Sportsman's horn.

cuernecico, illo, ito [coo-er-nay-thee'-co], *m. dim.* Cornicle, a small horn.

cuernezuelo [coo-er-nay-thoo-ay'-lo], *m.* 1. *(dim.)* Cornicle, a small horn. 2. A farrier's paring-knife.

cuerno [coo-err'-no], *m.* 1. Horn, the horn of quadrupeds. 2. Feeler, the horn or antenna of insects. 3. Horn, pointed end of the moon. 4. A button at the end of a rod about which a manuscript was rolled. 5. A huntsman's horn. 6. *(Bot.)* A spur or outgrowth resembling a horn. 7. *(Naut.)* An outrigger. 8. *(Vet.)* A disease of horses, occurring below where the saddle rests; callosity, presumably. 9. **Cuerno de ciervo**, hart's horn. **Verse en los cuernos del toro**, to be in the most imminent danger. **Poner los cuernos**, to cuckold: applied to a wife who wrongs her husband by unchastity. **Saber a cuerno quemado**, to be suspicious. **Irse al cuerno**, to fail, to fall through. **Mandar a uno al cuerno**, to tell somebody to go to hell. **Mandar algo al cuerno**, to consign something to hell.

cuero [coo-ay'-ro], *m.* 1. Pelt, the skin of an animal. 2. Leather. 3. Goat skin dressed entire, which serves as a bag to carry wine or oil. 4. *(Met.)* Toper, a great drinker. 5. *(And. Carib.)* Whore; *(And.)* Old maid (soltera); *(Carib.)* Old bag (vieja); *(And. Mex.)* Mistress (amante). 6. *(CAm. Carib.)* Cheek (descarado). 7. Wallet (cartera). **Cuero de suela**, sole leather. **En cueros** or **cueros vivos**, stark naked. **Cueros**, hangings or drapery of gilded or painted leather. **Cuero cabelludo**, scalp. **Estar hecho un cuero**, to be as drunk as a Lord. **Arrimar el cuero a uno**, *(LAm.)* to give somebody a beating.

cuerpada [coo-ayr-pah'-dah], *f.* **Tiene buena cuerpada**, *(Cono Sur)* she's got a good body.

cuerpear [coo-ayr-pay-ar'], *vn. (Cono Sur)* To dodge.

cuerpecico, illo, ito, cuerpezuelo [coo-er-pay-thee'-co], *m. dim.* A small body or carcass.

cuerpo [coo-err'-po], *m.* 1. Body, material substance. 2. Body of an animal; also more narrowly, the trunk. 3. Cadaver, a corpse, a dead body. 4. Body, matter; opposed to spirit. 5. Body, corporation, guild, any corporate body. 6. *(Geom.)* Body, any solid figure. 7. *(Arch.)* Floor or story in a building. 8. Volume, book. **Su librería contiene dos mil cuerpos de libros**, his library contains two thousand volumes. 9. The whole of a book, except the preface and index. 10. *(Law.)* Body, a collection of laws. **Cuerpo de doctrina**, body of teaching. **Cuerpo de leyes**, body of laws. 11. Degree of thickness of silks, woollens, or cottons. 12. Body, size; strength, thickness of liquids. **Un vino de mucho cuerpo**, a strongbodied wine. 13. Body; a collective mass. Body, in several other senses; as a body of a musical instrument, of ore, of scientific or diplomatic persons, etc. 14. Personal disposition; *(Acad.)* **Cuerpo del ejército**, the main body of an army. **Cuerpo de batalla de una escuadra**, the center division of a fleet. **Cuerpo a cuerpo**, hand to hand; in single combat. **A cuerpo descubierto**, 15. without cover or shelter.

16. manifestly. **Cuerpo del delito**, corpus delicti. **Cuerpo de Dios, de mí, de tal**; an exclamation denoting anger or vexation. **Cuerpo de guardia**, a guardroom. **Tratar a cuerpo de rey**, to feast like a king. **Tomar cuerpo**, to increase to enlarge. **En cuerpo y alma**, *(Coll).* totally, wholly. **Ester de cuerpo presente**, to be actually present; also, to lie in state after death. **Misa de cuerpo presente**, a mass said while the corpse of the deceased is present in the church. **Cantar cuando lo pide el cuerpo**, to sing when one has a mind to. **Luchar cuerpo a cuerpo**, to fight hand-to-hand. **Con el cuerpo en tierra**, to fall down. **Ir a cuerpo**, to go without a coat. **Cuerpo estatal**, public body. **Cuerpo de intendencia**, service corps. **Cuerpo compuesto**, compound.

cuerpo aéreo [coo-err'-po ah-ay'-ray-o], *m.* Air corps.

cuerudo [coo-ay-roo'-do], *a.* 1. *(LAm).* Slow, sluggish (caballo); lazy. 2. *(LAm).* Annoying (persona). 3. *(Cono Sur)* brave, tough. 4. *(CAm. Carib.)* Impudent, cheeky.

cuerva [coo-err'-vah], *f.* 1. *(Orn).* Crow, rook. 2. A fish very common on the Cantabrian, Biscay, coasts.

cuervo [coo-err'-vo], *m.* 1. *(Orn).* Raven, crow. 2. **Cuervo marino**, cormorant. 3. *(Astr.)* A southern constellation. **No poder ser el cuervo más negro que las alas**, the crow cannot be blacker than its wings; greater evil is not to be feared; the worst is over.

cuesco [coo-es'-co], *m.* 1. Kernel, the stone or core of pulpy fruit. 2. Millstone of an oilmill. 3. Wind from behind. 4. Punch, bash. 5. Loud fart (pedo).

cuesquillo [coo-es-keel'-lyo], *m. dim.* A small kernel or stone of fruit.

cuesta [coo-es'-tah], *f.* 1. Hill, mount. 2. Any ground rising with a slope. 3. Quest, gathering, charity, money collected by begging. 4. Coast. **Ir cuesta abajo**, to go downhill. **Ir cuesta arriba**, to go uphill. **Cuesta arriba**, painfully; with great trouble and difficulty. 5. **A cuestas**, on one's shoulders or back. 6. To one's charge or care. **Hemos vencido la cuesta ya**, we're over the hump now. **Echar algo a cuestas**, to put something o one's back, *(fig).* to take on the burden of something.

cuestación [coo-es-tah-the-on'], *f.* Petition, solicitation for a charitable purpose.

cuestero [coo-es-tay'-ro], *m.* One who collects alms or charity.

cuestión [coo-es-te-on'], *f.* 1. Question, inquiry. **Cuestión clave**, key question. **La cosa en cuestión**, the matter at issue. **Eso es otra cuestión**, that's another matter. 2. Question, dispute, quarrel. **La cuestión es que...**, the trouble is that... **No quiero questiones con los empleados**, I don't want trouble with the staff. 3. Problem. 4. Dough, money.

cuestionable [coo-es-te-o-nah'-blay], *a.* Questionable, problematical.

cuestionamiento [coo-es-te-o-nah-me-ayn'-to], *m.* Questioning.

cuestionar [coo-es-te-o-nar'], *va.* To question, to dispute.

cuestionario [coo-es-te-o-nah'-re-o], *m.* Questionnaire.

cuestor [coo-es-tor'], *m.* 1. Questor, a magistrate of ancient Rome. 2. Mendicant, one who collects alms.

cuestor, ra [coo-ays-tor'], *m. & f.* Charity collector.

cuestuoso, sa [coo-es-to-o-so, sah], *a.* Lucrative, productive.

cuete [coo-ay'-tay], *a. (Mex.)* Drunk. -*m.* 1. *(And. CAm. Mex.)* Pistol. 2. *(CAm. Mex.)* V. COHETE. 3. *(Mex.)* Drunkeness. 4. *(Mex.) (Culin.)* Steak.

cuetearse [coo-ay-tar'-say], *vr. (And.)* 1. To go off, to explode. 2. To kick the bucket.

cueto [coo-ay'-to], *m.* A lofty place, defended.

cuetzale [coo-et-thah'-lay], *m. (Orn.)* A large Mexican bird of golden green plumage. V. QUETZAL.

cueva [coo-ay'-vah], *f.* 1. Cave, grot, grotto, a subterraneous cavity. 2. Cellar. **Cueva de ladrones**, nest of thieves. **Cueva de fieras**, den of wild beasts.

cuévano [coo-ay'-vah-no], *m.* 1. A basket, or hamper, somewhat wider at the top than below. 2. *(Min.)* Sump basket.

cuevero [coo-ay-vay'-ro], *m.* One who makes caves and grottoes.

cuezo [coo-ay'-tho], *m.* 1. Hod for carrying mortar. 2. Skirt, petticoat; *(Acad.)* **Meter el cuezo**, to put in an oar, to intrude.

cúfico, ca [coo'-fe-co, cah], *a.* Cufic, relating to Cufa; said of the characters in which Arabic was written before the 10th century.

cuguar [coo-goo-ar'], *m. (Zool.)* Puma, cougar.

cugujada [coo-goo-hah'-dah], *f. (Orn.)* Common field-lark, skylark.

cugulla [coo-gool'lyah], *f.* Cowl. V. COGULLA.

cuí [coo-e'], *m. (LAm.)* Guinea-pig.

cuica [coo-e-cah], *f. (And.)* Earthworm.

cuico [coo-e'-co], *a. (And.)* Thin; *(Carib.)* Rachitic, feeble. -*m.* 1. *(Cono Sur)* foreigner, outsider. 2. *(And. Cono Sur)* Bolivian. 3. *(Carib.)* Mexican. 4. *(Mex.)* Policeman.

cuida [coo-ee'-dah], *f.* In ladies' seminaries, a young lady who takes care of another of tender age.

cuidadero, ra [coo-e-day'-ro], *m. & f. (Zool.)* Keeper.

cuidado [coo-e-dah'-do], *m.* 1. Care, solicitude, attention, heed, heedfulness. 2. Care, keeping, custody, charge or trust conferred. 3. Care, caution, fear, apprehension, anxiety. 4. Followed by prep. **con** and the name of a person, denotes vexation. **Estar con cuidado**, to be anxious. **Eso me trae sin ciudado**, I'm not worried about that. **Andarse con cuidado**, to go carefully. **Poner mucho cuidado en algo**, to take great care over something. **Hay que tener cuidado con él**, you have to handle him carefully. -*int.* **¡Cuidado!** Look out! stop! beware! **Está al cuidado de la computadora**, he's in charge of the computer. **Los niños están al cuidado de la abuela**, the children are in their grandmother's charge.

cuidador [coo-e-dah-dor'], *m.* Second (boxeo); trainer. **Cuidador de campo**, groundsman.

cuidadora [coo-e-dah-do'-rah], *f. (Mex.)* Nursemaid, nanny.

cuidadosamente [coo-e-dah-do-sah-men'-tay], *adv.* Carefully, attentively, heedfully, mindfully, cautiously, providently.

cuidadoso, sa [coo-e-dah-do'-so, sah], *a.* Careful, solicitous; vigilant, heedful, mindful, painstaking, currious, observing.

cuidaniños [coo-e-dah-nee'-nyos], *m. & f.* Babysitter.

cuidar [coo-e-dar'], *va.* To heed, to care; to execute with care, diligence, and attention; to keep, to mind, to look after. **Ella cuida a los niños**, she looks after the children. **No cuidan la casa**, they don't look after the house. -*vn.* 1. **Cuidar de**, to take care of. **Cuide de que no pase nadie**, see that nobody gets in. **Cuide de no caer**, take care not to fall. 2. **Cuida conesa gente**, be wary of those people. -*vr.* 1. To look after oneself. 2. **Cuidarse de algo**, to worry about something. 3. **Cuidar muy bien de**, to take good care not to.

cuido [coo-e'-do], *m.* Care, minding. **Para su cuido**, for your own good.

cuita [coo-e'-tah], *f.* (1.) Care, grief, affliction, trouble. 2. *(Ant.)* Ardent desire, craving. **Contar sus cuitas**, to tell one's troubles.

cuitadamente [coo-e-tah-dah-men'-tay], *adv.* Slothfully, afflictedly.

cuitadico, ica, illo, illa, ito, ita [coo-e-tah-dee'-co], *a. dim.* 1. Timid, chicken-hearted. 2. Having some slight trouble or affliction.

cuitado, da [coo-e-tah'-do, dah], *a.* 1. Anxious, wretched, miserable. 2. Chicken-hearted, pusillanimous, timid.

cuja [coo'-hah], *f.* 1. Bag, formerly fastened to the saddle, into which a spear or flagstaff was put for easier carriage. 2. Bedstead. 3. *(Obs.)* Thigh. 4. *(CAm. Mex.)* Envelope.

cujarda [coo-har-dah], *f. (Bot.)* V. CORONILLA DE FRAILE.

cuje [coo'-hay], *m. (Cuba)* Withe, each of three slender flexible rods, made of any wood, of which a kind of crane, or gallows, is made for suspending the stems in gathering tobacco. **Cujes** *pl.* Hoop-poles.

cujinillos [coo-he-nel-lyos], *m. & pl. (Mex.)* Saddlebags.

culada

culada [coo-lah'-dah], *f.* 1. Stroke with the backside or breech of anything. 2. Fall on one's backside. **Culadas,** *(Naut.)* Shocks and rollings of a ship.

culamen [coo-lah'-men], *m.* Bottom.

culandrón [coo-lahn-drone'], *m.* Queer.

culantrillo, or **Culantrillo de pozo** [coo-lan-treel'-lyo], *m.* Maiden's hair.

culantro [coo-lahn'-tro], *m.* *(Bot.)* Coriander. V. CORIANDRO and CILANTRO.

culata [coo-lah'-tah], *f.* 1. Breech of a gun, buttend of a musket. 2. Screwpin, which fastens the breech of a gun to the stock. 3. The back part of anything. **Dar de culata,** to recoil, among coachmen and carriage makers. **Dar la culata,** means to lift the back of the vehicle in order to remove it without disturbing the front part. 4. *(Conno Sur)* Shelter, hut.

culatada [coo-lah-tah'-dah], *f.* Kick, recoil of a firearm.

culatazo [coo-lah-tah'-tho], *m.* Recoil of a gun or musket.

culazo [coo-lah'-tho], *m. aug.* A large backside.

culcusido [cool-coo-see'-do], *m.* Botch-work, anything clumsily sewed. V. CORCUSIDO.

culear [coo-lay-ar'], *va.* *(And. Cono Sur, Mex.)* To fuck. -*vn.* 1. To waggle one's bottom (mover el culo). 2. *(And. Cono Sur, Mex.)* To fuck.

culebra [coo-lay'-brah], *f.* 1. Snake. 2. Trick, fun, joke. V. CULEBRAZO. 3. The worm, spiral part of a still. 4. Disorder, confusion suddenly made by a few in a peaceful assembly. **Sabe más que las culebras,** *(Coll.)* he is very crafty and cunning. **Culebra de cascabel,** a rattlesnake. 5. *(And.)* Debt, bill. 6. *(Mex.)* Waterspout. 7. *(Mex.)* Hosepipe (manga).

culebrear [coo-laybray-ar'], *vn.* 1. To move like a snake; to crankle. 2. *(Carib.)* To stall, to hedge.

culebreo [coo-lay-bray'-o], *m.* Wriggling; zigzag; winding, meandering.

culebrilla [coo-lay-breel'-lyah], *f.* 1. Tetter, ringworm; a cutaneous disease. 2. Rocking-staff of a loom. 3. Fissure in a gunbarrel.

culebrina [coo-lay-bree'-nah], *f.* *(Mil.)* Culverin.

culebrino, na [coo-lay-bree'-no, nah], *a.* Snake, snaky.

culebrón [coo-lay-brone'], *m.* 1. A crafty fellow; a double dealer. 2. A long T. V. serial.

culebrona [coo-lay-bro'-nah], *f.* An intriguing woman.

culeco [coo-lay'-co], *a.* 1. *(LAm.)* Broody (gallina). 2. *(LAm.)* Home-loving. 3. **Estar culeco,** *(And, Carib, Cono Sur)* to be head over heels in love. 4. **Estar culeco con algo,** *(And. CAm. Carib, Mex.)* To be very pleased about something.

culera [coo-lay'-rah], *f.* 1. Stain of urine in children's underwear. 2. A patch on the seat of drawers or trousers. *(Acad.)*.

culeras [coo-lay'-ras], *m. & f.* Coward.

culero [coo-lay'-ro], *m.* 1. Clout, diaper, a cloth for keeping children clean. 2. Disease in birds. 3. *(Mex.)* Coward. 4. *(CAm.)* Poof (maricón).

culero, ra [coo-lay'-ro, rah], *a.* Slothful, lazy.

culí [coo-le'], *m.* Coolie.

culibajo [coo-le-bah'-ho], *a.* Short, dumpy.

culícidos [coo-lee'-the-dose], *m. pl.* Culicidae, the family of gnats and mosquitoes.

culillera [coo-lel-lay'-rah], *f.* *(CAm.),* **culillo** *m.* 1. *(And. CAm. Carib.)* Fear, fright. 2. **Tener culillera,** *(Carib.)* To be in a hurry.

culinario, ia [coo-le-nah'-reo, ah], *a.* Culinary, belonging to the kitchen.

culipandear [coo-le-pan-day-ar'], *vn. vr.* *(Carib.)* To stall, to hedge.

culito [coo-lee'-to], *m. dim.* A small breech or backside.

culmífero, ra [cool-mee'-fay-ro, rah], *a.* *(Bot.)* Culmiferous.

culminación [cool-me-nah-the-on'], *f.* 1. *(Astr.)* Culmination, the transit of a planet through the meridian. 2. *(Naut.)* High tide.

culminancia [cool-me-nahn'-the-ah], *f.* *(Poet.)* Height, elevation, peak.

culminante [cool-me-nahn'-tay], *a.* Highest, topmost, culminating; culminating (momento); outstanding.

culminar [cool-me-nar'], *vn.* 1. *(Astr.)* To culminate, to be in the meridian. 2. To be raised or elevated. 3. *(Naut.)* To reach high water.

culo [coo'-lo], *m.* 1. Breech, backside, buttock. 2. Bottom, socket. 3. Anus. 4. The lower or hinder extremity of anything. **Culo de mona,** very ugly and ridiculous thing. **Ser un culo de mal asiento,** to be restless. **Ir con el culo a rastras,** to be in a jam. **Ir de culo,** to be overloaded with work. **Ser culo de vaso,** to be false.

culón [cool-lone'], *m.* *(Coll.)* An invalided or retired soldier. -*a.* V. CULIGORDO.

culpa [cool'-pah], *f.* Fault, offence, slight crime, failure, guilt. **Por culpa de,** through the fault of. **Echar la culpa a uno,** to blame somebody. **Nadie tiene la culpa,** nobody is to blame. **La culpa fue de los frenos,** the brakes were to blame. **Pagar las culpas ajenas,** to pay for somebody else's sins.

culpabilidad [cool-pah-be-le-dahd'], *f.* Culpability.

culpable [cool-pah'-blay], *a.* Culpable; faulty, condemnable, accusable. **Declarar culpable a uno,** to find somebody guilty. **Es culpable no hacerlo,** it is criminal not to do it. -*m. & f.* Culprit; offender, guilty party.

culpablemente [cool-pah-blay-men'-tay], *adv.* Culpably.

culpadamente [cool-pah-dah-men'-tay], *adv.* Culpably.

culpado, da [cool-pah'-do, dah], *n. & a.* Guilty. -*pp.* of CULPAR.

culpar [cool-par'], *va.* To blame, to impeach, to accuse, to condemn, to reproach. **Culpar a uno de algo,** to blame somebody for something.

cultamente [cool-tah-men'-tay], *adv.* 1. Neatly, elegantly, affectedly, politely.

cultedad [cool-tay-dahd'], *f.* Affected elegance and purity of style.

culteranismo [cool-tayrah-nees'-mo], *m.* Sect of purists who are affectedly nice in the use of words and phrases.

culterano, na [cool-tay-rah'-no, nah], *m. & f.* Purist with affectation.

culterano, na [cool-tay-rah'-no, nah], *a.* Relating to affected elegance and purity of style.

cultero [cool-tay'-ro], *m.* Purist with affectation.

cultiparlar [cool-te-par-lar'], *vn.* To speak with affected elegance.

cultiparlista [cool-te-par-lees'-tah], *a.* Speaking much with affected elegance and purity of language.

cultipicaño, ña [cool-te-pe-cah'-nyo, nyah], *a.* (Humorous) Speaking with affected elegance, and in a jeering manner.

cultismo [cool-tes'-mo], *m.* *(Ling.)* Learned word (palabra culta); gongorism.

cultivable [cool-te-vah'-blay], *a.* Cultivable, manurable, capable of cultivation.

cultivación [cool-te-vah-the-on'], *f.* Cultivation, culture.

cultivador, ra [cool-te-vah-dor'], *m. & f.* 1. Cultivator. **Cultivador de vino,** winegrower. 2. Kind of plough.

cultivar [cool-te-var'], *va.* 1. To cultivate the soil, to farm, to husband; to manure, to labor. 2. To cultivate, to preserve, to keep up: speaking of friendship, acquaintances, etc. 3. To cultivate, to exercise the memory, the talent, etc. 4. To cultivate the arts or sciences.

cultivo [cool-tee'-vo], *m.* 1. Cultivation, cultivating and improving the soil. 2. Cultivation, improvement. 3. Act of cultivating one's acquaintance or friendship. 4. Culture of the mind, elegance of manners. **El cultivo principal de la región,** the chief crop of the area. **Cultivo de secano,** dry farming.

culto, ta [cool'-to, tah], *a.* 1. Pure, elegant, correct (estilo, lenguaje). 2. Affectedly elegant. 3. Polished, enlightened, civilized (persona bien informada, nación).

culto [cool'-to], *m.* 1. Speaking in general, respect or veneration paid to a person, as a testimony of his superior excellence and worth. 2. Worship, adoration, religious act of reverence. **Culto divino**, public worship in churches. **Culto externo**, external demonstrations of respect to God and his saints, by processions, sacrifices, offerings, etc. **Culto sagrado o religioso**, honor or worship to God and the saints. **Culto superfluo**, worship by means of vain useless things. **Culto supersticioso**, worship paid either to whom it is not due, or in an improper manner.

cultro [cool'-tro], *m. (Prov.)* Plough with which the first fallow ploughing is performed.

cultrún [cool-troon'], *m. (Conso Sur) (Mus.)* Drum.

cultura [cool-too'rah], *f.* 1. Culture, improvement or amelioration of the soil. 2. Culture and improvement of the mind. 3. Elegance of style or language. 4. Urbanity, polish of manner, politeness. **Cultura física**, physical culture. **La cultura popular**, popular culture. **Persona de cultura**, cultured person. **No tiene cultura**, he has no manners.

cultural [cool-too-rahl'], *a.* Cultural.

culturar [cool-too-rar'], *va. (Prov.)* To cultivate. *V.* CULTIVAR.

culturismo [cool-too-res'-mo], *m.* Body-building.

culturista [cool-too-res'-tah], *m. & f.* Body-builder.

culturizar [cool-too-re-thar'], *va.* To educate, to enlighten. - *vr.* To educate oneself.

cuma [coo'-mah], *f. (S. Amer.)* 1. Godmother. 2. Crony, female friend or neighbor. 3. *(CAm.)* Long knife.

cumarú [coo-mah-roo'], *m.* The Tonquin or Tonka bean, used for flavoring tobacco and perfuming snuff.

cumbancha [coo-bahn'-chah], *f. (Carib.)* Spree, drinking bout.

cumbé [coom-bay'], *m.* Sort of dance among the negroes, and the tune to which it is performed.

cumbia [coom-be-ah], *f. (And.)* Colombian dance music; popular Colombian dance.

cúmbila [coom'-be-lah], *m. (Carib.)* Pal, buddy.

cumbo [coom'-bo], *m.* 1. *(CAm.)* Top hat; bowler hat (hongo). 2. *(CAm.)* Narrow-mouthed cup.

cumbre [coom'-bray], **cumbrera** [coom-bray'rah], *f.* 1. Ridgepole, tiebeam, summit, top. 2. Top, summit, cop, culmination. 3. *(Met.)* The greatest height of favor, fortune, science, etc. **Conferencia cumbre**, summit conference. **está en la cumbre de su poderío**, he is at the height of his power. **Momento cumbre**, culminating point.

cume [coo'-may], *m.* **cumiche** *m. (CAm.)* Baby of the family.

cumero [coo-may'-ro], *m.* A tree of Guiana.

cumia [coo'me-ah], *f.* Fruit of the cumero-tree, and the resin which is used for incense in the churches of Guiana.

cumíneo, nea [coo-mee'-nay-o, ah], *a.* Cumin-like.

cuminol [coo-me-nole'], *m.* Oil of cumin.

cumpa [coom'-pah], *m. (LAm.)* 1. Godfather. 2. Comrade, companion.

cúmplase [coom'-plah], *m.* 1. The countersign of a superior officer upon commissions in the army, or certificate of retirement. 2. A permit.

cumpleaños [coom-play-ah'-ny-os], *m.* Birthday.

cumplidamente [coom-ple-dah-men'tay], *adv.* Completely, complimentally.

cumplidero, ra [coom-ple-day'-ro, rah], *a.* 1. That which must be fulfilled or executed. 2. Convenient, fit, suitable, accomplishable.

cumplido, da [coom-plee'-do, dah], *a.* 1. Large, plentiful, high. **Un abrigo cumplido**, a full coat. **Una comida cumplida**, a plentiful dinner. 2. Gifted with talents, worthy of esteem, faultless. 3. Polished, polite, civil, courteous. 4. **Tiene 60 años cumplidos**, he is 60 (years old). -*pp.* of CUMPLIR.

cumplido, *m.* 1. Compliment; courtesy. **Visita de cumplido**, formal visit. **Andarse con cumplidos**, to stand on ceremony. **He venido por cumplido**, I came out of a sense of duty. 2. *(Naut.)* The length of the thing in question compared with the unit, as a cable's length.

cumplidor [coom-ple-dor'], *m.* One who executes a commission or trust.

cumplimentar [coom-ple-men-tar'], *va.* 1. To compliment or congratulate. 2. *(Law.)* To carry out superior orders.

cumplimentero, ra [coom-ple-men-tay'-ro, rah], *a. & n.* 1. *(Coll.)* Full of compliments, complimental, complaisant. 2. *complimentary.*

cumplimiento [coom-ple-meen'-to], *m.* 1. Act of complimenting or paying a compliment, complaisance, civility. 2. Compliment, accomplishment, completion, perfection, fulfilling. **Al cumplimiento del tiempo** or **del plazo**, at the expiration of the time. 3. Compliment, an expression of civility, course. **No se ande Vd. en cumplimientos**, do not stand upon compliments. 4. Complement.

cumplir [coom-pleer'], *va.* 1. To execute, discharge, or perform one's duty, fulfil. 2. To have served the time required in the militia. **Cumplir años** or **días**, to reach one's birthday. **Hoy cumple 8 años**, she's 8 today. **Cuando cumplas los 21 años**, when you're 21. **Cumplir de palabra**, keep one's word. **Cumplir por otro**, to do something in the name of another. **Cumpla Vd. por mí**, do it in my name. -*vn.* 1. To be fit or convenient. 2. To suffice, to be sufficient. 3. To mature, to be the time (or day) when an obligation, undertaking, ends. 4. To be realized, verified. **Por cumplir**, for mere courtesy, outward show. **El plazo se ha cumplido**, the time has expired. **Cumplir con la iglesia**, to fulfil one's religious obligations. -*vr.* 1. To be fulfilled. 2. To expire, to end (plazo). 3. **Se obedece pero no se cumple**, the letter of the law is observed but not its spirit.

cumucho [coo-moo'-cho], *m. (Cono Sur)* 1. Gathering, mob, crowd (multitud). 2. Hut, hovel (cabaña).

cumulador [coo-moo-lah-dor'], *m. V.* ACUMULADOR.

cumular [coo-moo-lar'], *va.* To accumulate, to compile or heap together. *V.* ACUMULAR.

cumulativamente [coo-moo-lah-te-vah-men'-tah], *adv.* In heaps.

cumulativo, va [coo-moo-lah-tee'-vo, vah], *a.* Cumulative.

cúmulo [coo'-moo-lo], *m.* 1. Heap or pile; congeries. 2. *(Met.)* Throng of business; variety of trouble and difficulties.

cuna [coo'-nah], *f.* 1. Cradle. **Cuna portátil**, carrycot. 2. *(Prov.)* Foundling hospital 3. *(Met.)* The native soil or country. 4. Family, lineage. **De humilde** or **de ilustre cuna**, of an humble or illustrious family. 5. Origin, beginning of anything. **Cuna del famoso poeta**, the birthplace of the famous poet.

cunar, cunear [coo-nar', coo-nay-ar'], *va.* To rock a cradle. To move, rock, like a cradle.

cunasiri [coo-nah-see'-ree], *m.* Peruvian tree of pinkish aromatic wood.

cuncuna [coon-coo'-nah], *f.* Caterpillar of Chili, resembling the silkworm.

cunchos [coon'-chose], *m. pl.* Indigenous independent race in Chili.

cundido [coon-dee'-do], *m.* 1. The provision of oil, vinegar, and salt given to shepherds. 2. Honey or cheese given to boys to eat with their bread -**Cundido, da**, *pp.* of CUNDIR.

cundir [coon-deer'], *va. (Obs.)* To occupy, to fill. -*vn.* 1. To spread (líquidos). 2. To yield abundantly. 3. To grow, to increase, to propagate. **Cunde el rumor que…**, there's a rumor going round that… **Hoy no me ha cundido el trabajo**, work did not go well for me today.

cunear [coo-nay-ar'], *va.* To rock, to craddle. -*vr.* To rock, to sway; to swing along, to walk with a roll.

cuneario, ia [coo-nay-ah'-reo, ah], *a. (Bot.)* Wedge-shaped.

cuneco [coo-nay'-co], *m. (Carib.)* Baby of the family.

cuneiforme [coo-nay-e-for'-may], *a.* Cuneiform, in the form of a wedge.

cúneo [coo'-nay-o], *m.* 1. *(Obs. Mil.)* Triangular formation of troops. 2. Space between the passages in ancient theaters.

cuneo [coo-nay'-o], *m.* 1. Rocking. 2. *(Naut.)* Rolling, pitching.

cunero ra [coo-nay'-ro, rah], *m. & f. (Prov.)* A foundling.

cuneta [coo-nay'-tah], *f. (Mil.)* A small trench made in a dry ditch or moat of a fortress, to drain off the rainwater, side culvert.

cunicultura [coo-ne-cool-too-rah], *f.* Rabbit breeding.

cuña [coo'-nyah], *f.* 1. Wedge, quoin. 2. Any object employed in splitting or dividing a body. 3. A chip, splinter, driven with a hammer. **Cuñas de mango**, *(Naut.)* Horsing-irons. **Cuñas de puntería**, *(Mil.)* Gun-quoins. **4**. Meter cuña, to sow discord. 5. *(LAm.)* Influential person. 6. Influence, pull. **Tener cuñas**, to have pull. 7. *(CAm. Carib.) (Aut.)* Two-seater car. 8. (Rad, TV) spot, slot.

cuñadería [coo-nyah-day-ree'-ah], *f.* Spiritual affinity contracted by being godfather to a child.

cuñadía, *f.* **cuñadío**, *m.* [coo-nyah-dee'-ah, coo-nyah-dee'-o]. Kindred by affinity.

cuñadismo [coo-nay-des'-mo], *m.* Nepotism, old boys network.

cuñado da [coo-nyah'-do, dah], *m. & f.* A brother or sister-in-law.

cuñete [coo-nyay'-tay], *m.* Keg, firkin.

cuño [coo'-nyo], *m.* 1. Die for coining money. 2. Impression made by the die. 3. Mark put on silver. 4. A triangular formation of troops.

cuociente [cwo-the-en'-tay], *m. V.* COCIENTE.

cuedlibético, ca [kwod-le-bay'-te-co, cah], *a.* Quodlibetic, not restricted to a particular subject.

cuodlibeto [kwo-dle-bay'-to], *m.* 1. A debatable point; discussion upon a scientific subject chosen by the author. 2. A thesis, scholastic dissertation in ancient universities. 3. A pungent saying, sharp sometimes, trivial and flat at others, not directed to a useful end.

cuoto [coo-o'-tah], *f.* Quota, contingent, fixed share. **Cuota de enseñanza**, school fees. **Cuota de socio**, membership fee. **cuotidiano** [coo-o-te-de-ah'-no], *a. V.* COTIDIANO.

cupano [coo-pah'-no], *m.* A great tree of the Philippine Islands, the bark yielding a dye-stuff and the wood fit for building.

cupé [coo-pay'], *m.* 1. Landau, a fourwheeled carriage. 2. Coupé, a car with two doors.

cupido [coo-pee'-do], *m.* 1. Bit of steel taken out of the eye of a needle. 2. Cupid. 3. A gallant, wooer, lover.

cupitel [coo-pe-tel'] **Tirar de cupitel**, to throw a bowl archwise.

cuplé [coo-play'], *m.* Pop song.

cupletista [coo-play-tes'-tah], *f.* Cabaret singer.

cupo [coo'-po], *m.* 1. Quota; share. **Cupo de azúcar**, sugar quota. 2. *(Mex.)* Space, room, capacity; *(And. Carib. Mex.)* Empty seat, vacancy. **No hay cupo**, there's no room.

cupón [coo-pone'], *m.* Coupon, a voucher for interest attached to a bond. **Cupón de los ciegos**, ticket for the lottery for the blind. **Cupón de dividendos**, dividend voucher.

cuprero [coo-pray'-ro], *a. (Cono Sur)* copper.

cupresino na [coo-pray-see'-no, nah], *a. (Poet.)* Belonging to the cypress-tree, or made of cypress-wood.

cúprico, ca [coo'-pre-co, cah], *a.* Cupric, belonging to copper.

cuproso, sa [coo-pro'-so, sah], *a.* Cuprous, like copper. Cuprous, combining in a lower equivalence than cupric.

cúpula [coo'-poo-lah], *f.* 1. Cupola, dome. 2. The turret of a monitor. 3. *(Bot.)* Cupule, cup, a sort of involucre. 4. *(Pol.)* Party, leadership, leading members.

cupulífero, ra [coo-poo-lee'-fay-ro, rah], *a.* Cupuliferous, cupbearing.

cupulino [coo-poo-lee'no], *m.* Lantern a small cupola raised upon another, which serves to light the vault.

cuquería [coo-kay-re'-ah], *f.* Craftiness.

cuquillero [coo-keel-lyay'-ro], *m. (Prov.)* Baker's boy, who fetches the paste of bread, and carries it back when baked.

cuquillo [coo-keel'lyo], *m.* 1. *(Orn.)* Cuckoo. *V.* CUCLILLO. 2. *(Ent.)* Insect which consumes the vines.

cura [coo'-rah], *m.* 1. Parish priest, rector, curate. **Cura párroco**, parish priest. 2. In Castile, it is commonly used to denote any clergyman, priest, or parson. -*f.* 1. Cure, healing, the act and effect of healing or of restoring to health. **Primera cura**, first aid. **Cura de reposo**, rest cure. **No tiene cura**, there's no remedy. 2. Guardianship. 3. Parsonage, the benefice of a parish. **Los derechos de cura**, the dues or fees of a rector, parson, or curate, with a parochial charge.

curable [coo-rah'-blay], *a.* Curable, healable.

curaca [coo-rah-cah], *f.* 1. *(And.)* Priest's housekeeper. 2. *(And.)* Indian chief, Indian native authority.

curación [coo-rah-the-on'], *f.* Cure, healing.

curadero [coo-rah-day'-ro], *m.* Place for bleaching woven goods and other objects.

curadillo [coo-rah-deel'-lyo], *m.* 1. *(Prov.)* Codfish, lingfish. 2. *(Tec.)* Bleached linen.

curado, da [coo-rah'-do, dah], *a.* Rectorial, belonging to the rector of a parish; relating to a rectory or parsonage. -*a. & pp.* of CURAR. 1. Cured, strengthened, restored to health. 2. Hardened, strengthened, or tanned. 3. Cured, salted.

curador [coo-rah-dor'], *m.* 1. Overseer. **Curador de bacalao**, codsalter. 2. Guardian, one who has the care of minors and orphans. 3. Physician, surgeon, healer. 4. Curator, administrator.

curadora [coo-rah-do'-rah], *f.* 1. Guardianess, a female guardian. 2. Healer.

curaduría [coo-rah-doo-ree'-ah], *f.* Guardianship.

curalle [coo-rahl'-lyay], *m.* Physic administered to a hawk.

curanderismo [coo-rahn-day-res'-mo], *m.* Quack medicine.

curandero [coo-ran-day'-ro], *m.* Quack, medicaster, an artful and tricking practitioner in physic.

curar [coo-rar'], *va. & vn.* 1. To cure, to heal, to restore to health, to administer medicines. 2. To prescribe the medicine or diet of a patient. 3. To salt, to cure meat or fish, to preserve. 4. To bleach thread, linen, or clothes. 5. To season timber. 6. To recover from sickness. 7. *(Met.)* To remedy an evil. **Curarse en salud**, *(Coll.)* 1. To guard against evil, when there is little or no danger. 2. To defend oneself, without being accused. 3. To confess a fault, to avoid reproach. -*vr.* 1. *(Med.)* To recover, to get better; to heal up (herida etc.). 2. **Curarse de**, to take notice of. 3. *(And. Cono Sur)* to get drunk, to get tight.

curare [coo-rah'-ray], *m.* Curare, or woorari, an extract obtained from Strychnos toxifera, a powerful blood-poison, used by South American Indians as an arrow-poison.

curatela [coo-rah-tay'-lah], *f. (Law.) V.* CURADURÍA.

curativo, va [coo-rah-tee'-vo, vah], *a.* Curative.

curato [coo-rah'-to], *m.* 1. The charge of souls. 2. Parish, the district committed to the care of a rector or parson. **Curato anejo**, a small parish, annexed to another.

curca [coor-cah], *f. (And. Cono Sur)* Hump.

curco [coor'-co], *a. (And. Cono Sur)* Hunchbacked.

curculiónido, da [coor-coo-le-o'-ne-do, dah], *a.* Curculionid, like the curculio.

cúrcuma [coor'-coo-math], *f.* 1. Turmeric, a root resembling ginger. 2. Turmeric, the yellow coloring-matter obtained from curcuma, useful in chemistry for testing for alkalies, which turn it brown.

curcumáceo, cea [coor-coo-mah'-thay-o, ah], *a.* Resembling turmeric.

curcumina [coor-coo-mee'-nah], *f.* Turmeric yellow, the coloring-matter of curcuma.

curcuncho [coor-coon-cho], *a.* 1. *(LAm.)* Hunchbacked (jorobado). 2. Fed up; annoyed (molesto). -*m. (LAm.)* Hunchback.

curda [coor'-dah], *m.* Drunk, sot. -*f.* Drunkenness. **Agarrar una curda**, to get sozzled. **Estar en curda**, *(Cono Sur)* to be sozzled.

cureña [coo-ray'-nyah], *f.* 1. Guncarriage. 2. Stay of a crossbow. 3. A gunstock in the rough. **A cureña rasa**, 4. Without a parapet or breastwork (militar). 5. *(Coll. Met.)* without shelter or defence. **Tirar a cureña rasa**, to fire at random.

cureñaje [coo-ray-nyah'-hay], *m*. Collection of gun carriages.

curesca [coo-res'-cah], *f*. Shearwool cut off by a clothier with shears when the cloth has been combed.

curia [coo'-reah], *f*. 1. A tribunal, court, more often used of ecclesiastical matters. 2. Care, skill, nice attention. 3. An ancient Roman division of people.

curial [coo-re-ahl'], *a*. Relating to the Roman *curia*, or tribunal for ecclesiastical affairs.

curial [coo-re-al], *m*. 1. A member of the Roman *curia*. 2. One who employs an agent in Rome to obtain bulls or rescripts. 3. One in a subaltern employ in the tribunals of justice, or who is occupied with other's affairs.

curiana [coo-re-ah'-nah], *f*. A cockroach. *V*. CUCARACHA.

curiche [coo-re'-chay], *m*. (*Cono Sur*) negro.

curiosamente [coo-re-o-sah-men'-tay], *adv*. 1. Curiously. 2 Neatly, cleanly. 3. In a diligent; careful manner.

curiosear [coo-re-o-say-ar'], *vn*. To busy oneself in discovering what others are doing and saying. **Curiosear por las tiendas**, to wander round the shops. **Curiosear por los escaparates**, to go window-shopping. -*va*. To glance at, to look over.

curiosidad [coo-re-o-se-dahd'], *f*. 1. Curiosity, inquisitiveness, curiousness. **Despertar la curiosidad de uno**, to arouse somebody's curiosity. **Estar muerto de curiosidad**, to be dying of curiosity. 2. Neatness, cleanliness. 3. An object of curiosity, rarity.

curioso, sa [coo-re-oh'-so, sah], *a*. 1. Curious, inquisitive, desirous of information. **Estar curioso por**, to be curious to. 2. Neat, clean. 3. Careful, attentive, diligent. 4. Odd, curious, exciting attention.

curiosón, sona [coo-re-o-sone'], *m*. & *f*. Busybody.

curita [coo-re'-tah], *f*. (*LAm.*) Plaster.

currante [coor-rahn'-tay], *m*. & *f*. Worker, laborer.

currar, currelar [coor-rahr'], *vn*. To work.

currele, currelo [coor-ray-lo], *m*. Work; job; activity.

currículo [coor-re'-coo-loom], *m*. Curriculum.

currinche [coor-ren'-chay], *m*. 1. (*Typ.*) Apprentice journalist, cub reporter. 2. Little man (persona insignificante).

curro [coor-ro], *a*. 1. Smart; showy, flashy. 2. Cocky, brashy, confident. -*m*. 1. Work; job. 2. Bashing, beating (golpes). **Dar un curro a uno**, to beat somebody up.

curroadicto, ta [coor-ro-a-dec'-to], *m*. & *f*. Workaholic.

curruca [coor-roo'-cah], *f*. (*Orn.*) Linnet, babbling warbler.

currutaca [coo-rroo-tah'-cah], *f*. A woman fond of show, dress, and flutter.

currutaco [coor-roo-tah'-co], *m*. 1. Beau, fop, dandy, coxcomb, dude. 2. Insignificant little man. 3. (*CAm.*) Curratos, diarrhoea.

currutaco, ca, *a*. 1. Belonging to a person affectedly nice in his or her dress. 2. Loud, showy, flashy (ostentoso). 3. Short, squat (bajito).

currutaquería [coor-roo-tah-kay-ree'-ah], *f*. Dandyism, coxcombry.

cursado, da [coor-sah'-do, dah], *a*. Accustomed, habituated, inured. -*pp*. of CURSAR.

cursante [coor-san'-tay], *pa*. 1. Frequenting; assiduous. 2. One who hears lectures in a university; student, scholar.

cursar [coor-sar'], *va*. 1. To frequent a place, to repeat a thing. 2. To follow the schools, or to follow a course of lectures in the universities. -*vn*. **El mes que cursa**, the present month.

curseta [coor-say'-tah], *f*. A snake of the island of Martinique.

cursi [coor'-se], *a*. Pretentious, vulgar, shoddy.

cursilería [coor-se-lay-re'-ah], *f*. Bad taste, vulgarity; pretentiousness; loudness, showiness, flashiness; poshness; gentility.

cursillo [coor-seel'-lyo], *m. dim*. A short course of lectures on any science in a university.

cursilón, ona [coor-se-lone'], *m*. & *f*. Common but pretentious person; flashy type; posh sort, genteel individual.

cursivo, va [coor-see'vo, vah], *a*. Relating to Italic characters in printing; cursive, script.

curso [coor'-so], *m*. 1. Course, direction, career. 2. Course of lectures in universities. **Los de segundo curso**, those in the second year. **Curso por correspondencia**, correspondence course. 3. Course, a collection of the principal treatises used in instruction in some branch in the universities. 4. Course, a series of sucessive and methodical procedures. 5. Laxity or looseness of the body: generally used in the plural. **Curso de la corriente**, (*Naut.*) The current's way. **Curso de la marea**, (*Naut.*) the tide's way. 6. (*fig.*) Course. **El curso de la enfermedad**, the course of the disease. **Dejar que las cosas sigan su curso**, to let matters take their course. **El proceso está en curso**, the process is going on.

cursor [coor-sor'], *m*. Slider, slide.

curtación [coor-tah-the-on'], *f*. (*Astr.*) The curtate distance. *V*. ACORTAMIENTO.

curtidero [coor-te-day'-ro], *m*. Ground tanbark.

curtido, da [coor-tee'-do, dah], *a*. 1. Accustomed; dexterous, expert. 2. Weather-beaten, tanned. 3. **Estar curtido en**, (*fig.*) To be expert at. -*m*. 1. Tanning (acto). 2. Tanned leather, tanned hides.

curtidor [coor-te-dor'], *m*. Tanner, Currier, leather-dresser.

curtidos [coor-tee'-dose], *m. pl*. Tanned leather; sometimes singular.

curtiduría [coor-te-doo-ree'-ah], *f*. Tanyard, tannery.

curtiente [coor-te-en'-tay], *a*. A powdery astringent substance serving to tan hides.

curtimbre [coor-teem'-bray], *f*. 1. Tanning 2. The total of the hides tanned.

curtimiento [coor-te-meen'-to], *m*. Tanning.

curtir [coor-teer'], *va*. 1. To tan leather. 2. To imbrown by the sun, to tan the complexion: commonly used in its reciprocal sense. 3. To inure to hardships, to harden. **Estar curtido**, (*Coll.*) to be habituated, accustomed, or inured. -*vr*. 1. To become tanned, to become bronzed. 2. To become inured. 3. (*LAm.*) To get oneself dirty.

curto, ta [coor'-to, tah], *a*. (*Prov.*) Short' docktailed.

curú [coo-roo'], *m*. (*Peru*) Clothes moth.

curuca, curuja [coo-roo'-cah' coo-roo-hah], *f*. (*Orn.*) Eagle-owl.

curucucú [coo-roo-coo-coo'], *m*. A disease caused by the bite of a certain South American snake.

curul [coo-rool'], *a*. Curule, belonging to a senatorial or triumphal chair in ancient Rome. Edile.

curva [coor'-vah], *f*. 1. Curve, a curved line. 2. (*Naut.*) Knee, timber hewed like a knee. **Curva cuadrada**, square knee. **Curvas verticales de las cubiertas**, hanging knees of the decks. **Curva de la felicidad**, paunch, beer belly. **Curva de nivel**, contour line.

curva cerrada [coor'-vah ther-rah'-dah], *f*. Sharp bend (road sign).

curva doble, curva completa or **curva en U**, *f*. U-turn (road sign).

curvativo, va [coor-vah-tee'-vo, vah], *a*. (*Bot.*) Involute, rolling inward.

curvato [coor-vah'-to], *m*. Bastinado, whipping the feet, an oriental punishment.

curvatón [coor-vah-tone'], *m*. (*Naut.*) Little knee or small knee.

curvatura, curvidad [coor-vah-too'-rah, coor-ve-dahd'], *f*. 1. Curvature, inflexion. 2. (*Naut.*) Curvature of any piece of timber.

curvilíneo, nea [coor-ve-lee'-nay-o, ah], *a*. (*Geom.*) Curvilinear.

curvo, va [coor'-vo, vah], *a*. 1. Curved, crooked, bent. 2. (*And.*) Bow-legged. 3. (*Carib.*) Left-handed.

cusca [coos'-cah], *f.* 1. **Hacer la cusca a uno**, to playa dirty trick on somebody; to harm somebody. 2. *(CAm.)* To flirt (coqueta). 3. *(Mex.)* Whore.

cuscurrante [coor-roos-cahn'-tay], *a.* Crunchy, crisp.

cuscurro [coos-coor'-ro], *m.* Crouton.

cuscus [coos-coos]. Couscous.

cuscha [coos'-chah], *f. (CAm.)* Liquor, rum.

cusir [coo-seer'], *va. (Coll.)* To sew or stitch clumsily.

cusita [coo-see'-tah], *a.* Cushite, descended from Cush, son of Ham.

cusma [coos-mah], *f. (And.)* Sleeveless shirt, tunic.

cuspa [coos-pah], *f. (And.) (Agri.)* Weeding.

cuspar [coos-pahr], *va. (And.) (Agri.)* To weed.

cúspide [coos'-pe-day], *f.* 1. Cusp, the sharp end of a thing; vertex of a pyramid or cone. 2. Peak of a mountain.

cuspídeo, dea [coos-pee'-day-o, ah], *a. (Bot.)* Cuspidate.

custodia [coos-to'-de-ah], *f.* 1. Custody, keeping; hold. **Bajo la custodia de**, in the care of. 2. Monstrance, the casket or reliquary in which the consecrated Host is manifested to public veneration in Catholic churches. 3. Guard, keeper. 4. Tabernacle. 5. In the order of St. Francis, a number of convents not sufficient to form a province.

custodiar [coos-to-de-ar'], *va.* Take care of; to guard, to watch over. *V.* GUARDAR.

custodio [coos-to'-de-o], *m.* Guard, keeper, watchman. **Ángel custodio**, guardian angel.

cususa [coo-soo'-sah], *f. (CAm.)* Home-made liquor.

cutama [coo-tah'-mah], *f. (Cono Sur)* bag, sack.

cutáneo, nea [coo-tah'-nay-o, ah], *a.* Cutaneous; of the skin.

cutaras [coo-tah'-rahs], *f. pl. (CAm. Carib. Mex.)* Sandals, rough shoes.

cúter [coo'-ter], *m. (Naut.)* Cutter, a small vessel rigged as a sloop.

cutí [coo-tee'], *m.* Bed-ticking. *V.* COTÍ.

cutícula [coo-tee'-coo-lah], *f.* The cuticle, epidermis.

cuticular [coo-te-coo-lar'], *a.* Cuticular. *V.* CUTÁNEO.

cutio [coo'-te-o], *m.* Labor, work. **Trabajo cutio**, short work.

cutir [coo-teer'], *va.* To knock or dash one thing against another.

cutis [coo'-tis], *m. & f.* The skin of the human body.

cutitis [coo-tee'-tis], *f.* Dermatitis, inflammation of the skin.

cuto, ta [coo'-to, tah], *a. (LAm.)* Handless, one-handed, maimed.

cutral [coo-trahl'], *com.* An old wornout ox, or cow, past usefulness, generally, destined to the slaughterhouse.

cutre [coo'-tray], *m. (Coll.)* A pitiful, miserable fellow.

cuyo, ya [coo'-yo, yah], *pron. pos.* Of which, of whom, whose, whereof. **El asunto, cuyos detalles conoces**, the matter of which you know the details. **En cuyo caso**, in which case.

cuyo [coo'-yo], *m. (Coll.)* Gallant, lover, wooer, sweetheart.

cuz, cuz [cooth, cooth], *m.* A term for calling dogs.

cuzma [cooth'-mah], *f. (Peru)* A sleeveless shirt used by some forest Indians of Peru. (Kechuan.)

cuzqueño, ña [cooth-kay'-nyo, nyah], or **cuzquense**, *a.* Belonging to Cuzco and its inhabitants.

C. *V. abr.* de **caballos de vapor** (horsepower).

czar [thar], *m. V.* ZAR.

czarevitz [thah-ray-veets'], *m. V* ZAREVITZ.

czariano, na [thah-re-ah'-no, nah], *a. V.* ZARIANO.

czarina [thah-ree'-nah], *f. V.* ZARINA.

D

d [day] is the fourth letter of the Spanish alphabet. **D** has the same unvaried sound it has in English in the words *dedicate, fed*. In pronouncing this letter the tongue must not touch the palate at all, and barely come in contact with the teeth. In some provinces of Spain it is wrongly sounded as *th* in *although*, and at the end of a word as *th* lisped in *path*, or as *t*. In Andalusia and some parts of America it is by some made silent in the termination *ado, ido*, and they say *compráo, vendío*, instead of *comprado, vendido*. **D**. is a contraction for *Don, Doña*, and Doctor; **DD**., doctors. As a Roman numeral, **D**. is 500.

dabaji [dah-bah'-he], *m.* An Arabic word used by Cervantes, meaning corporal of a squad.

dable [dah'-bray], *a.* Possible, feasible, practicable. **No es dable hacerlo**, it is not possible to do it.

dabna [dahb'-nah], *f. (Zool.)* A kind of African viper, which attacks venomous serpents and destroys pernicious insects.

dabuti [dah-boo'-te], *a.* Funny, killing; super, smashing. -*adv.* **Pasarlo dabuti**, to have a great time.

dacá [dah-cah'], *adv.* This here, this side, on this side here. **Dacá, or de acá**, from this.

daca [dah'-cah], *v. def.* Give here. **Daca acá**, give hither. **Daca, or da acá**, or **dame acá**, give me here.

dacio, cia [dah'-the-o, the-ah], *a.* Dacian, relating to Dacia. -*m.* Tribute, tax.

dación [dah-the-on'], *f. (Law.)* Yielding something or giving something up, esp. in payment of a debt; delivery.

dacriocistitis [dah-cre-o-this-tee'-tis], *f.* Inflammation of the lachrymal sac; dacryocystitis.

dacrióideo, dea [dah-cre-o'-i-day-o, dayah], *a.* Like a tear: applied to seeds.

dacrón [dah-crone'], *m.* Dacron (trademark); polyester fiber.

dactílado, da [dac-te'-lah'-do, dah], *a.* Finger-shaped.

dactilar [dahc-te-lar'], *a.* Finger. **Huella dactilar**, fingerprint.

dactílico, ca [dac-tee'-le-co, cah], *a.* Dactylic.

dactilio [dac-tee'-le-o], *m. (Zool.)* A worm parasitic in man, found in the bladder.

dactilión [dac-te-leon'], *m.* 1. Webbed fingers or toes. 2. An apparatus devised for finger-gymnastics.

dáctilo [dahc'-te-lo], *m.* 1. Dactyl, a poetic foot. 2. Kind of shell.

dactilografía [dac-te-lo-grah-fee'-ah], *f.* Typewriting.

dactilógrafo, fa [dac-te-lo-grah'-fo], *m & f.* Typist.

dactilograma [dac-te-lo-grah'-mah], *m. (Mex.)* Fingerprints.

dactitología [dac-te-tolo-hee'-ah], *f.* Dactylology, the art of talking by manual signs.

dactilóptero [dac-te-lop'-tay-ro], *m.* The flyingfish.

dactiloscopia [dac-te-los-co'-pe-ah], *f.* Dactyloscopy, identification and classification of fingerprinting.

dadaísmo [dah-dah-es'-mo], *m.* Dadaism.

dadaíso [dah-dah-ees'-mo], *m.* Dadaism, a literary movement.

dadista [dah-des'-tah], *m. (Mex.)* Gambler.

dádiva [dah'-de-vah], *f.* Gift, present, gratification, grant, keepsake.

dadivosamente [dah-de-vo-sah-men'-tay], *adv.* Liberally, plentifully, bountifully

dadivosidad [dah-de-vo-se-dahd'], *f.* Liberality, magnificence, bounty.

dadivoso, sa [dah-de-vo'-so, sah], *a.* Bountiful, magnificent, liberal, frank, generous.

dado [dah'-do], *m.* 1. Die, *pl.* dice. **Dado falso**, cogged or false dice, filled with quicksilver, with which sharpers play. **A una vuelta de dado**, at the cast of a die. 2. *(Arch.)* Dado. *V.* NETO. 4. *V.* DONACIÓN. **Dados de las velas**, *(Naut.)* tablings of the bowline cringles. -*pp.* of DAR. **Dado a su corta edad**, in view of his youth. **Dadas estas circunstancias**, since these circumstances exist. **Ser dado a**, to be given to. **Dado que...**, provided that....

dador, ra [dah-dor', rah], *m. & f.* 1. Donor, giver; one who gives or bestows; God. 2. Drawer of a bill of exchange. 3. *m.* Carrier of a letter from one individual to another, bearer.

dafnáceo, cea [daf-nah'-thay-o, thay-ah], *a.* Like the daphne, or laurel.

dafne [dahf'-nay], *m. (Bot.)* Daphne, laurel.

daga [dah'-gah], *f.* 1. Dagger. 2. Stove or furnace of a brick-kiln.

dagazo [dah-gah-tho], *m. (Carib. Mex.)* Stab wound.

daguerrotipia [dah-gher-ro-tee'-pe-ah], *f.* The art of making daguerreotypes.

daguerrotipo [dah-gher-ro-tee'-po], *m.* Daguerreotype, a portrait made upon a prepared metal plate, and the process by which it was obtained. Important, historically, as the precursor of the photograph.

daguilla [dah-geel'-lyah], *f.* 1. *(Dim.)* Small dagger. 2. *(Prov.)* V. PALILLO.

daifa [dah'-e-fah], *f.* Mistress, concubine.

daiquirí [dah-e-ke-ree], *m.* Daiquiri, mixed alcoholic drink.

dala [dah'-lah], *f. (Naut.)* Pump-dale of a ship.

dale [dah'-lay], *int.* A word expressive of displeasure at the obstinacy of another. V. DAR.

dalgo. Hacer mucho dalgo, to receive anyone with great attention and respect.

dalia [dah'-le-ah], *f. (Bot.)* The dahlia.

dálmata [dahl'-ma-tah], or **dalmático, ca** [dal-mah'-te-co, cah], *a.* Dalmatian, belonging to or native of Dalmatia.

Dalmacia [dal-mah'-the-ah], *f.* Dalmatia.

dalmática [dahl-mah'-te-cah], *f.* Dalmatica, vestment worn by the deacons in the Roman Catholic church.

daltoniano, na [dahl-to-ne-ah'-no, nah], *a.* Affected with daltonism, color-blind.

daltonismo [dahl-to-nees'-mo], *m.* Color-blindness, especially red-blindness; daltonism.

dallá, *adv. (Obs.)* V. DE ALLÁ.

dallador [dal-lyah-dor'], *m. (Prov.)* A mower of grass.

dallar [dal-lyar'], *va. (Prov.)* To mow.

dalle [dahl'-lyay], *m.* Scythe, sickle.

dallén [dal-lyen'], *adv.* From the other side there, from the other side. **dama** [dah'-mah], *f.* 1. Lady, dame; a noble or distinguished woman. 2. Lady courted by a gentleman. 3. A lady of honor at court. 4. A mistress or concubine. 5. Queen in the game of chess: king in the game of draughts or checkers. **Dama de palacio,** lady of honor at court. 6. Any woman affectedly nice. **Es muy dama,** she is excessively nice, difficult, or scrupulous. 7. American fallow deer. **Juego de damas,** game of draughts. 8. The actress who performs the principal parts: she is also called. **Primera dama,** or first actress, to distinguish her from *la segunda,* the second, or even *la* **tercera dama,** the third actress, who acts the secondary female parts in a play.

damajuana [dah-ma-hoo-ah'-nah], *f.* Demijohn.

damascado, da [dah-mas-cah'-do, dah], *a.* V. ADAMASCADO.

damascena [dah-mas-thay'-nah], *f.* Damson, damascene, damaskplum, a small black plum.

damasceno, na [dah-mas-thay'-no, nah], *a.* Damascene, native of or belonging to Damascus.

damasco [dah-mahs'-co], *m.* 1. Damask, figured silk stuff. **Damasco de lana,** woollen damask. 2. The Brussels apricot. 3. Damson, a small black plum.

damasina [dah-ma-see'-nah], *f.* Silk stuff resembling damask.

damasquillo [dah-mas-keel'-lyo], *m.* 1. Kind of cloth, silk or wool, resembling damask. 2. *(Prov.)* V. ALBARICOQUE.

damasquinado [dah-mahs-ke-nah'-do], *m. (Tec.)* Damascene.

damasquinar [dah-mas-ke-nar'], *va.* To damascene, to ornament (steel) by etching or by inlaying, usually with gold or silver.

damasquino, na [dah-mas-kee'-no, nah], *a.* 1. Damaskeened (hierro y acero). 2. Belonging to Damascus. **A la damasquina,** damascus fashion.

damero [dah-may'-ro], *m.* Checkerboard, draughtboard.

damesana [dah-may'-sah], *f. (LAm.)* Demijohn.

damil [dah-meel'], *a. (Obs.)* Female, feminine.

damisela [dah-me-say'-lah], *f.* 1. A young gentlewoman: applied to girls that give themselves the air of high ladies. 2. *(Coll.)* A courtesan.

damita [dah-me'-tah], *f. (CAm.)* Young lady.

damnificador, ra [dam-ne-fe-cah-dor', rah], *m. & f.* One who damnifies.

damnificar [dam-ne-fe-car'], *va.* To hurt, to damage, to injure.

danchado, da [dan-chah'-do, dah], *a. (Her.)* Dentate, indented.

dandí [dahn—de'], *m.* Dandy, fop.

dandismo [dahn-des'-mo], *m.* Foppishness, foppish ways; extreme elegance.

danés, sa [dahness', sah], *a.* Danish.

dánico, ca [dah'ne-co, cah], *a.* Dane, Danish.

dango, *m. (Orn.)* V. PLANOA.

danta [dahn'-tah], *f. (Zool.)* Tapir.

dantellado, da [dan-tayl-lyah'-do, dah], *a.* Dentated, having the form of teeth.

dantesco [dahn-tes'-co], *a.* 1. *(Liter.)* Of Dante, relating to Dante. 2. *(Fig.)* Dantesque; horrific, weird, macabre.

Danubio [dah-noo'-be-o], *m.* Danube.

danza [dahn'-thah], *f.* 1. Dance. **Danza de espadas,** sword dance. 2. A set, or number of dancers. 3. *(Coll.)* A quarrel. 4. An entangled affair. **Meter en la danza,** *(Met.)* to involve another in some business or dispute. **¿Por dónde va la danza?** *(Met.)* to which side does the wind blow? 5. Row, rumpus. **Armar una danza,** to kick up a row. **No metas los perros en danza,** let sleeping dogs lie.

danzador, ra [dan-thah-dor', rah], *m. & f.* Dancer.

danzante, ta [dan-thahn'-tay, tah], *m. & f.* 1. Dancer. 2. A knowing person. 3. A fickle, airy person. **Hablar danzante,** to stammer.

danzar [dan-thar'], *vn.* 1. To dance. 2. To whirl a thing round. **Sacar a danzar,** a) to invite or engage a lady to dance. b) to cite or to oblige one to take part in any business. 3. to make public the share which a person has taken in a business. 4. *(Coll.)* To introduce oneself into any business.

danzarín, na [dan-thah-reen', nah], *m. & f.* 1. A fine dancer. 2. *(Met.)* Giddy, meddling person.

dañable [dah-nyah'-blay], *a.* Prejudicial, condemnable.

dañado, da [dah-nyah'-do, dah], *a.* Eternally damned. *-pp.* of DAñAR.

dañador, ra [dah-nyah-dor', rah], *m. & f.* Offender.

dañar [dah-nyar'], *va.* 1. To hurt, to harm. 2. To damage, to injure, to mar, to impair; to spoil. 3. To weaken, to damnify. 4. To condemn. *-vr.* To get damaged, to get hurt.

dañinear [dah-nye-nay-ar'], *va.* 1. *(Cono Sur)* V. DAñAR. 2. *(Cono Sur)* To steal.

dañino, na [dah-nyee'-no, nah], *a.* Noxious, hurtful, injurious, mischievous, harmful. *-m. (Cono Sur)* Thief.

daño [dah'-nyo], *m.* 1. Damage, hurt, injury, prejudice, harm, mischief, maim, nuisance, loss, hindrance. **Hacer daño a,** to damage. **El ajo me hace daño,** garlic disagrees with me. **Los médicos no saben donde está el daño,** the doctors cannot tell where the trouble is. 2. *(LAm.)* Spell, curse (maleficio).

dañosamente [dah-nyo-sah-men'-tay], *adv.* Hurtfully, mischievously, harmfully.

dañoso, sa [dah-nyo'-so, sah], *a.* Hurtful, noxious, injurious, mischievous, harmful.

DAO *abr.* de **Diseño Asistido por Ordenador** (Computer Aided Design).

dar [dar], *va. & vn.* 1. To give. 2. To give, to supply, to minister, to afford. 3. To minister, to give medicines, to administer a remedy. 4. To give, to deliver, to confer, to bestow. 5. To consign, to give to another in a formal manner. 6. To hit, to strike, to beat, to knock. 7. To give, to impart, to extend, to communicate. 8. To suppose erroneously. 9. To consider an affair as concluded. 10. To give, to allow, to grant a position, to coincide in opinion. 11. To persist obstinately in doing a thing. 12. To appoint. 13. To sacrifice.

14. To explain, to elucidate. 15. To be situated, to look toward. 16. With *creer, imaginar,* and analogous verbs, to simply execute the action implied. **Dar contra alguna cosa,** to hit against. **Dar crédito,** a) to accredit, to believe. b) to trust, to sell on trust. **Dar cuenta de,** to account. **Dar de comer,** to feed. **Dar de,** to fall in the manner shown by the noun. **Dar en,** to engage, bind oneself, persist in. **Dar bien,** to have good fortune. **Dar consigo,** to cause to fall, to throw down, to stop. **Dar en el blanco,** to hit the mark. **Dar fiado,** to give credit. **Dar que hacer,** to give trouble. **Dar licencia,** to give leave. **Dar memorias,** to give one's respects. **Dar razón,** to inform, to give an account of anything. **Dar prestado,** to lend. **Dar que reír,** to set laughing. **Dar que llorar,** to fall crying. **Mi ventana da al campo,** my window overlooks the field. **Dar de traste,** *(Naut.)* to run aground. **Dar al traste,** to give up a thing, an undertaking; to lose, to destroy. **Dar largas,** to prolong an affair. **Dar que decir,** to give occasion to censure. **Dar de barato,** to allow it for peace' sake. **Dar fuego,** *(Naut.)* to bream a ship. **Dar calda,** to heat the iron. **Dar con uno,** to meet a person one is looking out for. **Dar de comer al diablo,** to wrangle, to quarrel; literally, to prepare food for the devil. **Dar de sí,** to stretch. **Dar el sí,** to grant anything; to consent to marry a person. **Dar fiador** or **fianza,** to find bail, to give security. **Dar guerra,** to wage war; to torment; to be very troublesome. **Dar la cara,** to go to the defence of someone. **Dar** or **echar luz,** to recover health. **Dar margen,** to occasion, to cause, to give opportunity. **Dar la enhorabuena,** to rejoice in another's happiness, to congratulate. **Dar la paz,** to give an embrace, to give an image to be kissed as a token of peace and fraternity. **Dar los días,** to congratulate one on his birthday. **Dar los buenos días,** to wish good day. **Dar madrugón,** to get up early. **Dar mal rato,** to give uneasiness. **Dar parte,** to share with. **Dar puerta y silla,** to invite a person to come in and sit down. **Dar señal,** to give earnest money, in token that a bargain is ratified. **Dar tras uno,** to persecute one. **Dar vez,** to give one his turn. **Dar voces,** to call, cry, or scream. **Dar vuelco a un coche,** to overturn a car. **Dar golpe alguna cosa,** to be surprised or struck with the beauty or rarity of a thing. **Dar de mano,** to depreciate or despise. **Dar a luz,** a) to be delivered of a child. b) to print, to publish. **Dar de baja,** to dismiss from the army. **No dar pie, ni patada,** to take no trouble to gain an end. **Dar entre ceja y ceja,** to strike between the eyes; to make an unpleasant announcement. **Dar pie con bola,** to guess rightly. **Dar el pésame,** to express condolence. **Dado que,** supposing that …, granted that … (argumentos). **Lo que cada uno cada puede dar de sí,** what each one can contribute. **Dan un 7 por 100 de interés,** they yield 7% interest. **Le dio un fuerte dolor de costado,** he felt a sharp pain in his side. **El reloj dio las 3,** the clock struck 3. **Lo podemos dar por terminado,** we shall be able to consider it finished. **Le ha dado por no venir a clase,** he has begun to cut classes. **Han dado en llamarle Boko,** they've taken to calling him Boko.

dardabasí [dar-dah-bah-see'], *m.* *(Orn.)* Hawk, kite.

dardada [dar-dah'-dah], *f.* Blow with a dart.

dárdano, na [dar'-dah-no, nah], *a.* Trojan, Dardanian.

dardo [dar'-do], *m.* 1. Dart, a missile. 2. A freshwater fish, about a foot long, easy of digestion, but full of spines. **Dardo de pescador,** fishgig, fizgig, a kind of harpoon.

dares y tomares [dah'-rays e to-mah'-rays], *m. pl.* 1. Quantity given and received. *(Acad.)* 2. *(Coll.)* Altercations, disputes.

darse [dar'-say], *vr.* 1. To yield, to cease resistance, to give in. **Darse a,** with noun or infinitive, to execute quickly or repeatedly the action of the verb. 2. To give oneself up to virtue or vice. 3. **Darse a la vela.** *(Naut.)* to set sail. 4. **Darse a merced,** *(Mil.)* to surrender at discretion, in hunting (pájaros), to halt fatigued. 5. To concern, to interest. **Darse por vencido,** to surrender. **Me doy por vencido,** I give it up. **Darse las manos,** to shake hands. **Darse maña,** to manage one's affairs in an able manner; to contrive. **Darse

prisa,** to make haste, to hasten, to accelerate. **Darse una panzada,** *(Coll.)* to be fed to satiety and sickness. **Darse una vuelta,** to scrutinize one's own conduct, to find out one's own faults. **Si se da el caso,** if that happéns. **El cultivo se da bien este año,** the crop is coming on well this year. **Darse por perdido,** to give oneself up for lost. **Se le dan muy bien las matemáticas,** she's pretty good at maths. **Dársela a uno,** to fool somebody.

dársena [dar'-sa-nah], *f.* Place in a harbor for preserving and repairing ships; dock, basin.

darvinista, darwinista [dahr-ve-nes'-tah], *a.* Darwinist; Darwinian. *-m & f.* Darwinist.

data [dah'-tah], *f.* 1. Date the time at which a letter is written, or any instrument drawn up. 2. Item or article in an account. 3. An aperture or orifice made in reservoirs in order to let out a definite quantity. **La cosa está de mala data,** the affair is in a bad state. 4. Written permission to do anything.

datable [dah-tah'-blay], *a.* Datable, that can be dated.

datación [dah-tah-the-on'], *f.* Date, dating. **De difícil datación,** hard to date.

datáfono [dah-tah'-fo-no], *m.* Dataphone.

datar [dah-tar'], *va. & vn.* 1. To date, to note with the time at which anything is written or done. 2. To date, to reckon. **Esto data de muy atrás,** this dates back a long time.

dataría [dah-tah-ree'-ah], *f.* Datary, an office of the chancery at Rome where the Pope's bulls are expedited.

datario [dah-tah'-re-o], *m.* The principal officer of the datary.

dátil [dah'-teel], *m.* 1. *(Bot.)* Date, the fruit of the common date-palm. **Dátil de raposa,** the fruit of the dwarf fan palm. 2. Belemnites, arrow-head or finger stone.

datilado, da [dah-te-lah'-do, dah], *a.* Resembling a date.

datilera [dah-te-lay'-rah], *f.* Common datepalm.

datilillo [dah-te-leel'lyo], *m. dim.* A small date.

dativa, *f.* The thing given.

dativo [dah-tee'-vo], *m.* Dative, the third case of nouns.

dato [dah'-to], *m.* 1. Datum, a fact, a truth granted and admitted, the basis of an opinion. **Un dato interesante,** an interesting fact. **No tenemos todos los datos,** we do not have all the facts. 2. A title of high dignity in some oriental countries. 3. *(Comput.)* **Datos de entrada,** input data. **Datos de salida,** output data. **Datos semipermanentes,** semipermanent data.

daturina [dah-too-ree'-nah], *f.* Daturine, the alkaloid of datura. *V.* ATROPINA.

dauco [dah'-oo-co], *m. (Bot.)* Carrot.

DC *f. (Pol.) abr.* de **Democracia Cristiana.**

dcha, *abr.* de **derecha** (right hand).

d. de J.C. *abr.* de **después de Jesucristo** (Anno Domini, in the year of our Lord).

de [day], *prep.* 1. Of, the sign of a genitive or possessive case, as **La ley de Dios,** the law of God. **El poder de la mente,** mind's power. 2. It serves to point out the matter of which a thing is made. **Vaso de plata,** a silver cup. 3. It is the sign of the ablative case. **Vengo de Flandes,** I come from Flanders. 4. It serves sometimes instead of the preposition *con.* **De intento,** on purpose. 5. It is used in place of *por.* **De miedo,** from fear. 6. It is of the same import as *desde.* **Vamos de Madrid a Toledo,** we go from Madrid to Toledo. 7. It sometimes governs the infinitive mood. **Hora de comer,** dinner time. 8. It is placed before adverbs of time. **De día,** by day. **De noche,** by night. 9. Sometimes marks an inference. 10. In familiar style it is used to give energy to an expression. 11. It is used after many verbs to denote some, a little, a portion, etc. **Comió del pescado,** he ate some fish. **Bebió del vino,** he drank some wine. 12. It is prefixed to many verbs, nouns, etc., altering their sense, as from *poner,* to put or to place, is formed *deponer,* to depose, etc. 13. *(Obs.)* To. **Bueno de comer,** good to eat. **De balde,** for nothing, free. **El coche de mi amigo,** the car of my friend, my friend's car. **Es de ellos,** it's theirs. **El peor alumno de la clase,** the worst pupil in the class. **Dolores no es de aquí,** Dolores is not from here. **De esto se deduce que…,** from this one deduces that. **Tiene tres hijos de su primera mujer**, he has 3 children by his first wife. **Hablaba de política**, he was talking about politics. **Una tacita de café**; a cup of coffee. **Un libro de Cela**, a book by Cela. **Máquina de coser**, sewing machine. **Pintado de negro**, painted in black. **De puerta en puerta**, from door to door. **Dar un salto**, in one bound. **Estar loco de contento**, to be crazy with joy. **Paralizado de las dos piernas**, paralysed in both legs. **De niño**, as a child. **Una persona amada de todos**, a person loved by all. **El bueno de Juan**, good old John

dea [day'-ah], *f. (Poet.)* Goddess. *V.* DIOSA.

deal [day-ahl], *a.* Like a goddess, divine (rare).

dealbación [day-ahl-bah-the-on'], *f.* (Chem.) Making white by means of fire.

deambular [day-ahn-boo-lar'], *vn.* To saunter, to stroll, to wander.

deán [day-ahn'], *m.* Dean, an ecclesiastical dignitary.

deanato, deanazgo [day-ah-nah'-to, day-ah-nahth'-go], *m.* Deanship.

debacle [day-bah'-clay], *f.* Disaster.

debajo [day-bah'-'ho], *adv.* Under, underneath, below. **Debajo de la mesa**, under the table. **Por debajo de**, under. Underhand, privately. *-prep.* Under, subordinate, dependent.

debate [day-bah'-tay], *m.* Debate, altercation, expostulation, discussion, contention.

debatir [day-bah-teer'], *va.* 1. To debate, to argue, to discuss. 2. To combat, to engage with arms. 3. To expostulate. *-vr, vn.* To struggle.

debe [day'-bay], *m. (Com.)* The debtor-side of an account, debit. **Debe y haber**, debit and credit.

debelar [day-bay-lar'], *va.* To debellate, to conquer.

deber [day-berr'], *m.* 1. Obligation, duty. 2. Debt. **Hacer su deber**, to fulfil one's duty.

deber [day-berr'], *va.* To owe, not to pay a debt which is due. **Me debes cinco dólares**, you owe me five dollars. **Esto lo debe a la influencia francesa**, he owes this to French influence. *-vn.* To be obliged to, to be to, must, ought, would, have to. **Debía ser**, must have been. **Deber de**, must. **Debo hacerlo**, I must do it. **He debido perderlo**, I must have lost it. **Debe de ser así**, it must be like that. **No debe de ser muy caro**, it can't be very dear. *-vr.* **Deberse a**, to be owing to. **Se debe al mal tiempo**, it's on account of the bad weather. **Puede deberse a que**..., it may be because....

debidamente [day-be-dah-men'-tay], *adv.* 1. Justly, with moderation and justice. 2. Duly, exactly, perfectly. **Un documento debidamente redactado**, a properly drawn up document.

debido, da [day-bee'-do, dah], *a.* Due, proper. **En forma debida**, in due or proper form. **Como es debido**, as is proper. **Debido a las circunstancias**, due to circumstances. **Debido a la falta de agua**, because of the water shortage.

débil [day'-beel], *a.* 1. Feeble, weak, extenuated, debilitated, faintly, sickly, infirm. 2. Feeble, weak. 3. Fragile, frail. 4. Pusillanimous, mean spirited.

debilidad [day-be-le-dahd'], *f.* 1. Debility, weakness, languor. 2. Weakness, feebleness, want of strength. 3. (Met.) Pusillanimity, fondness, craziness: frailty. **Tener una debilidad por el chocolate**, to have a weakness for chocolate.

debilitación [day-be-le-tah-the-on']; *f.* Debilitation, extenuation.

debilitar [day-be-le-tar'], *va.* To debilitate, to weaken, to extenuate, to enfeeble, to enervate. *-vr.* To grow weak(er), to weaken.

débilmente [day'-beel-men-tay], *adv.* Weakly, feebly, faintly, lamely.

débito [day'-be-to], *m.* Debt. **Débito** or **débito conyugal**, conjugal duty.

debitorio [day-be-to'-re-o], *m.* Contract of bargain and sale upon credit, by virtue of a partial payment, until settlement of the debt.

debó [day-bo'], *m.* Instrument used for scraping skins, scraper.

debocar [day-bo-car'], *va. vn.* To vomit.

debut [day-boo'], *m.* Debut.

debutanta, tante [day-boo-tahn'-tah], *m. & f.* Debutant.

debutar [day-boo-tar'], *vn.* To make one's debut, to present for the first time.

deca [day'-cah], **Greek prefix**, meaning ten.

década [day'-cah-dah], *f.* Decade, the number or sum of ten.

decadencia [day-cah-den'-the-ah], *f.* Decay, decline, fading, failing, decaying. **Ir en decadencia**, to be on the decline.

decadente [day-cahn'-tay], *pa.* Decaying, declining.

decáedro, dra [day-cah'-ay-dro, drah], *m. & f.* Decahedron, a solid of ten faces.

decaer [day-cah-err'], *vn.* 1. To decay, to decline, to fail, to languish, to grow weak, to fade. **Ella ha decaído en belleza**, her beauty is not what it was. 2. (Naut.) To fall to leeward. (*Yo decaigo, yo decaí, yo decaiga*, from *Decaer. V.* CAER.)

decágono [day-cah'-go-no], *m.* Decagon, a polygon of ten sides or angles.

decagramo [day-cah-grah'-mo], *m.* Decagram, the weight of ten grams.

decaído, da [day-cah-ee'-do, dah], *a.* Crestfallen, dejected, dispirited.

decaimiento [day-cah-e-me-an'to], *m.* Decay, failing, decline, weakness.

decalitro [day-cah-lee'-tro], *a.* Decaliter, ten liters.

decálogo [day-cah'logo], *m.* Decalogue, the Ten Commandments.

decámetro [day-cah'-may-tro], *m.* Decameter, the length of ten meters.

decampamento [day-cam-pahmen'to], *m.* Decampment, the act of shifting the camp.

decampar [day-cam-par'], *vn.* To decamp.

decanato [day-cahnah'to], *m.* Dignity of the senior of any community.

decandrio, dria [day-cahn'-dreo, ah], *a.* Decandrous, having ten stamens. *-f. pl.* Decandria, plants whose flowers have ten stamens.

decano [daycah'no], *m.* Senior, the most ancient member of a community or corporation.

decantación [daycantah-the-on'], *f.* Decantation, pouring off.

decantar [day-can-tar'], *va.* 1. To cry up, to exaggerate or magnify a thing. **El tan decantado edificio**, this building which has been so effusively praised. 2. To turn anything from a right line and give it an oblique direction. 3. To decant, to draw off liquor. *-vr.* **Decantarse hacia**, to move towards. **Decantarse por algo**, to show preference for something.

decapétalo, la [day-cah-pay'-tah-lo, lah], *a.* Having ten petals; decapetalous.

decapitación [day-cah-pe-tah-theon'], *f.* Decapitation, beheading.

decapitar [day-cah-pe-tar'], *va.* To behead, to decapitate.

decasílabo [day-cah-see'-lah-bo], *a.* (Poet.) Having ten syllables.

decastilo [day-cas-tee'-lo], *m.* (Arch.) Decastyle, an assemblage of ten pillars.

deceleración [day-thay-lay-rah-the-on'], *f.* (Phys.) Deceleration.

decena [day-thay'-nah], *f.* 1. Ten. **Una decena de barcos**, about ten ships. **Contar por decenas**, to count in tens. 2. (Prov.) Company or party of ten persons. 3. (Mus.) Consonance made of an octave and a third; a tenth.

decenal [day-thay-nahl'], *a.* Decennial, a space of ten years.

decenar [day-they-nar'], *m.* A squad or crew of ten.

decencia [day-then'-the-ah], *f.* 1. Decency, propriety of form or conduct. 2. Decency, reservedness, honesty, modesty.

decenio [day-thay'-neo], *m.* Space of ten years; decennial.

deceno, na [day-thay-no, nah], *a.* Tenth, ordinal of ten.

decentar [day-then-tar'], *va.* 1. To commence the use of things not before used. 2. To begin to lose that which had been preserved. *-vr.* To wound, to gall or injure the skin or body; to be bedridden.

decente [day-then'-tay], *a.* 1. Decent, just, honest, becoming, fit, suitable, decorous. 2. Convenient, reasonable. 3. Decent, modest, grave, genteel. 4. Of honest, but not noble parents.

decentemente [day-tehn-t-ay-men'-tay], *adv.* 1. Decently, fairly, honorably. 2. Decently, without immodesty, comely 3. Abundantly.

decenvirato [day-then-ve-rah'-to], *m.* Decemvirate.

decepción [day-thep-the-on'], *f.* Deception, illusion; disappointment.

decepcionante [day-thep-the-o-nahn'-tay], *a.* Disappointing.

decepcionar [day-thep-the-onar], *va.* To disappoint, to disillusion. *-vr.* To be disappointed.

deceso [day-thay'-so], *m.* Decease, a natural death.

dechado [day-chah'-do], *m.* 1. Sample, pattern, design, standard. 2. Linen, on which young girls perform several sorts of needlework. 3. Example, pattern, or model of virtue and perfection.

deci [day'-the], A Latin prefix, signifying one tenth.

deciárea [day-the-ah'-ray-ah], *f.* Decire, one tenth of an âre: 10 sq. meters.

decibel [day-the-bel], or **decibelio** [daythe-bay'-le-o], *m.* *(Phys.)* Decibel.

decible [day-thee'-blay], *a.* Expressible, that which may be expressed.

decidero, ra [day-the-day'-ro, rah], *a.* What may be said without inconvenience or impropriety.

decididamente [day-ce-de-dah-men'tay], *adv.* Decidedly.

decidido, da [day-the-dee'-do, dah], *a.* Determined, decided. **De carácter decidido**, firm, strong-willed.

decidir [day-the-deer'], *va.* To decide, to determine, to resolve, to conclude. **Esto le decidió a dejarlo**, this decided him to give it up. *-vn.* To decide, to make one's mind. **Decidir en favor de uno**, to decide in somebody's favor. *-vr.* To decide, to be determined.

decidor, ra [day-the-dor', rah], *m. & f.* 1. One who speaks with fluency and elegance. 2. A wit. 3. Versifier, poet.

decigramo [day-the-grah'-mo], *m.* Decigram, one tenth of a gram.

decilitro [day-the-lee'-tro], *m.* Decilitre, one-tenth of a liter.

décima [day'the-mah], *f.* 1. *(Poet.)* A Spanish stanza consisting of ten verses of eight syllables. 2. Tenth, tithe, the tenth part.

decimal [day-the-mahl,], *a.* 1. Decimal. 2. Pertaining to tithes. **Rentas decimales**, tithes or tithe rents. **Decimal codificado en binario**, *(Comput.)* binary coded decimal.

décimanovena [day'-the-mah-no-vay'-nah], *f.* One of the registers of the pipes of an organ.

decimar [day-the-mar'], *va.* V. DIEZMAR.

decímetro [day-thee'-may-tro], *m.* Decimeter, one-tenth of a meter.

décimo, ma [day'-the-mo, mah] *a.* Tenth, ordinal of ten.

décimoctavo va [day'-the-moc-tah'-vo, vah], *a.* Eighteenth.

décimocuarto, ta [day-the-mo-koo-ahr'-to], *a.* Fourteenth.

decimonónico [day-the-mo-no'-ne-co], Nineteenth-century; Victorian; *(fig.)* outdated, antiquated.

décimonono, na [day'-the-mo-no-no, nah], *a.* Nineteenth.

décimonoveno, na [day'-the-mo-no-vay' no, nah], *a.* V. DÉCIMONONO.

décimoquinto, ta [day'-the-mo-keen'-to, tah], *a.* Fifteenth.

décimoséptimo, ma [day'-the-mo-sep'-temo, mah], *a.* Seventeenth.

décimosexto, ta [day-the-mo-sex'-to, tah], *a.* Sixteenth.

decimotercio, cia [day'-the-mo-terr'-theo, ah], *a.* Thirteenth.

deciochono, na [day-the-o-chay'-no, nah], *a.* 1. Eighteenth. 2. Kind of cloth having a warp of 1,800 threads. 3. V. DIECIOCHENO.

decir [day-theer'], *va.* 1. To say or utter, to tell, to speak, to express by words. 2. To assure, to persuade. 3. To name, to give a name to a person or place. 4. To be conformable, to correspond. 5. To denote, to mark, to be a sign of. 6. To declare or depose upon oath. 7. To verify. **Decir bien**, to

speak fluently or gracefully; to explain a thing well. **¡Digo!** I say; hark; used in calling or speaking to. **Decir que sí**, to affirm something. **Decir que no**, to deny. **Decir por decir**, to talk for the sake of talking. **Como dijo el otro**, used of an unknown author, or when a name cannot be recalled. **Decir alguna cosa con la boca chica**, to offer a thing merely for form's sake. **No sé qué decir**, how can I tell?. **¿Qué quiere decir eso?**, what does that mean?. **Por más que Vd. diga**, you may say what you will. **No dijo nada**, he said nothing. **Decir a uno que se calle**, to tell somebody to be quiet. **Pero dice mal**, but he is wrong. **Como quien no dice nada**, quite casually. **Me dijo de todo**, he called me all the names under the sun. **Es mucho decir**, that's saying a lot. **Querer decir**, to mean. **Dar que decir**, to make people talk. **Por decirlo así**, so to speak. **El qué dirán**, public opinion. **Digan lo que digan**, whatever they say. **No estuvo muy cortés que digamos**, actually he wasn't all that polite. **No es que digamos muy guapa**, she's not really that pretty. **Su cara dice lo que es**, his face shows him up for what he is. *-vr.* 1. **Yo sé lo que me digo**, I know what I'm talking about. 2. To be called, to be named. **Esta plaza se dice de la Revolución**, this is called Revolution Square. 3. **Se dice**, it is said. **Se me ha dicho que…**, I have been told that. 4. **Esto es lo que se dice un queso**, this is a real cheese.

decir [day-theer'], *m.* A notable saying. **Decires**, idle talk, false rumors, scandal, slander. **Es un decir**, it's just a phrase.

decisión [day-the-se-on'], *f.* 1. Decision, determination, resolution, issue. **Tomar una decisión**, to make a decision. 2. Decision, judgment by court of justice. 3. Verdict by a jury. 4. Disposition.

decisivamente [day-the-se-vah-men'-tay], *adv.* Decisively.

decisivo, va [day-the-see'-vo, vah], *a.* Decisive, final, conclusive, decretory.

decisorio, ria [day-the-so're-o, ah], *a. (Law.)* Decisive, concluding, decisory.

declamación [day-clah-mah-the-on'], *f.* 1. Declamation, harangue, oration, discourse. 2. A speech delivered, an oratorial invective. 3. Declamation, a discourse addressed to the passions. 4. Delivery. 5. The manner of reciting theatrical compositions. 6. Panegyric.

declamador, ra [day-clah-mah-dor', rah], *m. & f.* Declaimer, exclaimer.

declamar [day-clah-mar'], *vn.* To declaim, to harangue. *-va.* To declaim, to recite (versos).

declamatorio, ria [day-clah-ma-to're-o, ah], *a.* Declamatory.

declaración [day-clah-rah-the-on'], *f.* 1. Declaration. 2. Declaration, interpretation, exposition. **Declaración conjunta**, joint declaration. **Declaración de derechos**, bill of rights 3. Manifest, manifestation; account. 4. Overture, proposal. 5. *(Law.)* Deposition. **Declaración de culpabilidad**, confession of guilt. **Prestar declaración**, to make a statement.

declaradamente [day-clah-rah-dah-men'-tay], *adv.* Declaredly, avowedly.

declarado, da [day-clah-rah'-do, dah], *a. & pp.* of DECLARAR. 1. Declared. 2. Applied to a person who speaks too plainly.

declarador, ra [day-clah-rah-dor, rah], *m. & f.* Declarer, expositor.

declarante [day-clah-rahn'-tay], *m.* 1. Declarer, one who declares or explains; a witness in the act of being examined. **Juan declarante**, a talkative person, who speaks his mind too freely. 2. Bidder (naipes).

declarar [day-clah-rar'], *va.* 1. To declare, to manifest, to make known. 2. To expound, to explain, to exemplify. 3. *(Law.)* To determine and decide, to find. **Declarar culpable a uno**, to find somebody guilty. 4. *(Law.)* To witness or depose upon oath. *-vn.* 1. To declare. **Según él mismo declara**, as he himself declares. 2. To bid, to declare (naipes). 3. To make a statement; to testify. *-vr.* 1. To declare one's opinion, to explain one's mind. **Declararse a una joven**, to say to a girl that one loves her. 2. **Declararse culpable**, to plead guilty.

declarativo, va [day-clah-ra-tee'-vo, vah], *a.* Declarative, assertive.

declaratorio, ria [day-clah-rah-to'-re-o, ah], *a.* Declaratory, explanatory.

declinable [day-cle-nah'-blay], *a.* (*Gram.*) Declinable, having variety of terminations.

declinación [day-cle-nah-the-on'], *f.* 1. Declination, descent, decay, fall, decline, falling. 2. (*Gram.*) Declination, the declension of nouns. 3. (*Astr.*) Declination, distance of a star or planet from the equator. 4. Deviation of a wall or building from facing one of the cardinal points of the compass. 5. Magnetic variation of the needle from the pole.

declinante [day-cle-nahn'-tay], *a.* Declining, bending down.

declinar [day-cle-nar'], *vn.* 1. To decline, to lean downward. 2. To decline, to sink, to be impaired, to decay, to degenerate, to abate, to diminish (de enfermedad). 3. To be finished or reach the last. 4. (*Naut.*) To vary from the true magnetic meridian. **Va declinando el día**, it is near twilight. -*va.* 1. (*Gram.*) To decline a word by various determinations. 2. To challenge a judge, to transfer a cause to another tribunal: in this last sense it is always used with the word *jurisdicción*.

declinatoria [day-cle-nah-to'-re-ah], *f.* (*Law.*) Plea which attacks the competency of a judge.

declinatorio [day-cle-nah-to'-re-o], *m.* Declinator, or declinatory, an instrument used in dialing.

declive, declivio [day-clee'-vey, day-clee'-veo], *m.* 1. Declivity, inclination downward, slope, fall. 2. Gradient, grade. **Tierra en declive**, sloping ground. **Estar en declive**, to slope.

declividad [day-cle-ve-dahd'], *f.* Declivity.

decocción [day-co-co-the-on'], *f* Decoction.

decoctivo, va [day-coc-tee'-vo, vah], *a.* Digestive.

decodificador [day-co-de-fe-cah-dor], *m.* (*Comput.*) Decoder.

decolación [day-co-lah-the-on'], *f.* 1. Separation of the parts of an organ which ought to act together. 2. Decapitation of the foetus.

desoloración [day-colo-rah-the-on'], *f.* Decoloration, loss of color; decolorization, bleaching, blanching.

decolorante [day-co-lo-rahn'-tay], *m.* Bleaching agent.

decolorar [day-colo-rar'], *va.* To remove the color from any substance, to decolorize. -*vr.* To lose color.

decolorímetro [day-co-lo-re-e'-may-tro], *m.* Decolorimeter.

decombustión [day-com-boos-te-on'], *f.* An operation to destroy the oxidation of a body which has undergone combustion.

decomisar [day-co-me-sar'], *va.* To confiscate, to seize, to forfeit.

decomiso [day-co-me-e'-so], *m.* Confiscation, forfeiture, seizure.

decoración [day-co-rah-the-on'], *f.* Decoration, ornament. **Decoración de escaparate**, window display. **Decoración de interiores**, interior decorating. -*pl.* The scenery and curtains of a theater.

decorado [day-co-rah-do], *m.* Scenery, set (cine, teatro).

decorador, ra [day-co-rah-dor'], *m.f.* Decorator.

decorar [day-co-rar'], *va.* 1. To decorate, to adorn, to embellish, to furnish. 2. To illustrate, to ennoble, to honor, to exalt. 3. To learn by heart. 4. To recite, to repeat.

decorativo, va [day-co-rah-te-vo], *a.* Decorative, ornamental.

decoro [day-co'-ro], *m.* 1. Honor, respect, reverence due to any person. 2. Circumspection, gravity, integrity. 3. Purity, honesty. 4. Decorum, decency, civility.

decorosamente [day-co-ro-sah-men'-tay], *adv.* Decently, decorously.

decoroso, sa [day-co-ro'-so, sah], *a.* Decorous, decent.

decorticación [day-cor-tee-cah-the-on'], *f.* Decortication, the act of stripping the bark or husk.

decrecer [day-cray-therr'], *vn.* To decrease, to diminish.

decreciente [day-cray-the-ayn'-tay], *a.* Decreasing, diminishing.

decrecimiento [day-cray-the-me-ayn'-to], *m.* Decrease, diminution; fall; shortening.

decremento [day-cray-men'-to], *m.* Decrement, decrease, diminution, declension, wane.

decrepitación [day-cray-pe-tah-the-on'], *f.* (*Chem.*) Decrepitation, a crackling noise as made by suit when heated.

decrepitante [day-cray-pe-tahn'tay], *pa.* (*Chem.*) Decrepitant.

decrepitar [day-cray-pe-tar'], *va. & vn.* 1. To decrepitate, to calcine salt until it has ceased to crackle in the fire. 2. To decrepitate, to crackle when put over the fire (sal).

decrépito, ta [day-cray'-pe-to, tah], *a.* Decrepit, worn with age.

decrepitud [day-cray-pe-tood'], *f.* Decrepitude, the last stage of decay; old age.

decretación [day-cray-tah-the-on'], *f.* Determination, establishment.

decretal [day-cray-tahl'], *f.* Decretal, letter or rescript of the Pope. **Decretales**, decretals, a collection of letters and decrees of the Popes.—*a.* Docretal.

decretalista [day-cray-tah-lees'-tah], *m.* Decretist, one that draws up or studies the rescripts, letters, and decrees of Popes.

decretar [day-cray-tar'], *va.* 1. To decree, to determine, to resolve. 2. (*Law.*) To give a decree or a determination in a suit. 3. To award (premio). -*vn.* To deliver a judgment.

decretero [day-cray-tay'-ro], *m.* 1 Catalogue or list of the names and offences of criminals. 2. Decretal, collection of decrees.

decretista [day-cray-tees'-tah], *m.* Decretist, one who expounds or explains the decretals.

decreto [day-cray'-to], *m.* 1. Decree, decision resolution. 2. Decree, order or determination issued in the king's name. 3. A judical decree. **Por real decreto**, royal decree. 4. In canon law, decree or ordinance enacted by the Pope with the advice of his cardinals. 5. Opinion, vote, advice.

decreto-ley [cay-cray'-to lay-e], *m. pl.* **decretos-leyes**, decree law.

decretorio, ria [day-cray-to'-re-o, ah], *a.* Decretory, critical: applied to the days when a judgment may be formed on the issue of a fit of illness.

decúbito [day-coo'-be-to], *m.* 1. (*Med.*) Decubitus, the position of a patient in bed. **Decúbito prono**, prone position. **Úlcera de decúbito**, bedsore.

décuplo, pla [day'-coo-plo, plah], *a.* Decuple, tenfold.

decuria [day-coo'-re-ah], *f.* Ten Roman soldiers under a decurion.

decurrente [day-coor-ren'-tay], *a.* Decurrent, applied to the stem: said of leaves.

decursas [day-coor'-sa], *f. pl.* (*Law.*) Arrears of rent.

decurso [day-coor'-so], *m.* Course, succession of movement or time. **En el decurso de los años**, over the years.

decusación [day-coo-sah-the-on'], *f.* 1. Decussation, intercrossing of nervefibers. 2. The spot of intersection of such fibers.

decusado, da [day-coo-sah'-do, dah], *a.* Intersected.

dedada [day-dah'-dah], *f.* 1. That which can be taken up with the finger at once, a pinch. **Dedada de miel**, adulation, flattery, wheedling. **Dar a uno una dedada de miel**, (*Met.*) to put a cheat on one, to deceive; literally, to give one a fingerful of honey 2. Triglyph of a Doric frieze.

dedal [day-dahl'], *m.* 1. Thimble. 2 A leather fingerstall used by calkers on the little finger of the left hand.

dedalera [day-dah-lay'-rah], *f.* (*Bot.*) Foxglove.

dédalo [day'-dah-lo], *m.* 1. A labyrinth, an entanglement. 2. (*Fig.*) Tangle, mess.

dedicación [day-de-cah-the-on'], *f.* Dedication, the act of dedicating, consecration; inscription. **Estar en dedicación exclusiva**, to work full-time; **dedicación plena**, full-time.

dedicante [day-de-cahn'-tay], *pa.* Dedicating, dedicator.

dedicar [day-de-car'], *va.* 1. To dedicate, to devote, to consecrate. **Dedico un día a la semana a pescar**, I spend one day a week fishing. 2. To dedicate a literary work to someone. **Dedicarse a alguna cosa**, to apply oneself to a thing. **Se dedicó a la cerámica**, he devoted himself to pottery.

dedicativo, va [day-de-cah-tee'-vo, vah], *a.* V. DEDICATORIO.

dedicatoria [day-de-cah-to'-re-ah], *f.* Dedication, an address by which a literary composition is inscribed to a patron or friend.

dedicatorio, ria [day-de-cah-to'-re-o, ah], *a.* Dedicatory, containing or serving as a dedication.

dedición [day-de-the-on'], *f.* Unconditional surrender of a town to ancient Rome.

dedil [day-deel'], *m.* Thumbstall of linen or leather used by reapers.

dedillo, ito [day-deel'-lyo], *m. dim.* A little finger. **Saber una cosa al dedillo**, to know a thing perfectly.

dedo [day'-do], *m.* 1. Finger. 2. Toe. 3. The forty-eighth part of a Spanish yard, or *vara.* 4. A finger's breadth, a small bit. **Meter los dedos**, to pump one. **Señalarle con el dedo**, to point at another with the finger. **Dedo pulgar**, thumb. **Dedo índice** or **saludador**, the index or forefinger. **Dedo del corazón, cordial** or **de en medio**, middle finger. **Dedo anular**, the ringfinger. **Dedo meñique** or **auricular**, the little finger. **A dos dedos de**, very near to. **Chuparse los dedos**, to eat, say, do, or hear something with delight. **Meter a uno los dedos**, to pretend to believe the contrary of what one knows certainly. **Morderse los dedos**, to be revengefully angry. **Se le escapó entre los dedos**, it slipped through his fingers. **Pillarse los dedos**, *(fig.)* to get caught red-handed. **No tienes dos dedos de frente**, he's pretty dim.

deducción [day-dooc-the-on'], *f.* 1. Deduction, derivation, origin, consequence. 2. Deduction, that which is deducted. 3. *(Mus.)* The natural progression of sounds.

deducible [day-doo-thee'-blay], *a.* Deducible, inferable.

deducir [day-doo-theer'], *va.* 1. To deduce, to collect, to infer as a consequence; to fetch, to devise, to draw. 2. To allege in pleading, to offer as a plea. 3. To subtract, to deduct, to extract.

deductivo, va [day-dooc-tee'-vo, vah], *a.* Deductive.

defácile [day-fah'-the-lay], *adv.* Easily.

defacto [day-fac'-to], *adv.* In fact, actually, effectually. = DE HECHO.

defalcar [day-fal-car'], *va.* V. DESFALCAR.

defecación [day-fay-cah-the-on'], *f.* 1. Defecation, purification of a liquid from less or sediment. 2. Defecation, voiding of excrement.

defecadora [day-fay-cah-do'-rah], *f.* In sugar refining, defecating pan, second boiler.

defecar [day-fay-car'], *va.* 1. To defecate, purify from lees, dregs, or polluting matter. 2. To defecate, void excrement.

defección [day-fec-the-on'], *f.* Defection, apostasy; revolt.

defectible [day-fec-tee'-blay], *a.* Defectible, imperfect, deficient.

defectillo [day-fec-teel'-lyo], *m. dim.* Slight fault or defect.

defectivo, va [day-fec-tee'-vo, vah], *a.* Defective, imperfect.

defecto [day-fec-to], *m.* 1. Defect, failing, fault. 2. Defect, any natural imperfection. **Defecto físico**, physical defect. **Defecto de palabra**, speech defect. *-pl. (Print.)* Sheets remaining after a day's work in order to complete the full number. **Poner defectos**, to find fault.

defectuosamente [day-fec-too-o-sah-men'-tay], *adv.* Defectively, faultily, deficiently.

defectuoso, sa [day-fec-too-oh'-so, sah], *a.* Defective, imperfect, faulty.

defendedoro, ra [day-fen-day-day'-ro, rah], *a.* Defensible.

defendedor, ra [day-fen-day-dor', rah], *a. & m. & f.* V. DEFENSOR.

defender [day-fen-derr'], *va.* 1. To defend, to protect, to guard. 2. To defend, to make good, to justify, to assert, to maintain. 3. To defend, to vindicate. 4. To veto, to prohibit, to forbid. 5. To resist, to oppose. 6. To defend a place, a cause, etc.; to fence. *-vr.* 1. To defend oneself. **Defenderse bien**, to resist firmly. 2. *(Fig.)* **Me defiendo en inglés**, I can manage in English. **Gana poco pero se defiende**, she doesn't earn much but she manages.

defendible [day-fen-dee'-blay], *a.* Defensible.

defendido, da [day-fen-dee'-do], *m.f.* A client.

defenecimiento [day-fay-nay-the-me-en'-to], *m. (Com. Prov.)* Settlement of an account.

defensa [day-fen'-sah], *f.* 1. Defence, safeguard, arms. **Defensa de**, defence against. 2. Defence, vindication, justification, apology. 3. Defence, guard, shelter, protection; fence. 4. Defence, in law, the defendant's reply. 5. (Sports) Defense. 6. Tusk. 7. Horn. **Legítima defensa**, *(For.)* self defense. **Defensas**, 1. Fortifications, defenses. 2. *(Naut.)* Skids. 3. *(Naut.)* Fenders.

defensa [day-fen'-sah], *m.* (Sports) Back.

defensa civil [day-fen'-sah the-veel'], *f.* Civil defense.

defensión [day-fen-se-on'], *f.* Safeguard, defence.

defensiva [day-fen-see'-vah], *f.* Defensive. **Estar a la defensiva**, or **ponerse sobre la defensiva**, to be upon the defensive, to put oneself upon the defensive.

defensivo [day-fen-see'-vo], *m.* 1. Defence, safeguard, preservative. 2. Piece of linen steeped in any medicated liquor, and applied to some part of the body, to refresh and strengthen it.

defensivo, va [day-fen-see'-vo, vah], *a.* Defensive, that which serves as a defence or safeguard; justificatory, defensory.

defensor, ra [day-fen-sor', rah], 1. Defender or keeper, maintainer, conservator, protector, supporter. **Defensor del pueblo**, public defender. 2. *(Law.)* A lawyer appointed by a court of justice to defend one absent, or one who cannot pay a defender. V. ABOGADO DE POBRES.

defensoría [day-fen-so-ree'-ah], *f.* The duty and office of a lawyer appointed by a judge to defend a person who is absent, or who has no defender.

defensorio [day-fen-so-re'-o], *m.* Defence, an apologetic writing in favor of any person or thing; a memoir, a manifesto.

deferencia [day-fay-ren'-the-ah], *f.* Deference, complaisance, condescension.

deferente [day-fay-ren'-tay], *a.* Assenting, deferring to the opinion of another; deferent.

deferir [day-fay-reer'], *vn.* To defer, to pay deference to another's opinion, to yield to another's judgment. *-va.* To communicate, or share in the jurisdiction or power.

defibríneo, a [day-fe-bree'-nay-o, ah], *a.* Defibrinated.

deficiencia [day-fe-the-en'-the-ah], *f.* Deficiency, imperfection. *(Antiq.).* **Deficiencia mental**, mental deficiency.

deficiente [day-fe-the-en'-tay], *a.* Defective, faulty, deficient. **Deficiente mental**, mental defective.

déficit [day'-fe-theet], *m.* Deficit. **Déficit comercial**, trade deficit.

deficitario [day-fe-the-ah'-re-o], *a.* 1. *(Fin.)* Deficit; in deficit, showing a deficit. 2. **Ser deficitario en**, to be short of.

definible [day-fe-nee'-blay], *a.* Definable.

definición [day-fe-ne-the-on'], *f.* 1. Definition. 2. Decision, determination. **Definiciones**, statutes of military orders.

definido, da [day-fe-nee'-do, dah], *a.* Definite. **Bien definido**, well defined. **Definido por el usuario**, user defined. *-pp.* of DEFINIR.

definidor [day-fe-ne-dor'], *m.* 1. Definer. 2. In some religious orders, one of the members who compose, under the presidency of their superior, a chapter or assembly to govern the order.

definir [day-fe-neer'], *va.* 1. To define, to describe, to explain. 2. To decide, to determine. 3. *(Pict.)* To conclude any work, finishing all its parts, even the least important, with perfection.

definitivamente [day-fe-ne-te-vah-men'-tay], *adv.* Definitively

definitivo, va [day-fe-ne-tee'-vo, vah], *a.* Definitive, determinate. **En definitiva**, definitively.

definitorio [day-fe-ne-to're-o], *m.* 1. Chapter or assembly of the chiefs of religious orders, to deliberate on the affairs of the order. 2. House or hall where the above chapters are held.

deflagración [day-flah-grah-the-on'], *f.* Deflagration, sudden burning.

deflagrador [day-flah-grah-dor'], *m.* Deflagrator, ignitor.

deflagrar [day-fla-grar'], *va.* To deflagrate, to cause to burn.

deflegmación [day-fleg-mah-the-on'], *f.* *(Med.)* Expectoration.

deflegmar [day-fleg-mar'], *vn.* To become free from water, as spirituous liquors; to dephlegmate, concentrate.

deflujo [day-floo'-ho], *m.* *(Astr.)* The recession of the moon from any planet.

defoliación [day-fo-le-ah-the-on'], *f.* Defoliation, the shedding of leaves.

defoliante [day-fo-lle-ahn'-tay], *m.* Defoliant.

deformación [day-for-mah-the-on'], *f.* Deformation; defacing.

deformador [day-for-mah-dor'], *m.* One who deforms or disfigures.

deformar [day-for-mar'], *va.* To deform, to disfigure, to misshape. *-vr.* To become deformed; to get distorted.

deformatorio, ria [day-for-mah-to'-re-o, ah], *a.* Deforming, disfiguring.

deforme [day-for'-may], *a.* Deformed, disfigured, ugly, hideous.

deformemente [day-for-may-men'-tay], *adv.* Deformedly.

deformidad [day-for-me-dahd'], *f.* 1. Deformity, hideousness, ugliness. 2. A gross error.

defraudación [day-frah-oo-dah-the-on'], *f.* Defraudation, fraud, deceit, usurpation. **Defraudación de impuestos**, tax evasion.

defraudador [day-fra-hoo-dah-dor'], *m.* Defrauder, defaulter.

defraudar [day-fra-hoo-dar'], *va.* 1. To defraud, to rob or deprive by wile or trick. 2. To defraud, to cheat, to trick, to usurp what belongs to another. 3. *(Met.)* To intercept the light of the sun; to spoil the taste; to disturb the sleep.

defuera [day-foo-ay'-rah], *adv.* Externally, outwardly on the outside.

defunción [day-foon-the-on'], *f.* *(Prov.)* 1. Death. 2. Extinction, transition from being to not being.

degeneración [day-hay-nay-rah-the-on'], *f.* Degeneration, degeneracy.

degenerado, da [day-hay-nay-rah'-do, dah], *a.* Degenerate. *-pp.* of DEGENERAR.

degenerar [day-hay-nay-rar'], *vn.* 1. To degenerate, to fall from its kind, to grow wild or base (plantas). 2. To degenerate, to fall from the virtue of our ancestors. 3. *(Pict.)* To disfigure anything. **La manifestación degeneró en una sangrienta revuelta**, the demonstration degenerated into a bloody riot.

deglución [day-gloo-the-on'], *f.* *(Med.)* Deglutition, swallowing.

deglutir [day-gloo-teer'], *va.* To swallow.

degollación [day-gol'-lyah-the-on'], *f.* Decollation, beheading.

degolladero [day-gol-lyah-day'-ro], *m.* 1. Throttle, windpipe. 2. Shambles, slaughterhouse. 3. In theaters, a place in the pit farthest from the stage, with no seats, where men are admitted at a very low price. It is separated from the pit by a partition as high as one's neck, from which it takes its name. **Degolladero de bolsas**, cut purse; also a shop where goods are sold at an extravagant price, or bad measure or weight is given. **Llevar al degolladero**, *(Met.)* to put one in very great danger.

degollado [day-gol-lyah'-do], *m.* A dart in women's waists or jackets.

degollador [day-gol-lyah-dor'], *m.* Executioner.

degolladura [day-gol-lyah-doo'-rah], *f.* 1. Cutting of the throat. 2. Interstice between two bricks filled up with mortar. 3. A slope out of women's jackets. 4. Slender part of balusters.

degollar [day-gol-lyar,], *va.* 1. To behead, to decapitate; to guillotine. 2. *(Met.)* To destroy, to ruin, to annihilate. 3. *(Coll.)* To tease, to importune. **Esta persona me degüella**, this person troubles and harasses me.

degollina [day-gol-lyee'-nah], *f.* *(Coll.)* Slaughter, butchery.

degradación [day-grah-dah-the-on'], *f.* 1. Degradation, dismission from an office or dignity; fall. 2. Degradation, degeneracy. 3. *(Pict.)* Degradation, diminution.

degradante [day-grah-dahn'-tay], *a.* Degrading.

degradar [day-grah-dar'], *va.* To degrade, to deprive one of his place, dignity, or honors. *-vr.* To degrade or demean oneself.

degüello [day-goo-ayl'-lyo], *m.* 1. Decollation, the act of beheading or cutting one's throat. 2. Neck or narrow part of many things. 3. Destruction, ruin. **Tirar a degüello**, to endeavor to destroy a person; to seek one's ruin.

degustación [day-goos-tah-the-on'], *f.* Tasting, sampling.

degustar [day-goos-tar'], *va.* To taste, to sample; to drink, to take.

dehesa [day-ay'-sah], *f.* Pasture-ground. **Dehesa concejil**, common, a pasture-ground.

dehesar [day-ay-sar'], *va.* To turn arable land into pasture-ground.

dehesero [day-ay-say'-ro], *m.* Keeper of a pasture-ground.

dehiscencia [day-is-then'-the-ah], *f.* *(Bot.)* Dehiscence.

deicida [day-e-thee'-dah], *m.* Deicide: a term applied by some writers to those who concurred in the crucifixion of Jesus.

deicidio [day-e-thee'-deo], *m.* Deicide, murder of Christ.

deidad [day-e-dahd'], *f.* 1. Deity, divinity. 2. Deity, goddess: a term of flattery addressed to women.

deificación [day-e-fe-ca-the-on'], *f.* Deification, apotheosis.

deificar [day-e-fe-car'], *va.* To deify, or praise excessively or extravagantly.

deífico [day-ee'-fe-co], *a.* Deifical, making divine; belonging to God.

deiforme [day-e-for'-may], *a.* Deiform, of a godlike form; godlike.

deípara [day-ee'-pa-rah], *f.* Deiparous, that brings forth a God: applied to the blessed Virgin.

deisidemonía [day-e-se-day-mo-nee'-ah], *f.* Superstitious fear.

deismo [day-ees'-mo], *m.* Deism.

deista [day-ees'-tah], *m.f.* Deist.

deja [day'-hah], *f.* Prominence between two fissures.

dejación [day-hah-the-on'], *f.* 1. Act of leaving, relinquishing, or giving up. 2. Abdication, resignation. **Dejación de bienes**, the act of resigning one's property to his creditors.

dejada [day-hah'-dah], *f.V.* DEJACIóN.

dejadez [day-hah-deth'], *f.* Slovenliness, neglect, laziness, lassitude.

dejado, da [day-hah'-do, dah], *a.* 1. Slovenly, idle, indolent. 2. Dejected, low-spirited. *-pp.* of DEJAR.

dejamiento [day-hah-me-en'-to], *m.* 1. Act of leaving, relinquishing, or giving up. 2. Indolence, idleness, carelessness. 3. Languor, decay of spirits. 4. Abdication, resignation.

dejar [day-har'], *va.* 1. To leave, to let, to relinquish, to quit, to come from, to go from. 2. To omit saying or doing anything. 3. To permit, to allow, not to obstruct. 4. To leave, to forsake, to desert. 5. To yield, to produce. 6. To commit, to give in charge. 7. To nominate, to appoint. **Dejar cargado**, to debit. **Dejar dicho**, to leave word or orders. **Dejar escrito**, to leave in writing. **Déjale que venga**, let him come. 8. To fling up, to give up. 9. To lay away. 10. To forbear, to leave off, to cease. 11. To leave a legacy to one absent. **Dejar atrás**, to excel, to surpass. **Dejar a uno a oscuras**, not to grant a request; to leave one in doubt. **Dejarse de cuentos**, to come to the point. **Dejar en cueros**, to strip one of his property. **Dejar para mañana**, to delay, to procrastinate. *-vn.* **Dejó de cantar**, she stopped singing. **No puedo dejar de fumar**, I can't give up smoking. *-vr.* 1. Not to take care of oneself. 2. To allow or suffer oneself to. 3. To become languid. 4. To abandon oneself to. **Dejarse llevar**, to suffer oneself to be led by another. **Dejarse rogar**, to extend the concession required, that the favor may be more estimable.

Dejarse vencer, to yield oneself to the opinion of another.

Dejarse caer abajo por un río, (*Naut.*) to drop down a river. **Dejarse caer a la popa**, (*Naut.*) to fall astern. **Dejarse caer a sotavento**, (*Naut.*) to fall to leeward. **Dejarse alguna cosa en el tintero**, to omit something necessary to the subject.

dejillo [day-heel'-lyo], *m. dim.* Slight relish or taste which remains after eating or drinking.

dejo [day'-ho], *m.* 1. End, termination. Negligence, carelessness, laziness. *V.* ABNEGACIóN. 4. Relish or taste which remains after eating or drinking. 5. Result, effect, or remains of a passion 6. Particular accentuation on the last syllable of words, of each province or country. 7. Recollection, echo.

dejugar [day-hoo-gar'], *va.* To extract the juice or substance of something.

del [del]. Of the, a contraction of the preposition *De* and the masculine article *el*; as, **el mérito del libro**, instead of *el mérito* de el *libro*.

Del. *abr.* de **Delegación**.

delación [day-lah-the-on'], *f.* 1. Delation, accusation, impeachment. 2. Information.

delantal [day-lan-tahl'], *m.* Apron; dashboard of a carriage. **Delantal de cuero**, leather apron.

delante [day-lahn'-tay], *adv.* 1. Before, in the presence of, in the sight of, in front of. **La casa no tiene nada delante**, the house has nothing opposite. **La parte de delante**, the front part. 2. Before, anteriorly, preceding in time. **Tenemos todavía 4 horas por delante**, we still have 4 hours in front of us. 3. Before, in preference to, prior to.

delantera [day-lan-tay'-rah], *f.* 1. Fore front, fore end, the fore part of anything. 2. The front seats, behind the barriers of a place, where bullfeasts are held. 3. Fore skirts of clothes. 4. Advantage obtained over another. 5. Vanguard of an army. **Coger la delantera**, to get the start of a person. **Ir en la delantera**, to take the lead. 6. (*Anat.*) Tits. 7. **Delanteras**, chaps (calzones).

delantero, ra [day-lan-tay'-ro, rah], *a.* Foremost, first.

delantero [day-lahn-tay'-ro], *m.* The first, one who takes the lead. **Delantero centro**, center forward, **delantero extremo**, outside forward. -*m. pl.* Linemen (en fútbol).

delatable [day-lah-tah'-blay], *a.* Accusable, blamable.

delatante [day-lah-tahn'-tay], *pa.* Informer, accuser.

delatar [day-lah-tar'], *va.* To inform, to accuse, to denounce, to impeach.

delator, ra [day-lah-tor'], *m.f.* Accuser, informer, denouncer.

delco [dayl'-co], *m.* (*Aut.*) Distributor.

del crédere [del cray'-day-ray], *m.* A guarantee by a merchant for another's payment.

delectación [day-lec-tah-the-on'], *f.* Delectation, pleasure, delight. **Delectación morosa**, the deliberate indulgence of some sensual pleasure.

delectar [day-lec-tar'], *va.* To delight.

delecto [day-lec'-to], *m.* Election, choice. *V.* ELECCIóN.

delegación [day-lay-gah-the-on'], *f.* 1. Delegation, substitution. 2. Power conferred upon someone to act in behalf of others; a proxy. **Delegación de poderes**, devolution. **La delegación fue a cumplimentar al Ministro**, the delegation went to pay its respects to the minister.

delegado, da [day-lay-gah'-do], *m.f.* Delegate, deputy, commissioner, minister. -**Delegado; da**, *pp.* of DELEGAR.

delegante [day-lay-gahn'-tay], *pa.* Constituent, one that delegates.

delegar [day-lay-gar'], *va.* To delegate, to substitute.

deleitabilidad [day-lay-e-tah-be-le-dahd'], *f.* Delectableness, delightfulness.

deleitable [day-lay-tah'-blay], *a.* Delectable, delightful.

deleitación [day-lay-tah-the-on'], *f.* Delectation, pleasure, delight.

deleitamiento [day-lay-tah-me-en'-to], *m.* Delight, pleasure.

deleitante [day-lay-tahn'-tay], *pa.* Delighting.

deleitar [day-lay-tar'], *va.* To delight to please, to content. -*vr.* To delight, to have delight or pleasure in.

deleite [day-lay'-e-tay], *m.* 1. Pleasure, delight, gratification. **Deleite sexual**, sexual pleasure. 2. Lust, carnal appetite.

deleitosamente [day-lay-te-so-sah-men'-tay], *adv.* Delightfully, pleasantly, cheerfully.

deleitoso, sa [day-lay-e-to'-so, sah], *a.* Delightful, agreeable, pleasing.

deletéreo, ea [day-lay-tay'-ray-o, ah], *a.* (*Med.*) Deleterious, deletory.

deletreador [day-lay-tray-ah-dor'], *m.* Speller.

deletrear [day-lay-tray-ar'], *va.* 1. To spell, to read by spelling. 2. To find out and explain the meaning of what is difficult and obscure; to examine. to scrutinize.

deletreo [day-lay-tray'-o], *m.* 1. Spelling. 2. Teaching to read by spelling the letters.

deleznable [day-leth-nah'-blay], *a.* 1. Slippery, smooth. 2. Brittle, fragile.

deleznadero [day-leth-nah-day'ro], *m.* A slippery place.

deleznamiento [day-leth-nah-me-en'-to], *m.* Act of slipping.

délfico, ca [del'-fe-co, cah], *a.* Delphic, of Delphi.

delfín [del-feen'], *m.* 1. Dolphin, a cetaceous animal. 2. Dolphin, a northern constellation. 3. Dauphin, formerly the title of the eldest son of the King of France. 4. (*Pol.*) Heir apparent, designated successor.

delfina [del-fee'-nah], *f.* 1. Dauphiness, the wife or widow of the dauphin of France. 2. An alkaloid extracted from larkspur and stavesacre.

delfinela [del-fe-nay'-lah], *f.* (*Bot.*) *V.* DELFINIO.

delfinio [del-fee'-neo], *m.* (*Bot.*) Larkspur.

delgadez [del-gah-deth'], *f.* 1. Thinness, tenuity. 2. (*Met.*) Acuteness, ingenuity. 3. Slenderness, leanness, smallness.

delgado, da [del-gah'-do, dah], *a.* 1. Thin, tenuous, delicate, light. **Delgado como un fideo**, as thin as a rake. 2. Thin, exiguous, slender, lean, lank, gaunt. 3. (*Met.*) Acute, fine, ingenious. 4. Short, little, scanty, poor, extenuate. **Delgados de un navío**, (*Naut.*) the narrowing or rising of a ship's floor.

delgado [del-gah'-do], *m.* A strait place. **Delgados**, flanks of animals.

delgaducho, cha [del-gah-doo'-cho, chah], *a.* Thin, delicate (with a sense of depreciation).

delgazar, *va.* (*Obs.*) *V.* ADELGAZAR.

deliberación [day-lebay-rah-the-on'], *f.* 1. Deliberation, consideration, reflection. 2. Resolution, determination. 3. Liberation.

deliberadamente [day-le-be-rah-dah-men'-tay], *adv.* Deliberately.

deliberado [day-le-bay-rah'-do], *a.* Deliberate.

deliberador [day-le-bay-rah-dor'], *m.* Deliverer.

deliberamiento [day-le-bay-rah-me-en'-to], *m.* Deliverance.

deliberar [day-le-bay-rar'], *vn.* 1. To consider, to deliberate, to discourse. 2. To consult or take counsel together. -*vr.* To have delight or pleasure in.-*va.* 1. To deliberate, to think in order to choose, to ponder. 2. To rescue from captivity. 3. (*Obs.*) To emancipate.

deliberativo, va [day-le-bay-rah-tee'-vo, vah], *a.* Deliberative.

delibrar [day-le-brar'], *va.* 1. To deliberate, to determine. 2. To liberate. 3. *V.* DESPACHAR.

delicadamente [day-le-cah-dah-men'-tay], *adv.* Delicately.

delicadez [day-le-cah-deth'], *f.* 1. Delicacy, weakness of constitution. 2. (*Met.*) Delicacy, tenderness, scrupulousness, mercifulness. 3. Gentleness of manners, sweetness of temper.

delicadeza [day-le-cah-day'-thah], *f.* 1. Delicateness, tenderness, softness, effeminacy; nicety, exquisiteness. 2. Delicacy, nicety in the choice of food, daintiness. 3. Subtlety, dexterity. 4. Fineness, tenuity. 5. (*Met.*) Acuteness of understanding, refinement of wit; perspicacity; curiosity; mellifluence. 6. Idleness, negligence.

delicado, da [day-le-cah'-do, dah], *a.* 1. Delicate, sweet, pleasing, tender. 2. Weak, faint, effeminate, finical, feminine, ladylike. 3. Delicate, exquisite, nice, delicious, dainty, pleasing to the taste; of an agreeable flavor. 4. Thin, slender, subtile. 5. Nice, scrupulous, fastidious. 6. Arduous, difficult, perplexing. 7. Captious, easy of annoyance, suspicious. **Está delicado del estómago**, he has a delicate stomach. **Es muy delicado en el comer**, he's very choosy about food. **Es muy delicada para la limpieza**, she's very particular about cleanliness.

delicia [day-lee'-the-ah], *f.* 1. Delight, comfort, satisfaction. **El país es una delicia**, the country is delightful. 2. A lively sensual pleasure. *(Acad.).* **El libro que ha hecho las delicias de muchos niños**, a book which has been the delight of many children.

deliviarse [day-le-the-ar'-say], *vr.* To delight, to have delight or pleasure in. *(Acad.)*

deliciosamente [day-le-the-o-sah-men'-tay], *adv.* Deliciously, daintily, delightsomely.

delicioso, sa [day-le-the-oh'-so, sah], *a.* Delicious, delightful, pleasing.

delictivo [day-lec-te-vo], *a.* Criminal.

delicuescencia [day-le-coo-es-then'-the-ah], *a.* *(Chem.)* Deliquescence.

delicuescente [day-le-coo-es-then'-tay], *a.* *(Chem.)* Deliquescent.

deligación [day-le-gah-the-on'], *f.* The art of preparing and applying bandages and other external applications.

deliminación [day-le-me-nah-the-on'], *f.* Delimitation.

delimitar [day-le-me-tar'], *va.* To delimit.

delincuencia [day-lin-coo-en'-the-ah], *f.* Delinquency, offence, failure in duty. **Delincuencia de menores**, juvenile delinquency. **Cifras de la delincuencia**, figures of crimes committed.

delincuente [day-lin-coo-en-tay], *pa.* Delinquent, offender. **Delincuente habitual**, hardened criminal. **Delincuente juvenil**, juvenile delinquent.

delineación [day-le-nay-ah-the-on'], *f.* Delineation, draft, sketch.

delineador, ra [day-le-nay-ah-dor', rah], *m. & f.* Delineator, draftsman.

delineamento, delineamiento [day-le-nay-ah-men'-to], *m.* Delineament. *V.* DELINEACIóN.

delineante [day-le-ne-ahn'-tay], *m.* Draughtsman.

delinear [day-le-nay-ar'], *va.* 1. To delineate, to draw the first draft of a thing; to sketch, to figure. 2. *(Met.)* To describe, in prose or verse.

delinquimiento [day-lin-kee-me-en'-to], *m.* Delinquency, fault, transgression.

delinquir [day-lin-keer'], *vn.* To transgress the law, to offend.

delintar, delinterar, *va.* *(Obs.)* *V.* CEDER and TRASPASAR.

delio [day'-leo], *m.* Of Delos. (Applied to Apollo.)

deliquio [day-lee'-keo], *m.* 1. Swoon, a fainting-fit, ecstasy. 2. State of a body wich has become more or less fluid; deliquescence.

deliramento [day-le-rah-men'-to], *m.* Delirium.

delirante [day-le-rahn'-tay], *pa.* Delirious, light-headed; raving.

delirar [day-le-rar'], *vn.* 1. To be delirious, to dote, to rave. 2. *(Met.)* To rant, to talk nonsense.

delirio [day-lee'-re-o], *m.* 1. Delirium, alienation of mind, dotage. 2. *(Met.)* Rant, nonsense, idle talk. 3. Frenzy; mania. **Delirio de grandezas**, megalomania. 4. **Con delirio**, madly. **Me gusta con delirio**, I'm crazy about it.

delirium tremens [day-lee'-re-oom tray'-mens], *m.* Delirium tremens (provoked by alcoholism).

delitescencia [day-le-tes-then'-the-ah], *f.* 1. Delitescence, a sudden subsidence of a local inflammation. 2. *(Chem.)* A sudden loss, by a crystallized body, of its water of crystallization, and consequent bursting asunder.

delito [day-lee'-to], *m.* Transgression of a law; fault, crime, guilt, delinquency. **Delito de mayor cuantía**, felony. **Delito de sangre**, violent crime. **Delitos informáticos**, *(Comput.)* computer-related crime.

della, dello [dayl'-lyah, dayl'-lyo]. Contractions of the words *de ella, de ello*, of her, of it. **Della con dello**, reciprocally, alternatively, one with the other, good and bad as they come.

delta, *f.* Delta, the fourth letter of the Greek alphabet. *-m.* A triangular island at the mouth of certain rivers, named from resembling the Greek letter of same name.

deltoides, dea [del-to'-e-des, day-ah], *a.* Deltoid, like a Greek delta.

delusivo, va [day-loo-see'-vo, vah], *a.* Delusive, fallacious.

delusor [day-loo-sor'], *m.* Cheat, impostor, deluder.

delusoriamente, *adv.* Delusively, deceitfully.

delusorio, ria [day-loo-so'-reo, ah], *a.* Deceitful, fallacious.

demacración [day-mah-crah-the-on'], *f.* Wasting away in flesh (of men and animals) marasmus.

demacrado, da [day-mah-rah'-do, dah], *a.* Emaciated. **Rostro demacrado**, wan, haggard countenance.

demacrar [day-mah-crar'], *vr.* To waste away. *-va.* To cause wasting.

demagogia [day-mah-go'-heah], *f.* 1. Demagogism, ambition to rule in a popular faction. 2. The predominance of the rabble.

demagógico, ca [day-mah-go'-he-co, cah], *a.* Demagogical.

demagogo [day-mah-go'-go], *m.* Demagogue.

demagrar [day-mah-grar'], *vn.* To waste away. *V.* DEMACRAR.

demanda [day-mahn'-dah], *f.* 1. Demand, claim, pretension, complaint. **Demanda de pago**, demand for payment. 2. Judicial suit, lawsuit. **Entablar una demanda**, to sue. **Salir a la demanda**, to appear in one's own defense. 3. Request petition. 4. Interrogation. **La ley de la oferta y la demanda**, the law of demand and supply. **Ese producto no tiene demanda**, there is no demand for that product.

demandadero, ra [day-man-dah-day'-ro, rah], *m. & f.* 1. A servant man or woman who attends at the door of a nunnery or convent, to run errands. 2. A servant in a jail.

demandado, da [day-man-dah'-do, dah], *m. & f.* Defendant, the person accused. *-pp.* of DEMANDAR.

demandador [day-man-dah-dor'], *m.* 1. One who goes about asking charity for pious uses. 2. Claimant, plaintiff. 3. One who solicits a woman in marriage.

demandadora [day-man-dah-do'-rah], *f.* A female plaintiff or petitioner.

demandante [day-man-dahn'-tay], *pa.* Claimant, complainant, plaintiff.

demandar [day-man-dar'], *va.* 1. To demand, to ask, to petition. 2. To claim, to enter an action. **Demandó al periódico por calumnia**, he sued the paper for libel. **Demandar a uno por daños y perjuicios**, to sue somebody for damages.

demarcación [day-mar-cah-the-on'], *f.* Demarcation.

demarcador [day-mar-cah-dor'], *m.* Designator, surveyor.

demarcar [day-mar-car'], *va.* To mark out confines or limits, to survey. **Demarcar el terreno de un campamento,** to trace out the ground of a camp.

demarrarse [day-mar-rar say], *vr.* To mislead, to deviate from the right way.

demás [day-mahs'], *adv.* Over and above a certain quantity, measure, or number; besides, moreover.

demás [day-mahs'], *a.* It is almost always used with the article prefixed to it, except sometimes in the plural. **Lo demás**, the rest. **Los demás** or **las demás**, the rest, the others. **Y así de lo demás**, and so on; so with the rest. **Estar demás**, to be over and above; to be useless or superfluous. **Por demás**, uselessly, in vain, to no purpose. *V.* ADEMÁS.

demases [day-mah'-ses], *m. pl.* *(Prov.)* Abundance, copiousness.

demasía [day-mah-see'-ah], *f.* 1. Excess, superabundance. 2. Badness, iniquity, quilt. 3. A bold, arduous undertaking. **En demasía**, excessively.

demasiadamente [day-mah-se-ah-dah-men'-tay], *adv.* Excessively; too.

demasiado, da [day-mah-se-ah'-do, dah], *a.* 1. Excessive, more than enough, too much. **Eso es demasiado**, that's too much. **Con demasiado cuidado**, with excessive care. 2. Bold, daring, enterprising.

demasiado [day-mah-seah'-do], *adv.* Enough, too, sufficiently, excessively. **Comer demasiado**, to eat too much. **Es demasiado pesado para levantar**, it is too heavy to lift.

demasié [day-mah-se-ay'], *adj, adv. V.* DEMASIADO.

dembo [dem'-bo], *m.* A kind of drum which the natives of the Congo use.

demediar [day-may-de-ar'], *va.* 1. To split, to divide into halves. 2. To wear a thing until it has lost half its value. 3. To complete half its age, or course. *-vn.* To reach half the duration of a thing. **Demediar la confesión**, to confess but half one's sins.

demencia [day-men'-the-ah], *f.* Dementia, loss of mind, insanity.

demencial [day-men-the-al'], *a.* Mad, crazy, demented.

dementar [day-men-tar'], *va.* To render insane: almost always used in its reciprocal sense. *-vr.* to go mad, to become demented.

demente [day-men'-tay], *a.* Demented, mad, distracted, infatuated, insane.

demergido [day-mer-hee'-do], *a. V.* ABATIDO.

demérito [day-may'-re-to], *m.* 1. Demerit. 2. The act of demeriting.

demeritorio, ria [day-may-re-to'-re-o, ah], *a.* Without merit.

demisión [day-me-se-on'], *f.* Submission, humility.

demiurgo [day-me-oor'-go], *m.* Demiurge, in Plato's philosophy, a spirit intermediate between God and the creature.

demo [day'-mo], *m.* (*Prov.*) Demon, a spirit; generally an evil spirit.

democracia [day-mo-crah'-the-ah], *f.* Democracy.

damócrata [day-mo'-cra-tah], *m.* Democrat.

democráticamente [day-mo-crah'-te-cah-men-tay], *adv.* Democratically.

democrático, ca [day-mo-crah'-te-co, cah], *a.* 1. Democratical, popular, liberal. 2. (*Met.*) Modest, without pretensions. 3. Rabble.

democratización [day-mo-crah-te-thah-the-on'], Democratization.

democratizar [day-mo-cra-te-thar'], *va.* To propagate or spread democratic ideas.

demografía [day-mo-grah-fee'-ah], *f* Demography.

demográfico, ca [day-mo-grah'-fe-co, cah] *a.* Demographic. **La explosión demográfica**, the population explosion.

demógrafo, fa [day-mo'-grah-fo], *m & f.* Demographer.

demoledor [day-mo-lay-dor'], *a.* (*Fig.*) Powerful, overwhelming; shattering (ataque).

demoler [day-mo-lerr'], *va.* To demolish, to overthrow.

demonche [day-mo-ne'-chay], *m.* Little devil: a vulgarism in form of the diminutive.

demolición [day-mo-le-the-on'], *f.* Demolition.

demoniaco, ca [day-mo-ne-ah'-co, cah], *a.* 1. Demoniacal, devilish. 2. Demoniacal. 3. Demonian.

demonio [day-mo'-ne-o], *m.* 1. Demon, familiar. 2. The devil. **Ir como el demonio**, to go like the devil. **Tener el demonio en el cuerpo**, to be always on the go. **Esto sabe a demonios**, this tastes awful. 3. *int.* The deuce! **Estudiar con el demonio**, to show signs of great genius and acuteness for evil, or of great knavery. **¿Dónde demonios lo habré dejado?**, where the devil can I have left it?.

demontre [day-mone'-tray], *m. V.* DEMONIO. Used as an exclamation: The deuce!

demoñuelo [day-mo-nyoo-ay'-lo], *m. dim.* A little demon or devil.

demora [day-mo'-rah], *f.* 1. Delay, procrastination, protraction, demurrer. 2. Demurrage, an allowance made for the detention of a ship in a port. **Sin demora**, without delay.

demorar [day-mo-rar'], *vn.* 1. To remain, to continue long in a place. 2. (*Naut.*) To bear, to be situated in regard to a ship. **La costa demora norte**, the coast bears north. 3. *va.* To retard, to delay. *-vr.* To take a long time.

demostrable [day-mos-trah'-blay], *a.* Demonstrable, manifestable.

demostrablemente [day-mos-trah-blay-men'-tay], *adv.* Demonstrably, ostensibly.

demostración [day-mos-trah-the-on'], *f.* 1. Demonstration; manifestation. **Demostración de cariño**, show of affection. 2. (*Mil.*) Demonstration, a feigned attack upon an enemy, to divert his attention.

demostrador, ra [day-mos-trah-dor', rah], *m.* & *f.* Demonstrator.

demostrar [day-mos-trar'], *va.* 1. To demonstrate, to prove, to manifest, to lay open, to make out. 2. To teach. **Demostrar cómo se hace algo**, to demonstrate how something is done. **Demostrar que...**, to show that....

demostrativamente [day-mos-trah-te-vah-men'-tay], *adv.* Demonstratively.

demostrativo, va [day-mos-trah-tee'-vo, vah], *a.* Demonstrative.

demótico, ca [day-mo'-te-co, cah], *a.* Demotic, belonging to the common people: especially used of Egyptian writing.

demudación [day-moo-dah-the-on'], *f.* Change, alteration.

demudar [day-moo-dar'], *va.* 1. To alter, to change, vary. 2. To cloak, disguise. *-vr.* To be changed; to change color suddenly, or the expression of countenance. **Continuó sin demudarse**, he went on quite unaffected.

demulcente [day-mool-then'-tay], *a.* & *m.* (*Med.*) Demulcent, emollient.

demultiplexor [day-mool-te-playc-sor], *m.* (*Comput.*) Demultiplexer.

denante, denantes, *adv.* (*Prov. Obs.*) *V.* ANTES.

denario [day-nah'-re-o], *m.* 1. Roman denarius, the penny of the New Testament, a small silver coin. 2. Denary, decimal or tenth number. 3. Money paid to laborers for one day's labor.

denario, ria [day-nah'-re-o, ah], *a.* Tenth, containing the number of ten.

dende [den'-day], *adv.* Hence, from *V.* DESDE.

dendrita, dendrite [den-dree'-tah, den-dree'-tay], *f.* Dendrite, a mineral representing the figures of plants.

dendrítico, ca [den-dree'-te-co, cah], *a.* Dendritic, showing markings like foliage.

dendrografía [den-dro-grah-fee'-ah], *f.* Dendrology, a description of trees.

dendrómetro [den-dro'-may-tro], *m.* (*Math.*) An instrument which resolves in a graphic manner problems of plane geometry.

denegación [day-nay-gah-the-on'], *f.* Denial, refusal, denegation.

denegar [day-nay-gar'], *va.* To deny, to refuse, to denegate.

denegrecer [day-nay-gray-therr'], *va.* 1. To blacken, to darken, to denigrate. 2. *V.* DENIGRAR.

denegrido, da [day-nay-gree'-do, dah], *a.* Blackened, denigrated. *-pp.* of DENEGRIR.

denegrir [day-nay-greer'], *va. V.* DENEGRECER.

dengoso, sa [den-go'-so, sah], *a.* Fastidious, overnice, scrupulous.

dengue [den'-gay], *m.* 1. Fastidiousness, 2. Prudery. 3. A sort of woman's cape with long points. 4. A boat used in the sardine fishery. 5. Dengue, or breakbone fever. 6. Affectation. **Andar en dengues**, to be overnice, to be too punctilious. **No andar en dengues**, not to mind trifles.

denguero, ra [den-gay'-ro, rah], *a.* Prudish, affected. *V.* DENGOSO.

denigración [day-ne-grah-the-on'], *f.* Denigration, stigma, disgrace.

denigrante [day-ne-grahn-tay], *a.* Insulting; degrading.

denigrar [day-ne-grar'], *va.* 1. To denigrate or blacken the character of a person, to calumniate, to defame, to expose, to censure. 2. To insult.

denigrativamente [day-ne-grah-te-vah-men'-tay], *adv.* Injuriously, infamously.

denigrativo, va [day-ne-grah-tee'-vo, vah], *a.* Blackening, stigmatizing.

denigratorio [day-ne-grah-to-re-o], *a.* Denigratory.

denodado, da [day-no-dah'-do, dah], *a.* Bold, intrepid, audacious.

denominable [day-no-me-nah'-blay], *a.* Denominable.

denominación [day-no-me-nah-the-on'], *f.* Denomination. **Monedo de baja denominación**, low value coin. **Denominación social**, *(Mex.)* Firm's official name. **Denominación de origen**, mark of origin.

denominadamente [day-no-me-nah-dah-men'-tay], *adv.* Distinctly, definitively.

denominado [day-no-me-nah'-do], *a.* Named, called; so-called.

denominador [day-no-me-nah-dor'], *m.* *(Arith.)* Denominator. **Denominador común**, *(Math.)* Common denominator.

denominar [day-no-me-nar'], *va.* To denominate, to give a name.

denominativo, va, *a.* Denominative.

denostadamente [day-nos-tah-dah-men'-tay], *adv.* Ignominiously, insultingly.

denostador [day-nos-tah-dor'], *m.* Vilifier, railer, reviler.

denostar [day-nos-tar'], *va.* To insult a person with foul language, to revile, to abuse.

denotación [day-no-tah-the-on'], *f.* Designation, denotation.

denotar [day-no-tar'], *va.* 1. To denote, to signify, to express. 2. To explain.

denotativo, va [day-no-tah-tee'-vo, vah], *a.* Denoting, denotative.

densamente [dayn-sah-men'-tay], *adv.* Closely, densely.

densidad [den-se-dahd'], *f.* 1. Density, closeness, compactness, grossness. 2. Obscurity, confusion, darkness. **Densidad de integración**, integration density.

densifoliado, da [den-se-fo-le-ah'-do, dah], *a.* Thick-leaved, of crowded foliage.

densímetro [den-see'-may-tro], *m.* Densimeter, an apparatus for determining the relative density of a substance.

denso, sa [den'-so, sah], *a.* 1. Dense, thick. 2. Close, compact. **El argumento es algo denso**, the reasoning is somewhat confused.

dentado, da [den-tah'-do, dah], *a.* 1. Furnished with teeth. 2. Denticulated, dentated, toothed. 3. Crenated, indented. -*pp.* of DENTAR. **Dentado** is sometimes used as a substantive.

dentadura [den-tah-doo'-rah], *f.* 1. A set of teeth. **Dentadura postiza**, false teeth. **Tener mala dentadura**, to have bad teeth. 2. Number and quality of the cogs or teeth of a wheel.

dentagra [den-tah'-grah], *f.* Toothache.

dental [den-tahl'], *m.* 1. Bed to which the plough-share is fixed. 2. A wooden fork, used to separate the straw from corn.

dental [den-tahl'], *a.* 1. Dental, belonging to the teeth. 2. *(Gram.)* Dental pronounced principally by the agency of the teeth.

dentar [den-tar'], *va. & vn.* 1. To tooth, to furnish with teeth, to indent; to cut into teeth. 2. To teeth, to cut teeth.

dentaria [den-tah'-re-ah], *f. (Bot.)* Toothwort.

dentecillo [den-tay-theel'-lyo], *m. dim.* Small tooth.

dentejón [den-tay-hone'], *m.* Yoke-tree, with which oxen are yoked to the cart.

dentelaria [den-tay-lah'-re-ah], *f. (Bot.)* Leadwort.

dentelete [den-tay-lay'-tay], *m.* Dentil, or dental, of a cornice of some Ionic entablatures.

dentellada [den-tel-lyah'-dah], *f.* 1. Gnashing of teeth. 2. Nip, a pinch with the teeth. 3. Impression made by the teeth. **A dentelladas**, snappishly, peevishly. **Dar o sacudir dentelladas**, to speak surlily and uncivilly.

dentellado, da [den-tel-lyah'-do, dah], *a.* 1. Denticulated, dented. 2. Bit or wounded with the teeth. -*pp.* of DENTELLAR.

dentellar [den-tel-lyar'], *vn.* To gnash, to grind or collide the teeth. **Estaba dentellando**, his teeth were chattering.

dentellear [den-tel-lyay-ar'], *va.* To bite, to fix the teeth in anything.

dentellón [den-tel-lyone'], *m.* 1. Moulding or ornament of the Corinthian cornice. 2. Piece of a doorlock which represents a large tooth.

dentera [den-tay'-rah], *f.* 1. An unpleasant, sensation, or tingling pain in the teeth. **Dar dentera a uno**, to set somebody's teeth on edge. 2. *(Met.)* V. ENVIDIA. **Le da dentera que hagan fiestas al niño**, it makes him jealous when they make a fuss of the baby.

dentezuelo [den-tay-thoo-ay'-lo], *m. dim.* A little tooth.

dentición [den-te-the-on'], *f.* 1. Dentition, cutting the teeth. 2. Dentition, the time at which children's teeth are cut.

denticular [den-te-coo-lar'], *a.* Like teeth, as a tooth; denticulated, toothed.

dentículo [den-tee'-coo-lo], *m. (Arch.)* Denticle, dentil.

dentífrico [den-tee'-fre-co], *m.* Dentifrice, toothpaste.

dentirrostros [den-teer-ros'-tros], *m. pl. (Zool.)* An order of birds with the upper mandible notched near the tip.

dentista [den-tees'-tah], *m & f.* Dentist.

dentivano, na [den-te-vah'-no, nah], *a.* Having long and large teeth: applied to horses.

dentolabial [den-to-lah-be-ahl'], *a. (Gram.)* Dentilabial, articulated by placing the lips and teeth together, as f.

dentón, na [den-tone', nah], *a.* Having large uneven teeth.

dentón [den-tone'], *m. (Zool.)* 1. Dental, a small shellfish. 2. A seafish of the sparus family, like a bream, remarkable for its strong, conical teeth.

dentrambos [den-trahm'-bos]. Contraction of *De entrambos*.

dentro [den'-tro], *adv.* Within. **Dentro del año**, in the course of the year. **Dentro de poco**, shortly. **Allí dentro**, in there. **Vamos dentro**, let's go in. -*prep.* 1. **Dentro de**, in, inside. **Dentro de la casa**, inside the house. 2. **Lo metió dentro del cajón**, he put it into the drawer. 3. Into, inside (tiempo). **Dentro de tres meses**, inside three months. 4. **Dentro de lo posible**, as far as one can.

dentudo, da [den-too'-do, dah], *a.* Having large uneven teeth.

denudación [day-noo-dah-the-on'], *f.* 1. Denudation, laying bare. 2. *(Geol.)* Erosion of mineral matters which form beds of auriferous sands.

denuedo [day-noo-ay'-do], *m.* Boldness, audaciousness, courage, intrepidity.

denuesto [day-noo-es'-to], *m.* Affront, insult.

denuncia [day-noon'-the-ah], *f.* 1. Denunciation. 2. Information laid against another person. **Hacer una denuncia**, to report an accident. **Falsa denuncia**, false accusation.

denunciable [day-noon-the-ah'-blay], *a.* Fit to be denounced. V. DELATABLE.

denunciación [day-noon-the-ah-the-on'], *f.* Denunciation, accusation. V. DENUNCIA and DELACIÓN.

denunciador [day-noon-the-ah-dor'], *m.* Denunciator, informer, accuser.

denunciar [day-noon-the-ar'], *va.* 1. To report, to give notice. 2. To denounce, to lay an information against another. 3. To prognosticate, to foretell. 4. To pronounce, to denunciate, to proclaim, to publish solemnly. **El accidente fue denunciado a la policía**, the accident was reported to the police.

denunciatorio, ria [day-noon-the-ah-to'-re-o, ah], *a.* Denunciatory.

denuncio [day-noon'-the-o], *m. (Prov.) V.* DENUNCIA.

deñar [day-nyar'], *va.* To deign, to deem worthy.

deontología [day-on-to-lo-hee'-ah], *f.* Deontology, ethics, the science of moral obligation.

deontólogo [day-on-toh'-lo-go], *m.* A writer on ethics or deontology.

deoperculado, da [day-o-per-coo-lah'-do, dah], *a.* Deoperculate, deprived of the operculum.

Dep. 1. *abr. de* **Departamento** (Department, Dept.). 2. *abr. de* **Depósito** (deposit, depot, dep.).

deparar [day-pa-rar'], *va.* To offer, to furnish, to present. **Los placeres que el viaje nos deparó**, the pleasures which the trip afforded us.

departamento [day-par-tah-men'-to], *m.* 1. Apartment. 2. Department, separate part, office or division. **Departamento de primera**, first-class compartment. 3. A part or division of the executive government. 4. A province, district, or subdivision of a country.

departidor, ra [day-par-te-dor', do'-rah], *m. & f.* Distributor, divider.

departimiento [day-par-te-me-en'-to], *m. (Obs.)* 1. Division, separation. 2. Distance; difference. 3. Dispute.

departir [day-par-teer'], *vn.* To speak, to converse, to commune. *-a.* 1. To divide, to separate. 2. To distinguish by notes of diversity. 3. To argue, to contend, to dispute. 4. To teach, to explain; to mark out, to impede, to obstruct.

depauperar [day-pah-oo-pay-rar'], *va.* 1. To impoverish. 2. To debilitate, to weaken, to exhaust.

dependencia [day-pen-den'-the-ah], *f.* 1. Dependence, dependency, the state of dependence on another. 2. Dependence, subordination to superior power. 3. Relations by consanguinity or affinity. 4. Business, affair, trust, charge. **Pedro tiene muchas dependencias**, Peter has a deal of business on his hands. 5. Dependence, relation of one thing to another.

depender [day-pen-derr'], *vn.* 1. To depend, to rest upon anything as its cause. 2. To depend, to be in a state of dependence or servitude. 3. To hang, to be dependent on. **Depender de**, to depend on. **Depende de lo que haga él**. It depends on what he does. **Todos dependemos de ti**, we are all relying on you.

dependienta [day-pen-de-ayn'-tah], *f.* Salesgirl, saleswoman, shop assistant.

dependiente [day-pen-de-en'-tay], *pa. & m.* 1. A dependent, one subordinate to or at the disposal of another. 2 *(Amer.)* A clerk.

dependientemente [day-pen-de-ayn-tay-men'-tay], *adv.* Dependently.

depilación [day-pe-lah-the-on'], *f.* Depilation.

depilar [day-pe-lar'], *va.* To strip of hair, to depilate.

depilatorio, a [day-pe-lah-to'-re-o, ah], *a.* Depilatory, used to remove hair.

depletivo, va [day-play-tee'-vo, vah], *a.* Depletive, evacuant.

deplorable [day-plo-rah'-blay], *a.* Deplorable, lamentable, calamitous, hopeless, mournful.

deplorablemente [day-plo-rah-blay-men'-tay], *adv.* Deplorably, mournfully, sorrowfully.

deplorar [day-plo-rar'], *va.* To deplore, to lament, to bewail, to bemoan, to condole, to mourn.

deponente [day-po-nen'-tay], *m. & f.* Deponent, a witness.

deponer [day-po-nerr'], *va.* 1. To lay by, separate, to put aside from oneself. 2. To depose, to remove from office. 3. To declare judicially, to depose, to declare upon oath. 4. To take down, to remove a thing from the place in which it is. 5. To evacuate the bowels. *-vn.* 1. *(Jur.)* To give evidence, to make a statement. 2. *(CAm. Mex.)* To vomit. (*Yo depongo, yo deponga, from Deponer. V.* PONER.)

deponible [day-po-nee'-blay], *a.* Declarable, capable of affirmation.

depopulador [day-po-poo-lah-dor'], *m.* Depopulator, devastator of a country or city.

deportación [day-por-tah-the-on'], *f.* Deportation, transportation, banishment.

deportar [day-por-tar'], *va.* To transport, to exile, to banish. *-vr.* 1. To take a diversion. 2. To rest.

deporte [day-por'-tay], *m.* 1. Sports, athletics. 2. Diversion, pastime, recreation. **Deportes acuáticos**, water sports. **El fútbol es un deporte**, football is a game. **Es muy aficionado a los deportes**, he is very fond of sport.

deportista [day-por-tees'-tah], *m.* Sportsman, athlete. *-f.* Sportswoman, athlete.

deportividad [day-por-te-ve-dahd'], *f.* Sportsmanship.

deportivo, va [day-por-tee'-vo, vah], *a.* Athletic, connected with sports. **Espíritu deportivo**, sportsmanship.

deposición [day-po-se-the-on'], *f.* 1. Deposition, testimony upon oath. 2. Declaration, assertion, affirmation. 3. Deposition, degradation from dignity or station. 4. Alvine evacuation. 5. *(Med.)* Depression.

depositador, ra [day-po-se-tah-dor'], *m. f.* One who leaves anything in trust with another, depositor.

depositante [day-po-se-tahn'-tay], *pa.* Depositor.

depositar [day-po-se-tar'], *pa.* 1. To deposit, to confide, to trust. 2. To commit or to put in any place for safekeeping. 3. To put a person in a position where he may freely manifest his will. 4. To inclose, to contain. *-vr.* To settle.

depositaría [day-po-se-tah-ree'-ah], *f.* Depository, the place where a thing is lodged.

depositario, ria [day-po-se-tah'-re-o, ah], *m. & f.* Depositary, the person with whom a thing is lodged in trust; trustee, receiver.

depositario, ria [day-pose-tah'-re-o, ah], *a.* Relating to a depository.

depósito [day-po'-se-to], *m.* 1. The thing deposited; deposit, trust. 2. Depository, the place where a thing is lodged. 3. The wind chest and windtrunks of organs. 4. *(Gil.)* A recruiting station. 5. *(Chem.)* Deposit, precipitate. 6. *(Geol.)* Layers of aqueous rocks formed by sluggish waters. **Depósito de animales perdidos**, pound. **En depósito**, in bond. **Depósito bancario**, bank deposit. **Depósito de libros**, book stack. **Depósito de basura**, rubbish dump. **Depósito de agua**, water tank. **Depósito de gasolina**, gas tank. **Depósito adicional**, bonus tank.

depravación [day-prah-vah-the-on'], *f.* Depravation, depravity.

depravado, da [day-prah-vah'-do, dah], *a.* Bad, depraved, lewd. *-pp.* of DEPRAVAR.

depravador [day-prah-vah-dor'], *m.* Depraver, corrupter.

depravar [day-prah-var'], *va.* To deprave, to vitiate, to corrupt, to contaminate, used chiefly of immaterial things. *-vr.* To become depraved.

depre [day-pray], *f.* Depression. **Tiene la depre**, she's feeling a bit low.

deprecación [day-pray-cah-the-on'], *f.* Petition, prayer, deprecation, conjuration.

deprecar [day-pray-car'], *va.* To entreat, to implore, to deprecate.

deprecativo, va, deprecatorio, ria [day-pray-cah-tee'-vo, vah], *a.* Deprecative, deprecatory.

depreciación [day-pray-the-ah-the-on'], *f.* Depreciation, decrease in price.

depreciar [day-pray-the-ar'], *va.* To depreciate, to reduce the value of. *-vr.* To depreciate, to lose value.

depredación [day-pray-dah-the-on'], *f.* 1. Depredation, plundering, laying waste, pillage. 2. Malversation committed by guardians or trustees.

depredador, ra [day-pray-dah-dor', rah], *m. & f.* A robber, destroyer, predator.

depredar [day-pray-dar'], *va.* To rob, to pillage, to defraud, to be predatory on.

deprensión [day-pren-se-on'], *f.* A basement, humiliation.

depresión [day-pray-se-on'], *f.* 1. Depression, pressing down. 2. Depression, abasement. 3. Lowering; drop, fall. **Depresión del mercurio**, fall in temperature.

depresivo, va [day-pray-see'-vo, vah], *a*. Depressive, lowering.

depresor [day-pray-sor'], *m*. 1. Depressor, an oppressor. 2. *(Anat.)* Depressor, a name given to muscles which depress the part on which they act.

depresorio, ria [day-pray-so'-re-o, ah], *a*. Depressor.

depreterición [day-pray-tay-re-the-on'], *f. (Obs. Law)* Preterition. *V.* PRETERICION.

deprimación [day-pre-mah-the-on'], *f*. Act and effect of cropping frostbitten grass.

deprimado, da [day-pre-mah'-do, dah], *a*. Applied to the fields or meadow in which the animals have eaten the tips of grass frostbitten by dews.

deprimar [day-pre-mar'], *va*. To make horses crop off the ends of grass frostbitten by the first spring dews.

deprimente [day-pre-men'-tay], *a*. Depressing. *-m*. Depressant.

deprimido, da [day-pre-mee'-do, dah], *a*. 1. Compressible, disappearing under the pressure of the finger, said of the pulse. 2. Flattened or hollowed at the middle; said of a tumor. 3. Depressed.

deprimir [day-pre-meer'], *va*. To depress, to humble, to deject, to sink; to depreciate, to belittle. *-vr*. To get depressed.

depurable [day-poo-rah'blay], *a*. Purifiable, capable of cleansing.

depuración [day-poo-rah-the-on'], *f*. Depuration, purification.

depurado, da [day-poo-rah'-do, dah], *a*. Depurate, cleansed, purified. *-pp*. of DEPURAR.

depuradora [day-poo-rah-do'-rah], *f*. Purifying plant.

depuramiento [day-poo-rah-meen'-to], *m. V.* DEPURACIÓN.

depurar [day-poo-rar'], *va*. To depurate, to cleanse, to purify, to filter.

depurativo, va [day-poo-rah-tee'-vo, vah], *a*. Depurant, depurative, purifying; antiscorbutic. *-m*. Blood tonic.

depuratorio, ria [day-poo-rah-to'-re-o, ah], *a*. Depuratory, purifying.

derecha [day-ray-chah], *f*. 1. Right hand, right side. 2. *(Obs.)* Pack of hounds, or the path they pursue in the chase. **A derechas** or **a las derechas**, right; well done, as it ought to be, honestly, rightly, justly. **No hacer cosa a derechas**, not to do anything right; to do everything wrong. **Torcer a la derecha**, to turn right. **Seguir por la derecha**, to keep right.

derechamente [day-ray-chah-men'-tay], *adv*. 1. Directly, full, straight. 2. Rightly, prudently, justly. 3 Expressly, formally, legally.

derechera [day-ray-chay'-rah], *f*. The direct road.

derechero [day-ray-chay'-ro], *m*. Clerk appointed to collect taxes.

derechista [day-ray-chees'-tah], *m*. Rightist (in political tendencies); rightwing.

derecho, cha [day-ray'-cho, chah], *a*. 1. Right, straight. **Todo derecho**, straight-forward. 2. Just, lawful, well-grounded, reasonable. legitimate. **Hecho y derecho**, perfect, absolute, complete; true, certain; without doubt. 3. Right, opposite to the left. *(Obs.)* Certain; directed.

derecho [day-ray'-cho], *m*. 1. Right, justice, law, equity. **Derecho civil**, civil law. **Derecho penal**, criminal law. 2. A just claim. 3. Tax, duty, impost, custom, toll. **Sujeto a derechos**, subject to duty. **Derechos de aduana, derechos arancelarios**, customs duty. 4. Due, fee, payment claimed by persons in office; in the last two senses it is almost always used in the plural. 5. The right side of cloth. 6. Exemption, freedom, privilege. 7. *(Obs.)* Road, path. **Derecho administrativo**, a collection of ordinances, regulations, etc.. **En derecho de su dedo** or **sus narices**, selfish care for one's own interest. **Derecho de gentes**, natural law, such as prevails among outside nations, as contrasted with the Roman law. **Derecho no escrito**, unwritten law, established custom. **Derecho de propiedad**

literaria, copyright. **Derecho de visita**, right of search. **Tener derechos a**, to have a right to.

derecho [day-ray'-cho], *adv. V.* DERECHAMENTE.

derecho de vía [day-ray'-cho day vee'-ah], *m*. Right of way.

derechuelo, derechuelos [day-ray-choo-ay'-lo], *m*. One of the first seams taught to little girls.

derechura [day-ray-choo'-rah], *f*. 1. Rectitude; right way. 2. Salary, pay. 3. *(Obs.)* Right; dexterity. **En derechura**, 1. By the most direct road. 2. Without delay, directly, immediately.

deriva [day-ree'-vah], *f*. 1. *(Naut.)* Ship's course. **Ir a la deriva**, to be adrift. 2. *(Aer.)* Deviation, drift.

derivable [day-re-vah'-blay], *a*. Derivable, deducible.

derivación [day-re-vah-the-on'], *f*. 1. Derivation, descent. 2. Derivation, a draining of water, a turning of its course. 3. *(Gram.)* Derivation, the tracing of a word from its original. 4. Shunt (en electricidad). 5. The act of separating one thing from another. 6. Diversion, turn-off (de una carretera).

derivado [day-re-vah-do], *m*. 1. Derivative. 2. Byproduct.

derivar [day-re-var'], *va*. 1. To derive, to separate one thing from another. 2. To derive, to deduce, or to trace anything from its origin. *-vn. (Naut.)* To derive or deflect from the course. *-vr*. To derive, to come from, to descend from.

derivativo, va [day-re-vah-tee'-vo, vah], *a*. Derivative.

dermalgia [der-mahl'-he-ah], *f*. Neuralgia of the skin.

dermatitis [der-mah-tee'-tis], *f*. Dermatitis, inflammation of the skin.

dermatología [der-mah-to-lo-hee'-ah], *f*. *(Anat.)* Dermatology, science of skin diseases.

dermatológico, ca [der-mah-to-lo'-he-co, cah], *a*. Dermatological, skin (as adjective).

dermatologista, or **dermatólogo** [der-mah-to-lo-hees'-tah, der-mah-toh'-lo-go], *m*. Dermatologist, specialist in skin diseases.

dermatoponte [der-mah-to-pon'-tay], *a. (Zool.)* Breathing by the skin.

dermesto [der-mes'-to], *m*. Dermestid, a genus including the bacon beetle and carpet beetle; very destructive warehouse pests.

dermico, ca [dayr'-me-co, cah], *a*. Dermic, relating to the skin.

dermis [dayr'-mis], *f*. Derma, dermis, the corium or true skin.

dermitis [der-mee'-tis], *f*. Inflammation of the skin.

dermodonte [der-mo-don'-tay], *a. (Zool.)* With teeth set below the skin.

dermografía [der-mo-gra-fee'-ah], *f*. Dermography, a scientific description of the skin.

dermóideo, a [der-mo'-e-dayo, ah], *a*. Dermoid, resembling skin.

dermología, dermologista [der-mo-lo-he'-ah], etc. *V.* DERMATOLOGÍA, etc.

derogable [day-ro-gah'-blay], *a*. Abolishable, annullable.

derogación [day-ro-gah-the-on'], *f*. 1. Derogation or abolition of a law, or of one of its clauses. 2. Deterioration, diminution.

derogado, da [day-ro-gah'-do, dah], *a. pp*. of DEROGAR. Derogate, derogated.

derogar [dar-ro-gar'], *va*. 1. To derogate, to abolish or annul any legal disposition. 2. To reform, to remove.

derogatorio, ria [day-ro-gah-to'-re-o, ah], *a*. Derogatory, derogative.

derrabadura [der-rah-bah-doo'-rah], *f*. The wound made in docking the tail of an animal.

derrabar [der-rah-bar'], *va*. To dock the tail.

derraigar [dayr-rah-e-gar'], *va. V.* DESARRAIGAR.

derrama [der-rah'-mah], *f*. Assessment of a tax, duty, or impost.

derramadamente [dar-rah-mah-dah-men'-tay], *adv*. 1. Profusely, lavishly. 2. Depravedly, corruptly.

derramadero, ra [der-rah-mah-day'-ro, rah], *a*. *V.* VERTEDERO.

derramador [der-rah-mah-dor'], *m*. Prodigal, waster, spendthrift.

derramamiento [der-rah-mah-me-en'-to], *m.* 1. Pouring out, wasting, or lavishing something. 2. Effusion, waste, spilling or shedding. 3. Dispersion, scattering, spreading. **Derramamiento de lágrimas**, flood of tears.

derramar [der-rah-mar'], *va.* 1. To pour, to-let out of a vessel, as liquids. 2. To leak, to let any liquid in or out. 3. To publish, to spread. 4. To spill, to scatter, to waste, to shed. **Derramar una taza de café**, to spill a cup of coffee. 5. To assess taxes. **Derramar doctrina**, *(Met.)* to diffuse a doctrine. -*vr.* 1. To be scattered or spread, to fly abroad. 2. To abandon oneself to sensual pleasures. 3. To disembogue itself (río), as a river. 4. *(Obs.)* To escape.

derrame [der-rah'-may], *m.* 1. The portion of liquor or seed lost in measuring. 2. Leakage, allowance for accidental loss in liquid measures. 3. Bevel of a wall at a window or door, to facilitate the entrance of light. 4. Declivity. 5. Subdivision of a ravine or valley in narrow outlets. 6. *(Mod.)* Accumulation of a liquid in a cavity, or its issuing from the body. **Derrame cerebral**, brain haemorrhage.

derramo [der-rah'-mo], *m.* The sloping of a wall in the aperture for door or window.

derrapar [dayr-rah-par'], *vn. (Aut.)* To skid. -*vr.* To slip.

derrape [dayr-rah'-pay], *m.* 1. *(Aut.)* Skip. 2. *(Carib.)* Uproar (alboroto).

derraspado [der-ras-pah'-do], *a.* Beardless (trigo).

derredor [der-ray-dor'], *m.* Circumference, circuit; round about: generally used in the plural, or with the article *al*, or the preposition *en*. **Al derredor** or **en derredor**, round about.

derrenegar [der-ray-nay-gar'], *vn. (Coll.)* To hate, to detest.

derrengada [der-ren-gah'-dah], *f. (Prov.)* Step in dancing.

derrengado, da [der-ren-gah'-do, dah], *a.* Incurvated, bent, crooked, lame, crippled. -*pp.* of DERRENGAR.

derrengadura [der-ren-gah-doo'-rah], *f.* Weakness in the hip, dislocation of the hip; lameness.

derrengar [der-ren-gar'], *va.* 1. To sprain the hip, to hurt severely the spine or loins of a person or animal; to cripple. 2. *(Prov.)* To knock off the fruit of a tree. -*vn. (Low.)* To abominate, to detest.

derrengo [der-ren'-go], *m. (Prov.)* Stick with which fruits are knocked off.

derretido, da [der-ray-tee'-do, dah], *a.* Melted (hielo, mantequilla). Madly in love (enamorado). -*pp.* of DERRETIR.

derretimiento [der-raytemeen'-to], *m.* 1. Thaw, liquefaction. fusion, melting (nieve). 2. Violent affection.

derretir [der-ray-teer'], *va.* 1. To liquefy, to melt (hielo, manteca), to dissolve, to fuse. 2. *(Coll.)* To change money. 3. To consume, to expend. -*vr.* 1. To be deeply in love. 2. To fall in love very easily. 3. To liquefy, to fuse, to melt or to be melted, to become liquid. 4. To melt, to grow tender or loving. 5. To be full of impatience. *(Acad.)* 6. To smelt, to found.

derribado [der-re-bah'-do], *a.* Applied to horses having the croup or buttocks rounder and lower than usual.-*pp.* of DERRIBAR.

derribar [der-re-bar'], *va.* 1. To demolish, to level with the ground. 2. To throw down, to knock down, to fell, to bring to the ground; to flatten; to lay flat, to lodge, to prostrate. **Fue derribado sobre el Canal**, he was shot down over the Channel. 3. To depose, to displace, to divest, to make a person lose protection, estimation, or acquired dignity. 4. *(Met.)* To subject, to subdue disordered passions of the mind. -*vr.* To tumble down, to throw oneself on the ground.

derribo [der-ree'-bo], *m.* 1. Demolition, as of a building. 2. Ruins of a demolished building.

derrisorio, a [der-re-so'-reo, ah], *a.* Derisive. *V.* IRRISORIO.

derrocadero [der-ro-cah-day'-ro], *m.* A very rocky and precipitous place, whence there is danger of falling.

derrocar [der-ro-car'], *va.* 1. To precipitate or fling down from a rock. 2. To pull down, to demolish, to fell, to lay. 3. *(Met.)* To rob one of his fortune or happiness. 4. To precipitate, to distract from anything spiritual or intellectual. -*vn.* To tumble, to fall down.

-*vr.* **Derrocarse por un precipicio**, to throw oneself over a cliff.

derrochado, ra [der-ro-chah-dor', rah], *m. f.* A prodigal, a spendthrift.

derrochamiento [der-ro-chah-me-en'-to], *m. (Antiq.)* Waste, squandering. *V.* DERROCHE.

derrochar [der-ro-char'], *va.* To dissipate, to waste or destroy property, to make way with.

derroche [der-ro'-chay], *m.* Waste, dissipation, destruction. **No se puede tolerar tal derroche**, such extravagance is not, to be tolerated.

derrota [der-ro'-tah], *f.* 1. *(Naut.)* Ship's course, the tack on which a ship sails; **seguir en directa derrota**, *(Naut.)* to steer a straight course. 2. Road, path. 3. Rout or defeat of an army; overthrow. **Sufrir una grave derrota**, to suffer a serious defeat.

derrotado [dayr-ro-tah'-do], *a.* 1. Defeated (vencido); defeated (equipo), beaten, losing. 2. Shabby (persona). **Un actor derrotado**, a shabby old actor.

derrotar [der-ro-tar'], *va.* 1. *(Naut.)* To cause to drive or fall off (viento, tormentas). 2. To destroy health or fortune. 3. To rout, to defeat. -*vn.* To arrive in a place in a ruined state, or in the utmost confusion and disorder. -*vr.* To cough (delincuente), to sing.

derrote [der-ro'-tay], *m.* 1. Defeat, rout, destruction. 2. *(Prov.)* Dilapidation.

derrotero [der-ro-tay'-ro], *m.* 1. *(Naut.)* Collection of seacharts. 2. *(Naut.)* Ship's course. 3. *(Met.)* Course, way or plan of life, conduct, or action.

derrotismo [der-ro-tees'-mo], *m.* Defeatism.

derrotista [der-ro-tees'-tah], *m. & f.* Defeatist.

derrubiar [der-roo-be-ar'], *va.* To break the bounds of a river or rivulet insensibly; to undermine or wash away the ground.

derrubio [der-roo'-be-o], *m.* The insensible overflow of water from a river or rivulet over the level grounds near to its bed, and the earth which falls or moulders away by this means.

derruir [der-roo-eer'], *va.* To demolish, to destroy, to ruin. *V.* DERRIBAR.

derrumbadero [der-room-bah-day'-ro], *m.* 1. Precipice; craggy, steep, and broken ground. 2. *(Met.)* A thorny or arduous affair.

derrumbamiento [der-room-bah-me-en'-to], *m.* Precipitation.

derrumbar [der-room-bar'], *va.* To precipitate, to throw down headlong. -*vr.* 1. To precipitate oneself head-long. 2. To sink down, crumble away, tumble down (edificio). 3. *(Fig.)* **Se han derrumbado los precios**, prices have tumbled.

derrumbe [der-room-bay'], *m.* 1. A tumbling down, collapse. 2. A landslide.

derviche [der-vee'-chay], *m.* Dervish, a Mohammedan monk or friar.

des [dess]. 1. A preposition, corresponding with the Latin *dis*; never used but in compound words. 2. *(Obs.)* A contraction of *de ese*, of this, of that.

desabarrancar [des-ah-bar-ran-car'], *va.* 1. To drag, to draw, or to pull out of a ditch. 2. *(Met.)* To disentangle from a state of perplexity, to extricate from difficulties.

desabastecer [des-ah-bas-tay-therr'], *va.* Not to supply a place with provisions, either through neglect or in consequence of a prohibition.

desabastecido [des-ah-bas-tay-the'-do], *a.* **Estar desabastecido de**, to be out of. **Nos cogió desabastecidos de gasolina**, it caught us without gas.

desabastecimiento [des-ah-bas-tay-the-me-ayn'-to], *m.* Shortage, scarcity.

desabejar [des-ah-bay-har'], *va.* To remove bees from their hive.

desabido, da [day-sah-bee'-do, dah], *a. (Obs.)* 1. Ignorant, illiterate. 2. Excessive, extraordinary.

desabillé [des-ah-beel-lyay'], *m.* Dishabille, undress; a loose dress for women:

desabitar [des-ah-be-tar'], *va. (Naut.)* To unbitt. **Desabitar el cable**, to unbitt a cable; that is, to remove the turns of a cable from the bitts.

desabollador [des-ah-bol-lyah-dor'], *m.* 1. An instrument used by tinworkers to take bulges out of pewter dishes, plates, or vessels. 2. Tinker.

desabollar [des-ah-bol-lyar], *va.* To tinker.

desabonarse [des-ah-bo-nar'-say], *vr.* To revoke a season-ticket or subscription.

desabono [des-ah-bo'-no], *m.* 1. Prejudice, injury. 2. Cancellation of one's subscription.

desabor [day-sah-bor'], *m.* 1. Insipidity, want of taste. 2. *(Met. Obs.)* Dullness, dejection, lowness of spirits.

desaborar [day-sah-bo-rar'], *va.* 1. To render a thing tasteless, to make it insipid or disgusting. 2. *(Met.)* To disgust, to vex.

desabordarse [des-ah-bor-dar'-say], *vr. (Naut.)* To get clear of a ship which has run foul of one's vessel.

desaborido, da [day-sah-bo-ree'-do, dah], *a.* 1. Tasteless, insipid. 2. Without substance.

desabotonar [des-ah-bo-to-nar'], *va.* To unbutton. *-vn.* To blow, to bloom, to blossom. *-vr.* To come undone.

desabozar [des-ah-bo-thar'], *va. (Naut.)* To unstopper.

desabrazar [des-ah-brah-thar], *va.* To separate one thing from another; to loosen, release what is embraced.

desabridamente [day-sah-bre-dah-men'-tay], *adv.* Bitterly, rudely, harshly.

desabrido, da [day-sah-bree'-do, dah], *a.* 1. Tasteless, insipid. 2. Sour, peevish, severe. 3. Hard, difficult (armas de fuego). 4. Bleak, sharp (aire, viento). 5. Disgusted, dissatisfied, at variance with.

desabrigadamente [de-sah-bri-gah-dah-men'-tay], *adv.* 1. Nakedly, without covering 2. Without shelter, without harbor.

desabrigado, da [des-ah-bre-gah'-do, dah], *a.* 1. Uncovered, wanting covering or clothes. 2. Shelterless; harborless, unsheltered. *-f.* An open roadstead. *(Met.)* Abandoned, without support. *-pp.* of DESABRIGAR.

desabrigar [des-ah-bre-gar'], *va.* 1. To uncover, to divest of covering; to strip, or to take off covering. 2. To deprive of shelter or harbor. *-vr.* To take off one's clothing; to leave oneself bare. **Desabrigarse en la cama**, to throw off one's bedcovers.

desabrigo [des-ah-bree'-go], *m.* 1. Nudity, nakedness. 2. Want of shelter or harbor. 3. *(Met.)* Destitution, want of support or protection.

desabrimiento [day-sah-bre-me-en'-to], *m.* 1. Insipidity, want of taste or flavor, flatness. 2. Severity or asperity of temper, rudeness of manners, acerbity. 3. Despondency, dejection, lowness of spirits. 4. The rebound of guns when discharged.

desabrir [day-sah-breer'], *va.* To vex, to plague, to torment, to harass.

desabrochar [des-ah-bro-char'], *va.* 1. To unclasp. 2. To unbutton. 3. To open, to burst open. *-vr.* To unbosom, to reveal in confidence, to disclose.

desacabalar [des-ah-cah-bah-lar'], *va.* To pilfer. V. DESCABALAR.

desacalorarse [des-ah-cah-lo-rar'-say], *vr. (Met.)* To grow less warm.

desacatadamente [des-ah-cah-tah-dah-men'-tay], *adv.* Disrespectfully.

desacatado, da [des-ah-cah-tah'-do, dah], *a.* Acting in a disrespectful manner. *-pp.* of DESACATAR.

desacatador, ra [des-ah-cah-tah-dor', rah], *m. & f.* An irreverent, uncivil, or disrespectful person.

desacatamiento [des-ah-cah-tah-me-en'-to], *m.* Disrespect.

desacatar [des-ah-cah-tar'], *va.* 1. To treat in a disrespectful manner: generally used in its reciprocal sense. 2. To desecrate, to profane, to dishonor.

desacato [des-ah-cah'-to], *m.* 1. Disrespect, incivility, want of reverence. 2. Desecration, profanation, dishonor. **Desacato de la autoridad**, contempt.

desaceitado, da [des-ah-thay-e-do, dah], *a.* Destitute of the necessary quantity of oil.

desaceitar [des-ah-thay-e-tar'], *va.* To remove oil from wollen stuffs; to remove fat.

desaceleración [des-ah-teh-lay-rah-the-on'], *f.* Deceleration, slowing down. **desacelerar** [des-ah-teh-lay-rar'], *vn.* To decelerate, to slow down.

desacerar [des-ah-thay-rar'], *va.* To unsteel, reduce from the state of steel.

desacerbar [des-ah-ther-bar'], *va.* 1. To temper, to sweeten, to take away harshness and bitterness. 2. *(Met.)* To pacify, to tranquillize, to calm.

desacertadamente [des-ah-ther-t-ah-dah-men'-tay], *adv.* Inconsiderately.

desacertado, da [des-ah-ther-tah'-do, dah], *a.* Inconsiderate, imprudent, without reflection. *-pp.* of DESACERTAR.

desacertar [des-ah-ther-tar'], *va.* To be wrong, to make a mistake.

desacidificar [des-ah-the-de-fe-car'], *va.* To remove the acid from a substance, to neutralize an acid state; to deacidify.

desacierto [des-ah-the-err'-to], *m.* Error, mistake, blunder. **Ha sido un desacierto elegir tal sitio**, it was a mistake to choose such a place. *(Yo desacierto, from Desacertar. V. ACERTAR.)*

desacobardar [des-ah-co-bar-dar'], *va.* To remove fear or cowardice, to inspire courage.

desacollar [des-ah-col-lyar'], *va. (Prov.)* To dig up the ground about vines, to cultivate vines.

desacomodadamente [des-ah-como-dah-dah-men'-tay], *adv.* Incommodiously, inconveniently.

desacomodado, da [des-ah-co-mo-dah'-do, dah], *a.* 1. Destitute of the conveniences of life. 2. Out of place or employment; out of service. 3. That which causes trouble or inconvenience. *-pp.* of DESACOMODAR.

desacomodar [des-ah-co-mo-dar'], *va.* 1. To incommode, to molest. 2. To deprive of ease or convenience. 3. To turn out of place. *-vr.* To lose one's place, to be out of place.

desacomodo [des-ah-co-mo'-do], *m.* Loss of a place or position.

desacompañamiento [des-ah-com-pa-nyah-me-en'to], *m.* Want of company or society.

desacompañar [des-ah-com-pa-nyar'], *va.* To leave the company, to retire.

desaconsejado, da [des-ah-con-say-hah'-do, dah], *a.* Acting without prudence or reflection, inconsiderate, ill-advised. *-pp.* of DESACONSEJAR.

desaconsejar [des-ah-con-say-har'], *va.* To dissuade, to disapprove of.

desacoplar [des-ah-co-plar'], *va.* To unfasten, to separate two similar things.

desacordadamente [des-ah-cor-dah-dah-men'-tay], *adv.* Inconsiderately, unadvisedly.

desacordado, da [des-ah-cor-dah'-do, dah], *a. (Art.)* Discordant. *-pp.* of DESACORDAR.

desacordamiento [des-ah-cor-dah-me-ayn'-to], *m.* V. DESACUERDO.

desacordanza, *f.* V. DISCORDANCIA.

desacordar [des-ah-cor-dar'], *va.* To untune: said of musical instruments. *-vn.* V. DISCORDAR. *-vr.* 1. To be forgetful, or of short memory. 2. To be at variance, to disagree.

desacorde [des-ah-cor'-dar], *a.* Discordant.

desacordonar [des-ah-cor-do-nar'], *va.* To uncord, to remove strings; to untie, to unfasten.

desacorralar [des-ah-cor-rah-lar'], *va.* 1. To let the flock or cattle out of the penfold. 2. To bring a bull into the open field. 3. *(Met.)* To inspirit, to animate, to encourage.

desacostumbradamente [des-ah-cos-toom-brah-dah-men'-tay], *adv.* Unusually.

desacostumbrado, da [desah-cos-toom-brah'-do, dah], *a.* Unusual, unaccustomed. *-pp.* of DESACOSTUMBRAR.

desacostumbrar [des-ah-cos-toom-brar'], *va.* To disuse, to drop or to lose the custom. *-vr.* **desacostumbrarse de**, to break oneself of the habit of.

desacotar [des-ah-co-tar'], *va.* 1. To lay open a pasture-ground which was before inclosed. 2. To raise or withdraw a prohibition. 3. To relinquish a contract, to withdraw from an agreement. 4. Among boys, to play without conditions or rules.

desacoto [des-ah-co'-to], *m.* The act of withdrawing the prohibition to enter a pasture-ground.

desacreditar [des-ah-cray-de-tar'], *va.* 1. To discredit, to impair one's credit or reputation, to cry down. 2. To dissemble or conceal the merits of anything. *-vr.* To become discredited.

desactivar [des-ac-te-var'], *va.* To desactivate, to switch off.

desactualizado [des-ac-too-ah-le-tah'-do], *a.* Out of date.

desacuerdo [des-ah-coo-err'-do], *m.* 1. Forgetfulness, oblivion. 2. Derangement of the mental faculties. 3. Discordance, disagreement, disunion. **Estar en desacuerdo**, to be out of keeping. 4. Error, mistake, blunder. 5. Want of accuracy and exactness. *(Yo desacuerdo, yo desacuerde, from Desacordar. V.* ACORDAR.)

desacuñador [des-ah-coo-nyah-dor'], *m. (Typ.)* A shooting-stick.

desacuñar [des-ah-coon-yar'], *va.* To unwedge, to remove the quoins.

desachispar [des-ah-chees-par'], *va. (Coll.)* To remove intoxication.

desaderezar [des-ah-day-ray-thar'], *va.* To undress, to divest of ornaments, to ruffle, to disarrange.

desadeudar [des-ah-day-oo-dar'], *va.* To pay one's debts.

desadorar [des-ah-do-rar'], *va.* To cease to worship or love.

desadormecer [des-ah-dor-may-therr'], *va.* 1. To wake, to rouse from sleep. 2. To rouse from mental stupor. *(Yo desadormezco, yo desadormezca, from Desadormecer. V.* ABORRECER.)

desadornar [des-ah-dor-nar'], *va.* To divest of ornaments or decorations.

desadorno [des-ah-dor'-no], *m.* Want of embellishments and charms.

desadvertidamente [des-ad-ver-te-dah-men'-tay], *adv.* Inadvertently, inconsiderately.

desadvertido, da [des-ad-ver-tee'-do, dah], *a.* Inconsiderate, imprudent. *-pp.* of DESADVERTIR.

desadvertimiento [des-ad-ver-te-me-en'-to], *m.* Want of prudence and reflection.

desadvertir [des-ad-ver-teer'], *va.* To act inconsiderately, to proceed without judgment or prudence.

desafear [des-ah-fay-ar'], *va.* To remove, or to diminish ugliness.

desafección [des-ah-fec-the-on'], *f.* Disaffection.

desafectación [des-ah-fec-tah-the-on'], *f.* Unaffectedness.

desafecto, ta [des-ah-fec'-to], *a.* Disaffected.

desafecto [des-ah-fec'-to], *m.* Disaffection, disaffectedness.

desaferrar [des-ah-fer-rar'], *va.* 1. *(Naut.)* To raise, weigh the anchors, so that the ship may sail. 2. To loosen anything which was tied or fastened. 3. To make one change an opinion which he has strenuously maintained.

desafiador, ra [des-ah-fe-ah-dor'], *m. f.* 1. A challenger, duellist. 2. Darer, one who dares or defies.

desafiante [des-ah-fe-ahn'-tay], *a.* Challenging; defiant (actitud).

desafianzador, ra [des-ah-fe-ahn-thah-dor', rah], *m. & f.* One who withdraws security.

desafianzar [des-ah-fe-ahn-thar'], *va.* 1. To withdraw the security given in favor of someone. 2. *vr.* To become impaired, to deteriorate.

desafiar [des-ah-fe-ar'], *va.* 1. To challenge, to defy, to dare. 2. To try one's strength against another. 3. To rival, to oppose, to struggle. 4. To decompose, to dissolve; to rescind; to discharge.

desafición [des-ah-fe-the-on'], *f.* Disaffection.

desaficionar [des-ah-fe-the-onar'], *va.* To destroy one's desire, wish, or affection for a thing. *-vr.* To come to dislike, to take a dislike to.

desafijar [des-ah-fe-har'], *va.* 1. V. DESFIJAR. 2. To deny the filiation of a son.

desafilado [des-ah-fe-lah'-do], *a.* Blunt.

desafilar [des-ah-fe-lar'], *va.* To blunt, to dull. *-vr.* To get blunt.

desafinadamente [des-ah-fe-nah-dah-men'-tay], *adv.* Dissonantly, discordantly.

desafinado [des-ah-fe-nah-do], *a.* Flat, out of tune.

desafinar [des-ah-fe-nar'], *va. & vn.* 1. To be inharmonious, to be out of tune. 2. To untune.

desafío [des-ah-fee'-o], *m.* 1. Challenge, duel. **Es un desafío a todos nosotros**, it is a challenge to us all. 2. Struggle, contest, combat. 3. Dismissal.

desaforado, da [des-ah-fo-rah'-do, dah], *a.* 1. Huge, uncommonly large. 2. Disorderly, lawless, impudent, outrageous. *-pp.* of DESAFORAR.

desaforar [des-ah-fo-rar'], *va.* 1. To encroach upon one's rights, to infringe one's privileges. 2. To deprive anyone of the rights or privileges belonging to his birth, profession, or character. *(Mil.)* To cashier. 3. To redeem a property. *-vr.* 1. To relinquish one's rights and privileges. 2. To be outrageous or disorderly.

desaforo [des-ah-fo'-ro], *m.* The act and effect of redeeming a perpetual lease.

desaforrar [des-ah-for-rar'], *va.* 1. To remove the lining of anything. 2. **Desaforrar los cables**, *(Naut.)* to unserve the cables.

desafortunado, da [des-ah-for-too-nah'-do, dah], *a.* Unfortunate, unlucky.

desafuero [des-ah-foo-ay'-ro], *m.* Excess; outrage, open violence, downright injustice, infraction of law.

desagarrar [des-ah-gar-rar'], *va. (Coll.)* To release; to let loose.

desagitadera [des-ah-he-tah-day'-rah], *f. (Agri.)* An instrument used in separating honeycombs from the hive.

desagitar [des-ah-he-tar'], *va.* To remove honeycombs from the hive with the *desagitadera*.

desagotar [des-ah-go-tar'], *va.* V. DESAGUAR.

desagraciado, da [de-sah-grah-the-ah'-do, dah], *a.* Ungraceful, inelegant. *-pp.* of DESAGRACIAR.

desagraciar [des-ah-grah-the-ar'], *va.* To deform, to disfigure, to make ungraceful or inelegant.

desagradable [des-ah-grah-dah'-blay], *a.* Disagreeable, unpleasant; uncomfortable.

desagradablemente [des-ah-grah-dah-blay-men'-tay], *adv.* Disagreeably.

desagradar [des-ah-grah-dar'], *va.* To displease, to offend, to make angry. **Me desagrada ese olor**, I don't like that smell. *-imp.* It does not suit.

desagradecer [des-ah-grah-day-therr'], *va.* To be ungrateful.

desagradecidamente [des-grah-the-ah-dah-men'-tay], *adv.* Ungratefully

desagradecido, da [des-ah-grah-day-thee'-do, dah], *a.* Ungrateful. *-pp.* of DESAGREDECER.

desagradecimiento [des-ah-grah-day-the-me-en'-to], *m.* Ingratitude.

desagrado [des-ah-grah'-do], *m.* 1. Asperity, harshness. 2. Discontent, displeasure. **Ser del desagrado del rey**, to have incurred the king's displeasure.

desagraviar [des-ah-grah-ve-ar'], *va.* 1. To give satisfaction, or make amends for an injury done; to relieve. 2. To vindicate. *-vr.* To get one's own back; to exact an apology.

desagravio [des-ah-grah'-veo], *m.* 1. Relief, satisfaction, or compensation for an injury done. 2. Vindication, justice, vengeance.

desagregación [des-ahgraygah-the-on'], *f.* 1. Separation, disintegration. *(Min.)* Separation of the mineral parts by means of a force which reduces the metal to grains or powder. 2. Separation of the molecules of a body.

desagregar [des-ah-gray-gar'], *va.* To disjoin, to separate. -*vr.* To desintegrate.

desagriar [des-ah-gre-ar'], *va.* 1. To neutralize acidity. 2. To sweeten, mollify, soften the character of someone. 3. To appease, remove anger.

desaguadero [des-ah-goo-ah-day'-ro], *m.* 1. Channel, drain for drawing off superfluous water. 2. *(Met.)* Drain of money.

desaguador [des-ah-goo-ah-dor'], *m.* Waterpipe, channel or conduit for water.

desaguar [des-ah-goo-ar'], *va.* 1. To drain, to draw off water. 2. *(Met.)* To waste money in extravagant expenses. -*vn.* To empty or flow into the sea (ríos). -*vr. (Met.)* To discharge by vomits or stools.

desaguazar [des-ah-goo-ah-thar'], *va.* To drain the water from any part.

desagüe [des-ah'-goo-ay], *m.* 1. Channel, drain, outlet. 2. Extraordinary expense. 3. Drainage.

desaguisado, da [des-ah-gee-sah'-do, dah], *a.* 1. Injurious, unjust. 2. Disproportionate, exorbitant. 3. Intrepid, bold.

desaguisado [des-ah-ges-ah'-do], *m.* Offence, injury, wrong.

desahijar [des-ah-eh-ar'], *va.* To wean, to separate the young from the dams. -*vr.* To swarm (abejas).

desahitarse [des-ah-e-tar'-say], *vr.* To relieve indigestion, to unload the stomach.

desahogadamente [des-ah-o-gah-dah-men'-tay], *adv.* 1. Freely, without embarrassment or obstruction. 2. In an impudent or brazen-faced manner.

desahogado, da [des-a-ho-gah'-do, dah], *a.* 1. Petulant, impudent, brazen-faced, licentious. 2. Having plenty of room, free, unencumbered (lugares). 3. *(Naut.)* Having sea room. -*pp.* of DESAHOGAR.

desahogamiento [des-ah-o-gah-me-ayn'-to], *m.* V. DESAHOGO.

desahogar [des-ah-o-gar'], *va.* To ease pain, to alleviate distress. -*vr.* 1. To recover from fatigue or disease. 2. To unbosom, to disclose one's grief. 3. To expostulate or debate with one against wrong received. 4. To vent, to utter. 5. To extricate oneself from debt. 6. To give a horse liberty, so that he may vent his passion and become obedient to the bridle.

desahogo [des-aho'-go], *m.* 1. Ease, alleviation from pain or affliction. **Es un desahogo de tantas cosas malas**, it's an outlet for so many unpleasant things. 2. The unbosoming or disclosing one's troubles or grief. 3. Freedom of speech, vent. **Expresarse con cierto desahogo**, to express oneself with a certain freedom. 4. Laxity. 5. Domestic convenience.

desahuciado, da [des-ah-oo-the-ah'-do, dah], *a.* Given over, despaired of. -*pp.* of DESAHUCIAR.

desahuciar [des-ah-oo-the-ar'], *va.* 1. To despair, to take away all hopes of obtaining a thing. **Con esa decisión le desahuciaron definitivamente**, by that decision they finally put an end to his hopes. 2. To give over, to declare a patient past recovery. 3. To dismiss a tenant or renter, at the expiration of his agreement. 4. To drive away cattle from a pasture-ground, at the expiration of a fixed term. -*vr.* To lose all hopes.

desahucio [des-ah-oo'-theo], *m.* The act of dismissing a tenant, or of driving away cattle from a pasture-ground, at the expiration of the stipulated time.

desahumado, da [des-ah-oo-mah'-do, dah], *a.* Mild, faded, vapid, applied to liquor which has lost its strength. -*pp.* of DESAHUMAR.

desahumar [des-ah-oo-mar'], *va.* To free from smoke, to expel smoke.

desainadura [day-sah-e-nah-doo'-rah], *f. (Vet.)* Disease in horses, occasioned by liquefying their fat through overheating them.

desainar [day-sah-e-nar'], *va.* To remove the fat of an animal; to lessen or diminish the thickness or substance of anything. -*vr.* To lose a great quantity of blood.

desairadamente [des-ah-e-rah-dah-men'-tay], *adv.* Unhandsomely, gracelessly.

desairado, da [des-ah-e-rah'-do, dah], *a.* 1. Unattractive, graceless. 2. *(Met.)* Disregarded, slighted, unrewarded. -*pp.* of DESAIRAR.

desairar [des-ah-e-rar'], *va.* To disregard, to slight, to take no notice, to disrespect, to rebuff.

desaire [des-ah'-ee-ray], *m.* 1. Slight, rebuff, disdain, disrespect. **Fue un desaire sin precedentes**, it was an unprecedented snub. **Sufrir un desaire**, to suffer a rebuff. 2. Awkwardness. 3. *(Met.)* Frown of fortune or power.

desaislarse [des-ah-is-lar'-say], *vr.* To cease to be insulated.

desajustar [des-ah-hoos-tar'], *va.* To mismatch, to unfit, to make unsuitable; not to adjust, not to be fit. -*vr.* 1. To disagree, to withdraw from an agreement. 2. To be out of order; as a door, a shutter, etc.

desajuste [des-ah-hoos'-tay], *m.* 1. The act of making a thing unfit, unsuitable, or out of order. 2. Disagreement, breaking of a contract.

desalabanza [des-ah-la-bahn'-thah], *f.* Vituperation, depreciation.

desalabar [des-ah-lah-bar'], *va.* To dispraise, to censure, to depreciate.

desalabear [des-ah-lah-bay-ar'], *va.* To straighten a warped plank or board.

desaladamente [des-ah-lah-dah-men'-tay], *adv.* Anxiously, swiftly.

desaladura [day-sah-lah-doo'-rah], *f. (Chem.)* V. DESALAZóN.

desalar [des-ah-lar'], *va.* To cut off the wings. -*vr.* 1. *(Met.)* To run up to one with open arms. 2. To toil with excess to obtain something: to hurry. 3. *(Naut.)* To take away the stowage or heavy part of the cargo which served as ballast.

desalar [day-sah-lar'], *va.* To take the salt out of fish, meat, etc., by steeping it in fresh water. -*vr.* 1. *(Chem.)* To precipitate from solutions (as salts), to fall as a precipitate. 2. *(Naut.)* To make sea-water drinkable.

desalazón [day-sah-lah-thone'], *f. (Chem.)* Removal from a liquid of a part or all of its contained salts.

desalbardar [des-al-bar-dar'], *va.* To take off the packsaddle from a beast of burden.

desalentador, ra [des-ah-len-tah-dor', rah], *a.* Dispiriting, discouraging.

desalentar [des-ah-len-tar'], *va.* 1. To put one out of breath by dint of labor. 2. *(Met.)* To discourage, to dismay, to damp. -*vr.* To jade, to lose heart.

desalfombrar [des-al-fom-brar'], *va.* To remove carpets from a room or house.

desalforjar [des-al-for-har'], *va.* To take off the saddlebags from horses or mules. -*vr. (Met. Coll.)* To take off one's accoutrements, to make oneself easy.

desalhajar [des-al-ah-har'], *va.* To strip a house or room of furniture.

desaliento [des-ah-le-en'-to], *m.* 1. Dismay, depression of spirits, discouragement, dejection. 2. Faintness, languor. (*Yo desaliento, yo desaliente*, from *Desalentar*. V. ACERTAR.)

desalinear [des-ah-le-nay-ar'], *va.* To destroy the lineation, to disorder, to separate from the line.

desaliñadamente [des-ah-le-nyah-dah-men'-tay], *adv.* Slovenly, uncleanly.

desaliñado [des-ah-le-nyah-do], *m.* 1. Slovenly, dirty, down-at-heel; shabby (raído); untidy. 2. Careless (negligente).

desaliñar [des-ah-le-nyar'], *va.* To disarrange, to disorder, to ruffle; to make one slovenly or dirty.

desaliño [des-ah-lee'-nyo], *m.* 1. Slovenliness, indecent negligence of dress. 2. Carelessness, want of attention.

desalivación [day-sah-le-vah-the-on'], *f.* Salivation, profuse flow of saliva.

desalivar [day-sah-le-var'], *vn.* To salivate.

desalmadamente [de-sal-mah-dah-men'-tay], *adv.* Soullessly, inhumanly.

desalmado, da [de-sal-mah'-do, dah], *a.* 1. Soulless, inhuman, merciless. 2 Impious, profligate. 3. Inanimate, abject. -*pp.* of DESALMAR.

desalmamiento [de-sal-mah-me-en'-to], *m.* Inhumanity, impiety, profligacy. *(Ant.)*

desalmar [des-al-mar'], *va. (Met.)* To speak with ingenuity and candor. -*vr.* To desire something very anxiously.

desalmenado, da [de-sal-may-nah'-do, dah], *a.* 1. Stripped of turrets (castillos, fortalezas). 2. Wanting an ornament or capital.

desalmidonar [des-al-me-do-nar'], *va.* To take the starch out of linen.

desalojamiento [des-ah-lo-hah-me-en'-to], *m.* 1. Dislodging, ejection, ousting. 2. Evacuation; abandonment; clearing.

desalojar [des-ah-lo-har'], *va.* 1. To dislodge the enemy's troops, to dispossess them of a place or post. 2. To remove, to expel (gas etc.). 3. To evacuate, to abandon, to move out of, to move away from. **Desalojar un tribunal de público**, to clear a court, to clean the public from a court. -*vn.* To quit one's house or apartments.

desalquilado, da [de-sal-ke-lah'-do, dah], *a.* Untenanted, unrented.

desalquilar [de-sal-kee-lar'], *va. & vr.* To leave a room or house for which a rent was paid.

desalterar [de-sal-tay-rar'], *va.* To allay, to assuage, to settle.

desalumbradamente [de-sah-loom-brah-dah-men'-tay], *adv.* Blindly, erroneously.

desalumbrado, da [des-ah-loom-brah'-do, dah], *a.* 1. Dazzled, overpowered with light; stricken with astonishment; surprised with splendor. 2. *(Met.)* Groping in the dark.

desalumbramiento [des-ah-loom-brah-me-en'-to], *m.* Blindness, want of foresight or knowledge, error.

desamable [des-ah-mah'-blay], *a.* Unamiable.

desamador [de-sah-mah-dor'], *m.* One who does not love, or has ceased loving; one who dislikes persons or things.

desamar [des-ah-mar'], *va.* 1. To love no more, not to love or esteem as formerly. 2. To hate, to detest.

desamarrar [des-ah-mar-rar'], *va.* 1. *(Naut.)* To unmoor a ship. 2. To untie. **Desamarrar un cabo**, *(Naut.)* to unbend a rope.

desamasado, da [des-ah-mah-sah'-do, dah], *a.* Dissolved, disunited, unkneaded.

desamelgamiento [des-ah-mel-ah-me-en'-to], *m.* Rotation, variation of crops.

desamelgar [des-ah-mel-gar'], *va. (Agri.)* To rotate crops, to vary the order of cultivation, alternating with lying fallow.

desamigado, da [des-ah-me-gah'-do, dah], *a.* Unfriendly, unconnected.

desamistad [des-ah-mis-tahd'], *f.* Unfriendliness.

desamistarse [des-ah-mis-tar'-say], *vr.* To fall out, to quarrel.

desamodorrar [des-ah-mo-dor-rar'], *va.* To remove lethargy or drowsiness. -*vr.* To emerge from lethargy or drowsiness; to recover oneself.

desamoldar [des-ah-mol-dar'], *va* 1. To unmould, to change as to the form. 2. *(Met.)* To change the proportion or symmetry of a thing; to disfigure.

desamor [des-ah-mor'], *m.* 1. Disregard, disaffection. 2. Lack of sentiment and affection which certain things generally inspire. 3. Enmity, hatred.

desamoradamente [des-ah-mo-rah-dah-men'-tay], *adv. (Obs.)* Unfriendly, harshly.

desamorado, da [des-ah-mo-rah'-do, dah], *a.* 1. Loveless, cold-hearted. 2. Harsh, rude, disdainful. -*pp.* of DESAMORAR.

desamorar [des-ah-mo-rar'], *va.* To extinguish love, to cease loving.

desamoroso, sa [des-ah-mo-ro'-so, sah], *a.* Unloving, destitute of regard or love.

desamorrar [des-ah-mor-rar'], *va. (Coll.)* To cheer up, to make one give up his obstinacy.

desamortajar [des-ah-mor-tah-har'], *va.* To unshroud, to remove the shroud.

desamortecer [des-ah-mor-tay-therr'], *va.* To remove torpor; to recover from a swoon.

desamortización [des-ah-mor-te-thah-the-on'], *f. (Jur.)* Disentailment.

desamortizar [des-ah-mor-te-thar'], *va.* To disentail, to break an entail.

desamotinarse [des-ah-mo-te-nar'-say], *vr.* To withdraw from mutiny and sedition.

desamparado [des-am-pah-rah'-do], *a.* 1. Helpless, defenceless; abandoned (niño, etc.). **Los niños desamparados de la ciudad**, the city's waifs and strays. 2. Exposed (lugar). 3. Lonely, deserted (lugar).

desamparador, ra [des-am-pa-rah-dor', rah], *m. & f.* Deserter, one who abandons.

desamparar [des-am-pa-rar'], *va.* 1. To forsake, to abandon, to leave, to relinguish, to desert. 2. To quit a place. 3. *(Naut.)* To dismantle, dismast a ship. **Desamparar los bienes**, to give up one's property, in order to avoid being molested by creditors.

desamparo [des-am-pah'-ro], *m.* 1. Abandonment, desertion, want of protection, helplessness, forlornness. 2. Dereliction, the state of being forsaken.

desamueblado, da [des-ah-moo-ay-blah'-do, dah], *a.* Unfurnished. -*pp.* of DESAMUEBLAR.

desamueblar [des-ah-moo-ay-blar'], *va.* To unfurnish, to deprive or strip of furniture.

desanclar, desancorar [des-an-clar'-de-san-co-rar'], *va. (Naut.)* To weigh anchor.

desandadura [des-an-dah-doo'-rah], *f.* Going back over the same road.

desandar [des-an-dar'], *va.* To retrograde, to go back the same road by which one came. **Desandar lo andado**, to undo what has been done.

desandrajado, da [des-an-drah-hah'-do, dah], *a.* Ragged, in tatters.

desangramiento [day-san-grah-me-en'-to], *m.* Bleeding to excess.

desangrar [day-an-grar'], *va.* 1. To bleed one to excess. 2. To draw a large quantity of water from a river. 3. *(Met.)* To exhaust one's means, to make poor. -*vr.* To lose much blood.

desanidar [des-ah-ne-dar'], *vn.* To forsake the nest (pájaros). -*va.* 1. *(Met.)* To dislodge from a post. 2. To apprehend fugitives in their place of concealment.

desanimadamente [des-ah-ne-mah-dah-men'-tay], *adv.* Spiritlessly.

desanimado, da [des-ah-ne-mah'-do, dah], *a.* 1. Despondent, dejected, discouraged. 2. Dull, lifeless, flat. **Fue una fiesta de lo más desanimada**, it was a terrible, dull party.

desanimar [des-ah-ne-mar'], *va.* 1. To dishearten, to dispirit, to discourage; to put a damper upon one's spirits. 2. To damp, to pall, to daunt. -*vr.* To jade. **No hay que desanimarse**, we must not lose heart.

desánimo [des-ah-ne-mo], *m.* 1. Despondency, depression, dejection. 2. Dullness, lifelessness (flojedad).

desanudar [des-ah-noo-dar'], *va.* 1. To untie, to loosen a knot. 2. *(Met.)* To extricate, to disentangle, to clear up what was obscure. **Desanudar la voz**, to pronounce clearly and distinctly, to articulate freely.

desañudadura [des-ah-nyoo-dah-doo'-rah], *f.* The untying or loosening of a knot; disentanglement.

desapacibilidad [des-ah-pa-the-be-le-dahd'], *f.* Rudeness, churlishness, peevishness.

desapacible [des-ah-pa-thee'-blay], *a.* Sharp, rough, disagreeable, unpleasant, harsh.

desapaciblemente [des-ah-pa-the-blay-men'-tay], *adv.* Sharply, disagreeably.

desapadrinar [des-ah-pah-dre-nar'], *va. (Met.)* To disprove, to contradict.

desaparear [des-ah-pa-ray-ar'], *va.* To unmatch, to disjoin.

desaparecer [des-ah-pa-ray-therr'], *va.* To remove from sight, to hide. -*vn. & vr.* To disappear.

desaparecido [des-ah-pah-r-ay-the'-do], *a.* Missing; extinct (especie). **El libro desaparecido**, the missing book. **Uno de los animales desaparecidos**, one of the extinct animals. 2. *m. pl.* **Los desaparecidos**, the missing.

desaparecimiento [des-ah-pa-ray-the-me-en'-to], *m.* The act of disappearing or vanishing out of sight.

desaparejar [des-ah-pa-ray-har'], *va.* 1. To unharness beasts of draught or burden. 2. *(Naut.)* To unrig a ship.

desaparición [des-ah-pah-re-the-on'], *f.* Disappearance, vanishing from sight. *(Astr.)* Occultation.

desaparroquiar [des-ah-par-roke-ar'], *va.* To remove someone from his parish. *-vr.* 1. To change one's parish, to remove from one parish to another. 2. *(Met.)* To cease to be a customer of a shop.

desapasionadamente [des-ah-pah-se-o-nah-dah-men'tay], *adv.* Impartially.

desapasionado [des-ah-pah-se-o-nah'-do], *a.* Dispassionate, impartial.

desapasionarse [des-ah-pah-se-o-nar'-say], *vr.* To root out a passion, or strong affection for anything.

desapegarse [des-ah-pay-gar'-say], *vr.* To be alienated from natural affection.

desapego [des-ah-pay'-go], *m.* 1. Alienation of love or affection, coolness. 2. Impartiality, disinterestedness, indifference.

desapercibidamente [des-ah-per-the-bah-men'-tay], *adv.* Inadvertently, carelessly.

desapercibido, da [des-ah-per-the-bee'-do, dah], *a.* 1. Unprovided, unprepared, unguarded, careless. 2. **Pasar desapercibido**, to go unnoticed.

desapercibimiento, desapercibo [des-ah-per-the-be-me-en'-to, des-ah-per-the-e'-bo], *m.* Unpreparedness.

desapestar [des-ah-pes-tar'], *va.* 1. To cure persons infected with the plague. 2. To disinfect.

desapiadadamente [des-ah-pe-ah-dah, dah-men'-tay], *adv.* Unmercifully, impiously.

desapiadado, da [des-ah-pe-ah-dah'-do, dah], *a.* Merciless, impious, inhuman.

desapiolar [des-ah-pe-o-lar'], *va.* To loosen the strings with which game is tied.

desaplicación [des-ah-ple-cah-the-on'], *f.* Inapplication, indolence.

desaplicadamente [des-ah-ple-cah-dah-men'-tay], *adv.* Indolently.

desaplicado, da [des-ah-ple-cah'-do, dah], *a.* Indolent, careless, neglectful, lazy.

desaplomar [des-ah-plo-mar'], *va.* To put out of plumb.

desapoderado, da [des-ah-po-day-rah'-do, dah], *a.* Furious, impetuous, ungovernable. *-pp.* of DESAPODERAR.

desapoderamiento [des-ah-po-day-rah-me-en'-to], *m.* 1. The act of depriving or ejecting. 2. Excessive boldness, extreme audacity.

desapoderar [des-ah-po-day-rar'], *va.* 1. To dispossess, to rob one of his property. 2. To repeal or revoke a power of attorney.

desapolillar [des-ah-po-leel-lyar'], *va.* To free and clear of moths. *-vr.* 1. *(Coll.)* To take the air when it is cold and sharp. 2. To get rid of moths.

desaporcar [des-ah-por-car'], *va.* To take away from plants earth which had been heaped about them.

desaposentar [des-ah-pos-en-tar'], *va.* 1. To turn one out of his lodgings, to force him to move. 2. To expel a thing from one's mind.

desaposesionar [des-ah-po-say-se-o-nar'], *va.* To dispossess.

desapostura [des-ah-pos-too'-rah], *f.* Inelegance, deformity, indecency.

desapoyar [des-ah-po-yar], *va.* To remove the foundation of something. *V.* DESAPUNTALAR.

desapreciar [des-ah-pray-the-ar'], *m.* To depreciate, to undervalue, to cry down.

desaprecio [des-ah-pray-theo], *m.* *(Prov.)* Depreciation, lessening the worth or value of a thing.

desaprender [des-ah-pren-derr'], *va.* To unlearn, to forget what one has learned by heart.

desaprensar [de-sah-pren-sar'], *va.* 1. To take away the gloss which clothes or other things obtain in the press. 2. *(Met.)* To extricate oneself from a pressing difficulty.

desaprensión [des-ah-pren-se-on'], *f.* Unscrupulousness, lack of scruple.

desaprensivamente [des-aph-pren-se-vah-men'-tay], *adv.* Unscrupulously.

desaprensivo [des-ah-pren-se'-vo], *a.* Unscrupulous.

desapretador [des-ah-pray-tah-dor'], *m.* Screwdriver.

desapretar [des-ah-pray-tar'], *va.* 1. To slacken, to loosen, to loose. 2. *(Met.)* To ease, to free from anxiety or uneasiness. *(Yo desaprieto, yo desapriete, from Desapretar. V.* ACERTAR.)

desaprisionar [des-ah-pre-se-onar'], *va.* To release from confinement, to set at liberty. *-vr.* *(Met.)* To extricate oneself from difficulties, to remove an impediment.

desaprobación [des-ah-pro-bah-the-on'], *f.* Disapprobation, censure.

desaprobar [des-ah-pro-bar'], *va.* To disapprove, to censure, to reprove, to condemn, to find fault.

desapropiación, *f.* **desapropiamiento**, *m.* [des-ah-pro-pe-ah-the-on', me-en'-to]. Alienation. *V.* ENAJENAMIENTO.

desapropiar [des-ah-pro-pe-ar'], *va.* To deprive someone of ownership. *-vr.* To alienate, to transfer one's right and property to another, to expropriate.

desapropio [des-ah-pro'-peo], *m.* Alienation, transfer of property.

desaprovechadamente [des-ah-pro-vay-chah-dah-men'-tay], *adv.* Unprofitably.

desaprovechado, da [des-ah-pro-vay-chah'-do, data], *a.* 1. Unprofitable, useless. 2. Backward. *-pp.* of DESAPROVECHAR.

desaprovechamiento [des-ah-pro-vay-chah-me-en'-to], *m.* 1. Backwardness, waste. 2. Inapplication, negligence.

desaprovechar [des-ah-pro-vay-char'], *va.* To waste, to misspend, to turn to a bad use. *-vn.* To be backward, to make little or no progress.

desapuntalar [des-ah-poon-tah-lar'], *va.* To take away the props or supports.

desapuntar [des-ah-poon-tar'], *va.* 1. To unstitch, to rip up. 2. To aim badly. 3. To efface the days of absence from the choir.

desarbolar [des-ar-bo-lar'], *va.* 1. *(Naut.)* To unmast a ship, to cut down the masts. 2. *-vn.* *(Naut.)* To loosen the masts by accident. 3. *(Agri.)* To root up or cut down the trees of a grove.

desarbolo [des-ar-bo'-lo], *m.* The act of unmasting a ship or laying her up in ordinary.

desarenar [des-ah-ray-nar'], *va.* To take away sand, to clear a place of sand.

desareno [des-ah-ray'-no], *m.* Clearing a place of sand.

desarmable [des-ar-mah'-blay], *a.* Demountable, collapsible.

desarmado, da [des-ar-mah'-do, dah], *a.* Unarmed, defenceless, bare.*-pp.* of DESARMAR.

desarmador [des-ar-mah-dor'], *m.* He, who discharges a gun.

desarmadura, *f.* **desarmamiento**, *m.* [des-ar-mah-doo'-rah, des-ar-mah-me-en'-to], Disarming, the act and effect of disarming.

desarmar [des-ar-mar'], *va.* 1. To disarm. 2. To prohibit the carrying of arms. 3. To undo a thing, to take it asunder. 4. To disband a body of troops. 5. To dismount a crossbow; to dismount cannon. 6. To butt, to strike with the horns. 7. *(Met.)* To pacify, to disarm wrath or vengeance. *-vn.* To disarm.

desarme [des-ar'-may], *m.* 1. Disarming of ships or troops. 2. Disarmament. **Desarme total**, total disarmament. **Desarme nuclear**, nuclear disarmament.

desarraigar [des-ar-rah-e-gar'], *va*. 1. To eradicate, to root out, to deracinate. 2. *(Met.)* To extirpate, to destroy, to exterminate. 3. *(Law.)* To expel from the country.

desarraigo [des-arrah-'e-go], *m*. 1. Eradication. 2. *(Law.)* Expulsion from a country.

desarrancarse [des-ar-ran-car'-say], *vr*. To desert, to separate from a body or association.

desarrapado, da [des-ar-rah-pah'-do, dah], *a*. Ragged.

desarrebozar [des-ar-ray-bo-thar'], *va*. 1. To unmuffle. 2. *(Met.)* To lay open, to manifest, to discover.

desarrebujar [des-ar-ray-boo-har'], *va*. 1. To unfold, to spread out. 2. To uncover. 3. To explain, to clear up.

desarregladamente [des-ahr-re-glah-dah-men'-tay], *adv*. Disorderly.

desarreglado, da [des-ar-ray-glah'-do, dah], *a*. 1. Immoderate, intemperate. 2. Extravagant, excessive. 3. Lawless, unruly. 4. Out of order; upset (estómago etc.). -*pp*. of DESARREGLAR.

desarreglar [des-ar-ray-glar'], *va*. To disorder, to discompose; to disarrange. **El viento le desarregló el peinado**, the wind made a mess of her hairdo. **No desarregles la cama**, don't mess up your bed. -*vr*. To get disarranged; to get untidy.

desarreglo [des-ar-ray'-glo], *m*. 1. Disorder, confusion, irregularity, mismanagement. 2. Licentiousness, license, disorder. 3. Derangement.

desarrendarse [des-ar-ren-dar'-say], *vr*. To shake off the bridle applied to a horse.

desarrimar [des-ar-re-mar'], *va*. 1. To remove, to separate. 2. To dissuade, to move away.

desarrimo [des-ar-ree'-mo], *m*. Want of props or support.

desarrollado [des-ahr-rolyah'-do], *a*. Well-developed.

desarrollar [des-ar-rol-lyar'], *va*. 1. To unroll, to unfold. 2. To develop (fotos). 3. To expand. 4. *(Mech.)* **El coche desarrolla 30 caballos**, the engine develops 30 hp. -*vr*. 1. To unfold, to develop (semillas). 2. To develop, expand, acquire growth and vigor. **La industria se desarrolla rápidamente**, the industry is developing rapidly. **La acción se desarrolla en Roma**, the scene is set in Rome.

desarrollo [de-sar-rol'-lyo], *m*. Unfolding, development, evolution. **Un país en desarrollo**, a developing country. **La industria está en pleno desarrollo**, the industry is making rapid growth.

desarropar [des-ar-ro-par'], *va*. To uncover, to undress. -*vr*. To undress, to uncover oneself. **Todavía el tiempo no es para desarroparse**, it's not yet weather for leaving off any clothes.

desarrugar [des-ar-roo-gar'], *va*. To take out wrinkles.

desarrumar [des-ar-roo-mar'], *va*. *(Naut.)* 1. To unload a ship, to discharge the cargo. 2. To remove the ballast in order to inspect the bottom.

desarticulación [des-ar-te-coo-lah-the-on'], *f*. Taking to pieces; separation; dislocation; breaking up.

desarticulado [des-ar-te-coo-lah'-do], *a*. Disjointed.

desarticular [des-ar-te-coo-lar'], *va*. To disarticulate, sever a joint. *(Naut.)* To loosen.

desartillar [des-ar-teel-lyar'], *va*. To take the guns out of a ship or a fortress.

desarzonar [des-ar-tho-nar'], *va*. To throw from the saddle, to unhorse.

desasado, da [des-ah-sah'-do, dah], *a*. 1. Without handles. 2. *(Cant.)* Without ears. *(Acad.)*.

desaseadamente [des-ah-say-ah-dah-men'-tay], *adv*. Uncleanly.

desasear [des-ah-say-ar'], *va*. To make dirty or unclean; to discompose, to disorder.

desasegurar [des-ah-say-goo-rar'], *va*. 1. To lose the security of something. 2. *(Amer.)* To cancel life or fire insurance.

desasentar [des-ah-sen-tar'], *va*. *(Met.)* To disagree with, to displease, not to suit or not to set well. -*vr*. To stand up.

desaseo [des-ah-say'-o], *m*. Uncleanliness, dirtiness, carelessness.

desasimiento [des-ah-se-me-en'-to], *m*. 1. The act of loosening or letting loose. 2. *(Met.)* Alienation of affection or love, disregard. 3. Disinterestedness.

desasir [des-ah-seer'], *va*. To loosen, to disentangle, to give up. -*vr*. 1. To disengage or extricate oneself. 2. *(Met.)* To disregard, to look with indifference or contempt. 3. To give up the possession of property.

desasnar [des-as-nar'], *va*. *(Met. Coll.)* To instruct, to polish one's manners. -*vr*. To grow sharp, to learn wit, to become polite.

desasociable [des-ah-so-the-ah'-blay], *a*. Unsociable.

desasosegadamente [des-ah-so-say-gah-dah-men'-tay], *adv*. Uneasily.

desasosegado [des-ah-so-say-gah'p-do], *a*. Uneasy, anxious; restless.

desasosegar [des-ah-so-say-gar'], *m*. To disquiet, to disturb. -*vr*. To become uneasy, to get perturbed.

desasosiego [des-ah-so-se-ay'-go], *m*. Restlessness, want of tranquillity, uneasiness. (*Yo desasosiego*, from *Desasosegar*. V. ACERTAR.)

desastrado, da [des-as-trah'-do, dah], *a*. 1. Wretched, miserable, unfortunate. 2. Ragged, tattered.

desastre [des-ahs'-tray], *m*. Disaster, catastrophe, misfortune. **La boda fue un desastre**, the wedding was a disaster.

desastroso, sa [des-as-tro'-so, sah], *a*. Unfortunate, disastrous.

desatacar [des-ah-tah-car'], *va*. To loosen, to untie.

desatado, da [des-ah-tah'-do, dah], *a*. Loose, unbound, untied.-*pp*.. of DESATAR.

desatador [des-ah-tah-dor'], *m*. He who unties, absolver.

desatadura, *f*. **desatamiento**, *m*. [des-ah-tah-doo'-rah, des-ah-tah-me-en'-to]. Untying, loosening.

desatancar [des-ah-tan-car'], *va*. 1. To clear sewers and conduits.

desatar [des-ah-tar'], *va*. 1. To untie, to undo, to unfasten, to loosen or unbind, to separate, to detach. 2. To loosen, to separate. 3. To solve, to find out, to unravel. 4. To liquefy, to dissolve.-*vr*. 1. To give loose rein to one's tongue. 2. To lose all reserve, fear, or bashfulness. 3. **Desatarse de un compromiso**, to get out of an agreement. 4. *(Fig.)* To break, to burst; to break out. **Desatarse en injurias**, to let rip with a torrent of abuse. 5. *(Fig.)* To spark off, give rise to, unleash.

desatascar [des-ah-tas-car'], *va*. 1. To pull or draw out of the mud. 2. *V*. DESATANCAR.. 3. *(Met.)* To extricate one from difficulties.

desataviar [des-ah-tah-ve-ar'], *va*. To strip off ornaments and decorations.

desatavio [des-ah-tah-vee'-o], *m*. Uncleanliness, negligence in dress.

desate [des-ah'-tay], *m*. 1. Disorderly proceeding. 2. Loss of fear, of reserve, of bashfulness. **Desate de vientre**, looseness of the bowels.

desatención [des-ah-ten-the-on'], *f*. 1. Inattention, absence of mind, abstraction. 2. Disrespect, want of respect 3. Incivility, want of politeness.

desatender [des-ah-ten-derr'], *va*. 1. To pay no attention to what is said or done. 2. To disregard, to neglect. 3. To take no notice of a person or thing.

desatendible [des-ah-ten-dee'-blay], *a*. What ought to be neglected or disregarded; mean, despicable, inconsiderate.

desatentado, da [des-ah-ten-tah'-do, dah], *a*. 1. Inconsiderate, unadvised, acting in an absurd and unreasonable manner. 2. Excessive, rigorous, disordered. -*pp*. of DESATENTAR.

desatentamente [des-ah-ten-tah-dah-men'-tay], *adv*. Disrespectfully, uncivilly.

desatentar [des-ah-ten-tar'], *va*. To perturb the mind, to perplex the understanding.

desatento, ta [des-ah-ten'-to, tah], *a*. 1. Inattentive, careless, heedless, thoughtless. 2. Rude, unmannerly, uncivil.

desatesorar [des-ah-tay-so-rar'], *va*. To remove or spend the treasure.

desatestar [des-ah-tes-tar'], *va*. To contradict a testimony. *-vr*. To retract from the testimony given.

desatiento [des-ah-te-en'-to], *m*. Inconsiderateness, thoughtlessness, absence of mind. *(Yo desatiento, yo desatiente, from Desatentar. V.* ACRECENTAR.)

desatinadamente [des-ah-te-nah-dah-men'-tay], *adv*. 1. Inconsiderately, indiscreetly. 2. Extravagantly, disproportionately.

desatinado, da [des-ah-te-nah'-do, dah], *a*. Extravagant, nonsensical, crazy, foolish, irregular, wild. *-pp*. of DESATIMAR.

desatinado [des-ah-te-nah-do], *m*. Idiot, fool, madman.

desatinar [des-ah-te-nar'], *va. & vn.* 1. To do foolish things, to act in an incoherent manner. 2. To disorder or derange one's mind. 3. To throw into a violent passion, to make one mad. 4. To talk nonsense. 5. To reel, to stagger, to totter, to dote.

desatino [des-ah-tee'-no], *m*. 1. Extravagance, irregularity, wildness; headiness. 2. Reeling, staggering. 3. Madness, craziness; nonsense.

desativar [des-ah-te-var'], *va*. To free a mine from heaps of rubbish.

desatolondrado, da [des-ah-to-lon-drah'-do, dah], *a*. 1. Recovery from stupor. 2. *(Peru.)* Extravagant, foolish. *-pp*. of DESATOLONDRAR.

desatolondrar [des-ah-to-lon-drar'], *va*. To bring one to his senses. *-vr*. To recover one's senses.

desatollar [des-ah-tol-lyar'], *va*. To pull out of the need or mire. V. DESATASCAR.

desatontarse [des-ah-ton-tar'-say], *vr*. To recover oneself from stupefaction.

desatornillador [des-tor-neel-lyah-dor'], *m*. *(LAm.)* Screwdriver.

desatornillar [des-ah-tor-neel-lyar'], *va*. To unscrew, to remove the screws.

desatrabillar [des-ah-trah-beel-lyar'], *va*. To unstrap, to unbuckle.

desatracar [des-ah-trah-car'], *va*. *(Naut.)* To sheer off, to bear away.

desatraer [des-ah-trah-err'], *va*. To disjoin, to separate, to remove one thing from another.

desatraillar [des-ah-trah-eel-lyar'], *va*. To uncouple hounds, to untie the leash with which they are coupled.

desatrampar [des-ah-tram-par'], *va*. 1. To clear a conduit, sink, or sewer. 2. V. DESATASCAR.

desatrancar des-ah-tran-car'], *va*. 1. To unbar. 2. To clear a well or spring.

desatufarse [des-ah-too-far'-say], *vr*. To grow calm, to allay one's passion.

desaturdir [des-ah-toor-deer'], *va*. To rouse from a state of dizziness or stupor, to animate.

desautoridad [des-ah-oo-to-re-dahd'], *f*. Want of authority.

desautorización [des-ah-oo-to-re-thah-the-on], *f*. 1. Discrediting; disapproval; repudiation. 2. Denial.

desautorizado [des-ah-oo-to-re-thah'-do], *a*. Unauthorized; unofficial.

desautorizar [des-ah-oo-to-re-thar'], *va*. To disauthorize.

desavahado, da [de-sah-va-hah'-do, dah], *a*. *(Ant.)* Uncovered, free from fogs, clouds, or vapors: applied to places where the sky is commonly very clear. *-pp*. of DESAVAHAR.

desavahar [des-ah-vah-ar'], *va*. *(Ant.)* To expose to the air, to evaporate, to send forth a fume or vapor. *-vr*. To grow lively or sprightly.

desavecindado, da [des-ah-vay-thin-dah'-do, dah], *a*. Deserted, unpeopled: applied to a place abandoned by its inhabitants. *-pp*. of DESAVECINDARSE.

desavecindarse [des-ah-vay-thin-dar'-say], *vr*. To change one's domicile; to leave the place where one was living.

desavenencia [des-ah-vay-nen-the-ah], *f*. Discord, disagreement, misunderstanding, misintelligence.

desavenido, da [des-ah-vay-nee'-do, dah], *a*. Discordant, disagreeing. *-pp*. of DESAVENIR.

desavenimiento [des-ah-vay-ne-me-en'-to], *m*. *(Obs.)* V. DESAVENENCIA.

desavenir [des-ah-vay-neer'], *va*. To discompose, to disconcert, to unsettle. *-vr*. To disagree, to quarrel.

desaventajadamente [des-ah-vayn-tah-hah-dah-men'-tay], *adv*. Disadvantageously, unprofitably.

desaventajado, da [des-ah-ven-tah-hah'-do, dah], *a*. Disadvantageous, unprofitable.

desaviar [des-ah-ve-ar'], *va*. 1. To deviate from the high road, to lead astray. 2. To strip of necessaries or conveniences. *-vr*. 1. To go astray, to miss one's way. 2. To lose the means of acquiring necessaries, conveniences, etc.

desavío [des-ah-vee'-o], *m*. 1. The act of going astray, or losing one's road. 2. Want of the necessary means for attaining some end or purpose.

desavisado, da [des-ah-ve-sah'-do, dah], *a*. Ill-advised, unadvised, misguided. *-pp*. of DESAVISAR.

desavisar [des-ah-ve-sar'], *va*. To give a contrary account, to contradict former advice, to countermand.

desayudar [des-ah-yoo-dar'], *va*. Not to assist, but oppose one with regard to his claims or rights. *-vr*. To be negligent or careless in the performance of one's duty.

desayunar [des-ah-yoo-nar'], *va*. To give the first intelligence of something unknown *-vr*. 1. To have breakfast. 2. *(Met.)* To have the first intelligence of anything.

desayuno [des-ah-yoo'-no], *m*. Light breakfast.

desayuntamiento [des-ah-yoon-tah-me-en'-to], *m*. *(Agri.)* Unyoking, uncoupling.

desayuntar [des-ah-yoon-tar'], *va*. To disunite, to dissolve, to separate; to uncouple a working span.

desayustar [des-ah-yoos-tar'], *va*. *(Naut.)* To unbend a rope or cable.

desazogar [des-ah-tho-gar'], *va*. To take off the quicksilver from a looking-glass or any other thing. *-vr*. *(Peru.)* To become unquiet, restless.

desazón [days-ah-thone'], *f*. 1. Insipidity, want of taste or flavor. 2. Disgust, displeasure. 3. *(Met.)* Disquietness, uneasiness, affliction, restlessness. 4. Unfitness of a soil for agricultural purposes.

desazonado, da [days-ah-tho-nah'-do, dah], *a*. 1. Ill-adapted, unfit for some purpose (tierra). 2. Peevish, impertinent, passionate, ill-humored. 3. Poorly, indifferent in health. *-pp*. of DESAZONAR.

desazonar [days-ah-tho-nar'], *va*. 1. To render tasteless, to infect with an unpleasant taste. 2. To disgust, to vex, to mortify. *-vr*.. To become indisposed in health, to be sick.

desazufrar [des-ah-thoo-frar'], *va*. *(Chem.)* To desulphurize, to desulphur.

desbabador [des-bah-bah-dor'], *m*. A mouthing bit, put on a horse to excite salivation.

desbabar [des-bah-bar'], *vn*. To drivel, to slaver. *-vr*. *(Coll.)* To be deeply in love, to regard with excessive fondness, to dote upon.

desbagar [des-bah-gar'], *va*. To extract the flaxseed from the capsule.

desbalijamiento [des-bah-le-hah-me-en'-to], *m*. The plundering of a portmanteau.

desbalijar [des-bah-le-har'], *va*. To plunder a portmanteau of its contents.

desballestar [des-bal-lyes-tar'], *va*. To unbend a crossbow, to take it asunder.

desbancar [des-ban-car'], *va*. 1. To clear a room of the benches, etc. 2. To win all the money staked by a gambler, who holds a basset or faro-table. 3. *(Met.)* To circumvent one in the frienship and affection of another.

desbandada [des-bahn-dah'-dah], *f*. Rush. **Hubo una desbandada general de turistas**, there was a mass exodus of tourists. **A la desbandada**, in disorder.

desbandarse [des-ban-dar'-say], *vr.* 1. To disband, to desert the colors (soldados). 2. To flee in disorder; to go off in all directions.

desbarajustar [des-bah-rah-hoos-tar'], *va.* To disorder, to confuse, to mix things.

desbarajuste [des-bah-rah-hoos'-tay], *m.* Disorder, confused medley of things.

desbaratadamente [des-bah-rah-tah-dah-men'-tay], *adv.* Disorderly.

desbaratado, da [des-bah-rah-tah'-do, dah] *a.* Debauched, corrupted with lewdness and intemperance. *-pp.* of DESBARATAR.

desbaratador, ra [des-bah-rah-tah-dor', rah], *m. & f.* 1. Destroyer, confounder, disturber. 2. Debaucher.

desbaratamiento [des-bah-rah-tah-me-en'to], *m.* Perturbation, commotion descomposition.

desbaratar [des-bah-rah-tar'], *va.* 1. To destroy or break up anything. 2. To defeat or rout an army. 3. To waste, to misspend, to dissipate, to cross. 4. To impede, disturb. **Desbaratar la paz**, to break the peace. *-vn.* To speak foolishly, to talk nonsense. *-vr.* To be confounded, to be disordered in mind, to be deranged.

desbarate, desbarato [des-bah-rah'-tay, des-bah-rah'-to], *m.* 1. The act of routing or defeating. 2. Ignorance, folly, madness, misgovernment.

desbarbado, da [des-bar-bah'-do, dah], *a.* Beardless. *pp.* of DESBARBAR.

desbarbar [des-bar-bar'], *va.* 1. (*Coll.*) To shave. 2. (*Met.*) To trim, to cut off the filaments of plants, to loosen threads of stuff, or other things. *-vr.* To shave.

desbarbillar [des-bar-beel-lyar'], *va.* (*Agri.*) To prune the roots which spring from the stems of young vines.

desbardar [des-bar-dar'], *va.* To uncover a wall or fence, to remove the brushwood or straw placed on the top of a mud wall to preserve it from injury.

desbarrar [des-bar-rar'], *vn.* 1. To throw (with an iron bar) as far as the strength permits, without taking aim. 2. To slip, to rove, to go beyond limits. 3. (*Met.*) To ramble beyond proper bounds. 4. To err, mistake in what is said or done.

desbarretar [des-bar-ray-tar'], *va.* To unbar, to unbolt.

desbarrigado, da [des-bar-re-gah'-do, dah], *a.* Little-bellied. *-pp.* of DESBARRIGAR.

desbarrigar [des-bar-re-gar'], *va.* To rip open the belly.

desbarro [des-bar'-ro], *m.* 1. The act of slipping or falling into fault or error. 2. Nonsense, madness, extravagance, frenzy.

desbastadura [des-bas-tah-doo'-rah], *f.* The act of planing, trimming, or polishing.

desbastar [des-bas-tar'], *va.* 1. To plane, to smooth the surface of boards. 2. To trim, to polish. 3. To waste, to consume, to weaken. 4. To purify one's morals and manners. *-vr.* (*Fig.*) To acquire some polish.

desbaste [des-bahs'-tay], *m.* The act of hewing, polishing, or trimming.

desbastecido, da [des-bas-tay-thee'-do, dah], *a.* Unprovided.

desbautizarse [des-bah-oo-te-thar'-say], *vr.* 1. (*Coll. Met.*) To be irritated, to fly into a passion. 2. To change one' name, to renounce the baptismal name. 3. (*Coll.*) To fall from a height and break one's head.

desbazadero [des-bah-thah-day'-ro], *m.* Humid, slippery place.

desbeber [des-bay-berr'], *va.* (*Coll.*) To urinate.

desbecerrar [des-bay-ther-rar'], *va.* To wean young animals.

desbituminación [des-be-too-me-nah-the-on'], *f.* Removal of bitumen from a body.

desbituminizar [des-be-too-me-ne-thar'], *va.* To remove bitumen.

desblandir [des-blan-deer'], *va.* To remove grease from skins in running water in order to curry them better.

desblanquecido, da [des-blan-kay-thee'-do, dah], *a.* Blanched. *V.* BLANQUECINO.

desblanquiñado [des-blan-ke-nyah'-do], *m. V.* DESBLANQUECIDO.

desbloquear [des-blo-kay-ar'], *va.* 1. (*Mil.*) To break the blockade of. 2. (*Com. Fin.*) To unfreeze, to unblock. 3. To unblock (caño etc.), to free (tráfico).

desbocadamente [des-bo-cah-dah-men'tay], *adv.* Impudently, ungovernedly.

desbocado, da [des-bo-cah'-do, dah], *a.* 1. Open-mouthed, wide at the mouth. 2. Wild (caballo). 3. Broken-lipped or mouthed, mouthless. 4. (*Met.*) Foul-mouthed, indecent. *-pp.* of DESBOCAR.

desbocamiento [des-bo-cah-me-en'-to], *m.* Impertinence, impudence.

desbocar [des-bo-car'], *va.* To break the brim of a mug, jar, or other vessel. *-vn.* To disembogue. *V.* DESEMBOCAR. *-vr.* 1. To be hard-mouthed, to be insensible of the bridle. 2. To use injurious or abusive language. 3. To be wild, not to obey the bridle (caballo).

desbonetarse [des-bo-nay-tar'-say], *vr.* (*Coll.*) To take off the cap or bonnet, to be uncovered.

desboquillar [des-bo-keel-lyar'], *va.* To break the mouth of a vessel.

desbordamiento [des-bor-dah-me-en'-to], *m.* 1. Inundation. 2. Overflowing. 3. (*Fig.*) Eruption, outburst. **Un tremendo desbordamiento de entusiasmo**, a great upsurge of enthusiasm.

desbordante [des-bor-dahn'-tay], *a.* Overflowing; (*fig.*) Overwhelming; excessive.

desbordar [des-bor-dar'], *vn.vr.* 1. To overthrow, to inundate, to run over the brim of a vessel. 2. To erupt, to burst forth (entusiasmo etc.). 3. To give free rein to one's feelings (persona); to get carried away (pasarse); to lose one's self-control. *-va.* To pass, to go beyond; to exceed, to surpass. **Desbordaron las líneas enemigas**, they burst through the enemy lines.

desboronar [des-bo-ro-nar'], *va.* (*Prov.*) *V.* DESMORONAR.

desborrar [des-bor-rar'], *va.* 1. To cut off the loose threads of stuff when it comes out of the loom. 2. (*Prov.*) To lop off the branches of trees, particularly of the mulberry.

desboscar [des-bos-car'], *va.* To deforest, to destroy the trees and woods of mountains particularly.

desbozar [des-bo-thar'], *va.* To take off the reliefs, carvings, or mouldings of a statue.

desbragado, da [des-brah-gah'-do, dah], *a.* Unbreeched.

desbraguetado, da [des-brah-gay-tah'-do, dah], *a.* 1. Having the forepart of the breeches unbuttoned and open. 2 Careless, heedless.

desbravar, desbravecer [des-brah-var'], *va.* To break in, to tame. *-vn.* 1. To tame, to break in (caballos). 2. To diminish the strength or force of anything, to mollify, to moderate; to lose some part of the fierceness.

desbrazarse [des-brah-thar'-say], *vr.* To extend one's arms, to stretch out the arms violently.

desbrevarse [des-bray-var'-say], *vr.* To evaporate, to lose body and strength (vino, licores).

desbridar [des-bre-dar'], *va.* 1. To break or remove a bridle. 2. (*Med.*) To pare away parts which prevent widening a wound and allowing pus to escape.

desbriznar [des-brith-nar'], *va.* 1. To chop or mince meat. 2. To cut or divide a thing, into small parts. 3. To pluck the stamens of saffron.

desbroce [des-bro'-thay], *m.* Clippings, cuttings from pruning trees; and the clearing of lands or trenches.

desbrozar [des-bro-thar'], *va.* To clear away rubbish.

desbrozo [des-bro'-tho], *m.* The act of clearing away rubbish.

desbruar [des-broo-ar'], *va.* To clean cloth of grease, to put it in the fulling-mill.

desbrujar [des-broo-har'], *va. V.* DESMORONAR.

desbuchar [des-boo-char'], *va.* 1. To disclose one's secrets, to tell all one knows. 2. To ease the stomach (pájaros). 3. *V.* DESAINAR.

desbulla [des-bool'-lyah], *f.* The part of an oyster that remains on the shell.

desbullar [des-bool-lyar'], *va.* To extract an oyster from its shell.

descabal [des-cah-bahl'], *a.* Imperfect, incomplete.

descabaladura [des-cah-bah-lah-doo'-rah], *f.* Diminution, impairment of a thing.

descabalar [des-cah-bah-lar'], *va.* 1. To make incomplete, to take away some necessary part; to unmatch. 2. To pilfer; to diminish the weight, quantity, or number of things, by petty thefts. 3. To impair the perfection of anything.

descabalgadura [des-cah-bal-gah-doo'-rah], *f.* The act of dismounting or alighting from a horse.

descabalgar [des-cah-bal-gar'], *vn.* To dismount, to alight from a horse. *-va.* To dismount. **Descabalgar la artillería de las cureñas,** to dismount the guns, to take them from carriages.

descaballar [des-cah-bal-lyar'], *va.* Among gardeners, to take away the leaves and superfluous buds of plants.

descabelladamente [des-cah-bayl-lyah-dah-men'-tay], *adv.* Without order or regularity.

descabellado, da [des-cah-bel-lyah'-do, dah], *a.* 1. Dishevelled (pelo). 2. *(Met.)* Disorderly, out of all rule and order. 3. Lavish, wild, unrestrained. 4. Disproportional. 5. Preposterous, absurd. *-pp.* of DESCABELLAR.

descabelladura [des-cah-bel-lyah-do'-rah], *f.* The act and effect of tossing the hair.

descabellamiento [des-cah-bel-lyah-me-en-to], *m.* V. DESPROPÓSITO.

descabellar [des-cah-bel-lyar'], *va.* 1. To disorder and undress the hair; commonly used as reciprocal. 2. To kill the bull by pricking it in the back of the neck with the point of the sword.

descabestrar [des-cah-bes-trar'], *va.* To unhalter. V. DESENCABESTRAR.

descabezado, da [des-cah-bay-thah'-do, dah], *a.* 1. Beheaded. 2. Lightheaded, injudicious, void of judgment, giddy. *-pp.* of DESCABEZAR.

descabezamiento [des-cah-bay-thah-me-en'-to], *m.* 1. The act of beheading. 2. The state of a person who is bewildered, or does not know how to act.

descabezar [des-cah-bay-thar'], *va.* 1. To behead. 2. To revoke an assessment which towns have made. 3. To cut the upper parts or points of some things; to head, top, poll. 4. To begin, to let the beginning of a thing pass over. 5. *(Naut.)* To break a mast through its neck. **descabezar la misa,** to let the beginning of the mass be over, before one enters church. *-vn.* To terminate, to join another property: speaking of the part of an estate or piece of land which adjoins another, belonging to a different person. *-vr.* 1. To screw one's wits, to batter one's brains. 2. To take the grain from the ears of corn.

descabritar [des-cah-bre-tar'], *va.* To wean goats.

descabullirse [des-cah-bool-lyeer'-say], *vr.* 1. To sneak off, to steal away, to scamper. 2. *(Met.)* To elude the strength of an argument, to avoid a difficulty by artifice.

descacilar [des-cah-the-lar'], *va. (Prov.)* To cut the extreme ends of bricks equally.

descaderar [des-cah-day-rar'], *va.* To hip, to sprain or dislocate the hip.

descadillar [des-cah-deel-lyar'], *va.* In woollen factories, to cut off the loose threads of the warp.

descaecer [des-cah-ay-therr'], *vn.* 1. To decline, to droop, to languish, to decay. 2. *(Naut.)* To edge away.

descaecido, da [des-cah-ay-thee-'do, dah], *a.* Weak, feeble, languishing. *-pp.* of DESCAECER.

descaecimiento, descaimiento [des-cah-ay-the-me-en'-to], *m.* 1. Weakness, debility, decay. 2. Despondency, lowness of spirits, languor.

descafeinado [des-cah-fay-e-nah'-do], *a.* Decaffeinated.

descalabazarse [des-cah-lah-bah-thar'-say], *vr. (Coll.)* To puzzle one's brains, to screw one's wits.

descalabrado, da [des-cah-lah-brah'-do, dah], *a. & pp.* of DESCALABRAR. Injured; wounded on the head. **Salir descalabrado,** to be a loser in any suit, game, or business.

descalabradura [des-cah-lah-brah-doo'-rah], *f.* 1. Contusion or wound in the head. 2. The scar remaining after such wound.

descalabrar [des-cah-lah-brar'], *va.* 1. To break or wound the head slightly. 2. To attack or impeach one's character. 3. To hurt, to injure. *(Naut.)* To cause a ship considerable damage. To occasion losses to the enemy 4. To cause annoyance. 5. To annoy by screams. *-vr.* To fall from a height and break one's skull. *(Peru.)* To be ruined, violently destroyed. **Vd. me descalabra con esto,** you will neither do what you offer nor give what you promise. Literally: you break my head with your proposal.

descalabro [des-cah-lah'-bro], *m.* A calamitous event, a considerable loss; misfortune.

descalandrajar [des-cah-lan-drah-har'], *va.* To rend or tear one's clothes.

descalar [des-cah-lar'], *va. (Naut.)* To unship the helm, to unhang the rudder.

descalcador [des-cal-cah-dor'], *m. (Carp.)* Ripping-iron, claw; *(Naut.)* ravehook.

descalcar [des-cal-car'], *va.* To take out old oakum from the seams of a boat.

descalcañalar [des-cal-cah-nyah-lar'], *va.* 1. *(Prov.)* To smooth, to take out the flutings or furrows. 2. *(Coll.)* To run shoes down at the heel.

descalcez [des-cal-theth'], *f.* 1. Nudity of the feet. 2. Barefootedness (monjes descalzos).

descalcificación [des-cal-the-fe-cah-the-on'], *f. (Med.)* Lack of calcium, calcium deficiency.

descalificación [des-cal-le-fe-cah-the-on'], *f.* Discrediting; *(Dep.)* Disqualification.

descalificar [des-cal-le-fe-car'], *va.* To discredit; *(Dep.)* To disqualify.

descalorarse [des-cah-lo-rar'-say], *v. (Prov.)* V. DESACALORARSE.

descalostrado, da [des-cah-los-trah'-do, dah], *a.* Having passed the days of the first milk (bebés).

descalzadero [des-cal-thah-day'-ro], *m. (Prov.)* Little door of a pigeon-house.

descalzado, da [des-cal-thah'-do, dah] *a. & pp.* of DESCALZAR. Barefooted.

descalzador [des-cal-thah-dor'], *f.* Bootjack. 2. *(Mas.)* Crowbar.

descalzadura [des-cal-thah-doo'-rah], *f.* Laying bare, the uncovering (pies, fundación, raíces)

descalzamiento [des-cal-thah-me-en'-to], *m.* 1. The act of baring the feet. 2. *(Agri.)* Removal of soil, in part, about the roots of plants.

descalzar [des-cal-thar'], *va.* 1. To take off shoes and stockings. 2. To remove an impediment, to surmount an obstacle: applied only to the impediment or obstacle used to prevent the motion of a wheel. 3. To take away the bits of thin boards put under tables to make them stand fast. 4. To lose or cast a shoe or shoes (caballos). *-vr.* To pull off one's own shoes and stockings. **Descalzarse los guantes,** to pull off one's gloves.

descalzo, za [des-cahl'-tho, thah], *a.* 1. Barefoot, barefooted, shoeless. **Estar con los pies descalzos,** to be barefooted, to have one's shoes off. 2. Barefooted (monjes). In this last sense it is frequently used as a substantive. 3. *(Fig.)* Destitute. **Su padre le dejó descalzo,** his father left him without a dime.

descamación [des-cah-mah-the-on'], *f.* 1. Removal of scales or layers from bulbous roots. 2. *(Med.)* Desquamation of epidermis.

descambiar [des-cam-be-ar'], *va.* To cancel an exchange or barter. V. DESTROCAR.

descambio [des-cam'-bio], *m.* Swap, change back; *(Com.)* Exchange.

descaminadamente [des-c-ah-me-nah-dah-men'-tay], *adv.* Absurdly, unreasonably, out of order.

descaminado, da [des-cah-me-nah'-do, dah], *a. & pp.* of DESCAMINAR. Ill-advised; misguided. **Ir descaminado,** to deviate from rectitude, reason, or truth; to take a wrong way.

descaminar [des-cah-me-nar'], *va.* 1. To misguide, to mislead, to lead astray. 2. To seduce one from his duty. 3. To seize upon smuggled goods. -*vr.* To go astray.

descamino [des-cah-mee'-no], *m.* 1. Seizure of smuggled goods. 2. The goods thus seized. 3. Deviation from the high road. 4. Error, blindness: deviation from justice, truth, and reason. 5. Duty imposed on things seized.

descamisado, da [des-cah-me-sah'-do, dah], *a.* Shirtless, naked (pobres). -*m.* **Es un descamisado,** *(Coll.)* He is a mean, poor fellow, a ragamuffin.

descampado, da [des-cam-pah'-do, dah], *a.* Disengaged, free, open, clear. **En descampado,** in the open air, exposed to wind and weather.-*pp.* of DESCAMPAR.

descansadamente [des-cahn-sah-dah-men'-tay], *adv.* Easily, without toil or fatigue.

descansadero [des-can-sah-day-ro], *m.* Resting place.

descansado, da [des-can-sah'-do, dah], *a.* Rested, refreshed. **Vida descansada,** a quiet, easy life. -*pp.* of DESCANSAR.

descansar [des-can-sar'], *vn.* 1. To rest from labor and fatigue, to recover strength by repose. **Necesito descansar un rato,** I need to rest a bit. **Podemos descansar aquí,** we can rest here. 2. To have some relief from cares, to give respite (said of evils). 3. To rest, to lean upon, as a joist does upon a beam. 4. To rest, to be satisfied, to trust or place confidence in the power, kindness, activity, etc., of another. 5. To repose, to sleep. **El enfermo ha descansado dos horas,** the patient has slept two hours. **Descansar las tierras,** to lie at rest (tierras). 6. To repose in the sepulchre. -*va.* 1. To aid or alleviate another in labor or fatigue. **Esto descansa la vista más,** this rests one's eyes better. 2. To help. -*vr.* **Descansarse en uno,** to rely on somebody.

descansillo [des-can-seel'-lyo], *m. (Arquit.)* Landing.

descanso [des-cahn'-so], *m.* 1. Rest, repose from labor or fatigue. **Tomarse unos días de descanso,** to take a few days' rest. **Trabajar sin descanso,** to work without a rest. 2. Quiet, tranquility, peace, stillness, sleep. 3. Cause of tranquility and rest. 4. Landing-place of stairs; seat, bench, or support of anything. 5. Day of rest. 6. Parade rest. 7. *(Naut.)* A strong chock in which the claw of the anchor rests. 8. *(Naut.)* Partner of the bowsprit. **Descanso exterior del bauprés,** *(Naut.)* pillow of the bowsprit.

descantar [des-can-tar'], *va.* To clear from stones.

descantear [des-can-tay-ar'], *va.* To smooth angles or corners.

descanterar [des-can-tay-rar'], *va.* To take off the crust of anything (pan).

descantillar, descantonar [des-can-teel-lyar'], *va.* 1. To pare off, to break off part of a thing. 2. To subtract part from a total. 3. *(Met.)* To lessen, to speak ill of someone, to murmur at one's neighbor.

descantillón [des-can-teel-lyone'], *m.* A small line marking the proper scantling to which anything is to be cut.

descañar [des-cah-nyar'], *va.* To pull up by the roots the canes from a piece of ground in order to utilize it; to break the stem or branch of something.

descañonar [des-cah-nyo-nar'], *va.* 1 To pluck out the feathers of a bird or fowl. 2. To shave close. 3. *(Met.)* To trick one out of his money at gambling or otherwise.

descaperuzar [des-cah-pay-roo-thar'], *va.* To take off the cowl or hood from another's head.-*vr.* To take off one's cowl or hood to salute another; to uncover one's head.

descaperuzo [des-cah-pay-roo'-tho], *m.* Taking off the cowl, hood, or huntingcap, in saluting.

descapillar [des-cah-peel-lyar'], *va.* To take off the hood. V. DESCAPERUZAR.

descapirotar [des-cah-pe-ro-tar'], *va.* To take off the *capirote* or ancient headcover, now used by doctors of some universities.

descapotable [des-cah-po-tah'-blay], *(Aut.) a.* Convertible. -*m.* Convertible.

descaradamente [des-cah-rah-dah-men'-tay], *adv.* Impudently, saucily, barefacedly.

descarado, da [des-cah-rah'-do, dah], *a.* Impudent, barefaced, saucy, pert, petulant. -*pp.* of DESCARARSE.

descararse [des-cah-rar'-say], *vr.* To behave in an impudent or insolent manner.

descarburar [des-car-boo-rar'], *va.* To decarbonize, to remove carbon from a body containing it.

descarcañalar [des-car-cah-nyah-lar'], *va. & vr.* To run down the heel of a shoe.

descarga [des-car'-gah], *f.* 1. Unburdening, unloading. 2. The act of mitigating the pressure. 3. Volley, a general discharge of great or small guns, flight, shooting. 4. **Descarga de aduana,** *(Com.)* clearance at the custom-house, permit to unload a vessel. **Descarga general del costado del navío,** *(Naut.)* broadside of a man-of-war. 5. Unloading or discharge of the cargo of a ship. 6. Exoneration.

descargadero [des-car-gah-day'-ro], *m.* Wharf, unloading-place.

descargado [des-car-gah'-do], *a.* Empty, unloaded; flat (pila).

descargador [des-car-gah-dor'], *m.* Discharger, unloader.

descargadura [des-car-gah-doo'-rah], *f.* Taking bones out of meat, to render it more useful.

descargar [des-car-gar'], *va.* 1. To unload, to discharge, to disburden, to ease, to take off or alleviate a burden, to lighten. 2. To take off the flap and bones of meat. 3. To fire, to discharge firearms, to unload firearms, to draw out the charge of powder and ball. **Descargar un golpe en uno,** to let fly a blow at somebody. 4. To unload a cargo. *(Naut.)* 5. To brace a lee, to clear the sails or yards. 6. To put the rudder in the middle or on an even keel, in a line with the keel. 7. To lower slightly the sheets, so as to diminish the surface and angle which the sails present to the wind. 8. To make port by degrees. 9. To acquit, to clear from a charge of guilt. 10. To acquit, to exonerate, to liberate from a charge, obligation, or debt. -*vn.* To disembogue or disgorge waters into the sea. **Descargar o meter en viento una vela,** *(Naut.)* to fill a sail again. -*vr.* 1. *(Law.)* To give a plea or answer to an impeachment or accusation; to assign or allege a cause of nonappearance when summoned. 2. To resign one's place or employment. 3. In painting, to lose brightness and lustre: applied to colors.

descargo [des-car'-go], *m.* 1. Exoneration, discharge, acquittal. 2. Acquittance, receipt. 3. Plea or answer to an impeachment or action, acquitted from blame. 4. *(Jur.)* **Pliego de descargo,** evidence, depositions.

descargue [des-car'-gay], *m.* 1. Unloading. 2. License to discharge vessels. 3. The last and largest metal plate of those which come from the furnace.

descariñarse [des-cah-ree-nyar'-say], *vr.* To withdraw the love or affection for a thing, to become cool.

descariño [des-cah-ree'-nyo], *m.* Coolness, indifference.

descarnado [des-car-nah'-do], *a.* Thin (flaco), lean, scrawny; cadaverous; *(fig.)* Bare.

descarnador [des-car-nah-dor'], *m.* Scraper, an instrument with which the flesh is removed from a tooth that is to be drawn.

descarnadura [des-car-nah-doo, rah], *f.* Excarnification, clearing from flesh.

descarnar [des-car-nar'], *va.* 1. To excarnate, to clear from flesh. 2. To take away part of a thing. **Descarnar los pellejos,** among curriers, to scrape hides or skins with the drawing-knife. 3. To remove one from earthly things. -*vr.* 1. To lose flesh, emaciate. 2. *(Naut.)* To destroy, undermine a spot of ground (mar). 3. To become uncovered (tierras, playas). 4. *(Agri.)* To prune too severely.

descaro [des-cah'-ro], *m.* 1. Impudence, barefacedness, effrontery. 2. Sauciness, forwardness, assurance.

descarriamiento [des-carre-ah-meen'-to], *m.* 1. The act of losing one's way or going astray. 2. The act of making anyone lose his way.

descarriar [des-car-rear'], *va.* 1. to take out of the right road, to lead astray, to misguide, to mislead. 2. To separate cattle. **Ser una oveja descarriada**, to be like a lost sheep. -*vr.* 1. To be disjoined or separated. 2. *(Met.)* To deviate from justice or reason. 3. To go astray, to become vitiated, corrupted; to acquire bad habits.

descarrilamiento [des-car-relah-me-en'-to], *m.* Derailment of cars.

descarrilar [des-car-re-lar'], *va.* & *vr.* To derail a train; to run off the track.

descarrilo [des-cahr-re'-lo], *m.* Derailment.

descarrillar [des-car-reel-lyar'], *va.* To tear the jaws asunder.

descarrío [des-car-ree'-o], *m.* The act of losing one's way or going astray.

descartar [des-car-tar'], *va.* To discard, to fling away, to dismiss, to eject, to put aside, to lay out. -*vr.* 1. To discard or to throw out of the hand such cards as are useless. 2. To excuse oneself; to refuse doing what is solicited or required.

descarte [des-car'-tay], *m.* 1. The cards discarded or thrown out as useless. 2. The act of discarding. 3. *(Met.)* Evasion, subterfuge.

descarzar [des-car-thar'], *va.* 1. To remove fungous matter from the trunks of trees. 2. To remove empty combs from a beehive.

descasamiento [des-cah-sah-me-en'-to], *m.* 1. Unmarrying. 2. Divorce, repudiation.

descasar [des-cah-sar'], *va.* 1. To unmarry, to divorce: to declare a marriage null. 2. *(Met.)* To remove or disturb the order of things. 3. *(Typ.)* To alter the position of the pages of a sheet, in order to suitably rearrange them.

descascar [des-cas-car'], *va.* To decorticate. -*vr.* To break into pieces.

descascarador [des-cas-cah-rah-dor'], *m.* Sheller, husker.

descascarar [des-cas-cah-rar'], *va.* 1. To peel, to decorticate, to flay. 2. *(Met.)* To boast or talk much, to bluster, to bully. -*vr.* To fall or come off (superficies).

descaspar [des-cas-par'], *va.* 1. Among curriers, to scrape off the fleshy parts of a half-dressed hide. 2. To take dandruff from the head.

descastado, da [des-cas-tah'-do, dah], *a.* Showing little natural affection to relatives, or others to whom it is due.

descastar [des-cas-tar'], *va.* 1. To lose caste, to deteriorate a race or lineage. 2. To make an end of a caste (hormigas, chinches). *V.* DESENCASTAR.

descaudalado, da [des-cah-oo-dah-lah'-do, dah], *a.* Penniless.

descebar [des-thay-bar'], *va.* To unprime firearms, to take away the priming of guns.

descendencia [des-then-den'-the-ah], *f.* Descent, origin, offspring, extraction, house. **Morir sin dejar descendencia**, to die without issue.

descendente [des-then-den'-tay], *pa.* Descending.

descender [des-then-derr'], *va.* & *vn.* 1. To descend, to get or to go down, to walk downward. 2. To flow or run as liquids. 3. To descend to, to proceed from, to be derived from. 4. To let down, to lower anything. 5. To descend from. **La tribu desciende de la región central**, the tribe comes from the central region. **De esa palabra descienden otras muchas**, many other words derive from that one.

descendida [des-then-dee'-dah], *f.* 1. Descent. 2. Maritime expedition and disembarkment.

descendiente [des-then-de-en'-tay], *pa.* & *m.* 1. Descending. 2. Descendant, the offspring of an ancestor. 3. Lineal, allied by lineal descent.

descendimiento. [des-then-de-me-en'-to], *m.* 1. Descent. 2. Descension. 3. Defluxion from the head to the breast.

descensión [des-then-se-on'], *f.* 1. Descension, descent. 3. *V.* DESCENDENCIA.

descenso [des-then'-so], *m.* 1. Descent. **Las cifras han experimentado un brusco descenso**, the figures show a sharp fall. 2. The act of putting one from his degree or of reducing from a higher to a lower state; degradation. 3. The rapid flight of a bird of prey in order to fall upon its prey. 4. A conducting tube. 5. *(Med.)* Hernia, rupture. 6. Prolapse of the womb.

descentración [des-then-trah-the-on'], *f.* Maladjustment.

descentrado [des-tehn-trah'-do], *a.* 1. *(Lit.)* Off-center. 2. *(Fig.)* Out of focus; wrongly adjusted, maladjusted. **Parece que el problema está descentrado**, the problem seems to be out of focus.

descentralización [des-then-trah-le-thah-the-on'], *f.* Decentralization.

descentralizar [des-then-trah-le-thar'], *va.* 1. To decenter. 2. To decentralize, to divide the powers and authority of the state. 3. To grant local autonomy.

desceñir [des-thay-nyeer'], *va.* To ungird, to loosen or take off the girdle or belt with which clothes are tied.

descepar [des-thay-par'], *va.* 1. To eradicate, to pull up by the roots. 2. *(Naut.)* To remove the anchor-stocks.

descerar [des-thay-rar'], *va.* To take the empty combs from a beehive.

descercado, da [des-ther-cah'-do, dah], *a.* Open, unfortified, undefended (lugares). *pp.* of DESCERCAR.

descercador [des-ther-cah-dor'], *m.* He that forces the enemy to raise a siege.

descercar [des-ther-car'], *va.* 1. To destroy or pull down a wall. 2. To oblige the enemy to raise a siege.

descerco [des-therr'-co], *m.* The act of raising a siege.

descerebrado [des-they-ray-brah-do], *a.* Brainless.

descerrajado, da [des-ther-rah-hah'-do, dah], *a.* Corrupt, vicious, wicked, ill-disposed. -*pp.* of DESCERRAJAR.

descerrajadura [des-ther-rah-hah-doo'-rah], *f.* The act of taking off locks or bolts.

descerrajar [des-ther-rah-har'], *va.* 1. To take off the lock of a door, chest, trunk, etc. 2. To discharge fire-arms.

descerrumarse [des-ther-roo-mar'-say], *vr.* To be wrenched or distorted (músculos).

descifrable [des-the-frah'-blay], *a.* Decipherable.

descifrador [des-the-frah-dor'], *m.* Decipherer.

descifrar [des-the-frar'], *va.* 1. To decipher, to explain writings in cipher. 2. *(Met.)* To unravel, to interpret the obscure, intricate, and of difficult understanding. 3. To translate a language or an unknown, strange inscription.

descinchar [des-thin-char'], *a.* To ungirt a horse.

desclasificación [des-cla-se-fe-cah-the-on'], *f.* *(Dep.)* Disqualification.

desclasificar [des-cla-se-fe-car'], *va.* To disqualify.

desclavador [des-cla-vah-dor'], *m.* Nailpull, drawer.

desclavar [des-clah-var'], *va.* To draw out nails; to unnail.

descoagulable [des-co-ah-goo-lah'-blay], *a.* Redissolvable after coagulation.

descoagulación [des-co-ah-goo-lah-the-on'], *f.* Solution, liquefaction of a clot or curd.

descoagular [des-co-ah-goo-lar,], *va.* To liquefy, to dissolve.

descobajar [des-co-bah-har'], *va.* To pull the stem from a grape.

descobijar [des-co-be-har'], *va.* To uncover, to undress.

descocadamente [des-co-cah-dah-men'-tay], *adv.* Impudently, boldly, brazen-facedly.

descocado, da [des-co-cah'-do, dah], *a.* Bold, impudent, licentious (mujeres). -*pp.* of DESCOCAR.

descocar [des-co-car'], *va.* To clean, to clear trees from insects. -*vr.* To be impudent, saucy, or petulant.

descocer [des-co-therr'], *va.* To digest, to concoct in the stomach.

descoco [des-co'-co], *m.* Barefacedness, impudence, boldness, sauciness.

descodar

descodar [des-co-dar'], *va. (Prov.)* To rip, to unstitch.

descodificar [des-co-de-fi-car'], *va. (Ling.)* To decode.

descoger [des-co-herr'], *va.* To unfold, to extend, to spread, to expand.

descogollar [des-co-gol-lyar'], *va.* To take out the heart or bud of a plant; to strip the summit.

descogotado, da [des-co-go-tah'-do, dah], *a.* Having the neck naked and exposed. *-pp.* of DESCOGOTAR.

descogotar [des-co-go-tar'], *va. (Obs.)* 1. To kill a beast by one blow on the nape. 2. To knock off with one blow on the nape. 3. To knock off the horns of a stag at one blow.

descojonante [des-co-ho-nahn'-tay], *a.* 1. Wildly funny (gracioso). 2. Immensely impressive (impresionante).

descojonarse [des-co-ho-har'-say], *vr.* 1. To die laughing. 2. To kill oneself.

descolar [des-co-lar'], *va.* 1. To cut off an animal's tail, to dock. 2. To cut off the fag-end of a piece of cloth.

descolchar [des-col-char'], *va. (Naut.)* To untwist a cable.

descolgar [des-col-gar'], *va.* 1. To take down what has been hung up. 2. To unhang, to take down hangings or tapestry. *-vr.* 1. To come down gently, to slip down by means of a rope or any other thing. **Descolgarse por una pared**, to climb down a wall. 2. *(Met.)* To glide flow, or run down (ríos, riachuelos). 3. **Descolgarse con una estupidez**, to come out with a silly remark.

descolmar [des-col-mar'], *va.* 1. To strike corn in a measure with strickle. 2. *(Met.)* To diminish.

descolmillar [des-col-meel-lyar'], *va.* To pull out or break the eye-teeth.

descolocado [des-co-lo-cah'-do], *a.* Out of a place.

descoloración [des-co-lo-rah-the-on'], *f.* 1. Discoloration. 2. *(Chem.)* Discolorizing.

descoloramiento [des-co-lo-rah-me-en'-to], *m.* Paleness, discoloration.

descolorar [des-co-lo-rar'], *va.* To discolor, to pale, to change from the natural hue. *-vr.* To lose the natural hue, to become discolored or pale.

descolorido, da [des-co-lo-ree'-do, dah], *a.* Discolored, pale, colorless, pallid. *-pp.* of DESCOLORIR.

descolorir [des-co-lo-reer'], *va.* To discolor, to change from the natural hue.

descolladamente [des-col-lyah-dah-men'-tay], *adv.* Loftily, haughtily; with an air of authority.

descollamiento [des-col-lyah-me-ayn'-to], *m. V.* DESCUELLO.

descollar [des-col-lyar'], *vn.* To overtop, to excel, to surpass. *-vr.* To exceed, to outdo, to be superior to others.

descombrar [des-com-brar'], *va.* To remove obstacles or encumbrances.

descomedidamente [des-co-may-de-dah-men'-tay], *adv.* 1. Rudely, coarsely, unmannerly; haughtily. 2. Excessively, immoderately.

descomedido, da [des-co-may-dee'-do, dah], *a.* 1. Excessive, disproportionate, immoderate. 2. Rude, impudent, insolent. *-pp.* of DESCOMEDIRSE.

descomedimiento [des-co-may-de-me-en'-to], *m.* Rudeness, incivility.

descomedirse [des-co-may-deer'-say], *vr.* To be rude or disrespectful, to act or speak unmannerly.

descomer [des-co-merr'], *vn. (Coll.)* To evacuate waste matter from the bowels; to shit.

descomodidad [des-co-mo-de-dahd'], *f.* Incommodity, inconvenience, uncomfortableness.

descompadrar [des-com-pah-drar'], *vn.* To disagree, to fall out with one.

descompaginar [des-com-pah-ge-nar'], *va.* To disarrange, to disorganize, to mess up.

descompás [des-com-pahs'], *m.* Excess, redundance, want of measure or proportion.

descompasadamente [des-com-pah-sah-dah-men'-tay], *adv. V.* DESCOMEDIDAMENTE.

descompasado, da [des-com-pah-sah'-do, dah], *a.* 1. Excessive, extravagant, beyond rule and measure, disproportionable. 2. Out of tune or time. *-pp.* of DESCOMPASARSE.

descompasarse [des-com-pah-sar'-say], *vr.* 1. To exceed all rule and measure, to transgress all bounds and proportion. 2. To be out of tune or time. 3. *(Met.)* To insult a person.

descompensar [des-com-pen-sar'], *va.* To unbalance.

descomponer [des-com-po-nerr'], *va.* 1. To discompose, to alter the order or composition of a thing. **Descomponer el peinado a una**, to mess up somebody's hair. 2. To discompose, to destroy harmony and friendship, to set at odds, to disconcert. 3. To decompound. 4. *(Chem.)* To decompose bodies. *-vr.* 1. To be out of temper, to transgress the rules of modesty and good behavior. **Descomponerse con uno**, to fall out with somebody. 2. To be indisposed or out of order. 3. To change for the worse (tiempo). 4. **Se le descompuso la cara**, her face fell. (*Yo descompongo*, from *Descomponer.* V. PONER.)

descomposición [des-com-po-se-the-on'], *f.* 1. Disagreement, disaccord. 2. Discomposure, disorder, confusion. 3. *(Chem.)* Breakdown, analysis. 4. **Descomposición de vientre**, *(Med.)* Upset stomach.

descompostura [des-com-pos-too'-rah], *f.* 1. Disagreement. 2. Discomposure, disorder, confusion, perturbation. 3. Slovenliness, uncleanliness. 4. Forwardness, impudence, want of modesty, disrespectful conduct.

descompresión [des-com-pray-se-on'], *f.* Decompression.

descompuestamente [des-com-poo-ays-tah-men'-tay], *adv.* Audaciously, impudently, insolently.

descompuesto, ta [des-com-poo-es-to, tah], *a.* 1. Audacious, impudent, insolent, immodest, out of order. 2. *(Bot.)* Branching much at the base (tallos); decompound (hojas, pétalos). *-pp.* of DESCOMPONER.

descomulgado, da [des-co-mool-gah'-do, dah], *a.* Perverse, nefarious, wicked. *-pp.* of DESCOMULGAR.

descomulgador [des-co-mool-gah-dor'], *m.* Excommunicator. *V.* EXCOMULGADOR.

descomulgar [des-co-mool-gar'], *va.* To excommunicate.

descomunal [des-co-moo-nahl'], *a.* Extraordinary, monstrous, enormous, colossal.

descomunalmente [des-co-moo-nahl'-men-tay], *adv.* Uncommonly, immoderately, extraordinarily.

descomunión [des-co-moo-ne-on'], *f.* Excommunication. *V.* EXCOMUNIÓN.

desconcentración [des-con-then-trah-the-on'], *f.* Decentralization, breaking-up.

desconcentrar [des-con-then-trar'], *va.* To decentralize (industria); to break up; to distribute over a wider area.

desconcertadamente [des-con-ther-tah'-dah-men-tay], *adv.* Disorderly, confusedly.

desconcertado, da [des-con-ther-tah'-do, dah], *a.* Disorderly, slovenly. *-pp.* Of DESCONCERTAR.

desconcertador [des-con-ther-tah-dor'], *m.* Disturber, disconcerter.

desconcertante [des-con-ther-tahn'-tay], *a.* Disconcerting.

desconcertar [des-con-ther-tar'], *va.* 1. To discompose, to disturb the order of things, to confound, to confuse. 2. To disconcert, to defeat machinations, measures, etc. *-vr.* 1. To disagree. 2. To luxate, to put out of joint, to disjoint. 3. To exceed the limits of prudence. 4. To be disconcerted, to be upset, to get embarrassed. **Siguió sin desconcertarse**, he went on quite unruffled.

desconcierto [des-con-the-err'-to], *m.* 1. Discomposure, disagreement of parts. 2. Discomposure, disorder, confusion. 3. Want of prudence and circumspection. 4. Flux, or looseness of the body. 5. *(Fig.)* Uneasiness; uncertainty; embarrassment; bewilderment (perplejidad). **Sembrar el desconcierto en el partido**, to sow confusion in the party. (*Yo desconcierto*, from *Desconcertar.* V. ACERTAR.)

desconchado [des-con-chah'-do], *m.* Place where plaster has broken away.

desconchar [des-con-char'], *va.* To strip off a surface of varnish, stucco, plaster. etc. -*vr.* To peel off, to flake off, to chip.

desconcordia [des-con-cor'-de-ah], *f.* Discord, disagreement, variance, disunion.

desconectar [des-co-nec-tar'], *va.* To disconnect; to uncouple; to switch off.

desconfiadamente [des-con-fe-ah-dah-men'-tay], *adv.* Diffidently, mistrustfully.

desconfiado, da [des-con-fe-ah'-do, dah], *a.* Diffident, distrustful, mistrustful, jealous. -*pp.* of DESCONFIAR.

desconfianza [des-con-fe-ahn'-thah], *f.* 1. Diffidence, distrust, mistrust. 2. Jealousy, suspicious fear.

desconfiar [des-con-fe-ar'], *vn.* 1. To distrust, to have no confidence in. 2. To mistrust, to suspect, to regard with distrust. **¿Desconfía Vd. de mi integridad?,** do you doubt my integrity? **Desconfía de las imitaciones,** beware of imitations.

desconformar [des-con-for-mar'], *vn.* To dissent, to disagree, to differ in opinion. -*vr.* To discord, to disagree, not to suit with.

desconforme [des-con-for-may], *a.* 1. Discordant, disagreeing, contrary. 2. Unequal, unlike.

desconformidad [des-con-for-me-dahd'], *f.* 1. Disagreement, opposition, contrariety of opinion, nonconformity. 2. Inequality, dissimilitude, unlikeness.

descongelación [des-con-hay-lah-the-on'], *f. (Aer.)* De-icing; freeing (de salarios), unfreezing.

descongelador [des-con-hay-la-dor'], *m.* Defroster, deicer.

descongelar [des-con-hay-lar'], *va.* To defrost. -*vn.* To melt.

descongestionar [des-con-hays-te-o-nar'], *va.* To relieve; to clear (cabeza); to make less crowded (ciudad); to relieve the traffic problems, to make less crowded.

desconocer [des-co-no-therr'], *va.* 1. Not to preserve the idea which was held of something. 2. To recognize the notable change which is found in some person or thing. 3. To disown, to disavow. 4. To mistake, to be totally ignorant of a thing, not to know a person. **Desconocer la tierra,** to be unacquainted with a country. **Desconocer a uno por hijo,** not to own one as a son. **Desconocer el beneficio,** not to acknowledge a favor received; to be ungrateful.

desconocidamente [des-co-no-the'-dah-men-tay], *adv.* 1. Ignorantly. 2. Ungratefully.

desconocido, da [des-co-no-thee'-do, dah], *a.* 1. Strange, unknown, ungrateful. **Por razones desconocidas,** for reasons which are not known. 2. Much changed. **Está desconocido,** he is much altered. -*m. & f.* Stranger.

desconocimiento [des-co-no-the-me-en'-to], *m.* 1. Ungratefulness, ingratitude. 2. Ignorance.

desconsentir [des-con-sen-teer'], *va.* To dissent, to disagree, not to acquiesce.

desconsideradamente [des-con-se-day-rah'-dah-men-tay], *adv.* Inconsiderately, rashly.

desconsiderado, da [des-con-se-day-rah'-do, dah], *a.* Inconsiderate, imprudent, thoughtless, rash.

desconsolación [des-con-so-lah-the-on'], *f.* Disconsolateness.

desconsoladamente [des-con-so-lah'-dah-men-tay], *adv.* Inconsolably, disconsolately.

desconsolado, da [des-con-so-lah'-do, dah], *a.* 1. Disconsolate, comfortless. 2. Disconsolate, heartsick, sorrowful, melancholy.

desconsolador, ra [des-con-so-lah-dor', rah], *a.* Disconsolate, disappointing, disconcerting, lamentable.

desconsolar [des-con-so-lar'], *va.* To afflict, to put in pain, to treat rudely. -*vr.* To lose one's cheerfulness; to become low-spirited or afflicted.

desconsuelo [des-con-soo-ay'-lo], *m.* 1. Affliction, trouble, disconsolateness. *(Yo desconsuelo,* from *Desconsolar.* V. ACORDAR.

descontado [des-con-tah'-do], *a.* **Por descontado,** of course.

descontagiar [des-con-tah-he-ar'], *va.* To purity, to disinfect.

descontaminación [des-con-tah-me-nah-the-on'], *f.* Decontamination.

descontaminar [des-con-tah-me-nar'], *va.* To decontaminate.

descontar [des-con-tar'], *va.* 1. To discount. 2. *(Met.)* To abate, to lessen, to diminish. 3. To detract from merit or virtues.

descontentadizo, za [des-con-ten-tah-dee'-tho, thah], *a.* Fastidious, too nice.

descontentamiento [des-con-ten-tah-me-en'-to], *m.* Discontentment, displeasure, grief.

descontentar [des-con-ten-tar'], *va.* To discontent, to dissatisfy, to displease.

descontento [des-con-ten'-to], *m.* Discontent, uneasiness, dissatisfaction, disgust, grumbling. **Estar descontento de,** to be dissatisfied with.

descontento, ta [des-con-ten'-to, tah], *a.* Discontent, dissatisfied, uneasy, displeased.

descontinuar [des-con-te-noo-ar'], *va.* To discontinue, to leave off, to forbear, to give over.

descontinuo, ua [des-con-tee'-noo-o, ah], *a.* Disjoined, discontinued.

descontrol [des-con-trol], *m.* Lack of control.

descontrolado [des-con-tro-lah-do], *a.* 1. Wild, undisciplined (desordenado). **Desarrollo descontrolado,** uncontrolled development. 2. *(LAm.)* Upset, irritated (perturbado).

descontrolarse [des-con-tro-lar'-say], *vr.* 1. To lose control. 2. To blow one's top, to go up the wall (enojarse).

desconveniencia [des-con-vay-ne-en'-the-ah], *f.* Inconvenience, incommodity, disadvantage, prejudice.

desconveniente [des-con-vay-ne-en'-tay], *pa.* Inconvenient, discording; incongruous.

desconvenir [des-con-vay-neer']' *vn.* 1. To disagree, to discord. 2. To be unlike, to dissimilar; not to suit.

desconvidar [des-con-ve-dar'], *va.* 1. To cancel or to retract an invitation. 2. To revolve, to annul, to rescind.

desconvocación [des-con-vo-cah-the-on'], *f.* Calling-off, cancellation.

desconvocar [des-con-vo-car'], *va.* To call off, to cancel.

desconvocatoria [des-con-vo-cah-to'-re-ah], *f.* Calling off, cancellation.

descopar [des-co-par'], *va.* To lop off the branches of a tree.

descorazonado, da [des-co-rah-tho-nah'-do, dah], *a.* Depressed, dejected, dispirited.

descorazonamiento [des-co-rah-tho-nah-me-ayn'-to], *m.* Lowness of spirits, depression, dejection.

descorazonar [des-co-ra-tho-nar'], *va.* 1. To tear out the heart 2. *(Met.)* To dishearten, to discourage. -*vr.* To lose heart, to get discouraged.

descorchador [des-cor-chah-dor'], *m.* Uncorker. **Descorchador de colmena,** one who breaks the hive to steal the honey.

descorchar [des-cor-char'], *va.* 1. To decorticate a corktree, to uncork. 2. To break a beehive to steal the honey. 3. To break open a chest or trunk to take out the contents. 4. To uncork (botellas).

descordar [des-cor-dar'], *va.* To uncord an instrument.

descorderar [des-cor-day-rar'], *va.* To wean lambs.

descordonar [des-cor-do-nar'], *va.* To remove or strike off by blows of a hammer the crusty string which sticks to the mallets in a fulling-mill.

descornar [des-cor-nar'], *va.* To dishorn, to knock off the horns of an animal. -*vr.* 1. To break the skull by a fall. 2. *(Fig.)* To work like a slave.

descoronar [des-co-ro-nar'], *va.* To take away the top or crown from a thing.

descorrear [des-cor-rayar'], *vn.* To loosen the skin that covers the tenderlings of a deer.

descorregido, da [des-cor-ray-hee'-do, dah], *a.* Incorrect, disarranged.

descorrer [des-cor-rerr'], *va.* 1. To flow, as liquids. 2. To retrograde. **Descorrer la cortina,** to draw the curtain.

descorrimiento [des-cor-re-me-en'-to], *m.* The fluxion of any liquid.

descortés [des-cor-tes'], *a.* Impolite, uncivil, unmannerly, ill-bred, coarse, misbehaved, impudent.

descortesía [des-cor-tay-see'-ah], *f.* Incivility, impoliteness, churlishness.

descortésmente [des-cor-tays'-men-tay], *adv.* Uncivilly, discourteously, rudely.

descortezador [des-cor-tay-thah-dor'], *m.* One who strips off the bark; decorticator.

descortezadura, *f.* **descortezamiento**, *m.* [des-cor-tay-thah-doo'rah]. Decortication, excortication.

descortezar [des-cor-tay-thar'], *va.* 1. To decorticate, to divest of the bark or husk. 2. To flay, to take off the crust of bread, to strip off the bark of trees, etc. 3. *(Met.)* To polish or civilize. *-vr.* To become civil and polite.

descosedura [des-co-say-doo'-rah], *f.* Ripping, unseaming.

descoser [des-co-serr'], *va.* 1. To rip, to unseam, to cut open. 2. *(Met.)* To separate, to disjoin. **No descoser los labios**, to keep a profound silence. *-vr.* 1. *(Met.)* To loosen one's tongue, to babble incessantly and indiscreetly. 2. *(Coll.) V.* VENTOSEAR

descosidamente [des-co-se'-dah-men-tay], *adv.* Excessively, immoderately.

descosido [des-co-see'-do], *m.* 1. Babler, an idle talker, a teller of secrets. 2. *V.* DESCOSEDURA. **Comer o beber como un descosido**, to eat or drink inmoderately.

descosido, da [des-co-see'-do, dah], *a. & pp.* of DESCOSER. Ripped, unseamed, unstitched.

descostillar [des-cos-til-lyar'], *va.* 1. To give many blows to anyone on the ribs. 2. To take out the ribs; to break the ribs. *-vr.* To fall with violence on one's back.

descostrar [des-cos-trar'], *va.* To take off the crust.

descotar [des-co-tar'], *va.* 1. To remove a restriction from the use of any road, boundary, or property. 2. *vr.* To expose the neck and shoulders.

descote [des-co'-tay], *m.* The nakedness or exposure of the neck and shoulders. *V.* ESCOTE.

descoyuntamiento [des-co-yoon-tah-me-en'-to], *m.* 1. Luxation, the act of disjointing bones. 2. Dislocation, a joint put out. 3. A pain or uneasiness felt in many parts of the body, in consequence of over-exertion.

descoyuntar [des-co-yoon-tar'], *va.* 1. To luxate or disjoint bones. **Descoyuntarse un hueso**, to put a bone out of joint. 2. To vex, to molest, to displease. *-vr.* To experience some violent motion. **Descoyuntarse de risa**, to split one's sides with laughing.

descrecencia [des-cray-then'-the-ah], *f.* Decrement, decreasing.

descrecer [des-cray-therr'], *va. & vn.* 1. To decrease, to make less, to diminish. 2. To decrease, to grow less. 3. To fall, to subside (mareas, ríos). 4. To grow short (día).

descrecimiento [des-cray-the-me-en'-to], *m.* Decrease, diminution, decrement.

descrédito [des-cray'-de-to], *m.* Discredit, loss of reputation. **Caer en descrédito**, to fall into disrepute.

descreer [des-cray-err'], *va.* 1. To disbelieve. 2. To deny due credit to a person; to disown or abjure.

descreído, da [des-cray-ee'-do, dah], *a.* Incredulous, infidel, miscreant. *-pp.* of DESCREER.

descreimiento [des-cray-ee-me-en'-to], *m.* Infidelity, unbelief, want of religious faith.

descremar [des-cray-mar'], *va.* To skim (leche).

descrestar [des-cres-tar'], *va.* To take off the crest.

descriarse [des-cre-ar'-say], *vr.* To weaken, to extenuate; to pine with desire or anxiety.

describir [des-cre-beer'], *va.* 1. To draw, to delineate. 2. To describe, to relate minutely. 3. *(Log.)* To give a description.

descripción [des-crip-the-on'], *f.* 1. Delineation, design. 2. Description, narration, account, relation. 3. *(Log.)* Description, imperfect definition. 4. *(Law.) V.* INVENTARIO.

descriptible [des-crep-te-blay], *a.* Describable.

descriptivo, va [des-crep-tee'-vo, vah], *a.* Descriptive.

descripto, ta [des-creep'-to, tah], *pp.* of DESCRIBIR. Described.

descriptor, ra [des-crip'-tor, rah], *m. & f.* Describer, narrator.

descrismar [des-cris-mar'], *va.* 1. *(Coll.)* To knock someone's block off. 2. To remove the chrism. *-vr.* To lose patience, to be enraged.

descristianar [des-cris-te-ah-nar'], *va. V.* DESCRISMAR.

descrito, ta [des-cre'-to], *pp. irr.* of DESCRIBIR. Described.

descruzar [des-croo-thar'], *va.* To undo the form or figure of a cross: used chiefly by the hands.

descuadernar [des-coo-ah-der-nar'], *va.* 1. To unbind (libros). 2. *(Met.)* To discompose, to disconcert, to disorder.

descuadrillado [des-coo-ah-dril-lyah'-do], *m. (Vet.)* Sprain in the haunch of animals.

descuadrillado, da [des-coo-ah-drel-lyah'-do], *a.* Separated from the rank or lines. *-pp.* of DESCUADRILLAR.

descuadrillarse [des-coo-ah-dril-lyar'-say], *vr.* To be sprained in the haunches (animales).

descuajado, da [des-coo-ah-hah'-do, dah], *a.* Dispirited, disheartened.

descuajar [des-coo-ah-har'], *va.* 1. To dissolve, to liquefy. 2. To eradicate, to pluck up weeds. 3. *(Met.)* To extirpate, to uproot.

descuajo [des-coo-ah'-ho], *m.* Eradication, destroying or eradicating weeds.

descuartelado [des-coo-ar-tay-lah'-do]. **A un descuartelado**, *(Naut.)* abaft the beam (viento fuerte).

descuartelar [des-coo-ar-tay-lar'], *va.* 1. To remove troops from winter quarters. 2. *(Naut.)* To undo the quartering of the sails.

descuartizar [des-coo-ar-te-thar'], *va.* 1. To quarter. 2. To carve, to cut eatables at the table.

descubierta [des-coo-be-err'-tah], *f.* 1. Pie without an upper crust. 2. *(Mil.)* Recognition, inspection made in the morning, before opening the gates of a citadel, or the passes of an encampment, to prevent surprises or ambuscades. 3. *(Naut.)* Scanning of the horizon at sunrise and sunset. **A la descubierta**, openly, clearly.

descubiertamente [des-coo-be-ay'r-tah-men-tay], *adv.* Manifestly, openly.

descubierto [des-coo-be-err'-to], *m.* 1. The solemn exposition of the sacrament. 2. Balance of accounts. **Vender al descubierto**, to sell short. 3. A deficit. **Al descubierto**, openly, manifestly. **Dejar en descubierto**, to leave others to pay a debt. **Estar** or **quedar en descubierto**, to be a defaulter.

descubierto, ta [des-coo-be-err'-to, tah], *a.* Patent, manifest, unveiled. **A descubierto**, *(Com.)* in blank. *-pp.* of DESCUBRIR.

descubridero [des-coo-bre-day'-ro], *m.* Eminence from which the adjacent country can be overlooked.

descubridor, ra [des-coo-bre-dor', rah], *m. & f.* 1. Discoverer, finder. 2. Investigator, searcher, seeker. 3. *(Mil.)* Scout, spy. 4. A vessel on a voyage of discovery.

descubrimiento [des-coo-bre-me-en'-to], *m.* 1. Discovery. 2. Discovery, disclosure. 3. Country or thing discovered.

descubrir [des-coo-breer'], *va.* 1. To discover, to disclose, to show, to bring, to light, to uncover. 2. To discover, to make visible, to expose to view, to lay open. 3. To discover, to find out. 4. To discover, to reveal, to communicate, to make known. 5. To discover things or places before unknown. 6. To expose the sacrament to public adoration or worship. 7. *(Mil.)* To overlook any place in a fortification. **Descubrir una vía** or **abertura de agua** *(Naut.)* to discover a leak. **Descubrir la tierra**, *(Naut.)* To make the land. **Descubrir por la popa** or **por la proa**, *(Naut.)* to descry astern or ahead. **Descubrir su pecho**, to unbosom, to communicate secrets to another. **Descubrir el cuerpo**. 1. To expose to danger any part of the body. 2. *(Met.)* To favor a perilous undertaking. **Descubrir quién es**, to find out who he is. **Descubrir sus intenciones**, to reveal one's intentions.

Fue la criada la que les descubrió a la policía, it was the servant who gave them away to the police. -*vr*. To uncover oneself, to take off the hat to anyone. 2. **Descubrirse a uno**, to confess to somebody. 3. To come out.

descuello [des-coo-ayl'-lyo], *m*. 1. Excessive stature or height. 2. *(Met.)* Pre-eminence, superiority. 3. *(Met.)* Loftiness, haughtiness.

descuento [des-coo-en'-to], *m*. 1. Deduction. 2. Discount. 3. Allowance. **Descuento en efectivo**, cash discount. **Descuento por no declaración de siniestro**, no claims bonus. *(Yo descuento, from Descontar. V.* ACORDAR.)

descuernacabras [des-coo-er-nah-cah-bras], *m*. Cold north wind.

descuerno [des-coo-err'-no], *m. (Coll)* V. DESAIRE.

descuidadamente [des-coo-e-dah-dah-men'-tay], *adv*. Carelessly, negligently, idly.

descuidado, da [des-coo-e-dah'-do, dah], *a*. 1. Careless, negligent, thoughtless, heedless, absent, listless, forgetful. 2. Slovenly, unclean. 3. *V*. DESPREVENIDO. -*pp*. of DESCUIDAR. 4. Easy in one's mind, without worries. **Puedes estar descuidado**, you needn't worry.

descuidar [des-coo-e-dar'], *va. & vn*. 1. To neglect, to forget, to overlook, to lay aside. 2. To relieve from care, to make easy. 3. To render careless or indolent; to want attention or diligence. **Ha descuidado mucho su negocio**, he has neglected his business a lot. **A poco que te descuides te cobran el doble**, you've got to watch them all the time or they'll charge you double. -*vr*. 1. To be forgetful of duty. 2. To make oneself easy. **Descuide Ud.**, make yourself easy. **Descuidarse de hacer algo**, not to bother to do something.

descuido [des-coo-ee'-do], *m*. 1. Carelessness, indolence, negligence, omission, forgetfulness. 2. Heedlessness, abstraction, absence. 3. Oversight. 4. Want of attention, incivility, coldness, disesteem. 5. Improper or disgraceful action. 6. Imprudence, inmodesty. **Al descuido**, affectedly or dissemblingly careless. **Al descuido y con cuidado**, studiously careless, a dissembling carelessness.

descular [descoolar'], *va*. To break the bottom or end of a thing.

descumbrado, da [des-coom-brah'-do, dah], *a*. Level, plain.

descurtir [des-coor-teer'], *va*. To remove tan from the complexion.

desdar [des-dar'], *va*. Among ropemakers, to untwist a rope.

desde [des'-day], *prep*. From, since, after, as soon as. **Desde aquí**, from this place. **Desde luego**, thereupon, immediately. **Desde entonces**, from that time forward, ever since. **Desde niño**, from or since one's childhood. **Desde allí**, thence, from that period. **Desde abajo**, from below. **Desde el martes**, since Tuesday. **Desde hace 2 años no le vemos**, we haven't seen him for 2 years. -*adv*. *V*. DESPUÉS DE.

desdecir [des-day-theer'], *va*. To give the lie to, to charge with falsehood. -*vn*. 1. To fail to live up to, not to be equal to. 2. To differ, to disagree. **Esta novela no desdice de las otras**, this novel is well up to the standard of the others. -*vr*. To renege, to retract, to recant. **Desdecirse de algo**, to go back on something.

desdén [des-dayn'], *m*. 1. Disdain, scorn, contempt, fastidiousness, neglect. **Al desdén**, affectedly careless. 2. Affront, insult. **Desdenes de la fortuna**, *(Met.)* the frowns of fortune.

desdentado, da [des-den-tah'-do, dah], *a*. Toothless.

desdentados, *m. pl*. The edentates; mammals having no cutting teeth, e.g. sloths, anteaters. -*pp*. of DESDENTAR.

desdentar [des-den-tar'], *va*. To draw teeth.

desdeñable [des-day-nyah'-blay], *a*. Contemptible: despicable.

desdeñadamente [des-day-nyah'-dah-men-tay], *adv*. Disdainfully, scornfully.

desdeñador, ra [des-day-nyah-dor', rah], *m. & f. (Obs.)* Scorner.

desdeñar [des-day-nyar'], *va*. 1. To disdain, to scorn. **La tierra le desdeña**, he is universally despised. 2. To vex, to exasperate. -*vr*. To be disdainful; to be reserved.

desdeñosamente [des-day-nyo-sah-men'-tay], *adv*. Disdainfully, contemptuously.

desdeñoso, sa [des-day-nyo'-so, sah], *a*. Disdainful; fastidious; contemptuous.

desdevanar [des-day-vah-nar'], *va*. To unwind or to undo a clew.

desdibujado [des-de-boo-hah'-do], *a*. Blurred (contorno); unclear (nada claro); faded (descolorado).

desdibujar [des-de-boo-har'], *va*. To blur. -*vr*. To blur, to get blurred, to fade away. **El recuerdo se ha desdibujado**, the memory has become blurred.

desdicha [des-dee'-chah], *f*. Misfortune, calamity, unhappiness, ill luck, misery, infelicity.

desdichadamente [des-de-chah-dah-men'-tay], *adv*. Unfortunately, unhappily.

desdichado, da [des-de-chah'-do, dah], *a*. Unfortunate, unhappy, unlucky, distressed, wretched, miserable, calamitous. **Es un desdichado**, *(Coll.)* he is a sorry, pitiful creature; he is a good-for-nothing fellow.

desdicho, cha [des-dee'-cho, chah], *pp. irr*. of DESDECIR.

desdoblado [des-po-blah'-do], *a. (Fig.)* Split (personalidad); two-lane (carretera).

desdoblar [des-do-blar'], *va*. 1. To unfold, to spread open. 2. To resume the thread of a speech or discourse. 3. *(Prov.)* To explain, to clear up. 4. *(Fig.)* To double, to divide. 5. *(Quim.)* To break down. -*vr*. To divide, to split into two.

desdorar [des-do-rar'], *va*. 1. To take off the gilding of a thing. 2. *(Met.)* To tarnish or sully one's reputation.

desdoro [des-do'-ro], *m*. Dishonor, blemish, blot, stigma.

deseable [day-say-ah'-blay], *a*. Desirable.

deseablemente [des-ay-ah'-blay], *adv*. Desirously.

desear [day-say-ar'], *va*. To desire, to wish, to long for, to covet. **Os deseo toda clase de éxito**, I wish you every success. **Estoy deseando que esto termine**, I wish this would end.

desecación [day-say-cah-the-on'], *f*. Desiccation, drying up; withering (plantas).

desecado, da [day-say-cah'-do, dah], *a*. Dried, desiccated.

desecador [day-say-cah-dor'], *m*. A room destined for drying medicinal substances.

desecamiento [day-say-cah-me-en'-to], *m*. Desiccation, drying.

desecante [day-say-cahn'-tay], *pa. & m. & f*. Drying, drier; desiccant.

desecar [day-say-car'], *va*. 1. To dry, to draw the moisture from anything, to desiccate. 2. To stop, to detain.

desecativo, va [day-say-cah-tee'-vo, vah], *a*. Desiccative. -*m*. Healing plaster.

desechable [des-ay-chah-blay], *a*. Disposable, throwaway. **Envases desechables**, non-returnable empties.

desechadamente [des-ay'-chah-men-tay], *adv*. Vilely, despicably.

desechado, da [des-ay-chah'-do, dah], *a. & pp*. of DESECHAR. Refused, excluded, expelled, rejected; outcast.

desechar [des-ay-char'], *va*. 1. To exclude, reprobate. 2. To depreciate, undervalue, disesteem. 3. To renounce, not admit. 4. To refuse not to admit. 5. To put aside sorrow, fear, etc. 6. To lay aside, fling away, not to use or wear; to reject.

desecho [des-ay'-cho], *m*. 1. Depreciation, renunciation. 2. Residue, overplus, remainder, rubbish. **Desecho de hierro**, scrap iron. **Producto de desecho**, waste product. 3. Refuse, offal. 4. *(Met.)* Disregard, contempt. **El desecho de la sociedad**, the scum of society. **Ese tío es un desecho**, that fellow is a disaster.

desedificación [des-ay-de-fe-cah-the-on'], *f*. Scandal, bad example.

desedificar [des-ay-de-fe-car'], *va*. To scandalize, to offend by some criminal or disgraceful action.

desegregación [day-say-gray-gah-the-on'], *f.* Desegregation.

desegregar [day-say-gray-gar'], *va.* To desegregate.

desejecutar [des-ay-hay-coo-tar'] *va. (Law.)* To raise a sequestration, execution, or seizure.

deselladura [day-sel-lyah-doo'-rah], *f.* Unsealing or taking off the seals.

desellar [day-sel-lyar'], *va.* To unseal, to take off the seals.

desembalaje [des-em-bah-lah'-hay], *m.* Unpacking, opening of bales.

desembalar [des-em-bah-lar'], *va.* To unpack, to open bales of goods.

desembaldosar [des-em-bal-do-sar'], *va.* To take away the flagstones or tiles.

desemballestar [des-em-bal-lyes-tar'], *va. (Falc.)* To prepare to bring a hawk down when it is ascending.

desembanastar [des-em-bah-nas-tar'], *va.* 1. To take out the contents of a basket. 2. *(Met.)* To talk much and at random. 3. *(Coll.)* To draw the sword. *-vr.* To break out or break loose (escapar).

desembarazadamente [des-em-bah-rah-thah-dah-men'-tay], *adv.* Freely, without embarrassment.

desembarazado, da [des-em-bah-ra-thah'-do, dah], *a.* Free, disengaged; unrestrained. **Modales desembarazados**, easy manners. *-pp.* of DESEMBARAZAR.

desembarazar [des-em-bah-ra-thar'], *va.* 1. To disembarrass, to free, to disengage, to remove an impediment or obstruction. 2. To remove an encumbrance. 3. To extricate. 4. To disencumber. 5. To unburden, to expedite. *-vr.* To be extricated from difficulties or embarrassments.

desembarazo [des-em-bah-rah'-tho], *m.* 1. Disembarrassment. 2. Disencumbrance, extrication. 3. Disengagement. 4. Freedom or liberty to do anything.

desembarcadero [des-em-bar-cah-day'-ro], *m.* Landing-place; dock, quay; platform.

desembarcar [des-em-bar-car'], *va.* To unship, to disembark. *-vn. vr.* 1. To land, to go on shore. 2. *(Met.)* To alight from a coach. 3. *(Coll.)* To be confined, to lie in. 4. To end at a landing place: said of a staircase.

desembarco [des-em-bar'-co], *m.* 1. Landing, disembarkation, unshipment. 2. Landing-place at the top of stairs.

desembargador [des-em-bar-gah-dor'], *m.* Chief magistrate and privy councillor in Portugal.

desembargar [des-em-bar-gar'], *va.* 1. *(Law.)* To raise an embargo or attachment. 2. To remove impediments, or clear away obstructions.

desembargo [des-em-bar'-go], *m. (Law.)* The act of raising an embargo or sequestration; removal of an attachment.

desembarque [des-em-bar'-kay] *m.* Landing, the act of coming onshore; clearance.

desembarrancar [des-em-bar-rahn-car'], *va. V.* DESABARRANCAR.

desembarrar [des-em-bar-rar'], *va.* To clear a thing from mud or clay.

desembastar [des-em-bas-tar'], *va.* 1. To give a suitable form to any object of metal, filing it to suit. 2. *(Mil.)* To remove the packsaddles from the horses which draw the field-pieces.

desembaste [des-em-bahs'-tay], *m.* Trimming a metallic object.

desembaular [des-em-bah-oo-lar'], *va.* 1. To empty a trunk, to take out its contents. 2. To empty a box, bag, chest, etc. 3. *(Met.)* To speak one's mind freely; to disclose one's secret thoughts.

desembebecerse [des-em-bay-bay-therr'-say], *vr.* To recover the use of one's senses.

desembelesarse [des-em-bay-lay-sar'-say], *vr.* To recover from amazement or abstraction.

desemblanza [day-sem-blahn'-thah], *f. V.* DESEMEJANZA.

desembocadero [des-em-bo-cah-day'-ro], *m.* 1. Exit, outlet. 2. The mouth of a river or canal, or the point where it empties into the sea; disemboguement.

desembocadura [des-em-bo-cah-doo'-rah], *f. V.* DESEMBOCADERO.

desembocar [des-em-bo-car'], *vn.* 1. *(Naut.)* To disembogue, to sail out of a strait. 2. To disembogue, to flow out at the mouth (río). **Desembocar la calle**, to go from one street into another. **Todas las calles que desembocan en la plaza estaban empalizadas**, all the streets that terminate in the square were barricaded. 3. *(Fig.)* To end in, to result in, to produce. **Esto desembocó en una tragedia**, this ended in tragedy.

desembolsar [des-em-bol-sar'], *va.* 1. To empty a purse. 2. To disburse, to expend, to lay out.

desembolso [des-em-bol'-so], *m.* 1. Disbursement, expenditure. 2. An advance with the object of speculating.

desemboque [des-em-bo'-kay], *m. V.* DESEMBOCADERO.

desemborrachar [des-em-bor-rah-char'], *va.* To sober up, to make sober, to cure of intoxication. *-vr.* To grow sober.

desemborrar [des-em-bor-rar'], *va.* To take away the nap from wool, silk, cotton, etc.

desemboscada [des-em-bos-cah'-dah], *f.* 1. The coming out of the game into the open. 2. Sound of horns to give notice that the game has gone into the open.

desemboscarse [des-em-bos-car'-say], *vr.* To get out of the woods, to get clear of an ambuscade.

desembotar [des-em-bo-tar'], *va.* To remove dullness from the understanding.

desembozar [des-em-bo-thar'], *va.* 1. To unmuffle or uncover the face. 2. To unmask, show oneself in one's true colors. Also *vr.*

desembozo [des-em-bo'-tho], *m.* Uncovering or unmuffling the face.

desembragar [des-em-brah-gar], *va.* 1. To unbind from the cable. 2. *(Mech.)* To ungear, disconnect. *-pp.* **desembragado**, out of gear.

desembrague [des-em-brah-gay], *m.* Disengagement; *(Aut.)* Declutching; clutch release (pieza).

desembravecer [des-em-brah-vay-therr'], *va.* To tame, to domesticate. *-vr.* To calm down.

desembravecimiento [des-em-brah-vay-the-me-en'-to], *m.* Taming, or reclaiming from wildness.

desembrazar [des-em-brah-thar'], *va.* 1. To dart or throw weapons; to throw from the arms. 2. To take anything from the arms.

desembriagar [des-em-bre-ah-gar'], *va.* To sober up, to cure from intoxication. *-vr.* To grow sober, to recover from drunkenness.

desembridar [des-em-bre-dar'], *va.* To unbridle a horse.

desembrollar [des-em-brol-lyar'], *va.* To unravel, to disentangle, to clear, to extricate.

desembuchar [des-em-boo-char'], *va.* 1. To disgorge, to turn out of the maw (pájaros). 2. *(Met.)* To unbosom, to disclose one's sentiments and secrets. *-vn. (Fig.)* To reveal a secret, to spill the beans.

desemejable [day-say-may-hah'-blay], *a.* 1. Dissimilar. 2. Strong, large, violent.

desemejado, da [day-say-may-hah'-do, dah], *a. & pp.* of DESEMEJAR.

desemejante [day-say-may-hahn'-tay], *a.* Dissimilar, unlike.

desemejantemente [day-say-may-han'-tah-men-tay], *adv.* Dissimilarly.

desemejanza [day-say-may-hahn'-thah] *f* Dissimilitude, unlikeness, dissimilarity.

desemejar [day-say-may-har'], *vn.* To be dissimilar or unlike. *-va. V.* DESFIGURAR.

desempacar [des-em-pah-car'], *va.* To unpack. *-vr. (Coll.)* To grow calm, to be appeased.

desempachar [des-em-pah-char'], *va.* To make the stomach discharge crudities or undigested material. *-vr. (Met.)* To grow bold, to lose all bashfulness.

desempacho [des-em-pah'-cho], *m.* Ease, alleviation.

desempalagar [des-em-pah-lah-gar'], *va.* 1. To remove nausea or loathing, to restore the appetite. 2. To clear a mill of stagnant water.

desempañar [des-em-pah-nyar'], *va.* 1. To take away the swaddling-clothes of children. 2. To clean a glass, looking-glass, or anything which is tarnished.

desempapelar [des-em-pah-pay-lar,], *va.* To unwrap, to unfold anything wrapped up in paper.

desempaquetar [des-em-pah-kay-tar'], *va.* To unpack, to open a packet.

desemparejar [des-em-pah-ray-har'], *va.* To unmatch, to make things unequal. -*vn.* 1. To become inimical. 2. To part, to be separated.

desemparentado, da [des-em-pah-ren-tah'-do, dah], *a.* Without relatives.

desemparvar [des-em-par-var'], *va.* To gather the thrashed corn in heaps.

desempastelar [des-em-pas-tay-lar'], *va. (Print.)* 1. To compose disarranged type. 2. To distribute, or mix letters. 3. To undo a secret meeting, political machination. 4. To disentangle, to extricate, to clear up.

desempatar [des-em-pah-tar'], *va.* 1. To make unequal, to do away existing equality. **Volvieron a jugar para desempatar**, they held a play-off (to resolve the earlier tie). 2. *(Met.)* To explain, to clear up, to facilitate.

desempate [des-em-pah'-tay], *m.* Play-off (fútbol, etc.).

desempedrar [des-em-pay-drar'], *va.* To unpave.

desempeñado, da [des-em-pay-nyah'-do dah], *a. & pp.* of DESEMPEÑAR, Free or clear of debt.

desempeñar [des-em-pay-nyar'], *va.* 1. To redeem, to recover what was in another's possession, to take out of pawn. 2. To clear or extricate from debt. **Sus estados están desempeñados**, his estates are clear of debt. 3. To perform any duty or promise, to discharge, to transact. **Desempeñar el asunto**, to prove a subject completely. **Desempeñó el negocio a satisfacción**, he accomplished the business satisfactorily. 4. To acquit, to free from an obligation. 5. To disengage from a difficult or arduous affair. -*vr.* 1. To extricate oneself from debt, to pay all debts. 2. In bullfighting, to disengage oneself from the attack of a bull.

desempeño [des-em-pay'-nyo], *m.* 1. The act of redeeming a pledge. 2. *(Met.)* Proof or confirmation of a statement. 3. Performance of an obligation or promise; fulfilment, discharge.

desemperezar [des-em-pay-ray-thar'], *va.* To relinquish habits of laziness and indolence.

desempernar [des-em-per-nar'], *va.* To take out the bolts or spikes.

desempiolar [des-em-pe-o-lar'], *va.* To remove the leash from falcons.

desempleada [des-em-play-dah'-dah], *f.* Unemployed woman.

desempleado [des-em-play-dah'-do], *a.* Unemployed, out of work. -*m.* Unemployed man.

desempleo [des-em-play'-o], *m.* Unemployment.

desemplomar [des-em-plo-mar']; *va.* To remove a leaden seal placed on goods (aduanas).

desemplumar [des-em-ploo-mar'], *va.* V. DESPLUMAR.

desempobrecer [des-em-po-bray-therr'], *va.* To relieve from poverty. -*vr.* To extricate oneself from poverty.

desempolvar [des-em-pol-var'], *va.* To remove dust or powder.

desempolvoradura [des-em-pol-vo-rah-doo'-rah], *f.* Dusting.

desempolvorar [des-em-pol-vo-rar'], *va.* To crust, to remove dust.

desemponzoñar [des-em-pon-tho-nyar'], *va.* 1. To heal from the effects of poison, to expel poison. 2. *(Met.)* To cure any disordinate passion or affection.

desempotrar [des-em-po-trar'], *va.* To remove the stays or props which support anything.

desempulgadura [des-em-pool-gah-doo'-rah], *f.* The unbending of a bow.

desempular [des-em-pool-gar'], *va.* To unbend a bow.

desenalbardar [des-ay-nal-bar-dar'], *va.* To take off a packsaddle.

desenamorar [des-ay-nah-mo-rar'], *va.* To destroy love or affection. -*vr.* 1. To lose love or affection. 2. To relinquish or yield up one's opinion.

desenastar [des-ay-nas-tar'], *va.* To remove the handle of a weapon or iron tool.

desencabalgar [des-en-cah-bal-gar'], *va. (Mil.)* To dismount cannon.

desencabestradura [des-en-cah-bes-trah-doo'-rah], *f.* The disentangling of a beast from the halter.

desencabestrar [des-en-cah-bes-trar'], *va.* To disentangle a beast from the halter, in which the forefeet are entangled.

desencadenamiento [des-en-cah-day-nah-me-ayn'-to], *f. (Fig.)* Unleashing; bursting. **Desencadenamiento de hostilidades**, outbreak of hostilities.

desencadenar [des-en-cah-day-nar'], *va.* 1. To unchain, to break the chain, to break loose. 2. *(Met.)* To dissolve all connection or obligation. -*vr.* 1. To break loose, to free oneself from chains. 2. To become infuriated (personas, pasiones, elementos). **Se desencadenaron los aplausos**, a storm of clapping broke out.

desencajado [des-en-cah-hah'-do], *a.* Twisted (cara), contorted; wild (ojos).

desencajadura [des-en-cah-hah-doo', rah], *f.* The part or place which remains unjoined, when the connection is removed; unjointing.

desencajamiento, desencaje [des-en-cah-hah-me-en'-to, des-en-cah'-hay], *m.* Disjointedness, luxation.

desencajar [des-en-cah-har'], *va.* 1. To disjoint, to take a thing out of its place; to disfigure. 2. To luxate. -*vr.* To become distorted (cara); to look wild (ojos).

desencajonar [des-en-cah-ho-nar'], *va.* 1. To unpack, to take out the contents of a box. 2. *(Mil.)* To separate the wings from the main body in a line of battle.

desencalabrinar [des-en-cah-lah-bre-nar'], *va.* 1. To remove dizziness, to free from stupidity. 2. To remove wrong impressions.

desencalcar [des-en-cal-car'], *va.* To loosen or dissolve what was caked, or close pressed.

desencallar [des-en-cal-lyar'], *va. (Naut.)* To set a ship afloat which has struck on rocky ground.

desencaminar [des-en-cah-me-nar'], *va.* 1. To lose one's way, to go astray. 2. To deviate from rectitude.

desencantamiento [des-en-cahn-tah-me-ayn'-to], *m.* V. DESENCANTO.

desencantar [des-en-can-tar'], *va.* To disenchant, to counter-charm.

desencantaración [des-en-can-ta-rah-the-on'], *f.* Act and effect of drawing lots or balloting for anything.

desencantarar [des-en-can-ta-rar'], *va.* 1. To draw lots for candidates. 2. To be withdrawn as incompetent, to withdraw a name on account of incapacity or privilege.

desencanto [des-en-cahn'-to], *m.* Disenchantment.

desencapillar [des-en-cah-pil-lyar'], *va. (Naut.)* To unrig, to take off the rigging.

desencapotadura [des-en-cah-po-tah-doo'-rah], *f.* Act of stripping on a cloak or a greatcoat.

desencapotar [des-en-cah-po-tar'], *va.* 1. To strip one of his cloak or greatcoat. 2. *(Met. Coll.)* To uncover, to make manifest. 3. *(Met.)* To raise and keep up the head of a horse. **Desencapotar las orejas**, to cock up the ears. -*vr.* 1. To lay aside frowns; to put on a pleasing countenance. 2. To clear up (cielo).

desencaprichar [des-en-cah-pre-char'], *va.* To dissuade from error or prejudice, to cure one of conceit. -*vr.* To desist, to yield, to get over a whim.

desencarcelar [des-en-car-thay-lar'], *va*. 1. To disincarcerate, to release from confinement, to set at liberty. 2. *(Met.)* To free from oppression, to extricate from difficulties.

desencarecer [des-en-cah-ray-therr'], *va*. To lower the price of anything offered for sale.

desencarnar [des-en-car-nar'], *va*. 1. To prevent dogs from eating game. 2. *(Met.)* To lose an affection for anything, or to divert the mind from it. 3. *(Art.)* To soften flesh color in figures.

desencastar [des-en-cas-tar'], *va*. To destroy insects, to end their race.

desencastillar [des-en-cas-til-lyar'], *va*. 1. To expel or drive out of a castle. 2. To manifest, to make appear, to discover.

desencenagar [des-en-thay-nah-gar'], *va*. 1. *V.* DESATASCAR. 2. To extricate one from a den of vice or crime.

desencentrar [des-en-then-trar'], *va*. To take anything from its center: to decenter.

desenceparse [des-en-thay-par'-say], *vr*. To unloosen folds of cable from the anchor stock.

desencerrar [des-en-ther-rar'], *va*. 1. To free from confinement. 2. To open, to unclose. 3. To disclose what was hidden or unknown. *(Yo desencierro*, from *Desencerrar. V.* ALENTAR.).

desenchufar [des-en-choo-far'], *va*. To disconnect, to unplug. -*vr*. To relax, to unwind, to switch off.

desencintar [des-en-thin-tar'], *va*. To untie, to loosen.

desenclavar [des-en-clah-var'], *va*. 1. To draw out nails. *V.* DESCLAVAR. 2. To put one violently out of his place.

desenclavijar [des-en-clah-ve-har'], *va*. To take out pins or pegs of a musical instrument.

desencoger [des-en-co-herr'], *va*. To unfold. -*vr*. 1. *(Met.)* To lay aside bashfulness or reserve, to grow bold. 2. To make merry.

desencogimiento [des-en-co-he-me-en'-to], *m*. Disembarrassment, freedom from perplexity.

desencolar [des-en-co-lar'], *va*. To unglue.

esencolerizarse [des-en-co-lay-re-thar'-say], *vr*. To grow calm, to be appeased.

desenconar [des-en-co-nar'], *va*. 1. To remove an inflammation. 2. *(Met.)* To moderate, to check or appease one's passion. 3. To make mild and begging. -*vr*. To become milder, to be appeased, to forget injuries.

desencono [des-en-co'-no], *m*. Mitigating anger or passion.

desencordar [des-en-cor-dar'], *va*. To unstring, to loosen or untie strings.

desencordelar [des-en-cor-day-lar'], *va*. To loosen, to untie or take away ropes.

desencorvar [des-en-cor-var'], *va*. To straighten, to untwist.

desencrudecer [des-en-croo-day-therr'], *va*. 1. To prepare silk or thread for receiving the dye. 2. To boil cocoons so as to be able to unwind the silk more readily. 3. To clean fabrics from matter which might alter them.

desencrudecimiento [des-en-croo-day-the-me-en'-to], *m*. Cleansing of silk (with lye).

desencuadernar [des-en-coo-ah-der-nar'], *va*. 1. To unbind, to take off the binding of a book. 2. *V.* DESCUADERNAR.

desendemoniar, desendiablar [des-en-day-mo-ne-ar', des-en-de-ah-blar'], *va*. To exorcise, to drive out an evil spirit. **Desendiablarse,** *(Met.)* to moderate one's fury or passion.

desendiosar [des-en-de-o-sar'], *va*. To humble vanity, to pull down presumption and haughtiness

desenfadaderas [des-en-fah-dah-day'-ras], *f. pl.* **Tener desenfadaderas,** *(Coll.)* to take means to extricate oneself from difficulties, or to liberate oneself from oppression.

desenfadado, da [des-en-fah-dah'-do-dah], *a*. 1. Free, unembarrassed. 2. Wide, spacious, capacious (lugares). -*pp.* of DESENFADAR.

desenfadar [des-en-fah-dar'], *va*. To abate anger, to appease passion.-*vr*. To be entertained or amused.

desenfado [des-en-fah'-do], *m*. 1. Freedom, ease, facility. 2. Calmness, relaxation.

desenfaldar [des-en-fal-dar'], *va*. To let fall the train of a gown.

desenfamar, [des-en-fa-mar'] *va. V.* DISFAMAR.

desenfangar [des-en-fan-gar'], *va*. To cleanse, to clear from mud, mire, car filth.

desenfardar, desenfardelar [des-en-far-dar', des-en-far-day-lar'], *va*. To unpack bales of goods.

desenfardelamiento [des-en-far-day-lah-me-en'-to], *m*. Unpacking of bales.

desenfardo [des-en-far'-do], *m. V.* DESENFARDELA-MIENTO.

desenfatuar [des-en-fah-too-ar'], *va*. *(Prov.)* To undeceive, to free from error.

desenfilada [des-en-fe-lah'-dah], *a*. *(Mil.)* Under cover from fire. -*f*. Part of a fortification protected against being fired upon from adjoining high lands.

desenfilar [des-en-fe-lar'], *va*. 1. To put the troops under cover from flank fire. 2. To unthread.

desenfocado [des-en-fo-cah'-do], *a*. Out of focus.

desenfrailar [des-en-frah-e-lar'], *vn*. *(Coll.)* To leave the monastic life, to become secularized. -*vr*. 1. To come out from subjection. 2. To rest from business for a time. -*va. (Prov. Agri.)* To lop off, to mutilate trees.

desenfrenadamente [des-en-fray-nah-dah-men'-tay], *adv*. Ungovernably, licentiously.

desenfrenado, da [des-en-fray-nah'-do, dah], *a. & pp*. of DESENFRENAR. Ungoverned, unbridled, outrageous, licentious, wanton.

desenfrenamiento [des-en-fray-nah-me-en'-to], *m*. Unruliness, rashness, wantonness, licentiousness, boundless liberty or license; libidinousness.

desenfrenar [des-en-fray-nar'], *va*. To unbridle. -*vr*. 1. To give loose rein to one's passions and desires. 2. To fly into a violent passion. 3. To be mad or wild.

desenfreno [des-en-fray'-no], *m. V.* DESENFRENAMIENTO. **Desenfreno de vientre,** sudden and violent looseness.

desenfundar [des-en-foon-dar'], *va*. To take out of a bag, bolster, pillow-case, etc.

desenfurecerse [des-en-foo-ray-therr'-say], *vr*. To grow calm or quiet, to lay aside anger.

desengalanar [des-en-gah-lah-nar'], *va*. To remove trappings or adornments.

desengalgar [des-en-gal-gar'], *va*. 1. To remove the (wooden) brake of a cart, to unscotch. 2. *(Naut.)* To remove anchorstakes.

desenganchar [des-en-gan-char'], *va*. To unhook, to take down from a hook. **Desenganchen los caballos** (del coche), let the horses be unharnessed. -*vr*. To come off drugs, to free oneself from drug addiction.

desengañadamente [des-en-gah-nyah-dah-men'-tay], *adv*. 1. Truly, clearly, ingenuously. 2. Awkwardly, without care or address, scurvily.

desengañado, da [des-en-gah-nyah'-do, dah], *a*. 1. Undeceived, disabused, knowing from experience. **Él está desengañado de eso,** he is aware of that. 2. Despicable, illexecuted. -*pp.* of DESENGAñAR.

desengañador [des-en-gah-nyah-dor'], *m*. Undeceiver.

desengañar [des-en-gah-nyar'], *va*. 1. To undeceive, to free from error, to disabuse, to set right. **Es mejor no desengañarla,** it is best not to disillusion her. 2. *(Tec.)* To accustom a horse to every kind of noise, and to objects which frighten him.

desengañilar [des-en-gah-nye-lar'], *va*. To free or disengage from grasp claws, or fangs of a person or beast.

desengaño [des-en-gah'-nyo], *m*. 1. Detection or discovery of an error by which one was deceived: undeceiving, the disabusing or freeing from error, disillusion; disappointment. **Sufrir un desengaño amoroso,** to be disappointed in love. 2. Censure, reproof, reproach, upbraiding. 3. Warning, admonition.

desengarrafar [des-en-gar-rah-far'], *va*. To unfasten or disengage from claws or clinched fingers.

desengarzar [des-en-gar-thar'], *va*. To unravel, to unstring.

desengastar [des-en-gas-tar'], *va*. To take a stone out of its setting.

desengoznar [des-en-goth-nar'], *va*. To unhinge; to disjoint. *V*. DESGOZNAR.

desengranar [des-en-grah-nar'], *va*. To uncog, to separate two cog-wheels; to ungear. *-vr*. To get out of gear.

desengrasador [des-en-grah-sah-dor'], *m*. A wringing-machine; scourer, wiping clout.

desengrasar [des-en-grah-sar'], *va*. 1. To take out the grease. 2. To remove the taste of fat.

desengrase [des-en-grah'-say], *m*. Removal of grease.

desengrosar [des-en-gro-sar'], *va*. To extenuate, to make lean, to debilitate, to make thin or fine.

desengrudamiento [des-en-groo-dah-me-en'-to], *m*. The rubbing off of cement or paste.

desengrudar [des-en-groo-dar'], *va*. To scrape or rub off paste.

desenhebrar [des-en-ay-brar'], *va*. To unthread.

desenhornar [des-en-or-nar'], *va*. To take out of the oven.

desenjaezar [des-en-hah-ay-thar'], *va*. To unharness mules or horses, to unsaddle.

desenjalmar [des-en-hal-mar'], *va*. To unharness mules or horses; to take off a packsaddle from a beast of burden.

desenjaular [des-en-hah-oo-lar'], *va*. 1. To uncage. 2. To remove someone from a jail.

desenlabonar [des-en-lah-bo-nar'], *va*. To unlink.

desenlace [des-en-lah'-thay], *m*. 1. *(Poet.)* Catastrophe of a play or dramatic poem. 2. *(Met.)* Conclusion, end, unravelling of an affair. **Desenlace trágico**, tragic ending. **Desenlace feliz**, happy ending.

desenladrillar [des-en-lah-dril-lyar'], *va*. To take up floortiles or bricks.

desenlazar [des-en-lah-thar'], *va*. 1. To unlace, to untie knots; to loosen. 2. To distinguish. 3. *(Fig.)* To solve (problema). *-vr*. 1. To come undone (desatarse). 2. *(Liter.)* To end, to turn out.

desenlodar [des-en-lo-dar'], *va*. 1. To remove, to clean off mud. 2. To separate earthy parts from any mineral or ore.

desenlosar [des-en-lo-sar'], *va*. To take up a floor made of flags.

desenlutar [des-en-loo-tar'], *va*. 1. To leave off mourning. 2. To banish sorrow.

desenmangar [des-en-mahn-gar'], *va*. To unhaft, to remove the handle of something. *V*. DESENASTAR.

desenmarañar [des-en-mah-ra-nyar'], *va*. 1. To disentangle. 2. *(Met.)* To extricate from impediments or difficulties, to explain.

desenmascarar [des-en-mas-cah-rar'] *va*. 1. To remove the mask. 2. To reveal the hidden intentions of someone.

desenmohecer [des-en-mo-ay-therr'], *va*. 1. To clear from rust. 2. *(Met.)* To clear up, to make manifest.

desenmudecer [des-en-moo-day-therr'], *va*. 1. To remove an impediment of speech. 2. To break a long silence.

desenojar [des-ay-no-har'], *va*. To appease anger, to allay passion. *-vr*. To recreate, to amuse oneself. *(Coll.)* To make friends.

desenojo [des-ay-no'-ho], *m*. Reconcilableness, appeasableness.

desenojoso, sa [des-ay-no-ho'-so, sah], *a*. Appeasing, reconciling.

desenredar [des-en-ray-dar'], *va*. 1. To disentangle, to free from perplexities, to outwind, to extricate, to loosen, to clear. 2. To put in order, to set to rights. *-vr*. To extricate oneself from difficulties.

desenredo [des-en-ray'-do], *m*. 1. Disentanglement. 2. *(Poet.)* Catastrophe of a play or poem.

desenrizar [des-en-re-thar'], *va*. To uncurl hair, to take out the curls.

desenrollar [des-en-ro-lyar'], *va*. To unroll. *V*. DESARROLLAR.

desenroñecer [des-en-ro-nyay-therr'], *va*. 1. To remove rust from metal. 2 *(Met.)* To polish manners, to cultivate the mind.

desenronquecer [des-en-ron-kay-therr'], *va*. To free from hoarseness.

desenroscar [des-en-ros-car'], *va*. To untwist.

desensabanar [des-en-sah-ba-nar'], *va*. 1. *(Coll.)* To change or take off the sheets. 2. *(Met. Coll.)* To remove an impediment or obstacle.

desensañar [des-en-sah-nyar'], *va*. 1. To appease, to pacify. 2. To mitigate irritation.

desensartar [des-en-sar-tar'], *va*. To unthread, to unstring.

desensebar [des-en-say-bar'], *va*. 1. To strip of fat. 2. *(Met.)* To change occupation in order to render one's work more endurable, to draw breath. 3. *(Met.)* To take away the taste of fat of a thing just eaten.

desensenar [des-en-say-nar'], *va*. To take out of the breast of bosom.

desensillar [des-en-se-lyar'], *va*. To unsaddle.

desensoberbecer [des-en-so-ber-bay-therr'], *va*. To humble, to take away pride. *-vr*. To become humble, to moderate one's pride.

desensortijado, da [des-en-sor-te-hah'-do, dah], *a*. Dislocated, displaced.

desentablar [des-en-tah-blar'], *va*. 1. To rip up or off planks or boards. 2. *(Met.)* To discompose, to disturb, to confuse. 3. To embroil an affair, to break off a bargain, to interrupt friendly intercourse. *-vr*. **Una discusión se desentabló, a** row broke out.

desentalengar [des-en-tah-len-gar'], *va. (Naut.)* To unbend a cable.

desentarquinar [des-en-tar-ke-nar'], *va*. To free a ditch or trench from mud, mire, or filth.

desentenderse [des-en-ten-derr'-say], *vr*. 1. To feign not to understand a thing. 2. To pass by a thing without taking notice of it. **Se ha desentendido de todo eso**, he has ceased to take any part in that.

desentendido, da [des-en-ten-dee'-do, dah], *a*. Unmindful, pretending or feigning ignorance. *-pp*. of DESENTENDERSE. **Hacerse el desentendido** or **darse por desentendido**, *(Coll.)* to wink at a thing; to pretend not to have taken notice, or to be ignorant of it.

desenterrador [des-en-ter-rah-dor'], *m*. He who disinters or digs up.

desenterramiento [des-en-ter-rah-me-en'-to], *m*. Disinterment.

desenterrar [des-en-ter-rar'], *va*. 1. To disinter, to unbury, to exhume, to dig up, to unearth. 2. *(Met.)* To recall to one's memory things forgotten. **Desenterrar los muertos** *(Met.)* to slander the dead.

desentierramuertos [des-en-te-er-rah-moo-err'-tos], *m*. Calumniator of the dead.

desentoldar [des-en-tol-dar'], *va*. 1. To take away awning. 2. *(Met.)* To strip a thing of its ornaments.

desentonación [des-en-to-nah-the-on'], *f*. Dissonance.

desentonadamente [des-en-to-nah-dah-men'-tay], *adv*. Unharmoniously.

desentonado, da [des-en-to-nah'-do, dah], *a. & pp*. of DESENTONAR. Out of tune, inharmonical, discordant.

desentonamiento [des-en-to-nah-me-en'-to], *m*. Dissonance, excess in the tone of the voice.

desentonar [des-en-to-nar'], *va*. To humble, to wound the pride of anyone. *-vn*. To be out of tune, to be inharmonious. *-vr*. To be of a coarse address, to be rude or uncouth; to raise one's voice in disrespect.

desentono [des-en-toh'-no], *m*. 1. Disharmony, discord. 2. A harsh, rude tone of voice. 3. Musical discord; false note.

desentornillar [des-en-tor-nil-lyar'], *va*. To unscrew.

desentorpecer [des-en-tor-pay-therr'], *va*. To free from torpor, to restore motion to torpid limbs. *-vr*. 1. To be freed from torpor, to be restored from numbness. 2. To become lively, smart, or pert. *(Yo desentorpezco.* from *Desentorpecer. V.* ABORRECER.)

desentrampar [des-en-tram-par'], *va.* To free from debts; or to take away traps set for mischievous animals. *-vr.* To get out of the red.

desentrañamiento [des-en-tra-nyah-me-en'-to], *m.* The act of giving anything as a proof of love and affection.

desentrañar [des-en-tra-nyar'], *va.* 1. To eviscerate, to disembowel. 2. *(Met.)* To penetrate or to dive into the most hidden and difficult matters. 3. *(Naut.)* To remove loops, twists, from ropes. *-vr. (Met.)* To give away all one's fortune and property, out of love and affection for a person.

desentrenado [des-en-tray-nah'-do], *a.* Out of practice; off form; untrained (soldado).

desentristecer [des-en-tris-tay-therr'], *va.* To banish sadness and grief.

desentronizar [des-en-tro-ne-thar'], *va.* 1. *V.* DESTRONAR. 2. To deprive anyone of his power or authority.

desentumecer [des-en-too-may-therr'], *va. V.* DESENTORPECER. *-vr.* To be freed from numbness.

desentumir [des-en-too-meer'], *va.* To free from torpor.

desenvainar [des-en-vah-e-nar'], *va.* To unsheath, as a sword. 2. *(Coll.)* To expose to view anything which was hidden or covered. 3. To stretch out the claws: applied to animals having talons.

desenvelejar [des-en-vay-lay-har'], *va. (Naut.)* To strip a vessel of her sails.

desenvendar [des-en-ven-dar'], *va.* To take off fillets or bands.

desenvenenar [des-en-vay-nay-nar'], *va.* To extract, to remove poison; to destroy the poisonous qualities of a substance.

desenvergar [des-en-ver-gar'], *va. (Naut.)* To unbend a sail.

desenvoltura [des-en-vol-too'-rah], *f.* 1. Sprightliness, cheerfulness. 2. Impudence, effrontery, boldness. 3. A lewd posture or gesture in women. 4. A graceful and easy delivery of one's sentiments and thoughts.

desenvolvedor [des-en-vol-vay-dor'], *m.* Unfolder, investigator.

desenvolver [des-en-vol-verr'], *va.* 1. To unfold, to unroll. 2. *(Met.)* To decipher, to discover, to unravel. *-vr.* To be forward, to behave with too much assurance. *(Yo desenvuelvo,* from *Desenvolver. V.* ABSOLVER.)

desenvueltamente [des-en-voo-el-ta-men'-tay], *adv.* 1. Impudently, licentiously. 2. Expeditiously.

desenvuelto, ta [des-en-voo-el-to, tah], *a.* Forward, impudent, licentious. *-pp.* of DESENVOLVER.

desenyesar [des-en-yay-sar'], *va.* To remove plaster from a wall. *-vr.* To fall, as plaster, from a wall.

desenzarzar [des-en-thar-thar'], *va.* 1. To disentangle from brambles. 2. To appease, to reconcile those who quarrel. *-vr.* To get well out of some entangled matter.

deseo [day-say'-o], *m.* Desire, wish, mind, liking. **A medida del deseo,** according to one's wish. **Arder de deseos de algo,** to yearn for something. **Tener deseos de,** to want, to yearn for.

deseoso, sa [day-say-oh'-so, sah], *a.* 1. Desirous, longing. 2. Greedy, eager.

desequilibrado [des-ay-ke-le-brah'-do], *a.* 1. Unbalanced; badly balanced, out of true. 2. *(Med.)* Unbalanced (mentalmente).

desequilibrar [des-ay-ke-le-brar'], *va.* To unbalance.

desequilibrio [des-ay-ke-lee'-bre-o], *m.* Unstable equilibrium; an unbalanced state.

deserción [day-ser-the-on'], *f.* 1. Desertion. 2. *(Law.)* Abandonment of a suit by a plaintiff.

desertar [day-ser-tar'], *va.* 1. To desert. **Desertar de sus deberes,** to neglect one's duties. 2. To go over to another party. 3. To separate from a body or company. 4. *(Law.)* To abandon a cause. **Desertarse a,** to fall over.

desértico [de-sayr'-te-co], *a.* Arid, desert-like; deserted (vacío).

desertización [de-sayr-te-thah-the-on'], *f.* Turning land into a desert; *(fig.)* Depopulation.

desertor, ra [day-ser-tor'], *m. f.* 1. Deserter. 2. Deserter, forsaker, fugitive, the person that has forsaken his cause, post etc.

deservicio [day-ser-vee'-the-o], *m.* Disservice, fault committed against a person who has a claim to services or devotion.

deservidor [day-ser-ve-dor'], *m.* He who fails in serving another.

deservir [day-ser-veer'], *va. (Ant.)* Not to perform one's duty, to disserve.

desescamar [des-es-cah-mar'], *va.* To scale, to remove scales.

desescombrar [des-es-com-brar'], *va.* To remove the garbage.

desescombro [des-es-com-bro], *m.* Clearing-up, clean-up.

desesalabonar [des-es-lah-bo-nar'], *va.* To cut the links of a chain.

desespaldar [des-es-pal-dar'], *va.* To wound the shoulder.

desespaldillar [des-es-pal-dil-lyar'], *va.* To wound in the shoulder blade. *-vr.* To receive a lesion in this bone.

desesperación [des-es-pay-rah-the-on'], *f.* 1. Despondency, despair, desperation. 2. *(Met.)* Displeasure, anger, passion, fury. **Es una desesperación,** *(Coll.)* It is unbearable. **Nadar con desesperación,** to swim furiously.

desesperadamente [des-es-pay-ra-dah-men'-tay], *adv.* 1. Despairingly, hopelessly. 2. Desperately, furiously, madly.

desesperado, da [des-es-pay-rah'-do, dah], *a. & pp.* of DESESPERAR. 1. Desperate, despaired, hopeless. 2. Desperate, furious. *-f.* **Hacer algo a la desesperada,** to do something as a last hope.

desesperado [des-es-pay-rah'-do], *m.* Desperate, despairer, desperado, a desperate man. **Como un desesperado,** like mad.

desesperante [des-es-pay-rahn'-tay], *a.* Maddening, infuriating.

desesperanzar [des-es-pay-ran-thar'], *va.* To deprive one of hope, to make him despair, to deprive of all hope. *-vr.* To lose hope.

desesperar [des-es-pay-rar'], *vn.* To despair, to be cast down. *-va.* To make one despair, to deprive him of all hope. *-vr.* 1. To sink into the utmost despair, to despond. 2. To fret, to be desperate.

desespigar [des-es-pe-gar'], *va.* To thrash grain.

desespigo, desespigue [des-es-pee'-go, gay], *m.* Thrashing of grain by the trampling of animals, or of suitable instruments.

desesponjarse [des-es-pon-har'-say], *vr.* To lose porosity or sponginess.

desestabilizar [des-es-tah-be-le-thar'], *va.* To destabilize.

desestacar [des-es-tah-car'], *va.* To take away stakes or props from vines, after the vintage.

desestancar [des-es-tan-car'], *va.* To take away a monopoly; to declare an article open to trade.

desesterar [des-es-tay-rar'], *va.* 1. To take off the mats. 2. *(Met.)* To lay aside winter clothes.

desestimación [des-es-te-mah-the-on'], *f.* Disesteem, disrespect; crying down.

desestimador, ra [des-es-te-mah-dor', rah], *m. & f.* Contemner, despiser.

desestimar [des-es-te-mar'], *va.* 1. To disregard, to contemn, to undervalue. 2. To reject, to deny.

desestivar [des-es-te-var'], *va. (Naut.)* To alter the stowage.

desfacedor [des-fah-thay-dor'], *m. (Obs.)* Destroyer. **Desfacedor de entuertos,** undoer of injuries.

desfacer [des-fah-therr'], *va. V.* DESHACER.

desfachatado, da [des-fah-chah-tah'-do, dah], *a.* Impudent, saucy.

desfachatez [des-fah-chah-teth'], *f. (Neol. Coll.)* Impudence, effrontery.

desfajar [des-fah-har'], *va.* To ungird.

desfalcador, ra [des-fahl-cah-dor'], *m & f.* Embezzler.

desfalcar [des-fal-car'], *va.* 1. To take away part of something, to cut off, to lop. 2. To peculate, to defalcate. 3. To oust one from his protection or patronage.

desfalcazar [des-fal-ca-thar'], *va. (Naut.)* To untwist a rope to make oakum.

desfalco [des-fahl'-co], *m.* **1.** Defalcation, shortage, deficit. 2. Diminution, diminishing, detracting.

desfallecer [des-fal-lyay-therr'], *vn.* 1. To pine, to fall away, to grow weak. 2. To swoon, to faint. -*va.* To weaken, to debilitate.

desfallecido [des-fahl-lyay-the'-do], *a.* Weak; faint.

desfalleciente [des-fal-lyay-the-en'-tay], *pa,* Pining, languishing.

desfallecimiento [des-fal-lyay-the-me-en'-to], *m.* 1. Languor, fainting, decline; dejection of mind. 2. A swoon, fainting fit.

desfasado [des-fah-sah'-do], *a. (Mech.)* Out of phase, badly adjusted; *(fig.)* Out of step; behind the times, antiquated. **Estar desfasado**, *(Aer.)* To be suffering from jet lag.

desfasar [des-fah-sar'], *va.* To change the phase of; *(fig.)* To put out of phase; to unbalance, to upset.

desfase [des-fah-say], *m.* Being out of phase; imbalance; gap, difference; *(Aer.)* Jet lag.

desfavor [des-fah-vor'], *m.* Disfavor.

desfavorable [des-fah-vo-rah'-blay], *a.* Unfavorable, contrary.

desfavorecedor, ra [des-fah-vo-ray-thay-dor', rah], *m. & f.* Disfavorer: contemner.

desfavorecer [des-fah-vo-ray-therr'], *va.* 1. To disfavor, to discountenance. 2. To despise, to contemn. 3. To injure, to hurt;. 4. To contradict, to oppose.

desfertilizar [des-fer-te-le-thar'], *va.* To destroy fertility. -*vr.* To lose fertility.

desfiguración, *f.* **desfiguramiento**, *m.* [des-fe-goo-rah-the-on'], Deformation, disfiguration, disfigurement.

desfigurado [des-fe-goo-rah'-do], *a.* Disfigured; deformed; distorted (sentido), misrepresentation.

desfigurar [des-fe-goo-rar'], *va.* 1. To disfigure, to deform, to misshape, to misform. **Una cicatriz le desfigura la cara**, a scar disfigures his face. 2. To disguise. 3. To misrepresent, to misstate. 4. *(Met.)* To cloud, to darken. -*vr.* To be disfigured by passion, or an accident.

desfijar [des-fe-har'], *va.* To remove a thing from its place.

desfilachar [des-fe-lah-char'], *va. V.* DESHILACHAR.

desfilada [des-fe-lah'-dah], *f. (Mil.)* Single file.

desfiladero [des-fe-lah-day'-ro], *m.* 1. Narrow passage where troops pass, single file. 2. Canyon.

desfilar [des-fe-lar'], *va. (Obs.)* To ravel, to unweave, to parade. **Desfilaron ante el general**, they paraded before the general. -*vn. (Mil.)* 1. To defile; to march off by files; to file off. 2. To march in review before an officer of high rank.

desfile [des-fee'-lay], *m.* 1. Parade, procession, marching in files. 2. *(Moda)* Fashion show.

desflecar [des-flay-car'], *va.* To remove the flakes of wool or frettings of cloth.

desflemación [des-flay-mah-the-on'], *f. (Chem. Obs.)* Dephlegmation.

desflemar [des-flay-mar'], *va.* To dephlegmate. -*vn. (Prov.)* To brag, to boast.

desflocar [des-flo-car'], *va.* To ravel out the ends of stud. *V.* DESFLECAR.

desfloración [des-flo-rah-the-on'], *f.* Defloration.

desfloramiento [des-flo-rah-me-en'-to], *m.* Violation, constupration, ravishment,

desflorar [des-flo-rar'], *va.* 1. To pull up or cut up flowers. 2. To constupate, to violate, to deflower. 3. To tarnish, to stain or sully. 4. To write or speak very superficially.

desflorecer [des-flo-ray-therr'], *vn.* To lose its bloom.

desflorecimiento [des-flo-ray-the-me-en'-to], *m.* Falling of flowers.

desfogar [des-fo-gar'], *va.* 1. To vent, to make an opening for fire. 2. To vent the violence of passion. 3. To temper or moderate passion or desire. 4. To give loose rein to a horse. -*vr.* To vent one's anger.

desfogonadura [des-fo-go-nah-doo', ran], *f.* Disproportionate width of the vent of a cannon.

desfogonar [des-fo-go-nar'], *va.* To widen or burst the vent of a cannon.

desfogue [des-fo'-gay], *m.* The venting or foaming out of passion.

desfollonar [des-fol-lyo-nar'], *va.* To strip off useless leaves.

desfondar [des-fon-dar'], *va.* 1. To break or take off the bottom of a vessel. 2. *(Naut.)* To penetrate the bottom of a ship. -*vr. (Fig.)* To go to pieces.

desforado, da [des-fo-rah'-do, dah], *a.* Outlawed; unjudicial. *V.* DESAFORADO.

desforestación [des-fo-rays-tah-the-on'], *f.* Deforestation.

desforestar [des-fo-rays-tar'], *va.* To deforest.

desformar [des-for-mar'], *va.* To disfigure, to deform. *V.* DEFORMAR.

desfortalecer, or **desfortificar** [des-for-tah-lay-therr'], *va. (Mil.)* To dismantle, to demolish the works of a fortress.

desfrenar [des-fray-nar'], *va.* To unbridle. *V.* DESENFRENAR.

desfundar [des-foon-dar'], *va. V.* DESENFUNDAR.

desfusión [des-foo-se-on'], *f.* Dilution, diffusion, attenuation. Quaint and rare form for *Difusión*.

desgaire [des-gah'-e-ray], *m.* 1. A graceless mien or deportment, slovenliness, affected carelessness in dress. 2. Gesture, indicating scorn or contempt. **Al desgaire**, affectedly careless, disdainfully, contemptuously.

desgajado [des-gah-hah-do], *a.* Separated, unconnected.

desgajadura [des-gah-hah-doo'-rah], *f.* Disruption, tearing off the branch of a tree.

desgajar [des-gah-har'], *va.* 1. To lop off the branches of trees. 2. To break or tear in pieces. -*vr.* 1. To be separated or disjointed. 2. To be rent or torn in pieces (ropa). 3. To tear oneself away from.

desgalgadero [des-gal-gah-day'-ro], *m.* A rugged declivitous place.

desgalgado, da [des-gal-gah'-do, dah], *a. & pp.* of DESGALGAR. 1. Precipitated. 2. Light, thin, small-waisted.

desgalgar [des-gal-gar'], *va.* To precipitate; to throw headlong. -*vr.* To flee by rough roads.

desgalichado, da [des-gah-le-chah'-do, dah], *a. (Coll.)* Ungainly, ungraceful.

desgana [des-gah'-nah], *f.* 1. Disgust, want of appetite. 2. Aversion, repugnance, reluctance. **Hacer algo a desgana**, to do something reluctantly. 3. *V.* CONGOJA.

desganado [des-gah-nah'-do], *a.* **Estar desganado**, to have no appetite.

desganar [des-gah-nar'], *va.* To deprive of the idea, desire, or pleasure of doing something. -*vr.* 1. To do with reluctance what was done before with pleasure. 2. To lose the appetite or desire for food.

desganchar [des-gan-char'], *va.* To lop off the branches of trees.

desgañifarse, desgañitarse [des-gah-nye-far'-say, des-gah-nye-tar'-say], *vr.* To shriek, to scream, to bawl.

desgarbado, da [des-gar-bah'-do, dah], *a.* Ungraceful, ungenteel, inelegant, ungainly.

desgargamillado, da [des-gar-gah-mil-lyah'-do, dah], *a. (Prov.) V.* DESIDIOSO and MANDRIA.

desgargantarse [des-gar-gan-tar'-say], *vr. (Coll.)* To become hoarse with bawling or screaming.

desgargolar [des-gar-go-lar'], *va.* To shed the seed (cáñamo).

desgaritar [des-gah-re-tar], *vn. (Naut.)* To lose the course (barco). -*vr.* 1. *(Naut.)* To lose the course. 2. *(Met.)* To give up a design or undertaking.

desgarradamente [des-gar-rah-dah-men'-tay], *adv.* impudently, barefacedly, shamelessly.

desgarrado, da [des-gar-rah'-do, dah], *a.* 1. Licentious, dissolute: impudent, shameless, bold. -*pp.* of DESGARRAR.

2. Irregularly segmented upon the border (hojas, alas de insectos).

desgarrador, ra [des-gar-rah-dor', rah], *m. & f.* Tearer, heart-breaking (escena), uncontrollable (emoción), piercing (grito).

desgarradura [des-gar-rah-doo'-rah], *f. (Prov.)* Rent, laceration, break.

desgarrar [des-gar-rar'], *va.* 1. To rend, to tear; to claw. 2. (Cuba) To expectorate, to cough up (phlegm). -*vr.* 1. To withdraw from one's company; to retire. 2. To give a loose rein to one's passions, to lead a licentious life.

desgarro [des-gar'-ro], *m.* 1. Laceration, rent, break, breach. 2. Impudence, effrontery. 3. Looseness, criminal levity. 4. Fanfaronade, idle boast, brag. 5. Solution of continuity, in a tissue by being overstretched.

desgarrón [des-gar-rone'], *m.* 1. *(aug.)* A large rent. 2. Piece of cloth torn off. 3. A big tear.

desgastamiento [des-gas-tah-me-en'-to], *m.* Prodigality, profusion.

desgastar [des-gas-tar'], *va.* 1. To consume, to waste by degrees. 2. To corrode, to gnaw, to eat away. 3. *(Met.)* To pervert, to vitiate. 4. To wear down. -*vr.* To ruin oneself by extravagant expenses; to debilitate oneself. 2. To wear away; to erode; to chafe, to fray; to corrode; to get worn out.

desgavilado, da [des-gah-ve-lah'-do, dah], *a. (Coll.)* Unkempt, ungainly.

desglosar [des-glo-sar'], *va.* 1. To blot out a note or comment on a thing. 2. To take off; to separate.

desglose [des-glo'-say], *m.* Act of blotting out a comment or gloss.

desgobernado, da [des-go-ber-nah'-do, dah], *a.* Ill-governed or regulated, ungovernable (personas). -*pp.* of DESGOBERNAR.

desgobernadura [des-go-ber-nah-doo'-rah], *f. (Vet.)* Act of confining a vein in animals.

desgobernar [des-go-ber-nar'], *va.* 1. To disturb or overturn the order of government; to misgovern. 2. To dislocate or disjoint. 3. To bar a vein on a horse's leg. 4. *(Naut.)* Not to steer steadily the right course. -*vr.* To affect ridiculous motions in dancing.

desgobierno [des-go-be-err'-no], *m.* 1. Mismanagement, misgovernment, misrule, want of conduct and economy; ill administration of public affairs. 2. *(Vet.)* Act of barring a vein on a horse's leg.

desgolletar [des-gol-lyay-tar'], *va.* 1. To break off the neck of a bottle or other vessel. 2. To cut off slopingly the fore part of a woman's gown.

desgonzar [des-gon-thar'], *va.* 1. *V.* DESGOZNAR. 2. To uncase, to unhinge, to discompose, to disjoint.

desgorrarse [des-gor-rar'-say], *vr.* To pull off one's bonnet, hat, or huntingcap.

desgotar [des-go-tar'], *va.* To drain off water. *V.* AGOTAR.

desgoznar [des-goth-nar'], *va.* To unhinge, to disjoint. -*vr.* 1. To be dislocated or disjointed. 2. To be torn to pieces. 3. To distort the body with violent motions.

desgrabar [des-grah-bar'], *va.* To wipe (cinta).

desgracia [des-grah'-the-ah], *f.* 1. Misfortune, adversity, mishap, fatality. 2. Misadventure, mischance, harm. 3. Enmity, unfriendly disposition. 4. Disgrace, state of being out of favor. 5. Unpleasantness, rudeness of language and address. **Correr con desgracia**, to be unfortunate in a design or undertaking. **Caer en desgracia**, to be disgraced or put out of favor. **La familia ha tenido una serie de desgracias**, the family has had a series of misfortunes.

desgraciadamente [des-grah-the-ah-dah-men'-tay], *adv.* Unfortunately, unhappily.

desgraciado, da [des-grah-the-ah'-do, dah], *a.* 1. Unfortunate, unhappy, unlucky, miserable, subject to misfortunes. **Desgraciado en amores**, unlucky in love. 2. Misadventured, luckless, hapless. 3. Out of work. 4. Disagreeable, ungrateful. -*m. f.* Wretch, poor devil. -*pp.* of DESGRACIAR.

desgraciar [des-grah-the-ar'], *va. (Obs.)* To displease, to disgust, to offend. -*vn. V.* MALOGRAR. -*vr.* 1. To disgrace, to fall out with one. 2. To be out of order; not to enjoy good health. 3. To lose the perfection formerly possessed, to degenerate; to die young. **Este negocio se desgració a sus principios**, this business failed at its commencement. **Se desgració con esta acción**, by this action he disgraced himself.

desgramar [des-grah-mar'], *va.* To pull up the panic-grass by the root.

desgranadera [des-grah-nah-day'-rah], *f.* An instrument for separating grapes from the stems.

desgranamiento [des-grah-nah-me-en'-to], *m.* 1. *(Agri.)* Shaking out grain. 2. *(Mil.)* Grooves which the expansive force of powder forms on the inner orifice of the vent-hole.

desgranar [des-grah-nar'], *va.* 1. To shake out the grain from the ears of corn, or other fruits. 2. *(Met.)* To kill. 3. *(Met.)* To scatter about. 4. **Desgranar mentiras**, to come out with a string of lies. 5. *(Fig.)* To sort out, to distinguish between. 6. *(Fig.)* To spell out (sentido). -*vr.* To wear away: applied to the vent of firearms.

desgranzar [des-gran-thar'], *va.* 1. To separate the husks or chaff from the grain. 2. *(Pict.)* To give colors the first grinding.

desgrasar [des-grah-sar'], *va.* To remove the fat (from).

desgravable [des-grah-vah'-blay], *a.* Tax-deductible.

desgravación [des-grah-vah-the-on'], *f.* **Desgravación fiscal**, tax relief.

desgravar [des-grah-var'], *va.* To reduce the tax on; to exempt from tax.

desgreñadura [des-gray-nyah-doo'-rah], *f.* The act and effect of dishevelling.

desgreñar [des-gray-nyar'], *va.* 1. To dishevel hair, to pull it out by the roots. 2. To discompose, to disturb.

desguace [des-goo-ah'-they], *m.* 1. Breaking up; scrapping; stripping. 2. Scrapyard (parque).

desguarnecer [des-goo-ar-nay-therr'], *va..* 1. To strip clothes of trimmings and other ornaments. 2. To deprive something of its strength, to strip it of all accessories; to take away what is necesary for the use of some mechanical instrument. 3. To disgarnish, to deprive of ornament or lustre. 4. To disgarrison. (*Yo desguarnezco, yo desguarnezca* from *Desguarnecer. V.* CONOCER.)

desguarnir [des-goo-ar-neer'], *va. (Naut.)* To unrig the capstan.

desguazar [des-goo-ah-thar'], *va.* To cut asunder timber or wood.

desguince [des-geen'-thay], *m.* 1. The knife which cuts lags in paper-mills. 2. *V.* ESQUINCE.

desguindar [des-geen-dar'], *va. (Naut.)* To take and bring down. -*vr.* To slide down a rope.

desguinzar [des-geen-thar'], *a.* To cut cloth or rags in papermills.

deshabitado [des-ah-be-tah-do], *a.* Uninhabited; deserted; empty, vacant.

deshabitar [des-ah-be-tar'], *va.* 1. To quit one's house or habitation. 2. To unpeople, to depopulate, to desert a place.

deshabituación [des-ah-be-too-ah-the-on'], *f.* Disuse, disusage, desuetude.

deshabituar [des-ah-be-too-ar], *va.* To disaccustom, to disuse, to destroy the force of habit. -*vr.* To lose the habit, to get out of the habit.

deshacedor [des-ah-thay-dor'], *m.* **Deshacedor de agravios**, undoer of injuries.

deshacer [des-ah-ther], *va.* 1. To undo or destroy the form or figure of a thing; to undo what has been done. 2. To consume, to diminish. 3. To cancel, to blot or scratch out, to efface. 4. To rout an army, to put to flight. 5. To melt, to liquefy. 6. To cut up, to divide. 7. To dissolve in a liquid. 8. To violate a treaty or agreement. 9. To discharge troops from service. **Deshacer algo en agua**, to dissolve something in water. **Deshacer el camino**, to go back over one's route. -*vr.* 1. To be wasted or destroyed. 2. To grieve, to mourn. 3. To disappear, to get out of one's sight. 4. To do anything with vehemence. 5. To grow feeble or meagre. 6. To be crippled, grievously maltreated. 7. To remove a hindrance to the carrying out of a project. 8. To transfer, to sell. **Deshacerse como el humo**, to vanish like smoke. **Deshacerse en lágrimas**, to burst into a flood of tears. **Deshacerse de una cosa**, to give a thing away, to dispose of. **Cuando se deshizo la reunión**, when the meeting broke up. **Deshacerse de algo**, to get rid of something. **Deshacerse por hacer algo**, to strive to do something, to struggle to do something. (*Yo deshago, yo deshice, yo deshaga*, from *Deshacer. V.* HACER.)

desharrapado, da [des-ar-rah-pah'-do, dah], *a.* Shabby, ragged, in tatters.

desharrapamiento [des-ar-rah-pah-me-en'-to], *m.* Misery, meanness.

deshebillar [des-ay-bil-lyar'], *va.* To unbuckle.

deshebrar [des-ay-brar'], *va.* 1. To unthread, to ravel into threads. 2. *(Met.)* To separate into filaments. 3. *(Met.)* To shed a flood of tears.

deshecha [des-ay'-chah], *f.* I. Simulation, fiction, evasion, shift. 2. A genteel departure, a polite farewell. 3. Step in a Spanish dance. **A la deshecha**, dissemblingly; deceitfully.

deshechizar [des-ay-che-thar'], *va.* To disenchant.

deshechizo [des-ay-chee'-tho], *m.* Disenchantment.

deshecho, cha [des-ay'-cho', chah], *a. & pp.* of DESHACER. 1. Undone, destroyed, wasted; melted: in pieces. 2. Perfectly mixed (colores). **Borrasca deshecha**, a violent tempest. **Tener un brazo deshecho**, to have a badly injured arm.

deshelador [des-ay-lah-dor'], *m.* De-icer.

deshelar [des-ay-lar'], *va.* 1. To thaw. 2. To overcome one's obstinacy. 3. *(Met.)* To invite, to inspirit. *-vr.* To thaw, to melt.

desherbar [des-er-bar'], *va.* To pluck up or extirpate herbs.

desheredación [des-ay-ray-dah-the-on'], *f.* Disheritance, disinheriting.

desheredamiento [des-ay-ray-dah-me-en'-to], *m.* Disinheriting.

desheredar [des-ay-ray-dar'], *va.* 1. To disinherit, to deprive of an inheritance; to disinherit, to cut off from an hereditary right. 2. *(Met.)* To deprive of influence or favor. *-vr.* To degenerate, to fall from the dignity and virtue of one's ancestors.

deshermanar [des-er-mah-nar'], *va.* *(Met.)* To unmatch things which were similar or equal. *-vr.* To violate the love due to a brother.

desherradura [des-er-rah-doo'-rah], *f.* *(Vet.)* Surbating, injury done to a horse's foot by being unshod.

desherrar [des-er-rar'], *va.* 1. To unchain. 2. To rip off the shoes of horses.

desherrumbrar [des-er-room-brar'], *va.* To clear a thing of rust.

deshidratado, da [des-e-drah-tah'-do, dah], *a.* Dehydrated.

deshidratación [des-e-drah-tah-the-on'], *f.* Dehydration.

deshidratado [des-e-drah-tah'-do], *a.* Dehydrated.

deshidratar [des-e-drah-tar'], *va.* To dehydrate.

deshielo [des-ay-e'-lo], *m.* Thaw. (*Yo deshielo*, from *Deshelar. V.* ACRECENTAR.)

deshilachar [des-e-lah-char'], *va.* To ravel, to uncord.

deshilado [des-e-lah'-do], *m.* Openwork, a kind of embroidery; drawn work.

deshilado, da [des-e-lah'-do dah], *a.* Marching in a file. **A la deshilada**, 1. In file, one after another, stealthily. 2. Deceitfully, dissemblingly.-*pp.* of DESHILAR.

deshiladura [des-e-lah-doo'-rah], *f.* Ripping, ravelling out.

deshilar [des-e-lar'], *va.* 1. To draw out threads from cloth, to ravel. 2. To reduce, to convert into filaments or lint. 3. To distract bees, in order to lead them from one hive to another. *-vn.* To grow thin, by reason of sickness.

deshilo [des-e-e'-lo], *m.* Obstructing the communication of bees, to get them into a new hive.

deshilvanar [des-eel-vah-nar'], *va.* To remove the basting-threads.

deshincadura [des-in-cah-doo'-rah], *f.* Act of drawing out anything nailed or fixed.

deshincar [des-in-car'], *va.* To draw a nail, to remove what is fixed.

deshinchadura [des-in-chah-doo'-rah], *f.* Act of abating a swelling.

deshinchar [des-in-char'], *va.* 1. To reduce a swelling. 2. To let out the air, or fluid, with which something is inflated. 3. To appease anger or annoyance. *-vr.* 1. To be removed (inflamación). 2. *(Met.)* To abate presumption.

deshipotecar [des-e-po-tay-car'], *va.* To lift, to satisfy a mortgage.

deshojado [des-o-hah'-do], *a.* Leafless (rama etc.); Stripped of its petals (flor).

deshojador [des-oh-hah-dor'], *m.* A stripper of leaves.

deshojadura [des-oh-hah-doo'-rah], *f.* Stripping a tree of its leaves.

deshojar [des-oh-har'], *va.* 1. To strip off the leaves. 2. *(Met.)* To display rhetorical elegance in discussion. 3. *(Met.)* To deprive of all hopes.

deshoje [des-oh'-hay], *m.* The fall of leaves from plants.

deshollejar [des-ol-lyah-har'], *va.* To peel, to pare, to strip off the husk.

deshollinador [des-ol-lyee-nah-dor'], *m.* 1. Chimney-sweeper. 2. Any instrument for sweeping chimneys. 3. *(Met. Coll.)* He who examines and inspects carefully and curiously.

deshollinar [des-ol-lyee-nar'], *va.* 1. To sweep or clean chimneys. 2. To clean what is dirty. 3. *(Met.)* To shift, to change clothes. 4. *(Met. Col.)* To view and examine with attention.

deshombrecerse [des-om-bray-therr'-say], *vr.* *(Prov.)* To shrug up the shoulders.

deshonestamente [des-o-nes-tah-men-tay], *adv.* 1. Dishonorably, disgracefully. 2. Lewdly, dishonestly.

deshonestar [des-o-nes-tar'], *va.* 1. To dishonor, to disgrace. 2. *(Obs.)* To disfigure, to deform. *-vr.* To be insolent, to be saucy.

deshonestidad [des-o-nes-te-dahd'], *f.* Immodesty, indecency, lewdness in actions or words.

deshonesto, ta [des-o-nes'-to, tah], *a.* 1. Immodest, lewd, unchaste, libidinous, lustful, dishonest. 2. Unreasonable, not conformable to reason. 3. *(Obs.)* Saucy, rude, rustic.

deshonor [des-o-nor'], *m.* 1. Dishonor, disgrace. 2. Injury, insult, affront.

deshonorar [des-o-no-rar'], *va.* 1. To deprive of office or employment. 2. *(Obs.)* To dishonor, to disgrace.

deshonra [des-on'-rah], *f.* 1. Dishonor, discredit. 2. Disgrace or infamy, obloquy, opprobrium. 3. Seduction or defloration of a woman. **Tener a deshonra alguna cosa**, to consider a thing unworthy, and beneath the rank or character of a person.

deshonradamonte [des-onr-rah'-dah-men-tay], *adv.* Dishonorably, shamefully, disgracefully.

deshonrador [des-on-rah-dor'], *m.* 1. One who dishonors, violator of chastity. 2. One who disgraces.

deshonrar [de-son-rar'], *va.* 1. To affront, to insult, to defame, to dishonor, to disgrace. 2. To scorn, to despise. 3. To seduce an honest woman.

deshonrible [des-on-ree'-bley], *a.* Shameless, despicable.

deshonroso, sa [des-on-ro'-so, sah], Dishonorable, indecent, disgraceful, low.

deshora [des-oh'-rah], *f.* An unseasonable or inconvenient time. **A deshora** or **a deshoras**, untimely, unseasonably; extemporary.

deshorado, da [des-o-rah'-do, dah], *a.* Untimely, unseasonable; unpropitious, fatal.

deshornar [des-or-nar'], *va.* To take out of the oven. *V.* DESENHORNAR.

deshuesamiento [des-oo-ay-sah-me-en'-to], *m.* Removal of bones.

deshuesar [des-oo-ay-sar'], *va.* To rid of bones.

deshumanizar [des-oo-mah-ne-thar'], *va.* To dehumanize.

deshumedecer [des-oo-may-day-therr'], *va.* To dehumidify, to deprive of humidity. *-vr.* To grow dry.

desiderable [day-se-day-rah'-blay], *a.* Desirable.

desiderativo, va [day-se-day-rah-tee'-vo, vah], *a.* Desiderative, expressing desire.

desidia [day-see'-de-ah], *f.* Idleness, laziness, indolence.

desidiosamente [day-se-de-o-sah-men'-tay], *adv.* Indolently, idly.

desidioso, sa [day-se-de-oh'-so, sah], *a.* Lazy, idle, indolent, heavy.

desierto, ta [day-se-err'-to, tah], *a.* Deserted, uninhabited, lonesome, solitary, desert, waste. **La calle estaba desierta**, the street was deserted.

desierta [day-se-ayr'-tah], *f.* (*Law.*) Withdrawal of an appeal.

desierto [day-se-err'-to], *m.* Desert, wilderness.

designación [day-sig-nah-the-on'], *f.* Designation.

designar [day-sig-nar'], *va.* 1. To design, to purpose, to intend anything. 2. To appoint a person for some determined purpose. 3. To express, to name.

designativo, va [day-sig-nah-tee'-vo, vah], *a.* Designative.

designio [day-sig'-ne-o], *m.* Design, purpose, intention, contrivance, mind.

desigual [des-e-goo-ahl'], *a.* 1. Unequal, dissimilar, unlike. 2. Uneven, unlevelled, broken, craggy, cragged. 3. Arduous, difficult, perious. 4. Variable; abrupt. 5. Excessive, extreme.

desigualar [des-e-goo-ah-lar'], *va.* To make unequal or to mismatch. *-vr.* To excel, to surpass.

desigualdad [des-e-goo-al-dahd'], *f.* 1. Inequality, odds, dissimilitude. 2. Variableness, levity, inconstancy. 3. Wrong, injury, injustice. 4. Knottiness, unevenness, craggedness, cragginess, unevenness of the ground, anfractuosity.

desigualmente [day-se-goo-ahl-men'-tay], *adv.* **Unequally**, oddly.

desilusión [des-e-loo-se-on'], *f.* Disillusion, disappointment. **Sufrir una desilusión**, to suffer a disappointment.

desilusionar [des-e-loo-se-o-nar'], *va.* 1. To destroy an illusion, to cause it to vanish. 2. To undeceive. *-vr.* 1. To lose an illusion. 2. To be disabused, undeceived.

desimaginar [des-e-mah-he-nar'], *va.* To blot out or obliterate in the mind. *-vn.* To be thoughtless or unconcerned about what may happen.

desimanarse [des-e-mah-nar'-say], *vn.* To lose its magnetism.

desimpresionar [des-im-pray-se-o-nar'], *va.* To undeceive.

desinclinar [des-in-cle-nar'], *va.* To disincline.

desincorporación [des-in-cor-po-rah-the-on'], *f.* Disincorporation, end of corporate existence.

desincorporar [des-in-cor-po-rar'], *va. & vr.* To separate what was before united or incorporated; to disincorporate.

desinencia [day-se-nen'-the-ah], *f.* (*Gram.*) Termination, ending.

desinfatuación [des-in-fah-too-ah-the-on'], *f.* Disinfatuation.

desinfatuar [des-in-fah-too-ar'], *va. & vr.* To disinfatuate, to become freed from infatuation.

desinfección [des-in-fec-the-on'], *f.* Disinfection, act of disinfecting.

desinfectante [des-in-fec-than'-tay], *pa & m.* Disinfectant; capable of destroying or neutralizing infection.

desinfectar [des-in-fec-tar'], *va.* To disinfect, to destroy the poison of disease.

desinficionar [des-in-fe-the-o-nar'], *va.* To free from infection.

desinflación [des-in-flah-the-on'], *f.* 1. Deflation. 2. Depression, dejection.

desinflado [des-en-flah-do], *a.* Flat (neumático).

desinflamar [des-in-flah-mar'], **va.** To cure or remove an inflammation.

desinflar [des-in-flar'], *va.* To deflate. **Desinflarse**, (*fig.*) to be deflated, to come down to earth.

desinformación [des-in-for-mah-the-on'], *f.* 1. Desinformation, misleading information. 2. Ignorance, lack of information.

desinformado [des-in-for-mah-do], *a.* Uninformed.

desinformar [des-in-for-mar'], *va.* To misinform.

desintegrable [des-in-tay-grah'-blay], *a.* Fissionable.

desintegración [des-in-tay-grah-the-on'], *f.* Disintegration. **Desintegración del átomo**, splitting of the atom.

desintegrador de átomos [des-in-tay-grah-dor' day ah'-to-mos], *m.* (*Phys.*) Atom smasher.

desintegrar [des-in-tay-grar'], *va.* To disintegrate, to decompose. *-vr.* To disintegrate; to split.

desinterés [des-in-tay-res'], *m.* Disinterest, indifference.

desinteresadamente [des-in-tay-ray-sah'-da-men-tay], *adv.* Disinterestedly.

desinteresado, da [des-in-tay-ray-sah'-do, dah], *a.* Disinterested, impartial.

desintoxicación [des-in-toc-se-cah-the-on'], *f.* Curing of poisoning; curing of drug addiction.

desintoxicar [des-in-toc-se-car'], *va.* To cure of poisoning.

desinvernar [des-in-ver-nar'], *vn.* To leave winter quarters: used of troops.

desistimiento [day-sis-te-me-en'-to], *m.* Desistance, the act of desisting.

desistir [day-sis-teer'], *vn.* 1. To desist, to cease, to give out, to go back. 2. To leave, to abandon, to flinch. 3. (*For.*) To abdicate a right.

desjarretar [des-har-ray-tar'], *va.* 1. To hough, to hamstring. 2. (*Met. Coll.*) To weaken, to debilitate, to leave powerless.

desjarrete [des-har-ray'-tay], *m.* Act of houghing.

desjugar [des-hoo-gar'], *va.* To extract the juice from anything.

desjuntamiento [des-hoon-tah-me-en'-to], *m.* Separation, disjunction.

desjuntar [des-hoon-tar'], *va.* To divide, to separate, to part.

desjurar [des-hoo-rar'], *va.* To retract an oath, to forswear.

deslabonar [des-lah-bo-nar'], *va.* 1. To unlink, to separate one link from another. 2. (*Met.*) To disjoin, to destroy. *-vr.* To withdraw from a company, to retire.

desladrillar [des-lah-dril-lyar'], *va.* V. DESENLADRILLAR.

deslamar [des-lah-mar'], *va.* To clear of mud.

deslastrar [des-las-trar'], *va.* To unballast a ship.

deslatar [des-lah-tar'], *va.* To take the laths or small joists out of a house or other building.

deslavado, da [des-lah-vah'-do, dah], *a.* Impudent, barefaced. *-pp.* of DESLAVAR.

deslavadura [des-lah-vah-doo'-rah], *f.* Washing, rinsing.

deslavar [des-lah-var'], *va.* 1. To wash or cleanse superficially, to rinse. 2. To wet, to spoil by wetting. 3. To take away the color, force, or vigor of a thing. **Cara deslavada**, a pale, puny face.

deslavazar [des-lah-vah-thar'], *va.* 1. V. DESLAVAR. 2. (*Agri.*) To expose hay to the action of rain.

deslave [des-lah'-vay], *m.* Washout, overflowing.

deslazamiento [des-lah-thah-me-en'-to], *m.* Disjunction, dissolution.

deslazar [des-lah-thar'], *va.* To unlace, to untie a knot.

desleal [des-lay-ahl'], *a.* Disloyal; perfidious, faithless; traitorous.

deslealmente [des-lay-ahl'-men-tay], *adv.* Disloyally, treacherously.

deslealtad [des-lay-al-tahd'], *f.* Disloyalty, treachery, faithlessness.

deslechar [des-lay-char'], *va.* (*Prov.*) To remove the leaves and dirt from silkworms.

deslecho [des-lay'-cho], *m.* (*Prov.*) Act of cleansing silkworms.

deslechugador [des-lay-choo-gah-dor'], *m.* Vine-dresser, pruner.

deslechugar, deslechuguillar [des-lay-choo-gar'], *va.* *(Agri.)* To cut and prune the branches of vines.

desleidura [des-lay-e-doo'-rah], *f.* **desleimiento**, *m.* Dilution, making thin or weak.

desleír [des-lay-eer'], *va.* To dilute, to make thin or weak, to dissolve. *-vr.* To dissolve; to become diluted; to get weaker. *(Yo deslío, yo desleí, el deslió, el disliera; from Desleír. V. PEDIR.)*

deslendrar [des-len-drar'], *va.* To clear the hair of nits.

deslenguado, da [des-len-goo-ah'-do, dah], *a.* Loquacious, impudent, foul-mouthed, scurrilous. *-pp.* of DESLENGUAR.

deslenguamiento [des-len-goo-ah-me-en'-to], *m.* Loquacity, impudence.

deslenguar [des-len-goo-ar'], *va.* To cut out the tongue. *-vr.* To talk ill of, to slander.

desliar [des-le-ar'], *va.* To untie, to loose. *-vr.* To come undone.

desligadura, *f.* or **desligamiento**, *m.* [des-le-gah-doo'-rah]. Disjunction, untying.

desligar [des-le-gar'], *va.* 1. To loosen, to untie, to unbind. 2. *(Met.)* To disentangle, to extricate, to unravel something not material. 3. *(Met.)* To absolve from ecclesiastical censure. 4. To remove from a ship part of its knees, or futtock timbers, or the spikes which hold them. 5. *(Med.)* To unfasten bandages or ligatures. 6. *(Mus.)* To separate notes very clearly. **Desligar el maleficio**, to dissolve a spell which prevented a husband from enjoying the marriage rights. **Desligar el primer aspecto del segundo**, to separate the first aspect from the second. *-vr.* To come undone, to get unfastened; to extricate oneself.

deslindable [des-lin-dah'-blay], *a.* Surveyable, capable of demarcation.

deslindador [des-lin-dah-dor'], *m.* He who marks limits or boundaries.

deslindamiento [des-lin-dah-me-en'-to], *m.* Demarcation.

deslindar [des-lin-dar'], *va.* 1. To mark the limits and bounds of a place or district. 2. *(Met.)* To clear up a thing.

deslinde [des-leen'-day], *m.* 1. Demarcation. 2. *(Fig.)* Definition.

deslingar [des-lin-gar'], *va.* To unsling.

desliñar [des-le-nyar'], *va.* To clean cloth before it goes to the press.

desliz [des-leeth'], *m.* 1. Slip, the act of slipping or sliding. 2. *(Met.)* Slip, a false step, frailty, weakness, failure, fault. **Los deslizes de la juventud**, the indiscretions of youth. 3. The mercury which escapes in melting silver ore.

deslizable [des-le-thah'-blay], *a.* That which can slip or slide.

deslizadero [des-le-thah-day'-ro], *m.* A slippery place.-*a.* V. DESLIZADIZO.

deslizadero, ra, or **deslizadizo, za** [des-le-thah-dee'-tho, thah], *a.* Slippery, slippy, lubricous.

deslizador [des-le-thah-dor'], *m.* 1. *(Aer.)* Glider. 2. Scooter (de niño). 3. *(Naut.)* Small speedboat. 4. *(Dep.)* Surfboard, aquaplane, water ski.

deslizamiento [des-le-thah-me-en'-to], *m.* 1. Slip, slipping. 2. Gliding.

deslizar [des-le-thar'], *vn. & vr.* 1. To slip, to slide, to glide. **Deslizar una mesa por el suelo**, to slide a table along the floor. **El insecto se deslizó fuera del agujero**, the insect wriggled out of the hole. **Deslizar la mano por la mesa**, to run one's hand over the table. **Deslizarse en un cuarto**, to slip into a room. 2. To act or speak carelessly, to make a slip of the tongue.

deslodaje [des-lo-dah'-hay], *m.* Cleansing of a mineral substance from mud which enwraps it.

deslomadura [des-lo-mah-doo'-rah], *f.* Act of breaking the back. *(Vet.)* Violent extension and even rupture of the fleshy fibres or of the aponeuroses of the muscles of the loins of horses.

deslomar [des-lo-mar'], *va.* To break the back, to distort or strain the loins, to chine. **No se deslomará**, he is sure not to overwork himself. *-vr. (Fig.)* To get worn out.

deslucidamente [des-loo-the'-dah-men-tay], *adv.* Ungracefully, inelegantly.

deslucido, da [des-loo-thee'-do, dah], *a.* 1. Unadorned, ungraceful, inelegant, awkward. 2. Useless, fruitless. 3. Flat, dull, lifeless. **Hizo un papel deslucido**, he was dull in the part. 4. **Quedó muy deslucido**, he did very badly, he made a very poor showing. *-pp.* of DESLUCIR.

deslucimiento [des-loo-the-me-en'-to], *m.* Disgrace, dishonor, want of splendor.

deslucir [des-loo-theer'], *va.* 1. To tarnish or impair the lustre and splendour of a thing. **La lluvia deslució el acto**, the rain ruined the ceremony. 2. *(Met.)* To obscure one's merit. *-vr. (Fig.)* To do badly; to make a poor showing.

deslumbrador, ra [des-loom-brah-dor', rah], *a.* Dazzling, brilliant, glaring.

deslumbramiento, deslumbre [des-loom-brah-me-en'-to], *m.* 1. Glare, overpowering lustre; dazzling. 2. Confusion of sight or mind; hallucination.

deslumbrante [des-loom-brahn'-tay], *a.* Dazzling.

deslumbrar [des-loom-brar'], *va.* 1. To dazzle the sight, to glare. 2. *(Met.)* To puzzle, to leave in doubt and uncertainty. **Deslumbró a todos con su oratoria**, he captivated everyone with his oratory.

deslustrador, ra [des-loos-trah-dor', rah], *m. & f.* Tarnisher.

deslustrar [des-loos-trar'], *va.* 1. To tarnish or sully the brilliancy of a thing, to take away the lustre. 2. To obscure, to make less beautiful or illustrious. 3. *(Met.)* To blast one's reputation, to impeach one's character or merit.

deslustre [des-loos'-tray], *m.* 1. Spot or stain which obscures the lustre or splendor of a thing. 2. Disgrace, ignominy, stigma.

deslustroso, sa [des-loos-tro'-so, sah], *a.* Unbecoming, ugly.

desmadejamiento [des-mah-day-hah-me-en'-to], *m.* Languishment, languidness.

desmadejar [des-mah-day-har'], *va.* To enervate, to produce languor. *-vr.* To languish, to be enervated and weak.

desmadrado [des-mah-drah-do], *a.* 1. Unruly (desenfrenado), rebellious; uninhibited (desinhibido). 2. Confused; disoriented, lost.

desmadrarse [des-mah-drahr'-say], *vr.* To rebel; to get out of control, to go too far, to run wild. **Los gastos se han desmadrado**, costs have gone right over the top.

desmadre [des-mah'-dray], *m.* 1. Excess; excess of emotion. **Esto va de desmadre total**, this is really getting out of hand. 2. Chaos, confusion; mess; outrage. 3. Wild party, rave-up.

desmajolar [des-mah-ho-lar'], *va.* 1. To pull up vines by the roots. 2. To loosen or untie the shoestrings.

desmallador [des-mal-lyah-dor'], *m.* He who breaks a coat of mail.

desmalladura [des-ma-lyah-doo'-rah], *f.* Act of ripping up or breaking a coat of mail.

desmallar [des-mal-lyar'], *va.* To cut and destroy a coat of mail.

desmamar [des-mah-mar'], *va.* V. DESTETAR.

desmamonar [des-mah-mo-nar'], *va.* To cut off the young shoots of vines or trees.

desmán [des-mahn'], *m.* 1. Misfortune, disaster, mishap, calamity. 2. Misbehavior. 3. Excess in actions or words. 4. Shrewmouse.

desmanarse [des-mah-nar'-say], *vr.* To stray from a flock or herd.

desmanche [des-mahn'-chay], *m.* Excessive movement in a rider, want of firmness in the saddle.

desmandado, da [des-man-dah'-do, dah], *a.* V. DESOBEDIENTE.-*pp.* of DESMANDAR.

desmandamiento [des-man-dah-me-en'-to], *m.* 1. Act of countermanding or disbanding. 2. Disorder, irregularity, neglect of rule.

desmandar [des-man-dar'], *va.* 1. To repeal an order, to countermand, to revoke an offer. 2. To revoke a legacy. *-vr.*

1. To transgress the bounds of justice and reason. 2. To disband (tropas). 3. To stray from the flock. 4. To go astray.

desmanear [des-mah-nayar'], *va.* To unfetter, to take off fetters or shackles (caballos, mulas).

desmangamiento, desmangue [des-man-gah-me-en'-to], *m.* Taking off the handle of a thing.

desmangar [des-man-gar'], *va.* To take off the handle of a thing.

desmanotado, da [des-mah-no-tah'-do, dah], *a.* Unhandy, awkward.

desmantecar [des-man-tay-car'], *va.* To take off the butter.

desmantelado, da [des-man-tay-lah'-do, ah], *a. & pp.* of DESMANTELAR. Dismantled, ruinous, dilapidated.

desmantelamiento [des-mahn-tay-lah-me-ayn'-to], *m.* 1. Dismantling; abandonment. 2. Dilapidation.

desmantelar [des-man-tay-lar'], *va.* 1. To dismantle. 2. To abandon, to desert, to forsake. 3. *(Naut.)* To unmast. *-vr.* To fall into disrepair, to become dilapidated.

desmaña [des-mah'-nyah], *f.* 1. Awkwardness, clumsiness. 2. Idleness, laziness.

desmañado, da [des-mah-nyah-do, dah], *a.* 1. Unhandy, clumsy, awkward, clownish. 2. Lazy, idle, indolent.

desmañar [des-mah-nyar'], *va. (Ant.)* To impede, to obstruct.

desmaquillador [des-mah-kel-lyah-dor'], *m.* Make-up remover.

desmarañar [des-mah-rah-nyar'], *va.* To disentangle. *V.* DESENMARAÑAR.

desmarcar [des-mar-car'], *va.* To remove, to efface, to obliterate marks. *-vr.* To shake off one's attacker; to avoid an opponent; to get clear; *(fig.)* To step out of line.

desmaridar [des-mah-re-dar'], *va.* To separate husband and wife.

desmarojador [des-mah-ro-hah-dor'], *m.* He who takes off the rind of olives.

desmarojar [des-mah-ro-har'], *va.* To take the glutinous rind from olives.

desmarrido, da [des-mar-ree'-do, dah], *a.* Sad, languid, dejected, exhausted.

desmayadamente [des-mah-yah'-dah-men-tay], *adv.* Weakly, dejectedly.

desmayado da [des-mah-yah'-do dah], *a. & pp.* of DESMAYAR. 1. Pale, weak, faint of lustre. 2. Dismayed, appalled.

desmayar [des-mah-yar'], *vn.* To be dispirited or faint-hearted, to want strength and courage. *-vn.* To dismay, to depress, to discourage. *-vr.* To faint, to swoon.

desmayo [des-mah'-yo], *m.* 1. Swoon, fainting fit. **Sufrir un desmayo**, to have a fainting fit. 2. Decay of strength and vigor. **Hablar con desmayo**, to speak falteringly. **Tenía un desmayo en todo el cuerpo**, he felt limp all over. 3. Dismay, discouragement.

desmazalado, da [des-mah-thah-lah'-do, dah], *a.* Weak, dejected, faint-hearted, spiritless.

desmedidamente [des-may-de'-dah-men-tay], *adv.* Disproportionably, disproportionately.

desmedido, da [des-may-dee'-do, dah], *a.* Unproportionable, out of proportion or measure. *-pp.* of DESMEDIRSE.

desmedirse [des-may-deer'-say], *vr. V.* DEMANDARSE and EXCEDERSE.

desmedrar [des-may-drar'], *vn.* To decrease, to decay.*-va.* To impair, to deteriorate.

desmedro [des-may'-dro], *m.* Diminution. decay, detriment.

desmejora [des-may-ho'-rah], *f.* Deterioration, depreciation, diminution, loss.

desmejorado [des-may-ho-rah'-do], *a.* **Queda muy desmejorada**, she's lost her looks.

desmejorar [des-may-ho-rar'], *va.* 1. To debase, to make worse. 2. *(Med.)* To weaken, to affect the health of. *-vr.* 1. To decay, to decline, to grow worse. 2. To lose one's looks, to look less attractive; *(Med.)* To lose one's health.

desmelancolizar [des-may-lan-co-le-thar'], *va.* To cheer, to enliven, to gladden.

desmelar [des-may-lar'], *va.* To take the honey from a hive.

desmelenado [des-may-lay-nah'-do], *a.* Dishevelled, tousled.

desmelenar [des-may-lay-nar'], *va.* To dishevel, to disarrange the hair. *-vr.* 1. To spruce up, to pull one's socks up. 2. To sail into action.

desmembración, desmembradura [des-mem-brah-the-on', des-mem-brah-doo'-rah], *f.* Dismemberment, division.

desmembrador, ra [des-mem-brah-dor', rah], *m. & f.* Divider, one who dismembers or divides.

desmembrar [des-mem-brar'], *va.* 1. To dismember, to divide limb from limb, to tear asunder, to curtail. 2. To separate, to divide.

desmemoriado, da [des-may-mo-re-ah'-do, dah], *a.* Forgetful, having a poor memory.

desmemoriarse [des-may-mo-re-ar'-say], *vr.* To be forgetful, to forget.

desmenguar [des-men-goo-ar'], *va.* 1. To lessen; to defalcate. 2. *V.* MENGUAR.

desmentida [des-men-tee'-dah], *f.* or **desmentido**, *m.* The act of giving the lie.

desmentidor, ra [des-men-te-dor', rah], *m. & f.* One who convicts of a falsehood.

desmentir [des-men-teer'], *va.* 1. To give the lie, to convince of a falsehood. 2. To counterfeit, to conceal, to dissemble. 3. To do things unworthy of one's birth, character, or profession. 4. To lose the right line, to warp or to change from the true situation. 5. To fold a lady's handkerchief so that one point may fall short of the other. **Desmentir rotundamente una acusación**, to deny a charge flatly. *-vr.* 1. To recant, retract. 2. Not to behave in accord with what has been said, to be lie.

desmenuzable [des-may-noo-thah'-blay], *a.* Friable, brittle, crisp, crimp, easily crumbled.

desmenuzador, ra [des-may-noo-thah-dor', rah], *m. & f.* A scrutator or investigator; a purifier.

desmenuzar [des-may-noo-thar'], *va.* 1. To crumble, to comminute, to crumb, to chip, to mill, to fritter. 2. *(Met.)* To sift, to examine minutely. *-vr.* To crumble, to fall into small pieces.

desmeollado, da [des-may-ol-lyah'-do, dah], *a.* Silly, simple, crackbrained.

desmeollar [des-may-ol-lyar'], *va.* To take out the marrow or pith.

desmerecedor [des-may-ray-thay-dor'], *m.* An unworthy, undeserving person.

desmerecer [des-may-ray-therr']. *va.* To demerit, to become unworthy or undeserving of a thing. *-vn.* 1. To lose part of its worth. 2. To grow worse, to deteriorate. 3. **Desmerecer de**, to compare unfavorably with.

desmerecimiento [des-may-ray-the-me-en'-to], *m.* Demerit, unworthiness.

desmesura [des-may-soo'-rah], *f.* 1. Excess, want of moderation and order. 2. Impudence, insolence; rudeness.

desmesuradamente [des-may-soo-rah'-dah-men-tay], *adv.* 1. Immeasurably. 2. Uncivilly, impudently.

desmesurado, da [des-may-soo-rah'-do, dah], *a.* 1. Immeasurable. 2. Huge, of gigantic stature or size. 3. Unmeasurable. *-pp.* of DESMESURAR.

desmesurar [des-may-soo-rar'], *va.* To disorder, to discompose, to perturbate. *-vr.* To be forward, to act or talk with impudence or insolence, to be rude.

desmidiáceo, cea [des-me-de-ah'-thay-o, theah], *a.* Like a desmid, desmidaceous.

desmigajar [des-me-gah-har'], *va.* To crumble, to comminute. *-vr.* To crumble.

desmigar [des-me-gar'], *va.* To crumble bread.

desmilitarización [des-me-le-tah-re-thah-the-on'], *m.* Demilitarization.

desmilitarizar [des-me-le-tah-re-thar'], *va.* To demilitarize.

desmirriado, da [des-mir-re-ah-do, dah], *a. (Coll.)* 1. Lean, extenuated, exhausted. 2. Melancholy,

desmocha [des-mo'-chah], *f.* 1. Lopping or cutting off. 2. Diminution or destruction of a great part of a thing.

desmochadura [des-mo-chah-doo'-rah], *f. V.* DESMOCHE.

desmochar [des-mo-char'], *va..* 1. To lop or cut off, to mutilate. 2. To unhorn (venado).

desmoche [des-mo'-chay], *m.* Truncation, mutilation.

desmocho [des-mo'-cho], *m.* Heap of things lopped or cut off.

desmogar [des-mo-gar'], *vn.* To cast the horns (venados).

desmografía [des-mo-grah-fee'-ah], *f.* Desmography, a description of the ligaments.

desmogue [des-mo'-gay], *m.* Act of casting the horns (vendados).

desmolado, da [des-mo-lah'-do, dah], *a.* Toothless, having no grinders.

desmoldamiento [des-mo-le-dah-men'-to], or **desmolde** [des-mo-le'-day], *m.* Removal of a casting from the mould.

desmoldar [des-mo-le-dar'], *va.* To remove from the mould, to strike the frame.

desmología [des-mo-lo-hee'-ah], *f.* Desmology, anatomical description of ligaments.

desmonetizar [des-mo-nay-te-thar'], *va.* 1. To convert money into bullion for other purposes. 2. To demonetize, deprive of legal-tender value.

desmontable [des-mon-tah'-blay], *a.* Detachable; sectional, in sections, which takes apart. *-m.* Tire level.

desmontador, ra [des-mon-tah-dor', rah], *m. & f.* 1. One who fells wood. 2. Dismounter.

desmontadura [des-mon-tah-doo'-rah], *f.* Felling timber, clearing from shrubbery.

desmontar [des-mon-tar'], *va.* 1. To fell or cut down wood. 2. To remove a heap of dirt or garbage. 3. To uncock firearms, to take an instrument to pieces. 4. To dismount a troop of horse, to dismount cannon. 5. **Desmontar el timón**, *(Naut.)* To unhang the rudder. *-vn.* To dismount, to alight from a horse, mule, etc.

desmonte [des-mon'-tay], *m.* 1. Felling, the act of cutting down, as timber. 2. The timber remaining on the spot. 3. Clearing a wood from trees, shrubbery, etc.

desmonterado, da [des-mon-tay-rah'-do, dah], *a.* Without the sort of cap named *montera.*

desmoñar [des-mo-nyar'], *va. (Coll.)* To undo the toupee of the hair, to loosen the hair.

desmoralización [des-mo-rah-le-thah-the-on'], *f.* Demoralization, corruption or depravation of morals; depravity.

desmoralizado, da [des-mo-rah-le-thah'-do, dah], *a. & pp.* of DESMORALIZAR. Demoralized, depraved, corrupted.

desmoralizador [des-mo-rah-le-thah-dor'], *a.* Demoralizing.

desmoralizar [des-mo-rah-le-thar'], *va.* To demoralize, to corrupt, to deprave. *-vr. (Mil.)* To relax the discipline of an army.

desmoronadizo, za [des-mo-ro-nah-dee'-tho, trah], *a.* Easily mouldered.

desmoronado [des-mo-ro-nah'-do], *a.* Tumbledown, ruinous, dilapidated.

desmoronamiento [des-mo-ro-nah-me-ayn'-to], *m.* Crumbling, dilapidation, decay; collapse.

desmoronar [des-mo-ro-nar'], *va.* 1. To destroy little by little, to ruin by insensible degrees. 2. *(Met.)* To cause to dwindle or moulder off. *-vr.* To moulder, to fall, to decay.

desmoso, sa [des-mo'-so, sah], *a.* Ligamentous.

desmostar [des-mos-tar'], *va.* To separate the must from the grapes. *-vn.* To ferment.

desmotadera [des-mo-tah-day'-rah], *f.* 1. Woman employed to take off knots and coarse naps from cloth. 2. An instrument used for removing knots from cloth; cloth nipper.

desmotar [des-mo-tar'], *va.* To clear cloth of knots and coarse naps.

desmovilización [des-mo-ve-le-thah-the-on'], *f.* Demobilization.

desmovilizar [des-mo-ve-le-thar'], *va.* To demobilize.

desmueblar [des-moo-ay-blar'], *va. V.* DESAMUEBLAR.

desmuelo [des-moo-ay'-lo], *m.* Want or loss of grinders.

desmugrador [des-moo-grah-dor'], *m.* Instrument which serves to clean wool or cloth of grease.

desmugrar [des-moo-grar'], *va.* To clean wool or cloth of grease.

desmuir [des-moo-eer'], *va.* To pick olives.

desmullir [des-mool-lyeer'], *va.* To discompose anything soft or bland.

desnacionalizar [des-nah-the-o-nah-le-thar'], *va. (Neol.)* To denationalize, to cause the loss of national characteristics.

desnarigar [des-nah-re-gar'], *va.* To cut off the nose.

desnatadora [des-nah-tah-do'-rah], *f.* Cream separator.

desnatar [des-nah-tar'], *va.* 1. To skim milk. **Leche sin desnatar**, whole milk. 2. To take the flower or choicest part of a thing.

desnaturalización [des-nah-too-rah-le-tha-the-on'], *f.* Expatriation, denaturalization.

desnaturalizado, da [des-nah-too-rah-le-thah'-do, dah], *a.* 1. Denatured. **Alcohol desnaturalizado**, denatured alcohol. 2. Unnatural; cruel, inhuman (persona).

desnaturalizar [des-nah-too-rah-le-thar'], *va.* To divest of the rights of naturalization, to deprive of the privileges of a citizen. *-vr.* To abandon one's country.

desnegar [des-nay-gar'], *va.* To contradict, to retract. *-vr.* To unsay, to retract, to recant.

desnervar [des-ner-var'], *va.* To enervate.

desnevado, da [des-nay-vah'-do, dah], *a.* Thawed, free from snow. *-pp.* of DESNEVAR.

desnevar [des-nay-var'], *va.* To thaw, to dissolve.

desnivel [des-ne-vel'], *m.* 1. Unevenness, inequality of the ground. 2. *(Fig.)* Inequality, difference, gap; lack of adjustment.

desnivelación [des-ne-vay-lah-the-on'], *f.* Making uneven.

desnivelado [des-ne-vay-lah'-do], *a.* 1. Uneven (terreno). 2. *(Fig.)* Unbalanced, badly adjusted (instrumento).

desnivelar [des-ne-vay-lar'], *va.* To make uneven or unequal. *-vn.* To lose its level.

desnucar [des-noo-car'], *va.* 1. To break the neck, to disjoint the nape. 2. To kill by a blow upon the nape. *-vr.* To break one's neck.

desnuclearizar [des-noo-clay-ah-re-thar'], *va.* To denuclearize. **Región desnuclearizada**, nuclear-free area.

desnudador [des-noo-dah-dor'], *m.* One that denudes.

desnudamente [des-noo-dah-men'-tay], *adv.* Nakedly; manifestly, plainly.

desnudar [des-noo-dar'], *va.* 1. To denudate, to denude, to strip off clothes or coverings; to fleece. 2. *(Met.)* To discover, to reveal. 3. *(Naut.)* To unrig. *-vr.* 1. To undress, to take off one's clothes. **Desnudarse hasta la cintura**, to strip to the waist. 2. *(Met.)* To deprive oneself of a thing.

desnudez [des-noo-deth'], *f.* Nudity, nakedness.

desnudismo [des-noo-dees'-moh], *m.* Nudism.

desnudo, da [des-noo'-do, dah], *a.* 1. Naked, bare, uncovered, ill-clothed. **En las paredes desnudas**, on the bare wall. **La ciudad quedó desnuda**, the town was flattened. 2. *(Met.)* Plain, evident, apparent. **Estar desnudo de**, to be devoid of. 3. Empty-handed, destitute of merit, interest, etc. **Y ahora están desnudos**, and now all they've got is what they stand up in.

desnudo [des-noo'-do], *m.* 1. *(Pict.)* A picture or statue without drapery; the nude. 2. Metal free from all foreign matter.

desnutrición [des-no-tre-the-on'], *f.* Malnutrition.

desnutrido [des-noo-tre'-do], *a.* Undernourished.

desobedecer [des-o-bay-day-therr'], *va.* To disobey. *(Yo desobedezco, yo desobedezca, from Desobedecer. V.* CONOCER.)

desobedecimiento [de-so-bay-day-the-me-en'-to], *m.* 1. Disobedience, incompliance. 2. Contempt of court.

desobediencia [de-so-bay-de-en'-the-ah], *f.* Disobedience; lawlessness. **Desobediencia civil**, civil disobedience.

desobediente [de-so-bay-de-en'-tay], *pa.* Disobedient.

desobedientemente [des-o-bay-de-ayn'-tay], *adv.* Disobediently.

desobligar [des-o-ble-gar'], *va.* 1. To release from an obligation. 2. To disoblige, to offend; to alienate the affections.

desobstruir [des-obs-troo-eer'], *va.* 1. To remove obstructions. 2. *(Med.)* To deobstruct.

desocupación [des-o-coo-pah-the-on'], *f.* Leisure, want of business or occupation.

desocupadamente [des-o-coo-pah'-dah-men-tay], *adv.* Deliberately, leisurely.

desocupado [des-o-coo-pah'-do], *a.* 1. Empty, vacant, unoccupied (silla, etc.). 2. Spare, free (tiempo). 3. Free, not busy; at leisure (persona).

desocupar [des-o-coo-par'], *va.* To evacuate, to quit, to empty. *-vr.* To disengage oneself from a business or occupation, to withdraw from.

desodorante [des-o-do-rahn'-tay], *m. & a.* Deodorant.

desofuscar [des-o-foos-car'], *va.* 1. To remove obscurity. 2. *(Met.)* To remove anyone's confusion.

desoir [des-o-eer'], *va.* To pretend not to hear.

desojar [des-o-har'], *va.* To break or burst (ojo de aguja). *-vr.* To strain one's eyes by looking steadily at a thing; to look intently.

desolación [day-so-lah-the-on'], *f.* 1. Desolation, destruction, havoc, extermination; fall. 2. Want of consolation or comfort, affliction.

desolado, da [day-so-lah'-do, dah], *a.* Desolate, disconsolate. **Estoy desolado por aquello**, I'm terribly grieved about that. *-pp.* of DESOLAR.

desolador, ra [day-so-lah-dor', rah], *m. & f.* Grieving.

desolar [day-so-lar'], *va.* To desolate, to lay waste, to harass. *-vr.* To grieve, to be distressed, to be disconsolate.

desolladamente [des-ol-lyah-dah-men'-tay], *adv. (Coll.)* Impudently, petulantly.

desolladero [des-ol-lyah-day'-ro], *m.* 1. A place where hides are taken off; slaughter-house. 2. An inn or shop, where exorbitant prices are charged.

desollado, da [day-sol-lyah'-do, dah], *a. (Coll.)* Forward, impudent, insolent. *-pp.* of DESOLLAR.

desollador [day-sol-lyah-dor'], *m.* 1. Flayer. 2. *(Prov.)* Slaughterhouse, a place where beasts are skinned. 3. *(Met.)* Extortioner. 4. Butcher-bird.

desolladura [day-sol-lyah-doo'-rah], *f.* Excoriation.

desollar [day-sol-lyar'], *va.* 1. To flay, to skin, to strip off the skin, to excoriate. 2. *(Met.)* To extort an immoderate price. 3. *(Naut.)* To pull at the creases of a sail, to reduce them to regular folds. **4.** Desollar vivo a uno, *(fig.)* To fleece somebody, to make somebody pay through the nose.

desonce [des-on'-thay], *m.* The discount of an ounce or ounces in each pound. *(Ant.)*

desonzar [des-on-thar'], *va.* To discount or deduct an ounce or ounces in the pound. *(Ant.)*

desopilar [des-o-pel-ar'], *va.* 1. To clear away obstructions. 2. *(Med.)* To remove retention or suppression of menstruation.

desopilativo, va. [des-o-pe-lah-tee'-vo, vah], *a.* Deobstruent.

desopinar [des-o-pe-nar'], *va.* To impeach one's characer, to defame.

desoprimir [des-o-pre-meer'], *va.* To free from oppression.

desorbitado [des-or-be-tah-do], *a.* 1. Disproportionate, excessive; exorbitant (precio); exaggerated (pretension etc.). 2. **Con los ojos desorbitados**, wild-eyed, pop-eyed.

desorbitante [des-or-be-tah'-dah-men-tay], *a.* Excessive, overwhelming.

desorbitar [des-or-be-tar'], *va.* 1. To carry to extremes; to exaggerate. 2. **Desorbitar un asunto**, to misinterpret. *-vr.* To go to extremes (persona).

desorden [desor'den], *m.* 1. Disorder, confusion, irregularity. 2. Lawlessness, license, excess, abuse. 3. Lack of symmetry of connection, in lyric poetry.

desordenadamente [des-or-day-nah-dah-men'-tay], *adv.* Disorderly, irregularly, confusedly.

desordenado, da [des-or-day-nah'-do, dah], *a.* 1. Disorderly, irregular, disordered, orderless. 2. Disorderly, lawless, licentious. *-pp.* of DESORDENAR.

desordenar [des-or-day-nar'], *va.* To disorder, to throw into confusion, to disturb, to confound or confuse. *-vr.* 1. To exceed or go beyond all rule: to be out of order, to be irregular. 2. To get unruly, to be unmanageable (caballo).

desorejado, da [des-o-ray-hah'-do, dah], *a. (Coll.)* Licentious, dissolute, degraded.

desorejador, ra [des-o-ray-hah-dor', ran], *m. & f.* One who crops off the ears.

desorejamiento [des-o-ray-hah-me-en'-to], *m.* Cropping the ears.

desorejar [des-o-ray-har'], *va.* To crop ears.

desorganización [des-or-gah-ne-thah-the-on'], *f.* Disorganization.

desorganizador [des-or-gah-ne-thah-dor'], *m.* Disorganizer.

desorganizar [des-or-gah-ne-thar'], *va.* 1. To disorganize. 2. To disconcert in the highest degree. 3. *(Chem.)* To decompose. 4. *(Mil.)* To disband an army. 5. To relax discipline. *-vr. (Med.)* To be altered, changed in texture, disorganized.

desorientado, da [des-o-re-en-tah'-do, dah], *a.* Disorientated, turned from the right direction. *-pp.* Of DESORIENTAR.

desorientar [des-o-re-en-tar'], *va.* 1. To lose or cause to lose one's bearings so as not to know one's position, geographically or morally. 2. To turn from the right direction, confuse. 3. To lose the way. **El nuevo cruce me desorientó**, the new junction made me lose my bearings. *-vr.* 1. To lose one's way, to lose one's bearings. 2. *(Fig.)* To go wrong, to go astray, to get off the track.

desorillar [des-o-reel-lyar'], *va.* 1. To cut off the selvage of cloth or other things. 2. To stretch skins well, so as not to form folds at the ends.

desortijado, da [day-sor-te-hah'-do, dah], *a. (Vet.)* Sprained (músculos de mulas y caballos). *-pp.* of DESORTIJAR.

desortijar [day-sor-te-har'], *va. (Agri.)* To hoe or weed plants the first time.

desosado, da [des-o-sah'-do, dah], *a.* Deprived of the bones. *-pp.* of DESOSAR.

desosar [des-o-sar'], *va.* To deprive of the bones. *-vn.* To be cowardly or fearful.

desoterrar [des-o-tayr-rahr'], *va.* To unbury, to dig up.

desovar [des-o-var'], *va.* To spawn.

desove [des-o'-vay], *m.* 1. Spawning. 2. The time in which fishes cast their spawn.

desovillar [des-o-vil-lyar'], *va.* 1. To unclew. 2. *(Met.)* To unravel, to disentangle, to clear up. 3. *(Met.)* To encourage, to animate.

desoxidación [des-ok-se-dah-the-on'], *f.* Deoxydization, removal of oxygen.

desoxidar [des-ok-se-dar'], *va.* To deoxydize, to remove oxygen from any compound.

desoxigenación [des-ok-se-hay-nah-the-on'], *f.* Deoxydation.

desoxigenar [des-ok-se-hay-nar'], *va.* To remove from a body the oxygen which it holds, to deoxydize.

despabiladeras [des-pah-be-lah-day'-ras], *f. pl.* Snuffers.

despabilado, da [des-pah-be-lah'-do, dah], *a. & pp.* of DESPABILAR. 1. Snuffed (velas). 2. *(Met.)* Watchful, vigilant in sleeping hours. 3. Lively, active, smart.

despabilador, ra [des-pah-be-lah-dor', rah], *m. & f.* Candlesnuffer; he who snuffs.

despabiladura [des-pah-be-lah-doo'-rah], *f.* Snuff of the candle.

despabilar [des-pah-be-lar'], *va.* 1. To snuff a candle. 2. *(Met.)* To cut off a superfluity. 3. *(Met.)* To despatch briefly or expeditiously. 4. *(Met.)* To rouse, to enliven. 5. *(Coll.)* To kill. **Despabilar el ingenio**, to sharpen the wits. *-vr.* To rouse, to wake from slunder, to be excited. **Vd. le verá despabilarse**, you will see him brighten up.

despacio [des-pah'-the-o], *adv.* 1. Slowly, leisurely; gently. 2. Insensibly, little by little. 3. Continually, without interruption.

¡despacio! *int.* Softly, gently.

despacito [des-pah-thee'-to], *adv.* 1. Very gently, softly. 2. Leisurely, very slowly.

despachado, da [des-pah-chah'-do, dah], *a.* 1. *(Coll.)* Impudent, bold-faced, brazen. 2. Resourceful, quick; business-like; practical. **Ir bien despachado de**, to be well off for. -*pp.* of DESPACHAR.

despachador [des-pah-chah-dor'], *m.* Expediter, one who despatches.

despachar [des-pah-char'], *va.* 1. To despatch, to expedite, to abridge, to facilitate. 2. To despatch, to pack, to send in a hurry; to lay by. 3. To despatch, to perform a business quickly, to cut off delays. 4. To decide and expedite suits and causes. 5. To dispose of goods and merchandise, to sell. 6. *(Met.)* To despatch, to send out of the world. **Despachar un barco**, to clear a vessel at the custom-house. **Despachar géneros** or **mercaderías en la aduana**, to clear, or take out goods or merchandise at the custom-house. **Despachar asuntos con el gerente**, to do business with the manager, -*vr.* 1. To accelerate, to make haste. 2. To finish off. **Suelo despacharme a las 5**, I finish at 5. **Despacharse a su gusto con uno**, to say what one really thinks to somebody. -*vn.* 1. In offices, to carry papers drawn up for the signature of the principal. 2. *(Com.)* To expend, to let goods go for money or barter. 3. To serve a shop. **No despacha los domingos**, he doesn't do business on Sundays. 4. To hurry up. 5. To finish things off.

despacho [des-pah'-cho], *m.* 1. Expedient, determination. 2. Despatch expedition. 3. **Custom, application from buyers**. 4. Cabinet, office, counting-house. 5. Commission, warrant, patent. 6. Despatch, correspondence by telegraph. **Secretario del despacho**, sectetary of state. 7. Resourcefulness, quickness of mind; business sense; efficiency. **Tener buen despacho**, to be very efficient. 8. Sale. **Géneros sin despacho**, unsaleable goods.

despachurrado, da [des-pah-choor-rah'-do, dah], *a.* Pressed to leave one. **Dejar a uno despachurrado**, *(Coll.)* to leave one stupefied. **Es un despachurrado**, *(Coll.)* he is a ridiculous, insipid fellow. -*pp.* of DESPACHURRAR.

despachurrar [des-pah-choor-rar'], *va.* *(Coll.)* 1. To press together, to squash, to rush. 2. *(Met.)* To make a speech, to obscure a subject by a bad explanation. 3. *(Met.)* To confound one by a smart repartee. **Despachurrar el cuento**, to interrupt a story and prevent its conclusion.

despajador, ra [des-pah-hah-dor', rah], *m. & f.* One who winnows.

despajadura [des-pah-hah-doo-rah], *f.* Winnowing.

despajar [des-pah-har'], *va.* To winnow.

despaje [des-pah'-hay], **despajo** [des-pah'ho], *m.* Winnowing or cleaning grain.

despaldillar [des-pal-dil-lyar'], *va.* To dislocate or break the shoulder or back of an animal. -*vr.* To disjoint or dislocate one's shoulder-blade.

despalillar [des-pah-leel-lyar'], *va.* To remove the stems from raisins, to strip tobacco, etc.

despalmador [des-pal-mah-dor'], *m.* *(Naut.)* Careening-place, dockyard.

despalmadura [des-pahl-mah-doo'-rah], *f.* or **despalme** [des-pahl'-may], *m.* Calking, paying the bottom.

despalmar [des-pal-mar'], *va.* 1. *(Naut.)* To grave, to calk. 2. To pare off a horse's hoof.

despampanador [des-pam-pah-nah-dor'], *m.* Pruner of vines.

despampanadura [des-pam-pah-nah-doo'-rah], *f.* Act of pruning vines.

despampanante [des-pahm-pah.-nahn'-tay], *a.* Stunning.

despampanar [des-pam-pah-nar'], *va.* 1. To prune vines. 2. *(Met. Coll.)* To unbosom, to give vent to one's feelings. 3. *vr.* *(Coll.)* To pity much, to be very sorry, to grieve.

despampanillar [des-pam-pah-nil-lyar'], *va.* To prune grapevines.

despamplonador, ra [des-pam-plo-nah-dor', rah], *m. & f.* One who separates vine-stems.

despamplonar [des-pam-plo-nar'], *va.* To make space between the shoots of the vine or shrub when they are very close. -*vr.* *(Met.)* To get dislocated (mano).

despanado da [des-pan-nah'-do, dah], *a.* *(Prov. Coll.)* Breadless, in want of bread. -*pp.* of DESPANAR.

despanar [des-pan-nar'], *va.* *(Prov.)* To remove the reaped corn from the field.

despancijar, despanzurrar [des-pan-the-har', des-pan-thoor-rar'], *va.* *(Coll.)* To burst the belly.

despapar [des-pah-par'], *vn.* To carry the head too high (caballo).

desparcir [des-par-theer'], *va.* *(Prov.)* To scatter, to disseminate.

desparecer [des-pah-ray-therr'], *vn.* To disappear. *V.* DESAPARECER. -*vr.* To be unlike or dissimilar.

desparejar [des-pah-ray-har'], *va.* To make unequal or uneven.

desparpajado, da [des-par-pah-hah'-do, dah], *a. & pp.* of DESPARPAJAR. Pert, petulant, garrulous.

desparpajar [des-par-pah-har'], *va.* 1. To undo in a disolderly manner. 2. *(Coll.)* To rant, to prattle at random.

desparpajo [des-par-pah'-ho], *m.* 1. *(Coll.)* Pertness of speech or action, self-confidence; naturalness; charm. 2. Savoir-faire, practical know-how; sharpness, quickness of mind. 3. *(CAm.)* Disorder, muddle. 4. *(And.)* Flippant remark (comentario).

desparramado, da [des-par-rah-mah'-do, dah], *a.* Wide, open. -*pp.* of DESPARRAMAR.

desparramador, ra [des-par-rah-mah-dor', rah], *m. & f.* Disperser, dilapidator; prodigal, waster, spendthrift.

desparramamiento [des-par-rah-ma-me-en'-to], *m.* Squandering, extravagance, dissipation.

desparramar [des-par-rah-mar'], *va.* 1. To scatter, to disseminate, to overspread. 2. To squander, to dissipate, to lavish. -*vr.* To give oneself up to pleasures with extravagance and excess, to be dissipated.

despartidor [des-par-te-dor'], *m.* Pacificator.

despartir [des-par-teer'], *va.* 1. To dispart, to part, to divide. 2. To conciliate.

desparvar [des-par-var'], *va.* To take the sheaves of corn out of the stack or rick to be thrashed.

despasar [des-pah-sar'], *va.* 1. To draw a cord or ribbon from a button-hole or seam. 2. *(Naut.)* To unreeve a cable from the blocks. 3. When sailing along the coast to keep the course until the wind is received in the same position on the opposite side.

despasmarse [des-pas-mar'-say], *vr.* To recover oneself from a stupor or spasm.

despatarrado, da [des-pah-tar-rah'-do, dah], *a.* **Quedar** or **dejar a uno despatarrado**, *(Coll.)* to leave one astonished, abashed, or stupefied. -*pp.* of DESPATARRAR.

despatarrar [des-pah-tar-rar'], *va.* To silence, to oblige one to be silent. -*vr.* 1. To slip and fall on the ground. 2. To be stupefied, to remain motionless.

despavorido [des-paha-vo-re'-do], *a.* **Estar despavorido**, to be utterly terrified.

despatillar [des-pah-til-lyar'], *va.* 1. To cut grooves or mortises in wood. 2. *(Naut.)* To break off the arm of an anchor by its getting caught in rocks on the bottom. 3. -*vr.* *(Coll.)* To shave oneself.

despavesadura [des-pah-vay-sah-doo'-rah], *f.* The act of snuffing the candle.

despavesar [des-pah-vay-sar'], *va.* To snuff the candle.

despavoridamente [des-pah-vo-red-ah-men'-tay], *adv.* Terrifiedly, aghast.

despavorir [des-pah-vo-reer'], *vn. & vr.* To be terrified, to be frightened, to be aghast. Defective verb: it is used only in the infinitive and past participle.

despearse [des-pay-ar'-say], *vr.* To bruise the feet or make them sore by much walking.

despectivamente [des-pec-tee'-vah-men-tay], *adv.* Contemptuously, scornfully; in derogatory terms.

despectivo, va [des-pec-tee'-vo, vah], *a.* Depreciatory; denoting contempt.

despechadamente [des-pay-chah-dah-men'-tay], *adv.* Angrily, spitefully.

despechado [des-pay-chah-do], *a.* Angry, indignant; spiteful.

despechador [des-pay-chah-dor'], *m.* Extortioner, tormentor, oppressor.

despechamiento [des-pay-chah-me-en'-to], *m.* Act of enraging or overburdening.

despechar [des-pay-char'], *va.* 1. To enrage, to excite indignation. 2. To overwhelm with taxes. *-vr.* 1. To fret, to be peevish. 2. To lose all hope, to despair.

despecho [des-pay'-cho], *m.* 1. Indignation, displeasure, wrath. 2. Asperity, harshness of temper. 3. Despite spite, defiance. **Por despecho**, out of spite. 4. Dejection, dismay, despair. 5. Disrespect, insolence. 6. Deceit, infidelity. 7. Derision, scores. **A despecho**, in spite of, in defiance of, against one's will.

despechugadura [des-pay-choo-gah-doo'-rah], *f.* Act of cutting of or uncovering the breast.

despechugar [des-pay-choo-gar'], *va.* To cut off the breast of a fowl. *-vr.* To uncover the breast, to walk with the breast open.

despedazador, ra [des-pay-dah-thah-dor', ah], *m. & f.* Dissector, lacerator, mangler.

despedazamiento [des-pay-dah-thah-me-en'-to], *m.* Laceration, dissection, cutting to pieces; mangling.

despedazar [des-pay-dah-thar'], *va.* 1. To cut into bits, to tear into pieces, to cut asunder, to limb, to claw. 2. *(Met.)* To lacerate, to destroy, to mangle. **Despedazarse de risa**, to burst into a fit of laughter.

despedida [des-pay-dee'-dah], *f.* 1. Leave-taking, farewell, leave. **Cena de despedida**, farewell dinner. **Regalo de despedida**, parting gift. 2. Dismission, dismissal. 3. *(Liter. etc.)* Envoi; *(Mus.)* Final verse; closing formula (en carta).

despedir [des-pay-deer'], *va.* 1. To emit, to discharge, to dart. 2. To dismiss from office, to discard. 3. To remove, to lay by. 4. To accompany through courtesy a departing guest. **Fuimos a despedirle a la estación**, we went to see him off at the station. 5. To diffuse, disperse odour, rays of light, etc. **Despedir la vida**, to die. *-vr.* 1. To take leave, to say, some expression of courtesy. **Se despidieron**, they said goodbye to each other. 2. To renounce something temporarily or perpetually. 3. To go out from service, to leave one's occupation.

despedrar [des-pay-drar'], *va. (Prov.) V.* DESPEDREGAR.

despedregar [des-pay-dray-gar'], *va.* To clear a field or other place of stones.

despegable [des-pay-gah'-blay], *a.* Dissoluble, dissolvable.

despegadamente [des-pay-gah-blay], *adv.* Roughly, harshly, disgustingly.

despegado, da [des-pay-gah'-do, dah], *a. & pp.* of DESPEGAR. Rough, morose, sullen, sour of temper, disgusting, unpleasant, harsh; separated.

despegadura [des-pay-gah-doo'-rah], *f.* Dissolving, separating.

despegamiento [des-pay-gah-me-en'-to], *m. V.* DESAPEGO.

despegar [des-pay-gar'], *va.* To unglue, to separate, to disjoin. **Despegar los labios**, to speak, to open one's lips, to break silence. *-vn.* To take off (avión). *-vr.* 1. To grow apart, to withdraw one's affections (from someone). 2. To become alienated, to become detached. **Despegarse de los amigos**, to break with one's friends.

despego [des-pay'-go], *m.* 1. Asperity, moroseness, coyness. 2. Displeasure, aversion. 3. Coldness, indifference.

despegue [des-pay'-gay], *m. (Aer.)* 1. Take off. 2. Blast-off. **Despegue de emergencia**, *(Aer.)* scramble. **Despegue vertical**, vertical take-off.

despeinado [des-pay-e-nah'-do], *a.* Dishevelled, tousled; unkempt.

despeinar [des-pay-e-nar'], *va.* To disarrange the hair of. *-vr. (Fig.)* To make a great effort, to get really involved.

despejadamente [des-pay-hah-dah-men'-tay], *adv.* Expeditiously, readily, freely

despejado, da [des-pay-hah'-do, dah], *a.* 1. Sprightly, smart, quick, vivacious, sagacious, dexterous, clean. 2. Clear, disengaged. 3. Wide-awake; *(Med.)* Free of fever; lucid. *-pp.* of DESPEJAR.

despejar [des-pay-har'], *va.* To remove impediments, to surmount obstacles to clear away obstructions. **Despejen la sala**, clear the room. **Los bomberos despejaron el teatro**, the firemen cleared the theater. *-vr.* 1. To cheer up, to amuse oneself. 2. To acquire or show looseness in behavior. 3. To be relieved of pain (paciente). 4. *(Math.)* To discover the unknown. **Despejarse el cielo, el día, el tiempo**, to become clear, serene weather.

despeje [des-pay-hay], *m.* 1. *(Dep.)* Clearance. 2. Clarity (de mente).

despejo [despay'ho], *m.* 1. The act of removing obstacles or clearing away impediments. 2. Sprightliness, smartness, liveliness, vivacity, briskness; grace, ease.

despelotar [des-pay-lo-tar'], *va.* 1. To dishevel the hair. 2. To strip, to undress, *-vr.* To strip off, to undress.

despelote [des-pay-lo-tay], *m.* 1. Nudity, nakedness; strip. 2. *(Carib.)* Big spree (juerga).

despeluzamiento [des-pay-loo-thah-me-en'-to], *m.* Act of making hair stand on end, horripilation.

despeluzar, despeluznar [des-pay-loo-thar', des-pay-looth-nar'], *va.* To make hair stand on end (miedo, terror). *-vr.* 1. To stand on end (pelo). 2. To be horrified (persona).

despellejadura [des-pel-lyay-hah-doo'-rah], *f.* 1. Scratch, a slight wound. 2. Skinning.

despellejar [des-pel-lyay-har'], *va.* 1. To skin. **Despellejar un conejo**, to uncase a rabbit. 2. *(Fig.)* To flay, to criticize unmercifully (criticar). 3. **Despellejar a uno**, to fleece somebody.

despenador, ra [des-pay-nah-dor', rah], *m. & f.* One who relieves pain.

despenalización [des-pay-nah-le-thah-the-on'], *f.* Legalization; decriminalization.

despenalizar [des-pay-nah-le-thar'], *va.* To legalize; to decriminalize.

despenar [des-pay-nar'], *va.* 1. To relieve from pain. 2. *(Met.)* To kill.

despendedor, ra [des-pen-day-dor', rah]. *m. & f.* Spendthrift, prodigal.

despender [des-pen-derr'], *va.* To spend, to expend, to waste, to squander.

despensa [des-pen'-sah], *f.* 1. Pantry, larder. 2. Store of provisions for a journey. 3. Butlership. 4. The provisions that are bought for daily use; marketing. 5. Contract to provide a horse with hay, straw, and barley, all year. 6. *(Naut.)* Steward's room.

despensería [des-pen-say-ree'-ah], *f.* Office of steward.

despensero, ra [des-pen-say'-ro, rah], *m. & f.* 1. Butler, caterer; *(Naut.)* steward on board of ships. 2. Dispenser, distributer.

despeñadero [des-pay-nyah-day'-ro], *m.* 1. Precipice, crag. 2. *(Met.)* A bold and dangerous undertaking.

despeñadero, ra [des-pay-nyah-day-ro, rah], *a.* Steep, precipitous, headlong.

despeñadizo, za [des-pay-nyah-dee'-tho, thah], *a.* 1. Steep, precipitous. 2. Glib, slippery.

despeñar [des-pay-nyar'], *va*. To precipitate, to fling down a precipice. *-vr*. To precipitate oneself, to throw oneself headlong.

despeño, despeñamiento [des-pay'-nyo, des-pay-nyah-me-en'-to], *m*. 1. A precipitate fall. 2. Destruction of character or credit. 3. Diarrhoea.

despepitador [des-pay-pe-tah-dor'], *m*. An instrument for removing cores or stones of fruit. *-va*. To remove the seeds from a melon or other fruit; to stone.

despepitar [des-pay-pe-tar'], *vr*. To give license to one's tongue, to vociferate, to speak rashly and inconsiderately, to act imprudently. *-va*. To remove the pips from.

despercudir [des-per-coo-deer'], *va*. To clean or wash what is greasy.

desperdiciadamente [des-per-de-the-ah'-dah-men-tay], *adv*. Profusely, wastefully.

desperdiciado, da [des-per-de-the-ah'-do, dah], *a. & pp*. of DESPERDICIAR. Wasted, destroyed, squandered.

desperdiciador, ra [des-per-de-the-ah-dor', rah], *m. & f*. Spendthrift, squanderer, lavisher.

desperdiciar [des-per-de-the-ar'], *va*. 1. To squander, to misspend, to fling away. 2. To lose, not to avail oneself of, not to utilize.

desperdicio [des-per-dee'-the-o], *m*. 1. Prodigality, profusion, waste. 2. Residuum, relics, remains, garbage. **Desperdicios de cuero**, furrier's waste. **El muchacho no tiene desperdicio**, he's a fine lad.

desperdigar [des-per-de-gar'], *va*. To separate, to disjoin, to scatter. *-vr*. To scatter, to separate.

desperecerse [des-pay-ray-therr'-say], *vr*. To crave, to desire eagerly. **Desperecerse de risa**, to laugh heartily.

desperezarse [des-pay-ray-thar'-say], *va*. To put away sloth. *-vr*. To stretch one's limbs on being roused from sleep.

desperezo [des-pay-ray'-tho], *m. V*. ESPEREZO.

desperfecto [des-per-fec'-to], *m*. 1. Deterioration, loss. 2. Injury which possessions suffer by the neglect or fault of the owner. **Sufrió algunos desperfectos en el accidente**, it suffered slight damage in the accident.

desperfilar [des-per-fe-lar'], *va. (Pict.)* To soften the lines of a painting. *-vr*. To lose the posture of a profile line or contour.

despergaminar [des-per-gah-me-nar'], *va*. To hull, to decorticate.

despernada [des-per-nah'-ah], *f*. A motion in dancing.

despernado, da [des-per-nah'-do, dah], *a*. Weary, fatigued, tired. *-pp*. of DESPERNAR.

despernar [des-per-nar'], *va*. To maim, to cripple, or cut off one's legs. *-vr*. To be worn out, to crippled from walking.

desperpentar [des-per-pen-tar'], *va. (Prov.)* To cut off with one stroke.

despertador, ra [des-per-tah-dor', rah], *m. & f*. 1. Awakener, one who awakes or rouses out of sleep. 2. Alarm bell in clocks: an alarm-clock. 3. Causing wakefulness, care, or anxiety.

despertamiento [des-per-tah-me-en'-to], *m*. Awakening. 2. Excitation, the act of rousing or awakening.

despertar [des-per-tar'], *va*. 1. To awake, to awaken. 2. To awaken, to excite, to put in motion. 3. To enliven, to make lively or sprightly. 4. To call to recollection. *-vn*. 1. To awake, to break from sleep. 2. To revive, to grow lively or sprightly.

despesar [des-pay-sar'], *m*. Displeasure, aversion, dislike.

despestañarse [des-pes-tah-nyar'-say], *va*. To pluck out eyelashes. *-vr*. 1. To look steadfastly at anything, to inspect it closely. 2. *(Met.)* To apply oneself attentively to business.

despezar [des-pay-thar'], *va*. 1. To dispose and arrange stones at a proper distance. 2. To make thinner at the end, applied to tubes and pipes.

despezo [des-pay'-tho], *m*. Diminution of one end of a tube or pipe. **Despezos**, faces of stone, where they join each other.

despezonar [des-pay-tho-nar'], *va*. 1. To cut off the end of a thing, to break off the stalk of fruit. 2. To divide, to separate. *-vr*. To break off (tallos de fruta).

despiadadamente [des-pe-ah-dah-dah-men-tay], *adv*. Cruelly; mercilessly, relentlessly; heartlessly.

despiadado, da [des-pe-ah-dah'-do, dah], *a*. Impious, cruel. *V*. DESAPIADADO.

despicar [des-pe-car'], *va*. To satisfy, to gratify. *-vr*. To take revenge.

despicarazar [des-pe-cah-ra-thar'], *va. (Prov.)* To pick figs (pájaros).

despichar [des-pe-char'], *va*. 1. *(Prov.)* To pick grapes; to seed grapes before pressing them. 2. To expel or discharge moisture or humor. 3. *(Coll.)* To die.

despidida [des-pe-dee'-dah], *f. (Prov.)* Gutter, a passage for water.

despido [des-pee'-do], *m*. 1. Despatch. 2. Dismissal. **Despido improcedente**, wrongful dismissal. *(Yo despido, él despidió, yo despida, from Despedir. V. PEDIR.)*.

despiertamente [des-pe-er-tah-men'-tay], *adv*. Acutely, ingeniously, cleverly.

despierto, ta [des-pe-err'-to, tah], *a*. 1. Awake. 2. Vigilant, watchful, diligent. 3. Brisk, sprightly, lively, smart, clearsighted. *(Yo despierto, yo despierte, from Despertar. V. ACERTAR.)*

despiezo [des-pe-ay'-tho], *m. (Arch.)* Juncture or bed of one stone on another.

despilarar [des-pe-lah-rar'], *va. (Min.)* To take away the pillars of ore-bearing rock.

despilfarradamente [des-pel-fahr-rah-dah'-men-tay], *adv*. Wastefully; slovenly.

despilfarrado, da [des-peel-far-rah'-do, dah], *a*. 1. Prodigal, wasteful. 2. Ragged, in tatters. *-pp*. of DESPILFARRAR.

despilfarrador, ra [des-peel-far-rah-dor', rah], *a*. Spendthrift, wasteful.

despilfarrar [des-peel-far-rar'], *va*. To destroy or waste with slovenliness, of prodigality.

despilfarro [des-peel-far'-ro], *m*. 1. Slovenliness, uncleanliness. 2. Waste, mismanagement, lavishness. 3. Misgovernment in public affairs.

despimpollar [des-pim-pol-lyar'], *va*. To prune away useless stems from plants.

despinces [des-peen'-thays], *m. pl*. Tweezers. *V*. PINZAS.

despintar [des-pin-tar'], *va*. 1. To blot or efface what is painted. 2. *(Met.)* To obscure things or make them less intelligible; to mislead. *-vn*. To degenerate. *-vr*. 1. To be deceived by mistaking one card for another. **No despintársele a uno alguna person o cosa**, not to forget the appearance of a person or thing. 2. To wash off (con la lluvia etc.); To lose its color.

despinzadera [des-pin-thah-day'-rah], *f*. 1. Woman that plucks the knots off cloth. *-pl*. 2. Tweezers.

despinzar [des-pin-thar'], *va*. To pick off the knots, hair, or straw from clothes.

despiojar [des-pe-o-har'], *va*. 1. To louse, to clean of lice. 2. *(Met. Coll.)* To trim or dress, to relieve from misery.

despique [des-pee'-kay], *m*. Vengeance, revenge.

despiritado, da [des-pe-re-tah'-do, dah], *a*. Languid, spiritless.

despistado, da [des-pes-tah-do], *a. m & f*. Vague, absent-minded; unpractical; hopeless. 2. Confused, out of touch; off the beam. **Ando muy despistado con todo esto**, I'm terribly muddled about all this.

despistar [des-pis-tar'], *va*. 1. To turn from the right trail. 2. *(Fig.)* To put off the scent; to mislead. **Esa pregunta está hecha para despistar**, that question is designed to mislead people. *-vr. (Fig.)* To go wrong; to take the wrong route.

despiste [des-pis'-tay], *m*. 1. *(Aut. etc.)* Swerve. 2. Mistake. 3. Absent-minded; muddle; confusion, bewilderment. **Tiene un terrible despiste**, he's terribly absent-minded.

despizcar [des-pith-car'], *va*. To comminute, to break or cut into small bits. -*vr*. To make the utmost exertions, to use one's best endeavors.

desplacer [des-plah-therr'], *m*. Displeasure, disgust, disobligation.

desplacer [des-plah-therr'], *va*. To displease, to disgust.

desplantación [des-plan-tah-the-on'], *f*. Eradication, displantation.

desplantador, ra [des-plan-tah-dor', rah], *m*. & *f*. One who eradicates, eradicator. -*m*. A trowel, scoop trowel.

desplantar [des-plan-tar'], *va*. To eradicate. *V*. DESARRAIGAR. -*vr*. To lose one's erect posture in fencing or dancing; to dismount artillery.

desplante [des-plahn'-tay], *m*. 1. An oblique posture in fencing. 2. Outspoken remark; impudent remark, cutting remark. **Me dio un desplante**, he left me stunned. 3. Lack of respect.

desplatar [des-plah-tar'], *va*. To separate silver from other substances with which it is mixed.

desplate [des-plah'-tay], *m*. The act of separating silver from other metals or substances.

desplazado, da [des-plah-thah-do], *a*. *m* & *f*. 1. Displaced, wrongly placed (objeto). 2. Badly adjusted (persona). **Sentirse un poco desplazado**, to feel rather out of place.

desplazamiento [des-plah-thah-me-en'-to], *m*. 1. (*Obs.*) Displacement, change of place. 2. (*Naut.*) Displacement of a vessel. 3. Journey, trip. **Reside en Madrid aunque con frecuentes desplazamientos**, she lives in Madrid but is often away.

desplazar [des-plah-thar'], *va*. 1. (*Ant.*) To displace. 2. (*Naut.*) To displace. 3. To displace (persona). -*vr*. 1. To move (objeto). 2. To go, to travel; to move away, to move out. **Tiene que desplazarse todos los días 25 kms**, he has to travel 25 kms every day.

desplegable [des-play-gah-blay], *m*. Folder, brochure.

desplegadura [des-play-gah-doo'-rah], *f*. Explication, unfolding, elucidation.

desplegar [des-play-gar'], *va*. 1. To unfold, to display, to expand, to spread, to lay out, to lay before. 2. (*Met.*) To explain, to elucidate. 3. (*Naut.*) To unfurl. **Desplegar las velas**, to unfurl the sails. **Desplegar la bandera**, to hoist the flag. -*vr*. 1. To open, unfold (flores). 2. To spread out (tropas). 3. To execute a maneuvre. 4. To acquire ease and freedom in his movements by good teaching (caballos).

despleguetear [des-play-gay-tay-ar'], *va*. (*Agri.*) To remove the folds from the tendrils of vines.

despliegue [des-ple-ay'-gay], *m*. 1. Unfurling, unfolding. 2. (*Mil.*) Change from the order of march to that of battle, or to form in line fronting a given position. 3. (*Fig.*) Manifestation, display, show.

desplomar [des-plo-mar'], *va*. To make a wall, building, etc., to bulge out. -*vr*. 1. To deviate from a perpendicular line, to sag (pared). **Se ha desplomado el techo**, the ceiling has fallen in. 2. (*Met.*) To fall flat to the ground.

desplome [des-ploh'-may], *m*. Collapse, downfall, toppling.

desplomo [des-plo'-mo], *m*. The bulging or jutting out of a wall.

desplumadura [des-ploo-mah-doo'-rah], *f*. Deplumation.

desplumar [des-ploo-mar'], *va*. 1. To deplume, to pluck, to strip off feathers. 2. (*Met.*) To despoil or strip one of his property. 3. (*Naut.*) To dismast an enemy's ship. -*vr*. To moult feathers.

despoblación, despoblada [des-po-blah-the-on'], *f*. Depopulation. **Desploblación rural**, rural depopulation.

despoblado [des-po-blah-do'], *m*. Desert, an uninhabited place. **Despoblado, da**, *a*. & *pp*. of DESPOBLAR, Depopulated.

despoblador, ra [des-po-blah-dor', rah], *a*. Which depopulates.

despoblar [des-po-blar'], *va*. 1. To depopulate, to dispeople. 2. To despoil or desolate a place. **Despoblar una zona de árboles**, to clear an area of trees. -*vr*. To depopulate, to become deserted.

despojador, ra [des-po-hah-dor', rah], *m*. & *f*. Despoiler, spoiler.

despojar [des-po-har'], *va*. 1. To despoil or strip one of his property. 2. To deprive of, to cut off from, judicially. 3. To dismiss, to turn out of a place or employment. -*vr*. 1. To undress. 2. To relinquish, to forsake.

despojo [des-po'-ho], *m*. 1. Despoliation, spoliation. 2. Plunder, spoils. **La hermosura es despojo del tiempo**, beauty is the spoil of time. 3. Slough, the cast-off skin of a serpent. 4. Head, pluck, and feet of animals. -*pl*. 1. Leavings, scraps of the table. **Despojos de hierro**, scrap iron. 2. Giblets, the wings, neck, heart, and gizzard of fowls

despolarización [des-po-lah-re-thah-the-on'], *f*. Depolarization.

despolarizar [des-po-lah-re-thar'], *va*. To depolarize.

despolitización [des-po-le-te-thah-the-on'], *f*. Depoliticization.

despolitizar [des-po-le-te-thar'], *va*. To depoliticize.

despolvar [des-pol-var'], *va*. To remove the dust.

despolvorear [des-pol-vo-ra-yar'], *va*. 1. To dust. 2. (*Met.*) To separate, to scatter, to dissipate. (*Coll.*) To sprinkle.

desponerse [des-po-nerr'-say], *vr*. To cease laying eggs (aves).

despopularizar [des-po-poo-lah-re-thar'], *va*. & *vr*. To deprive of; or to lose one's popularity.

desportillar [des-por-til-lyar'], *pa*. To break the neck of a bottle, pot, etc. (*Arch.*) To splay.

desposado, da [des-po-sah'-do, dah], *a*. Handcuffed. -*pp*. of DESPOSAR.

desposar [des-po-sar'], *va*. To marry, to betroth, to mate, to match. -*vr*. 1. To be betrothed, to get married. 2. (*Met.*) To be paired or coupled.

desposeer [des-po-say-err'], *va*. To dispossess, to oust. **Desposeer a uno de su autoridad**, to remove somebody's authority. -*vr*. **Desposeerse de algo**, to give something up.

desposeimiento [des-po-say-e-me-en'-to], *m*. Dispossession.

desposorio [des-po-so'-re-o], *m*. 1. A mutual promise to contract marriage: almost always used in the plural. 2. Betrothal, the act of betrothing.

déspota [des'-po-tah], *m*. 1. A despot, absolute sovereign. 2. A tyrant.

despóticamente [des-po'-te-cah-men-tay], *adv*. Despotically.

despótico, ca [des-po'-te-co, cah], *a*. Despotic, despotical.

despotismo [des-po-tees'-mo], *m*. Despotism, absoluteness.

despotricar [des-po-tre-car'], *vn*. (*Coll.*) To talk inconsiderately.

despreciable [des-pre-the-ah'-blay] *a*. Contemptible, despicable or despisable, worthless, abject, mean, paltry, miserable, lowly.

despreciador, ra [des-pray-the-ah-dor', rah], *m*. & *f*. Depreciator, asperser, despiser, scorner, contemner.

despreciar [des-pray-the-ar'], *va*. To depreciate, to despise, to scorn, to contemn, to reject, to lay aside, to neglect. **No hay que despreciar tal posibilidad**, one should not understimate such a possibility. -*vr*. **Despreciarse de**, to think it beneath oneself.

despreciativo, va [des-pray-the-ah-tee'-vo, vah], *a*. 1. Depreciative, depreciatory. 2. Offensive.

desprecio [des-pray'-the-o], *m*. 1. Disregard, scorn, contempt, despising, neglect, contumely, irrision. **Lo miró con desprecio**, he looked at it contemptuously. 2. Dispraise.

desprender [des-pren-derr'], *va*. To unfasten, to loose, to disjoin, to separate. -*vr*. 1. To give way, to fall down. 2. To extricate oneself, to disposses oneself, to give away. **Desprenderse de un estorbo**, to extricate oneself from a difficulty. **Desprenderse de algo**, to give something up. **Tendremos que desprendernos del coche**, we shall have to get rid of the car. 3. To be deduced, to be inferred. **Se desprende de esta declaración que…**, it is clear from this statement that…

desprendido, da [des-pren-dee'-do, dah], *a.* Disinterested, generous, uncovetous.

desprendimiento [des-pren-de-me-en'-to], *m.* 1. Alienation, disinterestedness. 2. A landslide, landslip.

desprensar [des-pren-sar'], *va.* To remove from the press.

despreocupación [des-pray-o-coo-pah-the-on'], *f.* Non-prejudice, freedom from bias, enlightenment.

despreocupado, da [des-pray-o-coo-pah'-do, dah], *a. pp.* of DESPREOCUPAR. Unconcerned, carefree, unconventional. **Despreocupado en el vestir,** careless in his attire.

despreocupar [des-pray-o-coo-par'], *va.* To unprepossess, to unpreoccupy. -*vr.* To be disabused of a prejudice or error, be set right.

desprestigiar [des-pres-te-he-ar'], *va.* To remove reputation, prestige. -*vr.* To lose prestige; to lose caste.

desprestigio [des-pres-tee'-he-o], *m.* Loss of reputation or prestige. **Campaña de desprestigio,** smear campaign. **Esas cosas que van en desprestigio nuestro,** those things which are to our discredit.

desprevención [des-pray-ven-the-on'], *f.* Improvidence, improvision, want of caution.

desprevenidamente [des-pray-vay-ne'-dah-men-tay], *adv.* Improvidently.

desprevenido, da [des-pray-vay-nee'-do, dah], *a.* 1. Unprovided, unprepared. 2. Improvident.

desproporción [des-pro-por-the-on'], *f.* Disproportion, want of symmetry, disparity; disproportionableness.

desproporcionadamente [des-pro-por-the-o-nah-dah-men'-tay], *adv.* Disproportionately.

desproporcionado, da [des-pro-por-the-o-nah'-do, dah], *a. & pp.* of DESPROPORCIONAR. Disproportionate, disproportional, unsymmetrical, unsuitable, unbecoming.

desproporcionar [des-pro-por-the-o-nar'], *va.* To disproportion, to mismatch things, to misproportion.

despropositado, da [des-pro-po-se-tah'-do, dah], *a.* Absurd.

despropósito [des-pro-po'-se-to], *m.* Absurdity, oddity.

desprotección [des-pro-tec-the-on'], *f.* Deprotection.

desprotegido [des-pro-tay-he-do], *a.* Unprotected.

desproveer [des-pro-vay-err'], *va.* To deprive of provisions, to despoil of the necessaries of life.

desproveído, da [des-pro-vey-ee'-do, dah], *a.* Unprovided, unprepared. -*pp.* of DESPROVEER.

desproveimiento [des-pro-vay-e-me-en'-to], *m.* Penury, poverty.

desprovisto, ta [des-pro-vees'-to, tah], *a. & pp. irreg.* of DESPROVEER. *V.* DESPROVEÍDO.

despueble [des-poo-ay'-blay], or **despueblo** [des-poo-ay'-blo], *m.* Depopulation.

después [des-poo-es'], *adv.* After, posterior in time; afterward, next, then. **Después de Dios,** under or after God. **Primero lo negó y después lo confesó,** he first denied it, then he confessed it. **Después de esa fecha,** since that date. **Mi nombre está después del tuyo,** my name comes next to yours. **Después que lo escribí,** after I wrote it.

despulir [des-poo-leer'], *va.* To tarnish. to frost, to grind (glass). **Vidrio despulido,** ground glass.

despulsar [des-pool-sar'], *va.* To leave without vigor or pulse. -*vr.* 1. To be sorely vexed. 2. To be violently affected with any passion; to eagerly desire.

despumación [des-poo-mah-the-on'], *f.* Despumation, the skimming of liquors.

despumar [des-poo-mar'], *va. V.* ESPUMAR.

despuntado [des-poon-tah'-do], *a.* Blunt.

despuntadura [des-poon-tah-doo'-rah], *f.* The act of blunting or taking off the point.

despuntar [des-poon-tar], *va.* 1. To blunt. 2. To cut away the dry combs in a beehive. 3. *(Naut.)* To double a cape. -*vn.* 1. To advance or make progress in the acquisition of talents and knowledge: to manifest wit and genius. **Despunta en matemáticas,** he shines at math. **Despunta por su talento,** her talent shines out. 2. To begin to sprout or bud, as plants.

3. To surpass, excel, morally. 4. To begin to dawn: said of the day or the sun.

desque [des'-key], *adv. (Vulg.)* Since, then, presently. *V.* DESDE QUE.

desquebrajar [des-kay-brah-har'], *va. & vr.* To break, to split, to crack.

desquejar [des-kay-har'], *va.* To pluck up a shoot near the root of a plant.

desqueje [des-kay'-hay], *m.* Pulling up a shoot near the root of a plant.

desquiciamiento [des-kee-the-ah-me-en'-to], *m.* Unhingeing, disjoining.

desquiciado [des-kee-the-ah-do], *a. (Fig.)* Deranged, unhinged.

desquiciar [des-ke-the-ar'], *va.* 1. To unhinge. 2. *(Met.)* To discompose, to disorder. 3. *(Met.)* To deprive of favor or protection.

desquijaramiento [des-ke-ha-rah-me-en'-to], *m.* Act of breaking the jaws.

desquijarar [des-ke-ha-rar'], *va.* 1. To break the jaws. 2. *(Naut.)* To break the cheek of a block.

desquijerar [des-ke-hay-rar'], *va.* To cut timber on both sides to make a tenon.

desquilatar [des-ke-lah-tar'], *va.* To diminish the intrinsic value of gold.

desquitar [des-ke-tar'], *va.* To retrieve a loss. -*vr.* 1. To win one's money back again. **Desquitarse de una pérdida,** to make up for a loss. 2. To retaliate, to take revenge; to meet with one.

desquite [des-kee'-tay], *m.* 1. Compensation, recovery of a loss. 2. Revenge, satisfaction retaliation. **Tomar el desquite,** to have one's revenge.

desrabotar [des-rah-bo-tar'], *va.* To cut off the tails of lambs or sheep, in order to fatten them.

desrancharse [des-ran-char'-say], *vr.* To withdraw oneself from a mess.

desramillar [des-rah-mil-lyar'], *va. (Agri.) V.* DESLECHUGAR.

desraspado [des-ras-pah'-do], *a. V.* CHAMORRO, as a kind of wheat. -*pp.* of DESRASPAR.

desraspar [des-ras-par'], *va. V.* RASPAR.

desrastrojar [des-ras-tro-har'], *va. (Agri.)* To remove the stubble.

desrastrojo [des-ras-tro'-ho], *m.* Removal, collection of stubble.

desrayadura [des-rah-yah-doo'-rah], *f.* 1. The last furrow of tillage in a field. 2. A deep boundary furrow between two fields.

desrayar [des-rah-yar'], *va.* 1. To open furrows for irrigation of a tilled field. 2. To make a boundary furrow to divide one field from another.

desrazonable [des-rah-tho-nah'-blay], *a.* Unreasonable, idle-headed.

desreglado, da [des-ray-glah'-do, dah], *a.* Disorderly, irregular. *V.* DESARREGLADO.

desreglarse [des-ray-glar'-say], *vr.* To be irregular, or ungovernable.

desrelingar [des-ray-lin-gar'], *va.* To take away the boltropes from the sails. -*vr. (Naut.)* To be blown from the boltrope (velas).

desreputación [des-ray-poo-tah-the-on'], *f.* Dishonor, ignominy.

desriñonarse [des-re-nyo-nahr'-say], *vr.* To slog one's guts out, *(fig.)* To break one's back.

desrizar [des-re-thar'], *va.* To uncurl.

desroblar [des-ro-blar'], *va.* To take off the rivets.

desroñar [des-ro-nyar'], *va. (Agri.)* To lop off decayed branches.

destacado [des-tah-cah'-do], *a.* Notable, outstanding, distinguished.

destacamento [des-tah-cah-men'-to], *m.* 1. Detachment, a body of troops detached on some particular service. 2. Station, or military post.

destacar [des-tah-car'], *va.* 1. To detach a body of troops from the main army on some particular service. 2. To make stand out; *(fig.)* To emphasize, to show up, to point up, to bring out. **Quiero destacar que**…, I wish to emphasize that… *-vr.* 1. To stand out. **Destacarse en**, to stand out against.

destaconar [des-tah-co-nar'], *va.* To wear out, or to break, the heels of footwear.

destajador [des-tah-hah-dor'], *m.* A kind of smith's hammer.

destajamiento [des-tah-hah-me-en'-to], *m.* (*Obs.*) 1. (*Met.*) Diminution, reduction. 2. Current taking a new course.

destajar [des-tah-har'], *va.* 1. To hire or undertake a job by the bulk, to do task work. 2. To stipulate the terms and conditions on which an undertaking is to be performed. 3. (*Obs.*) To prevent, to interrupt, to mislead.

destajero [des-tah-hay'-ro], *m.* One who undertakes a work by task or by the job.

destajista [des-tah-hes'-tah] *m. V.* DESTAJERO.

destajo [des-tah'-ho], *m.* 1. Job. 2. Undertaking the completion of a job within a certain time. **A destajo**, by the job, by the lump: earnestly, diligently. **Hablar a destajo**, to talk much and at random.

destallar [des-tal-lyar'], *va. V.* DESBORRAR.

destalonar [des-tah-lo-nar'], *va.* 1. To deprive of talons or heels. 2. (*Vet.*) To level horses' hoofs.

destapada [des-tah-pah'-dah], *f.* A kind of pie.

destapar [des-tah-par'], *va.* To uncover. *-vr.* 1. To be uncovered. 2. (*Fig.*) To cause surprise, to do something unexpected. 3. (*Fig.*) To speak frankly, to come into the open. 4. To lose control.

destape [des-tah-pay], *m.* 1. State of undress, nudity. 2. (*Fig.*) Permissiveness: process of liberalization.

destapiar [des-tah-pe-ar'], *va.* To pull down mud walls.

destapo [des-tah'-po], *m.* (*Prov.*) Act of uncovering or unstopping.

destaponar [des-tah-po-nar'], *va.* To uncork, to remove the stopper.

destarar [des-tah-rar'], *va.* To diminish the tare allowed in weighing a thing.

destartalado, da [des-tar-tah-lah'-do, dah], *a.* Huddled, rambling, in disorder, ruinous, tumbledown.

destazador [des-tah-thah-dor'], *m.* He who cuts dead things in pieces.

destazar [des-tah-thar'], *va.* To cut things in pieces.

deste, ta, to [des'-tay, tah], *pron.* A contraction formerly used for *De este, de esta, de esto*.

destechar [des-tay-char'], *va.* To unroof.

destejar [des-tay-har'], *va.* 1. To untile, to take off the tiles. 2. To leave a thing defenceless.

destejer [des-tay-herr'], *va.* To unweave, to ravel, to undo a warp prepared for the loom.

destellar [des-tel-lyar'], *va.* To throw out or scatter rays of light.

destello [des-tayl'-lyo], *m.* 1. The act of flowing out drop by drop. 2. Sparkle; flash; gleam; glint. 3. (*Fig.*) Atom, particle. **No tiene un destello de verdad**, there's not an ounce of truth in it. 4. **Destellos**, (*fig.*) Glimmer. **Tiene a veces destellos de inteligencia**, he sometimes shows a glimmer of intelligence.

destempladamente [des-tem-plah-dah-men'-tay], *adv.* Intemperately.

destemplado, da [des-tem-plah'-do, dah], *a.* 1. (*Art.*) Inharmonious, incongruous (cuadros). 2. Disharmonious, unharmonious, out of tune. 3. Intemperate. *-pp.* of DESTEMPLAR.

destemplanza [des-tem-plahn'-thah], *f.* 1. Unsettledness. 2. Disorder, intemperance; excess in the desires, or in the use of certain things. 3. Indisposition, an alteration in the pulse, not approaching fever symptoms. 4. Disorder, alteration in words or actions, lack of moderation.

destemplar [des-tem-plar'], *va.* 1. To distemper, to alter, to disconcert. 2. To put to confusion. 3. To untune. *-vr.* 1. To be ruffled, to be discomposed. 2. To be out of order (pulso).

3. To grow blunt, to lose the temper (instrumentos). 4. To act improperly or rashly; to lose moderation in actions or words. 5. To melt glue or other cement. 6. To anneal, to take out the temper of metals.

destemple [des-tem'-play], *m.* 1. Discordance, disharmony. 2. Discomposure, disorder. 3. Intemperance, distemperature. 4. (*Pict.*) Distemper. 5. Distemper, a slight indisposition.

destender [des-ten-derr'], *va.* (*Prov.*) To fold, to double.

desteñido [des-tay-ñye-do], *a.* Faded, discolored.

desteñir [des-tay-nyeer'], *va.* To discolor, to change from the natural hue. *-vn & vr.* 1. To fade, to discolor, to take the color out of. 2. To run (colores de tela). **Esta tela no destiñe**, this fabric will not run.

desternillarse [des-ter-nil-lyar'-say], *vr.* To break one's cartilage or gristle. **Desternillarse de risa**, to laugh violently.

desterradero [des-ter-rah-day'-ro], *m.* A retired part of the town.

desterrado, da [des-ter-rah'-do, dah], *a. & pp.* of DESTERRAR. Banished, outcast.

desterrado, da [des-ter-rah'-do, dah], *m. & f.* Exile, outcast.

desterrar [des-ter-rar'], *va.* 1. To banish, to transport, to exile. 2. To lay, or put aside. **Desterrar una sospecha**, to banish a suspicion from one's mind. 3. To take the earth from a thing. **Desterrar del mundo**, to be the outcast of the world.

desterronador, ra [des-ter-ro-nah-dor', rah], *m. & f.* Clodcrusher.

desterronar [des-ter-ro-nar'], *va.* To break clods with a harrow or spade.

destetadera [des-tay-tah-day'-rah], *f.* Pointed instrument placed on the teats of cows, to prevent calves from sucking.

destetar [des-tay-tar'], *va.* To wean, to ablactate. *-vr.* To wean oneself from an evil habit or custom.

destete [des-tay'-tay], *m.* The act of weaning from the breast.

desteto [des-tay'-to], *m.* 1. Number of weanlings (ganado). 2. The place where newly weaned mules are kept.

destiempo [des-te-em'-po], *m.* An unseasonable time. **A destiempo**, unseasonably, untimely.

destierro [des-te-er'-ro], *m.* 1. Exile, banishment, transportation. 2. The place where the exile lives. 3. Any remote and solitary place. 4. Judicial banishment. (*Yo destierro, yo destierre* from *Desterrar. V.* ACERTAR.)

destilación [des-te-lah-the-on'], *f.* 1. Distillation, act of dropping or falling in drops. 2. Distillation, the act of extracting by the fire or still. 3. Distillation, the substance drawn by the still.

destiladera [des-te-lah-day'-rah], *f.* 1. Still, alembic, a vessel for distillation. 2. An ingenious device or stratagem for obtaining one's end.

destilador [des-te-lah-dor'], *m.* 1. Distiller. 2. Filtering-stone. 3. Alembic, retort.

destilar [des-te-lar'], *va.* 1. To distil. 2. (*Fig.*) To exude; to reveal. **La carta destilaba odio**, the letter exuded hatred. *-vn.* 1. To distil, to drop, to fall in drops. 2. To distil, to filter though a stone.

destilatorio [des-te-lah-to'-reo], *m.* 1. Distillery. 2. Alembic.

destinación [des-te-nah-the-on'], *f.* 1. Destination. 2. Destiny, fate.

destinar [des-te-nar'], *va.* 1. To destine, to appoint for any use or purpose. **Ir destinado a**, to be bound for. **Una carta que viene destinada a ti**, a letter for you. 2. To destinate, to design for any particular end; to allot, assign. **Le han destinado a Lima**, they have appointed him to Lima. 3. (*Naut.*) To station strips.

destinatario, ria [des-te-nah-tah'-re-o], *m & f.* Addressee.

destino [des-tee'-no], *m.* 1. Destiny. 2. Fate, doom, fortune, force. **Es mi destino no encontrarlo**, I am fated not to find it. 3. Destination, appointment for any use or purpose. **Van con destino a Londres**, they are going to London. **Salir con destino a**, to leave for. 4. Profession, business. **Buscarse un destino de cartero**, to look for a job as a postman. 5. (*Naut.*) Station. **Con destino a**, bound for.

destiño [des-tee'-nyo], *m.* Piece of unfinished yellow or green and dry honeycomb in a beehive. (*Yo destiño, él destiñó*, from *Desteñir. V.* PEDIR.)

destitución [des-te-too-the-on'], *f.* 1. Privation of an employment, office or charge. 2. Destitution, dereliction, abandonment.

destituido, da [des-te-too-ee'-do, dah], *a. & pp.* of DESTITUIR. Destitute, forsaken, friendless, helpless.

destituir [des-te-too-eer'], *va.* To deprive, to make destitute. **Destituir a uno de algo**, to deprive somebody of something.

destocar [des-to-car'], *va.* 1. To uncoif, to pull off the cap or headdress. 2. (*Prov.*) To uncover the head.

destorcedura [des-tor-thay-doo'-rah], *f.* Untwisting, uncurling.

destorcer [des-tor-therr'], *va.* 1. To untwist, to uncurl. 2. To rectify what was not right. *-vr.* (*Naut.*) To deviate from the track, to lose the way.

destorgar [des-tor-gar'], *va.* (*Prov.*) To break the branches of evergreen oaks, taking off their acorns.

destornillado, da [des-tor-nil-lyah'-do, dah], *a.* Inconsiderate, heedless, rash. *-pp.* of DESTORNILLAR.

destornillador [des-tor-nil-lyah-dor'], *m.* Unscrewer, he or that which unscrews; screwdriver, wrench, turn-screw.

destornillar [des-tor-nil-lyar'], *va.* To unscrew. *-vr.* To act rashly, or without judgment or prudence.

destoserse [des-to-serr'-say], *vr.* To feign a cough, to cough needlessly.

destostarse [des-tos-tar'-say], *vr.* To gradually remove the tanning of the skin by the sun.

destrabar [des-trah-bar'], *va.* 1. To unfetter, to unbind. 2. To untie, to loosen, to separate; to break the barriers.

destrados [des-trah'-dos], *m. pl.* (*Prov.*) A coarse sort of woollen carpets, or rugs.

destraillar [des-tra-hil-lyar'], *va.* To unleash dogs.

destral [des-trahl'], *m.* A small axe or hatchet.

destraleja [des-trah-lay'-hah], *f.* A very small hatchet.

destralero [des-trah-lay'-ro], *m.* One who makes axes and hatchets.

destramar [des-trah-mar'], *va.* 1. To unweave, to undo the warp. 2. (*Mil.*) To dissolve a conspiracy or intrigue.

destrenzar [des-tren-thar'], *va.* To undo a tress of hair.

destreza [des-tray'-thah], *f.* 1. Dexterity, address, handiness, expertness, mastery, knowledge, cunning. 2. Nimbleness, adroitness. 3. Skill in fencing.

destrincar [des-trin-car'], *va. & vr.* (*Naut.*) To loose, to unlash.

destripacuentos [des-tre-pah-coo-en'-tos], *com.* One who often interrupts the person who is talking.

destripador [des-tre-pah-dor'], *m.* (*Fig.*) Butcher; murderer.

destripar [des-tre-par'], *va.* 1. To disembowel, to gut, to eviscerate. 2. *V.* DESPACHURRAR. 3. (*Met.*) To draw out the inside of a thing. **Destripar una botella**, to crack a bottle.

destripaterrones [des-tre-pah-ter-ro'-nes], *m.* (*Coll.*) Harrower, day laborer who harrows the land, clodbeater.

destripular [des-tre-poo-lar'], *va.* To discharge the crew of a vessel.

destriunfar [des-tre-oon-far'], *va.* To extract all the trumps in games at cards.

destrizar [des-tre-thar'], *va.* To mince, to crumble. *-vr.* To break the heart, to wear away with grief.

destrocar [des-tro-car'], *va.* To return a thing bartered.

destrocos [des-tro'-cose], *m. pl.* Ruins, remains.

destrón [des-trone'], *m.* A blind man's guide.

destronamiento [des-tro-nah-me-en'-to], *m.* Dethronement.

destronar [des-tro-nar'], *va.* To dethrone, to divest of legality.

destroncamiento [des-tron-cah-me-en'-to], *m.* Detruncation, amputation, lopping trees.

destroncar [des-tron-car'], *va.* 1. To detruncate, to lop, to cut short. 2. To maim, to dislocate, to cut a body in pieces. 3.

(*Met.*) To ruin, to destroy anyone; obstruct his affairs or pretensions. 4. (*Met.*) To cut short a discourse.

destronque [des-tron'-kay], *m.* DESTRONCAMIENTO.

destroquerio [des-tro-kay'-re-o], *m.* (*Her.*) The right arm, clothed or bare, but always armed, upon crests of arms.

destrozado [des-tro-thah'-do], *a.* Smashed, shattered, ruined.

destrozador, ra [des-tro-thah-dor', rah], *m. & f.* Destroyer, mangler.

destrozar [des-tro-thar'], *va.* 1. To destroy, to break into pieces. 2. To rout, to defeat to massacre. 3. (*Met.*) To spend much inconsiderately. **Destrozar la armonía**, to ruin the harmony. **Le ha destrozado el que no quisiera casarse con él**, he was shattered when she wouldn't marry him.

destrozo [des-tro'-tho], *m.* 1. Destruction. 2. Havoc, rout, defeat, massacre.

destrozón, na [des-tro-thone', nah], *m. & f.* One who is destructive of apparel, shoes, etc.

destrucción [des-trooc-the-on'], *f.* 1. Destruction, extermination, extinction, overthrow. 2. Destruction, ruin, havoc, loss.

destructible [des-trooc-te-blay], *a.* Destructible.

destructivamente [des-trooc-te-vah-men'-tay], *adv.* Destructively.

destructividad [des-trooc-te-vee-dahd'], *f.* Destructiveness, a phrenological term: its supposed seat is above the auditory canal.

destructivo, va [des-trooc-tee'-vo, vah], *a.* Destructive, wasteful, consumptive.

destructor, ra [des-trooc-tor', rah], *m. & f.* Destructor, destroyer (barco), consumer, harasser.

destructorio, ria [des-trooc-toh'-re-o, ah], *a.* Destroying.

destrueco, destrueque [des-troo-ay'-co, des-troo-ay'-kay], *m.* The mutual restitution of things bartered or exchanged. (*Yo destrueco, yo destrueque*, from *Destrocar. V.* ACORDAR.)

destruible [des-troo-ee'-blay], *a.* Destructible.

destruidor, ra [des-troo-e-dor', rah], *m. & f.* Destroyer, devastator.

destruir [des-troo-eer'], *va.* 1. To destroy, to ruin, to lay level. 2. To destroy, to waste or lay waste, to harass; to overthrow. 3. To misspend one's fortune. 4. To deprive one of the means of earning a livelihood.

destruyente [des-troo-yen'-tay], *va.* Destroying.

desturbar [des-toor-bar'], *va.* To turn out, to drive away. *V.* ECHAR.

destutanarse [des-too-tah-nar'-say], *va.* (*Amer. Cuba*) To kill oneself with work, either physical or mental.

desubstanciar [day-soobs-tan-the-ar'], *va.* To enervate, to deprive of strength and substance.

desucación [day-soo-ca-the-on'], *f.* Act of extrating the juice.

desucar [day-soo-car'], *va. V.* DESJUGAR. (*Lat.* succus, juice.)

desudar [day-soo-dar'], *va.* To wipe off sweat.

desuelar [day-soo-ay-lar'], *va.* To take off the sole. *-vr.* To be wrenched off or fall off (suela de zapato).

desuellacaras [day-soo-el-lyah-cah'-ras], *m.* 1. (*Prov. Coll.*) A bad barber. 2. (*Coll.*) An impudent, shameless person.

desuello [day-soo-ay'-lyo], *m.* 1. The act of flaying, fleecing, or skinning. 2. Forwardness, impudence, insolence. 3. Extortion, or an exorbitant price. (*Yo desuello, yo desuelle*, from *Desollar. V.* ACORDAR.)

desulfuración [day-sool-foo-rah-the-on'], *f.* Removal of sulphur from a compound.

desulfurar [day-sool-foo-rar'], *va.* To desulphurize.

desuncir [des-oon-theer'], *va.* To unyoke, to abjugate.

desunidamente [des-oo-ne-dah-men-tay], *adv.* Separately, severally.

desunión [des-oo-ne-on'], *f.* 1. Separation disunion, disjuction. 2. Discord, disunion, dissension, feud.

desunir [des-oo-neer'], *va.* To separate, to part, to disunite; to occasion discord. *-vr.* To loosen, to come asunder; to set at odds; to disunite, to become separated.

desuñar [des-oo-nyar], *va.* 1. To tear off the nails. 2. To pull out the roots of trees. *-vr.* To plunge into vice and disorder.

desurcar [day-soor-car'], *va.* To remove or undo furrows.

desurdir [des-oor-deer'], *va.* 1. To unweave cloth. 2. To unravel a plot.

desusadamente [des-oo-sah'-dah-men-tay], *adv.* Unusually, out of use, contrary to custom.

desusado, da [des-oo-sah'-do, dah], *a. & pp.* of DESUSAR. Disused, obsolete, out of date, archaic.

desusar [des-oo-sar'], *va.* To disuse, to discontinue the use of. *-vr.* To become disused or obsolete.

desuso [des-oo'-so], *m.* Disuse, obsoleteness, desuetude.

desustanciar [day-soos-tan-the-ar'], *va.* 1. To enervate. 2. To deprive of strength and substance.

desvahar [des-vah-ar'], *va. (Agri.)* To take away the dry or withered part of a plant.

desvaído, da [des-vah-ee'-do, dah], *a.* 1. Tall and graceless. 2. Dull, lustreless, matt (of colors). 3. *(Naut.)* Gaping: applied to the sheathing of ships; when its joints separate.

desvainar [des-vah-e-nar'], *va.* 1. To husk, to strip off the outward integument. 2. To unsheath.

desvalido, da [des-vah-lee'-do, dah], *a.* Helpless, destitute, unprotected. **Niñez desvalida**, underprivileged children.

desvalijar [des-vah-leh-ar'], *va.* 1. To take out the contents of a valise or gripsack. 2. To rob one of what he was carrying in a valise or satchel.

desvalimiento [des-vah-le-me-en'-to], *m.* Dereliction, abandonment, want of favor or protection.

desvalorar [des-vah-lo-rar'], *va.* 1. To devalue, to depreciate. 2. To discredit.

desvalorización [des-vah-lo-re-thah-the-on'], *f.* Devaluation.

desvalorizar [des-vah-lo-re-thar'], *va.* To devalue, to depreciate. *-vr.* 2. To depreciate.

desván [des-vahn'], *m.* Garret; loft. **Desván gatero**, cockloft, a room over the garret.

desvanar [des-vah-nar'], *va.* To wind to a skein. *V.* DEVANAR.

desvanecer [des-vah-nay-therr'], *va.* 1. To divide into imperceptible parts. 2. To cause to vanish or disappear, to take away from the sight. 3. To undo, to remove. 4. To swell with presumption or pride. *-vr.* 1. To pall, to grow vapid, to become insipid. 2. To vanish, to evaporate, to exhale. 3. To be effected with giddiness or dizziness; to fall. (*Yo me desvanezco, or desvanezca*, from *Desvanecerse. V.* CONOCER.)

desvanecidamente [des-vah-nay-the-dah-men'-tay], *adv.* Vainly, haughtily, proudly.

desvanecido [des-vah-nay-the'-do], *a.* 1. *(Med.)* Faint; giddy, dizzy. **Caer desvanecido**, to fall in a faint. 2. *(Fig.)* Vain (engreído); proud (orguñoso).

desvanecimiento [des-vah-nay-the-me-en'-to], *m.* 1. Pride, haughtiness, loftiness. 2. Giddiness, dizziness. 3. *(Med.)* Fainting fit, swoon. 4. *(Quim.)* Evaporation; melting.

desvano [des-vah'-no], *m.* Garret. *V.* DESVÁN.

desvaporizar [des-vah-po-re-thar'], *va. V.* EVAPORAR.

desvarar [des-vah-rar'], *va. vn. & vr.* 1. *V.* RESBALAR. 2. *(Naut.)* To set afloat a ship that was aground.

desvariadamente [des-vah-re-ah'-dah-men-tay], *adv.* 1. Ravingly, foolishly, madly. 2. Differently, diversely, dissimilarly.

desvariado, da [des-vah-re-ah'-do, dah], *a.* 1. Delirious, raving. 2. Disorderly, irregular. 3. Extravagant, nonsensical. 4. Long, luxuriant: applied to the branches of trees. *-pp.* of DESVARIAR.

desvariar [des-vah-re-ar'], *vn.* 1. To rave, to be delirious, to dote. 2. To make extravagant demands. *-vr.* To deviate, go wrong, go astray.

desvarío [des-vah-ree'-o], *m.* 1. An extravagant action or speech. 2. Delirium, raving, giddiness. 3. Inequality, inconstancy, caprice. 4. Monstrousness, extravagancy; derangement; disunion.

desvedado, da [des-vay-dah'-do, dah], *a.* Unprohibited, free from prohibition, having been prohibited before. *-pp.* of DESVEDAR.

desvedar [des-vay-dar'], *va.* To remove or revoke a prohibition against a thing.

desveladamente [des-vay-lah'-dah-men-tay], *adv.* Watchfully, vigilantly.

desvelado, da [des-vey-lah'-do, dah], *a.* Watchful, vigilant, careful. *-pp.* of DESVELAR.

desvelamiento [des-vay-lah-me-en'-to], *m.* Watchfulness. *V.* DESVELO.

desvelar [des-vay-lar'], *va.* 1. To keep awake. 2. To solve, to explain (misterio). *-vr.* To be or watchful or vigilant or zealous. 2. To stay awake, to keep awake; to go without sleep.

desvelo [des-vay'-lo], *m.* 1. Watching, want or privation of sleep. 2. Watch, forbearance of sleep. 3. Watchfulness, vigilance. 4. Anxiety, uneasiness.

desvenar [des-vay-nar'], *va.* 1. To separate or clear the veins of flesh. 2. To extract anything from the veins of mines or the filaments of plants. 3. To raise the bit of a bridle, so as to form an arch of mouth.

desvencijado, da [des-ven-the-hah'-do, dah], *a.* Rickety, loose-jointed.

desvencijar [des-ven-the-har'], *va.* To disunite, to weaken, to divide, to break. *-vr.* 1. To be ruptured; to be relaxed. 2. *(Coll.)* To be exhausted.

desvendar [des-ven-dar'], *va.* To take off a bandage, to unbandage.

desveno [des-vay'-no], *m.* Arch of the mouth; a kind of bridle-bit.

desventaja [des-ven-tah'-hah], *f.* 1. Disadvantage, misfortune, damage, loss: **Estar en desventaja con respecto a otros**, to be at a disadvantage compared with others. 2. Disfavor, which results from comparing two persons or things.

desventajado, da [des-ven-tah-hah'-do], *a.* Disadvantaged.

desventajosamente [des-ven-tah-ho-sah-men-tay], *adv.* Disadvantageously, unprofitably.

desventajoso, sa [des-ven-tah-ho'-so, sah], *a.* Disadvantageous, unfavorable, unprofitable, detrimental.

desventar [des-ven-tar'], *va.* To vent, to let out air.

desventura [des-ven-too'-rah], *f.* Misfortune, calamity, mishap, mischance; misery.

desventuradamente [des-ven-too-rah-dah-men'-tay], *adv.* Unhappily, unfortunately.

desventurado, da [des-ven-too-rah'-do, dah], *a.* 1. Unfortunate, calamitous, wretched, unlucky, unhappy, miserable. 2. Chicken-hearted, pusillanimous, timid. 3. Mean (tacaño). *-m. f.* Wretch, unfortunate.

desvergonzadamente [des-ver-gon-thah-dah-men'-tay], *adv.* Impudent, shamelessly.

desvergonzado, da [des-ver-gon-thah-do, dah], *a.* Impudent, shameless, immodest.

desvergonzarse [des-ver-gon-thar'-say], *vr.* To speak or act in an impudent or insolent manner. **Desvergonzarse a pedir algo**, to have the nerve to ask for something.

desvergüenza [des-ver-goo-en'-thah], *f.* 1. Impudence, effrontery, assurance, grossness. 2. Shameless word or action. **Esto es una desvergüenza**, this is disgraceful. (*Yo me desvergüenzo, yo me desvergüence*, from *Desvergonzarse. V.* ACORDAR.).

desvertebrar [des-ver-tay-brar'], *va. (Fig.)* To dislocate; to disturb, to upset, to throw off balance.

desvestir [des-ves-ter'], *va.* To undress. *-vr.* To undress.

desvezar [des-vay-thar'], *va. (Agr. Prov.)* To cut the young shoots of vines near the roots.

desviación [des-ve-ah-the-on'], *f.* 1. Deviation, deflection, separation. **Es una desviación de sus principios**, it is a deviation from his principles. 2. *(Med.)* Vicious direction of some parts of the body, especially the limbs and the bones: applied also to extravasation of fluids. 3. *(Astr.)* Wrong position of a telescope out of the plane of the meridian. 4. The quantity by which a body, falling freely, deviates from the perpendicular, and the variation of the magnetic needle. 5. Shunt (ferrocarril). 6. Detour; diversion (tráfico); bypass, ring road. **Desviación de circulación**, traffic diversion.

desviadero [des-ve-ah-day'-ro], *m.* A railway switch, siding, side-track, passing-place.

desviado, da [des-ve-ah'-do, dah], *a.* Devious, out of the common trach askew. -*pp.* of DESVIAR.

desviar [des-ve-ar'], *va.* 1. To divert from the right way, to lead off, to avert, to turn aside. **Desviar el cauce de un río**, to alter the course of a river. **Desviar a uno del buen camino**, to lead somebody astray. 2. To dissuade, to discourage someone, to put someone off. 3. To parry a thrust (esgrima). -*vr.* To deviate, to turn away, to turn off. **Desviarse de un tema**, to digrees from a theme.

desviejar [des-ve-ay-har'], *va.* Among shepherds, to separate the old ewes or rams from the flock.

desvigorizar [des-ve-go-re-thar'], *va.* To take away or diminish vigor.

desvincular [des-ven-coo-lar'], *va.* To detach; to disentail (finca). -*vr.* **Desvincularse con**, to break with.

desvío [des-vee'-o], *m.* 1. Turning away, going astray, deviation, aberrance. 2. The act of diverting. 3. Aversion, displeasure. 4. Coldness, indifference.

desvirar [des-ve-rar'], *va.* 1. To pare of the fore part of a sole. 2. In book-binding to trim a book. 3. *(Naut.)* To turn the capstan the other way from that used in winding, the cable; to reverse the capstan.

desvirgar [des-virr-gar'], *va.* *(Low.)* To deflower a maid.

desvirtuar [des-virr-too-ar'], *va.* To pall, to make insipid or vapid, to take the substance, virtue, or strength from anything. -*vr.* To spoil, to go off, to decline in quality.

desvivirse [des-ve-veer'-say], *vr.* To love excessively; to desire anxiously. **Desvivirse por los amigos**, to do one's utmost for one's friends.

desvolvedor [des-vol-vay-dor'], *m.* A screw tap.

desvolver [des-vol-verr'], *va.* 1. To alter a thing, to give it another shape. 2. To plough, to till the ground.

desyemar [des-yay-mar'], *va.* 1. *(Agri.)* To remove buds from plants. 2. To separate the yolk from the white of an egg.

desyerbar [des-yer-var'], *va.* To pluck up herbs, to weed, to grub.

desyuncir [des-yoon-theer'], *va.* 1. To unyoke. 2. To free from oppression or servitude.

deszafrar [des-thah-frar'], *va.* To carry away the ore from an excavation.

deszocar [des-tho-car'], *va.* To wound or hurt the foot.

deszumar [des-thoo-mar'], *va.* To extract the juice or substance.

detalladamente [day-tahl-lyah-dah'-men-tay], *adv.* In detail.

detallado [day-tahl-lyah'-do], *a.* Detailed.

detallar [day-tal-lyar'], *va.* To detail, to relate particularly or minutely, to particularize, to enumerate.

detalle [day-tahl'-lyay], *m.* 1. Detail, enumeration. **Con todos los detalles**, in detail. **Hasta en sus menores detalles**, down to the last detail. **No pierde detalle**, he misses nothing. 2. *(Fig.)* Token, gesture. **Tiene muchos detalles**, he is very considerate.

detectable [day-tec-tah'-blay], *a.* Detectable.

detectar [day-tec-tar'], *va.* To detect.

detective [day-tec-tee'-vay], *m. & f.* Detective, sleuth.

detector [day-tec-tor'], *m.* Detector. **Detector de humo**, smoke detector. **Detector de metales**, metal detector.

detención [day-ten-the-on'], *f.* 1. Detention, delay, stopping. **Detención de juego**, stoppage of play. 2. *(Naut.)* Demurrage. 3. Arrest. **Detención sin procedimiento**, imprisonment without trial.

detenedor, ra [day-tay-nay-dor', rah], *m. & f.* Detainer, one that detains.

detener [day-tay-nerr'], *va.* 1. To stop, to detain, to hinder, to fix. **Detener el progreso de**, to hold up the progress of. 2. To arrest, to imprison, to constrain. 3. To keep, to keep back, to retain, to reserve. -*vr.* 1. To tarry, to stay, to continue, to forbear, to give over. 2. To be detained, to stop, to be at leisure. **Se detuvo a mirarlo**, he stopped to look at it. 3. To consider a thing maturely. (*Yo detengo, yo detuve*, from *Detener. V.* TENER.)

detenidamente [day-tay-ne-dah-men'-tay], *adv.* Dilatorily, cautiously, attentively.

detenido, da [day-tay-nee'-do, dah], *a.* 1. Sparing, niggardly, parsimonious. 2. Embarrassed, of little resolution, dilatory, -*pp.* of DETENER.

detenimiento [day-tay-ne-me-en'-to], *m.* 1. *V.* DETENCIÓN. 2. Care, circumspection, reflection, tact.

detentación [day-ten-tah-the-on'], *f.* *(Law.)* Deforcement, detention, the act of keeping what belongs to another.

detentar [day-ten-tar'], *va.* To detain, to retain, to keep unlawfully the property or rights belonging to another.

detentor [day-ten-tor'], *m.* *(Com.)* Holder.

detergente [day-ter-hen'-tay], *a.* Detergent. **Jabón detergente**, detergent soap. -*m.* Detergent.

deterger [day-ter-herr'], *va.* To wash or cleanse an ulcer, a wound, etc.

deterior [day-tay-re-or'], *a.* Worse, of an inferior quality.

deterioración [day-tay-re-orah-the-on'], *f.* Deterioration, detriment, damage.

deteriorado [day-tay-re-o-rah'-do], *a.* Spoiled, damaged; worn; shopsoiled (géneros).

deteriorar [day-tay-re-o-rar'], *va. & vr.* To deteriorate, to impair.

deterioro [day-tay-re-oh'-ro], *m.* Deterioration, impairment, injury. **En caso de deterioro de las mercancías**, should the goods be damaged in in any way.

determinable [day-ter-me-nah'-blay], *a.* Determinable, conclusible.

determinación [day-ter-me-nah-theon'], *f.* 1. Determination, resolution, decision. 2. Conclusion or final decision. 3. Resolution, firmness, boldness, audaciousness.

determinadamente [day-ter-me-nah-dah-men'-tay], *adv.* 1. Determinately, resolutely. 2. Definitively, expressly, especially.

determinado, da [day-ter-me-nah'-do, dah], *a.* 1. Determinate, determined, resolved, decided; fixed, resolute. **Un día determinado**, on a certain day. **En momentos determinados**, at certain times. 2. Determinate, settled, definite, determined.-*pp.* of DETERMINAR.

determinante [day-ter-me-nahn'-tay], *pa.* Determining. -*a.* Determinate, determinative.

determinante [day-ter-me-nahn'-tay], *m.* 1. *(Gram.)* The determining verb. 2. Determiner, determinator, he who determines.

determinar [day-ter-me-nar'], *va.* 1. To determine, to resolve, to fix in a determination. **Determinar el peso de algo**, to determine the weight of something. 2. To distinguish, to discerns. 3. To appoint, to assign. 4. To cause, to produce. **Aquello determinó la caída del gobierno**, that brought about the fall of the government. 5. To classify. 6. To decide, to conclude. **Determinar un pleito**, to decide a lawsuit. -*vr.* To determine, to resolve, to take a resolution, or to come to a resolution.

determinativo, va [day-ter-me-nah-tee'-vo, vah], *a.* Determinative.

determinismo [day-ter-me-nees'-mo], *m.* Determinism, fatalism; a philosophy according to which the actions of men obey irresistible motives, mostly not suspected by the individual.

determinista [day-ter-me-nees'-tah], *m.* A fatalist.

detersión [day-tar-se-on'], *f.* 1. Detersion, the act of cleansing a sore. 2. Cleansing. 3. The act and effect of cleansing.

detersivo, va [day-ter-see'-vo, vah], *a.* Detersive, fit for a cleansing surgical application.

detersorio, ria [day-ter-so'-reo, ah], *a.* Detersive, cleansing.

detestable [day-tes-tah'-blay], *a.* Detestable, hateful, heinous, loathsome.

detestablemente [day-tes-tah'-blay-men-tay], *adv.* Detestably, hatefully, confoundedly.

detestación [day-tes-tah-the-on'], *f.* Detestation, hatred, abhorrence, horror, abomination.

detestar [day-tes-tar'], *va.* To detest, to abhor, to hate, to abominate, to loathe.

detienebuey [day-te-ay-nay-boo-ay'-e], *m. (Bot.)* Common rest-harrow, cammoc, groundfurze.

detonatión [day-to-nah-the-on'], *f.* Detonation, noise.

detonador [day-to-nah-dor'], *m.* Detonator.

detonar [day-to-nar'], *va. (Chem.)* To flash, to detonate.

detorsión [day-tor-se-on'], *f.* Violent extension, wrenching of a muscle, tendon, or ligament.

detracción [day-trac-the-on'], *f.* 1. Detraction, defamation, slander, obloquy. 2. Detraction, a withdrawing, a taking away.

detractar [day-trac-tar'], *va.* To detract, to defame, to slander.

detractor, ra [day-trac-tor', rah], *m. & f.* Detractor, slanderer.

detraer [day-tra-herr'], *va.* 1. To detract, to remove, to take away, to withdraw. 2. To detract, to slander to vilify.

detrás [day-trahs'], *adv.* 1. Behind. **Detrás de la puerta,** behind the door. **Por detrás,** behind. **Salir de detrás de un árbol,** to come out from behind a tree. 2. In the absence.

detrimento [day-tre-men'-to], *m.* Detriment, damage, loss, harm.

detrítico, ca [day-tree'-te-co, cah], *a.* Composed of detritus; detrital, detritic.

detritus [day-tree'-toos], *m. (Neol.)* 1. Detritus, remnants of the destruction of rocks and plants. 2. Inorganic residue replacing tissue in degenerated parts of the body. 3. Filth, excrements.

detumescencia [day-too-mes-then'-the-ah], *f.* Detumescence, resolution of a swelling.

detumescente [day-too-mes-then'-tay], *a.* Having power to disperse a swelling.

deturbadora (Fuerza) [day-toor-bah-do'-rah], *a.* 1. A force perpendicular to the plane of the orbit of the disturbed planet. 2. *V.* PERTURBACIÓN.

deuda [day'-oo-dah], *f.* 1. Debt, that which one man owes to another. 2. Fault, offence. 3. That which has relationship or affinity. **Deudas activas,** assets. **Deudas pasivas,** liabilities. **Deuda a largo plazo,** long-term debt. **Contraer deudas,** to contract debts. **Estar en deuda,** to be in debt.

deudo, da [day'-oo-do, dah], *m. & f.* 1. Parent, relative. 2. Kindred, relation. *V.* DESDÉN and PARENTESCO.

deudor, ra [day-oo-dor', rah], *m. & f.* Debtor. **Deudor moroso,** slow payer.

deuterio [day-oo-tay'-re-o], *m. (Chem.)* Deuterium.

deuterogarmia [day-oo-tay-ro-gah'-me-ah], *f.* State of second marriage.

deuterógamo, ma [day-oo-tay-ro'-gah-mo, mah], *a.* One who marries a second time.

deuteronomio [day-oo-tay-ro-no'-me-o], *m.* Deuteronomy, the fifth book of the Pentateuch.

devalar [duy-vah-lar'], *vn. (Naut.)* To be driven out of the right course by a current (barcos).

devaluación [day-vah-loo-ah-the-on'], *f. (Fin).* Devaluation.

devaluar [day-vah-loo-ar'], *va.* To devaluate, to depreciate.

devanadera [day-vah-nah-day'-rah], *f.* 1. A reel, spool, bobbin. **Devanadera de golpe,** clockreel, snapreel. 2. A movable picture or decoration on the stage. 3. *(Naut.)* Logreel.

devanador, ra [day-vah-nah-dor', rah], *m. & f.* 1. Winder, one who reels yarn. 2. Quill, bit of paper, or other thing, on which yarn is wound; spool.

devanar [day-vah-nar'], *va.* 1. To reel, as yarn. 2. *(Met.)* To wrap up one thing, in another. **Devanar las tripas,** to importune one with some impertinent affair. **Devanarse**

lossesos, to screw one's wits, to fatigue oneself with intense thinking, to hammer one's brains.

devanear [day-vah-nay-ar'], *vn.* To rave, to talk nonsense; to dote, to be delirious.

devaneo [day-vah-nay'-o], *m.* 1. Delirium, alienation of mind, giddiness; frenzy. 2. Idle or mad pursuit; dissipation.

devantal [day-van-tahl'], *m.* Apron. *V.* DELANTAL.

devastación [day-vas-tah-the-on'], *f.* Devastation, destruction, desolation, waste.

devastador, ra [day-vas-tah-dor', rah], *m. & f.* Desolator, harasser, spoiler. -*a.* Devastating.

devastar [day-vas-tar'], *va.* To desolate, to waste or to lay waste, to harass.

develar day-vay-lar'], *va.* To blockade a port.

devengar [day-ven-gar'], *va.* To obtain as the reward of labor, to deserve, to acquire a right to a thing as a reward for services, etc.

devisa [day-vee'-sah], *f.* 1. *V.* DIVISA. 2. Part of the tithes which belong to a plebeian heir. 3. Ancient patriots in Castile.

devoción [day-vo-the-on'], *f.* 1. Devotion, piety. **Con devoción,** devoutly; piously. 2. Godliness, observance of religious duties. 3. Prayer, act of religion. 4. *(Met.)* Strong affection, ardent love. **Sienten devoción por su general,** they feel devotion to their general. 5. *(Div.)* Devoutness, promptitude in obeying the will of God. **Estar a la devoción de alguno,** to be at one's disposal, to attend his orders.

devocionario [day-vo-the-o-nah'-re-o], *m.* Prayer-book.

devocionero, ra [day-vo-the-o-nay'-ro, rah], *a.* Devotional.

devolución [day-vo-loo-the-on'], *f. (Law.)* Devolution, restitution. **Pidió la devolución de los libros,** he asked for the books to be given back. **No se admiten devoluciones,** no refund will be given.

devoluta [day-vo-loo'-ta], *f.* In canonical law, the bestowal by the Pope of a vacant benefice.

devolutario [day-vo-loo-tah'-re-o], *m.* A person who receives a benefice from the Pope.

devolutivo [day-vo-loo-tee'-vo], *a. (Law.)* 1. What may be returned (causas). 2. What may be restored to a former state (derechos).

devolutorio, ria [day-vo-loo-toh'-re-o, ah], *a. V.* DEVOLUTIVO.

devolver [day-vol-verr'], *va.* To return, to refund, to restore. **Devolver el estómago,** *(coll.)* to vomit. **Devolver una carta al remitente,** to return a letter to the sender. **El espejo devuelve la imagen,** the mirror sends back the image. **Han devuelto el castillo a su antiguo esplendor,** they have restored the castle to its former glory.

devorador, ra [day-vo-rah-dor', rah], *m. & f.* Devourer. **Una mujer devoradora de hombres,** a man-eating woman.

devorar [dayvorar'], *va.* To devour, to swallow up, to consume ravenously, to glut. **Todo lo devoró el fuego,** the fire consumed everything. **Le devoran los celos,** he is consumed with jealously.

devotamente [day-vo-tah-men'-tay], *adv.* Devoutly, piously.

devoto, ta [day-vo'-to, tah], *a.* 1. Devout, pious, devotional, religious, godly. 2. Exciting devotion. 3. Strongly attached. **Devoto de monjas,** he who frequently visits and converses with nuns. **Su devoto amigo,** your devoted friend. **Es devoto de ese café,** he is much attached to that café.

devuelto, ta [day-voo-el'-to, tah], *pp. irr.* of DEVOLVER. Returned, restored.

dexiocardia [dek-se-o-car-de-ah], *f.* Deviation of the heart to the right side of the thoracic cavity.

dextrina [dex-tree'-nah], *f.* Dextrine.

dextrosa [dex-tro'-sah], *f. (Chem.)* Dextrose.

dezmable [deth-mah'-blay], *a.* Tithable, subject to tithes.

dezmar [deth-mar'], *va. V.* DIEZMAR.

dezmatorio [deth-mah-to'-re-o], *m.* 1. Place in which tithes are collected. 2. Tithing.

dezmero, ra [dayth-may'-ro], *a.* Belonging to tithes.

dezmería, dezmía [deth-may-ree'-ah, deth-mee'-ah], *f.* Titheland.

dezmero [deth-may'-ro], *m.* 1. One who pays tithes. 2. Tithegatherer; a tither.

día [dee'-ah], *m.* 1. Day: the space of twenty-four hours. 2. Day: the time between the rising and setting of the sun. 3. Daylight, sunshine. -*pl.* 1. Certain lapse of time, a certain epoch. 2. Existence, life. **Día de cumpleaños**, birthday. **Día de ayuno o de vigilia**, fasting-day or fastday. **Día de viernes**, day on which fish is eaten instead of meat. **Día de trabajo**, working-day. **Día de descanso**, 1. Day of rest. 2. The Sabbath-day. **Día del juicio**, doomsday. **Día laborable**, working-day. **Día natural**, from midnight to midnight. **De día**, by day. **De un día para otro** or **de día en día**, from day to day. **Un día sí y otro no**, or **cada tercer día**, every other day. **Hasta el día de hoy**, to this day. **El día de hoy** or **hoy en día**, the present day. **El mejor día**, some fine day. **Día pesado**, a dull, gloomy day. **Luz del día**, daylight. **Entre día**, in the daytime. **Tener días**, *(Coll.)* 1. To vary in one's physiognomy or countenance. 2. To be full of days, to be old. **De hoy en ocho días**, this day week. **Días complementarios**, complementary days which the Aztecs added at the end of the year to complete it. **Días de gracia**, days of grace allowed for the payment of bills. **Buenos días**, good morning. **En cuatro días**, in a short time. **Hace buen día**, it's a fine day. **Parece que no pasan por ti los días**, you don't look a day older. **Un día de éstos**, one of these days. **Todos los días**, every day. **7 veces al día**, 7 times a day. **Poner al día**, to enter up, to write up. **Día festivo**, vacation. **Día libre**, free day, day off. **Día señalado**, special day.

diabetes [de-ah-bay'-tes], *f.* Diabetes, a disease whose chief symptom is the abundant excretion of sugar in the urine.

diabético, ca [de-ah-bay'-te-co, cah], *a.* Diabetic, relating to diabetes.

diabla (A la) [de-ah'-blah (ah'lah)], *adv.* Carelessly; rudely. *f.* 1. A machine for carding wool of cotton. **Cosido a la diabla**, bound in paper. 2. A truck.

diablazo [de-ah-blah'-tho]; *m. aug.* A great devil.

diablear [de-ah-blay-ar'], *vn. (Coll.)* To commit deviltries, play pranks.

diablesa [de-ah-blay'-sah], *f. (Coll.)* A she-devil.

diablillo [de-ah-bleel'-lyo], *m.* 1. *(Dim.)* Deviling, devilkin, a little devil. 2. An acute, clever man.

diablo [de-ah'-blo], *m.* 1. Devil, Satan. **Ése es el diablo**, that's the devil of it. 2. Person of a perverse temper. 3. An ugly person. 4. A cunning, subtle person. **Ser la piel** or **de la piel del diablo**, to be a limb of the devil. **Pobre diablo**, poor devil. **Algún pobre diablo de cartero**, some poor devil of a postman.

diablotín, diabolín [de-ah-blo-teen', de-ah-bo-leen'], *m.* A sort of sweetmeat.

diablura [de-ah-bloo'-rah], *f.* A diabolical undertaking, devilishness, deviltry, mischief, wild prank.

diabólicamente [de-ah-bo'-le-cah-men-tay], *adv.* Diabolically, devilishly.

diabólico, ca [de-ah-bo'-le-co, cah], *a.* Diabolical, devilish.

diabrosis [de-ah-bro'-sis], *f.* Ulceration, erosion, corrosion.

diabrótico, ca [de-ah-bro'-te-co, cah], *a.* Corrosive, erosisve. -*m.* **Diabrótico**, a beetle destructive to vegetation.

diacasis [de-ah-cah'-sis], *m.* A purgative prepared from Cassia fistula (related to senna).

diacatalicón [de-ah-cah-tah-le-cone'], *m.* Diacatholicion, a universal medicine or purge.

diacitrón [de-ah-the-trone'], *m.* Lemon-peel preserved in sugar.

diaco [de-ah'-co], *a. & m.* A cleric of the order of Malta, who reached a chaplaincy only after twelve years of service.

diaconado [de-ah-co-nah'-do], *m. V.* DIACONATO.

diaconal [de-ah-co-nahl'], *a.* Diaconal.

diaconato [de-ah-co-nah'-to], *m.* Deanconship.

diaconía [de-ah-co-nee'-ah], *f.* Deaconry.

diaconisa [de-ah-co-nee'-sah], *f.* Deaconess.

diácono [de-ah'-co-no], *m.* Deacon, clergyman next in order below a priest.

diácope [de-ah'-co-pay], *m.* 1. *(Glam.)* Hyperbaton. 2. Incision, longitudinal fracture of a bone.

diacorético, ca [de-ah-co-ray'-te-co, cah], *a.* Having the property of producing evacuations.

diacrítico, ca [de-ah-cree'-te-co, cah], *a.* Diacritic, diacritical; distinguishing, diagnostic.

diacroción [de-ah-cro-the-on'], *m.* A collyrium prepared from saffrom.

diacústica [de-ah-coos'-te-cah], *f.* Diacoustics, the doctrine of sounds.

diadelfia [de-ah-del'-fe-ah], *f.* A plant having the stamens united into two sets.

diadelfo, fa [de-ah-del'-fo, fah], *a.* Diadelphous, with stamens in two sets.

diadema [de-ah-day'-mah], *f.* 1. Diadem, crown. 2. Crown, glory, a circle of metal put round the heads of images; represented in pictures by luminous circles.

diademado, da [de-ah-day-mah'-do, dah], *a. (Her.)* Diademed, adorned with a diadem.

diafanidad [de-ah-fah-ne-dahd'], *f.* Disphaneity, transparency, pellucidiness.

diáfano, na [de-ah'-fah-no, nah], *a.* 1. Transparent, pellucid, clear, lucid, diaphanous. 2. *(Amer.)* Finical, timid, and affected.

diafiláctico, ca [de-ah-fe-lahc'-te-co, cah], *a. (Med.)* Prophylactic.

diaforesis [de-ah-fo-ray'-sis], *f.* Diaphoresis, gentle perspiration.

diaforético. ca [de-ah-fo-ray'-te-co, cah], *a. (Med.)* Diaphoretic.

diafragma [de-ah-frahg'-mah], *m.* 1. Diaphragm, the midriff. 2. Cartilaginous partition of the nostrils. 3. A perforated disk used to cut off marginal rays in some optical instruments, or the vibrating disk of a telephone. 4. The porous cup of a voltaic cell.

diafragmático, ca [de-ah-frag-mah'-to-co, cah], *a.* Diaphragmatic, relating to the diaphragm.

diagnosis [de-ahg-no'-ses], *f.* Diagnosis.

diagnosticar [de-ag-nos-te-car'], *va.* To diagnosticate, form the diagnosis.

diagnóstico [de-ag-nos'-te-co], *m. & a. (Med.)* Diagnostic, a distinguishing symptom; diagnosis.

diagonal [de-ah-go-nahl'], *a.* Diagonal.

diagonalmente [de-ah-go-nal-men'-tay], *adv.* Diagonally.

diagráfica [de-ah-grah'-fe-cah], *f.* Sketch, design.

diagráfico, ca [de-ah-grah'-fe-co, cah], *a.* Diagraphic, showing by lines.

diagrafita [de-ah-grah-fee'-tah], *f.* Graphite, from which drawing-pencils are made.

diagrama [de-ah-grah'-mah], *f.* Diagram. **Diagrama de barras**, bar chart. **Diagrama circular** *(Comput.)*, pie chart. **Diagrama de Venn** *(Comput.)*, Venn diagram.

dialage [de-ah-lah'-hay], *m.* Diallage, the use of many arguments to prove one proposition.

dialéctica [de-ah-lec'-te-cah], *f.* Logic, dialectic.

dialéctico [de-ah-lec'-te-co], *m.* Dialectician, logician.

dialéctico, ca [de-ah-lec'-te-co, cah], *a.* Dialectical, logical.

dialecto [de-ah-lec'-to], *m.* Dialect, phraseology, speech.

diálisis [de-ah'-le-sis], *f.* Dialysis.

dialogal [de-ah-lo-gahl'], *a.* Relating to dialogue; written in dialogue.

dialogar [de-ah-lo-gar'], *vn.* 1. To speak a dialogue. 2. To sing responsively.

dialogismo [de-ah-lo-he-es'-mo], *m.* Dialogism.

dialogístico, ca [de-ah-lo-hees'-te-co, cah], *a.* Colloquial.

dialogizar [de-ah-lo-he-thar'], *vn.* To dialogize, to discourse in dialogue.

diálogo [de-ah'-lo-go], *m.* Dialogue.

dialoguista [de-ah-lo-gees'-tah], *m.* Dialogist.

diamantazo [de-ah-man-tah'-tho], *m. aug.* A large diamond.

diamante [de-ah-mahn'-tay], *m.* 1. Diamond. **Diamante en bruto**, uncut diamond. **Ser un diamante en bruto**, *(fig.)* To be a rough diamond. 2. Hardness, resistance.

diamantino, na [de-ah-man-tee'-no, nah], *a.* Adamantine, diamantine.

diamantista [de-ah-man-tees'-tah], *m.* V. LAPIDARIO.

diametral [de-ah-may-trahl'], *a.* Diametrical.

diametralmente [de-ah-may-tral-men'-tay], *adv.* Diametrically.

diámetro [de-ah'-may-tro], *m. (Geom.)* Diameter.

diana [de-ah'-nah], *f. (Mil.)* 1. Reveille, the beating of the drum at daybreak. 2. The moon.

dianche, diantre [de-ahn'-chay, de-ahn'-tray], *m. & int. (Coll.)* Deuce, the devil.

diantero [de-an-tay'-ro, rah], *a.* Having two anthers.

dianto, ta [de-ahn'-to, tah], *a.* Having two flowers, biflorous.

diapasón [de-ah-pah-so-ne'], *m.* 1. Diapason, an octave (from ancient Greek music). 2. A rule provided with scales of equal parts. 3. A tuning-fork, or the standard pitch given by the tuningfork. 4. Measure, compass.

diapente [de-ah-pen'-tay], *m. (Mus.)* A perfect fifth.

diapiema, diapiesis [de-ah-pe-ay'-mah, deah-peay'sis], *f.* Suppuration.

diapositiva [de-ah-po-se-tee'-vah], *f. (Phot.)* Plate, slide. **Diapositiva en color**, color slide.

diaprea [de-ah-pray-ah], *f.* Sort of round plum.

diaquea [de-ah-kay'-ah], *f.* A small fungus which grows on decayed wood.

diaquilón [de-ah-ke-lo-ne'], *m.* Lead plaster, diachylon.

diaria [de-ah'-re-ah], *f. (Naut.)* Supply of provisions and arms for a fortnight.

diariamente [de-ah-re-ah-men'-tay], *adv.* Daily.

diario, ria [de-ah'-re-o, ah], *a.* Daily.

diario, *m.* 1. Journal, diary; daily newspaper. **Diario dominical**. Sunday paper. 2. Diary, a daily account. **Nuestro mantel de diario**, our tablecloth for everyday. **Para diario**, for everyday use. 3. Daily expense. 4. Log. **Diario de navegación**, log-book.

diarista [de-ah-rees'-tah], *com.* Journalist.

diarrea [de-ar-ray'-ah], *f.* Diarrhoea.

diasfixia [de-as-feek'-se-ah], *f. (Med.)* Rapid pulse, palpitation of the heart.

diáspero, diaspro [de-ahs'-pay-ro, de-ahs'-pro], *m.* Jasper.

diastasia [de-as-tah'-se-ah], *f.* Diastase, a proximate principle discovered in cereals after germination.

diastema [de-as-tay'-mah], *m.* 1. Diasteme, name of pores scattered over the surface of bodies, which can be demonstrated only by the penetration of liquids. 2. *(Mus.)* A simple interval, in contrast to a complex. 3. Interspace between two consecutive teeth.

diástole [de-ahs'-to-lay], *m.* 1. *(Anat.)* Diastole, the dilatation of the heart. 2. *(Rhet.)* Diastole, a figure by which a short syllable is made long.

diastólico, ca [de-as-toh'-le-co, cah], *a.* Diastolic, relating to the diastole.

diatérmano. na [de-ah-terr'-mah-no, nah], *f.* Diathermanous, allowing free passage to rays of heat.

diatermia [de-ah-ter'-me-ah], *f.* Diathermy.

diatesarón [de-ah-tay-sah-ron'], *m.* 1. The harmony of the four Gospels. 2. *(Mus.)* Diatessaron, the interval of a fourth.

diatéstico, ca [de-ah-tay'-se-co, cah], *a. (Med.)* Diathetic, belonging to a diathesis.

diátesis [de-ah'-tay-sis], *f. (Med.)* Diathesis, organic disposition to contract certain diseases.

diatónico [de-ah-toh'-ne-co], *a. (Mus.)* Diatonic.

diatriba [de-ah-tree'-bah], *f.* Diatribe, a dissertation or discourse on polemic matters; a severe criticism on works of genius.

dibit [de-beet], *(Comput.)* Dibit.

dibujador, ra [de-boo-hah-dor', rah], *m. & f.* 1. Delineator. 2. Graver, a tool used in graving.

dibujante [de-boo-hahn'-tay], *m. & pa.* Designer, sketching. **Comerciante de publicidad**, commercial artist.

dibujar [de-boo-har'], *va.* 1. To draw, to design, to delineate, to sketch. 2. *(Met.)* To paint any passion of the mind. -*vr.* 1. To throw a shadow upon a surface. 2. To show, to appear. **El sufrimiento se dibuja en su cara**, suffering showed in his face.

dibujo [de-boo'-ho], *m.* 1. Design, drawing, sketch, draught. 2. Delineation, description. **Es un dibujo**, it is a picture (cara bonita). **Dibujos animados**, cartoon. **Un papel con dibujos a rayas**, a wallpaper with a stripped pattern.

dicacidad [de-ca-the-dahd'], *f.* 1. Pertness, sauciness, loquacity. 2. Jesting sarcasm.

dicaz [de-cath'], *a.* Keen, biting (said of speech).

dicción [dic-the-on'], *f.* Diction, style, language, expression.

diccionario [dic-the-o-nah'-re-o], *m.* Dictionary, lexicon. **Diccionario de bolsillo**, pocket dictionary.

dicha [dee'-chah], *f.* Happiness, felicity, fortune, good luck, good fortune. **Por dicha** or **a dicha**, by chance. **Para completar su dicha**, to complete her happiness.

dicharacho [de-chah-rah'-cho], *m. (Coll.)* A vulgar, low, or indecent expression.

dichido, dichito [de-chee'-do, de-chee'-to], *m. (Coll.)* A sharp or pert expression, small talk.

dicho [dee'-cho], *m.* 1. Saying, expression, sentence. 2. Declaration, deposition. 3. Promise of marriage. **Dicho y hecho**, no sooner said than done. **Del dicho al hecho hay gran trecho**, (prov.) saying and doing are two very different things. **Es un dicho**, it's just a saying. -*a.* Said. **Dichos animales**, the said animals. **En dicho país**, in this country. —**Dicho, cha**, *pp. irr.* of DECIR.

dichosamente [de-cho-sah-men-tay], *adv.* Happily, fortunately, luckily.

dichoso, sa [de-cho'-so, sah], *a.* Happy, fortunate, prosperous, successful, lucky. **Hacer dichoso a uno**, to make somebody happy. **Me siento dichoso de**, I feel happy to.

diciembre [de-the-em'-bray], *m.* December.

diciente [de-the-en'-tay], *pa.* of DECIR. Saying, talking.

dicotiledón, dicotiledóneo, a [de-co-te-lay-done'], *a. (Bot.)* Dicotyledonous, having two seedleaves.

dicotomal [de-co-to-mahl'], *a.* Dichotomal.

dicotomía [de-co-to-mee'-ah], *f.* 1. State of the moon when the sun illuminates no more than half its disk. 2. The angle formed by two dichotomous branches.

dicotómico, ca, or **dicótomo, ma** [de-co-to'-me-co], *a. (Bot.)* Subdividing into two; dichotomous. *(Astr.)* Halflighted (Moon, Venus y Mercury).

dicroismo [de-cro-ees'-mo], *m.* Dichroism, the property of showing different colors when viewed in different directions.

dicrónico, ca [de-cro'-ne-co, cah], *a.* Having two epochs or seasons in vegetation.

dicroto, ta [de-cro'-to, tah], *a. (Med.)* Dicrotic, dicrotous, showing two beats to each systole.

dictado [dic-tah'-do], *m.* 1. A title of dignity or honor. **Dictado, da**, *pp.* of DICTAR. 2. Dictation. **Escribir al dictado**, to take dictation.

dictador [dic-tah-dor'], *m.* Dictator, an ancient magistrate of Rome, invested with absolute authority.

dictadura [dic-tah-doo'-rah], *f.* Dictatorship, dictature.

dictáfono [dic-tah'-fo-no], *m.* Dictaphone, dictating machine.

dictamen [dic-tah'-men], *m.* 1. Opinion, sentiments, notion, judgment, mind. 2. Suggestion, insinuation, dictate.

dictaminar [dic-tah-me-nar'], *va.* To pass (sentencia). -*vn.* To pass judgement, to give an opinion.

díctamo [deec'-tah-mo], *m. (Bot.)* Dittany. **Díctamo blanco** or **real**, white flaxinella. **Díctamo crético**, dittany of Crete, marjoram. **Díctamo bastardo**, shrubby white horehound.

dictar [dic-tar'], *va.* 1. To dictate, to deliver one's opinions with authority. **Lo que dicta el sentido común**, what common sense suggests. 2. To dictate, to pronounce what another is to say or write.

dictatorio, ria [dic-tah-to'-re-o, ah], *a.* Dictatorial.

dicterio [dic-tay'reo], *m.* Sarcasm, taunt, keen reproach, insult.

didáctica [de-dahc'-te-cah], *a.* The art of teaching, pedagogy.

didáctico, ca, didascálico, ca [de-dahc'-te-co, cah, de-das-cah'-le-co, cah], *a.* Didactic, didactical, preceptive, giving precepts.

didascalia [de-das-cah'-le-ah], *f.* Pedagogy, the science and rules of teaching.

didelfo [de-del'-fo], *m.* The opossum.

didínamo, ma [de-dee'-nah-mo, mah], *a.* Didynamous: said of stamens arranged in two pairs of different sizes.

diecinueve [de-ay-the-noo-ay'-vay], *a. & m.* Nineteen.

diecinueveavo, va [de-ay-the-noo-ay-vay-ah'-vo, vah], *a.* Nineteenth.

dieciochavo, va [de-ay-the-o-chah'-vo, vah], *a. & m.* 1. An eighteenth part. 2. *(Typ.)* 18°, octodécimo, a sheet folding into 18 parts, or 36 pages.

dieciocheno, na [de-ay-the-o-chay'-no, nah], *a. & m.* 1. Eighteenth 2. A kind of cloth.

dieciséis [de-ay-the-say'-es], *a.* Sixteen; sixteenth.

diecisiete [de-ay-the-se-ay'-tay], *a.* Seventeen; seventeenth.

dieciseisavo [de-ay-the-say-es-ah'-vo], *m.* Décimo-sexto: applied to a book printed on a sheet folded into 16 leaves.

dieciseiseno, na [de-ay-the-say-es-ay'-no, nah], *a.* Sixteenth.

diecisieteavo, va [de-ay-the-se-ay-tay-ah'-vo, vah], *a.* Seventeenth.

diedro, dra [de-ay'-dro, drah], *a.* Dihedral, formed by or having two plane faces, as a dihedral angle.

diente [de-ayn'-tay], *m.* 1. Tooth. 2. Prop used by founders to secure the founding-frame. 3. Fang or tusk of wild boars. **Diente molar**, *V.* MUELA. **Diente incisivo**, incisor, foretooth. 4. Jag, a protuberance or denticulation. **Diente de lobo**, burnisher, a burnishing or polishing instrument. **Dientes de elefante**, elephant's tusks. **Dientes de jabalí**, wild boar's teeth. **Dientes postizos**, artificial teeth. **Diente de perro**, sampler, a piece worked by young girls. **Diente de león**, *(Bot.)* dandelion or lion's tooth. **Diente de perro**, *(Bot.)* dog's tooth violet. -*pl.* 1. The indented edges of different instruments, jags. 2. The prominent parts of wheels. **Dientes de ajo**, cloves of garlic. **Crujir de dientes**, to grind the teeth. **Tomar a uno entre dientes**, to have an antipathy against a person. **Pelear hasta con los dientes**, *(Coll.)* to fight tooth and nail. **Hablar** or **decir entre dientes**, to mumble, to mutter. **Hincar el diente**, to appropriate property to oneself. *(Coll.)* To censure, to grumble at. **Mostrar los dientes**, to oppose a person, to growl at him, to show spunk. **Diente de leche**, milk tooth.

dientecico, illo, ito [de-en-tay-thee'-co, theel'-lyo, ee'-to], *m. dim.* Little tooth.

diéresis [de-ay'-ray-sis], *f.* 1. *(Rhet.)* Diaeresis, poetical figure. 2. The two points placed over a vowel to show that it does not form a diphthong with the following vowel, as flu *argüir*.

diesel [de-ay'-sayl], **Motor diesel**, diesel engine.

diesi [de-ay'-se], *f. (Mus.)* The smallest and simplest part into which a tone is divided.

diestra [de-es'-trah], *f.* 1. The right hand. 2. *(Met.)* Favor, support, protection. **Juntar diestra con diestra**, To shake hands, to make up matters.

diestramente [de-es-trah-men-tay], *adv.* Dexterously, cleverly, neatly.

diestro, tra [de-es-tro, trah], *a.* 1. Right, dexter. 2. Dexterous, skillful, handy. 3. Sagacious, prudent, knowing, learned. 4. Sly, artful, cunning. 5. Favorable, propitious. **A diestro y siniestro**, right or wrong. **Llevar del diestro**, to lead a beast by the helter or bridle. **Repartir golpes a diestro y siniestro**, to lash out wildy.

diestro [de-es-tro], *m.* 1. A skilful fencer. 2. Halter or bridle for horses.

dieta [de-ay'-tah], *f.* 1. Diet, regimen, food regulated by the rules of medicine. **Dieta láctea**, milk diet. 2. Diet, the assembly of the ministers of the states of Germany. 3. *(Law.)*

One day's journey of ten leagues by land. 4. Daily salary of judges and other officers of the law. **Dietas**, *(Naut.)* cattle put on board a fleet, to furnish fresh provisions for the sick.

dietética [de-ay-tay'-te-cah], *f.* Dietetics, that branch of hygiene which treats of diet.

dietético, ca [de-ay-tay'-te-co, cah], *a.* Dietetic, dietetical.

diéxodo [de-ek'-so-do], *m.* Every secretory passage; emunctory, some use this term as synonymous of dejection, evacuation.

diez [de-eth'], *m.* Ten. **Las diez**, ten oclock.

diezma [de-eth'-mah], *f. (Prov.)* V. DÉCIMA and DIEZMO.

diezmador [de-eth-mah-dor'], *m. (Prov.)* V. DIEZMERO.

diezmal [de-eth-mahl'], *a.* Decimal tenth.

diezmar [de-eth-mar'], *va.* 1. To decimate, to take the tenth, to tithe. 2. To tithe, to pay the tithe to the church. 3. *(Mil.)* When there are many offenders, to punish one in ten.

diezmero [de-eth-may'-ro], *m.* 1. He who pays the tithe. 2. Tither, he who gathers the tithe.

diezmesino, na [de-eth-may-see'-no, nah], *a.* That which is ten months, or belongs to that tine.

diezmo [de-eth'-mo], *m.* 1. Tithe, the tenth part. 2. Duty of ten per cent paid to the king. 3. Tithe, the tenth part of the fruits of the earth assigned to the maintenance of the clergy. 4. Decimation.

difamación [de-fah-mah-the-on'], *f.* Defamation, libelling.

difamador [de-fah-mah-dor'], *m.* Defamer, libeller.

difamar [de-fah-mar'], *va.* To defame, to discredit; to libel. To divulge.

difamatorio, ria [de-fah-mah-to'-re-o, ah], *a.* Defamatory, scandalous, calumnious, contumelious, libellous.

difarreación [de-far-ray-ah-the-on'], *f.* Diffarreation, the parting of a cake, a sacrifice performed between man and wife at their divorce, among the Romans.

diferencia [defay-ren'-the-ah], *f.* 1. Difference. 2. Dissimilarity, dissimilitude. 3. Controversy, contrariety, mutual opposition. **A diferencia**, with the difference. **Diferencia de edades**, difference in ages. **Hacer diferencia entre**, to make a distinction between. **Partir la diferencia**, to split the difference.

diferencial [de-fay-ren-the-ahl'], *a.* Differential, different. **Cálculo diferencial**, differential calculus. -*m. (Mech.)* Differential, differential gear. -*f. (Math.)* Differential.

diferenciar [de-fay-ren-the-ar'], *va.* 1. To differ, to make different, to differentiate. 2. To change or alter the use or destination of things. -*vn.* To differ, to dissent, to disagree in opinion. -*vr.* 1. To differ, to be distinguished from. 2. To distinguish oneself. **No se diferencian en nada**, they do not differ at all. **Se diferencian en que…**, they differ in that…

diferente [de-fay-ren'-tay], *a.* Different, dissimilar, unlike. **Por diferentes razones**, for various reasons.

diferentemente [de-fay-ren-tay-men'-tay], *adv.* Differently, diversely.

diferido [de-fay-re-do], *a.* **Emisión diferida, emisión en diferido**, recorded program.

diferir [de-fay-reer'], *va.* To defer, to delay, to put off. **Diferir algo para otro tiempo**, to defer anything to another time. -*vn.* 1. To differ, to be different. 2. *(Naut.)* To remove the gaskets of a sail.

difícil [de-fee'-theel], *a.* 1. Difficult, arduous, hard, laborious. **Difícil de vencer**, hard to beat. **Creo que lo tiene difícil**, I think he's got a tough job on. **Es un hombre difícil**, he is a difficult man. 2. Unlikely. **Es difícil que…**, it is unlikely that…. 3. Odd, ugly (cara).

difícilmente [de-fee'-theel-men-tay], *adv.* Difficultly, hardly.

dificultad [de-fe-cool-tahd'], *f.* 1. Difficulty, embarrassment, hardness. 2. Difficulty, objection, adverse argument. **Sin dificultad alguna**, without the least difficulty. **Ha tenido dificultades con la policía**, he's been in trouble with the police. **Poner dificultades**, to raise objections.

dificultador [de-fe-cool-tah-dor'], *m.* One who starts or raises difficulties.

dificultar [de-fe-cool-tar'], *va*. 1. To start or raise difficulties. 2. To render difficult.

dificultosamente [de-fe-cool-to-sah-men'-tay], *adv*. Difficultly.

dificultoso, sa [de-fe-cool-to-so, sah], *a*. 1. Difficult, hard, troublesome, tiresome, laborious, painful. 2. Ugly, deformed: applied to the face.

difidación [de-fe-dah-the-on'], *f*. Manifesto, a declaration issued in justification of a war.

difidencia [de-fe-den'-the-ah], *f*. Distrust, doubtfulness.

difidente [de-fe-den'-tay], *a*. Disloyal, distrustful.

difluir [de-floo-eer'], *vn*. To be diffused, to spread out, to be shed.

difracción [de-frac-the-on'], *f*. Diffraction.

difractar [de-frac-tar'], *va*. To diffract a ray of light.

difractivo, va [de-frac-tee'-vo, vah], *a*. Diffractive, causing diffraction.

difrige [de-free'-hay], *m*. Dross of melted copper, gathered in the furnace.

difteria [dif-tay'-reah], *f*. Diphteria, a disease characterized by the formation of false membranes.

diftérico, ca [dif-tay'-re-co, cah], *a*. Diphtheritic, belonging to diphtheria.

difugio [de-foo'-he-o], *m*. V. EFUGIO.

difuminado [de-foo-me-nah'-do], *a*. Slurred, husky (voz).

difuminar [de-foo-me-nahr'], *va*. To blur. -*vr*. 1. To shade into. 2. (*Fig*.) To fade away.

difumino [de-foo-mee'-no], *m*. V. ESFUMINO.

difundido, da [de-foon-dee'-no, nah], *a. & pp*. of DIFUNDIR. Diffuse, diffused, scattered.

difundir [de-foon-deer'], *va*. 1. To diffuse, to extend, to outspread. **Difundir la alegría**, to spread happiness. 2. (*Met*.) To divulge, to publish. -*vr*. To spread; to become diffused.

difunto, ta [de-foon'-to, tah], *a*. 1. Defunct, dead; late. **El difunto ministro**, the late minister. 2. (*Met*.) Decayed, withered. **Día de los difuntos**, all-souls' Day, celebrated on Nov. 2nd by the Roman church. Instituted in 998. -*m*. V. CADÁVER.

difusamente [de-foo-sah-men'-tay], *adv*. Diffusely, diffusedly.

difusible [de-foo-see'-blay], *a*. Diffusible, of rapid diffusion.

difusión [de-foo-se-on'], *f*. 1. Diffusion, diffusiveness, dispersion. 2. (*Met*.) Diffusion, copiousness or exuberance of style.

difusivo, va [de-foo-see'-vo, vah], *a*. Diffusive.

difuso, sa [de-foo'-so, sah], *a*. Diffuse, diffusive, copious, ample, wide-spread.

digástrico, ca [de-gahs'-tre-co, cah], *a*. Digastric, of two muscular bands.

digerible [de-hay-ree'-blay], *a*. Digestible.

digerir [de-hay-reer'], *va*. 1. To digest. 2. (*Met*.) To bear with patience any loss or affront. 3. (*Met*.) To examine carefully into a thing. 4. (*Met*.) To digest, to adjust, to arrange methodically in the mind. **No puedo digerir a ese tío**, I can't stand that chap. 5. (*Them*.) To digest, to soften by heat, as in a boiler.

digestible [de-hes-te-on'], *a*. Digestible.

digestión [de-hes-te-on'], *f*. 1. Digestion. 2. Digestion, preparation of matter by chemical heat. **Hombre de mala digestion**, a man of a peevish, fretful temper. **Negocio de mala digestión**, a perplexed affair.

digestivo [de-hes-tee'-vo], *m*. (*Surg*.) Digestive, an application which disposes a wound to generate matter.

digestivo, va [de-hes-tee'-vo, vah], *a*. Digestive, assisting digestion.

digesto [de-hes'-to], *m*. Digest.

digino, na [de-hee'-no, nah], *a*. Digynous, having two pistils.

digitación [de-he-tah-the-on'], *f*. The art which teaches the use of the fingers upon some instrument.

digitado, da [de-he-tah-do, dah], *a*. Digitate, arranged like fingers. (*Bot. and Zool*.)

digital [de-ne-tahl'], *a*. Digital, belonging to or like fingers. **Huellas digitales**, fingerprints. -*f*. Digitalis, foxglove, a medicinal plant.

digitalina [de-he-tah-lee'-nah], *f*. Digitalin, a poisonous alkaloid procured from digitalis.

digitígrado, da [de-he-tee'-grah-do, dah], *a*. Digitigrade, walking on the toes; opposed to plantigrade.

dígito [dee'-he-to], *m*. (*Ast*.) Digit, the twelfth part of the diameter of the sun or moon.

dignación [dig-nah-the-on'], *f*. Condescension, voluntary humiliation.

dignamente [dig-nah-men'-tay], *adv*. 1. Worthily; fittingly, properly, appropriately. 2. Honorably. 3. With dignity. 4. Decently.

dignarse [dig-nar'-say], *vr*. To condescend, to deign, to vouchsafe.

dignatario [dig-nah-tah'-re-o], *m*. A dignitary, one who holds high rank, especially ecclesiastical.

dignidad [dig-ne-dahd'], *f*. 1. Dignity, rank, honor, greatness. **Herir la dignidad de uno**, to offend somebody's self-respect. 2. Dignity, grandeur of mien, nobleness. 3. Dignity, advancement, high place. 4. Among ecclesiastics, the prebend of a cathedral superior to a simple canonry, and the dignitary who possesses it. 5. The dignity of an archbishop or bishop. 6. (*Astrol*.) Dignity, the state of a planet being in any sign.

dignificante [dig-ne-fe-cahn'-tay], *pa*. (*Theol*.) Dignifying, that which dignifies.

dignificar [dig-ne-fe-car'], *va*. To dignify.

digno, na [deeg'-no, nah], *a*. 1. Meritorious, worthy, deserving. **Digno de**, worthy of. **Digno de mención**, worth a mention. 2. Condign, suitable, correspondent. **Digno de alabanza**, worthy to be praised. **Es digno**, it is worthwhile.

digresión [de-gray-se-on'], *f*. 1. Digression, deviation from the main scope of a speech or treatise. 2. (*Astr*.) Departure of a planet from the equinoctial line.

digresivamente [de-gray-se'-vah-men-tay], *adv*. Digressively.

digresivo, va [de-gray-see'-vo, vah], *a*. Digressive.

dije (or**dij**) [dee'-hay], *m*. 1. A trinket put upon a child. 2. *pl*. Trinkets relics, used for personal adornment. *Dije*, 1st pers. sing, past tense, of **decir**: I said.

dilaceración [de-lah-thay-rah-the-on'], *f*. Dilaceration.

dilacerar [de-lah-thay-rar'], *va*. To dilacerate, to tear.

dilacion [de-lah-theon'], *f*. 1. Delay, dilation, procrastination. 2. Dilatation, expansion.

dilapidación [de-lah-pe-dah-the-on'], *f*. Dilapidation.

dilapidador [de-lah-pe-dah-dor'], *m*. Dilapidator.

dilapidar [de-lah-pe-dar'], *va*. To dilapidate, to waste.

dilatable [de-lah-tah'-blay], *a*. Dilatable.

dilatación [de-lah-tah-the-on'], *f*. 1. Dilatation, extension, amplification. 2. Evenness, greatness of mind, calmness.

dilatadamente [de-lah-tah-dah-men'-tay], *adv*. With dilatation.

dilatado, da [de-lah-tah'-do, dah], *a. & pp*. of DILATAR. 1. Large, numerous, great. 2. Prolix, long, not concise. 3. Spacious, extensive, vast.

dilatador, ra [de-lah-tah-dor', rah], *m. & f*. 1. One who dilates or extends. 2. Dilator, an instrument for stretching.

dilatar [de-lah-tar'], *va*. 1. To dilate, to expand, to enlarge, to lengthen, to spread out. 2. To defer, to retard to delay, to put off, to protract. 3. (*Met*.) To comfort, to cheer up. -*vr*. To expatiate or enlarge on any subject. **El valle se dilata en aquella parte**, the valley widens at that point.

dilatativo, va [de-lah-tah-tee'-vo, vah], *a*. That which dilates.

dilatoria [de-lah-to'-re-ah], *f*. V. DILACIóN. A term given by a court of judge to a debtor. **Andar con dilatorias**, to waste time by deceiving with false promises.

dilatorio, ria [de-lah-to'-re-o, ah], *a*. Dilatory, delaying, long.

dilección [de-lec-the-on'], *f*. Love, affection.

dilecto, ta [de-lec'-to, tah], *a*. Loved beloved.

dilema [de-lay'-mah], *m.* Dilemma, an argument equally conclusive by contrary suppositions. **Estar en un dilema**, to be in a dilemma.

dilemático, ca [de-lay-mah'-te-co, cah], *a.* Belonging to a dilemma, dilemmatic.

diligencia [de-le-hen'-the-ah], *f.* 1. Diligence, assiduity, laboriousness. 2. Haste, hastiness, speed, diligence, activity, briskness in the performance of a thing. 3. *(Coll.)* Affair, business, something to be transacted, obligation. **Tengo que ir a una diligencia**, I must go upon some business. **Hacer diligencias**, to do business. 4. Return of a writ, judicial formalties procedure. **Hacer las diligencias de cristiano**, to perform the duty of a Christian. **Hacer diligencia**, to try, to endeavor. 5. Stage-coach, diligence.

diligenciar [de-le-hen-the-ar'], *va.* To exert oneself; to endeavor.

diligenciero [de-le-hen-the-ay'-ro], *m.* 1. Agent, attorney. 2. Apparitor, summoner; the lowest officer of an ecclesiastical court.

diligente [de-le-hen'-tay], *a.* 1. Diligent, assiduous, careful, laborious, active. 2. Prompt, swift, ready. **Diligente en aprender**, diligent to learn.

diligentemente [de-le-hen'-tay-men-tay], *adv.* Diligently, assiduously.

dilíndilín [de-leen'-de-leen'], *m.* The sound of a bell; dingdong. (Imitative.)

dilogía [de-lo-hee'-ah], *f.* 1. Ambiguity, double sense. 2. Drama with two actions at once.

dilucidación [de-loo-the-dah-the-on'], *f.* Elucidation, explanation, illustration.

dilucidador [de-loo-the-dah-dor'], *m.* Elucidator.

dilucidar [de-loo-the-dar'], *va.* To elucidate, to explain.

dilucidario [de-loo-the-dah'-re-o], *m.* Explanatory writing.

dilución [de-loo-the-on'], *f.* Dilution, solution.

diluente [de-loo-en'-tay], *pa.* Diluent.

diluición [de-loo-e-the-on'], *va.* Dilution.

diluido [de-loo-e'-do], *a.* Dilute; diluted, weak; watered-down.

diluir [de-loo-eer'], *va.* To dilute anything.

diluviano [de-loo-ve-ah'-no], *a.* Diluvian; relating to the deluge.

diluviar [de-loo-ve-ar'], *vn. imp.* To rain like a deluge.

diluvio [de-loo'-ve-o], *m.* 1. Deluge overflow, inundation, flood. 2. *(Met.)* Vast abundance.

dimanación [de-mah-nah-the-on'], *f.* Act of springing or issuing from, origin.

dimanante [de-mah-nahn'-tay], *pa.* Springing or proceeding from, originating.

dimanar [de-mah-nar'], *vn.* To spring or proceed from; to originate, to flow. **Dimanar de**, to originate from.

dimensión [de-men-se-on'], *f.* 1. Dimension, extent, capacity, bulk. **De grandes dimensiones**, of great size. 2. *(Mus.)* Compass, range. 3. *(Math.)* Either of the three geometrical properties, length, breadth, and depth. 4. Power, or grade of an equation. 5. Quaintity which enters as a factor of an algebraic expression.

dimensional [de-men-se-o-nahl'], *a.* Belonging to the dimension.

dimes [dee'-mes], *m. pl.* **Andar en dimes y diretes**, to use *ifs* and *buts*, or quibbles and quirks; to contend, to use altercations.

dimidiar [de-me-de-ar'], *va.* To dimidiate, to divide into halves. *V.* DEMEDIAR.

diminución [de-me-noo-the-on'], *f.* 1. Diminution, losing; exhaustion. 2. Contraction of the diameter of a column as it ascends. **Ir en diminución**, 1. To grow tapering to the top. 2. *(Met.)* To be losing one's character or credit.

diminuir [de-me-noo-eer'], *va.* To diminish. *V.* DISMINUIR.

diminutamente [de-me-noo-te-vah-men-tay], *adv.* 1. Diminutively. 2. Minutely, by retail.

diminutivo, va [de-me-noo-tee'-vo vah], *a.* Diminutive. *-m.* A noun which decreases the meaning of the primitive.

diminuto, ta [de-me-noo'-to, tah], *a.* Defective, faulty; tiny, minute.

dimisión [de-me-se-on'], *f.* Resignation, the act of resigning a place, employment, or commission. **Hacer dimisión de su empleo**, to resign one's place or employment.

dimisorias [de-me-so'-re-as], *f. pl.* Dimissory letters, given by the bishop to a candidate for holy orders that he may be lawfully ordained. **Dar dimisorias**, *(Coll.)* to dismiss anyone, driving him away ungraciously. **Llevar dimsorias**, to get dismissed, to get packed off.

dímite [dee'-me-tay], *m.* Dimity. *V.* COTONÍA.

dimitir [de-me-teer'], *va.* 1. To give up, to relinquish, to resign, to abdicate. **Dimitir la jefatura del partido**, to resign the party leadership. 2. To dismiss, to sack.

dimoño [de-mo'-nyo], *m. (Coll.)* Demon. *V.* DEMONIO.

dimorfismo [de-mor-fees'-mo], *m.* Dimorphism, two different crystallizations.

dina [dee'-nah], *f. (Phys.)* Dyne.

dinamarques, sa [de-nah-mar-kes', sah], *a.* Dane, Danish.

dinamia [de-nah'-me-ah], *f.* 1. Dynam, a foot-pound; a unit of effective force. 2. *(Med.)* Dynamia, vigor, robustness.

dinámica [de-nah'-me-cah], *f.* Dynamics, the science of moving powers.

dinámico, ca [de-nah'-me-co, cah], *a.* Dynamic.

dinamita [de-nah-mee'-tah], *f.* Dynamite; nitroglycerine combined with inert matter, a terrific explosive.

dinamo [de-nah'-mo], *m.* A dynamo-electric machine; a dynamo.

dinamómetro [de-nah-mo'-me-tro], *m.* Dynamometer, an instrument for measuring force exerted or power expended.

dinastía [de-nas-tee'-ah], *f.* Dynasty, sovereignty, race or family of rulers; time of their rule.

dinerada [de-nay-rah'-dah], *f. (Coll.)* A large sum of money.

dineral [de-nay-rahl'], *m.* 1. A large sum of money. **Habrá costado un dineral**, it must have cost a fortune. 2. Weight used by assayers to fix the purity of precious metals; a gold **dineral** is divided into 24 *quilates* or carats, each of which is 4 grains, a silver **dineral** is divided into 12 *dineros* of 24 grains each.

dinerillo [de-nay-reel'-lyo], *m. (Coll.)* A round sum of money.

dinero [de-nay'-ro], *m.* 1. Money. 2. An ancient Spanish copper coin. 3. Standard of silver, the twelfth of a dineral, penny-weight. **Dinero llama dinero**, money gets money. **Tener dinero**, to be rich. **Por el dinero baila** or **salta el perro**, *(Prov.)* Money makes the mare go. **Dinero contante**, cash. **El dinero lo puede todo**, money can do anything. **Andar mal de dinero**, to be badly off. **El negocio no da dinero**, the business does not pay.

dineroso, sa [de-nay-ro-so, sah], *a.* Moneyed, rich.

dineruelo [de-nay-roo-ay'-lo], *m. dim.* Small coin.

dinosaurio, or **dinosauro** [de-no-sah'-oo-re-o], *m.* Dinosaur, a fossil reptile, or reptile of enormous size.

dinoterio [de-no-tay'-re-o], *m.* Dinotherium, a gigantic mammal of the miocene epoch.

dintel [din-tel'], *m.* Lintel, part of a doorframe.

dintelar [din-tay-lar'], *va.* To make lintels.

dintorno [din-tor'-no], *m. (Art.)* Delineation of the parts of a figure contained within the contour.

diocesano, na [de-o-thay-sah'-no, nah], *a.* Diocesan.

diocesano [de-o-thay-sah'-no], *m.* Diocesan, a bishop as he stands related to his own clergy or flock.

diócesi, diócesis [de-o'-thay-se, de-o'-thay-sis], *f.* Diocese, the circuit of a bishop's jurisdiction.

diodo [de-o-do], *m (Comput.)* Diode. **Diodo emisor luz**, light emitting diode.

diodón [de-o-don'], *m.* Sea-urchin.

dióico, ca [de-o'-e-co, cah], *a.* 1. Dicecious, plants whose reproductive organs are borne upon different individuals. 2. Similarly applied to cephalopod mollusks.

diónea [de-o'-nay-ah], *f.* Dioaena, the Venus's flytrap of North Carolina.

dionisia [de-o-nee'-se-ah], *f.* Blood stone, a black stone, variegated with red spots; hematites.

dióptrica [de-op'-tre-cah], *f.* Dioptrics.

dióptrico, ca [de-op'-tre-co, cah], *a.* Dioptric.

diorama [de-o-rah'-mah], *m.* Diorama, an optical contrivance consisting of a series of views placed vertically, in which by means of arranged lights, objects are seen of natural size and distance without lenses.

diorámico, ca [de-o-rah'-me-co, cah], *a.* Dioramic, relating to a diorama.

diorita [de-o-ree'-tah], *f.* Diorite, a crystalline plutonic rock, very esteemed by the ancient Egyptians.

Dios [de-os'], *m.* 1. God, the Supreme Being. 2. God, a false god, an idol. 3. *(Met.)* God, any person or thing passionately beloved or adored. **A Dios** or **anda con Dios**, farewell, adieu. **Después de Dios**, under God. **Vaya usted con Dios**, farewell, God be with you. **Dios dará**, God will provide: used to stimulate alms-giving. **Oh, santo Dios**, oh, gracious God. **Por Dios**, for God's sake. **No lo quiera Dios**, God forbid. **Quiera Dios**, please God. **Sea como Dios quiera**, God's will be done. **Dios los cría y ellos se juntan**, birds of a feather flock together. **Dios lo quiera** or **lo haga**, God grant. **Mediante Dios**, God willing. **¡Válgame Dios!**, bless me!, **¡Válgate Dios!**, God preserve you or bless you. **A Dios rogando y con el mazo dando**, trust in God but keep your powder dry. **Vaya con Dios**, goodbye.

diosa [de-o'-sah], *f.* Goddess.

diosecillo, diosecito [de-o-say-theel'-lyo, de-o-say-thee'-to], *m. dim.* A godling, a little divinity.

diosecita [de-o-say-thee'-tah], *f. dim.* A little goddess.

diostedé [de-os-tay-day'], *m. (Amer.)* A bird of the toucan family whose note sounds like *¡Dios te dé*! it abounds in Venezuela, Peru, etc.

dióxido (or bioxido) de carbono [de-oc'-se-do, be-oc'-se-do day car-bo'-no], *m.* Carbon dioxide

dipétalo, la [de-pay-tah-lo, lah], *a.* Dipetalous, having two petals.

diplaco [de-plah'-co], *m.* A scrophulariaceous plant from California, highly esteemed in the gardens of Europe for the beauty of its flowers.

diplejia espástica [de-play'-he-ah es-pahs'-te-ca], *f.* Cerebral palsy.

diploe [de-plo'-ay], *m.* Diploe.

diploma [de-plo'-mah], *m.* 1. Diploma, patent, license. 2. *(Chem.)* A double-walled vessel in which water is put, and can replace the waterbath.

diplomacia [de-plo-may-the-ah], *f.* 1. Diplomacy, the management of international relations. 2. *(Coll.)* Simulated and interested courtesy.

diplomado, da [de-plo-mah'-do], *a. m. & f.* Qualified, trained, having a diploma.

diplomarse [de-plo-mar'-say], *vr.* To graduate, to obtain a diploma.

diplomática [de-plo-mah'-te-cah], *f.* Diplomatics, the science of diplomas, or of ancient writings, literary and public documents, etc., especially concerned with their authenticity.

diplomáticamente [de-plo-mah'-te-cah-men-tay], *a.* Diplomatically.

diplomático, ca [de-plo-math'-te-co, cah], *a.* 1. Diplomatic, relating; to diplomas. 2. Diplomatical. - *m.* 3. Diplomatist.

diplónomo, ma [de-plo'-no-mo, mah], *a.* Obeying two laws simultaneously.

diplóstomo [de-plos'-to-mo], *m.* A worm found in the eyes of certain fishes, but more often among the whales.

dípneo, nea, dipneumóneo, nea [deep'-na-yo, ah, dip-na-yoo-mo'-nay-o, ah], *a.* Having two lungs.

dípodo, da [dee'-po-do, dah], *a.* Dipodous, biped, having two (hind) feet.

diprósopo, pa [de-pro'-so-po, pah], *a.* A term applied to fishes having both eyes on the same side.

dipsaca [dip-sah'-cah], *f. (Bot.)* Teasel. *V.* CONDENCHA.

dipsas [deep'-sas], *m.* Serpent whose bite is said to produce great thirst.

díptero, ra [deep'-tay-ro, rah], *a.* 1. *(Arch.)* Having two wings, or a double colonnade. 2. *(Entom.)* Dipterous, two winged. -*m. pl.* The diptera, two-winged insects, embracing the host of flies, mosquitoes, midges, etc.

dipterólogo [dip-tay-ro'-lo-go], *m.* Dipserologist, a naturalist who devotes himself to the study of the diptera.

díptica [deep'-te-cah], *f.* Diptych, register of bishops and martyrs.

díptico [deep'-te-co], *m. V.* DÍPTICA.

diptongar [dip-ton-gar'], *va.* 1. To unite two vowels. 2. *(Met.)* To combine two or more things so as to form one whole.

diptongo [dip-ton'-go], *m.* Diphthong.

diputación [de-poo-tah-the-on'], *f.* 1. Deputation, the act of deputing on a special commission. 2. Deputation, the body of persons deputed; committee. 3. The object of a deputation. **Diputación permanente**, standing committee. **Diputación provincial**, county council.

diputado [de-poo-tah'-do], *m.* 1. Deputy, one appointed or elected to act for another, a representative, delegate. **Diputado a Cortes**, parliamentary deputy. 2. *(Com.)* Assignee. **Diputado, da**, *pp.* of DIPUTAR.

diputar [de-poo-tar'], *va.* 1. To depute, to commission, to constitute. 2. To depute, to empower one to act for another.

dique [dee'-kay], *m.* 1. Dike, dam. 2. Dock. **Dique de carena** or **dique seco**, dry dock. **Dique flotante**, floating dock.

dirección [de-rec-the-on'], *f.* 1. Direction, guiding or directing; tendency of motion. 2. Guidance, direction, goverment, administration. 3. Direction, order, command, prescription. 4. The board of directors appointed to supervise the management of some business or organization. **De dos direcciones**, two-way. **Dirección de viento**, wind direction. **Dirección prohibida**, no entry. **Calle de dirección obligatoria**, one-way street. **Cambiar de calle**, to change direction. **Bajo la dirección de**, under the direction of. **Me han confiado la dirección de la obra**, I have been put in charge of the work. **Dirección asistida**, power steering. **Dirección General de Turismo**, State Tourist Office. **Dirección de memoria**, *(Comput.)* memory adress.

directamente [de-rec-the-on'], *adv.* Directly.

directamento [de-rec-tah-men'-tay], *adv.* Directly, rectilineally.

directiva [de-rec-tee'-vah], *f.* 1. Governing body; management. 2. Directive.

directivo, va [de-rec-tee'-vo, vah], *a.* Managing, governing. -*m.* Manager, executive. **Un congreso de los directivos de la industria**, a conference of executives from the industry.

directo, ta [de-rec-to, tah], *a.* 1. Direct, in a straight line, non-stop. 2. Clear, open, apparent, evident. 3. Live. **Transmitir en directo**, to broadcast live. -*m.* Straight punch (boxeo); forehand shot (tenis).

director [de-rec-tor'], *m.* 1. Director, one that has authority over others. 2. Conductor, controller, guide, corypheus. 3. President in some institutions for public business. 4. Director, manager, one who has the management of the concerns of a trading company. 5. Overruler, overseer. **Director** or **director espiritual**, confessor, who guides the conscience of a person. **Director gerente**, managing director. **Director de hotel**, hotel manager. **Director de personal**, personnel manager. **Director de automatización de la oficina**, *(Comput.)* office automation director. **Director de procesamiento de datos**, director of data processing. **Director del centro de información**, *(Comput.)* information center director. **Director del departamento de informática**, *(Comput.)* computer manager.

directora [de-rec-to'-rah], *f.* 1. Directress, governess. 2. *(Geom.)* Directrix, a line determining the motion of another line or point in order to produce a definite curve or surface.

directorial [de-rec-to-re-ahl'], *a.* Relating to a directory.

directorio, ria [de-rec-to'-re-o, ah], *a.* 1. Directive, directorial.

directorio [de-rec-to'-re-o], *m.* 1. Directory, a book which serves as a guide in certain sciences or business matters. 2. The governing body of five men organized in the fourth year of the French republic, Oct., 1795. 3. *(Com.)* A body of directors, directorate. 4. Directors, board of directors. 5. Directory. **Directorio de teléfonos**, telephone directory. 6. Directory *(Comput.)* **Directorio principal**, root directory.

dirigible [de-re-hee'-blay], *m.* Dirigible. -*a.* Pliable, manageable, easily directed.

dirigido [de-re-he'-do], *a.* Guided.

dirigir [de-re-heer'], *va.* 1. To direct, to aim, to lead or to drive in a straight line; to level. 2. To guide, to direct, to conduct. 3. To dedicate a work. 4. To direct, to regulate, to head, to govern, to give rules or laws for the management of anything. 5. **Dirigir el rumbo**, *(Naut.)* to steer. -*vr.* 1. To address, to apply, to resort to. **Se dirigió a mí en la calle**, he spoke to me in the street. 2. To go to (ir hacia), to make one's way to; to head for. **Dirigirse hacia**, to head for.

dirimente [de-re-men'-tay], *pa.* Breaking off, dissolving.

dirimir [de-re-meer'], *va.* 1. To dissolve, to disjoin, to separate. 2. To adjust or accommodate differences. 3. To annul, to declare void.

dirradiación [dir-rah-de-ah-the-on'], *f.* Radiation of the light proceeding, from a body.

dirradiar [dir-rah-de-ar'], *va.* To radiate, to scatter luminous rays.

dirruir [dir-roo-eer'], *va.* To ruin, to destroy. *V.* DERRUIR.

dis [dees], *prep.* From the Latin, changed often into **Des**; it is used only in compound words; it has the meaning of the English prefixes **Dis** and **Un**, and implies separation, division, but commonly privation or negation; as, *armar*, to arm; *desarmar*, to disarm; *atar*, to tie; *desatar*, to untie; *gusto*, pleasure; *disgusto*, displeasure.

disafia [de-sah'-fe-ah], *f. (Met.)* Alteration of the sense of touch.

discantar [dis-can-tar'], *va.* 1. To chant, to sing. 2. To compose or recite verses. 3. To descant, to discourse copiously. 4. To quaver upon a note.

discante [dis-cahn'-tay], *m.* 1. Treble. *V.* TIPLE. 2. Concert, especially of stringed instruments. 3. A small guitar.

discapacitado [dis-cah-pah-the-tah'-do], *a.* Incapacitated, handicapped.

discapacitar [dis-cah-pah-the-tar'], *va.* To incapacitate, to handicap.

discataposis [dis-cah-tah-po'-sis], *f. (Med.)* Dysphagia, difficulty in swallowing.

disceptación [dis-thep-tah-the-on'], *f.* Argument, controversy, dispute.

disceptar [dis-thep-tar'], *va.* To dispute, to argue.

discernidor [dis-ther-ne-dor'], *m.* Discerner.

discernimiento [dis-ther-ne-me-en'-to], *m.* 1. Discernment, judgment. 2. Choice, the power of distinguishing. 3. Appointment of a guardian by the proper magistrates.

discernir [dis-ther-neer'], *va.* 1. To discern, to distinguish, to comprehend, to judge, to know. 2. To appoint a guardian.

disciforme [dis-the-for'-may], *a.* Disciform, having the shape of a disk.

discinesia [dis-the-nay'-se-ah], *f. (Med.)* Paralysis of voluntary movements.

disciplina [dis-the-plee'-nah], *f.* 1. Discipline, education, instruction. 2. Discipline, any art or science taught. 3. Discipline, rule of conduct, order. 4. Correction or punishment inflicted upon oneself. **Disciplinas**, scourge, a cat-of-nine-tails. 5. Flagellation.

disciplinable [dis-the-ple-nah'-blay], *a.* Disciplinable, capable of instruction.

disciplinadamente [dis-the-ple-nah'-dah-men-tay], *adv.* With discipline.

disciplinado, da [dis-the-ple-nah'-do dah], *a.* Marbled, variegated. -*pp.* of DISCIPLINAR.

disciplinal [dis-the-ple-nahl'], *a.* Relative to discipline, disciplinal.

disciplinante [des-the-ple-nahn'-tay], *pa.* Flagellator.

disciplinar [dis-the-ple-nar'], *va.* 1. To discipline, to educate, to instruct, to bring up. 2. To drill, to teach the manual exercise or the military regulations. 3. To chastise, to correct. -*vr.* To scourge oneself as penance.

disciplinario, ria [dis-the-ple-nah'-re-o, ah], *a.* Disciplinary, belonging to discipline.

discipulado [dis-the-poo-lah'-do], *m.* 1. Number of scholars who frequent the same school. 2. Education, instruction.

discípulo, la [dis-thee'-poo-lo, lah], *m. & f.* Disciple, scholar, learner, follower.

disco [dees'-co], *m.* 1. Disk, a round piece of iron thrown in the ancient sports; a quoit. **Disco volante**, flying saucer. 2. Face of the sun or moon, as it appears to the eye. 3. A plate of glass, of circular form, which serves for an electric machine, etc. **Disco de larga duración**, long-playing record. **Disco de marcar**, dial. 4. A cylinder whose base is very large as compared with its height: as the telescope lens. 5. A railway signal-disk, semaphore. 6. *(Comput.)* **Disco de arranque**, boot disk. **Disco duro; disco flexible**, floppy disk, diskette, floppy; **disco** virtual, RAM disk. **Disco grabable**, writable disk. **Disco magnético desmontable**, removable magnetic disk. **Disco óptico digital**, digital optical disk. **Disco WORM**, WORM disk (Write Once Read Many s). **Disco de Winchester**, Winchester disk.

disco [dis-co], *f.* Disco (sala de baile).

discóbolo [dis-co'-bo-lo], *m.* Discus thrower.

discografía [dis-co-grah-fe'-ah], *f.* 1. Records; collection of records. **La discografía de Ecles**, the complete recordings of Eccles. 2. Record company.

discográfico [disd-co-grah'-fe-co], *a.* Record. **Casa discográfica**, record company. **El momento discográfico actual**, the present state of the record industry.

díscolo, la [dees'-co-lo, lah], *a.* Ungovernable; wayward, peevish, froward.

disconforme [dis-con-for'-may], *a.* Differing. **Estar disconforme**, to be in disagreement.

disconformidad [dis-con-for-me-dahd'], *f.* Disagreement.

discontinuar [dis-con-te-noo-ar'], *va.* *V.* DESCONTINUAR.

discontinuo, a [dis-con-tee'-noo-o, ah], *a.* Discontinued.

disconveniencia [dis-con-vay-ne-en'-the-ah], *f.* Discord, disunion.

disconveniente [dis-con-vay-ne-en'-tay], *a.* *V.* DESCONVENIENTE.

discordancia [dis-cor-dahn'-the-ah], *f.* Disagreement, contrariety of opinion; discordance.

discordante [dis-cor-dahn'-tay], *pa. & a.* Dissonant, discordant.

discordar [dis-cor-dar'], *vn.* To discord, to disagree.

discorde [dis-cor'-day], *a.* 1. Discordant, contrary, not conformable. 2. *(Mus.)* Dissonant.

discordia [dis-cor'-de-ah], *f.* 1. Discord, disagreement, mis-intelligence. 2. Contrariety of opinion, opposition.

discoteca [dis-co-tay'-cah], *f.* 1. Record library. 2. Record store. 3. Discotheque.

discrasia [dis-crah'-se-ah], *f. (Med.)* Dyscrasia, ill-health due to constitutional disease; general bad health.

discreción [dis-cray-the-on'], *f.* 1. Discretion, prudence, judgment. 2. Acuteness of mind, sharpness of wit, liveliness of fancy. **Con vino a discreción**, with as much wine as one wants. **Comer a discreción**, to eat as much as one likes. 3. Discretion, liberty of acting at pleasure. **A discreción**, 1. At the discretion or will of another. 2. According to one's own will or fancy.

discrecional [dis-cray-the-o-nahl'], *a.* Discretional, discretionary.

discrepancia [dis-cray-pahn'-the-ah], *f.* Discrepancy, difference, contrariety.

discrepante [dis-cray-pahn'-tay], *pa.* Disagreeing, discrepant. **Hubo varias voces discrepantes**, there were some dissenting voices.

discrepar [dis-cray-par'], *vn.* To differ, to disagree.

discretamente [dis-cray-tah-men'-tay], *adv.* Discreetly, sensibly, prudently.

discretear [dis-cray-tay-ar'], *vn.* To be discreet, to talk with discretion: used ironically.

discreto, ta [dis-cray'-to, tah], *a.* 1. Discreet, circumspect, considerate, prudent. 2. Ingenious, sharp, witty, eloquent. 3. Discrete, distinct, separate. **Es más delicado que discreto**, he is more nice than wise. **Le daremos un plazo discreto**, we'll allow him a reasonable time.

discreto, ta [dis-cray'-to, tah], *m. & f.* A person elected assistant in the council of some religious houses.

discretorio [dis-cray-to'-re-o], *m.* Meeting or council of the seniors of religious bodies.

discriminación [dis-cre-me-nah-the-on'], *f.* Discrimination. **Discriminación racial**, racial discrimination.

discriminado [dis-cre-me-nah'-do], *a.* **Sentirse discriminado**, to feel that one has been unfairly treated.

discriminar [dis-cre-me-nar'], *va.* To discriminate.

disculpa [dis-cool'-pah], *f.* 1. Apology, excuse, exculpation. 2. *(Law.)* Plea.

disculpabilidad [dis-cool-pah-be-le-dahd'], *f.* Excusability, palliation, pardonableness.

disculpable [dis-cool-pah'-blay], *a.* Excusable, pardonable.

disculpablemente [dis-cool-pah'-blay-men-tay], *adv.* Pardonably, excusably.

disculpadamente [dis-cool-pah'-dah-men-tay], *adv.* Excusably.

disculpar [dis-cool-par'], *va.* To exculpate, to excuse, to palliate. **Disculpa el que venga tarde**, forgive me for coming late. *-vr.* To excuse oneself. **Disculparse con uno por haber hecho algo**, to apologize to somebody for having done something.

discurrir [dis-coor-reer'], *vn.* 1. To gad, to ramble about, to run to and fro, to pass, to flow by. **El verano discurrió sin grandes calores**, the summer passed without great heat. 2. To discourse upon a subject. 3. To discuss. **Discurre menos que un mosquito**, he just never thinks. *-va.* 1. To invent, to plan, to contrive, to consult, to meditate, to scheme. 2. To discourse, to infer, to deduce.

discursar [dis-coor-sar'], *vn.* To discourse, to treat upon, to converse.

discursista [dis-coor-sees'-tah], *m.* One who discusses a subject.

discursivo, va [dis-coor-see'-vo, vah], *a.* Discursive, reflective; cogitative.

discurso [dis-coor'-so], *m.* 1. Discourse. 2. Ratiocination, reasoning. 3. Discourse, conversation, speech. **Discurso de clausura**, closing speech. **Pronunciar un discurso**, to make a speech. 4. Discourse, dissertation, treatise, tract. 5. Space of time. **En el discurso del tiempo**, with the passage of time. 6. Ramble.

discusión [dis-coo-se-on'], *f.* Discussion, argument, dispute. **Tener una discusión**, to have an argument.

discusivo, va [dis-coo-see'-vo, vah], *a. (Med.)* Resolvent.

discutible [dis-coo-tee'-blay], *a.* Susceptible of discussion or examination; controvertible.

discutidor, ra [dis-coo-te-dor', rah], *m. & f.* Prone to discuss, fond of disputing.

discutir [dis-coo-teer'], *va.* To discuss, to investigate, to examine, to debate. **Discutir a uno lo que está diciendo**, to contradict what somebody is saying. *-vn.* To discuss, to talk; to argue. **Discutir de política**, to argue about politics.

disecación [de-say-cah-the-on'], *f.* Dissection, anatomist.

disecador [de-say-cah-dor'], *m.* Dissector, anatomist.

disecar [de-say-car'], *va.* 1. To dissect (cuerpos de animales). 2. To make an autopsy for study. 3. To preserve dead animals

with the appearance of life. 4. *(Met.)* To analyze minutely; to criticise.

disecativo, va [de-say-cah-tee'-vo, vah], *a.* Desiccative, desiccant, drying.

diseceión [de-sec-the-on'], *f.* Dissection, anatomy.

disector [de-sec-tor'], *m.* Dissector, anatomist.

diseminable [de-say-me-nah'-blay], *a.* Disseminable, capable of being spread or propagated.

diseminación [de-say-me-nah-the-on'], *f.* Dissemination, publishing; scattering of ripe seeds.

diseminador, ra [de-say-me-nah-dor, rah], *m. & f.* Disseminator, spreader.

diseminar [de-say-me-nar'], *va.* To disseminate, to propagate.

disensión [de-sen-se-on'], *f.* 1. Dissension, misunderstanding, contention, contest, strife. 2. The cause or motive of dissension.

disenso [de-sen'-so], *m.* Dissent, disagreement.

disentería [de-sen-tay-ree'-ah], *f.* Dysentery, a disease.

disentérico, ca [de-sen-tay'-re-co, cah], *a.* Belonging to dysentery.

disentimiento [de-sen-te-me-en'-to], *m.* Dissent, disagreement, declaration of difference of opinion.

disentir [de-sen-teer'], *vn.* To dissent, to disagree, or to differ in opinion.

diseñador, ra [de-say-nyah-dor'], *m & f.* Designer, delineator.

diseñar [de-say-nyar'], *va.* To draw, to design.

diseño [de-say'-nyo], *m.* 1. Design, sketch, draft, plan. 2. Delineation, description. 3. Picture, image. V. DESIGNIO. 4. Pattern, model. **Diseño asistido por ordenador**, *(Comput.)* Computer Aided Design (CAD).

disépalo, la [de-say'-pah-lo, lah], *a.* Having two sepals.

disepimento [de-say-pe-men'-to], *m.* Dissepiment, a partition of a compund ovary.

disertación [de-ser-tah-the-on'], *f.* Dissertation, a discourse, a disquisition, discussion.

disertador [de-ser-tah-dor'], *m.* Dissertator, debater.

disertar [de-ser-tar'], *va.* To dispute, to debate, to argue.

disestesia [di-ses-tay'-se-ah], *f.* Dysmaesthesia, numbness, loss of sensation.

disfagia [des-fah'-ge-ah], *f.* Dysphagia, difficulty in swallowing.

disfamación [dis-fah-mah-the-on'], *f.* Defamation, slander: censure.

disfamador, ra [dis-fah-mah-dor', rah], *m. & f.* Defamer, detractor, slanderer.

disfamar [dis-fah-mar'], *va.* 1. To defame, to slander. 2. To discredit.

disfamatorio, ria [dis-fah-mah-to'-re-o, ah], *a.* Defamatory, calumnious, libellous.

disfavor [dis-fah-vor'], *m.* 1. Disregard, want of favor. 2. Discountenance, cold treatment.

disfonía [dis-fo-nee'-ah], *f. (Med.)* Sensible alteration of the voice and speech, dysphonia.

disformar [des-for-mar'], *va.* V. DEFORMAR and AFEAR.

disforme [dis-for'-may], *a.* 1. Deformed, ugly, monstrous, formless. 2. Huge, big.

disformidad [dis-for-me-dahd'], *f.* Deformity, excessive bigness.

disfraz [dis-frath'], *m.* 1. Mask, disguise. **Baile de disfraces**, fancy-dress ball. 2. *(Met.)* Dissimulation, dissembling.

disfrazado [dis-frah-thah'-do], *a.* **Disfrazado de**, disguised as. **Ir disfrazado de duque**, to be made up like a duke.

disfrazar [dis-frah-thar'], *va.* 1. To disguise, to conceal. **Disfrazar a uno de lavandera**, to disguise somebody as a washerwoman. 2. To cloak, to dissemble, to cover; to misrepresent. *-vr.* 1. To masquerade, to go in disguise. 2. To feign.

disfrutar [dis-froo-tar'], *va.* 1. To gain fruit or advantage, to gather the fruit or products. 2. To enjoy, to reap benefit from a thing, without caring for its preservation or betterment. 3.

To enjoy health, convenience. 4. To avail oneself of, to profit by, the favor, friendship, or protection of some one. -*vn.* 1. To enjoy oneself; to have a good time. **Disfrutar con algo,** to enjoy something. **Siempre disfruto con los libros así,** I always enjoy books of that sort. 2. **Disfrutar de,** to enjoy; to have, to possess. **Disfrutar de una buena salud,** to enjoy good health.

disfrute [des-froo'-tay], *m.* Use, enjoyment.

disgregable [dis-gray-gah'-blay], *a.* Separable, segregable.

disgregación [dis-gray-gah-the-on'], *f.* 1. Separation, disjunction. 2. Dispersion of light rays.

disgregar [dis-gray-gar'], *va.* 1. To separate, to disjoin. 2. To disperse the rays of light.

disgregativo, va [dis-gray-gah-tee'-vo, vah], *a.* Disjunctive.

disgustadamente [dis-goos-tah'-dah-men-tay], *adv.* Disgustingly.

disgustar [dis-goos-tar'], *va.* 1. To disgust, to distaste, to disrelish. 2. To disgust, to strike with dislike, to offend. **Es un olor que me disgusta,** it's a smell which upsets me. **Me disgusta tener que repetirlo,** it annoys me to have to repeat it. -*vr.* 1. To be displeased; to fall out, to be at variance with another. 2. To get tired, fatigued, to be bored.

disgustillo [dis-goos-teel'-lyo], *m. dim.* Displeasure, slight disgust.

disgusto [dis-goos'-to], *m.* 1. Disgust, aversion, of the palate, loathing. 2. Ill-humor; offence conceived. 3. Grief. sorrow. **A disgusto,** in spite of, contrary to one's will and pleasure. **Me causó un gran disgusto,** it was a great blow to me. **Nunca nos dio un disgusto,** he never gave us any trouble. **Matar a uno a disgustos,** to wear somebody out with burdens.

disidencia [de-se-den'-the-ah], *f.* Dissidence, non-conformity.

disidente [de-se-den'-tay], *a. & m. & f.* Dissident, dissenter, non-conformist, schismatic.

disidio [de-see'-de-o], *m. (Poet.)* Discord.

disidir [de-se-deer'], *vn.* 1. To dissent, to separate from a (religious) belief before held. 2. To be of a distinct opinion, especially in matters of belief.

disilábico, ca [de-se-lah'-be-co, cah], *a.* Dissyllabic, of two syllables. Also **disílabo, ba**.

disílabo [de-see'-lah-bo], *m.* Dissyllable.

disímil [de-see'-mil], *a.* Dissimilar.

disimilar [de-se-me-lar'], *a.* Unequal, dissimilar.

disimilitud [de-se-me-le-tood'], *f.* Dissimilitude.

disimulable [de-se-moo-lah'-blay], *a.* What may be dissembled or feigned.

disimulación [de-se-moo-lah-the-on'], *f.* 1. Dissimulation, the act of dissembling; simulation, hypocrisy, mask, feint. 2. Reserve, reservedness.

disimuladamente [de-se-moo-lah-dah-men'-tay], *adv.* Dissemblingly; reservedly.

disimulado, da [de-se-moo-lah'-do, dah], *a.* 1. Dissembling. 2. Reserved, sullen, not open, not frank. 3. Dissembled, sly, cunning. -*pp.* of DISIMULAR. **A lo disimulado,** dissemblingly; reservedly. **Hacer la disimulada,** to feign ignorance.

disimulador, ra [de-se-moo-lah-dor', rah], *m. & f.* Dissembler.

disimular [de-see-moo-lar'], *va.* 1. To dissemble, to conceal one's real intentions. 2. To cloak, to conceal artfully any bent of the mind. 3. To hide. 4. To tolerate, to allow so as not to hinder, to overlook, to let pass. **Disimula mi atrevimiento,** forgive me if I have been too bold. 5. To color, to misrepresent.

disimulo [de-se-moo'-lo], *m.* 1. Dissimulation, reservedness. **Con disimulo,** cunningly, craftily. *V.* DISMULACIÓN. 2. Tolerance.

disipable [de-se-pah'-blay], *a.* Dissipable, easily scattered, easily dissipated.

disipación [de-se-pah-the-on'], *f.* 1. Separation of the parts which composed a whole. 2. Resolution of anything into

vapor. 3. Dissolute living. 4. Dissipation, the act of spending one's fortune; licentiousness, extravagance, waste.

disipado, da [de-se-pah'-do, dah], *a.* 1, Dissipated, devoted to pleasure. 2. Prodigal, lavisher. 3. Licentious, dissolute. -*pp.* of DISIPAR.

disipador, ra [de-se-pah-dor', rah], *m. & f.* Spendthrift, a prodigal, a lavisher.

disipar [de-se-par'], *va.* 1. To dissipate, to disperse, to scatter. 2. To misspend, to lavish. 3. To drive away, to put to flight. -*vr.* To vanish; to evaporate.

disjunto, ta [dis-hoon'-to, tah], *a. (Mus.)* Disjoined, not followed but separated by another interval.

diskette [dis-kay-tay], *m. (Comput.)* Floppy disk.

dislacerar [dis-lah-thay-rar'], *va.* To lacerate.

dislate [dis-lah'-tay], *m.* Nonsense, absurdity. *V.* DISPARATE.

dislexia [dis-lec'-se-ah], *f.* Dyslexia.

dislocación, dislocadura [dis-lo-ca-the-on', dis-lo-ca-doo'-rah], *f.* 1. Dislocation. 2. Dislocation, a luxation, a joint put out. 3. Separation of the different parts which form a machine.

dislocar [dis-lo-car'], *va.* To dislocate, to displace; to luxate, to disjoint. -*vr.* To be dislocated, to come asunder.

dismembración [dis-mem-brah-the-on'], *f. V.* DESMEMBRACIÓN.

dismenia [dis-may'-ne-ah], *f. V.* DISMENORREA.

dismenorrea [dis-may-no-rray'-ah], *f.* Dysmenorrhoea, painful menstruation.

disminución [dis-me-noo-the-on'], *f.* 1. *V.* DIMINUCIóN. **Proceso de disminución de réditos,** law of diminishing returns. 2. Disease in horses' hoofs.

disminuido, da [dis-me-noo-ee'-do], *a. m & f. (Med.)* Crippled, handicapped.

disminuir [dis-me-noo-eer'], *va.* 1. To diminish, to lessen, to lower, to abridge, to cut short. 2. To detract from. -*vr.* To lessen, to lower, to grow less.

disnea [dis-nay'-ah], *f.* Dyspnoea, difficulty in respiration.

disociación [de-so-the-ah-the-on'], *f.* Disjunction, separation.

disociar [de-so-the-ar'], *va.* To disjoin, to separate things.

disodila [de-so-dee'-lah], *f. (Min.)* A papyraceous coal, kind of bituminous earth in plates, found in Sicily.

disolubilidad [de-so-loo-be-le-dahd'], *f.* Dissolubility.

disoluble [de-so-loo'-blay], *a.* Dissoluble.

disolución [de-so-loo-the-on'], *f.* 1. Dissolution, the resolution of a body into its constituent elements. 2. Dissoluteness, dissipation, libertinism, lewdness, licentiousness.

disolutamente [de-so-loo-tah-men'-tay], *adv.* Dissolutely, licentiously.

disolutivo, va [de-so-loo-tee'-vo, vah], *a.* Dissolvent, solvent.

disoluto, ta [de-so-loo'-to, tah], *a.* Dissolute, loose, licentious, lewd, libidinous, libertine.

disolvente [de-sol-ven'-tay], *m.* Dissolvent, dissolver.

disolver [de-sol-verr'], *va.* 1. To loosen, to untie. 2. To dissolve, to separate, to disunite. 3. To melt, to liquefy. 4. To interrupt. -*vr.* To dissolve, to be melted.

disoma [de-so'-mah], *f.* An arsenosulphide of nickel; greynickel.

disón [de-sone'], *m. (Mus.)* Harsh, dissonant tone; discord.

disonancia [de-so-nahn'-the-ah], *f.* 1. Dissonance. 2. Disagreement, discord. **Hacer disonancia a la razón,** to be contrary to reason.

disonante [de-so-nahn'-tay], *a.* 1. Disonant, inharmonious, discrepant. 2. *(Met.)* Discordant, unsuitable.

disonar [de-so-nar'], *vn.* 1. To disagree in sound, to be disharmonious. 2. To discord, to disagree. 3. To be contrary or repugnant.

dísono, na [dee'-so-no, nah], *a.* Dissonant, inconstant.

dispar [dis-par'], *a.* Unlike, unequal.

disparado [dis-pah-r-ah'-do], *a.* **Entrar disparado,** to shoot in. **Salir disparado,** to shoot out, to be off like a shot.

disparador [dis-pah-rah-dor'], *m.* 1. Shooter. 2. Trigger of a gunlock. 3. Ratch, ratchet, or ratchet-wheel, in clock-work. 4. *(Naut.)* Anchor-tripper. 5. A machine like a musket for setting off rockets.

disparar [dis-pa-rar'], *va. & vn.* 1. To shoot, to discharge a thing with violence. **Disparar desde un sitio oculto**, to snipe. 2. To fire, to discharge fire-arms; to let off. 3. To cast or throw with violence. 4. *(Coll.)* To talk nonsense, to blunder. *-vr.* 1. To run headlong. 2. To stoop, to dart down on prey (halcón). 3. To run away disobeying the bridle (caballo). 4. *(Naut.)* To turn violently (cabr. estante). 5. To get loose from tiller ropes (timón).

disparatadamente [dis-paah-rah-tah'-dah-men-tay], *adv.* Absurdly, nonsensically.

disparatado, da [dis-pa-rah-tah'-do, dah], *a.* Inconsistent, absurd, extravagant, silly, foolish. *-pp.* of DISPARATAR.

disparatar [dis-pa-rah-tar'], *va.* 1. To act or talk in an absurd and inconsistent manner. 2. To blunder, to talk nonsense.

disparate [dis-pa-rah'-tay], *m.* Nonsense, blunder, absurdity, extravagance. **Hiciste un disparate protestando**, it was silly of you to complain.

disparatón [dis-pa-rah-tone'], *m. aug.* A great piece of nonsense, a very great blunder.

disparatorio [dis-pa-rah-to'-re-o], *m.* Speech or discourse full of nonsense.

disparidad [dis-pa-re-dahd'], *f.* Disparity, inequality, dissimilitude

disparo [dis-pah'-ro], *m.* 1. Shot (tiro). 2. Firing (acción de disparar un arma). 3. Shot (fútbol) 4. Discharge, explosion. 5. Nonsense, absurdity.

dispendio [dis-pen'-de-o], *m.* 1. Excessive or extravagant expense. 2. *(Met.)* Voluntary loss of life, honor, or fame.

dispendioso, sa [dis-pen-de-o'-so, sah], *a.* Costly, expensive.

dispensa [des-pen'-sah], *f.* 1. Dispense, exemption, dispensation. 2. Diploma granting a dispensation.

dispensable [dis-pen-sah'-blay], *a.* Dispensable.

dispensación [dis-pen-sah-the-on'], *f.* 1. Dispensation, exception. 2. *V.* DISPENSA.

dispensador, ra [dis-pen-sah-dor', rah], *m. & f.* 1. One who grants a dispensation. 2. Dispenser, distributor.

dispensar [dis-pen-sar'], *va.* 1. To dispense, to exempt, to absolve or set free from an engagement. 2. *(Coll.)* To excuse, to dispense with, to do without. **Dispensar a uno de una obligación**, to excuse somebody from an obligation. **Dispensar a uno de**, to excuse somebody from. 3. To deal out, to distribute. *-vr.* **No puedo dispensarme de esa obligación**. I cannot escape that duty.

dispensario [des-pen-sah'-re-o], *m.* 1. Pharmacopoeia. 2. Laboratory of medicaments. 3. Dispensary, clinic.

dispepsia [dis-pep'-se-ah], *f.* Dyspepsia.

dispéptico, ca [dis-pep'-te-co, cah], *a.* Dyspeptic.

dispermo, ma [dis-perr'-mo, mah], *a.* *(Bot.)* Having only two seeds.

dispersar [des-per-sar'], *va.* 1. To separate the things or persons who were joined. 2. *(Mil.)* To put to flight, to disperse. 3. *(Comput.)* To scramble *-vr.* To disperse, to scatter.

dispersión [dis-per-se-on'], *f.* Dispersion.

disperso, sa [dis-per'-so, sah], *a.* 1. Dispersed, separated. 2. Applied to military men who do not belong to a body of forces, and reside where they please.

dispertador, ra [dis-per-tah-dor', rah], *m. & f. V.* DESPERTADOR.

dispertar [dis-per-tar'], *va. V.* DESPERTAR. (*Yo dispierto, yo dispierte*, from *Dispertar. V.* ACERTAR.)

displacer [dis-plah-therr'], *va. V.* DESPLACER.

displicencia [dis-ple-then'-the-ah], *f.* Displeasure, discontent, dislike.

displicente [dis-ple-then'-tay], *a.* 1. Displeasing, unpleasing, 2. Angry, peevish, fretful.

dispondeo [dis-pon-day'-o], *m.* *(Poet.)* Dispondee, a foot of prosody consisting of four long syllables.

disponedor, ra [dis-po-nay-dor', rah], *m. & f.* Disposer; distributer.

disponer [dis-po-nerr'], *va. & vn.* 1. To arrange, to order, to place things in order. 2. To dispose, to make fit, to prepare. 3. To dispose of, to give, to distribute. 4. To deliberate, to resolve, to direct, to command. 5. To act freely, to dispose of property. **Disponer sus cosas**, to make a last will. **Disponer las velas al viento**, to trim the sails to the wind (barcos). **La ley dispone que...**, the law provides that... **Disponemos de poco tiempo**, we have very little time. *-vr.* To prepare oneself, to get ready, to resolve. (*Yo dispongo, yo dispuse*, from *Disponer. V.* PONER.)

disponible [dis-po-nee'-blay], *a.* Disposable (propiedad).

disposición [dis-po-se-the-on'], *f.* 1. Disposition, arrangement or distribution of things, ordering. 2. Disposition, natural fitness. 3. Disposition, tendency to any act or state. 4. Proportion, symmetry, measure. 5. Resolution, order, command. 6. Power, authority 7. Disposition, inclination, temper of mind. 8. *(Naut.)* Trim of a ship. 9. Elegance of person. 10. Despatch of business. **A la disposición**, at the disposal or will of another. **Según las disposiciones del código**, according to the provisions of the statue. **Tener algo a su disposición**, to have something at one's disposal. **Estar en disposición de**, to be ready to. **No tener disposición para**, to have no aptitude for. **Disposición de la página**, *(Comput.)* page layout.

dispositivo, va [dis-po-se-tee'-vo, vah], *a.* Preparatory, readying, preliminary. *-m.* Device, mechanism. **Dispositivo de arranque**, starting mechanism. **Dispositivo de seguridad**, safety catch. **Dispositivo de lecturas multiventana**, *(Comput.)* multiwindow readout device. **Dispositivo de comportamiento**, *(Comput.)* behavioral device. **Dispositivo de devolución de llamada**, *(Comput.)* callback device. **Dispositivo de seguridad biométrico**, *(Comput.)* biometric security device. **Dispositivo fisiológico**, *(Comput.)* physiological device.

dispositorio, ria [dis-po-se-to'-re-o, ah], *a. V.* DISPOSITIVO.

dispuesto, ta [dis-poo-es'-to, tah], *a.* 1. Disposed, fit, ready, minded. **Dispuesto según ciertos principios**, arranged according to certain principles. 2. Comely, genteel, graceful. **Bien dispuesto**, quite well, with regard to health. **Mal dispuesto**, indisposed, ill. 3. **Estar dispuesto a**, to be prepared to. **Estar poco dispuesto a**, to be reluctant to. *-pp. irr.* of DISPONER.

disputa [dis-poo'-tah], *f.* 1. Dispute, controversy, arguement. 2. Dispute, contest, conflict; contention, clash, fray, odds. **Sin disputa**, beyond dispute.

disputable [dis-poo-tah'-blay], *a.* Disputable, controvertible, contestable.

disputador [dis-poo-tah-dor'], *m.* Disputant, disputer.

disputar [dis-poo-tar'], *va. & vn.* 1. To dispute, to controvert, to contend, to contest. 2. To dispute, to question, to reason about. 3. To dispute, to debate, to argue. 4. To dispute, to jar, or to clamor. 5. To strive; to resist. **Disputar sobre algo**, to dispute on something. **Disputar con uno por un premio**, to contend with somebody for a prize. *-vr.* **Disputarse un premio**, to contend for a prize.

disputativamente [dis-poo-tah-te-vah-men'-tay], *adv.* Disputingly.

disquete [dis-ke-tay], *m.* Floppy disk, diskette, floppy.

disquisición [dis-ke-se-the-on'], *f.* Disquisition, examination.

distancia [dis-tahn'-the-ah], *f.* 1. Distance, interval of time or place. 2. Remoteness, length. 3. Difference, disparity. **Acortar distancias**, to reduce the distance. **Tomar distancias**, to calculate the longitude of a vessel. **Distancia del suelo**, height of the ground. **A larga distancia**, long-distance. **Mantener a uno a distancia**, to keep somebody at a distance. **Guardar las distancias**, to keep one's distance. **Distancia de Hamming**, *(Comput.)* Hamming distance.

distanciado [dis-tahn-the-ah'-do], *a.* 1. Remote; widely separated, isolated (aislado). 2. *(Fig.)* Far apart. **Estamos algo distanciados**, we are not particularly close. **Ella está distanciada de su familia**, she has grown apart from her family.

distanciar [dis-tahn-the-ar'], *va.* 1. To space out (objetos), to separate; to put further apart. 2. To out-distance (rival). 3. To cause a rift between. *-vr.* 1. **Distanciarse de un rival**, to get ahead of a rival. 2. To fall out, to become estranged; to become remote from each other.

distante [dis-tahn'-tay], *a.* 1. Distant, remote. 2. *(Naut.)* Off, offward.

distar [dis-tar'], *vn.* 1. To be distant or remote with regard to time or place. **Dista 5 kms de aquí**, it is 5 kms from here. 2. To be different, to vary.

distender [dis-ten-derr'], *va. (Med.)* To cause violent stretching in tissues, membranes, etc.

distensión [dis-ten-se-on'], *f.* Violent stretching.

distesia [dis-tay'-se-ah], *f. (Med.)* General discomfort and impatience in disease; dysthesia.

dístico [de-es'-te-co], *m.* Distich, couplet.

distilo, la [dis-tee'-lo, lah], *a.* Having two styles or pistils.

distinción [dis-tin-the-on'], *f.* 1. Distinction, difference, diversity. **Obrar sin distinción**, to act arbitrarily. **Sin distinción de edades**, irrespective of differences of age. 2. Prerogative, privilege. 3. Distinction, honorable note of superiority. 4. Order, clarity, precision. **Persona de distinción**, a person of superior rank. **A distinción**, in contradistinction.

distinguible [dis-tin-gee'-blay], *a.* Distinguishable.

distinguido, da [dis-tin-gee'-do, dah], *a. & pp.* of DISTINGUIR. 1. Distinguished, conspicuous. *-m.* 2. **Distinguido**, refined (modales). Gentlemanly (caballero). **Distinguido** or **soldado distinguido**, a nobleman serving as a private, who was allowed to wear a sword, and was exempted from menial labor.

distinguir [dis-tin-geer'], *va.* 1. To distinguish. **No distingo cuál es el mío**, I can't tell which is mine. 2. To distinguish. 3. To see clearly, and at a distance. 4. To discern, to discriminate, to know; to judge. 5. To set a peculiar value on things or persons. **Me distingue con su amistad**, he honors me with his friendship. 6. To clear up, to explain. *-vn.* **No distinguir**, to have no critical sense. **Es un hombre que sabe distinguir**, he is a discerning person. *-vr.* 1. To distinguish oneself, especially by warlike exploits. 2. To differ, to be distinguished from.

distintamente [dis-tin-tah-men'-tay], *adv.* Distinctly, diversely.

distintivo, va [dis-tin-tee'-vo, vah], *a.* Distinctive.

distintivo *m.* 1. A distinctive mark, as the badge of a military order. 2. A particular attribute, characteristic feature.

distinto, ta [dis-teen'-to, tah], *a.* 1 Distinct, different, diverse. **Son muy distintos**, they are very different. 2. Distinct, clear; intelligible. 3. **Distintos**, several, various.

distracción [dis-trac-the-on'], *f.* 1. Distraction, want of attention; heedlessness, absence; ecstasy, reverie. **Por distracción**, through sheer forgetfulness. 2. Amusement, pastime, sport. **Es mi distracción favorita**, it's my favorite amusement. 3. Licentiousness, dissolute living; want of constraint.

distráctil [dis-trahc'-teel], *a. (Bot.)* Applied to the connective, when it sensibly divides the cells of the anthers, as in the sage; distractile.

distraer [dis-trah-err'], *va.* 1. To distract, to harass the mind; to perplex, to divert. **Distraer a uno para robarle algo**, to distract somebody's attention so as to steal something from him. 2. To seduce from a virtuous life. 3. To amuse, to relax, to entertain. **La música me distrae**, music relaxes me. *-vr.* To amuse, to be absent of mind, inattentive. **Me distraigo pescando**, I relax when I fish. **Me distraje un momento**, I allowed my attention to wander for a moment.

distraídamente [dis-trah-ee'-dah-men-tay], *adv.* Distractedly, licentiously.

distraído, da [dis-trah-ee'-do, dah], *a.* 1. Absent, inattentive, heedless, mopish. **Iba yo algo distraído**, I was rather absorbed in other things. **Con aire distraído**, idly, casually. 2. Dissolute, licentious. 3. Amusing, entertaining. 4. Dissolute (vida). *-pp.* of DISTRAER. *(Yo distraigo, yo distraje,* from *Distraer. V.* TRAER.)

distraimiento [dis-trah-e-me-en'-to], *m.* 1. Distraction. *V.* DISTRACCIóN. 2. A licentious life.

distribución [dis-tre-boo-the-on'], *f.* 1. Distribution; division, separation. **Distribución de premios**, prize giving. 2. Proper collocation, arrangement. 3. Distribution of type in the printer's cases. 4. *(Arch.)* The art of economical employment and good selection of building materials.

distribuido [dis-tre-boo-ee'-dah], *a.* **Una casa bien distribuida**, a well-designed house.

distribuidor, ra [dis-tre-boo-e-dor', rah], *m. & f.* Distributor, divider.

distribuir [dis-tre-boo-eer'], *va.* 1. To distribute, to divide, to deal out. 2. To dispose, to range; to compart; to lot. 3. To allot, to measure. 4. *(Print.)* To distribute types.

distributivamente [dis-tre-boo-tee'-vah-men-tay], *adv.* Distributively.

distributivo, va [dis-tre-boo-tee'-vo, vah], *a.* Distributive.

distributor, ra [dis-tre-boo-tor', rah], *m. & f.* Distributer.

distribuyente [dis-tre-boo-yen'-tay], *pa.* Distributer, giver.

distrito [dis-tree'-to], *m.* 1. District, circuit of authority, province. 2. District, region, country, territory. **Distrito postal**, postal district.

distrofia muscular [dis-tro'-fe-ah moos-coo-lar], *f.* Muscular dystrophy.

disturbar [dis-toor-bar'], *va.* To disturb, to interrupt, to perturb.

disturbio [dis-toor'-be-o], *m.* Disturbance, outbreak, interruption. **Los disturbios**, the disturbances.

disuadir [de-soo-ah-deer'], *va.* To dissuade, to deter.

disuasión [de-soo-ah-se-on'], *f.* Dissuasion, determent.

disuasivo, va [de-soo-ah-see'-vo, vah], *a.* Dissuasive.

disuelto, ta [de-soo-el'-to, tah], *a. & pp. irr.* of DISOLVER. Dissolved, melted.

disuria [de-soo'-re-ah], *f. (Med.)* Dysuria, difficulty in urinating.

disyunción [dis-yoon-the-on'], *f.* 1. Disjunction, separation. 2. *(Gram.)* A disjunctive particle.

disyunta [dis-yoon'-tah], *f. (Mus.)* Change of the voice.

disyuntivamente [dis-yoon-tee'-vah-men-tay], *adv.* Disjunctively, separately.

disyuntivo, va [dis-yoon-tee'-vo, vah], *a.* 1. Disjunctive. 2. Disjunctive, applied to the insertion of stamens when the petals are united below the receptacle, but not to it.

disyunto, ta [dis-yoon'-to, tah], *a.* Separated, disjoined, distant.

disyuntor [dis-yoon-tor'], *m. (Elec.)* Circuit breaker.

dita [dee'-tah], *f.* 1. Securer, bonds-man; security, bond. 2. *(Prov. Amer.)* Debt.

ditirámbica [de-te-rahm'-be-cah], *f.* Dithyrambic, a hymn in honor of Bacchus, sung, danced, and placed at the same time.

ditirámbico, ca [de-te-rahm'-bee-co, cah], *a.* Dithyrambical.

ditirambo [de-te-rahm'-bo], *m.* 1. *(Poet.)* Dithyrambie, a dithyramb. 2. Exaggerated eulogy.

dito [dee'-to], *m. & pp. obs. V.* DICHO.

dítono [dee'-to-no], *m. (Mus.)* An interval of two tones, ditone, major third.

ditorno [de-tor'-no], *m.* A name which engravers give to the intermediate parts of a figure.

diuresis [de-oo-ray'-sis], *f.* Diuresis.

diurético, ca [de-oo-ray'-teco, cah], *a. (Med.)* Diuretic; also used as a substantive.

diurno, na [de-oor'-no, nah], *a.* Diurnal. -*f. pl.* Butterflies, lepidoptera. -*m. pl.* Insects which live but twenty-four hours; dayflies.

diurno [de-oor'-no], *m.* Diurnal, prayerbook, among Roman Catholics, which contains the canonical hours, except matins.

diuturnidad [de-oo-toor-ne-dahd'], *f.* Diuturnity, long duration.

diuturno, na [de-oo-toor'-no, nah], *a.* Diuturnal, lasting.

diva [dee'-vah], *f.* 1. (*Poet.*) Goddess. 2. (*Neol.*) A prima donna, star.

divagación [de-vah-gah-the-on'], *f.* Wandering, digression.

divagante [de-vah-gahn'-tay], *pa.* Rambling.

divagar [de-vah-gar'], *vn.* 1. To ramble. *V.* VAGAR. 2. To digress.

diván [de-vahn'], *m.* 1. Divan, the supreme council among the Turks. 2. The place of its meetings. 3. By extension, the Sublime Porte, the Ottoman govermnent. 4. Divan, a low, cushioned sofa.

divaricado, da [de-vah-re-cah'-do, dah] *a.* (*Bot.*) Divaricate, widely diverging.

divaricar [de-vah-re-car'], *va.* To separate, to cause to spread.

divergencia [de-ver-hen'-the-ah], *f.* 1. Divergence. 2. Diversity or difference in opinions.

divergente [de-ver-hen'-tay], *a.* 1. Divergent. 2. Dissenting, opposed, contrary.

divergir [de-ver-heer'], *vn.* 1. (*Phys.*) To diverge. 2. To differ, to be opposed, to clash (opiniones).

diversamente [de-ver-sah-men'-tay] *adv.* Diversely, differently.

diversidad [de-ver-se-dahd'], *f.* 1. Diversity, dissimilitude, unlikeness. 2. Diversity, distinct being. 3. Diversity, variety of things, abundance, plenty.

diversificar [de-ver-se-fe-car'], *va.* To diversify, to vary.

diversión [de-ver-se-on'], *f.* 1. Diversion. 2. Diversion, sport, merriment, fun, amusement. 3. (*Mil.*) Diversion, an attack made upon the enemy, to withdraw his attention from the real attack.

diversivo, va [de-ver-see'-vo, vah], *a.* Divertive.

diverso, sa [de-ver'-so], *a.* 1. Diverse, different from another. **Se trata de diverso asunto**, it's about a different matter. 2. Diverse, different from itself; various; multiform. -*pl.* Several, sundry, many. **Está en diversos libros**, it figures in several books.

divertículo [de-ver-tee'-coo-lo], *m.* A blind pouch, a diverticulum; a vertical appendix.

divertido, da [de-ver-tee'-do, dah], *a. & pp.* of DIVERTIR. Amused, amusive, merry, divertive, diverted, festive, funny, absent, inattentive. **Andar divertido**, to be engaged in love affairs.

divertimiento [de-ver-te-me-en'-to], *m.* 1. Diversion, sport, merriment, fun. 2. Amusement, entertainment of the mind, pastime, sport.

divertir [de-ver-teer'], *va.* 1. To turn aside, to divert, turn away. 2. To amuse, to entertain, to exhilarate, to divert, to make merry. 3. (*Mil.*) To draw the enemy off from some design, by threatening or attacking a distant part.-*vr.* To sport, to play, to frolic, to wanton, to dally, to fool, to amuse. **Divertirse haciendo algo**, to amuse oneself doing something. **Divertirse con el amor de uno**, to toy with somebody's affections.

dividendo [de-ve-den'-do], *m.* 1. (*Arith.*) Dividend, the number to be divided. 2. Dividend, share, the interest received for money placed in the public stocks or in a partnership.

dividir [de-ve-deer'], *va.* 1. To divide, to disjoin, to disunite, to cut. 2. To divide, to distribute, to separate. 3. To divide, to disunite by discord. **Dividir 12 por 4**, to divide 12 by 4. -*vr.* 1. To divide, to part, to cleave. 2. To divide, or to be of different opinions. 3. To divide, to break friendship, to withdraw oneself from the company and friendship of anyone. **Dividir por la mitad**, to divide into halves.

dividuo, dua [de-vee-doo-o, ah], *a.* (*Law.*) Divisible.

divieso [de-ve-ay'-so], *m.* (*Med.*) Furuncle, boil.

divinamente [de-ve-nah-men'-tay], *adv.* Divinely, heavenly, admirably.

divinidad [de-ve-ne-dahd'], *f.* 1. Divinity; deity, godhead, godship, divine nature. **Divinidad marina**, sea god. 2. The Supreme Being. 3. False god.

divinizable [de-ve-ne-thah'-blay], *a.* Worthy of being deified.

divinizado. da [de-ve-ne-thah'-do, dah], *a. & pp.* of DIVINIZAR. Deified.

divinizar [de-ve-ne-thar'], *va.* 1. To deify. 2. (*Met.*) To sanctify.

divino, na [de-vee'-no, nah], *a.* 1. Divine. 2. Heavenly, heaven-born, godlike. 3. Excellent in a supreme degree. **Es un ingenio divino**, he is a man of uncommon talents.

divino, na [de-vee'-no, nah], *m. & f. V.* ADIVINO.

divisa [de-vee'-sah], *f.* 1. Badge, emblem, identifying mark. 2. (*Her.*) Motto, device. 3. (*For.*) Share of the paternal inheritance. 4. Foreign exchange. **Control de divisas**, exchange control.

divisar [de-ve-sar'], *va.* 1. To distinguish at a distance, to perceive indistinctly, to make out, to discern. 2. (*Her.*) To make a difference, to vary.

divisero [de-ve-say'-ro], *m.* Heir who is not of noble extraction.

divisibilidad [de-ve-se-be-le-dahd'], *f.* Divisibility.

divisible [de-ve-see'-blay], *a.* Divisible.

división [de-ve-se-on'], *f.* 1. Division, the act of dividing a thing into parts. 2. Division, partition, distribution. compartment. 3. Division, disunion, difference, diversity of opinion. 4. Hyphen. 5. Division; one of the parts into which a thing is divided: used technically, especially in the army and navy. 6. (*Arith.*) Division, a rule in arithmetic.

divisional [de-ve-se-o-nahl'], *a.* Divisional.

divisivo, va [de-ve-see'-vo, vah], *a.* Divisible, divisive.

diviso, sa [de-vee'-so, sah], *a. & pp. & rr.* of DIVIDIR. Divided, disunited.

divisor [de-ve-sor'], *m.* 1. Divisor. 2. Anything which divides another.

divisorio, ria [de-ve-o'-re-o, ah], *a.* Divisive, forming division.

divo, va [dee'-vo, vah], *a.* (*Poet.*) Divine, godlike. -*m.* Movie star.

divorciado, da [de-vor-the-ah'-do], *a. m & f.* 1. Divorced. 2. **Las opiniones están divorciadas**, (*fig.*) Opinions are divided.

divorciar [de-vor-the-ar'], *va.* To divorce, to separate, to part, to divide. -*vr.* To be divorced.

divorcio [de-vor'-the-o], *m.* 1. Divorce, separation, disunion. 2. Rupture among friends.

divulgable [de-vool-gah'-blay], *a.* That which may be divulged.

divulgación [de-vool-gah-the-on'], *f.* Divulgation, publication.

divulgador, ra [de-vool-gah-dor', rah] *m. & f.* Divulger.

divulgar [de-vool-gar'], *ra.* To publish, to divulge, to report, to give out, to reveal. -*vr.* To go abroad.

divulsión [de-vol-se-on'], *f.* Divulsion, rupture.

DMA (*Comput.*) DMA (Direct Memory Access).

do [doh], *m.* First note of the musical scale.

dobla [do'-blah], *f.* An ancient Spanish gold coin.

dobladamente [do-blah-dah-men'-tay], *adv.* 1. Doubly. 2. Deceitfully, artfully.

dobladilla [do-blah-deel'-lyah], *f.* Ancient game of cards. **A la dobladilla**, doubly, repeatedly.

dobladillo, lla [do-blah-deel'-lyo, lyah], *a.* Squat and broad, short and thick.

dobladillo [do-blah-deel'-lyo], *m.* 1. Hem, the edge of a garment. 2. A strong thread commonly used to make stockings.

doblado [do-blah'-do], *m.* 1. Measure of the fold in cloth. 2. (*Med.*) A sort of asphyxia which attacks those who clean out privies.

doblado, da [do-blah'-do, dah], *a.* 1. Strong, robust, thickset. 2. *(Met.)* Deceitful, dissembling. **Tierra doblada**, a broken, mountainous country. *-pp.* of DOBLAR.

doblador [do-blah-dor'], *m.* A machine which serves to pass sugarcane a second time between the cylinders of the mill.

dobladura [do-blah-doo'-rah], *f.* 1. Fold, mark of a fold. 2. Anciently, an extra horse, for emergencies, which warriors had to take along. 3. Dish consisting of fried meat, bread, onions, nuts, etc. 4. *(Obs.)* Malicious fabrication.

doblaje [do-blah'-hay], *m.* Dubbling (cine).

doblamiento [do-blah-me-en'-to], *m.* Doubling, bending, as act and effect.

doblar [do-blar'], *va. & vn.* 1. To double, by addition of the same quantity. **Doblar el sueldo a uno**, to double somebody's salary. 2. To double, to fold. 3. To double, to contain twice the quantity. 4. To bend, to make crooked, to crook. 5. To toll or ring the passing bell. 6. To induce someone to do the contrary of what he had thought. **Doblar la rodilla**, to kneel. 7. To turn, to go round. 8. **Doblar dos papeles**, to take two parts (teatro). *-vr.* 1. To bend, to flow, to stoop, to submit. 2. To be led away by the opinion of another. 3. To change one's opinion.

doble [do'-blay], *a.* 1. Double, twice as much, duplicate; *(Chem.)* binary. 2. Thick and short. 3. Strong, robust. 4. Double, artful, deceitful. **Al doble**, doubly. *(Mus.)* **Espacios dobles** are intervals which exceed octaves. **Doble o nada**, double or quits. **Doble densidad** *(Comput.)*, double density.

doble [do'-blay], *m.* 1. Fold, crease. 2. Dissimulation, double-dealing. 3. Toll of the passing-bell. 4. Step in Spanish dance. 5. Double. **El doble**, twice the quantity. **Su sueldo es el doble del mío**, his salary is twice mine. 6. **Dobles**, doubles (tenis). **Dobles masculinos**, men's doubles. **Dobles mixtos**, mixed doubles. *-m & f.* Double. **Ser el doble de uno**, *(fig.)* to be somebody's double (cine).

doblegable [do-blay-gah'-blay], *a.* 1. Flexible, flexile. 2. Plaint. 3. That which may be doubled.

doblegar [do-blay-gar'], *va.* 1. To bend, to incurvate, to inflect. 2. To gain by persuasion, to reclaim. **Doblegar a uno**, *(fig.)* To be somebody's double. *-vr.* 1. To bend, to be incurvated. 2. To bend, to submit, to be submissive.

doblel [do-blel'], *m.* Bag, satchel.

doblemano [do-blay-mah'-no], *f. (Mus.)* Octave-coupler.

doblemente [do-blay-men'-tay], *adv.* Deceitfully, doubly, artfully.

doblero [do-blay'-ro], *m. (Prov.)* A small loaf of bread.

doblete [do-blay'-tay], *a.* That which is between double and single. *-m.* 1. Factitious gem. 2. A play in billiards.

doblez [do-bleth'], *m.* 1. Crease, a mark made by folding; fold; duplication, duplicature. *(Anat.)* A fold which forms a membrane by being turned back upon itself. 2. Duplicity, doubleness, disingenuity, dissimulation, double-dealing.

doblo [do'-blo], *m. (Law.)* Double.

doblón [do-blone'], *m.* 1. Doubloon, a Spanish gold coin. **Doblón de oro**, gold coin. 2. **Doblón de vaca**, tripes of a bullock or cow.

doblonada [do-blo-nah'-dah], *f.* Heap of doubloons or money. **Echar doblonadas**, to exaggerate one's revenues.

dobrao [do-brah'-o], *m.* A Portuguese gold coin, corresponding to the doubloon.

doce [do'-thay], *m. & a.* 1. Twelve. 2. Twelfth, as **El doce de Abril**, the 12th of April.

doceavo [do-thay-ah'-vo], *a.* Twelfth. *-m.* Twelfth.

docena [do-thay'-nah], *f.* Dozen. **Docena de fraile**, baker's dozen. **A docenas**, abundantly, in great quantities. **Por docenas**, by the dozen.

docenal [do-thay-nahl'], *a.* That which is sold by dozens.

docenario, ria [do-thay-nah'-re-o, ah], *a.* Containing twelve.

docente [do-then'-tay], *a.* Teaching. **Iglesia docente**, the body of prelates and clergy. **Personal docente**, teaching staff.

doceno, na [do-thay'-no, nah], *a.* Twelfth.

doceno [do-thay'-no], *m. & a.* A kind of cloth, the warp of which consists of twelve hundred threads.

doceñal [do-thay-nyahl'], *a.* That which consists of twelve years.

dócil [do'-theel], *a.* 1. Docile, mild, tractable, gentle. 2. Obedient, pliant, flexible, governable. 3. Ductile, pliable, malleable, flexible.

docilidad [do-the-le-dahd'], *f.* 1. Docility. 2. Flexibleness, compliance, easiness to be persuaded. 3. Manageableness, tractableness. 4. Gentleness, meekness.

dócilmente [do'-theel-men-tay], *adv.* Tractably, obediently.

docimástica [do-the-mahs'-te-cah], *f.* Assay, the docimastic art, the art of assaying minerals or ores.

doctamente [doc-tah-men'-tay], *adv.* Learnedly.

doctilocuo, cua [doc-te-lo'-coo-o, ah], *a.* Fluent and elegant in speech.

docto, ta [doc'-to, tah], *a.* Learned.

doctor [doc-tor'], *m.* 1. Doctor in medicine, law, physics, or philosophy. **Doctor en derecho**, doctor of laws. 2. Any able or learned teacher. 3. *(Coll.)* A physician.

doctora [doc-to'-rah], *f.* 1. Doctoress, she who professes the skill of a doctor; a vain, impertinent, or assuming woman. 2. A female medical practitioner. 3. Title given to Saint Theresa.

doctorado [doc-to-rah'-do], *m.* Doctorate, doctorship. **Estudiante de doctorado**, research student.

doctoral [doc-to-rahl'], *a.* Doctoral.

doctoral [doc-to-rahl'], *f.* The canonry called **doctoral** in the Spanish cathedrals. *-m.* The canon who possesses the **doctoral** canonry, councillor of the cathedral.

doctoramiento [doc-to-rah-me-en'-to], *m.* 1. The act of taking the degree of doctor. 2. Doctorate, doctorship.

doctorando [doc-to-rahn'-do], *m.* One who is on the point of taking out his degree as doctor.

doctorar [doc-to-rar'], *va.* To doctorate, to dignify with the degree of a doctor. *-vr.* To take one's doctor's degree.

doctorcillo [doc-tor-theel'-lyo], *m. dim.* 1. A little doctor: commonly used in a jocular style. 2. Quack, a petty physician.

doctorismo [doc-to-rees'-mo], *m. (Hum.)* The body of doctors.

doctrina [doc-tree'-nah], *f.* 1. Doctrine, instruction, lore. 2. Doctrine, the principles or positions of any sect or master. 3. Science, wisdom. 4. Discourse on the tenets of the Christian faith.

doctrinador, ra [doc-tre-nah-dor', rah], *m. & f.* Instructor, teacher.

doctrinal [doc-tre-nahl'], *m.* Catechism, an abridgment of Christian doctrine. *-a.* Doctrinal, relating to doctrine.

doctrinar [doc-tre-nar'], *pa.* 1. To teach, to instruct. 2. To break in horses.

doctrinero [doc-tre-nay'-ro], *m.* 1. Teacher of Christian doctrine. 2. Curate or parish priest in America. 3. One who accompanies a missionary in his teaching.

doctrino [doc-tree'-no], *m.* 1. An orphan child received into some college. 2. *(Met.)* A person of small talent and too free manners.

documentación [do-coo-men-tah-the-on'], *f.* 1. Documentation. 2. Papers, documents. **Documentos del barco**, ship's papers.

documental [do-coo-men-tahl'], *a.* Documental. *-m.* Documentary.

documentar [do-coo-men-tar'], *va.* 1. To document. 2. To inform, to acquaint. *-vr.* To get the necesary information.

documento [do-coo-men'-to], *m.* 1. Instruction, advice to avoid evil. 2. Document; writing, record. 3. Voucher, schedule. 4. *(Com.)* Any transferable paper, representing value; security. **Documentos del coche**, car papers, insurance papers of the car. **Documento de trabajo**, working paper.

dodecaedro [do-day-cah-ay'-dro], *m.* Dodecahedron.

dodecágono [do-day-cah'-go-no], *m.* Dodecagon.

dodecasílabo, ba [do-day-cah-see'-lah-bo, bah], *a.* Dodecasyllable, having twelve syllables.

dogal [do-gahl'], *m.* 1. Rope tied round the neck. 2. Halter, a rope to hang malefactors.

dogma [dog'-mah], *m.* 1. Dogma, established principle. 2. Act article of faith.

dogmáticamente [dog-mah'-te-cah-men tay], *adv.* Dogmatically, in a dogmatic manner.

dogmático, ca [dog-mah'-te-co, cah], *a.* Dogmatical or dogmatic.

dogmático [dog-mah'-te-co], *m.* Dogmatic.

dogmatismo [dog-mah-tees'-mo], *m.* 1. Dogmatism, disposition to affirm and believe in contrast to scepticism. Dogmatism admits an absolute certainty. 2. Dogmatic assertion, affirmation without proof. 3. Name of an ancient medical theory.

dogmatista [dog-mah-tees'-tah], *m.* 1. Dogmatist; a teacher of new dogmas. 2. An upholder of dogmatism.

dogmatizador, dogmatizante [dog-mah-te-thah-dor', dog-mah-te-thahn'-tay], *m.* Dogmatizer, dogmatist.

dogmatizar [dog-mah-te-thar'], *va.* To dogmatize, to teach or assert false dogmas.

dogo [do'-go], *m.* 1. Terrier. 2. A kind of small dog.

dogre [do'-gray], *m.* A Dutch boat for the herring-fishery, two-masted and like a smack; a dogger.

doladera [do-lah-day'-rah], *a.* A cooper's adze.

dolador [do-lah-dor'], *m.* Joiner, one who planes and polishes wood or stone.

doladura [do-lah-doo'-rah], *f.* Adzing, shavings from planing.

dolaje [do-lah'-hay], *m.* The wine imbibed by pipe-staves.

dolamas [do-lah'-mas, do-lah'-mes], *f. pl.* **dolames**, *m. pl.* Hidden vices and defects incident to horses.

dolar [do-lar'], *va.* To plane or smooth wood or stone.

dólar [do'lar], *m.* Dollar.

dolencia [do-len'-the-ah], *f.* 1. Disease, affliction. 2. *(Met. Obs.)* Danger; dishonor. **La dolencia de la economía**, the ills of the economy.

doler [do-lerr'], *vn.* 1. To feel pain, to ache or be in pain. **Me duele el brazo**, my arm hurts. **No me ha dolido nada**, it didn't hurt at all. 2. To cause sorrow or distress in the mind. **Le duele aún la pérdida**, the loss still grieves him. **No me duele el dinero, I** don't mind about the money. *-vr.* 1. To be in pain about anything, to be sorry; to repent. 2. To feel for the sufferings of others. 3. To lament, to complain. **Dolerse de**, to grieve. **Lo sufre todo sin dolerse**, he puts up with everything without complaining.

dolerita [do-lay-ree'-tah], *f.* Dolerite, an igneous rock.

dolerítico, ca [do-lay-ree'-te-co, cah], *a.* Doleritic, containing dolerite or resembling it.

doliente [do-le-en'-tay], *a.* Suffering or laboring under a complaint or affliction; sorrowful. —*m.* 1. Pall-bearer 2. Mourner.

dolimán [do-le-mahn'], *m.* Kind of long robe worn by the Turks.

dolo [do'-lo], *m.* Fraud, deceit, imposition, vulgarly, humbug. **Poner dolo**, to judge ill of a person.

dolomía [do-lo-mee'-ah], *f.* Dolomite, a brittle marble, phosphorescent upon rubbing.

dolomítico, ca [do-lo-mee'-te-co, cah], *a.* Dolomitic.

dolor [do-lor'], *m.* 1. Pain, sensation of uneasiness, aching, ache. **Dolor de cabeza**, headache. **Dolor de muelas**, toothache. **Dolor de tripas**, gripping. **Dolor de oídos**, earache. **Dolor de estómago**, stomachache. **Tener mucho dolor**, to be in great pain. 2. Affliction, anguish, grief, painfulness. **Le causa mucho dolor**, it causes him great distress. 3. Repentance, contrition. 4. Pain, the throes of childbirth. **Estar con dolores**, to be in labor.

dolorcillo, ito [do-lor-theel'-lyo, thee'-to], *m. dim.* A slight pain.

dolorido, da [do-lo-ree'-do, dah], *a.* Doleful, afflicted, painful, heartsick. *V.* DOLIENTE.

dolorido [do-lo-ree'-do], *m.* 1. The chief mourner, the nearest relation of a person deceased. 2. One in pain.

dolorosamente [do-lo-ro-sah-men'-tay], *adv.* Painfully, sorrowfully, miserably.

doloroso, sa [do-lo-ro'-so, sah], *a.* Sorrowful, afflicted, dolorous, dismal, doleful; painful.

dolosamente [do-lo'-sah-men-tay], *adv.* Deceitfully.

doloso, sa [do-loh'-so, sah], *a.* Deceitful, knavish.

domable [do-mah'-blay], *a.* Tamable, conquerable.

domador, ra [do-mah-dor', rah], *m. & f.* 1. Tamer, subduer. 2. Horse-breaker.

domadura [do-mah-doo'-rah], *f.* Act of taming or subduing.

domar [do-mar'], *va.* 1. To tame: to break or to break in. 2. To subdue, to overcome, to master, to conquer.

dombo [dom'-bo], *m.* Dome, cupola.

domeñar [do-may-nyar'], *va.* To reclaim, to make tractable, to tame, to master, to subdue.

domesticable [do-mes-te-cah'-blay], *a.* Tamable.

domesticado [do-mes-te-cah'-do], *a.* Tame; pet.

domésticamente [do-mes'-te-cah-men-tay], *adv.* Domestically.

domesticar [do-mes-te-car'], *va.* To render gentle, to domesticate. *-vr.* To grow tame.

domesticidad [do-mes-te-the-dahd'], *f.* Domesticity, affability.

doméstico, ca [do-mes'-te-co, cah], *a.* 1. Domestic, domestical. **Economía doméstica**, home economy. **Gastos domésticos**, household expenses. 2. Domestic, inhabiting the house. 3. Domesticant, forming part of the same family.

doméstico [do-mes'-te-co], *m.* Domestic, menial.

domestiquez [do-mes-te-keth'], *f.* Meekness, tameness.

domiciliación [do-me-the-le-ah-the-on'], *f. (Fin.)* Automatic payment (a través de banco).

domiciliado, da [do-me-the-le-ah'-do, dah], *a. & pp.* of DOMICILIARSE. Received as a denizen or citizen of a place; domiciliated.

domiciliar [do-me-the-le-ar'], *va.* 1. To domicile, to establish; to house. 2. *(Com.)* To place. 3. **Domiciliar su cuenta**, to give the number of one's account. *-vr.* To establish oneself, to take up residence.

domiciliario [do-me-the-le-ah'-re-o], *m.* Inhabitant, citizen.

domiciliario, ria [do-me-the-le-ah'-re-o ah], *a.* Domiciliary, intruding into private houses.

domiciliarse [do-me-the-le-ar'-say], *vr.* To establish oneself in a residence.

domicilio [do-me-thee'-le-o], *m.* Habitation, abode, domicile, home, dwelling-house. **Domicilio particular**, private residence. **Servicio a domicilio**, delivery service.

dominación [do-me-nah-the-on'], *f.* 1. Dominion, domination, authority, power. 2. *(Mil.)* Commanding ground. *-pl.* Dominations, some angelic beings.

dominador, ra [do-me-nah-dor', rah], *m. & f.* Dominator.

dominante [do-me-nahn'-tay], *a.* 1. Dominant, domineering, dictatory ascendant; prevailing, excelling. **La tendencia dominante**, the dominant tendency. 2. Dominative, imperious, masterful. 3. *(Mus.)* Dominant, the fifth in the scale.

dominar [do-me-nar'], *va.* 1. To dominate, to rule, to act without control, to oversway. **Le domina la envidia**, he is ruled by envy. 2. To master, to lord, to lead, to command. 3. *(Met.)* To moderate one's passions, to correct one's evil habits. 4. To have a good grasp of. **Domina 7 idiomas**, he knows 7 languages well. *-vn.* To dominate (edificio); to tower above, to look down on. *-vr.* 1. To rise above others (colinas). 2. To control oneself.

dominativo, va [do-me-nah-tee'-vo, vah], *a.* Dominative. *V.* DOMINANTE.

dómine *m.* Latin teacher.

domingo [do-meen'-go], *m.* Sunday, the first day of the week, the Christian Sabbath. **Domingo de Adviento**, Advent Sunday. **Domingo de Pasión** or **de Lázaro**, Passion Sunday. **Domingo de Ramos**, Palm Sunday. **Domingo de Resurrección**, Easter Sunday. **Hacer domingo**, to pass a working day idling.

dominguero, ra [do-min-gay'-ro, rah], *a.* Belonging to the Sabbath, done or worn on Sunday. **Traje dominguero**, Sunday clothes, Sunday suit.

dominguillo [do-min-geel'-lyo], *m.* Figure of a boy made of straw, and used at bull-feasts to frighten the bulls. **Hacer su dominguillo de uno**, (*Coll.*) to make one a laughing-stock; to sport at some one's expense.

domínica [do-mee'-ne-cah], *f.* Sunday, in ecclesiastical language. **Domínica in Albis**, Low Sunday. *V.* Domingo.

dominical [do-me-ne-cahl'], *a.* 1. Manorial (derechos feudales). 2. Dominical, belonging to the Lord's day. **Oración dominical**, lord's prayer. 3. A veil used by women in the old days for receiving communion. 4. Sunday. **Periódico dominical**, Sunday newspaper. *f.* Discourse of the Sundays of Advent and Lent.

dominicano, na, dominico, ca [do-me-ne-cah'-no, nah], *a.* 1. Dominican, belonging to the Dominican friars. 2. Native of the island of Santo Domingo.

dominico [do-me-nee-co], *m.* Jacobin, a friar of the order of Saint Dominic.

dominicatura [do-me-ne-cah-too'-rah]*f.* (*Prov.*) Certain duty of vassalage paid to the lord of the manor.

dominio [do-mee'-ne-o], *m.* 1. Dominion, domination, power, right of possession or use. **Dominio público**, public property. 2. Dominion, authority. 3. Dominion, territory, region. 4. Domain, possession, estate.

dominó [do-me-no'], *m.* 1. Domino, a masquerade garment. 2. The game of dominoes. **Juego de dominó**, dominoes.

Don [don], *m.* 1. Don, the Spanish title for a gentleman. It is equivalent to *Mr.* in English, but used only before Christian names, as **Don Juan** or **Don Andrés Pérez**, Mr. John or Mr. Andrew Perez. 2. **Don** alone or with an adjective or epithet, was formerly equivalent to *Señor.* **Don Guindo**, one who boasts of learning which he does not possess. **Don Lindo**, a dandy.

don, *m.* 1. Gift, present. 2. Gift, faculty, dexterity, knack, gracefulness, ability. **Dones sobrenaturales**, supernatural gifts, as prophecy, etc. **Don de gentes**, an habitual skill to win the goodwill of those persons with whom anyone is acquainted. **Don de acierto**, habitual dexterity in doing everything in the most successful manner. **Don de lenguas**, gift for languages. **Don de palabra**, gift of oratory.

dona [do'-nah], *f.* 1. Woman, lady. 2. *pl.* Wedding presents which the groom makes to the bride. (*Acad.*)

donación [do-nah-the-on'], *f.* 1. Donation. 2. Donation, gift, grant. **Donación piadosa**, pious donation.

donadío [do-nah-dee'-o], *m.* 1. (*Obs.*) *V.* DON. 2. (*Prov.*) Property derived from royal donations.

donado, da [do-nah-do, dah], *m. & f.* Lay brother or lay sister of a religious community. *-pp.* of DONAR.

donador, ra [do-nah-dor', rah], *m. & f.* Donor, bestower, giver.

donaire [do-nah'-e-ray], *m.* 1. Grace, elegance, gracefulness, gentility. 2. Witty saying, facetiousness. 3. Gracefulness, ease, activity in walking. **Hacer donaire de alguna cosa**, to make little of anything.

donairosamente [do-nah-e-ro'-sah-men-tay], *adv.* Facetiously, wittily.

donairoso, sa [do-nah-e-ro'-so, sah], *a.* 1. Pleasant. 2. Graceful, elegant. 3. Witty, facetious.

donante [do-nan'-tay], *pa.* Donor; giver.

donar [do-nar'], *va.* To make free gifts, to bestow.

donatario [do-nah-tah'-re-o], *m.* Donee, grantee, a person in whose favor a donation is made.

donativo [do-nah-tee'-vo], *m.* Donative.

doncel [don-thel'], *m.* 1. An appellation formerly given to the king's pages. 2. A man who has not carnally known a woman. 3. (*Obs.*) The son of noble parents. 4. The youth who was not yet armed as a knight. **Pino doncel**, timber of young pines without knots. *-adj.* Mild, mellow in flavor. **Vino doncel**, wine of a mild flavor.

doncella [don-thayl'-lyah], *f.* 1. Maid, virgin, maiden, lass. 2. Lady's maid, waiting-maid. 3. **Doncella de Numidia**, (*Or.*) the Numidian heron. 4. (*Zool.*) Snakefish. 5. (*Bot.*) The sensitive plant, humble plant. **Doncella jamona**, an old maid.

doncelleja [don-thel-lyay'-hah], *f. dim.* Little maid.

doncellería [don-thel-lyay-ree'-ah], *f.* (*Coll.*) Maiden-head, virginity.

doncellez [don-thel-lyeth'], *f.* Virginity, maidenhood.

doncellica, ita [don-thel-lyee'-cah, ee'-tah], *f. dim.* A young maid, a girl.

donde [don-day], *adv.* 1. *V.* ADONDE. 2. Where, in what place? 3. Whither, to what place? **¿De dónde?**, from what place? **Dondequiera**, Anywhere. **¿Hacia dónde?**, towards what place? **¿Por dónde?**, by what way or road?, by what reason or cause? **Fue adonde estaban**, he went to where they were. **No hay por donde cogerle**, there's no way to catch him. *-inter.* **¿Dónde lo dejaste?**, where did you leave it? **¿Adónde vas?**, where are you going?

dondequiera [don-day-ke-ay'-rah], *adv.* Anywhere. **Por dondequiera**, everywhere. *-conj.* Anywhere, wherever. **Dondequiera que lo busques**, wherever you look for it.

dondiego [don-de-ay'-go]. (*Bot.*) The morning-glory; jalap, marvel of Peru.

donceillo [do-nay-theel'-lyo], *m. dim.* A small present.

dongola [don-go'-lah], *f.* A beverage, like beer, made in Ethiopia.

dongón [don-gone'], *m.* A tree of the Philippine Islands, whose wood is of stony hardness and serves to make keels and other resisting parts of vessels.

donguindo [don-geen'-do], *m.* A pear-tree of larger fruit than the ordinary.

donillero [do-nil-lyay'-ro], *m.* Swindler, sharper, a tricking gambler.

donjuán [don-hoo-ahn'], *m.* (*Bot.*) *V.* DONDIEGO.

donosamente [do-no'-sah-men-tay], *adv.* Gracefully, pleasing, comelily.

donosidad [do-no-se-dahd'], *f.* Gracefulness, wittiness, festivity.

donosilla [do-no-seel'-lyah], *f.* Piece of plaited muslin, which ladies used to wear around their necks.

donoso, sa [do-no'-so, sah], *a.* Gay, witty, pleasant.

donosura [do-no-soo'-rah], *f.* Gracefulness, grace, elegance, gentility.

donpedro [don-pay'-dro], *m.* Morning glory. *V.* DOMPEDRO.

doña [do'-nyah], *f.* Lady, mistress.

doñear [do-nyay-ar'], *vn.* (*Coll.*) To pass the time or converse much with women.

doñegal, doñigal [do-nyay-gahl', do-nye-gahl'], *a.* Applied to a kind of figs, red inside.

dopado [do-pah'-do], *a.* Doped, doped-up.

dopar [do-par'], *va.* To dope, to drug.

doping [do'-peen], *m.* Doping, drugging.

doquier, doquiera [do-ke-err', do-ke-ay'-rah], *adv. V.* DONDEQUIERA.

dorada, doradilla [do-rah'-dah, do-rah-deel'-lyah], *f.* (*Zool.*) Gilthead, giltpoll.

doradilla [do-rah-deel'-lyah], *f.* 1. (*Bot.*) Common ceterach. 2. Gilthead (fish).

doradillo [do-rah-deel'-lyo], *m.* 1. Fine brass wire. 2. Wagtail, a small bird.

dorado, da [do-rah'-do, dah], *a.* Gilt. **Sopa dorada**, a high-colored soup. *-pp.* of DORAR.

dorado [do-rah'-do], *m.* 1. Gilding. *V.* DORADURA. 2. (*Zool.*) *V.* DORADA.

dorador [do-rah-dor'], *m.* Gilder.

doradura [do-rah-doo'-rah], *f.* Gilding.

doral [do-rahl'], *m.* (*Orn.*) Flycatcher.

dorar [do-rar'], *va.* 1. To gild, as with gold. 2. (*Met.*) To palliate, to excuse. 3. (*Poet.*) To gild, to illuminate with the rays of the sun, as a mountain top. 4. To coat pastry with the yolk of egg, to yellow it.

dórico, ca [do'-re-co, cah], *a.* Doric.

dorífora [do-ree'-fo-rah], *f.* The Colorado potato beetle, a noxious pest.

doríforo [do-ree'-fo-ro], *m.* A beetle of the chrysomelid group, of equinoctial America, of brilliant coloring.

dormán [dor-mahn'], *m.* Dolman, a lady's jacket; named from a huzzar's jacket.

dormida [dor-mee'-dah], *f.* 1. Time during which the silkworm sleeps and rests before each molt. In general, time spent in sleep. 2. The place where animals repose. 3. (*Amer.*) Alcove, bed.

dormidera [dor-me-day'-rah], *f.* (*Bot.*) Garden-poppy. *-pl.* Sleepiness, drowsiness. *V.* ADORIMIDERA.

dormidero, ra [dor-me-day'-ro, rah], *a.* Sleepy, soporiferous, narcotic, somniferous.*-m.* Place where cattle repose.

dormidor [dor-me-dor'], *m.* A great sleeper.

dormidos [dor-mee'-dos], *m. pl. V.* DURMIENTES.

dormiente [dor-me-en'-tay], *pa. V.* DURMIENTE.

dormilón, na [dor-me-lone', nah], *m. & f.* A dull, sleepy person, one who sleeps much.

dormir [dor-meer'], *vn.* 1. To sleep. 2. To sleep, to be inattentive, to neglect one's business. 3. To be calm or still or torpid. 4. (*Naut.*) Used of the magnetic needle, to lose its virtue. 5. To be slow and heavy in moving (barcos). 6. To be in the pupa state. 7. Among Freemasons, to cease to be an active member of any lodge. **Dormir la siesta**, to take a nap after dinner. **Dormir al sereno**, to sleep in the open. **Dormir a pierna suelta, a pierna tendida** or **a sueño suelto**, (*Coll.*) To sleep carelessly. **Dormir como un lirón**, to sleep like a log. **Dormir con uno**, to sleep with somebody. *-vr.* To be overcome by sleep, to fall asleep.

dormitar [dor-me-tar'], *vn.* To doze, to nap, to mope.

dormitivo [dor-me-tee'-vo], *m.* Dormitive, a soporiferous potion.

dormitorio [dor-me-to'-re-o], *m.* 1. In convents and colleges, a large room where novices or collegians sleep. 2. Dormitory, bedroom.

dornajo [dor-nah'-ho], *m.* A trough.

dorsal [dor-sahl'], *a.* Dorsal, belonging to the back.

dorsífero, ra [dor-see'-fay-ro, rah], *a.* (*Bot.*) Dorsiferous, dorsiparous.

dorso [dor'-so], *m.* The back part of anything; dorsum. **Al dorso**, on back, on the other side. **Escribir algo al dorso**, to write something on the back.

dos [dose], *m. & a.* 1. Two. 2. Second. **Dos de Abril**, the 2nd of April. 3. Deuce. 4. **A dos manos**, with both hands, with open arms. **Dos a dos**, two by two. **De dos en dos**, two by two, by couples. **Dos veces**, twice, double. **Las dos**, two o'clock. **Como ése no hay dos**, they don't come any better than that.

dosañal [dos-ah-ñyahl'], *a.* Biennial, of two years.

doscientos, tas [dos-the-en'-tos, tas], *a. pl. & n.* Two hundred.

dosel [dosel'], *m.* A canopy.

doselera [do-say-lay'-rah], *f.* Valance, the drapery of a canopy.

doselico [do-say-lee'-co], *m. dim.* A small canopy.

dosier [do-se-ayr'], *m.* Dossier.

dosificación [do-se-fe-cah-the-on'], *f.* Dosage.

dosificar [do-se-fe-car'], *va.* To measure out (medicina); to put up in doses.

dosis [do'-sis], *f.* 1. Dose, as of medicine. 2. Quantity.

dotación [do-tah-the-on'], *f.* 1. Dotation, endowment, foundation, a revenue established for any purpose. 2. Dotation, the act of giving a dowry. **Dotación de navíos**, (*Naut.*) fund appropriated to the repairing of ships. 3. **Dotación de un buque**, the complement of a crew. 4. (*Prov.*) Stock. 5. Munition and garrison of a fortress.

dotado, da [do-tah'-do, dah], *a. & pp.* of DOTAR. Dowered, portioned. **Dotado de**, endowed with, gifted with. **Bien dotado**, highly talented.

dotador, ra [do-tah-dor', rah], *m. & f.* One who portions or endows; donor, instituer.

dotal [do-tahl'], *a.* Dotal, relating to a portion or dowry.

dotar [do-tar'], *va.* 1. To portion, to endow with a fortune, to give a portion. **La dotó con un millón**, he gave her a million as a dowry. 2. To gift, to endow with powers or talents. **La naturaleza le dotó de buenas cualidades**, nature endowed him with good qualities. 3. To settle a sum for a particular purpose (beca); to endow: **La Academia ha dotado 2 premios**, the Academy has established 2 prizes. 4. (*Mech. etc.*) To supply, to fit, to provide. **Dotar un avión de todos los adelantos modernos**, to equip a plane with all the latest devices.

dote [doh'tay], *m. & f.* 1. Dower, dowry, the fortune or portion given with a wife. 2. Stock of counters to play with. *-m. pl.* 1. The choicest gifts of the blessed. 2. Gifts, blessings, talents received from nature. **Tiene excelentes dotes**, she has great gifts. 3. Endowments.

dovela [do-vey'-lah], *f.* The curved sides of the keystone of an arch; keystone.

dovelaje [do-vay-lah'-hay], *m.* Series of curved stones for an arch.

dovelar [do-vay-lar'], *va.* To hew a stone in curves for an arch or keystone.

dozavado, da [do-thah-vah'-do, dah], *a.* Twelve-sided.

dozavo, va [do-thah'-vo, vah], *m. & f.* The twelfth part.

Dpto. *abr. de* **Departamento** (department, dept.).

Dr. *abr. de* **doctor** (Doctor, Dr.).

Dra. *abr. de* **doctora** (Doctor, Dr.).

draba [drah'-bah], *f.* (*Bot.*) Whitlow.

dracena [drah-thay'-nah], *f.* Dracaena, a palm-like plant belonging to the lily family.

dracma [drahc'-mah], *f.* 1. Drachm, the eighth part of an ounce. 2. Greek silver coin.

draconiano, na [drah-co-ne-ah'-no, nah], *a.* Draconian, hence barbarous and cruel.

dracúnculo [drah-coon'-coo-lo], *m.* (*Ent.*) Dracunculus, long worm which breeds between the skin and flesh, guinea-worm.

draga [drah'-gah], *f.* Dredge, dredger: applied to the machine and the barge which carries it.

dragaminas [drah-gah-mee'-nas], *m.* (*Mil., Naut.*) Mine sweeper.

dragar [drah-gar'], *va.* To dredge, to use the dredging-machine to deepen a channel.

dragante [drah-gahn'-tay], *m.* 1. (*Bot.*) Goat's thorn. 2. Tragacanth, a sort of gum. 3. (*Naut.*) Pillow of the bowsprit.

drago [drah'-go], *m.* (*Bot.*) Dragon-tree, a tree of America and the Canary Islands, from which the resin called dragon's blood is obtained.

dragomán [drah-go-mahn'], *m.* Dragoman, an interpreter among the Turks.

dragón [drah-gone'], *m.* 1. An old serpent; a fabulous monster. 2. An herb, about three feet high, of red or white flowers, which serves for ornament. 3. (*Mil.*). Dragoon, a horse-soldier who serves occasionally on foot. 4. White spots in the pupils of horses' eyes. 5. Kind of exhalation or vapor. 6. A chimney of a reverberatory furnace. 7. (*Astr.*) A constellation of the northern hemisphere, consisting of forty-nine stars. 8. (Head and tail of the dragon.) The two opposite points in which the orbit of the moon cuts the ecliptic.

dragona [drah-go'-nah], *f.* 1. Shoulder-knot worn by military officers. 2. Female dragon.

dragonal [drah-go-nahl'], *m.* (*Bot.*) V. DRAGO.

dragonazo [drah-go-nah'-tho], *m. aug.* A large dragon.

dragoncillo [drah-gon-theel'-lyo], *m.* 1. Drake, a kind of ancient gun. 2. (*Dim.*) A little dragon or dragoon.

dragonero [drah-go-nay'-ro], *m. V.* DRACENA.

dragontea, dragontía [drah-gon-tay'-ah, drah-gon-tee'-ah], *f.* (*Bot.*) Common dragon.

dragontino, na [drah-gon-tee'-no, nah], *a.* Dragonish.

drama [drah'-mah], *m.* Drama.

dramática [drah-mah'-te-cah], *f.* The dramatic art.

dramáticamente [drah-mah-te-cah-men-tay], *adv.* Dramatically.

dramático, ca [drah-mah'-te-co, cah], *a.* Dramatical, dramatic.

dramatizar [drah-mah-te-thar'], *va.* To dramatize.

dramaturgo, ga [drah-ma-toor'-go, gah], *m. & f.* An author of dramas especially if tragic.

drao [drah'-o], *m. (Naut.)* A monkey, ram, pile-driver.

drapa [drah'-pah], *f. (Arch.) V.* GRAPA.

drástico, ca [drahs'-te-co, cah], *a.* Drastic, acting powerfully.

drecera [dray-thay'-rah], *f.* A row of houses, trees, etc., which form a straight line.

drenaje [dray-nah'-hay], *m.* Drainage by means of subterranean pipes, subsoil drainage.

dríada, dríade [dree'-ah-dah, dree'-ah-day], *f.* Dryad, wood-nymph.

dril [dreel], *m.* Drilling, a strong cloth; drill.

drino [dree'-no], *m.* Kind of venemous serpent.

drizar [dre-thar'], *va. (Naut.)* To hoist up the yards.

driza [dree'-thah], *f. (Naut.)* Halliard. **Drizas del foque mayor**, throat-halliards.

droga [dro'-gah], *f.* 1. Drug, any ingredient used in physic. **Droga dura**, hard drug. **El peligro de las drogas**, the drug menace. 2. *(Met.)* Stratagem, artifice, deceit. 3. Nuisance (molestia). 4. Drug on the market, unsaleable article.

drogadicción [dro-gah-deec-the-on'], *f.* Drug addiction.

drogadicto, ta [dro-gah-deec'-to], *m & f.* Drug addict.

drogado [dro-gah'-do], *m.* Drugging; drug taking.

drogar [dro-gar'], *va.* To drug. *-vr.* To drug oneself, to take drugs.

drogmán [drog-mahn'], *m.* Dragoman.

drogodependencia [dro-go-day-pen-den'-the-ah], *f.* Dependence on drugs, drug addiction.

drogodependiente [dro-go-day-pen-de-ayn'-tay], *m & f.* Person dependent on drugs.

droguería [dro-gay-ree'-ah], *f.* A druggist's shop; trade in drugs.

droguero [dro-gay'-ro], *m.* 1. Druggist. 2. Cheat, bad paymaster.

droguete [dro-gay'-tay], *m.* Drugget, kind of woollen stuff.

droguista [dro-gees'-tah], *m.* 1. Druggist. 2. Cheat, impostor.

dromedario [dro-may-dah'-re-o], *m.* 1. Dromedary. 2. *(Met.)* An unwieldy horse or mule.

dropacismo [dro-pah-thees'-mo], *m.* Ointment for taking off hairs.

drope [dro'-pay], *m. (Coll.)* Vile, despicable man.

druida [droo-ee'-dah], *m.* Druid.

drupa [droo'-pah], *f. (Bot.)* Drupe, a stone fruit with fleshy exterior and nut within.

drusa [droo'-sah], *f. (Min.)* A kind of incrustation in a mineral formed of distinct crystals.

Dtor. *abr.* de **Director** (Director, Dir.).

Dtora. *abr.* de **Directora** (Director, Dir.)

dúa [doo'-ah], *f. (Obs.)* Kind of personal service.

dual [doo-ahl'], *a. (Gram.)* Dual, belonging to two. **Duales**, Incisors. *V.* CORTADORES.

dualismo [doo-ah-lees'-mo], *m.* 1. A philosophy which recognizes two active principles in the universe, a spirit of good and one of evil, in perpetual conflict. 2. Antagonism.

duba [doo'-bah], *f. (Prov.)* Wall or inclosure of earth.

dubio [doo'-beo], *m. (Law.)* Doubt.

dubitable [doo-be-tah'-blay], *a.* Doubtful, dubitable, dubious.

dubitación [doo-be-tah-the-on'], *f.* Dubitation, doubt.

dubitativo, va [doo-be-tah-tee'-vo, vah], *a. (Gram.)* Used to express a doubt, doubtful, dubious (conjunciones).

ducado [doo-cah-do], *m.* 1 Duchy, dukedom. 2. Ducat, an ancient gold and silver coin.

ducal [doo-cahl'], *a.* Ducal.

ducentésimo, ma [doo-then-tay'-se-mo, mah], *a.* Two-hundredth.

ducha [doo'-chah], *f.* 1. Shower. 2. Straight piece of land reaped by a reaper. 3. Douche, a jet of water, used for medicinal effect upon the body. **Tomarse una ducha**, to have a shower. 4. The instruments by which the jet is applied.

duchar [doo-chahr'], *va.* To give a shower, to douche. *-vr.* To have a shower.

ducho, cha [doo'-cho, cha], *a.* Dexterous, accustomed, skillful.

dúcil [doo'-theel], *m. (Prov.) V.* ESPITA.

dúctil [doc'-teel], *a.* Ductile.

ductilidad [dooc-te-le-dahd'], *f.* Ductility.

ductivo, va [dooc-tee'ₓ-vo, vah], *a.* Conducing. *(Acad.)*

ductor [dooc-tor'], *m.* 1. Guide, conductor. 2. *(Med.)* Probe.

ductriz [dooc-treeth'], *f.* Conductress

duda [doo'-dah], *f.* 1. Doubt, uncertainty of mind, suspense, fluctuation, hesitation, irresolution. **Fuera de toda duda**, beyond all doubt. **Ello constituye una duda importante**, this is a big question mark. 2. Doubtfulness, dubiousness. 3. Doubt, question, point unsettled. **Sin duda** or **sin duda alguna**, certainly, doubtlessly, without doubt. **No cabe duda**, there is no doubt about it.

dudable [doo-dah'-blay], *a.* Dubitable, dubious, doubtful.

dudar [doo-dar'], *vn. & va.* 1. To doubt, to hesitate, to be in suspense; to fluctuate. **No dudo de su talento**, I don't question his talent. **No lo dudo**, I don't doubt it. 2. To doubt, to fear. **Dudar de algo**, to doubt something.

dudosamente [doo-do-sah-mayn-tay], *adv.* Doubtfully, dubiously.

dudoso, sa [doo-do'-so, sah], *a.* 1. Doubtful, dubious, uncertain. 2. Dubious, hazardous.

duela [doo-ay'-lah], *f.* Stave. **Duelas para toneles**, hogshead staves. **Duelas para pipas**, pipe staves. **Duelas para barriles**, barrel staves.

duelaje [doo-ay-lah'-hay], *m. V.* DOLAJE.

duelista [doo-ay-lees'-tah], *m.* 1. Duellist. 2. Duellist, fighter, a single combatant.

duelo [doo-ay'-lo], *m.* 1. Duel, challenge. **Batirse en duelo**, to fight a duel. 2. Sorrow, pain, grief, affliction. 3. Mourning, funeral; lamentation, condolement. **Duelos**, troubles, vexations, afflictions. **Sin duelo**, abundantly. *(Yo me duelo, yo me duela, from Dolerse. V.* MOVER.)

duende [doo-en'-day], *m.* 1. Elf, fairy, goblin or hobgoblin, ghost. **Tener duende**, to be hypocondriac, to be restless. 2. A kind of glazed silk.

duendecillo [doo-en-day-theel'-lyo], *m. dim.* A little fairy.

duendo, da [doo-en'-do, dah], *a.* Domestic, tame (palomas).

dueña [doo-ay'-nyah], *f.* 1. Owner proprietress, mistress. 2. Duenna, a widowed woman who used to be in the principal houses for authority, respect, and care of the maid-servants. 3. A married lady. 4. A single woman who has lost her virginity.

dueña de casa [doo-ay'-nyah day cah'-sah], *f.* 1. Housewife. 2. Lady of the house.

dueñaza [doo-ay-nyah'-thah], *f. aug.* A very old duenna, and also the duenna who was very strict.

dueñesco [doo-ay-nyes'-co], *a. (Coll.)* Belonging to a duenna.

dueño [doo-ay'-nyo], *m. & f.* Owner, proprietor, master or mistress. *-m.* Master, with respect to a servant. **Ser dueño de**, to be the owner of. **Ser dueño de sí mismo**, to be self-possessed. **Ser dueño de**, to be free to. **Hacerse dueño de**, to take over.

duermevela [doo-err-may-vay'-lah], *m. (Acad.)* 1. *(Coll.)* Dozing, a nap. 2. *(Coll.)* Labored, interrupted sleep; a catnap.

duerna [doo-err'-nah], *f. V.* ARTESA.

duerno [doo-err'-no], *m.* Double sheet, two, sheets of printed paper, one within another.

dueto [doo-ay'-to], *m.* Duet, a short composition for two voices or two instruments.

dula [doo'-lah], *f. (Prov.)* 1. Herd of black cattle belonging to different persons. 2. Horses and mules which graze on the same pasture. **Vete a la dula**, *(Coll.)* begone, get out of my sight.

dulcamara [dool-cah-mah'-rah], *f.* *(Bot.)* Woody night-shade.

dulce [dool'-thay], *a.* 1. Sweet, pleasing to the taste, luscious, honeyed. 2. Sweet, not salty; not sour; fresh; without flavor. 3. Sweet, mild, soft, gentle, meek. 4. Confortable, pleasing, sweet, pleasant, agreeable. 5. Soft, ductile. **Un instrumento dulce,** a sweet-sounding instrument. **Con el acento dulce del país,** with the soft accent of the region. -*m.* 1. Confiture, sweetmeat, confection, candied or dried fruits. **Dulce de almíbar,** preserves, fruit preserved in sirup. 2. *V.* DULZURA.

dulcecillo, illa, ito, ita [dool-thay-theel'-lyo], *a. dim.* Sweetish, somewhat sweet.

dulcedumbre [dool-thay-doom'-bray], *f.* Sweetness. *V.* DULZURA.

dulcémele [dool-thay'-may-lay], *m.* Dulcimer, a musical instrument.

dulcemente [dool-thay-men'-tay], *adv.* Sweetly, delightfully, mildly, gently.

dulcenta [dool-cen'-tah], *f.* A large kind of apple, red and savory, suited for making cider.

dulcería [dool-thay-ree'-ah], *f.* Confectionery-shop.

dulcera [dool-thay'-rah], *f.* A preserve dish, generally of glass.

dulcero, ra [dool-thay'-ro, rah], *m. & f.* Confectioner.

dulcificación [dool-the-fe-cah-the-on'], *f.* Dulcification.

dulcificante [dool-the-fe-cahn'-tay], *pa.* Dulcifying; sweetener.

dulcificar [dool-the-fe-car'], *va.* To sweeten, to dulcify. -*vr.* To turn mild.

dulcinea [dool-the-nay'-ah], *f.* Mistress, beloved one, in allusion to the celebrated character of this name in Don Quixote.

dulcir [dool-theer'], *va.* To grind plate-glass, to remove the inequalities of the surface, to polish.

dulcísono, na [dool-thee'-so-no, nah], *a.* Sweet toned.

dulero [doo-lay'-ro], *m.* *(Prov.)* Herdsman.

dulía [doo-lee'-ah], *f.* Dulia, worship of the saints.

dulimán [doo-le-mahn'], *m.* Long robe worn by the Turks.

dulzaina [dool-thah'-e-nah], *f.* 1. A musical wind instrument. 2. *(Mex.)* A lute. 3. *(Coll.)* Quantity of sweetmeats.

dulzamara [dool-thah-mah'-rah], *f.* *(Bot.)* *V.* DULCAMARA.

dulzarrón, na [dool-thar-rone', nah], *a.* Cloying, sickening, by being too sweet.

dulzor [dool-thorr'], *m.* *V.* DULZURA.

dulzorar [dool-tho-rar'], *va.* *(Prov.)* To sweeten, to dulcify.

dulzura [dool-thoo'-rah], *f.* 1. Sweetness. 2. Sweetness, meekness, gentleness, graciousness, agreeableness. 3. Comfortableness, pleasure. 4. Forbearance. 5. A graceful and pleasing manner of speaking or writing.

dulzurar [dool-thoo-rar'], *va.* 1. *(Chem.)* To free from saltness, to dulcify. 2. *(Obs.)* To soften, to mitigate.

dulleta [dool-lyay'-tah], *f.* A loose wrapper, for use in cold weather over the house-dress.

duna [doo-nah], *f.* Dune.

dunas [doo'-nas], *f. pl.* Downs, banks of sand which the sea forms on a coast, dunes.

duneta [doo-nay'-tah], *f.* *(Naut.)* The highest part of the poop.

dungarra [doon-gar'-rah], *f.* A sort of white cotton stuff, made in Persia.

dúo [doo'-o], *m.* *(Mus.)* Duo, duet, a musical composition.

duodecaedro [doo-o-day-cah-ay'-dro], *m.* *(Geom.)* Dodecahedron, a solid body of twelve faces.

duodecágono, na [doo-o-day-cah'-go-no, nah], *a. & m. & f.* Dodecagon, a polygon of twelve sides.

duodecasílabo, ba [doo-o-day-cah-see'-lah-bo, bah], *a.* Consisting of twelve syllables.

duodécima [doo-o-day'-the-mah], *f.* *(Mus.)* A twelfth, octave of the fifth.

duodecimal [doo-o-day-the-mahl'], *a.* 1. The last of twelve. 2. Duodecimal, a sistem of enumeration employing twelve distinct characters, and having more common divisors than the decimal.

duodecimo, ma [doo-o-day'-the-mo, ma], *a.* Twelfth.

duodécuplo, pla [doo-o-day'-coo-plo, plah], *a.* Duodecuple, twelve fold.

duodenal [doo-o-day-nahl'], *a.* Duodenal, relating to the duodenum.

duodenario, ria [doo-o-day-nah'-re-o, ah], *a.* 1. Lasting twelve days. 2. Divided into twelve parts.

duodeno, na [doo-o-day'-no, nah], *a.* Twelfth.

duodeno [doo-o-day'-no], *m. & a.* *(Anat.)* Duodenum, the first of the small intestines.

duomesino, na [doo-o-may-see'-no, nah], *a.* Of two months, or relating to that space of time.

dupa [doo'-pah], *m.* Dupe.

dupla [doo'-plah], *f.* In colleges, an allowance of provision larger than usual.

duplex [doo-plex], *m.* 1. Split level flat; semidetached house. 2. *(Telec.)* Link up. 3. *(Comput.)* Duplex.

dúplica [doo'-ple-cah], *f.* A writing in which the defendant replies to the complaint of the plaintiff.

duplicación [doo-ple-cah-the-on'], *f.* 1. Duplication; the act of multiplying by two. 2. Conduplication, a doubling.

duplicadamente [doo-ple-cah-dah-men'-tay], *adv.* Doubly.

duplicado [doo-ple-cah'-do], *m.* Duplicate, counterpart. **Por duplicado,** in duplicate.

duplicado, da [doo-ple-cah'-do, dah], *a. & pp.* of DUPLICAR. Duplicate, doubled.

duplicador [doo-ple-cah-dor'], *m.* An instrument for estimating the particular state of a given volume of air, and its electricity, positive or negative.

duplicar [doo-ple-car'], *va.* 1. To double, to duplicate. 2. To repeat, to do or say the same thing twice. -*vr.* To double.

duplicatura [doo-ple-cah-too'-rah], *f.* *V.* DOBLADURA.

dúplice [doo'-ple-thay], *a.* Double: applied to ancient monasteries with separate cells for friars and nuns.

duplicidad [doo-ple-the-dahd'], *f.* Duplicity, deceit, foul dealing, falseness.

duplo [doo'-plo], *m.* Double, twice as much; duple.

duque [doo'-kay], *m.* Duke.

duquecito [doo-kay-thee'-to], *m. dim.* A pretty duke; a young duke.

duquesa [doo-kay'-sah], *f.* 1. Duchess. **La señora Duquesa,** Her Grace the Duchess. 2. Sort of couch.

dura [doo'-rah], *f.* Duration, continuance.

durable [doo-rah'-blay], *a.* Durable, lasting.

duración, durada [doo-rah-the-on', doo-rah-dah], *f.* Duration, continuance, durableness, durability. **De larga duración,** long-lasting.

duraderamente [doo-rah-day'-rah-men-tay], *adv.* Durably.

duraderas [doo-rah-day'-ras], *f.pl.* Lasting; lasting prunella.

duradero, ra [doo-rah-day'-ro, rah], *a.* Lasting, durable.

duramater [doo-rah-mah'-ter], *f.* *(Anat.)* Dura mater, membrane inclosing the brain.

duramente [doo-rah-men'-tay], *adv.* Hardy, rigorously.

durando [doo-rahn'-do], *m.* Kind of cloth formerly used in Spain.

durante [doo-rahn'-tay], *prep.* During, in the meantime. **Durante muchos años,** for many years. **Habló durante una hora,** he spoke for an hour.

durar [doo-rar'], *vn.* To last, to continue, to endure. **Duró 5 años,** it lasted 5 years.

duraznero [doo-rath-nay'-ro], *m.* *(Bot.)* *V.* DURAZNO for the tree.

durazno [doo-rath'-no], *m.* 1. *(Bot.)* Common peach-tree. 2. Peach, the fruit of a peach-tree.

dureto [doo-ray'-to], *m.* A variety of apple.

dureza [doo-ray'-thah], *f.* 1. Hardness, solidity, firmness. 2. Acerbity or sharpness of temper, obduracy, hardness of heart, cruelty. 3. Steadiness, perseverance, obstinacy. 4. Want of softness or delicacy in paintings. 5. Tumor or callosity.

Dureza de vientre, costiveness. **Dureza de oído,** dullness of hearing. **Dureza de estilo,** harshness of style.

duriagra [doo-re-ah'-grah], *f.* A sort of cotton striped stuff, white and blue.

durillo, lla [doo-reel'-lyo, lyah], *a. dim.* Rather hard, hardish. *-m.* 1. *(Bot.)* Common laurustine, viburnum. 2. Callosity upon a horse, arising from the rubbing of some part of the harness or saddle. 3. **Durillo relevante,** bombast, fustian.

durmiente [door-me-en'-tay], *pa.* Sleeping, sleeper, dormant. *-m.* 1. In buildings, dormant or dormer, a piece of timber which rests on another; girder, stringer. 2. A sleeper (ferrocarril) 3. *(Naut.)* Clamp, shelf, a thick plank nailed to the ship's side within.

duro, ra [doo'-ro, rah], *a.* 1. Hard, solid, firm, knotty. **Más duro que una piedra,** as hard as nails. Tough (alimentos). Stale (pan). **Más duro que un mendrugo,** as tough as old boots. 2. Hard, vexatious, unbearable, unjust. 3. Hard, oppressive, rigorous, cruel, hard-hearted, unmerciful. **Ser duro con uno,** to be tough with somebody. 4. Stubborn, obstinate. **Duro de mollera,** dense (lerdo); pig-headed (terco). 5. Miserable, avaricious. 6. Rude, ill-natured, harsh, peevish, rough, rugged of temper. 7. *(Naut.)* Carrying a stiff sail (barco). 8. *(Pict.)* Harsh and rough, opposite of delicate and soft. Harsh, unsonorous (música). **A duras penas,** with difficulty and labor.

duro [doo'-ro], *m.* A five-peseta coin. **Estar sin un duro,** to be broke.

dutka [doot'-kah], *f.* A double flute, with three holes in each of the tubes, which are unequal. Used in Rusia.

duunvir [doo-oon-veer'], *m.* Roman judge.

duunvirato [doo-oon-ve-rah'-to], *m.* Duumvirate.

dux [doocs], *m.* Doge, magistrate in the republics of Venice and Genoa.

duz [dooth], *-a.* Sweet (dulce). Mild, gentle.

dzohara [dtho-ah'-rah], *f.* An Arabian divinity, corresponding to Venus.

E

e [A or ay] is the fifth letter of the alphabet, and the second of the vowels. **E** is pronounced in Spanish as in the English words they, **eh;** when unaccented, much like **e** in red. E was formerly used as a copulative conjunction, corresponding to **and,** but it is now in general replaced by *y,* yet retained when it precedes a word which begins with the vowel *i* or *hi;* as, **Sabios e ignorantes,** wise and ignorant men. **Padre e hijo,** father and son.

ea [ay'-ah], *m.* A kind of aspiration used to awaken attention. **Ea pues,** an interjection of inference or inquiry, equal to, *well then! Let us see.*

ebanista [ay-bah-nees-tah], *m.* Cabinet-maker, ebonist.

ebanistería [ay-bah-nees-tay-ree'-ah], *f.* Cabinet-work, cabinet-maker's shop.

ebanizar [ay-bah-ne-thar'], *va.* To ebonize, to give wood the color of ebony.

ébano [ay'-bah-no], *m.* Ebony, a hard, black wood.

ebonita [ay-bo-nee'-tah], *f.* Vulcanite, ebonite.

ebriedad [ay-bre-ay-dahd'], *f. V.* EMBRIAGUEZ.

ebrio, ria [ay'-bre-o, ah], *a.* Inebriated, intoxicated, tipsy.

ebrioso, sa [ay-bre-o'so, sah], *a.* Intoxicated, drunken.

ebullición [ay-bool-lye-the-on'], *f.* 1. Ebullition. **Punto de ebullición,** boiling point. 2. *(Fig.)* Movement, activity. **La juventud está en ebullición,** young people are in a state of ferment.

ebúrneo, nea [ay-boor'-nay-o, ah], *a. (Poet.)* Made of ivory, resembling ivory.

eccehomo [ec-thay-oh'-mo], *m.* Ecce Homo. Behold the man: the name of any painting which represents Jesus given up to the mob by Pilate.

eccema, *f.* or **eczema,** *m.* [ec-thay'-mah], *(Med.)* Eczema, a disease of the skin.

ecdémico, ca [ec-day'-me-co, cah], *a. (Med.)* Non-contagious.

ecdora [ec-do'-rah], *f. (Med.)* Excoriation.

ecfora [ec-fo'-rah], *f. (Arch.)* Ecphora, the projection of any member beyond that immediately below it.

eclécticamente [ay-clec'-te-cah-men-tay], *adv.* Eclectically.

eclecticismo [ay-clec-te-thees'-mo], *m.* Eclecticism.

ecléctico [ay-clec'-te-co], *m.* Eclectic, ancient philosophers who professed not to belong to any sect but who chose what was good from all sects.

ecléctico, ca [ay-clec'-te-co, cah], *a.* Eclectic.

eclesiástico [ay-clay-se-ahs'-te-co], *m.* 1. Clergyman, ecclesiastic, priest. 2. Ecclesiasticus, one of the books of Scripture.

eclesiástico, ca [ay-clay-se-ahs'-te-co, cah], *a.* Ecclesiastical, ecclesiastic.

eclesiastizar [ay-clay-se-as-te-thar'], *va. V.* ESPIRITUALIZAR.

eclipsable [ay-clip-sah'-blay], *a.* That may be eclipsed.

eclipsar [ay-clip-sar'], *va.* To eclipse, to darken a luminary, to outshine.

eclipse [ay-cleep'-say], *m.* Eclipse.

eclipsis [ay-cleep'-sis], *f.* Ellipsis.

eclíptica [ay-cleep'-te-cah], *f.* Ecliptic, a circle supposed to run obliquely through the equator.

eclíptico, ca [ay-cleep'-te-co, cah], *a.* Ecliptic, belonging to the eclipse.

eclisa [ay-clee'-sah], *f.* A rail coupling fishplate, shin.

écloga [ay'-clo-gah], *f.* Eclogue, pastoral poem. *V.* EGLOGA.

eco [ay'-co], *m.* 1. Echo. *Hacer eco,* to echo. 2. The repetition of the last syllables of verse. 3. A confused remembrance or idea of the past. 4. Hole or hollow in a horse's sole, occasioned by a frush or other humor. **Hacer eco,** to accord, to agree; to do something great or notable. **Hacerse eco de una opinión,** to echo an opinion. **Encontrar un eco,** to produce a response.

ecóico, ca [ay-co'-e-co, cah], *a. (Poet.)* Relating to echoes.

ecología [ay-co-lo-ge'-ah], *f.* Ecology.

ecológico, ca [ay-co-lo'-he-co, cah], *a.* Ecological.

ecologista [ay-co-lo-hes'-tah], *a. m. & f.* Conservation; environmental, conservationist; environmentalist.

ecólogo, ga [ay-coh'-lo-go, gah], *m. & f.* Ecologist.

ecometría [ay-co-may-tree'-ah], *f.* Arch. Echometry.

ecómetro [ay-co'-may-tro], *m.* Echometer.

economato [ay-co-no-mah'-to], *m.* 1. Guardianship, trusteeship. 2. Cooperative store.

economía [ay-co-no-mee'-ah], *f.* 1. Economy, prudent management, moderation, frugality. **Economía de mercado,** market economy. **Economía dirigida,** planned economy. 2. Economy, the disposition of time and many other things. 3. *(Pict.)* The disposition of figures. 4. Scantiness, misery. 5. Economy, a political science.

economía doméstica [ay-co-no-mee'-ah do-mes'-te-cah], *f.* Home economics; domestic science.

económica [ay-co-no'-me-cah], *f.* Economics, household management.

económicamente [ay-co-no'-me-cah-men-tay], *adv.* Economically.

económico, ca [ay-co-no'-me-co, cah], *a.* 1. Economical, economic. 2. Economical frugal, avaricious.

economista [ay-co-no-mees'-tah], *m.* 1. Economist. 2. One who is a good manager of affairs.

economizar [ay-co-no-me-thar'], *va.* To economize. *-vn.* To economize, to save; to save up.

ecónomo [ay-co'-no-mo], *m.* 1. Curator or guardian, trustee. 2. An administrator of ecclesiastical livings which are under litigation.

ecosistema [ay-co-ses-tay'-mah], *m.* Ecosystem.

éctasis [ec'-tah-sis], *f. (Gram.)* Ectasis, the lengthening of a short syllable for the due measure of the verse.

ectipo [ec-tee'-po], *m.* Ectype, copy from an original.

ectropión [ec-tro-pe-on'], *m.* (*Med.*) Ectropion, eversion of the eyelids, as a morbid state.

ecuable [ay-coo-ay'-blay], *a.* 1. Equable, equal to itself. 2. (*Obs.*) Just, right.

ecuación [ay-coo-ah-the-on'], *f.* 1. Equation. the difference between the time marked by the sun's apparent motion, and that measured by its real motion. 2. Equation, expression of equality between two algebraic quantities. **Ecuación de segundo grado,** quadratic equation. 3. Equalization.

ecuador, ecuator [ay-coo-ah-dor', ay-coo-ah-tor'], *m.* 1. Equator, a great circle of the celestial and terrestrial spheres. 2. The line.

ecualizador [ay-coo-ah-le-thah-dor'], *m.* (*Tec.*) Equalizer.

ecualizar [ay-coo-ah-le-thar'], *va.* To equalize.

ecuanimidad [ay-coo-ah-ne-me-dahd'], *f.* Equanimity; evenness of mind.

ecuatorial [ay-coo-ah-to-re-ahl'], *a.* Equatorial, relating to the equator, -*m.* Equatorial telescope.

ecuatoriano, na [ah-coo-ah-to-re-ah'-no, nah], *a.* Ecuadorian, belonging to Ecuador.

ecuestre [ay-coo-es'-tray], *a.* Equestrian.

ecuménico, ca [ay-coo-may'-ne-co, cah], *a.* Ecumenical, universal.

ecuóreo, rea [ay-coo-o'-ray-o, ah], *a.* (*Poet.*) Belonging to the sea.

eczema [ec-thay'-mah], *m.* V. **ECCEMA.**

echacantos [ay-chah-cahn'-tos], *m.* (*coll.*) A rattlebrained fellow.

echacorvear [ay-chah-cor-vay-ar'], *vn.* (*coll.*) To pimp, to procure.

echacuervos [ay-chah-coo-err'-vos], *m.* (*coll.*) 1. Pimp, procurer. *V.* ALCAHUETE. 2. Cheat, impostor.

echada [ay-chah'-dah], *f.* 1. Cast, throw. 2. The act of throwing oneself on the ground.

echadero [ay-chah-day'-ro], *m.* Place of rest or repose.

echadillo [ay-chah-deel'-lyo], *m.* A foundling.

echadizo, za [ay-chah-dee'-tho, thah], *m. & f.* 1. A Spy. 2. One who is employed in cautiously circulating reports. 3. Foundling.

echadizo, za [ay-chah-dee'-tho, thah], *a.* 1. That which is indirectly reported with the object of discovering some secret. 2. Applied to a person suborned to pry into other people's actions. 3. Supposititious, fictitious.

echador, ra [ay-chah-dor', rah], *m. & f.* Thrower, boaster, braggart.

echadura [ay-chah-doo'-rah], *f.* 1. The act of laying oneself down in a place. 2. Brooding, hatching, the act of sitting on eggs.

echamiento [ay-chah-me-en'-to], *m.* 1. Cast, throw, casting or throning. 2. Projection, the act of throwing away, rejection. 3. Ejection, casting out, expulsion.

echapellas [ay-chah-pel'-lyas], *m.* A woolsoaker.

echar [ay-char'], *va.* 1. To cast, to throw, to dart, to jet. 2. To turn or drive away, to eject, to reject, to cast away, to throw out or expel from an office or profession. 3. To shoot, to bud, to issue, to sprout, to burst out. 4. To put, to apply. 5. To lay on or impose as a tax. 6. (*coll.*) To eat, to drink. 7. To couple male and female animals for procreating. 8. To impute, to ascribe. 9. To perform for a wager. 10. To deal out, to distribute. 11. To publish, to give out, to issue. 12. With *por* and the name of a calling, to follow it. 13. With the words *rayos, centellas, fuego,* etc., to show much annoyance, to be very angry. 14. With the name of a punishment, to condemn to it. 15. With the infinitive of a verb and the preposition *a,* it signifies to begin the action denoted by the verb. **Echar a reír,** to burst out laughing. 16. **Echar por,** to go by one side or the other. 17. Speaking of horses, coaches, clothing, to use them, put into service. The *verb* **echar** is well described by a Spanish lexicographer as a verb of general utility. It serves frequently to assist the meaning of another verb, and enters into many phrases. **Echar carnes,** to become fat.

Echar por otra parte, to differ in opinions from another. **Echar de menos,** to miss. **Echar a perder,** to lose its good taste, to spoil. **Echar fuego,** to be the cause of a dispute. **Echar los hígados,** to be very much fatigued. **Echar a alguno a patadas,** to kick one out. **Echar al camino,** to take to the road, to become a highway robber. **Echar a fondo or a pique,** (*Naut.*) to sink a vessel. **Echar abajo, en tierra, por tierra or por el suelo,** to throw down, to demolish. **Echar el agua a un niño,** to baptize a child. **Echar en saco roto,** (*Met.*) to labor to no purpose, not to follow one's advice. **Echar de menos una persona o cosas,** to miss a person or thing. **Echar a uno la pierna encima,** to surpass or outshine a person. **Echar tierra a alguna cosa,** to bury an affair in oblivion. **Echar al mundo,** to create, to bring forth. **Echar mano,** to give assistance. **Echar a uno a pasear,** to send one abruptly about his business. **Echar suertes,** to draw lots. **Echar a correr,** to run away. **Echar en cara, a la cara or en la cara,** to reproach to one's face, to throw something in one's teeth. **Echar la ley a uno,** to judge and condemn a person to the utmost rigor of the law. **Echar a perder,** to spoil, to mar, not to utilize a thing. **Echarlo todo a rodar,** to spoil or mar utterly an affair. **Echar mano,** to lay hold of a thing; to make use of it, to seize, to catch. **Echar por en medio,** to cut short any difference. **Echar el pie adelante,** (*Met.*) to progress, to be foremost. **Echar el pie atrás,** to retrograde, to be last. **Echar una mano,** to lend a hand, to assist. **Echar un jarro de agua,** (*Met.*) to cut short a person's discourse, or throw a damper on it by an unexpected dry remark. **Echar or echarse un borrón,** (*Met.*) to disgrace oneself. **Echar el guante,** to arrest a person. **Echar en tierra,** (*Naut.*) to land, to disembark. **Echar raíces.** a) to take root. b) to become fixed or established in a place. c) to be rooted or confirmed in something by inveterate habit or custom. - *vr.* 1. To lie, to rest, to stretch oneself to full length; of birds, to sit on eggs. 2. To throw oneself down. 3. To apply oneself to a business. 4. To yield, to desist; of the wind, to grow calm, to abate. **Echarse un pitillo,** to have a smoke. **Echarse una siestecita,** to have a doze. **Echarse atrás,** to throw oneself back. **Echarse en brazos de uno,** to throw oneself into somebody's arms. **Echárselas de,** to boast of.

echazón [ay-chah-thon'], *f.* (*Law.*) Jetson or jettison, act of throwing goods overboard.

echeno [ay-chay'-no], *m.* In foundries, the pouring hole.

edad [ay-dahd'], *f.* 1. Age, the length of life. 2. Age, a particular generation or epoch of time. 3. Era, the time when a particular group of men or animals lived. **Edad de la aviación,** air age. **Edad atómica,** atomic age. **Edad media,** the Middle Ages. **Mayor de edad,** of age. **Menor edad.** a) minority. b) infancy. **Ser menor de edad,** to be a minor; to be under age. **Un señor de edad,** an older man. **Tener la edad de diez años,** to be ten years old. **Edad adulta,** adult age. **Persona de la tercera edad,** senior citizen. **Edad escolar,** school age. **Ella no aparenta la edad que tiene,** she doesn't look her age. **De edad,** elderly.

edecán [ay-day-cahn'], *m.* (*Mil.*) Aide-de-camp.

edema [ay-day'-mah], *f.* Oedema, a general puffiness of parts, due to effusion of serum.

Edén [ay-dayn'], *m.* Eden, paradise.

edeografía [ay-day-o-grah-fee'-ah], *f.* Description of the organs of generation.

éder [ay'-der], *m.* (*Zool.*) Eider-duck.

edición [ay-de-the-on'], *f.* 1. Edition. **Edición aérea,** airmail edition. **Edición de bolsillo,** pocket edition. **Edición semanal,** weekly edition. 2. Publication, issue. 3. **Ediciones Ramírez,** Ramírez Publications. 4. (*Fig.*) Event, occasion. **Es la tercera edición de este festival,** this is the third occasion on which this festival has been held. **Edición asistida por ordenador,** (*Inform.*) desktop publishing. **Edición informática,** (*Inform.*) desktop publishing.

edicto [ay-deec'-to], *m.* 1. Edict, proclamation. 2. Poster, placard.

edificación [ay-de-fe-cah-the-on,], *f.* 1. Construction, the art of raising any building. 2. Edification, edifying.

edificador, ra [ay-de-fe-cah-dor', rah], *m.* & *f.* Edifier, constructor, builder.

edificante [ay-de-fe-cahn'-tay], *a.* Edifying; erecting.

edificar [ay-de-fe-car'], *va.* 1. To edify, to build, to raise or construct a building. 2. To edify, to instruct.

edificativo. va [ay-de-fe-cah-tee'-vo, vah], *a.* Exemplary, instructive.

edificatorio, ria [ay-de-fe-cah-to'-re-o, ah], *a.* Edificatory.

edificio [ay-de-fee'-the-o], *m.* Edifice, structure, fabric.

edil [ay-deel'], *m.* 1. Edile, a Roman magistrate. 2. *(Neol.) V.* CONCEJAL.

edilidad [ay-de-le-dahd'], *f.* Edileship.

editar [ay-de-tar'], *va.* 1. To publish. 2. To edit, to correct. 3. To edit (texto). 4. *(Inform.)* To edit.

editor, ra [ay-de-tor', rah], *m.* Publishing. -*m.* & *f.* 1. Publisher. **Casa editora,** publishing house. 2. Editor. **Editor responsable,** editor (article). **Editor de textos,** *(Inform.)* text editor.

editorial [ay-de-to-re-al'], *a.* Publishing. 2. Editorial. -*m.* (Article) Editorial. -*f.* Publishing house.

edredón [ay-dray-done'], *m.* 1. Eiderdown, the down of an eiderduck. 2. Feather-pillow.

educación [ay-doo-cah-the-on'], *f.* 1. Education (enseñanza), instruction. **Educación física,** physical education. **Educación sexual,** sex education. 2. Manners (modales). **Falta de educación,** bad manners. **Es una persona sin educación,** he's a badly-bred person. **No tener educación,** to have no manners, to lack breeding. **Tiene muy mala educación,** he has very bad manners.

educado [ay-doo-cah'-do], *a.* Well-mannered, polite; nicely behaved; cultivated (culto). **Mal educado,** ill-mannered.

educador, ra [ay-doo-cah-dor', rah], *m.* & *f.* Instructor, educator, teacher (profesor).

educando, da [ay-doo-cahn'-do, dah], *m.* & *f.* Young person that enters a college to be educated.

educar [ay-doo-car'], *va.* To educate, to instruct, to nourish.

educativo, va [ay-doo-cah-tee'-vo, vah], *a.* Educational.

educción [ay-dooc-the-on'], *f.* Eduction, the act of bringing out.

educir [ay-doo-theer'], *va.* To educe, to extract, to bring out.

edulcoración [ay-dool-co-rah-the-on'], *f.* Edulcoration, removal of acidity.

edulcorar [ay-dool-co-rar'], *va. (Chem.)* To sweeten, to remove acidity or acridity.

efe [ay'-fay], *f.* Spanish name of the letter F.

efebo, ba [ay-fay'-bo, bah], *a.* Name which the Athenians gave to youths of eighteen to twenty years.

efectivamente [ay-fec-te-vah-men'-tay], *adv.* Effectually, powerfully; certainly, actually.

efectividad [ay-fec-te-ve-dahd'], *f.* Effectiveness.

efectivo, va [ay-fec-tee'-vo, vah], *a.* 1. Effective, true, certain, effectual. 2. *(Com.)* Specie, cash, in coin. **Efectivo en caja,** cash on hand. **Hacer efectiva una letra,** to cash a draft. **Con 50 libras en efectivo,** with 50 pounds in cash.

efecto [ay-fec'-to], *m.* 1. Effect, result (resultado); operation. **Efectos sonoros,** sound effects. **Hacer efecto,** to take effect (medicina). 2. Effect, consequence. **Tener por efecto,** to have as a result. 3. Effect, purpose, meaning; general intent. **A este efecto,** to this end. **Al efecto de que,** in order that… -*pl.* 1. Assets. 2. Effects, goods, movables. -*pl. (Com.)* Drafts. **Efectos públicos,** public securities. **Efectos en cartera,** bills in hand. **Efectos a pagar,** bills payable. **Efectos a recibir,** bills receivable. **En efecto,** in fact, in truth, actually.

efectuar [ay-fec-too-ar], *va.* To effectuate, to bring, to pass, to accomplish, to effect.

efemérides [ay-fa'-may'-re-des], *f. pl.* Ephemeris, a journal; an account of daily transactions.

efémero [ay-fay'-may-ro], *m. (Bot.)* Iris. Iris sylvestris.

efervescencia [ay-fer-ves-then'-the-ah], *f.* 1. Effervescence, ebullition. 2. *(Met.)* Ardor, fervor.

efervescente [ay-fer-vays-then'-tay], *a.* 1. Effervescent. 2. Seething.

eficacia [ay-fe-cah'-the-ah], *f.* Efficacy, activity.

eficaz [ay-fe-cath'], *a.* Efficacious, active, powerful, forcible, effective.

eficazmente [ay-fe-cath-men'-tay], *adv.* Efficaciously, actively, effectively.

eficiencia [ay-fe-the-en'-the-ah], *f.* Efficiency, effectiveness.

eficiente [ay-fe-the-en'-tay], *a.* Efficient, effective, effectual.

eficientemente [ay-fe-the-ayn'-tay-men-tay], *adv.* Efficiently, effectively.

efigie [ay-fee'-he-ay], *f.* Effigy, image.

efímera [ay-fee'-may-rah], *f.* 1. Ephemera, a fever that terminates in one day. 2. Ephemera, ephemerid, dayfly or Mayfly, an insect that lives but a day.

efímero, ra [ay-fee'-may-ro, rah], *a.* Ephemeral, ephemerous, diurnal, beginning and ending in one day.

eflorecer [ay-flo-ray-therr], *vr. (Chem.)* To effloresce, to fall into powder when exposed to air.

eflorescencia [ay-flo-res-then'-the-ah], *f. (Chem.)* Efflorescent.

eflorescente [ay-flo-res-then'-tay], *a. (Chem.)* Efflorescent.

efluencia [ay-floo-en'-the-ah], *f.* Effluence, emanation.

efluente [ay-floo-en'-tay], *f.* Effluent, emanant.

efluvio [ay-floo'-veo], *m.* 1. Effluvium or effluvia. 2. Exhalation.

efugio [ay-foo'-he-o], *m.* Subterfuge, evasion, shift.

efundir [ay-foon-deer'], *va.* To effuse, to pour out, to spill.

efusión [ay-foo-se-on'], *f.* 1. Effusion, efflux. 2. Confidential disclosure of sentiments. **Efusiones amorosas,** amorous excesses.

efusivo [ay-foo-se-vo], *a.* Effusive; extrusive, warm; effusive (manera). **Mis más efusivas gracias,** my warmest thanks.

efuso, sa [ay-foo'-so, sah], *a.* & *pp. irr.* of EFUNDIR. Effused

égida [ay'-he-dah], *f.* 1. Egis, the shield of Minerva 2. *(Met.)* Protection, defense.

egílope [ay-hee'-lo-pay], *f. (Bot.)* Wild bastard oat.

egipcio [ay-hip-the-o], *a.* Egyptian.

egiptólogo [ayhiptoh'logo], *m.* Egyptologist.

égira [ay'-he-rah], *f.* Hegira, the Mohammedan epoch.

égloga [ay'-glo-gah], *f.* Eclogue, a pastoral poem.

egocéntrico [ay-go-then'-tre-co], *a.* Egocentric, self-centered.

egoísmo [ay-go-ees'-mo], *m.* 1. Selfishness, self-love. 2. Egoism.

egoísta [ay-go-ees'-tah], *a.* Selfish, attentive only to one's own interest or case. -*m.* Egoist, one of a class of philosophers who professed to be sure of nothing but their own existence.

egotismo [ay-go-tees'-mo], *m.* Egotism, selfishness.

egotista [ay-go-tees'-tah], *m.* & *a.* Egotist, one who talks too much of himself.

egregiamente [ay-gray'-he-ah-men-tay], *adv.* Illustriously, egregiously.

egregio, gia [ay-gray'-heo, ah], *a.* Egregious, eminent.

egrena [ay-gray'-nah], *f.* An iron clamp.

egreso [ay-gray'-so], *m.* Item of expense, outgo.

egrisador [ay-gre-sah-dor'], *m.* A box in which lapidaries preserve the powder for grinding diamonds.

egrisar [ay-gre-sar'], *va.* To grind and polish diamonds.

eidero [ay-e-day'-ro], *m.* Eider-duck.

ej. abr de **ejemplo** (example, ex.).

ejarrar [ay-har-rar'], *va.* To scrape the bristles from a hide.

eje [ay'-hay], *m.* 1. Axis. 2. Axle tree, axle. **Eje delantero,** front axle. 3. Center. 4. Wrist pin. **Eje vertical,** *(Aer.)* vertical axis. **Naciones del Eje,** axis Nations.

ejecución [ay-hay-coo-the-on'], *f.* 1. Execution, completion, performance. **Poner en ejecución,** to carry out, to carry into effect. **Ejecución secuencial,** *(Inform.)* sequential execution. 2. Execution, the act of the law, by which possession is given of body or goods. 3. Death inflicted by forms of law. **Pelotón de ejecución,** firing squad. 4. *(Mus.)* Execution, technical skill in playing or singing. **Poner en ejecución,** to put into execution, to carry out.

ejecutable [ay-hay-coo-tah'-blay], *a.* Executable, performable.

ejecutante [ay-hay-coo-tahn'-tay], *m. & a.* One who compels another to pay a debt by legal execution.

ejecutar [ay-hay-coo-tar], *va.* 1. To execute, to perform, to make, to do, to act, to carry out (proyecto). 2. *(Met.)* To impel, to urge to importune, to incite. 3. To oblige one to pay what he owes. 4. To put to death according to the form of justice (condenado).

ejecutivamente [ay-hay-coo-te-vah-men'-tay], *adv.* Executively, promptly.

ejecutivo, va [ay-hay-coo-tee'-vo, vah], *a.* 1. Executive, active. 2. Executory.

ejecutor, ra [ay-hay-coo-tor', rah], *m. & f.* 1. Executor or executer, one that performs or executes something. 2. Officer of justice who serves executions. **Ejecutor or ejecutor de la justicia,** executioner, executer. *V.* VERDUGO.

ejecutoria [ay-hay-coo-to'-re-ah], *f.* 1. *(Law.)* A writ or decree of execution. 2. Letters patent of nobility, pedigree. 3. Executorship.

ejecutoría [ay-hay-coo-to-ree'-ah], *f.* The post or office of an executioner.

ejecutorial [ay-hay-coo-to-re-ahl'], *a.* Applied to the execution of the sentence of an ecclesiastical tribunal.

ejecutoriar [ay-hay-coo-to-re-ar'], *va.* 1. To obtain a verdict or judgment in one's favor. 2. To establish the truth of a thing.

ejecutorio, ria [ay-hay-coo-to'-re-o, ah], *a. (Law.)* Executory, belonging to an execution or seizure.

ejemplar [ay-hem-plar'], *m.* 1. Exemplar, a pattern, model; original, prototype. **Ejemplar gratuito,** free copy. 2. Precedent, example. 3. Copy of a work. 4. An example warning. *-a.* Exemplary, worthy of imitation. **Sin ejemplar,** a) not to be a precedent: used in conceding special grants. b) without precedent.

ejemplarmente [ay-hem-plar-men-tay], *adv.* 1. Exemplarily. 2. Exemplarily, in a manner to warn others. 3. Edifyingly

ejemplificación [ay-hem-ple-fe-cah-the-on'], *f.* Exemplification, illustration by examples.

ejemplificar [ay-hem-ple-fe-car'], *va.* To exemplify.

ejemplo [ay-hem'-plo], *m.* 1. Example, precedent, instance; comparison. 2. Pattern, copy; exemplar, exemplarity, footstep. **Por ejemplo,** for instance. **Dar ejemplo,** to set an example for the imitation of others.

ejercer [ay-her-therr'], *va.* To exercise, to practice, to perform, to use. *-vn.* To practise; to be in office, to hold office.

ejercicio [ay-her-thee'-the-o], *m.* 1. Exercise. 2. Employment, exercise, office, task; ministry. **Durante el ejercicio actual,** during the current financial year. 3. Exercise, labor of the body, labor considered as conducive to health. 4. Military evolutions. **Hacer ejercicio.** 1. To drill troops, to train to military operations. **Ejercicio de defensa contra incendios,** fire drill. 2. To take a walk; to labor for health. **Estar en or tomar ejercicios,** to be in a spiritual retreat; to devote some days to meditation, prayer, etc. **El ejercicio hace maestro,** practice makes perfect.

ejercitación [ay-her-the-tah-the-on'], *f.* Exercitation, practice.

ejercitador, ra [ay-her-the-tah-dor', rah], *m. & f.* 1. Exerciser, practiser.

ejercitante [ay-her-the-tahn'-tay], *m.* 1. The person who is in a spiritual retreat. 2. One who maintains a thesis in disputation or for an academic degree. *-pa.* Exerciser, exercising.

ejercitar [ay-her-the-tar'], *va.* 1. To exercise, to put into practice. 2. To exercise troops, to teach by practice. **Ejercitar la paciencia de alguno,** to try the patience of someone. *-vr.* To practise, to do repeatedly in order to acquire skill.

ejercitativo, va [ay-her-the-tah-tee'-vo vah], *a.* That which may be exercised.

ejército [ay-herr'-the-to], *m.* An army. **Ejercito de ocupación,** army of occupation.

ejido [ay-hee'-do], *m.* Common, a public inclosed space of land.

ejión [ay-he-on'], *m. (Arch.)* Corbel, purlin.

ejotes [ay-ho'-tes], *m. pl.* (Mexican) String-beans.

el [el]. An article of the masculine gender. The. **El General Prim,** General Prim. **El tío ese,** that guy. **El de Pepe es mejor,** Joe's is better.

él, ella, ello [ayl' ayl'-lyah, ayl'-lyo], *pron.* He, she, it. **Él es alto,** he is tall. **Ella es guapa,** she is pretty.

elaboración [ay-lah-bo-rah-the0-on'], *f.* Elaboration.

elaborado, da [ay-lah-bo-rah'-do, dah], *a.* Elaborate. *-pp.* of ELABORAR.

elaborador, ra [ay-lah-bo-rah-dor', rah], *m. & f.* One who or that which elaborates.

elaborar [ay-lah-bo-rar'], *va.* To elaborate, to finish with care.

elación [ay-lah-the-on'], *f.* 1. Elation, haughtiness, pride. 2. Magnanimity generosity. 3. Affected elevation or sublimity of style.

elaína [ay-lah-ee'-nah], *f.* Olein or triolein; absolute oil.

elaiometría [ay-lah-e-o-may-tree'-ah], *f.* The measurement of the density of oils.

elaiómetro [ay-lah-e-o'-may-tro], *m.* Elaeometer, a hydrometer for determining the density of oils.

elaiso [ay-lah'-e-so], *m.* 1. Greek name of the olive-tree. 2. A kind of palm, from the fruit of which in S. America an oil is obtained.

elamí [ay-lah-mee'], *m.* The note in music named mi. *(Ant.)*

elamita [ay-lah-mee'-tah], *a. & m.* Elamite, belonging to Elam.

elasticidad [ay-las-te-the-dahd'], *f.* 1. Elasticity. 2. Facility of being adapted to every use and necessity.

elástico, ca [ay-lahs'-te-co, cah], *a.* Elastic, elastical. *-f.* An undershirt. *-m.* A spring. *(Mech.)*

elaterina [ay-lah-tay-ree'-nah], *f.* Elaterin, a crystallizable principle obtained from elaterium.

elaterio [ay-lah-tay-re-o], *m.* Elaterium, violent purge.

elatine [ay-lah-tee'-nay], *f. (Bot.)* Smooth speedwell.

elche [el'-chay], *m.* Apostate, renegade.

eldorado [el-do-rah'-do], *m.* An imaginary paradise of riches and abundance.

ele [ay'-lay], *f.* Spanish name of the letter L.

eleborina [ay-lay-bo-ree-nah], *f. (Bot.)* Helleborine.

eléboro, elebor [ay-lay'-bo-ro, ay-lay-bor'], *m. (Bot.)* Hellebore.

elección [ay-lec-the-on'], *f.* 1. Election, the act of choosing. **Una elección acertada,** a sensible choice. 2. Election, the ceremony of a public choice. **Elecciones generales,** general election. 3. Election, voluntary preference, liberty of action. 4. Election, discernment, choice, distinction, mind.

electivo, va [ay-lec-tee'-vo, vah], *a.* Elective.

electo, ta [ay-lec'-to, tah], *a. & pp. irr.* of ELEGIR. Elect, chosen.

electo [ay-lec'-to], *m.* Elect, a person chosen, nominee.

elector [ay-lec-tor'], *m.* 1. Elector, voter (elecciones). 2. Elector (antiguo príncipe alemán).

electoral [ay-lec-to-rahl'], *a.* Electoral.

electricidad [ay-lec-tre-the-dahd'], *f.* Electricity.

electricista [ay-lec-tre-thees'-tah], *m.* Electrician.

eléctrico, ca [ay-lec'-tre-co, cah], *a.* Electric or electrical.

electrificación [ay-lec-tre-fe-cah-the-on'], *f.* Electrification.

electrificar [ay-lec-tre-fe-car'], *va.* To electrify.

electrización [ay-lec-tre-tha-the-on'], *f. (Phys.)* Electrification, electrization.

electrizar [ay-lec-tre-thar'], *va.* 1. To electrify (cargar de electricidad), to make electric, to impart electricity. 2. To fill with enthusiasm. *-vr.* To electrize.

electro [ay-lec'-tro], *m.* 1. Electron or amber. 2. Electrum, a mixed metal of gold and silver. *a.* Electromagnetic.

electrocardiógrafo [ay-lec-tro-car-de-o'-grah-fo], *m.* Electrocardiograph.

electrocardiograma [ay-lec-tro-car-de-o-grah'-mah], *m.* Electrocardiogram.

electrocución [ay-lec-tro-coo-the-on'], *f.* Electrocution.

electrocutar [ay-lec-tro-coo-tar'], *va.* To electrocute.

electrochoque [ay-lec-tro-cho'-kay], *m.* Electroshock therapy.

electrodinámica [ay-lec-tro-de-nah' -me-cah], *f.* Electrodynamics.

electrodinámico, ca [ay-lec-tro-de-nah'-me-co, cah], *a.* Electrodynamic.

electrodo [aylectro'-do], *m.* Electrode.

electrodoméstico, ca [ay-lec-tro-do-mes'-te-co, cah], *a.* **Aparato electrodoméstico,** home appliance.

electróforo [ay-lec-tro'-fo-ro], *m.* Electrophorus.

electrógrafo [ay-lec-tro'-grah-fo], *m.* Electrograph.

electroimán [ay-lec-tro-ee-mahn'], *m.* Electromagnet.

electrólisis [ay-lec-tro'-le-sis], *f.* Electrolysia

electrólito [ay-lec-tro'-le-to], *m.* Electrolyte.

electrolizable [ay-lec-tro-le-thah'-blay], *a.* Electrolyzable, decomposable by electricity.

electolización [ay-lec-tro-le-thah-the-on'], *f.* Electrolyzation, decomposing by electricity.

electrolizar [ay-lec-tro-le-thar'], *va.* To electrolyze, to decompose a chemical compound by electricity.

electromagnético, ca [ay-lec-tro-mag-nay'-te-co, cah], *a.* Electromagnetic.

electromagnetismo [ay-lec-tro-mag-may-trees'-mo], *m.* Electromagnetism.

electrometría [ay-lec-tro-may-tree'-ah], *f.* Electrometry, the science or art of making electrical measurements.

electrómetro [ay-lec-tro'-may-tro], *m.* Electrometer, an instrument for measuring electricity.

electromotor, ra [ay-lec-tro-mo-tor', rah], *a.* Electromotor. -*m.* An electric motor.

electrón [ay-lec-trone'], *m.* Electron.

electronegativo, va [ay-lec-tro-nay-gah-te'-vo, vah], *a.* Electronegative.

electrónica [ay-lec-tro'-nee-cah], *f.* Electronics.

electrónico, ca [ay-lec-tro'-ne-co, cah], *a.* Electronic.

electropositivo, va [ay-lec-tro-po-se-tee'-vo, vah], *a.* Electropositive.

electropuntura [ay-lec-tro-poon-too'-rah], *f.* Electropuncture.

electroscopio [ay-lec-tros-co'-peo], *m.* Electroscope.

electrotecnia [ay-lec-tro-tec'-ne-ah], *f.* Electrotechnics.

electroterapia [ay-lec-tro-tay-rah'-pe-ah], *f.* Electrotherapy.

electrotipia [ay-lec-tro-tee'-pe-ah], *f.* Electrotyping.

electrotípico, ca [ay-lec-tro-tee'-pe-co, cah], *a.* Electrotypic, relating to electrotyping.

electrotipista [ay-lec-tro-te-pees'-tah], *m.* Electrotyper.

electuario [ay-lec-too-ah'-re-o], *m.* Electuary, a kind of medicinal conserve.

elefancía [ay-lay-fan-thee'-ah], *f.* Elephantiasis.

elefante, ta [ay-lay-fahn'-tay, tah], *m. & f.* Elephant.

elefantíasis [ay-lay-fan-tee'-ah-sis], *f.* Elephantiasis.

elefantino, na [ay-lay-fan-tee'-no, nah], *a.* Elephantine.

elegancia [ay-lay-gahn'-the-ah], *f.* 1. Elegance, smartness, beauty of style. 2. Elegance, gracefulness; neatness.

elegante [ay-lay-gahn'-tay], *a.* Elegant, smart, gallant, fine, accomplished, nice, dainty, man of fashion (hombre). Fashionable woman (mujer).

elegía [ay-lay-hee'-ah], *f.* Elegy.

elegibilidad [ay-lay-he-be-le-dahd'], *f.* Eligibility.

elegible [ay-lay-hee'-blay], *a.* Eligible, preferable.

elegido, da [ay-lay-hee'-do, dah], *a.* 1. Elected, chosen. 2. Select, choice (selecto). **El presidente elegido,** the president-elect. -*m. & f.* Elected person. One chosen (escogido). -*pp.* of ELEGIR.

elegir [ay-lay-heer'], *va.* To choose, to elect, to name, to nominate. **Te toca elegir a ti,** the choice is yours.

élego, ga [ay'-lay-go, gah], *a.* Mournful, plaintive.

elemental [ay-lay-men-tahl'], *a.* 1. Elemental. 2. Essential, fundamental. 3. Constitutive, constituent.

elemento [ay-lay-men'-to], *m.* 1. Element. **Los cuatro elementos,** the four elements. 2. Element, the first or constituent principle of something. 3. Element, the proper sphere of something. **Elementos,** elements, rudiments (literatura, ciencia).

elemí [ay-le-mee'], *m.* Elimi, a resin.

elenco [ay-len'-co], *m.* I. Table index. **Elenco de artistas,** cast of characters (obra teatral).

elevación [ay-lay-vah-the-on'] *f.* 1. Elevation, the act of raising something. 2. Highness, loftiness. 3. Elevation, exaltation, dignity, advancement. 4. Elevation, rise, ascent; height. 5. Elevation, exaltation of mind, ecstasy, rapture. 6. Haughtiness, presumption, pride. 7. Altitude, the elevation of the pole above the horizon.

elevadamente [ay-lay-vah'-dah-men-tay], *adv.* With elevation, loftily.

elevado, da [ay-lay-vah'-do, dah], *a. & pp.* of ELEVAR. 1. Elevate, elevated, exalted, raised aloft. 2. Elevated, sublime, majestic, high, grand, lofty.

elevador [ay-lay-vah-dor'], *m.* Elevator. **Elevador de granos,** grain elevator.

elevalunas [ay-lay-vah-loo'-nahs], *m. (Aut.)* Electrically-operated window system.

elevamiento [ay-lay-vah-me-en'-to], *m.* Elevation, ecstasy, rapture.

elevar [ay-lay-var'], *va.* 1. To raise, to elevate, to heave, to lift up. 2. *(Met.)* To elevate, to exalt to a high station. -*vr.* 1. To be enraptured. 2. To be elated with presumption or pride. **La cantidad se eleva a...,** the quantity amounts to ... **Los precios se han elevado mucho,** prices have risen a lot.

elidir [ay-le-deer'], *va.* 1. To weaken, to enervate, to debilitate. 2. *(Gram.)* To elide.

elijar [ay-le-har'], *va. (Pharm.)* To seethe or digest vegetable substances.

eliminación [ay-le-me-nah-the-on'], *f.* Elimination, exclusion.

eliminador, ra [ay-le-me-nah-dor', rah], *m. & f.* One who or that which eliminates.

eliminar [ay-le-me-nar'], *va.* 1. To eliminate, to remove one thing from another. 2. To remove a name from a list, a quantity from a calculation, etc.

elipse [ay-leep'-say], *f. (Geom.)* Ellipse, a conic section.

elipsis [ay-leep'-sis], *f. (Gram.)* Ellipsis.

elíptico, ca [ay-leep'-te-co, cah], *a.* Elliptic or elliptical.

elíseos [ay-lee'-say-os], *m.pl.* Elysian. **Campos Elíseos,** Elypsean fields.

elisión [ay-le-se-on'], *f. (Gram.)* Elision.

elite [ay'-le-tay], *f.* Elite.

élitro [ay'le-tro], *m.* 1. Elytron, a thickened wing-cover. 2. *(Bot.)* A common conceptacle.

elixir [ay-lic-seer'], or **elíxir** [ay-leec'-seer], *m.* Elixir (medicina).

ella [ayI'-lyah], *pr. f.* She (sujeto, personas). **Ella vino anoche,** she came last night. 2. Her, herself (enfático, personas). **Es ella,** it's her. **Lo hizo ella,** she did it herself. **Hablo de ella,** I'm talking about her. **Mañana será ella,** there will be trouble tomorrow. **Mi libro y el de ella,** my book and hers.

ellas pron. pers. pl. V. ELLOS.

elle [ayl'-lyay], *f.* Name of the letter *Ll.*

ello[ayl'-lyo], *pron.* 1. It; this business, that whole affair. **Ello es difícil,** it's awkward. **Ello no me gusta,** I don't like it. 2. **Es que ello...,** the fact is that. **Es por ello que...,** that is why... **Por ello no quiero,** that's why I don't want to.

ellos [ayl'-lyos], *pron pers. m. pl.* 1. They. 2. Them (tras *prep.*). 3. Theirs (tras de).

elocución [ay-lo-coo-the-on'], *f.* 1. Elocution. 2. Language, expression, style.

elocuencia [ay-lo-coo-en'-the-ah], *f.* Eloquence.

elocuente [ay-lo-coo-en'-tay], *a.* Eloquent. **Un dato elocuente,** a significant fact.

elocuentemente [ay-lo-coo-en-tay-men'-tay], *adv.* Eloquently.

elogiador, ra [ay-lo-he-ah-dor', rah], *m & f.* Eulogist, encomiast, praiser. *-a.* laudatory, eulogitic.

elogiar [ay-lo-he-ar'], *va.* To praise, to extol, to eulogize, to laud.

elogio [ay-lo'-he-o], *m.* Eulogy, panegyric. **Hacer elogio de,** to praise. **Hizo un caluroso elogio del héroe,** he paid a warm tribute to the hero.

elote [ay-lo'-tay], *m. (Mex.)* A tender ear of maize. Also written *Helote.*

elucidación [ay-loo-the-dah-the-on'], *f.* Elucidation, explanation.

eludible [ay-loo-de-blay], *a.* Avoidable.

eludir [ay-loo-deer'], *va.* To elude, to avoid by artifice.

elzevir [ayl-thay-veer'], *m.* Elzevir (libro).

emaciación [ay-mah-the-ah-the-on'], *f. (Med.)* Emaciation, emaceration.

emanación [ay-mah-nah-the-on'], *f.* 1. Emanation. 2. Emanation, effluvium.

emanante [ay-mah-nahn'-tay], *pa.* Emanating, emanant, emanative.

emanar [ay-mah-nar'], *vn.* To emanate, to proceed from.

emancipación [ay-man-the-pah-the-on'], *f.* Emancipation.

emancipador, ra [ay-man-the-pah-dor', rah], *m. & f.* Emancipator.

emancipar [ay-man-the-par'], *va.* To emancipate. *-vr.* 1. To recover liberty. 2. To go out from tutelage. 3. To shake off a yoke.

emasculación [ay-mas-coo-lah-the-on'], *f.* Emasculation, castration.

emascular [ay-mas-coo-lar'], *va.* To castrate, to emasculate.

embabiamiento [em-bah-be-ah-me-en'-to], *m.* 1. Stupidity, foolishness. 2. Distraction, absence of mind.

embachar [em-bah-char'], *va.* To pen sheep, to be shorn.

embadurnar [em-bah-door-nar'], *va.* To besmear, to bedaub.

embaidor, ra [em-bah-e-dor', rah], *m. & f.* Sharper, impostor, swindler.

embaimiento [em-bah-e-me-en'-to], *m.* 1. Delusion, illusion. 2. Deceit, imposition, imposture.

embair [em-bah-eer'], *va.* To impose upon, to deceive.

embajada [em-bah-hah'-dah], *f.* 1. Embassy, a public or solemn message, legation. 2. Embassy, an ambassador's house.

embajador [em-bah-hah-dor'], *m.* Ambassador.

embajadora, embajatriz [em-bah-hah-do'-rah, em-bah-hah-treeth'], *f.* Ambassadress, ambassador's lady.

embajatorio, ria [em-bah-hah-to'-re-o, ah], *a.* Belonging to an ambassador.

embalador [em-bah-lah-dor'], *m.* Packer.

embalar [em-bah-lar'] *va.* To bale, to make up into bundles, to pack.

embalaje [em-bah-lah'-hay], *m.* Packing, package, baling.

embaldosado [em-bal-do-sah'-do], *m.* Tiled floor. *-a.* Tiled **Embaldosado, da,** *pp.* of EMBALDOSAR.

embaldosar [em-bal-do-sar'], *va.* To floor with tiles, to tile (con baldosas).

embalijar [em-bah-le-har'], *va.* To pack up into a portmanteau.

emballenador [em-bal-lyay-nah-dor'], *m.* Staymaker.

emballenar [em-bal-lyay-nar'], *va.* To stiffen with whalebone (ballenas).

emballestado [em-bal-lyes-tah'-do], *m.* Contraction of the nerves in the feet of animals. **-Emballestado, da,** *pp.* of EMBALLESTARSE.

emballestarse [em-bal-lyes-tar'-say], *vr.* To be on the point of discharging a cross-bow.

embalsadero [em-bal-sah-day-ro], *m.* Pool of stagnant rainwater.

embalsamador, ra [em-bal-sah-mah-dor', rah], *m.* Embalmer.

embalsamadura, *f.* **embalsamamiento,** *m.* [em-bal-sah-mah-doo'-rah] Embalming.

embalsamar [em-bal-sah-mar'], *va.* To embalm, to dam up; to retain, to collect.

embalsamiento [em-bal-sah-me-en-to], *m.* 1. Act of putting something into a pool of water. 2. The stoppage of water, forming a pool.

embalsar [em-bal-sar'], *va.* 1. To dam, to dam up (agua). 2. To sling, to hoist (izar). 3. To put something into a pool of still water. 4. To drive cattle into a pool of water to refresh them.

embalse [em-bahl'-say], *m.* 1. Dam (presa), damming, damming up (acción de embalsar); reservoir, dam(lago artificial) 2. Slinging, hoisting (izar). 3. Act of putting anything into a pool of water. 4. Act of driving cattle into water.

embalumar [em-bah-loo-mar'], *va.* To load a horse unequally. *-vr.* To embarrass oneself with business.

embanastar [em-bah-nas-tar'], *va.* To put into a basket.

embancadura [em-ban-cah-doo'-rah], *f.* The benches, collectively, of a rowboat.

embancar [em-ban-car'], *va.* To move to the center the spool of the spindles in looms, in order to begin to lay the warp. *-vr.* to run aground.

embaracillo [em-bah-rah-theel'-lyo], *m. dim.* A slight embarrassment.

embarazada [em-bah-rah-thah'-dah], *a.* Pregnant. **Dejar embarazada a una,** to get a girl pregnant. *-f.* Pregnant woman.

embarazadamente [em-bah-rah-thah-dah-men'-tay], *adv.* Perplexedly, with embarrassment, awkwardly.

embarazado, da [em-bah-rah-thah'-do, dah], *a.* Embarrassed, perplexed, mazy. *-pp.* of EMBARAZAR. **Embarazada,** pregnant.

embarazador, ra [em-bah-rah-thar-dor', rah], *m. & f.* Embarrasser.

embarazar [em-bah-rah-thar'], *va.* 1. To embarrass, to perplex, to hinder, to obstruct, to cumber. 2. To make pregnant.

embarazo [em-bah-rah'-tho], *m.* 1. Impediment, embarrassament, vexation, obstruction, obstacle. 2. Confusion, perplexity. 3. Pregnancy, time of gestation.

embarazosamente [em-bah-rah-tho'-sah-men-tay], *adv.* Difficultly, cumbersomely.

embarazoso, sa [em-bah-rah-tho-so, sah], *a.* Difficult, intricate, entangled, cumbersome, troublesome, vexatious, obstructive.

embarbascado, da [em-bar-bas-cah'-do, dah], *a.* Difficult, intricate, involved, complicated. *-pp.* of EMBARBASCAR.

embarbascar [em-bar-bas-car'] *va.* 1. To throw hellebore, mullein, etc., into water, to stupefy fish. 2. *(Met.)* To perplex, to confound, to embarrass. *-vr.* To be entangled among the roots of plants.

embarbecer [em-bar-bay-therr'], *vn.* To have a beard appearing, at the age of puberty.

embarbillar [em-bar-beel-lyar'], *va.* To join planks or beams together.

embarcación [em-bar-cah-the-on'], *f.* 1. Vessel or ship of any size or description. **Embarcación de arrastre,** trawler. 2. Embarkation. *V.* EMBARCO. 3. Navigation.

embarcadero [em-bar-cah-day'-ro], *m.* 1. Wharf, quay, or key. 2. Port, harbor.

embarcador [em-bar-cah-dor'], *m.* One who embarks or ships goods.

embarcar [em-bar-car'], *va.* 1. To embark, to ship, to put on shipboard. 2. *(Met.)* To embark, to engage another in an affair or enterprise. **Embarcar a uno en una empresa,** to involve somebody in an enterprise. *-vr.* 1. To embark, to go on shipboard. 2. *(Met.)* To embark, to engage in an affair. **Embarcarse en un asunto,** to get involved in a matter.

embarco [em-bar-co], *m.* Embarcation(personas), embarking, shipping(mercancías).

embargador [em-bar-gah-dor'], *m.* One who sequestrates or lays on an embargo; sequestrator.

embargante [em-bar-gahn'-tay], *pa.* Arresting, impeding, restraining. **No embargante,** notwithstanding, nevertheless.

embargar [em-bar-gar'], *va.* 1. *(Law.)* To sequestrate, to seize (juzgada), to attach, to lay an embargo upon. 2. *(Met.)* To impede, to restrain, to suspend. 3. To overcome (emoción, dolor)

embargo [em-bar'-go], *m.* 1. Embargo on shipping, sequestration. 2. *(Law.)* Extent, execution, distraint, seizure attachment. 3. Access (emoción). 4. Indigestion. **Sin embargo,** notwithstanding. **Sin embargo de,** despite the fact that.

embarnecer [em-bar-nay-therr'], *vn. (Obs.)* To grow plump, full, or fat.

embarnizador [em-bar-ne-thah-dor'], *m.* Varnisher.

embarnizadura [em-bar-ne-thah-doo'-rah], *f.* Varnishing.

embarnizar [em-bar-ne-thar'], *va.* 1. To varnish, to japan, to glaze. 2. *(Met.)* To adorn, to embellish, to set off.

embarque [em-bar'-kay], *m.* Putting goods and provisions on shipboard.

embarrado [em-bar-rah'-do], *a.* Muddy.

embarrador [em-bar-rah-dor'], *m.* Plasterer, dauber.

embarradura [em-bar-rah-doo'-rah], *f.* Overlaying with plaster or mortar.

embarrancarse [em-bar-ran-car'-say], *vr.* 1. To get mired in a deep hole. 2. *(Naut.)* To run aground.

embarrar [em-bar-rar'], *va.* 1. To daub or overlay with plaster, clay, or mortar. 2. *(Met.)* To confound or perplex an affair. 3. To besmear with mud. 4. To cover with plaster. *-vr.* To collect or mount upon trees, as partridges when pursued.

embarrillar [em-bar-re-lar'], *va.* To barrel, to put in a barrel.

embarrotar [em-bahr-ro-tar'], *va. V.* ABARROTAR.

embarullar [em-bah-rool-lyar'], *va. (coll.)* 1. To confuse, to mix things in disorder. 2. To act without order or plan. *-vr.* To be confounded, overwhelmed.

embasamiento [em-bah-sah-me-en'-to]. *m. (Arch.)* Basis or foundation of a building.

embastar [em-bas-tar'], *va.* 1. To baste linen, silk, etc., to secure it in a frame to be embroidered. 2. To put stitches in a mattress. 3. *(Prov.)* To put a packsaddle on a beast of burden.

embaste [em-bahs'-tay], *m.* Basting.

embastecer [em-bas-tay-therr'], *vn.* To become corpulent; to become fat or gross. *-vr.* To become gross.

embatada [em-bah-tah'-dah], *f. (Naut.)* A sudden dash of the sea or wind against the course being followed.

embate [em-bah'-tay], *m.* 1. The dashing of the sea against something. 2. A sudden impetuous attack. **Embates,** sudden reversal of fortune.

embaucador, ra [em-bah-oo-cah-dor], *m. & f.* Sharper, impostor, abuser.

embaucamiento [em-bah-oo-cah-me-en'-to], *m.* Deception, illusion.

embaucar [em-bah-oo-car'], *va.* To deceive, to delude, to humbug, to impose upon.

embaular [em-ba-hoo-lar'], *va.* 1. To pack in a trunk. 2. *(Met. coll.)* To cram with food.

embausamiento [em-bah-oo-sah-me-en'-to], *m.* Amazement, astonishment, absence of mind.

embazador [em-bah-thah-dor'], *m.* One who shades or darkens a color.

embazadura [em-bah-thah-doo'-rah], *f.* 1. The art of shading or darkening colors. 2. *(Met.)* Amazement, astonishment.

embazar [em-bah-thar'], *va.* 1. To tinge, to shade. 2. *(Met.)* To astonish, to strike with amazement. 3. *(Met.)* To impede the execution of a thing. *-vn.* To be amazed or astonished, to remain without action. *-vr.* 1. To become tired, disgusted, or satiated. 2. To blush.

embebecer [em-bay-bay-therr'], *va.* 1. To astonish, to stupefy. 2. To entertain, to amuse. *-vr.* To be struck with amazement.

embebecidamente [em-bay-bay-the'-dah-men-tay], *adv.* Amazedly.

embebecimiento [em-bay-bay-the-me-en'-to], *m.* Amazement, astonishment.

embebedor, ra [em-ba'-bay-dor', rah], *m. & f.* Imbiber.

embeber [em-bay-berr'], *va.* 1. To imbibe, to drink in. 2. To imbibe, to drench, to saturate. 3. To incorporate, to introduce, to include. 4. To shrink or make to shrink, to squeeze, to press. 5. Among curriers, to oil a hide. *-vn.* 1. To shrink, to contract itself. 2. To row thick and close. *-vr.* 1. To be enraptured or ravished, to be wrapt up in thought. 2. To imbibe, to admit or retain firmly in the mind.

embebimiento [em-bay-be-me-en'-to], *m.* Imbibition.

embecaduras [em-bay-cah-doo'-ras], *f. pl. (Arch.)* Spandrel.

embelecador, ra [em-bay-lay-cah-dor rah], *m. & f.* Impostor, sharper.

embelecar [em-bay-lay-car'], *va.* To impose upon, to deceive, to humbug.

embeleco [em-bay-lay'-co], *m.* Fraud, delusion, imposition, humbug.

embeleñado, da [em-bay-lay-nyah'-do, dah], *a. & pp.* of EMBELEÑAR. 1. Enraptured, ravished. 2. Stupefied, besotted.

embeleñar [em-bay-lay-nyar'], *va.* To stupefy, to besot.

embelesamiento [em-bay-lay-sah-me-en'-to], *m.* Amazement, astonishment, rapture.

embelesar [em-bay-lay-sar'], *va.* 1. To amaze, to astonish. 2. To charm, to subdue the mind by pleasure. *-vr.* To be charmed, ravished or delighted.

embeleso [em-bay-lay'-so], *m.* 1. Amazement, astonishment, ravishment. 2. Charm, charmer.

embellaquecerse [em-bel-lyah-kay-therr'-say], *vr.* To become low-minded or mean-spirited; to have wicked or worthless ideas.

embellecedor [em-bel-lyay-the-dor'], *m. (Aut.)* Hub cap.

embellecer [em-bel-lyay-therr'], *va.* To embellish, to adorn, to decorate, to flourish.

emberar [em-bay-rar'], *vn. (Prov.)* To begin to have a ripe color (uvas).

embermejar [em-ber-may-har'], *va.* To give a red color.

embermejecer [em-ber-may-hay-therr'] *va.* 1. To dye red. 2. To put to blush, to shame. *-vr.* To blush.

embermellonar [em-ber-mayl-lyo-nar'], *va.* To apply vermilion, to paint scarlet.

embere [em-bay'-ray], *m. (Prov.)* Color of grapes which are ripening.

emberrincharse [em-ber-rin-char'-say] *vr. (coll.)* To fly into a violent passion (niños).

embestida [em-bes-tee-dah], *f.* 1. Assault, violent attack, onset. 2. *(Met.)* Importunate demand by way of charity, loan, etc.

embestidor [em-bes-te-dor'], *m.* One who makes importunate demands.

embestidura [em-bes-te-doo'-rah], *f.* Attack, assault, onset.

embestir [em-bes-teer'], *va.* 1. To assail, to attack, to offend. 2. To importune with unseasonable demands. 3. *(Naut.)* To collide against something, or against another vessel. *-va. & vr.* 1. To entangle the parts of a harness or to get entangled. 2. *(Mil.)* To invest a place.

embetunar [em-bay-too-nar'], *va.* To cover with gum-resin or bitumen.

embicador [em-be-cah-dor'], *m. (Amer.)* Cup and ball.

embicar [em-be-car'], *va.* **Embicar las vergas,** *(Naut.)* To top the yards. *-vn.* 1. To be inclined toward the horizon: said of something which has arms. 2. To strike straight upon the shore or beach with the lifeboat. 3. To luff, to haul to the wind. 4. *(Mil.)* To point downward the mouths of cannon as much as possible.

embijar [em-be-har'], *va.* To paint with minium or red lead.

embión [em-be-on'], *m.* A shove.

embioncillo [em-be-on-theel'-lyo], *m. dim.* A slight shove.

embizarrarse [em-be-thar-rar'-say], *vr.* In the jocular style, to brag, to boast of courage, to bully.

emblandecer [em-blan-day-therr'], *va.* To moisten, to soften with moisture. *-vn. (Met.)* To soften, or move to pity. *-vr.* To soften, to get soft.

emblanquecer [em-blan-kay-ther'], *va.* To bleach or whiten. *-vr.* To grow white, to be bleaching.

emblanquecimiento, emblanquimiento [em-blan-kay-the-me-en'-to, em-blan-ke-me-en'to], *m. (Obs.)* Whitening, bleaching.

emblema [em-blay'-mah], *m.* 1. Emblem. 2. All occult representation, an allusive picture.

emblemático, ca [em-blay-mah'-te-co, cah], *a.* Emblematic.

embobamiento [em-bo-bah-me-en'-to], *m.* Admiration, astonishment, enchantment; stupefying.

embobar [em-bo-bar'], *va.* To amuse, to entertain the mind, to divert from, to distract. *-vr.* To be in suspense, to stand gaping or gazing, to muse. **Reírse embobado,** to laugh like mad.

embobecer [em-bo-bay-therr'], *va.* To stultify, to stupefy, to make foolish. *-vr.* To become stupefied or stultified.

embobecimiento [em-bo-bay-the-me-en'-to], *m.* Stupefaction.

embocadero, embocador [em-bo-cah-day'-ro, em-bo-cah-dor'], *m.* Mouth of a channel, by which water is conveyed through a mill-dam. **Estar al embocadero,** to be at the point of attaining something.

embocado, da [em-bo-cah'-do, dah], *a.* Applied to wine which is pleasant to the taste. *-pp.* of EMBOCAR.

embocadura [em-bo-cah-doo'-rah], *f.* 1. The mouth or entrance by a narrow passage. 2. Mouthpiece of a bridle. 3. Mouthpiece of a musical instrument.

embocar [em-bo-car'], *va.* 1. To enter by the mouth. **Embocar una cosa en un agujero,** to insert something into a hole. 2. *(Met.)* To enter by a pass or narrow passage. 3. To swallow in haste, to cram food. **Embocar la comida,** to cram one's food. 4. *(Met.)* To give news agreeable or sad, without preparation or warning.

embocinado, da [em-bo-the-nah'-do, dah], *a.* V. ABOCINADO.

embodarse [em-bo-dar'-say], *vr. (Obs.)* To be married.

embojar [em-bo-har'], *va.* To arrange branches for silkworms, for forming their webs and cocoons.

embojo [em-bo'-ho], *m.* The operation of arranging branches for silkworms, and the branches so arranged.

embolar [em-bo-lar'], *va.* 1. To put balls on the tips of bulls' horns. 2. To apply the gilding-size.

embolia [em-bo'-lee-ah], *f.* Embolism, obstruction of a blood-vessel by a clot or plug. **Embolia cerebral,** clot on the brain.

embolismador, ra [em-bo-lis-mah-dor', rah], *m. & f. & a.* Detractor, reviler, reviling.

embolismal [em-bo-lis-mahl'], *a.* Applied to the intercalary year, composed of thirteen lunations.

embolismar [em-bo-lis-mar'], *va.* To propagate malicious sarcasms and rumors.

embolismo [em-bo-lees'-mo], *m.* 1. Embolism, intercalation; insertion of days or years to produce regularity and equation of time. 2. The time inserted, intercalary time. 3. Confusion, mixture of things. 4. Maze. 5. Falsehood.

émbolo [em'-bo-lo], *m.* 1. Embolus, the piston or plunger in a pump. 2. Forcer, the embolus of a force-pump.

embolsar [em-bol-sar'], *va.* 1. To put money into a purse. 2. To reimburse, to recover money advanced.

embolso [em-bol'-so], *m.* The act of putting money into a purse.

embonar [em-bo-nar'], *va.* 1. To make good or firm. 2. *(Naut.)* To cover a ship's bottom and sides with planks.

embones [em-bo'-nes], *m. pl. (Naut.)* Planks which are employed in covering the ship's bottom.

embono [em-bo'-no], *m.* 1. *(Naut.)* The act of doubling a ship's bottom and soles with planks. 2. Lining, stiffening.

emboñigar [em-bo-nye-gar'], *va.* To plaster with cow-dung.

emboque [em-bo'-kay], *m.* I. Passage of a thing through an arch or strait part. 2. Deception, cheat, fraud. **Eso no tiene emboque,** *(Amer.)* that has not the least appearance of truth.

emboquillar [em-bo-keel-lyar'], *va.* To make the entrance of a shaft in mines.

embornal [em-bor-nahl'], *m. (Naut.)* Scupperhole.

emborrachador, ra [em-bor-rah-chah-dor', rah], *a.* Intoxicating, producing drunkenness. *-n.* One who makes drunk.

emborrachamiento [em-bor-rah-chah-me-en'-to], *m. (coll.)* Intoxication, drunkenness.

emborrachar [em-bor-rah-char'], *va.* To intoxicate, to inebriate, to fuddle, to get drunk. *-vr.* To inebriate, to be intoxicated, to overdrink oneself.

emborrada [em-bor-rah'-dah], *f.* Portion of wool which is passed through the carder.

emborradura [em-bor-rah-doo'-rah], *f.* 1. Recarding of wool. 2. What serves to recard.

emborrar [em-bor-rar'], *va.* 1. To stuff with goat's hair. 2. In woollen manufactories, to card the wool a second time.

emborrascar [em-bor-ras-car'], *va. &; vr.* To provoke, to enrage.

emborrazamiento [em-bor-rah-thah-me-en'-to], *m.* Act of basting a fowl while roasting.

emborrazar [em-bor-rah-thar'], *va.* To tie pieces of pork on a fowl, to serve as basting.

emborricarse [em-bor-re-car'-say], *vr. (coll.)* To be stupefied, or to grow stupid.

emborrizar [em-bor-re-thar'], *va.* To give the first combing to wool.

emborrullarse [em-bor-rool-lyar'-say], *vr.* In jocular style, to be at variance, to dispute noisily.

emboscada [em-bos-cah'-dah], *f.* 1. Ambuscade. 2. *(Mil.)* Ambush, ambuscade. **Tender una emboscada,** to lay an ambush for.

emboscadura [em-bos-cah-doo'-rah], *f.* Ambush, ambuscade.

emboscar [em-bos-car'], *va.* 1. *(Mil.)* To place in ambush. 2. To emboss. 3. *(Met.)* To conceal in some secret place. *-vr.* 1. To retire into the thickest part of a forest. 2. To ambush, to lie in ambush. **Estaban emboscados cerca del camino,** they lay in ambush near the road.

embosquecer [em-bos-kay-therr'], *vn.* To become woody, to convert into shrubberies.

embotado, da [em-bo-tah'-do, dah], *a.* Blunt, dull. *-pp.* of EMBOTAR.

embotador [em-bo-tah-dor'], *m.* He who blunts the points or edges of swords, etc.

embotadura [em-bo-tah-doo'-rah], *f.* Blunting (acción), dullness, bluntness (estado) of swords and other edged weapons.

embotamiento [em-bo-tah-me-en'-to], *m.* 1. Blunting edged weapons; obtusion. 2. Bluntness, obtuseness, dullness. 3. *(Met.)* Stupefaction, the act of making dull or stupid.

embotar [em-bo-tar'], *va.* 1. To blunt, to dull an edge or point, to break off the edges or points of edged tools or weapons, to foil. 2. *(Met.)* To enervate, to debilitate. 3. To dull, to stupefy. *-vr.* 1. To dull, to become dull. 2. *(coll.)* To put on the boots.

embotellado [em-bo-tayl-lyah'-do], *a.* Bottled; prepared (discurso). *-m.* Bottling.

embotellamiento [em-bo-tayl-lyah-me-ayn'-to], *m.* 1. *(Aut.)* Traffic jam. 2. *(Fig.)* Bottleneck.

embotellar [em-bo-tel-lyar'], *va.* To bottle wine or other liquors.

embotijar [em-bo-te-har'], *va.* 1. To lay a stratum of small earthen jars, before a tile flooring is put down. 2. To fill jars with oil or other liquids. *-vr.* To swell, to expand. 2. To be in passion, to be inflated with arrogance.

embovedado, da [em-bo-vay-dah'-do, dah], *a.* Arched, vaulted.

embovedar [em-bo-bay-dar'], *va.* To cover with an arch or vault.

emboza [em-bo'-thah], *f.* Inequalities in the bottom of barrels or casks.

embozado, da [em-bo-thah'-do, dah], *a.* Covered, involved. *-pp.* of EMBOZAR.

embozalar [em-bo-thah-lar'], *va.* To muzzle animals.

embozar [em-bo-thar'], *va.* 1. To muffle the greater part of the face. 2. To cloak, to dissemble. 3. To muzzle. *-vr.* To muffle oneself by throwing the right fold of the cape over the left shoulder.

embozo [em-bo'-tho], *m.* 1. The part of a cloak, veil, or any other thing with which the face is muffled. 2. The act of muffling the greater part of the face. 3. *(Met.)* An artful way of expressing one's thoughts, so as to keep them in part concealed.

embozo (De) [em-bo'-tho], *adv.* Incognito, unknown, private.

embracilado, da [em-brah-the-lah'-do, dah], *a.* *(coll.)* Constantly carried about in one's mother's arms.

embragar [em-brah-gar'], *vn.* To let out the clutch. *-va.* 1. *(Naut.)* To sling. 2. To put in gear, to engage.

embrague [em-brah'-gay], *m.* 1. Clutch. 2. Letting out the clutch. **Embrague automático,** Automatic transmission.

embravar, embravecer [em-brah-vay', em-brah-vey-therr'], *va.* To enrage, to irritate, to make furious. *-vn.* To become strong (plantas). *-vr.* 1. To become furious, to enraged. 2. *(Naut.)* To be extremely boisterous (el mar).

embravecimiento [em-brah-vey-the-me-en'-to], *m.* Fury, rage, passion.

embrazadura [em-brah-thah-do'-rah], *f.* 1. Clasping of a shield or buckler. 2. Embracing, clasping.

embrazar [em-brah-thar'], *va.* 1. To clasp a shield, as in the posture of fighting. 2. To engage the teeth of two wheels in each other.

embreado [em-bray-ah'-do], *m.* **embreadura** [em-bray-ah-doo'-rah], *f.* *(Naut.)* Tarring, paying a ship with pitch.

embrear [em-bray-ar'], *va.* *(Naut.)* To pay with pitch, to tar.

embregarse [em-bray-gar'-say], *vr.* To quarrel, to wrangle, to dispute.

embreñarse [em-bray-nyar'-say], *vr.* To hide oneself among brambles or in thickets.

embriagado, da [em-bre-ah-gah'-do, dah], *a.* & *pp.* of EMBRIAGAR. Intoxicated, drunk.

embriagador [em-bre-ah-gah-dor'], *a.* Intoxicating (olor); Heady, strong (vino etc.).

embriagar [em-bre-ah-gar'], *va.* 1. To intoxicate, to inebriate. 2. To transport, to enrapture. *-vr.* To inebriate, to grow drunk.

embriaguez [em-bre-ah-geth'], *f.* 1. Intoxication, drunkenness, inebriety. 2. *(Met.)* Rapture, transport of the mind.

embridar [em-bre-dar'], *va.* 1. To bridle, to guide by a bridle. 2. *(Met.)* To govern, to restrain.

embriogenia [em-bre-o-hay'-ne-ah], *f.* Formation and development of the foetus in its intrauterine existence.

embriología [em-bre-o-lo-hee'-ah], *f.* Embryology.

embriologo, ga [em-bre-o'-lo-go, gah], *m.* & *f.* Embryologist.

embrión [em-bre-on'], *m.* 1. Embryo or embryon, the first rudiment of a plant or an animal. 2. The beginning of a thing, still shapeless. 3. *(Met.)* Assemblage of confused ideas, without method or order.

embrionario, ria [em-bre-o-nah'-re-o, ah], *a.* Embryonal, rudimentary.

embroca, embrocación [em-bro'-cah, em-bro-cah-the-on'], *f.* *(Pharm.)* Embrocation.

embrocar [em-bro-car'], *va.* 1. To pour out of one vessel into another. 2. With embroiderers, to wind thread or twist upon quills. 3. To fasten with tacks to the last (zapateros). 4. To catch the bull between the horns.

embrochado, da [em-bro-chah'-do, dah], *a.* Embroidered.

embrochalar [em-bro-chah-lar'], *va.* To sustain with a crosspiece or a bar of iron the beams which rest on the walls.

embrolla [em-brol'-lyah], *f.* *(coll.)* V. EMBROLLO.

embrollador, ra [em-brol-lyah-dor', rah], *m.* & *f.* 1. Entangler, confounder. 2. *V.* EMBROLLÓN.

embrollar [em-brol-lyar'], *va.* 1. To entangle, to twist, to overlace, to comber. 2. *(Met.)* To entangle, to ensnare, to confound with artful subtleties, to embroil. *-vr.* To get into a muddle, to get into a mess. **Embrollarse en un asunto,** to get involved in a matter.

embrollo [em-brol'-lyo], *m.* Fraud, imposture, snare, deception; embroiling; knot.

embrollón, na [em-brol-lyone', nah], *m.* & *f.* 1. Liar, talebearer; impostor. 2. Entangler.

embromado, da [em-bro-mah'-do, dah], *a.* *(Prov. Naut.)* Misty, hazy, foggy. *-pp.* of EMBROMAR.

embromador, ra [em-bro-mah-dor', rah], *m.* & *f.* & *a.* 1. Applied to one who is tumultuously merry. 2. Wheedler, one who deceives by artful tricks.

embromar [em-bro-mar'], *va.* 1. To make fun, to tease (burlarse de). 2. To hoax, to fool (engañar). 3. To jest, to joke. 4. To repair provisionally the damaged seams of a ship, to chinse.

embroquelarse [em-bro-kay-lar'-say], *V.* ABROQUELARSE.

embroquetar [em-bro-kay-tar'], *va.* To skewer the legs of birds, in order to roast them.

embrujado [em-broo-hah'-do], *a.* Bewitched (persona); Haunted (lugar). **Una casa embrujada,** a haunted house.

embrujar [em-broo-har'], *va.* To bewitch. **La casa está embrujada,** the house is haunted. *V.* HECHIZAR.

embrujo [em-broo'-ho], *m.* 1. Bewitching (acto). 2. Curse (maldición). 3. Spell, charm (ensalmo). **El embrujo de la Alhambra,** the enchantment of the Alhambra.

embrutecer [em-broo-tay-therr'], *va.* To stupefy. *-vr.* 1. To grow stupid, to become brutish. 2. To lose refined manners.

embrutecimiento [em-broo-tay-the-me-en'-to], *m.* The act of making brutish stupefaction.

embuchado [em-boo-chah'-do], *m.* Large sausage made of pork, with salt and spice. **—Embuchado, da,** *pp.* Of EMBUCHAR.

embuchar [em-boo-char'], *va.* 1. To stuff with minced meat: to make pork sausages. 2. To cram the maw of animals. 3. *(Met.)* To swallow food without chewing.

embudador [em-boo-dah-dor'], *m.* Filler, one who fills vessels with a funnel.

embudar [em-boo-dar'], *va.* 1. To put a funnel into a vessel to pour liquors through. 2. *(Met.)* To scheme, to ensnare.

embudista [em-boo-dees'-tah], *m.* Intriguer, deceiver.

embudito [em-boo-dee'-to], *m. dim.* A little funnel.

embudo [em-boo'-do], *m.* 1. Funnel. 2. Among wax-chandlers, tail of a wax-candle mould. 3. The basin of a water-closet. 4. *(Met.)* Fraud, deceit artifice.

embullarse [em-bool-lyar'-say], *vr.* *(Prov. Cuba and Canary Islands.)* To carouse, to revel, to be gay.

embullo [em-bool'-lyo], *m.* Carousal, gaiety, revelry. *(Cuba and Canary Islands.)*

emburujar [em-boo-roo-har'], *va.* *(coll.)* To jumble, to mix confusedly.

embuste [em-boos'-tay], *m.* 1. An artful tale; a lie, fiction. 2. Fraud, imposition. 3. *(Met.)* Pleasing quibble of children. **Embustes,** gewgaws, baubles, trinkets.

embustear [em-boos-tay-ar'], *vn.* 1. To lie, to impose upon, to gab. 2. To make frequent use of frauds, tricks, and deceits.

embustería [em-boos-tay-ree'-ah], *f* Deceit, imposture, trick.

embustero, ra [em-boos-tay'-ro, rah], *m.* & *f.* 1. Liar, talebearer, tale-teller. 2. Impostor, cheat. 3. Hypocrite, dissembler. 4. *(coll.)* Cajoler, coaxer.

embusterón, na [em-boos-tay-rone', nah], *a. aug. V.* EMBUSTERO.

embutidera [em-boo-te-day'-rah], *f.* Instrument for riveting tin-work.

embutido [em-boo-tee'-do], *m.* Inlaid work. *-pl.* Large sausage filled with minced meat. **-Embutido, da,** *pp.* of EMBUTIR.

embutidor [em-boo-te-dor'], *m.* A riveting set, a punch.

embutidura [em-boo-te-doo'-rah], *f. (Naut.)* Worming, filling the grooves of a rope with material.

embutir [em-boo-teer'], *va.* 1. To inlay, to encase. 2. To mix confusedly, to jumble, to insert. 3. *(Met.)* To cram, to eat much. 4. *(Obs.)* To imbue. **Embutir algo a uno,** to make somebody swallow something. *-vr.* To stuff oneself.

eme [ay'-may], *f.* Spanish name of the letter M.

emenagogo [ay-may-nah-go'-go], *m.* Emmenagogue, an agent promoting the menstrual flow.

emendable [ay-men-dah'-blay], *a. (Ant.)* Amendable, corrigible.

emendación [ay-men-dah-the-on'], *f.* 1. Emendation, amendment, correction. 2. Satisfaction, chastisement.

emendador [ay-men-dah-dor'], *m. (Ant.)* Emendator.

emendadura, *f.* **emendamiento,** *m.* [ay-men-dah-doo'-rah, ay-men-dah-me-en'-to]. *(Obs.) V.* ENMIENDA.

emendar [ay-men-dar'], *va. (Ant.)* 1. To amend, to correct, to emend. 2. **Emendar un aparejo,** *(Naut.)* to overhaul a tackle.

emergencia [ay-mer-hen'-the-ah], *f.* 1. Emergency. 2. Emergence. **Aterrizaje de emergencia,** forced landing, emergency landing.

emergente [ay-mer-hen'-tay], *a.* Emergent, resulting, issuing from something.

emerger [ay-mer-her'], *a.* 1. To emerge; to appear; to surface (submarino).

emérito [ay-may'-re-to], *a.* 1. Emeritus, an epithet applied to a professor in a university, public teacher, or religious order, who, having well discharged his duties for a stated time, is allowed to retire, receiving the whole or part of his appointment, and retaining the honors and exemptions belonging to it. 2. A Roman soldier allowed to retire after having done sufficient public service.

emersión [ay-mer-se-on'], *f. (Ast.)* Emersion.

emético, ca [ay-may'-te-co, cah], *m. & a.* Emetic. *-m.* Tartar emetic, tartrate of antimony and potassa.

emetina [ay-may-tee'-nah], *f.* Emetin, an alkaloid procured from ipecacuanha.

emetizar [ay-may-te-thar'], *va.* 1. To add an emetic to any substance whatever. 2. To produce vomiting.

emienda [ay-me-en'-dah], *f. (Ant.) V.* ENMIENDA.

emigración [ay-me-grah-the-on'], *f.* 1. Emigration, immigration. 2. Sum total of emigrants. 3. Periodical migration of certain animals.

emigrado [ay-me-grah'-do], *m.* Emigrant, immigrant.

emigrado, da [ay-me-grah'-do, dah], *a. & m. & f.* Emigrated, immigrated. *-pp.* of EMIGRAR.

emigrante [ay-me-grahn'-tay], *m.* Emigrant.

emigrar [ay-me-grar'], *vn.* To emigrate, to immigrate.

emina [ay-mee'-nah], *f.* 1. Measure containing the fourth part of a Spanish bushel. 2. Ancient tax.

eminencia [ay-me-nen'-the-ah], *f.* 1. Eminence, eminency, height, a hill. 2. *(Met.)* Eminence, excellence, conspicuousness. 3. Eminence, greatness, power. 4. Eminence, title given to cardinals. **Con eminencia,** eminently.

eminencial [ay-me-nen-the-ahl'], *a.* Eminential.

eminente [ay-me-nen'-tay], *a.* 1. Eminent, high, lofty. 2. Eminent, eximious, conspicuous.

eminentemente [ay-me-nen'-tay-men-tay], *adv.* Eminently, conspicuously.

eminentísimo [ay-me-nen-tee'-se-mo], *a.* Most eminent (título de cardenales).

emir [ay-meer'], *m.* 1. Emir, or ameer. 2. Prince, lord 3. A title of dignity among the Turks.

emisario [ay-me-sah'-re-o], *m.* 1. Emissary, spy. 2. Outlet, discharge. 3. *(Med.)* Emunctory.

emisión [ay-me-se-on'], *f.* 1. Emission, vent. 2. Issue of paper money. 3. Scattering of atoms. 4. *(Med.)* Emission. 5. Broadcasting (radio); broadcast (programa). **Emisión deportiva,** sports program.

emisivo, va [ay-me-see'-vo, vah], *a.* Having the faculty of spreading or scattering warmth or light.

emisor, ra [ay-me-sor, rah], *a.* Emitting, issuing. *-f.* Broadcasting station (radio).

emitir [ay-me-teer'], *va.* 1. To emit, to send forth, to let go. 2. To issue, to put into circulation (dinero). 3. To show, manifest an opinion, to give a vote. 4. To broadcast (radio, TV).

emoción [ay-mo-the-on'], *f.* 1. Emotion, agitation of mind. **Nos comunica una emoción de nostalgia,** it gives us a nostalgic feeling. 2. Excitement, thrill; tensión, suspense. **Al abrirlo sentí gran emoción,** I felt very excited on opening it.

emocionado [ay-mo-the-o-nah-do], *a.* Deeply moved, deeply stirred.

emocional [ay-mo-the-o-nahl'], *a.* Emotional.

emocionalismo [ay-mo-the-o-nah-lees'-mo], *m.* Emotionalism.

emocionante [ay-mo-the-o-nahn'-tay], *a.* Emotional, thrilling, exciting.

emocionar [ay-mo-the-o-nar'], *va.* To excite, to thrill. *-vr.* To get excited, to be thrilled. **¡No te emociones tanto!,** don't get so excited.

emoliente [ay-mo-leen'-tay], *m. & a.* Emollient, softening, healing.

emolumento [ay-mo-loo-men'-to], *m.* 1. Emolument, fee, profit, advantage. 2. Perquisite. Mostly used in the plural.

emotivo [ay-mo-tee'-vo], *a.* Emotional.

empacar [em-pah-car'], *va.* To pack up in chests; to wrap up in hides or skins. *-vr.* To be sullen, to be displeased.

empachadamente [em-pah-chah'-dah-men-tay], *adv. (Prov.)* Cumbersomely

empachado, da [em-pah-chah'-do, dah], *a. & pp.* of EMPACHAR. 1. Clumsy, awkward (torpe). 2. Surfeited, glutted, fed to satiety. **Estar empachado,** to have indigestion (estómago).

empachar [em-pah-char'], *va.* 1. To impede, to embarrass, to clog, to disturb. 2. To perplex, to confound. 3. To overload, to cram, to cause indigestion (estómago). 4. To disguise. *-vr.* 1. To be ashamed, to be confounded. 2. To be fed to satiety.

empacho [em-pah'-cho], *m.* 1. Bashfulness, timidity. 2. Embarrassment, obstacle. 3. Surfeit, indigestion.

empachoso, sa [em-pah-cho'-so, sah], *a. V.* VERGONZOSO.

empacón [em-pah-cone'], *a. (Prov. S. Amer.)* Obstinate, stubborn, contumacious.

empadronador [em-pah-dro-nah-dor'] *m.* Enroller, censustaker.

empadronamiento [em-pah-dro-nah-me-en'-to], *m.* 1. Census, an official enumeration of the inhabitants of a country. 2. List or register of persons liable to pay taxes. *V.* PADRÓN.

empadronar [em-pah-dro-nar'], *va.* 1. To make, or take the census of a country. 2. To enter in a register the names of those who are liable to pay taxes. *-vr.* To register.

empajar [em-pah-har'], *va.* To cover something or to fill it with straw.

empalagamiento [em-pah-lah-gah-me-en'-to], *m.* Loathing, surfeit, cloying.

empalagar [em-pah-lah-gar'], *va.* 1. To loathe, to cause the disgust of satiety, to cloy. 2. To disgust in a high degree, to offend, to trouble. *-vr.* 1. To loathe, to feel abhorrence or disgust. 2. To be cloyed, to be disgusted or displeased.

empalago [em-pah-lah'-go], *m. V.* EMPALAGAMIENTO.

empalagoso, sa [em-pah-lah-go'-so, sah], *a.* Squeamish, cloying, loathsome, loathful, fastidious, troublesome.

empalamiento [em-pah-lah-me-en'-to], *m.* Empalement, empaling.

empalar [em-pah-lar'], *va.* To empale.

empaliar [em-pah-le-ar'], *va. (Prov.)* To hang with tapestry a church cloister, or other place, through which a procession passes.

empalizada [em-pah-le-thah'-dah], *f. (Mil.)* Palisade or palisado.

empalizar [em-pah-le-thar'], *va*. 1. To palisade, to inclose with palisades. 2. To pale.

empalmadura [em-pal-mah-doo'-rah], *f*. Dovetailing, the junction of two pieces of wood. *V*. EMPALME.

empalmar [em-pal-mar'], *va*. 1. To scarf, to dovetail. 2. *(Naut.)* To splice cables. *3.* To join, to connect; to splice (cuerdas). *-vn*. To join, to meet, to come together (ferrocarril).

empalme [em-pahl'-may], *m*. 1. Scarf, joining, connection (conexión). 2. A splicing. 3. Junction of a branch line of railway with the main line.

empalmillar [em-pal-mil-lyar'], *m. (Arch.)* A wall of stone, unhewed, for procuring the filtering of river water, which is to be turned into irrigating trenches.-*va*. To glue the inner sole of the shoe.

empalmo [em-pahl'-mo], *m*. Shank, a piece of wood which goes under the head of a beam.

empalomadura [em-pah-lo-mah-doo'-rah], *f. (Naut.)* Marline.

empalomar [em-pah-lo-mar'], *va. (Naut.)* To sew the boltrope to the sail.

empalletado [em-pal-lyay-tah'-do], *m. (Naut.)* A kind of quilting as a defence in fight to those who are on deck.

empalletar [em-pal-lyay-tar'], *va*. To form the parapet called *empalletado*.

empamparse [em-pam-par'-say], *vr. (Amer.)* 1. To be absent of mind, to be in suspense. 2. To get lost on a pampa.

empanada [em-pah-nah'-dah], *f*. 1. Meat pie. 2. **Empanada mental,** confusion.

empanadilla [em-pah-nah-deel'-lyah], *f*. 1. *(dim.)* A small pie. 2. *(Prov.)* Movable footstep put in coaches.

empanado [em-pah-nah'-do], *a*. 1. Receiving light from another room. 2. Covered in breadcrumbs (cocina). **Empanados,** limber boards; planks laid over the well in a ship. -**Empanado, da,** *pp*. of EMPANAR.

empanar [em-pah-nar'], *va*. 1. To cover with paste, to bake in paste. 2. To sow grain. -*vr*. To be choked by too much seed having been sown (agricultura).

empandar [em-pan-dar'], *va*. To bend into an arch.

empandillar [em-pan-dil-lyar'], *va*. To remove by stealth, to hide.

empantanado [em-pahn-tah-nah'-do], *a*. Flooded, swampy.

empantanar [em-pan-tah-nar'], *va*. 1. To submerge, to make a pond or lake. 2. To bemire. 3. To embarrass the course of an affair. -*vr*. 1. To be flooded, to get swamped. 2. *(Fig.)* To be obstructed, to be held up.

empañado [em-pah-nyah'-do], *a*. Misty, steamy, steamed-up (ventana); dim, blurred (contorno); tarnished (superficie); faint (voz).

empañadura [em-pah-nyah-doo'-rah], *f*. Swaddling of children.

empañar [em-pah-nyar'], *va*. 1. To swaddle, to wrap in swaddling clothes. 2. *(Met.)* To soil a glass with one's breath, to darken, to obscure. 3. *(Met.)* To denigrate, to impeach one's character or reputation. -*vr*. 1. To film over, to get misty; to cloud over.

empañicar [em-pah-nye-car'], *va. (Naut.)* To hand or furl (barcos).

empapar [em-pah-par'], *va*. To imbibe, to saturate, to soak, to drench. -*vr*. 1. To imbibe, to be soaked, to be surfeited. 2. To imbue oneself with the principles of doctrine, science etc. 3. To surfeit. 4. To boast of something without reason.

empapelado [em-pah-pay-lah'-do], *m*. Papering, paperhanging.

empapelador [em-pah-pay-lah-dor'], *m*. A person who wraps something up in paper.

empapelar [em-pah-pay-lar'], *va*. 1. To wrap up in paper. 2. *(Prov.)* To waste paper. 3. **Empapelar a uno,** *(Jur.)* To lay a charge against somebody.

empapirolado, da [em-pah-pe-ro-lah'. do, dah], *a. (coll.)* Full, satisfied.

empapirotado, da [em-pah-pe-ro-tah'. do, dah], *a. (coll.)* Lofty, haughty, puffed up.-*pp*. of EMPAPIROTAR.

empapirotar [em-pah-pe-ro-tar'], *va. (coll.)* To adorn carefully, to deck nicely.

empapujar [em-pah-poo-har'], *va*. To make one eat too much. *(Acad.)*

empaque [em-pah'-kay], *m*. 1. Packing. 2. *(And. and Amer.)* Air, semblance, look: generally in bad part. Appearance and aspect of a person, according to which he pleases us, or displeases, at first sight. *(Acad.)*

empaquetador, ra [em-pah-kay-tah-dor', rah], *m. & f.* Packer. -*f*. Packing machine.

empaquetadura [em-pah-kay-tah-doo'-rah], *f*. Packing, gasket.

empaquetar [em-pah-kay-tar'], *va*. To pack, to bind goods into bales; to clap together.

emparamentar [em-pah-rah-men-tar'], *va*. To adorn, to set off.

emparchar [em-par-char'], *va*. To cover with a plaster.

emparedado, da [em-pah-ray-dah'-do, dah], *m. & f.* 1. Cloisterer: applied to a devotee who lives in a cloister without the vows. 2. A sandwich. 3. Confinement. -*pp*. of EMPAREDAR.

emparedamiento [em-pah-ray-dah-me-en'-to], *m*. 1. Confinement, the act of shutting up between walls. 2. Cloister, religious retirement.

emparedar [em-pah-ray-dar'], *va*. To confine, to immure, to shut up between walls.

emparejador [em-pah-ray-hah-dor'], *m*. Matcher, fitter.

emparejadura [em-pah-ray-hah-doo'-rah], *f*. Equalization.

emparejamiento [em-pah-ray-hah-me-en'-to], *m*. Act of matching or making equal.

emparejar [em-pah-ray-har'], *va. & vn.* 1. To level, to reduce to a level. 2. To match, to fit, to equal. 3. To put abreast, to put on a level, to be equal. -*vr*. To pair off.

emparentar [em-pah-ren-tar'], *vn*. To be related by marriage.

emparentado, da [em-pah-ren-tah'-do, dah], *a. & pp*. of EMPARENTAR. Related by marriage. **Estar bien or muy emparentado,** have respectable relatives.

emparentar [em-pah-rayn-tar'], *vn*. To become related by marriage. **Emparentar con una familia,** to marry into a family.

emparrado [em-par-rah'-do], *m*. Arbor or bower made with the branches of primped vines. -**Emparrado, da,** *pp*. of EMPARRAR.

emparrar [em-par-rar'], *va*. To embower, to form bowers with the branches of vines.

emparrillar [em-par-reel-lyar'], *va*. To broil on the grill.

emparvar [em-par-var'], *va*. To put grain in order to be thrashed.

empasma [em-pahs'-mah], *m*. A perfumed toilet powder.

empastado [em-pas-tah'-do], *a*. 1. *(Typ.)* Clothbound, bound. 2. Filled (diente).

empastador [em-pas-tah-dor'], *m*. 1. A painter who gives a liberal coat of color to his works. 2. Pastebrush. 3. *(Amer.)* Binder of books in leather.

empastadura [em-pas-tah-doo'-rah], *f*. Dental filling.

empastar [em-pas-tar'], *va*. 1. To bind (books, etc.) 2. To fill with paste. 3. To fill (muela). 4. To cover with paint.

empaste [em-pahs'-tay], *m*. 1. Filling (diente). 2. *(Typ.)* Binding.

empastelar [em-pas-tay-lar'], *va. & vr. (Fig. and coll.)* 1. To transact a matter without regard to justice in order to get out of a difficulty. 2. *(Typ.)* To pie, to distribute wrongly, to jumble together.

empatadera [em-pah-tah-day'-rah], *f. (coll.)* Checking, impeding; suspension of anything.

empatar [em-pah-tar'], *va*. 1. To draw, to tie. **Empatar a dos,** to tie two to two. **Smith empató en el minuto veinte,** Smith equalized in the twentieth minute. To tie, to have a dead hit (carreras). **Han empatado a dos,** they tied two to two. **Estar empatados,** to be equal or tying. **Han empatado,** they tied, or drew.

empate [em-pah'-tay], *m.* 1. Equality, equal number of votes. 2. Stop, suspension.

empatronamiento [em-pah-tro-nah-me-en'-to], *m.* Stamping as standard.

empatronar [em-pah-tro-nar'], *va.* To stamp a certain mark upon weights and measures, to certify that they are standard.

empavesada [em-pah-vay-sah'-dah], *f. (Naut.)* Waist clothes, painted linen or close netting spread on the sides of ships to obstruct the enemy's sight.

empavesar [em-pah-vay-sar'], *va.* 1. *(Naut.)* To spread waist clothes on the sides of a ship. 2. *(Naut.)* To dress ships.

empecatado, da [em-pay-cah-tah'-do, dah], *a.* Very wily, evil-minded, incorrigible. *(Acad.)*

empecer [em-pay-therr'], *va.* 1. To hurt, to offend, to injure. 2. To prevent.

empecinado [em-pay-the-nah'-do], *m. (Acad.)* 1. *V.* PEGUERO. 2. *(Peru)* Stubborn, inexorable, incorrigible.

empecinar [em-pay-the-nar'], *va.* 1. To fill with mud. 2. *V.* EMPEGAR. *-vr. (Amer.)* To be obstinate, to be given over to vice. **Empecinarse en algo,** to be stubborn.

empedernido [em-pay-der-ne'-do], *a.* 1. Heartless; obdurate (persona); flinty, stony (corazón). 2. Hardened, inveterate (en un vicio). **Un fumador empedernido,** a strongly addicted smoker.

empedernimiento [em-pay-der-ne-me-en'-to], *m.* Hardness of heart.

empedernir [em-pay-der-neer'], *va.* To indurate, to harden. -*vr.* 1. To be petrified, to grow hard as stone. 2. *(Met.)* To be obstinate, to be inflexible.

empedrado [em-pay-drah'-do], *m.* Pavement. **Empedrado, da,** *pp.* of EMPEDRAR.

empedrador [em-pay-drah-dor'], *m.* Paver or pavier.

empedrar [em-pay-drar'], *va.* 1. To pave, to floor with stones. 2. To form small holes or cavities in any superficies.

empega [em-pay'-gah], *f.* 1. Varnish of pitch. 2. Mark of pitch.

empegadura [em-pay-gah-doo'-rah], *f.* The varnish of pitch which is put on vessels.

empegar [em-pay-gar'], *va.* 1. To pitch, to cover with pitch. 2. To mark sheep with pitch.

empego [em-pay'-go], *m.* 1. Marking sheep with pitch. 2. *(Amer.)* The disagreeable taste which some wines have.

empeguntar [em-pay-goon-tar'], *va.* To mark sheep with pitch.

empeine [em-pay'-e-nay], *m.* 1. The groin. 2. The instep. 3. Hoof of a beast. 4. Tetter, ringworm. 5. *(Prov.)* Flower of the cotton plant. 6. *(Bot. Ant.)* Lichen, an order of cryptogramous plants.

empeinoso, sa [em-pay-e-no'-so, sah], *a.* Full of fetters or ringworms.

empelar [em-pay-lar'], *vn.* To get hair, to begin to be hairy.

empelechar [em-pay-lay-char'], *va.* To join or unite marble blocks.

empelotarse [em-pay-lo-tar'-say], *vr.* 1. To be at variance, to quarrel. 2. To be vexed, to be uneasy.

empeltre [em-pel'-tray], *m. (Prov.)* Small olive-tree or sapling springing from an old trunk.

empella [em-pel'-lyah], *f.* 1. The fat of fowls, the lard of swine. 2. Upper leather of a shoe.

empellar, empeller [em-pel-lyar' em-pel-lyerr'], *va.* To push, to impel.

empellejar [em-pel-lyay-har'], *va.* To cover with skins.

empellón [em-pel-lyone'], *m.* Push, heavy blow. **A empellones,** rudely, with pushes.

empenachar [em-pay-nah-char'], *va.* To adorn with plumes.

empenar [em-pay-nar'], *va.* To feather an arrow, to dress with feathers.

empenta [em-pen'-tah], *f.* Prop, stay, shore.

empentar [em-pen-tar'], *va. (Prov.)* To push, to impel. *V.* EMPUJAR.

empeña [em-pay'-nyah], *f. (Obs.)* Upper leather of a shoe. *V.* PELLA.

empeñadamente [em-pay-nyah-dah-men'-tay], *adv.* Strenuously, in a courageous or spirited manner.

empeñado [em-pay-nyo], *a.* 1. Pawned (objeto). 2. **Estar empeñado hasta los ojos,** to be deeply in debt. 3. Determined (persona). **Estar empeñado en,** to be determined to.

empeñar [em-pay-nyar'], *va.* 1. To pawn, to pledge, to gage, to impignorate. 2. To engage, to oblige. *-vr.* 1. To bind oneself, to fulfil a contract or to pay debts. 2. To persist in a determination or resolution. 3. To encounter dangers with courage and spirit. 4. To intercede, to mediate. 5. *(Naut.)* To be embayed on a leeshore. **Empeñarse por alguno,** to recommend anyone, or to exert oneself in favor of anyone. **Empeñarse en algo,** to take a fancy, to undertake a thing eagerly.

empeño [em-pay'-nyo], *m.* 1. Obligation contracted by pledging. 2. Engagement, contract. 3. Earnest desire, ardent love. 4. Boldness; courage and perseverance in overcoming difficulties. 5. Firmness, constancy. 6. Protection, favor, recommendation. 7. Recommender, the person who protects or favors. **Con empeño,** with great ardor, diligence, eagerness. **Tengo un empeño con Vd, I** have a particular favor to ask you. **Tiene empeño en que su amigo salga bien,** he is bent on his friend's success.

empeoramiento [em-pay-o-rah-me-en'-to], *m.* Deterioration.

empeorar [em-pay-o-rar'], *va.* To impair, to deteriorate. *-vn. -vr.* To grow worse.

empequeñecer [em-pay-kay-nyay-therr'], *va.* To make smaller, to diminish.

emperador [em-pay-rah-dor'], *m.* 1. An emperor. 2. A name given to certain animals on account of their great size and beauty; for example, the golden-crested wren, the emperor moth, etc.

emperatriz [em-pay-rah-treeth'], *f.* Empress.

emperchar [em-per-char'], *va.* To suspend on a perch,

emperdigar [em-per-de-gar'], *va. V.* PERDIGAR.

emperejilar [em-pay-ray-he-lar'], *va.* To adorn, or to dress with a profusion of ornaments. *-vr.* To be adorned, to be dressed out.

emperezar [em-pay-ray-thar'], *vn. & vr.* 1. To be lazy or indolent. 2. To be dilatory, tardy, slow.

empericado, da [em-pay-re-cah'-do, dah], *a.* To be dressed in style; to wear false hair.

emperifollar [em-pay-re-fol-lyar'], *va. & vr.* To decorate excessively, to cover with ribbons and bows, to deck with flowers, to ornament a discourse with flowers of rhetoric.

empernar [em-per-nar'], *va.* 1. To nail, to spike, to peg. 2. *(Naut.)* To bolt, to fasten with bolts.

empero [em-pay'-ro], *conj.* Yet, however. *V.* PERO.

emperramiento [em-per-rah-me-ayn'-to], *m.* Stubbornness.

emperrar [em-per-rar'], *va.* To irritate, to enrage. *-vr.* To grow mad or furious, to be obstinate or stubborn. **Emperrarse en algo,** to be stubborn about something.

empesador [em-pay-sah-dor'], *m.* Handful of rushes used by weavers for trimming their yarn.

empetro [em-pay'-tro], *m. (Bot.)* Crow-berry. **Empetro blanco,** white-berried crowberry. **Empetro negro,** Blackberried crowberry.

empezar [em-pay-thar'], *va.* To begin, to commence. **Obra empezada, medio acabada,** well begun is half done. **Empezar por,** to begin by. **Empezó diciendo que…,** he began by saying that…

empicarse [em-pe-car'-say], *vr.* To be too much attached to something.

empicotadura [em-pe-co-tah-doo, rah], *f.* Act of pillorying.

empicotar [em-pe-co-tar'], *va.* To pillory, to put in the pillory; to picket.

empiedro [em-pe-ay'-dro], *m.* Paving: a dry wall. *(Yo empiedro, yo empiedre, from Empedrar. V.* ACERTAR.)

empiema [em-pe-ay'-mah], *m.* 1. A serous, bloody, or purulent accumulation in any part of the body, but especially in the thoracic region. 2. Name of the surgical operation employed to withdraw such fluid, it is called also paracentesis of the thorax.

empiezo [em-pe-ay'-tho], *m. (Prov.)* Beginning of a thing. (*Yo empiezo, you empiece,* from *Empezar. V.* ACERTAR.).

empinado [em-pe-nah'-do], *a.* 1. Steep (cuesta); high, lofty (edificio). 2. (*Fig.*) Proud (orgulloso); stiff (tieso).

empinador, ra [em-pe-nah-dor', rah], *m. & f. (coll.)* One who drinks much wine or liquors.

empinadura [em-pe-nah-doo'-rah], *f.* Exaltation, elevation, raising.

empinamiento [em-pe-nah-me-en'-to] *m.* Erection, elevation.

empinar [em-pe-nar'], *va.* 1. To raise to exalt. 2. (*coll.*) To drink much. -*vr.* 1. To stand on tiptoe. 2. To tower, to rise high.

empingorotar [em-pin-go-ro-tar'], *va. (coll.)* To raise something and put it upon another.

empino [em-pee'-no], *m.* Elevation, height.

empiolar [em-pe-o-lar'], *va.* 1. To tie the legs of hawks with jesses. 2. (*Met.*) To bind, to subject, to imprison. 3. *V.* APIOLAR.

empíreo [em-pee'-ray-o], *m.* 1. Empyrean, the highest heaven. 2. Happiness, paradise.

empíreo, rea [em-pee'-ray-o, ah], *a.* Empyreal, celestial.

empireuma [em-pe-ray'-oo-mah], *f. (Chem.)* Empyreum, empyreuma.

empireumático, ca [em-pe-ray-oo-mah'-te-co, cah], *a. (Chem.)* Empyreumatic, empyreumatical.

empírico [em-pee'-re-co], *m.* Quack, empiric, medicaster.

empírico, ca [em-pee'-re-co, cah], *a.* Empiric, empirical.

empirismo [em-pe-rees'-mo], *m.* 1. Empiricism, quackery. 2. A philosophical doctrine according to which all human knowledge is due to experience.

empizarrado [em-pe-thar-rah'-do], *m.* All of the slates which cover a building. -**Empizarrado, da,** *pp.* of EMPIZAR.

empizarrar [em-pe-thar-rar'], *va.* To slate, to roof a building with slates.

emplastadura, *f.* **emplastamiento,** *m.* [em-plas-tah-doo'-rah]. Plastering.

emplastar [em-plas-tar'], *va.* 1. To plaster, to apply plasters. 2. To paint the face. 3. To suspend, to obstruct. -*vr. V.* EMBADURNARSE.

emplastecer [em-plas-tay-therr'], *va. (Art.)* To level the surface in order to paint something.

emplasto [em-plahs'-to], *m.* 1. Plaster or emplaster. **Estar hecho un emplasto,** to be in a bad state of health. 2. A sickly and extremely delicate person.

emplástrico, ca [em-plahs'-tre-co, cah], *a.* 1. Glutinous, resembling a plaster. 2. (*Med.*) Suppurative.

emplazador [em-plah-thah-dor'], *m. (Law.)* Summoner; messenger of a court who serves summonses.

emplazamiento, emplazo [em-plah-thah-me-en'-to, em-plah'-tho], *m.(Law.)* Summons, citation.

emplazar [em-plah-thar'], *va.* 1. (*Law.*) To summon, to cite. 2. To convene, to summon judicially. **Emplazar la caza,** to arrange or set the chase. 3. (*coll.*) To cite to appear before the judgment seat of God. -*vr.* In bullfights, for the bull to plant himself in the midst of the ring, and to show no disposition to charge.

empleado [em-play-ah'-do], *m.* Employee, clerk (oficinista). **Funcionarios o empleados del estado,** civil servants. **Empleado, da,** *pp.* of EMPLEAR. **Empleado de confianza,** confidential clerk. **Empleado bancario,** bank clerk.

empleador [em-play-ah-dor'], *m.* Employer.

emplear [em-play-ar'], *va.* 1. To employ, to use (usar), to exercise, to occupy. 2. To employ, to give a place or employment, to commission, to entrust with the management of affairs. 3. To purchase, to lay out, to employ one's money in the purchase of property. 4. To employ, to make use of. 5. To employ, to fill up, to lead, to pass, or spend in a certain manner (tiempo). **Emplear mal el tiempo,** to waste time. -*vr.* To be employed, to occupy, to follow business.

Emplearse haciendo algo, to occupy oneself doing something.

empleita [em-play'-e-tah], *f. V.* PLEITA.

emplenta [em-plen'-tah], *f.* 1. Piece of mudwall made at once. 2. (*Obs.*) Impression.

empleo [em-play'-o], *m.* 1. Employ, job, employment, business, occupation. 2. Employment or employ, public place or station, office. 3. Employment, calling, vocation, profession. 4. Aim or object of our desires. 5. Lady courted, sweetheart. **Empleo del dinero or fondos, en algún negocio,** investment of money or capital in some business. **Buscar un empleo,** to look for a job. **Estar sin empleo,** to be unemployed.

empleomanía [em-play-o-mah-nee'-ah], *f.* Rage for public office.

emplomado [em-plo-mah'-do], *m.* Roof covered with lead. **Emplomado, da,** *pp.* of EMPLOMAR.

emplomador [em-plo-mah-dor'], *m.* Plumber, he who fits with lead in any way.

emplomar [em-plo-mar'], *va.* To lead, to fit with lead.

emplumar [em-ploo-mar'], *va.* 1. To feather, or dress in feathers, as a punishment. 2. To feather, to adorn with feathers or plumes. 3. To swindle (estafar). -*vr.* To mew, to moult, to shed the feathers.

emplumecer [em-ploo-may-ther'], *vn.* To begin to get feathers, to fledge. (*Yo emplumezco, yo emplumezca,* from *Emplumecer. V.* CONOCER.)

empobrecer [em-po-bray-therr'], *va.* To impoverish. -*vr.* To become poor. (*Yo empobrezco, yo empobrezca,* from *Empobrecer. V.* CONOCER.

empobrecimiento [em-po-bray-the-me-en'-to], *m.* Impoverishment, depauperation.

empodrecer [em-po-dray-therr'], *vn.* To corrupt, to reduce to a state of putrefaction. -*vr.* To corrupt, to become putrid.

empolvar [em-pol-var'], *va. & vr.* 1. To cover with dust. 2. To sprinkle powder upon, as the hair; to powder.

empolvoramiento [em-pol-vo-rah-me-en'-to], *m.* The act of covering with dust.

empolvorizar [em-pol-vo-re-thar'], **empolvorar** [em-pol-vo-rar'], *va.* To cover with dust or powder.

empollado, da [em-pol-lyah'-do, dah], *a.* 1. Hatched. 2. (*Met.*) Confined, pent up in the house. -*pp.* of EMPOLLAR

empolladura [em-pol-lyah-doo'-rah], *f.* Brood of bees.

empollar [em-pol-lyar'], *va.* 1. To brood, to hatch. 2. *V.* AMPOLLAR.

empollón, ona [em-pol-lyon'], *m & f.* Swot, bookworm (estudiante).

emponzoñador, ra [em-pon-tho-nyah-dor', rah], *m. & f.* Poisoner.

emponzoñamiento [em-pon-tho-nyah-me-en'-to], *m.* Poisoning, the act of administering or killing by poison.

emponzoñar [em-pon-tho-nyar'], *va.* 1. To poison, to infect with poison. 2. (*Met.*) To poison, to taint, to corrupt one's morals.

empopar [em-po-par'], *va. (Naut.)* To give the stern to the wind. -*vn. & vr.* To sail before the wind.

emporcar [em-por-car'], *va.* To soil, to dirty, to foul.

emporio [em-po'-re-o], *m.* 1. Emporium, a mart for the sale of merchandise. 2. A place which has made itself famous for sciences, arts, etc.

emporrado [em-por-rah'-do], *a.* **Estar emporrado,** to be high (drogas).

empotrado, da [em-po-trah'-do, dah], *a.* Built-in. **Muebles empotrados,** built-in furniture.

empotramiento [em-po-trah-me-en'-to], *m.* The act of scarfing two timbers together.

empotrar [em-po-trar'], *va.* 1. To mortise, to join with a mortise. 2. To scarf, to splice. 3. To put beehives in a pit (to divide the hives). 4. (*Naut.*) To fasten the cannon so that they shall not run back on firing. 5. To prevent the turning of the wheels of a guncarriage. -*vr.* **El coche se empotró en la tienda,** the car embedded itself in the shop.

empozar [em-po-thar'], *va.* To throw into a well. To stagnate, (estancarse). *-vr.* To be pigeonholed (papel normal).

empradizarse [em-prah-de-thar'-say], *vr.* To become a meadow.

emprendedor [em-pren-day-dor'], *m.* 1. Enterpriser, one who undertakes a great thing. 2. Undertaker, one who engages in projects and affairs.

emprender [em-pren-derr'], *va.* 1. To undertake, to engage in an arduous undertaking. 2. To attempt, to go about any business. **Emprender con alguno,** to address or accost one, either to trouble, to reprimand, to supplicate, or to quarrel with him. **Emprender la retirada,** to begin to retreat.

empreñar [em-pray-nyar'], *va.* To impregnate; to beget.

empresa [em-pray'-sah], *f.* 1. Symbol, motto. 2. Enterprise, undertaking. **Empresa privada,** private enterprise. **Empresa funeraria,** undertaker's. **Empresa de servicios públicos,** public utility company. 3. Design, an intention, a purpose. **Empresa de venta por correspondencia,** mailorder firm.

empresarial [em-pray-sah'-re-ah], *a.* Owners', manager's; managerial (función, clase). **Estudios empresariales,** business studies.

empresario [em-pray-say'-re-o], *m.* 1 The person who undertakes to do or perform, on his own account, some business of great importance. **Pequeño empresario,** small businessman. 2. Manager of a theater.

emprestillar [em-pres-til-lyar'], *va.* To borrow frequently, to ask the use of any thing.

empréstito [em-prays'-te-to], *m.* Loan, something lent. **Un empréstito del gobierno,** a government loan. **Lanzar un empréstito,** to float a loan.

emprimado [em-pre-mah'-do], *m.* Last combing to wool. **—Emprimado, da,** *pp.* of EMPRIMAR.

emprimar [em-pre-mar'], *va.* 1. To print linen or cotton. 2. In woollen manufactories, to card the wool several times, to prepare it for spinning. 3. *(coll.)* To abuse one's candor, to deceive, to mock.

emprimerar [em-pre-may-rar'], *va.* To place one in the first rank at a feast, or on any other occasion.

empringar [em-prin-gar'], *va. V.* PRINGAR.

emprisionar [em-pre-se-o-nar'], *vn. V.* APRISIONAR.

empsícosis [emp-see'-co-sis], *f. (Phil.)* 1. Animation. 2. Union of the soul with the body.

empuchar [em-poo-char'], *va.* To cut skeins of thread into a lye, or to buck them before they are bleached.

empujamiento [em-poo-hah-me-en'-to], *m.* 1. The act of pushing away. 2. The force employed for that purpose.

empujar [em-poo-har'], *va.* 1. To push, to force by constant violence, to press forward. **Empujar el botón a fondo,** to press the button down hard. 2. To push away, to shove off. *-vn. (Fig.)* To intrigue, to work behind the scenes.

empuje [em-poo'-hay], *m.* 1. Impulse, push, driving force. 2. *(Aer.)* Thrust. 3. *(Fig.)* Push, drive. **Le falta empuje,** he hasn't got any go to him, he lacks drive.

empujón [em-poo-hone'], *m.* Push, a violent shove. **A empujones,** pushingly, rudely.

empulgar [em-pool-gar'], *va.* To stretch the cord of a crossbow.

empulgueras [em-pool-gay-ras], *f. pl.* 1. Wings of a crossbow, through which the ends of the cord run, 2. Instrument with which the thumbs were tied together. **Apretar las empulgueras a uno,** to put one in a difficult situation, to compel him.

empuntador [em-poon-tah-dor'], *m.* One who makes the points of needles or pins.

empuntadura [em-poon-tah-doo'-rah], *f.* Pointing of needles or pins.

empuntar [em-poon-tar'], *va.* To point, form the point of a needle or pin.

empuñador, ra [em-poo-nyah-dor', rah], *m. & f.* Grasper.

empuñadura [em-poo-nyah-doo'-rah], *f.* Hilt of a sword. **Empuñaduras,** *(Naut.)* earrings, thin ropes fastened to the four corners of a sail, in the form of a ring.

empuñar [em-poo-nyar'], *va.* 1. To clinch, to clutch, to grasp, to gripe with the fist. **Empuñar el bastón,** *(Fig.)* To take command.

empuñir [em-poo-nyeer'], *va. (Naut.)* To pull on the sheets until the fists touch the block where the topsail sheet works.

emulación [ay-moo-lah-the-on'], *f.* Emulation, envy, jealousy.

emulador, ra [ay-moo-lah-dor', rah], *m.* Emulator, rival.

emular [ay-moo-lar'], *va.* To emulate, to rival, to contest.

emulgente [ay-mool-hen'-tay], *a.* Emulgent.

émulo [ay'-moo-lo], *m.* Competitor, rival, emulator.

emulsina [ay-mool-see'-nah], *f.* Emulsin or synaptase, an albuminous principle of almonds, which forms an emulsion with water and acts as a ferment.

emulsión [ay-mool-se-on'], *f.* Emulsion.

emulsivo, va [ay-mool-see'-vo, vah], *a.* Emulsive.

emunctorio [ay-moonc-to'-re-o], *m.* Emunctory, excretory gland.

emundación [ay-moon-dah-the-on'], *f.* Cleansing.

emuselado, da [ay-moo-say-lah-do', dah], *a.* Muzzled to prevent biting (oso, perro).

en [en], *prep.*

1. Tiempo. -IN. **Estar en 1999,** to be in 1999. **En un año,** in a year's time. **Estamos en invierno,** we are in winter. **Estábamos en enero,** we were in January. **In mis tiempos,** in my time. **En vísperas de,** on the eve of. **En esto,** thereupon. **No dormí en toda la noche,** I didn't sleep a wink all night. **En 1997,** in 1997. **En agosto,** in August, -ON. **Lo hicimos el domingo,** we did it on Sunday. **El día de Nochebuena,** on Christmas eve. -AT. **En aquella época,** at that time. **En el momento de su llegada,** at the time of his arrival. **Al anochecer,** at nightfall.

2. Lugar. -IN. **Está en la habitación,** it's in the room. **Trabaja en la tienda,** she works in the shop. **En la cama,** in bed. **En un sillón,** in an armchair. **En un coche,** in a car. **En la calle del Oeste,** in West street. **en los Alpes,** in the Alps. -ON. **En el autobús,** on the bus. **En el avión,** on the plane. **En la costa,** on the coast. **Sobre el río,** on the river. **Sobre la mesa,** on the table. **En la silla,** on the chair. -AT. **Está en casa,** he is at home. **En el semáforo,** at the traffic lights. **Nos encontramos en la estación,** we met at the station. **La vi en el supermercado,** I saw her at the supermarket.

3. Modo. -IN. **En pantalones cortos,** in shorts. **En voz alta,** in a loud voice. -BY. **La conocí al andar,** I recognized her by her gait. **Ir en tren, bicicleta, autobús,** to go by train, bicycle, bus.

4. Locuciones. En cuanto podamos, as soon as we can. **En un rincón,** in a corner. **En la esquina,** on/at the corner. **En la parte de atrás,** at the back. **En el concierto,** at the concert. **En la peluquería,** at the hairdresser's. **De vez en cuando,** from time to time. **De casa en casa,** from house to house. **En la colina,** on the hill.

enaceitarse [ay-nah-thay-e-tar'-say], *vr.* To become oily or rancid.

enacerar [ay-nah-thay-rar'], *va.* To steel, to edge with steel.

enaguachar [ay-nah-goo-ah-char'], *va.* To fill or load with water; used only to denote the state of the stomach after drinking a great deal.

enaguas [ay-nah'-goo-as], *f.pl.* 1. Petticoat, underskirt. **Enaguas blancas,** the inner skirt. 2. A gown or tunic of black baize, formerly worn by men as mourning.

enaguar [ay-nah-goo-ar'] *va.* To flood, to drench, to soak.

enaguazar [ay-nah-goo-ah-thar'], *va.* To irrigate; to cover with water (la tierra).

enagüillas, tas [ay-nah-goo-eel'-lyas, ee'-tas], *f.pl.* 1. *(dim.)* Short linen under-petticoats. 2. *V.* ENAGUAS for a gown or tunic.

enajenable [ay-nah-hay-nah'-blay], *a.* Alienable.

enajenación, *f.* **enajenamiento,** *m.* [ay-nah-hay-nah-the-on', ay-nah-hay-nah-me-en'-to]. 1. Alienation, the act of transferring property. 2. Change of affection, want of friendly intercourse. 3. Absence of mind; distress of mind; rapture, astonishment; overjoy. 4. Disorder of the mental faculties. **Enajenación mental,** mental derangement.

enajenar [ay-nah-hay-nar'], *va.* 1. To alienate, to transfer or to give away property. 2. To transport, to enrapture. *-vr.* 1. To withdraw one's affection. 2. To be deprived of reason. 3. To be restless or uneasy.

enálage [ay-nah-'lah-hay], *f. (Gram.)* Enallage, the use of one part of speech or inflection for another.

enalbar [ay-nal-bar'], *va.* To heat iron to a white heat.

enalbardar [ay-nal-har-dar'], *va.* 1. To lay a packsaddle on beasts of burden. 2. To cover meat or any other dish with a batter of eggs, flour, and sugar, and fry it afterward in oil or butter.

enalforjar [ay-nal-for-har'], *va.* To put into a saddlebag.

enalmagrado, da [ay-nal-mah-grah'-do, dah], *a. & pp.* of ENALMAGRAR. 1. Colored with ochre. 2. Vile, despicable.

enalmagrar [ay-mal-mah-grar'], *va.* To cover with ochre.

enalmenar [ay-nal-may-nar'], *va.* To crown a wall with indented battlements.

enaltecer [ay-nal-tay-therr'], *va.* V. ENSALZAR.

enamarillecer [ay-nah-mah-reel-lyay-therr'], *va.* To dye yellow, to make yellow. *-vr. (Ant.)* 1. To become yellow. 2. To grow pale.

enamoradamente [ay-nah-mo-rah-dah-men'-tay], *adv.* Lovingly, in a loving manner.

enamoradizo, za [ay-nah-mo-rah-dee'-tho, thah], *a.* Inclined to love, of an amorous disposition.

enamorado, da [ay-nah-mo-rah'-do-dah], *a. & pp.* of ENAMORAR. In love, enamoured, lovesick. **Es muy enamorado de ella,** he is madly in love with her. *-m. y f.* Sweetheart, lover. **Es un enamorado de la buena música,** he is a lover of good music.

enamorador [ay-nah-mo-rah-dor'], *m.* Lover, wooer.

enamoramiento [ay-nah-mo-rah-me-en'-to], *m.* Act of enamouring, lovesuit.

enamorar [ay-nah-mo-rar'], *va.* 1. To excite or inspire love. 2. To make love, to woo, to court, to enamour. **Por fin la enamoró,** eventually he got her to fall in love with him. *vr.* To fall in love.

enamoricarse [ay-nah-mo-re-car'-say], *vr. (coll.)* To be slightly in love.

enanchar [ay-nan-char'], *va. (coll.)* To widen, to enlarge.

enangostar [ay-nan-gos-tar'], *va.* V. ANGOSTAR.

enanito, ita [ay-nah-nee'-to, tah], *a. dim.* Little, minute.

enano, na [ay-nah'-no, nah], *a.* Dwarfish, low, small, little.

enano [ay-nah'-no], *m.* Dwarf.

enarbolar [ay-nar-bo-lar'], *va.* To hoist, to raise high; to hang out. **Enarbolar la bandera,** *(Naut.)* to hoist the colors. *-vr. V.* ENCABRITARSE.

enarcar [ay-nar-car'], *va.* 1. To hoop barrels. 2. V. ARQUEAR.

enardecer [ay-nar-day-therr'], *va.* To fire with passion, to kindle, to inflame. *-vr.* To be kindled, inflamed, or animated, with anger.

enarenación [ay-nah-ray-nah-the-on'], *f.* Lime and sand, or plaster, used to whiten walls before painting them.

enarenar [ay-nah-ray-nar'], *va.* To fill with sand, to choke with sand. *-vr. (Naut. Obs.)* To run onshore.

enarme [ay-nar'-may], *m. (Prov.)* A framework in fishingnets, or the method of fitting them up.

enarmonar [ay-nar-mo-nar'], *va.* To raise, to rear. *-vr.* To rise on the hind feet.

enarmonía [ay-nar-mo-nee'-ah], *f. (Mus.)* Enharmonic modulation, a change in notation without a change in sound.

enarmónico, ca [ay-nar-mo'-ne-co, cah], *a.* Enharmonic, proceeding by quarter tones.

enarración [ay-nar-rah-the-on'], *f.* Narration, relation.

enarrar [ay-nar-rar'], *va.* To narrate.

enastar [ay-nas-tar'], *va.* To put a handle to an instrument.

enastillar [ay-nas-teel-lyar'], *va.* To put handles to forging-hammers.

encabalgamiento [en-cah-bal-gah-me-en'-to], *m.* Gun-carriage.

encabalgar [en-cah-bal-gar'], *vn.* 1. To be upon (something else); to be mounted. 2. *(Obs.)* To parade on horseback. *-va.* To provide horses.

encaballadura [en-cah-bal-lyah-doo-rah], *f.* Lapping over.

encaballar [en-cah-bal-lyar'], *va.* To lap over, to imbricate, to lay so that the object rests upon the end of another, as tiles or shingles upon a roof.

encabellecer [en-cah-bel-lyay-therr'], *vn. & vr.* To begin to have hair on a part of the head where there was none before. *(Yo encabellezco, yo encabellezca,* from *Encabellecer.* V. CONOCER.)

encabestradura [en-cah-bes-trah-doo'-rah], *f.* An injury to a horse by a halter.

encabestrar [en-cah-bes-trar'], *va.* 1. To put a halter to a beast. 2. *(Met.)* To force to obedience. *-vr.* To be entangled in the halter.

encabezador [en-cah-bay-thah-dor'], *m.* Header, a reaping-machine which removes the heads of grain.

encabezadura [en-cah-bay-thah-doo'-rah], *f.* Scarfing, heading.

encabezamiento, encabezonamiento [en-cah-bay-thah-me-en'-to], *m.* 1. List, roll, or register of persons liable to pay a tax; census. 2. The act of enrolling persons liable to pay taxes. 3. Tax tribute, or imposts. 4. Headline, heading.

encabezar, encabezonar [en-cah-bay-thar'], *va.* 1. To make a roll or register of all those subject to any tax or tribute, to take a census of the inhabitants. 2. To register, to enroll, to set down in a list of taxes. *-vr.* 1. To compound for taxes. 2. To compound, to bargain in the lump. 3. To put the beginning of a formula to certain writings, as a will. 4. *(Amer.)* To put at the head, or in the first line. 5. To strengthen a wine, to add other stronger, or some brandy. 6. **Encabezar un terreno,** *(Agr.)* To put fresh earth at the top of a slope. 7. *(Carp.)* To join top and top, to scarf, to head. 8. *(Naut.)* To mend the furring of a ship.

encabillar [en-cah-beel-lyar'], *va. (Naut.)* To scotch, to pin, to bolt.

encabrahigar [en-cah-brah-e-gar'], *va.* V. CABRAHIGAR.

encabriar [en-cah-bre-ar'], *va.* To preserve and fashion timber for roofing.

encabritarse [en-cah-bre-tar'-say], *vr.* To rise on the hind feet (caballos).

encachar [en-cah-char'], *va.* To thrust anything in a wall or box, to imbed.

encadenadura, f. encadenamiento, *m.* [en-cah-day-nah-doo'-rah, en-cah-day-nah-me-en'-to]. 1. Catenation, the act of linking together. 2. State of being linked or connected, concatenation. 3. Chainging. **Encadenamiento en margarita,** daisy chaining.

encadenar [en-cah-day-nar'], *va.* 1. To chain, to link, to fetter, to enchain, to shackle. 2. To concatenate, to link together. 3. *(Met.)* To leave anyone without movement or action. **Los negocios le encadenan al escritorio,** business ties him to his desk. 4. To subject, to subjugate, to oppress. 5. To captivate, to gain the will. 6. To cast the chains which close the entrance of harbors, docks, etc.

encajador [en-cah-hah-dor'], *m.* 1. He who encases or inserts. 2. Instrument for encasing.

encajadura [en-cah-hah-doo'-rah], *f.* Encasing, inserting or inclosing one thing into another.

encajar [en-cah-har'], *va.* 1. To encase, to infix, to drive in, to inclose one thing in another, to insert. 2. To thrust with violence one into another. 3. *(Met.)* To do or say something inopportunely. 4. Of firearms, to shoot, fire. **Encajar bien,** to be to the purpose, to come to the point, to be opportune. **Encajar las manos,** *(coll.)* to join or shake hands. *-vn.* 1. To fit well. 2. To chuck (lanzar). 3. *(Fig.)* To fit, to match, to correspond. **Esto no encaja con lo que dijo antes,** this does not square with what he said before. *-vr.* 1. To thrust oneself into some narrow place. 2. To intrude. 3. To squeeze in; to intrude.

encaje [en-cah'-hay], *m.* 1. The act of adjusting or fitting one thing to another. 2. The place or cavity in which anything is inlaid or inserted; groove. 3. The measure of one thing to adjust with another. 4. Encasing. 5. Joining together. 6. Lace. **Encaje de oro, de plata, de kilo, etc.,** gold silver, thread lace, etc. 7. Inlaid work. **Ley del encaje,** an arbitrary law.

encajera [en-cah-hay'-rah], *f.* Lace-woman, she who makes lace.

encajerado, da [en-cah-hay-rah'-do dah], *a. (Naut.)* Fouled or entangled on the sheave of a block or pulley (cuerda).

encajerarse [en-cah-hay-rar'-say], *vr. (Naut.)* To get caught between the brook and the pulley-wheel (cuerda).

encajonado [en-cah-ho-nah'-do], *m.* Mudwall supported by pillars of bricks and stones.-**Encajonado, da,** *pp.* of ENCAJONAR.

encajonamiento [en-cah-ho-nah-me-en'-to], *m.* Act of packing up in a box.

encajonar [en-cah-ho-nar'], *va.* 1. To box, to pack up in a box, to lay up in a chest. 2. To squeeze in (meter con dificultad). *-vr.* To run through a narrow place (río).

encalabozar [en-cah-lah-bo-thar'], *va. (coll.)* To put one into a dungeon.

encalabrinado, da [en-cah-lah-bre-nah'-do, dah], *a.* Headstrong, stubborn, obstinate. *-pp.* ENCALABRINAR.

encalabrinar [en-cah-lah-bre-nar'], *va.* To affect the head with some unpleasant smell or vapor. *-vr.* To become headstrong, obstinate, or stubborn; to be confused.

encalada [en-cah-lah'-dah], *f.* Piece of the trimmings of a saddle.

encalador [en-cah-lah-dor'], *m.* In tanneries, the lime pit or vat, into which hides are put.

encaladura [en-cah-lah-doo'-rah], *f.* The act of whitening with lime; whitewashing.

encalar [en-cah-lar'], *va.* 1. To whitewash. 2. To cover with plaster or mortar. 3. To thrust into a pipe or tube. 4. To put hides into the lime vats or pits.

encalipto [en-cah-leep'-to], *m.* A kind of moss belonging to the northern hemisphere.

encalmadura [en-cal-mah-doo'-rah], *f.* A disease in horses occasioned by much work in times of great heat.

encalmarse [en-cal-mar'-say], *vr.* 1. To be worn out with fatigue. 2. *(Naut.)* To be becalmed (barco).

encalostrarse [en-cah-los-trar'-say], *vr.* To make the young sick by sucking the first milk.

encalvecer [en-cal-vay-therr'], *vn.* To grow bald. (*Yo encalvezco, yo encalvezca, from Encalvecer. V.* CONOCER.)

encallada [en-cal-lyah'-dah], *f. V.* ENCALLADURA.

encalladero [en-cal-lyah-day'-ro], *m. (Naut.)* Shoal, sandbank.

encalladura [en-cal-lyah-doo'-rah], *f. (Naut.)* Striking on a sandbank.

encallar [en-cal-lyar'], *vn.* 1. *(Naut.)* To run aground, to stand, to hit against. 2. To be checked in the progress of an enterprise, not to be able to proceed.

encalle [en-cahl'-lyay], *m. V.* ECALLADURA.

encallecer [en-cal-lyay-therr'], *vn.* To get corns on the feet. 2. To attain much experience in something. *-vr.* To harden, to be confirmed in wickedness.

encallecido, da [en-cal-lyay-thee'-do, dah], *a. & pp.* of ENCALLECER. 1. Troubled with corns. 2. *(Met.)* Hardened in wickedness and iniquities.

encallejonar [en-cal-lyay-ho-nar'], *va.* To enter or put something into a narrow street.

encamación [en-cah-mah-the-on'], *f.* Scaffolding for sustaining the galleries in mines.

encamarados [en-cah-mah-rah'-dos], *m. pl.* Chambers in cannon and mortars.

encamarar [en-cah-mah-rar'], *va. (Colt.)* To store up grain in granaries.

encamarse [en-cah-mar'-say], *vr.* 1. *(coll.)* To keep oneself in bed. 2. To lie down, to stretch themselves out to rest (animales). 3. To be laid or laid flat by rain, wind, etc. (maíz).

encambijar [en-cam-be-har'], *va.* To conduct water by means of arched reservoirs.

encambrar [en-cam-brar'], *va.* To put in a store.

encambrillonar [en-cam-breel-lyo-nar'], *va.* To put the first narrow sole, called *encambrillonado,* upon a shoe.

encambronar [en-cam-bro-nar'], *va.* 1. To inclose witty hedges of briers and brambles. 2. To strengthen with iron.

encaminadura [en-cah-me-nah-doo'-rah], *f.* **Encaminamiento,** *m.* The act of putting on the right road.

encaminar [en-cah-me-nar'], *va.* 1. To guide, to put on the right road, to show the way. 2. *(Met.)* To direct or manage an affair or business. **El proyecto está encaminado a,** the plan is directed towards. *-vr.* To take a road, to proceed in a road, to go to.

encamorrarse [en-cah-mor-rar'-say], *vr.* To embroil oneself in disputes.

encampanado, da [en-cam-pah-nah'-do, dah], *a.* Bellshaped (morteros).

encanalar, encanalizar [en-cah-nah-lar', en-cah-nah-le-thar'], *va.* To convey through pipes or conduits.

encanallarse [en-cah-nal-lyar'-say], *vr. (Acad.)* 1. To contract a habit of committing mean and vile acts. 2. To associate with depraved and base people.

encanarse [en-cah-nar'-say], *vr.* To grow senseless with fear or crying (niños).

encanastar [en-cah-nas-tar'], *va.* 1. To pack up in canisters, baskets or hampers. 2. *(Naut.)* To put the topsails In the roundhouse or top.

encancerarse [en-can-thay-rar'-say], *vr. V.* CANCERARSE.

encandecer [en-can-day-therr'], *va.* To heat something white-hot.

encandelar [en-can-day-lar'], *vn.* To bud, as trees, instead of flowering.

encandiladera, encandiladora [en-can-de-lah-day'-rah, en-can-de-lah-do'-rah], *f.* Procuress, bawd.

encandilado, da [en-can-de-lah'-do dah], *a.* 1. Sharp or high-cocked (sombreros). **Trae el sombrero muy encandilado,** he wears his hat fiercely cocked. 2. *(Naut.)* Raised vertically. *-pp.* of ENCANDILAR.

encandilar [en-can-de-lar'], *va.* 1. To dazzle with the light of a candle or lamp. 2. *(Met.)* To dazzle or deceive with false appearances. 3. *(coll.)* To stir the fire. *-vr.* 1. To inflame one's eyes, as with drink, to be dazzled. 2. To get excited, to become emotional (persona).

encanecer [en-cah-nay-therr'], *vn.* 1. To grow gray. 2. To mould. 3. To grow old. 4. To possess much experience and knowledge. (*Yo encanezco, yo encanezca, from Encanecer. V.* CONOCER.)

encanijamiento [en-cah-ne-hah-me-en'-to], *m.* Weakness, meagreness; the act of growing weak and lean; extenuation.

encanijar [en-cah-ne-har'], *va.* To weaken a baby by giving him bad milk. *-vr.* 1. To pine, to be emaciated, to grow weak and thin, to fall away (niños mal amamantados). 2. To grow weak.

encanillar [en-cah-nil-lyar'], *va.* To wind silk, wool, or linen on a quill made of cane.

encantado, da [en-can-tah'-do, dah], *a.* 1. Haunted, enchanted, charmed. **Casa encantada,** a haunted house. **Hombre encantado,** a man who is habitually absent or musing. 2. Delighted, pleased (persona). **Estoy encantado de conocerle,** I'm delighted to meet you. *-pp.* of ENCANTAR.

encantador [en-can-tah-dor'], *m.* Enchanter, sorcerer, conjurer; charmer.

encantadora [en-can-tah-doo-rah], *f.* Sorceress, enchantress; charming, bewitching.

encantamiento [en-can-tah-me-en'-to], *m.* 1. Magic (mágia). **Como por encantamiento,** as if by magic. 2. Bewitchment, witchcraft (hechizo). 3. Spell, charm, enchantment, incantation (invocación mágica).

encantar [en-can-tar'], *va.* 1. To enchant, to charm, to conjure, to bewitch, to cast a spell on (con magia). 2. To fascinate, to delight in a high degree. **Nos encanta la casa,** we are delighted with the house.

encantarar [en-can-tah-rar'], *va.* To put something into a jar or pitcher.

encante [en-cahn'-tay], *m.* Auction, public sale: the place where it is held.

encanto [en-cahn'-to], *m.* Enchantment, charm, spell. 2. Fascination. **Es un encanto,** it is truly charming, it is bewitching. **El niño es un encanto,** the child is a little treasure.

encantorio [en-can-to'-re-o], *m. (coll.)* Enchantment.

encantusar [en-can-too-sar'], *va.* To coax, to wheedle, to deceive by flatteries.

encañado [en-cahn-yah'-do], *m.* 1. Conduit of water. 2. Hedge formed with canes or reeds. *-a.* Piped, tubed. **Encañado, da,** *pp.* of ENCAÑAR.

encañador, ra [en-cah-nyah-dor', rah], *m. & f.* One who spools or winds silk on quills made of cane.

encañadura [en-cah-nyah-doo'-rah], *f.* 1. Hedge made of cane or reeds. 2. Strong rye-straw not broken.

encañar [en-cah-nyar'], *va.* 1. To inclose a plantation with a hedge of cane. 2. To convey water through conduits or pipes. 3. To wind silk on quills of reed or cane. *-vn.* To form or grow into stalks (maíz).

encañizada [en-cah-nye-thah'-dah], *f.* Inclosure made of cane and reeds for catching mullets.

encañonado [en-cah-nyo-nah'-do], *a.* 1. Goffering, crimping (planchado). 2. Applied to the wind blowing through a narrow passage. **-Encañonado, da,** *pp.* of ENCAÑONAR.

encañonar [en-cah-nyo-nar'], *va. & vn.* 1. To begin to grow fledged, to get feathers and wings (aves). 2. To put into tubes or pipes (agua). 3. To plait, to fold. 4. To wind silk on quills of cane. 5. To aim at, to point at (armas).

encañutar [en-cah-nyoo-tar'], *va.* To flute, to mould into the form of tubes and pipes.

encapacetado, da [en-cah-pah-thay-tah'-do, dah], *a.* Covered with a helmet.

encapachadura [en-cah-pah-chah-doo'-rah], *f.* In oil-mills, number of baskets full of olives to be pressed.

encapachar [en-cah-pah-char'], *va.* 1. To put into a flail or basket. 2. *(Agr. Prov.)* To guard bunches of grapes from the sun by covering them with the shoots.

encapado, da [en-cah-pah'-do, dah], *a.* Cloaked, wearing a cloak.

encapazar [en-cah-pah-thar'], *a.* To collect and put into a basket.

encaperuzado, da [en-cah-pay-roo-thah'-do, dah], *a.* Hooded, wearing a hood.

encaperuzarse [en-cah-pay-roo-thar'-say], *vr.* To cover one's head with a hood.

encapilladura [en-cah-pil-lyah-doo'-rah], *f. (Naut.)* Tie of a shroud or stay; top-rigging.

encapillar [en-cah-pil-lyar], *va.* 1. *(Naut.)* To fix the standing rigging to the mast-head. 2. To rig the yards. **Encapillarse el agua,** *(Naut.)* to ship a head sea. *-vr.* To put on clothes over the head.

encapirotado, da [en-cah-pe-ro-tah'-do, dah], Wearing a cloak of hood. *-pp.* of ENCAPIROTAR.

encapirotar [en-cah-pe-ro-tar'], *va.* To hood a hawk.

encapotado, da [en-cah-po-tah'-do], *a.* 1. Cloaked, wearing a cloak. 2. Cloudy, overcast (cielo).

encapotadura [en-cah-po-tah-doo'-rah], *f.* **encapotamiento** [en-cah-po-tah-me-en'-to], *m.* Lower, frown, cloudiness.

encapotar [en-cah-po-tar'], *va.* 1. To cloak, to cover with a cloak or great-coat. 2. To cover with a veil, to muffle the face. *-vr.* 1. To lower, to gloom, to be clouded (cielo). 2. To lower the head too much and press upon the bit (caballos).

encaprichamiento [en-cah-pre-chah-me-en'-to], *m.* Headstrongness, stubbornness.

encapricharse [en-cah-pre-char'-say], *vr.* 1. To indulge in whims and fanciful desires, to become obstinate or stubborn. 2. *(coll.)* To be somewhat enamoured.

encapsulado [en-cap-soo-lah-do], *a. (Inform.)* Encapsulated.

encapuchar [en-cah-poo-char'], *va.* To cover a thing with a hood.

encapuzado, da [en-cah-poo-thah'-do, dah], *a.* Covered with a hood or cowl. *-pp.* of ENCAPUZAR.

encapuzar [en-cah-poo-thar'], *va.* To cover with a long gown.

encarado, da [en-cah-rah'-do, dah], *a.* 1. Faced. **Bien or mal encarado,** well or ill faced. 2. *(Amer.)* Haughty, threatening. *-pp.* of ENCARAR.

encaramadura [en-cah-rah-mah-doo'-. rah], *f. (Obs.)* 1. Height, eminence. 2. The act of climbing up an eminence.

encaramar [en-cah-rah-mar'], *va. & vr.* 1. To raise; to elevate. 2. To extol, to exaggerate. 3. To climb. 4. To reach an eminent post.

encaramianto [en-cah-rah-me-en'-to], *m.* The act of facing or aiming.

encarar [encahrar'], *vn.* To face, to confront, to be opposite. **Encararse con,** to face. **Tendrá que encararse con los electores,** he will have to face the electorate. *-va.* 1. To aim, to point or level a firelock. 2. To face, to confront (problema). 3. To bring face to face (dos cosas).

encaratularse [en-cah-rah-too-lar'-say], *vr.* To mask or disguise oneself.

encaraxis [en-ca-rahk'-sis], *f.* Scarification.

encarbo [en-car'-bo], *m.* Pointer, a pointer dog.

encarcavinar [en-car-cah-ve-nar'], *va.* 1. To infect with a pestilential smell. 2. To put one into a ditch.

encarcelación [en-car-thay-lah-the-on'], *f.* Incarceration.

encarcelado, da [en-car-thay-lah'-do dah], *a. & pp.* of ENCARCELAR. Confined, imprisoned.

encarcelar [en-car-thay-lar'], *va.* 1. To imprison, to commit to prison. 2. To compress newly glued timbers in a clamp. 3. To fasten something with mortar (jambas de puerta). 4. *(Naut.)* To woold; to fasten two cables which cross each other.

encarecedor [en-cah-ray-thay-dor'], *m.* Praiser, extoller; one who exaggerates.

encarecer [en-cah-ray-therr'], *va. & vn. & vr.* 1. To raise the price of commodities, to overrate, to overvalue. 2. *(Met.)* To enhance, to exaggerate. 3. To recommend earnestly.

encarecidamente [en-cah-ray-the-dah-men'-tay], *adv.* Exceedingly, highly, hyperbolically.

encarecimiento [en-cah-ray-the-me-en'-to], *m.* 1. Enhancement, augmentation of value. 2. Exaggeration, hyperbolical amplification. **Con encarecimiento,** ardently, earnestly.

encargado [en-car-gah'-do], *a.* **El empleado encargado de estos géneros,** the employee in charge of these stocks. *-m & f.* Agent, representative. **Encargado de campo,** groundsman. **Encargado de vestuario,** costume designer.

encargado de negocios [en-car-gah'-do day nay-go'-the-os], *m.* 1. Chargé d'affaires 2. *(Mex.)* Agent, attorney, commissioner.

encargar [en-car-gar'], *va.* To recommend, to charge, to commission, to commit. **Encargarse de alguna cosa,** to take charge of something.

encargo [en-car'-go], *m.* 1. Charge, command, trust conferred, commission, request. **Hacer encargos,** to run errands. 2. Office, place, employ. 3. *(Com.)* Order.

encariñado [en-c-ah-re-nyah'-do], *a.* **Estar encariñado con,** to be fond of.

encariñar [en-cah-re-nyar'], *va.* To inspire affection, fondness or love. *-vr.* To become passionately fond of.

encarna [en-car'-nah], *f.* Act of giving the entrails of dead game to the dogs.

encarnación [en-car-nah-the-on'], *f.* 1. Incarnation, the act of assuming a body (Jesucristo). 2. Carnation, the natural flesh color. 3. A certain adhesive cement which serves to repair chinaware, etc. 4. *(Med.)* Making of tissue in a wound.

encarnadino, na [en-car-nah-dee'-no, nah], *a.* Incarnadine, of a reddish color.

encarnado, da [en-car-nah'-do, dah], *a. & pp.* of ENCARNAR. 1. Incarnate, anything tinged of a deep red color. 2. Dyed flesh color. 3. Covered with flesh.

encarnado [en-car-nah'-do], *m.* Flesh color given to pieces of sculpture.

encarnadura [en-car-nah-doo'-rah], *f.* 1. The natural state of flesh in living bodies, with respect to the cure of wound. 2. The effect produced by an edged weapon on the flesh.

encarnamiento [en-car-nah-me-en'-to], *m.* Incarnation, the act of breeding flesh (herida).

encarnar [en-car-nar'], *vn.* To incarn, to incarnate, to breed flesh. *-va.* To incarnadine, to give a flesh color to pieces of sculpture. 2. To make a strong impression upon the mind. 3. To fill a wound with new flesh. 4. To wound, to pierce the flesh with a dart. 5. To embody. 6. To entice or allure dogs; to feed sporting dogs with flesh. *-vr.* To unite or incorporate one thing with another.

encarnativo [en-car-nah-tee'-vo, vah], *m. & a.* Incarnative, a medicine suposed to generate flesh.

encarne [en-car'-nay], *m.* First feed given to dog of the entrails of game.

encarnecer [en-car-nay-therr'], *vn.* To grow fat and fleshy.

encarnizado, da [en-car-ne-thah'-do, dah], *a.* Bloodshot, inflamed (ojos). *-pp.* of ENCARNIZAR.

encarnizamiento [en-car-ne-thah-me-en'-to], *m.* 1. The act of fleshing or satiating with flesh. 2. Cruelty, rage, fury.

encarnizar [en-car-ne-thar'], *va.* 1. To flesh, to satiate with flesh. 2. To provoke, to irritate. *-vr.* 1. To be glutted with flesh. 2. To be cruelly bent against one; to fall foul upon one.

encaro [en-cah'-ro], *m.* 1. The act of viewing steadfastly. 2. *(Prov.)* Blunderbuss, a wide-mouthed short handgun. **Encaro de escopeta,** aiming, the act of levelling a musket or fire-lock aim.

encarrilar, or encarrillar [en-car-ril-yar'], *va.* 1. To direct, to guide, to put on the right road, to conduct a carriage in a proper track, to place in the rails. 2. *(Met.)* To arrange again what had been deranged. *-vr. (Naut.)* To be fouled or entangled on the sheave of a block (cuerda).

encarroñar [en-car-ro-nyar'], *va. (coll.)* To infect, to corrupt. *-vr.* To be infected or corrupted.

encarrujado [en-car-roo-hah'-do], *m.* Ancient kind of silk stuff. *-pp.* of ENCARRUJAR.

encarrujar [en-car-roo-har'], *va.* To plait, to flute, to mangle. *-vr.* To be corrugated, curled, or wrinkled.

encartación [en-car-tah-the-on'], *f.* 1. Enrolment. *V.* ENPADRONAMIENTO. 2. Vassalage, the state of a vassal; tenure at will; servitude. 3. The people or places which enter into a state of vassalage, or knowledge one as a lord.

encartamiento [en-car-tah-me-en'-to], *m.* 1. Outlawry, proscription. 2. Vassalage. *V.* ENCARTACIŌN.

encartar [en-car-tar'], *va.* 1. To outlaw, to proscribe. 2. To summon to judgment. 3. To include, to enrol. 4. To enter in the register of taxes. *-vr.* To be unable to discard in a game (naipes).

encarte [en-car'-tay], *m.* In cards, the fortuitous order in which the cards remain at the close of a hand.

encartonador [en-car-to-nah-dor'], *m.* One who applies boards to books for binding.

encartonar [en-car-to-nar'], *va.* 1. To apply (binder's) boards to books. 2. To bind in boards only.

encartuchar [en-car-too-char'], *va.* To fill cartridges with powder.

encasamento [en-cah-sah-men'-to], *m.* Niche, place in a wall for a statue.

encasamiento [en-cah-sah-me-en'-to], *m.* 1. An ornament of fillets and mouldings. 2. Reparation of ruinous houses. 3. Niche.

encasar [en-cah-sa'], *va.* To set a dislocated bone.

encascabelado, da [en-cas-cah-bay-lah'-do, dah], *a.* Filled or adorned with bells.

encascotar [en-cas-co-tar'], *va.* To cover with a layer of rubbish.

encasillado [en-cah-se-lyah'-do], *m.* Set of pigeon-holes.

encasillar [en-cah-se-lyar'], *va.* 1. To place in pigeon-holes. 2. To classify persons or things and assign them to their places.

encasquetar [en-cas-kay-tar'], *va.* 1. To clap on one's hat close to the head. 2. *(Met.)* To induce one to adopt an opinion. *-vr.* To persist, to be head-strong.

encastar [en-cas-tar'], *va.* 1. To improve a race of animals. 2. *V.* PROCREAR.

encastillado, da [en-cas-til-lyah'-do, dah], *a. (Met.)* Elated, lofty, haughty. *-pp.* of ENCASTILLAR.

encastillador, ra [en-cas-til-lyah-dor', rah], *m. & f.* 1. One who shuts himself up in a castle. 2. A potter's workman who piles up the pieces which ought to be aired before going into the furnace.

encastillamiento [en-cas-til-lyah-me-en'-to], *m.* Act of shutting up in a castle.

encastillar [en-cas-til-lyar'], *va.* To fortify with castles. *-vn.* To make the cell of the queen-bee in beehives. *-vr.* 1. To shut oneself up in a castle, by way of defence. 2. *(Met.)* To persevere obstinately in maintaining one's opinion.

encastrar [en-cas-trar'], *va.* 1. *(Naut.)* To mortise or scarf pieces of timber. 2. To let in, to imbed.

encastre [en-cahs'-tray], *m.* Fitting in, groove; socket.

encatusar [en-cah-too-sar'], *va. V.* ENGATUSAR.

encauchado [en-cah-oo-chah'-do], *m.* An India-rubber poncho.

encauma [en-cah'-oo-mah], *f. (Med.)* 1. A pustule produced by a burn, and the scar which remains. 2. Corroding ulcer of the cornea.

encausado, da [en-cah-oo-sah'-do], *m & f. (Jur.)* Accused, defendant.

encausar [en-cah-oo-say], *va.* To prosecute, to sue; to put on trial.

encáustico, ca [en-cah'-oos-te-co, cah] *a.* Encaustic, belonging to enamel-painting.

encausto [en-cah'-oos-to], *m.* 1. *(Pict.)* Enamelling. **Pintar al encausto,** to paint in colors requiring firing. 2. A red ink with which emperors alone used to write.

encauzar [en-cah-oo-thar'], *va.* 1. To channel (agua). 2. *(Fig.)* To channel, to direct, to guide. **Las protestas se pueden encauzar a fines buenos,** the protests can be directed towards good objectives.

encavarse [en-cah-var'-say], *vr.* To incave oneself, to hide in a hole.

encebadamiento [en-thay-bah-dah-me-en'-to], *m.* Surfeit, repletion of horses.

encebadar [en-thay-bah-dar'], *va.* To surfeit with barley, and water drunk immediately after it. (animales). *-vr.* To be surfeited by eating barley and drinking water (caballos).

encebollado [en-thay-bol-lyah'-do], *m.* Fricassee of beef or mutton and onions seasoned with spice.

encefálico, ca [en-thay-fah'-le-co, cah], *a.* Encephalic, relating to the brain.

encefalitis [en-thay-fah-lee'-tis], *f.* Encephalitis, inflammation of the brain. **Encefalitis letárgica,** sleeping sickness.

encéfalo [en-thay'-fah-lo], *m.* The encephalon, the brain as a whole; cerebrum, cerebellum, and medulla oblongata.

encefalograma [en-thay-fah-lo-grah'-mah], *m.* Encephalogram.

encefalóideo, dea [en-thay-fah-lo'-e-day-o, ah], *a.* Encephaloid, resembling brain matter in aspect. *-f.* Encephaloid, a variety of cancer resembling the brain in consistency.

encelar [en-thay-lar'], *va.* To excite jealousy. -*vr.* To become jealous or suspicious in love.

encelitis [en-thay-lee'-tis], *f. (Med.)* Intestinal inflammation.

encellar [en-thel-lyar'], *va.* To mould curds or cheese in a wattle.

encenagado, da [en-thay-nah-gah'-do, dah], *a.* Mixed or filled with mud. -*pp.* of ENCENAGARSE.

encenagar [en-thay-nah-gar'], *va.* To mull, to mire. -*vr.* 1. To wallow in dirt or mire, to dirty oneself with mud or mire. 2. *(Met.)* To wallow in crimes and vices: it is seldom used but in its reflexive sense.

encencerrado, da [en-then-ther-rah'-do, dah], *a.* Carrying a wetherbell.

encendedor, ra [en-then-day-dor', rah], *a.* Lighting. -*m.* 1. Lighter. 2. Cigarette lighter. **Encendedor de gas,** gas lighter.

encender [en-then-derr'], *va.* 1. To light (vela, cigarrillo), to make burn. 2. To set fire to, to set on fire. 3. To heat, to produce heat, to glow. 4. *(Met.)* To inflame, to inspirit, to incite. 5. *(Met.)* To foment a party, to sow discord. 6. To switch on, to turn on, to put on (luz, aparato eléctrico). 7. To strike, to light (cerilla). -*vr.* To fire, to take fire, to be kindled. **Encenderse en cólera,** to fly into a passion. **Encenderse en ira,** to kindle with anger. **¡Cuándo se encienden las luces?,** when is lighting up time?

encendidamente [en-then-de-dah-men'-tay], *adv.* Vividly, ardently; efficaciously.

encendido, da [en-then-dee'-do, dah], *a. & pp.* of ENCENDER. 1. Lit (fuego, cigarrillo). 2. On, switched on (luz, aparato eléctrico). **La luz está encendida,** the light is on. 3. Flushed, red, inflamed. **Encendido de color,** high colored. -*m.* 1. Lighting. **El encendido de las farolas,** lighting of the lamps. 2. Ignition (coche). Firing (cohete).

encendimiento [en-then-de-me-en'-to] *m.* 1. Incension, the act of kindling and the state of being on fire. 2. Incandescence, glow. 3. *(Met.)* Inflammation. 4. *(Met.)* Liveliness and ardor of human passions and affections.

encenizar [en-thay-ne-thar']. *va.* To fill or cover with ashes.

encensar, encensuar [en-then-sar', en-then-soo-ar'], *va.* To give or take at lawful interest, to lease.

encentador [en-then-tah-dor'], *m.* The person who begins to use things not before used.

encentadura [en-then-tah-doo'-rah], *f.* **encentamiento,** *m.* The act of beginning the use of a thing not before used.

encentar [en-then-tar'], *va..* To start, to begin.

encepador [en-thay-pah-dor'], *m.* Stocker, gun-stocker.

encepar [en-thay-par'], *va.* 1. *(coll.)* To put in the stocks. 2. To stock a gun; to stock the anchor. -*vn.* To take root (planta).

encerado [en-thay-rah'-do], *m.* 1. Oil-cloth, oilskin. 2. Window-blind. 3. *(Naut.)* Tarpauling. 4. Sticking-plaster. 5. A square of oil-skin, used as a slate or black board in schools.

encerado, da [en-thay-rah'-do, dah], *a.* Waxed, like wax. -*pp. de Encerar.* **Papel encerado,** wax paper.

enceramiento [en-thay-rah-me-en'-to], *m.* Act of waxing, paper, cloth, etc.

encerar [en-thay-rar'], *va.* 1. To fasten or stiffen with wax. 2. To fill or stain with wax.

encernada [en-ther-nah-dar'], *va.* V. ACERNADAR.

encerotar [en-thay-ro-tar'], *va.* To wax thread.

encerradero [en-ther-rah-day'-ro], *m.* 1. Place for keeping sheep before or after shearing. 2. V. ENCIERRO.

encerrado, da [en-ther-rah'-do, dah], *a. (Obs.)* Brief, succinct. -*pp.* of ENCERRAR.

encerrador [en-ther-rah-dor'], *m.* 1. One who shuts or locks up. 2. Driver of black cattle.

encerradura [en-ther-rah-doo'-rah], *f.* Cloister, enclosure, closure.

encerramiento [en-ther-rah-me-en'-to], *m.* 1. Cloister, retreat, place of retirement. 2. Prison, jail, dungeon. 3. The locking up of a thing.

encerrar [en-ther-rar'], *va.* 1. To lock or shut up, to confine, to get in or to close in. 2. To emboss. 3. To contain, to conclude, to comprehend. **El libro encierra profundas verdades,** the book contains deep truths. -*vr.* 1. To retire or withdraw from the world. 2. To be locked or shut up, to be closeted. **Se encerró en el cuarto,** she shut herself in her room.

encerrona [en-ther-ro'-nah], *f.* A voluntary retreat, a spontaneous retirement.

encespedar [en-thes-pay-dar'], *va. (Mil.)* To line or cover the sides of a moat with sods.

encestar [en-thes-tar'], *va.* 1. To gather and put in a basket; to toss in basket, to hamper. 2. To make a basket (basketball).

enchabetar [en-chah-bay-tar'], *va.* **Enchabetar un perno,** *(Naut.)* to forelock a bolt.

enchalecar [en-chah-lay-car'], *va. (Prov. Amer.)* To put in the straitjacket (locos).

enchamarrado, da [en-chah-mar-rah'-do, dah], *a.* Clothed in coarse frieze or sheepskin.

enchancletar [en-chan-clay-tar'], *va.* 1. To put on slippers. 2. To wear shoes in the manner of slippers.

enchapar [en-chah-par'], *va.* To veneer; to plate (con metal).

enchapinado, da [en-chah-pe-nah'-do dah], *a.* 1. Made in the manner of patters. 2. Built and raised upon a vault or arch.

encharcada [en-char-cah'-dah], *f.* A pool of water.

encharcar [en-char-car'], *va.* To swamp, to flood (terreno); to cover with puddles, to turn into pools.

encharcarse [en-char-car'-say], *vr.* To be covered with water, to be inundated.

enchicar [en-che-car'], *va.* V. ACHICAR.

enchilada [en-che-lah'-dah], *f.* A cake of corn dressed with peppers, a Mexican dish.

enchiquerar [en-che-kay-rar'], *va.* 1. To shut the bull in the pen called *chiquero,* 2. *(Met. coll.)* To imprison.

encía [en-thee'-ah], *f.* The gum of the mouth.

enciclia [en-thee'-cle-ah], *f.* Concentric circles formed in water when a solid and heavy body falls into it.

encíclica [en-thee'-cle-cah], *f.* An encyclical letter from the Pope to all the world.

encíclico, ca [en-thee'-cle-o, cah], *a.* Encyclic, circular (cartas pastorales).

enciclopedia [en-the-clo-pay'-de-ah], *f.* Encyclopedia, cyclopedia, the circle of sciences.

enciclopédico, ca [en-the-clo-pay'-de-co, cah], *a.* Encyclopedic.

enciclopedista [en-the-clo-pay-dees'-tah], *a. & n.* Encyclopedist.

encierro [en-theer'-ro], *m.* 1. Closure, confinement, closeness. 2 Inclosure. 3. Cloister, religious retreat. 4. Prison, close confinement, custody. 5. The act of driving bulls into the penfold for the bullfighting. *(Yo encierro, yo encierre,* from *Encerrar.* V. ACRECENTAR.)

encima [en-thee'-mah], *adv.* 1. Above, over. 2. At the top. 3. Over and above, besides. 4. On. 5. Overhead. **Encima de la mesa,** over the table. **El avión pasó encima,** the plane passed over. **Echarse algo encima,** to take something upon oneself. **La guerra está encima,** war is upon us. **Por encima de,** over.

encimar [en-the-mar'], *va. (Obs.)* To place at the top, to raise high. -*vr.* To raise oneself upon.

encimero, ra [en-the-may'-ro, rah], *a.* That which is placed over or upon.

encina [en-thee'-nah], *f. (Bot.)* Evergreen oak, live-oak.

encinal, encinar [en-the-nahl', enthe-nar'], *m.* Wood, consisting of evergreen oak.

encinta [en-theen'-tah], *a.* Pregnant.

encintado [en-thin-tah'-do], *m.* Curb.

encintar [en-thin-tar'], *va.* 1. To ribbon. 2. To curb (acera).

encismar [en-this-mar'], *va. (coll.)* To set a schism or division.

encisto [en-thees'-to], *m.* An encysted tumor.

enclaustrado, da [en-clah-oos-trah'-do, dah], *a.* Shut up in cloisters.

enclaustrar [en-clah-oos-trar'], *va.* To cloister; to hide away.

enclavación [en-clah-vah-the-on'], *f. (Obs.)* Act of nailing or fixing.

enclavadura [en-clah-vah-doo'-rah], *f.* 1. The part where two pieces of wood are joined. 2. *V.* CLAVADURA.

enclavar [en-clah-var'], *va.* 1. To nail, to fasten with nails. 2. To prick horses in shoeing. *V.* TRASPASAR. **Enclavar la artillería,** to spike up guns.

enclavijar [en-clah-ve-har'], *va.* To unite or join closely. **Enclavijar un instrumento,** to put pegs in a musical instrument. *(Naut.) V.* EMPERNAR.

enclenque [en-clen'-kay], *m. & a.* One who is of a weak or feeble constitution, an emaciated person.

encliquitaje [en-cle-ke-tah'-hay], *m.* Gearing, cogging.

enclítico, ca [en-clee'-te-co, cah], *a.* Enclitic.

encloclar, encloquecer [en-clo-clar', en-clo-kay-therr'], *vn. & vr.* To cluck, to manifest a desire to hatch eggs (aves).

encobar [en-co-bar'], *vn.* To cover or hatch eggs.

encobijar [en-co-be-har'], *va. V.* COBIJAR.

encobrado, da [en-co-brah'-do, dah], *a.* Coppery; copper-colored, copper-plated.

encoclar [en-co-clar'], *vn.* To cluck, to show a desire; to lay eggs (aves).

encocorar [en-co-co-rar'], *va. (coll.)* To molest, to vex, to annoy.

encofrado [en-co-frah'-do], *m. (Min.)* Plank lining timbering.

encofrar [en-co-frar'], *va. (Min.)* To plank, to line with sheeting.

encoger [en-co-herr'], *va.* 1. To contract, to draw together, to shorten. 2. To shrink, to make to shrink. 3. *(Met.)* To discourage, to dispirit. *-vr.* 1. To be low-spirited, to be dismayed. 2. To humble oneself, to be dejected. 3. To shrink, to contract itself into less room. **Encogerse de hombros,** to shrink the shoulders with fear; to put an end to a debate, to occasion silence.

encogidamente [en-co-he'-dah-men-tay], *adv.* Meanly, abjectly.

encogido, da [en-co-hee'-do, dah], *a.* Pusillanimous, timid, fearful, narrow-minded. *-pp.* of ENCOGER.

encogimiento [en-co-he-me-en'-to], *m.* 1. Contraction, contracting, drawing together or shortening; constriction, corrugation. 2. Pusillanimity, want of resolution. 3. Lowness of spirits. 4. Humility, submission, resignation. **Encogimiento de los costados,** *(Naut.)* the tumbling home or housing in of the sides of a ship.

encojar [en-co-har'], *va.* To cripple, to lame, to make lame. *-vr.* 1. To grow lame. 2. To feign sickness in order to avoid doing some business.

encoladura [en-co-lah-doo'-rah], *f.* **encolamiento** [en-co-lah-me-en'-to], *m.* Gluing, the act and effect of gluing.

encolar [en-co-lar'], *va.* To glue, to fasten with cement; to glutinate.

encolerizar [en-co-lay-re-thar'], *va.* To provoke, to anger, to irritate. *-vr.* To be in a passion, to be vexed or displeased; to be in a rage.

encolpismo [en-col-pees'-mo], *m. (Med.)* Vaginal injection.

encomendable [en-co-men-dah'-blay], *a.* Recommendable, commendable.

encomendado [en-co-men-dah'-do], *m.* Vassal of a military chief. **-Encomendado, da,** *pp.* of ENCOMENDAR.

encomendamiento [en-co-men-dah-me-ayn'-to], *m. V.* ENCOMIENDA.

encomendar [en-co-men-dar'], *va.* 1. To recommend, to commend, to commit, to charge. 2. To praise, to applaud. *-vn.* To hold a commandery in a military order. *-vr.* 1. To commit oneself to another's protection. 2. To send compliments and messages. **Sin encomendarse a Dios ni al diablo,** proverb used to signify fool-hardiness in throwing oneself into some desperate affair: literally, without commending oneself to God or the devil.

encomendero [en-co-men-day'-ro], *m.* 1. Agent who receives and executes commissions and orders. 2. Pensioner or annuitant. 3. One who holds a commandery in a military order.

encomiador, ra [en-co-me-ah-dor', rah], *m. & f.* One who praises.

encomiar [en-co-me-ar'], *va.* 1. To offer encomiums or praises. 2. To eulogize, to extol.

encomiasta [en-co-me-ahs'-tah], *m.* Encomiast.

encomiástico, ca [en-co-me-ahs'-te-co, cah], *a.* Encomiastic, panegyrical, laudatory.

encomienda [en-co-me-en'-dah], *f.* 1. Commission, charge. 2. Message, compliment sent to an absent person. 3. Commandery in a military order: land or rent belonging to a commandery. 4. The embroidered cross worn by knights of military orders. 5. Patronage, protection, support. 6. Recommendation. 7. *(Com.)* Charge or commission for negotiation. **Encomiendas,** compliments, invitations, respects. **Encomienda de Santiago,** *(Bot.)* daffodil.

encomio [en-co'meo], *m.* Praise, encomium, eulogy, commendation.

encompadrar [en-com-pah-drar'], *vn. (coll.)* 1. To contract affinity by godfather. 2. To be close friends.

enconado, da [en-co-nah'-do, dah], *a. & pp.* of ENCONAR. 1. Inflamed, swollen. 2. Tainted, stained, spotted.

enconamiento [en-co-nah-me-en'-to], *m.* 1. Inflammation, a morbid swelling. 2. *(Met.)* Provocation, the act of exciting passion or anger. 2. *(Obs.)* Venom.

enconar [en-co-nar'], *va.* 1. To inflame, to irritate, to provoke. 2. To increase the state of inflammation in a wound. *-vr.* To rankle, to fester (herida).

encono [en-co'-no]. *m.* Malevolence, rancor, ill-will, steadfast implacability.

enconoso, sa [en-co-no'-so, sah], *a.* 1. Apt to cause or produce an inflammation. 2. Hurtful, prejudicial, malevolent.

enconrear [en-con-ray-ar'], *va.* To oil wool that is to be carded.

encontradizo, za [en-con-trah-dee'-tho, thah], *a.* That which may be met on the way. **Hacerse encontradizo con alguno,** to go to meet someone as if by chance.

encontrado, da [en-con-trah'-do, dah], *a.* 1. Opposite, in front. 2. Hostile, opposed. 3. *(Naut.)* One of the classes of blocks, the contrary course of two vessels, and everything, which is moved or is situated opposite to that with which it is compared. *-pp.* of ENCONTRAR.

encontrar [en-con-trar'], *va. & vn.* 1. To meet, to encounter. 2. To meet, to encounter unexpectedly, to hit upon, to find by chance, to fall in with, to light upon. 3. To meet, to assemble, to come together. **Lo encontró bastante fácil,** he found it pretty easy. **No lo encuentro en ninguna parte,** I can't find it anywhere. *-vr.* 1. To meet, to encounter in a hostile manner, to clash. 2. To be of opposite opinions. 3. To meet at the same place, to meet with. **Encontrarse con uno,** to meet somebody. **Encontrarse con un obstáculo,** to run into an obstacle.

encontrón [en-con-trone'], *m.* Collision, clash, push, shock, violent concourse, a sudden stroke.

encopetado, da [en-co-pay-tah'-do, dah], *a.* Presumptuous, boastful. *-pp.* of ENCOPETAR.

encopetar [en-co-pay-tar'], *va. (Obs.)* To raise the hair high, as in a toupee.

encorachar [en-co-rah-char'], *va.* To put in a leather bag.

encorado, da [en-co-rah'-do, dah], *a. & pp.* of ENCORAR. Wrapped up in leather.

encorajado, da [en-co-rah-hah'-do, dah], *a. & pp.* of ENCORAJAR. 1. Bold, audacious, adventurous. 2. Angry, furious, in a rage.

encorajar [en-co-rah-har'], *va.* To animate, to give courage, to inflame. *-vr.* To be furious, to be in a rage.

encoramentar [en-co-rah-men-tar'], *va. (Naut.)* To bolt, to coak, to fay.

encoramento, encoramiento [en-co-rah-me-en'-to], *m. (Naut.)* Bolting, coaking, faying.

encorar [en-co-rar'], *va. & vn.* 1. To cover with leather. 2. To wrap up in leather. 3. To get a skin (heridas). 4. To skin, to heal the skin.

encorazado, da [en-co-rah-thah'-do, dah], *a.* 1. Covered with a cuirass. 2. Covered with leather in the cuirass fashion. 3. Iron-clad, armored. *Acorazado* is more commonly used.

encorchadura [en-cor-chah-doo'-rah], *f.* 1. The act of hiving bees. 2. The corks or floats, collectively, of fishing nets.

encorchar [en-cor-char'], *va.* 1. To hive bees, to put them into hives made of cork. 2. To buck (caballo).

encorchetar [en-cor-chay-tar'], *va.* To hook, to put on hooks or clasps.

encordar [en-cor-dar'], *va.* 1. To string or chord musical instruments. 2. To halter, to lash or bind with cords or ropes.

encordelar [en-cor-day-lar'], *va.,* To bind with cords. **Encordelar una cama,** to cord a bed.

encordonado, da [en-cor-do-nah'-do, dah], *a.* Adorned with cords. *-pp.* of ENCORDONAR.

encordonar [en-cor-do-nar'], *va.* To put running strings to a purse or other thing; to tie with strings.

encorecer [en-co-ray-therr'], *va. & vn.* 1. To skin, to heal the skin. 2. To get a skin (heridas).

encoriación [en-co-re-ah-the-on'], *f.* Act of skinning over a sore, healing a wound.

encornar [en-cor-nar'], *va.* 1. To inlay with horn. 2. To gore or wound with the horns. 3. *(Arch.)* To ornament the ends of an arch with tips of horn.

encornijamiento [en-cor-ne-hah-men'-to], *m. V.* CORNIJAMENTO.

encornudar [en-cor-noo-dar'], *vn.* To begin to get horns (ganado), *-va.* To cuckold, to hornify.

encorozar [en-co-ro-thar'], *va.* To cover the head with a *coraza,* or cone-shaped cap, worn by criminals as a punishment.

encorralar [en-cor-rah-lar'], *va.* To inclose and keep in a yard (ganado).

encortinar [en-cor-te-nar'], *va.* To provide with curtains.

encorvada [en-cor-vah'-dah], *f.* 1. The act of bending or doubling the body. 2. A graceless and awkward manner of dancing. 3. *(Bot.)* Hatchet wetch coronilla. **Hacer la encorvada,** *(Met.)* to feign disease to avoid something.

encorvadura, *f.* **encorvamiento,** *m.* [en-cor-vah-doo'-rah]. 1. Act of bending or reducing to a crooked shape, crouching. 2. Crookedness; falcation, hookedness.

encorvar [en-cor-var'], *va.* To bend, to incurvate, to crook, to curve. *-vr.* To bend, to curb; to go crooked.

encosadura [en-co-sah-doo'-rah], *f. (Prov.)* The act of sewing or joining fine linen to some of a coarser sort.

encostarse [en-cos-tar'-say], *(Naut.)* To stand inshore, to near the coast.

encostradura [en-cos-trah-doo'-rah], *f.* Incrustation, crust.

encostrar [en-cos-trar'], *va.* 1. To crust, to incrust, to envelope or cover with a crust. 2. To roughcast with mortar, made of lime and sand.

encovadura [en-co-vah-doo'-rah], *f.* Act of depositing in a cellar.

encovar [en-co-var'], *va.* 1. To put or lay up in a cellar. 2. *(Met.)* To guard, to conceal, to inclose. *-vr.* 1. To go down into a cellar or cave. 2. To hide oneself.

encrasar [en-crah-sar'], *va.* To fatten; to thicken.

encrespado [en-cres-pah'-do], *a.* Curly (pelo); choppy (mar).

encrespador [en-cres-pah-dor'], *m.* Crisping-pin, crisping-iron, curling-iron.

encrespadura [en-cres-pah-doo'-rah], *f.* Crispation, the act of curling.

encrespamiento [en-cres-pah-me-en'-to], *m.* Crispation, crispness, curliness, curledness.

encrespar [en-cres-par'], *va.* To curl, to frizzle, to crimp. *-vr.* 1. *(Naut.)* To become rough and boisterous (mar). 2. To be rude or unpolite. 3. To be involved in quarrels and disputes.

encrespo [en-cres-po], *m. (Obs.)* Crispation, the act and effect of curling.

encrestado, da [en-cres-tah'-do, dah], *a. & pp.* of ENCRESTARSE. 1. Adorned with a crest or comb. 2. *(Met.)* Haughty, lofty.

encrestarse [en-cres-tar'-say], *vr.* 1. To get the crest or comb (gallo). 2. *(Met.)* To be proud, elated, or haughty.

encrinita [en-cre-nee'-tah], *f.* Encrinite, a fossil crinoid.

encruce [en-croo-thay], *m.* 1. Crossing of threads. 2. Shed, lease, the plane in which the warp-threads cross.

encrucijada [en-croo-the-hah'-dah], *f.* Crossway, crossroad, intersection, junction. *(Fig.)* **Estamos en la encrucijada,** we are at the crossroads.

encrudecer [en-croo-day-therr'], *va.* 1. To make a wound worse or raw. 2. To exasperate, to irritate. *-vr.* To be enraged, to become furious with passion. *(Yo me encrudezco, yo me encrudezca, from Encrudecerse. V. CONOCER.)*

encruelecer [en-croo-ay-lay-therr'], *va.* To excite to cruelties, to make cruel. *(Yo me encruelezco, yo me encruelezca, from Encruelecer. V. CONOCER.)*

encruzar [en-croo-thar'], *va.* To cross the threads of the warp, to twill.

encuadernación [en-coo-ah-der-nah-the-on'], *f.* Binding (libros) **Encuadernación en cantoné,** paste-board binding. **Encuadernación en tela,** cloth binding.

encuadernador [en-coo-ah-der-nah-dor'], *m.* Binder or bookbinder.

encuadernar [en-coo-ah-der-nar'], *va.* 1. To bind books, pamphlets, etc. 2. *(Met.)* To join again what was disjoined. 3. To reconcile.

encuadrar [en-coo-ah-drar'], *va.* 1. To frame, to encase. 2. To fit, to insert (encajar). 3. *(Fig.)* To contain, to comprise.

encubar [en-coo-bar'], *va.* 1. To put liquids into casks, barrels, etc. 2. *(Ant.)* To put a criminal into a butt, by way of punishment.

encubertado [en-coo-ber-tah'-do], *m. (Zool.)* A kind of South American armadillo.

encubertar [en-coo-ber-tar'], *va.* To overspread with a covering of cloth or silk. *-vr.* To dress and arm oneself for defence of the body.

encubierta [en-coo-be-err'-tah], *f.* Fraud, deceit, imposition.

encubiertamente [en-coo-be-ayr'-tah-men-tay], *adv.* 1. Hiddenly, secretly. 2. Deceitfully, fraudulently.

encubierto, ta [en-coo-be-err'-to, tah], *a. & pp.* of ENCUBRIR. 1. Hidden concealed. 2. *V.* CUBIERTO. *(Yo encubierto, yo encubierta, from Encubertar. V. ACRECENTAR.)*

encubridor, ra [en-coo-bre-dor', rah], *m. & f.* Concealer, hider, harborer. **Encubridor de hurtos,** receiver of stolen goods.

encubrimiento [en-coo-bre-me-en'-to], *m.* Concealment, hiding, the act of hiding or concealing.

encubrir [en-coo-breer'], *va.* To hide, to conceal, to cloak, to mask, to palliate.

encucar [en-coo-car'], *va. (Prov.)* To gather nuts and filberts, and store them up.

encuentro [en-coo-en'-tro], *m.* 1. Knock, a sudden stroke, chock, jostle, clash. 2. Encounter, accidental congress; sudden meeting. 3. Encounter, fight. 4. The act of going to meet and see anyone. 5. Opposition, difficulty. 6. Joint of the wings, in fowls or birds, next to the breast. 7. In the larger quadrupeds, the points of the shoulder-blades. 8. *(Arch.)* An angle formed by two beams, two walls, etc. **Salir al encuentro,** a) to go to meet a person in a certain place. b) to encounter. c) to prevent a person in what he is to say or observe. **Encuentros,** temples of a loom. **Un encuentro fortuito,** a chance meeting. **Ir al encuentro de lo desconocido,** to go out to face the unknown. *(Yo encuentro, yo encuentre, from Encontrar. V. ACORDAR.)*

encuesta [en-coo-ays'-tah], *f.* Poll, opinion poll, survey (opinión pública). **Hacer una encuesta,** to carry out an opinion poll. 2. Inquiry, investigation (investigación).

encuestador, ra [en-coo-ays-tah-dor'], *m & f.* Pollster.

encuestar [en-coo-ays-tar'], *va.* To poll, to take a poll of.

encuitarse [en-coo-e-tar-say], *vr.* To grieve, to afflict oneself.

enculatar [en-coo-lah-tar'], *va.* To put on the covering or cap of a hive.

encumbrado, da [en-coom-brah'-do, dah], *a.* High, elevated, lofty, stately. *-pp.* of ENCUMBRAR.

encumbramiento [en-coom-brah-me-en'-to], *m.* 1. The act of raising or elevating. 2. Height, eminence.

encumbrar [en-coom-brar'], *va.* 1. To raise, to elevate. 2. To mount or ascend a height. 3. *(Met.)* To elevate to dignities or honors. *-vr.* 1. To be raised or elevated. 2. To be proud, to rate himself high.

encunar [en-coo-nar'], *va.* 1. To put a child in the cradle. 2. *(Met.)* To catch the bullfighter between the horns (toro).

encuñar [en-coo-nyar'], *va.* To coin. *V.* ACUñAR.

encureñado, da [en-coo-ray-nyah'-do, dah], *a.* Put into the carriage or stock.

encurtidos [en-coor-tee'-dos], *m. pl.* Pickles of small cucumbers and peppers.

encurtir [en-coor-teer'], *va.* To souse in pickle or vinegar.

enchironar [en-che-ro-nar'], *va.* To jug, to jail.

enchufado, da [en-choo-fah'-do], *m & f.* Creep; teacher's pet (en escuela).

enchufar [en-choo-far'], *vn.* To fit, as the orifice of a tube into another. *-va.* 1. To join, to connect, to fit together (técnica). 2. *(Com, Fin.)* To merge. *-vr.* To wangle oneself a job (puesto).

enchufe [en-choo'-fay], *m.* 1. Socket joint (unión). 2. Plug (clavija). 3. *(coll.)* Additional job obtained through political influence. **Tiene un enchufe en el ministerio,** he's got a contact in the ministry. **Hay que tener enchufes,** you've got to have contacts.

endeble [en-day'-blay], *a.* Feeble, weak, flaccid, flimsy, forceless.

endeblez [en-day-bleth'], *f.* Feebleness, flaccidity, flimsiness.

endecágono [en-day-cah'-gono], *m.* Hendecagon, a figure of eleven angles or sides.

endecasílabo, ba [en-day-cah-see'-lah-bo, bah], *a.* Applied to metrical lines consisting of eleven syllables. **Verso endecasílabo,** hendecasyllable verse.

endecha [en-day'-chah], *f.* Dirge, a doleful ditty.

endechar [en-day-char'], *va.* To sing funeral songs in honor and praise of the dead. *-vr.* To grieve, to mourn.

endemia [en-day'-me-ah], *f.* Endemia, any disease produced and propagated by local conditions.

endémico, ca [en-day'-me-co, cah], *a.* Endemic, chronic, peculiar to a climate.

endemoniado, da [en-day-mo-ne-ah'-do, dah], *a.* 1. Possessed with the devil, fiendful (poseído). 2. Devilish, extremely bad, perverse or hurtful (endiablado). *-pp.* of ENDEMONIAR.

endemoniar [en-day-mo-ne-ar'], *va.* 1 To· possess with a devil (endiablar). 2. *(Met.)* To irritate, to provoke, to enrage. *-vr.* To get riled.

endentar [en-den-tar'], *va.* 1. To join with a mortise. 2. *(Naut.)* To insert one thing in another. 3. To snake the teeth on a wheel.

endentecer [en-den-tay-therr'], *vn.* To cut teeth, to teeth, to tooth. *(Yo endentezco, yo endentezca, from Endentecer. V.* CONOCER.)

endeñado, da [en-day-nyah'-do, dah], *a.* Damaged, hurt, inflamed.

enderezadamenete [en-day-ray-thah-dah-men'-tay], *adv.* Justly, rightly; directly.

enderezado [en-day-ray-thah'-do], *a.* Appropriate; favorable, opportune.

enderezador [en-day-ray-thah-dor'], *m.* Guide, director; governor.

enderezadura [en-day-ray-thah-doo'-rah], *f.* The straight and right road.

enderezamiento [en-day-ray-thah-me-en'-to], *m.* Guidance, direction, the act of guiding or setting right.

enderezar [en-day-ray-thar'], *va.* 1. To erect, to place perpendicularly to the horizon what is not upright, to make straight (poner vertical). 2. To rectify, to set right. 3. To address, to dedicate (dedicar). 4. To go and meet a person. **Las medidas están enderezadas a corregirlo,** the measures are designed to correct it. *-vn.* To take the direct road. *-vr.* 1. To erect, to rise upright. 2. *(Met.)* To fix or establish oneself in a place or employment. **Enderezar el genio,** to break a bad temper.

endérmico, ca [en-derr'-me-co, cah], *a.* Endermic, said of a remedy applied directly to the skin.

endeudarse [en-day-oo-dar'-say], *vr.* To get in debt, to contract debts. *V.* ADEUDARSE. **Endeudarse con uno,** to become indebted to somebody.

endiablada [en-de-ah-blah'-dah], *f.* Masquerade, a diversion in which the company is dressed in masks.

endiabladamente [en-de-ah-blah-dah-men-tay], *adv.* Uglily, abominably, devilishly.

endiablado, da [en-de-ah-blah'-do, dah], *a. & pp.* of ENDIABLAR. 1. Devilish, diabolical, diabolic (diabólico). 2. Ugly, deformed (feo); perverse, wicked. 3. Furious, angry (enojado).

endiablar [en-de-ah-blar'], *va.* 1. *(Obs.)* To possess with the devil (endemoniar). 2. *(Met.)* To pervert, to corrupt (corromper). *-vr.* 1. To be possessed with a devil. 2. *(Met.)* To be furious, to be beside oneself.

endíadis [en-dee'-ah-dis], *f.* *(Rhet.)* Hendiadys, a figure by which two words are used to express a single idea.

endibia [en-dee'-be-ah], *f.* *(Bot.)* Endive, succory.

endilgador, ra [en-deel-gah-dor', rah] *m. & f. (coll.)* Pander; inducer, adviser.

endilgar [en-deel-gar'], *va. (coll.)* 1. To pander, to induce, to persuade. 2. To procure, to facilitate, to accommodate. 3. To show the way, to direct (encaminar).

endiñar [en-de-nyahr'], *va.* 1. To fetch (tortazo), to deal, to land (golpe). 2. **Endiñarla,** to put it in.

endiosamiento [en-de-o-sah-me-en'-to] *m.* 1. Haughtiness, loftiness, pride (engreimiento). 2. Ecstasy, abstraction; disregard of worldly concerns.

endiosar [en-de-o-sar'], *va.* To deify, to adore as a god, to glorify. *-vr.* 1. To be elated, to be puffed up with pride (engreírse). 2. To be in a state of religious abstraction or fervent devotion.

endoblado, da [en-do-blah'-do, dah], *a.* Applied to a lamb that sucks its own mother and another ewe.

endocardio [en-do-car'-de-o], *m.* Endocardium, the serous lining membrane of the heart.

endocarditis [en-do-car-dee'-tis], *f.* Endocarditis, inflammation of the lining of the heart.

endocarpo [en-do-car'-po], *m. (Bot.)* Endocarp, the inner membrane of the pericarp.

endógeno, na [en-do'-hay-no, nah], *a.* Endogenous, growing by internal additions.

endorsar, endosar [en-dor-sar', en-do-sar'], *va.* To endorse a bill of exchange.

endorso, endoso [en-dor'-so, en-do'-so], *m.* Endorsement of a bill of exchange.

endosador, endosante [en-do-sah-dor', en-do-sahn'-tay], *m.* Endorser.

endoselar [en-do-say-lar'], *va.* To hang, to make hangings or curtains.

endósmosis [en-dos'-mo-sis], *f.* Endosmosis, transudation.

endospermo [en-dos-perr'-mo], *m.* Endosperm, the albumen of a seed.

endotérmico, ca [en-do-terr'-me-co, cah], *a. (Chem.)* Endothermic.

endragonarse [en-drah-go-nar'-say], *vr.* In the jocular style, to grow furious as a dragon.

endriago [en-dre-ah'-go], *m.* A kind of fabulous monster.

endrina [en-dree'-nah], *f.* Sloe, the fruit of the blackthorn or sloetree.

endrino [en-dree'-no], *m. (Bot.)* Black-thorn, sloetree.

endrino, na [en-dree'-no, nah], *a.* Of a sloe-color.

endulzmientio [en-dool-thah-me-en'-to], *m.* **endulzadura** [en-dool-thah-doo'-rah], *f.* Dulcification, act of sweetening.

endulzante [en-dool-than'-tay], *m.* Sweetening, sweetener.

endulzar, endulzorar [en-dool-thar', en-dool-tho-rar'], *va.* 1. To sweeten, to make sweet. 2. (Met.) To soften, to make mild; to alleviate the toils of life.

endurador, ra [en-doo-rah-dor', rah], *m. & f. & a.* Miser, a mean, avaricious person.

endurar [en-doo-rar'], *va* 1. To harden, to indurate, to make hard. 2. To live in a parsimonious manner. 3. To endure, to bear, to suffer. 4. To delay, to put off.

endurecer [en-doo-ray-therr'], *va.* 1. To harden, to indurate, to make hard. 2. (Met.) To accustom the body to labor and hardships, to inure. 3. (Met.) To render one steady in his sentiments and opinions. 4. To exasperate, to irritate. **Endurecer a uno a los peligros,** to inure somebody to danger. -*vr.* 1. To harden, to grow hard, to grow cruel. 2. To hammer metals. 3. In the manufacture of needles, to temper then. *(Yo endurezco, yo endurezca, from Endurecer. V. CONOCER.)*

endurecidamente [en-doo-ray-the-dah-men'-tay], *adv.* Pertinaciously.

endurecido, da [en-doo-ray-thee'-do, dah], *a.& pp.* of ENDURECER. 1. Hard (duro), hardy. 2. Indurated, hardened (lodo), obdurate. 3. Tutored by experience, inured.

endurecimiento [en-doo-ray-the-me-en-to], *m.* Hardness; obstinacy, tenacity, hardness of heart, obdurateness. **Endurecimiento de las arterias,** hardening of the arteries.

ene [ay'-nay], *f.* Spanish name of the letter N.

enea [ay-nay'-ah], *f. (Bot.)* Cat's tail, reedmace, rush.

eneágono [ay-nay-ah'-go-no], *m.* A plain figure with nine sides and nine angles.

eneático, ca [ay-nay-ah'-te-co, cah], *a.* Belonging to the number nine.

enebral [ay-nay-brahl'], *m.* Plantation, of the juniper-tree.

enebrina [ay-nay-bree'-nah], *f.* Fruit of the juniper-tree.

enebro [ay-nay'-bro], *m. (Bot.)* Common juniper.

eneida [ay-nay'-e-dah], *f.* The Aeneid, an epic poem by Virgil.

enejar [ay-nay-har'], *va.* 1. To put an axle-tree to a cart or carriage. 2. To put anything in an axle-tree.

eneldo [ay-nel'-do], *m. (Bot.)* Common dill.

enema [ay-nay'-mah], *f.* Enema, injection, clyster.

enemiga [ay-nay-mee'-gah], *f.* Enmity, malevolence, aversion, ill-will.

enemigamente [ay-nay-mee'-gah-men-tay], *adv.* Inimically, in a hostile manner.

enemigarse [ay-nay-me-gar'-say], *vr.* To be in a state of enmity.

enemigo, ga [ay-ne-mee'-go, gah], *a.* Inimical, hostile, contrary, unfriendly, adverse. **Ser enemigo de,** to be hostile to.

enemigo, ga [ay-nay-mee'-go, gah], *m. & f.* Enemy, antagonist, foe, foeman. **El enemigo,** the fiend, the devil.

enemistad [ay-nay-mis-tahd'], *f.* Enmity, hatred.

enemistar [ay-nay-mis-tar'], *va.* To make an enemy. -*vr.* To become an enemy. **Enemistarse con uno,** to become an enemy of somebody.

eneo, ea [ay-na-yo, ah], *a. (Poet.)* Brazen, belonging to brass.

enerar [ay-nay-rar'], *va.* To kill plants by frost.

energético [ay-nayr'-he-co], *a.* 1. (Tec.) Energy, fuel, power. **La crisis energética,** the energy crisis.

energía [ay-ner-hee'-ah], *f.* 1. Energy, power, vigor (vigor). **Obrar con energía,** to act energetically. 2. Strength of expression, force of meaning. 3. Comprehensiveness. 4. Pep (coll.). **Energía atómica,** atomic energy. **Energía solar,** Solar power. **Energía eólica,** wind power.

enérgicamente [ay-nerr'-he-cah-men-tay], *adv.* Energetically, expressively.

enérgico, ca [ay-nerr'-he-co, cah], *a.* Energetic, energetical, energic (persona), forcible, active, vigorous (esfuerzo), expressive, lively, strenuous (esfuerzo).

energúmeno, na [ay-nayr-goo'-may-no], *m. & f.* Person possessed of the devil; (Fig.) demon, wild person, madman. **Ponerse como un energúmeno,** to get mad (enfadarse).

enero [ay-nay'-ro], *m.* January, the first month of the year.

enervación [ay-ner-vah-the-on'], *f.* 1. Enervation. 2. (Vet.) Section of two tendons in the head of a horse.

enervado, da [ay-ner-vah'-do], *a. & pp.* of ENERVAR. Enervate, enervated, weakened.

enervador, ra [ay-ner-vah-dor', rah], *a.* Weakening, enervating.

enervamiento [ay-ner-vah-me-en'-to], *m.* 1. Enervation. 2. Effeminacy.

enervar [ay-ner-var'], *va.* 1. To enervate, to deprive of force. 2. To weaken the reasons or arguments. -*vr.* 1. To grow weak, to lose force. 2. To become effeminate. 3. To become dull (sentidos). 4. To cut the tendon of the muscles which raise the upper lip of horses.

enésimo, ma [ay-nay'-se-mo], *a. m & f.* **Por enésima vez,** for the umpteenth time.

enético, ca [ay-nay'-te-co, cah], *a.* Lethal, mortal.

enfadadizo za [en-fah-dah-dee'-tho, thah], *a.* Irritable, irascible, peevish, waspish, easily offended, soon angry.

enfadar [en-fah-dar'], *va.* To vex, to molest, to trouble, to fret, to offend (ofender), to make angry, to cut to the heart, to anger (enojar). -*vr.* To fret, to become angry (enojarse). **No te enfades,** don't be cross. **De nada sirve enfadarse,** it's no good getting cross.

enfado [en-fah'-do], *m.* 1. Trouble, vexation, molestation, fret, crossness, anger, gall, fastidiousness (enojo). 2. V. AFÁN and TRABAJO.

enfadoso, sa [en-fah-do'-so, sah], *a.* Vexatious, troublesome, heavy, cumbersome, molestful.

enfaldar [en-fal-dar'], *va.* To lop off the lower branches of trees. -*vr.* To tuck or truss up the skirts of one's clothes.

enfaldo [en-fahl'-do], *m.* Act of tucking up one's clothes.

enfangar [en—fahn-gar'], *va.* To cover with mud.

enfangarse [en-fan-gar'-say], *vr. (Naut.)* To touch ground in a miry or muddy place. (coll.) To get into difficulties.

enfardador [en-far-dah-dor], *m.* Packer, a person who packs up bales and packages.

enfardar [en-far-dar'], *va.* To pack, to bale, to make packages.

enfardelador [en-far-day-lah-dor'], *m.* Packer, one who makes up bales.

enfardeladura [en-far-day-lah-doo'-rah], *f.* Packing, act of packing merchandise.

enfardelar [en-far-day-lar'], *va.* To bale, to make up into bales, to pack.

énfasis [en'-fah-sis], *m.* Emphasis, a remarkable stress laid on a word or sentence. **Hablar con énfasis,** to speak emphatically.

enfáticamente [en-fah'-te-cah-men-tay], *adv.* Emphatically.

enfático, ca [en-fah'-te-co, cah], *a.* Emphatical, emphatic, impressive, heavy (discurso).

enfatizar [en-fah-te-thar'], *va.* To emphasize, to stress. -*vn.* To emphasize.

enfelpar [en-fel-par'], *va.* V. AFELPAR.

enfermamente [en-fer-mah-men'-tay], *adv.* Weakly, feebly.

enfermar [en-fer-mar'], *vn.* To be seized with a fit of illness, to fall ill. -*va.* 1. To make sick. 2. To cause damage or loss. 3. To weaken, to enervate.

enfermedad [en-fer-may-dahd'], *f.* 1. Infirmity, indisposition (indisposición), illness, complaint, disease, malady, distemper. **Durante esta enfermedad,** during this illness. **Enfermedad de la piel,** skin disease. **Enfermedad de transmisión sexual,** sexually transmitted disease. 2. Damage, disorder, risk.

enfermería [en-fer-may-ree'-ah], *f.* Infirmary, lodgings for the sick, sanatorium; hospital.

enfermero, ra [en-fer-may'-ro, rah], *m. & f.* Overseer or nurse, who has the care of the sick.

enfermizo, za [en-fer-mee'-tho, thah], *a.* 1. Infirm, sickly, in bad health. 2. Morbifical, morbific, causing diseases.

enfermo, ma [en-ferr'-mo, mah], *a.* 1. Sick, diseased, infirm, indisposed, unhealthy. 2. Weak, feeble. 3. Of little importance or consideration. 4. Corrupted, tainted. **Enfermo de amor,** love-sick. **Ponerse enfermo,** to fall ill. *m. & f.* Sick person, invalid; patient (hospital).

enfervorizar [en-fer-vo-re-thar'], *va.* To heat, to inflame, to incite. *-vr.* To overheat oneself.

enfeudación [en-fay-oo-dah-the-on'], *f.* Infeudation, enfeoffment, the act of putting one in possession of a fee or estate.

enfeudar [en-fay-oo-dar'], *va.* To feoff, to enfeoff, to invest with a right or estate.

enfielar [en-fe-ay-lar'], *va.* To put in balance.

enfilar [en-fe-lar'], *va.* 1. To continue as if united in a file or line (alinear). 2. To enfilade, to pierce in a right line; to carry off by a cannon shot a whole file of the enemy's troops; to keep straight forward (rumbo). **El piloto trató de enfilar la pista,** the pilot tried to line the aircraft up with the runway.

enfisema [en-fe-say'-mah], *m.* Emphysema, infiltration of the cellular tissue with air.

enfisematoso, sa [en-fe-say-ma-to'-so, sah], *a.* Emphysematous, affected by emphysema.

enfiteusis, enfiteósis [en-fe-tay'-oo-sis, en-fe-tay'-o-sis], *m. & f.* A species of alienation, by which the use and usufruct are transferred, but not the whole right of property.

enfiteuta [en-fe-tay'-oo-tah], *m.* A tenant by emphyteusis.

enfitéutico, ca [en-fe-tay'-oo-te-co, cah], *a.* Emphyteutic, taken on hire.

enflaquecer [en-flah-kay-therr'], *va.* To weaken, to diminish, to make thin and lean, to extenuate, to fade. *-vr.* To become thin and lean (adelgazarse), to fall away or fall off.

enflaquecidamente [en-flah-kay-the-dah-men'-tay], *adv.* Weakly, feebly, faintly, without strength.

enflaquecimiento [en-flah-kay-the-me-en'-to], *m.* 1. Extenuation, a general decay in the muscular flesh of the whole body (adelgazamiento). 2. Attenuation, debilitation, maceration.

enflautado, da [en-flah-oo-tah'-do, dah] *a.* Turgid, inflated. *-m.* 1. (*Naut.*) The row of cannon mouths which show upon a vessel's side. 2. (*Amer.*) The flutestops of act organ, collectively. 3. A sound which imitates the flute.

enflautador, ra [en-flah-oo-tah-dor', rah], *m. & f.* Procurer, pimp.

enflautar [en-flah-oo-tar'], *va.* To procure.

enflechado, da [en-flay-chah'-do, dah], *a.* Applied to a bent bow or arrow ready to discharge.

enflechastes [en-flay-chahs'-tes], *m. pl.* (*Naut.*) Ratlines.

enfocar [en-fo-car'], *va.* 1. To focus. 2. To size up or weigh the aspects (de un problema o negocio). **Podemos enfocar este problema de tres maneras,** we can approach this problem in three ways.

enfoque [en-fo'-kay], *m.* Focus.

enfornar [en-for-nar'], *va.* V. ENHORNAR.

enfoscado, da [en-fos-cah'-do, dah], *a. & pp.* of ENFOSCARSE. 1. Brow-beaten. 2. Confused, entangled.

enfoscar [en-fos-car'], *va. & vr.* 1. To be uneasy, to be troubled or perplexed. 2. To be immersed in business. 3. To be cloudy (cielo). 4. To stop up the holes in a wall after it is constructed.

enfrailar [en-frah-e-lar'], *va. & vr.* To make one a monk or a friar, to induce him to take the vows of a religious order; to become a friar.

enfranquecer [en-fran-kay-therr'], *va.* To frank, to make free.

enfrascamiento [en-fras-cah-me-en'-to], *m.* The act of being entangled between brambles and briers.

enfrascar [en-fras-car'], *va.* To put liquid in a flask or bottle. *-vr.* 1. To be entangled between brambles and briers. 2. (*Met.*) To be involved in difficulties and to troubles, to engage deeply in an object. **Enfrascarse en un problema,** to get deeply involved in a problem. **Estaba enfrascado en la lectura,** he was buried in a book.

enfrenador [en-fray-nah-dor'], *m.* Bridler, one who puts on a bridle.

enfrenamiento [en-fray-nah-me-en'-to], *m.* 1. Putting on the brake (automóvil). 2. Bridling (caballo).

enfrenar [en-fray-nar'], *va.* 1. To put on the brake (automóvil) 2. To curb, to restrain. 3. To bridle, to put on the bridle (caballo).

enfrentamiento [en-fren-tah-me-ayn'-to], *m.* Clash, confrontation.

enfrentar [en-fren-tar'], *va.* 1. To put face to face (carear). 2. To face, to confront (problema). *-vn.* To face. *-vr.* **enfrentarse con,** to face, to confront. **Hay que enfrentarse con el peligro,** one must face up to the danger.

enfrente [en-fren'-tay], *adv.* Over against, opposite, in front, front to front. **Enfrente de casa,** opposite to the house.

enfriadera [en-fre-ah-day'-rah], *f.* Back, cooler or keelfat, the vessel for cooling any liquid; refrigerator.

enfriadero, enfriador [en-fre-ah-day'-ro, en-fre-ah-dor'], *m.* Cooling-place; refrigerator.

enfriamiento [en-fre-ah-me-en'-to], *m.* Refrigeration, the act of cooling, the state of being cooled (refrigeración).

enfriar [en-fre-ar'], *va.* 1. To cool (helar), to make cool, to allay, to heat out of, to refrigerate. 2. (*Met.*) To cool, to allay the heat of passion, to calm the mind. *-vr.* 1. To cool, to grow less hot. 2. (*Met.*) To cool, to grow less warm with regard to passion.

enfundar [en-foon-dar'], *va.* 1. To case, to put into a case (instrumento); to sheathe (espada). 2. To fill up to the brim, to cram, to stuff (llenar).

enfuñarse [en-foo-nyar'-say], *vr.* (*Prov. Cuba*) To get excited, worried. V. AMOHINARSE.

enfurecer [en-foo-ray-therr'], *va.* 1. To irritate, to enrage, to madden, to make furious. 2. V. ENSOBERBECER. *-vr.* 1. To rage, to grow boisterous or furious (viento y mar). 2. To become furious or enraged. (*Yo me enfurezco, yo me enfurezca,* from *Enfurecerse,* V. CONOCER.)

enfurruñarse [en-foor-roo-nyar'-say], *vr.* (*coll.*) To grow angry, to tiff, to sulk (enfadarse), to frown.

enfurtir [en-toor-teer'], *va.* 1. To full or mill clothes. 2. Among hatters; to felt.

engace [en-gah'-thay], *m.* Catenation, connection. V. ENGARCE.

engaitador, ra [en-gah-e-tah-dor', rah], *m. & f.* Coaxer, wheedler.

engaitar [en-gah-e-tar'], *va.* To coax, to wheedle.

engalanado [en-gah-lah-nah'-do], *m.* The banners and bunting with which a ship is adorned.

engalanar [en-gah-lah-nar'], *va.* 1. To adorn, to deck. 2. (*Naut.*) To dress a ship, to display a variety of colors, ensigns, or pendants. *-vr.* To adorn oneself; to dress up.

engalgar [en-gal-gar'], *va.* To pursue closely, not to lose sight of (galgos).

engallado, da [en-gal-lyah'-do, dah], *a.* 1. Erect, upright. 2. Haughty, elated, arrogant (arrogante).

engalladura [en-gal-lyah-doo'-rah], *f.* V. GALLADURA.

engallarse [en-gal-lyar'-say], *vr.* To affect gravity.

enganchador [en-gan-chah-dor'], *m.* One who decoys others into military service, vulgarly a crimp.

enganchamiento [en-gan-chah-me-en'-to], *m.* 1. Accroachment, the act of drawing as with a hook, hooking. 2. The act of entrapping, alluring, or decoying someone, particularly to make him enlist in the military service.

enganchar [en-gan-char'], *va.* 1. To hook, to catch with a hook, to accroach (con gancho). 2. To entrap, to ensnare. 3. To decoy into the military service, vulgarly to crimp. 4. To couple, to connect. **Enganchar los caballos al coche,** to harness the horses to the carriage. *-vr.* 1. To engage, to enlist or enroll in military service. 2. **Engancharse a las drogas,** to get hooked (prenderse).

enganche [en-gahn'-chay], *m.* 1. Enlistment, enrollment. 2. Bounty money (pago). 3. Coupler, coupling, connecting link. 4. (*Mex. coll.*) Down payment on a purchase.

engañabobos [en-gah-nyah-bo'bos], *m. (coll.)* 1. Impostor. 2. Fooltrap, a snare to catch fools in.

engañadizo, za [en-gah-nyah-dee'-tho, thah], *a.* Deceptible, easily deceived.

engañado, da [en-gah-nyah'-do, dah], *a. & pp.* of ENGAÑAR. Mistaken, deceived, overseen.

engañador, ra [en-gah-nyah-dor', rah] *m. & f.* Cheat, impostor, deceiver, cozener, colluder, abuser.

engañadura [en-gah-nyah-doo'-rah], *f. (Naut.)* Seizing truck, shroud, double wall knot.

engañapastor [en-gah-nyah-pas-tor'], *m. (Orn.)* Wagtail, a bird.

engañar [en-gah-nyar'], *va.* 1. To deceive (embaucar), to cheat, to mock, to mislead (despistar). **A mí no me engaña nadie,** you can't fool me. **Engaña a su marido,** she's unfaithful to her husband. 2. To cheat, to delude, to impose upon, to trick. 3. To fool, to hoax, to abuse, to gull. -*vr.* To be deceived, to mistake, to make a mistake. **Ser malo de engañar,** *(coll.)* to be not easily deceived, to be sagacious. **Se engaña con falsas esperanzas,** she deludes herself with false hopes.

engañifa [en-gah-nyee'-fah], *f. (coll.)* 1. Deceit, trick, fraudulent action. 2. A catchpenny.

engaño [en-gah'-nyo], *m.* 1. Mistake, mistaking, misunderstanding (malentendido), misapprehension, misconception. 2. Deceit (cualidad), fraud, imposition, falsehood (cosa fingida). 3. Hoax, lure. **Todo es engaño,** it's all a sham. **Aquí no hay engaño,** there is no attempt to deceive anybody here. **Padecer engaño,** to labor under a misunderstanding.

engañosamente [en-gah-nyo'-sah-men-tay], *adv.* Deceitfully, fraudfully, guilefully; mistakenly.

engañoso, sa [en-gah-nyo'-so, sah], *a.* Deceitful (persona), artful, fallacious, false, fraudulent, mendacious.

engarabatar [en-gah-ra-bah-tar'], *va. (coll.)* To hook, to seize with violence. -*vr.* To grow crooked.

engarabitarse [en-gah-ra-be-tar'-say], *vr. (coll.)* To climb, to mount, to ascend (subir).

engarbarse [en-gar-bar'-say], *vr.* To perch on the highest branch of a tree (pájaros).

engarbullar [en-gar-bool-lyar'], *va. (coll.)* To entangle, to involve.

engarce [en-gar-thay], *m.* 1. Catenation, link. 2. Close union or connection. 3. Setting, mount of jewellery.

engargantar [en-gar-gan-tar'], *va.* 1. To put something into the throat. 2. To thrust the foot into the stirrup, quite to the instep. 3. *vn.* To gear, to fit into each other: used of cogwheels.

engargolar [en-gar-go-lar'], *va.* To fit the end of one waterpipe into that of another.

engaripolar [en-gah-re-po-lar'], *va. (coll.)* To adorn with trifles and baubles.

engaritado, da [en-gah-re-tah'-do, dah], *a.* 1. Cheated, deceived. 2. Surrounded with sentry-boxes. -*pp.* of ENGARITAR.

engaritar [en-gah-re-tar'], *va.* 1. To fortify, to adorn with sentry-boxes. 2. To impose upon or deceive in an artful or dexterous manner.

engarrafador [en-gar-rah-fah-dor'], *m.* Grappler.

engarrafar [en-gar-rah-far'], *va. (coll.)* 1. To claw, to seize with the claws or talons. 2. To grapple with hooks.

engarrotar [en-gar-ro-tar'], *va.* To squeeze and press hard. V. AGARROTAR. -*vr. (LAm.)* To get stiff, to go numb (pierna).

engarzador [en-gar-thah-dor'], *m.* One who links or enchains; stringer of beads.

engarzar [en-gar-thar'], *va.* To enchain, to link; to curl (pelo), to set (joya).

engastador [en-gas-tah-dor'], *m.* Encaser, incloser.

engastar [en-gas-tar'], *va.* To inclose one thing in another without being screened, such as a diamond in gold; to set, to mount.

engaste [en-gahs'-tay], *m.* 1. The setting of stones, the act of setting or infixing. 2. The hoop or envelope. 3. A pearl flat on one side.

engatado, da [en-gah-tah'-do, dah], *a. & n.* A petty robber, a sharper, a petty thief. -*pp.* of ENGATAR.

engatar [en-gah-tar'], *va. (coll.)* To cheat in a dexterous manner, to wheedle.

engatillado, da [en-gah-til-lyah'-do, dah], *a.* Thick, high-necked (caballos y toros). -*pp.* of ENGATILLAR.

engatillar [en-gah-til-lyar'], *va. (Arch.)* To bind with a crampiron.

engatusador, ra [en-gah-too-e-ah-dor', rah], *m. & f.* One who coaxes; wheedler.

engatusamiento [en-gah-too-sah-me-en'-to], *m. (coll.)* Deception, cheat, coaxing.

engatusar [en-gah-too-sar'], *va. (coll.)* To trick without intention; to rob or hurt, to coax. **Engatusar a uno para que haga algo,** to coax somebody into doing something.

engavillar [en-gah-vel-lyar'], *va.* V. AGAVILLAR.

engazador, ra [en-gah-thah-dor', rah], *m. & f.* V. ENGARZADOR.

engazadura [en-gah-tha-doo'-rah], *f. (Naut.)* 1. Splicing in form of a ring. 2. Spot in a cable where a round splice is made.

engazamiento [en-gah-thah-me-ayn'-tao], *m.* V. ENGARCE.

engazar [engahthar'], *va.* 1. To enchain, to link. 2. *(Naut.)* To stop or splice an end of a rope in a circular form about a block. 3. To dye in the cloth.

engendrable [en-hen-drah'-blay], *a.* That may be engendered.

engendramiento [en-hen-drah-me-en'-to], *m.* Begetting, generating.

engendrador, ra [en-hen-drah-dor', rah], *m. & f.* Engenderer, one who engenders or produces.

engendrar [en-hen-drar'], *va.* 1. To beget, to engender, to gender, to generate. 2. To produce, to bear fruit; to create.

engendro [en-hen'-dro], *m.* 1. Foetus, a shapeless embryo. 2. Abortive. **Mal engendro,** a low breed; a perverse youth. 3. Bungled job (chapuza); idiotic scheme (proyecto); brainchild (idea).

engestado [en-hes-tah'-do], *a. (Amer.)* **Bien or mal engestado,** well or gruff-looking.

engestarse [en-hes-tar'-say], *vr. (Amer.)* To address abruptly and uncivilly.

engibar [en-he-bar'], *va.* To crook, to make gibbous.

engilmar [en-heel-mar'], *va. (Naut.)* To pick up a mast which is floating in the sea.

engimelgar [en-he-mel-gar'], *va. (Naut.)* To fish a mast, to mend a spar.

englandado, da [en-glan-dah'-do, dah], *a. (Her.)* Covered with acorns (roble).

englobar [en-glo-bar'], *va.* 1. To include, to comprise (abarcar). 2. To lump together, to put all together (unir).

engolado, da [en-go-lah'-do, dah], *a.* Collared, wearing a collar.

engolfar [en-gol-far'], *vn. (Naut.)* To enter a gulf or deep bay. -*vr.* 1. To be engaged in arduous undertakings or difficult affairs. 2. To be lost in thought, to be absorbed in meditation.

engolondrinarse [en-go-lon-dree-nar'-say], *vr.* 1. *(coll.)* To be elated, to be puffed up with pride. 2. *(Low.)* To fall in love, to be smitten with love (amorosamente).

engolosinar [en-go-lo-se-nar'], *va.* To tempt, to entice. -*vr.* To delight, or to have delight or pleasure in.

engollar [en-gol-lyar'], *va.* To make a horse carry his head and neck by means of the bridle.

engolletado da [en-gol-lyay-tah'-do, dah], *a. (coll.)* Elated, puffed up, presumptuous, haughty. -*pp.* of ENGOLLETARSE.

engolletarse [en-gol-lyay-tar'-say], *vr.* To elate, to become haughty.

engomadero, ra [en-go-mah-day'-ro, rah], *a.* That may be stiffened with starch or gum.

engomadura [en-go-mah-doo-rah], *f.* 1. Gumming, act of gumming. 2. Coat which bees lay over their hives before making the wax.

engomar [en-go-mar'], *va.* To gum, to stiffen with gum.

engominar [en-go-me'-nah], *va.* To put hair-cream on (pelo).

engorar [en-go-rar'], *va.* To addle. *V.* ENHUERAR.

engordadero [en-gor-dah-day'-ro], *m.* 1. Stall or sty to fatten hogs. 2. Time for fattening them.

engordador [en-gor-dah-dor'], *m.* One who makes it his sole business to pamper himself.

engordar [en-gor-dar'], *va.* To pamper, to fatten, to lard, to make fat. -*vn.* 1. To grow fat, to feed (ponerse gordo). 2. To grow rich, to amass a fortune (enriquecerse). 3. Of waves, to increase in size, to swell.

engorde [en-gor'-day], *m.* Fattening of herds, especially of hogs.

engorgetado, da [en-gor-hay-tah'-do, dah], *a.* Palisaded breast-high.

engorro [en-gor'-ro], *m. (coll.)* Impediment, embarrassment, obstacle.

engorroso, sa [en-gor-ro'-so, sah], *a.* Troublesome, tiresome, vexatious, cumbersome, cumbrous.

engoznar [en-goth-nar'], *va.* To hinge, to put hinges on doors and windows.

engranaje [en-grah-nah'-hay], *m.* 1. Gear, transmission gear. **Caja de engranaje,** gear case. 2. *(Fig.)* Adjustment, interlocking of ideas, circumstances, etc.

engranar [en-grah-nar'], *va.* To tooth, to connect; to gear, to throw into gear.

engrandar [en-grahn'-day], *va. V.* AGRANDAR.

engrandecer [en-gran-day-therr'], *va.* 1. To augment, to aggrandize, to increase. 2. To promote to a higher station, to exalt, to extol (ensalzar). 3. *(Met.)* To exaggerate, to magnify (exagerar). (*Yo engrandezco, yo engrandezca,* from *Engrandecer. V.* CONOCER.

engrandecimiento [en-gran-day-the-me-en'-to], *m.* 1. Increase, aggrandizement; aggrandization. 2. Exaggeration, hyperbolical amplification.

engranerar [en-grah-nay-rar'], *va.* To enclose in a granary.

engranujarse [en-grah-noo-har'-say], *vr.* 1. To be covered with pimples. 2. To become a rogue.

engrapar [en-grah-par'], *va.* To secure, to unite or bind with cramp-irons.

engrasación [en-grah-sah-the-on'], *f.* or **engrasamiento,** *m.* Lubrication, oiling, greasing.

engrasador [en-grah-sah-dor'], *m.* Oiler, lubricator (aceitera).

engrasar [en-grah-sar'], *va.* 1. To grease, to oil, to fat, to lubricate. 2. To stain with grease (manchar). 3. To dress cloth. 4. *(Met.)* To pickle. 5. *(Prov.)* To manure, to hearten.

engrase [en-g-rah'-say], *m.* 1. Greasing, lubrication. 2. Bribe.

engravedar [en-grah-vay-dar'], *va.* To assume an air of dignity, to affect gravity.

engredar [en-gray-dar'], *va.* To bedaub with marl or fuller's earth.

engreído, da [en-gray-ee'-do, dah], *a. & pp.* of ENGREÍR. Elated, lofty, haughty; petulant.

engreimiento [en-gray-e-me-en'-to], *m.* 1. Presumption, vanity, elation. 2. Vain pomp in dress.

engreír [en-gray-eer'], *va.* To encourage someone's pride and petulance, to make him pert and saucy, to lift, to flush, to pride. -*vr.* 1. *V.* ENSOBERBECERSE and ENVANECERSE. 2. To deck or attire oneself in style, to be extravagant in dress. (*Yo me engrío, yo me engría,* from *Engreirse. V.* PEDIR.)

engrifarse [en-gre-far'-say], *vr.* To tiff, to be in a pet, to be displeased, to sulk.

engrosar [en-gro-sar'], *va.* 1. To make a thing fat and corpulent, to increase its bulk. 2. To make strong or vigorous. 3. To augment, to make more numerous (cantidad). -*vn.* 1. To grow strong, to increase in vigor and bulk. -*vr.* 1. To fatten. 2. *(Naut.)* To increase in cloudiness, to increase in size (olas). (*Yo engrueso, yo engruese,* from *Engrosar. V.* ACORDAR.)

engrudador [en-groo-dah-dor'], *m.* Paster, one who pastes; gluer.

engrudamiento [en-groo-dah-me-en'-to], *m.* 1. Act of pasting. 2. Gluing.

engrudar [en-groo-dar'], *va.* To paste, to fasten with paste.

engrudo [en-groo'-do], *m.* 1. Paste, flour and water boiled together so as to make a cement. 2. *(Naut.)* Cement, made chiefly of pounded glass and cow-hair, used to stanch the planks of a ship.

engruesar [en-groo-ay-sar'], *va. V.* ENGORDAR and ENGROSAR.

engrumecerse [en-groo-may-therr'-say], *vr.* To clot.

engualdar [en-goo-ahl-dar'], *va.* To make like woad, or the color of woad.

engualdrapar [en-goo-al-drah-par'], *va.* To caparison a horse with rich trappings.

enguantado, da [en-goo-an-tah'-do, dah], *a.* Wearing gloves. -*pp.* of ENGUANTARSE.

enguantarse [en-goo-an-tar-say], *vr.* To put on glove

enguedejado, da [en-gay-day-hah'-do dah], *a.* 1. Curl-pated, having hair curled or braided, and growing in tufts and locks. 2. Crisped, curled.

enguijarrar [en-gee-har-rar'], *va.* To pave with pebbles.

enguillar [en-geel-lyar'], *va. (Naut.)* To wind a thin rope around a thicker one.

enguirnaldado, da [en-geer-nal-dah'-do, dah], *a.* Adorned with garlands.

enguirnaldar [en-geer-nal-dar'], *va.* To garland, to engarland, to adorn with garlands.

enguizgar [en-geeth-gar'], *va.* To excite, to incite, to set on.

engullidor, ra [en-gool-lye-dor', rah], *m. & f.* 1. Devourer, one who swallows without mastication. 2. Gobbler, one who devours in haste.

engullir [en-gool-lyeer'], *va.* To devour meat without chewing it, to gobble, to glut, to gorge.

engurriñarse [en-goor-re-nyar'-say], *vr. (coll.)* To be melancholy (pájaros).

engurruñarse [en-goor-roo-nyar'-say], *vr.* To get sad, to grow gloomy.

enharinar [en-ah-re-nar'], *va.* To cover or besprinkle with flour.

enhastiar [en-as-te-ar'], *va.* To disgust, to excite disgust, to cloy.

enhastillar [en-as-til-lyar'], *va.* To put arrows in a quiver.

enhatijar [en-ah-te-har'], *va.* To cover the mouths of hives with bassweed, in order to move them from one place to another.

enhebrar [en-ay-brar'], *va.* 1. To thread a needle. 2. *(Met. coll.)* To link, to unite or connect closely.

enhenar [en-ay-nar'], *va.* To cover with hay, to wrap up in hay.

enherbolar [en-er-bo-lar'], *va.* To poison with venomous herbs.

enhestador [en-es-tah-dor'], *m.* He who erects.

enhestadura [en-es-tah-doo'-rah], *f.* Erection.

enhestar [en-es-tar'], *va.* 1. To erect to set upright. -*vr.* To erect, to rise upright.

enhidro, dra [en-ee'-dro, drah], *a. (Miner.)* Hyaline quartz or fluorine which contains some drops of water.

enhielar [en-e-ay-lar'], *va.* To mix with gall or bile.

enhiesto, ta [en-e-ays'-to, tah], *a. & pp. irr.* of ENHESTAR. Erect, upright, erected.

enhilado, da [en-e-lah'-do, dah], *a.* Well arranged, disposed in good order. -*pp.* of ENHILAR.

enhilar [en-e-lar'], *va.* 1. To thread (aguja). 2. To direct, to tend; to take the way or road to anything or place. 3. To arrange. 4. *(coll.)* To enter or go through a long story.

enhorabuena [en-o-rah-boo-ay'-nah], *f.* Congratulation, felicitation, joy for the happiness or success of another. **Dar la enhorabuena a uno,** to congratulate somebody. **Estar de enhorabuena,** to be in luck. -*adv.* Well and good; all right.

enhoramala [en-o-rah-mah'-lah], f. A word used to express the act of scorning, despising, or contemning a thing. -adv. Its an evil hour. **Vete enhora mala,** (coll.) go to the devil.

enhornar [en-or-nar'], va. To put into an oven to be baked.

enhuecar [en-oo-ay-car'], va. V. AHUECAR.

enhuerar [en-oo-ay-rar'], va. To lay addle eggs, to addle.

enigma [ay-neeg'-mah], m. Enigma, a riddle; an obscure question; cross-purpose.

enigmático, ca [ay-nig-mah'-te-co, cah], a. Enigmatical, dark, obscure, ambiguously or darkly expressed.

enigmatista [ay-nig-mah-tess'-tah], m. Enigmatist.

enigmatizar [ay-nig-mah-te-thar'], va. To make enigmas. -vn. To talk ambiguously.

enipiotismo [ay-ne-pe-o-tees'-mo], m. Magnetic sleep, hypnotism.

enjabegarse [en-hah-bay-gar-say], vr. (Naut.) 1. To get entangled (cuerdas). 2. Among fishers, to be twisted.

enjabonadura [en-hah-bo-nah-doo'-rah], f. V. JABONADURA.

enjabonar [en-hah-bo-nar'], va. 1. To soap, to wash with soap. 2. (Met.) To insult with foul language and blows. 3. (coll.) To soft-soap one (dar coba a).

enjaezar [en-hah-ay-thar'], va. To caparison a horse with rich trappings; to harness.

enjagüe [en-hah'-goo-ay], m. Adjudication required by the creditors of a ship.

enjalbegador, ra [en-hal-bay-gah-dor', rah], m. & f. Whitewasher, a plasterer.

enjalbegadura [en-hal-bay-gah-doo'-rah], f. Act of whitewashing walls.

enjalbegar [en-hal-bay-gar'], va. 1. To whitewash walls. 2. (Met.) To paint, to paint the face.

enjalbiego [en-hal-be-ay'-go], m. Whitewashing.

enjalma [en-hahl'-mah], f. Kind of packsaddle.

enjalmar [en-hal-mar'], va. 1. To put the packsaddle on a horse, 2. To make pack-saddles.

enjalmos [en-hal'-mos], m. (Bot.) Crooked-meadow saxifrage.

enjalmero [en-hal-may'-ro], m. Packsaddle maker.

enjambradera [en-ham-brah-day'-rah], f. 1. (Prov.) Queenbee of a hive. 2. V. CASQUILLA.

enjambradero [en-ham-brah-day'-ro], m. Place where bees collect to form their hives.

enjambrar [en-ham-brar'], va. 1. To gather a scattered swarm of bees. 2. To form a new hive of bees, which left another hive. -vn. To breed a new hive of bees, to produce abundantly.

enjambrazón [en-ham-brah-thone'], f. Generation or swarming of bees.

enjambre [en-hahm'-bray], m. 1. Swarm of bees. 2. Crowd, multitude of people.

enjambrillo [en-ham-breel'-lyo], m. dim. A small swarm of bees.

enjarciadura [en-har-the-ah-doo'-rah], f. The act of rigging a ship.

enjarciar [en-har-the-ar'], va. To put the tackle aboard a ship.

enjardinar [en-har-de-nar'], va. 1. To set and trim the trees as they are in gardens. 2. (Fal.) To put a bird of prey into a meadow or green field.

enjaretado [en-hah-ray-tah'-do], m. (Naut.) Gratings, nettings, a kind of lattice-work between the main and foremast. **Enjaretado de proa,** the beak or head gratings.

enjaretar [en-hah-ray-tar'], va. 1. To draw through a seam. 2. (Met.) To order, to dispose a matter. -vr. (Met. coll.) To creep in by stealth, to be introduced subtly into some place, conversation, etc.

enjaular [en-ha-oo-lar'], va. 1. To cage. 2. (Met.) To imprison, to confine, to mew, to crib, to coop.

enjebar [en-hay-bar'], va. To steep in lye, to buck.

enjebe [en-hay'-bay], m. Lye in which cloth is put to be cleansed or scoured; act of bucking.

enjergar [en-her-gar'], va. (Colt.) To set about a business, to bring a thing on the tapis.

enjero [en-hay'-ro], m. (Prov.) Beam of a plough.

enjertación [en-her-tah-the-on'], f. Insertion, inoculation, budding.

enjertal [en-her-tahl'], m. Nursery of grafted fruit-trees.

enjertar [en-her-tar'], va. V. INJERTAR.

enjerto [en-herr'-to], m. 1. V. INJERTO 2. (Met.) Mixture of diverse things. -pp. irr. of ENJERTAR.

enjorguinar [en-hor-gee-nar'], va. To smear or cover with soot. -vr. To be blackened with soot.

enjoyado [en-ho-yah'-do], a. Bejewelled, set with jewels.

enjoyar [en-ho-yar'], va. 1. To adorn with jewels. 2. To set a ring with diamonds or other precious stones. 3. (Met.) To heighten the lustre and brilliancy of a thing, to give additional splendor.

enjoyelado, da [en-ho-yay-lah'-do, dah], a. Applied to gold or silver used in jewellery.

enjoyelador [en-ho-yay-lah-dor'], m. Enchaser, he who enchases.

enjuagadientes [en-hoo-ah-gah-de-en'-tes], m. (coll.) Mouthful of water or wine for rinsing the mouth after a meal.

enjuagadura [en-hoo-ah-gah-doo'-rah], f. Act of rinsing the mouth.

enjuagar [en-hoo-ah-gar'], va. 1. To rinse the mouth and teeth 2. To rinse clothes.

enjuague [en-hoo-ah'-gay], m. 1. Water, wine, or other liquid, used to rinse the mouth and teeth, and the act of rinsing the mouth with a liquid. 2. Finger-bowl. 3. (Met.) Plot to obtain an object, which cannot be attained openly.

enjugadero [en-hoo-gah-day'-ro], m. 1. V. ENJUGADOR, 1st def. 2. A place in which something is dried.

enjugador, ra [en-hoo-gah-dor', rah]. 1. Drier, one who dries. 2. Round-house for airing linen.

enjugar [en-hoo-gar'], va. 1. To dry in the air or at the fire, to make dry. 2. To wipe on moisture. -vr. To dry up; to grow lean.

enjuiciamiento [en-hoo-ee-the-ah-me-en'-to], m. 1. Preparation of a lawsuit. 2. A judge's charge; legal instruction upon the subject of a suit. **Enjuiciamiento criminal,** trial, criminal prosecution.

enjuiciar [en-hoo-e-the-ar'], va. (Law.) 1. To prepare a lawsuit for judgment (juzgar). 2. To make a pleading. 3. To pass judgment (sentenciar).

enjulio, or **enjullo** [en-hoo'-leo, en-hool'-lyo], m. The clothbeam of a loom.

enjuncar [en-hoon-car'], va. To tie with rush ropes. **Enjuncar un barco,** to ballast a vessel with kentledge or stones.

enjundia [en-hoon'-de-ah], f. 1. Fat in the ovary of fowls, and also the grease or fat of an animal. 2. Substance, force.

enjundioso, sa [en-hoon-de-o'-so, sah], a. Fat, fatty.

enjunque [en-hoon'-kay], m. (Naut.) The heaviest part of a cargo which serves as ballast.

enjuta [en-hoo'-tah], f. (Arch.) 1. Each of the spaces left by a circle inscribed within a square. 2. V. PECHINA.

enjutar [en-hoo-tar'], va. To dry.

enjutez [en-hoo-teth'], f. Dryness, aridity.

enjuto, ta [en-hoo'-to, tah], a. & pp. irr. of ENJUTAR. 1. Dried. 2. Lean, spare, slender. **A pie enjuto,** without pain or labor.

enjutos [en-hoo'-tos], m. pl. 1. Dry brushwood for lighting a fire. 2. Dry crust of bread.

enlabiador, ra [en-lah-be-ah-dor'-rah], m. & f. Wheedler, cajoler, seducer.

enlace [en-lah'-thay], m. 1. Connection or coherence of one thing with another; link, lacing (vinculación). 2. (Met.) Kindred, affinity. **El enlace de las dos familias,** the linking of the two families by marriage. **Enlace telefónico,** telephone link-up.

enlaciar [en-lah-the-ar'], *vn.* To be lax or languid. *-vr.* To wither, to become dry, to decay (plantas, fruta).

enladrillado [en-lah-dril-lyah'-do], *m.* Pavement made of bricks; brickwork. **—Enladrillado, da,** *pp.* of ENLADRILLAR.

enladrillador [en-lah-dril-lyah-dor'], *m.* One who bricks or paves with bricks.

enladrilladura [en-lah-dreel-lyah-doo'-rah], *f.* 1. The act and effect of paving with brick. 2. *V.* ENLADRILLADO.

enladrillar [en-lah-dril-lyar'], *va.* To pave a floor with bricks.

enlamar [en-lah-mar'], *va.* To cover land with slime (inundaciones).

enlanado, da [en-lah-nah'-do, dah], *a.* Covered or supplied with wool.

enlardar [en-lar-dar'], *va.* To rub with grease, to baste. *V.* LARDAR.

enlargues [en-lar'-gays], *m. pl. (Naut.)* Rope-ends fastened to the head of a sail, with which it is tied to the yard.

enlatado [en-lah-tah'-do], *a.* Canned, tinned; *(Mus.)* canned. *-m.* Canning, tinning.

enlatar [en-lah-tar'], *va.* To can, to tin; to pre-record (televisión).

enlazable [en-lah-thah'-blay], *a.* Which can be bound or fastened together.

enlazador, ra [en-lah-thah-dor', rah], *m. & f.* Binder, uniter.

enlazadura [en-lah-thah-doo'-rah], *f. V.* ENLAZAMIENTO.

enlazamiento [en-lah-thah-me-en'-to], *m.* 1. Connection, binding, uniting. 2. *(Met.) V.* ENLACE.

enlazar [en-lah-thar'], *va.* 1. To bind, to join, to unite; to connect 2. To knit, to lace. *-vr.* To link, to be linked; to be connected; to join; to interlock; to entwine; to marry (novios).

enlechuguillado, da [en-lay-choo-gil-lyah'-do, dah], *a.* Applied to one who wears a ruff round the neck.

enlejiar [en-lay-he-ar'], *va.* To make into lye.

enligarse [en-legar'-say], *vr.* To be joined by means of a glutinous substance, to stick, to adhere.

enlistonado [en-lis-to-nah'-do], *m.* Lathing, lath work.

enlistonar [en-lis-to-nar'], *va.* To lath, to batten.

enlizar [en-lee-thar'], *va.* To provide a loom with leashes.

enllantar [en-lyan-tar'], *va.* To rim, to shoe a wheel.

enllentecer [en-lyen-tay-therr'], *va.* To soften, to blandish.

enlodadura [en-lo-dah-doo'-rah], *f.* Act of daubing and filling up with mud.

enlodar [en-lo-dar'], *va.* 1. To bemire, to mire, to soil or bedaub with mud. 2. To stop up a vessel with loam or clay; to lute. 3. *(Met.)* To tarnish one's reputation.

enloquecer [en-lo-kay-ther'], *va.* To enrage, to madden. *-vn.* or *vr.* 1. To madden, to become mad, to become enraged. 2. To be vexed, to be annoyed. 3. To grow barren (árbol). *(Yo enloquezco, yo enloquezca, from Enloquecer. V.* CONOCER.)

enloquecimiento [en-lo-key-the-me-en'-to], *m.* Enraging, maddening.

enlosado [en-lo-sah'-do], *m.* Pavement made of flags; flagging. **-Enlosado, da,** *pp.* of ENLOSAR.

enlosar [en-lo-sar'], *va.* To lay a floor with flags.

enlozanarse [en-lo-thah-nar'-say], *vr.* To boast of one's dexterity or strength.

enlucido da [en-loo-thee'-do, dah], *a.* Whitewashed, plastered. *-m.* Whitewash, coat of plaster.

enlucidor [en-loo-the-dor'], *m.* Whitener.

enlucimiento [en-loo-the-me-en'-to], *m.* 1. The whitewashing of a wall. 2. The scouring of plate.

enlucir [en-loo-theer'], *va.* 1. To whitewash a wall (pared). 2. To scour plate with whiting or chalk. *(Yo enluzco, yo enluzca, from Enlucir.)*

enlustrecer [en-loos-tray-therr'], *va.* To clean, to brighten, to render bright.

enlutar [en-loo-tar'], *va.* 1. To put in mourning (persona). 2. To veil, to cover with a veil (vestido etc.) 3. To darken. *-vr.* To go into mourning.

enmacetar [en-mah-thay-tar'], *va.* To pot, to put in a pot (planta).

enmachambra [en-man-cham-brar'], *va.* To scarf pieces of timber together.

enmaderado [en-mah-day-rah-do], *va.* Timbered; boarded.

enmaderamiento, *m.* **enmaderación,** *f.* [en-mah-day-rah-me-en'-to], Work or cover of wood, wains-cotting.

enmaderar [en-mah-day-rar'], *va.* To roof a house with timber, to floor with boards.

enmadrado [en-mah-drah'-do], *a.* **Está enmadrado,** he's a mama's boy.

enmagrecer [en-mah-gray-therr'], *vn.* To grow lean; to lose fat.

enmalecer [en-mah-lay-therr'], *vn.* To fall sick.

enmallar [en-mahl-lyar'], *va. (Naut.)* To put meshes, to border a net.

enmalletado, da [en-mahl-lyay-tah'-do dah], *a. (Naut.)* Fouled (cables, cuerdas). *V.* ENREDADO.

enmanger [en-mahl-lyay-tar'], *va. (Naut.)* 1. To set partners; to secure masts. 2. *V.* ENDENTAR.

enmalletar [en-man-gar'], *va.* To put a handle to an instrument.

enmantar [en-man-tar'], *va.* To cover with a blanket. *-vr.* To be melancholy (pájaros).

enmarañamiento [en-mah-ra-nyah-me-en'-to], *m.* Entanglement, perplexity.

enmarañar [en-mah-ra-nyar'], *va.* 1. To entangle, to perplex (persona), to involve in difficulties (asunto). 2. *(Met.)* To puzzle, to confound. **Sólo logró enmarañar más el asunto,** he only managed to make a still worse mess of the matter. *-vr.* 1. To get tangled. 2. *(Fig.)* To get more involved; to get into a mess; to get confused.

enmararse [en-mah-rar'-say], *vr. (Naut.)* To get or take sea-room.

enmarcar [en-mar-car'], *va.* 1. To frame (cuadro). 2. *(Fig.)* To fit into a framework, to set in a framework.

enmaridar [en-mah-reel-dar'], *vn.* To marry, to take a husband.

enmarillecerse [en-mah-reel-lyay-therr'-say], *vr.* To become yellow.

enmaromar [en-mah-ro-mar'], *va.* To tie with a rope.

enmascarado, da [en-mas-cah-rah'-do], *m & f.* Masked person.

enmascarar [en-mas-cah-rar'], *va.* 1. To mask, to cover the face with a mask. 2. *(Met.)* To cloak, to give a false appearance. *-vr.* To masquerade, to go in disguise.

enmasillar [en-mah-seel-lyar'], *va.* To putty, to cement.

enmechar [en-may-char'], *va. (Naut.)* To rabbet, to fit and join two pieces of timber.

enmelar [en-may-lar'], *va.* 1. To bedaub or besmear with honey. 2. *(Met.)* To sweeten, to give a pleasing taste.

enmendación [en-men-dah-the-on'], *f.* Emendation, correction.

enmendadamente [en-men-dah-da-men'-tay], *adv.* Accurately, exactly.

enmendado [en-men-dah-dor'], *m.* Corrector, emendator, mender.

enmendar [en-men-dar'], *va.* 1. To correct, to reform (texto). 2. To repair, to compensate (pérdida). 3. *(Law.)* To revoke, to abrogate. 4. To put back a thing in the spot which it had before occupied. *-vr.* To mend, to grow better, to lead a new life. *(Yo enmiendo, yo enmiende, frown Enmendar. V.* ACRECENTAR.)

enmienda [en-me-en'-dah], *f.* 1. Emendation, correction, amendment. 2. Correction, emendation, that which is substituted in the place of something wrong. 3. Reward, premium. 4. *(Law.)* Satisfaction, compensation.

enmohecer [en-mo-ay-therr'], *va.* To mould, to must, to mildew, to make mouldy. *-vr.* 1. To mould, to grow mouldy or musty. 2. To rust, to gather rust (metal).

enmohecido, da [en-mo-ay-thee'-do, dah], *a. & pp.* of ENMOHECER. Musty, mouldy, spoiled with damp.

enmoldado, da [en-mol-dah'-do, dah], *a*. 1. Moulded, cast in a mould. 2. Figured, modelled.

enmollecer [en-mol-lyay-therr'], *va*. To soften, to make tender.

enmondar [en-mon-dar'], *va*. To clear cloth from knots.

enmoquetar [en-mo-kay-tar'], *va*. To carpet.

enmordazar [en-mor-dah-thar'], *va*. To gag. V. AMORDAZAR.

enmudecer [en-moo-day-therr'], *vn*. 1. To grow dumb, to be deprived of speech. 2. To be silent, to be still, -*va*. To impose silence, to hush. -*vr*. To be silent; to remain silent, to say nothing (callarse). *(Yo enmudezco, yo enmudezca,* from *Enmudecer. V.* CONOCER.)

ennatado, da [en-nah-tah'-do, dah], *a*. *(Agr.)* Recuperated: said of a field which has recovered its fertility by lying fallow.

ennegrecer [en-nay-gray-therr'], *va*. 1. To blacken, to make black (poner negro). 2. *(Met.)* To darken, to obscure (oscurecer). -*vr*. -*vn*. To turn black. *(Yo ennegrezco, yo ennegrezca,* from *Ennegrecer. V.* CONOCER.)

ennoblecer [en-no-blay-therr'], *va*. 1. To ennoble, to illustrate, to make noble. 2. *(Met.)* To adorn, to embellish. *(Yo ennoblezco, yo ennoblezca,* from *Ennoblecer. V.* CONOCER.)

ennoblecimiento [en-no-blay-the-me-en'-to], *m*. Ennoblement, the act of ennobling.

ennoviar [en-no-ve-ar'], *vn*. To contract marriage.

ennudecer [en-noo-day-therr'], *vn*. V. ANUDARSE.

enodación [ay-no-dah-the-on'], *f*. Illustration, explanation.

enodio [ay-no'-de-o], *m*. Fawn, a young deer.

enodrida [ay-no-dree'-dah], *a*. Barren (gallinas).

enoema [ay-no-ay'-mah], *f*. Fantastic idea, product of simple conception.

enofobia [ay-no-fo'-be-ah], *f*. Dread of wine.

enófobo, ba [ay-no'-fo-bo, bah], *m*. & *f*. One who hates wine.

enóforo [ay-no'-fo-ro], *m*. 1. A vessel for wine. 2. Name of a handsome statue of Praxiteles. 3. One charged with the service of wines or who used to sell them.

enojadamente [ay-no-hah-dah-men'-tay], *adv*. Fretfully, crossly, peevishly.

enojadizo, za [ay-no-hah-dee'-tho, thah], *a*. Fretful, peevish fractious.

enojado, da [ay-no-hah'-do, dah], *a*. Angry, fretful, peevish, out of humor. -*pp*. of ENOJAR.

enojante [ay-no-hahn'-tay], *pa*. He who vexes.

enojar [ay-no-har'], *va*. 1. To vex, to irritate, to anger, to fret, to make angry (enfadar). 2. To tease, to molest, to trouble. 3. To offend, to displease, to injure. -*vr*. 1. To be fretful or peevish. 2. To be boisterous. 3. To be offended, displeased.

enojo [ay-no'-ho], *m*. 1. Fretfulness, peevishness. 2. Anger, choler, passion (irritación). **Decir con enojo,** to say angrily.

enojosamente [ay-no-ho-sah-men'-tay], *adv*. Vexatiously, crossly.

enojoso, sa [ay-no-ho'-so, sah], *a*. Offensive, vexatious.

enojuelo [ay-no-hoo-ay'-lo], *m*. *dim*. Slight peevishness.

enología [ay-no-lo-hee'-ah], *f*. The art of making wine; enology.

enómetro [ay-no'-may-tro], *m*. Enometer, a hydrometer for determining the alcoholic strength of wines by their specific gravity.

enorgullecer [en-or-gool-lyay-therr'], *va*. To make proud or haughty. -*vr*. To be filled with pride or arrogance. **Enogullecerse de,** to be proud of.

enorgullecimiento [en-or-gool-lyay-the-me-en'-to], *m*. Arrogance, haughtiness.

enorgullecido, da [en-or-gool-lyay-thee'-do, dah], *a*. Haughty, arrogant, very proud.

enorme [ay-nor'-may], *a*. 1. Enormous, vast, huge, mighty, exorbitant. 2. Horrible, crying, grievous. 3. Wicked beyond common measure, heinous. **Delito enorme,** enormity.

enormemente [ay-nor'-may-men-tay], *adv*. Immoderately, enormously, hugely, horridly.

enormidad [ay-nor-me-dahd'], *f*. 1. Enormity, enormousness, monstrousness, exorbitance (inmensidad). 2. Grievousness, horridness, gravity. 3. An enormous deed, an atrocious crime (crimen).

enótera [ay-no'-tay-rah], *f*. *(Bot.)* Enothera, a generic name of plants, typical of the evening primrose family. **enótera bienal,** the evening-primrose. **Enótera florichica,** small-flowered enothera.

enuiciado, da [en-ke-the-ah'-do, dah], *a*. 1. Hung upon hinges. 2. *(Met.)* Built upon a solid foundation. -*pp*. of ENQUICIAR.

enquiciar [en-ke-the-ar'], *va*. To hinge, to put on hinges.

enquillotrarse [en-kil-lyo-trar'-say], *vr*. 1. To be jumbled together. 2. *(coll.)* To fall in love, to be enamoured.

enquimosis [en-ke-mo'-sis], *f*. *(Med.)* A sudden effusion of blood in the cutaneous vessels.

enquiridión [en-ke-re-de-on'], *m*. Compendium, summary, abridgment.

enquistado, da [en-kis-tah'-do, dah], *a*. *(Surg.)* Cysted, encysted.

enquistar [en-kis-tar'], *va*. *(Fig.)* To seal off, to shut off, to enclose. -*vr*. To develop a cyst.

enrabiarse [en-rah-be-ar'-say], *vr*. *(coll.)* To grow furious, to become enraged.

enraigonar [en-ra-he-go-nar'], *va*. *(Prov.)* To fix bassweed in the walls of sheds, for the silkworms to begin to spin.

enraizar [en-rah-e-thar'], *vn*. To take root.

enralecer [en-rah-lay-therr'], *va*. *(Agr.)* 1. To thin plants, to pluck away leaves or branches. 2. To prune.

enramada [en-rah-mah'-dah], *f*. 1. A decoration formed with the branches of trees. 2. A covering of branches for shade, a bower (cobertizo). 3. *(Poet.)* A thicket, a wood. 4. Undergrowth.

enramar [en-rah-mar'], *va*. 1. To cover with branches of trees. 2. To cover the ground with flowers, branches, and aromatic herbs in some festival. 3. *(Naut.)* To mast a vessel.

enranciarse [en-ran-the-ar'-say], *vr*. To grow rancid, to be stale.

enrarecer [en-rah-ray-therr'], *va*. To thin, to rarefy, to extenuate. -*vr*. 1. To become rarefied (aire). 2. To become scarce, to grow rare (escasear). 3. To deteriorate, to become tense (relaciones). *(Yo enrarezco, yo enrarezca,* from *Enrarecer. V.* CONOCER.)

enrarecido [en-rah-ray-the-do], *a*. 1. Rarefied. 2. Tense, difficult (relaciones).

enrarecimiento [en-rah-ray-the-me-en'-to], *m*. Rarefaction.

enrás [en-rahs'], *m*. 1. *(Arch.)* Bed, seat. 2. *(Mas.)* Last or levelling course.

enrasado, da [en-rah-sah'-do, dah], *a*. & *pp*. of ENRASAR. Smoothed, flush. **Puertas enrasadas,** plain doors.

enrasar [en-rah-sar'], *va*. 1. To smooth, to plane. 2. To even, to make even or level, to flush. -*vn*. To be bald.

enrastrar [en-ras-trar'], *va*. *(Prov.)* To string the silk cocoons.

enrayar [en-rah-yar'], *va*. To fix spokes in a wheel.

enredadera [en-ray-dah-day'-rah], *f*. *(Bot.)* 1. A name applied to all twining plants, particularly to the convolvulus, cultivated in gardens. 2. Small bindweed, bell-bind.

enredado, da [en-ray-dah'-do, dah], *a*. 1. Entangled, matted. 2. *(Naut.)* Foul (cables y cuerdas). -*pp*. of ENREDAR.

enredador, ra [en-ray-dah-dor', rah], *m*. & *f*. 1. Entangler, one who entangles, ensnares, or involves in difficulties. 2. Tattler, tale-bearer; busybody (entrometido), intermeddler, gossip (chismoso).

enredar [en-ray-dar'], *va*. 1. To entangle, to ensnare, to hamper, to lime, to knot. 2. To confound, to perplex, to involve in difficulties, to puzzle (asunto). 3. To catch in the net (animal etc.) 4. To lay snares for birds. 5. To sow discord. 6. To fumble, to play childishly. 7. To coil. -*vr*. 1. To tangle or to be entangled (enmarañarse). **No te enredes,** don't you get mixed up in this. **Enredarse de palabras,** to get involved in an argument. 2. *(coll.)* To live in concubinage.

enredo [en-ray'-do], *m.* 1. Entanglement, entangling, ensnaring (lío). 2. Perplexity, embarrassment, puzzle. 3. Complexity, complicateness. 4. Imposition, falsehood, intricate or mischievous lies (mentiras), circumvention. 5. Plot of a play. **Comedia de enredo,** comedy of intrigue.

enredoso, sa [en-ray-do'-so, sah], *a.* Full of snares and difficulties.

enrehojar [en-ray-o-har'], *va.* Among wax-chandlers, to remove the bleached leaves and thin cakes of wax.

enrejado [en-ray-hah'-do], *m.* 1. Trellis (de jardín), lattice (de ventana); grate, grillework. 2. Kind of open embroidery or lace worn by ladies. **Enrejado, da,** *pp.* of ENREJAR.

enrejar [en-ray-har'], *va.* 1. To fix a grating to a window. 2. To fix the ploughshare to the plough. 3. To make a trellis, to grate, to lattice. 4. To wound cattle's feet with a ploughshare.

enrevesado, da [en-ray-vay-sah'-do, dah], *a.* V. REVESADO.

enriado [en-re-ah'-do], *m.* Maceration, retting of flax or hemp.

enriador [en-re-ah-dor'], *m.* One who steeps or submerges.

enriar [en-re-ar'], *va.* To steep hemp and flax in water, in order to macerate its stalky parts; to ret.

enrielar [en-re-ay-lar'], *va.* To make ingots of gold or silver.

enripiado [en-re-pe-ah'-do], *m.* Filling, packing, rubble work.

enripiar [en-re-pe-ar'], *va.* To fill the chinks of a wall with small stones and mortar.

enriquecedor, ra [en-re-kay-thay-dor', rah], *m. & f.* One who enriches.

enriquecer [en-re-kay-therr'], *va.* 1. To enrich, to aggrandize. 2. To adorn. *-vn.* To gain, to grow rich. *-vr.* To get rich; to prosper; to enrich oneself. **Enriquecerse a costa ajena,** to do well at other people's expense. *(Yo enriquezco, yo enriquezca,* from *Enriquecer.* V. CONOCER.)

enriquecimiento [en-re-kay-the-me-ayn'-to], *m.* Enrichment.

enriscado, da [en-ris-cah'-do, dah], *a.* Mountainous, craggy; full of rocks and cliffs. *-pp.* of ENRISCAR.

enriscamiento [en-ris-cah-me-en'-to], *m.* Taking refuge among rocks.

enriscar [en-ris-car'], *va.* To place on the top of mountains or rocks. *(Met.)* To lift, to raise. *-vr.* To take refuge, among rocks.

enristrar [en-ris-trar'], *va.* 1. To couch the lance, or to fix it in the posture of attack. 2. To range, to file, to string (cebollas, ajos). 3. *(Met.)* To go directly to a place, to meet a difficulty. 4. To succeed finally in a difficult matter (dificultad).

enristre [en-rees'-tray], *m.* Act of couching a lance.

enrizamiento [en-re-thah-me-en'-to], *m.* 1. Act of curling. 2. Irritating.

enrizar [en-re-thar'], *va. (Ant. and Amer.)* 1. To curl, to turn into ringlets. 2. To irritate. V. RIZAR.

enrobrescido, da [en-ro-bres-thee'-do, dah], *a.* Hard and strong, like an oak.

enrobustecer [en-ro-boos-tay-therr'], *va.* To make robust.

enrocar [en-ro-dar'], *va.* At chess, to castle the king.

enrodar [en-ro-dar'], *va.* To break on the wheel. *(Yo enruedo, yo enruede,* from *Enrodar.* V. ACORDAR.)

enrodelado, da [en-ro-day-lah'-do, dah], *a.* Armed with a shield.

enrodrigonar [en-ro-dre-go-nar'], *va.* To prop vines with stakes.

enrojar, enrojecer [en-ro-har', en-ro-hay-therr'], *va.* 1. To tinge, to dye, or to give a red color (volver rojo). 2. To put to the blush (persona). *-vn. -vr.* To blush, to redden.

enrojecido, da [en-ro-hay-thee'-do, dah], *a.* Red.

enrollado [en-rol-lyah'-do], *a.* **Un tío muy enrollado,** a thoroughly turned-on guy.

enrollar [en-rol-lyar'], *va.* To wrap a thing within another or round about it (cuerda) *-vr.* 1. To go on a long time (al explicarse). **Cuando se enrolla no hay quien lo pare,** when he gets going there's no stopping him. 2. **Enrollarse en,** to get involved in.

enromar [en-ro-mar'], *va.* To blunt, to dull an edge or point.

enronar [en-ro-nar'], *va. (Prov.)* To throw rubbish in a place

enronquecer [en-ron-kay-therr'], *va.* To make hoarse.*-vn.* To grow hoarse.

enronquecimiento [en-ron-kay-the-me-en'-to], *m.* Hoarseness. V. RONQUERA.

enroñar [en-ro-nyar'], *va.* To fill with scabs or scurf.

enrosar [en-ro-sar'], *va.* To tinge, to dye or give a rose color.

enroscadamente [en-ros-cah-da-men'-tay], *adv.* Intricately.

enroscado [en-ros-cah-do], *a.* 1. Coiled; twisted; kinky. 2. *(And.)* Angry.

enroscadura [en-ros-cah-doo'-rah], *f.* Act of twisting; convolution, sinuosity, twist.

enroscar [en-ros-car'], *va.* 1. To twine, to twist (torcer). 2. To screw in (tornillo). *-vr.* To curl or twist itself.

enrubescer [en-roo-bes-therr'], *va.* To make red.

enrubiador, ra [en-roo-be-ah-dor', rah], *m. & f.* That which has the power of making red.

enrubiar [en-roo-be-ar'], *va.* To tinge, to dye, or give a bright reddish color.

enrubio [en-roo'-be-o], *m.* Rubefaction, reddening.

enrudecer [en-roo-day-therr'], *va.* To weaken the intellect, to make dull.

enruinecer, enruinescer [en-roo-e-nay-therr', en-roo-e-nes-therr'], *vn.* To become vile.

ensabanar [en-sah-ba-nar'], *va.* To wrap up in sheets.

ensacar [en-sah-car'], *va.* To sack up, to inclose or put in a sack.

ensaí [en-sa-hee'], *m. (Naut.)* A clear space between the frames.

ensalada [en-sah-lah'-dah], *f.* 1. Salad, a food of raw herbs, seasoned with salt, oil, vinegar, etc. **Ensalada de patatas,** potato salad. 2. Hodge-podge, medley.

ensaladera [en-sah-lah-day'-rah], *f.* Salad-dish or bowl.

ensaladilla [en-sah-lah-deel'-lyah], *f.* 1. Dry sweetmeats of different sorts and sizes. 2. Jewel made up of different precious stones.

ensalmador, ra [en-sal-mah-dor', rah], *m. & f.* 1. Bonesetter. 2. One who pretends to cure by charms.

ensalmar [en-sal-mar'], *va.* 1. To set dislocated or broken bones (hueso). 2. To enchant, to charm, to bewitch; to cure by spells (enfermedad). **Ensalmar a alguno,** to break the head.

ensalmo [en-sahl'-mo], *m.* Enchantment, spell, charm.

ensalobrarse [en-sah-lo-brar'-say], *vr.* To become putrid and corrupt, as stagnant water.

ensalvajar [en-sal-vah-har'], *va.* To brutalize, to brutify.

ensalzador [en-sal-thah-dor'], *m.* Exalter, praiser, extoller.

ensalzamiento [en-sal-thah-me-en'-to], *m.* Exaltation.

ensalzar [en-sal-thar'], *va.* 1. To extol, to exalt, to aggrandize. 2. To magnify, to exaggerate. *-vr.* To boast, to display one's own worth or actions.

ensambenitar [en-sam-bay-ne-tar'], *va.* To put on the *sambenito,* a gown worn by penitent convicts of the Inquisition.

ensamblado [en-sam-blah-do], *m.* Assembly (coches).

ensamblador [en-sam-blah-dor'], *m.* Joiner, worker in wood.

ensambladura [en-sam-blah-doo'-rah], *f.* 1. Joinery, the trade of a joiner. 2. Art of joining boards, planks, and timbers together.

ensamblaje [en-sam-blah'-hay], *m.* V. ENSAMBLADURA.

ensamblar [en-sam-blar'], *va.* To join or unite pieces of wood; to scarf, to dovetail, to mortise.

ensamble [en-sahm'-blay], *m.* V. ENSAMBLADURA.

ensancha [en-sahn'-chah], *f.* Extension, enlargement. V. ENSANCHE. **Dar ensanchas,** to give too much license or liberty.

ensanchador, ra [en-san-chah-dor', rah], *m. & f.* One who or that which makes a thing larger; stretcher, widener, expander, reamer.

ensanchamiento [en-san-chah-me-en'-to], *m.* 1. Widening, enlarging. 2. Dilation, augmentation.

ensanchar [en-san-char'], *va.* To widen, to extend, to enlarge. **Ensanchar el corazón,** to cheer up, to raise one's spirits, to unburden the mind. *-vr.* 1. To assume an air of importance, to affect grandeur and dignity. 2. To get wider, to spread, to expand.

ensanche [en-sahn'-chay], *m.* 1. Dilatation, augmentation, widening, extension. 2. Gore, a slip of cloth or linen to widen a garment. 3. Suburbs which are joined to the city (de ciudad). 4. Reaming.

ensandecer [en-san-day-therr'], *vn.* To grow crazy, to turn mad.

ensangrentado [en-san-grayn-tah'-do], *a.* Blood-stained; bloody, gory.

ensangrentamiento [en-san-gren-tah-me-en'-to], *m.* Bloodiness.

ensangrentar [en-san-gren-tar'], *va.* To imbrue, to stain with blood. *-vr.* To be too irritated, vexed, in a dispute. *(Yo ensangriento, yo ensangriente,* from *Ensangrentar. V.* ACRECENTAR.)

ensañar [en-sah-nyar'], *va.* To irritate, to enrage. *-vr.* **Ensañarse con,** to vent one's anger on.

ensarnecer [en-sar-nay-therr'], *vn.* To get the itch.

ensarta [en-sar'-tah], *f.* A string (perlas). *V.* SARTA.

ensartar [en-sar-tar'], *va.* 1. To string, to file on a string; to link (cuentas etc.) 2. *(Met.)* To make a string of observations (larga historia). *-vr.* To be shut up in a narrow place; to be piled one upon another.

ensay [en-sah'-e], *m.* Assay, trial, proof.

ensayado, da [en-sah-yah'-do, dah], *a.* Tested, tried, practiced.

ensayador [en-sah-yah-dor'], *m.* 1. Assayer, an officer of the mint. 2. Rehearser, prompter on the stage.

ensayar [en-sah-yar'], *va.* 1. To assay precious metals. 2. To instruct, to teach, to make dexterous. 3. To rehearse, to practise. 4. To examine, to prove, to try, to test(probar). *-vr.* To exercise oneself, or to train oneself by use to any act.

ensaye [en-sah'-yay], *m.* Assay, trial, proof.

ensayo [en-sah'-yo], *m.* 1. Assay, trial, proof (prueba). 2. Rehearsal of a play. **Ensayo general,** dress rehearsal. 3. Essay, a trial, an experiment (experimento), liking. **Viaje de ensayo,** trial run. **Vuelo de ensayo,** test flight. 4. Exercise, preparatory practice (ejercicio). 5. *(Com.)* Sample.

ensebar [en-say-bar'], *va.* To grease, to tallow.

ensedar [en-say-dar'], *va.* To join the thread with the bristle in order to sew shoes.

enseguida [en-say-gee'-dah], *adv.* Straight off; at once, right away. **Enseguida termino,** I've very nearly finished. **enseguida,** at once.

enselvado, da [en-sel-vah'-do, dah], Full of trees. *-pp.* of ENSELVAR.

enselvar [en-sel-var'], *va. V.* EMBOSCAR.

ensenada [en-say-nah'-dah], *f.* Creek, cove, fleet, a small bay.

ensenado, da [en-say-nah'-do, dah], *a.* Having the form of a bay, creek, or gulf. *-pp.* of ENSENAR.

enseña [en-say'-nyah], *f.* Standard, colors, ensign.

enseñable [en-say-nyah'-blay], *a.* Teachable.

enseñado [en-say-nyah'-do], *a.* Trained; informed; educated. **Bien enseñado,** house-trained (perro).

enseñador, ra [en-say-nyah-dor', rah], *m. & f.* Teacher, instructor.

enseñanza [en-say-nyahn'-thah], *f.* 1. Teaching, instruction, doctrine (doctrina), the act of teaching, the way or manner of teaching (acto, profesión). 2. Public instructions. **EnseÑanza primaria,** elementary education. **Enseñanza universitaria,** university education. **Enseñanza programada,** programmed learning.

enseñar [en-say-nyar'], *va.* 1. To teach, to instruct, to lecture, to lesson (asignatura). **Enseñar a uno a hacer algo,** to teach somebody to do something. 2. To show the way

(mostrar), to point out the road (señalar), to lead. **Nos enseñó el museo,** he showed us the museum. **Esto nos enseña las dificultades,** this reveals the difficulties to us. *-vr.* To accustom or habituate oneself; to be inured.

enseño [en-say'-nyo], *m. (coll.) V.* ENSEñANZA.

enseñoreador [en-say-nyo-ray-ah-dor'], *m.* He who domineers.

enseñorear [en-say-nyo-ray-ar'], *va.* To lord, to domineer. *-vr.* To possess oneself of a thing.

enserar [en-say-rar'], *va.* To cover with bassweed.

enseres [en-say'-res], *m. pl.* Chattels (efectos personales), marketable effects, fixtures, furniture, utensils. **Enseres de cocina,** kitchen utensils.

enseriarse [en-say-re-ar'-say], *vr. (Cuba and Amer.)* To become serious, to affect seriousness.

enserpentado, da [en-ser-pen-tah'-do, dah], *a.* Enraged, furious.

enserrinar [en-ser-re-nar'], *va.* To varnish.

ensifoliado, da [en-se-fo-le-ah'-do, dah], *a.* Having sword-shaped or ensiform leaves.

ensiforme [en-se-for'-may], *a.* Ensiform, having the shape of a sword.

ensilaje [en-se-lah'-hay], *m.* Ensilage, the process of preserving green fodder in a silo, and the fodder so stored.

ensilar [en-se-lar'], *va.* To preserve grain in a place under ground.

ensillado, da [en-se-lyah'-do, dah], *a.* Hollow-backed (caballos).*-pp.* of ENSILLAR.

ensilladura [en-sil-lyah-doo'-rah], *f.* The part on which a saddle is placed on a horse or mule.

ensillar [en-sil-lyar'], *va.* 1. To saddle.

ensimismado [en-se-mis-mah'-do], *a.* 1. Selfish. 2. Absorbed in thought.

ensimismarse [en-se-mis-mar'-say], *vr.* To be centred in oneself, to be abstracted.

ensoberbecer [en-so-ber-bay-therr'], *va.* To make proud, to puff up with haughtiness and pride. *-vr.* 1. To become proud and haughty, to be arrogant. 2. *(Naut.)* To become boisterous (mar). *(Yo me ensoberbezco, yo me ensoberbezca,* from *Ensoberbecerse. V.* CONOCER.)

ensoberbecimiento [en-so-ber-bay-the-me-en'-to], *m.* Haughtiness, arrogance, pride.

ensogar [en-so-gar'], *va.* To fasten with a rope.

ensolapar [en-so-lah-par'], *va.* To lap over, to overlap (de solapa).

ensolerar [en-so-lay-rar'], *va.* To fix stools to beehives.

ensolver [en-so-verr'], *va.* 1. To jumble, to mix confusedly together. 2. *(Med.)* To resolve, to discuss, to dissipate.

ensombrecer [en-som-bray-ther'], *va.* 1. To darken. 2. *(Fig.)* To overshadow, to put in the shade. *-vr.* 1. To darken, to get dark. 2. *(Fig.)* To get gloomy.

ensoñar [en-so-nyar'], *va. V.* SOÑAR.

ensopar [en-so-par'], *va.* To make soup by steeping bread in wine.

ensordecedor [en-sor-day-the-dor'], *a.* Deafening.

ensordecer [en-sor-day-therr'], *va.* To deafen, to make deaf, to cause deafness (persona). *-vn.* 1. To grow deaf, to be deprived of hearing. 2. To become silent, to observe silence.

ensordecimiento [en-sor-day-the-me-en'-to], *m.* Deafness, the act of deafening.

ensortijadura [en-sor-te-hah-doo'-rah], *f.* 1. A ring which looms have in the middle of the netting called *perchado.* 2. *(Vet.)* Dislocation.

ensortijamiento [en-sor-te-hah-me-en-to], *m.* Act of curling the hair, or ringing animals.

ensortijar [en-sor-te-har'], *va.* 1. To ring, to form into a ring, to encircle; to curl (pelo). 2. To ring hogs, buffaloes, or other beasts. 3. To fix a ring in (nariz).

ensotarse [en-so-tar'-say], *vr.* To conceal oneself in a thicket.

ensuciador, ra [en-soo-the-ah-dor', rah], *m. & f.* Stainer, defiler.

ensuciamiento [en-soo-the-ah-me-en'-to], *m.* Act of dirtying, staining, or polluting.

ensuciar [en-soo-the-ar'], *va.* 1. To stain, to dirty, to soil, to smear, to file, to daub, to sully, to focal. 2. *(Met.)* To defile, to pollute with vicious habits. *-vr.* To dirty one's bed, clothes, etc.

ensueño [en-soo-ay'-nyo], *m.* Sleep, fantasy. **Una cocina de ensueño,** a dream kitchen. **Mundo de ensueño,** dream world.

entablación [en-tah-blah-the-on'], *f.* A register in churches.

entablado [en-tah-blah'-do], *m.* Floor made of boards. - **Entablado, da,** *pp.* of ENTABLAR

entabladura [en-tah-blah-doo'-rah], *f.* Act of flooring with boards; wains-cotting.

entablamento [en-tah-blah-men'-to], *m.* 1. *(Arch.)* Entablature, entablement. 2. Roof of boards.

entablar [en-tah-blar'], *va.* 1. To cover with boards, to floor with boards. 2. To bring an affair on the tapis, to take the preparatory steps for attaining one's end (conversación). 3. *(coll.)* To claim something without right and with pretence. *(Amer.)* 4. To set up (ajedrez). 5. To enter into (contrato).

entable [en-tah'-blay], *m.* 1. *V.* ENTABLADURA. 2. *(Amer.)* Exaggerated pretence.

entablillado [en-tah-ble-lyah'-do], *m.* *(Surg.)* Splint.

entablillar [en-tah-ble-lyar'], *va.* To secure with small boards, to bind up a broken leg; to splint.

entalamado, da [en-tah-lah-mah'-do, dah], *a.* Hung with tapestry. *-pp.* of ENTALAMAR.

entalamadura [en-tah-lah-mah-doo'-rah], *f.* Awning of a boat, carriage, etc.

entalegar [en-tah-lay-gar'], *va.* To put in a bag or sack.

entalingar [en-tah-lin-gar'], *va.* *(Naut.)* To clinch the cable, to fasten it to the anchor.

entalpía [en-tal-pee'-ah], *f.* Enthalpy.

entallable [en-tal-lyah'-blay], *a.* Capable of being sculptured.

entallado, da [en-tah-lyah'-do, dah], *a.* Close fitting, tight fitting.

entallador [en-tal-lyah-dor'], *m.* 1. Sculptor, a cutter in wood or stone. 2. Engraver. 3. Carter.

entalladura [en-tal-lyah-doo'-rah], *f.* 1. Sculpture, carving (arte, objeto); engraving. 2. Slot (corte), notch, cut, groove.

entallamiento [en-tal-lyah-me-en'-to], *m.* 1. Sculpture, act of sculpturing, carving. 2. Among carpenters, a mortise or groove for receiving a piece. 3. *(Med.)* A deep incision by a cutting instrument.

entallar [en-tal-lyar'], *va.* 1. To sculpture, to carve; to cut figures in wood or stone (esculpir). 2. To engrave, to picture by incisions in copper (gravar). *-vn.* To cut or shape a thing so as to fit it to the body. **Traje que entalla bien,** a suit that fits well.

entalle [en-tahl'-lyay], *m.* The work of a sculptor or engraver; intaglio.

entallecer [en-tal-lyay-therr'], *vn.* To shoot, to sprout (plantas).

entamar [en-tah-mar'], *va.* *(Prov.)* 1. *V.* DECENTAR. 2. In woollen factories to label the cloth which belongs to a purchaser.

entapizado [en-tah-pe-thah'-do], *a.* 1. Upholstered; hung; covered. 2. *(Bot.)* Overgrown. *-m.* *(Mex.)* Wall-coverings, tapestries.

entapizar [en-tah-pe-thar'], *va.* 1. To hang or adorn with tapestry (pared). 2. To upholster (mueble). 3. To cover with fabric (butaca)

entarascar [en-ta-ras-car'], *va.* *(coll.)* To cover with too many ornaments.

entarimado [en-tah-re-mah'-do], *m.* Boarded floor (tablas), parquetry, inlaid floor (taracea).—**Entarimado, da,** *pp.* of ENTARIMAR.

entarimar [en-tah-re-mar'], *va.* To cover a floor with boards.

entarquinar [en-tar-ke-nar'], *va.* To bemire, to cover with mud or mire; to manure land with mud.

entasis [en'-tah-sis], *m.* The increase of diameter which some columns present in their first third: entasis.

ente [en'-tay] *m.* 1. Entity, being. 2. Ridiculous man.

enteco, ca [en-tay'-co, cah], *a.* 1. Infirm, weak, languid. 2. Timid, pusillanimous.

entejado, da [en-tay-hah'-do, dah], *a.* *(Prov.)* Made in the form or shape of tiles.

entelarañarse [en-tay-lah-ra-nyar'-say], *vr.* *(Prov.)* To be clouded or overcast (cielo).

entelequía [en-tay-lay-kee'-ah], *f.* *(Phil.)* Entelechy, (in the philosophy of Aristotle) actuality as opposed to potentiality.

entelerido, da [en-tay-lay-ree'-do, dah] *a.* Fearful (atemorizado), timid.

entena [en-tay'-nah], *f.* *(Naut.)* Lateen yard.

entenada [en-tay-nah'-dah], *f.* A step-daughter, a daughter of a former marriage.

entenado [en-tay-nah'-do], *m.* A stepson, a son of a former marriage.

entenallas [en-tay-nahl'-lyas], *f. pl.* A small hand-vise.

entendederas [en-ten-day-day'-ras], *f. pl.* *(coll.)* Understanding, judgment. **Ser corto de entendederas,** to be pretty dim, to be slow on the uptake. **Sus entendederas no llegan a más,** he has a brain the size of a pea, he's a bird-brain.

entendedor, ra [en-ten-day-dor', rah] *m. & f.* Understander, one who understands.

entender [en-ten-derr'], *va. & vn.* 1. To understand, to comprehend (comprender); to conceive, to relieve, to hear. 2. To remark, to take notice of, to realize (darse cuenta). 3. To reason, to think (creer), to judge. 4. To be employed about or engaged in something. **A mi entender,** in my opinion. **Lo mismo se debe entender este artículo,** the same construction is to be given to this article. **Entenderse con alguno,** to address or correspond with someone. **Tenga usted entendido, I** warn you, or, you must be aware, you must keep in mind. **Sólo me he entendido con él, I** have applied only to, or had correspondence only with him, I have known no other person but him. **No entiendo palabra,** it's Greek to me. **Hacer entender algo a uno,** to make somebody understand something. **Entender de carpintería,** to know all about carpentry. **Ella no entiende de coches,** she's hopeless with cars. *-vr.* 1. To have some motive for doing a thing (tener razones). **Él se entiende,** he knows what he is about. 2. To agree or be agreed. 3. To understand each other (dos personas). **Entender de alguna cosa,** to be skilful in anything. **Entenderse con alguna cosa,** to take the charge or management of a chair. **Ya te entiendo,** I know your intention. **Se entiende que…,** it is undertood that… **Entenderse con una mujer,** to have an affair with a woman. *(Yo entiendo, yo entienda,* from *Entender. V.* ATENDER.)

entendidamente [en-ten-de-dah-men'-tay], *adv.* Knowingly, prudently.

entendido, da [en-ten-dee'-do, dah], *a.* Wise (sabio), learned, prudent, knowing. **Darse por entendido,** to manifest by signs or words that the thing is understood; to answer any attention or compliment in the customary manner. **Tenemos entendido que…,** we understand that… **Según tenemos entendido,** as far as we can gather. **Según el juicio de los entendidos,** in the opinion of those who know.

entendimiento [en-ten-de-me-en'-to], *m.* 1. Understanding (comprensión), knowledge, judgment, mind (inteligencia); conceiving. 2. Explanation, illustration.

entenebrecer [en-tay-nay-bray-therr'], *va.* To obscure, to darken.

enténola [en-tay'-no-lah], *f.* *(Naut.)* A spare spar.

enteomanía [en-tay-o-mah-nee'-ah], *f..* A kind of religious insanity, which consists in believing oneself inspired by Heaven.

enterado [en-tay-rah'-do], *a.* 1. Knowledgeable; well-informed. **Estar enterado,** to be informed. **No darse por enterado,** to pretend not to understand. *-m. f.* Know-all.

enteralgia [en-tay-rahl'-ge-ah], *f.* Enteralgia, neuralgia of the intestines.

enteramente [en-tay-rah-men'-tay], *adv.* Entirely, fully, completely, full; clear, clean; quite.

enterar [en-tay-rar'], *va.* 1. To inform thoroughly, to acquaint, to instruct, to give intelligence. 2. *(Amer.)* To complete, to make entire, -*vr.* To find out, to get to know. **Enterarse de,** to find out about. **Seguir sin enterarse,** to remain ignorant. **Ya me voy enterando,** I'm beginning to understand.

entereza [en-tay-ray'-thah], *f.* 1. Entireness, integrity. 2. Rectitude, uprightness; perfection. 3. Fortitude, firmness. **Entereza virginal,** virginity.

enteritis [en-tay-ree'-tis], *f. (Med.)* Enteritis, inflammation of the mucous coat of the bowels.

enterizo, za [en-tay-ree'-tho, thah], *a.* Entire, complete; of one piece.

enternecedor, ra [en-ter-nay-the-dor', rah], *a.* Compassionate, pitiful.

enternecer [en-ter-nayt-herr'], *va.* 1. To soften, to make fonder or soft, to melt, to affect. 2. *(Met.)* To move to compassion. -*vr.* To be moved to compassion, to pity, to commiserate, to be affected. *(Yo enternezco, yo enternezca, from Enternecer. V.* CONOCER.)

enternecidamente [en-ter-nay-the-dah-men'-tay], *adv.* Compassionately.

enternecimiento [en-ter-nay-the-me-en'-to], *m.* Compassion, pity, melting.

entero, ra [en-tay'-ro, rah], *a.* 1. Entire, undiminished. 2. Perfect, complete. 3. Sound, without a flaw. 4. Just, right. 5. Honest, upright, pure, uncorrupted (honesto). 6. Strong, robust, vigorous. 7. Informed, instructed. 8. Uncastrated. 9. Strong, coarse (ropa de casa). 10. *(Arith.)* Whole. **Números enteros,** whole numbers. 11. Constant, firm. **Por entero,** entirely, fully, completely. -*m.* 1. *(Mat.)* Integer, whole number. 2. *(Com, Fin.)* Point. **Las acciones han subido dos enteros,** the shares have gone up two points.

enterorrafia [en-tay-ror-rah'-fe-ah, *f.* Enterorraphy, a suture for maintaining the edges of a wound of the intestines.

enterótomo [en-tay-ro'-to-mo], *m.* Enterotome.

enterrado [en-tayr-rah'-do], *a.* Buried; ingrowing (uña).

enterrador [en-ter-rah-dor'], *m.* 1. Gravedigger, burier, sexton. 2. The sexton beetle; necrophorus.

enterraje [en-ter-rah'-hay], *m.* In foundries, a bank of earth around a mould.

enterramiento [en-ter-rah-me-en'-to], *m.* 1. Interment, burial, funeral. 2. Tomb, burying place.

enterrar [en-ter-rar'], *va.* 1. To inter, to bury. 2. *V.* SOBREVIVIR.

enterronar [en-ter-ro-nar'], *va.* To cover with clods.

entesamiento [en-tay-sah-me-en'-to], *m.* The act of stretching, the effect of being stretched, fullness.

entesar [en-tay-sar'], *va.* To extend, to stretch out, to give greater force or vigor to a thing.

entestado, da [en-tes-tah'-do, dah], *a.* Obstinate, stubborn.

entibador [en-te-bah-dor'], *m.* One who shores up mines.

entibar [en-te-bar'], *vn.* To rest, to lean upon.-*va.* To prop, to shore up mines.

entibiadero [en-te-be-ah-day'-ro], *m.* Cooler, a bath in which something is cooled.

entibiar [en-te-be-ar'], *va.* 1. To cool, to make cool, to damp. 2. To temper, to moderate the passions. -*vr. (Met.)* To become cool, to slacken, to relax, to languish.

entibo [en-tee'-bo], *m.* 1. Stay, prop, shore. 2. Foundation.

entidad [en-te-dahd'], *f.* 1. Entity, a real being. 2. *(Met.)* Consideration, extimation, value, moment, consequence, import, matter, importance.

entierro [en-teer'-ro], *m.* 1. Burial, interment (acto), funeral (funeral). **Asistir al entierro,** to go to the funeral. 2. Tomb, grave (tumba), sepulture. *(Yo entierro, yo entierre, from Enterrar. V.* ACERTAR.)

entigrecerse [en-te-gray-therr'-say], *vr.* To be as enraged or furious as a tiger.

entimema [en-te-may'-mah], *f.* Enthymem, a syllogism which consists of two propositions.

entinar [en-te-nar'], *va.* 1. To tinge, to color. 2. To put wool into the clearing bath.

entintar [en-tin-tar'], *va.* 1. To stain with ink (manchar). 2. To tinge or give a different color.

entiznar [en-teeth-nar'], *va.* To revile, to defame. *V.* TIZNAR.

entoldado [en-tol-dah'-do], *m.* An awning.—**Entoldado, da,** *pp.* of ENTOLDAR.

entoldamieto [en-tol-dah-me-en'-to], *m.* Act of covering with an awning.

entoldar [en-tol-dar'], *va.* 1. To cover with an awning (cubrir con toldo). 2. To hang walls with cloths or silks (decorar). -*vr.* 1. To dress pompously. 2. To grow cloudy or overcast.

entomizar [en-to-me-thar'], *va.* To tie bass cords around posts or laths, that the plaster may stick to them.

entomófago, ga [en-to-mo'-fah-go, gah], *a.* Insectivorous, entomophagous.

entomófilo, la [en-to-mo'-fe-lo, lah], *a.* Entomophilous, fond of insects.

entomología [en-to-mo-lo-hee'-ah], *f.* Entomology.

entomológicamente [en-to-mo-lo'-he-cah-men-tay], *adv.* Entomologically.

entomológico, ca [en-to-mo-lo'-he-co, cah], *a.* Entomological, relating to the study of insects.

entomologista [en-to-mo-lo-hees'-tah], *m.* or **entomólogo,** *m.* An entomologist.

entomostráceo, cea [en-to-mos-trah'-thay-o, ah], *a.* Entomostracan.-*m. pl.* The entomostracans.

entonación [en-to-nah-the-on'], *f.* 1. Modulation, intonation. 2. The act of blowing the bellows of an organ. 3. *(Met.)* Haughtiness, presumption, pride.

entonadera [en-to-nah-day'-rah], *f.* The blow-lever of an organ.

entonado [en-to-nah'-do], *m.* The process of toning in photography.

entonado, da [en-to-nah'-do, dah], *a. & pp.* of ENTONAR. Haughty, puffed with pride (orgulloso).

entonador [en-to-nah-dor'], *m.* 1. Organ-blower. 2. One who tunes the first verse of a psalm. 3. One that sets the tune. 4. *(Med.)* A tonic.

entonamiento [en-to-nah-me-en'-to], *m.* 1. *V.* TONO. 2. Intoning. 3. Arrogance, haughtiness.

entonar [en-to-nar'], *va.* 1. To tune to modulate, to intonate (canción) 2. To commence or set a tune. 3. *(Pict.)* To harmonize colors. *(Phot.)* To tone prints. 4. To blow the bellows of an organ (órgano). 5. *(Med.)* To strengthen the muscular fibers by means of tonic medicines. -*vr. (Met.)* To grow haughty, to be puffed up with pride; to look big.

entonatorio [en-to-nah-to'-re-o], *m.* A book of sacred music used in Catholic churches.

entonces [en-ton'-thes], *adv.* Then, at that time, on that occasion. **Desde entonces,** since then. **Las costumbres de entonces,** the customs of the time. **Fue entonces que…,** it was then that… **No fue hasta entonces,** it wasn't till then.

entonelar [en-to-nay-lar'], *va.* To barrel.

entono [en-toh'-no], *m.* 1. The act of intoning. 2. *V.* ENTONACIÓN. 3. *(Met.)* Arrogance, haughtiness, pride.

entontecer [en-ton-tay-therr'], *va.* To mope, to fool, to craze. -*vn. & vr.* To grow foolish, to be stupid. *(Yo me entontezco, yo me entontezca, from Entontecerse. V.* CONOCER.)

entontecimiento [en-ton-tay-the-me-en'-to], *m.* Act of growing foolish or stupid.

entorchado [en-tor-chah'-do], *m.* A twisted gold or silver cord, for embroideries. **Entorchados,** cords for a musical instrument covered with silver wire, bass strings.

entorchar [en-tor-char'], *va.* 1. To twist a cord. 2. To cover cords for musical instruments with wire.

entorilar [en-to-re-lar'], *va.* To put the bull in the *toril,* or stall.

entornar [en-tor-nar'], *va.* To turn, to half-close (ojos); to half-close (puerta); to upset (volcar).

entornillar [en-tor-nil-lyar'], *va.* To make something in the form of a screw or ring.

entorno [en-tor'-no], *m.* Setting, milieu, ambience; climate; scene. **El entorno cultural,** the cultural scene.

entorpecer [en-tor-pay-therr'], *va.* 1. To benumb (entendimiento), to dampen, to render torpid (aletargar). 2. To stupefy, to obscure the understanding. (*Yo me entorpezco, yo me entorpezca,* from *Entorpecerse.* V. CONOCER.

entorpecimiento [en-tor-pay-the-me-en'-to], *m.* 1. Torpor, benumbedness, numbness, stupefaction, dullness. 2. Stupidity, thickness.

entortadura [en-tor-tah-doo'-rah], *f.* Crookedness, curvity.

entortar [en-tor-tar'], *va.* 1. To bend, to make crooked. 2. To pull out an eye.

entortijar [en-tor-te-har'], *va.* V. ENSORTIJAR.

entosigar [en-to-se-gar'], *va.* V. ATOSIGAR.

entozoario, ria [en-to-tho-ah'-re-o, ah], *a. & n.* Entozoarian, entozoic; entozoa.

entrada [en-trah'-dah], *f.* 1. Entrance, entry (lugar). 2. Entrance, entry, coming in, ingress (acto). **La entrada de las tropas en 1940,** the entry of the troops in 1940. **Su entrada en la Academia,** his admission to the Academy. 3. Entrance, prerogative of certain authorities to enter places forbidden to the public (público). 4. Beginning of a musical clause. 5. Entry, the act of publicly entering a city. 6. The act of admitting a person into a community or society. 7. Concourse of people. **Hubo una grande entrada aquel día en la comedia,** the play-house was crowded on that day. 8. Entrance fee, admission, ticket (billete). **Entrada de regalo,** complimentary ticket. 9. The means or power to do something. 10. Familiar access, intimacy. 11. *(Naut.)* The rising, beginning of a wind, a soft breeze, or a storm. 12. A good hand at cards. 13. Each of the more substantial dishes which are served at table (comidas). 14. Receipts, property vested in any concern. **Derechos de entrada,** import duty. **Entradas,** temples, the upper parts of the sides of the head. 15. **Entrada furtiva en una casa, forzándola para robar,** *(Law.)* burglary. 16. Beginning. **La entrada de la primavera,** the start of spring. 17. *(Fin.)* Receipts, takings; income. **Entradas familiares,** family income. **Entradas brutas,** gross receipts. **Entradas y salidas,** income and expenditure. **Entrada de reloj (validación, muestreo),** *(Inform.)* clock input, enable, strobe.

entradero [en-trah-day'-ro], *m. (Prov.)* A narrow entrance.

entrado [en-trah'-do], *a.* 1. **Entrado en años,** elderly, advanced in years. 2. **Hasta muy entrada la noche,** until late at night.

entramado [en-tra-mah'-do], *m. (Carp.)* Framework, studwork, bay-work.

entramar [en-tra-mar'], *va.* To make stud-work, framework.

entrambos, bas [en-trahm'-bos, bas], *pron. pl.* Both. V. AMBOS.

entrampar [en-tram-par'], *va.* 1. To entrap, to ensnare, to catch in a trap. 2. *(Met.)* To involve in difficulties, to perplex. 3. To ensnare, to deceive; to noose, to circumvent, to hamper. 4. *(Met.)* To encumber an estate with debts, to contract debts. -*vr.* To borrow money, to become indebted.

entrante [en-trahn'-tay], *pa.* 1. Entering, coming in. **El mes entrante,** the coming month.-*m.* One who is entering (persona). 2. The coming month. - *m & pl.* **Entrantes y salientes,** people coming to and leaving a house.

entraña [en-trah'-nyah], *f.* An entrail, a bowel, any principal organ or part which has an appropriate use; very seldom used in the singular in either language. -*pl.* 1. Entrails, bowels. 2. *(Met.)* Entrails, the internal parts of anything; center of a city, heart of a country. 3. *(Met.)* Mind, affection (sentimientos); disposition (temperamento); idiosyncrasy. 4. The inmost recess of something. **Dar las entrañas,** or **dar hasta las entrañas,** to give one's very heart-blood away. **Esto me llega a las entrañas,** that goes to my heart.

entrañable [en-trah-nyah'-blay], *a.* Intimate, affectionate (afectuoso), charming (simpático).

entrañablemente [en-trah-nyah-blay-men'-tay], *adv.* Affectionately.

entrañar [en-trah-nyar'], *vn.* To penetrate to the core, to know profoundly. -*vr.* 1. To contract intimacy and familiarity. 2. V. EMBUTIR. *(Naut.)*

entrapada [en-trah-pah'-dah], *f.* A coarse crimson cloth.

entrapajar [en-trah-pah-har'], *va.* To tie with rags.

entrapar [en-trah-par'], *va.* 1. To powder the hair to clean it. 2. *(Agr.)* To put woollen rags to the roots of plants, as manure. -*vr.* To be covered with dust.

entrar [en-trar'], *va. & vn.* 1. To enter, to go in, to march in, to come in and *fig.,* to penetrate. 2. To inclose one thing in another, to introduce it (objeto). 3. To commence, to begin, to win a trick at cards. 4. To undertake. 5. *(Geog.)* To disembogue, to join (ríos). 6. To thrust or put one thing upon another. 7. To take possession of a place by force of arms. 8. To set down, or place to account. **Entrar en una partida de trigo, lana, etc.,** to purchase a quantity of wheat, wool, etc. 9. To be classed or ranked, to conduce, or to be employed for some end (número de cosas). 10. Followed by the prepositions *a* or *en,* it signifies to begin or commence, as, **entrar a cantar,** to begin to sing in concert. **Entrar en recelo,** to begin to suspect. **Este abrigo no entra en la maleta,** this coat doesn't fit in the suitcase. **Entrar de por medio,** to settle a scuffle, to adjust, to reconcile disputants. 11. To dedicate or consecrate oneself to something. 12. To find place, to take possession of the mind (pasión, afecto). 13. In fencing to advance a step. 14. *(Naut.)* To gain upon a vessel steering the same course, to begin to rise (la marea) or to blow (el viento). **Entrar bien alguna cosa,** to come to the point. **Entrar dentro de sí** or **en sí mismo,** to reflect upon one's own conduct in order to improve it. **No entrar (a alguno) alguna cosa,** not to believe a thing; to have a repugnance for it. **Entrar y salir,** to be clever in business or conversation. **Entrar como por su casa,** to fit loosely. **Juan entró tercero,** John came in third. **El paquete no entra en el saco,** the parcel won't go into the bag. **Entrar en detalles,** to go into details. **Le entraron deseos de,** he felt a sudden urge to. **Estos zapatos no me entran,** these shoes don't fit. **No me entra la lógica,** I can't get the hang of logic. **La letra con sangre entra,** those who would succeed must work with a will. **Me entra por un oído y por el otro me sale,** it goes in one ear and out of the other.

entre [en'-tray], *prep.* 1. Between (dos cosas). **Entre año, semana, día, etc.,** in the course of the year, week, day; etc. **Entre dos aguas,** wavering, irresolute. **Trae a uno entre dientes,** to take a dislike to somebody. 2. In, or in the number of things, among (más de dos cosas). **Entre tanto,** in the interim. **Entre manos,** in hand. **Traer una cosa entre manos,** to be doing something. **Tomar entre manos,** to take in hand. 3. In composition with another word it weakens or limits the signification, as **entrefino,** middling fine. **Lo cogió entre sus manos,** he took it in his hands. **Dicho sea entre nosotros,** between ourselves. **Estaba entre la vida y la muerte,** he was at death's door. **Entre tanto,** meanwhile, in the meantime. **Entre el ruido y el calor no he dormido,** what with the noise and the heat I didn't sleep. **Entre todos había 30 personas,** there were 30 people all together.

entreabierto [en-tray-ah-be-ayr'-to], *a.* Half-open; ajar.

entreabrir [en-tray-ah-breer'], *va.* To half open a door, to leave it ajar.

entreacto [en-tray-ahc'-to], *m.* Interval.

entreancho, cha [en-tray-ahn'-cho, chah], *a.* Neither wide nor narrow.

entrecalle [en-tray-cahl'-lyay], *m.* Clear between two mouldings, quirk.

entrecanal [en-tray-cah-nahl'], *f. (Arch.)* Space between the striae or flutings of a column.

entrecano, na [en-tray-cah'-no, nah], *a.* Between black and gray, grayish (pelo, barba).

entrecava [en-tray-cah'-vah], *f.* A very shallow digging.

entrecavar [en-tray-cah-var'], *va.* To dig shallow, not to dig deep.

entrecejo [en-tray-thay'-ho], *m.* 1. The space between the eyebrows. 2. A frowning, supercilious look, show of annoyance. **Arrugar el entrecejo,** to frown.

entrecerca [en-tray-ther'-cah], *f.* Space between inclosures.

entrecielo [en-tray-the-ay'-lo], *m.* Awning. V. TOLDO.

entreclaro, ra [en-tray-clah'-ro, rah], *a.* Slightly clear.

entrecogedura [en-tray-coh-ay-doo'-rah], *f.* Act of catching.

entrecoger [en-tray-co-herr'], *va.* 1. To catch, to intercept. 2. To compel by arguments or threats.

entrecomillar [en-tray-co-mel-lyar'], *va.* To place in inverted commas, to put inverted commas, quotes.

entrecoro [en-tray-co'-ro], *m.* Space between the choir and the chief altar; chancel.

entrecortado, da [en-tray-cor-tah'-do, dah], *a.* 1. *(Med.)* Short of breath, dyspneal (respiración). 2. *(Geol.)* Broken.

entrecortadura [en-tray-cor-tah-doo'-rah], *f.* Cut made in the middle of anything without dividing it.

entrecortar [en-tray-cor-tar'], *va.* To cut a thing in the middle without dividing (cortar).

entrecorteza [en-tray-cor-tay'-thah], *f.* An imperfection in timbers through the union of the branches to the trunk, with interior defects.

entrecot [en-tray-cot'], *m. (Culin.)* Sirloin steak.

entrecriar [en-tray-cre-ar'], *va.* To rear plants among others.

entrecruzar [en-tray-croo-thar'], *va.* To interlace, to interweave. -*vr. (Bio.)* To interbreed.

entrecubiertas, entrepuentes [en-tray-coo-be-err'-tas, en-tray-poo-en'-tes], *m. & f. pl. (Naut.)* Between decks.

entrecuesto [en-tray-coo-es'-to], *m.* Back-bone.

entredecir [en-tray-day-theer'], *va.* To interdict, to prohibit.

entredicho [en-tray-dee'-cho], *m.* 1. Interdiction, prohibition. **Estar en entredicho,** to be under a ban (prohibido). 2. Ecclesiastical censure or interdict.—**Entredicho, cha,** *pp. irr.* of ENTREDECIR.

entredoble [en-tray-do'-blay], *a.* Neither double nor single.

entredós [en-tray-dose'], *m.* 1. A strip of lace between two hems; insertion. 2. The size of type called long primer. 3. *(Arch.)* The keystone of an arch. Plancher.

entrefino, na [en-tray-fee'-no, nah], *a.* Middling fine.

entreforro [en-tray-for'-ro], *m.* 1. Doublet, waistcoat, jerkin. 2. *(Naut.)* Parceling, a canvas wrapping, usually tarred, applied to protect a rope.

entrega [en-tray'-gah], *f.* 1. Delivery, the act of delivering, conveyance. **Entrega contra reembolso,** cash on delivery. **Hacer entrega de,** to hand over. 2. Part, installment (novela); part, number, fascicule (revista).

entregadamente [en-tray-gah-dah'-men-tay], *adv.* Really, perfectly.

entregadero, ra [en-tray-gah-day-ro, rah], *a. (Com.)* To be supplied; deliverable.

entregado [en-tray-gah'-do], *a.* Committed, devoted. **Entregado a,** absorbed in. **Entregado en,** committed to.

entregador [en-tray-gah-dore'], *m.* 1. Deliverer. 2. Executor.

entregamiento [en-tray-gah-me-en'-to], *m.* Delivery.

entregar [en-tray-gar'], *va.* 1. To deliver, to put into the hands of another (dar), to give, to give way, or to give up (ceder): *(Com.)* to transfer, to pay. **Entregar algo a un abogado,** to refer something to a lawyer. **No quiso entregármelo,** he refused to hand it over to me. 2. To insert by the point or sidewise, part of one body into another. -*vr.* 1. To deliver oneself up into the hands of another. **Entregarse a vicios,** to abandon oneself to vices. 2. To devote oneself wholly to something (dedicarse). **A entregar,** to be supplied; supply expected.

entregerir [en-tray-hay-reer'], *va.* To insert, to intermix.

entrego [en-tray'-go], *m.* Delivery.

entrejuntar [en-tray-hoon-tar'], *va.* To nail or join the panels of a door to the crossbars or ledges.

entrelazado [en-tray-lah-tha'-do], *a.* Entwined, interlaced; criss-crossed; interlocking.

entrelazar [en-tray-lah-thar'], *va.* To interlace, to intermix, to interweave, to entwine. -*vr.* To entwine, to interlace; to interlock.

entreliño [en-tray-lee'-nyo], *m.* Space of ground between the rows of vines or olives.

entrelistado, da [en-tray-lis-tah'-do, dah], *a.* Striped or variegated.

entrelucir [en-tray-loo-theer'], *vn.* To glimmer, to shine faintly (relucir). *(Yo entreluzco, yo entreluzca,* from *Entrelucir.* V. DESLUCIR).

entremedias [en-tray-may'-de-as], *adv.* In the meantime.

entremés [en-tray-mess'], *m.* 1. A playlet, an interlude, entertainment. 2. Entrée, side dish. **Entremés salado,** savory. **Entreméses,** hors d'oeuvres.

entremesear [en-tray-may-say-ar'], *va.* To act a part in a farce or interlude.

entremesista [en-tray-may-sees'-tah], *m.* Player of farces or interludes.

entremeter [en-tray-may-terr'], *va.* 1. To put one thing between others. 2. To put on a clean cloth without undressing children, or taking off the swaddling clothes. -*vr.* 1. To thrust oneself into a place without being called or invited. 2. To take charge of. 3. To intermeddle, to meddle, to pry, to interpose officiously.

entremetido [en-tray-may-tee'-do], *m.* Meddler, obtruder, intermeddler; a busy-body, a go-between.

entremetido, da [en-tray-may-tee'-do, dah], *a. & pp.* of ENTREMETER. Meddling or intermeddling, officious, meddlesome.

entremetimiento [en-tray-may-te-me-en'-to], *m.* Interposition, interjection, intermeddling, meddlesomeness, obtrusion.

entremezcladura [en-tray-meth-clah-doo'-rah], *f.* Intermixture.

entremezclar [en-tray-meth-clar'], *va.* To interweave, to intermix.

entremiso [en-tray-mee'-so], *m.* A long bench on which cheeses are formed.

entremorir [en-tray-mo-reer'], *vn.* To die away by degrees, to be nearly extinguished (llama).

entrenador, ra [en-tray-nah-dor', rah], *m. & f.* Coach, trainer, instructor, instructress.

entrenamiento [en-tray-nah-me-ayn'-to], *m.* Training, coaching.

entrenar [en-tray-nar'], *va. (Dep.)* To train, to coach; to exercise (caballo). **Estar entrenado,** to be in training. -*vr.* To train.

entrencar [entren-car'], *va.* To put rods in a beehive.

entrenervios [en-tray-nerr'-ve-ose], *m. pl.* Among bookbinders the spaces between the bands of the back of a book.

entrenudos [en-tray-noo'-dos], *m. pl. (Bot.)* Internodes, the spaces between the nodes of a stem.

entrenzar [en-tren-thar'], *va.* To plait hair.

entreoír [en-tray-o-eer'], *va.* To hear without perfectly understanding what is said. *(Yo entreoigo, yo entreoiga; él entreoiga, entreoyera;* from *Entreoír.* V. OÍR).*

entreordinario, ria [en-tray-or-de-nah'-re-o, ah], *a.* Middling, between good and bad.

entrepalmadura [en-tray-pal-mah-doo'-rah], *f. (Vet.)* Disease in horses, hoofs.

entrepanes [en-tray-pah'-nes], *m. pl.* Pieces of unsown ground between others that are sown.

entrepañado, da [en-tray-pa-nyah'-do, dah], *a.* Composed of several panels (puertas).

entrepaño [en-tray-pah'-nyo], *m.* 1. Panel. 2. Space between pilasters. 3. Pier.

entreparecerse [en-tray-pa-ray-therr'-say], *vr.* 1. To be transparent, to shine through. 2. To have traces of resemblance to some other thing, to be like.

entrepechuga [en-tray-pay-choo'-gah], *f.* Small piece of flesh on the breast of birds.

entrepeines [en-tray-pay'-e-nes], *m. pl.* The wool which remains in the comb after combing.

entrepelado, da [en-tray-pay-lah'-do, dah], *a.* Spotted with white upon a dark ground, pied (colores de mulas y caballos).

entrepelar [en-tray-pay-lay'], *va.* To variegate hair, or mix it with different colors.

entrepernar [en-tray-per-nar'], *vn.* To put legs between those of others for ease in sitting.

entrepiernas [en-tray-pe-er'-nas], *f. pl.* 1. Opening between the legs; the inner surface of the thighs. 2. Pieces put into the fork of a pair of breeches.

entreponer [en-tray-po-nerr'], *va.* To interpose.

entrepretado, da [en-tray-pray-tah'-do, dah], *a. (Vet.)* Applied to a mule or horse with a weak breast or shoulder.

entrepuentes [en-tray-poo-en'-tes], *m. pl. (Naut.)* Between decks.

entrepunta [en-tray-poon'-tah], *f.* One of the pieces of a crane.

entrepuzadura [en-tray-poon-thah-doo'-rah], *f.* Pricking pain of an unripe tumor.

entrerrenglón [en-tray-ren-glone'], *m.* Interline, space between lines.

entrerenglonadura [en-tray-ren-glo-nah-doo'-rah], *f.* Something written within lines: interlineal note.

entrerenglonar [en-tray-ren-glo-nar'], *va.* To interline.

entresaca, entresacadura [en-tray-sah'-cah, en-tray-sah-cah-doo'-rah], *f.* 1. The act of cutting down trees, in order to thin a wood. 2. Selection of branches at the time of pruning.

entresacar [en-tray-sah-car'], *va.* 1. To pick or choose out of a number or parcel of things (seleccionar). 2. *(Agr.)* To cut away branches of trees, to make a clearing. 3. To clip hair close to the head.

entrescuro, ra [en-tres-coo'-ro, rah], *a. (Prov.)* Somewhat obscure.

entresemana [en-tray-say-mah'-nah], *f.* Midweek; working days of the week. **Cualquier día de entresemana,** any day midweek.

entresijo [en-tray-see'-ho], *m.* 1. Mesentery (mesenterio); secret, mystery (misterio). **Tener muchos entresijos,** to be very complicated. 2. *(Met.)* Something occult, hidden (parte oculta).

entresuelo [en-tray-soo-ay'-lo], *m.* A small room between two stories; floor between the first floor and the second floor; entresol, mezzanine.

entresurco [en-tray-soor'-co], *m.* Space between furrows.

entretalla, entretalladura [en-tray-tahl'-lyah, en-tray-tallyah-doo'-rah], *f.* Sculpture in bas-relief.

entretallar [en-tray-tal-lyar'], *va.* 1. To sculpture or carve in bas-relief. 2. To cut, to slash, or to mangle. 3. *(Met.)* To intercept or obstruct the passage.

entretanto [en-tray-tahn'-tao], *a.* Meanwhile, meantime. *-m.* Meantime. *-conj.* **Entretanto esto se produce,** until this happens.

entretejedura [en-tray-tay-hay-doo'-rah], *f.* Intertexture, a work interwoven with another.

entretejer [en-tray-tay-herr'], *va.* 1. To tissue, to variegate. 2. To interweave, to intermix, to knit. 3. To insert words, verses, etc., in a book or writing.

entretejimiento [en-tray-tay-he-me-en'-to], *m.* Intertexture, interweaving; variegation.

entretela [en-tray-tay'-lah], *f.* Interlining (sastrería).

entretelar [en-tray-tay-lar'], *va.* To put buckram between the lining and cloth.

entretenedor [en-tray-tay-nay-dor'], *m.* Entertainer, he that pleases, diverts, or amuses.

entretener [en-tray-tay-nerr'], *va.* 1. To feed or to keep in hope or expectation. 2. To allay pain, to make less troublesome. 3. To amuse (distraer), to entertain (divertir). 4. To delay (demorar), to put off, to postpone (aplazar). **Nos entretuvo en conversación,** he engaged us in conversation. *-vr.* To amuse oneself. (*Yo entretengo, yo entretuve; yo entretenga, entretuviera;* from *Entrener.* V. TENER.)

entretenido, da [en-tray-tay-nee'-do, dah], *a.* 1. Entertaining, pleasant, amusing. 2. Doing business in an office, in hopes of obtaining a place. 3. *(Naut.)* The prisoner who cannot set foot on land. **Dar a uno con la entretenida,** to put one off with excuses, for not giving what is asked for, *-pp.* of ENTRETENER.

entretenimiento [en-tray-tay-ne-me-en'-to], *m.* 1. Amusement, entertainment. **Es un entretenimiento más,** it's just an amusement. 2. Pay, allowance, appointment. 3. Delay, procrastination. 4. Game or sport of any kind, fun, jest, joke.

entretiempo [en-tray-te-em-po], *m.* The middle season between the beginning and end of spring or autumn.

entreuntar [en-tray-oon-tar'], *va.* To anoint slightly.

entrevenarse [en-tray-vay-nar'-say], *vr.* To diffuse through the veins.

entreventana [en-tray-ven-tah-nah], *f.* Space between windows.

entrever [en-tray-verr'], *va.* To have a glimpse of, to see imperfectly.

entreverado, da [en-tray-vey-rah'-do, dah], *a.* Interlined with fat and lean (carne). *-pp.* of ENTREVERAR.

entreverar [en-tray-vay-rar'], *va..* To intermix, to insert one thing in another, to mix with others.

entrevía [en-tray-vee'-ah], *f.* Railway gauge, space between rails.

entrevista [en-tray-vees'-tah], *f.* 1. Interview. 2. Conference. **Entrevista de fondo,** interview in depth.

entrevistador, ra [en-tray-vees-tah-dor', rah], *m. & f.* Interviewer.

entrevistar [en-tray-vees-tar'], *va.* To interview.

entrevistarse [en-tray-vees-tar'-say], *vr.* To confer. **Entrevistarse con,** to interview, to have an interview with.

entrincado, da [en-trin-cah'-do, dah], *a.* Intricate. V. INTRINCADO.

entripado, da [en-tree-pah'-do, dah], *m.f.* Contained in the entrails or intestines.

entripado [en-tree-pah'-do], *m.* 1. *(coll.)* Dissembled anger or displeasure. 2. An indigestion. 3. *(Mex.)* A game of cards. 4. A dead animal from which the intestines have not been removed.

entristecer [en-tris-tay-therr'], *va.* To sadden, to grieve, to afflict, to make melancholy. *-vr.* 1. To grieve, to fret, to grow sad. 2. To wither, to decay (plantas). (*Yo entristezco, yo entristezca,* from *Entristecer.* V. CONOCER.)

entristecimiento [en-tris-tay-the-me-en'-to], *m.* Gloominess, heaviness of mind, sadness (tristeza), sorrowfulness; mournfulness, dejection; fretting.

entrojar [en-tro-har'], *va.* 1. To gather grain in barns. 2. To mow, to gather the harvest.

entrometer [en-tro-may-terr'], *va. & vn.* V. ENTREMETER in all its meanings.

entrometido [en-tro-may-tee'-do], *a.* Meddlesome, interfering. *-m.f.* Meddler, intruder.

entrometimiento [en-tro-may-te-me-en'-to], *m.* Intermeddling.

entronar [en-tro-nar'], *va.* To enthrone. V. ENTRONIZAR.

entroncar [en-tron-car'], *vn.* 1. To be descended from the same stock, to belong to the same family. 2. To contract relationship.

entronerar [en-tro-nay-rar'], *va.* To drive the ball into the hole of a truck or billiard-table.

entronización [en-tro-ne-thah-the-on'], *f.* Elevation to a throne.

entronizar [en-tro-ne-thar'], *va.* 1. To enthrone, to place on the throne. 2. To exalt, to raise to a distinguished rank or station. *-vr.* 1. To be elated or puffed up with pride. 2. To take possession of, to seat oneself in a post.

entronque [en-tron'-kay], *m.* 1. Cognation, relationship with the chief of a family. 2. A railway junction.

entropía [en-tro-pee'-ah], *f.* Entropy.

entruchada [en-troo-chah'-dah], *f.* Clandestine operation, an underhand business *(coll.)* Plot, intrigue.

entruchar [en-troo-char'], *va.* To decoy, to lure into a snare.

estruchón, na [es-troo-chone', nah], *m. & f.* Decoyer, plotter.

entruejo [en-troo-ay'-ho], *m.* V. ANTRUEJO.

entruesca [en-troo-es'-cah], *f.* In some mills, the cogged wheel.

entrujar [en-troo-har'], *va.* 1. To keep olives in the store-room. 2. V. ENTROJAR. 3. *(Fig. Coll.)* To reimburse.

entuerto [en-too-err'-to], *m.* V. AGRAVIO and TUERTO. *-pl.* Afterpains.

entullecer [en-tool-lyay-therr'], *vn.* To be crippled or maimed. *-va.* To stop, to check, to obstruct. *(Yo entullezco, yo entullezca, from Entullecer. V. CONOCER.)*

entumecer [en-too-may-therr'], *va.* 1. To swell, to make tumid. 2. To benumb, to make torpid (miembro). *-vr.* To swell, to surge (mar), to rise high.

entumecimiento [en-too-may-the-me-en'-to], *m.* 1. Swelling. 2. Torpor, deadness, numbness.

entumescencia [en-too-mes-then'-the-ah], *f. (Med.)* Intumescence, swelling.

entumirse [en-too-meer'-say], *vr.* To become torpid.

entunicar [en-too-ne-car'], *va.* To give two coats of plaster to a wall before painting it (fresco).

entupir [en-too-peer'], *va.* 1. To obstruct, to block up. 2. To compress, to tighten, to press.

enturbiar [en-toor-be-ar'], *va.* 1. To muddle, to make muddy or turbid (agua). 2. To obscure, to confound (asunto). *-vr.* To disorder to derange a thing.

entusiasmado, da [en-too-se-as-mah'-do, dah], *a. & pp.* of ENTUSIASMAR Enthusiastical, enthusiastic.

entusiasmar [en-too-se-as-mar'], *va.* To transport, to enrapture, to fill with enthusiasm. **No me entusiasma mucho la idea,** I'm not very keen on the idea. *-vr.* To become enthsiastic, to be enraptured. **Se ha quedado entusiasmada con el vestido.** she was delighted with the dress.

entusiasmo [en-too-se-ahs'-mo]. *m.* Enthusiasm, heat of imagination, ardor; fanaticism, caprice.

entusiasta [en-too-se-ahs'-tah], *m. & f.* Enthusiast, a visionary.

entusiástico, ca [en-too-se-ahs'-te-co, cah], *a.* Enthusiastic, fanatical.

enucleación [ay-noo-clayah-the-on'], *f.* 1. Enucleation, extraction of the kernel of a stone-fruit. 2. Enucleation, extirpation of a tumor. 3. Excision of a bone.

enuclear [ay-noo-clay-ar'], *va.* 1. To enucleate. 2. To excise a bone.

énula campana [ay'-noo-lah cam-pah'-nah], *f. (Bot.)* Elecampane, a tall herb of the aster family.

enumerable [ay-noo-may-rah'-blay], *a.* Numerable, capable of being counted.

enumeración [ay-noo-may-ra-the-on'], *f.* 1. Enumeration. 2. Recapitulation of the points of a discourse.

enumerar [ay-noo-may-rar'], *va.* 1. To enumerate (nombrar). 2. To count (contar).

enunciación [ay-noon-the-ah-the-on'], *f.* Enunciation, declaration.

enunciar [ay-noon-the-ar'], *va.* To enunciate, to declare, to proclaim.

enunciativo, va [ay-noon-the-ah-tee'-vo, vah], *a.* Enunciative.

enuresis, or **enuresia** [ay-noo-ray'-sis], *f.* Enuresis, incontinence of urine.

envagarar, or **envagrar** [en-vah-ga-rar'], *va. (Naut.)* To set the cross-pawls, or rib-bands, upon the frames of a ship.

evainador, ra [en-vah-e-nah-dor', rah], *a.* Sheathing. *(Bot.)* Clasping the stem.

envainar [en-vah-e-nar'], *va.* To sheathe (espada); to plunge.

envalentonar [en-vah-len-to-nar'], *va.* To encourage, to inspirit, to render bold. *-vr.* To become courageous.

envanecer [en-vah-nay-therr'], *va.* To make vain; to lift, to swell with pride. *-vr.* To become proud or haughty. *(Yo envanezco, yo envanezca, from Envanecer. V. CONOCER.)*

envarado, da [en-vah-rah'-do, dah], *a. & pp.* of ENVARAR. Deadened, benumbed, numbed (entumecido).

envaramiento [en-vah-rah-me-en'-to], *m.* 1. Deadness, stiffness, numbness 2. A number of bailiffs or petty officers of justice.

envarar [en-vah-rar'], *va.* To benumb, to numb (entumecer) to make torpid, to stupefy. *-vn.* To go numb (entumecerse), to go stiff (ponerse tieso).

envasado [en-vah-sah'-do], *m.* Packaging.

envasador [en-vah-sah-dor'], *m.* 1. Filler, one whose employment is to fill vessels of carriage. 2. Funnel.

envasar [en-vah-sar'], *va.* 1. To funnel, to put liquor into casks, to barrel (en tonel), to bottle. 2. To drink liquor to excess. 3. To put grain into sacks (en saco). *4.* To pack, to wrap (en paquete).

envase [en-vah'-say], *m.* 1. The recipient or vessel in which liquids are preserved or transported. 2. Packing, wrapping; packaging (acto). 3. Container (recipiente); package (papel), wrapping; bottle. **Recipiente de hojalata,** tin can. **Géneros sin envase,** unpackaged goods.

envedijarse [en-vay-de-har'-say], *vr.* 1. To get entangled. 2. *(coll.)* To wrangle.

envejecer [en-vay-hay-therr'], *va.* To make old, to make a person or thing look old. *-vn.* To grow old (persona). *-vr.* 1. To be of an old date or fashion (objeto). 2. To hold out a long time, to be of long duration. 3. To grow out of use. **En dos años ha envejecido mucho,** he's got very old these last two years. *(Yo envejezco, yo envejezca, from Envejecer. V. CONOCER.)*

envejecido, da [en-vay-hay-thee'-do, dah], *a. & pp.* of ENVEJECER. 1. Grown old, looking old. 2. Accustomed, habituated.

envejecimiento [en-vay-hay-the-me-en'-to], *m.* Oldness, age.

envenenador, ra [en-vay-nay-nah-dor', rah], *m. & f.* A poisoner.

envenenamiento [en-vay-nay-nah-me-en'-to], *m.* Poisoning.

envenenar [en-vay-nay-nar'], *va.* 1. To envenom, to poison; to infect with poison, to pollute (el aire). 2. To reproach, to judge ill of one. 3. To embitter one's own talk or another's. *-vr.* To poison oneself, to take poison.

enverdecer [en-ver-day-therr'], *vn.* To grow green. *(Yo enverdezco, yo enverdezca, from Enverdecer. V. CONOCER.)*

enveredar [en-vay-ray-dar'], *va.* To put on the right road, to guide.

envergadura [en-ver-ga-doo'-rah], *f.* 1. Bending the sails. 2. The rope bands of a sail collectively. 3. Breadth of the sails. 4. V. GRATIL. 5. Expanse, spread, extent. 6. *(Fig.)* Scope, compass; magnitude. **Un programa de gran envergadura,** a program of considerable scope. **La obra es de envergadura,** the plan is ambitious.

envergar [en-ver-gar'], *va. (Naut.)* To bend the sails.

envergues [en-ver'-gays], *m. pl. (Naut.)* Rope-bands, used to fasten sails to the yards.

envés [en-vays'], *m.* 1. The wrong side of anything (tela) V. REVÉS. 2. Back, shoulders.

envesado [en-vay-sah'-do], *m.* Among leather-dressers, the fleshy part of hides.

envestidura [en-ves-te-doo'-rah], *f.* Act of investing one with an office or place.

envestir [en-ves-teer'], *va.* 1. To invest, to put in possession of a place or office. 2. To adorn, to set off. 3. To illuminate, to enlighten. 4. To cover. V. REVESTIR. *-vr.* 1. To accustom or habituate oneself, to contract a habit. 2. To introduce oneself, or to interfere in something. 3. V. REVESTIRSE. *(Yo envisto, yo envista, envistiera or envistiese, from V. PEDIR.)*

enviada [en-ve-ah'-dah], *f.* 1. Message, errand. 2. Skiff, or smack, for carrying fish to land.

enviadizo, za [en-ve-ah-dee'-tho, thah], *a.* Missive, designed to be sent.

enviado [en-ve-ah'-do], *m.* 1. Envoy, representative, a public minister sent from one power to another. 2. Envoy, messenger (periodista).

enviador [en-ve-ah-dor'], *m.* A sender.

enviajado, da [en-ve-ah-hah'-do, dah], *a.* (Arch.) Oblique, sloped.

enviar [en-ve-ar'], *va.* 1. To send, to transmit, to convey. 2. To send, to give, to bestow. 3. To exile. **Enviar a pasear,** *(Met.)* to send someone about his business; to give one his walking-ticket; to dismiss contemptuously. **Enviar de vuelta,** *(Com.)* to return. **Enviar a uno a hacer algo,** to send somebody to do something.

enviciar [en-ve-the-ar'], *va.* To vitiate, to corrupt, to make vicious. *-vn.* To have luxurious foliage and little fruit (plantas). *-vr.* To be immoderately addicted to, to be excessively fond of.

envidador [en-ve-dah-dor'], *m.* He who invites at cards, or opens the game by staking a sum.

envidar [en-ve-dar'], *va.* Among gamesters, to invite, or to open the game by staking a certain sum.

envidia [en-vee'-de-ah], *f.* 1. Envy. 2. Emulation.

envidiable [en-ve-de-ah'-blay], *a.* Enviable.

envidiador, ra [en-ve-de-ah-dor', rah], *m. & f.* Envier, envious person.

envidiar [en-ve-de-ar'], *vn.* 1. To envy, to feel envy, to grudge, to malign. 2. *(Met.)* To covet, to desire what is lawful and honorable.

envidiosamente [en-ve-de-o'-sah-men-tay], *adv.* Enviously.

envidioso, sa [en-ve-de-oh'-so, sah], *a.* Envious; invidious, jealous, malignant.

envigotar [en-ve-go-tar'], *va.* (Naut.) To strap dead-eyes.

envilecer [en-ve-lay-therr'], *va.* To vilify, to debase, to make contemptible. *-vr.* To degrade oneself, to be disgraced.

envilecimiento [en-ve-lay-the-me-en'-to], *m.* Vilification, debasement.

envinado, da [en-ve-nah'-do, dah], *a.* Having the taste of wine. *-pp.* of ENVINAR.

envinagrar [en-ve-nah-grar'], *va.* To put vinegar into something.

envinar [en-ve-nar'], *va.* To mix wine with water.

envío [en-ve-e'-o], *m.* Remittance (dinero), consignment of goods (mercancías), sending (acto), dispatch. **Gastos de envío,** postage and packing. **Envío contra reembolso,** cash on delivery. Shipment *(Inform.)*

enviperado, da [en-ve-pay-rah'-do, dah], *a.* In jocular style, viperlike, enraged, furious.

envirar [en-ve-rar'], *va.* To clasp or unite together cork wood to form a beehive.

enviscamiento [en-vis-cah-me-en'-to], *m.* Act of gluing.

enviscar [en-vis-car'], *va.* 1. To glue, to fasten with glue. 2. To irritate, to anger. *-vn.* To be glued with birdlie (pájaros e insectos).

envite [en-vee'-tay], *m.* 1. The act of inviting at cards, or opening the game by staking a certain sum (apuesta). 2. Invitation; any kind of polite offer (oferta).

enviudar [en-ve-oo-dar'], *vn.* To become a widower or widow. **Enviudar de su primera mujer,** to lose one's first wife.

envoltorio [en-vol-to'-re-o], *m.* 1. Bundle of clothes. 2. Fault in cloth, arising from the mixture of inferior material.

envoltura [en-vol-too'-rah], *f.* 1. Wrapper, jacket (libro). 2. Wrapping, covering.

envolturas [en-vol-too'-ras], *f. pl.* 1. Swaddling cloth, swaddling band, cloth wrapped round a baby. 2. (Anat.) The coverings, commonly membranous, which serve as a protection to certain organs.

envolvedero, envolvedor [en-vol-vay-day'-ro, en-vol-vay-dor'], *m.* Wrapper, wrapping, envelope, cover.

envolver [en-vol-verr'], *va.* 1. To wrap up, to wrap around with paper, cloth, or other analogous thing: to convolve; to inwrap. **Dos paquetes envueltos en papel,** two parcels wrapped in paper. 2. *(Met.)* To convince by reasoning. 3. To put things into confusion. 4. *(Mil.)* To attack an enemy on all sides, to surround, so as to force a surrender. *-vr.* 1. To be implicated in an affair. 2. To be unlawfully connected with women. *(Yo envuelvo, yo envuelva,* from *Envolver. V.* MOVER.)

envolvimiento [en-vol-ve-me-en'-to], *m.* 1. Envelopment, inwrapping or enveloping. 2. *V.* REVOLCADERO.

envuelto, ta [en-voo-el'-to, tah], *pp. irr.* of ENVOLVER. 1. Wrapped. 2. **Envuelta,** a cord matted.

enyerbarse [en-yer-bar'-say], *vr.* (Amer. Cuba) To be clothed or covered with grass.

enyesado [en-yay-sah'-do], *m.* Plastering; plaster cast.

enyesadura [en-yay-sah-doo'-rah], *f.* Plastering with gypsum.

enyesar [en-yay-sar'], *va.* To plaster, to cover with plaster; to whitewash.

enyugar [en-yoo-gar'], *va.* To yoke cattle. *-vr. (Met. Obs.)* To marry.

enzamarrado, da [en-thah-mar-rah'-do, dah], *a.* Dressed in a shepherd's greatcoat, made of sheep skins with the wool on.

enzarzada [en-thar-thah'-dah], *f. (Mil.)* A light fortification; breastworks at the entrance of forests, defiles, and crags, aiding to defend an important pass.

enzarzado, da [en-thar-thah'-do, dah], *a.* Curled, matted (pelo). *-pp.* Of ENZARZAR.

enzarzar [en-thar-thar'], *va.* 1. To throw among brambles and briers. 2. *(Met.)* To sow discord, to excite dissensions. 3. To put hurdles for silkworms. *-vr.* 1. To be entangled among brambles and briers. 2. *(Met.)* To be involved in difficulties. 5. To squabble, to wrangle.

enzima [en-thee'-mah], *f.* Enzyme.

enzimático, ca [en-the-mah'-te-co, cah], *a.* Enzymic, enzymatic.

enzimología [en-the-mo-lo-hee'-ah], *f.* Enzymology.

enzootía [en-thoo-tee'-ah], *f.* Epizootic, a contagious disease among cattle.

enzurdecer [en-thoor-day-therr'], *vn.* To become left-handed.

enzurronar [en-thoor-ro-nar'], *va.* 1. To put in a bag. 2. *(Met.)* To inclose one thing in another.

eñe [ay'-nyay], *f.* Spanish name of the letter ñ.

eoceno, na [ay-o-thay'-no, nah], *a. (Geol.)* Eocene.

eólico [ay-o'le-co], *a.* æolian, æolic. 2. The æolian dialect.

eolio, lia [ay-o'-leo, ah], *a.* æolian, Eolian; used of the dialect.

eolipilo [ay-o-le-pee'-lo], *m.* A ventilator for cleaning chimneys.

eón [ay-on'], *m. (Geol.)* Eon.

epacta [ay-pahc'-tah], *f.* 1. Epact, the excess of the solar year over twelve lunar months. 2. *V.* AÑALEJO.

epactilla [ay-pac-teel'-lyah], *f.* A small calendar for the performance of divine service, which is published every year.

epagómeno [ay-pa-go'-may-no], *a.* Epagomenal, intercalary: said of the five days which the Egyptians and Chaldeans added to the 360 of the vague year, after the establishment of the lunar cycle.

epéntesis [ay-pen'-tay-sis], *f. (Gram.)* Epenthesis.

eperlano [ay-per-lah'-no], *m. Zool.)* Smelt, a small sea-fish.

epi, a Greek preposition signifying on, used as a prefix.

épicamente [ay-pe'-cah-rah-men-tay], *adv.* In an epic or heroic manner.

epicarpo [ay-pe-car'-po], *m.* Epicarp, a membrane which covers the pericarp.

epicedio [ay-pe-thay'-de-o], *m.* Epicedium, elegy, eulogy of the dead.

epiceno, na [ay-pe-thay'-no, nah], *a.* Epicene, belonging to both genders.

epicentro [ay-pe-then'-tro], *m.* Epicenter.

epiciclo [ay-pe-thee'-clo], *m.* Epicycle, a small circle, whose center is supposed to be upon the circumference of another.

epicicloide [ay-pe-the-clo'-e-day], *f. (Goons.)* Epicycloid.

épico, ca [ay'-pe-co, cah], *a.* Epic, narrative, containing narrations. **Poema épico,** epic, epopee, an epic poem.

epicúreo, rea [ay-pe-coo'-ra-yo, ah], *a.* Epicurean.

epidemia [ay-pe-day'-me-ah], *f.* 1. An epidemic disease. 2. A multitude of ills or misfortunes.

epidémico, ca [ay-pe-day'-me-co, cah], *a.* Epidemical, epidemic.

epidendro [ay-pe-den'-dro], *m.* Epidendrum, a large genus of tropical American epiphytic orchids often cultivated for their beautiful flowers.

epidérmico, ca [ay-pe-derr'-me-co, cah], *a.* Epidermic, belonging to the outer covering.

epidermis [ay-pe-derr'-mis], *f.* Epidermis, the scarf-skin, the cuticle.

epidídimo [ay-pe-dee'-de-mo], *m. (Anat.)* Epididymis.

epifanía [ay-pe-fah-nee'-ah], *f.* Epiphany.

epifaringe [ay-pe-fah-reen'-hay], *f.* Epipharynx, a little valve which closes the pharynx of certain hymenoptera.

epifillo, lla [ay-pe-feel'-lyo, lyah], *a. (Bot.)* Budding and growing upon the surface of leaves.

epifilospermo, ma [ay-pe-fe-los-perr'-mo, mah], *a. (Bot.)* Epiphyllospermous.

epífisis [ay-pee'-fe-sis], *f. (Anat.)* Epiphysis.

epífito, ta [ay-pee'-fe'-to, tah], *a.* Epiphytal, growing upon other plants, but not extracting nutriment from them.

epifonema [ay-pe-fo-nay'-ma], *f. (Rhet.)* Epiphonema, an exclamation made after recounting something.

epífora [ay-pee'-fo-rah], *f.* 1. Epiphora, watering of the eye. 2. *(Rhet.)* A kind of amplification.

epigástrico, ca [ay-pe-gahs'-tre-co, cah], *a.* Epigastric.

epiglotis [ay-pe-glo'-tis], *f.* Epiglottis, a cartilage of the larynx.

epígrafe [ay-pee'-grah-fay], *m.* Epigraph, title (encabezamiento), inscription (inscripción); motto (lema).

epigrama [ay-pe-grah'-mah], *m. & f.* Epigram.

epigramatario, ria, or **epigramático, ca** [ay-pe-grah-mah-tah'-re-o, ah], *a.* Epigrammatic.

epigramático, epigramatista, epigramista [ay-pe-grah-mah'-te-co, ay-pe-grah-mah-tees'-tah], *m.* Epigrammatist.

epilepsia [ay-pe-lep'-se-ah], *f.* Epilepsy.

epiléptico, ca [ay-pe-lep'-te-co, cah], *a.* Epileptic epileptical.

epilogación [ay-pe-lo-gah-the-on'], *f. V.* EPÍLOGO.

epilogal [ay-pe-lo-gahl'], *a.* Epilogistic, compendious, summary.

epilogar [ay-pe-lo-gar'], *va.* To recapitulate, to sum up.

epilogismo [ay-pe-lo-hees'-mo], *m.* Epiloglism, calculation, computation.

epílogo [ay-pee'-lo-go], *m.* 1. A conclusion or close of a speech. 2. Epilogue. 3. Recapitulation, a brief or compendious statement.

epipedometría [ay-pe-pay-do-may-tree'-ah], *f.* Epipedometry, the mensuration of figures standing on the same base.

epiqueya [ay-pe-kay'-yah], *f.* A mild and prudent interpretation of the law.

episcopado [ay-pis-co-pah'-do], *m.* Episcopacy; episcopate (período), bishopric (oficio), the dignity of a bishop.

episcopal [ay-pis-co-pahl'], *a.* Episcopal, relating to bishops.

episódico, ca [ay-pe-so'-de-co, cah], *a.* Episodic, episodical.

episodio [ay-pe-so'-de-o], *m.* 1. Episode, an incidental narrative or digression in a poem. 2. *V.* DIGRESIÓN.

epispástico, ca [ay-pis-pahs'-te-co, cah], *a.* Epispastic, blistering, reddening the skin.

epispermo [ay-pis-perr'-mo], *m.* Episperm, an envelope which inwraps the seed.

epistaxis [ay-pis-tak'-sis], *f.* Epistaxis, nose-bleed.

epistemología [ay-pis-tay-mo-lo-hee'-ah], *f.* Epistemology.

epistilo [ay-pis-tee'-lo], *m. (Arch.)* Epistyle.

epístola [ay-pees'-to-lah], *f.* 1. Epistle, letter. 2. Epistle, a part of the mass. **Epístola** or **orden de epístola,** subdeaconship, subdeaconry.

epistolar [ay-pis-to-lar'], *a.* Epistolary.

epistolario [ay-pis-to-lah'-re-o], *m.* 1. Collection of epistles read or sung at the mass. 2. Volume of letters.

epistolero [ay-pis-to-lay'-ro], *m.* Epistler, the subdeacon or any priest who sings the epistle.

epitafio [ay-pe-tah'-fe-o], *m.* Epitaph, inscription on a tomb.

epitalamio [ay-pe-tah-lah'lmelo], *m.* Epithalamium, a nuptial song; a compliment upon marriage.

epítasis [aylpee'ltahlsis], *f.* Epitasis the most complex part of the plot of a play.

epitelio [aylpeltay'llelo], *m.* Epithelium, the epidermis of mucous membranes.

epítema, or **epítima** [ay-pee'-te-mah], *f.* Epithem, a lotion.

epíteto [ay-pee'-tay-to], *m.* Epithet.

epitimar [ay-pe-te-mar'], *va.* To apply an epithem.

epítimo [ay-pee'-te-mo], *m. (Bot.)* Lesser dodder.

epitomar [ay-pe-to-mar'], *va.* To epitomize, to abstract, to contract into a narrow space.

epítome [ay-pee'-to-may], *m.* Epitome, abridgment, extract, summary, compend or compendium.

epizoario, a [ay-pe-tho-ah'-re-o, ah], *a. (Zool.)* Epizoic, epizoan, parasitic on the body of other animals, like lice.

epizóico, ca [ay-pe-tho'-eco, cah], *a.* 1. *V.* EPIZOARIO. 2. *(Geol.)* Denoting upper primitive lands which contain remain of organized bodies.

epizootia [ay-pe-tho-o'-te-ah], *f. (Vet.)* Epizooty, epidemic influenza.

época [ay'-po-cah], *f.* 1. Epoch. 2. Date of an event. **En la época de Carlos III,** in Charles III's time. **En aquella época,** at that time. **Coche de época,** vintage car. **Todos tenemos épocas así,** we all go through spells like that.

épodo [ay-po-do], *m.* Epode.

epopeya [ay-po-pay'-yah], *f.* Epopee, an epic poem.

epsomita [ep-so-mee'-tah], *f.* Epsom salts.

epulia, epúlida [ay-poo'-le-ah, ay-poo'-le-dah], *f.* Epulis, a tumor of the gums.

epulón [ay-poo-lon'], *m.* An epicure or great eater.

equeno [ay-kay'-no], *m.* A rectangular earthen trough, for pouring melted metal into a mould, used in casting statues.

equiángulo, la [ay-ke-ahn'-goo-lo, lah], *a. (Geom.)* Equiangular.

equiáxeo, a [ay-kee-ak'-say-o, ah], *a.* Equiaxe, having equal axes.

equidad [ay-ke-dahd'], *f.* 1. Equity, equitableness, right, honesty. 2. Equity, impartiality, justice. 3. Conscionableness; conscientiousness. 4. Moderation in the execution of laws, or in the price of things bought or sold (precio)

equidistancia [ay-ke-dis-tahn'-the-ah], *f.* Equidistance.

equidastante [ay-ke-dis-tahn'-tay], *pa.* Equidistant.

equidistar [ay-ke-dis-tar'], *vn.* To be equidistant.

equidna [ay-keed'-nah], *m.* Echidna, the porcupine ant-eater.

equidnita [ay-keed-nee'-tah], *f.* A kind of agate with spots like those of the viper.

equilateral [ay-ke-lah-tay-rahl'], *a. V.* EQUILÁTERO.

equilátero, ra [ay-ke-lah'-tay-ro, rah], *a.* Equilateral.

equilibrado, da [ay-ke-le-brah'-do, dah], *a.* 1. Balanced. 2. Sensible, fair, just. **Dieta equilibrada,** balanced diet.

equilibrar [ay-ke-le-brar'], *va.* 1. To equilibrate, to balance in a scale. 2. *(Met.)* To balance equally. 3. To counterpoise, to counterbalance.

equilibre [ay-ke-lee'-bray], *a.* Balanced, equilibrious.

equilibrio [ay-ke-lee'-bre-o], *m.* Equilibrium, equilibrity, equipoise (social), equality of weight, counterpoise, counterbalance, equilibration. **Perder el equilibrio,** to lose one's balance. **Equilibrio político,** balance of power.

equilibrista [ay-ke-le-brees'-tah], *m.* 1. Balancer, tight-rope walker. 2. Turn-coat, one who changes political opinions often.

equimosis [ay-ke-mo'-sis], *m.* *(Med.)* Ecchymosis, subcutaneous effusion of blood, caused by a blow.

equinita [ay-ke-nee'-tah], *f.* Sea-urchin, sea-hedgehog, echinus.

equino, na [ay-kee'-no, nah], *a.* *(Poet.)* Belonging to a horse, equine.

equino [ay-kee'-no], *m.* 1. *(Zool.)* Echinus, a shellfish set with prickles. 2. *(Arch.)* Echinus, an ornament.

equinoccial [ay-ke-noc-the-ahl'], *a.* Equinoctial. **Línea equinoccial,** the equinoctial line.

equinoccio [ay-ke-noc'-the-o], *m.* The equinox. **Equinoccio otoñal,** autumnal equinox.

equinodermo, ma [ay-ke-no-derr'-mo, mah] *a.* Echinodermatous.

equipaje [ay-ke-pah'-hay], *m.* 1. Luggage, baggage. **Equipaje de mano,** hand luggage. **Facturar el equipaje,** to register one's luggage. 2. *(Naut.)* The crew (tripulación). 3. *(Mil.)* Baggage train, supply wagons. 4. Storehouse. 5. Equipment (avíos).

equipamento [ay-ke-pah-men'-to], *m.* *(Naut.)* Fitting out, accoutrement, for navigation and military operations.

equipamiento [ay-ke-pah-me-ayn'-to], *m.* Equipment.

equipar [ay-ke-par'], *va.* 1. To fit out, to supply with everything necessary. 2. To equip, to furnish, to accoutre; to gird.

equiparable [ay-ke-pah-rah'-blay], *a.* Comparable; applicable.

equiparación [ay-ke-pa-rah-the-on'], *f.* Comparison, collation.

equiparar [ay-ke-pa-rar'], *va.* To compare (comparar), to match. *-vr.* **Equipararse con,** to be on a level with.

equipo [ay-kee'-po], *m.* 1. *(Mil.)* Fitting out, accoutrement, equipment (conjunto de cosas). 2. Trappings. **Equipo de alpinismo,** climbing kit. **Equipo de caza,** hunting gear. **Equipo de primeros auxilios,** first-aid kit. **Equipo de reparaciones,** repair kit. *(Ferro.)* **Equipo rodante,** rolling stock. 3. Team (personas); side. **Equipo de fútbol,** football team. 4. *(Comput.)* **Equipo interferente,** infringing equipment. **Equipo para copias de seguridad,** backup equipment.

equipolencia [ay-ke-po-len'-the-ah], *f.* Equipollence, equality of force or power.

equipolente [ay-ke-po-len'-tay], *a.* Equivalent, equipollent.

equiponderación, or **equiponderancia** [ay-ke-pon-day-rahn'-the-ah], *f.* Equality of weight, balance.

equiponderante [ay-ke-pon-day-rahn'-tay], *pa.* & *a.* Equiponderating; equiponderant.

equiponderar [ay-ke-pon-day-rar'], *vn.* To equiponderate.

equis [ay'-kis], *f.* Spanish name of the letter X. **Estar hecho una equis,** to be intoxicated and staggering. **Tenía que hacer equis cosas,** I had to do any amount of things.

equitación [ay-ke-tah-the-on'], *f.* Horsemanship (arte): equitation.

equitativamente [ay-ke-tah-te-vah-men'-tay], *adv.* Equitably.

equitativo, va [ay-ke-tah-tee'-vo, vah], *a.* 1. Equitable (juicio justo). 2. Just, honorable. **A precio muy equitativo,** very cheap.

equivalencia [ay-ke-vah-len'-the-ah], *f.* Compensation; equivalence.

equivalente [ay-ke-vah-len'-tay], *a.* 1. Equivalent. 2. Compensatory, compensative.

equivaler [ay-ke-vah-lerr'], *vn.* 1. To be of equal value and price. 2. To equiponderate, to be equal to. (*Yo equivalgo, yo equivalga; equivaliera, equivaliese, equivaliere;* from *Equivaler.* V. VALER.)

equivocación [ay-ke-vo-cah-the-on'], *f.* 1. Mistake (error), misconception, error, misapprehension, misunderstanding (malentendido), oversight (olvido). 2. Blunder, hallucination.

equivocadamente [ay-ke-vo-cah'-dah-men-tay], *adv.* Mistakenly, by mistake.

equivocado, da [ay-ke-vo-cah'-do, dah], *a.* & *pp.* of EQUIVOCAR. Mistaken. **Estás equivocado,** you're mistaken.

equívocamente [ay-kee'-vo-cah-men-tay], *adv.* Ambiguously, equivocally.

equivocar [ay-ke-vo-car'], *va.* To mistake, to take one thing for another; to conceive wrong. **Equivocar el camino,** to take the wrong road, *-vr.* To mistake, to be mistaken, to make a mistake. **Pero se equivocó,** but he was wrong.

equívoco, ca [ay-kee'-vo-co, cah], *a.* Equivocal, ambiguous.

equívoco [ay-kee'-vo-co], *m.* Equivocation (ambigüedad), equivoque, a quibble.

equivoquillo [ay-ke-vo-keel'-lyo], *m. dim.* A quibble, a slight cavil; a sort of pun.

era [ay'-rah], *f.* 1. Era, computation from any date or epoch. 2. Age, or long space of time. **Era atómica,** atomic age. **Era cristiana,** Christian era. 3. Thrashing-floor. 4. Bed or plot in a garden, sown with salad-seeds, etc.

eradicación [ay-rah-de-cah-the-on'], *f.* Eradication, thorough cure.

eradicativo, va [ay-rah-de-cah-tee'-vo, vah], *a.* Eradicative, radically curative.

eraje [ay-rah'-hay], *m.* *(Prov.)* Virgin honey.

eral [ay-rahl'], *m.* A two-year-old ox.

erar [ay-rar'], *va.* To lay out ground for growing garden-stuff.

erario [ay-rah'-re-o], *m.* Exchequer public treasury.

erección [ay-rec-the-on'], *f.* 1. Foundation, erection, establishment. 2. Erection, erectness, elevation.

eréctil [ay-rayk'-teel], *a.* Erectile, capable of erection.

erectilidad [ay-rec-te-le-dahd'], *f.* Erectility, power of erection.

erector, ra [ay-rec-tor', rah], *m.* & *f.* Erecter, founder.

eremita [ay-ray-mee'-tah], *m.* V. ERMITAÑO.

eremítico, ca [ay-ray-mee'-te-co, cah], *a.* Hermitical, eremitical, solitary.

eretismo [ay-ray-tees'-mo], *m.* Erethism, abnormal excitability.

ergio [er'-he-o], *m.* *(Phys.)* Erg.

ergotear [er-go-tay-ar'], *vn.* *(coll.)* To argue, to debate without reason.

ergoteo [er-go-tay'-o], *m.* *(coll.)* Sophistry, debate on trifling things.

erguido, da [er-gee'-do, dah], *a.* 1. Erect, straight. 2. Swelled with pride.

erguir [erg-eer'], *va.* To erect, to raise up straight (enderezar). *(Fig.)* **Erguir la cabeza,** to hold one's head high. *-vr.* To be elated or puffed up with pride.

erial, eriazo, za [ay-reahl', ay-re-ah'-tho, thah], *a.* Unploughed, untilled, uncultivated: it is commonly used as a substantive to express a piece of uncultivated ground.

erica [ay-ree'-cah], *f.* *(Bot.)* Heath, heather.

ericáceo, cea [ay-re-cah'-thay-o, ah], *a.* Ericaceous of the heath family.

ericera [ay-re-thay'-rah], *f.* *(Prov.)* Kind of hut without a roof.

erigeron [ay-re-hay'-ron], *m.* *(Bot.)* Erigeron.

erigir [ay-re-heer'], *va.* 1. To erect, to raise, to build. 2. To erect, to establish anew.

eringe [ay-reen'-hay], *f.* *(Bot.)* V. ERINGIO.

eringio [ay-reen'-he-o], *m.* *(Bot.)* Field eringo.

erío, ría [ay-ree'-o, ah], *a.* Unploughed, untilled. V. ERIAL.

erísimo [ay-ree'-se-mo], *m.* *(Bot.)* Hedgemustard.

erisipela [ay-re-se-pay'-lah], *f.* *(Med.)* Erysipelas, a disease.

erisipelar [ay-re-se-pay-lar'], *va.* To cause erysipelas.

erisipelatoso, sa [ay-re-se-pay-lah-to'-so, sah], *a.* *(Med.)* Erysipelatous, belonging to erysipelas.

eristalo [ay-ris-tah'-lo], *m.* The dronefly, eristalis; much resembling a drone-bee in appearance.

eritema [ay-re-tay'-mah], *f.* *(Med.)* Erythema, congestion of the skin.

eritematoso, sa [ay-re-tay-ma-to'-so, sah], *a.* Erythematous, relating to or characterized by erythema.

eritreo, trea [ay-ree-tray'-o, ah], *a. (Poet.)* Erythraean, belonging to the Red Sea.

erizado da [ay-re-thah'-do, dah], *a.* Covered with bristles. -*pp.* of ERIZAR.

erizamiento [ay-re-thah-me-en'-to], *m.* Act of setting on end, as the hair.

erizar [ay-re-thar'], *va.* To set on end; to bristle (pelo). **El gato erizó el pelo,** the cat bristled, -*vr.* 1. To stand on end (pelo). 2. To bristle, to stand erect.

erizo [ay-ree'-tho], *m.* 1. Hedgehog. 2. Sea-hedgehog, or urchin. 3. Echinus, the prickly husk of a chestnut and other fruits. 4. *(Mech.)* In weaving, an urchin, a carding roller; a sprocket wheel, a rag wheel, spar-toothed wheel.

ermita [er-mee'-tah], *f.* Hermitage.

ermitaña [er-me-tah'-nyah], *f.* Hermitess.

ermitaño [er-me-tha'-nyo], *m.* Hermit, one who takes care of a hermitage.

ermitorio [er-me-to're-o], *m. V.* EREMITORIO.

ermunia [er-moo'-ne-ah], *f.* A certain kind of earth which needs constant moisture in order to be productive.

ermunio [er-moo'-ne-o], *m.* Name formerly given to persons exempted from every kind of tribute and service.

erogar [ay-ro-gar'], *va.* To distribute (bienes), to divide, to apportion, to spend in fees or judicial proceedings.

erogatorio [ay-ro-gah-to'-re-o], *m.* Pipe through which liquor is drawn.

erosión [ay-ro-se-on'], *f.* Erosion, corosion.

erosionar [ay-ro-se-o-nar'], *va.* To erode, -*vr.* To erode, to be eroded.

eróticamente [ay-ro'-te-cah-men-tay], *adv.* Erotically, in an erotic manner.

erótico, ca [ay-ro'-te-co, cah], *a.* Erotical, erotic, belonging to love (poesía); voluptuous, sensual.

erótilo [ay-ro'-te-lo], *m.* A beetle of Mexico and South America.

erótema [ay-ro'-tay-mah], *f. (Rhet.)* Interrogation.

erotismo [ay-ro-tees'-mo], *m.* 1. A violent love. 2. Sensuality.

erotomanía [ay-ro-to-mah-nee'-ah], *f.* Erotomania, love-madness.

erpetología [er-pay-to-lo-hee'-ah], *f.* Herpetology, that branch of zoology which treats of reptiles.

errabundo, da [er-rah-boon'-do, dah], *a.* Wandering, strolling about.

errada [er-rah'-dah], *f.* A miss, in billiards.

erradamente [er-rah-da-men'-tay], *adv.* Erroneously, falsely, faultily, mistakenly, erratically.

erradicación [er-rah-de-ca-the-on'], *f.* Eradication, extirpation.

erradicar [er-rah-de-car'], *va.* To eradicate, to pull up by the roots.

erradizo, za [er-rah-dee'-tho, thah], *a.* Wandering to and fro.

errado, da [ar-rah'-do], *a. & pp.* of ERRAR. Mistaken, erring, erroneous.

erraj [er-rah'], *m.* Fine coal made from the stones of olives.

errante [er-rahn'-tay], *pa. & a.* Errant, erring, roving, wandering, rambling; excursive, nomadic.

errar [er-rar'], *va.* 1. To err, to commit errors. 2. To misjudge, to make mistakes, to mistake. 3. To offend anyone. -*vn.* To wander about without knowing one's way (vagar). **Errar el camino,** to miss the right way. **Errar el golpe,** to miss a blow. *(Met.)* To miss one's aim.

errata [er-rah'-tah], *f.* Error in writing or printing; erratum. **Erratas** or **fe de erratas,** errata, the faults of the printer.

errático, ca [er-rah'-te-co, cah], *m.* Wandering, vagabond, vagrant, errant or, erratical.

errátil [er-rah'-teel], *a. (coll.)* Wavering, not firm or steady.

erre [er'-ray], *f.* The Spanish name of the letter R. **Erre que erre,** pertinaciously, obstinately.

erróneamente [er-ro'-nay-ah-men-tay], *adv.* Erroneously, mistakenly, faultily, falsely.

erróneo, nea [er-ro'-nay-o, ah], *a.* Erroneous, mistaken, not conformable to truth (doctrinas y opiniones).

erronía [er-ro-ne'-ah], *f. (coll.)* Opposition, hatred.

error [er-ror'], *m.* 1. Error, stale, involuntary deviation from truth, misapprehension, misbelief, misconception, hallucination, fallacy (de teoría) 2. Mispersuasion, misguidance. 3. Deceit, falsity, illusion, fault (defecto). 4. Deficiency, fault, defect. **Error de copia,** clerical error. **Error de imprenta,** writing error. **Por error,** by mistake. **Caer en un error,** to fall into error. **Error de paridad,** *(Inform.)* parity error. **Error intencionado,** *(Inform.)* willful misconduct.

erubescencia [ay-roo-bes-then'-the-ah], *f.* Erubescence, the act of blushing. **eructación** [ay-rooc-tah-the-on'], *f.* Eructation, belching.

eructar [ay-rooc-tar'], *vn.* To belch, to eructate.

eructo [ay-rooc'-to], *m.* Belching, eructation.

erudición [ay-roo-de-the-on'], *f.* Erudition, learning, knowledge, letters.

eruditamente [ay-roo-de'-tah-men-tay], *adv.* Learnedly.

erudito, ta [ay-roo-dee'-to, tah], *a.* Erudite, learned, lettered.

eruginoso sa [ay-roo-he-no'-so, sah], *a.* That which is thick, coarse, and knotty.

erupción [ay-roop-the-on'], *f.* Eruption, outbreak, bursting forth. **Estar en erupción,** to be erupting.

eruptivo, va [ay-roop-tee'-vo, vah], *a.* Eruptive.

erutación [ay-roo-tah-the-on'], *f.* Eructation, belching.

erutar [ay-roo-tar'], *vn. V.* ERUCTAR.

eruto [ay-roo'-to], *m. V.* ERUCTO.

ervato [er-vah'-to], *m. (Bot.)* Sea sulphur-wort, hog's-fennel.

ervellada [er-vel-lyah'-da], *f. (Bot.)* Bean-trefoil.

ésa [ay'-sah], A demonstrative pronoun of the feminine gender. That, that one.

esa [ay-sah], Demonstrative adjective, feminine. That.

esbatimentar [es-bah-te-men-tar'], *va. (Art.)* To delineate a shadow. -*vn.* To cast the shadow of one body on another.

esbatimento [es-bah-te-men'-to], *m.* Shade in a picture.

esebeltez [es-bel-teth'], *f.* Slenderness, gracefulness.

esbelto, ta [es-bel'-to, tah], *a.* Slender, svelte, graceful.

esbirro [es-bir'-ro], *m.* Bailiff (alguacil), apparitor; a petty officer of courts of justice, a myrmidon, henchman (ayudante), killer (sicario).

esbozar [es-bo-thar'], *va.* To outline, to sketch, to make a plan.

esbozo [es-bo'-tho], *m. (Pict.)* Sketch, outline; a rough draught.

esca [ays'-cah], *f.* 1. Food, nourishment. 2. Bait for hunting or fishing.

escabechar [es-cah-bay-char'], *va.* To souse, to steep in pickle, to pickle.

escabeche [es-cah-bay'-chay], *m.* Souse pickle (de escabechar); pickled fish (pescado).

escabel [es-cah-bel'], *m.* 1. Foot-stool; small seat. 2. A small seat of boards without back.

escabelillo [es-cah-bay-leel'-lyo], *m. dim.* A small foot-stool.

escabelón [es-cah-be-lone'], *m. (Arch.)* A kind of pedestal.

escabiosa [es-cah-be-o'-sah], *f. (Bot.)* Field-scabious.

escabioso, sa [es-cah-be-o'-so, sah], *a. (Med.)* Scabious; relating to scabies, or the itch.

escabro [es-cah'-bro], *m.* 1. A kind of scab, itch, or mange in sheep. 2. The large amphibious crab. 3. A roughness, like mange, which grows upon the bark of trees and vines.

escabrosamente [es-cah-bro-sah-men'-tay], *adv.* Roughly, ruggedly.

escabrosidad [es-cah-bro-se-dahd], *f.* 1. Roughness, unevenness. 2. Difficulty, hardness. 3. Sharpness.

escabroso, sa [es-cah-bro'-so, sah], *a.* 1. Rough, uneven (terreno). 2. Very difficult, thorny (problema). 3. Scabrous.

escabullimiento [es-cah-bool-lyee-me-en'-to], *m.* Evasion, slipping away, act of escaping.

escabullirse [es-cah-bool-lyeer'-say], *vr.* To escape, to evade; to slip away, to slip through one's hands.

escacado, da [es-cah-cah'-do, dah], *a. (Her.)* Checkered, variegated, like a chess-board.

escachar [es-cah-char'], *va. (Prov.)* To smash, to squash. *-vr.* To prick.

escacharrar [es-cah-char-rar'], *va.* 1. To break, to smash. 2. *(Fig.)* To ruin, to wreck

escachifollar [es-cah-che-fol-lyar'], *va.* To humiliate.

escafandra, *f.* **escafandro,** *m.* [es-cah-fahn'-drah, es-cah-fahn'-dro], Diving suit. **Escafandra autónoma,** scuba. **Escafandra espacial,** space suit. **Escafandra rígida,** rigid diving suit.

escafandrero [es-cah-fan-dray'-ro], *m.* Deep-sea diver.

escafóideo, dea [es-cah-fo'-day'-o, ah], *m.* Scaphoid, skiff-like.

escala [es-cah-lah], *f.* 1. Ladder, scale. 2. Scale, a figure subdivided by lines to measure proportions. 3. Scale, the series of harmonic or musical proportions. 4. Scale, regular graduation. 5. Any port, bay, or road for stripe to ride in, in order to get provisions, etc (parada). **Modelo a escala,** scale model. **A escala nacional,** on a national scale. **Un plan en gran escala,** a large-scale plan. **Vuelo sin escalas,** non-stop flight.

escalada [es-cah-lah'-dah], *f.* 1. Escalade (con escalera de mano), scaling (pared, acantilado). **Escalada a escala vista,** a daylight escalade. **Escalada de precios,** price escalade. 2. Climb (alpinismo) **Escalada en rocas,** rock climbing.

escalado, da [es-cah-lah'-do, dah], *a.* Applied to fish cut open to be salted or cured. *-pp.* of ESCALAR.

escalador, ra [es-cah-lah-dor'], *m. & f.* Climber, person who scales walls (alpinista).

escalafón [es-cah-lah-fon'], *m.* 1. Seniority scale, grade scale (de personas). 2. Company roster.

escalamera [es-cah-lah-may'-rah], *f.* Bar rowlock.

escalamiento [es-cah-lah-me-en'-to], *m.* Act of scaling walls.

escálamo [es-cah'-lah-mo], *m. (Naut.)* Thole or thowl, or tholepin; row-lock.

escalamotes [es-cah-lah-mo'-tes], *m. pl. (Naut.)* Timber-heads, kevelheads.

escalante [es-cah-lahn'-tay], *pa.* Scaling, climbing.

escalar [es-cah-lar'], *va.* 1. To scale, to climb (montaña) *(Fig.)* **Escalar puestos,** to move up. 2. To burgle, to break into (casa). *-vn.* To climb; *(Fig.)* to climb the social ladder.

escaldada [es-cal-dah'-dah], *f.* A woman very abusive, loose, and lewd in her behavior.

escaldado, da [es-cal-dah'-do], *a.* Cautious, suspicious, wary, *-pp.* of ESCALDAR.

escaldar [es-cal-dar'], *va.* 1. To burn, to scald (quemar); to bathe with very hot water. 2. To make iron red-hot. *-vr.* 1. To get scalded. 2. To chafe.

escaldrantes [es-cal-drahn'-tes], *m. pl. (Naut.)* Kevels, wooden pin on which tackle and sails are put to dry.

escaldufar [es-cal-doo-far'], *va. (Prov.)* To take broth out of the pot when it is too full.

escaleno [es-cah-lay'-no], *a. (Geom.)* Scalene.

escalentamiento [es-cah-len-tah-me-en'-to], *m.* Inflammation, disease in the feet of animals.

escalera [es-cah-ley'-rah], *f.* 1. Staircase. 2. Stair (de casa). **Escalera de caracol,** a winding stair. **Escalera de incendios,** fire escape. 3. Ladder (escalera de mano). 4. Sloats of a cart.

escalera mecánica [es-cah-lay'-rah may-cah'-ne-cah], *f.* Escalator.

escalereja, escalerilla [es-cah-la-ray'-hah, es-cah-lay-reel'-lyah], *f.* 1. *(dim.)* A small ladder. 2. *(Mech.)* Rack. 3. Drenching instrument. **En escalerilla,** in degrees.

escalerón [es-cah-lay-rone'], *m. aug.* A large staircase.

escaleta [es-cah-lay'-tah], *f.* Engine for raising cannons and mortars on their carriages.

escalfado, da [es-cal-fah'-do, dah], *a.* Applied to whitewashed walls full of blisters. *-pp.* of ESCALFAR.

escalfador [es-cal-fah-dor'], *m.* 1. A barber's pan for keeping water warm. 2. Chafing-dish.

escalfar [es-cal-far'], *va.* 1. To poach eggs. 2. To warm. **Escalfar el pan,** to put bread into an oven which is too hot, and scorches it.

escalfarote [es-cal-fah-ro'-tay], *m.* A kind of wide boot lined with hay.

escalfeta [es-cal-fay'-tah], *f.* 1. Small pan, used to hold live coals. 2. Chafing-dish. V. ESCALFADOR. 3. Water-dish or water-plate, for keeping meat hot.

escalimarse [es-cah-le-mar'-say], *m. (Naut.)* To be split or worked out of the seams of a ship (estopa).

escalinata [es-cah-le-nah'-tah], *f.* A stone staircase in front of an edifice.

escalio [es-cah'-le-o], *m.* Land abandoned for tillage.

escalmo [es-cahl'-mo], *m. V.* ESCÁLAMO.

escalofriado, da [es-cah-lo-fre-ah'-do, dah] *a.* Shivering.

escalofriante [es-cah-lo-fre-ahn'-tay], *a.* Hair-raising, chilling, frightening.

escalofrío [es-cah-lo-free'-o], *m.* Indisposition attended with shivering; cold stage of a fever.

escalón [es-cah-lo-ne'], *m.* 1. Step of a stair (peldaño). 2. Degree of dignity. 3. *(Mil.)* Echelon.

escalonar [es-cah-lo-nar'], *va.* 1. *(Mil.)* To echelon. 2. To scale, to place at intervals. 3. To stagger (horas de trabajo, etc.)

escalope [es-cah-lo'-pay], *m. (Culin.)* Escalope. **Escalope de ternera,** escalope of veal.

escalpelo [es-cal-pay'-lo], *m. (Med.)* Scalpel, a surgeon's instrument.

escalplo [es-cahl'-plo], *m.* Currier's knife.

escaluña [es-cah-loo'-nyah], *f. (Bot.)* Eschalot, shallot, scallion.

escama [es-cah'-mah], *f.* 1. Scale, horny plate, forming the coat of fishes (pez) 2. Scale, something exfoliated, a thin lamina. 3. A small scaly piece, many of which, lapping one over another form a coat of mail. 4. *(Met.)* Resentment, grudge, deep sense of injury. 5. *(Bot.)* Scale, an abortive, rudimentary leaf.

escamada [es-cah-mah'-dah], *f.* Embroidery in figure of scales.

escamado [es-cah-mah'-o], *m.* Work wrought with the figure of scales.

escamado, da [es-cah-mah'-do, dah], *a. & pp.* of ESCAMAR. Tutored by experience.

escamdura [es-cah-mah-doo'-ra], *f.* Act of embroidering like scales.

escamar [es-cah-mar'], *va.* 1. To scale fish. 2. *(Met.)* To offend, to irritate, to molest. **Eso me escama,** that makes me suspicious, *-vn.* To embroider scale or shell fashion. *-vr.* To be tutored by painful experience, to resent, to take ill. **Y luego se escamó,** and after that he was on his guard.

escambronal [es-cam-bro-nahl'], *m.* Plantation of buckthorns.

escamel [es-cah-mel'], *m.* Instrument used by sword-makers; long arm of an anvil on which the sword is laid to beat it out.

escamilla, ita [es-cah-meel'-lyah, ee'-tah], *f. dim.* A little scale.

escamochear [es-cah-mo-chay-ar'], *vn. (Prov.)* V. PAVORDEAR.

escamocho [es-cah-mo'-cho], *m.* 1. Broken victuals, leavings. 2. *(Prov.)* A rickety and languid person.

escamonda [es-cah-mon'dah], *f.* The act of pruning trees.

escamondadura [es-cah-mon-dah-doo'-rah], *f.* Useless branches of trees.

escamondar [es-cah-mon-dar'], *va.* 1. To prune or clear trees of noxious excrescences. 2. To clean, to cleanse.

escamondo [es-cah-mon'-do], *m.* Clearing trees of useless branches.

escamonea [es-cah-mo-nay'-a], *f. (Bot.)* Scammony.

escamoneado, da [es-cah-mo-nay-ah'-do, dah], *a.* Relating to scammony. *-pp.* of ESCAMONEARSE.

escamonearse [es-cah-mo-nay-ar'-say], *vr. (coll.)* To resent, to take ill, to be offended.

escamoso, sa [es-cah-mo'-so, sah], *a.* Scaly (pez), ostraceous, squamous.

escamotar [es'-cah-mo-tar'], *va.* In jugglery, to palm, to make a thing disappear from among the hands.

escamoteador, ra [es-cah-mo-tay-ah-dor', rah], *m. & f.* A juggler, prestidigitateur.

escamotear [es-cah-mo-tay-ar'], *va.* V. ESCAMOTAR.

escamoteo [es-cah-mo-tay'-o], *m.* Jugglery, sleight of hand (destreza).

escampada [es-cam-pah'-dah], *f.* Stampede.

escampado, da [es-cam-pah'-do, dah], *a.* V. DESCAMPADO. *-pp.* of ESCAMPAR.

escampar [es-cam-par'], *vn.* 1. To cease raining. 2. To leave off working, *-va.* To clean or clear out a place.

escampavía [es-cam-pa-vee'-ah], *f. (Naut.)* A light craft.

escamudo, da [es-cah-moo'-do, dah], *a.* V. ESCAMOSO.

escamujar [es-cah-moo-har'], *va.* To prune olive trees, to lop off the superfluous branches.

escamujo [es-cah-moo'-ho], *m.* 1. A lopped-off branch of an olive tree. 2. Time of pruning olive trees.

escanciador, ra [es-can-teah-dor', rah], *m. & f.* Cup bearer, the person that serves wine at feasts.

escanciar [es-can-the-ar'], *va.* To pour wine, to serve wine.

escanda [es-cahn'-dah], *f. (Bot.)* Spelt-wheat.

escandalar [es-can-dah-lar'], *m.* Apartment for the compass.

escandalizador, ra [es-can-dah-le-thah-dor', rah], *m. & f.* One who scandalizes.

escandalizante [es-can-dah-le-thahn'-tay], *a.* Scandalous, shocking.

escandalizar [es-can-dah-le-thar'], *va.* To scandalize, to offend by a scandalous action. *-vr.* 1. To be scandalized. 2. To be irritated. 3. To be amazed, to wonder (at). **Se escandalizó ante la pintura,** he threw up his hands in horror at the picture.

escandalizativo, va [es-can-dah-le-tha-tee'-vo, vah], *a.* Scandalous.

escandallar [es-can-dal-lyar'], *va. (Naut.)* To sound.

escandallo [es-can-dahl'lyo], *m.* 1. *(Naut.)* Deep sea lead. 2. *(Met.)* Proof, trial.

escándalo [es-cahn'-dah-lo], *m.* 1. Scandal, offence given by the faults of others. 2. Admiration, astonishment (asombro). 3. Tumult, commotion (alboroto). **El escándalo del año,** the scandal of the year. **Es un escándalo cómo suben los precios,** it is scandalous the way prices are rising. **Armar un escándalo a uno,** to give someone a dressing down.

escandalosa [es-can-dah-lo'-sah], *f. (Naut.)* Gaff-sail.

escandalosamente [es-can-dah-lo'-sah-men-tay], *adv.* Scandalously, shamefully.

escandaloso, sa [es-can-dah-lo'-so, sah], *a.* 1. Scandalous, giving public offence. 2. Scandalous (vida), shameful, disgraceful. 3. Turbulent, flagrant (crimen)

escandencencia [es-can-day-then'-the-ah], *f.* 1. Candescence, the state of growing hot. 2. Heat, anger, passion. V. EXCANDECENCIA.

escandecer [es-can-day-therr'], *va.* V. EXCANDECER.

escandelar [es-can-day-lar'], *m. (Naut.)* The second cabin in a row-galley.

escandelarete [es-can-day-lah-ray-tay], *m. (Naut.)* A small cabin in a row-galley.

escandia [es-cahn'-deah], *f. (Bot.)* Cienfuegos wheat.

escandinavo, va [es-can-de-nah'-vo, vah], *a.* Scandinavian.

escáner [es-cah'-nayr], *m. (Med.)* Scanner.

escantillar [es-can-til-lyar'], *va.* To trace lines on walls, to make them of different colors.

escantillón [es-can-teel-lyon'], *m.* 1. Gauge, pattern, template, rule. 2. Angle forested by two walls. 3. *(Mil.)* Semi-circular modelling-board to measure the exterior diameters of pieces of artillery.

escaña [es-cah'-nyah], *f. (Bot.)* Saint Peter's corn, or one-grained wheat.

escañero [es-cah-nyay'-ro], *m.* Seat-keeper, one who takes care of seats and benches in council chambers or courts.

escañillo [es-cah-nyeel'-lyo], *m. dim.* A small bench or form with a back.

escaño [es-cah'-nyo], *m.* 1. Bench or form with a back. 2. *(Naut.)* Sheer-rail, which divides the quick works from the dead works. 3. *(Parl.)* Seat.

escañuelo [es-cah-nyoo-ay'-lo], *m.* Small bench placed at the feet.

escapada, *f.* **escapamiento,** *m.* [es-cah-pah'-dah]. Escape (huida), flight, escapade. **Haré la comida en una escapada,** I'll get the meal right away.

escapar [es-cah-par'], *va.* To liberate from danger; to slip from the memory, to ride hard (caballo). *-vn. & vr.* To escape (persona), to flee, to get out of danger, to avoid punishment, to flee away or to get away off, to make off, to make one's escape. **Escapar de la cárcel,** to escape from prison. **Escaparse con algo,** to make off with something. **Escaparse por un pelo, to have a narrow escape.**

escaparate [es-cah-pa-rah'-tay], *m.* 1. Press, case, cupboard (vitrina). 2. Shop window (de tienda).

escaparatico [es-cah-pa-rah-tee'-co], *m. dim.* A little cupboard.

escaparatista [es-cah-pa-rah-tees'-tah], *m & f.* Window dresser.

escapatoria [es-cah-pa-to'-re-ah], *f.* 1. Escape, flying, flight. 2. Escape, excuse, evasion, subterfuge, loophole.

escape [es-cah'-pay], *m.* 1. Escape, flight, escaping (huida). 2. Flying, flight. 3. Escape, subterfuge, evasion. 3. Leak, leakage (de gas) **A todo escape,** at full speed. 4. Leak. 5. Exhaust valve, exhaust. **Tubo de escape,** exhaust pipe.

escapo [es-cah'-po], *m.* 1. *(Arch.)* Shaft of a column without base or capital. 2. *(Bot.)* Scape, a stem rising from the root, and bearing nothing but flowers.

escápula [es-cah'-poo-lah], *f. (Anat.)* Scapula, shoulder blade.

escapular [es-cah-poo-lar'], *va. (Naut.)* To double or clear a cape. *-a.* Scapular, relating to the shoulder blade.

escapulario [es-cah-poo-lah'-re-o], *m.* 1. Scapulary, a part of the habit of various religious orders. 2. Scapular. 3. *(Med.)* Shoulder-strap.

escaque [es-cah'-kay], *m.* 1. Any of the squares of a chess-board. 2. *(Her.)* Any of the squares of a coat of arms. *-pl.* 1. Checker work of a draught or chessboard. 2. Any work resembling the checkers of a draught or chess-board. 3. The game of chess.

escaqueado, da [es-cah-kay-ah'-do, dah], *a.* Checkered, variegated with alternate colors. *-pp.* of ESCAQUEAR.

escara [es-cah'-rah], *f. (Med.)* 1. The scurf or crust of a sore. 2. Eschar, a hard crust or scar made by caustics.

escarabajear [es-cah-rah-bah-ha-yar'], *vn.* 1. To crawl to and fro like insects. 2. To scrawl, to scribble (escribir mal). 3. *(coll.)* To sting, to give pain, to disquiet, to harass.

escarabajo [es-cah-rah-bah'-ho], *m.* 1. *(Ent.)* The common black beetle, tumble bug, dung beetle. 2. Nickname given to a thick, short, ill-shaped person (enano). 3. Flaw (en un tejido); fault in the bore (de un cañón).

escarabídeo, dea [es-cah-rah-bee'-day-o, ah], *a.* Scarabaeid, like a tumble bug.

escarafullar [es-cah-rah-fool-lyar'], *vn.* To deceive, to gloss over.

escaramucear [es-cah-rah-moo-thay-ar'], *vn.* To skirmish.

escaramujo [es-cah-rah-moo'-ho], *m.* 1. *(Bot.)* Dog rose. 2. *(Zool.)* A kind of small marine snail which clings to the hull of vessels.

escaramuza [es-cah-rah-moo'-thah], *f.* 1. Skirmish, slight engagement. 2. *(Met.)* Skirmish, contest, dispute, quarrel, contention.

escaramuzador [es-cah-rah-moo-thah-dor'], *m.* 1. Skirmisher. 2. *(Met.)* Disputer.

escaramuzar [es-cah-rah-moo-thar'], *vn.* 1. To skirmish, to fight loosely. 2. *(Met.)* To dispute, to quarrel; rarely used in this sense.

escarapela [es-cah-rah-pay'-lah], *f.* 1. Dispute which terminates in blows: applied commonly to a fray among women. 2. Cockade worn in the hat.

escarapelar [es-cah-rah-pay-lar'], *vn. & vr.* 1. To dispute (discutir), to wrangle, to quarrel (mujeres). 2. *vr. (Peru. and S. A.)* To have hair stand on end; to cringe upon hearing sharp noises.

escarbadero [es-car-bah-day'-ro], *m.* Place where boars, wolves, and other animals scrape or scratch the ground.

escarbadientes [es-car-bah-deen'-tes], *m. V.* MONDADIENTES.

escarbador [es-car-bah-dor'], *m.* Scratcher, scraper.

escarbadura [es-car-bah-doo'-rah], *f.* Act and effect of scratching.

escarbajuelo [es-car-bah-hoo-ay'-lo], *m. (Ent.)* Vine-fretter.

escarbaorejas [es-car-bah-o-ray'-has], *m.* Earpick.

escarbar [es-car-bar'], *va.* 1. To scrape or scratch the earth, as fowls (tierra). 2. *(Met.)* To inquire minutely, to investigate.

escarbo [es-car'-bo], *m.* Act and effect of scraping or scratching.

escarcela [es-car-thay'-lah], *f.* 1. A large pouch fastened to the belt; sportsman's net for catching game. 2. Cuisse, armor which covers the thigh. 3. Kind of head-dress for women.

escarceo [es-car-thay'-o], *m.* Small broken waves occasioned by currents (olas). **Escarceos,** bounds and windings of spirited horses.

escarcha [es-car'-chah], *f.* 1. Hoar frost, rime. 2. The frozen watery vapors observable on windows and other articles of glass; frost work.

escarchada [es-car-chah'-dah], *f. (Bot.)* Ice plant, *fig.* marigold.

escarchado [es-car-chah'-do], *m.* 1. A kind of gold or silver twist. 2. Frosting upon cakes and confectionery.

escarchado, da [es-car-chah'-do], *a. & pp.* of ESCARCHAR. Hoary, white with frost.

escarchador [es-car-chah-dor'], *m.* Freezing tool, a device in mints for thinning the nibs of ingots so as to make them pass through the gauge plate.

escarchar [es-car-char'], *vn.* To be frozen or congealed (rocío, vapor). *-va.* 1. To dilute potter's clay with water. 2. To put frostwork, shining points, upon confections. 3. To thin nibs of ingots, in mints.

escarche [es-car'-chay], *m.* A kind of gold or silver flat wire for embroidery.

escarcho [es-car'-cho], *m. (Zool.)* Red surmullet.

escarchosa [es-car-cho'-sah], *f. (Bot.)* Ice plant, fig-marigold.

escarda [es-car'-dah], *f.* 1. Weed hook (herramienta). 2. The act of weeding cornfields.

escardadera [es-car-dah-day'-rah], *f.* 1. Woman employed to clear cornfields of weeds or noxious herbs. 2. A gardener's hoe.

escardador, ra [es-car-dah-dor', rah], *m. & f.* Weeder, a man or woman who weeds cornfields.

escardadura [es-car-dah-doo'-rah], *f.* or **escardamiento,** *m.* Weeding.

escardar [es-car-dar'], *va.* 1. To weed cornfields. 2. *(Met.)* To weed, to part good from bad; to root out vice. **Enviar a escardar,** *(coll.)* to refuse harshly.

escardillar [es-car-deel-lyar'], *va. V.* ESCARDAR.

escardillo, lla [es-car-deel'-lyo, lyah], *m. & f.* 1. Small weed hook. 2. Thistledown.

escariador [es-cah-reah-dor'], *m.* Kind of punch used by coppersmiths; reamer.

escariar [es-cah-re-ar'], *va.* To ream, to widen a hole or the interior of a tube, by using the reamer.

escarificación [es-cah-re-fe-cah-the, on'], *f. (Med.)* Scarification.

escarificador [es-cah-re-fe-cah-dor'], *m. (Med.)* Scarifier, scarificator; cupping glass.

escarificar [es-cah-re-fe-car'], *va. (Surg.)* To scarify.

escarioso, sa [es-cah-re-o'-so, sah], *a. (Both.)* Scarious, like a thin scale.

escarizar [es-cah-re-thar'], *va. (Surg.)* To clean a sore by taking away the scurf or scab.

escarlador [es-car-lah-dor'], *m.* Iron instrument for polishing combs.

escarlata [es-car-lah'-tah], *f.* 1. Scarlet (color). 2. Scarlet, cloth dyed with a scarlet color. 3. Scarlet fever, scarlatina (emfermedad).

escarlatina [es-car-lah-tee'-nah], *f.* 1. *(Com.)* A red or crimson woollen fabric. 2. *(Med.)* Scarlatina, scarlet fever, a contagious eruptive fever.

escarmenador [es-car-may-nah-dor'], *m. V.* ESCARPIDOR.

escarmenar [es-car-may-nar'], *va.* 1. To comb, to pick wool, silk, etc.; to disentangle what is twisted. 2. To punish anyone by depriving him of his money. 3. To cheat.

escarmentado, da [es-car-men-tah'-do, dah], *a.* Punished (por experiencia).

escarmentar [es-car-men-tar'], *vn.* To be tutored by experience, to take warning. **Yo escarmenté y no lo volví a hacer,** I learned my lesson and never did it again. *-va.* 1. To correct severely, to inflict an exemplary punishment.

escarmiento [es-car-me-en'-to], *m.* 1. Warning, caution, lesson (aviso), punishment (castigo). 2. Fine, chastisement. **Que esto te sirva de escarmiento,** let this be a lesson to you. *(Yo escarmiento, yo escarmiente, from Escarmentar. V.* ACRECENTAR.)

escarnecedor, ra [es-car-nay-thay-dor', rah], *m. & f.* Scoffer, scorner, jeerer, giber, mocker, flinger.

escarnecer [es-car-nay-therr'], *va.* To scoff; to mock, to ridicule, to jeer, to gibe, to laugh at. *(Yo escarnezco, yo escarnezca, from Escarnecer. V.* CONOCER.)

escarnecidamente [es-car-nay-the'-dah-men-tay], *adv.* Scornfully.

escarnecimiento [es-car-nay-the-me-en'-to], *m.* Scoffing; derision.

escarnido, da [es-car-nee'-do, dah], *a. V.* DESCARNADO.

escarnio [es-car'-ne-o], *m.* 1. Scoff, contemptuous, ridicule. 2. Gibe, jeer, jeering, mock, flout.

escaro [es-cah'-ro], *m.* 1. *(Zool.)* A kind of mutton fish. 2. One who has crooked feet.

escarola [es-cah-ro'-lah], *f.* 1. *(Bot.)* Endive, garden-succory. 2. Plaited frill round the neck, ruff.

escarolado, da [es-cah-ro-lah'-do, dah], *a.* 1. Of the endive color. 2. Curled. *-pp.* of ESCAROLAR.

escarolar [es-cah-ro-lar'], *va. V.* ALECHUGAR.

escarolero, ra [es-cah-ro-lay'-ro, rah], *m. & f.* One who sells endives.

escarolita [es-cah-ro-lee'-tah], *f. dim.* A small endive.

escarótico, ca [es-cah-ro'-te-co, cah], *a.* Escharotic, caustic.

escarpa [es-car'-pah], *f.* 1. Declivity or gradual descent of a place. 2. *(Mil.)* Scarp, or escarp, the talus or slope on the inside of a ditch toward the rampart.

escarpado, da [es-car-pah'-do, dah], *a.* Sloped, craggy, rugged, crabbed. *-pp.* of ESCARPAR. *-m.(Arch.) V.* ESCARPE.

escarpar [es-car-par'], *va.* 1. *(Naut.)* To scarf or join timbers. 2. To rasp or cleanse works of sculpture. 3. *(Mil.)* To escarp, to slope down.

escarpe [es-car'-pay], *m.* 1. Declivity, sloped bank. 2. *(Arch.)* The scarf of a wall, a lapped joint. 3. *(Naut.)* A scarf joint.

escarpelar [es-car-pay-lar'], *va. (Anat.)* To scalp.

escarpelo [es-car-pay'-lo], *m.* Rasp, a coarse file.

escarpia [es-car'-pe-ah], *f.* 1. Tenterhook. 2. Meat hook, flesh hook.

escarpidor [es-car-pe-dor'], *m.* Comb with large wide teeth.

escarpín [es-car-peen'], *m.* 1. Sock, half hose (calcetín). 2. Shoe with a thin sole and low heel, a pump (zapatilla).

escarpión [es-car-pe-on'], *adv.* In the form of a tenter or hook.

escartivana [es-car-te-vah'-nah], *f.* A strip of paper or linen for binding maps or engravings.

escarza [es-car'-thah], *f.* 1. A sore in the hoofs of horses or mules. 2. An opening for discovering a tumor.

escarzamiento, *m.* or **escarzadura,** *f.* [es-car-thah-me-en'-to, es-car-thah-doo'-rah]. Act and effect of removing honey-combs.

escarzano, na [es-car-thah'-no, nah], *a. (Arch.)* Applied to an arch which is less than a semicircle.

escarzar [es-car-thar'], *va.* To remove the honeycomb from a hive in February.

escarzo [es-car'-tho], *m.* 1. Blackish green honeycomb found in the hive without honey. 2. Operation and time of removing honey from a hive. 3. Fungi on the trunks of trees. 4. Floss silk.

escarzo, za [es-car'-tho, thah], *a.* Lame on account of sores in the hoof (mulas, caballos).

escasamente [es-cah-sah-men'-tay], *adv.* 1. Scantily, sparingly, miserably. 2. Hardly, scarcely, difficultly; narrowly.

escaseada [es-cah-say-ah'-dah], **escaseadura,** *f. (Naut.)* Lack of wind.

escasear [es-cah-say-ar'], *va.* 1. To give sparingly and grudgingly. 2. To spare, to live in a frugal manner. *-vn.* 1. To grow less, to decrease, to be wanting. 2. *(Naut.)* To grow scanty (viento).

escasez, escaseza [es-cah-seth', es-cah-say'-thah], *f.* 1. Scantiness, meagreness; hardiness. 2. Want, lack (falta). 3. Poverty (pobreza).

escaso, sa [es-cah'-so, sah], *a.* 1. Small, short, limited, little. 2. Sparing, parsimonious, not in us. 3. Scanty, defective, narrow; hard; churlish. **Escaso de población,** thinly populated. **Escaso de recursos naturales,** poor in natural resources. **Andar escaso de dinero,** to be short of money.

escatimado, da [es-cah-te-mah'-do, dah], *a.* Little, scanty. *-pp.* of ESCATIMAR.

escatimar [es-cah-te-mar'], *va.* 1. To curtail (reducir), to lessen, to clip. 2. To haggle, to be tedious in a bargain. 3. To corrupt the meaning of words.

escatimosamente [es-cah-te-mo'-sah-men-tay], *adv.* Maliciously, viciously.

escatimoso, sa [es-cah-te-mo'-so, sah], *a.* Cunning, malicious.

escatofagio, gia [es-cah-to-fah'-heo, ah], *a.* Scatophagous, dungeating.

escaupil [es-cah-oo-peel'], *m.* Armor used by the Mexicans before the conquest.

escayola [es-cah-yo'-lah], *f.* 1. Paste or composition resembling marble in appearance. 2. *(Med.)* Plaster.

escayolar [es-cah-yo-lar'], *va.* To put in plaster. **Con la pierna escayolada,** with his leg in plaster. **Tener el cuello escayolado,** to have one's neck in plaster.

escena [es-thay'-nah], *f.* 1. The stage (escenario). **Entrar en escena,** to enter. **Poner en escena,** to stage. 2. Scene, part of a play. **Escena muda,** by-play. 3. *(Met.)* Revolution, vicissitude. 4. Bed and shepherd's hut made of branches. 5. A spectacle.

escenario [es-thay-nah'-re-o], *m.* 1. The stage. 2. *(Fig.)* Scene; setting. **El escenario del crimen,** the scene of the crime. **Desapareció del escenario político,** he disappeared from the political scene.

escénico, ca [es-thay'-ne-co, cah], *a.* Scenic, belonging to the stage.

escenificación [es-thay-ne-fe-cah-the-on'], *f.* Dramatization, adapting for stage or movies.

escenificar [es-thay-ne-fe-car'], *va.* To dramatize (novela), to stage (comedia).

escenita [es-thay-nee'-tah], *f. dim.* A short scene.

escenografía [es-thay-no-grah-fee'-ah], *f.* Scenography, the art of perspective.

escenográfico, ca [es-thay-no-grah'-fe-co, cah], *a.* Scenographic, perspective.

escenógrafo [es-thay-no'-grah-fo], *m.* An instrument for representing perspective views.

escépticamente [es-thep'-te-cah-men-tay], *adv.* Sceptically.

escepticismo [es-thep-te-thees'-mo], *m.* Scepticism.

escéptico, ca [es-thep'-te-co, cah], *a.* Sceptic, sceptical.

esciadofillo, lla [es-the-ah-do-feel'-lyo, lyah], *a.* Having parasol-shaped leaves.

esciagrafía [es-the-ah-grah-fee'-ah], *f.* 1. *(Arch.)* Sciagraph, the plan of a building in vertical section. 2. The art of correct shading. 3. *(Ast.)* Sciagraphy, the art of finding the hour by the shadows of heavenly bodies.

esciágrafo [es-the-ah'-grah-fo], *m.* Sciagrapher.

esciarro [es-the-ar'-ro], *m.* A stream of lava.

esciatérico, ca [es-the-ah-tay'-re-co, cah], *a.* Sciatheric, relative to a sundial.

esciatorio [es-the-ah-tay'-reo], *m.* 1. Gnomon, triangular piece of a sundial. 2. Among quarrymen, a dialplate.

esciátero [es-the-ah'-tay-ro], *m.* A kind of sundial of the ancients.

escibalario, ria [es-the-bah-lah'-re-o, ah], *a.* Living in excrement.

escible [es-thee'-blay], *a.* Worthy of being known.

esciena [es-the-ay'-nah], *f. (Zool.)* A species of crawfish.

escífula [es-thee'-foo-lah], *f.* A kind of funnel with which certain lichens are provided.

escila marítima [es-thee'-lah ma-ree'-te-mah], *f. (Bot.)* Squill.

esciografía [es-the-o-grah-fe'-ah], etc. *V.* ESCIAGRAFÍA, etc.

escisión [es-these-on'], *f.* Scission, splitting, fission.

esclarecedor [es-cla-ray-they-dor'], *a.* Illuminating (explicación).

esclarecer [es-clah-ray-therr'], *va.* 1. To lighten, to produce light; to illuminate. 2. *(Met.)* To illustrate, to ennoble (ennoblecer). *-vn.* To dawn.

esclarecidamente [es-clah-ray-the'-dah-men-tay], *adv.* Illustriously, conspicuously.

esclarecido, da [es-clah-ray-thee'-do, dah], *a.* Illustrious, noble, conspicuous, eminent, honorable. *pp.* of ESCLARECER.

esclarecimiento [es-clah-ray-the-me-en'-to], *m.* 1. Dawn, the morning dawn. 2. Ennoblement, illustriousness, conspicuousness.

esclava [es-clah'-vah], *f.* 1. Slave, drudge. **Esclava blanca,** white slave. 2. Slave bangle (pulsera).

esclavillo, illa; ito, ita [es-clah-veel'-lyo, lyah, vee'-to, vee'-tah], *m.* & *f. dim.* A little slave.

esclavina [es-clah-vee'-nah], *f.* 1. A long robe worn by pilgrims. 2. Pilgrim's pall, to which shells are fixed. 3. Collar formally worn by priests. 4. Kind of cloth formally worn over women's shoulders in winter; tippet. 5. Cape of a cloak.

esclavista [es-clah-vees'-tah], *a.* Proslavery.

esclavitud [es-clah-ve-tood'], *f.* 1. Slavery, bondage, servitude, enslavement, mancipation, slavishness. 2. *(Met.)* Brotherhood, congregation. 3. *(Met.)* Servile subjection of passions and sentiments. 4. Ornament of jewels, worn by women on the breast.

esclavizar [es-clah-ve-thar'], *va.* 1. To enslave, to reduce to slavery. 2. *(Met.)* To drive, to overwork.

esclavo, va [es-clah'-vo, vah], *m.* & *f.* 1. Slave, captive, helot. **Vender a uno como esclavo,** to sell somebody into slavery. 2. Member of a brotherhood or confraternity. 3. Fag, one who works hard. 4. *(Met.)* Slave of one's own desires and passions. **Ser esclavo del tabaco,** to be a slave to tobacco.

esclavón, na [es-clah-vo-ne', nah], *a.* Slavonian, belonging to Slavonia, Slavonic language.

esclerosis [es-clay-ro'-sis], *f. (Med.)* Sclerosis. **Esclerosis múltiple,** multiple sclerosis.

esclerótica [es-clay-ro'-te-cah], *f.* Sclerotic, the exterior white coat of the eye.

esclusa [es-cloo'-sah], *f.* Lock, sluice, floodgate, milldam.

escoa [es-co'-ah], *f. (Naut.)* Rung-head, floor-head, floor-timber of the head.

escoba [es-co'-bah], *f.* 1. Broom, a besom. 2. A tall shrub from which brooms are made.

escobada [es-co-bah'-dah], *f.* The act of sweeping slightly.

escobadera [es-co-bah-day'-rah], *f.* A woman who sweeps, or cleans, with a broom.

escobajo [es-co-bah'-ho], *m.* 1. The remains of an old broom. 2. The stalk of a bunch of grapes.

escobar [es-co-bar'], *m.* A place where broom grows.

escobar [es-co-bar'], *va.* To sweep with a broom.

escobazar [es-co-bah-thar'], *va.* To sprinkle water with a broom or brush.

escobazo [es-co-bah'-tho], *m.* Stroke or blow with a broom (golpe). **Dar un escobazo,** to have a quick sweep-up (barrido).

escobera [es-co-bay'-rah], *f. V.* RETAMA.

escobenes [es-co-bay'-nes], *m. pl. (Naut.)* Hawses or hawseholes.

escobero, ra [es-co-bay'-ro, rah], *m.* 1. One who makes or sells brooms. 2. A broom used by masons for cleaning stones. *-f. V.* RETAMA.

escobeta [es-co-bay'-tah], *f.* 1. A small brush. 2. *(Bot.)* Sweet sultan centaury.

escobilla [es-co-beel'-lyah], *f.* 1. Brush. 2. A small broom or besom; a whisk. 3. *(Bot.)* The head of the plume-thistle with which silk is carded. 4. Sweepings of gold or silver in the workshop of a gold or silversmith 5. A swab for cleaning the touch-hole of a gun.

escobillón [es-co-beel-lyone'], *m. (Mil.)* Sponge of a cannon.

escobina [es-co-bee'-nah], *f.* Chips or dust made in boring something.

escobo [es-co'-bo], *m.* Brushwood, briers, brambles.

escobón [es-co-bone'], *m.* 1. *(Aug.)* A large broom (escoba). 2. Brush, with which a smith sprinkles the fire in his forge (bruza). *-pl. (Naut.)* Hawses.

escocer [es-co-therr'], *va.* 1. To cause a sharp pain, as if the part had been burnt. 2. *(Met.)* To make one smart or feel a poignant pain. 3. *(Met.)* To irritate, to provoke. *-vr.* To smart.

escocés, sa [es-co-thes', thay'-sah], *a.* Scotch, Scottish.

Escocia [es-co'-the-ah], *f. (Arch.)* Scotia, a semicircular concave moulding around the base of a column. Scotland.

escoda [es-co'-dah], *f.* An edged hammer, used by stonecutters.

escodadero [es-co-dah-day'-ro], *m.* Place where cattle rub their horns.

escodar [es-co-dar'], *va.* To hew stones with an edged hammer.

escofia [es-co'-fe-ah], *f. V.* COFIA.

escofiar [es-co-fe-ar'], *va.* To dress the head with a net.

escofieta [es-co-fe-ay'-tah], *f.* Coif, head-tire, women's head-dress.

escofina [es-co-fee'-nah], *f.* 1. Rasp, a coarse file used by carpenters. 2. Nailfile, file for corns.

escofinar [es-co-fe-nar'], *a.* To rasp, to mould wood with a large file.

escogedor, ra [es-co-hay-dor', rah], *m. & f.* Selecter, chooser.

escoger [es-co-herr'], *va.* To choose (entre), to select, to pick out, to excerpt, to cull, to elect (por voto).

escogidamente [es-co-he-dah-men'-tay], *adv.* 1. Choicely, selectly. 2. Elegantly, nicely.

escogido, da [es-co-hee'-do, dah], *a.* 1. Select, choice (en calidad). 2. Chosen.

escolar [es-co-lar'], *m.* Scholar, student, clerk, learner. *-a.* Scholastic, scholastical.

escolar [es-co-lar'], *vn. V.* COLAR.

escolaridad [es-co-lah-re-dahd'], *f.* Schooling. **Escolaridad obligatoria,** compulsory schooling.

escolarizar [es-co-lah-re-thar'], *va.* To enrol in school. **Niños sin escolarizar,** children not in school.

escolásticamente [es-co-lahs'-te-cah-men-tay], *adv.* Scholastically.

escolasticismo [es-co-las-te-thees'-mo], *m.* Scholasticism, Aristotelian philosophy.

escolástico, ca [es-co-lahs'-te-co, cah], *a.* Scholastic, scholastical, pertaining to schools.

escolástico [es-co-lahs'-te-co], *m.* A professor of theology.

escoliador [es-co-le-ah-dor'], *m.* Scholiast, a writer of explanatory notes.

escoliar [es-co-le-ar'], *va.* To gloss, to explain, to comment.

escolimado, da [es-co-le-mah'-do, dah], *a.* Weak, delicate.

escolimoso, sa [es-co-le-mo'-so, sah], *a.* Difficult, severe, hard to please.

escolio [es-co'-leo], *m.* 1. Scholion or scholium, a brief explanatory observation. 2. Gloss, commentary. 3. *(Geom.)* Note which refers to a preceding proposition.

escoliosis [es-co-le-o'-sis], *f. (Med.)* Scoliosis, lateral curvature of the spinal column.

escolopendra [es-co-lo-pen'-drah], *f.* 1. *(Ent.)* Scolopendra, centipede, a myriapod insect. 2. A fish. 3. *(Bot.)* Spleenwort, common hart's tongue.

escolta [es-col'-tah], *f.* Escort (persona), convoy, guard. **Dar escolta a,** to escort.

escoltar [es-col-tar'], *va.* To escort, to convoy, to guard (proteger).

escollera [es-col-lyay'-rah], *f. (Naut.)* Rocky place or cliff.

escollo [es-col'-lyo], *m.* 1. A shelf in the sea, or a rock under shallow water; a reef. 2. *(Met.)* Embarrassment, difficulty, danger (peligro oculto).

escombra [es-com'-brah], *f.* Purgation, removal of obstacles.

escombrar [es-com-brar'], *va.* To remove obstacles, to free from obstructions; to purify.

escombro [es-com'-bro], *m.* 1. Rubbish, fragments of materials used in building. 2. *(Zool.)* Mackerel.

escomerse [es-co-merr'-say], *va.* To be wasted or worn out with use or time.

esconce [es-con'-thay], *m.* Corner, angle.

esconderero [es-con-day-ray'-ro], *m.* A hiding or lurking place.

esconder [es-con-derr'], *va.* 1. To hide, to conceal, to keep in, to keep out of sight. 2. *(Met.)* To disguise, to dissemble. 3. To include, to contain. *-vr.* To hide, to lie hid, to be concealed, to skulk.

escondidamente [es-con-de-dah-men'-tay], *adv.* Privately, secretly, hiddenly.

escondidas (A), A escondidillas [es-con-dee'-das, ah escon-de-deel'-lyas], *adv.* Privately, in a secret manner.

escondimiento [es-con-de-me-en'-to], *m.* Concealment, concealing, the act of hiding or concealing something.

escondite [es-con-dee'-tay], *m.* Concealment, hold, a lurking place, a hiding place (escondrijo). **Juego de escondite,** hide and seek.

escondrijo [es-con-dree'-ho], *m.* Concealment, a hiding or lurking place.

escontrete [es-con-tray'-tay], *m. (Naut.)* Prop, stay, shore.

esconzado, da [es-con-thah'-do, dah], *a.* Angular, oblique.

escoñarse [es-co-nyar'-say], *vr.* 1. To hurt oneself (persona). **Estoy escoñado,** I'm knackered. 2. *(Med.)* To break, to get broken.

escopa [es-co'-pah], *f.* A kind of a chisel for chipping or cutting stones.

escoperada [es-co-pay-rah'-dah], *f.* Gunwale.

escopero [es-co-pay'-ro], *m. (Naut.)* Pitch-brush for paying the seams of ships; swab.

escopeta [es-co-pay'-tah], *f.* A shotgun, a gun. **Escopeta de viento,** an air-gun. **A tiro de escopeta,** 1. Within gunshot. 2. *(Met.)* At first view, easily. **Escopeta de aire comprimido,** popgun. **Escopeta de dos cañones,** double-barrelled gun.

escopetar [es-co-pay-tar'], *va.* To dig out goldmines.

escopetazo [es-co-pay-tah'-tho], *m.* 1. Gun or musket-shot (disparo). 2. Wound made by a gunshot (herida).

escopetear [es-co-pay-tay-ar'], *va.* To discharge a firelock or gun repeatedly. *-vr.* 1. To discharge firelocks at each other. 2. *(Met.)* To insult each other with foul language.

escopeteo [es-co-pay-tay'-o], *m.* Act of discharging volley of shots (disparos).

escopetería [es-co-pay-tay-ree'-ah], *f.* 1. Infantry armed with muskets. 2. Multitude of gunshot wounds.

escopetero [es-co-pay-tay'-ro], *m.* Gunsmith, armorer.

escopetilla [es-co-pay-teel'-lyah], *f. dim.* A small gun.

escopetón [es-co-pay-tone'], *m. aug.* A large gun.

escopleadura [es-co-play-ah-doo'-rah], *f.* Mortise-hole.

escoplear [es-co-play-ar'], *va.* To chisel, to cut with a chisel.

escoplillo, ito [es-co-pleel'-lyo, ee'-to], *m. dim.* A small chisel.

escoplo [es-co'-plo], *m.* Chisel.

escora [es-co'-rah], *f.* 1. Stanchion, prop, outrigger. 2. *(Naut.)* That part of a ship's side which makes the most resistance (apoyo); the central line of a vessel (línea). **Navío de escora baja,** a ship which carries a stiff sail. **Escoras,** *(Naut.)* shores, outriggers.

escorar [es-co-rar'], *va.* 1. *(Naut.)* To prop, to shore up. 2. To bank (avión). 3. *(Naut.)* To wedge. -*vn.* To reach low tide.

escorbútico, ca [es-cor-boo'-te-co, cah], *a.* Scorbutic, scorbutical; it is sometimes used as a substantive for a person affected with scurvy.

escorbuto [es-cor-boo'-to], *m.* Scurvy, a disease.

escorchapín [es-cor-chah-peen'], *m.* Passageboat, ferry.

escorchar [es-cor-chahr'], *va. V.* DESOLLAR.

escorche [es-cor'-chay], *m.* Decrease of a tuberous body.

escordio [es-cor'-deo], *m. (Bot.)* Water germander.

escoria [es-co'-re-ah], *f.* 1. Dross slags, scoria (metal). 2. Lee. 3. *(Met.)* Any mean or worthless thing. -*pl.* Scoriae, volcanic ashes.

escoriáceo, cea [es-co-re-ah'-thay-o, ah], *a.* Scoriaceous, ensembling scoria.

escoriación [es-co-re-ah-the-on'], *f.* Incrustation, scurf formed on a sore. *V.* EXCORIACIóN.

escorial [es-co-re-ahl'], *m.* 1. Place where a mine has been exhausted. 2. Place where the dross of metals is thrown.

escoriar [es-co-re-ar'], *va. V.* EXCORIAR.

escorificación [es-co-re-fe-cah-the-on'], *f.* Scorification, smelting an ore with lead.

escorificar [es-co-re-fe-car'], *va.* To scarify, to separate (oro y plata) by the process of scorification.

escorificatorio [es-co-re-fe-cah-to-tre-o], *m.* Scorifier. 1. A small flat dish used for scarifying. 2. A furnace for the same purpose.

escorodonia [es-co-ro-do'-ne-ah], *f. (Bot.)* Wood sage termander.

escorpena, escorpina [es-cor-pay'-nah, es-cor-pee'-nah], *f.* Grouper, a small sea food fish.

escorpiaco [es-cor-pe-ah'-co], *m.* An antidote against scorpion bites.

escorpioide [es-cor-pe-o'-e-day], *f. (Bot.) V.* ALACRANERA.

escorpión [es-cor-pe-on'], *m.* 1. Scorpion. Scorpio. 2. Scorpion (pez). 3. An ancient war-like machine. 4. Scorpion (zodíaco). 5. Instrument of torture, armed with metal points.

escorpiónido, da [es-cor-pe-o'-ne-do, dah], *a.* Scorpion-like. -*m. pl.* Scorpionidea, the scorpion family.

escorpiuro [es-cor-pe-oo'-ro], *m.* Scorpiurus, an herb of the bean family.

escorroso [es-cor-ro'-so], *m. (Prov. Cuba)* 1. Clamor, vociferation. 2. *V.* CACAREO.

escorrozo [es-cor-ro'-tho], *m. (coll.)* Pleasure, enjoyment.

escorzado [es-cor-thah'-do], *m. (Art.) V.* ESCORZO. **Escorzado, da,** *pp.* of ESCORZAR. Fore-shortened.

escorzar [es-cor-thar'], *va.* 1. *(Pict.)* To contract the size of a figure; to fore-shorten. 2. To form a depressed arch.

escorzo [es-cor'-tho], *m. (Art.)* Contraction or decrease of a figure in perspective.

escorzón [es-cor-thone'], *m. V.* ESCUERZO.

escorzonera [es-cor-tho-nay'-rah], *f. (Bot.)* Viper-root or garden viper-grass. **Escorzonera laciniada,** cut-leaved viper-grass.

escoscarse [es-cos-car'-say], *vr. V.* CONCOMERSE.

escota [es-co'-tah], *f.* 1. *(Agr. Prov.)* A kind of mattock or grubbing axe. 2. *(Naut.)* Sheet, a rope fastened to the lower corners of a sail for the purpose of extending or retaining it in a particular position. **Escotas mayores,** main-sheets. **Escotas de las velas de estay,** stay-sail sheets. **Escotas volantes,** flowing-sheets.

escotado [es-co-tah'-do], *m.* Neck, neckline (escotadura). -*a.* low-necked, low-cut (vestido). **Iba muy escotada,** she was wearing a very low-cut dress.

escotadura [es-co-tah-doo'-rah], *f.* 1. Sloping of a jacket or a corset. 2. The large trap-door of a theater or stage. 3. *(Mil.)* In the breast-plate of armor, the armhole to enable the arms to be moved.

escotar [es-co-tar'], *va.* 1. To cut out a thing so as to make it fit. 2. To slope. 3. To hollow a garment about the neck. 4. To club, to contribute to a common expense. 5. To draw water from (río).

escote [es-co'-tay], *m.* 1. Neck, neckline (corte del cuello). Low cut, low neckline. 2. Tucker, lace frill (adorno). 3. One's share (cuota). **Comprar algo a escote,** to club together to buy something. **Pagar a escote,** to pay Dutch (una pareja). **Cada uno pagó su escote,** each one paid his share.

escotera [es-co-tay'-rah], *f. (Naut.)* Sheet-hole, through which the main and fore-sheets are reeved.

escotero, ra [es-co-tey'-ro, rah], *a.* Free, disengaged.

escotilla [es-co-teel'-lyah], *f. (Naut.)* Hatchway. **Escotilla mayor,** the main hatchway. **Escotilla de proa,** fore-hatchway. **Escotilla de popa,** magazine hatchway.

escotillón [es-co-teel-lyone'], *m.* Scuttle, trap-door.

escotín [es-co-teen'], *m. (Naut.)* Tow sail-sheet, fastened to the lower corners of top-sails and topgallant-sails.

escotmía [es-co-to-mee'-ah], *f.* Dizziness or swimming in the head.

escoznete [es-coth-nay'-tay], *m. (Prov.)* A nutpick.

escozor [es-co-thor'], *m.* 1. A smart pungent pain. 2. *(Met.)* A lively sensation or perception of the mind.

escriba [es-cree'-bah], *m.* Scribe, among the Hebrews.

escribanía [es-cre-bah-nee'-ah], *f.* 1. Office or employment of a notary or scrivener (oficina). 2. Office or place where contracts and other notarial deeds and instruments are drawn up. 3. Secretary, escritoire, a case of drawers for writings, with a desk (mueble). 4. Portable writing-case (enseres).

escribano [es-cre-bah'-no], *m.* 1. Notary public; scrivener. **Escribano de cámara,** the clerk of a high court of justice, who must be also a notary public. **Escribano de número, or del número,** one of a certain number of notaries public, before whom only certain deeds can be executed. 2. Purser of a vessel. 3. *(Zool.)* An insect, shaped like a small spider, which is in continual movement upon the surface of slow streams or fountains. A (agua) skater. Gerris. **Es un gran escribano,** he writes a very neat hand, he writes like copper plate. **Escribano or escribanillo del agua,** water-skater.

escribiente [es-cre-be-en'-tay], *m.* Amanuensis, a clerk.

escribir [es-cre-beer'], *va.* 1. To write. **Escribir a mano,** to write in longhand. **Escribir a máquina,** to type. 2. To write, to compose literary works (escritor). 3. To write, to tell by letters. -*vr.* 1. To enrol oneself, to enter one's name in a register or roll. 2. To keep up an epistolary correspondence. **Escribir en la arena,** to bury in oblivion.

escriño [es-cree'-nyo], *m.* 1. Sort of hamper made of straw, and matted together with osier. 2. *(Prov.)* A jewel box, casket of jewels.

escrita [es-cree'-tah], *f.* A kind of fish, having marks like letters upon the back. *V.* ESCUADRO.

escritillas [es-cre-teel'-yas], *f. pl.* Lamb's testicles.

escrito [es-cree'-to], *m.* 1. Book or other literary composition. 2. *(Law.)* Allegation or petition exhibited in a court of justice. **Acuerdo por escrito,** written agreement. **Poner algo por escrito,** to commit something to paper. —**Escrito, ta,** *pp. irr.* of ESCRIBIR.

escritor, ra [es-cree-tor'], *m & f.* 1. Writer, author, composer. 2. Copyist.

escritorcillo [es-cre-tor-theel'-lyo], *m. dim.* A bad writer.

escritorillo [es-cre-to-reel'-lyo], *m. dim.* A small scrutoire.

escritorio [es-cre-to'-re-o], *m.* 1. A writing desk (mueble), secretary. 2. Counting-house, office (despacho). 3. Press, a large chest of drawers, or sort of cupboard, adorned with inlaid ivory, ebony, etc. 4. In printing offices every composing-case.

escritorzuelo, la [es-cre-tor-thoo-ay'-lo, lah], *m. & f. dim.* A poor writer.

escritura [es-cre-too'-rah], *f.* 1. Writing, the act of putting something on paper. 2. Deed, instrument, bond, contract. 3. Writing, a work or treatise written. **Escritura de seguro,** policy of insurance. 4. Art of writing. **Tiene malísima escritura,** her writing is terrible. **No acierto a leer su escritura,** I can't read his writing.

escriturar [es-cre-too-rar'], *va.* To bind oneself by a public instrument; to sign articles, to formalize legally (documentos). **Estar escriturado,** to be under articles.

escriturario [es-cre-too-rah'-re-o], *m.* One who professes to explain the holy Scripture, a professor of divinity.

escrófula [es-cro'-foo-lah], *f.* Scrofula, king's evil.

escrofularia [es-cro-foo-lah'-re-ah], *f. (Bot.)* Figwort.

escrofuloso, sa [es-cro-foo-lo'-so, sah], *a.* Scrofulous.

escrotal [es-cro-tahl'], *a.* Scrotal, relating to the scrotum.

escroto [es-cro'-to], *m.* Scrotum.

escrudriñar [es-croo-de-nyar'], *va. V.* ESCUDRIÑAR.

escrupulear [es-croo-poo-lay-ar'], *v. V.* ESCRUPULIZAR.

escrupulete [es-croo-poo-lay'-tay], *m. dim. (coll.)* A slight doubt or scruple.

escrupulillo [es-croo-poo-leel'-lyo], *m.* 1. *(dim.)* Slight doubt, scruple, or hesitation. 2. Small piece of metal put into a hollow brass globe, to ring as a bell for animals.

escrupulizar [es-croo-poo-le-thar'], *vn.* To scruple, to doubt, to hesitate.

escrúpulo [es-croo'-poo-lo], *m.* 1. Doubt, scruple, hesitation (duda). **Falta de escrúpulos,** unscrupulousness. 2. Scrupulosity, a great nicety or tenderness of conscience; conscience (cualidad). 3. Scruple, a small weight, the third part of a drachm. 4. *(Ast.)* Minute on a graduated sphere.

escrupulosamente [es-croo-poo-lo'-sah-men-tay], *adv.* Scrupulously.

escrupulosidad [es-croo-poo-lo-se-dah'], *f.* 1. Scrupulosity, minute and nice doubtfulness. 2. Scrupulosity, conscientiousness.

escrupuloso, sa [es-croo-poo-lo'-so, sah], *a.* 1. Scrupulous, characterized by careful observation of what is morally right, conscientious. 2. Scrupulous, nice, cautious, exact; narrow; critical.

escrutador, ra [es-croo-ta-dor', rah], *m & f.* 1. Examiner, scrutator, inquirer, searcher. 2. Inspector of an election.

escrutar [es-croo-tar'], *va.* 1. To count votes (votos). 2. To search (examinar), to pry into.

escrutinio [es-croo-tee'-ne-o], *m.* Scrutiny, inquiry, close examination. **Escrutinio electoral,** election returns, counting of electoral votes (votación).

escrutiñador [es-croo-te-nyah-dor'], *m.* Scrutator, censor.

escuadra [es-coo-ah'-drah], *f.* 1. Square, an instrument for measuring right angles. 2. Socket in which the pivot or spindle of a door turns. 3. A small number of horses or foot soldiers commanded by a corporal; a squad. 4. Squadron, fleet (de coches etc.), or more properly a part of a fleet. **A escuadra,** in a square manner. **Jefe de escuadra,** *(Naut.)* rear-admiral.

escuadrador [es-coo-ah-drah-dor'], *m.* Groover, a tool for opening the moulds of wax-candles.

escuadrar [es-coo-ah-drar'], *va.* 1. To square; to reduce to a square. 2. To fix the trunnions horizontally in a piece of ordenance.

escuadreo [es-coo-ah-dray'-o], *m.* Dimension, valuation of the square contents of a piece of ground.

escuadría [es-coo-ah-dree'-ah], *f.* Square, a measure having or forming right angles.

escuadrilla [es-coo-ah-dree'-lyah], *f.* Squadron of ships or planes.

escuadro [es-coo-ah'-dro], *m.* Species of dogfish.

escuadrón [es-coo-ah-dro-ne'], *m.* Squadron, troop of horses, a small body of horses. **Escuadrón de la muerte,** death squad.

escuadronar [es-coo-ah-dro-nar'], *va.* To draw up troops in rank and file, to form troops in squadrons.

escuadroncillo, ito [es-coo-ah-dron-theel'-lyo, ee'-to], *m. dim.* A small party of troops.

escuadronista [es-coo-ah-dro-nees'-tah] *m. (Mil.)* He who forms squadrons.

escualidez [es-coo-ah-le-deth'], *f.* Squalor, wretchedness.

escuálido, da [es-coo-ah'-le-do, dah], *a.* 1. Very weak, languid (débil). 2. Squalid, filthy (sucio), nauseous. 3. Like the spotted dogfish.

escualino, na [es-coo-ah-lee'-no, nah], *a. V.* ESCUÁLIDO, 3d def.

escualo [es-coo-ah'-lo], *m.* The spotted dogfish; a shark.

escucha [es-coo'-hah], *f.* 1. Sentinel, sentry. 2. **Escucha, or madre escucha,** a nun who is sent with another to the grate, to listen to what is said. 3. Scout, one who is sent privily to observe the motions of the enemy. 4. A small window, made for listening. 5. Servant who sleeps near her mistress, in order to wait on her. 6. Listening (acto). **Escucha telefónica,** telephone tapping. **Estar a la escucha,** to listen in.

escuchador, ra [es-coo-chah-dor', rah], *m. & f.* Hearer, hearkener, listener.

escuchante [es-coo-chahn'-tay], *pa. & m. & f.* Listener; hearkening.

escuchar [es-coo-char'], *va.* To listen (consejo), to give ear, to attend, to hear. *-vr.* To hear oneself with complacency, to be highly gratified with one's eloquence.

escudar [es-coo-dar'], *va.* 1. To shield, to defend with a shield. 2. To guard from danger. *-vr. (Met.)* To depend on some means of evading danger.

escuderaje [es-coo-day-rah'-hay], *m.* The office and service of a lady's page.

escuderear [es-coo-day-ray-ar'], *va.* To perform the service of a page; to perform the functions of a squire.

escudería [es-coo-day-ree'-ah], *f.* Service of a squire or shield-bearer.

escuderil [es-coo-day-reel'], *a.* Belonging to the office of a shield bearer, or to the place of a page.

escudero [es-coo-day'-ro], *m.* 1. Shield-bearer, squire or attendant on a warrior, a custrel. 2. Gentleman descended from an illustrious family. 3. Page who attends a lady. 4. A maker of shields and other defensive armor. **Escudero de a pie,** a servant kept to carry messages.

escuderón [es-coo-day-rone'], *m.* Squire puffed up with vanity and pride.

escudete [es-coo-day'-tay], *m.* 1. Gusset, a piece of lace sewn on a surplice under the armpit, to strengthen it. 2. A stain on the olive's fruit, from damage received in consequence of falls of rain. 3. Budding or inoculating. 4. *(Bot.)* White waterlily. *V.* NENÚFAR.

escudilla [es-coo-deel'-lyah], *f.* Bowl (recipiente), bowlful (contenido), crock; a soup-plate, porringer.

escudillar [es-coo-deel-lyar'], *va.* 1. To pour broth into porringers, to distribute broth. 2. *(Met.)* To lord, to domineer.

escudillo, ito [es-coo-deel'-lyo, ee'-to], *m. dim.* A small shield.

escudo [es-coo'-do], *m.* 1. Shield, buckler. 2. Plate on which arms are engraved. 3. Scutcheon of a lock. 4. Shield, patronage, protection, defense. 5. Back of a wild boar. 6. The bandage used in bleeding. 7. Sideplate of a gun. **Escudo de bote,** *(Naut.)* The backboard of a boat. 8. Crown, a coin of a different value in different countries.

escudriñador, ra [es-coo-dre-nyah-dor', rah], *m. & f.* Prier, scrutator; a person who inquires into the secrets of others.

escudriñamiento [es-coo-dre-nyah-me-en'-to], *m.* Investigation, scrutiny.

escudriñar [es-coo-dre-nyar'], *va.* To search, to pry into; to inquire after (investigar), to examine into (examinar); to consult.

escudriño [es-coo-dree'-nyo], *m. V.* ESCUDRIÑAMIENTO.

escuela [es-co-ay'-lah], *f.* 1. School, a house of discipline and instruction. 2. School, university, a place of literary education. 3. School, a state of instruction or the instruction given in schools. 4. School, a system of doctrine; style of a teacher. **Escuela de párvulos,** infant school. **Escuela de Bellas Artes,** Art school. **Escuela automovilista,** driving school. **Escuela elemental,** primary school. **Escuela naval,** naval academy. **Escuela de equitación,** riding school. **Estar en la escuela,** to be at school. **Formarse en una escuela dura,** to learn in a tough school. **Tener buena escuela,** to be well trained.

escuerzo [es-coo-err'-tho], *m.* Toad.

escueto, ta [es-coo-ay'-to, tah], *a.* 1 Concise (conciso), simple, unadorned, plain. **Un informe muy escueto,** a very concise report. **La verdad escueta,** the plain truth. 2. *(Amer. Peru)* Solitary, uninhabited.

escueznar [es-coo-eth-nar'], *va. (Prov.)* To extract the kernel of nuts.

escuezno [es-coo-eth'-no], *m. (Prov.)* Pulp or soft kernel of a nut fit for eating.

esculina [es-coo-lee'-nah], *f.* Esculin, a substance obtained from the horse-chestnut.

escullador [es-cool-lyah-dor'], *m.* In oilmills, a vessel for carrying off the oil.

escullirse [es-cool-lyeer'-say], *V. (Prov.)* To slip, to slide.

esculpir [es-cool-peer'], *va.* To sculpture, to engrave in wood or stone, to cut (inscripción).

esculto, ta [es-cool'-to, tah], *pp. irr. obs.* of ESCULPIR.

escultor [es-cool-tor'], *m.* Sculptor, carver.

escultora [es-cool-to'-rah], *f.* Female sculptor, sculptress.

escultura [es-cool-too'-rah], *f.* 1. Sculpture, the art of cutting wood or stone into images. 2. Carved work, the work made by a sculptor. **Escultura en madera,** wood carving.

escultural [es-cool-too-rahl'], *a.* Sculptural; belonging to the art of sculpture.

escupidera [es-coo-pe-day'-rah], *f.* Spittoon, cuspidor.

escupidero [es-coo-pe-day'-ro], *m.* 1. Spitting place. 2. *(Met.)* Despicable or abject situation.

escupido [es-coo-pee'-do], *m. V.* ESPUTO.—**Escupido, da, pp.** of ESCUPIR.

escupidor, ra [es-coo-pe-dor', rah], *m. & f.* A great spitter (persona).

escupidura [es-coo-pe-doo'-rah], *f.* 1. The act of spitting. 2. Spittle. 3. (En labios) Cracking.

escupir [es-coo-peer'], *va.* 1. To spit, to spit out (palabra, comida). **Escupir en el suelo,** to spit on the ground. 2. To break out in the skin (sangre). 3. *(Met. Poet.)* To discharge balls from firearms. 4. *(Met.)* To dart, to flash. 5. *(Met.)* To depreciate, to underrate the value of a thing. **Escupir en la cara,** to deride to the face, to ridicule. 6. To cough (confesar). 7. To cough up (pagar).

escupita, escupitina [es-coo-pee'-tah, es-coo-pe-tee'-nah], *f. (coll.) V.* SALIVA.

escupitajo [es-coo-pee-tah-ho], *m.* Spit.

escurar [es-coo-rar'], *va.* To scour cloth, to cleanse it from grease before it is milled.

escurina [es-coo-ree'-nah], *f. (Prov.)* Obscurity, darkness.

escurreplatos [es-coor-ray-plah'-tos], *m.* Plate rack.

escurribanda [es-coor-re-bahn'-dah], *f.* 1. Evasion, subterfuge. 2. Diarrhoea (vientre); bowel complaint. 3. Scuffle, bustle.

escurridizo, za [es-coor-re-dee'-tho, thah], *a.* 1. Slippery, not affording firm footing (superficie). 2. Hard to hold, hard to keep, easily escaping (objeto). **Lazo escurridizo,** a running knot.

escurridor [es-coor-re-dor'], *m.* Wringer (ropa); plate rack (de loza); colander, strainer (cocina).

escurriduras, escurrimbres [es-coor-re-doo'-ras, es-coor-reem'-bress], *f. pl.* Dregs, the sediment of liquors; the lees, the grounds. **Llegar a las escurriduras,** to reach the end of a festival, the remains of a dinner.

escurrimiento [es-coor-re-me-ayn'-to], *m. V.* DESLIZ.

escurripa [es-coor-ree'-pah], *f. (Bot.)* Cardinal flower.

escurrir [es-coor-reer'], *va.* To drain off liquor to the dregs (líquido), -*vn.* 1. To drop, to fall in drops (líquido). 2. To slip, to slide (objeto). 3. To lapse, to glide slowly. -*vr.* To escape from danger (persona); to slip out (observación), or to slip away; to creep, to skulk. **Se me escurrió de entre las manos,** it slipped out of my hands.

escutas, escutillas [es-coo'-tas, es-coo-teel-lyas], *f. pl. (Naut.)* Scuttles. *V.* ESCOTILLAS.

escutelaria [es-coo-tay-lah'-re-ah], *f.* (Scutellaria), skullcap, a herb of the mint family.

escuteliforme [es-coo-tay-le-for'-may], *a. (Bot.)* Shield-shaped, platter-shaped.

escúter [es-coo'-tayr], *m.* Scooter (motor).

escutiforme [es-coo-tefor'-may], *a.* Shield-shaped. *m.* The thyroid cartilage.

escuyer [es-coo-yerr'], *m.* Purveyor of meat to the palace.

esdrújula [es-droo'-hoo-lo], *f.* A Spanish word of more than two syllables, the last two of which are short, e.g. *cántaro.*

ese [ay'-say], *f.* 1. Spanish name of the letter **S.** 2. Link of a chain of the figure of this letter. **Hacer eses,** to zigzag.

ése, ésa, eso [ay'-say], *dem. pron.* That, that one. (plural: **ésos, ésas;** those). **Ni por ésas,** on no account. **No es una chica de ésas,** she's not one of those. **Ésos son tus padres,** those are your parents. **Ése lo sabe,** he knows. **Llegaremos a ésa mañana,** we'll get there tomorrow. **¡No me vengas con ésas!,** don't come to me with that story! **¡Conque ésas tenemos!,** so that's it! **Eso es lo que me dijo,** that's what he told me. **Ésa es la que vino,** that's the one who came.

ese, esa, *dem. adj.* That. (plural: **esos, esas;** those). **Esa mujer,** that woman. **Ese hombre,** that man. **Esos hombres,** those men. **Esos libros,** those books.

esecilla [ay-say-theel'-lyah], *f. dim.* Small link of a chain.

esencia [ay-sen'-the-ah], *f.* 1. Essence, formal existence (problema) 2. *(Chem. and Phar.)* Essence, a volatile oil; a solution in alcohol of an aromatic, or volatile oil. **Quinta esencia,** quintessence, an extract. **Ser de esencia,** to be indispensable, necessary.

esencial [ay-sen-the-ahl'], *a.* 1. Essential, necessary, constituent. 2. Essential, important in the highest degree; material; principal, main: formal.

esencialmente [ay-sen-the-ahl'-men-tay], *adv.* Essentially, principally, naturally, materially.

esenciarse [ay-sen-the-ar'-say], *vr.* To be intimately united, to grow essential.

esfacelado, da [es-fah-thay-lah'-do, dah], *a. (Med.)* Sphacelated, gangrenous.

esfacelar [es-fah-thay-lar'], *va.* To cause sphacelus, or gangrene.

esfacelo [es-fah-thay'-lo], *m. (Med.)* Sphacelus, gangrene of an entire member.

esfeciforme [es-fay-the-for'-may], *a.* Wasp-shaped, like a sphex (avispa).

esfenoidal [es-fay-no-ee-dahl'], *a.* Sphenoidal, belonging to the sphenoid bone.

esfenoides [es-fay-no'-e-days], *m.* The sphenoid bone.

esfera [es-fay'-rah], *f.* 1. Sphere, a globe or orb. 2. Globe, representing the earth or sky. 3. Quality, character, condition, state, rank. 4. *(Post.)* Heaven. **Está fuera de mi esfera,** that is out of my reach. **En forma de esfera,** spherical.

esferal [es-fay-rahl'], *a. V.* ESFÉRICO.

esféricamente [es-fay'-re-cah-men-tay], *adv.* Spherically.

esfericidad [es-fay-re-the-dahd'], *f.* Sphericity, rotundity, orbicularness, globosity.

esférico, ca [es-fay'-re-co, cah], *a.* Spherical, globular, globous, globated.

esferoidal [es-fay-ro-e-dahl'], *a.* Spheroidical, spheroidal.

esferoide [es-fay-ro'-e-day'], *f.* Spheroid. **Bóveda esferoide,** elliptical arch.

esférula [es-fay'-roo-lah], *f.* A rounded conceptacle, whether oblong or conical, which is porous in its upper part.

esfinge [es-feen'-hay], *f.* Sphinx, a fabulous monster. *-m.* Sphinx, hawk-moth, or humming bird moth.

esfíngido, da [es-feen'-he-do, dah], *a.* Sphinx-like.

esfínter [es-feen'-ter], *m. (Anat.)* Sphincter.

esflorecer [es-flo-ray-therr'], *vn. (Chem.)* To effloresce, to fall into powder when exposed to the air.

esforrocino [es-for-ro-thee'-no], *m.* Sprig shooting from the trunk of a vine.

esforzadamente [es-for-thah-dah'-men-tay], *adv.* Strenuously, vigorously, valiantly.

esforzado [es-for-thah'-do], *m.* One of the books of the civil law which deals with testaments and last wills.

esforzado, da [es-for-thah'-do, dah], *a.* Strong (fuerte), vigorous, valiant (valiente). *-pp.* of ESFORZAR.

esforzador, ra [es-for-thah-dor', rah], *m. & f.* Exciter, animater.

esforzar [es-for-thar'], *va.* 1 To strengthen (fortalecer), to invigorate, to exert, to enforce or to force. 2. *(Met.)* To aid, to corroborate, to encourage (animar). *-vr.* 1. To exert oneself, to make efforts. **Hay que esforzarse más,** you must try harder. 2. To be confident, to assure oneself.

esfuerzo [es-foo-err'-tho], *m.* 1 Courage (valentía), spirit, vigor (vigor), heart, manfulness. 2. Effort (imaginación), strong endeavor, exertion, contention, laboring. **Sin esfuerzo,** effortlessly, without strain. **Bien vale el esfuerzo,** it's well worth the effort. 3. Confidence, faith. 4. Help, aid. (*Yo esfuerzo, yo esfuerce,* from *Esforzar. V.* ACORDAR.)

esfumado [es-foo-mah'-do], *m.* The first sketch of a painting, drawn with a pencil or charcoal. *-a.* Sfumato, having hazy outlines. **Esfumado, da,** *pp.* of ESFUMAR.

esfumar [es-foo-mar'], *va. (Pict.)* To shade over the pencilled outlines of a picture.

esfumarse [es-foo-mar'-say], *vr.* To disappear, to fade away (esperanzas)

esfumino [es-foo-mee'-no], *m. (Art.)* A stump for shading with charcoal or powdered pigments. *Cf.* DIFUMINO.

esgarrar [es-gar-rar'], *m. (Prov. Amer.) V.* GARGAJEAR.

esgarro [es-gar'-ro], *m. (Amer.) V.* GARGAJO.

esgorbia [es-gor'-be-ah], *f.* An auger for tin workers.

esgrima [es-gree'-mah], *f.* Fencing, the art of manual defence (arte). **Maestro de esgrima,** fencing master.

esgrimidor [es-gre-me-dor'], *m.* Fencer or fencing master. **Casa de esgrimidor,** *(Met.)* house without furniture.

esgrimidura [es-gre-me-doo'-rah], *f.* The act of fencing.

esgrimir [es-gre-meer'], *va.* 1. To practise the use of weapons (espada). 2. To fence, to fight according to art.

esguazable [es-goo-ah-thah'-blay], *a.* Fordable.

esguazar [es-goo-ah-thar'], *va.* To ford, as a river.

esgucio [es-goo'-the-o], *m. (Arch.)* Concave moulding.

esguín [es-geen'], *m.* Young salmon before entering the sea.

esguince [es-geen'-thay], *m.* 1. Movement of the body to avoid a blow or a fall (movimiento). 2. Frown (ceño). 3. A twist or sprain of a joint.

esgüízaro [es-goo-ee'-thah-ro], *a.* A miserable fellow, a ragamuffin.

eskol [es'-kole], *m.* A fabulous wolf.

eslabón [es-lah-bone'], *m.* 1. Link of a chain, chain links (cadena). 2. Steel for striking fire with a flint. 3. Steel for sharpening knives. 4. A very poisonous scorpion.

eslabonador [es-lah-bo-nah-dor'], *m.* Chain maker.

eslabonamiento [es-la-bo-nah-me-en'-to], *m.* 1. Linking, uniting. 2. A chain, concatenation of various things.

eslabonar [es-lah-bo-nar'], *va.* To link, to join one ring to another. 2. *(Met.)* To add, to unite.

eslavo, va [es-lah'-vo, vah], *a* Slavic, Slavonic *-m. & f.* Slav *-m.* Slavic language.

eslinga [es-leen'-gah], *f. (Naut.)* Sling, a rope with which bales or casks are hoisted.

eslingar [es-lin-gar'], *va. (Naut.)* To sling, to throw with a sling.

eslogan [es-lo'-gahn], *m. V.* SLOGAN.

eslora [es-lo'-rah], *f.* Length of a ship on the deck from the stem to the sternpost. **Esloras,** beams running from stem to stern.

esmaltador [es-mal-tah-dor'], *m.* Enameller.

esmaltadura [es-mal-tah-doo'-rah], *f.* 1. Enamelling. 2. Enamel work.

esmaltar [es-mal-tar'], *va.* 1. To enamel (metal), to be scattered over, to varnish (uñas) 2. *(Met.)* To adorn, to embellish.

esmalte [es-mal'-tay], *m.* 1. Enamel, something enamelled. 2. An azure color, made of paste. 3. Smalt. **Esmalte de uñas,** nail polish. *V.* LUSTRE.

esmarchazo [es-mar-chah'-tho], *m.* A bully.

esmectita [es-mec-tee'-tah], *f.* Name of some clays like fuller's earth.

esmeradamente [es-may-rah-dah-men'-tay], *adv.* Nicely, correctly, accurately.

esmerado, da [es-may-rah'-do, dah], *a.* Careful, neat, executed with care, painstaking, precise (trabajo). *-pp.* of ESMERAR.

esmeralda [es-may-rahl'-dah], *f.* Emerald, a precious stone.

esmerar [es-may-rar'], *va.* To polish, to brighten by attrition. *-vr.* To endeavor, to attain eminence or excellence, to take great pains.

esmerejón [es-may-ray-hone'], *m.* 1. *(Orn.)* Merlin, the yellow-legged falcon. 2. Small piece of artillery.

esmeril [es-may-reel'], *m.* 1. Emery, a mineral used in polishing. 2. Small piece of ordnance.

esmerilar [es-may-re-lar'], *va.* To burnish, to polish with emery.

esmerilazo [es-may-re-lah'-tho], *m.* Shot of a gun called *esmeril.*

esmero [es-may'-ro], *m.* Careful attention, elaborate effort, niceness, correctness, accuracy. **Poner esmero en algo,** to take great care over something.

esmilacina [es-me-lah-thee'-nah], *f.* 1. *(Bot.)* Smilacina, false Solomon's seal. 2. An alkaloid obtained from the inner pith of the sarsaparilla.

esmirriado [es-mer-re-ah'-do], *a.* Puny, thin (enclenque); scraggy.

esmodita [es-mo-dee'-tah], *f.* A pulverulent material produced by volcanoes.

esmoladera [es-mo-lah-day'-rah], *f.* Whetstone.

esmoquin [es-mo'-keen], *m.* Dinner jacket.

esmuciarse [es-moo-the-ar'-say], *vr. (Prov.)* To slip from the hands.

esnifar [es-ne-far'], *va.* To sniff.

esnob or **snob** [es-nob'], *m.* Snob (persona); posh (coche, restaurante).

esnobismo [es-no-bees'-mo], *m.* Snobbery, snobbishness.

esnón [es-none'], *m. (Naut.)* A spencer mast, trysail mast.

eso [ay'-so], *dem. pron.* That. (plural: **Esos,** those). **Eso es,** that is it. **No es eso,** it is not that. **A eso de,** toward, about. **No me gusta eso,** I don't like that. **Nada de eso,** nothing of the kind. **Antes de eso,** before that. **Después de eso,** after that. **Es por eso que no vino,** that's why she didn't come.

esófago [ay-so'-fah-go], *m. (Anat.)* Esophagus, gullet; the throat.

esotérico, ca [ay-so-tay'-re-co, cah], *a.* Esoteric; confidential, secret.

esotro, tra [ay-so'-tro, ay-so'-trah], *pron dem.* This or that other; pointing out not the first, but the second, third, etc., person or thing.

espabiladeras [es-pah-be-lah-day-ras], *f. pl.* Snuffers.

447

espabilar [es-pah-be-lar'], *va.* 1. To snuff a candle (vela). 2. To nick (robar). 3. To do in (matar). -*vr.* To wake up; to look lively, to get a move on; to pull one's socks up. V. DESPABILAR.

espachurrar [es-pah-choor-rhar'], *va.* To squash, to flatten.

espaciador [es-pah-the-ah-dor'], *m.* Spacer (máquina de escribir).

espacial [es-pah-the-al'], *a.* Relating to space. **Cápsula espacial,** space capsule.

espaciar [es-pah-the-ar'], *va.* 1. To extend, to dilate, to spread. 2. To space, to separate the lines in writing or printing. 3. To stagger (horas de trabajo). -*vr.* 1. To expand (en escritura y hablado). **Espaciarse en un tema,** to enlarge on a subject. 2. To amuse oneself.

espacio [es-pah'-the-o], *m.* 1. Space, capacity; distance between objects. **Espacio libre,** clear space. 2. Space, interval of time. **En el espacio de tres generaciones,** in the space of three generations. 3. Slowness, delay (tardanza), procrastination. 4. *(Obs.)* Recreation, diversion. 5. Musical interval. 6. In printing, space, type which separates words. **A dos espacios,** doubled-space. 7. *(Ast.)* V. DESCAMPADO.

espacio interastral [es-pah-the-o in-ter-as-trahl'], *m.* Outer space.

especiosamente [es-pay-the-o'-sah-men-tay], *adv.* Deliberately, spaciously.

espaciosidad [es-pah-the-o-se-dahd'], *f.* Spaciousness, capacity.

espacioso, sa [es-pah-the-oh'-so, sah], *a.* 1. Spacious, capacious, wide, roomy, large, extensive (cuarto). 2. Slow, deliberate (movimiento).

espada [es-pah'-dah], *f.* 1. Sword (arma). 2. Swordsman (persona). 3. Ace of spades, or any card in the suit of spades. 4. *(Zool.)* Swordfish. 5. The bullfighter who kills the bull with a sword. **Espada blanca,** sword. **Espada negra** or **de esgrima,** foil, a blunt sword used in fencing. **Entrar con espada en mano,** to attack sword in hand; to enter upon an affair supporting one's own business strongly. **Hombre de capa y espada,** a person of no profession. **Primer espada,** the head bullfighter. **Verse entre la espada y la pared,** to be driven to the wall, to be surrounded by danger. **Es una buena espada,** he is a good or dexterous swordsman. **Espada ancha** or **espada de a caballo,** Broadsword; dragoon's sabre.

espadachín [es-pah-dah-cheen'], *m.* Bully, hackster, one who affects valor.

espadadero [es-pah-dah-day'-ro], *m.* Braking floor, scutch-blade, a table for braking flax or hemp.

espadado, da [es-pah-dah'do, dah], *a.* Armed with a sword. -*pp.* of ESPADAR.

espadador [es-pah-dah-dor'], *m.* One who brakes flax or hemp with a swingle.

espadaña [es-pah-dah'-nyah], *f.* 1. *(Bot.)* Reedmace, great cat-tail. 2. Spire.

espadaña [es-pah-dah-nya], *f.* Sudden flow of blood, water, etc., from the mouth.

espadañal [es-pah-dah-nyahl'], *m.* The place where reedmace is growing.

espadañar [es-pah-dah-nyar'], *va.* To divide into long thin slips, resembling flags.

espadar [es-pah-dar'], *va.* To brake hemp or flax with a swingle.

espadarte [es-pah-dar'-tay], *m.* *(Zool.)* Swordfish. V. ESPADA.

espadazo [es-pah-dah-tho], *m.* Sword thrust, slash with a sword.

espadería [es-pah-day-ree'-ah], *f.* Sword-cutler's shop.

espadero [es-pah-day'-ro], *m.* Swordsmith.

espádice [es-pah'de-thay], *m.* Spadix, a common receptacle of several flowers inclosed in a spathe.

espadilla [es-pah-deel'-lyah], *f.* 1. Red insignia of the order of Santiago in the shape of a sword. 2. Swingle used in braking hemp and flax, a scutching handle. 3. *(Naut.)* A small oar, or helm for boats. 4. Ace of spades. 5. *(Bot.)* Cornflag.

espadillar [es-pah-deel-lyar'], *va.* To brake or scutch hemp or flax with a swingle.

espadillazo [es-pah-dil-lyah'-tho], *m.* Adverse fortune at cards, where the ace is lost.

espadín [es-pah-deen'], *m.* A small short sword (espada).

espadita [es-pah-dee'-tah], *f. dim.* A small sword.

espadón [es-pah-done'], *m.* 1. *(Aug.)* A large sword. 2. Eunuch, one that is castrated.

espadrapo [es-pah-drah'-po], *m.* V. ESPARADRAPO.

espagírica [es-pah-hee'-re-cah], *f.* Metallurgy, the art of refining metals.

espagírico, ca [es-pah-he'-re-co, cah], *a.* Belonging to the art of metallurgy.

espaguetis [es-pah-gay'-tees], *m. pl.* Spaghetti.

espalda [es-pahl'-dah], *f.* 1. Shoulder, the upper part of the back. 2. *(Mil.)* Shoulder of a bastion. **Espaldas,** a) back or back part. b) *(Met.)* aid, protection. **A espaldas,** at one's back, in one's absence. **Echar a las espaldas,** to forget on purpose, to abandon. **Sobre mis espaldas,** at my expense. **Tornar** or **volver las espaldas,** 1. To avoid someone; to turn one's back in contempt. 2. To fly, to run away. **A espaldas de uno,** behind somebody's back. **Atar las manos a la espalda,** to tie somebody's hands behind his back. **Cubrir las espaldas,** *(Fig.)* to cover oneself.

espaldar [es-pal-dar'], *m.* 1. Back piece of an armor, shoulder piece of a coat of mail. 2. Place where one puts his back to rest against (silla). 3. Espalier in gardens. **Espaldares,** pieces of tapestry against which chairs lean.

espaldarazo [es-pal-dah-rah'-tho], *m.* Blow with the flat of a sword, or of the hand, on the shoulders.

espaldarón [es-pal-dah-rone'], *m.* Ancient armor for the shoulders.

espaldear [es-pal-day-ar'], *va.* *(Naut.)* To break (olas) with impetuosity against the poop of a vessel.

espalder [es-pal-derr'], *m.* The first of stern rower in a galley.

espaldera [es-pal-day'-rah], *f.* Espalier, trees planted and cut so as to join; wall trees.

espaldilla [es-pal-deel'-lyah], *f.* 1. Shoulder blade. 2. Hind quarter of a waistcoat or jacket. 3. *(Anat.)* Omoplate, scapula.

espalditendido, da [es-pal-de-ten-dee'-do, dah], *a. (coll.)* Stretched on one's back.

espaldón [es-pal-done'], *m.* 1. *(Arch.)* V. RASTRO. 2. Intrenchment or barrier to defend one from an attack. 3. *(Naut.)* A hawsepiece. 4. A barrier of, baskets, bags, etc., to guard the artillery and sappers during a siege. 5. Half bulwark, generally of one face and one flank.

espaldonarse [es-pal-do-nar'-say], *vr* To get under cover, to guard oneself from the fire of the enemy.

espaldudo, da [es-pal-doo'-do, dah], *a.* Broad-shouldered.

espalmadura [es-pal-mah-doo'-rah], *f.* Hoofs of quadrupeds.

espalmar [es-pal-mar'], *va. (Naut.)* To clean and pay a ship's bottom. V. DESPALMAR.

espalto [es-pahl'-to], *m.* 1. Dark-colored paint. 2. *(Mil.)* Esplanade. 3. Spalt, a scaly whitish mineral used as a flux for metals.

espantable [es-pan-tah'-blay], *a.* 1. Frightful, horrid, terrible. 2. Marvellous, wonderful.

espantablemente [es-pan-tah-blay-men'-tay], *adv.* Horribly, terribly, frightfully.

espantadizo, za [es-pan-tah-dee'-tho, thah], *a.* Timid, easily frightened.

espantado [es-pan-tah'-do], *a.* Frightened, scared, terrified.

espantador, ra [es-pan-tah-dor', rah], *m. & f.* Bugbear, one that frightens or terrifies (espantador).

espantajo [es-pan-tah'-ho], *m.* 1. Scarecrow, set up to frighten birds. 2. One who cuts grimaces for the purpose of frightening.

espantalobos [es-pan-tah-lo'-bos], *m.* *(Bot.)* Bladder or bastard senna. **Espantalobos arborescente,** common bladder senna.

espantamocas [es-pan-tah-mos'-cas], *m.* Net put on horses to scare away flies.

espantanublados [es-pan-tah-noo-blah'-dos], *m.* Rake, vagabond begging in long robes, who is thought by the vulgar to have power over the clouds.

espantapájaros [es-pan-tah-pah'-hah-ros], *m.* Scarecrow.

espantar [es-pan-tar'], *va.* 1. To frighten (asustar), to terrify, to fright, to daunt, to shock. 2. To chase or drive away (ahuyentar). *-vr.* To be surprised or astonished, to marvel (asombrarse).

espantavillanos [es-pan-tah-vil-lyah', nos], *m.* Sort of shining or glittering gaudy stuff.

espanto [es-pahn'-to], *m.* 1 Fright (miedo), consternation (consternación), frightfulness. 2. Menace, threat (amenaza). 3. Admiration, wonder, surprise; horror. 4. Hideousness, grimness. **Hace un frío de espanto,** it's terribly cold.

espantosamente [es-pah-to'-sah-men-tay], *adv.* Dreadfully, marvellously, frightfully, ghastfully.

espantoso, sa [es-pan-to'-so, sah], *a.* 1. Frightful, dreadful, horrid, horrible; fearful. 2. Marvelous, wonderful.

español, la [es-pah-nyole', lah], *a.* Spanish, relating to Spain. **A la española,** in the Spanish manner.

español [es-pah-nyole'], *m.* Spanish language.

españolado, da [es-pah-nyo-lah'-do, dah], *a.* Applied to a foreigner who in his manners, etc., is like a Spaniard, or who follows Spanish customs. *-pp.* of ESPAÑOLAR.

españolar [es-pah-nyo-lar'], *va.* V. ESPAÑOLIZAR.

españolería [es-pah-nyo-lay-ree'-ah], *f.* *(Obs.)* Spanish taste, manners, and customs.

españoleta [es-pah-nyo-lay'-tah], *f.* Ancient Spanish dance.

españolismo [es-pah-nyo-lees'-mo], *f.* Love, devotion, to Spain; patriotism.

españolizado, da [es-pah-nyo-lee-thah'-do, dah], *a.* & *pp.* of *Españolizar.* V. ESPAÑOLADO.

españolizar [es-pah-nyo-le-thar'], *va.* To make Spanish, to render conformable to the Spanish language or Spanish analogies. *-vr.* To adopt the customs and manners of Spain.

espar [es-par'], *m.* Spar, a kind of aromatic drug.

esparadrapo [es-pah-rah-drah'-po], *m.* Adhesive plaster, court plaster.

esparagón [es-pah-rah-gone'], *m.* Grogram, a coarse stuff.

esparamarín [es-pah-rah-ma-reen'], *m.* Serpent which mounts trees to dart on its prey.

esparaván [es-pah-rah-vahn'], *m.* 1 *(Vet.)* Bone-spavin, tumor in the legs of horses. 2. *(Orn.)* Sparrow-hawk.

esparavel [es-pah-rah-vel'], *m.* 1. Kind of fishing net. 2. Carpenter's mortarboard.

esparceta [es-par-thay'-tah], *f.* *(Bot.)* Saintfoin hedysarum.

esparciata [es-par-the-ah'-tah], *a.* Spartan.

esparcidamente [es-par-the'-dah-men-tay], *adv.* Distinctly, separately; gayly.

esparcido, da [es-par-thee'-do, dah], *a.* 1. Scattered (desparramado). 2. *(Met.)* Merry, festive, gay (alegre). *-pp.* of ESPARCIR.

esparcilla [es-par-theel'-lyah], *f.* *(Bot.)* Spurrey. **Esparcilla arvense,** rough-seeded spurrey.

esparcimiento [es-par-the-me-en'-to], *m.* 1. Scattering, dissemination. 2. Amusement (recreo). 3. *(Met.)* Frankness, openness (franqueza). 4. *(Met.)* Liberality of sentiments, generosity of mind.

esparcir [es-par-theer'], *va.* 1. To scatter (desparramar), to disseminate (divulgar), to fling. 2. *(Met.)* To divulge, to spread abroad. *-vr.* To amuse oneself (distraerse), to make merry.

espardeña [es-par-day'-nyah], *f.* *(Prov.)* V. ESPARTEÑA.

esparganio [es-par-gah'-ne-o], *m.* *(Bot.)* Bur-reed.

esparo [es-pah'-ro], *m.* *(Zool.)* Gilt-head, a seafish.

esparragado [es-par-rah-gah'-do], *m.* A dish of asparagus.

esparragador [es-par-rah-gah-dor'], *m.* He who collects and takes care of asparagus.

esparragar [es-par-rah-gar'], *va.* To guard or collect asparagus. **Anda or vete a esparragar,** *(coll.)* expression, to dispatch or dismiss one contemptuously or angrily.

esparragíneo, nea [es-par-rah-hee'-nay-o, ah], *a.* Asparagoid, like asparagus.

espárrago [es-par'-rah-go], *m.* 1. *(Bot.)* Sprout of asparagus. **Solo como el espárrago,** *(coll.)* As lonely as asparagus; every stalk growing by itself. **Espárrago triguero,** wild asparagus. **Mandar a uno a freír espárragos,** to tell somebody to go to hell. 2. Pole to support an awning.

esparragón [es-par-rah-gone'], *m.* Silk stuff that forms a cord thicker and stronger than taffeta.

esparraguera [es-par-rah-gay'-rah], *f.* 1. Asparagus plant; stem of this plant. 2. An asparagus bed.

esparraguero, ra [es-par-rah-gay'-ro, rah], *m.* & *f.* One who gathers and sells asparagus.

esparrancado, da [es-par-ran-cah'-do, dah], *a.* Bow-legged, bandy-legged, divaricated. *-pp.* of ESPARRANCARSE.

esparrancarse [es-par-ran-car'-say], *vr.* *(coll.)* To straddle, to bestride.

espartal [es-par-tahl'], *m.* Field on which feathergrass is growing.

espartano, na [es-par-tah'-no, nah], *a.* Spartan, belonging to Sparta.

esparteña [es-par-tay'-nyah], *f.* A sort of sandal made of feathergrass.

espartería [es-par-tay-ree'-ah], *f.* Place where mats of tough feather-grass are made or sold.

espartero, ra [es-par-tay'-ro, rah], *m.* & *f.* One who makes and sells articles of feathergrass.

espartilla [es-par-teel'-lyah], *f.* Handful of feathergrass which serves as brush for cleaning animals.

espartizal [es-par-te-thahl'], *m.* Field on which feathergrass is growing.

esparto [es-par'-to], *m.* *(Bot.)* Feather grass; Spanish grass hemp. **Esparto basto,** rush-leaved lygeum.

espasmo [es-pahs'-mo], *m.* V. PASMO. Spasm.

espasmódico, ca [es-pas-mo'-de-co, cah], *a.* Spasmodic, convulsive.

espástico, ca [es-pahs'-te-co, cah], *a.* Spastic, spasmodic.

espata [es-pah'-tah], *f.* *(Bot.)* Spathe, a large bract sheathing a fowercluster.

espático, ca [es-pah'-te-co, cah], *a.* Spathic, of spar.

espato [es-pah'-to], *m.* Spar, a calcareous mineral.

espátula [es-pah'-too-lah], *f.* 1. Spatula, or slice used by apothecaries and surgeons. 2. A palette knife. 3. *(Bot.)* A kind of fetidiris. 4. *(Zool.)* The spoonbill, a long-shanked bird common in S. America.

espaviento [es-pah-ve-en'-to], *m.* V. ASPAVIENTO.

espavorido, da, espavorecido, da [es-pah-vo-ree'-do, dah, es-pah-ro-ray-thee'-do, dah], *a.* V. DESPAVORIDO.

especería [es-pay-thay-ree'-ah], *f.* The more colloquial form. V. ESPECIERÍA. Spicery.

especia [es-pay'-the-ah], *f.* Spice. *-pl.* Medicinal drugs.

especial [es-pay-the-ahl'], *a.* Special, particular (persona). **En especial,** specially.

especialidad [es-pay-the-ah-le-dahd'], *f.* Speciality or specialty, particularity.

especialista [es-pay-the-ah-lees'-tah], *a.* & *m.* Specialist, one who cultivates or excels in a science. **Especialista en telecomunicaciones,** *(Inform.)* telecommunications specialist.

especialización [es-pay-the-ah-le-thah-the-on'], *f.* Specialization.

especializado [es-pay-the-ah-le-thah-do], *a.* Specialized; skilled (obrero), trained. **Mano de obra especializada,** skilled labor.

especializarse [es-pay-the-ah-le-thar'-say], *vr.* To specialize.

especialmente [es-pay-the-al-men'-tay], *adv.* Especially, in particular, namely, nominally.

especiar [es-pay-the-ar'], *va.* To spice broth or food.

especie [es-pay'-the-ay], *f.* 1. Species; a kind, a sort; a subdivision of a general term; nature (clase). 2. Species, any sensible representation. 3. Image or idea of any object in the mind (idea). 4. Event, incident. 5. Pretext, show. 6. *(Chem.)* A collection of properties which only belong to one body. 7. Feint in fencing. 8. *pl. (Phys.)* Luminous rays diversely reflected. 9. *pl.* **Especies sacramentales,** the accidents of color, taste, and smell, which remain in the sacrament, after the conversion of the bread and wine into the body and blood of Christ.

especiería [es-pay-the-ay-ree'-ah], *f.* 1. A grocer's shop, grocery. 2. A shop where spices are sold. 3. Spices and all sorts of aromatic drugs. *(Acad.)*

especiero [es-pay-the-ay'-ro], *m.* A dealer in spices and aromatic drugs, a grocer.

especificación [es-pay-the-fe-ca-the-on'], *f.* Specification, a minute enumeration of things.

específicamente [es-pay-the'-fe-cah-men-tay], *adv.* Specifically, distinctly, expressly.

especificar [es-pay-the-fe-car'], *va.* To specify, to state minutely, to name; to show by some particular mark of distinction.

especificativo, va [es-pay-the-fe-cah-tee'-vo, vah]. *a.* That which has the power of specifying or distinguishing.

específico [es-pay-thee'-fe-co], *m.* Specific, a remedy for some particular disease.

específico, ca [es-pay-thee'-fe-co, cah], *a.* Specific.

espécimen [es-pay'-the-men], *m.(Neol.)* Specimen, sample. *-pl.* The known kinds of letters in ancient times.

especioso, sa [es-pay-the-oh'-so, sah], *a.* 1. Neat, beautiful, gay; finished with care. 2. Superficial, apparent, specious, plausible, colorable; glossy.

espectacular [es-payc-tah-coo-lar'], *a.* Spectacular.

espectacularmente [es-payc-tah-coo-lahr'-men-tay], *adv.* Spectacularly, in spectacular fashion.

espectáculo [es-pec-tah'-coo-lo], *m.* 1. Spectacle, show; a pageant. **Espectáculo de variedades,** variety show. 2. Spectacle, anything to be looked on, or anything exhibited as eminently remarkable. **Dar un espectáculo,** to make a scene.

espectador [es-pec-tah-dor'], *m.* Spectator. **Los espectadores.** the spectators.

espectral [es-pec-trahl'], *a.* 1. Spectral, phantom-like, ghost-like. 2. *(Phys.)* Spectral.

espectro [es-pec'-tro], *m.* 1. Specter, phantom, ghost (fantasma). 2. A vampire bat.

espectroscópico, ca [es-pec-tros-co'-pe-co, cah], *a.* Spectroscopic, relating to the solar spectrum.

espectroscopio [es-pec-tros-co'-pe-o], *m.* Spectroscope.

especulación [es-pay-coo-lah-the-on'], *f.* 1. Speculation, contemplation (meditación), mental view. 2. A commercial scheme or adventure. 3. Theory, as opposed to practice.

especulador, ra [es-pay-coo-lah-dor', rah], *m. & f.* Speculator.

especular [es-pay-coo-lar'], *va.* 1. To behold, to view, to examine(examinar). 2. To speculate, to meditate (meditar), to contemplate. 3. To form commercial schemes.

especular, *adj.* 1. Specular, relating to a mirror. 2. Transparent, diaphanous.

especulativa [es-pay-coo-lah-tee'-vah], *f.* Faculty of viewing or speculating understanding.

especulativamente [es-payc-tah-coo-lah-te'-vah-men-tay], *adv.* Speculatively.

especulativo, va [es-pay-coo-lah-tee'-vo, vah], *a.* Speculative, thoughtful.

espéculo [es-pay'-coo-lo], *m.* 1. Speculum, an instrument to aid in the inspection of cavities of the body. 2. A code of laws compiled by order of Alfonso the Wise.

espejado, da [es-pay-hah'-do, dah], *a.* Mirror-like, resembling or consisting of looking glasses.

espejería [es-pay-hay-ree'-ah], *f.* 1. Glass-shop, a place where looking glasses are sold. 2. Glasshouse, where plate-glass is made.

espejero [es-pay-hay'-ro], *m.* One whose trade is to make or sell mirrors.

espejico, illo, ito [es-pay-hee'-co, eel'-lyo, ee'to], *m. dim.* Little mirror.

espejismo (or **espejeo**) [es-pay-hees'-mo, es-pay-hay'o], *m.* Looming, mirage.

espejo [es-pay'-ho], *m.* 1. Looking glass, mirror; a glass which shows forms reflected. **Limpio como un espejo,** as clean as a penny. **Espejo de cuerpo entero,** full-length mirror. **Espejo retrovisor,** driving mirror. 2. **Espejo de popa,** *(Naut.)* Sternframe.

espejuela [es-pay-hoo-ay'-lah], *f.* A kind of sharp bit for a horse, forming an arch.

espejuelo [es-pay-hoo-ay'-lo], *m.* 1. *(dim.)* A small looking glass. 2. Specular stone, selenite, a kind of transparent lamellated gypsum. 3. Transparent leaf of mica. 4. Instrument used by bird catchers in catching larks.**Espejuelos,** crystal lenses, of which spectacles are made; glasses.

espelta [es-pel'-tah], *f. (Bot.)* 1. V. ESCANDIA. 2. V. ESCAÑA.

espélteo, ea [es-pel'-tay-o-ah], *a.* Belonging to spelt.

espeluznante [es-pay-looth-nahn'-tay], *a.* Hair-raising, horrifying.

espeluznarse [es-pay-looth-nar'-say], *vr.* To have the hair dishevelled, or set on end with fear.

espeque [es-pay'-kay], *m.* Handspike, wooden lever.

espera [es-pay'-rah], *f.* 1. Expectation, the act of expecting. 2. Expectance or expectancy, the state of expecting. 3. Stay, the act of waiting (período). 4. Pause, stop. 5. Stay, restraint, prudence, caution, steadiness. 6. *(Law.)* Respite, adjournment, pause, interval. 7. A kind of heavy ordnance. 8. A letter of license. **Estar a la espera,** to be in expectation of. **En espera de su contestación,** awaiting your reply. **La cosa no tiene espera,** the matter brooks no delay. **Sala de espera,** waiting room.

esperable [es-pay-rah'-blay], *a.* That which may be expected or hoped.

esperador, ra [es-pay-ra-dor', rah], *a.* Expectant.

esperanza [es-pay-rahn'-thah], *f.* Hope, expectance, expectancy. **No hay esperanza,** there is no chance. **Esperanza de vida,** life expectancy. **Hay pocas esperanzas de que venga,** there is little prospect of his coming. **Tener esperanzas de,** to have hopes of.

esperanzador [es-pay-ran-thah-dor'], *a.* Hopeful, encouraging.

esperanzar [es-pay-ran-thar'], *va.* To give hope.

esperar [es-pay-rar'], *va.* 1. To hope (tener esperanza). **Esperar que,** to hope that… **Espero que sea así,** I hope it is so. **Espero que vengas,** I hope you'll come. 2. To expect, to have a previous apprehension of either good or evil. **Esperamos que llegue a la hora,** we expect it to arrive on time. 3. To wait, to stay, to wait for (aguardar, esperar a), to attend the coming, to look for. **Esperar el avión,** to wait for the plane. **Ir a esperar a uno,** to go and meet somebody. **No me esperes después de las 7,** don't wait for me after 7. 4. To fear. *-vr.* To expect, to wait, to stay (aguardar). **Como podía esperarse,** as it might be expected. **Se espera que todo esté listo,** it is hoped that all will be ready.

esperezarse, or **desperezarse** [es-pay-ray-thar'-say], *vr.* To stretch oneself.

esperezo [es-pay-ray'-tho], *m.* The act of stretching one's arms and legs after being roused from sleep.

esperiego, ga [es-pay-re-ay'-go, gah], *a.* V. ASPERIEGA. **Esperiego,** tart apple-tree, pippin.

esperlán [es-per-lahn'], *m. (Zool.)* Smelt, a small sea-fish.

esperma [es-perr'-mah], *f.* Sperm. V. SEMEN. **Esperma de ballena,** spermaceti.

espermeceti [es-per-may-thay'-te], *m.* Spermaceti.

espermático

espermático, ca [es-per-mah'-te-co, cah], *a.* Spermatic, seminal, belonging to the sperm.

espermatorrea [es-per-ma-tor-ray'-ah], *f.* Spermatorrhoea, involuntary loss of semen.

espermatozoide [es-per-mah-to-thoy'-day], *m.* Spermatozoid.

espérmido, da [es-perr'-me-do, dah], Producing seeds,

espernada [es-per-nah'-dah], *f.* End of a chain.

espernible [es-per-nee-blay], *a.* (*Prov.*) Despicable.

esperón [es-pay-rone'], *m.* (*Naut.*) The forecastle head.

esperonte [es-pay-ron'-tay], *m.* Kind of ancient fortification.

esperpento [es-per-pen'-to], *m.* 1. Fright, sight (persona). 2. Absurdity (disparate), nonsense. 3. Macabre story (cuento), grotesque tale. 4. (*Teat.*) Play which focuses on the grotesque.

esperriaca [es-per-re-ah'-cah], *f.* (*Prov.*) The last must or juice drawn from grapes.

espesamiento [es-pay-sah-me-en'-to], *m.* (*Prov.*) Coagulation.

espesar [es-pay-sar'], *va.* 1. To thicken, to inspissate, to condense what is fluid (líquido). 2. To coagulate, to curdle, to concrete. 3. To mass, to assemble. 4. To close, to join, as silk or stuff does (tejido). *-vr.* To condensate, to grow thicker.

espesartina [es-pay-sar-tee'-nah], *f.* Spessartite or spessartin, a hyacinthred garnet.

espesativo, va [es-pay-sah-tee'-vo, vah], *a.* That which has the power of thickening.

espeso, sa [es-pay'-so, sah], *a.* 1. Thick, condensed, dense (bosque), gross, crass; curdy. 2. Close, contiguous. 3. Frequent, often repeated. 4. Slovenly, dirty (sucio).

espesor [es-pay-sor'], *m.* Thickness, grossness, crassitude; corpulence.

espesura [es-pay-soo'-rah], *f.* 1. Thickness (espesor), density, closeness, crassitude. 2. (*Fort.*) Thickness, solidity of the works of a fortress. 3. Thicket, a close wood. **Se refugiaron en las espesuras,** they took refuge in the forest. 4. Slovenliness, negligence of dress.

espetamiento [es-pay-tah-me-en'-to], *m.* (*coll.*) Stiffness, formality, stateliness of mien or deportment.

espetar [es-pay-tar'], *va.* 1. To spit, to put upon a spit. 2. To run through with a sword (persona). 3. To tell, to relate (lección, sermón). **Le espetó fuertes razones,** he gave strong reasons. *-vr.* 1. To be stiff and stately, to be puffed up with pride. 2. (*Met. coll.*) To slide or thrust oneself into some narrow place.

espatera [es-pay-tay'-rah], *f.* 1. Rack, a board with hooks, on which kitchen utensils are hung. 2. Kitchen furniture.

espetón [es-pay-tone'], *m.* 1. Spit, a long iron prong (broqueta). 2. A large pin (clavija). 3. (*Zool.*) Seapike, spit-fish. 4. Blow given with a spit.

espía [es-pee'-ah], *m. & f.* A spy. **Espía doble,** double agent. 2. (*Naut.*) Warp, a rope used in moving a ship, a towrope of twisted bark (cabo).

espiar [es-pe-ar'], *va.* 1. To spy, to watch closely (vigilar). 2. To lurk, to lie in wait. 3. (*Naut.*) To warp, to move a ship by means of a warp.

espibia [es-pee'-be-ah], *f.* (*Vet.*) Incomplete dislocation of the vertebrae.

espibio, espibión [es-pee'-be-o, es-pe-be-on'], *m.* (*Vet.*) Dislocation or contraction in the nape of the neck of animals.

espicanardi [es-pe-cah-nar'-de], *f.* (*Bot.*) Spikenard.

espichar [es-pe-char'], *va.* 1. To prick (pinchar). V. PINCHAR. 2. (*coll.*) To give up the ghost, to die (morir).

espiche [es-pee'-chay], *m.* A sharp-pointed weapon. **Espiches,** (*Naut.*) pegs, small pointed pieces of wood driven into the holes of the planks of ships, dowel, spire.

espichón [es-pe-chone'], *m.* Wound with a pointed weapon.

espicifloro, ra [es-pe-the-flo'-ro, rah], *a.* (*Bot.*) Spicate, having flowers arranged in spikes.

espículeo, a [es-pe-coo'-lay-o, ah], *a.* (*Bot.*) Spiculate, divided into spikelets.

espiculífero, ra [es-pe-coo-lee'-fay-ro, rah], *a.* (*Bot.*) Spiculiferous, bearing spikelets.

espiga [es-pee'-gah], *f.* 1. Ear, the spike or head of corn (trigo); that part which contains the seed. 2. Tenon, the end of a piece of timber fitted into another (clavija). 3. Fuse of a bomb or shell. 4. (*Naut.*) Distance between the last collar of the top-gallant masts and the summit or acorn; sail of a galley. **Espiga céltica,** a valerian. **Espiga de agua,** (*Bot.*) pondweed.

espigadera [es-pe-gah-day'-rah], *f.* Gleaner, a woman who gathers corn after the reapers.

espigado, da [es-pe-gah'-do, dah], *a.* 1. Tall, graceful, slender (delgado, esbelto). 2. Acrospired.*-pp.* of ESPIGAR.

espigadora [es-pe-gah-do'-rah], *f. V.* ESPIGADERA.

espigar [es-pe-gar'], *vn.* 1. To ear, to shoot into ears (trigo). 2. (*Met.*) To grow, to increase in bulk and stature. *-va.* 1. To glean, to gather corn left by the reapers. 2. (*Prov.*) To make presents to a bride. 3. To make a tenon.

espigelia [es-pe-hay'-le-ah], *f.* Spigelia, pinkroot, an anthelmintic herb.

espigón [es-pee-gone'], *m.* 1. Ear of corn. 2. Sting, as of bees, wasps, etc. 3. Point of a dart or javelin. 4. Sharp point of a hill without trees. **Ir con espigón or llevar espigón,** (*Met.*) to retire indignant or irritated.

espiguilla, ta [es-pe-geel'-lyah, gee'-tah], *f.* 1. Small edging of lace, tape, or inkle. 2. Flower of some trees. 3. (*dim.*) A small ear of corn; spikelet.

espilo [es-pee'-lo], *m.* A small spot upon grasses below the first membrane, at its inner base.

espilorchería [es-pe-lor-chay-ree'-ah], *f.* (*Low.*) Sordid avarice.

espín [es-peen'], *m.* Porcupine.

espina [es-pee'-nah], *f.* 1. A thorn. 2. A fishbone (de pez). 3. Spine, the back bone. 4. A small splinter of wood, esparto, etc (astilla). 5. (*Met.*) Scruple, doubt, suspicion. **Espina blanca,** (*Bot.*) woolly cotton thistle. **Mala espina,** resentment. **Me da mala espina,** it worries me. **Sacarse la espina,** (*Fig.*) to pay off an old score, to get even. **Tener una espina en el corazón,** to have a spine in one's side.

espinaca [es-pe-nah'-cah], *f.* (*Bot.*) Spinage.

espina dorsal [es-pee'-nah dor-sahl'], *f.* Spinal column.

espinadura [es-pe-nah-doo'-rah], *f.* Act of pricking with a thorn.

espinal, espinar [es-pe-nahl', es-pe-nar'], *m.* 1. Place full of thornbushes, brambles, and briers. 2. (*Met.*) A dangerous undertaking, an arduous enterprise.

espinal [es-pe-nahl'], *a.* Spinal, dorsal.

espinar [es-pe-nar'], *va.* 1. To prick with thorns (punzar). 2. To surround trees with briers and thornbushes. 3. (*Met.*) To nettle, to make uneasy, to abuse, to provoke.

espinazo [es-pe-nah'-tho], *m.* Spine, the backbone.

espinel [es-pe-nel'], *m.* A fishing-line with many hooks, to catch congereels and other large fishes.

espinela [es-pe-nay'-lah], *f.* 1. A piece of Spanish poetry, consisting of ten verses of eight syllables. 2. Spinel-ruby, a precious stone.

espineta [es-pe-nay'-tah], *f.* 1. Spinet, a small harpsichord. 2. The bit of a bridle.

espingarda [es-pin-gar'-dah], *f.* 1. A small piece of ordnance. 2. A long handgun or musket used in Morocco.

espinica, illa [es-pe-nee'-cah, eel'-lyah], *f. dim.* A small thorn.

espinilla [es-pe-neel'-lyah], *f.* 1. Shin or shin bone. 2. Blackhead.

espinita [es-pe-nee'-tah], *f. dim.* A little thorn.

espino [es-pee'-no], *m.* (*Bot.*) Thorn, a prickly tree of several kinds; hawthorn. **Espino albar or blanco,** white-thorn. **Espino negro,** boxthorn like buckthorn.

espinoso, sa [es-pe-no'-so, sah], *a.* 1. Spiny, thorny (planta). 2. (*Met.*) Arduous, dangerous. 3. Bony (pez).

espinoso [es-pe-no'-so], *m.* (*Zool.*) Three-spined stickleback.

espinulífero, ra [es-pe-noo-lee'-fay-ro, rah], *a.* (*Bot.*) Spinuliferous, thorn-bearing.

espinuloso, sa [es-pe-noo-lo'-so, sah], *(Bot.)* Spinulous, thorny.

espinzar [es-pin-thar'], *va.* To burl; to dress cloth after it has been milled.

espión [es-pe-on'], *m.* Spy. *V.* ESPÍA.

espionaje [es-pe-o-nah'-hay], *m.* Espionage, the action of spying. **Novela de espionaje,** spy story.

espiote [es-pe-o'-tay], *m.* A sharp pointed weapon.

espique [es-pee'-kay], *m. V.* ESPICANARDI.

espira [es-pee'-rah], *f.* 1. A spiral line, a spire, a helix. 2. Spire, a winding staircase. 3. Part of the base of a column, above the plinth. 4. Each turn of a conical shell.

espiración [es-pe-rah-the-on'], *f.* Expiration, respiration.

espiráculo [es-pe-rah'-coo-lo], *m.* Spiracle, breathing pore.

espiradero [es-pe-rah-day'-ro], *m. V.* RESPIRADERO.

espirador [es-pe-rah-dor'], *m.* He who expires or breathes.

espiral [es-pe-rahl'], *a.* Spiral, winding, helical, helispherical. -*f.* Spiral, corkscrew (forma); *(Tec.)* whorl; hairspring (reloj). **El humo subía en espiral,** the smoke went spiralling up.

espiralmente [es-pe-ral-men'-tay], *adv.* Spirally.

espirante [es-pe-rahn'-tay], *pa.* Expiring, respiring.

espirar [es-pe-rar'], *vn.* 1. To expire, to breathe the last. 2. To make an emission of the breath, to expire. 3. To finish, to come to an end. 4. To fly out with a blast. -*va.* 1. To exhale (aire). 2. To infuse a divine spirit.

espirativo, va [es-pe-rah-tee'-vo, vah], *a.* That which can breathe or respire.

espirea [es-pe-ray'-ah], *f. (Bot.)* Spiraea. **Espira ulmaria,** meadow sweet spiraea. **Espirea opulifolia,** guelder roseleaved spiraled.

espiratar [es-pe-ra-tar'], *va.* 1. To irritate or agitate. 2. *V.* ENDEMONIAR. -*vr.* To be possessed with an evil spirit.

espiritillo [es-pe-re-teel'-lyo], *m. dim.* A little spirit.

espiritismo [es-pe-re-tees'-mo], *m.* Spiritualism, spiritism, the belief that the spirits of the dead communicate in various ways with men, usually through a medium.

espiritista [es-pe-re-tees'-tah], *m. & f.* A spiritualist.

espiritosamente [es-pe-re-to'-sah-men-tay], *adv.* Spiritedly, ardently.

espiritoso, sa [es-pe-re-to'-so, sah]. *a.* 1. Spiritious (licor). 2. *(Met.)* Spirited, lively, active, ardent (persona).

espíritu [es-pee'-re-too], *m.* 1. Spirit, an immaterial substance. 2. Soul of man. 3. Genius, vigor of mind; power of mind, moral or intellectual. 4. Spirit, ardor, courage, life, manhood. 5. That which gives vigor or cheerfulness to the mind or body. 6. Inclination, turn of mind (talento). 7. Spirit, inflammable liquor, raised by distillation (alcohol). 8. True sense or meaning. **El Espíritu Santo,** the Holy Ghost. **Espíritu maligno,** the devil. **Dar el espíritu,** to give up the ghost, to die. **Cobrar espíritu,** to take courage. **Espíritus,** 1. Spirits, demons, hobgoblins. 2. Spirits, ether. **Pobre de espíritu,** poor in spirit. **Con espíritu amplio,** with an open mind.

espiritual [es-pe-re-too-ahl'], *a.* Spiritual, ghostly (fantasmal).

espiritualidad [es-pe-re-too-ah-le-dahd'], *f.* 1. Spirituality, incorporality, intellectual nature. 2. Principle and effect of what is spiritual. **Espiritualidades de un obispo,** revenue of a bishop arising from his jurisdiction.

espiritualismo [es-pe-re-too-ah-lees'-mo], *m.* Spiritualism, as a philosophic system, opposed to materialism.

espiritualista [es-pe-re-too-ah-lees'-tah], *m.* He who treats of the vital spirits.

espiritualizar [es-pe-re-too-ah-le-thar'], *va.* 1. To spiritualize, to purify from the feculencies of the world. 2. To refine the intellect.

espiritualmente [es-pe-re-too-al-men-tay], *adv.* Spiritually.

espirituoso, sa [es-pe-re-too-oh'-so, sah], *a.* 1. Spirituous, having the quality of spirit; ardent, inflammable. 2. Spirituous, vivid, airy, lively.

espirómetro [es-pe-ro'-may-tro], *m.* Spirometer, instrument for measuring the breathing capacity of the lungs.

espita [es-pee'-tah], *f.* 1. A faucet. 2. Tippler, a drunkard. 3. Span, the space from the end of the thumb to the end of the little finger extended.

espitar [es-pe-tar'], *va.* To put a faucet in a tub or other vessel.

espito [es-pee'-to], *m.* Peel, a piece of wood used to hang up paper to dry.

esplendente [es-plen-den'-tay], *pa. (Poet.)* Shining, glittering, resplendent.

espléndidamente [es-plen'-de-dah-men-tay], *adv.* Splendidly, nobly, magnificently, gloriously, brightly, glitteringly.

esplendidez [es-plen-de-deth'], *f.* Splendor, magnificence, ostentation.

espléndido, da [es-plen'-de-do, dah], *a.* 1. Splendid (magnífico), magnificent, grand, sumptuous, pompous. 2. *(Poet.)* Resplendent.

esplendor [es-plen-dor'], *m.* 1. Splendor, brilliancy, luster, glory, magnificence, grandeur. 2. Fulgency, glitter, lucidity. 3. Excellence, eminence, nobleness, gallantry. 4. Finery, fineness, gorgeousness. 5. White paint made of pounded egg-shells.

esplendoroso, sa [es-plen-do-ro'-so, sah], *a. (Poet.)* Brilliant, refulgent, luminous.

esplenético, ca [es-play-nay'-te-co, cah], *a.* Splenic, belonging to the spleen or milt.

espliego [es-ple-ay'-go], *m. (Bot.)* Lavender.

esplín [es-pleen'], *m. (coll.)* Spleen, melancholy.

esplique [es-plee'-kay], *m.* Machine for catching birds.

espodio [es-po'-deo], *m.* 1. Calx found in copper furnaces. 2. Ashes of burnt ivory or reeds.

espodito [es-po-dee'-to], *m.* Whitish ashes of volcanoes.

espodolenco, ca [es-po-do-len'-co, cah], *a. (Zool.)* Ashen in color, of a mixed gray and white.

espolada [es-po-lah-dah], *f.* Prick with a spur (espolazo). **Espolada de vino,** *(coll.)* a large draught of wine.

espolazo [es-po-lah'-tho], *m.* A violent prick with a spur.

espoleadura [es-po-lay-ah-doo'-rah], *f.* Wound made with a spur.

espolear [es-po-lay-ar'], *va.* 1. To spur, to drive with a spur (caballo). 2. To spur, to instigate, to incite, to urge forward.

espoleta [es-po-lay'-tah], *f.* 1. Fuse of a bomb or a handgrenade. **Espoletas de cubierta,** *(Naut.)* fuses of a fireship. 2. Small bone between the wings of birds.

espolín [es-po-leen'], *m.* 1. A small spool for raising flowers on stuff. 2. Silk stuff; on which flowers are raised, like brocade.

espolinado, da [es-po-le-nah'-do, dah], *a.* Flowered (material de seda). -*pp.* of ESPOLINAR.

espolinar [es-po-le-nar'], *va.* To weave flowers in silk.

espolio [es-po'-le-o], *m.* The property which a prelate leaves at his death.

espolique [es-poo-lee'-kay], *m.* Footman.

espolista [es-po-lees'-tah], *m.* 1. A servant who travels on foot before the horse or mule of his master, a running footman. 2. One who farms the fruits of the ecclesiastical benefice of a diseased bishop.

espolón [es-po-lone'], *m.* 1. Spur, the sharp point on the legs of a cock (gallo). 2. The acute angle of the pier of a stone bridge, to break the force of the current. 3. *(Arch.)* Stay, prop. 4. *(Naut.)* The ram of a man-of-war. 5. *(Naut.)* Fender-beam, knee of the head, a curve which is put upon vessels which lack a cut water, in order to fit the bowsprit to it. 6. Part of a causeway or dock which juts into the sea 7. *(Fort.)* Kind of a salient angle. 8. Chilblain.

espolvorear [es-pol-vo-ray-ar'], *va.* 1. To powder, to sprinkle with powder. 2. To dust, to brush off the dust. 3. *(Met.)* To separate, to scatter, to dissipate.

espolvorizar [es-pol-vo-re-thar'], *va.* To scatter powder.

espondaico, ca [es-pon-dah'-ee-co, cah], *a.* Spondaic, of spondees.

espondeo [es-pon-day'-o], *m.* Spondee, a foot of verse consisting of two long syllables.

espondilitis [es-pon-de-lee'-tis], *f. (Med.)* Spondylitis, inflammation of the spinal column.

espóndilo [es-pon'-de-lo], *m.* 1. Vertebra. 2. A ball which was used in ancient Greece for elections.

esponja [es-po-ne'-hah]. *f.* 1. Sponge. **Esponja de baño,** bath sponge. **Beber como una esponja,** to drink like a fish. 2. *(Met.)* Sponger (gorrón), one who by mean arts lives on others.

esponjado [es-pon-hah'-do], *m. (Prov.)* A sponge made of sugar which instantly dissolves.-**Esponjado, da,** *pp.* of ESPONJAR.

esponjadura [es-pon-hah-doo'-rah], *f.* 1. Act of sponging. 2. Cavity or defect in cast metal.

esponjar [es-pon-har'], *va.* To sponge, to soak or imbibe. -*vr.* To be puffed up with pride (engreírse).

esponjilla [es-pon-hel'-lyah], *f. (Bot.)* A fruit of the size of a turkey's egg which abounds in Venezuela, Colombia, and Ecuador.

esponjilla, ita, uela [es-pon-heel'-lyah], *f. dim.* A small piece of sponge.

esponjosidad [es-pon-ho-se-dahd'], *f.* Sponginess.

esponjoso, sa [es-pon-ho'-so, sah], *a.* Spongy (materia), porous.

esponsales [es-pon-sah'-les], *m. pl.* Espousals, betrothal, a mutual promise of marriage.

esponsalicio, cia [es-pon-sah-lee'-the-o, ah], *a.* Belonging to espousals, nuptial, spousal.

esponsor [es-pon-sor'], *m. (Com. Dep. etc.)* Sponsor.

espontáneamente [es-pon-tah'-nay-ah-men-tay], *adv.* Spontaneously, voluntarily.

espontanearse [es-pon-tah-nay-ar'-say], *vr. & vn.* To avow or declare spontaneously (confesar).

espontaneidad [es-pon-tah-nay-e-dahd'], *f.* Spontaneity, spontaneousness, the state of being spontaneous, voluntariness.

espontáneo, nea [es-pon-tah'-nay-o, ah], *a.* Spontaneous, voluntary, willing.

espontón [es-pon-tone'], *m.* Spontoon, a half-pike.

espontonada [es-pon-to-nah'-dah], *f.* Salute to royal personages or generals with a spontoon.

esporádico, ca [es-po-rah'-de-co, cah], *a.* Sporadic, isolated (enfermedad).-*adv.* **Esporádicamente.**

espora, *f.* or **esporo,** *m.* [es-po-rah, roh], *(Bot.)* Spore.

esportear [es-por-tay-ar'], *va.* To carry something in frails, panniers, or baskets.

esportilla [es-por-teel'-lyah], *f. dim.* A small frail, pannier, or wicker vessel.

esportillero [es-por-til-lyay-ro], *m.* Porter, one who carries burdens for hire.

esportillo [es-por-teel'-lyo], *m.* Pannier, fail, a wicker vessel.

esportón [es-por-tone'], *m.* A large pannier.

espórtula [es-por'-too-lah], *f. (Prov.)* Judicial fees.

esposa [es-po'-sah], *f.* Spouse, wife, consort, matron. -*pl.* Manacles, handcuffs, fetters, or chains for the hands. **Poner las esposas a uno,** to handcuff somebody.

esposo [es-po'-so], *m.* Spouse, husband, consort.

esprilla [es-preel'-lyah], *f. (Both.)* V. ESCAÑA.

espuela [es-poo-ay'-lah], *f.* 1. Spur, a goading instrument worn off a horseman's heel. 2. *(Met.)* Spur, stimulus, incitement. **Mozo de espuela,** *V.* ESPOLISTA. **Poner espuela.** *(Met.)* to incite, to urge on.

espuenda [es-poo-en'-dah], *f. (Naut.)* Margin of a river.

espuerta [es-poo-err'-tah], *f.* Pannier, basket, frail, with two handles.

espulgar [es-pool-gar'], *va.* 1. To rid of, to clean from lice or fleas (quitar las pulgas). 2. To examine closely, to scrutinize.

espulgo [es-pool'-go], *m.* The act of cleaning from lice or fleas.

espuma [es-poo'-mah], *f.* 1. Froth (sobre cerveza), spume, foam (sobre agua); the bubbles caused in liquors by agitation.

Espuma de mar, meerschaum. **Crecer como la espuma,** to flourish like the green bay tree. 2. Scum (residuos). **Hacer espuma,** to foam.

espumadera [es-poo-mah-day'-rah], *f.* 1. Skimmer, a sort of ladle with holes. 2. Vessel used by confectioners to clarify sugar. 3. *(Naut.)* Pitchskimmer.

espumajear [es-poo-mah-hay-ar'], *vn.* To foam at the mouth.

espumajo [es-poo-mah'-ho], *m.* Froth, spume; saliva.

espumajoso, sa [es-poo-mah-ho'-so, sah], *a.* Foamy, frothy, spumous.

espumante [es-poo-mahn'-tay], *pa.* Foaming at the mouth, like enraged animals.-*a.* Sparkling.

espumar [es-poo-mar'], *va.* To skim or to scum, to take off the scum.-*vn.* To froth, to foam.

espumear [es-poo-may-ar'], *va.* To raise foam.

espumarajo [es-poo-ma-rah'-ho], *m.* Foam, frothy substance thrown from the mouth. **Echar espumarajos por la boca,** to foam at the mouth with passion.

espumero [es-poo-may-ro], *m.* Place where salt water is collected to crystallize.

espumescente [es-poo-mes-then'-tay], *a.* Spumescent.

espumilla [es-poo-meel'-lyah], *f.* Thread crape, a sort of thin cloth loosely woven.

espumillón [es-poo-mil-lyone'], *m.* Silk crape or gauze.

espumosidad [es-poo-mo-se-dahd'], *f.* Frothiness, foaminess.

espumoso, sa [es-poo-mo'-so, sah], *a.* Frothy, foamy, lathery (jabón), sparkling (vino).

espundia [es-poon'-de-ah], *f. (Vet.)* A cancerous ulcer.

espurcílocuo, cua [es-poor-thee'-lo-kwo, kwah], *a.* Of foul, disgusting talk.

espúreo, rea, or **espurio, ria** [es-poo'-ray-o, ah, re-o, ah], *a.* 1. Spurious, not legitimate. 2. *(Met.)* Spurious, adulterated, corrupted, not genuine.

espurriar, or **espurrear** [es-poor-re-ar'], *va.* To spurt, to moisten a thing with water.

espurrir [es-poor-reer'], *va.* To stretch out something, chiefly said of the feet.

esputo [es-poo'-to], *m.* Spittle, saliva; sputum.

esquebrajar [es-kay-brah-har'], *va.* To split, to cleave. -*vr.* To become open, to be split or full of chinks, as wood.

esqueje [es-kay'-hay], *m.* Among gardeners, a cutting, slip.

esquela [es-kay'-lah], *f.* Billet, a small letter or paper, a note (nota). **Esquela amatoria,** a love-letter.

esquelético [es-kay-lay'-te-co], *a.* Skeletal; thin, skinny.

esqueleto [es-kay-lay'-to], *m.* 1. Skeleton, the bones of the body preserved in their natural situation. 2. Person very thin and meager. 3. Watch, the works and movements of which are exposed to view. 4. *(Naut.)* Carcass or framework of a ship without cover or sheathing. **En esqueleto,** unfinished, in an incomplete manner. **Menear el esqueleto,** to shake a hoof. **Estar hecho un esqueleto,** to be like a skeleton.

esquelita [es-kay-lee'-tah], *f.* 1. A small note, a billet. 2. Tungstate of calcium.

esquema [es-kay'-mah], *m.* Plan (proyecto), sketch (esbozo), outline, diagram (diagrama). **Esquema del vuelo,** *(Aer.)* flight pattern.

esquemático, ca [es-kay-mah'-te-co, cah], *a.* Schematic. -*m. pl.* Sectarians who believed that the body of Jesus Christ was only apparent.

esquena [es-kay'-nah], *f.* Spine of fishes.

esquero [es-kay'-ro], *m.* A leather bag or pouch.

esquerro, ra [es-ker'-ro, rah], *a. V.* IZQUIERDO.

esquí [es-kee'], *m.* Ski. **Esquí acuático,** water ski. **Hacer esquí,** to go skiing.

esquiador, ra [es-kee-ah-dor'], *m & f.* Skier.

esquiar [es-ke-ar'], *vn.* To ski.

esquiciado, da [es-ke-the-ah'-do, dah], *a.* Sketched, traced, delineated. -*pp.* of ESQUICIAR.

esquiciar [es-ke-the-ar'], *va.* To sketch, to draw the outlines of a painting; to trace, to delineate.

esquicio [es-kee'-the-o], *m.* Sketch, outline, line.

esquifada [es-ke-fah'-dah], *f.* 1. A skiff or boat load. 2. Vault of a cistern.

esquifar [es-ke-far'], *va.* 1. *(Naut.)* To arm a boat with oars. 2. To fit out a ship.

esquifazón [es-ke-fah-thone'], *f. (Naut.)* 1. A boat's crew. 2. A set of sails, written also *Esquifación.*

esquife [es-kee'-fay], *m.* 1. A skiff, a small boat. 2. *(Arch.)* Cylindrical vault.

esquila [es-kee'-lah], *f.* 1. Hand bell, a small bell, also a bell carried by cattle (campanilla). 2. The act and time of sheep shearing. *V.* ESQUILEO. 3. *(Zool.)* Shrimp. 4. *(Ent.)* Water-spider. 5. *(Bot.)* V. ESCILLA.

esquilada [es-ke-lah'-dah], *f. (Prov.)* V. CENCERRADA.

esquilador [es-ke-lah-dor'], *m.* Sheep-shearer, clipper.

esquilar [es-ke-lar'], *va.* 1. To shear or to fleece sheep, to cut off the wool or hair of animals. 2. *(Prov.)* To climb a tree with the hands and feet only.

esquileo [es-ke-lay'-o], *m.* Sheep-shearing time; also, the act and place of shearing.

esquilimoso, sa [es-ke-le-mo'-so, sah], *a. (coll.)* Fastidious, over nice.

esquilmar [es-keel-mar'], *va.* To gather and get in the harvest (cosecha). **Esquilmar la tierra,** to impoverish the earth (árboles).

esquilmeño, ña [es-keel-may'-nyo, nyah], *a.* Fruitful, productive (árboles, plantas).

esquilmo [es-keel'-mo], *m.* 1. Harvest, the corn garnered. 2. Produce of vines. 3. Produce of cattle.

esquilo [es-kee'-lo], *m.* 1. Shearing time; also, the act of shearing. 2. Kind of squirrel.

esquilón [es-ke-lone'], *m.* 1. A small bell. 2. Large bell worn by cattle.

esquimal [es-kee-mahl'], *a.* Eskimo.

esquina [es-kee'-nah], *f.* Corner, the outward angle formed by two lines, coin, edge, angle. **En la esquina de la calle,** on the corner of the street. **La tienda de la esquina,** the corner shop.

esquinado, da [es-ke-nah'-do, dah], *a.* Cornered (que tiene esquinas), angled. *-pp.* of ESQUINAR.

esquinal [es-ke-nahl'], *m.* Corner plate, angle iron; iron knee, corner casting.

esquinante, esquinanto [es-ke-nahn'-tay], *m.* Kind of aromatic or medicinal rush.

esquinar [es-ke-nar'], *va.* 1. *(Prov.)* To make a corner (hacer esquina), to form into an angle. 2. To square (madera). 3. To swerve, to slice (pelota). 4. To set at odds (personas), *-vr.* 1. To quarrel, to fall out. 2. To get a chip on one's shoulder (estar resentido).

esquinazo [es-ke-nah'-tho], *m.* 1. Corner (esquina), a very acute outward angle. 2. *(coll.)* Quinsy. **Dar a uno esquinazo,** to dodge somebody.

esquinela [es-ke-nay'-lah], *f.* Armor for the legs.

esquinzador [es-kin-thah-dor'], *m.* Large apartment in paper-mills for putting the rags in, after cutting them.

esquinzar [es-kin-thar'], *va.* To cut rags in small pieces, in paper-mills.

esquipado, da [es-ke-pah'-do, dah], *a.* Made boat-fashion. *-pp.* of ESQUIPAR.

esquipar [es-ke-par'], *pa. (Naut.)* To equip, to fit out a ship. *V.* EQUIPAR.

esquiraza [es-ke-rah'-thah], *f.* Kind of ancient ship.

esquirla [es-keer'-lah], *f. (Surg.)* Splinter of a bone.

esquirol [es-ke-rol'], *m.* 1. Squirrel. 2. Strike-breaker.

esquirro [es-keer'-ro], *m. (Med.)* Scirrhus, hard cancer.

esquirrogastria [es-kir-ro-gahs'-tre-ah], *f.* Cancerous degeneration of the stomach.

esquisar [es-ke-sar'], *va. (Obs.)* To search, to investigate.

esquisto [es-kees'-to], *m.* Schist.

esquistoso, sa [es-kis-to'-so, sah], *a.* Schistose.

esquitar [es-ke-tar'], *va. (coll.)* To pardon, to remit a debt.

esquivar [es-ke-var'], *va.* To shun, to avoid, to evade, to escape. **Esquivar un golpe,** to dodge a blow. *-vr.* To disdain, to scorn, to view with contempt, to coy.

esquivez [es-ke-veth'], *f.* Disdain, scorn, asperity, coyness, coldness.

esquivo, va [es-kee'-vo, vah], *a.* 1. Scornful, severe, stubborn, fastidious. 2. Shy (tímido), reserved, difficult, coyish, cold, haggard.

esquizado, da [es-ke-thah'-do, dah], Applied to spotted marble.

esquizofrenia [es-ke-tho-fray'-ne-ah], *f.* Schizophrenia.

esquizofrénico, ca [es-ke-tho-fray'-ne-co cah], *a. & m. & f.* Schizophrenic.

esquizomicetes [es-ke-tho-me-thay'-tays], *m. pl.* Schizomycetes, a class of minute unicellular plants allied to the algae; it comprises the bacteria.

estabilidad [es-tah-be-le-dahd'], *f.* Stability, duration, permanence, constancy, firmness, consistence, fixedness.

estabilización [es-tah-be-le-thah-the-on'], *f.* Stabilization.

estabilizar [es-tah-be-le-thar'], *va.* To stabilize, to hold steady, to prevent fluctuations. *-vr.* To become stable, to settle down (en la vida).

estable [es-tah'-blay], *a.* Stable (firme), permanent, durable, steady, firm, fast, consistent.

establear [es-tah-blay-ar'], *va.* To tame, to domesticate, to accustom to the stable.

establecedor [es-tah-blay-thay-dor'], *m.* Founder, he that establishes an institution or law; confirmer.

establecer [es-tah-blay-therr'], *va.* 1. To enact, to establish by law, to decree, to confirm. 2. To establish, to found, to fix immovably. 3. To fortify; to constitute. 4. To establish, to fix or settle in an opinion, to ground. *-vr.* To establish or fix oneself in a place. (*Yo establezco, yo establezca,* from *Establecer. V.* CONOCER.)

estableciente [es-tah-blay-the-en'-tay], *pa. & m. & f.* Establisher: establishing.

establecimiento [es-tah-blay-the-me-en'-to], *m.* 1. Statute, law, ordinance. 2. Establishment, foundation, settlement. 3. Establishment, footing, settlement or fixed state of a person. 4. *(coll.)* Manufactory, place where handicraft business is carried out. **Establecimiento comercial,** commerical establishment.

establemente [es-tah'-blay-men-tay], *adv.* Stably, firmly.

establillo [es-tah-bleel'-lyo], *m. dim.* A small stable.

establo [es-tah'-blo], *m.* Stable for horses and mules; barn (granero).

estaca [es-tah'-cah], *f.* 1. A stake (poste), picket. 2. Slip of a tree put into the ground to grow. 3. Stick, cudgel, bludgeon. *-pl.* 1. *(Naut.)* Thowls or tholes. *V.* TOLETES. 2. Divisions or partitions made in mines. 3. Clampnails, large nails used by carpenters. **Estar a la estaca,** *(coll.)* to live very poorly, to be indigent or oppressed with want.

estacada [es-tah-cah'-dah], *f.* 1. *(Mil.)* Palisade or stockade. 2. Paling, a kind of fence-work for parks, gardens, and grounds (cerca). 3. A place to fight in, place for a duel. **Dejar en la estacada,** to abandon one in peril, to sacrifice him.

estacado [es-tah-cah'-do], *m.* Place for a duel. —**Estacado, da,** *pp.* of ESTACAR.

estacar [es-tah-car'], *va.* 1. To put stakes into the ground; to enclose a spot with stakes (tierra, propiedad). 2. To tie to a stake (animal). *-vr.* To be enclosed or surrunded with stakes.

estacazo [es-tah-cah'-tho], *m.* Blow given with a stake.

estacha [es-tah'-chah], *f.* Rope fastened to a harpoon, to give the whale room to dive.

estación [es-tah-the-on'], *f.* 1. State, situation, position. 2. Season of the year (temporada). **Las cuatro estaciones,** the four seasons. 3. Hour, moment, time. 4. Station, a railway stopping place. 5. Stations of the cross (Vía Crucis). 6. Apparent motion in the stars. 7. A party of persons posted at some place. 8. Business, duty, one's obligations. **Estación astral,** *(Aer.)* space station. **Estación de servicio,** car service station. **Estación de vehículos,** cab stand, parking lot. **Red de estaciones,** radio network. **Estación de ferrocarril,** railway station. **Estación de gasolina,** gas station. **Estación**

terminal, terminus. **Estación invernal,** winter sports resort. **Estación de autobuses,** bus station.

estacional [es-tah-theo-nahl'], *a.* 1. Pertaining to the seasons. 2. Seasonal, occurring at a specified time. 3. *(Ast.)* Stationary.

estacionamiento [es-tah-the-o-nah-me-en'-to], *m.* Parking (vehículo).

estacionar [es-tah-the-o-nar'], *va.* To park (vehículo). -*vn.* & *vr.* To be motionless or stationary.

estacionario, ria [es-tah-the-o-nah'-re-o, ah], *a.* Stationary, fixed, not progressive.

estacte [es-tahc'-tay]. *m.* Odoriferous liquor extracted from fresh myrrh.

estada [es-tah'-dah], *f.* Stay, sojourn, residence.

estadal [es-tah-dahl'], *m.* 1. Land measure, containing about three square yards and two thirds, or eleven feet. 2. Kind of ornament or holy ribbon worn at the neck. 3. *(Prov.)* Fathom of wax taper.

estadía [es-tah-dee'-ah], *f.* 1. An instrument used for levelling. 2. *(Com. and Naut.)* Stay (estancia), detention; demurrage. Cost of such stay.

estadio [es-tah'-de-o], *m.* 1. Race-course. 2. Stadium (pl: stadia), ancient measure of 125 paces, furlong. 3. Stage, phase (fase).

estadista [es-tah-dees'-tah], *m.* Statist, statesman, politician.

estadística [es-tah-dees'-te-cah], *f.* Statistics, the science so called.

estadístico, ca [es-tah-dees'-te-co, cah], *a.* Statistical, statistic, political.

estadizo, za [es-tah-dee'-tho, thah], *a.* Stagnant, corrupted (agua).

estado [es-tah'-do], *m.* 1. State, the actual condition of a thing. 2. State, condition, circumstances of nature or fortune, footing, station in life. 3. Rank, state, estate, quality, condition (status). 4. State, the commonwealth. 5. Stature or height of a person. 6. Statement, account, report (informe). 7. Suite, attendants. **Estado general or llano,** community or peasantry of any district, not including the nobles. **Materias de estado,** state affairs. **Estado mayor,** *(Mil.)* staff, generals and commanders of an army. **Hombre de estado,** statesmam. **Estado de emergencia,** state of emergency. **Estado de sitio,** state of siege. **Estar en estado,** to be pregnant. **Estar en malísimo estado,** to be in a terrible condition. 8. *(Inform.)* **Estado de espera,** wait state. **Estado flotante,** floating state.

estadounidense, estadunidense [es-tah-do-oo-nee-denn'-say], *m.* & *f.* Native of United States of America. -*a.* From the United States.

estafa [es-tah'-fah], *f.* Trick, deceit, imposition.

estafador, ra [es-tah-fah-dor', rah], *m.* & *f.* Impostor, swindler, chiseler, cheat. -*a.* Chiseling, swindling.

estafar [es-tah-far'], *va.* 1. To deceive, to defraud. **Estafar algo a uno,** to swindle something out of somebody. 2. Among sculptors, to size a statue with a white coat in order to gild it.

estafermo [es-tah-ferr'-mo], *m.* 1. A wooden movable figure of an armed man. 2. *(Met.)* An idle fellow, who affects importance.

estafeta [es-tah-fay'-tah], *f.* 1. Courier (persona), express, estafet. 2. General postoffice for letters (oficina).

estafetero [es-tah-fay-tay'-ro], *m.* Postmaster, director of the post office.

estafilea piñada [es-tah-fe-lay'-ah pe-nyah'-dah], *f.* 1. *(Bot.)* Five-leaved bladder-nut. 2. **Estafilea,** a nymph converted by Bacchus into a cluster of grapes.

estafisagra [es-tah-fe-sah'-grah], *f.* *(Bot.)* Stavesacre, lousewort.

estagnación [es-tag-nah-the-on'], *f.* Stagnation, want of circulation in fluids or in business. *V.* ESTACACIÓN.

estala [es-tah'-lah], *f.* 1. Stable. 2. Seaport.

estalación [es-tah-lah-the-on'], *f.* Class, rank, order.

estalactita [es-tah-lac-tee'-tah], *f.* Stalactite, a rocky concretion, in form of an icicle, hanging from the vaults of caves.

estalagmita [es-tah-lag-mee'-tah], *f.* Stalagmite, a cylindrical or conical deposit on the floor of a cavern, formed by a dropping from the roof.

estalingadura [es-tah-lin-gah-doo'-rah], *m.* *(Naut.)* The bending of a cable, or fastening it to the ring of the anchor

estalingar [es-tah-lin-gar'], *va.* *(Naut.)* To bend a cable.

estallar [es-tal-lyar'], *vn.* 1. To crack (látido), to burst into chinks with a loud sound (bomba, neumático), to creak. 2. *(Met.)* To break out into fury or rage. **Estallar en llanto,** to burst into tears. **Hacer estallar,** to set off; *(Fig.)* to spark off.

estallido, estallo [es-tal-lyee'-do, es-tahl'-lyo], *m.* 1. Crack, crackling, creaking, crashing, the sound of something bursting or falling. 2. The report of firearms. **Dar un estallido,** to publish; to expose; to make a noise or confusion. *(coll.)* To fail dishonestly.

estambor [es-tam-bor'], *m.* *(Naut.)* Sternpost.

estambrado [es-tam-brah'-do], *m.* *(Prov.)* Kind of cloth made of worsted.

estambrar [es-tam-brar'], *va.* To twist wool into yarn, to spin worsted.

estambre [es-tahm'-bray], *m.* 1. Fine worsted or woollen yarn. 2. Fine wool. 3. *(Bot.)* Stamen of flowers. **Estambre de la vida,** *(Poet.)* the thread of life. 4. Warp. *V.* URDIMBRE.

estamento [es-tah-men'-to], *m.* 1. Name given to each of the estates of Spain, or to the clergy, nobility, and commons, who composed the assembly of the Cortes. 2. Body (cuerpo); stratum (estrato); class (clase).

estameña [es-tah-may'-nyah], *f.* Serge, a kind of woollen stuff.

estaminal [es-tah-me-nahl'], *a.* Staminal, pertaining to stamens.

estamíneo, nea [es-tah-mee'-nay-o, ah], or **estaminífero, ra** [es-ta-me-nee'-fay-ro, rah], *a.* Staminate, having stamens.

estampa [es-tahm'-pah], *f.* 1. Print, a figure or image printed (imagen); stamp; cut. **De estampa poco agradable,** of disagreable appearance. 2. The first sketch or design of a drawing or painting. 3. Press of printing machine for printing books (imprenta). 4. Track, an impression left by the foot.

estampado [es-tam-pah'-do], *m.* Impression, act and effect of stamping (impresión).

estampado, da [es-tam-pah'-do, dah], *a.* 1. Stamped (lino, algodón). 2. Embossed, figured: in speaking of printed dry goods. -*pp.* of ESTAMPAR.

estampador [es-tam-pah-dor'], *m.* 1. One who makes or sells prints. 2. Printer.

estampar [es-tam-par'], *va.* 1. To print (imprimir), to stamp (marcar). 2. To leave in the ground an impression of the foot. 3. *(Met.)* To fix in one's mind or memory.

estampería [es-tam-pay-ree'-ah], *f.* Office for printing or selling prints.

estampero [es-tam-pay'-ro], *m.* He who makes or sells prints or stamps.

estampida [es-tam-pee'-dah], *f.* 1. *(Amer.)* Stampede, a general scamper of animals. 2. *(coll.)* **Dar una estampida,** to run away; to run away in debt.

estampido [es-tam-pee'-do], *m.* 1. Report of a gun or piece of ordinance. 2. Crack, crash, crashing, the sound of anything bursting or falling. **Dar estampido,** to publish, to propagate, to make a noise.

estampilla [es-tam-peel'-lyah], *f.* 1. *(dim.)* A small print. 2. A small press. 3. Signet, a seal manual, used instead of a signature. 4. *(Amer.)* A postage-stamp (sello).

estampita [es-tam-pee'-tah], *f. dim.* A small print or stamp.

estancación [es-tan-cah-the-on'], *f.* Stagnation of circulating fluids or of business matters.

estancado [es-tan-cah'-do], *a.* 1. Stagnant (agua). 2. *(Fig.)* Static. **Estar éstancado,** to be held up.

estancamiento [es-tan-cah-me-ayn'-to], *m.* 1. Stagnancy, stagnation (de agua). 2. *(Fig.)* Stagnation; blockage, stoppage, suspension.

estancar [es-tan-car'], *va.* 1. To stop, to check, to stem a current. 2. *(Naut.)* To caulk a leak. 3. To monopolize, to hinder the free sale of merchandise. 4. To interdict, to prohibit, to suspend (negocio). *-vr.* 1. To stagnate, to become stagnant (agua). 2. *(Fig.)* To stagnate.

estancia [es-tahn'-the-ah], *f.* 1. Stay (permanencia), sojourn, continuance in a place. 2. Mansion, dwelling (domicilio), habitation; a sitting-room, a bedroom (cuarto). 3. *(Poet.)* Stanza, a division of a song or poem. 4. *(Amer.)* Farm; farm for grazing cattle; a country house. 5. *(Anger.)* Landed property.

estanciero [es-tan-the-ay'-ro], *m.* Overseer of a farm, mansion, or domain.

estanco [es-tahn'-co], *m.* 1. Forestalling, monopoly. 2. Place where privileged goods are sold exclusively. 3. Stop, stay, detention. 4. Repository, archives, 5. Tank.

estanco, ca [es-tahn'-co, cah], *a. (Naut.)* Stanch, well-repaired (barco).

estandar [es-tahn'-dar], *a. m.* Standard.

estandardización [es-tan-dar-de-thah-the-on'], *f.* Standardization.

estandarte [es-tan-dar'-tay], *m.* 1. Banner, standard, colors. 2. **Estandarte real,** *(Naut.)* Royal standard, used only by the commanding admiral of a fleet. 3. The upper petal of a papilionaceous corolla.

estangurria [es-tan-goor'-re-ah], *f.* 1. Strangury, difficulty in evacuating urine. 2. Catheter, an instrument to assist in voiding urine.

estánnico, estanífero [es-tahn'-ne-co], *a.* Stannic, containing tin.

estannolita [es-tan-no-lee'-tah], *f.* Oxide of tin.

estanque [es-tahn'-kay], *m.* Pond, basin, dam of water. **Estanque para chapotear,** paddling pool.

estanquero, ra [es-tan-kay'-ro], *m.* 1. Keeper of reservoirs. 2. Retailer of privileged goods, as tobacco in Spain.

estanquillero [es-tan-keel-lyay'-ro], *m.* A tobacconist.

estantal [es-tan-tahl'], *m.* Buttress. V. ESTRIBO.

estante [es-tahn'-tay], *m.* 1. Shelf, bookshelf (para libros). 2. *(Prov.)* He who carries, in company with others, images in processions. *-pa. & a.* 1. Being, existing in a place; extant. 2. Fixed, permanent: applied to sheep which are not driven to the mountains in summer.

estantería [es-tan-tay-ree'-ah], *f.* 1. A series of bookshelves. 2. Shelving.

estanterol [es-tan-tay-rol'], *m.* Center of a galley, where the captain stands in an engagement.

estantigua [es-tan-tee'-goo-ah], *f.* 1. Phantom, vision, hobgoblin. 2. A deformed person in a ridiculous garb.

estantío, tía [es-tan-tee'-o, ah], *a.* 1. Standing still and immovable on a spot. 2. *(Met.)* Dull, stupid; without life or spirit.

estañadera [es-tah-nyah-day'-rah], *f.* Soldering receiver or holder of tin plate.

estañado [es-tah-nyah'-do], *m.* Vessel or bath with melted pewter, in which copper or iron plates are immersed to be tinned.-**Estañado, da,** *pp.* OF ESTAÑAR.

estañador [es-tah-nyah-dor'], *m.* Tinman, a manufacturer of tin or tinned iron.

estañadura [es-tah-nyah-doo'-rah], *f.* Act of tinning.

estañar [es-tah-nyar'], *va.* To tin, to cover with tin.

estañero [es-tah-nyay'-ro], *m.* A person who works and sells tinware, a metalman.

estaño [es-tah'-nyo], *m.* 1. Tin, a primitive metal. 2. Tin, iron plates covered with tin.

estaquero [es-tah-kay'-ro], *m.* Buck or doe of a year old.

estaquilla, ita [es-tah-keel'-lyah, ee'-tah], *f.* 1. In shoe making, a peg (madera). 2. Any wooden pin which fastens one piece of timber to another. 3. Beam of a velvet-loom.

estaquillador [es-tah-keel-lyah-dor'], *m.* An awl to bore for pegs.

estaquillar [es-tah-keel-lyar'], *va.* To peg, to fasten with pegs.

estaquis [es-tah'-kees], *f. (Bot.)* Stachys, hedge-nettle, a plant resembling hoarhound.

estar [es-tar'], *vn.* 1. To be in a place (permanecer). 2. To understand or comprehend (comprensión). **Estoy en lo que Vd. me dice,** I understand what you tell me. 3. To be in favor of, to answer for (acuerdo). 4. To be of the opinion. **Estoy en que,** I am of the opinion that. 5. To be: an auxiliary verb, derived from the Latin *stare,* to stand, and used always with reference to existing or being in a place. **Estar escribiendo,** to be writing, 6. To undertake, to oblige or subject oneself to. 7. To stand. 8. To cost (precio) 9. With the preposition *en,* it signifies cause, motive. **En eso está,** in this it consists, on this it depends. 10. With the preposition *por* and the infinitive of some verbs it sometimes means that something is not done, and sometimes that something will be done immediately. **Estar por** or **para partir,** to be ready to set out. 11. With *a* and some nouns it signifies to be obliged or disposed to execute what the noun signifies. 12. With *con* and a person's name, to live in company with. 13. To see another in order to treat with him of a matter. 14. With *de* to be executing a thing or understanding in it, in whatever way. **Estar de gaita,** to be merry, in high spirits. **Estar algo por suceder,** to expect something to happen. **Estar a erre,** to be doing something with the utmost care. **Estar alerta,** to be on the watch, to be vigilant. **Estar bajo de llave** or **cerrado con llave,** to be under lock and key. **Estar de buen humor,** to be in good humor or spirits. **Estar de mal humor,** to sulk, to be angry. **Estar de pie** or **en pie; estar levantado** or **derecho,** to stand. **Estar de prisa,** to be in haste, to haste, to hasten. **Estar de por medio,** to interpose, to mediate. **Estar sobre sí,** to be tranquil or serene; to be greatly elated. **Estar para ello,** to be ready, to be disposed to do anything. **¡Dónde estamos!** An expression of admiration or disgust at what we see or hear. **Estar bien con,** to have regard for a person, to be in concord with him. **Estar bien una cosa,** to suit, to agree, to fit. **Estar mal con,** to have a bad opinion of. **Estar mal,** not to suit, to show bad looks. **¿Está Vd.?** or **Estamos?** Are you aware? Have you understood well? **Estar con el pie en el aire,** to be unsettled. **Está enfermo,** he is ill. **Dos vueltas más y ya está,** two more turns and that's it. **Para las cinco estará terminado,** it will be finished by 5 o'clock. **Las uvas están a 50 pesos,** grapes are 50 pesos. **Estar de vacaciones,** to be on vacation. **Está por llover,** it's about to rain. **Están sin vender,** they remain unsold, *-vr.* To be detained; to stay (quedarse). **Estarse parado or quieto,** to stand still.

estarcido [es-tar-thee'-do], *m.* Stencil.

estarcir [es-tar-theer'], *va.* To stencil.

estarna [es-tar'-nah], *f. (Orn.)* Kind of small partridge.

estatal [es-tah-tahl'], *a.* State.

estatera [es-tah-tay'-rah], *f.* 1. Balance, steel-yard. 2. An ancient Grecian coin.

estática [es-tah'-te-cah], *f.* (Radio) Static.

estátice [es-tah'-te-thay], *f. (Bot.)* Sea-lavender. **Estátice sinuada,** scallop-leaved sea-lavender.

estático, ca [es-tah'-te-co, cah], *a.* 1. (Radio) Static. 2. Static, motionless. 3 Dumbfounded.

estatificar [es-tah-te-fe-car'], *va.* To nationalize.

estatismo [es-tah-tees'-mo], *m.* 1. Static condition. 2. Statism, government control.

estatua [es-tah'-too-ah], *f.* 1. A statue. 2. A dull, stupid fellow.

estatuaria [es-tah-too-ah'-re-ah], *f.* Statuary.

estatuario [es-tah-too-ah'-re-o], *m.* Statuary, one who makes statues.

estatuir [es-tah-too-eer'], *va.* To establish (ordenar), to ordain, to enact, to prove (probar).

estatura [es-tah-too'-rah], *f.* Stature, the height of a person. **De regular estatura,** of average height.

estatutario, ria [es-tah-too-tah'-re-o, ah], *a.* Belonging to a statute or law.

estatuto [es-tah-too'-to], *m.* 1. Statute, law (de ciudad), ordinance. 2. Form of government established by laws and customs.

estay [es-tah'-e], *m. (Naut.)* Stay. **Estay mayor,** the main stay. **Estay de trinquete,** the fore stay. **Estay del mastelero mayor,** the maintop stay.

este [es'-tay], *m.* East, one of the four cardinal points of the compass. **Este cuarto** or **cuarta al nordeste,** East-by-north. **Este nordeste,** East-north-east. **Este cuarto al sudeste,** East-by-south. **Este sudeste,** East-south-east. **Viento del este,** easterly wind.

éste, ésta, esto [es'-tay, tah, to], *pron, dem.* This, this one (pl: **éstos, éstas,** these). **En esto,** at this time. **Ésta lo vio, Nos gusta más esa casa que ésta,** we prefer that house to this one. **Ese problema es fácil, éste es más difícil,** that problem is easy, this one is more difficult.

este, esta *adj. dem.* (pl: **estos, estas;** these). **Este coche es el más grande,** this car is the biggest. **Esta casa es la más bonita,** this house is the nicest. **Estos hombres llevan aquí todo el día,** these men have been here all day. **Estas chicas son muy atractivas,** these girls are very attractive.

estearato [es-tay-rah'-to], *m.* Stearate, a salt of stearic acid.

esteárico, ca [es-tay-ah'-re-co, cah], *a.* Stearic, relating to stearine.

estearina [es-tay-ah-ree'-nah], *f. (Chem.)* Stearine, a white crystalline component of fats.

estearona [es-tay-ah-ro'-nah], *f.* Stearone, a crystalline compound the ketone of stearic acid.

esteatita [es-tay-ah-tee'-tah], *f.* Steatite, soap stone, massive talc.

esteba [es-tay-bah], *f.* 1. A plant of prickly leaves and stem, growing in ponds and marshy places. 2. A stout pole, used on boats for pushing bales of wool close together.

estebar [es-tay-bar'], *va.* With dyers, to put cloth into the caldron to dye it.

esteclar [es-tay-clar'], *va.* To change the combs of looms for silk fringe, when they can no longer serve.

esteirosis [es-tay-e-ro'-sis], *f. (Med.)* Barrenness, sterility.

estela [es-tay'-lah], *f.* 1. The wake of a ship. 2. The trail of a meteor. **Estela de vapor,** *(Aer.)* contrail.

estelar [es-tay-lar'], *a.* 1. Stellar, sideral. 2. *(Teat. etc.)* Star. **Cargo estelar,** star role. **Combate estelar,** star bout (boxeo).

estelaria [es-tay-lah'-re-ah], *f.* 1. *(Bot.)* An old name given to the silvery ladiesmantle.

estelión [es-tay-le-on'], *m.* 1. Stellion, a small spotted lizard. 2. Toadstone.

estelionato [es-tay-le-o-nah'-to], *m. (Law.)* Stellionate, the crime of maliciously defrauding the unwary.

estelón [es-tay-lone'], *m.* Toadstone.

estelulado, da [es-tay-loo-lah'-do, dah], *a.* Stellular, starshaped.

estemenaras [es-tay-may-nah-ras], *f. pl. (Naut.)* Futtock timbers. *V.* LIGAZONES.

estemple [es-tem'-play], *m. (Mining.)* Stempel, a beam helping to support a platform.

estenografía [es-tay-no-grah-fee'-ah], *f.* Stenography, shorthand; in particular, phonography.

estenografiar [es-tay-no-grah-fe-ar'], *va.* To write in stenography.

estenográfico, ca [es-tay-no-grah'-fe-co, cah], *a.* Stenographic, relating to shorthand.

estenógrafo, fa [es-tay-no'-grah-fo, fah], *m. & f.* Stenographer, one who writes shorthand.

estenomecanografía [es-tay-no-may-cah-no-grah-fee'-ah], *f.* Stenotyping.

estenomecanógrafa [es-tay-no-may-cah-no'-grah-fah], *f.* Stenotypist.

estenotipía [es-tay-no-te-pee'-ah], *f.* Stenotyping.

estepa [es-tay'-pah], *f.* 1. *(Bot.)* Rock rose. **Estepa común,** laurel-leaved rock-rose. 2. Steppe, an immense uncultivated plain of Russia and certain regions of Asia.

estepar [es-tay-par'], *m.* Place filled with rock-roses.

estepilla [es-tay-peel'-lyah], *f. (Bot.)* White-leaved rock-rose.

ester [es'-ter], *m. (Chem.)* Ester.

estera [es-tay'-rah], *f.* Mat, a texture of sedge, flags, or rushes.

esterar [es-tay-rar'], *va.* To mat, to cover with mats. *-vn. (Met. coll.)* To keep oneself warm with clothes.

estercolar [es-ter-co-lar'], *va.* To dung, to muck, to manure, etc. *-vn.* To void the excrements (animales).

estercolero [es-ter-co-lay'-ro], *m.* 1. Boy or servant who drives the muckcart, or carries dung into the fields. 2. Dunghill, muckhill. 3. Laystall, a heap of dung.

estercorácea [es-ter-co-rah'-tha-yah], *f. adj.* Fistula of the anus.

estercuelo [es-ter-coo-ay-lo], *m.* The act of manuring the earth.

estéreo [es-tay'-ray-o], *m. (Arith.)* Stere, a unit of cubic measurement; one cubic meter. *-a.* Stereo. **Un disco estéreo,** a stereo record.

estereofónico, ca [es-tay-ray-o-fo'-ne-o, cah], *a.* Stereophonic. **Sonido estereofónico,** stereophonic sound.

estereografía [es-tay-ray-grah-fee'-ah], *f.* Stereography, representation of solids on a plane.

estereográfico, ca [es-tay-ray-o-grah'-fe-co, cah], *a.* Stereographic.

estereometría [es-tay-ray-o-may-tree'-ah], *f.* Stereometry, art of measuring solids.

estereómetro [es-tay-ray-o'-may-tro], *m.* Stereometer, an instrument for measuring the volume of a body.

estereoscópico [es-tay-ray-os-co'-pe-co], *m.* Stereoscope.

estereoscopio [es-tay-ray-os-co'-pe-o], *m.* Stereoscope, an optical instrument, showing two slightly different pictures, blended into one, in relief.

estereotipa [es-tay-ray-o-tee'-pah], *f. V.* ESTEREOTIPIA.

estereotipar [es-tay-ray-o-tee-par'], *va.* To stereotype or print with solid plates.

estereotipia [es-tay-ray-tee'-pe-ah], *f.* Stereotype, stereotyping.

estereotípico, ca [es-tay-ray-o-tee'-pe-co, cah], *a.* Stereotype, stereotypic, belonging to stereotype.

estereotipo [es-tay-re-o-te-po], *m.* Stereotype.

esterero [es-tay-ray'-ro], *m.* Mat-maker, mat-seller.

estéril [es-tay'-reel], *a.* Sterile, barren (terreno), unfruitful, unproductive, fruitless (esfuerzo).

esterilidad [es-tay-re-le-dahd'], *f.* 1. Sterility, barrenness (terreno), unfruitfulness, jejuneness. 2. Scarcity, the want of crops.

esterilización [es-tay-re-le-thah-the-on'], *f.* Sterilization, sterilizing.

esterilizar [es-tay-re-le-thar'], *va.* To sterilize, to make sterile.

esterilla [es-tay-reel'-lyah], *f.* 1. *(dim.)* Small mat (alfombrilla). 2. Ferret lace, made of gold, silver, or thread. **Paños de esterilla,** saved lists. **Esterilla de cerda para forrar sillas, etc.,** haircloth.

estérilmente [es-tay'-reel-men-tay], *adv.* Barrenly, unfruitfully, meagerly.

esterlino, na [es-ter-lee'-no, nah], *a.* Sterling (dinero).

esternón [es-ter-none'], *m. (Anat.)* Sternum, the breast-bone.

estero [es-tay'-ro], *m.* 1. A large lake near the sea, a salt marsh (pantano). 2. Matting, the act of covering with matting; also, the season in which matting is laid down. 3. *(Geog.)* A small creek, into which the tide flows (estuario). 4. A certain fishing-net.

esteroide [es-tay-ro'-e-day], *m.* Steroid.

estertor [es-ter-tor'], *m.* Rattle in the throat of agonizing persons; stertor.

estertoroso, sa [es-ter-to-ro'so, sah], *a.* Stertorous, accompanied by a snoring sound.

esteta [es-tay'-tah], *m. & f.* Aesthete or esthete.

estética [es-tay'-te-cah], *f.* aesthetics; the science of the beautiful.

esteticista [ess-tay-te-this'-tah], *m.* Beauty consultant, beauty specialist.

estético, ca [es-tay'-te-co, cah], *a.* æsthetic.

estetoscopio [es-tay-tos-co'-peo], *m. (Med.)* Stethoscope.

esteva [es-tay'-vah], *f.* 1. Plough-handle. 2. Curved bar of wood on the bottom, of coaches, connected with the shafts.

estevado, da [es-tay-vah'-do, dah], *a.* Bow-legged.

estezado [es-tay-thah'-do], *m. V.* CORREAL.

estiaje [es-te-ah'-hay], *m.* The lowest stage of water in a river, by reason of heat.

estiba [es-tee'-bah], *f.* 1. Rammer. *V.* ATACADOR. 2. Stowage, the arrangement of a ship's cargo. 3. Place where wool is compressed.

estibador [es-te-bah-dor'], *m.* Stevedore.

estibar [es-te-bar'], *va.* 1. To compress wool (lana). 2. To stow a cargo (meter).

estibio [es-tee'-be-o], *m.* Antimony stibium.

estíctico, ca [es-teec'-te-co, cah], *a. (Biol.)* Marked with points, punctate.

estiércol [es-te-ayr'-col], *m.* 1. Dung, excrement, ordure. 2. Dung or compost to fatten lands, manure.

estigma [es-teeg'-mah], *m.* 1. Stigma, brand (marca), mark of a slave or criminal. 2. Stigma, every mark of infamy. 3. *(Bot.)* Stigma, the upper extremity of the pistil for receiving the pollen. 4. A miraculous mark upon the body (marca de nacimiento).

estigmatizar [es-tig-ma-tee-thar'], *va.* To stigmatize, to mark with a brand.

estilar [es-te-lar'], *vn. & va.* 1. To use, to be accustomed (usar). 2. To draw up in writing according to the usual style or practice. -*vr.* To be in fashion. **Ya no se estila la chistera,** top hats aren't in fashion any more.

estilbita [es-teel-bee'-tah], *f.* Stilbite hydrous aluminum-calcium silicate.

estilista [es-te-lees'-tah], *m.* Stylist (escritor).

estilito [es-te-lee'-to], *m. dim.* A small style or gnomon.

estilizar [es-te-lee-thar'], *va.* To stylize; to design, to style. -*vn.* To cut a dash, to show off.

estilo [es-tee'-lo], *m.* 1. Style, a pointed iron formerly used to write on tables of wax. 2. Gnomon or style of a dial (reloj del sol). 3. Style, the manner of talking or writing, with regard to language. 4. Form or manner of proceeding in suits at law. 5. Use, custom. 6. *(Bot.)* Style, prolongation of the ovary and support of the stigma. **Estilo castizo,** a correct style. **Estilo de vida,** life-style. **Al estilo antiguo,** in the old style. **Los dictadores y otros por el estilo,** dictators and others of that sort.

estilográfico, ca [es-te-lo-grah'-fe-co, cah], *a.* Stylographic. **Pluma estilográfica,** fountain pen.

estilóideo [es-te-lo'-e-day-o], *a.* Styloid, like a style.

estima [es-tee'-mah], *f.* 1. Esteem, respect (aprecio). 2. *(Naut.)* Dead reckoning.

estimabilidad [es-te-mah-be-le-dahd'], *f.* Estimableness.

estimable [es-te-mah'-blay], *a.* Estimable, valuable, creditable; worthy of honor and esteem; computable.

estimación [es-te-mah-the-on'], *f.* 1. Estimation, valuation (evaluación), esteem, regard (aprecio). 2. Estimation, estimate, valuation, account. **Estimación propia,** self-esteem.

estimador, ra [es-te-mah-dor', rah], *m. & f.* Esteemer, estimator.

estimar [es-te-mar'], *va.* 1. To estimate (evaluar), to value; to set a value on a thing; to compute or to computate (calcular), to make of. 2. To esteem, to respect (apreciar), to regard, to honor, to make account of, or to make much of. **Estimar a uno en mucho,** to have a high regard for somebody. **Se lo estimo mucho,** I am much indebted to you for it. 3. To judge, to form an opinion. 4. To thank, to acknowledge. 5. To look into.

estimativa [es-te-mah-tee'-vah], *f.* 1. Power of judging and forming an opinion. 2. Instinct, natural propensity or aversion.

estimulante [es-te-moo-lahn'-tay], *pa. & a.* Stimulating, exciting. -*m.* Stimulant, excitant.

estimular [es-tee-moo-lar'], *va.* 1. To sting, to stimulate (apetito), to irritate, to excite, to goad. 2. To incite, to encourage (esfuerzo, industria).

estímulo [es-tee'-moo-lo], *m.* Sting, stimulus; incitement; stimulation, encouragement.

estinco [es-teen'-co], *m.* Skink, kind of lizard.

estío [es-tee'-o], *m.* The summer.

estiomenado, da [es-te-o-may-nah'-do, dah], *a.* Mortified, corrupted. -*pp.* of ESTIOMENAR.

estiomenar [es-te-o-may-nar], *va.* To corrode, to mortify.

estiómeno [es-te-o'-may-no], *m.* Mortification, gangrene.

estipa [es-tee'-pah], *f.* Stipa, a genus of tall, tufted grasses.

estipendiar [es-te-pen-de-ar'], *va.* To give a stipend.

estipendiario [es-te-pen-de-ah'-re-o], *m.* Stipendiary, one who performs a service for a settled payment.

estipendio [es-te-pen'-de-o], *m.* Stipend, salary (sueldo), pay, wages, fee (derechos).

estípite [es-tee'-pe-tay], *m. (Arch.)* Plaster in form of a reversed pyramid.

estipticar [es-tip-te-car'], *va.* To use or apply a styptic.

estipticidad [es-tip-te-the-dahd'], *f.* 1. Stypticity, the power of stanching blood.

estíptico, ca [es-teep'-te-co, cah], *a.* 1. Styptic, astringent: having the power of stanching. 2. Costive, bound in the body. 3. *(Met.)* Miserly, avaricious. 4. *(Met.)* Difficult to be obtained.

estiptiquez [es-tip-te-keth'], *f.* 1. Costiveness. 2. Niggardliness.

estípula [es-tee'-poo-lah], *f. (Bot.)* Stipule, a foliaceous appendage at the base of the petiole.

estipulación [es-te-poo-lah-the-on'], *f.* Stipulation, promise, clause, covenant, bargain.

estipulante [es-te-poo-lahn'-tay], *pa.* Stipulator, stipulating.

estipular [es-te-poo-lar'], *va.* To stipulate, to contract, to bargain, to settle terms, to covenant.

estique [es-tee'-kay], *m.* Stick, a wooden instrument used by sculptors for modelling in clay.

estira [es-tee'-rah], *f.* Kind of knife used by curriers.

estirace [es-te-rah'-tha], *m. (Bot.)* Styrax, the typical genus of the storax family; one species yields benzoin, another storax.

estiracear [es-te-rah-thay-ar'], *va. (coll.)* To pull, to tug, to stretch.

estiráceo, cea [es-te-rah'-thay-o, ah], *a.* Like styrax, styracaceous.

estiradamente [es-terah-dah-men'-tay], *adv.* 1. Scarcely, difficultly. 2. Violently, forcibly.

estirado, da [es-te-rah'-do, dah], *a.* 1. Extended, dilated, expanded. 2. Excellent. 3. *(Met.)* Grave, stiff (tieso), lofty; full of affected dignity. -*pp.* of ESTIRAR.

estirador [es-te-rah-dor'], *m.* 1. Stretcher (cortinas) 2. Drawing table.

estirar [es-te-rar'], *va.* 1. To dilate, to stretch out (extender), to lengthen. 2. To fit, to adjust. 3. To extend a discourse, to enlarge upon a subject (discurso) 4. *(Naut.)* To row slowly, to continue the tack. **Estirar la pierna,** *(coll.)* to die. -*vr.* 1. To stretch, to be extended, to bear extension (cuerpo, miembro). 2. To hold up one's head with affected gravity.

estirón [es-te-rone'], *m.* 1. Pull, the act of pulling (tirón); pluck, haul or hauling. 2. Pain produced by the violent extension of any part. 3. *(Naut.)* The distance gained in the course pursued. **Dar un estirón,** *(coll.)* to grow rapidly.

estirpe [es-teer'-pay], *f.* Race, origin, stock.

estitiquez [es-te-te-keth'], *f.* Costiveness. *V.* ESTIPTIQUEZ.

estivador [es-te-vah-dor'], *m.* Packer of wool at shearing.

estival [es-te-vahl'], *a.* Estival, pertaining to the summer.

esto [es'-to], *pron. dem.* This. **A esto,** hereto, hereunto. **Con esto,** herewith. **En esto,** herein, hereinto. **Sobre esto,** hereon, hereupon. **Por esto,** hereby. **Todo esto es inútil,** all this is useless. **Antes de esto,** before this. **Esto es todo lo que sé,** this is all I know.

estocada [es-to-cah'-dah], *f.* Stab (golpe), a thrust with a sword, lunge. **Estocada de vino,** breath of a person intoxicated. **Estocada por cornada,** *(coll.)* injury which one receives in striking another.

estoequiometría [es-to-ay-ke-o-may-tree'-ah], *f.* Stoichiometry, the mathematics of chemistry.

estoequiométrico, ca [es-to-ay-ke-o-may'-tre-co, cah], *a.* Stoichiometric, belonging to chemical calculations.

estofa [es-toh'-fah], *f.* 1. Quilted stuff. 2. *(Met.)* Quality, condition. **Hombre de estofa,** a person of consideration.

estofado, da [es-to-fah'-do, dah], *a. & pp.* of ESTOFAR. 1. Quilted. 2. Stewed.

estofado, *m.* Stewed meat.

estofador [es-to-fah-dor'], *m.* Quilter.

estofar [es-to-far'], *va.* 1. To quilt. 2. To paint relievos on a gilt ground. 3. To stew meat with wine, spice, or vinegar.

estoicamente [es-to-e-cah-men'-tay], *adv.* Stoically.

estoicidad [es-to-e-the-dahd'], *f.* Imperturbability.

estoicismo [es-to-e-thees'-mo], *m.* 1. Stoicism, the doctrine and sect of the Stoics. 2. A philosophical school founded in Athens by Zeno, 308 B.C., and whose motto was, "Suffer and abstain."

estoico, ca [es-to'-e-co, cah], *a.* Stoic, stoical. -*m.* Stoic.

estola [es-to'-lah], *f.* 1. Stole, a garment worn by priests. **Derechos de estola,** surplice fees. 2. Stole, woman's scarf. **Estola de piel,** fur stole.

estolidez [es-to-le-deth'], *f.* Stupidity, incapacity.

estólido, da [es-toh'-le-do, dah], *a.* Stupid, foolish.

estolón [es-to-lone'], *m. aug.* 1. A large stole. 2. *(Bot.)* Stolon, a runner or offset.

estomacacia [es-to-ma-cah'-the-ah], *f. (Med.)* Ulceration of the mouth; also scurvy.

estomacal [es-to-mah-cahl'], *a.* Stomachic, belonging to the stomach.

estomagar [es-to-mah-gar'], *vn. & va.* 1. To stomach, to resent, to remember with anger or malignity. 2. To enrage, to make angry.

estómago [es-toh'-mah-go], *m.* The stomach. **Tener buen estómago,** *(coll.)* to bear insults patiently. **Dolor de estómago,** stomach ache.

estomaguero [es-to-mah-gay'-ro], *m.* Stomacher, a piece of baize applied to the stomach of children.

estomaguillo [es-to-mah-geel'-lyo], *m.* 1. *(dim.)* A small stomach. 2. A weak stomach.

estomatical [es-to-mah-te-cahl'], *a.* Stomachic.

estomaticón [es-to-mah-te-cone'], *m.* Stomach-plaster.

estomatitis [es-to-mah-tee'-tis], *f.* Stomatitis, inflammation of the membranes of the mouth.

estopa [es-toh'-pah], *f.* 1. Tow, the coarsest part of hemp and flax. 2. Coarse cloth made of tow (del cáñamo). 3. *(Naut.)* Oakum.

estopada [es-to-pah'-dah], *f.* Quantity of tow for spinning.

estopear [es-to-pay-ar'], *va.* .1. To calk. 2. *(Naut.)* To stuff oakum in a sail to catch water.

estopeño, ña [es-to-pay'-nyo, nyah], *a.* Of tow; belonging to tow.

estopero [es-to-pay'-ro], *m.* That part of the piston of a pump round which tow is wound.

estoperol [es-to-pay-role'], *m.* 1. *(Naut.)* Short, round-headed tarpaulin nails. 2. Match or wick made of tow (mecha).

estopilla [es-to-peel'-lyah], *f.* 1. Cheese cloth. 2. Finest part of heron or flax.

estopín [es-to-peen'], *m.* Quick match, to fire off a gun.

estopón [es-to-pone'], *m.* Coarse tow.

estoposo, sa [es-to-po'-so, sah], *a.* Belonging to tow; filaceous, filamentous.

estoque [es-toh'-kay], *m.* 1. Estoc, rapier, a long, narrow sword (espada). 2. *(Bot.)* V. ESPADILLA.

estoqueador [es-to-kay-ah-dor'], *m.* Thruster (toreros) who use a long, narrow sword.

estoquear [es-to-kay-ar'], *va.* To thrust with a rapier.

estoqueo [es-to-kay'-o], *m.* Act of thrusting or stabbing.

estoraque [es-to-rah'-kay], *m.* 1. *(Bot.)* Official storax. 2. Gum of the storax-tree. **Estoraque líquido,** sweet gum tree, or sweet gum liquid ambar.

estorbador, ra [es-tor-bah-dor', rah], *m. & f.* Hinderer, obstructer.

estorbar [es-tor-bar'], *va.* To hinder (obstaculizar), to impede, to obstruct, to cumber, to hamper, to forbid, to lead off or out of, to be in one's way.

estorbo [es-tor'-bo], *m.* Impediment, hindrance, obstruction, nuisance. **No hay estorbo para que se haga,** there is no obstacle to its being done.

estornija [es-tor-nee'-hah], *f.* 1. An iron ring round the end and arms of an axle tree, which secures the linch-pin holes. 2. *(Prov.)* Boys' play.

estornino [es-tor-nee'-no], *m. (Orn.)* Starling.

estornudar [es-tor-noo-dar'], *vn.* To sneeze.

estonudo [es-tor-noo'-do], *m.* Sternutation, sneeze.

estornutatorio [es-tor-noo-tah-toh'-re-o], *m.* Sternutatory, medicine that provokes sneezing.

estotro, tra [es-to'-tro, trah]. A compound pronoun of *esto* and *otro,* this other.

estovar [es-to-var'], *va.* V. REHOGAR.

estrabismo [es-trah-bees'-mo], *m.* Squint, strabismus.

estracilla [es-trah-theel'-lyah], *f.* Kind of fine brown paper; fine blotting paper.

estrada [es-trah'-dah], *f.* Causeway, paved road; turnpike road (carretera). **Estrada encubierta,** *(Mil.)* covert-way.

estradiota [es-trah-de-o'-tah], *f.* 1. Ancient mode of riding with long stirrups and stiff legs. 2. Kind of lance.

estradiote, ta [es-trah-de-oh'-tay, tah], *a.* Relating to riding with long stirrups. **Estradiote,** soldier mounted with long stirrups.

estrado [es-trah'-do], *m.* 1. Drawing-room where company is received, guest chamber. 2. Carpets and other embellishments of a drawing-room. **Entrados,** halls where courts of justice hold their sittings. 3. Baker's table for holding the loaves to be put into the oven. 4. A platform on which the royal throne is placed.

estrafalariamente [es-trah-fah-lah-re-ah-men'-tay], *adv.* *(coll.)* Carelessly, slovenly, extravagantly, wildly.

estrafalario, ria [es-trah-fah-lah'-re-o, ah], *a.* 1. Slovenly, uncleanly dressed; indecently neglectful of dress; estravagant, wild (ropa). 2. Odd, queer, eccentric (excéntrico).

estragadamente [es-trah-gah-dah-men'-tay], *adv.* Depravedly.

estragador, ra [es-trah-gah-dor', rah], *m. & f.* Corrupter, destroyer.

estragamiento [es-trah-gah-meen'-to], *m.* 1. Ravage, waste, ruin. 2. *(Met.)* Disorder, corruption of morals.

estragar [es-trah-gar'], *va.* 1. To deprave, to vitiate, to corrupt, to spoil (gusto), to make less pure, to disfigure. 2. *(Obs.)* To destroy, to ruin, to waste, to harass.

estrago [es-trah'-go], *m.* 1. Ravage, waste, ruin, havoc. **Los estragos del tiempo,** the ravages of time. 2. Wickedness, corruption of morals, depravity.

estragón [es-trah-gone'], *m. (Bot.)* Tarragon wormwood.

estrambosidad [es-tram-bo-se-dahd'], *f.* Distortion of the eyes.

estrambote [es-tram-bo'-tay], *m.* Burden of a song.

estrambótico, ca [es-tram-bo'-te-co, cah], *a.* 1. Strange, extravagant, irregular. 2. Eccentric, eccentrical.

estramonio [es-trah-mo'-ne-o], *m. (Bot.)* Common thornapple; used as a remedy for asthmatic attacks.

estrangol [es-tran-gole'], *m. (Vet.)* Inflammation in a horse's tongue.

estrangul [es-tran-gool'], *m.* A reed for an oboe or any other winding strument, of cane or of metal.

estrangulación [es-tran-goo-lah-the-on'], *f.* 1. Strangling, as act and effect. 2. Strangulation, constriction of the neck by a circular ligature. 3. Stoppage of a hydraulic apparatus.

estrangulado, da [es-tran-goo-lah'-do, dah], *a. (Med.)* Strangulated.

estrangulador [es-tran-goo-lah-dor'], *m.* 1. Strangler (persona). 2. *(Mech.)* Throttle.

estrangulamiento [es-tran-goo-lah-me-ayn'-to], *m. (Aut.)* Narrow stretch of road, bottleneck.

estrangular [es-tran-goo-lar'], *va.* 1. To strangle (persona), to kill by compressing the trachea. 2. *(Med.)* To strangulate. 3. *(Mech.)* To throttle; to choke.

estraperlo [es-trah-payr-lo], *m.* Black market.

estrapontina [es-trah-pon-tee'-nah], *f.* Kind of hammock.

estratagema [es-trah-tah-hay'-mah], *f.* 1. Stratagem in war. 2. Trick, artful deception; craftiness; finesse; fetch.

estrategia [es-trah-tay'-he-ah], *f. (Mill.)* Strategy, military science.

estratégico, ca [es-trah-tay'-he-co, cah], *a. (Mil.)* Strategic, strategical, belonging to strategy.

estratificación [es-trah-te-fe-cah-the-on'], *f. (Min.)* Stratification, arrangement of layers.

estratificar [es-trah-te-fe-car'], *va. (Min.)* To stratify, to dispose in strata.

estratiforme [es-trah-te-for'-may], *a.* Stratiform, disposed in strata.

estrato [es-trah-to], *m. (Geol.)* Stratum, layer, bed.

estratosfera [es-trah-tos-fay'-rah], *f.* Stratosphere.

estrave [es-trah'-vey], *m. (Naut.)* End of a ship's keel.

estraza [es-trah-thah], *f.* Rag, fragment of cloth. **Papel de estraza,** brown paper.

estrazar [es-trah-thar'], *va. (Obs.)* To tear or break into pieces.

estrechamente [es-tray-chah-men'-tay], *adv.* 1. Narrowly, tightly (apretadamente), closely, fast, compactly, close, nearly. 2. *(Met.)* Exactly, punctually. 3. *(Met.)* Strongly, forcibly. 4. *(Met.)* Strictly (severamente), rigorously. 5. *(Met.)* Scantily, penuriously.

estrechamiento [es-tray-chah-me-en'-to], *m.* Act of tightening, tightness, narrowing.

estrechar [es-tray-char'], *va.* 1. To tighten, to make narrow (hacer estrecho). 2. To contract, to constringe, to constrict, to curtail, to compress. 3. *(Met.)* To confine, to pin up. 4. *(Met.)* To constrain, to compel (presionar). 5. *(Met.)* To restrain, to obstruct. -*vr.* 1. To bind oneself strictly. 2. *(Met.)* To reduce one's expenses (gastos). **Estrecharse en los gastos,** to stint oneself, to economize. 3. *(Met.)* To act in concert with another. 4. *(Met.)* To relate or communicate in confidence (amistad). 5. *(Met.)* To be dejected. 6. To be intimate with. **Se estrecharon la mano,** they shook hands.

estrechez [es-tray-cheth'], *f.* 1. Straitness, narrowness, compactness, closeness. 2. *(Met.)* Intimate union. 3. *(Met.)* Intimacy, friendship (amistad). 4. *(Met.)* Arduous or dangerous undertaking. 5. *(Met.)* Austerity (austeridad), abstraction from worldly objects. 6. *(Met.)* Property. 6. Financial stringency. **Estrechez del dinero,** tightness of money. **Estrecheces,** financial difficulties. **Vivir con estrechez,** to live in straitened circumstances.

estrecho [es-tray'-cho], *m.* 1. Strait or frith, a narrow arm of the sea. 2. Pass, a narrow passage between two mountains. 3. *(Met.)* Peril, danger, risk.

estrecho, cha [es-tray'-cho, chah], *a.* 1. Narrow, close, dense. 2. Straight, tight. **Estos zapatos me están muy estrechos,** these shoes are too small for me. 3. *(Met.)* Intimate, familiar (relación). 4. *(Met.)* Rigid (actitud), austere (carácter). 5. *(Met.)* Exact, punctual. 6. *(Met.)* Narrow-minded, illiberal. **Es muy estrecha,** she's very strait-laced. 7. *(Met.)* Poor, indigent, penurious, needy, necessitous. -*m.* Narrows, channel. **Estrecho de Gibraltar.** Straits of Gibraltar.

estrechura [es-tray-choh'-rah], *f.* 1. Narrowness, straitness; narrowing. 2. *(Met.)* Austerity, abstraction from the world. 3. *(Met.)* Distress, danger. 4. Intimate familiarity.

estregadera [es-tray-gah-day-rah], *f.* A kind of brush used for rubbing off dirt (fregasuelos, bruza).

estregadero [es-tray-gah-day'-ro], *m.* 1. Place where beasts rub themselves against a tree, stone, etc. 2. Place for washing clothes.

estregadura [es-tray-gah-doo'-rah], *f.* Friction, act of rubbing.

estregamiento [es-tray-gah-me-en'-to], *m.* Friction.

estregar [es-tray-gar'], *m.* 1. To rub one thing against another, to scour (con cepillo), to fray, to grind. 2. To scratch.

estrella [es-trayl'-lyah], *f.* 1. A star. **La estrella de Belén,** star of Bethlehem. **Estrella del norte,** north star. **Estrella polar,** polar star. 2. *(Met.)* A white mark on a horse's face. 3. Asterisk, a mark in printing. 4. *(Met.)* Fate, lot, destiny. **Tener estrella,** to be fortunate. 5. *(Mil.)* Star-fort, a work with five or more faces, having salient and re-entering angles. **Tomar la estrella,** *(Naut.)* to take the altitude of a star. **Estrellas errantes** or **erráticas,** planets, satellites. **Con estrellas,** after night or before sunrise.

estrellada [es-trehl-lyah'-dah], *f. (Bot.)* Ladies' mantle. *V.* ALQUIMILA.

estrelladera [es-trel-lyah-day'-rah], *f.* Kind of ladle for frying eggs.

estrelladero [es-trel-lyah-day'-ro], *m.* Kind of frying-pan for dressing eggs without breaking the yolks.

estrellado, da [es-trel-lyah'-do, dah], *a.* Starry (con estrellas). **Huevos, estrellados,** eggs fried in oil or butter; fried eggs. -*pp.* of ESTRELLAR.

estrellamar [es-trel-lyah-mar'], *f.* 1. *(Bot.)* Buckthorn plantain. 2. Starfish.

estrellar [es-trel-lyar'], *a.* Stellated, starry.

estrellar [es-trel-lyar'], *va.* 1. To smash, to dash to bits (romper). **Lo estrelló contra la pared,** he smashed it against the wall. **Estrelló el balón en el poste,** he crashed the ball into the goal-post. 2. To fry (huevos). -*vr.* 1. *(Aer. and Naut.)* To crash. 2. To smash, shatter. 3. *(Fig.)* To be ruined, to fail utterly. 4. To fill with stars. **Estrellarse con,** to conflict violently with.

estrellato [es-trel-lay-to], *m.* Stardom.

estrellera [es-trel-lyay'-rah], *f. (Naut.)* Plain rigging without runners.

estrellón [es-trel-lyone'], *m.* 1. *(Aug.)* Large star (estrella). 2. Star ball used in artificial fireworks (fuegos artificiales).

estremecedor, ra [es-tray-may-thay-dor', rah], *a.* Frightful, terrifying.

estremecer [es-tray-may-therr'], *va.* 1. To shake (sacudir), to make tremble. 2. *(Naut.)* To work or labor hard (barco). -*vr.* To shake (edificio), to tremble (persona: miedo), to shudder (horror), to be uncommonly agitated. (*Yo me estremezco, yo me estremezca,* from *Estremecer. V.* CONOCER.)

estremecimiento [es-tray-may-the-me-en'-to], *m.* Trembling, quaking, shaking.

estremiche [es-tray-mee'-chay], *m. (Naut.)* A piece of timber which is notched into the knee of a ship.

estrena [es-tray'-nah], *f.* 1. A new year's gift. 2. *(Arch.)* Handsel, the first act of using anything; the first act of sale. 3. Treat on wearing a new suit of clothes.

estrenar [es-tray-nar'], *va.* 1. To handsel, to use or to do something the first time (ropa) 2. To commence, to begin. -*vr.* To begin to put something in execution. **No se estrena,** he hasn't done a hand's turn.

estreno [es-tray'-no], *m.* Debut (persona), premier, first presentation; new play (comedia), new film, new release (película). **Cine de estreno,** first-run cinema. **Su estreno como vendedor fue un éxito,** his debut as a salesman was quite a success.

estrenque [es-tren'-kay], *m. (Naut.)* Rope made of bass or sedge.

estrenuidad [es-tray-noo-e-dahd'], *f.* Strength, valor, strenuousness. *(Acad.)*

estrenuo, nua [es-tray'-noo-o, ah], *a.* Strong, agile, valorous, strenuous. *(Acad.)*

estreñido, da [es-tray-nyee'-do, dah], *a.* 1. Close bound, costive, hard bound. 2. Miserable, niggardly. *-pp.* of ESTREÑIR.

estreñimiento [es-tray-nye-me-en'-to], *m.* Obstruction: the act of binding or restraining; confine, confinement.

estreñir [es-trey-nyeer'], *va.* To bind, to tie close, to restrain. *-vn.* To restrain oneself. **Estreñirse el vientre,** to constipate, to be costive. (*Yo estriño, yo estriña,* from *Estreñir. V.* PEDIR.)

estrepa, estrepilla [es-tray'-pah, es-tray-peel'-lyah], *f. (Bot.)* V. ESTEPILLA.

estrepitarse [es-tray-pe-tar'-say], *vr. (Coll. Cuba.)* To be noisily merry, to carouse wildly.

estrépito [es-tray'-pe-to], *m.* Noise, clamor, bustle, noisiness, racket, din (ruido fuerte); clatter, clash (ruido brusco).

estrepitosamente [es-tre-pe-to'-sah-men-tay], *adv.* Noisily, with a din.

estrepitoso, sa [es-tray-pe-toh'-so, sah], *a.* Noisy, boisterous, loud, clamorous, deafening; rowdy (persona).

estreptococo [es-trep-to-co'-co], *m.* Streptococcus.

estreptomicina [es-trep-to-me-thee'-nah], *f. (Med.)* Streptomycin.

estrés [es-tress'], *m. (Med.)* Stress.

estresante [es-tray-sahn'-tay], *a.* Stressful.

estría [es-tree'-ah], *f. (Arch.)* Fluting, channel cut along half the length of shafts or pilasters. Stria.

estriadura [es-tre-ah-doo'-rah], *f. (Arch.)* Fluting.

estriar [es-tre-ar'], *va. (Arch.)* To flute, to cut columns into channels and grooves, to gutter. *-vr.* To be grooved, striated.

estribadero [es-tre-bah-day'-ro], *m.* Prop, stay.

estribar [es-tre-bar'], *vn.* 1. To prop, to support with props. 2. *(Met.)* To found, to build upon; to be supported. **La dificultad estriba en el texto,** the difficulty lies in the text.

estribera [es-tre-bay'-rah], *f.* 1. Buttress, arch, pillar. 2. Joiner's bench.

estribería [es-tre-bay-ree'-ah], *f.* Place where stirrups are kept.

estriberón [es-tre-bay-rone'], *m.* Prominences made on earth or wood by cross-bars, to serve as steps.

estribillo [es-tre-beel'-lyo], *m.* 1. Introduction or beginning of a song, chorus, refrain. 2. Tautology, a needless and superfluous repetition of the same words.

estribo [es-tree'-bo], *m.* 1. Buttress, abutment arch, pillar. 2. Stirrup (jinete). 3. Step on the side of a coach (apoyapié). 4. Staple fixed at the end of a cross-bow. 5. Bone of the ear resembling a stirrup; the stapes. 6. V. ESTRIBILLO. 7. *(Gunn.)* Clasp on the felloes of gun-carriage wheels. **Estribos,** *(Naut.)* stirrups of a ship, pieces of timber fastened to the keel with iron plates. **Perder los estribos,** *(Fig.)* to fly off the handle.

estribor [es-tre-bor'], *m. (Naut.)* Starboard.

estribordarios [es-tre-bor-dah'-re-os], *m. pl.* People on the starboard hand.

estricnina [es-tric-nee'-nah], *f. (Med.)* Strychnine, an alkaloid obtained from nux vomica; an important medicine and a violent poison.

estricote (Al) [es-tre-co'-tay], *adv.* Without rule or order. **Tener a uno al estricote,** to amuse one with vain promises.

estrictamente [es-treec'-tah-men-tay], *adv.* Strictly.

estricto, ta [es-treec'-to, tah], *a.* 1. Strict, exact, accurate, rigorously nice. 2. Strict, severe, rigorous, extreme.

estridente [es-tre-den'-tay], *a. (Poet.)* That which causes noise or creaking; strident.

estridor [es-tre-dor'], *m.* Noise, creak, screech, stridor.

estrige [es-tree'-hay], *f.* Night-bird, said to be an unlucky omen; screechowl, vampire.

estrigila [es-tre-hee'lah], *f.* Strigil, a scraper of bronze which Roman gladiators used to clean off the oil and dust of combat, and which passed for a specific for certain diseases.

estringa [es-treen'-gah], *f. V.* AGUJETA.

estripar [es-tre-par'], *va. (Prov.) V.* DESTRIPAR.

estriptís *m.* **estriptise** *m.* [es-trip-tees'], Striptease.

estrobilífero, ra [es-tro-be-lee'-fay-ro, rah], *a.* Cone-bearing, strobiliferous.

estróbilo [es-tro'-be-lo], *m.* Strobile, cone of the pine family.

estroboscopio [es-tro-bos-co'-pe-o], *m.* Stroboscope.

estrofa [es-tro'-fah], *f. (Poet.)* Strophe.

estrógeno [es-tro'-hay-no], *m. (Biol.)* Estrogen.

estronciana [es-tron-the-ah'-nah], *f.* Strontia, an alkaline earth.

estroncio [es-tron'-the-o], *m.* Strontium, a metallic element.

estropajear [es-tro-pah-hay-ar'], *va.* To clean a wall with a dry brush or rubber.

estropajo [es-tro-pah'-ho], *m.* 1. Dishcloth (trapo). 2. Brush, made of bass or sedge, to clean culinary vessels. **Estropajo de acero,** steel wool. 3. *(Met.)* A worthless, trifling thing (objeto inútil).

estropajosamente [es-tro-pah-ho'-sah-men-tay], *adv.* Stammeringly.

estropajoso, sa [es-tro-pah-ho'-so, sah], *a.* 1. Ragged, despicable, low, mean (vil). 2. *(Met.)* Troublesome, useless. 3. *(Met.)* Stuttering, stammering (habla).

estropalina [es-tro-pah-lee'-nah], *f.* Refuse of wool.

estropeado, da [es-tro-pay-ah'-do, dah], *a. & pp.* of ESTROPEAR. Lame. **Está muy estropeada,** she looks older than she is.

estropeamiento [es-tro-pay-ah-me-en'-to], *m.* Act of maining, wounding, or laming.

estropear [es-tro-pay-ar'], *va.* 1. To damage (objeto), to ruin, to cripple (persona), to mutilate, to mangle (texto etc.), to cut. 2. To mix lime and sand. *-vr.* To get damaged; to spoil, to go bad; to deteriorate, to fail (plan).

estropecillo [es-tro-pay-theel'-lyo], *m. dim.* A slight stumble or impediment.

estropeo [es-tro-pay'-o], *m. (Prov.)* Maim, hurt, injury.

estropicio [es-tro-pee'-the-o], *m. (Acad. Coll.)* 1. Clatter, crash (rotura estrepitosa), destruction, with noise, of table service, etc. 2. Damage (destrozo), rumpus (jaleo).

estrovo [es-tro'-vo], *m. (Naut.)* Strap, a piece of rope used for strapping blocks.

estructura [es-trooc-too'-rah], *f.* 1. Structure, constructure, manner of building or constructing an edifice. 2. Order, method, arrangement (orden).

estructurar [es-trook-too-rar'], *va.* 1. To distribute, to organize the parts (projecto). 2. To construct.

estruendo [es-troo-en'-do], *m.* 1. Clamor, noise (ruido), outcry, clatter. 2. Confusion, bustle, uproar (alboroto) 3. Pomp, ostentation (fig.: pompa), show.

estruendoso, sa [es-troo-en-do'-so, sah], *a.* 1. Noisy, clamorous. 2. Pompous, full of ostentation.

estrujadura [es-troo-hah-doo'-rah], *f.* Pressing, squeezing, pressure, compressing.

estrujamiento [es-troo-hah-me-en'-to], *m. V.* ESTRUJADURA.

estrujar [es-troo-har'], *va.* To press, to squeeze the juice (exprimir). **Estrujar el dinero,** to be avaricious or extremely covetous.

estrujón [es-troo-hone'], *m.* 1. The last pressing of grapes, which gives a miserable wine. 2. Pressing, squeezeing, expression.

estrupador [es-troo-pa-dor'], *m. V.* ESTUPRADOR.

estrupar [es-troo-par'], *va. V.* ESTUPRAR.

estuante [es-too-ahn'-tay], *a.* Very hot, boiling, scorching.

estuario [es-too-ah'-re-o], *m.* A low ground, overflowed by the sea at high tides; an estuary.

estucador [es-too-cah-dor'], *m.* A stucco-plasterer.

estucar [es-too-car'], *va.* To stucco or plaster something.

estuco [es-too'-co], *m.* Stucco, a kind of fine plaster.

estuche [es-too'-chay], *m.* 1. Case for scissors or other instruments (caja). **Estuche de aseo,** toilet case. **Estuche**

de joyas, jewel box. 2. The ace of spades, the deuce of spades or clubs, and ace of clubs in certain games of cards. 3. Small comb. 4. *(Met.)* One who knows a little of everything, or is capable of anything. **Ser estuche** or **es un estuche de habilidades,** *(Met. Coll.)* he is a very clever fellow.

estudiador [es-too-de-ah-dor'], *m. (coll.)* Student.

estudiantazo [es-too-de-an-tah'-tho], *m.* He who is reputed a great scholar.

estudiante [es-too-de-ahn'-tay], *m.* 1. Scholars; one who learns of a master (universidades); a student. **Estudiante de medicina,** medical student. 2. A kind of prompter to players.

estudiantil [es-too-de-an-teel'], *a. (coll.)* Scholastic, belonging to scholar.

estudiantillo [es-too-de-an-teel'lyo], *m. dim.* A little scholar.

estudiantino, na [es-too-de-an-tee'-no, nah], *a.* Belonging to a scholar or student. **A la estudiantina,** in the manner of students.

estudiantón [es-too-de-an-tone'], *m. aug.* A big student.

estudiar [es-too-de-ar'], *va.* 1. To study, to acquire knowledge. 2. To muse, to ponder, to contemplate, to commit, to memory. 3. To make a drawing after a model or nature. 4. To attend the clases in a university. **Estudiar para abogado,** to study to become a lawyer. **Tengo que ir a estudiar,** I must go and work.

estudio [es-too'-de-o], *m.* 1. Study, application to books and learning. 2. Study (dibujo, arte). 3. Study, apartment (cuarto). 4. Hall where models, prints, and plans are kept to be copied or studied. 5. *(Met.)* Study, attention, meditation, contemplation. **Hacer estudio de alguna cosa,** *(Met.)* to act with art, cunning, or crafty reflection. **Estudio general,** university. **Un estudio del mercado,** a market survey or reasearch. *-pl.* 1. Time, trouble, and core applied to the study of the sciences. 2. Sciences, letters. **Dar estudios a uno,** to maintain one at his studies. **Hizo sus estudios en París,** he studied in Paris. **Estudios de tiempo y movimiento,** time and motion study. 6. Studio (arte, cine). **Estudio de cine,** film studio. **Estudio de televisión,** television studio.

estudiosamente [es-too-de-o-sah-men'-tay], *adv.* Studiously, with care and reflection.

estudioso, sa [es-too-de-oh'-so, sah], *a.* 1. Studious, given to study and reflection. .2. *(Met.)* Studious, careful solicitous, contemplative.

estufa [es-too'-fah], *f.* 1. A stove, heater (calentador). **Estufa de gas,** gas heater. **Estufa eléctrica,** electric heater. 2. A warm, close room, a hothouse. 3. A drying-chamber, hot closet, dry bath. 4. A small brazier used to warm the feet.

estufador [es-too-fah-dor'], *m.* Vessel in which meat is stewed.

estufar [es-too-far'], *va. (Obs.)* 1. To warm something. 2. *V.* ESTOFAR.

estufero [es-too-fay'-ro], or **estufista,** *m.* He who makes stoves.

estufilla [es-too-feel'-lyah], *f.* 1. Muff a cover made of fur to keep the hands warm. 2. A small brasier, used to warm the feet on (brasero).

estultamente [es-tool-tah-men'-tay], *adv. (coll.)* Foolishly, sillily.

estulticia [es-tool-tee'-the-ah], *f. (coll.)* Folly, silliness.

estulto, ta [es-tool'-to, tah], *a. (coll.)* Foolish, silly.

estuosidad [es-too-o-se-dahd'], *f.* Burning, excessive hotness.

estuoso, sa [es-too-oh'-so, sah], *a.* Very hot, ardent, burnt by the heat of the sun.

estupefacción [es-too-pay-fac-the-on'], *f.* Stupefaction, numbness.

estupefacientes [es-too-pay-fah-the-en'-tess], *m. pl.* Narcotics, narcotic drugs.

estupefactivo, va [es-too-pay-fac-tee'-vo, vah], *a.* Stupefying.

estupefacto [es-too-pay-fahc'-to], *a. (coll.)* Motionless, petrified, immovable with astonishment.

estupendamente [es-too-pen-dah-men'-tay], *adv.* Wonderfully, stupendously.

estupendo, da [es-too-pen'-do, dah], *a.* Stupendous, wonderful, marvellous. **Esas chicas son estupendas,** those girls are terrific. **Tiene un coche estupendo,** he's got a marvelous car.

estúpidamente [es-too'-pe-dah-men-tay], *adv.* Stupidly, dully, lumpishly.

estupidez [es-too-pe-deth'], *f.* Stupidity (cualidad), insensibility, dullness, sluggishness, stupidness.

estúpido, da [es-too'-pee-do, dah], *a.* Stupid, insensible, dull, crackbrained, gross, heavy, mopish.

estupor [es-too-por'], *m.* 1. Stupor, suspension of sensibility. 2. Amazement, admiration, astonishment.

estuprador [es-too-prah-dor'], *m.* Ravisher, deflowerer, violator.

estuprar [es-too-prar'], *va.* To ravish, to violate, to deflower.

estupro [es-too'-pro], *m.* Ravishment, rape, constupration.

estuque [es-too'-kay], *m. V.* ESTUCO. **Estuquista** [es-too-kees'-tah], *m.* Plasterer, stucco-worker.

esturar [es-too-rar'], *va.* 1. To dry by the force of fire. 2. To overdo meat by the force of fire.

esturión [es-too-re-on'], *m. (Zool.)* Sturgeon.

ésula [ay'-soo-lah], *f. (Bot.)* Leafy-branched spurge.

esviaje [es-ve-ah'-hay], *m. (Arch.)* 1. The inclination of a vertical with respect to a line which crosses it. 2. Oblique direction of the sides of an arch or vault.

etanún [ay-tah-noon'], *m.* The seventh month of the Hebrew ecclesiastical year.

etapa [ay-tah'-pah], *f.* 1. *(Mil.)* The ration of necessaries to troops in the field or traveling (de viaje). **A cortas etapas,** in easy stages. 2. Stage (cohete). 3. *(Fig.)* Stage, phase. **En la segunda etapa del plan,** in the second phase of the plan. **Lo haremos por etapas,** we'll do it in stages.

etcétera [et-thay'-tay-rah], *f.* Etcetera, the rest, and so on. Commonly abbreviated to *etc.*

éter [ay'-ter], *m.* 1. *(Chem.)* Ether, ethyl ether. 2. Ether or aether, a supposed medium, filling all space, through which the vibrations of light, heat, and electricity are propagated. 3. Ether, the upper air, the sky.

etéreo, rea [ay-tay'-ray-o, ah], *a.* 1. Ethereal, etherous, formed of ether. 2. *(Poet.)* Ethereal, ethereous, heavenly.

eterióscopo [ay-tay-re-os-co-po], *m.* An instrument for measuring the force of solar radiation.

eterización [ay-tay-re-thah-the-on'], *f.* Etherization, the administration of ether for anaesthesia.

eterizar [ay-tay-re-thar'], *va.* 1. To etherize, to cause anaesthesia by inhalation of ether. 2. To convert into ether (eterificar).

eternal [ay-ter-nahl'], *a.* Eternal.

eternamente [ay-ter'-nah-men-tay], *adv.* 1. Eternally, forever, everlastingly, evermore. 2. *(Met.)* For a long time. 3. Never.

eternidad [ay-ter-ne-dahd'], *f.* 1. Eternity. 2. Duration or length of continuance, which comprehends many ages.

eternizar [ay-ter-ne-thar'], *va.* 1. To eternize, to perpetuate. 2. To prolong for a great length of time.

eterno, na [ay-tayr'-no, nah], *a.* 1. Eternal, endless, never-ending, everlasting. 2. Durable, lasting.

eteromancia [ay-tay-ro-mahn'-the-ah], *f.* Divination by the flight or song of birds.

ética [ay'-te-cah], *f.* Ethics, morals, morality, or the doctrine of morality.

ético, ca [ay'-te-co, cah], *a.* Ethical, moral, treating on morality.

etileno [ay-te-lay'-no], *m. (Chem.)* Ethylene.

etilo [ar-tee'-lo], *m. (Chem.)* Ethyl.

etimología [ay-te-mo-lo-hee'-ah], *f.* Etymology.

etimológicamente [ay-te-mo-lo'-he-cah-men-tay], *adv.* Etymologically.

etimológico, ca [ay-te-mo-lo'-he-co, cah], *a.* Etymological.

etimologista [ay-te-mo-lo-hees'-tah], *m.* Etymologist, etymologer.

etíope, etiópico, ca, etiopio, a [ay-tee'-pay, ay-te-o'-pe-co, cah], *a.* Ethiopian.

etiópide [ay-te-oh'-pe-day], *f. (Bot.)* Clary, Ethiopian mullein.

etiqueta [ay-te-kay'-tah], *f.* 1. Etiquette, ceremony, formality (formalistmo). **De etiqueta,** formal, full-dress. **Baile de etiqueta,** dress ball. 2. Compliments in conversation. 3. *(Com.)* Label showing price and class of merchandise (rótulo); in this sense it is Gallicism. 4. *(Inform.)* Label. **Etiqueta opaca,** opaque sticker.

etiquetado [ay-te-kay-tah'-do], *m.* Labelling.

etiquetar [ay-te-kay-tar'], *va.* To label.

etiquetero, ra [ay-te-kay-tay'-ro, rah], *a.* Ceremonious, civil and formal to a fault: it is used frequently as a substantive to express an observer of etiquette, or a very ceremonious person.

etites [ay-tee'-les], *f.* Eaglestone, hydroxide of iron.

etmoides [ayt-mo'-e-days], *m. (Anat.)* The ethmoid bone.

etnia [ayt'-nee-ah], *f.* Ethnic group; race.

étnico, ca [ayt'-ne-co, cah], *a.* Ethnic. *V.* GENTIL.

etnografía [et-no-grah-fee'-ah], *f.* Ethnography, the study of races of men.

etnográfico, ca [et-no-grah'-fe-co, cah], *a.* Ethnographic, relating to ethnography.

etnógrafo [et-no'-grah-fo], *m.* Ethnographer.

etnología [et-no-lo-hee'-ah], *f.* Ethnology, the science of the natural races or families of men. **Etnólogo,** *m.* Ethnologist.

etografía [et-to-grah-fee'-ah], *f.* Ethology, the science of the formation of human character.

etólico, ca, or **etolio, lia** [ay-toh'-le-co, cah], *a.* Etolian.

etrusco, ca [ay-troos'-co, cah], *a.* Etruscan

eubolia [ay-oo-bo'-leah], *f.* The act of expressing one's thoughts with propriety.

eucalipto [ay-oo-cah-leep'-to], *m.* Eucalyptus, the Australian gum tree.

Eucaristía [ay-oo-cah-ris-tee'-ah], *f.* The Eucharist.

eucarístico, ca [ay-oo-cah-rees'-te-co, cah], *a.* 1. Eucharistical. eucharistic. 2. Eucharistical, belonging to works in prose or verse containing acts of thanksgiving.

euclorina [ay-oo-clo-ree'-nah], *f.* Euchloring, chlorous oxide gas, an explosive mixture of chlorine dioxide and chlorine.

eucologio, eucólogo [ay-oo-co-lo'-he-o, ay-oo-co'-lo-go], *m.* Euchology, book containing the service for all the Sundays, and festivals in the year; eucholgion.

eucrasia [ay-oo-crah'-se-ah], *f. (Med.)* Eucrasy, sound health.

eucrático, ca [ay-oo-crah'-te-co, cah], *a.* Euchratical.

eudiometría [ay-oo-de-o-may-tree'-ah], *f.* Eudiometry.

eudiómetro [ay-oo-de-o'-may-tro], *m. (Chem.)* Eudiometer.

eufemismo [ay-oo-fay-mees'-mo], *m.* Euphemism, a suave style in words and expressions; the toning down of what would otherwise sound harsh or offensive.

eufonía [ay-oo-fo-nee'-ah], *f.* Euphony.

eufónico, ca [ay-oo-fo'-nee-co, cah], *a.* Euphonic, euphonious.

eufono [ay-oo-fo'-no], *m.* Euphonium, a musical instrument composed of 42 glass cylinders.

euforbio [ay-oo-for'-beo], *m. (Bot.)* Officinal spurge.

euforia [ay-oo-fo'-re-ah], *f.* Euphoria; exuberance, elation.

eufórico [ay-oo-fo'-re-co], *a.* Euphoric; exuberant.

eufrasia [ay-oo-frah'-se-ah], *f. (Bot.)* Eyebright. **Euphrasia oficinal,** common eyebright.

eugenesia [ay-oo-hay-nay'-se-ah], *f.* Eugenics.

eumenes [ay-oo-may'-nes], *m.* Eumenes, a genus of solitary wasps.

eunuco [ay-oo-noo'-co], *m.* Eunuch.

eupatorio [ay-oo-pah-to'-re-o], *m. (Bot.)* Eupatorium. **Eupatorio cañameño,** hempagrimony eupatorium.

euritmia [ay-oo-reet-'me-ah], *f.* 1. *(Arch.)* Eurythmy, proportion and harmony in an edifice. 2. Happy selection of musical rhythm and movement. 3. Skill in the handling of surgical instruments. 4. Regularity in arterial pulsations, normal pulse.

euro [ay'-oo-ro], *m.* 1. Eurus, the cast wind. **Euro austro** or **Euro noto,** southeast wind. 2. European currency.

eurodiputado, da [ay-oo-ro-de-poo-tah'-do], *m. & f.* Euro MP, member of the European Parliament.

Europa [ay-oo-ro'-pah], *f.* Europe.

europeo, a [ay-oo-ro-pay'-o, ah], *a.* European.

éuscaro, ra [ay'-oos-cah-ro, rah], *a.* Pertaining to the Basques or their language. *-n.* A Basque, a native of Biscay.

eutanasia [ay-oo-tah-nah'-se-ah], *f.* 1. Euthanasia, a painless, peaceful death. 2. A means for producing a gentle, easy death. 3. Death in a state of grace.

eutaxia [ay-oo-tahc'-se-ah], *f. (Med.)* A perfectly organized constitution.

eutiquiano, na [ay-oo-te-ke-ah'-no, nah], *a.* Eutychian, belonging to the sect of Eutyches.

eutrapelia, eutropelia [ay-oo-trah-pay'-leah, ay-oo-tro-pay'- le-ah], *f.* 1. Moderation in jests, jokes, and pleasures. 2. Pastime, sport.

eutrapélico, ca, eutropélico, ca [ay-oo-trah-pay'-le-co, cah], *a.* Moderate, temperate.

evacuación [ay-vah-coo-ah-the-on'], *f.* Evacuation.

evacuante [ay-vah-coo-ahn'-tay], *pa. & a.* Evacuant, evacuating: it is used sometimes as a substantive.

evacuar [ay-vah-coo-ar'], *va.* 1. To evacuate, to empty. 2. To quit, to leave. **Evacuar un negocio,** to finish or complete a business.

evacuativo, va [ay-vah-coo-ah-tee'-vo, vah], *a.* Evacuative, that which has the power of evacuating.

evacuatorio, ria [ay-vah-coo-ah-to'-re-o, ah], *a.* 1. That which evacuates. 2. Public lavatory.

evadir [ay-vah-deer'], *va.* 1. To evade, to escape, to flee from danger. 2. To evade (dinero), to elude by sophistry, to avoid, to decline by subterfuge. *-vr.* 1. To evade, to escape, to slip away, to make one's escape. 2. To evade, to practise sophistry or evasions.

evagación [ay-vah-gah-the-on'], *f.* Evagation, the act of wandering; excursion.

evaluación [ay-vah-loo-ah-the-on'], *f.* 1. *(Gen.)* Evaluation. 2. *(Escol.)* Report, assessment.

evaluar [ay-vah-loo-arl'], *va.* To evaluate.

evalúo [ay-vah-loo'-o], *m.(Com.)* Valuation, appraisement.

evangélicamente [ay-vah-he'-le-cah-men-tay], *adv.* Evangelically.

evangélico, ca [ay-van-hay'-le-co, cah], *a.* Evangelical.

evangelio [ay-van-hay'-le-o], *m.* 1. Gospel. 2. Small book, containing the first chapters of St. John and the other evangelists, placed between relics, and formerly worn by children around their necks.

evangelismo [ay-van-hay-lees'-mo], *m.* 1. Evangelism, the religious and humanitarian system of the Gospel. 2. Spirit of reform among Protestant sects who call themselves evangelical.

evangelista [ay-van-hay-lees'-tah], *m.* 1. Evangelist. 2. Gospeller, one who chants the gospels in churches.

evangelistero [ay-van-hay-lis-tay'-ro], *m.* 1. Gospeller, a priest or deacon who chants the books of the evangelists at solemn masses. 2. Gospel bookstand, on which the gospel book is laid to sing the gospel at high mass.

evangelizar [ay-van-hay-le-thar'], *va.* To evangelize, to preach the gospel.

evaporable [ay-vah-po-rah'-blay], *a.* Evaporable, that may be evaporated.

evaporación [ay-vah-po-rah-the-on'], *f.* 1. Evaporation, exhalation of vapor. 2. Act of damping cloth, or placing it over steam, to render the wool softer.

evaporado, da [ay-vah-po-rah'-do, dah], *a.* Evaporated. **Leche evaporada,** evaporated milk.

evaporar [ay-vah-po-rar'], *vn.* To evaporate, to fly off in vapors or fumes. *-va.* To evaporate, to drive away in fumes, to disperse in vapors: to flat, to flatten, to pall, to make vapid. *-vr.* 1. To vanish, to pass away. 2. To pall, to grow vapid.

evaporatorio [ay-vah-po-rah-toh'-re-o], *a.* Having the power of evaporating.

evaporizar [ay-vah-po-re-thar'], *vn. & va.* To evaporate.

evasión [ay-vah-se-on'], *f.* Evasion, escape, subterfuge. **Evasión de impuestos,** tax evasion.

evasiva [ay-vah-see'-vah], *f.* Subterfuge, evasion: loophole (escapatoria), way out.

evasivamente [ay-vah-se'-vah-men-tay], *adv.* Evasively.

evasivo, va [ay-vah-see'-vo, vah], *a.* Evasive, elusive, sophistical.

evata [ay-vah'-tah], *f.* Kind of black wood resembling ebony.

evección [ay-vec-the-on'], *f. (Ast.)* Evection, the largest inequality in the motion of the moon, as an effect of solar attraction.

evento [ay-vayn'-to], *m.* Event, accident, issue, unforeseen happening (incidente).

eventración [ay-ven-trah-the-on'], *f.* 1. Eventration, ventral hernia, or relaxation of the abdominal walls. 2. Disemboweling.

eventual [ay-ven-too-ahl'], *a.* 1. Eventual, fortuitous (casual); possible (posible). 2. Temporary (obrero, trabajo); stopgap (solución).

eventualidad [ay-ven-too-ah-le-dahd'], *f.* Contingency.

eventualmente [ay-ven-too-al-men'-tay], *adv.* 1. Fortuitously, by chance (accidentalmente). 2. Possibly (posiblemente), depending upon circumstances.

eversión [ay-ver-se-on'], *f.* Eversion, destruction, ruin, desolation.

evicción [ay-vic-the-on'], *f.* Eviction, security, convictiveness.

evidencia [ay-ve-den'-the-ah], *f.* Evidence (pruebas), manifestation, proof, obviousness, conspicuity, nakedness, cogency. **Evidencia por pruebas** or **causas comitantes,** circumstantial evidence.

evidenciar [ay-ve-den-the-ar'], *va.* To evidence, to prove, to render evident.

evidente [ay-ve-den'-tay], *a.* Evident, clear, manifest, open, naked, palpable, obvious, plain, glaring.

evidentemente [ay-ve-den'-tay-men-tay], *adv.* Evidently, plainly, clearly, manifestly, glaringly, notoriously.

evilasa [ay-ve-lah'-sah], *f.* Kind of ebony which grows in the island of Madagascar.

evisceración [ay-vis-thay-rah-the-on'], *f.* Evisceration, removal of the viscera in an autopsy, or embalming.

eviscerar [ay-vis-thay-rar'], *va.* To eviscerate, to remove the viscera.

evitable [ay-ve-tah'-blay], *a.* Avoidable, extricable, evitable.

evitación [ay-ve-tah-the-on'], *f.* Evitation, act of avoiding.

evitado, da [ay-ve-tah'-do, dah], *a. & pp.* of EVITAR. Avoided.

evitar [ay-ve-tar'], *va.* To avoid, to escape (peligro), to forbear, to help: to fly, to shun, to decline, to avoid (peligro). **Para evitar tales dificultades,** in order to avoid such difficulties. *-vr.* **Para evitarse trabajo.** in order to save onself trouble.

eviterno, na [ay-ve-terr'-no, nah], *a. (Theol.)* Imperishable, lasting, without end.

evo [ay'-vo], *m.* 1. *(Poet.)* Age, a long period of time. 2. *(Theol.)* Eternity, endless duration.

evocación [ay-vo-cah-the-on'], *f.* Evocation, pagan invocation.

evocar [ay-vo-car'], *va.* 1. To call out. 2. To invoke, to solicit a favor, to implore assistance.

evolución [ay-vo-loo-the-on'], *f.* 1. Evolution, changing the position of troops or ships. 2. Evolution, gradual development of things and of ideas, slow transformation. 3. *(Met.)* Change of political ideas.

evolucionar [ay-vo-loo-the-o-nar'], *m. (Mil. Naut.)* To perform evolutions or tactical movements.

evoluta [ay-vo-loo'-tah], *f.* 1. *(Math.)* Volute. 2. *(Naut.)* A snail-shell.

evolutivo, va [ay-vo-loo-tee'-vo, vah], *a.* Evolutive.

evulsión [ay-vool-se-on'], *f. (Med.)* Evulsion, plucking out, forcible extraction.

ex [ex], *prep.* Used in Spanish only in composition, where it either amplifies, the signification, as exponer, or serves as a negative, as *exámine. Exprovincial,* Former or late provincial.

ex abrupto [ex ah-broop'-to], *adv.* Abruptly, violently.

exacción [ek-sac-the-on'], *f.* 1. Exaction, the act of levying taxes. 2. Impost, tax, contribution, levy.

exacerbación [ek-sah-ther-bah-the-on'], *f. (Med.)* Exacerbation, paroxysm.

exacerbar [ek-sah-ther-bar'], *va.* To irritate, to exasperate, to exacerbate.

exactamente [ek-sac-tah-men'-tay], *adv.* Exactly, minutely, just, justly, accurately, faithfully, circumstantially, critically, nicely, to a hair.

exactitud [ek-sac-te-tood'], *f.* Exactness, exactitude, punctuality, accuracy, correctness, justness, niceness.

exacto, ta [ek-sahc'-to, tah], *a.* Exact, punctual (puntual), assiduous, nice, heedful, faithful, observant, critical, just, precise (preciso), right (correcto).

exactor [ek-sac-tor'], *m.* Tax-gatherer, exactor.

exactora [ek-sac-to'-rah], *f.* Exactress.

exageración [ek-sah-hay-rah-the-on'], *f.* Exaggeration, hyperbolical amplification.

exageradamente [ek-sah-hay-rah'-dah-men-tay], *adv.* In an exaggerated way; excessively, exorbitantly; over-demonstratively, theatrically.

exagerado [ek-sah-hay-rah'-do], *a.* 1. Exaggerated (pretensión). 2. Highly-colored (relato). 3. Excessive (precio). 4. Theatrical.

exagerador, ra [ek-sah-hay-rah-dor', rah], *m. & f.* Amplifier, one that exaggerates.

exagerante [ek-sah-hay-rahn'-tay], *pa. & m. (Poet.)* Amplifier; exaggerating.

exagerar [ek-sah-hay-rar'], *va.* To exaggerate, to amplify, to heighten by misrepresentation, to magnify, to hyperbolize, to overstate.

exagerativamente [ek-sah-hay-rah-te'-vah-men-tay], *adv.* With exaggeration.

exagerativo, va [ek-sah-hay-rah-tee'-vo, vah], *a.* Exaggerating, exaggeratory.

exágono, na [ek-sah'-go-no, nah], *a.* Hexagonal. *V.* HEXÁGONO.

exaltación [ek-sal-tah-the-on'], *f.* 1. Exaltation (ensalzamiento), elevation. 2. *(Chem.)* Sublimation.

exaltado, da [ek-sal-tah'-do, dah], *a.* 1. *(Neol.)* Exaggerated and violent in political ideas (fanático). 2. Exalted (elevado). 3. Over-excited (humor), worked up; elated; excitable (carácter).

exaltar [ek-sal-tar'], *va.* 1. To exalt, to elevate (elevar); to magnify; to lift, to heave. 2. To praise, to extol (elogiar); to cry up. *-vr.* To get excited (emocionar), to get worked up; to get carried away; to get heated (discusión), to become very intense.

examen [ek-sah'-men], *m.* 1. Examination, disquisition, exploration, consideration. 2. Trial, inquiry (encuesta). 3. Examination. **Examen de conductor**, driving test. **Examen de fin de curso,** final examination. 4. Care and diligence in searching out something.

exámetro [ek-sah'-may-tro], *m.* Hexameter verse.

examinación [ek-sah-me-nah-the-on'], *f.* Examination.

examinado, da [ek-sah-me-nah'-do], *m & f.* examinee, candidate.

examinador, ra [ek-sah-me-nah-dor', rah], *m & f.* Examiner, explorator; examinator.

examinando [ek-sah-me-nahn'-do], *m.* Examinant, he who is to be examined.

examinante [ek-sah-me-nahn'-tay], *pa. & n.* 1. Examining.

examinar [ek-sah-me-nar'], *va.* 1. To examine (poner a prueba), to investigate (inspeccionar). 2. To consider (problema), to explore, to look into (indagar), to look over, to fathom; to feel, to consult. 3. To inquire into books or writings. *-vr.* To take an examination.

esangüe [ek-sahn'-goo-ay], *a.* 1. Bloodless, without blood; pale from the loss of blood, exsanguious. 2. *(Met.)* Weak, without strength.

exángulo, la [ek-sahn'-goo-lo, lah], *a.* Having six angles.

exanimación [ek-sah-ne-ma-the-on'], *f.* Examination.

exánime [ek-sah'-ne-may], *a.* Spiritless, exanimous, weak, without force or vigor.

exantema [ek-san-tay-mah], *f.* Exanthema, an eruptive disease of the skin.

exantemático, ca, or **exantematoso, sa** [ek-san-tay-mah'-co, cah, ek-san-tay-mah-to'-so, sah], *a.* Exanthematous, or exanthematic.

exantropía [ex-san-tro-pee'-ah], *f. (Med.)* The last stage of melancholy.

exápodo, da [ek-sah'-po-do, dah], *a.* Hexapod, six-footed. - *m. pl.* Hexapods, the true insects, with six feet.

exarcado [ek-sar-cah'-do], *m.* Exarchate or vice royalty.

exarco [ek-sar'-co], *m.* 1. Exarch, viceroy. 2. A dignitary in the Greek church.

exasperación [ek-sas-pay-rah-the-on'], *f.* Exasperation.

exasperado, da [ek-sas-pay-rah'-do, dah], *a. & pp.* of EXASPERAR. Exasperate, exasperated.

exasperante *a.* [ek-sas-pay-rahn'-tay], Exasperating, infuriating.

exasperar [ek-sas-pay-rar'], *va.* To exasperate, to irritate, to offend, to acerbate. *-vr.* To get exasperated.

exastilo [ex-sas-tee'-lo], *m. (Arch.)* Hexastyle, a portico of six columns in front.

excandecencia [ex-can-day-then'-the-ah], *f.* 1. Candescence, incandescence. 2. Anger, passion.

excandecer [ex-can-day-therr'], *va.* To irritate, to provoke, to put into a passion. *-vr.* To be in a passion.

excarcelación [ex-car-thay-lah-the-on'], *f.* Release (cárcel).

excarcelado, da [ex-car-the-lah'-do], *m. & f.* Ex-prisoner, former prisoner.

excarcelar [ex-car-thay-lar'], *va.* To remove a prisoner from the jail by command of the judge.

ex cáthedra *(Acad.)* A phrase from Latin to denote a tone of mastery and finality. To speak, or decide, **ex cáthedra.**

excava, excavación [ex-cah'-vah, es-cah-vaht-he-on'], *f.* Excavation.

excavador, ra [es-cah-vah-dor'-rah], *a.* Excavating. *-f.* Excavating machine.

excavar [ex-cah-var'], *va.* To escavate, to dig out, to hollow.

excavillo [ex-cah-veel'-lyo], *m. (Prov.)* A little spade used in making excavations.

excedencia [ex-the-den'-the-ah], *f.* Leave of absence, **Excedencia por maternidad,** maternity leave.

excedente [ex-thay-den'-tay], *pa. & a.* Excessive, exceeding.

exceder [ex-thay-derr'], *va.* To exceed (superar), to surpass (sobrepasar), to excel, to go beyond, to outrun, to outgo, to overtop. *-vr.* To exceed, to overgo. **Excederse a sí mismo,** to surpass one's own actions. **Excederse en sus funciones,** to exceed one's duty.

excelencia [ex-thay-len'-the-ah], *f.* 1. Excellence, eminence, height, exquisiteness, superior worth or merit. 2. Excellency, a title of honor applied in Spain to grandees, councillors of state, etc. **Por excelencia,** *(coll.)* par excellence.

excelente [ex-thay-len'-tay], *a.* Excellent, exquisite.

excelentemente [ex-the-len'-tay-men-tay], *adv.* Exceptionally.

excelentísimo, ma [ex-the-len-tee'-se-mo, mah], *a. superl.* Most excellent: applied in courtesy to persons receiving the title of *Excellency.*

excelsamente [ex-thel-sah-men'-tay], *adv.* Sublimely.

excelsitud [ex-thel-se-tood'], *f.* Excelsitude, loftiness.

excelso, sa [ex-thel'-so, sah], *a.* Elevated, sublime, lofty.

excéntrica [es-then'-tre-cah], *f. (Mech.)* Cam.

excéntricamente [ex-then'-tre-cah-men-tay], *adv.* Eccentrically.

excentricidad [ex-then-tre-the-dahd'], *f.* Eccentricity; deviation from the center; excursion from the proper orb.

excéntrico, ca [ex-then'-tre'-co, cah], *a.* 1. Eccentric, eccentrical, having a different center. 2. Extravagant, odd, eccentric.

excepción [ex-thep-the-on'], *f.* 1. Exception, exclusion from things comprehended. 2. Exception, thing excepted or specified in exception. 3. *(Law.)* Demurrer, exception, a stop or stay to an action. **Excepción de la regla,** exception to the rule. **A excepción de,** with the exception of.

excepcional [ex-thep-the-o-nahl'], *a.* Exceptional, unusual, contrary to rule.

excepcionar [ex-thep-theo-nar'], *va. (Law.)* To except, to object, to demur.

excepto [ex-thep'-to], *adv.* Except that, besides that, excepting.

exceptuación [ex-thep-too-ah-the-on'], *V.* EXCEPCIÓN.

exceptuar [ex-thep-too-ar'], *va.* To except, to exempt, to exclude, to leave out.

excerta [ex-therr'-tah], *f.* Excerpt, extract, citation.

excesivamente [ex-the-see'-vah-men-tay], *adv.* Excessively,

excesivo, va [ex-thay-see'-vo, vah], *a.* Excessive, inmoderate, exorbitant, overgreat, extreme, unreasonable (indebido).

exceso [ex-thay'-so], *m.* 1. Excess, overmuch; superfluity (de comida), excessiveness, exuberance. 2. Excess, intemperance in eating or drinking. 3. Excess, irregularity, transgression of due limits. 4. Great wickedness, enormity of crime. 5. Excess, violence of passion. **En exceso,** excessively. **Exceso de equipaje,** excess luggage. **Exceso de peso,** excess weight. **Cuidadoso en exceso,** excessively careful. **Llevar algo al exceso,** to carry something to excess.

excipiente [ex-the-pe-en'-tay], *m. (Med.)* Excipient, a substance serving to incorporate, or to dissolve others in a medicine; a vehicle.

excisión [ex-the-se-on'], *f.* 1. Uprising, mutiny. 2. Altercation, quarrel.

excitabilidad [ex-the-tah-be-le-dahd'], *f.* Excitability.

excitable [ex-the-tah'-blay], *a.* Excitable.

excitación [ex-the-tah-the-on'], *f.* Excitation, exciting, the act of exciting; excitement (estado).

excitante [ex-the-tahn'-tay], *a.* Exciting (emocionante), stimulating. *-m.* Stimulant, excitant.

excitar [ex-the-tar'], *va.* 1. To excite, to move, to stimulate. 2. To excite (emoción), to stir up, to rouse, to animate, to fire, to flame. 3. To incite, to urge on (incitar). **Excitar al pueblo a la rebelión,** to incite the populace to rebellion.

excitativo, va [ex-the-tah-tee'-vo, vah], *a.* Exciting, stimulative, excitative.

esclamación [ex-clah-ma-the-on'], *f.* 1. Exclamation, vehement outcry, clamour. 2. Exclamation, an emphatical utterance.

exclamar [ex-clah-mar'], *vn.* To exclaim, to cry out, to clamor. *-vr.* To complain, to protest.

exclamativo, va [ex-clah-mah-tee'-vo, vah], *a.* Exclaiming.

exclamatorio, ria [ex-clah-mah-to'-re-o, ah], *a.* Exclamatory.

exclaustrado [ex-clah-oos-trah'-do, da], *m.* The cleric who has ceased to live in a cloister, chiefly by supression of his order; a secularized monk.

excluir [ex-cloo-eer'], *va.* 1. To exclude, to shut out, to expel, to foreclose, to cut out. 2. To exclude (posibilidad), to debar, to hinder from participation.

exclusión [ex-cloo-se-on'], *f.* 1. Exclusion, shutting out or denying admission, rejection, ejection. 2. Exclusion, exception.

exclusiva [ex-cloo-se'-vah], *f.* 1. Refusal of place or employment; rejection of an application to become member of a community (negativa); exclusion. 2. A special privilege. *(Acad.)* 3. *(Com.)* Sole right, sole agency. **Tener la exclusiva de un producto,** to have the sole right to sell a product. 4. **Trabajar en exclusiva para,** to work exclusively for.

exclusivamente, exclusive [ex-cloo-se-vah-men'-tay], *adv.* Exclusively.

exclusivo, va [ex-cloo-see'-vo, vah], *a.* Exclusive.

excluso [ex-cloo'-so], *pp. irr.* From EXCLUIR.

excogitable [ex-co-he-tah'-blay], *a.* Imaginable, possible to be conceived.

excogitar [ex-co-hetar'], *va.* To excogitate, to meditate; to strike out by thinking.

excombatiente [ex-com-bah-tee-ayn'-tay], *m.* Ex-service man, veteran.

excomulgación, excomunicación [ex-co-mool-gah-the-on', ex-co-moo-ne-cah-the-on'], *f. V.* EXCOMUNICACIÓN.

excomulgado, da [ex-co-mool-gah'-do, dah], *a. & pp.* of EXCOMULGAR. Excommunicate, excommunicated, accursed.

excomulgador [ex-co-mool-gah-dor'], *m.* Excommunicator.

excomulgar [ex-co-mool-gar', *va.* 1. To excommunicate, to eject from the communion of the church, and the use of the sacraments. 2. To fulminate ecclesiastical censure. 3. *(Met.)* To treat with foul language, to use ill, to accurse (maldecir).

excomunión [ex-co-moo-ne-on'], *f.* Excommunication, exclusion from the fellowship of the church.

excoriación [ex-co-re-ah-the-on'], *f.* Excoriation, privation of skin, the act of flaying.

excoriar [ex-co-re-ar'], *va. (Med.)* To excoriate, to flay: it is almost always used in its reciprocal sense.

excrecencia [ex-cray-then'-the-ah], *f.* Excrescence or excrescency.

excreción [ex-cray-the-on'], *f.* Excretion.

excrementar [ex-cray-men-tar'], *va.* To excrementize, to purge, to void by stool.

excrementicio, cia [ex-cray-men-tee'-the-o, ah], *a.* Excrementitious, excremental.

excremento [ex-cray-men'-to], *m.* 1. Excrement, flux. 2. Particles separated from plants by putrefaction.

excrementoso, sa [ex-cray-men-to'-so, sah], *a.* Excremental, excrementitious.

excretar [ex-cray-tar'], *vn.* To excrete; to eject the excrements.

excreto, ta [ex-cray'-to, tah], *a.* That which is ejected.

excretor, ra, or **excretorio, ria** [ex-cray-to're-o, ah], *a.* Excretory, excretive, having the quality of ejecting superfluous parts.

excursión [ex-coor-se-on'], *f.* 1. Excursion, expedition into the enemy's country. 2. *(Law.)* Liquidation of the estate of a debtor for paying off his debts. 3. Excursion, outing, trip. **Excursión de caza,** hunting trip. **Ir de excursión,** to go on a trip.

excursionista [ex-coor-se-o-nees'-tah] *m. & f.* Excursionist, traveler.

excusa [ex-coo'-sah], *f.* 1. Excuse, apology or plea offered in extenuation. 2. Excuse, the act of excusing or apologizing. 3. Excuse, cause for which one is excused. 4. Allowance, excusableness, color, cloak, loop-hole. **Excusas,** exemptions, immunities or emoluments granted to certain persons. **Buscar excusa,** to look for an excuse. **Presentar sus excusas,** to make one's excuses.

excusabaraja [ex-coo-sah-ba-rah'-hah], *f.* Basket or pannier with a cover of osiers.

excusable [ex-coo-sah'-blay], *a.* Excusable, pardonable.

excursación [ex-coo-sah-the-on'], *f. V.* EXCUSA.

excusadamente [ex-coo-sah-dah'-men-tay], *adv.* Uselessly, voluntarily, without necessity; not to the purpose.

excusado [ex-coo-sah'-do], *a.* 1. Exempted, privileged. 2. Superfluous, useless (inútil). 3. Preserved, laid up as useless.-*pp.* of EXCUSAR.

excusado [ex-coo-sah-do], *m.* Toilet.

excusador, ra [ex-coo-sah-dor', rah], *m. & f.* 1. One who performs another's functions in his stead. 2. Vicar or curate of a parish church. 3. *(Law.)* Excuser, one who excuses the non-appearance of a defendant in court.

excusalí [ex-coo-sah-lee'], *m.* Small apron.

excusar [ex-coo-sar'], *va.* 1. To excuse (disculpar), to extenuate by apology, to exculpate, to color, to palliate. 2. To exempt from taxes. 3. To obstruct, to hinder, to prevent. **Excusamos decirle que...,** we don't have to tell you that... 4. To shun, to avoid. -*vr.* To decline or reject a request, to

apologize. **Escusarse de haber hecho algo,** to apologize for having done something.

excusión [ex-coo-se-on'], *f. (Law.)* 1. Liquidation of the estate of a debtor for paying his debts. 2. *(Med.)* Concussion, a violent shaking.

ex diámetro [ex de-ah'-may-tro], *adv.* Diametrically.

execrable [ek-say-crah'-blay], *a.* Execrable, detestable, hateful, accursed.

execrablemente [ek-say-crah'-blay-men-tay], *adv.* Execrably.

execración [ek-say-crah-the-on'], *f.* Execration, detestation, cursing, abhorrence.

execrador, ra [ek-say-crah-dor', rah], *m. & f.* Execrater.

execrar [ek-say-crar'], *va.* To execrate, to detest, to curse, to imprecate ill upon. -*vr.* To mutually hate one another.

execratorio [ek-say-crah-to'-re-o], *a.* **Juramento execratorio,** execratory.

exégesis [ek-say'-hay-sis], *f.* Exegesis, explanation in general, and in particular of the Bible.

exegético, ca [ek-say-hay'-te-co, cah], *a.* Exegetical, explanatory.

exención [ek-sen-the-on'], *f.* 1. Exemption, immunity, privilege, freedom from imposts. 2. Franchise, exemption from any onerous duty.

exentado, da [ek-sen-tah'-do, dah], *a. & pp.* of EXENTAR. Exempt, exempted.

exentamente [ek-sen-tah-men'-tay], *adv.* 1. Freely. 2. Clearly, simply, sincerely.

exentar [ek-sen-tar'], *va.* 1. To exempt, to grant immunity from, to privilege, to franchise. 2. To absolve, to acquit, to excuse, to disengage from an obligation. -*vr.* To except oneself.

exento, ta [ek-sen'-to, tah], *a.* 1. Exempt (libre), free, freed, disengaged. 2. Exemptible, exempt, free, privileged. **Exento de derechos,** duty-free. 3. Clear, open, isolated, free from impediment. **Estar exento de cuidados,** to be free of worries. -*pp. irr.* of EXIMIR.

exequátur [ek-say-koo-ah'-toor] *m.* Exequatur.

exequias [ek-say'-ke-as], *f. pl.* Exequies, funeral rites.

exequible [ek-say-kee'-blay], *a.* Attainable.

exerción [ek-ser-the-on'], *f. (Neol. Med.)* Irritation, animation, activity, or contraction of fibrous tissues.

exergo [ek-serr'-go], *m.* Exergue, the space left on the face sides of medals for the inscription.

exfoliación [ex-fo-le-ah-the-on'], *f. (Med.)* Desquamation, scaling.

exfoliar [ex-fo-le-ar'], *va. (Med.)* To exfoliate. -*vr.* To become exfoliated.

exfoliativo, va [ex-fo-le-ah-tee'-vo, vah], *a. (Surg.)* Exfoliative, producing exfoliation.

exhalación [ex-ah-lah-the-on'], *f.* 1 Exhalation, the act of exhaling. 2. Exhalation, that which rises in vapors. 3. An electrical or other fire accustomed to be seen in the atmosphere; a shooting star.

exhalador, ra [ex-ah-lah-dor', rah], *m. & f.* Exhaler, one who exhales.

exhalar [ex-ah-lar'], *va.* To exhale, to send or draw out vapors or fumes. -*vr.* 1. To exhale, to evaporate. 2. To be consumed or wasted gradually. 3. To be consumed or wasted by violent exercise of the body.

exhalatorio, ria [ex-ah-lah-to'-re-o, ah], *a.* Exhalant. -*m.* An apparatus for evaporating fresh water in salt-works.

exhaución [ex-ah-oo-the-on'], *f.* Exhaustion, a method of establishing the equality of two numbers by proving that they differ by less than any assignable quantity.

exhaustivo [ex-ah-oos-te'-vo], *a.* Exhaustive; comprehensive.

exhausto, ta [ex-ah'-oos-to, tah], *a.* Exhausted, totally drained or drawn out.

exheredación [ex-ay-ray-dah-the-on'], *f.* Disinheritance, privation of an inheritance.

exheredar [ex-ay-ray-dar'], *va.* To disinherit.

exhibición [ex-e-be-the-on'], *f.* Exhibition, the act of exhibiting, display, show (cine). **Exhibición folklórica,** folk festival. **Una impresionante exhibición de fuerza,** an impressive show of strength.

exhibicionismo [ex-e-be-the-o-nees'-mo], *m.* 1. Exhibitionism. 2. Indecent exposure (sexual).

exhibicionista [ex-e-be-the-o-nees'-tah], *a.* Exhibitionist. *-m & f.* Exhibitionist.

exhibir [ex-e-beer'], *va.* To exhibit, to prevent, to make manifest, to lay, to show, to show (pasaporte), to show off (mostrar con orgullo). *-vr.* 1. To show oneself. 2. To expose oneself (sexualmente).

exhortación [ex-or-tah-the-on'], *f.* 1. Exhortation, admonition. 2. A short and familiar sermon.

exhortador, ra [ex-or-tah-dor', rah], *m. & f.* Exhorter, monitor.

exhortar [ex-or-tar'], *va.* To exhort, to excite by words to a good action.

exhortatorio, ria [ex-or-tah-to'-re-o, ah], *a.* Exhortatory, hortative.

exhorto [ex-or'-to], *m.* Letters requisitorial sent by one judge to another.

exhumación [ex-oo-mah-the-on'], *f.* Exhumation, disinterment.

exhumar [es-oo-mar'], *va.* To disinter, to unbury, to exhume.

exigencia [ek-se-hen'-the-ah], *f.* Exigence, want, pressing necessity, exaction, demand (requerimiento). **Según las exigencias de la situación,** as the situation requires.

exigente [ek-se-hen'-tay], *a.* Demanding, exacting, exigent. **Ser exigente con uno,** to be hard on somebody. **Es muy exigente en la limpieza,** she is very particular about cleanliness.

exigible [ek-se-hee'-blay], *a.* Capable of being demanded or required.

exigir [ek-se-heer'], *va.* 1. To exact (contribución), to demand (requirir), to require. **Exigir el pago,** to demand payment. **Esto exige mucho cuidado,** this needs a lot of care. 2. To wish for, to desire, to beg of.

exigüidad [ek-se-goo-e-dahd'], *f.* Exiguity, smallness.

exiguo, ua [ek-see'-goo-o, a], *a.* Exiguous, small.

exiliado [ek-se-le-ah'-do], *a. m & f.* Exile, in exile.

exiliar [ek-se-le-ahr'], *va.* To exile.

exilio [ek-se'-le-o], *m.* Exile. **Estar en el exilio,** to be in exile.

eximio, mia [ek-see'-me-o, ah], *a.* Eximious, famous, eminent.

eximir [ek-se-meer'], *va.* 1. To exempt, to free from an obligation, to clear from a charge. **Esto me exime de toda obligación con él,** this frees me from any obligation with him. 2. To exempt, to privilege, to excuse, to except. *-vr.* **Eximirse de,** to excuse oneself from.

exinanición [ek-se-nah-ne-the-on'], *f.* Inanition, want of vigor and strength, debility.

exinanido, da [ek-se-nah-nee'-do, dah], *a.* Debilitated, very weak, very feeble.

existencia [ek-sis-ten'-the-ah], *f.* Existence (vida), existency, state of being; actual possession of being. **Existencias,** stock in hand, articles or goods remaining unsold. **Amargar la existencia a uno,** to make somebody's life a misery.

existencialismo [ek-sis-ten-the-ah-lees'-mo], *m.* Existentialism.

existente [ek-sis-ten'-tay], *pa. & a.* Existing, extant (texto), existent, on hand. **La situación existente,** the existing situation.

existimación [ek-sis-te-ma-the-on'], *f.* Estimation, opinion, esteem.

existimar [ek-sis-tee-mar'], *va.* To hold, to form an opinion, to judge.

existir [ek-sis-teer'], *vn.* To exist, to be, to have a being. **Dejar de existir,** to pass out of existence.

éxito [ek'-se-to], *m.* 1. Result (resultado), outcome. **Buen éxito,** happy outcome. 2. Success (logro), good fortune.

Con éxito, successfully. **Tener éxito en,** to be successful in. 3. *(Mus. Teat. fig.)* Success, hit. **Éxito editorial,** bestseller.

exitoso, sa [ek-se-to'-so, sah], *a.* Successful.

éxodo [ek'-so-do], *m.* Exodus, the second of Moses. **El éxodo rural,** the depopulation of the countryside.

exoftalmía [ex-of-tahl-me'-ah], *f.* Exophthalmia, or exophthalmus, abnormal protrusion of the eyeball from the orbit.

exoneración [ek-so-nay-rah-the-on'], *f.* Exoneration, the act of disburdening.

exonerar [ek-so-nay-rar'], *va.* To exonerate (de culpa), to unload; to disburden, to lighten, to exempt (de un impuesto). **Exonerar a uno de un deber,** to free somebody from a duty.

exopilativo, va [ek-so-pe-lah-tee'-vo, vah], *a.* Deobstruent.

exorable [ek-so-rah'-blay], *a.* Exorable, to be moved by entreaty.

exorbitancia [ek-sor-be-tahn'-the-ah], *f.* Exorbitance.

exorbitante [ek-sor-be-tahn'-tay], *a.* Exorbitant, enormous, excessive, extravagant.

exorbitantemente [ek-sor-be-tahn'-tay-men-tay], *adv.* Exorbitantly, extravagantly.

exorcismo [ek-sor-thees'-mo], *m.* Exorcism.

exorcista [ek-sor-thees'-tah], *m.* Exorciser, exorcist.

exorcizante [ek-sor-the-thahn'-tay], *pa. & com.* Exorcising; exorciser.

exorcizar [ek-sor-the-thar'], *va.* To exorcise, to adjure by some holy name, to drive away by adjurations.

exordio [ek-sor'-de-o], *m.* Exordium, the proemial part of a composition; origin, beginning.

exornación [ek-sor-nah-the-on'], *f. (Rhet.)* Exornation, ornaments in waiting or speaking.

exornar [ek-sor-nar'], *va.* To adorn or embellish a discourse with rhetorical figures.

exortación [ek-sor-tah-the-on'], *f.* Exhortation, familiar admonition to piety; monition.

exostosis [ek-sos-to'-sis], *f.* 1. Exostosis, a disease of the bones. 2. *(Bot.)* Excrescence on the trunk of trees of very hard wood, whose fibres cross in all directions.

exotérico, ca [ek-so-tay'-re-co, cah], *a.* Exoteric, public, common.

exótico, ca [ek-so'-te-co, cah], *a.* 1. Exotic, foreign, extraneous. 2. Extravagant, odd.

expandir [ex-pan-deer'], *va.* To expand; to spread out (ropa); *(comm.)* to expand, to enlarge; *(Fig.)* to expand, to extend; to spread (noticia). **Expandir el mercado de un producto,** to expand the market for a product. *-vr.* To expand; to extend, to spread.

expansibilidad [ex-pan-se-be-le-dahd'], *f.* Expansibility.

expansión [ex-pan-se-on'], *f.* 1. Expansion, extension, spreading. **La expansión económica,** economic growth. 2. *(Fig.)* To relax (relajarse). 3. *(Fig.)* Expansiveness (efusión).

expansionar [ex-pan-see-o-nar'], *va.* To expand (mercado). *-vr.* 1. To expand. 2. *(Fig.)* To relax (relajarse). 3. *(Fig.)* To unbosom oneself (desahogarse).

expansivo, va [ox-pan-see'-vo, vah], *a.* 1. Expansive, capable of extension. 2. Affable, communicative.

expanso [ex-pahn'-so], *m.* 1. Expanse, a body widely expanded. 2. Space between the superior sphere of the air and the empyrean or highest heaven.

expatriación [ex-pah-tre-ah-the-on'], *f.* Expatriation.

expatriado, da [ex-pah-tre-ah-do], *m. & f.* Expatriate; exile.

expatriar [ex-pah-tre-ar'], *va.* To expatriate, to go into exile. *-vr.* To be exiled.

expectable [ex-pec-tah'-blay], *a.* Conspicuous, eminent, illustrious.

expectación [ex-pec-tah-the-on'], *f.* Expectation (esperanza), expectance, expectancy, anxious desire, hope, looking. **Joven de expectación,** a hopeful youth. **Hombre de expectación,** a celebrated man.

expectativa [ex-pec-tah-tee'-vah], *f.* 1. Right or claim respecting some future thing. 2. Hope of obtaining a reward, employment, or other thing. 3. Expectation, expectance. **Estar a la expectativa,** to wait and see.

expectoración [ex-pec-to-rah-the-on'], *f.* Expectoration, the act and effect of expectorating; sputum.

expectorante [ex-pec-to-rahn'-tay], *pa.* Expectorting. -*a.* & *n.* (*Med.*) Expectorant, a medicine which provokes expectoration.

expectorar [ex-pec-to-rar'], *va.* To expectorate, to spit out.

expedición [ex-pay-de-the-on'], *f.* 1. Readiness, facility, or freedom in saying, or doing. 2. Expedition, haste, speed (prontitud), activity, nimbleness. 3. Brevet or bull despatched by the See of Rome. 4. Expedition, a warlike enterprise. **Expedición militar,** military expedition. 5. Excursion, jaunt, journey.

expedicionero [ex-pay-de-the-o-nay'-ro], *m.* He who superintends expeditions or despatches.

expedido [ex-pay-dee'-do], *a.* & *pp.* of EXPEDIR. Expedite, quick, prompt, nimble.

expedidor [ex-pay-de-dor'], *m.* (*Com.*) Agent, shipper.

expediente [ex-pay-de-en'-tay], *m.* 1. The collection of all the papers belonging to a business matter (dossier, ficha). 2. Despatch, course of business. 3. Expedient, measure, means to an end contrived in an exigency or difficulty. 4. Facility or dexterity in the management of affairs. 5. Dismissal (despido).

expedienteo [ex-pay-de-en-tay'-o], *m.* (*coll.*) Red tape.

expedir [ex-pay-deer'], *va.* 1. To expedite, to facilitate, to free from impediment. 2. To despatch (negocio), to issue from a public office (orden, pasaporte), to forward, to transit (mercancías).

expeditamente [ex-pay-de'-tah-men-tay], *adv.* Expeditiously, expeditely, easily.

expeditivo, va [ex-pay-de-tee'-vo, vah], *a.* Expeditive, performing with speed, expeditious, speedy, quick; apt in expedients.

expedito, ta [ex-pay-dee'-to, tah], *a.* Prompt, expeditious, speedy, quick (pronto).

expeler [ex-pay-lerr'], *va.* To expel, to eject, to throw with violence.

expeliente [ex-pay-leen'-tay], *pa.* & *m.* & *f.* Expelling, expulser.

expendedor, ra [ex-pen-day-dor', rah], *m.* & *f.* 1. Spendthrift, lavisher. 2. One who sells publicly and disposes of some merchandise. 3. One who passes counterfeit money, knowing it to be so. 4. Agent, commission merchant; one who sells goods for another (agente). **Expendedor de billetes,** ticket clerk.

expendeduría [ex-pen-day-doo-ree'-ah], *f.* A shop in which tobacco and other wares are retailed.

expender [ex-pen-derr'], *va.* 1. To expend, to spend, to lay out (dinero). 2. (*For.*) To pass counterfeit money or stolen goods in trade.

expendio [ex-pen'-de-o], *m.* Expense, outlay, consumption, (*Acad.*)

expensas [ex-pen'-sas], *f. pl.* Expenses, charges, costs. **Estar a expensas de otro,** to live by favor, at the cost of another, or to depend upon him.

experiencia [ex-pay-reen'-the-ah], *f.* 1. Experience, knowledge gained by practice. 2. Experience, experiment (expèrimento), practice, trial. **Una triste experiencia,** a sad experience. **Aprender por la experiencia,** to learn by experience.

experimentado, da [ex-pay-re-men-tah'-do, dah], *a.* & *pp.* of EXPERIMENTAR. Experienced, conversant.

experimentador, ra [ex-pay-re-men-tah-dor', rah], *m.* & *f.* Experimenter, experimentalist.

experimental [ex-pay-re-men-tahl'], *a.* Experimental; attained by experience.

experimentalmente [ex-pay-re-men-tahl'-men-tay], *adv.* Experimentally.

experimentar [ex-pay-re-men-tar'], *va.* 1. To experience, to learn or know by practice. 2. To experiment, to search out

by trial. **Están experimentando un nuevo helicóptero,** they are testing a new helicopter. 3. To experience, to undergo, to go through (sufrir cambio); to suffer (pérdida); to feel (emoción). **No experimenté ninguna sensación nueva, I** felt no new sensation.

experimento [ex-pay-re-men-to], *m.* Experiment, trial of something. **Hacer experimentos,** to experiment.

expertamente [ex-perr'-tah-men-tay], *adv.* Expertly, cunningly.

experto, ta [ex-perr'-to, tah], *a.* Expert, able, experienced, conversant. clever, cunning.

expiación [ex-pe-ah-the-on'], *f.* 1. Expiation, the act of atoning for any crime. 2. Atonement, purification. 3. Reparation, compensation for damage.

expiar [ex-pe-ar'], *va.* 1. To expiate, to pay for a crime. 2. To purify, to free from profanation.

expiativo, va [ex-pe-ah-tee'-vo, vah], *a.* That which serves for expiation, expiatory.

expiatorio, ria [ex-pe-ah-to'-re-o, ah], *a.* Expiatory.

explanación [ex-plah-nah-the-on'], *f.* Explanation, elucidation, exposition.

explanada [ex-plah-nah'-dah], *f.* (*Mil.*) 1. A slope. 2. Esplanade (paseo), glacis, raised area (plataforma); levelled area (zona nivelada).

explanar [ex-plah-nar'], *va.* 1. To level. V. ALLANAR. 2. (*Met.*) To explain, to elucidate, to clear up.

explayamiento [ex-plah-yah-me-en'-to], *m.* The act of dilating or dwelling upon a subject.

explayar [ex-plah-yar'], *va.* To extend, to dilate, to enlarge. -*vr.* 1. To enlarge or dwell upon a subject (discurso). 2. To amuse oneself, by taking a walk or any other amusement (relajarse). 3. To be extended or enlarged (extender).

expletivo, va [ex-play-tee'-vo, vah], *a.* Expletivo.

explicable [ex-ple-cah'-blay], *a.* Explicable, explainable. **Cosas no fácilmente explicables,** things not easily explained.

explicación [ex-ple-cah-the-on'], *f.* Explanation, explication, elucidation, exposition, interpretation, comment. **Sin dar explicaciones,** without giving any reason.

explicadamente [ex-ple-cah-dah-men'-tay], *adv.* Explicitly.

explicaderas [ex-ple-cah-day'-ras], *f. pl.* (*coll.*) Manner in which something is explained; facility of explaining. (Irónico.)

explicador, ra [ex-ple-cah-dor', rah], *m.* & *f.* 1. One who explains. 2 Commentator, glossarist, glossator.

explicar [ex-ple-car'], *va.* To explain, to clear up, to expound (teoría), to comment, to construe. -*vr.* 1. To explain or speak one's mind with propriety and freedom. **Explicar el porqué de una cosa,** to account. 2. To be explained (ser explicable). **Esto no se explica fácilmente,** this cannot be explained easily.

explicativo, va [ex-ple-cah-tee'-vo, vah], *a.* Explicative, explicatory, exegetical.

explícitamente [ex-ple'-the-tah-men-tay], *adv.* Explicitly, manifestly.

explícito, ta [ex-plee'-the-to, tah], *f.* Explicit, clear, distinct, manifest.

exploración [ex-plo-rah-the-on'], *f.* Exploration; scanning (radar); Skin diving (deporte).

explorador, ra [ex-plo-rah-dor', rah], *f.* 1. Explorator, explorer. 2. (*Med.*) Probe; scanner (radar)

explorar [ex-plo-rar'], *va.* To explore, to search into, to examine by trial.

exploratorio [ex-plo-rah-to'-re-o], *m.* Probe, catheter.

explosión [ex-plo-se-on'], *f.* 1. Explosion, outburst. **Explosión demográfica,** population explosion. 2. (*Fig.*) Explosion, blast. **Hacer explosión,** to explode.

explosivo, va [ex-plo-see-vo, vah], *a.* Explosive, capable of producing an explosion.

explotable [ex-plo-tah-blay], *a.* Workable, exploitable.

explotación [ex-plo-tah-the-on'], *f.* 1. Exploiting, exploitation, improvement of mines, or of lands. 2. Exploitation, unfair utilization (de algo, de alguien).

explotar [ex-plo-tar'], *va.* 1. To work or develop mines (veta). 2. To till lands. 3. *(Met.)* To exploit, to get all the benefit possible out of a thing (recursos etc). 3. To exploit (obreros); to exploit (situación). -*vn. (Mil. etc.)* To explode; to go off. **Explotaron 2 bombas,** 2 bombs exploded.

expoliación [ex-po-le-ah-the-on'], *f.* Despoiling, spoliation.

expolio [ex-po'-lee-o], *m.* 1. Pillaging, sacking. 2. **Armar un expolio,** to cause a hullaballoo.

exponencial [ex-po-nen-the-ahl'], *a. (Alg.)* Exponential.

exponente [ex-po-nen'-tay], *pa. & m. & f.* Expositor. 2. *(Arith.)* Exponent. 3. *(Com.)* Exhibitor; manufacturer, inventor or artist who exhibits a product in public exhibitions.

exponer [ex-po-nerr'], *va.* 1. To expose, to lay before the public, to show, to exhibit (cuadro) 2. To expound, to explain (argumento). 3. To expose, to, lay open, to make bare. 4. To expose, to put in danger, to hazard, to occasion, to chance. 5. To expose a young child, or to cast him out to chance. -*vr.* To hazard, to adventure, to try the chance.

exportación [ex-por-tah-the-on'], *f.* 1. Exportation, sending commodities to other countries. 2. Export (artículo); exported article; exports (mercancías). **Géneros de exportación,** exports.

exportar [ex-por-tar'], *va.* To export, to carry out of a country.

exposición [ex-po-se-the-on'], *f.* 1. Exposition, explanation, interpretation (de hechos) 2. Making manifest. 3. Solicitude lifted into petition or allegation. 4. Exposition, a public display of industrial products, agricultural, artistic (arte). **Exposición de modas,** fashion show. 5. Peril, risk.

expositivo, va [ex-po-se-tee'-vo, vah], *a.* Explanatory, expositive.

expósito, ta [ex-po'-se-to, tah], *a.* Exposed (niños abandonados).

expositor, ra [ex-po-se-tor'], *m. & f.* Expounder, interpreter, explainer, explicator, exhibitor (arte); exponent (de teoría).

expremijo [ex-pray-mee'-ho], *m.* Cheesevat, a wooden case in which cheeses are formed and pressed.

exprés [ex-press'], *m.* Black coffee.

expresado, da [ex-pray-sah'-do, dah], *a.* Before mentioned, cited, aforesaid. **Según las cifras expresadas,** according to these figures.

expresamente [ex-pray-sah-men'-tay], *adv.* Expressly, in direct terms, plainly.

expresar [ex-pray-sar'], *va.* 1. To express, to declare one's sentiments clearly and distinctly, to word (redactar); to state (declarar); to quote (citar). **Expresa las opiniones de todos,** he is voicing the opinions of us all. 2. To delineate, to sketch, to design. -*vr.* 1. To express oneself (persona). 2. To be stated (cifra, dato), **Como se expresa abajo,** as is stated below.

expresión [ex-pray-se-on'], *f.* 1. Expression, declaration of one's sentiments and opinions. **Esta expresión de nuestro agradecimiento,** this expression of our gratitude. 2. Expression, the form of language in which thoughts are uttered. 3. Expression phrase, a mode of speech. 4. Expression, the act of squeezing out the juice from succulent fruits. 5. Present, gift. 6. Expression, the act of representing something.

expresivamente [ex-pray-see'-vah-men-tay], *adv.* 1. Expressively. 2. Tenderly, affectionately (cariñosamente).

expresividad [ex-pray-see-ve-dahd], *f.* Expressiveness.

expresivo, va [ex-pray-see'-vo, vah], *a.* 1. Expressive (personas, cosas). 2. Affectionate, kind, gracious (afectuoso).

expreso, sa [ex-pray'-so, sah], *a. & pp.irr.* of EXPRESAR. Expressed: express (explícito), clear, manifest, not dubious (exacto).

expreso [ex-pray'-so], *m.* 1. Express, extraordinary messenger, a courier (persona). 2. *(Naut.)* Packet-boat, advice-boat. 3. A rapid train for passengers and mails.

exprimidera [ex-pre-me-day'-rah], *f.* A small press used by apothecaries to squeeze out the juice of herbs.

exprimidero [ex-pre-me-day'-ro], *m.* A press or any other thing, by which, something is crushed or squeezed.

exprimido, da [ex-pre-mee'-do, dah], *a. & pp.* of EXPRIMIR Squeezed: dry, extenuated.

exprimidor [ex-pre-me-dor], *m.* Wringer, presser, squeezer. **Exprimidor de limones,** lemon squeezer.

exprimir [ex-pre-meer'], *va.* 1. To squeeze or press out (fruta). 2. To express, to declare clearly and distinctly.

ex profeso [ex-pro-fay'-so], *adv. (Lat.)* Avowedly, designedly, on purpose.

expropiación [ex-pro-pe-ah-the-on'], *f.* Expropriation, dispossession from ownership for public use.

expropiar [ex-pro-pe-ar'], *va.* To expropriate, to take property from a private owner for public use.

exprovincial [ex-pro-vin-the-ahl'], *m.* Exprovincial, a late provincial.

expuesto, ta [ex-poo-es'-to, tah], *a. & pp. irr.* of EXPONER. **Exponer; según lo arriba expuesto,** according to what has been stated above. Exposed, liable, obnoxious.

expugnable [ex-poog-nah'-blay], *a.* Expugnable.

expugnación [ex-poog-nah-the-on'], *f.* Expugnation.

expugnador [ex-poog-nah-dor'], *m.* Expugner, he who takes by assault.

expugnar [ex-poog-nar'], *va.* To expugn, to conquer, to reduce a place by force of arms.

expulsar [ex-pool-sar'], *va.* To expel, to eject, to drive out, to force away, to send off (jugador).

expulsión [ex-pool-se-on'], *f.* Expulsion, the act of driving out.

expulsivo, va [ex-pool-see'-vo, vah], *a.* Expulsive.

expulso, sa [ex-pool-so, sah], *a. & pp. irr.* of EXPELER and EXPULSAR. *(Acad.)* Ejected, driven out, expelled: outcast.

expurgación [ex-poor-gah-the-on'], *f.* Expurgation, purification from bad mixture or error.

expurgar [ex-poor-gar'], *va.* 1. To expurgate, to expunge, to purge away, to cleanse, to purify. 2. *(Lit.)* To correct, to emend, to remove errors.

expurgativo, va [ex-poor-gah-tee'-vo, vah], *a.* Expurgatory, expurgatorious.

expurgatorio [ex-poor-gah-to'-re-o], *m.* Index of the books prohibited by the Inquisition.

expurgo [ex-poor'-go], *m. (Prov.)* Expurgation, purification from bad mixture.

exquisitamente [ex-ke-see'-tah-men-tay], *adv.* Exquisitely; deliciously, delightfully; excellently.

exquisitez [ex-ke-see-tayth'], *f.* 1. Exquisiteness; excellence. 2. Affection.

exquisito, ta [ex-ke-see'-to, tah], *a.* Exquisite, consummate, excellent, delicious (excelente).

éxtasis, [ex'-tah-sis], *m.* 1. Ecstasy, enthusiasm. 2. *(Med.)* Catalepsy, or hypnotic sleep, with the eyes open (de médium).

extático, ca [ex-tah'-te-co, cah], *a.* 1. Ecstatic, absorbed. 2. *(Med.)* Cataleptic.

extemporáneamente [ex-tem-po-rah'-nay-ah-men-tay], *adv.* Extemporaneously, extempore, without premeditation.

extemporáneo, nea [es-tem-po-rah'-nay-o, ah], *a.* Extemporaneous, unpremeditated, out of time.

extender [ex-ten-derr'], *va.* 1 To extend, to stretch out or stretch forth, to hold out (brazo, mano), to stretch out, to spread (crema, mantequilla) 2. To extend, to expand, to unfold, to unwrap. 3. Speaking of a message, writing, etc. (documento), to record it in the ordinary form. -*vr.* 1. To be extended or enlarged; to increase in bulk; to propagate (en el espacio). **Delante de nosotros se extendía la mar,** the sea stretched out before us. **Sus terrenos se extienden sobre muchos kilómetros,** his lands spread over many miles. 2. To extend (tiempo). 3. To spread, to extend (conocimiento, costumbre); to escalate, to widen, to broaden (guerra). **Su venganza se extendió hasta matar a las mujeres,** in his vengeance he even killed the women.

extendidamente [ex-ten-de'-dah-men-tay], *adv.* Extensively.

extendido, da [ex-ten-dee'-do, dah], *a. & pp.* of EXTENDER. Extended, stretched out (brazos), extent, extensive, spacious, roomy.

extendimiento [ex-ten-de-me-en'-to], *m.* Extension, dilatation.

extensamente [ex-ten-sah-men-tay], *adv.* 1. Extensively (viajar, leer). 2. Fully, in full, with full details (tratar).

extensible [ex-ten-see'-blay], *a.* Extensible, extensile.

extensión [ex-ten-se-on'], *f.* 1. Extension (acto). 2. Extension, extent, length, space or degree to which something is extended; extensiveness (dimensiones). **Un solar de mayor dimensión** a site of greater size. 3. Length, duration; span (de tiempo). 4. *(Mus.)* Range, compass. 5. **Extensión de cable,** extension lead.

extensivamente [ex-ten-see'-vah-men-tay], *adv.* Amply, extensively, widely, largely.

extensivo, va [ex-ten-see'-vo, vah], *a.* Extensive, ample, wide, large, extensible. **Hacer extensivo a,** to extend to.

extenso, sa [ex-ten'-so, sah], *pp. irr.* of EXTENDER, and *a.* Extensive (grande). **Por extenso,** at large; clearly and distinctly.

extensor, ra [ex-ten-sor', rah], *a.* Extending. *(Med.)* Extensor, as used of certain muscles.

extenuación [ex-tay-noo-ah-the-on'], *f.* Extenuation, a general decay in the muscular flesh of the whole body; feebleness, wasting.

extenuado, da [ex-tay-noo-ah'-do, dah] *a. & pp.* of EXTENUAR. Extenuated, extenuate, weak.

extenuar [ex-tay-noo-ar'], *va.* To extenuate, to diminish, to debilitate, to make lean, to wear away. *-vr.* To languish, to grow feeble, to lose strength, to decay.

extenuativo, va [ex-tay-noo-ah-tee'-vo, vah], *a.* That which extenuates.

exterior [ex-tay-re-or'] *a.* Exterior, external, formal, extrinsic, extrinsical, outward (aspecto); outside (cuarto).

exterior [ex-tay-re-or'], *m.* 1. Exterior, outside (parte de casa etc.); composure. **Con el exterior pintado de azul,** with the outside painted blue. 2. Foreign parts (países extranjeros). **Noticias del extranjero,** foreign news. 3. *(Pol.)* **Exteriores,** foreign affairs.

exterioridad [ex-tay-re-o-re-dahd'], *f.* 1. Exteriority, outwardness, outward or external form: outward appearance. 2. Outside (superficies), surface, external part. 3. Pomp, ostentation, pageantry.

exteriorizar [ex-tay-re-o-re-thar'], *va.* To express (expresar), to reveal outwardly (mostrar).

exteriormente [ex-tay-re-or-men'-tay], *adv.* 1. Externally, outwardly. 2. Externally, in appearance. 3. Exteriorly.

exterminación [ex-ter-me-nah-the-on'], *f. V.* EXTERMINIO.

exterminador, ra [ex-ter-me-nah-dor' rah], *m. & f.* Exterminator. *-a.* Exterminatory.

exterminar [ex-ter-me-nar'], *va.* 1. To banish, to drive away. 2. To exterminate, to root out, to tear up, to destroy, to confound.

exterminio [ex-ter-mee'-ne-o], *m.* 1. Expulsion, banishment. 2. Extermination, desolation, extirpation, destruction.

externo, na [ex-terr'-no, nah], *a.* 1. External, visible, outward. 2. A day-pupil, one who attends classes at a school or college, but does not board there.

extestamento [ex-tes-tah-men'-to], By will or testament in contrast to ab intestato.

extinción [ex-tin-the-on'], *f.* 1. Extinction, quenching or extinguishing. 2. Extinction, suppression. 3. Extinguishment, obliteration.

extinguible [ex-tin-gee-blay], *a.* Extinguishable.

extinguido [ex-tin-gee'-do], *a.* 1. **Estar extinguido** (incendio), to be out, to be extinguished. 2. Extinct (animal, volcán).

extinguir [ex-tin-geer'], *va.* 1. To quench, to extinguish, to put out (incendio). 2. To extirpate, to suppress, to destroy. *-vr.* 1. To go out (fuego). 2. *(Bio.)* To die out, to become extinct.

extinto, ta [ex-teen'-to, tah], *a. & pp. irr.* of EXTINGUIR. Extinguished, extinct.

extintor [ex-tin-tor'], *m.* Extinguisher, fire extinguisher. **Extintor de incendios,** fire extinguisher.

extirpación [ex-teer-pah-the-on'], *f.* Extirpation, eradication, extermination, excision.

extirpador [ex-teer-pah-dor'], *m.* Extirpator.

extirpar [ex-teer-par'], *va.* 1. To extirpate, to root out, to eradicate, to exscind. 2. To destroy.

extorsión [ex-tor-se-on'], *f.* 1. Extortion. *(coll.)* Shake down. 2. Inconvenience (molestia).

extorsionar [ex-tor-se-o-nar'], *va.* 1. To extort (usurpar), to extract. 2. *(Fig.)* To pester, to bother.

extra [ex-trah], *prep.* Out, without, besides. *-a.* Extra. **Vino extra,** high-quality wine. **Extra de,** in addition to.

extracción [ex-trac-the-on'], *f.* 1. Exportation. 2. Extraction, the act ot drawing one part out of a compound. 3. *(Surg.)* Extraction, the taking of extraneous substances out of the body. 4. Drawing numbers in the lottery **Extracción de fondos,** *(Com.)* The secreting of effects. 5. *(Math.)* The procces of finding the root of a number.

extractador [ex-trac-tah-dor'], *m.* Extractor.

extractar [ex-trac-tar'], *va.* To extract, to abridge, to select an abstract from a longer writing (resumir).

extractivo, va [ex-trac-tee'-vo, vah], *a.* Extractive.

extracto [ex-trahc'-to], *m.* 1. Extract, an abridgment or compendium of a large work, book, or writing. 2. *(Pharm.)* Extract, any substance obtained by the evaporation of a vegetable solution. **Extracto de Saturno,** white lead. **Extractos,** excerpts. 3. A number drawn in a lottery.

extractor [ex-trac-tor'], *m.* Extractor.

extradición [ex-tra-de-the-on'], *f.* Extradition.

extraer [ex-trah-err'], *va.* 1. To extract, to remove, to export. 2. To extract, to draw out the chief parts of a compound. 3. *(Law.)* To extract from any document. 4. To discover the root of a number. *(Yo extraigo, yo extraiga, extraje, extrajera,* from *Extraer. V.* TRAER.)

extraescolar [ex-trah-ays-co-lar'], *a.* **Actividad extraescolar,** out-of-school activity.

extrajudicial [ex-trah-hoo-de-the-ahl'], *a.* Extrajudicial.

extrajudicialmente [ex-trah-hoo-de-the-ahl-men-tay], *adv.* Extrajudicially.

extramuros [ex'-trah-moo'-ros], *adv.* Outside the walls of a town.

extranjería [ex-tran-hay-ree'-ah], *f.* 1. The quality of being a stranger or foreigner. 2. The manner, use, and customs of a foreigner. **Ley de extranjería,** law on aliens.

extranjerismo [ex-tran-hay-rees'-mo], *m.* Fondness for foreign customs.

extranjero [ex-tran-hay'-ro], *m.* Any foreign land. **En el extranjero,** abroad, in a foreign land. **No me siento a gusto en el extranjero,** I don't feel at ease abroad.

extranjero, ra [ex-tran-hay'-ro, rah], *m. & f.* Stranger, foreigner, alien. *-a.* Foreign, outlandish, exotic.

extranjía [ex-tran-hee'-ah], *f.* or **Extranjis.** 1. *(coll.)* V. EXTRANJERÍA. **De extranjía or de extrajis,** foreign. 2. *(Fig.)* A strange or unexpected thing (secretamente).

extrañamente [ex-trah-nyah-men'-tay], *adv.* Wonderfully, extraordinarily, oddly.

extrañamiento [ex-trah-nyah-me-en'-to], *m.* 1. Alienation, rejection, aversion. 2. Expulsion.

extrañar [ex-trah-nyar'], *va.* 1. To alienate, to banish from one's sight and intercourse. 2. To admire, to wonder (asombrar). **Me extrañaba que no hubieras venido,** I was surprised that you had not come. 3. To censure, to chide, to reprimand. **No hay que extrañar,** no wonder. 4. To miss (echar de menos). *-vr.* 1. To refuse (negarse), to decline; to break off any engagement. 2. To be amazed, to be surprised (asombrarse); to marvel (maravillarse). **Extrañarse de que…,** to be surprised that…

extrañeza [ex-trah-nyay'-thah], *f.* 1. Alienation or change of affection, aversion (amigos). 2. Singularity, irregularity (rareza). 3. Admiration, surprise (asombro). **Me miró con extrañeza,** he looked at me in surprise.

extraño, ña [ex-trah'-nyo, nyah], *a.* 1. Foreign, extraneous (extranjero). 2. Rare, monstrous, singular, marvelous (raro). 3. Extravagant, irregular, wild. 4. Unwelcome, not well received. **Es muy extraño,** it is very odd. **País extraño,** Foreign country.

extraoficial [ex-trah-o-fe-the-ahl'], *a.* Unofficial.

extraordinariamente [ex-trah-or-de-nah'-re-ah-men-tay], *adv.* Extraordinarily, uncommonly, remarkably.

extraordinario, a [ex-trah-or-de-nah'-re-o, ah], *a.* Extraordinary, uncommon (insólito), rare, odd, outstanding (destacado). **Por sus servicios extraordinarios,** for his outstanding services.

extraordinario [ex-trah-or-de-nah'-re-o], *m.* The dish or dishes which are used only on a particular day or occasion. **Extraordinario** or **correo extraordinario,** an extraordinary courier.

extrapolar [ex-trah-po-lar'], *va. & vn. (Math.)* Extrapolate.

extrarradio [ex-trahr-rah'-de-o], *m.* Outer parts (ciudad).

extrasecular [ex-trah-say-coo-lar'], *a.* 1. Who has lived beyond a century. 2. Of another century, of remote times, antique.

extrasensorial [ex-trah-sen-so-re-ahl], *a.* Extrasensory.

extrasensorio, ria [ex-tra-sen-so'-re-o, ah], *a.* Extrasensory. **Percepción extrasensoria,** extrasensory perception.

extratémpora [ex-trah-tem'-po-rah], *f.* Dispensation for receiving orders out of the time specified by the church.

extraterrestre [ex-trah-ter-res-tray], *a.* Extraterrestrial.

extraterritorial [ex-trah-ter-re-to-re-ahl'], *a.* Extraterritorial, outside territorial limits of a jurisdiction.

extravagancia [ex-trah-vah-gahn'-the-ah], *f.* 1. Extravagance (cualidad), irregularity, oddness, folly, freak. 2. Extravagance, waste, vain and superfluous expense (capricho).

extravagante [ex-trah-vah-gahn'-tay], *a.* 1. Extravagant, irregular, wild, humorous, frantic, freakish. 2. *(coll.)* Odd (raro), out of the way, outlandish (estrafalario).

extravagante [ex-trah-vah-gahn'-tay], *f.* Extravagant, a papal constitution not included in the body of the canon law almost always used in the plural.

extravagantemente [ex-trah-vah-gahn'-tay-men-tay], *adv.* Extravagantly; eccentrically.

extravasación [ex-trah-vah-sah-the-on'], *f. (Med.)* Extravasation.

extravasarse [ex-trah-vah-sar'-say], *vr.* To extravasate, to exude.

extravenado, da [ex-trah-vay-nah'-do, dah], *a.* Extravenate, forced out of the veins. *-pp.* of EXTRAVENARSE.

extravenarse [ex-trah-vay-nar'-say], *vr.* To let out of the veins.

extraviar [ex-trah-vear'], *va.* To mislead, to lead out of the way; to embezzle (dinero), secrete. **Extraviados,** *(Mil.)* Men missing. *-vr.* 1. To lose one's way, to deviate from the right or common way (persona). 2. To stray from rectitude, to err.

extravío [ex-trah-vee'-o], *m.* 1. Misplacement, loss (pérdida). 2. Deviation. 3. Irregularity, disorder, misguidance. 4. Frenzy.

extremadamente [ex-tray-mah'-dah-men-tay], *adv.* Extremely, in the utmost degree, greatly, hugely.

extremadas [ex-tray-mah'-das], *f. pl.* The time of making cheese.

extremado, da [ex-tray-mah'-do, dah], *a.* 1. Extreme, absolute, consummate in good or bad, intense (intenso); extremely good (muy bueno); extremely bad (muy malo). 2. Facetious, cheerful, gay. *-pp.* of EXTREMAR.

extremamente [ex-tray-mah-men'-tay], *adv.* Extremely, exceedingly, mightily.

extremar [ex-tray-mar'], *va.* 1. To reduce to an extreme; generally used in a bad sense. 2. To finish, to complete, to give the finishing stroke. **Sin extremar el sentimentalismo,** without overdoing the sentimentality. *-vr.* 1. To be punctual or exact in the performance of something. 2. To persist obstinately in an undertaking. *-vn.* To winter in Extremadura (oveja).

extremaunción [ex-tray-mah-oon-the-on'], *f.* Unction or extreme unction.

extremidad [ex-tray-me-dahd'], *f.* 1. The end or extremity of something (punta). 2. The edge, brink, border, or brim of any thing (borde).

extremismo [ex-tray-mees'-mo], *m.* Extremism.

extremista [ex-tray-mees'-tah], *a.m. & f.* Extremist.

extremo, ma [ex-tray'-mo, mah], *a.* 1. Extreme, last, that beyond which there is nothing (lugar). 2. Extreme, greatest, of the highest degree. 3. Extreme, excessive, utmost. **Con extremo, en extremo, por extremo, extremely,** in the utmost degree.

extremo [ex-tray'-mo], *m.* 1. Extreme, utmost point, highest degree (punto maás alto). **Hasta el extremo de,** to the point of. 2. Extreme, the point at the greatest distance from the center, extremity (cabo, limite). **Pasar de un extremo a otro,** to go from one end to another. 3. *(Met.)* Extreme care or application (asunto). **Hacer extremos,** to caress, to fondle; to manifest grief and displeasure. 4. The winter or summer of emigrating flocks.

extremoso, sa [ex-tray-mo'-so, sah], *a.* Extreme, impassioned, unbridled, gushing (persona); vehement (vehemente).

extrínseco, ca [ex-treen'-say-co, cah], *a.* Extrinsic, outward, external, eastern.

extrovertido [ex-tro-vayr-te'-do], *a.* Extrovert; outgoing. *m. f.* Extrovert.

extumescencia [ex-too-me-then'-the-ah], *f. (med.)* Swelling, tumefaction.

exuberancia [ek-soo-bay-rahn'-the-ah], *a.* Exuberance, utmost, plenty, abundance.

exuberante [ek-soo-bay-rahn'-tay], *a.* Exuberant, overabundant.

exuberar [ek-soo-bay-rar'], *vn.* To be exuberant, to exuberate.

exudación [ek-soo-dah-the-on'], *f.* Sweating, a critical sweat.

exudar [ek-soo-dar'], *vn.* To exude, to ooze like sweat.

exulceración [ek-sool-thay-rah-the-on'], *f.* Exulceration, ulceration.

exulcerar [ek-sool-thay-rar'], *va.* To exulcerate, to ulcerate, to disuse with sores.

exultación [ek-sool-tah-the-on'], *f.* Exultation, demonstration of joy.

exutorio [ek-soo-toh'-re-o], *m. (Med.)* Issue, an ulcer artificially made and maintained for a curative purpose.

exvoto [ex-vo'-to], *m. (Lat.)* Offering to God in consequence of a vow, consisting of relics, pictures, images, etc., hung up in churches.

eyaculación [ay-yah-coo-lah-the-on'], *f. (Neol.)* 1. *(Med.)* Ejaculation, the rapid emission of certain secretions. 2. *(Zool.)* Rapid expulsion of water from the gills of certain fishes (para escapar). 3. Rapidity with which the chameleon darts its tongue upon the insects which cling to it.

eyaculador, ra [ay-yah-coo-lah-dor', rah], *a.* Ejaculatory, serving for ejaculation.

eyacular [ay-yah-co-lar'], *va.* To ejaculate, to expel fluid secretions.

eyector [ay-yec-tor'], *m.* Ejector (maquina).

ézula [ay'-thoo-lah], *f. (Bot.)* Spurge. *V.* ÉSULA.

F

f [ay'-fay]. Sixth letter of the Spanish alphabet. Its name is *efe.* This letter is pronounced in Spanish, as in English. In law works, *ff* signifies digest or pandect of the civil law. *F* stood for 40 in the middle ages, and with a dash above, 40,000. In music, *f* stands for **fuerte,** loud. In works of art, **fecit** or **faciebat.**

fa [fah], *m. (Mus.)* Fourth note in the gamut.

faba [fah'-bah], *f.* (*Prov.*) V. HABA.

fabacrasa [fah-bah-crah'-sah], *f.* (*Bot.*) Common orpine, stone-crop.

fabada [fah-bah'-dah], *f.* Rich stew of beans, pork, etc.

faber [fah-bayr'], *m.* A fish, the gilthead.

fábrica [fah'-bre-cah], *f.* 1. Factory, works; still, distillery. **Fábrica de cerveza,** brewery. **Fábrica de papel,** paper mill. 2. Fabrication, manufacture (acto). **Marca de fábrica,** trademark. **Trabajo de fábricas,** factory work. 3. Make (origen). **De fábrica alemana,** of German make. 4. (*Arch.*) Building, structure.

fabricación [fah-bre-cah-the-on'], *f.* Manufacture, construction. **Fabricación en serie** or **en gran escala,** mass production. **Fabricación de coches,** car manufacture. **Estar en fabricación,** to be in production. **Fabricación asistida por ordenador,** (*Comput.*) computer-aided manufacturing.

fabricador, ra [fah-bre-cah-dor', rah], *m.* & *f.* 1. V. FABRICANTE. 2. Inventor, contriver, deviser, coiner, framer. 3. (*Naut.*) Constructor.

fabricante [fah-bre-cahn'-tay], *m.* 1. Builder, architect, fabricator. 2. Maker, manufacturer, master workman, artificer (industria). 3. Operative, artisan.

fabricar [fah-bre-car'], *va.* 1. To build (construir), to make, to construct, to frame, to fabricate. 2. To manufacture (producir). 3. To fabricate, to contrive, to devise. **Fabricar a piedra perdida,** to build upon a false foundation.

fabril [fah-breel'], *a.* 1. Belonging to manufacturers, artisans, or workmen. 2. Febrile, belonging to the craft of a smith, mason, or carpenter.

fabriquero [fah-bre-cay'-ro], *m.* 1. Manufacturer, artisan, artificer (fabricante). 2. Person charged with the care of cathedrals and church buildings.

fabuco [fah-boo'-co], *m.* Beechmast, the fruit of the beech tree.

fabueno [fah-boo-ay'-no], *m.* Westerly wind.

fábula [fah'-boo-lah], *f.* 1. Fable, a feigned story, to enforce some moral precept. 2. Rumor, report, common talk (rumor, chisme). 3. Fable, a fiction, a lie, a false-hood (mentira). 4. Fable, the series of events which constitute a poem: a legend. 5. Mockery, derision. **Está hecho la fábula del mundo,** he is become the laughing-stock of the whole world. 6. V. MITOLOGÍA. 7. **Un negocio de fábula,** a splendid piece of business.

fabulador [fah-boo-lah-dor'], *m.* Fabulist, author of fables, dealer in fictions.

fabular [fah-boo-lar'], *va.* To invent fables or deal in fictions.

fabulilla, ita [fah-boo-leel'-lyah, ee'-tah], *f. dim.* A little fable.

fabulista [fah-boo-lees'-tah], *m.* Fabulist, a writer of fables.

fabulosamente [fah-boo-lo-sah-men'-tay], *adv.* Fabulously.

fabuloso, sa [fah-boo-lo-so, sah], *a.* Fabulous (estupendo, mítico), feigned, fictitious (ficticio), legendary, romantic.

faca [fah'-cah], *f.* A curved knife.

facción [fac-the-on'], *f.* 1. Military exploit, engagement, action. 2. Faction, a turbulent party in a state. 3. Party, faction. 4. Feature, countenance, favor: in this last sense it is generally used in the plural. 5. An act of military service, as guard, patrol, etc. **Facción de testamento,** faculty of testating. **Facciones,** features; the lineaments, cast or form of the face.

faccionario, ria [fac-the-o-nah'-re-o, ah], *a.* Belonging to a party or faction. -*m.* & *f.* Factionary, a party man.

faccioso, sa [fac-the-o'-so, sah], *a.* Factious, turbulent, unruly, mutinous: it is used as a substantive. **Los facciosos,** the rebels.

faceta [fah-thay'-tah], *f.* Facet, face or side of a precious stone cut into a number of angles.

faceto, ta [fah-thay'-to, tah], *a.* Merry, witty, gay, lively.

facha [fah'-chah], *f.* (*coll.*) Appearance, aspect, look (aspecto), mien, face (cara). **Ser un facha** or **una facha,** to be ridiculous. **Tiene facha de poli,** he looks like a cop. **Tiene facha de buena gente,** he looks OK.

fachada [fah-chah'-dah], *f.* 1. Facade, face, front, or fore part of a building. 2. (*coll.*) V. PRESENCIA for figure. 3. (*Met.*) Broad or plump face. 4. Frontispiece of a book. 5. Front-age (medida). **Con fachada al parque,** looking towards the park. 6. (*Fig.*) Facade, outward show. **No tiene más que fachada,** it's all just show with him. 7. Mug, face (cara).

fachenda [fah-chen'-dah], *a.* (*coll.*) Vain, ostentatious (hombre de negocios), -*f.* Vanity, boasting.

fachendear [fah-chen-day-ar'], *va.* To affect having much important business, to make an ostentatious parade of business.

fachendista [fah-chen-dees'-tah], *a.* & *m.* & *f.* (*coll.*) A vain and ostentatious person, a busybody.

fachendón, na [fah-chen-done', nah], *a. aug.* Very vain and ostentatious

fachín [fah-cheen'], *m.* (*Prov.*) Porter carrier.

fachinal [fah-che-nahl'], *m.* (*Prov. Amer.*) A salt marsh, swamp, place liable to be overflowed.

facial [fah-the-ahl'], *a.* Facial, belonging to the face. **Ángulo facial,** the facial angle.

facie [fah'-the-ay], *f.* (*Min.*) A face of a crystal.

facies [fah'-the-ays], *m.* (*Med.*) Facies, physiognomy in disease.

fácil [fah'-theel], *a.* 1. Facile, easy, light, performable with little trouble (sencillo). **Fácil para el usuario,** user-friendly. **Fácil de hacer,** easy to do. 2. Pliant, flexible, compliant, familiar, easily persuaded (persona). 3. Easy of access (mujeres). 4. Frail, weak of resolution.

facilidad [fah-the-le-dahd'], *f.* 1. Facility, easiness to be performed; freedom from difficulty. **Con la mayor facilidad,** with the greatest ease. 2. Facility, easiness to be persuaded, vicious docility (docilidad), ready compliance. 3. **Facilidades,** facilities. **Facilidades de crédito,** credit facilities.

facilillo, illa, ito, ita [fah-the-leel'-lyo, eel'-yah, ee'-to, ee'-tah], *a. dim.* Rather easy. **Facilillo es eso,** (Iron.) that is easy enough: meaning that it is extremely difficult.

facilitación [fah-the-le-tah-the-on'], *f.* Facility, expedition, facilitation.

facilitar [fah-the-le-tar'], *va.* 1. To facilitate, to make easy (hacer fácil), to free from difficulties, to expedite (agilizar). 2. To supply, to deliver (proporcionar). **Me facilitó un coche,** he supplied me with a car.

fácilmente [fah'-theel-men-tay], *adv.* Easily, lightly, without difficulty, facilely.

facilitón, na [fah-the-le-tone', nah], *a.* One who assumes to make everything easy.

facineroso [fah-the-nay-ro'-so], *a.* Wicked, atrocious, flagitious: it is also used as a substantive, speaking of highwaymen.

facistol [fah-this-tole'], *m.* Chorister's desk or stand on which choirbooks are placed.

facistor, ra [fah-this-tor', rah], *a.* (Cuban). V. FACHENDA.

faco [fah'-co], *m.* (*Coll.*) 1. Pony, a little nag. 2. Francis (apodo).

facsímile [fac-see'-me-lay], *m.* Facsimile.

factible [fac-tee'-blay], *a.* Feasible, practicable.

facticio, cia [fac-tee'-the-o, ah], *a.* Factitious, made by art.

factor [fac-tor'], *m.* 1. Factor, an agent for another. 2. Factor (aritmética). 3. Factor, constituting element (elemento). **Factor Rh,** (*Med.*) Rh factor. **Factor humano,** human factor. **El factor suerte,** the luck factor.

factoraje [fac-to-rah'-hay], *m.* Factorage, commission for agency in purchasing goods.

factoría [fac-to-ree'-ah], *f.* 1. Factory, foreign traders in a distant country; also the district where they reside; trading houses. 2. Factorage, the commission of factor, agency (agencia). 3. Foundry (fundición).

factorizar [fac-to-re-thar'], *va.* To establish commerce by factors.

factótum [fac-to'-toom], *m.* 1. Factotum, a man of all work (empleado). 2. One who officiously intermeddles in everything.

factura [fac-too'-rah], *f.* 1. Invoice of merchandise. **Según factura,** as per invoice. **Presentar factura,** to send an invoice. 2. Among organ-builders, the quality, length, breadth, and thickness of the pipes.

facturación [fac-too-rah-the-on'], *f.* 1. Invoicing (acto). 2. *(Com.)* Sales (ventas). 3. *(Aer.)* Check-in.

facturar [fac-too-rar'], *va.* 1. To note on merchandise the amount of the prime cost. 2. To check baggage.

fácula [fah'-coo-lah], *f. (Ast.)* Bright spot on the sun's disk.

facultad [fah-cool-tahd'], *f.* 1. Faculty, power of doing something. 2. Faculty, privilege, authority, right to do anything (autoridad). **Tener la facultad de,** to have the power to. 3. Science, art. 4. Faculty, in a university, denotes the body of the professors teaching a science. 5. *(Med.)* Faculty, the power of performing an action, natural, vital, or animal (de mente). **Facultades metales,** mental powers. 6. License, permission. *-pl.* **Facultades,** fortune, wealth, means of living. **Facultades del alma,** powers of the mind. **Facultad mayor,** in universities, divinity, civil and canonical law, or medicine.

facultado, da [fah-cool-tah'-do, dah], *a.* Authorized, empowered.

facultador, ra [fah-cool-tah-dor', rah], *m. & f.* One who commissions or empowers.

facultar [fah-cool-tar'], *va. (Law.)* To empower, to authorize, to commision.

facultativamente [fah-cool-tah-te-vah-men'-tay], *adv.* According to the principles, rules, or axioms of a science or art.

facultativo, va [fah-cool-tah-tee'-vo, vah], *a.* 1. Belonging to some faculty, art, or science. 2. Granting power, faculty, leave, or permision. 3. That which may be done or omitted at pleasure (opcional).

facultativo [fah-cool-tah-tee'-vo], *m.* 1. Master of a science or art (profesional). 2. A person skilful, intelligent, or conversant with an art, trade, or business; connoisseur (doctores).

facundia [fah-coon'-de-ah], *f.* Eloquence, the power of speaking with fluency and elegance.

facundo, da [fah-coon'-do, dah], *a.* Eloquent, fluent.

fada [fah'-dah], *f.* 1. A small apple of the pippin kind. 2. Witch.

fadiga [fah-dee'-gah], *f. (Prov.)* Leave granted to sell a feudal estate.

faena [fah-ay'-nah], *f.* 1. Work, labor, fatigue (trabajo). **Faena doméstica,** house-work. 2. *(Naut.)* Duty on board of ships. 3. **Mala faena,** dirty trick. **Hacer una faena a uno,** to lay a dirty trick on somebody. 4. Play with the cape; performance (tauromaquia). **Hizo una faena maravillosa,** he gave a splendid performance.

faenar [fah-ay-nar'], *va.* To slaughter (ganado). *-vn.* To fish (pescar), to work.

faetón [fah-ay-tone'], *m.* 1. Phaeton, a kind of open carriage. 2. An omnibus, with seats along the sides.

fagina [fah-hee'-nah], *f.* 1. Fascine, a small bundle of branches bound up. 2. Fagot, a bundle of sticks or brush-wood for fuel. 3. Stock or rick of corn piled up in sheaves. 4. Fatigue, work, labor. 5. *(Mil.)* A war-call.

faginada [fah-he-nah'-dah], *f.* Collection of fascines or fagots.

fagocitos [fah-go-thee'-tos], *m. pl. (Biol.)* Phagocytes, a type of white corpuscle.

fagot [fah-gote'], *m.* Bassoon (instrumento).

fagotista [fah-go-tees'-tah], *m.* Bassoon player.

faisán [fah-e-sahn'], *m. & f.* Pheasant (pájaro).

faja [fah'-hah], *f.* 1. Band, bandage (tira de tela), roller, fillet; a swathing band. 2. Border, a line which divides any superficies. 3. *(Arch.)* Fascia, belt, fillet. 4. A belt, sash, girdle (prenda). **Faja pantalón,** panty girdle. 5. *(Mil.)* Scarf, the principal insignia of a general. 6. *(Naut.)* A reefband.

fajadura [fah-hah-doo'-rah], *f. (Naut.)* Patched clothes rolled round a rope to preserve it.

fajamiento [fah-hah-me-en'-to], *m.* Act of rolling or swathing.

fajar [fah-har'], *va.* 1. To swathe (envolver), to bind a child with bands and rollers; to fillet. 2. To fall on, to attack (atacar). 3. To bandage (vendar); to wrap up (correos). *-vr.* To put on one's belt (ponerse una faja).

fajardo [fah-har'-do], *m.* A kind of minced pie.

fajeado, da [fah-hay-ah'-do, dah], *a.* That which has girdles, bands, or rollers.

fajero [fah-hay'-ro], *m.* A knitted swaddling band for children.

fajín [fah-heen'], *m.* Sash (militar). **El fajín rojo del general,** the general's red sash.

fajo [fah'-ho], *m.* 1. Bundle (papeles); roll (billetes). 2. Baby's clothes (de bebé). V. HAZ. *-pl.* Swaddling clothes.

fajón [fah-hone'], *m. aug.* A large band or roller.

fajuela [fah-hoo-ay'-lah], *f. dim.* A small bandage or roller.

fakir [fah-keer'], *m.* Fakir (faquir).

falacia [fah-lah'-the-ah], *f.* Fallacy (error), fraud (engaño), sophism, deceitful argument, hollowness, fallaciousness.

falange [fah-lahn'-hay], *f.* 1. Phalanx, a closely embodied troop. 2. Phalanx, *pl.* phalanges, small bones of the fingers and toes.

falangia, *f.* **falangio,** *m.* [fah-lahn'-he-ah, fah-lahn'-he-o]. A venomous spider with a red head and a black body.

falangista [fah-lan-hees'-tah], *m. & f.* Falangist.

fálaris [fah'-la-ris], *f. (Orn. Acad.)* V. FOJA.

falaz [fah-lath'], *a.* Deceitful (persona), fraudulent; frustrative, fallacious (doctrina), disappointing, deceptive (aspecto)

falbalá [fal-bah-lah'], *m.* 1. Flounce, furbelow, an ornament sewed to a garment and hanging loose. V. FARCALÁ. 2. Skirt of a gown or coat plaited.

falca [fahl'-cah], *f.* 1. *(Naut.)* A waistboard, or washboard. 2. *(Prov.)* A small wedge of wood used by carpenters.

falcada [fal-cah'-dah], *f.* Falcade, a curvet made by horses.

falcado, da [fal-cah'-do, dah], *a. & pp.* of FALCAR. Hooked, curvated, falcated. A scythed chariot.

falcario [fal-cah'-re-o], *m.* Roman soldier armed with a falchion.

falce [fahl'-thay], *f.* 1. Sickle, reaping-hook, scythe, billhook. 2. Falchion, a short crooked sword.

falcidia [fal-thee'-de-ah], *f.* 1. Fourth part of an inheritance. 2. The Roman law which established such division.

falciforme [fal-the-for'-may], *a.* Falciform, sickle-shaped.

falcinelo [fal-the-nay'-lo], *m. (Orn.)* Gray ibis, sicklebill.

falcón [fal-cone'], *m.* Ancient piece of artillery.

falconete [fal-co-nay'-tay], *m.* Falconet, a small piece of ordnance.

falda [fahl'-dah], *f.* 1. Skirt (prenda), the loose edge of a garment: that part which hangs loose below the waist; train; flap. **Falda escocesa,** kilt. **Haberse criado bajo las faldas de mamá,** to have led a very sheltered life. 2. The lap. **Sentarse en la falda de una,** to sit on somebody's lap. 3. Brow of a hill, that part of an eminence which slopes into the plain. 4. Loin of beef, mutton, etc. 5. The brim of a brazier where the hinge is fixed. 6. Brim (de sombrero). 7. Table cover (de camilla). **Perrillo faldero,** lap-dog.

faldamento [fal-dah-men'-to], *m.* Fold, flap, skirt. V. FALDA.

faldar [fal-dar'], *m.* Tassel, armor for the thighs.

faldellín [fal-del-lyeen'], *m.* 1. A skirt or underpetticoat used formerly by women (falda). 2. V. REFAJO.

falderillo, illa [fal-day-reel'-lyo, lyah], *a. dim.* 1. Small lap. 2. Little lap-dog.

faldero, ra [fal-day'-ro, rah], *a.* 1. Belonging to the lap. **Perrillo faldero,** lap-dog. 2. Fond of being constantly among women, and busy with women's affairs.

faldeta [fal-day'-tah], *f. dim.* Small skirt.

faldetes [fal-day'-tes], *f. pl.* 1. Tassels. 2. Fringes, trimmings.

faldicorto, ta [fal-de-cor'-to, tah], *a.* Having short skirts.

faldilla [fal-deel'-lyah], *f. dim.* V. FALDETA. *-pl.* Small skirts of a jacket.

faldistorio [fal-dis-to'-re-o], *m.* Stool on which bishops sit during the performance of church functions.

faldón [fal-done']. *m.* 1. A long flowing skirt, flap (devestido). 2. The flap of a saddle. 3. A millstone of a horsemill put upon another to increase the weight. 4. *(Arch.)* A sloping, side, gable; also the cap-piece and walls of the entrance of chimneys.

faldriguera [fal-dre-gay'-rah], *f.* Pocket. *V.* FALTRIQUERA.

falena [fah-lay'-nah]. *f. (Zool.)* Moth, a nocturnal lepidopterous insect; a tent-caterpillar.

falencia [fah-len'-the-ah], *f.* Want of security, uncertainty, mistake.

faleris [fah-lay'-ris], *m.* Coot, a bird of the family of the penguins. It inhabits Behring Strait and adjacent waters.

falibilidad [fah-le-be-le-dahd], *f.* Fallibility.

falible [fah-lee'-blay], *a.* Fallible.

falimiento [fah-le-meen'-to], *m.* Deception, deceit, falsehood.

falla [fahl'-lyah], *f.* 1. *(Naut.)* Defect, deficiency; lack of wood for the finishing of a certain figure. *V.* FALTA. 2. A sort of light loose cover, worn by women over their headdress at night. 3. *(Geol.)* Fault, dislocation of a seam or layer.

fallar [fahl-lyar'], *va,* 1. *(Law.)* To give sentence, to judge. 2. To ruff (naipes), to trump, to win a trick with trumps. *-v. impers.* To be deficient or wanting. *-vn.* To fail (cosecha, freno, memoria); to go wrong (plan); to miss (tiro); to break (apoyo, cuerda); to misfire (fusil). **Algo falló en sus planes,** something went wrong with his plans.

falleba [fal-lyay'-bah]. *f.* An iron bar for fastening doors and windows.

fallecedor, ra [fal-lyay-thay-dor', rah], *a.* Perishable.

fallecer [fal-lyay-therr'], *vn.* To die. *(Yo fallezco, yo fallezca, from Fallecer. V.* ABORRECER.)

fallecido, da [fahl-lay-the'-do], *m. & f.* Deceased, person who has lately died.

fallecimiento [fal-lyay-the-me-en'-to], *m.* Decease, death.

fallido, da [fal-lyee'-do, dah], *a.* 1. Deceived, disappointed, frustrated. 2. Bankrupt.

fallo [fahl'-lyo], *m.* 1. Judgment, decision of a judge in a lawsuit or trial. 2. In some games of cards not to have a card of the suit played. 3. Shortcoming (defecto); *(Med.)* failure: error. mix-up. **Debido a un fallo de los frenos.** because of a break failure. **Fallo del equipo,** *(Comput.)* equipment failure.

falo [fah'-lo], *m.* 1. Phallus the generative organ, the penis (clítoris) 2. Phallus, a genus of fungi.

falordía [fah-lor-dee'-ah], *f. (Prov.)* Deception, imposition, deceit, fable.

falsa or falsa escuadra [fal'-sah, es-coo-ah'-drah], *f.* Bevel rule, bevel square.

falsamarra [fal-sah-mar'-rah], *f. (Naut.)* Preventer-rope, employed to support another which suffers an unusual strain.

falsamente [fal-sah-men'-tay]. *adv.* Falsely; deceitfully, lyingly, fallaciously, counterfeitly, untruly.

falsario, ria [fal-sah-re-o.ah], *a.* 1. Falsifying, forging, counterferting. 2. Accustomed to tell falsehoods. *-m. & f.* 1. Faisifier (mentiroso);har, 2. Forger (falseador), counterfeiter.

falsarregla [fal-sahr-ray'-glah]. *f.* Bevel rule. bevel square.

falseable [fal-say-ah'-blay], *a.* Falsifiable, capable of being counterfeited.

falseador [fal-say-ah-dor'], *m.* Forger, counterfeiter, falsifier.

falsear [fal-say-ar'], *va.* 1. To falsify (falsificar), to adulterate, to counterfeit (moneda): to forge (firma). 2. To pierce, to penetrate. **Falsear la llave,** to counterfeit a key. *-vn.* 1. To slacken, to lose strength and firmness. 2. Not to agree in sound (instrumentos musicales). 3. To leave a hollow in saddles to make easy.

falsedad [fal-say-dahd'], *f.* 1. Falsehood, falsity, untruth, mendacity, fiction, fable, fib. 2. Deceit, malicious dissimulation.

falsete [fal-say'-tay], *m.* 1. Falsetto voice, the register of head tones. 2.*(Prove.)* Spigot.

falsía [fal-see'-ah], *f. V.* FALSEDAD.

falsificación [fal-se-fe-cah-the-on']. *f.* Falsification (acto), falsifying or counterfeiting forgery (objeto), counterfeit.

falsificador, ra [fal-se-fe-cah-dor'-rah], *m. & f.* Falsifier, counterfeiter, forger.

falsificar [fal-se-fe-car'], *va.* To falsify to counterfeit (moneda), to forge (cuadro, sello), to foist, imitation (joya); false (declaración, testimonio); hollow (persona).

falsilla [fal-seel'-lyah], *f.* Ruled pattern to guide in writing.

falsío [fal-see'-o], *m. (Prov.)* Kind of sausage.

falso, sa [fahl'-so, sah], *a.* 1. False (moneda), false, untrue (testimonio), uncertain, not real. 2. False, false-hearted, hypocritical, deceitful, treacherous, perfidious, traitorous (amigo). 3. False, counterfeit, supposititious, supposed. 4. Feint; mock. **Piedras falsas,** mock jewellery. 5. Vicious (caballos, mulas). 6. Producing no fruit (flores). 7. Defective, false. **De falso,** falsely deceitfully. **En falso,** without due security. **No levantarás falso testimonio,** thou shalt not bear false witness against thy neighbor. **Cerrar en falso la puerta,** to miss shutting the door, or to leave the door purposely unlocked. **Dar un** paso **en falso,** to step on something that is not there.

falta [fahl'-tah], *f.* 1. Fault, defect, want, absence, lack (carencia), mistake (dictado, escrito). **Falta de asistencia,** non-attendance. **Falta de peso,** short weight. **Echar algo en falta.** 2. Fault (culpa), offence, slight crime, defect (defabricación), faultiness, failing, misdoing, failure, flaw. 3. Want or stoppage of the catamenia in pregnant women. **Tiene cuatro faltas,** she is in the fifth month of her pregnancy. 4. Deficiency in the weightof coin. 5. Default, non-appearance in court at day assigned. **Sin falta,** without fail. **A falta de,** in want or for want of. **Hacer falta,** to be absolutely necessary to anything; not to be punctual to the fixed time; to be in want of a thing, to disappoint. *(Com.)* **Falta de aceptación, de pago,** for non-acceptance. **Acusar de falta,** to find fault with.

faltar [fartar'], *vn.* 1. To be deficient, to be wanting (ser necesario). 2. To fail (fallar), to falter, to fault, to flinch. 3. To be consumed, to fall short. 4. Not to fulfil one's promise, not to perform one's engagement. 5. To need, to lack, to be in want of. 6. To die. **Faltar a su palabra,** to fall back. **Le falta dinero,** he lacks money. **Nos falta tiempo para hacerlo,** we lack the time to do it. **Faltaron 3 en la reunión,** there were 3 missing in the meeting. **Fatar al trabajo,** to stay away. **Faltar en hacer algo,** to fail to do something, **Faltan pocos minutos para el comienzo,** there's only a few minutes to go till the start. **Falta poco para terminar,** it's almost over.

faltilla [fal-teel'-lyah], *f. dim.* A slight fault or defect.

falto, ta [fahl'-to, tah], *a.* 1. Wanting, deficient, defective (deficiente). **Estar falto de,** to be short of. 2. Miserable, wretched (moralmente). 3. Mad, insane.

faltrero, ra [fal-tray'-ro, rah]. Pickpocket, petty thief.

faltriquera [fal-tre-kay-rah], *f.* Pocket (bolsillo), as in clothes; fob, watch pocket (de reloj); handbag (bolso).

falúa, faluca [fah-loo'-ah, fah-loo'cah], *f. (Naut.)* Felucca, a small open boat, or a long boat with oars.

falucho [fah-loo'-cho], *m.* A small boat with oars, and one lateen sail.

fama [falh'-mah]. *f.* 1. Fame, report, rumor (rumor). 2. Fame (renombre), reputation (reputación), repute, name; glory. **Mala fama,** bad reputation. **El libro que le dio fama,** the book which made him famous.

fame [falh'-may]. *f. (Prov.)* Hunger. *V.* HAMBRE.

famélico, ca [fah-may'leco, cah], *a.* Hungry. *V.* HAMBRIENTO.

familia [fah-mee'-le-ah], *f.* 1. Family, the people who live in the same house together. 2. Family, those that descend from one common progenitor: a race, a generation, a house, a clan. **Familia política,** relatives by marriage. **De buena familia,** of good family. **Ser como de la familia,** to be one of the family. 3. Religious order. 4. Number of servants or retainers.

familiar [fah-me-le-ar'], *a.* 1. Familiar, domestic, belonging to the family (de la familia). **Los lazos familiares,** the family bond. 2. Familiar, common, frequent. 3. Familiar, well known. well acquainted with (conocido). 4. Agreeable, conformable, useful, observant, conversant, **Estilo familiar,** colloquial, familiar style; an easy, unconstrained style.

familiar. *m.* 1. Domestic, one belonging to a family, one kept in the same house. 2. Servant, especially of the clergy. 3. College servant, who waits upon all the collegians collectively. 4. Demon, a familiar spirit. 5. Familiar or intimate friend, one long acquainted. 6. One of the officers of the Inquisition.

familiarcito [fah-me-le-ar-thee'-to], *m.* 1. *(dim.)* Servant-boy, a little servant. 2. One who affects great familiarity or intimacy.

familiaridad [fah-me-le-ah-re-dahd'], *f.* 1. Familiarity, easiness of conversation or intercourse. 2. Familiarity, acquaintance, habitude. 3. *V.* FAMILIATURA.

familiarizar [fah-me-le-ah-re-thar'], *va.* To familiarize, to render familiar, to make easy by habitude. -*vr.* To become familiar, to descend from a state of distant superiority.

familiarmente [fah-me-le-ar-men'-rah], *adv.* Familiarly.

familiatura [fah-me-le-ah-too'-rah], *f.* 1. Place and employment of a *familiar* of the Inquisition. 2. Place of one of the college-servants called *familiares.*

famis [fah'-mis], *f.* A kind of gold cloth or brocade from Smyrna.

famosamente [fah-mo-sah-men'-tay], *adv.* Famously, excellently.

famoso, sa [fah-mo'-so-sah], *a.* 1. Famous, celebrated. renowned, conspicuous, great, splendid (estupendo). 2. Noted (ladrones) 3. Notorious.

fámula [fah'-moo-lah], *f. (coll.)* Maid-servant.

famulato, famulicio [fah-moo-lah'-to,-fah-moo-lee'-the-o], *m.* Servitude.

fámulo [fah'-moo-lo], *m.* Servant of a college.

fan [fahn], *m.* & *f.* Fan *(Cine, Mus.etc.)*

fanal [fah-nahl'], *m.* 1. *(Naut.)* Pooplantern of a commodore's ship. 2. Lantern (linterna), a lighthouse to guide ships (faro). 3. A kind of lantern of crystal in the form of a conoid.4. *(Met.)* Guide, friend, adviser in difficulties and dangers.

fanáticamente [fah-nah'-te-cah-men-tay], *adv.* Fanatically.

fanático, ca [fah-nah'-te-co, cah], *a.* Fanatic, fanatical, enthusiastic, superstitious. **Es un fanático del aeromdlismo.** he's mad about model aeroplanes.

fanatismo [fah-nah-tees'-mo], *m.* Fanaticism, mysticism, religious frency.

fanatizar [fah-nah-te-thar'], *va.* To spread or instil fanaticism.

fandango [fan-dahn'-go], *m.* 1. Fandango, a lively Spanish dance the music to this dance. 2. Festive entertainment; dance with eastanets or balls in the hands. 3. Row (jaleo).

fandanguear [fan-dan-gayar'], *va. (coll.)* To revel, to carouse.

fandanguero [fan-dan-gay'-ro], *m.* 1. Fandango-dancer. 2. One fond of festive entertainments.

faneca [fah-nay'-cah]. *f. (Zool.)* Pout, whiting pout.

fanega [fah-nay'-gah], *f.* 1. A measure of grain and seed of about a hundred weight, or an English bushel: it has been sometimes called faneague in English. 2. The quantity of seed contained in a **fanega** or Spanish bushel, and the vessel containing it. **Fanega de tierra,** extent of arable and, generally of four hundred fathoms square, and of pasture land five hundred. **Fanega de cacao,** a measure of one hundred and ten pounds of cocoa.

fanegada [fah-nay-gahn'-dah]. *f. V.* FANEGA DE TIERRA. **A fanegadas,** in great plenty or abundance.

faneranto, ta [fah-nay-rahn'-to, tah], *a.* Flowering, having visible flowers.

fanerocarop, pa [fah-nay-ro-car'-po, pah], *a.* Flowering, having visible flowers.

fanerógamo, ma [fah-nay-ro'-gah-mo, mah], *a.* Phanerogamous, flowering.

fanerrear [fan-far-ray-ar'], *vn.* To bully, to brag.

fanfarria [fan-far'-re-ah], *f.* 1. *(coll.)* Empty arrogance of a braggart. 2. *(Mus.)* Fanfare.

fanfarrón [fan-far-rone'], *m.* Fanfaron, a bully, a hector.

fanfarrón, na [fan-far-rone', nah], *a. (coll.)* Boasting, vaunting; inflated.

fanfarronada [fan-far-ro-nah'-dah], *f.* Fanfaronade, boast, brag, a bravado.

fanfarronazo, za [fan-far-ro-nah'-tho, thah], *a.* Applied to a great swank, boasting, vaunting.

fanfarronear [fan-far-ro-nay-ar'], *vn.* To bully, to brag, to show off, to swank.

fanfarronería [fan-far-ro-nay-ree'-ah], *f.* Fanfaronade, braggartism, bragging, show off.

fanfarronesca [fan-far-ro-ness'-cah], *f.* Manner of a fanfaron.

fanfurriña [fan-foor-ree'-nyah], *f.* Passion or displeasure, arising from a slight motive.

fangal [fan-gahl'], *m.* Slough, a miry place, a fen, a marsh, a place full of mud or mire.

fango [fahn'-go], *m.* 1. Mire, mud at the bottom of still water. 2. *(Naut.)* Oozy bottom of the sea.

fangoso, sa [fan-go'-so, sah], *a.* Muddy, miry.

fanón [fah-none'], *m.* 1. *(Med.)* A cylindrical splint made of barley-straw, and used in fractures of the thigh. 2. *(Vet.)* The tuft of hairs back of a horse's head. 3. A fold in the lower part of the neck of the ox and the sheep.

fantasear [fan-tah-say-ar'], *vn.* To fancy, to imagine.

fantasía [fan-tah-see'-ah], *f.* 1. Fancy, imagination. 2. Fantasy, the power of imagining. (facultad). **Es obra de la fantasía,** it is a work of the imagination. 3. Fancy, caprice, humor, whim, conceit (capricho). 4. Fancy, an opinion bred rather by the imagination than the reason. 5. Fancy, fiction, conception, image. 6. Presumption, vanity (afectación). 7. *pl.* A string of pearls. 8. *(Naut.) V.* ESTIMA. *(Mus.)* A kind of composition whose origin dates from the 16th century.

fantasioso, sa [fan-tah-se-o'-so, sah], *a. (coll.)* Fantastic, vain, conceited.

fantasma [fan-tahs'-mah], *m.* 1. Phantom, a fancied vision. 2. A vain, presumptuous man (presumido). 3. Image of some object which remains impressed on the mind. -*f.* 1. Ghost, Specter, apparition, a scarecrow to frighten simple folks. 2. *(Med.)* Lesion or defect of the visual organs.

fantasmada [fan-tahs-mah'-dah], *f.* Bluster, bravado.

fantasmagoría [fan-tahs-mah-go-ree'-ah], *f.* Phantasmagoria, an optical illusion.

fantasmagórico, ca [fan-tas-mah-go'-re-co, cah], *a.* Phantasmagoric.

fantasmal [fan-tahs'-mah], *a.* Ghostly; phantom.

fantasmón [fan-tas-mone'], *m. aug.* presumptuous coxcomb, a vain pretender.

fantásticamente [fan-tahs'-te-cah-men-tay], *adv.* Fantastically, fallaciously, pompously, conceitedly, grotesquely.

fantástico, ca [fan-tahs'-te-co, cah], *a.* 1. Fantastic, whimsical, fanciful (caprichoso). 2. Fantastic, imaginary. fantasied, subsisting only in the fancy. 3. Fantastic, unreal (extraño). 4. Fantastic, conceited, vain, presumptuous (vanidoso).

fantoche [fan-to-chay], *m.* 1. Puppet, marionette (muñeco). 2. Mediocrity, nonentity (mediocre); braggart (presumido).

faquín [fah-keen'], *m.* Porter, carrier.

faquir [fat-keer'], *m.* Fakir. *(Acad.)*

fara [fah'-rah], *f.* A kind of serpent of Africa.

farachar [fah-rah-char'], *va (Prov.)* To beat or clean hemp.

faralá [fah-rah-lah'], *m.* 1. Flounce. *V.* FARFALÁ, VUELO. 2. Rufflet, frill.

farallón [fah-ral-lyone'], *m. (Naut.)* Small rocky island in the sea.

faramalla [fah-rah-mahl'-lyah], *f.* Bluff, deceitful chatter. -*m.* & *f.* Bluffer, deceitful person.

faramallear [fah-rah-mahl-lyay-ar'], *va.* To tattle, to babble.

faramallero, faramallón [fah-rah-mal-lyay'-ro, lyon'], *m. (coll.)* Tattling, deceitful man, busybody.

farándula [fah-rahn'-doo-lah], *f.* 1. Profession of a low comedian. 2. Artful trick, stratagem; humbug (labia); pack of lies (mentiras); confidence trick (trampa); wicked gossip (chisme).

farandulero [far-ran-doo-lay'-ro], *m.* 1. Actor, player. 2. Idle tattler, deceitful talker (timador).

farandúlico, ca [fah-ran-doo'-le-co, ca], *a.* Relating to a low comedian.

faraón [fah-rah-on'], *m.* 1. Faro, game of cards. 2. An ancient dance. 3. Pharaoh, the scriptural name of Egyptian kings.

faraute [fah-rah'-oo-tay], *m.* 1. Messenger, he who carries messages. 2. *(coll.)* Principal manager or director. 3. *(coll.)* A noisy, meddling fellow. 4. Player who recites the prologue of a play.

farcinador [far-the-nah-dor'], *m. (Prov.)* One who stuffs or fills something.

farda [fahr'-dah], *f.* 1. A kind of tax or tribute formerly paid by foreigners in Spain. 2. Bundle of clothing. 3. Notch in a timber for joining with another.

fardacho [far-dah'-cho], *m. (Prov.) V.* LAGARTO.

fardada [far-dah'-dah], *f.* Show, display; piece of showmanship. **Pegarse una fardada**, to swank.

fardaje [far-dah'-hay], *m.* Luggage.

fardar [far-dar'], *va.* To furnish or supply with clothes. -*vn.* 1. To give tone, to be classy (objecto). **Es un coche que farda mucho**. it's a car with a lot of class. 2. To show off (persona). 3. To boast.

fardel [far-del'], *m.* 1. Bag, knapsack. 2. Parcel, bundle (bulto).

fardería [far-day-ree'-ah], *f.* A collection of bundles or packages, luggage. *V.* FARDAJE.

fardillo [far-deel'-lyo], *m. dim.* A small bundle, a parcel.

fardo [far'-do], *m.* Bale of goods, parcel, bundle, pack, package.

farellón [fah-rel-lyone'], *m.* 1. Point, cape, headland. 2. Rock, cliff in the sea.

farfalá [far-fah-lah'], *f.* Flounce, ornament of a gown or curtain; furbelow. *V.* VUELO.

farfallás [far-fal-lyahs'], *f. pl. (Bot. Prov.) V.* BARBAJAS.

farfalloso, sa [far-fal-lyo'-so, sah], *a. (Prov.)* Stammering.

farfán [far-fahn'], *m.* A name given to Christian horsemen who served Mohammedan princes.

farfante, farfantón [far-fahn'-tay, far-fan-tone'], *m.* A boasting babbler.

farfantonada, farfantonería [far-fan-to-nah'-dah], *f.* Idle boast.

fárfara [far'-fah-rah], *f.* 1. *(Bot.)* Colt's foot. 2. Membrane which covers the white of an egg.

farfulla [far-fool'-lyah], *m.* Mumbler, a stammering, talkative person (tartamudez).

farfulladamente [far-fool-lyah'-dah-men-tay], *adv.* Stammeringly.

farfullador, ra [far-fool-lyah-dor', rah], *m. & f.* Stammerer, mumbler, jabberer.

farfullar [far-foo-lyar'], *va.* 1. To talk quickly and stammeringly, to talk low and quick. 2. *(Met.)* To do in a hurry with confusion.

farfullero, ra [far-fool-lyay'-ro, rah], *a.* 1. Mumbling, talking unintelligibly 2. Hurried and confused in action.

fargallón, na [far-gal-lyone', nah], *a. & m. & f. (coll.)* Applied to those who are careless or dirty in their dress, and to those who do things hurriedly.

farináceo, [fah-re-nah-thay-o, ah], *a.* Farinaceous, mealy, starchy.

farinetas [fah-re-nay'-tas], *f. pl. (Prov.)* Fritters made of flour, honey, and water.

faringe [fah-reen'-hay], *f. (Anat.)* Pharynx.

faríngeo, gea [fah-reen'-hay-o, ah], *a.* Pharyngeal, relating to the pharynx.

faringitis [fah-rin-hee'-tis], *f. (Med.)* Pharingitis.

farisaico, ca [fah-re-sah'-e-co, cah], *a.* Pharisaical, pharisaic.

farisaismo [fah-re-sah-ees-mo], *m.* Pharisaism.

fariseo [fah-re-say'-o], *m.* 1. A Pharisee.

farmacéutico, ca [far-mah-thay' -oo-te-co, cah], *a.* Pharmaceutical.-*m.* Pharmacist.

farmacia [far-mah'-the-ah], *f.* 1. Pharmacy, the art of preparing medicines (ciencia). 2. Pharmacy, the shop where they are prepared and sold. 3. A collection of medications.

fármaco [far'-mah-co], *m. V* MEDICAMENTO.

farmacología [far-mah-co-lo-hee'-ah], *f.* Pharmacology, the knowledge of medicines.

farmacológico, ca [far-mah-co-lo'-he-co, cah], *a.* Pharmacological, relating to drugs.

farmacólogo [far-mah-co'-lo-go], *m.* Pharmacologist, a writer upon medicines.

farmacopea [far-mah-co-pay'-ah], *f.* Pharmacopoeia.

farmacópola [far-mah-co'-po-lah], *m. (coll.)* Apothecary, pharmaceutist, pharmacopolist.

farmacopólico, ca [far-mah-co-po'-le-co, cah] *a. (coll.)* Pharmaceutical, pharmaceutic.

farnero [far-nay'-ro], *m. (Prov.)* Receiver of rents.

faro [fah'-ro], *m.* 1. Pharos, a lighthouse (torre); beacon (señal). 2. *(Naut.)* Light, lantern; *(Aut.)* headlamp, headlight. **Faro antiniebla**, fog-lamp. **Faro piloto**, rear light.

farol [fah-ro-le'], *m.* 1. A lantern (linterna); headlamp. **Farol de la calle**, streetlamp. 2. Lamppost (farola); handstand (gimnasia). 3. Wrapping of tobacco packet (envase). 4. Swank (ostentación). **Echarse un farol**, to shoot a line. 5. Lie, fib (mentira). 6. Bluff (juego).

farola [fah-ro'-lah], *f.* A lantern of great size.

farolear [fah-ro-lay-ar'], *vn. (coll.)* To strut, to make an ostentatious parade.

farolero [fah-ro-lay'-ro], *m.* 1. One who makes lanterns. 2. Lamplighter. *(coll.) V.* FAROLÓN.

farolico [fah-ro-lee'-co], *m. dim.* Small lantern. **Farolico de jardín**, Indian heartseed, smooth-leaved heartseed.

farolillo, ito [fah-ro-leel'-lyo, ee'to], *m. dim.* Small lantern. **Farolillo de jardín**, *(Bot.) V.* FAROLICO DE JARDÍN.

farolón [fah-ro-lone'], *m.* 1. *(Coll.)* A boasting person 2. *(Aug.)* A large lantern.

farota [fah-ro-tah], *f. (Prov.)* A brazen-faced woman, without sense or judgment.

farotón [fah-roh-tone'] *m. (Prov.)* A brazen-faced, stupid fellow.

farotona [fah-roh-to'-nah], *f.* Tall slovenly woman.

farpa [far'-pah], *f. pl.* Any of the notches, hollows, or segments of circles marked on the edge of a thing.

farpado, da [far-pah'-do, dah], *a.* Scalloped, notched.

farra [far'-rah], *f. (Zool.)* A kind of salmon.

farra [far-rah], *f.* 1. Spree, party, carousal (juerga). **Ir de juerga**, to go on a spree. 2. Mockery, teasing (mofa).

fárrago [far'-rah-go], or **farrago** [far-rah'-go], *m.* Farrago, a confused mass of ingredients; a medley.

farraguista [far-rah-gees'-tah], *m.* A pedantic scholar; one vain of useless learning.

farro [far'-ro], *m.* 1. Peeled barley, barley freed from the husk. 2. A sort of husked wheat.

farropea [far-ro-pay'-ah], *f. (Prov.) V.* ARROPEA.

farruco [far-roo'-co], *a.* Pig-headed (agresivo).

farsa [far'-sah], *f.* 1. Farce, a ludicrous dramatical composition, or representation 2. Company of players.

farsanta [far-sahn'-tah], *f.* An actress.

farsante [far-sahn'-tay], *m.* 1. An actor, a player. 2. A pretender, a deceiver.

farsista [far-sees'-tah], *com.* A writer of farces.

fartal, farte [far-tahl, far-tay], *m. (Prov.)* Fruit-tart or pie.

fartriquera [far-tre-kay'-rah], *f. (Prov.) V.* FALTRIQUERA.

fas(por), o por nefas [por fas oh por nay'-fas], *adv.* Justly or unjustly.

fascal [fas-cahl'], *m. (Prov.)* Shock, a pile of sheaves of corn.

fasciculado, da [fas-the-coo-lah'-do, dah], *a.* Fasciculate, composed of or growing in bundles.

fascicular [fas-the-coo-lar'], *a. (Bot.)* Fascicular, disposed in bundles.

fascículo [fas-thee'-coo-lo], *m.* 1. A bundle, armful, the quantity of plants which may be carried under the arm. 2. Fascicle, a number of printed sheets stitched together.

fascinación [fas-the-nah-the-on'], *f.* 1. Fascination, the power or act of bewitching; enchantment. 2. Imposition, deceit.

fascinador, ra [fas-the-nah-dor, rah], *m. & f.* Fascinator, charmer. *-a.* Fascinating.

fascinante [fas-the-nahn'-tay], *pa. & m,* ×*& f.* Fascinator, fascinating.

fascinar [fas-the-nar'], *va.* 1. To fascinate, to bewitch (hechizar), to enchant. 2. To deceive, to impose upon.

fascismo [fas-thees'-mo], *m.* Fascism.

fascista [fas-thees'-tah], *a. & m. & f.* Fascist.

fase [fah'-say], *f:* 1. (*Ast.*) Phase of the moon or planets. 2. (*Dep.*) Half. **Estar en fase ascendente**, to be on one's way up.

fasma [fahs'-mah], *f.* (*Zool.*) Walking stick, phasma.

fásoles [fah'-so-les], *m. pl.* Kidney-beans, haricots.

fastbus [fast-boos], *m.* Fastbus.

fastial [fas-te-ahl'], *m.* Pyramid placed on the top of an edifice.

fastidiar [fas-te-de-ar'], *va.* 1. To excite, to disgust. 2. To look on with dislike or abhorrence (dar asco a). 3. To grate, to offend by something harsh or vexatious. 4. To annoy, to bother, to vex (molestar); to bore (aburrir). **Eso me fastidia terriblemente**, it annoys me no end. *-vr.* 1. To loathe, to feel disgust or abhorrence, to weary, to be weary (aburrirse). 2. To suffer damage or loss. 3. To get cross (enojarse). **¡Para que te fastidies!** so there!

fastidio [fas-tee'-de-o], *m.* 1. Squeamishness, arising from a weak or disordered stomach, or from a bad smell. 2. Weariness, lassitude, fatigue, ennui. 3. Distaste, disgust, fastidiousness (molestia). 4. Disgust, repugnance (asco). 5. Loathing.

fastidiosamente [fas-te-de-o-sah-men'-tay], *adv.* Fastidiously.

fastidioso, sa [fas-te-de-o'-so, sah], *a.* 1. Fastidious, squeamish, delicate to a vice. 2. Loathsome, nauseous, mawkish, 3. Tedious, livelong (aburrido). 4. Disdainful, disgusted (asqueroso).

fastigio [fas-tee'-he-o], *m.* (*Arch.*) 1. Pinnacle, the top of anything which ends in a point. 2. The top of trees. 3. Summit, meridian.

fasto [fahs'-to], *m.* 1. Haughtiness, pride. 2. Splendor, pageantry, pomp, grandeur.

fastosamente [fas-to-sah-men'-tay], *adv.* Pompously, gaudily, magnificently.

fastoso, fastuoso, sa [fas-to'-so, fas-too-o' so, sah], *a.* Proud, haughty, ostentatious: gaudy.

fatal [fah-tahl'] *a.* 1. Fatal, ominous, proceeding by destiny. 2. Fatal(mortal), deadly, mortal, destructive. 3. Unfortunate. 3. Irrevocable; unavoidable (inevitable). 4. Awful, ghastly, rotten (horrible). **Tiene un inglés fatal**, he speaks awful English.

fatalidad [fah-tah-le-dahd'] *f.* 1. Fatality, predetermined order of things and events (destino). 2. Fatality, tendency to danger, mischance, ill luck, ill fortune (desdicha).

fatalismo [fah-tah-lees'mo], *m.* Fatalism.

fatalista [fah-tah-lees'-tah], *m.* Fatalist, predestinarian.

fatalmente [fah-tal-men'-tay], *adv.* Fatally, ominously.

fatídicamente [fah-tee'-de-cah-men-tay], *adv.* 1. Prophetically. 2. Fatefully, ominously.

fatídico, ca [fah-tee'-de-co, cah], *a.* Fatidical, prophetic of gloom (profético). 2. Fateful (de mal agüero).

fatiga [fah-tee'-gah], *f.* 1. Toil, hard labor, fatigue, lassitude (cansancio). 2. Hardship oppression. 3. Anguish, grief, painfulness, importunity. **Fatiga cerebral**, mental fatigue.

fatigadamente [fah-te-gah-dah-men'-tay], *adv.* With difficulty.

fatigador, ra [fah-te-gah-dor', rah], *m. & f.* Molester.

fatigar [fah-te-gar'], *va.* 1. To fatigue, to tire (cansar), to molest (molestar), to weary, to harass, to gall. 2. To desolate

or lay waste by warlike incursion or invasion. *-vr.* To tire or be tired, to fail with weariness.

fatigosamente [fah-te-go-sah-men-tay]. *adv.* Painfully, wearisomely, tediously.

fatigoso, sa [fah-te-go'-so, sah], *a.* 1. Tiresome (molesto), troublesome. 2. Anxious, painful. 3. Tiring, exhausting, fatiguing (que cansa).

fatuidad [fah-too-e-dahd'], *f.* 1. Fatuity, foolishness, weakness of mind. 2. A stupid speech, a foolish action.

fatuo, tua [fah'-too-o, ah], *a.* Fatuous (necio), stupid, foolish, coxcombical, foppish, conceited (vanidoso), crazy.

fauces [fah'-oo-thes], *f. pl.* Fauces, gullet.

fauna [fah'-oo-nah], *f.* 1. Fauna, the whole of the animals belonging to a region or country. 2. A work in which these are described.

fausto, ta [fah'-oos-to, tah], *a.* Happy, fortunate, prosperous, successful.

fausto [fah'-oos-to], *m.* Splendor, pomp, pageantry, ostentation, gaudiness, gaiety; grandeur, greatness; luxury.

faustoso sa [fah-oos-to'-so, sah], *a.* Fastuous, haughty, proud, ostentatious, gaudy.

fautor, ra [fah-oo-tor', rah], *m. & f.* Countenancer, abetter, furtherer, favorer, supporter.

fautoría [fa-oo-to-ree'-ah], *f.* Aid, favor, auxiliary.

favo [fah'-vo], *m.* (*Med.*) V. AVISPERO. Favus; carbuncle.

favonio [fah-vo-ne-o], *m.* Westerly wind, zephyr.

favor [fah-vor'], *m.* 1. Favor, protection, support (apoyo), countenance, help. 2. Favor, kindness granted, good turn, gift (regalo), grace (gracia); comfort. 3. Compliment, an expression of civility and kindness. 4. Favor, love-favor, something given by a lady to be worn. **A favor de**, on behalf of, on account of. **Por favor**, please. **Haga el favor de no fumar**, please be so good as to refrain from smoking. **Estar en favor**, to be in favor. **A favor de la marea**, helped by the tide. **Gozar del favor de alguien**, to be in somebody's favor. **Tener algo en su favor**, to have something in one's favor.

favorable [fah-vo-rah'-blay], *a.* Favorable, advantageous, propitious, kind, friendly, gracious.

favorablemente [fah-vo-rah-blay-men'-tay], *adv.* Favorably.

favorcillo [fah-vor-theel'-lyo], *m. dim.* A small favor.

favorecedor, ra [fah-vo-ray-thay-dor', rah], *m. & f.* Favorer, countenancer, friend, helper, well-wisher.

favorecer [fah-vo-ray-therr'], *va.* 1. To favor, to protect, to help (amparar), to countenance, to accredit, to abet. 2. To grant favors. **Favorecerse de alguno o de alguna cosa**, to avail oneself of a person's favor or support, or of any other kind of protection. *-vr.* To help one another. (*Yo favorezco, yo favorezca,* from *Favorecer. V.* ABORRECER.)

favoritismo [fah-vo-tees'-mo], *m.* Favoritism, nepotism.

favorito, ta [fah-vo-ree'-to, tah], *a.* Favorite, beloved, regarded with favor, darling.

favorito, ta [fah-vo-ree'-to, tah], *m. & f.* 1. Favorite, one chosen as a companion by a superior. 2. Favorite, court minion. 3. Favorite, darling. fondling.

fax [fax], *m.* Fax.

fayado [fah-yah'-do], *m.* (*Prov.*) A small garret or lumberroom.

fayanca [fah-yahn'-cah], *f.* Position of the body, in which it does not stand firm and steady.

fayanco [fah-yahn'-co], *m.* A flat basket made of osier.

faz [fath], *f.* 1. Face. *V.* ROSTRO. 2. Front, the fore part of a building or any other thing. *V.* HAZ. **Faz a faz**, face to face. **A prima faz**, at first sight.

fe [fay], *f.* 1. Faith, belief of the revealed truths of religion. 2. Faith, trust in God. 3. Faith, testimony, credit, credence, confidence, trust. 4. Promise given. 5. Assertion, asseveration. 6. Certificate (certificado), testimony. **Dar fe**, to attest, to certify. **Poseedor de buena fe**, a bona fide possessor, one who thinks himself the right owner, although he is not. **De buena fe**, with truth and sincerity. **A fe**, in truth, in good earnest. **A fe mía** or **por mi fe**, upon my honor. **A la buena fe**, with candor and sincerity without malice. **En fe,** consequently. **De mala fe,** craftily, deceitfully, cunningly, fallaciously. **Fe de bautismo,** certificate of baptism.

fea [fay-ah], *f.* Ugly woman, plain girl. **Ser la fea del baile,** to be a wallflower.

fealdad [fay-al-dahd'], *f.* 1. Ugliness, deformity; disproportion of the parts which compose a whole. 2. Homeliness; hard favoredness: hideousness. 3. *(Met.)* Turpitude, dishonesty, foulness, moral depravity.

feamente [fay-ah-men'-tay], *adv.* 1. Uglily, deformedly. 2. *(Met.)* Brutally, inordinately.

feazo, za [fay-ah-tho, thah], *a. aug.* Very ugly or deformed.

febeo, bea [fay-bay'-o, ah], *a. (Poet.)* Relating to Phoebus, or the sun.

feble [fay'-blay], *a.* 1. Weak, faint, feeble. 2. Among jewellers, mintmen, and silversmiths, deficient in weight or quality (plata, diamantes).

feble [fay'-blay], *m.* Light money or coin.

feblemente [fay-blay-men'-tay], *adv.* Feebly.

febo [fay-bo], *m. (Poet.)* Phoebus, the sun.

febrero [fay-bray'-ro], *m.* February.

febricitante [fay-bre-the-tahn'-tay], *a. V.* CALENTURIENTO.

febrífugo. ga [fay-bree'-foo-go, gah], *a.* Febrifuge: also used as a substantive.

febril [fay-breel'], *a.* Febrile.

fecal [fay-cahl'], *a.* Feculent, excrementitious, fecal.

fécula [fay'-coo-lah], *f.* Fecula, a substance obtained by bruising vegetables in water; starch.

feculencia [fay-coo-len'-the-ah], *f.* Feculence, dregs, lees.

feculento. ta [fay-coo-len'-to, tah], or **feculoso, sa,** *a.* Feculent, foul, dreggy.

fecundación [fay-coon-dah-the-on'], *f.* Fecundation, making fruitful or prolific.

fecundamente [fay-coon-dah-men'-tay], *adv.* Fertilely, fruitfully.

fecundante [fay-coon-dahn'-tay], *a. & pa.* Fructifying, making fruitful.

fecundar [fay-coon-dar'], *va.* To fertilize, to make fruitful, to fructify.

fecundativo, va [fay-coon-dah-tee'-vo, vah], *a.* Fertilizing, fructifying.

fecundidad [fay-coon-de-dahd'], *f.* Fecundity, fertility, fruitfulness.

fecundizar [fay-coon-de-thar], *va.* To fecundate, to fertilize, to fructify.

fecundo, da [fay-coon'-do, dah], *a.* 1. Fecund, fruitful, fertile, prolific. 2. *(Fig.)* Fruitful; copious (copioso), abundant; productive (productivo). **Fecundo de palabras,** fluent. **Un libro fecundo en ideas,** a book full of ideas.

fecha [fay'-chah], *f.* Date of a letter or other writing. **Fecha tope,** closing date. **A partir de esta fecha,** from today. **En fecha próxima,** soon. **¿Cuál es la fecha de hoy?** What is the date today? **El año pasado por estas fechas,** this time last year.

fechar [fay-char'], *va.* To date, to put the date to a letter or other writing.

fecho [fay'-cho], *m.* **Fecho de azúcar,** chest of sugar, containing not more than twelve *arrobas* or about three hundredweight.

fecho, cha [fay'-cho, chah], *pp. irr.* of FACER. Hecho.

fechoría [fay-cho-ree'-ah], *f.* Misdeed, misdemeanor. **Cometer fechorías,** to commit misdeeds; mischief. **Los niños hicieron fechorías,** the children got up to mischief.

fechuría [fay-choo-re'-ah], *f. V.* FECHORÍA.

federación [fay-day-rah-the-on'], *f.* Federation, confederated.

federado [fay-day-rah'-do], *m.* Federate. *a.* Federate, federated.

federal [fay-day-rahl'], *a.* Federal.

federalismo [fay-day-rah-lees-mo], *m.* Federalism, political autonomy of various provinces or states.

federativo, va [fay-day-rah-tee'-vo, vah], *a.* Federative.

fehaciente [fay-ah-the-en'-tay], *a.* Authentic.

feldespato, or **feldspato** [fel-des-pah'-to, or fel-des-pah'-to], *m.* Feldspar, a common constituent of rocks; silicate of aluminum and an alkali.

feldmariscal [feld-mah-ris-cahl'], *m. (Gil.)* Fieldmarshal.

felice [fay-lee'-thay], *a. (Poet.) V.* FELIZ.

felicidad [fay-le-the-dahd'], *f.* Felicity, happiness (alegría), success, luckiness, blissfulness, blessedness, prosperity. **Felicidades, best** wishes, congratulations. **Os deseo toda clase de felicidades, I** wish you every kind of happiness. **La curva de la felicidad,** potbelly.

felicitación [fay-le-the-tah-the-on] *f.* Congratulation, felicitation, professing, joy for the happiness or success of another.

felicitar [fay-le-the-tar'], *va.* To congratulate, to compliment upon any happy event, to felicitate.

feligrés, sa [fay-le-grays', sah], *m. & f.* Parishioner, one who belongs to a parish.

feligresía [fay-le-gray-see'-ah], *f.* District of a parish, and the inhabitants of the same.

felino [fay-le'-no], *a.* Feline, cat-like.

feliz [fay-leeth'], *a.* Happy, fortunate, lucky (afortunado), prosperous, felicitous, **Y vivieron felices,** and they lived happily. **La cosa tuvo un final feliz,** the affair had a happy ending. **¡Feliz Año Nuevo!** Happy New Year! **Feliz** desenlace; happy ending. **¡Feliz viaje!** have a good journey!

felizmente [fay-leeth'-men-tay], *adv.* Happily, fortunately, luckily, felicitously.

felonía [fay-lo-nee'-ah], *f.* Treachery, disloyalty, felony.

felpa [fayl'-pah], *f.* 1. Plush. a silk stuff. 2. In jocular style, a good drubbing.

felpado, da [fel-pah'-do, dah], *a.* Shaggy, villous.

felpilla [fel-peel-lyah], *f.* Corded silk for embroidering; chenille.

felposo, sa [fel-po'-so, sah], *a.* 1. Felted, with interlaced fibres. 2. Plush-covered.

felpudo [fel-poo'-do], *m.* Mat. doormat (alfombrilla).

felpudo, da [fel-poo'-do, dah], *a.* Plushy, velvety. *V.* FELPADO.

femenil [fay-may-neel'], *a.* Feminine, womanish, womanly.

femenilmente [fay-may-neel'-men-tay], *adv.* Falsely, fallaciously.

femenino, na [fay-may-nee'-no, nah], *a.* 1. Feminine, belonging to women, female (sexo). 2. Feminine, of the feminine gender. **Equipo femenino,** women's team. **Del género femenino,** of the feminine gender.

fementídamente [fay-men-tee'-dah-men-tay], *adv.* Falsely, fallaciously.

fementido, da [fay-men-tee'-do, dah], *a.* False, unfaithful, deficient in the performance of one's promise.

feminidad [fay-me-ne-dahd'], *f.* Femininity.

feminismo [fay-me-nees'-mo], *m.* Feminism, women's liberation.

feminista [fay-me-nees'-tah], *a. & m. & f.* Feminist.

femoral [fay-mo-rahl'], *a.* Femoral, belonging to the thighs.

fémur [fay'-mor], *m.* Femur.

fenacetina [fay-nah-thay-tee'-nah], *f. (Med.)* Phenacetin.

fenda [fen'-dah], *f.* A crack in the bark of trees.

fendiente [fen-de-en'-tay], *m.* Gash, a deep cut or wound.

fenecer [fay-nay-therr'], *vn.* 1. To terminate, to be at an end (terminar). 2. To degenerate, to decline. 3. To die (morir). - *va.* To finish, to conclude, to close. (*Yo fenezco, yo fenezca,* from *Fenecer. V.* ABORRECER.)

fenecimiento [fay-nay-the-me-en'-to], *m.* 1. Close, finish, termination, end. 2. Settling of an account. 3. Dying.

fenedal [fay-nay-dahl'], *m. (Prov.)* Hay-loft.

fenicio, cia [fay-nee'-the-o, ah], *a.* Phoenician.

fénico [fay'-ne-co], *a.* Phenic, carbolic. **Ácido fénico,** Phenol, carbolic acid.

fénix [fay'-nix], *m.* 1. Phoenix, fabulous bird. 2. *(Met.)* That which is exquisite or unique of its kind.

fenol [fay-nole'], *n.* Phenol, carbolic acid.

fenomenal [fay-no-may-nahl'], *a.* 1. Phenomenal. 2. Tremendous, terrific (estupendo).

fenomenalismo [fay-no-may-nah-lees'-mo], *m.* Phenomenalism, materialism, a doctrine which gives importance only to what can affect our senses.

fenomenalmente [fay-no-may-nal'-men-tay], *adv.* Terrifically.

fenómeno [fay-no'-may-no], *m.* Phenomenon. -*a.* Great, marvelous. **Una chica fenómena,** a smashing girl. -*adv.* **Lo hemos pasado fenómeno,** we had a terrific time.

feo, ea [fay' -o, ah], *a.* 1. Ugly, deformed, hideous (aspecto), haggard, grim: homely. **Más feo que Picio,** as ugly as sin. 2. Causing horror or adversion. 3. Bad, nasty (olor); dirty (jugada); nasty, awful (tiempo); nasty (situación). **Eso es muy feo,** that's nasty. **Esto se está poniendo feo,** this is beginning to look bad, -*m.* Insult, slight, **Hacer un feo a uno,** to insult somebody.

feracidad [fay-rah-the-dahd'], *f.* Feracity, fecundity, fruitfulness, fertility.

feral [fay-rahl'], *a.* Cruel, bloodthirsty.

feraz [fay-rath'], *a.* 1. Fertile, fruitful, feracious, 2. Abundant, copious, plentiful.

féretro [fay'-ray-tro], *m.* Bier, coffin, hearse.

feria [fay-re-ah], *f.* 1. Any day of the week, exempting Saturday and Sunday. 2. Fair, an annual or stated meeting of sellers and buyers (mercado). 3. Rest, repose. 4. Carnival (carnaval). **Feria de libros,** book fair. **Feria de muestras,** trade show. 5. Holiday (descanso). 6. Fun fair.

feriado, da [fay-re-ah'-do, dah], *a.* **Día feriado,** a holiday. -*pp.* of FERIAR.

ferial [fay-re-ahl'], *a.* 1. Belonging to fairs. 2. Ferial, relating to the days of the week. -*m. & f.* Market, fair.

feriante [fay-re-ahn'-tay], *m. (Prov.)* One who trades at fairs (vendedor).

feriar [fay-re-ar'], *va.* 1. To sell, to buy; to exchange one thing for another (comerciar). 2. To give fairings, to make presents at a fair. 3. *V.* SUSPENDER.

ferino, na [fay-ree'-no, nah], *a.* Ferine, wild, savage, ferocious.

fermata [fer-mah'-tah], *f. (Mus.)* A pause or hold.

fermentación [fer-men-tah-the-on'], *f.* Fermentation.

fermentar [fer-men-tar'], *vn. & vn.* To ferment. **Hacer fermentar,** to ferment or to cause to ferment, to heat.

fermentativo, va [fer-men-tah-tee'-vo, vah], *a.* Fermentative.

fermentescible [fer-men-tes-thee'-blay], *a.* Fermentable, capable of fermentation.

fermento [fer-men'-to], *m.* 1. Ferment. 2. Leaven, leavening. 3. Ferment, intestine motion, tumult.

fernambuco [fer-nah-mboo-'co], *m.* A dyewood of Brazil.

fernandina [fer-nan-dee'-nah], *f.* Kind of linen.

ferocidad [fay-ro-the-dahd'], *f.* Ferocity, wildness, ferociousness, fierceness, savageness, fury.

feróstico, ca [fay-ros'-te-co, cah], *a. (coll.)* Irritable, wayward.

feroz [fay-roth'], *a.* Ferocious, cruel, savage, fierce, ravenous, heathenish. **El lobo feroz,** the big bad wolf. **Tener un hambre feroz,** to be ravenous.

ferozmente [fay-roth-men'-tay], *adv.* Ferociously, folly, savagely.

ferrada [fer-rah'-dah], *f.* Iron club, used formerly as an offensive and defensive weapon.

ferrado [fer-rah'-do], *m. (Prov.)* 1. Measure for corn, which makes about the fourth part of a bushel. 2. Measure for land of twelve yards square.

ferrar [fer-rar'], *va.* 1. To garnish with points of iron; to strengthen with iron plates. 2. *V.* HERRAR.

férreo, rea [fer-ray-o, ah], *a.* 1. Ferreous, made of iron or containing iron. 2. Iron (época). 3. Iron, harsh, stern, severe. 4. *(Ferro.)* Rail. **Volutad férrea,** iron will. **Vía férrea,** railroad.

ferrería [fer-ray-ree'-ah], *a.* Iron works, where iron is manufactured.

ferrete [fer-ray'-tay], *m.* 1. Burnt copper or brass used to color glass. 2. Marking-iron.

ferretear [fer-ray-tay-ar'], *va.* To bind, to fasten, to mark, or work with iron.

ferretería [fer-ray-tay-ree-ah], *f.* Hardware store, ironmongery (objetos).

ferretero, ra [fer-ray-tay'-ro], *m & f.* Ironmonger, hardware dealer.

férrico, ca [fer'-re-co, cah], *a.* 1. Ferric, containing iron. 2. Ferric, pertaining to iron in its higher combinations.

férridos, das [fer'-re-dos, das], *a. pl.* Simple bodies whose type is iron.

ferro [fer'-ro], *m. (Naut.)* Anchor.

ferrocarril [fer-ro-car-reel'], *m.* Railroad, railway. **Ferrocarril funicular,** cable railroad. **Ferrocarril subterráneo,** subway. **Ferrocarril de vía estrecha,** narrow-gauge railroad.

ferrocarrilero, ra [fer-ro-car-re-lay'-ro, rah], *a.* Railway. -*m.* Railroad man, railroad worker.

ferrón [fer-rone'], *m. (Prod.)* 1. Iron manufacturer. 2. Ironmonger.

ferroso, sa [fer-ro'-so, sah], *a.* Ferrous, obtained from iron, pertaining to iron in its lower combinations.

ferrotipia [fer-ro-tee'-pe-ah], *f.* Tintype, ferrotype.

ferroviario, ria [fer-ro-ve-ah'-re-o, re-ah], *a.* Railroad, pertaining to a railroad. -*a.* Railroadman, railroad employee.

ferrugiento, ta [fer-roo-he-en'-to, tah], *a.* Irony, belonging to or containing iron.

ferrugíneo, nea [fer-roo-hee'-nay-o, ah], *a.* Ferruginous.

ferruginoso, sa [fer-roo-he-no'-so, sah], *a.* Ferruginous.

ferry [fer'-ree], *m.* Ferry.

fértil [fayr'-teel], *a.* Fertile, fruitful, copious, plentiful, fertile (imaginación).

fertilidad [fer-te-le-dahd'], *f.* Fertility, copiousness, plenty, fruitfulness.

fertilizantes [fer-te-le-thahn'-tess], *m. pl.* Fertilizers, fertilizing agents.

fertilizar [fer-te-le-thar'], *va.* To fertilize, to fructify, to make the soil fruitful.

fértilmente [fayr'-teel-men-tay], *adv.* Fertilely.

férula [fay'-roo-lah], *f.* 1. Ferule (del maestro), cane. 2. *(Met.)* Rule, yoke, authority 3. *(Bot.)* Ferula, a genus of umbelliferous plants.

feruláceo, ea [fay-roo-lah'-thay-o, ah], *a.* Like a ferule.

ferventísimo, fervientísimo [fer-ven-tee'-se-mo, mah], *a. sup.* Fervent, ardent in piety, warm in zeal.

férvido, da [fayr'-ve-do, dah], *a.* Fervid, ardent.

ferviente [fer-ve-en'-tay], *a.* Fervent, ardent. *V.* FERVOROSO.

fervor [fer-vor'], *m.* 1. Fervor, violent heat, warmth. 2. Fervor, fervidness, zeal, ardor, eagerness. 3. Fervor, fervency, ardor of piety.

fervorizar [fer-vo-re-thar'], *va.* To heat, to inflame, to incite.

fervorosamente [fer-vo-ro-sah-men' -tay], *adv.* Fervently, ardently.

fervoroso, sa [fer-vo-ro'-so, sah], *a.* Fervent, ardent in piety, warm in zeal; active, officious.

festejador, ra [fes-tay-hah-dor', rah], *m. & f.* Feaster, courtier, entertainer.

festejar [fes-tay-har'], *va.* 1. To entertain, to feast (persona). 2. To court, to woo (mujer), to make love. 3. To celebrate or solemnize an event (aniversario, ocasión etc).

festejo, festeo [fes-tay'-ho, fes-tay'-ho], *m.* 1. An expression of joy for the happiness of another. 2. *(Coll.)* Courtship, solicitation of a woman in marriage (cortejo). 3. Feast, entertainment (fiesta). 4. Obsequiousness. **Hacer festejos a uno,** to make a great fuss of somebody.

festero [fes-tay'-ro], *m.* Director of church music on festive occasions.

festín [fes-teen'], *m.* Feast, entertainment, banquet.

festinación [fes-te-nah-the-on'], *f.* Speed, haste, hurry.

festival [fes-te-vahl'], *m. (Neol.)* Festival, a great vocal and instrumental concert.

festivamente [fes-te-vah-men'-tay], *adv.* Festively, wittily, jovially.

festividad [fes-te-ve-dahd'], *f.* 1. Festivity, rejoicing, gaiety, merrymaking (actos). 2. Solemn manner of celebrating an event.

festivo, va [fes-tee'-vo, vah], *a.* 1. Festive, gay, joyful, light-hearted (alegre). 2. Festival, festal, pertaining to feasts. 3. Witty, facetious, humorous (gracioso). **Día festivo,** a holiday.

festón [fes-tone'], *m.* 1. Garland, wreath of flowers. 2. Festoon.

festonear [fes-to-nay-ar'], *va.* To embellish with festoons.

festuca [fes-too'-cah], *f. (Bot.) V.* CAÑUELA. Fescue-grass, valuable for pasturage.

fetal [fay-tahl'], *a.* Foetal.

fetichismo [fay-te-chees'-mo], *m.* Fetishism.

fetichista [fay-te-chees'-tah], *m & f.* Fetishistic.

fétido, da [fay'-te-do, dah], *a.* Fetid, stinking, foul-smelling.

feto [fay'-to], *m.* 1. *(Bio.)* Foetus. 2. Abortion, monster (monstruo).

feúcho, cha [fay-oo'-cho, chah], *a.* Ugly, repulsive.

feudal [fay-oo-dahl'], *a.* Feudal, feodal.

feudalidad [fay-oo-dah-le-dahd'], *f.* Feodality, feudality.

feudalismo [fay-oo-dah-lees'-mo], *m.* Feudalism.

feudar [fay-oo-dahr'], *va. V.* ENFEUDAR.

feudatario [fey-oo-dah-tah'-re-o], *m.* Feudatary, feodatary.

feudatario, ria [fay-oo-dah-tah'-re-o, ah], *a.* Feudatary, feudary.

feudista [fay-oo-dees'-ah], *m.* Feudist, a writer upon feudal law.

feudo [fay'-oo-do], *m.* 1. Fief, all lands or tenements held by acknowledgment of a superior lord, feod, feud, manor. 2. Tribute or rent paid to a feudal lord.

fez [feth]. *m.* Fez, a woollen cap, white or red, used in the Orient and in Northern Africa.

fiabilidad [fe-ah-be-le-dahd'], *f.* Reliability, trustworthiness; credibility.

fiable [fe-ah'-blay], *a.* Trustworthy, reliable.

fiado, da [fe-ah'-do-dah], *a & pp.* of FIAR. Confident, trusting. **Al fiado,** upon trust. **En fiado,** upon bail. **Comprar géneros, al fiado,** to buy goods on credit. **Dar fiado,** to give credit.

fiador, ra [fe-ah-dor', rah], *m. & f.* 1. One who trusts another. 2. Bondsman, guarantor, surety, one who becomes security for another. *m.* 3. The loop of a cloak. 4. *(Falcon.)* Creance. 5. Bolt or instrument with which something is made fast; stop, catch, safety catch, ratchet, detent, tumbler of a lock.

fiambrar [fe-am-brar'], *va.* To boil or roast meat, and leave it to cool for eating.

fiambre [fe-ahm'-bray], *m,* 1. Cold meat preserved for use. 2. Corpse, stiff (cadáver). **El pobre está fiambre,** the poor chap is stone dead. 3. *-a.* 1. Cold (carne). 2. *(coll.)* Of a long standing.

fiambrera [fe-am-bray'-rah], *f.* 1. Pannier or basket in which cold meat is carried into the country (canasto). 2. *(coll.)* Stupid or foolish speech.

fiambrero [fe-am-bray'-ro], *m.* One who takes care of the larder, or of the cold meat preserved for use.

fiancilla [fe-an-theel'-lyah], *f.* Binding ring of a carriage.

fianza [fe-ahn'-thah], *f.* 1. Caution, guarantee, security given for the performance of engagements (garantía). 2. Reversion. 3. Bond, security. **Fianza bancaria,** bank security given in Rome to insure pensions charged on ecclesiastical works. **Dar fianza,** to give bail or a pledge. **Bajo fianza,** on bail.

fiar [fe-ar'], *va.* 1. To bail, to give bail. 2. To trust, to sell upon trust to give credit. 3. To place confidence in another, to commit to another, to credit. *-vn,* To confide, to be sure of a thing. **Ser de fiar,** to be reliable. *-vr.* **Fiarse de uno,** to trust somebody. **No me fío de él,** I don't trust him:

fiasco [fe-ahs'-co], *m.* Failure. **Hacer fiasco,** to result in humiliating failure (teatro).

fíat [fee'-at], *m,* Fiat, blessing. **Dar el fíat,** to give one's blessing.

fibra [fee'-brah], *f.* 1. Fiber, filament, staple. **Fibra artificial,** man-made fiber. 2. Fiber, a delicate root. 3. *(Met.)* Energy of character, firmeness, vigor. **Despertar la fibra sensible,** to strike a sympathetic cord. 4. *(Min.)* Vein of ore.

fibrazón [fe-brah-thone'], *f.* The whole of the ore-veins of a mine.

fibrila [fe-bree'-lah], *f. (Bot.)* Fibril, a capillary rootlet.

fibrilar [fe-bre-lar'], *a.* Fibrillar, disposed in fibrils or fine fibers.

fibrina [fe-bree'-nah], *f. (Chem.)* Fibrin, fibrine.

fibrinoso, sa [fe-bro-no'-so, sah], *a.* Fibrinous.

fibroso, sa [fe-bro'-so, sah], *a.* 1. Fibrous. 2. Energetic, firm, or vigorous in character.

ficción [fic-the-on'], *f.* 1. Fiction, the act of feigning or inventing. 2. Fiction, figment, an invention, and the thing feigned or invented. 3. Fiction, falsehood, lie. 4. Grimace, gesture. 6. Stratagem, artifice.

fice [fee'-thay], *m. (Zool.)* Whiting.

ficha [fee'-chah], *f.* 1. Counter, used in reckoning (en juegoes); chip (póquer); *(Com. Fin.)* token, tally. **Ficha del dominé,** domino. 2. Card (tarjeta); registration form (hotel). **Ficha policíaca,** police record.

fichaje [fee-chah'-hay], *m.* 1. *(Dep.)* Signing-up (nuevo jugador). 2. **Buenos fichajes,** new good players, new supporters.

fichar [fee-chahr'], *va.* 1. To file, to index (ficha). 2. To file the personal (persona); to record (dato). **Le tenemos fichado,** we have his record. 3. To play (dominó). 4. To sign up (deporte).

fichero [fe-chay-ro], *m.* File (informática); filling cabinet. **Fichero fotográfico de delincuentes,** photographic records of criminals.

ficticio, cia [fee-tee'-the-o, ah], *a.* Fictitious.

ficto, ta [feec'c-to, tah], *a.* 1. Feigned, counterfeited 2. Vain, useless, of no value.

fidedigno, na [fe-day-deeg'-no], *a.* Worthy or credit, deserving of belief.

fideicomisario [fe-day-e-co-me-sah'-re-o], *m.* Trustee, fiduciary, one who holds something in trust for another.

fideicomiso [fe-day-e-co-mee'-so], *m.* Trusteeship of any executor.

fidelidad [fe-day-le-dahd'], *f.* 1. Fidelity (lealtad), honesty, veracity, faith, constancy, honor. 2. Fidelity, faithful adherence, fealty, loyalty. 3. Punctuality in the execution or performance of anything. 4. Accuracy (exactitud). 5. *(Rad.)* **Alta fidelidad,** high fidelity.

fidelísimo, ma [fe-day-lee'-se-mo, mah], *a. aug.* of FIEL.

fideos [fe-day'-os], *m. pl.* Vermicelli, noodles, spaghetti.

fiducial [fe-do-the-ahl'], *a.* 1. *(Math.)* Passing through the center of graduation, referring to a fixed line. 2. Belonging to faith or credit.

fiduciario, ria [fe-doo-the-ah'-re-o, ah], *-a.* Fiduciary, belonging to a position of trust or confidence.

fiebre [fe-ay'-bray], *f.* Fever. **Fiebre amarilla,** yellow fever. **Fiebre mediterránea or de Malta,** undulant fever. **Fiebre del oro,** gold rush. **Tener fiebre,** to have a temperature.

fiebrecilla [fe-ay-bray-theel'-lyah], *f. dim.* Feveret. *V.* CALENTURILLA.

fiel [fe-ayl'], *a.* 1. Faithful, honest (fiable), loyal, upright. 2. True, right. 3. Faithful, observant of compact or promise.

fiel [fe-ayl'], *m.* 1. Inspector, supervisor (verificador) of the market, a person appointed to inspect weights and measures. 2. Needle of a balance. 3. Pivot of a steelyard. 4. Pin which keeps the blades of scissors together. 5. Catholic Christian who lives in obedience to the Church.

fielmente [fe-ayl-men'-tay], *adv.* 1. Faithfully. 2. Accurately, exactly (exactamente).

fieltro [fe-ayl'-tro], *m.* 1. Felt, a stuff used to make hats (tela). 2. A kind of hat used to keep off rain. 3. Surtout, a large great coat.

fieme [fe-ay'-may], *m. (Vet.)* Fleam, a heart-shaped lancet.

fiemo [fe-ay'-mo], *m. (Prov.)* Dung, manure.

fiera [fe-ay'-rah], *f.* 1. A wild beast (animal). 2. An inhuman, haughty and excessively choleric man, a savage. -*m & f.* (*Fig.*) Fiend; virago, dragon; ball on fire (en buen sentido). highly energetic person. **Como una fiera enjaulada**, like a caged tiger. **Es un fiera para el trabajo**, he's a demon for work.

fierabrás [fe-ay-rah-brahs'], *m.* (*coll.*) Bully, braggart, blusterer.

fieramente [fe-ay-rah-men'-tay], *adv.* Fiercely, savagely, ferociously, haughtily.

fiereza [fe-ay-ray'-thah], *f.* 1. Fiercely, cruelty, ferocity, hardness (ferocidad). 2. Fierceness, heat of temper. 3. (*Her.*) Attitude of an animal showing its teeth. 4. Deformity, ugliness (fealdad).

fiero, ra [fe-ay'-ro, rah], *a.* 1. Fierce (feroz), cruel (cruel), bloodthirsty; ferocious, fiery. 2. Ugly, deformed (feo). 3. Rough, rude. 4. Great, huge enormous. 5. Furious, terrible: wild, savage. -*m.pl.* **Fieros**, fierce threats and bravadoes.

fierro [fe-er'-ro], *m. V.* HIERRO Brand, the mark of ownership on an animal, and frequently on other articles.

fiesta [fe-ess'-tah], *f.* 1. Feast, entertainment, rejoicing feasting, merriment (de la ciudad). 2. Feast, festivity, festival, a church feast holiday; the day of some ecclesiastical festival. 3. Merrymaking, festivities, fun and games (juerga). **Fiesta de guardar**, day of obligation to hear mass. **Estar de fiesta**, to be merry, to be in a good mood. **Aguar la fiesta**, to spoil the fun. **No sabe de qué va la fiesta**, he hasn't a clue. **Fiesta nacional**, public holiday. **La fiesta continuó hasta muy tarde**, the festivities went on very late. -*pl.* 1. Vacations. **No estar para fiestas**, to be out of humor. **Fiestas reales**, royal festivals. **2. Fiestas de pólvora**, artificial fireworks; a bonfire. 3. Caresses, nets of endearment. **Hacer fiestas**, to caress, to wheedle, to fawn. **Hacer fiesta**, to take the day off. **Auguar la fiesta**, to be a wet blanket.

figala [fe-gah'-lah], *f.* An East Indian oared boat with one mast.

figle [fee'-glay], *m.* (*Mus.*) Ophicleide, a bass brass instrument of 12 keys.

figón [fe-gone'], *m.* Eating house, chop house.

figonero [fe-go-nay'-ro], *m.* Keeper of an eating house.

figueral [fe-gay-rahl'], *m.* Plantation of fig trees.

figulino, na [fe-goo-lee-no, nah], *a.* Made of potter's clay.

figura [fe-goo'-rah], *f.* 1. Figure, the form of anything. **De figura entera**, full-length. 2. The shape, the particular external appearance of a thing (forma). 3. Face, mien, countenance. 4. Figure, statue, image, anything formed in resemblance of something else. 5. (*Law.*) Form, mode. 6. (*Mus.*) 1. A musical note; 2. motive, theme, subject. 7. (*Gram.*) Figure, any deviation from the rules of analogy or syntax. 8. (*Geom.*) Figure, a space included in certain lines. 9. (*Rhet.*) Figure, any mode of speaking in which words are distorted from their literal and primitive sense (personaje). **Natural or genio y figura hasta la sepultura**, (*Prov.*) what is bred in the bone will never come out of the flesh. 10. Figure (baile, patinaje). 11. Marionette (títere). 12. Picture card (naipes). -*m.* A foolish person assuming an air of importance and dignity. **Ser un figura**, to be a big name. -*com.* Person of a mean or ridiculous appearance. -*f. pl.* In games of cards, the king, queen, and knave.

figurable [fe-goo-rah'-blay], *a.* Figurable, that which may be figured.

figuradamente [fe-goo-rah-men-tay], *adv.* Figuratively.

figurado, da [fe-goo-rah'-do, dah], *a.* Figurative, typical; not literal; rhetorical. -*pp.* of FIGURAR.

figural [fe-goo-rahl'], *a.* Figural, belonging to figures; represented by delineation.

figuranza [fe-goo-rahn'-thah], *f.* (*Prov.*) Resemblance.

figurar [fe-goo-rar'], *va.* 1. To figure, to form into a determinate shape. 2. To adorn with figures. -*vn.* 1. To figure (incluirse). **Los nombres no figuran aquí**, the names do not appear here. 2. (*Fig.*) To show off, to cut a dash. -*vr.* To fancy, to imagine, to believe without being able to prove.

Ya me lo figuraba, I thought as much. **Me figuro que es caro**, I fancy it's dear.

figurativamente [fe-goo-rah-te-vah-men'-tay], *adv.* Figuratively.

figurativo, va [fe-goo-rah-tee'-vo, rah], *a.* 1. Fugurative, typical; not literal, explanatory. 2. Symbolical, emblematic. 3. Representational (arte).

figurería [fe-goo-ray'-ah], *f. V.* MUECA.

figurero, ra [fe-goo-ray'-ro, rah], *m. & f.* Mimic, a ludicrous imitator; a buffoon who copies another's actions.

figurilla, ita [fe-goo-reel'], -lyah, ee'tah], *f. dim* A small figure.

figurín [fe-goo-reen'], *m.* Fashion plate, or small model for dresses.

figurón [fe-goo-rone'], *m.* 1. (*Aug.*) A huge or enormous figure of a ridiculous appearance. 2. A low-bred person assuming an air of dignity and importance (presumido).

fija [fee'-hah], *f.* Kind of hinge.

fijación [fe-hah-the-on'], *f.* 1. Fixation, stability, firmness. 2. The act of posting up printed bills, edicts, etc. 3. Fixation, the net of fixing mercury or any other volatile spirit.

fijador ra [fe-hah-dor', rah], *a.* 1. (*Phot.*) Fixer; fixing bath. **2. Fijador para el pelo**, hair lotion.

fijamente [fe-hah-men-tay], *adv.* 1. Firmly, assuredly. 2. Intensely, attentively. 3. Fixedly, steadfastly.

fijar [fehar'], *va.* 1. To fix, to fasten (clavar), to make fast, firm, or stable. 2. To fix, to settle, to establish (residencia), to clinch. 3. To fix, to direct without variation. 4. To fix, to deprive of volatility. 5. (*Fig.*) To settle on, to decide, to determine (determinar). **La fecha no se puede fijar con precisión**, the date cannot exactly be determined. -*vr.* 1. To fix or settle itself in a place (establecerse), to stare at (observar). 2. To fix, to determine, to resolve. **Lo malo es que no se fija**, the trouble is he doesn't pay attention. **Fíjese bien**, pay close attention. **Fijarse en algo**, to observe something.

fijenes [fe-hay'-nes], *m. pl.* Cheeks of a press.

fijeza [fe-hay'-thah], *f.* Firmness, stability.

fijo, ja [fee-ho, hah], *a. & pp. irr.* of FIJAR. 1. Fixed, firm, secure 2. Settled, permanent.

fila [fee'-lah], *f.* 1. A long row or series of persons or things (cola, asientos) **Una fila de coches**, a line of cars. **En fila**, in a row. 2. A line of soldiers ranged abreast or side by side. **En fila**, in a line, in a row. **Estar en filas**, to be with the colors. **Llamar a uno a filas**, to call somebody up. **Romper filas**, to break ranks.

filacteria [fe-lac-tay'-re-ah], *f.* Phylactery.

filada [fe-lah-dah], *f.* A slaty, schistose, micaceous rock, at times containing other varieties.

filagrama [fe-lah-grah-mah], *f.* A wire mould for a water-mark. *cf.* FILIGRAMA.

filamento [fe-lah-men'-to], *m.* Filament, fiber, thread.

filamentoso, sa [fe-lah-men-to'-so, sah], *a.* Filamentous.

filandria [fe-lahn'-dre-ah], *f.* Worm bred in the intestines of birds of prey.

filantropía [fe-lan-tro-pee'-ah], *f.* Philanthropy, good nature.

filantrópicamente [fe-lan-tro'-pe-cah-men-tay], *adv.* Humanely.

filantrópico [fe-lan-tro'-pe-co], **ca**, *a* Philanthropical, philanthropic.

filántropo [fe-lahn'-tro-po], *m.* Philanthropist.

filar [fe-lar'], *a.* **Triángulo filar**, a mathematical instrument serving as a sector, for various uses.

filarete [fe-lah-ray'-tay], *m.* (*Naut.*) Netting put on the waist or sides of a ship.

filariosis [fe-lah-re-o'-sis], *f.* (*Med.*) Filariasis.

filarmonía [fe-lar-mo-nee'-ah], *f.* Love of harmony, passion for music.

filarmónico, ca [fe-lar-mo'-ne-co, cah], *a.* Philharmonic, devoted to music.

filástica [fe-lahs'-te-cah], *f.* (*Naut.*) Rope-yarn, yarn made of untwisted ropes. **Filástica fina para maniobras**, fine rope-yarn for running rigging.

filatelia [fe-lah-tay'-le-ah], *f.* Philately, stamp collecting.

filatélico, ca [fe-lah-tay'-le-co, cah], *a.* Philatelic.

filatelista [fe-lah-tay-lees'-tah], *m. & f.* Philatelist, stamp collector.

filatería [fe-lah-tay-ree'-ah], *f.* Verbosity, exuberance or superfluity of words.

filatero [fe-lah-tay'-ro], *m.* A verbose speaker.

filatura [fe-lah-too'-rah], *f.* The art of spinning wool, cotton, etc.

filbán [feel-bahn'], *m.* The rough edge of a knife, scissors, etc.

filderretor [fil-der-ray-tor'], *m.* Sort of superfine camlet.

filelí [fe-lay-lee'], *m.* A very thin woollen stuff; superfine flannel. It comes from Barbary.

fileno, na [fe-lay'-no, nah], *a. (coll.)* Delicate, effeminate, soft.

filera [fe-lay'-rah], *f.* 1. A fishing net apparatus with small weights at the ends. 2. Spinneret of weaving spiders.

filete [fe-lay'-tay], *m.* 1. *(Arch.)* Fillet, a small member which appears in ornaments and mouldings, otherwise called *listel.* 2. Hem, the edge of a garment doubled and sewed. 3. A thin and small spit for roasting. 4. Welt of a shoe. 5. A twist-like ornament raised on plate. 6. Tenderloin, loin of beef (carne), fillet (pescado). **Darse el filete con,** to feel, touch up.

filetear [fe-lay-tay-ar'], *va.* To adorn with fillets.

filetón [fe-lay-tone'], *m.* 1 *(Aug.)* In architecture, a large fillet or listel 2. Kind of embroidery.

filiación [fe-leah-the-on'], *f.* 1. Filiation, the relation of a son to a father (relación); connection, relationship (de ideas etc.) 2. Dependence of some things upon others. 3. *(Mil.)* Regimental register of a soldier's height, physiognomy, age, etc. 4. Personal description; characteristics (señas).

filial [fe-le-ahl'], *a.* Filial, befitting a son.

filiar [fe-le-arl'], *vn.* To prove one's descent. *-va.* To enrol a soldier.

filiatra [fe-le-ah-trah], *a. & n.* Devoted to the study of medicine. Philiater.

filiatría [fe-le-ah-tree'-ah], *f.* Love of the study of medicine.

filibote [fe-le-bo-tay], *m.* Fly-boat, light vessel of 100 tons burden.

filibustero [fe-le-boos-tay'-ro] *m.* 1. Name given to freebooters or buccaneers (bucanero), who plundered America in the 17th century. 2. Filibuster, an armed adventurer invading unlawfully other people's territory.

filiforme [fe-le-for-may], *a.* Filiform, slender like a thread.

filigrana [fe-le-grah'-nah], *f.* 1. Filigree, filigrane, fine work made of gold and silver threads. 2. *(Met.)* Anything neatly wrought.

filípica [fe-lee'-pe-cah], *f.* Philippic, invective, declamation.

filipichín [fe-le-pe-cheen'], *m.* Kind of damask, moreen, woollen cloth.

filipino, na [fe-le-pee'-no, nah], *a.* Philippine, belonging to the Philippine Islands.

filis [fee'-lis], *f.* 1. Grace, a graceful manner of doing or saying a thing. 2. Gewgaw made of clay.

filisteo, tea [fe-lis-tay' o, ah], *m. & f.* 1. *(coll.)* A very tall and corpulent person (gigante). 2. Philistine.

film, filme [feelm, feel'-may], *m.* Film, movie.

filmación [feel-mah-the-on'], *f.* Filming, shooting.

filmador [feel-mah-dor'], *m.* Film maker.

filmadora [feel-mah-do'-rah], *f.* Film studio (estudio); film camera (aparato).

filmar [feel-mar'], *va.* To film.

filmina [feel-mee'-nah], *f.* Slide (diapositiva); short film (película).

filmografía [feel-mo-graha-fee'-ah], *f.* 1. Study of the film (estudio). **La filmografía de la estrella,** the star's film history. 2. Films (filmes).

filmoteca [feel-mo-tay'-cah], *f.* Film library.

filo [fee'-lo], *m.* Edge of a sword or other cutting instrument (de herramienta), blade; dividing line (línea); ridge (cresta). **De doble filo,** double-edged. **Dar un filo a,** to sharpen.

filogenitura [fe-lo-hay-ne-too'-rah], *f.* Philoprogenitiveness.

filogía, filológica [fe-lo-lo-hee'-ah, fe-lo-lo'-he-cah], *f.* Philology, linguistics.

filógico, ca [fe-lo-lo'-he-co, cah], *a.* Philological.

filólogo [fe-lo'-lo-go], *m.* Philologist.

filomena [fe-lo-may'-nah], *f.* Nightingale, philomel, philomela.

filón [fe-lone'], *m. (Geol.)* Vein, lode, mineral layer; gang.

filonio [fe-lo'-ne-o], *m. (Pharm.)* Kind of opiate.

filopos [fe-lo'-pos], *m. pl.* Pieces of linen used to drive game into a place assigned for that purpose.

filoseda [fe-lo-say'-dah], *f.* Vesting, silk and worsted or cotton cloth.

filosofador, ra [fe-lo-so-fah-dor', rah], *m. &f.* Philosopher.

filosofal [fe-lo-so-fahl'], *a.* **Piedra filosofal,** Philosopher's stone. *(Ant.)*

filosofar [fe-lo-so-far'], *va.* 1. To philosophize, to examine as a philosopher. 2. To play the philosopher, to assume the critic.

filsofastro [fe-lo-so-fahs-tro], *m.* A pretended philosopher, a smatterer in philosophy, philosophaster.

filosofía [fe-lo-so-fee'-ah], *f.* 1. Philosophy, a science which treats of the essence and affections of things and beings. 2. Philosophy, a particular doctrine or system of opinions. **Filosofía moral,** ethics or moral philosphy. **Filosofía natural,** physics or natural philosophy.

filosóficamente [fe-lo-so'-fe-cah-men-tay], *adv.* Philosophically.

filosófico, ca [fe-lo-so'-fe-co, cah], *a.* Philosophical, philosophic.

filosofismo [fe-lo-so-fee'-mo], *m. (Iron.)* Philosophism, sophistry, free thinking.

filosofista [fe-lo-so-fees'-tah], *m. (Iron.)* Philosophist, sophist.

filósofo [fe-lo'-so-fo], *m.* Philosopher.

filósofo, fa [fe-lo'-so-fo, fah], *a.* 1. Philosophic, philosophical. 2. *V.* AFILOSOFADO.

filoxera [fe-loc-say'-rah], *f.* Phylloxera, an insect of the aphis family, terrible in the destruction it causes to vineyards.

filtración [fil-trah-the-on'], *f.* 1. Filtration, leakage, loss. 2. Leak(age), leaking (información).

filtrador [fil-trah-dor'], *a.* Filtering. *-m.* filter.

filtrar [fil-trar'], *va.* 1. To filter, to filtrate, to defecate. 2. To filter, to strain. 3. To leak (información). *-vn. -vr.* 1. To filter. **Filtrarse por,** to filter through. 2. *(Fig)* To dwindle, to disppear bit by bit.

filtro [feel'-tro], *m.* 1. Filter, a piece of cloth, linen, or paper, through which liquids are strained. **Filtro de aceite,** oil filter. **Filtro de aire,** air filter. 2. Philter, a love-potion.

fimbria [feem'-bre-ah], *f.* Edge or lower part of a garment doubled in.

fimo [fee'-mo], *m.* Manure. *V.* FIEMO.

fin [feen], *m.* 1. End (final), close, termination, conclusion, issue. 2. Limit, boundary. 3. End, object, purpose (objetivo). 4. Goal, the end to which a design tends. **Al fin,** at last, at length, upon the main. **En fin** or **por fin,** finally, lastly, in fine. **Dar fin,** to die. **Dar fin a alguna cosa,** to finish, to conclude a thing. **Dar fin a alguna cosa,** to destory a thing completely. **A fin de,** in order that. **Por cualquier fin,** prompted by any motive, or end. **Fin de fichero,** end-of-file. **Hacia finales del siglo,** towards the end of the century. **Poner fin a,** to stop. **A tal fin,** with this aim in view. **Con fines deshonestos,** with an immoral purpose.

finado, da [fe-nah'-do, dah], *a. & pp.* of FINAR. Dead, deceased. **Día de los finados,** All Souls' Day. *-m. & f.* Person dead.

final [fe-nahl'], *a.* Final, ultimate, conclusive.

final [fe-nahl'], *m.* End, termination, conclusion. **Por final,** in fine, ultimately, lastly. **Final feliz,** happy-ending. **Al final de la calle,** at the end of the street.

finalizar [fe-nah-le-thar'], *va*. To finish, to conclude. **Dar algo por finalizado,** to consider something finished. *-vn*. To be finished or concluded.

finalmente [fe-nal-men'-tay], *adv*. Finally, at last, ultimately, lastly.

finamente [fe-nah-men-tay], *adv*. Finely, nicely, delicately.

finamiento [fe-nah-me-en'-to], *m*. Death, decease.

financiamiento [fe-nan-the-ah-me-en'-to], *m*. Financing.

financiar [fe-nan-the-ar'], *va*. To finance.

financiero [fe-nan-the-ay-ro], *m. & a*. Financer, financial. **El mundo financiero,** the financial world.

finanzas [fe-nahn'-thas], *f. pl*. Finances.

finar [fe-nar'], *vn*. To die. To long for.

finca [feen'-cah], *f*. Any kind of property, but especially land, which yields a regular income; tenement, building, house, real estate (propiedad). **Propiedad urbana,** town property. **Propiedad cafetera,** coffee plantation. **Penetrar en propiedad ajena,** to trespass.

fincar [fin-car'], *vn. & va*. 1. To buy real estate. 2. *(Fig. Peru.)* To lean on, to have confidence in something.

fin de semana [feen day say-mah-nah], *m*. Weekend.

finés, sa [fe-nays, sah], *a*. Finnie, or Finnish, relating to the Finns.

fineza [fe-nay'-thah], *f*. 1. Fineness, goodness, purity, perfection (calidad). 2. Kindness, expression of friendship or love. 3. Delicacy, beauty. 4. Friendly activity and zeal. 5. A small, friendly gift (regalo), a favor.

fingidamente [fin-he-dah-men-tay], *adv*. Feignedly, fictitiously, counterfeitly.

fingido, da [fin-hee'-do, dah], *a*. Feigned, dissembled, false. **Nombre fingido,** false name.

fingidor, ra [fin-he-dor', rah], *m. & f*. Dissembler, simulator, feigner.

fingimiento [fin-he-me-en'-to], *m*. Simulation, deceit, false appearance.

fingir [fin-heer'], *va*. 1. To feign, to dissemble, to counterfeit, to pretend, to affect. 2. To fancy, to imagine what does not really exist. **Fingir mucha humildad,** to pretend to be very humble. *-vn*. To pretend, to feign. **Fingir dormir,** to pretend to be asleep.

finiquitar [fi-ne-ke-tar'], *va*. To give a final receipt, close an account (cuenta).

finiquito [fi-ne-kee'-to], *m*. 1. Quittance, close of an account. 2. Final receipt or discharge.

finítimo, ma [fi-nee'-te-mo, mah], *a*. Bordering, contiguous, near.

finito, ta [fi-nee'-to, tah], *a*. Finite, limited, bounded.

finlandés, sa [fin-lan-days'., sah], *a*. Of Finland, Finnish. *m*. A Finn.

fino, na [fee'-no, nah], *a*. 1. Fine, perfect, pure (de buena calidad). 2. Delicate, nice (sutil). 3. Excellent, eminent. 4. Affectionate, true. 5. Acute, sagacious, cunning (inteligencia). 6. Of polished education and choice manners (cortés).

finta [feen'-tah], *f*. 1. A tax formerly paid to government. 2. Feint, a deceptive movement in fencing.

finura [fe-noo'-rah], *f*. 1. Fineness (calidad de fino), purity, delicacy. 2. In horsemanship, attention and obedience of a horse to the least wish of the rider. 3. Politeness, courtesy, refinement (cortesía). 4. Shrewdness, acuteness (astucia).

fiordo [fe-or'-do], *m*. Fiord or fjord.

fique [fee'-kay], *m*. A filaceous substance, resembling hemp, made of the leaves of the maguey tree.

firma [feer'-mah], *f*. 1. Signature. 2. A commercial house and its firm name. 3. *(Law. Prov.)* Order or rescript of a tribunal for keeping possession. **Firma en blanco,** blank signature. **Buena firma,** a house of standing, solvent.

firmamento [fir-mah-men'-to], *m*. Firmament, sky, heaven. *V.* EMPÍREO.

firmán [fir-mahn'], *m*. Firman, a grant or license given by oriental potentates.

firmante [fir-mahn-tay], *pa. & m. & f*. Supporter, subscriber.

firmar [fir-mar'], *va*. To sign, to subscribe. **Firmado y sellado,** signed and sealed. *-vr*. To style oneself, to assume a title or appellation.

firme [feer'-may], *a*. 1. Firm, stable (estable), strong, secure, fast, hard (duro), compact. **Estar en lo firme,** to be in the right. 2. Firm, unshaken, constant, consistent, resolute. 3. Steady (mercado); firm (precio), stable. 4. Staunch (persona), steadfast, resolute. 5. **De firme,** firmly. **Batir de firme,** to strike hard. **Oferta en firme,** firm offer. **Ponerse firmes,** to come to attention. **Sentencia firme,** final judgement.

firmemente [fir-may-men-tay], *adv*. 1. Firmly, strongly, unmovably. 2. Firmly, faithfully, steadily, constantly. 3. Staunchly, steadfastly (lealmente).

firmeza [fir-may'-thah], *f*. 1. Firmness, stability, hardness, compactness. 2. Firmness, steadiness, constancy. 3. Gold or silver clasp, ornament made of a precious stone in a triangular form. 3. Firmness (moral); steadfastness, resolution.

fisalia [fe-sah'-le-ah], *f*. *(Zool.)* Physalia, an acaleph; the Portuguese man of-war.

fiscal [fis-cahl'], *m*. 1. Attorney-general, a ministerial officer, who acts for the government by which he is appointed, and who, *ex oficio* personates the state or the people. 2. **Fiscal** or **abogado fiscal,** a public attorney, a prosecutor. 3. *(coll.)*. Censurer, critical.

fiscal [fis-cahl'], *a*. Fiscal, belonging to the exchequer. **Año fiscal,** fiscal year.

fiscalear [fis-cah-lay-ar'], *va*. *(coll.)* To become a public accuser, to censure.

fiscalía [fis-cah-lee'-ah], *f*. Office and business of the magistrate called *fiscal*.

fiscalizar [fis-cah-le-thar'], *va*. To accuse of a criminal offence, to criticize, to censure, to control (controlar).

fisco [fees'-co], *m*. National treasury, exchequer. **Declarar algo al fisco,** to declare something for tax purposes.

fiseter [fe-say-terr'], *m*. *(Zool.)* The small blunt-headed whale or cachalot.

fisga [fees'-gah], *f*. 1. Harpoon with three hooks for catching large fish. 2. *(Met.)* Raillery, jest, scoff. 3. *(Prov.)* Wheat of the finest quality; bread of spelt-wheat.

fisgador, ra [fis-gah-dor', rah], *m. & f*. Harpooner; one who burlesques. *V.* FISGÓN.

fisgar [fis-gar'], *va*. 1. To mock, to scoff, to jeer (mofarse). 2. To fish with a harpoon (pez). 3. To peep, to pry.

fisgón, one [fis-gone', nah], *a*. 1. Prying, peeping, snooping (curioso). 2. Jesting, mocking (mofador). *-m. & f*. 1. Busybody, Peeping Tom. 2. Jester, buffoon.

fisgonear [fis-go-nay-ar'], *va*. FISGAR.

física [fee'-se-cah], *f*. Physics. **Física de bajas energías,** high-energy physics. **Física de bajas temperaturas,** lowtemperature physics. **Física del estado sólido,** solid-state physics. **Física del plasma,** plasma physics.

físicamente [fee'-se-cah-men-tay], *adv*. Physically; corporeally; really.

físico [fee'-se-co, cah], *a*. 1. Physical, relating to nature or natural philosophy. 2. Natural, really existing.

físico, ca [fee'-se-co], *m*. 1. Physicist. 2. Physique, constitution. 3. *(coll.)* Face, appearance (aspecto).

fisicoquímico, ca [fee-se-co-kee'-me-co, cah], *a*. Physicochemical.

fisiografía [fe-se-o-grah-fee'-ah], *f*. Physiography, a description of nature.

fisiográfico, ca [fe-seo-grah'-fe-co, cah], *a*. Physiographic.

fisiología [fe-se-o-lo-hee'-ah], *f*. Physiology, the science of vital phenomena. **fisiológico, ca** [fe-se-o-lo'-he-co, cah], *a*. Physiological. *-adv*. **Fisiológicamente.**

fisiologista [fe-se-o-lo-hees'-tah], *m*. Physiologist.

fisiólogo [fe-se-o'-lo-go], *m*. Phisiologist: used also as adjective.

fisión [fe-se-on'], *f*. *(Phy.)* Fission. **Fisión nuclear,** nuclear fission.

fisionable [fe-se-o-nah'-blay], *a*. Fissionable.

fisionomía [fe-se-o-no-mee'-ah], *V.* FISONOMÍA. *(Acad.)*

fisioterapeuta [fe-se-o-tay-rah-pay'-oo-tah], *m & f.* Physiotherapist.

fisioterapia [fe-se-o-tay-rah'-pe-ah], *f.* Physiotherapy.

fisioterapista [fe-se-o-tay-rah-pees'-tah], *m & f.* Physiotherapist.

fisonomía [fe-so-no-mee'-ah], *f.* 1. Physiognomy, lineaments, features. 2. Physiognomy, the art of discovering the temper and talents by the features of the face.

fisonómico, ca [fe-so-no'-me-co, cah], *a.* Physiognomical.

fisonomista, fisónomo [fe-so-no-mees'-tah], *m.* Physiognomist.

fistol [fis-tole'], *m.* 1. A crafty person, specially a gambler. 2. *(Mex.)* A stickpin.

fístola [fees'-to-lah], *f.* 1. *(Surg.)* Fistula, a narrow channel not disposed to heal. 2. *V.* FÍSTULA for a pipe. 3. *V.* CAÑAFÍSTULA.

fístula [fees'-too-lah], *f.* 1. Waterpipe or conduit. 2. Musical wind-instrument, resembling a flute or flageolet. 3. *(Surg.)* Fistule.

fistular [fis-too-lar'], *a.* *(Med.)* Fistular, fistulous.

fistuloso, sa [fis-too-lo'-so, sah], *a.* Fistulous.

fisura [fe-soo-rah], *f.* 1. *(Geol.)* Fissure, cleft. 2. *(Med.)* Fissure, a shallow and narrow break of continuity. 3. Fissure, a longitudinal fracture of a bone.

fitobiología [fe-to-be-o-lo-hee'-ah], *f.* Phytobiology, the branch of biology which treats of plants.

fitogenesia [fe-to-hay-nay'-se-ah], *f.* Phytogenesis, the doctrine of the origin of plants.

fitografía [fe-to-grah-fee'-ah], *f.* Phytography, plant geography; description of plant life.

fitología [fe-to-lo-hee'-ah], *f.* Phytology, botany.

fitonisa [fe-to-nee'-sah], *f.* *V.* PITONISA.

flabelación [flah-bay-lah-the-on'], *f.* Action of agitating the air to refresh it.

flabelado, da [flah-bay-lah'-do, dah], *a.* 1. Like a flyflap. 2. *(Bot.)* Fan-shaped.

flacamente [flah-cah-men-tay], *adv.* Languidly, weakly, feebly.

flacidez [flah-the-deth'], *f.* *(Med.)* Flaccidity, laxity, limberness, want of tension.

flácido, da [flah'-the-do, dah], *a.* *(Med.)* Flaccid, limber, lax.

flaco, ca [flah'-co, cah], *a.* 1 Lank, lean, meagre, flaccid. 2. Feeble, languid. 3. Dejected, low-spirited. 4. Frail, weak of resolution. **Ponerse flaco**, to get thin.

flacura [flah-coo'-rah], *f.* 1. Meagreness, leanness, weakness (debilidad). 2. Thinness (delgadez).

flagelación [flah-hay-lah-the-on'], *f.* Flagellation, scourging.

flagelar [flah-hay-lar'], *va.* 1. To lash (azotar), to scourge. *V.* AZOTAR. 2. *(Fig.)* To flay, to criticize severely.

flagelo [flah-hay'-lo], *m.* 1. Lash (azote), scourge, chastisement. 2. *(Biol.)* Flagellum, a lash-like locomotive appendage of certain infusoria; a large cilium. 3. *(Amer.)* An epidemic.

flagicio [flah-hee'-the-o], *m.* Flagitousness, wickedness; an enormous crime.

flagicioso, sa [flah-he-the-o'-so, sah], *a.* Flagitious, wicked.

flagrante [flah-grahn'-tay], *a. & pa.* Flagrant, resplendent. **En flagrante delito**, in the very act, red-handed (in fraganti).

flagrar [flah-grar'], *vn.* *(Poet.)* To flagrate, to burn, to glow, to flame.

flajolé [flah-ho-lay'], *m.* Flageolet, a beakflute.

flama [flah'-mah], *f.* 1. Flame, excessive ardor. 2. An ornament upon the upper part of caps, shakos, etc., in the army.

flamante [flah-mahn'-tay], *a.* 1. Flaming, bright, resplendent. 2. Quite new (nuevo), spick and span; luxurious (lujoso); superb (estupendo).

flamear [flah-may-ar'], *vn.* *(Naut.)* To shiver, to flutter (vela).

flamenco [flah-men'-co], *m.* *(Orn.)* Flamingo.

flamenco, ca [flah-men'-co, cah], *a.* 1. Flemish, relating to Flanders. 2. Andalusian gipsy. **Cantante flamenco,**

flamenco singer. 3. **Ponerse flamenco**, to get cocky (engreído); to get on one's high horse (satisfecho).

flamenquilla [flah-men-keel'-lyah], *f.* *(Prov.)* 1. Dish of a middling size. 2. Marigold.

flámeo [flah'-may-o], *m.* A kind of yellow veil, with which the face of a bride was formerly covered during the marriage ceremony.

flameo [flah-may'-o], *m.* Flapping or fluttering of banners, sails, etc.

flamígero, ra [flah-mee'-hay-ro, ra], *a.* *(Poet.)* Flamiferous, emitting, flames.

flamín [flah-meen'], *m.* Flamen, a Roman priest.

flámula [flah'-moo-lah], *f.* 1. *(Bot.)* Sweet-scented virgin's bower. 2. *(Naut.)* Streamer, pennon

flan [flahn], *m.* Caramel custard (crema); baked custard (pastel).

flanco [flahn'-co], *m.* 1. *(Fort.)* Flank, flanker the part of a bastion which reaches from the curtain to the face. 2. *(Mil.)* Flank of an army. 3. *(Naut.)* Side of a ship.

Flandes [flahn'-des], *m.* Flanders.

flanela [flah-nay'-lah], *f.* Flannel.

flanquear [flan-kay-ar'], *va.* *(Fort.)* To flank; to defend by lateral fortifications.

flanqueo [flan-kay'-o], *m.* A flank attack.

flaón [flah-on'], *m.* 1. A custard. 2. Piece of gold or silver ready to be coined.

flaquear [flah-kay-ar'], *vn.* 1. To flag, to grow feeble, to lose vigor. 2. To grow spiritless or dejected, to be disheartened (moralmente). 3. To slacken in the ardor with which an enterprise was commenced (esfuerzo). 4. To decline (salud).

flaqueza [flah-kay'-thah], *f.* 1. Leanness, extenuation of the body, want of flesh, meagreness, lankness. 2. Feebleness, faintness, languishment. 3. Weakness, frailty, foible. 4. Importunity, molestation.

flash [flash], *m. pl.* Flashed, flashs 1. News flash (noticia). 2. Flash, flashlight. **Con flash**, by flashlight. 3. *(Fig.)* Surprise.

flato [flah'-to], *m.* Flatus, wind gathered in a cavity of the body.

flatoso, flatuoso, sa [flah-to'-so, flah-too-o'-so, sah], *a.* Flatuous, windy; full of wind.

flatulencia [flah-too-len'-the-ah], *f.* Flatulency.

flatulento, ta [flah-too-len'-to, tah], *a.* Flatulent, turgid with air, windy.

flauta [flah'-oo-tah], *f.* A flute (instrumento).

flautado, da [fla-hoo-tah'-do, dah], *a.* Resembling a flute.

flautado [flah-oo-tah-do], *m.* Stop in an organ, which produces the sound of a flute.

flautero [flah-oo-tay'-ro], *m.* One who makes flutes.

flautillo [flah-oo-teel'-lyo], *m.* *V.* CARAMILLO.

flautín [flah-oo-teen'], *m.* 1. Octave flute, piccolo, a small flute of high pitch. 2. *-m -f.* Piccolo player (persona).

flautista [flah-oo-tees'-tah], *m.* Player of the flute. **El flautista de Hamelin**, the Pied Piper of Hamelin.

flavo, va [flah'-vo, vah], *-a.* Of a fallow or honey color.

flébil [flay'-beel], *a.* Mournful, deplorable, lamentable.

flebolito [flay-bo-lee'-to], *m.* Phlebolith, a concretion formed in a vein: vein-stone.

flebotomía [flay-bo-to-mee-ah], *f.* Phlebotomy, blood-letting.

flebotomiano [flay-bo-to-me-ah'-no], *m.* Phlebotomist, one who lets blood for medical purposes.

flebotomista [flay-bo-to-mees'-tah], *m.* *V.* FLEBOTOMIANO.

flebotomizar [flay-bo-to-me-thar'], *va.* To bleed, to let blood.

flebótomo [flay-bo'-to-mo], *m.* *V.* FLEBOTOMIANO.

fleco [flay'-co], *m.* 1. Fringe, an ornamental appendage to dress and furniture. 2. Flounce. 3. Fringe (pelo).

flecha [flay'-chah], *f.* 1. Arrow, dart. 2. A sign which serves to indicate the north, or the current of rivers, upon a map. 3. *(Fort.)* A work of two faces and two sides. 4. *(Naut.)* Front piece of the cutwater. 5. The principal piece of those which compose the beakhead of a galley. 6. *(Min.)* Variety of hydroxide of iron called "lov's dart." 7. Sagitta, a northern constellation. **Flecha de dirección**, Trafficator. **Como una flecha**, like an arrow.

flechador [flay-chah-dor'], *m*. Archer.

flechaduras [flay-chah-doo-ras'], *f. pl. (Naut.)* Ratlines. *V.* FLECHASTES.

flechar [flay-char'], *va*. 1. To dart, to shoot an arrow or dart (arco). 2. To wound or kill with a bow and arrow. 3. *(Prov. Mex.)* To point out, without fear, in gambling. *-vn*. To have a bow drawn ready to shoot.

flechaste [flay-chas'-tay], *m. (Naut.)* Ratline.

flechazo [flay-chah'-tho], *m*. 1. Blow or stroke given with a dart or arrow. 2. Love at first sight (amor). **Con nosotros fue el flechazo**, with us it was love at first sight.

flechera [flay-chay'-rah], *f. (S. Am.)* A long, narrow, sharp canoe.

flechería [flay-chay-ree'-ah], *f*. A number of darts or arrows darted at a time, shower of arrows.

flechero [flay-chay'-ro], *m*. 1. Archer, bowman. 2. Fletcher, an arrow maker.

flegmasía [fleg-mah-see'-ah], *f*. Inflammation, phlegmasia.

fleje [flay'-hay], *m*. Hoop. **Flejes de hierro** or **fierro**, iron hoops. **Flejes**, twigs for barrels.

flema [flay'-mah], *f*. 1. Phlegm. 2. Thick spittle ejected from the mouth. 3. Phlegm, coolness, dullness, sluggishness.

flemático, ca [flay-mah'-te-co, cah], *a*. 1. Phlegmatic, generating phlegm; abounding in phlegm. 2. Phlegmatic, dull, cold, sluggish.

fleme [flay'-may], *f*. Fleam, an instrument used to bleed cattle.

flemón [flay-mo-ne'], *m*. 1. Phlegmon, an inflammation of the cellular tissue. 2. A gumboil, a tumor of the gum ending in suppuration.

flemoso, sa [flay-mo'-so, sah], *a*. Mucous, consisting of phlegm.

flemudo, da [flay-moo'-do, dah], *a. (Prov.)* Dull, sluggish, cold, frigid.

flequillo [flay-keel'-lyo], *m*. Fringe.

flerecín [flay-ray-theen'], *m. (Med.)* Gout.

flet, flez [flet, fleth], *m. (Zool.)* Halibut.

fletador [flay-tah-dor'], *m*. Freighter, charterer of a ship.

fletamento [flay-tah-men'-to], *m*. Freightment, the act of freighting a ship; chartering. **Cerrar el fletamento**, to charter, to make out the charter-party.

fletante [flay-tahn'-tay], *m*. 1. Ship owner. 2. Shipper.

fletar [flay-tar'], *va*. To freight a ship, to charter (avión, barco).

flete [flay'-tay], *m*. 1. Charter (alquiler). **Vuelo flete**, charter flight. 2. Freight (carga). 3. Freightage (gastos).

flexibilidad [flec-se-be-le-dahd'], *f*. 1. Flexibility, pliableness, ductility, flexibleness. 2. Flexibility, easiness to be persuaded, ductility of mind, managableness, obsequiousness, mildness of temper.

flexibilizar [flec-se-be-le-thar'], *va*. To make flexible; to adjust.

flexible [flec-see-blay], *a*. 1. Flexible, ductile, pliant, possible to be bent. 2. Flexible, manageable, docile. 3. Soft (sombrero). 3. Open-minded, open to argument (persona).

flexión [flec-se-on'], *f*. Flexion, flexure, act of bending.

flexionar [flec-se-o-nar'], *va*. To bend; to flex (músculo).

flexor [flec-sor'], *a*. Flexor, used of the muscles which bend a joint.

flexuoso, sa [flec-soo-o-so, sah], *a. (Bot.)* Flexuose, changing its direction in a curve from joint to joint or from bud to bud in the stem, or from flower to flower in the peduncle.

flibote [fle-bo'-tay], *m*. Flyboat, a small fast-sailing vessel.

flictena [flic-tay'-nah], *f. (Med.)* Phlyctena, a small blister, or vesicle, filled with a serous or watery fluid.

flin [fleen'], *m*. Stone used for edging and polishing steel; a kind of emery.

flinflón [flin-flon'], *m*. A fresh-colored, corpulent man.

flipante [fle-pahn-tay], *a*. Attractive, cool.

flipar [fle-pahr'], *vn*. 1. To freak out (desmadrarse); to go round the twist (volverse loco): to get stoned (drogarse,

emborracharse). 2. **Flipar por algo,** to be dying for something.

flirtear [flir-tay-ar'], *vn*. To flirt, to have a light-hearted affair.

flocadura [flo-cah-doo'-rah], *f*. A trimming made with fringes as an ornament of dress.

flogosis [flo-go'-sis], *f*. Inflammation, phlegmasia.

flojamente [floh-ah-men'-tay], *adv*. Slowly, carelessly, laxly, loosely (sueltamente), weakly (débilmente), lightly (ligeramente).

flojear [flo-hay-ar'], *vn*. To slacken, to grow weak. *V*. FLAQUEAR.

flojedad [flo-hay-dahd'], *f*. 1. Weakness, feebleness, laxity. 2. Sloth, laziness, negligence, slackness.

flojel [flo-hel'], *m*. 1. Wool shorn from cloth by the shearer. 2. Down, soil feathers.

flojera [flo-hay'-rah], *f. (coll.)* Weakness. *V*. FLOJEDAD.

flojo, ja [flo'-ho, hah], *a*. 1. Slack; loose (tuerca) **Vino flojo,** flaggy, insipid wine. 2. Feeble, weak, flaccid (esfuerzo). 3. Slack, remiss, lazy, slothful, negligent, cold, cool, spiritless (actitud). 4. Low, weak (precio). 5. Soft, limp (carne). **Me la trae floja,** it leaves me stone-cold.

floqueado, da [flo-kay-ah'-do, dah], *a*. Fringed.

flor [flor'], *f*. 1. Flower, that part of a plant which contains the organs of generation; a blossom. 2. The down of fruits newly gathered. 3. Flower, prime, the most excellent or valuable part of a thing; bloom. 4. Cuticle or thin skin formed, on the surface of liquors. 5. *(Chem:)* Flos, the most subtle part of mineral separated in sublimation. 6. Virginity, maidenhood. 7. The face or surface of the earth. 8. Smart or witty saying: commonly used in plural. 9. Grain, the outside of tanned leather. 10. Trick or artifice among gamesters or gamblers. 11. Figures of rhetoric. **Flor de canela,** cassia buds. **Flor de la miel,** *(Bot.)* great honeyflower. **Flor de lis,** 1. Flower-de-luce. 2. *(Bot.)* Jacobea lily, amaryllis. **Flor del sol,** *(Bot.)* V. CORONA REAL. **En flor,** in a state of infancy, imperfect, in blossom, in flower. **En la flor de su edad,** *(Met.)* in his bloom. **La flor y nata de la sociedad,** the cream of society. **En la flor de la vida,** in the prime of life. **Decir flores a una,** to pay pretty compliments to a girl (piropo). **A flor de agua,** awash, even with the surface of the water. **La flor y nata,** the cream, the best. **Tienda de flores,** florist's shop.

flora [flo'-rah], *f. (Bot.)* Flora, the description of the plants of some district, region, etc.

florada [flo-rah-da'h], *f. (Prov.)* The season of flowers with bee-masters.

florales [flo-rah'-les], *a. pl*. Floral; feasts in honor of Flora.

florar [flo-rar'], *vn*. To flower. *(Acad.)*

flordelisado, da [flor-day-le-sah'-do, dah], *a*. Adorned with iris. *-pp*. of FLORDELISAR.

floreado, da [flo-ray-ah'-do, dah], *a. & pp*. of FLOREAR. 1. Flowered (tela). 2. Applied to things made of the finest flour or meal. **Rasos, sedas, u otros efectos or géneros floreados,** silks, or any other figured goods.

florear [flo-ray-ar'], *va*. 1. To adorn with flowers (tela) 2. To flourish a sword. 3. *(Mus.)* To flourish, to play the guitar without rule. 4. *(Amer.)* V. FLORAR.

florecer [flo-ray-therr'], *vn*. 1. To flower, to bloom, to blossom. 2. To flourish, to thrive, to prosper. 3. To flourish in any age. *-vr*. To mould, to become mouldy.

florecica [flo-ray-thee'-cah], *f. dim*. Floweret.

floreciente [flo-ray-the-en'-tay], *pa. & a*. Flourishing, blossoming, flowery.

florecilla, ita [flo-ray-theel'-lyah, ee'-tah], *f*. 1. *(dim.)* A small flower. 2. *(Bot.)* The partial or separate little flower of an aggregate flower.

florentina, *f*. **florentin,** *m*. [flo-ren-tee'-nah, flo-ren-teen']. A silk stuff first manufactured at Florence; florentines.

floreo [flo-ray'-o], *m*. 1. Flourish made by fencers before they engage. 2. Flourish on the guitar; flourish (esgrima). 3. A luxuriant redundancy of words (cumplido). 4. Cross caper, a movement in dancing. 5. Idle pastime.

florera [flo-ray'-rah], *f.* Flower girl, female flower vendor.

florero [flo-ray'-ro], *m.* 1. Vase(recipiente). 2. One who makes or deals in artificial flowers. 3. Painting representing flowers. 4. Case destined for artificial flowers. 5. One who makes use of florid, empty language (persona). 6. A chaplet of flowers.

florescencia [flo-res-then'-the-ah], *f.* 1. *(Bot.)* Florescence or the flowering season. 2. Efflorescence, manner of flowering.

floresta [flo-res'-tah], *f.* 1. Forest, shrubbery, thicket. 2. A delightful, rural place (lugar atractivo). 3. Collection of fine things pleasing to the taste; beauties.

florestero [flo-res-tay'-ro], *m.* Forester, keeper of a forest.

floreta [flo-ray'-tah], *f.* 1. Border of morocco leather on the edge of a girth. 2. In paper mills, pile, heap.

florete [flo-ray'-tay], *m.* Foil, floret, a blunt sword used in learning to fence (esgrima).

florete [flo-ray'-tay], *a.* Very white and fine (papel).

floretear [flo-ray-tay-ar'], *va.* To garnish with flowers.

floricultura [flo-re-cool-too'-rah], *f.* Floriculture, cultivation of flowers.

floridamente [flo-re-dah-men'-tay], *adv.* Elegantly, floridly, flourishingly.

florídeas [flo-ree'-day-as], *f. pl.* Floridae, a very large class of marine algae, purple and red. The color is enhanced upon drying.

floridez [flo-re-deth'], *f.* Floridity, floridness.

florido, da [flo-ree'-do, dah], *a.* 1. Florid, flowery; full of flowers (campo) 2. Choice, elegant, slect. 3. Flowery, florid (estilo).

florífero, ra [flo-ree'-do, dah], *a* Floriferous, bearing flowers.

florilegio [flo-re-lay-he-o], *m.* Florilegium, anthology, select writings.

florín [flo-reen'], *m.* Florin, a silver coin.

floripondio, floripundio [flo-re-pon'-de-o, flo-re-poon'-de-o], *m.* 1. Magnolia, tree of great beauty, with very large white fragrant flowers. 2. *(Bot.)* Floripondium, smooth-stalked brugmansia.

florisado, da [flo-re-sah'-do, dah], *a.* V. FLORDELISADO.

florista [flo-rees'-tah], *com.* 1. Florist. 2. One who makes or deals in artificial flowers.

floristería [flo-rees-tay-ree'-ah], *f.* Florist's (tienda).

florión [flo-ro-ne'], *m.* 1. *(Aug.)* A large flower. 2. Flower work, an ornament resembling a large flower.

flósculo [flos'-coo-lo], *m. (Bot.)* The separate little flower of an aggregate one; floret.

flosculoso, sa [flos-coo-lo'-so, sah], *a. (Bot.)* Flosculous, composed of flowers or florets.

flota [flo'-tah], *f.* 1. *(Naut.)* Fleet of merchant ships. **Flota mercante,** merchant marine. **La flota pesquera,** the fishing fleet. 2. Fleet, squadron. Nowadays the term *escuadra* or *armada* is used.

flotable [flo-tah'-blay], *a.* 1. Capable of floating. 2. A navigable river. *(Acad.)*

flotacion [flo-tah-the-on'], *f.* 1. Floating, the act of floating. 2. Friction, rubbing. 3. *(Min.)* Flotation. **Línea de flotación,** *(Naut.)* Waterline.

flotador, ra [flo-tah-dor', rah], *a.* Floating. -*m.* 1. Float. 2. *(Aer.)* Pontoon. 3. Ballcock (de cisterna). 4. Rubber ring (de niño).

flotamiento [flo-tah-me-en'-to], *m.* Stroking, gentle friction.

flotante [flo-tahn'-tay], *pa.&a.* 1. Floating, floaty. 2. *(Bot.)* Rooted upon the bottom of a stream and whose leaves follow the course of the current.

flotar [flo-tar'], *vn.* 1. To float. 2. To hang, to hang loose (pieza); to flutter (bandera) **Flotar en el aire,** to float in the air. **Flotar al viento,** to stream in the wind. -*va. (Ant.)* To stroke, to rub gently.

flote [flo-tay'], *m.* V. FLOTADURA. *Afloat,* afloat; *(fig.)* escaping happily. **Estar a flote,** to be afloat.

flotilla [flo-teel'-lyah], *f.* 1. Flotilla, a number of small vessels. 2. *(Dun.)* A small fleet.

flox [flox], *m. (Bot.)* Phlox.

fluatado, da [floo-ah-tah'-do, dah], *a.* Fluorid, fluorate.

fluato [floo-ah'-to], *m.* Fluorate, compound of hydrofluoric acid.

fluctuación [flooc-too-ah-the-on'], *f.* 1. Fluctuation, motion of the waves. 2. Fluctuation, uncertainty, indetermination, irresolution (indecisión). 3. *(Med.)* Fluctuation.

fluctuamiento [flooc-too-ah-me-ayn'-to], *m.* V. FLUCTUACIÓN.

fluctuante [flooc-too-ahn'-tay], *pa. & a.* Fluctuating, fluctuant; floating (población).

fluctuar [flooc-too-ar'], *vn.* 1. To fluctuate, to float backward and forward, to oscillate. 2. To be in danger of being lost or destroyed. 3. To fluctuate, to hesitate, to be irresolute, to vacillate (vacilar). 4. To fluctuate, to be in an uncertain state.

flutícola [flooc-tee'-co-lah], *a. (Zool.).* Inhabiting the waters.

fluctígena [flooc-tee'-hay-nah], *a. (Zool.)* Born on the water.

fluctuoso, sa [flooc-too-o'-so, sah], *a.* Fluctuant, wavering.

fluente [floo-en'-tay], *pa. & a.* Fluent, flowing.

fluidez [floo-e-deth'], *f.* Fluidity, liquidity, **Fluidez de stilo,** fluency.

fluidificable [floo-e-de-fe-cah'-blay], *a.* Liquefiable.

fluidificación [floo-e-de-fe-cah-the-on'], *f.* Liquefaction, rendering fluid.

fluidificar [floo-e-de-fe-car'], *va. & vr.* To convert into fluid, to liquefy.

fluido, da [floo-ee'-do, dah], *a.* 1. Fluid, not solid (líquido). 2. *(Met.)* Fluent (estilo); fluent (lenguaje). **La circulación es bastante fluida,** traffic is moving quite freely. -*pp.* of FLUIR.

fluido [floo-ee'-do], *m.* 1. Fluid, not solid. 2. *(Med.)* Fluid, any animal juice.

fluir [floo-eer'], *vn.* To flow. **El fluir del agua,** the flow of water.

flujo [floo'-ho], *m.* 1. Flux, the motion of liquids. 2. *(Med.)* Flux, a flow or discharge. 3. Flowing, haemorrhage. 4. *(Naut.)* Flow, rising tide. 5. *(Chem.)* Flux, a substance aiding the fusion of another substance. **Flujo de palabras,** flow of words, volubility. **Flujo de risa,** fit of laughter. **Flujo de sangre,** haemorrhage. **Flujo de vientre,** diarrhoea.

fluor [floo'-or], *m.* Fluorine, a gaseous element.

fluorescencia [floo-o-res-then'-the-ah], *f.* Flourescence.

Fluorescente, ca [floo-o-res-then-tay], *a.* Flourescente.

fluorhídrico, ca [floo-o-ree'-dre-co, cah], *a.* Fluorhydric, hydrofluoric.

fluórico, ca [floo-o'-re-co, cah], *a. (Chew.)* Fluoric, containing fluorine.

fluorita, fluorina [floo-o-ree'-nah, floo-ree'-nah], *f.* Fluor(spar), fluorite.

fluoroacopio [flo-oo-ros-co'-pe-o], *m.* Fluoroscope.

fluoruración [floo-o-roo-rah-the-one'], *f.* Fluoridation.

fluvial [floo-ve-ahl'], *a.* Fluvial, pertaining to rivers. **Navegación fluvial,** river navigation.

flux [floocs], *m.* Flush, a run of cards of the same suit (naipes). **Hacer flux,** *(Colt.)* to spend one's whole fortune without paying a debt.

fluxión [flooc-se-on'], *f.* 1. A flow or discharge; flux. 2. *(Amer.)* A cold, catarrh. 3. *(Hex.)* A very painful toothache.

Fo [fo], The Chinese name of Buddha.

foca [fo'-cah], *f.* Seal. **Foca de trompa,** sea elephant.

focal [fo-cal'], *a.* Focal.

foco [fo-co], *m.* 1. Focus, the point of convergence (centro). 2. The principal spot where an insurrection has broken out. 3. Center of action, origin, source (de calor, de luz). 4. The seat of a purulent process; core or center of an abscess (de incendio). 6. *(Mil.)* Touch-hole of a gun. 7. The focus of an ellipse. 7. *(Chom.)* Firebox, furnace; place for combustibles.

fóculo [fo'-coo-lo], *m.* A small fire place.

focha [fo'-chah], *f. (Zool.)* Rail; mudhen.

fodolí [fo-do-lee'], *a.* Meddlesome, intrusive.

fofo, fa [fo'-fo, fah], *a.* Spongy, soft, bland (esponjoso); flabby (carnes). 2. Fat, plump (rechoncho).

fogaril [fo-gah-reel'], *m.* Combustibles which serve for signal lights.

fogata [fo-gah'-tah], *f.* 1. Blaze, the light of a flame. 2. A small mine under some attackable point.

fogón [fo-gone'], *m.* 1. Hearth, the fireside. 2. Vent or touch-hole of a gun (de cañon, máquina). 3. *(Naut.)* Caboose, a cooking stove for a ship. 4. *(Naut.)* Galley, cook room, the kitchen in ships.

fogonadura [fo-go-nah-doo'-rah], *f. (Naut.)* Partner, piece of timber round the holes into which mats are set.

fogonazo [fo-go-nah'-tho], *m.* Flame of the priming of a gun, a flash in the pan (estallido).

fogonero [fo-go-nay'-ro], *m.* Fireman, stoker.

fogosidad [fo-go-se-dahd'], *f.* Excessive vivacity, fieriness, heat of temper.

fogoso, sa [fo-go'-so, sah], *a.* 1. Fiery, vehement, ardent. 2. Fervent, hot in temper, ardent in love, impetuous, lively, choleric.

fogote [fo-go´-tay], *m.* A live coal, match.

fogueación [fo-gay-ah-the-on'], *f.* Enumeration of hearths or fire.

foguear [fo-gay-ar'], *va.* 1. To habituate persons or horses to the discharge of fire-arms. 2. To cleanse fire-arms with a charge of gunpowder. *-vr.* To have one's baptism of fire.

fogueo [fo-gay'-o], *m.* **Bala de fogueo,** blank cartridge.

foja [fo'-hah], *f.* 1. *(For.)* A sheet of paper. 2. *(Orn.)* Coot or common coot.

fole [fo'-lay], *m.* A leather bag, especially of the Galician bagpipe.

folgo [fol'-go], *m.* Foot-warmer, bag of skin to cover the feet and legs when sitting.

foliáceo [fo-le-ah'-the-o], *a. (Bot)* Foliaceous.

foliación [fo-le-ah-the-on'], *f.* 1. Numbering the pages of a book. 2. The numeration of the pages of a book. 3. *(Bot.)* Foliation.

foliar [fo-le-ar'], *va.* To page, to number the leaves of a book.

foliatura [fo-le-ah-too'-rah], *f.* 1. Numbering the pages of a book. 2. Numeration of the pages of a book.

folículo [fo-lee'-coo-lo], *m.* 1. *(Bot.)* Follicle, a seed-vessel or pericarp. 2. *(Anat.)* Follicle, a membraneous sac.

folio [fo'-le-o], *m.* Folio, leaf of a book (hoja). **Al primer folio,** at first sight. **En folio,** in folio.

folklore [fo-clor'], *m.* Folklore.

folklórico [fol-clo'-re-co], *a.* Folklore; folk; popular, traditional. **Es muy folklórico,** it's very quaint. *-m & f.* Folk singer.

folla [fol'-lyah], *f.* 1. An irregular conflict in a tournament. 2. Medley of a variety of things confusedly jumbled together; olio.

follada [fol-lyah'-dah], *f.* 1. Sort of hollow paste. 2. Fuck.

follados [fol-lyah'-dos], *m. pl.* Ancient kind of pants.

follaje [fol-lyah'-hay], *m.* 1. Foliage. 2. Leafiness: leafage. 3. Gaudy ornament of trifling value. 4. Fucking.

follar [fol-lyar'], *va.* 1. To blow with bellows. 2. To form in leaves. 3. To fuck. 4. To bother, to annoy. *-vr.* 1. *(coll.)* To discharge wind without noise. 2. To fuck.

follero [fol-lyay'-ro], *m.* One who makes or sells bellows.

folleta [fol-lyay'-tah], *f.* Wine measure nearly equal to an English pint.

folletín [fol-lyay-teen'], *m.* The story, novel, etc., inserted in many periodicals.

folletinista [fol-lyay-te-nees'-tah], *m.* One who edits *folletines.*

folletista [fol-lyay-tees'-tah], *m.* Pamphleteer, a writer of pamphlets.

folleto [fol-lyay'-to], *m.* A pamphlet; folder, brochure, leaflet.

follón, na [fol-lyone', nah], *a.* Feeble, inert, lazy (perezoso), negligent, mean, blustering (fanfarrón).

follón [fo-lyone'], *m.* 1. Rogue, villain, a mean, despicable fellow. 2. Rocket which discharges without noise (cohete).

3. Bud or branch from the root or trunk of a tree. 4. Breaking wind without noise. 5. Rumpus, row, shindy (jaleo); mess (lío).

follonería [fol-yo-nay-ree'-ah], *f.* Knavishness.

foma [fo'-mah], *f. (Bot.)* A fungus growing generally in small tubercles upon branches or leaves of plants.

fomentación [fo-men-tah-the-on']. *f.* Fomentation.

fomentador, ra [fo-men-tah-dor', rah], *m. & f.* Fomenter.

fomentar [fo-men-tar'], *va.* 1. To foment, to produce warmth by fomentation. 2. *(Met.)* To foment, to protect, to favor, to patronize, to countenance, to encourage.

fomento [fo-men'-to], *m.* 1. Fomentation. 2. Fuel. 3. Patronage, protection, support, encouragement.

fomes [fo'-mes], *m.* 1. Incentive, generally applied to that which excites to sin. 2. Lust, concupiscence.

fonación [fo-nah-the-on'], *f.* 1. Phonation, emission of the voice. 2. Pronunciation.

fonas [fo'-nas], *f. pl.* Pieces sewed to a cloak.

fonda [fon'-dah], *f.* Hotel, inn, tavern, lodging house (pensión), small restaurant (restaurante).

fondable [fon-dah'-blay], *a.* That may be sounded with a plummet.

fondado, da [fon-dah'-do, dah], *a.* Applied to pipes or barrels, the bottoms of which are secured with cords or nails.

fondeadero [fon-day-ah-day'-ro], *m. (Naut.)* Anchoring-ground.

fondear [fon-day-ar'], *va.* 1. To sound, to explore the depth of water (profundidad). 2. To bring up from the bottom of water. 3. *(Naut.)* To search a ship for prohibited goods (registrar). 4. To examine closely. *-vn. (Naut.)* To cast anchor.

fondeo [fon-day'-o], *m.* The act of searching a ship.

fondillón [fon-del-lyone'], *m.* 1. The dregs and lees at the bottom of a cask of liquor. 2. Rancid Alicant wine.

fondillos [fon-deel'-lyos], *m. pl.* The seat of underwear or wide pants. *(Acad.)*

fondista [fon-dees'-tah], *m.* Inn-keeper, hotel-keeper, tavern-keeper.

fondo [fon'-do], *m.* 1. Bottom of a hollow thing (de caja) 2. Bottom, the ground under the water (de mar). 3. Bottoms of a hill or valley. 4. Ground of silks and other stuffs. 5. Plain or cut velvet. 6. Thickness of a diamond. 7. Bottom, the extent of a man's capacity (carácter). 8. The principal or essential part of a thing. 9. Stock, quantity, store (virtudes, vicios) 10. Stock, fund, capital, effects. **Fondos públicos,** stute securities. 11. Every hollow to be gilded. 12. *(Mil.)* Space occupied by files of soldiers. **Dar fondo,** *(Naut.)* to cast anchor. **Echar a fondo,** to sink a vessel. **Irse a fondo,** to go to the bottom, to founder. **A fondo,** perfectly, completely. **Fondos vitalicios,** life annuities. **Fondos de un navío,** *(Naut.)* the floor or flat of a ship. **A fondo,** deeply, **El fondo,** the background. **Conocer algo a fondo,** to know something thoroughly. **Corredor de medio fondo,** middle-distance runner. **Bajos fondos sociales,** dregs of society. **Estar sin fondos,** to have no fund. **Reunir fondos,** to get money together.

fondón [fon-done'], *m.* 1. *V.* FONDILLÓN. 2. Ground of silk or velvet.

fondona [fon-do'-nah], *a.* Old and ungraceful (mujer).

fondura [fon-doo'-rah], *f.* Profundity, depth.

fonema [fo-nay'-mah], *m.* Phonema.

fonética [fo-nay'-te-cah], *f.* Phonetics.

fonético, ca [fo-nay'-te-co, cah], *a.* Phonetic, relating to, or representing sounds.

fónica [fo'-ne-cah], *f.* Phonics, the science of articulate sound.

fónico [fo'-ne-co, cah], *a.* Phonic, relating to sound: phonetic. *(Arch.)* An elliptic arch for repeating echoes; the foci are called phonic, and there are placed the speaker and the listener. A whispering gallery.

fonil [fo-neel'], *m. (Naut.)* Funnel, an instrument for filling hogsheads of water.

fonje [fon'-hay], *a.* Bland, soft, spongy.

fonografía [fo-no-grah-fee'-ah], *f.* Phonography, representation of sound by signs: the chief mode of stenography.

fonográfico, ca [fo-no-grah'-fe-co, cah], *a.* Phonographic, belonging to phonography.

fonógrafo [fo-no'-grah-fo], *m.* Phonograph, an apparatus invented by Edison, for fixing and recording sounds.

fonología [fo-no-lo-hee'-ah], *f.* Phonology, the science of the letters and pronunciation of a language.

fonoteca [fo-no'-tay-cah], *f.* Record library, sound archive.

fontal [fon-tahl'], *a. (Ant.)* Main, chief, principal.

fontana [fon-tah'-nah], *f. (Poet.)* Fountain.

fontanal [fon-tah-nahl'], *m.* 1. Source or spring of water. 2. Place abounding in springs. *-a.* Belonging to fountain.

fontanar [fon-tah-nar'], *m.* A spring of water.

fontanela [fon-tah-nay'-lah], *f.* Surgeon's instrument for opening issues.

fontanería [fon-tah-nay-ree'-ah], *f.* 1. The art of conducting water through pipes to make fountains. 2. The collection of pipes conduits through which water is conducted for a fountain 3. Plumber's shop (tienda).

fontanero [fon-tah-nay'-ro], *m.* He that makes fountains, by conducting water through pipes and conduits.

fontezuela [fon-tay-thoo-ay'-lah], *f. dim.* A small fountain.

fontícola [fon-tee'-co-lah], *a. (Biol.)* Living in fountains or on their borders.

footing [foo'-teen], *m.* Jogging. **Hacer footing,** to jog, to go jogging.

foque [fo'-kay], *m. (Naut.)* Jib. **Foque mayor** or **foque de caza,** the standing jib.

forajido, da [fo-rah-hee'-do, dah], *a.* 1. Outlawed. 2. Wicked, villainous: used as a substantive.

foral [fo-rahl'], *a. (Law.)* Belonging to the statute law of a country, or to the civil rights of its inhabitants. **Bienes forales,** lands and tenements held by acknowledgment of superiority to a higher lord.

foralmente [fo-ral-men'-tay], *adv.* In the manner of courts.

foramen [fo-rah'-men], *m.* Hole in the under stone of a mill.

foraminíferos [fo-rah-me-nee'-fay-ros], *m. pl.* Foraminifera, microscopic protozoa, having calcareous shells.

foráneo, nea [fo-rah'-nayo, ah], *a.* Stranger, foreign.

forastería [fo-ras-tay-ree'-ah], *f.* Place for strangers, inn for strangers.

forastero, ra [fo-ras-tay'-ro, rah], *a.* 1. Strange, not living in the town or place. 2. Exotic, not produced in the country.

forastero, ra [fo-ras-tay'-ro, rah], *m. & f.* Stranger, guest: applied to persons belonging to another town, but of the same nation.

forbante [for-bahn'-tay], *m. V.* FILIBUSTERO.

forcejar [for-thay-har'], or **Forcejear,** *vn.* 1. To struggle, to strive, to labor. 2. To strive, to contest, to contend to struggle in opposition. *-va. V.* FORZAR.

forcejo [for-thay'-ho], *m.* Struggling, striving, laboring in opposition.

forcejón [for-thay-hone'], *m.* Push effort to disengage oneself from another.

forcejudo, da [for-thay-hoo'-do, dah], *a.* Strong, robust, of great strength.

fórceps [for'-theps], *m.* Forceps, ordinary and surgical.

forchina [for-chee'-nah], *f.* war-like instrument in shap of a fork.

forcina [for-thee'-nah], *f.* Swelling of a tree in the angle formed by a thick branch with the trunk.

forense [fo-ren'-say], *a.* Forensic, belonging to the courts.

forero, ra [fo-ray'-ro, rah], *a.* Conformable to the statute law of a country.

forestación [fo-rays-tah-the-on'], *f.* Afforestation.

forestal [fo-rays-tah', *a.* Forest.

forja [for'-hah], *f.* 1. Forge, the place where silver is beaten into form (fundición). 2. Forging, fabricating, manufacturing. 3. Mortar, cement.

forjable [for-hah'-blay], *a.* Forgeable.

forjador [for-hah-dor'], *m.* Smith gold-beater; franker, forger.

forjadura [for-hah-doo'-rah], *f.* 1. Forging, beating a metal into form or shape. 2. Trap, snare, imposition. 3. Forgery; falsification.

forjar [for-har'], *va.* 1. To forge, to hammer, to bend metal into shape (hierro) 2. To finale, to form or fabricate by orderly construction. 3. To forge, to counterfeit, to falsify (falsificar). 4. To frame, to invent, to fabricate. **Forjar un plan,** to make a plan.

forlón [for-lone'], *m.* Old kind of coach with four seats.

forma [for'-mah], *f.* 1. Form, shape, a figure abstractedly considered, free, make, fashion. 2. Form, stated method, established practice, ritual, prescribed manner of doing something. 3. Hand, form or cast of waiting. 4. Form, the essential modification of matter, by which it has existence. 5. Form, regularity, method, order. 6. form, particular model or modifation, mould, matrix. 7. *(Print.)* Form, a frame containing the pages arranged for press, as they appear on one side of a planted sheet. 8. The unleavened bread which serves for the communion of the laity. 9. Form, ceremony, external rights. **De forma que,** in such a manner that. **En forma** or **en debida forma,** formally, according to law or established rules, legally. **En forma** or **en toda forma,** perfectly, completely, carefully, heedfully, exactly. **Dar forma,** to regulate or arrange that which was disordered. **Tener buenas formas:** a) to be of fine figure, wellproportined, especially said of women. b) to be polite, affable and discreet in speech and action. **La única forma de hacerlo es…,** the only way to do it is. **De esta forma,** in this way. **De todas formas,** at any rate. **Forma de pago,** means of payment.

formable [for-mah'-blay], *a.* That which may be formed.

formación [for-mah-the-on'], *f.* 1. Formation, the act of forming or generating. 2. Formation, the manner in which something is formed; form, shape, figure. 3. *(Mil.)* Array of troops. 4. Twisted cord of silk, gold, silver, etc., used by embroiderers. 5. Training, education (educación). **Sin la debida formación en la investigación,** without the proper research.

formador, ra [for-mah-dor', rah], *m. & f.* Former, one that forms, fashions, or shapes.

formaje [for-mah'-hay], *m.* Cheesevat, cheese. *Cf.* Fr. fromage.

formal [for-mahl'], *a.* 1. Formal, regular, methodical. 2. Proper, genuine. 3. Formal (promesa etc.), serious (serio), grave, steady, sedate, punctual (puntual), dignified (grave). **Es una persona muy seria,** he is a perfectly reliable sort. **Siempre estuvo muy formal conmigo,** he was always very correct towards me.

formalidad [for-mah-le-dahd'], *f.* 1. Formality, the quality by which something is what it is. 2. Exactness, punctuality. 3. Formality, ceremony; established mode of behavior. 4. Gravity, seriousness (seriedad), solemnity. 5. Established form of judicial proceedings, or legal precedent (requisito). **Son las formalidades de costumbre,** these are the usual formalities. **Con formalidad,** in earnest.

formalismo [for-mah-lees'-mo], *m.* 1. Formalism, a metaphysical system which denies the existence of matter and recognizes only the form. 2. Rigorous application of method, adhesion to routine; red tape (burocrático).

formalizar [for-mah-le-thar'], *va.* 1. To form or make complete or perfect (cosas no materiales). *-vr* 1. To grow formal (relación), to affect gravity, to be regulized (situación). 2. To grow serious (ponerse serio). 3. To take offence (ofenderse).

formalmente [for-mal-men'-tay], *adv.* 1. Formally, according to established rules. 2. Formally, seriously.

formar [for-mar'], *va.* 1. To form, to shape, to fashion, to frame, to make up, to cut out, to build up (existenciar, reserva) 2. To form, to make out of materials (integrar). 3. To form, to model to a particular shape. 4. To form or draw up troops; to put in order; to arrange in a particular manner. 5. To train, to educate (educar). *-vn.* 1. To adjust the edges of embroidery work. 2. To shape, to develop (desarrollarse). 3. To be trained, to be educated (educarse). **Formar concepto,** to form judgment. **Está formado por,** it is formed by. **Se formó en la escuela de Praga,** he was trained in the Prague school.

formatear [for-mah-tay-ar'], *va. (Comput.)* To format.

formateo [for-mah-tay'-o], *m. (Comput.)* Formating.

formativo, va [for-mah-tee'-vo, vah], *a.* Formative.

formato [for-mah'-to], *m.* 1. *(TIP.)* Format; size (tamaño de papel). **Periódico de formato reducido,** tabloid newspaper. 2. *(Comput.)* **Formato del hardware,** hardware formatting. **Formato del software,** software formatting. **Formato opcional,** optional formatting.

formatriz [for-mah-treeth'], *a.* Forming.

formejar [for-may-har'], *va. (Naut.)* To arrange things in order on board ships; to trim the hold.

formero [for-may'-ro], *m. (Arch.)* Side arch of a vault.

formicante [for-me-cahn'-tay], *a.* Applied to a low, weak, and frequent pulse.

formicarios, formícidos [for-me-cah'-re-os, for-mee'-the-dos], *m. pl: (Et.)* Hymenoptera which carry a string; bees, wasps, sandwasps, etc.

fórmico [for'-me-co], *m.* 1. Formic, (ácido, éter). 2. A certain hard tumor like a wart.

formicular [for-me-coo-lar'], *a.* Relating to ants.

formidable [for-me-dah'-blay], *a.* 1. Formidable (terrible), dreadful, tremendous, terrific (estupendo). 2. Uncommonly large (enorme).

formidablemente [for-me-dah-blay-men'-tay], *adv.* Formidably.

formidoloso, sa [for-me-do-lo'-so, sah], *a.* 1. Timorous, timid, fearful. 2. Dreadful, frightful, horrible.

formillón [for-meel-lyon'], *m.* A hatform.

formón [for-mone'], *m.* 1. Paring chisel, used by carpenters and joiners. 2. Punch, an instrument used to cut wafers for consecration.

fórmula [for'-moo-lah], *f.* 1. Formula, a prescribed model or rule. 2. Recipe. 3. An algebraical expression. 4. Profession of faith. 5. Formulary. **Una fórmula para conseguir el éxito,** a formula to ensure success.

formular [for-moo-lar'], *va.* To formulate; to draw up, to make out; to frame, to pose (pregunta); to file, to put in (reivindicación).

formulario [for-moo-lah'-re-o], *m.* Formulary, a book containing models, rules, or formulas. **Formulario de inscripción,** application form.

formulista [for-moo-lees'-tah], *m.* One who punctually observes the prescribed models.

fornáceo, cea [for-nah'-thay-o, ah], *a. (Poet.)* Belonging to or like a furnace.

fornaz [for-nath'], *m. (Poet.)* V. FRAGUA.

fornecino, na [for-nay-thee'-no, nah], *a.* Bastard, illegitimate (niños).

fornelo [for-nay'-lo], *m.* A portable little oven or furnace.

fornicación [for-ne-cah-the-on'], *f.* 1. Fornication. 2. In Scripture, sometimes idolatry.

fornicador, ra [for-ne-cah-dor', rah], *m. &f.* Fornicator.

fornicar [for-ne-car'], *va.* To fornicate, to commit lewdness.

fornicario, ria [for-ne-cah'-re-o, ah], *a.* Relating to fornication.

fornicio [for-nee'-the-o], *m. (Ant.)* Fornication.

fornido, da [for-nee'-do, dah], *a.* Robust, corpulent, lusty, stout.

fornitura [for-ne-too'-rah], *f.* 1. Leather straps worn by soldiers. 2. *(Print.)* Types cast to complete sorts.

foro [fo'-ro], *m.* 1. Court of justice, the hall where tribunals hold their sittings. 2. Bar, the legal profession. 3. Lordship, the right of a superior lord, or whom lands or tenements are held. 4. Background of the stage or theatre. 5. Forum (reunión), meeting.

forofo, fa [fo-ro'-fo], *m &f.* Fan, supporter.

forrado [for-rah'-do], *a. &pp.* of FORRAR. Lined. **Un libro forrado de pergamino,** a book bound in parchment.

forraje [for-rah'-hay], *m.* 1. Forage (pienso); grain, hay, or grass for horses; foraging (acto). 2. *(coll.)* Abundance of things of little value.

forrajeador, forrajero [for-rah-hay-ah-dor'], *m.* Forager, a soldier detached in search of forage; fodderer.

forrajear [for-rah-hay-ar'], *va.* To forage, to collect forage for the horses of soldiers.

forrar [for-rar'], *va.* 1. To line (ropa). 2. To cover (libro). 3. To upholster (coche). 4. To lag (cubo, cisterna). *-vr.* 1. To line one's pocket (enriquecerse). 2. To stuff oneself (de comida).

forro [for'-ro], *m.* 1. Linning. 2. *(Naut.)* Furring of a ship, double planks laid on the sides, sheathing. 3. Cover of a book. **Con forro de piel,** with a fur lining. **Ni por el forro,** not in the slightest.

fortachón, na [for-tah-chon', nah], *a.* Applied to a person possessed of uncommon strength.

fortalecedor, ra [for-tah-lay-thay-dor', rah], *m. & f.* Fortifier.

fortalecer [for-tah-lay-therr'], *va.* 1. To fortify, to strengthen, to corroborate. 2. To fortify a place. 3. To aid, to encourage, to support (moralmente). *-vr.* 1. To fortify oneself. 2. To become stronger (opinión). (*Yo fortalezco, yo fortalezaca,* from *Fortalecer.* V. ABORRECER.

fortalecimiento [for-tah-lay-the-me-en'-to], *m.* 1. Act of fortifying. 2. Works raised for the defence of a place.

fortaleza [for-tah-lay'-thah], *f.* 1. Fortitude, firmness. 2. Fortitude, courage. 3. Strength, vigor, nerve, force, manhood (cualidad). 4. Stronghold, fortress.

forte [for'-tay], *int. (Naut.)* Avast! *-a. (Mus.)* Loud.

fortificable [for-te-fe-cah'-blay], *a.* Fortifiable.

fortificación [for-te-fe-cah-the-on'], *f.* 1. Fortification, the science of military architecture. 2. Fortification, place built for strength. 3. Works raised for the defence of a place.

fortificador [for-te-fe-cah-dor'], Fortifier.

fortificante [for-te-fe-cahn'-tay], *pa.* Fortifying.

fortificar [for-te-fe-car'], *va.* 1. To strengthen, to fortify, to corroborate, to invigorate. 2. To fortify a place.

fortín [for-tran], *m.* 1. *(dim.)* Fortin, fortler, a small fort. 2. Field or temporary fortifications for the defence of troops.

FORTRAN [for-tran], *m. (Comput.)* FORTRAN (FORmula TRANslator).

fortuitamente [for-too-ee-tah-men'-tay], *adv.* Fortuitously; by chance.

fortuito, ta [for-too-ee'-to, tah], *a.* Fortuitous, accidental, unexpected.

fortuna [for-too'-nah], *f.* 1. Fortune, chance, fate. 2. Good luck (suerte), success. 3. Storm, tempest. 4. Chance, unforeseen event. **Probar fortuna,** to try one's fortune. **Por fortuna,** luckily.

fortunón [for-too-none'], *m. (Aug.)* Great fortune, immense riches.

forzadamente [for-thah-dah-men-tay], *adv.* Forcibly, violently, forcefully. **Sonreír forzadamente,** to force a smile.

forzado, da [for-thah'-do, dah], *a. & pp.* of FORZAR. 1. Forced, constrained, necessitated. 2. Indispensable, necessary. **Sonrisa forzada,** forced smile.

forzado [for-thah'-do], *m.* Criminal sentenced to the galleys.

forzador [for-thah-dor'], *m.* 1. Ravisher. 2. Forcer, one who commits acts of violence to attain some purpose.

forzal [for-thahl'], *m.* The middle part of a comb between the two rows of teeth.

forzamiento [for-thah-me-en'-to], *m.* The act of forcing.

forzar [for-thar'], *va.* 1. To force, to overpower by strength, to draw or push by main strength (obligar). 2. To force, to compel, to constrain. 3. To enforce, to urge. 4. To subdue by force of arms. 5. To force, to ravish, to commit a rape (mujer). 6. To force, to oblige or enforce, to urge. 7. To force (puerta); to break into (casa); to force (cerradura).

forzosa [for-tho'-sah], *f.* 1. A decisive move at the game of draughts. 2. Necessity of acting against one's will.

forzosamente [for-tho-sah-men'-tay], *adv.* Forcibly, necessarily; violently, forcedly. **Tuvieron forzosamente que venderlo,** they had no choice but to sell it.

forzoso, sa [for-tho'-so, sah], *a.* Indispensable, necessary (necesario), needful, requisite, compulsory (obigatorio); forced (aterrizaje)

forzudo, da [for-thoo'-do, dah], *a.* Strong, vigorous, potent, lusty, stout, able-bodied.

fosa [fo'-sah], *f.* 1. Grave, tomb (sepultura). **Fosa común,** common grave. 2. *(Anat.)* Fossa. **Fosa séptica,** septic tank.

fosar [fo-sar'], *va.* To make a pit, ditch, or fosse round something.

fosca [fos'-cah], *f. (Prov.)* A thick wood or grove.

fosco, ca [fos'-co, cah], *a.* Brow-beaten, frowning. V. HOSCO.

fosfático, ca [fos-fah'-te-co, cah], *a.* Phosphatic.

fosfato [fos-fah'-to], *m.* Phosphate, salt of phosphoric acid.

fosfito [fos-fee'-to], *m.* Phosphite, a salt of Phosphorous acid.

fosforado, da [fos-fo-rah'-do, dah], *a.* Phosphated, containing phosphorous.

fosforera [fos-fo-ray'-rah], *f.* A match-box.

fosforero, ra [fos-fo-ray'-ro, rah], *m. & f.* A vender of matches.

fosforescencia [fos-fo-res-then'-the-ah], *f.* Phosphorescence.

fosforescente [fos-fo-res-then'-tay], *a.* Phosphorescent.

fosforescer [fos-fo-res-therr'], *vn.* To be phosphorescent, to shed a phosphoric light.

fosfórico, ca [fos-fo'-re-co, cah], *a.* Phosphoric.

fósforo [fos'-fo-ro], *m.* 1. Phosphorus, one of the elements. 2. A friction match (cerilla).

fosforoso, sa [fos-fo-ro'-so, sah], *a.* Phosphorous, relating to the lower equivalents of phosphorus.

fósfuro [fos-foo'-ro], *m.* Phosphide, a compound of phosphorus, not acid.

fosgeno [fos-hay'-no], *m. (Chem.)* Phosgene.

fósil [fo'-seel], *a.* Fossil, dug out of the earth, and mineral in nature. *-m* Fossil, petrifaction, organic remains.

fosilizarse [fo-se-le-thar'-say], *vr.* To become fossilized, petrified.

foso [fo'-so], *m.* 1. Pit, hole dug in the ground. V. HOYO. 2. Bog, a marshy ground covered with water. 3. Moat, ditch fosse. 4. Pit (escenario).

foto [fo-to], *f.* Photo; snap, snapshot. **Foto de conjunto,** group photo. **Sacar una foto,** to take a photo.

fotocélula [fo-to-thay'-loo'-lah], *f.* Electric eye.

fotocopia [fo-to-co'-pe-ah], *f.* 1. Photocopy. 2. Photocopying (acto).

fotocopiadora [fo-to-co-pe-ah'-do-rah], *f.* Photocopier.

fotocopiar [fo-to-co-pe-ar'], *va.* To photocopy.

fotoeléctrico, ca [fo-to-ay-lec'-tre-co, cah], *a.* Photoelectric.

fotofobia [fo-to-fo'be-ah], *f.* Photophobia, dread of light (enfermedad).

fotogénico, ca [fo-to-hay'-ne-co, cah], *a.* Photogenic, lightproducing.

fotograbado [fo-to-grah-bah'-do], *m.* A photo engraving, photo gravure.

fotografía [fo-to-grah-fee'-ah], *f.* 1. Photography, the art of fixing an image by the chemical rays of light. 2. A photograph, the picture obtained by this process. **Fotografía aérea,** aerial photography. **Fotografía en colores,** color photography.

fotografiar [fo-to-grah-fe-ar'], *va.* To photograph.

fotográfico, ca [fo-to-grah'-fe-co, cah], *a.* Photographic, relative to photography.

fotógrafo [fo-to'-grah-fo], *m.* Photographer. **Fotógrafo aficionado,** amateur photographer.

fotograma [fo-to-grah-mah], *m.* (Cine) Shot, still.

fotolitografía [fo-to-le-to-grah-fee'-ah], *f.* 1. Photolithography, the art of imprinting a photograph upon a lithographic stone. 2. Photolithograph, each of the prints obtained by this process.

fotomatón [fo-to-mah-tone'], *m.* 1. Photograph booth (quiosco). 2. Passport-type photo (foto).

fotometría [fo-to-may-tree'-ah], *f.* Photometry.

fotométrico, ca [fo-to-may'-tre-co, cah], *a.* Photometric, measuring light.

fotómetro [fo-to'-may-tro], *m.* Photometer.

fotonovela [fo-to-no-vay'-lah], *f.* Romance illustrated with photos.

fotsíntesis [fo-to-seen'-tay-sis], *f.* Photosynthesis.

fotostático, ca [fo-tos-tah'-te-co, cah], *a.* Photostatic.

fototipia [fo-to-tee'-pe-ah], *f.* Phototype.

foulard [foo-lar'], *m.* Scarf (cabeza).

fovila [fo-vee'-lah], *f. (Bot.)* Fovilla, a substance emitted from the pollen of flowers.

foya [fo'-yah], *f. (Prov.)* An oven full of charcoal.

frac [frahc], *m.* A dress-coat.

fracasado, da [frah-cah-sah'-do], *a.* Unsuccessful, failed. *-m & f.* Failure, person who is a failure.

fracasar [frah-cah-sar'], *vn.* 1. To crumble, to break in pieces (barcos). 2. To be lost or destroyed. 3. To be unsuccessful.

fracaso [frah-cah'-so], *m.* 1. Downfall, ruin, destruction. 2. Calamity, an unfortunate event. **Es un total fracaso,** it's a complete disaster.

fracción [frac-the-on'], *f.* 1. Fraction, the act of breaking into parts. 2. Fraction, a broken part of an integral. 3. *(Math.)* Fraction. **Fracción decimal,** fraction.

fraccionar [frac-the-o-nar'], *va.* To divide into fractions, to break up, to split up.

fraccionario, ria [frac-theo-nah'-re-o, ah], *a.* Fractional. **Número fraccionario,** a mixed number.

fracmasón [frac-mah-son'], *m.* Freemason, mason.

fractura [frac-too'-rah], *f.* 1. Fracture, breach, separation of the contiguous parts. 2. *(Surg.)* Fracture, the separation of the continuity of a bone. **Fractura complicada,** compound fracture.

fracturar [frac-too-rar'], *va.* To fracture, to break a bone. *-vr.* To fracture, to break.

fraga, fragaria [frah'-gah, frah-gah'-re-ah], *f.* Species of raspberry.

fragancia [frah-gahn'-the-ah], *f.* 1. Fragrance, sweetness of smell. 2. Good name, good reputation. 3. Actual commission of a crime.

fragante [frah-gahn'-tay], *a.* 1. Fragrant, odoriferous. 2. Flagrant, notorious. **En fragante,** in the act itself, red-handed (en flagrante delito). V. FLAGRANTE.

franganti (in) *adv.* Red-handed, in the act.

fragata [frah-gah'-tah], *f.* 1. A frigate. **Fragata ligera,** a light fast-sailing vessel. 2. The frigate bird.

frágil [frah'-heel], *a.* 1. Brittle, tangible, fragile. 2. Frail, weak of resolution, liable to error or seduction. 3. Decaying, perishable.

fragilidad [frah-he-le-dahd'], *f.* 1. Fragility, brittleness. 2. Fragility, frailty, liableness to a fault. 3. Sin of infirmity, sensual pleasure, folly.

frágilmente [frah'-heel-men-tay], *adv.* Frailly.

fragmentación [frag-men-tah-the-on'], *f.* Fragmentation.

fragmento [frag-men'-to], *m.* 1. Fragment, a small part separated from the whole. 2. Fragment, a part of some book or writing.

fragor [frah-gor'], *m. (Archaic.)* Noise, clamor, crash.

fragoroso, sa [frah-go-so], *a. (Poet.)* Noisy, obstreperous.

fragosidad [frah-go-se-dahd'], *f.* Unevenness or roughness of the road; imperviousness of a forest; craggedness, cragginess.

fragoso, sa [frah-go'-so, sah], *a.* Craggy, rough, uneven; full of brambles and briers; noisy; difficult (terreno); dense (bosque).

fragua [frah'-goo-ah], *f.* 1. Forge, as for iron. 2. Place where intrigues are plotted.

fraguador [frah-goo-ah-dor'], *m.* Schemer, one who plans an intrigue; one who counterfeits or forges.

fraguar [frah-goo-ar'], *va.* 1. To forge, to reduce iron or other metal into shape (hierro) 2. *(Met.)* To plan, to plot, to contrive, to brew, to hatch.-*vr.* To unite in a mass (mortero)

fragura [frah-goo'-rah], *f.* Roughness of the road, imperviousness of a forest.

fraile [frah'-e-lay], *m.* 1. Friar, brother; appellation of the members of religious orders. **Fraile predicador,** friar preacher. *V.* RELIGIOSO. 2. Fold or plait in petticoats. 3. *(Print.)* That part of a printed page which is pale for want of ink. 4. The upright post of a floodgate in watermills.

frailecillo [fra-he-lay-theel'-lyo], *m.* 1. *(dim.)* A little frair, or a child which wears a friar's habit. 2. *(Orn.)* Lapwing. 3. Wedge securing the spindle of a silkreel.

frailería [fra-he-lay-ree'-ah], *f.* *(coll.)* Number of friars assembled together.

frailero, ra [frah-e-lay'-ro, rah], *a.* Very fond of friars.

frailesco, ca [frah-e-less'-co, cah], *a.* Monkish, belonging to friars, friar-like.

frailía [frah-e-lee'-ah], *f.* 1. State of monks, monastic life. 2. Regular clergy.

frailuno, na [frah-e-loo'-no, nah], Belonging or proper to a friar.

frambuesa [fram-boo-ay'-sah], *f.* The raspberry.

frambueso [fram-boo-ay'-so], *m.* *(Bot.)* Raspberry bush.

frámea [frah'-may-ah], *f.* *(Obs.)* Javelin, dart.

francachela [fran-cah-chay'-lah], *f.* *V.* COMILONA.

francalete [fran-cah-lay'-tay], *m.* Strap, slip of leather with a buckle.

francamente [fran-cah-men'-tay], *adv.* 1. Frankly, openly, freely, nakedly (hablar) 2. Frankly; really, definitely (realmente). **Francamente no lo sé,** frankly I don't know.

francés, sa [fran-thays', sah], *a.* French. -*m.* The French language. **A la francesa,** after the French fashion. **Despedirse a la francesa,** *(Coll.)* to take French leave.

francesilla [fran-thay-seel'-lyah], *f.* *(Bot.)* Common yard crowfoot.

franchipán [fran-che-pahn'], *m.* Frangipani, a perfume.

franciscano, na [fran-this-cah'-no, nah], *a.* 1. Franciscan, belonging to the order of St. Francis. 2. Gray-colored, like the dress of the Franciscans.

francmasón [franc-mah-sone'], *m.* (free) mason.

francmasonería [franc-mah-so-nay-ree'-ah], *f.* (Free) masonry, a secret society of mutual protection.

franco [frahn'-co], *m.* 1. Franc, a French coin. 2. Fairtime, when merchandise is sold free of duty.-*pl.* Franks, an appellation given by the Turks, Arabs, and Greeks to the people of the west of Europe.

franco, ca [frahn'-co, cah], *a.* 1. Frank, open generous, liberal, open-hearted, bountiful (directo). **Si he de ser franco,** frankly, to tell the truth. 2. Free, disengaged. 3. Exempt, privileged. 4. Ingenuous, plain, sincere (sincero), fair, generous. 5. Free, exempt from duty. **Puerto franco,** a free port. **Franco de porte,** carriage-free.

francófono [fran-do-fo'-no], *a.* French-speaking. -*m* & *f.* French speaker.

franco-hispano [fran-co-ees-pah'-no], *a.* Franco-Spanish.

francolín [fran-co-leen'], *m.* *(Orn.)* Francolin, the African or Indian partridge. **francotirador** [fran-co-tee-rah-dor'], *m.* 1. Sniper, sharp shooter. 2. Freelance (periodista)

franela [frah-nay'-lah], *f.* Flannel (tela).

frange [frahn'-hay], *m.* *(Her.)* Division of the field of a shield.

frangente [fran-hen'-tay], *m.* Accident, disaster.

frangible [fran-hee'-blay], *a.* Brittle, frangible.

frangollar [fran-gol-lyar'], *va.* To do a thing carelessly.

frangollo [fran-gol'-lyo], *m.* 1. Pottage made of wheat boiled in milk. 2. *(Peru and Chili)* A stew of many ingredients or which is poorly made. 3. *(coll.)* Disorder, confusion.

frangote [fran-go'-tay], *m.* Bale of goods.

frángula [frahn'-goo-lah], *f.* *(Bot.)* Berrybearing alder, alder buckthorn.

franja [frahn'-hah], *f.* 1. Fringe, an ornamental border, stripe. 2. Fringe, strip, band (zona). **Franja de tierra,** strip of land.

franjar [fran-har'], *va.* To fringe, to trim with fringe, to adorn with fringes.

franjear [fran-hay-ar'], *va.* *V.* FRANJAR.

franquear [fran-kay-ar'], *va.* 1. To exempt, to grant immunity from, to enfranchise. 2. To pay the postage on letters, books, etc (Correos). **Una carta franqueada,** a post-paid letter. 3. To gratify, to make liberal grants or gifts. 4. To disengage, to extricate; to clear from obstacles or impediments (obstáculo). 5. To free a slave. *(Acad.)* -*vr.* 1. To give oneself easily to the desire of others. **Franquearse con uno,** to unbosom oneself to somebody. 2. To unbosom oneself, to reveal in confidence one's secrets or thoughts. 3. To become liberal. 4. *(Naut.)* To be ready for sailing.-*vn.* *(Naut.)* To be situated at a point whence may be seen clearly and openly a work, harbor-entrance, etc.

franqueo [fran-kay'-o], *m.* 1. Franking letters, printed matter, etc. 2. Postage, that is paid on mail matter; also postage stamps.

franqueza [fran-kay'-thah], *f.* 1. Freedom, liberty, exemption, enfranchisement, freeness. 2. Frankness, generosity, open-heartedness; liberality of sentiment. 3. Frankness, ingenuousness, sincerity. **Lo digo con toda franqueza, I** say so quite frankly. **Con franqueza,** frankly.

franquía [fran-kee'-ah], *f.* *(Naut.)* In the stream. Readiness for sailing.

franquicia [fran-kee'-the-ah], *f.* 1. Immunity or exemption from taxes, liberty, franchise (exención). 2. A privileged place, which enjoys exemption from taxes and imposts. **Franquicia postal,** privilege of franking letters.

fraque [frah'-kay], *m.* *V.* FRAC.

frasca [frahs'-cah], *f.* *(Prov.)* Dry leaves or small branches of trees.

frasco [frahs'-co], *m.* 1. Flask, a bottle with a narrow neck. **Frasco de bolsillo,** hip flask. **Frasco de perfume,** scent bottle. 2. Powder-horn or flask.

frase [frah'-say], *f.* 1. Pharse, a mode of speech (locución). 2. Idiomatic expression, style of any writer (oración). 3. An energetic expression, generally metaphorical, signifying more than is expressed. **Frase compleja,** complex sentence. **Diccionario de frases,** dictionary of quotations.

frasear [frah-say-ar'], *va.* 1. To phrase, to employ idiomatic expressions. 2. *(Mus.)* To pharse, to give the proper expression to each musical phrase.

fraseología [frah-say-olo-hee'-ah], *f.* 1. Phraseology, the style of a writer. 2. Verbosity, pomposity.

frasquera [fras-kay'-rah], *f.* Bottle-case, liquor-case.

frasquerilla, ita [fras-kay-reel'-lyah, ee'-tah], *f. dim.* Small bottle-case.

frasqueta [fras-kay'-tah], *f.* Frisket of a printing press.

frasquillo, ito [fras-keel'-lyo], *m. dim.* A small flask.

fraterna [frah-terr'-nah], *f.* *(coll.)* A severe reprimand, lecture, lesson.

fraternal [frah-ter-nahl'], *a.* Fraternal, brotherly.

fraternalmente [frah-ter-nal-men'-tay], *adv.* Fraternally.

fraternidad [frah-ter-ne-dahd'], *f.* Fraternity, the state or quality of a brother, brotherhood.

fraternizar [fra-ter-ne-thar'], *vn.* To live in harmony, to fraternize.

fraterno, na [frah-terr'-no, nah], *a.* Fraternal, brotherly.

frates [frah'-tes], *m.* 1. A glass instrument, mushroom-shaped, for polishing stockings after they are washed. 2. A mason's wooden trowel.

fratesar [frah-tay-sar'], *va.* To polish or smooth with the frates.

fratricida [frah-tre-thee'-dah], *m.* & *f.* Fratricide, murderer of a brother.

fratricidio [frah-tre-thee'-de-o], *m.* Fratricide, murder of a brother.

fraude [frah'-oo-day], *m.* Fraud, deceit, cheat, trick, artifice, imposture, craft, gull, dishonestly (cualidad).

fraudulencia [frah-oo-doo-len'-the-ah], *f.* Fraudulence, trickiness, deceitfulness.

fraudulentamente [frah-oo-doo-len-tah-men'-tay], *adv.* Fraudulently, knavishly.

fraudulento, ta [frah-oo-doo-len'-to, tah], *a.* Fraudulent, deceitful, artful, knavish.

fraudulosamente [frah-oo-doo-lo-sah-men'-tay], *adv.* Fraudulently, deceitfully, knavishly.

fraustina [frah-oos-tee'-nah], *f.* A wooden head for fashioning ladies' headdresses.

fraxinela [frac-se-nay'-lah], *f. (Bot.)* White dittany.

fray [frah'-e], *m.* A contracted appellation of respect addressed to religious men; brother. V. FRAILE.

frazada [frah-thah'-dah], *f.* A blanket.

frazadilla [frah-thah-deel'-lyah], *f. dim.* A small or light blanket.

frecuencia [fray-coo-en'-the-ah], *f.* Frequency. **Con frecuencia**, frequently.

frecuentación [fray-co-en-tah-the-on'], *f.* Frequentation, frequenting, visiting often.

frecuentador, ra [fray-coo-en-tah-dor', rah], *m. & f.* Frequenter.

frecuentar [fray-coo-en-tar'], *va.* 1. To frequent, to haunt, to visit often. 2. To repeat an act often.

frecuentativo [fray-coo-en-tah-tee'-vo], *a. (Gram.)* Frequentative (verbos).

frecuente [fray-coo-en'-tay], *a.* Frequent, often done (costumbre) or seen, often occurring. -*adv.* V. FRECUENTEMENTE.

frecuentemente [fray-coo-en-tay-men', tay], *adv.* Frequently, often, commonly.

fregadero [fray-gah-day'-ro], *m.* Kitchen sink (recipiente).

fregado [fray-gah'-do], *m.* 1. The act of scouring or cleaning kitchen utensils (de cocina). 2. A complicated subject or matter (lío); nasty affair (asunto turbio). **-Fregado, da,** *pp.* of FREGAR.

fregador [fray-gah-dor'], *m.* 1. Scullery. V. FREGADERO. 2. Dishcloth (trapo).

fregadura [fray-gah-doo'-rah], *f.* The act of rubbing or scouring.

fregajo [fray-gah'-ho], *m.* V. ESTROPAJO

fregamiento [fray-gah-me-en'-to], *m.* V. FRICACIÓN

fregar [fray-gar'], *va.* 1. To rub one thing against another (estregar). 2. To scour kitchen utensils (platos).

fregatriz [fray-gah-treet'], *f.* Kitchen maid, kitchen-wench.

fregona [fray-go'-nah], *f.* Kitchen maid (persona), kitchenwench, mop (utensilio).

fregoncilla [fray-gon-theel'-lyah], *f. dim.* A little kitchen maid.

fregonil [fray-go-neel'], *a.* Belonging to or becoming a kitchen maid.

fregonzuela [fray-gon-thoo-ay'-lah], *f. dim.* A little kitchen-girl.

freidura [fray-doo'-rah], *f.* Act of frying or dressing in a pan.

freír [fray-eer'], *va.* 1. To fry or dress in a frying pan. 2. *(Fig.)* To annoy (molestar); to torment (atormentar); to bore (aburrir). -*vr.* To fry, to be frying. **Freírse de calor**, to be excessively hot.

freje [fray'-hay], *m. (Prov.)* A hoop of osier to bind things with.

fréjol [fray'-ho-le], *m.* French bean, kidney bean.

frejol [fray-ho-le'], *m. (Amer.)* V. FREJOL and FRÍSOL.

frelo, la [fray'-lo, lah], *a.* Delicate, weakly, sickly. *(Prov. Andal.)*

frémito [fray'-me-to], *m.* V. BRAMIDO.

frenar [fray-nar'], *va.* 1. *(Aut.)* To Brake; to put the brake on. 2. *(fig.)* To Check.

frenazo [fray-nah-tho], *m* Sudden braking; sudden halt. **Dar un frenazo**, to brake suddenly.

frenería [fray-nay-ree'-ah], *f.* 1. Business of bridle making. 2. Place in which bridles are made or sold.

frenero [fray-nay'-ro], *m.* One who makes the bits of a bridle, a bridle maker.

frenesí [fray-nay-see'], *m.* 1. Frenzy, madness, distraction. 2. *(Met.)* Folly, extravagant caprice.

frenéticamente [fray-nay'-te-cah-men-tay], *adv.* Madly, furiously, distractedly, franticly.

frenético, ca [fray-nay'-te-co, cah], *a.* Mad, distracted, frantic, furious, lunatic.

frénico, ca [fray'-ne-co, cah], *a.* 1. Phrenic, relating to the diaphragm. 2. Relating to the intelligence or thought (phrenic).

frenillar [fray-neel-lyar'], *va. (Naut.)* To bridle the oars.

frenillo [fray-neel'-lyo], *m.* 1. Frenum of the tongue; tongue-tie. 2. *(Naut.)* Bridle of the oars, a rope with which oars are tied.

frenitis [fray-nee'-tis], *f.* Inflammation of the diaphragm.

freno [fray'-no], *m.* 1. Brake (coche). **Meter el freno**, to put on the brake. **Soltar el freno**, to release the brake. 2. Curb, check, restraint. **Poner frenos a las malas lenguas**, to stop the gossip. 3. Bridle or bit (de caballo). 4. Brace (dientes).

frenología [fray-no-lo-hee'-ah], *f.* Phrenology, cranioscopy; (formerly) the branch of science concerned with localization of functions of the human brain, esp. by examination of the shape and size of the skull.

frenológico, ca [fray-no-lo'-he-co, cah], *a.* Phrenological.

frenólogo [fray-no'-lo-go], *m.* Phrenologist.

frental [fren-tahl'], *a.* Frontal (frente). V. FRONTAL.

frentaza [fran-tah'-thah], *f. aug.* A broad forehead.

frente [fren'-tay], *f.* 1. The forehead. **Arrugar la frente**, to knit one's brow. **Frente a frente**, face to face. **Ir de frente**, to go foward. **Hacer frente a unos grandes gastos**, to meet considerable expenses. 2. Blank space at the beginning of a letter or other document. *(Acad.)* 3. *com.* Front, the forepart of a building or any other thing (parte delantera). **Frente, en frente**, opposite, over the way. -*m.* 4. *(Mil.)* Front rank of a body of troops. **Frente de batalla**, battle front. 5. Face of a bastion. -*prep.* Opposite, facing; in front of; *(fig.)* as opposed to.

frentero [fren-tay'-ro], *m.* Band worn on the forehead of children, to protect their face in case of falling.

freo [fray'-o], *m. (Naut.)* 1. A narrow channel between an island and the mainland. 2. *(Prov.)* Gorge, canyon, ravine between mountains.

fresa [fray'-sah], *f.* Strawberry, the fruit of the strawberry plant.

fresada [fray-sah'-dah], *f.* A dish formerly made of flour, milk and butter.

fresadora [fray-sah-do'-rah], *f.* Milling or drilling machine,

fresal [fray-sahl'], *m.* 1. *(Bot.)* Strawberry plant. 2. Ground bearing strawberry plants.

fresca [fres'-cah], *f.* 1. V. FRESCO. **Tomar la fresca**, to take the air (aire). **Salir con la fresca**, to go out during the fresh air in the evening or very early in the morning (período). 2. *(coll.)* (impertinencia) A cheeky remark. 3. Shameless woman, brazen woman (descarada).

frescachón, na [fres-cah-chone', nah], *a.* 1. Stout, good looking (robusto). 2. *(Naut.)* Fresh, cool (viento).

frescal [fres-cahl'], *a.* Not entirely fresh, but preserved with little salt (pescado).

frescamente [fres-cah-men'-tay], *adv.* 1. Freshly, recently, lately. 2. Coolly, resolutely, without passion.

frescar [fres-car'], *vn. (Naut.)* V. REFRESCAR.

fresco, ca [fres'-co, cah], *a.* 1. Fresh, coolish, rather cool. 2. Fresh, recent, newly come, just made (nuevo). **Cosas todavía frescas en la memoria**, things still fresh in the memory. 3. Plump, ruddy. 4. Fresh, bold in manner (descarado). **Estar más fresco que una lechuga**, to be as cool as a cucumber. **Dinero fresco**, ready money, cash paid off-hand. **Viento fresco**, *(Naut.)* a fresh breeze. 5. Light, thin (vestido, tela) 6. Fresh, ruddy, healthy (tez).

fresco [fres'-co], *m.* 1. Cool, refreshing air (aire). **Tomar el fresco**, to get some fresh air. 2. Fresh guy (sinvergüenza). V. FRESCURA. 3. *(Peru)* A cold iced drink, prepared from pineapple.

frescón, na [fres-cone', nah], *a. aug.* Very fresh; blooming.

frescor [fres-cor'], *m.* 1. Cool, refreshing air. 2. *V.* FRESCURA. 3. Flesh-color (pintura).

frescote, ta [fres-co'-tay, tah], *a.* 1. Aug. of FRESCO. 2. Ruddy, youthful, and strong.

frescura [fres-coo'-rah], *f.* 1. Freshness, coolness (frío), cool, gentle cold, cheek (descarado). 2. Amenity, agreeableness of situation. 3. Frankness, openness. 4. Freedom, ease, disengagement. 5. Serenity (serenidad), tranquility, coolness of mind. **Con la mayor serenidad**, with the greatest unconcern.

fresera [fray-say'-rah], *f.* A rosaceous plant with fibrous roots, resembling the strawberry and cinquefoil.

fresita [fray-see'-tah], *f.* The service-berry.

fresnal [fres-nahl'], *m. V.* FRESNEDA.

fresneda [fres-nay'-dah], *f.* Grove or plantation of ash trees.

fresnillo [fres-neel'-lyo], *m. V.* DÍCTAMO BLANCO. White fraxinella.

fresno [fres'-no], *m.* 1. *(Bot.)* Ash tree. 2. *(Poet.)* Staff of a lance, a spear. **Fresno florido or de flor**, *(Bot.)* Flowering ash tree.

fresón or **fresón de Chile** [fray-sone'], *m. (Bot.)* Chili strawberry (fruta).

fresquecito, ita, fresquillo, lla [fres-kay-thee'-to, ee'-tah, fres-keel'-lyo, lyah], *a. dim. V.* FRESQUITO.

fresquista [fres-kees'-tah], *m.* A painter employed in painting in fresco.

fresquito, ta [fres-kee'-to, tah], *a. dim.* Cool, foolish, approaching to cold.

fresquito [fres-kee'-to], *m.* Cool, fresh air.

frey [fray'-e], *m.* Father, if a religious person; or brother, if a secular man.

frez, freza [freth, fray'-thah], *f.* Dung, the excrement of animals.

freza [fray-thah], *f.* 1. The time when silkworms eat (estación), 2. Ground turned up by the snout of a hog or other animal. 3. Track, trace of fish in spawning (huevos).

frezada [fray-thah'-dah], *f.* A blanket. *V.* FRAZADA.

frezar [fray-thar'], *vn.* 1. To eject excrements (animales). 2. To eject the droppings of grubs from hives.

frezar [fray-thar'], *va.* 1. To nibble the leaves of mulberry trees (gusanos de seda). 2. To rub in order to spawn (peces). 3. To turn up the ground, as hogs. 4. To be disposed to rise like worms after moulting.

fría [free'-ah], *a. (Pros.)* Applied to dead fowls, paid as tribute.

friabilidad [free-ah-be-le-dahd'], *f.* Friability, brittleness.

friable [fre-ah'-blay], *a.* Friable, fragile, brittle.

frialdad [fre-al-dahd'], *f.* 1. Frigidity, coldness, want of warmth. 2. Frigidity, coldness, unconcern, coolness, want of affection. 3. Frigidity, insipidity, dullness. 4. A silly observation or saying. 5. *(Med.)* Impotence (impotencia), inability to procreate.

fríamente [free'-ah-men-tay], *adv.* In a heavy, stupid, and graceless manner; coldly, frigidly, coolly, flatly.

friático, ca [fre-ah'-te-co, cah], *a.* 1. Foolish, graceless, silly. 2. Chilly.

fricación [fre-cah-the-on'], *f.* Friction.

fricandó [fre-can-do'], *m.* Scotch collop; veal cut into small pieces and stewed.

fricar [fre-car'], *va.* To rub, to scour.

fricasé [fre-cah-say'], *m.* Fricassee.

fricción [fric-the-on'], *f.* 1. Friction. *V.* FRICACIÓN. 2. Embrocation, liniment.

friega [fre-ay'-gah], *f.* Friction, rubbing with flesh-brush, etc. *(Yo friego, yo friegue*, from *Fregar. V.* ACERTAR.)

friera [fre-ay'-rah], *f.* Chilblain.

frigidez [fre-he-dayth'], *f. V.* FRIALDAD.

frígido, da [free'-he-do, dah], *a. (Poet.)* Cold, frigid.

frigo [free'-go], *m.* Fridge, refrigerator.

frigorífero, ra [fre-go-ree'-fay-ro, rah], *a.* Cooling, chilling.

frigorífico, ca [fre-go-ree'-fe-co, cah], *a.* Cooling, refrigerating, chilling. **Cámara frigorífica**, cooler, freezer. -*m.* 1. Cold storage. 2. Refrigerator, freezer. 3. Refrigerator van or ship.

friísimo, ma [free-e'-se-mo, mah], *a. sup.* Extremely cold.

fríjol [free'-hol], *m.* Kidney bean, French bean. **Fríjol de soja**, soy bean.

frío, ía [free'-o, ah], *a.* 1. Cold, frigid, tepid. **Más frío que el hielo**, as cold as ice. 2. Cold, frigid, impotent by nature (impotente). 3. Cold, frigid, indifferent, heartless, without warmth of affection. **Eso me deja frío**, that leaves me cold. 4. Frigid, dull, graceless, inefficacious.

frío [free'-o], *m.* 1. Cold, the effect of coldness. 2. Cool, fresh air. 3. Iced drinks. **Hace frío**, it's cold. **Pasar frío**, to be cold.

friolento, ta [fre-o-len'-to, tah], *a.* Chilly; very sensible to cold.

friolera [fre-o-lay'-rah], *f.* An insignificant speech or act; a trifle.

friolero, ra [fre-o-lay'-ro, rah], *a. V.* FRIOLENTO.

frisa [free'-sah], *f.* Frieze, a coarse woollen stuff (tela).

frisado [fre-sah'-do], *m.* Silk plush or shag. -**Frisado, da**, *pp.* of FRISAR.

frisador [fre-sah-dor'], *m.* Frizzler, one who frizzles or raises the nap on frieze or cloth.

frisadura [fre-sah-doo'-rah], *f.* Act of frizzling or shagging.

frisar [fre-sar'], *va.* To frizzle or frizz, to raise the nap on frieze or other woollen stuff (tela); to rub against the grain. -*vn.* To resemble, to be like; to assimilate, to approach.

friso [free'-so], *m.* 1. *(Arch.)* Frieze, the part of a column between the architrave and cornice. 2. Wainscot.

frísol [free'-sol], *m. (Bot.)* French or kidney bean.

frisón [fre-sone'], *m.* 1. A large draught horse, a cart or dray horse. 2. Any animal of a large size.

frita [free'-tah], *f.* 1. Frit, the ingredients of which glass is made; partially fused sand and fluxes. 2. The time employed in fusing glass.

fritada [fre-tah'-dah], *f.* Dish of fried meat or fish.

fritilaria [fre-te-lah'-re-ah], *f. (Bot.)* Fritillary.

fritillas [fre-teel'-lyas], *f. pl. (Prov.)* Fritters, pancakes.

frito [free'-to], *m.* Fry, fried (plato). **Fritos variados**, mixed fry. *V.* FRITADA.

frito, ta [free'-to, tah], *pp. irr.* of FREÍR. Fried.

frito [free-to], *a.* 1. Fried. 2. **Tener frito a uno**, to worry, somebody to death (acosar). 3. **Estar frito**, to be kipping (dormido); to be a goner (muerto).

frituras [fre-too'-rahs], *f. pl.* Fritters (plato frito). **Frituras de maíz,** *(Mex.)*, corn fritters.

frivolamente [free'-vo-lah-men-tay], *adv.* Frivolously, triflingly, without weight.

frivolidad [fre-vo-le-dahd'], *f.* Frivolity, frivolousness, triflingness, emptiness, frothiness.

frivolité [fre-vo-le-tay'], *f.* Tatting.

frívolo, la [free'-vo-lo, lah], *a.* Frivolous, slight, trifling, vain, empty, frothy, light, futile.

froga [fro'-gah], *f.* Brickwork, masonry.

fronda [fron'-dah], *f (Bot.)* Frond, a name given to the leaves of ferns and hepaticae.

frondescencia [fron-des-then'-the-ah], *f.* 1. *(Bot.)* The leafing process, frondescence. 2. *(Zool.)* Disposition of a polipary in leafy branches.

frondescente [fron-des-then'-tay], *a. (Bot.)* Frondescent.

frondífero [fron-dee'-fay-ro], *a. (Bot.)* Frondiferous, bearing leaves.

frondosidad [fron-do-se-dahd'], *f.* 1. Luxuriance of the branches and leaves of trees; foliage. 2. Redundancy of words or phrases.

frondoso, sa [fron-do'-so, sah], *a.* Leafy, abounding with leaves, frondose or full of leaves, luxuriant.

frontal [fron-tahl'], *a.* Frontal, relating to the forehead. -*m.* 1. Frontlet, a fillet with the name of God or a biblical text, which the Jews used to wear upon the forehead. 2. Frontal, a rich hanging for the front of an altar. 3. Chisel used by guitar makers to finish the frets. 4. Headstall of a bridle. 5. Piece of black baize, put as mourning over a horse's head.

frontalmente [fron-tal'-men-tay], *adv.* Frontally. **Chocar frontalmente,** to collide head-on.

frontalera [fron-tah-lay'-rah], *f.* Ornament for the front of an altar, and the place where such ornaments are kept.

frontera [fron-tay'-rah], *f.* 1. Frontier, limit, confine, the border (zona), the marches. 2. Fillet of a bridle; binder of a frail basket. 3. *V.* FACHADA. 4. Ornament for the control of a riding saddle.

fronterizo, za [fron-tay-ree'-tho, thah], *a.* 1. Limitaneous, belonging to a frontier. 2. Frontier, bounding or bordering upon. 3. Fronting, opposite, over against (en frente).

frontero [fron-tay'-ro], *m.* 1. Governor or magistrate of a frontier town. 2. Frontlet, frontal, or browband. *-adv.* In front.

frontero, ra [fron-tay'-ro, rah], *a* FFrontier, placed in front

frontil [fron-teel'], *m.* Bassweed matting on the foreheads of draught-oxen, to preserve them from injury.

frontino, na [fron-tee'-no, nah], *a.* Applied to animals marked in the face.

frontis [fron'-tis], *m.* Frontispiece, facade.

frontispicio [fron-tees-pe'-the-o], *m.* 1. Front, the fore part of a building, or any other thing which meets the eye. 2. *(coll.)* Face, visage (cara). 3. Title page of a book.

frontón [fron-tone'], *m.* 1. Pelota court; wall of a pelota court (pared). 2. Court where Jai alai is played. 3. *(Arch.)* Pediment, a triangular gable of the principal entrance of a building.

frontudo, da [fron-too'-do, dah], *a.* Broad-faced.

frontura [fron-too'-rah], *f.* Front of a stocking frame.

frotación, frotadura [fro-tah-the-on', fro-tah-doo'-rah], *f.* Friction.

frotador, ra [fro-tah-dor', rah], *m. & f.* 1. One who rubs. 2. Kind of old brushes which hatters use to clean the sadiron.

frotar [fro-tar'], *va.* 1. To rub one thing against another. **Quitar algo frotando,** to rub something off. 2. To stroke gently with the hand. 3. To strike (cerilla). *-vr.* To rub, to chafe. **Frotarse las manos,** to rub one's hands.

fructescencia [frooc-tes-then'-the-ah], *f. (Bot.)* Frutescence or the fruiting season, the time when vegetables scatter their ripe seeds.

fructíferamente [frooc-tee'-fay-rah-men-tay], *adv.* Fruitfully.

fructífero, ra, [frooc-tee'-fay-ro, rah], *a.* Fructiferous, frugiferous, fruit-bearing-fruitful.

fructificación [frooc-te-fe-cah-the-on'] *f. (Bot.)* Fructification, fertilization.

fructificador, ra, [frooc-te-fe-cah-dor', rah], *m. & f.* Fertilizer.

fructificar [frooc-te-fe-car'], *va.* 1. To fructify, to fertilize, to make fruitful. 2. *(Met.)* To profit or give profit, to benefit. 3. *(Met.)* To edify, to promote piety and morality.

fructívoro, ra [frooc-tee'-vo-ro, rah], *a.* Frugivorous, fruiteating.

fructosa [frooc-to'-sah], *f.* fructose.

fructuosamente [frooc-too-o-sah-men-tay], *adv.* Fruitfully.

fructuoso, sa [frooc-too-o'-so, sah], *a.* Fruitful, fructuous, useful.

frugal [froo-gahl'], *a.* Frugal, parsimonious, sparing, thrifty.

fruglidad [froo-gah-le-dahd'], *f.* Frugality, parsimony, thrift, economy.

frugalmente [froo-gal-men'-tay], *adv.* Frugally, sparingly, thriftily.

frugívoro, ra [froo-hee'-vo-ro. rah], *a.* Frugivorous, herbivorous, plant-eating.

fruición [froo-e-the-on'], *f.* 1. Fruition, enjoyment of possession. 2. Fruition, satisfaction, gratification, taste.

fruir [froo-eer'], *vn.* To live in happiness, to enjoy.

fruitivo, va [froo-e-tee'-vo, vah], *a.* Fruitive, enjoying.

frumentario, ria [froo-men-tah'-re-o, ah], *a.* Cereal, relating to cereal grains in respect to their supply and to commerce.

-m. A Roman official charged with conveying wheat to the army.

frumenticio, cia [froo-men-tee'-the-o, ah], *a. (Bot.)* Frumentaceous, cereal.

frunce [froon'-thay], *m.* Plait, fold.

fruncido, da [froon-thee'-do, dah], *a.* Frizzled, corrugated, wrinkled (frente); frowning (cara). *-pp.* of FRUNCIR.

fruncidor [froon-the-dor'], *m.* Plaiter, folder.

fruncimiento [froon-the-me-en'-to], *m.* 1. The act of pursing up into corrugations. 2. Fiction, deceit, imposture.

fruncir [froon-theer'], *va.* 1. To gather the edge of cloth into plaits. 2. *(Met.)* To reduce to a smaller compass. 3. *(Met.)* To conceal the truth. 4. To affect modesty and composure. 5. To wrinkle (frente); to purse (labios). **Fruncir las cejas,** to knit the eyebrows. **Fruncir los labios,** to curl the lips.

fruslera [froos-lay'-rah], *f.* Brass turnings or clippings.

fruslería [frus-lay-ree'-ah], *f.* Trifle, a thing of no value, frivolity.

fruslero, ra [froos-lay'-ro, rah], *a.* Trifling, frivolous, insignificant, futile.

frustración [fross-trah-the-on], *f.* Frustration.

frustráneo, nea [froos-trah'-nay-o, ah], *a.* Vain, useless, nugatory.

frustrante [froos-trahn-tay], *f.* Frustrating.

frustrar [froos-trar'], *va.* To frustrate, to disappoint, to balk, to defeat, to mock, to elude, *-vr.* To miscarry, to fail (plan), to be balked.

frustratorio, ria [froos-trah-to'-re-o', ah], *a. V.* FRUSTRÁNEO.

fruta [froo'-tah], *f.* Fruitage, fruit, the eatable fruit of a tree or plant. **Fruta del tiempo,** 1. Fruit eaten in the season in which it is produced. 2. *(Met.)* Anything incident or peculiar to a season. **Fruta prohibida,** forbidden fruit.

frutaje [froo-tah'-hay], *m.* A painting of fruits and flowers.

frutal [froo-tahl'], *a,* Fruitful, fruit bearing (árboles).-*m.* Fruit tree.

frutar [froo-ter'], *va. (Prov.)* To fertilize.

frutería [froo-tay-ree'-ah], *f.* Fruitery, place where fruit is kept or preserved (tienda).

frutero, ra [froo-tay'-ro, rah], *m. & f.* 1. Fruiterer, one who deals in fruit (persona). 2. Fruit basket served up at table (recipiente). 3. Piece of painting representing various sorts of fruit.

frutescente [froo-tes-then'-tay], *a. (Bot.)* Frutescent: applied to stems from herbaceous becoming shrubby.

frútice [froo'-to-thay], *m.* Any perennial shrub.

fruticultura [froo-te-cool-too-rah], *f.* Fruit growing, fruit farming.

fruticoso, sa [froo-te-co'-so, sah], *a.* 1. *(Bot.)* Fruiticant, frutescent; applied to a plant with many branches from its root. 2. Shrubby: applied to vegetables bearing woody stems. **Tallo fruticoso,** shrubby stem.

frutilla [froo-teel'-lyah], *f.* 1. *(dim.)* Small fruit. 2. In Peru, strawberry. 3. Round shell or nut of which rosaries are made.

frutillar [froo-teel-lyar'], *m.* Strawberry bed.

fruto [froo'-to], *m.* 1. Fruit, the product of a tree or plant in which the seeds are contained. **Dar fruto,** bear fruit. 2. Any useful produce of the earth. 3. Fruit, benefice (beneficio), profit, advantage gained by an enterprise or conduct (resultado). **El fruto de esta unión,** the offspring of this marriage. *-pl.*. 1. Seeds, grain. 2. Produce of an estate, place, or employment.

fu [foo], *interj.* 1. Of disgust. 2. Sound imitating the snarling of a cat.

fucáceo, cea [foo-cah'-thay-o, ah], *a.* Fucaceous, relating to fucus, or great sea weeds.

fúcar [foo'-car], *m.* A rich, opulent man.

fucsia [fooc'-se-ah], *f.* Fuchsia, an ornamental plant with pendent blossoms.

fucha [foo'-chah], *int. (Mex.)* Exclamation denoting neatness.

fuego [foo-ay'-go], *m.* 1. Fire. **Fuegos artificiales,** fireworks. **Apagar el fuego,** to put out the fire. **Jugar con fuego,** to play with fire. 2. Fire, anything burning. 3. Fire, a conflagration. 4. Signal given with smoke from the coast; beacon fire. 5. *(Met.)* Force, life, vigor, animation. 6. (Cocina) Burner, ring. 7. Firing of soldiers. 8. Hearth, fireplace (hogar). 9. Ardor, heat of an action. 10. Flame, heat (calor). **Hervir a fuego lento,** to simmer. 11. Light (para cigarro). **Le pedí fuego,** I asked him for a light. 12. Burner, ring (degas). **Una cocina a gas de cuatro fuegos,** a gas cooker with 4 burners. **¡Fuego!** the military command to shoot. **Estar entre dos fuegos,** to be between two fires. **Jugar con fuego,** to play with fire. **Fuego nutrido,** heavy fire. **Marcar a fuego,** to brand (reses). **Fuego a discreción,** fire at will. **Arma de fuego,** firearm. **Poner las manos en el fuego por,** to stake one's life on. **Romper el fuego,** to open fire. **Echar leña al fuego,** to add fuel to the fire.

fuel [foo-ayl'], *m.* Paraffin, kerosene.

fuellar [foo-el-lyar'], *m.* Paper ornament around wax tapers

fuelle [foo-ayl'-lyar], *m.* 1. Bellows (de soplar). 2. *(coll.)* Tell-tale (soplón). 3. Leather curtain of an open chaise. 4. Puff for powdering hair. **Fuelles,** puckers or corrugations in clothes.

fuente [foo-en'-tay], *f.* 1. Fountain, fount, a spring of water (manantial). **Fuente de beber,** drinking fountain. 2. Jet, a spout of water. 3. *(Met.)* Original, first principle, first cause, source. **De fuente desconocida,** from an unknown source. 4. Dish, platter, a broad wide vessel in which food is served up at table (recipiente). 5. A small ulcer, an issue. 6. *(Comput.)* Character set. **Fuente de caracteres,** characters font.

fuentecica, illa, ita, zuela [foo-en-tay-thee'-cah, eel'lyah, ee'tah, thoo-ay'-lah], *f. dim.* A small fountain.

fuer(A) [foo-ayr'], *adv.* **A fuer de caballero,** upon the word of a gentleman.

fuera [foo-ay'-rah], *adv.* 1. Out, speaking of a person or thing which is not a place. 2. Without, out of the place where one is. 3. *V.* AFUERA. 4. Over and above. 5. **Estar Fuera.** to be out of town (persona). 6. Away (de casa). **Los de fuera,** the away team. **Fuera de sí,** absent of mind; deranged, beside oneself, aghast. **De fuera,** exteriorly. **Fuera de,** out of, forth. **Fuera de eso,** besides, moreover. **Estar fuera,** not to be at home, not to be in some place. **Fuera de esto,** short of this, besides this. **Fuera de que,** besides over and above. -prep. 1. Outside (lugar). **Estaba fuera de su jaula,** it was outside its cage. 2. *(Fig.)* In addition to, besides, beyond.

¡fuera! [foo-ay'-rah], *int.* Away, get out!, out of the way, clear the way.

fuera-borda [foo-ay-rah bor'-dah], *m.* Outboard engine, outboard motor.

fuercecilla, ita [foo-er-thay-theel'-lyah], *f. dim.* Little strength.

fuero [foo-ay'-ro], *m.* 1. Statute law of a country. 2. Jurisdiction, judicial power (autoridad). 3. Privilege or exemption granted to a province (de grupo). 4. A compilation of laws. **Fuero exterior or externo,** canon and civil laws. **A fuero,** according to law.

fuerte [foo-err'-tay], *m.* 1. Fortification, intrenchment, fort, hold. *-f.* 2. Coin over weight. 3. *(Mus.)* Forte, the loudness of the voice or notes marked. *-f.* 4. The buckle from which the stirrup hangs.

fuerte [foo-err'-tay], *a.* 1. Vigorous, able, hardy, lusty, stout, healthy, hale. 2. Strong (defensa, fe, objectión). 3. Strong (té, vino), firm, compact, 4. Strong, forcible, resistless, cogent, efficacious. 5. Manly, manlike, firm. 6. Hard, not malleable. 7. Terrible, grave (crisis). **Eso es muy fuerte,** that's a very serious thing to say. **Fuerte como un roble, as** strong as a horse.

fuerte [foo-err'-tay], *adv.* Strongly; hard (golpear); loud (tocar, hablar). **Poner la radio más alta,** to turn the radio up. **Toca muy alto,** she plays very loud.

fuertecico, illo, ito [foo-er-tay-thee'-co, eel-lyo, ee'-to], *m. dim.* Small fortress, a block-house.

fuertemente [foo-er-tay-men'-tay], *adv.* Strongly, lustily, firmly, fast, forcible, vehemently.

fuerza [foo-err'-thah], *f.* 1. Force, strength (de persona), might, vigor, cogency. 2. Fortitude, valor, courage, manliness, constancy. 3. Force (obligación), violence, coercion, compulsion, constraint. 4. Force (argumento), violence (violencia), defloration, rape. 5. Force, virtue, efficacy, mental power or strength. 6. Force, moment, impulsive weight, actuating power. 7. Force, armament, war-like preparation: commonly used in the plural. 8. Fortress, a strong place: used commonly in the plural. 9. The natural force, power, or faculty of things. 10. *V.* RESISTENCIA. 11. The strongest part of a thing. 12. Proneness, strong propensity. 13. The third of a sword next the hilt. **A fuerza de,** by dint of; by force of. **Por fuerza** or **de por fuerza,** by force, head and shoulders, violently, forcibly; by sheer necessity, necessarily; without excuse. **Fuerza de voluntad,** will-power. **Írsele a uno la fuerza por la boca,** to be all talk and no action. **En fuerza de,** by virtue of. **Sin usar fuerza,** without using force. **Fuerzas aéreas,** air force. **Fuerzas armadas,** armed forces. **Fuerzas del orden público,** forces of law and order.

fuete [foo-ay'-tay], *m. (Cuba)* A whip.

fufú [foo-foo'], *m. (Cuba)* Mass made of yam, plantain, or other nutritious root, and pounded.

fuga [foo'-gah], *f.* 1. Flight, escape (huida), elopement (de amantes). 2. State of the utmost perfection of a thing. 3. *(Mus.)* Fugue, a musical composition in which a theme introduced by one part is repeated and imitated by the others in succession. 4. *(Naut.)* Force, violence, velocity of the wind. 5. Leak, escape (de gas) **Fuga de la cárcel,** escape from prison. **Darse a la fuga,** to flee.

fugacidad [foo-gah-the-dahd'], *f.* Fugacity. volatility, fugitiveness, fugaciousness, brevity.

fugado, da [foo-gah'-do, dah], *a.* Written in the style of a fugue, without following the strict rules for the latter.

fugar [foo-gar'], *va.* To cause to fly or escape.-*vr.* To escape, to fly, to run away, to get out of danger (huir).

fugaz [foo-gahth'], *a.* 1. Fugacious, volatile, apt to fly away. 2. Fugitive, running away. 3. *(Met.)* Perishable, decaying. 4. Fleeting (momento). 5. Elusive (esquivo).

fúgido [foo'-he-do], **da,** *a. (Poet.) V.* FUGAZ.

fugitivo, va [foo-he-tee'-vo, vah], *m. & f.* A fugitive

fugitivo [foo-he-te'-vo], **va,** *a.* 1. Fugitive, running, from danger, flying from duty (que huye). 2. Fugitive, unsteady, unstable.

fuina [foo-ee'-nah], *f. V.* GARDUÑA.

fulanito, ta [foo-lah-nee'-to, tah], *m. &f. dim.* Little master, little miss.

fulano, na [foo-lah'-no, nah], *m. & f.* Such a one; so-and-so.

fulero [foo-lay'-ro], *a.* 1. Useless (inútil); sham (falso); poor-quality (pobremente hecho). 2. Tricky, sly (taimado). 3. Blundering (torpe).

fulgecer [fool-hay-therr'], *vn. (Poet.)* To shine, to be resplendent.

fulgente [fool-hen'-tay], *a. (Poet.)* Refulgent, brilliant.

fúlgido [fool'-he-do, dah], *a. (Poet.)* Resplendent.

fulgor [fool-gor'], *m.* Fulgency, resplendence, brilliancy.

fulgora [fool-go'-rah], *f.* Fulgora, the lantern-fly, a homopterous insect, with ocelli and antennae beneath the compound eyes.

fulgurante [fool-goo-rahn'-tay], *pa. & a. (Poet)* Resplendent, shining (brillante).

fulgurar [fool-goo-rar'], *vn. (Poet.)* To fulgurate, to emit flashes of light, to yield splendor and brilliancy.

fuliginoso, sa [foo-le-he-no'-so, sah], *a.* Fuliginous, dark, obscure.

fullería [fool-lyay-ree'-ah], *f.* 1. Cheating at games (naipes, etc.) 2. Cunning, arts used to deceive (cualidad). 3. Cogging, cheat, fallacy (tramposo).

fullerito [fool-lyay-ree'-to], *m. dim.* A little sharper.

fullero [fool-lyay'-ro], *m.* Sharper, cheater at games (naipes), gamester, gambler.

fullet [fool-lyet'], *m.* A very small saw.

fullona [fool-lyo'-nah], *f. (coll.)* Dispute, quarrel.

fulminación [fool-me-nah-the-on'], *f.* Fulmination, the act of thundering.

fulminado [fool-me-nah'-do], *a.* Wounded by lightning. **-Fulminado, da,** *pp. of* FULMINAR.

fulminador [fool-me-nah'-dor'], *m.* Thunderer.

fulminante [fool-me-nahn'-tay], *pa. & a.* Fulminating (polvo), thundering. -*m.* Detonator, percussion cap (cápsula fulminante).

fulminar [fool-me-nar'], *va.* 1. To fulminate, to emit lightning (con rayo). 2. To throw out as an object of terror, to express wrath. **Fulminar a uno con la mirada,** to look daggers at somebody.

fulminato [fool-me-nah'-to], *m.(Chem.)* Fulminate, a salt of fulminic acid.

fulmíneo, nea [fool-mee'-nay-o, ah], *a. (Poet.)* Belonging to thunder and lightning.

fulmínico [fool-mee'-ne-co], *a. (Chem.)* Fulminic (ácido), a compound of cyano gen and oxygen; its salts are explosive.

fulminoso, sa [fool-me-no'-so, sah], *a. (Poet.)* Fulminatory, thundering, striking horror.

fumada [foo-mah'-dah], *f.* The quantity of smoke taken at once in smoking tobacco; whiff.

fumadero [foo-mah-day'-ro], *m. (coll.)* A place particularly used for smoking tobacco, smoking room.

fumador, ra [foo-mah-dor', rah], *m. & f. (coll.)* Smoker, one who smokes tobacco.

fumante [foo-mahn'-tay], *pa.* Fuming, smoking.

fumar [foo-mar']. *pa.* To disperse in vapors; to smoke (tabaco.) **Fumar como una chimenea,** to smoke like a chimney. **Está fumando su pipa,** he is smoking his pipe. -*vr.* To dissipate (dinero); to cut, to miss (clase).

fumarada [foo-mah-rah'-dah], *f.* 1. Blast of smoke (fumada). 2. A pipeful of tobacco (en pipa).

fumaria [foo-mah'-re-ah], *f. (Bot.)* Fumitory.

fumear [foo-may-ar'], *va. (Prov.)* V. HUMEAR.

fumífero, ra [foo-mee'-fay-ro, rah], *a. (Poet.)* Smoking, emitting smoke.

fumífugo, ga [foo-mee'-foo-go, gah], *a.* Smoke dispersing.

fumigación [foo-me-gah-the-on'], *f.* 1. Fumigation, fumes raised by fire. 2. Fumigation, application of medicines to the body in fumes.

fumigador [foo-me-gah-dor'], *m.* Fumigator, one who or that which fumigates.

fumigar [foo-me-gar'], *va.* 1. To fumigate, to smoke. 2. To fumigate, to medicate or purify by vapors (cosecha).

fumigatorio, ria [foo-me-gah-to'-re-o, ah], *a.* Fumigatory.

fumívoro, ra [foo-mee'-vo-ro, rah], *a.* Smoke consuming.

fumorola [foo-mo-ro'lah], *f.* Cavity in the earth which emits a sulphureous smoke.

fumosidad [foo-mo-se-dahd'], *f.* Smokiness.

fumoso, sa [foo-mo'-so, sah], *a.* Full of smoke or fume, fumid, smoky.

funámbulo, la [foo-nahm'-boo-lo, lah], *m. & f.* Funambulist, a rope dancer.

función [foon-the-on'], *f.* 1. Function, fulfilling the duties of any employment, profession, or office (puesto). **Presidente en funciones,** acting president. 2. *(Med.)* Function, vital action. 3. Solemnity, festival, feast, party, rout. **Función de la tarde,** matinée. **Mañana no hay función,** there will be no performance tomorrow. 4. Festive concourse of people, a public act. 5. Fight, engagement, battle. 6. Function; functioning (de máquina). 5. *(Comput.)* **Función aritmética,** arithmetic function. **Función condicional,** conditional function. **Función de fecha,** date function. **Función de macro,** macro facility. **Función estadística,** statistical function. **Función financiera,** financial function. **Función "engaño",** cheat function.

funcionamiento [foon-the-nah-me-en'-to], *m.* Functioning, operation, action. **Máquina en funcionamiento,** machine in working order. **Entrar en funcionamiento,** to come into operation. **Funcionamiento erróneo,** *(Comput.)* defective operation.

funcionar [foon-the-o-nar'], *vn.* To work, to perform duly, to functionate (maquinarias, personas). **Hacer funcionar una máquina,** to operate a machine.

funcionario [foon-the-o-nah'-re-o], *m.* Functionary, a public official.

funda [foon'-dah], *f.* A case, a sheath, a covering, generally of linen or leather. **Funda de almohada,** pillow-case.

fundación [foon-dah-the-on'], *f.* 1. Foundation, groundwork. 2. Foundation, the act of fixing the basis of an edifice, etc. 3. Foundation, rise, beginning, or origin of a thing. 4. Foundation, revenue established for any purpose.

fundadamente [foon-dah-dah-men'-tay], *adv.* Fundamentally.

fundado [foon-dah-do], *a.* Firm, well-founded, justified.

fundador, ra [foon-dah-dor', rah], *m. & f.* Founder.

fundamental [foon-dah-men-tahl'], *a.* 1. Fundamental, serving for the foundation. 2. Fundamental, essential, principal.

fundamentalmente [foon-dah-men-tal-men'-tay], *adv.* Fundamentally.

fundamentar [foon-dah-men-tar'], *va.* 1. To found (sentar las bases), to lay the foundation of a building. 2. *(Met.)* To found (argumento), to establish, to fix firm.

fundamento [foon-dah-men'-to], *m.* 1. Foundation, groundwork. 2. Fundamental, lending proposition. 3. Foundation, ground, the principles on which any notion is raised. **Eso carece de fundamento,** that is groundless. 4. Reason, cause, ground or principle. 5. Source, origin, root. 6. Weft, the woof of cloth.

fundar [foon-dar'], *va.* 1. To found, to lay the foundation of a building. 2. To found, to establish (crear). 3. To found (teoría), to ground, to raise upon, as on a principle, maxim, or ground. **Fundarse en algo,** to go upon or to take as a principle.

fundible [foon-dee'-blay], *a.* Fusible.

fundibulario [foon-de-boo-lah'-re-o], *m.* In the Roman militia, the soldier who was armed with a sling.

fundíbulo [foon-dee'-boo-lo], *m.* An ancient war-like machine for throwing stones: a sling.

fundición [foon-de-the-on'], *f.* 1. Fusion, melting of metals (acto). **Fundición de hierro,** iron foundry. 2. Foundry, a place where melted metal is cast into form; a casting house (fábrica). 3. A complete set of printing types; font.

fundidor [foon-de-dor'], *m.* Founder, melter, one who casts metals.

fundilario [foon-de-lah'-re-o], *m.* Slinger, Roman soldier who used a sling.

fundir [foon-deer'], *va.* 1. To found or melt metals. 2. *(Met.)* To unmake a thing in order to make it anew. 3. To fuse (fusionar). 4. To melt (nieve). 5. To throw away (dinero). -*vr.* 1. To fuse; to join, to unite; to merge (colores, efectos) 2. To melt (derretirse).

fundo [foon'-do], *m.* 1. *(Law and Amer.)* V. HEREDAD. 2. A large estate.

funebre [foo'-nay-bray], *a.* 1. Mournful, sad, lamentable. 2. Funeral, funereal, mourning (sonido) 3. Funeral (pompa).

fúnebremente [foo'-nay-bray-men-tay], *adv.* Mournfully, sorrowfully, lamentably.

funeral [foo-nay-rahl'], *a.* Funeral.

funeral [foo-nay-rahl'], *m.* Funeral, the solemnization of a burial; generally used in the plural.

funeraria [foo-nay-rah'-re-ah], *f.* Funeral parlor.

funerario, ria [foo-nay-rah'-re-o, ah], *a.* Funeral, funereal.

funéreo, rea [foo-nay'-ray-o, ah], *a. (Poet.)* Mournful, sad. V. FÚNEBRE.

funestar [foo-nes-tar'], *va.* To blot, to stain, to profane.

funestamente [foo-nay'-tah-men-tay], *adv.* Mournfully.

funesto, ta [foo-ness'-to, tah], *a.* Funest, doleful, lamentable, untoward; mournful, sad, dismal.

fungiforme [foon-he-for'-may], *a.* Fungiform, like a mushroom.

fungir [foon-heer'], *vn. (Amer.)* To affect importance.

fungita [foon-hee'-tah], *f.* Fungite, a fossil like a fungioid coral.

fungívoro, ra [foon-hee'-vo-ro, rah], *a.* Fungivorous, devouring fungi.

fungo [foon'-go], *m. (Surg.)* Fungus, fleshy excrescence.

fungóideo, dea [foon-go'-e-day-o, ah], *a. (Med.)* Fungoid, like a fungus.

fungón [foon-gone'], *m. (coll.)* A great snuff-taker.

fungosidad [foon-go-se-dahd'], *f. (Surg.)* Fungosity, excrescence.

fungoso, sa [foon-go'-so, sah], *a.* Fungous, excrescent, spongy.

funicular [foo-ne-coo-lar'], *a.* 1. Funicular, consisting of cords or fibres. 2. Funicular machine, machines with a cord attached at one point and passing over a pulley, weights being added to demonstrate certain mechanical principles. 3. *(Naut.)* Tackle, rigging.

funículo [foo-nee'-coo-lo], *m. (Bot.)* Funicle, or funiculus, a filament which connects the ovule or seed with the placenta.

funiculoso, sa [foo-ne-coo-lo'-so, sah], *a. (Zool.)* Provided with prominent lines (cáscaras).

funífero, ra [foo-nee'-fay-ro, rah], *a. (Bot.)* Having appendages like cords.

furcia [foor'-the-ah], *f.* Tart, whore, prostitute.

furgón [foor-gone'], *m.* 1. A military covered transport wagon.2. A freight car or box car. **Furgón entero,** a carload.

furgoneta [foor-go-nay'-tah], *f. (Com.)* Van; transit van, pick-up truck; estate car (coche particular).

furia [foo'-re-ah], *f.* 1. Fury, rage. 2. Fury, one of the deities of vengeance, and thence a stormy, violent woman. 3. Hurry, velocity and vigor, used in the performance of a thing. **A toda furia,** with the utmost speed. 4. Zeal, ardor. 5. A Roman law which prohibited the manumission of more than one hundred slaves at once..

furial [foo-re-ahl'], *a. (Poet.)* Belonging to the Furies.

furibundo, da [foo-re-boon'-do, daha], *a.* Furious, enraged, frantic, raging.

furiosamente [foo-re-o-sah-men'-tay], *adv.* Furiously.

furioso, sa [foo-re-o'-so, sah], *a.* 1. Furious, mad, frantic, frenetic. 2. Furious, raging, violent. 3. Very great, excessive. **Estar furioso,** to be furious.

furo, ra [foo'-ro, rah], *a.* 1. Shy, reserved. 2. *(Prov.)* Ferocious, fierce; severe.

furor [foo-ror'], *m.* 1. Fury (ira), madness, franticness. 2. Fury, rage, anger, approaching to madness (locura). 3. *(Poet.)* Fury, enthusiasm, exaltation of fancy.

furtivamente [foor-te-vah-men'-tay], *adv.* By stealth, clandestinely.

furtivo, va [foor-tee'-vo, vah], *a.* Furtive, clandestine; pirated (edición).

furúnculo [foo-roon'-coo-lo], *m. (Surg.)* Furuncle, boil.

furunculoso, sa [foo-roon-coo-lo'-so, sah], *a.* Furunculose, prone to suffer a succession of boils.

fusa [foo'-sah], *f.* Demi-semiquaver, a note in music.

fusado, da, fuselado, da [foo-sah'-do, dah], *a. (Her.)* Charged with fusils or spindles.

fusca [foos'-cah], *f.* A kind of dark-colored duck.

fusco, ca [foos'-co, cah], *a.* Fuscous, brown, of a dim or dark color.

fuselaje [foo-say-lah'-hay], *m.* Fuselage (avión).

fusible [foo-see'-blay], *m. (Elec.)* Fuse.

fusible, fúsil [foo-see'-blay, foo'-seel], *a.* Fusible.

fusiforme [foo-se-for'-may], *a.* Fusiform, spindle-shaped.

fusil [foo-seel'], *m.* Gun, rifle. **Fusil de juguete,** toy gun. **Fusil ametrallador,**, automatic rifle. **Fusil de chispa,** flintlock. **Fusil de repetición,** magazine rifle.

fusilador, ra [foo-se-lah-dor', rah], *m. & f.* One who shoots and who commands to shoot.

fusilamiento [foo-se-lah-me-en'-to], *m.* The act and effect of shooting.

fusilar [foo-se-lar'], *va.* 1. To kill by shooting (ejecutar, matar). 2. To shoot, to execute by shooting.

fusilazo [foo-se-lah'-tho], *m.* Musket shot, blow with a musket.

fusilería [foo-se-lay-ree'-ah], *f.* Body of fusileers or musketeers.

fusilero [foo-se-lay'-ro], *m.* Fusileer, musketeer.

fusión [foo-se-on'], *f.* 1. Fusion, melting together (de metal). 2. Alliance, mingling of parties, systems, etc. 3. Liquefaction.

fusionar [foo-se-o-nar'], *va.* To fuse; to merge, to amalgamate. *-vr.* To fuse; to merge, to amagamate.

fusique [foo-see'-kay], *m.* Kind of snuff-box in the shape of a small bottle.

fuslina [foos-lee'-nah], *f.* Smelting works.

fuslor [foos-lor'], *m.* Smelting ladle, a vessel for melting.

fusta [foos'-tah], *f.* 1. Small vessel, with lateen sails. 2. Thin boards of wood (leña). 3. Kind of woollen cloth. 4. Whip (látigo).

fustán [foos-tahn'], *m.* 1. Fustian, a kind of cotton stuff (tela). 2. *(Peru)* A woman's white skirt (falda).

fustanero [foos-tah-nay'-ro], *m.* Fustian manufacturer.

fuste [foos'-tay], *m.* 1. Wood, timber (madera). 2. Tree and bows of a saddle (silla). 3. *(Poet.)* A saddle. 4. Shaft of a lance (arma). 5. Foundation of something, not material. 6. Substance of anything. 7. *(Arch.)* Fust or body of a column (columna, chimenea). 8. An instrument of silversmiths.

fustero, ra [foos-tay'-ro, rah], *a.* Belonging to a fuss, foundation, etc.

fustero [foos-tay'-ro], *m.* Turner or carpenter.

fustete [foos-tay'-tay], *m. (Bot.)* Red or Venice sumach-tree. Fustic, a wood from the West Indies, used in dyeing. *V.* FUSTOC.

fustigar [foos-te-gar'], *va.* To whip, to fustigate.

fustina [foos-tee'-nah], *f.* Place for fusing metals.

fustoc [foos-toc'], *m.* Fustic, a yellow dye-wood, Venie sumach.

fútbol [foot-ball'], *m.* Soccer. **Fútbol americano,** American football.

futbolín [foot-bo-leen'], *m.* Table soccer, bar soccer.

futbolista [foot-bo-lees'-tah], *m. & f.* Soccer player.

futesa [foot-tay'-sah], *f. (coll.)* Trifle, bagatelle.

fútil [foo'-teel], *a.* Futile, trifling, worthless, flimsy.

futileza [foo-te-lay'-thah], *f. V.* FUTILIDAD.

futilidad [foo-te-le-dahd'], *f.* Futility, weakness, groundlessness.

futura [foo-too'-rah], *f.* 1. Survivor-ship, survival. 2. *(coll.)* Intended bride (novia).

futurismo [foo-too-rees'-mo], *m.* Futurism.

futurista [foo-too-rees'-tah], *a.* Futuristic.

futuro, ra [foo-too'-ro, rah], *a.* Future. **Futura madre,** mother-to-be.

futuro [foo-too'-ro], *m.* 1. Future, futurity. 2. *(Gram.)* Future tense. **Para el futuro,** for the future. **En un futuro próximo,** in the very near future.

futurología [foo-too-ro-lo-he'-ah]. *f.* Futurology.

futurólogo, ga [foo-too-ro'-lo-go], *m & f.* Futurologist.

G

g [hay], before the vowels *a, o* and *u,* has the same sound in Spanish as in English, but before *e* and *i* is the same as the Spanish *j,* or the English *h* strongly aspirated, as in *hay, her, he.* Before the diphthongs *ue, ui,* as in **guerra, guión,** the *u* becomes liquid, and the *g* has the hard sound as in the English word *give;* with a diaeresis over the *ü,* both letters have their proper sound as in **agüero.**

gabacho, cha [gah-bah'-cho, chah], *a.* 1. Applied to the natives of some places at the foot of the Pyrenees; used also in derision to the French. 2. Frenchified (afrancesado), given to Gallicisms.

gabán [gah-bahn'], *m.* 1. Great-coat with a hood and close sleeves. 2. Overcoat.

gabanzo [gah-bahn'-tho], *m. (Bot.)* Dogrose. *V.* GAVANZO.

gabaonita [gah-bah-o-nee'-tah], *a. & n.* Gibeonite.

gabarda [gah-bar'-dah], *f.* Wild rose.

gabardina [gah-bar-dee'-nah], *f.* Gabardine (tela), cassock with close-buttoned sleeves (prenda).

gabarra [gah-bar'-rah], *f.* 1. *(Naut.)* Lighter, a large boat. 2. A ferry-boat. 3. A fishing boat.

gabarrero [gah-bar-ray'-ro], *m.* 1. Dealer in wood and timber. 2. *(Naut.)* Lighterman.

gabarro [gah-bar'-ro], *m.* 1. A morbid swelling on the pastern of horses. 2. Pip, a horny pellicle on the tongue of fowls (de gallina). 3. Flaw or defect in cloth (tela). 4. Error or mistake in accounts (error). 5. Defect discovered in goods after they have been bought. 6. *(Met.)* Obligation, burdensome change, error in accounts.

gábata [gah'-bah-tah], *f.* Bowl, a small wooden basin.

gabazo [gah-bah'-tho], *m.* In sugarmills, bruised sugar-cane. *V.* BAGAZO

gabela [gah-bay'-lah], *f.* 1. Gabelle, tax or duty paid to government. 2. Load, heavy service.

gabesina [gah-bay-see'nah], *f.* Ancient kind of arms.

gabinete [gah-be-nay'-tay], *m.* 1. Cabinet, a meeting of ministers of state and privy councillors. 2. Cabinet, a private room for consultation (estudio). 3. Cabinet, a closet or small room for retirement (cuarto de estar). 4. A dressing room for ladies (tocador). 5. Collection of curiosities, museum (museo). **Gabinete de historia natural,** natural history section. **Gabinete de lectura,** reading room.

gabón [gah-bon'], *m.* 1. *(Naut.)* Lodging quarters. in the hold of a galley. 2. Powder magazine.

gabote [gah-bo'-tay], *m. (Prov.)* Shuttle-cock.

gacel [gah-thel'], *m.* **Gacela** [gah-thay'-lah], *f.* Gazelle, antelope.

gaceta [gah-thay'-tah], *f.* Gazette (boletín), newspaper (diario); an official publication.

gacetero [gah-thay-tay'-ro], *m.* 1. Gazetter, news-writer (periodista). 2. A seller of newspapers (vendedor).

gacetilla [gah-thay-tee'-lyah]. *f.* 1. A section of a newspaper devoted to news generally non political (notas de sociedad). 2. *a. & n.* Newsmonger.

gacetillero [gah-thay-teel-lyay'-ro], *m.* 1. Editor of a *gacetilla.*. 2. A wretched writer, penny-a-liner.

gacetista [gah-thay-tees'-tah], *m.* 1. One who delights in reading newspapers. 2. Newsmonger, gossip of news.

gacha [gah'-chah], *f. (Amer. Cuba)* 1. An unglazed crock for preparing salt, and which the Indians use for eating and drinking. 2. *(Naut.)* V.GATA.

gachas [gah'-chahs], *f. pl.* 1. Sort of fritters, made of flour, honey, and water. 2. Any sort of soft pap. 3. *(Prov. Andal.)* Caresses, pettings. **Hacerse unas gachas,** to manifest extraordinary emotion in the presence or at the recollection of something; also, to grant a favor first refused. **¡Ánimo a las gachas!** Cheer up! take courage!

gacheta [gah-chay-tah], *f.* 1. Spring in large locks. 2. *(Prov.)* V. ENGRUDO.

gacho, cha [gah'-cho, chah], *a.* 1. Curvated, bent downward. 2. Having horns curved downward (ganado). 3. Slouching (sombreros).

gachón, na [gah-chone', nah], *a. & m. & f.* 1. *(coll.)* Graceful, sweet, attractive. 2. *(Andal.)* Pampered, spoiled, petted (niños).

gachondo, da [gah-chon'-do, dah], *a.* V. GACHÓN, second definition.

gachonería, gachonada [gah-cho-na-ree'-ah], *f.* Caress, endearment, fondness.

gachumbo [gah-choom'-bo], *m. (Almer.)* The woody, tough rind of various fruits, from which cups and other vessels are made.

gachupín [gah-choo-peen'], *m.* Name given in Mexico to a native of Spain who in Lima is called *Chapetón* and in Buenos Ayres *Maturrango.*

gádidos [gah'-de-dos], *pl.* Gadidae, codfishes and allied species.

gaditano, na [gah-de-tah'-no, nah], *a.* Native of or belonging to Cadiz.

gaélico, ca [ga-hay'-le-co, cah], *a.* Gaelic.

gafa [gah'-fah], *f.* A kind of hook, used to bend a crossbow. *-pl.* 1. *(Naut.)* Can-hooks, used to raise or lower casks. 2. Spectacles. **Gafas ahumadas,** smoked glasses. **Gafas negras,** dark glasses. 3. Spectacle-bows. 4. Grapple (grapa); clamp (abrazadera).

gafar [gah-far'], *va.* 1. To hook (agarrar), to catch with a hook. 2. To bring bad luck (mala suerte).

gafe [gah-fay], *a.* **Ser gafe,** to have constant bad luck.

gafedad [gah-fay-dahd'], *f.* 1. Kind of leprosy. 2. Contraction of the nerves.

gafete [gah-fay'-tay], *m.* Clasp, a hook and eye. V. CORCHETE.

gafo, fa [gah'-fo, fah], *a.* 1. Infected with leprosy. 2. Indisposed with a contraction of the nerves. 3. *(Peru)* Paralytic, tremulous.

gafón [gah-fone'], *m. (Orn.)* Green-finch.

gago [gah-go], **ga,** *a.* V. TARTAMUDO.

gaguear [gah-gay-ar'], *vn. (Peru. Cuba)* V. TARTAMUDEAR.

gaillardia [gah-eel-lyar'-de-ah], *f. (Bot.)* Gaillardia, a showy composite flower of the gardens.

gaita [gah'-ee-tah], *f.* 1. Bagpipe; hornpipe. 2. Flageolet (flauta). 3. Hand-organ. 4. *(coll.)* The neck (cuello). 5. Bother, nuisance (molestia); tough job (trabajo). **Estar de gaita,** *(coll.)* to be very merry, in high spirits.

gaitería [gah-e-tay-ree'-ah], *f.* A gay and gaudy dress.

gaitero [gah-e-tay'-ro], *m.* Piper, one who plays the bagpipe (persona).

gaitero, ra [gah-e-tay'-ro, rah], *a.* Applied to a person who is more facetious or lively than is proper to his character or profession.

gaje [gah'-hay], *m.* 1. Challenge, a summons to fight. 2. Salary, pay, wages. *-pl.* Perquisites, fees, above the settled wages: sometimes used in the singular. **Los gajes del oficio,** the occupational hazards.

gajo [gah'-ho], *m.* 1. Branch of a tree (rama). 2. Part of a bunch of grapes torn off (uvas) 3. Pyramidal raceme of any fruit.

gajoso, sa [gah-ho'-so, sah], *a.* Branchy; spreading.

gala [gah'-lah], *f.* 1. Gala, full, or court-dress (traje de etiqueta). **Día de gala,** court day; holiday. 2. Graceful, pleasing address. 3. Parade, ostentation. 4. Choicest part of a thing. 5. In America, the present or premium given to anyone as a reward of merit. **Hacer gala,** to glory in having done something. 6. Finery, trappings; jewels, adornments (lujos). **Galas de novia,** bridal attire. 7. Elegance (elegancia). 8. Speciality (especialidad), special accomplishment.

galactite [gah-lac-tee'-tay], *f.* Fuller's-carth, alumina.

galactófago, ga [gah-lac-to'-fah-go, gah], *a,* Living upon milk in the first period of life.

galactóforo, ra [gah-lac-to'-fo-ro, rah], *a.* 1. Galactiferous, conducting milk. 2. *(Med.)* Galactogog(ue), increasing the flow of milk. 3. *m.* Breast-pump.

galactómetro [gah-lac-to'-may-tro], *m.* Galactometer, lactometer, an instrument for determining the density of milk.

galafate [gah-lah-fah'-tay], *m.* 1. An artful thief, a cunning rogue. 2. Hangman, executioner. 3. Porter who carries burdens. 4. *(Naut.)* Calker. V. CALAFATE.

galafatear [gah-lah-fah-tay-ar'], *(Naut.)* V. CALAFATEAR.

galaico, ca [gah-lah'-e-co, cah], *a.* V. GALLEGO. *(Acad.)*

galamero, ra [gah-lah-may'-ro, rah], *a.* Dainty. V. GOLOSO.

galán [gah-lahn'], *m.* 1. Gallant, a spruce, well-made man (joven). 2. Gentleman in full dress. 3. Gallant (novio), suitor (pretendiente); lover, wooer. 4. Actors who perform serious characters in plays are distinguished in order, as first, second, etc., *galán.* **Primer galán,** leading man. **Joven galán,** juvenile lead.

galán, na [gah-lahn', nah], *a.* 1. Gallant, gay, fine, neat, well-dressed. 2. Elegant, lively, ingenious. 3. Gallant, courtly, with respect to ladies.

galana [gah-lah'-nah], *f.* 1. (*Bot.*) Flat-podded lathyrus. 2. A woman very showily dressed.

galanamente [gah-lah-nah-men'-tay], *adv.* Gallantly, elegantly.

galancete [gah-lan-thay'-tay], *m. dim.* A spruce little man, a buck, a spark, a little gallant.

galanga [gah-lahn'-gah], *f.* (*Bot.*) **Galanga mayor,** officinal galangal. **Galanga menor,** smaller galangal.

galano, na [gah-lah'-no, nah], *a.* 1. Gallant, fine, gay, genteel, splendidly dressed (gallardo). 2. Elegant (elegante), ingenious, lively, sprightly.

galante [ga-lahn'-tay], *a.* 1. Gallant (hombre), courtly with respect to ladies. 2. Brave, generous, liberal. 3. Elegant, handsome; witty, facetious.

galanteador [gah-lan-tay-ah-dor'], *m.* Wooer, lover.

galantear [gah-lan-tay-ar'], *va.* To court, to woo (cortejar); to solicit favor, to flirt with (coquetear con).

galantemente [gah-lan-tay-men'-tay], *adv.* Gallantly, civilly.

galanteo [gah-lan-tay'-o], *m.* 1. The act of soliciting favor. 2. Gallantry, courtship, refined address to women.

galantería [gah-lan-tay-ree'-ah], *f.* 1. Gallantness, gallantry, elegance. 2. Splendor of appearance, show, magnificence; a graceful manner. 3. Liberality, munificence, generosity. 4. Compliment (cumplido); charming thing (piropo).

galanto [gah-lahn'-to], *m.* (*Bot.*) Snowdrop.

galanura [gah-lah-noo'-rah], *f.* 1. A showy, splendid dress or ornament. 2. Gracefulness, elegance.

galápago [gah-lah'-pah-go], *m.* 1. Fresh-water tortoise. 2. Bed of a plough-share. 3. Frame for boring guns. 4. A kind of shed which soldiers once formed with shields joined together. 5. A horns saddle. 6. A pig of copper, lead, or tin. 7. A convex frame, on which vaults are formed. 8. Cleft in a horse's foot. 9. Ancient military machine.

galapo [gah-lah'-po], *m.* Frame for twisting ropes.

galardón [gah-lar-done'], *m.* Guerdon, reward, recompense.

galardonador, ra [gah-lar-do-nah-dor', rah], *m. & f.* Remunerator, rewarder.

galardonar [gah-lar-do-nar'], *va.* To reward, to recompense, to requite. **Obra galardonada por la Academia,** work which won an Academy prize.

gálata [gah'-lah-tah], *a.* Galatian, of Galatia.

galatea [gah-lah-tay'-ah], *f.* 1. (*Bot.*) A composite plant common in North America and North Asia. 2. A crustacean of the Mediterranean and of the coasts of Chili.

galato [gah-lah'-to], *m.* (*Chem.*) Gallate.

galatite [gah-lah-te'-tay], *f. V.* GALACTITE.

galaxía [gah-lac-see'-ah], *f.* 1. (*Ast.*) Galaxy, the milky way. 2. Soap stone.

galbana [gal-bah'-nah], *f.* 1. (*Bot.*) V. GULANA. 2. Sloth, laziness, slothfulness, idleness, indolence.

galbanado, da [gal-bah-nah'-do, dah], *a.* Of the color of galbanum.

galbanero, ra [gal-bah-nay'-ro, rah], *a.* (*coll.*) Lazy indolent, careless, inattentive.

gálbano [gahl'-bah-no], *m.* (*Pharm.*) Galbanum, a resinous gum.

galbanoso, sa [gal-bah-no'-so, sah], *a.* Indolent, lazy, shiftless.

gálbulo [gahl'-boo-lo], *m.* The nut of the cypress-tree.

galdrope [gal-dro'-pay], *m.* (*Naut.*) Wheel-rope, the rope of the steering-wheel.

gálea [gah'-lay-ah], *f.* An ancient morion or helmet.

galeato, ta [gah-lay-ah'-to, tah], *a.* Applied to the prologue or preface of any work, in which a reply or defence is made to the objections against it.

galeaza [gah-lay-ah'-thah], *f.* (*Naut.*) Galeas, a kind of vessel.

galega [gah-lay-gah], *f.* (*Bot.*) Officinal goat's-rue.

galena [gah-lay'-nah], *f.* Galena sulphur of lead.

galénico, ca [gah-lay'-ne-co, cah], *a.* Galenic, galenical.

galenismo [gah-lay-ness'-mo], *m.* Galenism, doctrine of Galen.

galenista [gah-lay-nees'-tah], *m.* Galenist, physician who follows the doctrine of Galen.

galeo [gah-lay'-o]. *m.* (*Zool.*) Swordfish.

galeón [gah-lay-on'], *m.* (*Naut.*) Galleon, aimed ship of burden, formerly used in Spain for trade in time of war.

galeota [gah-lay-o'-tah], *f.* (*Naut.*) Galliot, a smaller galley of sixteen to twenty oars on a side.

galeote [gah-lay-o'-tay], *m.* Galley-slave.

galera [gah-lay'-rah], *f.* 1. Galley, a vessel with oars, in use in the Mediterranean. 2. Wagon (carro), a heavy covered carriage for burdens. 3. House of correction for women. 4. (*Print.*) Galley, an oblong square frame with ledges, to preserve together a column of types as they were composed. 5. (*Arith.*) Line cutting off the quotient in division. 6. (*Mil.*) A subterranean gallery under a fortress. 7. A room for keeping the common metals. 8. An organ-builder's plane. 9. A furnace for distilling sulphur. *-pl.* Punishment of rowing on board of galleys.

galerada [gah-lay-rah'-dah], *f.* 1. (*Print.*) Galley of types composed, or the proof of a galley for correction. 2. Wagonload (carga).

galerero [gah-lay-ray'-ro], *m.* A wagoner.

galería [gah-lay-ree'-ah], *f.* 1. Gallery, lobby. 2. (*Fort.*) A narrow covered passage across a moat. 3. **Galería de popa,** (*Naut.*) stern-gallery or balcony, into which there is a passage out of the great cabin. **Galería secreta,** secret passage.

galerilla [gah-lay-reel'-lyah], *f. dim.* A small gallery.

galerín [gah-lay-reen'], *m. dim..* A wooden galley in printing offices.

galerita [gah-lay-ree'-tah], *f.* (*Orn.*) Crested lark.

galerna [gah-lerr'-nah], *f.* (*Naut.*) A stormy northwest wind which blows on hot summer days upon the northern coast of Spain.

galfarro [gal-far'-ro], *m.* 1. Rogue, swindler. 2. (*Prov.León*) V. GAVILÁN.

galga [gahl'-gah], *f.* 1. Greyhound bitch, the female of the *Canis grajus, L.* 2. Wheel of the stone of an oilmill. 3. Kind of itch. 4. (*Naut.*) Back of an anchor. 5. Drag, Scotch brake for a wheel.

galgo [gahl'-go], *m.* Greyhound (perro). **Correr como un galgo,** to run like a hare.

galgo [gahl-go], **ga,** *a.* (*Amer.*) Hungry, anxious for something.

galgueño, ña [gal-gay'-nyo, nyah], *a.* Resembling or concerning a greyhound.

gálugulo [gal'-goo-lo], *m.* (*Orn.*) Roller.

galiambo [gah-le-ahm'-bo], *m.* Song of the Gallic priest of Cybele.

galibar [gah-le-bar'], *va.* (*Naut.*) To mould.

gálibo [gah'-lee-bo], *m.* (*Naut.*) Model of a ship.

galicado, da [gah-le-cah'-do, dah], *a.* (*coll.*) V. GALICOSO.

galicana [gah-le-cah'-nah], *a.* **La iglesia galicana,** the Gallican church.

galicismo [gah-le-thees'-mo], *m.* Gallicism, French phraseology.

gálico [gah'-le-coh], *m.* Venereal disease, syphilis. *-a.* Gallic.

galicoso, sa [gah-le-co'-so, sah], *a.* (*coll.*) Infected with syphilis.

galileo, lea [gah-le-lay'-o, ah], *a.* Galilean, of Galilee.

galillo [gah-leel'-lyo], *m.* Uvula, hanging palate.

galimatías [gah-le-mah-tee'-ahs], *m.* (*coll.*) 1. Gibberish, confused speech, jive. 2. A tangled, confused matter.

galio [gah'-le-o], *m.* 1. (*Bot.*) Cheese-rennet bed-straw. 2. (*Chem.*) Galium.

galiopsis [gah-le-op'-sis], *f.* (*Bot.*) Common hedge-nettle.

galipodio [gah-le-po'-de-o], *m.* White frankincense, or the white rosin which distils from the pine-tree or fir; galipot.

galivos [gah-lee'-vos], *m. pl.* Compassings, bevellings, pieces of timber incurvated in the form of an arch.

galizabra [gah-le-thah'-brah], *f.* Kind of vessel with lateen sails in the Levant trade.

galladura [gal-lyah-doo'-rah], *f.* Tread, cicatricula, a ruddy spot in the yolk of an egg.

gallarda [gal-lyar'-dah], *f.* A kind of airy Spanish dance.

gallardamente [gal-lyar-dah-men-tay], *adv.* Elegantly, gracefully, gallantly.

gallardear [gal-lyar-day-ar'], *vn.* To do something with grace or elegance (con elegancia).

gallardete [gal-lyar-day'-tay], *m.* (*Naut.*) Pennant, streamer.

gallardetón [gal-lyar-day-tone'], *m.* (*Naut.*) Broad pennant.

gallardía [gal-lyar-dee'-ah], *f.* 1. A graceful air and deportment. 2. Genteelness, elegance, gracefulness. 3. Gallantry, bravery, nobleness. 4. Activity, briskness in the execution or performance of a thing. 5. Liberality of sentiments, disinterestedness. 6. Magnanimity, greatness of mind.

gallardo, da [gal-yar'-do, dah], *a.* 1. Gay, graceful, elegant, genteel (elegante). 2. Magnanimous, great of mind, exalted in sentiments. 3. Generous, disinterested, high-spirited; pleasant, lively. 4. Brave (valiente), daring, bold, gallant, noble (noble).

gallareta [gal-lyah-ray'-tah], *f.* (*Orn.*) Widgeon.

gallarón [gal-lyah-ron'], *m.* (*Orn.*) A kind of bustard.

gallarito [gal-lyah-ree'-to], *m.* (*Bot.*) Lousewort.

gallaruza [gal-lyah-roo'-thah], *f.* A coarse garment, worn by country people.

gallear [gal-lyay-ar'], *va.* 1. To tread, to copulate as birds (gallo). 2. (*Met.*) To assume an air of importance. -*vn.* 1. To raise the voice with a menace or call; to become irritated (gritar). 2. To crow, to bully (envalentonarse).

gallegada [gal-lyay-gah'-dah], *f.* 1. Number of natives of Galicia assembled together. 2. Manners or behavior of the natives of Galicia. 3. A Galician dance.

gallera [gal-lyay'-rah], *f.* (*Sp. Am.*) Cock fighting ring.

galleta [gal-lyay'-tah], *f.* 1. Cracker. 2. Cookie. 3. Sea biscuit. 4. (*coll.*) Slap in the face (puñetazo). 5. Small bowl with a spout.

gallillo [gal-lyeel'lyo (generally pronounced gah-leel'-lyo)], *m.* (*Anat.*) Uvula. V. GALILLO.

gallina [gal-lyee'-nah], *f.* 1. Hen, a domestic fowl. **Gallina de agua,** coot. **Gallina clueca,** broody hen. 2. (*Met.*) Coward, a chicken-hearted fellow. In this sense used as masculine. **Eres un gallina,** you're chicken, you're yellow. 3. In some universities, second orator or student destined to deliver the eulogium at graduating. **Gallina ciega,** blindman´s-buff, or hoodman's blind: a play among children. **Gallina de río,** V. GALLINETA.

gallináceo, cea [gah-lye-nah'-thay-o, ah], *a.* Gallinaceous, relating to domestic fowls.

gallinaza [gal-lye-nah'-thah], *f.* 1. Hendung. 2. (*Orn.*) Carrion vulture, kite.

gallinería [gal-lye-nay-ree'-ah], *f* I. (*Prov.*) Poulterer's shop (tienda). 2. Hen-coop or hen-house. 3. (*Met.*) Cowardice, pusillanimity.

gallinero, ra [gal-lrye-nay'-ro, rah], *a.* (*Falc.*) Praying or feeding upon fowls.

gallinero [gal-lye-nay'-ro], *m.* 1. Poulterer, one who deals in poultry (persona). 2. Henyard, hen-coop, henroost, hen-house (criadero). 3. Basket in which fowls are carried to market (cesta). 4. (*Met.*) Place where many women meet. 5. (*coll.*) The gallery of a Spanish play-house.

gallineta [gal-lye-nay'-tah], *f.* 1. (*Orn.*) Sand-piper. 2. Buffed grouse.

gallipavo [gal-lye-pah'-vo], *m.* 1. (*Orn.*) Turkey. 2. A false, unpleasant note in singing.

gallipollo [gal-lye-pol-lyo], *m.* Cockerel, a young cock.

gallipuente [gal-lye-poo-en'tay], (*Prov.*) Bridge without rails.

gallito [gal-lyee'-to], *m.* 1. Beau, coxcomb. 2. (*Dim.*) Small cock. **Gallitos,** shaggy-leaved toad-flax. 3. The yellow violet of California.

gallo [gahl'-lyo], *m.* 1. (*Orn.*) Cock, rooster, the male to the hen. **Gallo de pelea,** game cock. **Estar como gallo en gallinero,** to be much esteemed. **Otro gallo me cantara,** that would be quite a different matter. 2. (*Zool.*) Dory, a seafish (pez). 3. (*Met.*) Chief of a village or parish (jefe). 4. Float of cork serving as a mark to fishers, so that they may draw their nets. 5. V. GALLIPAVO. 6. (*Carp.*) Wall-board in the roofing of a house. 7. (*Mus.*) False note, squeak, squawk. **Soltó un gallo,** his voice cracked.

gallobosque [gal-lyo-bos'-kay], *m.* (*Orn.*) Wood-grouse.

gallocresta [gal-lyo-cres'-tah], *f.* (*Bot.*) Annual clary sage.

gallofa [gal-lyo'fah], *f.* 1. Morsel of bread or other food given to pilgrims. 2. Greens used for salad and pottage. 3. An idle tale. 4. (*Prov.*) Directory of divine service.

gallofear [gal-lyo-fay-ar'], *vn.* To saunter about and live upon alms.

gallofero, ra [gal-lyo-fay'-ro, rah], *a.* Idle, lazy, vagabond: applied to a beggar, without a home.

gallofo, fa [gal-lyo'-fo, fah], *a.* V. GALLOFERO.

gallón [gal-lyo-ne'], *m.* 1. (*Prov.*) Green sod, turf; a clod covered with grass. 2. Local bass (cacique).

gallonada [gal-lyo-nah'-dah], *f.* Wall made of sods.

galluda [gal-lyoo'-dah], *f.* (*Zool.*) Tope, dogfish, a small shark.

gallumbos [gal-loom'-bos], *m. pl.* Pants, trousers.

galo, la [gah'-lo, lah], *a.* Gaul, native of Gaul; French (moderno).

galocha [gah-lo'-chah], *f.* 1. Galosh, clog, a wooden shoe. 2. Patten, an over-shoe of wood with an iron ring.

galón [gah-lone'], *m.* 1. Gallon, a texture of silk, thread, gold or silver. 2. Lace. 3. Gallon, a liquid measure (medida). 4. (*Naut.*) Wooden ornament on the sides of ships. **La acción le valió 2 galones,** the action got him a couple of stripes.

galonazo [gahlo-nah'-tho], *m.* 1. (*aug.*) Large galloon. 2. Excessive ornament.

galoneadura [gah-lo-nay-ah-doo'-rah], *f.* Garnishing with lace or galloons.

galonear [gah-lo-nay-ar'], *va.* To lace, to adorn with lace.

galonero [gah-lo-nay'-ro], *m.* Lace or galloon maker.

galop [gah-lop'], *m.* (*Acad.*) A Hungarian dance, and the music to which it is set.

galopada [gah-lo-pah'-dah], *f.* The space over which a horse gallops.

galopante [gah-lo-pahn'-tay], *a.* (*Med. fig.*) Galloping.

galopar [gah-lo-par'], *vn.* To gallop. **Echar a galopar,** to break into a gallop.

galope [gah-lo'-pay], *m.* 1. Gallop, motion of a horse. 2. Hasty execution of a thing. **A gallope** or **de galope,** gallopingly.

galopeado, da [gah-lo-pay-ah'-do, dah], *a. & pp.* of GALOPEAR. Done in a hurry.-*m.* Whipping, flogging.

galopear [gah-lo-pay-ar'], *vn.* V. GALOPAR.

galopín [gah-lo-peen'], *m.* 1. (*Naut.*) Swabber, a boy who swabs the deck; a cabin boy. 2. Scullion, a kitchen boy. 3. A contemptible rogue. 4. Boy meanly dressed. 5. A clever knave. 6. Ragamuffin (pícaro). 7. Scroundel, rogue (bribón); smart-aleck (sabelotodo).

galopo [gah-lo'-po], *m.* Rogue.

galopinada [gah-lo-pe-nah'-dah], *f.* Action of a cunning, crafty person; knavery.

galpito [gal-pee'-to], *m.* A weak, sickly chicken.

galpón [gal-pone'], *m.* (*Peru*) dormitory for the laborers of a farm.

galván (proper name). **No lo entenderá Galván,** an intricate, difficult thing.

galvánico, ca [gal-vah'-ne-co, cah], *a. (Phys.)* Galvanic.

galvanismo [gal-vah-nees'-mo], *m.* Galvanism, electricity of metals.

galvanizar [gal-vah-ne-thar'], *(Phys.)* To galvanize.

galvanómetro [gal-vah-no'-may-tro], Galvanometer.

galvanoplastia, or **galvanoplástica** [galvah-no-plahs'-te-ah], *f.* Galvanoplasty, electrotypy.

gama [gah'-mah], *f.* 1. Gamut, the scale of musical notes. 2. Doe, the female to a buck.

gama globulina [gah'-mah glo-boo-lee'-nah], *f. (Med.)* Gammaglobulin.

gamalote [gah-mah-lo'-tay], *m.* A grass of South America; arrowgrass.

gamarra [gah-mar'-rah], *f.* Martingale, a strap used to prevent a horse from rearing.

gamarza [gah-mar'-thah], *f. (Bot.)* Wild Syrian rue, peganum.

gamba [gam'-bah], *f. (Zool.)* Prawn.

gambaj, or **gambax** [gam-bah', gam-box'], *m.* A quilted jacket of wool.

gambalúa [gam-bah-loo'-ah], *f. (coll.)* A tall, ill-shaped man, without life or spirit.

gámbaro [gahm'-bah-ro], *m.* A kind of small craw-fish.

gambesina [gam-bay-see'-nah], *f.* or **gambesón** [gambayson'], *m.* A kind of jacket worn under the armor for comfort.

gamberrada [gam-bayr-rah'-dah], *f.* Piece of hooliganism, loutish thing.

gamberrismo [gam-bayr-rees'-mo], *m.* Hooliganism; loutishness.

gamberro [gam-bayr'-ro], *f.* Ill-bread, loutish, rough. *-m.* Lout, hooligan, troublemaker.

gambeta [gam-bay'-tah], *f.* 1. Cross caper in dancing; ancient dolce. 2. Affected language or tone of voice. 3. **Gambeta de mar,** scaled center shell.

gambetear [gam-bay-tay-ar'], *vn.* To caper like a horse.

gambeto [gam-bay'-to], *m.* A quilted great-coat.

gambo [gahm'-bo], *m.* Cap for a new born child.

gambotes [gam-bo'-tes], *m. pl. (Naut.)* Counter timbers, arched timbers (Also **Gambotas,** *f.*)

gambux [gam-boocs'], *m.* A small bonnet or cap for children.

gamela [gah-may'-lah], *f.* Kind of basket.

gamelo [gah-may'-lo], *m.* Name given by the Indians to balsam copaiba.

gamella [gah-mel'-lyah], *f.* 1. Yoke for oxen and mules. 2. A large wooden trough. 3. *V.* CAMELLÓN. 4. Shecamel. *(Acad.)*

gamelleja [gah-mel-lyay'-hah], *f. dim.* A small yoke.

gamellón [gah-mel-lyone'], *m.* 1. *(aug.)* A large yoke for oxen and mules. 2. *(Prov.)* Trough in which grapes are trodden.

gamezno [gah-meth'-no], *m.* Little young buck.

gamino [gah-mee'-no], **m.** *(Vet.)* A tumor which attacks sheep and goats.

gamo [gah'-mo], *m.* 1. Buck of the fullow-deer. 2. *V.* GAMINO. 3. An iron hook in a wooden handle for hooking fishes already caught. 4. *(coll.)* A restless, quick-moving individual.

gamogastro [gah-mo-gahs'-tro], *a. (Bot.)* Gamogastrous, having the ovaries united.

gamón [gah-mone'], *m. (Bot.)* Asphodel.

gamonal [gah-mo-nahl'], *m.* Place in which asphodels flourish.

gamoncillo [gah-mon-theel'-lyo], *m. (Bot.)* Onion-leaved asphodel.

gamonito [gah-mo-nee'-to], *m.* 1. Young shoots springing round trees or shrubs. 2. *(Dim.)* Young asphodel. 3. *(Bot.) V.* MARTAGÓN.

gamonoso, sa [gah-mo-no'-so, sah], *a.* Abounding in asphodels.

gamopétalo, la [gah-mo-pay'tah-lo, lah], *a.* Gamopetalous.

gamosépalo, la [gah-mo-say'-pah-lo, lah], *a.* Gamosepalous.

gamucería [gah-moo-thay'-ree'-ah], *f.* The factory where chamois skins are curried and prepared.

gamuno, na [gah-moo'-no, nah], *a.* Skins (ciervos).

gamuza [gah-moo'-thah], *f.* 1. Chamois. 2. Chamois or chamois leather (piel).

gamuzado, da [gah-moo-thah'-do, dah], *a.* Chamois color.

gamuzón [gah-moo-thon'], *m. dim.* A kind of coarse chamois.

gana [gah'-nah], *f.* 1. Appetite (apetito), keenness of stomach; hunger. 2. *(Prov.)* A healthy disposition of body. 3. Inclination (afán), desire (deseo), mind, list. **De buena gana,** with pleasure, willingly, voluntarily. **De mala gana,** unwillingly, with reluctance, with dislike. **De gana,** designedly, on purpose. **Tenar gana,** to have a mind. **Comer con gana,** to eat with an appetite. **Hacer algo con ganas,** to do something reluctantly. **Como te dé la gana,** just as you wish. **Quedarse con las ganas,** to fail. **Tengo pocas ganas de,** I don't much feel like.

ganadería [gah-nah-day-ree'-ah], *f.* 1. Breeding cattle (raza). 2. Stock of cattle (crianza).

ganadero, ra [gah-nah-day'-ro, rah], *a.* Cattle (animal), stock; cattle-raising. *-m.* Stock-breeder (persona), rancher; cattle dealer.

ganado [gah-nah'-do], *m.* 1. Herd of domesticated animals of the same kind; flock, drove. **Ganado mayor,** cattle: it is also said of mules. **Ganado menor,** sheep. **Ganado asnal,** donkeys. **Ganado ovejuno,** sheep. **Ganado cabrío,** goats. 2. Cattle, word of contempt applied to men and women. 3. Collection of bees of a beehive.—**Ganado, da,** *pp.* of GANAR.

ganador, ra [gah-nah-dor', rah], *m. & f.* 1. Winner. 2. Gainer. 3. Earner. **El equipo ganador,** the winning team.

ganancia [gah-nahn'the-ah], *f.* 1. Gain (beneficio), earnings, profit. 2. Winnings. 3. Earning, profiting. **Ganancia bruta,** gross profit. **Gananancias y perdidas,** profit and loss.

ganancial [gah-nan-the-ahl'], *a.* Lucrative. **Bienes gananciales,** property acquired during marriage.

ganancioso, sa [gah-nan-the-o'-so, sah], *a.* Lucrative, gainful (lucrativo).

ganapán [gah-nah-pahn'], *m.* 1. A porter (recadero). 2. A rude, coarse man (patán). *(Acad.)* A shiftless fellow, a ne'erdo well.

ganapierde [gah-nah-pe-err'-day], *m.* A mode of playing draughts, where he who loses all his men wins the game; give away or losing game.

ganar [gah-nar'], *va.* 1. To gain, to get or obtain (adquirir), as profit or advantage. 2. To gain, to win (premio). 3. To gain, to have the overplus in comparative computation. 4. To win, to conciliate, to allure to kindness or compliance. 5. To attain, to acquire. 6. To conquer. 7. To surpass. **Ganar la vida,** to gain a living. **Ha ganado mucho dinero,** she has made a great deal of money. **Ganar unas oposiciones para un puesto,** to win a post by public competition. **No hay quien le gane,** there's nobody who can beat him. *-vn.* 1. *(Dep. etc.)* To win; to gain. 2. To thrive, to improve; to do well (prosperar). **Ha ganado mucho en salud,** he has much improved in health.

ganchero [gan-chay'-ro], *m.* Conductor of a raft of timber.

ganchillo [gan-cheel'-lyo], *m. dim.* A little hook or crotch.

gancho [gahn'-cho], *m.* 1. Hook, which remains after a branch of a tree has been broken off. 2. Hook, an incurvated piece of iron; a crotch. 3. Crook, a sheephook. 4. An allurer, one who insinuates himself into the favor of another to attain some purpose. 5. Pimp, procurer, pander (persona). 6. *(Naut.)* An iron hook with an eye. 6. Appeal, attraction (atractivo). **Gancho de aparejo,** tacklehook. **Gancho de carnicero,** butcher's hook. **Echar el gancho a,** *(Fig.)* to hook.

ganchoso, sa [gan-cho'-so, sah], *a.* Hooked, curved.

ganchuelo [gan-choo-ay'-lyo], *m. dim. V.* GANCHILLO.

gándara [gahn'-dah-rah], *f.* A low range of mountains, or rough, uncultivated ground.

gandaya [gan-dah'-yah], *f.* 1. Laziness, idleness. 2. *V.* COFIA.

gandido, da [gan-dee'-do, dah], *a.* 1. *(Prov.)* Seduced, led astray. 2. *(Amer. Peru.)* Hungry, gluttonous.

gandinga [gan-deen'-gah], *f. (Cuba)* A stew made from the liver of a hog or other animal.

gandir [gan-deer'], *va.* To eat.

gandujado [gan-doo-hah'-do], *m.* Ornament or ruffle of a woman's dress.—**Gandujado, da** *pp.* of GANDUJAR.

gandujar [gan-doo-har'], *va.* To bend, to plait, to fold.

gandul, la [gan-dool', lah], *m. dim.* Vagabond, vagrant, tramp.

gandulear [gan-doo-lay-ar'], *vn.* To lounge, to be idle.

ganfalonero [gan-fah-lo-nay'-ro], *m.* Gonfalonier, Pope's standard-bearer.

ganfanón [gan-fah-non'], *m.* Gonfalon, ensign of the Romish church, and of some Italian states.

ganforro, ra [gan-for'-ro, rah], *m. & f. (coll.)* Vagrant, vagabond.

ganga [gahn'-gah], *f.* 1. *(Orn.)* The little pintailed grouse. 2. Anything valuable acquired with little labor (cosa fácil). 3. Bargain price. **Precio de ganga,** bargain price. **Esto es una ganga,** this is a cinch.

ganga [gahn'-gah], *f. (Min.)* Gangue, bed or matrix of minerals.

gangarilla [gan-gah-reel'-lyah], *f.* Ancient company of strolling players.

ganglio [gahn'-gle-o], *m.* 1. *(Anat.)* Ganglion. 2. *(Med.)* Ganglion, a small tumor of the sheath of a tendon.

ganglionar [gan-gle-o-nar'], *a.* Ganglionic, provided with ganglions.

gangoso, sa [gan-go'-so, sah], *a.* Snuffling, or speaking through the nose (acento).

gangrena [gan-gray'-nah], *f.* Gangrene, mortification.

gangrenar [gan-gray-nar'], *va.* To cause gangrene or mortification; to corrupt, to rot. -*vr.* To become gangrenous or mortified.

gangrenoso, sa [gan-gray-no'-so, sah], *a.* Gangrenous.

gán(g)ster [gahns'-tayr], *m.* Gangster, gunman.

ganguear [gan-gay-ar'], *vn.* To snuffle, to speak through the nose.

gánguil [gahn'-gee!], *m.* 1. A barge used for fishing, or in the coasting trade; lighter. 2. A fishing net broader than that called *tartana.*

ganil [gah-neel'], *m.* A granular, calcareous rock.

ganoso, sa [gah-no'-so, sah], *a.* Desirous, full of desire; longing after (afanoso).

gansa [gahn'-sah], *f.* 1. *(Orn.)* Goose. 2. Goose, silly girl.

gansarón [gan-sah-ron'], *m.* 1. A gosling. 2. A tall, thin man.

gansería [gan-say-ree'-ah], *f.* Folly, stupidity.

ganso, sa [gahn'-so, sah], *m. & f.* 1. *(Orn.)* Gander, goose. 2. Tall, slender person. 3. *(coll.)* A goose or goose-cap, a silly person. -*pl.* Giblets of a goose.

gánster [gahns'-tayr], *m.* Gangster.

gante [gahn'-tay], *m.* A kind of linen manufactured in Ghent.

ganzúa [gan-thoo'-ah], *f.* 1. Picklock, an instrument with which locks are opened. 2. Thief who picks locks (ladrón).

ganzuar [gan-thoo-ar'], *va.* To pick a lock, to open it with a picklock.

gañán [gah-nyahn'], *m.* Day laborer; teamster, rustic.

gañanía [gah-nyah-nee'-ah], *f.* Number of day-laborers.

gañido [gah-nyee'-do], *m.* Yelping or howling of a dog. **Gañido, da** *pp.* of GAÑIR.

gañiles [gah-nyee'-les], *m. pl.* The cartilaginous larynx, organ of the voice.

gañir [gah-nyeer'], *va.* 1. To yelp or howl (perro). 2. To croak (pájaro), to cackle, to crow. 3. To talk hoarsely (persona).

gañón, gañote [gah-nyon', gah-nyo'-tay], *m.* 1. The throat. 2. *(Prov.)* Kind of fritters.

gaón [gah-on'], *m.* 1. A substitute for the oar in the Indian vessels known as barangays and virreys. 2. Title of honor which was once given to rabbis or Jews who distinguished themselves in the sciences.

garabatada [gah-rah-bah-tah'-dah], *f. (coll.)* Act of throwing a hook.

garabatear [gah-rah-bah-tay-ar'], *va.* 1. To hook, to catch with a hook. 2. To scrawl, to scribble. 3. To use tergiversations. -*vn.* 1. To scribble, to scrawl (escribiendo). 2. To beat about the bush (andar con rodeos).

garabateo [gah-rah-bah-tay'-o], *m.* Act of hooking.

garabatillo [gah-rah-bah-teel'-lyo], *m.* 1. *(Dim.)* A small hook. 2. Difficulty of evacuating any peccant matter from the lungs.

garabato [gah-rah-bah'-to], *m.* 1. Pot-hook (escritura); grapnel, creeper. **Garabatos,** scribble. 2. Hook to hang meat on (gancho). 3. A graceful gait and deportment. -*pl* 1. Ill-formed or scrawling letters or characters; pot-hooks. 2. Improper gestures or movements of the hands and fingers.

garabatoso, sa [gah-rah-bah-to'-so, sah], *a.* 1. Full of scrawls. 2. *(Met.)* Elegant charming, attractive.

garabeta [gah-rah-bay'-tah], *f.* A stick armed with one or more hooks at the end to catch cuttle-fish.

garabito [gah-rah-bee'-to], *m.* A linen cover spread over fruit stalls (mercado).

garaje [gah-rah'-hay], *m.* Garage.

garamón [gah-rah-mone'], *m.* In printing, a small Roman type.

garante [gah-rahn'-tay], *m.* 1. Guarantee, a power who undertakes to see stipulations performed (responsable). 2. Warranter. *V.* FIADOR.

garantía [gah-ran-tee'-ah], *f.* 1. Warranty, guarant, the act of securing the performance of articles or stipulations (seguridad); undertaking (compromiso).

garantir [gah-ran-teer'], *va.* To guarantee.

garantizado [gah-rahn-tee-thah'-do], *a.* Guaranteed.

garantizar [gah-rahn-tee-thar'], To guarantee, to warrant; to vouch for. *V.* GARANTIR.

garañón [gah-rah-nyone'], *m.* 1. Jackass kept for breeding (asno). 2. A man much given to lust; lecher. 3. Male breeding camel. *(Acad.)*

garapacho [gah-rah-pah'-cho], *m.* Kind of dressed meat.

garapiña [gah-rah-pee'-nyah], *f.* 1. The congealed particles of any liquid. 2. A kind of black lace.

garapiñado, da [gah-rah-pe-nyah'-do, dah], *a.* Glacé, candied.

garapiñar [gah-rah-pe-nyar'], *va.* To ice, to turn, to ice (pastel), to cover with ice, to freeze (helado), to clot (nata).

garapiñera [gah-rah-pe-nyay'-rah], *f.* Vessel in which liquids are congealed; a cooler, refrigerator.

garapita [gah-rah-pee'-tah], *f.* Fishing net with small meshes.

garapito [gah-rah-pee'-to], *m.* Small insect, like a tick.

garapullo [gah-rah-pool'-lyo], *m.* 1. Dart made of paper (rehilete). 2. A shuttle-cock. 3. Banderilla (toros).

garatura [gah-rah-too'-rah], *f.* Scraper, an instrument used by curriers of leather.

garatusa [gah-rah-too'-sah], *f.* 1. A sort of card game. 2. *(coll.)* Caress, act of endearment.

garavito [gah-rah-vee'-to], *m.* Stall, a small shed, in which greens, fruit, etc., are sold at market.

garay [gah-rah'-e], *m.* A Philippine craft.

garba [gar'-bah], *f.* Sheaf, as of corn. *(Bot.)* Hairy bastard vetch.

garbancera [gar-ban-thay'-rah], *f. (Bot.) V.* GARBANCILLO.

garbanzal [gar-ban-thahl'], *m.* A piece of ground sown with chick-peas.

garbanzo [gar-bahn'-tho], *m. (Bot.)* Chick-pea or common chick-pea. **Ganarse los garbanzos,** to earn one's living.

garbanzuelo [gar-ban-thoo-ay'-lo], *m. dim.* 1. *(Dim.)* Small chick-pea. 2. *(Vet.)* Disease in horses' feet. *V.* ESPARAVÁN.

garbar [gar-bar'], *va. (Prov.)* To form sheaves, to tie stalks of corn into bundles.

garbear [gar-bay-ar'], *va.* 1. (*Prov.*) *V.* GARBAR. 2. To seize, to lay hold of something eagerly. -*vn.* To affect an air of dignity and grandeur (afectar garbo).

garbeo [gar-bay'-o], *m.* Affected elegance, show. **Darse un garbeo**, to go for a walk.

garbeña [gar-bay'-nyah], *f.* (*Bot.*) Common heath.

garbias [gar'-be-as], **pl.** A ragout, made of herbs, cheese, flour, eggs, sugar, and butter.

garbillador [gar-beel-lyah-dor'], *m.* Sifter, riddler.

garbillar [gar-beel-lyar'], *va.* To garble, to sift; to separate the bad from the good.

garbillo [gar-beel'-lyo], *m.* Riddle, a coarse sieve made of bass or sedge.

garbín [gar-been'], *m.* Coif made of net-work.

garbino [gar-bee'-no], *m.* South-west wind.

garbo [gar'-bo], *m.* 1. Gracefulness, gentility, elegance of manner, jauntiness (aire); grace (elegancia). 2. A clover and genteel way of doing things. 3. A gentleman-like air and deportment. 4. Frankness, disinterestedness, generosity (largueza); liberality of sentiments; cleverness. **Andar con garbo.** to walk gracefully. **Hacer algo con garbo**, to do something with grace.

garbosamente [gar-bo-sah-men'-tay], *adv.* Gallantly, nobly, generously, liberally.

garboso, sa [gar-bo'-so, sah], *a.* 1. Genteel, graceful (elegante), elegant, comely, gallant, springly, gay. 2. Liberal, generous, magnanimous (generoso).

garbullo [gar-bool'-lyo], *m.* Crowd, a multitude confusedly pressed together.

garcero, ra [gar-thay'-ro, rah], *m. & f.* (*Orn.*) Heron-hawk.

garceta [gar-thay'-tah], *f.* 1. A young heron. 2. Hair which falls in locks on the cheeks and temples. 3. (*Naut.*) Point or reef-band, a small rope which serves to furl the sails. **Garcetas**, tenderlings, the first horns of a deer.

gardenia [gar-day'-nyah], *f.* (*Bot.*) Gardenia.

garduja [gar-doo'-hah], *f.* Barren stone thrown away in quicksilver mines.

garduña [gar-doo'-nyah], *f.* Marten.

garduño [gar-doo'-nyo], *m.* 1. He or male marten. 2. (*coll.*) Filcher, a petty thief.

garete [gah-ray'-tay], *m.* **Ir al garete**, to be adrift.

garfa [gar'-fah], *f.* 1. Claw, as of an animal or bird (sarcastically) a hand. 2. An ancient tax.

garfada, garfiada [gar-fah'-dah.gar-fe-ah'-dah], *f.* Clawing or seizing with the nails.

garfear [gar-fay-ar'], *vn.* To use a drag-hook for getting something out of a well or river.

garfio [gar'-feo], *m.* Hook, drag-hook; gaff, climbing iron (alpinismo).

gargajeada [gar-gah-hay-ah'-dah], *f.* Spitting, ejecting phlegm.

gargajear [gar-gah-hay-ar'], *vn.* To spit, to expectorate.

gargajeo [gar-gah-hay'-o], *m.* Spitting, ejecting phlegm.

gargajiento, ta [gar-gah-he-en'-to, tah], *a.* Spitting, ejecting expectorate matter.

gargajo [gar-gah'-ho], *m.* Phlegm or mucus brought up by coughing, expectorated matter, sputum.

gargajoso, sa [gar-gah-ho'-so, sah], *a. V.* GARGAJIENTO.

garganchón [gar-gahn-chone'], *m. V.* GARGÜERO.

garganta [gar-gahn'-tah], *f.* 1. Throat, gullet. 2. The instep (pie). 3. Mountain-flood, torrent. 4. A narrow pass between mountains or rivers. 5. The shaft of a column or balustrade. 6. Neck (botella). 7. Shaft (columna). **Tener buena garganta**, to be a good singer. **Tener el agua a la garganta**, to be in imminent danger.

gargantada [gar-gan-tah'-dah], *f.* Quantity of water, wine, or blood, ejected at once from the throat.

gargantear [gar-gan-tay-ar'], *vn.* To quaver, to warble.

garganteo [gar-gan-tay'-o], *m.* Quavering, a tremulous modulation of the voice.

gargantilla [gar-gan-teel'-lyah], *f.* Necklace worn by women.

gárgara [gar'-gah-rah], *f.* Noise made by gargling the throat. **Mandar a uno a hacer gárgaras**, to tell somebody to go to hell.

gargarismo [gar-gah-rees'-mo], *m.* 1. Gargarism, gargle (líquido). 2. Gargling.

gargarizar [gar-gah-re-thar'], *va.* To gargle, to gargarize.

gárgol [gar'-gol], *m.* Groove. *V.* RANURA. **Gárgoles**, grooves of casks, where the head and bottom pieces come in, chimes.

gárgol [gar'-gol], *a.* (*Prov.*) Empty, addle (huevos).

gárgola [gar'-go-lah], *f.* 1. Spout of a gutter in the form of a lion or other animal; gargoyle. 2. Linseed.

gargüero, garguero [gar-goo-ay'-ro, gar-gay'-ro], *m.* 1. The gullet. 2. Windpipe.

garico [gah-ree'-co], *m.* A kind of medicinal fungus of Canada which grows among the pines.

gariofilea [gah-re-o-fe-lay'-ah], *f.* (*Bot.*) Common avens or herb bennet.

garita [gah-ree-tah], *f.* 1. Sentry box. 2. A porter's lodge (consejería). 3. A seat in a privy. 4. Look-out post (de vigilancia).

garitear [gah-re-tay-ar'], *vn.* (*coll.*) To gamble.

garitero [gah-re-tay'-ro], *m.* 1. Owner of a gambling-house (dueño). 2. Gamester, gambler (jugador).

garito [gah-ree'-to], *m.* Gambling-house, gambling-den (casa), profits of gaming (ganancias).

garla [gar'-lah], *f.* (*coll.*) Talk, chatter.

garlador, ra [gar-lah-dor', rah], *m. & f.* (*coll.*) Babbler, prattler.

garlante [gar-lahn'-tay], *pa.* (*coll.*) Babbling, prater.

garlar [gar-lar'], *va.* (*coll.*) To babble, to prattle, to chatter.

garlito [gar-lee'-to], *m.* 1. A wicker snare or trap for fish. 2. Snare, trap, or gin.

garlocha [gar-lo'-chah], *f.* Goad, with which oxen are driven; oxgoad. *V.* GARROCHA.

garlopa [gar-lo'-pah], *f.* Jack plane, a long plane.

garnacha [gar-nah'-chah], *f.* 1. Robe, a dress worn by councillors. 2. Dignity or employment of a councillor. 3. A liquor made of honey and wine. 4. A large red grape and the wine made from it (vino). 5. Company of strolling players. *V.* GARGARILLA.

garo [gah'-ro], *m.* 1. A kind of lobster. 2. Brine for fish or meat.

garra [gar'-rah], *f.* 1. Claw of a wild beast, talon of a bird of prey, a clutch a fang. 2. Hand, in contempt. **Echarle a uno la garra**, (*coll.*) to grasp, to seize, to imprison anyone. 3. (*Tec.*) Claw, tooth, hook. 4. (*Fig.*) Bite, penetration; (*Dep.*) sharpness, edge. **Esta canción no tiene garra**, that song has no bite to it.

garrafa [gar-rah'-fah], *f.* Vessel for cooling liquors; carafe (de vino, licor).

garrafal [gar-rah-fahl'], *a.* 1. Applied to a kind of cherries larger and sweeter than the common ones. 2. Great, vast, huge; monumental (error).

garrafilla [gar-rah-feel'-lyah], *f. dim.* A small vessel for cooling liquids.

garrafinar [gar-rah-fee-nar'], *va.* (*coll.*) To grapple, to snatch away.

garrafón [gar-rah-fone'], *m. aug.* 1. A large vessel for cooling liquids. 2. Demijohn, carboy.

garrama [gar-rah'-mah], *f.* 1. Tax or duty anciently paid by the Moors. 2. Imposition, fraud, robbery.

garramar [gar-rah-mar'], *va.* 1. To rob, to plunder and pillage. 2. To collect an ancient tax.

garrancho [gar-rahn'-cho], *m.* Branch of a tree broken off; splinter.

garrapata [gar-rah-pah'-tah], *f.* 1. Tick, the louse of dogs and sheep. 2. A short, little person.

garrapatear [gar-rah-pah-tay-ar'], *vn.* To scribble, to scrawl.

garrapatilla [gar-rah-pah-teel'-lyah], *f. dim.* A small tick.

garrapato [gar-rah-pah'-to], *m.* Pot-hook, ill-formed character or letter.

garrar, garrear [gar-rar' gar-ray-ar'], *vn. (Naut.)* To drag, to be driven from the moorings (barco). **El ancla garra**, the anchor drags.

garridamente [gar-re-dah-men'-tay], *adv.* Gracefully, neatly.

garrido, da [gar-ree'-do, dah], *a.* Handsome (bien parecido), neat (elegante), graceful.

garroba [gar-ro-bath], *f. V.* ALGARROBA.

garrobal [gar-ro-bahl'], *m.* Plantation of carob-trees.

garrobilla [gar-ro-beel'-lyah], *f.* Chips of carob-trees used to tan leather.

garrobo [gar-ro'-bo], *m.* 1. *(Bot.)* Carob-tree, or St. Johns bread. 2. Small alligator (caimán).

garrocha [gar-ro'-chah], *f.* 1. A sort of javelin with a hooked head. 2. A kind of dart used to prick bulls.

garrochada [gar-ro-chah'-dah], *f.* or **Garrochazo**, *m.* Prick with a javelin or dart.

garrocheador [gar-ro-chay-ah-dor'], *m.* Goader, pricker.

garrochear [gar-ro-chay-ar'], *va. V.* AGARROCHAR.

garrochón [gar-ro-chone'], *m.* Spear, used by bullfighters on horseback.

garrofa, or **garroba** [gar-ro'-fah, gar-ro'-bah], *f. (Prov.)* A fruit of the carob-tree. *V.* ALGARROBA.

garrofal [gar-ro-fah'], *m. V.* GARROBAL.

garrón [gar-rone'], *m.* 1. Spur of cocks and birds. 2. Talon of a bird of prey. 3. *V.* CALCAÑAR.

garrotazo [gar-ro-tah'-tho], *m.* 1. Blow with a cudgel. 2. *(aug.)* A large cudgel.

garrotal [gar-ro-tahl'], *m.* A plantation of olive-trees, made with crossed slips of large olive-trees put into the ground to grow.

garrote [gar-ro'-tay], *m.* 1. Cudgel, a strong stick (bastón). 2. A capital punishment used in Spain, consisting in strangling a criminal with an iron collar. 3. The scaffold where the capital punishment called **garrote** is inflicted. 4. *V.* GARROTAZO. 5. The act of tying a rope or cord very tight. 6. *(Prov.)* Hazel basket or pannier. **Dar garrote a uno**, to garrotte somebody.

garrotillo [gar-ro-teel'-lyo], *m.* Inflammation in the throat, croup, diphtheria.

garrubia [gar-roo'be-ah], *f. V.* ALGARROBA.

garrucha [gar-roo'-chah], *f.* 1. Pulley, one of the mechanical powers. 2. Horse or board on which the card is fixed for combing wool.

garruchón [gar-roo'-chone'], *m.* Body of a coach without straps and buckles.

garrucho [gar-roo'-cho], *m. (Naut.)* Cringle, a sort of ring for a variety of uses on board of ships.

garruchuela [gar-roo-choo-ay'-lah], *f. dim.* A small pulley.

garrudo, da [gar-roo'-do, dah], *a.* Nervous, brawny, strong.

garrulador, ra [gar-roo-lah-dor', rah], *m. & f.* A garrulous person.

garrulería [gar-roo-lay-re'-ah], *f.* Chatter.

gárrulo, la [gar'-roo-lo, lah], *a.* 1. Chirping, making a cheerful noise, as birds. 2. Chattering, prattling; garrulous (persona). 3. Noisy (viento).

garú [gah-roo'], *m.* A plant of the mozereum family, of disagreeable smell, whose bark is used as a sinapism or mustard plaster by moistening it in vinegar.

garúa [gah-roo'-ah], *f. (Peru)* Drizzle (lloviznar).

garuar [gah-roo-ar'], *vn. (Peru)* To drizzle.

garufo [gah-roo'-fo], *m.* Concrete. *V.* HORMIGÓN.

garulla [gah-rool'-lyah], *f.* 1. Ripe grapes which remain in the basket (uvas). 2. *(coll.)* Rabble, crowd (gentío). *(Per.)*

garullada [gah-rool-lyah'-dah], *f.* Gang of rogues.

garvier [gar-ve-ayr'], *m.* A small pouch anciently in use.

garza [gar'-thah], *f. (Orn.)* Heron.

garzo [gar'-tho], *m.* Agaric.

garzo, za [gar-tho', thah], *a.* Blue-eyed (persona).

garzón [gar-thone'], *m.* Lad, boy; stripling.

garzonear [gar-tho-nay-ar'], *vn.* To make a parade of boyish actions; to solicit, to court.

garzota [gar-tho'-tah], *f.* 1. *(Orn.)* Night-heron. 2. Plumage worn as an ornament. 3. Crest of a helmet.

garzul [gar-thool'], *m. (Prov.)* A kind of wheat.

gas [gahs], *m.* Gas, fumes (vapores). **Gas combustible**, inflammable gas. **Gas lacrimógeno**, tear gas. **Gas venenoso**, poison gas. **Gas natural**, natural gas. **Asfixiar con gas**, to gas.

gasa [gah'-sah], *f.* Gauze, a very thin, transparent cloth, nappy-liner (pañal), crêpe (luto). **Gasa rayada**, striped muslin. **Gasa higiénica**, sanitary towel.

gascón, na, nés [gas-con', nah, nes'], *a.* Gascon, belonging to or native of Gascony.

gasconada [gas-co-nah'-dah], *f.* Gasconade, boast, a bravado.

gaseiforme [gah-say-e-for'-may], *a.* Aeriform, gaseous.

gaseoso, sa [gah-say-o'-so, sah], *a.* Gaseous gas. *-f.* Soda water.

gasífero, ra [gah-see'-fay-ro, rah], *a.* Gasconducting.

gasificable [gah-se-fe-cah'-blay], *a.* Convertible into gas.

gasificación [gah-se-fe-cah'-the-on'], *f.* Gasification, conversion into gas.

gasificar [gah-se-fe-car'], *va.* To gasify, to convert into gas.

gas-oil [gah-so'-el], *m.* Diesel oil.

gasóleo [gah-so'-lay-o], *m.* Diesel oil.

gasolina [gah-so-lee'-nah], *f.* Gasoline, petrol, motor spirit. **Estación de gasolina**, gas station. **Gasolina super**, three star petrol.

gasolinera [gah-so-le-nay'-rah], *f.* 1. Motor launch. 2. Gas station.

gasómetro [gah-so'-may-tro], *m.* 1. Gasholder, gas-storage tank. 2. Gasometer.

gasoquimia [gah-so-kee'-me-ah], *f.* Gas chemistry.

gastable [gas-tah'-blay], *a.* That may be wasted or spent.

gastadero [gas-tah-day'-ro], *m.* 1. Waster, spender. 2. Wasting, spending.

gastado, da [gas-tah'-do, dah] *a. & pp.* of GASTAR. Wornout (decaído), useless, shabby (ropa), hackneyed (trillado).

gastador, ra [gas-tah-dor', rah], *m. & f.* 1. Spendthrift (derrochador), prodigal. 2. Pioneer in military operations. 3. Persons sentenced to public labor. 4. *(Met.)* Corrupter, destroyer.

gastadura [gas-tah-doo'-rah], *f.* The murk which remains upon any object as an effect of friction.

gastamiento [gas-tah-me-en'-to], *m.* Consumption of something.

gastar [gas-tar'], *va.* 1. To expend, to lay out money, to spend (dinero, esfuerzo, tiempo) **Han gastado un** dineral, they've spent a fortune. 2. To waste or make way with, to melt, to consume or wear out gradually (ropa, zapatos) 3. To apply to some purpose. 4. To plunder, to pillage, to sack. 5. To digest, to concoct in the stomach. 6. **Gastar bromas**, to play practical jokes. **Gastar saliva**, to waste one's breath. **Ya verás tú cómo las gasto**, you'll see what stuff I'm made of. **Ya sé cómo las gasta usted. I** know what you are like. 7. To have, to wear (vestir): **Antes no gastaba gafas**, didn't use to wear glasses. *-vr.* 1. To be sold or disposed of. 2. To grow old or useless. 3. To become rotten or corrupted.

gasterópodo, da [gas-tay-ro'-po-do, dah], *a.* Gasteropod.

gasto [gahs'-to], *m.* 1. Expenditure, expense, cost, consumption (consumo). 2. Act of spending or consuming (acto). *-pl.* Expenses, charges, disbursements, outlay, commission. **Gastos de administración**, administrative costs. **Gastos comerciales**, business expenses. **Gastos de explotación**, operating costs. **Gastos de viaje**, traveling expenses.

gástrico, ca [gahs'-tre-co, cah], *a.* Gastric, belonging to the stomach.

gastritis [gas-tree'-tis], *f.* Gastritis, inflammation of the stomach.

gastroenteritis [gas-tro-en-tay-ree'-tees], *f,* Gastroenteritis.

gastrología [gas-tro-lo-hee'-ah], *f.* Gastrology, a treatise on the kitchen and culinary art.

gastronomía [gas-tro-no-mee'-ah], *f.* Gastronomy, epicurism.

gastronómico, ca [gas-tro-no'-me-co, cah], *a.* Gastronomic, belonging to epicurism.

gastrónomo, ma [gas-tro'no-mo], *m & f.* 1. Epicure, gourmet, gastronomer, a judge of good eating. 2. A writer on epicurism.

gastrorrectomía [gas-tror-rec-to-mee'-ah], *f.* Gastrectomy.

gastrotomía [gas-tro-to-mee'-ah], *f. (Surg.)* Gastrostomy.

gástrula [gahs'-troo-lah], *f. (Surg.)* Gastrula.

gata [gah'-tah], *f.* 1. She-cat, puss. 2. *(Bot.)* V. GATUÑA. 3. *(Naut.)* A toothed bar from which is suspended the floodgate of a dam. 4. *(Mil.)* A machine which served to protect those who were scaling a wall against the besieged. 5. *(Naut.)* The crossjack yard. **A gatas**, on all fours.

gatada [gah-tah'-dah], *f.* 1. Clawing, wounding with claws (arañazo). 2. Turn of a hare which is closely pursued. 3. Theft or robbery effected in an artful manner (ladrón). 4. *(coll.)* An artful action or doing; scurvy trick (trampa).

gatafura [gah-tah-foo'-rah], *f.* Cake made of herbs and sour milk.

gatallón [gah-tal-lyone'], *m. (coll.)* Rogue, cheat.

gatatumba [gah-tah-toom'-bah], *f. (coll.)* Affected civility or submission.

gatazo [gah-tah'-tho], *m.* 1. *(aug.)* A large cat. 2. A clumsy joke. 3. An artful trick (trampa).

gateado, da [gah-tay-ah'-do, dah], *a.* Feline, catlike (gatuno). *-pp.* of GATEAR.*-m.* A very compact American wood, employed in rich furniture. 2. Crawl, crawling (movimiento). 3. Scratch, clawing (arañazos).

gateamiento [gah-tay-ah-me-en'to], *m.* Scratching, tearing with the nails.

gatear [gah-tay-ar'], *vn.* To climb up (trepar), to clamber, to go upon all fours (andar a gatas).*-va. (coll.)* 1. To scratch or claw (arañar). 2. To steal, to rob (robar).

gatera [gah-tay'-rah], *f.* 1. A cat's hole, through which cats go in and out. (apertura) 2. *(Bot.)* Common catmint.

gatería [gah-tay-ree'-ah], *f.* 1. Number of cats brought together in a place (gatos). 2. Cringing submission, mean servility. 3. Rabble, assembly of low people; a number of mischievous ill-bred boys brought together (pandilla).

gatica, illa, ita [gah-tee'-cah. eel'-lyah, ee'-tah], *f. dim.* A little she-cat.

gaticida [gah-te-thee'-dah], *m.* Cat killer.

gatico, illo, ito [gah-tee'-co, eel'-lyo, ee'-to], *m. dim.* A little cat.

gatillazo [gah-teel-lyah'-tho], *m.* The noise made by a trigger at firing.

gatillo [gah-teel'-lyo], *m.* 1. *(Dim.)* A little cat, a kitten. 2. Pelican, an instrument for drawing teeth. 3. Trigger of a gun. 4. Nape of a bull or ox. 5. Filcher, a petty thief or robber.

gato [gah'-to], *m.* 1. Cat, tomcat. 2. Skin of a cat used as a purse, and its contents. 3. A pickpocket, petty thief (ladrón), filcher. 4. Tongs used for hooping casks. 5. Crampiron. 6. Instrument used for examining the bore of a cannon. 7. (de coche) Jack. **Gato montés** or **de clavo**, mountain cat. **Gato de Angora**, Angora cat. **Aquí hay gato encerrado**, I smell a rat. **Llevar el gato al agua**, to pull off something difficult.

gatuna, gatuña [gah-too'-nah, gah-too'-nyah], *f. (Bot.)* Restharrow, cammock.

gatunero [gah-too-nay'-ro], *m. (Prov.)* A person who sells smuggled meat.

gatuno, na [gah-too'-no, nah], *a.* Catlike, feline.

gatuperio [gah-too-pay'-re-o], *m.* 1. Mixture of liquors without art and proportion (mezcla). 2. Fraud (fraude), snare, intrigue.

gauchada [gah-oo-chah'-dah], *f. (Rep. Arg.)* 1. Artifice. 2. Action of a gaucho.

gaucho, cha [gah'-oo-cho, chah], *a. (Arch.)* Applied to unlevel superficies.*-m. & f. (Arg.)* 1. Rustic, herdsman, or Indian of the pampas of the Argentine Republic. 2. A man of the humble people, of rude manners.

gaudeamus, gaudete [gah-oo-day-ah'-moos, gah-oo-day'-tay], *m.* Feast, entertainment, merry making.

gaulteria [gah-ool-tay'-re-ah], *f.* Gaultheria, a heath-plant of the hot lands of South America.

gavanza [gah-vahn'-thah], *f.* Flower of the dog-rose.

gavanzo [gah-vahn'-tho], *m.* Dog-rose. V. ESCARAMUJO.

gaveta [gah-vay'-tah], *f.* Drawer of a desk, locker.

gavetilla [gah-vay-teel'-lyah], *f. dim.* A small drawer of a desk.

gavia [gah'-ve-ah], *f.* 1. *(Naut.)* Main topsail. 2. Place where madmen are confined. 3. Pit or hole into which a tree is transplanted with its roots. 4. V. GAVIOTA. *-pl. (Naut.)* Topsails of the main and foremast.

gavial [gah-ve-ahl'], *m.* A crocodile of the Ganges.

gaviero [gah-ve-ay'-ro], *m. (Naut.)* Seaman who works at the top-masts.

gavieta [gah-ve-ay'-tah], *f. (Naut.)* Scuttle.

gaviete de las lanchas [gah-ve-ay'-tay], *m. (Naut.)* Davit in a long boat.

gavilán [gah-ve-lahn'], *m.* 1. *(Orn.)* Sparrow-hawk. 2. Fine hairstroke in letters; either side of the nib of a pen (plumilla). 3. An iron hook. 4. Among tailors, the point which each pant-leg forms at the crotch. 5. The part which projects under the chisel in turning with the lathe.*-pl.* 1. *(Naut.)* Tholes, V. TOLETES. 2. Dry flowers of artichokes or thistles.

gavilancillo [gah-ve-lan-theel'-lyo], *m.* 1. *(Dim.)* A young hawk. 2. The incurvated point of an artichoke leaf.

gavilla [gah-veel'lyah], 1. Sheaf of corn; a bundle of vineshoots. 2. Gang of suspicious persons.

gavillero [gah-veel-lyay'-ro], *m.* 1. Place where suspicious persons assemble; a nest of thieves. 2. Place where the sheaves of corn are collected.

gavina [gah-ve-nah], *f. (Prov.)* V. GAVIOTA.

gavión [gah-ve-on'], *m.* 1. *(Mil.)* Gabion, a wicker basket filled with earth to protect against the fire of the enemy. 2. A large hat.

gavioncillo [gah-ve-on-theel'-lyo], *m. dim. (Mil.)* A small gabion.

gaviota [gah-ve-o'-tah], *f. (Orn.)* Gull, sea-gull.

gavitel [gah-ve-tel'], *m. (Naut.)* A small buoy.

gavota [gah-vo'-tah], *f.* Gavot, a French dance.

gaya [gah'-yah], *f.* 1. Stripe of different colors on stuffs, silks, ribbons, etc (tela). 2. V. PICAZA.

gayado, da [gah-yah'-do, dah], *a. & pp.* of GAYAR. Motley, mingled of various colors.

gayadura [gah-yah-doo'-rah], *f.* Garniture, an ornamental trimming of various colors.

gayar [gah-yar'] *va.* To garnish or adorn with trimming of a different color from the stuff; to variegate, to checker.

gayata [gah-yah'-tah], *f. (Prov.)* Crook, sheep-hook.

gayo [gah'-yo], *m.* 1. *(Orn.)* Jay. 2. Merry, gay (alegre). 3. Bright, showy (vistoso).

gayola [gah-yo'-lah], *f.* 1. *(Naut.)* V. JAULA. 2. *(Prov.)* Kind of hut raised for watching vineyards.

gayomba [gah-yom'-bah], *f. (Bot.)* White single-seed broom.

gayuba [gah-yoo'-bah], *f. (Bot.)* Strawberry-tree, red berried arbutus.

gayubal [gah-yoo-bahl'], *m.* Place where there is an abundance of the strawberry-tree.

gaza [gah'-thah], *f. (Naut.)* Strap, spliced in a circular form, and used to fasten blocks to the masts, yards, and rigging.

gazafatón, gazapatón [gah-thah-fah-tone', gah-thah-pah-tone'], *m.* Nonsense, foolish talk.

gazapa [gah-thah'-pah], *f. (Prov.)* Lie, falsehood.

gazapela [gah-thah-pay'-lah], *f.* Clamorous wrangling or quarrelling.

gazapera [gah-thah-pay'-rah], *f.* 1. Warren for rabbits (conejera). 2. A hiding place where people meet for unlawful purposes.

gazapico, illo, ito [gah-thah-pee'-co, eel'-lyo, eer-to], *m. dim.* A small rabbit.

gazapina [gah-thah-pee'-nah], *f.* 1. Assembly of vile people. 2. Confusion, disorder, wrangling.

gazapo [gah-thah'-po], *m.* 1. A young rabbit. 2. A dissembling, artful knave. 3. *(coll.)* A great lie (mentira). 4. Sly fellow (taimado).

gazi [gah-thee'], *a.* Applied formerly to a Moor who changed his religion.

gazmiar [gath-me-ar'], *va.* To steal and eat tid-bits. *-vn. (coll.)* To complain, to resent.

gazmol [gath-mole'] *m.* Kind of cancer on the tongue of hawks.

gazmoñada, gazmoñería [gath-mo-nyah'-dah, gath-mo-nyay-re'-ah], *f.* Hypocrisy, false devotion.

gazmoñero, ra, gazmoño, ña [gath-mo-nyah'-ro, rah, gathmo'-ny-o, nyah], *a.* Hypocritical (hipócrita), dissembling, hypocrite.

gaznápiro [gath-nah'-pe-ro], *a. & m.* Churlish, a simpleton, dolt, clown.

gaznar [gath-nar'], *vn. V.* GRAZNAR.

gaznatada [gath-nah-tah'-dah], *f.* Blow or stroke on the throttle.

gaznate [gath-nah'-tay], *m.* Throttle, windpipe, gorge, **Remojar el gaznate,** to have a drink.

gaznatón [gath-nah-tone'] *m.* 1. Blow on the throat. 2. Pancake, fritter.

gazofia [gah-tho'-fah], *f. V.* BAZOFIA.

gazpacho [gath-pah'-cho], *m.* 1. Dish made of bread, oil, vinegar, onions, salt, and red pepper, mixed together in water. 2. Crumbs of bread fried in a pan.

gazuza [gah-thoo'-thah], *f. (coll.)* Keenness of stomach, violent hunger.

ge [hey], *f.* Spanish name of the letter G.

geato [hay-ah'-to], *m. (Chem.)* Geate, or humate, a salt of humic acid.

gehena [hay-ay'-nah], *m.* Hell. *(Heb.)*

geico, ca [hay'-e-co, cah], *a. (Chem.)* Geic. humic, ulmic.

geiger, contador de [gah'-e-ger, con-tah-dor'-day], *m.* Geiger counter.

géiser [hay'-ser], *m.* Geyser, gusher.

gelasino, na [hay-lah-see'-no. nah], *a.* Seen on laughing (dientes frontales).

gelatina [hay-lah-tee'-nah], *f.* 1. Gelatine, jelly. 2. A compound jelly made of animal substances, with fruit and sugar.

gelatiniforme [hay-lah-te-ne-for'-may], *a.* Gelatiniform, like gelatine.

gelatinoso, sa [hay-lah-te-no'-so, sah], *a.* Gelatinous, glutinous.

gelatinudo, da [hay-lah-te-noo'-do, dah], *a. (Peru)* 1. Gelatinous, 2. Phlegmatic, lazy, without energy.

gelberda [hel-bayr'-tah], *f.* An argilaceous variety of ochre belonging to the silicates of iron.

gelenita [hay-lay-nee'-tah], *f. (Mill.)* Stilbite, a hydrous aluminum-calciumferrous silicate.

gelfe [hel'-fay], *m.* A black slave.

gélido, da [hay'-le-do, dah], *a. (Poet.)* Gelid, frigid.

gema [hay'-mah], *f.* 1. A short and deep cut in a piece of wood. 2. Gem, precious stone (joya). 3. *(Bot.)* Bud. *V.* YEMA. 4. **Sal gema,** rock -salt.

gemación [hay-mah-the-on'], *f.* Gemation, the first development of the bud.

gemebundo, da [hay-may-boon'-do, dah], *a. (Poet.)* Groaning, moaning, howling.

gemela [hay-may'-lah], *f.* Flower exhaling the odour of orange and jessamine; jasmine.

gemelo, la [hay-may'-lo, lah], *a. & m. & f.* Twin. **Hermanas gemelas,** twin sisters. *-m. pl.* 1. Binocular telescope, opera glasses, field glasses. 2. Cuff links.

gemido [hay-mee'-do], *m.* 1. Groan. 2. Lamentation, moan. 3. Howl, the cry of a wolf or dog. **Gemido, da,** *pp.* of GEMIR.

gemidor, ra [hay-me-dor', rah], *m. & f.* Lamenter, mourner: also used as an adjective, applied to one who groans, or to anything which makes a noise like a groan.

gemificación [hay-me-fe-cah-the-on'], *f.* Gemmation, the mode or time of development of the buds of plants.

geminífloro, ra [hay-me-nee'-flo-ro, rah], *a.* Twin-flowered; bearing flowers set in pairs.

Géminis [hay'-me-nis], *m.* 1. Gemini, a sign of the zodiac. 2. A kind of resolving and healing plaster.

gemir [hay-meer'], *vn.* 1. To groan, to moan, to grieve (quejarse). 2. To howl, as a wolf or dog (animal). 3. To roar, to whistle, as the sea or wind. 4. To grunt.

gen [hen], *m. (Biol.)* Gene.

genciana [hen-the-ah'-nah], *f. (Bot)* Gentian.

gencianáceo, cea [hen-the-ah-nah'-thay-o, ah], *a.* Gentianaceous, belonging to the gentian family.

genciáneo, a, gencianoideo, a, *a. V.* GENCIANÁCEO.

gendarme [hen-dar'-may], *m.* 1. Gendarme, French policeman. 2. Policeman.

gendarmería [hen-dar-may-ree'-ah], *f.* Gendarmery, French police.

gene [hay'-nay], *m.* Gene.

genealogía [hay-nay-ah-lo-hee'-ah], *f.* Genealogy (ascendientes), lineage.

genealógico, ca [hay-nay-ah-lo'-he-co, cah], *a.* Genealogical, heraldic.

genealogista [hay-nay-ah-lo-hees'-tah], *m.* Genealogist.

geneantropía [hay-nay-an-tro-pee'-ah], *f.* A treatise on the origin of the human race.

geneático, ca [hay-nay-ah'-te-co, cah], *a.* Genethliacal, relating to divination by nativities.

geneo [hay-nay'-o], *m.* A banana of Peru.

generable [hay-nay-rah'-blay], *a.* Generable, that may be produced or begotten.

generación [hay-nay-rah-the-on'], *f.* 1. Generation, act of begetting (acto). 2. Generation, progeny (descendencia), race, offspring. 3. Generation (grupo), age. **La generación del 98,** the 1898 generation. 4. *V.* NACIÓN. 5. Generation, succession (sucesión), lineage. 6. Generation, a single succession.

generador, ra [hay-nay-rah-dor', rah], *m. & f.* 1. Generator. **Generador, de códigos,** *(Comput.)* code generator. 2. *(Math.)* Every extension which by its movement produces another. 3. *pl.* The genital organs.

general [hay-nay-rahl'], *a.* 1. General, comprehending many species or individuals. 2. General, universal, relating to a whole class or body of men. 3. General, common (común), usual (frecuente). **En general,** generally, in general. **Es general por todo Méjico,** it is common throughout Mexico. **El mundo en general,** the world in general.

general [hay-nay-rahl'], *m.* 1. Hall or room in a public school where the sciences are taught (habitación). 2. A general (militar). 3. *(Prov.)* Custom-house. 4. General, superior of a religious order.

generala [hay-nay-rah'-lah], *f.* 1. General (llamamiento), a beat of the drum, which calls troops to arms. 2. The wife of a general (mujer). 3. *(Naut.)* Signal to join convoy.

generalato [hay-nay-rah-lah'-to], *m.* 1. Generalship, commission or dignity of a general (órdenes religiosas). 2. Generals (personas).

generalero [hay-nay-rah-lay'-ro], *m. (Prov.) V.* ADUANERO.

generalidad [hay-nay-rah-le-dahd'], *f.* 1. Generality, the whole, totality. **La generalidad de los hombres,** the mass of ordinary people. 2. *(Prov.)* Community corporation. 3. *(Prov.)* Custom duties on goods. **generalidades,** *(Prov.)* custom-house fees; discourse consisting of only general principles. 4. Vague answer (vaguedad).

generalísimo [hay-nay-rah-lee'-se-mo], *m.* 1. Generalissimo, the commander-in-chief of an army or of a fleet of ships of war. 2. *V.* GENERAL, for a superior of a religious order.

generalización [hay-nay-rah-le-thah-the-on'], *f.* 1. Generalization (acto). 2. Widening, escalation (conflicto).

generalizar [hay-nay-rah-le-thar'], *va.* To generalize. *-vr.* 1. To become general or usual. 2. To be divulged.

generalmente [hay-nay-ral-men'-tay], *adv.* Generally.

generante [hay-nay-rahn'-tay], *pa.* & *a.* Generating, engendering; generant.

generar [hay-nay-rar'], *va.* To generate.

generativo, va [hay-nay-rah-tee'-vo, vah], *a.* Generative, having the power of propagation.

generatriz [hay-nay-rah-treeth'], *a.* (*Math.*) Generatrix.

genéricamente [hay-nay'-re-cah-men-tay], *adv.* Generically.

genérico, ca [hay-nay'-re-co, cah], *a.* Generic.

género [hay'-nay-ro], *m.* 1. Genus, a class comprehending many species. 2. Kin, the same generical class: speaking of the relation between two or more different beings. **Género humano,** human nature, mankind. 3. Manner, way, kind, sort, or mode of doing something (manera). 4. Sex, gender. 5. (*Gram.*) Gender. 6. Something to be bought or sold (productos). **Géneros,** goods, merchandise, wares, or commodities. **Género para chalecos,** vestings. **Géneros de algodón fino,** cotton shirtings. 7. (*Arte, Liter.*) Genre; type. **Género novelístico,** novel genre.

generosidad [hay-nay-ro-se-dahd'], *f.* 1. Hereditary, nobility. 2. Generosity (larguesa), magnimity, liberality, frankness munificence, open-heartedness. 3. Valor and fortitude in arduous undertakings.

generoso, sa [hay-nay-ro'-so, sah], *a.* 1. Noble (noble), generous, of good extraction. 2. Generous, magnanimous, honorable, freehearted. 3. Generous (liberal), liberal, frank, openhanded, munificent. 4. Generous, strong, vigorous (vinos). 5. Excellent.

genesíaco, ca [hay-ne-see'-ah-co, cah], *a.* 1. Genesiacal, belonging to Genesis. 2. Genesial, belonging to the origin or creation of something.

génesis [hay'-nay-sis], *m.* 1. Genesis, the first book of the Old Testament. 2. Origin.

genética [hay-nay'-te-cah], *f.* (*Biol.*) Genetics.

genético [hay-nay'-te-co], *a.* Genetic.

genetliaca [hay-net-leah'-cah], *f.* Genethliacs, the science of casting nativities.

genetliaco, ca [hay-net-leah'-co, cah], *a.* Genethliacal, prognosticating by nativities.

gengibre [hen-hee'-bray], *m.* V. JENGIBRE.

genial [hay-ne-ahl'], *a.* 1. Inspired, brilliant (brillante). **Escritor genial,** writer of genius. 2. Pleasant (agradable), cheerful, genial; cordial (afable); witty (divertido). 3. In character, characteristic (propio); individual (singular); typical (típico).

genialidad [han-ne-ah-le-dahd'], *f.* Habits or disposition of a person produced by his natural temper (genio).

genialmente [hay-ne-al-men'-tay], *adv.* Genially (con genio).

geniculado, da [hay-ne-coo-lah-on'], *f.* Geniculation, curvature in the shape of a knee.

geniculado, da [hay-ne-coo-lah-do, dah], *a.* Geniculate, bent like a knee-joint.

genio [hay'-ne-o], *m.* 1. Genius, peculiar mental power or faculties (talento). **¡Eres un genio!,** you' re a genius! 2. Genius, the protecting power of men, places, and things; its plural is genii. 3. Nature, genius, peculiar characteristic, disposition of a person, temper, character, inclination, humor (temperamento). **Genio alegre,** cheerful nature. **De mal genio,** bad-tempered. **Tiene genio,** he's temperamental. **Estar de mal genio,** to be in a bad temper. 4. (*Pict.*) Little angel.

genipa [hay-nee'-pah], *f.* (*Bot.*) Silky mugwort or wormwood.

geniquén (or **henequén**) [hay-nee'-kayhn], *m.* (*Mex.*) Sisal hemp, the fibre of Agave Ixtli, of Mexico and Yucatan. V. HENEQUÉN.

genista [hay-nees'-tah], *f.* (*Bot.*) 1. V. RETAMA DE OLOR. 2. V. GINESTA.

genital [hay-ne-tahl'], *a.* Genital. *-m.* V. TESTÍCULO.

genitivo, va [hay-ne-tee'-vo, vah], *a.* Having the power of generation. *-m.* (*Gram.*) The genitive or possessive case.

genitura [hay-ne-too'-rah], *f.* 1. Generation, procreation. 2. (*Ast.*) Horoscope.

genízaro, ra [hay-nee'-thah-ro, rah], *a.* 1. Begotten by parents of different nations. 2. Composed of different species.

genocidio [hay-no-thee'-de-o], *m.* Genocide, extermination of a racial, political or cultural group.

génoli, génuli [hay'-no-le], *m.* A light yellow paste made of sandarach, used by painters.

genovés, sa [hay-no-vays', sah], *a.* Genoese.

gentalla [hen-tahl'-lyah], *f.* Rabble, mob. V. GENTUALLA.

gente [hen'-tay], *f.* 1. People, persons in general, folk. 2. Nation, those who compose a community (nación). 3. (*coll.*) A family (parientes). 4. Army, troops (séquito). **Gente de bien** or **de buen proceder,** honest people. **Gente común** or **gente vulgar,** common people. **Gente de pluma,** notaries, attorneys. **Gente fina,** well-educated persons. **Gente de razón,** educated persons. **Son gente inculta,** they're rough people. **No me gusta esa gente,** I don't like those people. **Gente de color,** colored people. **Gente de mar,** seafaring men, seamen. **Gente de pelo,** well-to-do people. **Gente gorda,** people of influence. **Gente menuda,** children. **Gente humilde,** humble people.

gentecilla [hen-tay-theel'-lyah], *f.* Mob, rabble.

gentil [hen-teel'], *m.* Gentile, pagan, heathen.

gentil [hen-tee'], *a.* 1. Genteel, elegant (elegante), graceful, handsome, charming (encantador). 2. Excellent, exquisite.

gentileza [hen-tee-lay'-thah], *f.* 1. Gentility, gracefulness of mien, elegance of behavior (elegancia), genteel deportment and address, charm (encanto). 2. Easiness, freedom from constraint. 3. Ostentation, pageantry. 4. Civility, politeness, genteelness.

gentil hombre [hen-teel' om'-bray], *m.* 1. Fine fellow: my good man. 2. Gentleman, the servant who waits about the person of a man of rank.

gentilicio, ia [hen-te-lee'-the-o, ah], *a.* 1. Gentilitious, peculiar to a nation. 2. Gentilitious, hereditary, entailed on a family; tribal.

gentílico, ca [hen-tee'-leco, cah], *a.* Heathen, gentile, pagan, heathenish, hellenic.

gentilidad [hen-te-le-dahd'], *f.* Gentilism, gentility, heathenism, paganism, religion of the heathens; the body of heathens or gentiles.

gentilismo [hen-te-lees'-mo], *m.* V. GENTILIDAD.

gentilizar [hen-te-le-thar'], *vn.* To observe the rites of gentiles or heathens; to gentilize.

gentilmente [hen-teel-men'-tay], *adv.* Genteelly; heathenishly, elegantly (con elegancia); charmingly (con encanto); prettily (con gracia).

gentío [hen-tee'-o], *m.* Crowd, multitude. **Había un gentío,** there were lots of people.

gentualla, gentuza [hen-too-ahl'-lyah, hen-too'-thah], *f.* Rabble, mob.

genuflexión [hay-noo-flec-se-on'], *f.* Genuflexion, bending the knee.

genuino, na [hay-noo-ee'-on, nah], *a.* Genuine, pure, real, legitimate, natural, good.

geocéntrico [hay-o-then'-tree-co], *a.* (*Ast.*) Geocentric.

geoda [hay-o'-dah], *f.* Geode, a nodule of stone containing crystals.

geodesia [hay-o-day'-se-ah], *f.* Geodesia, the doctrine or art of measuring surfaces; land surveying.

geodésico, ca [hay-o-day'-se-co, cah], *f.* Geodaesia, **Cúpula geodésica,** geodesic dome.

geófago, ga [hay-o'-fah-go, gah], *a.* Geophagous, earth-eating. *-m. f.* Geofagia.

geofísica [hay-o-fee'-se-cah], *f.* (*Geol.*) Geophysics.

geognosia [hay-og-no'-se-ah], *f.* Geognosy, structural geology.

geografía [hay-ograh-fee'-ah], *f.* Geography. **En toda la geografía nacional,** all over the country.

geográficamente [hay-o-grah'-fe-cah-men-tay], *adv.* Geographically.

geográfico, ca [hay-o-grah'-fe-co, cah], *a.* Geographical.

geógrafo, fa [hay-o'-grah-fo], *m & f.* Geographer.

geología [hay-o-lo-hee'-ah], *f.* Geology.

geológico, ca [hay-o-lo'-he-co, cah], *a.* Geologic(al); relating to geology.

geólogo, ga [hay-o'-lo-go], *m & f.* Geologist.

geomagnético, ca [hay-o-mag-nay'-te-co, cah], *a.* Geomagnetic.

geomancia [hay-o-mahn'-the-ah], *f.* Geomancy, foretelling by figures.

geomántico [hay-o-mahn'-te-co], *m.* Geomancer. *-a.* Geomantic.

geómetra [hay-o'-may-trah], *m.* Geometer, a geometrician.

geometral [hay-o-may-tral'], *a. V.* GEOMÉTRICO.

geometría [hay-o-may-tree'-ah], *f.* Geometry. **Geometría del espacio**, solid geometry. **Geometría plana**, plane geometry.

geométricamente [hay-o-may'-tre-cah-men-tay], *adv.* Geometrically.

geométrico, ca [hay-o-may'-tre-co, cah], *a.* Geometrical, geometric.

geometrinos [hay-o-may-tree'-nos], *m. pl.* The geometric moths, whose larva are called measuring worms.

geopolítica [hay-o-po-lee'-te-cah], *f.* Geopolitics.

geopónica [hay-o-po'-ne-cah], *f.* Geoponics, the science of agriculture; gardening.

georama [hay-o-rah'-mah], *f.* Georama, a large hollow globe, on the side of which are represented the natural divisions of the earth.

georgiano, na [hay-or-he-ah'-no, nah], *a.* Georgian, relating to Georgia.

geórgica [hay-or'-he-cah], *f.* Georgic, a poem upon husbandry.

geranio [hay-rah'-ne-o], *m. (Bot.)* Crane's-bill. Geranium.

gerapliega [hay-rah-ple-ay'-gah], *f. (Pharm.)* Hierapicra, a bitter purgative medicine.

gerbo [herr'-bo], *m.* The jerboa.

gerencia [hay-ren'-the-ah], *f.* 1. Administration. 2. Management (de negocios) 3. Management (dirección). 4. Managership (cargo). 5. Manager's office (oficina).

gerente [hay-ren'tay], *m. (Com.)* Manager, director. **Gerente de fábrica**, works manager.

geriatra [hay-re-ah'-trah], *m.* Geriatrician.

geriatría [hay-re-ah-tree'-ah], *f. (Med.)* Geriatrics.

geriátrico [hay-re-ah'-tre-co], *a. m & f.* Geriactric.

gericaya [hay-re-cah-yah], *f. (Mex.)* Custard.

gerifalto [hay-re-fahl'-tay], *m. (Orn.)* Gerfalcon.

germanesco, ca [her-mah-ness'-co, cah], *a.* Belonging to the jargon of the gipsies.

germanía [her-mah-nee'-ah], *f.* 1. Jargon or cant of the gipsies, thieves, etc.; slang. 2. Concubinage.

germánico, ca [her-mah'-ne-co, cah], *a.* Germanic, German; of Germany.

germanismo [her-mah-nees'-mo], *m.* Germanism, a German idiom employed in another language.

germen [her'-men], *m.* 1. Germ. **Germen plasma**, germ plasma. 2. Sprout, shoot.

germicida [her-me-thee'-da], *a.* Germicidal.*-m.* Germicide.

germicultura [her-me-cool-too'-rah], *f.* Culture or medium for the growth of bacteria.

germífugo, ga [her-mee'-foo-go, gah], *a.* Germicidal.

germinación [her-me-nah-the-on'], *f. (Bot.)* Germination, the first act or vegetation in a seed.

germinar [her-me-nar'], *vn.* To germinate, to bud.

germinativo, va [her-me-nah-tee'-vo, vah], *a.* Germinative.

gerundiada [hay-roon-deah'-dah], *f. (coll.)* An emphatical, pompous, and unmeaning expression.

gerundio [hay-roon'-de-o], *m.* 1. *(Gram.)* Gerund, a verbal noun. 2. The person who affects to speak or preach in a pompous and emphatical manner.

gesta [hess'-tah], *f. (Bot.) V.* RETAMA.

gestación [hes-tah-the-on'], *f.* 1. Gestation, the term of pregnancy. 2. An exercise practised among the Romans for the confirmation of health, and the place where it was carried out. 3. Superstition of wearing rings to preserve oneself from evil.

gestar [hes-tar'], *va. (Bio.)* To gestate; *(Fig.)* to prepare, to hatch. *-vr. (Bio.)* To gestate; *(Fig.)* to be in preparation.

gestatorio, ria [hes-tah-to'-re-o, ah], *a.* Proper to gestation (estado, ejercicio).

gestero, ra [hes-tay'-ro, rah], *a.* Playing antic tricks, making grimaces; it is also used as a substantive for one who distorts his countenance from habit or affectation; a gesticulator.

gesticulación [hes-te-coo-lah-the-on'], *f.* Gesticulation (ademán), gesture (mueca).

gesticular [hes-te-coo-lar'], *va.* To gesticulate (hacer ademanes), to make gestures or grimaces (hacer muecas).

gesticular [hes-te-coo-lar'], *a.* Relating to gestures or gesticulation; gesticulatory.

gestión [hes-te-on'], *f.* 1. *(Com.etc.)* Management, conduct. 2. Negotiation (negociación). 3. Measure (medida), step; action (acción); effort (esfuerzo); operation (operación). **Gestiones**, measures. **Hacer las gestiones preliminares**, to do the ground work.

gestionar [hes-te-o-nar'], *va.* 1. To manage (conducir). 2. To negotiate (negociar). 3. To try to arrange (procurar).

gesto [hess'-to], *m.* 1. Face (cara), visage. 2. Grimace (mueca), a distortion of the countenance, a gesture. 3. Aspect, appearance (semblante). 4. Likeness, resemblance. **Estar de buen gesto**, to be in good humor. **Hacer un gesto**, to make a face. **Hacer gestos**, to make gestures. **Con un gesto de cansancio**, with a weary gesture.

gestor [hes-tor'], *m.* 1. *(Com.)* Superintendent, manager. 2. *(for.)* Proxy, representative, one who executes another's business and require his principal's ratification.

gestora [hes-to'-rah], *f.* Committee of management.

gestoría [hes-to-ree'-ah], *f.* Agency.

gestudo, da [hes-too'-do, dah], *a.* Humored, cross.

gialomina [he-ah-lo-mee'-nah], *f.* Sort of yellow ochre.

giba [hee'-bah], *f.* 1. Hump, crooked back, hunch, gibbosity. 2. *(coll.)* Importunity, tiresomeness.

gibado, da [he-bah'-do, dah], *a.* Crooked, hump-backed. *V.* GIBOSO. *-pp.* of GIBAR.

gibar [he-bar'], *va. V.* JIBAR.

gibón [he-bon'], *m.* Gibbon, an anthropoid ape.

gibosidad [he-boo-se-dahd'], *f.* 1. *(Bot.)* A hump, gibbosity. 2. *(Med.)* A hump on the back.

giboso, sa [he-bo'-so, sah], *a.* Gibbous, crook-backed, hump-backed.

gicama [hee'-cah-mah], *f. (Mex.).* A palatable root resembling yucca.

giganta [he-gahn'-tah], *f.* 1. Giantess 2. *(Bot.)* Smooth bear's breech.

gigantazo, za [he-gan-tah'-tho, thah], *m. & f. aug.* A huge giant.

gigante [he-gahn'-tay], *m.* 1. Giant, one unnaturally large. 2. One superior in courage, talents, or virtues. *-a.* Gigantic.

gigantesco, ca [he-gan-tays'-co, cah], *a.* Gigantic, giant-like.

gigantez [he-gan-teth'], *f.* Gigantic tallness.

gigantilla [he-gan-teel'-lyah], *f.* A figure made of paste or paste-board, with a very large head.

gigantón, na [he-gan-tone', nah], *m. & f. aug.* Giant of enormous size. **Gigantones**, gigantic figures of pasteboard.

gijas [hee'-has], *f. pl. (Prov.) V.* GUIJAS.

gilí [he-lee'], *a.* 1. Stupid, silly (tonto). 2. Stuck-up (vanidoso); presumptuous (presumido). *-m & f.* 1. Berk (tonto), idiot. 2. Conceited individual (vanidoso).

gilia [hee'-leah], *f.* Gilia, a plant of the phlox family.

gilicopa [he-lo-co'-pah], *f. V.* JILOCOPO.

gilipollas [he-le-po'-yahs], *m & f. V.* GILÍ.

gilipollez [he-le-po-yeth'], *f.* 1. Idiocy (idiotez); silliness. 2. Conceit (vanidad), presumption.

gilvo, va [heel'-vo, vah], *a.* 1. Honey-colored, or between white and red.

gimelga [he-mel'-gah], *f. (Naut.)* Fish, a piece of timber used to strengthen masts and yards.

gimnanto, ta [him-nahn'-to, tah], *a. (Bot.)* Naked, without floral envelopes.

gimnasia [him-nah'-se-ah], *f.* Gymnastics; physical training. **Hacer gimnasia,** to do gymnastics. *V.* GIMNÁSTICA.

gimnasiarca [him-nah-se-ar'-cah], *m.* Gymnasiarch, head of an academy, college, or school.

gimnasio [him-nah'-se-o], *m.* 1. School, academy, gymnasium. 2. Gymnasium, a place for athletic training and exercises.

gimnasta [him-nahs'-tah], *m.* Master of athletic exercises.

gimnasterio [him-nas-tay'-re-o], *m.* Wardrobe of a gymnasium.

gimnástica [him-nahs'-te-cah], *f.* Gymnastics.

gimnástico, ca [him-nahs'-te-co, cah], *a.* Gymnastic, gymnastical.

gímnica [heem'-ne-cah], *f.* Gymnics, athletic exercises and the art of teaching them.

gímnico, ca [heem'-ne-co, cah], *a.* Gymnastical.

gimnobranquio, ia [him-no-brahn'-ke-o, ah], *a.* Having naked gills, gymnobranchiate.

gimnocarpeo, a [him-no-car'-pay-o, ah], *a.* Gymnocarpous, having naked fruit.

gimnoclado [him-no-clah'-do], *m.* The Kentucky coffee tree: gymnocladus.

gimnópodo, da [him-no'-po-do, dah], *a.* Gymnopodous, naked-footed.

gimnoto [him-no'-to], *m.* Gymnotus, the electrical eel.

gimnosofista [him-no-so-fees'-tah], *m.* Gymnosophist, one of a sect of Indian philosophers.

gimnospermo, ma [him-nos-perr'-mo, mah], *a.* Gymnospermous, having the seeds naked.

gimotear [he-mo-tay-ar'], *vn.* 1. *(coll.)* To be always crying (lamentar, lloriquear). 2. To whine (gemir), to whimper.

gimoteo [he-mo-tay'-o], *m.* 1. The act of crying very frequently (lamento, lloriqueo). 2. Whine, whining (gemido)

ginantropo [he-nan-tro'-po], *m.* Hermaphrodite.

ginebra [he-nay'-brah], *f.* 1. Rattle, an instrument popular among the Moors;. 2. Gin or geneva. 3. *(Met.)* Confusion, disorder. 4. A confused noise. 5. Game of cards. 6. Geneva.

ginebrada [he-nay-brah'-dah], *f.* Sort of puff paste.

ginebrés, sa, or **ginebrino, na** [he-nay-brays', sah, he-nay-bree'-no, nah], *a.* Genevan, relating to Geneva.

gineceo [he-nay-thay'-o], *m.* Gyneceum, the part of an ancient Greek house reserved for women.

ginecocracía [he-nay-co-crah-thee'-ah], *f.* Gynaeocracy or gynecocracy, gynarchy, female government.

ginecografía [he-nay-co-grah-fee'-ah], *f.* Gynaeocracy, a treatise on the diseases of women.

ginecología [he-nay-co-lo-hee' -ah], *f. (Med.)* Gynecology, study of women's diseases.

ginecólogo, ga [he-nay-co'-lo-go, gah], *m. & f.* Gynecologist, specialist in women's diseases.

gineta [he-nay'-tah], *f.* Genet, a kind of weasel. *V.* JINETA.

ginete [he-nay'-tah], *m. V.* JINETE.

gingivitis [hin-he-vee'-tis], *f. (Med.)* Gingivitis.

ginizo [he-nee'-tho], *m.* The moist, viscous surface of the stigma of orchids.

ginología [he-no-lo-hee'-ah], *f.* Gynecology.

ginseng [hin-seng'], *m. (Bot.)* Ginseng, Aralia ginseng.

gipaeto [he-pah-ay'-to], *m.* A diurnal bird of prey resembling the vulture and the eagle.

gips [heeps], *m.* A bird of the vulture family, of a brownish color.

gipsífero, ra [hip-see'-fay-ro, rah], *a.* Gypseous, containing gypsum.

gira [hee'-rah], *f. V.* JIRA.

girada [he-rah'-dah], *f.* 1. Gyration; pirouette, a turn on one foot in dancing. 2. Reciprocal motion of a tuft of wool from one comb to another in wool-shops.

girado [he-rah'-do], *m. (Com.)* Drawee.

girador, girante [he-rah-dor', he-rahn'-tay], *m. (Com.)* Drawer.

girafa [he-rah'-fah], *f.* Giraffe, camelopard.

giralda [he-rahl'-dah], *f.* 1. Vane or weather-cock in the form of a statue; derived from the statue of a woman on the spire of the cathedral church of Seville. 2. Common name of this tower.

giralete [he-ral-day'-tay], . Rochet or surplice without sleeves.

giraldilla [he-ral-deel'-lyah], *f. dim.* A small vane or weather-cock in the form of a statue.

girándula [he-rahn'-doo-lah], *f.* 1. In artificial fireworks, box of rockets, which turns swiftly and emits a quantity of rockets. 2. Girandole, a branched candle-stick.

girar [he-rar'], *vn.* 1. To turn round (voltearse), to make a gyre, to circumgyrate, to hurdle, to rotate (dar vueltas). **Girar hacia la derecha,** to turn right. **El satélite gira alrededor de la tierra,** the satellite circles the earth. 2. To remit, by bills of exchange, to draw. 3. To swing (balancear); to swivel; to pivot (en equilibrio). *-va.* To turn (dar vuelta a), to turn round, to rotate; to twist (torcer); to spin (revolverse). **Girar la manilla 2 veces,** to turn the crank twice.

girasol [he-rah-sole'], *m. (Bot.)* Sunflower.

giratorio, ria [he-rah-to'-re-o, ah], *a.* Rotating, gyrating, revolving (puerta) **Silla giratoria,** swivel chair.

girel [he-rel'], *m.* Caparison, trappings for a horse. *V.* JIREL.

girifalte [he-re-fahl'-tay], *m. V.* GERIFALTE.

girimiquiar [he-re-me-ke-ar'], *vn. (Cuba)* To sob.

girino [he-ree'-no], *m.* 1. Embryo of a frog. 2. Gyrinus, whirligig beetle.

giro [hee'-ro], *m.* 1. *(Com.)* Draft. **Giro a la vista,** sight draft. **Giro postal,** money order. 2. Gyration, rotation. 3. Turn (vuelta), trend (tendencia), turn of events. **Tomar otro giro,** to change intent or resolution, to change the aspect of the matter. **Giro regular de los negocios,** a fair run of business.

giromancia [he-ro-man'-the-ah], *f.* Gyromancy.

giroscopio [he-ros-co'-pe-o], *m.* Gyroscope.

gis [hees], *m. (Pict.)* Crayon.

gitana [he-tah-nah], *f.* Gipsy; fortune teller (de feria)

gitanada [he-tah-nah'-dah], *f.* Blandishment, wheedling like gipsies, caress, flattery.

gitanamente [he-tah-nah-men'-tay], *adv.* In a sly, winning manner.

gitanear [he-tah-nay-ar'], *va.* To flatter, to wheedle, to caress, to entice by soft words.

gitanería [he-tah-nay-ree'-ah], *f.* 1. Band of gipsies (gítanos). 2. Gipsy (vida). 3. Gipsy saying (dicho).

gitanesco, ca [he-tah-ness'-co, cah], *a.* Gipsy-like, gipsy.

gitanillo, lla [he-tah-neel'-lyo, lyah], *m. & f. dim.* Little gipsy.

gitanismo [he-tah-nees'-mo], *m.* The gipsies taken as a body, gipsyism, customs and manners which characterize gipsies.

gitano, na [he-tah'-no, nah], *m. &f.* 1. Gipsy. 2. A sly, artful fellow, or of a genteel pleasing address (zalamero).

gitón [he-tone'], *m.* Ancient copper coin used only as the title of unity. *V.* GUITÓN.

glacial [glah-the-ahl'], *a.* Glacial. **Mar glacial,** the frozen sea.

glaciar [glah-the-ar'], *m.* Glacier.

glacis [glah'-this], *m.* 1. *(Mil.) V.* EXPLANADA. 2. Ends which join the bar in lacework. 3. Union of colors, scumbling, in a picture to give it tone and harmony (cuadro). 4. *(Arch.)* The slope of a cornice to turn off water.

gladiador [glah-de-ah-dor'], or **Gladiator** [glah-de-ah-tor'], *m.* Gladiator a sword-player; a prize-fighter.

gladiatorio, ria [glah-de-ah-to'-re-o, ah], *a.* Gladiatorial, gladiatory.

gladiolo [glah-de-o'-lo], *m. (Bot.)* Common corn-flag.

glaglar [glah-glar'], *va. (coll.)* To gaggle, to talk in a voice resembling the cry of a goose.

glande [glahn-day], *m.* The glans penis, or clitoridis.

glandífero, ra, glandígero, ro [glan-dee'-fay-ro, rah], *a.* 1. Glandiferous, bearing acorns. 2. Bearing tubercles in the form of acorns.

glándula [glan'-doo-lah], *f.* 1. Gland, a soft, spongy substance. 2. *(Bot.)* Gland, a little tumor discharging a fluid. **Gládula endocrina,** endocrine gland. **Glándula tiroides,** thyroid.

glandular [glan-doo-lar'], *a.* Glandular.

glandulífero, ra [glan-doo-lee'-fay-ro, rah], *a.* Glanduliferous, gland-bearing.

glandulilla [glan-doo-leel'-lyah], *f. dim.* Glandule, a small gland.

glanduloso, sa [glan-doo-lo'-so, sah], *a.* Glandulous, glandular, pertaining to the glands.

glasé [glah-say'], *m.* Glacé finish.

glaseado, da [glah-say-ah'-do, dah], *a.* Variegated, embroidered, glossy.

glasear [glah-say-ar'], *va.* To glaze (papel); to glaze (repostería).

glasto [glash'-to], *m. (Bot.)* Woad or common dyers' woad.

glaucio [glah'-oo-the-o], *m. (Bot.)* Celandine.

glauco, ca [glah'-oo-co, cah], *a. (Bot.)* Glaucous, sea-green, pale bluish green.

glauco [gah'-oo-co], *m.* A kind of oyster with equal shells.

glaucoma [glah-oo-co'-mah], *m.* Glaucoma, a disease of the eye characterized by increased tension, advancing farsightedness, dimness of vision and ultimate blindness.

gleba [glay'-bah], *f.* 1. Sod of earth turned up by the plough; glebe; fief; heritage. 2. A slave anciently joined to a piece of land and transferred with it to another owner.

gleboso, sa [glay-bo'-so, sah], *a. (Prov.)* Glebous, turfy.

glenóideo, dea [glay-no'-e-day-o, ah], *a.* Glenoid, every deep cavity which receives the head of a bone.

glicerina [gle-thay-ree'-nah], *f.* Glicerine.

glicónico [gle-co'-ne-co], *m.* A kind of Latin verse.

glifo [glee'-fo], *m. (Arch.)* Glyph, a concave ornament.

glíptica [gleep'-te-cah], *f.* Glyptics, the art of engraving fine stones and the like.

gliptografía [gleep-to-grah-fee'-ah], *f,* Glyptography, a description of the art of engraving upon gems.

global [glo-bahl'], *a.* Global (en conjunto); total (completo), complete, overall; full (investigación, informe), comprehensive; total (suma).

globalizar [glo-bah-le-thar'], *va.* To encompass, to include.

globalmente [glo-bahl'-men-tay], *adv.* As a whole (considerar, examinar).

globiforme [glo-be-for'-may], *a.* Globe shaped, globiform, spherical.

globo [glo'-bo], *m.* 1. Globe, a spherical body. 2. Sphere, a terrestrial or celestial globe on which the various regions of the earth are geographically delineated, or the constellations and stars depicted. 3. Orb. **Globo aerostático,** a balloon. **Globo terráqueo,** globe. **Globo dirigible,** dirigible.

globoso, sa [glo-bo'-so, sah, *a.* Globular, spherical, orbicular.

globular [glo-boo-lar'], *a.* Globular spherical.

glóbulo [glo'-boo-lo], *m.* 1. Globule. 2. Conceptacle of the reproductive bodies of certain lichens. **Glóbulo blanco,** white corpuscle.

globuloso, sa [glo-boo-lo'-so, sah], *a.* Globulous.

glomerula [glo-may'-roo-lah], *f. (Bot.)* Glomerule, head of flowers.

glomerulado, da [glo-may-roo-lah'-do, dah], *a.* Glomerulate, in small clusters.

gloria [glo'-re-ah], *f.* 1. Glory (fama), honor, fame. 2. Paradise, state of blessedness. 3. Pleasure, delight in something (delicia). 4. Majesty, splendor. 5. Glory, blessedness, that which ennobles or illustrates. 6. A sort of tart or pie. 7. In painting, an opening in the sky representing angels,

splendors, etc. **Oler a gloria,** to smell divine. **Saber a gloria,** to taste heavenly. **Una vieja gloria,** a has-been, a great figure.

gloriarse [glo-re-ar'-say], *vr.* 1. To glory, to boast in, to be proud of, to flourish. 2. To take a delight in something.

glorieta [glo-re-ay'-tah], *f.* Summer house (cenador), bower (pérgola), arbor. 2. Roundabout, traffic circle (encrucijada). 3. Square (plaza ajardinada).

glorificación [glo-re-fe-cah-the-on'], *f.* 1. Glorification, giving glory. 2. Praise.

glorificador [glo-re-fe-cah-dor'], *m.* Glorifier, he that glorifies: an appellation given to God.

glorificante [glo-re-fe-cahn'-tay], *pa. & m. & f.* Glorifying; glorifier.

glorificar [glo-re-fe-car'], *va.* 1. To glorify, to pay honor in worship. 2. To exalt to glory or dignity; to praise, to honor, to extol. -*vr. V.* GLORIARSE.

gloriosamente [glo-re-o-sah-men'-tay], *adv.* Gloriously.

glorioso, sa [glo-re-o'-so, sah], *a.* 1. Glorious, excellent, worthy of honor or praise. 2. Enjoying the bliss of heaven, blessed. 3. Glorious, boastful, ostentatious, proud, elate.

glosa [glo'-sah], *f.* 1. Gloss, a scholium; a comment or commentary. 2. Note added to a document, or inserted in a book of accounts, to explain its contents. 3. *(Poet.)* Amplification of a verse. 4. *(Mus.)* Variation in a tune.

glosador, ra [glo-sah-dor', rah], *m. & f.* Commentator, glosser, a writer of glosses.

glosalgia [glo-sahl'-he-ah], *f.* Glossalgia, neuralgia of the tongue.

glosantrace [glo-san-trah'-thay], or **Glosántrax,** *m.* Glossanthrax, carbuncle of the tongue.

glosar [glo-sar'], *va.* 1. To gloss, to explain by comment. 2. To palliate by specious exposition or representation. 3. *(Poet.)* To amplify the sense of a verse. 4. *(Mus.)* To vary notes.

glosario [glo-sah'-re-o], *m.* 1. A glossary; a special lexicon. 2. The mouth parts of insects.

glose [glo'-say], *m.* Act of glossing or commentating.

glosilla [glo-seel'-lyah], *f.* 1. *(Dim.)* A short gloss, comment, or note. 2. *(Print.)* Minion type. 7. Point.

glositis [glo-see'-tis], *f.* Glossitis, inflammation of the tongue.

glotis [glo'-tis], *f. (Anai.)* Glottis, opening of the larynx.

glotón, na [glo-to-ne', nah], *m. & f.* 1. A glutton, gormandizer. 2. Glutton woiverene, a carnivore. -*a.* Gluttonous, given to excessive feeding.

glotonazo, za [glo-to-nah'-tho, thah], *m & f. aug.* Great glutton, great eater.

glotoncillo, illa [glo-ton-theel'-lyoh, lyah], *m. & f. dim.* Little glutton.

glotonear [glo-to-nay-ar'], *vn.* To indulge too much in eating, to devour, to gormandize.

glotonería, glotonía [glo-to-nay-ree'-ah], *f.* Gluttony, greediness.

gloxinia [gloc-see'-ne-ah], *f.* Gloxinia, a perennial plant, having large, handsome flowers.

glucina [gloo-thee'-nah], *f.* Glucina, aluminum oxide.

glucinio [gloo-thee'-ne-o], *m.* Glucinum, a hard, silver, white metallic element.

glucosa [gloo-co'-sah], *f.* Glucose.

gluma [gloo'-mah], *f. (Bot.)* Glume, the chaff-like bract of the blossom of grasses and sedges.

glumáceo, cea [gloo-mah'-thay-o, ah], *a.* Glumaceous.

glumal [gloo-mahl'], *a. V.* GLUMÁCEO.

glumífero, ra [gloo-mee'-fay-ro, rah], *a.* Glumaceous, bearing glumes.

gluten [gloo'-ten], *m.* Gluten.

gluteo, tea [gloo-tay'-o, ah], *a.* Glutèal, relating to the buttocks.

glutinosidad [gloo-te-nose-dahd'], *f.* Glutinousness, viscosity.

glutinoso, sa [gloo-te-no'-so, sah], *a.* Glutinous, viscous, mucous.

gneis [nay'-is], *m.* Gneiss, a rock resembling granite, composed of quartz, feldspar, and hornblende.

gnómico, ca [no'-me-co, cah], *a.* Sententious, gnomic.

gnomo [no'-mo], *m.* 1. Aphorism, apothegm. 2. Gnome, a fabulous being.

gnomon [no'-mon], *m.* 1. Gnomon, the hand of a dial. 2. Bevel square, composed of two movable rules.

gnomónica [no-mo'-ne-cah], *f.* Gnomonics, the science which teaches the art of making sun-dials.

gnomónica, ca [no-mo'-ne-co, cah], *a.* Gnomonic, gnomonical. relating to dialing.

gnosticismo [nos-te-thees'-mo], *m.* Gnosticism, the philosophy of the gnostics, prevailing from the 1st to the 6th century.

gnóstico [nos'-te-co], *m. & a.* Gnostic: applied to one of the earliest heretics.

goa [go'-ah], *f.* Pig iron.

gobernable [go-bayr-nah'-blay], *a.* 1. *(Pol.)* Gobernable. **Un pueblo difícilmente gobernable,** people hard to govern. 2. *(Naut.)* Navigable.

gobernación [go-ber-nah-the-on'], *f.* 1. Government, governing (acto). **Ministro de la gobernación,** Department of the Interior. 2. Governor's residence (residencia); governor's office (oficina). V. GOBIERNO.

gobernado, da [go-ber-nah'-do, dah], *a. & pp.* of GOBERNAR. Governed.

gobernador [go-ber-nah-dor'], *m.* Governor, ruler, muster. **Gobernador civil,** civil governor.

gobernadora [go-ber-nah-do'-rah], *f.* Governess, directress.

gobernalle [go-ber-nahl'-lyay], *m.* Rudder, helm.

gobernante [go-ber-nahn'-tay], *m. (coll.)* A person assuming the management of a thing. *-pa.* Governing (que gobierna).

gobernar [go-ber-nar'], *va.* 1. To govern, to rule as a first magistrate. 2. To regulate to govern, to command, to lead, to head, to control (controlar), to manage: to guide (dirigir), to direct. 3. To entertain, to maintain. **Gobernar el timón,** to steer the ship.

gobernativo, va [go-ber-nah-tee'-vo, vah], *a.* V. GUBERNATIVO.

gobernoso, sa [go-bayr-no'-so, sah], *a.* Methodical, systematic, loving good order.

gobierno [go-be-ayr'-no], *m.* 1. Government, form of a community with respect to the disposition of the supreme authority. 2. Government, administration of public affairs, executive power. 3. Government, district or province under the command of a governor. 4. The space of time which the administration of a governor lasts, and the manner in which he governs. 5. Government, regularity of behavior, guidance (en general), conduct, management, direction. **Gobierno autónomo,** autonomous government. **Gobierno militar,** military government. **Gobierno de la casa,** house keeping. *(Yo gobierno, yo gobierne, from Gobernar.V.* ACERTAR.)

gobio [go'-be-o], *m. (Zool.)* Gudgeon.

goce [go'-thay], *m.* Enjoyment; possession.

gocete [go'-thay-tay], *m.* Ancient armor for the head.

gocha [go'-chah], *f.* Sow.

gocho [go'-cho], *m.* Pig (cerdo), hog.

gociano, na [go-the-ah'-no, nah], *a.* Gath, Gothic.

godeño, ña [go-day'-nyo, nyah], *a.* Rich, renowned.

godentia [go-day'-te-ah], *f.* Godetia, a genus of showy flowers, belonging to the evening-primrose family of California and Chili.

godo, da [go'-do, dah], *a. & m. & f.* Gothic; a Goth.

gofio [go'-fe-o], *m. (Cuba)* Parched corn-meal, maize, or other cereal.

gofo, fa [go'-fo, fah], *a.* Stupid; ignorant, rude. **Gofo,** *(Pict.)* a little figure or image.

gofrador [go-frah-dor'], *m. (Neol.)* Leaf-marker, a florist's copper tool for stamping in relief the veins of leaves. 2. The one who uses this tool.

gofrar [go-frar'], *va.* To mark leaves for artificial flowers.

gol [gol], *m.* Goal. **Meter un gol,** *(Fig.)* to score a point against somebody.

gola [go'-lah], *f.* 1. Gullet, throat, oesophagus. 2. Goriget, a piece of silver or brass worn by officers of foot when on duty. 3. *(Fort.)* Gorge, the entrance of a bastion, ravelin, or other work. 4. *(Arch.)* Gola, cymatium, a moulding, the profile of which represents an S.

goleada [go-lay-ah'-dah], *f.* Quantity of goals, high score.

goleador [go-lay-ah-dor'], *a. m & f.* **El equipo más goleador,** the team which has scored most goals.

golear [go-lay-ar'], *va.* To score a goal against. **El portero menos goleado,** the keeper who has let in fewest goals.

goleta [go-lay'-tah], *f. (Naut.)* A schooner.

golf [golf], *m.* Golf, golf game (juego); golf course (pista).

golfa [gol-fah], *f.* Tart, whore.

golfan [gol-fahn'], *m.* V. NENUFAR.

golfería [gol-fay-ree'-ah], *f.* 1. Loafers (golfos). 2. Loafing (acto); life of idleness (estilo de vida).

golín [gol-feen'], *m.* V. DELFÍN.

golfista [gol-fees'-tah], *m & f.* Golfer.

golfo [gol'-fo], *m.* 1. Gulf, bay (bahía). 2. Gulf, abyss. 3. Hoodlum, rake, vagabond.

golilla [go-leel'-lyah], *f.* 1. A kind of collar, forming part of the dress of the magistrates of some superior courts of justice in Spain. 2. *(coll.)* The magistrate of said superior courts. **Levantar la golilla,** to become passionate. **Bajar la golilla,** to be pacified.

golillero, ra [go-leel-lyay'-ro, rah], *m. & f.* Collar-maker.

gollería, golloría [go-lyay'-ro, rah], *f.* 1. A dainty dish (golosina). 2. Delicacy, superfluity, excess.

gollete [gol-lyay'-tay], *m.* 1. Throttle, the superior part of the throat (garganta). 2. The neck of a bottle.

gollizo [gol-lyce'-tho], *m.* Narrow passage of mountains or rivers.

golmajo, ja [gol-mah'-ho, hah], *(Prov.)* V. GOLOSO.

golondrina [go-lon-dree'-nah], *f.* 1. *(Orn.)* Swallow. **Golondrina de mar,** tern. 2. *(Zool.)* Sapphire gurnard, tub-fish.

golodrinera [go-lon-dre-nay'-rah], *f. (Bot.)* Swallow-wort, celandine.

golondrino [go-lon-dree'-no], *m.* 1. A male swallow. 2. Vagrant, deserter (vagabundo). 3. Tub-fish. 4. A large tumor in the arm-pit.

golondro [go-lon'-dro], *m.* Desire, longing. **Campar de golondro,** *(coll.)* to live at another's expense. **Andar en golondro,** *(coll.)* to feed on vain hopes.

golosamente [go-lo-sah-men'-tay], *adv.* Daintily.

goloserazo [go-lo-sah'-tho], *m. aug.* Applied to a person extremely fond of dainties or delicacies.

goloserazo [go-lo-say-ar'], *va.* V. GOLOSINAR.

golosina [go-lo-see'-nah], *f.* 1. Dainty, something nice or delicate, a titbit (manjar). 2. Daintiness, fondness of dainties. 3. Something more agreeable than useful. 4. Cupidity, desire (deseo). *-pl.* Niceties, dainties, delicacies.

golosinar, golosinear, golosmear [go-lo-se-nar', go-lo-se-nay-ar', golos-may-ar'], *va.* 1. To eat titbits, dainties, or sweatmeats, and also to look for them. 2. To be fond of tasting or trying the relish of nice things. 3. To guzzle dainties.

goloso, sa [go-lo'-so, sah], *a. & m. & f.* Applied to a person very fond of dainties, nicotine, or sweetmeats; sweet tooth, lickerish.

golpazo [gol-pah'-tho], *m. aug.* A great blow.

golpe [gol'-pay], *m.* 1. Blow (impacto), stroke, hit; knock, dash; wound, hurt. 2. Action, push, act. 3. Crowd, throng of people, abundance (multitud). 4. An unfortunate accident, 5. Spring bolt of a lock. 6. V. LATIDO. 7. A pocket flap (abrigo). 8. Movements of attack in fencing. 9. Admiration, surprise (sorpresa). 10. Opportunity concluding in some business. 11. With gardeners, a hole for planting; also the depth, of a foot or more, to which a thing is plumed. 12. *(Naut.)* Any point which does not follow rigorously the direction of a given line. 13. *(Mus.)* The action of striking a string, key, etc. **Golpe de música,** band of music. **Golpe de remo,** stroke in rowing. **Golpe de fortuna,** A fortunate event, a jump. **El golpe del reloj,** the tick of the watch, or clock. **De golpe,** plump, all at once. **De un golpe,** once, all at once. **Golpe de Estado,** a stroke of policy, **Darse golpes de pecho,** to beat one's breast. **Golpe aplastante,** crushing blow. **Dar golpes en la puerta,** to thump the door. **No dar golpe,** not to do a stroke. **Preparaba su primer golpe,** he was planning his first job. **Golpe de viento,** gust of wind. **Cerrar una puerta de golpe,** to slam a door.

golpeadero [gol-pay-ah-day'-ro], *m.* 1. Place much beaten. 2. Noise made by striking a thing repeatedly.

golpeado, da [gol-pay-ah'-do, dah], *a.* Done a stroke, with a free brush and masterfully (pintura).

golpeador, ra [gol-pay-ah-dor', rah], *m. & f.* Striker, person or thing that strikes, beater.

golpeadura [gol-pay-ah-doo'-rah], *f.* Percussion, the act of beating, hammering or striking.

golpear [gol-pay-ar'], *va.* 1. To beat, to strike, to hit (desastre natural), to knock, to hammer, to give blows; to bruise, to tap (suavemente), to punch (puñetazos), to thump (mesa). 2. To tick, like a watch. *-vn.* To throb (latir), to tick.

golpecico, illo, ito [gol-pay-thee'-co], *m. dim.* A slight blow.

golpeo [gol-pay'-o], *m.* Striking, knocking, hitting; beating, pounding; punching. V. GOLPEADURA.

golpeteo [gol-pay-tay'-o]. *m.* Lively and continued striking; constant hammering. *(Acad.)*

golusmear [go-loos-may-ar'], *vn.* V. GOLOSINEAR.

goma [go'-mah], *f.* 1. Gum. 2. Rubber. 3. Rubber band. **Goma araábiga,** arabic gum. **Goma de borrar,** eraser. **goma elástica,** rubber.

gomal [go-mahl'], *m. (Sp. Am.)* Grove of rubber trees.

gomero, ra [go-may'-ro, rah], *a.* Rubber.-*m. & f.* Rubber plantation worker (obrero).

gomía [go-mee'-ah], *f.* 1. Bugbear to frighten children. 2. Glutton, a voracious eater. **Gomía del caudal,** spendthrift.

gomífero, ra [go-mee'-fay-ro, rah], *a.* Bearing or containing gum; gummiferous.

gomina [go-mee'-nah], *f.* Hair cream (brillantina); gel (fijador).

gomorresina [go-mor-ray-see'-nah], *f.* Gum-resin.

gomosidad [go-mo-se-dahd'], *f.* Gumminess, viscosity.

gomos [go'-mos], *m.* A gummatous tumor.

gomoso, sa [go-mo'-so, sah], *a.* Gummy, productive of gum.

gomuto [go-moo'-to], *m* An East Indian palm-tree yielding an edible fruit highly prized.

gonagra [go-nah'-grah], *f. (Med.)* Gout which attacks the knees.

gonce [gon'-thay], *m.* V. GOZNE.

góndola [gon'-do-lah], *f.* 1. Gondola, a Venetian flat boat with an awning. 2. A certain carriage in which several can ride together.

gondolero [gon-do-lay'-ro], *m.* Gondolier, rower of a gondola.

gonela [go-nay'-lah], *f.* A tunic or outer garment, sleeveless, and reaching to the calf of the leg, worn over the armor and bearing the arms, in embroidery, of the knight who wore it.

gonfalón [gon-fah-lon'], *m.* 1. Banner, pennant. 2. *(Her.)* Standard of the church.

gonfaloniero [gon-fah-lo-ne-ay'-ro], *m.* 1. Title of the chiefs of some of the small republics in Italy. 2. Standard bearer.

gongorino, na [gon-go-ree'-no, nah], *a. (coll.)* Applied to a pompous, lofty style of writing.

gongorismo [gon-go-rees'-mo], *m. (coll.)* Altiloquence, pompous language (poesía).

gongorista [gon-go-rees'-tah], *f.* One who affects to write poetry in a pompous style.

gongorizar [gon-go-re-thar'], *vn.* To affect loftiness of style in poetry.

goniometría [go-ne-o-may-tree'-ah], *f.* Goniometry, art of measuring angles.

goniométrico, ca [go-ne-may'-tre-co, cah], *a.* Goniometric, belonging to goniometry.

goniómetro [go-ne-o'-may-tro], *m.* Goniometer, instrument for measuring angles.

gonóideo, dea [go-no'-e-day-o, ah], *a.* Resembling sperm or semen.

gonorrea [go-nor-ray'-ah], *f. (Med.)* 1. Spermatorrhoea *(Acad.)* 2. Gonorrhoea, a venereal disease; specific urethritis.

gonorreico, ca [go-nor-ray'-e-co, cah], *a.* Gonorrhoeal, relating to gonorrhoea.

gorbión [gor-be-on'], *m.* 1. A kind of edging for embroidering. 2. Gum euphorbium.

gordal [gor-dahl'], *a.* Fat, big, fleshy.

gordana [gor-dah'-nah], *f.* Oil extracted in India from the testicles of oxen, and used for wool.

gordazo, za [gor-dah'-tho, thah], *a. aug.* Very fat and big.

gordico, ica, illo, illa, ito, ita [gor-dee'-co, cah, etc.], *m. & f. dim.* Not very fat, rather plump.

gordiflón, na [gor-de-flone', nah], *m. f.* A very corpulent, flabby person.

gordo, da [gor'-do, dah], *a.* 1. Fat, corpulent, plump, fleshy, obese (persona). **Está más gordo que nunca,** he's fatter than ever. 2. Fat, rich, gray, oily (comida, sustancia). **Tocino gordo,** fat pork. 3. Coarse, thick (hilo, tela) **Lienzo gordo,** coarse linen. 4. Great, large, big. 5. Torpid, stupid. **Mentira gorda,** a gross falsehood. 6. Unpleasant. **Ese tipo me cae gordo,** that chap gets on my nerves. **Lo más gordo fue...,** the most outrageous was...

gordo [gor'-do], *m.* Fat, suet, lard.

gordolobo [gor-do-lo'-bo], *m. (Bot.)* Great-mullein.

gordón, na [gor-done', nah], *a. aug. (coll.)* Very fat and corpulent.

gordura [gor-doo'-rah], *f.* 1. Grease, fat (obesidad). 2. Fatness, corpulence (corpulencia).

gorfe [gor'-fay], *m.* A deep hole in a river forming a whirlpool or eddy.

gorga [gor'-gah], *f.* 1. Food of hawks. 2. *(Prov.)* Whirlpool.

gorgojarse [gor-go-har'-say], *vr.* V. AGORGOJARSE.

gorgojo [gor-go'-ho], *m.* 1. Grub, weevil. 2. A dwarfish little boy.

gorgojoso, sa [gor-go-ho'-so, sah], *a.* Full of grubs or weevils.

gorgona [gor-go'-nah], *f.* 1. Gorgonia, sea-fan, a zoophyte. 2. *(Amer.)* A whirlpool near the island of this name, S.W. of the coast of Colombia, in lat. 3° N.

gorgorán [gor-go-rahn'], *m.* Sort of silk program.

gorgorear [gor-go-ray-ar'], *en. (Prov.)* To cry like a turkey-cock.

gorgorita [gor-go-ree'-tah], *f.* Bubble formed on water by the fall of rain.

gorgoritear [gor-go-re-tay-ar'], *vn.* To warble, to gargle, to quiver the voice.

gorgoritos [gor-go-ree'-tos], *m. pl. (coll.)* Quivers of the voice.

gorgorotada [gor-go-ro-tah'-dah], *f.* The quantity of liquid swallowed at once.

gorgotero [gor-go-tay'-ro], *m.* Peddler, hawker.

gorguera [gor-gay'-rah], *f.* 1. A kind of neckcloth, formerly worn by ladies of fashion. 2. Armor of the neck.

gorguerín [gor-gay-reen'], *f.* Small kind of ruff or frill for the neck.

gorguz [gor-gooth'], *m.* Javelin, a missile weapon.

gorila [go-ree'-lah], *m.* 1. Gorilla. 2. Tough (matón), bruiser, thug; henchman (guardaespaldas), bodyguard.

gorja [gor'-hah], *f.* 1. Throat, throttle. 2. Rejoicing, merry making. 3. *(Naut.)* Head of the keel.

gorjal [gor-hahl'], *m.* 1. Collar of a doublet. 2. Armor to defend the neck or throat.

gorjeador, ra [gor-hay-ah-dor', rah], *m. & f.* Warbler, modulator.

gorjear [gor-hay-ar'], *vn.* To warble, to quaver, to shake the voice in a melodious manner; to chirp, to twitter.-*vr.* To gabble (niño).

gorjeo [gor-hay'-o], *m.* 1. Trilling, quaver; a melodious shake of the voice; chirp, twitter. 2. Chatter of a child which begins to talk.

gorjería [gor-hay-ree'-ah], *f. V.* GORJEO for chatter of a child.

gorra [gor'-rah], *f.* 1. Cap, bonnet (de bebé), a covering of the head. **Gorra de montar,** riding cap. **Gorra de visera,** peaked cap. 2. **Gorra de señora,** lady's hat or bonnet. 3. Hunting cap. 4. Intrusion at feasts without invitation. **Colarse de gorra,** to gatecrash. **Entrar de gorra,** to get in free. 5. Parasite, sponger.

gorrada [gor-rah'-dah], *f. V.* GORRETADA.

gorrero [gor-ray'-ro], *m.* 1. Cap-maker. 2. Parasite, sponger.

gorretada [gor-ray-tah'], *f.* Salute with a cap.

gorrete [gor-ray'-tay], *m. dim.* Small cap or bonnet.

gorrica, ills, ita [gor-ree'-cah, eel'-lyah, ee'-tah], *f. dim.* Small cap or bonnet.

gorrico, illo, ito [gor-ree'-co, eel'-lyo, ee'-to], *m. dim.* Small round cap.

gorrín, gorrino [gor-reen', gor-ree'-no], *m.* 1. A small pig (cochinito), a sucking pig. 2. *(Prov.)* Pig (cerdo).

gorrinada, or **gorrinera** [gor-re-nah'-dah, gor-re-nay'-rah], *f.* 1. Pigs (cerdos). 2. Dirty trick (mala pasada).

gorrinería [gor-re-nay-ree'-ah], *f.* 1. A pigsty. 2. *(Met.)* Filthiness, bestiality. 3. A dirty trick (mala pasada). 4. A disgusting thing.

gorrinillo, ito [gor-re-neel'-lyo, ee'-to], *m. dim.* A small sucking pig.

gorrión [gor-re-on'], *m. (Orn.)* Sparrow.

gorrioncillo [gor-re-on-theel'-lyo], *m. dim.* A small sparrow.

gorrionera [gor-re-o-nay'-rah], *f.* Rendez-vous or hiding place of rogues.

gorrista [gor-rees'-tah], *m.* Parasite, sponger.

gorro [gor'-ro], *m.* A night-cap, bonnet (de mujer, niño). **Gorro de baño,** bathing cap. **Estar hasta el gorro de,** to be fed up with.

gorrón [gor-rone'], *m.* 1. A poor student who goes from house to house to get his dinner; parasite. 2. Spindle, pivot, or gudgeon of a gate or door; pillow, swing-block. 3. Lazy, unhealthy silkworm. 4. A round, smooth pebble (guijarro). 5. Man given to debauchery and lewdness. 6. An iron staff which aids in turning flee capstan. 7. Peg serving as a hinge in flood-gates.

gorrona [gor-ro'-nah], *f.* Strumpet, prostitute.

gorronal [gor-ro-nahl'], *m.* Place full of pebbles or coarse gravel.

gorronazo [gor-ro-nah'-tho], *m. (aug.)* A great lecher or rake.

gorronear [gor-ro-nay-ar'], *va.* To scrounge. **Gorronear algo a uno,** to scrounge something from somebody. *-vn.* To cadge, to sponge.

gorronería [gor-ro-nay-re'-ah], *f.* 1. Cadging (sablear), sponging. 2. Avarice, greed (avaricia).

gorullo [go-rool'-lyo], *m.* A small button or ball of wool, or other matter which sticks together.

gosipífero, ra [go-se-pee'-fay-ro, rah], *a.* Cotton producing.

gosipino, na [go-se-pee'-no, nah], *a.* Of a cottony surface.

gosipio [go-see'-pe-o], *m.* Goseypium, the cotton plant.

gota [go'-tah], *f.* 1. Drop, a globule of moisture which falls at once. 2. A small quantity of any liquor. 3. Gout, a disease. 4. A small portion taken from a smelting of gold or silver for assaying. 5. In clock work, the small steel plate put at the end of the fuse and sometimes of the barrel arbor. 6. A variety of topaz called "water drop." **Gota a gota,** drop by drop. **Sudar la gota gorda,** to sweat blood. **La gota que colma el vaso,** the straw that breaks the camel's back, the last straw. *-pl. (Arch.)* Ornaments of the Doric order. **Unas gotas de coñac,** a few drops of brandy.

goteado, da [go-tay-ah'-do, dah], *a. & pp.* of GOTEAR. Guttated, sprinkled, spotted, speckled.

gotear [go-tay-ar'], *vn.* 1. To drop, to fall drop by drop, to drip (destilar), to trickle (escurrir). 2. To give by driblets or intermittently: to leak (salirse).

goteo [go-tay'-o], *m.* 1. Leak, leakage. 2. Dribbling.

gotera [go-tay'-rah], *f.* 1. Gutter, a passage made by water on the roofs of houses. 2. Leak, the water which drops or runs through the passage, the place where the water falls, and the mark left by the dropping of rain (agujero). 3. Fringe of bed-hangings, valance (colgadura). 4. Invalidism. *V.* ACHAQUE.

goterón [go-tay-ron'], *m.* 1. A large drop of rain-water. 2. Throating in a cornice.

goteroncillo [go-tay-ron-theel'-lyo], *m.* A drop of rain-water not much larger than usual.

gotica, illa, ita [go-tee'-cah, eel'-lyah, ee'-tah], *f. dim.* Droplet, a small drop.

gótico, ca [go'-te-co, cah], *a.* Gothic: chiefly applied to the pointed style of building. **Letra gótica,** gothic characters.

gotón, na [go-ton', nah], *a. & m. pl.* Goth.

gotoso, sa [go-to'-so, sah], *a.* Gouty.

gozada [go-thah'-dah], *f.* Pleasure, delight.

gozador, ra [go-thah-dor', rah], *m. & f.* Enjoyer.

gozante [go-thahn'-tay], *pa.* Enjoying; enjoyer.

gozar [go-thar'], *va.* 1. To enjoy (disfrutar), to have possession or fruition of (poseer). 2. To enjoy, to seduce (mujer). *-vr.* To rejoice.

gozne [goth'-nay], *m.* Hinge.

gozo [go'-tho], *m.* 1. Joy (alegría), pleasure (placer), satisfaction, glee, merriment, mirth gladfulness, gladness, cheerfulness. **Es un gozo para los ojos,** it's a joy to see. **No caber de gozo,** to be beside oneself with joy. 2. A sudden blaze of dry chips of wood. 3. *pl.* Verses in praise of the Virgin or the saints in which certain words are repeated at the end of every couplet.

gozosamente [go-tho-sah-men'-tay], *adv.* Joyfully, cheerfully.

gozoso, sa [go-tho'-so, sah], *a.* Joyful, cheerful, content, glad, festive, mirthful, merry.

gozque [goth'-kay], *m.* A cur-dog.

gozquejo [goth-kay'-ho], *m. dim.* A small cur-dog.

grabación [grah-bah-the-on'], *f.* Recording. **Grabación en cinta,** tape recording.

grabado [grah-bah'-do], *m.* 1. Engraving, the art of engraving. 2. Engraving, the copy printed from an engraved plate. **Grabado en madera,** woodcut. **Grabado al agua tinta,** aquatint. *-a.* Recorded (música); on tape (en cinta). **Grabado, da,** *pp.* of GRABAR.

grabador, ra [grah-bah-dor', rah], *m. & f.* Engraver, a cutter in stone, metal or wood. *-m.* Tape recorder.

grabadura [grah-bah-doo'-rah], *f.* Act of engraving, sculpture.

grabar [grah-bar'], *va.* 1. To engrave (arte), to picture by incisions in stone, wood, or metal; to grave. **Grabar al agua fuerte** or **de agua fuerte,** to etch. 2. To record (cinta, disco).

grabazón [grah-bah-thone'], *f.* Engraving, sculpture.

gracejo [grah-thay'-ho], *m.* 1. Joke, jest, mirth, facetiousness, cheerful wit (chispa). 2. A graceful or pleasing delivery in speaking, charm (encanto).

gracia [grah'-the-ah], *f.* 1. Grace (garbo), favorable influence of God in the human mind, and the effect of this influence. 2. Grace, natural excellence, gracefulness, gentility, elegance of mien or manner; cleverness. 3. Grace, favor confered (favor), gift, benefaction, kindness, concession; graciousness (benevolencia), condescension. 4. Benevolence, courtesy, pleasing manners (agrado). 5. Grace, pardon, mercy. 6. Elegance (elegancia), beauty. 7. Remission of a debt. 8. A witty saying or expression. 9. *(coll.)* Name, the discriminative appellation of an individual. 10. Gratitude for favors received. **Dar gracias,** to thank, or to give thanks. **Caer en gracia,** to become a favorite. **Gracias,** grants or concessions. **Gracia de Dios,** *(coll.)* the bread. **En gracia de,** for the sake of. *-interj.* **¡Qué gracia!** What a wonder! A fine thing indeed!

Golpe de gracia, finishing stroke. **Me cayó en gracia**, I took to him. **Ahí está la gracia**, that's what's so funny about it. **Tener gracia**, to be funny. **Gracias a la ayuda de otros**, thanks to the help of others.

graciable [grah-theah'-blay], a. 1. Good natured, affable (afable). 2. Easily obtained (favor).

grácil [grah'-thee;], a. Gracile, slender (esbelto), small (fino).

graciola [grah-the-o-sah-men'-tay], f. (Bot.) Hedge hyssop.

graciosamente [grah-the-o-sah-men'-tay], adv. Graciously, gratefully, kindly, gratuitously.

graciosidad [grah-the-o-se-dahd'], f. 1. Gracefulness, beauty, perfection, elegance and dignity of manners. 2. Facetiousness, cheerful wit.

gracioso, sa [grah-the-o'-so, sah], a. 1. Graceful (garboso), beautiful, accomplished, 2. Facetious, witty, funny (chistoso), pleasing (atractivo). **Una situación muy graciosa**, a very amusing situation. 3. Benevolent, inclined to grant favors, gracious. 4. Gratuitous (gratuito), granted without claim. 5. Ridiculous, extravagant.

gracioso, sa [grah-the-o'-so, sah], m. & f. 1. Merry-andrew, buffoon, harlequin, mime. 2. Comic actor or actress, generally in the character of servants in Spanish plays.

grada [grah'-dah], f. 1. Step of a staircase (peldaño). 2. In nunneries, a room where the nuns are allowed to hold conversation with their friends through a grate. 3. An older of steps before a church, gradatory. 4. Harrow, to break the clods after ploughing. **Grada de construcción** (Naut.) stocks for ship building. -pl. 1. Bar, the place where legal cases are tried. 2. Seats of an amphitheater.

gradación [grah-dah-the-on'], f. 1. A harmonious gradation (progresión) or scale of music. 2. (Rhet.) Climax.

gradado, da [grah-dah'-do, dah], a. Applied to the building with an order of steps around it. -pp. of GRADAR.

gradar [grah-dar'], va. (Prov.) To harrow, to break with the harrow.

gradatim [grah-dah'-tim], adv. (Lat.) Gradually, by degrees.

gradería [grah-day-ree'-ah], f. Series of seats or steps (asientos, escalones).

gradilla [grah-deel'-lyah], f. 1. (Dim.) Small step or seat. 2. Tile-mould. 3. A step-ladder, a small portable ladder.

gradinar [grah-de-nar'], va. To cut off with a chisel.

gradino [grah-dee'-no], m. 1. Chisel, an edged tool used by stone-cutters. 2. Graver, the tool used in graving.

gradiolo [grah-de-o'lo], m. (Bot.) V. GLADIOLO.

grado [grah'-do], m. 1. Step of a staircase (peldaño). 2. Value or quality of a thing (cualidad). 3. Degree of kindred, order of lineage (punto). 4. Will, pleasure. 5. Degree, an academical title of honor conferred by universities. 6. (Mil.) Rank. 7. (Geom.) Degree, the three hundred and sixtieth part of the circumference of a circle (medida). 8. Degree, the division of the lines upon mathematical instruments. 9. Degree, grade, the measure of the quality or state of a thing. 10. (Mus.) Degree, the intervals of sounds. **De grado en grado**, gradually, by degrees, in regular progression. **El grado que ahora hemos alcanzado**, the stage we have now reached. **Est' en el segundo grado de elaboración**, it is now in the second stage of production. **Grado** universitario, university degree. **En un ángulo de 45 grados**, at an angle of 45 degrees. **De buen grado**, willingly.

graduación [grah-doo-ah-the-on'], f. 1. The act and effect of measuring or comparing different things. 2. Graduation, regular progression by succession of degrees. 3. Rank, condition or quality of a person. **De alta graduación**, of high rank. 4. (Mil.) Rank. 5. (Univ.) Gradation (acto). 6. Grading (regulación).

graduado, da [grah-doo-ah'-do, dah], a. (Mil.) Brevet: applied to officers enjoying higher rank than they possess. -pp. of GRADUAR. -m. Graduate, one who has obtained an academical degree.

graduador [grah-doo-ah-dor'], m. Graduator, graduating instrument, gauge.

gradual [grah-doo-ahl'], a. Gradual, proceeding by degrees.

gradual [grah-doo-ahl'], m. A verse read between the epistle and gospel at the celebration of mass.

gradualmente [grah-doo-al-men'-tay], adv. Gradually, by degrees.

graduando [grah-doo-ahn'-do], m. Candidate for academical degrees.

graduar [grah-doo-ar'], va. 1. To measure or compare different things (medir). 2. To graduate, to dignify with an academical degree. 3. To give military rank. 4. To divide into degrees. (coll.) To calculate, to appraise (evaluar).-vr. 1. To graduate, to take an academical degree. 2. (Mil.) To take a commission.

gráfica [grah'-fe-cah], f. Diagram (diagrama), sketch, illustration.

gráficamente [grah'-fe-cah-men-tay], adv. Graphically, in a picturesque manner.

gráfico, ca [grah'-fe-co, cah], a. Graphic, graphical, relating to engravings; well delineated.

gráfila [grah'-fe-lah], f. The little border on the edge of a coin.

grafio [grah'-fe-o], m. Graver, a tool used in making grafitto or scratch-work.

grafioles [grah-fe-o'-les], m. pl. Kind of biscuits made in the form of an S.

grafito [grah-fee'-to], m. Graphite, plumbago.

grafolita [grah-fo-lee'-tah], f. Grapholite, a variety of slate suitable for writing on.

grafología [grah-fo-lo-hee'-ah], f. Graphology, study of handwriting.

grafólogo, ga [grah-fo'-lo-go], m & f. Graphologist.

grafómetro [grah-fo'-may-tro], m. Graphometer, circumferentor, a surveying instrument with sights for measuring angles.

graja [grah'-hah], f. (Orn.) 1. Female jackdaw. 2. Jay.

grajal [grah-hahl'], a. Belonging to crows, ravens, or magpies.

grajea [grah-hay'-ah], f. A very small sugar-plum.

grajear [grah-hay-ar'], vn. To caw, as crows; to chatter, as magpies.

grajero, ra [grah-hay'-ro, rah], a. Applied to rookeries.

grajo [grah'-ho], m. 1. (Orn.) Jackdaw. 2. (Peru. Coll.) Strong sweat, particularly in the armpits.

grajuelo [grah-hoo-ay'-lo], m. dim. A small jackdaw.

grama [grah'-mah], f. (Bot.) Creeping cynodon.

gramal [grah-mahl'], m. Place where couch-grass or dog's-grass grows.

gramalla [grah-mahl'-lyah], f. 1. A long scarlet gown anciently worn by the magistrates of Aragon. 2. Coat of mail.

gramallera [grah-mal-lyay'-rah], f. (Prod.) Pothanger. V. LLARES.

gramar [grah-mar'], va. (Prov.) To knead the dough of bread.

gramática [grah-mah'-te-cah], f. Grammar.

gramatical [grah-mah-te-cahl'], a. Grammatical, grammar.

gramaticalmente [grah-mah-te-cahl'-men-tay], adv. Grammatically.

gramático [grah-mah'-te-co], m. Grammarian.

gramaticón [grah-mah-te-cone'], m. One who believes himself a great grammarian, or he who knows nothing but grammar.

gramaticuelo [grah-mah-te-coo-ay'-lo], m. dim. Grammaticaster, a smatterer in grammar, a pedant.

gramatista [grah-mah-tees'-tah], f. Teacher of grammar.

gramil [grah-meel'], m. A joiner's marking gauge.

gramilla [grah-meel'-lyah], f. Brake, a wooden, instrument for dressing hemp or flax.

gramíneo, ea [grah-mee'-nay-o, ah], a. (Poet.) Gramineous, grassy.

graminívoro, ra [grah-me-nee'-vo-ro, rah], a. Graminivorous, grass eating, living upon grass.

gramo [grah'-mo], m. Gram, unit of weight in the metrical system: the weight of a cubic centimeter of distilled water.

gramófono [grah-mo'-fo-no], *m.* Gramophone, talking machine.

gramómetro [grah-mo'-may-tro], *m.* A type-gauge.

grampa [grahm'-pah], *f. (Naut.)* A hook for sustaining light weights.

gramuro, ra [grah-moo'-ro, rah], *a.* Having a long, slender tail.

Gran [grahn], *a.* 1. Great. *V.* GRANDE. It is used only before substantives in the singular, as **Gran cosa**, great thing; **Gran miedo**, great fear. 2. Grand, as chief or principal: used also before substantives as **Gran maestre**, grandmaster. **Gran señor**, grand signior.

grana [grah'-nah], *f.* 1. Grain, the seed of plants (semilla). 2. The time when corn, flax, etc., form their seed (estación). 3. Cochineal. 4. Scarlet grain. 5. Fine scarlet cloth (tela). 6. Fresh red color of the lips and checks (color). **Ponerse como la grana**, to turn scarlet.

granada [grah-nah-dah], *f.* 1. Pomegranate (fruta). 2. *(Mil.)* Hand-grenade. **Granada de mano**, hand grenade. **Granada de metralla**, shrapnel shell.

granadera [grah-nah-day-rah], *f. (Mil.)* A grenadier's pouch.

granadero [grah-nah-day'-ro], *m. (Mil.)* Grenadier, a footsoldier, formerly employed to throw grenades.

granadilla [grah-nah-deel'-lyah], *f. (Bot.)* Passion-flower; passion fruit (fruta).

granadino, na [grah-nah-dee'-no, nah], *a.* Native of or belonging to Granada, or the U. S. of Colombia, formerly New Granada. *-m.* The flower of the pomegranate-tree.

granado, da [grah-nah'-do, dah], *a.* 1. Large, remarkable. 2. Principal, chief; illustrious; select (selecto). 3. Seedy, abounding with seed. *-pp.* OF GRANAR.

granado [grah-nah'-do], *m. (Bot.)* Pomegranate-tree.

granador [grah-nah-dor'], *m.* A sieve for granulating gunpowder, and the spot destined for this operation.

granaje [grah-nah'-hay], *m.* The act of granulating powder.

granalla [grah-nahl'-lyah], *f.* Granulation, grains of metal.

granar [grah-nar'], *vn.* 1. To seed, to grow to maturity so as to shed the seed. 2. To seed, to shed the seed. 3. To grain, to granulate.

granate [grah-nah'-tay], *m.* Garnet, a precious stone resembling a ruby.

granático, ca [grah-nah'-te-co, cah], *a.* Scarlet, garnet; characteristic of cochineal or the garnet.

granatín [grah-nah-teen'], *m.* Kind of ancient cloth.

granazón [grah-nah-thone'], *f.* Seeding, shedding the seed.

gran bestia [gran bes'-te-ah], *f.* Tapir.

grancé [gran-thay'], *a.* Madder colored.

grande [grahn'-day], *a.* 1. Great, large in bulk or number, extensive, huge, big (tamaño), big, tall (estatura), old (persona). **Grande como una montaña**, as big as a house. **Los zapatos le están muy grandes**, the shoes are too big. 2. Great, having any quality in a high degree, impressive (impresionante). 3. Grand, principal. 4. As a whole (en conjunto), on a grand scale, in a big way. **Estar en grande**, to be going strong. **Pasarlo en grande**, to have a tremendous time.

grande [grahn'-day], *m.* 1. Grandee, Spanish nobleman of the first rank. 2. **Los grandes**, the great.

grandecico, ica, illo, illa, ito, ita, [gran-day-thee'-co], *a.* Growing rather big; pretty large or big.

grandemente [grahn-day-men-tay], *adv.* Greatly; very well; extremely; grandly.

grandeza [gran-day'-thah], *f.* 1. Greatness, bigness (gran tamaño). 2. Greatness (impresionante), grandeur, magnificence, grandness, nobleness. 3. Grandeeship, the preeminence and dignity of a grandee of Spain (rango). 4. The body of grandees (personas).

grandilocuencia [gran-de-lo-coo-en'-the-ah], *f.* Grandiloquence.

grandilocuente [gran-dee-lo-coo-en', tay], *a. V.* GRANDILOCUO.

grandílocuo, cua [gran-dee'-lo-coo-o, coo-ah], *a.* Grandiloquent, making use of a lofty or pompous style.

grandillón, na [gran-deel-lyone', nah], *a. aug.* Excessively large and big.

grandiosamente [gran-de-o-sah-men'-tay], *adv.* Magnificently.

grandiosidad [gran-de-o-se-dahd'], *f.* Greatness, grandeur; magnificence; abundance.

grandioso, sa [gran-de-o'-so, sah], *a.* Grand, great, magnificent, splendid.

grandísimo [gran-dee'-se-mo], *a.* Superl. De grande, great, big. **Un coche grandísimo**, a whacking great car.

grandor [gran-dor'], *m.* Size and bigness of things, magnitude, greatness, extensiveness.

grandullón, na [gran-dool-lyone', nah], *a.* Large in proportion to age.

graneado, da [grah-nay-ah'-do, dah], *a.* 1. Reduced to grains; spotted, granulous. 2. *(Peru)* Select, choice. *-pp.* of GRANEAR.

graneador [grah-nay-ah-dor'], *m.* A kind of graver or tool for engraving.

granear [grah-nay-ar'], *va.* 1. To sow grain in the earth. 2. To engrave.

granel [grah-nel'], *m. (Prov.)* Heap of corn (montón); in abundance (abundancia); by the score (a montones); lavishly; at random (al azar). **A granel**, 1. In a heap. 2. *(Naut.)* In bulk. 3. *(Amer. Peru.)* The *gacetilla* of some periodicals.

granelar [grah-nay-lar'], *va.* In tanneries, to grain leather.

graneo [grah-nay'-o], *m.* The act of shedding seed, or sowing seed.

granero [grah-nay'-ro], *m.* 1. Granary, grange, cornloft. 2. A fruitful country.

granete [grah-nay'-tay], *m. (Mech.)* Marking-awl; countersink punch.

granevano [grah-may-vah'-no], *m. (Bot.)* Goat's-thorn.

granguardia [gran-goo-ar'-de-ah], *f. (Mil.)* Grandguard, an advanced guard in front of an army.

granico [grah-nee'-co], *m. dim.* Granule, small grain.

granífero, ra [gra-nee'-fay-ro rah], *a. (Bot.)* Bearing seeds in the form of grains.

granilla [grah-neel'-lyah], *f.* Rough nap on cloth.

granillero, ra [grah-neel-lyay'-ro, rah], *a. (Prov.)* Applied to hogs that feed on what they find in the fields.

granillo [grah-neel'-lyo], *m.* 1. *(Dim.)* Granule, small grain. 2. Gain or profit frequently obtained. 3. Pimple growing at the extremity of the rump of canary birds and linnets.

granilloso, sa [grah-neel-lyo'-so, sah], *a.* Granulous, granular.

granítico, ca [grah-nee'-te-co, cah], *a.* Granitic, formed of granite.

granito [grah-nee'-to], *m.* 1. Granite, a hard stone composed of quartz, feldspar, and mica. 2. Hairs, streaks, or points which diminish the brilliancy and price of diamonds. 3. (Pharmacy) Granule. 4. *(Prov. Murcia)* Small egg of a silkworm.

granitulino, na [grah-ne-too-lee'-no, nah], *a. (Min.)* Nodular; granulous.

granívoro, ra [grah-nee'-vo-ro, rah], *a.* Granivorous, eating grain, living upon grain.

granizada [grah-ne-thah'-dah], *f.* 1. Copious full of hail. 2. *(Met.)* Multitude of things which fall in abundance.

granizado, da [grah-ne-thah'-do, dah], *a.* 1. Fall of hail, destroyed by hail. 2. Iced drink. *-pp.* of GRANIZAR.

granizar [grah-ne-thar'], *vn.* 1. To hail. 2. To pour down with violence (lluvia).

granizo [grah-nee'-tho], *m.* 1. Hail, rain frozen in falling. 2. Cloud or web in the eyes. *V.* GRANIZADA.

granja [grahn'-hah], *f.* Grange, farm, farm-house (cortijo); a country-house, a villa, a manse, dairy (lechería). **Granja avícola**, chicken farm.

granjear [gran-hay-ar'], *va.* 1. To gain, to get, to obtain, to win. 2. To conciliate or gain the good-will of another.

granjeo [gran-hay'-o], *m*. 1. The act of getting or acquiring. 2. Gain, profit, advantage, advancement in interest, influence, etc.

granjería [gran-hay-ree'-ah], *f*. Gain, profit, advantage.

granjero, ra [gran-hay'-ro, rah], *m. & f*. 1. Farmer, husbandman, granger. 2. Dealer in profitable commodities.

grano [grah'-no], *m*. 1. Grain, the seed of corn (semilla). 2. Grain, a single seed of corn. 3. Grain, any minute particle (particula). 4. Grain, the direction of the fibres of wood or other fibrous matter. 5. *(Pharm.)* Grain, the smallest weight in physic, twenty of which make an English scruple, and twenty four a Spanish one. 6. The bushing of a cannon. 7. Pimple, a pustule on the skin, furuncle. **Grano de arroz,** grain of rice. **Grano de café,** coffee bean. **Ir al grano,** to get to the point. **Poner su grano de arena,** *(Fig.)* to make one's contribution.

granoso, sa [grah-no'-so, sah], *a*. Granulous, grainy, granular.

granudo, da [grah-noo'-do, dah], *a.V.* GRANOSO.

granuja [grah-noo'-hah], *f*. 1. Ripe grapes separated from the branches. 2. Grapestone, the stone or seed contained in the grape. 3. Little rogue, scoundrel, knave, rascal (canalla). 4. Urchin (pilluelo).

granujado, da [grah-noo-hah'-do, dah], *a*. 1. Full of pimples. 2. Full of stones, full of seeds.

granujiento, ta [grah-noo-heen'-to, tah], *a*. Grainy, full of grain.

granujo [grah-noo'-ho], *m*. *(coll.)* Pimple or tumor in the flesh.

gránula [grah'-noo-lah], *f*. *(Bot.)* Spore, reproductive body of cryptogamous plants.

granulación [grah-noo-lah-the-on'], *f*. *(Chem.)* 1. Granulation, the act of being reduced into small particles. 2. Granulation, the act of reducing metal into grains by pouring it, when melted, into cold water.

granular [grah-noo-lar'], *va*. To granulate, to reduce to small pieces like grains. *-vr.* 1. To granulate. 2. To be covered with granules.

granular [grah-noo-lar'], *a*. Granular.

gránulo [grah'-noo-lo], *m*. 1. Granule, a small grain. 2. Pellet, a medicated granule.

granulosidad [grah-noo-lo-se-dahd'], *f*. Granularity, the state of being granular.

granuloso, sa [grah-noo-lo'-so, sah], *a*. Granulous, granular.

granza [grahn'-thah], *f*. Madder. *V.* RUBIA. *-pl*. 1. Siftings, the refuse of corn which has been winnowed and sifted. 2. Dross of metals.

granzón [gran-thone'], *m*. Fragment of ore which does not pass through the screen; screenings. *(Acad.) -pl*. Refuse of straw not eaten, but left by the cattle.

granzoso, sa [gran-tho'-so, sah], *a*. Applied to grain, having much refuse.

grañón [grah-nyone'], *m*. 1. Pap made of boiled wheat. 2. *V.* GRANO.

grao [grah'-o], *m*. Strand, shore.

grapa [grah'-pah], *f*. 1. Staple; clip, fastener (para papeles). 2. Kind of mangy ulcers in the joints of horses.

grapadora [grah-pah-do'-rah], *f*. Stapler, stapling machine.

grapar [grah-pahr'], *va*. To staple (papeles).

grapón [grah-pone'], *m. aug*. A large cramp-iron.

graptolita [grap-to-lee'-tah], *f*. Dendrite, generic name of stones exhibiting markings upon the surface.

grasa [grah-sah], *f*. 1. Suet (sebo); fat; grease; kitchen stuff. **Grasa de ballena,** blubber. **Grasa de pescado,** fish oil. 2. Gum of juniper-trees. 3. Grease of clothes. 4. *(Naut.)* Compound of rosin, pitch, and tallow used for preserving masts and yards. 5. Slag of metals. 6. The base of an ointment or pomade.

grasera [grah-say'-rah], *f*. 1. An ointment jar. 2. Vessel for fat or grease; a dripping pan.

grasería [grah-say-ree'-ah], *f*. 1. Tallow-chandler's shop. 2. A disease of silk-worms.

graseza [grah-say'-thah], *f*. Quality of fat or grease.

grasiento, ta [grah-seen'-to, tah], *a*. Greasy (grasoso); filthy, grimy.

grasilla [grah-seel'-lyah], *f*. 1. Pounce, a powder made of gum sandarach. 2. *(Bot.)* The odoriferous resin which the juniper produces.

graso, sa [grah'-so, sah], *a*. Fat, unctuous, lardy, oily (comida).

graso [grah'-so], *m*. Fat, grease.

grasones [grah-so'-nes], *m. pl*. 1. Fast dish, made of flour, milk of almonds, sugar, and cinnamon.

grasoso, sa [grah-so-so], *a*. Fatty (graso); greasy (grasiento).

grasura [grah-soo'-rah], *f. V.* GROSURA.

grata, grataguja [grah'-tah, grah-tah-goo'-hah], *f*. Instrument for burnishing silver or silver gilt.

gratamente [grah-tah-men'-tay], *adv*. Graciously, gratefully, in a kind of benevolent manner.

gratar [grah-tar'], *va*. To burnish silver or silver gilt.

gratel [grah-tel'], *m*. A braid, made by hand, with the number of skeins of yarn suited to its use.

gratificación [grah-te-fe-cah-the-on'], *f*. 1. Gratification, reward (recompensa), recompense, gratuity, fee, tip (propina), allowance to officers for expenses. 2. Indulgence.

gratificador, ra [grah-te-fe-cah-dor', rah], *m. & f*. Gratifier; pleasurable.

gratificante [grah-te-fe-cahn'-tay], *a*. Gratifying.

gratificar [grah-te-fe-car'], *va*. 1. To gratify, to reward, to requite, to recompense. 2. To gratify (satisfacer), to indulge (anhelo), to delight.

gratil [grah-teel'], *m*. 1. *(Naut.)* Head of a sail. 2. Body of the yard where the sail is tied.

gratis [grah'-tis], *adv*. Gratis, for nothing.

gratisdato, ta [grah-tis-dah'-to, tah], *a*. Gratuitious.

gratitud [grah-te-tood'], *f*. Gratitude, gratefulness.

grato, ta [grah'-to, tah], *a*. 1. Graceful, pleasing (placentero), pleasant, luscious, acceptable. 2. Grateful (agradecido). **Recibir una impresión grata,** to get a pleasing impression.

gratonada [grah-to-nah'-dah], *f*. Kind of ragout or fricassee, made of chickens half roasted, bacon, almonds, rich broth, fresh eggs, spice, and greens.

gratuitamente [grah-too-ee-tah-men'-tay], *adv*. Gratuitously, free (gratis).

gratuito, ta [grah-too-ee'-to, tah], *a*. 1. Gratuitous, gratis, free (gratis). 2. Gratuitous (observación), uncalled-for; unfounded; unjustified (acusación).

gratular [grah-too-lar'], *vn*. To congratulate. *-vr.* To rejoice.

gratulatorio, ria [grah-too-lah-to'-re-o, ah], *a*. Congratulatory.

grava [grah'-vah], *f*. Gravel (guijarros), coarse sand, crushed stone (piedra molida); road metal (carretera).

gravamen [grah-vah'-men], *m*. 1. Charge, obligation to perform or execute something. 2. Hardship, load, inconvenience, nuisance. 3. Encumbrance, burden. 4. *(Law.)* Mortgage.

gravar [grah-var'], *va*. To burden (cargar), to oppress, to fatigue, to molest, to assess for tax. **Gravar con impuestos,** to burden with taxes.

gravativo, va [grah-vah-tee-vo, vah], *a*. Grievous, injurious.

grave [grah'-vay], *a*. 1. Weighty, ponderous, heavy (pesado). 2. Grace, important (importante), momentous, of weight, of great consequence, dangerous. *(Met.)* Mortal, deadly. 3. Great, huge, vast. 4. Grave, circumspect. 5. Haughty, lofty. 6. Troublesome, vexatious, grievous; arduous, difficult (pérdida). **Ponerse grave,** to assume an air of importance. 7. *(Mus.)* Grave tone (nota, tono). 8. *(Gram.)* Grave accent (acento). **Delito grave,** a heinous crime. **Enfermedad grave,** a dangerous disease. **Estar grave,** to be seriously ill. **La situación es grave,** the situation is grave.

gravear [grah-vay-ar'], *vn*. To weigh, to gravitate, to sink.

gravedad [grah-vay-dahd'], *f*. 1. Gravity, weight, heaviness. 2. Gravity, modesty, composure, circumspection. 3. Graveness, seriousness, sobriety of behavior, importance;

severity (severidad). 4. Gravity, enormity, atrociousness. 5. Vanity, pride (grandeza). 6. Seriousness, dignity (dignidad).
Estar de gravedad, to be seriously ill. **Estar herido de gravedad**, to be severely injured.

gravemente [grah-vay-men'-tay], *adv.* Gravely, seriously. **Estar gravemente enfermo**, to be critically ill.

gravidez [grah-ve-deth'], *f.* Pregnancy.

grávido, da [grah'-ve-do, dah], *a.* 1. Full, abundant. 2. Gravid, pregnant (embarazado).

gravilla [grah-vel'-lyah], *f.* Gravel.

gravímetro [gra-vee'-may-tro], *m.* Gravimeter, an instrument for learning specific weight.

gravitación [grah-ve-tah-the-on'], *f.* Gravitation.

gravitar [grah-ve-tar'], *va.* To gravitate, to weigh down (caer sobre), to tend to some part slightly.

gravívolo, la [grah-vee'-vo-lo, lah], *a. (Zool.)* Of heavy flight.

gravoso, sa [grah-vo'-so, sah], *a.* 1. Grievous, offensive, afflictive, painful, onerous. 2. Unbearable.

graznador, ra [grath-nah-dor', rah], *m. & f.* Croaker; cawing, cackling.

graznar [grath-nar'], *vn.* To croak, to caw (cuervo), to cackle (ganso), to quack (pato).

graznido [grath-nee'-do], *m.* 1. A croak, caw, or cackle. 2. Croaking.

greba [gray'-bah], *f.* Ancient armor for the leg; greave(s).

greca [gray'-cah], *f.* Grecian fret, ornament consisting of a line forming many right angles.

greciano, na [gray-the-ah'-no, nah], or **grecisco** [gray-thees'- co], *a.* Greek, Grecian (fuego griego).

grecismo [gray-thees'-mo], *m.* Grecism, hellenism, Greekism.

grecizante [gray-the-thahn'-tay], *pa.* Grecianizing, Hellenizing.

grecizar [gray-the-thar'], *vn.* To Grecianize, to hellenize, to play the Grecian, to speak Greek.

Greco, ca [gray'-co, cah], *a.* Greek. In the form *Greco* it enters into composition, as: **Grecolatino**, written in Greek and Latin. **A la greca**, in the Grecian style.

greda [gray'-dah], *f.* 1. Chalk, marl. 2. Fuller's earth.

gredal [gray-dahl'], *m.* Pit where chalk, marl or fuller's earth is found.

gredal [gray-dahl'], *a.* Chalky.

gredoso, sa [gray-do'-so, sah], *a.* Chalky, marly, cretaceous.

green [green], *m.* (Golf) Green.

gregal [gray-gahl'], *m.* Northeast wind in the Mediterranean.

gregal [gray-gahl'], *a.* Gregarious, going in flocks.

gregalizar [gray-gah-lee-thar'], *vn. (Naut.)* To be northeasting, to drive or decline to north-east.

gregario, ria [gray-gah'-re-o, ah], *a.* Gregarian, of the common sort, ordinary.

gregoriano, na [gray-go-re-ah'-no, nah], *a.* Gregorian.

gregorillo [gray-go-reel'-lyo], *m.* Neck cloth formerly worn by women.

greguería [gray-gay-ree'-ah], *f.* 1. Out-cry, confused clamor. 2. V. GUIRIGAY.

gregüescos [gray-goo-ays'-cos], *pl.* A wide sort of breeches made in the Grecian fashion.

greguisco, ca [gray-gees'-co, cah], *a.* Greek, belonging to Greece.

greguizar [gray-gee-thar'], *va.* 1. To Grecianize, to talk Greek. 2. To Grecize, to convert into Greek.

gremial [gray-me-ahl'], *m.* Lap cloth, used by bishops when they officiate at divine service.

gremial [gray-me-ahl'], *a.* Belonging or relating to a body, corporation, or guild; it is also used as a substantive for a member of the corporation. -m & f. Union member (miembro).

gremio [gray'-me-o], *m.* 1. The lap. 2. Body, society, company, guild, corporation; fraternity. 3. Trade-union (sindical). **El gremio de la iglesia**, the pale of the church. **El gremio de una universidad**, the professors, doctors, and scholars, belonging to a university, considered as a body.

greña [gray'-nyah], *f.* 1. Entangled or matted hair (cabellos revueltos). 2. Something entangled. 3. *(Prov.)* Heap of grain laid to be thrashed. 4.*(prov)* First leaves of a vine-shoot.

greñudo, da [gray-nyoo'-do, dah], *a.* Dishevelled, having entangled hair.

greñuela [gray-nyoo-ay'-lah], *f. (Prov.)* The first shoots of a vine.

gres [grays], *m.* Generic name of every rock of grainy texture.

gresca [grays'-cah], *f.* 1. Carousal, revelling, clatter. 2. Wrangle, quarrel.

grey [gray'-e], *f.* 1. Flock, as of sheep or goats. 2. *(Met.)* Flock, congregation of the faithful.

grial [gre-ahl'], *m.* Grail, the legendary holy chalice of the Last Supper.

griego, ga [gre-ay'-go, gah], *a.* Greek; belonging to or native of Greece. -m. 1. The Greek language. 2. Incomprehensible language.

grieta [gre-ay'-tah], *f.* 1. Crevice, crack, cleft. 2. Chink, fissure, cranny, flaw. 3. Scratch or fissure in the skin. **Grieta en las manos**, chapped hands.

grietado, da [gre-ay-tah'-do, dah], *a.* Fissured, cleft, showing flaws.

grietarse [gre-ay-tar'-say], *vr.* To crack in the form of a star: said of ingots or metal plates.

grietecilla [gre-ay-tay-theel'-lyah], *f. dim.* A small fissure or scratch; a small crevice.

grietoso, sa [gre-ay-to'-so, sah], *a.* Full of cracks or crevices, flawy.

grifa [gree'-fah], *f.* Italics, in printing.

grifado, da [gre-fah'-do, dah], *a.* Italic (type).

grifalto [gre-fahl'-to], *m.* Small kind of culverin.

grifo, fa [gree'fo, fah], *a.* 1. Applied to the letters invented by Haldus Pius Manutius, which superseded the Gothic characters; Italic. 2. Kinky (pelo).

grifo [gree'-fo], *m.* 1. Griffin or griffon, a fabled animal. 2. *(Amer.)* The child of a negro and an Indian. **Grifos**, frizzled hair. 3. Tap, faucet. **Cerveza al grifo**, draught beer.

grifón [gre-fone'], *m.* A stop-cock for water; faucet, spigot.

gril [greel'], *m.* Grilse, Scotch name of a young salmon on its first return from sea.

griliforme [gre-le-for'-may], *a. (Zool.)* Shapped like a cricket.

grilla [greel'-lyah], *f.* 1. Female cricket. V. GRILLO. 2. A piece of the mechanism of a stocking loom. **Esa es grilla**, there is no such a thing: vulgar expression of doubt.

grillado [greel-lah'-do], *a.* Barmy.

grillar [greel-lyar'], *vn.* To chirp or squeak (grillo). -vr. To shoot, to sprout.

grillera [greel-lyay'-rah], *f.* Cricket cage, a place where crickets are kept (jaula).

grillero [greel-lyay'-ro], *m.* He who takes off prisoners' irons.

grillete [greel-lyay'-tay], *m.* Shackle, fetter.

grillo [greel'-lyo], *m.* 1. Cricket, an insect. 2. Shoot issuing from seed in the earth, germ. **Grillos**, 1. Fetters, irons, shackles or chains for the feet. 2. Any impediment which prevents motion.

grillones [greel-lyo'-nes], *m. pl. aug.* Large fetters or irons.

grillotalpa [greel-lyo-tahl'-pah], *m.* Mole-cricket, fen-cricket.

grima [gree'-mah], *f.* Fright, horror, astonishment, grimness, aversion (aversión), uneasiness (inquietud); annoyance (molestia).

grimazo [gre-mah'-tho], *m.* A grotesque posture, or contortion of the face.

grímpola [greem'-po-lah], *f. (Naut.)* Vane, a sort of weather-cock on the top-mast head. 1. Pennant, streamer.

grinalde [gre-nahl'day], *m.* Machine of artificial firework.

gringo [green'-go], *a. (coll.)* Unintelligible, gibberish (idioma). -m. *(Vulg.)* Yankee (norteamericano). **Hablar en gringo**, to speak double Dutch.

griñón [gre-nyone'], *m.* 1. A wimple worn by nuns and religious women.

gripe [gree'-pay], *f.* Influenza, flu, grippe.

gris [grees], *m.* 1. Mixture of white and black, grizzle, gray. 2. Miniver, a grizzle-colored squirrel or weasel. 3. *(coll.)* Cold, sharp air or weather.

gris [grees], *a.* Gray, grizzled (día, tiempo). **Gris marengo** (telas), dark gray. **Gris perla**, pearl-gray.

grisa [gree'-sah], *f. (Amer.) V.* CHINCHILLA.

grisáceo [gree-sah'-thay-o], *a.* Grayish.

grisalla [gre-sahl'-lyah], *f.* Grisaille, a style of painting in grayish tints imitating the effect of relief.

grisar [gre-sar'], *va.* To polish the diamond.

griseta [gre-say'-tah], *f.* 1. Kind of flowered silk. 2. *(Neol.)* A French grisette.

grisú [gree-soo'], *m.* A French and Belgian name of firedamp, or methane gas, which in coal mines produces an explosive mixture with atmospheric air.

grita [gree'-tah], *f.* 1. Clamor, outcry, vociferation. 2. Halloo; a word of encouragement to dogs. 3. Exclamations of applause or censure.

gritador, ra [gre-tah-dor', rah], *m. & f.* Clamorer, exclaimer; bawler.

gritar [gre-tar'], *vn.* 1. To exclaim, to cry out, to clamor, to clatter, to halloo, to shout, to hoot. 2. To talk very loud. 3. To bawl. 4. To shriek.

gritería [gre-tay-ree'-ah], *f.* 1. Outcry, clamor, confused noise, shout, exclamation, screaming; hooting. 2. Confused cry of many voices.

grito [gree'-to], *m.* Cry, scream, howling; hoot. **Estar en un grito**, to be in continual pain. **Dar un grito**, to raise an outcry, to set up a shout, a hurrah. **Llorar a gritos**, to weep and wail. Es **el último grito**, it's the very latest.

gritón, na [gre-tone', nah], *a.* Vociferous, clamorous.

gro [gro], *m.* Grosgrain, a twilled silk fabric; a stout silk.

groenlandés, sa [gro-en-lan-days', sah], *a. m. & f.* Greenlander.

gromo [gro'-mo], *m. (Bot.)* Leafy bud, young shoot.

gropos [gro'-pos], *m. pl.* Cotton put in ink-stands or ink-horns.

gros [gros], *m.* Ancient coin of small value.

grosca [gros'-cah], *f.* Kind of venomous serpent.

grosella [gro-sayl'-lyah], *f. (Bot.)* The fruit of the red currant. **Grosella blanca**, white currant, the fruit of a variety of red currant. **Grosella negra**, fruit of the black currant.

grosellero [gro-sel-lyay'-ro], *m. (Bot.)* Currant. **Grosellero rojo or común**, red currant. **Grosellero blanco**, white red currant. **Grosellero negro**, black currant.

groseramente, [gro-say-rah-men'-tay], *adv.* Grossly, coarsely (ordinariamente), rudely (descortésmente), clownishly, in a rude, unmannerly way.

grosería [gro-say-ree'-ah], *f.* 1. Grossness, homeliness, plainness, coarseness (ordinariez), churlishness, clumsiness, clownishness, rudeness, ill-breeding. 2. Grossness, shameless word or action.

grosero, ra [gro-say'-ro, rah], *a.* 1. Gross, coarse (ordinario), rough (maleducado), plain, homely, homespun, not elegant, not fine. 2. Gross, thick, fat, bulky. 3. Gross, rude, unpolished, churlish, clownish, uncivil, rough, brutal. 4. Gross, indelicate (indecente), indecent, smutty.

grosísimo, ma [gro-see'-se-mo, mah], superlative of GRUESO.

groso [gro'-so], *a.* Coarse snuff, badly powdered.

grosor [gro-sor'], *m.* Thickness, density, closeness, compactness.

grosularina, or **grosulina** [gro-soo-lah-ree'-nah, gro-soo-lee'-nah], *f. (Chem.)* Grossaline, a vegetable jelly found in acid fruits.

grosura [gro-soo'-rah], *f.* 1. Suet, tallow, fat of animals. 2. Extremities, heart, liver, and lungs of an animal.

grotesco, ca [gro-tes'-co, cah], *a.* Grotesque, laughable.

grúa [groo'-ah], *f.* 1. Crane, a machine for raising heavy weights. 2. An ancient military machine. 3. *(Naut.)* Bend of a curved piece of timber. 4. Hoist, derrick, **Grúa corredera**, traveling crane. **Grúa de torre**, tower crane.

grueras [groo-ay'-ras], *f. pl. (Naut.)* Rope holes.

gruero, ra [groo-ay'-ro, rah], *a.* Belonging to birds of prey, trained to pursue cranes.

gruesa [groo-ay'-sah], *f.* 1. Gross, twelve dozen. 2. Chief part of a prebend. 3. Bottomry.

gruesamente [groo-ay-sah-men-tay], *adv.* Grossly, coarsely by wholesale.

grueso, sa [groo-ay'-so, sah], *a.* 1. Bulky (voluminoso), corpulent, thick (espeso), fleshy, fat, fullfed, plump, gross. 2. Large, great, big (grande, pesado). 3. Coarse, plain, homespun, not fine. 4. Dense, compact. 5. *(Met.)* Heavy, dull, stupid, dim, not quick in any of the senses.

grueso [groo-ay'-so], *m.* 1. Corpulence, bulkiness of body (tamaño). 2. Thickness (calidad), density, space taken up by matter interposed. 3. Gross, the main body, the bulk, the chief part (parte principal). 4. Size body of type.

gruir [groo-eer'], *vn.* To crank or crankle: to cry like a crane.

grujidor [groo-he-dor'], *m.* Steel instrument used by glaziers for rounding glass.

grujir [groo-heer'], *va.* To chip away angles and inequalities of glass with a *grujidor*.

grulla [grool'-lyah], *f.* 1. *(Orn.)* Crane. 2. Crane, the name of a southern constellation.

grullada [grool-lyah'-dah], *f. (coll.)* 1. Crowd of people going together to any place. 2. Crowd of constables or police officers.

grullero, ra [grool-lyay'-ro, rah], *a.* Applied to falcons or birds of prey in chase of cranes.

grumete [groo-may'-tay], *m. (Naut.)* Younker, ship's boy.

grumillo [groo-meel'-lyo], *m. dim.* A small grume, clot, or curd.

grumo [groo'-mo], *m.* 1. Grume, a thick viscid consistence in a fluid; a clot (coágulo). **Grumo de leche**, curd. 2. Cluster, bunch (de uvas) 3. Heart or pith of trees. **Grumos**, pinions, the joints of the wings remotest from the body.

grumoso, sa [groo-mo'-so, sah], *a.* Grumy, grumous, clotty; full of grumes.

gruñido [groo-nyee'-do], *m.* 1. Grunt, the noise of a hog. 2. Growl, maundering, the murmur of a discontented person. **Gruñido, da**, *pp.* of GRUÑIR.

gruñidor, ra [groo-nye-dor', rah], *m. & f.* Grunter, grumbler, murmurer, mutterer.

gruñimiento [groo-nye-me-en'-to], *m.* Grunting, murmuring, grumbling.

gruñir [groo-nyeer'], *vn.* 1. To grunt like a hog. 2. To creak (puerta) 3. *(Met.)* To grumble, to growl, to snarl.

gruñón, na [groo-nyone', nah], *m. & f. (coll.) V.* GRUÑIDOR.

grupa [groo'-pah], *f.* 1. Croup, the buttocks of a horse. 2. A cavalry call to saddle the horses. **Cargar la grupa**, to pass the tail of a horse through the crupper.

grupada [groo-pah'-dah], *f.* 1. Squall or gust of wind. 2. Croupade, leap of a horse.

grupera [groo-pay'-rah], *f.* 1. Cushion at the back of a saddle for carrying a satchel, etc (de caballo). 2. Crupper, a looped strap for a horse's tail. 3. *V.* RETRANCA.

grupo [groo'-po], *m.* 1. Group, assemblage. 2. Clump of sprigs growing out of the same root. 3. Cluster (árboles) **Reunirse en grupos**, to gather in groups. **Grupo de trabajo**, working party.

gruta [groo'-tah], *f.* Cavern, cavity between rocks; a grotto, a grot. **Gruta de fieras**, menagerie. **Grutas**, crypts, vaults, subterranean edifices.

grutesco [groo-tes'-co], *m.* Grotesque, a kind of ornament in painting, composed of leaves, shells, etc.

gruyere [groo-yerr'], *m.* A kind of rich cheese, made at Gruyere in France.

¡gúa! [goo'-ah]. Interjection of surprise and depreciation used in Peru and Bolivia. Come now!

guaba [goo-ah'-bah], *f.* Abbreviated form of *guayaba*.

guaca [goo-ah'-cah], *f.* A grave mound of the ancient Peruvians (tumba).

guacal [goo-ah-cahl'], *m. (Mex.)* An oblong hamper for carrying fruit (cajón).

guacamayo [goo-ah-cah-mah'-yo], *m. (Orn.)* Macao or macaw.

guacamole [goo-ah-cah-mo'-lay], *m. (Cuba)* Salad of alligator pear.

guachapear [goo-ah-chah-pay-ar'], *va.* To daddle, to play with the feet in water (agua). *-vn.* To clap, as horses' shoes when loose; to clatter.

guachapelí [goo-ah'-chah-pay-lee'], *m.* Solid strong wood, which grows in Guayaquil, used for ships.

guácharo, ra [goo-ah'-chah-ro, rah], *a.* 1. Sickly, not in health. 2. Dropsical, diseased with dropsy.

guachí [goo-ah-chee'], or **guají** [goo-a-hee'], *m. (Mex.)* Fool, dolt, simpleton.

guachinango, ga [goo-ah-che-nahn'-go, gah], *m. & f.* A name given by the inhabitants of Cuba to the natives of Mexico, and in Vera Cruz to those of the interior (persona astuta).

guacho, cha [goo-ah'-cho, chah], *a. (W. S. Amer.)* 1. Orphan (huérfano), foundling. 2. Solitary, forlorn.*-m.* Birdling of a sparrow. *(Acad.)*

guacia [goo-ah'-the-ah], *f.* 1. *V.* ACACIA. 2. Gumarabic.

guaco [goo-ah'-co], *m. (Amer.)* A plant of South America, eminent as an antidote for the bite of venomous snakes.

guadafiones [goo-ah-dah-fe-o'-nes], *m. pl.* Fetters with which the legs of horses are shackled.

guadamacil [goo-ah-dah-mah-theel'], *m.* Printed leather, gilt and adorned with figures.

guadamacilería [goo-ah-dah-mah-the-lay-ree'-ah], *f.* Manufactory of glit or printed leather.

guadamacilero [goo-ah-dah-mah-the-lay'-ro], *m.* Manufacturer of printed leather.

guadaña [goo-ah-dah'-nyah], *f.* 1. Scythe for mowing. 2. *(Met.)* Death, as depicted with a scythe. 3. A knife used by manufacturers of leather wine-bags.

guadañadora [goo-ah-dah-nyah-do'-rah], *f.* Mowing machine.

guadañar [goo-ah-dah-nyar'], or **guadañear**, *va. (Prov.)* To mow, to cut grass.

guadañero [goo-ah-dah-nyeel'], *m.* 1. Mower, one who cuts grass. 2. The owner or manager of a *guadaño*.

guadañil [goo-ah-dah-nyeel'], *m.* Mower who cuts down hay; haymaker.

guadaño [goo-ah-dah'-nyo], *m.* 1. A small boat with an awning used in the traffic of the port of Havana. 2. Name given at Cadiz and other sea-ports to transport vessels.

guadañón [goo-ah-dah-nyone'], *m.* Mower. *V.* GUADAÑERO.

guadapero [goo-ah-dah-pay'-ro], *m.* 1. *(Bot.)* Wild common pear. 2. A boy who carries victuals to reapers or mowers.

guadarn's [goo-ah-dar-nays'], *m.* 1. Harness-room, a place where harness is kept. 2. Harness keeper, an officer of the king's mews.

guadijeño [goo-ah-de-hay'-nyo], *m.* Poniard, stiletto, knife. - *a.* Belonging to Guadix.

guadramaña [goo-ah-drah-mah'-nyah], *f.* Trick, deceit, imposition.

guadua [goo-ah'-doo-ah], *f.* Gadua bamboo-cane of Ecuador and Colombia. **guadual** [goo-ah-doo-ahl'], *m* Plantation of large reeds.

guagua [goo-ah'-goo-ah]. 1. *f.* Nursing baby. *(In Ecuad.)* Both *f.* and *m.* 2. *(Cuba)* A kind of insect. 3. *(Cuba)* A kind of bus. 4. **(De)** *adv.* Free, for nothing (gratis).

guainambí [goo-ah-e-nam-bee'], *m. (Medic. C. A.)* A humming-bird.

guaira [go-ah'-e-rah], *f. (S. Amer.)* 1. A triangular sail. 2. A tall furnace which the Peruvians used in smelting metals.

guairo [goo-ah'-e-ro], *m. (Ecu.)* 1. One of the seven faces of a dice used by the Indians. 2. A small two-masted craft with sails called *guairas. V. supra.*

guajalote, or **guajolote** [goo-ah-hah-lo'-tay], *m. (Mex.)* Turkey.

guajamón, na [goo-ah-hah-mone', nah], *a. (Cuba)* Orange-colored, speaking of horses.

guájaras [goo-ah'-hah-ras], *f. pl.* Fastnesses, the roughest part of a range of mountains.

guaje [goo-ah'-hay], *m. (Mex.)* A calabash which serves for learning to swim. In Peru, called *mate*; in Cuba, *güiro*.

guajiro, ra [goo-ah-hee'-ro, rah], *a. (Cuba)* 1. Rustic, rural. 2. Rustic, rude, boorish.

gualá! [goo-ah-lah'], *int.* Assuredly.

gualatina [goo-ah-lah-tee'-nah], *f.* Dish made of boiled apples, milk of almonds and broth, and beaten up with spice and rose water.

gualda [goo-ahl'-dah], *f. (Bot.)* Weld, wild woad, dye's weed, reseda, a plant which dyer's yellow.

gualdado, da [goo-al-dah'-do, dah], *a.* Weld-colored, yellowish.

gualderas [goo-al-day'-ras], *f. pl.* The sides, cheeks or brackets of a gun-carriage. **Gualderas de las garlingas**, *(Naut.)* checks of the mast-steps.

gualdo, da [goo-ahl'-do, dah], *a.* Weld, yellow or gold color.

gualdón [goo-al-done'], *m. (Bot.)* Base rocket, reseda.

gualdrapa [goo-al-drah'-pah], *f.* 1. Horse-cloth, housing, foot-cloth. 2. Tatter rag hanging from clothes.

gualdrapazo [goo-al-drah-pah'-tho], *m. (Naut.)* Flap of the sails against the masts.

gualdrapear [goo-al-drah-pay-ar'], *va.* To put one thing upon another.*-vn. (Naut.)* To flap against the masts (vela).

gualdrapeo [goo-al-drah-pay'-o], *m.* Flapping of the sails.

gualdrapero [goo-al-drah-pay'-ro], *m.* Ragamuffin, a ragged fellow.

gualdrín [goo-al-dreen'], *m.* Weather-strip.

gualputra [goo-al-poo'-trah], *f. (Amer.)* Name given to the creeping clover.

guama [goo-ah'-mah], *f.* Fruit of the *guamo*.

guamo [goo-ah'-mo], *m.* A tall, branching tree of narrow leaves, planted to shade the coffee-tree.

guambra [goo-ahm'-brah], *f. (S. Amer.)* A child-servant.

guanábana [goo-ah-nah'-ba-nah], *f.* 1. Fruit of the *guanábana* tree, very sweet and white. 2. A beverage common in Havana made from same.

guanábano [goo-ah-nah'-ba-no], *m.* A fruit-tree of America, a variety of chirimoya.

guanaco [goo-ah-nah'-co], *m. (Zool.)* Guanaco, S. American mammal related to the llama.

guanajo [goo-ah-nah'-ho], *m. (Cuba)* A turkey.

guano [goo-ah'-no], *m.* 1. Kind of American palm tree (árbol). 2. Guano, sea birds' dung, an excellent fertilizing material from the Peruvian Islands.

guantada [goo-an-tah'-dah], *f.* Slap or blow with the palm or inner part of the hand.

guante [goo-ahn'-tay], *m.* 1. Glove, a cover of the hands. **Guantes de ante**, buff gloves. **Guante de goma**, rubber glove. **Se ajusta como un guante**, it fits like a glove. 2. Gauntlet, an iron glove used for defence, and thrown down in challenges. 3. Familiarly, the hand. **Echar el guante**, *(coll.)* to catch or lay hold on with the hand. **Echar el guante a otro**, to grasp, to seize, to imprison. **Echar** or **arrojar el guante**, to challenge or to send a challenge.

guantelete [goo-an-tay-lay'-tay], *m.* 1. Gauntlet. 2. A bandage for the hand.

guantera [goo-ahn-tay-rah], *f. (Aut.)* Glove compartment.

guantería [goo-an-tay-ree'-ah], *f.* A glover's shop and the art of a glover (tienda, fabricación); glove factory (fábrica).

guantero [goo-an-tay'-ro], *m.* Glover, one who makes gloves.

guañín [goo-ah-nyeen'], *a.* Applied to gold under legal standard.

guao [goo-ah'-o], *m.* A tree of the island of Santo Domingo whose smell is fatal.

guapamente [goo-ah-pah-men'-tay], *adv. (coll.)* Bravely, courageously.

guapear [goo-ah-pay-ar'], *vn. (coll.)* 1. To boast of courage (fanfarronear). 2. To take pride in fine dress (ostentarse).

guaperas [goo-ah-pay'-ras], *a.* Excessively good-looking. - *m.* Excessively good-looking youth.

guapeza [goo-ah-pay'-thah], *f. (coll.)* 1. Bravery, courage. 2. Ostentation in dress (ostentación). 3. Good looks (atractivo). 4. Smartness (elegancia), elegance.

guapinal [goo-ah-pe-nahl'], *m.* A resin-yielding tree of Central America.

guapo, pa [goo-ah'-po, pah], *a. (coll.)* 1. Stout, courageous, valiant, bold (valiente), enterprising, good, clever. 2. Spruce, neat, elegant (elegante), ostentatious, vain. 3. Gay, sprightly, fond of courting women. 4. Good-looking, handsome (hombre). **Va de guapo por la vida**, he goes through life with every confidence in his good looks. **¡Hombre, qué guapo estás!**, how smart you're looking!

guaquero [goo-ah-key'-ro], *m.* Earthenware. Vessel for drinking *chicha* found in ancient Peruvian tombs.

guaracha [goo-ah-rah'-chah], *f.* 1. A kind of dance (baile). 2. *(Mex.)* A sandal (alboroto).

guarana [goo-ah-rah'-nah], *f. (Bot.)* Paullinia; and the agreeable drink made in Brazil from its seeds.

guarango [go-ah-rahn'-go], *m.* A shrub used for dyeing; a species of prosopis. (Ecuador.)

guarapo [goo-ah-rah'-po], *m.* Sub-acid drink made in sugar-mills with the fermented cane-liquor. *(Cuba)* **Menear el guarapo**, to chastise.

guarda [goo-ar'-dah], *com.* Guard (persona), keeper (cuidador); anything that preserves others from injury. *-f.* 1. Custody, wardship, guard, keeping (acto). 2. Observance of a law or ordinance. 3. Nun who accompanies men through convents. 4. Each of the outside ribs or guards of a fan. 5. Sheet of paper placed at the beginning and end of volumes to guard the printed sheets in binding. 6. The ward of a lock or of a key. **Guarda de la aduana**, an officer of the custom-house. **Guardacosta**, *(Naut.)* custom-house cutter, a vessel employed to clear the coast of smugglers. **Guarda de coto**, gamekeeper. **Guardafuego**, 1. Screen for a chimney-fire. 2. Fender. **Guardajoyas**, place where jewels or other precious things are kept. **Guardamayor**, chief-guard. **Guarda jurado**, security guard. **Guarda nocturno**, night watchman.

¡guarda! [goo-ar'-dah], *int.* Take care! beware!

guardaaguja [goo-ar-dah-ah-goo'-hah], *m.* A railway switchman.

guardaalmacén [goo-ar-dah-ahl-mah-then'], *m.* Storekeeper.

guardabosque [goo-ar-dah-bos'-kay], *m.* Keeper of a forest, gamekeeper.

guardabrazo [goo-ar-dah-brah'-tho], *m.* A part of the armor to defend the arm.

guardabrisa [goo-ar-dah-bree'-sah], *m.* Windshield.

guardacabras [goo-ar-dah-cah'-bras], *m.* Goatherd.

guardacantón [goo-ar-dah-can-tone'], *m.* A spur-stone, a check-stone.

guardacostas [goo-ar-dah-cos'-tahs], *m.* Coast-defense ship

guardadamente [goo-ar-dah-dah-men'-tay], *adv.* Guardedly.

guardador, ra [goo-ar-dah-dor', rah], *m. & f.* 1. A very careful, watchful, and provident man, one who keeps his property with great care, protective (protector). 2. Keeper. 3. One who observes a law. 4. Miser. 5. Mean, stingy.

guardaespaldas [goo-ar-dah-ays-pahl'-das], *m.* Bodyguard.

guardafango [goo-ar-dah-fahn'-go], *m.* Fender (vehículo).

guardafrenos [goo-ar-dah-fray'-nos], *m.* A brakeman.

guardafuego [goo-ar-dah-foo-ay'-go], *(Naut.)* Breaming board.

guardainfante [goo-ar-dah-in-fahn'-tay], *m.* Farthingale, ladies' hoop.

guardaja [goo-ar-dah'-hah], *f.* V. GUEDEJA.

guardalado [goo-ar-dah-lah'-do], *m.* Battlement of a bridge.

guardamangel [goo-ar-dah-man-hel'], *m.* Pantry, buttery.

guardamano [goo-ar-dah-mah'-no], *f.* Guard of a sword.

guardamateriales [goo-ar-dah-mah-tay-re-ah'-les], *m.* Person appointed to purchase bullion and other necessaries for a mint.

guardameta [goo-ar-dah-may'-tah], *m.* Goalkeeper, goalie.

guardamonte [goo-ar-dah-mon'-tay], *m.* 1. Guard of a gunlock, sword, etc. 2. Forester, keeper of a forest.

guardamozo, or **guardamancebo** [goo-ar-dah-mo'-tho, goo-ar-dah-man-thay'-bo], *m. (Naut.)* Man-rope, entering rope.

guardamuebles [goo-ar-dah-moo-ay'-blays], *m.* 1. Store-room for furniture in great houses. 2. Guard over the furniture of a palace.

guardamujer [goo-ar-dah-moo-herr'], *f.* Servant of the queen, next to the ladies of honor.

guardapapo [goo-ar-dah-pah'-po], *m.* Ancient piece of armor for the face.

guardapelo [goo-ar-dah-pay'-lo], *m.* A locket.

guardapiés [goo-ar-dah-pe-ays'], *m.* 1. A petticoat commonly used under the upper garment. 2. *V.* BRIAL.

guardapolvo [goo-ar-dah-pol'-vo], *m.* 1. A piece of cloth or leather to guard against dust (ropa). 2. The inner lid of a watch (reloj). 3. The dust-guard of a carriage or railway car (cubierta).

guardapuerta [goo-ar-dah-poo-err'-tah], *f.* Storm door (puerta), door curtain (cortina).

guardar [goo-ar-dar'], *va.* 1. To keep, to preserve in a state of security (preservar), to keep from, to look to, to guard (cuidar), to protect. 2. To keep, to take care of, to watch (proteger), to guard, to preserve from damage. 3. To lay up, to store, to deposit for future use. 4. To lay by, to reserve for some future time, to conserve, to keep back, to maintain. 5. To keep, to hold for another. 6. To observe, to respect (mandamiento) 7. To fulfil one's duty. 8. To be on one's guard, to avoid (evitar), to abstain from, to guard against, to fence. **Guardársela a alguno**, to delay vengeance for a favorable opportunity. **Lo guardó en el bolsillo**, he put it away in his pocket. **Guardo los mejores recuerdos**, I have the nicest memories. *-vr.* 1. To be on one's guard (precaverse). 2. **Guardarse de algo**, to avoid something (evitar); to look out for something (cuidarse); to refrain from something (abstenerse); to protect oneself against something. **Guárdate de no ofenderle**, take care not to upset him.

guardarraya [goo-ar-dar-rah'-yah], *f. (Cuba)* 1. An avenue of trees or shrubs upon a plantation of sugar-cane or coffee. 2. Boundary which marks the end of a drill-hole in mines, after it has been measured.

guardarrío [goo-ar-dah-ree'-o], *m. (Orn.)* Kingfisher.

guardarropa [goo-ar-dar-ro'-pah], *f.* Wardroom, checkroom (habitación). *-m.* Checkroom attendant, wardrobe (ropero).

guardarruedas [goo-ar-dar-roo-ay'-das], *m. V.* GUARDACANTÓN.

guardasol [goo-ar-dah-sol'], *m. V.* QUITASOL.

guardavajilla [goo-ar-day-vah-heel'-yah], *f.* A room for keeping the (royal) plate or table-service.

guardaventana [goo-ar-dah-ven-tah'-nah], *f.* Storm window.

guardería [goo-ar-day-ree'-ah], *f.* 1. Occupation of a guard. 2. Day nursery.

guardia [goo-ar'-de-ah], *f.* 1. Guard, a body of soldiers or armed men to watch by way of defence (defensa). **Cuerpo de guardia**, guard-room. 2. *(Naut.)* Watch. *(Mil.)* **Estar de guardia**, to be on duty. **Montar la guardia**, to mount guard. **Salir de guardia**, to come off guard. *-m & f.* 1. Soldier belonging to the guards. **Guardia marina**, midshipman. **Guardia de circulacion**, traffic policeman. **Guardia forestal**, game warden.

guardián, na [goo-ar-de-ahn', nah], *m. & f.* 1. Keeper, one who has charge of something, caretaker (edificio). 2. Guardian, watchman. *-m.* 1. The local superior of convents (franciscanos). 2. *(Naut.)* Keeper of the arms and storeroom. **Guardián de parque**, park keeper. **Guardián de prisiones**, warder.

guardianía [goo-ar-de-ah-nee'-ah], *f.* Guardianship.

guardilla [goo-ar-deel'-lya], *f.* 1. Garret, skylight. 2. With seamstresses, ornament and guard of a seam.

guardín de la caña [goo-ar-deen' day lah cah'-nyah], *m* *(Naut.)* Tiller-rope.

guardoso, sa [goo-ar-do'-so, sah], *a.* 1. Frugal, parsimonious. 2. Mean, stingy.

guare [goo-ah'-ray], *m. (Ec.)* Raft made of great rushes, with a square sail.

guarecer [goo-ah-ray-therr'], *va.* 1. To aid, to succour, to assist. 2. To guard, to preserve; to cure. *-vr.* To take refuge, to escape from danger.

guarentigio, gia [goo-ah-ren-tee'-he-o, ah], *a. (Law.)* Applied to a contract, writing, or clause, which empowers the justices to cause it to be executed.

guarida [goo-ah-ree'-dah], *f.* 1. Den, the cave or couch of a wild beast. 2. Haunt, the place where one is frequently found (de persona). 3. Protection, aid, shelter, a lurking-place, a cover.

guarín [goo-ah-reen'], *m.* Young pig, last born of a litter.

guarir [goo-ah-reer'], *va. & vn.* To subsist.

guarismo [goo-ah-rees'-mo], *m.* Figure, cipher, an arithmetical character.

guarismo, ma [goo-ah-rees'-mo, mah], *a.* Arithmetical.

guarne [goo-ar'-nay], *m. (Naut.)* Each turn of a cable or tackle.

guarnecedor [goo-ar-nay-thay-dor'], *m.* 1. Hatter who cocks hats. 2. One who garnishes or surrounds a thing with ornamental appendages.

guarnecer, guarnescer [goo-ar-nay-therr'], *va.* 1. To garnish, to surround with ornamental appendages. 2. To set a diamond or stone in gold, silver, etc. 3. To trim, to adorn (adornar). 4. To harness horses or mules. 5. To garrison a town or other place. 6. To line (frenos), to plaster (pared). (*Yo guarnezco, yo guarnezca*, from *Guarnecer.* V. CONOCER.)

guarnés [goo-ar-ness'], **m.** Harness-room (para arneses). V. GUADARNÉS.

guarnición [goo-ar-ne-the-on'], *f.* 1. Flounce, furbelow, trimming. 2. Setting of anything in gold or silver (joyas). 3. Guard of a sword (espada). 4. Garrison, a body of soldiers in a fortified town to defend it. 5. Garniture, garnish, any ornamental hem, lace or border. 6. Marines, naval troops. 7. **Guarnición de la bomba,** *(Naut.)* the upper or spear-box of a pump. *-pl.* 1. Ancient steel armor of defence. 2. Gears or traces of mules and horses; harness (de caballo). 3. Gear (equipo): fittings (de casa). **Guarniciones de alumbrado,** light fittings.

guarnicionería [goo-ar-ne-the-o-nay-ree'-ah], *f.* Shop of a harness-maker.

guarnicionero [goo-ar-ne-the-o-nay'-ro], *m.* Harness-maker.

guarniel [goo-ar-ne-el'], *m.* 1. Leather purse used by carriers, with divisions for paper, money, and other things. 2. *(Mex.)* A powder-flask.

guarnir [goo-ar-neer'], *va.* To reeve, to pass a rope through the eyes of blocks, to form a tackle. **Guarnir el cabrestante,** to rig the capstan.

guaro [goo-ah'-ro], *m.* A small, very talkative parrot. *(Acad.)*

guarra [goo-ar'-rah], *f.* A sow.

guarrada [goo-ahr-rah'-dah], *f.* Dirty trick (trampa); rotten thing (dicho); indecent act (indecencia), vulgar thing.

guarrillo [goo-ar-reel'-lyo], *m. dim.* A small pig.

guarro [goo-ar'-ro], *m.* Hog, pig, whether large or small, dirty person. *-a.* Dirty, filthy.

guaruba [goo-ah-roo'-bah], *f.* 1. An American parrot with a red neck. 2. A howling ape.

guasa [goo-ah'-sah], *f. (coll.)* 1. Jest, satire, irony, joke (broma). 2. Insipidity, dullness (sosería).

guasanga [goo-ah-sahn'-gah], *(Cuba)* Noisy mirth.

guasanguero, ra [goo-ah-san'-gay-ro, rah], *a. (Cuba)* Jolly, merry, noisy.

guasca [goo-ahs'-cah], *f. (Peru)* Cord, thong, whip (látigo). **Dar guasca,** to whip, to scourge.

guaso [goo-ah'-so], *m.* 1. V. GAUCHO. 2. Lasso.

guasón, na [goo-ah-sone', nah], *a. (Coll. Andal.)* Jocose, witty (gracioso), satirical, joking (burlón). **Dijo burlón,** he said jokingly.

guasquear [goo-as-kay-ar'], *va. (Amer.)* To whip (azotar), to scourge.

guata [goo-ah'-tah], *f.* Raw cotton (algodón); padding (relleno); twine, cord.

guataca [goo-ah-tah'-cah], *f. (Cuba)* 1. Spade. 2. Applied ironically to a large ear.

guataquear [goo-ah-tah-kay-ar'], *va. (Cuba)* To spade, to clear sowed ground with the spade.

guatemalteco, ca [goo-ah-tay-mal-tay'-co, cah], *a.* Guatemalan, of Guatemala.

guateque [goo-ah-tay'-kay], *m.* Party, celebration, binge.

guatuse [goo-ah-too'-say], *m.* A Nicaraguan animal with reddish-brown fur.

¡guay! [goo-ah'-e], *int.* Oh! an exclamation of pain or grief. V. AY. **Tener muchos guayes,** to labor under many afflictions.

guaya [goo-ah'-yah], *f.* Grief, sorrow, affliction.

guayaba [goo-ah-yah'-bah], *f.* Fruit of the guava tree. **Guayaba blanca,** white guava. **Guayaba roja,** red guava.

guayabal [goo-ah-yah-bahl'], *m.* An orchard of guava trees.

guayabo [goo-ah-yah'-bo], *m. (Bot.).* Guava-tree.

guayacán [goo-ah-yah-cahn'], *m. (Bot.)* V. GUAYACO.

guayacana [goo-ah-yah-cah'-nah], *f. (Bot.)* Dateplum.

guayaco [goo-ah-yah'-co], *m. (Bot.)* Lignumvitae tree, guaiacum. **Guayaco oficinal,** officinal guaiacum, or lignumvitae tree.

guayapil, guayapín [goo-ah-yah-peel', goo-ah-yah-peen'], *m.* A loose Indian dress for women.

guayusa [goo-ah-yoo'-sah], *f.* A tall shrub of the Napo River, Ecuador; an ilex. The leaves are used for tea.

gubán [goo-bahn'], *m.* Kind of large boat used in the Philippines. It is made without nails, clinker-built, rowed rapidly and easily taken on land.

gubernamental [goo-ber-nah-men-tahl'], *a.* Gubernamental; loyalist (de facción), -m & f. Loyalist, government supporter; government soldier.

gubernativo, va [goo-ber-nah-tee'-vo, vah], *a.* Administrative, relating to government; gubernative.

gubia [goo'-be-ah], *f.* Gouge, a round hollow chisel.

gubiadura [goo-be-ah-doo'-rah], *f. (Naut.)* Notch, channel.

gubilete [goo-be-lay'-tay], *m. (Prove.)* Kind of vase. V. CUBILETE.

guedeja [gay-day'-hah], *f.* 1. Lock of hair falling on the temple, forelock. 2. Lion's mane.

guedejilla [gay-day-heel'-lyah], *f. dim.* A small lock of hair.

guedejón, na, guedejoso, sa [gay-day-hone', nah], *a.* V. GUEDEJUDO.

guedejudo, da [gay-day-hoo'-do, dah], *a.* Bushy, clotted (pelo).

guelde [gayl'-day], *m. (Bot.)* Water-elder, guelder-rose, viburnum.

güelfo, fa [goo-el'-fo, fah], *a.* Guelph, partisan of the popes, and opponents of the Ghibellines.

gueltre [gayl'-tray], *m.* A cant word for money or cash.

güembé [goo-em-bay'], *m.* Manila-hemp. V. ABACÁ.

guerindola [gay-rin-do'-lah], *f.* V. GUIRINDOLA.

güermeces [goo-ayr'-may-thes], *m.* A morbid swelling in the throat of hawks, and other birds of prey.

güero, ra [goo-ay'-roh, rah], *a. & m. & f. (Men.)* Blond, blonde (pelo).

guerra [gayr'-rah], *f.* 1. War. 2. Art of war, military science. 3. War, profession of arms. 4. War, hostility, conflict of passions. **Guerra fría,** cold war. **Estado de guerra,** state of war. **Hacer guerra,** to wage war. **Guerra mundial,** world war. **Guerra nuclear,** nuclear war. **Guerra química,** chemical warfare. **Guerra de guerrillas,** guerilla warfare. **Dar guerra,** to be troublesome, to annoy (niño). **Guerra de la Independencia,** War of independence. **Segunda Guerra Mundial,** Second World War.

guerreador, ra [gayr-ray-ah-dor', rah], *m. & f.* Warrior, one passionately fond of military fame.

guerreante [gayr-ray-ahn'-tay], *pa. & m. & f.* Warrior, warring.

guerrear [gayr-ray-ar'], *va. 1.* To war, to wage war, to fight. 2. To oppose, to be in a state of hostility.

guerrera [gayr-ray'-rah], *f.* Military jacket.

guerreramente [gayr-ray-rah-men'-tay], *adv.* Warlikely.

guerrero [gayr-ray'-ro], *m. 1.* Warrior. *V.* GUERREADOR. 2. A soldier, a military man.

guerrero, ra [gayr-ray'-ro, rah], *a. 1.* Martial, warlike (carácter). 2. Warring (contrario). 3. Fighting (belicoso).

guerrilla [gayr-reel'-lyah], *f. dim. 1.* Band of guerrillas (grupo). **Guerra de guerrillas**, guerrilla warfare. 2. Game of cards between two persons, each with twenty cards.

guerrillear [gayr-reel-lyay-ar'], *vn.* To take part in guerrilla warfare.

guerrillero, ra [gayr-reel-lay'-ro], *m & f. 1.* The commander of a skirmish force. 2. A civilian who serves in guerilla warfare.

guía [gee'-a], *m. & f. 1.* Guide, one who directs another in his way (persona). 2. Guide, conductor, leader, director, regulator, one who directs another in his conduct. *-f. 3.* Permit, docket; a writing or letter of safe conduct, proving that the customs and duty are paid at the custom house. 4. A young shoot or sucker of a vine. 5. A certain timber in the water-wheels called norias. 6. An instrument of jewellers for guiding drills. 7. *(Naut.)* Guy, a small rope, to keep weighty things in their places. 8. Earth which indicates the vein of a mine. 9. Guard of a fan. 10. *m.* Sergeant or corporal who attends to dressing the line. 11. Guidance, guiding (acto). **Para que te sirva de guía**, for your guidance. 12. Guide book; hand book (manual). **Guía oficial de ferrocarriles**, official railway guide. **Guía telefónica**, telephone directory, *-pl. 1.* Trains of powder in rockets or fireworks. 2. Horses or mules which go before flee wheel horses or mules; leaders. 3. Guide-lines, reins for controlling the leader horses.

guiadera [gee-ah-day'-rah], *f.* Guide or conductor in mills. **Guiaderas**, two upright pieces of wood in oilmills.

guiado, da [gee-ah'-do, dah], *a. & pp.* of GUIAR. Guided.

guiador, ra [gee-ah'-dor, dah], *a. & m. & f.* Guide, director.

guiamiento [gee-ah-meen'-to], *m.* Guidance, the act of guiding, security.

guiar [gee-ar'], *va. 1.* To guide, to conduct, to show the way. 2. To govern by counsel, to lead (dirigir), to teach, to direct, to manage (controlar). 3. To lead a dance. *-vr.* **Guiarse por**, to be guided by.

guija [gee'-hah], *f. 1.* Pebble (piedra), pebble-stone, cobble (camino), coarse gravel. 2. *(Bot.) V.* ALMORTA.*-pl. (coll.)* Strength, force, vigor.

guijarral [gee-har-rahl'], *m.* Heap of pebble-stones, a place abounding in pebbles.

guijarrazo [gee-har-rah'-tho], *m.* Blow with a pebble-stone.

guijarreño, ña [gee-har-ray'-nyo, nyah], *a 1.* Pebbly, gravelly, 2. Hardy, strong and rude.

guijarro [gee-hahr'-ro], *m.* Pebble; cobble (camino), cobblestone.

guijarrillo, ito [gee-har-reel'-lyo, ee'-to], *m. dim.* A small pebble.

guijarro [gee-har'-ro], *m.* Pebble or smooth stone, cobblestone.

guijarroso, sa [gee-har-roso, sah], *a.* Pebbly.

guijeño, ña [gee-hay'-nyo, nyah], *a. 1.* Full of pebbles or coarse gravel. 2. Hard, sour, difficult.

guijo [gee'-ho], *m.* Small pebbles or gravel for roads (grava).

guijón [gee'-hone'], *m. V.* NEGUIJóN.

guijoso, sa [gee-ho'-so, sah], *a. 1.* Gravelly, 2. *V.* GUIJEñO.

guilalo [gee-lah'-lo], *m.* A Philippine bark, intended for the postal service.

guilla [geel'-lyah]. *f.* A plentiful harvest.

guillame [geel-lyah'-may], *m.* Rabbet plane, a carpenter's tool.

guilledín [geel-lyay-deen'], *m.* Gelding.

guillemote [geel-lyay-mo'-tay], *m. (Zool.)* A puffin.

guillote [geel-lyo'-tay], *m. 1.* Husbandman who enjoys the produce of a farm. 2. Tree-nail or iron pin. 3. Vagrant, sponger, an idle fellow, 4. *(coll.)* A simpleton.

guillotina [geel-lyo-tee'-nah], *f.* Guillotine, a machine for decapitating.

guillotinar [geel-lyo-te-nar'], *va.* To guillotine.

guimbalete [geem-bah-lay'-tay], *m. (Naut.)* Brake or handle of a pump.

guimbarda [geem-bar'-dah], *f. 1.* An ancient dance. 2. A plane like a rabbet plane. 3. A jew's harp.

guinchar [geen-char'], *a.* To prick; to stimulate.

guincho [geen'-cho], *m. 1.* Goad, pike. 2. *(Cuba)* Seagull.

guinda [geen'-dah], *f. 1.* Cherry (fruta). 2. Height of the masts and topmasts. **guindado, da** [geen-dah'-do, dah], *a.* Hoisted, set up.

guindajos [geen-dah'-hos], *m. pl.* Fringe or small tassels for ornament.

guindal [geen-dahl'], *m. (Bot.)* Cherry-tree. *V.* GUINDO.

guindalera [geen-dah-lay'-rah], *f.* Cherry orchard, a plantation of cherry-trees.

guindaleta [geen-dah-lay'-tah], *f. 1.* Crank-rope a rope, used to raise materials to the top of a building. 2. Fulcrum of a balance.

guindaleza [geen-dah-lay'-thah], *f. (Naut.)* Hawser.

guindamaina [geen-dah-mah'-e-nah], *f. (Naut.)* Salute between ships or squadrons.

guindar [geen-dar'], *va. 1.* To lift, to elevate, to raise, to hoist. 2. To procure in concurrence with others. 3. *(coll.)* To hang. *V.* AHORCAR.*-vr.* To be suspended, to hang by or on something.

guindastes [geen-dahs'-tes], *m. pl. (Naut.)* Gears or jeers, an assemblage of tackles.

guindilla [geen-deel'-lyah], *f. 1.* Small kind of red pepper. 2. *(Dim.)* A small cherry.

guindillo [geen-deel'-lyo], *m.* Indian cherry-tree.

guindo [geen'-do], *m. (Bot.)* Cherry-tree. **Guindo griego**, large cherry-tree.

guindola [geen'-do-lah], *f. (Naut.)* A triangular hanging stage.

guinea [gee-nay'-ah], *f.* Guinea, an English gold coin (moneda). **Cochino de Guinea**, Guinea pig.

guineo [gee-nay'-o], *m.* Dance used amongst negroes. **Plátano guineo**, a short kind of banana. *-a.* Native of or belonging to Guinea

guinga [geen'-gah], or **guingans** [geen-gahns'], *f.* Ginghams.

guinja, *f.* **guinjo**, *m.* [geen'-hah, ho], *V.* AZUFAIFA and AZUFAIFO.

guinjolero [geen-ho-lay'-ro], *m. V.* AZUFAIFO.

guiñada, guiñadura [gee-nyah'-dah, gee-nyah-doo'-rah], *f. 1.* Wink, a hint given by the eye. 2. *(Naut.)* Yaw, the deviation of a ship from her course.

guiñador, ra [gee-nyah-dor', rah], *m. & f.* Winker.

guiñapo [gee-nyah'-po], *m. 1.* Tatter, rag (andrajo). **Poner a uno como un giñapo**, to shower insults on somebody. 2. Ragamuffin, tatterdemalion; a ragged fellow (persona).

guiñaposo, sa, guiñpiento, ta [gee-nyah-po'-so, sah, gee-nyah-pe-en'to, tah], *a.* Ragged, tattered, torn.

guiñar [gee-nyar'], *va. 1.* To wink (parpadear), to hint or direct by a motion of the eyelids. 2. *(Naut.)* To yaw or make yaws; not to steer in a steady manner.

guiño [gee'-nyo], *m. 1.* Wink (parpadeo); grimace (mueca), wry face. **Hacer giños**, to wink at; to make eyes at (amantes).

guión [gee'-nyo], *m. 1.* Hyphen, division in writing. 2. Cross, the standard carried before prelates and corporations or communities. 3. Repeat, in music. 4. Scenario of a play, etc. 5. Leader (persona). 6. Script (Cine: texto); subtitle (Cine: traducción).

guionista [gee-o-ness'-tah], *m & f.* (Cine) Screenwriter; writer of subtitles.

guipar [gee-par'], *va. (coll.* and vulgar) 1. To see (ver). 2. To spot (observar).

guirigay [gee-re-gah'-e], *m.* Gibberish; meaningless words, jargon.

guirindola [gee-rin-do'-lah], *f.* Bosom of a shirt, frill.

guirlache [geer-lah'-chay], *m.* Roast almond caramel (turrón).

guirnalda [geer-nahl'-dah], or **guirlanda**, *f.* 1. Garland, a wreath or open crown interwoven with flowers (funeral). 2. *(Naut.)* Puddening, a wreath of cordage put around a variety of things on board of ships.

guirnaldar [geer-nal-dar'], *va. (Prov.)* To surround a thrashing place with trees.

güiro [gee-ee'-ro], *m. (Cuba)* Fruit of disagreeable odor and harsh taste, much like a gourd. *Cf.* GUAJE.

guirre [geer'-ray], *m.* Vulture (islas Canarias).

guisado [gee-sah'-do], *m.* 1. A stew, or made dish; ragout, fricassee. 2. *(Met. Coll.)* Action or deed performed under very remarkable circumstances.

guisador, ra [gee-sah-dor', rah], *m. & f. V.* GUISANDERO.

guisandero, ra [gee-san-day'-ro, rah], *m. & f.* A cook.

guisantal [gee-san-tahl'], *m.* A pea patch; ground planted with peas.

guisante [gee-sahn'-tay], *m. (Bot.)* Pea. **Guisante de olor** or **oloroso,** sweet pea, lathyrus.

guisar [gee-sar'], *va.* 1. To cook or dress victuals; to cure meat. 2. *(Met.)* To arrange, to adjust.

guiso [gee'-so], *m.* The seasoning of a dish (aliño); sauce of meat, or any other victuals; condiment.

guisopillo [gee-so-peel, lyo], *m. V.* HISOPILLO.

guisote [gee-so'-tay], *m.* Dish of meat dressed country fashion.

guita [gee'-tah], *f.* Pack-thread, a small hempen cord.

guitar [gee-tar'], *va.* To sew with pack-thread.

guitarra [gee-tar'-rah], *f.* 1. Guitar, a stringed musical instrument played with the fingers (instrumento). 2. Pounder, a pestle for pounding gypsum or whiting. **Ser buena guitarra,** *(Met. Coll.)* to be very artful and cunning.

guitarrear [gee-tar-ray-ar'], *vn.* To play the guitar.

guitarrero, ra [gee-tar-ray'-ro, rah], *m. & f.* 1. Guitar maker. 2. Player of the guitar.

guitarresco, ca [gee-tar-res'-co, cah], *a. (Joc.)* Belonging to the guitar.

guitarrista [gee-tar-rees'-tah], *m.* Player of the guitar, guitarist.

guitarrón [gee-tar-rone'], *m.* 1. *(ang.)* A large guitar. 2. *(coll.)* An acute knave.

guito, ta [gee'-to, tah], *a.* Treacherous, vicious (mula).

guitón, na [gee-tone', nah], *m. & f.* Mendicant, vagrant, vagabond.

guitonazo [gee-to-nah'-tho], *m. aug.* A great vagabond.

guitonear [gee-to-nay-ar'], *vn.* To loiter or idle about, to lead a vagabond life; to tramp it.

guitonería [gee-to-nay-ree'-ah], *f.* Idleness; a vagrant or vagabond life.

guizgar [geeth-gar'], *va.* To excite, to invite.

guizque [geeth'-kay], *m.* 1. *(Prov.)* Hook of a hanging lamp. 2. *(Prov.)* Sting of a wasp.

guja [goo'-hah], *f.* Arm used by archers.

gula [goo'-lah], *f.* Gluttony, inordinate desire of eating, and drinking.

gulchenita [gool-chay-nee'-tah], *a. & n.* A member of one of the Muslim monastic orders.

gules [goo'-les], *m. pl. (Her.)* Gules, red.

guloso, sa [goo-lo'-so, sah], *a.* Gluttonous, greedy.

gulusmear [goo-loos-may-ar'], *vn. (coll.) V.* GOLOSINEAR.

gullería [gool-lyay-ree'-ah], *f.* Dainty.

gulloría [gool-lyo-ree'-ah], *f.* 1. *(Orn.)* A kind of lark. 2. *V.* GOLLERÍA.

gúmena [goo'-may-nah], *f.* Cable.

gumeneta [goo-may-nay'-tah], *f. dim.* A small cable.

gumía [goo-mee'-ah], *f.* Kind of dagger or poniard.

gumífero, ra [goo-mee'-fay-ro, rah], *a.* Gum-producing, gummiferous.

gur [goor], *m.* A white cotton fabric which comes from India.

gurbión [goor-be-on'], *m.* 1. Twisted silk, of a coarse quality. 2. Silk stuff resembling grogram. 3. Gumresin extracted from the officinal spurge.

gurbionado, da [goor-be-o-nah'-do, dah], *a.* Made of twisted coarse silk.

gurrar [goor-rar'], *vn.* 1. *(Naut.)* To get clear of another ship. 2. To retrograde, to fall back.

gurrufero [goor-roo-fay'-ro], *m.* A deformed nag or horse.

gurrumina [goor-roo-mee'-nah], *f. (coll.)* Uxoriousness, unbecoming submission to a wife.

gurrumino [goor-roo-mee'-no], *m. (coll.)* Indulgent husband.

gurullada [goo-rool-lyah'-dah], *f.* 1. A crowd of people (multitud). 2. Crowd of constables or police officers.

gurullo [goo-rool'-lyo], *m.* Lump or knot. *V.* BURUJO.

gurullón [goo-rool-lyone'], *m.* A knot of wool in cloths.

gurumete [goo-roo-may'-tay], *m.* Ship's boy. *V.* GRUMETE.

gurupa [goo-roo'-pah], *f.* Croup of horse *V.* GRUPA.

gurupera [goo-roo-pay'-rah], *f.* Crupper. *V.* GRUPERA.

gurupetín [goo-roo-pay-teen'], *m. dim.* A small crupper.

gurvio, a [goor'-ve-o, ah], *a.* Curved, arched, incurvated.

gusanear [goo-sah-nay-ar'], *vn.* To itch. *V.* HORMIGUEAR.

gusanera [goo-sah-nay'-rah], *f.* 1. Place or spot where maggots or vermin are bred. 2. *(Met.)* The passion which reigns most in the mind.

gusanico, ito [goo-sah-nee'-co, ee'-to], *m. dim.* A small worm or maggot.

gusaniento, ta [goo-sah-ne-en'-to, tah], *a.* Troubled with maggots or vermin, maggoty, worm-eaten.

gusanillo [goo-sah-neel'-lyo], *m.* 1. *(Dim.)* A small worm or maggot. 2. A kind of embroidery. 3. Bit of a gimlet or auger. **Me anda el gusanillo, I** feel peckish. **Matar el gusanillo,** to have a snack.

gusano [goo-sah'-no], *m.* Maggot, worm, grub, caterpillar (mariposa, polilla). 2. A meek person. 3. Distemper among sheep. **Gusano de seda,** silkworm. **Gusano de luz,** *V.* LUCIÉRNAGA. **Matar el gusano,** to have a drink (beber).

gusanoso, sa [goo-sah-no'-so], *a. V.* GUSANIENTO.

gusarapa [goo-sah-rah'-pah], *. (Prov.) V.* GUSARAPO.

gusarapiento, ta [goo-sah-rah-peen'-to, tah], *a.* Wormy, corrupted.

gusarapillo, ito [goo-sah-rah-peel'-lyo, ee'-to], *m. dim.* A small water-worm.

gusarapo [goo-sah-rah'-po], *m.* Water-worm, an aquatic insect.

gusil [goo-seel'], *m.* A kind of harp of horizontal strings in use among the Russians.

gustable [goos-tah'-blay], *a.* 1. Tastable, capable of being tasted or relished. 2. *V.* GUSTOSO.

gustadura [goos-tah-doo'-rah], *f.* Gustation, tasting.

gustar [goos-tar'], *va.* 1. To taste. 2. To preceive by the taste. *-vn.* 3. To like, to love. 4. To enjoy a thing. **Gustar de,** to like to. 5. To experience, to examine. 6. To take pleasure or delight in a thing, to be pleased with. **La comedia no gustó,** the play was not a success. 7. **Me gusta el té, I** like tea. **No le gusta que le llamen Pepe,** he doesn't like to be called Joe. **Me gusta como anda,** I like the way she walks.

gustativo [goos-tah-tee'-vo], *a.* Lingual: applied to a branch of the inferior maxillary nerve.

gustazo [goos-tah'-tho], *m. aug.* A great pleasure; unhealthy pleasure (malsano), nasty pleasure.

gustillo [goos-teel'-lyo], *m.* 1. Relish. 2. *(Dim.)* Agreeable, delicate taste.

gusto [goos'-to], *m.* 1. Taste, the sense of tasting (sentido). 2. The sensation of tasting (sabor). 3. Pleasure (placer), delight, gratification, complacence, contentment. 4. Liking (agrado). 5. One's own will and determination. 6. Election, choice. 7. Taste, intellectual relish or discernment. 8. Caprice, fancy (antojo), diversion. **Por dar gusto a,** for the sake or gratification of, to please. **Gustos**, sensual pleasures; evil habits; vices. **Dar gusto**, to gratify. **Tiene un gusto amargo**, it has a bitter taste. **Mal gusto**, bad taste. **Para mi gusto**, to my taste. **Tiene gusto para vestir**, she dresses elegantly. **Con mucho gusto**, with pleasure. **Estar a gusto**, to be at ease. **Tener gusto en**, to be glad to. **El gusto es mío**, how do you do? **Tengo mucho gusto en conocerle**, I'm pleased to meet you. **Tomar gusto a**, to take a liking to.

gustosamente [goos-to'-sah-men-tay], *adv.* Tastefully, gladly, acceptably.

gustoso, sa [goos-to'-so, sah], *a.* 1. Gustable, dainty, pleasing to the taste. 2. Tasty (sabroso). 3. Cheerful, merry, content, joyful. 4. Pleasing, pleasant (agradable), entertaining. **Lo hizo gustoso**, he did it gladly.

gutagamba, gutiámbar [goo-tah-gahm'-bah, goo-te-ahm'-bar], *m.* Gamboge. *(Malay.)*

gutapercha [goo-tah-perr'-chah], *f.* 1. Guttapercha. 2. Caoutchouc, Indian-rubber.

gutífero, ra [goo-tee'-fay-ro, rah], *a.* Guttiferous, gum-yielding.

gutiforme [goo-te-for'-may], *a.* In the shape of a drop.

gutural [goo-too-rahl'], *a.* 1. Guttural, pronounced in the throat. 2. Guttural, belonging to the throat.

guturalmente [goo-too-ral-men'-tay], *adv.* Gutturally.

guturoso, sa [goo-te-ro'-so, sah], *a.* 1. *(Bot.)* Throated (musgo). 2. *(Zool.)* Throaty, having a large or capacious throat. 3. Pouter pigeon, vulgarly called *buchona.*

guzla [gooth'-lah], *f.* 1. A soft, harmonious musical instrument among the Greeks and the Asiatics. 2. A fiddle with a single string.

guzmán [gooth-mahn'], *m.* Nobleman who formerly served as midshipman in the navy or cadet in the army.

H

h [ah'-chay], *f.* eighth letter of the Castilian alphabet, is now treated as a mere aspiration. The moderns use *h* to soften the pronunciation of many words, as *facer, fijo*, are now written **hacer, hijo**. For the same purpose it is placed before *u*, followed by *e*, in many words derived from the Latin; as **huevo**, from ovum, an egg; **hueso**, from *os*. The *h* is never sounded in the Spanish language except by the people in Andalusia, Extremadura, and the former Spanish possessions in America. The words in which *h* was preceded by a *p*, and took the sound of *f*, are now written as pronounced, thus: *fenómeno*, phenomenon. After *r* and *t* the *h* is entirely omitted, as in, *reuma*, rheum, *teatro*, theater; but it is retained, but not aspirated, in all words which originally began with *h*, or between two vowels, as **honor, almohaza**. Symbol of hydrogen.

¡ha! [ah], *int.* 1. Ha! 2. Ah, alas! 3. *(Naut.)* Haul away!

haba [ah'-bah], *f.* 1. *(Bot.)* Bean, a kind of pulse, bean (de café) **Haba común**, garden beach vetch. **Haba de soja**, soy bean. **En todas partes cuecen habas**, it's the same the whole world over.

habanero, ra [ah-bah-nay'-ro, rah], *a.* Havanese, of Havana.

habano, na [ah-bah'-no, nah], *a.* Applied to Havana tobacco.

habar [ah-bar'], *m.* Bean field.

habascón [ah-bas-cone'], *m.* A kind of root, like parsnip, in use as a food in most South American towns.

Habeas corpus [ah'-bay-as cor'-poo], *m. (for.)* Habeas corpus.

habenaria [ah-bay-nah'-re-ah], *f.* Habenaria, rein-orchid, a large genus of American orchids.

haber [ah-berr'], *va.* 1. To possess (tener). 2. To have, an auxiliary verb (tiempos compuestos). 3. To take, to recover. 4. To happen, to fall out, to befall. 5. To exist. -*v. impers.* V.

ACAECER. **Tomará lo que haya**, he'll take whatever there is. -*vr.* To behave, to act, to conduct oneself; to become, to pretend, to feign. **Hay**, there is, there are. **Había, hubo**, there was, there were. So also with other tenses. **Ha**, it is, since, ago. **Ha más de que**, it is more than since. **Haber que**, it is necessary. **Hay que**, you are welcome; don't mention it. **No haber más que pedir**, it leaves nothing to be desired. **Lo hubiéramos hecho**, we would have done it. **Ha de haberse perdido**, it must have got lost. **No hay plátanos**, there are no bananas. **Hay que trabajar**, one has to work. **Hay que hacerlo**, it has to be done. **Hay que ser fuertes**, we must be strong. **Habérselas con uno**, to be up against somebody.

haber [ah-berr'], *m.* Property, income (ingresos), fortune, assets, credit side (balance). **Pasar algo al haber de uno**, to credit something to somebody. **Haberes**, assets.

habichuela [ah-be-choo-ay'-lah], *f. (Bot.)* French bean or kidney bean. **Habichuela común**, common kidney bean. **Habichuela multiflora**, scarlet bean. **Ganarse las habichuelas**, to earn one's living.

hábil [ah'-beel], *a.* 1. Clever (listo), skillful (diestro), dexterous, expert, knowing, cunning. 2. Capable, intelligent, learned, able to understand. 3. Agile, active, ready. 4. Apt, fit, handy, able (capaz), qualified for.

habilidad [ah-be-le-dahd'], *f.* 1. Ability (capacidad), skill, dexterity in performing. **Hombre de gran habilidad política**, a man of great political skill. 2. Cleverness, expertness (destreza), mastery, knowledge, talent; cunning. 3. Nimbleness, quickness, speed. 4. Instinct. -*pl.* Accomplishments.

habilidoso, sa [ah-be-le-do'-so, sah], *a. (Andal. and Amer. coll.)* Accomplished.

habilitación [ah-be-le-tah-the-on'], *f.* 1. Habilitation, qualification (título). 2. Fitting out, equipment (de casa).

habilitado, da [ah-be-le-tah'-do, dah], *a. & pp.* of HABILITAR. Habilitate, qualified.

habilitado [ah-be-le-tah'-do], *m.* An officer in every Spanish regiment charged with the agency of his regiment, a paymaster.

habilitador, ra [ah-be-le-tah-dor', rah], *m. & f.* Qualifier, one who makes fit or able.

habilitar [ah-be-le-tar'], *va.* 1. To qualify, to enable (permitir). 2. To provide, to supply. 3. To fit out, to equip (casa), to furnish means. 4. To finance.

hábilmente [ah'-beel-men-tay], *adv.* Dexterously, ably, knowingly, cleverly.

habitable [ah-be-tah'-blay], *a.* Habitable, lodgeable.

habitación [ah-be-tah-the-on'], *f.* 1. Habitation (vivienda), abode, lodging (alquilado). 2. Set of rooms (cuartos), that part of a house intended to be inhabited. **Habitación de matrimonio**, double room. **Habitación individual**, single room.

habitáculo [ah-be-tah'-coo-lo], *m. (coll.)* A cramped, incovenient dwelling.

habitado [ah-be-tah-do], *a.* Inhabited; live-in; manned (satélite), carrying a crew.

habitador, ra [ah-be-tah-dor', rah], *m & f.* Inhabitant, resident, dweller; abider.

habitante [ah-be-tahn'-tay], *pa.* Inhabiting. -*m. & f.* Inhabitant or habitant, dweller, resident (vecino), occupant (inquilino). **Una ciudad de 10.000 habitantes**, a town of 10.000 inhabitants.

habitar [ah-be-tar'], *va.* To inhabit, to live, to reside, to lodge or lie in a place.

habitico, illo, ito [ah-be-tee'-co], *m. dim.* A small dress or habit.

hábito [ah'-be-to], *m.* 1. Dress, habit, habiliment, garment, **Hábitos**, dress of ecclesiastics. 2. Habit, habitude, custom, customariness. **Tener el hábito de**, to be in the habit of. 3. The robes of the military orders. **Colgar los hábitos**, *(coll.)* To throw off the cowl.

habituación

habituación [ah-be-too-ah-the-on'], *f.* Habitude, custom.

habitual [ah-be-too-ahl'], *a.* Habitual, accustomed, inveterate, customary, common, frequent, regular (cliente, lector), incorrigible (mentiroso), besetting (pecado). **Su restaurante habitual**, one's usual restaurant.

habitualmente [ah-be-too-al-men'-tay], *adv.* Habitually, customarily, by habit.

habituar [ah-be-too-ar'], *va.* To accustom, to habituate, to inure. -*vr.* To become accustomed, to accustom oneself.

habitud [ah-be-tood'], *f.* Habitude, the respect or relation which one thing bears to another.

habla [ah'-blah], *f.* 1. Speech (facultad), idiom, language (nacional) 2. Discourse, argument. 3. Talk (acto), conversation. **Estar sin habla** or **perder el habla**, to be speechless. **Negar** or **quitar el habla**, to refuse to speak to a person. **Ponerse al habla**, 1. To come within speaking distance (entre barcos). 2. *(coll.)* To talk with anyone by means of the telephone.

hablado [ah-blah'-do], *ptp.* de *hablar*, spoken. **El lenguaje hablado**, the spoken language. -*a.* **Bien hablado**, nicely-spoken.

hablador, ra [ah-blah-dor', rah], *m. & f.* An impudent prattler, a trifling talker, a gabbler, a prattler, a chattering fellow (parlanchín).

habladorcillo, lla [ah-blah-dor-theel'-lyo, lyah], *m. & f. dim.* A babbling dandiprat.

habladuría [ah-blah-doo-ree'-ah], *f.* An impertinent speech, rumor (rumor); nasty remark (injuria), sarcastic remark, idle chatter (chisme), piece of gossip.

hablantín, na, hablanchín, na [ah-blan-teen', nah, ah-blan-cheen', nah], *a. (coll.)* A talkative person.

hablar [ah-blar'], *va.* 1. To speak (lengua), to express thoughts by words. 2. To talk, to speak in conversation, to commune, to reason, to converse. 3. To harangue, to address, to make a speech. 4. To advise, to admonish. **Hablar disparates** or **necedades**, to talk nonsense. **Hablar alto**, to talk loud. **Hablar en plata**, to speak clearly, without ambiguity. **Hablar por hablar**, to talk for the sake of talking. **Hablar entre dientes**, to mutter, to mumble. **Hablar de la mar**, to talk on an endless subject. **Hablar de memoria**, to talk without reflection, without knowledge of the matter. **No dejar que hablar**, to convince anyone, to impose silence. **Hablar de veras**, to speak in earnest. **No hablarse**, not to speak to each other, from enmity or aversion. **Habla bien el portugués**, he speaks good Portuguese. **Y no hay más que hablar**, so there's no more to be said about it. **Hablar claro**, to speak plainly. **Dar que hablar a la gente**, to make people talk. **Se habla de que van a comprarlo**, there is talk of their buying it. **No se hablan**, they are not on speaking terms.

hablatista [ah-blah-tees'-tah], *m. (Joc.)* A trifling prattler, an idle talker.

hablilla [ah-bleel'-lyah], *f.* 1. Rumor, report, little tale. 2. Bubbling, a foolish talk.

hablista [ah-blees'-tah], *m.* A person who speaks or writes with great correctness.

habón [ah-bone'], **m. aug.** Large kind of bean.

habrotamno [ah-bro-tahm'-no], *m.* Habrothamnus, a solanaceous shrub, native of Mexico.

haca [ah'-cah], *f.* Pony, pad, a small horse. **¿Qué haca?** or **¿qué haca morena?**, for what good? to what purpose?

hacán [ah-cahn'], *m.* A learned man among the Jews.

hacanea [ah-cah-nay'-ah], *f.* Nag, a small horse somewhat bigger than a pony.

hacecico, illo, ito [ah-thay-thee'-co], *m. dim.* A small sheaf.

hacedero, ra [ah-thay-day'-ro, rah], *a.* Feasible, practicable; easily effected.

hacedor, ra [ah-thay-dor', rah], *m. & f.* 1. Maker, author; factor. 2. Steward, one who manages the estate of another. 3. A good workman, an able performer.

hacendado [ah-then-dah-do], *m.* A land-holder, a farmer.

hacendado, da [ah-then-dah'-do, dah], *a. & pp.* of HACENDAR. 1. Acred, landed, having a fortune in land, having a real property. 2. Rich.

hacendar [ah-then-dar'], *va.* To transfer or make over the property of an estate. -*vr.* To make a purchase of land in order to settle in a place.

hacendeja [ah-then-day'-hah], *f. dim.* A small farm.

hacendera [ah-then-day'-rah], *f.* Public work, at which all the neighborhood assists.

hacendero, ra [ah-then-day'-ro, rah], *a.* Industrious, laborious.

hacendilla, hacenduela [ah-then-deel'-lyah, ah-then-doo-ay'-lah], *f. dim.* 1. A small farm. 2. A trifling work.

hacendoso, sa [ah-then-do'-so, sah], *a.* Assiduous, diligent, industrious (trabajador), busy (ocupado).

hacer [ah-therr'], *va. & vn.* 1. To make, to form, to produce. 2. To do, to practice, to act something good or bad, to make, to perform (realizar). 3. To put in execution, to carry into effect; to effect. 4. To make, to cause to have any quality, to bring into any new state or condition, to prepare (preparar), to dispose, to compose. 5. To make up a number, to complete. 6. To make, to raise as profit from something, to gain (ganar). 7. To make, to turn to some use. 8. To habituate, to accustom (acostumbrar). 9. To give, to grant. 10. To include, to contain (incluir). 11. To cause (causar), to occasion. 12. To resolve, to determine, to judge, to consider. 13. To assemble, to convoke: to correspond. 14. To make, to compel, to force, to constrain, to oblige (obligar): in this sense it is followed by an infinitive verb. **Hacer venir**, to oblige to come. 15. To dress: applied to hawks or cocks for fighting. -*vn.* 16. To grow, to increase or receive anything. 17. To matter, to import (importar). 18. To be, to exist. **Hace frío**, it is cold. 19. To accord, to agree, to fit, to answer, to suit. 20. Joined with the particle *a*, it signifies to be ready or disposed. **Hacer a todo**, to be ready or disposed to do anything. 21. Joined with the particle *de*, and the names of offices or professions, it signifies to perform their duties. **Hacer de escribano**, to act as scrivener or notary. **Hacer de portero**, to act as a porter. 22. Joined with *de, se, el, la, lo*, it signifies to represent, to counterfeit, or to show what is not in reality. **Hacer de bobo**, to counterfeit an idiot. 23. With *por* or *para*, joined to an infinitive verb, it signifies taking pains and care in executing the import of such verb. **Hacer por llegar**, to endeavor to arrive. **Hacer para** or **por salvarse**, to strive to save oneself. 24. Followed by substantives it gives them a verbal signification. **Hacer estimación**, to esteem. **Hacer pensar**, to put in mind, to give cause to suspect. **Hacer avergonzar**, to put one to the blush, to frown anyone down. **Hacer bajar los ojos**, to make one abashed. **Hacer bajar las orejas**, to humble anyone. **Hacer de capitán**, to personate or act the captain. **Haz por venir**, try to come. **Hacer cuerpo presente**, to attend a meeting without taking part in it. **Hacer a uno con alguna cosa**, *(coll.)* to procure a thing for anyone. **No hacer alto**, to overlook, not to mind. **No hagas caso**, never mind. **Hacer el papel**, to personate or act the part of another person. **Hacer la vista gorda**, to wink at, to connive at. **Hacer alarde**, to muster; to boast of. **Hacer aire**, to blow: speaking of the wind. **Hacer alguna cosa a la moda**, to fashion. **Hacer a uno perder los estribos**, to make anyone lose his temper: literally, to make a man lose his stirrups. **Hacer bancarrota**, to fail, to break, to become bankrupt. **Hacer caso de**, to pay attention to, to mind, to care. **Hacer cara**, to make head against, to face, to resist. **Hacer de tripas corazón**, to pluck up courage, to bluster and show much boldness when one is afraid, to pluck up heart. **Hacer de figura** or **hacer figura**, to make a figure or cut a figure. **Hacer fermentar**, to heat. **Hacer frente a**, to make head against, to face, to resist. **Hacer fiesta**, to take a day off. **Hacer fiestas**, to fondle, to endear, to flatter, to cajole, to fawn. **Hacer gasto**, to spend. **Hacer humo**, 1. To smoke. 2. *(Met.)* To continue long in a place. **Hacer opinión**, to form an opinion, to be an authority. **Hace ocho días**, eight days ago. So with other phrases of time. **Hacer juego**, to be well matched. **Hacer la comida**, to dress the dinner. **Hacer limosna**, to give alms. **Hacer las amistades**, to make it up. **Hacer mal de ojo**, *(coll.)* to fascinate. **Hacer memoria**, to recollect, to remember. **Hacer milagros**, to do wonders. **Hacer niebla**, to haze. **Hacer un papel**, to act a part; to make or to cut a figure; to acquit oneself well. **Hacer por**, to try, to do one's best. **Hacer progresos**, to gain ground, to improve. **Hacer pedazos**, to pull to pieces. **Hacer pucheros**, to make wry faces, as children do before they begin to cry. **Hacer pie**, to find the bottom of water without swimming; to be firm and secure in anything; to stop, to reside in a place. **Hancer que hacemos**, to act officially, to affect doing some business, to fidget about for no purpose. **Hacer saber**, to acquaint, to make known. **Hacer sombra**, *(Met.)* to protect, to support; to impede, to obscure. **Hacer su agosto**, to make hay while the sun shines: literally, to make one's harvest. **Hacer ventaja**, to exceed, to surpass. **No hay que hacer** or **eso no tiene que hacer**, it is only to act, it is easily done. **Hacer que**, to feign, to pretend, to affect. **Hágame Vd. el favor**, pray. **Haga buen o mal tiempo**, rain or shine. **Hacer el pelo a una**, to do somebody's hair. **El ábol hace sombra**, the tree gives shade. **No sé que hacer**, I don't know what to do. **La ha hecho buena**, a fine mess he's made of it. **Él protestó y yo hice lo mismo**, he protested and I did the same. **Hacer el cuerpo al frío**, to inure the body to cold. **Les hice venir**, I made them come. **Me lo hizo saber**, he told me it. **Éste hace 100**, this one makes 100. **Hacer el tonto**, to act the fool. **Dar que hacer**, to cause trouble. **Está perdido desde hace 15 días**, it's been lost for a fortnight. **Hace poco**, a short while back. **Hacer "clic"**, *(Inform.)* to clic.

hacerse [ah-therr'-say], *vr.* 1. To recede, to separate. 2. To become, to enter into some new state or condition (llegar a ser). 3. To accustom oneself (acostumbrarse). **Hacerse de miel**, to treat one gently, not to be very severe. **Hacerse con algo** or **de algo**, to acquire, to attain; to purchase anything which is wanting. **Hacerse lugar**, to gain a name or reputation. **Hacerse memorable**, to become memorable, famous, notorious, etc. **Hacerse añicos**, to take great pains in doing anything. **Hacerse chiquito**, to pretend to be modest; to conceal one's knowledge. **Se hace de noche**, night falls. **Hacerse con una cosa**, to obtain a thing rightly or wrongly. **Se hará de ladrillos**, it will be built of brick. **Todavía no se ha hecho**, it still has not been done. **Hacer cortesías** (mutuamente), to exchange courtesies. **Hacerse un retrato**, to have one's portrait painted. **Hacerse enfermera**, to become a nurse. **Hacerse el sueco**, to pretend not to hear. **Esto se hace pesado**, this is becoming tedious. **Hacerse grande**, to grow tall, to get tall. **Se me hace imposible trabajar**, it's becoming impossible for me to work. **Hacerse a una idea**, to get used to an idea. **Hacerse con algo**, to get hold of something. **Logró hacerse con una copia**, he managed to get hold of a copy. **Hacerse a un lado**, to stand aside.

hacia [ah'-the-ah], *adv.* 1. Towards (lugar), in a direction to, near to, about (cerca). **Hacia adelante**, forward. **Hacia acá or hacia esta parte**, hitherward, hitherwards. **Hacia dónde**, whither, toward which, to what place, to where. **Hacia casa, hacia su país**, homeward, homeward. 2. About (tiempo). **Hacia mediodía**, about noon. 3. Towards (actitud). **Su hostilidad hacia la idea**, his hostility towards the idea.

hacienda [ah-the-en'-dah], *f.* 1. Landed property (finca), lands, tenements. 2. Estate, fortune, wealth (fortuna). 3. Farm. 4. Domestic work done by the servants of the house. **Ministro de hacienda** (en España), and **Secretario de hacienda** (en S. América), the Secretary of the Treasury, or Chancellor of the Exchequer. **Hacienda pública**, public treasury, finances.

hacina [ah-thee'-nah], *f.* 1. Stack or rick of corn piled up in sheaves. 2. Any collection of things placed one over another.

hacinador, ra [ah-the-nah-dor', rah], *m. & f.* Stack-maker, one who piles up the sheaves of corn. **Hacinador de riquezas**, hoarder of riches.

hacinamiento [ah-the-nah-me-en'-to], *m.* 1. Accumulation, act of heaping or hoarding up. 2. Acervation, coacervation, heaping together.

hacinar [ah-the-nar'], *va.* 1. To stack or pile up sheaves of corn. 2. To hoard (ahorrar), to make hoards. 3. To accumulate (acumular); to coacervate.

hacino, na [ah-thee'-no, nah], *a.* V. AVARO and TRISTE.

hacha [ah'-chah], *f.* 1. A large taper with four wicks. 2. An axe or hatchet. **Hacha de armas**, battleaxe. 3. Ancient Spanish dance. 4. *(Fig.)* Genius. **Es un hacha para el bridge**, he's a genius at bridge.

hachazo [ah-chah'-tho], *m.* Blow or stroke with an axe (golpe).

hache [ah'-chay], *f.* Name of the letter H.

hachear [ah-chay-ar'], *va.* To cut with an axe; to hew. *-vn.* To strike with an axe.

hachero [ah-chay'-ro], *m.* 1. Torch stand, a large candlestick for tapers or torches. 2. *(Mil.)* V. GASTADOR. 3. Wood-cleaver or wood-cutter; a laborer employed to fell wood and cut timber. 4. *(Prov.)* Carpenter.

hacheta [ah-chay'-tah], *f. dim.* 1. A small hatchet. 2. A small torch or link.

hachis [ah-chees'], *m.* Hashish.

hacho [ah'-cho], *m.* Fagot, or bundle of straw or feather grass, covered with pitch or resin.

hachón [ah-chone'], *m.* 1. A large torch made of bass and pitch. 2. Kind of altar, on which bonfires are lighted for illuminations.

hachuela [ah-choo-ay'-lah], *f. dim.* A small hatchet or axe. **Hachuela, de abordar**, *(Naut.)* boarding axe.

hada [ah'-dah], *f.* Fairy. **Cuento de hadas**, fairy tale. **Hada encantada**, enchanted fairy.

hadado, da [ah-dah'-do, dah], *a. & pp.* of HADAR. Fortunate, lucky.

hado [ah'-do], *m.* Fate, destiny, inevitable doom.

hagiógrafo [ah-he-o'-grah-fo], *m.* Hagiographer, a writer of lives of the saints.

haitiano, na [ah-e-te-ah'-no, nah], *a.* Haitian (de Haiti).

haje [ah'-hay], *f.* The African cobra or asp: it has the power of inflating the neck.

halacabullas, halacuerdas [ah-lah-cah-bool'-lyas, ah-lah-coo-err'-das], *m. (coll.)* Fresh-water sailors.

halagador, ra [ah-lah-gah-dor', rah], *m. & f.* Cajoler, flatterer.

halagar [ah-lah-gar'], *va.* To cajole, to flatter (lisonjear); to caress, to dandle, coax, to coy, to allure, to make much of, to wheedle, to hug, to fondle, to treat with tenderness (mostrar afecto).

halago [ah-lah'-go], *m.* Cajolery, flattery, caress, adulation, cooing, pleasure, delight.

halagüeñamente [ah-lah-goo-ay-nyah-men'-tay], *adv.* Endearingly, fatteringly.

halagüeño, ña [ah-lah-goo-ay'-nyo, nyah], *a.* Endearing, attractive, alluring (atrayente), fawning, flattering (opinión, observación), meek, gentle.

halar [ah-lar'], *va. (Naut.)* To haul, to pull by a rope. **Halar al viento**, to haul the wind.

halcón [al-cone'], *m. (Orn.)* Falcon, a hawk trained for sport. **Halcón común**, peregrine. **Los halcones y las palomas**, the hawks and the doves.

halconado, da [al-co-nah'-do, dah], *a.* Falcon or hawk-like.

halconcico, illo, ito [al-con-thee'-co, eel'-lyo, ee'-to], *m. dim.* Jashawk, a young falcon or hawk.

halconear [al-co-nay-ar'], *va. (coll.)* To look and inveigle (mujeres de ciudad).

halconera [al-co-nay'-rah], *f* Place where falcons are kept.

halconería [al-co-nay-ree'-ah], *f.* Falconry.

halconero [al-co-nay'-ro], *m.* Falconer, one who rears or trains hawks for sport.

halda [ahl'-dah], *f.* 1. Bag or sack made of sack-cloth (arpillera). 2. Skirt of a garment (falda). **Haldas en cinta,** *(coll.)* disposed and ready for anything.

haldear [al-day-ar'], *vn.* To run along with the skirts flying loose.

haldica, illa, ita [al-dee'-cah], *f. dim.* A small skirt.

haldudo, da [al-doo'-do, dah], *a.* Having flying skirts.

haleche [ah-lay'-chay], *m.* Horse-mackerel, a kind of mackerel. *V.* ESCOMBRO.

halía [ah-lee'-ah], *f.* 1. *(Bot.)* A papilionaceous plant of the Cape of Good Hope. 2. *(Ent.)* An European moth. 3. A nereid, a sea-nymph.

haliéntica [ah-le-en'-te-cah], *f.* Angling, the art of fishing.

haliéntico, ca [ah-le-en'-te-co, cah], *a.* Angling, belonging to the art of angling.

halieto [ah-le-ay'-to], *m.* Sea-eagle.

halinatrón [ah-le-nah-tron'], *m.* Native soda.

haliquedón [ah-le-kay-don'], *a.* Like the sea-swallows.

hálito [ah'-le-to], *m..* 1. The breath (aliento). 2. Vapor (vapor). 3. *(Poet.)* Soft air.

hall [hall], *m.* Hall (teatro) foyer, lounge (hotel).

hallado, da [ah-lyah'-do, dah], *a.* Found. **Bien hallado,** very familiar, welcome, easy, contented. **Mal hallado,** uneasy, not at ease, conetrained.-*pp.* of HALLAR.

hallador, ra [al-lyah-dor', rah], *m. & f.* Finder, discoverer.

hallar [ahl-lyar'], *va.* 1. To find, to obtain by searching or seeking, to locate (localizar). 2. To find, to hit on, to hit upon by chance, to perceive by accident. 3. To find, to meet with, to fall upon. 4. To find out (averiguar), to discover (descubrir). 5. To find, to gain by any mental endeavor, to invent, to excogitate. 6. To find, to remark, to observe, to note, to compare, to verify. 7. To find, to discover something hidden. 8. To find, to detect, to catch, to understand, to comprehend .9. To manifest, to show anything unexpected. -*vr.* 1. To meet occasionally in any place, to light, to happen to find, to fall upon by chance. 2. To be content or pleased in any place. 3. To be somewhere. 4. To find oneself, to be, to fare with regard to ease or pain. **Se hallaba fuera,** he was away at the time. **Se halla sin dinero,** he has no money. **Hallarse enfermo,** to be ill. **Hallarse con un nuevo obstáculo,** to encounter an obstacle.

hallazgo [al-lyath'-go], *m.* 1. The act of finding or recovering anything lost. 2. Reward given for finding anything lost (premio). 3. Thing found (cosa).

hallulla [al-lyool'-lyah], *f.* 1. A kind of paste made and used to feed fowls. 2. *V.* HALLULLO.

hallullo [al-lyool'-lyo], *m.* Cake baked on or under cinders.

halo, halón [ah'-lo, ah-lone'], *m. (Ast.)* Halo, a red circle round the sun or moon.

halodendro, dra [ah-lo-den'-dro, drah], *a. (Bot.)* Growing in earth impregnated with salts.

halógeno, na [ah-lo'-hay-no, nah], *a. (Chem.)* Halogen, producing saline compounds.

halografía [ah-lo-grah-fee'-ah], *f. (Chem.)* The section of chemistry which deals with salts, halography.

halomancia [ah-lo-mahn'-the-ah], *f.* Halomancy, divination with salt.

haloquimia [ah-lo-kee'-me-ah], *f.* The branch of chemistry which treats of salts and their properties.

haloza [ah-loh'-thah], *f.* Wooden shoe.

haltera [al-tay'-rah], *f.* Barbell, dumbbell.

halterofilia [al-tay-ro-fee'-lyah], *f.* Weight lifting.

halurgia [ah-loor'-he-ah], *f.* Preparation of salts and the art of preparing them.

hamaca [ah-mah'-cah], *f.* Hammock, a kind of suspended bed.

hamaquero [ah-mah-kay'-ro], *m.* Person who carries a hammock.

hamano [ah-mah'-no], *m.* A kind of pink cotton stuff from the Levant.

hambre [ahm'-bray], *f.* 1. Hunger, appetite; the pain felt from fasting. **Tener hambre,** to be hungry, to have an appetite. 2. Scarcity of provisions, famine (de población entera). 3. Greediness, eagerness of appetite or desire. **Muerto de hambre,** starved with hunger. **Vengo con mucha hambre,** I'm terribly hungry. **Hambre canina,** ravenous hunger.

hambrear [am-bray-ar'], *vn.* To hunger, to be hungry.-*va.* 1. To hunger, to cause hunger. 2. To starve, to famish, to kill with hunger, to subdue by famine.

hambrientamente [am-bre-en-tah-men'-tay], *adv.* Hungrily.

hambriento, ta [am-bre-en'-to, tah], *a.* 1. Hungry, starved, greedy, ravenous. 2. Greedy, eager, vehemently desirous.

hambrón, na [am-brone', nah], *m. & f. (coll.)* A hungry person, one who is often hungry.

hamburguesa [am-boor-gay'-sah], *f.* Hamburger.

hampa [ahm'-pah], *f.* 1. Underworld. **El hampa de Chicago,** the Chicago underworld.

hampesco, ca [am-pes'-co, cah], *a.* Vagabond, villainous, vainglorious.

hampo, hampón [ahm'-po, am-pone'], *a.* Bold, valiant, licentious.

hanega [ah-nay'-gah], *f.* A dry measure. *V.* FANEGA.

hanegada [ah'-nay-gah'-dah], *f.* Quantity of land sown with a *fanega* of corn.

hangar [an-gar'], *m. (Aer.)* Hangar.

hanguilla [an-keel'-lyah], *f.* A kind of boat.

hao [ah'-o], *m.* Noise.

haquilla, ita [ah-keel'-lyah, ee'-tah], *f. dim.* Very little pony.

haragán, na [ah-rah-gahn', nah], *m. & f. & a.* 1. Idler, loiterer, lingerer, lounger, lubbard, an idle, lazy person. 2. Idle, slothful, inactive, indolent.

haraganamente [ah-rah-gah-nah-men'-tay], *adv.* Idly, lazily, slothfully, indolently.

haraganazo, za [ah-rah-gah-nah'-tho, thah], *a. aug.* Very idle.

haraganear [ah-rah-gah-nay-ar'], *vn.* To lead an idle life, to be lazy, to act the truant, to lounge, to idle, to loiter.

haraganería [ah-rah-gah-nay-ree'-ah], *f.* Idleness, laziness, sluggishness, inactivity, slothfulness.

harapiento [ah-rah-pe-ayn'-to], *a.* Ragged, tattered, in rags, in tatters.

harapo [ah-rah'-po], *m.* Rag, tatter; fringe. **Estar hecho un harapo,** to go about in rags.

haraposo, sa [ah-rah-po'-so, sah], *a.* Ragged, tattered.

harem, harén [ah-rem', ahren'], *m.* Harem.

harija [ah-ree'-hah], *f.* Mill-dust, the flour which flies about in a corn-mill.

harina [ah-ree'-nah], *f.* 1. Flour, the edible part of corn and meal. **Harina de avena,** oatmeal. **Harina de patata,** potato flour. **Harina de pescado,** fish meal. 2. *(Met.)* Powder, dust.

harinado [ah-re-nah'-do], *m.* Flour dissolved in water.

harinero [ah-re-nay'-ro], *m.* 1. Flour merchant (persona). 2. Place where meal or flour is kept (recipiente).

harinero, ra [ah-re-nay'-ro, rah], *a.* Made of flour, belonging to flour.

harinoso, sa [ah-re-no'-so, sah], *a.* Mealy, containing meal, floury.

harkisa [ar-kee'-sah], *f.* Nickel sulphide.

harma [ar'-mah], *f. (Ant. Bot.)* Wild rue. *V.* GAMARZA.

harmaga [ar-mah'-gah], *f. (Bot.) V.* GAMARZA and ALHÁRGAMA.

harmonía [ar-mo-nee'-ah], *f.* Harmony. *V.* ARMONÍA and its adjuncts.

harmonista [ar-mo-nees'-tah], *m.* Musician.

harnerico, illo, ito [ar-nay-ree'-co], *m. dim.* A small sieve.

harnero [ar-nay'-ro], *m.* Sieve; properly, of fine meshes and small diameter. *V.* CRIBA. **Estar hecho un harnero,** to be covered with wounds.

harón, na [ah-ron', nah], *a.* 1. Slow, inactive, sluggish. 2. Balky.

haronear [ah-ro-nay-ar'], *vn.* 1. To dawdle, to move sluggishly; to be tardy or slow. 2. To balk, to stop short (caballo).

haronía [ah-ro-nee'-ah], *f.* Sluggishness, laziness, idleness.

harpado, da [ar-pah'-do, dah], *a.* V. ARPADO.

harpía [ar-pee'-ah], *f.* Harpy, V. ARPÍA.

harpillera [ar-peel'-lyay'rah], *f.* Sacking, sack cloth.

harria [ar'-re-ah], *f. (Amer.)* Drove of beasts of burden.

hartada [ar-tah'-dah], *f.* V. HARTAZGO.

hartar [ar-tar'], *va.* 1. To stuff with eating and drinking, to glut. 2. To satiate, to gratify desire. 3. To satiate (calmar el hambre), to satisfy (un deseo), to tire (cansar), to annoy (fastidiar) to cloy, to fill to uneasiness, to fill beyond natural desire. **Hartar de palos,** to shower with blows. *-vr.* 1. To eat one's fill, to gorge, to be satiated. **Comer hasta hartarse,** to eat to repletion. 2. *(Fig.)* To weary, to get weary. **Hartarse de reír,** to laugh, fit to burst. **Hartarse de esperar,** to get tired of waiting.

hartazgo [ar-tath'-go], *m.* Satiety, the act of glutting or filling beyond natural desire.

harto [ar'-to], *adv.* Enough.

harto, ta [ar'-to, tah], *a. & pp. irr.* of HARTAR. 1. Satiate, satiated, glutted. 2. Sufficient, full, complete. **Estar harto de,** to be fed up with.

hartura [tar-too'-rah], *f.* 1. Satiety, fullness beyond desire or pleasure, glut. 2. Plenty, abundance (abundancia).

hasiz [ah-seeth'], *m.* Guard or keeper of silk.

hasta [ahs'-tah], *prep.* Until, as far as (lugar); also, even, until (tiempo). **Hasta no más,** to the highest pitch. **Hasta ahora, hasta aquí,** hitherto. **Hasta el fin de la calle,** down to the end of the street. **No me levanto hasta las 9, I** don't get up until 9 o'clock. **No iré hasta después de la reunión,** I shan't go till after the meeting.

hastial [as-te-ahl'], *m.* 1. A gable end. 2. *(Fig.)* A coarse, rude man. 3. Lateral face of an excavation, in mining.

hastiar [as-te-ar'], *va.* To loathe, to create disgust, to weary (fastidiar), to sicken (asquear).

hastío [as-tee'-o], *m.* Loathing, want of appetite; disgust, abhorring.

hataca [ah-tah'-cah], *f.* 1. A large kind of wooden ladle. 2. Rolling pin, with which paste is moulded.

hatajar [ah-tah-har'], *va.* To divide cattle into flocks or herds.

hatajo [ah-tah'-ho], *m.* 1. A small herd of cattle. 2. Assemblage, collection; abundance.

hatear [ah-tay-ar'], *vn.* To collect one's clothes necessary for traveling, when on a journey.

hatería [ah-tay-ree'-ah], *f.* Allowance of provisions and clothes for shepherds, when traveling with their flocks.

hatero [ah-tay'-ro], *m.* 1. Shepherd or other person who carries provisions to those who attend a flock of sheep. 2. *(Cuba)* Cow-boy, herder of cattle, or keeper of a cattle-farm.

hatero, ra [ah-tay'-ro, rah], *a.* Applied to the animals that carry the shepherd's baggage.

hatijo [ah-tee'-ho], *m.* Covering of straw or feather-grass over beehives.

hatillo [ah-teel'-lyo], *m. dim.* A small bundle; a few clothes. **Echar el hatillo al mar,** to irritate, to vex oneself.

hato [ah'-to], *m.* 1. A large herd of cattle (animales). **Un hato de carneros,** a flock or fold of sheep. *(Amer.)* A farm for rearing cattle. 2. Fold, place chosen by shepherds to eat and sleep near their flocks (choza). 3. Provisions for shepherds, for some days' consumption (víveres). 4. Clothes, wearing apparel (ropa). 5. Heap, cluster, number driven together. 6. Herd, in contempt, a company of men; a crowd, multitude, or meeting of suspicious people. 7. Assemblage, collection, abundance. 8. *(coll.)* V. CORRILLO.

hay [ah'-ee], Impersonal form, from **haber,** there is, there are.

haya [ah'-yah], *f. (Bot.)* Beech tree. **Haya común or silvática,** common beech.

hayal, hayedo [ah-yahl'], *m.* Plantation of beech trees.

hayo [ah'-yo], *m. (Cuba)* Coca, the shrub and its leaves.

hayucal [ah-yoo-cahl'], *m. (Prov.)* Grove of beech trees.

hayuco [ah-yoo'-co], *m.* Beech-mast, fruit of the beech.

haz [ahth'], *m.* Fagot, fascine, a bundle (lío) of brushwood or sticks a bundle of hay or grass; a sheaf of corn.

haz [ahth], *f.* 1. Face, visage. 2. Right side or outside of cloth (tela). 3. *(Arch.)* Facing. V. PARAMENTO. **Sobre la haz de la tierra,** upon the face of the earth.

haza [ah'-thah], *f.* Piece of cultivable land.

hazada [ah-thah'-dah], *f.* V. AZADA.

hazadón [ah-thah-done'], *m.* V. AZADÓN.

hazaleja [ah-thah-lay'-hah], *f. (Prov.)* A towel.

hazán [ah-thahn'], *m.* The cantor of a synagogue.

hazaña [ah-thah'-nyah], *f.* 1. Exploit, achievement, an heroic feat. **Las hazañas del héroe,** the hero's exploits. 2. *(Iron.)* Ignoble action.

hazañería [ah-thah-nyay-ree'-ah], *f.* Show or affectation of scrupulosity.

hazañero, ra [ah-thah-nyay'-ro, rah], *a.* Prudish, affectedly grave and scrupulous, dramatic (persona), histrionic (acción), exaggerated.

hazañero, ra [ah-thah-nyay'-ro, rah], *m. & f.* Affected, prudish person.

hazañosamente [ah-thah-nyo-sah-men'-tay], *adv.* Valorously.

hazañoso, sa [ah-thah-nyo'-so, sah], *a.* Valient, courageous, heroic (persona, acción).

hazcona [ath-co'-nah], *f.* Dart. V. DARDO.

hazmerreír [ath-may-ray-eer'], *m.* Ridiculous person, laughing-stock, gazing-stock, or jesting-stock.

¡he! [ay], *int.* 1. Ho! hey! a sudden exclamation to give notice of something. 2. Hark! list! hear! listen! Behold! look here. 3. What? Eh? It is used with pronouns, as *te, lo, los,* etc., and *aquí* or *allí.*

hebdómada [eb-do'-mah-dah], *f.* 1. Hebdomad, a week, seven days. 2. Seven years.

hebdomadario, ria [eb-do-mah-dah'-re-o, ah], *m. & f.* Hebdomadary, a member of a chapter or convent. *-a.* Weekly.

hebe [ay'bay], *f.* 1. The down which grows upon the pubis. 2. The age of puberty. 3. An asteroid of this name. 4. A moth.

hebén, [ay-ben'], *a.* Applied to white grapes, like muscatels.

hebepétalo, la [ay-bay-pay'-tah-lo, lah], *a.* Downy-petaled.

hebetina [ay-bay-teeh'-nah], *f.* Willemite, silicate of zinc.

hebilla [ay-beel'-lyah], *f.* A buckle, a clasp.

hebillaje [ay-beehl-lyah'-hay], *m.* Collection of buckles, or mounting of horses, accoutrements.

hebillita [ay-beel-lyee'-tah], *f. dim.* Small buckle.

hebillar [ay-beel-lyar'], *va.* To buckle.

hebillón [ay-beehl-lyone'], *m. aug.* A large buckle.

hebillona, ota [ay-beel-lyo'-nah, oh'-tah], *f. aug.* V. HEBILLÓN.

hebra [ay'-brah], *f.* 1. A needleful of thread of linen, yarn, worsted, or silk. 2. Pistil of the flower or blossom of saffron and other plants. 3. Fiber, filament, thread (de gusano). 4. Vein, layer, stratum. 5. *pl. (Poet.)* Hair. **Tabaco de hebra,** loose tobacco.

hebraico, ca [ay-brah'-eco, cah], *a.* Belonging to the Hebrews.

hebraísta [ay-brah-ees'-tah], *m.* Hebraist, one who is proficient in Hebrew.

hebreo [ay-bray'-o], *m.* 1. A Hebrew. 2. *(coll.)* A merchant, a tradesman.

hebreo, ea [ay-bray'-o, ah], *a.* Hebraic, Judaical. **A la hebrea,** in the Hebrew manner.*-m.* 1. Hebrew language (idioma). 2. *(coll.)* Trader. 3. *(coll.)* Usurer.

hebroso, sa [ay-bro'-so, sah], *a.* Fibrous; consisting of many fibers and threads, stringy (carne).

hecatombe [ay-cah-tom'-bay], *f.* 1. Hecatomb. 2. Massacre, slaughter.

hechiceresco, ca [ay-che-thay-res'-co, cah], *a.* Relating to witchcraft.

hechicería [ay-che-thay-ree'-ah], *f.* 1. Witchcraft, the practices of witches. 2. Witchery, enchantment. 3. Charmingness, the power of pleasing.

hechicero, ra [ay-che-thay'-ro, rah], *m. & f. & a.* 1. Witch, wizard; hag. 2. Charmer, enchanter, bewitcher. 3. Charming, bewitching, attractive in the highest degree.

hechizar [ay-che-thar'], *va.* 1. To bewitch, to enchant, to injure by witchcraft. 2. To charm, to fascinate.

hechizo [ay-chee'-tho], *m.* 1. Bewitchment, fascination. 2. Enchantment, irresistable power of pleasing, enchanter, charmer (de mujer) 3. Entertainment, amusement.

hechizo, za [ay-chee'-tho, thah], *a.* Made or done on purpose, artificial, factitious, imitated, well-adapted (falso).

hecho, cha [ay'-cho, chah], *pp. irr.* of HACER. 1. Made, done. 2. Accustomed, inured, used (acostumbrado). **Hecho al trabajo**, inured to labor and hardship. **Hecho un león**, like a lion, furiously angry. **A lo hecho pecho**, *(Prov.)* we must make the best of what we have done. **Hombre hecho**, a man of experience. -*a.* 1. Complete, finished (acabado); Mature (hombre, queso, vino); perfect; ready-made. **Hecho y derecho**, complete, right and true. **Un hombre hecho y derecho**, a real man.

hecho [ay'-cho], *m.* 1. Action, well or ill performed. 2. Act, feat. 3. Event, incident (suceso). 4. Subject or matter discussed (asunto). 5. *(Law.)* Point litigated. **De hecho**, in fact, actually, effectually. **Hecho consumado**, fait accompli, accomplished fact. **Esto es un hecho**, this is a fact. **Volvamos al hecho**, let's get back to the facts. **Hechos de los Apóstoles**, facts of the Apostles.

Hecho a la medida [ay'-cho ah lah may-dee'-dah], *a.* Tailormade, custom-made, custom-built.

hechura [ay-choo'-rah], *f.* 1. Act of performing or doing something (acto). 2. The work done or made, and the price of making it. 3. Form, cut (traje), shape, fashion, make, figure or form given to a thing (forma). 4. Workmanship. 5. Creature, client, a person who owes his rise or fortune to another. **De exquisita hechura**, of exquisite workmanship.

hectárea [ec-tha'-ray-ah], *f.* Hectare, a measure of surface.

héctico, ca [ec'-te-co, cah], *a.* Hectic. *Cf.* HÉTICO.

hecto [ec'-to], *m.* Greek prefix, signifying one hundred.

hectógrafo [ac-to'-grah-fo], *m.* Hectograph.

hectogramo [ec-to-grah'-mo], *m.* Hectogram, the weight of 100 grams.

hectolitro [ec-to-lee'-tro], *m.* Hectoliter, 100 liters.

hectómetro [ec-to'-may-tro], *m.* Hectometer, 100 meters.

hectóreo, ea [ec-to'-ray-o, ah], *a.* Belonging to Hector.

hedentina [ay-den-tee'-nah], *f.* Stench, stink.

heder [ay-derr'], *vn.* 1. To stink, to emit an offensive smell. 2. *(Met.)* To vex, to fatigue, to be intolerable.

hederáceo, cea [ay-day-rah-thay-o, ah], *a.* Hederaceus, relating to ivy.

hediondamente [ay-de-on-dah-men'-tay], *adv.* Stinkingly.

hediondez [ay-de-on-deth'], *f.* A strong stench or stink (olor); thing stinking; fetidness (cosa).

hediondo, da [ay-de-on'-do, dah], *a.* 1. Fetid, mephitical, stinking (maloliente). 2. Irascible, pettish, unpleasant. **Este es un hediondo**, he is a stinkard.

hediondo [ay-do-on'-do], *m.* *(Bot.)* V. GAMARZA.

hedonismo [ay-do-nees'-mo], *m.* Hedonism, theory of living for pleasure.

hedor [ay-dor'], *m.* Stench, stink, fetor, smell.

hedrar [ay-drar'], *va.* *(Prov.)* To dig a second time about the vines.

hegemonía [ay-hay-mo-nee'-ah], *f.* Hegemony, pre-eminence, leadership.

hégira [ay'-ge-rah], *f.* Hegira, the Mohammedan epoch.

hejotes, or **eotes** [ay-ho'-tes], *m. pl.* *(Mex.)* String-beans.

helable [ay-lah'-blay], *a.* Congealable.

helada [ay-lah'-dah], *f.* Frost (escarcha); freeze (fenómeno atmosférico). **Helada blanca**, hoarfrost.

heladería [ay-lah-day-ree'-ah], *f.* Ice-cream parlor, ice-cream stall.

heladero [ay-lah-day-ro], *m.* Ice-cream man.

heladizo, za [ay-lah-dee'-tho, thah], *a.* Easily congealed.

helado, da [ay-lah'-do, dah], *a. & pp.* of HELAR. 1. Gelid, frigid. 2. Frozen, congealed, frost-bitten, glacial, icy. 3. Frozen, chill in affection, indifferent. 4. Astonished, astounded. **Dejar helado a uno**, to dumbfound somebody. **Quedarse helado**, to be scared stiff.

helado [ay-lah'-do], *m.* 1. Ice-cream, frozen custard. 2. In Andalusia, pink sugar.

helamiento [ay-lah-meen'-to], *m.* Congelation, frostiness.

helar [ay-lar'], *va. & vn.* 1. To congeal (líquido), to ice (bebida), or to turn to ice. 2. To freeze, to congeal or be congealed with cold. 3. To freeze, to chill by the loss of power or motion. 4. To astound, to astonish, to amaze (pasmar). 5. To dispirit, to discourage (desalentar).-*vr.* 1. To freeze, to be congealed with cold (líquido), to be frozen. 2. To glaciate, to turn into ice. 3. To congeal, to concrete, to gather into a mass by cold; to be coagulated. 4. To grow motionless, to remain without action; to be stupefied to be dispirited. **Se me heló la sangre or se me heló la sangre en las venas**, *(Met.)* my blood curdled.

héle, hétele, aquí [ay'-lay, ay'-tay-lay, ah-kee'], *int.* Behold it, look here. *V.* HE.

helear [ay-lay-ar'], *va.* *(Prov.)* To point with the finger.

helechal [ay-lay-chahl'], *m.* A fernery.

helecho [ay-lay'-cho], *m.* *(Bot.)* Fern. **Helecho macho**, male fern. **Helecho hembra**, female fern.

helena [ay-lay'-nah], *f.* *(Naut.)* Castor and Pollux, a meteor, called also night-fire, or jack-o'-lantern.

helénico, ca [ay-lay'-ne-co, cah], *a.* Hellenic, Greek.

helanismo [ay-lay-nees'-mo], *m.* 1. Hellenism, Greek idiom. 2. Imitation, or study of Greek civilization.

helenista [ay-lay-nees'-tah], *m.* Hellenist, a name given to the Jews of Alexandria, who spoke Greek, or to the Greeks who professed Judaism.

helenístico, ca [ay-le-nees'-te-co, cah], *a.* 1. Hellenistic, pertaining to the Hellenists. 2. The Alexandrine Greek dialect, and particularly that of the Septuagint.

helera [ay-lay'-rah], *f.* Pip, disease in fowls.

helgado, da [el-gah'-do, dah], *a.* Jag-toothed.

helgadura [el-gah-doo'-rah], *f.* Irregularity of the teeth.

heliaco, ca [ay-le-ah'-co, cah], *a.* Heliacal, rising or setting of a star.

helianto [ay-le-ahn'-to], *m.* *(Bot.)* Sun-flower.

hélice [ay'-le-thay], *f.* 1. Propeller (barcos, aviones). 2. *(Ast.)* Northern constellation of Ursa Major. 3. *(Geom.)* Helix, spiral.

helicóptero [ay-le-cop'-tay-ro], *m.* Helicopter.

helio [ay'-le-o], *m.* Helium.

heliocéntrico, ca [ay-le-o-then'-tre-co, cah], *a.* *(Ast.)* Heliocentric, appearing from the center of the sun.

heliograbado [ay-le-o-grah-bah'-do], *m.* Photogravure.

heliografía [ay-le-o-grah-fee'-ah], *f.* Blueprint.

heliómetro [ay-le-oh'-may-tro], *m.* Heliometer.

helioscopio [ay-le-os-co'-pe-o], *m.* Helioscope, telescope fitted for viewing the sun.

helioterapia [ay-le-o-tay-rah'-pe-ah], *f.* Heliotherapy, treating of disease by sunbaths.

heliotropio, heliotropo [ayle-o-tro, pe-o], *m.* 1. *(Bot.)* Turnsole, heliotrope. 2. Heliotrope, bloodstone, a precious stone. 3. Heliotrope, an instrument for reflecting solar light to an observer at a long distance.

helmíntico, ca [el-meen'-te-co, cah], *a.* Helminthic: applied to medicines against worms.

helota [ay-lo'-tah], *a. & n.* Helot, a bondman of Sparta.

helote [ay-lo'-tay], *m.* *(Mex.)* Green maize.

helvecio, cia [el-vay'-the-o, ah], *a.* Helvetic, Swiss

helvético, ca [el-vay'-te-co, cah], *a.* Helvetic, Swiss (persona).

hemacrimo, ma [ay-mah-cree'-mo, mah], *a.* Cold-blooded.

hemafobia [ay-mah-fo'-be-ah], *f.* Dread of blood.

hematemesis [ay-mah-tay-may'-sis], *f.* Hematemesis, vomiting of blood.

hematoma [ay-mah-to-mah], *m.* Bruise.

hemefóbico, ca [ay-mah-fo'-be-co, cah], *a.* Hemaphobic, having an aversion to blood.

hematina [ay-mah-tee'-nah], *f.* 1. Hematoxylin, the coloring matter of logwood. 2. Hematine, the coloring matter of the blood.

hematites [ay-mah-tee'-tes], *f.* Hematites, ore of iron.

hematosis [ay-mah-to'-sis], *f.* Haematosis, conversion of venous blood into arterial.

hematuria [ay-mah-too'-re-ah], *f.* Hematuria, blood in the urine.

hembra [em'-brah], *f.* 1. Female, she (de animales). **El pájaro hembra**, the female bird. **El elefante hembra**, the female elephant, the she-elephant. Nut of a screw. 3. Eye of a hook. 4. *V.* MUJER.

hembrear [em-bray-ar'], *vn.* 1. To be inclined to females (machos). 2. To generate or produce females only, or chiefly.

hembrilla [em-breel'-lyah], *f.* 1. A sort of wheat of very fine grain. 2. (*Mech.*) Any piece into which another is fitted. 3. (*Prov.*) Leather trace of horses for ploughing.

hemeroteca [ay-may-ro-tay'-kah], *f.* Newspaper archive.

hemicarpo [ay-me-car'-po], *m.* The half of a fruit divided naturally, as seen in the umbelliferae.

hemiciclo [ay-me-thee'-clo], *m. V.* SEMICÍRCULO.

hemicilíndrico, ca [ay-me-the-leen'-dre-co, cah], *a.* Semicylindrical.

hemicránea [ay-me-crah'-nay-ah], *f.* Hemicrania, migraine, headache of one side of the head.

hemina [ay-mee'-nah], *f.* 1. A measure containing the third part of a fanega. 2. Hemina, a Greek liquid measure.

hemiope [ay-me-o'-pay], *a. & n.* Hemiope, one who is affected with hemiopia.

hemiopía [ay-me-o-pee'-ah], *f.* Hemiopia, partial obliteration of the field of vision.

hemiplejia [ay-me-play'-he-ah], *f.* (*Med.*) Hemiplegia, paralysis of one side of the body.

hemíptero, ra [ay-meep'-tay-ro, rah], *a.* Hemipterous. -*m. pl.* The hemiptera; true bugs.

hemisférico, ca [ay-mis-fay'-re-co, cah], *a.* Hemispheric, hemispherical, half-round.

hemisferio [ay-mis-fey'-re-o], *m.* Hemisphere.

hemisferoidal [ay-mis-fay-ro-e-dahl'], *a.* Hemispheroidal.

hemistiquio [ay-mis-tee'-ke-o], *m.* Hemistich, half a verse.

hemofilia [ay-mo-fee'-le-ah], *f.* (*Med.*) Haemophilia.

hemoglobina [ay-mo-glo-bee'-nah], *f.* Haemoglobin.

hemómetro [ay-mo'-may-tro], *m.* Hemometer, an instrument for measuring the tension of a blood vessel.

hemopatía [ay-mo-pah-tee'-ah], *f.* (*Med.*) Disease of the blood.

hemoptisis [ay-mop-tee'-sis], *f.* Haemoptysis; spitting of blood.

hemorragia [ay-mor-rah'-he-ah], *f.* Hemorrhage, flux of blood. **Morir por hemorragia**, to bleed to death.

hemorrágico [ay-mor-rah'-he-co], *a.* Hemorrhagic, relating to bleeding.

hemorroide [ay-mor-ro'-e-day], *f.* (*Med.*) Piles, hemorrhoids.

hemorroidal [ay-mor-ro-e-dahl'], *a.* Hemorrhoidal.

hemostático, ca [ay-mos-tah'-te-co, cah], *a.* Hemostatic, serving to staunch bleeding.

henal [ay-nahl'], *m.* Hayloft.

henar [ay-nar'], *m.* Meadow of hay.

henchidor, ra [en-chee-dor', rah], *m. & f.* Filler, satiator, one who fills.

henchidura [en-chee-doo'-rah], *f.* Repletion, act of filling.

henchimiento [en-chee-me-en'-to], *m.* Abundance, repletion.

henchir [en-cheer'], *va.* 1. To fill up. 2. To stuff or fill with mingled ingredients, to farce. 3. To sow discord, to produce mischief. -*vr.* To fill oneself (persona). **Henchirse de orgullo**, to swell with pride.

hendedor, ra [en-day-dor', rah], *m. & f.* Divider, one who divides or splits something.

hendedura [en-day-doo'-rah], *f.* Fissure, crack, rent, chink, cleft, cranny, crevice, cut.

hender [en-derr'], *va.* 1. To chink, to break into apertures or chinks, to crack, to flaw, to break, to fissure, to cleave (cortar), to split. 2. To go through: to open a passage (abrirse paso). 2. To break into pieces. -*vr.* To gape, to open in fissures or holes.

hendible [en-dee'-blay], *a.* Fissile, capable of being split.

hendido, da [en-dee'-do, dah], *a. & pp.* of HENDER. Crannied, full of chinks, cleft.

hendrija [en-dree'-hah], *f.* (*Prov.*) A small fissure or crack.

henequén [ay-nay-ken'], *m.* (*Mex.*) 1. Maguey, American agave (planta). 2. Fiber of this plant, used for making hammocks, etc (fibra).

henil [ay-neel'], *m.* Hayloft.

heno [ay'-no], *m.* 1. Hay. 2. (*Amer.*) Moss, used for filling mattresses.

heñir [ay-nyeer'], *va.* To knead dough. **Hay mucho que heñir**, (coll.) there is much to do.

heparina [ay-pah-ree'-nah], *f.* Heparin.

hepática [ay-pah'-te-cah], *f.* (*Bot.*) Liverwort.

hepático, ca [ay-pah'-te-co, cah], *a.* Hepatic, hepatical, belonging to the liver.

hepatitis [ay-pah-tee'-tis], *f.* (*Med.*) Hepatitis, inflammation of the liver.

hepatizacion [ay-pah-te-thah-the-on'], *f.* Hepatization.

hepatizarse [ay-pah-te-thar'-say], *vr.* To become hepatized; to be transformed into a liver-like substance.

heptacordo [ep-tah-cor'-do], *m.* Heptachord, a musical instrument.

heptagonal [ep-tah-go-nahl'], *a.* (*Math.*) Heptagonal. *V.* HEPTAGONO, which is more used.

heptágono, na [ep-tah'-gono, nah], *a.* Heptagonal, having seven angles or sides.

heptágono [ep-tah'-go-no], *m.* Heptagon, a figure of seven sides and angles.

heptamerón [ep-tah-may-ron'], *m.* A literary work divided into seven parts.

heptámetro [ep-tah'-may-tro], *m.* Heptameter, verse of seven feet.

heptanemo [ep-tah-nay'-mo], *a.* Having seven tentacles.

heptangular [ep-tan-goo-lar'], *a.* Having seven angles.

heptapétalo, la [ep-tah-pay'-tah-lo], *a.* Seven petaled, heptapetalous.

heptarquía [ep-tar-kee'-ah], *f.* Heptarchy, a seven-fold government.

heráldica [ay-rahl'-de-cah], *f.* Heraldry, the art and office of a herald.

heráldico, ca [ay-rahl'-de-co, cah], *a.* Heraldic, relating to a herald.

heraldo [ay-rahl'-do], *m.* Herald, an officer who registers genealogies and adjusts armorial ensigns.

heraprica [ay-rah-pree'-cah], *f.* (*Pharm.*) Hierapicra, a bitter purgative medicine.

herbáceo, cea [er-bah'-thay-o, ah], *a.* 1. Herby, having the nature of herbs. 2. Herbaceous, belonging to herbs.

herbajar [er-bah-har'], *va.* To put flocks to graze, to pasture. -*vn.* To graze, to browse.

herbaje [er-bah'-hay], *m.* 1. Herbage, grass, pasture, feeding. 2. Payment for pasturage. 3. (*Prov.*) Tribute for cattle. 4. Kind of ancient coarse cloth made of herbs.

herbajero [er-bah-hay'-ro], *m.* One who rents meadows or pastures; one who lets pasturage.

herbar [er-bar'], *va.* To dress skins with herbs.

herbario [er-bah'-re-o], *m.* 1. *V.* BOTÁNICO. 2. Herbarium, a hortus siccus, collection of dried plants (colección). 3. Herbalist's (tienda).

herbario, ria [er-bah'-re-o, ah], *a.* Herbaceous, of or belonging to herbs.

herbazal [er-bah-thahl'], *m.* A place herbaged or covered with herbs or grass; a pasture ground for cattle.

herbecer [er-bay-therr'], *vn.* To begin to grow (hierba).

herbítero, ra [er-bee'-tay-ro, rah], *a.* Herbiferous, bending herbs.

herbívoro, ra [er-bee'-vo-ro, rah], *a.* Herbivorous, herbaceous, feeding on herbs.

herbolado, da [er-bo-lah'-do, dah], *a.* Applied to things poisoned with the juice of plants, as daggers, darts.

herbolario [er-bo-lah'-re-o], *m.* 1. Herbalist, herbarist, herbist, a person skilled in herbs (persona). 2. Herbman, a person who sells herbs. 3. A ridiculous, extravagant man.

herborización [er-bo-re-thah-the-on'], *f.* Herborization, botanizing.

herborizador, herborizante [er-bo-re-thah-dor'], *m.* Herbalist, herbarist, one who herborizes.

herborizar [er-bo-re-thar'], *vn.* To herborize, to go in search of herbs and plants (como coleccionista).

herboso, sa [er-bo'-so, sah'], *a.* Herbous, herby, grassy, abounding in herbs.

hercúleo, ea [er-coo'-lay-o, ah], *a.* Herculean.

hércules [err'-coo-les], *m.* 1. A man of great strength. 2. *(Ast.)* A northern constellation. 3. Name of a gigantic beetle.

heredad [ay-ray-dahd'], *f.* 1. Piece of ground which is cultivated and bears fruit. 2. Hereditament.

heredado, da [ay-ray-dah'-do, dah], *a.* V. HACENDADO. **Estar heredado**, to be in possession of one's family property. *-pp.* of HEREDAR.

heredamiento [ay-ray-dah-me-en'-to], *m.* Landed property, lands, tenements.

heredar [ay-ray-dar'], *va.* 1. To inherit, to heir (propiedad). 2. To make over property to another, to be possessed by himself and his heirs or successors. 3. To possess the disposition or temperament of their parents (niños).

heredero, ra [ay-ray-day'-ro, rah], *m. & f.* 1. Heir, heiress, inheritor to something left by a deceased person. 2. Heir, one possessing the same propensities as his predecessors. 3. *(Prov.)* Vintager, one who gathers the vintage. **Heredero forzoso**, general heir. **Heredero presuntivo**, heir apparent.

heredípeta [ay-ray-dee'-pay-tah], *com.* Legacy-seeker; one who artfully plots to procure legacies or inheritances. *(Acad.)*

hereditario, ria [ay-ray-de-tah'-re-o, ah], *a.* Hereditary, derived from ancestors; entailed on a family.

hereje [ay-ray'-hay], *com.* A heretic. **Cara de hereje**, hideous or deformed aspect.

herejía [ay-ray-hee'-ah], *f.* 1. Heresy. 2. Literary error, contrary to the principles of a science. 3. Injurious expression against anyone (injuria). 3. Dirty trick (trampa).

herejote, ta [ay-ray-ho'-tay, tah], *m. & f.* 1. *(coll.)* A great heretic.

herén [ay-ren'], *m.* *(Bot.)* Vetch. V. YERO.

herencia [ay-ren'-the-ah], *f.* Inheritance, hereditament, heritage, heirship, heirdom.

heresiarca [ay-ray-se-ar'-cah], *m.* Heresiarch, a leader in heresy.

heretical [ay-ray-te-cahl'], *a.* Heretical, containing heresy.

herético, ca [ay-ray'-te-co, cah], *a.* Heretical.

hergoma [er-go'-mah], *f.* An Irish linen made with threads of a spider's web.

heria [ay'-re-ah], *f.* 1. Strolling vagrant. V. HAMPA.

herida [ay-ree-'ah], *f.* 1. Wound. 2. Affliction, anything which afflicts the mind. 3. Injury, outrage, mischief. 4. Place where the game perches when pursued by the hawk.

herido, da [ay-ree'-do, dah], *a. & pp.* of HERIR. 1. Wounded, injured, hurt. **Mal herido**, badly wounded. 2. Bloody, cruel. **A grito herido**, with loud cries. *-m.* Injured man; wounded man. **Los heridos**, the wounded (guerra), the injured (accidente). **El número de los heridos en el accidente**, the number of people hurt in the accident.

heridor, ra [ay-re-dor', rah], *m. & f.* Wounder, striker.

herimiento [ay-re-me-en'-to], *m.* 1. Act of wounding. 2. Conjunction of vowels in a syllable; elision.

herir [ay-reer'], *va.* 1. To wound, to break the continuity of any part of the body. 2. To wound, to hurt by violence, to cause either bodily or mental pain, to harm, to mischief (dañar). 3. To shine upon, to cast his beams upon, to irradiate (sol). 4. To knock, to dash together, to strike (golpear), to collide. 5. To strike, or to make an impression upon the mind or upon the senses, to affect, to touch, to move (corazón etc.) 6. To play on a stringed instrument. 7. To offend (ofender), to pique, to irritate. *-vr.* V. AGRAVIARSE. **Un sonido me hirió el oído**, a sound reached my ear. **Es un color que hiere la vista**, it's a color which offends the eye. *(Yo hiero, él hirió, hiriera, from Herir. V. ASENTIR.)*

hermafrodita, hermafrodito [er-mah-fro-dee'-tah, to], *m.* Hermaphrodite, androgyne, an animal or plant uniting two sexes.

hermana [er-mah'-nah], *f.* 1. Sister. **Media hermana**, half-sister. **Hermana gemela**, twin sister. 2. Sister-in-law. 3. *(Ecl.)* Sister. **Hermana lega**, lay sister. V. HERMANO.

hermanable [er-mah-nah'-blay], *a.* Fraternal (hermano), brotherly.

hermanablemente [er-mah-nah-blay-men'-tay], *adv.* Fraternally.

hermanamiento [er-mah-naha-me-ayn'-to], *m.* **Hermanamiento de ciudades**, town-twinning.

hermanar [er-mah-nar'], *va.* 1. To match (para formar par), to suit, to proportion, to fellow, to pair, to harmonize (armonizar). 2. To combine (combinar). *-vn.* To join (unir), to unite. *-vr.* To love one another as brothers.

hermanastro, tra [er-mah-nahs'-tro-trah], *m. & f.* Step-brother, step-sister.

hermanazgo [er-mah-nath'-go], *m.* Fraternity, brotherhood.

hermandad [er-man-dahd'], *f.* 1. Fraternity, the state or quality of a brother. 2. Conformity, resemblance. 3. Amity, friendship. 4. Brotherhood (cofradía, gremio), confraternity, an association of men, fraternity. **La Santa Hermandad**, Spanish militia, formed in the XVIIth century to maintain public order. **Hermandad de ganaderos**, association of cattlemen.

hermanear [er-mah-nay-ar'], *va.* To treat as a brother.

hermanita [er-mah-nee'-tah], *f. dim.* A little sister.

hermanito [er-mah-nee'-to], *m. dim.* A little brother.

hermano, na [er-mah'-no, nah], *a.* Matched, suitable, having resemblance.

hermano [er-mah'-no], *m.* 1. Brother, born of the same parents. 2. Brother-in-law. 3. Similarity: as among the members of a religious community. **Hermano carnal**, brother by the same father and mother. **Hermano de leche**, foster-brother. **Hermano político**, brother-in-law. **Primo hermano**, first cousin. **Medio hermano**, half-brother. *-pl.* 1. Members of the same religious confraternity. 2. Lay-brothers of a religious order.

hermanuco [er-mah-noo'-co], *m.* Name given in contempt to lay-brothers of some religious orders.

herméticamente [er-may'-te-cah-men-tay], *adv.* Hermetically.

hermético, ca [er-may'-te-co, cah], *a.* Hermetical; airtight, watertight; self-contained; reserved (persona), secretive; watertight (teoría); impenetrable (misterio).

hermodátiles [er-mo-dah'-te-les], *m. pl.* Hermodactyl, a bulbous root formerly used as a cathartic.

hermosamente [er-mo-sah-men'-tay], *adv.* Beautifully, handsomely, lovely; perfectly, properly.

hermoseador, ra [er-mo-say-ah-dor', rah], *m. & f.* Beautifier.

hermosear [er-mo-say-ar'], *va.* 1. To beautify, to embellish, to adorn. 2. To glamorize, to add glamor or luster.

hermoso, sa [er-mo'-so, sah], *a.* Beautiful (bello), handsome (hombre), graceful, lovely, comely, neat, goodly, fine (espléndido), beauteous, fair. **Un día hermoso**, a fine day. **Seis hermosos toros**, six magnificent bulls.

hermosura [er-mo-soo'-rah], *f.* 1. Beauty, that assemblage of graces which pleases the eye. 2. Handsomeness (de un hombre), goodliness, fineness, fairness, freshness. 3. Symmetry, agreement of one part with another. 4. Beauty (persona), a beautiful person. **¡Qué hermosura!**, what a beauty!

hernia [ayr'-ne-ah], *f.* Hernia, rupture.

herniario [er-ne-ah'-re-o], *a.* Hernial, relating to hernia. **Saco herniario**, hernial sac.

herniarse [er-ne-ahr'-say], *vr.* To rupture oneself.

hernista [er-nees'-tah], *m.* Surgeon who applies himself to the cure of ruptures.

héroe [ay'-ro-ay], *m.* 1. Hero, a man eminent for bravery and valor. 2. Hero, the principal person in a poem. 3. Among the ancient pagans, one whom they believed to be born of a god or goddess and a human being.

heroicamente [ay-ro-e-cah-men'-tay], *adv.* Heroically.

heroicidad [ay-ro-e-the-dahd'], *f.* Quality or character which constitutes an heroic action (cualidad). *V.* HEROÍSMO.

heroico, a [ay-ro'-e-co, cah], *a.* 1. Heroic, eminent for bravery. 2. Heroical, befitting a hero. 3. Reciting the feats of heroes.

heroína [ay-ro-ee'-nah], *f.* A heroine.

heroína [ay-ro-ee'-nah], *f.* Heroin, a narcotic.

heroinómano, na [ay-ro-ee-no'-mah-no], *m & f.* Heroin addict.

heroísmo [ay-ro-ees'-mo], *m.* Heroism.

herpe [err'-pay], *m.* or *f.* Herpes, tetter, a cutaneous disease: commonly used in the plural.

herpético, ca [er-pay'-te-co, cah], *a.* Herpetic.

herpil [er-peel'], *m.* Sack of esparto netting with wide meshes, made for carrying straw, melons, etc.

herrada [er-rah'-dah], *f.* A pail.

herrada [er-rah'-dah], *a.* Applied to water in which red-hot iron has been cooled.

herradero [er-rah-day'-ro], *m.* 1. Place destined for marking cattle with a hot iron. 2. Marking cattle with a hot iron.

herrador [er-rah-dor'], *m.* Farrier, a shoer of horses.

herradura [er-rah-doo'-rah], *f.* 1. Shoe (animales). **Herradura de caballo**, horse-shoe. 2. Collar or necklace in the form of a horse-shoe. 3. The horse-shoe shape commonly given to the galleries of a theatre, or like audience-chamber.

herraj [er-rah'], *m.* Stones of olives after extracting the oil. *V.* ERRAX.

herraje [er-rah'-hay], *m.* 1. Ironwork, pieces of iron used for ornament and strength. **Herraje de un navío**, ironwork of a ship. 2. Horse-shoe. 3. *V.* HERRAJ.

herramental [er-rah-men-tahl'], *m. & a.* Bag with instruments for shoeing horses.

herramienta [er-rah-me-en'-tah], *f.* 1. Tool, set of tools, tool kit (equipo). **Herramienta mecánica**, power tool. 2. Ironwork. 3. Horns of a beast (de toro). 4. *(coll.)* Teeth (dientes), grinders. 5. Weapon (arma). 6. *(Inform.)* **Herramienta de ayuda en la toma de decisiones**, decision support tool.

herrar [er-rar'], *va.* 1. To garnish with iron. 2. To shoe horses (caballo). 3. To brand cattle with a hot iron (ganado). (*Yo hierro, yo hierre*, from *Herrar. V.* ACRECENTAR.)

herrén [er-ren'], *m.* 1. Maslin, mixed corn for feeding horses. 2. *V.* HERRENAL.

herrenal, or **herreñal** [er-ray-nahl', er-ray-nyahl'], *m.* Piece of ground in which maslin is sown.

herrería [er-ray-ree'-ah], *f.* 1. Ironworks, where iron is manufactured and moulded into pigs or bars (fábrica). 2. Forge (taller). 3. Clamor, confused noise.

herrerico, herrerillo [er-ray-ree'-co, eel'lyo], *m.* Small bird.

herrero [er-ray'-ro], *m.* Smith, one who forges iron.

herrerón [er-ray-rone'], *m.* A bad smith.

herreruelo [er-ray-roo-ay'-lo], *m.* 1. *(Orn.)* Wagtail, a bird whose note resembles the sound of hammering and betokens rain. 2. *V.* FERRERUELO. 3. *(Dim.) V.* HERRERICO.

herrete [er-ray'-tay], *m.* Tag, point of metal at the end of a cord.

herretear [er-ray-tay-ar'], *va.* To tag a cord, to string, or to ribbon.

herretero, ra [er-ray-tay'-ro, rah], *m. & f.* Tag-maker.

herrezuelo [er-ray-thoo-ay'-lo], *m.* Light piece of iron.

herrial [er-re-ahl'], *a.* Applied to a kind of large black grapes, and to the vines which bear them.

herrín [er-reen'], *m.* Rust of iron.

herrón [er-rone'], *m.* 1. A ring, in the middle of which is a hole, which boys pitch at a stake; a quoit. 2. A washer.

herronada [er-ro-nah'-dah], *f.* 1. A violent blow or stroke. 2. *(Met.)* Blow with a bird's beak.

herrugiento, ta [er-roo-he-en'-to, tah], *a.* Rusty.

herrumbre [er-room'-bray], *f.* Rust of iron; irony taste.

herrumbroso, sa [er-room-bro'-so, sah], *a.* 1. Rusty, drossy, scaly. 2. Participating of the qualities of iron.

herventar [er-ven-tar'], *va.* To boil something.

hervidero [er-ve-day'-ro], *m.* 1. Ebullition, the agitation of a boiling fluid (acto). 2. Kind of water-clock or small spring, from which water bubbles out (manantial). 3. Rattling in the throat. 4. Multitude, great quantity or number. **Un hervidero de gente**, a swarm of people.

hervir [er-veer'], *vn.* 1. To boil; to bubble (burbujear); to seethe (mar) **Hervir a fuego lento**, to simmer. (*Yo hiervo, el hirvió, hirviera*; from *Hervir. V.* ASENTIR.) **Empezar a hervir**, to begin to boil. 2. *(Met.)* To swarm with vermin, to be crowded with people. 3. To be fervent, vehement.

hervor [er-vor'], *m.* 1. Ebullition, the agitation of boiling fluids (acto). 2. Fervor, heat, vigor, fret. 3. *(Met.)* Noise and movement of waters. **Alzar or levantar el hervor**, to begin to boil.

hervoroso, sa [er-vo-ro'-so, sah], *a. V.* FOGOSO.

hespéride, hespérido, da [es-pay'-re-day, es-pay'-re-do, dah], *a.* 1. Relating to the Pleiades. 2. *(Poet.)* Western.

hespérides [es-pay'-re-des], *f. pl. V.* PLÉYADES.

héspero [ays'-pay-ro], *m.* The planet Venus, as evening star.

heteróclito, ta [ay-tay-ro'-cle-to, tah], *a.* 1. *(Gram.)* Heteroclite, inflected irregularly. 2. Irregular, abnormal.

heterodino, na [ay-tay-ro-dee'-no, nah], *a.* Heterodyne.

heterodoxia [ay-tay-ro-doc'-se-ah], *f.* Heterodoxy, misbelief.

heterodoxo, xa [ay-tay-ro-doc'-so, sah], *a.* Heterodox, not orthodox.

heterodromo [ay-tay-ro-dro'-mo], *m.* A lever whose fulcrum is between the power and the weight.

heterogamia [ay-tay-ro-gah'-me-ah], *f.* Heterogamy.

heterógamo, mah [ay-tay-ro'-gah-mo, mah], *a.* Heterogamous, bearing flowers of two sexual kinds.

heterogeneidad [ay-tay-ro-hay-nay-ee dahd'], *f.* Heterogeneousness, heterogeneity.

heterogéneo, nea [ay-tay-ro-hay'-nay-o, ah], *a.* Heterogeneous, dissimilar in nature, heterogene, heterogeneal.

heteromorfo, fa [ay-tay-ro-mor'-fo, fah], *a.* Heteromorphic, or morphous; of diverse form in several of its parts.

heterónomo, ma [ay-tay-ro'-no-mo, mah], *a.* Heteronymous, differing from the common type.

heterópsido, da [ay-tay-rop'-se-do, dah], *a.* (Metals) in a state of alkaline earth.

heterosexual [ay-tay-ro-sec-soo-al'], *a. m & f.* Heterosexual.

heterosexualidad [ay-tay-ro-sec-soo-ah-le-dahd'], *f.* Heterosexuality.

hética, hetiques [ay'-te-cah, ay-te-keth'], *f.* Phthisis, consumption, hectic (tísico).

hético, ca [ay'-te-co, cah], *a.* 1. Pertaining or related to tuberculosis. 2. Weak, emaciated (flaco).

heu [ay'-oo], *m.* Sloop, with one sail, of 300 tons, used in northern seas.

heurística [ay-oo-rees-te-cah]. *(Inform.)* Heuristics.

hexacordo [ec-sah-cor'-do], *m. (Mus.)* Hoxachord.

hexaedro [ec-sah-ay'-dro], *m.* Hexahedron a cube.

hexagonal [ec-sah-go-nahl'], *a.* Hexagonal.

hexágono [ec-sah'-gono], *m.* Hexagon, a figure of six sides.

hexágono, na [ec-sah'-gono, nah], *a.* Hexagonal, having six sides.

hexámetro [ec-sah'-may-tro], *m.* Hexameter, a verse of six feet.

hexápeda

hexápeda [ec-sah'-pay-dah], *f. V.* TOESA.

hexástilo [ec-sahs'-te-lo], *m. (Arch.)* Hexastyle, a building with six columns in front.

hez [eth], *f.* 1. Scum, lee, the dregs of liquors. 2. Dross of metals. 3. Grains of malt. **La hez del pueblo**, the scum of the people. **Heces**, faeces, excrements.

híadas, híades [ee'-ah-das, ee'-ah-des], *f. pl. V.* PLÉYADES.

hialino, na [e-ah-lee'-no, nah], *a.* Hyaline, transparent.

hialitis [e-ah-lee'-tis], *f.* Hyalitis, inflammation of the vitreous body.

hialóideo, dea [e-ah-lo'-e-day-o, ah], *a.* Vitreous, glass-like.

hialoides [e-ah-lo'-e-des], *f.* Hyaloid membrane, inclosing the vitreous body of the eye.

hialosomo, ma [e-ah-lo-so'-mo, mah], *a. (Zool.)* Transparent in body; hyaline.

hialurgia [e-ah-loor'-hee-ah], *f.* The art of making glass.

hialúrgico, ca [e-ah-loor'-he-co, cah], *a.* Glass working, belonging to glass making.

hiante [e-ahn'-tay], *a.* Applied to a verse with a hiatus.

hiato [e-ah'-to], *m.* Hiatus, panes or cacophony, by the succession of an initial to a final vowel.

hibernación [e-bayr-nah-the-on'], *f.* Hibernation.

hibernal, hibernizo, za [e-ber-nahl', e-ber-nee'-tho, thah], *a.* Hibernal, wintry.

hibernar [e-ber-nar'], *vn. (Prov.)* To winter, to live in a place during winter.

hibernés, sa [e-ber-nays', sah], *a.* Hibernian, Irish.

hibierno [e-be-err'-no], *m.* Winter. *V.* INVIERNO.

hibisco [e-bees'-co], *m. (Bot.)* Syrian mallow.

híbrido, da [ee'-bre-do, dah], *m. & f.* Hybridous animal, as a mule; hybridous words. -*a.* Hybridous, hybrid.

hibridación [e-bre-dah-the-on'], *f.* Hybridization, hybridism.

hicocervo [e-co-therr'-vo], *m.* Fabulous animal; chimera, a wild fancy.

hidalgamente [e-dal-gah-men'-tay], *adv.* Nobly, in a gentleman-like manner.

hidalgarse [e-dal-gar'-say], *vr. (coll.)* To assume the nobleman, to affect the gentleman.

hidalgo, ga [e-dahl'-go, gah], *a.* Noble, illustrious, excellent, exalted.

hidalgo, ga [e-dahl'-go, gah], *m. & f.* Hidalgo, a noble man or woman, a person of noble descent, one who is ennobled.

hidalgón, na, hidalgote, ta [e-dal-gone', nah], *m. & f. aug.* An old noble man or woman, proud of the rights and privileges of their class.

hidalguejo, ja, hidalguete, ta, hidalguillo, lla [e-dal-gay'-ho, hah], *m. & f. dim.* A petty country squire, a poor gentleman or lady.

hidalguía [e-dal-gee'-ah], *f.* 1. Nobility, the rights and privileges of noble men. 2. Nobleness of mind, liberality of sentiments.

hidátide [e-dah'-te-day], *f.* 1. Hydatid, a cyst containing a larval tapeworm. 2. *(Min.)* A stone esteemed as precious by the ancients: used also as an adjective.

hidatidiforme [e-dah-te-de-for'-may], *a.* Hydatidiform, bladder-shaped.

hidra [ee'-drah], *f.* 1. Hydra, a fabulous monster. 2. A poisonous serpent. 3. *(Met.)* Seditions, plots. 4. Hydra, a fresh-water polyp.

hidragogo [e-drah-go'-go], *m. & a. (Med.)* Hydragogue.

hidrargírido, da [e-drar-hee'-re-do, dah], *a.* Resembling mercury.

hidrargirio [e-drar-hee'-re-o], *m.* An amalgam of mercury with another metal.

hidrárgiro [e-drar'-he-ro], *m.* Ancient name of mercury (hydrargyrum); entering into composition.

hidratado, da [e-drah-tah'-do, dah], *a.* Hydrate(d), containing water in composition.

hidratar [e-drah-tar'], *va.* To hydrate, to combine with water.

hidrato [e-drah'-to], *m.* Hydrate, a compound with water or hydrogen peroxide. **Hidrato de carbono**, carbohydrate.

hidráulica [e-drah'-oo-le-cah], *f.* Hydraulics, a branch of hydrodynamics.

hidráulico, ca [e-drah'-oo-le-co, cah], *a.* Hydraulical, hydraulic. **Fuerza hidráulica**, water power.

hidráulico [e-drah'-oo-le-co], *m.* Professor of hydraulics.

hidrazina [e-drah-thee'-nah], *f.* Hydrazine (combustible).

hidremia [e-dray'-me-ah], *f.* Hydramia, an excess of water in the blood.

hidria [ee'-dre-ah], *f.* Jar or pitcher for water.

hidro [ee'-dro], *m.* Water in Greek.

hidroavión [e-dro-ah-ve-on'], *m.* Hydroplane, sea-plane.

hidrocarburo [e-dro-car-boo'-ro], *m. (Chem.)* Hydrocarbon.

hidrocéfalo [e-dro-thay'-fah-lo], *m. (Med.)* Hydrocephalus, dropsy in the head.

hidrocerámico, ca [e-dro-thay-rah'-me-co, cah], *a.* Hydroceramic, porous.

hidroclórico, ca [e-dro-clo'-re-co, cah], *a.* Hydrochloric.

hidrodinámica [e-dro-de-nah'-me-cah], *f.* Hydrodynamics, science which relates to the motion of fluids.

hidroeléctrico, ca [e-dro-ay-lec'-tre-co, cah], *a.* Hydroelectric.

hidrofilacio [e-dro-fe-lah'-the-o], *m.* Great cavern full of water.

hidrófilo, la [e-dro'-fe-lo, lah], *a.* Water loving.

hidrofobia [e-dro-fo'-be-ah], *f.* Hydrophobia, a disease; rabies.

hidrófobo [e-dro'-ho-bo], *m.* Person suffering hydrophobia.

hidrófugo, ga [e-dro'-foo-go, gah], *a. (Zool.)* Hydrofuge, shedding water.

hidrogenar [e-dro-hay-nar'], *va.* To hydrogenate.

hidrógeno [e-dro'-hay-no], *m. (Chem.)* Hydrogen. **Hidrógeno líquido**, liquid hydrogen.

hidrogogía [e-dro-go-hee'-ah], *f.* The art of science of canalizing water.

hidrografía [e-dro-grah-fee'-ah], *f.* Hydrography, the description of the watery part of the globe.

hidrográfico, ca [e-dro-grah'-fe-co, cah], *a.* Hydrographical.

hidrógrafo [e-dro'-grah-fo], *m.* Hydrographer.

hidrólisis [e-dro'-le-sis], *f.* Hydrolysis.

hidrolizar [e-dro-le-thar'], *va.* To hydrolyze.

hidrología [e-dro-lo-hee'-ah], *f.* Hydrology, description of the nature and properties of water.

hidromático, ca [e-dro-mah'-te-co, cah], *a.* Hydromatic.

hidromel, hidromiel [e-dro-mel', me-el'], *m.* Hydromel, mead, metheglin.

hidrómetra [e-dro'-may-trah], *m.* Professor of hydrometry.

hidrometría [e-dro-may-tree'-ah], *f.* Hydrometry.

hidrometro [e-dro'-may-tro], *m.* Hydrometer, instrument for measuring the weight of fluids.

hidrónica [e-dro'-ne-cah], *f.* Hydronics.

hidrópata [e-dro'-pah-tah], *m.* Hydropath, follower of hydropathy.

hidropatía [e-dro-pah-tee'-ah], *f.* Hydropathy, hydrotherapy.

hidropático, ca [e-dro-pah'-te-co, cah], *a.* Hydropathic.

hidropesía [e-dro-pay-see'-ah], *f.* Dropsy.

hidrópico, ca [e-dro'-peco, cah], *a.* Hydropic, hydropical, dropsical.

hidroplano [e-dro-plah'-no], *f.* Hydroplane.

hidrópota [e-dro'-po-tah], *a. & n.* A person who drinks only water: a water-drinker.

hidróscopo [e-dros'-co-po], *m.* One who detects the presence of water under ground.

hidrosita [e-dro-see'-tah], *f.* A geode of chalcedony which contains water.

hidrostática [e-dros-tah'-te-cah], *f.* Hydrostatics.

hidrostáticamente [e-dros-tah'-te-cah-men-tay], *adv.* Hydrostatically.

hidrostático, ca [e-dros-tah'-te-co, cah], *a.* Hydrostatical.

hidrosulfúrico, ca [e-dro-sool-foo'-re-co, cah], *a.* Hydrosulphuric, or sulphhydric.

hidrotecnia [e-dro-tec'-ne-ah], *f.* Hydraulics, hydraulic engineering.

hidroterapia [e-dro-tay-rah'-pe-ah], *f.* Hydrotherapeutics.

hidrotórax [e-dro-to'-rax], *f.* Hydrothorax, dropsy of the chest.

hidróxido [e-droc'-se-do], *m.* Hydroxide.

hiedra [e-ay'-drah], *f.* 1. (*Bot.*) Ivy. 2. (*Local*) Poison-vine. **Hiedra terrestre**, ground ivy. (*Yo hiedro, yo hiedre*, from *Hedrar. V.* ACRECENTAR.

hiel [eel'], *f.* 1. Gall, bile, an animal juice. 2. (*Met.*) Bitterness, asperity. **No tener hiel**, to be meek, simple, and gentle. **Hieles**, calamities, misfortunes, toils.

hiel de la tierra [e-el' day lah te-ay'-rah], *f.* 1. (*Bot.*) Common fumitory or earth-smoke. 2. Common erythraea centaurium.

hielo [e-ay'-lo], *m.* 1. Ice. 2. Frost. 3. Congealment. **Hielo seco**, dry ice. **Hielo movedizo**, drift ice. 4. (*Fig.*) Coolness, indifference. **Ser más frío que el hielo**, to be as cold as ice.

hiena [e-ay'-nah], *f.* Hyena, a fierce animal.

hierarca [e-ay-rar'-cah], *m.* Hierarch, among the Greeks, the chief of a sacred order.

hierático, ca [e-ay-rah'-te-co, cah], *a.* Hieratic, sacerdotal.

hierba [e-err'-bah], *f.* 1. Herb, a plant not possessing a woody stem, but dying down to the ground after flowering. 2. Green food for cattle, herbage, grass (chiefly in plural). 3. Flaw in the emerald which tarnishes its lustre. -*pl.* 1. Poison given in food; a poisonous plant. 2. Among the clergy, greens, gardenstuff. 3. Grass, pasturage. **Crecer como la mala hierba**, to grow like weeds. **Hierbas** grass. **Hierba cana**, groundsel. **Y otras hierbas**, (*Fig.*) and so forth.

hierbabuena [e-ayr-bah-boo-ay'-nah], *f.* (*Acad.*) Peppermint, mint. *V.* YERBABUENA.

hierbajo [e-ayr-bah'-ho], *m.* Weed.

herogenia [e-ay-ro-hay'-ne-ah], *f.* Origin of different religions and the science which treats of such origin.

hieroglífico, ca [e-ay-ro-glee'-fe-co, cah], *a.* Hieroglyphic, hieroglyphical, emblematical. -*m.* (*Acad.*) *V.* JEROGLÍFICO.

hieroscopia [e-ay-ros-co'-pe-ah], *f. V.* ARUSPICINA.

hierro [e-ayr'-ro], *m.* 1. Iron, a malleable metal (metal). 2. Any iron tool (herramienta). 3. Brund, a mark made by burning with a hot iron. 4. An iron instrument to wound with. **Hierro colado or fundido**, cast-iron. **Hierro forjado**. forged iron. **Es de hierro**, he is indefatigable, or as hardy as steel. **Hierros**, irons, fetters, jail. **Como el hierro**, like iron. **Hierro en lingotes**, pig iron.

hietómetro [e-ay-to'-may-tro], *m.* Hyetometer, rain-guage, or pluviometer.

hi-fi [e'-fe], *m.* Hi-fi.

higa [ee-gah], *f.* 1. A fist-shaped, amulet, charm, hung about the neck for preventing or curing disease. 2. An obscene gesture. 3. Ridicule, derision. **Dar higas**, to despise a thing.

higadillo [e-gah-deel'-lyo], *m. dim.* A small liver; the liver of birds, fishes, and other small animals.

hígado [ee'-gah-do], *m.* 1. Liver, one of the entrails. 2. (*Met. Coll.*) Courage, valor, bravery. **Tener malos hígados**. 1. To be white-livered, to be ill-disposed. 2. (*Met.*) To hate. **Echar los hígados**, to be very tired or fatigued. **Hasta los higados**, (*coll.*) to the heart. **¡Qué hígados tiene!**, what guts he has!

higate [e-gah'-tay], *m.* Pottage, formerly made of figs, pork, and fowl. boiled together, and seasoned with sugar, ginger, cinnamon, pimento, and other spices.

higiene [e-he-ay'-nay], *f.* (*Med.*) Hygiene.

higiénicamente [e-he-ay'-ne-cah-men-tay], *adv.* Hygienically.

higiénico, ca [e-he-ay'-ne-co, cah], *a.* Hygienic.

higo [ee'go], *m.* 1. Fig, the fruit of the fig-tree. **Higo chumbo or de pala**, fruit of the nopal or Indian fig-tree. **Pan de higos**, cake made of figs. 2. A kind of piles.

higrometría [e-gro-my-tree'-ah], *m.* Hygrometry.

higrométrico, ca [e-gro-may'-tre-co, cah], *a.* Hygrometric, measuring moisture.

higrómetro [e-gro'-may-tro], *m.* Hygrometer, an instrument for measuring the degrees of moisture.

higroscopia [e-gros-co'-pe-ah], *f.* Hygroscopy, hygrometry.

higroscopio [e-gros-co'-pe-o], *m.* Hygroscope, a device for indicating the humidity of the air.

higuera [e-gay'-rah], *f.* (*Bot.*) Fig-tree. **Higuera infernal**, castor-oil plant. **Higuera de Indias or de las Indias**, Indian fig-tree, prickly-pear cactus. **Caer de la higuera**, to come down to earth with a bump. **Estar en la higuera**, to be miles away, to be in the clouds.

higueral [e-gay-rahl'], *m.* Plantation of fig-trees.

higuerón [e-gay-rone'], *m.* Large tree in America.

higuito [e-gee'-to], *m. dim.* A small fig.

hija [ee'-hah], *f.* 1. Daughter. 2. Daughter-in-law. *V.* HIJO, JA.

hijar [e-har', *m. V.* IJAR.

hijastro, tra [e-hahs'-tro, trah], *m. & f.* Step-child.

hijezna [e-heth'-nah], *m.* The young of any bird.

hijito, ita [e-hee'-to, tah], *m. & f. dim.* Little child, little dear.

hijo [ee'-ho], *m.* 1. Son. 2. Son-in-law.

hijo, ja [ee'-ho, hah], *m. & f.* 1. Child. 2. Young of all animals. 3. Son or native of a place. 4. Child, son, daughter, anything which is the product or effect of another. **Hijo de familia**, 1. A minor. 2. A son of noble parents. 5. Bud or root of the horns of animals. **Hijo de leche**, foster child. **Hijo bastardo, hijo de su madre**, (*coll.*) bastard. **Hijo natural**, illegitimate child. **Como cada hijo de vecino**, everyone. **Ser hijo de papá**, to be daddy's boy. **Nombrar a uno hijo predilecto** de la ciudad, to give the freedom of the city. **Hijo único**, only child. **Hacerle a una un hijo**, to get someone pregnant. **Hijo adoptivo**, adopted child. **Hijo político**, son-in-law. **El Hijo de Dios**, the Son of God.

hijodalgo, hijadalgo [e-ho-dahl'-go, e-hah-dahl'-go], *m. & f. V.* HIDALGO.

hijuela [e-hoo-ay'-lah], *f.* 1. Piece of cloth or linen joined to another which is too short or narrow. 2. A small mattress, put between others, to make the bed even. 3. Pall, a square bit of linen or pasteboard put over the chalice. 4. A small drain for drawing off water from an estate. 5. Schedule or inventory delivered in Spain to parties entitled in distribution to the estate of a person deceased, containing an exact account of their distributive share. 6. An inventory, a catalogue of the articles which belong to the estate of a deceased person. 7. Crossroad. 8. Postman who delivers letters from the office. 9. Palm-seed. 10. Fascine of wood. 11. Cord made of the gut of silkworms.

hijuelo, la [e-hoo-ay'-lo, lah], *m. & f. dim.* 1. A young child (niño). 2. (*Bot.*) Sucker.

hila [ee'-lah], *f.* 1. Row (fila), line. *V.* HILERA. 2. Thin gut (cuerda). 3. Act of spinning. 4. Lint to lay on sores. 5. Small trench for dividing the water destined for the irrigation of different pieces of ground.

hilacha [e-lah'-chah], *f.* Filament or thread ravelled out of cloth.

hilachoso, sa [e-lah-cho'-so, sah], *a.* Filamentous.

hilada [e-lah'-dah], *f.* 1. Row or line of bricks or stones in a building. 2. *V.* HILERA.

hiladillo [e-lah-deel'-ly-o], *m.* 1. Ferret silk. 2. Narrow ribbon or tape.

hilado [e-lah'-do], *m.* Spun flax, hemp, wool, silk, or cotton. **Hilado, da**, *pp.* Of HILAR.

hilador, ra [e-lah-dor', rah], *m. & f.* Spinner, spinster.

hilandera [e-lan-day'-rah], *f.* Spinster, woman who spins.

hilandería [e-lan-day-ree'-ah], *f.* Place where hemp is spun.

hilandero [e-lan-day'-ro], *m.* 1. Spinner. 2. Spinning room, a rope-walk.

hilanderilla [e-lan-day-reel'-lyah], *f. dim.* A little spinster.

hilanza [e-lahn'-thah], *f.* (*Prov.*) Thread, line, mode of spinning.

hilar [e-lar'], *va.* 1. To spin, to draw silk, cotton, etc., into thread. 2. To argue, to discuss. **Hilar delgado**, to split hairs. 3. To spin a cocoon (gusanos de seda). **Máquina de hilar**, spinning machine.

hilaracha [e-lah-rah'-chah], *f.* Filament. *V.* HILACHA.

hilarante [e-lah-rahn'-tay], *a.* Nitrous oxide gas; so called laughing gas.

hilaridad [e-lah-re-dahd'], *f.* Hilarity, laughter, jollity.

hilaza [e-lah'-thah], *f.* 1. Anything spun or drawn out into thread. *V.* HILADO. 2. Yarn. **Hilazas**, filaments of plants.

hilera [e-lay'-rah], *f.* 1. Row, line. 2. *(Mech.)* Wiredrawer. 3. Fine thread. 4. *(Mil.)* File, single file. 5. *(Arch.)* Ridge-pole. 6. *(Zool.)* Spinneret. 7. *(Mas.)* Course. 8. Fine yarn.

hilero [e-lay'-ro], *m.* 1. Sign of currents in the sea. 2. Thread-seller.

hilete [e-lay'-tay], *m. dim.* of HILO.

hilo [ee'-lo], *m.* 1. Thead, a small line of cotton, silk, etc (tela). 2. Wire, metal drawn into threads (metal). 3. A slender thread, formed by liquids falling in drops (líquido) 4. *(Met.)* Continuation, series. 5. Fine thread of spider or silkworms. 6. *V.* FILO. 7. *(Fig.)* Thread, theme (conversación, discurso), curse (vida), train (pensamiento). **Hilo a hilo**, drop by drop. **Hilo de zapatero**, shoemaker's thread. **Hilo de oro** or **de plata**, gold or silver thread. **Hilo para sastre**, tailors' thread. **Hilo en ovillos**, thread in balls. **Hilo de torzal** or **de pelos**, cotton yarn. **Hilo de zurcir**, darning wool. **Hilo de humo**, thin line of smoke. **Traje de hilo**, linen dress. **Coger el hilo**, to pick up the thread. **Perder el hilo**, to lose the thread.

hilván [eel-vahn'], *m.* Basting, long stitches set in clothes to keep them in order for sewing.

hilvanar [eel-vah-nar'], *va.* 1. To baste, to sew slightly. 2. To act or perform in a hurry (trabajo).

himen [ee'-men], *m.* Hymen, the virginal membrane.

himeneo [e-may-nay'-o], *m.* 1. *(Poet.)* Marriage, matrimony. 2. Epithalamium, hymeneal, hymenean. 3. Hymen, the god of marriage.

himenocarpo, pa [e-may-no-car'-po, pah], *a. (Bot.)* Bearing a membranous fruit.

himenófilo [e-may-no'-fe-lo], *m.* Hymenophyllum, filmy fern, lace fern.

himenópteros [e-may-nop'tay-ros], *m. pl.* The hymenoptera: the order of insects which contains those of the highest intelligence, as bees and ants, and others which are indirectly beneficial to husbandmen.

himnario [im-nah'-re-o], *m.* Hymnal, hymnary.

hímnico, ca [eem'-ne-co, cah], *a.* Hymnic, pertaining to hymns; lyric.

himnista [im-nees'-tah], *m. (coll.)* Composer of hymns.

himno [eem'-no], *m.* Hymn.

himnología [im-no-lo-hee'-ah], *f.* Hymnology, the study of hymns; a treatise on hymns.

himplar [im-plar'], *vn.* To roar or bellow.

himpón [im-pon'], *m.* Name of one of the tribunals of the Chinese empire.

hin [een or heen], *m.* Sound emitted by mules or horses; whinny.

hincadura [in-cah-doo'-rah], *f.* Act of fixing something.

hincapié [in-cah-pe-ay'], *m.* An effort made with the foot by fixing it firmly on the ground. **Hacer hincapié**, to make a strenuous attempt.

hincar [in-car'], *va.* 1. To thrust in (meter), to drive into, to nail one thing to another. **Hincar la rodilla**, to kneel down. 2. *(Prov.)* To plant. **Hincar el diente**, to appropriate property to oneself: to censure, to calumniate. **Hincó la mirada en ella**, he fixed his gaze on her. **Hincó el bastón en el suelo**, he stuck his stick in the ground.

hincha [een'-chah], *f. (coll.)* Hatred, displeasure, emnity. **Tener hincha a uno**, to have a grudge against somebody.

hinchable [in-chah'-blay], *a.* Inflatable.

hinchado, da [in-chah'-do, dah], *a. & pp.* of HINCHAR. 1. Swollen, tumefied swelled. 2. Vain, arrogant (persona), presumptuous. 3. Inflated, turgid, tumid, pompous (estilo).

hinchante [in-chan'-tay], *a.* 1. Annoying (molesto), tiresome. 2. Funny (gracioso).

hinchar [in-char'], *va.* 1. To inflate, to swell with wind. 2. To fill a musical instrument with air. 3. To swell, to raise to arrogance. 3. To blow up (neumático).-*vr.* 1. To swell, to grow turgid, to be tumefied. 2. To be elated with arrogance or anger. 3. To make a pile (enriquecerse). 4. **Hincharse a correr**, to run hard. **Hincharse a reír**, to laugh a lot.

hinchazón [in-chah-thone'], *m.* 1. Swelling, tumefaction, a tumid inflammation. 2. Ostentation, vanity, pride; inflation, pomposity (estilo)

hincón [in-cone'], *m.* Post to which cables are fastened on the banks of rivers.

hindú [in-doo'], *a. m & f.* Hindu.

hinduismo [in-doo-ees'-mo], *m.* Hinduism.

hiniesta [he-nees'-tah], *f. (Bot.)* Spanish broom.

hiniestra [e-ne-es'-trah], *f. (Prov.)* Window. *V.* VENTANA.

hinnible [in-nee'-blay], *a.* Capable of neighing.

hinojal [e-no-hah'], *m.* Bed or place full of fennel.

hinojo [e-no'-ho], *m.* 1. Knee. *V.* RODILLA. 2. *(Bot.)* Fennel. 3. **Hinojo marino**, *(Bot.)* samphire.

hintero [in-tay'-ro], *m.* Table on which bakers knead their dough.

hiñir [e-nyeer'], *va. (Prov.)* V. HEMIR. (*Yo hiño, yo hiña; él hiñó, hiñera*; from *Heñir V.* PEDIR.)

hióideo, dea [e-o'-e-day-o, ah], *a.* Hyoid, like a Y in shape.

hipar [e-par'], *vn.* 1. To hiccup. 2. To be harassed with anxiety and grief. 3. To pant (perro), to desire eagerly, to be anxious. 4. To follow the chase by the smell (perros).

hiparca [e-par'-cah], *m.* Name given by the Greeks to the satraps and their lieutenants.

hipear [e-pay-ar'], *vn.* To hiccup. *V.* HIPAR.

hipecoo [e-pay-co'-o], *m. (Bot.)* Horned cumin.

hiperactividad [e-per-ac-te-ve-dahd'], *f.* Hyperactivity.

hiperactivo [e-per-ac-tee'-vo], *a.* Hyperactive.

hipérbola [e-per'-boh-lah], *f. (Geom.)* Hyperbola, section of a cone.

hipérbole [e-per'-boh-lay], *f.* Hyperbole, a figure in rhetoric.

hiperbólicamente [e-per-bo'-ly-cah-men-tay], *adv.* Hyperbolically.

hiperbólico, ca [e-per-bo'-le-co, cah], *a.* Hyperbolical.

hiperbolizar [e-per-bo-le-thar'], *m.* To use hyperboles.

hiperboloide [e-per-bo-lo'-e-day], *f.* Hyperboloid.

hiperbóreo, rea [e-per-bo'-ray-o, ah], *a.* Hyperborean.

hiperconversación [e-per-con-ver-sah-the-on']. *(Inform.)* Hypertalk.

hipercrítico, ca, [e-per-cree'-te-co, cah], *a.* Hypercritical, censorious

hiperdrulía [e-per-droo-lee'-ah], *f.* Hyperdulia, worship of the Virgin Mary.

hiperemesia or **hiperemesis** [e-per-ay-may'-se-ah], *f.* Hyperemesis, excessive vomiting.

hipergólico, ca [e-per-go'-ne-co, cah], *a.* Hypergolic.

hipérico hipericón [e-pay'-re-co, e-pay-re-cone'], *m. (Bot.)* St. John's wort. **hiperinflación** [e-per-in-fla-the-on'], *f.* Runaway inflation.

hipermercado [e-per-mer-cah'-do], *m.* Hypermarket.

hipersensibilidad [e-per-sen-se-be-le-dahd'], *f.* Hypersensitivity.

hipersensible [e-per-sen-se-blay], *a.* Hypersensitive.

hipersónico, ca [e-per-so'-ne-co, cah], *a.* Hypersonic.

hipertensión [e-per-ten-se-on'], *f.* Hypertension, high blood pressure.

hipertrofia [e-per-tro'-fe-ah], *f.* Hypertrophy, undue growth.

hipertrofiarse [e-per-tro-fe-ar'-say], *m.* To hypertrophy, to become hypertrophied.

hipertrófico, ca [e-per-tro'-fe-co, cah], *a.* Hypertrophic, relating to hypertrophy.

hípico, ca [ee'-pe-co, cah], *a.* Relating to horses.

hipio [ee'-pe-o], *m.* Surname of Mars and Neptune, meaning *equestrian.*

hipnal [ip-nahl'-], *m.* Kind of serpent said to produce sleep.

hipnosis [ip-no'-sis], *f.* Hypnosis.

hipnótico, ca [ip-no'-te-co, cah], *a. & m. (Med.)* Hypnotic.

hipnotismo [ip-no-tees'-mo], *m.* Hypnotism, mesmerism, hypnotic suggestion.

hipnotizador [ip-no-te-thah-dor'], *a.* Hypnotizing.

hipnotizar [ip-no-te-thar'], *va.* To hypnotize.

hipo [ee'-po], *m.* 1. Hiccough. **Quitar el hipo a uno**, to cure somebody's hiccups. 2. Wish, desire, anxiety (deseo). 3. Anger, displeasure, fury. 4. Disgust (asco); grudge (rencor).

hipocampo [e-po-cahm'-po], *m.* Hippocampus, sea horse.

hipocentauro [e-po-then-tah'-oo-ro], *m.* Hippocentaur, a fabulous monster.

hipocondría [e-po-con-dree'-ah], *f.* Hypochondria, melancholy, hypochondriasis, hypochondriac affection or passion.

hipocondríaco, ca [e-po-con-dre-ah'-co, cah], *a.* Hypochondriasis, hypochondriacal, melancholy, fanciful.

hipocóndrico, [e-po-con'-dre-co], **ca, m. & f.** Hypochondriac, melancholist.

hipocóndrico, ca [e-po-con'-dre-co, cah], *a.* Hypochondriac, hypochondriacal.

hipocondrio [epo-con'-dre-oh], *m. (Anat.)* Hypochondrium, that part of the body which lies under the cartilages of the false ribs: more generally used in its plural, hypocondres.

hipocras [e-po-crahs'], *m.* Hippocras, medicated wine.

hipocrático, ca [e-po-cra'-te-co, cah], *a.* 1. Hippocratic, relating to Hippocrates. 2. Cadaveric countenance.

hipocrenides [e-po-cray-nee'-des], *f. pl. (Poet.)* Epithet applied to the muses of Parrassus.

hipocresía [e-po-cray-see'-a], *f.* Hypocrisy, dissimulation.

hipócrita [e-po'-cre-tah], *a.* Hypocritical, dissembling, insincere.

hipócrita [e-po'-cre-tah], *com.* Hypocrite, a dissembler.

hipócritamente [e-po'-cre-tah-men-tay], *adv.* Hypocritically.

hipocritilla [e-po-cre-teel'-lyah], *f. dim.* A sly hypocrite.

hipócrito, ta [e-po'-cre-to, tah], *a.* Feigned, dissembled, hypocritical.

hipocritón, na [e-po-cre-tone', nah], *a. aug.* Extremely hypocritical or dissembling.

hipodérmico, ca [e-po-der'-me-co, cah], *a.* Hypodermic.

hipódromo [e-po'-droh-mo], *m.* Hippodrome, race track, arena.

hipofosfito [e-po-fos-fee'-to], *m.* Hypophosphite, a salt of hypophosorus acid.

hipofosforoso, sa [e-po-fos-fo-ro'-so, sah], *a.* Hypophosphorous (acido). -H3 PO2.

hipogástrico, ca [e-po-gahs'-tre-co, cah], *a.* Hypogastric.

hipogastro [e-po-gahs'-tro], *m.* Hypogastrium, the lower part of the belly.

hipogeo [epo-hay'-o], *m.* 1 Subterranean vault where the ancient Greeks kept their dead without cremating them. 2. Hypogeum, an underground chapel or structure.

hipogloso, sa [e-po-glo'-so, sah], *a.* Hypoglossal.

hipogrifo [e-po-gree'-fo], *m.* Hippogriff, a winged horse.

hipohema [e-po-ay'-mah], *m.* Hyphaemia, effusion of blood in the eye.

hipomanes [e-po-mah'-nes], *m.* A vaginal discharge from the mare when in heat.

hipomoclio, hipomoclión [e-po-mo'-cle-o, epo-mo-cle-on'], *m.* Fulcrum of a lever; part on which the beam of a balance revolves.

hiponitrato [e-po-ne-trah'-to], *m.* Subnitrate.

hipopión [e-po-pe-on'], *m. (Med.)* Hypopyon, a collection of pus in the chambers of the eye.

hipopo, pa [e-po'-po, pah], *a.* Hoofed like a horse.

hipopótamo [e-po-po'-tah-mo], *m.* Hippopotamus, a river-horse.

hipóstasis [e-pos'-tah-sis], *f. (Theol.)* Hypostasis, anyone of the persons of the Holy Trinity.

hipostático, ca [e-pos-tah'-te-co, cah], *a.* Hypostatical.

hiposulfato, furo, fito [e-po-sool-fah'-to, foo'-ro, fee'-to], *m. (Chem.)* Hyposulphite. Hyposulphite of soda, so called (properly thiosulphate), is important in photography.

hipoteca [e-po-tay'-cah], *f.* Mortgage, pledge; security given for the performance of an engagement. **Levantar una hipoteca**, to raise a mortgage.

hipotecable [e-po-tay-cah'-blay], *a.* Capable of being pledged.

hipotecar [e-po-tay-car'], *va.* To hypothecate, to pledge, to mortgage.

hipotecario, ria [e-po-tay-cah'-re-o, ah], *a.* Belonging to a mortgage.

hipotensión [e-po-ten-se-on'], *f. (Med.)* Hypotension.

hipotenusa [e-po-tay-noo'-sah], *f.* Hypotenuse.

hipótesis [e-po'-tay-sis], *f.* Hypothesis, a supposition.

hipotético, ca [e-po-tay'-te-co, cah], *a.* Hypothetic, hypothetical, conditional.

hipsómetro [ep-so'-may-tro], *m.* Hypsometer, an instrument for measuring altitude by determining the boiling point of water at a given altitude.

hipúrico [e-poo'-re-co], *a. (Chem.)* Hippuric (ácido).

hirma [eer'-mah], *f.* Edge of cloth.

hirsuto, ta [ir-soo'-to, tah], *a.* 1. Hirsute, covered with rough hairs. 2. *(Poet.)* Rough, rugged (brusco).

hirundinaria [e-roon-de-nah'-re-ah], *f. (Bot.)* V. CELIDONIA and GOLONDRINERA.

hirviente [ir-ve-en'-tay], *pa.* Boiling.

hisca [ees'-cah], *f.* Bird-lime, a glutinous substance by which the feet of birds are entangled.

hiscal [is-cahl'], *m.* A rope of three strands made of esparto.

hisopada [e-so-pah'-dah], *f.* Water sprinkled with a water-sprinkler.

hisopear [e-so-pay-ar'], *va.* To sprinkle water with a sprinkler.

hisopillo [e-so-peel'-lyo], *m.* 1. A small water-sprinkler. 2. Bit of soft linen at the end of a stick, used to wash and refresh the mouth of a sick person. 3. *(Bot.)* winter-savory.

hisopo [e-so'-po], *m.* 1. *(Bot.)* Hyssop. 2. Water-sprinkler, with which holy water is sprinkled made of a lock of horse-hair fastened to the end of a stick. **Hisopo húmedo**, *(Pharm.)* grease collected in washing fleeces of wool.

hispalense [is-pah-len'-say], *a.* Native of or belonging to Seville.

hispánico, ca [is-pah'-ne-co, cah], *a.* Spanish.

hispanidad [is-pah-ne-dahd'], *f.* 1. Spanish culture, Spanish spirit. 2. Spanish speaking world.

hispanismo [is-pah-nees'-mo], *m.* A Spanish idiom.

hispanizado, da [is-pah-ne-thah-do, dah], *a. & pp.* of HISPANIZAR. V. ESPAÑOLIZADO.

hispanizar [is-pah-ne'-thar], *va.* V. ESPAÑOLIZAR.

hispano, na [is-pah'-no, nah], *a.* Spanish, Hispanic. -*m. & f. (Poet.)* A Spaniard.

hispanoamericano, na [is-pah-no-ah-may-re-cah'-no, nah], *m. & f. & a.* Spanish American, Latin American.

hispanohablante [is-pah-no-ha-blahn'-tay], *a. m & f.* Spanish-speaking, Spanish speaker.

híspido, da [ees'-pe-do, dah], *a.* Bristly like hogs.

histerectomía [is-tay-rec-to-mee'-ah], *f. (Med.)* Hysterectomy, surgical removal of the uterus.

histeria [is-tay'-re-ah], *f.* Hysteria, hysterics.

histéricamente [is-tay'-re-cah-men-tay], *adv.* Hysterically.

histérico [is-tay'-re-co], *m.* Hysterics. V. HISTERISMO.

histérico, ca [is-tay'-re-co, cah], *a.* Hysteric, hysterical; relating to the womb, or to hysteria.

histerismo [is-tay-rees'-mo], *m.* Histeria.

histología [is-to-lo-hee'-ah], *f.* Histology, the science of the tissues, or a treatise upon them.

histológico, ca [is-to-lo'-he-co, cah], *a.* Histological.

histólogo [is-to'-lo'-go], *m.* Histological.

historia [is-to'-re-ah], *f.* 1. History, a narration of events (narración). 2. *(coll.)* Tale (cuento), story, table. 3. Historypiece, an historical painting. **Meterse en historias**, to meddle in things without possessing sufficient knowledge thereof, or being concerned in them. **No me vengas con historias**, don't give me that. 4. History (humana) **En toda la historia humana**, in the whole of human history. **Historia universal**, world history.

historiado, da [is-to-re-ah'-do, dah], *a.* Applied to a painting consisting of various parts harmoniously united. -*pp.* of HISTORIAR.

historiador, ra [is-to-re-ah-dor', rah], *m. & f.* Historian, historiographer, chronicler, a writer of history or of facts and events.

historial [es-to-re-ahl'], *a.* Historical, historic. *-m.* 1. Background, history. 2. Employment record.

historialmente [is-to-re-al-men'-tay], *adv.* Historically.

historiar [is-to-re-ar'], *va.* 1. To historify, to record in history. 2. To represent historical events in paintings or tapestry (arte).

históricamente [is-to'-re-cah-men-tay], *adv.* Historically.

histórico, ca [is-to'-re-co, cah], *a.* Historical, historic.

historieta [is-to-re-ay'-tah], *f. dim.* Short story or tale, short novel or anecdote, mixed with fact and fable. **Historieta cómica**, comic strip.

historiografía [is-to-re-o-grah-fee'-ah], *f.* Historiography.

historiógrafo [is-to-re-oh'-grah-fo], *m.* Historigrapher, historian.

historión [is-to-re'-on'], *m.* A tedious, long-winded story.

histrión [is-tre-on'], *m.* 1. Actor, player; used only in contempt. 2. Buffoon, juggler.

histriónico, ca [is-tre-o'-ne-co, cah], *a.* Histrionic, histrionical.

histrionisa [is-tre-oh-nee'-sah], *f.* An actress.

histrionismo [is-tre-o-nees'-mo], *m.* In contempt, histrionism, the art and profession of an actor or player.

hita [ee'-tah], *f.* A sort of nail without a head; stub-nail.

hito, ta [ee'-to, tah], *a.* Fixed, firm; importunate. **Dar en el hito**, to hit the nail on the head.

hito [ee'-to], *m.* 1. Landmark, anything set up to mark boundaries. 2. Guide-post, milestone. 3. Pin, or mark at which quoits are cast; mark to shoot at. **A hito**, fixedly, firmly. **Dar en el hito** or **dar en el hito de la dificultad**, to hit the nail on the head, to come to the point. **Mirar de hito en hito**, to view with close attention.

hitón [e-ton'], *m.* A large square nail without a head. *(Acad.)*

hobachón, na [o-bah-chone', nah], *a.* Sluggish, fat, and lazy.

hobby [ho'-be], *m.* Hobby.

hobechos [o-bay'-chos], *m. pl.* Soldiers armed with pikes: pikemen.

hoblonera [o-blo-nay'-rah], *f.* Hop-ground, hop-yard, hop-garden, any place where hops are cultivated.

hocicada [o-the-cah'-dah], *f.* 1. A blow given with the snout of a beast and sometimes also with the mouth. 2. Fall upon the face, or headlong on the ground. 3. *(coll.)* A smart reprimand.

hocicar [o-the-car'], *va.* To break up the ground with the snout (cerdo), to nuzzle (persona). *-vn.* 1. To fall headlong with the face to the ground (cerdo), to nuzzle (persona), to pet (amantes). 2. To stumble or slide into errors.

hocico [o-thee'-co], *m.* 1. Snout, the nose of a beast. 2. Mouth of a man who has very prominent lips (persona). 3. Anything disproportionably big or prominent. 4. Gesture of thrusting out the lips, pouting. 6. *(Met.)* The face (cara). **Meter el hocico en todo**, to meddle in everything. **Estar de hocico**, to be at variance.

hocicudo, da, or **hocicón, na** [o-the-coo'-do, dah, o-the-cone', nah], *a.* 1. Long-snouted. 2. Blubber-lipped, flap-mouthed. 3. Looking sullen by thrusting out the lips.

hocino [o-thee'-no], *m.* 1. Bill, a sort of hatchet with a hooked point. 2. The narrow bed of a river which flows between mountains.

hociquillo, ito [o-the-keel'lyo, ee'to], *m. dim.* A little snout.

hockey [ho'-kay-e], *m.* Hockey. **Hockey sobre hielo**, ice hockey.

hodometría [o-do-may-tree'-ah], *f.* Odometry, mechanical measurement of distance.

hodómetro [o-do'-may-tro], *m.* Odometer, an instrument for measuring distance traveled.

hogañazo [o-gah-nyah'-tho], *adv. (coll.)* V. HOGAÑO.

hogaño [o-gah'-nyo], *adv. (coll.)* This present year; in this epoch.

hogar [o-gar'], *m.* 1. Hearth, fire-place; the pavement of a room where fire is kindled. 2. *(Met.)* House, residence, home. **No tienen hogar**, they have no home. **Los que han quedado sin hogar**, the homeless.

hogareño [o-gar'], *a.* Home, family; fireside, home-loving (persona), stay-at-home.

hogaza [o-gah'-thah], *f.* 1. A large loaf of household bread. 2. Any large loaf.

hoguera [o-gay'-rah], *f.* 1. Bonfire. 2. Any blaze produced by burning things heaped together.

hoja [o'-hah], *f.* 1. Leaf of trees and plants. 2. Leaf, anything foliated or thinly beaten; scales (metal). 3. **Hoja de puerta**, leaf, one side of a double door. **Hoja de ventana**, shutter. 4. Blade of a sword or knife. 5. Ground cultivated one year, and lying at rest for another. 6. Half of each of the principal parts of a coat, etc. **Hoja de servicios**, *(Mil.)* a certificate setting forth the rank and services of a military officer. **Hoja de papel**, leaf of paper. **Hoja de un libro**, leaf of a book. **Hoja de estaño**, sheet of bismuth, tin, and quicksilver, laid on the back of a looking glass. **Volver la hoja**, to turn over a new leaf to alter one's sentiments and proceedings. **Hoja de afeitar**, razor blade. **Hoja de cálculo**, *(Inform.)* electronic spreadsheet. **Hoja de trabajo**, *(Inform.)* worksheet. *-pl.* 1. Leaves, greens. 2. Lamina, thin plates, one coat laid over another. **Hoja de ruta**, flight plan (avión). **Hoja de trebol**, cloverleaf, clover leaf, highway intersection.

hojalata or **hoja de lata** [o-hah-lah'-tah, o'-hah day lah'-tah], *f.* Tin plate.

hojalatería [o-ha-lah-tay-ree'-ah]. 1. The art of making tinplate, or utensils of it. 2. A tin-shop.

hojalatero [o-hah-lah-tay'-ro], *m.* Tin-man, a manufacturer of tin.

hojaldrado [o-hal-drah'-do], *a.* Laminated, foliate, resembling thin cakes. -**Hojaldrado, da**, *pp.* of HOJALDRAR.

hojaldrar [o-hal-drar'], *va.* To make something of puff paste.

hojaldre [o-hahl'-dray], *m.* or *f.* A sort of pancake or paste.

hojaldrista [o-hal-drees'-tah], *m.* Maker of buttered cakes.

hojarasca [o-hah-rahs'-cah], *f.* 1. Withered leaves; redundancy of leaves; foliage. 2. Useless trifles (palabras), rubbish (basura).

hojear [o-hay-ar'], *va.* To turn the leaves of a book. *-vn.* To form metal into sheets; to foliate.

hojica, illa, ita [o-hee'-cah, eel'-lyah, ee'-tah], *f. dim.* A small leaf.

hojica, sa, hojudo, da [o-ho'-so, sah, o-hoo'-do, dah], *a.* Leafy, full of leaves.

hojuela [o-hoo-ay'-lah], *f.* 1. *(Dim.)* A small leaf, a leaflet. 2. Puff paste, composed of thin flakes lying one on another (hojas delgadas). 3. Flat gold or silver thread in spools for embroidery. 4. Skins of olives after pressing.

¡hola! [oh'-lah], *int.* 1. Hello!, hallo! (saludo, sorpresa), hullo! (por teléfono). 2. A word used in calling to someone at a distance. 2. Ho! ho! a sudden exclamation of wonder or astonishment (sorpresa). 3. *(Naut.)* Hoy! Ahoy!

holán, holán batista [o-lahn'], *m. (coll.)* Cambric: the finest cambric, batiste.

Holanda [o-lahn'-dah], *f.* Holland, fine Dutch linen.

holandés, sa [o-lan-days', sah], *a.* Dutchman.

holandilla, holandeta [o-lan-deel-lyah, o-lan-day'-tah], *f.* 1. A lead-colored glazed linen, used for lining. 2. Tobacco of inferior quality. *(Acad.)*

holgachón, na [ol-gah-chone', nah], *a.* Fond of ease and little work.

holgadamente [ol-gah-dah-men'-tay], *adv.* 1. Widely, amply, fully, loosely. **Caben holgadamente**, they fit easily. 2. Quietly, carelessly.

holgado, da [ol-gah-do, dah], *a. pp.* of HOLGAR. 1. Loose (ropa), lax, disproportionately wide or broad. 2. Loose, disengaged, at leisure (sin trabajo). 3. Well off, in easy circumstances, free from want. **Andar** or **estar holgado**, to be well off.

holganza [ol-gahn'-thah], *f.* 1. Repose, ease, tranquility of mind, quiet. 2. Diversion, recreation, amusement (diversión), entertainment. 3. *V.* ASUETO.

holgar [ol-gar'], *vn.* 1. To rest (descansar), to cease from labor (obrero etc.), to lie at rest. 2. To spend one's time free from business. 3. *(Acad.)* To take pleasure or satisfaction in. To be unnecessary, to be superfluous. *-vr.* To sport, to dally, to trifle, to idle, to toy, to play the fool.

holgazán, na [ol-gah-thahn', nah], *m. & f.* Idler, loiterer, vagabond, lounger, *-a.* Idle, lazy, slothful, inactive, indolent.

holgazanear [ol-gah-thah-nay-ar'], *vn.* To idle or to be idle, to lead an idle life, to be lazy to loiter, to lounge.

holgazanería [ol-gah-thah-nay-ree'-ah], *f.* Idleness, laziness, sluggishness, slothfulness, inactivity, indolence.

holgín, na [ol-heen', nah], *a. V.* HECHICERO.

holgorio [ol-go'-re-o], *m.* *(coll.)* Mirth, jollity, noisy merriment.

holgueta [ol-gay'-tah], *f. (coll.)* A feast, a merry-making.

holgura [ol-goo'-rah], *f.* 1. Country, feast, an entertainment in the country. 2. Width, breadth. 3. Ease (confort), repose. 4. Freedom (ocío). 5. Enjoyment (goce), merriment (alegría).

holladura [oh-lyah-doo'-rah], *f.* 1. Act of trampling. 2. Duty paid for the run of cattle.

hollar [ol-lyar'], *va.* 1. To tread upon, to trample under foot. 2. To trample on or to tread in contempt, to pull down, to humble, to depress.

holleca [ol-lyay'-cah], *f. (Orn.) V.* HERRERILLO.

hollecico, illo, ito, uelo [ol-lyay-thee'-co], *m. dim.* A small pellicle or peel of grapes and some other fruits.

hollejo [ol-lyay'-ho], *m.* Pellicle, peel, the thin skill which covers grapes and other fruit.

hollí [ol-lyee'], *m.* Balsam or resinous liquor distilled from a tree of Mexico and which is used mixed with chocolate.

hollín [ol-lyeen'], *m.* Soot, condensed smoke.

holliniento, ta [ol-lye-ne-en'-to, tah], *a.* Fuliginous, sooty.

holocausto [o-lo-cah'-oos-to], *fah*], *m.* 1. Holocaust (desastre), a burnt sacrifice. 2. *V.* SACRIFICIO.

hológrafo, fa [o-lo'-grah-fo, fah], *a.* Holographic, holograph, written entirely by the testator.

holómetro [o-lo'-may-tro], *m.* Holometer, an instrument for making all kinds of angular measurements.

holoturias [o-lo-too'-re-as], *a. f. pl.* Holothurian(s), belonging to the Holothuridea; a division of echinoderms, including sea-cucumbers, etc.

homarrache [o-mar-rah'-chay], *m.* Buffoon, jack-pudding, a merry-andrew.

hombracho [om-brah'-cho], *m.* A squat and square thick man.

hombrachón [om-brah-chone'], *m. aug.* A very tall, square, thick man.

hombrada [om-brah'-dah], *f.* 1. A manly action. 2. It is used also in an ironical sense for a ridiculous action.

hombrazo [om-brah'-tho], *m. aug.* A large man.

hombre [om'-bray], *m.* 1. Man, mankind. 2. Man, a male human being as distinguished from woman. 3. Man not a boy: one who has reached adult age. 4. Man, one of uncommon qualifications, qualified in a particular manner. 5. Man, a word of familiarity bordering on contempt. 6. Husband, among the populace. 7. Ombre, game at cards. **Hombre de bien**, an honest man. **Hombre de corazón** or **de gran corzón**, a courageous man. **Hombre de pro** or **de provecho**, a worthy, useful man. **Hombre hecho**, a grown man. **Hombre honrado**, an honest, worthy man. **Hombre de negocios**, businessman. **Hombre de su palabra**, a man of his word. **Ser muy hombre**, to be a man of spirit and courage. **Hombre de cabeza**, a talented man. **¡Hombre!** an exclamation of surprise (sorpresa). **¡Hombre al agua!** man overboard! **Una charla de hombre a hombre**, a man-to-man talk. **El hombre del montón**, the average man. **Hombre blanco**, white man. **El hombre de la calle**, the man in the street. 8. Dear me! (compasión). 9. Come now! (protesta).

hombrear [om-bray-ar'], *vn.* To assume the man before the time (joven).*-vn. & vr.* To vie with another; to put oneself upon a level with.

hombrecillo [om-bray-theel'-lyo], *m. dim.* Manikin, manling, a pitiful little fellow. **Hombrecillos**, *(Bot.)* hops.

hombrecito [om-bray-thee'-to], *m.* Youth, a young man.

hombrera [om-bray'-rah], *f.* Piece of ancient armor for the shoulders (almohadilla).

hombre rana [om'-bray rah'-nah], *m.* Frogman.

hombría de bien [om-bree'-ah day been'], 1. Probity, honesty.

hombrillo [om-breel'-lyo], *m.* Gusset, an angular piece of cloth.

hombro [om'-bro], *m.* Shoulder. **Encogerse de hombros**, to shrug up the shoulders. **A hombro** or **sobre los hombros**, on the shoulders. **Llevar en hombros**, to support, to protect. **Arrimar el hombro**, to work with a will; to lend a hand. **Echar al hombro**, to shoulder, to become responsible for. **Mirar sobre el hombro**, to cast a contemptuous look. **Sacar a uno en hombros**, to carry somebody out on shoulders.

hombrón [om-brone'], *m.* 1. *(aug.)* A big, lusty man. 2. A man distinguished for talents, knowledge, and valor.

hombronazo [om-bro-nah'-tho], *m. aug.* A huge, vulgar man.

hombruno, na [om-broo'-no, nah], *a.* 1. Manlike, virile; belonging to man. 2. Relating to the shoulders.

homecillo [o-may-thee'-lyo], *m. (Bot.)* Hops.

homenaje [o-may-nah'-hay], *m.* Homage, service to a superior lord, obeisance. **Rendir homenaje**, to pay homage, to profess fealty. **Partido homenaje**, benefit match.

homenajeado, ada [o-may-nah-hay-ah'-do], *m & f.* **El homenajeado**, the person being honored.

homenajear [o-may-nah-hay-ar'], *va.* To honor.

homeópata [o-may-o'-pah-tah], *m.* Homoeopath(ist).

homeopatía [o-may-o-pah-tee'-ah], *f.* Homoeopathy; the medical system of Hahnemann.

homeopático, ca [o-may-o-pah'-te-co, cah], *a.* Homoeopathic, relating to homoeopathy.

homérico, ca [o-may'-re-co, cah], *a.* Homeric.

homicida [o-me-thee'-dah], *com.* Murderer, homicide. **El arma homicida**, the murder weapon.

homicida [o-me-thee'-dah], *a.* Homicidal, murderous.

homicido [o-me-thee'-de-o], *m.* 1. Murder, homicide. 2. Ancient tribute.

homilía [o-me-lee'-ah], *f.* Homily, a discourse read in a congregation.

homilista [o-me-lees'-tah], *m.* Author or writer of homilies.

homocéntrico, ca [o-mo-then'-tre-co, cah], *a.* Homocentric, having a common center.

homófono, na [o-mo'-fo-no, nah], *a.* Of like sound, homophonous.

homógamo, ma [o-mo'-gah-mo, mah], *a.* Homogamous, having flowers of one sex only.

homogeneidad [o-mo-hay-e-dahd'], *f.* Homogeneity, homogeneosness.

homogeneizar [o-mo-hay-nay-thar'], *va.* To homogenize (leche).

homogéneo, nea [o-mo-hay'-nay-o, ah], *a.* Homogoneous.

homógrafo, fa [o-mo'-grah-fo, fah], *a.* Homonymous, written alike. *Cf.* HOMÓFONO.

homologación [o-mo-lo-gah-the-on'], *f.* Homologation, publication, or confirmation of a judicial act, to render it more valid.

homologado [o-mo-lo-gah'-do], *a.* Officially approved, authorized.

homologar [o-mo-lo-gar'], *va.* 1. To coordinate (coordinar), to bring into line (estandarizar). 2. To compare (comparar). 3. To check and approve (aprobar).

homólogo, ga [o-mo'-lo-go, gah], *a.* Homologous, having the same ratio; synonymous.

homonimia [o-me-nee'-me-ah], *f.* Homonymy, sameness of name where there is difference of meaning; ambiguity, equivocation.

homónimo, ma [o-mo'-ne-mo, mah], *a.* Homonymous, equivocal.

homosexual [o-mo-sek-soo-ahl'], *a. & m.f.* Homosexual.

homosexualidad [o-mo-sec-soo-ah-le-dahd'], *f.* Homosexuality.

honda [on'-dah], *f.* 1. Sling, a stringed instrument for casting stones.

hondable [on-dah'-blay], *a.* (*Naut.*) Soundable.

hondamente [on-dah-men'-tay], *adv.* 1. Deeply, profoundly, to a great depth. 2. Deeply profoundly, with deep concern; with deep insight.

hondarras [on-dar'-ras], *f. pl.* (*Prov.*) Dread or less or any liquor remaining in the vessel which contained it.

hondazo [on-dah'-tho], *m.* Cast or throw with a sling.

hondear [on-day-ar'], *va.* To unload a vessel (descargar).

hondero [on-day'-ro], *m.* Slinger, a soldier armed with a sling.

hondica, illa, ita [on-dee'-cah], *f. dim.* A small sling to cast stones.

hondijo [on-dee'-ho], *m.* V. HONDA.

hondillos [on-deel'-lyo], *m. pl.* The crotch (de los calzones).

hondo, da [on'-do, dah], *a.* 1. Profound, deep, far below the surface. 2. Profound, low with respect to neighboring places. 3. (*Met.*) V. PROFUNDO. **Con hondo pesar**, with deep regret.

hondo [on'-do], *m.* (*Prov.*) V. FONDO for bottom.

hondón [on-done'], *m.* 1. Bottom of a vessel or jar where the dregs of liquor settle (taza) 2. Any deep or broken ground. 3. A deep hole. 4. Eye of a needle (aguja).

hondonada [on-do-nah'-dah], *f.* 1. Dale, raving, bottom of a steep place (barranco) 2. Comb, a valley surrounded by hills.

hondura [on-doo'-rah], *f.* Depth (medida, lugar), profundity.

honestamente [o-nes-tah-men'-tay], *adv.* Honestly, modestly.

honestar [o-nes-tar'], *va.* 1. To honor, to dignify. 2. To excuse, to palliate.

honestidad [o-nes-te-dahd'], *f.* 1. Honesty, composure, modesty, moderation. 2. Honesty, purity of sentiments and principles, honorableness; urbanity.

honesto, ta [o-nes'-to, tah], *a.* 1. Honest, decent (decente), honorable (honrado), creditable, handsome, hrave. 2. Honest, comely, pure (casto), chaste, virtuous. 3. Honest, reasonable, just.

hongo [on'-go], *m.* 1. (*Bot.*) Mushroom (comestible). 2. Fungus, an excrescence which grows upon the bark of trees, and serves for tinder. 3. A fleshy excrescence growing on the lips of wounds. **Crecen como hongos**, they grow like mushrooms.

honor [o-nor'], *m.* 1. Honor, a public mark of respect to virtue or merit. 2. Honor, reputation, fame, celebrity. 3. Honor (de mujer). 4. Honor, dignity rank, employment: more commonly used an the plural. **Palabra de honor**, word of honor. **Señoras de honor**, maids of honor. **Honores**, 1. Honors, privileges of rank or birth. 2. Honors, or privileges conferred without gain. 3. Public marks of respect to a person of rank. **En honor de uno**, in somebody's honor. **Hacer los honores de la casa**, to do the honors of the house.

honorable [o-no-rah'-blay], *a.* Honorable, illustrious, noble.

honorablemente [o-no-rah-blay-men-tay], *adv.* Honorably, creditably.

honorario, ria [o-no-rah'-re-o, ah], *a.* 1. Honorary, bestowing honor without gain. **Consejero honorario**, honorary counsellor, one who has the rank and title of a counsellor without the pay.

honorario [o-no-rah'-re-o], *m.* 1. Salary or stipend given for labor (profesional). 2. Fees of counsellors, notaries, or physicians.

honorcillo [o-nor-theel'-lyo], *m. dim.* V. HONRILLA.

honoríficamente [o-no-ree'-fe-cah-men'-tay], *adv.* Honorably.

honorificencia [o-no-re-fe-then'-the-ah], *f.* The act of honoring or doing honor.

honorífico, ca [o-no-ree'-fe-co, cah], *a.* Creditable, honorable, liberal, that which gives honor.

honra [on'-rah], *f.* 1. Honor, reverence, respect. 2. Honor, reputation, celebrity, fame, glory. 3. Honor, chastity (mujer). 4. Honor, mark of respect, favor conferred or received. **Honras**, funeral honors. **Tener algo a mucha honra**, to be proud of something.

honradamente [on-rah-dah-men'-tay], *adv.* Honorably, reputably, honestly.

honradez [on-rah-deth'], *f.* Honesty, probity, integrity, fairness, faithfulness.

honrado, da [on-ra'-do, dah], *a.* 1. Honest, honorable, reputable, just, fair. 2. Honest, exact in the performance of engagements. 3. In an ironical sense, refined in point of roguery and fraud.

honrador, ra [on-rah-dor', rah], *m. & f.* Honorer, one that honors.

honramiento [on-rah-me-en'-to], *m.* Act of honoring.

honrar [on-rar'], *va.* 1. To honor, to reverence, to respect (respetar). 2. To cajole, to caress, to fondle. 3. To dignify, to illustrate, to exalt, to glorify. 4. To praise, to applaud. 5. To credit, to grace to adorn. -*vr.* **Me honro con su amistad, I** am honored by his friendship.

honrilla [on-ree'-lah], *f. dim.* Concern for one's reputation; almost always used with the adjective *negra*, black. **Por la negra honrilla he omitido hacerlo**, I have left it undone from some little point of honor or bashfulness.

honrosamente [on-ro-sah-men'-tay], *adv.* Honorably, honestly, creditably.

honroso, sa [on-ro'-so, sah], *a.* 1. Honorable, decent, decorous, creditable. 2. Just, equitable, honest. 3. Jealous of one's honor.

honrudo, da [on-roo'-do, dah], *a.* Firm in maintaining one's honor, and acting conformably to it.

hontanal [on-tah-nahl'], *m.* V. ONTANAR. **Hontanales**, feasts of the ancients held at fountains.

hontanar [on-tah-nar'], *m.* Place in which water rises, source of springs and rivers.

hopa [oh'-pah], *f.* 1. A long cassock with sleeves. 2. The sack of those who are executed for crime.

hopalanda [o-pah-lahn'-dah], *f.* Tail or train of a gown worn by students.

hopear [o-pay-ar'], *vn.* To wag the tail (animales).

hopeo [o-pay'-o], *m.* (*coll.*) Volatile, coxcomb.

hopo [o'-po], *m.* Tail with a tuft of hair, similar to that of a fox or squirrel. **Seguir el hopo**, to dog, to pursue closely.

hoque [oh-kay], *m.* Treat given to celebrate the completion of a bargain or contract.

hora [o'-rah], *f.* 1. Hour, the twenty-fourth part of a day. 2. Hour, particular time for doing something (tiempo). 3. Hour, the time as marked by the clock. 4. (*Prov.*) Way made in an hour, a league. 6. Time between twelve and one o'clock on the day of the ascension, during which that mystery is celebrated in Catholic churches. **A la hora de esta** or **a la hora de ahora**, (*coll.*) at this moment. **Cada hora**, every hour, continually. **A buena hora**, at a seasonable time. **A la hora**, at the nick of time, then. **En hora buena**, it is well. **Por horas**, by instants. **En la hora de su muerte**, at the moment of his death. **Es hora de irnos**, it's time we went. **A una hora avanzada**, at a late hour. **Hora del cierre**, closing time. **A la hora de comer**, at lunch-time. **Hora de recreo**, play-time. **A última hora**, at the last moment. **Dar la hora**, to strike. **No ver la hora de algo**, to be scarcely able to wait for something. -*pl.* 1. Hours or canonical hours, the stated times of devotion of the Catholic church. 2. Book which contains the office of the blessed Virgin and other devotions.

hora [o'-rah], *adv.* Now, at this time, at present. -*conj.* V. ORA.

horadable [o-rah-dah'-blay], *a.* Capable of being pierced.

horadación [o-rah-dah-the-on'], *f.* Act of boring or piercing.

horadado [o-rah-dah'-do], *m.* Silkworm's cocoon bored through.-**Horadado, da**, *pp.* of HORADAR.

horadar [o-rah-dar'], *va.* To bore or pierce from side to side.

horado [o-rah'-do], *m.* 1. Hole bored from side to side. 2. Cavern, grotto; niche or cavity in a wall.

horambre [o-ram'-bray], *m.* Hole in the cheeks of mills.

horario, ria [o-rah'-re-o, ah], *a.* Horary, horal, relating to an hour, continuing for an hour.

horario [o-rah'-re-o], *m.* Hour hand of a clock or watch (del reloj). **Puesto de horario partido**, part-time job.

horca [or'-cah], *f.* 1. Gallows, gibbet (ejecución). 2. Sort of yoke for dogs or hogs, to prevent them from doing mischief; also used formerly as a punishment. 3. Fork with two wooden prongs, used by farmers for lifting straw, corn, hay, etc. 4. Rope or string of onions or garlic (ajos).

horcado, da [or-cah'-do, dah], *a.* Forked into different branches; forky.

horcadura [or-cah-doo'-rah], *f.* Fork (árbol).

horcajadas (a), or **a horcajadillas** [ah or-cah-hah'-das], *adv.* Astride on horseback.

horcajadura [or-cah-hah-doo'-rah], *f.* Fork formed by the two things.

horcajo [or-cah'-ho], *m.* 1. Yoke or collar put on the neck of mules, when employed in drawing. 2. In oil-mills, the Y-shaped division of the beam. 3. Confluence of two streams (de árbol, de río).

horcate [or-cah'-tay], *m.* 1. A yoke or collar of a horse. 2. Hame, collar of a draught-horse.

horco [or'-co], *m.* Rope or string of onions or garlic.

horcón [o-cone'], *m.* A forked pole set upright, to support the branches of fruit-trees (frutales).

horchata [or-chah'-tah], *f.* An emulsion, usually made of melon or pumpkin seeds, or of almonds.

horchatero, ra [or-chah-tay'-ro, rah], *m. & f.* One who makes or sells almond emulsion.

horda [or'-dah], *f.* Horde, clan, tribe. V. ADUAR.

hordeáceas [or-day-ah'-thay-as], *f. pl.* (*Bot.*) Pertaining to barley, hordeaceous.

hordeína [or-day-ee'-nah], *f.* 1. The finest bran of barley. 2. Hordein, a proximate principle from barley.

hordeolo [or-day-o'-lo], *m.* Hordeolum, stye.

hordiate [or-de-ah'-tay], *m.* 1. Beverage of barley water. 2. *f.* (*Bot.*) Barley without awns or beard. 3. (*Bot.*) Spring naked barley.

horizontal [o-re-thon-tahl'], *a.* Horizontal, parallel to the horizon; on a level.

horizontalmente [o-re-thon-tal-men'-tay], *adv.* Horizontally, flatly.

horizonte [o-re-thon'-tay], *m.* 1. Horizon, the line which terminates the view. 2. (*Geog.*) Horizon, the largest circle of the sphere, which divides it into two equal parts.

horma [or'-mah], *f.* Mould, model in which anything is cast, formed or modeled. **Horma de zapatero** shoemaker's last. **Hallar la horma de su zapato**, 1. (*coll.*) to meet one's wishes, to accommodate or satisfy anyone. 2. To meet with his match, someone who understands his artifices and can oppose his designs. **Horma de sombrero**, hat block.

hormazo [or-mah'-tho], *m.* (*Prov.*) House and garden.

hormero [or-may'-ro], *m.* Last-maker.

hormiga [or-mee'-gah], *f.* 1. Ant, pismire, or emmet. **Hormiga blanca**, white ant. 2. A cutaneous eruption, producing an itching which resembles the bitting of an ant. 3. **Ser una hormiga**, to be hard (trabajador).

hormigón [or-me-gone'], *m.* Concrete. **Hormigón armado**, reinforced concrete. **Hormigón para bloques**, block concrete.

hormigonera [or-me-go-nay'-rah], *f.* Concrete mixer.

hormigos [or-mee'-gos], *m. pl.* 1. Dessert of hazelnuts and honey. 2 Coarse remains of sifted wheat.

hormigoso, sa [or-me-go'-so, sah], *a.* Relating to ants.

hormigueamiento [or-me-gay-ah-me'-en-to], *m.* Formication, act of itching or moving like ants.

hormiguear [or-me-gay-ar'], *vn.* 1. To itch (piel). 2. To run about like ants.

hormigueo [or-me-gay'-o], *m.* Formication, a sensation like that of the creeping or stinging of ants.

hormiguero [or-me-gay'-ro], *m.* 1. Ant hill or hillock, formicarium. 2. Place where there are a crowd of people moving. 3. *pl.* Pile of weeds covered with earth in which ants breed, and after being burned serve as manure. 4. An anteater.

hormiguero, ra [or-me-gay'-ro, rah], *a.* Relating to the cutaneous eruption called *hormiga*.

hormiguita [or-me-gee'-tah], *f. dim.* A small ant.

hormiguillo [or-me-geel'-lyo], *m.* 1. Distemper which affects the hoofs of horses. 2. People ranged in a line who pass from hand to hand the materials for a work to be raised. 3. In Mexico, a beverage made of pounded cookies, sugar, and spice, boiled together. 4. Mixture of salts with silver. 5. (*Prov.*) V. HORMIGUEO.

hormilla [or-meel'-lyah], *f.* 1. (*Dim.*) A small last.

hormona [or-moh'-nah], *f.* Hormone.

hornabeque [or-nah-bay'-kay], *m.* (*Fort.*) Hornwork, an outwork, composed of a front and two demi-bastions, joined by a curtain.

hornacero [or-nah-thay'-ro], *m.* Person who watches crucible with silver and gold in the furnace.

hornacina [or-nah-thee'-nah], *f.* Vaulted niche in the wall of an altar.

hornacho [or-nah'-cho], *m.* 1. Shaft of a mine, an excavation formed in a hill. 2. Furnace in which metal is melted for casting statues.

hornachuela [or-nah-choo-ay'-lah], *f.* Hole made in a wall.

hornada [or-nah'-dah], *f.* Batch, the bread balled at one time.

hornaguear [or-nah-gay-ar'], *va.* To open the ground in search of pitcoals.

hornaguera [or-nah-gay'-rah], *f.* Pit-coal, hard coal.

hornaguero, ra [or-nah-gay'-ro, rah], *a.* 1. Wide, spacious. 2. Coaly: applied to ground containing coals.

hornaje [or-nah'-hay], *m.* (*Prov.*) Money paid to a baker for baking bread.

hornaza [or-nah'-thah], *f.* 1. A small furnace, used by gold and silver-smiths, and other founders, to melt and cast metal. 2. A light yellow color, in painting: a yellow glazing.

hornazo [or-nah'-tho], *m.* Cake made with a batter of eggs and butter (pastel).

hornblenda [orn-blen'-dah], *f.* Horn-blende, a greenish-black variety of amphibole.

hornear [or-nay-ar'], *va.* To carry on the trade of a baker.

hornería [or-nay-ree'-ah], *f.* Trade of a baker.

hornero, ra [or-nay'-ro, rah], *m. & f.* Baker.

hornija [or-nee'-hah], *f.* Brush wood burnt in an oven, to heat it for baking bread.

hornijero [or-ne-hay'-ro], *m.* Person who supplies the oven with fuel.

hornilla [or-neel'-lyah], *f.* 1. Small furnace, stew-hole, a small stove in a kitchen-hearth on which something is put to boil or stew. 2. Pigeon-hole, a hole for pigeons to make their nests and breed in.

hornillo [or-neel'-lyo], *m.* 1. (*Dim.*) A small stove. 2. (*Mil.*) Chamber of a mine. 3. A portable furnace. 4. (*Mil.*) Fougade, a small mine dug under some work or fortification, in order to blow it up.

hornito [or-nee'-to], *m.* (*Mex.*) A mud-volcano.

horno [or'-no], *m.* 1. Oven. 2. Kiln (alfarero). 3. (*Fig.*) Furnace. **Alto horno**, blast furnace. **No estar el horno para bollos**, not to be the right moment.

horología [o-ro-lo-hee'-ah], *f.* Horology.

horón [o-rone'], *m.* (*Prov.*) Large round hamper or frail.

horópter, horóptero [o-rop'-tayr, tay'-ro], *m.* A straight line through the point where the optical axes meet.

horóscopo [o-ros'-co-po], *m.* Horoscope, the configuration of the planets at the hour of birth.

horqueta [or-kay'-tah], *f.* 1. (*dim.* of HORCÓN.) A little fork. 2. (*Naut.*) V. HORQUILLAS.

horquilla [or-keel'-lyah], *f.* 1. Forked stick, for hanging up and taking down things from an elevated place. 2. Disease which causes the hair of the head to split. 3. A hair-pin (pelo). 4. A pitchfork. 5. The upper extremity of the sternum. 6. (*Anat.*) The fourchette, inferior commissure of the labia majora. 7. Instrument for operating on tongue-tie. 8. (*Mil.*) An instrument which arquebusiers used to sustain the weapon and fix the aim. 9. (*Vet.*) The frog of a horse's foot. 10. Fork (de bicicleta). 11. Footrest (zanco). **Horquilla de cavar**, garden fork.

horquilladura [or-kee'-lyah-doo'-rah], *f.* (*Prov.*) Forkedness.

horra [or'-rah], *a.* Among graziere, applied to females not with young; also to the head of cattle given to herds to keep at the expense of their owners.

horrendamente [or-ren-dah-men'-tay], *adv.* Dreadfully.

horrendo, da [or-ren'-do, dah], *a.* 1. Vast, enormous; dreadful, hideous, monstrous, fearful, horrible, grim. 2. Extraordinary, uncommon.

hórreo [or'-ray-o], *m.* A kind of granary built upon pilasters, to prevent rats and mice from injuring the grain.

horrero [or-ray'-ro], *m.* One who has the care of a granary; store-keeper.

horribilidad [or-re-be-le-dahd'], *f.* Horribleness, dreadfulness.

horrible [or-ree'-blay], *a.* Horrid, dreadful, hideous, horrible, heinous. **La película es horrible**, the film is dreadful.

horriblemente [or-re-blay-men'-tay], *adv.* Horribly, heinously, horridly, formidably, damnably.

hórrido, da [or'-re-do, dah], *a.* Horrid, vast, enormous, hideous.

horrífico, ca [or-ree'-fe-co, cah], *a.* (*Poet.*) Horrific, causing horror.

horripilación [or-re-pe-lah-the-on'], *f.* (*Med.*) Horripilation, a symptom of the approach of fever.

horripilante [or-re-pe-lahn'-tay], *pa.* Horrifying, harrowing, hair-raising.

horripilar [or-re-pe-lar'], *va.* 1. To cause bristling of the hair. 2. To inspire horror. **Horripilar a uno**, to make somebody's hair stand on. -*vr.* To feel horripilation. **Era para horripilarse**, it was enough to make your hair stand on end.

horripilativo, era [or-re-pe-lah-tee'-vo, vah], *a.* (*Med.*) Causing horripilation, or belonging to it.

horrísono, na [or-ree'-so-no, nah], *a.* (*Poet.*) Horrisonous, sounding dreadfully.

horro, ra [or'-ro, rah], *a.* 1. Enfranchised, set at liberty. 2. Free (exento), disengaged.

horror [or-ror'], *m.* 1. Horror, consternation, fright. 2. Horror, hate, abhorrence. 3. Horridness, enormity, hideousness, grimness, frightfulness, the cause of fright or astonishment. **¡Es un horror!** (*coll.*) it is a wonder; that is to say, a great deal of something. **Tener horror a algo**, to have a horror of something. **Hoy he trabajado un horror**, today I worked awfully. **Se divirtieron horrores**, they had a tremendous time.

horrorizar [or-ro-re-thar'], *va.* To cause horror, to terrify. -*vr.* To be terrified.

horrorosamente [or-ro-ro-sah-men'-tay], *adv.* Horribly, frightfully.

horroroso, sa [or-ro-ro'-so, sah], *a.* 1. (*coll.*) Horrid, hideous, frightful. 2. Horrid, dreadful, shocking, offensive, awful (feo).

horrura [or-roo'-rah], *f.* 1. Scoria dross, recrement. 2. Dreariness of a thicket or close wood. 3. Filth, dirt, obscenity.

hortaliza [or-tah-lee'-thah], *f.* Garden stuff, pot-herbs, all sort of esculent plants produced in a garden.

hortatorio, ria [or-tah-to'-re-o], *a.* V. EXHORTATORIO.

hortelanear [or-tay-lah-nay-ar'], *vn.* (*Prov.*) To cultivate an orchard.

hortelana [or-tay-lah'-nah], *f.* A gardener's wife.

hortelano [or-tay-lah'-no], *m.* Gardener, horticulturist. Hortelano, (*Orn.*) ortolan.

hortense [or-ten'-say], *a.* Hortensial, hortulan, relating to gardens.

hortensia [or-ten'-se-ah], *f.* (*Bot.*) Hydrant.

hortera [or-tay'-rah], *f.* A wooden bowl. -*m.* 1. Shop assistant, grocer's boy. 2. (*Fig.*) Rough type (inculto), coarse person, fraud (fingido). -*a.* Common (ordinario), vulgar; crude, tasteless; flashy (ostentoso).

horterada [or-tay-rah'-dah], *f.* Crude thing; coarse remark; vulgarity. **Ese vestido es una horterada**, that dress is a disgrace.

hortícola [or-tee'-co-lah], *a.* Horticultural.

horticultor, ra [or-te-cool-tor'], *m.* & *f.* Horticulturist.

horticultura [or-te-cool-too'-rah], *f.* Horticulture, culture of orchards.

hosco, ca [os'-co, cah], *a.* 1. Dark brown (oscuro), livercolored. 2. Sullen (persona), gloomy. 3. Boastful, ostentatious, vainglorious, arrogant.

hoscoso, sa [os-co'-so, sah], *a.* Crisp, rough.

hospedado, da [os-pay-dah'-do, dah], *a.* Applied to a house receiving guests. -*pp.* of HOSPEDAR.

hospedaje [os-pay-dah'-hay], *m.* 1. Kind reception of guests and strangers. 2. Price paid for lodging.

hospedamiento [os-pay-dah-me-en'-to], *m.* Reception of guests.

hospedar [os-pay-dar'], *va.* To receive, to lodge and entertain strangers and travelers, to harbor. -*vr.* To host, to take up entertainment; to lodge or take a temporary residence. -*vn.* To lodge collegians who have finished their studies, though they live in the college, but at their own expense.

hospedería [os-pay-day-ree'-ah], *f.* 1. Hospice, a house close to a monastery, a convent or a college, for the reception and accommodation of travelers and strangers. 2. Hospitium, a house kept in some places, at the expense of communities, to lodge their members. 3. V. HOSPEDAJE.

hospedero [os-pay-day'ro], *m.* 1. One who kindly receives guests and strangers. 2. Hospitaller, he whose trade is to receive and accommodate travelers and strangers.

hospiciano, na [os-pe-the-ah'-no, nah], *m.* & *f.* Poor person who lives in a house of charity.

hospicio [os-pee'-the-o], *m.* 1. Hospitium, charitable institution, house of charity. 2. Work-house. 3. (*Prov.*) House of correction. 4. Kind reception to guests and strangers. 5. In monasteries, the same as *hospedería*.

hospital [os-pe-tahl'], *a.* Hospitable, affable. **Hospital de aislamiento**, isolation hospital.

hospital [os-pe-tahl'], *m.* Hospital, infirmary, a place for the reception of the sick or support of the poor. **Hospital de sangre**, a field hospital for first aid to the wounded.

hospitalario, ria [os-pe-tah-lah'-re-o, ah], *a.* Applied to the religious communities which keep hospitals.

hospitalero, ra [os-pe-tah-lay'-ro, rah], *m.* & *f.* 1. Person entrusted with the care and direction of a hospital. 2. Any hospitable person.

hospitalidad [os-pe-tah-le-dahd'], *f.* 1. Hospitality, hospitage, the practice of kindly entertaining travelers and strangers. 2. Hospitableness, kindness to strangers. 3. The days which a person remains in an hospital.

hospitalización [os-pe-tah-le-thah-the-on'], *f.* Hospitalization.

hospitalizar [os-pe-tah-le-thar'], *va.* To hospitalize.

hospitalmente [os-pe-tal-men'-tay], *adv.* Hospitably.

hosquillo, lla [os-keel'-lyo, lyah], *a. dim.* Darkish, somewhat gloomy.

hostal [os-tahl'], *m.* Boarding house, cheap hotel.

hostelero, ra [os-tay-lay'-ro, rah], *m.* & *f.* An inn-keeper, tavern-keeper.

hostería [os-tay-ree'-ah], *f.* Inn, tavern, hostelry.

hostia [os'-te-ah], *f.* 1. Host, victim, sacrifice offered on the altar. 2. Host, the wafer prepared for the sacrifice of the mass.

hostiario [os-te-ah'-re-o], *m.* Waferbox, in which the bread is preserved that is to be consecrated.

hostiero [os-te-ay'-ro], *m.* Person who prepares the host.

hostigamiento [os-te-gah-me-en'-to], *m.* Chastisement, vexation, molestation.

hostigar [os-te-gar'], *va.* To vex, to trouble, to harass, to molest, to gall, to tire.

hostigo [os-tee'-go], *m.* 1. That part of a wall which the rain and winds beat on. 2. The beating of rain and winds against a wall.

hostil [os-teel'], *a.* Hostile, adverse.

hostilidad [os-te-le-dahd'], *f.* Hostility, opposition in war.

hostilizar [os-te-le-thar'], *va.* To commit hostilities; to hostilize.

hostilmente [os-teel-men'-tay], *adv.* Hostilely.

hotel [o-tel'], *m.* 1. (*Neol.*) Hotel. **Hospedarse en un hotel**, to put up at a hotel. 2. Detached house, suburban house.

hotelero [o-tay-lay-ro], *a.* Hotel. **La industria hotelera**, the hotel trade.

hotentote, ta [o-ten-to'-tay], *m. & f. & a.* Hottentot.

hoy [oh'-e], *adv.* 1. Today, this present day. 2. The present time, the time we live in. **Hoy día, hoy en el día** or **hoy en día**, nowadays. **Hoy por hoy**, this very day. **De hoy en adelante** or **de hoy más**, henceforward in future. **Antes hoy que mañana**, rather today than tomorrow, the sooner the better. **De hoy a mañana**, any time now. **De hoy en ocho días**, a week today.

hoya [oh'-yah], *f.* 1. Hole, cavity, pit in the earth (agujero). 2. V. SEPULTURA. 3. (*Amer, Peru.*) Bed of a river.

hoyada [o-yah'-dah], *f.* The lowest part of a field.

hoyito [o-yee'-to], *m. dim.* A small hole, cavity, pit, or excavation.

hoyo [o'-yo], *m.* 1. Hole (agujero), pit, excavation. 2. V. SEPULTURA. 3. Inequality or unevenness of a surface. 4. (Golf) Hole. **En el hoyo 18**, at the 18th hole.

hoyoso, sa [oh-yo-so, sah], *a.* Pitted, full of holes.

hoyuelo [oh-yoo-ay'-lo], *m.* 1. (*Dim.*) A little hole, a dimple in the chin or cheek. 2. A boy's play.

hoz [oth], *f.* 1. Sickle, a reaping hook, with which corn is cut. 2. Defile, ravine: a narrow pass. 3. (*Anat.*) Every membranous fold of a sickle shape. **De hoz y de coz**, headlong.

hozadero [o-thah-day'-ro], *m.* Place where hogs turn up the ground.

hozadura [o-thah-doo'-rah], *f.* Rooting, turning up the ground, as hogs do with their snouts.

hozar [o-thar'], *va.* To root, to turn up the ground, as hogs (cerdos).

huaca [oo-ah'-cah], *f.* (Peru) Burial place, ruins, etc., of the ancient Indians of Peru. V. GUACA.

huacal [oo-ah-cahl'], *m.* (*Amer.*) 1. Create for crockery or fruit. 2. (*Mex.*) A small hen-coop, carried on the back. V. GUACAL.

huaquero [oo-ah-kay'-ro], *m.* (*Peru*) A pitcher of fine earthenware found in the huacas.

huasicama [oo-ah-se-cah'-mah], *m.* (*S. Amer. Indian*) A door keeper.

huasipongo [oo-ah-se-pon'-go], *m.* (*Ec.*) An Indian hut.

huaso [oo-ah'-so], *m.* V. GUASO. (Vulgar.)

hucha [oo'-chah], *f.* 1. A large chest, trunk (arca). 2. Moneybox (alcancía), piggy bank. 3. Money kept and saved, savings (ahorros). **Tener una buena hucha**, to have money laid by.

húchoho [oo'-cho-o], *m.* Word used to call birds.

huebra [oo-ay'-brah], *f.* 1. Extent of ground which a yoke of oxen can plough every day. 2. Pair of mules with a ploughman hired or let our for a day's work. 3. (*Prov.*) V. BARBECHO.

hueca [oo-ay'-cah], *f.* Notch at the small end of a spindle.

hueco, ca [oo-ay'-co, cah], *a.* 1. Hollow (vacío), empty, concave. 2. Empty, vain, ostentatious. 3. Tumid, resonant, inflated (sonido, voz). **Voz hueca**, sonorous and hollow voice. 4. Soft, spongy: applied to ground, or to short wool fit only for carding. **Se ha puesto muy hueco**, he has become very vain or ostentatious.

hueco [oo-ay'-co], *m.* 1. Notch or nick of a wheel, into which the leaves of a pinion or the teeth of a wheel hitch and set it in motion. 2. Interval of time or place. 3. Hollowness. 4. Hollow, gap (brecha), hole. 5. Any vacant space or aperture in a house or other building (de escalera, de ascensor) 6. V. MUESCA. 7. (*Met.*) Office or post vacant (vacante). **Deja un hueco que será difícil llenar**, he leaves a gap which will be hard to fill.

huélfago [oo-el'-fah-go], *m.* Difficulty of breathing in beasts and hawks, or other birds.

huelga [oo-el'-gah], *f.* 1. Strike, go on strike. 2. Rest (descanso), repose; relaxation from work; recreation (recreo), merry-making. 3. Fallow, ground lying at rest. 4. The quitting of work by a body of laborers to enforce compliance with some demand. **Huelga de brazos caídos**, sit-down strike. **Huelga de hambre**, hunger strike. **Huelga patronal**, lock out. **Los obreros en huelga**, the workers on strike.

huelgo [oo-el'-go], *m.* 1. Breath (aliento), respiration. **Tomar huelgo**, to breathe, to respire. 2. V. HOLGURA. (*Yo huelgo, yo huelgue*, from *Holgar.* V. ACORDAR.)

huelguista [oo-ayl-gees'-tah], *m & f.* Striker.

huella [oo-el'-lyah], *f.* 1. Track, footstep; the print of the foot of a man or beast (de pie). 2. The horizontal width of the steps of a staircase (escalera). 3. Act and effect of treading or trampling (acto). 4. Impression of a plate or other thing on paper. 5. An impression morally or physically speaking. **Sin dejar huella**, without leaving a trace. **Seguir las huellas de uno**, to follow in somebody's footsteps.

huellas digitales [oo-el'-lyahs de-he-tah'-less], *f. pl.* Fingerprints.

huello [oo-el'-lyo], *m.* 1. Ground, the floor or level of a place. 2. Step, pace. 3. Lower part of an animal's hoof. (*Yo huello, yo huelle*, from *Hollar.* V. ACORDAR.)

huembe [oo-em'-bay], *m.* (*Amer.*) A liana so tough as to sustain great weights. *Cf.* GÜEMBÉ.

huequecito [oo-ay-kay-thee'-to], *m. dim.* A small cavity or space.

huérfago [oo-er'-fah-no], *m.* V. HUÉLFAGO.

huerfanito, ita [oo-er-fah-nee'-to, tah], *m. & f. dim.* A little orphan.

huérfano, na [oo-err'-fah-no, nah], *m. & f.* Orphan, a child who has lost a father or mother or both. **Huérfano de padre**, Fatherless. *-a.* Orphan, bereft of parents.

huero, ra [oo-ay'-ro, rah], *a.* 1. Empty, addle (huevo). 2. (*Met.*) Addle, empty, void. *-m.* (*Mex.*) A person with lightcolored hair.

huerta [oo-er'-tah], *f.* 1. A large orchard, fruit garden, or kitchen garden. 2. (*Prov.*) Land which can be irrigated.

huerto [oo-err'-to], *m.* A small orchard or kitchen garden (de verduras), generally near the house; orchard (de frutales); back garden (de casa pequeña).

huesa [oo-ay'-sah], *f.* Grave, sepulture.

huesarrón [oo-ay-sar-rone'], *m. aug.* A large bone.

huesecico, illo, ito [oo-ay-say-thee'-co], *m. dim.* A little bone.

hueso [oo-ay'-so], *m.* 1. Bone. **Hueso de la alegría**, funny bone. **Sin hueso**, boneless. **Estar en los huesos**, to be nothing but skin and bones. 2. Stone, core, the case which contains the seeds and kernels of fruit. 3. The part of a limestone which remains unburnt in the kiln. 4. Anything which produces more pain than profit. 5. Any useless or unprofitable thing. 6. Piece of ground of little value and bad quality. 7. Hard work (trabajo); stumbling block (obstáculo). 8. Very strict person (persona). **Su profesor es un hueso**, his teacher is terribly strict.

huesoso, sa [oo-ay-so'-so, sah], *a.* Bony, osseous.

huésped, da [oo-ays'-ped, dah], *m. & f.* 1. Guest (invitado), lodger (pensión), one entertained in the house of another. 2. Host (anfitrión), hostess, he who entertains others in his house. 3. Inn-keeper, tavern-keeper. 4. Stranger.

hueste [oo-ays'-tay], *f.* Host, army to campaign. **Huestes**, hosts, armies.

huesudo, da [oo-ay-soo'-do, dah], *a.* Bony, having large bones.

hueva [oo-ay'-vah], *f.* Egg or spawn of fishes.

huevar [oo-ay-var'], *vn.* To lay egs.

huevecico, illo, ito, zuelo [oo-ay-vay-thee'co], *f. dim.* A small egg.

huevera [oo-ay-vay'-rah], *f.* 1. Ovarium of birds. 2. Egg stand.

huevero, ra [oo-ay-vay'-ro, rah], *m. & f.* Dealer in eggs.

huevo [oo-ay'-vo], *m.* 1. Egg. 2. Spawn, sperm. 3. Hollow piece of wood used by shoemakers for shaping shoes. 4. Small waxen vessel filled with scented drops. 5. Ball (testículo), testicle. **A huevo**, for a trifle, at a low price. **Huevos estrellados**, fried eggs. **Huevos pasados por agua**, soft-boiled eggs. **Huevos escalfados**, poached eggs. **Huevos revueltos**, buttered eggs. **Nos lo han puesto a huevo** they've made it easy for us. **Me costó un huevo**, it cost me an arm and a leg (precio).

huevón [oo-ay-vone'], *(LAm.) a.* 1. Idle (vago), lazy; dim (tonto); slow (lento); chicken-livered (cobarde). 2. Brave (valiente).

hugonote, ta [oo-gono'-tay, tah], *m. & f. & a.* Huguenot, a French Protestant.

huída [oo-ee'-dah], *f.* 1. Flight, escape, outleap. V. FUGA. 2. Hole made to put in or draw out something with facility. *-pl.* Evasions, subterfuges.

huidero [oo-ee-day'-ro], *m.* 1. Place of retreat, where game retires. 2. Laborer in quicksilver mines, who opens the holes in which the beams of the mine are fixed.

huidizo, za [oo-e-dee'-tho, thah], *a.* Fugitive, fleeing (impresión), shy (persona).

huido [oo-ee'-do], *a.* 1. Fugitive, on the run (que ha huido).

huiñapu [oo-e-nyah'-poo], *m. (Amer.)* Maize moistened and spread upon a bed of straw until it begins to germinate for making chicha.

huir [oo-eer'], *vn.* 1. To flee, to escape; to pack, to go, to flinch or get away, to get off. 2. To give the slip, to slip away; with words denoting time, to pass rapidly, to fly (tiempo). 3. To shun, to avoid doing a bad thing, to flee from, *-vr.* To run away, to escape, to take to one's heels, to make one's escape.

huito [oo-e'-to], *m. (Ec.)* A vegetable dye used for skin diseases.

hulanos [oo-lah'-nos], *m. pl.* Uhlans, name of a light Asiatic cavalry introduced into Europe.

hule [oo'-lay], *m.* 1. Rubber (goma). 2. Oil cloth (tela). **Zapatos de hule**, rubber shoes.

hulero [oo-lay'-ro], *m.* A collector of rubber or caoutchouc.

hulla [ool'-lyah], *f.* Pit-coal, hard goal.

hullera [ool-lyay'-rah], *f.* A coal-mine.

humada [oo-mah'-dah], *f. V.* AHUMADA.

humanado, da [oo-mah-nah'-do, dah], *a. & pp.* of HUMANAR. Humanate, invested with humanity (hijo de Dios).

humanamente [oo-mah-nah-men'-tay], *adv.* 1. Humanely (humanidad), kindly, mercifully. 2. Humanly (en términos humanos), in the power of men. **Eso humanamente no se puede hacer**, that cannot possibly be done.

humanar [oo-mah-nar'], *va.* 1. To humanize, to soften. 2. *(Poet.)* To transform or convert into man. *-vr.* 1. To become man (hijo de Dios). 2. To become humane or meek: to grow familiar; to be humbled, to be lowered.

humanidad [oo-mah-ne-dahd'], *f.* 1. Humanity, the nature of man (género humano). 2. Humanity (cualidad), human kind, the collective body of mankind. 3. Humanity, benevolence, tenderness, kindness, benignity. 4. *(coll.)* Corpulence (gordura), bulkiness of body, fleshiness. 5. Human weakness, *-pl.* Philology, grammatical studies.

humanista [oo-mah-nees'-tah], *m.* Humanist, philologer, grammarian.

humanitario, ria [oo-mah-ne-tah'-re-o, ah], *a.* 1. Humanitarian, philanthropic. 2. Interesting to the generality of mankind, or tending toward their well-being.

humanizar [oo-mah-ne-thar'], *va. & vr. V.* HUMANAR.

humano, na [oo-mah'-no, nah], *a.* 1. Human, peculiar to man (humano). 2. Humane, kind, merciful, benevolent (benévolo), gracious. **En lo humano**, as regards human power or agency.

humareda [oo-mah-ray'-dah], *f.* 1. A great deal of smoke. 2. Confusion, perplexity.

humazga [oo-math'-gah], *f.* Hearth-money, fumage, tax paid on fireplaces.

humazo [oo-mah'-tho], *m.* Smoke; fume proceeding from burning paper which is doubled and twisted.

humeante [oo-may-ahn'-tay], *va.* Fuming, fumant.

humear [oo-may-ar'], *vn.* 1. To smoke (humo), to emit smoke. 2. To vapor, to emit or exhale fumes or vapors (vapor). 3. *(Met.)* To inflame, to fire (pasiones). 4. *(Met.)* To kindle or stir up a tumult, quarrel, or lawsuit.

humectación [oo-mec-tah-the-on'], *f.* 1. Preparation of a medicine by moistening with water. 2. Dampness of the surface. 3. *(Med.)* Action of fomentations.

humectante [oo-mec-tahn'-tay], *pa. (Med.)* Moistening.

humectar [oo-mec-tar'], *va. (Med.)* To moisten, to wet.

humectativo, va [oo-mec-tah-tee'-vo, vah], *a.* Humective, causing moisture.

humedad [oo-may-dahd'], *f.* Humidity, moisture, dampness, moistness. **A prueba de humedad**, damp-proof.

humedal [oo-may-dahl'], *m.* Humid soil, a marsh.

humedecer [oo-may-day-therr'], *va.* To moisten, to wet (mojar), to soak, to steep, to dampen. *(Yo humedezco, yo humedezca, from Humedecer. V.* CONOCER.)

humedecido, da [oo-may-day-thee'-do, dah], *a.* Dampened, moistened, humidified.

húmedo, da [oo'-may-do, dah], *a.* Humid, wet, mist, watery, damp.

humeral [oo-may-rahl'], *a. (Anat.)* Humeral, belonging to the humerus.

húmero [oo'-may-ro], *m.* Humerus, a bone situated between the scapula and forearm.

humero [oo-may'-ro], *m.* Tunnel, funnel, the shaft of a chimney; the passage for the smoke.

humildad [oo-meel-dahd'], *f.* 1. Humility, modesty, meekness. 2. Lowliness, meanness, lowness of mind or birth, submission.

humilde [oo-meel'-day], *a.* 1. Humble (carácter), modest, submissive, meek. 2. Humble, low (clase), not high, not great, not tall. 3. Base, ignoble, of little worth or account. **Son gente humilde**, they are humble people.

humildemente [oo-meel-day-men'-tay], *adv.* Humbly, submissively; modestly, meekly.

humildito, ita [oo-meel-dee'-to, tah], *a. dim.* Very humble or modest.

humillación [oo-meel-lyah-the-on'], *f.* 1. Humiliation, submission, abatement of pride. 2. Humiliation, act of humility, abjectness, humbling: obsequiousness. 3. Humiliation, mortification, self-contempt.

humillador, ra [oo-meel-lyah-dor', rah], *m. & f.* Humiliator.

humilante [oo-meel-lyahn'-tay], *pa. & a.* Humbling, indecorous, unbecoming, degrading.

humillar [oo-meel-lyar'], *va.* 1. To humble, to lower; to bend, to bow (cabeza). 2. To humiliate, to crush (enemigos), to subdue, to bring down from loftiness and pride, to degrade, to depreciate. **Humillar a alguno**, to humiliate someone. *-vr.* To humble oneself, to become humble or submissive.

humillo [oo-meel'-lyo], *m.* 1. *(Dim.)* Smoke or vapor which is not dense. 2. Vanity, petty pride: commonly used in the plural. 3. Disease of sucking pigs.

humita [oo-mee'-tah], *f. (Amer. Peru.)* 1. A small cake made of tender maize and sugar. It is wrapped in maize leaves and cooked in an oven or a water-bath. 2. A rocky substance found in small crystals.

humo [oo'-mo], *m.* 1. Smoke, the visible effluvium from something burning. 2. Vapor (vapor), steam, fumes (gases). 3. Thin, clear, black silk stuff. **Hacer humo**, to smoke. *-pl.* 1. Families or houses in a town or village (hogares). 2. (*Met.*) Vanity, petty pride, haughtiness, presumption (presunción). **Bajar los humos a uno**, to take somebody down a peg. **Tener humos para**, to have the nerve to. **Cortina de humo**, smoke screen. **¡Cuántos humos tiene!**, how presumptuous he is! **Hacerse humo**, to vanish into thin air. **Se le bajaron los humos**, he was put in his place. **Se le han subido los humos a la cabeza**, he's got on his high horse. **Tener muchos humos**, to put on airs.

humor [oo-mor'], *m.* 1. Humor, a general name for any fluid of the body. 2. Humor, the disposition of a person to act in any way. 3. Humor, general turn or temper of mind, mood. **Buen humor**, good-nature, pleasant disposition. **Mal humor**, ill-temper. **Hombre de buen humor**, a good-humored man. **Estar de buen humor**, to be in good humor, to be gay. **Tener sentido del humor**, to have a sense of humor. **Humor de todos los diablos**, very bad temper. **Seguirle el humor a uno**, to humor someone, to go along with somebody. **Si estás de humor**, if you feel like it.

humorada [oo-mo-rah'-dah], *f.* 1. Graceful sprightliness 2. A witty saying, stroke of wit.

humorado, da [oo-mo-rah'-do, dah], *a.* 1. Full of humors. 2. Well or ill disposed.

humoral [oo-mo-rahl'], *a.* Humoral, procceding from the humors.

humorcico, illo, ito [oo-mor-thee'-co], *m. dim.* of HUMOR. Generally used to denote a bad-tempered person.

humorismo [oo-mo-rees'-mo], *m.* Humor, humorousness.

humorista [oo-mo-rees'-tah], *m. f.* Humorist.

humoroso, sa [oo-mo-ro'-so, sah], *a.* Watery, containing fluid.

humoso, sa [oo-mo'-so, sah], *a.* Smoky, fumy.

humus [oo'-moos], *m.* Vegetable mould, humus.

hundible [oon-dee'-blay], *a.* Sinkable, capable of submersion or destruction.

hundido [oon-dee-do], *a.* Sunken; deep-set (ojos), hollow.

hundimiento [oon-de-me-en'-to], *m.* 1. Submersion, immersion, the act of sinking. 2. Downfall, destruction of fabrics (edificio). 3. Cave-in (tierra).

hundir [oon-deer'], *va.* 1. To submerge (sumergir), to immerge, to put under water. 2. To sink, to crush, to overwhelm, to beat down. 3. To refute, to confound. 4. To sink, to make to fall, to pull or bear down, to destroy, to ruin, (edificio). *-vr.* 1. To sink, to fall down, to fall to a level. 2. To sink (arena, lodo), to go to the bottom. 3. (*coll.*) To hide, to lie hidden: applied to things which cannot be found. 4. To have dissensions and quarrels. **Se hundió la economía**, the economy collapsed. **Se hundió en la meditación**, he became lost in meditation.

húngaro, ra [oon'-gah-ro, rah], *a.* Hungarian, pertaining to Hungary.

huno, na [oo'-no, nah], *a.* Hun, one of an obscure Asiatic warlike race. *-m.* The Huns.

hupe [oo'-pay], *f.* A white spongy substance which results from the decomposition of certain woods, and serves as tinder.

hura [oo'-rah], *f.* 1. Furuncle, an angry pustule on the head. 2. A tree of the Antilles, known as the American walnut. 3. A carbuncle.

huracán [oo-rah-cahn'], *m.* Hurricane, a violent storm. (*Carib.*)

huracanado [oo-rah-cah-nah-do], *a.* **Viento huracanado**, hurricane wind.

hurañamente [oo-rah-nyah-men'-tay], *adv.* 1. Wildly, in a savage and intractable manner. 2. Diffidently, disdainfully.

huraño, ña [oo-rah'-nyo, nyah], *a.* 1. Shy (tímido), diffident; intractable. 2. Disdainful. 3. Cold-hearted, loveless. 4. Wild (salvaje).

hurción [oor-the-on'], *f. V.* INFURCIÓN.

hurgar [oor-gar'], *va.* 1. To stir, to move with a stick or iron. 2. To stir up disturbances, to excite quarrels.

hurgón [oor-gone'], *m.* 1. Poker for stirring the fire (fuego); a fire-fork. 2. Thrust in fencing (con arma).

hurgonada [oor-go-nah'-dah], *f. V.* ESTOCADA.

hurgonazo [oor-go-nah'-tho], *m.* A violent thrust.

hurgonear [oor-go-nay-ar'], *va.* 1. To stir the fire with a poker (fuego). 2. To make a thrust in fencing (adversario).

hurgonero [oor-go-nay'-ro], *m.* Poker. *V.* HURGÓN.

hurí [oo-ree'], *f.* Houri, a Mohammedan nymph of paradise.

hurón, na [oo-ro-ne', nah], *m. & f.* 1. Ferret. 2. Ferreter, one who pries into others' secrets. *-a.* Cold-hearted, loveless, shy, intractable, disdainful.

huronear [oo-ro-nay-ar'], *va.* 1. To ferret, to hunt with a ferret. 2. To pry, snoop, ferret (escudriñar).

huronera [oo-ro-nay'-rah], *f.* 1. Ferret hole. 2. Lurking place.

huronero [oo-ro-nay'-ro], *m.* Ferret keeper.

¡hurra! [oor'-rah], *int.* Hurrah!

hurraca [oor-rah'-cah], *f.* (*Orn.*) Magpie.

hurtable [oor-tah'-blay], *a.* Capable of being stolen.

hurtadillas (a) [oor-tah-deel'-lyas], *adv.* By stealth, slyly, artfully, privately, in a hidden manner.

hurtadineros [oor-tah-de-nay'-ros], *m.* (*Prov.*) *V.* ALCANCÍA.

hurtador, ra [oor-tah-dor', rah], *m. & f.* Robber, thief.

hurtagua [oor-tah'-goo-ah], *f.* (*Prov.*) *V.* REGADERA.

hurtamano (de) [oor-tah-mah'-no], *adverbial phrase.* Without consideration or pity.

hurtar [oor-tar'], *va.* 1. To steal (robar), to rob, to make way with. 2. To cheat in weight or measure. 3. To recover a piece of ground from the sea or a river (mar) 4. To separate, to part. **Hurtar el cuerpo**, to flee, to avoid a difficulty. 5. To commit plagiarism. *-vr.* To remove or withdraw (retirarse), to abscond.

hurtarropa [oor-tar-ro'-pah], *f.* Boy's play.

hurto [oor'-to], *m.* 1. Theft (acto), robbery, stealing. 2. Theft, the thing stolen (cosa robada). 3. In mines, passage between the principal apartments. **A hurto**, by stealth.

husada [oo-sah'-dah], *f.* A spindleful of thread or worsted.

husaño [oo-sah'-nyo], *m.* A large spindle.

húsar [oo'-sar], *m.* Hussar, originally a Hungarian horse soldier.

husillero [oo-see'-lyay'-ro], *m.* One who attends the spindle in oil-mills.

husillo [oo-seel'-lyo], *m.* 1. (*Dim.*) A small spindle. 2. A hollow cylinder running round in a spiral nut; a screq-pin. *-pl.* Drains, small channels for draining fens.

husita [oo-see'-tah], *m.* Hussite, a follower of John Huss.

husma [oos'-mah]. *f.* **Andar a la husma**, (*coll.*) to peep narrowly in order to discover secrets.

husmeador, ra [oos-may-ah-dor', rah], *m. & f.* Scenter, smeller.

husmeadorcillo, lla [oos-may-ah-dor-theel'-lyo, lyah], *m. & f. dim.* Little smeller.

husmear [oos-may-ar'], *va.* 1. To scent, to find out by smelling. 2. To pry, to peep, or inspect curiously, officiously, or impertinently. *-vn.* To begin to smell bad (carne).

husmo [oos'-mo], *m.* Smell of meat somewhat tainted. **Estar al husmo**, to be on the scent; to watch for a favorable opportunity to do something.

huso [oo'-so], *m.* Spindle, the pin by which the thread is formed, and on which it is wound.

huta [oo'-tah], . Hut, kind of shed in which huntsmen hide, in order to start their dogs at the chase.

hutía [oo-tee'-ah], *f.* Cuban rat.

¡hug! [oo'-e]. Interjection of surprise (sorpresa), astonishment, grief (dolor), on seeing or hearing something.

huyuyo, ye [oo-yoo'-yo, yah], *a.* (*Cuba*) Untractable, shy, diffident.

I

i [ee], the third of the Spanish vowels called the Latin *i*, to distinguish it from they *y* called Greek. *I* in Spanish is sounded like the English *e* in *even*, or *i* in *idiotism*. As a numeral, it stands for one. In chemistry, it is the symbol for iodine. (I.)

Iberia [e-bay'-re-ah], *f.* 1. An ancient region of Asia, now transcaucasian Georgia. 2. Name given by the ancient Greeks to Spain and Portugal.

ibérico, ca [e-bay'-re-co, cah], *a.* or **íbero** [ebay'-ro], *m.* Spaniard. -*a.* Spanish, Iberian.

iberoaméricano [e-bay-ro-ah-may-re-cah'-no], *a. m & f.* Latin-American.

íbice [ee'-be-thay], *m.* Ibex, kind of goat.

ibidem [e-bee'-dem]. Ibidem. Latin word, meaning *in the same place.* In the same writing of an author.

ibis [ee'-bes], *f. (Orn.)* Ibis, a kind of bird.

icaco [e-cah'-co], *m. (Bot.)* West Indian cocoaplum.

iceberg [e-thay-ber'], *m.* Iceberg.

icneumón [ic-nay-oo-mon'], *m.* 1. Ichneumon, a small animal; a mongoose. The Egyptian ichneumon devours the eggs of the crocodile, and was held sacred by the ancient Eygptians. 2. The ichneumonfly, a hymenopterous insect predatory upon other insects.

icnografía [ec-no-grah-fee'-ah], *f.* 1. Ichnography, ground plan, a delineation of the length, breadth, angles, and lines of a fortification or building. 2. Ground-plot, the ichnography of building.

icnográfico, ca [ec-no-grah'-fe-co, cah], *a.* Ichnographical.

icónico, ca [e-co'-ne-co, cah], *a.* Exactly conformable to the model; a perfect image.

icono [e-co-no], *m.* Ikon, icon.

iconoclasta, iconómaco [e-co-no-clahs'-tah, e-co-no'-mah-co], *m.* Iconoclast, image breaker, heretic who denies the worship due to holy images.

iconografía [e-co-no-grah-fee'-ah], *f.* Iconography, the art of describing by pictures.

iconográfico, ca [e-co-no-grah'-fe-co, cah], *a.* Relating to iconography.

iconólatra [e-co-no'lah-trah], *m.* Iconolater, a worshipper of images.

iconología [e-co-no-lo-hee'-ah], *f.* Iconology, representation by figures.

iconoscopio [e-co-nos-co'-pe-o], *m.* Iconoscope.

icoroso, sa [e-co-ro'-so, sah], *a.* Ichorous, serous.

icosaedro [e-co-sah-ay'-dro], *m.* Icosahedron, a solid bounded by twenty plane faces.

ictericia [ic-tay-ree'-the-ah], *f.* Jaundice, a disease.

ictericiado, da, icotérico, ca [ic-tay-re-the-ah'-do, dah, ectay'-re-co, cah], *a.* Icterical, jaundiced.

ictiofagia [ic-te-o-fah'-he-ah], *f.* Ichthyophagy, diet of fish.

ictiófago, ga [ec-te-o'-fah-go, gah], *a.* Fish-eating, relating to the ichthyophagists.-*m. & f.* Ichthyophagist.

ictiología [ic-te-o-lo-he'-ah], *f.* Ichthyology, the science of the nature of fishes.

ictiopetra [ic-te-o-pay'-trah], *f.* A petrified fish.

ictiosauro [ic-te-o-sah'-oo-ro], *m.* Ichthyosaurus.

ictiosis [ic-te-o'-sis], *f.* Ichthyosis, a scaly disease of the skin.

ictita [ic-tee'-tah], *f.* A stone which preserves the impression of a fish.

icho, or **ichu** [ee'-cho, ee'-choo], *m.* Grass in the Andes. *(Peru)*

ida [ee'-dah], *f.* 1. Departure, act of going from one place to another (partida). 2. *(Met.)* Impetuosity, rash, inconsiderate, or violent proceeding, silly. 3. Act of driving a ball out of the truck-table. 4. Mark or impression of the foot or game on the ground. **Ida y vuelta**, out and home, round-trip, excursion. **Dejar las idas por las venidas**, to miss the boat. **Viaje de ida**, outward journey.

idea [e-day'-ah], *f.* 1. Idea, a mental image. 2. Notion (noción), conception. **Idea genial**, bright idea. **Meterse una idea en la cabeza**, to get an idea into one's head. 3. Contrivance, design, intention (propósito), plan, project, scheme. **Con la idea de**, with the idea of. **Cambiar de idea**, to change one's mind. 4. Thread of a discourse. 5. Model, example. 6. Genius, talent. 7. Fancy, conceit, extravagant notion, impression: in this sense it is used commonly in the plural.

ideal [e-day-ahl'], *a.* Ideal, mental, intellectual, imaginary, notional: not physical.

idealidad [e-day-ah-le-dahd'], *f.* 1. Ideality, the ideal. 2. Ideality, the sentiment of the beautiful, the poetic, the eloquent.

idealismo [e-day-ah-lees'-mo], *m.* 1. Idealism, generic name of the philosophic systems which consider the idea as the essence of things. 2. Aptitude of the artist, poet, orator, etc., to raise above reality the objects which he describes.

idealista [e-day-ah-lees'-tah], *a.* Idealistic, striving after the ideal. -*m.* Idealist, believer in idealism.

idealizar [e-day-ah-le-thar'], *va.* To idealize.

idealmente [e-day-al-men'-tay], *adv.* Ideally, intellectually.

idear [e-day-ar'], *va.* 1. To form or conceive an idea. 2. To think, to contrive, to invent, to imagine, to plan, to scheme, to meditate. 2. To discuss a subject on futile grounds, to indulge in airy conceptions.

idem [ee'-dem], *prom. (Lat.)* Idem, the same.

idénticamente [e-den'-te-cah-men'-tay], *adv.* Identically.

idéntico, ca [e-den'-te-co, cah], *a.* Identic, identical, congenerous, the same, implying the same thing.

identidad [e-den-te-dahd'], *f.* Identity, sameness, identicalness.

identificación [e-den-te-fe-cah-the-on'], *f.* Identification. **Identificación errónea**, mistaken identity.

identificar [e-den-te-fe-car'], *va.* To identify; to ascertain the sameness of two objects.-*vr.* To become the same.

ideográfico, ca [e-day-o-grah'-fe-co, cah], *a.* Ideographic, presenting ideas by symbolic characters.

ideografía [e-day-o-gra-fee'-ah], *f.* Ideography, representation of thought by signs especially phonetic.

ideología [e-day-o-lo-hee'-ah], *f.* Ideography, ideas.

ideológico, ca [e-day-o-lo'-he-co, cah], *a.* Ideological.

idílico, ca [e-dee'-le-co, cah], *a.* Idyllic, having the qualities of an idyl.

idilio [e-dee'-le-o], *m. (Poet.)* Idyl, a pastoral poem, romance (amor).

idioma [e-de-o'-mah], *m.* 1. Language, tongue, idiom, the language peculiar to a nation or country. 2. Idiom, mode of speaking peculiar to a dialect or language. **No hablamos el mismo idioma**, we just don't speak the same language.

idiomático, ca [e-de-o-mah'-te-co, cah], *a.* Idiomatic, proper to a language.

idiopatía [e-de-o-pah-tee'-ah], *f.* Idiopathy, a primary disease distinctive in character.

idiopático, ca [e-de-o-pah'-to-co, cah], · *a.* Idiopathic, primary, independent (enfermedades).

idiosincrasia [e-de-o-sin-crah'-se-ah], *f.* Idiosyncrasy, a peculiar disposition.

idiota [e-de-o'-tah], *m.* Idiot, a fool, an ignorant person.

idiotez [e-de-o-teth'], *f.* Idiotism, silliness, ignorance, idiocy.

idiotismo [e-de-o-tees, mo], *m.* 1. Idiom (gramática), idiotism, peculiarity of expression. 2. Idiocy, folly, natural imbecility of mind.

ido, da [ee'-do, dah], *pp.* of IR. Gone. 1. *(LAm.)* Absent-minded (despistado). 2. *(LAm.)* Nuts, crazy (chiflado). 3. *(CAm. Mex.)* **Estar ido**, to be drunk.

idólatra [e-do'-lah-trah], *a.* Idolatrous, heathen, paganish.

idolatra [e-do'-lah-trah], *m.* 1. Idolater, a worshipper of idols. 2. One who idolizes a woman, or loves her with excessive fondness.

idolatradamente [e-do-lah-trah-dah-men'-tay], *adv.* Idolatrously.

idolatrar [e-do-lah-trar'], *va.* 1. To idolatrize. 2. To idolize, to love excessively.

idolatría [e-do-lah-tree'-ah], *f.* 1. Idolatry. 2. Inordinate love, excessive fondness.

idolito, illo [e-do-lee'-to], *m. (Dim.)* 1. A little idol. 2. Darling, favorite, the object of fondness.

idolo [ee'-do-lo], *m.* 1. Idol, an image worshipped as God. 2. *(Col.)* Idol, a person or thing loved with the utmost affection.

idoneidad [e-do-nay-e-dahd'], *f.* Aptitude (capacidad), fitness, capacity.

idóneo, nea [e-doh'-nay-o, ah], *a.* Fit, convenient, proper. neat, suitable (apropiado); *(Mex.)* genuine (genuino).

idus [ee'-doos], *m.* Ides, last of the three parts into which the Romans divided the month.

iglesario [e-glay-sah'-re-o], *m.* The total of the lands which used to belong to the churches.

iglesia [e-glay'-se-ah], *f.* 1. Church, the collective body of Christians. 2. Church, body of Christians adhering to some particular form of worship. 3. Church, place which Christians consecrate to the worship of God 4. Temple, place where Christian worship. 5. Ecclesiastical state; chapter; diocese. 6. Right of immunity enjoyed in churches. **Iglesia Anglicana**, Church of England. **Iglesia Católica**, Catholic Church. **Casarse por la iglesia**, to get married in church.

iglú [e-gloo'], *m.* Igloo.

ignaro, ra [ig-nah'-ro, rah], *a.* Ignorant, unlearned, uninstructed.

ignavia [ig-nah'-ve-ah], *f.* Idleness, laziness, carelessness.

igneo, ea [eeg'-nay-o, ah], *a.* Igneous, fiery.

ignescente [ig-nes-then'-tay], *a.* Scintillating, burning, ignescent.

ignición [ig-ne-the-on'], *f.* Ignition, the act of kindling or setting on fire.

ignícola [ig-nee'-co-lah], *m.* Fire-worshipper.

ignífero, ra [ig-nee'-fay-ro, rah], *a. (Poet.)* Igniferous, ignifluous, containing or emitting fire.

ignipotente [ig-ne-po-ten'-tay], *a. (Poet.)* Ignipotent, having power over fire.

igniscencia [ig-nis-then'-the-ah], *f.* Incandescence.

igniscente [ig-nis-then'-tay], *a.* Incandescent, glowing with heat.

ignoble [ig-no'-blay], **a.** *(Ant.)* V. INNOBLE.

ignografía [ig-no-grah-fe'-ah], *f.* V. ICNOGRAFÍA.

ignominia [ig-no-mee'-ne-ah], *f.* Ignominy, infamy, public disgrace, opprobrium.

ignominiosamente [ig-no-me-neo-sah-men'-tay], *adv.* Ignominiously, opprobriously.

ignominioso, sa [ig-no-me-ne-o'-so, sah], *a.* Ignominious, opprobrious. reproachful, disgraceful.

ignorado, da [ig-no-rah'-do, dah], *a. & pp.* of IGNORAR. Unknown. occult, fameless.

ignorancia [ig-no-rahn'-the-ah], *f.* Ignorance, unlearnedness, want of knowledge, illiterateness; idiotism; folly; darkness.

ignorante [ig-no-rahn'-tay], *pa. & a.* 1. Ignorant, stupid, unlearned, uninstructed. 2. Ignorant, without knowledge of some particular. -*m.* Ignorant.

ignorantemente [ig-no-ran-tay-men'-tay], *adv.* Ignorantly.

ignorantón, na [ig-no-ran-tone', nah], *a. aug.* Grossly ignorant.

ignorar [ig-no-rar'], *va.* To be ignorant of, not to know (desconocer). **Lo ignoro en absoluto**, I don't know at all. **Ignoramos su paradero**, we don't know his whereabouts.

ignoto, ta [ig-no'-to, tah], *a.* Unknown, undiscovered.

igorrote [e-go-rro'-tay], *m.* Name of a tribe of savage Indians of the island of Luzón (Philippines), and of their language.

igual [e-goo-ahl'], *a.* 1. Equal, similar, the same, alike (seme-jante), coequal, like another in any quality that admits comparison. **No vi nunca cosa igual**, I never saw the like. **Me es igual**, it's all the same to me. 2. Level, even (llano), flat. **Ir iguales**, to be level. 3. Like, resembling, similar, uniform,

equable. 4. Constant (constante), firm, determined, equanimous, consistent. -*m.* The sign of equality, *viz.* =. **En igual de**, instead of. **Al igual**, equally. **No tiene igual**, he has not his like; it is matchless. **Por igual** or **por un igual**, equally, with equality. **Sin igual**, not to be equalled. -*m & f.* Equal. **Al igual**, equally. **Ser el igual de**, to be the equal of. **No tener igual**, to be unrivalled.

iguala [e-goo-ah'-lah], *f.* 1. Agreement, convention, stipulation, contract, commutation. 2. Equalizing, equalling, the act of equalling. 3. Level, an instrument with which masons adjust their work. 4. Stipend or gratuity given in settlement, and especially a yearly or monthly stipend given in rural districts to doctors and apothecaries for the right to services and medicines.

igualación [e-goo-ah-lah-the-on'], *f.* 1. Equalling, equalizing, equalization, levelling, the act and effect of making equal or even. 2. Agreement, stipulation, contract. 3. *(Alg.)* Equation. 4. Counter-gauge, a trimming of one piece of wood into another.

igualado, da [e-goo-ah-lah'-do, dah], *pp.* of IGUALAR. Equalled. Said of some birds which have shed their down and have even plumage. **Dejar a uno igualado**, *(coll.)* to give one a severe drubbing. -*a. (CAm. Mex.)* Cheeky (irrespetuoso); sly (astuto).

igualador, ra [e-goo-ah-lah-dor', rah], *m. & f.* 1. Equalizer, leveller. 2. A kind of sieve of fine skin for refining the grain of powder.

igualamiento [e-goo-ah-lah-me-en'-to], *m.* Equalizing, equalization, act of equalling.

igualar [e-goo-ah-lar'], *va.* 1. To equalize (hacer igual), to match, to mate. 2. To judge without partiality, to hold in equal estimation. 3. To flatten, to make even or level, to level the ground (allanar). 4. To rake the ground. 5. To adjust differences, to agree upon. -*vn.* To be equal. -*vr.* To level, to efface distinction or superiority, to place oneself upon a level with others. 2. *(Met.)* To give a second blow. 3. *(CAm. Mex.)* To be familiar, to be cheeky (faltar al respeto).

igualdad [e-goo-al-dahd'], *f.* 1. Equality, similitude. 2. Conformity, consimilitude, likeness. 3. Levelness, evenness (superficie), equality of surface. 4. Equality, uniformity. **Igualdad de ánimo**, evenness of mind; constancy, equability.

igualmente [e-goo-al-men'-tay], *adv.* Equally, uniformly, equably, evenly (modo uniforme); likewise (también); constantly.

iguana [e-goo-ah'-nah], *f.* Iguana, a kind of lizard, a native of America.

iguarandi [e-goo-ah-rahn'-de], *m. (Amer.)* Pellitory.

igüedo [e-goo-ay'-do], *m.* V. CABRÓN.

ijada [e-hah-dah], *f.* 1. Flank, the lateral part of the lower belly. 2. Pain in the side, colic (dolor). **Tener su ijada**, *(Met.)* to have a weak side.

ijadear [e-hah-day-ar'], *vn.* To pant, to palpitate.

ijal [e-hahl'], *m. (Cuba)* V. IJADA.

ijar [e-har'], *m.* Flank. V. IJADA.

ilación [e-lah-the-on'], *f.* Inference, illation, conclusion drawn.

ilativo, va [e-lah-tee'-vo, vah], *a.* Illative, that which denotes illation or conclusion.

ilegal [e-lay-gahl'], *a.* Illegal, unlawful.

ilegalidad [e-lay-gah-le-dahd'], *f.* Illegality, unlawfulness.

ilegalizar [e-lay-gah-le-thar'], *va.* To outlaw, to declare illegal.

ilegalmente [e-lay-gal-men'-tay], *adv.* Illegally, lawlessly, unlawfully.

ilegible [e-lay-hee'-blay], *a*, Illegible.

ilegítimamente [e-lay-hee'-te-mah-men-tay], *adv.* Illegitimately, foully.

ilegitimar [e-lay-he-te-mar'], *va.* To illegitimate, to render or prove a person illegitimate.

ilegitimidad [e-lay-he-te-me-dahd'], *f.* Illegitimacy.

ilegítimo, ma [e-lay-hee'-te-mo, mah], *a*. 1. Illegal, contrary to law. 2. Illegitimate, unlawfully begotten. 3. False (falso).

ileo [e'-lay-o], *m*. Ileus, severe colic due to intestinal obstruction.

ileon [ee'-lay-yon], *m*. Ileum, the third division of the small intestines.

ileosía [e-la-yo-see'-ah], *f. V*. ILEO.

ileso, sa [e-lay'-so, sah], *a*. Unhurt, free from damage, harmless. **Salió ileso del accidente**, he came out of the accident unharmed. **Los pasajeros resultaron ilesos**, the passengers were unhurt.

ilíaco, ca [e-lee'-ah-co, cah], *a*. Belonging or relating to Ilium or Troy.

iliberal [e-le-bay-rahl'], *a*. Illiberal.

ilícitamente [e-lee'-the-tah-men'-tay], *adv*. Illicitly, forbiddenly.

ilícito, ta [e-lee'-the-to, tah], *a*. Illicit, unlawful.

ilimitado, da [e-le-me-tah'-do, dah], *a*. Unlimited, boundless, limitless, unconditional.

ilion [ee'-le-on], *m*. Ilium, the upper part of the innominate bone.

ilíquido, da [e-lee'-ke-do, dah], *a*. Unliquidated (cuentas, deudas).

iliterato [e-le-tay-rah'-to], *a*. Illiterate, unlearned.

illutar [ee-llyoo-tar'], *va*. To cover a part of the body with mud or mineral sediment; to illutate; to take a mud bath.

ilógico, ca [e-lo'-he-co, cah], *a*. Illogical.

ilota [e-lo'-tah], *m*. 1. A slave of Lacedemonia; a Helot. 2. One deprived of the rights and privileges of a citizen.

iludir [e-loo-deer'], *va. V*. BURLAR.

iluminación [e-loo-me-nah-the-on'], *f*. 1. Illumination, the act of supplying with light. **Iluminación indirecta**, indirect lighting. 2. Illumination, festive lights, hung out as a token of joy. 3. Illumination, infusion of intellectual light, knowledge, or grace.

iluminado, da [e-loo-me-nah'-do, dah], *a. & pp*. of ILUMINAR. Illuminate, enlightened (en mal sentido).

iluminado, da [e-loo-me-nah'-do], *m & f*. Illuminate, visionary; illuminist.

iluminador [e-loo-me-nah-dor'], *m*. Illuminator, one who illumines; one who adorns with colors. *-a*. Illuminating.

iluminar [e-loo-me-nar'], *va*. 1. To illumine or illuminate (alumbrar), to light, to fill with light, to supply with light. 2. To illuminate, to adorn with festal lamps or bonfires. 3. To illuminate, to enlighten intellectually, to infuse knowledge or grace. 4. To give light and shade to a painting; to color, to illumine books. 5. To render transparent.

iluminativo, va [e-loo-me-nah-tee'-vo, vah], *a*. Illuminative.

ilusión [e-loo-se-on'], *f*. 1. Illusion (noción falsa), false show, counterfeit appearance; fallaciousness. **Todo es Ilusión**, it's all an illusion. 2. A sort of smart and lively irony. 3. *(coll.)* Apprehension. 4. Hope, dream (esperanza, suello). **Con ilusión**, hopefully. **No te hagas ilusiones**, don't get any false ideas. 5. Excitement (emoción), thrill; eagerness; hopeful anticipation (expectación). **Trabajar con ilusión**, to work with will.

ilusionado [e-loo-se-o-nah'-do], *a. m & f*. Hopeful; excited, eager. **El viaje me trae muy ilusionado**, I am so looking forward to the trip.

ilusionar [e-loo-se-o-nar'], *va*. 1. To cause illusion (alentar). 2. To fascinate. *-vr*. To suffer illusions.

ilusivo, va [e-loo-see'-vo, vah], *a*. Delusive, illusive, false, deceitful.

iluso, sa [e-loo'-so, sah], *a*. 1. Deluded, deceived, ridiculed. 2. Bigoted. *-m & f*. Dreamer, visionary.

ilusoriamente [e-loo-so-re-ah-men'-tay], *adv*. Illusively.

ilusorio, ria [e-loo-so'-re-o, ah], *a*. 1. Delusive, illusory, deceptive, 2. *(Law.)* Null, void of effect, of no value.

ilustración [e-loos-trah-the-on'], *f*. 1. Illustration, explanation, elucidation, exposition, explication. 2. *pl*. The engravings of a book or periodical.

ilustrado, da [e-loos-trah'-do, dah], *a*. Wise, intelligent, of abundant knowledge.

ilustrador, ra [e-loos-trah-dor', rah], *m. & f*. Illustrator, explicator.

ilustrar [e-loos-trar'], *va*. 1. To illustrate, to clear up, to explain (aclarar), to enlighten, to elucidate. 2. To inspire, to infuse supernatural light. 3. To aggrandize, to ennoble, to illustrate, to heighten. 4. To provide printed matter with plates or engravings. 5. To make famous (hacer famoso). *-vr*. 1. To acquire knowledge (instruirse). 2. To become celebrated (hacerse famoso).

ilustre [e-loos'-tray], *a*. Illustrious, noble, celebrated, conspicuous, glorious, honorable, magnificent.

ilustremente [e-loos-tray-men'-tay], *adv*. Illustriously, greatly.

ilustrísimo, ma [e-loos-tree'-se-mo, mah], *a*. Appellation of honor given to bishops and other persons of a certain dignity. **Su ilustrísima**, His Grace.

imadas [e-mah'-das], *f. pl. (Naut.)* Ways, sliding planks used in launching ships.

imagen [e-mah'-hen], *f*. 1. Image, figure, any corporeal representation, imagery, statue, effigy. 2. Image, show appearance, fancy, conception. 3. *(Rhet.)* Picture or lively description. **Ser la viva imagen de**, to be the living image of. **Imagen fantasma**, ghost image.

imagencita, illa [e-mah-hen-thee'-tah, thee-llyah], *f. dim*. A little image.

imaginable [e-mah-he-nah'-blay], *a*. Imaginable, contrivable, conceivable.

imaginación [e-mah-he-nah-the-on'], *f*. 1. Imagination, fancy; the power of forming ideal, pictures. 2. Imagination, conception, image of the mind. 3. Conceit, fantasy; any unsolid or fanciful opinion or idea. **Ni por imaginación**, on no account. **Ella se deja Ilevar por la imaginación**, she lets her imagination run away with her.

imaginar [e-mah-he-nar'], *va*. 1. To imagine, to fancy, to image, to paint in the mind (visualizar). 2. To imagine, to scheme, to contrive, to excogitate, to conceive; to find out. 3. To form erroneous suppositions. **Cosas que nadie imagina**, things that no-one imagines. *-vn. V* FIGURARSE.

imaginaria [e-mah-he-nah'-re-ah], *f. (Mil.)* Reserve guard.

imaginariamente [e-mah-he-nah-reah-men'-tay], *adv*. In a visionary manner.

imaginario [e-mah-he-nah'-re-o], *m*. Painter or sculptor of images.

imaginario, ria [e-mah-he-nah'-re-o], *a*. Imaginary, fancied, visionary.

imaginativa [e-mah-he-nah-tee'-vah], *f*. Imagination, fancy.

imaginativo, va [e-mah-he-nah-tee'-vo, vah], *a*. Imaginative, fantastic, fanciful.

imaginerís [e-mah-he-nay-ree'-ah], *f*. Imagery, an embroidery representing flowers, birds, or fishes.

imán [e-mahn'], *m*. 1. Loadstone, the magnet. 2. The mariner's compass. 3. Charm, attraction. 4. Electromagnet.

imanación [e-ma-nah-the-on'], *f. V*. IMANTACIÓN.

imanar [e-mah-nar'], *va*. To magnetize, to communicate the property of a loadstone.

imantación [e-man-tah-the-on'], *f*. Magnetization. *V*. MAGNETIZACION.

imantar [e-man-tar'], *va*. To touch the mariner's compass needle with loadstone. 2. To magnetize.

imbatible [em-bah-te-blay], *a*. Unbeatable.

imbécil [im-bay'-theel], *a*. 1. Weak, feeble, imbecile. 2. Simple, silly, stupid.

imbecilidad [im-bay-the-le-dahd'], *f*. 1. Imbecility, weakness, debility. 2. Simplicity, silliness. **Decir imbecilidades**, to say silly things.

imbele [im-bay'-lay], *a. (Poet.)* Feeble, weak: unfit for war.

imberbe [im-bayr'-bay], *m*. Beardless youth.

imbibición [im-be-be-the-on'], *f*. Imbibition.

imbornal [im-bor-nahl'], *m. (Naut.)* Scupper-hole. **Irse por los imbornales**, *(LAm. Fig.)* to go off on a tangent.

imborrable [im-bor-rah'-blay], *a.* Indelible, unforgettable (recuerdo).

imbricación [im-bre-cah-the-on'], *f.* Imbrication, overlapping of scales.

imbricado, da [im-bre-cah'-do, dah], *a.* Imbricated, indented with concavities.

imbricativo, va [im-bre-cah-tee'-vo, vah], *a.* (*Bot.*) Imbricate, overlapping in the bud.

imbuir [im-boo-eer'], *va.* To imbue, to admit into the mind, to infuse into the mind, to instruct.

imbursación [im-boor-sah-the-on'], *f.* (*Prov.*) Act of putting into a sack.

imbursar [im-boor-sar'], *va.* (*Prov.*) To put into a sack or bag.

imilla [e-meel'-lyah], *f.* (*S. Amer.*) The girl sent by each settlement of Indians to the curate, to serve him for a week.

imitable [e-me-tah'-blay], *a.* Imitable.

imitación [e-me-tah-the-on'], *f.* 1. Imitation (copiar); mimicry (parodía). 2. Imitation, that which is offered as copy. **A imitación**, after the example, in imitation of. **Desconfíe de las imitaciones**, beware of imitations.

imitado, da [e-me-tah'-do, dah], *a. & pp.* OfIMITAR. Copied, imitated, imitative.

imitador, ra [e-me-tah-dor', rah], *m.&f.* Imitator, follower.

imitante [e-me-tahn'-tay], *pa.* of IMITAR. Imitator.

imitar [e-me-tar'], *va.* To imitate, to copy, to follow (copiar); to counterfeit (falsificar).

imitativo, va [e-me-tah-tee'-vo, vah], *a.* Imitative, aiming at resemblance.

imóscapo [e-mos'-cah-po], *m.* (*Arch.*) Apophyge, a concave curve in a column where the shaft rises from the base.

impaciencia [im-pah-the-en'-the-ah], *f.* 1. Impatience, inability to suffer pain; rage under suffering. 2. Impatience, inability to suffer delay, eagerness, hastiness. 3. Impatience, peevishness, vehemence of temper, heat of passion.

impacientar [im-pah-the-en-tar'], *va.* To vex, to irritate, to make one lose all patience. -*vr.* To become impatient, to lose all patience.

impaciente [im-pah-the-en'-tay], *a.* Impatient, fidgety, restless, peevish, not able to endure delay. **Impaciente por empezar**, impatient to start.

impacientemente [im-pah-the-en-tay-men'-tay], *adv.* Impatiently, longingly, peevishly, eagerly, ardently, with great desire.

impactante [im-pahc-tahn'-tay], *a.* Impressive; shattering, crushing, overwhelming.

impactar [im-pahc-tar'], *va.* To impress (impresionar), to have an impact on; to please (gustar).

impacto, ta [im-pahc'-to, tah], *a.* Impacted, thrust into, packed tight, incidence (repercusión); hit; (*LAm.*) punch, blow (boxeo).

impagado [im-pah-gah-do], *a.* Unpaid, still to be paid.

impago [im-pah-go], (*LAm.*) -*a.* Unpaid, still to be paid. -*m.* Non-payment.

impalpabilidad [im-pal-pa-be-le-dahd'], *f.* Impalpability.

impalpable [im-pal-pah'-blay], *a.* Impalpable, not to be perceived by the touch.

impar [im-par'], *a.* 1. Unequal, dissimilar, odd. 2. Uneven, not divisible into equal numbers. **Los números impares**, the odd numbers.

imparable [im-pah-rah'-blay], *a.* Unstoppable.

imparcial [im-par-the-ahl'], *a.* 1. Impartial, equitable. 2. Impartial, indifferent, disinterested, just. 3. Unprejudiced, imprejudicate.

imparcialmente [im-par-the-ah-le-dahd'], *f.* Impartiality, equitableness, justice; indifference.

imparcialidad [im-par-the-al-men'-tay], *adv.* Impartially, equitably, justly, honestly.

imparidad [im-pa-re-dahd'], *f.* Inequality, imparity, dissimilarity.

impartible [im-par-tee'-blay], *a.* 1. Indivisible. 2. (*Law.*) Impartible, communicable, what can be bestowed or conferred.

impartir [im-par-teer'], *va.* 1. To demand or require assistance; chiefly applied to courts of judicature, which demand one another's assistance for the effectual administration of justice. 2. To grant, to impart (instrucción).

impasable [im-pah-sah'-blay], *a.* Impassable.

impasibilidad [im-pah-se-be-le-dahd'], *f.* Impassibility, impassiveness, insusceptibility of suffering, exemption from pain.

impasible [im-pah-see'-blay], *a.* 1. Impassible, incapable of suffering. 2. Impassible, exempt from external impression, insensible to pain.

impastar [im-pas-tar'], *va.* To reduce ground material to paste.

impávidamente [im-pah'-ve-dah-men-tay], *adv.* 1. Intrepidity, undauntedly. 2. (*LAm.*) Cheekily.

impavidez [im-pah-ve-deth'], *f.* 1. Intrepidity, courage, boldness. 2. (*LAm.*) Cheek, cheekiness.

impávido, da [im-pah'-ve-do, dah], *a.* 1. Dauntless, intrepid (valiente), undaunted (impasible). 2. (*LAm.*) Cheeky (insolente).

impecabilidad [im-pay-cah-bele-dahd'], *f.* Impeccability, impeccancy, incapacity for sin.

impecable [im-pay-cah'-blay], *a.* Impeccable, exempt from possibility of sin.

impecablemente [im-pay-cah-blay-men-tay], *adv.* Impeccably, faultlessly.

impedido, da [im-pay-dee'-do, dah], *a.* Invalid, handicapped, impeded, sick, valetudinarian, crippled; having lost the use of the limbs. -*pp.* of IMPEDIR.

impedidor, ra [im-pay-de-dor', rah], *m. & f.* Obstructer, one who impedes.

impediente [im-pay-de-en'-tay], *pa.* Hindering, that which impedes.

impedimento [im-pay-de-men'-to], *m.* Impediment (obstáculo), obstacle, hindrance, obstruction, let, clog, cumbrance, cumbersomeness, impeachment. (*Met.*) Shackles.

impedir [im-pay-deer'], *va.* 1. To impede (dificultar), to hinder, to obstruct, to prevent, to clog, to keep back from, to forbid. 2. To constrain, to restrain, to cohibit; to counteract, to preclude. 3. (*Poet.*) To suspend. 4. To stop (prohibir), to prevent; to thwart (frustrar). **Impedir a uno hacer algo**, to stop somebody from doing something. **Me veo impedido para ayudar, I** find it impossible for me to help.

impeditivo, va [im-pay-de-tee'-vo, vah], *a.* Impeding, hindering, impeditive.

impeler [im-pay-lerr'], *va.* 1. To impel, to give an impulse. 2. To incite, to stimulate, to move. 3. To impel, to press on, to urge forward, to propel.

impenetrabilidad [im-pay-nay-trah-be-le-dahd'], *f.* Impenetrability, impenetrableness.

impenetrable [im-pay-nay-trah'-blay], *a.* 1. Impenetrable, impervious, that cannot be pierced or penetrated. 2. Impenetrable, incomprehensible, not to be conceived by the mind; fathomless.

impenetrablemente [im-pay-nay-trah'-blay-men-tay], *adv.* Impenetrably, imperviously.

impenitencia [im-pay-ne-ten'-the-ah], *f.* Impenitence.

impenitente [im-pay-ne-ten'-tay], *a.* Impenitent, obdurate, hard-hearted.

impensa [im-pen'-sah], *f.* (*for.*) Expense.

impensable [im-payn-sah'-blay], *a.* Unthinkable.

impensadamente [im-pen-sah-dah-men'-tay], *adv.* 1. Unexpectedly. 2. At random, by chance. 3. Inadvertently (sin querer).

impensado, da [im-pen-sah'-do, dah], *a.* 1. Unexpected (imprevisto), unforeseen, fortuitous. 2. Random (casual).

imperante [im-pay-rahn'-tay], *pa.* Commanding (*Astrol.*) Ruling: applied to a star. Formerly it was used as a substantive.

imperar [im-pay-rar'], *vn.* To command (mandar), to reign (prevalecer). -*va.* To command a person, to direct his actions.

imperativamente [im-pay-rah-te-vah-men'-tay], *adv.* Imperatively, authoritatively.

imperativo, va [im-pay-rah-tee'-vo, vah], *a.* Imperative (necesidad), commanding, expressive of command; a mood in grammar. *-f.* The tone or gesture of command (tono).

imperatoria [im-pay-rah-to'-re-ah], *f. (Bot.)* Masterwort.

imperatorio, ria [im-pay-rah-to'-re-o, ah], *a.* 1. Imperial, royal, belonging to an emperor or monarch. 2. Eminent, possessed of superior qualities.

imperceptible [im-per-thep-tee'-blay], *a.* Imperceptible.

imperceptiblemente [im-per-thep-te-blay-men'-tay], *adv.* Imperceptibly.

impercuso, sa [im-per-coo'-so, sah], *a.* Unstruck: used of coins where a side remains blank.

imperdible [im-per-dee'-blay], *a.* Safety pin.

imperdonable [im-per-do-nay'-blay], *a. (coll.)* Unpardonable, irremissible.

imperecedero, ra [im-pay-ray-thay-day'-ro, rah], *a.* Imperishable, unforgettable.

imperfección [im-per-fec-the-on'], *f.* Imperfection, fault, slight failure or defect.

imperfectamente [im-per-fec-tah-men'-tay], *adv.* Imperfectly, faultily, lamely, inadequately.

imperfecto, ta [im-per-fec'-to, tah], *a.* 1. Imperfect (objeto), not complete (tarea); defective, faulty, crippled, broken. 2. Imperfect, in grammar: referring to past time.

imperforación [im-per-fo-rah-the-on'], *f. (Med.)* Imperforation, the state of being closed.

imperforado, da [im-per-fo-rah'-do, dah], *a. (Med.)* Imperforate, closed up.

imperial [im-pay-re-ahl'], *f.* 1. Roof (autobús). 2. *(Naut.)* Poop-royal, a platform which serves as a covering of the poop-gallery of a ship.

imperial [im-pay-re-ahl'], *a.* 1. Imperial, belonging to an emperor or monarch. 2. Applied to a kind of small black plum.

imperialismo [im-pay-re-ah-lees'-mo], *m.* Imperialism, government by empire.

imperialista [im-pay-re-ah-lees'-tah], *m.* Imperialist.

impericia [im-pay-ree'-the-ah], *f.* Unskilfulness, want of knowledge or experience.

imperio [im-pay'-re-o], *m.* 1. Empire, dominion, command. 2. Dignity of an emperor. 3. Empire, the dominions of an emperor. 4. Kind of linen made in Germany. **Imperio Británico**, British Empire. **Vale un imperio**, it's worth a fortune.

imperiosamente [im-pay-re-o'-sah-men'-tay], *adv.* Imperiously, lordly, masterly.

imperiosidad [im-pay-re-ose-dahd'], *f* Imperiousness.

imperioso, sa [im-pay-re-o'-so, sah], *a.* 1. Imperious (porte, tono), commanding arrogant, haughty. 2. Powerful, overbearing, magisterial.

imperitamente [im-pay-re-tah-men'-tay], *adv.* Unskillfully, ignorantly.

imperito, ta [im-pay-ree'-to, tah], *a.* Unlearned, unskilled (inhábil); deficient in the knowledge of art and science, inexperienced (inexperto).

impermeabilidad [im-per-may-ah-be-le-dahd'], *f.* Impermeability.

impermeable [im-per-may-ah'-blay], *a.* Waterproof. *-m.* Raincoat (prenda de vestir).

impermutable [im-per-moo-tah'-blay], *a.* Immutable.

impersonal [im-per-so-nahl'], *a.* 1. Impersonal (verbos). 2. Mode of speaking impersonally. **En** or **por impersonal**, impersonally.

impersonalmente [im-per-so-nal-men'-tay], *adv.* Impersonally.

impersuasible [im-per-soo-ah-se'-blay], *a.* Not to be moved by persuasion.

impertérrito, ta [im-per-tayr'-re-to, tah], *a.* Intrepid, unterrified, dauntless.

impertinencia [im-per-te-nen'-the-ah], *f.* 1. Impertinence (insolencia), folly, nonsense. 2. Peevishness, humorousness. 3. Impertinence, troublesomeness, intrusion. 4. Minute accuracy in the performance of a thing.

impertinente [im-per-te-nen'-tay], *a.* 1. Impertinent, intrusive (intruso), importunate, meddling. 2. Impertinent (insolente), nonsensical, trifling. 3. Peevish, fretful, cross, froward, ill-humored (malhumorado).

impertinentemente [im-per-te-nen'-tay-men-tay], *adv.* Impertinently.

imperturbable [im-per-toor-bah'-blay], *a.* Imperturbable, not to be disturbed.

imperturbablemente [im-per-toor-bah'-blay-men-tay], *adv.* Imperturbably.

imperturbar [im-per-toor-bar'], *va. (Ven.)* To disturb.

impervio, via [im-payr'-ve-o, ah], *a.* Impervious, impassable, impenetrable.

impetra [im-pay'-trah], *f.* 1. Diploma, license, permission. 2. Bull by which dubious benefices are granted.

impetrable [im-pay-trah'-blay], *a. (Law.)* Impetrable, possible to be obtained.

impetración [im-pay-trah-the-on'], *f.* Impetration, the act of obtaining by prayer or entreaty.

impetrado, da [im-pay-trah'-do, dah], *a. & pp.* of IMPETRAR. Impetrate, impetrated, granted.

impetrador, ra [im-pay-trah-dor', rah], *m. & f.* One who impetrates.

impetrante [im-pay-trahn'-tay], *pa.* Impetrating. *-m. (Law.)* Grantee; impetrator.

impetrar [im-pay-trar'], *va.* To impetrate, to obtain by entreaty (obtener).

ímpetu [eem'-pay-too], *m.* 1. Impetus, a violent tendency to any point: a violent effort. 2. Impetuosity (impetuosidad), fit, impulse, sally, start, violence or vehemence of passion (violencia).

impetuosamente [im-pay-too-o'-sah-men-tay], *adv.* Impetuosly, vehemently, violently.

impetuosidad [im-pay-too-o-se-dahd'], *f.* Impetuosity, vehemence.

impetuoso, sa [im-pay-too-o'-so, sah], *a.* 1. Impetuous (persona), violent, forcible, fierce. 2. Impetuous, vehement, passionate, heady, hasty (acto).

impía or **flor impía** [im-pee'-ah], *f.* Scarlet-flowered pentapetes, an herb like rosemary.

impiedad [im-pe-ay-dahd'], *f.* 1. Impiety; irreligion, contempt of religion. 2. Impiety, any act of wickedness, impiousness; cruelty.

impío, pía [im-pee'-o, ah], *a.* Impious, irreligious, wicked, profane, godless.

impla [ee'-plah], *f.* Woman's veil anciently used, and the fabric of which it was made.

implacabilidad [im-plah-cah-be-le-dahd'], *f.* Implacability.

implacable [im-plah-cah'-blay], *a.* Implacable, not to be pacified: inexorable.

implacablemente [im-plah-cah'-blay-men-tay], *adv.* Implacably, relentlessly.

implantación [im-plan-tah-the-on'], *f.* Implantation, act of implanting. Implementation *(Comput.)*

implantar [im-plan-tar'], *va.* To implant, to set for growth; to inculcate, to introduce (costumbre).

implaticable [im-plah-te-cah'-blay], *a.* Intractable, unmanageable.

implexo, a [im-plec-so, sah], *a.* Said of epic or dramatic poems which present vicissitudes in the fortune of the heroes.

implicación [im-ple-cah-the-on'], *f.* 1. Implication; contradiction (contradicción); implicitness. 2. Complicity (complicidad). 3. *(LAm.)* Implication (significado).

implicado, da [im-ple-cah'-do, dah], *a. & pp.* of IMPLICAR. Implicit, entangled, implicated.

implicar [im-ple-car'], *vn.* To oppose, to contradict one another: applied to terms and propositions. *-va.* To implicate (involucrar), to imply (significar), to involve; to entangle, to embarrass. **Esto no implica que**…, this does not imply that…

implicatorio, ria [im-ple-cah-to'-re-o, ah], *a.* Implicative.

implícitamente [im-plee'-the-tah-men-tay], *adv.* Implicitly.

implícito, ta [im-plee'-the-to, tah], *a.* Implicit, inferred; tacitly comprised, not expressed.

imploración [im-plo-rah-the-on'], *f.* Entreaty, imploration, the act of imploring.

implorar [im-plo-rar'], *va.* 1. To implore, to call upon in supplication, to solicit. 2. To implore, to ask with eagerness, to crave, to entreat, to beg.

impolítica [im-po-lee'-te-cah], *f.* 1. Incivility, lack of courtesy, clownishness, rudeness, coarseness. 2. Impolicy.

impolíticamente [im-po-le'-te-cah-men-tay], *adv. (coll.)* Impolitically, impoliticly.

impolítico, ca [im-po-lee'-te-co, cah], *a.* 1. Impolitic or impolitical (imprudente), indiscreet, imprudent. 2. Impolite (descortés), rude, coarse, unpolished.

impoluto, ta [im-po-loo'-to, tah], *a.* Unpolluted, pure, free from stain, clean.

imponderabilidad [im-pon-day-rah-be-le-dahd'], *f.* Imponderability (calor).

imponderable [im-pon-day-rah'-blay], *a.* Inexpressible, unutterable, imponderable.

imponedor [im-po-nay-dor'], *m.* He who imposes or charges.

imponente [im-po-nen'-tay], *a.* 1. Imposing (impresionante), awe-inspiring. 2. Terrific (estupendo), tremendous, smashing.

imponer [im-po-nerr'], *va.* 1. To lay, to put, or set in or upon (carga). 2. To impose or lay a tax, a duty, etc. (tarea, impuesto). 3. To impose, to lay on as a burden or penalty. 4. To charge upon or impute falsely (achacar). 5. To advise, to give notice, to acquaint, to instruct someone (instruir). 6. To infuse respect or fear. 7. *(Print.)* To impose, to arrange pages of types for the press. *-vr.* 1. **Imponerse un deber**, to assume a duty. 2. To assert oneself (hacerse obedecer), to get one's way. 3. To prevail (prevalecer); to grow up (costumbre). **Se impondrá el buen sentido**, good sense will prevail. 4. To be necessary (ser inevitable), to impose itself. **La conclusión se impone**, the conclusion is inescapable. 5. *(Mex.)* To get accustomed (acostumbrarse).

impopular [im-po-poo-lar'], *a.* Unpopular.

impopularidad [im-po-poo-lah-re-dahd'], *f* Unpopularity.

imporosidad [im-po-ro-see-dahd'], *f.* Imporosity, state of being without pores.

imporoso, sa [im-po-ro'-so, sah], *a.* Imporous, without pores, solid.

importable [im-por-tah'-blay], *a.* What can be imported from abroad: importable.

importación [im-por-tah-the-on'], *f.* Importation (acto), importing. **Artículo de importación**, imported article. **Comercio de importación**, import trade.

importador [im-por-tah-dor'], *m & f.* Importer.

importancia [im-por-tahn'-the-ah], *f.* 1. Importance, import, consequence, moment, concern. 2. Importance, considerableness, a claim to notice; claim to respect. **De cierta importancia**. of some importance. **Carecer de importancia**, to be unimportant. **Restar importancia a**, to diminish the importance of.

importante [im-por-tahn'-tay], *a.* Important, momentous, weighty, material, considerable. **Lo más importante es**…, the main thing is…

importantemente [im-por-tahn'-tay-men-tay], *adv.* Importantly, usefully, materially, essentially.

importar [im-por-tar'], *v. imp.* 1. To import, to be important or convenient, to concern, to matter. **Esto importa mucho**, this is very important. **No le importa**, he doesn't care. **No le importa conducir todo el día**, he doesn't mind driving all day. 2. To amount, or amount to. **No importa**, no matter, it is no matter, it matters not. **¿Qué importa? or ¿qué importa eso?** what does it matter? what of that? what does it signify? **Importa mucho**, it matters much. *-va.* 1. To import, to carry into any country from abroad. **Este país importa carne**, this country imports meat. 2. To carry along with, to be a consequence of.

importe [im-por'-tay], *m.* Amount or gross amount, value (coste); total (total). **Importe total**, final total. **Hasta el importe de**, up to the amount of. **El importe de la factura**, the amount of this bill.

importunación [im-por-too-nah-the-on'], *f.* Importunity, incessant solicitation.

importunadamente [im-por-too-nah-dah'-men-tay], *adv.* Importunately.

importunador, ra [im-por-too-nah-dor's, rah], *m. & f.* Importunator, importuner.

importunamente [im-por-too'-nah-men-tay], *adv.* 1. Importunely, with importunity. 2. Importunely, unseasonably.

importunar [im-por-too-nar'], *va.* 1. To importune, to disturb by reiteration of the same request; to crave. 2. To vex, to molest, to harass, to tease, to disturb by reiteration of the same request.

importunidad [im-por-too-ne-dahd'], *f.* Importunity (acto), importunacy, importunateness.

importuno, na [im-por-too'-no, nah], *a.* 1. Importune (molesto), importunate, unseasonable, happening at the wrong time. 2. Importune (inoportuno), troublesome, vexatious, heavy.

imposibilidad [im-po-se-be-le-dahd'], *f.* Impossibility, impracticability, impracticableness.

imposibilitado [im-po-se-be-le-tah'-do], *a. & pp.* of IMPOSIBILITAR. 1. Helpless, without means, poor. 2. Disabled, weakened, unfit for service. **Estar imposibilitado para**, to be unable to.

imposibilitar [im-po-se-be-le-tar'], *va.* To disable, to render impossible (impedir), to weaken, to make unfit for service (incapacitar). **Esto me imposibilita hacerlo**, this makes it impossible for me to do it.

imposible [im-po-see'-blay], *a.* 1. Impossible, impracticable, unfeasible. 2. Extremely difficult. 3. Impossible; intolerable (inaguantable), unbereable. **Es imposible**, it's impossible. **Es imposible de predecir**, it's impossible to forecast. 4. Difficult, awkward, impossible (persona). 5. *(LAm.)* Slovenly (descuidado). *-m.* The impossible.

imposiblemente [im-po-se'-blay-men-tay], *adv.* Impossibly.

imposición [im-po-se-the-on'], *f.* 1. imposition, the act of laying anything on another. 2. Imposition, the act of laying, putting, or setting in or upon. 3. Imposition, the act of imposing taxes or duties, and the tax, charge, or duty imposed. 4. Injunction of anything as a law or duty. 5. Among printers, imposition, the arrangement of pages for the press.

imposta [im-pos'-tah], *f.* *(Arch.)* Impost, that part of a pillar in vaults and arches on which the weight of the whole building lies.

impostor, ra [im-pos-tor', ah], *m. & f.* Impostor (charlatán), juggler, slanderer (calumniador).

impostura [im-pos-too'-rah], *f.* 1. A false imputation or charge. 2. Imposture (fraude), fiction, deceit, cheat, fraud.

impotable [im-po-tah'-blay], *a.* Not drinkable, unpotable.

impotencia [im-po-ten'-the-ah], *f.* 1. Impotence or impotency, inability, weakness. 2. Impotence, frigidity, incapacity of propagation.

impotente [im-po-ten'-tay], *a.* 1. Impotent, weak, feeble, wanting force. 2. Impotent, frigid, without power of propagation.

impracticable [im-prac-te-cah'-blay], *a.* 1. Impracticable, impossible, unfeasible. 2. Impassable (carreteras).

imprecación [im-pray-cah-the-on'], *f.* Imprecation, curse.

imprecar [im-pray-car'], *va.* To imprecate, to curse.

imprecatorio, ria [im-pray-cah-to'-re-o, ah], *a.* Imprecatory.

imprecaución [im-pray-ca-hoo-the-on'], *f.* Imprevision, want of foresight.

imprecisión [im-pray-the-se-on'], *f.* Lack of precision, vagueness.

impreciso [im-pray-the'-so], *a.* Imprecise, vague.

impredecible [im-pray-day-the'-blay], *a. (LAm.)* Unpredictable.

impregnación [im-preg-nah-the-on'], *f.* Impregnation.

impregnar [im-preg-nar'], *va.* To impregnate, to saturate with any matter or quality. *-vr.* To be impregnated.

impremeditación [im-pray-may-de-tah-the-on'], *f.* Unpremeditation, absence of plan.

impremeditado, da [im-pray-may-de-tah'-do, dah], *a.* Unpremeditated, unforeseen.

imprenta [im-pren'-tah], *f.* 1. Printing, the art of printing (arte). 2. Printing office, press (aparato). 3. Print, the form, size, etc., of the types used in printing books.

imprescindible [im-pres-thin-de'-blay], *a.* That which cannot be prescinded or put aside. **Cosas imprescindibles**, essential things.

imprescriptible [im-pres-crip-tee'-blay], *a.* Imprescriptible, without the compass of prescription.

impresentable [im-pray-sen-tah'-blay], *a.* Unpresentable.

impresión [im-pray-se-on'], *f.* 1. Impression, the act of pressing one body upon another. 2. Impression, impress, mark made by pressure, stamp. 3. Print, the form, size, etc., of the types used in printing books. 4. Impression, edition, number printed at one time (tirada). 5. Impression, efficacious agency, influence, or operation of one body upon another. 6. Impression (desagradable), impress, image fixed in the mind. **Cambiar impresiones**, to exchange impressions. **Hacer buena impresión**, to make a good impression. **Su muerte me causó una gran impresión**, her death was a great shock to me. 7. *(Astrol.)* Influence of the stars; impression or effect. 8. *(Inform.)* **Impresión en modo gráfico**, dot bit, image mode, graphic mode.

impresionable [im-pray-se-o-nah'-blay], *a.* Emotional, impressionable.

impresionado [im-pray-se-o-nah'-do] *a.* 1. Impressed. 2. Exposed.

impresionante [im-pray-se-o-nahn'-tay], *a.* Impressive, aweinspiring, striking (espectacular), moving (commovedor).

impresionar [im-pray-se-o-nar'], *va.* 1. To imprint or fix on the mind or memory. **Me impresionó mucho**, it greatly impressed me. 2. To cut (disco); to expose. *-vn.* To impress, to make a good impression. **Lo hace sólo para impresionar**, he just does it to impress. *-vr.* To be impressed; to be moved.

impresionismo [im-pray-se-o-nees'-mo], *m. (Lit. & Art)* Impressionism.

impreso [im-pray'-so], *m.* 1. Pamphlet, a short treatise. 2. Form (formulario). **Formulario de solicitud**, application form.

impreso, sa [im-pray'-so, sah], *pp. irr. of* IMPRIMIR. Printed.

impresor [im-pray-sor'], *m.* Printer.

impresora [im-pray-so'-rah], *f. (Inform.)* Printer. **Impresora de línea**, line-printer. **Impresora de margarita**, daisywheel printer. **Impresora calidad pseudo-courrier**, near letter quality printer. **Impresora de cadena**, chain printer. **Impresora de impacto**, impact printer. **Impresora de inyección de tinta**, ink jet printer. **Impresora de matriz de puntos**, dot matrix printer. **Impresora de procesador de textos**, wordprocessing printer. **Impresora de puntos**, dot printer. **Impresora láser**, laser printer. **Impresora térmica**, thermal printer. **Impresora trazadora**, printer plotter.

imprestable [im-pres-tah'-blay], *a.* That cannot be lent.

imprevisible [im-pray-ve-se'-blay], *a.* Unforeseeable.

imprevisión [im-pray-ve-se-on'], *f.* Imprevision, improvidence.

imprevisto, ta [im-pray-vees'-to, tah], *a.* Unforeseen, unexpected, unprovided against.

imprimación [im-pre-mah-the-on'], *f.* Priming, the act of laying on the first colors on canvas or boards to be painted; stuff for priming.

imprimadera [im-pre-mah-day'-rah], *f.* The instrument used in priming, or laying on the first colors in painting.

imprimador [im-pre-mah-dor'], *m.* One who lays the first colors on a piece of linen or board to be painted.

imprimar [im-pre-mar'], *va.* To prime, to lay the first colors on in painting.

imprimir [im-pre-meer'], *va.* 1. To print, to stamp. 2. To imprint, to fix an idea on the mind or memory. 3. To put a work to press, to get it printed.

improbabilidad [im-pro-bah-be-le-dahd'], *f.* Improbability, unlikelihood, difficulty to be believed.

improbable [im-pro-bah'-blay], *a.* Improbable, unlikely, difficult to be proved.

improbablemente [im-pro-bah'-blay-men-tay], *adv.* Improbably.

improbar [im-pro-bar'], *va.* To disapprove, to dislike, to censure.

improbidad [im-pro-be-dahd'], *f.* Improbity, dishonesty.

ímprobo, ba [eem'-pro-bo, bay], *a.* 1. Corrupt (poco honrado), wicked. 2. Laborious (tarea), painful.

improcedencia [eem-pro-thay-den'-the-ah], *f.* 1. Wrongness, inapplicability. 2. *(Jur.)* Inadmissibility.

improcedente [eem-pro-thay-dayn'-tay], *a.* 1. Wrong (incorrecto), not right; inappropriate (inadecuado). 2. Unfounded, inadmissible; out of order.

improductivo, va [im-pro-dooc-tee'-vo, vah], *a.* 1. Unproductive, unfruitful. 2. Useless.

impronta [im-pron'-tah], *f.* Cast, or reproduction in any soft substance, like wax, papier-maché, etc., of images in relief or intaglio.

improperar [im-pro-pay-rar'], *va.* To upbraid, to gibe, to taunt.

improperio [im-pro-pay'-re-o], *m.* Contemptuous reproach, injurious censure.

impropiamente [en-pro-pe-ah-men'-tay], *adv.* Improperly.

impropiedad [im-pro-pe-ay-dahd'], *f.* Impropriety, unfitness, want of justness.

impropio, pia [im-pro'-pe-o, ah], *a.* 1. Improper, unfit; not conducive to the right end; unqualified. 2. Improper, unbecoming. **Impropio para**, inappropriate for.

improporción [im-pro-por-the-on'], *f.* Disproportion.

improporcionado, da [im-pro-por-the-o-nah'-do, dah], *a.* Disproportionate, unsymmetrical, unsuitable in terms of quality or quantity.

impropriedad [im-pro-pre-ay-dahd'], *f.* Impropriety.

improrrogable [im-pror-ro-gah'-blay], *a.* That which cannot be prorogued.

impróspero, ra [im-pro'-ve-do, dah], *a.* Unfortunate, unprosperous, unhappy.

impróvidamente [im-pro'-ve-dah-men-tay], *adv.* Improvidently.

impróvido, da [im-pro'-ve-do, dah], *a.* Improvident, wanting forecast or care to provide, thoughtless.

improvisación [im-pro-ve-sah-the-on'], *f.* Improvisation; extemporization; *(Mus.)* Imprompty; *(Teat.)* Ad-lib.

improvisado [im-pro-ve-sah'-do], *a* Improvised; makeshift (reparación); *(Mus.)* extempore, impromptu.

improvisamente [im-pro-ve-sah-men'-tay], *adv.* Unexpectedly, improvidently

improvisar [im-pro-ve-sar'], *va.* To extemporize, to speak extempore, *(Teat.)* to ad-lib. **Improvisar una comedia**, to rustle up a meal.

improviso, sa [im-pro-vee'-so, sah], **Improvisto, ta**, *a.* Unexpected (imprevisto), unforeseen, not provided against. **De improviso**, unexpectedly, all of a sudden. **Hablar de improviso**, to play impromptu.

imprudencia [im-proo-den'-the-ah], *f.* Imprudence, indiscretion, heedlessness; impolicy; improvidence. **Imprudencia temeraria**, criminal negligence. **Ser acusado de conducir con imprudencia temeraria**, to be charged with dangerous driving.

imprudente [im-proo-den'-tay], *a.* Imprudent, indiscreet (indiscreto), improvident, unwise (precipitado).

imprudentemente [im-proo-den-tay-men-tay], *adv.* Imprudently.

impúber [im-poo'-ber], *a.* V. IMPÚBERO.

impúbero, ra [im-poo-bay'-ro, rah], *a.* Impuberal, not having reached puberty.

impudencia [im-poo-den'-the-ah], *f.* Impudence, shamelessness, immodesty.

impudente [im-poo-den'-tay], *a.* Impudent, shameless.

impúdicamente [im-poo'-de-cah-men-tay], *adv.* Lewdly (obscenamente), impudently.

impudicicia [im-poo-de-thee'-the-ah], *f.* Unchastity, lewdness (obscenidad), incontinence, lustfulness, impudicity.

impúdico, ca [im-poo'-de-co, cah], *a.* 1. Unchaste, lewd (obsceno), lustful, obscene. 2. Impudent, shameless.

impuesto [im-poo-ays'-to], *m.* 1. Tax. 2. Duty, impost. **Impuesto sobre la renta**, income tax. **Sujeto a impuesto** taxable. **Impuesto de plusvalía**, capital gains tax. **Impuesto de venta**, sales tax.

impuesto, ta [im-poo-ays'-to, tah], *a. & pp. irr.* of IMPONER. Imposed. **Estar or quedar impuesto de alguna cosa**, to have full knowledge of some business or command.

impugnable [im-poog-nah'-blay], *a.* Impugnable.

impugnación [im-poog-nah-the-on'], *f.* Opposition, contradiction, refutation, impugnation.

impugnador, ra [im-poog-nah-dor', rah], *m. & f.* One who refutes, attacks or contradicts; impugner, objector.

impugnar [im-poog-nar'], *va.* To impugn (teoría), to contradict, to oppose, to confute.

impugnativo, va [im-poog-nah-tee'-vo, vah], *a.* Impugning.

impulsar [im-pool-sar'], *va.* To impel, to give an impulse, to urge on.

impulsión [im-pool-se-on'], *f.* 1. Impulsion, impulse, momentum (fuerza existente), drive (empuje), communicated force, the effect of one body acting upon another. 2. Impulsion, impulse, influence acting upon the mind, motive.

impulsivo, va [im-pool-see'-vo, vah], *a.* Impulsive.

impulso [im-pool'-so], *m.* Impulsion; impulse. V. IMPULSIÓN. **Los impulsos del corazón**, the promptings of the heart. **No resisto al impulso de decir que…**, I can't resist saying that…

impulsor, ra [im-pool-sor', rah], *m. & f.* Impeller, *(Mec.)* drive, *(Aer.)* booster.

impune [im-poo'-nay], *a.* Exempt from punishment, unpunished.

impunemente [im-poo-nay-men'-tay], *adv.* With impunity.

impunidad [im-poo-ne-dahd'], *f.* Impunity, freedom from punishment.

impuramente [im-poo-rah-men'-tay], *adv.* Obscenely, impurely.

impureza [im-poo-ray'-thah], *f.* 1. Impurity, foul with extraneous mixtures. 2. Impurity, dishonesty, unchastity. 3. Obscenity, obsceneness, foulness.

impuro, ra [im-poo'-ro, rah], *a.* Impure, foul.

imputable [im-poo-tah'-blay], *a.* Imputable, chargeable.

imputabilidad [im-poo-tah-be-le-dahd'], *f.* Imputableness.

imputación [im-poo-tah-the-on'], *f.* Imputation, attribution of anything, generally of ill.

imputador, ra [im-poo-tah-dor', rah], *m. & f.* Imputer.

imputar [im-poo-tar'], *m.* To impute, to charge upon, to attribute, to father.

in [een], *prep. Lat.* Used only in composition, where it has generally a negative signification, as **incapaz**, incapable.

inabarcable [in-ah-bar-cah'-blay], *a.* Not capable of being embraced.

inacabable [in-ah-cah-bah'-blay], *a.* Interminable, inconsumptible, that cannot be brought to an end.

inacabado [in-ah-cah-bah'-do], *a.* Unfinished.

inaccesibilidad [in-ac-thay-see'-be-le-dahd'], *f.* Inaccessibility.

inaccesible [in-ac-thay-see'-blay], *a.* inaccessible, not to be approached.

inaccesiblemente [in-ac-thay-se'-blay-men-tay], *adv.* Inaccessibly.

inacción [in-ac-the-on'], *f.* Inaction, cessation from labor.

inaceptable [in-ah-thayp-tah'-blay], *a.* Unacceptable.

inactividad [in-ac-te-ve-dahd'], *f.* Inactivity, laziness, idleness.

inactivo, va [in-ac-tee'-vo, vah], *a.* Inactive, lazy, iddle.

inadaptable [in-ah-dap-tah'-blay], *a.* Not adaptable.

inadaptación [in-ah-dap-tah-the-on'], *f.* Inadequacy; unsuitability, inappropriateness.

inadaptado [in-ah-dap-tah-do], *a.* Maladjusted, who fails to adjust. *-m & f.* Misfit; person who fails to adjust.

inadecuado, da [in-ah-day-coo-ah'-do, dah], *a.* Inadequate, unsuitable.

inadherente [in-a-day-ren'-tay], Unadherent.

inadmisible [in-ad-me-see'-blay], *a.* Inadmissible, unacceptable.

inadvertencia [in-ad-ver-ten'-the-ah], *f.* Inadvertence, carelessness, inattention, heedlessness.

inadvertidamente [in-ad-ver-te-dah'-men-tay], *adv.* Inadvertently.

inadvertido, da [in-ad-ver-tee'-do, dah], *a.* 1. Inadvertent, inconsiderate, careless (descuidado). 2. Unseen, unnoticed (no visto).

inafectado, da [in-ah-fec-tah'-do, dah], *a.* Natural, free from affectation.

inagotable [in-ah-go-tah'-blay], *a.* 1. Inexhaustible, exhaustless. 2. Unexhausted: applied to the powers of the mind. 3. Never-failing.

inaguantable [in-ah-goo-an-tah'-blay], *a.* Insupportable.

inajenable [in-ah-hay-nah'-blay], *a.* Inalienable, that cannot be alienated.

inalámbrico, ca [in-ah-lahm'-bre-co, cah], *a.* Wireless. **Telegrafía inalámbrica**, wireless telegraphy.

inalcanzable [in-ahl-can-thah'-blay], *a.* Unattainable.

inalienable [in-ah-le-ay-nah'-blay], *a.* Inalienable.

inalterable [in-al-tay-rah'-blay], *a.* Unalterable, unchanging; immature; impassive (cara); fast (color); permanent (lustre).

inalterablemente [in-al-tay-rah'-blay-men-tay], *adv.* Unalterably.

inalterado, da [in-al-tay-rah'-do, dah], *a.* Unchanged, stable.

inamisible [in-ah-me-see'-blay], *a.* Which cannot be lost.

inamovible [in-ah-mo-vee'-blay], *a.* Immovable, fixed.

inamovibilidad [in-ah-mo-ve-be-le-dahd'], *f.* Immovability.

inanición [in-ah-ne-the-on'], *f. (Med.)* Inanition, extreme weakness from want of nourishment.

inanidad [in-ah-ne-dahd'], *f.* 1. Emptiness. 2. Vanity, uselessness.

inanimado, da [in-ah-ne-mah'-do, dah], *a.* Inanimate, lifeless.

inánime [in-ah'-ne-may], *a.* V. INANIMADO.

inapagable [in-ah-pah-gah'-blay], *a.* Inextinguishable, unquenchable.

inapeable [in-ah-pay-ah'-blay], *a.* 1. That cannot be lowered or levelled. 2. Incomprehensible (oscuro), inconceivable. 3. Obstinate (terco), stubborn.

inapelable [in-ah-pay-lah'-blay], *a.* Without appeal, not admitting appeal.

inapetencia [in-ah-pay-ten'-the-ah], *f.* Inappetence or inappetency, want of appetite or desire of food.

inapetente [in-ah-pay-ten'-tay], *a.* 1. Having no appetite or desire of food. 2. Disgusted.

inaplacable [in-ah-plah-cah'-blay], *a.* Implacable, unappeasable.

inaplicable [in-ah-ple-cah'-blay], *a.* Inapplicable.

inaplicación [in-ah-ple-ca-the-on'], *f.* Indolence, inapplication.

inaplicado, da [in-ah-ple-cah'-do, dah], *a.* Indolent, careless, inactive.

inapreciable [in-ah-pray-the-ah'-blay], *a*. Inestimable, invaluable (valor), inappreciable.

inaptitud [in-ap-te-tood'], *f. (Prov.) V.* INEPTITUD.

inarticulado, da [in-ar-te-coo-lah'-do, dah], *a*. Inarticulate, not uttered with distinctness.

inasequible [in-ah-say-kee'-blay], *a*. That which cannot be followed, out of reach.

inasimilable [in-ah-se-me-lah'-blay], *a*. Unassimilable.

inastillable [in-as-te-lyah'-blay], *a*. Shatter-proof.

inatacable [in-ah-tah-cah'-blay], *a. (coll.)* That which cannot be attacked.

inaudito, ta [in-ah-oo-dee'-to, tah], *a*. Unheard of, strange, most extraordinary.

inauguración [in-ah-oo-goo-rah-the-on'], *f*. 1. Inauguration, investiture by solemnities. 2. Exaltation or elevation to royal dignity. 3. Auguration, the practice of augury.

inaugural [in-ah-oo-goo-rahl'], *a*. Inaugural, opening, maiden (viaje).

inaugurar [in-ah-oo-goo-rar'], *va*. 1. To divine by the flight of birds. 2. To inaugurate, to invest with a new office by solemnities, to open (canal, puente, exposición).

inaveriguable [in-ah-vay-re-goo-ah'-blay], *a*. That cannot be ascertained, that cannot be easily proved.

inca [een'-cah], *m*. Inca.

incalculable [in-cal-coo-lah'-blay], *a*. Incalculable.

incalificable [in-cah-le-fe-cah'-blay], *a*. Unqualifiable, downright.

incamerar [in-cah-may-rar'], *va*. To unite to the Apostolic Chamber, or ecclesiastical dominion.

incandescencia [in-can-des-then'-the-ah], *f*. Incandescence, white heat.

incadescente [in-can-des-then'-tay], *a*. 1. Incandescent, glowing with heat. 2. Burning (mirada).

incansable [in-can-sah'-blay], *a*. Indefatigable, unwearied.

incansablemente [in-can-sah'-blay-men-tay], *adv*. Indefatigably, tirelessly.

incantable [in-can-tah'-blay], *a*. That which cannot be sung.

incapacidad [in-cah-pah-the-dahd'], *f*. 1. Incapacity, inability, want of power or strength. 2. Incapability, incapableness, natural inability, want of comprehensiveness of mind. 3. Incapability, legal disqualification. **Su incapacidad para**, his inability to.

incapacitado [in-cah-pah-the-tah-do], *a*. 1. Incapacitated; unfitted. 2. *(Mex.)* Disabled, handicapped (minusválido).

incapacitar [in-cah-pah-the-tar'], *va*. To incapacitate, to render incapable.

incapaz [in-cah-path'], *a*. 1. Incapable, unable, not equal to anything, unfit (no apto), inadequate (inadecuado). 2. Incapable, wanting power to do anything. 3. Incapable, wanting understanding, wanting talent. **Incapaz de**, unable to.

incardinación [in-car-de-nah-the-on'], *f. (Law.)* Administration of church revenues without ownership.

incasable [in-cah-sah'-blay], *a*. 1. Unmarriageable. 2. Averse or opposed to marriage.

incautación [in-cah-oo-tah-the-on'], *f*. Seizure, confiscation.

incautamente [in-cah-oo-tah-men'-tay], *adv*. Unwarily, incautiously.

incauto, ta [in-cah'-oo-to, tah], *a*. Incautious, unwary, heedless.

incendiar [in-then-de-ar'], *va*. To kindle, to set on fire, to inflame. **El acto de incendiar maliciosamente una casa**, *(Law.)* arson. *-vr*. To catch fire.

incendiario, ria [in-then-de-ah'-re-o, ah], *m. & f*. 1. Firebug, incendiary, one who sets fires compulsively. 2. Firebrand, agitator, one who inflames factions or promotes quarrels.

incendio [in-then'-de-o], *m*. 1. Fire, conflagration, burning. **Incendio intencionado**, arson. **Echar incendios a uno**, *(And. Cono Sur)* to sling or throw mud at somebody. 2. Inflammation, the act of setting on flame; the state of being in flame.

incensación [in-then-sah-the-on'], *f*. The act of perfuming with incense.

incensar [in-then-sar'], *va*. 1. To perfume, to incense, to offer incense on the altar. 2. To bestow fulsome praise or adulation.

incensario [in-then-sah'-re-o], *m*. Incensory, thurible, the vessel in which incense is burnt.

incensurable [in-then-soo-rah'-blay], *a*. Unblamable, not culpable.

incentivo [in-then-tee'-vo], *m*. Incentive, incitement, spur; encouragement.

inceración [in-thay-rah-the-on'], *f*. Inceration, the act of covering with or mixing with wax.

incertidumbre [in-ther-te-doom'-bray], *f*. Incertitude, uncertainty, doubtfulness, hesitancy, fluctuation.

incesable [in-thay-sah'-blay], *a*. Incessant, unceasing.

incesablemente [in-thay--sah-blay-men-tay], *adv*. Incessantly, without intermission.

incesante [in-thay-sahn'-tay], *a*. Incessant, unceasing, continual, uninterrupted.

incesantemente [in-thay-sahn'-tay-men-tay], *adv*. Incessantly, continually.

incesto [in-thes'-to], *m*. Incest.

incestuosamente [in-thes-too-o-sah-men'-tay], *adv*. Incestuously.

incestuoso, sa [in-thes-too-o'-so, sah], *a*. Incestuous.

incidencia [in-the-den'-the-ah], *f*. 1. Incidence or incidency, an accident, hap, casualty, incident (suceso). 2. Incidence, the direction with which one body strikes upon another. 3. **La huelga tuvo escasa incidencia**, the strike was not widely supported.

incidental [in-the-den-tahl'], *a*. Incidental, dependent, subsidiary.

incidente [in-the-den'-tay], *a*. Incident, casual, incidental, happening by chance.

incidente [in-the-den-'tay], *m*. Incident (suceso), hap, accident, casualty, occurrence, accidental event (suceso accidental). *-pl. (Com.)* Appurtenances.

incidentemente [in-the-den-tahl'-men-tay], *adv*. Incidentally.

incidir [in-the-deer'], *vn*. To fall in or upon, to meet with, to influence, to affect. **Incidir en un error**, to fall into error. **El impuesto incide más en ellos**, the tax falls most heavily on them.

incienso [in-the-en'-so], *m*. 1. Incense, an aromatic gum used to perfume the altar. 2. Peculiar reverence and veneration paid to a person. 3. Court paid to a person out of flattery or interested views.

inciertamente [in-the-ayr'-tah-men-tay], *adv*. Uncertainly.

incierto, ta [in-the-ayr'-to, tah], *a*. 1. Untrue, false, contrary to reality. 2. Uncertain, doubtful. 3. Unstable, inconstant; unknown (desconocido).

incineración [in-the-nay-rah-the-on'], *f*. Incineration, the act of buring a thing to ashes.

incinerar [in-the-nay-rar'], *va*. To incinerate, to burn to ashes, to cremate (cadáver).

incipiente [in-the-pe-en'-tay], *a*. Beginning, incipient, inceptive, inchoative.

incircunciso, sa [in-theer-coon-thee'-so, sah], *a*. Incircumcised.

incircunscripto, ta [in-theer-coons-creep'-to, tah], *a*. Uncircumscribed.

incisión [in-the-se-on'], *f*. 1. Incision, a cut; a wound with a sharp instrument. 2. *V.* CESURA.

incisivo, va [in-the-see'-vo, vah], *a*. Incisive. **Dientes incisivos**, incisors, cutting teeth.

inciso [in-thee'-so], *m*. 1. Comma. *V.* COMA. 2. Partial meaning of a clause. 3. Parenthetical(observación). 4. Interjection (conversación).

inciso, sa [in-thee'-so, sah], *a*. Incised. *V.* CORTADO.

incisorio, ria [in-the-so'-re-o, ah], *a*. Incisory, that which cuts.

incitación [in-the-tah-the-on'], *f*. Incitation, incitement.

incitador, ra [in-the-tah-dor', rah], *m. & f*. Instigator, inciter, exciter.

incitamento, incitamiento [in-the-tah-men'-to], *m.* Incitement, impulse, inciting power, incentive.

incitar [in-the-tar'], *va.* To incite, to excite, to spur, to stimulate. **Incitar a uno a hacer algo**, to urge somebody to do something.

incitativa [in-the-tah-tee'-vah], *f. (Law.)* Writ from a superior tribunal to the common judges, that justice may be administered.

incitativo, va [in-the-tah-tee'-vo, vah], *a.* 1. Incentive, inciting, incensive. 2. *(Law.)* V. AGUIJATORIO.

incitativo [in-the-tah-te-vo], *m.* Incitement.

incivil [in-the-veel'], *a.* Uncivil, unpolished, incivil.

incivilidad [in-the-ve-le-dahd'], *f.* Incivility, rudeness, coarseness, grossness.

incivilmente [in-the-veel-men'-tay], *adv.* Uncivilly, rudely, incivilly.

inclasificable [in-clah-se-fe-cah'-blay], *a.* Unclassifiable, difficult to classify.

inclemencia [in-clay-men'-the-ah], *f.* 1. Inclemency, severity, harshness, rigor, unmercifulness. 2. Inclemency of the weather. **La inclemencia del tiempo**, the inclemency of the weather.

inclemente [in-clay-men'-tay], *a.* Inclement, cruel, severe.

inclinación [in-cle-nah-the-on'], *f.* 1. Inclination, the act of inclining and the state of being inclined, slope (pendiente); stoop (cuerpo). **Inclinación lateral**, *(Aer.)* bank. 2. Inclination, propension of mind, favorable disposition, love, affection, liking, fancy. **Tener inclinación hacia la poesía**, to have a penchant for poetry. 3. Inclination, tendency toward any point. 4. A bow, an act of reverence (reverencia). 5. *(Math.)* Inclination, the angle between two lines or planes; in gunnery, the angle between the axis of the piece and the horizon. **Inclinación magnética**, the angle of magnetic dip.

inclinado, da [in-cle-nah'-do, dah], *a. & pp.* of INCLINAR. 1. Inclined to any part (ángulo). 2. *(Met.)* Inclined, disposed, affected, minded.

inclinador, ra [in-cle-nah-dor', rah], *m. & f.* One who inclines.

inclinante [in-cle-nahn'-tay], *pa.* Inclining, bending, drawing to.

inclinar [in-cle-nar'], *va.* 1. To incline, to slope (sesgar), to bow (bajar), to bend; to give a tendency or direction to any place or state. 2. To incline, to influence, to turn the desire toward anything. **Inclinar a uno a hacer algo**, to induce somebody to do something. *-vn.* To resemble, to be alike. *-vr.* 1. To incline (estar inclinado), to lean, to bend to, to tend toward any part. 2. To incline, to lean, to be favorably disposed to. 3. To bend the body (encorvarse), to bow (hacer reverencia). 4. To have a particular reason to follow some opinion or do something. **Inclinarse a hacer algo**, to be inclined to do something. 5. *(Naut.)* To heel.

Inclinativo, va [in-cle-nah-tee'-vo, vah], *a.* Inclinatory.

inclito, ta [een'-cle-to, tah], *a.* Famous, renowned, conspicuous, illustrious.

incluir [in-cloo-eer'], *va.* 1. To include, to comprise, to enclose (carta); to comprehend, to contain. 2. To allow one a share in a business.

inclusa [in-cloo'-sah], *f.* Foundling hospital.

inclusero, ra [in-cloo-say'-ro, rah], *m. & f. & a.* Foundling.

inclusión [in-cloo-se-on'], *f.* 1. Inclusion, the act of inclosing or containing a thing. 2. Easy access, familiar intercourse.

inclusivamente, inclusive [in-cloo-se-vah-men'-tay], *adv.* Inclusively.

inclusivo, va [in-cloo-see'-vo, vah], *a.* Inclusive.

incluso, sa [in-cloo'-so, sah], *a & pp. irr.* of INCLUIR. Inclosed, *-adv.* Even, actually. **Incluso la pegó**, he even hit her.

incluyente [in-cloo-yen'-tay], *pa.* Including.

incoado, da [in-co-ah'-do, dah], *a. & pp.* of INCOAR. Inchoate, begun, commenced.

incoagulable [in-co-ah-goo-lah'-blay], *a.* Incoagulable, uncoagulable.

incoar [in-co-ar'], *va.* To commence, to begin, to inchoate.

incoativo, va [in-co-ah-tee'-vo, vah], *a.* Inchoative, inceptive, noting inchoation or beginning.

incobrable [in-co-brah'-blay], *a.* Irrecoverable, irretrievable.

incoercible [in-co-er-thee'-blay], *a.* 1. Incoercible, which cannot be forced or restrained. 2. Incoercible, used of imponderable agents, as light, heat, electricity, magnetism.

incógnito, ta [in-cog'-ne-to, tah], *a.* Unknown. **De incógnito**, 1. Incog or incognito. 2. Hiddenly, or clandestinely. *-f. (Math.)* An unknown quantity, the quantity sought. **Despejar la incógnita**, to clear the unknown quantity of coefficients, exponents, or divisor.

incognoscible [in-cog-nos-thee-blay], *a.* Imperceptible.

incoherencia [in-co-ay-ren'-the-ah], *f.* Incoherence.

incoherente [in-co-ay-ren-tay], *a.* Incoherent, inconsistent.

íncola [een'-co-lah], *m.* Inhabitant.

incoloro, ra [in-co-lo'-ro, rah], *a.* Free of color, colorless.

incólume [in-co'-loo-may], *a.* Sound, safe, unharmed.

incolumidad [in-co-loo-me-dahd'], *f.* Security, safety.

incombinable [in-com-be-nah'-blay], *a.* Uncombinable, which cannot be combined.

incombustibilidad [in-com-boos-te-be-le-dahd'], *f.* Incombustibility.

incombustible [in-com-boos-tee'-blay], *a.* Incombustible.

incomerciable [in-co-mer-the-ah'-blay], *a.* Contraband, unlawful, prohibited. (artículos de comercio).

incomible [in-co-me'-blay], *a.* Uneatable, inedible.

incómodamente [in-co'-mo-dah-men-tay], *adv.* Incommodiously.

incomodar [in-co-mo-dar'], *va.* To incommode, to trouble, to put out. *-vr.* 1. To put oneself out (tomarse molestia). 2. To get cross (enfadarse), to get annoyed. **Estar incomodado con**, to be cross with.

incomodidad [in-co-mo-de-dahd'], *f.* 1. Incommodiousness, inconvenience (inoportunidad) 2. Weariness: annoyance (fastidio). *(Acad.)*

incómodo, da [in-co'-mo-do, dah], *a.* Incommodious, inconvenient (inoportuno), uncomfortable (nada cómodo), tiresome (molesto), annoying. **Un bulto incómodo**, an awkward package. **Sentirse incómodo**, to feel uncomfortable.

incomparable [in-com-pa-rah'-blay], *a.* Incomparable, matchless.

incomparablemente [in-com-pah-rah'-blay-men-tay], *adv.* Incomparably.

incomparado, da [in-com-pa-rah'-do, dah], *a. V.* INCOMPARABLE.

incompartible [in-com-par-tee'-blay], *a.* Indivisible.

incompasible [in-com-pa-see'-blay], *a. V.* INCOMPASIVO.

incompasivo, va [in-com-pa-see'-vo, vah], *a.* Uncompassionate, void of pity.

incompatibilidad [in-com-pah-te-be-le-dahd'], *f.* Incompatibility, contrariety. **Incompatibilidad de intereses**, conflict of interests.

incompatible [in-com-pah-tee'-blay], *a.* Incompatible, inconsistent.

incompensable [in-com-pen-sah'-blay], *a.* Incompensable, that cannot be compensated.

incompetencia [in-com-pay-ten'-the-ah], *f.* Incompetency, inability.

incompetente [in-com-pay-ten'-tay], *a.* 1. Incompetent, not proportionate, not adequate. 2. *(Law.)* Unqualified. 3. Unsuitable.

incompetentemente [in-com-pay-ten'-tay-men-tay], Incompetently, unduly, unsuitably.

incomplejo, ja [im-com-play'-ho, hah], *a.* Incomplex, simple.

incompletamente [in-com-play-tah-men-tay], *adv.* Incompletely.

incompleto, ta [in-com-play'-to, tah], *a.* Incomplete, inconsummate.

incomplexo, xa [in-com-plec'-so, sah], *a.* Disunited, without connection, non-adherent.

incomponible [in-com-po-nee'-blay], *a.* Incompoundable.

incomportable [in-com-por-tah'-blay], *a.* Intolerable, unbearble.

incomposibilidad [in-com-po-se-be-le-dahd'], *f.* Incompossibility, quality of being not possible, but by the negation or destruction of something.

incomposible [in-com-po-see'-blay], *a.* Incompossible, not possible together.

incomposición [in-com-po-se-the-on'], *f.* 1. Want of proportion, or defective comparison. 2. *V.* DESCOMPOSTURA.

incomprehensible [in-com-pray-en-see'-blay], *a. (Acad.) V.* IMCOMPRENSIBLE.

incomprendido [in-com-pren-de'-do], *a.* Misunderstood (persona); not appreciated. *-m & f.* Misunderstood person.

incomprensibilidad [in-com-pren-se-be-le-dahd'], *f.* Incomprehensibility.

incomprensible [in-com-pren-see'-blay], *a.* 1. Incomprehensible, that cannot be comprehended. 2. Incomprehensible, expressing thoughts in an obscure or confused manner.

incomprensiblemente [in-com-pren-see'-blay-men-tay], *adv.* Inconceivably, incomprehensibly.

incomprensión [in-com-pren-se-on'], *f.* Incomprehension, lack of understanding; lack of appreciation.

incomprimible [in-com-pre-mee'-blay], *a.* Incompressible.

incomunicabilidad [in-co-moo-ne-cah-be-le-dahd'], *f.* Incommunicability.

incomunicable [in-co-moo-ne-cah'-blay], *a.* Incommunicable.

incomunicación [in-co-moo-ne-cah-the-on'], *f.* Isolation; lack of communication; *(Jur.)* solitary confinement. **Ello permite la incommunicación de los detenidos**, it allows those detained to be held incommunicado.

incomunicado, da [in-co-moo-ne-cah'-do, dah], *a.* Incommunicated, incommunicating; having no intercourse. *-m.* A prisoner deprived of intercourse with anyone.

incomunicar [in-co-moo-ne-car'], *va.* To deprive a prisoner of intercourse with anyone, to leave without communications; to cut off, to isolate. **Incomunicar un detenido**, to refuse a prisoner access to a lawyer. *-vr.* To isolate oneself.

inconcebible [in-con-thay-bee'-blay], *a.* Inconceivable, unthinkable.

inconciliable [in-con-the-leah'-blay], *a. V.* IRRECONCILIABLE.

inconcino, na [in-con-thee'-no, nah], *a.* Disordered, disarranged.

inconcusamente [in-con-coo'-sah-men-tay], *adv.* Certainly, indubitably.

inconcuso, sa [in-con-coo'-so, sah], *a.* Incontrovertible, incontestable.

incondicional [in-con-de-the-o-nahl'], *a.* 1. Unconditional, absolute, without restriction. 2. *(LAm.)* Servile, fawning. *-m. & f.* 1. Staunch (partidario, adepto), staunch supporter; diehard, hardliner. 2. *(LAm.)* Today, yes-man.

incondicionalmente [in-con-de-theo-nal-men'-tay], *adv.* Unconditionally, unreservedly.

inconducente [in-con-doo-then'-tay], *a.* Incongruous.

inconexión [in-co-nec-se-on'], *f.* 1. Incoherency, incongruity, want of dependence of one part upon another. 2. Lack of connection, self-contradiction.

inconexo, xa [in-co-nec'-so, sah], *a.* 1. Unconnected, disconnected (desarticulado), unrelated (no relacionado), incoherent, inconsequential, having no dependence of one part upon another. 2. Independent, not supported by any other.

inconfesable [in-con-fay-sah'-blay], *a.* Which cannot be told, unconfessable; shameful, disgraceful.

inconfeso, sa [in-con-fay'-so, sah], *a.* Unconfessed, applied to a criminal who does not confess his guilt.

inconfidencia [in-con-fe-den'-the-ah], *f.* 1. Distrust, mistrust, want of confidence. 2. Disloyalty, want of fidelity to the sovereign.

inconforme [in-con-for'-may], *a.* Non-conformist. **Estar inconforme con algo**, *(CAm.)* to disagree with somebody.

inconformista [in-con-for-mees'-tah], *a. m & f.* Nonconformist.

inconfundible [in-con-foon-de'-blay], *a.* Unmistakable.

incongruamente [in-con-groo-ah-men'-tay], *adv.* Incongruously.

incongruencia [in-con-groo-en-the-ah], *f.* Incongruence, want of symmetry or proportion; unsuitableness, want of adaptation.

incongruente [in-con-groo-en'-tay], *a.* Incongruous, incongruent.

incongruentemente [in-con-groo-ayn'-tay-men-tay], *adv.* Incongrously, incompatibly.

incongruo, grua [in-con'-groo-o, ah], *a.* 1. Incongruous, disproportionate, unsuitable. 2. Applied to ecclesiastical livings which do not yield a competent income, and to the priests who perform the duties of those livings.

inconjugable [in-con-hoo-gah'-blay], *a.* Inconjugable, that cannot be conjugated.

inconmensurable [in-con-men-soo-rah'-blay], *a.* Incommensurable, not to be reduced to any measure.

inconmovible [in-con-mo-vee'-blay], *a.* Unshakable, inflexible, relentless.

inconmutabilidad [in-con-moo-tah-be-le-dahd'], *f. V.* INMUTABLIDAD.

inconmutable [in-con-moo-tah'-blay], *a.* 1. Incommutable, that cannot be exchanged, commuted, or bartered. 2. *V.* INMUTABLE.

inconquistable [in-con-kis-tah'-blay], *a.* Unconquerable, impregnable, inexpugnable, invincible. 2. Incorruptible (persona).

inconsciencia [in-cons-the-en-the-ah], *f.* 1. Unconsciousness. 2. Irresponsibility, unawareness (ignorancia), thoughtlessness (irreflexión).

inconsciente [in-cons-the-en'-tay], *a.* 1. *(Med.)* Unconscious. **Le encontraron inconsciente**, they found him unconscious. 2. Irresponsible, thoughtless (irreflexivo), carefree. **Son gente inconsciente**, they're thoughtless people. 3. Unconscious (ignorante), unaware.

inconsecuencia [in-con-say-coo-en-the-ah], *f.* Inconsequence, inconclusiveness, want of just inference; unsteadiness, changeableness.

inconsecuente [in-con-say-coo-en'-tay], *a.* Inconsequent, changeable.

inconservable [in-con-ser-vah-blay], *a.* Unpreservable.

inconsiderable [in-con-se-day-rah'-blay], *a.* Valueless, worthless.

inconsideración [in-con-se-day-rah-the-on'], *f.* Inconsideration, want of thought, inattention, inadvertency, abruptness.

inconsideradamente [in-con-se-day-rah'-dah-men-tay], *adv.* Inconsiderately, thoughtlessly.

inconsiderado, da [in-con-se-day-rah'-do, dah], *a.* Inconsiderate, thoughtless, inattentive.

inconsiguiente [in-con-se-gee-en'-tay], *a.* Inconsequent, without just conclusion, without regular inference, contradictory.

inconsistencia [in-con-sis-ten'-the-ah], *f.* 1. Inconsistency, self-contradiction, incongruity, contrariety (contrariedad). 2. Inconsistence, unsteadiness, changeableness.

inconsistente [in-con-sis-ten'-tay], *a.* Inconsistent, incongruous, absurd, lacking firmness (poco sólido), uneven (irregular), loose (tierra); flimsy (tela).

inconsolable [in-con-so-lah'-blay], *a.* Inconsolable.

inconsolablemente [in-con-so-lah'-blay-men-tay], *adv.* Inconsolably.

inconstancia [in-cons-tahn'-the-ah], *f.* Inconstancy, fickleness, unsteadiness, levity, lightness, frailty.

inconstante [in-cons-tahn'-tay], *a.* Inconstant, changeable, mutable, variable, fickle (caprichoso), unsteady (poco firme).

inconstantemente [in-cons-tan'-tay-men-tay], *adv.* Inconstantly, fickly, giddily.

inconstitucional [in-cons-te-too-the-o-nahl'], *a.* Unconstitutional.

inconstitucionalidad [in-cons-te-too-the-o-nah-le-dahd'], *f.* Unconstitutionality.

inconstitucionalismo [in-cons-te-too-the-o-nah-lees'-mo], *m.* Disobedience to the principles of the constitution.

inconstruible [in-cons-troo-ee'-blay], *a.* 1. *(coll.)* Whimsical, fantastical, fanciful, variable, fickle. 2. *(Gram.)* Obscure, unintelligible, difficult to be construed.

inconsútil [in-con-soo'-teel], *a.* Seamless, having no seam.

incontable [in-con-tah'-blay], *a.* Innumerable, countless.

incontaminado, da [in-con-tah-me-nah'-do, dah], *a.* Undefiled, uncontaminated.

incontenible [in-con-tay-ne'-blay], *a.* Uncontrollable, unstoppable, uncontainable.

incontestable [in-con-tes-tah'-blay], *a.* Incontestable, indisputable, incontrovertible.

incontestablemente [in-con-tays-tah-blay-men-tay], *adv.* Incontestably.

incontinencia [in-con-te-nen'-the-ah], *f.* Incontinence or incontinency; unchastity, lewdness. **Incontinencia de orina** *(Med.)* Incontinence of urine, a disease.

incontinente [in-con-te-nen'-tay], *a.* 1. Incontinent: applied to one who has no command of his passions. 2. Incontinent, unchaste.

incontinente [in-con-te-nen'-tay], *adv.* Instantly, immediately, incontinently.

incontinentemente [in-con-te-nayn'-tay-men-tay], *adv.* Incontinently, unchastely.

incontinenti [in-con-te-nen'-te], *adv.* Incontinently, instantly, immediately.

incontrastable [in-con-tras-tah'-blay], *a.* 1. Insurmountable, irresistible, incontrollable, insuperable (dificultad). 2. Inexpugnable, unconquerable. 3. Inconvincible.

incontratable [in-con-trah-tah'-blay], *a.* *V.* INTRATABLE.

incontrolado [in-con-tro-lah'-do], *a.* Uncontrolled; violent, wild. *-m & f.* Violent person.

incontrovertible [in-con-tro-ver-tee'-blay], *a.* Incontrovertible, indisputable.

inconvencible [in-con-ven-thee'-blay], *a.* 1. Inconvincible, not capable of conviction. 2. *V.* INVENCIBLE.

inconvenible [in-con-vay-nee'-blay], *a.* 1. Discordant, inconsistent, opposite. 2. Inconvenient.

inconveniencia [in-con-vay-ne-en'-the-ah], *f.* 1. Inconvenience, incommodity, unfitness. 2. Incongruence, unsuitableness. 3. Impoliteness (descortesía). 4. Impropriety (incorrección), wrongness. 5. Silly remark (disparate).

inconveniente [in-con-vay-ne-en'-tay], *a.* 1. Inconvenient (inoportuno), incommodious, troublesome, unsuitable (impropio). 2. Impolite (descortés). 3. Improper (incorrecto).

inconveniente [in-con-vay-ne-en'-tay], *m.* Difficulty, obstacle (dificultad), obstruction, impediment, disadvantage (desventaja). **El inconveniente es que...**, the trouble is that... **No hay inconveniente en**, there is no objection to.

inconversable [in-con-ver-sah'-blay], *a.* Unsociable, incommunicative.

inconvertible [in-con-ver-tee'-blay], *a.* Inconvertible, that which cannot be converted or changed.

incordiar [in-cor-de-ar'], *va.* To bother, to annoy.

incordio [in-cor'-de-o], *m.* Nuisance. *-a. (Vul.)* Wearisome, vexing.

incorporación [in-cor-po-rah-the-on'], *f.* Incorporation, the act of uniting in one mass.

incorporadero [in-cor-po-rah-day'-ro], *m.* The spot where mercury is mixed with metals.

incorporado [in-cor-po-rah'-do], *a. (Tec.)* Built-in. **Con antena incorporada**, with built-in antenna.

incorporal [in-cor-po-rahl'], *a.* Incorporeal.

incorporalmente [in-cor-po-rahl'-men-tay], *adv.* Incorporeally, incorporally.

incorporamiento [in-cor-po-rah-me-en'-to], *m. V.* INCORPORACIÓN.

incorporar [in-cor-po-rar'], *va.* 1. To incorporate, to unite in one mass, to embody, to include (incluir), to involve (involucrar). 2. To incorporate, to form into a corporation. 3. To raise or to make a patient sit up in his bed. *-vr.* 1. To incorporate, to mingle. 2. To become incorporated or united in one mass or body. **Incorporarse en la cama**, to sit up in bed. 3. *(Naut.)* To sail in company, to join the convoy. 4. To join (sociedad, regimiento). **Incorporarse al trabajo**, to go to work.

incorporeidad [in-cor-po-ray-e-dahd'], *f.* Incorporeity, incorporality, immateriality.

incorpóreo, rea [in-cor-po'-ray-o, ah], *a.* Incorporeal, immaterial, unbodied.

incórporo [in-cor'-po-ro], *m. V.* INCORPORACIÓN.

incorrección [in-cor-rec-the-on'], *f.* 1. Incorrectness (datos), inaccurate. 2. Irregularity (irregularidad). 3. Discourtesy (descortesía). **Cometer una incorrección**, to do something improperly.

incorrectamente [in-cor-rec'-tah-men-tay], *adv.* Inaccurately.

incorrecto, ta [in-cor-rec'-to, tah], *a.* 1. Incorrect (cálculo, dato), inaccurate. 2. Irregular (facciones). 3. Discourteous (conducta), bad-mannered. **Ser incorrecto con una**, to take liberties with somebody.

incorregibilidad [in-cor-ray-he-be-le-dahd'], *f.* Incorrigibleness, hopeless depravity.

incorregible [in-cor-ray-hee'-blay], *a.* Incorrigible, forward.

incorregiblemente [in-cor-ray-he'blay-men-tay], *adv. (coll.)* Incorrigibly, obstinately.

incorrupción [in-cor-roop-the-on'], *f.* 1. Incorruption, incapacity of corruption. 2. Incorruptness, purity of manners, integrity, honesty.

incorruptamente [in-cor-roop-tah-men'-tay], *adv.* Incorruptly.

incorruptible [in-cor-roop-tee'-blay], *a.* Incorruptible.

incorrupto, ta [in-cor-roop'-to, tah], *a.* 1. Incorrupt, free from depravation. 2. Uncorrupt or uncorrupted, pure of manners, honest, good, incorruptible. **Incorrupta**, applied to a virgin.

incrasar [in-crah-sar'], *va.* To inspissate, to thicken.

increado da [in-cray-ah'-do, dah], *a.* Uncreated, increate: a divine attribute.

incredibilidad [in-cray-de-be-le-dahd'], *f.* Incredibility, incredibleness, the quality of surpassing belief.

incredulidad [in-cray-doo-le-dahd'], *f.* Incredulity, incredulousness.

incrédulo, la [in-cray'-doo-lo, lah], *a.* Incredulous, hard to believe, refusing credit. *-m. & f.* A miscreant.

increíble [in-cray-ee'-blay], *a.* Incredible, not to be credited. **Es increíble que...**, it is unbelievable that...

increíblemente [in-cray-ee'-blay-men-tay], *adv.* Incredibly.

incrementar [in-cray-men-tar'], *va.* To increase, to intensify. *-vr.* To increase.

incremento [in-cray-men'-to], *m.* Increment, increase, act of growing greater, cause of growing more. **Incremento de temperatura**, rise in temperature.

increpación [in-cray-pah-the-on'], *f.* Severe, reprimand, reproach.

increpador, ra [in-cray-pah-dor', rah], *m. & f.* Chider, rebuker, scolder.

increpar [in-cray-par'], *va.* To chide, to reprehend, to scold, to reproach, to rebuke.

incriminar [in-cre-me-nar'], *va.* 1. To incriminate, to accuse (persona). 2. To exaggerate a fault or defect. 3. To magnify (falta). *V.* ACRIMINAR.

incristalizable [in-cris-tah-le-thah'-blay], *a.* Uncrystallizable.

incruento, ta [in-croo-en'-to, tah], *a.* Unstained with blood, bloodless.

incrustación [in-croos-tah-the-on'], *f.* Incrustation.

incrustar [in-croos-tar'], *va.* To incrust or incrustate, to cover with an additional coat, to inlay (joyas). *-vr.* **Incrustarse en**, to lodge in (bomba).

incuartación [in-coo-ar-tah-the-on'], *f.* Inquartation, or quartation, the adding of silver to a button of gold (usually in the proportion of three-fourths to one-fourth) in the process of refining gold.

incubación [in-coo-bah-the-on'], *f.* 1. Incubation, the process of hatching eggs. 2. Incubation, the time intervening between exposure and the outbreak of a disease. 3. *(Met.)* Secret preparation of a design.

incubadora [in-coo-bah-do'-rah], *f.* 1. Incubator. 2. Brooder.

incubar [in-coo-bar'], *va.* To incubate, to hatch eggs. *V.* ENCOBAR.

incubo [een'-coo-bo], *m.* 1. Incubus, nightmare. 2. Incubus, a pretended fairy or demon.

incuestionable [in-coo-ays-te-o-nah-blay], *a.* Blameless, guiltless.

inculcación [in-cool-ca-the-on'], *f.* 1. Inculcation, enforcing. 2. *(Print.)* Act of binding or wedging in a form.

inculcar [in-cool-car'], *va.* 1. To inculcate, to impress by frequent admonitions. 2. To make one thing tight against another. 3. *(Print.)* To lock up types. *-vr.* To be obstinate, to conform oneself in an opinion or sentiment.

inculpabilidad [in-cool-pah-be-le-dahd'], *f.* Inculpableness, unblamableness.

inculpable [in-cool-pah'-blay], *a.* Inculpable, unblamable.

inculpablemente [in-cool-pah'-blay-men-tay], *adv.* Inculpably.

inculpación [in-cool-pah-the-on'], *f.* Charge, accusation.

inculpadamente [in-cool-pah'-dah-men-tay], *adv.* Faultlessly.

inculpado, da [in-cool-pah'-do, dah], *a.* Faultless.-*pp.* of INCULPAR.

inculpar [in-cool-par'], *va.* To accuse, to blame. **Los crímenes que se le inculpan**, the crimes with which he is charged.

incultamente [in-cool-tah-men'-tay], *adv.* Rudely, without culture.

incultivable [in-cool-te-va'-blay], *a.* Incapable of cultivation, uncultivable.

inculto, ta [in-cool'-to, tah], *a.* 1. Incult, uncultivated, untilled. 2. Uncivilized, unpolished, unrefined, clownish, clumsy.

incultura [in-cool-too'-rah], *f.* Inculture, want or neglect of culture.

incumbencia [in-coom-ben'-the-ah], *f.* 1. Incumbency. 2. Duty imposed upon a person; ministry. **Eso no es de la incumbencia de usted**, that does not concern you; it is not your business.

incumbir [in-coom-beer'], *vn.* To be incumbent upon someone, to have anything imposed as a duty. **No me incumbe a mí**, it is not my job.

incumplido [in-coom-ple-do], *a.* Unfulfilled.

incumplimiento [in-coom-ple-me-ayn-to], *m.* Non-fulfilment; non-completion. **Incumplimiento de contrato**, breach of contract.

incumplir [in-coom-pler'], *va.* To break (regla), to disobey, to fail to observe; to break a promise (promesa).

incunable [in-coo-nah'-blay], *m.* Incunable, incunabulum.

incurable [in-coo-rah'-blay], *a.* Incurable, immedicable; irremediable, hopeless.

incuria [in-coo-re-ah], *f.* Negligence, indolence, inaccuracy.

incurioso, sa [in-coo-re-o'-so, sah], *a.* Negligent, indolent, incurious, inattentive.

incurrimiento [in-coo-rre-me-en'-to], *m.* Act of incurring.

incurrir [in-coo-rreer'], *vn.* To incur (deuda, ira, odio), to become liable to punishment or reprehension: to deserve.

incursión [in-coor-se-on'], *f.* 1. Incurring. 2. Incursion, raid, overrunning an enemy's country. **Incursión aérea or ataque aéreo**, air raid, air attack.

incurso, sa [in-coor'-so, sah], *pp. irr.* of INCURRIR.

incurvación [in-coor-vah-the-on'], *f. V.* ENCORVADURA.

indagación [in-dah-gah-the-on'], *f.* Search, inquiry, examination, inquest.

indagador, ra [in-dah-gah-dor', rah], *m. & f.* Investigator, inquirer, an examiner.

indagar [in-dah-gar'], *va.* To search, to inquire, to examine into; to investigate (examinar).

índar [een'-dar], *m.* A kind of mattock for clearing out shrubs, grubbing of the ground and like uses.

indebidamente [in-day-be'-dah-men-tay], *adv.* Unjustly, illegally, wrongfully.

indebido, da [in-day-bee'-do, dah], *a.* Undue, illegal, unlawful, void of equity and moderation.

indecencia [in-day-then'-the-ah], *f.* 1. Indecency, indecorum, obscenity (obscenidad). 2. Nuisance. 3. Filth (porquería); wretchedness. 4. Indecent act; indecent thing (palabra).

indecente [in-day-then'-tay], *a.* 1. Indecent, dishonest, unbecoming. 2. Filthy (asqueroso); miserable (despreciable), wretched; low (vil), mean. **Un cuchitril indecente**, a miserable pigsty of a place. **Es una persona indecente**, he's a low sort, he's a mean character.

indecentemente [in-day-then'-tay-men-tay], *adv.* Indecently, fulsomely.

indecible [in-day-thee'-blay], *a.* Inexpressible, unutterable. **Sufrir lo indecible**, to suffer terribly.

indeciblemente [in-day-the'-blay-men-tay], *adv.* Inexpressibly, unspeakably.

indecisamente [in-day-the'-sah-men-tay], *adv.* Irresolutely.

indecisión [in-day-the-se-on'], *f.* Irresolution, indecision, want of firmness of mind.

indeciso, sa [in-day-thee'-so, sah], *a.* 1. Irresolute, indecisive (resultado), not constant in purpose. 2. Undecided (persona), not settled.

indeclinable [in-day-cle-nah'-blay], *m.* 1. Incapable of decline or decay, firm, unshaken. 2. *(Gram.)* Indeclinable, not varied by terminations.

indecoro [in-day-co'-ro], *m.* Indecorum, indecorousness, indecency.

indecorosamente [in-day-co-ro'-sah-men-tay], *adv.* Indecorously, indecently.

indecoroso, sa [in-day-co-ro'-so, sah], *a.* Indecorous, indecent, unbecoming.

indefectibilidad [in-day-fec-te-be-le-dahd'], *f.* Indefectibility, quality of suffering no decay or defect.

indefectible [in-day-fec-tee'-blay], *a.* Indefectible, unfailing.

indefectiblemente [in-day-fec-tee'-blay-men-tay], *adv.* Indefectibly.

indefendible [in-day-fen-dee'-blay], *a.* Indefensible, that cannot be defended.

indefensible [in-day-fen-see'-blay], *a.* Indefensible.

indefenso, sa [in-day-fen'-so, sah], *a.* Defenceless, indefensive.

indeficiente [in-day-fee-the-en'-tay], *a.* Indefectible, unfailing.

indefinible [in-day-fe-nee'-blay], *a.* Indefinable.

indefinidamente [in-day-fe-ne-dah-men-tay], *adv.* Indefinitely.

indefinido, da [in-day-fe-nee'-do, dah], *a.* 1. Indefinite, not defined. 2. Indefinite not determined. 3. Indefinite, large beyond the comprehension of man. 4. Indefinite, not limited. **Por tiempo indefinido**, for an indefinite time.

indefinito, ta [in-day-fe-nee'-to, tah], *a.* Indefinite, without limits.

indehescencia [in-day-es-then'-the-ah], *f. (Bot.)* Indehiscence, lack of the power to open spontaneously.

indehiscente [in-day-es-then'-tay], *a.* Indehiscent, not splitting spontaneously.

indeleble [in-day-lay'-blay], *a.* Indelible, not to be blotted out.

indeleblemente [in-day-lay-blay-men-tay], *adv.* Indelibly.

indeliberación [in-day-le-bay-rah-the-on'], *f.* 1. Indetermination, irresolution. 2. Inadvertency.

indeliberadamente [in-day-le-bay-rah'-dah-men-tay], *adv.* Inadvertently, indeliberately.

indeliberado, da [in-day-le-bay-rah'-do, dah], *a.* Indeliberate or indeliberated, unpremeditated; done without sufficient consideration.

indemne [in-dem'-nay], *a.* Undamaged, unhurt, unharmed (persona).

indemnidad [in-dem-ne-dahd'], *f.* Indemnity, exemption from damage.

indemnizable [in-dem-ne-thah'-blay], *a.* What can be made good, or indemnified.

indemnización [in-dem-ne-thah-the-on'], *f.* 1. Indemnification (acto), reimbursement. 2. Indemnity (pago), compensation. **Indemnización de despido**, severance pay. **Indemnización por enfermedad**, sick pay.

indemnizar [in-dem-nee-thar'], *va.* To indemnify, to secure against loss; to manitain unhurt, to make amends; to compensate, to make good to one.

indemostrable [in-day-mos-trah'-blay], *a.* Indemonstrable, incapable of demonstration.

independencia [in-day-pen-den'-the-ah], *f.* Independence, freedom from reliance or control.

independiente [in-day-pen-de-ayn'-tay], *a.* Independent, free: it is sometimes used as a substantive. **Independiente de eso**, Independent of that, besides that. *-m. & f.* Independent.

independientemente [in-day-pen-de-ayn'-tay-men-tay], *adv.* Independently.

independizar [in-day-pen-de-thar'], *va.* To emancipate, to free; to make independent. *-vr.* To become free, to become independent.

indescifrable [in-des-the-frah'-blay], *a.* Undecipherable, impenetrable (misterio).

indescribible [in-des-cre-bee'-blay], or **Indescriptible**, *a.* Indescribable.

indeseable [in-day-say-ah'-blay], *a.* Undesirable. *m. & f.* Undesirable (persona). **Es un indeseable**, he's an unsavory sort.

indesignable [in-day-sig-nah'-blay], *a.* That which cannot be designed.

indestructibilidad [in-des-trooc-te-be-le-dahd'], *f.* Indestructibility.

indestructible [in-des-trooc-tee'-blay], *a.* Indestructible, imperishable.

indeterminable [in-day-ter-me-nah'-blay], *a.* 1. Indeterminable. 2. Irresolute, undecided.

indeterminación [in-day-ter-me-nah-the-on'], *f.* Indetermination or indeterminateness, irresolution.

indeterminadamente [in-day-ter-me-nah'-dah-men-tay], *adv.* Indeterminately.

indeterminado, da [in-day-ter-me-nah'-do, dah], *a.* 1. Indeterminate, not defined. 2. Indetermined, irresolute (persona), doubtful. 3. Pusillanimous, chicken-hearted. 4. Indefinite, general; loose.

indevoción [in-day-vo-the-on'], *f.* Indevotion, want of devotion.

indevoto, ta [in-day-vo'-to, tah], *a.* Indevout, irreligious.

India [een'-de-ah], *f. (Met. Coll.)* 1. Great wealth, abundance of money and other precious things. 2. India (País).

indiana [in-de-ah'-nah], *f.* Chintz.

indianismo [in-de-ah-nees'-mo], *m.* 1. Interest in or knowledge of West Indian culture. 2. East Indian idiom.

indianista [in-de-ah-nees'-tah], *m. & f.* 1. Indianist. 2. Person versed in West Indian cultures.

indiano, na [in-de-ah'-no, nah], *a. & m. & f.* 1. East Indian. 2. West Indian. 3. Spanish emigrant who returns rich from Latin America.

indicación [in-de-ca-the-on'], *f.* 1. Indication (señal), any mark, token, sign or note. 2. *(Med.)* Indication, the sign or

symptom which indicates what is to be done (síntoma). 3. Hint, suggestion (sugerencia). **Por indicación de, at the suggestion of. Seguiré sus indicaciones,** I will follow your suggestion.

indicado [in-de-cah'-do], *a.* Right, suitable, proper; obvious; likely. **El sitio más indicado**, the most obvious place. **Es el más indicado para el puesto**, he is the most suitable man for the job.

indicador [in-de-ca-dor'], *m.* 1. Indicator, pointer, hand (aguja). 2. The forefinger. 3. Electrical indicator. **Indicador de dirección**, *(Aer.)* direction indicator. **Indicador de velocidade**, speedometer.

indicante [in-de-cahn'-tay], *pa.* Indicating. *-m. (Med.)* Indicant, anything from which an indication is drawn in a disease.

indicar [in-de-car'], *va.* 1. To indicate, to show (mostrar), to point out (señalar). 2. *(Med.)* To indicate, to point out a remedy, to read (termómetro).

indicativo, va [in-de-cah-tee'-vo, vah], *a.* Indicative, pointing.

indicativo [in-de-cah-tee'-vo], *m. (Gram.)* Indicative, one of the modes of verbs.

indicción [in-dic-the-on'], *f.* Indiction, the convening of a synod, council, etc.

índice [een'-de-thay], *m.* 1. Mark, sign, index. 2. Hand of a watch or clock. 3. Pin that casts the shade on a sundial. 4. Index, table of contents to a book. 5. Index, forefinger. **Índice del coste de vida**, cost-of-living index. **Índice de mortalidad**, death rate.

indicación [in-de-cah-the-on'], *f.* Indexing.

indiciado, da [in-de-the-ah'-do, dah], *a.* Suspected of a crime or vice. *-pp.* of INDICIAR. Suspicious, liable to be suspected.

indiciador, ra [in-de-the-ah-dor, rah], *m. & f.* 1. One who entertains suspicions. 2. Informer, one who discovers offenders to the magistrates.

indiciar [in-de-the-ar'], *va. (Law.)* 1. To give reasons, to suspect or surmise. 2. To discover offenders to the magistrates. 3. *V.* INDICAR.

indicio [in-dee'-the-o], *m.* Indication, mark, sign, token, trace (vestigio). **Dar indicios de sorpresa**, to show surprise. **Es indicio de**, it is an indication of.

Índico, ca [een'-do-co, cah], *a.* Indian.

indicolita [in-de-co-lee'-tah], *f.* A variety of tourmaline of indigo-blue color, found in Sweden.

indiferencia [in-de-fay-ren'-the-ah], *f.* 1. Indifference, incuriosity. 2. Neglect, unconcern, coldness, lukewarmness, listlessness. 3. Neutrality, suspension.

indiferente [in-de-fay-ren'-tay], *a.* 1. Indifferent, neutral, apathetic (apático), uninterested. 2. Unconcerned, inattentive, regardless. 3. Lukewarm, cool, frigid, listless. **Eso es indiferente**, *(coll.)* that is immaterial, that makes no difference.

indiferentemente [in-de-fay-ren'-tay-men-tay], *adv.* Indifferently, impartially, coolly.

indígena [in-dee'-hay-nah], *a.* Indigenous, native; *(LAm.)* Indian. *-m. & f.* An Indian.

indigencia [in-de-hen'-the-ah], *f.* Indigence, want, penury, poverty, need.

indigenismo [in-de-hay-nees'-mo], *m.* Study of or interest in West Indian culture.

indigenista [in-de-hay-nees'-tah], *a.* Treating of or defending West Indian culture. *-m. & f.* Supporter of West Indians and their culture.

indigente [in-de-hen'-tay], *a.* Indigent, necessitous, poor, needy.

indigerible [in-de-hay-ree'-blay], *a.* Not possible of digestion.

indigestar [in-de-hays-tar'], *va.* To cause indigestion to. *-vr.* To get indigestible (persona). 2. To cause indigestion (comida). **Esa carne se me indigestó**, that meat gave me indigestion. 3. *(Fig.)* To be insufferable. 4. *(LAm.)* To get worried (inquietarse).

indigestible [in-de-hes-tee'-blay], *a.* Indigestible, hard to digest.

indigestión [in-de-hes-te-on'], *f.* 1. Indigestion. 2. Rudeness of temper, ill-nature.

indigesto, ta [in-de-hes'-to, tah], *a.* 1. Hard to digest, indigestible. 2. Indigest, confused, not separated into distinct parts, not methodized, not well considered. 3. *(coll.)* Rude, ill-natured.

indignación [in-dig-nah-the-on'], *f.* Indignation, anger.

indignado, da [in-dig-nah'-do, dah], *a. & pp.* of INDIGNAR. Provoked, teased, indignant, angry.

indignamente, *adv.* Unworthily (no merecedor), unsuitably.

indignante [in-dig-nahn'-tay], *pa.* Indignant, irritating, infuriating.

indignar [in-dig-nar'], *va.* To irritate, to provoke, to tease. -*vr.* To be inflamed with anger and disdain, to become angry or indignant. **Indignarse con uno**, to get indignant with somebody.

indignidad [in-dig-ne-dahd'], *f.* 1. Indignity (ofensa), want of merit. 2. An unworthy action (acto), meanness. 3. Indignation, passion.

indigno, na [in-deeg'-no, nah], *a.* 1. Unworthy (sin mérito), undeserving. 2. Unbecoming, incongruous, unsuitable. 3. Unworthy, bringing indignity, disgraceful, vile (vil), mean, despicable.

índigo [een'-de-go], *m. (Bot.)* V. AÑIL.

indiligencia [in-de-le-hen'-the-a], *f.* Lack of diligence, carelessness.

indio, ia [een'-de-o, ah], *a.* 1. East or West Indian. 2. Blue, azure (azul). -*m. & f.* East or West Indian. -*m.* 1. *(Chem.)* Indium. 2. **Hacer el indio**, to play the fool. 3. **Indio viejo**, *(CAm. Mex.)* stewed meat with maize and herbs.

indirecta [in-de-rec'-tah], *f.* Innuendo, an oblique hint, a cue, a surmise. **Soltar una indirecta**, to drop a hint.

indirectamente [in-de-rec'-tah-men-tay], *adv.* 1. Indirectly, obliquely. 2. Indirectly, not in express terms.

indirecto, ta [in-de-rec'-to, tah], *a.* Indirect, not direct: oblique.

indisciplina [in-dis-the-plee'-nah], *f.* Want of discipline, insubordination.

indisciplinable [in-dis-the-ple-nah'-blay], *a.* Indisciplinable, incapable of discipline.

indisciplinado, da [in-dis-the-ple-nah'-do, dah], *a.* Untaught, undisciplined.

indiscreción [in-dis-cray-the-on'], *f.* Indiscretion, imprudence, rashness, in consideration, folly, tactless thing (falta social). **Si no es indiscreción…**, if you don't mind my saying…

indiscretamente [in-dis-cray-tah-men'-tay], *adv.* Indiscreetly.

indiscreto, ta [in-dis-cray'-to, tah], *a.* Indiscreet, imprudent, incautious, foolish; injudicious, inconsiderate.

indiscriminado [in-dis-cre-me-nah'-do], *a.* Indiscriminate.

indisculpable [in-dis-cool-pah'-blay], *a.* Inexcusable.

indiscutible [in-dis-coo-tee'-blay], *a.* Unquestionable, beyond discussion.

indisolubilidad [in-de-so-loo-be-le-dahd], *f.* Indissolubility, indissolubleness.

indisoluble [in-de-so-loo'-blay], *a.* Indissoluble, indissolvable.

indisolublemente [in-de-so-loo'-blay-men-tay], *adv.* Indisolubly.

indispensable [in-dis-pen-sah'-blay], *a.* Indispensable, needful.

indispensablemente [in-dis-pen-sah'-blay-men-tay], *adv.* Indispensably, necessarily.

indisponer [in-dis-po-nerr'], *va.* 1. To disable, to indispose, to render unfit. 2. To indispose, to disincline, to make verse or unfavorable. 3. To indispose or disorder slightly with regard to health: commonly used in its reciprocal sense. -*vr.* 1. To be indisposed; to grow ill. 2. To become peevish or fretful.

indisponible [in-dis-po-nee'-blay], *a.* Not available.

indisposición [in-dis-po-se-the-on'], *f.* 1. Indisposition, disinclination, dislike. 2. Indisposition, slight disorder.

indisposicioncilla [in-dis-po-se-the-on-theel'-lyah], *f. dim.* Slight indisposition.

indispuesto, ta [in-dis-poo-ays'-to, tah], *a. & pp. irr.* of INDISPONER. 1. Indisposed, disordered in health. 2. Indisposed, at variance.

indisputable [in-dis-poo-tah'-blay], *a.* Indisputable, in controvertible.

indisputablemente [in-dis-poo-tah'-blay-men-tay], *adv.* Indisputably.

indistinción [in-dis-tin-the-on'], *f.* 1. Indistinction, indiscrimination (falta de discriminación). 2. Lack of distinction (igualdad).

indistinguible [in-dis-tin-gee'-blay], *a.* Undistinguishable, indistinguishable.

indistintamente [in-dis-tin-tah-men'-tay], *adv.* Indistinctly, indiscriminately.

indistinto, ta [in-des-teen'-to, tah], *a.* Indistinct (pococlaro), indiscriminate (indiscriminado), faint (borroso).

individuación [in-de-ve-doo-ah-the-on'], *f.* V. INDIVIDUALIDAD.

individual [in-de-ve-doo-ahl'], *a.* 1. Individual; peculiar (particular), special; single (cama, habitación). 2. *(And. Cono Sur)* Identical (idético). -*m. (Dep.)* Singles, match.

individualidad [in-de-ve-doo-ah-le-dahd'], *f.* Individuality.

individualismo [in-de-ve-doo-ah-lees'-mo], *m.* Individualism.

individualista [in-de-ve-doo-ah-lees'-tah], *a.* Individualistic. -*m. & f.* Individualist.

individualizar [in-de-ve-doo-ah-le-thar'], *va.* To individualize.

individualmente [in-de-ve-doo-ahl-men-tay], *adv.* 1. Individually, numerically. 2. Individually, not separably.

individuar [in-de-ve-doo-ar'], *va.* To individuate, to distinguish; to particularize, to specify individually.

individuo [in-de-vee'-doo-o], *m.* Individual, a single person or thing. **El individuo en cuestión**, the person in question.

individuo, dua [in-de-vee'-doo-o, ah], *a.* Individual, indivisible, inseparable.

indivisamente [in-de-ve-sah-men'-tay], *adv.* Indivisibly.

indivisibilidad [in-de-ve-se-be-le-dahd'], *f.* Indivisibility.

indivisible [in-de-ve-see'-blay], *a.* Indivisible.

indivisiblemente [in-de-ve-see'-blay-men-tay], *adv.* Inseparably, indivisibly.

indiviso, sa [in-de-vee'-so, sah], *a.* Undivided, individuate, not separated into parts.

indo, da [een'-do, dah], *a.* Indian. *(Acad.)* V. INDIO. -*m.* The river Indus, now the Sind.

indócil [in-do'-theel], *a.* 1. Indocile, unteachable. 2. Inflexible, not to be prevailed upon; headstrong, forward

indocilidad [in-do-the-le-dahd'], *f.* 1. Indocility, refusal of instruction. 2. Inflexibility, stubbornness of mind.

indócilmente [in-do'-theel-men-tay], *adv.* Inflexibly.

indocto, ta [in-doc'-to, tah], *a.* Ignorant, uninstructed, unlearned.

indocumentado [in-do-coo-men-tah'-do], *a.* Without identifying documents, who carries no identity papers. -*m & f.* Person who carries no identity papers; *(Mex.)* illegal immigrant.

indoeuropeo, a [in-do-ay-oo-ro-pay'-o, ah], *a.* Indo-European.

indogermánico, ca [in-do-her-mah'-ne-co, cah], *a.* IndoGermanic.

índole [een'-do-lay], *f.* Disposition, temper, inclination, peculiar genius, idiosyncrasy, humor, nature (naturaleza).

indolencia [in-do-len'-the-ah], *f.* Indolence, indifference, laziness; insensibility to grief or pain.

indolente [in-do-len'-tay], *a.* Indolent, indifferent.

indolentemente [in-do-len'-tay-men-tay], *adv.* Indolently, inertly.

indoloro [in-do-lo'-ro], *a.* Painless.

indomable [in-do-mah'-blay], *a.* 1. Untamable, indomitable (espíritu), unmanageable (animales salvajes). 2. Inflexible, unconquerable (pasiones).

indomado, da [in-do-mah'-do, dah], *a.* Untamed.

indomesticable [in-do-mes-te-cah'-blay], *a.* Untamable.

indoméstico, ca [in-do-mays'-te-co, cah], *a.* Untamed, fierce, intractable.

indómito, ta [in-do'-me-to, tah], *a.* Untamed, ungoverned, wild.

indostánico, ca [in-dos-tah'-ne-co, cah], *a.* Hindu or Hindoo, belonging to Hindustan

indostano, na [in-dos-tah'-no, nah], *m. & f.* Hindu, a native of Hindustan.

indotación [in-do-tah-the-on'], *f. (Law.)* Want of a wife's portion.

indotado, da [in-do-tah'-do, dah], *a.* 1. Unendowed, wanting endowments or talents. 2. Portionless (mujeres).

indrí [in-dree'], *m. (Zool.)* A mammal of the lemur family, greatly resembling an anthropoid ape.

indubitable [in-doo-be-tah'-blay], *a.* Indubitable, unquestioned, irrefutable, unquestionable.

indubitablemente [in-doo-be-tah'-blay-men-tay], *adv.* Undoubtedly, indubitably, unquestionably.

indubitado, da [in-doo-be-tah'-do, dah], *a.* Undoubted, indubitate.

inducción [in-dooc-the-on'], *f.* 1. Induction, inducement (persuasión), persuasion. 2. Induction, the act of infering a general proposition from several particular ones. **Por inducción,** inductively.

inducidor, ra [in-doo-the-dor', rah], *m. & f.* Inducer, persuader.

inducimiento [in-doo-the-me-en'-to], *m.* Inducement, motive to anything.

inducir [in-doo-theer'], *va.* To induce (persuadir), to persuade, to influence, to attract. **Inducir a uno a hacer algo,** to induce somebody to do something.

inductancia [in-dooc-tahn'-the-ah], *f. (Elec.)* Inductance.

indúctil [in-dooc'-teel], *a.* Not ductile.

inductivo, va [in-dooc-tee'-vo, vah], *a.* Inductive.

indudable [in-doo-dah'-blay], *a.* Undoubted, indubitable.

indulgencia [in-dool-hen'-the-ah], *f.* 1. Indulgence, forbearance, tenderness, clemency, forgiveness. 2. Fond kindness. 3. Indulgence, release of the penalty due to sin.

indulgente [in-dool-hen'-tay], *a.* Indulgent, kind, mild, gentle.

indulgentemente [in-dool-hen'-tay-men-tay], *adv.* Indulgently.

indultar [in-dool-tar'], *va.* 1. To pardon, to forgive. 2. To free, to exempt (eximir). -vr. 1. *(And.)* To meddle, to pry (entrometerse). 2. *(Carib.)* To get oneself out of a jam.

indultario [in-dool-tah'-re-o], *m.* He who in virtue of a pontifical privilege can dispense eclesiastical benefices.

indulto [in-dool'-to], *m.* 1. Pardon, forgiveness, amnesty. 2. Indult, privilege, exemption (exención). 3. Impost, tax or duty on merchandise imported into Spain.

indumentaria [in-doo-men-tah'-re-ah], *f.* 1. Clothing (ropa), apparel, dress. 2. Costume (estudio).

induración [in-doo-rah-the-on'], *f. (Med.)* Induration, a morbid hardness of any part.

industria [in-dos'-tre-ah], *f.* 1. Industry, diligence, assiduity (dedicación). 2. Ingenuity (maña), subtility, acuteness. **Industria algodonera,** cotton industry. **Industria pesada,** heavy industry. **Industria siderúrgica,** iron and steel industry.

industrial [in-doos-tre-al'], *a.* Industrial.

industrialismo [in-doos-tre-ah-lees'-mo], *m.* Industrialism, a social system which considers industry as the principal and most important of the objects of mankind.

industrialista [in-doos-tre-ah-lees'-tah], *a. (LAm.)* Industrialist.

industrialización [in-doos-tre-ah-le-thah-the-on'], *f.* Industrialization.

industrializar [in-doos-tre-ah-le-thar'], *va.* To industrialize. -vr. To become industrialized.

industriar [in-doos-tre-ar'], *va.* To teach, to instruct.

industriosamente [in-doos-tre-o-sah-men'-tay], *adv.* Industriously.

industrioso, sa [in-doos-tre-o'-so, sah], *a.* 1. Industrious (trabajador), skillful (mañoso), dexterous; painstaking, laborious, assiduous. 2. Made with ingenuity, skillfully or finely done.

inebriativo, va [in-ay-bre-ah-tee'-vo, vah], *a.* Inebriating.

inedia [in-ay'-de-ah], *f.* Fast, abstinence from food.

inédito, ta [in-ay'-de-to, tah], *a.* Not published, unedited, inedited.

ineducado [in-ay-doo-cah'-do], *a.* 1. Uneducated (sin instrucción). 2. Ill-bred (maleducado).

inefabilidad [in-ay-fah-be-le-dahd'], *f.* Ineffability, unspeakableness; impossibility of being explained.

inefable [in-ay-fah'-blay], *a.* Ineffable, unspeakable.

inefablemente [in-ay-fah-blay-men'-tay], *adv.* Ineffably.

ineficacia [in-ay-fe-cah'-the-ah], *f.* Inefficacy, want of effect, ineffectualness, inefficiency (proceso).

ineficaz [in-ay-fe-cath'], *a.* Inefficacious, ineffectual, ineffective, inefficient.

ineficazmente [in-ay-fe-cath'-men-tay], *adv.* Inefficaciously.

ineficiencia [in-ay-fe-the-ayn'-the-ah], *f.* Inefficiency.

ineficiente [in-ay-fe-the-ayn'-tay], *a.* Inefficient.

inelegancia [in-ay-lay-gahn'-the-ah], *f.* Inelegance.

inelegante [in-ay-lay-gahn'-tay], *a.* Inelegant.

ineluctable [in-ay-looc-tah'-blay], *a.* Inevitable, irresistible.

inenarrable [in-ay-nar-rah'-blay], *a.* Inexplicable, inexpressible.

inepcia [in-ep'-the-ah], *f.* (Rare) *V.* NECEDAD. -*a.* 1. Idiocy, incompetence; stupidity. 2. Unsuitability (impropiedad). 3. Silly thing (necedad).

ineptamente [in-ep-tah-men'-tay], *adv.* Unfitly, ineptly.

ineptitud [in-ep-te-tood'], *f.* Ineptitude, inability, unfitness.

inepto, ta [in-ep'-to, tah], *a.* Inept (incompetente), unfit, useless; foolish.

inequívoco, ca [in-ay-kee'-vo-co, cah], *a.* Unequivocal, unmistakable.

inercia [in-ayr'-the-ah], *f.* 1. Inertia, the passive principle in matter; inertness, want of motion. 2. Inactivity, inertia, dulness, indolence.

inerme [in-ayr'-may], *a.* Disarmed, without arms, defenceless.

inerrable [in-er-rah'-blay], *a.* Inerrable, exempt from error.

inerrante [in-er-rahn'-tay], *a. (Ast.)* Fixed (estrellas).

inerte [in-ayr'-tay], *a.* 1. Inert, dull, sluggish. 2. Unskilful. 3. *(Med.)* Paralytic paralyzed.

inerudito ta [in-ay-roo-dee'-to, tah], *a.* Inerudite, unlearned.

inervación [in-er-vah-the-on'], *f.* Innervation, the act of giving nervous stimulus and control to an organ.

inescrutable [in-es-croo-tah'-blay], *a.* Inscrutable, unsearchable.

inescudriñable [in-es-coo-dree-nyah'-blay], *a.* Inscrutable.

inesperadamente [in-es-pay-rah-dah-men'-tay], *adv.* Unexpectedly, suddenly.

inesperado, da [in-es-pay-rah'-do, dah], *a.* Unexpected, unforeseen.

inestabilidad [in-es-tah-be-le-dahd'], *f.* Instability, inconstancy, fickleness, mutability, giddiness.

inestable [in-es-tah'-blay], *a.* Unstable, unsteady.

inestimabilidad [in-es-te-mah-be-le-dahd'], *f.* Inestimableness.

inestimable [in-es-te-mah'-blay], *a.* Inestimable, invaluable.

inestimado, da [in-es-te-mah'-do, dah], *a. (Law.)* That which has not been rated or valued.

inevitable [in-ay-ve-tah'-blay], *a.* Inevitable, unavoidable, fatal.

inevitablemente [in-ay-ve-tah'-blay]. *adv.* Inevitably.

inexactitud [in-ec-sahc-te-tood'], *f.* Inaccuracy, want of exactness.

inexacto, ta [in-ec-sac'-to, tah], *a.* Inexact, inaccurate.

inexcusable [in-ex-coo-sah'-blay], *a.* 1. Inexcusable (imperdonable). 2. Inevitable, indispensable 3. Excuseless.

inexcusablemente [in-ex-coo-sah-blay-men'-tay], *adv.* Inexcusably.

inexhausto, ta [in-ec-sah'-oos-to, tah], *a.* 1. Unexhausted, unemptied, unspent. 2. Full, abundant, plentiful.

inexistencia [in-ec-sis-ten'-the-ah], *f.* Non-existence.

inexistente [in-ec-sis-ten'-tay], *a.* Inexistent, non-existent.

inexorable [in-ec-so-rah'-blay], *a.* Inexorable, relentless, hard-hearted.

inexperiencia [in-ex-pay-re-en'-the-ah], *f.* Inexperience.

inexperto, ta [in-ex-per'-to, tah], *a.* Inexpert, unskillful, inexperienced.

inexpiable [in-ex-pe-ah'-blay], *a.* Inexpiable.

inexplicable [in-ex-ple-cah'-blay], *a.* Inexplicable, inexplainable.

inexplicablemente [in-ex-ple-cah'-blay-men-tay], *adv.* Inexplicably, unaccountably.

inexplorado, da [in-ex-plo-rah'-do, dah], *a.* Unexplored.

inexpresivo [in-ex-pray-see'-vo], *a.* Inexpressive; dull, flat, wooden.

inexpugnable [in-ex-poog-nah'-blay], *a.* 1. Inexpugnable, impregnable. 2. Firm, constant; obstinate, stubborn.

inextinguible [in-ex-tin-gee'-blay], *a.* Inextinguishable, unquenchable; perpetual.

inextricable [in-ex-tre-cah'-blay], *a.* Inextricable.

infacundo, da [in-fah-coon'-do, dah], *a.* Ineloquent, not persuasive, not oratorical.

infalibilidad [in-fah-le-be-le-dahd'], *f.* Infallibility.

infalible [in-fah-lee'-blay], *a.* Infallible; certain, sure; unerring (puntería).

infaliblemente [in-fah-le-blay-men-tay], *adv.* Infallibly.

infamable [in-fah-mah'-blay], *a.* Capable of infamy, calumnious.

infamación [in-fah-mah-the-on'], *f.* Slander, calumny, defamation, the defaming of another.

infamador, ra [in-fah-mah-dor', rah], *m. & f.* Defamer, libeller.

infamante [in-fah-mahn'-tay], *pa. & a.* Defaming; opprobrious, offensive (injurioso), slanderous (difamatorio).

infamar [in-fah-mar], *va.* To defame, to make infamous, to dishonor by reports.

infamativo, va [in-fah-mah-tee'-vo, vah], *a.* That which defames.

infamatorio, ria [in-fah-mah-to'-re-o, ah], *a.* Defamatory, libellous, foul-spoken.

infame [in-fah'-may], *a.* Infamous, vile, despicable, damnable.

infamemente [in-fah-may-men'-tay], *adv.* Infamously, vilely.

infamia [in-fah'-me-ah], *f.* Infamy, dishonor, public reproach or opprobrium: meanness, baseness.

infancia [in-fahn'-the-ah], *f.* 1. Infancy, the first part of life. 2. Infancy, the first age of anything; beginning, commencement (edad).

infando, da [in-fahn'-do, dah], *a.* So abominable as not to be expressed, too bad to be mentioned.

infanta [in-fahn'-tah], *f.* 1. Infant, a female child under seven years of age (niña). 2. Infanta, a princess (princesa). 3. Wife of a prince royal.

infante [in-fahn'-tay], *m.* 1. Infant, a male child under seven years of age (niño). 2. Infante, prince (principe). 3. A foot-soldier. *-pl.* Choristers, boys brought up to sing in cathedral churches.

intantería [in-fan-tay-ree'-ah], *f.* Infantry, foot-soldiers.

infanticida [in-fan-te-thee'-dah], *com.* Infanticide, the murderer of an infant.

infanticidio [in-fan-te-thee'-de-o], *m.* Infanticide (acto), the murder of a child or infant.

infantil [in-fan-teel'], *a.* 1. Infantile, infantine (niño). 2. Child-like (inocente).

infanzón [in-fan-thone'], *m.* Nobleman.

infanzonado, da [in-fan-tho-nah'-do, dah], *a.* Pertaining to a noble.

infanzonazgo [in-fah-tho-nath'-go], *m.* Territory of a nobleman.

infanzonía [in-fah-tho-nee'-ah], *f.* Nobility.

infartación [in-far-tah-the-on'], *f.* Infarction, the stoppage of a channel.

infarto [In-far'-to], *m.* Infarct, that which composes an infarction, heart attack.

infatigable [in-fah-te-gah'-blay], *a.* Indefatigable, unwearied.

infatigablemente [in-fah-te-gah'-blay-men-tay], *adv.* Indefatigably.

infatuado, da [in-fah-too-ah'-do, dah], *a. & pp.* of INFATUAR. Infatuate, infatuated, stupefied; infatuating.

infatuar [in-fah-too-ar'], *va.* To infatuate, to deprive of understanding. *-vr.* 1. To become stupefied. 2. In religious matters, to be or become a bigot.

infaustamente [in-fah-oos-tah-men'-tay], *adv.* Unluckily.

infausto, ta [in-fah'-oos-to, tah], *a.* Unlucky, unhappy, unfortunate, accursed.

infección [in-fec-the-on'], *f.* Infection.

infeccioso [in-fec-the-o'-so], *a.* Infectious.

infectar [in-fec-tar'], *va.* 1. To infect, to hurt by infection. 2. To corrupt, to vitiate, to pervert. *-vr.* To catch, to take by infection.

infectivo, va [in-fec-tee'-vo, vah], *a.* Infective, infectious.

infecto, ta [in-fec'-to, tah], *a. & pp. irr* of INFECIR. Infected, tainted.

infecundidad [in-fay-coon-de-dahd'], *f.* Infecundity, sterility, infertility.

infecundo, da [in-fay-coon'-do, dah], *a* Infecund, barren, unfruitful, infertile. **La época infecunda de la mujer**, the woman's infertile period.

infelice [in-fay-lee'-thay], *a. (Poet.)* V. INFELIZ.

infelicidad [in-fay-lee-the-dahd'], *f.* Misfortune, calamity, disgrace, misery, unhappiness, infelicity.

infeliz [in-fay-leeth'], *a.* 1. Unhappy (desgraciado), unfortunate (desdichado), luckless, miserable. 2. *(coll.)* Applied to a man of excessive softness and goodnature (mujer). 3. *(Cono Sur, Mex.)* Trifling, insignificant (nimio). *-m & f.* 1. Wretch, poor devil. 2. Simpleton (inocentón).

infelizmente [in-fay-leeth'-men-tay], *adv.* Unhappily, unluckily, unfortunately.

inferaxilar [in-fay-rac-se-lar'], *a. (Bot.)* Infraaxillary, situated below the axil.

inferencia [in-fay-ren'-the-ah], *f.* Inference, illusion.

inferior [in-fay-re-or'], *a.* 1. Inferior lower in place (situación). 2. Inferior, lower in value or excellency (calidad). **De calidad inferior**, of inferior quality. **No ser inferior a nadie**, to be inferior to none. 3. Inferior, lower in station or rank (rango). 4. Inferior, subordinate, subject. 5. *(Mat.)* Lower. **Cualquier número inferior a 9**, any number under 9.

inferioridad [in-fay-re-o-re-dahd'], *f.* Inferiority, subjection.

inferir [in-fay-reer'], *va.* To infer (deducir), to deduce, to draw conclusions, to collect, to gather. -*vr.* To follow, to be consequential, as inference to premises.

infernáculo [in-fer-nah'-coo-lo], *m.* Kind of boyish play, called in America *rayuela*; hop scotch.

infernal [in-fer-nahl'], *a.* 1. Infernal, hellish. 2. Extremely hurtful. **Máquina infernal**, a machine arranged to throw many projectiles at once.

infernalmente [in-fer-nahl'-men-tay], *adv.* (*coll.*) Hellishly, infernally.

infernar [in-fer-nahr'], *va.* 1. To damn, to doom to eternal torments. 2. To tease, to vex, to provoke.

inferno, na [in-fer'-no, nah], *a.* (*Poet.*), Infernal.

ínfero, ra [een'-fay-ro, rah], *a.* Combining form of inferior; and in botany and poetry for inferior.

infértil [in-fer'-teel], *a.* Infertile.

infestación [in-fes-tah-the-on'], *f.* Act of harassing, infestation, annoyance.

infestar [in-fes-tar'], *va.* 1. To infest (infectar), to overrun (invadir), to harass an enemy by incursions. 2. *V.* INFICIONAR. 3. *V.* APESTAR.

infeudar [in-fay-oo-dar'], *va. V.* ENFEUDAR.

infición [in-fe-the-on'], *f.* Infection. *V.* INFECCIÓN.

inficionar [in-fe-the-o-nar'], *va.* 1. To infect, to hurt by infection. 2. To corrupt, to defile, to pervert by bad maxims or bad example. 3. To defile the honors of a noble descent, to taint the purity of noble blood; to vitiate.

infidelidad [in-fe-day-le-dahd'], *f.* 1. Infidelity (adulterio), treachery, deceit, faithlessness. 2. Miscreance, unbelief, want of faith, disbelief of Christianity. 3. The whole body of infidels.

infidelísimo, ma [in-fe-day-lee'-se-mo, mah], *a. super.* of INFIEL.

infidencia [in-fe-den'-the-ah], *f.* 1. Unfaithfulness, faithlessness (cualidad); treason. 2. (*Law.*) Misfeasance.

infidente [in-fe-den'-tay], *a.* Unfaithful.

infiel [in-feel'], *a.* Unfaithful (desleal), infidel; faithless, disloyal; godless; pagan: it is also used as a substantive. **Fue infiel a su mujer**, he was unfaithful to his wife.

infielmente [in-fe-el'-men-tay], *adv.* Unfaithfully.

infiernillo, infernillo [en-fe-er-neel'-lyo, en-fer-neel'-lyo], *m.* Chafing dish.

infierno [in-fe-err'-no], *m.* 1. Hell, the place of the devil and wicked souls; torment of the wicked. 2. Limbo. 3. Anything which causes confusion, pain, or trouble; discord, dispute. **Mandar a uno al quinto infierno**, to tell somebody to go to hell. 4. Refectory or eating room in some convents. 5. A large retort or other chemical vessel.

infigurable [in-fe-goo-rah'-blay], *a.* That which cannot be represented by any figure.

infiltración [in-feel-trah-the-on'], *f.* (*Med.*) Infiltration.

infiltrar [in-feel-trar'], *va.* To infiltrate; to inculcate.

infiltrarse [in-feel-trar'-say], *vr.* To infiltrate, to insinuate by filtration.

ínfimo, ma [een'-fe-mo, mah], *a.* 1. Lowest, lowermost, most inferior, the least. 2. Abject, vile, low-bred.

infinidad [in-fe-ne-dahd'], *f.* 1. Infinity, infiniteness, immensity, boundlessness. 2. Infinity, endless number. **Durante una infinidad de días**, for days on end.

infinitamente [in-fe-ne-tah-men'-tay], *adv.* Infinitely, immensely.

infinitesimal [in-fe-ne-tay-se-mahl'], *a.* (*Mat.*) Infinitesimal (fracciones).

infinitésimo, ma [in-fe-ne-tay'-se-mo, mah], *a.* (*coll.*) Infinitely small.

infinitivo [in-fe-ne-tee'-vo], *m.* (*Gram.*) Infinitive, one of the modes of verbs.

infinito, ta [in-fe-nee'-to, tah], *a.* Infinite, unbounded, unlimited, immense. 2. Infinite, very numerous, excessive. **Hasta lo infinito**, ad infinitum.

infinito [in-fe-nee'-to], *adv.* Infinitely, immensely.

inflación [in-flah-the-on'], *f.* 1. Inflation, the state of being swelled with wind; flatulence. 2. Inflation, conceit, vanity, haughtiness, vaingloriousness.

inflamabilidad [in-flah-mah-be-le-dahd'], *f.* Inflammability.

inflamable [in-flah-mah'-blay], *a.* Inflammable, easy to be set on flame.

inflamación [in-flah-mah-the-on'], *f.* 1. Inflammation, setting on flame, the state of being in flame. 2. (*Med.*) Inflammation, a morbid state characterized by heat, pain, etc. 3. Inflammation, excitement of passions or of fervor of mind.

inflamar [in-flah-mar'], *va.* 1. To inflame, to kindle, to set on fire. 2. To inflame, to kindle desire. -*vr.* To become red, to become inflamed or heated. **Se inflama fácilmente**, it is highly inflammable.

inflamatorio, ria [in-flah-mah-to'-re-o, ah], *a.* Inflammatory.

inflar [in-flar'], *va.* 1. To inflate (inchar), to swell with wind. 2. (*Met.*) To elate, to inflate, to puff up with pride. -*vr.* To jet, to strut. -*vn.* (*Mex.*) To booze (beber).

inflexibilidad [in-flec-se-be-le-dahd'], *f.* 1. Inflexibility, stiffnes, rigidity. 2. Inflexibility, inflexibleness, obstinacy, tenacity.

inflexible [in-flec-see'-blay], *a.* 1. Inflexible, not to be bent. 2. Inflexible, not to be prevailed upon, immovable; contumacious. **Inflexible a los ruegos**, unmoved by appeals.

inflexiblemente [in-flec-see'-blay-men-tay], *adv.* Inflexibly, inexorable; invariably.

inflexión [in-flec-se-on'], *f.* 1. Inflection, the act of bending or turning. 2. (*Gram.*) Inflection, variation of a noun or verb. 3. Inflection, modulation of the voice.

inflictivo, va [in-flic-tee'-vo, vah], *a.* (*Law.*) Inflictive, used as punishment.

infligir [in-fle-heer'], *va.* To inflict, to condemn.

inflorescencia [in-flo-res-then'-the-ah], *f.* Inflorescence; habit or axis of flowering.

influencia [in-floo-en'-the-ah], *f.* 1. (*Ant.*) Influence, the power of the celestial bodies upon terrestrial bodies and affairs. 2. (*Met.*) Influence, influx, influencing, credit, consequence, holding ascendent power, power of directing or satisfying. **Bajo la influencia de**, under the influence of. 3. (*Met.*) Inspiration of divine grace.

influenciar [in-floo-en-the-ar'], *va.* To influence.

influente [in-floo-en'-tay], *pa. & a.* Influencing, influential.

influenza [in-floo-en'-thah], *f.* Flu, influenza.

influir [in-floo-eer'], *va.* 1. To influence, to modify; to prevail upon, to guide. 2 To interfere; to inspire with grace. -*vn.* 1. To have influence, to carry weight. **Es hombre que influye**, he's a man of influence. 2. **Influir en**, to influence.

influjo [in-floo'-ho], *m.* Influx, influence, power, credit.

influyente [in-floo-yen'-tay], *a.* Influential, effective.

infolio [in-fo'-le-o], *m.* A book in folio form. (*Acad.*)

información [in-for-mah-the-on'], *f.* 1. Information, news (noticias), data (informática), report (informe), account, intelligence given; instruction: hint. **Información secreta**, secret information. **Información deportiva**, sports section. 2. Information, charge or accusation exhibited. 3. Judicial inquiry and process. 4. Brief, the writing given to the pleaders, containing the case. 5. Inquiry, investigation.

informado [in-for-mah-do], *a.* Informed.

informador, dora [in-for-mah-dor'], *m & f.* Informant. **Informador gráfico**, reporter. **Los informadores de la prensa**, the representatives of the media.

informal [in-for-mahl'], *a.* 1. Informal, irregular (incorrecto). 2. Applied to persons who do not keep their word, or who have no regard for the established forms of society (conducta), unreliable (poco fiable), offhand (maleducado), frivolous (frívolo).

informalidad [in-for-ma-le-dahd'], *f.* Informality, want of attention to established forms.

informalmente [in-for-mahl'-men-tay], *adv.* 1. Irregularity; badly; unconventionally. 2. Unreliable; shiftily. 3. Informally, unofficially.

informante [in-for-mahn'-tay], *pa.* Informing, instructing. - *m.* 1. Informant, informer, one who gives information. 2. Informant, one who is peculiarly charged to collect information respecting the descent and quality of a person.

informar [in-for-mar'], *va.* 1. To inform (enterar), to instruct, to supply with intelligence or knowledge, to acquaint, to report. 2. To inform, to animate, to actuate by vital powers. 3. To state a case to a counsellor or judge. -*vn.* 1. To report (acerca de). **El profesor informará de su descubrimiento**, the professor will report on his discovery. 2. *(Jur.)* To plead (abogado). -*vr.* To take cognizance, to make an inquiry, to ask for information. **Informarse de**, to find out about. **Informarse sobre algo**, to gather information about something.

informática [in-for-mah'-te-cah], *f.* Information science, computer science. **Informática en grupo**, workgroup computing, shareware, groupware.

informativo, va [in-for-mah-tee'-vo, vah], *a.* 1. Instructive, that which informs. 2. Animative, informative, having power to animate.

informatización [in-for-mah-te-tha-the-on'], *f.* Computerization.

informatizar [in-for-mah-te-thar'], *va.* To computerize.

informe [in-for'-may], *m.* 1. Information, the act of communicating intelligence or imparting knowledge; a report (declaración). 2. Brief. 3. Piece of information. **Según mis informes**, according to my information. **Dar informes sobre**, to give information about. 4. *(Jur.)* Plea, pleading.

informe [in-for'-may], *a.* 1. Informous, shapeless, formless. 2. Not performed in a regular manner. 3. **Informe de inventario (existencias)**, inventory stock status report.

infortificable [in-for-te-fe-cah'-blay], *a.* That which cannot be fortified.

infortuna [in-for-too'-nah], *f.* *(Astrol.)* Sinistrous influence of the stars.

infortunado, da [in-for-too-nah'-do, dah], *a.* Unfortunate, unlucky, unhappy.

infortunio [in-for-too'-ne-oh], *m.* Infortune, ill luck, calamity, mischance; misery; fatality.

infosura [in-fo-soo'-rah], *f.* Surfeit in cattle and other animals.

infracción [in-frac-the-on'], *f.* 1. Infraction, the act of breaking. 2. Infraction, breach, contravention, infringement, violation of a compact; misdemeanor, trespass.

infracto, ta [in-frahc'-to, tah], *a.* Steady, not easily moved.

infractor, ra [in-frac-tor', rah], *m. & f.* Violator.-*a.* Violating.

infraestructura [in-frah-es-trooc-too'-rah], *f.* 1. Substructure, foundation. 2. *(Aer.)* Ground installations. 3. (R.W.) Roadbed and installations. 4. *(Mil.)* Infrastructure. 5. Groundwork, base, underpinnings.

in fraganti [in-frah-gahn'-tee], *adv. V.* EN FLAGRANTE.

infrahumano [in-fran-oo-mah'-no], *a.* Subhuman.

infrangible [in-fran-hee'-blay], *a.* Infrangible, not to be broken; inviolable.

infranqueable [in-fran-kay-ah'-blay], *a.* Unsurmountable, inextricable.

infraoctava [in-frah-oc-tah'-vah], *f.* Six days comprehended in any church festival of eight days, not counting the first and the last.

infrarrojo, ja [in-fra-rro'-ho, hah], *a.* Infrared.

infrascripto, ta [in-fras-creep'-to, tah], or **Infrascrito, ta** [in-fras-cree'-to, tah], *a.* Underwritten, undersigned (nombres).

infravalorar [in-frah-vah-lo-rar'], *va.* To under value.

infrecuencia [in-fray-coo-en'-the-ah], *f.* Infrequency.

infrecuente [in-fray-coo-en'-tay], *a.* Infrequent.

infringir [in-frin-heer'], *va.* To infringe, to violate or break: to infract.

infrucción [in-frooc-the-on'], *f. V.* INFURCIÓN.

infructífero, ra, infrugífero, ra [in-frooc-tee'-fay-ro, rah], *a.* Unfruitful, not producing fruit: useless.

infructuosamente [in-frooc-too-o-sah-men-tay], *adv.* Unfruitfully, fruitlessly.

infructuoso, sa [in-frooc-too-oh'-so, sah], *a.* Fruitless, unproductive, unprofitable, gainless, abortive; unsuccessful.

ínfulas [een'-foo-las], *f. pl.* 1. Ornaments or marks of a sacerdotal or pontifical dignity. 2. Presumption, ostentation, conceit (vanidad).

infundadamente [in-foon-dah'-dah-men-tay], *adv.* Groundlessly, without reason or cause.

infundado, da [in-foon-dah'-do, dah], *a.* Groundless, void of reason, unfounded.

infundible [in-foon-dee'-blay], *a.* Infusible, incapable of fusion.

infundibuliforme [in-foon-de-boo-le-for'-may], *a.* Infundibuliform, funnel-shaped. *(Bot.)*

infundíbulo [in-foon-dee'-boo-lo], *m.* 1. Infundibulum, a funnel shaped prolongation from the base of the brain to the pituitary body. 2. The expanded end of the ureter, of the Fallopian tube, etc.

infundir [in-foon-deer'], *va.* 1. To infuse, to pour liquor into a vessel. 2. To infuse, to make an infusion with any ingredient. 3. To infuse, to inspire with. 4. To infuse, to pour into the mind, to instil. **Infundir ánimo a uno**, to encourage somebody. **Infundir miedo a uno**, to scare somebody.

infurtir [in-foor-teer'], *va. V.* ENFURTIR.

infusibilidad [in-foo-se-be-le-dahd'], *f.* Infusibility, resistance to melting.

infusible [in-foo-see'-blay], *a.* Infusible, incapable of being melted.

infusión [in-foo-se-on'], *f.* 1. Infusion, the act and effect of infusing. 2. *(Med.)* Infusion, the act of pouring water of any required degree of temperature on substances of a loose texture and suffering it to stand a certain time; and the liquor obtained by the above process. 3. The act of sprinkling water on the person baptized. 4. Infusion, influxion, inspiration; the act of pouring into the mind.

infuso, sa [in-foo'-so, sah], *a. & pp.* of INFUNDIR. Infused, introduced: applied solely to the grace of God in the soul.

infusorio, ria [in-foo-so'-re-o, ah], *a.* *(Zool.)* Infusorian. -*pl.* The infusoria, protozoans occurring in infusions.

ingenerable [in-hay-nay-rah'-blay], *a.* Ingenerable, not to be produced or brought into being.

ingeniador, ra [in-hay-ne-ah-dor', rah], *m. & f.* Inventor, contriver.

ingeniar [in-hay-ne-ar'], *va.* To conceive, to contrive, to strike out. -*vr.* To work in the mind, to endeavor to find out, to try by all means to obtain or do something; to manage skillfully. **Ingeniarse con algo**, to manage with something.

ingeniatura [in-hay-ne-ah-too'-rah], *f.* *(coll.)* 1. Ingenuity, subtility, acuteness; skillful management. 2. *(Amer.)* Engineering.

ingeniería [in-hay-ne-ay-ree'-ah], *f.* Engineering. **Ingeniería eléctrica**, electrical engineering. **Ingeniería mecánica**, mechanical engineering.

ingeniero [in-hay-ne-ay'-ro], *m.* 1. Engineer, one versed in engineering, the science and art of making or using machines and public works. Civil, military, mining, electrical, hydraulic, engineers. **Ingeniero agrónomo**, agronomist. **Ingeniero forestal**, forestry expert. **Ingeniero de aplicaciones**, *(Comput.)* application engineer. **Ingeniero de campo / de mantenimiento**, *(Comput.)* maintenance / field engineer. **Ingeniero de equipos**, *(Comput.)* hardware engineer. **Ingeniero de instalaciones**, *(Comput.)* site application engineer. **Ingeniero de programas**, *(Comput.)* software engineer. **Ingeniero de sistemas**, *(Comput.)* systems engineer. **Ingeniero de telecomunicaciones**, *(Comput.)* computer engineer. **Ingeniero informático**, *(Comput.)* computer engineer. 2. *(LAm. Univ.)* Graduate.

ingenio [in-hay'-ne-o], *m.* 1. Genius, talent (talento), skill, cleverness, creative ability. 2. Ingenuity (inventiva). 3. Engine, any mechanical complication in which various movements and parts concur to one effect. 4. Clever person, talented person (persona). **Aguzar el ingenio**, to sharpen one's wits. **Ingenio nuclear**, nuclear device.

ingeniosidad [in-hay-ne-o'-se-dahd'], *f.* Ingenuity (maña), ingeniousness, invention, wittiness (agudeza).

ingenioso, sa [in-hay-ne-o'-so, sah], *a.* 1. Ingenious (mañso), inventive. 2. Made with ingenuity.

ingénito, ta [in-hay'-ne-to, tah], *a.* 1. Unbegotten, not generated. 2. Innate, inborn, ingenerate.

ingente [in-hen'-tay], *a.* Very large, huge, prodigious.

ingenuamente [in-hay'-noo-ah-men-tay], *adv.* Ingenuously, fairly, simply.

ingenuidad [in-hay-noo-e-dahd'], *f.* Ingenuousness, candor, frankness, openness, open-heartedness.

ingenuo, nua [in-hay'-noo-o, ah], *a.* 1. Ingenuous, open, candid, fair, open-hearted. 2. *(Law.)* Ingenuous, freeborn, not of servile extraction.

ingerencia [in-hay-ren'-the-ah], *f.* Interference, intermeddling.

ingeridor [in-hay-re-dor'], *m.* A grafting knife.

ingeridura [in-hay-re-doo'-rah], *f.* 1. Grafting. 2. The place where a tree is grafted.

ingerir [in-hay-reer'], *va.* 1. To insert, to place in or among other things. 2. To introduce, to inclose within another. 3. To graft. **El automovilista había ingerido 3 litros de alcohol**, the motorist had drunk 3 liters of alcohol. *-vr.* To interfere officiously, to intermeddle.

ingerto, ta [in-her'-to, tah], *a. & pa. irr.* of INGERIR. Grafted, ingrafted.

ingestión [in-hes-te-on'], *f. (Med.)* Ingestion, taking in or introducing into the stomach.

ingina [in-hee'-nah], *f. V.* QUIJADA.

ingle [een'-glay], *f.* Groin, the part next to the thigh.

inglés, sa [in-glays', sah], *a.* English, belonging to or native of England. **A la inglesa**, in the English fashion.

inglés, *m.* English language.

inglesar [in-glay-sar'], 1. *va. & vr.* To anglicize, to acquire English tastes. 2. *va.* To dock a horse's tail.

inglete [in-glay'-tay], *m.* Diagonal, oblique line which divides a square into two triangles.

inglosable [in-glo-sah'-blay], *a.* That admits no gloss or comment.

ingobernable [in-go-ber-nah'-blay], *a.* Ungovernable, uncontrollable.

ingraduable [in-grah-doo-ah'-blay], *a. (coll.)* That cannot be graduated.

ingramatical [in-grah-mah-te-cahl'], *a.* Ungrammatical. **-mente**, *adv.*

ingratamente [in-grah'-tah-men-tay], *adv.* Ungratefully.

ingratitud [in-grah-te-tood'], *f.* Ingratitude.

ingrato, ta [in-grah'-to, tah], *a.* 1. Ungrateful (persona). 2. Unpleasant (sabor), disagreeable. 3. Unproductive. harsh.

ingravidez [in-grah-ve-deth'], *f.* Weightlessness.

ingrávido, da [in-grah'-ve-do, dah], *a.* Weightless.

ingrediente [in-gray-de-en'-tay], *m.* Ingredient.

ingresar [in-gray-sar'], *vn.* To enter, to come in. **Ingresar en una sociedad**, to join a club. **Ingresar en el hospital**, to be admitted to hospital. *-vr.* 1. To deposit, to place. 2. *(Mex.)* To become a member. *-va.* 1. To deposit (dinero); to receive (ganancias). **Ingresar dinero en una cuenta**, to pay money to an account.

ingreso [in-gray'-so], *m.* 1. Ingress, entrance. **Examen de ingreso**, entrance examination. 2. Commencement of a work. 3. Entry, any sum of money received which is to be charged in accounts. **Ingresos anuales**, annual income. **Ingresos brutos**, gross receipts. 4. Surplice fees.

inguinal [in-gee-nahl'], *a. (Med.) V.* INGUINARIO.

inguinario, ria [in-gee-nah'-re-o, ah], *a.* Inguinal, belonging to the groin.

ingurgitación [in-goor-he-tah-the-on'], *f.* 1. Ingurgitation. 2. Introduction of fluids by a tube or syringe.

inhábil [in-ah'-beel], *a.* 1. Unable, incapable, unqualified; disqualified, unfit (no apto). 2. Unskillful (torpe), clumsy, awkward.

inhabilidad [in-ah-be-le-dahd'], *f.* Inability, unskillfullness, incapacity, unfitness.

inhabilitación [in-ah-be-le-tah-the-on'], *f.* 1. Act of disabling or disqualifying. 2. Disqualification; disability.

inhabilitar [in-ah-be-le-tar'], *va.* 1. To disqualify, to make unfit, to disable by some natural or legal impediment. 2. To disqualify, to deprive of a right or claim.*-vr.* To lose a right or claim.

inhábilmente [in-ah'-beel-men-tay], *adv.* Unskillfully.

inhabitable [in-ah-be-tah'-blay], *a.* Uninhabitable.

inhabitado, da [in-ah-be-tah'-do, dah], *a.* Uninhabited.

inhabituado, da [in-ah-be-too-ah'-do, dah], *a.* Unhabituated, unaccustomed.

inhalación [in-ah-lah-the-on'], *f. (Med.)* Inhalation.

inhalador [in-ah-lah-dor'], *m. (Med.)* Inhaler.

inhalar [in-ah-lar'], *va.* To inhale, to absorb.

inhartable [in-ar-tah'-blay], *a.* Insatiable.

inherencia [in-ay-ren'-the-ah], *f.* Inherence or inherency.

inherente [in-ay-ren'-tay], *a.* Inherent.

inhestar [in-es-tar'], *va. V.* ENHESTAR.

inhibición [in-e-be-the-on'], *f.* Inhibition, prohibition. **Orden de inhibición**, writ to forbid a judge from further proceeding in the cause before him.

inhibir [in-e-beer'], *va.* 1. To inhibit, to prohibit. 2. *(Law.)* To prohibit an infector court from proceeding further in a cause depending before them.

inhibitorio, ria [in-e-be-to'-re-o, ah], *a.* Prohibitory.

inhiesto, ta [in-e-ays'-to, tah], *a.* Entangled, perplexed. *V.* ENHIESTO.

inhonestamente [in-o-nes-tah-men'-tay], *adv.* Dishonestly.

inhonestidad [in-o-nes-te-dahd'], *f.* Dishonesty; indecency.

inhonesto, ta [in-o-nays'-to, tah], *a.* 1. Dishonest. 2. Indecent, immodest.

inhonorar [in-o-no-rar'], *va. V.* DESHONRAR.

inhospedable, inhospitable [in-os-pay-dah'-blay], *a.* Inhospitable, repulsive.

inhospital [in-os-pe-tahl']. *a. V.* INHOSPITALARIO.

inhospitalario, ria [in-os-pe-tah-lah'-re-o, ah], *a.* Unhospitable, reluctant to entertain guests.

inhospitalidad [in-os-pe-tah-le-dahd'], *f.* Inhospitality, inhospitableness, want of courtesy to strangers.

inhumanación [in-oo-mah-nah-the-on'], *f.* Burial, inhumation.

inhumanamente [in-oo-ma-nah-men'-tay], *adv.* Inhumanly.

inhumanidad [in-oo-mah-ne-dahd'], *f.* Inhumanity, cruelty.

inhumano, na [in-oo-mah'-no, nah], *a.* Inhuman, savage, cruel. *(Cono Sur)* dirty.

inhumar [in-oo-mar'], *va.* To bury, to inter.

iniciación [e-ne-the-ah-the-on'], *f.* Initiation, introduction, beginning.

inicial [e-ne-the-ahl'], *a.* Initial, placed at the beginning. **Letras iniciales or las iniciales**, initials.

iniciar [e-ne-the-ar'], *va.* To initiate, to instruct in the rudiments of an art, to put into a new society. *-vr.* To be initiated, to receive the first orders. **Iniciar sesión, conectarse**, *(Comput.)* to sign-in; to log-in.

iniciativo, va [e-ne-the-ah-tee'-vo, vah], *a.* Initiating or producing initiation, initiatory.-*f.* Initiative, the right of proposing laws, etc., lead (liderazgo), plans (propósitos). **Tomar la iniciativa**, to be first in doing or saying something.

inicio [e-ne'-the-o], *m.* Start, beginning. **Inicio del juego**, book opening.

inicuamente [in-e-coo-ah-men'-tay], *adv.* Iniquitously.

inicuo, cua [in-ee'-coo-o, ah], *a.* Iniquitous, wicked, unjust.

inigualable [in-ee-goo-ah-lah'-blay], *a.* Unsurpassable.

inimaginable [in-e-mah-he-nah'-blay], *a.* Unimaginable, inconceivable.

inimitable [in-e-me-tah'-blay], *a.* Inimitable, above imitation; not to be copied.

inimitablemente [in-e-me-tah'-blay-men-tay], *adv.* Inimitably.

ininteligible [in-in-tay-le-hee'-blay], *a.* Unintelligible, that cannot be understood.

ininterrumpidamente [in-in-tayr-room-pee'-dah-men-tay], *adv.* Uninterruptedly; continuously.

ininterrumpido [in-in-tayr-room-pee'-do], *a.* Uninterrupted; continuous, without a break.

iniquidad [in-e-ke-dahd'], *f.* Iniquity, injustice, unrighteousness.

iniquísimo, ma [en-e-kee'-se-mo, mah], *a.* Superlative of INICUO.

injeridura [in-hay-re-doo'-rah], *f. V.* INGERIDURA.

injerir [in-hay-reer'], *va. V.* INGERIR.

injertar [in-her-tar'], *va.* To ingraft a tree, to graft, to inoculate.

injerto [in-her'-to], *m.* 1. Grafting, the action of transplanting a section of one plant to another. 2. Graft, the part transplanted. **Injerto de órganos**, *(Med.)* medical transplant.

injuria [in-hoo'-re-ah], *f.* 1. Injury, offence, wrong, insult (insulto), outrage. 2. Injury, annoyance, hardship, contumely, mischief. 3. Injury, contumelious language, reproachful appellation. **Llenar a uno de injurias**, to heap abuse on somebody.

injuriado, da [in-hoo-re-ah'-do, dah], *a. & pp.* of INJURIAR. Injured, wronged.

injuriador, ra [in-hoo-re-ah-dor', rah], *m. & f.* Aggressor, injurer, wrongdoer.

injuriante [in-hoo-re-ahn'-tay], *pa.* Injuring, injurer.

injuriar [in-hoo-re-ar'], *va.* To injure, to wrong, to annoy, to harm or hurt unjustly (dañar), to offend.

injuriosamente [in-hoo-re-o'-sah-men-tay], *adv.* Injuriously, offensively, hurtfully.

injurioso, sa [in-hoo-re-oh'-so, sah], *a.* Injurious, contumelious, reproachful, hurtful, opprobrious, offensive, insulting (ofensivo), harmful (dañoso).

injustamente [in-hoos-tah-men'-tay], *adv.* Unjustly.

injusticia [in-hoos-tee'-the-ah], *f.* Injustice, iniquity, wrong. **Una gran injusticia**, a terrible injustice.

injustificable [in-hoos-te-fe-cah'-blay], *a.* Unjustifiable.

injustificadamente [in-hoos-te-fe-cah'-dah-men-tay], *adv.* Unjustifiably.

injustificado [in-hoos-te-fe-cah'-do], *a.* Unjustified, unwarranted.

injusto, ta [in-hoos'-to, tah], *a.* Unjust, wrongful, unfair. **Ser injusto con uno**, to be unjust to somebody.

inlegible [in-lay-hee'-blay], *a.* Illegible.

inllevable [in-lya-vah'-blay], *a.* Insupportable.

inmaculadamente [in-mah-coo-lah'-dah-men-tay], *adv.* Immaculately.

inmaculado, da [in-mah-coo-lah'-do, dah], *a.* Immaculate, holy, pure, spotless.

inmadurez [in-mah-doo-reth'], *f.* Immaturity.

inmaduro, ra [in-mah-doo'-ro, rah], *a.* Immature (individuo), unripe, unripened (fruta).

inmaleable [in-mah-lay-ah'-blay], *a.* Unmalleable.

inmanejable [in-mah-nay-hah'-blay], *a.* Unmanageable; intractable.

inmanente [in-mah-nan'-tay], *a.* Immanent, inherent.

inmarcesible [in-mar-thay-see'-blay], *a.* Unfading, unwithering, imperishable.

inmaterial [in-mah-tay-re-ahl'], *a.* Immaterial, incorporeal.

inmaterialidad [in-mah-tay-re-ah-le-dahd'], *f.* Immateriality.

inmaturo, ra [in-mah-too'-ro, rah], *a.* Immature.

inmediación [in-may-de-ah-the-on'], *f.* Contiguity, contact.

inmediatamente [in-may-de-ah'-tah-men-tay], *adv.* Immediately, forthwith, at once.

inmediatez [in-may-de-ah-teth'], *f.* Immediacy.

inmediato, ta [in-may-de-ah'-to, tah], *a.* Contiguous, meeting so as to touch, close, hard by, next. **De inmediato**, immediately, at once. **Inmediato a**, close to, next to.

inmedicable [in-may-de-cah'-blay], *a.* Incurable.

inmejorable [in-may-ho-rah'-blay], *a.* Unimprovable, not capable of improvement, unsurpassable. **Inmejorables recomendaciones**, excellent references. *adv.* **-mente.**

inmemorable [in-may-mo-rah'-blay], *a.* Immemorable.

inmemorablemente [in-may-mo-rah'-blay-men-tay], *adv.* Immemorably.

inmemorial [in-may-mo-re-ahl'], *a.* Immemorial, past time, out of memory; so ancient that the beginning cannot be traced.

inmensamente [in-men-sah-men'-tay], *adv.* Immensely, infinitely, hugely.

inmensidad [in-men-se-dahd'], *f.* Immensity, unbounded greatness.

inmenso, sa [in-men'-so, sah], *a.* Immense, unlimited, unbounded, infinite. **Sentir una tristeza inmensa**, to be terribly sad.

inmensurable [in-men-soo-rah'-blay], *a.* Immensurable, measureless; not to be counted.

inmergir [in-mer-heer'], *va.* To submerge, to souse (implying immediate withdrawal of the body acted on).

inméritamente [in-may'-re-tah-men-tay], *adv.* Immeritedly.

inmeritorio, ria [in-may-re-to'-re-o, ah], *a.* Immeritorious, underserving.

inmersión [in-mer-se-on'], *f.* 1. Immersion, dive (buzo). 2. The entry of a planet into the shadow of another during an eclipse.

inmigración [in-me-grah-the-on'], *f.* Immigration.

inmigrado, da [in-me-grah'-do], *m & f.* Immigrant.

inmigrante [in-me-grahn'-tay], *a. m & f.* Immigrant.

inmigrar [in-me-grar'], *vn.* To immigrate.

inminencia [in-me-nayn'-the-ah], *f.* Imminence.

inminente [in-me-nen'-tay], *a.* Imminent, impending, at hand.

inmiscible [in-mis-thee'-blay], *a.* Immiscible, incapable of being mixed.

inmiscuir [in-mis-coo-eer'], *va.* To mix.-*vr.* To interfere in, to intermeddle.

inmobiliaria [in-mo-be-le-ah'-re-ah], *f.* Construction company, builder; property company.

inmoble [in-mo'-blay], *a.* 1. Unmovable, immovable (inmóvil), motionless. 2. Unmovable, immovable, unshaken, unaffected, constant.

inmoderación [in-mo-day-rah-the-on'], *f.* Immoderation, immoderateness; *(Cono Sur)* excess.

inmoderadamente [in-mo-day-rah-dah-men'-tay], *adv.* Immoderately.

inmoderado, da [in-mo-day-rah'-do, dah], *a.* Immoderate, excessive.

inmodestamente [in-mo-des-tah-men-tay], *adv.* Immodestly.

inmodestia [in-mo-days'-te-ah], *f.* Immodesty, indecency, indelicacy.

inmodesto, ta [in-mo-days'-to, tah], *a.* Immodest.

inmodificable [in-mo-de-fe-cah'-blay], *a.* Unmodifiable.

inmolación [in-mo-lah-the-on'], *f.* Immolation, the act of sacrificing, a sacrifice offered.

inmolador, ra [in-mo-lah-dor', rah], *m. & f.* Immolator.

inmolar [in-mo-lar'], *va.* To immolate, to sacrifice.

inmoral [in-mo-rahl'], *a.* Immoral.

inmoralidad [in-mo-rah-le-dahd'], *f.* Immorality; unethical nature.

inmorigerado, da [in-mo-re-hay-rah'-do, dah], *a.* Of bad habits: not self-controlled.

inmortal [in-mor-tahl'], *a.* 1. Immortal, exempt from death. 2. Immortal, endless.

inmortalidad [in-mor-tah-le-dahd'], *f.* Immortality, exemption from death and oblivion.

inmortalizar [in-mor-tah-le-thar'], *va.* 1. To immortalize, to make immortal. 2. To exempt from oblivion, to perpetuate.

inmortalmente [in-mor-tal-men'-tay], *adv.* Immortally.

inmortificación [in-mor-te-fe-cah-the-on'], *f.* Immortification, want of subjection of the passions, licentiousness.

inmortificado, da [in-mor-te-fe-cah'-do, dah], *a.* Unmortified, free from mortification.

inmotivado, da [in-mo-te-vah'-do, dah], *a.* Without reason or cause.

inmoto, ta [in-mo'-to, tah], *a.* Unmoved.

inmovible, inmóvil [in-mo-vee'-blay, in-mo'-veel], *a.* Immovable. **Quedar inmóvil**, to remain motionless. *V.* INMOBLE.

inmovilidad [in-mo-vele-dahd'], *f.* 1. Immobility, unmovableness, resistance to motion. 2. Immovability, incapacity of being removed. 3. Immovableness, the state or quality of being immovable; firmness, constancy.

inmovilizar [in-mo-ve-le-thar'], *vr.* To immobilize; to stop, to paralyze, to bring to a standstill; to tie up (capital).

inmudable [in-moo-dah'-blay], *a.* Inmutable. *V.* INMUTABLE.

inmueble [in-moo-ay'-blay], *a.* Immovables or immovable estate: applied to lands. **Bienes inmuebles**, real estate.

inmundicia [in-moon-dee'-the-ah], *f.* 1. Uncleanliness, nastiness, dirtiness, filthiness. 2. Uncleaness, impurity.

inmundo, da [in-moon'-do, dah], *a.* 1. Unclean, filthy, dirty. 2. Obscene, unchaste.

inmune [in-moo'-nay], *a.* 1. Free, exempt. 2. Enjoying immunity.

inmunidad [in-moo-ne-dahd'], *f.* Immunity, privilege, exception, franchise, freedom; liberty. **Inmunidad parlamentaria**, parliamentary immunity.

inmunizar [in-moo-ne-thar'], *va.* To immunize, to render immune.

inmunología [in-moo-no-lo-hee'-ah], *f.* Immunology.

inmutabilidad [in-moo-tah-be-le-dahd'], *f.* Immutability, immutableness.

inmutable [in-moo-tah'-blay], *a.* Immutable, invariable, unalterable.

inmutación [in-moo-tah-the-on'], *f.* Change, alteration.

inmutar [in-moo-tar'], *va.* To change, to alter. *-vr.* To change one's appearance, turn pale. **Se inmutó**, his face fell. **Siguió sin inmutarse**, he carried on unperturbed.

inmutativo, va [in-moo-tah-tee'-vo, vah], *a.* That which changes or causes alterations.

innatismo [in-nah-tees'-mo], *m.* Philosophical system of those who claim ideas are innate.

innato, ta [in-nah'-to, tah], *a.* Innate, inborn, natural.

innatural [in-nah-too-rahl'], *a.* Unnatural.

innavegable [in-nah-bay-gah'-blay], *a.* 1. Innavigable, not to be passed by sailing. 2. Unfit for sea, unseaworthy (barcos).

innecesariamente [in-nay-thay-sah-re-ah-men-tay], *adv.* Unnecessarily.

innecesario, ria [in-nay-thay-sah'-re-o, ah], *a.* Unnecessary.

innegable [in-nay-gah'-blay], *a.* Incontestable, incontrovertible, undeniable.

innervación [in-ner-vah-the-on'], *f.* Innervation, the nervous control of an organ.

innoble [i-no'-blay], *a.* Ignoble, mean of birth; not of noble descent.

innocivo, va [in-no-thee'-vo, vah], *a.* Innoxious.

innocuo, ua [in-no-coo-o, ah], *a.* Innocuous, harmless.

innominado, da [in-no-me-nah'-do, dah], *a.* Nameless. **Hueso innominado**, innominate bone.

innovación [in-no-vah-the-on'], *f.* Innovation (acto), innovation (novedad), novelty.

innovador, ra [in-no-vah-dor', rah], *m. & f.* Innovator.

innovar [in-no-var'], *va.* 1. To innovate, to bring in something not known before. 2. To pursue a cause while an appeal or decree of inhibition is pending.

innumerabilidad [in-noo-may-rah-be-le-dahd'], *f.* Innumerability, innumerableness.

innumerable [in-noo-may-rah'-blay], *a.* Innumerable, numberless, countless.

innumerablemente [in-noo-may-rah-blay-men-tay], *adv.* Innumerably.

innutrición [in-noo-tre-the-on',], *f.* Innutrition, failure of nourishment.

innutritivo, va [in-noo-tre-tee'-vo, vah], *a.* Innutritious, not nourishing.

inobediencia [in-o-bay-de-en'-the-ah], *f.* Disobedience.

inobediente [in-obay-de-en'-tay], *a.* 1. Disobedient. 2. Inflexible (cosas inanimadas).

inobservable [in-ob-ser-vah'-blay], *a.* Unobservable, inobservable.

inobservado [in-ob-ser-vah-do], *a.* Unobserved.

inobservancia [in-ob-ser-vahn'-the-ah], *f.* Inadvertency, neglect, inobservance.

inobservante [in-ob-ser-vahn'-tay], *f.* Inobservant.

inocencia [e-no-then'-the-ah], *f.* 1. Innocence, untainted integrity. 2. Innocence, harmlessness, guiltelessness, innocuousness. 5. Innocence, freedom from guilt imputed. 4. Innocence, sincerity, simplicity.

inocentada [e-no-then-tah'-dah], *f. (coll.)* 1. A simple or silly speech or action. 2. Practical joke (trastada).

inocente [e-no-then'-tay], *a.* 1. Innocent (sin culpa), pure, candid, harmless (sin malicia), lamb-like, just. 2. Innocent, free from particular guilt. 3. Innocent, simple (ingenuo), easily imposed upon.

inocentemente [e-no-then-tah-dah-men-tay], *adv.* Innocently, guiltlessly, harmlessly, innocuously, innoxiously.

inocentón, na [e-no-then-tone', nah], *a. aug.* Very simple and credulous.

inoculación [e-no-coo-lah-the-on'], *f.* 1. Inoculation. 2. Vaccination.

inoculador [e-no-coo-lah-dor'], *m.* Inoculator.

inocular [e-no-coo-lar'], *va.* 1. To inoculate, to propagate by incisions or insertions. 2. To contaminate, to pervert by bad examples or doctrines.

inodoro, ra [in-o-do'-ro, rah], *a.* Odorless, *-m.* 1. Deodorizer. 2. Toilet, water-closet.

inofensivo, va [in-o-fen-see'-vo, vah], *a.* Inoffensive.

inoficioso, sa [in-o-fe-the-oh'-so, sah], *a. (Law.)* Done at an improper time, and not in the manner prescribed by the law; irregular; inofficious.

inojeta [in-o-hay'-tah], *f.* Top of a boot.

inolvidable [in-ol-ve-dah'-blay], *a.* Unforgettable, not to be forgotten.

inoperable [in-o-pay-rah'-blay], *a. (Med.) (CAm. Cono Sur, Mex.)* Inoperable, not admitting on oration.

inopia [in-o'-pe-ah], *f.* Indigence, poverty, penury. **Estar en la inopia**, to be in the dark, to have no idea.

inopinable [in-o-pe-nah'-blay], *a.* 1. Unthought of, not to be foreseen or expected. 2. Indisputable, incontrovertible.

inopinadamente [in-o-pe-nah-dah-men'-tay], *adv.* Unexpectedly.

inopinado, da [in-o-pe-nah'-do, dah], *a.* Inopinate, unexpected, unforeseen.

inoportunamente [in-o-por-too-nah-men-tay], *adv.* Inopportunely.

inoportuno, na [in-o-por-too'-no, nah], *a.* 1. Inopportune (intempestivo), untimely. 2. Inconvenient (molesto); inexpedient (imprudente); inappropriate (no apto).

inordenadamente [in-or-day-nah-dah-men-tay], *adv.* Inordinately.

inordenado, da [in-or-day-nah'-do, dah], *a.* Inordinate, irregular, disorderly.

inorgánico, ca [in-or-gah'-ne-co, cah], *a. (Med.)* Inorganic.

inoxidable [in-oc-se-dah'-blay], *a.* 1. Stainless. 2. Rustproof. **Acero inoxidable**, stainless steel.

in promptu [inpromp'-too], *adv.* Off hand, impromptu, extempore.

inquebrantable [in-kay-bran-tah'-blay], *a.* 1. Inviolable, irrevocable, unbreakable. 2. Unswerving. **Fe inquebrantable**, unswerving faith.

inquietador, ra [in-ke-ay-tah-dor', rah], *m. & f.* Disturber.

inquietamente [in-ke-ay-tah-men'-tay], *adv.* Disquietly, uneasily, anxiously (con ansiedad), restlessly (agitadamente).

inquietante [in-ke-ay-tahn'-tay], *a.* Worrying, disturbing.

inquietar [in-ke-ay-tar'], *va.* 1. To disquiet, to trouble, to disturb. 2. To molest, to vex, to pain. 3. To stir up or excite disturbances. *-vr.* To become uneasy or restless.

inquieto, ta [in-ke-ay'-to, tah], *a.* 1. Restless, turbulent. 2. Noisy, troublesome, clamorous. 3. Anxious (preocupado), solicitous, uneasy, fidgety, disquiet. **Estar inquieto por**, to be anxious about.

inquietud [in-ke-ay-tood'], *f.* Inquietude, restlessness, uneasiness, vexation, anxiety.

inquilinato [in-ke-le-nah'-to], *m.* 1. *(Law.)* Right acquired by the tenant of a house. 2. Rent (alquiler). 3. *(Cono Sur)* Tenement house (casa pobre).

inquilino, na [in-ke-lee'-no, nah], *m. & f.* 1. Tenant (arrendatario), the inhabitant of a house that is hired from another. 2. One that has temporary possession and use of the property of another; an innate, a lodger. 3. *(Cono Sur. Agr.)* Tenant farmer.

inquina [in-kee'-nah], *f. (coll.)* Aversion, hatred, dislike.

inquiridor, ra [in-ke-re-dor', rah], *m. & I.* Inquirer, inquisitor.

inquirir [in-kee-reer'], *va.* 1. To inquire, to look for carefully or anxiously, to look after. 2. To ascertain by research and inquiry.

inquisición [in-ke-se-the-on'], *f.* 1. Inquisition, examination, judicial inquiry. 2. Inquisition, a court for the detection of heresy. 3. Building where the Inquisition held its sittings.

inquisidor, ra [in-ke-se-dor', rah], *m. & f.* 1. Inquirer, examiner. 2. Inquisitor, a member of the tribunal of Inquisition.

inquisitivo, va [in-ke-se-tee'-vo, vah], *a.* Inquisitive, curious; busy in search.

inquisitorial [in-ke-se-to-re-ahl'], *a.* Inquisitorial, inquisitorious.

insaciabilidad [in-sah-the-ah-be'-le-dahd'], *f.* Insatiableness, greediness.

insaciable [in-sah-the-ah'-blay], *a.* Insatiable, greedy beyond measure, craving.

insaciablemente [in-sah-the-ah'-blay-men-tay], *adv.* Insatiably.

insaculación [in-sah-coo-lah-the-on'], *f. (Law.)* Act of casting lots or balloting for names.

insaculador [in-sah-coo-lah-dor'], *m. (Law.)* Balloter.

insacular [in-sah-coo-lar'], *va.* To ballot, to vote by ballot.

insalivación [in-sah-le-vah-the-on'], *f.* Insalivation, the mixing of saliva with food.

insalivar [in-sah-le-vahr'], *f.* To mix with saliva in the mouth.

insalubre [in-sah-loo'-bray], *a.* Insalubrious, unhealthy.

insalubridad [in-sah-loo-bre-dahd'], *f.* Insalubrity, unhealthfulness.

insalvable [in-sahl-vah'-blay], *a.* Insuperable (obstáculo).

insanable [in-sah-nah'-blay], *a.* Incurable, irremediable.

insania [in-sah'-ne-ah], *f.* Insanity. *V.* LOCURA.

insano, na [in-sah'-no, nah], *a.* 1. Insane (loco), mad. 2. Unhealthy (malsano).

insatisfacción [in-sah-tees-fac-the-on'], *f.* Dissatisfaction.

insatisfactorio [in-sah-tees-fac-to'-re-o], *a.* Unsatisfactory.

insatisfecho [in-sah-tees-fay'-cho], *a.* Unsatisfied.

inscribir [ins-cre-beer'], *va.* 1. To inscribe (grabar), to mark with writing. 2. *(Geom.)* To inscribe, to draw a figure within another. 3. To enrol (matricular), to register (registrar).

inscripción [ins-crip-the-on'], *f.* 1. Inscription (acto); enrolment, registering. *-vr.* To enrol, to register.

inscrito, ta [ins-cree'-to, tah], *pp. irr.* of INSCRIBIR.

inscrutable [ins-croo-tah'-blay], *a. V.* INESCRUTABLE.

insculpir [ins-cool-peer'], *va.* To insculp, to engrave, to cut.

insecable [in-say-cah'-blay], *a. (Prov.)* Not to be dried, that cannot be dried.

insecticida [in-sec-te-thee'-dah], *m.* Insecticide, insect-killer.

insectil [in-sec-teel'], *a.* Insectile.

insectívoro [in-sec-tee'-vo-ro], *a. (Nat. Hist.)* Insectivorous.

insecto [in-sec'-to], *m.* Insect.

insectólogo, ga [in-sec-to'-lo-go, gah]. *m. & f.* Entomologist.

insectología [in-sec-to-lo-he'-ah], *f.* Entomology.

inseguridad [in-say-goo-re-dahd'], *f.* Insecurity, uncertainty, unsafeness. **Inseguridad ciudadana**, lack of safety in the streets.

inseguro, ra [in-say-goo'-ro, rah], *a.* Insecure, uncertain, unsafe (peligroso); unsteady (paso).

insembrado, da [in-sem-brah'-do, dah], *a.* Unsowed or unsown.

inseminación [in-say-me-nah-the-on'], *f.* Insemination. **Inseminación artificial**, artificial insemination.

inseminar [in-say-me-nar'], *va.* To inseminate.

insenescencia [in-say-nes-then'-the-ah], *f.* Quality of not becoming old.

insensatamente [in-sen-sah-tah-men'-tay], *adv.* Madly, stupidly.

insensatez [in-sen-sah-teth'], *f.* Insensateness, stupidity, folly.

insensato, ta [in-sen-sah'-to, tah], *a.* Insensate, stupid, mad, fatuous, out of one's wits.

insensibilidad [in-sen-se-be-le-dahd'], *f.* 1. Insensibility, inability to perceive, dulness of mind. 2. Insensibility, want of feeling, hard-heartedness.

insensible [in-sen-see'-blay], *a.* 1. Insensitive (persona), void of feeling, either mental or corporeal; callous, stupid. 2. Imperceptible (imperceptible), not discoverable by the senses. 3. Hard, stupid, unfeeling, obdurate, cold, cold-hearted, loveless.

insensiblemente [in-sen-se-blay-men-tay], *adv.* Insensitively; unfeelingly.

inseparabilidad [in-say-pa-rah-be-le-dahd'], *f.* Inseparableness, inseparability.

inseparable [in-say-pa-rah'-blay], *a.* Inseparable, not easily separated or disjoined.

inseparablemente [in-say-pah-rah'-blay-men-tay], *adv.* Inseparably.

insepulto, to [in-say-pool'-to, tah], *a.* Unburied, uninterred, graveless.

inserción [in-ser-the-on], *f.* Insertion.

insertar [in-ser-tar'], *va.* To insert, to introduce.

inserto, ta [in-ser'-to, ta], *a. & pp. irr.* of INSERTAR. Inserted. *V.* INGERTO.

inservible [in-ser-vee'-blay], *a.* Unserviceable, useless.

insidia [in-see'-de-ah], *f.* Ambush, snare (trampa), contrivance, maliciousness (cualidad).

insidiador, ra [in-se-de-a-dor', rah], *m. & f.* Plotter, conspirator, intriguer.

insidiar [in-se-de-ar'], *va.* To plot, to waylay.

insidiosamente [in-se-de-oh'-sah-men-tay], *adv.* Insidiously, guilefully.

insidioso, sa [in-se-de-oh'-so, sah], *a.* Insidious, sly, circumventive, guileful.

insigne [in-seeg'-nay], *a.* Notable, remarkable, flagrant, noted.

insignemente [in-seeg'-nay-men-tay], *adv.* Notably, signally, conspicuously.

insignia [in-seeg'-ne-ah], *f.* A distinctive mark of honor, a badge (señal). **Insignias**, insignia, distinguishing marks of office or honor.

insignificación [in-sig-ne-fe-cah-the-on'], *f.* Insignificance.

insignificancia [in-sig-ne-fe-cahn'-the-ah], *f,* Insignificance.

insignificante [in-sig-ne-fe-cahn'-tay], *a.* Insignificant, unimportant.

insignificativo, va [in-sig-ne-fe-cah-tee'-vo, vah], *a.* Insignificant; insignificativo.

insincero [in-seen-thay'-ro], *a.* Insincere.

insinuación [in-se-noo-ah-the-on'], *f.* 1. Insinuation, innuendo. 2. Insinuation, power of pleasing, or stealing upon the affections. 3. *(Law.)* Exhibition of a public instrument before a judge. 4. *(Met.)* Kind of exordium.

insinuador [in-se-noo-ah-dor'], *a.* Insinuating.

insinuante [in-se-noo-ahn'-tay], *pa. & a.* Insinuant, insinuating (que insinúa), having the power to gain favor.

insinuar [in-se-noo-ar'], *va.* 1. To insinuate, to hint. 2. To touch slightly on a subject. *-vr.* 1. To insinuate, to ingratiate, to wheedle, to gain on the affections by gentle degrees; to gain another's favor by artful means. 2. To insinuate, to get in, to creep in, to steal into imperceptibly: speaking of the insinuation of a virtue or vice into the mind. **Insinuarse con uno**, to ingratiate oneself. **Insinuarse en**, to worm one's way into.

insípidamente [in-see'-pe-dah-men-tay], *adv.* Insipidly, without taste; without spirit.

insipidez [in-se-pe-deth'], *f.* Insipidity, insipidness, tasteless.

insípido, da [in-see'-pe-do, dah], *a.* Insipid, tasteless, unpleasant; spiritless, flat.

insipiencia [in-se-pe-en'-the-ah], *f.* Ignorance, want of knowledge or taste.

insipiente [in-se-pe-en'-tay], *a.* Ignorant, tasteless, uninformed.

insistencia [in-sis-ten'-the-ah], *f.* Persistence, steadiness, constancy, obstinacy.

insistente [in-sis-ten'-tay], *a.* Insistent; persistent.

insistentemente [in-sis-ten'-tay-men-tay], *adv.* Insistently.

insistir [in-sis-teer'], *vn.* 1. To insist, to persist. 2. To insist, to dwell upon in discourse. **Insistir en algo**, to insist on something. **Insistir en hacer algo**, to insist on doing something.

ínsito, ta [een'-se-to, tah], *a.* Ingrafted, natural.

insociabilidad [in-so-the-ah-be-le-dahd'], *f.* Unsociability, unsociableness.

insociable [in-so-the-ah'-blay], *a.* Unsociable, averse to conversation and society.

insocial [in-so-the-ahl'], *a. V.* INSOCIABLE.

insolación [in-so-lah-the-on'], *f.* 1. Sunshine, sunlight. 2. *(Med.)* Sun-stroke, heat-stroke. **Horas de insolación**, hours of sunshine.

insolar [in-so-lar'], *va.* To insolate, to dry in the sun; to expose to the action of the sun. *-vr.* To fall ill by the heat of the sun.

insoldable [in-sol-dah'-blay], *a.* 1. That cannot be soldered. 2. Irreparable, irretrievable.

insolencia [in-so-len'-the-ah], *f.* 1. Insolence (descaro), impudence, effrontery, malapertness, haughtiness. 2. Effrontery, barefacedness. 3. Insulting.

insolentar [in-so-len-tar'], *va.* To make bold. *-vr.* To become insolent.

insolente [in-so-len'-tay], *a.* 1. Insolent (descarado), impudent, froward, haughty (altivo). 2. Performing uncommon things. 3. Unusual, uncommon; unaccustomed: it is also used as a substantive, for a bare-faced or shameless man.

insolentemente [in-so-len'-tay-men-tay], *adv.* Insolently, haughtily, insultingly.

insolidario [in-so-le-dah'-re-o], *a.* Unsupportive, uncooperative.

in sólidum [in so'-le-doom], *adv. (Law.)* Jointly, so as to be answerable for the whole.

insólito, ta [in-so'-le-to, tah], *a.* Unusual, unaccustomed, insolite.

insolubilidad [in-so-loo-be-le-dahd'], *f.* Insolubility.

insoluble [in-so-loo'-blay], *a.* 1. Indissoluble, insoluble. 2. Insolvable, that cannot be paid.

insolutundación [in-so-loo-toon-dah-the-on'], *f. (Law.)* Assignment of goods or effects in payment of a debt.

insolvencia [in-sol-ven'-the-ah], *f.* Insolvency.

insolvente [in-sol-ven'-tay], *a.* Insolvent.

insomne [in-some'-nay], *a.* Insomnious, sleepless.

insomnio [in-some'-ne-o], *m.* Insomnia, sleeplessness.

insondable [in-son-dah'-blay], *a.* 1. Unfathomable, not to be sounded, fathomless. 2. Inscrutable, unsearchable. 3. Abysmal.

insonorización [in-so-no-re-thah-the-on'], *f.* Sound-proofing.

insonorizado [in-so-no-re-thah'-do], *a.* Sound-proof.

insonorizar [in-so-no-re-thar'], *va.* To sound-proof.

insonoro, ra [in-so-no'-ro, rah], *a.* Insonorous, not clear, soundless.

insoportable [in-so-por-tah'-blay], *a.* Insupportable, intolerable.

insoportablemente [in-so-por-tah'-blay-men-tay], *adv.* Insupportably.

insospechable [in-sos-pay-chah'-blay], *a.* Beyond suspicion.

insospechado [in-sos-pay-chah'-do], *a.* Unsuspected.

insostenible [in-sos-tay-nee'-blay], *a. (coll.)* Indefensible.

inspección [ins-pec-the-on'], *f.* 1. Inspection, survey, superintendence: control. 2. The house or office of an inspector. 3. Union of five consistorial churches forming an ecclesiastical district in the French organization of the Protestant worship.

inspeccionar [ins-pec-the-o-nar'], *va.* To inspect (examinar), to examine, to oversee, to supervise (supervisar).

inspector, ra [ins-pec-tor', rah], *m. & f.* Inspector, a careful examiner; superintendent, controller, *(Cono Sur)* Conductor (autobus).

inspiración [ins-pe-rah-the-on'], *f.* 1. Inspiration, the act of drawing in the breath. 2. *(Met.)* Inspiration, infusion of ideas into the mind by a superior power.

inspirador, ra [ins-pe-rah-dor', rah], *m. & f.* Inspirer, one who inspires.

inspirante [ins-pe-rahn'-tay], *pa.* Inspiring.

inspirar [ins-pe-rar'], *va.* 1. To inspire, to draw air into the lungs, to inhale. 2. To infuse with fortitude, courage, etc. 3. To inspire, to infuse into the mind, to instill, to induce. 4. To inspire, to animate by supernatural infusion. *-vn. (Poet.)* To blow. *-vr.* To be inspired by.

inspirativo, va [ins-pe-rah-tee'-vo, vah], *a.* Inspiratory, producing inspiration.

instabilidad [ins-tah-be-le-dahd'], *f. V.* INESTABILIDAD.

instable [ins-tah'-blay], *a.* Unstable, inconstant, changing, mutable, fickle.

instalación [ins-tah-lah-the-on'], *f.* Installation (acto, equipo), installment; induction. **Instalaciones deportivas**, sports facilities.

instalador [ins-tah-lah-dor'], *m.* Installer; fitter.

instalar [ins-tah-lar'], *va. (Law.)* 1. To install, to give possession of a rank or employment. 2. To induct, to put into actual possession of a benefice. 3. To install; to set up.

instancia [ins-tahn'-the-ah], *f.* 1. Instance or instancy, importunity, persistency, urgency. 2. Instance, prosecution or process of a suit. 3. Instance, pressing argument. **De primera instancia**, instantly, on the first impulse; first, in the first place. **A instancia de**, at the request of. *V.* JUEZ and JUZGADO.

instantánea [ins-tan-tah'-nay-ah], *f.* Snapshot.

instantáneamente [ins-tan-tah'-nay-ah-men-tay], *adv.* Instantly, instantaneously.

instantáneo, nea [ins-tan-tah'-nay-o, ah], *a.* Instantaneous, instant.

instante [ins-tahn'-tay], *m.* Instant, a point in duration, a moment. **Al instante**, immediately. **Por instantes**, incessantly, continually. **En un instante**, in a flash.

instante [ins-tan'-tay], *pa. & a.* Instant, pressing, urgent.

instantemente [ins-tahn'-tay-men-tay], *adv.* Instantly, with urgent importunity.

instar [ins-tar'], *va.* 1. To press or urge a request or petition. 2. In schools, to impugn the solution of a question. **Instar a uno a hacer algo**, to urge somebody to do something. *-vn.* To urge the prompt execution of something.

instauración [ins-ta-hoo-rah-the-on'], *f.* 1. Instauration, restoration. 2. Establishment.

instaurar [ins-ta-hoo-rar'], *va.* To renew, to re-establish, to rebuild, to restore (renovar).

instaurativo, va [ins-tah-oo-rah-tee'-vo, vah], *a.* Restorative.

instigación [ins-tee-gah-the-on'], *f.* Instigation, incitement, impulse, encouragement.

instigador, ra [ins-te-gah-dor', rah], *m. & f.* Instigator, abetter.

instigar [ins-te-gar'], *va.* To instigate, to incite, to provoke, to urge to ill.

instilación [ins-te-lah-the-on'], *f.* Instillation, pouring in by drops.

instilar [ins-te-lar'], *va.* 1. To instill, to infuse by drops. 2. To instill, to insinuate imperceptibly into the mind.

instintivo, va [ins-tin-tee'-vo, vah], *a.* Instinctive, determined by natural impulse. **-amente**, *adv.*

instinto [ins-teen'-to], *m.* 1. Instinct, natural desire or aversion, natural tendency. 2. Instinct, the power determining the will of brutes. 3. Divine inspiration. 4. Encouragement, incitement, impulse. **Por instinto**, instinctively.

institución [ins-te-too-the-on'], *f.* 1. Institution (organismo), establishment, settlement. 2. Institution (acto), education, instruction. 3. Collation or bestowing of a benefice. **Instituciones**, institutes of any science. **Institución pública**, public institution.

institucional [ins-te-too-the-o-nahl'], *a.* Institutional.

institucionalizar [ins-te-too-the-o-nah-le-thar'], *va.* To institutionalize.

instituente [ins-te-too-en'-tay], *pa.* Instituting: founder.

instituidor, ra [ins-te-too-e-dor', rah], *m. & f.* Institutor, founder.

instituir [ins-te-too-eer'], *va.* 1. To institute, to establish, to found. 2. To institute, to teach, to instruct. 3. To nominate, to appoint; to determine or resolve.

instituta [ins-te-too'-tah], *f.* Institute, a part or section of the Roman law.

instituto [ins-te-too'-to], *m.* Institute, established law; settled order; design, object, end. **Instituto de belleza**, beauty parlor. **Instituto laboral**, technical school.

institutor, ra [ins-te-too-tor', rah], *m. & f. V.* INSTITUIDOR.

institutriz [ins-te-too-treeth'], *f.* Governess, child's private instructress.

instituyente [ins-te-too-yen'-tay], *pa.* Institutor; foundling.

instrucción [ins-trooc-the-on'], *f.* 1. Instruction, the art of teaching; lesson. 2. Precepts conveying knowledge (conocimientos); knowledge. 3. *(Comput.)* Statement, instruction. **Instrucción memoria a memoria**, memory to memory instruction. **Instrucción registro a memoria**, register to memory instruction. **Instrucción registro a registro**, register to register instruction. **Instrucción única, flujo de datos individual**, single instruction, single data stream. **Instrucción única, flujo de datos múltiples**, single instruction, multiple data stream. **Instrucción oculta**, concealed instruction. 4. **Instrucciones** (órdenes), instructions, orders, drill, training (ejército). **De acuerdo con sus instrucciones**, in accordance with your instructions. **Instrucciones para el uso**, directions for use.

instructivamente [ins-trooc-te-vah-men'-tay], *adv.* Instructively.

instructivo, va [Ins-trooc-tee'-vo, vah], *a.* Instructive; educational (película).

instructor [ins-trooc-tor'], *m & f.* 1. Instructor, teacher, lecturer, monitor. 2. *(Comput.)* Trainer

instructora [ins-trooc-to'-rah], *f.* Instructress.

instruir [ins-troo-eer'], *va.* 1. To instruct, to teach, to lecture, to acquaint. 2. To civilize. 3. To inform authoritatively. 4. *(Law.)* To instruct, to model a cause according to established rules.

instrumentación [ins-troo-men-tah-the-on'], *f.* Instrumentation.

instrumental [ins-troo-men-tahl'], *a.* 1. Instrumental, produced by instruments, not vocal. 2. *(Law.)* Belonging to legal instruments.

instrumentalmente [ins-troo-men-tahl'-men-tay], *adv.* Instrumentally.

instrumentista [ins-troo-men-tees'-tah], *m.* Player on an instrument of music (músico).

instrumento [ins-troo-men'-to], *m.* 1. Instrument, a tool, an engine or machine (herramienta). 2. Instrument, the agent or means of something. 3. *(Law.)* Instrument, a writing containing a contract, or serving as proof or evidence. 4. *(Mus.)* Instrument, any musical instrument. 5. *(coll.)* Instrument, one who acts merely for another. **Instrumento de viento**, a wind instrument. **Instrumento de cuerda**, a stringed instrument. **Tablero de instrumentos**, instrument panel. **Instrumento de precisión**, precision instrument. **Instrumentos científicos**, surgical instruments.

insuave [in-soo-ah'-vay], *a.* Unpleasant, disagreeable.

insubordinación [in-soo-bor-de-nah-the-on'], *f.* Insubordination, disorder, want of obedience.

insubordinado, da [in-soo-bor-de-nah'-do, dah], *a. & pp.* of INSUBORDINARSE. Insubordinate, rebellious, resisting authority.

insubordinar [in-soo-bor-de-nar'], *va.* To incite, to resist authority. *-vr.* To rebel against authority (militares).

insubsistencia [in-soob-sis-ten'-the-ah], *f.* Instability, inconstancy.

insubsistente [in-soo-sis-ten'-tay], *a.* 1. Unable to subsist, incapable of duration. 2. Instable, inconstant, changing.

insubstancial [in-soobs-tan-the-ahl'], *a.* Unsubstantial, of little substance or worth, or of none.

insuficiencia [in-soo-fe-the-en'-the-ah], *f.* 1. Insufficiency, inadequateness. **Debido a la insuficiencia de personal**, through shortage of stafff. 2. Incompetence. 3. *(Med.)* **Insuficiencia cardíaca**, heart failure.

insuficiente [in-soo-fe-the-en'-tay], *a.* Insufficient (inadecuado), inadequate; wanting abilities.

insuficientemente [in-soo-fe-the-en'-tay-men-tay], *adv.* Insufficiently.

insuflación [in-soo-flah-the-on'], *f.* Insufflation, the blowing into the air-passages of air, a powder, etc.

insuflar [in-soo-flar'], *va.* 1. To blow. V. SOPLAR. 2. To suggest, to prompt. 3. *(Med.)* To insufflate, to blow or breathe into.

insufrible [in-soo-free'-blay], *a.* Intolerable, insufferable, overbearing, insupportable.

insufriblemente [in-soo-fre-blay-men'-tay], *adv.* Insufferably.

ínsula [een'-soo-lah], *f. (Archaic.)* 1. Isle. V. ISLA. 2. *(Joo.)* A petty state or government.

insular, insulano, na [in-soo-lar', in-soo-lah'-no, nah], *a.* Insular V. ISLEÑO.

insulina [in-soo-lee'-nah], *f.* Insulin.

insulsamente [in-sool-sah-men'-tay], *adv.* Insipidly.

insulsez [in-sool-seth'], *f.* Insipidity, flatness, want of taste (insipidez).

insulso, sa [in-sool'-so, sah], *a.* 1. Insipid, tasteless (insípido). 2. *(Met.)* Dull, heavy; flat cold.

insultador, ra [in-sool-tah-dor', rah], *m. & f.* Insulter.

insultante [in-sool-tahn'-tay], *pa.* Insulting, insulter.

insultar [in-sool-tar'], *va.* To insult, to treat with insolence or contempt. *-vr (coll.)* To meet with an accident, to be suddenly attacked with disease.

insulto [in-sool'-to], *m.* 1. Insult (ofensa), act of insulting. 2. A sudden and violent attack. 3. A sudden fit of illness. 4. *(Mex.)* Belly-ache (indigestión).

insumable [in-soo-mah'-blay], *a.* Incalculable, unnumberable.

insumergible [in-soo-mer-hee'-blay], *a.* Not submersible, incapable of being submerged.

insumiso [in-soo-me'-so], *a.* Unsubmissive, rebellious.

insuperable [in-soo-pay-rah'-blay], *a.* Insuperable, insurmountable, overbearing, not to be overcome, unsurpassable (calidad).

insupurable [in-soo-poo-rah'-blay], *a.* That which cannot suppurate or form pus.

insurgente [in-soor-hen'-tay], *m.* Insurgent, one who rises in rebellion against the goverment of his country: it is also used as an adjective.

insurrección [in-soor-rec-the-on'], *f.* Insurrection, a seditious rising, a rebellious commotion.

insurrecionar [in-soor-rec-the-o-nar'], *va.* To promote an insurrection. *-vr.* To rebel against the constituted authorities.

insurrecto, ta [in-soor-rec'-to, tah], *a.* Rebellious. *-m. & f.* Rebel, insurgent.

insustancial [in-soos-tan-the-ahl'], *a.* V. INSUBSTANCIAL.

insustituible [in-soos-te-too-ee'-blay], *a.* Irreplaceable.

intáctil [in-tahc'-teel], *a.* Intangible, intactible, not perceptible to touch.

intacto, ta [in-tahc'-to, tah], *a.* 1. Untouched not touched. 2. Untouched, not meddled with, not spoken of. 3. Pure, unmingled; entire; intact.

intachable [in-tah-chah'-blay], *a.* Irreproachable.

intangible [in-tan-hee'-blay], *a.* Intangible, not to be touched.

integérrimo, ma [in-tay-her'-re-mo, mah], *a. super.* Very sincere.

integración [in-tay-grah-the-on'], *f.* Integration.

integrado [in-tay-grah'-do], *a.* 1. Integrated (entero); in one piece; integrated (sociedad). 2. **Un grupo integrado por**, a group made up of. 3. *(Comput.)* Encapsulated, built-in.

integral [in-tay-grahl'], *a.* Integral, whole, complete, total.

integralmente [in-tay-grahl'-men-tay], *adv.* Integrally.

íntegramente [een'-tay-grah-men-tay]; *adv.* V. ENTERAMENTE.

integrante [in-tay-grahn'-tay], *a.* Integral, integrant. **Los integrantes del conjunto**, the members of the group.

integrar [in-tay-grar'], *va.* 1. To integrate, to make up a whole (formar). 2. To find the integral of a differential quantity. 3.

(Fin.) To repay, to reimburse; *(And. Cono Sur, Mex.)* To hang over, to pay up (pagar).

integridad [in-tay-gre-dahd'], *f.* 1. Integrality, wholeness (entereza), completeness. 2. Integrity, honesty, purity of manners, uprightness (honradez). 3. Virginity (virginidad), maidenhead. 4. Confidence, honor.

integrista [in-tay-gres'-tah], *a.* Reactionary; traditionalist. *-m & f.* Reactionary.

íntegro, gra [een'-tay-gro, grah], *a.* 1. Integral, entire, complete, not fractional. **La cantidad íntegra**, the whole sum. 2. Candid, upright, honest, disinterested, just.

intelección [in-tay-lec-the-on'], *f.* Intellection, the act of understanding.

intelectiva [in-tay-lec-tee'-vah], *f.* Intellect, the power of understanding.

intelectivo, va [in-tay-lec-tee'-vo, vah], *a.* Intellective, having power to understand.

intelecto [in-tay-lec'-to], *m. (Ant.)* Intellect, understanding.

intelectual [in-tay-lec-too-ahl'], *a.* Intellectual, relating to the understanding: mental, ideal, belonging to the mind.

intelectualmente [in-tay-lec-too-ahl'-men-tay], *adv.* Intellectually, mentally, ideally.

inteligencia [in-tay-le-hen'-the-ah], *f.* 1. Intelligence (intelecto), commerce of information: mutual communication, comprehension, knowledge, knowing. 2. Intelligence, direction or government understanding, skill, ability, experience. 3. Intelligence, friendly intercourse. 4. Sense, signification of a passage. 5. Intelligence, spirit. **En inteligencia**, in the understanding, suppositively. **La buena inteligencia entre los pueblos**, good understanding between peoples. 6. *(LAm. Mil.)* Intelligence. 7. *(Imform.)* **Inteligencia incorporada**, builtin intelligence. **Inteligencia integrada**, built-in intelligence.

inteligenciado, da [in-tay-le-hen-the-ah'-do, dah], *a. (coll.)* Instructed, informed.

inteligente [in-tay-le-hen'-tay], *a.* Intelligent, skillful (hábil), clever (listo), learned, knowing. **-mente**. *adv.*

inteligibilidad [in-tay-le-he-be-le-dahd], *f.* Intelligibility, capacity of being understood.

inteligible [in-tay-le-hee'-blay], *a.* Intelligible, conceivable, perspicuous, to be perceived by the senses.

inteligiblemente [in-tay-le-hee'-blay-men-tay], *adv.* Intelligibly.

intemperancia [in-tem-pay-rahn'-the-ah], *f.* Intemperance, want of moderation; excess.

intemperante [in-tem-pay-rahn'-tay], *a.* Intemperate. V. DESTEMPLADO.

intemperie [in-tem-pay'-re-ay], *f.* Intemperateness, unseasonableness of weather: inclemency. **Estar a la intemperie**, to be out in the open. **Aguantar la intemperie**, to put up with wind and weather.

intempesta [in-tem-pays'-tah], *a. (Poet.)* Excessively dark, dreary: applied to the dead of night.

intempestivamente [in-tem-pays-tee'-vah-men-tay], *adv.* Unseasonable, abortively, intempestively.

intempestivo, va [in-tem-pes-tee'-vo, vah], *a.* Unseasonable, not suited to the time or occasion: abortive.

intención [in-ten-the-on'], *f.* 1 Intention, design, meaning, mind, view. 2. Instinct of brutes. **Segunda intención**, duplicity. **Con intención**, deliberately. **Tener la intención de**, to intend to.

intencionadamente [in-ten-the-o-nah-dah-nen'-tay], *adv.* Designedly.

intencionado, da [in-ten-the-o-nah'-do, dah], *a.* Inclined, disposed, meaningful (significativo).

intencional [in-ten-the-o-nahl'], *a.* Intentional, designed.

intencionalmente [in-ten-the-o-nahl'-men-tay], *adv.* Intentionally.

intendencia [in-ten-den'-the-ah], *f.* 1. Administration, management (dirección). 2. Place, employment, or district of an intendant. 3. Manager's office (oficina). 4. *(Cono Sur)* Mayoralty (alcaldía); governorship (gobernador).

intendenta [in-ten-den'-tah], *f.* Lady of an intendant.

intendente [in-ten-den'-tay], *m.* 1. Manager (gerente). 2. *(Cono Sur)* Mayor (alcalde); governor (gobernador). **Intendente de provincia**, the governor of a province under a viceroy or captain general. **Intendente del ejército**, quarter-master general. **Intendente de marina**, the commandant of a navy-yard.

intensamente [in-ten-sah-men'-tay], *adv.* Intensely, strongly, powerfully.

intensidad [in-ten-se-dahd'], *f.* Intensity; vehemence, power, strength.

intensificar [in-ten-se-fe-car'], *va.* To intensify, to heighten, to deepen.

intensión [in-ten-se-on'], *f.* Intenseness, vehemence, ardency; earnestness, great attention.

intensivo, va, intenso, sa [in-ten'-see-vo, vah, in-ten'-so, sah], *a.* Intense (emoción, sentimiento), intensive, vehement, ardent, lively.

intentar [in-ten-tar'], *va.* 1. To try (probar), to attempt, to endeavor. 2. To intend, to mean (proponerse), to design. 3. To enter an action, to commence a lawsuit.

intento [in-ten'-to], *m.* 1. Intention (propósito), intent, object. 2. Attempt (tentativa). **Intento golpista**, attempted coup. **Intento de suicidio**, attempted rape.

intentona [in-ten-to'-nah], *f.* Foolhardy attempt.

interacción [in-ter-ac-the-on'], *f.* Interaction.

interactivo [in-ter-ac-tee'-vo], *a.* *(Comput.)* Interactive.

interamericano, na [in-ter-ah-may-re-cah'-no, nah], *a.* Inter-American.

interarticular [in-ter-ar-te-col-lar'], *a.* Interarticular, between joints.

interbranquial [in-ter-bran-ke-ahl'], *a.* *(Zool.)* Interbranchial, between the branchiae or gills.

intercadencia [in-ter-cah-den'-the-ah], *f.* 1. Interruption, interposition. 2. Inconstancy. 3. *(Med.)* Intermission or inequality of the pulse.

intercadente [in-ter-cah-den'-tay], *a.* Changeable, variable.

intercadentemente [in-ter-cah-den'-tay-men-tay], *adv.* Changeably.

intercalación [in-ter-cah-lah-the-on'], *f.* Intercalation, the act of inserting amongst other things.

intercalar [in-ter-cah-lar'], *va.* To intercalate, to insert among other things.

intercalar [in-ter-cah-lar'], *a.* Intercalary.

intercambiable [in-ter-cam-be-ah-blay], *a.* Interchangeable.

intercambiar [in-ter-cam-be-ahr'], *va.* To change over, to interchange; to exchange (prisioneros, revistas); to exchange (sellos).

intercambio [in-ter-cahm'-be-o], *m.* Interchange, mutual exchange, reciprocity.

interceder [in-ter-thay-derr'], *vn.* 1. To intercede, to mediate, to entreat for another. 2. To intercede, to interpose, to place between.

intercelular [in-ter-thay-loo-lar'], *a.* Intercellular.

interceptación [in-ter-thep-tah-the-on'], *f.* Interception, stop-page, the act of intercepting. *(Acad.)*

interceptar [in-ter-thep-tar'], *va.* To intercept, to cut off, to obstruct.

intercesión [in-ter-thay-se-on'], *f.* Intercession, mediation, interposition, interceding.

intercesor, ra [in-ter-thay-sor', rah], *m. & f.* Intercessor, interceder, mediator, excuser, solicitor.

intercesorio, ria [in-ter-thay-so'-re-o, ah], *a.* Intercessory, intervening between two parties; entreating for another.

intercolumnio [in-ter-co-loom'-ne-o], *m.* Intercolumniation, the space between pillars or columns.

intercomunicación [in-ter-co-moo-ne-cah-the-on'], *f.* Intercommunication.

interconectar [in-ter-co-nec-tar'], *va.* To interconnect.

intercostal [in-ter-cos-tahl'], *a.* Intercostal, between the ribs.

intercurrente [in-ter-coor-rayn'-tay], *a.* Intercurrent, intervening.

intercutáneo, nea [in-ter-coo-tah'-nay-o, ah], *a.* Intercutaneous, between the skin and flesh.

interdecir [in-ter-day-theer'], *va.* To interdict, to prohibit.

interdentario, ria [in-ter-den-tah'-re-o, ah], *a.* Interdental, between the teeth.

interdicción [in-ter-dec-the-on'], *f.* Interdiction, prohibition; interdict.

interdicto [in-ter-deec'-to], *m.* 1. A judgment of summary possession. 2. Prohibition, interdiction.

interés [in-tay-res'], *m.* 1. Interest, concern, advantage, concernment. 2. Interest, share or participation in any profit (participación). 3. Interest, any surplus of advantage. 4. Interest, money paid for the use of money. 5. Interest, part taken for or against any person. 6. *(Poet.)* Pathos or interest of dramatic incidents. **Dar a interés**, to put on interest. **Llevar cinco por ciento de interés**, to bear five per cent interest. **De gran interés**, of great interest. **Sentir interés por**, to be interested in. **Intereses creados**, vested interests. **Interés compuesto**, compound interest. **Intereses por pagar**, interest payable.

interesable [in-tay-ray-sah-blay], *a.* Avaricious, mercenary.

interesadamente [in-tay-re-sah'-dah-men-tay], *adv.* Selfishly.

interesado, da [in-tay-ray-sah'-do, dah], *a. & pp.* of INTERESAR. 1. Interested, concerned. **Estar interesado en**, to be interested in. 2. Interested, selfish (egoísta), sordid, mercenary, avaricious. 3. Blessed, prejudiced (parcial). **Actuar de una manera interesada**, to act in a biased way.

interesado, da [in-tay-ray-sah'-do, dah], *m. & f.* A person concerned in any undertaking or business, a partner. **Los interesados**, the concern, persons connected in business, or their affairs in general.

interesante [in-tay-ray-sahn'-tay], *a.* Interesting (de interés), useful (útil), convenient, profitable (provechoso).

interesar [in-tay-ray-sar'], *vn. & vr.* To be concerned or interested in (tener interés en), to have a share in or to take a part in any concern. **La idea no interesó**, the idea was of no interest. *-va.* 1. To interest, to concern, to give a share in. 2. To interest, to concern, to engage by feeling or sentiment (afectar). 3. *(Poet.)* To interest, to affect or touch with pardon: speaking of a poem. **No me interesan los toros**, I'm not interested in bull-fighting. **El asunto interesa a todos**, the matter concerns everybody.

interescolar [in-ter-es-co-lar'], *a.* Inter-scholastic, interschool.

interesillo [in-tay-ray-seel'-lyo], *m. dim.* A slight interest.

interestelar [in-ter-ays-tay-lar'], *a.* Interstellar.

interfaz *(Comput.)* Interfacing.

interferencia [in-ter-fay-ren'-the-ah], *f.* 1. *(Opt.)* Interference of rays of light; crossing. 2. *(Fis. Rad.)* Interference, jamming (con intención).

interferir [in-ter-fay-reer'], *va.* 1. *(Fis. Rad.)* To interfere with, to jam (con intención). 2. To interfere with (injerirse en), to upset, to affect. **Su acción ha interferido en nuestras operaciones**, his action has interfered with our operations. *-vn.* To interfere. *-vr.* To interfere.

interfoliar [in-ter-fo-le-ar'], *va.* To interleave a book.

ínterin [een'-tay-rin], *m* V. INTERINIDAD.

ínterin, or en al ínterin [een'-tay-rin], *adv.* In the interim, in the meantime. V. INTERINAMENTE.

interinamente [in-tay-re-nah-men'-tay], *adv.* In the intervening time (entretanto), in the interim, meantime, provisionally.

interinidad [in-tay-re-ne-dahd'], *f.* Quality of holding temporary charge or office.

interino, na [in-tay-ree'-no, nah], *a.* Provisional, appointed provisionally, having the temporary charge of an employ or office.

interior [in-tay-re-or'], *a.* Interior, internal, inward (pensamiento), inner, domestic (comercio, política). **Habitación interior**, room without a view.

interior, *m.* 1. The interior, the inside, the inner part. 2. Mind, soul. 3. That which is only felt in the soul. 4. In coaches with three compartments, the middle one. 5. *(Geog.)* Interior. **Política interior**, domestic policy.

interioridad [in-tay-re-o-re-dahd'], *f.* 1. Inside, interior part. 2. The act of concealing something, and the thing hidden. **En su interioridad, sabe que...**, in his heart he knows that... **Desconocen las interioridades del mercado**, they don't know all the ins and outs of the market.

interiorizar [in-tay-re-o-re-thar'], *va.* 1. *(Psic.)* To internalize. 2. *(LAm.)* To look into, to investigate closely.

interiormente [in-tay-re-or'-men-tay], *adv.* In the interior, internally, inwardly, interiorly. **Lo que pasa interiormente**, what goes on inside.

interjección [in-ter-hec-the-on'], *f. (Gram.)* Interjection, a part of speech.

interlineación [in-ter-le-nay-ah-the-on'], *f.* Interlineation.

interlineal [in-ter-le-nay-ahl'], *a.* Interlineal.

interlinear [in-ter-le-nay-ar'], *va.* V. ENTRERRENGLONAR.

interlocución [in-ter-lo-coo-the-on'], *f.* Interlocution, dialogue, interchange of speech.

interlocutor, ra [in-ter-lo-coo-tor', rah], *m. & f.* 1. Interlocutor, one who speaks in the name of another. 2. Collocutor, colloquist, one of the speakers in a dialogue.

interlocutoria, ria [in-ter-lo-coo-to'-re-o, ah], *a.* Interlocutory, preparatory to a definitive decision.

intérlope [in-ter'-lo-pay], *a.* 1. Interloping, defrauding in commerce between a nation and the colonies of another. 2. *(Mex.)* Fraudulent (fraudulento).

interlunio [in-ter-loo'-ne-o], *m.* Time when the moon, being about to change, is invisible.

intermediar [in-ter-may-de-ar'], *va.* To interpose, to be in the middle.

intermediario [in-ter-may-de-ah'-re-o], *a.* 1. Intermediary. 2. Mediating (mediador). -*m.* 1. Intermediary, go-between. 2. Mediator (árbitro).

intermedio, dia [in-ter-may'-de-o, ah], *a.* Intermediate (etapa), intervening, interposed, intermedial.

intermedio [in-ter-may'-de-o], *m.* 1. Interval, intermedium, time passing between (tiempo); interim. **El período intermedio**, the intervening period. 2. Interlude, an entertainment between the acts of a play; farce interval; middle.

interminable [in-ter-me-nah'-blay], *a.* Interminable, endless.

intermisión [in-ter-me-se-on'], *f.* Intermission, interruption, forbearance.

intermitencia [in-ter-me-ten'-the-ah], *f.* Discontinuance of an intermittent fever; the interval between the fits.

intermitente [inter-me-ten'-tay], *a.* Intermittent, intermissive, coming by fits. -*m. (Aut.)* Directional light.

intermitir [in-ter-me-teer'], *va.* To intermit, to discontinue.

intermundo [in-ter-moon'-do], *m.* Space between the worlds.

intermuscular [in-ter-moos-coo-lar'], *a.* Intermuscular, between the muscles.

internación [in-ter-nah-the-on'], *f.* Importation.

internacional [in-er-nah-the-o-nahl'], *a.* International.

internacionalizar [in-ter-nah-the-o-nah-le-thar'], *pa.* To internationalize.

internado, da [in-ter-nah'-do, dah], *a.* Interned. -*m.* Boarding school (colegio), boarding pupils (alumnos).

internamente [in-ter-nah-men'-tay], *adv.* Internally. V. INTERIORMENTE.

internar [in-ter-nar'], *va.* To pierce, to penetrate beyond the surface, to penetrate into the interior of a country. -*vr.* 1. To insinuate, to gain upon the affections by degrees; to wheedle. 2. To advance (avanzar); to penetrate. 2. **Internarse en** (avanzar). 3. **Internarse en un estudio**, to go deeply into a subject.

interno, na [in-ter'-no, nah], *a.* Interior, internal, inward, intern. **La política interna**, internal politics. -*m. & f.* 1. Boarder (alumno). 2. Prisoner (preso). -*m. (Cono Sur, Telec.)* Extension.

internuncio [in-ter-noon'-the-o], *m.* Internuncio, an agent of the court of Rome; interlocutor.

interpolación [in-ter-po-lah-the-on'], *f.* 1. *(Law.)* Interpellation, summons. 2. Interpellation, an earnest address, a demand for an official statement.

interpelar [in-ter-pay-lar'], *va.* 1. To appeal to, to implore the aid of. 2. *(Law.)* To summon, to cite (citar). 3. To interrogate as to the truth or falsity of an act. 4. To interpellate, to officially interrogate a member of a government, as in continental legislatures. 5. To address (dirigirse).

interplanetario, ria [in-ter-plah-nay-tah'-re-o, ah], *a.* Interplanetary.

interpolación [in-ter-po-lah-the-on'], *f.* 1. Interpolation, something added to the original. 2. Act of adding something to the original.

interpoladamente [in-ter-po-lah'-dah-men-tay], *adv.* In an interpolating manner.

interpolar [in-ter-po-lar'], *va.* 1. To interpolate, to foist in. 2. To interpose, to intermix, to intermit. 3. To interpose, to interrupt.

interponer [in-ter-po-nerr'], *va.* 1. To interpose (insertar), to place between. 2. To thrust in as an interruption or obstruction. 3. **Interponer la autoridad**, *(Law.)* to sanction, to approve, or confirm by the authority of the law. -*vr.* To go between, to interpose.

interposición [in-ter-po-se-the-on'], *f.* 1. Interposition (inserción), the state of being placed between other things or persons. 2. Interposition, intervenient agency, interference, mediation, meddling. 3. Interval, time passing between.

interpósita persona [in-ter-po'-se-ta per-so'-nah]. *(Lat. exp. Law)* Intermediary, agent, one who acts for another.

interpresa [in-ter-pray'-sah], *f.* Military enterprise, a sudden undertaking or attempt.

interpretable [in-ter-pray-tah'-blay], *a. (coll.)* Interpretable.

interpretación [in-ter-pray-tah-the-on'], *f.* 1. Interpretation, the act of interpreting (teatro). 2. Interpretation, elucidation, explanation, exposition, construction, commentary; the sense given by an interpreter. **Mala interpretación**, misinterpretation.

interpretador, ra [in-ter-pray-tah-dor', rah], *m. & f.* Interpreter, translator.

interpretante [in-ter-pray-tahn'-tay], *pa. & m. & f.* Interpreting, translator.

interpretar [in-ter-pray-tar'], *va.* 1. To interpret, to explain, to expound. **Interpretar mal**, to misinterpret. 2. To translate, to interpret, to construe. **Interpretar del chino al ruso**, to translate from Chinese into Russian. 3. To interpret, to take or understand the meaning in a particular sense or manner. 4. To attribute. 5. *(Mus.)* To render, to perform; *(Teat.)* to perform; to play (papel).

interpretativamente [in-ter-pre-tah-tee'-vah-men-tay], *adv.* Interpretatively.

interpretativo, va [in-ter-pray-tah-tee'-vo, vah], *a.* Interpretative.

intérprete [in-ter-pray'-tay], *com.* Interpreter, expounder, translator; indication, sign.

interpuesto, ta [in-ter-poo-ays'-to, tah], *a. & pp. irr.* of INTERPONER. Interposed, intervening, placed between, mediate.

interregno [in-ter-reg'-no], *m.* Interreign, interregnum, the time in which the throne is vacant; vacancy of the throne.

interrogación [in-ter-ro-gah-the-on'], *f.* 1. Question (pregunta). 2. Questioning. 3. Question marks (signo). 4. Interrogation (policía).

interrogador, ra [in-ter-ro-gah-dor'], *m. & f.* Interrogator; questioner.

interrogante [in-ter-ro-gahn'-tay], *a.* Questioning. -*m. & f.* Questioner (persona). **La gran interrogante**, the real issue. **Punto interrogante**, question marks.

interrogar [in-ter-ro-gar'], *va.* To question, to interrogate.

interrogativamente [in-ter-ro-gah-tee'-vah-men-tay], *adv.* Interrogatively.

interrogativo, va [in-ter-ro-gah-tee'-vo, vah], *a.* Interrogative.

interrogatorio [in-ter-ro-gah-to'-re-o], *m.* Interrogatory, questionnaire, questioning.

interrumpidamente [in-ter-room-pee'-dah-men-tay], *adv.* Interruptedly.

interrumpido, da [in-ter-room-pee'-do, dah], *a. & pp.* of INTERRUMPIR. Interrupted, broken.

interrumpir [in-ter-room-peer'], *va.* 1. To interrupt, to hinder or obstruct the continuance of a thing. 2. To interrupt, to hinder from proceeding, to cut off (electricidad, servicio), to cut short.

interrupción [in-ter-roop-the-on'], *f.* Interruption, interpellation, discontinuance. *(Comput.)* Interrupt.

interruptor [in-ter-roop-tor'], *m. (Elec.)* Switch. **Interruptor DIP** *(Comput.),* DIP switch.

intersecarse [in-ter-say-car'], *-vr. (Geom.)* To intersect each other.

intersección [in-ter-sec-the-on'], *f.* 1. Intersection; the point where lines cross each other. 2. A line common to two surfaces which cut one another.

intersectario, ria [in-ter-sec-tah'-re-o, ah], *a.* Interdenominational.

intersticio [in-ters-tee'-the-o], *m.* Interstice, interval (intervalo).

intertropical [in-ter-tro-pe-cahl'], *a.* Intertropical, placed or produced between the tropics.

interuniversitario, ria [in-ter-oo-ne-ver-se-tah'-re-o, ah], *a.* Intercollegiate.

intervalo [in-ter-vah'-lo], *m.* 1. Interval (espacio), space between places. 2. Interval (tiempo), time passing between two assignable points, interlapse.

intervención [in-ter-ven-the-on'], *f.* 1. Intervention (participación), supervision (control), *(LAm.)* government takeover (sindicato), assistance, mediation, interposition; knowledge, consent. 2. *(Med.)* Operation. **Intervención quirúrgica**, surgical operation. 3. *(Telec.)* Taping.

intervenir [in-ter-ve-neer'], *vn.* 1. To intervene, to come between things or persons, to mediate; to intercur, to intermediate. 2. To assist, to attend, to supervise (controlar); *(LAm.)* to install government appointees in (sindicato), to superintend. *-vn.* 1. To intervene (tomar parte); to take part, to participate; to contribute. **No intervino en el debate**, he did not take part in the debate. 2. To intercede (interceder); to mediate (mediar).

interventor, ra [in-ter-ven-tor', rah], *m. & f.* Comptroller, supervisor, inspector, superintendent.

intervertebral [in-ter-ver-tay-brahl'], *a.* Invertebral, between the vertebrae.

interyacente [in-ter-yah-then'-tay], *a.* Interjacent, intervening, lying between.

intestable [in-tes-tah'-blay], *a.* 1. Intestable, legally disqualified to make a will. 2. Legally disqualified to testify.

intestedo, da [in-tes-tah'-do, dah], *a.* Intestate, dying without a will.

intestinal [in-tes-te-nahl'], *a.* Intestinal.

intestino, na [in-tes-te'-no, nah], *a.* Intestine, internal; civil, domestic.

intestino [in-tes-tee'-no], *m.* Intestine, the gut; the bowels.

intimación [in-te-mah-the-on'], *f.* Intimation, hint, notification.

íntimamente [en'-temah-men-tay], *adv.* Intimately.

intimar [in-te-mar'], *va.* To intimate (notificar), to hint, to make known, to order (ordenar).*-vr.* 1. To pierce, to penetrate. 2. To gain on the affections, to insinuate. **Ahora intiman mucho**, they're very friendly with somebody.

intimidación [in-te-me-dah-the-on'], *f.* Intimidation.

intimidad [in-te-me-dahd'], *f.* 1. Intimacy (amistad), close familiarity or connection, friendship, consociation, inwardness. 2. Privacy, private life (vida privada). **La ceremonia se celebró en la intimidad**, the wedding took place privately.

intimidar [in-te-me-dar'], *va.* To intimidate, to daunt, to fright. *-vr.* To be intimidated, to be overawed.

íntimo, ma [een'-te-mo, mah], *a.* 1. Internal, innermost. 2. Intimate (relación), familiar, conversant, near, closely acquainted. **Una boda íntima**, a quiet wedding. **Es íntimo amigo mío**, he is a close friend of mine.

intitular [in-te-too-lar'], *va.* 1. To entitle, to prefix a title to a book or writing. 2. To entitle, to grace, or dignify with a title or honorable appellation. *-vr.* To use a title or honorable appellation.

intolerabilidad [in-to-lay-rah-be-le-dahd'], *f.* Intolerableness.

intolerable [in-to-lay-rah'-blay], *a.* Intolerable, insufferable.

intolerancia [in-to-lay-rahn'-the-ah], *f.* Intolerance, narrow-mindedness.

intolerante [in-to-lay-rahn'-tay], *a.* Intolerant, not favorable to toleration, narrow-minded.

intonso, sa [in-tone'-so, sah], *a. (Poet.)* 1. Unshorn, having the hair uncut. 2. Ignorant, unpolished. 3. A book bound with uncut leaves.

intorsión [in-tor-se-on'], *f. (Bot.)* Intorsion, turning of a plant out of the vertical position.

intoxicación [in-toc-se-cah-the-on'], *f. (Med.)* Intoxication, poisoning caused voluntarily or involuntarily.

intoxicar [in-toc-se-car'], *va. (Med.)* To poison.

intradós [in-trah-dos'], *m.* The concave face of an arch or vault; intrados.

intraducible [in-trah-doo-thee'-blay], *a.* Untranslatable.

intramitable [in-trah-me-tah'-blay], *a. (Law.)* Not capable of advancement upon the calendar.

intramuros [in-trah-moo'-ros], *adv.* Within the walls.

intranquilidad [in-tran-ke-le-dahd'], *f.* Worry, uneasiness, disquiet.

intranquilizar [in-tran-ke-le-thar'], *va.* To disquiet, to make uneasy. *-vr.* To worry.

intranquilo, la [in-tran-kee'-lo, lah], *a.* 1. Uneasy, restless. 2. Worried, discomfited.

intransferible [in-trans-fay-re'-blay], *a.* Untransferable, not transferable.

intransigencia [in-tran-se-hayn'-the-ah], *f.* Intransigence; uncompromising attitude.

intransigente [in-tran-se-hayn'-tay], *a.* Intransigent; uncompromising, intolerant.

intransitable [in-tran-se-tah-blay], *a.* Impassable, impenetrable.

intransitivo, va [in-tran-se-tee'-vo, vah], *a. (Gram.)* Intransitive.

intrasmutabilidad [in-tras-moo-tah-be-le-dahd'], *f.* Immutability.

intrasmutable [in-tras-moo-tah'-blay], *a.* Intransmutable.

intratable [in-trah-tah'-blay], *a.* 1. Intractable (problema), ungovernable, stubborn, obstinate, unmanageable. 2. Intractable, unsociable (persona), rude, hard to deal with. 3. Impassable.

intrauterino, na [in-trah-oo-tay-ree'-no, nah], *a.* Intrauterine, existing or occurring in the uterus.

intravenoso [in-trah-vay-noh'-so], *a.* Intravenous.

intrépidamente [in-tray'-pe-dah-men-tay], *adv.* Intrepidly, fearlessly.

intrepidez [in-tray-pe-deth'], *f.* 1. Intrepidity, courage, boldness, fearlessness, dauntlessness, hardiness. 2. Temerity.

intrépido, da [in-tray'-pe-do, dah], *a.* Intrepid, daring, fearless, courageous, dauntless, gallant, hardy.

intriga [in-tree'-gah], *f.* 1. Intrigue, a (complicated) plot or scheme. 2. Entanglement, embroilment.

intrigante [in-tre-gahn'-tay], *m.* Intriguer, cunning meddler. *-a.* 1. Intriguing, scheming. 2. Intriguing (interesante).

intrigar [in-tre-gar'], *vn.* To intrigue, to form plots. *-va.* 1. To intrigue, to interest, to puzzle. 2. *(LAm.)* To conduct in a surprising way (asunto). *-vr. (LAm.)* To be intrigued.

intrincable [in-trin-cah'-blay], *a.* Intricate, perplexed, easily entangled.

intrincación [in-trin-cah-the-on'], *f.* Intricacy, intricateness.

intrincadamente [in-trin-cah-day-men'-tay], *adv.* Intricately.

intrincado, da [in-trin-cah'-do, dah], *a. & pp.* of INTRINCAR. Intricate (complicado), entangled, perplexed, knotty, obscure, impenetrable.

intrincamiento [in-trin-cah-me-en'-to], *m.* Intricateness, intrication.

intrincar [in-trin-car'], *va.* To perplex, to intricate, to entangle, to knot, to involve, to confound, to obscure.

intríngulis [in-treen'-goo-list], *m.* 1. *(coll.)* Crafty intention, hidden motive (motivo). 2. *(Peru)* Mystery, enigma, puzzle (misterio).

intrínsecamente [in-treen'-say-cah-men-tay], *adv.* Intrinsically, essentially.

intrínseco, ca [in-treen'-say-co, cah], *a.* 1. Intrinsic, intrinsical, internal, hidden. 2. Close, habitually silent *V.* ÍNTIMO. 3. *(Law.) V.* JUDICIAL.

introducción [in-tro-dooc-the-on'], *f.* Introduction, the art of conducting or ushering to any place or person, intromission. 2. Access, intercourse. 3. Introduction, the act of bringing any new thing into notice or practice. 4. Introduction, the preface of a book.

introducir [in-tro-doo-theer'], *va.* 1. To introduce, to conduct or usher into a place, to lead in. 2. To introduce, to bring into notice or practice. 3. To induce, to facilitate, to conciliate. *-vr.* To insinuate, to gain on the affections: to interfere, to find one's way, to get into (meterse).

introductor, ra [in-tro-dooc-tor', rah], *m. &f.* 1. Introducer, anyone who brings a thing into notice. 2. Introductor, introducer, one who introduces another to a person or place.

introductivo, va [in-tro-dooc-tee'-vo, vah], *a.* Introductory, introductive.

introductorio, ria [in-tro-dooc-to'-re-o, rah], *a. (for.)* Introductory.

introito [in-tro'-e-to], *m.* 1. Entrance, entry. 2. Introit, the beginning of the mass; the commencement of public devotions.

intromisión [in-tro-me-se-on'], *f.* Introduction (inserción), inserting, intromission.

introspección [in-tros-pec-the-on'], *f.* Introspection, examination of the interior.

introspectivo, va [in-tros-pec-tee'-vo, vah], *a.* Introspective.

introversión [in-tro-ver-se-on'], *f.* Introversion.

introverso, sa [in-tro-vayr'-so, sah], *a.* Introverted, self-contemplating.

introvertido [in-tro-vayr-tee'-do], *a.* Introvert, introverted; inward-looking. *-m & f.* Introvert.

intrusamente [in-troo'-sah-men-tay], *adv.* Intrusively.

intrusarse [in-troo-sar'-say], *vr.* To obtrude oneself in a place or office.

intrusión [in-troo-se-on'], *f.* Intrusion, obtrusion, the act of intruding or obtruding oneself into any place, state, or office, without right or welcome.

intruso [in-troo'-so], *m.* Intruder, obtruder, one who forces himself into any place, office, company, etc., without right or welcome; squatter.

intruso, sa [in-troo'-so, sah], *a* Intruded, intrusive, obtrusive.

intuición [in-too-e-the-on'], *f.* Intuition, knowledge not obtained by deduction of reason.

intuitivamente [in-too-e-te-vah-men'-tay], *adv.* Intuitively.

intuir [in-too-eer'], *va.* To know by intuition; to intuit; to sense, to feel, to have an intuition of. *-vr.* **Eso se intuye**, that can be guessed.

intuitivamente [in-too-e-tee'-vah-men-tay], *adv.* Intuitively.

intuitivo, va [in-too-e-tee'-vo, vah], *a.* Intuitive, evident; perceived without ratiocination.

intumescencia [in-too-mes-then'-the-ah], *f. V.* HINCHAZÓN.

intumescente [in-too-mes-then'-tay], *a.* Intumescent, swollen.

intususcepción [in-too-soos-thep-the-on'], *f.* *(Med.)* Introsusception, intussusception.

inulina [in-oo-lee'-nah], *f.* Inulin, a substance like starch.

inulto, to [in-ool'-to, tah], *a. (Poet.)* Unrevenged, unpunished.

inundación [in-oon-dah-the-on'], *f.* 1. Food, inundation, overflow of waters, deluges 2. Confluence of any kind.

inundante [in-noon-dhan'-tay], *pa.* Inundating; inundant, that which inundates.

inundar [in-oon-dar'], *va.* 1. To inundate, to overflow, to deluge, to flood. 2. To overrun with numbers. **Se le inundaron los ojos en lágrimas**, a flood of tears fell from her eyes. **Inundar el mercado de un producto**, to flood the market with a product. **La lluvia inundó la campiña**, the rain flooded the countryside.

inurbanamente [in-oor-bah-nah-men'-tay], *adv.* Incivilly, uncivilly.

inurbanidad [in-oor-bah-ne-dahd'], *f.* Incivility, want of education, inurbanity.

inurbano, na [in-oor-bah'-no, nah], *a.* Uncivil, want, unpolished, inurbane.

inusitadamente [in-oo-se-tah-dah-men'-tay], *adv.* Unusually.

inusitado, da [in-oo-se-tah'-do, dah], *a.* Unusual, not in use, not accustomed.

inusual [in-oo-soo-ahl'], *a.* Unusual.

inútil [in-oo'-teel], *a.* Useless, unprofitable, inutile, fruitless, needless, frivolous, idle, vain (esfuerzo, tentativa).

inutilidad [in-oo-te-le-dahd'], *f.* Inutility, uselessness, unprofitableness, needlessness.

inutilizar [in-oo-te-le-thar'], *va.* To render useless, to disable (barco); to spoil (estropear); to nullify (esfuerzo). *-vr.* To become useless.

inútilmente [in-oo'-teel-men-tay], *adv.* Uselessly, idly.

invadeable [in-vah-day-ah'-blay], *a.* Not fordable, impassable without swimming.

invadir [in-vah-deer'], *va.* To invade, to attack a country.

invaginación [in-vah-he-nah-the-on'], *f.* Invagination.

invalidación [in-vah-le-dah-the-on'], *f.* Invalidation, invalidity.

inválidamente [in-vah'-le-dah-men'-tay], *adv.* Invalidly.

invalidar [in-vah-le-dar'], *va.* To invalidate, to deprive of force or efficacy, to irritate, to nullify.

invalidez [in-vah-le-dayth'], *f.* 1. *(Med.)* Disablement; unfitness; disability. **Invalidez permanente**, permanent disability.

inválido, da [in-vah'-le-do, dah], *a.* Invalid, without force; feeble, weak, null. **Declarar inválida una elección**, to declare an election invalid.

inválido [in-vah'-le-do], *m.* 1. *(Mil.)* Invalid, a soldier who has retired from the service in consequence of age or disability. 2. *(coll.)* Invalid, any person weakened by sickness.

invariabilidad [in-vah-re-ah-be-le-dahd'], *f.* Invariability.

invariable [in-vah-re-ah'-blay], *a.* Invariable, constant.

invariablemente [in-vah-re-ah-blay-men'-tay], *adv.* Invariably.

invariación [in-vah-re-ah-the-on'], *f.* Immutability, invariableness.

invariado, da [in-vah-re-ah'-do, dah], *a.* Unvaried, constant, invaried.

invasión [in-vah-se-on'], *f.* Invasion, hostile entrance, attack.

invasor, ra [in-vah-sor', rah], *m. & f.* Invader. *-a.* Invading.

invectiva [in-vec-tee'-vah], *f.* Invective, harsh censure.

invencible [in-ven-thee'-blay], *a.* Invincible, insuperable, unconquerable.

invenciblemente [in-ven-the-blay-men'-tay], *adv.* Invincibly.

invención [in-ven-the-on']. *f.* 1. Invention (invento), excogitation, the act or power of inventing (descubrimiento). 2. Invention, discoverer, the thing invented. 3. Invention, contrivance, fiction, artifice.

invencionero, ra [in-ven-the-o-nay'-ro, rah], *m. & f* 1. Inventor. 2. Plotter. 3. Boaster, decider. 4. *(coll.)* Gesticulator, mimic.

invendible [in-ven-dee'-blay], *a.* Unmerchantable; not marketable, unsaleable.

inventar [in-ven-tar'], *va.* 1. To invent, to discover, to find out, to excogitate, to device (idear). 2. To invent, to forge, to frame, to contrive falsely.

inventariar [in-ven-tah-re-ar'], *va.* 1. To make an inventory, to inventory, to register. 2. *(coll.)* To commemorate the doings of a person.

inventario [in-ven-tah'-re-o], *m.* Inventory, catalogue, stock. **Hacer inventario de**, to make an inventory of.

inventiva [in-ven-tee'-vah], *f.* The faculty of invention.

inventivo, va [in-ven-tee'-vo, vah], *a.* Inventive, quick at contrivance, ready at expedients: inventful.

invento [in-ven'-to], *m.* Invention, discovery.

inventor, ra [in-ven-tor', rah], *m & f.* Inventor, contriver, framer.

inverecundo, da [in-vay-ray-coon'-do, dah], *a.* Shameless, impudent.

inverísimil [in-vay-re-see'-meel], *a.* V. INVEROSÍMIL.

invernálo [in-ver-nah'-coo-lo], *m.* Green-house, hothouse, conservatory.

invernada [in-ver-nah'-dah], *f.* 1. Winter Season (estación). 2. Wintering (etapa invernal); hibernation (hibernación). 3. *(And. Cono Sur)* Winter pasture (pasto). 4. *(Carib.)* Heavy rainstorm (tempestad).

invernadero [in-ver-nah-day'-ro], *m.* 1. Winter-quarters: applied generally to wintering places for sheep. 2. V. INVERNÁCULO.

invernal [in-ver-nahl'], *a.* Hibernal, wintry.

invernar [in-ver'-nar'], *vn.* To winter, to pass the winter; to be in the winter season, to hibernate.

invernizo, za [in-ver-nee'-tho, thah], *a.* 1. Winterly suited to the winter: hibernal. 2 Winter-beaten, harassed by frost and severe weather.

inverosímil [in-vay-ro-see'-meel], *a.* Unlikely, improbable.

inverosimilitud [in-vay-ro-se-me-le-tood'], *f.* Improbability, unlikelihood.

inversamente [in-ver-sah-men'-tay], *adv.* Inversely: contrariwise.

inversión [in-ver-se-on'], *f.* 1. Inversion; change of order, time, or place. 2. Investment, the act of employing or spending a sum of money. **Inversión de capital**, capital investment.

inversionista [in-ver-se-o-nees'-tah], *m. & f.* Investor.

inverso, sa [in-ver'-so, sah], *a. & pp. irr.* of INVERTIR. Inverse, inverted, reciprocal. **A la inversa**, on the contrary.

invertebrado, da [in-ver-tay-brah'-do, dah], *a.* Invertebrate, without a backbone.

invertido [in-ver-tee'-do], *a.* Inverted (volcado); reversed (alrevés). *-m & f.* Homosexual.

invertir [in-ver-teer'], *va.* 1. To invert (volcar), to turn upside down; to change the order of time or place (cambiar el orden). 2. To employ, to spend (esfuerzo, tiempo), or lay out money, to invest (dinero). **Invirtieron 5 días en el viaje**, they spent 5 days on the journey.

investidura [in-ves-te-doo'-rah], *f.* Investiture, the act of giving possession of a manor office, or benefice.

investigable [in-ves-te-gah'-blay], *a.* Investigable.

investigación [in-ves-te-gah-the-on'], *f.* Investigation (indicación), research; inquest. **Investigación policíaca**, police investigation.

investigador, ra [in-ves-te-gah-dor', rah], *m. & f.* Investigator.

investigar [in-ves-te-gar'], *va.* To investigate (indagar), to search out; to look after.

investir [in-ves-teer'], *va.* To invest, to confer some dignity.

inveterado, da [in-vay-tay-rah'-do, dah], *a. & pp.* of INVETERARSE. Inveterate, old, chronic, obstinate.

inveteradamente [in-vay-tay-rah-dah-men'-tay], *adv.* Inveterately.

inveterarse [in-vay-tay-rar'-say], *vr.* To become antiquated, to grow old, to become chronic: it has been used, though seldom, as an active verb.

invictamente [in-vic-tah-men'-tay], *adv.* Unconquerably, valiantly.

invicto, ta [in-veec'-to, tah], *a.* Unconquerable, unconquered.

invidente [in-ve-den'-tay-men-tay], *a.* Sightless, blind. *-m & f.* Sightless person, blind person.

invierno [in-ve-er'-no], *m.* 1. Winter. 2. *(And. CAm. Carib.)* Rainy season (meses de lluvia). 3. *(Carib.)* Heavy shower (aguacero).

invigilancia [in-ve-he-lahn'-the-ah], *f.* 1. Want of vigilance. 2. Watching, observant attention.

invigilar [in-ve-he-lar'], *vn.* To watch, to be observant, to be attentive.

inviolabilidad [in-ve-o-lah-be-le-dahd'], *f.* Inviolability, inviolableness.

inviolable [in-ve-o-lah'-blay], *a.* Inviolable.

inviolablemente [in-ve-o-lah-blay-men-tay], *adv.* Inviolably, holily: infallibly.

inviolado, da [in-ve-o-lah'-do, dah], *a.* Inviolate, unhurt, uninjured.

invisibilidad [in-ve-se-be-le-dahd'], *f.* Invisibility.

invisible [in-ve-see'-blay], *a.* Invisible, not perceptiable. **En un invisible**, *(coll.)* in an instant. *-m. (And. Cono Sur)* Hairpin.

invisiblemente [in-ve-see'-blay-men-tay], *adv.* Invisibly.

invitación [in-ve-tah-the-on'], *f.* Invitation.

invitado, da [in-ve-tah'do, dah], *m. & f.* Guest. *-a.* Invited.

invitador, ra [in-ve-tah-dor', rah], *m. & f.* One who invites, an inviter.

invitar [in-ve-tar'], *va.* 1. To invite. 2. To excite, to stimulate, to execute a thing. **Invitar a uno a hacer algo**, to invite somebody to do something. **Nos invitó a cenar fuera**, he took us out for a meal.

invitatorio [in-ve-tah-to'-re-o], *m.* Invitatory, psalm or anthem sung at the beginning of matins or morning worship.

invocación [in-vo-cah-the-on'], *f.* 1. Invocation, the act of calling upon in prayer. 2. *(Poet.)* Invocation, the form of calling for the assistance or presence of any being.

invocador, ra [in-vo-cah-dor', rah], *m. & f.* One who invokes.

invocar [in-vo-car'], *va.* To invoke (llamar en ayuda), to implore, to cry into. **Invocar la ley**, to invoke the law.

invocatorio, ria [in-vo-cah-to'-re-o, ah], *a.* That which invocates.

involucela [in-vo-loo-they'-lah], *f. (Bot.)* Involucel.

involución [in-vo-loo-the-on'], *f. (Bot.)* State of being rolled in; involution.

involucral [in-vo-loo-crahl'], *a. (Bot.)* Involucral, relating to an involucre.

involucrar [in-vo-loo-crar'], *va.* 1. To wrap up, to cover. 2. To mingle, to confuse, to upset. 3. To insert in writings questions or subjects foreign to their principal object. 4. To involve (implicar). **Involucrar uno en algo**, to involve somebody in something. 5. To jumble up, to mix up. *-vr.* To meddle, to interfere; to get involved. **Las personas involucradas en el caso**, the people involved in the affair.

involucro [in-vo-loo'-cro], *m. (Bot.)* Involucre. **Involucro partial**, V. INVOLUCELA.

involuntariamente [in-vo-loon-tah'-re-ah-men-tay], *adv.* Involuntarily.

involuntariedad [in-vo-loon-tah-re-ay-dahd'], *f.* Involuntariness.

involuntario, ria [in-vo-loon-tah'-re-o, ah], *a.* Involuntary.

involute [in-vo-loo'-tah], *f. (Arch.)* Volute. V. VOLUTA.

invulnerabilidad [in-vool-nay-rah-be-le-dahd'], *f.* Invulnerability.

invulnerable [in-vool-nay-rah'-blay], *a.* Invulnerable.

inyección [in-yec-the-on'], *f.* 1. Injection, the art of injecting. 2. The liquid injected, shot. **Inyección estimulante**, *(Med.)* booster shot.

inyectador, ra [in-yec-tah-dor', rah], *m. &f.* 1. One who injects. 2. *(Med.)* Any instrument which serves for making injections.

inyectar [in-yec-tar'], *va.* **To inject.**

inyector [in-yec-tor'], *m. (Mech.)* Injector. **Inyector del combustible,** *(Aer.)* afterburner.

ion [e-on'], *m. (Chem. & Phy.)* Ion.

iónico, ca [e-o' -ne-co, cah] *a.* Ionic.

ionización [e-o-ne-thah-the-on'], *f.* Ionization.

ionizar [e-o-ne-thar'], *va.* To ionize.

ionosfera [e-o-nos-fay' -rah], *f.* Ionosphere.

iota [e-o'-tah], *f.* Ninth letter of the Greek alphabet. *(Cf. Jot.)*

ipso facto [eep'-so fahc' -to], *(Law.)* An adverbial phrase; immediately, without delay; also, by the very fact.

ipso juro [eep' -so yoo'-ray], *(Law.)* An adverbial pharse used in courts of law, to denote that a thing does not require the declaration of the judge, as it constitutes the law itself.

ir [eer], *vn.* 1. To go, to move, not to stand still. 2. To go, to walk (a pie), to move step by step. 3. To be, to exist. 4. To bet, to lay a wager. 5. To consist, to depend on. 6. To import (importar), to concern. **Nada se me va en ello,** I have no concern in it, I do not care for it. 7. To differ, to be different (differencia), to be distant. 8. To lead (carretera). 9. To devote oneself to a calling, to follow a profession: In this last sense it is used with *por* **Ir por letras,** to study letters. 10. To proceed, to act. 11. To decline a noun or conjugate a verb for another. *Ir* joined to present participles implies the existence or actual execution of the action designated; joined with past participles it signifies to suffer their action; with the preposition *a* and infinitive mode, it implies disposition toward, as **ir a misa,** to go to mass; followed by *con,* it gives the noun an adverbial import, and accompanied by the preposition *contra or fuera de,* it signifies to persever, or act contray to. *-vr.* 1. To go, to go off or go away (marcharse), to depart or remove from a place. 2. To be dying. 3. To go off, to go out of life, to be gone (morir). 4. To leak (recipiente), to ooze. 5. To exhale, to evaporate. 6. To discharge wind. 7. To break: to grow old. **Ir a caballo,** to ride. **Ir agua arriba,** to work up stream. **Ir a una,** to act with one accord, harmoniously. **Ir y venir,** to turn something in one's mind. **Íresele a uno el alma por alguna cosa,** to long for. **Irse de boca,** to speak without reflection. **Ir (or andar) de capa cal'da,** to be crestfallen, to decline in fortune or credit. **Ni va, ni viene,** indecision, want of resolution. **Ir de campo,** to go on a picnic. **Ir or irse a pique or por ojo,** *(Naut.)* to founder, to go to the bottom. **Ir adelante,** to go on. **Ir a pie,** to walk. **Ir de una parte a otra,** to go up and down. **Ir en contra de,** to go against. **Ir en decadencia or ir empobreciendo,** to go down the wind. **Ir en busca de or ir por algo,** to go for. **Ir otra vez,** to go back or to go again. **Ir separadamente,** to go asunder. **Ir sobre seguro,** to go upon sure grounds. **Ir tras la corriente,** to go down the stream. **Ir bien or mal,** speaking of a business, it means that it is going prosperously or unprosperously. **Ir con alguno,** 1. To be of the same opinion as another. 2. To be of the same party as another. 3. To accompany. **Iísele a alguno la cabeza,** to perturb the mind, to confuse the reason. **¿Quién va? or ¿quién va allá?,** who is there?, or who goes there? **Vaya usted con Dios,** farewell; God be with you. **Ir pagando,** *(coll.)* to pay by degrees. **Ir pasando or mejorando,** to be recovering by degrees. **Él se mete en lo que no le va, ni le viene,** he meddles in what does not concern him at all. **Ir delante or por delante,** to go ahead. **No hay que irse atrás,** flinch not. *(Met).* To treat or discuss, to look for. **Mucho va de Pedro a Pedro,** *(Prove.)* there is a wide difference between man and man. **A donde fueres, haz lo que vieres,** when you are in Rome, do as the Romans do. **Irse los ojos tras de una persona or cosa,** to have an admiring eye, or longing after a person or thing; to look after it with anxiety. **Me voy de con usted,** *(CAM.)* I'm leaving you.

Ir hasta Córdoba, to go as far as Cordoba. **Va para viejo,** he's getting old. **El enfermo va mejor,** the patient is better. **Eso no va por ti,** (intención) I wasn't referring to you. **Va mucho en esto,** a lot depends on it. **Va para ingeniero,** (carrera) he's going to become an engineer. **Vamos, no es difícil,** come now. **Iban fumando,** they were smoking. **Iba cansado,** he was tired. **Vamos a hacerlo,** we are going to do it. **Es hora de irnos,** it's time we went. **Se nos fue hace 3 años,** he departed from us 3 years ago, he passed away 3 years ago.

ira [ee'-rah], *f.* 1. Ire, anger, passion, indignation, wrath, fury (viento), choler, rage. 2. Ire, desire of vengeance, chastisement. 3. *(Met.)* Violence of the elements or weather. **La ira es mala consejera,** wrath is a bad advisor. **¡Ira de Dios!,** by thunder!

iracundia [e-rah-coon' -de-ah], *f.* Irascibility, ire, irascibleness.

iracundo, da [e-rah-coon'-do, dah], *a.* 1. Passionate, ireful. 2. *(Poet.)* Enraged, furious (viento).

iranio, nia [e-rah'-ne-o, ah], *a.* Iranian, relating to Persia or Iran.

irascible [e-ras-thee'-blay], *a.* Irascible, impetuous, determined.

irenarca [e-ray-nar'-cah], *m.* Irenarch, an officer of the Greek empire, employed to preserve public tranquility.

iridáceo, cea [e-re-dah'-thay-o, thay-ah], *a.* Iridaceous, iris-like.

íride [ee'-re-day], *f. (Boat.) V.* EFÉMERO.

iridectomía [e-re-dec-to-mee'-ah], *f.* Iridectomy, excision of a portion of iris.

irídeo dea [e-ree'-day-o, ah], *a.* Irideous, like the iris or flower-deluce.

iridescente [e-re-des-then'-tay], *a.* Iridescent, rainbow-hued.

iridio [e-ree'-deo], *m. (Min.)* Iridium, a metallic element.

iris [ee'-ris], *m.* 1. Iris, the rainbow. 2. Iris, the circle round the pupil of the eye. 3. Mediator, peace-maker. 4. *(Bot.) V.* LIRIO PAJIZO or ESPADANAL. 5. Prim. 6. *(LAm.)* To wink (guiñar el ojo).

irisado, da [e-re-sah'-do, dah], *a.* Rainbow-hued.

irisar [e-re-sar'], *va.* To throw out rainbow-hued scintillations.

irlanda [ir-lahn'-dah], *f.* 1. Cloth made of cotton and woollen yarn. 2. Fine Irish linen.

irlandés, esa [ir-lan-days', sah], *a.* Irish, relating to Ireland. *-m.* The Irish language. *-f.* Irish woman.

ironía [e-ro-nee'-ah], *f.* Irony, the use of words designed to convey a meaning opposite to the literal sense. A rhetorical figure.

irónicamente [e-ro'-ne-cah-men-tay], *adv.* Ironically.

irónico, ca [e-ro'-ne-co, cah], *a.* Ironical.

irracional [i-rrah-the-o-nahl'], *a.* Irrational, void of reason, absurd: sometimes used as a substantive for an irrational animal.

irracionalilad [ir-rah-the-o-nah-le-dahd'], *f.* Irrationality, absurdness.

irracionalmente [ir-rah-the-o-nahl'-men-tay], *adv.* Irrationally, absurdly.

irradiación [ir-rah-de-ah-the-on'], *f.* 1. Irradiation, the act of emitting light; irradiance. 2. Illumination, intellectual light.

irradiar [ir-rah-de-ar'], *va.* To irradiate, to emit beams of light.

irrazonable [ir-rah-the-nah'-blay], *a.* Unreasonable.

irreal [ir-ray-ahl'], *a.* Unreal.

irrealista [ir-ray-ah-lees'-tah], *a.* Unrealistic.

irrealizable [ir-ray-ah-le-thah-blay], *a.* Unrealizable, unworkable (trabajo), impossible to carry out, unattainable (meta).

irrebatible [ir-ray-bah-tree'-blay], *a.* Indisputable.

irreconciliable [ir-ray-con-the-le-ah'-blay], *a.* Irreconciliable, unappeasable.

irreconciliablemente [ir-ray-con-the-le-ah'-blay-men-tay], *adv.* Irreconcilably.

irreconocible [ir-ray-co-no-thee'-blay], *a.* Unrecognizable.

irrecuperable [ir-ray-coo-pay-rah'-blay], *a.* Irrecoverable, irretrievable.

irrecusable [ir-ray-coo-sah'-blay], *a.* 1. Not to be refused or declined, unimpeachable. 2. Inevitable.

irredimible [ir-ray-de-mee'-blay]. *a.* Irredeemable, irretrievable, irreparable.

irreducible [ir-ray-doo-thee'-blay], *a.* 1. Irreducible (mínimo). 2. Stubborn, obstinate.

irreemplazable, irremplazable [ir-ray-em-plah-thah'-blay, rem-plah-thah'-blay], *a.* Irreplaceable.

irreflexión [ir-ray-flec-se-on'], *f.* Rashness, indiscretion, inconsideration.

irreflexivo, va [ir-ray-flec-see'-vo, vah], *a.* Inconsiderate, indiscreet, unreflecting.

irreformable [ir-ray-for-mah-blay], *a.* Not to be reformed or reclaimed.

irrefragable [ir-ray-frah-gah'-blay], *a.* Irrefragable, irrefutable.

irregular [ir-ray-goo-lar'], *a.* 1. Irregular, disorderly, abnormal. 2. Irregular, immethodical.

irregularidad [ir-ray-goo-lah-re-dahd'], *f.* Irregularity, deviation from rule, disorder, misgovernance, abnormity.

irregularmente [ir-ray-goo-lar'-men-tay], *adv.* Irregularly, loosely.

irrelevante [ir-ray-lay-vahn'-tay], *a.* Irrelevant.

irreligión [ir-ray-le-he-on'], *f.* Irreligion, impiety, unbelief.

irreligiosidad [ir-ray-le-he-o-se-dahd'], *f.* Irreligiousness, impeity.

irreligioso, sa [ir-ray-le-he-o'-so, sah], *a.* Irreligious, impious.

irremediable [ir-ray-may-de-ah'-blay], *a.* Irremediable, incurable: helpless.

irremediablemente [ir-ray-may-de-ah'-blay-men-tay], *adv.* Irremediably, helplessly, irrecoverably.

irremisible [ir-ray-me-see'-blay], *a.* Irremissible, unpardonable.

irremisiblemente [ir-ray-me-see'-blay-men-tay], *adv.* Unpardonably, irremissibly.

irremunerado, da [ir-ray-moo-nay-rah'-do, dah], *a.* Unremunerated.

irreparable [ir-ray-pah-rah'-blay], *a.* Irreparable, irretrievable.

irreparablemente [ir-ray-pah-rah'-blay-men-tay], *adv.* Irreparably, irretrievably, irrecoverably.

irrepetible [ir-ray-pay-tee'-blay], *a.* One-and-only, unique.

irreprensible [ir-ray-pen-see'-blay], *a.* Irreprehensible, irreproachable, irreprovable.

irreprensiblemente [ir-ray-pren-see'-blay-men-tay], *adv.* Irreprehensibly, irreproachably.

irreprochable [ir-ray-pro-chah'-blay], *a.* Irreproachable.

irresistibilidad [ir-ray-sis-te-be-le-dahd'], *f.* Irresistibility.

irresistible [ir-ray-sis-tee'-blay], *a.* Irresistible; impossibly strong (demasiado fuerte).

irresistiblemente [ir-ray-sis-tee'-blay-men-tay], *adv.* Irresistibly.

irresoluble [ir-ray-so-loo'-blay], *a.* 1. Indeterminable, not to be defined; not to be resolved, irresoluble. 2. Irresolute, not constant in purpose.

irresolución [ir-ray-so-loo-the-on'], *f.* Irresolution, want of firmness, irresoluteness, hesitation.

irresoluto, ta, irresuelto, ta [ir-ray-so-loo'-to, tah, ir-ray-soo-el'-to, tah], *a.* Irresolute (carácter), unsteady, unresolved (problema).

irrespetuoso, sa [ir-res-pay-too-o'-so, sah], *a.* Unrespectful, wanting in respect.

irrespirable [ir-res-pe-rah'-blay], *a.* Irrespirable, not fit to be breathed.

irresponsabilidad [ir-res-pon-sah-be-le-dahd'], *f.* Irresponsibility.

irresponsable [ir-res-pon-sah'-blay], *a.* Irresponsible.

irreverencia [ir-ray-vay-ren'-the-ah], *f.* Irreverence, want of respect or veneration.

irreverente [ir-ray-vay-ren'-tay], *a.* Irreverent.

irreverentemente [ir-ray-vay-ren-tay-men-tay], *adv.* Irreverently.

irreversible [ir-ray-ver-see'-blay]. *a.* Irreversible.

irrevocabilidad [ir-ray-vo-cah-be-le-dahd'], *f.* Irrevocability.

irrevocable [ir-ray-vo-cah'-blay], *a.* Irrevocable, irreversible.

irrevocablemente [ir-ray-vo-cah'-blay-men-tay], *adv.* Irrevocably.

irrisible [ir-re-see'-blay], *a.* Risible, laughable.

irrisión [ir-re-se-on'], *f.* Irrision, the art of laughing at another, mockery.

irrisoriamente [ir-re-so-re-ah-me'-tay], *adv.* Laughingly, derisively.

irrisorio, ria [ir-re-so'-re-o, ah], *a.* Derisive, risible, ridiculous, absurd; absurdly low, bargain (precio).

irritatilidad [ir-re-tah-be-le-dahd'], *f.* Irritability.

irritable [ir-re-tah'-blay], *a.* 1. That can be rendered void or annulled. 2. Irritable, easily provoked. 3. Irritable, easily irritated.

irritación [ir-re-tah-the-on'], *f.* 1. Irritation, commotion, agitation. 2. Invalidation, abrogation. 3. (*Med.*) Irritation, morbid action of the organs.

irritador, ra [ir-re-tah-dor', rah], *m. &f.* Irritator, stimulator. -a. Irritating.

irritamiento [ir-re-tah-me-en'-to], *m.* Irritation; abrogation.

irritante [ir-re-tahn'-tay], *a. & pa.* 1. Annulling or making void. 2. Irritative, irritant, stimulating.

irritante [ir-re-tahn'Tay], *m.* (*Med.*) Stimulant, irritant.

irritar [ir-re-tar'], *va.* 1. To annual, to render void. 2. To irritate, to exasperate, to agitate violently, to nettle, to offend, to make angry. 3. To alter, to produce a change.

írrito, ta [eer'-re-to, tah], *a.* Null, void.

irrogar [ir-ro-gar'], *va.* To cause, to occasion.

irrompible [ir-rom-pee'-blay], *a.* Unbreakable.

irrupción [ir-roop-the-on'], *f.* Irruption, inroad, invasion.

isagoge [e-sah-go'-hay], *f.* Introduction, preliminary remarks.

isagógico, ca [e-sah-go'-he-co, cah], *a.* Isagogical, introductive, introductory.

iságono [e-sah'-go-no], *m.* (*Geom.*) Isagon.

isanto, ta [e-sahn'-to, tah], *a.* (*Bot.*) Having floral envelopes just alike.

isatina [e-sah-tee'-nah], *f.* Isatin, a crystalline compound obtained by oxydizing indigo.

iscofonía [is-co-fo-ne'-ah], (*Med.*) A defect of the the voice, difficulty in pronouncing certain consonants.

isla [ees'-lah], *f.* 1. Isle, island. 2. A remote or retired spot. 3. Square, an area of four sides, with houses on each side. 4. (*Mex*). Isolated dump of trees (árboles). **En isla**, insulated. **Islas de barlovento**, windward islands. **Islas de sotavento**, leeward islands.

islam [is-lahm'], *m.* Islamism, the religion of Muslims.

islámico, ca [es-lah'-me-co, cah], *a.* Islamic.

islamismo [is-lah-mees'-mo], *m.* Mohammedanism.

islamita [is-lah-mee'-tah], *a. & m. f.* Islamite.

islán [is-lahn'], *m.* A kind of veil anciently worn by women.

islandés, sa [is-lan-day'-sah], *a.* Icelandic, relating to Iceland.

isleño, ña [is-lay'-nyo, nyah], *m. & f.* Islander.

isleo [is-lay'-o], *m.* Island formed by rocks.

isleta [is-lay'-tah], *f. dim.* A small isle, islet.

islilla [is-leel'-lyah], *f.* Flank, part of the body from the hip to the armpit.

islote [es-lo'-tay], *m.* A small barren island.

ismaelita [is-mah-ay-lee'-tah], *a.* Ishmaelite, Mohammedan, Arab.

isobárico, ca [e-so-bah'-re-co, cah], *a.* (*Phy.*) Isobaric.

isócrono, na [e-so'-cro-no, nah], *a.* Isochronal, having equal times.

isoglos [e-so'-glos], *m.* Isoglos.

isógono, na [e-so' -go-no, nah], *a.* Having two equal angles.

isomérico, ea [e-so-may-re-co, cah], *a.* Isomeric, relating to isomerism.

isomerismo [e-so-may-rees'-mo], *m. (Chem.)* Isomerism, the condition of having different properties, but the same molecular composition, or same atomic weight.

isómero, ra [e-so'-may-ro, rah], *a.* 1. Isomerous, equal in number. 2. Isomeric.

isometría [e-so-may-tree'-ah], *f.* Isometrics.

isométrico, ca [e-so-may'-tre-co, cah], *a.* Isometric.

isomorfismo [e-so-mor-fees'-mo], *m.* Isomorphism, identical crystallization.

isomorfo, fa [e-so-mor'-fo, fah], *a.* Isomorphous, isomorphic, of the same construction.

isonomía [e-so-no-mee'-ah], *f.* Equality of civil rights, isonomy.

isónomo, ma [e-so' -no-mo, mah], *a.* Governed by the same law.

isoperimétrico, ca [e-so-pay-re-may-tre-co, cah], *a.* Isoperimetrical.

isósceles [e-sos'-thay-les], *a (Geom.)* Isosceles, a triangle having two sides equal.

isotermo, ma [e-so-ter' -mo, mah], *a* Isothermal, of equal temperature.

isótopo [e-so'-to-po], *m (Phy. & Chem.)* Isotope.

israelí [is-rah-ay-lee'], *a. & m. & f.* Israeli.

israelita [is-ra-hay-lee' -tah], *m.* Israelite, Jew.

israelítico, ca [is-rah-ay-lee' -te-co, cah], *a.* Israelitish, Jewish.

ístmico, ca [eest' -me-co, cah], *a.* Isthmian, belonging to the isthmus.

istmo [eest' -mo], *m.* Isthmus.

italianismo [e-tah-le-ah-nees'-mo], *m.* Italianism, an Italian idiom or expression.

italianizar [e-tah-le-ah-ne-thar'], *va.* To Italianize.

italiano [e-tah-le-ah'-no], *a.* Italian, -*m.* The Italian language.

itálico, ca [e-tah'-le-co, cah], *a.* Italic. -*f.* Italic type.

ítem [ee' -tem], *m.* Item, near article. -*adv.* Also, moreover.

iterar [e-tay-rar'], *va.* To iterate, to repeat. *V.* REPETIR.

iterativo, va [e-tay-rah-tee'-vo, vah], *a.* Iterative, repeating, redoubling.

itinerario [e-te-nay-rah'-re-o], *m.* Itinerary, book of travels; guide for traveling; march, route.

itinerario, ria [e-te-nay-rah'-re-o, ah], *a.* Itinerary.

itria [ee'-tre-ah], *f. (Min.)* Yttria, a white insoluble earth.

itrio [ee'-tre-o], *m.* Yttrium, a rare element belonging to the cerium group.

iza [ee'-thah], *f. (Naut.)* Hoisting, hauling up.

izaga [e-thah'-gah], *f.* Place abounding in rushes and reeds.

izamiento [e-thah-me-en' -to], *m.* Hoisting, raising (bandera).

izar [e-thar'], *va. (Naut.)* To hoist, to raise up on high. **La bandera está izada**, the flag is flying.

izquierdear [ith-ke-er-day-ar'], *vn.* To degenerate, to fall from its kind; to grow wild.

izquierdista [ith-ke-er-dees'-tah], *a. & m. & f.* Leftist, left-wing.

izquierdo, da [ith-keer'-do, dah], *a.* 1. Left-handed (zurdo), left; sinister. **A la izquierda**, to the left. 2. Crooked, not right or straight.

izquierdo, da [ith-keer'-do, dah], *m. & f* A left-handed (persona).

J

j [ho'-tah], It is always a consonant in Spanish, and its pronunciation is guttural, or like the sound of *h* strongly aspirated, as in *ham, her, him, home, who.* **J** is used in some cases in preference to **G** to represent the guttural sound before *e*, thus: *mujer, tejer.*

jaba [hah'-bah], *f.* 1. *(Cuba)* A basket made of the leaves of *yarey.* **Llevar or tener la jaba**, *(coll.)* to be unpolished, uneducated. 2. *(Carib.)* Poverty. 3. *(Carib.)* Beggar's bag. **Llevar algo en la jaba**, to have something up one's sleeve.

jabalcón [hah-bal-co-ne'], *m.* Bracket, purlin.

jabalconar [hah-bal-co-nar'], *va.* To support the roof of a house with brackets.

jabalí [hah-bah-lee'], *m.* Wild boar.

jabalina [hah-bah-lee'-nah], *f.* 1. Sow of a wild boar. 2. Javelin, a kind of spear.

jabalonar [hah-bah-lo-nar'], *va V.* JABALCONAR.

jabardear [hah-bar-day-ar'], *va.* To swarm, to rise as bees in a body.

jabardillo [hah-bar-deel'-lyo], *m. V.* JABARDO for a crowd.

jabardo [hah-bar'-do], *m.* 1. A small swarm of bees. 2. Any crowd or assembly of low people; mob, rabble.

jabato [hah-bah'-to], *m.* A young wild boar. -*a.* 1. Brave, bold. 2: *(Carib. Mex.)* Rude (grosero), gruff; ill-tempered (malhumorado).

jabeca [hah'-bay-cah], *f.* 1. Sweep-net, a large net for fishing. 2. *V.* JÁBEGA.

jabega [hah'-bay-gah], *f.* A Moorish wind instrument, somewhat like a flute.

jabeguero [hah-bay-gay' -ro], *m.* Fisher-man who fishes with a sweep-net.

jabeque [hah-bay'-kay], *m. (Naut.)* 1. Xebec, a small Mediterranean three-masted vessel. 2. A wound made in the face with a knife or other cutting weapon.

jabí [hah-bee'], *m.* 1. Small wild apple or crab. 2. Small kind of grapes. 3. A hard-wood tree of Yucatan.

jabladera [hah-blah-day'-rah], *f.* Crozer, a cooper's tool.

jable [hah'-blay], *m.* Croze, the groove in the staves of casks which receives the heads.

jabón [hah-bo-ne'], *m.* 1. Soap, bar of soap (pastilla de jabón). **Jabón de afeitar.** shaving soap. **Jabón en polvo**, soap powder. 2. *(Met.)* Any saponaceous mass or matter. 3. *(coll.)* Smart stroke with a batlet. 4. Soft soap (adulación). 5. *(Carib. Cono Sur, Mex.)* Fright, scare. **Dar un jabón**, to reprimand severely.

jabonado, da [hah-bo-nah'-do, dah], *a. & pp.* of JABONAR. Soaped, cleansed with soap.

jabonado [hah-bo-nah'-do], *m.* 1. Wash, the act of washing with soap. 2. Parcel of linen washed with soap (ropa).

jabonadura [hah-bo-nah-doo'-rah], *f.* The act of washing (acto). **Jabonaduras**, 1. Suds or soapsuds. 2. Lather. **Echarle or darle a uno una jabonadura**, *(coll.)* to reprimand somebody.

jabonamiento [hah-bo-nah-me-en'-to], *m. V.* JABONADURA.

jabonar [hah-bo-nar'], *va.* 1. To soap, to cleanse with soap. 2. *(coll.)* To reprimand severely.

jaboncillo, jabonete, or **jabonete de olor** [hah-bon-theel'-hah-bo-nay'-tay], *m.* 1. Bar of soap; shaving soap. 2. Soap-stone or French chalk used by tailors. 3. Mixture of oils and alkali, especially ammonia, hardly saponified.

jabonera [hah-bo-nay'-rah], *f.* 1. Box or case for a bar of soap. 2. *(Bot.)* Soapwort.

jabonería [hah-bo-nay-ree'-ah], *f.* Soap-manufactory, soap-house.

jabonero [hah-bo-nay' -ro], *m.* Soap maker or seller.

jabonoso, sa [hah-bo-no' -so, sah], *a.* Soapy.

jabuco [hah-boo'-co], *m. (Cuba)* A round basket in the form of a very large decanter with a narrow neck.

jaca [hah'-cah], *f.* 1. Nag, pony, mare(jegua). *V.* HACA. 2. A name of the bread-fruit tree.

jacal [hah-cahl'], *m. (Max.)* 1. An Indian hut, a wigwam. 2. *(Zool.)* Jackal. *V.* CHACAL.

jacamar [hah-cah-mar'], *m.* Jacamar, an insectivorous bird of South America, notable for its beauty.

jacana [hah-cah'-nah], *f.* A tropical South American wading bird.

jácara [hah'-cah-rah], *f.* 1. A sort of romance. 2. A kind of rustic tune for singing or dancing; a kind of dance. 3. Company of young men who walk about at night time singing *jácaras* (personas). 4. Molestation, vexation (molestia). 5. Idle talk or prattle, story, tale (cuento); fable, lie, vainglorious fiction.

jacarandina, jacarandana [hah-cah-ran-dee'-nah, hah-cah-ran-dah'-nah], *f.* 1. Low, foul language, slang, the language of ruffians and prostitutes; bullies. 2. Singing of jácaras or boastings. 3. (*Low.*) Assembly of ruffians and thieves.

jacarear [hah-cah-ray-ar'], *vn.* 1. To sing *jácaras.* 2. To go about the streets with singing and noise. 3. To be troublesome and vexatious (armar un lío); to be rude (insultar).

jacarero [hah-cah-ray'-ro], *m.* 1. Ballad-singer. 2. Wag or merry droll, a facetious person.

jacarilla [hah-cah-reel'-ly-ah], *f. dim.* of JÁCARA.

jácaro [hah'-cah-ro], *m.* Boaster, bully.

jácaro, ra [hah'-cah-ro, rah], *a.* Belonging to boasters or noisy singers. **A lo jácaro.** in a boastful or bragging manner.

jacena [hah-thay'-nah], *f.* Girder, a beam on which joists rest.

jacerina [hah-thay-ree'-nah], *f.* Mail, a coat of steel network for defence.

jacilla [hah-theel'-lyah], *f.* Mark which a thing leaves upon the ground where it has been for some time.

jacinto [hah-theen'-to], *m.* 1. Hyacinth (planta). 2. Hyacinth (piedra preciosa).

jacio [hah'-the-o], *m.* (*Naut.*) A dead calm.

jaco [hah'-co], *m.* 1. Nag, pony. 2. A short jacket, formerly used by soldiers. 3. *V.* JAQUE.

jacobínico, ca [hah-co-bee'-ne-co, cah], *a.* Jacobin, Jacobinical, belonging to Jacobins.

jacobinismo [hah-co-be-nees'-mo], *m.* Jacobinism, the principles of a Jacobin.

jacobino [hah-co-bee'-no], *m.* Jacobin, one of a faction in the French revolution, a downright democrat; an infidel.

jacra, or **jagra** [hah'-crah], *f.* A kind of sugar obtained from the wine of the palm-tree or the cocoanut.

jactancia [hac-tahn'-the-ah], *f.* Jactation, boasting, arrogance, ostentation.

jactanciosamente [hac-tan-the-o-sah-ment' -tay], *adv.* Boastingly.

jactancioso, sa [hac-tan-the-o'-so, sah], *a.* Boastful, vainglorious: arrogant, glorious, ostentatious.

jactarse [hac-tar'-say], *vr.* To vaunt, to boast, to display with ostentation, to glory, to flourish, to brag, to gasconade.

jaculatoria [hah-coo-lah-to'-re-ah], *f.* Ejaculation, a short prayer.

jaculatorio, ria [hah-coo-lah-to'-re-o, ah], *a.* Jaculatory.

jachalí [hah-chah-lee'], *m.* The custard apple, a tropical shrub or low tree valued for its hard wood.

jada [hah'-dah], *f.* (*Prov.*) *V.* AZADA.

jade [hah'-day], *m.* Jade (mineral).

jadeante [hah-day-ahn'-tay], *a.* Panting, breathless, gasping.

jadear [hah-day-ar'], *vn.* To pant, to palpitate, to have the breast heaving as for want of breath; to jade.

jadeo [hah-day'-o], *m.* Pant; palpitation, gasping.

jadiar [hah-de-ar'], *va.* (*Prov.*) To dig up with a spade.

jaecero, ra [hah-ay-thay'-ro, rah], *m. &f.* Harness-maker.

jaén [hah-en'], *m.* A kind of large white grape, with thick rind.

jaez [hah'-eth], *m.* 1. Harness, the traces of draught-horses. 2. Manner or quality in which several things resemble each other. **Jaeces**, ornaments or harness of horses in processions.

jafético, ca [hah-fay'-te-co, cah], *a.* Japhetic, Indo-Germanic, descended from Japhet.

jagua [hah'-goo-ah], *f.* Fruit of the custard-apple, of a sweet, agreeable taste. (*Cuba*)

jaguar, or **jaguarete** [hah-goo-ar', or hah-goo-ah-ray'- tay], *m.* The Jaguar, a ferocious beast resembling the leopard.

jagüey [hah-goo-ay'-e], *m.* 1. In Peru and Mexico, a large pool or lake. Also, a reservoir for rain-water, when no spring water is at hand. 2. (*Cuba*) The matador liana, a climbing plant which kills the tree which it clasps.

jaharrar [ha-har-rar'], *va.* To plaster, to overlay or make even with plaster.

jaharro [ha-har'-ro], *m.* Plaster, the act of plastering.

jai alai [hah-e ah-lah'-e], *m.* Jai alai, Basque ball game.

jaiba [hah'-e-bah], *f.* (*Cuba & Mex.*) Certain type of crab (cangrejo). 2. (*And.*) Mouth (boca). -*m & f.* (*Carib. Mex.*) Sharp customer. -*f.* (*Mex.Zool.*) Crab; (*CAm.*) fresh-water or river crab (de río).

jabol [hah-e-bol'], *m.* (*Mex.*) High-ball.

jaire [hah'-e-ray], *m.* 1. The curved line made in a timber which is joined to another for greater solidity. 2. Among shoemakers, the outward inclination of the knife in splitting leather.

¡ja, ja, ja! [hah, hah, hah], *int.* Exclamation, denoting laughter.

jalapa [hah-lah'-pah], *f.* (*Bot.*) 1. Jalapa. 2. Jalap, the root of the jalap, plant frequently used in medicine.

jalar [hah-lahr'], *va.* 1. (*LAm.*) To pull (tirar de). 2. (*LAm.*) to work hard. 3. (*And. Carib.*) To make, to do (hacer). 4. To guzzle. 5. (*LAm.*) To pull (conquistar). -*vn.* 1. (*LAm.*) To pull (tirar). 2. (*LAm.*) To work hard. 3. (*LAm.*) To go off, to go (irse). 4. (*CAm. Mex.*) To be courting (amantes). 5. (*Mex.*) To exaggerate (exagerar). -*vr.* 1. (*CAm.*) To be courting (amantes). 2. (*LAm.*) To get drunk.

jalbegar [hal-bay-gar'], *va.* 1. To whiten, to whitewash. 2. To paint excessively, to lay too much white on the face.

jalbegue [hal-bay'-gay], *m.* 1. Whitewash. 2. Whitewashing, whitening a wall with lime. 3. Whitewash, a paint or wash to make the skin seem fair.

jaldado, da, jaldo, da [hal-dah'-do, dah, hahl'-do, dah], *a.* Of a bright yellow color.

jalde [hahl'-day], *a.* Bright yellow, crocus-colored.

jaldre [hahl'-dray], *m.* A bright yellow color, peculiar to birds.

jalea [hah-lay'-ah], *f.* Jelly, the inspissated juice of fruit, boiled with sugar. **Hacerse una jalea**, (*Met.*) to love with excessive fondness.

jalear [hah-lay-ar'], *va.* 1. To encourage hounds to follow the chase (perro). 2. To animate dancers, by clapping hands (bailarines). 3. To quaver the voice, to use the vibrato. -*vn.* (*Mex.*) To have a high old time.

jaleo [hah-lay'-o], *m.* 1. Spree, binge (juerga). **Estar de jaleo**, to make merry. 2. Row, uproar (ruido); hassle (confusión). **Armar un jaleo**, to kick up a row. 3. Hallooing (caza). 4. (*Mus.*) Shouting and clapping.

jaletina [hah-lay-tee'-nah], *f.* 1. Calf's foot jelly. 2. Gelatine.

jalma [hahl'-mah], *f.* A kind of packsaddle.

jalmero [hal-may'-ro], *m.* One whose trade is to make packsaddles and harness for mules.

jaloque [hah-lo'-kay], *m.* South-east wind. *V.* SIROCO.

jamaicano, na [hah-mah-e-cah'-no, nah], *a.* Jamaican, pertaining to Jamaica.

jamaiquense, jamaiqués, sa [hah-mah-e-ken'-say, keys', sah], *a, & m. &f.* Jamaican.

jamar [hah-mar'], *vn.* To eat, to stuff oneself. -*vr.* **Se lo jamó todo**, he scoffed the lot.

jamás [hah-mahs'], *adv.* Never, at no time. **Para siempre jamás**, forever. (*Vulg.*) For ever and a day. **Jamás, por jamás or nunca jamás**, never, nevermore.

jamba [hahm'-bah], *f. (birch.)* Door-jamb, window-post, which supports the lintel or head-piece.

jambaje [ham-bah'-hay], *m. (Arch.)* Collection of jambs.

jámbico, ca [hahm'-be-co, cah]. *a.* Iambic. *V.* YÁMBICO.

jamerdana [hah-mer-dah'-nah], *f.* Sewer which runs from a slaughterhouse.

jamerdar [hah-mer-dar'], *va.* 1. To clean the guts of animals. 2. To wash hastily.

jamete [hah-may'-tay], *m.* A sort of stuff formerly worn in Spain.

jametería [hah-may-tay-ree'-ah], *f. (Prov.) V.* ZALAMERÍA.

jamilla [hah-meel'-lyah], *f. V.* ALPECHÍN.

jamón [hah-mone'], *m.* 1. Ham, the salted thigh of a hog. **Jamón York**, boiled ham. **Jamón serrano**, cured ham. 2. *(Carib.)* Bargain (ganga). 3. *(Carib.)* Difficulty (conflicto).

jamona [hah-mo'-nah], *a.* A stout middle-aged woman.

jamuga, or **jamugas** [hah-moo'-gah], *f.* A kind of side saddle for women.

jándalo, la [hahn'-dah-lo, lah], *a.* Having the gait and dialect of an Andalusian; particularly in giving the *h* a strong guttural sound.

jangada [han-gah'-dah], *f.* Raft, a frame or float.

jantio [hahn'-te-o], *m. (Bot.)* Lesser burdock.

japonés, sa [hah-po-nays', sah], *a.* Japanese, relating to Japan.

jaque [hah'-kay], *m.* 1. Braggart, boaster. 2. Check, in the game of chess (ajedrez). **Jaque mate**, checkmate. 3. Saddlebag. 4. Sort of smooth combing of the hair. **Dar jaque** a, to check.

jaquear [hah-kay-ar'], *va.* To give or make check at chess.

jaqueca [hah-kay'-cah], *f.* Migrain headache, a severe headache; *(Cono Sur)* hangover (resaca).

jaquel [hah-kayl'], *m.* Chessboard.

jaquelado, da [hah-kay-lah'-do, dah], *a.* Checkered: applied to cut diamonds or precious stones.

jaquero [hah-kay'-ro], *m.* Fine-toothed comb.

jaquetón [hah-kay-tone'], *m. aug.* 1. A large, wide coat. 2. Great swaggerer, boaster.

jáquima [hah'-ke-mah], *f.* Headstall of a halter.

jaquimazo [hah-ke-mah'-tho], *m.* 1. Stroke with the headstall of a halter. 2. Displeasure; an unfair trick, ill turn.

jara [hah'-rah], *f.* 1. *(Bot.)* Cistus or rock-rose, labdanumtree. 2. A kind of dart or arrow (dardo). *Java cerval, (Bot.)* round-leaved cistus.

jarabe [hah-rah'-bay], *m.* 1. Sirup, vegetable juice with sugar. 2. Any very sweet mixed drink, especially if not very cool. **Jarabe de palo**, beating. **Jarabe de arce**, maple syrup. 3. *(Mex.)* Popular dance.

jarabear [hah-rah-bay-ar']. *va.* To prescribe sirups very often. *-vr.* To take sirups or sweet beverages frequently.

jaraiz [hah-rah'-eeth], *m.* Pit for pressing grapes.

jaral [hah-rahl'], *m.* 1. Place planted with the cistus or labdanum shrub (maleza). 2. A very intricate or puzzling point.

jaramago [hah-rah-mah'-go], *m. (Bot.)* All the species of cruciferous plants bearing yellow flowers; mustards.

jarameño, ña [hah-rah-may'-nyo, nyah], *a.* Applied to bulls reared on the banks of the Jarama, a river in Spain.

jaramugo [hah-rah-moo'-go], *m.* Small fish used as bait for others.

jarana [hah-rah'-nah], *f.* 1. Carousel, reverly, romping. 2. *(coll.)* Scuffle, contest. 3. Outcry, row, spree (juerga). **No querer meterse en jaranas**, not to like to get into scrapes. 4. Trick, deceit (trampa); *(LAm.)* joke, practical joke. 5. *(And. Carib. Mex.)* Folk dance (baile); *(Carib.)* dance band (banda). 6. *(Mex.)* Small guitar. 7. *(CAm. Fin.)* debt.

jarano [hah-rah'-no], *m.* Mexican wide-brimmed felt hat.

jarapastroso, sa [hah-rah-pas-tro'-so, sah], *a.* Dialectic for *zarrapastroso* ragged.

jarapote [hah-rah-po'-tay], *m. (Prov.) V.* JAROPEO.

jarapotear [hah-rah-po-tay-ar'], *va. (Prove.)* To stuff or fill with medicinal drugs.

jarazo [hah-rah'-tho], *m.* Blow or wound with a dart.

jarcia [har'-the-ah], *f.* 1. Parcel or bundle of a variety of things laid by for use. 2. A multitude of things without order (montón). 3. *(Naut.)* Tackle (pesca), rigging and cordage belonging to a ship, the shrouds. 4. A complete fishing-tackle. 5. *(Carib.Mex.)* Rope (cuerda). 6. *(CAm. Mex.)* Agave; rope (cuerda). **Almacén de jarcias**, rigging-house, store-house for rigging. **Tablas de jarcia**, suit or set of rigging. **Jarcia mayor**, the main shrouds.

jardín [har-deen'], *m.* 1. A garden. 2. Spot which disfigures an emerald. 3. Privy on board of ships. 4. *(LAm.)* Kindergarten, nursery school.

jardincito, jardinito [har-din-thee'-to, har-de-nee'-to], *m. dim.* A small garden.

jardinería [har-de-nay-ree'-ah], *f.* Gardening, the art of cultivating gardens.

jardinero, ra [har-de-nay'-ro, rah], *m. & f.* Gardener. *-f.* 1. Flower stand, jardiniere. 2. A basket carriage. 3. *(Cono Sur)* Handcart (carrito). 4. *(And.)* Jacket (saco).

jareta [hah-ray'-tah], *f.* 1. Seam made by doubling the edge of cloth, through which a string or lace may be drawn. 2. *(Naut.)* Netting, harpings. 3. *(CAm. Cono Sur)* Pants files (de pantalón). 4. *(Carib.)* Snag, setback (contratiempo).

jaretera [hah-ray-tay'-rah], *f. V.* JARRETERA.

jarife [hah-ree'-fay], *m. V.* JERIFE.

jarifo, fa [hah-ree'-fo, fah], *a.* Showy, full-dressed, adorned, elegant.

jaripeo [ha-re-pay'-o], *m.* Rodeo, horse show.

jaro, ra [hah'-ro, rah], *a.* Resembling a wild boar (cerdos).

jarocho [hah-ro'cho], *m.* 1. *(Mex.Coll.)* A rough, stout countryman. 2. Mulatto or negro.

jaropar, jaropear, or **jaropotear** [hah-ro-par', hah-ro-po-tay-ar'], *va.* To stuff or fill with medicinal drugs; to give any liquor as a medical draught, to medicine.

jarope [hah-ro'-pay], *m.* 1. Medical draught or potion. 2. Any kind of bitter **beverage**. 3. Sirup.

jaropeo [hah-ro-pay'-o], *m.* The excessive and frequent use of bitters or medical potions; the drug habit.

jarra [har'-rah], *f.* 1. Jug, jar, pitcher, mug (cerveza), churn (leche), of earthenware. 2. *(Prove.)* Ancient equestrian order. **En jarra** or **de jarras**, akimbo.

jarrear [har-ray-ar'], *vn. (coll.)* To take out often water or wine with a jug; to drink often.

jarrero [har-ray'-ro], *m.* Vender or maker of jugs or jars.

jarreta, illa, ita [har-ray-tah, eel'-lya, ee'-tah], *f. dim.* 1. A small jar. 2. *(Naut.)* Gratings.

jarrete [har-ray'-tay], *m.* Ham, the upper part of the leg, hock (caballo).

jarretera [har-ray-tay'-rah], *f.* 1. Garter. 2. Garter, the highest order of English knighthood.

jarrito [har-ree'-to], *m. dim.* A small jug or pot with one handle.

jarro [har'-ro], *m.* 1. Jug or pot with one handle only, pitcher. **Caer como un jarro de agua fría**, to come as a complete shock. 2. *(Prov.)* A chatterer.

jarrón [har-rone'], *m. aug.* A large jug or pitcher, an urn.

jaspe [hahs'-pay], *m.* Jasper, a precious stone

jaspeado, da [has-pay-ah'-do, dah], *a. & pp.* of JASPEAR. Spotted, like jasper; marbled, mottled; variegated.

jaspeadura [has-pay-ah-doo'-rah], *f.* Marbling, the act of marbling.

jaspear [has-pay-ar'], *va.* To marble, to paint, to vein or speckle with variegated colors in imitation of jasper. *-vr. (Carib.)* To get cross.

jasteo, tea [has-tay'-o, ah], *a.* Chasing the fox (perros).

jastial [has-te-ahl'], *m.* Facade of an edifice.

jato, ta [hah'-to, tah], *m. & f.* 1. *V.* BECERRO. 2. *(Carib.)* Stray dog (perros). 3. *(Mex.)* Load (carga). 4. *(Mex.)* Stopping place (parada). 5. *(And.)* Saddle (silla de montar).

¡jau! [hah'-oo], *int.* Exclamation to incite animals, especially bulls. Repeated signifies noisy applause.

jauja [hah'-oo-hah], *pr. n.* **¿Estamos aquí, o en Jauja?**, a rebuke or caution: take care!

jaula [hah'-oo-lah], *f.* 1. Cage, an inclosure for birds. 2. Cell for insane persons (locos). 3. Lock-up (tienda, garaje). 4. *(Mex. Ferro.)* Cattle truck.

jaulón [hah-oo-lone'], *m. aug.* A large cage for birds.

jauría [hah'-oo-ree'-ah], *f.* Pack of hounds.

jauto, ta [hah'-oo-to, tah], *a. (Prov.) V.* SOSO.

javanés, sa [hah-vah-nays', sah], *a.* Javanese, relating to java.

javia, or **javio aronillero** [hah-ve-ah, or hah'-ve-o-ah-ray-neel-lay'ro], *m.* The sandbox tree.

jayán, na [hah-yahn', nah], *m. & f.* A tall, strong, and robust person.

jayanazo [hah-ya-nah'-tho], *m. aug.* A huge, big fellow

jazilla [hah-theel'-lyah], *f.* Vestige mark, trace. *V.* JACILLA.

jazmín [hath-meen'], *m. (Bot.)* Jessamine or jasmine, a fragrant flower. **Jazmín real**, catalonian jessamine. **Jazmín amarillo**, Italian jessamine. **Jazmín de Virginia**, ashleaved trumpet flower.

jazminorro [hath-me-nor'-ro], *m. (Bot.)* Common yellow jessamine.

jazz [yath], *m. (Mus.)* Jazz. **Jazz progresivo**, progressive jazz.

jebe [hay'-bay], *m.* 1. *(Prov.)* Rockalum. *(Acad.)* 2. *(Peru)* Caoutchouc, Indianrubber. 3. Arse (trasero).

jeep [jeep], *m.* Jeep.

jeera [hay-ay'-rah], *f.* Piece of drained marshy ground.

jefatura [hay-fah-too'-rah], *f.* 1. The dignity of a chief, or governor of a province (liderato). 2. The place where the different offices of that government are kept (sede). **Bajo la jefatura**, under the leadership of.

jefe, fa [hay'-fay, fah], *m. & f.* Chief, boss (de un empleado), head superior, lender (líder), manager (gerente). **Jefe de escuadra.** *(Naut.)* Rear admiral. **Jefe de bomberos**, fire officer. **Jefe de estación**, station master. **Jefe de estudios**, deputy head. **Jefe de obras**, project manager. **Jefe supremo**, commander-in-chief.

Jehová [hay-o-vah']. Hebrew word for God. Properly Yahweh.

¡je, je, je! [hay], *int.* Denoting laughter.

jema [hay'-mah], *f.* The part of a beam which is badly squared.

jemal [hay-mahl'], *a.* Of the length of a *jeme*.

jeme [hay'-may], 1. The distance from the end of the thumb to the end of the forefinger (both extended). 2. *(coll.)* A woman's face.

jenabe, jenable [hay-nah'-bay, hay-nah'-blay]. *m.* Mustard. *V.* MOSTAZA.

jengibre [hen-hee'-bray], *m.* Ginger, the pungent, spicy rootstock of Zingiber officinale. Used as medicine and as a spice.

jeniquén [hay-ne-ken'], *m.* Sisal hemp. *V.* HENEQUÉN.

jeque [hay'-kay], *m.* 1. An old man; a governor or chief among the Moors. 2. Portmanteau.

jera [hay'-rah], *f. (Prov.)* Extent of ground which can be ploughed in a day with a pair of oxen.

jerapellina [hay-rah-pel-lyee'-nay], *f.* An old ragged suit of clothes.

jerarca [hay-rar'-cah], *m.* Hierarch.

jerarquía [hay-rar-kee'-ah], *f.* 1. Hierarchy, order among the various choirs of angels and ranks of the chruch. 2. By extension, a rank or grade of importance.

jerárquico, co [hay-ray-ke-co, cah], *a.* Hierarchical, belonging to a hierarchy.

jerez [hay-rayth'], *m.* Sherry.

jerezano, na [hay-ray-thah'-no, nah], *a. & m. & f.* Native of or belonging to Jerez de la Frontera.

jerga [herr'-gah], *f.* 1. Course frieze, any coarse cloth. 2. Jargon, gibberish, unintelligible talk, slang. **Jerga informática**, computer jargon. *V.* JERIGONZA. 3. Large sack.

jergón [her-gone'], *m.* 1. Large course mattress or sack, filled with straw or paper cuttings. 2. Suit of clothes ill made. 3. An illshaped person (persona). 4. Kidderminster carpeting. 5. *(coll.)* Paunch, belly.

jerguilla [her-geel'lyah], *f.* A sort of serge made of silk or worsted.

jerigonza [hay-re-gon'-thah], *f.* 1. Jargon, gibberish, especially of gipsies. 2. Language difficult to understand. 3. Strange and ridiculous action (estupidez).

jeringa [hay-reen'-gah], *f.* 1. Syringe, an instrument for injecting liquids into animal bodies, wounds, etc. 2. *(LAm.)* Pest, nuisance (persona).

jeringación [hay-rin-gah-the-on'], *f.* Syringing, the action and effect of the syringe; the liquid injected by this action.

jeringar [hay-rin-gar'], *va.* To syringe, to inject by means, of a syringe; to wash and cleanse by injections from a syringe.

jeringazo [hay-rin-gah'-tho], *m.* 1. The act of injecting a liquid with the syringe. 2. Clyster, injection, the liquid substance injected with a syringe.

jeringuilla [hay-rin-geel'-lyah], *f.* 1. *dim.* A little syringe. 2. Mock orange, syringa.

jeroglífico [hay-ro-glee-fe-co], *m.* Hieroglyph, the symbol for a word; an ideograph, especially the sacred writing of the Egyptians.

jeroglífico, ca [hay-ro-glee'-fe-co], *a.* Hieroglyphic, hieroglyphical.

jerpa [herr'-pah], *f.* Sterile shoot of a vine.

jerricote [her-re-co'-tay], *m.* A pottage of almonds, sugar, sage and ginger, in chicken broth.

jesucristo [hay-soo-crees'-to], *m.* Jesus Christ.

jesuita [hay-soo-ee'-tah], *m.* Jesuit.

Jesús [hay-soos'], *m.* Jesus. Bless you! (al estornudar).

jet [jet], *m.* Jet, jet plane. -f. Jet-set.

jeta [hey'-tah], *f.* 1. Thick, heavy lips; blobber-lip. 2. A hog's snout; *(Cono Sur)* To kick the bucket (morir). 3. Frown (ceño). 4. Cheek (descaro), nerve. **Lo hace por la jeta**, he gets away with it by sheer cheek.

jeto [hay'-to], *m. (Prov.)* An empty beehive rubbed with honey to attract the bees.

jetudo, da [hay-too'do, dah], *a.* Thick-lipped.

jiba [hee'-bah], *f.* 1. A hump, 2. Bother, tiresomeness.

jibado, da [he-bah'-do, dah], *a.* Hump-backed, crooked.

jibar [he-bar'], *va. (coll.)* To vex, to molest, to annoy.

jíbaro, ra [hee'-bah-ro, rah], *a. (Cuba)* 1. Run wild. 2. Rustic (rústico), rude. -m. Countryman.

jibia [hee'-be-ah], *f. (Zool.)* Cuttle-fish.

jibión [he-be-on'], *m.* Cuttle-fish bone used by gold and silversmiths.

jiboso, sa [he-bo'-so, sah], *a.* Gibbous, hump-backed.

jícama [hee'-ca-mah], *f. (Amer.)* A farinaceous root.

jícara [hee'-ca-rah], *f.* 1. Chocolate-cup (tacita). 2. Gourdtree (calabaza).

jicarazo [he-ca-rah'-tho], *m. aug.* A large chocolate cup. *(Amer. Coll.)* **Dar un jicarazo**, to give poison to a person.

jicotea [he-co-tay'-ah], *f. (Amer.)* A mud-turtle.

jifa [hee'-fah], *f.* Refuse of slaughtered beasts.

jiferada [he-fay-rah'-dah], *f.* Stroke with a butcher's knife.

jifería [he-fah-ree'-ah], *f.* Slaughtering.

jifero, ra [he-fay'-ro, rah], *a.* Belonging to the slaughter-house.

jifero [he-fay'-ro], *m.* 1. Butcher's knife. 2. Butcher.

jifia [hee-fe-ah], *f. (Zool.)* Xiphias, the swordfish.

jiga [hee'-gah], *f.* Jig. a lively dance and tune.

jigote [he-go'-tay], *m.* 1. Minced meat, stewed and dressed with butter; a hash. 2. Any other dish minced.

jijallo [he-hahl'-lo], *m. (Bot.)* Prickly broom, hairy cytisus.

jijene [he-hay'-nay], *m. (S. Amer.)* Sandfly.

jijona [he-ho'-nah], *f.* A variety of flinty wheat. -m. Soft nougat.

jilguero [heel-gay'-ro], *m*, Gold-finch.

jilocopo [he-lo-co'-po], *m*. The carpenter bee, xylocopa.

jilote [he-lo'-tay], *V*. HILOTE.

jimagua [he-nah'-goo-ah], *m & f. (Cuba)* Twin.

jimelga [he-mel'-gah], *f. (Naut.)* The fish of a mast.

jimenzar [he-men-thar'], *va. (Prov.)* To ripple flax or hemp.

jinestada [he-nes-tah'-dah], *f*. Sauce made from milk, rice-flour, dates, spices and other things.

jineta [he-nay'-tah], *f*. 1. A kind of short lance. 2. Art of horsemanship. 3. The office of a sergeant. 4. Ancient tribute imported upon cattle. *Andar a la jineta*, to go at a short trot. **Cabalgar a la jineta**, to ride with very short stirrups.

jinete [he-nay'-tay], *m*. 1. Trooper, cavalryman. 2. One mounted on horseback, a horseman, cavalier.

jinetear [he-nay-tay-ar'], *va*. 1. *(Mex.)* To tame wild horses by riding them (domar). 2. To ride on horseback (montar), publicly, with ostentation. 3. *(Mex.)* To misappropriate (fondos). -*vr*. 1. *(And. Mex.)* To stay in the saddle (no caer). 2. *(And.)* To be vain (ser presumido).

jinglar [hin-glar'], *vn*. To move from one side to another as if hung in a swing.

jinoísmo [hin-go-ees'-mo], *m*. Jingoism, exaggerated patriotism.

jingoísta [hin-go-ees'tah], *a*. Jingoistic.-*m. & f*. Jingoist. ardent patriot.

jinjol [heen-hole'], *m*. Jujube. *V*. AZUFAIFA.

jipar [he-par'], *va*. **Le tengo jipado**, I've got him taped.

jipato. ta [he-pah'-to, tah], *a. (Cuba)* 1. Pale, of sickly countenance. 2. Full, replete with eating.

jipi [he'-pe], *m & f*. Hippy.

jipijapa [he-pe-hah'-pah], *f*. 1. Fine straw (paja), flexible and durable, used in weaving hats, cigar cases, dippers, etc. 2. Panama hat (sombrero). **Sombrero de jipijapa**, panama hat.

jira [hee'-rah], *f*. 1. Strip of cloth (de tela). 2. Shred, tatter, scrap. 3. Picnic, outing. 4. Tour, excursion.

jirafa [he-rah'-fah], *f*. 1. Giraffe. 2. Boom (micrófono).

jirapliega [he-rah-ple-ay'-gah], *f*. A purgative confection.

jirasal [he-rah-sahl'], *f*. Fruit of the lactree.

jirofina [he-ro-fee'-nah], *f*. A kind of sauce or gravy.

jiroflé [he-ro-flay'], *m*. The clove-tree.

jirón [he-rone'], *m*. 1. Facing of a skirt. 2. Piece torn from a gown or other clothing (andrajo). 3. Banner, pennant. 4. Small part of any whole. 5. *(Peru)* A long street, a row of houses (calle).

jironado, da [he-ro-nah'-do, dah], *a*. 1. Torn into strips or fragments. 2. Garnished with triangular pieces of cloth.

jirpear [heer-pay-ar'], *va*. To dig about vines.

jisca [hees'-cah], *f. (Bot.)* Cylindrical sugar-cane. *V*. CARRIZO.

jiste [hees'-tay], *m*. Yeast, barm, leaven. Froth of beer. *(Acad.)*

jitar [he-tar'], *va. (Prov.)* To emit, to turn out.

jito [hee'-to], *m*. The channel by which melted metal runs, and the hole where it enters the mould.

¡jo! [ho]. *int*. Whoa!

jocosamente [ho-co-sah-me'-tay], *adv*. Jocosely, jocularly, waggishly, humorously, good humoredly.

jocoserio, ria [ho-co-say'-reo, ah], *a*. Jocoserious, partaking of mirth and seriousness.

jocosidad [ho-co-se-dahd'], *f*. Jocularity, Jocoseness, jocosity, humor.

jocoso, sa [ho-co'-so, sah], *a*. Jocose, jocular, waggish, facctious, ludicrous, good-humored.

jocoyote [ho-co-yo'-tay], *m. (Amer.)* The youngest child, best loved by the parents.

joder [ho-dayr'], *va*. 1. *(Esp.)* To fuck; damn it! (enfadado). 2. *(Fig.)* To annoy (fastidiar), to upset; to harm (dañar); to pester (acosar); to mess up (estropear). **Esto me jode**, I'm fed up with this. **Son ganas de joder**, they're just trying to be awkward. 3. To pinch, to steal (robar). -*vr*. 1. To flop (fracasar); to get spoiled (estropearse). **Se jodió todo**, everything was spoiled.

jodido, da [ho-dee'-do], *a*. 1. Awkward, difficult (difícil). **Es un libro jodido**, it's a very difficult book. 2. Bloody (condenado). **Ni un jodida peso**, not a dime. 3. *(LAm.)* Selfish (egoísta); evil (malo), wicked (quisquilloso).

jofaina [ho-fah'-e-nah], *f*. A china bowl. *V*. ALJOFAINA.

jogging [jo-ggin], *m*. 1. Jogging. **Hacer jogging**, to jog. 2. *(Cono Sur)* Jogging suit (ropa).

jojoto [ho-ho'-to], *m. (Ven.)* Corn in milk.

jolgorio [hol-go'-re-o], *m. (coll.)* 1. Recreation, relaxation. 2. Mirth, jollity, fun (juerga).

jolito [ho-lee'-to], *m*. Rest, leisure, calm.

jónico, ca, jonio nia [ho'-ne-co, cah, ho'-ne-o, ah], *a*. Ionic (arquitectura). -*m*. A foot in poetry.

jonuco [ho-noo'-co], *m. (Mex.)* A dark, damp corner under a staircase.

jordán [hor-dahn'], *m. (Prov.)* Anything which revives, or gives a fresh bloom.

jorfe [hor'-fay], *m*. 1. A wall made of dry stones only. 2. A high, solitary rock; a tor.

jorfear [hor-fay-ar'], *va*. To form a floor without arches.

jorguín [hor-geen'], *m. (Prov.)* Soot, condensed smoke.

jorjina [hor-hee'-nah], *f*. Witch, sorceress, whose charms consist in soporiferous draughts.

jornada [hor-nah'-dah], *f*. 1. March or journey performed in one day (viaje). 2. Journey, travel by land. 3. A military expedition. 4. Opportunity, occasion, circumstance. 5. Passage through life (etapa). 6. Act, one of the parts into which Spanish plays are divided. 7. Number of sheets printed off in a day. **Al fin de la jornada**, *(Met.)* at the end, at last. **Jornada de 8 horas**, 8 hour day. **Trabajar en jornadas reducidas**, to work short-time. **Hay jornada limitada en la industria**, there is short-time working in the industry.

jornal [hor-nahl'], *m*. 1. Day-work (trabajo), day-labor, the work done by a workman hired by the day. 2. Day-wages (sueldo), or wages paid to day-laborers for one day's work. **Mujer que trabaja a jornal**, charwoman. **A jornal**, by the day. 3. *(Com.)* Journal, diary, a book used by merchants.

jornalero [hor-nah-lay'-ro], *m*. Day-laborer.

joroba [ho-ro'-bah], *f*. 1. Hump, a prominence on the back. 2. *(coll.)* Importunity, incessant, troublesome solicitation. -*m. & f*. A worry, a bore.

jorobado, da [ho-ro-bah'-do, dah], *a*. Crooked, gibbous, humpbacked or crook-backed.-*pp*. of JOROBAR.

jorobar [ho-ro-bar'], *va*. 1. *(coll.)* To importune, to worry, to tease or harass by frequent repetition of the same request (fastidiar). **Esto me joroba**, I'm fed up with this. 2. To break (estropear). -*vr*. 1. To get cross (enfadarse), to get worked up; to get fed up (cansarse). 2. To put up with (aguantar). 3. To fail (fracasar), to go down the drain. 4. To break, to smash (romperse).

jorro [hor'-ro], *m. (Cuba)* Bad tobacco.

josa [ho'-sah], *f*. Piece of ground planted with vines and fruit-trees.

jostrado, da [hos-trah'-do, dah], *a*. Round-headed (dardo, flecha).

jota [ho'-tah], *f*. 1. Name of the letter J. 2. Jot, little. 3. Spanish dance. **No saber una jota**, to be very ignorant. **No entendió ni jota**, he didn't understand a word of it. 4. *(And. Cono Sur)* Vulture.

jovada [ho-vah'-dah], *f. (Prov.)* Ground which may be tilled by a pair of mules in one day.

joven [ho'-ven], *a*. Young, youthful (aspecto), juvenile. -*m. & f*. Youth, a stripling, a young man; a young woman; a young person. **Los jovenes**, young people. 2. *(Cono Sur)* Waiter.

jovenado [ho-vay-nah'-do], *m*. The time or place in which young persons, after taking the vows, are under the direction of a master in convents.

jovencillo, illa [ho-ven-thee-llyo, eel'-lya], *m. & f. dim.* Youngster.

jovial [ho-ve-ahl'], *a.* 1. Jovial, under the influence of Jupiter. 2. Jovial, gay, airy, merry, cheerful.

jovialidad [ho-ve-ah-le-dahd'], *f.* Joviality, jollity, mirth, merriment, gaiety, good-humor, festivity.

joya [ho'-yah], *f.* 1. Jewel, a precious stone set in gold or silver. 2. Anything well polished and finished. 3. Present, gift. 4. Astragal, a convex architectural moulding. *-pl.* Jewels, trinkets: all the wearing apparel and ornaments of women, especially of brides. **Joyas de imitación**, imitation jewellery.

joyante [ho-yahn'-tay], *a.* Extremely glossy (sedas).

joyel [ho-yel'], *m.* A small jewel.

joyera [ho-yay'-rah], *f.* Woman who keeps a jeweller's shop.

joyería [ho-yay-ree'-ah], *f.* Jeweller's shop (tienda).

joyero [ho-yay'-ro], *m.* 1. Jeweller (persona). 2. Jewel case (estuche).

joyita [ho-yee'-tah], *f. dim. V.* JOYUELA.

joyo [ho'-yo], *m. (Bot.)* Bearded darnel, darnelgrass.

joyuela [ho-yoo-ay'-lah], *f. dim.* Jewel of small value.

juaguarzo [hoo-ah-goo-ar'-tho], *m. (Bot.)* Montpellier rock-rose.

Juan [hoo-ahn'], *m.* John. **San Juan Bautista**, St John the Baptist. **El Papa Juan Pablo II**, Pope John Paul II.

juanete [hoo-ah-nay'-tay], *m.* 1. The knuckle-bone of the great toes, especially when it sticks out more than usual (pie). A bunion. 2. Prominent cheek-bones (pómulo). 3. (*Naut.*) A gallant sail. 4. (*And. CAm.*) Hip (cadera).

juanetero [hoo-ah-nay-tay'-ro], *m.* A young marine apprentice who is occupied in furling and loosening the top-gallant sails.

juanetudo, da [hoo-ah-nay-too'-do, dah], *a.* Applied to persons who have the knuckle-bone of the great toes very protuberant.

juarda [hoo-ar'-dah], *f.* Stain in cloth, occasioned by the wool having imbibed too much oil before it was carded and spun.

juardoso, sa [hoo-ar-do'-so, sah], *a.* Stained, spotted (ropa de lana).

jubarba [hoo-bar'-bah], *f.* Houseleek.

jubertar [hoo-ber-tar'], *va. (Naut.)* To hoist the boat on board.

jubetería [hoo-bay-tay-ree'-ah], *f.* Shop where jackets and doublets are sold; a slop-shop.

jubetero [hoo-bay-tay'-ro], *m.* One who makes and sells jackets and doublets.

jubilación [hoo-be-lah-the-on'], *f.* 1. Retirement (acto, estado). **Jubilación anticipada** early retirement. 2. Pension (pago), retirement pension.

jubilado [hoo-be-lah'-do], *a.* 1. Retired. 2. (*And. Carib.*) Wise (sagaz). 3. (*And.*) Thick, slow witted. *-m & f.* Retired person.

jubilar [hoo-be-lar'], *va.* 1. To pension off; to superannuate; to exempt anyone from the duties of a charge (persona). 2. To exempt from toil and labor. 3. To lay aside as useless (persona). *-vn.* To become a pensioner in consequence of having been exempted from the labor or burden of a charge, office, or ministry. *-vr.* 1. To retire. 2. (*CAm.*) To play truant (hacer novillos). 3. (*Carib.*) To gain experience (ponerse listo). 4. (*And.*) To deteriorate (deteriorar).

jubileo [hoo-be-lay'-o], *m.* Jubilee, a public festivity; concession of plenary indulgence; an ecclesiastical solemnity. celebrated by the Jews every fifty years. **por jubileo**, rarely, happening seldom.

júbilo [hoo'-be-lo], *m.* Glee, joy, merriment, rejoicing, festivity, hilarity, mirth.

jubiloso, sa [hoo-be-lo'-so, sah], *a.* Gleeful, joyful.

jubón [hoo-bone'], *m.* 1. Doublet (de hombre), jacket. 2. The waist in female dress.

juboncito [hoo-bon-thee'-to], *m. dim.* A small jupon or jacket, a doublet of little value.

jubonero [hoo-bo-nay'-ro], *m.* Maker of jackets, doublets, or jupons.

jucla [hoo'-clah], *f.* A sign which the Arabs place over consonants to replace the vowels which they lack.

judaico, ca [hoo-dah'-e-co, cah], *a.* Judaical, Jewish, relating to the Jews.

judaísmo [hoo-dah-ees'-mo], *m.* Judaism, religion of the Jews.

jadaizante [hoo-dah-e-thahn'-tay], *pa. & m.* Judaizing, Judaizer, one who Judaizes.

judaizar [hoo-dah-e-thar'], *va.* To Judaize, to observe the rites of the Jews.

Judas [hoo'-das], *m.* 1. Judas. 2. One that treacherously deceives his friend, an impostor, traitor. 3. Silkworm that does not spin. 4. (*LAm.*) Peephole (en puerta). 5. (*Cono Sur*) Snooper.

judería [hoo-day-ree'-ah], *f.* 1. Jewry (judíos); a quarter of the town where the Jews live (barrio); tax on Jews. 2. (*CAm. Mex.*) Prank (travesura).

judía [hoo-dee'-ah], *f.* 1. (*Bot.*) French bean, kidneybean. **Judía colorada**, runner bean. **Judía verde**, French bean. 2. Jewess, a Hebrew woman.

judiada [hoo-de-ah'-ah], *f.* 1. An inhuman action (actocruel). 2. Excessive and scandalous profit.

judicante [hoo-de-cahn'-tay], *m. (Prov.)* Judge appointed to inquire into the conduct and proceedings of officers of justice.

judicatura [hoo-de-cah-too'-rah], *f.* 1. Judicature, the power and act of administering justice (cargo). 2. Dignity of a judge.

judicial [hoo-de-the-ahl'], *a.* Judicial, juridical, practised in the distribution of justice or used in courts of justice.

judicialmente [hoo-de-the-al-men'-tay], *adv.* Judicially.

judiciaria [hoo-de-the-ah'-re-ah], *f.* Judiciary astrology.

judiciario, ria [hoo-de-the-ah'-re-o, ah], *a.* Astrological, professing the art of foretelling future events.

judiega [hoo-de-ay'-gah], *f.* Kind of olives, good for making oil, but not for eating.

judihuelo, la [hoo-de-oo-ay'-lo, lah], *m. & f.* 1. A young Jew or Jewess. 2. French bean.

judío, día [hoo-dee'-o, ah], *a.* Judaical, Jewish.

judío [hoo-dee'-o], *m.* 1. Jew. 2. Appellation given by boys to the trumpeters who attend the processions in the holy week.

judión [hoo-de-on'], *m.* A large sort of French beans. Dutch kidney-beans.

judo [joo-do], *m.* Judo.

juego [hoo-ay'-go], *m.* 1. Play (acto), amusement, diversion, sport. **Los niños en el juego**, children at play. **Juego duro**, rough play. **Juego de bolos**, nine pins. **Juego de destreza**, game of skill. **Juego de palabras**, a pun, a quibble. **Juegos de palabras**, word games. 2. Game, gaming, gambling (apuestas). **Juego de suerte y ventura**, game of hazard or chance. 3. A set of good cards. 4. Manner of acting of an engine. 5. Set, a number of things suited to each other; or a number of things of which one cannot conveniently be separated from the rest (conjunto). **Juego de mesa**, dinner service. **Juego de café**, coffee set. 6. Disposition, ability, or artfulness to obtain or prevent any end or object. 7. Method, convenient order. 8. Running gear of a vehicle. 9. Play (luces). 10. (*Fig.*) Game. **Le conozco el juego**, I know his little game. **Juego de manos**, juggling feat, legerdemain. **Juego de pelota**, pelota game. **Juego de niños**, play-game. **Entrar en juego**, to come into play. **Hacer juego**, to match, to suit, to fit. **El juego es un vicio**, gambling is a vice. **Seguirle el juego a alguien**, to play along with somebody. **El juego de los colores**, the interplay of the colors. **Juego de caracteres**, *(Comput.)* character set. **Juegos**, *(Comput.)* recreational software. *(Yo juego, yo juegue, from Jugar. V. JUGAR.)*

jueguecico, illo, ito [hoo-ay-gay-thee'-co, eel'-lyo, ee'to], *m.* A little game, a bit of play.

juerga [hoo-er'-gah], *f. (coll.)* Carousal, revel, spree. **Correr las grandes juergas**, to live it up. **Ir de juerga**, to go on a spree.

juerguista [hoo-er-gees-tah], *m & f,* Reveller.

jueves [hoo-ay'-ves], *m.* Thursday. **Jueves Santo**, Maundy Thursday.

juez [hoo-eth'], *m & f.* 1. Judge, one invested with power and authority to decide and determine causes and lawsuits. 2. Judge, one who has sufficient skill to form a correct opinion or judgment of the merit of anything. **Juez árbitro**, arbitrator, umpire. **Juez de letras** or **juez letrado**, a justice of the peace of a small district, who, being a counsellor at law, has more authority in certain cases than other justices. **Juez de primera instancia**, judge of the primary court of claims. **Juez de línea**, linesman. **Juez de salida**, starter.

jugada [hoo-gah'-dah], *f.* 1. Play, the act of playing, a throw (echada). 2. The act of playing a card. 3. Ill turn, dirty trick. **Una bonita jugada**, a pretty piece. **Hacer una jugada**, to make a move.

jugadera [hoo-gah-day'-rah], *f.* Shuttle used to make network. *V. LANZADERA.*

jugador, ra [hoo-gah-dor', rah], *m. & f.* 1. Player, one who plays. 2. Gamester, gambler (de apuestas). **Jugador de manos**, juggler, one who practices sleight of hand, or plays tricks by legerdemain. **Jugador de bolsa**, speculator, gambler on the stock exchange. **Jugador dor de fútbol**, footballer.

jugano [hoo-gah'-no], *m. (Ec.)* A solid wood of Guayaquil employed in ship-building.

jugar [hoo-gar'], *va. & vn.* 1. To play, to sport, to frolic, to trifle, to toy. 2. To play, to game, to contend at some game. 3. To gamble (apostar), to game, to play extravagantly for money, to lose at play. 4. To put in action or motion: speaking of a part of the body. 5. To make use of weapons (armas). 6. To move on joints or hinges. 7. To intervene; to take an active part in an affair, to exercise. 8. To mock, to make gone of. **Jugar 5 dólares a una carta**, to stake 5 dollars on a card. **Jugar al tenis**, to play tennis. **La niña juega a ser madre**, the little girl plays at being mother. **Solamente está jugando contigo**, he's just trifling with you. *-vr.* 1. To gamble, to risk. **Se jugó 200 dólares**, he staked 200 dollars. 2. **Jugársela**, to be unfaithful.

jugarreta [hoo-gar-ray'-tah], *f.* 1. *(coll.)* Bad play, unskillful manner of playing. 2. Bad trick (trampa). **Hacer una jugarreta a uno**, to play a dirty trick on somebody.

juglándeo, dea [hoo-glahn'-day-o, ah], *a.* Belonging to the walnut family.

jugular [hoo-goo-lar'], *m.* Buffoon, mimic, juggler, mountebank.

juglar [hoo-glar'], *m.* Minstreel, jongleur; juggler, tumbler, entertainer.

juglara, juglaresa [hoo-glah'-rah, hoo-glah-ray'-sah], *f.* A female buffoon or mimic.

jugo [hoo'-go], *m.* 1. Sap, juice of plants. 2. Juice, moisture. 3. *(Met.)* Marrow, pith, substance of anything. **Jugo de naranja**, orange juice. **Jugos digestivos**, digestive juices.

jugosidad [hoo-go-se-dahd'], *f.* Sappiness, succulence, juiciness (suculencia).

jugoso, sa [hoo-go'-so, sah], *a.* 1. Sappy, juicy (suculento), succulent. 2. *(Fig.)* Substantial, pithy; meaty, full of good stuff, full of solid sense; profitable (rentable).

juguete [hoo-gay'-tay], *m.* 1. Toy (de niño), plaything, gewgaw, trinket. **Un coche de juguete**, a toy car. 2. Jest, joke (chiste). 3. Carol, a song of joy and exulation.

juguetear [hoo-gay-tay-ar'], *vn.* To trifle, to fool, to toy, to frolic, to sport, to dally, to wanton, to play childish tricks.

juguetón, na [hoo-gay-tone', nah], *a.* Playful, acting the buffoon, wanton, playsome.

juicio [hoo-ee'-the-o], *m.* 1. Judgment (facultad), the power of judging; the act of judging. 2. Sense (sentido), soundness of faculties, strength of natural reason. 3. Judgement, notion, opinion (opinión). 4. Prudence, wisdom (práctica). 5. Judgment, the act of exercising judicature (veredicto). 6. Forecast of the events of a year made by astrologers. **Pedir en juicio**, to sue at law. **No estar en su juicio**, to be out of one's senses. **Tener mucho juicio**, to be sedate, steady, well-behaved. **No tener juicio**, to be wild; to be a harum-scarum fellow. **Sano de juicio**, *(Law.)* perfectly sound in mind. **Lo dejo a su juicio**, I leave it to your discretion. **Estar fuera de juicio**, to be out of one's mind.

juiciosamente [hoo-e-the-o-sah-men'-tay], *adv.* Judiciously, considerately.

juicioso, sa [hoo-e-the-o'-so, sah], *a.* Judicious, prudent, mature, clear-sighted.

julepe [hoo-lay'-pay], *m.* 1. Julep, a sirup-like medical potion. 2. *(Fig. and Boll.)* Reprimand, punishment. 2. *(LAm.)* Scare, fright (susto). 4. *(Carib. Mex.)* Bind (trabajo).

juliano, na [hoo-le-ah'-no, nah], *a.* Julian, relating to Julius Caesar, or instituted by him.

julio [hoo'-lee-o], *m.* July, the seventh month of the year.

julo [hoo'-lo], *m.* 1. Bell-mule, that takes the lead of a sumpter's or carrier's mules. 2. Male which guides the flocks of goats, sheep, or cattle. 3. Iulus, a myriapod.

jumá [hoo-mah'], *m.* Mohammedan name of Friday (i.e., day of assembly).

jumenta [hoo-men'-tah], *f.* Female ass.

jumental, or **jumentil** [hoo-men-tahl', teel'], *a.* Belonging to the ass.

jumentillo, illa, ito, ita [hoo-men-teel'-lyo, lyah, ee'-to, tah], *m. & f. dim.* A little ass or beast of burden.

jumento [hoo-men'-to], *m.* 1. Beast of burden. 2. Ass, jument. 3. A stupid person. *V. ASNO.*

juncada [hoon-cah'-dah], *f.* 1. Kind of fritters. 2. A horse medicine against the glanders.

juncago [hoon-cah'-go], *m. (Bot.)* Bastard rush.

juncal, juncar [hoon-cahl'], *m.* Marshy ground full of rushes.

júnceo, a [hoon'-thay-o, ah], *a.* Rush-like.-*f. pl.* The rush family.

juncia [hoon'-the-ah], *f. (Bot.)* Cyperus, a sedge, the root of which serves for fumigation. **Juncia olorosa**, sweet cyperus, English galangal. **Juncia avellanada or redonda**, round-rooted cyperus, the round cyperus. **Juncia comestible.** *V. CHUFAS.*

junciana [hoon-the-ah'-nah], *f.* Brag, boast.

junciera [hoon-the-ay'-rah], *f.* An earthen vessel with a perforated lid, in which aromatics are kept.

juncino, na [hoon-thee'-no, nah], *a.* Rushy, consisting of rushes.

junco [hoon'-co], *m.* 1. *(Bot.)* Rush. **Junco de esteras**, soft rush. **Junco de flor or florido**, umbelled flowering rush. 2. Junk, Chinese ship.

juncoso, sa [hoon-co'-so, sah], *a.* 1. Full of rushes, resembling rushes; juncous. 2. Covered in rushes (lugar).

jungla [hoon'-glah], *f.* Jungle.

junio [hoo'-ne-o], *m.* June, the sixth month of the year.

junior [hoo'-ne-or], *m.* Novice (monje). -*m* & *f.* (*Dep*). Junior (el más joven).

junípero [hoo-ne'-pay-ro], *m. V.* ENEBRO.

junquera [hoon-kay'-rah], *f.* (*Bot.*) Rush.

junqueral [hoon-kay-rahl'], *m. V.* JUNGAL.

junquillo [hoon-keel'-lyo], *m.* 1. (*Bot.*) Jonquil. 2. A small round moulding.

junta [hoon'-tah], *f.* 1. Junta or junto, a congress, an assembly, a council (consejo), a convention, tribunal. 2. Any meeting of persons to speak about business (asamblea). 3. Conjunction, union, junction (punto de unión), concession, fraternity. 4. Each lateral surface of a square hewed stone. 5. Joint; coupling (acoplamiento). **Junta de médicos**, a consultation. **Junta de comercio**, board of trade. **Junta de sanidad**, board of health. **Junta directiva**, board of management. **Junta de portavoces**, (*Parl.*) House business committee.

juntador, ra [hoon-tah-dor', rah], *pl.* & *f.* Jointer, one who joins.

juntamente [hoon-tah-men-tay], *adv.* Jointly; at, the same time, conjunctively.

juntar [hoon-tar'], *va.* 1. To join (unir), to conjoin, to combine, to coalesce, to connect, to unite. 2. To join, to convoke to couple; to associate, to consociate, to congregate. 3. To amass, to collect, to heap, to gather, to lay up. -*vr.* 1. To join, to meet, to assemble (montar), to concur. 2. To be closely united. 3. To copulate. -*vr.* 1. To join (unirse), to come together; to meet (gente), to assemble, to gather. 2. (*Zool.*) To mate, to copulate. 3. To live together (personas).

juntera [hoon-tay'-rah], *f.* Carpenter's plane, jointer.

junterilla [hoon-tay-reel'-lyah], *f. dim.* Small plane.

junto, ta [hoon'-to, tah], *a.* & *pp. irr.* Of JUNTAR. United, conjoined, annexed. **Fuimos juntos**, we went together. **Vivir juntos**, to live together.

junto [hoon'-to], *adv.* Near, close to, at hand, near at hand, at the same time. **Por junto** or **de por junto**, in the bulk, by the lump, wholesale. **En junto**, together, in all. **Demasiado junto**, too close.

juntura [hoon-too'-rah], *f.* 1. Juncture, the part at which two things are joined together, joining. 2. Joint, articulation of limbs, juncture of movable bones in animal bodies. 3. (*Naut.*) Scarf.

Júpiter [hoo'-pe-ter], *m.* 1. Jupiter, a planet. 2. Among chemists, tin.

jura [hoo'rah], *f.* 1. Oath, an affirmation, negation, or promise, corroborated by the attestation of the Divine Being. 2. Oath of allegiance. **Jura de bandera**, oath of loyalty. -*m.* (*CAm. Carib.*) Cop.

jurado [hoo-rah'-do], *m.* 1. Jury (cuerpo), a certain number of persons sworn to declare the truth upon such evidence as shall be given before them. 2. Juror (persona), juryman, one serving in a jury. 3. Jurat, a magistrate in some corporations.

jurador, ra [hoo-rah-dor', rah], *m.* & *f.* Swearer, profane swearer.

juraduría [hoo-rah-doo-ree'-ah], *f.* Office of a jurat.

juramentar [hoo-rah-men-tar'], *va.* To swear, to put to an oath. -*vr.* To bind oneself by an oath, to obtest by an oath.

juramento [hoo-rah-men'-to], *m.* 1. Oath, an affirmation, negation, or promise, corroborated by the attestation of the Divine Being. 2. Oath, curse, imprecation: commonly used in the plural in this last sense. **Bajo juramento**, on oath. **Prestar juramento**, to take the oath. **Decir juramentos a uno**, to swear at somebody.

jurar [hoo-rar'], *va.* To obtest some superior power; to attest the great name; to promise upon oath; to swear,

to make oath. **Jurar decir la verdad**, to swear to tell the truth. **Jurar como un carretero**, to swear like a trooper.

jurásico, ca [hoo-rah'-se-co, cah], *a.* Jurassic, relating to the mountains of Jura.

juratoria [hoo-rah-to'-re-ah], *f.* (*Prov.*) Plate of silver containing the holy evangelists, on which magistrates lay their hands in taking an oath.

jurdía [hoor-dee'-ah], *f.* Kind of fishing net.

jurel [hoo-rel'], *m.* A spiny sea-fish of the mackerel family.

jurguina, or **jurgina** [hoor-gee' -nah, hoor-hee' -nah], *f.* Witch, sorceress.

jurídicamente [hoo-ree'-de-cah-men'-tay], *adv.* Lawfully, legally, juridically.

jurídico, ca [hoo-ree'-de-co, cah], *a.* Lawful, legal, judicial; done according to law.

jurisconsulto [hoo-ris-con-sool'-to], *m.* 1. Jurisconsult, one who gives his opinion in law. 2. Civilian, civilist. 3. Jurist, a lawyer.

jurisdicción [hoo-ris-dic-the-on'], *f.* 1. Jurisdiction, legal authority, extent of judicial power, power, authority. 2. Jurisdiction, district to which any judicial authority extends (distrito). 3. Boundary of some place or province.

jurisdiccional [hoo-ris-dic-the-o-nahl'], *a.* Jurisdictional, relating to jurisdiction.

jurisperito, ta [hoo-ris-pay-ree'-to], *m.* A professor of jurisprudence.

jurisprudencia [hoo-ris-proo-den'-the-ah], *f.* Jurisprudence, law, or the science of law.

jurisprudente [hoo-ris-proo-den'-tay], *m. V.* JURISCONSULTO.

jurista [hoo-rees'-tah], *m.* 1. Jurist, lawyer, a man who professes the science of law. 2. Pensioner, one who has an annuity assigned to him upon the revenue of the crown.

juro [hoo'-ro], *m.* 1. Right of perpetual property (derecho). 2. Annuity assigned upon the revenue of the crown. **De juro**, certainly.

jusbarba [hoos-bar'-bah], *f.* (*Bot.*) Field myrtle.

jusello [hoo-sel'-lyo], *m.* Pottage made of broth, parsley, grated cheese, egg, and spice.

jusi [hog'-se], *m.* A delicate vegetable fiber of the Philippine Islands used for dresses.

justa [hoos'-tah], *f.* 1. Joust, tilt, tournament. 2. Literary contest in poetry or prose.

justador [hoos-tah-dor'], *m.* Titter, one who pays at jousts.

justamente [hoos-tah-men'-tay], *adv.* Justly (con justicia), just (precisamente), exactly; precisely, fairly. **De eso se trata justamente**, that's just the point. **Son justamente las que no están en venta**, they are precisely the ones which are not for sale.

justar [hoos-tar'], *vn.* To joust, to tilt.

justicia [hoos-tee'-the-ah], *f.* 1. Justice, giving to every man his due. 2. Justice, the attribute of God according to which he arranges all things. 3. Reason, honesty; equity; right (derecho). 4. Retribution, punishment.-*m.* Justice, magistrate or tribunal. **Hacer justicia a**, to do justice to. **Tomarse la justicia por su mano**, to take the law into one's own hands.

justiciero, ra [hoos-te-the-ay'-ro, rah], *a.* One who rigorously observes justice; one who chastises crimes with rigid justice.

justificable [hoos-te-fe-cah'-blay], *a.* Justifiable.

justificación [hoos-te-fe-cah-the-on'], *f.* 1. Justification, defence, maintenance, support. 2. Production of the documents or instruments tending to establish a claim or right. 3. Equity, conformity with justice. 4.

Sanctification by grace 5. *(Print.)* Adjustment of lines in a page of types.

justificadamente [hoos-te-fe-cah-dah-men'tay], *adv.* Justly, correctly, justifiably.

justificado, da [hoos-te-fe-cah'-do, dah], *a.* Equal, justified, conformable to justice.-*pp.* of JUSTIFICAR.

justificador [hoos-te-fe-cah-dor'], *m.* Justifier, Justificator. *V.* SANTIFICADOR.

justificante [hoos-te-fe-cahn'-tay], *pa.* Justifying; justifier.

justificar [hoos-te-fe-car'], *va.* 1. To justify, to free from past sin, to render just. 2. To justify, to clear from imputed guilt (sospechoso); to absolve from an accusation;to exculpate. 3. To prove or establish a claim in a court of judicature. 4. To prove or show by argument or testimony.5. To justify, to rectify, to adjust, to arrange, to regulate exactly. 6.*(Print.)* To justify or equalize the spaces between the words in a line of types. -*vr.* To vindicate one's character, to clear oneself from imputed guilt.

justificativo, va [hoos-te-fe-cah-tee'-vo, vah], *a.* Justificative, justifying, justificatory.

justillo [hoos-teel'-lyo], *m.* Jacket without sleeves; inner waist of a dress; corset-cover.

justipreciar [hoos-te-pray-the-ar'], *va.* To estimate anything.

justipreciador [hoos-te-pray-the-ah-dor'], *m* A praiser, a person appointed to set price upon things.

justiprecio [hoos-te-pray'-thear'], *m.* Appraisement, just valuation.

justo, ta [hoos'-to, tah], *a.* 1. Just (correcto), comformable to justice, rightful, lawful; fair. **Una decisió justa**, a just decision. 2. Just, upright. 3. Just, honest, honorable, good, faithful. 4. Just exact (exacto), strict, punctual.5. Just, fit, tight (ropa), close, exactly proportioned. **El traje me viene muy justo**, the suit is rather tight for me. 6. Just, good, pious.

justo [hoos'-to], *m.* A just and pious man.

justo [hoos'-to], *adv.* 1. Tightly (con dificultad), straitly. **Vivir muy justo**, to be hard up. 2. Right, just (exactamente), **Vino justo a tiempo** he came just time.

juta [hoo'tah], *f.(Orn.)* A kind of American goose.

jutía [hoo-tee'-ah], *f V.* HUTÍA.

juvenil [hoo-vay-neel'], *a.* juvenile, young, youthful; girlish. **Equipo juvenil**, youth team. **En los años juveniles**, in one's early years.

juventud [hoo-ven-tood'], *f.* Youthfulness, youth (época), juvenility, young people (jóvenes). **La juventud de hoy**, young people today.

juzgado [hooth-gah'-do], *m.* Tribunal, court of justice; judicature.

juzgador, ra [hooth-gah-dor', rah], *m. & f.* Judge, one who judges.

juzgamundo [hooth-gah-moon'do.] *m. & f.* One who censures the actions of everyone but himself.

juzgante [hooth-gahn'-tay], *pa.* Judging; judge.

juzgar [hooth'-gar'], *va & vn.* 1. To judge, pass sentence upon, to give judgement.2. To judge, to apprehend, to form or give an opinion, to opine, to hold. **Juzgar mal**, to misjudge. **A juzgar según lo que hemos visto**, to judge by what we have seen.

K

k The eleventh letter of the alphabet, and eighth of the consonants. It has little use in Spanish except in words taken from other languages. It has the same sound as in English. **K** in chemistry is the symbol of potassium. *(Kalium.)*

ka [kah], *f.* Name of the letter K.

kabila [kah-bee'-lah], *f.* A tribe of Barbary, living in the Atlas region.

kahué [ka-hoo-ay'], *m.* Arabic name of coffee.

Káiser [kah'-e-ser], *m.* kaiser.

kaki or **caqui** [kah'-ke], *a.* Khaki.

kaleidoscopio [ka-lay-e-dos-co'-pay-o], *m. V.* CALIDOSCOPIO.

kalenda [ka-len'-dah], *f.* kalends. *V.* CALENDA.

kalmuco, ca [kal-moo'-co, cah], *a. & n.* kalmuck, a race of western Mongols. *V.* CALMUCO.

kamikaze [ka-me-kah'-they], *m.* kamikaze.

kan [kahn], or **khan**, *m.* khan, prince among the Tartars.

kanna [kahn'-nah], *f.* Canna, a root very esteemed by the Hottentots as the best of stomachics. It resembles ginseng.

kantiano, na [kan-te-ah'-no, nah], *a.* kantian, relating to the philosophy of kant.

Kantismo [kan-tees'-mo], *m* Kantism, the philosophic system of Kant.

kárate [kah'-rah-tay], *m.* karate.

keralila [kay-rah-lee'-lah], *f.(Mex.)* Horny flint.

kermes [kerr'-mes], *m.*1. *V.* QUÉRMES. kermes mineral, an impure antimony sulphide.

kg. abr de **kilogramo.**

kilo [kee'-lo], *m.* A prefix from the Greek signifying a thousandfold.-*m. (Com.)* kilogram, an abbreviation.

kilociclo [ke-lo-thee'-clo], *m* kilocycle.

kilográmetro [ke-lo-grah'-may-tro], *m.* kilogrammeter, the unit of force required to raise a kilogram one meter in one second (7.2 foot-pounds).

kilogramo [ke-lo-grah'-mol], *m.* kilogram, a metric unit of weight, 1,000 (2 **1/5**lbs.).

kilolitro [ke-lo-lee'-tro], *m.* kiloliter, the measure of 1,000 liters.

kilometraje [ke-lo-may-trah'-hay], *m.* Length or distance in kilometers, mileage.

kilométrico [ke-lo-may'-tre-co, cah], *a.* kilometric. **Discurso kilométrico** long-winded speech.

kilómetro [ke-lo'-may-tro], *m.* kilometer, the distance of 1,000 meters chief unit of long distance in the metric system; about five-eighths of a mile. A Spanish league slightly exceeds five and a half kilometers.

kilotón [ke-lo-ton'], *m.* or **kilotonelada** [ke-lo-to-nay-lah'-da], *f.* kiloton.

kilovatio [ke-lo-vah'-te-o], kilowatt.

kilovoltamperio [ke-lo-vol-tam-pay'-re-o], *m.* kilovolt-tampere.

kilovoltio [ke-lo-vol'o], *m.* Kilovolt.

kinoscopio [ke-nos-co'-pe-o], *m.* Kinescope.

kiosco [ke-os'-co], *m.* 1. kiosk, an open, small pavil-ion, designed, according to the custom of Orientals; for taking refreshment in the middle of the day. 2. Kisok, a news-stand, etc., in imitation of the foregoing.

kirie [kee'-re-ay], *m.* Kyrie, the first movement in the mass, after the introit.

kirieleisón [ke-re-ay-lay-e-sone'], *m.* 1. *V.* KIRIE. 2. *(coll.)* Funeral chant.

kiwi [kee'-wee], *m.* Kiwi (fruta).

kirsch [keerch], *m.* Kirschwasser, a cordial distilled from the European wild cherry.

kopú [ko-poo'], *m.* A Chinese fabric.

krausismo [kra-hoo-sees'-mo], *m.* Krausism, the philosophic system of Krause.

kremlin [krem'leen], *m.* A Slavic word which signifies fortress. In particular the citadel of this name in Moscow.

kurdo, da [coor'-do, dah], *a.* kurdish, or kurd; native of or belonging to kurdistan.

L

l [ay'-lay], L (letra). The *l* always keeps the same sound as in English. **L** as a numeral stands for fifty.

la [lah], *def. art. fem. sing.* The. **La cabeza**, the head. **La casa**, the house.

la [lah], *pron. pers. acc. f. sing.* Her (persona). **Yo la vi ayer**, I saw her yesterday. It (objeto). **La leí el domingo**, I read it on Sunday.

la [lah], *pron. dem.* **Mi casa y la de Vd**, my house and yours. **La de Pedro es mejor**, Peter's is better. **La de Juan**, John's. **Ir a la de Pepe**, to go to Pepe's place.

La [lah], *m. (Mus.)* La, the sixth, sound of the hexachord.

L.A.B., Abbreviation of **Libre a bordo.** F.O.B. free on board.

laberinto [lah-bay-reen'-to], *m.* 1. Labyrinth, maze. 2. An intricate and obscure matter, hard to be understood; maze, uncertainty, perplexity. 3. *(Anat.)* Labyrinth of the ear. 4. *(LAm.)* Row, racket (griterío).

labia [lah'-be-ah], *f. (coll.)* Sweet, winning eloquence. **Tener mucha labia**, to have the gift of the gab.

labiado, da [lah-be-ah'-do, dah], *a. (Bot.)* Labiate.

labial [lah-be-ahl'], *a.* Labial, uttered by the lips.

labiérnago [lah-be-ayr'-nah-go], *m.* A shrub with lanceolate, shining leaves.

labihendido, da [lah-be-en-dee'-do, dah], *a.* Harelipped.

labio [lah'-be-o], *m.* 1. The lip. 2. Lip, the edge of anything. **Labio hendido**, hare-lip. **Labio inferior**, lower lip. **No morderse los labios**, to be outspoken. **Sin despegar los labios**, without uttering a word.

labiodental [lah-be-o-den-tahl'], *a.* Labiodental.

labionasal [lah-be-o-nah-sahl'], *a.* Labionasal.

labor [lah-bor'], *f.* 1. Labor (trabajo), task, the act of doing what requires an exertion of strength. 2. Labor, work to be done, work done. 3. Symmetry, adaptation of parts to each other; design. 4. A seamstress's work, any kind of needlework, embroidery (bordado). 5. A thousand tiles or bricks. 6. Cultivation, husbandry, tillage, ploughing (arada). 7. *V.* LABRANZA. 7. *(Prov.)* Egg of a silkworm. 8. *(Amer.)* The works of a mine. **Campo de labor**, a cultivated field. **Sus labores**, housewife. **Labor de equipo**, teamwork. **Una labor**, a piece of needlework. **Labor de ganchillo**, crochet.

laborable [lah-bo-rah'-blay], *a.* Tillable (cultivable), working (día), work. **Día laborable**, working day.

laborador [lah-bo-rah-dor'], *m. V.* TRABAJADOR and LABRADOR.

laboral [lah-bo-rahl'], *a.* Labor; technical.

laborar [lah-bo-rar'], *pa.* To work, to till.-*vn.* To scheme, to plot.

laborativo, va [lah-bo-rah-tee'-vo, vah]. **Día laborativo**, *(Com.)* clear day.

laboratorio [lah-bo-rah-to'-re-o], *m.* Laboratory, a chemist's work-room.

laborcica, illa, ita [lah-bor-thee'-cah], *f. dim.* 1. An insignificant work or task. 2. Pretty needle-work.

laborear [lah-bo-ray-ay'], *va.* 1. To cultivate, to till the ground. 2. *(Naut.)* To work a ship, to direct her movements. *V.* MANIOBRAR.

laboreo [lah-bo-ray'-o], *m.* 1. *(Prov.)* Culture, labor. 2. The working of mines. 3. *(And. Cono Sur)* Foreman (capataz).

laboriosamente [lah-bo-re-o-sah-men'-tay], *adv.* Laboriously, painfully.

laboriosidad [lah-bo-re-o-se-dahd'], *f.* Laboriousness (pesadez), industry (trabajo), assiduity.

laborioso, sa [lah-bo-re-o'-so, sah], *a.* 1. Laborious, assiduous, industrious. 2. Laborious, requiring much toil and labor; tiresome, painful.

labra [lah'-brah], *f.* 1. The action of working or chiselling stone. 2. Carving, or other work given to materials before placing them, especially if rough stone.

labrada [lah-brah'-dah], *f.* Land ploughed and fallowed to be sown.

labradero, ra [lah-brah-day'-ro, rah], *a.* Suited to labor, capable of labor.

labradío, día [lah-brah-dee'-o, ah], *a. V.* LABRANTÍO.

labrado, da [lah-brah'-do, dah], *a.* Worked (tela), wrought (metal), carved (madera). -*pp.* of LABRAR.

labrado [lah-brah'-do], *m.* Land cultivated: commonly used in the plural.

labrador, ra [lah-brah-dor', rah], *a.* Industrious, laborious, fit for work.-*m. & f.* 1. Laborer, one who works at the plough or spade. 2. Cultivator, farmer (granjero), a husbandman or woman. 3. Rustic, peasant (campesino).

labradoresco, ca [lah-brah-do-ress'-co, cah], *a.* Belonging or relating to a laborer: rustic, clownish.

labradorita [lah-brah-do-ree'-tah], *f. (Min.)* Labradorite.

labrandera [lah-bran-day'-rah], *f.* Seamstress, embroiderer.

labrante [lah-brahn'-tay], *m.* Stone-cutter, sculptor.

labrantín [lah-bran-teen'], *m.* A petty farmer, who cultivates a small farm.

labrantío, tía [lah-bran-tee'-o, ah], *a.* Producing grain: applied to arable land fit for the culture of grain.

labranza [lah-brahn'-thah], *f.* 1. Tillage, the cultivation of the ground, ploughing, farming (cultivo). 2. Husbandry, the employment of a cultivator or farmer. 3. Farm (granja), land let to a tenant; tilled land; an estate applied to the purposes and pursuits of agriculture.

labrar [lah-brar'], *va.* 1. To work (metales), to labor. 2. To till, to cultivate (tierra). *V.* ARAR. 3. To build, to construct buildings. 4. To do needlework, to embroider (tela). 5. To inform, to instruct. 6. To finish, to polish to the degree of excellence intended or required. 7. To make designs in fabrics, stones, arms, etc. 8. To carve (madera). 9. To plow (tierras). -*vn.* To make a strong impression on the mind.

labrero, ra [lah-bray'-ro, rah], *a.* Applied to a kind of fishing net.

labriego, ga [lah-bre-ay'-go], *m & f.* Peasant.

labro [lah'-bro], *m.* The upper lip, labrum, of the mouth of animals.

labrusca [lah-broos'-cah], *f.* A wild grape-vine.

laburno [lah-boor'-no], *m. (Bot.)* Laburnum.

laca [lah'-cah], *f.* 1. Lac, or gumlac, a red, brittle, resinous substance, brought from India, and used for dyeing and making sealing wax. 2. Red color, lake (color), a pigment; *e.g.* madder lake. 3. Lacquer (barniz), a kind of varnish. *(Per.)* **Laca de uñas**, nail polish. **Laca para el pelo**, hair spray.

lacar [lah-car'], *va.* To lacquer.

lacayo [lah-cah'-yo], *m.* 1. Lackey, footman, servant, foot boy. 2. Knot of ribbons worn by women.

lacayuelo [lah-cah-yoo-ay'-lo], *m. dim.* Foot-boy.

lacayuno, na [lah-cah-yoo'-no, nah], *a.* Belonging to a lackey or foot-boy.

lacear [lah-thay-ar'], *va.* 1. To adorn with ribbons tied in bows (adornar); to lace. 2. To pin up the game or drive it into an appointed place. 3. (Cono Sur) To whip (zurrar). 4. To snare, to trap (coger); to beat (ojear), to drive.

lacedemónico, ca [lah-thay-day-mo'-ne-co, cah], or **lacedemonio, a** [lah-thay-day-mo'-ne-o, ah], *a.* Lacedemonian, relating to Lacedemonia.

laceración [lah-thay-rah-the-on'], *f.* Laceration, lancination, tearing.

lacerado, da [lah-thay-rah'-do, dah], *a.* 1. Unfortunate, unhappy. 2. Leprous.-*pp.* of LACERAR.

lacerar [lah-thay-rar'], *va.* To mangle, to tear to pieces, to lacerate.

laceria [lah-thay'-re-ah], *f.* 1. Misery, poverty (pobreza), wretchedness. 2. Labor, fatigue, trouble, distress (sufrimiento).

lacería [la-thay-ree'-ah], *f.* A set of nets.

lacerioso, sa [lah-thay-re-o'-so, sah], *a.* Miserable: scrofulous.

lacha [lah'-chah], *f. V.* HALECHE.

lacinia [lah-thee'-ne-ah], *f. (Bot.)* 1. Lacinia, a narrow, deep, slender lobe. 2. The fringe of a Roman toga.

laciniado, da [lah-the-ne-ah'-do, dah], *a. (Bot.)* Laciniate, slashed irregularly.

lacio, cia [lah'-the-o, ah], *a.* Faded, withered, dried up; flaccid, languid.

lacónicamente [lah-co'-ne-cah-men'-tay], *adv.* Laconically, concisely.

lacónico, ca [lah-co'-ne-co, cah], *a.* Laconic, brief, concise.

laconismo [lah-co-nees'-mo], *m.* Laconism, conciseness, brevity, concise expression or style.

lacra [lah'-crah], *f.* 1. Mark left by some wound or disorder; *(LAm.)* sore (llaga). 2. Fault, vice, wickedness. **La prostitución es una lacra social**, prostitution is a blot on society.

lacrar [lah-crar'], *va.* 1. To injure or impair the health. 2. To hurt or injure in point of property or money. 3. To seal with sealing wax.

lacre [lah'-cray], *m.* Sealing wax.

lacrimal [lah-cre-mahl'], *a.* Lachrymal.

lacrimatorio, ria [lah-cre-mah-to'-re-o-ah], *a. & m. & f.* Lachrymatory.

lacrimógeno [lah-cre-mo'-hay-no], *a.* Tear-producing. **Bomba lacrimógena**, tear bomb.

lacrimoso, sa [lah-cre-mo'-so, sah], *a.* Weeping, shedding tears, lachrymose.

lacris [lah'-cris], *m.* Fruit of rose-mary.

lactación [lac-tah-the-on'], *f.* Lactation, the act of suckling.

lactancia [lac-tahn'-the-ah], *f.* Lactation, the act or time of giving suck.

lactante [lac-tahn'-tay], *m.* Sucker, one who sucks milk.

lactar [lac-tar'], *va.* To suckle, to give suck, to feed on milk.

lactario, ria [lac-tah'-re-o, ah], *a.* Lactary, lacteous, lactescent.

lactato [lac-tah'-to], *m. (Chem.)* Lactate.

lácteo, tea [lac'-tay-o, ah], *a.* Lacteous, milky, lacteal, lactean, lactescent. **Vía láctea**, *(Ast.)* galaxy, the milky way.

lactescente [lac-tes-then'-tay], *a.* Lactescent, having a milky juice.

lacticinio [lac-te-thee'-ne-o], *m.* Milk-pottage, and, in general, all sorts of food prepared with milk.

lacticinoso, sa [lac-te-the-no'-so, sah], *a. V.* LÁCTEO.

láctico, ca [lahc'-te-co, cah], *a.* Lactic, relating to milk.

lactífago, ga [lac-tee'-fah-go, gah], *a.* Feeding upon milk, galactophagous.

lactífico, ca [lac-tee'-fe-co, cah], *a.* Lactific, yielding milk.

lactífero, ra [lac-tee'-fay-ro, rah], *a.* Lactiforous, lacteal, milky.

lactómetro [lac-to'-may-tro], *m.* Lactometer, a hydrometer for determining the density of milk.

lactosa [lac-to'-sah], *f.* Lactose, milk sugar.

lactumen [lac-too'-men], *m.* Scab breaking out on the head of sucking children.

lacustre [lah-coos'-tray], *a.* Marshy, belonging to lakes.

lada [lah'-dah], *f. V.* JARA.

ládano [lah'-da-no], *m.* Labdanun, a resin which exudes from a shrub.

ladeado, da [lah-day-ah'-do, dah], *a. & pp.* of LADEAR. 1. Turned to one side, inclined, lopsided (inclinado). 2. *(ConoSur)* Slovenly (descuidado). 3. *(Cono Sur)* **Andar ladeado**, to be in a bad temper.

ladeamiento [lah-day-ah-me-en'-to], *m. V.* LADEO.

ladear [lah-day-ar'], *va.* To move or turn to one side; to go side by side; to go along rails. *-vn.* 1. *(Naut.)* To incline: applied to the needle of the mariner's compass. 2. To go by the side, to incline to one side. 3. To tilt (inclinarse). 4. To turn aside (apartarse). *-vr.* 1. To incline toward an opinion or party. 2. To lean, to incline (inclinarse). 3. *(Cono Sur)* To fall in love (enamorarse).

ladeo [lah-day'-o], *m.* Inclination or motion to one side.

ladera [lah-day'-rah], *f.* Declivity, gradual descent. *-pl.* 1. Rails or staves of a common cart. 2. Cheeks of a guncarriage.

laderica, illa, ita [lah-day-ree'-cah, eel'-lyah, ee'tah], *f. dim.* A small declivity of the ground.

ladierno [lah-de-err'-no], *m. (Bot.)* Buckthorn.

ladilla [lah-deel'-lyah], *f.* 1. Crab-louse. 2. *(Bot.)* Common barley.

ladinamente [lah-de-nah-men'-tay], *adv.* Sidewise, artfully, sagaciously.

ladino, na [lah-dee'-no, nah], *a.* 1. Sagacious, cunning (taimado), crafty. 2. *(LAm.)* Smooth-tongued (adulador). 3. *(Mex.)* High-pitched (voz).

lado [lah'-do], *m.* 1. Side, that part of the human body which extends from the armpit to the hipbone. 2. Side or half of an animal. 3. Side, the right or left. 4. Side, part of any body opposed to another part. 5. Side, any part placed in contradistinction or opposition to another. 6. Side, the margin, edge, or verge of anything. 7. *(Met.)* Side, party, faction, interest. 8. *(Met.)* Companion, comrade. 9. Mat used to cover carts, etc. 10. *(Met.)* Patron, protector. 11. Course, manner; mode of proceeding. 12. Side: it is used to note consanguinity. **Al lado**, just by, at hand, or near at hand. **Lado débil**, weak spot. **Al lado**, near. **Estuvo a mi lado**, she was at my side. **Viven al lado de nosotros**, they live next door to us. **Estar de un lado para otro**, to be up and down. **Por todos lados**, on all sides. **Dejar a un lado**, to skip. **Me da de lado**, I don't care. **Por el lado de la madre**, on the mother's side.

ladón [lah-don'], *m. V.* LADA.

ladra [lah'-drah], *f.* 1. Barking. 2. Cry of hounds after the game.

ladrador, ra [lah-drah-dor', rah], *m. & f.* 1. Barker, one that barks. 2. *(coll.)* Talker, one who talks much and to no purpose.

ladrante [lah-drahn'-tay], *pa.* Barking, latrant; barker.

ladrar [lah-drar'], *vn.* 1. To bark, to howl (perro). 2. To use empty threats. 3. To clamor, to vociferate, to make outcries.

ladrear [lah-dray-ar'], *vn.* To bark often and without object.

ladrería [lah-dray-ree'-ah], *f.* 1. Lazaretto, a hospital for the treatment of lepers. 2. Elephantiasis, or leprosy of the Arabs. 3. *(Vet.)* A certain disease of swine and another of horses. 4. *(And. Carib. Mex.)* Brickworks.

ladrido [lah-dree'-do], *m.* 1. Barking or howling of a dog. 2. Vociferation, outcry; calumny; incitement.

ladrillado [lah-dreel-lyah'-do], *m.* Floor made with bricks, tile floor (azulejos).

ladrillador [lah-dreel-lyah-dor'], *m. V.* ENLADRILLADOR.

ladrillal, ladrillar [lah-dreel-lyahl', lah-dreellyar'], *m.* Brickfield, brick kiln, a place where bricks are made.

latrillazo [lah-dreel-lyah'-tho], *m.* Blow with a brickbat.

ladrillera [lah-dreel-lyay'-rah], *f.* Brick kiln.

ladrillero [lah-dreel-lyay'-ro], *m.* Brick-maker.

ladrillo [lah-dreel'-lyo], *m.* A brick, tile (azulejo), block (chocolate). **Ladrillo de chocolate**, chocolate cake. **ladrillo de fuego**, fire brick.

ladrilloso, sa [lah-dreel-lyo'-so, sah], *a.* Made of brick.

ladrón, na [lah-drone', nah], *m. & f.* 1. Thief, robber, highwayman, cut-purse. **Ladrona de corazones**, lady killer. 2. Lock, sluice-gate. 3. Snuff of a candle that makes it melt.

ladronamento [lah-dro-nah-men'-to], *adv.* Thievishly, dissemblingly.

ladroncillo [lah-dron-theel'-lyo], *m. dim.* Of LADRÓN. Petty thief, filcher.

ladronera [lah-dro-nay'-rah], *f.* 1. Nest of rogues, den of robbers. 2. Filching, stealing; defrauding, extortion. 3. Sluicegate in a mill. 4. Money-box. *V.* ALCANCÍA.

ladronería [lah-dro-nay-ree'-ah], *f. V.* LADRONICIO.

ladronesco, ca [lah-dro-nes'-co, cah], *a. (coll.)* Belonging to thieves.

ladronicio [lah-dro-nee'-the-o], *m.* Larceny, theft, robbery. *V.* LATROCINIO.

lafría [lah-free'ah], *f.* A robber-fly.

laga [lah'-gah], *f.* A large black bean of the Orient which serves for weighing gold.

lagaña [lah-gah'nyah], *f.* A slimy fluid running from the eyes.

lagañoso, ha [lah-gah-nyo'-so, sah], *a.* Bleary-eyed, troubled with running of the eyes.

lagar [lah-gar'], *m.* 1. Place where grapes are pressed. 2. Wine-press (de vino), an engine for squeezing the juice from grapes.

lagarada [lah-gah-rah'dah], *f.* A wine-pressful; each filling of a winepress.

lagarejo [lah-gah-rah'-ho], *m.* A small wine-press.

lagarero [lah-gah-ray'-ro], *m.* 1. Wine presser, one employed in pressing grapes. 2. One employed in pressing the juice of olives.

lagareta [lah-gah-ray'-tah], *f.* Small wine-press.

lagarta [lah-gar'-tah], *f.* 1. Female lizard. 2. Sly woman (mujer).

lagartado, da [lah-gar-tah'-do, dah], *a. V.* ALAGARTDADO.

lagartera [lah-gar-tay'-rah], *f.* Lizard hole, a place under ground where lizards breed.

lagartija [lah-gar-tee'-hah], *f.* Small lizard, eft. **Se mueve más que el rabo de una lagartija**, he has ants in his pants, he's very fidgety.

lagartijero, ra [lah-gar-te-hay'-ro, rah], *a.* Catching efts (animales).

lagartillo [lah-gar-teel'-lyo], *m. dim.* A small lizard.

lagarto [lah-gar'-to], *m.* 1. Lizard; (*LAm.*) Alligator (caimá). 2. A large muscle of the arm. 3. A sly crafty person. 4. (*CAm. Mex.*) Get-rich-quick (codicioso). 5. (*Mex.*) Sharp customer (astuto).

lago [lah'-go], *m.* A lake; a large quantity of any liquid. **Los Grandes Lagos**, the Great Leaks.

lagostín [lah-gos-teen'], *m. V.* LANGOSTÍN.

lagotear [lah-go-tay-ar'], *vn.* (*coll.*) To flatter, to wheedle, to cajole.

lagotoría [lah-go-tay-ree'-ah], *f.* (*coll.*) Flattery, adulation.

lagotero, ra [lah-go-tay'-ro, rah], *a.* (*coll.*) Flattering, soothing.

lágrima [lah'-gre-mah], *f.* 1. A tear. 2. Any moisture trickling in drops; a drop or small quantity (gota). 3. (*Hot.*) Graymill, gromwell. 4. Wine extracted from the grape by very slight pressure, in order to have the purest juice. **Lágrimas de S. Pedro**, pebbles, stones thrown at any person. **Lágrimas de cocodrilo**, crocodile tears. **Llorar a lágrama viva**, to sob one's heart out.

lagrimable [lah-gre-mah'blay], *a.* Lachrymable, lamentable; worthy of tears.

lagrimal [lah-gre-mahl'], *m.* Corner of the eye near the nose.

lagrimar, lagrimear [lah-gre-mar'], *vn.* To weep, to shed tears.

lagrimeo [lah-gre-may'-o], *m.* The act of shedding tears.

lagrimón [lah-gre-mone'], *m. jug.* A large tear.

lagrimoso, sa [lah-gre-mo'-so, sah], *a.* 1. Weeping, shedding tears. 2. Watery; lachrymary.

laguna [lah-goo'-nah], *f.* 1. Pond, lake, a large diffusion of stagnant water marsh, lagoon (de atolón). 2. An uneven country, full of marshes. 3. Blanks in a book or writing (en escritos).

lagunajo [lah-goo-nah'-ho], *m.* Small pool of water in a field after rain.

lagunar [lah-goo-nar'], *m.* Timber-roof.

lagunero, ra [lah-goo-nay'-ro, rah], *a.* Belonging to marshes or lakes.

lagunoso, sa [lah-goo-no'-so, sah], *a.* Marshy, fanny, abounding in lakes; laky.

laical [lah-e-cahl'], *a.* Laical, belonging to the laity or people, as distinct from the clergy.

laicismo [la-he-thees'-mo], *m.* Laicism, exclusion of the clergy from teaching and all positions of the state.

laico, ca [lah'-e-co, cah], *a. V.* LEGO.

lairén [la-he-ren'], *a.* Applied to a kind of grapes, and to the vines which produce them.

laja [lah'hah], *f.* A shill flat stone.

lama [lah'-mah], *f.* 1. Mud, slime, ooze. 2. (*Prov.*) A flat even country. 3. (*Prov.*) Fine sand used for mortar. 4. Foam on the surface of water. 5. Dust of ores in mines. 6. (*Mex.*) Moss (musgo).

lambel [lam-mel'], *m.* (*Her.*) Lambel, label, a bar with three pendants.

lambrequines [lam-bray-kee'-nes], *m. pl.* (*Her.*) Ornaments which hang from helmets.

lambrija [lam-bree'-hah], *f.* 1. Worm bred in the human body. *V.* LOMBRIZ. 2. (*coll.*) Meager, slender person.

lamedal [lah-may-dahl'], *m.* A musty, miry place.

lamedero [lah-may-day'-ro], *m.* A salt-lick.

lamedor, ra [lah-may-dor', rah], *m. & f.* 1. Licker, one that laps and licks. 2. (*Pharm.*) A kind of syrup. 3. (*Mets.*) Enticement, allurement, wheedling.

lamedura [lah-may-doo'-rah], *f.* Act of licking.

lamelar [lah-may-lar'], *va.* To roll copper into sheets.

lamelibranquio [lah-may-le-brahn'-ke-oh], *a.* Lamellibranchiate, having lamellate gills.

lamelicornios [lah-may-le-cor'-ne-os], *a. & m. pl.* Lamellicorn beetles.

lameliforme [lah-may-le-for'-may], *a.* Lamelliform, in thin layers or plates.

lamentable [lah-men-tah'-blay], *a.* Lamentable, deplorable.

lamentablemente [lah-men-tah-blay-men'-tay], *adv.* Lamentably.

lamentación [lah-men-tah-the-on'], *f.* Lamentation, lamenting, groaning.

lamentador, ra [lah-men-tah-dor', rah], *m. & f.* Lamenter, weeper, mourner, complainer.

lamentar [lah-men-tar'], *va.* To lament (pérdida), to mourn (muerte), to bewail, to moan, to complain (quejarse). *-vn. & vr.* To lament, to grieve, to wail, to complain (quejarse), to cry.

lamento [lah-men'-to], *m.* Lamentation, lament, moan, groaning, mourning, cry.

lamentoso, sah [lah-men-to'-so, sah], *a.* Lamentable, mournful, to be lamented.

lameplatos [lah-may-plah'-tos], *m & f.* 1. Lick-plate, nickname given to the servants who attend at table. 2. (*Mex.*) Toady (adulón); scrounger (parásito); disaster (inútil).

lamer [lah-merr'], *va.* 1. To lick, to pass over with the tongue. 2. To lick, to lap, to take in by the tongue. 3. To touch slightly (rozando).

lamerón, na [lah-may-ro-ne', nah], *m. & f.* (*coll.*) A person very fond of dainties or delicacies.

lameronazo, za [lah-may-ro-nah'-tho, thah], *m. & f. aug.* (*coll.*) A person extremely fond of dainties.

lamia [lah'-me-ah], *f.* 1. Lamia, a fabulous monster. 2. Kind of shark. 3. A longicorn beetle of Europe.

lamido, da [lah-mee'-do, dah], *a.* 1. Deformed, worn out with use. 2. Very thin (delgado); pale (pálido). 3. Prim (afectado). *-pp.* of LAMER.

lamiente [lah-me-en'-tay],. 1. Licking. 2. Lapping.

lámina [lah'me-nah], *f.* 1. Thin sheet (metal, vidrio). 2. Plate, engraving (gravado). 3. Print, illustration. 4. Thin layer. 5. (*Bot. & Zool.*) Lamina. **Láminas de acero**, steel in sheets.

laminable [lah-me-nah'-blay], *a.* Capable of lamination, laminable.

laminación [lah-me-nah-the-on'], *f.* 1. Rolling. 2. Lamination.

laminado, da [lah-me-nah'-do, dah], *a.* Laminated, laminate. *-m.* 1. Rolling. 2. Lamination.

laminador, ra [lah-me-nah-dor', rah], *a.* 1. Laminating. 2. Rolling. *-m.* 1. Rolling mill. 2. Laminator.

laminar [lah-me-nar'], *va.* 1. To roll (metales). 2. To laminate. *-a.* Laminar, laminal.

laminaria [lah-me-nah'-re-ah], *f. (Bot.)* Laminaria.

laminería [lah-me-nay-ree'-ah], *f.* Tidbit, choice morsel.

laminero, ra [lah-me-nay'-ro, rah], *m. & f.* 1. Laminator. 2. Decorator of containers for religious objects. *-a.* Fond of sweets.

laminoso, sa [lah-me-no'-so, sah], *a.* Laminose, laminous.

lamiscar [lah-mes-car], *va. (coll.)* To lick up greedily.

lamoso, sa [lah-mo'-so, sah], *a.* Muddy, slimy.

lampa [lahm'-pah], *f. (Per.)* Shovel for grain (agricultura).

lampacear [lam-pa-thay-ar'], *va. (Naut.)* To swab, to clean the decks with a swab.

lampar [lam-par'], *vn. & vr. V.* ALAMPA. To be eager for something.

lámpara [lahm'-pa-rah], *f.* 1. Light, aluminous body. 2. An oil lamp. 3. An electric light or lamp. 4. A spot of grease or oil. **Lámpara de arco**, arc light. **Lámpara de intermitencia**, flashlight. **Lámpara portátil**, emergency light. **Lámpara de radio**, radio tube. **Lámpara de rayos ultravioletas**, sunlamp. **Lámpara de seguridad**, miner's safety lamp. **Lámpara de soldar**, blowtorch. *-m & f. (Carib.)* Thief (ladrón).

lamparero, ra [lam-pa-ray'-ro, rah], *m. & f.* Lamp lighter.

lamparilla [lam-pa-reel'-lyah], *f.* 1. *(Dim.)* A small lamp (lámpara). 2. A night-taper. 3. A sort of coarse camlet.

lamparín [lam-pa-reen'], *m.* Case into which a glass lamp is put.

lamparista [lam-pah-rees'-tah], *n. com* Lamp-lighter.

lamparón [lam-pah-rone'], *m.* 1. *(aug.)* A large grease-spot. 2. King's evil, a scrofulous tumor in the neck.

lamparonoso, sa [lamp-pah-ro-no'-so, sah], *a.* Scrofulous.

lampazo [lam-pah'-tho], *m.* 1. *(Bot.)* Burdock. *V.* BARDANA. 2. *(Naut.)* Swab, a mop used to clean the decks and cabin of a ship. 3. *(LAm.)* Floor mop (estropajo). 4. *(And. Carib.)* Whiping (azotamiento).

lampiño [lam-pee'-nyo], *a.* Beardless; having little hair.

lampión [lam-pe-on'], *m.* A large lantern.

lampíride, lampiro [lam-pee'-re-day, lam-pee'-ro], *m. (Zool.)* Lampyris, the glow-worm, a sorricorn beetle. Also the firefly.

lampote [lam-po'-tay], *m.* Cotton cloth made in the Philippine Islands.

lamprea [lam-pray'-ah], *f. (Zool.)* Lamprey.

lamprear [lam-pray-ar'], *va.* 1. To marinate, to prepare a stew. 2. *(Mex.)* To dip in flour and beaten egg (antes de cocinar).

lamprehuela, lampreilla [lam-pray-oo-ay'-lah, lam-pray-eel'-lya], *f.* Kind of small lamprey.

lana [lah'-nah], *f.* 1. Wool, the fleece of sheep. 2. Short curled hair of some animal 3. Woollen manufacture in general. 4. *(coll.)* Cash, money. **Lana fieltrada**, felt wool. **Lana de camello**, camel's hair. **Hecho de lana**, woollen.

lanada [lah-nah'-dah], *f.* Sponge for cleaning cannons.

lanado, da [lah-nah'-do, dah], *a. V.* LANUGISO.

lanar [lah-nar'], *a.* Woolly, clothed with wool (oveja).

lanaria [lah-nah'-re-ah], *f. (Bot.)* Cud-weed, used in cleaning wool.

lance [lanh'-thay], *m.* 1. Cast, throw (red). 2. Casting of a net to catch fish (peces). 3. Favorable opportunity, critical moment (momento). 4. Chance, casualty, accident, fortuitous event, occurrence (suceso). *(Met.)* Transaction. 5. Sudden quarrel or dispute (riña). 6. Skill and industry of a player. 7. *(Cono Sur)* Duck, dodge (agachada). 8. *(Cono Sur, Arquit.)* Section, range. **Lance de honor**, affair of honor. **Lance de fortuna**, stroke of luck. *-pl.* 1. Missile weapons. 2. Blot or intrigues of a play.

lancear [lan-thay-ar'], *va.* To wound with a lance.

lancéola [lan-thay'-o-lah], *f. (Bot.)* Rib-grass plantain.

lanceolado, da [lan-thay-o-lah'-do, dah], *a.* Lance-shaped, lanceolate.

lancera [lan-thay'-rah], *f.* Hooks in an armory, on which arms are placed.

lancero [lan-thay'-ro], *m.* 1. Pikeman, lancer. 2. Maker of pikes. *-pl.* Type of square dance.

lanceta [lan-thay'-tah], *f.* 1. Lancet. 2. Potter's knife.

lancetada, *f.* **lancetazo**, *m.* [lan-thay-tah'-dah, lan-thay-tah'-tho]. Act of opening or wounding with a lancet.

lancetera [lan-thay-tay'-ro], *m.* A case for carrying lancets.

lancha [lahn'-chah], *f.* 1. Boat, barge, launch, lighter. **Lancha de motor**, motorboat. **Lancha de socorro**, lifeboat. **Lancha patrullera**, patrol boat. **Lancha de pesca**, fishing boat. 2. A thin and flat piece of stone. 3. Snare for partridges.

lanchaje [lan-chah'-hay], *m.* 1. Lighterage. 2. *(Mex.)* Ferry changes.

lanchar [lan-char'], *m.* A quarry from which flat stones are procured.

lanchero [lan-chay'-ro], *m.* 1. Boatman; lighterman. 2. *(Carib.)* Cuban refugee.

lanchón [lan-chone'], *m. (Naut.)* Lighter.

lanchonero [lan-cho-nay'-ro], *m.* Lighterman.

lancurdia [lan-coor'-de-ah], *f.* Small trout.

landre [lahn'-dray], *f.* 1. A morbid swelling of the glands. 2. A purse concealed in the clothes. 3. Acorn.

landrilla [lan-dreel'-lyah], *f.* Small grain which grows under the tongues of hogs.

lanería [lah-nay-ree'-ah], *f.* Shop where washed wool is sold (tienda).

lanero [lah-nay'-ro], *m.* 1. Dealer in wool. 2. Warehouse for wool (almacén).

langaruto, ta [lan-gah-roo'-to, tah], *a. (coll.)* Tall, lank, illshaped.

langosta [lan-gos'-tah], *f.* 1. Locust, a devouring insect (saltamonte). 2. Lobster, a marine crustacean (de mar). 3. One who extorts money.

langostera [lan-gos-tay'-rah], *f.* Name of a fishing-net.

langostín [lan-gos-teen'], *m.* Prawn, a shrimp-like crustacean.

langostino [lan-gos-tee'-no], *m.* Prawn V. LANGOSTÍN.

langüente [lan-goo-en'-tay], *a.* Infirm, weak.

lánguidamente [lahn'-gee-dah-men-tay], *adv.* Languidly, languishingly.

languidecer [lan-gee-day-ther'], *vn.* To languish, to pine, to wither.

languidez, languideza [lan-gee-deth'], *f.* 1. Languishment, languidness, languishing, heaviness, languor, weariness, faintness. 2. Decay of spirits, melancholy.

lánguido, da [lahn'-gee-do, dah], *a.* 1. Languid, faint, weak, languishing, feeble. 2. Dull, heartless.

lanífero, ra [lah-nee'-fay-ro, rah], *(Poet.)* Laniferous, woolly.

lanificio [lah-ne-fee'-the-o], *m.* Woollen manufacture, the art of manufacturing wool.

lanilla [lah-neel'-lyah], *f.* 1. Nap of cloth, down, villous substance. 2. Swan skin, a very fine flannel (tela). 3. *(Naut.)* Bunting, a thin woollen stuff of which flags are made. 4. *(Bot.)* Down.

lanosidad [lah-no-se-dahd'], *f.* Down of the leaves of plank.

lanoso, sa [lah-no'-so, sah], *a. V.* LANUDO.

lanteja [lan-tay'-hah], *f.* Lentil. *V.* LENTEJA.

lantajuela [lan-tay-hoo-ay'-lah], *f.* 1. Spangle, a small plate of shining metal. 2. Scurf left on the skin after a sore.

lanudo, da [lah-noo'-do, dah], *a.* Woolly (lanoso), consisting of wool, clothed with wool, lanigerous, fleecy. 2. *(And. Carib.)* Rustic, uncouth (maleducado). 3. *(Carib. Mex.)* Well off (rico).

lanuginoso, sa [lah-noo-he-no'-so, sah], *a.* Lanuginous, lanicerous, downy; covered with soft hair.

lanza [lahn'-thah], *f.* 1. Lance, spear, javelin. 2. Pole of a coach or wagon (carro). 3. Pikeman, soldier armed with a pike. **A punta de lanza**, strenuously, with all one's might.

lanzabombas [lan-thah-bom'-bahs], *m.* Bomber, bomb thrower, bomb release.

lanzacohetes [lan-thah-co-ay'-tes], *m.* Rocket launcher.

lanzada [lan-thah'-dah], *f.* Stroke with a lance, thrust with a spear.

lanzadera [lan-thah-day'-rah], *f.* Shuttle, a weaver's instrument.

lanzado, da [lan-thah'-do, dah], *a.* 1. *(Naut.)* Raking, overhanging. 2. Forward, brazen (ser). 3. Randy, in the mood. *-pp.* of LANZAR.

lanzador, ra [lan-thah-dor', rah], *m. & f.* 1. Thrower, ejecter, pitcher (béisbol). 2. Promoter. 3. *(Mil.)* Launcher (de cohetes).

lanzafuego [lan-thah-foo-ay'-go], *m. V.* BOTAFUEGO.

lanzallamas [lan-thahl-lyah'-mas], *m.* Flame thrower.

lanzamiento [lan-thah-me-en'-to], *m.* 1. Launch, launching. 2. Cast, throw. 3. Flinging, hurling. 4. Throwing off. 5. Publication, 6. *(for.)* Eviction. 7. Promotion. **Lanzamiento del disco**, discus throw. **Lanzamiento del martillo**, hammer throw. **Lanzamiento del peso**, shot put. **Lanzamiento de la jabalina**, javelin throw. **Oferta de lanzamiento**, promotional offer.

lanzaminas [lan-thah-mee'-nas], *m.* Mine layer, mine thrower.

lanzar [lan-thar'], *va.* 1. To lance, to throw, to dart, to launch, to fling (con violencia), to pitch (pelota), to throw out (desafío), to hurl (crítica). 2. To cast up, to vomit. 3. *(Law.)* To eject, to dispossess. 4. To let loose. *-vr.* 1. To rush or dart upon; to launch. 2. *(Com.)* To engage or embark on. **Lanzarse en paracaídas**, *(Aer.)* to bail out. **Se lanzó al río**, he jumped into the river. **Lanzar una bomba**, to drop a bomb.

lanzatorpedos [lan-thah-tor-pay'-dos], *m.* Torpedo boat.

lanzón [lan-thone'], *m. aug.* A short and thick lance.

laña [lah'-nyah], *f.* 1. Cramp or crampiron. 2. Green cocoanut.

lañar [lah-nyar'], *va.* 1. To vamp, to fasten two things together with a crampiron. *(Prov.)* To open and gut fish.

lapa [lah'-pah], *f.* 1. Scum or pellicle raised on the surface of some liquors. 2. *(Zool.)* A kind of shell-fish. Lepas. 3. *(Bot.)* Goose-grass, cleavers. 4. *(And. Cono Sur)* Half gourd. 5. *(And.)* Large flat-topped hat (sombrero).

lapachar [lah-pah-char'], *m.* Hole full of mud and mire.

lápade [lah'-pah-day], *f. (Zool.)* Acorn shell-fish.

lapaza [lah-pah'-thah], *f. (Prov.)* Rough panic-grass.

lapicero [lah-pe-thay'-ro], *m.* 1. A metal pencil case. 2. Pencil holder. 3. Mechanical pencil. 4. *(LAm.)* Fountain pen (pluma fuente).

lápida [lah'-pe-dah], *f.* A flat stone, on which inscriptions are engraved. **Lápida mortuoria**, head-stone. **Lapida mural**, tablet let into a wall.

lapidación [lah-pe-dah-the-on'], *f.* Lapidation, stoning to death.

lapidar [lah-pe-dar'], *va.* 1. To throw stones. 2. To stone to death.

lapidaria [lah-pe-dah'-re-ah], *f.* The art or profession of a lapidary, who deals in stones and gems.

lapidario [lah-pe-dah'-re-o], *m.* Lapidary, lapidist, one who deals in stones and gems.

lapidario, ria [lah-pe-dah'-re-o, ah], *a.* Lapidary.

lapideo, dea [lah-pee'-day-o, ah], *a.* Lapideous, stony of the nature of.

lapidificación [lah-pe-de-fe-ca-the-on'], *f.* Petrification, lapidification.

lapidífico, ca [lah-pe-dee'-fe-co, cah], *a.* Lapidescent, lapidific, growing or turning to stone.

lapidoso, sa [lah-pe-do'-so, sah], *a.* Lapideous, stony.

lapilla [lah-peel'-lyah], *f. (Bot.)* Hound's tongue.

lapislázuli [lah-pis-lah'-thoo-le], *m.* Lapis lazuli, an azure stone, of which the ultra-marine color is prepared by calcination.

lápiz [lah'-pith], *m.* Pencil, lead pencil, crayon. **Lápiz de labios** or **lápiz labial**, lipstick. **Lápiz de ojos**, eyeliner. **Escribir algo a lápiz**, to write something in pencil.

lapizar [lah-pe-thar'], *m.* Black-lead mine.

lapizar [lah-pe-thar'], *va.* To draw or delineate with black chalk or black lead.

lapo [lah'-po], *m.* 1. *(coll.)* Blow with the flat side of a sword. 2. *(And. Carib.)* Swig (trago). 3. *(Carib.)* Simple soul (inocente). 4. Spit (escupitajo).

lapón, na [lah-pone', nah], *a. & m. & f.* Laplander, relating to Lapland, Laplandish.

lapso [lahp'-so], *m. (Law.)* Lapse or course of time.

lapsus [lahp-soos], *m.* Lapse, mistake.

lapsus linguae [lap'-soos leen'-goo-ay], *m.* Slip of the tongue.

lar [lahr], *m.* A household god. *V.* LARES.

larario [lah-rah'-re-o], *m.* Place where the pagans worshipped their house-gods.

lardar, lardear [lar-dar', lar-day-ar'], *va.* 1. To lard, to baste meat on the spit (carne). 2. To beat with a stick.

lardero [lar-day'-ro], *a.* Applied to the Thursday before Lent.

lardo [lar'-do], *m.* Lard, the fat of swine and other animals.

lardón [lar-done'], *m.* A marginal note, observation, or addition, in a book or in a proof. Also a piece of paper clinging to the frisket and preventing the impression of some part of a sheet.

lardosico, ica, illo, illa, ito, ita [lar-do-see'-co, ee'-cah], *a. dim.* Greasy, dirty with grease.

lardoso, sa [lar-do'-so, sah], *a.* Greasy, fatty.

lares [lah'-res], *m. pl.* 1. House-gods of the ancient Romans. 2. Home.

larga [lar'-gah], *f.* 1. An added piece which shoemakers put on last, in order to lengthen a shoe. 2. Delay, procrastination: commonly used in the plural.

largamente [lar-gah-men'-tay], *adv.* Largely, copiously; completely; liberally, frankly; for a long time (de tiempo). 2. Generously (compensar, tratar). 3. Comfortably, at ease (vivir).

largar [lar-gar'], *va.* 1. To loosen, to slacken (aflojar). 2. To let go (soltar), to set at liberty. 3. *(Naut.)* To loosen a sail, to ease a rope. 4. To give, to fetch, to deal (vivir). 5. **Nos largó ese rollo de...**, he gave us the usual boring tale about... 6. *(And.)* To throw, to hurl (lanzar). 7. *(And.)* To hand over (entregar). **¡Vaya rollo!**, what a bore! *-vr.* 1. To beat it, to hop it; to quit. **¡Lárgate!**, clear off. 2. *(Naut.)* To set sail. 3. *(LAm.)* To start, to begin (empezar).

largo, ga [lar'-go, gah], *a.* 1. Long, of a certain measure in length (largo, medida). 2. Long, not short (espacio, tiempo). 3. Long, protracted, not soon ceasing or at an end. 4. Large, generous (generoso), free, liberal. 5. Copious (copioso). 6. Prompt, expeditious. 7. Sharp, shrewd; quick (astuto). **Largo de lengua**, too free and unguarded with the tongue, to be mordacious. **De largo a largo**, from one end to the other, length-wise. **Navegar a lo largo de la costa**, *(Naut.)* to navigate along the coast. **Pasar de largo**, to walk by without stopping. **A la corta o a la larga**, sooner or later. **A lo largo**, at length, slowly; in the long run; in course of time. **A lo largo**, 1. At a distance. 2. The long way, lengthwise. **Pasar de largo**, to pass by a person without taking notice of him. **Ese es cuento largo**, that is a long story. **A lo largo de**, along. **Dar largas a un asunto**, to delay a matter. *-m.* 1. Length. **El largo de las faldas**, the length of the skirts. 2. *(Mus.)* Largo. *-adv.* Largely, profusely.

largometraje [lar-go-may-trah'-hay], *m.* Full-length film, feature film.

largomira [lar-go-mee'-rah], *f.* Telescope.

largón, na [lar-gone', nah], *a. aug.* 1. Very long. 2. *(And. Cono Sur)* Delay (demora). 3. **Darse una largona**, *(Cono Sur)* to take a rest.

largor [lar-gor'], *m.* Length, the extent of something from end to end.

largueado, da [lar-gay-ah'-do, dah], *a.* Striped. *V.* LISTADO.

larguero [lar-gay'-ro], *m.* Jamb-post of a door or window. *V.* CABEZAL. *-a.* 1. *(Cono Sur)* Long (largo), lengthly; wordy (discurso); slow (persona). 2. *(Cono Sur)* Generous (generoso), lavish; abundant, copious (copioso).

largueza [lar-gay'-thah], *f.* 1. Length, extent, largeness, width. 2. Liberality, generosity, munificence, frankness.

larguito, ita [lar-gee'-to, tah], *a.* Not very long.

largura [lar-goo'-rah], *f.* Length, longness, stretch, extent.

lárice [lah'-re-thay], *m. (Bot.)* Larch-tree.

laricino, na [lah-re-thee'-no, nah], *a.* Belonging to the larch-tree.

larige [lah-ree'-hay], *a.* Applied to a kind of very red grapes.

laringa [lah-reen'-gah], *f.* Turpentine extracted from the larchtree; Venice turpentine.

laringe [lah-reen'-hay], *f. (Anat.)* Larynx, the upper part of the trachea, where the voice is formed.

laríngeo, gea [lah-reen'-hay-o, ah], *a.* Laringeal, relating to the larynx.

laringitis [lah-ren-hee-tis], *f.* Laryngitis, inflammation of the larynx.

laringología [lah-rin-go-lo-hee'-ah], *f.* Laryngology, scientific knowledge of the larynx.

laringoscopia [lah-rin-gos-co-pe-ah], *f.* Laryngoscopy, use of the laryngoscope; inspection of the larynx.

laringoscopio [lah-rin-gos-co'-pe-o], *m.* Laryngoscope, a reflecting mirror for examining the larynx.

laringotomía [lah-rin-go-to-mee'-ah], *f. (Surg.)* Laringotomy.

laro [lah'-ro], *m. (Orn.)* Gull, seagull.

larva [lar'-vah], *f.* 1. Mask. V. MASCARA and FANTASMA. 2. *(Ent.)* Larva, grub-state of an insect. **Larvas,** hobgoblins; lemures.

larvado, da [lar-vah'-do, dah], *a.* 1. *(Med.)* Larvate, masked. 2. Hidden, latent.

larval [lar-vahl'], *a.* 1. Frightful, ghastly. 2. Larvated, like a mask.

las [lahs], *pron.* of third person plural feminine. It does not admit a preposition, and should not be used for the dative. **Las de Méjico son las mejores,** those of Mexico are the best. **Éstas son las de usted,** these are yours. **Son ellas las que me lo dijeron,** they were the ones who told me. **Esas cortinas son las que quiero,** those curtains are the ones that I want.

las [lahs] *art. def.* The. **Las casas son muy bonitas,** the houses are very nice. **Son las nueve,** it is nine o'clock. **Me gustan las patatas fritas,** I like fritters.

lasaña [lah-sah'-nyah], *f.* A sort of paste fried in a pan.

láscar [lahs'-car], *m.* Lascar, a native seaman or gunner in India.

lascar [las-car'], *va.* 1. *(Naut.)* To ease off; to slacken. 2. *(Mex.)* To graze (piel); to chip (piedra).

lascivamente [las-the-vah-men'-tay], *adv.* Lasciviously, lustfully, libidinously.

lascivia [las-thee'-ve-ah], *f.* 1. Luxuriance, luxury; excess in delicious fare. 2. Lasciviousness, lewdness, lust.

lascivo, va [las-thee'-vo, vah], *a.* 1. Lascivious, lewd, lustful, libidinous. 2. Luxuriant, exuberant.

láser [lah'-ser], *m.* 1. *(Bot.)* Benzoin. 2. Laser.

laserpicio [lah-ser-pee'-the-o], *m. (Bot.)* Laserwort.

lasitud [lah-se-tood'], *f.* Lassitude, weariness, faintness.

laso, sa [lah'-so, sah], *a.* 1. Weary (cansado), tired with labor, subdued by fatigue. 2. Lax, flaccid.

lastar [las-tar'], *va.* To pay, to answer, or suffer for another.

lástima [lahs'-te-mah], *f.* 1. Grief, compassion, pity (sentimiento), condolence. **Es una lástima,** it's a shame. **Eso me da mucha lástima,** I feel very sorry about that. **Todos me dan lástima,** I feel sorry for them all. 2. Object of compassion or pity (objeto).

lastimar [las-te-mar'], *va.* 1. To hurt (lesionar), to wound (herir), to offend (ofender). 2. To move to compassion, to excite pity, to pity (apiadarse de). -*vr.* 1. To be moved to compassion, to grieve, to be sorry for (apiadarse); to complain (quejarse). 2. To hurt oneself. **Se lastimó el brazo,** he hurt his arm.

lastimeramente [las-te-may-rah-men'-tay], *adv.* Sadly, sorrowfully.

lastimero, ra [las-te-may'-ro, rah], *a.* Sad, doleful, mournful, miserable, moving, lamentable, grievous.

lastimosamente [las-te-mo-sah-men'-tay], *adv.* Miserably, pitifully, grievously, lamentably.

lastimoso, sa [las-te-mo'-so, sah], *a.* Doleful, sad, pathetic. V. LASTIMERO.

lasto [lahs'-to], *m.* Receipt given or belonging to him who has paid for another.

lastra [lahs'-trah], *f. (Naut.)* Boat, lighter. V. LANCHA.

lastrar [las-trar'], *va.* 1. *(Naut.)* To ballast a ship. 2. To keep something steady by means of a ballast.

lastre [lahs'-tray], *m.* 1. Rough stones used to ballast ships or build walls. 2. Ballast, a freight put at the bottom of ships to keep them steady, lastage. **Lastre grueso,** heavy ballast. **Lastre lavado,** washed ballast. **Ir en lastre,** to go in ballast. 3. Weight, motive, judgment.

lata [lah'-tah], *f.* 1. Tin, can (envase), tinplate (metal). **Sardinas en lata,** canned sardines. 2. *(coll.)* Annoyance, boredom. **Dar la lata,** to annoy, to bother, to bore. **Dar la lata a uno,** to annoy somebody. 3. Lath (madera). 4. **Estar sin latas,** *(And. CAm.)* to be penniless. 5. *(LAm.)* Drag (persona).

latamente [lah-tah-men'-tay], *adv.* Largely, amply.

latazo [lah-tah-tho], *m.* Nuisance, bore, bind.

latente [lah-ten'-tay], *a.* 1. Latent, obscure, hidden. 2. *(LAm.)* Alive, intense, vigorous.

lateral [lah-tay-rahl'], *a.* Lateral, belonging to the side.

látex [lah'-teks], *m. (Bot.)* Latex.

latido [lah-tee'-do], *m.* 1. Pant, palpitation; motion of the heart. 2. Howling or barking of a dog after game. -*pp.* of LATIR.

latiente [lah-teen'-tay], *pa.* Palpitating, fluttering.

latigadera [lah-te-gah-day'-rah], *f. (Prov.)* Strap or thong by which the yoke is fastened to the pole of a cart.

latigazo [la-te-gah'-tho], *m.* 1. Lash (golpe), crack of a whip (chasquido), a jerk. 2. Reprimand (reprimenda). 3. Drink, swig (beber). **Dar latigazos,** to lash, to whip.

látigo [lah'-te-go], *m.* 1. Whip; thong, or point of a whip. 2. Rope with which something to be weighed is fastened to the steel-yard. 3. The end of every strap which must be passed through a buckle. 4. Mast of a boat when it is extremely tall.

latiguear [lah-te-gay-ar'], *vn.* To smack or crack with the lash of a whip, to lash or ply the whip.

latiguera [lah-te-gay'-rah], *f.* Cord with which a girth is fastened.

latiguero [lah-te-gay'-ro], *m.* Maker or seller of whip thongs or lashes.

latiguillo [lah-te-geel'-lyo], *m. dim.* A small whip.

latín [lah-teen'], *m.* 1. Latin, the Latin tongue. 2. A Latin word or clause interposed in a Romance text. **Saber mucho latín,** to be full of wit and cunning. **Latín vulgar,** vulgar Latin.

latinajo [lah-te-nah'-ho], *m. (coll.)* Latin jargon.

latinamente [lah-te-nah-men'-tay], *adv.* In pure Latin.

latinidad [lah-te-ne-dahd'], *f.* Latinity, the Latin tongue.

latinismo [lah-te-nees'-mo], *m.* Latinism, a mode of speech peculiar to the Latin language.

latinizar [lah-te-ne-thar'], *va.* To Latinize, to give names a Latin termination. -*vn.* To use words borrowed from the Latin.

latino, na [lah-tee'-no, nah], *a.* 1. Latin, written or spoken in the language of the old Romans. 2. Belonging to the Latin language or to the country of Latium. 3. Applied to the Western church, opposed to the Greek. **A la latina,** in a lateen or triangular fashion.

latino, na [lah-tee'-no, nah], *m. & f.* 1. Latinist, one who knows the Latin language. 2. A native of Latium.

latinoamericano, na [lah-te-no-ah'-may-re-cah'-no, nah], *a. & m. & f.* Latin American, South American.

latir [lah-teer'], *m.* 1. To palpitate, to beat the heart (corazón); to flutter. 2. To yelp, to bark as a hound in pursuit of game.

latitud [lah-te-tood'], *f.* 1. Breadth (extensión), width, latitude, extent. 2. *(Geog.)* Latitude, the distance of any point from the equator.

latitudinal [lah-te-too-de-nahl'], *a.* Relating to the latitude.

lato, ta [lah'-to, tah], *a.* Large, diffuse, extensive.

latón [lah-tone'], *m.* 1. Brass (metal), latten. **Latón en hojas or planchas,** latten brass; sheet brass. 2. *(Cono Sur)* Big tin, large tin.

latonería [lah-to-nay-ree'-ah], *f.* 1. The art of working in brass. 2. A brass-worker's shop.

latonero [lah-to-nay'-ro], *m.* Brazier, a manufacturer who works in brass.

latones [lah-to'-nes], *m. pl. (Naut.)* Laths or ledges, used on board ships.

latoso, sa [lah-to'-so, sah], *a. (coll.)* Boring, annoying.

latría [lah-tree'-ah], *f.* Latria, worship, adoration due to God only.

latrina [lah-tree'-nah], *f.* Privy house. *V.* LETRINA.

latrocinio [lah-tro-thee'-ne-o], *m.* Robbery, frequent and repeated theft.

laúd [lah-ood'], *m.* 1. Lute, a stringed musical instrument. 2. Merchant vessel, craft.

laudable [lah-oo-dah'-blay], *a.* Laudable, praiseworthy.

laudablemente [lah-oo-dah-blay-men'-tay], *adv.* Laudably.

láudano [lah'-oo-dah-no], *m.* Laudanum, a tincture from opium.

laudar [lah-oo-dar'], *va.* To render a decision as an arbitrator or umpire.

laudatorio, ria [lah-oo-dah-to'-re-o, ah], *a.* Laudatory, acclamatory.

laude [lah'-oo-day], *f.* 1. A tombstone with an epitaph engraved on it. 2. *pl.* Lauds, that part of the divine service which is said after matins, and consists in praise of the Almighty. **A laudes,** at all hours, frequently.

laudemio [lah-oo-day'-me-o], *m. (Law.)* Dues paid to the lord of the manor on all transfers of landed property, within the manor.

launa [lah'-oo-nah], *f.* 1. Lamina, a thin plate of metal. 2. Schistose clay for covering houses.

laura [lah'-oo-rah], *f.* Solitary situation where the ancient monks had their detached cells.

lauráceo, cea [lah-oo-rah'-thay-o, ah]; *a.* Laurel-like.

láurea [lah'-oo-ray-ah], *f.* A laurel leaf or crown.

laureado, da [lah-oo-ray-ah'-do, dah], *a. & pp.* of LAUREAR. Laureate, laurelled.

laureando [lah-oo-ray-ahn'-do], *m.* He who is soon to receive a degree in a university.

laurear [lah-oo-ray-ar'], *pa.* 1. To crown with laurel. 2. To graduate, to dignify with a degree at universities.

lauredal [lah-oo-ray-dahl'], *m.* Plantation of laurel-trees.

laurel [lah-oo-rel'], *m.* 1. *(Bot.)* Laurel. 2. A crown of bays as a reward.

lauréola [lah-oo-ray'-o-lah], *f.* 1. A crown of laurel. **Lauréola macho,** spurge laurel. 2. Diadem.

laurífero, ra [lah-oo-ree'-fay-ro, rah], *a. (Poet.)* Lauriferous, producing or carrying laurel.

lauríneo, nea [lah-oo-ree'-nay-o, ah], *a. (Bot.)* Laurel-like.

laurino, na [lah-oo-ree'-no, nah], *a.* Belonging to laurel.

lauro [lah'-oo-ro], *m.* 1. Glory, honor, fame, triumph, 2. *(Bot.) V.* LAUROCERASO.

lauroceraso, lauroreal [lah-oo-ro-thay-rah'-so, lah-oo-ro-ray-ahl], *m. (Bot.)* Cherry-laurel or laurel plum-tree.

lautamente [lah-oo-tah-men'-tay], *adv.* Splendidly.

lauto, ta [lah'-oo-to, tah], *a.* Rich, wealthy.

lava [lah'-vah], *f.* 1. Washing of metals in mines. 2. Lava, a volcanic production.

lavable [lah-vah'-blay], *a.* Washable.

lavabo [lah-vah'-bo], *m.* 1. A washbasin (lavamanos); washstand (con soporte); washroom (cuarto de aseo). 2. *(Rel.)* Lavabo (lavatorio). 3. The napkin on which the priest dries his hands after washing. 4. Lavatory, toilet (retrete).

lavacaras [lah-vah-cah'-ras], *m. (Met.)* A flatterer.

lavación [lah-vah-the-on'], *f.* Lotion, wash.

lavada [lah-vah'-dah], *f.* 1. A large drawnet for fishing. 2. *(LAm.)* Washing.

lavadero [lah-vah-day'-ro], *m.* 1. Washing-place (público, al aire libre); wash house (edificio). 2. Vat or pit in which tanners clean their skins. 3. Laundry, the room in which clothes are washed. 4. Place where gold-bearing sands are washed.

lavado [lah-vah'-do], *m.* Wash (acto), washing. **Lavado bucal,** mouth wash. **Lavado intestinal,** enema. **Lavado en seco,** dry cleaning.

lavador, ra [lah-vah-dor', rah], *m. & f.* Washer, one who washes wool. 2. Burnisher, an instrument which serves to clean and brighten fire arms. 3. *(Cono Sur)* Washbasin (fregadero).

lavadora [lah-vah-do'-rah], *f.* Washing machine, washer (para la ropa).

lavadura [lah-vah-doo'-rah], *f.* 1. Wash, washing, lavation, the act of washing anything. 2. Composition of water, oil, and eggs, beaten together, in which glove-leather is prepared. 3. *V.* LAVAZAS.

lavaje [lah-vah'-hay], *m.* Washing of wools.

lavajo [lah-vah'-ho], *m.* Pool where cattle go to drink; morass.

lavamanos [lah-vah-mah'-nos], *m.* A washing-stand, lavatory.

lavanco [lah-vahn'-coh], *m.* A kind of wild duck.

lavanda [lah-vahn'-dah], *f.* Lavender; lavander water (agua).

lavandera [lah-van-day'-rah], *f.* 1. Laundress, a washer-woman. 2. *(Zool.)* Wagtail. *V.* AGUZANIEVE.

lavandería [lah-van-day-ree'-ah], *f.* 1. Laundry, laundering establishment. 2. Washing, laundering. **Lavandería automática** laundromat.

lavandero [lah-van-day'-ro], *m.* 1. Washer, he who washes, launderer. 2. One who carries and brings foul linen to be washed.

lavaojos [lah-vah-o'-hose], *m.* Eye-cup.

lavaplatos [lah-vah-plah'-tose], *m.* 1. Dishwasher (aparato). 2. *(Cono Sur)* Dishwasher (persona). 3. *(Cono Sur, Mex.)* Sink (fregadero).

lavar [lah-var'], *va.* 1. To wash, to cleanse by ablution, to rave, to launder. 2. To clear from an imputation or charge of guilt. 3. To white-wash a wall with lime or chalk. **Lavary marcar,** to shampoo and set. **Lavar la cabeza,** to wash one's hair. *-vr.* To wash, to have a wash. **Lavarse las manos,** to wash one's hands.

lavativa [lah-lya-tee'-vah], *f.* 1. Enema, clyster, a medicinal injection. 2. A clyster-pipe; a syringe. 3. *(Met.)* Vexation, annoyance (molestia).

lavatorio [lah-vah-to'-re-o], *m.* 1. Lavation, the act of washing. 2. Medicinal lotion with which diseased parts are washed. 3. Ceremony of washing the feet on Holy Thursday. 4. Lavatory. *V.* LAVAMANOS.

lavavajilla [lah-vah-vah-heel'-lyahs], *m.* Dishwasher.

lavazas [lah-vah'-thas], *f. .pl.* Foul water running from a washing-place.

lave [lah'-vay], *m.* Washing of metals in mines.

lavotear [lah-vo-tay-ar'], *va. & vr. (coll.)* To wash hurriedly and poorly. *(Acad.)*

lavoteo [lah-vo-tay'-o], *m.* Washing hurriedly and poorly performed.

laxacíon [lac-sah-the-on'], *f.* Loosening, laxation, slackening.

laxamiento [lac-sah-me-en'-to], *m.* Laxation, laxity, laxness, loosening.

laxante [lac-sahn'-tay], *pa.* Loosening, softening. *-m. & a. (Med.)* Laxative.

laxar [lac-sar'], *va.* To loosen (vientre), to soften.

laxativo, va [lac-sah-tee'-vo, vah], *a. & f.* Laxative, lenitive.

laxidad [lac-se-dahd'], *f. V.* LAXITUD.

laxitud [lac-se-tood'], *f.* 1. Lassitude, weariness. 2. Laxity, laxness.

laxo, xa [lac'-so, sah], *a.* 1. Lax, slack, not tense, feeble. 2. *(Met.)* Lax, vague; loose in opinions or morals.

laya [lah'-yah], *f.* 1. Quality, nature. 2. *(Prov.)* A two-pronged instrument, with which the ground is turned up.

layador [lah-yah-dor'], *m.* He who cultivates the soil with a two-pronged instrument.

layar [lah-yar'], *va.* To turn up the ground with a *laya.*

lazada [lah-thah' -dah], *f.* 1. Slip-knot formed with a ribbon, cord, thread, etc. 2. Any ornament made in the form of a knot. *(Amer.)* The knot or slip made with a *lazo* on an animal's horns or neck, to keep him fast.

lazador [lah-thah-dor'], *a.* He who catches with the lasso.

lazar [lah-thar'], *va. (Mex.)* To catch with a lasso.

lazareto [lah-thah-ray'-to], *m.* Lazaretto, lazaret, a public building for the reception of persons coming from places suspected of being infected with the plague, to perform quarantine.

lazarillo [lah-thah-reel'-lyo], *a.* Boy who guides a blind man; a blind person's guide.

lazarino, na [lah-thah-ree'-no, nah], *a.* Leprous, lazar-like, lazarly.

lázaro [lah'-tha-hro], *m.* Lazar, a person deformed and nauseous with filthy and pestiential diseases.

lazo [lah'-tho], *m.* 1. Bow, a slip knot. 2. Any knot or complication of thread, ribbon, string, etc. 3. Ornament in the shape of a knot. 4. Snare, trick, scheme. 5. Tie, bond, chain (vínculo). 6. The act of decoying or driving the game to a certain spot. 7. *(Arch.)* Interlaced lines and flowerwork. 8. Pattern made with box and other plants in a garden bed. 9. Cord with which a load is fastened. 10. *(Amer.)* Lasso, a line or rope for catching wild animals (caza). **Lazo de zapato**, bootlace. **Los lazos familiares**, the family bond. *-pl.* Figures in dancing.

lazulita [lah-thoo-lee'-tah]. *f.* Lazulite.

le [lay], *pron.* Him or her, to him, to her, dat. and accus. sing. of the personal pronoun *él*, he or it; and of its feminine, *ella*, she. **No le veo**, I don't see him. **Le hablé, I** spoke to him. **Le he comprado esto,** I bought this for him. **No se le conoce otra obra,** no other work of his is known. **Yo le dije, I** told him/her.

leal [lay-ahl], *a.* 1. Loyal, true to government. 2. Faithful, gentle, tame (animales).

leal [lay-ahl'], *m.* Loyalist.

lealmente [lay-al-men'-tay], *adv*, Loyally, faithfully.

lealtad [lay-al-tahd'], *f.* 1. Loyalty, fidelity, attachment to the laws and government, fealty. 2. Gentleness toward a master (bestias).

lebrada [lay-brah'-dah], *f.* Fricassee made of hare.

lebratico, illo, its [lay-brah-tee' -co, eel'-lyo, ee' -to], *m. dim.* A young hare, a leveret.

lebrato [lay-brah' -to], or **lebratón** [lay-brah-tone'], *m.* Young hare.

lebrel [lay-brel'], *m.* Greyhound.

lebrela [lay-bray'-lah], *f.* Greyhound bitch.

lebrero, ra [lay-bray'-ro, rah], *a.* Applied to dogs for hunting hares.

lebrillo [lay-breel'-lyo], *m.* A glazed earthenware tub or pan.

lebrón [lay-bro-ne'], *m.* 1. A large hare. 2. Coward, poltroon. 3. Sharp (listo). 4. Boastful, insolent (arrogante).

lebroncillo [lay-bron-theel'-lyo], *m.* V. LEBRATO.

lebruno, na [lay-broo'-no, nah], *a.* Leporine, of the hare kind.

lección [lec-the-on'], *f.* 1. Art of reading; reading. 2. Lesson, anything read or repeated to a teacher. 3. Lecture, a discourse upon any subject. 4. Lection, the letter or text of a work. 5. Warning, admonition, example. **Lección particular**, private lesson. **Dar una lección a uno**, to teach somebody a lesson.

leccionario [lec-the-o-nah'-re-o], *m.* Lesson book of the matins.

leccioncita [lec-the-on-thee'-tah], *dim.* A short lecture or lesson.

leccionista [lec-the-o-nees'-tah], *m.* One who gives lessons in private houses; a private tutor.

lecha, lechaza, [lay' -chah, lay-chah'-thah], *f.* 1. Seminal fluid of fishes. 2. Each of the two sacs which contain it.

lechada [lay-chah' -dah], *f.* 1. Lime slaked in water, whitewash. 2. Pulp for making paper (pulpa). 3. Lime water, 4. *(LAm.)* Milking.

Lechal [lay-chahl'], *a.* 1. Sucking (mamífero). **Cordero lechal**, baby lamb. 2. Lactiferous, milky.

lechar [lay-char'], *a.* 1. *V.* LECHAL. 2. Nursing: applied to a woman who has milk in her breasts. 3. Promoting the secretion of milk in female mammals. 4. *(LAm)*. To milk (ordeñar). 5. *(CAm. Mex.)* To whitewash (blanquear).

lechaza [lay-chah'-thah], *f. V.* LECHA.

lechazo [lay-chah'-tho], *m.* 1. A suckling, an unweaned mammal. 2. A weaned lamb.

leche [lay'-chay],. 1. Milk. 2. Milk or white fluid in plants. 3. Good luck (suerte). 4. Bash (golpe); bash, bang (choque). 5. Bore, pain (molestia). 6. Hell!, get away! **Cochinillo de leche**, sucking pig. **Vaca de leche**, milch cow. **Leche de canela**, oil of cinnamon dissolved in wine. **Hermano de leche**, foster brother. **Leche crema or quemada**, custard. **Leche en polvo**, powdered milk. **Un tío de mala leche**, a nasty sort. **Hay mucha mala leche entre ellos**, there's a lot of bad blood between them. **No entiende ni leches**, he doesn't understand a bloody thing. **Ir a toda leche**, to scorch along.

lechecillas [lay-chay-theel'-lyas], *f. pl.* 1. Sweetbread of calves, lambs, and kids. 2. Livers and lights.

lechera [lay-chay'-rah], *f.* 1. Milk-woman, milk-maid (persona), dairy-maid. 2. Milk pan, or vessel for serving milk (recipiente). 3. *(LAm.)* Cow. 4. Police can. 5. Milch cow (vaca de leche).

lechería [lay-chay-ree'-ah], *f.* 1. Cow-house, diary (edificio), lactary. 2. *(Cono Sur)* Cows, herd (vacas). 3. *(And, Mex.)* Meanness (tacañería).

lechero, ra [lay-chay' -ro, rah], *a.* 1. *(coll.)* Milky; containing milk. 2. *(LAm.)* Lucky (con suerte). 3. *(Mex.)* Mean, stingy (tacaño). 4. *(Carib.)* Greedy, grasping (codicioso).

lechero [lay-chay' -ro], *m.* 1. Milkman. 2. Tanpit, where the ooze of bark is prepared.

lecherón [lay-chay-rone'], *m.* 1. Milkman. 2. Tanpit, where the ooze of bark is prepared.

lecherón [lay-chay-rone'], *m.* *(Prov.)* 1. Milk-pail, milkvessel. 2. Flannel in which new-born infants are rolled.

lechetrezna [lay-chay-treth'-nah], *f. (Bot.)* Spurge.

lechigada [lay-che-gah'-dah], *f.* 1. Litter, a number of animals produced at a single birth. 2. A company of persons of the same kind of life or the same calling.

lechín [lay-cheen'], *m.* 1. Tent, pledget. 2. *(Prov.)* Olives rich in oil.

lechino [lay-chee'-no], *m.* 1. Tent, a roll of lint put into a sore. 2. Small tumor in horses.

lecho [lay'-cho], *m.* 1. Bed (cama), a couch. 2. Litter, straw laid under animals. **Lecho de lobo**, haunt of a wolf. 3. Bed of a river; horizontal surface of a seat. 4. Layer, a stratum or row.

lechón [lay-chone'], *m.* 1. A sucking pig; pig of any size. 2. A dirty fellow as regards dress or manner of living.

lechona [lay-cho'-nah], *f.* 1. Sucking female pig. 2. *(coll.)* A dirty woman.

lechoncico, illo, ito [lay-chon-thee'-col], *m. dim.* A very young pig.

lechoso, sa [lay-cho'-so, sah], *a. (Bot.)* Having a milky juice, *-m. (S. Amer.)* The papaw-tree; the juice has remarkable digestive properties.

lechuga [lay-choo'-gah], *f.* 1. *(Bot.)* Lettuce, 2. *V.* LECHUGUILLA for a frill. 3. *(Carib.)* Bank note.

lechugado, da [lay-choo-gah'-do, dah], *a.* Having leaves like lettuce.

lechuguero, ra [lay-choo-gay'-ro, rah], *m. & f.* Retailer of lettuce.

lechuguilla [lay-choo-geel'-lyah], *f.* 1. *(Dim.)* Small lettuce. 2. Frill formerly worn around the neck.

lechuguino [lay-choo-gee'-no], *m.* Plot of small lettuces. *(coll.) -m. & f.* Dandy, dandizette.

lechuza [lay-choo'-thah], *f.* Owl, barn owl. **Lechuza común**, barn owl. 2. *(Cono Sur, Mex.)* Albino, light blond. 3. *(Carib. Mex.)* Whore (prostituta).

lechuzo, za [lay-choo'-tho, thah], *a.* 1. Suckling: applied to mule colts less than a year old. 2. Collecting debts in trust for another. 3. Owlish; a nickname applied to persons.

lechuzo [lay-choo'-tho], *m.* 1. Nickname of an agent, collector, or commissioner who collects money or debts. 2. Nickname of persons resembling owls in any of their qualities.

lectisternio [lec-tis-terr'-ne-o], *m.* Banquet of the heathen gods.

lectivo, va [lec-tee'-vo, vah], *a.* Applied to the time of lecture in universities.

lector, ra [lec-tor', rah], *m. & f.* 1. Reader. 2. In monastic orders, a lecturer, teacher, or professor. 3. In the Roman Catholic church, the second of the four minor orders.

lectorado [lec-to-rah'-do], *m.* Institution of lecturer.

lectoral [lec-to-rah'], *f.* 1. A prebendary, dignity in cathedral churches of Spain. 2. *m.* The person who enjoys the prebend called *lectoral.*

lectoral [lec-to-rahl'], *a.* Applied to the prebend or canonry celled *lectoral* in Spain, and to the prebendary who enjoys it.

lectoría [lec-to-ree'-ah], *f.* Lectureship, in monastic orders; the place and office of a lecturer.

lectura [lec-too'-rah], *f.* 1. Reading, lecture, the act of reading. 2. The act of teaching by way of lectures. 3. Among printers, small pica, 11-point. **Una persona de mucha lectura,** a well-read person. **Dar lectura a,** to read.

ledamente [lay-dah-men'-tay], *adv. (Poet.)* Merrily, cheerfully.

ledo, da [lay'-do, dah], *a. (Poet.)* Gay, merry, cheerful, glad, joyful.

leer [lay-err'] *va.* 1. To read. 2. To lecture, to instruct publicly. 3. To read one's thoughts. **Leer entre líneas**, to read between the lines. **Leer la mano a uno**, to read somebody's palm.

lega [lay'-gah], *f.* A lay sister who serfes the community.

legacía, legación [lay-gah-thee'-ah, lay-gah-the-on'], *f.* 1. Embassy, legation, deputation. 2. Legateship, office of a legate. 3. Message sent by an ambassador or deputy. 4. Province of the ecclesiastical states governed by a legate. 5. Duration of a legate's embassy or government.

legado [lay-gah'-do], *m.* 1. Legacy, a particular thing given by last will and testament. 2. Deputy, ambassador, legate (enviado). 5. Commander of a Roman legion.

legador [lay-gah-dor'], *m. (Prov.)* Day laborer, who ties the feet of sheep, for shearing them.

legadura [lay-gah-doo'-rah], *f. (Ant.)* Ligature, cord, or strap for tying or binding.

legajico, illo, ito [lay-gah-hee'-co], *m. dim.* A small bundle of loose papers tied together.

legajo [lay-gah'-ho], *m.* Bundle of loose papers tied together.

legal [lay-gahl'], *a.* 1. Legal, lawful, constitutinal. 2. Loyal (persona), true, faithful in the performance of duty, punctual. 3. *(And).* Fine, marvellous.

legalidad [lay-gah-le-dahd'], *f.* Legality, fidelity, punctuality; lawfulness, legitimateness.

legalización [lay-gah-le-thah-the-on'], *f.* 1. Attestation of a signature or subscription by which an instrument or writing is legalized. 2. Notarial certificate.

legalizar [lay-gah-le-thar'], *va.* To legalize, to authorize, to make lawful.

legalmente [lay-gal-men'-tay], *adv.* Legally, lawfully; faithfully.

legamente [lay-gah-men'-tay], *adv.* Ignorantly, in an illiterate manner.

légamo [lay'-gah-mo], *m.* Slime, mud, or clay left by water (arcilla).

legamoso, sa [lay-gah-mo'-so, sah], *a.* Slimy, greasy.

legaña [lay-gah'-nyah], *f.* Lippitude, blearedness of eyes.

legar [lay-gar']. *va.* 1. To depute, to send on an embassy. 2. To bequeath, to leave by last will or testament.

legatario, ria [lay-gah-tah'-re-o, ah], *m. & f.* Legatee, a person to whom a legacy is left, legatory.

legatina [lay-gah-tee'nah], *f.* A stuff made of silk and wool.

legenda [lay-hen'-dah], *f.* Legend, traditional history of saints. *(Acad.)*

legendario [lay-hen-dah'-re-o], *m.* 1. Legend, a chronicle or register of the lives of saints. 2. Legendary, author of a legend.

legible [lay-hee'-blay], *a.* Legible, such as may be read.

legión [lay-he-on'], *f.* 1. Legion. **Legión Extranjera**, foreign Legion. 2. Legion, an indefinite number.

legionario, ria [lay-he-o-nah'-re-oh, ah], *a.* Legionary, belonging to a legion.

legislación [lay-hes-lah-the-on'], *f.* 1. Legislation, collection of the laws of a country. 2. Enactment of laws.

legislador, ra [lay-his-lah-dor', rah], *m. & f.* 1. Legislator, law-giver, law-maker. 2. Censor, censurer, he that blames or censures.

legislar [lay-his-lar'], *va.* 1. To legislate, to enact laws. 2. To censure, to criticise.

legislativo, va [lay-his-lah-tee'-vo, vah], *a* Legislative, lawgiving: constitutive.

legislatura [lay-his-lah-too'-rah], *f.* Legislature, the power that makes laws.

legisperito [lay-his-pay-ree'-to], *m.* V. JURISPERITO.

legista [lay-hees'-tah], *m.* Legist, one skilled in law; a professor of laws; a student of jurisprudence.

legítima [lay-hee'-te-mah], *f.* Portion or share of the paternal or maternal estate, which belongs to the children, according to law.

legitimación [lay-he-te-mah-the-on'], *f.* Legitimation, the act of investing with the privileges of lawful birth.

legítimamente [lay-he-te-may-men-tay], *adv.* Legitimately, lawfully.

legitimar [lay-he-te-mar'], *va.* 1. To prove, to establish in evidence. 2. To legitimate, to procure to any the rights of legitimate birth. 3. To make legitimate or adequate; to legalize.

legitimidad [lay-he-te-me-dahd'], *f.* Legitimacy, legitimateness; legality; lawfulness.

legitimista [lay-he-te-mees'-tah], *a. & m. & f.* Legitimist, upholding the divine right of kings, and of succession to the crown by rigorous order of primogeniture.

legítimo, ma [lay-hee'te-mo, mah], *a.* 1. Legitimate, legal, lawful, authentic, 2. True, certain.

lego [lay'-go], *m.* 1. Layman, laic, one of the people distinct from the clergy. 2. Lay-brother or lay-friar, a person admitted for the service of a religious body. -*a.* 1. Laical, lay, laic. 2. Ignorant, illiterate.

legón [lay-gone'], *m.* Spade.

legra [lay'-grah], *f.* Trepan, surgeon's instrument; a cylindrical saw, trephine.

legración, legradura [lay-grah-the-on', lay-grah-doo'rah], *f.* Act of trepanning.

legrar [lay-grar'], *va.* To trepan, to perforate the skull with a trepan; to trephine.

legua [lay'-goo-ah], *f.* League. **A legua, a la legua, a leguas, de cien lenguas, de muchas or desde media legua**, very far, at a great distance. **Legua marítima**, marine league. **Se ve a la legua**, it stands out a mile, you can see it a mile away.

leguilla [lay-goom'-lyah], *f. V.* LIGUILLA.

legumbre [lay-goom'-bray], *f.* 1. Pulse, leguminous plants. 2. Vegetables, garden-stuff, legume or legumen.

legúmina [lay-goo'-me-nah], *f.* Legumin, a proteid compound called also vetable casein.

leguminoso, sa [lay-goo-me-no'-so, sah], *a. (Bot.)* Leguminous: applied to plants which bear legumes or pods.

leíble [lay-ee'-blay], *a.* Legible, readable.

leído, da [lay-ee'-do, dah], *a.* Having read much, booklearned. -*pp.* of LEER.

leila [lay'-e-lah], *f.* A Moorish dance.

leima [lay'-e-mah], *m.* Interval of music.

lejanía [lay-hah-nee'-ah], *f.* Distance (distancia), remoteness in place.

lejano, na [lay-hah'-no, nah], *a.* Distant, remote, far.

lejía [lay-hee'-ah], *f.* 1. Lye, water boiled with ashes. 2. *(Met.)* Severe reprehension.

lejío [lay-hee'-o], *m.* Among dyers, lye.

lejivial [lay-he-ve-ahl'], *a.* Lixivial.

lejos [lay'-hos], *adv.* At a great distance, far off. **Desde lejos**, from afar. **Está muy lejos**, it's a long way. **Eso viene de lejos**, *(Fig.)* that's been going on for a long time.

lejos [lay'-hos], *m.* 1. Perspective, distant, prospect, background. 2. *(Met.)* Similarity, appearance, resemblance. **A lo lejos, de lejos, de muy lejos or desde lejos**, at a great distance.

lejos, jas [lay'-hos, has], *a.* Distant, very remote: generally used in the feminine.

lejuelos [lay-hoo-ay'-los], *adv. dim.* At a little distance.

leilí [lay-le-lee'], *m.* War-whoop of the Moors.

lelo, la [lay'-lo, lah], *a.* Stupid, ignorant, crazy.

lema [lay'-mah], *m.* 1. Argument of a poem explained in the title; motto. 2. Lemma, a proposition previously assumed.

lemosín, na [lay-mo-seen', nah], *a.* Relating to the Lemosin language, or that of the troubadors.

lemosín [lay-mo-seen'], *m.* The Lemosin language.

len [len], *a.* Applied to soft, untwisted silk.

lena [lay'nah], *f.* Spirit, vigor.

lencera [len-thay'-rah], *f.* A woman who deals in linen; the wife of a linen-draper.

lencería [len'-thay-ree'-ah], *f.* 1. An assortment of linen; plenty of linen (telas). 2. Linen draper's shop (tienda); linen hall, where linen is sold. 3. Linen trade. 4. Lingerie (ropa interior).

lencero, ra [len-thay'-ro, rah], *m. & f.* Linen-draper, linen merchant.

lendel [len-del'], *m.* Circle described by a horse turning a wheel to raise water out of a well.

lendrera [len-dray'-rah], *f.* A close toothed comb for taking out nits.

lendrero [len-dray'-ro], *m.* Place full of nits.

lendroso, sa [len-dro'-so, sah], *a.* Nitty, full of nits.

lene [lay'nay], *a.* 1. Mild, soft, bland. 2. Mild, pleasant, benevolent. 3. Light, of small weight or consideration.

lengua [len'-goo-ah], *f.* 1. The tongue. 2. Language (idioma), idiom. 3. Information, advice. 4. Speech. 5. Tongue or needle of a balance. 6. Clapper of a bell. **Lengua de tierra**, neck of land running out into the sea. **Tener algo en la punta de la lengua**, to have something on the tip of one's tongue. **Lengua sabia**, learned language. **Lengua de vaca**, cow's tongue. **De lengua en lengua**, from mouth to mouth. **Irse de la lengua**, to give loose rein to one's tongue. 7. *(Antiq.)* Interpreter. **Andar en lenguas**, to be much talked of. **Morderse la lengua**, *(Met.)* to curb one's speech sharply. **Dar a la lengua**, to chatter. **No morderse la lengua**, not to mince one's words. **Sacar la lengua a uno**, to poke one's tongue out at somebody.

lenguado [len-goo-ah'-do], *m.* *(Zoo.)* Sole, flounder.

lenguaje [len-goo-ah'-hay], *m.* 1. Language, idiom (forma de hablar), speech. 2. Language, style, manner of speaking or writing. **Lenguaje comercial**, business language. **Lenguaje del cuerpo**, body language. 3. *(Comput..)* **Lenguaje natural**, natural language. **Lenguaje de alto nivel**, high-level language. **Lenguaje de bajo nivel**, low-level language. **Lenguaje de cuarta generación (4GLs)**, fourth-generation language (4GLs). **Lenguaje de inteligencia artificial**, artificial-intelligence language. **Lenguaje de máquina**, machine language. **Lenguaje de muy alto nivel**, very-high-level language. **Lenguaje de programación orientado al objeto**, object-oriented programming language. **Lenguaje de recuperación y actualización**, retrieval and update language. **Lenguaje de tercera generación**, third-generation language. **Lenguaje ensamblador**, assembly language. **Lenguaje para procedimientos**, procedural language. **Lenguaje no procesal**, nonprocedural language. **Lenguaje de control de la impresora**, printer control language. **Lenguaje postcript**, postscript language.

lenguaraz [len-goo-ah-rath'], *a.* 1. Languaged, having various languages. Fluent, voluble. 3. Forward, petulant. 4. Talkative, free-tongued. It is sometimes used as a substantive for a linguist.

lenguaz [len-goo-ath'], *a.* Loquacious, garrulous.

lengüecica, illa, ita [len-goo-ay-thee'-cah, eel'-lyah], *f. dim.* A small tongue.

lengüeta [len-goo-ay-tah], *f.* 1. *(Dim.)* A small tongue. 2. Languet, anything cut in the form of a tongue; a free reed in wind instruments. 3. *(Anat.)* Epiglottis. 4. Needle of a balance. 5. Book-binder's cutting-knife (cortapapeles). 6. *(Mech.)* Feather, a thin wedge. 7. *(Arch.)* Buttress; moulding. 8. Borer used by saddlers and chair makers. 9. *(LAm.)* Chatterbox (hablador).

lengüetada [len-goo-ay-tah'-dah], *f.* The act of licking.

lengüetería [len-goo-ay-tay-ree'-ah], *f.* The reedwork of an organ. *-f. pl. (LAm.)* Gossip, title-tattle.

lengüezuela [len-goo-ay-thoo-ay'-lah], *f. dim.* A small tongue.

lenidad [lay-ne-dahd'], *f.* Lenity, mildness, favor.

lenificar [lay-ne-fe-car'], *va.* To lenify, to soften. *V.* SUAVIZAR.

lenificativo, va [lay-ne-fe-cah-tee'-vo, vah], *a.* Mollifying, softening.

lenitivo, va [lay-ne-tee'-vo, vah], *a.* Lenitive, lenient, mitigant.

lenitivo [lay-ne-tee'vo], *m.* Emollient, mitigator, lenient.

lenocinio [lay-no-thee'-ne-o], *m.* Pimping, pandering. *V.* ALCAHUETERÍA.

lentamente [len-tah-men'-tay], *adv.* Slowly, heavily, lazily, lingeringly.

lente [len'-tay], *com.* 1. Lens. 2. Eyeglass. **Lente angular**, wide-angle lens. **Lente telefotográfico**, telephoto lens. **Lentes bifocales**, bifocals, bifocal glasses. **Lentes de contacto**, contact lenses.

lentecer [len-tay-therr'], *vn. & vr.* To grow soft or tender.

lenteja [len-tay'-hah], *f.* *(Bot.)* Lentil. **Lenteja de agua**, gibbous duckweed. **lentejuela** [len-tay-hoo-ay'-lah], *f.* Spangle, a small plate of shining metal.

lenticular [len-te-coo-lar'], *a.* Lenticular, in the form of a lentil. **Hueso lenticular**, the smallest bone of the ear; stapes.

lentiforme [len-te-for'-may], *a.* *(Anat.)* Lens-shaped, lentiform.

lentillas [len-teel'-lyahs], *f. pl.* Contact lenses.

lentisco [len-tees'-co], *m.* *(Bot.)* Mastich-tree.

lentitud [len-te-tood'], *f.* Slowness, sluggishness, coldness.

lento, ta [len'-to, tah], *a.* 1. Slow, sluggish, tardy, heavy, long, lingering. 2. *(Met.)* Glutinous. 3. *(Mus.)* Largo. 4. *(Med.)* Slow.

lentor [len-tor'], *m.* Lentor, sluggishness.

leña [lay'-nyah], *f.* 1. Wood, fire-wood. 2. *(coll.)* Stick, beating. **Echar leña al fuego**, *(Met.)* to foment discord. **Llevar leña al monte**, to carry coals to Newcastle.

leñador, ra [lay-nyah-dor', rah], *m. & f.* Woodman, wood-cutter, dealer in wood.

leñar [lay-nyar'], *va.* To cut wood.

leñera [lay-nyay'-rah], *f.* Place for fire-wood.

leñazgo [lay-nyath'-go], *m.* Pile of wood or timber.

leñero [lay-nyay'ro], *m.* 1. Dealer in wood, timber-merchant. 2. Timber-yard. 3. A logman.

leño [lay'-nyo], *m.* 1. Block, a heavy piece of timber (madera), a log (tronco); the trunk of a tree cut down. 2. *(Poet.)* Ship, vessel. 3. *(Met.)* Person of little talent or ability. 4. *(Bot.)* Woody fibre. **Hacer leño del árbol caído**, to kick somebody when he's down.

leñoso, sa [lay-nyo'-so, sah], *a.* Woody, ligneous.

león [lay-on'], *m.* 1. Lion. Felis leo. **León marino**, sea lion. **Estar hecho un león**, to be furious. **Leó pardo**, *V.* LEOPARDO. 2. *(Ast.)* Leo, the fifth sign of the zodiac. 3. *(Met.)* An irritable and cruel person. 4. A neuropterous insect, dragonfly.

leona [lay-o'-nah], *f.* Lioness.

leonado, da [lay-o-nah'-do, dah], *a.* Lion colored, tawny.

leonera [lay-o-nay'-rah], *f.* 1. Cage (jaula) or place where lions are shut up; a menagerie 2. Gambling den (de juego); *And. Cono Sur)* communal prison cell (celda); *(And.)* noisy gathering.

leonero [lay-o-nay'-ro], *m.* 1. Keeper of lions. 2. Master of a gambling house.

leónica [lay-o'-ne-cah], *f.* Vein or gland under the tongue (caballos).

leonino, na [lay-o-nee'-no, nah], *a.* 1. Leonine, belonging to lions. 2. Leonine verses, the end of which rhymes to the middle.

leonina [lay-o-nee'-nah], *f.* Elephantiasis, a kind of leprosy.

leopardo [lay-o-par'-do], *m.* Leopard, panther.

leotardo [lay-tar'-do], *m.* Leotard, tights.

lépero, ra [lay'-pay-ro, rah], *a. (Mex.)* Of the lowest kind of people, ragged and wretched.

lepidio [lay-pee'-de-o], *m. (Bot.)* Pepper-grass.

lepidóptero, ra [lay-pe-dop'-tay-ro, rah], *a.* Lepidopterous, belonging to the lepidoptera. *-m. pl.* The lepidoptera, a class of insects having wings covered with dust-like scales. It includes butterflies, moths, and sphinxes.

lepisma [lay-pees'-mah], *f.* Lepisma, the bristle-tail, silver-fish or sugar louse.

leopoldina [lay-o-pol-dee'-nah], *f.* Watch fob.

leporino, na [lay-po-ree'-no, nah], *a.* Like a hare. **Labio leporino**, harelip.

lepra [lay'-prah], *f.* Leprosy.

leprosería [lay-pro-say-ree'-ah], *f.* A hospital for lepers.

leprosidad [lay-pro-se-dahd'], *f. (Med.)* Leprousness.

leproso, sa [lay-pro'-so, sah], *a.* Leprous, leperous. *-m. & f.* Leper.

lercha [lerr'-chah], *f. (Prov.)* A reed passed through the gills of fishes to hang them up.

lerdamente [ler-dah-men'-tay], *adv.* Slowly, heavily, lumpishly, obtusely.

lerdez [ler-deth'], *f.* Slowness, tardiness, heaviness.

lerdo, da [layr'-do, dah], *a.* Slow (lento), heavy (pesado); dull of comprehension, lumpish, obtuse.

lerdón [ler-done'], *m. (Vet.)* Tumor in a horse's pastern.

les [lays], *pron. pers.* 1. Them, to them (a ellos); you, to you (a usted, a ustedes). 2. Them (dativo); you. **Yo les vi**, I saw them. **Yo les presté (a ellas) dinero**, I lent them some money. **Yo les compré a ustedes una casa**, I bought a house from you.

lesbiano, na, lesbio, bia [les-be-ah'-no, nah, les'-be-o, ah], *a. & f. & m.* Lesbian.

lesbio, bia [les'-be-o, ah], *a.* Lesbian, of Lesbos.

lesión [lay-se-on'], *f.* Hurt, damage, wound; injury, wrong. **Lesión cerebral**, brain-damage.

lesionado [lay-se-o-nah-do], *a.* Hurt, injured; injured (jugador), unfit.

lesionar [lay-se-o-nar'], *va.* To hurt (dañar), to injure; to wound (herir). *-vr.* To get hurt.

lesivo, va [lay-see'-vo, vah], *a.* Prejudicial, injurious.

lesna [les'-nah], *f.* Awl, a pointed instrument to bore holes.

lesnordeste [les-nor-des'-tay], *m. (Naut.)* East-north-east wind.

leso, sa [lay'-so, sah], *a.* 1. Wounded, hurt (herido), damaged; perverted, injured (ofendido). 2. *(Cono Sur, And.)* Simple, stupid.

leste [les'-tay], *m.* East wind, east.

lesueste [lay-soo-es'-tay], *m. (Naut.)* East-south-east wind.

letal [lay-tahl'], *a.* Mortal, deadly destructive, lethal.

letanía [lay-tah-nee'-ah], *f.* 1. Litany, a form of prayer. **Letanías**, supplicatory processions. 2. *(coll.)* List or enumeration of things.

letárgico, ca [lay-tar'-he-co, cah], *a.* Lethargic, lethargical.

letargo [lay-tar'-go], *m.* Lethargy, a morbid drowsiness.

letargoso, sa [lay-tar-go'-so, sah], *a.* Causing lethargy, deadening.

leteo, a [lay-tay'o, ah], *a. (Poet.)* Lethean.

letífero, ra [lay-tee'-fay-ro, rah], *a.* Lethiferous, deadly, that which is the cause or sign of death.

letificante [lay-te-fe-cahn'-tay], *pa.* Exhilarating.

letífico, ca [lay-tee'-fe-co, cah], *a.* Cheering, bringing joy.

letra [lay'-trah], *f.* 1. Letter, a character of the alphabet. 2. Hand character, or peculiar manner of writing (escritura). 3. Type, a printing letter. 4. Motto, inscription. 5. Letter, the verbal expression, the literal meaning, the grammatical sense of a phrase. 6. A kind of Spanish poetical composition. 7. Words of a song. 8. An arithmetical character, a figure. **Letra** or **letra de cambio**, bill of exchange. **A la letra**, literally, punctually, entirely. **Letras**, 1. Letters, learning; the learned professions. 2. Rescript, despatch. 3. *(Prov.)* Certification, testimony. **Letras sagradas**, the Bible, the sacred Scriptures. **Letra gótica**, Gothic script. **Letra negrita**, bold type. **En letras de molde**, in print. **Tiene buena letra**, he writes a good hand.

letrada [lay-trah'-dah], *f. (coll.)* Lawyer's wife.

letradería, letraduría [lay-trah-day-ree'-ah], *f.* 1. *(Low.)* Body or society of lawyers, inn. 2. A foolish speech pompously uttered.

letrado, da [ly-trah'-do, dah], *a.* 1. Learned, erudite, lettered. 2. *(coll.)* Vain, presumptuous. **A lo letrado**, as a lawyer, like a counsellor.

letrado [lay-trah'-do], *m.* Lawyer, professor of law; advocate, counsellor.

letrero [lay-tray'-ro], *m.* An inscription, a title, sign (anuncio), label; a legend on medals or coins, placard (cartel).

letrilla [lay-treel'-lyah], *f.* 1. *(Dim.)* A small letter. 2. A short poem adapted to music.

letrina [lay-tree'-nah], *f.* Privy, water-closet, latrine.

letrón [lay-trone'], *m. aug.* A large letter.

letrones [lay-tro'-nes], *m. pl.* Capital letters or large characters written at the door of churches.

leucemia [lay-oo-thay'-me-ah], *f.* Leukaemia.

leucocito [lay-oo-co-thee'-to], *m. (Anat.)* Leucocyte.

leucoma [lay-oo-co'-mah], *f. (Med.)* Leucoma, disease of the cornea.

leucorrea [lay-oo-cor-ray'-ah], *f.* Leucorrhoea; colloquially, whites.

leucoris [lay-oo-co'-ris], *f.* Generic name of diseases which attack the lymphatic vessels.

leudar [lay-oo-dar'], *va.* To ferment dough with leaven; to raise bread.

leudo, da [lay'-oo-do, dah], *a.* Fermented, leavened (pan).

leva [lay'-vah], *f.* 1. *(Naut.)* Act of weighing anchor. **Pieza de leva**, shot fired as a signal for weighing anchor. 2. Levy, the act of raising men for military service; press. 3. *(Naut.)* Swell of the sea. **Hay mar de leva**, there is a swell in the offing. 4. Cog, tooth, cam, wiper. 5. Play of a piston. *-pl.* Tricks, artful devices. **Bajar la leva a uno**, *(And. Cono Sur)* To do somebody mischief. **Echar levas**, *(And, Mex.)* to boast.

levada [lay-vah'-dah], *f.* 1. Silkworm which moves from one place to another. 2. Salute or flourish made with the foil by fencers before they set to. *V.* LLEVADA.

levadero, ra [lay-vah-day'-ro, rah], *a.* That which is demanded.

levadizo, za [lay-vah-dee'-tho, thah], *a.* That can be lifted or raised.

levadura [lay-vah-doo'-rah], *f.* 1. Ferment, leaven, yeast. 2. *(Med.)* Ferment, septic matter.

levantada [lay-van-tah'-dah], *f. (coll.)* Rise, the act of rising.

levantadamente [lay-van-tah'-dah-men-tay], *adv.* In an elevated or exalted manner.

levantador, ra [lay-van-tah-dor', rah], *m. & f.* 1. One who raises or lifts up. 2. Disturber, rioter. 3. *(Surg.)* Levator, elevator.

levantamiento [lay-van-tah-me-en' -to], *m.* 1. Elevation, the act of raising; sublimity. **Levantamiento de pesas**, weight lifting. 2. Insurrection, revolt, rebellion, commotion. 3. *(Prov.)* Balance of accounts.

levantar [lay-van-tar'], *va.* 1. To raise, to lift or lift up, to heave, to get up, to hold up, to hang up, to mount, to set upright. 2. To build up, to raise, to erect a building. 3. To raise, to excite to tumult or war, to stir up. 4. To impute or attribute falsely. 5. To rouse, to raise, to excite to action. 6. To elevate, to aggrandize, to promote. 7. To rouse or start a game. 8. To cut the cards 9. To levy, to raise men for military service. 10. To increase, to enlarge. 11. To raise the voice, to utter loudly. 12. To cause, to occasion; to begin. 13. *(And.)* To nick, to arrest. 14. *(Cono Sur)* To pick up (persona). *-vr.* 1. To rise, to change a recumbent for an erect posture, to get up from a fall (incorporase). 2. To rise, to get up from a bed (de la cama). 3. To stand up. 4. To rise, to have more elevation than some other thing. 5. To rise, to break more break in commotions or insurrections. 6. To start or to rise suddenly (juego). 7. To conclude, to be concluded (sesión). **Levantar falso testimonio**, to accuse falsely. **Levantar la mesa**, to clear the table. **Levantó la mano**, he raised his hand. **Fue imposible levantarlo**, it was impossible to lift it. **Levantarse con el pie izquierdo**, to get out of bed on the wrong side.

levante [lay-vahn'-tay], *m.* 1. Levant, particularly the coasts of the Mediterranean east of Italy. 2. East, east wind (viento). 3. *(Carib.)* Driving of cattle (arreo). 4. *(And.)* Arrogance, haughtiness. 5. *(Cono Sur)* Pick-up (encuentro). **Hacer un levante a uno**, to pick somebody up. 6. **Hacer un levante**, *(Carib.)* To fall in love.

levantín [lay-van-teen'], *m.* Levantine: generally used in the plural.

levantino, na [lay-van-tee'-no, nah], *a.* Levantine, relating to the Levant.

levantisco, ca [lay-van-tees'-co, cah], *a.* 1. Turbulent, restless. 2. *V. LEVANTINO.*

levar [lay-var'], *va. (Naut.)* To weigh anchor. *-vr.* To set sail.

leve [lay'-vay], *a.* Light, of little weight; trifling, trivial (poco importante). **Una herida leve**, a slight wound.

leveche [lay-vay'-chay], *m. (Naut.)* The south-west wind.

levedad [lay-vay-dahd'], *f.* Lightness, levity: inconstancy.

levemente [lay-vay-men'-tay], *adv.* Lightly, gently; venially.

leviatán [lay-ve-ah-tahn'] *m.* Leviathan, a monstrous water animal.

levigación [lay-ve-gah-the-on'], *f.* Levigation, separation by washing of a finer powder from a coarser; elutriation.

levigar [lay-ve-gar'], *va.* To levigate, to free from grit, to elutriate.

levita [lay-vee'-tah], *m.* 1. Levite, one of the tribe of Levi. 2. *V. DIÁCONO.*

levita [lay-vee'-tah], *f.* Frock-coat, Prince Albert coat. **Gente de levita**, middle classes.

levítico [lay-vee'-te-co], *m.* 1. Book of Leviticus. 2. *(coll.)* Ceremonial used at a festival.

levítico, ca [lay-vee'-te-co, cah], *a. (coll.)* Levitical, priestly.

levitón [lay-ve-tone'], *m.* A long overcoat, like a frock-coat.

levulosa [lay-voo-lo'-sah], *f.* Fructose.

léxico, or **lexicón** [lec'-se-co, or lec-se-cone'], *m.* 1. Lexicon, an abridged or special dictionary, principally Greek or Latin. 2. Glossary, vocabulary.

lexicografía [lec-se-co-grah-fee'-ah], *f.* Lexicography, the art of writing dictionaries.

lexicográfico, ca [lec-se-co-grah'-fe-co, cah], *a.* Lexicographic, relating to compiling a lexicon or dictionary.

lexicógrafo [lec-se-co'-grah-fo], *m.* Lexicographer, author or writer of a dictionary.

lexicología [lec-se-co-lo-hee'-ah], *f.* Lexicology, the systematic study of the words of a language.

lexicólogo, ga [lec-se-co'-lo-go], *m & f.* Lexicologist.

ley [lay'-e], *f.* 1. Law, an ordinance, constitution or statute publicly established. 2. Law, a rule of action. 3. Loyalty, faithful attachment to a superior or master. 4. Religion. 5. A legal standard of quality, weight or measure. 6. A principle, or universal property. **Ley de la trampa**, fraud, deceit. **A la ley**, with propriety and neatness. **A toda ley**, perfectly, according to rule. *-pl.* 1. Body or collection of laws. 2. Study and profession of the law. **Ley escrita**, statute law, as opposed to custom or unwritten law. **Ley antigua**, the law of Moses. **Ley del embudo**, severity for others, indulgence for ourselves. **Ley orgánica**, constitutional law. **De acuerdo con la ley**, in accordance with the law. **Está fuera de la ley**, he's, outside the law. **Recurrir a la ley**, to go to law.

leyenda [lay-yen'-dah], *f.* 1. Reading, lecture, legend (historia), what is read. 2. Inscription on coins or models.

lezda [leth'-dah], *f.* Ancient tax on merchandise.

lezna [leth'-nah], *f. V.* LESNA.

lía [lee'-ah], *f.* 1. A thin bass-rope. 2. Husk of pressed grapes.

liana [le-ah'-nah], *f.* Liana, a twining or climbing plant of the tropical forest.

liar [le-ar'], *va.* To tie (atar), to bind, to fagot.*-vr.* 1. To contract an alliance. 2. To get tied up. 3. To get involved. 4. To get involved (amantes) **Estar liado con**, to live with.

liaza [le-ah'-thah], *f.* Collection of hoops used by coopers.

libación [le-bah-the-on'], *f.* Libation, pouring out wine for a sacrifice.

libamiento [le-bah-me-en'-to], *m.* The offering in ancient sacrifices.

libar [le-bar'], *va.* 1. To suck, to sip, to extract the juice; to taste. 2. To perform a libation. 3. To sacrifice. *-vn. (LAm.)* To booze, to drink.

libelar [le-bay-lar'], *va.* To petition, to sue at law.

libelático, ca [le-bay-lah'-te-co, cah], *a.* Applied to the Christians who renounced the Christian religion in a written declaration, for which the Roman emperors exempted them from persecution.

libelo [le-bay'-lo], *m.* 1. Petition, libel; a declaration of charge in writing against a person in court. 2. A defamatory writing, lampoon (sátira), libel.

libélula [le-bay'-loo-lah], *f.* The dragonfly, a neuropterous insect of the greater part of the globe.

líber [lee'-ber], *m.* Bast, liber, or inner bark of exogenous plants.

liberación [le-bay-rah-the-on'], *f.* 1. Setting at liberty, liberation. 2. *(Law.)* Remission of a debt.

liberado [le-bay-rah'-do], *a.* Paid-up, paid-in. *-m. (Pol.)* Agent (de un grupo terrorista).

liberal [le-bay-rahl'], *a.* 1. Liberal (caracter), generous, free, open, large, manificent, open-hearted. 2. Quick in the performance of a thing; brisk, active. 3. Liberal: applied to the arts, as opposed to mechanics.

liberalidad [le-bay-rah-le-dahd'], *f.* Liberality, generosity, largeness, munificence, frankness, open-heartedness; gallantry.

liberalismo [le-bay-rah-lees'-mo], *m.* Liberalism, profession of liberal doctrines favorable to political and religious liberty.

liberalizar [le-bay-rah-lee-thar'], *va.* To liberalize.

liberalmente [le-bay-ral-men'-tay], *adv.* Liberally, expeditiously; largely, munificently, generously, frankly.

liberar [le-bay-rar'], *va.* To free, to liberate. **Liberar a uno de una obligación**, to release somebody from a duty.

libérrimo, ma [le-ber'-re-mo, mah], *a. sup.* Most free.

libertad [le-ber-tahd'], *f.* 1. Liberty, freedom, the power of doing without inconvenience what is not contrary to the laws or established customs. 2. Liberty, freedom, as opposed to slavery. 3. Liberty, freedom, the state of one who is not a prisoner. 4. Liberty, freedom, license, assumed familiarity, relaxation of restraint. 5. Liberty, freedom, exemption, privilege, immunity. 6. Freedom, agility, address; independence, unconventionality. 7. Ransom. **Libertad académica**, academic freedom. **Libertad de comercio**, free trade. **Libertad de estado**, the unmarried state. **Libertad provisional**, freedom on bail. **Estar en libertad**, to be free. **Tomarse la libertad de**, to take the liberty of. **Poner a uno en libertad**, to set somebody free.

libertadamente [le-ber-tah'-dah-men-tay], *adv.* Freely, impudently.

libertado, da [le-ber-tah'-do, dah], *a.* 1. Libertine, impudent. 2. Free, ungoverned. 3. Idle, disengaged. *-pp.* of LIBERTAR.

libertador, ra [le-ber-tah-dor', rah], *m. & f.* Deliverer, liberator. *-a.* Liberating.

libertar [le-ber-tar'], *va.* 1. To free, to set at liberty, to liberate. 2. To exempt (eximir), to free, to excuse, to clear from an obligation or debt, to acquit. 3. To free, to rid from, to clear from anything ill. 4. To preserve.

liberticida [le-ber-te-thee'-dah], *m.* Liberticide, a destroyer of liberty.

libertinaje [le-ber-te-nah'-hay], *m.* Libertinism, licentiousness of opinion or practice; libertinage, license, irreligion.

libertino, na [le-ber-tee-no, nah], *m. & f.* Child of a freed man. *-a.* Libertine (juergista), irreligious, dissolute, impudent, licentious, lewd.

liberto [le-ber'-to], *m.* A freed man, an emancipated slave.

libi [lee'-be], *m.* A kind of linseed of Mindanao (P.I.), from which oil is obtained.

libídine [le-bee'-de-nay], *f.* Lewdness, lust.

libidinosamente [le-be-de-no-sah-men'-tay], *adv.* Libidinously.

libidinoso, sa [le-be-de-no'-so, sah], *a.* Libidinous, lewd, lustful.

libra [lee'-brah], *f.* 1. Pound, a weight of sixteen ounces. **Libra medicinal**, pound troy, of twelve ounces, apothecaries' weight, troy weight. 2. **Libra esterlina**, a pound sterling. 3. (*Ast.*) Libra, sign of the zodiac.

libración [le-brah-the-on'], *f.* Libration, the state of being balanced.

libraco [le-brah'-co], *m.* (*coll.*) An old worm-eaten book or pamphlet; a bad book.

librado [le-brah'-do], *m.* (*Com.*) Drawee.

librador, ra [le-brah-dor', rah], *m. & f.* 1. Deliverer. 2. The drawer of a bill of exchange. 3. Store keeper of the king's stables. 4. Metal scoop for handling dry sweetmeats, vegetables, etc.

libramiento [le-brah-me-en'to], *m.* 1. Delivery, the act of delivering. 2. Warrant, order of payment.

librancista [le-bran-thees'-tah], *m.* One who holds a warrant or order of payment.

libranza [le-brahn'-thah], *f.* Bank draft.

librar [le-brar'], *va.* 1. To free, to deliver, to extricate, to exempt, to preserve from ill. 2. To give a warrant or order for paying a certain sum. 3. To despatch, to expedite. 4. To commit, to intrust. 5. To place (confianza, esperanza). 6. To pass (sentencia), to issue (edicto), to reveal (secreto). 7. To make out (cheque). **Librar bien or mal**, to get over a thing well or ill. **Librar a uno de una obligación**, to free somebody from an obligation. *-vn.* 1. To give birth. 2. **Librar bien**, to fare well. 3. **Libro a las 3**, I'm free at 3 (tiempo). *-vr.* To free oneself, to escape. **Librarse de**, to escape from. **De buena nos hemos librado**, we did well to get out of that.

libratorio [le-brah-to'-re-o], *m.* V. LOCUTORIO.

librazo [le-brah'-tho], *m.* (*aug.*) A large book.

libre [lee'-bray], *a.* 1. Free, uncumbered, unrestrained, independent; unembrassed. 2. Free, at liberty, not enslaved, not a prisoner. 3. Free, exempt, privileged. 4. Free, innocent, guiltless. 5. Single, unmarried. 6. Free, libertine, loose, unrestrained, frank, licentious, impudent. 7. Rash, bold, forward, thoughtless. 8. Independent. 9. Free, clear from distress. 10. Isolated, alone. **Libre cambio**, free trade. **Esa plaza no está libre**, that seat is not free. **Cada cual es libre de hacer lo que quiera**, Everyone is free to do as he wishes. **Trabajar por libre**, to freelance.

librea [le-bray'-ah], *f.* Livery, clothes given to servants.

librear [le-bray-ar'], *va.* To weigh, to sell or distribute by pounds.

librecambista [le-bray-cam-bees'-tah], *m.* Freetrader. *-a* Advocating free trading.

librejo [le-bray'-ho], *m. dim.* A little book, a pamphlet.

libremente [le-bray-men'-tay], *adv.* Freely; boldly; audaciously; impudently.

librería [le-bray-ree'-ah], *f.* 1. Book-store, bookseller's shop (tienda). **Librería anticuaria**, antiquarian bookshop. 2. Bookcase (estante), library (biblioteca).

librero [le-bray'-ro], *m.* Book seller (persona).

libreta [le-bray'-tah], *f.* 1. The troy-weight pound. 2. Loaf of bread which weighs sixteen ounces. 3. Small memorandum book. **Libreta de banco**, bank book. **Libreta de ahorro**, savings book.

librete [le-bray'-tay], *m.* 1. (*Dim.*) A small book. 2. Small vessel with coals, used for warming the feet: foot-warmer.

libreto [le-bray'-to], *m.* (*Mus.*) Libretto (opera).

librico, ito [le-bree'-co, ee'-to], *m. dim.* A small book.

librilla [le-breel'-lyah], *f. dim.* A small pound.

librillo [le-breel'-lyo], *m.* 1. Small book. 2. Cigarette paper. **Librillo de cera**, a wax taper for carrying light.

libro [lee'-bro], *m.* 1. A book. 2. Book, a division or part of a work. 3. (*Met.*) Contribution, impost, tax. **Libro de caja**, a cash-book. **Libro de asiento** or **libro de cuentas**, account-book. **Libro de facturas**, invoice-book. **Libro del diario**, (*Naut.*) journal. **Libro en blanco**, a paper-book. **Libro mayor**, ledger. **Libro de memoria**, memorandum-book. **Libro de cocina**, cookery-book. **Libro de cheques**, check-book. **Libro escolar**, report-book. **Libro de texto**, textbook. **Libro de visitas**, visitors' book.

librote [le-bro'-tay], *m. aug.* Large book (mal libro).

licantropía [le-can-tro'-pee-co, cah], *a.* Lycanthropy, insanity in which the patient imagines himself transformed into a wolf. *V.* ZOANTROPÍA.

licantrópico, ca [le-can-tro'-pe-co, cah], *a.* Lycanthropic, relating to or affected by lycanthropy.

licencia [le-then-the-ah], *f.* 1. Permission, leave, license (permiso), liberty. (*Mil.*) Furlough. 2. Licentiousness (moral), contempt of just restraint, looseness, wantonness. 3. Degree of licentiate. 4. Licence, permit (documento). **Licencia de armas**, gun licence. **Licencia de conducir**, driving licence. **Licencia de utilización in situ**, site licence.

licenciadillo [le-then-the-ah-deel'-lyo], *m*, Nickname given to a little ridiculous person dressed in clerical habits.

licenciado [le-then-the-ah'-do], *m.* 1. Licentiate, a degree in Spanish universities, and the person who has taken that degree. 2. (*coll.*) Any scholar in the Spanish universities. 3. A title given to lawyers. **Licenciado en Filosofía y Letras**, Bachelor of Arts.

licenciado; da [le-then-the-ah'-do, dah], *a. & pp.* of LICENCIAR. Licensed; vainglorious.

licenciamiento [le-then-the-ah-me-en'-to], *m.* 1. The act of taking the degree of licentiate. 2. The disbandment of troops.

licenciar [le-then-the-ar'], *va.* 1. To permit (permitir), to allow, to license (dar permiso); to licentiate. 2. To license, to dismiss, to send away. 3. To make a licentiate. (*Mil.*) To break off, to disband. *-vr.* 1. To become dissolute. 2. To graduate, to take one's degree. **Licenciarse en Derecho**, to take a degree in Law.

licenciatura [le-then-the-ah-too'-rah], *f.* 1. The degree of licentiate (título), and the act of receiving it. 2. Degree course (estudios).

licenciosamente [le-then-se-o-sah-men'-tay], *adv.* Licentiously.

licencioso, sa [le-then-the-o'-so, sah], *a.* Licentious, dissolute, free, loose.

liceo [le-thay´-o], *m.* 1. Lyceum, a public school. 2. Name of certain literary societies. 3. *(Cono Sur, Mex)* Secondary school.

licio [lee'-the-o], *m. (Bot.)* Boxthorn.

licitación [le-the-tah-on'], *f.* Selling by auction.

lícitamente [lee'-the-tah-men-tay], *adv.* Lawfully, justly, licitly.

licitante [le-the-tahn'-tay], *m.* Bidder or buyer at auction.

licitar [le-the-tar'], *va.* To sell at auction.

lícito, ta [lee'-the-to, tah], *a.* Licit, lawful; just, fair (justo); permissible (permisible).

licnomancia [lic-no-mahn'-the-ah], *f.* Superstitious divination by means of flames.

licor [le-cor'], *m.* 1. Liquor, something liquid. 2. Liquor, strong drink, spirits (alcohol); liqueur (frutas).

licorera [le-co-ray'-rah], *f.* Liqueur bottle.

licorista [le-co-rees'-tah], *m. (Com.)* A manufacturer or dealer in spirituous liquors (fabricante, comerciante).

licoroso, sa [le-co-ro' -so, sha], *a.* Applied to generous wine.

lictor [lic-tor'], *m.* Lictor, a minister of justice in ancient Rome

licuable [le-coo-ah'-blay], *a.* Liquable, that may be melted.

licuación [le-coo-ah-the-on'], *f.* Liquation, liquefaction, the act of melting.

licuadora [le-coo-ah-do'-rah], *f. (Culin.)* Blender, liquidizer.

licuante [le-coo-ahn'-tay], *pa.* of LICUAR. Liquefying, dissolving, melting.

licuar [le-coo-ar'], *va.* To liquefy, to dissolve, to melt (nieve).

licuefacción [le-coo-ay-fac-the-on'], *f.* Liquefaction, conversion into the liquid state.

licuefacer [le-coo-ay-fah-therr'], *va. & vr.* V. LICUAR. *(Acad.)*

licuefactible [le-coo-ay-fac-tee'-blay], *a.* Liquefiable.

licuescencia [le-coo-es-then'-the-ah], *f.* Liquescence, aptness to melt.

licuescente [le-coo-es-then'-tay], *f.* Liquescent, melting.

lichera [le-chay'-rah], *f. (Prov)* Woollen cover of a bed.

lid [leed], *f.* Conflict, contest, fight; dispute, argument.

líder [lee'-der], *m.* Leader.

liderar [lee-day-rar'], *va.* To lead, to head.

lidia [lee'-de-ah], *f.* 1. *(Taur.)* Bullfight; bullfighting. **Toro de lidia**, fighting bull. 2. *(Mex.)* Trouble, nuisance (molestia).

lidiador [le-de-ah-dor'], *m.* Combatant; one who publicly disputes or argues: *(Taur.)* bullfighter.

lidiar [le-de-ar'], *vn.* 1. To fight, to oppose, to contend 2. *(Met).* To deal with annoying, vexing persons. 3. *(Archaic.)* To plead before a court.-*va.* To run or fight bulls.

lidio [lee'-de-o], *a. (Mus.)* Lydian, a species of ancient music.

liebrastón [le-ay-bras-tone's], *m*, Leveret, a small or young hare.

liebratico [le-ay-brah-tee'-co], *m.* Young hare.

liebre [le-ay'-bray], *f.* 1. Hare. 2. Coward, poltroon. **Coger una liebre**, to fall into mud or mire. 3. *(And. Cono Sur)* Minibus. -*pl.* 1. *(Naut.)* Racks or ribs. 2. *(Naut.)* Dead-eyes.

liebrecica, illa, ita [le-ay-bray-thee'-cah, el'-lyah, ee'-tah], *f. dim.* A young or small hare.

liebrecilla [le-ay-bray-theel'-lyah], *f. (Bot.)* V.AZULEJO.

liebrezuela [le-ay-bray-thoo-ay'-lah], *f. dim.* V. LIEBRECICA.

liencecico, illo, ito [leen-thay-thee'-co, eel'lyo, ee'-to], *m. dim.* Little linen cloth.

liendre [le-en'-dray], *f.* Nit, the egg of a louse.

lientera, lientería [le-en-tay'-rah, le-an-tay-ree'-ah], *f.* Lientery diarrhoea which carries off the food undigested.

lientérico, ca [le-en-tay'-re-co, cah], *a.* Lienteric.

liento, ta [le-en'-to, tah], *a.* Damp, moist.

lienza [le-en'-thah], *f.* A narrow strip of any cloth.

lienzo [le-en'-tho], *m.* 1. Linen (tela), cloth made of flax or hemp; canvas. **Lienzo encerado**, glazed linen. **Lienzo curado**, bleached linen. 2. Handkerchief (pañuelo). 3. Painting on linen. 4. *(Fort).* Curtain, part of a wall lying

between the two bastions. 5. Face or front of a building (fachada).

liga [lee'-gah], *f.* 1. A garter. 2. Bird-lime (trampa viscosa). 3. League, coalition, confederacy, combination, alliance. 4. Alloy for gold and silver (metal). 5. *(And.)* Bosom friend (amigo).

ligación [le-gah-the-on'], *f.* 1. Ligation, act of tying. 2. Union, mixture.

ligada [le-gah'-dah], *f. (Print.)* Ligature, logotype.

ligado, da [le-gah'-do, dah], *a. & pp.* of LIGAR. Tied, bound, leagued, confederate.

ligado [le-gah'-do], *m. (Mus.)* Slur.

ligadura [le-gah-doo'-rah], *f.* 1. Ligature, anything tied round another. 2 Ligation, ligature, flee act of binding. 3. Subjection. 4. *(Mus.)* A tie, a slur. 5. *(Arch.)* All the arcs made by crosstimbers in arches. 6. *(Mech.)* An iron wire which binds the strands of a wire cable. 7. *(Naut.)* Seizing, the fastening of two ropes with a thin line; lashing.

ligamaza [le-gah-mah'-thah], *f.* Viscous or glutinous matter around fruits.

ligamento [le-gah-men' -to], *m.* 1. *(Anat.)* Ligament; a cord. 2. Ligament, bond, chain, entanglement.

ligamentoso, sa [le-gah-men-to'-so, sah], *a.* Ligamentous, Ligamental.

ligamiento [le-gah-me-en'to], *m.* 1. Union, act of tying or uniting. 2. Union, concord. 3. Ligament.

ligar [le-gar'], *va.* 1. To tie, to bind, to fasten, to knit, to mix (bebidas). 2. To alloy gold or silver for coinage (metal). 3. To league, to coalesce, to confederate. 4. To render impotent by charms or spells. 5. To exorcise, to purify from the influence of malignant spirits. 6. To pick up, to get off with (chica). 7. To get (conseguir). 8. *(Carib.) (Agr.)* To contract in advance for. -*vn.* 1. To mix (ir juntos); to blend, to go well together. 2. *(Carib. Mex.)* To have a bit of luck (tener un poco de suerte). 3. *(Carib. Mex.)* To look, to stare (mirar). 4. **Ligar con una**, to flirt with somebody (flirtear), to pick a girl up (conocer). -*vr.* 1. To league, to conspire to conjoin, to be leagued, to be allied. 2. To bind oneself to the performance of a contract.

ligazón [le-gah-thone'], *f.* 1. Union, contexture, confixture, connection, ligament, bond. 2. *(Naut.)* Futtock-timbers.

ligeramente [le-hay-rah-men'-tay], *adv.* Swiftly, lightly, easily; giddily, slightly (conocer), hastily (juzgar).

ligereza [le-hay-ray'-thah], *f.* 1. Lightness, celerity, fleetness, agility, nimbleness. 2. Levity, unsteadiness, inconstancy, fickleness, flippancy, flirtation. 3. Lightness, want of weight. **Ligereza de espíritu**, light-heartedness. **Obrar con ligereza**, to act rashly.

ligero, ra [le-hay'-ro, rah], *a.* 1. Light, of little weight (de poco peso). 2. Light, thin (tela, ropa). 3. Swift (rápido), light, active, nimble, fleet. 4. Light, gay, airy, unsteady, giddy. 5. Light, trifling. 6. Easily digestible (comida). 7. Unsound, not calm (sueño). 8. Slight (modesto). 9. Superficial (carácter), shallow, flippant; frivolous, flighty. **A la ligera**, lightly, expeditiously. **Ligero de ropa**, lightly clad. **Un ligero conocimiento**, a slight acquaintance. **Ligero de cascos**, scatter-brained. **Juzgar a la ligera**, to judge hastily.

ligeruela [le-hay-roo-ay'-lah], *a.* Applied to early grapes.

ligio, a [lee'-he-o, ah], *a.* Liege, bound by some feudal tenure.

lignito [lig-nee'-to], *m.* Lignite, brown coal.

lignívoro, ra [lig-nee'-vo-ro, rah], *a.* Wood-eating. -*m. pl.* The longicorn beetles.

lignum crucis [lig-noom croo'-this], *m.* Relic of the cross of Christ.

ligomela [le-go-may'-lah], *a.* V. LIGERUELA.

ligón [le-gon'], *a.* 1. Flirtatious (persona). **Es muy ligón.** he's a great one for the girls. 2. Attractive; provocative, sexy (prenda). 3. Posh (distinguido). -*m.* Womanizer, wolf.

ligue [lee'-gay], *m.* 1. **Se dedica mucho al ligue**, he's always after the women (acto). 2. Pick-up (acto). 3. Pick-up (persona); boyfriend (chico), girlfriend (chica).

liguero [le-gay'-ro], *m.* Suspender belt, garter belt.

liguilla [le-geel'-lyah], *f.* Kind of narrow ribbon.

lígula [lee'-goo-lah], *f.* 1. *(Anat.)* Epiglottis, the cartilage which covers the larynx. 2. *(Bot.)* Ligule.

ligulado, da [le-goo-lah'-do, dah], *a. (Bot.)* Ligulate, strap-shaped.

ligurino, na [le-goo-ree'-no, nah], or **Ligústico, ca** [le-goos'-te-co, cah], *a.* Ligurian.

ligústico [le-goos'-te-co], *m. (Bot.)* Lovage.

ligustro [le-goos'-tro], *m. (Bot.)* Privet. *V.* ALHEÑA.

lija [lee'-hah], *f.* 1. Dog-fish, a small variety of shark. 2. Skin of the dog-fish used, dry, for polishing wood, lining boxes, etc. **Papel de lija**, sandpaper.

lijar [le-har'], *va.* 1. To smooth, to polish. 2. *(Prov.) V.* LASTIMAR.

lila [lee'-lah], *f.* 1. *(Bot.)* Lilac-tree. 2. Lilac flower. 3. A kind of light woollen stuff of various colors.

lilaila [le-lah-ee'-lah], *f.* 1. Thin woollen stuff. 2. Artifice, trick. wile.

liliáceo, cea [le-le-ah'-thay-o, ah], *a.* Liliaceous, of the lily family.

lililí [le-le-lee'], *m.* War-whoop of the Moors.

lima [lee'-mah], *f.* 1. *(Bot.)* Lime-tree. 2. Lime, the fruit of the lime-tree, also, the sweet lime, another variety of small lemon. 3. File (herramienta), an instrument for smoothing metals. 4. *(Met.)* Correction, finish, polish. 5. Channel in the roof of a house for the water to pass to the eaves. **Lima de uñas**, nail file. **Dar la última lima a una obra**, to give a work its final polish.

limación [le-mah-the-on'], *f.* The process of filing roughnesses of the teeth.

limadura [le-mah-doo'-rah], *f.* 1. Act of filing. 2. Filing, limature, metallic fragment rubbed off by the file.

limalla [le-mahl'-lyah], *f.* Filings.

limar [le-mar'], *va.* 1. To file, to cut with a file. 2. To file, to polish; to give the finishing stroke to literary productions.

limatón [le-mah'-tone'], *m.* Coarse round file.

limaza [le-mah'-thah], *f.* 1. Snail. 2. Archimedes' screw. 3. A disease of the feet of cattle.

limazo [le-mah-tho], *m.* Viscosity, sliminess.

limazón [le-mah-thone'], *m.* Slug, a snail or slimy animal without a shell.

limbo [leem'-bo], *m.* 1. Limbo, a region assigned to the souls of unbaptized children. 2. *(Ast.)* Limb, edge or border of the sun or moon. 3. Limb, exterior graduated border of a quadrant. 4. *(Zool.)* Circumference, or edge of a bivalve shell. **Estar en el limbo**, to be in limbo.

limen [lee'-men], *m. (Poet.) V.* UMBRAL.

limeño, ña [le-may'-nyo, nyah], *a.* Belonging to or native of the city Lima.

limera [le-may'-rah], *f.* 1. Shopwoman who sells files or limes. 2. *(Naut.)* Helmport, where the tiller is fastened to the rudder of the ship.

limero [le-may'-ro], *m.* 1. Shopkeeper who sells files or limes. 2. *(Bot.)* Lime-tree.

limeta [le-may'-tah], *f.* 1. Vial, a small bottle (botella). 2. *(Amer.)* Medium sized wine bottle. 3. *(Cono Sur)* Broad brow (frente).

limiste [le-mees'-tay], *m.* Cloth made of Segovia wool; cloth of the first quality.

limitación [le-me-tah-the-on'], *f.* 1. Limitation, restriction, modification, circumscription, corrective; conditionality. 2. Limit, district. **Limitación de velocidad**, speed restriction.

limitadamente [le-me-tah-dah-men'-tay], *adv.* Limitedly, finitely.

limitado, da [le-me-tah'-do, dah], *a.* Limited, possessed of little talent. *-f. (Com.)* Of limited liability.*-pp.* of LIMITER.

limitador, ra [le-me tah-dor', rah], *m. & f.* One who limits, circumscriber.

limitáneo, nea [le-me-tah'-nay-o, ah], *a.* 1. Limitary, placed on the boundaries. 2. Limitaneous, belonging to limits.

limitar [le-me-tar'], *va.* 1. To limit (restringir), to confine within bounds, to narrow. 2. To form boundaries, to establish limits. 3. To restrain, to circumscribe; to reduce expense. *-vr.* To limit oneself, to restrict oneself. **Limitarse a**, to limit oneself to.

límite [lee'-me-tay], *m.* Limit, boundary, bound, border, confine. **Límite forestal**, timber line. **Límite de velocidad**, speed limit. **Poner un límite a**, to set a limit to. **No tener límites**, to have no limits. *-adv.* **Caso límite**, extreme case. **Situaciones límites**, extreme situations.

limítrofe [le-mee'-tro-fay], *a.* Limiting, bounding, conterminous, limitary applied to frontier provinces.

limnea [lim-nay'-ah], *f.* Limnaea, the common pond-snail.

limo [lee'-mo], *m.* Slime (barro), mud.

limón [le-mone'], *m.* 1. Lemon, the fruit of the lemon-tree. 2. *(Bot.)* Lemon-tree. 3. *V.* LIMONERO. *(Per.)*

limonada [le-mo-nah'-dah], *f.* Lemonade. **Limonada de vino**, lemonade mixed with wine.

limonado, da [le-mo-nah'-do, dah], *a.* Lemon colored.

limonar [le-mo-nar'], *m.* Plantation of lemon-trees.

limoncillo [le-mon-theel'-lyo], *m. dim.* A small lemon.

limonera [le-mo-nay'-rah], *f.* Shaft of a cart.

limonero [le-mo-nay'-ro], *m. (Bot.)* Lemon-tree. *m. & f.* Dealer in lemons.*-a.* Applied to the shaft horses in carriages.

limonza [le-mon'-thah], *f.* The citron, or the bitter lemon.

limoscapo [le-mos-cah'-po], *m. (Arch.)* The part of the shaft of a column nearest the base, apophyge.

limosidad [le-mo-se-dahd'], *f.* 1. Sliminess. 2. Foul matter between teeth.

limosna [le-mos'-nah], *f.* Alms, charity. **Pedir limosna**, to beg. **Vivir de limosna**, to live by begging.

limosnero [le-mos-nay'ro], *m.* Almoner. *-a.* Charitable.

limoso, sa [le-mo'-so, sah], *a.* Slimy, muddy, limose.

limpia [leem'-pe-ah], *f.* 1. Cleansing, freeing from dirt. 2. Dredging of harbors. 3. A certain tax paid by ships in harbors where dredging is required. 4. *(CAm. Mex. Agr.)* Weeding, cleaning. *-m.* Boot-black.

limpiabotas [lim-pe-ah-bo'-tas], *m.* A shoe-cleaner.

limpiachimeneas [leem'-pe-ah-che-may-nay'-as], *m.* Chimney-sweeper.

limpiacristales [leem-pe-ah-cres-tah'-lays], *m.* Window-cleaner.

limpiadera [lim-pe-ah-day'-rah], *f.* 1. A clothes-brush. 2. Comb-brush; a plough-cleaner.

limpiadientes [lim-pe-ah-de-en'-tes], *m.* Toothpick.

limpiador, ra [lim-pe-ah-dor', rah], *m. & f.* Cleanser, scourer.

limpiadura [lim-pe-ah-doo'-rah], *f.* Cleaning, *-pl.* Dirt thrown away in cleaning anything.

limpiamente [lim-pe-ah-men'-tay], *adv.* Cleanly, neatly; purely; sincerely, faithfully.

limpiametales [lim-pe-ah-may-tah'-lays], *m.* Metal polish.

limpiamiento [lim-pe-ah-me-en'-to], *m.* Act of cleaning.

limpiaoídos [lim-pe-ah-o-ee'-dos], *m.* Earspoon, earpick.

limpiaojos [lim-pe-ah-o'-hos], *m.* An eyestone.

limpiaparabrisas [lim-pe-ah-pah-rah-bree'-sahs], *m.* Windscreen wiper.

limpiaplumas [lim-pe-ah-ploo'-mas], *m.* A penwiper.

limpiar [lim-pe-ar'], *va.* 1. To clean, to scour, to cleanse. **Limpiar en seco**, to dry-clean. 2. To purify, to clear from guilt. 3. To pursue, to persecute. 4. *(coll.)* To steal (robar). 5. To clean out (en el juego). 6. *(Mex.)* To hit, to bash (pegar). *-vr.* 1. To clear oneself from imputed guilt. 2. To clean oneself. **Limpiarse las narices**, to wipe one's nose.

limpiauñas [lim-pe-ah-oo'-nyas], *m.* Fingernail cleaner.

limpidez [lim-pe-deth'], *f.* Transparency, limpidity.

límpido, da [leem'-pe-do, dah], *a.* Limpid, crystal-clear, transparent.

limpieza [lim-pe-ay'-thah], *f.* 1. Cleanness (estado), cleanliness, neatness, purity, limpidness. 2. Chastity, purity of morals. 3. Integrity, rectitude; disinterestedness (cualidad). 4. Purity of blood. **Limpieza de bolsa**, emptiness of the purse. **Limpieza en seco**, dry-cleaning.

limpio, pia [leem'-pe-o, ah], *a.* 1. Clean, free from stain; cleanly, limpid. 2. Neat (ordenado), elegant. 3. Pure: applied to families unconnected with Moors or Jews. 4. Pure, unmingled (maíz). 5. Pure (agua), free, clear (despejado). 6. Clear of all charges, net. 7. Pure (moralmente); honest (honrado); fair (juego). 8. Alone (solo). 9. **Estar limpio**, Not to know a single thing. **Jugar limpio**, to deal fair, to act uprightly. **Poner en limpio**, to make a fair copy. **Tierra limpia**, even, flat country. **Costa limpia**, *(Naut.)* clear coast, without shoals, sand-banks, or shallows. **En limpio**, in substance; net price; clearly. **Más limpio que el oro**, as clean as can be. **50 dólares de ganancia limpia**, 50 dollars of clear profit. **Luchar a puñetazo limpio**, to fight with bare fists. *-adv.* Fair, clean. *-m.* En limpio, clearly. **No pude sacar nada en limpio**, I couldn't make anything of it.

limpión [lim-pe-on'], *m.* A hasty cleaning. **Date un limpión**, *(coll.)* ironical phrase telling someone he will not get what he wishes.

límulo [lee'-moo-lo], *m.* Limulus, king-crab.

limusina [lee-moo-see'-nah], *f.* Limousine.

lináceas [le-nah'-thay-as], *a. &f.* Linaceous, of the flax family.

linaje [le-nah'-hay], *m.* 1. Lineage (familia), race, progeny, offspring, family, house, kin, extraction, generation. 2. Class (clase), condition. 3. *(Prov.)* Nobless, nobility.

linajista [le-nah-hees'-tah], *m.* Genealogist, a writer of pedigrees.

linajudo, da [le-nah-hoo'-do, dah], *m. &f. & a.* 1. One who boasts of his origin or family. 2. *m.* Genealogist.

lináloe [le-nah'-lo-ay], *m.* Aloes. *V.* ÁLOE.

linar [le-nar']. *m.* Flax field, land on which flax is grown.

linaria [le-nah'-re-ah], *f. (Bot.)* Wild flax, yellow toad flax.

linaza [le-nah'-thah], *f.* Linseed, the seed of flax. **Aceite de linaza**, linseed oil.

lince [leen'-thay], *m.* 1. Lynx; *(CAm. Mex.)* wild cat. 2. Person of great acuteness and perspicacity. 3. *(LAm.)* Sharpness, intelligence.

lince [leen'-thay], *a.* 1. Sharp-sighted, quick-sighted. **Ojos de lince**, sharp eyes. 2. Acute, penetrating.

lincear [lin-thay-ar'], *va. (coll.)* To discover, to note what may be seen with difficulty.

linchamiento [lin-chah-me-ayn'-to], *m.* Lynching.

linchar [lin-char'], *va.* To lynch.

linches [leen'-chays], *m. pl. (Mex.)* Saddle-bags made from the fiber of the maguey (alforjas).

lindamente [lin-dah-men'-tay], *adv.* Neatly, elegantly (con elegancia).

lindar [lin-dar'], *vn.* To be contiguous, to be adjacent. **Lindar con**, to border on.

linde [leen'-day], *m. & f.* Landmark, boundary, limit.

linde [leen'-day], *a.* Contiguous, bordering upon.

lindero, ra [lin-day'-ro, rah], *a.* Contiguous, bordering upon.

lindero [lin-day'-ro], *m. V.* LINDE.

lindeza [lin-day'-thah], *f.* 1. Neatness, elegance (elegancia), prettiness (atractivo). 2. *pl. (Iron.)* Improprieties, insults. 3. Witticism (ocurrencia).

lindo, da [leen'-do, dah], *a.* 1. Neat, handsome (hombre), pretty (bonito), fine, genteel. 2. Complete, perfect. 3. Nice (precioso), lovely; fine (excelente). **De lo lindo**, perfectly, wonderfully. **Un lindo carro**, a lovely car. *-adv. (LAm.)* Nicely, well, marvellously. **Baila lindo**, she dances beautifully. *-m.* Beau, coxcomb, minion.

lindón [lin-done'], *m.* Ridge, ground thrown up between asparagus-beds.

lindura [lin-doo'-rah], *f. V.* LINDEZA.

línea [lee'-nay-ah], *f.* 1. Line, longitudinal extension. 2. *V.* RAYA. 3. *V.* RENGLÓN. 4. Line (genealogía), lineage, progeny, family ascending or descending. 5. Line, equator, equinoctial line. 6. Line, boundary, limit. 7. Class, order. 8. *(Mil.)* Trench or intrenchment. 9. *(Mil.)* Rank of soldiers. 10. Line, twelfth part of an inch. **Línea aérea**, airline. **Línea de batalla**, line of battle. **Línea de fuego**, firing line. **Primera línea**, front line. **En línea**, in line. **Leer entre líneas**, to read between the lines. **Guardar la línea**, to keep one's figure. 11. *(Inform.)* **Línea de bloqueo**, locking line. **"Línea caliente"**, "hot line". **Línea de fuego**, line of fire.

lineal [le-nay-ahl'], *a.* Lineal, composed of lines. **Lineal de partido**, party line.

lineamento [le-nay-ah-men'-to], *m.* Lineament, exterior feature of a body.

lineamiento [le-nay-ah-me-en'-to], *m.* Lineament, feature.

linear [le-nay-ar'], *va.* To draw lines, to form with lines.

linfa [leen'-fah], *f.* 1. Lymph, a fluid of the body. 2. *(Poet.)* Water.

linfático, ca [lin-fah'-te-co, cah], *a.* Lymphatic, pertaining to lymph (vasos y glándulas).

linfoquicia [lin-fo-kee'-the-ah], *f. (Med.)* Serous diarrhoea.

lingotazo [lin-go-tah'-tho], *m.* Swig, shot.

lingote [lin-go'-tay], *m. (Min.)* Ingot, a mass of gold or silver, lingot, a pig of metal.

lingual [lin-goo-ahl'], *a.* Lingual, relating to the tongue.

linguete [lin-gay'-tay], *m.* A pawl; a ratchet.

lingüista [lin-goo-ees'-tah], *m & f.* Linguist, one versed in languages.

lingüística [lin-goo-ees'-te-cah], *f.* Linguistics, the science of languages, comparative philology.

lingüístico, ca [lin-goo-ees'-te-co, cah], *a.* Linguistic, relating to language or linguistics.

linier [le-ne-ayr'], *m. (Dep.)* Linesman.

linimento [le-ne-men'-to], *m. (Med.)* Liniment.

linio [lee'-ne-o], *m. V.* LIÑO.

lino [lee'-no], *m.* 1. *(Bot.)* Flax. 2. Linen (tela fina). 3. Sailcloth, canvas (lona). 4. *(Carib. Cono Sur)* Linseed. **Géneros de lino**, linen goods.

linóleo [le-no'-layo], *m.* Linoleum.

linón [le-non'], *m.* Lawn.

linotipia [le-no-tee'-pe-ah], *f.* Linotype machine.

linotípico, ca [le-no-tee'-pe-co, cah], *a.* Linotype.

linotipista [le-no-te-pees'-tah], *m. & f.* Linotype operator.

linotipo [le-no-tee'-po], *m.* Linotype.

lintel [lin-tel], *m.* Lintel.

linterna [lin-terr'-nah], *f.* 1. Lantern. 2. *(Arch.)* Small tower, cupola. 3. *(Mech.)* Lantern pinion. 4. *(Arg.)* Firefly. **Linterna de proyección**, slide projector. **Linterna eléctrica**, flashlight. **Linterna mágica**, magic lantern. **Linterna de bolsillo**, torch.

linternazo [lin-ter-nah'-tho], *m.* 1. Blow with a lantern. 2. *(Coll.)* Wallop, crack.

linternero [lin-ter-nay'-ro], *m.* Lantern maker.

linternilla [lin-ter-neel'-lyah], *f dim.* A small lantern.

linueso [le-noo-ay'-so], *m. V.* LINAZA.

liño [lee'-nyo], *m.* 1. Row of trees or plants. 2. Ridge between furrows in ploughed land.

liñuelo [len-yoo-ay'-lo], *m.* Rope, cord.

lío [lee'-o], *m.* 1. Bundle, parcel, package (paquete). 2. *(coll.)* Entanglement, row (jaleo), mess (confusión), jam (aprieto). 3. Affair (amorío), liaison. 4. Tale (chisme), piece of gossip. **Armar un lío**, to start a fight. **Hacerse uno un lío**, to become entangled, to get all confused. **Ese lío de los pasaportes**, that fuss about the passports. **Se armó un tremendo lío**, there was an almighty row.

liorna [le-or-nah], *f. (coll.)* Uproar, hullabaloo, confusion.

lioso [le-o'-so], *a.* Gossipy.

lipia [lee'-pe-ah], *f.* Lippia, a plant of the verbena family. Lipia citriodora is the lemonscented verbena.

lipis [lee'-pis], *f.* Blue vitriol, copper sulphate.

liputud [le-pe-tood'], *f. (Med.)* Lippitude, blearedness of the eyes.

lipotimia [le-po-te'-me-ah], *f.* Faint, black-out.

liquen [lee'-ken], *m.* Lichen, a low cryptogamic plant.

líquida [le'-ke-dah], *f. (Ling.)* liquid.

liquidable [le-kee-dah'-blay], *a.* Liquefiable.

liquidación [le-kee-dah-the-on'], *f.* 1 Liquidation, settlement. 2. Balance. 3. Sale, clearance sale. **Vender en liquidación**, to sell out. 4. *(Pol.)* To liquidate, to eliminate.

líquidamente [lee'-ke-dah-men-tay], *adv.* In a liquid manner.

liquidar [le-kee-dar'], *va.* 1. To liquefy, to melt, to dissolve. **Liquidar cuentas**, to clear accounts, to liquidate debts. 2. *(Pol.)* To liquidate, to eliminate; *(LAm.)* to bump up (matar). 3. *(LAm.)* To destroy, to ruin (destrozar). -*vr.* 1. To liquefy, to liquate, to grow liquid. 2. To become liquid: used of letters.

liquidez [le-kee-deth'], *f.* Liquidness, fluidity.

liquidificar [le-ke-de-fe-car'], *va.* To dissolve, to liquify.

líquido, da [lee'-ke-do, dah], *a.* 1. Liquid, fluid, fluent. 2. Evident, clear. 3. Net, neat. **Ganancia líquida**, net profit. 4. *(LAm.)* Exact; accurate, right, correctly measured. -*m.* 1. Liquid, fluid. 2. *(Fin.)* Cash, ready money (efectivo).

lira [lee'-rah], *f.* 1. Lyre, á harp; a lyric poem. 2. Lyra, a northern constellation. 3. *(Fin.)* Lira.

liria [lee'-re-ah], *f. V.* LIGA, bird-lime.

lírico, ca [lee'-re-co, cah], *a.* Lyric, lyrical.

lirio [lee'-re-o], *m.* The lily. **Lirio blanco**, *V.* AZUCENA. **Lirio florentino**, Florentine iris.

lirón [le-rone'], *m.* 1. Dormouse; *(Fig.)* sleepy head. **Dormir como un lirón**, to sleep like a log. 2. *(Bot.) V.* ALISMA. 3. *(Naut.)* Jackscrew.

lirondo, da [le-ron'-do, dah], *a.* Pure, clean, neat.

lis [lees], *f.* Flor de lis, flower-deluce, iris.

lisa [lee'-sah], *f.* 1. A smooth stone for polishing paper. 2. A mixture for moulding the letters of a bell

lisamente [le-sah-men'-tay], *adv.* Smoothly, plainly. **Lisa y llanamente**, openly and frankly; without dispute or contention.

lisbonense [lis-bo-nen'-say], or **lisbonés, sa** [lis-bo-nays', sah], *a.* Belonging to or native of Lisbon.

lisera [le-say'-rah], *f.* Large cane used in silkworm sheds.

lisiado, da [le-se-ah'-do, dah], *a. (Met.)* Lamed (cojo), injured, hurt. *(Prov.)* Anxiously, desirous. -*pp.* of LISIAR.

lisiar [le-se-ar'], *va.* To lame; to hurt a limb, to injure (herir).

lisimaquia [le-se-mah'-ke-ah], *f. (Bot.)* Loose strife.

lisis [lee'-sis], *f.* Lysis, the gradual abatement of disease, opposed to crisis.

liso, sa [lee'-so, sah], *a.* 1. Plain, even, flat (carrera), glib, smooth, straight (liso). **Liso como la palma de la mano**, as smooth as glass. 2. Clear, evident. 3. *(And, Mex.)* Fresh, cheeky. **Liso y llano**, straightforward. -*m. (Cono Sur)* Tall beer glass.

lisonja [le-son'-hah], *f.* 1. Adulation. flattery, fawning, coaxing. 2. *(Her.)* Lozenge. 3. *(Geom.)* Rhomb or rhombus, -*m.* Lysol.

lisonjado, da [le-son-hah'-do, dah], *a. (Her.)* Lozenged; rhombic.

lisonjeador, ra [le-son-hay-ah-dor', rah], *m. & f.* Flatterer.

lisonjear [le-son-hay-ar'], *va.* 1. To flatter (halagar), to praise deceitfully, to coax, to wheedle, to fawn. 2. To delight, to please (agradar).

lisonjeramente [le-son-hay-rah-men'-tay], *adv.* Flatteringly, fawningly.

lisonjero, ra [le-son-hay'-ro, rah], *m. & f.* A flatterer, a fawner, a parasite. -*a.* 1. Parasitical, wheedling, fawning. 2. Flattering (halagüeño), pleasing (agradable), agreeable.

LISP [leesp], *(Inform.)* LISP (LISt Processor).

lista [lees'-tah], *f.* 1. Slip of paper, shred of linen, a list or strip of cloth (tela). 2. Selvage, the edge of cloth. 3. List, catalogue (catálogo). *(Law.)* Docket. 4. Stripe (raya). **Pasar lista**, to call over; to muster, to review troops, to call the roll. **Lista de gastos**, bill of expense and charges. **Lista de direcciones**, mailing list. **Lista de premios**, prize or honors list. **Tela a listas**, striped material.

listadillo [lis-tah-deel'-lyo], *m. (Amer.)* 1. Cotton cloth striped white and blue. 2. Striped gingham.

listado, da [lis-tah'-do, dah], *a.* Striped, listed. -*pp.* of LISTAR. -*m. pl.* **Listados**, striped checks, plaid.

listadura [lis-tah-doo'-rah], *f.* 1. The action of listing or applying strips. 2. The thing so listed.

listar [lis-tar'], *va.* 1. To list, to cover with srips of sloth. 2. *V.* ALISTAR.

listeado, da [lis-tay-ah'-do, dah], *a. V.* LISTADO.

listel, listelo [lis-tel', lis-tay'-lo], *m. (Arch.) V.* FILETE.

listero, ra [lis-tay'-ro], *m & f.* Time keeper, wages clerk.

listillo, lla [lis-teel'-lyo], *m & f.* Know-all.

listín [lis-teen'], *m. (Telec.)* List of numbers, *(Carib.)* newspaper.

listo, ta [lees'-to, tah], *a.* Ready, diligent, prompt, active, clever (carácter). **Todo está listo**, everything is ready. **Ser más listo que el hambre**, to be as smart as they come. **Van listos si piensan eso**, if they think that they've got another thing coming.

listón [lis-tone'], *m.* 1. Ribbon. 2. Ferret, tape. 3. Lath, cleat, strip (madera). 4. *(Arch.)* Fillet. 5. *(Dep.)* Bar (salto de altura).

listonado, da [lis-to-nah'-do, dah], *a. (Arch.)* Barred, striped, filleted.

listonar [lis-to-nar'], *va.* To batten, to lath.

listonería [lis-to-nay-ree'-ah], *f.* 1. Parcel of ribbons, tapes, and inkles. 2. A ribbon-store; ribbon-manufactory.

listonero, ra [lis-to-nay'-ro, rah], *m. & f.* Ribbon-maker.

lisura [le-soo'-rah], *f.* 1. Smoothness (superficie), evenness, flatness. 2. Sincerity, candor, plainness (sinceridad). 3. *(LAm.)* Shamelessness (descaro), brazenness.

lita [lee'-tah], *f.* Larva of an insect which fixes itself under the tongue of certain quadrupeds.

litación [le-tah-the-on'], *f.* Sacrificing.

litagogo, ga [le-tah-go'-go, gah], *a.* Lithagogue, solvent of urinary calculi; also, lithontriptic, destroying calculi (instrumentos médicos).

litar [le-tar'], *va.* To sacrifice to the divinity.

litarge, litargirio [le-tar'-hay, le-tar-hee'-re-o], *m.* Litharge. *V.* ALAMÁRTAGA.

lite [lee'-tay], *f.* Lawsuit, process. *V.* PLEITO.

litera [le-tay'-rah], *f.* Litter, stretcher, bed, bunk (cama). **Litera alta**, upper berth (en coche). **Litera baja**, lower berth.

literal [le-tay-rahl'], *a.* Literal.

literalmente [le-tay-rahl'-men-tay], *adv.* Literally.

literario, ria [le-tay-rah'-re-o, ah], *a.* Literary.

literatillo [le-tay-rah-teel'-lyo], *m. dim.* of LITERATO: commonly used in contempt.

literato, ta [le-tay-rah'-to, tah], *a.* Learned, lettered, literate, versed in sciences and letters.

literato [le-tay-rah'-to], *m.* A learned man, a literary man. -*pl.* Literati, the learned.

literatura [le-tay-rah-too'-rah], *f.* Literature, learning; skill in sciences and letters.

literero [le-tay-ray'-ro], *m.* One who drives a litter.

litiasis [le-te-ah'-sis], *f. (Med.)* Lithiasis, the formation of stones or gravel in the human body, especially in the urinary passages.

litigación [le-te-gah-the-on'], *f.* Litigation.

litigante [le-te-gahn'-tay], *pa. & n.* Litigating; litigant; a party concerned in a lawsuit.

litigar [le-te-gar'], *va.* 1. To litigate, to manage a suit at law. 2. To contend, to dispute. -*vn.* To go to law; to argue.

litigio [le-tee'-he-o], *m.* 1. Litigation, lawsuit. 2. Dispute, contest.

litigioso, sa [le-te-he-o'-so, sah], *a.* Litigious, contentious.

litina [le-tee'-nah], *f.* Lithia, lithium oxide.

litio [lee'-te-o], *m.* Lithium, an alkaline metal, the lightest solid element.

litis [lee'-tis], *f. V.* LITE.

litisconsorte [le-tis-con-sor'-tay], *com.* Associate in a lawsuit.

litiscontestación [le-tis-con-tes-tah-the-on'], *f. (Law.)* Answer to a juridical command.

litisexpensas [le-ti-sex-pen'-sas], *f. pl. (Law.)* Costs of suit.

litispendencia [le-tis-pen-den'-the-ah], *f.* The state of a lawsuit which is under judgment or pending.

litocálamo [le-to-ca'-lah-mo], *m.* Petrified or fossil reed.

litoclasto [le-to-clahs'-to], *m.* Lithoclast, an instrument for crushing stone in the bladder.

litocola [le-to-co'-lah], *f.* Lithocolla, lapidary's cement, composed of marble dust, glue, and white of egg.

litófago, ga [le-to'-fah-go, gah], *a.* Rock consuming.

litófilo, la [le-to'-fe-lo, lah], *a. (Bot.)* Growing on or attached to rocks.

litófito [le-to'-fe-to], *m.* Lithophyte, a stone plant, coral.

litofotografía [le-to-fo-to-grah-fee'-ah], *f. V.* FOTOLITOGRAFÍA.

litografía [le-to-grah-fee'-ah], *f.* Lithography, printing from prepared stone. Inv. 1799, by Senefelder.

litografiar [le-to-grah-fe-ar'], *va.* To lithograph.

litográfico, ca [le-to-grah'-fe-co, cah], *a.* Lithographic.

litógrafo [le-to'-grah-fo], *m.* Lithologist.

litoídeo, dea [le-to-ee'-day-o, ah], *a.* Lithoid, having the appearance of stone.

litolapaxia [le-to-lah-pahc'-se-ah], *f.* Litholapaxy, crushing of a stone and washing out at one operation.

litología [le-to-lo-hee'-ah], *f.* Lithology, natural history of stones.

litológico, ca [le-to-lo'-he-co, cah], *a.* Lithological, mineralogical.

litólogo [le-to'-lo-go], *m.* Lithologist.

litoral [le-to-rahl'], *a.* Littoral, seaboard, pertaining to the shore. *-m.* Coast line, littoral, seaboard.

litoscopio [le-tos-co'-pe-o], *m.* Lithoscope.

litosfera [le-tos-fay'-rah], *f.* Lithosphere.

litote [le-to'-tay], *f.* Litotes, a rhetorical figure: denial of the opposite.

litotricia [le-to-tree'-the-ah], *f.* Lithotrity, the crushing of a stone within the bladder.

litotritor [le-to-tre-tor'], *m.* Lithotrite, instrument for crushing vesical calculi.

litoxilo [le-toc-see'-lo], *m.* Petrified wood.

litrámetro [le-trah'-may-tro], *m.* Litrameter, an instrument for measuring the specific gravity of liquids.

litro [lee'-tro], *m.* Liter, a unit of capacity in the decimal system. One cubic decimeter.

lituano, no [le-too-ah'-no, nah], *a.* Lithuanian.

lituo [lee'-too-o], *m.* 1. Ancient military instrument of music. 2. Lituus, augur's staff.

liturgia [le-toor'-he-ah], *f.* Liturgy, form of prayers, manner of celebrating the mass.

litúrgico, ca [le-toor'-he-co, cah], *a.* Liturgical, liturgic, belonging to the liturgy.

livianamente [le-ve-ah-nah-men'-tay], *adv.* Licentiously; with levity; lightly.

liviandad [le-ve-an-dahd'], *f.* 1. Lightness, want of weight. 2. Levity, imprudence. 3. Incontinence, libidinousness.

liviano, na [le-ve-ah'-no, nah], *a.* 1. Light, of little weight. 2. Imprudent, light, unsteady. 3. Incontinent, unchaste, libidinous.

livianos [le-ve-ah'-nos], *m. pl.* Lungs. V. BOFES.

lividez [le-ve-deth'], *f.* 1. Lividity, lividness. 2. The black and blue color of a bruise. 3. *(LAm.)* Paleness, pallor.

lívido, da [lee'-ve-do, dah], *a.* 1. Livid (morado). V. AMORATADO. 2. Pale (pálido).

lixiviación [lec-se-ve-ah-the-on'], *f.* Leaching, or lixiviation of an alkali.

liza [lee'-thah], *f.* 1. Skate, a sea fish. 2. Arena for tournaments, prize ring.

lizo [lee'-tho], *m.* Skein of silk.

lizón [le-thone'], *m. (Bot.)* Water plaintain.

ll [el'-lyay], *f.,* It was formerly a letter of the Spanish alphabet. Though double in figure, it is considered simple in its sound. It should not, therefore, be divided at the end of a line, but added to the succeeding vowel with which it forms a complete syllable: as *hallar, seguidi-lla.* It has the liquid sound of *lli* in halliard.

llábana [lyah'-bah-nah], *f. (Prov.)* A natural flagstone, smooth and commonly slippery from the action of water.

llaga [lyah'-gah], *f.* 1. An ulcer (úlcera). 2. Wound (herida), sore. 3. Prick, thorn, tormenting thought. 4. Crack between the bricks of a wall.

llagar [lyah-gar'], *va.* To wound, to hurt, to injure.

llama [lyah'-mah], *f.* 1. Flame, light emitted from fire. 2. Flame, force and violence of passion. 3. *V.* ALPACA. In this sense *(lama),* though feminine in America, it is masculine according to the Spanish Academy. 4. *(Prov.)* Marshy ground. **Arder sin llama**, to smoulder. **Estallar en llamas**, to burst into flames. *-f. (Zool.).* Llama (animal).

llamada [lyah-mah'-dah], *f.* 1. Call, the act of calling (a la puerta). 2. Marginal note. 3. Any motion or sign to call attention (ademán). 4. *(Mil.)* A call by drum or trumpet; chamade. 5. *(Com.)* Notice, entry. 6. *(Mex.)* Cowardliness (cobardía). **La última llamada**, the last call. **Llamada a larga distancia**, long-distance call. **Llamada gratuita**, toll free number.

llamador, ra [lyah-mah-dor', rah], *m. & f.* 1. Caller, he who calls (persona). 2. Beadle, messenger. 3. Knocker of a door (aldaba). 4. Servant of a salesman, vulgarly called barker, clicker, or drummer.

llamamiento [lyah-mah-me-en'-to], *m.* 1. Calling, call, the act of calling. 2. Convocation, the act of convening the members of an assembly or corporation. 3. Calling, call, inspiration, divine vocation.

llamar [lyah-mar'], *va.* 1. To call to one (nombrar). 2. To call, to summon (convocar); to cite. 3. To call, or call upon, to invoke, to appeal to. 4. To call, to invoke with ardor of piety 5. To call, to name, to denominate. 6. To incline. 7. To call, to attract. 8. To excite thirst. 9. To knock (puerta). **Llamar a la puerta**, to knock or rap at the door. **Llaman**, someone is knocking. **Llamar por los nombres**, to call roll. **Llamar** or **dar voces para que se haga alguna cosa**, to call out orders to have something done. **¿Cómo le van a llamar?**, what are they going to call him? **Que me llamen a las 7**, please have them call me at 7. **Llamar al departamento de asistencia técnica**, *(Comput.)* service call. *-vn.* 1. To call. **Llamar por ayuda**, to call for help. 2. To knock (a la puerta). *-vr.* To be called, to be named. **Me llama Mimi**, my name is Mimi. **!Eso se llama cantar !**, that's what you really call singing.

llamarada [lyah-mah-rah'-dah], *f.* 1. A sudden blaze of fire, a flash. 2. Flash, a sudden burst of wit. 3. Sudden flush of the face.

llamativo, va [lyah-mah-tee'-vo, vah], *a.* 1. Exciting thirst. 2. Showy. **De modo llamativo**, in such a way as to draw attention.

llamazar [lyah-mah-thar'], *m.* Swamp.

llambria [lyahm'-bre-ah], *f.* Steep face of a rock difficult to pass. *(Acad.)*

llamear [lyah-may-ar'], *vn.* To blaze.

llana [lyah'-nah], *f.* 1. Trowel, a tool for spreading mortar. 2. Page of a book or writing. 3. Plain.

llanada [lyah-nah'-dah], *f.* A plain, a tract of level ground.

llanamente [lyah'-nah-men-tay], *adv.* Ingenuously, simply, sincerely; homely; plainly.

llanero, ra [lyah-nay'-ro, rah], *m. & f.* Plainsman or plainswoman, inhabitant of the plains.

llaneza [lyah-nay'-thah], *f.* 1. Plainness, sincerity, simplicity. 2. Want of attention and respect, familiarity. 3. Uncultivated style.

llano, na [lyah'-no, nah], *a.* 1. Plain, even, level (superficie), smooth, flat. 2. Meek, homely, affable. 3. Unmannerly, uncivil. 4 Plain (sencillo), open (franco), honestly rough. 5. Plain, simple, void of ornament. 6. Plain, clear, evident, discernible. 7. Plain, simple, not varied by art (estilo). 8. *V.* PECHERO. **En lenguaje llano**, in plain language. **De llano**, openly.

llano [lyah'-no], *m.* A level field, an even ground.

llanta [lyahn'-tah], *f.* 1. *(Bot.)* V. BERZA LLANTA. 2. Tire, the iron hoop or band of a wheel; *(Carib.)* large finger-ring (anillo).

llantén [lyan-ten'] *m. (Bot.)* Plaintain. **Llantén de agua**, *V.* LIZÓN.

llantina [lyan-tee'-nah], *f.* A violent fit of crying, especially in children.

llanto [lyahn'-to], *m.* Flood of tears, crying, weeping.

llanura [lyah-noo'-rah], *f.* 1. Evenness, equality; flatness (superficie), level. 3. A vast tract of level ground, a prairie.

llapa [lyah-pah], *f.* 1. An additional portion of mercury added to metal for working in a smelting furnace. 2. *(Peru)* A gratuity given to the buyer.

llapar [lyah-par'], *va.* To add an additional portion of quicksilver in extracting metals.

llares [lyah'-res], *m. pl.* Pot-hanger, an iron chain, on which pots are hung over the fire.

llave [lyah'-vay], *f.* 1. Key (de puerta). 2. Wrench. 3. Spigot, faucet, tap (grifo). 4. Lock, gunlock (de escopeta). 5. Bracket. 6. Hold (lucha). 7. *(Mus.)* Stop, key. **Bajo llave**, under lock and key. **Echar la llave a**, 1. To lock. 2. *(Fig.)* To put the finishing touches on. **Llave de percusión**, percussion lock. **Llave inglesa**, monkey wrench. **Llave maestra**, master key. **Llave de cambio**, shift key. **Cerrar una puerta con llave**, to lock a door. **Llave de paso**, stopcock.

llavero, ra [lyah-vay'-ro, rah], *m. & f.* 1. Keeper of the keys. 2. Ring in which keys are kept. 3. *(Prov.)* Housekeeper.

lle, *pron. obs. V.* LE.

llegada [lyay-gah'-dah], *f.* Arrival, coming.

llegar [lyay-gar'], *vn.* 1. To arrive, to come to any place. 2. To reach (alcanzar), to arrive at, to go as far as, to fetch. 3. To last, to continue. 4. To attain a purpose. 5. To suffice, to be enough (bastar). 6. To ascend; to amount to (sumar). *-va.* 1. To approach, to bring near to. 2. To join. *-vr.* 1. To approach, to draw near. 2. To proceed to some neighboring place. 3. To unite. **Llegar a**, to come to, to get to be, to succeed in. **Llegar a ser**, to come to be. **Llegar y besar**, no sooner said than done. **No llegar a uno la camisa al cuerpo**, to be terrified and anxious. **Llegar a las manos**, to come to blows, to fight. **Llegar a oír**, to hear. **Llegar a saber**, to find out, to be informed of. **No llegar**, to fall short, not to reach. *(Met.)* To be inferior. **Hacer llegar una carta a**, to send a letter to. **Cuando llegue eso**, when that happens. **El importe llega a 50 pesos**, the total is 50 pesos. **Por fin llegó a hacerlo**, he managed to do it eventually. **Si llego a saberlo**, if I had known it.

lleira [lyay'-e-rah], *f. (Prov.)* Place full of pebbles or gravel.

llena [lyay'-nah], *f.* Alluvion, overflow of rivers.

llenamente [lyay'-nah-men-tay], *adv.* Fully, copiously.

llenar [lyay-nar'], *va.* 1. To fill, to stuff. 2. To occupy a public place. 3. To fill, to satisfy (deseo), to content. 4 To make up a number. 5. To beget young. 6. To fill in (formulario), to cover (superficie). *-vr.* 1. To feed gluttonously. 2. To be irritated after having suffered long. **Llenar completamente**, to fill up. *(Fig.)* **Llenar a uno de elogios**, to heap praises on somebody.

llenero, ra [lyay-nay'-ro, rah], *a. (Law.)* Full, complete, absolute.

lleno [lyay'-no], *m.* 1. Glut, plenty, abundance (abundancia), full. 2. Perfection (perfección), completeness. 3. Full moon. 4. An organ-stop.

lleno, na [lyay'-no, nah], *a.* Full, replete, complete. **Lleno hasta el borde**, brimful. **Estar lleno a reventar**, to be full to bursting. **Estar lleno de polvo**, to be covered in dust. **De lleno**, fully.

llenura [lyay-noo'-rah], *f.* Fulness, plenty, copiousness, abundance.

lleta [lyay'-tah], *f.* Stalk of plants bearing fruit.

lleudar [lyay-oo-dar'], *va.* To ferment bread with leaven.

llevada [lyay-vah'-dah], *f.* or **Lleva.** Carriage, transport, act of carrying.

llevadero, ra [lyay-vah-day'-ro, rah], *a.* Tolerable, light.

llevador, ra [lyay-vah-dor', rah], *m. & f.* Carrier, conductor.

llevar [lyay'-var], *va.* 1. To carry, to convey, to transport. 2. To carry, to bear (nombre, título), to wear (ropa), to have about one. 3. To carry, to take, to have with one. 4. To exact, to demand, to ask a price for a thing. 5. To bear, to produce. 6. To excel, to exceed (exceder). 7. To bear, to suffer, to endure. 8. To lead, to guide. 9. To manage a horse. 10. To

cut off, to carry off (apartar). 11. To induce, to bring to any opinion (inducir). 12. To introduce. 13. To gain, to obtain. 14. To obtain possession. 15. To fetch away or fetch off. 16 To carry in accounts. 17. With the preposition *por*, it signifies to exercise whatever may be the import of the following noun. **Llevár(se)lo de calle**, to overpower another in argument. **Llevar mosca**, to go away offended and angry. **Llevar en peso**, to carry in the air. **Llevar consigo**, to carry along with, to be attached to, to be a consequence of. **Llevar una caída, golpe, porrazo, chasco, etc.** *(coll.)* to suffer a fall or blow; to be disappointed. **Llevar y conllevar**, to bear and forbear. **Llevar de conformidad,** *(Com.)* to find correct. **Llevar a uno adelante**, To carry forward (plan). **Llevaba puesto un sombrero raro**, she had an odd hat on. **El avión no llevaba paracaídas**, the plane had no parachutes. **Le llevamos al teatro**, we took him to the theater. **Llevar una vida tranquila**, to live a quiet life. **Llevar las desgracias con paciencia**, to bear misfortunes patiently. **El tren lleva una hora de retraso**, the train is an hour late. **Llevo estudiados 3 capítulos**, I have studied 3 chapters. **Ella me lleva dos años**, she's 2 years older than I am. **Esto me lleva a pensar que…**, this leads me to think that… *-vn.* To be reprimanded, to suffer chastisement. **Llevar a cuestas**, 1. To carry on one's shoulders or back. 2. *(coll.)* To burden oneself with others' affairs. *-vr.* To suffer oneself to be led away by passion. **Llevarse bien or mal**, to be on good or bad terms. **No llevarlas todas consigo**, to be suspicious, to be afraid. **Se lo llevaron al cine**, they took him off to the cinema. **Los ladrones se llevaron la caja**, the thieves took the safe away. **Se llevó el primer premio**, she carried off the first prize.

lloíca [lyo-ee'-cah], *f. V.* PECHICOLORADO. Robin red-breast.

lloradera [lyo-rah-day'-rah], *f.* Weeping from slight motives.

llorador, ra [lyo-rah-dor', rah], *m. & f.* Weeper, one who sheds tears.

lloraduelos [lyo-rah-doo-ay'-los], *m. (coll.)* Weeper, mourner.

llorar [lyo-rar'], *vn.* 1. To weep, to cry (persona). 2. To mourn (muerte, pérdida), to lament, to bewail. 3. To affect poverty and distress. 4. *(Met.)* To fall drop by drop. 5. *(Cono Sur)* To suit, to be becoming (quedar bien). 6. *(And. Carib. Cono Sur)* To be very unbecoming (quedar muy mal). **Llorar a moco tendido**, to sob one's heart out. **El que no llora no mama**, if you don't ask you don't get.

lloriquear [lyo-re-kay-ar'], *vn.* To be constantly crying.

lloro [lyo'-ro], *m.* Act of weeping or crying.

llorón [lyo-rone'], *m.* 1. Weeper, one apt to shed tears, mourner. 2. A weeping willow. *-a.* Crying with little cause.

lloronas [lyo-ro'-nas], *f. pl.* Weepers, mourners.

llorosamente [lyo-ro'-sah-men-tay], *adv.* Weepingly.

lloroso, sa [lyo-ro'-so, sah], *a.* Mournful, sorrowful, tearful.

llovediza (Agua) [lyo-vay-dee'-thah], *a.* Rainwater.

llover [lyo-verr'], *vn.* 1. To rain. 2. To pour down rain. 3. To shower, to abound, to come in abundance, as troubles. *-vr.* To penetrate the roof with rain. **Llover a cántaros** or **a chorros**, to rain bucketfuls. **Como llovido del cielo**, unexpectedly. **Llueva o no**, rain or shine. **Siempre que llueve escampa,** *(Carib.)* every cloud has a silver lining. *(Llueve, llueva, from Llover V.* ABSOLVER.)

llovida [lyo-vee'-dah], *f.* Rain.

llovioso, sa [lyo-ve-o'-so], *a. V.* LLUVIOSO.

llovizna [lyo-veeth'-nah], *f.* Mist, a fine rain.

lloviznar [lyo-veeth-nar'], *vn.* To drizzle.

llueco, ca [lyoo-ey-co, cah], *a. V.* CLUECO.

lluvia [lyoo'-ve-ah], *f.* 1. Rain, shower, water from the clouds. 2. Shower, abundance, copiousness. 3. Shower, storm. 4. Rainfall (cantidad), spray (insecticida), rose (regadera). **Lluvia artificial**, cloud seeding. **Lluvia ácida**, acid rain. **Lluvia torrencial**, torrential rain.

lluvioso, sa [lyoo-ve-o'-so, sah], *a.* Rainy, wet, showery.

lo, *indef. pron.* It: placed before or after verbs. It is used before adjectives, when by an ellipsis they are used in a general sense, referring to a thing either masculine or feminine, singular or plural. It is used also with reference to whole sentences. **Lo tengo aquí,** I have it here. **Lo veo, I** see it. **Guapa sí que lo es,** she's certainly very pretty.

lo. *pron. rel.* **Lo que,** what. **Lo que digo es…,** what I say is… **Con lo que él gana,** with what he earns. **Lo que se dice un hombre,** a real man.

lo, *art* "neutro". **Lo bello,** the beautiful. **Lo difícil,** what is difficult. **Defiendo lo mío,** I defend what is mine. **Lo mejor de la película,** the best part of the film. **No saben lo aburrido que es,** they don't know how boring it is. *-pron. pers. neut.* It. **No lo creo,** I don't believe it. **No lo he visto nunca,** I've never seen it. *-pron. pers. m.* him. **No lo conozco,** I don't know him.

loa [lo'-ah], *f.* 1. Prologue of a play. 2. Praise (elogio).

loable [lo-ah'-blay], *a.* Laudable, praiseworthy.

loablemente [lo-ah'-blay-men-tay], *adv.* Laudably, commendably.

loador, ra [lo-ah-dor', rah], *m. & f.* Praiser, lauder.

loán [lo-ahn'], *m.* A land measure of the Philippine Islands, equal to 3,600 square feet.

loanda [lo-ahn'-dah], *f.* Kind of scurvy.

loar [lo-ar'], *va.* To praise; to approve.

loasa [lo-ah'-sah], *f.* Loasa, a genus of South American climbing plants of elegant flowers.

loba [lo'-bah], *f.* 1. Ridge between furrows. 2. Long gown worn by clergymen and students. 3. She-wolf.

lóbado [lo'-bah-do], *m.* Morbid swelling incident to horses.

lobanillo [lo-bah-neel'-lyo], *m.* Wen, a callous excrescence.

lobato [lo-bah'-to], *m.* Young wolf.

lobelia [lo-bay'-le-ah], *f. (Bot.)* Lobelia.

lobera [lo-bay'-rah], *f.* Thicket where wolves make their lair.

lobero, ra [lo-bay'-ro, rah], *a.* Relating to wolves.

lobero [lo-bay'-ro], *m.* V. ESPANTANUBLADOS.

lobezno [lo-beth'-no], *m.* A young wolf.

lobina [lo-bee'-nah], *f.* Striped bass.

lobo [lo'-bo], *m.* 1. Wolf. **Lobo de mar,** sea dog. 2. Lobe, a division of the lungs, liver, etc. 3. *(Joc.)* Intoxication, inebriation. 4. Iron instrument for defending or scaling walls. **Ver las orejas del lobo,** *(Met.)* to find oneself in the greatest danger. **Son lobos de una camada,** they're birds of a feather. 5. *(Mex.)* Traffic cop. 6. *(LAm.)* Half-breed.

lobo marino [lo'-bo mah-ree'-no], *m.* Seal, sea-calf.

loboso, sa [lo-bo'-so, sah], *a.* Full of wolves (montes, bosques).

lóbrego, ga [lo'-bray-go, gah], *a.* Murky, obscure, sad, mirk.

lobreguecer [lo-bray-gay-therr'], *vn.* To grow dark, to be dark. *-va.* To make dark.

lobreguez [lo-bray-geth'], *f.* Obscurity, darkness.

lóbulo [lo'-boo-lo], *m.* Lobe or lobule, a division or distinct part of the lungs, liver, etc.

lobuno, na [lo-boo'-no, nah], *a.* Wolfish, resembling a wolf.

locación y conducción [lo-ca-the-on' ee con-dooc-the-on'], *f. (Law.)* Contract of letting on lease.

local [lo-cahl'], *a.* Local, relating to a particular place (sitio).

localidad [lo-cah-le-dahd'], *f.* 1. Locality, existence in place; location, place, town (pueblo). 2. Ticket, seat. **Sacar localidades,** to get tickets.

localizable [lo-cah-le-thah'-blay], *a.* **Fácilmente localizable,** easy to find. **El director no estaba localizable,** the director was not available.

localización [lo-cah-le-thah-the-on'], *f.* Localization, fixing in a definite place.

localizar [lo-cah-le-thar'], *va.* 1. To localize, to fix in a determined place, to locate (ubicar), to place (colocar), to find (encontrar). 2. *(Med.)* To localize. *-vr.* 1. *(Mex.)* To be located (situarse). 2. *(Med.)* To be localized (dolor).

localmente [lo-cahl'-men-tay], *adv.* Locally.

locamente [lo'-cah-men-tay], *adv.* Madly: immoderately, extravagantly; fondly.

locarias [lo-cah'-re-as], *m. (coll.)* A madcap, a wild, hot-brained fellow.

loción [lo-the-on'], *f.* 1. Lotion, a medicine used to wash any part with. 2. Wash, lavation, the act of washing. **loción capilar,** hair restorer.

loco, ca [lo'-co, cah], *a.* 1. Mad, crack-brained. 2. Fool. 3. Abundant, fertile, huge, tremendous (enorme). **A tontas y a locas,** inconsiderately, without reflection. **Estar loco de contento,** *(coll.)* to be mad with joy. **A palabras, locas, orejas sordas,** a silly question deserves no answer. **Loco de atar,** raving mad. **Más loco que una cabra,** as mad as a hatter. **Estar loco por hacer algo,** to be mad keen to do something. **Volverse loco,** to go mad. **He tenido una suerte loca,** I've been fantastically lucky.

loco [lo'-co], *m.* A madman, crazyman.

locomoción [lo-co-mo-the-on'], *f.* 1. *(Phys.)* Locomotion, power of moving. 2. *(LAm.)* Transport.

locomotivo, va [lo-co-mo-tee'-vo, vah], *a.* Locomotive, possessed of the power of moving.

locomotor, ra [lo-co-mo-tor', rah], *a.* Locomotor, having the power of producing motion.

locomotora [lo-co-mo-to'-rah], *f.* A locomotive engine. **Locomotora de maniobras,** shunting engine.

locomotriz [lo-co-mo-treeth'], *a.* Locomotive.

locomóvil [lo-co-mo'-veel], *a.* Locomotive.-*f.* Traction engine.

locro [lo'-cro], *m. (Peru. Ec.)* A stew composed chiefly of winter squash, potatoes, tender corn, meat or fish, etc.

locuacidad [lo-coo-ah-the-dahd'], *f.* Loquacity, talkativeness, garrulity, flippancy.

locuaz [lo-coo-ath'], *a.* Loquacious, talkative, garrulous, flippant.

locución [lo-coo-the-on'], *f.* Locution, manner of speech; phrase, expression.

locuela [lo-coo-ay'-lah], *f.* 1. Each one's particular mode of speaking. 2. Name commonly given to a giddy and conceited young girl.

locura [lo-coo'-rah], *f.* 1. Madness (cualidad, estado), frenzy, lunacy, craziness. 2. Fury; folly, absurdity. **Hacer locuras,** to act in an absurd, foolish manner. **Me gusta con locura,** I'm crazy about it. **Es capaz de cometer cualquier locura,** he is capable of any madness.

locutor [lo-coo-tor'], *m.* Speaker, announcer, commentator (comentarista), presenter (desfile de modelos). **Locutor de radio,** radio announcer, radio commentator. **Locutor de televisión,** television announcer or commentator.

locutorio [lo-coo-to'-re-o], *m.* Parlor, place in monasteries for receiving visits, visiting room (cárcel), telephone box.

locha, *f.* **loche,** *m.* [lo'-chah, lo'-chay]. *(Zool.)* Loach, groundling, a small fish.

locho, cha [lo'-cho, chah], *a. (Amer. coll.)* Red-bearded, bright red.

lodazal, lodazar [lo-dah-thahl', lo-dah-thar'], *m.* A muddy place.

lodo [lo'-do], *m.* Mud, mire.

lodoñero [lo-do-nyay'-ro], *m. (Bot.)* Guaiac, lignumvitae tree.

lodoso, sa [lo-do'-so, sah], *a.* Muddy, miry.

logarítmico, ca [lo-gah-reet'-me-co, cah], *a.* Logarithmic, logarithmical.

logaritmo [lo-gah-reet'-mo], *m.* Logarithm.

logia [lo'-he-ah], *f.* Lodge assembly of Freemasons and the place where they meet.

lógica [lo'-he-cah], *f.* Logic, dialectics. **Ser de una lógica aplastante,** to be as clear as day.

lógicamente [lo'-he-caa-men-tay], *adv.* Logically.

lógico, ca [lo'-he-co, cah], *a.* Logical; natural, right, reasonable. **Es lógico que…,** it is natural that…

lógico [lo'-he-co], *m.* Logician, dialectician, a professor of logic.

logístico, ca [lo-hees'-te-co, cah], *a.* Logistic. -*f.* Logistics.

logo [lo-go]. *(Comput.)* Logo.

logografía [lo-go-grah-fee'-ah], *f.* Shorthand.

logogrifo [lo-go-gree'-fo], *m.* Logograph, an enigma in which the different parts of a word are taken in divers meanings.

logomaquia [lo-go-mah'-ke-ah], *f.* Logomachy, dispute about words.

logoterapeuta [lo-go-tay-rah-pey'-oo-tah], *m & f.* Speech therapist.

logotipo [lo-go-tee'-po], *m.* Logo.

logrado [lo-grah'-do], *a.* Successful.

lograr [lo-grar'], *va.* 1. To gain (obtener), to obtain, to succeed, to procure, to compass. 2. To possess, to enjoy. 3. To avail oneself of. 4. To hit upon, to manage, to do well. **Lograr hacer algo,** to manage to do something. **Lograr que uno haga algo,** to get somebody to do something. *-vr.* To reap the benefit of one's labor and exertions.

logrear [lo-gray-ar'], *vn.* To borrow or lend on interest.

logrería [lo-gray-ree'-ah], *f.* Dealing in interest, usury.

logrero, ra [lo-gray'-ro, rah], *m. & f.* Lender at interest, usurer.

logro [lo'-gro], *m.* 1. Gain, benefit. 2. Attainment of some purpose (éxito). **Uno de sus mayores logros,** one of his greatest successes. 3. Interest; usury.

loma [lo'-mah], *f.* 1. Rising ground in the midst of a plain, a little hill or hillock. 2. Slope. 3. *(Cono Sur)* **En la loma del diablo,** at the back of beyond.

lombarda [lom-bar'-dah], *f.* 1. Lombardy gun. 2. *(Bot.)* Red cabbage.

lombardada [lom-bar-dah-dah], *f.* Shot from a Lombardy gun.

lombardear [lom-bar-day-ar'], *va.* To discharge Lombardy guns.

lombardería [lom-bar-day-ree'-ah], *f.* Park of Lombardy guns.

lombardero [lom-bar-day'-ro], *m.* Soldier appointed to Lombardy guns.

lombárdico, ca [lom-bar'-de-co, cah], *a.* Lombard, belonging to Lombardy.

lombardo, da [lom-bar'-do, dah], *a.* Lombard, belonging to Lombardy.

lombriguera [lom-bre-gay'-rah], *f.* Hole made by worms. 2. *(Bot.)* Southern-wood wormwood.

lombriz [lom-breeth'], *f.* Worm bred in the body, or in the earth. **Lombriz intestinal,** tapeworm.

lombrizal [lom-bre-thahl'], *a. (Anat.)* Vermiform.

lomear [lo-may-ar'], *vn.* To jerk or move the loins of horses in a circular manner.

lomento [lo-men'-to], *m. (Bot.)* Loment, a kind of legume falling in pieces when ripe.

lomera [lo-may'-rah], *f.* 1. Strap of harness which crosses the loins. 2. *(Prov.)* Ridge of a house.

lomiancho, a [lo-me-ahn'-cho, chah], *a.* Strong or broad-backed.

lomica, illa, ita [lo-mee'-cah], *f. dim.* A very little hill or hillock.

lomillo [lo-meel'-lyo], *m.* 1. *(Dim.)* A small loin. 2. A kind of needle work. 3. *(LAm.)* Pads.

lominhiesto, ta [lo-min-e-es'-to, tah], *a.* 1. High-cropped. 2. Presumptuous, arrogant.

lomo [lo'-mo], *m.* 1. Loin (carne). 2. Chine, a piece of the back of an animal. 3. Back of a book or cutting tool: double of any cloth, fold. 4. Ridge between furrows. **Llevar or traer a lomo,** to carry on the back. *-pl.* Ribs; loins.

lomudo, da [lo-moo'-do, dah], *a.* Large in the loins, broad-backed.

lona [lo'-nah], *f.* Canvas. **Lona para hacer velas,** duck-canvas, sail-cloth.

loncha [lone'-chah], *f.* 1. Thin flat stone. 2. Thin slice of meat.

lóndiga [lon'-de-gah], *f.* ALHÓNDIGA.

londinense [lon-de-nen'-say], *a.* Of London, Londonese.

londó [lon-do'], *m. (Com.)* A fabric made in Brittany.

londrina [lon-dree'-nah], *f.* A sort of woollen cloth from London.

loneta [lo-nay'-tah], *f.* Ravens' duck sail-cloth.

longa [lone'-gah], *f.* Long musical note.

longanimidad [lon-gah-ne-me-dahd'], *f.* Longanimity, forbearance.

longánimo, ma [lon-gah'-ne-mo, mah], *a.* Forbearing, generous, magnanimous.

longaniza [lon-gah-nee'-thah], *f.* 1. A kind of long sausage (salchicha). 2. *(Cono Sur)* String, series (serie).

longar [lon-gar'], *a.* Applied to long piece of honey-comb in the hive.

longazo, za [lon-gah'-tho, tha], *a. aug.* Very long.

longevidad [lon-hay-ve-dahd'], *f.* Longevity.

longevo [lon-hay'-vo], *a.* Longeval, long-lived.

longicornios [lon-he-cor'-ne-ose], *a. & m. pl.* Longicorn, the longicorn beetles have very long antennae, sometimes surpassing the entire length of the body. The larvae burrow in the hardest woods.

longifloro, ra [lon-he-flo'-ro, rah], *a.* Long-flowered, longiflorous.

longimetría [lon-he-may-tree'-ah], *f. (Geom.)* Longimetry, the art of measuring distances.

longincuo, cua [lon-heen'-coo-o, ah], *a.* Distant, remote.

longípedo, da [lon-hee'-pay-do, dah], *a.* Long-footed.

longirrostros [lon-hi-rros'-tro-se], *m. pl. a.* Longirostres, a family of birds including snipes, etc. As adjective, longirostral, long-billed.

longísimo, ma [lon-hee'-se-mo, mah], *a. sup.* of LUENGO. Longest, So, too, V. LONGUÍSIMO.

longitud [lon-he-tood'], *f.* 1. Length, longness. 2. Longitude.

longitudinal [lon-he-too-de-nahl'], *a.* Longitudinal.

longitudinalmente [lon-he-too-de-nahl'-men-tay], *adv.* Longitudinally, lengthwise.

longuera [lon-gay'-rah], *f.* Long and narrow strip of land.

longura [lon-goo'-rah], *f.* 1. Length. 2. Long lapse of time. 3. Delay.

lonja [lone'-hah], *f.* 1. Exchange, a public place where merchants meet. **Lonja de pescado,** fish market. 2. Slice or steak of ham, or any other eatable. 3. Grocer's shop (abacería), warehouse, sale-room. **Lonja cerrada** or **abierta,** shut or open shop or exchange. 4. Entrance hall of an edifice. 5. Leather strap, used in falconry.

lonjero [lon-hay'-ro], *m.* Grocer.

lonjista [lon-hees'-tah], *com.* Shopkeeper who deals in groceries.

lontananza [lon-tah-nahn'-thah], *f. (Art.)* Distance, background.

loor [loor'], *m. (Poet.)* Praise.

lopigia [lo-pee'-he-ah], *f.* Disease which makes the hair fall off. *V.* ALOPECIA.

loquear [lo-kay-ar'], *vn.* 1. To act the fool, to talk nonsense. 2. To rejoice, to exult, to revel, to frolic.

loquero, ra [lo-kay'-ro, rah], *m. & f.* 1. Keeper of a madhouse (manicomio). 2. Physician to a madhouse (persona). 3. *(Cono Sur)* **Esta oficina es un loquero,** this office is a madhouse.

loquesca [lo-kes'-cah], *f.* The frantic demeanor of mad people.

loquillo, illa, ito, ita [lo-keel'-lyo], *a dim.* Wild, almost mad.

loquios [lo'-ke-ose], *m. pl.* Lochia, the evacuations following childbirth for two to three weeks.

loran [lo'-rahn], *m.* Loran, contraction of Long Range Navigation.

lord, *m. (pl.* **Lores**). Lord, a title of honor given to the highest nobility in England.

lorenzana [lo-ren-thah'-nah], *f.* A sort of coarse linen.

loriga [lo-ree'-gah], *f.* 1. Coat of mail, cuirass. 2. Naveband, the hoop which surrounds the nave of a coach wheel.

lorigado, da [lo-re-gahh'-do, dah], *a.* Armed with a coat of mail, loricate.

loriguillo [lo-re-geel'-lyo], *m.* Shrub used by dyers.

loro, ra [lo'ro, rah], *a.* Tawny, dark brown.

loro [lo'-ro], *m.* 1. Parrot. 2. *(Bot.)* Portugal laurel. 3. Old bat (arpía). 4. *(Cono Sur)* Thieves' look-out man. 5. *(Cono Sur.*

Med.) Bedpan. 6. *(Cono Sur)* **Sacar los loros**, to pick one's nose. 7. **Estar al loro**, to be on the alert.

los art def *m.pl.* **las** *f.pl.* The. V. El. **Los árboles**, the trees. **Los niños**, the children.

los, las *pron.* Them. **Los hay**, there are some. **Dámelos**, give them to me. **¿Los libros?, ¡tómalos!**, the books?; take them!

los, las *pron. dem.* **Nuestros cines y los de París**, our cinemas and those of Paris. **Los de Juan son verdes**, John's are green. **Éstos son los nuestros y ésos los de Pedro**, these are ours, and those are Peter's.

losa [lo'-sah], *f.* 1. Flag, a square stone used for pavements. 2. Painter's block of marble on which colors are ground. 3. Trap for catching birds or rats.

losado [lo-sah'-do], *m.* V. ENLOSADO. **-Losado, da**, *pp.* of LOSAR.

losanje [lo-sahn'-hay], *m. (Her.)* Lozenge; rhomb.

losar [lo-sar'], *va.* V. ENLOSAR.

losica, ita [lo-see'-cah, ee'-tah], *f.dim.* A small flag or stone.

loseta, losilla [lo-say'-tah, lo-seel'-lyah], *f.* 1. A small trap or snare. 2. V. LOSICA.

lote [lo'-tay], *m.* 1. Lot, fortune, chance, portion (porción); *(LAm.)* Building site (solar). 2. *(Mex.)* About 100 hectares (medida). 3. *(Cono Sur)* Any old how. 4. Affair. **Darse el lote con**, to have it off with.

lotería [lo-tay-ree'-ah], *f.* 1. Lottery. 2. The game lotto. **Le tocó la lotería**, he won a big prize in the lottery.

loto [lo'-to], *m. (Bot.)* 1. Lotus, the Egyptian and Indian waterlily. 2. The loto-tree, or nettle-tree. V. ALMEZ. 3. Jujube-tree.

loza [lo'-thah], *f.* China, fine earthenware. **Loza refractaria**, pyrex ware.

lozanamente [lo-thah-nah-men'-tay], *adv.* 1. Luxuriantly. 2. In a self-assured way.

lozanear [lo-thah-nay-ar'], *vn.* To affect pomp and ostentation in words and actions.

lozanía [lo-thah-nee-ah], *f.* 1. Luxuriance of verdure, exuberant growth of plants. 2. Elegance; lustiness.

lozano, na [lo-thah'-no, nah], *a.* 1. Luxuriant. 2. Sprightly. 3. Self-assured (seguro); arrogant (arrogante).

lúa [loo'-ah], *f.* 1. Esparto glove (sin separación de los dedos) for cleaning horses. 2. *(Prov.)* A sort of crane for raising weights. 3. *(Naut.)* Lee. 4. *(Prov.)* Saffron-bag.

lubricación [loo-bre-cah-the-on'], *f.* Lubrication.

lubricador, ra [loo-bre-cah-dor', rah], *a.* Lubricating.

lubricante [loo-bre-cahn'-tay], *a.* 1. *(Tec.)* Lubricant, lubricating. 2. Oily (persona). *-m.* Lubricant.

lubricar, lubrificar [loo-bre-car', loo-bre-fe-car'], *va.* To lubricate.

lubricativo, va [loo-bre-cah-tee'-vo, vah], *a.* Lubricant, lubricative.

lubricidad [loo-bre-the-dahd'], *f.* 1. Lubricity, slipperiness. 2. Lewdness.

lúbrico, ca [loo'-bre-co, cah], *a.* Slippery (resbaladizo): lubricous; lewd.

lubrificación [loo-bre-fe-cah-the-on'], *f.* Lubrication.

lubrificador, ra [loo-bre-cah-dor', rah], *a.* Lubricating.

lubrificante [loo-bre-cahn'-tay], *a.* Lubricating.

lucano [loo-cah'-no], *m.* The stag-beetle, commonly called *cometa.*

lucas [loo'-cas], *m. pl.* 1. *(Cant.)* Playing-cards. 2. *(Mex.)* Crazy.

lucerna [loo-ther'-nah], *f.* 1. Glow-worm. 2. Lamp.

lucérnula [loo-therr'-noo'-lah], *f. (Bot.)* Lucern, lucerne, alfalfa.

lucero [loo-thay'-ro], *m.* 1. Morning star, Venus, day star, Lucifer. 2. Splendor. 3. Part of a window where light enters. 4. White spot on the forehead of certain quadrupeds. *(Acad.)* **Lucero de la tarde**, evening star. *-pl. (Poet.)* Eyes.

lucha [loo'-chah], *f.* 1. Struggle, strife, contest, wrestle. 2. Dispute, argument. **Lucha de clases**, class war.

luchador, ra [loo-chah-dor', rah], *m. & f.* Wrestler, fighter.

luchar [loo-char'], *va.* 1. To wrestle, to contend, to struggle. **Luchaba con los mandos**, he was struggling with the controls. 2. To discuss, to debate.

lucharniego, ga [loo-char-ne-ay'-go, gah], *a.* Applied to dogs used for catching hares at night.

luchillo [loo-cheel'-lyo], *m. (Naut.)* Gering, goring cloth.

lucidamente [loo-the-dah-men' -tay], *adv.* Lucidly, brightly.

lucidar [loo-the-dar'], *va.* To copy a picture on transparent paper.

lucidez [loo-the-deth'], *f.* 1. Brilliancy, brightness, lucidity (claridad). 2. *(CAm. Cono Sur)* Brilliance (brillantez).

lucido, da [loo-thee'-do, dah], *a.* Magnificent, splendid (brillante), brilliant in performance, elegant (elegante); successful (exitoso). *-pp.* of LUCIR.

lúcido, da [loo'-the-do, dah], *a.* 1. Lucid, clear in reason. 2. Brilliant, shining.

lucidura [loo-the-doo'-rah], *f. (coll.)* Whiteness of whitewashed walls.

luciente [loo-the-en'-tay], *pa.* Shining, lucid, luminous, bright.

luciérnaga [loo-the-err'-nah-gah], *f.* Glow-worm, firefly.

Lucifer [loo-the-ferr'], *m.* 1. Lucifer. Satan. 2. A very proud and wicked man. 3. V. LUCERO for the morning star.

luciferino, na [loo-the-fay-ree'-no, nah], *a.* Luciferian, devilish.

lucífero, ra [loo-thee'-fay-ro, rah], *a. (Poet.)* Resplendent, shining, luciferous.

lucífugo, ga [loo-thee'-foo-go, gah], *a.* Avoiding the light, lucifugous.

lucillo [loo-theel'-lyo], *m.* Tomb; sarcophagus.

lucimiento [loo-the-me-en'-to], *m.* 1. Lucidity, brightness. 2. Splendor, luster, applause.

lucio, cia [loo'-the-o, ah], *a.* Lucid, bright.

lucio [loo'-the-o], *m. (Zool.)* Common pike, luce.

lucir [loo-theer'], *va.* 1. To emit light, to glitter, to gleam, to glow. 2. To illuminate (iluminar), to enlighten. 3. To outshine, to exceed. 4. To show off, to display. **Lucía traje nuevo**, he was sporting a new suit. *-vn. & vr.* 1. To shine, to be brilliant. **Le luce el trabajo**, he enjoys the fruits of his labor. 2. To dress to advantage. **Lucirlo**, *(coll.)* to dash away, to sport. *(Yo luzco, yo luzca, from Lucir. V. DESLUCIR.)*

lucrarse [loo-crar'-say], *vr.* To get gain or profit from a business or charge.

lucrativamente [loo-crah-te'-vah-men-tay], *adv.* Profitably, lucratively.

lucrativo, va [loo-crah-tee'-vo, vah], *a.* Lucrative, productive of gain.

lucro [loo'-cro], *m.* Gain, profit, lucre.

lucroso, sa [loo-cro'-so, sah], *a.* Lucrific, gainful, profitable.

luctuosa [looc-too-o'-sah], *f.* Ancient tax paid to lords and bishops for the dead.

luctuosamente [looc-too-o'-sah-men-tay], *adv.* Mournfully, sorrowfully.

luctuoso, sa [looc-too-o'-so, sah], *a.* Sad, mournful.

lucubración [loo-coo-brah-the-on'], *f.* Lucubration, nocturnal study.

lucubrar [loo-coo-brar'], *va.* To lucubrate, to study by night.

lúcuma [loo'-coo-mah], *f.* Fruit of the *lúcumo*, a tree of Peru and tropical America.

ludia [loo'-de-ah], *f. (Prov.)* Ferment, yeast.

ludiar [loo-de-ar'], *va. & vr. (Prov.)* To ferment.

ludibrio [loo-dee'-bre-o], *m.* Mockery, derision, scorn.

ludimiento [loo-de-me-en'-to], *m. (Prov.)* V. COLISIÓN.

ludir [loo-deer'], *va.* To rub, to waste by friction, to collide.

ludria [loo'-dre-ah], *f.* V. NUTRIA.

lúe [loo'-ay], *f.* Infection. *(Acad.)*

luego [loo-ay'-go], *adv.* 1. Presently (pronto), immediately, outright, out of hand, *(CAm.)* later (después), *(And. Carib. Cono Sur, Mex.)* sometimes (de vez en cuando). **Luego vuelvo**, I'll be back at once. 2. Soon afterward. *-conj.* Then, therefore. **Pienso, luego existo, I** think, therefore, I am. *(LAm.)* **Luego que llegues avísame**, let me know the moment you arrive. **Desde luego**, of course.

lugano [loo-gah'-no], *m.* A linnet. *V.* JILGUERO.

lugar [loo-gar'], *m.* 1. Place, spot, situation, position (posición). 2. City, town, village (pueblo): properly speaking, it is applied to a village or a very small town. 3. Employment, office, dignity. 4. Time, opportunity (oportunidad), occasion. 5. Leisure, convenience of time. 6. Cause, motive, reason (razón). 7. Text, authority or sentiment of an author. **En lugar de**, instead of, in lieu of. **Lugar seguro**, safe place. **En primer lugar**, in the first place. **Estar fuera de lugar**, to be out of place. **Ocupar el lugar de**, to take the place of, **Tener lugar**, to take place. **Hacer lugar para**, to make room for. **Dar lugar a**, to give rise to.

lugarcico, illo, ito [loo-gar-thee'-co], *m. dim. V.* LUGARILLO.

lugarillo, lugarejo [loo-gah-reel'-lyo, loo-gah-ray'-ho], *m. dim.* Hamlet, a small village.

lugarño, ña [loo-gah-ray'-nyo, nyah], *m. & f. & a.* 1. Belonging to a village. 2. Inhabitant of a village.

lugarete [loo-gah-ray'-tay], *m. dim. V.* LUGARILLO.

lugarón [loo-gah-rone'], *m. aug. V.* LUGARAZO.

lugarote [loo-gah-ro'-tay], *m. aug. V.* LUGARAZO.

lugartenencia [loo-gar-tay-nen'-the-ah], *f.* Lieutenancy.

lugarteniente [loo-gar-tay-ne-en'-tay], *m.* 1. Deputy, substitute, delegate. 2. Lieutenant.

lugre [loo'-gray], *m.* Lugger, a small two or three masted vessel.

lugo [loo'-go], *m.* Kind of linen.

lúgubre [loo'-goo-bray], *a.* Sad, mournful, gloomy, melancholy, lugubrious, dismal.

luir [loo-eer'], *m. (Naut.)* To gall, or be galled or fretted, to wear away by friction. *-va (Prov.) V.* REDIMIR CENSOS.

lujación [loo-hah-the-on'], *f. V.* LUXACIÓN.

lujar [loo-har'], *va. (Cuba)* 1. To rub. *V.* LUDIR. 2. To smooth the sole of a shoe. 3. *(Med.)* To luxate, to dislocate.

lujo [loo'-ho], *m.* Profuseness, extravagance or excess in pomp, dresses, fare, etc.; superfluity, luxury, finery. **Vivir en el lujo**, to live in luxury.

lujoso, sa [loo-ho'-so, sah], *a.* Showy (vestidos), sumptuous, luxurious: profuse, lavish.

lujuria [loo-hoo'-re-ah], *f.* 1. Lechery, lubricity, lust, carnal pleasure. 2. Excess, profuseness, lavishness.

lujuriante [loo-hoo-re-ahn'-tay], *pa.* Lusting. *-a.* Luxuriant, exuberant.

lujuriar [loo-hoo-re-ar'], *vn.* 1. To be lecherous or libidinous, to lust. 2. To couple together: speaking of animals.

lujuriosamente [loo-hoo-re-o'-sah-men-tay], *adv.* Lecherously, lustfully, voluptuously.

lujurioso, sa [loo-hoo-re-o'-so sah], *a.* Lecherous, lustful, voluptuous, lewd, libidinous.

lumbago [loom-bah'-go], *m. (Med.)* Lumbago, lumbar rheumatism.

lumbar [loom-bar'], *a.* Lumbar, lumbary.

lumbrada, lumbrarada [loom-brah'-dah, loom-brah-rah'-dah], *f.* A great fire, a fierce conflagration.

lumbre [loom'-bray], *f.* 1. Fire (fuego), anything burning. 2. Spark from a flint. 3. Splendor, brigtness (brillo); lucidity, clearness. 4. Light (para cigarrillo). **Cerca de la lumbre**, near the fire, *-pl.* 1. Tinderbox, with the materials for striking fire. 2. Hammer, that part of a gun-lock which strikes fire from the flint. 3. Forepart of horse-shoes.

lumbrera [loom-bray'-rah], *f.* 1. Luminary, anybody which emits light. 2. Skylight. 3. Genius, whizz kid (persona). 4. *(Mex. Taur. Teat.)* Box.

luminar [loo-me-nar'], *m.* 1. Luminary, anybody which emits light. 2. Among painters, light, as opposed to shade. 3. Luminary, a man eminent in science.

luminaria [loo-me-nah'-re-ah], *f.* 1. Illumination, festival lights. 2. Lamp which is kept burning in Roman Catholic churches before the sacrament. *-pl.* Money paid for illuminations.

lumínico, ca [loo-mee'-ne-co, cah], *a. V.* LUMINOSO. *-m.* Light.

luminosamente [loo-me-no'-sah-men-tay], *adv.* Luminously.

luminosidad [loo-me-no-se-dahd'], *f.* 1. Brightness (brillantez), luminosity. 2. *(Fig.)* Brightness, brilliance.

luminoso, sa [loo-me-no'-so, sah], *a.* Luminous, shining, bright (brillante).

luna [loo'-nah], *f.* 1. The moon. 2. Glass plate for mirrors (espejo), glass for optical instruments. 3. Effect of the moon upon lunatic people. 4. **Media luna**, *(Mil.)* half-moon, a ravelin built before the angle or curtain of a bastion. 5. *(Prov.)* Open, uncovered court or hall. **Luna llena or menguante**, full or waning moon. **Estar en la luna**, to have one's head in the clouds.

lunación [loo-nah-the-on'], *f.* Lunation, the period of revolution of the moon.

lunado, da [loo-nah'-do, dah], *a.* Lunated, formed like a half-moon.

lunanco, ca [loo-nahn'-co, cah], *a.* Applied to animals with one quarter higher than another.

lunar [loo-nar'], *m.* 1. Mole, a natural spot or discoloration of the body. **Lunar postizo**, patch which ladies wear on the face as an ornament. 2. Note or stain of infamy (moral). *-a.* Lunar, lunary.

lunaria [loo-nah'-re-ah], *f. (Bot.)* Moonwort, honesty.

lunario [loo-nah'-re-o], *m. V.* CALENDARIO.

lunático, ca [loo-nah're-co, cah], *a.* Lunatic, moonstruck, mad.

lunecilla [loo-nay-theel'-lyah], *f.* Crescent worn by women.

lunes [loo'-nes], *m.* Monday. **No ocurre cada lunes y cada martes**, it doesn't happen every day of the week.

luneta [loo-nay'-tah], *f.* 1. The two or three rows of cushioned seats in the pit of a play-house, immediately behind the orchestra. 2. The spot where olives are pressed. 3. A saddler's knife, leather knife. 4. *(Ant.)* A spectacle lens (gafas). 5. Ornament in the shape of a half moon which women used to wear on the head and children on the shoes. 6. *(Arch.) V.* BOCATEJA and LUNETO.

luneto [loo-nay'-to], *m.* A skylight, of half-moon shape, in an arch, lunette.

lúnula [loo'-noo-lah], *f.* 1. A crescent, a figure formed by two arcs of a circle. 2. *(Opt.)* Meniscus, a lens or glass convex on one side and concave on the other.

lupa [loo'-pah], *f.* Magnifying glass.

lupanar [loo-pah-nar'], *m.* Brothel, a bawdy-house.

lupanario, ia [loo-pah-nah'-re-o, ah], *a.* Belonging to a brothel.

lupia [loo'-pe-ah], *f.* 1. Encysted tumor. 2. Wen (lobanillo). 3. *(And.)* Small amount of money.

lupino [loo-pee'-no], *m. (Bot.)* Lupine or lupin. *V.* ALTRAMUZ.

lupulina [loo-poo-lee'-nah], *f.* Lupulin the active principle of hops.

lúpulo [loo'-poo-lo], *m. (Bot.)* Hops.

luquete [loo-kay'-tay], *m.* 1. Zest, a slice of orange with the peel thrown into wine. 2. Match, a card, rope, or small chip dipped in melted sulphur. 3. Grease spot (mancha). 4. Bald patch (calva).

lusitano, na [loo-se-tah'-no, nah], *a.* Lusitanian, Portuguese.

lustración [loos-trah-the-on'], *f.* Lustration, purification by water.

lustrador [loos-trah-dor'], *m.* 1. Hot-press, mangler, a machine which gives a gloss to clothes. 2. Hot-presser. 3. Mirror-polisher.

lustral [loos-trahl'], *a.* Lustral: applied to water used in purifications.

lustramiento [loos-trah-me-en'-to], *m.* Action of decorating or honoring someone. *(Acad.)*

lustrar [loos-trar'], *va.* 1. To expiate, to purify. 2. To illustrate, to make brilliant. 3. To mangle, to fine. 4. To wander.

lustre [loos'-tray], *m.* 1. Gloss, luster, fineness. 2. Clearness, nobleness, splendor, glory. 3. Shoe-polish (sustancia).

lústrico, ca [loos'-tre-co, cah], *a. (Poet.)* Belonging to a lustrum, or to lustration.

lustro [loos'-tro], *m.* 1. Lustrum, the space of five years. 2. Lamp or chandelier for illumination.

lustrosamente [loos-tro'-sah-men-tay], *adv.* Brilliantly, splendidly, glitteringly.

lustroso, sa [loos-tro'-so, sah], *a.* Bright, brilliant, lustrous, shining, glossy, golden.

luten [loo'-ten], *m.* (*Chem.*) Lute, a kind of paste to make vessels airtight.

lúteo, tea [loo'-tay-o, ah], *a.* Miry, muddy.

luteranismo [loo-tay-rah-nees'-mo], *m.* Lutheranism.

luterano, na [loo-tay-rah'-no, nah], *a. & m. & f.* Lutheran.

luto [loo'-to], *m.* 1. Mourning, the dress of sorrow (ropa). **Medio luto**, half mourning. 2. Mourning, sorrow, condolement, grief (duelo).

lutria [loo'-tre-ah], *f. V.* NUTRIA.

luxación [looc-sah-the-on'], *f.* Luxation, dislocation of a joint.

luz [looth], *f.* 1. Light. 2. Daylight (de día). 3. Guiding light, inspiration. **Dar a luz**, 1. To give birth. 2. To bring out, to publish. **Luz blanca para marcha atrás**, backup light. **Luz intermitente**, 1. Directional signal. 2. Blinker. **Luz negra**, black light. **Luz roja**, stop light. **Luz trasera**, tail-light. **Salir a luz**, a) to come out, to be published. b) to come to light. **Ver la luz**, to see the light of day. **Luces**, 1. Windows, openings. 2. Cultural attainments. **A todas luces**, obviously. **Luces de carretera**, high beams, brights. **Luces de cruce**, low beams, dims. **Luces de población**, parking lights. **Luces de posición**, (*Aer.*) navigation lights. **Traje de luces**, bullfighter's costume. **Como la luz del día**, as clear as daylight. **Quitar la luz a uno**, to stand in somebody's light. **A la luz de**, in the light of. **Dar luz verde a un proyecto**, to give a plan the go ahead. **Luces de aterrizaje**, landing lights. **Luces de tráfico**, traffic lights.

Luzbel [looth-bel'], *m.* Lucifer, Satan.

M

m [ay'-may], *f.*, It has in the Spanish language the same sound as in English. *M* is never doubled in Spanish. M. 1. Sign for one thousand. 2. Abbr. for midday, noon. 3. Abbr. for misce, mix. 4. Abbr. for majesty, *merced* (grace), *metro*, (meter).

mabre [mah'-bray], *f.* Marver, a plate of iron used to shape a ball of glass upon.

maca [mah'-cah], *f.* 1. Bruise in fruit (fruta). 2. Spot, Stain. 3. Deceit, fraud, trick (defecto).

macabro, bra [mah-cah'-bro, brah], *a,* Macabre, gruesome.

macaco, ca [mah-cah'-co, cah], *m & f.* 1. Macaque, or macaco, a flat-headed monkey. 2. (*Mex.*) Hobgoblin, bogie for frightening children. *-a.* 1. Ugly (feo), ill-shaped, squat. 2. (*CAm. Carib.*) Silly (tonto). 3. (*Cono Sur*) Brazilian. 3. (*Carib.*) Big shot (persona importante). 4. (*Mex.*) Bogey.

macádam [mah-cah'-dam], *m.* Macadam, macadam paving.

macadamizar [mah-cah-dah-me-thar'], *va.* To macadamize (carretera).

macagua [mah-cah'-goo-ah], *f.* An American bird of prey whose hoarse cry resembles a laugh.

macaisa [mah-cah'-e-sah], *f.* (*Bot.*) A tree of the Philippine Islands, of very light wood.

macana [mah-cah'-nah], *f* 1. A wooden weapon in use among the ancient Indians of Mexico and Peru, generally edged with sharp flint. 2. (*And. Cono Sur*) Stupid comment (disparate). 3. (*Cono Sur*) Bad job (chapuza).

macaundo, da [mah-cah-noo'-do, dah], *a.* (*Sp. Am. coll.*) 1. Extraordinary, terrific. 2. Glaring, conspicuous.

macareno, na [mah-cah-ray'-no nah], *a.* (*coll.*) Applied to a bragging, boasting person.

macarra [mah-cahr'-rah], *m.* Thug (gamberro). Queer (marica); pimp; lout (bruto).

macarrón [mah-car-rone'], *m.* 1. Macaroni, a kind of paste. 2. (*Naut.*) Awning stanchions. *V.* CANDELEROS.

macarrónico, ca [mah-car-ro'-ne-co, cah], *a.* Macaronic.

macarronismo [mah-car-ro-nees'-mo], *m.* The macaronic style of poetry.

macarse [mah-car'-say], *vr.* To rot, to be spoiled in consequence of a bruise or hurt (macear).

macayo [mah-cah'-yo], *m.* (*Centr. Amer.*) Macaw.

maceador [mah-thay-ah-dor'], *m.* Beater, hammerer.

macear [mah-thay-ar'], *va.* To peat of drive with a mallet, to knock, to hammer down. *-vn.* To repeat frequently the same demand.

macedonia [mah-thay-do'-ne-ah], *f.* **Macedonia de frutas**, fruit salad.

maceración [mah-thay-rah-the-on'], *f.* 1. Maceration, steeping, infusion. 2. Mortification, maceration, corporeal severity.

macerar [mah-thay-rar'], *va.* 1. To macerate, to soften by steeping or by blows. 2. To mortify, to macerate, to harass with corporeal hardships. 3. (*Chem*). To bruise plants, to harass extract their juice.

macero [mah-thay'-ro], *m.* Mace-bearer, mace, macer.

maceta [mah-thay'-tah], *f.* 1. Flower-pot (tiesto). 2. Handle of a stick used at Spanish truck-tables. 3. Handle of many kinds of tools. 4. Haunch of mutton. 5. Two-clawed hammer (martillo). 6. (*Naut.*) Maul, mallet. **Maceta de ajustar.** A driving mallet. **Macetas**, mallets or beetles, with which ropeends are beaten to make oakum. *-a.* 1. (*And. Cono Sur*) Slow, thick. 2. (*Carib.*) Miserly (tacaño).

macetón [mah-thay-tone'], *m. aug.* of MACETA.

machaca [mah-chah'-cah], *com.* (*coll.*) A bore, tiresome person.

machacadera [mah-chah-cah-day'-rah], *f.* Instrument for pounding or breaking.

machacador, ra [mah-chah-cah-dor', rah], *m. & f.* Pounder, beetler, bruiser.

machacar [mah-chah-car'], *va.* To pound or break anything into small pieces, to crush (hacer polvo), to contuse. *-vn.* To importune, to harass, to molest, to go on (insistir). **Machacar en hierro frío**, to hammer cold iron; phrase indicating inutility. (*coll*) To brood upon a thing.

machacón, na [mah-chah-cone', nah], *a.* Heavy, monotonous (monótono), importunate, tiresome (pesado). **Con insistencia machacona**, with wearisome insistence.

machada [mah-chah'-dah], *f.* 1. Flock of he-goats. 2. (*coll.*) *V.* NECEDAD.

machado [mah-chah'-do], *m* A hatchet.—**Machado, da**, *PP.* of MACHAR.

machaque [mah-chah'-kay], *m.* The act of pounding or breaking.

machaquería [mah-chah-kay-ree'-ah], *f.* (*coll.*) Importunity, insistence.

machar [mah-char'], *va.* To pound. *V.* MACHACAR. **A macha martillo**, firmly, strongly; in a solid manner. *-vr.* (*Cono Sur*) To get drunk.

machear [mah-chay-ar'], *vn.* To beget more males than females.

machetazo [mah-chay-tah'-tho], *m.* 1. Blow or stroke with a cutlass. 2. (*LAm.*) Large *machete* (instrumento).

machete [mah-chay'-tay], *m.* Cutlass chopping-knife, caneknife.

machetear [mah-chay-tay-ar'], *va.* 1. To wound or cut with a machete. 2. (*Naut.*) To make slow headway against a heavy sea. *-vn.* 1. (*And. Mex.*) To dig on's heels in (obstinarse). 2. (*Mex.*) To hammer away (trabajar).

machetero [mah-chay-tay'-ro], *m.* 1. One who clears away bushes with a cutlass. 2. (*Mex.*) Porter (cargador). 3. (*Carib.*) Revolutionary. 4. (*Mex. Univ.*) Plodder.

machial [mah-che-ahl'], *m.* A wooded hill availed of for pasturing goats.

machiega [mah-che-ay'-gah], *a. V.* ABEJA MACHIEGA.

machihembrar [mah-che-em-brar'], *va.* To join or dovetail pieces of wood in a box with grooves.

machina [mah-chee'-nath], *f.* 1. Sheers, a machine for masting or unmasting a vessel. 2. A cutting compass for cutting out the brims of hats.

machismo [mah-chees'-mo], *m.* Manliness, male chauvinism, male pride (orgullo), virility (virilidad).

machista [mah-chees'-tah], *a.* 1. Full of machismo, full of male pride, very masculine.

macho [mah'-cho], *m.* 1. A male animal, in particular, a hemule or a he-goat. 2. A masculine plant. 3. A piece of some instrument which enters into another. 4. Hook to catch hold in an eye. 5. Screwpin. 6. An ignorant fellow (persona). 7. *(And.)* Splendid, terrific (fantástico). 8. *(CAm.)* U.S. marine (marino). **Macho cabrío**, he-goat. **Es muy macho**, he's very tough. 9. Pillar of masonary support a building. 10. Sledge hammer. 11. Block on which a smith's anvil is fixed. 12. A square anvil.

macho [mah'-cho], *a.* Masculine, vigorous, robust; male.

machón [mah-chone'], *m. (Arch.)* Buttress, an arched pillar to support a wall or building.

machorra [mah-chor'-rah], *f.* 1. A barren ewe. 2. A barren woman.

machota, *f.* **machute**, *m.* [mah-cho'-tah, mah-choo'-tay], 1. A kind of beetle or mallet. 2. Mannish woman (mujer). 3. *(And. Carib.)* Carelessly.

machote [mah-cho'-tay], 1. Tough guy, he-man. 2. *(LAm.)* Rough draft (borrador); model (modelo); pattern (pauta). 3. *(Mex.)* Blank form.

machucadura [mah-choo-cah-doo'-rah], *f.* The act of pounding or bruising.

machucamiento [mah-choo-cah-me-en'-to], *m. V.* MACHUCADURA.

machucar [mah-choo-car'], *va.* To pound (hacer polvo), to bruise. *V.* MACHACAR.

machucho, cha [mah-choo'-cho, chah], *a.* 1. Mature, ripe of age and understanding; judicious (juicioso). 2. *(And. Mex.)* Cunning (taimado), sly, shrewd.

machuelo [mah-choo-ay'-lo], *m.* 1. *(dim.)* A small he-mule. 2. Heart of an onion.

macicez [mah-the-theth'], *f. (Prov.)* Solidity, compactness.

macilento, ta [mah-the-len'-to, ta], *a.* Lean, extenuated; withered, decayed.

macis [mah'-this], *f.* Mace, a kind of spice.

macizamente [mah-the-tha'-men-tay], *adv.* In a firm and solid manner.

macizar [mah-the-thar'], *va.* 1. To close an opening or passage, to form into a compact body. 2. To support a proposition by argument.

macizo, za [mah-thee'-ho, thah], *a.* 1. Compact, close, solid (neumático, oro, puerta), massive (grande) certain. **De roble macizo**, of solid oak.

macizo [mah-thee'-tho], *m.* 1. Massiveness, bulk. 2. *(Geog.)* Massif. 3. *(Hort.)* Bed, plot. 4. *(Aut.)* Solid tire. 5. *(Arch.)* Stretch, section.

macla [mah'-clah], *f.* 1. *(Bot.)* Water-caltrops. 2. Wooden instrument to scotch flax or hemp.

macle [mah'-clay], *m.(Her.)* Mascle, a perforated lozenge.

macoca [mah-co'-cah], *f.* A large sort or early figs.

macolla [mah-col'-lyah], *f.* Bunch of flowers, etc., growing on one stalk.

macona, [mah-co'-nah], *f (Prov.)* Basket without handles.

macrocéfalo, la [mah-cro-thay-fah'-lo, lah], *a.* Macrocephalous, of a large head.

macrocomo, ma [mah-cro-co'-mo, mah], *a. (Biol.)* Long-haired.

macrocosmo [mah-cro-cos'-mo], *m.* Macrocosm, the whole world, or visible system in opposition to the microcosm, or little world of man.

macrogloso, sa [mah-cro-glo'-so, sah], *a.* Macroglossate. having a long tongue.

macruros [mah-croo'-rose], *m. pl.* Macrura, a division of the decapods, including lobsters and shrimps.

macuache [mah-coo-ah'-chay], *m.* 1. An impoverished Mexican Indian. 2. *(Fig.)* A brute, an animal.

macuba [mah-coo'-bah], *f.* Tobacco from the north of Martinique. *(m. in America).*

macuca [mah-coo'-cah], *f. (Bot.)* Kind of wild pear or pear-tree.

mácula [mah'-coo-lah], *f.* 1. Stain, spot, blemish, macula. 2. Trick, fraud (trampa).

macular [mah-coo-lar'], *va.* To mackle or make a double impression in printing, with types or copper plates.

maculatura [mah-coo-lah-too'-rah], *f. (Print.)* Sheet which has received a double impression in printing.

macuteno [mah-coo-tay'-no], *m. (Mex.)* An infamous man, a petty thief.

macuto [mah-coo'-to], *m.* 1. Knapsack (mochila); satchel. 2. *(Carib.)* Begging basket.

madama [mah-dah'-mah], *f.* Madam. *V.* SEÑORA.

medeja [mah-day'-hah], *f.* 1. Hank or skein of thread (lana), worsted, silk, or cotton. 2. Lock of hair. 3. A weak, lazy person. **Se está enredando la madeja**, the affair is getting complicated.

madejeta, ica, illa, ita [mah-day-hay'-tah], *f. dim.* A small skein.

madera [mah-day'-rah], *f.* 1. Wood, timber, lumber. **Madera de construcción**, timber for building. **Madera dura**, hard wood. **Madera laminada**, plywood. 2. Hoof of a horse or other beast. 3. Said of green or unripe fruit. 4. *(Fig.)* Nature, temperament; aptitude. **Tiene buena madera**, there's a lot in him. **Tiene madera de futbolista**, he'll make a soccer player. *-m.* Madeira wine.

maderable [mah-day-rah'-blay], *a.* Bearing timber, timber producing.

maderada [mah-day-rah'-dah], *f.* Raft, a wooden frame or float.

maderaje, maderamen [mah-day-rah'-hay, mah-day-rah'-men], *m.* The timber necessary for a building; a house in frame.

maderamen [mah-day-rah'-men], *m.* Lumber for construction.

madera terciada [mah-day'-rah-ter-the-ah'-dah], *f.* Plywood.

madería [mah-day-ray-ree'-ah], *f.* Timberyard.

maderero [mah-day-ray'-ro], *m.* 1. Timber merchant, lumber dealer. 2. Carpenter.

maderero, ra [mah-day-ray'-ro, rah], *a.* Pertaining to the lumber industry. **Industria maderera**, lumber industry.

maderista [mah-day-rees'-tah], *m. (Prov.)* Conductor of a raft or float.

madero [mah-day'-ro], *m.* 1. Beam (viga), any large piece of timber: sometimes applied to any piece of timber, log (tronco). **Maderos de cuenta**, the main timbers of a vessel. 2. Oaf (idiota). 3. *(Esp.)* cop (policía).

madia [mah'-de-ah], *f.* A plant of Chili, from the seed of which an edible oil is extracted.

madona [mah-do'-nah], *f.* Madonna.

madraza [mah-drah'-thah], *f. aug.* A very fond mother.

madrastra [mah-drahs'-trah], *f.* 1. Stepmother. 2. *(Met.)* Anything disagreeable.

madre [mah'-dray], *f.* 1. A mother. 2. Mother superior (convento). 3. Expectant mother (embarazada). 4. Mother, a title given to religious women 5. Matron (hospital). 6. Basis, foundation, origin. 7. Matrix womb, 8. Bed of a river (de río). 9. Sewer sink. 10. Mother, a substance concreted in liquors, or the less or scum concreted. 11. Mother, a familiar term of address to an old woman, 12. The principal irrigating ditch whence small branches issue. **Madre de leche**, a wet-nurse. **Mal de madre**, 1. Mother or hysterical passion. 2. The state of children spoiled by their mother. **Madre política**, mother-in-law. **Su señora madre**, your mother. **Sin madre** motherless. **Ciento y la madre**, hundreds of people. *-a.* 1. *(Lit.)* Mother. **Buque**

madre, mother ship. **Lengua madre**, parent language. 2. **La cuestión madre**, the chief problem. 3. *(LAm.)* Tremendous, terrific.

madrear [mah-dray-ar'], *va.* To construct sewers.

madrecilla [mah-dray-theel'-lyah], *f.* 1. Ovary of birds. 2. *(dim.)* V. MADRECITA.

madrecita [mah-dray-thee'-tah], *m. dim.* Of MADRE. Used as an endearing expression instead of mother.

madreclavo [mah-dray-clah'-vo], *m.* Clove, a spice which has remained on the tree two years.

madreperla [mah-dray-perr'-lah], *f.* Mother-of-pearl; pearloyster.

madrépora [mah-dray'-po-rah], *f.* Madrepore, white coral.

madrero, ra [mah-dray'-ro, rah], *a. (Prov. Coll.)* Fondling, caressing a mother.

madreselva [mah-dray-sel'-vah], *f. (Bot.)* Honeysuckle.

madrigada [mah-dre-gah'-dah], *a.* Applied formerly to a woman twice married.

madrigado, da [mah-dre-gah'-do, dah], *a.* 1. Practical, experienced. 2. Applied to a bull that has been a sire.

madrigal [mah-dre-gahl'], *m.* Madrigal, a light airy song.

madrigaleja, madrigalete [mah-dre-gah-lay'-hah, mah-dre-gah-lay'-tay], *m. dim.* A short madrigal.

madriguera [mah-dre-gay'-rah], *f.* 1 Burrow, the holes made in the ground by rabbits or conies. 2. Den, lurking-place.

madrileño, ña [mah-dre-lay'-nyo, nyah], *a.* Native of or belonging to Madrid.

madrilla [mah-dreel-lyay'-rah], *f. (Prov.)* A small river fish. V. BOGA.

madrillera [mah-dreel-lyay'-rah], *f. (Prov.)* Instrument for catching small fish.

madrina [mah-dree'-nah], *f.* 1. A godmother (bautizo). 2. Bridesmaid. 3. Protectress. 4. Prop, stanchion. 5. Straps or cords which yoke two horses. 6. *(Mex.)* Police informer.

madriz [mah-dreeth'], *f.* Place where quails nest or seaurchins grow.

madrona [mah-dro'-nah], *f.* 1. Mother overfond of her children, who spoils them by excessive tenderness. 2. *(Bot.)* Clandestine toothwort.

madroncillo [mah-dron-theel'-lyo], *m.* Strawberry.

madroñal [mah-dron-yahl'], *m.* A grove of madrone-trees.

madroñero, ra [mah-dron-nyay'-ro, rah], *m. & f.* One who sells silk tassels; also a seller of madrones. *-f.* V. MADROÑAL.*-m. (Bot.)* Madrone-tree.

madroño [mah-dro'-nyo], *m.* 1. The madrone, or strawberry-tree. 2. Fruit of the strawberry-tree. 3. Silk tassel.

madrugada [mah-droo-gah'-dah], *f.* 1. Dawn, the first appearance of light. 2. The act of rising early in the morning.

De madrugada, at break of day. **A las 4 de la madrugada**, at 4 0' clock in the morning.

madrugador, ra [mah-droo-gah-dor, rah], *m & f.* Early riser.

madrugar [mah-droo-gar'], *vn.* 1. To rise early (levantarse). 2. To contrive, to premeditate. 3. To anticipate, to get there first. *-va.* **Madrugar a uno**, to forestall somebody (adelantarse a).

madrugón [mah-droo-gone'], *m.* 1. Act of rising early in the morning. 2. Early riser.

maduración [mah-doo-rah-the-on'], *f.* Ripeness, maturity.

maduradero [mah-doo-rah-day'-ro], *m.* Place for ripening fruits.

madurador, ra [mah-doo-rah-dor', rah], *a.* That which matures or ripens.

maduramente [mash-doo'-rah-men-tay'], *adv.* Maturely, prudently, considerately.

madurante [mah-doo-rahn'-tay], *va.* Maturing, ripening.

madurar [mah-doo-rar'], *va.* To ripen (frutos), to mature (plan), to mellow. *(Med.)* To maturate. *-vn.* 1. To ripen, to grow ripe. 2. To attain the age of maturity. *-vr.* To ripen, to grow ripe.

madurativo, va [mah-doo-rah-tee'-vo, vah], *a.* Maturative.

madurativo [mah-doo-rah-tee'-vo], *m.* 1. Anything that matures. 2. Means employed to induce a person to yield to a request.

madurez [mah-doo-reth'], *f.* 1. Maturity, mellowness, ripeness. 2. Prudence, wisdom.

madurillo, IIa [mah-doo-reel'-lyo', yah], *a.* Beginning to ripen.

maduro, ra [mah-doo'-ro, rah], *a.* 1. Ripe, mature, perfect, mellow, full-grown. 2. Prudent, judicious. **Poco maduro**, unripe. **De edad madura**, of mature years. **La cosa está madura para la reforma**, the business is ripe for reform.

maelstrom [mah'-els-trom], *m.* Maelstrom, Norwegian whirlpool.

maesa [mah-ay'-sah], *f.* V. ABEJA MAESTRA.

maese [mah-ay'-say], *m.* V. MAESTRO. **Maestro coral**, a kind of game played with balls.

maesil [mah-ay-seel'], *m.* V. MAESTRIL.

maesillas [mah-ay-seel'-lyas], *f. pl.* Cords which serve in making trimmings to raise or lower the skeins.

maestra [mah-es'-trah], *f.* 1. Mistress, school-mistress, teacher. 2. Master's wife in all trades and professions. 3. Queen bee. 4. Whatever instructs. **La historia es maestra de la vida**, history is the instructress of life. 5. Among masons, a guide line for evening the surface. **Maestra de escuela**, school-teacher.

maestral [mah-es-trahl'], *a.* 1. Suiting or relating to a grandmaster of a military order, or to his dignity or jurisdiction. 2. Northwest: applied to the wind. **Mesa maestral**, the sheepwalk board. *-m.* Cell of the queen-bee.

maestralizar [mah-es-trah-le-thar'], *vn. (Naut.)* To vary or decline to west or northwest: applied to the compass needle (in the Mediterranean).

maestrante [mah-es-trahn'-tay], *m.* Any of the members of one of the societies called *maestranzas*.

maestranza [mah-es-trahn'-thah], *f.* 1. Society of noblemen in Spain for practicing equestrian exercises. 2. All the workmen of a navy-yard. 3. Workshop of naval furniture. 4. Factory or workshops for making weapons of war. 5. Spot which the workshops occupy; navy-yard, arsenal.

maestrazgo [mah-es-trath'-go], *m.* Dignity or jurisdiction of a grand-master of amilitary order.

maestrazo [mah-es-trah'-tho], *m. aug.* A great master. *-a.* Masterly, skilled, highly intelligent.

maestre [mah-es'-tray], *m.* 1. Grand-master of a military order: also called *gran maestro*. 2. *(Naut.)* Mate of a merchant-ship.

maestrear [mah-es-tray-ar'], *vn. (coll.)* To domineer, to act the master. *-va.* 1. To lop vines. 2. *(Prov.)* To adulterate, to falsify. 3. To level the surface of a wall. 4. To direct (dirigir).

maestresala [mah-es-tray-sah'-lah], *m.* The chief waiter, headwaiter, maître d'hôtel.

maestrescuela [mah-es-tres-coo-ay'-lah], *m.* 1. Cathedral dignitary who teaches divinity. 2. Chancellor in some universities.

maestría [mah-es-tree'-ah], *f.* 1. Mastery (dominio), mastership, complete knowledge, skill (habilidad). **Lo hizo con maestría**, he did it very skillfully. 2. In regular orders, the dignity or degree of a master.

maestril [mah-es-treel'], *m.* Cell in which the queen bee is bred; a queen-cell.

maestrillo [mah-es-treel'-lyo], *m. dim.* A little master. **Cada maestrillo tiene su librillo**, *(Prov.)* every one has his hobby.

maestro [mah-es'-tro], *m.* 1. Master, teacher (profesor), professor. 2. Master (aposición), a man eminently skillful in practice or science. 3. A title of respect in monastic orders. 4. Master, a title of dignity in some universities. 5. The main-mast of a vessel. 6. **Maestro de capilla**, a choirmaster, one who composes and directs church music. **Maestro de obras**, a contractor, or builder superintendent of construction. **Maestro de armas** or **de esgrima**, fencing master. **Maestro de maquillaje**, make-up expert.

maestro, tra [mah-es'-tro, trah], *a.* Masterly (genial), principal, first, main. **Llave maestra**, skeleton key. **Obra maestra**, masterpiece.

maestro de ceremonias [mah-es'-tro day thay-ray-mo'-ne-ahs], *m.* Master of ceremonies.

mafia [mah'-fe-ah], *f.* Mafia, criminal gang.

mafioso [mah-fe-o'-so], *m.* **Mafioso**, member of the Mafia.

magallánico, ca [mah-gah-lyah'-ne-co, cah], *a.* Magellanic, relating to the Straits of Magellan.

maganto, ta [mah-gahn'-to, tah], *a.* Spiritless, dull, faint, languid.

magaña [mah-gah'-nyah], *f.* 1. Honeycomb, a flaw in the bore of a gun. 2 *(coll.)* Cunning artifice, strategem.

magarzuela [mah-gar-thoo-ay'-lah], *f.* Stinking chamomile.

Magdalena [mag-dah-lay'-nah], *f.* 1. A paste composed of sugar, lemon-juice flour, eggs, almonds, and other ingredients. 2. Magdalen, a repentant woman.

magdaleón [mag-dah-layon'], *m.* Sticks of plaster, made up in small cylindrical rolls for use.

magia [mah'-he-ah], *f.* 1. Magic, the art of producing effects by the secret agency of natural powers: in this sense it is also called **magia blanca** or **magia natural.** 2. Magic, the pretended science of putting in action the power of spirits: in this sense it is generally called **magia negra.**

magiar, or **magyar** [mah-he-ar'], *a. & n.* 1. Magyar, of the race predominant in Hungary and Transylvania. 2. Their language.

mágicamente [mah'-he-cah-men-tay], *adv.* Magically.

mágico, ca [mah'-he-co, cah], *a.* Magic, magical, necromantic. *-m. & f.* Magician, one who professes magic.

magín [mah-heen'], *m. (coll.)* Fancy, idea. *V.* IMAGINACIÓN. **Se le ha metido en el magín**, he has gotten it into his head.

magisterial [mah-his-tay-re-al'], *a.* Magisterial.

magisterio [mah-his-tay'-re-o], *m.* 1. Magistery, rule of a master. 2. Mastership, the title and rank of a master in universities (enseñanza). 3. Teaching profession (profesión), body of teachers in a nation, city, etc. (personas). 4. *(fig.)* Affected gravity.

magistrado, da [mah-his-trah'-do], *m & f.* 1. A magistrate. 2. Magistracy, the office or dignity of a magistrate. 3. Court, tribunal.

magistral [mah-his-trahl'], *a.* 1. Magisterial, masterly (genial), oracular. 2. Applied to a prebend in Catholic cathedrals, called **magistral**, and to the person who enjoys it. 3. *(Mod.)* Magistral or magistralia: applied to such medicines as are extemporaneous or in common use. *-f.* Title of a prebendary, in the Roman Catholic church, whose functions consist in teaching and preaching.

magistralmente [mah-hes-trahl'-men-tay], *adv.* Magisterially, masterly.

magistratura [mah-his-trah-too'-rah], *f.* Magistracy, judicature, judgeship.

magnánimamente [mag-nah'-ne-mah-men'-tay], *adv.* Magnanimously, bravely; generously.

magnanimidad [mag-nah-ne-me-dahd'], *f.* Magnanimity, fortitude, greatness.

magnánimo, ma [mag-nah'-ne-mo, mah], *a.* Magnanimous, heroic, generous; honorable.

magnate [mag-nah'-tay], *m.* Magnate, a person of rank, opulence, etc. **Los magnates de la industria**, the top people in industry.

magnesia [mag-nay'-se-ah], *f.* Magnesia, a medicinal powder: magnesium oxide.

magnesiano, na [mag-nay-se-ah'-no, nah], *a.* Magnesian, containing magnesia.

magnesio [mag-nay'-se-o], *m.* Magnesium, a light, grayish-white metal.

magnesita [mag-nay-see'-tah], *f.* Magnesite.

magnéticamente [mag-nay'-te-cah-le], *adv.* Magnetically.

magnético, ca [mag-nay'-te-co, cah], *a.* Magnetic, magnetical, attractive.

magnetismo [mag-nay-tees'-mo], *m.* Magnetism.

magnetizable [mag-nay-te-thah'-blay], *a.* Magnetizable.

magnetización [mag-nay-te-thah-the-on'], *f.* Magnetizing.

magnetizar [mag-nay-te-thar'], *va.* To magnetize.

magneto [mag-nay'-to], *m.* Magneto.

magnetoeléctrico, ca [mag-nay-to-ay-lec'-tre-co, cah], *a.* Magnetoelectric.

magnetofónico, ca [mag-nay-to-fo'-ne-co, cah], *a.* Tape recording.

magnetófono, magnetofón [mag-nay-to'-fo-no, mag-nay-to-fon'], *m.* Tape recorder.

magnetohidrodinámica [mag-nay-to-e-dro-de-nah'-me-cah], *f.* Magneto-hydrodynamics.

magnetómetro [mag-nay-to'-may-tro], *m.* Magnetometer.

magnetrón [mag-nay-tron'], *m.* Magnetron.

magníficamente [mag-nee'-fe-cah-men'-tay], *adv.* Magnificently, loftily, nobly.

magnificar [mag-ne-fe-car'], *va.* To magnify, to extol, to exalt.

magníficat [mag-nee'-fe-cat], *m.* The solid of the blessed Virgin.

magnificiencia [mag-ne-fe-then'-the-ah], *f.* Magnificence, grandeur, splendor (esplendor); gorgeousness.

magnífico, ca [mag-nee'-fe-co, cah], *a.* 1. Magnificent, splendid, grand, costly; gaudy. 2. A title of honor. **Es un muchacho magnífico**, he's a fine boy.

magnitud [mag-ne-tood'], *f.* 1. Magnitude, comparative bulk. 2. Magnitude, greatness, grandeur.

magno, na [mahg'-no, nah], *a.* Great: used as an epithet in the Spanish language; *e. g.* **Alejandro Magno**, Alexander the Great.

magnolia [mag-no'-le-ah], *f. (Bot.)* Magnolia.

mago, ga [mah'-go, gah], *m. & f.* 1. A title formerly given in the east to philosophers, kings, or wise men, called magi. 2. Magician, one skilled in magic; a necromancer.

magra [mah'-grah], *f.* Rasher, slice of pork (lonja), bacon, or ham with eggs.

magro, gra [mah'-gro, grah], *a.* 1. Meagre, lean (persona). 2. Lean (carne). 3. Poor, thin (tierra).

magrura [mah-groo'-rah], *f.* Leanness, thinness.

magua [mah'-goo-ah], *f. (Cuba)* Jest, joke.

magüeto, ta [mah-goo-ay'-to, tah], *m. & f.* Young steer or heifer.

maguey [mah-gay'-e], *m. (Bot.)* American agave, the century plant. Agave Americana.

maguillo [mah-geel'-lyo], *m.* Wild apple-tree, used as grafting-stock in southern Spain.

magujo [mah-goo'-ho], *m. (Naut.)* Ravehook, an instrument with a crooked point, which serves to pick old oakum out of the seams of the ship's sides and decks.

magulladura [mah-goo-llyah-doo'-rah], *f.* Bruise, contusion; an injury with something blunt and heavy.

magullamiento [mah-goo-lyah-me-en'-to], *m.* Act of bruising: contusion.

magullar [mah-gool-lyar'], *va.* To bruise (amoratar), to mangle, to hurt (dañar), to batter (golpear); *(And, Carib.)* To crumple.

maharrana [ma-ha-rrah'-nah], *f. (Prov. Andal.)* Fresh bacon.

mahometano [mah-o-may-tah'-no], *a, m & a.* Mohammedan.

mahometismo [mah-o-may-tees'-mo], *m.* Mohammedanism.

mahometizar [mah-o-may-te-thar'], *vn.* To profess Mohammedanism.

mahón [mah-on'], *m.* Nankeen or nankin, a kind of light cotton. (Name derived from Port Mahón, in the Balearic Islands.)

mahona [mah-o'-nah], *f.* Turkish transport vessel.

mahonesa [mah-oh-nay'-sah], *f.* Mayonnaise.

maicena [mah-e-thay'-nah], *f. (LAm.)* Cornflor, corn starch.

maído [mah-ee'-do], *m.* Mewing. *V.* MAULLIDO.

maimona [ma-he-mo'-nah], *f.* Beam of a horse-mill in which the spindle runs.

maimonetes [ma-he-mo-nay'-tes], *m. pl. (Naut.)* Pins, placed near the main and foremast, to which ropes are fastened; belaying-pins.

maitinante [ma-he-te-nahn'-tay], *m.* Priest whose duty is to celebrate or attend matins.

maitinario [ma-he-te-nah'-re-o], *m.* Book containing the matins.

maitines [ma-he-tee'-nes], *m. pl.* Matins, earliest of the canonical hours in the Catholic church.

maíz [mah-eeth'], *m. (Bot.)* Maize, Indian corn. **Maíz machacado**, hominy.

maizal [ma-he-thahl'], *m.* Indian cornfield.

maizena [mah-e-thay'-nah], *f. (LAm.) V.* MAICENA.

maja [mah'-hah], *f.* Pestle of a mortar.

majá [mah-hah'], *m.* A thick-bodied snake of Cuba.

majada [mah-hah'-dah], *m.* 1. Sheep-cot, sheep-fold (corral). 2. Dung of animals (estiércol). *(Acad.)* 3. *(Cono Sur)* Flock of sheep (de ovejas); herd of goats (de chivos).

majadal [mah-hah-dahl'], *m.* Land which has been used for a sheep-fold and has been improved by the manure of the flock.

majadear [mah-hah-day-ar'], *m.* To take shelter in the night (ovejas).

majadería [mah-hah-day-ree'-ah], *f.* 1. Absurd speech, nonsense; lumpishness.

majaderico, ca, majaderillo, lla [mah-hah-day-ree'-co, cah, eel'-lyo, lyah], *a. dim.* Rather dull, somewhat silly, gawkish.

majaderillo [mah-hah-day-reel'-lyo], *m.* Bobbin for lace.

majadero, ra [mah-hah-day'-ro, rah], *a.* Dull, foolish, doltish, silly, sottish.

majadero [mah-hah-day'-ro], *m.* 1. Gawk, a foolish, troublesome fellow, a bore. 2. Pestle, an instrument with which something is broken in a mortar.

majaderón [mah-hah-day-rone'], *m. aug.* A great gawk, a great fool, a great bore.

majador, ra [mah-hah-dor', rah], *f.* Pounder, bruiser.

majadura [mah-hah-doo'-rah], *f.* The act of pounding or bruising.

majagranzas [mah-hah-grahn'-thas], *m. (coll.)* A stupid brute: nickname for an ignorant, troublesome fellow.

majagua [mah-hah'-goo-ah], *f.* A tree of Cuba and parts of South America, from the bark of which the strongest and most durable cordage is made.

maja martillo (Á) *adv. exp.* Hammer and tongs; strongly.

majamiento [mah-hay-me-en'to], *m. V.* MAJADURA.

majano [mah-hah'-no], *m.* A small heap of stones serving as a landmark.

majar [mah-har'], *va.* 1. To pound (aplastar), to break in a mortar. 2. To importune, to vex, to molest.

majara [mah-hah'-rah], *a. V.* MAJARETA.

majarete [mah-hah-ray'-tay], *m. (Cuba)* Corn-pudding, a dessert made from grated maize, milk, and sugar.

majarrana [mah-har-rah'-nah], *f. (Prov.)* Fresh pork.

majenca [mah-hen'-cah], *f. (Prov.)* Digging of vines. (Murcia.)

majencar [mah-hen-car'], *va. (Prov.)* To dig the earth about vines, and clear them of weeds.

majencia [mah-hen'-the-ah], *f. (Prov. Coll.)* Spruceness or fineness in one's dress.

majestad [mah-hes-tahd'], *f.* 1. Majesty, dignity; grandeur of appearance, loftiness: gravity. 2. Majesty, royalty, the title of emperors, kings, empresses, and queens. 3. Power, kingship, sovereignty, elevation. **Vuestra majestad**, your Majesty.

majestuosamente [mah-hes-too-o-sah-men'-tay], *adv.* Majestically, kingly.

majestuosidad [mah-hes-too-o-se-dahd'], *f.* Majesty, dignity.

majestuoso, sa [mah-hes-too-o'-so, sah], *a.* 1. Majestic, majestical, august, grand. 2. Stately, pompous, lofty. 3. Grave, solemn.

majeza [mah-hay'-thah], *f. (coll.)* 1. Spruceness, fineness in dress (elegancia). 2. Good looks (atractivo).

majo, ja [mah'-ho, hah], *m. & f.* Boaster, bragger. -*a.* Gallant, gay, spruce, fine, nice (agradable), pretty (guapa), attractive, good-looking (guapo).

majojo [mah-ho'-ho], *m.* Dry, half-thrashed straw and trodden stubble used as fodder.

majolar [mah-ho-lar'], *va.* To put straps to the shoes, to tie them tight.

majorca [mah-hor'-cah], *f. V.* MAZORCA.

majuela [mah-hoo-ay'-lah], *f.* 1. Fruit of the white hawthorn. 2. Strap with which shoes are tied, shoe lacing.

majuelo [mah-hoo-ay'-lo], *m.* 1. Vine newly planted. 2. The white hawthorn.

mal [mahl], *m.* 1. Evil, harm, hurt (daño), injury, mischief. 2. Illness, disease, complaint. 3. Imperfection. 4. Fault, trespass. -*a.* Evil (malvado), bad, wrong (equivocado). **Mal hombre**, an evil man. **El problema está mal**, the problem is wrong. **Es un chico malo**, he's a bad boy. -*adv.* Badly (de mala manera), injuriously, ill, wrongly (equivocadamente), hardly (apenas). **Anda mal**, he is a bad walker. **Mal hecho**, 1. Badly done, ill finished. 2. Unjust, contrary to equity and justice. **Mal que bien**, with good or ill will. **Mal por mal**, for want of something better. **De mal en peor**, worse and worse. **Mal de ojo**, evil eye. **Mal de ojos**, eyesore. **Mal de ánimo**, heart-sore. **Mal que le pese**, in spite of him. **Lo hace muy mal**, he does it very badly. **Oigo mal**, I don't hear well. **Me entendió mal**, he misunderstood me. **Menos mal que…**, it's just as well that… **El bien y el mal**, good and evil. **Caer en el mal**, to fall into evil ways. **Estar a mal con uno**, to be on bad terms with somebody. **El mal ya está hecho**, the harm is done now.

mala [mah'-lah], *f.* 1. Deuce of spades. 2. *(Amer.)* A mailsteamer. 3. *(And.)* Bad luck. 4. Mailbag (correo).

malabar [mah-lah-bar'], *a.* **Juegos malabares**, juggling.

malabarismo [mah-lah-bah-rees'-mo], *m.* 1. Juggling, conjuring. 2. **Malabarismos**, *(fig.)* Juggling; balancing act.

malabarista [mah-lah-bah-rees'-tah], *m & f.* Juggler, conjurer.

malacate [mah-lah-cah'-tay], *m.* Hoisting machine in mines.

malacología [mah-lah-co-lo-hee'-ah], *f.* Malacology, the science which treats of mollusks, especially their soft parts.

malaconsejado, da [mal-ah-con-say-hah'-do, dah], *a.* Ill-advised.

malaconsejar [mal-ah-con-say-har'], *va.* 1. To advise badly. 2. To incline to evil.

malacostumbrado, da [mah-lah-cos-toom-brah'-do, dah], *a.* Having bad habits or customs (vicioso).

malacostumbrar [mal-ah-cos-toom-brahr'], *va.* **Malacostumbrar a uno**, to get somebody into bad habits.

malacuenda [mah-lah-coo-en'-dah], *f.* Coarse cloth made of tow.

malagaña [mah-lah-gah'-nyah], *f. (Prov.)* Pole set up with dry furze to catch bees swarming.

malagradecido, da [ma-lah-grah-day-thee'-do, dah], *a.* Unappreciative, ungrateful.

malagradecimiento [ma-lah-grah-day-the-me-en'-to], *m.* Ungratefulness, lack of appreciation.

malagueño, ña [mah-lah-gay'-nyo, nyah], *a.* Native of or belonging to Malaga. -*f.* A song popular in the province of Malaga.

malagueta [mah-lah-gay'-tah], *f.* Tabasco pepper.

malamente [mah-lah-men'-tay], *adv.* Badly, wickedly, wrongly. **Estar malamente de dinero**, to be badly off for money.

malandante [mah-lan-dahn'-tay], *a.* Calamitous, unfortunate.

malandanza [mah-lan-dahn'-thah], *f.* Misfortune, calamity.

malandar [mah-lan-dar'], *m. (Prov.)* Wild hog.

malandrín [mah-lan-dreen'], *m.* High-wayman. -*a.* Malign, perverse.

malanga [mah-lahn'-gah], *f.* A farinaceous root of great consumption in Cuba.

malapata [mah-lah-pah'-tah], *m & f* Pest, nuisance, tedious individual; clumsy sort.

malaquita [mah-lah-kee'-tah], *f. (Min.)* Malachite precious stone: green copper carbonate.

malar [mah-lar'], *a.* Malar, relating to the cheek.

malaria [mah-lah'-re-ah], *f.* malaria.

malatía [mah-lah-tee'-ah], *f.* 1. Leprosy. 2. Disease in general.

malato, ta [mah-lah'-to, tah], *a.* 1. Leprous. 2. Sick, diseased. Also noun.

malato [mah-lah'-to], *m. (Chem.)* Malate.

malavenido, da [mah-lah-vay-nee'-do, dah], *a. & f.* Quarrelsome person, a sower of discord; curst, mischievous.

malaventura [mah-lah-ven-too'-rah], *f.* Calamity, misfortune.

malaventurado, da [mah-lah-ven-too-rah'-do, dah], *a.* Unfortunate ill-fated, luckless.

malaventuranza [mah-lah-ven-too-rahn'-thah], *f.* Infelicity, unhappiness.

malayo, a [mah-lah'-yo, yah], *a.* 1. Malay, belonging to Malacca. 2. The Malay tongue.

malbaratador, ra [mal-bah-rah-tah-dor', rah], *m. & f.* Spendthrift, prodigal.

malbaratar [mal-bah-rah-tar'], *va.* 1. To misspend, to lavish. 2. To disorder.

malbaratero, ra [mal-bah-rah-tay' -ro, rah], *a.* V. MALBARATADOR.

malbaratijo [mal-bah-rah-tee-ho], *m.* Bad sale, sale in a second-hand shop.

malbaratillo [mal-bah-rah-teel'-lyo], *m.* A cheap, second-hand shop.

malcarado, da [mal-cah-rah'-do, dah], *a.* Grim-faced, foulfaced.

malcasado, da [mal-cah-sah'-do, dah], *a. & pp.* of MALCASAR. Not well married.

malcasar [mal-cah-sar'], *va.* To make someone marry against his or her will: applied to parents, guardians, etc. -*vr.* To contract an improper or unfortunate marriage.

malcaso [mal-cah'so], *m.* 1. Treason, turpitude, crime.

malcocinado [mal-co-the-nah'do], *m.* 1. Tripes, liver, and lights of a quadruped. 2. Place where tripes are sold.

malcomer [mal-coh'-mar], *vn.* To have a poor meal, to eat badly.

malcomido, da [mal-co-mee'-do, dah], *a.* Hungry, destitute of wholesome food.

malcontento, ta[mal-con-ten'-to], *m.* 1. Malcontent; grumbler. 2. A game at cards.

malcontento, [mal-con-ten'-to, tah], *a.* Discountented, malcontent.

malcorte [mal-cor'-tay], *m.* Transgression of the mountain laws in cutting wood or making charcoal.

malcriado, da [mal-cre-ah'-do, dah], *a.* ill-bred, unmannerly, impolite, clownish; spoiled (niños).

malcriar [mal-cre-ar'], *va.* To spoil (niño).

maldad [mal-dahd'], *f.* 1. Wickedness, iniquity, corruption, abomination. 2. Guiltiness, criminality, mischievousness.

maldecidor, ra [mal-day-the-dor', rah], *m. & f.* Detractor; swearer.

maldecir [mal-day-theer'], *va.* 1. To curse (con maldición), to accurse, to execrate. 2. To detract. -*vn.* **Maldecir de**, to speak ill of, to slander (difamar); to disparage (denigrar). (*yo maldigo, yo maldiga,* from *Maldecir V.* BENDECIR.)

maldicho, cha [mal-dee'-cho, chah]. *pp. & irr. obs* of MALDECIR. Accurserd; caluminated.

maldiciente [mal-de-the-en'-tay], *pa & m & f.* Cursing; curser; grumbler, complainer, malcontent.

maldición [mal-de-the-on'], *f.*1. Malediction, curse, execration; imprecation. 2. Divine chastisement. **Parece que ha caído una maldición sobre este programa**, there seems to be a curse on this programme.

maldita [mal-dee'-tah], *f.* 1. *(coll).* The tongue (lengua). **Soltar la maldita**, *(coll).* to give a loose rein to one's tongue, to tell one's mind very freely. 2. *(Carib.)* Sore (llaga).

maldito, ta [mal-dee'-to, tah], *a.* 1. Perverse, wicked (maligno). 2. Chastised by Divine justice. 3. Damned (condenado), cursed, confounded. 4. *(coll).* None, not one. -*pp irr* of MALDECIR, accursed. **Ese maldito libro**, that dammed book. **No le encuentro maldita la gracia**, I don't find it in the least amusing. 5. *(Mex.)* Crafty (taimado). -*m.* 1. **El maldito**, the devil. 2. *(Teat.)* Extra.

maleabilidad [mah-lay-ah-be-le-dahd'], *f.* Malleability, malleableness.

maleable [mah-lay-ah'-blay], *a.* Malleable.

maleante [mah-lay-ahn'-tay], *m.* Corrupter, injurer, malefactor (malhechor), vragant (vago). -*pa.* Currupting.

malear [mah-lay-ar'], *va.* To pervert, to corrupt, to injure, to damnify. -*vr.* To spoil to be harmed; to be corrupted.

malecón [mah-lay-cone'], *m.* Dike, embankment, levee, jetty.

maledicencia [mah-lay-de-then'-the-ag], *f.* Slander, calumny.

maleducar [mahl-ay-doo-car'], *va.* To spoil (niños).

maleficencia [mah-lay-fe-then'-the-ah], *f.* Mischievousness, the habit of doing mischief.

maleficiador, ra [mah-lay-fe-the-ah-dor', rah], *m & f.* Adulterator, corrupter. **maleficiar** pmah-lay-fe-the-ar'], *va.* 1. To adulterate, to corrupt, to vitiate. 2. To betwitch (hechizar), to injure by witchcraft.

maleficio [mah-lay-fee'-the-o], *m.* Witchraft (brujería), charm, enchantment.

maléfio, ca [mah-lay'-fe-co, cah], *a.* Mischievous, malicious, injurious to others, especially by witchcraft.

malentendido [mah-layn-ten-dee'-do], *m.* Misunderstanding.

maleolar [mah-lay-o-lar'], *a.* Malleolar, relating to the ankle.

maleólo [mah-lay'-o-lo], *m.* Malleolus, each bony promience of the ankles.

malestar [mah-les-tar], *m.* 1. Discomfort, uneasiness. 2. Indisposition, physical disorder.

maleta [mah-lay'-tah], *f.* 1. Portmanteau, valise, gripsack. **Hacer la maleta**, to make preparations for a journey. 2. *(Aut.)* Boot, trunk. 3. *(CAm. Cono Sur)* Saddle-bag. 4. *(And. CAm. Cono Sur)* Bundle of clothes. 5. *(And, Carib.)* Hump (joroba).

maletero [mah-lay-tay'-ro], *m.* Harness-maker, saddler, portamanteau-maker 2. *(Ant.)* Boot, trunk.

maletilla [mah-lay-teel'-lyah], *f.* Satche, small handbag. -*m. (Taur.)* Itinerant aspiring bullfighter.

maletín [mah-le-teen'], *m. dim.* A satchel, small case.

maletón [mah-lay-tone'], *m.aug.* A large leather bag, portamanteau.

malevolencia [mah-lay-vo-len'-the-ah], *f.* Malevolence, illnature, ill-will, maligancy.

malévolo, la [mah-lay'-vo-lo, lah], *a.* Malevolent, malignant, mischievous, hateful.

maleza [mah-lay'-thah], *f.* 1. Piece of ground, rendered unfruitful by brambles and briers. 2. Undergrowth, thicket, coppice, scrub (arbustos), weeds (hierbas).

malformación [mah-for-mah-the-on'], *f.* Malformation.

malformado [mahl-for-mah'-do], *a.* Malformed.

malgama [mal-gah'-mah], *m. (Chem.) V.* AMALGAMA.

malgastador, ra [mal-gas-tah-dor', rah], *m. & f.* Spendthrift, squanderer.

malgastar [mal-gas-tar'], *va.* To misspend, to waste (tiempo, esfuerzo), to lavish, to lose, to throw away.

malhablado, da [mal-hah-blah'do, dah], *a.* Bold, impudent in speaking, foul-mouthed.

malhadado, da [mal-ah-dah-do, dah], *a.* Wretched, unfortunate.

malhecho [mal-hay'-cho], *m* Flagitious action: an evil deed.

malhecho, cha [mal-ay'-cho, chah], *a* Ill-shaped: applied to persons who are humpbacked or otherwise deformed.

malhechor, ra [mal-ay-chor', rah], *m. & f.* Malefactor, offender, misdoer.

malherido, da [mal-ay-ree'-do, dah], *a. & pp.* Of MALHERIR. Badly wounded.

malherir [mal-ay-reer'], *va* To wound badly.

malhojo [mal-o'-ho], *m (Naut.)* Vegetable refuse.

malhumorado, da [mal-oo-mo-rah'-do, dah], *a.* Ill-humored, peevish; bad-tempered. **Estar malhumorado,** to be in a bad mood.

malicia [mah-lee'-the-ah], *f.* 1. Malice, perversity, wickedness (maldad), malignity. 2. Malice, maliciousness, mischievousness, intention of mischief to another (intención). 3. Suspicion, apprehension. 4. Cunning, artifice. 5. Dissimulation, hypocrisy. 6. Gall, rancor, animosity. 7. Viciousness (carácter). 8. Roguishness (mirada, chiste), naughtiness. **Contó un chiste con mucha malicia,** he told a very naughty story.

maliciar [mah-le-the-ar'], *va.* To corrupt, to adulterate. -*vn.* To put a malicious construction on a thing; to discourse in a malicious manner; to suspect maliciously.

maliciosamente [mah-le-the-o-sah-men'-tay], *adv.* 1. Maliciously. 2. Wickedly. 3. Roguishly. 4. Viciously; mischievously.

maliciosico, ica, illo, illa, ito, ita [mah-le-the-o-see'co], *a. dim.* A little malicious.

malicioso, sa [mah-le-the-o'-so, sah], *a.* Malicious, suspicious, wicked (malo), knavish, mischievous (travieso), vicious (vicioso), ill-intentioned (malintencionado).

málico, ca [mah'-le-co, cah], *a.* Malic, belonging to or derived from apples.

malignamente [mah-lig-nah-men'-tay], *adv.* Malignantly, mischievously, hatefully, malevolently.

malignar [mah-lig-nar'], *va.* To vitiate, to corrupt, to deprave. -*vr.* 1. To become sore. 2. To grow worse.

malignidad [mah-lig-ne-dahd'], *f.* Malignity, malice (rencor); perverseness; mischievousness, hatred.

maligno, na [mah-leeg'-no, nah], *a.* Malignant, perverse, malicious (actitud, observación), ill-disposed, hateful.

malilla [mah-leel'-lyah], *f.* 1. Manille, the deuce of spades or clubs, or the seven of hearts or diamonds, in some games. 2. A game of cards like whist. 3. *(coll.)* Person full of wickedness and malice.

malinformar [mahl-en-for-mar'], *va.* To misinform.

malintencionado, da [mal-in-ten-the-o-nah'-do, dah], *a.* Bearing ill-will, ill disposed, with bad intentions.

malinterpretar [mahl-in-ter-pray-tar'], *va.* To misinterpret.

malísimo [mah-lee'-se-mo], *a.* Very bad, dreadful, appalling.

malla [mahl'-lyah], *f.* 1. Mesh, space between the threads of a net. **Hacer malla,** to knit. 2. *(Naut.)* Net-work of a ship. 3. Coat of mail.

mallar [mah-llyar'], *va.* To make net-work.

mallero [mah-llyay'-ro], *m.* Armorer, maker of coats of mail.

malletes [mal-llyay'-tes], *m. pl.* Partners, strong pieces of timber bolted to the beams, encircling the masts, to keep them steady in their steps.

mallo [mahl'-lyo], *m.* 1. Pallmall, game of bowls, skittles, or ninepins. 2. Mall, bowling-green, skittle-ground. 3. Mallet.

malmandado, da [mal-man-dah'-do, dah], *a. (coll.)* Disobedient, obstinate.

malmeter [mal-may-terr'], *vn. (coll.)* To incline, to induce to evil; to make one differ with another; to breed quarrels.

malmirado, da [mal-me-rah'-do, dah], *a.* 1. Impolite, inconsiderate. 2. Indiscreet, imprudent.

malnacido [mal-nah-the'-do], *a.* Rotten, awful.

malnutrido [mal-noo-tre'-do], *a.* Undernourished.

malo, la [mah'-lo, lah], *a.* 1. Bad, evil, not good. 2. Bad, vicious, wicked, mean, nasty, perverse, naughty (niño). 3. Imperfect, defective. 4. Artful, cunning, crafty, mischievous. 5. Sickly, disordered, ill. **Estar malo,** to be ill, to be sick. **Ser malo,** to be wicked. 6. Unhealthy, prejudicial to health. 7. Difficult (difícil), inquiet. 8. Wrong. **Ésta es una mala respuesta,** this is the wrong answer. **Andar a malas,** to go in enmity. **Este papel es malo para escribir,** this paper is bad for writing. **Es un animal malo de domesticar,** it's a difficult animal to tame. **Estar de malas,** to be in a bad mood. -*m.* **El malo,** the Evil. 2. *(Teat.)* Villain; *(Cine)* Bad guy.

malo [mah'-lo], *int.* Bad; so much the worse.

malogramiento [mah-lo-grah-me-en'-to], *m.* Disappointment.

malograr [mah-lo-grar'], *va.* 1. To disappoint, to disconcert. 2. *(Com.)* To waste or spoil goods (desperdiciar).-*vr.* 1. To be disappointed (decepcionar), to fail. 2. To die before one's time (persona). 3. *(And. Aut.)* To break down.

malogro [mah-lo'-gro], *m.* Disappointment, miscarriage, failure (fracaso), waste (desperdicio).

maloja [mah-lo'-hah], *f. (Cuba)* The leaves and stalks of Indian corn, used only for fodder.

maloler [mah-lo-lerr'], *vr.* To stink.

maloliente [mah-lo-le-en'-tay], *pa.* Stinking, foul-smelling.

malolor [mah-lo-lor'], *m.* Stench, stink, pestiferous smell.

malón [mah-lone'], *m.* *(Chili)* A hostile, predatory incursion of Indians.

maloquear [ma-lo-kay-ar'], *m. (Mex.)* 1. To make a predatory raid (by Indians). 2. To trade with Indians for stolen goods.

maloquero, ra [mah-lo-kay'-ro, rah], *a. & n. (Amer.)* 1. An Indian thief. 2. One who trades with Indian thieves.

malordenado, da [mah-lor-day-nah'-do, dah], *a.* Badly contrived, ill arranged.

malparado, da [mal-pah-rah'-do, dah], *a & pp.* of MALPARAR. Ill-conditioned, impaired, useless.

malparar [mal-pah-rar'], *va.* To ill-treat (maltratar), to impair, to damage (dañar), to hurt, to blemish.

malparecido, da [mal-pah-ray-thee'-do, dah], *a.* Of evil aspect or countenance, ugly.

malparida [mal-pah-ree'-dah], *f.* Woman who has miscarried.

malparir [mal-pah-reer'], *vn.* To miscarry.

malparto [mal-par'-to], *m.* Abortion, miscarriage.

malpaso [mal-pah'-so], *m.* 1. Exigency, tight place, grievous difficulty. 2. Reprehensible fault.

malpensado [mal-pen-sah'-do], *a.* Nasty, evil-minded.

malponer [mal-po-nerr'], *va.* 1. To indispose. 2. To excite quarrels.

malquerencia [mal-kay-ren'-the-ah], *f.* Ill-will, hatred.

malquerer [mal-kay-rerr'], *va.* To abhor, to hate, to bear ill-will.

malquistar [mal-kis-tar'], *va.* To excite disputes and quarrels among friends and others.-*vr.* To incur hatred and displeasure.

malquisto, ta [mal-kees'-to, tah], *a.* Hated, detested, abhorred.

malrotador, ra [mal-ro-tah-dor', rah], *m. & f.* Squanderer, spendthrift.

malrotar [mal-ro-tar'], *va.* To misspend, to lavish, to waste one's fortune.

malsano, na [mal-sah'-no, nah], *a.* 1. Unhealthy (clima, atmósfera), sickly, infirm. 2. Unwholesome, insalubrious, injurious to health.

malsín [mal-seen'], *m.* Tale-bearer, mischief-maker.

malsonante [mal-so-nahn'-tay], *a.* Ill-sounding, offensive, nasty (palabra).

malsufrido, da [mal-soo-free'-do, dah], *a.* Impatient of suffering, weak (débil).

Malta [mahl'-tah], *f.* 1. A bandage in the shape of a Maltese cross. 2. Asphalt, mineral pitch.

maltés, sa [mal-tays', sah], *a.* Maltese, of Malta.

maltosa [mal-to'-sah], *f.* Maltose.

maltrabaja [mal-trah-bah'-hah], *com. (coll.)* Idler, lounger.

maltraer [mal-trah-err'], *va.* 1. To treat ill (maltratar). 2. To insult (insultar). *V.* MALTRATAR.

maltratadamente [mal-trah-tah-dah-men'-tay], *adv.* Ill-used, in an abused manner.

maltratamiento [mal-trah-tah-me-en'-to], *m.* Ill treatment, bad usage; affliction.

maltratar [mal-trah-tar'], *va.* 1. To treat ill (persona), to abuse, to maltreat, to misuse. 2. To spoil, to destroy.

maltrato [mal-trah'-to], *m.* 1. Ill treatment (persona). 2. Abuse (abuso).

maltrecho [malñ-tray'-cho], *a.* Battered, damaged; injured. **Dejar maltrecho a uno,** to leave somebody in a bad way.

malucho, cha [mah-loo'-cho, chah], *a.* 1. *(coll.)* A sickly person. 2. Naughty, wayward.

malva [mahl'-vah], *f.* *(Bot.)* Mallows. **Malva blanca,** walteria hibiscus. **Malva rosa,** hibiscus mutabilis. **De color malva,** mauve.

malvadamente [mal-vah-dah-men'-tay], *adv.* Wickedly, naughtily, mischievously, hellishly; lewdly.

malvado, da [mal-vah'-do, dah], *a.* Malicious, wicked, insolent, vicious, nefarious.

malvar [mal-var'], *m.* Place covered with mallows.

malvasía [mal-vah-see'-ah], *f.* Malmsey or Malvoisie grape; malmsey wine.

malvavisco [mal-vah-vees'-co], *m.* *(Bot.)* Marshmallows.

malvender [mal-ven-der'], *va.* To sell off cheap.

malversación [mal-ver-sah-the-on'], *f.* Mis-application or mal-administration of money, malversation.

malversador, ra [mal-ver-sah-dor', rah], *m. & f.* Person who misapplies property.

malversar [mal-ver-sar'], *va.* To misapply, to apply money to wrong purposes.

malvis, malviz [mal-vees', mal-veeth'], *m.* Bird resembling a thrush; redwing.

mallorquín, na [mal-lyor-keen', nah], *a.* Majorcan.

mamá [mah-mah'], *f.* Ma, mamma, mum, mummy: a fond word for mother.

mama [mah'-ma], *f.* 1. The mammary gland, breast. 2. *(Prov. Andal.)* Mamma, mother.

mamacallos [mah-mah-cahl'-lyos], *m. (coll.)* Dolt, simpleton.

mamada [mah-mah'-dah], *f.* 1. *(coll.)* Time which a child takes in sucking (chupada). 2. *(LAm.)* Cinch (cosa fácil). 3. *(Cono Sur)* Drunkenness (borrachera).

mamadera [mah-mah-day'-rah], *f.* Breast-pump.

mamador, ra [mah-mah-dor', rah], *m. & f.* Sucker, suckling, one who sucks.-*n.* Feeding-bottle, nursing-bottle for artificial lactation.

mamahigos [mah-mah-ee'-gose], *a.* Silly, booby.

mamalón [mah-mah-lon'], *m.* *(Cuba)* Idler who tries constantly to live at another's expense; parasite.

mamante [mah-mahn'-tay], *a.* Sucking.

mamantón, na [mah-man-to-ne', nah], *a.* Sucking (animales).

mamar [mah-mar'], *va.* 1. To suck, to draw milk from the breast (pecho). 2. *(coll.)* To cram and devour victuals. 3. To acquire in infancy. 4. *(coll.)* To get, to obtain. 5. *(Mex.)* To suck off. -*vn.* 1. To suck. 2. *(Fig.)* To get something free. 3. To booze (beber). -*vr.* 1. To wangle (puesto, ventaja). 2. *(And.)* To go back on one's word.

mamario, ria [mah-mah'-re-o, ah], *a.* Mammary: relating to the breast.

mamarrachada [mah-mar-rah-chah'-dah], *f.* 1. A collection of rude or ridiculous figures. 2. A foolish action or speech.

mamarracho [mah-mar-rah'-cho], *m.* An ill-drawn figure of a man; a grotesque ornament.

mamayuca [mah-mah-yoo'-cah], *f.* Crust of bread put into a frying-pan or dish where many eat, to set bounds to or suspend a meal.

mambla [mahm'-blah], *f.* Isolated rounded hillock.

mamelón [mah-may-lon'], *m.* *(Anat.)* 1. Teat, nipple. 2. Any teat-shaped tubercle.

mameluco [mah-may-loo'-co], *m.* 1. Mameluke, Egyptian soldier. 2. Leotard, practice costume for dancing. 3. Child's rompers. 4. A fool, an idiot (idiota).

mamella [mah-mayl'-lyah], *f.* 1. Small teat, nipple. 2. A small teat-shaped appendage on the neck of goats, etc. *V.* MARMELLA.

mamellado, da [mah-mel-lyah'-do, dah], *a.* Mammellated: applied to animals having loose skins on their necks.

mamífero, ra [ma-mee'-fay-ro, rah], *a.* Mammiferous, having mammary glands: mammalian. -*pl.* Mammals.

mamiforme [mah-me-for'-may], *a.* Having the shape of a mammary gland. *V.* MASTÓIDEO.

mamila [mah-mee'-lah], *f.* 1. The chief part of a woman's breast round the nipple. 2. The nipple in men. *(Acad.)*

mamilar [mah-me-lar'], *a.* Mamillary.

mamografía [mah-mo-grah-fe'-ah], *f.* Mammography.

mamola [mah-mo'-lah], *f.* Chuck under the chin.

mamón, na [mah-mone', nah], *m. & f.* 1. A sucking animal. 2. A child that sucks too much, or for too long a time. 3. Sucker, young twig.

mamoso, sa [mah-mo'-so, sah], *a.* 1. Sucking. 2. Applied to panic grass.

mamotreto [mah-mo-tray'-to], *m.* 1. Memorandum-book, hefty tome (libro). 2. *(LAm.)* Contraption (aparato). 3. *(Mex.)* Dead loss (inútil).

mampara [mam-pah'-rah], *f.* Screen before a door or any other place.

mamparo [mam-pah'-ro], *m.* *(Naut.)* Bulkhead, partition in a ship. **Mamparos de quita y pon,** *(Naut.)* ship and unship bulkheads.

mamporro [mam-por'-ro], *m.* Bash, punch, clout; bump (al caer). **Atizar un mamporro a uno,** to give somebody a swipe.

mampostear [mam-pos-tay-ar'], *va.* To raise mason-work, to cement with mortar.

mampostería [mam-pos-tay-ree'-ah], *f.* 1. Rubble-work (sin labrar), masonry. 2. The employment of collecting alms or tithes.

mampostero [mam-pos-tay'-ro], *m.* 1. Mason, stone mason. 2. Collector of alms or tithes.

mampresar [mam-pray-sar'], *va.* *(Prov.)* To begin to break horses.

mampuesta [mam-poo-es'-tah], *f.* Row of bricks.

mampuesto [mam-poo-es'-to], *m.* Rubble, rough stone.

mamullar [mah-mool-lyar'], *va.* To eat or chew as if sucking; to mutter; to mumble.

mamut [mah-moot'], *m.* Mammoth, primitive elephant now extinct.

maná [mah-nah'], *m.* 1. Manna, food of the Israelites. 2. Manna, a gum obtained from ash-trees. 3. Tart made of blanched almonds, sugar, spice, etc. 4. Hired of small sugar-plums.

manada [mah-nah'-dah], *f.* 1. Flock, herd, drove of cattle. 2. Handful of corn, etc.; tuft, cluster. 3. Crowd, fry, multitude. **A manadas,** in troops or crowds.

manadera [mah-nah-day'-rah], *f.* Strainer, an instrument for filtration.

manadero [mah-nah-day'-ro], *m.* 1. Source, spring. 2. Shepherd, herdsman.

manadero, ra [mah-nah-day'-ro, rah], *a.* Springing, that which issues.

manadilla [mah-nah-deel'-lyah], *f. dim.* A small flock.

manante [mah-nahn'-tay], *pa.* Proceeding, issuing.

manantial [mah-nan-te-ahl'], *m.* 1. Source, spring. 2. Source, origin, principle, head. -*a.* Flowing, running (agua).

manar [mah-nar'], *va.* 1. To spring from; to distil from, as a liquor. 2. To drop or distil from. 3. To proceed, to issue, to arise. 4. To bound. **Manar sangre,** to run with blood. -*vn.* 1. To run, to flow (líquido). 2. To abound, to be plentiful.

manatí, manato [mah-nah-tee', mah-nah'-to], *m.* 1. Manati, manatee, sea-cow. 2. A whip made of the manati's hide.

manaza [mah-nah'-thah], *f. aug.* A large hand (mano), a mutton-fist.

manca [mahn'-cah], *f. V.* MANCO.

mancamiento [man-cah-me-en'-to], *m.* Want, defect, privation, deficiency, maimedness.

mancar [man-car'], *va.* 1. To maim (mutilar), to render useless an arm or hand. 2. To disable a man for business. 3. *(Cono Sur)* **Mancar el tiro,** to miss. -*vn.* *(And. Escol.)* To fail; to blow it (fracasar).

manceba [man-thay'-bah], *f.* Mistress, concubine.

mancebía [man-thay-bee'-ah], *f.* Brothel, bawdy-house.

mancebico, illo, ito [man-thay-bee'-co], *m. dim.* A little young man.

mancebo, ba [man-thay'-bo, bah], *m. & f.* 1. Young person, under forty years of age (joven). 2. Journeyman, a hired workman. 3. Bachelor (soltero).

mancera [man-thay'-rah], *f.* Ploughtail, handle of a plough.

mancerina [man-thay-ree'-nah], *f.* (*Prov.*) Saucer. *V.* MACERINA.

mancha [mahn'-chah], *f.* 1. Stain, spot, discoloration; blot, macula. 2. Stigma, mark of infamy. 3. Piece of ground distinct from those which adjoin it. 4. (*Met.*) Stigma, blemish, dishonor, either from mean birth or an ignominious act. 5. A spot on the sun or other heavenly body. **Mancha solar**, sunspot. 6. (*And, Carib.*) Cloud, swarm.

manchado, da [man-chah'-do, dah], *a.* Spotted (animal), speckled (ave), Smudged (papel). **Un abrigo manchado de barro**, a coat stained with mud. *-pp.* of MANCHAR.

manchar [man-char'], *va.* 1. To stain, to corrupt, to soil (persona), to contaminate; to daub; to darken, to cloud. 2. To defile one's character, to tarnish one's name and reputation (persona). **Manchar papel**, to scribble, to write much, and nothing to the purpose. 3. (*Pict.*) To lay in spots of light color before defining the figure. *-vr.* 1. To get dirty (ensuciarse). 2. (*Fig.*) To stain one's reputation.

manchega [man-chay'-gah], *f.* Garter of different colors, made of worsted, especially in La Mancha.

manchego, ga [man-chay'-go, gah], *a.* Native of or belonging to La Mancha, a province of Spain.

manchica, illa, ita [man-chee'-cah], *f. dim.* A small stain, spot, or macula.

manchón [man-chone'], *m.* 1. Spot where grain grows rank or thick. 2. (*Aug.*) A large stain or spot.

manchú [man-choo'], *a.* Belonging to Manchuria or its inhabitants; Manchurian.

mancilla [man-theel'-lyah], *f.* Spot, blemish.

mancillar [man-theel'-lyar], *va.* To spot, to stain. *V.* AMANCILLAR.

mancipar [man-the-par'], *va.* To subject, to enslave, to mancipate.

manco, ca [mahn'-co, cah], *a.* 1. Handless, one-handed (una mano), lacking one or both hands, or without the use of them. 2. Maimed, defective, faulty, imperfect. 3. (*Fig.*) **No ser manco**, to be useful (útil).

manco, ca [mahn'-co, cah], *m. & f.* 1. A handlers or a one-handed person (una mano). 2. (*Cono Sur*) Old horse, nag (caballo).

mancomún [man-co-moon'], *m.* Concurrence of two or more persons in the execution of a thing; it is now used only in the adverbial phrase, **de mancomún**, jointly, by common consent.

mancomunadamente [man-co-moo-nah'-dah-men-tay], *adv.* Conjointly, by common consent.

mancomunar [man-co-moo-nar'], *va.* 1. To associate, to unite (personas). 2. (*Law.*) To make two or more persons pay jointly the costs of a lawsuit. *-vr.* To act together, to join in the execution of a thing.

mancomunidad [man-co-moo-ne-dahd'], *f.* Union, conjunction, fellowship.

mancornar [man-co-moo-nar'], *va.* 1. To throw a young steer with its horns fixed in the ground, leaving it motionless. 2. To tie a pair of animals by the horns, so as to make them go together.

mancuerna [man-coo-err'-nah], *f.* 1. Pair of animals or things. 2. Thong for throwing a steer. 3. (*Cuba*) Stem with two or three leaves, which is cut from the plant in collecting tobacco.

manda [mahn'-dah], *f.* 1. Offer, proposal. 2. Legacy or donation left by virtue of last will.

mandadera [man-dahday'rah], *f. V.* DEMANDADERA.

mandadero, ra [man-dah-day'-ro, rah], *m. & f.* 1. Porter, messenger; one engaged to run errands. 2. *V.* DEMANDADERO.

mandado [man-dah'-do], *m.* 1. Mandate, precept, command. 2. Errand, message, advertisement, notice. **Muchacho de mandados**, errand-boy. **Mandado, da**, *pp.* of MANDAR.

mandamiento [man-dah-me-en'-to], *m.* 1. Mandate, precept, order (orden), command. 2. Commandment, one of the ten precepts of the Decalogue. 3. Peremptory order issued by a judge, respecting the execution of his sentence. *-pl.* (*coll.*) The five fingers of the hand. **Mandamientos de la ley de Dios**, the ten commandments. **Mandamientos de la Iglesia or de la Santa Madre Iglesia**, commandments of the church.

mandante [man-dahn'-tay], *pa.* Commanding.

mandar [man-dar'], *va.* 1. To command, to give orders, to order (ordenar), to ordain, to enact. 2. To lead, to head (grupo). 3. To leave or bequeath in a last will or testament (legar). 4. (*Prov.*) To send (enviar), to transmit. 5. To offer, to promise. 6. To ask for. 7. (*LAm.*) To throw (echar). 8. (*LAm.*) To give, to strike (golpe). 9. (*LAm.*) To break in (caballo). **Mandar hacer**, (*coll.*) to have made, to order or cause to be made, to bespeak.*-vr.* 1. In buildings, to communicate with. 2. To have free use of one's limbs, to manage oneself without the aid of others. 3. (*Carib. Cono Sur*) To go away (irse). 4. (*LAm.*) **Mándese entrar**, please come in. **Mandar a alguno a puntapiés, a puntillazos** or **a zapatazos**, to have complete ascendancy over anyone. **Mandar hacer un traje**, to order a suit. **Mandar salir a uno**, to order somebody out.

mandarín [man-dah-reen'], *m.* Mandarin, a Chinese magistrate.

mandarina [man-dah-ree'-nah], *f.* 1. (*Bot.*) Tangerine (fruta). 2. Mandarin language, Chinese dialect.

mandarria [man-dar'-re-ah], *f.* (*Naut.*) Iron maul, a large hammer or sledge.

mandatario [man-dah-tah'-re-o], *m.* 1. Attorney, agent. 2. Mandatory; mandatary. 3. (*Mex.*) Collector of religious confraternities.

mandato [man-dah'-to], *m.* 1. Mandate, precept, injunction, order (orden), ordinance 2. Charge, trust, commission. 3 Ecclesiastical ceremony of washing the feet of twelve persons on Maundy Thursday. 4. Mandate (gobierno). 5. Term (período). **Mandato judicial**, warrant. **Territoria bajo mandato**, mandated territory.

¡mande! [mahn'-day], *int.* (*Naut.*) Holla! a word of command on shipboard, enjoining attention.

mandíbula [man-dee'-boo-lah], *f.* Jawbone, mandible.

mandibular [man-de-boo-lar'], *a.* Mandibular, belonging to the jaw.

mandil [man-deel'], *m.* 1. Coarse apron used by men or women. 2. (*Low.*) Servant to a pimp or prostitute. 3. (*Cono Sur*) Horse blanket (de caballo).

mandilada [man-de-lah'-dah], *f.* 1. An apronful. 2. (*Low.*) A number of ruffians.

mandilar [man-de-lar'], *va.* To wipe a horse with a course apron or cloth.

mandilejo [man-de-lay'-ho], *m.* 1. (*dim.*) A small apron, a ragged apron. 2. (*Low.*) Servant of a rogue or prostitute, pimp, pander.

mandilete [man-de-lay'tay], *m.* (*Mil.*) Door of the porthole of a battery.

mandilón [man-de-lone'], *m.* (*coll.*) Coward, a mean, dastardly fellow.

mandioca [man-de-o'-cah], *f.* The Brazilian name of the yucca (manioc) or cassava, yielding tapioca.

mando [mahn'-do], *m.* 1. Command, authority, power, dominion, rule (de país), leadership (liderazgo). **Alto mando**, high command. **Ejercer el mando**, to be in command. **Entregar el mando**, to hand over command. 2. Lead (en carretera). **Tomar el mando**, to take the lead. 3. Leaders (personas). 4. (*Mec.*) Control. **Mando a distancia**, remote control. 5. (*Rad. Téc.*) Controls.

mandoble [man-do'-blay], *m.* 1. A two-handed blow (golpe) 2. A severe reprimand. 3. Large sword (espada).

mandolina [man-do-lee'-nah], *f.* Mandolin, a stringed instrument played with a plectrum.

mandón, na [man-done', nah], *a.* Imperious, domineering. *-m.* An imperious. haughty person.

mandrachero [man-drah-chay'-ro], *m.* Proprietor of a gaming-table.

mandracho

mandracho [man-drah'-cho], *m.* (*Prov.*) Gambling-house.

mandrágora [man-drah'-go-rah], *f.* (*Bot.*) Mandrake.

mandria [mahn'-dre-ah], *m.* Coward, poltroon. -*a.* Worthless.

mandril [man-dreel'], *m.* 1. (*Zool.*) Mandril, a West African baboon. 2. Mandrel, chuck, spindle of a lathe.

mandrín [man-dreen'], *m.* 1. Mandrel. 2. A hollow iron instrument which serves to join the ends of a metallic rod or to support the arms of a wheel.

manducación [man-doo-cah-the-on'], *f.* (*coll.*) Manducation, act of chewing or eating.

manducar [man-doo-car'], *va.* (*coll.*) To manducate, to cut, to chew.

manducatoria [man-doo-cah-to'-re'-ah], *f.* Dining-room, refectory.

manea [mah-nay'-ah], *f.* Shackles, fetters, hopple. *V.* MANIOTA.

manear [mah-nay-ar'], *va.* To hobble, to fasten with fetters or shackles (caballos, asnos).

manecica, ita [mah-nay-thee'-cah, ee'-tah], *f. dim.* A small hand (reloj).

manecilla [mah-nay-theel'-lyah], *f.* 1. (*dim.*) A small hand. 2. A mark or index, in grammar. 3. Book clasp. 4. Hand of a clock or watch (reloj).

manejable [mah-nay-hah'-blay], *a.* Manageable, tractable, handy (herramienta).

manejado [mah-nay-hah'-do], *a.* (*Pict.*) Handled.-*pp.* of MANEJAR.

manejar [mah-nay-har'], *va.* 1. To manage, to wield, to move with the hand. 2. To manage, to train a horse to graceful action. 3. To manage, to conduct, to govern, to contrive. 4. To handle (herramienta, lengua), to hand, to palm. 5. To manage (persona), to carry on. **Ella maneja a su marido**, she manages her husband. -*vr.* 1. To know how to conduct oneself (comportarse). 2. To be able to move after having been deprived of motion. 3. To manage (arreglárselas). **Se maneja bien con los chiquillos**, she manages all right with the kids.

manejo [mah-nay'-ho], *m.* 1. Employment of the hands to any purpose, handling (acto). **Manejo doméstico**, housekeeping. 2. Management, conduct, administration. 3. Horsemanship, manage. 4. Handling, cunning, trick; intrigue, device. **Hay que ver el manejo que tiene la chica**, you should see how quick the girl is.

maneota [mah-nay-o'-tah], *f.* Shackles, hobbles, fetters. *V.* MANIOTA.

manera [mah-nay'-rah], *f.* 1. Manner, form, figure; method, mode, kind, guise: manner of style. 2. Manner, or style, in painting, or carving in stone. 3. Ceremonious behavior, deportment. 4. Fore part or fall of breeches. 5. (*Ant.*) Quality, class of persons. 6. Manners (modales). **Manera de ser**, way of life. **No hay manera**, there's no solution. **De esta manera**, in this way. **De otra manera**, otherwise. **De tal manera que**, in such a way that. **De maneras muy groseras**, with very bad manners. **De manera** or **por manera**, so as, in such a manner.

manero, ra [mah-nay'-ro, rah], *a.* Tame: applied to hawks in falconry.

manes [mah'-nes], *m. pl.* Manes, ghost of the dead.

manezuela [mah-nay-thoo-ay'-lah], *f.* 1. (*dim.*) A small hand. 2. A clasp, a buckle.

manfla [mahn'-flah], *f.* (*coll.*) 1. A concubine. 2. (*Prov.*) Old sow.

manga [mahn'-gah], *f.* 1. Sleeve, part of a garment. 2. Arm of an axle-tree, on which the nave turns. 3. Kind of cloak-bag or portmanteau (bolso). 4. Stripe of cloth hanging from the shoulder of clerical cloaks. 5. Hose for water, firehose. (*Acad.*) 6. Body of troops in a line. 7. Fishing-net. 8. Bag made of woollen, linen, or paper, in the form of a sleeve, used to strain and clarify liquors; Hippocrates' sleeve. 9. **Manga or manga marina**, hurricane whirl-wind, water-spout. 10. (*Mex.*) Blanket or oblong piece of cloth, round at the ends, with a slit in the middle to put the head through, used as a covering when traveling on horseback. *V.* PONCHO. 11. (*LAm.*) Crowd (multitud) 12. (*LAm. Agr.*) Corral entrance. 13. (*CAm.*) Poncho, coarse blanket. 14. (*Mex.*) Condom (preservativo). 15. A variety of mango (árbol y fruta). **Manga de camisa**, shirtsleeve. **Estar en mangas de camisa**, to be in one's shirt-sleeves. **Ser de manga ancha**, to be easy-going. **Manga de agua**, rain cape.

manga de aire [mahn'-gah day ah'-e-ray], *f.* (*Aer.*) Jet stream.

mangana [man-gah'-nah], *f.* Lasso, lariat.

manganear [man-gah-nay-ar'], *va.* (*Amer. Mex.*) To throw a lasso at a running animal.

manganeo [man-gah-nay'-o], *m.* Sport in which lassoing is the chief diversion.

manganato [man-gah-nah'-to], *m.* Manganate, a salt of manganic acid.

manganesa, or **manganesia** [man-gah-nay'-sah], *f.* Peroxide of manganese, used in the manufacture of glass and paints, and in medicine.

manganeso [man-gah-nay'-so], *m.* Manganese, a hard, brittle, grayish-white metallic element.

mangánico, ca [man-gah'-ne-co, cah], *a.* Manganic, relative to manganese.

manganilla [man-gah-neel'-lyah], *f.* 1. Sleight of hand, a juggling trick. 2. (*Prov.*) Pole for gathering acorns.

manganoso [man-gah-no'-so], *a.* Manganous.

mangante [man-gahn'-tay], *a.* Brazen. -*m.* Beggar (mendigo); scrounger (gorrón); thief (ladrón); shoplifter (ratero); loafer (vago); rotter (caradura); villain.

mangar [man-gahr'], *va.* 1. To pinch (robar). 2. To beg (mendigar), to scrounge. -*vn.* To pilfer (robar); (*Cono Sur*) to scrounge.

mangla [mahn'-glah], *f.* Gum which exudes from the rock-rose or dwarf sunflower.

manglar [man-glar'], *m.* Plantation of mangrove trees.

mangle [mahn'-glay], *m.* (*Bot.*) Mangrove tree.

mango [mahn'-go], *m.* 1. Handle, haft, heft; helve, the handle of an axe. 2. (*Bot.*) Indian mango-tree.

mangonada [man-go-nah'-dah], *f.* Push with the arm.

mangonear [man-go-nay-ar'], *vn.* (*coll.*) 1. To wander about; to rove idly. 2. To intermeddle: to pry. 3. (*LAm.*) To pillage, to plunder (saquear). -*vn.* 1. To meddle (entrometerse). 2. To boss people about (ser mandón). 3. (*LAm.*) To graft, to be on the fiddle; to fix things.

mangoneo [man-go-nay'-o], *m.* 1. Meddling (entrometido), interference. 2. Bossing people about (con personas). 3. (*LAm.*) Graft, fiddling; (*Pol.*) fixing, fiddling of results.

mangorrero, ra [man-gor-ray'-ro, rah], *a.* 1. Wandering, roving, rumbling. 2. Hafted (cuchillo).

mangosta [man-gos'-tah], *f.* Mongoose, a quadruped noted for its ability to kill the most venomous snakes.

mangote [man-go'-tay], *m.* (*coll.*) A large and wide sleeve.

mangual [man-goo-ahl'], *m.* Weapon consisting of a pole with iron chains terminated by balls attached to it.

manguardia [man-goo-ar'-de-ah], *f.* Buttress of a bridge.

manguera [man-gay'-rah], *f.* 1. Hose, a tube for conveying liquids. 2. (*Naut.*) Piece of canvas tarred for various uses. 3. (*And.*) Bicycle tyre inner tube. 4. (*Met.*) Water-spout. 5. (*Cono Sur*) Corral, yard.

mangueta [man-gay'-tah], *f.* 1. Bladder and pipe for administering clystere. 2. Jamb of a glass-door. 3. Lever.

manguilla [man-geel'-lyah], *f. dim.* A small sleeve.

manguita [man-gee'-tah], *f.* 1. Sheath. *V.* FONDA. 2. (*dim.*) *V.* MAGUILLA.

manguitero [man-gee-tay'-ro], *m.* 1. Muff-maker, muffseller. 2. Leather dresser, one who dresses fine skins or white leather.

manguito [man-gee'-to], *m.* 1. Muff, a cover for the hands. 2. Sleeve which is tight from the elbow to the wrist.

maní [mah-nee'], *m.* (*Cuba, Peru, Chili*) Peanut. *V.* CACAHUATE.

manía [mah-nee'-ah], *f.* 1. Mania, frenzy, madness. 2. Extravagance, whimsical obstinacy. 3. Inordinate desires. **Tiene manías**, he's rather odd. **Tener manía a uno**, to dislike somebody.

maniaco, ca [mah-ne-ah'-co'cah], *a.* Maniac, magical, mad, frantic.*m & f.* Maniac, a mad person.

manialbo [mah-ne-ahl'-bo], *a.* White-footed (caballo).

maniatar [mah-ne-ah-tar'], *va.* To manacle, to handcuff.

maniático, ca [mah-ne-ah'-te-co, cah], *a. 1.* Maniacal; *(hum.)* fanatical. 2. *(Fig.)* Crazy (chiflado); odd (excéntrico), eccentric, peculiar; fussy (delicado). *-m. f.* 1. Maniac; *(hum.)* fanatic. 2. *(Fig.)* Maniac; odd individual.

manicero [mah-ne-thay'-ro], *m. (Cuba)* Peanut vendor.

manicomio [mah-ne-co'-me-o], *m.* Asylum or hospital for the mentally ill. *(Acad.)*

manicordio [mah-ne-cor'-de-o], *m.* Manichord, a musical instrument: a clavichord.

manicorto, ta [mah-ne-cor'-to, tah], *a.* Illiberal, parsimonious.

manicurista [mah-ne-coo-rees'-tah], *m. & f.* Manicurist.

manicuro, ra [mah-ne-coo'-ro, rah], *m. & f.* Manicurist.

manida [mah-nee'-dah], *f.* Resort, abode, nest, any place where persons or animals take shelter. **Manida de pícaros**, nest of thieves.

manido, da [mah-nee'-do, dah], *a.* 1. Hidden, concealed. 2. *(Peru)* Said of meats which smell bad; *-pp.* Of MANIR.

manifacero, ra [mah-ne-fah-thay'-ro, rah], *a. (Prov.)* Intriguing, meddlesome, intrusive.

manifestación [mah-ne-fes-tah-the-on'], *f.* 1. Manifestation (emoción), declaration, explication, statement (declaración). 2. A writ resembling the English habeas corpus. 3. Demonstration; mass meeting.

manifestador, ra [mah-ne-fes-tah-dor', rah], *m. & f.* Discoverer, publisher.

manifestante [mah-ne-fes-tahn'-tay], *com.* Demonstrator.

manifestar [mah-ne-fes-tar'], *va.* 1. To manifest, to make known, to show (emoción). 2. To state, to declare (política). *-vr.* 1. To show (emoción), to become apparent. 2. To demonstrate, to hold a mass meeting. *(Yo manifiesto, yo manifieste, from Manifestar. V. ACRECEMNTAR.)*

manifiestamente [mah-ne-fe-ays'-tah-men-tay], *adv.* Clearly.

manifiesto, ta [mah-ne-fe-es'-to, tah], *a.* Manifest (verdad), plain, open, obvious, clear (claro), overt, evident (patente). *-pp. irr.* of MANIFESTAR.

manifiesto [mah-ne-fe-es'-to], *m.* 1. Act of exposing the Holy Sacrament to public adoration. 2. Manifest or manifesto, public protestation or declaration. **Poner de manifiesto**, to manifest, to make public, to expose, to lay open.

manigua [mah-nee'-goo-ah], *f. (Cuba)*1. Thicket, jungle (selva). 2. Monte played for diversion.

manigueta [mah-ne-gay'-tah], *f.* Handle (mango), clasp.

manija [mah-nee'-hah], *f.* 1. Handle of an instrument or working tool. 2. Shackles, handcuffs. 3. Ring, brace. 4. *(And. Mex.)* Door handle (puerta). 5. *(Agr.)* Hobble. 6. *(ConoSur)* Mug (vaso). 7. *(Cono Sur, aut.)* Starting handle.

manilargo, ga [mah-ne-lar'-go, gah], *a.* 1. Large-handed, that is, having long hands. 2. Prone to fisticuffs, pugilistic.

maniluvio [mah-ne-loo'-ve-o], *m.* Bath for the hands used as a remedy.

manilla [mah-neel'-lyah], *f.* 1. *(dim.)* Small hand. 2. Bracelet for the arm or wrist (pulsera). 3. Manacle, handcuff (de hierro). 3. Hand (de reloj). 4. *(And. Mex.)* Door handle.

maniobra [mah-ne-o'-brah], *f.* 1. Work with the hand, handiwork. 2. Handling, artifice for obtaining a thing (acto). 3. *(Mil.)* Maneuver, evolution, movement of troops. 4. *(Naut.)* Working of a ship. 5. *(Naut.)* Gear, rigging (aparejo). **Maniobras de combate**, preventer rigging. **Hacer maniobras**, to maneuver. **Estar de maniobras**, to be on maneuver.

maniobrar [mah-ne-o-brar'], *va..* 1. To work with the hands. 2. *(Naut.)* To work a ship. 3. *(Met.)* To seek the means of effecting anything. 4. *(Mil.)* To maneuver troops. Also, *vn.*

maniobrista [mah-ne-o-brees'-tah], *m. (Naut.)* A skillful naval tactician.

maniota [mah-ne-o'-tah], *f.* Hobble or cord tied about the feet of beasts to prevent running away.

manipodio [mah-ne-po'-de-o], *m. (coll.)* Bawdry, pollution.

manipulación [mah-ne-poo-lah-the-on'], *f.* Manipulation: used in speaking of minerals. **Manipulación defectuosa**, *(Comput.)* mishandling. **Manipulación simbólica**, *(Inform.)* symbolic manipulation.

manipulador, ra [mah-ne-poo-lah-dor'], *m & f.* Manipulator; handler. *-m. (Elec. Telec.)* Key, tapper.

manipulante [mah-ne-poo-lahn'-tay], *m. (coll.)* Administrator, negotiator.

manipular [mah-ne-poo-lar'], *va. (coll.)* To manipulate, to handle, to manage business in a peculiar manner; to meddle with everything.

manípulo [mah-nee'-poo-lo], *m.* 1. Maniple, a fanon worn by the officiating priests of the Roman Catholic church. 2. Maniple, a division of the Roman army. 3. A handful, expressed in recipes by an M.

maniqueismo [mah-ne-kay-ees'-mo], *m.* Manicheism.

maniqueo, a [mah-ne-kay'-o, ah], *a.* Manichean.

maniquí [mah-ne-kee'], *m.* 1. Puppet, one governed by another's caprice. 2. Manikin, a movable figure, which can be put in different postures, for the study of drapery.

manir [mah-neer'], *va.* To keep meat until it grows tender; to mellow.*-vr.* To become tender or mellow (carne).

manirroto, ta [mah-nir-ro'-to, tah], *a.* Extravagant, wasteful.

manita [mah-nee'-tah], *f.* 1. The hour-hand of a watch or clock. 2. Small hand. **Manita de cerdo**, trotters. **Echar una manita a uno**, to lend somebody a hand.

manivacío, cía [mah-ne-vah-thee'-o, ah], *a. (coll.)* Emptyhanded, idle, lazy.

manivela [mah-ne-vay'-lah], *f.* Winch, handle, crank.

manjar [mah-har'], *m.* 1. Food, victuals. 2. *(Met.)* Refection or entertainment which recruits the spirits. 3. Any of the four suits of a pack of cards. **Manjar exquisito**, tasty morse. **Manjar espiritual**, food for the mind.

manjarria [man-har'-re-ah], *f. (Cuba)* The driving beam of a canemill.

manjelín [man-hay-leen'], *m.* Weight used for diamonds: carat.

manjolar [man-ho-lar'], *va.* To carry a hawk in the hand, in a basket or a cage.

manjorrada [man-hor-rah'-dah], *f.* Abundance of ordinary victuals.

mano [mah'-no], *f.* 1. The hand. 2. Fore foot of a quadruped. 3. Among butchers, the feet of cattle after being cut off. 4. Proboscis, the snout or trunk of an elephant. 5. Hand, side, right or left. 6. Hand of a clock or watch (reloj). 7. Pestle. 8. A long cylindrical stone, with which cocoa is ground, to make chocolate. 9. Quire of paper. 10. Command, power. 11. Reprimand, censure. 12. The musical scale. 13. First hand at play (cartas). 14. Workmanship; power or means of making or attaining something. 15. Hand, time or turn in correcting something. 16. Cover, or varnish, colors, coat, laid over a thing (pintura). 17. Industry. 18. *V.* PATROCINIO. 19. *V.* SOCORRO. *-pl.* 1. Handicraft, handiwork. 2. Works of the hand considered by themselves. 20. Lot, series (grupo). 21. Skill, dexterity (destreza). 22. *(LAm.)* Misfortune (desgracia), mishap; unexpected event (imprevisto). 23. *(LAm. Aut.)* One-way street. **Mano en el juego**, deal, in a game. **A la mano**, at hand, near at hand. **A mano**, at hand; with the hand, studiously. **Manos de carnero**, sheep's trotters. **Manos de vaca**, cow-heels. **¡Manos a la obra!** *(Naut.)* bar a hand! to work! **Manos libres**, emoluments annexed to an office or place. **A dos manos**; willingly, readily. **A manos llenas**, liberally, abundantly, copiously. **Ser sus pies y sus manos**, to be one's chief support and consolation in distress. **Venir con sus manos lavadas**, to usurp the fruit of another's labor. **Bajo mano** or **de mano**, underhandedly, secretly. **Estar a mano**, to be square, to be quits. **Alzar la mano**, *(Met.)* (1) to lift the hand, threatening to strike. (2) To cease protecting an individual. (3) To leave off attending to a business which one had begun to care for. **Mano de santo**, sure remedy. **Bordado a mano**, handembroidered. **Llegó a mis manos**, it reached me. **Coger a uno con las manos en la masa**, to catch somebody red-handed. **De segunda mano**, second-hand. **Ha hecho cuanto ha estado en su mano**, he has done all in his power. **Darse la mano**, to shake hands. **Se le fue la mano**, his hand slipped. **Llevarse las manos a la cabeza**, to throw one's hands in the air. **No hay quien le meta mano**, there's nobody to touch him. **Tener mano para**, to be clever at. **Mano de obra**, labor.

manobra [mah-no'-brah], *f. (Prov.)* Raw material.

manobre [mah-no'-bray], *m. (Prov.)* A hodman, hod-carrier.

manojico, illo, ito [mah-no-hee'-co], *m. dim.* A small bundle, a small fagot.

manojo [mah-no'-ho], *m.* 1. A bundle of herbs or other things which may be held in the hand. 2. A fuzot or bundle of twigs bound together for the fire. **Manojo de llaves**, hunch of keys. **Un manojo de apio**, a bunch of celery. **A manojos**, abundantly.

manómetro [mah-no'-may-tro], *m. (Phys.)* Manometer, an instrument for ascertaining the tension of gases; pressure gauge.

manopla [mah-no'-plah], *f.* 1. Gauntlet, a glove for defense. 2. Coachman's whip. 3. *(Carib. Cono Sur)* knuckle duster (puño de hierro). 4. *(Cono Sur)* Spanner (llave inglesa).

manosear [mah-no-say-ar'], *va.* 1. To handle (tocar), to touch, to feel. 2. To rumple clothes (ajar).

manoseo [mah-no-say'-o], *m.* Handling, fingering, touching; rumpling; pawing; *(LAm.)* feeling up, touching up.

manotada, *f.* **manotazo**, *m.* [mah-no-tah'-dah, mah-no-tah'-tho]. Blow with the hand, a cuff (golpe).

manotear [mah-no-tay-ar'], *va.* To strike with the hand. *-vn.* To wring the hands from emotion, to gesticulate.

manoteo [mah-no-tay'-o], *m.* 1. A blow with the hand. 2. Manual gesticulation (gestos). 3. *(Mex.)* Theft, robbery (robo).

manquear [man-kay-ar'], *vn.* To affect the cripple, to pretend to be maimed.

manquedad [man-kay-dahd'], *f.* or **Manquera**, *f.* 1. Lameness, an injury which prevents the use of the hands or arms. 2. Defect, imperfection.

mansalva, A [ah man-sahl'-vah], *adv.* Unsportsmanly, cowardly. **Tiro a mansalva**, pot shot.

mansamente [man'-sah-men-tay], *adv.* Meekly, gently, quietly.

mansedumbre [man-say-doom'-bray], *f.* Meekness, gentlelness (persona), peacefulness, mildness, manageableness.

mansejón, na [man-say-hone', nah], *a.* Tame (animales).

mansera [man-say'-rah], *f. (Cuba)* A vat placed below the hammers of a sugar-mill, which receives the cane-juice.

mansión [man-se-on'], *f.* 1. Mansion (casa suntuosa). 2. **Mansión señorial**, stately home.

manso, sa [mahn'-so, sah], *a.* 1. Tame (animales). 2. Meek, gentle (persona), tractable; soft, quiet, mild, gentle, lamblike.

manso [mahn'-so], *m.* Male, which guides the flocks of goats, sheep, or cattle; bellwether.

manta [mahn'-tah], *f.* 1. A woollen blanket (de cama); in some parts of America, domestic cotton skirting. **Manta blanca**, bleached cotton. **Manta eléctrica**, electric blanket. **Liarse la manta a la cabeza**, to decide to go the whole hog. 2. A horse-blanket. 3. *(Mil.)* Mantelet, a movable parapet. 4. Thrashing, drubbing. 5. *(Min.)* A bag of agave for loading ore in clearings. 6. The devilfish octopus. 7. *(S. Amer.)* A mantle. 8. A game of cards resembling *tresillo* or *ombre*.

manteador, ra [man-tay-ah-dor', rah], *m. & f.* Tosser, one who tosses in a blanket.

manteamiento [man-tay-ah-me-en'-to], *m.* Tossing in a blanket.

mantear [man-tay-ar'], *va.* To toss in a blanket. *-vn. (Prov.)* To gad frequently abroad in a mantle (mujeres).

manteca [man-tay'-cah], *f.* 1. Lard, fat. 2. Butter. 3. Pulpy and oily parts of fruits. 4. A name given to certain metallic chlorides, as of antimony, bismuth, and zinc. 5. Dough (dinero); goods (género). 6. *(LAm.)* Hash, marijuana. 7. *(And.)* Servant, girl.

mantecada [man-tay-cah'-dah], *f.* Buttered toast and sugar.

mantecado [man-tay-cah'-do], *m.* 1. Butter-cake. 2. Ice-cream (helado).

mantecón [man-tay-cone'], *m.* Milk-sop; sweet-tooth, a dainty person.

mantecoso, sa [man-tay-co'-so, sah], *a.* Buttery (como la mantequilla), consisting of butter, mellow.

mantel [man-tel'], *m.* 1. Table-cloth: commonly used in the plural. 2. Altar cloth. **Levantar los manteles**, to clear the table. **Poner los manteles**, to lay the table.

mantelería [man-tay-lay-ree'-ah], *f.* Table linen.

manteleta [man-tay-lay'-tah], *f.* Mantelet, a small mantle, cloak, or scarf (prenda de señora).

mantelete [man-tay-lay'-tay], *m.* 1. Mantelet, a short mantle worn by bishops. 2. Mantelet, a movable parapet. 3. *(Her.)* Mantling, the representation of a mantle or any drapery drawn about a coat of arms.

mantellina [man-te-lyee'-nah], *f.* A short cloak worn by women.

mantenedor [man-tay-nay-dor'], *m.* The principal in a tournament.

mantener [man-tay-nerr'], *va.* 1. To maintain, to support (idea, opinión), to keep up with the hand; to hold up. 2. To maintain, to support life, to nourish, to keep, to feed (alimentar). 3. To maintain, to continue, to keep up (costumbre, disciplina). 4. To be the first challenges at a tournament. 5. To persevere, to persist in a design. 6. To support a weight. 7. To pursue, to continue. 8. To maintain, to hold out, to defend or sustain an opinion. 9. To support anyone in the possession of a thing. **Mantener correspondencia**, to keep up a correspondence. **Mantener algo en equilibrio**, to keep something balanced. **Le mantiene la esperanza**, he is sustained by hope. **Mantener la comida caliente**, to keep the food hot. *-vr.* 1. To continue residing in a place. 2. To continue in the same condition without alteration. 3. To nourish or gain nourishment, to maintain oneself. **Mantenerse firme**, to stand one's ground. **Mantenerse en lo dicho**, to abide by.

manteniente [man-tay-ne-en'-tay], *m.* A violent blow with both hands.

mantenimiento [man-tay-ne-me-en'-to], *m.* Maintenance, sustenance, upkeep.

manteo [man-tay'-o], *m.* 1. A long cloak or mantle worn by priests and formerly by students. 2. Sort of woollen petticoat.

mantequera [man-tay-kay'-rah], *f* 1. A churn (para batir). 2. A butter dish or bowl (de mesa).

mantequero, ra [man-tay-kay'-ro, rah], *m. & f.* One who sells butter, dairy-man, dairy-maid.

mantequilla [man-tay-keel'-lyah], *f.* Butter (manteca de vaca). **Mantequilla fresca**, fresh butter. **Mantequilla derretida**, melted butter.

mantaquillera [man-tay-keel-lyay'-rah], *f.* Butter dish.

mantera [man-tay'-rah], *f.* Mantle-maker, one who makes or sells mantles.

mantero, ra [man-tay'-ro, rah], *m. & f.* One who sells or manufactures blankets.

mántide [mahn'-te-day], *f. (Zool.)* The praying mantis, an orthopterous insect.

mantilla [man-teel'-lyah], *f.* 1. Mantilla, or veil (de mujer). **Mantilla de encajes**, lace mantilla. 2. Housing, saddle-cloth.

-pl. The outer (long) clothes of little children (de bebé). 3. *(typ.)* A blanket. **Estar en mantillas**, to be in a state of infancy.

mantillo [man-teel'-lyo], *m.* Humus, dung, organic portion of soil.

mantillón, na [man-teel-lyone', nah], *a. (Prov.)* Dirty, slovenly.

manto [mahn'-to], *m.* 1. Silken veil for ladies, a mantle, a kirtle. 2. Cloak (capa), robe; a mantle of state. 3. Mantelpiece of a chimney. 4. In mines, a horizontal vein. 5. Veil, cover.

mantón [man-tone'], *m.* 1. *(Aug.)* A large cloak or mantle. 2. A kind of shawl; in Cuba, a woman's mantilla.

manuable [mah-noo-ah'-blay], *a.* Tractable, manageable.

manual [mah-noo-ahl'], *a.* 1. Manual, handy, performed by hand. 2. Easily handled or performed with the hand. 3. Tractable, pliant; light, prompt. **Tener habilidad manual**, to be clever with one's hands. **Trabajo manual**, manual labor.

manual [mah-noo-ahl'], *m.* 1. Manual, a portable book. 2. Book in which the heads of matters are set down; notebook, account-book. 3. Ritual, a book of rites. 4. Old name of the journal, a book of accounts recorded so as to be easily posted in the ledger. *(Acad.)* 5. *pl.* Extra fees given to the priests for being present in the choir. **Manual de instrucciones**, instruction book, servicing manual.

manualidad [mah-noo-ah-le-dahd'], *f.* Manual craft.

manualmente [mah-noo-al'-men-tay], *adv.* Manually, by hand.

manubrio [mah-noo'-bre-o], *m.* 1. Handlebar (de unabicicleta). 2. Handle (manivela). 3. *(Mus.)* Barrel organ.

manucodiata [mah-noo-co-de-ah'-tah], *f.* Bird of paradise.

manuella [mah-noo-el'-lyah], *f.* Hand-spike.

manufactura [mah-noo-fac-too'-rah], *f.* Manufacture, any mechanical work.

manufacturar [mah-noo-fac-too-rar'], *va.* To manufacture.

manufacturero, ra [mah-noo-fac-too-ray'-ro, rah], *a.* Belonging to manufacture.

manumisión [mah-noo-me-se-on'], *f.* Manumission.

manumiso, sa [mah-noo-mee'-so, sah], *pp. irr.* or MANUMITIR. Emancipated. *-a.* Free, disengaged.

manumisor [mah-noo-me-sor'], *m. (Law.)* Liberator.

manumitir [mah-noo-me-teer'], *va.* To manumit, to emancipate.

manuscrito, ta [mah-noos-cree'-to, tah], *a.* Manuscript, not printed.

manuscrito [mah-noos-cree'-to], *m.* Manuscript, a book written and not printed.

manutención [mah-noo-ten-the-on'], *f.* 1. Maintaining. 2. Maintenance, supply of the necessaries of life (sustento). 3. Maintenance, support, protection. 4. Conservation.

manutener [mah-noo-tay-nerr'], *va. (Law.)* To maintain, to support.

manzana [man-thah'-nah], *f.* 1. An apple. 2. Block of houses bounded on every side by a street; square. 3. *(Ant.)* Knob of a sword. **La manzana de la discordia**, *(fig.)* apple of discord. **Manzana silvestre**, wild apple.

manzanal [man-thah-nahl'], *m.* 1. *V.* MANZANAR. 2. *V.* MANZANO.

manzanar [man-thah-nar'], *m.* Orchard, a garden of apple-trees.

manzanil [man-thah-neel'], *a.* Like an apple.

manzanilla [man-thah-neel'-lyah], *f.* 1. *(Bot.)* Common chamomile. **Manzanilla fina**, golden cotula. 2. Small ball or knob at the top of coaches, bedsteads, etc. 3. Kind of small olive. 4. Lower part of the chin. 5. The pad, or cushion, of the feet of animals having claws. 6. *(dim.)* A small apple. 7. Manzanilla (jerez).

manzanillo, ito [man-thah-nee'-lyo, ee-to], *m. (Bot.)* Little apple-tree. **Olivo manzanillo**, a kind of olive-tree. *-m.* Manchineel, a tropical American tree, having an apple-like fruit reputed to be poisonous.

manzanita [man-thah-nee'-tah], *f.* 1. *(dim.)* Little apple. 2. Tame of a California shrub, or small tree, related to the *madroño.* Named from its fruit.

manzano [man-thah'-no], *m. (Bot.)* Apple-tree.

maña [mah'-nyah], *f.* 1. Handiness, skill, contrivance, dexterity, cleverness, expertness, ability, faculty. 2. Cunning, craftiness, artifice, craft. 3. An evil habit or custom. 4. Bundle of hemp or flax when reaped. **Darse maña**, to contrive, to bring about, to manage. **Tiene maña para hacerlo**, he's got the knack of doing it.

mañana [mah-nyah'-nah], *f.* 1. Morning. 2. The part of the day from twelve o'clock at night to twelve o'clock at noon. **Por la mañana**, in the morning. **Pasado mañana**, the day, after tomorrow. **Esta mañana**, this morning. **A la mañana siguiente**, the following morning. **A las tres de la mañana**, at three o'clock in the morning. *-adv.* 1. Tomorrow. 2. Soon. 3. Expression of negation. 4. In time to come. **Tomar la mañana** (1) To rise very early. (2) *(coll.)* To drink liquor before breakfast. **Muy de mañana**, very early. **A partir de mañana**, as from tomorrow. **Pasado mañana**, the day after tomorrow. **Hasta mañana**, see you tomorrow. **Muy de mañana**, very early. **No dejes para mañana lo que puedas hacer hoy**, do not put off till tomorrow what you can do today.

mañanear [mah-nyah-nay-ar'], *vn.* To rise early habitually.

mañanica, ita [mah-nyah-nee'-cah], *f.* Break of day, early morning (madrugada).

mañear [mah-nyay-ar'], *va.* To act with craft and address to attain one's end.

mañería [mah-nyay-ree'-ah], *f.* 1. Sterility. 2. Right of succeeding to the possessions of those who die without legitimate succession.

mañero, ra [mah-nyay'-ro, rah], *a.* 1. Dexterous, skillful, artful. 2. Meek, tractable. 3. *(Cono Sur)* Vicious (animal).

mañosamente [mah-nyo-sah-men'-tay], *adv.* Dexterously, neatly, handily, cleverly; subtly; maliciously, graftly.

mañoso, sa [mah-nyo'-so, sah], *a.* 1. Dexterous, skillful, handy, clever (hábil). 2. *(And.)* Lazy (perezoso). 3. *(And. CAm. Cono Sur, Mex.)* Vicious (animal); obstinate (terco).

mañuela [mah-nyoo-ay'-lah], *f.* Low cunning, mean trick.

maoísmo [mah-o-ees'-mo], *m.* Maoism.

maoísta [mah-o-ees'-tah], *a.* Maoist. *-m & f.* Maoist.

mapa [mah'-pah], *m.* Map, a geographical picture. **Mapa mural**, wall map. **El mapa político**, the political scene. **Mapamundi**, a map of the world.*-f.* Anything excellent and prominent in its line.

mapache [mah-pah'-chay], *m. (Zool.)* Racoon.

mápula [mah'-poo-lah], *f. (Min.)* A precious stone mined near Popayan in Colombia.

mapurite [mah-poo-ree'-tay], *m. (Amer. Ven.)* A skunk.

maque [mah'-kay], *m. (Mex.)* A certain varnish or lacquer.

maqueta [mah-kay'-tah], *f.* 1. Model; scale model. 2. Dummy (libro).

maquí [mah-kee'], *m.* 1. Kind of ginger. 2. A lemur of Madagascar.

maquiavélico, ca [mah-ke-ah-vay'-le-co, cah], *a.* Machiavelian.

maquiavelismo [mah-ke-ah-vay-lees'-mo], *m.* Machiavelism.

maquievelista [mah-ke-ah-vay-lees'-tah], *m.* Machievelian.

maquila [mah-kee'-lah], *f.* 1. Multure (tributo), toll-corn, corn which the miller takes for grinding. 2. Toll in general. 3. Corn measure, the 24th part of a *fanega.*

maquilar [mah-ke-lar'], *va.* 1. To measure and take the miller's dues for grinding corn. 2. To clip, to retrench, to cut off.

maquilero, maquilón [mah-ke-lay'-ro, mah-ke-lone'], *m.* One who measures or takes the miller's dues for grinding corn.

maquillaje [mah-keel-lyah'-hay], *m.* Make-up, cosmetics.

maquillar [mah-kel-lyahr'], *va.* To make up. *-vr.* to make up.

máquina [mah'-ke-nah], *f.* 1. Machine. 2. Engine. 3. A vast structure. 4. Project, imaginative scheme (projecto). 5. *(Cuba)* An automobile. **Máquina calculadora digital**, digital computer. **Máquina de coser**, sewing machine. **Máquina tragaperras**, fruit machine. **Má para hacer punto**, knitting machine. **Coser a máquina**, to machine. **Máquina de escribir**, typewriter. **Escribir a máquina**, to type. **Máquina de vapor**, steam engine. **Máquina de encauzamiento**, *(Comput)*. pipeline machine. **Máquina vectorial**, *(Comput.)* vector machine.

maquinación [mah-ke-nah-the-on'], *f.* Machination, artifice, contrivance.

maquinador, ra [mah-ke-nah-dor', rah], *m. & f.* Contriver, schemer, machinator; plotter.

maquinal [mah-ke-nahl'], *a.* Machinal, relating to machines, mechanical.

maquinalmente [mah-ke-nahl'-men-tay], *adv.* Mechanically; undesignedly.

maquinar [mah-ke-nar'], *va.* To machinate, to plan, to contrive, to hatch, to conspire, to compass.

maquinaria [mah-ke-nah'-re-ah], *f.* 1. Applied mechanics, the art of contriving and building machines. 2. Machinery. 3. Mechanics.

maquinista [mah-ke-nees'-tah], *m.* Machinist, mechanician, mechanist.

mar [mar], *m. y f.* 1. The sea 2. Sea (océano), some large lakes. 3. Sea, proverbially for any large quantity. 4. Swell (marejada). **Alta mar** or **mar ancha**, the main sea, the high seas. **Baja mar**, low water, ebbtide. **Mar llena, pleamar**, high water. **Correr los mares**, to follow the seas. **Salir a la mar**, to put to sea. **La mar está muy crecida**, the sea runs very high. **Un mar de confusiones**, a sea of confusion. **Estar hecho un mar de lágrimas**, to weep floods. **Está la mar de contento**, he's terribly happy.

marabú [mah-rah-boo'], *m.* Marabou, an African bird of the stork family and the white plumes from it.

maraca [mah-rah'-kah], *f.* 1. *(Mus.)* Maraca, rattle. 2. *(Conto Sur)* Whore (prostituta).

maranata [mah-rah-nah'-tah], *f.* Maranatha, a form of anathematizing.

maraña [mah-rah'-nyah], *f.* 1. Place rendered impassable by brambles or briers. 2. Entanglement of a skein of silk, thread, cotton, etc. 3. Silk waste and stuff made from it. 4. Perplexity, puzzle. 5. Fraud, imposition. 6. Intrigue, plot.

marañado, da [mah-rah-nyah'-do, dah], *a.* Entangled, perplexed.

marañero, ra [mah-rah-nyay'-ro, rah], **Marañoso, sa.** *a.* Entangling, insnaring, perplexing.

marañón [mah-rah-nyone'], *m. (Cuba)* The common cashew; also its fruit, the cashew-nut.

marasmo [mah-rahs'-mo], *m. (Med.)* Consumption, marasmus, wasting.

maratón [mah-rah-tone'], *f.* Marathon.

maravedí [mah-rah-vay-dee'], *m. (pl.* Maravedíes.*)* Maravedi, an old Spanish coin.

maravilla [mah-rah-veel'-lyah], *f.* 1. Wonder, an uncommon event; a marvel (objecto, asunto), admiration. 2. *(Bot.)* Common marigold. **A las (mil) maravillas**, uncommonly well; wonderfully. **Hacer maravillas**, to work wonders.

maravillar [mah-rah-vil-lyar'], *va.* To admire, to regard with wonder.-*vr.* To wonder, to marvel, to be astonished, to be struck with admiration.

maravillosamente [mah-rah-vel-lyo'-sah-men-tay], *adv.* Wonderfully, marvellously, miraculously.

maravilloso, sa [mah-rah-vil-lyo'-o-so sah], *a.* Wonderful, marvellous, monstrous, astonishing, admirable, miraculous; strange.

marbete [mar-bay'-tay], *m.* 1. Stamp, the manufacturers mark on cloth. 2. Label (etiqueta).

marca [mar'-cah], *f.* 1. A frontier province. 2. The due measure or weight of anything. 3. Marker, stamp, an instrument used for marking (herramienta). 4. Landmark, light-house. 5. A mark made upon a person or thing to distinguish it from another. 6. The act of marking. **De marca**, excellent of its kind. **Marca registrada**, registered

trademark. **Coches de 3 marcas distintas**, cars of 3 different makes.

marcadamente [mar-cah-dah-men'-tay], *adv.* Markedly, notably.

marca de fábrica [mar'-cah day fah'-bre-cah], *f.* Trade mark.

marcado [mar-cah'-do], *a.* Marked, strong, pronounced; distinct. **Con marcado acento argentino**, with a marked Argentinian accent. -*m.* Set (pelo).

marcador [mar-cah-dor'], *m.* Marker, assay-master, bookmark (de libro); high-lighter (para escribir). **Marcador de caminos**, road-sign. **Inaugurar el marcador**, to open the scoring.

marcapasos [mar-cah-pah'-sos], *m. (Med.)* Pacemaker.

marcar [mar-car'], *va.* 1. To mark, to brand; to embroider initials; to mark off (tierra). **Marcar el campo**, to mark the ground for a camp. 2. To mark (indicar), to observe, to note; to designate. **Las agujas marcan las 2**, the hands point to 2 o'clock. 3. To keep a tally of (números). 4. *(Mus.)* To mark (paso); to beat (compás). 5. *(Telec)*. To dial. 6. *(Dep.)* To score (gol, tanto). **Marcar un tanto en la discusión.** to score a point in the argument. 7. To put a price.

marcasita [mar-cah-se'-tah], *f.* Marcasite, a dimorphous iron sulphide.

marcear [mar-thay-ar'], *va.* To shear the wool, hair, or fur of animals.

marceo [mar-thay-o], *m.* Trimming away of the lower soiled parts of honey-combs in spring by beekeepers.

marcha [mar'-chah], *f.* 1. March, a solemn movement of troops: a journey of soldiers. **Marchas forzadas**, forced marches. **Abrir la marcha**, to come first. **Estar en marcha**, to be in motion. 2. March, signal to move. 3. Marching tune. **Marcha fúnebre**, funeral march. 4. *(Prov.)* Bonfire. 5. The movement of a watch. 6. Regularity, working order of a machine. **Tocar la marcha**, to strike up a march. 7. *(Dep.)* Walk; walk (excursión), hike. 8. Speed (velocidad). **A toda marcha**, at full speed. 9. Progress (progreso), march (avance); trend (rumbo); path (de huracán). **La marcha de los acontecimientos**, the march of events. **No le va la marcha**, he's not with it. 10. Charm (duende), magic, appeal, mystery (misterio); inipiration (inspiración); style (estilo). 11. *(Carib.)* Slow trot (caballo). 12. *(Mex. Aut.)* Self-starter.

marchamar [mar-chah-mar'], *va.* To mark goods at the custom-house.

marchamero [mar-chah-may'-ro], *m.* Custom-house officer who marks goods.

marchamo [mar-chah'-mo], *m.* Mark put on goods at the custom-house.

marchante [mar-chahn'-tay], *m.* 1. Shop-keeper, dealer (tratante). 2. *(Prov. Andal.)* Customer (cliente), buyer. 3. *(Cuba)* Sharper, trickster. -*a.* 1. *V.* MERCANTIL 2. Merchantable.

marchantear [mar-chan-tay-ar], *va.* To trade, especially in live-stock.

marchar [mar-char'], *vn. & vr.* 1. To go, to go away, to go off, to depart from a place, to move (viajar). 2. To march, to walk gravely. 3. *(Mil.)* To march, in military form. 4. *(Naut.)* To have much headway, to sail fast. 5. *(Mec.)* To go; to run, to function, to work; to run (tren). **El motor no marcha**, the engine isn't working. 6. To go, to proceed. **Todo marcha bien.** Everything is going well. 7. To go away, to leave. **Marcharse a otro sitio**, to go somewhere else.

marchazo [mar-chah'-tho], *m.* Braggadocio, boaster, braggart.

marchitable [mar-che-tah'-blay], *a.* Perishable, liable to wither.

marchitamiento [mar-che-tah-me-en'-to], *m.* The act of withering or fading.

marchitar [mar-che-tar'], *va.* 1. To wither, to make fade. 2. To fade, to wear away, to deprive of vigor. -*vr.* 1. To wither, to fade, to fall away; to dry up. 2. To pine away, to grow lean.

marchitez [mar-che-teth'], *f.* Withering, fading, marcidity.

marchito, ta [mar-chee'-to, tah], *a.* Faded, withered, decayed, marcid.

marchoso [mar-cho'-so], *a.* 1. Ultramoderm (moderno); trendy. 2. Lively (animado), fast-living. 3. Fun-loving (amigo de placeres).

marcial [mar-the-ahl'], *m.* Aromatic powder used anciently for dressing gloves.

marcial [mar-the-ahl'], *a.* 1. Martial, war-like. 2. *(Pharm.)* Martial, having iron. 3. Frank, unceremonious.

marcialidad [mar-the-ah-le-dahd'], *f.* 1. Martialness. 2. Freedom, assumed familiarity or liberty.

marciano [mar-the-ah'-no], *a.* Martian. -*m & f.* Martian.

marco [mar'-co], *m.* 1. Door-case, window-case. 2. Picture-frame. 3. Mark, a weight of eight ounces. 4. An instrument for measuring the length of shoes, etc. 5. A measure for liquids. 6. The necessary size of timber for being foiled. 7. Model, archetype. 8. Measure of ground which should have a *fanega* of grain. 9. Mark, the unit of German money-values. **Marco para cuadro**, picture frame. **Cuadro de ventana**, window frame. **márcola** [mar'-co-lah], *f.* Pruning hook for trimming trees.

marea [mah-ray'-ah], *f.* 1. The tide. 2. Sea shore; tidal area. 3. Soft wind. 4. Collection of street dirt. 5. Drizzle (llovizna); *(Cono Sur)* sea mist. **Marea creciente**, flood-tide. **Marea menguante**, ebb-tide. **Dirección de las mareas**, setting of the tide. **Ir contra marea**, to sail against the tide. **Navegar con la marea**, to tide up or down. **Mareas vivas**, springtides. **La marea crece**, the tide flows.

mareado [mah-ray-ah'-do], *a.* **Estar mareado** 1. To fell sick (nauseado); to feel dizzy (aturdido); to be seasick. 2. To be a bit drunk (bebido).

mareaje [mah-ray-ah'-hay], *m.* Art of navigating a ship.

mareamiento [mah-ray-ah-me-en'-to], *m.* Sea-sickness.

mareante [mah-ray-ahn'-tay], *a.* Skilled in navigating a ship.

marear [mah-ray-ar'], *va.* 1. To work a ship. 2. To molest and harass by impertinent questions (irritar). 3. To sell goods at auction. 4. *(Med.)* To make somebody feel sick (causarnáuseas). 5. *(Carib. Mex.)* To cheat. -*vr.* 1. To be sea sick. 2. To be damaged at sea; to be averaged (mercancía). 3. *(Carib. Cono Sur)* To fade (paño).

marecanita [mah-ray-cah-nee'-tah], *f. (Min.)* Marekanite, a variety of obsidian occurring in rounded globules.

marejada [mah-ray-hah'-dah], *f.* Swell of the sea, head sea, surf. **Tuvimos una marejada del noroeste**, we had a great sea from the north-west.

mare magnum [mah'-ray mahg'-noom], *m. (Let.)* Expressing the abundance or magnitude of anything; also confusion, disorder.

maremoto [mah-ray-mo'-to], *m.* Tidal wave.

mareo [mah-ray'-o], *m.* 1. Sea-sickness (en mar); sick feeling (náuseas); dizziness (aturdimiento). 2. *(coll.)* Molestation, vexation. 3. Nuisance, bore (lata). **Es un mareo que…**, it is a nuisance having to…

mareógrafo [mah-ray-o'-grah-fo], *m.* Stereograph, a recording tide-gauge.

marero [mah-ray'-ro], *a.* Sea-breeze, wind coming from the sea.

mareta [mah-ray'-tah], *f. (Naut.)* Slight commotion of the sea.

maretazo [mah-ray-tah'-tho], *m.* Surge of the sea.

márfaga, or **márfega** [mar'-fah-gah], *f.* 1. A coarse woollen frieze, or sack-cloth, anciently used for mourning. 3. *(Prov.)* Rug, a bed coverlet.

marfil [mar-feel'], *m.* Ivory. **Marfil vegetal**, vegetable ivory, the fruit of a palm-tree of equatorial America.

marfileño, ña [mar-fe-lay'-nyo, nyah], *a. (Poet.)* Belonging to ivory.

marfuz [mar-footh'], *a.* 1. Repudiated, rejected. 2. Fallacious, deceitful.

marga, marea [mar'-gah, mah-ray'-ah], *f.* 1. Marl, loam, clay-marl. 2. A coarse cloth, formerly used for mourning.

margaíta [mar-gah-e'-tah], *f.* Marl in which either the limestone or clay exceeds eighty parts.

margajita [mar-gah-hee'-tah], *f.* Iron pyrites.

margal [mar-gahl'], *m.* Soil chiefly clayey.

margallón [mar-gah-lyone'], *m. V.* PALMITO.

margar [mar-gar'], *va.* To manure with marl.

margarato [mar-gah-rah'-to], *m. (Chem.)* Margarate.

margárico, ca [mar-gah'-re-co, cah], *a.* **Acido margárico**, margaric acid.

margarina [mar-gah-ree'-nah], *f.* Margarine.

margarita [mar-gah-ree'-tah], *f.* 1. Daisy. **Criar margaritas**, to be pushing up the daisies. 2. Pearl. 3. Periwinkle.

margen [mar'-hen], *com.* 1. Edge, border (borde). 2. Margin (de papel). 3. Marginal notation. 4. *(Fig.)* Latitude. 5. *(Fig.)* Chance. 6. *(Fig.)* Margin; gap (intervalo), space; leeway (libertad de acción). **A media margen**, with a center margin. **Dar margen para**, to bring about. **Margen de beneficio**, profit margin. **Dejar a uno al margen**, to leave somebody out. **Mantenerse al margen**, to keep out.

margenar [mar-hay-nar'], *va.* 1. *V.* MARGINAR. 2. To leave a margin on paper.

marginación [mar-he-nah-the-on'], *f.* 1. Exclusion (acto). 2. Isolation (estado).

marginado, da [mar-he-nah'-do, dah], *a. & pp.* of MARGINAR. Marginated, having a margin. **Quedar marginado**, to be excluded. **Sentirse marginado**, to feel rejected.

marginal [mar-he-nahl'], *a.* Marginal, belonging to the margin.

marginar [mar-he-nar'], *va.* 1. To make annotations on the margin (página). 2. To exclude (persona), to leave out.

margoso, sa [mar-go'-so, sah], *a.* Marly, loamy.

margrave [mar-grah'-vay], *m.* Margrave, a German title of sovereignty.

marguera [mar-gay'-rah], *f.* Marlpit.

María [mah-ree'-ah], *f.* 1. *(coll.)* A white waxtaper, placed in the middle of eight shorter yellow wax-candles, in Roman Catholic churches. 2. An old silver coin worth twelve reals vellon. 3. Mary, a proper name. **María Antonieta**, Marie Antoinette.

mariachi [mah-re-ah'-che], *m.* 1. Mariachi, Mexican street band (conjunto). 2. Member of a mariachi. 3. Mariachi music (música).

marial [mah-re-ahl'], *a.* Praising the Virgin Mary.

marianismo [mah-re-ah-nees'-mo], *m.* Mariolatry.

mariano, na [mah-re-ah'-no, nah], *a.* Marian. **Año mariano**, Marian Year.

marica [mah-ree'-cah], *f.* 1. Magpie. 2. Jack of diamonds. -*m.* 1. Sissy. 2. *V.* MARICÓN.

maricastaña [mah-re-cas-tah'-nyah], *f.* **En tiempo de Maricastaña**, ages ago, in days of yore.

maricón [mah-re-con'], *m.* 1. Sissy. 2. *(coll.)* Fairy, queer, puff (sodomita).

mariconada [mah-re-co-nah'-dah], *f.* Dirty trick.

maridable [mah-re-dah'-blay], *a.* Conjugal, matrimonial, connubial, martial.

maridaje [mah-re-dah'-hay], *m.* 1. Marriage (unión), conjugal union. 2. Intimate connection or union.

maridanza [mah-re-dahn'-thah], *f. (Prov.)* Treatment of a wife.

maridar [mah-re-dar'], *vn.* To marry. -*va.* To unite, to join.

maridazo [mah-re-dah'-tho], *m. V.* GURRUMINO.

maridillo [mah-re-deel'-lyo], *m.* 1. A sorry, pitiful husband. 2. A brazier, used by women to warm the feet.

marido [mah-ree'-do], *m.* Husband, a married man.

mariguana or **marihuana** [mah-re-goo-ah'-nah, mah-re-oo-ah'-nah], *f.* Marihuana or marijuana.

marimacho [mah-re-mah'-cho], *m.* Virago, a robust, masculine woman.

marimanta [mah-re-mahn'-tah], *f.* Bug bear, a phantom.

marimba [mah-reem'-bah], *f.* 1. *(Mus.)* Marimba; *(Carib. Cono Sur)* out-of-tune instrument. 2. *(Cono Sur)* Beating (paliza). 3. *(And. Med.)* Large goitre.

marímbula [mah-reem'-boo-lah], *f.* The jew's-harp. *V.* BIRIMBAO.

marimorena [mah-re-mo-ray'-nah], *f. (coll.)* Dispute, difference, quarrel.

marina [mah-ree'-nah], *f.* 1. Shore, sea-coast. 2. *(Pict.)* Seapiece. 3. Sea-manship (marinería), nautical art, marine, sea affairs. 4. The navy. **Soldados de marina**, marines. **Departamento de marina**, naval department.

marinda [mah-re-nah'-dah], *f.* 1. A stew much in favor among sailors. 2. A ship's provisions and the brine (marinade) with which it is prepared.

marinaje [mah-re-nah'-hay], *m.* 1. Sea-manship, the art of working a ship. 2. Sailors, considered as a body.

marinar [mah-re-nar'], *va.* 1. To marinate, to salt fish. 2. To man a ship taken from the enemy.

marinear [mah-re-nay-ar'], *va.* To be a mariner.

marinerado, da [mah-re-nay-rah'-do, dah], *a.* Manned, equipped. *V.* TRIPULADO.

marinería [mah-re-nay-ree'-ah], *f.* 1. Seamanship (arte). 2. Profession of sea-faring men. 3. The body of seamen.

marinero [mah-re-nay'-ro], *m.* Mariner, seaman, sailor. **A lo marinero**, in a seaman-like manner.

marinero [mah-re-nay'-ro], **ra**, *a.* Ready to sail.

marinesco, ca [mah-re-nes'-co, cah], *a.* Nautical. **A la marinesca**, in a seaman-like manner, ship-shape.

marino, na [mah-ree'-no, nah], *a.* Marine, belonging to the sea. **Fauna marina**, marine life.

marino [mah-ree'-no], *m.* Mariner, seaman, seafaring man.

marión, marón [mah-re-on', mah-rone'], *m.* Sturgeon.

marioneta [mah-re-o-nay'-tah], *f.* Marionette, puppet.

mariposa [mah-re-po'-sah], *f.* 1. Butterfly. **Mariposa de la col**, cabbage-white. 2. A night-taper. 3. Butterfly stroke (natación). 4. *(And. CAm.)* Toy windmill (juguete). 5. *(And.)* Blindman's buff.

mariposear [mah-re-po-say-ar'], *vn.* To flit like a butterfly (revolotear); to be fickle and capricious (ser inconstante); to flirt (coquetear).

mariquita [mah-re-kee'-tah], *f.* Lady-bird, lady-cow, or lady-fly, a hemispherical beetle.

marisabidilla [mah-re-sah-be-deel'-lyah], *f.* Blue stocking, a woman who presumes on being learned.

mariscal [mah-ris-cahl'], *m.* 1. Marshal, a general officer of high rank in some armies. 2. Farrier, blacksmith. **Mariscal de campo**, field-marshal, major-general, a rank inferior to lieutenant-general.

mariscalato [mah-ris-cah-lah'-to], *m. V.* MARISCALÍA.

mariscalía [mah-ris-cah-lee'-ah], *f.* Marshalship, the dignity or office of a marshal.

mariscar [mah-ris-car'], *va.* To gather shellfish or the strand.

mariscos [mah-rees'-cos], *m. pl.* Seafood.

marisma [mah-rees'-mah], *f.* Lake formed by the overflow of the tide.

marismo [mah-rees'-mo], *m. (Bot.) V.* ORZAGA.

marisquería [mah-rees-kay-ree'-ah], *f.* Shellfish bar, seafood restaurant.

marital [mah-re-tahl'], *a.* Marital, pertaining to a husband.

marítimo, ma [mah-ree'-te-mo, mah], *a.* Maritime, maritimal, marine, shipping (agente). **Ciudad marítima**, seaside town. **Seguro marítimo**, marine insurance.

maritornes [mah-re-tor'-nes], *f. (coll.)* An ill-shaped, awkward woman.

marjal [mah-hahl'], *m.* Fen, marsh, moor, moorland, marshy ground.

marjoleta [mar-ho-lay'-tah], *f. (Prov.) V.* MAJUELA.

marjoleto [mar-ho-lay'-to], *m. V.* MAJUELO or ESPINO MAJUELO.

márketing [mar'-kay-teen], *m.* Marketing; marketing technique.

marlo [mar'-lo], *m. (Amer.).* An ear of Indian corn.

marlota [mar-lo'-tah], *f.* Robe, a kind of Moorish gown.

marmatita [mar-mah-tee'-tah], *f. (Min.)* Marmatite, a ferriferous variety of sphalerite.

marmella [mar-mel'-lyah], *f.* Each of two long oval warts which some goats have under the neck.

marmellado, da [mar-mel-lyah'-do, dah], *a.* Having warts *(marmellas)* under the throat.

marmita [mar-mee'-tah], *f.* Kettle, flesh-pot, porridge-pot, a small copper.

marmitón [mar-me-tone'], *m.* Scullion, one who is engaged to wash the dishes and plates in the kitchen.

mármol [mahr'-mol], *m.* 1. Marble. **Mármol pintado** spotted marble. **Mármol rayado**, streaked marble. 2. Pillar, column. 3. Marver, flatting-table. 4. *(typ.)* Imposing-stone.

marmolejo [mar-mo-lay'-ho], *m.* A small pillar or column of marble.

marmoleño, ña [mar-mo-lay'-nyo, nyah], *a.* Made of marble, resembling marble.

marmolería [mar-mo-lay-ree'-ah], *f.* Any work made of marble.

marmolista [mar-mo-lees'-tah], *m.* Worker in marble, sculptor.

marmóreo, ea, marmoroso, sa [mar-mo'-ray-o, ah, mar-mo-ro'-so, sah], *a.* Marbled, marble, marmorean, made of marble.

marmosete [mar-mo-say'-tay], *m.* Among printers; a vignette, or ornamental cut, at the end of a chapter, or of a volume.

marmota [mar-mo'-tah], *f.* 1. *(Zool.)* Marmot, ground-hog, wood-chuck. 2. *(fig.)* Sleepy-head. **Dormir como una marmota**, to sleep like a log.

maroma [mah-ro'-mah], *f.* 1. Rope (cuerda), a thick cord made of bass or hemp. **Andar en la maroma**, 1. To dance on a rope. 2. *(Met.)* To engage in a perilous undertaking. 2. *(LAm.)* Tight rope (cuerda floja); acrobatic performance (actuación); *(Carib.)* Circus.

marota [mah-ro'-tah], *f. (Amer. Mex.) V.* MARIMACHO.

marqués [mar-kess'], *m.* Marquis, marquess.

marquesa [mar-kay'-sah], *f.* 1. Marchioness, the lady of a marquis. 2. *V.* MARQUESINA.

marquesado [mar-kay-sah'-do], *m.* Marquisate.

marquesica, illa, ita [mar-kay-see'-cah], *f. dim.* A little marchioness, a young marchioness.

marquesina [mar-key-see'-nah], *f.* Marquee, tilt over an officer's tent, serving more effectually to keep out the rain.

marquesita [mar-kay-see'-tah], *f.* Marcasite, pyrite, mundic, a metallic sulphide.

marquesote [mar-kay-so'-tay], *m. (Mex.)* Caramel, burnt sugar.

marqueta [mar-kay'-tah], *f.* Crude cake of wax.

marquetería [mar-kay-tay-ree'-ah], *f.* 1. Cabinet-manufactory. 2. Marquetry, checkered or inlaid work.

marquida, marquisa [mar-kee'-dah], *f.* Cant; low Prostitute.

marquito [mar-kee'-to], *m. dim.* A photographic kit; holder for a smaller plate.

marra [mar'-rah], *f.* 1. Want, deficiency, defect. 2. Club, knobbed stick.

márraga [mar'-ah-gah], *f. V.* MARGA.

marrajo [mar-rah'-ho], *m.* White shark.

marrajo, ja [mar-rha'-ho, hah], *a.* Sly cunning, crafty, artful, wily.

marrana [mar-rah'-nah], *f.* Sow, a female pig.

marranada [mar-rah-nah'-dah], *f.* 1. Hoggish action. 2. Swinishness, brutishness, filthiness; dirty, low act.

marranada [mar-rah-nah'-dah], *f. V.* CANALLA.

marranamente [mar-rah-nah-men'-tay], *adv.* Piggishly, swinishly.

marranchón, na [mar-ran-chon'], *a. V.* MARRANO.

marranería [mar-rah-nay-ree'-ah], *f.* 1. *V.* MARRANADA. 2. Trade in hogs.

marraneta [mar-rah-nay'-tah], *f. (Prov.)* A young sow.

marrano [mar-rah'-no], *m.* 1. Pig, hog. 2. Rafter or woodwork which supports a floor or cistern.

marrano, na [mar-rah'-no], *a.* Dirty, indecent.

marrar [mar-rar'], *vn.* 1. To deviate from truth or justice. 2. V. ERRAR. *-va.* **Marrar el tiro**, to miss; to miss the mark.

marras [mar'-ras], *adv. (coll.)* Long ago, long since. **Es un problema de marras**, it's the same old problem. **Hace marras que no le veo**, *(And.)* it's ages since I saw him.

marrasquino [mar-ras-kee'-no], *m.* Maraschino, a cordial.

marregón [mar-ray-gone'], *m. (Prov.)* Strawsack. V. JERGÓN

marrilla [mar-reel'lyah], *f.* A rather slender club.

marrillo [mar-reel'-lyo], *m. (Prov.)* Thick short stick.

marro [mar'-ro], *m.* 1. Kind of game, quoits. 2. Slip given by a deer or hare in the course of the chase. 3. Disappointed; failure. 4. Crooked bat for striking a ball.

marrojar [mar-ro-har'], *va.* To lop off the useless branches of trees.

marrón [mar-rone'], *m.* 1. Quoit, pitcher. 2. *(Cuba)* A runaway slave. 3. Chestnut (color); brown. 4. *(Culin.)* Marron glacé. 5. *(And.)* Curipaper. 6. *(Carib.)* Coffee with milk. 7. *(Jur.)* Charge (acusación); sentence (condena). **Comerse un marrón**, to cough up. **Le pillaron de marrón**, they gave him 5 years' bird. *-a.* Chestnut, brown; brown (zapatos).

marroquí [mar-ro-kee'], **marroquín, na** [mar-ro-keen', nah], *a.* Morocco, belonging to Morocco.

marrubio [mar-roo'-be-o], *m. (Bot.)* Common white horehound.

marrueco, ca [mar-roo-ay'-oo, cah], *a.* Moroccan, belonging to Morocco.

marrullería [mar-rool-lyay-ree'-ah], *f.* Cunning, craft; artful tricks.

marrullero, ra [mar-rool-lyay'-ro, rah], *a.* Crafty, cunning.

marsellés [mar-sel-lyess'], *m.* A kind of short jacket.

marsellés, sa [mar-sel-lyess', sah], *a.* Relating to Marseilles. *-f.* Marseillaise, the French national hymn.

marsopa, or **marsopla** [mar-so'-plah], *f.* Blunt-headed cachalot, porpoise.

marsupiales [mar-soo-pe-ah'-less]. *a. m. pl.* The marsupial animals, such as opossums and kangaroos.

marta [mar'-tah], *f.* Pine marten. **Martas**, martens, creased marten-skins.

martagón, na [mar-tah-gone', nah], *m. & f.* 1. *(coll.)* Cumling, artful person. 2. *m. (Bot.)* Wild lily, Turk's-cap lily.

Marte [mar'-tay], *m.* Mars; iron.

martellina [mar-tel-lyee'-nah], *f.* Marteline, a marble-worker's hammer having a surface presenting rows of teeth.

martes [mar'-tes], *m.* Tuesday. **Martes de carnaval**, Shrove Tuesday. **El martes pasado**, last Tuesday, **El martes que viene**, next Tuesday. **Vendra' el martes**, he will come on Tuesday.

martillada [mar-til-lyah'-dah], *f.* Stroke with the hammer.

martillador, ra [mar-til-lyah-dor', rah], *m. & f.* Hammerer.

martillar [mar-til-lyar'], *va.* To hammer (golpear con martillo), to malleate, to pound (machacar).

martillego [mar-til-lyay'-ho], *m. dim.* A small hammer.

martilleo [mar-til-lyay'-o], *m.* Noise caused by hammering.

martillo [mar-teel'-lyo], *m.* 1. A hammer; claw-hammer. 2. Person who perseveres in something. 3. Tuning hammer. 4. Malleus (hammer) the largest of the ossicles of the car. **A martillo**, with strokes of a hammer. **Martillo mecánico**, power hammer.

martinete [mar-te-nay'-tay], *m.* 1. A swift or martin. 2. The crest of the king-fisher. 3. Jack in a harpsichord; hammer of a pianoforte. 4. Hammer in copper-works. 5. A pile-driver, drop-hammer.

martingala [mar-tin-gah'-lah], *f.* 1. Martingale, a strap fastened to the girth and noseband of a horse. 2. Ancient kind of breeches.

martini [mar-tee'-ne], *m.* Martini, mixed alcoholic drink.

mártir [mar'-teer], *com.* A martyr.

martirio [mar-tee'-re-o], *m.* Martyrdom.

martirizador, ra [mar-te-re-thah-dor', rah], *m. & f.* One who commits martyrdom.

martirizar [mar-te-re-thar'], *va.* 1. To martyr, to put to death as a martyr. 2. To inflict great sufferings; to martyrize.

martirologio [mar-te-ro-lo'-he-o], *m.* Martyrology, a register of martyrs.

marxismo [Mark-sees'-mo], *m.* Marxism, marxianism.

marxista [mark-sees'-tah], *a. & m. & f.* Marxist.

marzo [mar'-tho], *m.* March, the third month of the year.

mas [mahs], *conj.* But, yet. **Mas que**, although, even if. **Mas si**, perhaps if.

más [mahs], *adv.* 1. More, to a greater degree. 2. Plus; the sign 1. 3. Besides moreover. **A más correr**, with the utmost speed. **A más tardar**, at latest. **A más y mejor**, greatly, highly, at best; excellently. **De más a más**, still more and more. **Por lo más**, at most. **Por más que**, However much. **Más que** or **de**, more than, but. **Más de tres años**, more than three years. **Sin más ni más**, without further ado; heedlessly. **Más bien**, rather. **Los más**, the largest number. **Lo más antes**, as soon as possible. **Más vale** or **más valiera si…** It is better or would be better if… **Sin más acá ni más allá**, without ifs or ands. **Él es el más inteligente**, he is the most intelligent. **Un libro de lo más divertido**, a most amusing book. **Trabajar más**, to work harder. **Más o menos**, more or less. **Como el que más**, as well as anyone. **Nada más**, nothing else. **Nada más llegar te llamo**, I'll call you as soon as I arrive. **Cada vez viene más tarde**, he comes later and later. **Es más pobre que las ratas**, he is as poor as a church mouse. **Hay más de cien personas**, there are over a hundred people. **Más tarde o más temprano**, sooner or later. **¿Qué más da?**, What difference does it make? **Más vale hacerlo enseguida**, it's better to do it straight away. **Dame dos paquetes más**, give two more packets.

mas [mahs], *m.* 1. *(Prov.)* Farm-house and stock. 2. A weight for gold and silver used in the Philippines equal to 3.768 gm. or 58 grains. 3. The sign 1 (matemáticas).

masa [mah'-sah], *f.* 1. Dough. 2. Mortar. 3. Mass of gold, silver, or other metal. 4. The whole mass of a thing; the lump. 5. Mass, congeries, the union or concurrence of many things. 6. A gentle disposition. 7. *(Prov.)* Farm-house. 8. Estate of a bankrupt. 9. *(And. Cono Sur)* As a whole, altogether.

masacrar [mah-sah-crar'], *va.* To massacre.

masacre [mah-sah'-cray], *f.* Massacre.

masaje [mah-sah'-hay], *m.* Message. **Dar masaje a**, to massage.

masajista [mah-sah-hees'-tah], *m.* or *f.* Masseur, masseuse.

masar [mah-sar'], *va.* V. AMASAR.

masato [mah-sah'-to], *m.* A fermented liquor made from the yucca or plantain-tree by Indians bordering on the branches of the Amazon river.

mascabado, da [mas-cah-bah'-do, dah], *a.* Applied to inferior sugar; raw, unrefined, muscovado.

mascada [mas-cah'-dah], *f. (Mex.)* 1. A silk neckerchief (pañuelo de cuello). 2. The iron ring by which the neck of criminals condemned to death by the *garrote* is broken. 3. *(LAm.)* Quid (tabaco de mascar). 4. *(And. CAm.)* Buried treasure (tesoro). 5. *(CAm.)* Rebuke (reprimenda).

mascador, ra [mas-cah-dor', rah], *m. & f.* Chewer, masticator.

mascadura [mas-cah-doo-rah], *f.* Mastication, manduction, chewing.

mascar [mas-car'], *va.* 1. To chew (comida), to masticate. 2. To pronounce or talk with difficulty (palabras).

máscara [mahs'-cah-rah], *f.* 1. Mask, a cover to disguise the face. **Quitar la máscara a uno**, to unmask somebody. 2. Masquerade. 3. Mask, any pretence or subterfuge. 4. A face-mask used by beekeepers. 5. Mascara (rimel). *com.* Masker, masquerader, mummer; a person in a mask.

mascarada [mas-cah-rah'-dah], *f.* Masquerade, mummery.

mascarero [mas-cah-ray'-ro], *m.* Dealer in masks.

mascarilla [mas-cah-reel'-lyah], *f.* 1. *(dim.)* A small mask which covers only the forehead and eyes. **Quitarse la mascarilla**, to take off the mask, to declare one's sentiments boldly 2. Mould taken from the face of a dead person; deathmask. 3. Face pack (maquillaje).

mascarón [mas-cah-rone'], *m.* *(Aug.)* 1. A large hideous mask. 2. Hideous or grotesque forms: *e. g.*, satyrs' faces, used to adorn fountains and buildings. 3. Person ridiculously grave and solemn. **Mascarón de proa**, figure-head of a vessel.

mascota [mas-co'-tah], *f.* Mascot.

masculinidad [mas-coo-le-ne-dahd'], *f.* Masculinity, manhood.

masculino, na [mas-coo-lee'-no, nah], *a.* 1. Masculine, male, virile. 2. *(Gram.)* Masculine (género).

mascullar [mas-cool-lyar'], *va.* To falter in speaking.

masecoral, masejicomar [mah-say-co-rahl', mah-say-he-co-mar'], *m.* Sleight of hand, legerdemain.

masera [mah-say'-rah], *f.* A kneading trough.

masería, masía [mah-say-ree'-ah, mah-see'-ah], *f.* Farm-house. *V.* MASADA.

masetero [mah-say-tay'-ro], *m.* Masseter, a muscle of the lower jaw.

masica [mah-see'-cah], *f.* The breadnut tree of Central America.

masicote [mah-se-co'-tay], *m.* Massicot, oxide of lead prepared without fusion by the dry method.

masilla [mah-seel'-lyah], *f.* 1. Glaziers' putty (ventanas). 2. *(dim.)* A little mass.

masivamente [mah-se'-vah-men-tay], *adv.* Massively; on a large scale.

masivo [mah-see'-vo], *a.* Massive (ataque, dosis); large-scale (evacuación); mass (ejecución).

maslo [mahs'-lo], *m.* 1. Root of the tail of quadrupeds. 2. Shaft or stem of some plants.

masón [mah-sone'], *m.* 1. Mess of dough given to fowls. 2. *(Aug.)* A large mass. 3. *V.* FRANCMASÓN.

masonería [mah-so-nay-ree'-ah], *f.* Free masonry.

masónico, ca [mah-so-ne-co, cah], *a.* Masonic.

masoquismo [mah-so-kees',-mo], *m* Masochism.

masoquista [mah-so-kees',-tah], *a. m & f* Masochitic masochist.

masora [mah-so'-rah], *f.* Masorah, a Hebrew, work on the Bible. The tradition relied on by the Jews to preserve the text of the Old Testament from corruption.

masorético, ca [mah-so-ray'-te-co, cah], *a.* Masoretic.

masque [mahs-kay], *adv.* *(Mex.)* No matter, let it be so. *(mas and que.)*

massbus [mahs-boos]. *(Inform.)* Massbus.

mastelero [mas-tay-lay'-ro], *m.* *(Naut.)* Top-mast. **Mastelero mayor** or **de gavia**, main top-mast. **Mastelero de proa**, fore top-gallant-mast.

masticación [mas-te-cah-the-on'], *f.* Mastication.

masticar [mas-te-car'], *va.* 1. To masticate, to chew. 2. To ruminate or meditate.

masticatorio, ria [mas-te-cah-to'-re-o, ah], *a.* Masticatory.

mastigador [mas-te-gah-dor'], *m.* Instrument put into horses' mouths to prevent their chewing.

mástil [mahs'-teel], *m.* 1. *V.* MASTELERO. 2. Upright post of a bed or loom. **Mástil de barrena**, shank of an auger. 3. Trunk or stem of a tree. 4. Wide breeches worn by Indians. 5. The handle of some musical instruments. 6. Support (sostén). 7. Flag-pole (bandera).

mastín, na [mas-teen', nah], *m. & f.* 1. Mastiff, a dog of the largest size: bulldog. 2. A clumsy fellow; clown.

mastodonte [mas-to-don'-tay], *m.* The mastodon, a fossil mammal like the elephant.

mastoideo, dea [mas-to-e-day'-o, ah], *a.* Mastoid, nippleshaped.

mastoides [mas-to'-e-days], *m.* The mastoid prominence of the temporal bone.

mastoiditis [mas-toy-dee'-tis], *f.* *(Med.)* Mastoiditis, mastoid inflammation.

mastranto, mastranzo [mas-trahn'-to, mas-trahn'-tho], *m.* *(Bot.)* Round-leaved mint.

mastuerzo [mas-too-err'-tho], *m.* *(Bot.)* Common cress.

masturbación [mas-toor-bah-the-on'], *f.* Masturbation.

masturbarse [mas-toor-bar'-say], *vr.* To masturbate.

mata [mah'-tah], *f.* 1. Small bush (arbusto), shrub, undershrub. 2. Sprig (ramita), blade. 3. Grove, a cluster of trees of one species, copse. 4. The mastic-tree. 5. Lock of matted hair. 6. Piece of ore only partly fused. 7. *(Agr.)* Field, plot. **Mata de olivos**, field of olive trees. 8. **Mata de pelo**, head of hair. **Mata rubia**, kermes oak.

mata, *f.* 1. Game at cards. *V.* MATARRATA. 2. Slaughter. (From MATAR.)

matacán [mah-tah-cahn'], *m.* 1. A poisonous composition for killing dogs. 2. *(Bot.)* V. NUEZ VÓMICA. 3. A hare previously hunted. 4. Stone which may be grasped in the hand and thrown. 5. *(And, Carib.)* Fawn, young deer.

matacandelas [mah-tah-can-day'-las], *f.* Extinguisher.

matacandil [mah-tah-can-deel'], *m.* *(Prov. Murcia)* Lobster.

matachín [mah-tah-cheen'], *m.* 1. Merry andrew, jackpudding. 2. Dance performed by grotesque figures. 3. Slaughterman, butcher.

matadero [mah-tah-day'-ro], *m.* 1. Slaughterhouse; severe labor. 2. *(Mex. Cono Sur)* Brothel.

matador [mah-tah-dor'], *m.* 1. Murderer. 2. A card in the game of ombre. -*a.* Mortal; murderous, homicidal.

matadora [mah-tah-do'-rah], *f.* Murderess.

matadura [mah-tah-doo'-rah], *f.* Wound on a horse's back made by the harness; gall.

matafuego [mah-tah-foo-ay'-go], *m.* 1. Fire-engine, fire-extinguisher. 2. Fire-man.

matahambre [mah-tah-ahm'-bray], *m.* *(Cuba)* Marchpane, dainty made of yucca flour, sugar, etc.

matahormigas [mah-tah-or-mee'-gas], *a. & m. & f. (coll.)* Half-witted, doltish.

matalobos [mah-tah-lo'-bos], *m.* *(Bot.)* Wolf's-bane, aconite.

matalón, matalote [mah-tah-lone', mah-tah-lo'tay], *m.* An old worn-out horse.

matamoros [mah-tah-mo'-ros], *m.* Braggart, boaster. *V.* MATASIETE.

matamoscas [mah-tah-mos'-cahs], *m.* flyswat; flypaper.

matanza [mah-tahn'-thah], *f.* 1. The action of slaughtering. 2. Cattle to be slaughtered. 3. Massacre, butchery; slaughter in the field of battle. 4. Obstinacy, eagerness of pursuit. 5. *(Carib.)* Slaughterhouse (matadero); *(And.)* tienda; *(CAm.)* meat market.

mataperros [mah-tah-per'-ros], *m.* *(Met. and coll.)* A mischievous, street-lounging boy.

matapolvo [mah-tah-pol'-vo], *m.* Light rain which scarcely settles the dust.

matar [mah-tar'], *va.* 1. To kill, to put to death (persona); to make away with; to execute. 2. To murder, to assassinate. 3. To put out a light, to extinguish the fire. 4. To slake lime. 5. To worry, to vex, to molest (fastidiar). 6. To make a horse's back sore by the rubbing of the harness. **Matar de un golpe**, to knock on the head. **Matar de hambre**, to famish, to starve, to kill with hunger. **A mata caballo**, in the utmost hurry. -*vn.* 1. To kill. 2. To mate (ajedrez). -*vr.* 1. To commit suicide (suicidarse). 2. To make the utmost exertions to obtain a thing. **Matarse por**, to struggle to. 3. To be extremely concerned at a failure or disappointment. **Mátalas callando**, *(coll.)* by crafty silence, or underhand means, he obtains his end.

matarife [mah-tah-re'-fay], *m.* *(Prov.)* Slaughterman. *V.* MATACHÍN.

matarrata [mah-tar-rah'-tah], *f.* Game at cards.

matasanos [mah-tah-sah'-nos], *m.* Quack, charlatan: empiric.

matasellos [mah-tah-sayl'-lyos], *m.* Postmark.

matasiete [mah-tah-se-ay'-tay], *m.* Bully, braggadocio.

matasuegras [mah-tah-soo-ay'-gras], *m.* Streamer, blower (juguete).

mate [mah'-tay], *m.* 1. Checkmate in chess. **Dar mate**, to scoff at anyone. 2. Size, used by painters and gilders; gold or silver-sizing. 3. The leaves of a shrub of that name, used in South America as a substitute for tea. 4. Unpolished ore. 5. *(Amer.)* A dry gourd. **Entrar a mate**, *(Prov. Mex.)* to correspond or understand each other by signs (amor). 6. *(LAm.)* Maté (bebida). 7. *(CAm.)* To go crazy. *-a.* Unpolished, rough, matt; faded.

matear [mah-tay-ar'], *vn.* 1. *(Prov.)* To grow up into stalks (trigo, cebada). 2. *(Amer.)* To take mate-tea.

matemáticamente [mah-tay-mah'-te-cah-men-tay], *adv.* Mathematically.

matemáticas [mah-tay-mah'-te-cas], *f.* Mathematics. **Matemáticas puras**, pure mathematics.

matemático ca [mah-tay-mah'-te-co, cah], *a.* Mathematical.

matemático [mah-tay-mah'-teh-co], *m.* Mathematician.

materia [mah-tay'-re-ah], *f.* 1. Matter, substance. 2. Material of which something is made. **Prima** or **primera materia**, raw material. 3. Matter, subject, thing treated; cause, occasion. **En materia de**, in the matter of. 4. Matter, question considered, point discussed. **Será materia de muchas discusiones**, it will be the subject of a lot of arguments. 5. Matter, pus. 6. Matter, corporeal substance; opposed to spirit.

material [mah-tay-re-ahl'], *a.* 1. Material, not spiritual. 2. Rude, uncouth, ungenteel. 3. Real, true; literal (literal); physical. **El autor material del hecho**, the actual perpetrator of the deed. *-m.* 1. Ingredient, component, portion of which something is made. **Hecho de mal material**, made of bad material. 2. *(Tec.)* Equipment, plant; materials. **Material escolar**, teaching materials. **Material de oficina**, stationery. 3. *(Tip.)* Copy. 4. Leather (zapatos). 5. *(LAm.)* Made of bricks. **Material defectuoso**, *(Inform.)* faulty equipment.

materialidad [mah-tay-re-ah-le-dahd'], *f.* 1. Materiality, corporeity. 2. Surface or appearance of things; sound of words. 3. *(Theol.)* Materiality, physical fact of actions done in ignorance of right and wrong.

materialismo [mah-tay-re-ah-lees'-mo], *m.* Materialism.

materialista [mah-tay-re-ah-lees'-tah], *com.* Materialist.

materialmente [mah-tay-re-al-men-tay], *adv.* Materially, corporeally.

maternal [mah-ter-nahl'], *a.* Maternal. V. MATERNO.

maternalmente [mah-ter-nahl'-men-tay], *adv.* Maternally.

maternidad [mah-ter-ne-dahd'], *f.* 1. Maternity, the condition of being a mother. 2. *(Amer.)* Maternity, a hospital for women lying-in.

materno, na [mah-terr'-no, nah], *a.* Maternal (parentesco), motherly, mother (lengua).

mático [mah'-te-co], *m.* *(Acad.)* Matico, a shrub of the pepper family, native of Peru and Bolivia, the leaves containing an astringent, aromatic oil.

matinal [mah-te-nahl'], *a.* *(Pont.)* V. MATUTINAL.

matiné [mah-te-nay'] *f.* *(Th.)* Matinee, morning or afternoon performance.

matiz [mah-teeth'], *m.* 1. Shade of colors; mixture of a variety of colors. 2. Shade (de significado); touch (de ironía).

matizado, da [mah-te-thah'-do, dah], *a. & pp.* of MATIZAR. Variegated.

matizar [mah-te-thar'], *va.* 1. To mix colors agreeably. 2. To embellish, to adorn, to beautify. 3. To make more precise (aclarar); to go into fine detail over (sutilizar). **Se matizarán los cursos con deportes**, classes will be interspersed with sports.

mato [mah'-to], *m.* V. MATORRAL.

matojo [mah-toh'-ho], *m.* 1. A barrilla-producing bush about two feet high which grows in Spain. 2. *(Cuba)* Shoot which trees put out after being cut.

matón [mah-tone'], *m.* Bully, a noisy, quarrelsome fellow.

matorral [mah-tor-rahl'], *m.* 1. Field full of brambles and briers, a bushy place. 2. A thicket, copse.

matoso, sa [mah-to'-so, sah], *a.* Bushy, covered with bushes.

matraca [mah-trah'-cah], *f.* 1. A wooden rattle (objeto). 2. Jest, contemptuous joke (guasa). 3. *(And.)* Hash, pot. 4. *(Mex.)* Machine gun (metralleta). **Dar matraca**, to banter.

matraquear [mah-trah-kay-ar'], *va.* To jest, to scoff, to mock, to ridicule.

matraquista [mah-trah-kees'-tah], *com.* Wag, jester, punster.

matraz [mah-trath'], *f.* Matrass, vessel used by apothecaries.

matrería [mah-tray-ree'-ah], *f.* *(Mex. Cuba)* Penetration, shrewdness, suspiciousness.

matrero, ra [mah-tray'-ro, rah], *a.* Cunning (astuto), sagacious, knowing. *-m.* Artful knave; cunning, knavish soldier; fugitive from justice (fugitivo); trickster (tramposo).

matriarcado [mah-tre-ar-cah'-do], *m.* Matriarchy.

matricida [mah-tre-thee'-dah], *com.* Matricide, murderer of one's mother.

matricidio [mah-tre-thee'-de-o], *m.* Matricide, slaughter of a mother.

matrícula [mah-tree'-coo-lah], *f.* 1 Register (registro), list. 2. Matriculation. **Un barco con matrícula de Bilbao**, a boat registered in Bilbao. **Matrícula de honor**, prize (universidad). **Derechos de matrícula**, registration fees. 3. License plate (coches).

matriculación [mah-tre-coo-lah-the-on'], *f.* Matriculation, registration (coche, barco).

matriculador [mah-tre-coo-lah-dor'], *m.* He who matriculates.

matricular [mah-tre-coo-lar'], *va.* To matriculate, to register, to enroll, to enter a list.

matrimonial [mah-tre-mo-ne-ahl'], *a.* Matrimonial, connubial, nuptial. **Enlace matrimonial**, link by marriage.

matrimonialmente [mah-tre-mo-ne-ahl'-men-tay], *adv.* Matrimonially.

matrimonio [mah-tre-mo'-ne-o], *m.* 1, Marriage, matrimony. 2. *(coll.)* Husband and wife, couple (personas). **Matrimonio de conveniencia**, marriage of convenience. **Matrimonio por la iglesia**, church marriage.

matriz [mah-treeth'], *f.* 1. Mother church, metropolitan church. 2. Matrix, womb. 3. Mould, form, matrice. 4. The original draft of a writing. 5. A female screw. *-a.* First, principal, chief. 6. *(Inform.)* **Matriz lógica de campo programable**, programmable logic array, programmed logic array.

matrona [mah-tro'-nah], *f.* 1. A matron. 2. A midwife.

matronaza [mah-tro-nah'-thah], *f. aug.* A corpulent respectable matron.

maturrango, ga [mah-too-rahn'-go, gah], *m. & f.* Appellation given to a European in Buenos Aires. It means a bad horseman or bad horse.

Matusalén [mah-too-sah-layn'], *a.* *(coll.)* Old as Methuselah.

matute [ma-tooh'-tay], *m,* 1. Smuggling (acto). 2. Smuggled goods (géneros), a prohibited commodity.

matutear [mah-too-tay-ar'], *va.* To smuggle goods.

matutero, ra [mah-too-tay'-ro, rah], *m. & f.* Smuggler, contrabandist.

matutinal [mah-too-te-nahl'], *a.* Belonging to the morning; morning.

matutino, na [mah-too-tee'-no, nah], *a.* Matutinal, belonging to the morning.

maula [mah'-oo-lah], *f.* 1. Anything worthless (objeto); rubbish trumpery, trash. 2. Cunning, craft, deceitful tricks, imposition. *-com. (coll.)* Cheat, bad paymaster. **Es una buena maula**, *(coll.)* he is a good-for-nothing fellow. **Ella es buena maula**, she is a hussy: used jocularly.

maulería [mah-oo-lay-ree'-ah], *f.* 1. Frippery, old clothes-shop, a piece-broker's shop. 2. Craft, cunning.

maulero [mah-oo-lay'-ro], *m.* 1. Piece-broker, seller of old clothes. 2. Impostor, deceitful type (engañador), cheat (tramposo), swindler.

maullador, ra [mah-oo-llyah-dor', rah], *a.* Applied to a mewing cat.

maullar [ma-hoo-llyar'], *vn.* To mew (gatos).

maullido, maúllo [mah-oo-llyee'-do, mah-ool'-lyo], *m.* Mew, cry of a cat.

mauraca [mah-oo-rah'-cah], *f. (Prov. Andal.)* Act of roasting chestnuts, acorns, or ears of Indian corn over coals in the open air.

mauritano, na [mah-oo-re-tah'-no, nah], *a.* Mauritanian.

mauseolo [mah-oo-say-o'-lo], *m. V.* MAUSOLEO.

mausoleo [mah-oo-so-lay'-lo], *m.* Mausoleum.

maxilar [mac-se-lar'], *a.* Maxillary, maxillar.

máxima [mahc'-se-mah'], *f.* 1. A maxim, an axion. 2. Sentence, apothegm. 3. Idea, thought. 4. Musical point.

máximamente and **máxime** [mahc'-se-may], *adv.* Principally.

máximo, ma [mahc'-se-mo, mah], *a. sup.* Chief, principal; very great. **El máximo dirigente**, the top leader. **Su máximo esfuerzo**, their greatest effort.

máximum [mac-se-moom], *m.* Maximum, extreme limit.

maya [mah'-yah], *f.* 1. *(Bot.)* Common daisy. 2. May-queen, a little girl adorned with flowers. 3. Name of the native language of Yucatan and of its ancient civilization.

mayador, ra [mah-yah-dor', rah], *a.* Mewing.

mayal [mah-yahl'], *m.* 1. Flail, a thrashing instrument. 2. Lever in oilmills.

mayar [mah-yar'], *vn.* To mew. *V.* MAULLAR.

mayo [mah'-yo], *m.* 1. May, the fifth month. 2. Maypole.

mayólica [mah-yo'-le-cah], *f.* Majolica ware (loza esmaltada).

mayonesa [mah-yo-nay'-sah], *f.* Mayonnaise dressing; oil and yolks of eggs beaten together.

mayor [mah-yor'], *a.* Greater, larger. **Hombre mayor**, an elderly man, also a man of great age. 2. High (atar, calle; main, principal (plaza). 3. Main, major, larger (parte). 4. Head (en rango). 5. *(Superl.)* Biggest, largest (en tamaño). - *m.* 1. Superior, mayor or chief of a community. 2. Major, a field officer (rango). 3. *(Geog.)* Lake Maggiore, in northern Italy. 4. *(Arch.) V.* SILLAR.-*f. (Log.)* Major, first proposition in a syllogism.-*pl.* 1. Ancestors, forefathers (antepasados). 2. Superiors. 3. *(Naut.)* Three principal sails of a ship. 4. In grammar schools, the higher class. **Mayor or mayor de edad**, person of age. **Hermano mayor**, eldest brother. **Llegar a mayores**, to get out of hand. **Vender al por mayor**, to sell wholesale.

mayora [mah-yo'-rah], *f.* Mayoress.

mayoral [mah-yo-rahl'], *m.* 1. Head shepherd (pastor); leader. 2. Overseer, steward (mayordomo).

mayorana [mah-yo-rah'-nah], *f. V.* MEJORANA.

mayorazga [mah-yo-rath'-gah], *f.* 1. The wife of a person possessing an entailed estate. 2. She who possesses an entailed estate.

mayorazgo [mah-yo-rath'-go], *m.* 1. Primogeniture. 2. Entailed estate, (inherited by primogeniture). 3. Heir to an entailed estate (heredero).

mayorazguista [mah-yo-rath-gees'-tah], *m. (Law.)* Author who treats on entails.

mayordoma [mah-yor-do'-mah], *f.* Steward's wife.

mayordomía [mah-yor-do-mee'-ah], *f.* Administration, stewardship, controllership.

mayordomo [mah-yor-do'-moh], *m.* Steward (de casa), the principal servant of a nobleman or gentleman; majordomo, super intendent; *(Cono Sur)* foreman (capataz); *(And.)* servant (criado).

mayoría [mah-yo-ree'-ah], *f.* 1. Advantage, excellence, superiority. 2. Major's commission. 3. Majority, full age. **En la mayoría de los casos**, in most cases. **Por una mayoría arrolladora**, by an overwhelming majority. **Gobierno de la mayoría**, majority government.

mayoridad [mah-yo-re-dahd'], *f.* Superiority.

mayorista [mah-yo-rees'-tah], *m.* Student of the highest classes in grammar schools. -*m & f.* Wholesaler.

mayormente [mah-yor'-men-tay], *adv.* Principally, chiefly (principalmente), especially (especialmente).

mayúscula [mah-yoos'-coo-lah], *a.* Capital letter (letra).

maza [mah'-thah], *f.* 1. Club, a stick shod with iron. 2. Mace, an ensign of authority. 3. Engine or pile engine. 4. Nave or hub of a wheel. 5. Rag pinned to men or women's clothes to make a laughing-stock of them. 6. Beetle for flax or hemp. 7. An importunate or troublesome fellow. 8. The thick end of a billiard-cue. 9. Something noisy tied to a dog's tail (carnaval). **Maza de fraga**, hammer.

mazacote [mah-thah-co'-tay], *m.* 1. Kali, barilla. 2. Mortarcement. 3. Dry, tough mass. 4. Injurious nickname for a peevish person. 5. *(Amer.)* Antimony.

mazada [mah-thah'-dah], *f.* Blow with a mallet (golpe), offensive expression.

mazagatos [mah-thah-gah'-tos], *m.* Noise, dispute, contention.

mazamorra [mah-thah-mor'-rah], *f.* 1. Bread-dust; biscuit spoiled and broken in pieces. 2. Anything broken into small bits. 3. Sort of pap, made of the flour of Indian corn, honey, and sugar. 4. *(LAm.)* Blister (ampolla).

mazaneta [mah-thah-nay-tah], *f.* Apple-shaped ornament in jewels.

mazapán [mah-thah-pahn'], *m.* Marchpane, a sweet paste of almonds, sugar, churn milk.

mazar [mah-thar'], *va. (Prov.)* To churn milk.

mazarí [mah-thah-ree'], *m.* A tile-shaped brick.

mazmorra [math-mor'-rah], *f.* Moorish dungeon, underground.

mazo [mah'-tho], *m.* 1. Mallet, a wooden hammer (martillo). 2. Bundle, a quantity of ribbons or other things tied together (manojo). **Mazo de llaves**, bunch of keys. 3. An importunate, tiresome person.

mazonería [mah-tho-nay-ree'-ah], *f.* 1. Masonry, brickwork. 2. Relief or relievo-work.

mazorca [mah-thor'-cah], *f.* 1. Spindle full of thread, *spun* from the distaff in the shape of a cone. 2. Ear of corn the spike or cob of corn (de maíz). 3. Spindle-shaped work upon a balustrade.

mazorral [mah-thor-rahl'], *a.* Rude, uncouth, clownish.

mazote [mah-tho'-tay], *m.* 1. A kind of cement or mortar. 2. A block-head.

mazotear [mah-tho-tay-ar'], *va.* To strike with a club or mallet.

mazurca [mah-thoor'-cah], *f.* Mazurka.

me [may], *pron.* Me, the dative and accusative case of the pronoun I, placed either before or after a verb. **Me lo compró**, he bought it from me. **Me lavé**, washed.

meada [may-ah'-dah], *f.* 1. The quantity of urine made at one time (orinar), piss. **Echar una meada**, to have a piss. 2. Spot or mark left by making water (mancha).

meados [may-ah'-dos], *m. pl. V.* ORINES.

meajuela [may-ah-hoo-ayl'-lah], *f.* Small piece attached to the bits of a bridle.

mear [may-ar'], *vn.* 1. To urinate, to piss, to have a piss, to make water. -*va.* To walk all over (humillar).

meato [may-ah'-to], *m.* Passage or channel of the body; meatus.

meauca [may-ah-oo'-cah], *f.* A sea-fowl, so called from its cry; a gull.

meca [may'-cah], *f.* **Casa de meca**, house of noise and confusion. **Andar de Ceca en Meca**, to wander about.

mecánica [may-cah'-ne-cah], *f.* 1. Mechanics. *V.* MAQUINARIA. 2. *(coll.)* A mean, despicable action or thing. 3. *(Mil.)* Management of soldiers' affairs.

mecánicamente [may-cah'-ne-cah-men-tay], *adv.* Meanly, sordidly, mechanically.

mecánico, ca [may-cah'-ne-co, cah], *a.* 1. Mechanical, done by machinery (máquina). 2. Mean, servile; of mean occupation (oficio). **Potencias mecánicas**, mechanical powers.

mecánico [may-cah'-ne-co], *m.* I. Mechanician, mechanic, manufacturer, handicraftsman.

mecanismo [may-cah-nees'-mo], *m.* Mechanism, action performed according to mechanical laws.

mecanización [may-cah-ne-thah-the-on'], *f.* Mechanization.

mecanizar [may-cah-ne-thar'], *va.* To mechanize.

mecanografía [may-cah-no-grah-fee'-ah], *f.* Typewriting.

mecanografiar [may-cah-no-grah-fe-ar'], *va.* To type.

mecanógrafo, fa [may-cah-no'-grah-fo, fah], *m. & f.* Typist.

mecapal [may-cah-pahl'], *m. (Mes.)* Porter's leather strap, a kind of leather band with two cords attached, serving porters to carry a load more conveniently.

mecate [may-cah'-tay], *m. (Mex.)* Rope or cord made of the maguey or American agave.

mecatito [may-cah-tee'-to], *m.* Small cord, twine.

mecedero [may-thay-day'-ro], *m. V.* MECEDOR.

mecedor, ra [may-thay-dor', rah], *m. & f.* 1. Rocker, one who rocks something to and fro. 2. *m.* Stirrer, a pole with which wine is stirred in a hogshead, wort in a vat, and soap in a boiler. 3. Swing (columpio). 4. *(CAm. Mex.)* Rocking chair (asiento). 5. *(Carib.)* Stirrer (cuchara). **Mecedora**, *f.* Rocking-chair.

mecedura [may-thay-doo'-rah], *f.* Act of rocking something.

mecer [may-therr'], *va.* 1. To stir (líquido), to agitate, to jumble, to mix. 2. To rock (cuna), to shake. 3. To dandle a child (niño).

mecereón [may-thay-ray-on'], *m. (Bot.)* Mezereon.

mecha [may'-chah], *f.* 1. Wick, for candles, tapers, and torches. 2. Roll of lint put into a sore. 3. Match, match-cord, for firing ordnance. 4. Bacon, with which fowls and meat are larded. 5. A lock of hair; a bundle of threads or fibers. 6. *(And, Carib.)* Joke (broma). 7. *(Mex.)* Fear (miedo). 8. Shoplifting. (ratería). **Alargar la mecha**, to augment a salary; to protract a business: to allow a debtor time to discharge a debt. **A toda mecha**, at full speed.

mechar [may-char'], *va.* To lard fowls, game, or meat, with bacon; to force or stuff.

mechazo [may-chah'-tho], *m.* Burning of a slow match (fuse) without setting off the blast.

mechera [may-chay'-rah], *f.* Larding-pin.

mechero [may-chay'-ro], *m.* 1. Tube for the wick of a lamp; socket of a candle sticks. 2. Cigarette lighter (encendedor); burner (cocina). **Mechero piloto**, pilot light. **Mechero de gas**, gas burner.

mechificar [may-che-fe-car'], *va. (Peru Ven. coll.)* To annoy, to make fun of.

mechinal [may-che-nahl'], *m.* Square stones left projecting in a wall to be continued.

mechoacán [may-cho-ah-cahn'], *m. (Bot.)* Mechoacan bindneed, an inferior kind of jalap.

mechón [may-chone'], *m. aug.* 1. Large lock of hair; large match (pelo). 2. A large bundle of threads or fibers separated from the rest (hilos).

mechoso, sa [may-cho'-so, sah], *a.* Full of matches or wicks.

mecida [may-thee'-dah], *f. V.* MECEDURA.

meco, ca [may'-co, cah], *a. (Mex.)* Blackish red; copper-colored: used of animals. *-m. & f. (Mex.)* Savage Indian.

mecónico, ca [may-co'-ne-co, cah], *a.* Meconic acid, a white solid discovered in opium.

medalla [may-dahl'-lyah], *f.* 1. A medal. 2. *(Sculpt.)* A round or oval target on which a figure is carved in relief. 3. *(coll.)* Gold coin weighing an ounce.

medallón [may-dal-lyon'], *m. aug.* 1. Medallion (medalla). 2. *(Arch.)* Round or oval bas-relief placed on buildings. 3. A locket for a portrait or some souvenir.

médano, medaño [may'-dah-no, may-dah'-nyo], *m.* 1. Sandbank on the sea-shore, dune. 2. A mound of sand covered by shallow water.

media [may'-de-ah], *f.* 1. Stocking, hose. **Medias lisas**, plain hose. **Medias rayadas**, ribbed hose. **Medias-medias**, socks, half-hose. 2. Measure of about half a hundredweight.

mediacaña [may-de-ah-cah'-nyah], *f.* 1. *(Arch.)* A concave mouldings. 2. A strip of wood with mouldings. 3. A gouge, a chisel with a curved cutting edge. 4. A half-round file. 5. Curling-tongs for the hair.

mediación [may-de-ah-the-on'], *f.* Mediation (intercesión), intervention, interposition, intercession.

mediador, ra [may-de-ah-dor', rah], *m. & f.* Mediator, intercessor.

mediana [may-de-ah'-nah], *f.* 1. Flesh of the shoulder near the neck of animals. 2. Household bread. 3. *(Prov.)* Top of a fishing-rod. 4. *V.* BARZÓN. 5. *(Aut.)* Central reservation.

medianamente [may-de-ah-nah-men-tay], *adv.* Middlingly, moderately, meanly. **Un trabajo medianamente bueno**, a moderately good piece of work.

mediados de (A), *adv. (coll.)* About the midst of, in the midst of.

medianejo, ja [may-de-ah-nay'-ho, hah], *a. (coll.)* Barely middling or moderate; hardly mediocre.

medianería [may-de-ah-nay-ree'-ah], *f.* 1. A wall common to two contiguous houses. 2. Half of a piece of land or of a rent.

medianero, ra [may-de-ah-nay'-ro, rah], *a.* 1. Mediating, interceding, mediatory. 2. Intermediate; having the half of something. **Pared medianera**, partition wall.

medianero [may-de-ah-nay'-ro], *m.* 1. Mediator, go-between. 2. Owner of a house which has a common wall (de casa). 3. *(Carib. Mex.)* Partner; *(Agr.)* share-cropper.

medianta, medianidad [may-de-ah-nee'-ah, may-de-ah-ne-dahd'], *f.* 1. Moderation or temperance in the execution of a thing. 2. Mediocrity, mean, middle state; moderate means.

medianil [may-de-ah-neel'], *m. (Agr.)* Middle-piece of ground.

mediano, na [may-de-ah'-no, nah], *a.* Moderate, middling (regular), mediocre, indifferent (indiferente). **De tamaño mediano**, medium-sized.

medianoche [may-de-ah-no-chay], *f.* Midnight.

medianos [may-de-ah'-nos], *m. pl.* In grammar schools, the class in syntax.

mediante [may-de-ahn'-tay], *adv.* By means of, by virtue of.

mediar [may-de-ar'], *vn.* 1. To come to the middle of a thing, to be at the middle (estar en medio). 2. To intercede for another, to mediate (interceder). 3. To intervene (intervenir). 4. To come up (suceder). **Media un abismo entre los dos gobiernos**, there is a wide gap between the two governments. **Median relaciones cordiales entre los dos**, cordial relations exist between the two.

mediastino [may-de-as-tee'-no], *m. (Anat.)* 1. Mediastinum, the intervening space between the lungs. 2. *(Bot.)* Delicate septum of the silique of the mustard family.

mediatamente [may-de-ah-tah-men-tay], *adv.* Mediately.

mediato, ta [may-de-ah'-to, tah], *a.* Mediate.

mediator [may-de-ah-tor'], *m.* Ombre, game at cards.

médica [may'-de-cah], *f.* 1. Doctor's wife. 2. Doctress, female physician.

medicable [may-de-cah'-blay], *a.* Curable, medicable.

medicación [may-de-cah-the-on'], *f.* Medication, treatment.

medicamento [may-de-cah-men'-to], *m.* Medicament, medicine, physic.

medicar [may-de-car'], *va. V.* MEDICINAR.

medicastro [may-de-cahs'-tro], *m.* Quack, empiric in physic.

medicina [may-de-thee'-nah], *f.* 1. Medicine, the healing arts. 2. Medicine, a remedy. **Medicina alternativa**, alternative medicine.

medicinal [may-de-the-nahl'], *a.* Medicinal, healing, belonging to physic.

medicinar [may-de-the-nar'], *va.* To medicine, to administer medicines, to apply medicaments.

medición [may-de-the-on'], *f.* Measurement, measuration, measuring.

medicucho [may-de-coo'-cho], *a.* Quackish, quack (used adjectively).

médico [may'-de-co], *m & f.* Physician, doctor, medical practitioner. **Médico de cabecera**, family doctor. **Médico residente**, house physician.

médico, ca [may'-de-co, cah], *a.* Medical, medicinal.

medida [may-dee'-dah], *f.* 1. Measure, that by which something is measured; standard, gauge (sistema, recipiente). 2. Measuring (acto), measurement. 3. Height, length, breadth, or quantity measured. 4. Proportion, relation, correspondence. 5. *(Arith.)* Root, a number which, repeated various times, exactly produces another. 6. Measure, syllables metrically numbered. 7. Measure, means to an end. 8. Measure, moderation (moderación), prudence. 9. Girdle on the statues of saints bearing their name. 10. Size, fitting (camisa, zapato). **A medida** or **a sabor de su paladar**, to his health's content. **A medida que**, according as, in proportion; at the same time that, whilst. **En gran medida**, to a great extent. **Tomar las medidas a uno**, to measure somebody. **Medida para líquidos**, liquid measure. **Medida preventiva**, preventive measure. **Tomar medidas**, to take steps.

medidamente [may-de-dah-men-tay], *adv.* Moderately.

medidor, ra [mae-de-dor', rah], *m. & f.* Measurer, evaluator. *-m.* Meter, gauge. **Medidor de franqueo**, postage meter. **Medidor del gas**, gas meter.

mediero [may-day'-ro], *m.* 1. Hosier, dealer in stockings. 2. Knitter of stockings. 3. Share-cropper, co-partner in the cultivation of lands, etc.

medieval [may-de-ay-vahl'], *a. & m.* Mediaeval, pertaining to the middle Ages. *(Neol.)*

medio, dia [may'-de-o, ah], *a.* 1. Half, in part (mitad). 2. Mid, midway, middle (punto). 3. Mean, average. 4. *(LAm.)* Big, huge (grande). **Media noche**, midnight, twelve at night. **Medio día**, midday, noon. **Medio hermano**, half-brother or half-blood. **Medio borracho**, halfseas over. **Media naranja**, *V.* CÚPULA. **A medias**, by halves. **Ir a medias**, to go halves with one. **A media mañana**, mid-morning. **A media voz**, in a low voice. **Clase media**, middle class. **Oriente Medio**, Middle East. **Término medio**, average. **Media botella de vino**, half a bottle of wine.

medio [may'-de-o], *m.* 1. Middle (centro). 2. Medium. 3. Step, measure. 4. Means. 5. Surroundings, environment. 6. *(Math.)* Half. 7. Middle finger. 8. (Sports) Lineman. *-pl.* 1. Means (método), resources. 2. Center of the bull-ring. *-adv* Half (término medio). **A medio cocer**, half cooked. **Corto de medios**, short of funds. **De medio a medio**, 1. Right in the middle. 2. Absolutely. **De por medio**, 1. Halfway. 2. In the middle. **En medio de**, 1. In the middle of. 2. Despite. **Estar de por medio**, to mediate. **Por medio de**, by means of, through. **Medios de publicidad**, advertising media. **Medio dormido**, half asleep. **Hablaba a media voz**, she was speaking in a low voice. **En medio de la plaza**, in the middle of the square. **Quitar algo de en medio**, to remove something. **Meterse de por medio**, to intervene. **Los medios de comunicación**, the media.

mediocre [may-de-o'-cray], *a.* Middling, mean, moderate, mediocre.

mediocridad [may-de-o-cre-dahd'], *f.* Mediocrity, small degree, middle rate, middle state.

mediodía [may-de-o-dee'-ah], *m.* 1. Noon, midday, noonday, noontide, meridian. 2. South. 3. South wind.

mediopaño [may-de-o-pah'-nyo], *m.* Thin woollen cloth.

mediquillo [may-de-keel'-lyo], *m.* Indian of the Philippine Islands, having medical experience, but no title.

medir [may-deer'], *va.* 1. To measure, to ascertain the length, magnitude, or quantity of a thing. 2. To measure or examine the number or syllables of a verse. 3. To compare, to measure, to estimate the quality of things. 4. **Medir por millas**, to measure in miles. *-vn.* 1. To measure (objeto, persona). **La tela mide 90 cms**, the cloth measures 90 cms. *-vr.* 1. To be moderate, to act with prudence. **No perder la calma**, to keep one's head. 2. *(LAm.) (Dep.)* To play each other. 3. *(LAm.)* To try on (ropa).

meditabundo, da [may-de-tah-boon'-do, ah], *a.* Pensive, musing, thoughtful.

meditación [may-de-tah-the-on'], *f.* Meditation, cogitation, deep thought, contemplation. **Meditaciones**, meditations.

meditar [may-de-tar'], *va.* To meditate, to contemplate, to consider.

Mediterráneo, nea [may-de-ter-rah'-nay-o, ah], *a.* Mediterranean, encircled with land, midland.

médium [may'-de-oom], *m.* Medium, a person fit for spiritualistic communications.

medo, da [may'-do, dah], *a.* Mede, belonging to ancient Media.

medra [may'-drah], *f.* Proficiency, progress, amelioration, improvement.

medrar [may-drar'], *vn.* To thrive, to prosper, to grow rich, to improve (mejorar).

medriñaque [may-dre-nyah'-kay], *m.* 1. A Philippine stuff for lining and stiffening women's garments. 2. A short petticoat.

medro [may'-dro], *m. V.* MEDRA. *-pl.* Progress, improvement.

medrosamente [may-dro'-sah-men-tay], *adv.* Timorously, fearfully, faintly.

medroso, sa [may-dro'-so, sah], *a.* 1. Fearful, timorous, faint-hearted, cowardly. 2. Terrible, inspiring fear.

medula, or **médula** [may-doo'-lah, may'-doo-lah], *f.* 1. Marrow, medulla. 2. The substance or essence of anything.

medular [may-doo-lar'], *a.* Medullar, medullary.

meduloso, sa [may-doo-lo'-so, sah], *a.* Full of marrow, marrowish.

medusa [may-doo'-sah], *f.* Jelly-fish.

megabus [may-gah-boos]. *(Inform.)* Megabus.

megabyte [may-gah-bite], *m. (Inform.)* Megabyte.

megaciclo [may-gah-thee'-clo], *m.* Megacycle.

megáfono [may-gah'-fo-no], *m.* Megaphone.

magalomanía [meh-gah-lo-mah-nee'-ah], *f.* Megalomania, delusions of grandeur.

megalómano, na [me-gah-lo'-mah-no, nah], *a.* Megalomaniacal. *-m. & f.* Megalomaniac.

mego, ga [may'-go, gah], *a.* Gentle, mild, meek, peaceful.

mejana [may-hah'-nah], *f.* Islet in the middle of a river.

mejicano, na [may-he-cah'-no, nah], *a.* Mexican, native of or belonging to Mexico. *-m.* The Mexican language, Aztec.

mejido, da [may-hee'-do, dah], *a.* Beaten with sugar and water (huevos).

mejilla [may-hee'-lyah], *f.* The cheek.

mejillón, mijillón [may-hil-lyone'], *m.* A kind of cockle.

mejor [may-hor'], *a.* Better, *comp.* of BUENO. *-adv.* Better; more exactly. **A lo mejor**, when least expected. **El mejor día**, some fine day. **A cual mejor**, as well as could be wished. **Llevar lo mejor**, to come off victorious. **Mejor que mejor**, much better. **Lo mejor será**, the better way will be. **Tanto mejor**, so much the better. **Lo mejor de la novela**, the best part of the novel. **Está mucho mejor**, he's much better.

mejora [may-ho'-rah], *f.* 1. Improvement, amelioration, addition, growth. 2. Appeal to a superior court. 3. The act of leaving by will a larger share than the legatee by law had a right to. 4. Outbidding at a public sale (en subasta). **Mejora de la resolución en pantalla**, *(Comput.)* display enhancement.

mejorable [may-ho-rah'-blay], *a.* Improvable.

mejoramiento [may-ho-rah-me-en'-to], *m.* Improvement, amelioration.

mejorana [may-ho-rah'-nah], *f. (Bot.)* Sweet marjoram.

mejorar [may-ho-rar'], *va.* 1. To improve, to ameliorate, to heighten, to cultivate, to mend. 2. To outbid, or bid over. 3. To leave, by will, to a son or grandson an increased share beyond his legal right. 3. To enhance (realzar); to raise (postura); to improve (oferta). *-vn.* To recover from a disease or calamity. *-vr.* To improve, to grow better.

mejoría [may-ho-ree'-ah], *f.* 1. Improvement, amelioration, mending. 2. Repairs. 3. The state of growing better in health. 4. Advantage, superiority.

mejunje [may-hoon'-hay], *m. (coll.) V.* MENJURJE.

melada [may-lah'-dah], *f.* A slice of toasted bread soaked in honey.

melado, da [may-lah'-do, dah], *a.* Of the color of honey. *-pp.* of MELAR.

meladucha [may-lah-doo'-chah], *f.* A course, mealy apple.

meladura [may-lah-doo'-rah], *f. (Cuba)* Purified sap of the sugar-cane; sirup, treacle.

meláfiro [may-lah'-fe-ro], *m.* Melaphyre, a pre-tertiary basalt.

melaína [may-lah-ee'-nah], *f.* 1. Black coloring matter of cephalopod mollusks. 2. Pigment of the skin of colored people.

melancolía [may-lan-co-lee'-ah], *f.* Melancholy, gloomy madness, gloom, gloominess.

melancólico, ca [may-lan-co'-le-co, cah], *a.* Melancholy (triste), sad, gloomy, fanciful, cloudy, mournful, hypochondriacal, dreamy (soñador).

melancolizar [may-lan-co-le-thar'], *va.* To affect with melancholy, to render gloomy and dejected, to dispirit.

melandro [may-lahn'-dro], *m. (Prov. Ast.)* Badger.

melanesiano, na [may-lah-nay-se-ah'-no, nah], *a.* Melanesian, relating to the islands between New Guinea and the Fijis, called collectively Melanesia.

melanuro, ra [may-lah-noo'-ro, rah], *a.* Black-tailed.

melapia [may-lah'-pe-ah], *f.* Kind of apple, related to the pippin.

melar [may-lar'], *vn.* 1. In sugar-works to boil down the juice of the sugar-cane a second time until it obtains the consistency of honey. 2. To deposit honey as bees.

melaza [may-lah'-thah], *f.* 1. Molasses 2. *(Prov.)* Dregs of honey.

melca [layl-cah], *f. V.* ZAHINA.

melcocha [mel-co'-chah], *f.* Paste made with honey, flour, and spice; molasses candy (melaza).

melcochero [mel-co-chay'-ro], *m.* Molasses-candy maker or seller, ginger breed baker.

melele [may-lay'-lay], *a.* Foolish, silly *V.* MELILOTO.

melena [may-lay'-nah], *f.* 1. Dishevelled hair hanging loose over the eyes. 2. Foretop hair or mane that falls on a horse's face; also a lion's mane. 3. A soft, fleecy skin put on the forehead of working oxen to prevent their being hurt by the yoke. **Ester en melena**, to have one's hair down.

melena [may-lay'-nah], *f.* Black stools from intestinal hemorrhage.

melenudo, da [may-lay-noo'-do, dah], *a.* Hairy, having bushy hair.

melero [may-lay'-ro], *m.* 1. Dealer in honey. 2. Place destined to preserve honey.

melgacho [mel-gah'-cho], *m.* Dog-fish.

melgar [mel-gar'], *m.* Patch of wild alfalfa.

melgarejo [mel-gah-ray'-ho], *m.* The helmsman's post. *V.* TIMONERA.

mélico, ca [may'le-co, cah], *a.* Lyrical, belonging to song, or to lyric poetry. *(Acad.)*

melífero, ra [may-lee'-fay-ro, rah], *a.* Melliferous, productive of honey.

melificado, da [may-le-fe-cah'-do, dah], *a.* Mellifluous, mellificent. -*pp.* of MELIFICAR.

melificar [may-le-fe-car'], *va. & vn.* To make honey as bees.

melifluamente [may-le'-floo-ah-men-tay], *adv.* Mellifluently.

melifluidad [may-le-floo-e-dahd'], *f.* Mellifluence, suavity, delicacy.

melifluo, flua [may-lee'-floo-o, ah], *a.* Mellifluous, mellifluent, honey mouthed; flowing with honey.

meliloto [may-le-lo'-to], *m. (Bot.)* Bird's foot trefoil; melilot, a sweet clover.

meliloto [may-le-lo-to], **ta**, *a.* Silly, stupid.

melindre [may-leen'-dray], *m.* 1 Fritters made with honey and flour (bollo). 2. Prudery, affectation (mojigatería). 3. Fastidiousness.

melindrear [may-lin-dray-ar'], *vn.* To act the prude; indulge in affectation; to be squeamish.

melindrero, ra [may-lin-dray'-ro, rah]. *V.* MELINDROSO.

melindrillo [May-lin-dreel'-lyo], *m. (Prov.)* Ferret, narrow tape.

melindrizar [may-lin-dre-thar'], *vn. (coll.) V.* MELINDREAR.

melindroso, sa [may-lin-dro'-so, sah], *a.* Prudish, precise, finical, too nice, too formal, fastidious, dainty, very particular.

melisa [may-lee'-sah], *f.* Balm. **Agua de melisa**, balm-water distilled from the fresh leaves. *V.* TORONJIL.

mella [mel'-lyah], *f.* 1. A hollow or crack made in something by a blow which it has received. Notch, nick (rotura), in edged tools. 2. Gap (en dientes), empty space. **Hacer mella**, to make an impression upon the mind by reproach or advice.

mellado, da [mel-lyah-do, dah], *a. & pp.* Of MELLAR. 1. Notched, hacked. 2. Toothless, wanting teeth.

mellar [mel-lyar'], *va.* 1. To notch, to hack, to nick (hacer muecas), to cut in small hollows. 2. To deprive of luster and splendor. **Mellar la honra**, to wound one's character and honor.

mellica [mel-lyee'-cah], *f. (Prov.) V.* MELLIZA.

melliza [mel-lyee'-thah], *f.* Kind of sausage made of lean pork, almonds, pineapple kernels, and honey.

mellizo, za [mel-lyee'-tho, thah], *a. V.* GEMELO.

mellón [mel-lyone'], *m.* A handful of straw lighted as a torch.

melocotón [may-lo-co-tone'], *m.* 1. *(Bot.)* Common peachtree (árbol). 2. Peach, fruit of that tree (fruto).

melocotonero [may-lo-co-to-nay'-ro], *m.* 1. Peach-tree. 2. Vender of peaches.

melodía [may-lo-dee'-ah], *f.* 1. Melody, harmony, melodiousness. 2. Melody, sweetness of sound.

melódico [may-lo'-de-co], *a.* Melodic.

melodiosamente [may-lo-de-o-sah-men-tay], *adv.* Melodiously, harmoniously.

melodioso, sa [may-lo-de-o'-so, sah], *a.* Melodious, musical, harmonious.

melodrama [may-lo-drah'-mah], *m.* Melodious, musical, harmonious.

melodrama [may-lo-drah'-mah], *m.* Melodrama.

melodramático [may-lo-drah-mah-te-co], **ca**, *a.* Melodramatic.

meloe [may-lo'-ay], *m.* Meloe, oil-beetle, blister-beetle. *V.* also CANTÁRIDA.

melografía [may-lo-grah-fee'-ah], *f.* The art of writing music.

meloja [may-lo'-hah], *f.* Metheglin, honey boiled with water and fermented: mead.

melojo [may-lo'-ho], *m.* Plant like the white oak.

melomanía [may-lo-mah-nee'-ah], *f.* Melomania, a mania for music

melómano, na [may-lo'-mah-no], *a.* Music-mad, excessively fond of music.

melón [may-lone'], *m. (Bot.)* 1. Melon (fruit). *(Col.)* Nut (cabeza). **Melón de agua**, water melon.

melonar [may-lo-nar'], *m.* Field or bed of melons.

melonero, ra [may-lo-nay'-ro, rah], *m. & f.* One who raises or deals in melons.

melonífero, ra [may-lo-nee'-fay-ro, rah], *a.* 1. Melon-bearing. 2. Melon-shaped.

melosidad [may-lo-se-dahd'], *f.* 1. Sweetness arising from honey, lusciousness. 2. Meekness, gentleness of behavior.

meloso, sa [may-lo'-so, sah], *a.* 1. Having the taste or qualities of honey mellow (dulce). 2. Gentle, mild, pleasing.

melote [may-lo'-tay], *m.* 1. Molasses, treacle. 2. *(Prov.)* Conserve of honey.

melsa [mel'-sah], *f.* 1. *(Prov.) V.* BAZO. 2. Phlegm, lentor, slowness.

melusa [may-loo'-sah], *f. (Cuba)* Portion of honey, or of fruit-juice which sticks to clothing or to the fingers.

membrado, da [mem-brah'-do, dah], *a. (Her.)* Membered: applied to the beak and legs of a bird, when of a different tincture from the body.

membrana [mem-brah'-nah], *f.* 1. Membrane, a thin skin; a caul. 2. *(Anat.)* Membrane. **Membrana mucosa**, mucous membrane.

membranáceo, cea [mem-brah-nah'-thay-o, ah], *a.* Membranaceous, membrane-like.

membranoso, sa [mem-brah-no'-so, sah], *a.* Membranous, filmy.

membrete

membrete [mem-bray'-tay], *m.* 1. Short annotation or note written to remember a thing. 2. In letters or notes, a line in which the person's name is inserted to whom it is written. 3. A note or small bit of paper given as a memorandum to a person in office, to put him in mind of any one's pretentions. 4. A card of invitation.

membrilla [mem-breel'-lyah], *f. (Prov.)* The tender bud of a quince-tree.

membrillar [mem-bril-lyar'], *m.* Plantation of quince-trees.

membrillero, membrillo [mem-bril-yay'-ro, mem-breel'-lyo]. *m.* 1. (*Bot.*) Quince-tree. 2. Quince, the fruit of the quince-tree.

membrudamente [mem-broo'-dah-men-tay], *adv.* Robustly, strongly.

membrudo, da [mem-broo'-do, dah], *a.* Strong, robust, corpulent: membered.

memo, ma [may'-mo, mah], *a.* Silly, foolish. **Hacerse memo,** to pretend not to understand.

memorable, memorando, da [may-mo-rah'-blay, may-mo-rahn'-do, dah], *a.* Memorable, commemorable, notable, filmous.

memorablemente [may-mo-rah'-blay-men-tay], *adv.* Memorably.

memorándum [may-mo-rahn'-doom], *m.* 1. Memorandum, notebook (libreta). 2. Memorandum, diplomatic note of informal character, often not signed, set down for reference or explanation.

memorar [may-mo-rar'], *va.* To remember, to record, to mention.

memoratísimo, ma [may-mo-rah-tee'-se-mo, mah], *a. sup.* Worthy of eternal memory.

memoria [may-mo´-re-ah], *f.* 1. Memory, reminiscence, recollection. 2. Fame, glory. 3. Memory, memorial, monumental record. 4. An anniversary or pious work which anyone found to preserve his memory. 5. Memoir, an account of transactions familiarly written: commonly used in the plural (personales). 6. Bill, account. 7. Memorandum, a note to help the memory (memorándum). 8. Codicil. 9. (*Inform.*) Memory. **Memoria de acceso aleatorio,** random access memory. **Memoria de acceso aleatorio estable,** non volatile random access memory. **Memoria de sólo lectura,** read only memory. **Memoria de sólo lectura alterable eléctricamente,** electrically alterable read only memory. **Memoria de sólo, lectura programable borrable electrónicamente,** electrically erasable programmable read only memory. **Memoria intermedia,** buffer. **Memoria intermedia de interrupción,** interrupt buffer. **Memoria primaria,** primary storage. **Memoria principal,** main memory. **Hacer memoria,** to remember, to put in mind. **Saber de memoria,** to know by heart. **Hablar de memoria,** to speak from memory. **Set flaco de memoria,** to have a short memory, forgetful. **En memoria de,** in memory of. **Tener mala memoria,** to have a bad memory. **Traer algo a la memoria,** to recall something. **Memoria programable,** programmable memory. **Aprender de memoria,** to learn by heart. **Memoria del teclado,** key-board memory. *-pl.* 1. Compliments, expression of kindness and civility. 2. Memorandum-book. 3. Two or more rings put on the finger as a memorandum.

memorial [may-mo-re-ahl'], *m.* 1. Memorandum-book. 2. Memorial (petición), brief. 3. Bulletin (publicación).

memorialista [may-mo-re-ah-lees'-tah], *m.* An amanuensis; a person who writes petitions for others.

memorión [may-mo-re-on'], *m. aug.* A strong memory.

memorioso, sa [may-mo-re-o'-so, sah], *a.* Mindful, retentive (memoria).

memorizar [may-mo-re-thar'], *va.* To memorize.

mena [may'-nah]. *f.* 1. Small sea-fish, kind of anchovy. 2. A mineral vein ore. 3. *V.* VITOLA. Ball gauge. 4. (*Naut.*) Size of cordage.

ménade [may'-nah-day], *f.* 1. Bacchante, priestess of Bacchus. 2. A woman beside herself, in a frenzy.

menador, ra [may-nah-dor', rah], *m. &f (Prov.)* Winder, one who turns a wheel to wind silk.

menaje [may-nah'-hay], *m.* 1. Furniture, movables, house-stuff, furnishing (de una casa). 2. Furniture, fittings (escuela). 3. House keeping (economía doméstica). **Sección de menaje,** hardware and kitchen department (en almacenes).

menar [may-nar'], *va. (Prov. Murcia.)* To wind silk on a reel or spinning-jenny.

mención [men-the-on'], *f.* Mention, oral or written rectial of something. **Hacer mención de,** to mention.

mencionar [men-the-o-nar'], *va.* To mention, to name. **Dejar de mencionar,** to fail to mention.

mendicación [men-de-cah-the-on'], *f. V.* MENDIGUEZ.

mendicante [men-de-cahn'-tay], *a.* Mendicant, begging. *m.* Mendicant, one of a begging fraternity.

mendicidad [men-de-the-dad'], *f.* Mendicity, mendicancy, beggary.

mendigante, ta [men-de-gahn'-tay, tah], *m. & f.* Mendicant, beggar.

mendigar [men-de-gar'], *va.* To ask charity, to live upon alms, to beg, to mendicate; to crave, to entreat.

mendigo [men-dee'-go], *m.* Beggar. *-a. (Mex.)* Yellow (cobarde).

mendiguez [men-de-gheth'], *f.* Beggary, indigence, mendicancy.

mendosamente [men-do'-sah-men-tay], *adv.* Falsely, erroneously, equivocally.

mendoso, sa [men-do'-so, sah], *a.* False, mendacious.

mendrugo [men-droo'-go], *m.* Crust (pan).

mendruguillo [men-droo-geel'-lyo], *m. dim.* A small bit of bread.

meneador, ra [may-nay-ah-dor', rah], *m. & f.* Mover, manager, director.

menear [may-nay-ar'], *va.* 1. To move from place to place. 2. To manage, to direct. 3. To shake (cabeza); to wag (cola); to sway (caderas). **Sin menear el dedo,** without lifting a finger. 4. To get on with (asunto). *-vr.* 1. To be brisk and active, to stir about. 2. To wriggle, to waddle; to move from side to side; to shake (agitarse); to way (caderas).

meneo [may-nay'-o], *m.* 1. A wriggling or waddling motion of the body (movimiento). 2. Trade, business. **Dar un meneo a,** to jerk.

menester [may-nes-terr'], *m.* 1. Necessity, need, want. **Ser menester,** to be necessary, to be wanting. 2. Employment, business, occupation (trabajo), office; function (función). **Salir para un menester,** to go out on an errand. *-pl. (coll.)* 1. Natural or corporal necessities. 2. Implements, necessary tools of a workman.

menesteroso, sa [may-nes-tay-ro'-so, sah], *a.* Needy, necessitous.

menestra [may-nes'-trah], *f.* 1. Pottage made of different pulse and roots. 2. Vegetable soup.

menestral [may-nes-trahl'], *m.* Mechanic, handicraftsman, workman.

mengano, na [men-gah'-no, nah], *m. & f* Such a one; so and so (the second of two).

mengua [men'-goo-ah], *f.* 1. Decay (decadencia), decline. 2. Poverty (pobreza), indigence. 3. Disgrace arising from cowardly conduct (persona). 4. Discredit (descrédito).

menguadamente [men-goo-ah-dah-men-tay], *adv.* 1. Ignominiously. 2. Meanly (tacañería). 3. Foolishly (estúpidamente).

menguado [men-goo-ah'-do], *m.* 1. Coward, a silly, mean-spirited fellow. 2. An avaricious, miserable wretch. 3. Decrease, narrowing of stockings, etc.

menguado, da [men-goo-ah'-do, dah], *a.* 1. Diminished (disminuido), impaired, stunted. 2. Cowardly (cobarde), pusillanimous; foolish (tonto). **Hora menguada,** fatal moment. *-pp.* Of MENGUAR.

menguante [men-goo-ahn'-tay], *m.* 1. Ebb-tide, low-water, neap-tide. 2. Decline, decay. 3. Decrease of the moon. *-a.*

Decreasing (que disminuye); dwindling; decaying (decadente), waning (luna); ebb (marea).

menguar [men-goo-ar'], *va.* 1. To decay, to decline, to fall off. 2. To fail to be deficient. 3. To narrow stockings. -*vn.* To diminish (disminuir), to get less, to dwindle, to decrease; to go down (marea, número).

mengue [men'-gay], *m. (coll.)* To deuce, the devil.

menhir [men-neer'], *m.* Menhir, a great megalithic vertical stone.

menina [may-nee'-nah], *f.* Maid of honor.

meninge [may-neen'-hay], *f.* Meninges, membranes enveloping the brain and spinal cord.

meningitis [may-neen-hee'-tis], *f.* Meningitis, inflammation of the membranes of the brain.

menino [may-nee'-no], *m.* 1. Page of the queen and infants. 2. *(Prov.)* An affected, spruce little fellow.

menipea [may-ne-pay'-ah], *f.* Kind of satire in prose and verse.

menisco [may-nees'-co], *m.* 1. Meniscus (anatomía). 2. Glass concave on one side and convex on the other.

menjuí [men-hoo-ee'], *m. V.* BENJUÍ.

menjunje, menjurje [men-hoon'-hay, men-hoor'-hay], *m. (coll.)* Beverage composed of different ingredients, and of an unpleasant taste.

menologio [may-no-lo'-he-o], *m.* Menology, the martyrology of the Greeks divided into the months of the year.

menopausia [may-no-pah'-oo-se-ah], *f.* Menopause, cessation of menstruation, the change of life in women.

menor [may-nor'], *m & f.* 1. Minor, one under age. 2. Minor premise, the second proposition in a syllogism. 3. Minor, minorite, a Franciscan friar or nun. **Los menores de edad**, those who are under age. -*pl.* 1. The third class in a grammar-school. 2. Minor orders.

menor [may-nor'], *a. comp.* 1. Less, smaller (en tamaño), minor. 2. Minor, in music. **Menor edad**, minority, under age. **Hermano menor**, younger brother. **Por menor**, by retail, in small parts; minutely.

menorete [may-no-ray'-tay], *a. dim. coll.* **Al menorete** or **por el menorete**, at least.

menoría [may-no-ree'-ah], *f.* Inferiority (inferioridad), subordination (subordinación).

menorista [may-no-rees'-tah], *m.* Student of grammar in the third class. -*m & f.* Retailer.

menorquín, na [may-nor-keen', nah], *a.* Native of or belonging to the island Minorca.

menorragia [may-nor-rah'-he-ah], *f. (Med.)* Menorrhagia, excessive menstrual flow.

menos [may'-nos], *adv.* 1. Less, in a lower degree. 2. Except, with the exception of. **A lo menos or por lo menos**, at least, however. **Mucho menos**, much less. **Poco más o menos**. A little more or less. **Venir a menos**, to decay, to grow worse; to become poor. **Ni más, ni menos**, neither more nor less, just equal. **Lo menos 10**, 10 at least. **Ir a menos**, to come down in the world. **Cada vez menos**, less and less. **Poco menos de una libra**, little less than a pound. **Tener en menos**, to look down on. **Tanto menos**, so much the less. **Ha venido a menos**, he has come down in the world. **Hacer de menos a uno**, to be unfaithful to somebody. -*prep.* Except. **Todos menos él**, everybody except him. **Cualquier cosa menos eso**, anything but that. **Todo incluido menos el transporte**, everything included but the transport. **Cuatro menos uno son tres**, four minus one is three. **Son las cuatro menos diez**, it is ten to four.

menoscabador, ra [may-nos-cah-bah-dor', rah], *m. & f.* Detracter, lessener. **menoscabar** [may-nos-cah-bar'], *va.* 1 To impair, to lessen (disminuir), to make worse. 2. To reduce, to deteriorate.

menoscuenta [may-nos-cah'-bo], *m.* Diminution, deterioration, loss.

menoscuenta [may-nos-coo-en'-tah], *f.* Discount.

menospreciable [may-nos-pray-the-ah-blay], *a.* Despicable, contemptible.

menospreciablemente [may-nos-pray-the-ah-blay], *adv.* Comtemptuously.

menospreciador, ra [may-nos-pray-the-ah-dor', rah], *m. & f.* Contemner, despiser.

menospreciar [may-nos-pray-the-ar'], *va.* To underrate (subestimar), to undervalue, to despise (despreciar), to contemn, to neglect, to overlook, to make light of.

menosprecio [may-nos-pray'-the-o], *m.* Contempt, scorn (desdén); the act of undervaluing a thing, neglect, contumely.

mensaje [men-sah'-hay], *m.* 1. Message, despatch, errand. 2. Petition or congratulation which the Cortes addressed to the king. 3. An official communication between the legislative and the executive power. *(Acad.)* **Mensaje de buenos augurios**, goodwill message. **Mensaje de la corona**, King's speech.

mensajero, ra [men-sah-hay'-ro, rah], *m. & f.* 1. Messenger. 2. The secretary bird. 3. *(Naut.)* Bull's eye traveler. A wooden thimble. **Mensajero de buenas noticias**, bearer of good news.

ménsola [men'-so-lah], *f. (Arch.) V.* MENSULA.

menstruación [mens-troo-ah-the-on'], *f.* Menstruation.

menstrual [mens-troo-ahl'], *a.* Menstrual.

menstrualmente [mens-troo-ahl'-men-tay], *adv.* Monthly, menstrually.

menstruante [mens-troo-ahn'-tay], *a.* Menstruating.

menstruar [mens-troo-ar'], *vn.* To menstruate.

menstruo [mens'-troo-o], *m.* 1. Menses (producto), catamenia, courses. 2. *(Chem.)* Menstruous, any liquor used as a solvent. 3. Menstruation. -*a.* Menstruous, monthly, menstrual.

mensual [men-soo-ahl'], *a.* Monthly, menstrual.

mensualidad [men-soo-ah-le-dahd'], *f.* A month's pay; monthly salary.

mensualmente [men-soo-ahl-men-tay], *adv.* Monthly.

ménsula [men'-soo-lah], *f. (Arch.)* Cantilever, bracket.

mensura [men-soo'-rah], *f.* Measure.

mensurabilidad [men-soo-rah-be-le-dahd'], *f.* Mensurability.

mensurable [men-soo-rah'-blay], *a.* Mensurable.

mensurador, ra [men-soo-rah-dor', rah], *m. & f.* Measurer, meter.

mensural [men-soo-rahl'], *a.* Applied to something used to measure.

mensurar [men-soo-rar'], *va. V.* MEDIR and JUZGAR.

menta [men'-tah], *f. (Bot.)* Mint.

mentado, da [men-tah'-do, dah], *a.* Famous, celebrated, renowned.-*pp.* of MENTAR.

mental [men-tahl'], *a.* Mental, intellectual (capacidad, trabajo), ideal.

mentalidad [men-tah-le-dahd'], *f.* Mentality, mind.

mentalizar [men-tah-le-thar'], *va.* To prepare, condition; to sensitize, to make aware; to persuade (convencer). -*vr.* To prepare oneself (mentalmente).

mentalmente [men-tahl'-men-tay], *adv.* Mentally, intellectually, ideally.

mentar [men-tar'], *va.* To mention, to record.

mente [men'-tay], *f.* 1. Mind, understanding; intellectual power. 2. Sense, meaning; will, disposition. **Mente consciente**, concious mind. **No tengo mente**, it is not in my mind.

mentecatería [men-tay-cah-tay-ree'-ah], *f.* Folly, absurdity, nonsense.

mentecato, to [men-tay-cah'-to, tah], *a.* Silly, foolish, stupid, crack-brained.-*a.* Fool.

mentecatón, na [men-tay-cah-tone', nah], *a. aug.* Very silly.

mentidero [men-te-day'-ro], *m.* Talking corners, where idlers meet to tattle.

mentir [men-teer'], *va.* 1. To lie, to utter falsehoods. 2. To disappoint, to frustrate, to deceive (engañar), to feign. 3. To gainsay, to retract; to equivocate, to falsify.

mentira [men-tee'-rah], *f.* 1. Lie, falsehood, mendacity. 2. Error, mistake in writing. 3. White mark (señal). 4. **Sacar**

mentiras, *(And. Cono Sur)* to crack one's knuckles. 5. **De mentira**, *(LAm.)* Pretend, sham (artificial). **Una mentira como una casa**, a whopping great lie. **Aunque parezca mentira**, however incredible it seems.

mentirilla, ita [men-te-reel'-lyah, ee, tah], *f. dim.* Falsehood told in jest. **De mentirillas**, in jest.

mentirón [men-te-rone'], *m. aug.* Great lie.

mentirosamente [men-te-ro-sah-men-tay], *adv.* Falsely, deceitfully, lyingly.

mentirosito, ta [men-te-ro-see'-to, tah], *a. dim.* A little false, deceitful.

mentiroso, sa [men-te-ro'-so, sah], *a.* 1. Lying (que miente), mendacious. 2. Erroneous, equivocal, incorrect. -*m. yf.* Liar.

mentís [men-tees'], *m.* You lie, or thou liest. Term of insult.

mentol [men-tole'], *m.* Menthol.

mentolado, da [men-to-lah'-do, dah], *a.* Mentholated.

mentón [men-tone'], *m.* Chin.

mentor [men-tor'], *m.* Mentor, counsellor, guide.

menú [may-noo'], *m.* Menu (lista), bill of fare.

menudear [may-noo-day-ar'], *va.* To repeat (repetir), to detail minutely (narración).-*vn.* 1. To relate or describe little things (al explicarse). *(Com.)* To sell by retail. 2. *(Cono Sur, Mex.)* To abound (abundar).

menudencia [may-noo-den'-the-ah], *f.* Trifle (bagatela), littleness; minuteness (minuciosidad), minute, accuracy.

menudeo [may-noo-day'-o], *m.* Act of repeating minutely; retail.

menudero, ra [may-noo-day'-ro, rah], *m. & f.* Dealer in tripes, giblets, sausages, etc.

menudico, ica, ito, ita [may-noo-dee'-co, cah], *a.* Somewhat small.

menudillo [may-noo-deel'-lyo], *m.* Extremities of animals. **Menudillos**, giblets of fowls.

menudo, da [may-noo'-do, dah], *a.* 1. Small (pequeño), slender of body; minute. 2. Of no moment or value, worthless. 3. Common, vulgar. 4. Examining minutely into things. 5. Small money, change. 6. Exact, scrupulous (persona). **Hombre menudo**, a mean, miserable fellow. **A menudo**, repeatedly, frequently, continually, often.

menudo [may-noo'-do], *m.* 1. Intestines, viscera. 2. Tithe of fruits.

menura, or **menura-lira** [may-noo'-rah-lee'-rah], *f.* Lyre-bird.

meñique [may-nyee'-kay], *a.* Very small, tiny, diminute. **Dedo meñique**, little finger. -*m.* Little finger (dedo auricular).

meollar [may-ol-lyar'], *m. (Naut.)* Thin line of spun-yarn made of oakum or untwisted ropes.

meollo [may-ol-lyo], *m.* 1. Marrow. 2. Judgment, understanding. 3. Soft part of bread, crumb (pan). 4. The substance or essential part of something (asunto).

meón, na [may-on', nah], *a. (coll.)* Continually making water.

meona [may-o'-nah], *f. (coll.)* New-born female infant, in distinction from the male.

mequetrefe [may-kay-tray'-fay], *m.* Insignificant, noisy fellow, jackanapes, coxcomb.

meramente [may-rah-men'-tay], *adv.* Merely, solely, nakedly.

merar [may-rar'], *va.* To mix liquors: generally applied to the mixture of wine and water.

merca [merr'-cah], *f. (coll.)* A purchase. *V.* COMPRA.

mercachifle [mer-cah-chee'-flay], *m.* 1. Peddler, hawker (vendedor ambulante). 2. *(Fig.)* Money grubber.

mercadantesco, ca [mer-cah-dan-tes'-co, cah], *a.* Mercantile.

mercadear [mer-cah-day-ar'], *vn.* To trade, to traffic. -*va.* To market (vender); to haggle over (regatear).

mercader [mer-cah-der'], *m.* Dealer, trader, shop-keeper.

mercadera [mer-cah-day'-rah], *f.* Shop keeper's wife, tradeswoman.

mercadería [mer-cah-day-ree'-ah], *f.* 1. Commodity, merchandise. Trace, the business of a trader. -*pl.* Goods.

mercadillo [mer-cah-deel'-lo], *m.* Bazaar (caridad).

mercado [mer-cah'-do], *m.* 1. Market, marketing. 2. Market, market place, mart. **Mercado negro**, black market. **Mercado**

mundial, world market. **Mercado de valores**, stock market. **Mercado de vendedores**, seller's market.

mercadotecnia [mer-cah-do-tec'-ne-ah], *f.* Marketing, marketing techniques.

mercaduría [mer-cah-doo-ree'-ah], *f.* Merchandise, trade.

mercancía [mer-can-thee'-ah], *f.* 1. Trade, traffic. 2. Merchandise, salable goods.

mercante [mer-cahn'-tay], *m. & a.* Dealer, trader; mercantile, commercial. **Buque mercante**, a trading vessel.

mercantil [mer-can-teel'], *a.* Commercial, mercantile, merchant-like.

mercantilizar [mer-can-te-le-thar'], *va.* To commercialize.

mercantilmente [mer-can-teel'-men-tay], *adv.* Merchantly, in a commercial or mercantile manner.

mercar [mer-car'], *va. V.* COMPRAR.

merced [mer-thed'], *f.* 1. Gift, favor (favor), grace, mercy. 2. Wages, pay for services especially to day-laborers. 3. Will, pleasure. 4. Appellation of civility, with which untitled persons are addressed. **Vuestra or vuesa merced**, your honor, your worship, sir. 5. A religious military order, whose chief object is to redeem captives. **Estar a merced**, to live at another's expense. **Hágame usted la merced**, do me the favor.

mercenario [mer-thay-nah'-re-o], *m.* 1. Day-laborer. 2. Mercenary, hireling. 3. A friar of the religious order *la Merced*.

mercenario, ria [mer-thay-nah'-re-o, ah], *a.* Mercenary, hired, hireling.

mercería [mer-thay-ree'-ah], *f.* 1. Trade of a haberdasher (géneros), who deals in small wares, mercery. 2. *(Amer.)* Fine hardware store (tienda). 3. *(Cono Sur)* Ironmonger's (ferretería).

mercerizado, da [mer-thay-re-thah'-do, dah], *a.* Mercerized.

mercero, a [mer-thay'ro], *m. & f.* 1. Haberdasher. 2. The keeper of a fine hardware store.

mercurial [mer-coo-re-ahl'], *m. & a.* 1. *(Bot.)* All good, mercury. 2. Mercurial.

mercúrico [mer-coo'-re-co], *a.* Mercuric, of the higher combining equivalent of mercury.

mercurio [mer-coo'-re-o], *m.* 1. Mercury, quicksilver. 2. Planet Mercury.

mercurioso, sa [mer-coo-re-o'-so, sah], *a.* Mercurous, relative to mercury, especially in its lower valence.

mercurocromo [mer-coo-ro-cro'-mo], *m. (Med.)* Mercurochrome.

merchante [mer-chahn'-tay], *m.* Merchant, who buys and sells goods without keeping an open shop. -*a.* Merchant. *V.* MERCANTE.

merdellón, na [mer-del-lyone', nah], *a. (Low.)* Slovenly, unclean, dirty.

merdoso, sa [mer-do'-so, sah], *a.* Nasty, filthy.

merecedor, ra [may-ray-thay-dor', rah], *m. & f.* One who deserves reward or punishment. **Merecedor de confianza**, trustworthy.

merecer [may-ray-therr'], *vn.* 1. To deserve, to merit. 2. *V.* LOGRAR. 3. To owe, to be indebted for. **Merecer mucho**, to be very deserving. -*va.* 1. To do anything deserving reward or censure. **Merecer el trabajo**, to be worth the while. **Te lo tienes merecido**, it serves you right. 2. *(And.)* To catch (atrapar); to snatch (robar).

merecidamente [may-ray-the-dah-men-tay], *adv.* Worthily, meritoriously, condignly.

merecido, da [may-ray-thee'-do, dah], *a.* Meritorious, condign. -*pp.* of MERECER.

merecido [may-ray-thee'-do], *m.* Deserts, due, condign punishment. **Llevar su merecido**, to get one's deserts.

merecimiento [may-ray-the-me-en'-to], *m.* Condignity, merit (cualidad), deserts (lo merecido).

merendar [may-ren-dar'], *vn.* 1. To take a collation between dinner and supper. 2. *(Prov.)* To eat the principal meal at noon. -*va.* 1. To pry into another's writings or actions. 2. To anticipate, to be in advance of another. **Merendar lo que**

escribe otro, to peep at somebody else's cards. -vr. **Merendarse algo**, to wangle something. *(Yo meriendo, yo meriende*, from *Merendar. V.* ACERTAR.)

merendero, ra [may-ren-day'-ro, rah], *a.* Picking up the seeds in cornfields (cuervos). -*m.* Open-air café.

merendilla [may-ren-deel'-lyah], *f. dim.* of MERIENDA. A light lunch.

merendona [may-ren-do'-nah], *f. aug.* A plentiful or splendid collation.

merengue [may-ren'-gay], *m.* 1. Kiss sugar-plum, a confection of sugar and white of eggs; meringue. 2. *(And. Carib. Cono Sur)* Sickly person (enclenque). 3. *(Cono Sur)* Row (alboroto).

meretricio, cia [may-ray-tree'-the-o, ah], *a.* Meretricious, harlot, lustful.

meretricio [may-ray-tree'-the-o], *m.* Carnal sin.

meretriz [may-ray-treeth'], *f. V.* RAMERA.

merey [may-ray'-e], *f. (Bot.)* Cashew-tree.

mergánsar [mer-gahn'-sar], *m. (Orn.)* Goosander, merganser.

mergo [merr'-go], *m. (Orn.)* Diver.

merián [may-re-ahn'], *com. (Zool.)* Merianopossum of South America, a marsupial without a pouch.

meridiana [may-re-de-ah'-nah], *f.* Meridional line. **A la meridiana**, at midday, noon.

meridiano [may-re-de-ah'-no], *m.* Meridian, a large circle of the celestial sphere. -*a.* Meridional, noon.

meridional [may-re-de-o-nahl'], *a.* Southern, southerly, meridional.

merienda [may-re-en'-dah], *f.* 1. Luncheon, collation between dinner and supper, afternoon snack. 2. *(Prov.)* Principal meal eaten at noon. 3. *(coll.)* Hump-back. **Hacer merienda de negros**, free-for-all, bedlam. **Ir de merienda**, to go for a picnic.

merino [may-ree'-no], *m.* 1. Shepherd of merino sheep. 2. Merino (carnero, lana, tela). -*a.* 1. Moving from pasture to pasture (ovejas). 2. Applied to thick, curled hair.

méritamente [may'-re-tah-men-tay], *adv. V.* MERECIDAMENTE.

mérito [may'-re-to], *m.* Merit (valor), worth, excellence (excelencia), virtue. **Hacer mérito de**, to mention. **Restar méritos de**, to detract from.

meritoriamente [may-re-to'-re-ah-men-tay], *adv.* Meritoriously.

meritorio, ria [may-re-to'-re-o, ah], *a.* 1. Meritorious. 2. Employed in an office, without salary; emeritus.

merla [merr'-lah], *f. (Orn.)* Blackbird, merle.

merlán [merr-lahn'], *m.* The European whiting, a small fish of the cod family.

merlín [mer-leen'], *m. (Naut.)* Marline, a loosely twisted hempen line.

Merlín, *m.* Merlin, name of a famous enchanter. **Saber mas que Merlín**, to be very shrewd or keen.

merlo [merr'-lo], *m. (Zool.)* Black wrasse, a sea-fish very frequent in the Mediterranean.

merlón [mer-lone'], *m. (Mil.)* Merlon the solid part of a parapet between the embrasures.

merluza [mer-loo'-thah], *f.* Hake, a fish of the cod family.

merma [merr'-mah], *f.* Waste, leakage, soakage, decrease (disminución).

mermar [mer-mar'], *vn. vr.* To waste, to diminish, to dwindle, to lessen. -*va.* To reduce, to lessen; to cut down (pago, raciones).

mermelada [mer-may-lah'-dah], *f.* Marmalade, a conserve.

mero [may'-ro], *m.* Polluck, a Mediterranean foodfish of delicate flavor.

mero, ra [may'-ro, rah], *a.* 1. Mere, pure, simple, naked. 2. *(Mex.)* Precise, exact (preciso). 3. *(Mex.)* Right (justo). 4. *(Mex.)* **El mero centro**, the very center.

merodeador [may-ro-day-ah-dor'], *m.* Marauder, pillager.

merodear [may-ro-day-ar'], *vn.* To pillage, to maraud.

merodeo [may-ro-day'-o], *m.* The act of pillaging or marauding.

merodista [may-ro-dees'-tah], *m.* Pillager, marauder.

mes [mess], *m.* 1. Month. **Mes lunar**, lunar month. **El mes que viene**, next month. 2. Catamenia, menses, courses. **Al mes**, in a month's time, by the month, at the expiration of a month. **Dentro de un mes**, in a months' time. **El mes corriente**, the current month. **Pagar por meses**, to pay by the month.

mesa [may'-sah], *f.* 1. Table, an article of furniture. 2. Table, the fare or viands put on a table. 3. Table, a flat surface on the top of hills or mountains. 4. Landing place of a staircase. 3. In printing offices, a case for types. 4. The table of accounts of the rents of cathedral churches, prelates, or dignitaries in Spain. 7. Set or rubber, anyone of the games played at a truck-table. 8. Spanish truck-table or the hire of it. 9. The flat of a sword, of a shoe-maker's awl, etc. 10. Communion table. **Levantar la mesa**, to take away the cloth. **Sentarse a mesa puesta**, to live at other people's expense. **Mesa redonda**, (a) round table conference. (b) Table d'hote (en restaurantes). **Mesa de billar**, billiard table. **Bendecir la mesa**, to say grace. **Vino de mesa**, table wine.

mesada [may-sah'-dah], *f.* Monthly pay, wages, or allowance; stipend.

mesana [may-sah'-nah], *f. (Naut.)* Mizzenmast or sail.

mesar [may-sar'], *va.* To pluck off the hair with the hands.

meseguero [may-say-gay-ro], *m.* 1. Keeper of the fruits of the harvest. 2 *(Prov.)* The guard of the vineyard. -*a.* Relating to the harvest fruits.

mesentérico, ca [may-sen-tay'-re-co, cah], *a.* Mesenteric, relating to the mesentery.

mesenterio [may-sen-tay'-reo], *m.* Mesentery, a fold of the peritoneum enveloping the small intestine and connecting it to the abdominal wall posteriorly.

meseraica [may-say-rah'-e-cah], *a.* Mesenteric (vein). The portal vein with its branches.

meseta [may-say'-tah], *f.* 1. Landing place of a staircase. 2. Plateau, tableland, meseta (llanura).

Mesías [may-see'-as], *m.* Messiah, Jesus Christ.

mesilla [may-seel'-lyah], *f.* 1. *(dim.)* Small table; sideboard. 2. Screw. 3. Board-wages. 4. Censure by way of a jest. **Mesilla de chimenea**, mantelpiece. **Mesilla de noche**, bedside table.

mesita [may-see'-tah], *f. dim.* 1. A small table. 2. **Mesita de un pie**, stand.

mesmedad [mes-may-dahd'], *f.* Nature, actuality, used only in the pleonastic phrase: **Por su misma mesmedad**, by the very fact.

mesmerismo [mes-may-rees'-mo], *m.* Mesmerism, hypnotism.

mesocracia [may-so-crah'-the-ah], *f.* Mesocracy, government by the middle class.

mesón [may-sone'], *m.* 1. Inn, hostelry. 2. *(Phy. & Chem.)* Meson. 3. *(CAm.)* Lodging house.

mesonaje [may-so-nah'-hay], *m.* Street or place which contains numerous inns and public-houses.

mesoncillo [may-son-theel'-lyo], *m. dim.* A little inn.

mesonero, ra [may-so-nay'-ro, rah], *m. & f.* Inn-keeper, publican, landlord of an inn (dueño), host, hostess. -*a.* Waiting, serving in an inn.

mesonista [may-so-nees'-tah], *com.* Waiter in an inn or public-house.

mesopotámico, ca [may-so-po-tah'-me-co, cah], *a.* Mesopotamian, relating to Mesopotamia.

mesta [mes'-tah], *f.* 1. The proprietors of cattle and sheep, considered as a body. 2. Annual meeting of shepherds and owners of flocks, which bears the title of **El honrado concejo de la mesta**, the honorable board of **Mesta.**

mesteño, ña [mes-tay'-nyo, yah], *a.* 1. Belonging to the *mesta* or graziers. 2. *V.* MOSTRENCO.

mestizaje [mes-te-tha-hay], *m.* 1. Cross-breeding (acto). 2. Half-castes (personas).

mestizar [mees-te-thar'], *va.* To cross breeds or races of animals. *(Acad.)*

mestizo, za [mes-tee'-tho, thah], *a.* 1. Of a mongrel breed, hybrid, hybridous. 2. *(Amer.)* Mestee or mustee, the offspring of a white man and an Indian woman, or vice versa.

mesto [mes'-to], *m. (Bot.)* 1. Large, prickly oak. 2 Turkey oak. *V.* REBOLLO.

mestura [mes-too'-rah], *f. (Prov.)* Mashlin, mixed wheat and rye.

mesura [may-soo'-rah], *f.* 1. A grave deportment, a serious countenance. 2. Civility, politeness (cortesía). 3. Moderation (moderación); measure.

mesuradamente [may-soo-rah'-dah-men-tay], *adv.* Gently, prudently, measurably.

mesurado, da [may-soo-rah'-do, dah], *a.* Moderate (moderado), circumspect, modest; regular, temperate, regulated. *-pp.* of ·MESURAR.

mesurar [may-soo-rar'], *va.* To assume a serious countenance, to act with solemn reserve. *-vr.* To behave with modesty and prudence.

meta [may'-tah], *f.* 1. Boundary, limit. 2. *(Dep.)* Goal; winning post (de carrera), finishing line. -m. Goal-keeper.

metábola [may-tah'-bo-lah], *f.* 1. *(Med.)* Transformation of one disease into another. 2. Metabolism, the sum of the assimilative and destructive processes in the body. 3. *(Rhet.)* Pleonasm, bringing together several synonymous expressions to set forth a single idea.

metabolismo [may-tah-bo-lees'-mo], *m.* Metabolism.

metacarpiano, na [may-tah-car-pe-ah'-no, nah], *a.* Metacarpal, relating to the Metacarpus.

metacarpo [may-tah-car'-po], *m. (Anat.)* Metacarpus, the part of the hand between the wrist and the fingers.

metacronismo [may-tah-cro-nees'-mo], *m.* Metachronism, anachronism.

metafísica [may-tah-fee'-se-cah], *f.* 1. Metaphysic, metaphysics, ontology. 2. The art of subtilizing in any matter.

metafísicamente [may-tah-fe'-se-cah-men-tay], *adv.* Metaphysically.

metafísico, ca [may-tah-fee'-se-co, cah], *a.* Metaphysical, abstract, obscure.

metafísico [may-tah-fee'-se-co], *m.* Metaphysician, ontologist.

metáfora [may-tah'-fo-rah], *f.* Metaphor, a rhetorical figure.

metafóricamente [may-tah-fo'-re-cah-men-tay], *adv.* Metaphorically, figuratively.

metafórico, ca [may-tah-fo'-re-co, cah], *a.* Metaphorical.

metaforizar [may-tah-fo-re-thar'], *va.* To use metaphors.

metal [may-tahl'], *m.* 1. Metal. 2. Brass, latten. 3. The sound or tone (tono-color) of the voice. 4. Quality, nature or condition of a thing.

metalario, metálico, metalista [may-tah-lah'-re-o, may-tah'-le-co, may-tah-lees'-tah], *m.* Workman or dealer in metal, metallist, metallurgist.

metalescente [may-tah-les-then'-tay], *a.* Metallic in lustre.

metálica [may-tah'-le-cah], *f. V.* METALURGIA.

metálico, ca [may-tah'-le-co, cah], *a.* 1. Metallic. 2. Medallic, pertaining to medals.-m. Bullion. **Metálico en caja,** *(Com.)* cash on hand.

metalífero, ra [may-tah-lee'-fay-ro, rah], *a. (Poet.)* Metalliferous.

metalistería [may-tah-lis-tay-ree'-ah], *f.* Metal-working.

metalizado [may-tah-te-tha'-do], *a.* 1. Metallic (pintura). 2. *(Fig.)* Mercenary, dedicated to making money.

metalizar [may-tah-le-thar'], *va.* To make a body acquire metallic properties.-vr. 1. To be converted into or impregnated with metal. 2. *(Met.)* To be controlled by love of money.

metalografía [may-tah-lo-grah-fee'-ah], *f.* Metallography.

metaloide [may-tah-lo'-e-day], *m.* Metalloid, a simple body resembling the metals in some of its properties, such as sulphur carbon, phosphorus.

metalurgia [may-tah-loor'-he-ah], *f.* Metallurgy.

metalúrgico, ca [may-tah-loor'-he-co, cah], *a.* Relating to metallurgy.

metalúrgico [may-tah-loor'-he-co], *m.* Metallurgist.

metalla [may-tahl'-lyah], *f.* Small piece of gold leaf used to cover parts imperfectly gilt.

metamorfosear [may-tah-mor-fo-say-ar'], *va.* To metamorphose, to transform.

metamórfico, ca [may-tah-mor'-fe-co, cah], *a. (Geol.)* Metamorphic, igneous (rocas).

metamorfosis, metamorfosis [may-tah-mor-fo'-sis], *f.* Metamorphosis, transformation.

metaplasmo [may-tah-plahs'-mo], *m. (Gram.)* The changing, taking away, or adding to the letters of a word; metaplasm.

metástasis [may-tahs'-tah-sis], *f. (Med.)* Metastasis, translation or removal of a disease from one place to another.

metasticizar [may-tahs-te-the-thar'], *vn.* To metastasize.

metatarsiano, na [may-tah-tar-se-ah'-no, nah], *a. (Anat.)* Metatarsal.

metatarso [may-tah-tar'-so], *m. (Anat.)* Metatarsus, the part of the foot or limb between the ankle and the toes; it consists of five bones in man.

metate [may-tah'-tay], *m. (Mex.)* A curved stone in the shape of an inclined plane resting on three feet, used for grinding maize for *tortillas*, or cocoa for chocolate.

metátesis [may-tah-tay'-sis], *f. (Rhet.)* Metathesis, a transposition.

metedor, ra [may-tay-dor', rah], *m. & f.* 1. He who puts one thing into another. 2. Smuggler. 3. Clout of now-born children.

metedura [may-tay-doo'-rah], *f.* 1. Putting, placing (acto de meter). 2. **Metedura de pata,** bloomer.

meteduría [may-tay-doo-ree'-ah], *f.* Smuggling.

metemuertos [may-tay-moo-err'-tose], *m.* 1. Attendant in a play-house. 2. Busybody, a vain, meddling person.

meteórico, ca [may-tay-o'-re-co, cah], *a.* Meteoric, meteorous.

meteorismo [may-tay-o-rees'-mo], *m. (Med.)* Meteorism, distension of the abdomen by gases.

meteorita [may-tay-o-ree'-tah], *f.* Meteorite.

meteorizar [may-tay-o-re-thar'], *va.* To cause meteorism or tympanites.-vr. To suffer from this disorder.

meteoro [may-tay-o'-ro], *m.* An atmospheric phenomenon.

meteorología [may-tay-o-ro-lo-hee'-ah], *f.* Meteorology.

meteorológico, ca [may-tay-o-ro-lo'-he-co, cah], *a.* Meteorological. **Informe or boletín meteorológico,** weather report.

meteorologista [may-tay-o-ro-lo-hees'-tah], *m.* Meteorologist.

meter [may-terr'], *va.* 1. To place or to put in, to include one thing within another, to get on. 2. To smuggle goods into a country (géneros). 3. To make, to cause (causar), to occasion, to urge, to move. 4. To engage, to prevail upon, to induce. 5. To stake (dinero), to put to hazard. 6. To cram down victuals. 7. To put things close together, to cram or heap them together. 8. To impose upon, to deceive. 9. To compress, to straighten, to reduce. 10. *(coll.)* To eat. *V.* COMER. 11. To score (tanto). **Meter bulla,** to make a noise. **Meter cizaña,** to sow discord, to breed disturbances. **Meter prisa,** to urge, to hasten. **A todo meter,** full-speed. **Meter un susto a uno,** to put the wind up somebody. **Meter a uno a trabajar,** to put somebody to work. **Le metieron 5 años de cárcel,** they put him away for 5 years. -vr. 1. To meddle, to intermeddle, to interfere. 2. To be on terms of familiarity with a person. 3. To choose a profession or trade. 4. To be led astray, to plunge into vice. 5. To empty into the sea (ríos). 6. To attack sword in hand. 7. To go into, to get into (introducirse). 8. To extend, to project. 9. To provoke somebody (provocar). **Meterse con alguno,** to pick a quarrel. **Meterse donde no le llaman,** to thrust oneself where he is not called. **Meterse en vidas ajenas,** to dive into other people's affairs. **Meterse en todo,** to be jack of all trades. **Meterse soldado,** to become a soldier. **Meterse en un agujero,** to get into a hole. **Se metió en la cama,** she got into bed. **Meterse en peligro,** to get into danger. **El río se mete en el mar,** the river flows into the sea. **Meterse a escritor,** to become a writer.

metesillas [may-tay-seel'-lyas], *m. V.* METEMUERTOS.

meticulosamente [may-te-coo-lo'-sah-men-tay], *adv.* Meticulously, scrupulously.

meticuloso, sa [may-te-coo-lo'-so, sah], *a.* Meticulous, scrupulous, finicky.

metido, da [may-tee'-do, dah], *a. & pp.* of METER. 1. Placed or put in or into; engaged: deceived. **Estar muy metido en algún negocio**, to be deeply engaged in an affair. 2. *(LAm.)* Meddling, meddlesome (entrometido). 3. *(Carib. Cono Sur)* Half tight (bebido).

metileno [may-te-lay'-no], *m. (Chem.)* Methylene, an organic radical known only in combination.

metilo [may-tee'-lo], *m. (Chem.)* Methyl.

metimiento [may-te-me-en'-to], *m.* Inclusion, the act and effect of putting one thing into another.

metódicamente [may-to'-de-cah-men-tay], *adv.* Methodically, orderly.

metódico, ca [may-to'-de-co, cah], *a.* Methodical, formal.

metodismo [may-to-dees'-mo], *m.* 1. Systematic method. 2. Methodism, the system and practices of the Methodist church, developed by John Wesley and his followers.

metodista [may-to-dees'-tah], *n. com.* 1. Methodist, a religious sectary, follower of John Wesley. 2. *a. V.* METÓDICO.

método [may'-to-do], *m.* Method, manner, mode, custom, order, form.

metonimia [may-to-nee'-me-ah], *f.* Metonymy, a rhetorical figure.

metonímico, ca [may-to-nee'-me-co, cah], *a.* Metonymical, relating to metonymy.

metopa [may-to'-pah], *f. (Arch.)* Metope, the space between the triglyphs in the Doric order.

metraje [may-trah'-hay], *m.* Length in meters. **Película de largo metraje**, full length film.

metralla [may-trahl'-lyah], *f.* Grape-shot, case-shot, canister-shot.

metrallar [may-trahl-lyar'], *va.* To canister, to attack with grape-shot

metralleta [may-trahl-lyay'-tah], *f.* Submachine gun, tommy gun.

metreta [may-tray'-tah], *f.* A Greek and Roman measure of liquids.

métrica [may'-tre-cah], *f.* Metrical art, poetry.

métricamente [may'-tre-cah-men-tay], *adv.* Metrically.

métrico, ca [may'-tre-co, cah], *a.* Metrical, composed in verse.

metrificar [may-tre-fe-car'], *va. V.* VERSIFICAR.

metritis [may-tree'-tis], *f. (Med.)* Metritis, inflammation of the womb.

metro [may'-tro], *m.* 1. Meter, unit of measure in the decimal system (medida). 2. Metre, verse. 3. Subway train. **Metro cúbico**, cubic meter. **Metro cuadrado**, square meter.

metrología [may-tro-lo-hee'-ah], *f.* A treatise on weights and measures.

metrónomo [may-tro'-no-mo], *m.* Metronome.

metrópoli [may-tro'-po-le], *f.* 1. Metropolis, the chief city of a country. 2. Archiepiscopal church.

metropolitano [may-tro-po-le-tah'-no], *m.* 1. Metropolitan, archbishop. 3. Subway train.

México [may'-he-co], Mexico.

mezcal [meth-cahl]', *m. (Mex.)* 1. A species of maguey, or American agave. 2. An intoxicating liquor prepared from this plant.

mezcla [meth'-clah], *f.* 1. Mixture (sustancia), commixture, compound, composition, medley. 2. Mortar. 3. Mixed cloth.

mezcladamente [mayth-clah'-dah-men-tay], *adv.* In a mixed or promiscuous manner.

mezcladillos [meth-clah-deel'-lyos], *m. pl.* A kind of paste made by confectioners.

mezclador, ra [mezh-clah-dor', rah], *m. & f.* One who mixes, mingler, compounder.

mezclar [meth-clar'], *va.* 1. To mix, to mingle, to unite, to commix, to blend (armonizar), to merge (combinar). 2. To

spread false reports, to sow discord, to excite disturbances. **Mezclar a la iglesia en el debate**, to drag the Church into the debate. *-vr.* 1. To mix, to be united into a mass. 2. To marry a person of inferior rank. 3. To introduce oneself into anything. **Mezclarse con cierta gente**, to mix with certain people.

mezclilla [meth-clee'-lyah], *f.* Denim, coarse cotton drill.

mezcolanza [meth-co-lahn'-thah], *f. (coll.)* Bad mixture of colors, mishmash.

mezquinamente [meth-ke'-nah-men-tay], *adv.* Miserably, avariciously.

mezquindad [meth-keen-dahd'], *f.* 1. Penury, poverty, indigence. 2. Avarice, covetousness, paltriness, currishness, meanness (cualidad).

mezquino, na [meth-kee'-no, nah], *a.* 1. Poor, indigent, penurious; diminutive. 2. Avaricious, covetous, mean (tacaño), paltry; miserable (cualidad), lean. 3. Petty, minute, puny. *-m.* 1. Mean person (avaro); petty individual (miserable). 2. *(And. CAm. Mex.)* Wart (verruga).

mezquita [meth-kee-tah], *f.* Mosque, a Mohammedan temple or place of worship.

mezquite [meth-kee'-tay], *m.* The mezquite shrubs of Mexico. 1. The honey-mezquite. 2. The screw bean.

mí [mee], *pro.* Me; the oblique case of the pronoun *yo* when it is governed by any preposition other than *con*: as, *de mí*, from me. **Para mí no hay duda**, so far as I'm concerned there's no doubt. **Por mí mismo**, by myself.

mi [mee], *adj. pos.* My; placed before nouns. **Mi amor**, my love. **Ésta es mi casa**, this is my house. *-pl.* **mis**, my. **Éstos son mis padres**, these are my parents. **Ésos son mis libros**, those are my books.

mi. *m.* Mi, the third note of the scale.

miaja [me-ah'-hah], *f.* Crumb, minute portion.

miar [me-ar'], *m.* To mew, as a cat.

miasma [me-ahs'-mah], *m. (Med.)* Miasm or miasma. *-pl.* Miasmata.

miasmático, ca [me-as-mah'-te-co, cah], *a.* Miasmatic producing miasm.

miau [me-ah'-oo], *m.* Mew of a cat.

mica [mee'-cah], *f.* 1. Mica, a mineral cleaving in thin scales, transparent to translucent. Called also isinglass. 2. Female long-tailed monkey. *(Ame.)* **Agarrar una mica**, to get sloshed (emborracharse).

micáceo, cea [me-cah'-the-o, ah], *a.* Micaceous, mica-like.

micasquisto [me-cas-kees'-to], *m.* Micaschist.

micción [mic-the-on'], *f.* Micturition, the act of urinating.

mico [mee'-co], *m.* 1. Monkey, an ape with a long tail. 2. *(coll.)* Libidinist. 3. An ugly (feo), ill-shaped man; conceited person (engreído); flirt (mariposón); hot man (cachondo). 4. *(CAm.)* Cunt (vajina).

micología [me-co-lo-hee'-ah], *f.* 1. Mycology, the science of fungi.

micra [mee'-crah], *f.* Micron (unit of length).

micro [me-cro], *a.* A Greek word, signifying small, much used in combination.

micro [mee'-cro], *m. (coll.)* Mike.

microamperio [me-cro-am-pay'-re-o], *m.* Microampere.

microbiano, na [me-cro-be-ah'-no, nah], *a.* Microbial, microbic.

microbicida [me-cro-be-thee'-dah], *m.* Microbicide.-*a.* Microbicidal.

microbilanza [me-cro-be-lahn'-thah], *f.* Microbalance.

microbio [me-cro'-be-o], *m.* Microbe.

microbiología [me-cro-be-o-lo-hee'-ah], *f.* Microbiology.

microbiológico, ca [me-cro-be-o-lo'-he-co, cah], *a.* Microbiological.

microbiólogo [me-cro-be-o'-lo-go], *m.* Microbiologist.

microbús [me-cro-boos'], *m.* Minibus.

microcanal [me-cro-cah-nahl]. *(Inform.)* Microchannel.

microcéfalo, la [me-cro-thay'-fah-lo, lah], *a.* Microcephalous, microcephalic, having an unusually small skull.

microcircuito [me-cro-ther-coo-ee'-to], *m.* Microcircuit.

micrococo [me-cro-co'-co], *m.* Micrococcus.

micocosmo [me-cro-cos'-mo], *m.* Microcosm.

microchip [me-cro-cheep'], *m.* Microchip.

microfilm [me-cro-feelm'], *m.* Microfilm.

microfísica [me-cro-fee'-se-cah], *f.* Microphysics.

micrófono [me-cro'-fo-no], *m.* Microphone.

microfotografía [me-cro-fo-to-grah-fee'-ah], *f.* 1. Microphotography. 2. Microphotograph.

micrografía [me-cro-grah-fee'-ah], *f.* Micrography.

microinstrucciones [me-cro-ins-trooc-the-o-nays]. *(Inform.)* Firmware.

micrómetro [me-cro'-may-tro], *m.* Micrometer.

microómnibus, microbús [me-cro-om'-ne-boos, me-cro-boos'], *m.* Microbus.

microonda [mi-cro-on'-dah], *f.* Microwave.

microorganismo [me-cro-or-gah-nees'-mos], *m. pl.* Microorganisms.

microprocesador [me-cro-pro-thay-sah-dor'], *m.* Microprocesor. **Microprocesador modular de bits,** *(Comput.)* bit slice microprocessor.

microscópico [me-cros-co'-pe-co], *ca*, *a.* Microscopic, microscopical.

microscopio [me-cros-co'-pe-o], *m.* Microscope. **Microscopio electrónico,** electron microscope.

microsurco [me-cro-soor'-co], *m.* Microgroove.

michelín [me-chay-leen'], *m.* Spare tire, roll of fat.

michito [me-chee'-to], *m. dim.* Kitten, a young cat.

micho, cha [mee'-cho, chah], *m. & f.* Puss, name of a cat.

mida [mee'-dah], *m.* Mida, bean-fly, worm that breeds in vegetables. *(Yo mido, yo mida; el midió, midiera; from Medir. V.* PEDIR.*)*

miedo [me-ay'-do], *m.* Fear, dread, apprehension. **Morirse de miedo,** to die for fear. **No haya miedo,** there is nothing to be apprehended. **Por miedo a,** for fear of. **Hace un frío de miedo,** it's terribly cold.

miedoso, sa [me-ay-do'-so, sah], *a.* Fearful, timorous, easily afraid.

miel [me-el'], *f.* Honey. **Miel de caña,** Molasses. **Dejar a uno con la miel en los labios,** to deprive one of what he was just beginning to enjoy. **Las mieles del triunfo,** the sweets of success. **Hacerse de miel,** to snatch something away from somebody.

mielga [me-el'-gah], *f.* 1. *(Bot.)* Lucerne, when it grows wild. 2. A kind of dog-fish. 3. Rake, an instrument for raking hay, etc. 4. Stripe of ground.

melitis [me-ay-lee'-tis], *f.* Myelitis, inflammation of the spinal cord.

miembro [me-em'-bro], *m.* 1. Member, a limb of the body. 2. Member, one of a community or corporation. 3. Member, any branch or part of an integral. 4. Member, a head, a clause of a discourse or period. **Hacerse miembro de,** to become member of.

mienta [me-en'-tah], *f. (Bot.)* Mint. *V.* HIERBABUENA.

mientras [me-en'-tras], *adv.* In the meantime, in the meanwhile; when. **Mientras que,** whilst, during the time that, as long as, so long as.

miera [me-ay'-rah], *f.* 1. Juniper oil. 2. Resin.

miércoles [me-err'-co-les], *m.* Wednesday. **Miércoles de ceniza,** Ash Wednesday.

mierda [me-err'-dah], *f. (coll.)* 1. Excrement, faeces, ordure, shit. 2. Dirt, muck. **Es una mierda,** it's shit. **El libro es una mierda,** the book is crap. **Es una mierda de coche,** it's, an awful car.

mierdacruz [me-er-dah-crooth'], *f. (Bot. Prov.)* Ciliate sparrow-wort.

mierla [me-err'-lah], *f. (Orn.)* Blackbird. *V.* MERLA.

mies [me-ess'], *f.* 1. Wheat and other grain of which bread is made, corn (grano). 2. Harvest, the time of reaping (temporada). 3. *(Met.)* Multitude converted or ready for conversion.

miga [mee'-gah], *f.* 1. Crumb, the soft part of bread. 2. A small fragment of anything. 3. Marrow, substance, or principal part. **Migas,** crumbs of bread fried with oil, salt, and pepper. **Hacer buenas, or malas migas,** *(coll.)* to agree or disagree readily with one.

migaja [me-gah'-hah], *f.* 1. A small particle, scrap, or bit of bread. 2. Scrap, crumb, small particles of bread, meat, etc., left at the table. 3. A small bit of anything, ace. 4. *(coll.)* Nothing, little or nothing. *-pl.* Offals, leavings; broken victuals.

migajada [me-gah-hah'-dah], *f.* A small particle.

migajica, illa, ita, uela [me-gah-hee'-cah], *f. dim.* A very small particle of bread.

migajón [me-gah-hone'], *m.* Crumb, without crust; marrow core.

mígala [mee'-gah-lah], *f.* Mygale, bird-spider, a very huge species of spider.

migar [me-gar'], *va.* To crumble, to break into small bits.

migración [me-grah-the-on'], *f.* Migration.

migratorio, ria [me-grah-to'-re-o, ah], *a.* Migrating, migratory.

miguero, ra [me-gay'-ro, rah], *a.* Crummy, relating to crumbs fried in a pan.

mijar [me-har'], *m.* A millet-field.

mijero [me-hay'-ro], *m.* Milestone.

mijo [mee'-ho], *m.* 1. *(Bot.)* Millet or millet panic-grass. **Mijo alemán,** german panic-grass. 2. *(Bot.)* Turkey-millet. 3. (LOCAL) Maize.

mikado [me-kah'-do], *m.* Mikado, the sovereign of Japan.

mil [meel], *m.* One thousand or ten hundred. **Perdió muchos miles de pesos,** he lost several thousand dollars. **Tres mil coches,** three thousand cars. **Lo ha hecho mil veces,** he's done it hundreds of times.

milagrero, ra [me-lah-gray'-ro, rah], *m. & f.* Person fond of considering natural events as miracles, and publishing them as such; a miracle-monger.

milagro [me-lah'-gro], *m.* 1. Miracle, wonder, something above human power. 2. Offering of wax or any other substance, hung up in churches in commemoration of a miracle. **Vida y milagros,** *(coll.)* life, character, and behavior. **Hacer milagros,** *(fig.)* to work wonders.

milagrón [me-lah-grone'], *m. (coll.)* Dread, astonishment; extreme.

milagrosamente [me-lah-gro'-sah-men-tay], *adv.* Miraculously, marvellously.

milagroso, sa [me-lah-gro'-so, sah], *a.* Miraculous, done by miracle; marvellous, admirable.

milamores [meel-lah-mo'-res], *f.* Perennial plant, a species of valerian.

Milán [me-lahn'], *m.* 1. The city Milan. 2. Kind of linch cloth, so called from being made in Milan.

milanés, sa [me-la-nays', sah], *a.* Native of or belonging to Milan, Milanese.

milano [me-lah'-no], *m.* 1. Kite (ave), a bird of prey. **Mesa de milanos,** keen hunger and little to eat. 2. Flying gurnard (pez). **Cola de milano,** dovetail.

milenario, ria [me-lay-nah'-re-o, ah], *a.* Millenary, consisting of a thousand.

milenario [me-lay-nah'-re-o], *m.* 1. Millenary, the space of a thousand years. 2. Millennium. 3. Millenary, one who expects the millennium.

milenio [me-lay'-ne-o], *m.* Millennium.

mileno, na [me-lay'-no, nah], *a.* Applied to cloth, the warp of which contains a thousand threads.

milenrama [me-len-rah'-mah], *f. (Bot.)* Common milfoil or yarrow.

milésimo, ma [me-lay'-se-mo, mah], *a.* 1. Thousandth, millesimal, the ordinal of a thousand. 2. The thousandth part of anything. *-***Milésima,** *f.,* mill, the thousandth part of the monetary unit.

milhojas [mil-o'-has], *f. (Bot.)* Yarrow, milfoil. *V.* MILENRAMA.

mili [me'-le], *f.* Military service. **Estar en la. mili,** to do one's military service.

miliar [me-le-ar'], *a.* Miliary, having the size or form of a millet-seed.

miliárea [me-le-ah'-ray-ah], *f.* Milliare, one-thousandth of an acre.

milicia [me-lee'-the-ah], *f.* 1. Art and science of war, warfare (arte). 2. Military men in general, the militia or soldiery (soldados). 3. Militia, the trained bands of the inhabitants of a country: in this last sense it is almost always used in the plural.

miliciano [me-le-the-ah'-no], *m.* Militiaman (soldado),-*a.* Military, militar.

miligramo [me-le-grah'-mo], *m.* Milligram, the thousandth part of a gram.

mililitro [me-le-lee'-tro], *m.* Milliliter, the thousandth part of a liter.

milímetro [me-lee'-may-tro], *m.* Millimetre, the thousandth part of a meter, 25,4 to the inch.

militante[me-le-tahn'-tay], *a.* Militant; military.

militar [me-le-tar'], *m.* Soldier, a military man (soldado). -*pl.* Military, the soldiery.-*a.* Militar, military, soldierly, war-like (espíritu), martial.

militar [me-le-tar'], *vn.* 1. To serve in the army, to follow the profession of arms. 2. To hold, to militate, to stand good, to go against (razones, argumentos). **Militar en un partido**, to belong to a party. **Militar en favor de**, to speak for.

militarismo [me-le-tah-rees'-mo], *m.* Militarism, predominance in the goverment of state of the military spirit.

militarización [me-le-tah-re-thah-the-on'], *f.* Militarization.

militarizar [me-le-tah-re-thar'], *va.* To militarize.

militarmente [me-le-tar'-men-tay], *adv.* Militarily, in a military stile.

milla [meel'-lyah], *f.* 1. Mile, a linear measure, eight stadia, or one thousand geometric steps. 2. (*Naut.*) Knot.

millar [mil-lyar'], *m.* 1. Number of a thousand. 2. Thousand, proverbially a great number: in this last sense it is almost always used in the plural. 3. A certain quantity of cocoa, which in some parts is three pounds and a half, and in others more.

millarada [mil-lyah-rah'-dah], *f.* Several thousands. **Echar** millaradas, to brag of wealth and riches. **A millaradas**, Innumerable times.

millo [meel'-lyo], *m.* (*Prov.*) In the Canary Islands, and in Galicia, maize.

millón [mil-yone'], *m.* Million, ten hundred thousand. 2. Million, any very great number. **Un millón de sellos**, a million stamps. **Mil millones**, a billion. (GB, a thousand millions).

millonario [mil-lyo-nah'-re-o], *m.* Millionaire, a person very rich in money.

millonésimo, ma [mil-lyo-nay'-se-mo, mah], *a.* Millionth.

milmillonésimo, ma [mil-meel-lyo-nay'-se-mo, mah], *a.* Thousand millionth, billionth.

milo [mee'-lo], *m.* (*Prov. Ast.*) Earth-worm.

milocha [me-lo'-chah], *f.* (Local) Kite, a toy.

milpa [meel'-pah], *f.(Mex.)* A maize-field (plantación).

milpiés [mil-pe-ays'], *m.* Centipede, millipede.

milréis [mil-rays'], *m.* Milreis, Brazilian and Portuguese coin.

mimado, da [me-mah'-do, dah], *a.* Spoiled, humored.

mimar [me-mar'], *va.* To coax, to wheedle, to flatter, to fondle, to caress, to indulge, to humor, to pet.

mimbral [mim-brahl'], *m.* Plantation of osiers.

mimbre [meem'-bray], *m.* (*Bot.*) 1. Twig of an osier. 2. Osier, willow.

mimbrear [mim-bray-ar'], *vn.* V. CIMBRAR.

mimbrera [mim-bray'-rah], *f.* (*Bot.*) Osier.

mimbreral [mim-bray-rahl'], *m.* Plantation of osiers.

mimbroso, sa [mim-broh'-so, sah], *a.* Made of osiers.

mimeografiar [me-may-o-grah-fe-ar'], *va.* To mimeograph.

mimeógrafo [me-may-o'-grah-fo], *m.* Mimeograph.

mimetismo [me-may-tees'-mo], *m.* mimetism, protective coloring.

mímica [mee'-me-cah], *f.* Pantomime, sign-language (señas).

mímico, ca [mee'-me-co, cah], *a.* Mimic.

mimo [mee'-mo], *m.* 1. Mime, mimic. 2. Endearingness, fondness, indulgence. 3. Prudery, delicacy. 4. Ancient mimes or farcical representations. **Dar mimos a un niño**, to spoil a child.

mimología [me-mo-lo-hee'-ah], *f.* Act of imitating the voice and actions of others.

mimosa [me-mo'-sah], *f.* (*Bot.*) Mimosa, the sensitive-plant.

mimoso, sa [me-mo'-so, sah], *a.* Delicate, endearingly soft (blandengue), fond, foolishly nice or tender.

mina [mee'-nah], *f.* 1. Conduit, mine, a subterraneous canal or cavity in the ground. 2. Mine, a place which contains metals or minerals. 3. Spring, source of water. 4. Business which yields great profit and demands but little exertion. 5. (*coll.*) A large quantity of money. 6. (*Mil.*) Mine under a fortress. 7. Lead; refill (de lapicero).

minador, ra [me-nah-dor', rah], *m.* & *f.* Miner, one who works in mines; one who makes military mines; engineer.

minal [me-nahl'], *a.* Belonging to a mine.

minar [me-nar'], *va.* 1. To mine, to dig mines and burrows. 2. To mine, to sap, to ruin by mines. 3. To make uncommon exertions to attain some end or collect information.

minarete [me-nah-ray'-tay], *m.* Minaret, a spire in Saracen architecture.

mineraje [me-nay-rah'-hay], *m.* Labor of mining.

mineral [me-nay-rahl'], *a.* Mineral, consisting of inorganic bodies.

mineral [me-nay-rahl'], *m.* 1. Mineral, an inorganic substance, matter dug out of the earth, ore. 2. A spring of water, the mineral source or origin of fountains. 3. A source or origin which produces a plenty of something. 4. Mine which contains metals, minerals, or precious stones.

mineralización [me-nay-rah-le-thah-the-on'], *f.* (*Phys.*) Mineralization, the state of a metal in combination with another body.

mineralogía [me-nay-rah-lo-hee'-ah], *f.* Mineralogy.

mineralógico, ca [me-nay-rah-lo'-he-co, cah], *a.* Belonging to mineralogy, mineralogical.

mineralogista [me-nay-rah-lo-hees'-tah], *m.* Mineralogist.

mineralurgia [me-nay-rah-loor'-he-ah], *f.* Metallurgy.

mineralurgista [me-nay-rah-loor-hees'-tah], *m.* Metallurgist.

minería [me-nay-ree'-ah], *f.* 1. The art of mining. 2. Force of miners; the whole body of workers in a mine. 3. Body of mine-operators.

minero [me-nay'-ro], *m.* 1. Mine, place in the earth which contains metals or minerals. 2. Miner, one who digs for metals, or makes military mines. 3. Source, origin.

mingo [meen'-go], *m.* One of the three balls in the game of billiards, which is never struck by a cue, but by another ball: the red ball. **Poner el mingo**, to excel (sobresalir), to attract attention (llamar la atención).

minguito [min-gee'-to], *m.* Piece of bread, one-quarter of a loaf.

mini....*pref.* mini.... **Minibikini**, microscopic bikini.

miniar [me-ne-ar'], *va.* To paint in miniature.

miniatura [me-ne-ah-too'-rah], *f.* Miniature, a painting on vellum, ivory, or paper.

miniaturista [me-ne-ah-rees'-tah], *com.* Painter of miniatures.

miniaturización [me-ne-ah-too-re-thay-the-on'], *f.* Miniaturization.

mínima [mee'-ne-mah], *f.* (*Mus.*) Minim; half-note.

minimista [me-ne-mees'-tah], *m.* Student of the second class in grammar.

mínimo, ma [mee'-ne-mo, mah], *a.* Least, smallest (más pequeño). **Cifra mínima**, minimum number. -*m.* Minimum. **Como mínimo**, as a minimum.

minino, mino [me-nee'-no, mee'-no], *m.* Word used for calling a cat.

minio [mee'-ne-o], *m.* Minium, an oxide of lead.

ministerial [me-nis-tay-re-ahl'], *a*. Ministerial.

ministerialmente [me-nis-tay-re-ahl'-men-tay], *adv*. Ministerially.

ministerio [me-nis-tay'-re-o], *m*. 1. Ministry, office, public place, employment. 2. Manual labor. 3. Ministry, administration, the principal officers of government. 4. Ministry, the charge or office of a minister or secretary of state, and the time which he is in office.

ministra [me-nees'-trah], *f*. 1. Ministress, she who serves. 2. Wife of a cabinet minister.

ministrador, ra [me-nis-trah-dor', rah], *m. & f*. One who ministers.

ministrante [me-nis-trahn'-tay], *pa*. Serving, ministrating.

ministrar [me-nis-trar'], *va. & vn*. 1. To minister, to serve an office or employment, to perform the functions of a public place. 2. To minister, to supply, to furnish.

ministril [me-nis-treel'], *m*. 1. Apparitor, tipstaff; a petty officer of justice. 2. Minstrel, one who plays the flute and other musical wind-instruments. **Ministriles**, musical wind-instruments.

ministro [me-nees'-tro], *m*. 1. Minister, agent. 2. Minister employed in the administration of justice. 3. Secretary of state. **Ministro de Estado**, or **de relaciones exteriores**, the secretary of state or minister of foreign affairs. **Ministro de la Gobernación**, or **de relaciones interiores**, minister of the interior. **Ministro de Hacienda**, secretary of the treasury. 4. Minister or agent of a foreign power. 5. A petty officer of justice. 6. One of the heads of some religious communities.

minoración [me-no-rah-the-on'], *f*. Minoration.

minorar [me-no-rar'], *va*. To lessen, to reduce to a smaller compass, to diminish, to clip. *-vr*. To lower, to fall.

minorativo, va [me-no-rah-tee'-voh, vah], *a*. Lessening, that decreases or lessens.

minoría [me-no-ree'-ah], *f*. Minority, the smaller number.

minoridad [me-no-re-dahd'], *f*. Minority, nonage.

minoritario [me-no-re-tah'-re-o], *a*. Minority.

minotauro [me-no-tah'-oo-ro], *m*. Minotaur, fabulous monster.

minucia [me-noo'-the-ah], *f*. 1. Minuteness, smallness; mite, atom, anything of very little value. 2. Small tithes paid of wool, lambs, etc. *-pl*. Minutiae.

minuciosamente [me-noo-the-o'-sah-men-tay], *adv*. Thoroughly, meticulously; in a very detailed way.

minuciosidad [me-noo-the-o-se-dahd'], *f*. 1. Minute explanation of a thing. 2. A trifle.

minucioso, sa [me-noo-the-o'-so, sah], *a*. Superfluously exact, nice, scrupulously and minutely cautious, thorough (meticuloso), very detailed (detallado).

minué, minuete [me-noo-ay', me-noo-ay'-tay], *m*. Minuet, a kind of grave and stately dance.

minuendo [me-noo-en'-do], *m*. (*Arith*.) Minuend.

minúscula [me-noos'-coo-loh], *a*. Small, lower-case letters.

minúsculo [me-noos'-coo-lo], *a*. Tiny, minute, minuscule; (*Tip*.) small.

minusvalía [me-noos-vah-le'-ah], *f*. 1. Handicap (physical). 2. (*Com*.) Depreciation, capital loss.

minusvalidez [me-noos-vah-le-dayth'], *f*. State of being handicapped, disablement.

minusválido [me-noos-vah'-le-do], *a*. Handicapped, disabled. *-m & f*. Handicapped person.

minuta [me-noo'-tah], *f*. 1. Minute, first draft of an agreement in writing (borrador); an enumeration of the principal heads of a contract. 2. Papers containing brief notes or memorandums (apuntes). **Libro de minutas**, minute-book, memorandum-book, a common-place book. 3. (*culin*.) Menu. 4. (*Cono Sur*) Junk (basura). 5. (*CAm*.) Flavored ice drink (bebida).

minutar [me-noo-tar'], *va*. To take down the principal heads of an agreement; to make the first draft of a contract, to minute.

minutario [me-noo-tah'-re-o], *m*. The book in which public notaries keep a memorandum of the documents they authorize.

minutero [me-noo-tay'-ro], *m*. Minute hand of a watch or clock.

minutisa [me-noo-tee'-sah], *f*. (*Bot*.) Sweet-william pink.

minuto [me-noo'-to], *m*. 1. Minute, the sixtieth part of an hour; the sixtieth part of a degree; sixty seconds. 2. Minute, moment, any small space of time.

miñón [me-nyone'], *m*. 1. Name given to some troops of light infantry in Spain. 2. Minion, scoriae of iron ore.

miñona [me-nyo'-nah], *f*. (*typ*.) Minion, 7-point type.

mío, mía [mee'-o, mee'-ah], *pron. poss*. My, mine. **Es muy mío**, he is much my friend. **Los míos**, my people. **Es mío**, it is mine. **Éste es el mío**, this is mine.

miocardio [me-o-car'-de-o], *m*. Myocardium.

mioceno, na [me-o-thay'-no, nah], *a*. (*Geol*.) Miocene.

miografía [me-o-grah-fee'-ah], *f*. Myography. *V*. MIOLOGÍA.

miología [me-o-lo-hee'-ah], *f*. Myology, part of anatomy which treats of the muscles; a treatise on muscles.

miope [me-o'-pay], *a*. Myopic, near sighted.

miopía [me-o-pe'-ah], *f*. Myopia, near sightedness.

miosota [me-o-so'-tah], *f*. (*Bot*.) Myosotis, forget-me-not, a plant of the borage family.

miquelete [me-kay-lay'-tay], *m*. Miquelet, mountain soldier belonging to the militia of Catalonia and the Pyrenees.

mira [mee'-rah], *f*. 1. The sight of a gun. 2. A point of mathematical instruments to direct the sight. 3. Care: vigilance; expectation, design. **Estar a la mira**, to be on the lookout, to be on the watch. **Mira de bombardero**, bombsight. **Tener miras sobre**, to have designs on. **De miras estrechas**, narrow-minded.

¡mira! [mee'-rah], *int*. Look! behold! take care! see!

mirabel [me-rah-bel'], *m*. 1. (*Bot*.) Summer cypress goose-foot. 2. (*Prov*.) Sun flower.

mirabolano [me-rah-bo-lah'-no], *m*. (*Bot*.) Myrobalan, a dried astringent prune-like fruit of India, used as a cathartic.

mirada [me-rah'-dah], *f*. 1. Glance, a transient view. 2. Gaze, steadfast look. **Mirada fija**, stare. **Apartar la mirada**, to look away. **Clavar la mirada en**, to fix one's eyes on.

miradero [me-rah-day'-ro], *m*. Place exposed to view on all sides; watchtower, or any elevated spot which commands an extensive prospect.

mirado, da [me-rah'-do, dah], *a*. Considerate (considerado), circumspect, prudent, moderate, sensible (juicioso), cautious (cauto). **Ser mirado en los gastos**, to be sensible about what one spends. 2. **Bien mirado**, well thought of. 3. Finicky, fussy. *-pp*. of MIRAR.

mirador, ra [me-rah-dor', rah], *m. & f*. 1. Spectator, looker-on. 2. *m*. Mirador, gallery which commands an extensive view. 3. *m*. A kind of balcony (balcón). 4. A boat used in the tunny-fishery.

miradura [me-rah-doo'-rah], *f*. Act of looking. *V*. MIRADA.

miraje [me-rah'-hay], *m*. Mirage, looming.

miramiento [me-rah-me-en'-to], *m*. 1. Awe, reverence, dread. 2. Consideration (consideración), reflection; expectation. 3. Circumspection (circunspección), prudence. 4. Reverential civility, attentions. **Sin miramientos**, unceremoniously. **Tratar sin miramientos a uno**, to treat somebody without consideration.

mirar [me-rar'], *va*. 1. To look or look at, to look upon or toward, to give a look, to watch (observar). 2. To respect, to have regard for, to esteem, to appreciate, to look on (considerar). 3. To have some private end, to aim at, to have in view. 4. To look, to be directed with regard to any object. 5. To observe, to watch, to spy (vigilar). 6. To take notice, to notice. 7. To fool, to consider, to reflect, to meditate. 8. To inquire, to collect information. 9. To look, to take care, to attend, to protect. *-vn*. 1. To look; to glance. 2. (*Arch*.) To look on to, to face. 3. (*Fig*.) To have in mind. *-vr*. 1. To look at oneself. 2. To look at one another. **Mirar a uno con**

malos ojos, to look at one with an evil eye. **Mirar alrededor**, to look about. **Mirar por uno**, to take care of, to look after. **Mirar de reojo**, to squint. **Mirar por encima**, to examine slightly. **Mirar sobre el hombro**, to cast a contemptuous look or frown. **Lo hago mirando el porvenir**, I do it bearing the future in mind. **No mira las dificultades**, he doesn't take into account the difficulties. **Mirar a uno como**, to look on somebody as. **Mirar hacia otro lado**, to look the other way. **Mirar atrás**, to look back. **Mirarse al espejo**, to look at oneself in the mirror.

mirasol [me-rah-sole'], *m. (Bot.)* Turnsol, sunflower. *V.* GIRASOL.

miriagramo [me-re-ah-grah'-mo], *m.* Myriagram, ten thousand grams.

miriámetro [me-re-ah'-may-tro], *m.* Myriameter, ten thousand meters.

miriápodos [me-re-ah'-po-dos], *a. & m. pl.* Myriapods, centipedes, articulates which have a great number of feet.

mirífico, ca [me-ree'-fe-co, cah], *a.* Marvellous, wonderful.

mirilla [me-reel'-lyah], *f.* Peep-hole; spy-hole; *(Fot.)* viewer.

miriñaque [me-re-nyah'-kay], *f.* 1. Bauble, gewgaw, trifling articles. 2. Manila grass-cloth. 3. Hoop-skirt.

mirística [me-rees'-te-cah], *f.* The nutmeg-tree.

mirla [meer'-lah], *f. (Orn.)* Blackbird. *V.* MIRLO.

mirlamiento [meer-lah-me-en'-to], *m.* Air of importance, affected gravity.

mirlarse [meer-lar'-say], *vr.* To assume an air of importance, to affect gravity.

mirlo [meer'-lo], *m.* 1. *(Orn.)* Blackbird. 2. Air of importance, affected gravity. 3. Tongue (lengua).

mirmego, ga [meer-may'-go, gah], *a.* Like an ant.

mirón, na [me-rone', nah], *m. & f.* 1. Spectator, looker-on (espectador), bystander. 2. Prier, busybody, gazer. **Ir de mirón**, to go along just to see.

mirra [meer'-rah], *f.* Myrra, a resinous gum.

mirrado, da [mir-rah'-do, dah], *a.* Composed of myrrh, perfumed with myrrh; myrrhine.

mirrauste [mir-rah'-oos-tay], *m.* Pigeon sauce, made of bread, almonds, and other ingredients.

mirrino, no [mir-ree'-no, nah], *a.* Myrrhine, of or like myrrh. *(Acad.)*

mirtáceo, cea [meer-tah'-thay-o, ah], *a.* Myrtaceous, pertaining to the myrtle family.

mirtidano [meer-te-dah'-no], *m.* Sprout which springs at the foot of a myrtle.

mirtiforme [meer-te-for'-may], *a.* Myrtiforal, having the shape of myrtle.

mirtino, na [meer-tee'-no, nah], *a.* Resembling myrtle.

mirto [meer'-to], *m. (Bot.)* Myrtle. *V.* ARRAYÁN.

misa [mee'-sah], *f.* 1. Mass, the service of the Roman Catholic Church. 2. Music composed for a solemn mass. **Misa del gallo**. Midnight mass. **Misa mayor**, high mass. **Oír misa**, to go to mass. **No saben de la misa la media**, they don't know the half of it.

misacantano [me-sah-can-tanh'-no], *m.* 1. Priest who is ordained and says the mass. 2. Priest who celebrates the first mass.

misal [me-sahl'], *m.* 1. Missal, the mass-book. 2. *(typ.)* Twoline pica.

misantropía [me-san-tro-pee'-ah], *f.* Misanthropy.

misantrópico, ca [me-san-tro'-pe-co, cah], *a.* Misanthropic, misanthropical, hating mankind.

misántropo, pa [me-sahn'-tro-po], *m & f.* Misanthropist.

misar [me-sar'], *vn. (doll.)* To say mass; to hear mass.

misario [me-sah'-re-o], *m.* Acolyte, one who attends on the priest during mass.

miscelánea [mis-thay-lah'-ne-ah], *f.* Miscellany, mixture, medley.

miscibilidad [mis-the-be-le-dahd'], *f.* Miscibility, capacity for being mixed.

miscible [mis-thee'-blay], *a.* Miscible, such as can be mixed.

miserable [me-say-rah'-blay], *a.* 1. Miserable, wretched, hapless, unhappy, lamentable. 2. Exhausted, dejected. 3. Covetous, avaricious, niggard; hard. 4. Mean, stingy (persona). 5. Squalid, sordid (cuarto, lugar). 6. Rotten, vile (moralmente).

miserablemente [me-say-rah'-blay-men-tay], *adv.* Miserably, unhappily, covetously, sordidly.

míseramente [mee'-say-rah-men-tay], *adv.* Meanly. *V.* MISERABLEMENTE.

miserear [me-say-ray-ar'], *vn.* To act penuriously.

miserere [me-say-ray'-ray], *m.* 1. The psalm **miserere**. 2. A solemn Lenten service in which this psalm is sung. 3. *(Med.)* **Cólico miserere**, ileus.

miseria [me-say'-re-ah], *f.* 1. Misery, miserableness, calamity, wretchedness, forlornness, need; oppression. 2. Covetousness, avariciousness, narrowness, hardness, stinginess, meanness (tacañría). 3. Trifle, a very small matter. 4. Poverty (pobreza), want (carencia). 5. Squalor, squalid conditions (condiciones). **Caer en la miseria**, to fall into abject poverty.

misericordia [me-say-re-cor'-de-ah], *f.* Mercy, mercifulness, clemency, loving-kindness.

misericordiosamente [me-say-re-cor-de-o'-sah-men-tay], *adv.* Piously, clemently, mercifully.

misericordioso, sa [me-say-re-cor-de-oh'-so, sah], *a.* Pious, humane, compassionate, merciful.

misero, ra [me-say'-ro, rah], *a.* 1. Mass loving. 2. Applied to a priest who says mass very often.

mísero, ra [mee'-say-ro, rah], *a. V.* MISERABLE.

misérrimo, ma [me-ser'-re-mo, mah], *a. sup.* Very miserable.

misil [me-seel'], *m.* Missile. **Misil tierra-aire**, ground-to-air missile. **Misil de crucero**, cruise missile. **Misil de ataque**, attack missile. **"Misiles"** (Juego), "missile command".

misión [me-se-on'], *f.* 1. Mission, the act of sending. 2. Mission, travel undertaken by priests and other religious persons to propagate religion. 3. Country or province where missionaries preach the gospel among infidels. 4. Missionary sermon. 5. Charges, cost, expense. 6. Money and victuals allowed to reapers during the harvest.

misionar [me-se-o-nar'], *va. & vn.* To preach as a missionary. *(coll.)* To reprimand.

misionero, misionario [me-se-o-nay'-ro], *m.* Missionary, one sent to propagate religion.

misivo, va [me-see'-vo, vah], *a.* Missive: applied to a letter or small note sent to any person.

mismamente [mes'-mah-men-tay], *adv.* Only (sólo), just; literally (literalmente); even (hasta); really (en realidad).

mismísimo, ma [mis-mee'-se-mo, mah], *a. sup.* Very same.

mismo, ma [mees'-mo, mah], *a.* Same, similar, equal, selfsame, like. **Yo mismo lo hago**, I myself do it. **Viven en la misma calle**, they live in the same street. **Es lo mismo**, it's the same thing. **Lo mismo no vienen**, they may not come. **En ese mismo momento**, at that very moment. *-adv.* Right. **Aquí mismo**, right here. *-conj.* **Lo mismo que**, just like.

misoginia [me-so-hee'-ne-ah], *f.* Misogyny, hatred of women.

misógino, na [me-so'-he-no, nah], *a.* Misogynous, hating women.

miss [mees], *f.* Beauty queen.

mistar [mis-tar'], *vn.* To speak or make a noise with the mouth: used generally with a negative.

mistela [mis-tay'-lah], *f.* Drink made of wine, water, sugar, and cinnamon.

míster [mees'-tayr], *m.* 1. Briton. 2. *(Dep.)* Trainer, coach.

misterio [mis-tay'-re-o], *m.* 1. Mystery, something above human intelligence. 2. Mystery, anything artfully made difficult; abstruseness, abstrusity. **No hay misterio**, there is no mystery about it.

misteriosamente [mis-tay-re-o'-sah-men-tay], *adv.* Mysteriously, secretly.

misterioso, sa [mis-tay-re-o'-so, sah], *a.* Mysterious, dark, obscure, mysterial, mystic, mystical.

mística [mees'-te-cah], *f.* Mysticalness, mystical theology.

místicamente [mees'-te-cah-men-tay], *adv.* Mystically; spiritually; emblematically.

misticismo [mis-te-thees'-mo], *m.* Mysticism, the doctrine of a sect of philosophers: a modern word.

místico, ca [mees'-te-co, ah], *a.* 1. Mystic, mystical, sacredly obscure. 2. Mystical, emblematical. 3. Mystical, spiritual, belonging to mystical divinity, or to the contemplation of spiritual things.

místico [mees'-te-co], *m.* 1. A mystic, a person devoted to religious contemplation; a writer in mystical divinity. 2. Small coasting vessel in the Mediterranean.

misticón [mis-te-cone'], *m. aug.* A great mystic man; a person who affects a mystical or holy life in a high degree.

mistificar [mis-te-fe-cahr'], *va.* 1. To hoax (embromar), to play a practical joke on; to hoodwink (engañar). 2. To mix up (confundir). 3. To falsify (falsificar).

mistilíneo, nea [mis-te-lee'-nay-o, ah], *a.* (*Geom.*) V. MIXTILÍNEO.

mistión, misto, mistura, misturar. *V.* MIXTIÓN, MIXTO, MIXTURA, and MIXTURAR.

misturera [mis-too-ray'-rah], *f.* (*Mex. Peru*) Flower-girl who sells bouquets or mixed flowers.

mita [mee'-tah], *f.* Mita, ancient tribute. The number of Indians subjected to compulsory labor by terms, in conformity with the law of that name.

mitad [me-tahd'], *f.* 1. Half. **Por mitades**, by halves. **Mitad y mitad**, by equal parts. 2. Middle (centro). **A mitad de**, halfway along. **Estar a mitad de camino**, to be halfway there. 3. (*Dep.*) Half. **La primera mitad**, the first half.

mitayo [me-tah'-yo], *m.* Indian serving his turn of compulsory labor.

mítico, ca [mee'-te-co, cah], *a.* Mythical.

mitigación [me-te-gah-the-on'], *f.* Mitigation, moderation, extenuation.

mitigador, ra [me-te-gah-dor', rah], *m & f.* Mitigator, mollifier.

mitigar [me-te-gar'], *va.* 1. To mitigate, to soften, to mollify (ira), to lull. 2. To quench (sed), to assuage.

mitigativo, va, mitigatorio, ria [me-te-gah-tee'-vo, vah], *a.* Lenitive, mitigant, mitigative.

mitin [mee'-tin], *m.* Political or labor meeting.

mito [mee'-to], *m.* Myth, allegorical fiction, chiefly about a religious subject.

mitocondrio [me-to-con'-dre-o], *m.* Mitochondrion.

mitología [me-to-lo-hee'-ah], *f.* Mythology, the history of the fabulous gods of antiquity.

mitológico, ca [me-to-lo'-he-co, cah], *a.* Mythological. -*m.* Mythologist.

mitologista, mitólogo [me-to-lo'-he-co], *m.* Mythologist.

mitón [me-tone'], *m.* Mitt, a sort of ladies' glove without fingers.

mitosis [me-to'-sis], *f.* (*Biol.*) Mitosis.

mitote [me-to'-tay], *m.* 1. An Indian dance. 2. (*Amer.*) Household festival. 3. (*Amer.*) Fastidiousness, affectation. 4. (*Mex. Coll.*) Riot, uproar, disturbance, confusion.

mitotero, ra [me-to-tay'-ro, rah], *a. & n.* (*Mex. Amer.*) 1. Precise, finical, dainty, fastidious. 2. Jolly, fond of diversion.

mitra [mee'-trah], *f.* Miter, an ornament for the head, worn by bishops; the dignity of a bishop.

mitrado [me-trah'-do], *a.* Mitered: applied to a person bearing a miter at festivals. -*pp.* of MITRAR.

mitrar [me-trar'], *vn.* (*coll.*) To be mitered or wear a miter.

mitridato [me-tre-dah'-to], *m.* Mithridate, antidote.

mixtamente [mix'-tah-men-tay], *adv.* Belonging to both ecclesiastical and civil courts.

mixtilíneo, nea [mix-te-lee'-nay-o, ah], *a.* (*Geom.*) Mixtilinear.

mixtión [mix-te-on'], *f.* Mixtion, mixture, commixture.

mixtiori [mix-te-fo'-re], *a.* (*Lat. Law.*) Applied to a crime that may be tried either in ecclesiastical or secular courts.

mixto, ta [mix'-to, tah], *a.* 1. Mixed, mingled. 2. Mixed, composed of various simples. 3. Half-breed, of a crossbreed: of mixed breed, mongrel.-*m.* V. MIXTURA.

mixtura [mix-too'-rah], *f.* Mixture, a mass formed by mingled ingredients. 2. Meslin, mixed corn, as rye and wheat.

mixturar [mix-too-rar'], *va.* To mix, to mingle.

mixturero, ra [mix-too-ray'-ro, rah], *a.* 1. Mixing, which mixes.

miz [meeth], *m.* Puss, the common appellation of cats.

mizo, za [mee'-tho, thah], *m. & f.* V. MICHO, CHA.

mnemónico [nay-mo-en-co]. (*Inform.*) Mnemonic.

moaré [mo-ah-ray'], *m.* Moiré, watered silk.

mobiliario, ria [mo-be-le-ah'-re-o, ria], *a.* House-furnishing, relating to furniture.-*m.* Furniture (muebles), fitment, household goods (artículos domésticos).

moca [mo'-cah], *f.* Mocha coffee.

mocadero, mocador [mo-cah-day'-ro, mo-cah-dor'], *m.* (*Prov.*) Pocket-handkerchief.

mocarro [mo-car'-ro], *m.* Mucus of the nose, not cleaned away (vulgarly, snot).

mocasín [mo-ca-seen'], *m.* 1. Moccasin, an Indian shoe of soft leather: 2. The moccasin snake.

mocear [mo-thay-ar'], *va.* To act as a boy; to revel, to rake.

mocedad [mo-thay-dahd'], *f.* 1. Juvenility, youthfulness (juventud). 2. Light and careless kind of living (vida).

mocetón, na [mo-thay-tone', nah], *m. & f.* A young, robust person.

mochada [mo-chah'-dah], *f.* Butt, a stroke with the head of a horned animal.

mochar [mo-char'], *va.* 1. To cut, to lop off. V. DESMOCHAR. 2. (*Cono Sur*) To pinch. 3. (*And.*) To fire, to sack.

mochazo [mo-chah'-tho], *m.* Blow with the butt-end of a musket.

mochil [mo-cheel'], *m.* Farmer's boy.

mochila [mo-chee'-lah], *f.* Knapsack, a bag in which soldiers carry their linen and provisions. **Hacer mochila**, to provide provisions for a journey.

mochilera [mo-che-lay'-rah], *a.* Pouched.

mochilero [mo-che-lay'-ro], *m.* One who carries the baggage of soldiers.

mochín [mo-cheen'], *m.* Young shoot of a tree. V. VERDUGO.

mocho, cha [mo'-cho, chah], *a.* 1. Dishonored. 2. Cropped, shorn. 3. Lopped, having the branches cut off. 4. Maimed, mutilated. 5. (*Mex. Coll.*) Hypocritical.

mochuelo [mo-choo-ay'-lo], *m.* (*Orn.*) Red owl. **Tocar el mochuelo**, to get always the worst part of something.

moción [mo-the-on'], *f.* 1. Motion (movimiento), movement. 2. Leaning, inclination of mind. 3. Divine inspiration. 4. (*Neol.*) Motion, a proposal to be voted on in an assembly. **Moción de censura**, motion of censure.

mocito, ta [moth-ee'-to, tah], *a. dim.* Juvenile, youthful.-*m. & f.* A very young person.

moco [mo'-co], *m.* 1. Mucus, a viscid fluid secreted by mucous membranes. 2. Any viscid, glutinous matter. 3. Snuff of a lamp or candle (mecha). 4. Candle drippings. 5. Slag of iron. **Moco de pavo**, Crest which hangs over the forehead of a turkey. 2. Any worthless thing. **¿Es moco de pavo?** do you call that nothing? **No sabe quitarse los mocos**, the fellow does not know how to blow his nose. **Quitar a uno los mocos**, to knock off one's nose with a blow. **Llorar a moco tendido**, to sob one's heart out. **Tirarse el moco**, to hesitate (vacilar).

mocora [mo-co'-rah], *f.* A tree of Ecuador from which hats are sometimes made.

mocosidad [mo-co-se-dahd'], *f.* Mucosity, mucousness, viscosity.

mocoso, sa [mo-co'-so, sah], *a.* 1. Snively: running from the nose. 2. Despicable, worthless. 3. Ignorant, thoughtless.

mocoso, sa [mo-co'-so, sah], *m. & f.* An ignorant, thoughtless person; an inexperienced youth.

mocosuelo, la [mo-co-soo-ay'-lo, lah], *m. & f. dim.* A thoughtless, inexperienced youth.

moda [mo'-dah], *f.* Fashion, form, mode, custom; especially in dress. **Un sombrero a la moda**, a fashionable hat. **Pasado de moda**, old fashioned. **Ponerse de moda**, to become fashionable.

modales [mo-dah'-les], *m. pl.* Manners, breeding, education.

modalidad [mo-dah-le-dahd'], *f.* 1. Modality, method. 2. Character nature. 3. *(Mus.)* Mode and tone. 4. Form (clase), way (manera). **Una nueva modalidad teatral**, a new dramatic form.

modelar [mo-day-lar'], *va.* To model, to form (formar).

modelismo [mo-day-lees'-mo], *m.* Modelling (hobby).

modelo [mo-day'-lo], *m.* 1. Model, pattern (patrón), standard (norma), copy, exemplar, paragon, rule. 2. *(Mex.)* Blank form (forma). **Servir de modelo**, to serve as a model. **Modelo de tecla**, *(Inform.)* keystroke pattern. *-m & f.* Model (alta Costura).

módem [mo'-daym], *m. (Inform.)* Modem. **No hay módem instalado**, nul modem.

moderación [mo-day-rah-the-on'], *f.* Moderation, temperance, frugality; abstemiousness, circumspection, continence. **Con moderación**, in moderation.

moderadamente [mo-day-rah'-dah-men-tay], *adv.* Moderately, temperately, reasonably, measurably.

moderado, da [mo-day-rah'-do, dah], *a.* 1. Moderate, temperate, abstemious, abstinent, considerate; gentle, 2. In politics, conservative.

moderador [mo-day-rah-dor'], *m.* Moderator. *-m & f.* (TV) Presenter.

moderadora [mo-day-rah-do'-rah], *f.* Moderatrix.

moderante [mo-day-rahn'-tay], *m.* Moderator, in some colleges, he who presides over the studies of pupils.

moderantismo [mo-day-ran-tees'-mo], *m.* Conservatism in politics.

moderar [mo-day-rar'], *va.* To moderate, to regulate, to adjust, to restrain (violencia), to curb, to repress.-*vr.* To become moderate, to refrain from excesses.

moderativo, va [mo-day-rah-tee'-vo, vah], *a.* Moderating.

moderatorio, ria [mo-day-rah-to'-re-o, ah], *a.* That which moderates.

modernamente [mo-dayr'-nah-men-tay], *adv.* Recently (recientemente), lately, newly, freshly.

modernismo [mo-der-nees'-mo], *m.* Modernism.

modernización [mo-der-ne-thah-the-on'], *f.* Modernization.

modernizar [mo-der-ne-thar'], *va.* To modernize.

moderno, na [mo-derr'-no, nah], *a.* Late, recent, modern, new, novel.

modestamente [mo-days'-tah-men-tay], *adv.* Modestly, comelily, meekly, maidenly, honestly.

modestia [mo-des'-te-ah], *f.* Modesty, decency, chastity, meekness, maidenliness; coyness; humility.

modesto, ta [mo-des'-to, tah], *a.* Modest, decent, pure, chaste, maidenly, unpretending, unassuming.

módico, ca [mo'-de-co, cah], *a* Moderate in price.

modificación [mo-de-fe-cah-the-on'], *f.* Modification, the act of modifying.

modificador, ra [mo-de-fe-cah-dor', rah], *m. & f.* Modifier.

modificar [mo-de-fe-car'], *va.* To modify, to moderate.

modificativo, va [mo-de-fe-cah-tee'-vo, vah], *a.* Modificative, that which modifies.

modillón [mo-dil-lyone'], *m. (Arch.)* Modillion, bracket.

modio [mo'-de-o], *m.* Roman dry measure.

modiolo [mo-de-o'-lo], *m. (Arch.)* Intermodillion, the quadrangular space between the modillions of a column.

modismo [mo-dees'-mo], *m.* Particular phraseology in a language deviating from the rules of grammar; mannerism.

modista [mo-dees'-tah], *f.* Milliner, dressmaker, modiste.

modisto [mo-dees'-to], *m & f.* Fashion designer.

modo [mo'-do], *m.* 1. Mode (método), method, manner, form. 2. Moderation, temperance. 3. Civility, urbanity. 4. Mode or mood in grammar. 5. *(Mus.)* A system of dividing the intervals of an octave; a Greek or Gregorian mode. **Del modo, del mismo modo que** or **al modo que**, in the same manner as. **A modo**, after a similar manner. **De modo**, so that. **Modo de gobierno**, form of government. **De este modo**, this way. **Del mismo modo**, in the same way. **De diversos modos**, in various ways. **De un modo o de otro**, one way or another. **Modo de programa**, *(Inform.)* program mode. **Modo de programación conversacional**, *(Inform.)* conversational programming mode. **Modo ampliado**, *(Inform.)* emphasized mode. **Modo de doble impresión**, *(Inform.)* double strike printing mode. **Modo de espaciado proporcional**, *(Inform.)* proportional spacing mode. **Modo de impresión super / subscript**, *(Inform.)* super / subscript printing mode.

modorra [mo-dor'-rah], *f.* 1. Drowsiness (sueño), heaviness. 2. Dawn or approach of day. 3. Flabby softness of the pulp of fruit. 4. A disease in sheep arising from plethora: sturdy.

modorrar [mo-dor-rar'], *va.* To drowse, to render heavy with sleep. *-vr.* To become flabby: applied to the pulp of fruit.

modorrilla [mo-dor-reel'-lyah], *f.* The third night-watch.

modorro, ra [mo-dor'-ro, rah], *a.* 1. Drowsy (soñoliento), sleepy, heavy. 2. Drowsy, dull (tonto), stupid.

modoso, sa [mo-doh'-so, sah], *a.* Temperate, sedate, in manner and gestures.

modrego [mo-dray'-go], *m.* Dunce, dolt, thick-skull.

modulación [mo-doo-lah-the-on'], *f.* Modulation, agreeable harmony. **Modulación de frecuencia**, *(Inform.)* frequency modulation.

modulador, ra [mo-doo-lah-dor', rah], *m. & f.* Modulator.

modulante [mo-doo-lahn'-tay], *a.* Modulating.

modular [mo-doo-lar'], *vn.* To modulate, to sing with harmony and variety of sound.

módulo [mo'-doo-lo], *m.* 1. *(Arch.)* Module, measure of columns. 2. Modulation of voice. 3. Unit of measure of running water for household use, irrigation, and manufacturing application. 4. Size of coins and medals. 5. *(Cono Sur)* Shelf unit (estantería).

mofa [mo'-fah], *f.* Mockery, jeer, scoff, ridicule, sneer.

mofador, ra [mo-fah-dor', rah], *m. & f.* Scoffer, scorner, jeerer, jester, mocker.

mofadura [mo-fah-doo'-rah], *f.* Jeer, scoff; scorn, jesting.

mofar [mo-far'], *va.* To deride, to jeer, to scoff; to mock, to ridicule, to flout. *-vr.* To sneer, to scoff, to behave with contempt.

mofeta [mo-fay'-tah], *f.* 1. Mephitis, a pestilential exhalation in mines or other deep places. 2. Skunk or polecat (animal).

moflete [mo-flay'-tay], *m.* Chub-cheek (mejilla).

mofletudo, da [mo-flay-too'-do, dah], *a.* Chub-cheeked.

mogate [mo-gah'-tay], *m.* Varnish, glazing which covers anything. **A medio mogate**, carelessly, heedlessly.

mogato, ta [mo-gah'-to, tah], *a. V.* MOJIGATO.

mogol, la [mo'-gol, go'-lah] *(Acad.)*, or **Mongol, la**, *a.* Mongolian. **Gran Mongol**, Grand Mogul, title of the ancient Emperor of the Mongolians.

mogólico, ca [mo-go'-le-co, cah], *a.* Relating to Mongolia.

mogollón, na [mo-gol-lyone'], *m & f.* 1. A hanger-on, a trencher friend, a parasite. **Comer de mogollón**, to sponge upon others. 2. Fuss, row (lío). 3. Large amount (cantidad). **Un mogollón de gente**, a mass of people.

mogote [mo-go'-tay], *m.* 1. An insulated rock or cliff with a flat crown, appearing at sea. 2. Pointed stack of corn.

mogrollo [mo-grol'-lyo], *m.* 1. Parasite, sponger. 2. Clown, rustic.

moharra [mo-ar'-rah], *f.* The point in which an ensign or flag-staff terminates.

moharrache, moharracho [mo-ar-rah'-chay, mo-ar-rah'-cho], *m.* Jack-pudding; a low jester.

mohatra [mo-ah'-trah], *f.* The act of selling for high prices and buying on the lowest terms, in order to overreach the buyer or seller.

mohatrar [mo-ah-trar'], *va.* To buy under price and sell above it; to make a deceitful sale.

mohatrero, ra [mo-ah-tray'-ro, rah], *m. & f.* Extortioner.

mohatrón [mo-ah-trone'], *m.* Extorter.

mohecer [mo-ay-therr'], *va.* To moss, to cover with moss.

mohiento, ta [mo-e-en'-to, tah], *a.* V. MOHOSO.

mohín [mo-een'], *m.* Grimace. **Hacer un mohín**, to make a face.

mohina [mo-ee'-nah], *f.* Animosity, desire of revenge (rencor).

mohino, na [mo-ee'-no, nah], *a.* 1. Fretful, peevish (disciplente), 2. Begotten by a stallion and she-ass (mulas). 3. Black (caballos, mulas). 4. Sad (triste), mournful. —*m.* One who plays alone against several others.

moho [mo'-o], *m.* 1. (*Bot.*) Moss. 2. Mould, concreted matter; rust (en metal); mouldiness. 3. Bluntness occasioned for want of application. 4. Lazy feeling (pereza).

mohoso, sa [mo-o'-so, sah], *a.* Mouldy, musty, rusty (metal), mossy.

mojada [mo-hah'-dah], *f.* 1. The act of wetting or moistening; dampening (al mojarse). 2. Sop, a piece of bread steeped in liquor. 3. (*coll.*) Stab, a wound with a pointed weapon (herida).

mojado, da [mo-hah'-do, dah], *a.* Wet; drenched, soaked. **Llover sobre mojado**, to be quite unnecessary.

mojador, ra [mo-hah-dor', rah], *m. & f.* Wetter, moistener.

mojadura [mo-hah-doo'-rah], *f.* Act of moistening or wetting.

mojama [mo-hah'-mah], *f.* Salt tuna-fish, dried or smoked.

mojar [mo-har'], *va.* 1. To wet, to moisten, to damp (humedecer), to drench (empapar). 2. To meddle, to interfere. 3. To stab (apuñalar). 4. To celebrate (triunfo). 5. (*Carib.*) To tip; (*Carib.*) to bribe (sobornar). **La lluvia mojó a todos**, the rain soaked everybody. **Mojar la ropa en un líquido**, to soak clothes in a liquid. -*vn.* To be immersed in my business. -*vr.* To get wet.

mojarra [mo-har'-rah], *f.* 1. Sea-fish, small and very broad. 2. (*Amer.*) A heart-shaped, or short and broad dagger.

mojarrilla [mo-har-reel'-lyah], *m.* (*coll.*) Punster, jester.

moje [mo'-hay], *m.* (*coll.*) Sauce of fricassee, ragout, or any other dressed meat.

mojeles [mo-hay'-less], *m. pl.* (*Naut.*) Blocks, pulleys.

mojicón [mo-he-cone'], *m.* 1. Blow in the face with a clinched fist (bofetada). 2. Kind of biscuit.

mojiganga [mo-he-gahn'-gah], *f.* A morrice or morris dance; masquerade, mask, mummery.

mojigatería [mo-he-gah-tay-ree'-ah], *f.* Hypocrisy, religious fanaticism.

mojigatez [mo-he-gah-teth'], *f.* Bigotry. V. MOJIGATERÍA.

mojigato, ta [mo-he-gah'-to, tah], *m. & f.* Dissembler, hypocrite (hipócrita), a person who affects humility and servile submission to obtain his end.-*a.* Deceitful, hypocritical, hypocritic.

mojí, mojil [mo-hee', mo-heel'], *a.* V. CAZUELA.

mojón [mo-hone'], *m.* 1. Landmark (hito). 2. Heap, pile (montón). 3. Kind of game, like pitching. 4. Solid excrement. -*m & f.* (*Carib.*) Idiot (bruto); shortie (chaparro).

mojona [mo-ho'-nah], *f.* 1. Duty on wine sold by retails 2. Survey of land; the setting up of landmarks.

mojonación [mo-ho-nah-the-on'], *f.* V. AMOJONAMIENTO.

mojonar [mo-ho-nar'], *va.* V. AMOJONAR.

mojonera [mo-ho-nay'-rah], *f.* Landmark.

mojonero [mo-ho-nay'-ro], *m.* Gauger, a person appointed by government to measure wine.

mola [mo'-lah], *f.* 1. Mole, a formless concretion in the uterus, false conception commonly called **mola-matriz**. 2. Barley or flour mixed with salt and used in sacrifices.

molada [mo-lah'-dah], *f.* Quantity of colors ground at once.

molar [mo-lahr'], *a.* Molar, belonging to a mill-stone, or any other thing for grinding, as the teeth.

molar [mo-lahr'], *va.* **Lo que más me mola es**…, what I'm really into is…(gustar). **No me mola**, I don't go for that. -

vn. 1. To be in, to be fashionable. 2. To be classy (dar tono). 3. To swank (darse tono). 4. To be OK (valer).

molcajete, or **morcajete** [mol-cah-hay'-tay], *m.* (*Mex.*) A mortar, either of burnished clay or stone, used to pound spices and smell seeds.

moldar [mol-dar'], *va.* To mould. V. AMOLDAR.

molde [mol'-day], *m.* 1. Mould, the matrix in which anything is cast or receives its form: pattern (patrón), mould, block. 2. A form ready for printing. 3. A person who has reached the highest grade in anything; example, model. **De molde**, in print, printed or published; fitting, to the purpose.

moldeador [mol-day-ah-dor'], *m.* (*Prov.*) Moulder.

moldear [mol-day-ar'], *va.* To mould, to make moulds.

moldura [mol-doo'-rah], *f.* Moulding, an ornamental cavity in wood or stone.

moldurar [mol-doo-rar'], *va.* To make a moulding or ornament of something.

mole [mo'-lay] *a.* Soft, mild.-*f.* Vast size or quantity; massiness. **Se sentó con todo su mole**, he sat down with his full weight.

mole [mo'-lay], *m.* Mexican stew of meat or fowl with a special hot sauce.

molécula [mo-lay'-coo-lah], *f.* Molecule, invisible particle of bodies.

molecular [mo-lay-coo-lar'], *a.* Molecular, relating to molecules.

moledera [mo-lay-day'-rah], *f.* (*coll.*) Bother, annoyance. V. CANSERA.

moledero, ra [mo-lay-day'-ro, rah], *a.* That which is to be ground.

moledor, ra [mo-lay-dor', rah], *m. & f.* 1. Grinder, one who grinds and prepares colors. 2. Bore, a tiresome fellow (aburrido). 3. A tool employed by powder-makers for reducing powder to small grains. 4. Each of the crushing cylinders in a sugar-mill.

moledura [mo-lay-doo'-rah], *f.* The act of grinding. V. MOLIENDA.

molendero [mo-len-day'-ro], *m.* 1. Miller, grinder. 2. Chocolate manufacturer, one who grinds the cocoa and beats it with sugar and flavoring.

moler [mo-lerr'], *va.* 1. To grind, to pound (pulverizar), to pulverize, to mill (trigo). 2. To vex, to molest; to fatigue (cansar). 3. To waste, to consume by use. 4. To masticate, to chew. **Moler a azotes**, to lash, to whip.

molero [mo-lay'-ro], *m.* Maker or seller of mill-stones.

molestador, ra [mo-les-tah-dor', rah], *m. & f.* Disturber, vexer, molester.

molestamente [mo-lays'-tah-men-tay], *adv.* Troublesomely, vexatiously, grievously.

molestar [mo-les-tar'], *va.* To vex, to disturb, to molest, to trouble (dolor), to hurry, to tease, to grate, to cut to the heart, to annoy (fastidiar), to upset (incordiar). **Me molesta ese ruido**, that noise upsets me. **Me molesta tener que repetirlo**, I hate having to repeat it. -*vn.* To be a nuisance (fastidiar); to get in the way (estorbar). **No quiero molestar**, I don't want to intrude. -*vr.* To bother (darse trabajo); to go to trouble (incomodarse). **Molestarse en**, to bother to.

molestia [mo-les'-te-ah], *f.* Injury, molestation, hardship, grievance, nuisance, excruciation. **Es una molestia**, it's a nuisance.

molesto, ta [mo-les'-to, tah], *a.* Grievous, vexatious, oppressive, molestful, heavy, troublesome (que molesta), inconvenient (incómodo), discontented (descontento); restless (inquieto); ill-at-ease (incómodo). **Estar molesto con uno**, to be cross with somebody.

moleta [mo-lay'-tah], *f.* 1. Muller, a stone flat at the bottom and round at the top, used by painters to grind colors on marble. 2. An apparatus for smoothing and polishing flint glass. 3. Muller, grinder for printing-ink on the ink-table.

moletón [mo-lay-tone'], *m.* Milled flannel, canton or cotton flannel, swan's-down.

molibdato [mo-lib-dah'-to], *m.* Molibdate.

molibdeno [mo-lib-day'-no], *m.* Molybdenum, a white, brittle, lustreless metal.

molíbdico [mo-leeb'-de-co], *a.* Molybdic, relating to, derived from, or compounded with molybdenum.

molicie [mo-lee'-the-ay], *f.* 1. Tenderness, softness (blandura), effeminacy. 2. An unnatural crime.

molido, da [mo-lee'-do, dah], *a. & pp.* of MOLER. Ground (machacado); fatigued; flogged.

molienda [mo-le-en'-dah], *f.* 1. The act of grinding or pounding. 2. Quantity pounded or ground at once, grist. 3. Weariness (cansancio), fatigue, lassitude. 4. Season of grinding sugar-cane or olives (temporada).

moliente [mo-le-en'-tay], *pa.* Grinder, grinding. **Moliente y corriente**, *(coll.)* right, justly, exactly.

molificación [mo-le-fe-cah-the-on'], *f.* Mollification.

molificar [mo-le-fe-car'], *va.* To mollify, to soften, to mitigate.

molificativo, va [mo-le-fe-cah-tee'-vo, vah], *a.* That which mollifies, lenitive.

molimiento [mo-le-me-en'-to], *m.* 1. The act of grinding, pounding, or beating up. 2. Fatigue, weariness, lassitude.

molina [mo-lee'-nah], *f.* Oil-mill of large capacity. *(Recent.)*

molinar [mo-le-nar'], *m.* Place where there are mills; milling-plant.

molinejo [mo-le-nay'-ho], *m. dim.* A small mill.

molinera [mo-le-nay'-rah], *f.* 1. Miller's wife. 2. Woman who tends or works in a mill.

molinero [mo-le-nay'-ro], *m.* Miller, grinder.

molinero, ra [mo-le-nay'-ro, rah], *a.* Anything which is to be ground or pounded; anything belonging to a mill.

molinete [mo-le-nay'-tay], *m.* 1. *(Naut.)* Windlass. 2. Turnstile. 3. *(dim.)* A little mill. 5 Brandish, twirl about the head in fencing. 5. *(Mech.)* Friction roller; sway-plate of a vehicle; smoke dispeller.

molinillo [mo-le-neel'-lyo], *m.* 1. *(dim.)* A little mill; a handmill. 2. Churn-staff, chocolate-mill, a stick with which chocolate is beat up in a chocolate-pot. **Molinillo de café**, coffee mill.

molinismo [mo-le-nees'-mo], *m.* Molinism or quietism, principles of a sect.

molinista [mo-le-nees'-tah], *m.* Molinist, a follower of the doctrines of Molinism.

molinito [mo-le-nee'-to], *m. dim.* A small mill.

molino [mo-lee'-no], *m.* 1. Mill, an apparatus in which corn is ground; corn-mill (trituradora). **Molino de viento**, windmill. **Molino de agua**, water-mill. **Molino de mano**, handmill. **Molino de papel**, paper-mill. 2. A restless (inquieto), noisy fellow. 3. *(coll.)* Mouth.

molitivo, va [mo-le-tee'-vo, vah], *a.* Mollient.

molla [mol'-lyah], *f.* 1. Lean meat without bone. 2. *(Prov.)* Crumb of bread.

mollar [mol-lyar']. *a.* 1. Soft (fruta), tender, pappy, pulpous. 2. Fleshy, lean, without bone (carne). 3. Gullible (crédulo). 4. Cushy (trabajo). 5. Super (bueno).

mollear [mol-lyay-ar'], *vn.* To grow soft and pliable, to soften or to grow less hard, to yield easily.

molledo [mol-lyay'-do], *m.* 1. The fleshy part of a limb. 2. Crumb of bread.

molleja [mol-lyay'-hah], *f.* 1. Gland, particularly that which is seated at the root of the tongue. 2. Gizzard, the strong muscular stomach of a fowl; maw.

mollejón [mo-lyay-hone'], *m.* 1. *(Aug.)* A large gland. 2. A big, corpulent person.

mollejuela [mol-lyay-hoo-ay'-lah], *f. dim.* A small gland.

mollera [mol-lyay'-rah], *f.* Crown or top of the head. **Ser duro de mollera**, to be obstinate. **Cerrado de mollera**, rude, ignorant.

mollero [mol-lyay'-ro], *m.* *(Prov.)* Fleshy part of the arm.

molleta [mol-lyay'-tah], *f.* 1. Snuffers. 2. Bread made of the finest flour.

mollete [mol-lyay'-tay], *m.* Manchet, a small loaf made of the finest flour. **Molletes**, plump or round cheeks.

mollina, mollizna [mol-lyee'-nah, mol-lyeeth'-nah], *f* Mist, small rain.

mollizar, molliznear [mol-lyeeth-nar'], *vn.* To drizzle, to mizzle, to fall in small, slow drops.

molón [mo-lon'], *a.* 1. Super (bueno), smashing. 2. Posh (elegante).

molondro, molondrón [mo-lon'-dro, mo-lon-drone'], *m.* A sluggish, mean-spirited and ignorant fellow, poltroon.

moloquita [mo-lo-kee'-tah], *f. (Min.)* A variety of agate of dull-green hue.

molotov [mo-lo-tov], *m.* **Cóctel molotov**, Molotov cocktail.

moltura [mol-too'-rah], *f. V.* MOLIENDA.

molusco [mo-loos'-co], *m.* Mollusk, one of the mollusca, invertebrates having an unsegmented body, and usually a calcareous shell.

moma [mo'-mah], *f. (Mex.)* Blindman's-buff.

momentáneamente [mo-men-tah-nay-men-tay] *adv.* 1. Instantly. 2. Momentarily.

momentáneo, nea [mo-men-tah'-nay-o, ah], *a.* Momentous, momentary, of short duration.

momento [mo-men'-to], *m.* 1. Moment, the least space of time. 2. Moment, consequence, momentum, weight, importance. 3. *(Math.)* Difference. 4. *(Mech.)* Power, force. **Al momento**, in a moment, immediately. **Por momentos**, successively, continually. **En el momento actual**, at the present time.

momería [mo-may-ree'-ah], *f.* Mummery, a farcical entertainment, in which masked persons play frolics and antic tricks.

momia [mo'-me-ah], *f.* Mummy, a dead body preserved by embalming.

momificar [mo-me-fe-car'], *va.* To mummify, to convert into a mummy.-*vr.* To resemble a mummy.

momio, mia [mo'-me-o, ah], *a.* Meagre, lean (carne).

momo [mo'-mo], *m.* Buffoonery, low jests, scurrile mirth, wry faces (cara), grimaces.

momórdiga [mo-mor'-de-gah], *f. (Bot.) V.* BALSAMINA.

momperada [mom-pay-rah'-dah], *f.* A kind of glazed woollen stuff.

mona [mo'-nah], *f.* 1. Female monkey or ape (especie). 2. *(coll.)* A mimic, a ludicrous imitator. 3. In jocular style, drunkenness and drunkard (borrachera). 4. *(Prov.)* Cake made of flour, eggs, and milk. 5. Iron plate worn for protection on the right leg by bull-fighters on horseback. 6. *(And.)* Blonde. 7. *(LAm.)* Colombian golden marijuana. **Aunque la mona se vista de seda, mona se queda**, *(Prov.)* dress a monkey as you will, it remains a monkey still. **Dormir la mona**, to sleep off a hangover.

monacal [mo-nah-cahl'], *a.* Monachal, monastic, monkish, belonging to monks.

monacalmente [mo-nah-cahl'-men-tay], *adv.* Monastically.

monacato [mo-nah-cah'-to], *m.* Monkhood, monachism.

monacillo [mo-nah-theel'-lyo], *m.* Acolyte, acolithe, or aculotist, a boy who serves in a church.

monacordio [mo-nah-cor'-de-o], *m.* Spinet, an old-fashioned stringed musical instrument with keys.

monada [mo-nah'-dah], *f.* 1. Grimace (mueca), a ludicrous or ridiculous distortion of the countenance. 2. Monkeyism, monkey-shine, behavior characteristic of a monkey (comportamiento). 3. Fawning, flattery. 4. Lovely thing. **La casa es una monada**, the house is lovely.

mónada [mo'-nah-dah], *f.* 1. Monad, an indivisible thing. 2. A microscopic infusorian, monad.

monadelfo, fa [mo-nah-del'-fo, fah], *a.* Monadelphous, (stamens) united into one cluster.

monago, monaguillo [mo-nah'-go, mo-nah-geel'-lyo], *m. V.* MONACILLO.

monaguismo [mo-nah-gees'-mo], *m.* Monachism, monasticness.

monarca [mo-nar'-cah], *m.* Monarch, king, sovereign, lord.

monarquía [mo-nar-kee'-ah], *f.* Monarchy, the government of a single person, kingdom, empire, kingship.

monárquico, ca [mo-nar'-ke-co, cah], *a.* Monarchical, monarchal, kingly, king-like.

monasterial [mo-nas-tay-re-ahl'], *a.* Monastic.

monasterillo [mo-nas-tay-reel'-lyo], *m. dim.* A small monastery.

monasterio [mo-nas-tay'-re-o], *m.* Monastery, a house of religious retirement; convent, minster; cloister.

monásticamente [mo-nahs'-te-cah-men-tay], *adv.* Monastically.

monástico, ca [mo-nahs'-te-co, cah], *a.* Monastic, monastical, monachal, monkish.

monazo, za [mo-nah'-tho, thah], *m. & f. aug.* Large monkey or ape.

monda [mon'-dah], *f.* 1. Pruning of trees (acto); the pruning season (temporada). 2. Peel (piel), peelings, skin. 3. *(And. Carib. Mex.)* Beating. 4. *(Fig.)* **Fue la monda**, it was a scream. **Este nuevo baile es la monda**, this new dance is awful.

mondadientes [mon-dah-de-en'-tays], *m.* Toothpick.

mondador, ra [mon-dah-dor', rah], *m. & f.* Cleaner, purifier.

mondadura [mon-dah-doo'-rah], *f.* Cleaning (limpieza), cleansing, the act of freeing from filth. **Mondaduras**, parings, peelings, anything which comes off by cleaning.

mondaoídos [mon-dah-o-ee'dose], or **Mondaorejas** [mon-dah-o-ray'-has], *m.* Ear-spoon.

mondar [mon-dar'], *va.* 1. To clean (limpiar), to cleanse, to free from filth. 2. To husk, to strip off the husks of fruit, to peel (pelar), to decorticate; to deprive of money. 3. To cut the hair. 4. *(And, Carib.)* To beat (dar una paliza). **Mondar los huesos**, to pick bones quite clean.

mondejo [mon-day'-ho], *m.* Paunch or belly of a pig or sheep stuffed with minced meat.

mondo, da [mon'-do, dah], *a.* Neat, clean (limpio), pure (puro), unadulterated. **Mondo y lirondo**, *(coll.)* pure, without any admixture.

mondonga [mon-don'-gah], *f.* In contempt, a kitchen-wench or a maid-servant.

mondongo [mon-don'-go], *m.* Paunch, tripes, black pudding. **Hacer el mondongo**, *V.* MONDONGONIZAR.

mondongonizar [mon-don-go-ne-thar'], *va.* To dress tripe, to make black puddings.

mondonguero, ra [mon-don-gay'-ro, rah], *m. & f.* One who makes black puddings or deals in them.

mondonguil [mon-don-geel'], *a. (coll.)* Relating to tripes or puddings.

monear [mo-nay-ar'], *vn.* 1. To act in an affected, ridiculous, or preposterous manner (comportarse); to monkey (hacer muecas). 2. *(Cono Sur, Mex.)* To boast, to swank (jactarse).

moneda [mo-nay'-dah], *f.* Money, pieces of gold, silver, or copper, coined for the purpose of trade; coinage. **Moneda corriente**, current coin. **Pagar a uno con la misma moneda**, to pay somebody back with his own coin. **Una moneda de 5 dólares**, a 5-dollar piece.

monedaje [mo-nay-dah'-hay], *m.* Coinage, the charges paid for coining money.

monedar, monedear [mo-nay-dar'], *va.* To coin.

monedería [mo-nay-day-ree'-ah], *f.* Mint, factory of money.

monedero [mo-nay-day'-ro], *m.* 1. Officer of the mint who coins money, coiner, moneyer. **Monedero falso**, coiner or maker of base money. 2. Purse (portamonedas).

monedilla, ita [mo-nay-deel'-lyah], *f. dim.* A small piece of money.

monería [mo-nay-ree'-ah], *f.* 1. Grimace, a ludicrous or ridiculous distortion of the countenance; mimicry (imitación). 2. Trifle, gewgaw, bauble.

monesco, ca [mo-nes'-co, cah], *a.* Apish, having the qualities of a monkey.

monetario [mo-nay-tah'-re-o], *m.* 1. Cabinet of ancient coins and models. 2. Collection of coins and medals; the whole number of cases, tables or drawers which contain them. 3. Treasury-chamber, museum or place which holds such a collection.

monetario [mo-nay-tah-re-o], *a.* Monetary, pertaining to money or finance.

monotización [mo-nay-te-thah-the-on'], *f* Monetization, the act of legally declaring to be money.

monetizar [mo-nay-te-thar'], *va.* To monetize, to legalize as money.

mongol, la [mon-gol'], *a. V.* MOGOL.

moniato [mo-ne-ah'-to], *m.* A farinaceous root of which a kind of bread is made in some parts of South America.

monicaco, monicongo [mo-ne-cah'-co], *m.* A conceited, thoughtless person. *V.* CHUCHUMECO.

monición [mo-ne-the-on'], *f.* Admonition, publication of the bans of marriage.

monigote [mo-ne-go'-tay], *m. (coll.)* 1. Lay-brother of religious orders. 2. A person who is considered without knowledge or skill in his own profession. 3. *(Met. and coll.)* A poorly made painting or statue.

moniliforme [mo-ne-le-for'-may], *a.* Moniliform, like a string of beads.

monillo [mo-neel'-lyo], *m.* Waist, bodice, a jacket without sleeves, worn by women.

monipodio [mo-ne-poh'-de-o], *m.* Any combination or agreement among several persons with an unlawful object.

monismo [mo-nees'-mo], *m. (Phil.)* Monism.

mónita [mo'-ne-tah], *f.* 1. Artifice, artfulness, affected flattery. 2. *(Peru. Coll.)* Severs reproof.

monitor [mo-ne-tor'], *m.* 1. Monitor (profesor). 2. An armorclad vessel. 3. *(Inform. Tec.)* Monitor, display. **Monitor en color**, color monitor.

monitoria [mo-ne-to'-re-ah], *f.* Summons issued by an ecclesiastical judge to command the personal appearance and deposition of a witness.

monitorio, ria [mo-ne-to'-re-o, ah], *a.* Monitory, admonitory.

monja [mon'-hah], *f.* Nun, a religious woman confined in a cloister.-*pl.* Appellation given to sparks in burned papers.

monje [mon'-hay], *m.* 1. Monk: also, recluse, anchorite. 2. Brown peacock.

monjía [mon-hee'-ah], *f.* Proband, enjoyed by a monk in his convent.

monjil [mon-heel'], *m.* 1. Habit or dress of a nun (hábito). 2. Mourning dress or weeds of a widow.

monjío [mon-hee'-o], *m.* The day and ceremony of a lady's taking the veil.

mono, na [mo'-no, nah], *a. (coll.)* Cute, pretty. **Una chica muy mona**, a very attractive girl. -*m.* 1. Monkey. 2. *(Fig.)* Mimic (imitador). 3. Coveralls (de obrero). 4. Cocky youngster (engreído). 5. Joker (naipes). 6. Ugly devil (feo). 7. Pansy (maricón). 8. Cop (policía). 9. *(Carib.)* Debt (deuda). 10. Sign (señal). **Meter los monos a**, to scare the daylights out of someone. **Mono de imitación**, copycat (niño).

monoceronte, monocerote [mo-no-thay-ro'-tay], *m.* Unicorn.

monocordio [mo-no-cor-de-o], *m.* Monochord, an instrument of one string anciently used.

monocotiledóneo, ea [mo-no-co-te-lay-do'-nay-o, ah], *a. (Bot.)* Monocotyledonous.

monocromático, ca [mo-no-cro-mah'-te-co, cah], *a.* Monochromatic, of one color: applied to yellow light, and also to a painting done in one color.

monócromo [mo-no'-cro-mo], *m. y a.* Monochrome, a painting done in one color.

monóculo, la [mo-no'-coo-lo, lah], *a.* Monoculous, monocular, one-eyed.

monóculo [mo-no'-coo-lo], *m.* 1. Monocle. 2. Bandage for only one eye.

monodonte [mo-no-don'-tay], *m. (Zool.)* Narwhal, seaunicorn.

monogamia [mo-no-gah'-me-ah], *f.* Monogamy, marriage of one wife only.

monógamo [mo-no'-gah-mo], *m.* He who marries only one woman.

monogástrico, ca [mo-no-gahs'-tre-co, cah], *a. (Zool.)* Monogastric, having a single stomach.

monografía [mo-no-grah-fee'-ah], *f.* Monograph, a description of one genus, one species, etc.; an extended essay upon a single topic.

monográfico, ca [mo-no-grah'-fe-co, cah], *a.* Monographic, drawn in plain lines. **Programa monográfico**, program devoted to a single subject.

monograma [mo-no-grah'-mah], *m.* Monogram, a cipher or character compounded of several letters and standing for some name.

monoico, ca [mo-no'-e-co, cah], *a.* Monoecious, bearing distinct male and female flowers upon one stem.

monolito [mo-no'-lee'-to], *m.* Monolith, a stone monument in a single piece.

monólogo [mo-no'-lo-go], *m.* Monologue, soliloquy.

monomanía [mo-no-mah-nee'-ah], *f.* Monomania, insanity upon one subject.

monomaníaco, ca [mo-no-mah-nee'-ah-co, cah], *a.* Monomaniac.

monomio [mo-no'-me-o], *m. (Alg.)* Monomial; expression consisting of a single term.

monona [mo-no'-nah], *a. (coll.)* Graceful and pretty, especially if very young (mujer).

monopastos [mo-no-pahs'-tose], *m.* Pulley with one wheel.

monopatín [mo-no-pah-teen'], *m.* Skateboard.

monopétalo, la [mo-no-pay'-tah-lo, lah], *a.* Monopetalous, having only one flower-leaf; gamopetalous.

monoplano [mo-no-plah'-no], *m.* Monoplane.

monópodo, da [mo-no'-po-do, dah], *a.* Monopode, having but one foot.

monopolio [mo-no-po'-le-o], *m.* Monopoly, the exclusive privilege of selling anything, and the combination or agreement among tradesmen for selling a thing at a certain price.

monopolista [mo-no-po-lees'-tah], Monopolist, forestaller, monopolizer.

monopolizar [mo-no-po-le-thar'], *va.* To monopolize, to forestall.

monosilábico, ca [mo-no-se-lah'-be-co, cah], *a.* Monosyllabic, consisting of one syllable.

monosílabo, ba [mo-no-see'-lah-bo, bah], *m. & f.* Monosyllable.

monospermo, ma [mo-nos-perr'-mo, mah], *a. (Bot.)* Monospermous, single seeded.

monóstrofe [mo-nos'-tro-fay], *f.* A poetical composition of a single strophe; monostrophe.

monoteísmo [mo-no-tay-ees'-mo], *m.* Monotheism, belief in only one God.

monoteísta [mo-no-tay-ees'-tah], *a.* Monotheistic, holding or relating to monotheism. *-m.* Monotheist.

monotipia [mo-no-tee'-pe-ah], *f (typ.)* Monotyping.

monotipo [mo-no-tee'-po], *m.* Monotype.

monotonía [mo-no-to-ne'-ah], *f.* Monotony, uniformity of sound.

monótono, na [mo-no'-to-no, nah], *a.* Monotonous, monotonic.

monóxido [mo-noc'-see-do], *m.* Monoxide.

monseñor [mon-say-nyor'], *m.* Monsignor.

monserga [mon-ser'-gah], *f.* 1. *(coll.)* Gabble, confused language. 2. Drivel (disparates), tedious. **Dar la monserga**, to get on somebody's nerves.

monstruo [mons'-troo-o], *m.* 1. Monster, a production contrary to the order of nature, idol (del mundo pop), wonder boy. 2. *(Bio.)* Freak, monster. *-a.* Fantastic, fabulous.

monstruosamente [mons-troo-o'-sah-men-tay], *adv.* Monstruously.

monstruosidad [mons-troo-o-se-dahd'], *f.* Monstruosity, monstrosity, excessive ugliness, monstrousness.

monstruoso, sa [mons-troo-o'-so, sah], *a.* 1. Monstrous, contrary to or deviating from the stated order of nature. 2. Monstrous, too irregular, enormous: shocking.

monta [mon'-tah], *f.* 1. Amount, sum total. 2. Value, worth, price. 3. Signal given with a trumpet for the cavalry to mount their horses.

montacargas [mon-tah-car'-gas], *m.* Elevator hoist, freight elevator.

montada [mon-tah'-dah], *f.* The elevation given to the bit of a bridle.

montadero [mon-ta-day'-ro], *m.* One who mounts; mounting-stone.

montado [Mon-tah'-do], *a.* 1. Applied to a horse ready for being mounted (caballo). 2. Applied to a trooper or horseman.*-pp* of MONTAR.

montador [mon-tah-dor'], *m.* 1. Mounter (persona). 2. Mounting block (objeto). 3. Film editor (que hace el montaje).

montadura [mon-tah-doo'-rah], *f.* 1. Mounting (acto). 2. Setting (of a gem). 3. Harness, trappings.

montaescaleras [mon-tah-cah-lay'-ras], *m.* Chair lift.

montaje [mon-tah'-hay], *m.* 1. Assembly. 2. Editing (película). 3. Set-up (arreglo de antemano). 4. Fiddle (estafa). 5. *(Teat.)* Stage design.

montanera [mon-tah-nay'-rah], *m.* The feeding of hogs with acorns, driven for that purpose into groves of oak.

montanero [mon-tah-nay'-ro], *m.* Forester, keeper of a forest.

montano, na [mon-tah'-no, nah], *a.* Mountainous.

montantada [mon-tan-tah-dah], *f.* 1. Ostentation, boasting. 2. Multitude.

montante [mon-tahn'-tay], *m.* 1. A broadsword used by fencing-masters. 2. A kind of fireworks which, when lighted, forms this figure. 3. *(Naut.)* Flood tide. 4. *(Arch.)* Upright, standard, a piece of wood, stone, or metal which divides a window into various parts (de ventana). 5. *(Mil.)* Stempel, an upright timber used for support in a mine (poste).

montantear [mon-tan-tay-ar'], *vn.* 1. To wield the broadsword in a fencing-school. 2. To vaunt, to brag.

montantero [mon-tan-tay'-ro], *m.* He who fights with a broadsword.

montaña [mon-tah'-nyah], *f.* 1. Mountain, mount. *V.* MONTE. 2. *(And, Carib.)* Forest (selva). 3. *(CAm.)* Virgin jungle (selva virgen). *-pl.* Highlands; a ridge of mountains. **Montaña rusa**, roller coaster.

montañés, sa [mon-tah-nyes', sah], *a.* 1. Mountain, pertaining to the mountains. 2. Mountainous, inhabiting mountains, highlander. *-m. & f.* Mountaineer, mountainer, an inhabitant of the mountains, a highlander.

montañeta, montañuela [mon-tah-nyay'-tah, nyoo-ay'-lah], *f. dim.* A small mountain.

montañoso, sa [mon-tah-nyo'-so, sah], *a.* Mountainous, hilly.

montar [mon-tar'], *vn.* 1. To mount or go on horseback (en caballo). 2. To amount to, to be worth. 3. To cock a gun. 4. To be of importance. **Montar a caballo**, to ride, **Me ayudó a montar**, he helped me up. **Monta a**, to amount to. *-va.* 1. To impose a penalty for cattle entering a forest. 2. To mount (bicicleta, caballo), to set, to provide with a setting. 3. To mount, to set up, to put in place the parts of a machine or apparatus. 4. To cover, to copulate with: said of a horse or ass. 5. To mount, to carry, or be equipped with. 6. *(Mar.)* To double a cape or headland. 7. To edit (película). **Tanto monta**, it's all the same. **Vestido or traje de montar**, riding habit. **Montar un reloj**, to wind a watch or clock. **Montar a uno sobre un tronco**, to lift somebody on to a log. **Montar un color sobre otro**, to overlap one color with another. **Montar una tienda**, to open a shop. **Montar un número**, to make a scene.

montaraz [mon-tah-rath'], *m.* Forester, guard of woods or farms.

montaraz [mon-tah-rath'], *a.* 1. Mountain (de montaña), mountainous. 2. Wild (salvaje), untamed, haggard.

montazgar [mon-tath-gar'], *va.* To levy or collect the toll for cattle passing from one province into another.

montazgo [mon-tath'-go], *m.* 1. Toll to be paid for cattle passing from one province into another. 2. Place through which the cattle pass.

monte [mon'-tay], *m.* 1. Mountain (montaña), mount, a large hill, a vast protuberance of the earth. 2. Wood (bosque), forest, a woody place. 3. Difficulty, obstruction, obstacle (obstáculo). 4. A bushy head of hair much entangled. 5. Stock of cards which remain after each player has received his share. 6. *(Amer.)* A game at cards. 7. *(CAm. Carib.)* Outskirts (alrededores). 8. *(Mex.)* Grass (pasto). 9. *(LAm.)* Hash (droga). **Monte alto** or **de árboles**, a lofty grove or wood. **Creer que todo el monte es orégano**, to think everything in the garden is lovely.

montea [mon-tay'-ah], *f.* 1. Art or trade of cutting or hewing stone. 2. Plan or profile of a building. 3. *(Arch.)* Convexity of an arch.

montear [mon-tay-ar'], *va.* 1. To beat a wood in pursuit of game, to hunt. 2. To draw the plan or profile of a building. 3. To vault, to form arches.

montecillo [mon-tay-theel'-lyo], *m. dim.* 1. A small wood or forest. 2. Hillock, hummock, a small mount.

montepío or **monte de piedad**, *m.* Charitable pawnshop.

montera [mon-tay'-rah], *f.* 1. A kind of cap glade of cloth (sombrero). 2. Skylight, covering of glass over a gallery, court. etc. 3. Receiver, condenser of a still or alembic. 4. *(Naut.)* Skysail, skyscraper. 5. Hunter's wife.

monterería [mom-tay-ray-ree'-ah], *f.* Shop or place where caps are made or sold.

montería [mon-tay-ree'-ah], *f.* 1. Hunting (arte), hunt (cacería), chase. 2. Place where hunting-caps are made or sold. 3. Hunting party (personas). 4. *(And.)* Canoe. 5. *(CAm.)* Concession. 6. *(CAm. Mex.)* Timber camp (maderería).

montero [mon-tay'-ro], *m.* Huntsman, hunter.

monteruca [mon-tay-roo'-cah], *f.* An ugly cap.

monterrey [mon-ter-ray'-e], *m.* A kind of thin paste rolled up into spiral tubes.

montés, sa [mon-tes', sah], *a.* Montigenous, mountain, bred or found in a forest or mountain.

montesa [mon-tay'-sah], *f.* One of the military orders of Spain.

montescos [mon-tes'-cos], *m. pl.* **Haber Montescos y Capeletes**, to have great disputes and contentions (to be Montagues and Capulets).

montesino, na [mon-tay-see'-no, nah], *a.* Montigenous, bred or found in a forest or mountain.

monto [mon'-to], *m.* Amount, sum.

montón [mon-tone'], *m.* 1. Heap, pile. **Montón de gente**, crowd, multitude. 2. Congeries, mass, cluster. 3. A dirty, lazy fellow. **A montones**, abundantly, by heaps.

montuosidad [mon-too-o-see-dahd'], *f. (Prov.)* Mountainousness.

montuoso, sa [mon-too-o'-so, sah], *a.* Full of woods and thickets, mountainous, hilly.

montura [mon-too'-rah], *f.* 1. Horses and mules intended for the saddle. 2. Saddle (silla), trappings and accoutrements of horses (arreos). **Cabalgar sin montura**, to ride bareback.

monuelo [mo-noo-ay'-lo], *m. dim.* A coxcomb, a fop.

monumental [mo-noo-men-tahl'], *a.* Monumental (enorme), belonging to monuments.

monumento [mo-noo-men'-to], *m.* 1. Monument, anything by which the memory of persons or things is preserved, such as a statue, a tomb, a cenotaph, etc. 2. Altar raised in churches on Holy Thursday to resemble a sepulchre. **Monumentos**, monuments or remains of antiquity. 3. Pretty girl (chica).

monzón [mon-thone'], *m.* Monsoon, a periodical wind in the East Indian Ocean.

moñá [mo'-nyah], *f.* 1. Lay-figure of a woman to show a style of dress. 2. Peevishness, fretfulness. 3. An ornament of ribbons used on the head by bullfighters. 4. *(coll.)*

Drunkenness (borracho). 5. Very elaborate cap for nursing infants. 6. Hair ribbon (cinta). 7. Sash, prize ribbon (premio). 8. Doll (muñeca).

moño [mo'-nyo], *m.* 1. Hair on the crown of the head tied together; tuft. 2. Tuft of feathers on the heads of birds. 3. A bow of ribbons. 4. *(LAm.)* Pride, haughtiness (altivez). 5. *(Cono Sur)* To give in. **Estar hasta el moño**, to be fed up.

moñudo, da [mo-nyoo'-do, dah], *a.* Crested, topped.

moquear [mo-kay-ar'], *vn.* To snivel, to run at the nose; to blow the nose.

moqueo [mo-kay'-o], *m.* Runny nose.

moquero [mo-kay'-ro], *m. (coll.)* Pocket handkerchief.

moqueta [mo-kay'-tah], *f.* Moquette (alfombra), a woollen stuff, with a wool of hemp, from which carpets and rugs are made.

moquete [mo-kay'-tay], *m.* Blow on the face or nose.

moquetear [mo-kay-tay-ar'], *vn.* To discharge much mucus from the nose.-*va.* To give blows in the face.

moquillo [mo-keel'-lyo], *m.* 1. *(dim.)* A little mucus. 2. Pip, a disease in fowls.

moquita [mo-kee'-tah], *f.* Snivel, running from the nose in cold weather.

mora [mo'-rah], *f.* 1. *(Law.)* Delay, procrastination. 2. Mulberry (del moral), the fruit of the mulberry-tree.

morabita [mo-rah-bee'-tah], *m.* Member of a sect formed by a son-in-law of Mohammed.

morabito [mo-rah-bee'-to], *m.* 1. A Mohammedan hermit. 2. *V.* MORABITA.

moracho, cha [mo-rah'-cho, chah], *a.* Dark purple.

morada [mo-rah'-dah], *f.* Habitation, abode, residence, mansion, lodging, home, continuance (casa). **La eterna morada**, the great beyond. **Última morada**, resting place.

morado, da [mo-rah'-do, dah], *a.* Violet, mulberry-colored. **Ojo morado**, black eye. **Ponerse morado**, to do oneself well, to eat a lot.

morador, ra [mo-rah-dor', rah], *m. & f.* Inhabitant, lodger.

moraga [mo-rah'-gah], *f.* Handful or bundle formed by female gleaners.

morago [mo-rah'-go], *m. V.* MORAGA.

moral [mo-rahl'], *m. (Bot.)* Mulberry tree. -*f.* 1. Morale, buoyant spirits despite danger. 2. Moral ethics, morality (moralidad).-*a.* Moral. **Apoyo moral**, moral support.

moraleja [mo-rah-lay'-hah], *f.* A brief moral observation.

moralidad [mo-rah-le-dahd'], *f.* 1. Morality, the doctrine of the duties of life. 2. Morality, form of an action, which makes it the subject of reward or punishment.

moralista [mo-rah-lees'-tah], *m & f.* Moralist, one who teaches the duties of life.

moralizador, ra [mo-rah-le-thah-dor', rah], *m. & f.* Commentator, critic, moralizer.

moralizar [mo-rah-le-thar'], *va. & vn.* 1. To moralize, to apply to moral purposes; to explain in a moral sense. 2. To moralize, to speak or write on moral subjects.

moralmente [mo-rahl'-men-tay], *adv.* Morally, in the ethical sense; according to the rules of virtue; popularly, by common sense.

morar [mo-rar'], *vn.* To inhabit, to dwell, to reside, to lodge, to live; to continue.

moratón [mo-rah-tone'], *m.* Bruise.

moratoria [mo-rah-to'-re-ah], *f.* 1. Letters of license granted to a debtor. 2. *(Com.)* Delay (para pagar).

moravo, va [mo-rah'-vo, vah], *a.* Moravian.

morbidez [mor-be-deth'], *f.* Softness, delicacy.

mórbido, da [mor'-be-do, dah], *a.* 1. Morbid (enfermo). 2. Soft, delicate (arte).

morbilidad, morbididad [mor-be-le-dahd', mor-be-de-dahd'], *f.* 1. Morbidity. 2. Sickness rate.

morbo [mor'-bo], *m.* 1. Disease. 2. *(Fig.)* Unhealthy curiosity.

morboso, sa [mor-bo'-so, sah], *a.* 1. Diseased, morbid (enfermo). 2. *(Fig.)* Diseased, morbid.

morcajo [mor-cah'-ho], *m.* A low grade wheat cultivated in Old Castile.

morcella [mor-thel'-lyah], *f.* Spark from a lamp.

morcilla [mor-theel'-lyah], *f.* 1. Black pudding, hog's pudding; *(Mex.)* Tripe (callos). 2. *(Teat.)* Gag, unscriped lines. 3. Prick (pene). 4. *(Carib.)* Lie (mentira).

morcillero, ra [mor-theel-lyay'-ro, rah], *m. & f.* One who makes or deals in black puddings.

morcillo, lla [mor-theel'-lyo, lyah], *a.* Entirely black (caballos).

morcillo [mor-theel'-lyo], *m.* The fleshy part of the arm from the shoulder to the elbow.

morcón [mor-cone'], *m.* 1. A large black pudding made of the blind gut; a large sausage. 2. *(coll.)* A short, plumpy fellow (rechoncho). 3. Sloppy individual (descuidado).

mordacidad [mor-dah-the-dahd'], *f.* 1. Mordacity, biting quality. 2. Roughness, asperity, acrimony in unripe fruit. 3. Mordacity, a nipping, sarcastic language.

mordante [mor-dahn'-tay], *m. (Print.)* Guide, container: a frame used by compositors to keep their copy secure, and mark the place up to which their work is completed.

mordaz [mor-dath'], *a.* Corrosive, biting (crítica), nipping; sarcastic; acrimonious, satirical, keen.

mordaza [mor-dah'-thah], *f.* 1. Gag, to prevent speaking or crying (de boca). 2. Sort of nippers or pincers.

mordazmente [mor—dath'-men-tay], *adv.* Acrimoniously, nippingly.

mordedor, ra [mor-day-dor', rah], *m. & f.* 1. Biter, one who bites. 2. One who satirizes.

mordedura [mor-day-doo'-rah], *f.* Bite, wound made by biting; mordication.

mordente [mor-den'-tay], *m.* 1. Mordant, a substance used in dyeing for fixing the colors. 2. *(Mus.)* Mordent, or double appoggiatura, a musical embellishment. 3. *(Bus.)* Turn.

morder [mor-derr'], *va.* 1. To bite, to seize with the teeth, to nip (pinchar). 2. To be sharp or pungent to the taste; to make rough to the touch. 3. To seize or stick fast one thing in another. 4. To bite, to gnaw, to wear away gradually. 5. *(Met.)* To nip, to carp at, to taunt, to nibble (mordisquear), to find fault with, to satirize. 6. To gossip (denigrar). 7. To recognize (reconocer). **No morderse los labios,** *(coll.)* to speak one's opinions frankly and openly. **Morderse la lengua,** to refrain from saying what one is tempted to say. -*vn.* To bite. **Estoy que muerdo,** I'm simply furious. *(Yo muerdo, yo muerda, from Morder. V. MOVER.)*

mordicante [mor-de-cahn'-tay], *pa. & a.* Biting, pungent, acrid.

mordicar [mor-de-car'], *va.* To gnaw, to nibble; to smart, to sting.

mordicativo, va [mor-de-cah-tee'-voh, vah], *a.* Biting, gnawing, mordicant.

mordida [mor-dee'-dah], *f.* 1. Bite. 2. *(Mex. Coll.)* Bribe (soborno).

mordido, da [mor-dee'-do, dah], *a.* Diminished, wasted away.-*pp.* of MORDER.

mordido [mor-dee'-do], *m.* Bit, mouthful of meat.

mordiente [mor-de-en'-tay], *m.* 1. Gold size, mordant, used by painters. 2. Mordant. *V.* MORDENTE. 3. Mordant, the acid or other corrosive by which etching is done.

mordihuí [mor-de-oo-ee'], *m.* Weevil, a grub bred in wheat.

mordimiento [mor-de-me-en'-to], *m.* Bite, mordication, biting.

mordiscar [mor-dis-car'], *va.* 1. To nibble. 2. *V.* MORDER.

mordisco, mordiscón [mor-dees'-co], *m.* Bite, the act of seizing with the teeth; the piece bitten off. **Deshacer algo a mordiscos,** to bite something to pieces.

morel de sal [mo-rel' day sahl], *m. (Met.)* Purple red used for painting in fresco.

morena [mo-ray'-nah], *f* 1. Brown bread. 2. Moray, a muraenoid eel.

morenilla, morenita [mo-ray-neel'-lyah], *f.* A brunette.

morenill [mo-ray-neel'-lyo], *m.* A black powder, used by sheep-shearers for the wounds of sheep.

morenillo, illa, ito, ita [mo-ray-neel'-lyo], *a. dim.* of MORENO, brunette: used always as endearing.

moreno, na [mo-ray'-no, nah], *a.* 1. Brown, inclining to black. 2. Swarthy (persona). 3. Tanned (bronceado). 4. *(And, Carib.)* Mulatto. **Ponerse moreno,** to become sunburned.

morera [mo-ray'-rah], *f. (Bot.)* White mulberry-tree. -*pl. V.* MORERAL.

moreral [mo-ray-rahl'], *m.* Plantation of white mulberry-trees.

morería [mo-ray-ree'-ah], *f.* 1. Suburb or quarter where Moors reside (barrio). 2. A Moorish province or lands.

moretón [mo-ray-tone'], *m. (coll.)* Bruise, ecchymosis.

morfa [mor'-fah], *f.* Scale, disease produced by scale-insects on orange and lemon-trees.

morfema [mor-fay'-mah], *m.* Morpheme.

morfeo [mor-fay'-o], *m. (Myth.)* Morpheus.

morfina [mor-fee'-nah], *f.* Morphine, the chief alkaloid of opium.

morfología [mor-fo-lo-hee'-ah], *f.* Morphology, the science of organic forms.

morfológico, ca [mor-fo-lo'-he-co, cah], *a.* Morphologic, morphological.

morga [more'-gah], *f.* Indian berries.

morganático [mor-gah-nah'-te-co], *a.* Morganatic. *V.* MATRIMONIO.

moribundo, da [mo-re-boon'-do, dah], *a.* Dying, near death.

moriche [mo-ree'-chay], *m.* An American tree, like the coconut, useful to mankind.

moriego, ga [mo-re-ay'-go, gah], *a. (Prov.)* Moorish.

morigeración [mo-re-hay-rah-the-on'], *f.* Morigeration, obedience, obsequiousness, temperance.

morigerar [mo-re-hay-rar'], *va.* To endeavor to curb or restrain one's affections and passions; to moderate.

morillo [mo-reel'-lyo], *m.* 1. *(dim.)* A little Moor. 2. Andiron.

morir [mo-reer'], *vn.* 1. To die, to expire. 2. To die, to perish, to come to nothing. 3. To hanker, to desire excessively. 4. To perish or be lost for want of anything. 5. *(Ferro.)* To end (línea). 6. To die down (fuego). **Morir de sed,** to die with thirst. **Morir de frío,** to perish with cold. **Morir ahogado,** to drown. **Morir de hambre,** to die of starvation. **Moría el día,** the day was almost over. -*vr.* 1. To go out, to be extinguished or quenched (fuego, luz). 2. To go numb. **Morirse por,** to be excessively fond of. **Irse muriendo,** to die away gradually. **Me moría de vergüenza,** I nearly died of shame. **Me moría de miedo,** I was half-dead with fright. **Morirse por algo,** to be dying for something. *(Yo muero, yo muera; él murió, muriera, from Morir. V. DORMIR.)*

morisco, ca [mo-rees'-co, cah], *a.* Moorish, belonging to the Moors.-*m. & f.* 1. Name given to the Moors who remained in Spain after its restoration. 2. *(Mex.)* Quadroon.

morisma [mo-rees'-mah], *f.* Mohammedan sect, multitude of Moors.

morisqueta [mo-ris-kay'-tah], *f. (coll.)* 1. Moorish trick. 2. Deception, fraud, trick. 3. Rice boiled without salt, the ordinary food of the Indian natives of the Philippines.

morlaco, ca [mor-lah'-co, cah], *a.* Cunning, sly, fox (taimado). *m.* Sly fox, cunning person.

mormones [mor-mo'-nes], *m. pl.* Mormons, a sect founded by Joseph Smith in 1830.

mormullo, mormureo [mor-mool'-lyo, mor-moo-ray'-o], *m.* Mutter, murmur a low noise. *V.* MURMULLO.

mormuración [mor-moo-rah-the-on'], *f. V.* MURMURACIÓN.

mormurador [mor-moo-rah-dor'], *m.* Murmurer, detractor.

mormurar [mor-moo-rar'], *va.* To murmur. *V.* MURMURAR.

moro, ra [mo'-ro, rah], *a.* 1. Moorish, belonging to the Moors. 2. In jocular style, it is applied to wine not mixed with water or christened. 3. Dappled (caballo). -*m. & f.* 1. Moor, a native of Africa. 2. Domineering husband (marido). 3. Drug pusher (vendedor). **Haber moros y cristianos,** to have a great scuffle or dispute.

morocada [mo-ro-cah'-dah], *f.* Blow given by a ram with its horn, butt.

morocho, cha [Mo-ro'-cho, chah], *a. (Amer.)* 1. Fresh, vigorous, well preserved (persona). 2. Applied to a hard kind of Indian corn. 3. *V.* GEMELO.

morón [mo-rone'], *m.* Hill, hillock.

moroncho, cha [mo-ron'-cho, chah], *a. V.* MORONDO.

morondanga [mo-ron-dahn'-gah], *f. (coll.)* Hodge-podge, medley.

morondo, da [mo-ron'-do, dah], *a.* Bald (calvo), leafless (sin hojas).

moronía [mo-ro-nee'-ah], *f.* A dish made of a variety of vegetables. *V.* ALBORONÍA.

morosamente [mo-ro'-sah-men-tay], *adv.* Slowly, tardily.

morosidad [mo-ro-se-dahd'], *f.* Slowness (lentitud), tardiness, detention, delay, arrears (atrasos).

moroso, sa [mo-ro'-so, sah], *a.* Slow (lento), tardy, heavy. **Deudor moroso**, slow payer.

morquera [mor-kay'-rah], *f. (Bot.)* Spanish thyme.

morra [mor'-rah], *f.* 1. Upper part of the head, top, crown. 2. Vulgar game with the fingers; odd or even. **Andar a la morra**, to come to blows.

morrada [mor-rah'-dah], *f.* Butting of the heads by two persons (cabezazo).

morral [mor-rahl'], *m.* 1. A bag hung to the mouths of mules or horses out of which they eat when traveling 2. Game-bag (caza).

morralla [mor-rahl'-lyah], *f.* 1. Small fry (peces), little fish. 2. Heap or medley of useless things. 3. Rabble (personas).

morrear [mor-ray-ahr'], *va. vn.* To kiss.

morreo [mor-ray'-o], *m.* Kiss.

morrillo [mor-reel'-lyo], *m.* 1. Pebble. 2. Fat of the nape of a sheep.

morriña [mor-ree'-nyah], *f.* 1. Murrain, a disease among cattle. 2. Sadness, melancholy.

morrión [mor-re-on'], *m.* 1. Morion, steel helmet. 2. Vertigo, a disease in hawks.

morro [mor'-ro], *m.* 1. Anything that is round like the head. 2. Headland, head, bluff. 3. A prominent, overhanging lip. 3. *(Aer. Aut.)* Nose. 4. Pebble (guijarro). 5. Small rounded hill (cerro). **Beber a morro**, to drink from the bottle. **Estar de morros**, to be in a bad mood. **Poner morro**, to look cross. *-a.* Purring (gato).

morroncho, cha [mor-ron'-cho, chah], *a. (Prov.)* Mild, meek, tame.

morrocotudo, da [mor-ro-cotoo'-do, dah], *a.* 1. Strong (fuerte), stout, solid. 2. Of much importance or difficulty (difícil). 3. *(Cono Sur, Mex.)* Big (grande). 4. *(And.)* Rich (rico). 5. *(Cono Sur)* Clumsy (amazacotado).

morrudo, da [mor-roo'-do, dah], *a.* Blobber-lipped, flap-mouthed, having prominent lips.

morsa [mor'-sah], *f.* Walrus, morse, a large marine seal-like mammal.

mortadela [mor-tah-day'-lah], *f.* Bologna sausage.

mortaja [mor-tah'-hah], *f.* 1. Shroud (de muerto), windingsheet, grave-clothes. 2. Mortise, a hole cut into wood. 3. *(Amer.)* Cigarette paper. *(Acad.)*

mortal [mor-tahl'], *a.* 1. Mortal, subject to death (que muere). 2. Mortal, fatal (herida), deadly (golpe), destructive. 3. Mortal, deadly (distancia, espera), implacable. 4. One who has the appearance or symptoms of death.

mortal [mor-tahl'], *m.* Mortal, human being: commonly used in the plural.

mortalidad [mor-tah-le-dahd'], *f.* Mortality, liability to death.

mortalmente [mor-tahl'-men-tay], *adv.* Mortally.

mortandad [mor-tan-dhad'], *f.* Mortality, frequency of death; massacre, butchery.

mortecino, na [mor-tay-thee'-no, nah], *a.* 1. Dying a natural death, moribund. 2. Dying away or extinguishing; on the point of dying. 3. *(Low.)* Weak (débil), exhausted. **Hacer la mortecina**, to feign death. **Color mortecino**, a pale or deadly color. **La luz mortecina del crepúsculo**, the fading glow of twilight.

morterada [mor-tay-rah'-dah], *f.* 1. Sauce made at once in a mortar. 2. Quantity of stones thrown out at once by a stone mortar.

morterete [mor-tay-ray'-tay], *m.* 1. *(dim.)* A small mortar. 2. Piece of wax in shape of a mortar, with a wick in it, to serve as a lamp: it is placed in a glass with water. 3. *(Met.)* Hollow piece of iron used for firing gunpowder at fireworks.

morterico, illo, ito [mor-tay-ree'-co], *m. dim.* A small mortar.

mortero [mor-tay'-ro], *m.* 1. Mortar, a piece of ordnance. 2. Mortar, a vessel in which materials are pounded with a pestle. 3. Mortar, a building cement. **Mortero de una bomba de agua**, *(Naut.)* pump-box of a ship's pump.

morteruelo [mor-tay-roo-ay'-lo], *m.* 1. *(dim.)* A small mortar. 2. A kind of game of boys. 3. Fricassee of hog's liver.

mortífero, ra [mor-tee'-fay-ro, rah], *a.* Death-dealing, fatal.

mortificación [mor-te-fe-cah-the-on'], *f.* 1. Mortification of the body, by hardships and macerations. 2. Mortification, gangrene. 3. Mortification, vexation, trouble.

mortificar [mor-te-fe-car'], *va.* 1. To mortify, to destroy vital qualities. 2. To mortify, to subdue inordinate passions. 3. To mortify, to afflict, to disgust, to vex. **Estos zapatos me mortifican**, these shoes are killing me. *-vr.* 1. To mortify, to gangrene. 2. To mortify, to practice religious severities; to conquer one's passions.

mortuorio [mor-too-o'-re-o], *m.* Burial, funeral.-*a.* Mortuary, belonging to the dead. **Casa mortuoria**, house of the deceased.

morueca [mo-roo-ay'-cah], *f.* Heap of loose stones.

morueco [mo-roo-ay'-co], *m.* Ram, a male sheep.

moruno, na [mo-roo'-no, nah], *a.* Morish, belonging to the Moors.

morusa [mo-roo'-sah], *f. (coll.)* Cash, specie; money in hand.

mosa [mo'-sah], *f. (Zool.)* Moose.

mosaico, ca [mo-sah'-e-co, cah], *a.* Mosaic. **Obra mosaica**, mosaic work.

mosaísmo [mo-sah-ees'-mo], *m.* The Mosaic law or civilization.

mosca [mos'-cah], *f.* 1. Fly, a two-winged insect; the housefly. 2. *(coll.)* Cash, specie; money in hand (dinero). 3. An impertinent intruder. 4. Vexation, trouble. 5. *pl.* Sparks from a light (centellas). 6. *pl.* Exclamation of complaint or surprise. **Mosca de burro**, horse-fly. **Mosca muerta**, hypocrite. **Picarle la mosca**, to spend a bad quarter of an hour, to be disquieted. **Sacudir las moscas**, to shake off an incumbrance. **Tener la mosca detrás de la oreja**, to be wary. **Por si las moscas**, just in case.

moscada [mos-cah'-dah], *a. V.* NUEZ MOSCADA.

moscarda [mos-car'-dah], *f.* 1. Gadfly, horsefly. 2. *(Prov.)* Eggs of bees.

moscardear [mos-car-day-ar'], *vn. (Prov.)* To lay eggs as bees in the cells of their combs.

moscardón [mos-car-done'], *m.* 1. Large gadfly or horsefly. 2. A hornet (abejón). 3. An importuning, sly fellow, a cheat.

moscareta [mos-cah-ray'-tah], *f. (Orn.)* Fly-catcher.

moscatel [mos-cah-tel'], *a.* 1. Muscat or muscatel; musk-flavored: applied to a kind of grape and to the wine made from them. 2. A tiresome (pesado), ignorant fellow.

moscella [mos-thayl'-lah], *f. V.* MORCELLA.

mosco [mos'-co], *m. V.* MOSQUITO.

moscón [mos-cone'], *m.* 1. A large fly, a blow-fly. 2. A hanger-on, a crafty, deceitful fellow.

moscovita [mos-co-vee'-tah], *a.* Muscovite, Russian.

Moscú [mos-koo], Moscow.

mosqueado, da [mos-kay-ah'-do, dah], *a.* Spotted (moteado), painted.-*pp.* of MOSQUEAR.

mosqueador [mos-kay-ah-dor'], *m.* 1. Fly-trap, flap for killing flies. 2. *(coll.)* Tail of animals.

mosquear [mos-kay-ar'], *va.* 1. To flap, to frighten flies away with a flap, to catch flies. 2. To reply with a witticism.

-vr. (coll.) To become angry or cross (ofenderse); To smell a rat (sospechar)

mosqueo [mos-kay'-o], *m.* 1. The act of catching flies or driving them away with a flap. 2. Annoyance (enfado). 3. Hassle (lío).

mosquero [mos-kay'-ro], *m.* Fly-trap.

mosqueruela [mos-kay-roo-ay'-lah], *f.* Muscadine pear.

mosqueta [mos-kay'-tah], *f.* White musk-rose.

mosquetazo [mos-kay-tah'-tho], *m.* Musket-shot.

mosquete [mos-kay'-tay], *m.* Musket, blunderbuss, an ancient firearm which was jested upon a crotch to fire it.

mosquetería [mos-kay-tay-re'-ah], *f.* 1. A body of musketeers. 2. The company in the pit of a playhouse.

mosqueteril [mos-kay-tay-reel'], *a. (coll.)* 1. Belonging to musketeers. 2. Belonging to the crowd in the pit of a theater.

mosquetero [mos-kay-tay'-ro], *m.* 1. Musketeer, a foot-soldier. 2. Person who frequents the pit in a playhouse.

mosquil, mosquino, na [mos-keel', mos-kee'-no, nah], *a.* Belonging to flies.

mosquita [mos-kee'-tah], *f.* A small bird of Sardinia in whose nest the cuckoo lays an egg. **Mosquita muerta,** hypocrite. **Hacerse la mosquita muerta,** to look as if butter would not melt in one's mouth.

mosquitero, ra [mos-ke-tay'-ro, rah], *m. & f.* Mosquito bar or net, a gauze cover hung over a bed, to keep off gnats and mosquitoes.

mosquito [mos-kee'-to], *m.* 1. Gnat, mosquito. 2. Tippler.

mostacera [mos-tah-thay'-rah], *f.* Mustard-pot.

mostacilla [mos-tah-theel'-lyah], *f.* 1. Sparrow-shot, the smallest kind of bird-shot. 2. Seed bugle; very small glass, gold, silver, or steel beads.

mostacho [mos-tah'-cho], *m.* 1. *V.* BIGOTE. 2. Spot in the face, gloom in the countenance.

mostachón [mos-tah-chone'], *m.* A kind of ginger-bread.

mostachoso, sa [mos-tah-cho'-so, sah], *a.* Wearing a mustache.

mostajo [mos-tah'-ho], *m. (Bot.)* White beam-tree;

mostaza [mos-tah'-thah], *f.* 1. *(Bot.)* Mustard. 2. Mustard-seed. 3. Fine shot.

mostazo [mos-tah'-tho], *m. (Bot.)* Mustard; a plant. 2. *(Aug.)* Strong, thick must.

mostear [mos-tay-ar'], *vn.* 1. To yield must (uvas). 2. To put must into vats or earthen jars to ferment. 3. To mix must with old wine, in order to revive it. *V.* REMOSTAR.

mostela [mos-tay'-lah], *f. (Prov.)* Sprig or twig of vines.

mostelera [mos-tay-lay'-rah], *f.* Place where the sprigs or twigs of vines are laid up.

mostellar [mos-tel-lyar'], *m.* A tree having a white hard wood and a fleshy-red fruit.

mostillo [mos-teel'-lyo], *m.* 1. Cake made of must and other ingredients. 2. Sauce made of must and mustard.

mosto [mos'-to], *m.* 1. Must, the pressed juice of the grape not yet fermented. 2. Stum, must, new wine.

mostrable [mos-trah'-blay], *a.* That which may be shown.

mostrado, da [mos-trah'-do, dah], *a.* Accustomed, habituated, inured.*-pp.* Of MOSTRAR.

mostrador, ra [mos-trah-dor', rah], *m. & f.* 1. Demonstrator, one who demonstrates, one who shows.*-m.* 2. Pointer, hand of a clock or watch (reloj). 3. Counter, the table of a shop (tienda).

mostrar [Mos-trar'], *va.* 1. To show, to exhibit, to view, to point out (señalar), to lay before. 2. To show, to establish, to prove, to explain (explicar), to expound, to demonstrate (demostrar). 3. To show or make a thing appear what it is not, to feign, to dissemble. 4. To show any quality of the mind. **Mostrar en pantalla,** *(Comput.)* to display. *-vr.* To appear, to show oneself. **Se mostró muy amable,** he was very kind. **No se muestra muy imaginativa,** she does not seem to be very imaginative. *(Yo muestro, yo muestre,* from *Mostrar. V.* ACORDAR.)

mostrenco, ca [mos-tren'-co, cah], *a.* 1. Strayed, having no owner (sin dueño). 2. Vagabond, vagrant: applied to a stroller without house or home. 3. Dull, ignorant, stupid. 4. *(Prov.)* Fat (gordo), bulky. **Bienes mostrencos,** goods which have no known owner.

mota [mo'-tah], *f.* 1. A small knot on cloth, which is taken off with burling irons or scissors (nudillo en paño). 2. A bit of thread or anything similar sticking to clothes. 3. Mote, small particle of matter. 4. A slight defect or fault. 5. Bank or mound of earth. 6. Quota of each sailor to a common fund for subsistence stores, when the crew of a merchant vessel join together in trading. 7. Speck, tiny piece (partícula). 8. Dot (dibujo). 9. *(Agr.)* Ridge, boundary mark (mojón). 10. *(LAm.)* Lock of wavy hair (pelo). 11. *(And. Carib. Mex.)* Powder stuff (borla). 12. *(Mex. Bot.)* Marijuana plant (droga). **Mota de polvo,** speck of dust. **No hace mota de aire,** there isn't a breath of air.

motacilla [mo-tah-theel'-lyah], *f. V* AGUZANIEVE.

mote [mo'-tay], *m.* 1. Motto or sentence added to a device, or prefixed to anything written. 2. Nickname (apodo). 3. *(Peru, Bol.)* Popcorn.

motear [mo-tay-ar'], *vn.* To speckle, to mark with spots.

motejador, ra [mo-tay-hah-dor', rah], *m. & f.* Mocker, scoffer, censurer.

motejar [mo-tay-har'], *va.* To censure, to ridicule, to nickname.

motero [mo-tay'-ro], *m.* motorcyclist, motorcycle maniac.

motete [mo-tay'-tay], *m.* Motet or motetto, a short musical composition to be sung in church.

motil [mo-teel'], *m. V.* MOCHIL.

motilar [mo-te-lar'], *va.* To cut the hair, to crop.

motilón, na [mo-te-lone', nah], *a.* Poor, indigent. *-m. (coll.)* Lay-brother of a religious order.

motín [mo-teen'], *m.* Mutiny, insurrection, riot (disturbio).

motita [mo-tee'-tah], *f.* A small bit of thread sticking to cloths.

motivar [mo-te-var'], *va.* 1. To give a reason for anything, to assign a motive (causar). 2. To explain (explicar).

motivo [mo-tee'-vo], *m.* 1. Motive, cause, reason, occasion, impulse. 2. Motif, motive, or theme in a musical composition. **Motivo de divorcio,** grounds for divorce. **Por cuyo motivo,** for which reason. **Por motivos de salud,** for reasons of health.

motivo, va *a.* Motive, moving, causing motion, having the power to move. **De su motivo,** of one's own accord. **Con motivo de,** owing to, by reason of.

moto [mo'-to], *f.* Motorbike; scooter (escúter).

motocicleta [mo-to-the-clay'-tah], *f.* Motorcycle.

motociclismo [mo-to-the-clees'mo], *m.* Motorcycling.

motocilista [mo-to-the-clees'-tah], *m & f.* Motorcyclist.

moto-cross [mo'-to-cross], *m.* Moto-cross.

motolita [mo-to-lee'-tah], *f. V.* AGUZANIEVE.

motolito, ta [mo-to-lee'-to, tah], **Motolótico, ca,** *a.* Easily deceived, ignorant.

motón [mo-tone'], *m. (Naut.)* Block, pulley, tackle for ropes to run in. **Motón sencillo,** single-block. **Motón de gancho,** hook-block. **Motones,** *(Naut.)* pulleys with sheaves. **Motones herrados,** iron-bound blocks.

motonave [mo-to-nah'-vay], *f.* Motor ship.

motonería [mo-to-nay-ree'-ah], *f. (Naut.)* Blocks and pulleys in ships.

motonero [mo-to-nay'-ro], *m.* Block-maker.

motor, ra [mot-tor', rah], *a.* Motor, motive causing motion. *-m.* Motor, a prime mover, particularly an electrical machine. **Motor de aviación,** aircraft engine. **Motor delantero,** front-mounted engine. **Motor diesel,** diesel engine.

motorismo [mo-to-rees'-mo], *m.* Motorcycling.

motorista [mo-to-rees'-tah], *m.* 1. *(LAm.)* Motorman. 2. Motorcyclist (motociclista).

motorizado [mo-to-re-thah'-do], *a.* Motorized.

motril [mo-treel'], *m. V.* MOCHIL.

motriz [mo-treeth'], *a.* Motor, motive, moving cause. **Fuerza motriz,** moving cause.

movedizo, za [mo-vay-dee'-tho, thah], *a.* 1. Movable, easily moved (movible). 2. Variable, unsteady (poco seguro), inconstant, shifting (arenas).

movedor, ra [mo-vay-dor', rah], *m. & f.* Mover, motor, exciter, occasioner.

movedura [mo-vay-doo'-rah], *f. V.* MOVIMIENTO.

mover [mo-verr'], *va.* 1. To move, to put in motion (objeto). 2. To move, to prevail upon, to persuade, to induce. 3. To move, to stir passion, to touch pathetically, to cause or give occasion to. 4. To move, to stir up (descontento), to put into commotion. 5. To move, to excite, to commence a thing. 6. To move, to inspire (inspirar). **El agua mueve la rueda**, the water turns the wheel. **Mover a uno a hacer algo**, to move somebody to do something. -*vn.* 1. *(Arch.)* To spring an arch. 2. To bud, to begin to sprout. 3. To miscarry, to have an abortion.-*vr.* 1. To move, to be in a state of changing place, to walk. 2. To move, to have vital action. 3. To move, to go forward. **Hay que moverse**, we must get a move on. *(Yo muevo, yo mueva. V.* MOVER.)

movible [mo-vee'-blay], *a.* 1. Movable (no fijo), locomotive. 2. Variable.

movida [mo-vee'-dah], *f.* 1. Move (ajedrez). 2. *(Pol.)* Movement. 3. Thing (asunto), affair, business; gathering (concentración); happening (acontecimiento). **La movida cultural**, the cultural scene.

movido [mo-vee'-do], *a.* 1. Blurred (movimiento de camara). 2. Active (persona); restless (inquieto). 3. *(And. CAm. Cono Sur)* Soft-shelled (huevo). 4. *(And. CAm. Cono Sur)* Weak, feeble (débil).

moviente [mo-ve-en'-tay], *pa. & a.* Moving, motory.

móvil [mo'-veel], *a.* Movable, capable of moving or of being moved.-*m.* Mover, motor.

movilidad [mo-ve-le-dahd'], *f.* 1. Mobility, movableness, aptitude to be moved. 2. Mobility, inconstancy, unsteadiness, levity.

movilización [mo-ve-le-thah-the-on'], *f.* Mobilization.

movilizar [mo-ve-le-thar'], *va.* 1. To put in movement. 2. To mobilize (organizar), to make ready for active service.-*vr.* 1. To be set in motion. 2. To be mobilized, to go into active service.

movimiento [mo-ve-me-en'-to], *m.* 1. Movement, motion, moving, shake (negando), nod (asintiendo). **Movimiento continuo**, perpetual motion. **Estar en movimiento**, to be in motion. 2. Commotion, disturbance, sedition, revolt. 3. *(Arch.) V.* ARRANQUE. 4. Movement; activity; bustle (bullicio). **Una tienda de mucho movimiento**, a busy shop. 5. *(Liter. Teat.)* Action. 6. Tempo (compás). 7. Change, alteration (emociones). **Movimiento de ánimo**, perturbation.

moya [mo'-yah], *f. (Amer. Colom.)* A small, unglazed jar for boiling salt.

moyana [mo-yah'-nah], *f.* 1. A small culverin. 2. *(coll.)* Lie, falsehood. 3. Bread made of bran for feeding dogs.

moyo [mo'-yo], *m.* 1. Liquid measure of about 32 gallons or 129 liters. 2. Number of tiles fixed at 110.

moyuelo [mo-yoo-ay'-lo], *m.* Grits, pollard, coarse meal.

moza [mo'-thah], *f.* 1. Girl, a maid-servant engaged to do all kinds of work. **Moza de fortuna**, prostitute. **Moza de servicio**, domestic servant. 2. A clothes-pounder, used to beat linen when it is being washed. 3. Last or conquering game.

mozalbete, mozalbillo [mo-thal-bay'-tay, mo-thal-beel'-lyo], *m.* A lad, a beardless youth.

mozallón [mo-thahl-lyone'], *m.* A young, robust laborer.

mozcorra [moth-cor'-rah], *f. (Vulg.)* A common prostitute.

mozo, za [mo'-tho, thah], *a.* 1. Young, youthful (joven). 2. Applied to any unmarried person (soltero).

mozo [mo'-tho], *m.* 1. Youth, a young man, a lad. 2. Man-servant engaged to do all kinds of work in the house. 3. Bachelor, a man unmarried. 4. *(coll.)* Fellow. 5. Waiter. **Mozo de caballos**, groom, horse-boy. 6. Dumbwaiter. **Mozo de estación**, porter. **Buen mozo**, handsome lad.

mozón [mo-thone'], *m. aug.* A robust young man.

mozuela [mo-thoo-ay'-lah], *f. dim.* 1. A very young lass or woman: sometimes applied in contempt. 2. *(Vulg.)* A prostitute.

mozuelo [mo-thoo-ay'-lo], *m. dim.* A very young man or lad.

mozuelo, la [mo-thoo-ay'-lo, lah], *a. dim.* Young, youthful.

mu [moo], *f.* A child's word for sleep. 2. **No pasó ni mu**, nothing at all happened.

muaré [moo-ah-ray'], *m.* Moiré (tela).

mucamuca [moo-cah-moo'-cah], *f. (Peru.) V.* ZORRA MOCHILERA.

muceta [moo-thay'-tah], *f.* 1. Part of the dress worn by bishops when officiating. 2. A short cape worn by doctors.

mucilaginoso, sa [moo-the-lah-he-no'-so, sah], *a.* Mucilaginous, slimy.

mucílago *(Acad.)*, or **mucilago** [moo-thee'-lah-go], *m.* Mucilage, a solution of gum; any viscous or slimy body.

mucina [moo-thee'-nah], *f.* Mucin, an alkaline glutinous fluid.

mucíparo, ra [moo-thee'-pah-ro, rah], *a.* Muciparous, secreting mucus.

mucol [moo-cole'], *m.* Mucilage considered as an excipient.

mucor [moo-cor'], *m.* Mucor, mouldiness.

mucosidad [moo-co-se-dahd'], *f.* Mucosity, mucilaginousness.

mucoso, sa [moo-co'-so, sah], *a.* Mucous, slimy, viscous, mucilaginous.

mucronato, ta [moo-cro-nah'-to, tah], *a.* Mucronate, tipped with a sharp point.

múcura [moo'-coo-rah], *f.* A kind of pitcher or ewer used in Venezuela among Indians.

muchachada [moo-chah-chah'-dah], *f.* A boyish trick, a girlish trick, gaiety.

muchachear [moo-chah-chay-ar'], *vn.* To act in a boyish or childish manner, to fumble or play childishly.

muchachería [moo-chah-chay-ree'-ah], *f.* 1. Boyish trick. 2. Clamorous noise made by a crowd of boys.

muchachez [moo-chah-cheth'], *f.* Childhood; puerility; boyhood.

muchacha [moo-chah'-chah], *f.* Girl; lass, child.

muchacho [moo-chah'-cho], *m.* 1. Boy (chico), lad; servant (criado). 2. *(LAm.)* Clamp (abrazadera), holdfast; *(Cono Sur)* shoeborn (zapato); miner's lamp (lámpara). -*a.* Boyish, girlish, childish.

muchedumbre [moo-chay-doom'-bray], *f.* Multitude, many, a great number; plenty, abundance, much.

muchísimo, ma [moo-chee'-se-mo, mah], *a.* Superlative of MUCHO. Very much, very large; a great deal.

mucho, cha [moo'-cho, chah], *a.* Much, large in quantity, long in time, many in number; abundant, plentiful. **No es mucho**, it is no wonder. **Mucho tiempo**, a long time. **Hace mucho calor**, it's very hot. **Es mucha mujer**, what a woman she is! **Hay muchos conejos**, there are lots of rabbits. **Tengo mucho que hacer**, I have lots to do. -*adv.* Much, in a great degree; excessively, by far, often, long (tiempo): to a certain degree. **Mucho menos**, much less. **Correr mucho**, to run fast. **Con mucho el mejor**, far and away the best. **Es mucho difícil**, *(Mex.)* it's jolly difficult.

muda [moo'-dah], *f.* 1. Change, alteration. 2. Change of linen. 3. The act and time of moulting (temporada) and shedding feathers. 4. A transition of the voice in boys who come to maturity. 5. Roost of birds of prey. 6. A cosmetic. **Estar en muda**, to keep silence in company.

mudable [moo-dah'-blay], *a.* Changeable, variable, mutable, fickle (de carácter), light.

mudamente [moo'-dah-men-tay], *adv.* Silently, tacitly, mutely.

mudanza [moo-dahn'-thah], *f.* 1. Alteration, change; mutation, commutation. 2. Removal from place to place. 3. Inconstancy, levity. 4. Certain number of motions in a dance. **Estar de mudanza**, to be moving.

mudar [moo-dar'], *va.* 1. To change (cambiar), to put one thing in place of another, to remove, to deviate. 2. To change, to cause alteration, to vary, to alter. 3. To change one thing for another, or to quit something for the sake of another. 4. To shed the feathers, to moult. 5. To change the voice: applied to boys who come to maturity. 6. To change, to vary in a moral sense; to mend the disposition. **Me van a mudar la pluma**, they're going to change the pen for me. **Le mudan las sábanas todos los días**, they change his sheets every day. *-vr.* 1. To change, to undergo change. 2. To change the sentiments and manners. 3. To shift, to dress in fresh linen or clothes. 4. To move into another house (casa). 5. *(coll.)* To wander from the topic of conversation.

mudéjar [moo-day'-har], *a. & m. pl.* Used of a Mohammedan who, without changing his religion, became a subject of Christian sovereigns.

mudez [moo-deth'], *f.* Dumbness; impediment of speech.

mudo, da [moo'-do, dah], *a.* Dumb, silent (callado), still, mute. **Quedarse mudo de asombro**, to be dumbfounded. **Quedarse mudo de envidia**, to be green with envy.

mué, muer [moo-ay', moo-err'], *m.* Tabby, moiré, watered silk.

mueblaje [moo-ay-blah'-hay], *m.* Fitment, collection of furniture.

mueble [moo-ay'-blay], *m.* 1. Any movable piece of furniture. **Mueble combinado**, piece of unit furniture. *-pl.* Movable goods, chattels, furniture, household stuff. 2. *(Mex.)* Car (coche).

mueblista [moo-ay-blees'-tah], *m.* Furniture dealer, furniture maker.

mueca [moo-ay'-cah], *f.* Grimace, wry face, grin.

muedín [moo-ay-deen'], *m.* Muezzin, one who calls the Mohammedan faithful to prayer. *V.* ALMUÉDANO.

muela [moo-ay'-lah], *f.* 1. In cornmills, runner, the upper millstone (de molino). 2. Grindstone (de afilar), whetstone. 3. Water sufficient to set a mill in motion. 4. Hill, hillock; any artificial mound 5. Track or circle made with anything. 6. Grinder, one of the back teeth, molar teeth. **Al que le duele la muela, que se la saque**, it is none of my business. **Dolor de muelas**, toothache.

muellaje [moo-el-yah'-hay], *m.* Wharfage, dockage, a harbor tax.

muelle [moo-el'-lyay], *a.* 1. Tender, delicate (delicado), soft (blando). 2. Licentious luxurious.*-m.* 1. Spring, an elastic body (elástico). 2. Regulator, a small spring which regulates the movements of a watch. 3. *(Naut.)* Mole, pier; jetty; quay, wharf; a place in a seaport for shipping goods, etc.

muellear [moo-el-yay-ar'], *vn.* To bear against, to prop. A word much used by type-founders.

muellemente [moo-ayl'-lyay-men-tay], *adv.* Tenderly, gently, softly.

muérdago [moo-err'-dah-go], *m. (Bot.)* Mistletoe.

muermera [moo-er-may'-rah], *f. (Bot.)* Common virgin's-bower; traveler's-joy.

muermo [moo-err'-mo], *m.* Glanders, a contagious disease in horses, affecting the nose and accompanied by a pustular eruption.

muermo [moo-ayr'-mo], *a. (Esp.)* Boring (pesado); wet (débil), indecisive; slow (lento). *-m & f.* Crashing bore (pesado); drip, wet fish (débil); dolt (tonto). *-m.* Boredom (aburrimiento); blues (depresión).

muermoso, sa [moo-er-mo'-so, sah], *a.* Snoring, breathing with difficulty; glandered.

muerte [moo-err'-tay], *f.* 1. Death, the extinction of life. 2. Death, murder (homicidio), assassination (asesinato), the act of killing unlawfully. 3. Death, image of mortality, represented by a skeleton. 4. A violent affection that cannot be borne, labor, difficulty, severe affliction. **Muerte civil**, (1) *(Law.)* civil death. (2) *(coll.)* A miserable and painful life. **Buena muerte**, a good end, the contrite death of a person. **Bajo pena de muerte**, on pain of death. **Hasta la muerte**, until death. **A muerte o a vida**, kill or cure, at all risks. **Tomarse la muerte por su mano**, to imperil one's life, health, or welfare against good advice. **Muerte súbita**,

sudden death. **Dar muerte a**, to kill. **Luchar a muerte**, to fight to the death. **Un susto de muerte**, a terrible fright.

muerto [moo-err'-to], *m.* 1. Corpse (cadáver), a dead body. 2. *(Naut.)* The standing part of a running rope.*-pl.* 1. Stripes, strokes, blows. 2. *(Naut.)* Ground-ways.

muerto, ta [moo-err'-to, tah], *a. & pp. irr.* of MORIR. 1. Dead, extinguished, lifeless. 2. Languid, faded (colores). 3. Slaked (cal). **Más muerto que vivo**, half-dead. **No tener donde caerse muerto**, to be utterly destitute. **Estar muerto de cansancio**, to be dead tired. **Estar muerto de hambre**, to be dying of hunger.

muesca [moo-ays'-cah], *f.* 1. Groove cut in the staves of casks and baskets, in which the bottoms and headpieces are fixed; hack, nick, mortise. 2. An empty or void space. *V.* MELLA. 3. Dove-tail scarf.

muestra [moo-ays'-trah], *f.* 1. A small sample of cloth. 2. Outer piece of cloth where the stamp of the maker is put. 3. A shop sign (de tienda). 4. Any indicative sign or demonstration of a thing (demostración). 5. Specimen, design, model (pauta), copy. 6. Clock which does not strike (reloj). **Es muestra de cariño**, it is a token of affection. **Muestra gratuita**, free sample. **Muestra representativa**, cross-section sample.

muestrario [moo-es-trah'-re-o], *m.* Samples, set of samples.

mufla [moo'-flah], *f.* Muffle, an earthen cover placed over tests and coppels in the assaying of metals. **muflas**, thick winter gloves, which serve instead of a muff.

mufti [moof'-te], *m.* Mufti, the high-priest of the Mohammedans.

mugido [moo-hee'-do], *m.* The lowing of an ox, cow, or bull.

múgil [moo'-heel], *m.* Mullet. *V.* MÚJOL.

mugir [moo-heer'], *vn.* To low, to moo (vaca), to bellow like an ox.

mugre [moo'-gray], *f.* Grime, dirt, or filth which sticks to clothes and other things.

mugriento, ta [moo-gre-en'-to, tah], *a.* Greasy, dirty, filthy, grimy.

mugrón [moo-grone'], *m.* Sprig or shoot of a vine.

muguete [moo-gay'-tay], *m.* Lily of the valley.

mujer [moo-herr'], *f.* 1. Woman, the female of the human race. **Ser mujer**, to be a woman, to have attained the age of puberty. 2. Wife (esposa), mate. **Mujer de su casa** or **mujer de gobierno**, housewife, a woman skilled in female business. **Mujer varonil**, a manly woman. **Ser muy mujer**, to be very feminine. **Mujer fatal**, femme fatale.

mujeracha [moo-hay-rah'-chah], *f. (coll.)* A coarse woman of the lowest class.

mujercilla [moo-her-theel'-lyah], *f.* A worthless woman: jade, hussy; a strumpet.*-m.* Hilding, a sorry, paltry, cowardly fellow.

mujeriego, ga [moo-hay-re-ay'-go, gah], *a.* 1. Feminine, womanly, belonging to women. 2. Womanish, given to women.*-m.* Womankind; all the women of a place.

mujeril [moo-hay-reel'], *a.* Womanish, womanly, feminine.

mujerilmente [moo-hay-reel'-men-tay], *adv.* Effeminately.

mujerío [moo-hay-ree'-o], *m.* A gathering of women.

mujerona [moo-hay-ro'-nah], *f. aug.* A stout woman; a matron.

mujerzuela [moo-hayr-thoo-ay'-lah], *f.* Whore.

mula [moo'-lah], *f.* 1. She-mule. 2. A kind of thick soled shoe. 3. A certain Moorish vessel. 4. *(Mex.)* Trash, junk, unsaleable goods (trastos). 5. *(CAm.)* Shame (vergüenza). 6. *(And.)* Pipe (pipa). 7. *(And.)* Idiot (idiota). 8. *(Mex.)* Tough guy (duro). 9. *(Cono Sur)* Lie (mentira); trick (engaño).

muladar [moo-lah-dar'], *m.* 1. Place where the dirt and sweepings of houses are put. 2. Dung-heap: rubbish heap. 3. Anything very dirty or infectious.

muladí [moo-lah-dee'], *a.* Renegade Spanish Christian who lived among the Moors.

mular [moo-lar'], *a.* Belonging to mules.

mulatero [moo-lah-tay'-ro], *m.* Muleteer, mule-driver; a mule-boy.

mulato, ta [moo-lah'-to, tah], *a.* Mulatto, tawny.-*n.* Mulatto, the offspring of a white person and a black person.

múleo, muléolo [moo'-lay-o, moo-lay'-o-lo], *m.* Name of a pointed, purple-colored footwear used among the Roman patricians.

mulero [moo-lay'-ro], *m.* Mule-boy, who takes care of mules employed in agriculture; a muleteer.-*a.* Applied to a horse fond of mules.

muleta [moo-lay'-tah], *f.* 1. A young she-mule, not yet trained to work. 2. Crutch, prop, support (para andar). 3. An instrument of rope-makers. 4. *V.* MULETILLA.

muletada [moo-lay-tah'-dah], *f.* Herd of mules.

muletero [moo-lay-tay'-ro], *m.* Muleteer, mule-driver.

muletilla [moo-lay-teel'-lyah], *f.* 1. Word or phrase often repeated inadvertently in talking. 2. A wand or rod. 3. A rod with a cape (commonly red) which the bullfighter uses to provoke the bull when he is about to kill it. 4. A passementerie button (botón). 5. A cane (bastón), the head of which forms a kind of crutch.

muleto [moo-lay'-to], *m.* A young he-mule not yet broken.

mulilla [moo-leel'-lyah], *f. dim.* of MULA.

mulla [mool'-lyah], *f.* The act of digging around vines.

mullida [mool-yee'-dah], *f.* Ridge of soil between furrow and furrow.

mullido [mool-yee'-do], *m.* A soft cushion, or pillow.

mullidor, ra [mool-lye-dor', rah], *m. & f.* 1. Bruiser, mollifier. 2. *V.* MUÑIDOR.

mullir [mool-lyeer'], *va.* 1. To beat up anything, in order to make it soft and spongy (ablandar). **Mullir la cama**, to beat up the bed. 2. To call, to convene. *V.* MUÑIR. 3. To adopt proper measures for attaining one's purpose. 4. To dig about the roots of vines and trees.

mulo [moo'-lo], *m.* Mule.

mulso, sa [mool'-so, sah], *a.* Of mixed honey and sugar.

multa [mool'-tah], *f.* 1. Fine, ticket (aparcamiento). 2. A wild fruit-tree of Puerto Rico.

multar [mool-tar'], *va.* To penalize, to fine, or impose a fine.

multicaule [mool-te-cah'-oo-lay], *a.* (*Bot.*) Multicauline, having many stems.

multicoloro, ra [mool-te-co-lo'-ro, rah], *a.* Many-hued, many-colored.

multifacético, ca [mool-te-fah-thay'-te-co, cah], *a.* With many phases.

multifloro, ra [mool-te-flo'-ro, rah], *a.* Many-flowered.

multiforme [mool-tee-for'-may], *a.* Multiform.

multigrado [mool-te-grah'-do], *a.* Multigrade (aceite).

multígrafo [mool-tee'-grah-fo], *m.* Multigraph.

multilátero, ra [mool-te-lah'-tay-ro, rah], *a.* Multilateral.

multimillonario, ria [mool-te-mil-lyo-nah'-re-o, ah], *m. & f.* Multimillionaire.

multinomio, mia [mool-te-no'-me-o, ah], *a.* (*Alg.*) Polynomial.

múltiple [mool'-te-play], *a.* Multiple, complex; opposed to simple.

multiplexor [mool-te-plec-sor]. (*Comput.*) Multiplexor.

multiplicable [mool-te-ple-cah'-blay], *a.* Multiplicable, multipliable.

multiplicación [mool-te-ple-cah-the-on'], *f.* Multiplication.

multiplicador, ra [mool-te-ple-cah-dor', rah], *m. & f.* Multiplier; multiplicator.

multiplicando [mool-te-ple-cahn'-do], *m.* (*Arith.*) Multiplicand.

multiplicar [mool-te-ple-car'], *va. & vr.* To increase, to multiply.

multíplice [mool-tee'-plee-thay], *a.* Multiple; multiplex.

multiplicidad [mool-te-ple-the-dahd'], *f.* Multiplicity.

múltiplo, pla [mool'-te-plo, plah], *a.* Multiple, exactly divided by another quantity. *V.* MULTÍPLICE.

multiprocesador [mool-te-rpo-thay-sah-dor]. (*Comput.*) Multiprocessor.

multitud [mool-te-tood'], *f.* Multitude, a great number, crowd (gente). *V.* MUCHEDUMBRE. **La multitud**, the multitude, the mass.

multitudinario [mool-te-too-de-nah'-re-o], *a.* Massive; big (reunión); mass (manifestación).

multiuso [mool-te-oo'-so], *a.* For many uses.

multivalvo, va [mool-te-vahl'-vo, vah], *a.* (*Con.*) Multivalve: applied to a class of shell-fish.

mumiforme [moo-me-for'-may], *a.* Mummiform; like a mummy.

mundanalidad [moon-dah-nah-le-dahd'], *f.* Worldliness.

mundano, na [moon-dah'-no, nah], *a.* 1. Mundane, worldly (del mundo). **Mujer mundana**, common prostitute. 2. Society (de alta sociedad). **Son gente muy mundana**, they're high society people.

mundial [moon-de-ahl'], *a.* Worldwide; universal. **Las comunicaciones mundiales**, world communications.

mundialmente [moon-de-ahl'-men-tay], *adv.* Throughout the world.

mundificar [moon-de-fe-car'], *va.* To cleanse, to make clean.

mundificativo, va [moon-de-fe-cah-tee'-vo, vah], *a.* Mundificant, cleansing.

mundillo [moon-deel'-lyo], *m.* 1. An arched frame put over braziers to dry or air linen. 2. Cushion on which bone-lace is made. 3. Warming-pan. 4. World circle.

mundo [moon'-do], *m.* 1. World, the collective idea of all bodies whatever; terrestrial sphere, globe. 2. (*coll.*) Great multitude, great quantity. 3. (*Met.*) The manners of men; worldly desires and practices. 4. A dissipated life. **El nuevo mundo**, North and South America. **El otro mundo**, the next world, the world to come. **No ser de este mundo**, to live retired from the world, to be very innocent and simple. **Ver mundo**, to travel. **Medio mundo**, many people. **Desde que el mundo es mundo**, from the beginning of time. **Echar al mundo**, to create. **Echarse al mundo**, to plunge into dissipation. **Echar del mundo**, to banish from society, to send to Coventry. **No caber en el mundo**, to be inflated with pride. **Ponerse el mundo por montera**, to care nothing for what people will say. **Tener mundo or mucho mundo**, to be acute, not easily deceived. **En todo el mundo**, everywhere. **El mundo es un pañuelo**, it's a small world.

munición [moo-ne-the-on'], *f.* 1. Munition or ammunition, materials for war (balas etc.); war-like stores. 2. Charge of fire-arms. **Botas de munición**, army boots.

municionar [moo-ne-the-o-nar'], *va.* To supply with ammunition or war-like stores.

municipal [moon-ne-the-pahl'], *a.* Municipal, corporate.

municipalidad [moo-ne-the-pah-le-dahd'], *f.* Municipality; town council, the governing board of a city.

munícipe [moo-nee'-the-pay], *m.* Citizen, denizen; member of a corporation.

municipio [moo-ne-thee'-pe-o], *m.* 1. Place which enjoys the rights and privileges of a city. 2. Corporation (ayuntamiento).

munificencia [moo-ne-fe-then'-the-ah], *f.* Munificence, liberality.

munificentísimo, ma [moo-ne-fe-then-tee'-se-mo, mah], *a. super.* of MUNÍFICO.

munífico, ca [moo-nee'-fe-co, cah], *a.* Munificent, liberal.

muñeca [moo-nyay'-cah], *f.* 1. The wrist. 2. A doll (de niña). **Muñeca de trapo**, rag doll. 3. A small bundle of medicinal ingredients put into a decoction. 4. (*Cono Sur*) Pull, influence. -*pl.* In the mint, the screws that pinch the coin, and give it the due thickness.

muñeco [moo-nyay'-co], *m.* 1. Puppet (títere), representing a male figure (figura), doll (juguete). 2. A soft, effeminate fellow. 3. Puppet (instrumento). 4. Pretty little boy (niño). 5. Row (lío).

muñeira [moo-nyay'-e-rah], *f.* A popular dance of Galicia.

muñequear [moo-nyay-kay-ar'], *va.* To play with the wrist in fencing.

muñequera [moo-nyay-kay'-rah], *f.* Bracelet, an ornament for the wrist of dolls.

muñequería [moo-nyay-kay-ree'-ah], *f.* Excessive fondness for clothes and ornaments.

muñidor [moo-nye-dor'], *m.* 1. Bandle of a corporation or confraternity; apparitor, messenger. 2. *(Amer.)* Undertaker.

muñir [moo-nyeer'], *va.* To summon (convocar), to call to a meeting.

muñón [moo-nyone'], *m.* 1. Brawn, the fleshy part of the body. 2. Stump of an amputated arm or leg. 3. Trunnion of a cannon; gudgeon, lug, swing-block.

muñonera [moo-nyo-nay'-rah], *f.* Trunnion-plate, trunnion-socket, *(Mech.)* gudgeon-socket.

murajes [moo-rah'-hes], *m.* A medicinal herb of pungent taste.

mural [moo-rahl'], *a.* Mural, belonging to walls.

muralla [moo-rahl'-lyah], *f.* Rampart which surrounds a place; wall.

murar [moo-rar'], *va.* To wall, to surround with a rampart.

murciano, na [moor-the-ah'-no, nah], *a.* Murcian, of Murcia.

murciélago [moor-the-ay'-lah-go], *m (Zool.)* The bat.

murena [moo-ray'-nah], *f.* A kind of eel. *V.* MORENA.

murga [moor'-gah], *f.* 1. *V.* ALPECHÍN. 2. Street musicians who play for a gratuity. 3. Bore, nuisance (lata). **Dar la murga**, to be a pain.

muriático, ca [moo-ree-ah'-te-co, cah], *a. (Chem.)* Muriatic.

muriato [moo-re-ah'-to], *m. (Chem.)* Muriate.

múrice [moo'-re-thay], *m.* 1. Porcelain shell-fish; generic name of sea-shells which end in a straight canal; murex, Tyrian purple. 2. *(Poet.)* Purple.

múrido, da [moo'-re-do, dah], *a.* Mouse like.

murmujear [moor-moo-hay-ar'], *va.* To murmur, to mutter.

murmullar [moor-mool-lyar'], *vn. (Prov.) V.* MURMURAR, 2d def.

murmullo [moor-mool'-lyo], *m.* 1. Muttering, mumbling in speaking. 2. Murmuring (susurro), purling.

murmuración [moor-moo-rah-the-on'], *f.* Backbiting, privy calumny, slander, gossiping, obloquy.

murmurador, ra [moor-moo-rah-dor', rah], *m. & f.* Murmurer, detractor, backbiter (criticón). -*a.* Gossip (chismoso); backbiting (criticón).

murmurar [moor-moo-rar'], *va.* 1. To murmur (persona), to purl, to flow gently (corriente). 2. To murmur, to grudge, to grumble, to mutter (quejarse). 3. To backbite, to censure an absent person. 4. To rustle (hojas, viento), to hum (abejas, multitud). **Siempre están murmurando del jefe**, they're always grumbling about the boss.

murmurio [moor-moo'-re-o], *m.* The purling or murmuring of a stream.

muro [moo'-ro], *m.* Wall. *V.* PARED and MURALLA.

murria [moor'-re-ah], *f.* 1. Heaviness of the head, lowness of spirits, melancholy, mumps, reverie, spleen. 2. A former astringent medicament.

murrino, na [moor-ree'-no, nah], *a.* Applied to a cup or vase much esteemed in old times.

murrio, ria [moor'-re-o, ah], *a.* Sad, melancholy.

murta [moor'-tah], *f.* Myrtle. *V.* ARRAYÁN and MIRTO.

murtal [moor-tahl'], *m.* Grove of myrtles.

murtilla, murtina [moor-teel'-lyah, moor-tee'-nah], *f. (Bot.)* 1. A shrub growing in Chile. 2. The fruit of the same shrub. 3. The fruit of the myrtle.

murtón [moor-tone'], *m.* Myrtle-berry the fruit of myrtle.

murucuya [moo-roo-coo'-yah], *f. (Bot.)* Purple passion-flower.

murueco [moo-roo-ay'-co], *m. V.* MORUECO.

mus [moos], *m.* A card game.

musa [moo'-sah], *f.* 1. Muse, the goddess of poetry. 2. Poetic genius. 3. Musa, Latin name of the plantain and banana trees.

musaraña [moo-sah-rah'-nyah], *f.* 1. Fetid shrew-mouse. 2. Spirit, ghost, hobgoblin. 3. Any insect or small animal; vermin. *(Fig.)* **Pensar en las musarañas**, to go wool-gathering.

muscardina [moos-car-dee'-nah], *f.* Muscurdin(e), a disease of silkworms due to a fungus.

muscaria, or **muscícapa** [moos-cah'-re-ah, moos-thee'-cah-pah], *f. (Orn.)* Fly-catcher.

múscido, da [moos'-the-do, dah], *a.* Like a fly.

muscívoro, ra [moos-thee'-vo-ro, rah], *a.* Devouring flies; fly-catching.

musco [moos'-co], *m.* Moss.

musco, ca [moos'-co, cah], *a.* Chestnut color.

muscosidad [moos-co-se-dahd'], *f.* Mossiness.

musculado, da [moos-coo-lah'-do, dah], *a. (Met.)* Muscular, brawny.

muscular [moos-coo-lar'], *a.* Muscular.

musculatura [moos-coo-lah-too'-rah], *f.* Musculature, the entire muscular system.

músculo [moos'-coo-lo], *m.* 1. Muscle, a fleshy fibre susceptible of contraction and relaxation. 2. Whale of a prodigious size.

musculoso, sa [moos-coo-lo'-so, sah], *a.* Muscular, full of muscles.

muselina [moo-say-lee'-nah], *f.* Muslin, fine cotton cloth. **Muselina fina estampada**, French jaconet muslin.

museo [moo-say'-o], *m.* 1. Museum, a place set apart for the study of the sciences and arts. 2. Repository of learned curiosities. **Museo de arte**, art gallery.

muserola [moo-say-ro'-lah], *f.* The noseband of a horse's bridle.

musgaño [moos-gah'-nyo], *m.* 1. Shrew-mouse. *V.* MUSARAÑA. 2. Large field-spider.

musgo [moos'-go], *m.* Moss.

musgoso, sa [moos-go'-so, sah], *a.* 1. Mossy. 2. Moss-covered.

música [moo'-se-cah], *f.* 1. Music, the science of harmonical sounds. 2. Music, instrumental or vocal harmony. 3. Harmony, or melody modulated sound. 4. Company of musicians. 5. A musical composition. 6. Written sheets of music. 7. Music: applied by antiphrasis to a dissonant sound. **Música de campanas**, chimes. **Música celestial**, fine talk. **Música de fondo**, background. **Irse con la música a otra** parte, to take one's troubles elsewhere.

musical [moo-se-cahl'], *a.* Musical.

músico, ca [moo'-see-co, cah], *m. & f.* Musician, one skilled in harmony, harmonist; one who performs upon instruments of music.-*a.* Musical, harmonious, relating to music.

musicómano, na [moo-se-co'-mah-no, nah], *a.* Music-mad. *V.* MELÓMANO.

musitación [moo-se-tah-the-on'], *f.* Muttering, or whispering of a sick person, generally accompanying delirium.

musitar [moo-se-tar'], *vn.* To mumble, to mutter; also, to whisper.

muslera [moos-lay'-rah], *f.* Cuish, ancient armor for the thigh.

muslime [moos-lee'-may], *a.* Moslem.

muslímico, ca [moos-lee'-me-co, cah], *a.* Moslem, Mohammedan.

muslo [moos'-lo], *m.* 1. Thigh, which includes all between the buttocks and the knee. 2. Leg (pollo). 3. Drumstick.

musmón [moos-mone'], *m.* 1. Mouflon, a wild sheep with very large curved horns, native of Corsica and Sardinia, considered by some as the original type of the domestic sheep.

musquerola [moos-kay-ro'-lah], *f.* Muscadine pear.

mustelino, na [moos-tay-lee'-no, nah], *a.* Weasel-like.

mustelo [moos-tay'-lo], *m. (Zool.)* Fish without scales, having a hard rough skin, and of about five feet in length.

mustiamente [moos'-te-ah-men-tay], *adv.* In a sad and melancholic manner.

mustio, tia [moos'-te-o, ah], *a.* 1. Parched, withered; sad (triste), sorrowful. 2. *(Mex.)* Hypocritical.

musulmán [mo-sool-mahn'], *m.* Mussulman, Moslem, Muslim.

muta [moo'-tah], *f.* Pack of hounds.

mutabilidad [moo-tah-be-le-dahd'], *f.* Mutability, inconstancy, fickleness.

mutación [moo-tah-the-on'], *f.* 1. Mutation, change (cambio). *V.* MUDANZA. 2. A change of scene in a theater. 3. Unseasonable weather.

mutante [moo-tahn'-tay], *a. m & f.* Mutant.

mutila [moo-tee'-lah], *f.* Mutilla, a solitary ant.

mutilación [moo-te-lah-the-on'], *f.* Mutilation, maimedness.

mutilado [moo-te-lah'-do], *a.* Crippled, disabled. *-m & f.* Cripple, disabled person.

mutilar [moo-te-lar'], *va.* 1. To mutilate, to maim, to cripple (lisiar), to mangle. 2. *(Fig.)* To mutilate (texto); to deface (objeto, estatua).

mútilo, la [moo'-te-lo, lah], *a.* Maimed. *(Acad.)*

mutis [moo'-tees], *m.* A word used by theatrical prompters to signify that one or all of those in the scene are to go off. **¡Mutis!** *int.* Silence!

mutual [moo-too-ahl'], *a.* Mutual, reciprocal. *V.* MUTUO.

mutualidad [moo-too-ah-le-dahd'], *f.* 1. Mutuality (reciprocidad), state of being mutual. 2. *(Com.)* System of mutual insurance companies or societies (sociedad).

mutuamente [moo'-too-ah-men-tay], *adv.* Mutually, conversely, reciprocally.

mutuante [moo-too-ahn'-tay], *com.* Lender, loaner.

mutuo, tua [moo'-too-o, ah], *a.* Mutual, reciprocal, commutual.

mutuo [moo'-too-o], *m.* Loan.

muy [moo'-e], *adv.* Very; a particle which, being joined to a positive adjective, converts it into a superlative one; greatly, highly; too (demasiado). **Muy bueno**, very good. **Muy de noche**, very late at night. **Eso es muy de él**, that's just like him. **Es muy mujer**, she's very feminine.

muz [mooth], *m. (Naut.)* Extremity of the cutwater.

muzárabe [moo-thah'-rah-bay], *a. V.* MOZÁRABE.

muzo [moo'-tho], *m.* Wood of a tree of Columbia, veined black and red, much esteemed for handsome furniture.

my [me], *f.* Mu, twelfth letter of the Greek alphabet, corresponding to M.

mycin [me-theen]. *(Comput.)* Mycin. **Mycin vacía**, emycin (empty mycin).

N

n [ay'-nay], fourteenth letter of the alphabet, has the same pronunciation in Spanish as in the English language. 1. In maritime or geographical charts, *N* stands for north. 2. In medals and inscriptions, for Number or **Número.** 3. N (potencia). **Diez a la potencia n**, ten to the power of n. 4. X (fulano). **La condesa N**, Countess X.

naba [nah'-bah], *f (Bot.)* 1. Rutabaga, Swedish turnip. 2. The root of this plant.

nabal, nabar [nah-bahl', nah-bar'], *m.* Turnip field. *-a.* Belonging to turnips, made of turnips, pottage made of turnips.

nabería [nal-bay-ree'-ah], *f.* Turnip-pottage or heap of turnips.

nabillo [nah-beel'-lyo], *m. dim.* A small turnip.

nabina [nah-bee'-nah], *f.* Rape and turnip seed.

nabiza [nah-bee'-thah], *f. (Bot.)* 1. The lateral branches of the root of turnips. 2. The young shoots from the root or stem of turnips.

nabla [nah'-blah], *f.* Ancient instrument of music like a psaltery.

nabo, nabo común [nah'-bo], *m.* 1. *(Bot.)* Rape, turnip; the plant and the root. 2. Cylindrical timber, spindle, newel. 3. *(Naut.)* Mast.

naboria [nah-bo'-re-ah], *a. & n.* Free Indian who used to be employed in domestic service.

nácar [nah'-car], *m.* 1. Mother-of-pearl, nacre. 2. Pearl-color. *-a. (Amer.)* Scarlet.

nacarado, da [nah-cah-rah'-do, dah], *a.* Set with mother-of-pearl; of pearl color.

nacáreo, rea [nah-cah'-ray-o, ah], *a. V.* NACARINO.

nacarino, na [nah-cah-ree'-no, nah], *a.* Like nacre, nacreous.

nacarón [nah-cah-ron'], *m.* Large pearl shell of inferior quality.

nacencia [nah-then'-the-ah], *f. (LAm.)* 1. Birth. 2. Swelling, tumor, outgrowth.

nacer [nah-therr'], *vn.* 1. To be born, to come into the world. 2. To flower, to blossom (flores). 3. To hud, to shoot, to grow (plantas). 4. To rise, to appear on the horizon. 5. To take its rise, to have its beginning from. 6. To spring, to take its rise, to flow from (río). 7. To be reared in some habit. 8. To infer one thing from another. 9. To appear or start up all of a sudden 10. Followed by a preposition, it signifies natural propensity or destiny; as, **Nació para ser gran general**, he was born to be a great general. 11. To spring up (agua), to rise (estrella). **Nacer de pies**, to be born to good luck. **Haber nacido tarde**, to be deficient in experience or intelligence. **Nacer en tal día**, to escape from peril. **Entre ellos ha nacido una fuerte simpatía**, a strong friendship has sprung up between them. *-vr.* To be propagated by nature, not sown, as grass. *(Yo nazco, yo nazca, from Nacer. V.* CONOCER.)

nacido, da [nah-thee'-do, dah], *a.* Proper, apt, fit, connate. *-pp.* of NACER. **Nacido de padres ricos**, born of wealthy parents. **Recién nacido**, newborn.

nacido [nah-thee'-do], *m.* 1. A living man: generally used in the plural. 2. Pimple, pustule, tumor.

naciente [nah-the-en'-tay], *pa. & a.* 1. Growing (creciente), which grows or springs up; very recent (nuevo). 2. *(Her.)* Naissant. *-m.* 1. East (este). 2. *(Cono Sur)* Spring, source.

nacimiento [nah-the-me-en'-to], *m.* 1. Birth, nativity. 2. Growing of plants. 3. Beginning of a thing (origen). 4. Nativity, the place of birth. 5. Rising of the plants. 6. Nativity, the coming of our Lord into the world. 7. Origin, descent, lineage. 8. The origin or the physical or moral cause of a thing. **Nacimiento de un río**, head of a river. **De nacimiento**, from its birth.

nación [nah-the-on'], *f.* 1. *(coll.)* Birth, issue into life. 2. A nation. 3. *(coll.)* Foreigner. 4. *(Amer.)* A race, or tribe of Indians. **De nación**, native of.

nacional [nah-the-o-nahl'], *a.* National, gentile. **Vuelos nacionales**, domestic flights.

nacionalidad [nah-the-o-nah-le-dahd'], *f.* National manners and customs, nationality.

nacionalismo [nah-the-o-nah-lees'-mo], *m.* Patriotism, love of country.

nacionalista [nah-the-o-nah-lees'-tah], *a. m & f.* Nationalist.

nacionalización [nah-the-o-nah-le-thah-the-on'], *f.* Nationalization.

nacionalizar [nah-the-o-nah-le-thar'], *va., vn., & vr.* To nationalize, to become nationalized, to become a citizen (de un país).

nacionalmente [nah-thei-o-nahl'-men-tay], *adv.* Nationally.

nacionalsocialismo, Partido [nah-the-oh-nahl-so-the-ah-lees'-mo, par-tee'-do], *m.* Nazi party (National Socialist German Workers' Party).

nacrita [nah-cree'-tah], *f.* Variety of tale with a nacreous lustre.

nacho, cha [nah'-cho, chah], *a. V.* ROMO and CHATO.

nada [nah]-dah], *f.* Nothing, nothingness, naught; nonentity; little, or very little. **En menos de nada** or **en una nada**, in an instant. **Enfadarse por nada**, to be vexed by the most insignificant thing. **Más vale algo que nada**, *(Prov.)* half a loaf is better than no bread. **Nada de eso**, nothing of the kind. **Casi nada**, next to nothing. **No reparar en nada**, to stop at nothing. **Hace nada**, just a moment ago. **Por nada del mundo**, not for anything in the world. **No ha sido nada**, it's nothing.

nada [nah'-dah], *adv.* In no degree, by no means. **Nada menos**, nothing less: a particular negation.

nadaderas [nah-dah-day'-ras], *f. pl.* Corks or bladders used in learning to swim.

nadadero [nah-dah-day'-ro], *m.* Swimming-place.

nadador, ra [nah-dah-dor', rah], *m. & f.* Swimmer.

nadadora [nah-dah-do'-rah], *f.* Dragonfly.

nadante [nah-dahn'-tay], *pa.* 1. *(Poet.)* Natant, swimming. 2. *(Her.)* Naiant.

nadar [nah-dar'], *vn.* 1. To swim. 2. To float on the water, not to sink. 3. To be wide or loose. 4. *(Met.)* To abound, to be plentiful.

nadie [nah'-de-ay], *indef. prom.* Nobody, no-one, no one, none. **Apenas nadie**, hardly anybody. **No había nadie**, there was nobody. **A nadie se le ocurriría hacer tal cosa**, nobody would think of doing such a thing. **Nadie más**, nobody else. **No he hablado con nadie**, I haven't spoken to anyone.

nadir [nah-deer'], *m.* Nadir, the point opposite to the zenith.

nado (A) [nah'-do]. 1. Afloat. **Poner un bajel a nado**, to set a ship afloat. **Pasó el río a nado**, he swam across the river. 2. With difficulty and great toil. **Salir a nado**, to save oneself by swimming; to effect something with great difficulty and labor. **Echarse a nado**, to hazard, to undertake something boldly.

nafta [nahf'-tah], *f.* Naphtha, fluid bitumen; *(Cono Sur)* gasoline.

naftalina [naf-tah-lee'-nah], *f.* Naphthalene, a solid crystalline body obtained from coal-tar by distillation.

naguaclato, naguatate [nah-goo-ah-clah'-to], *m. (Mex.)* Interpreter.

naguas [nah'-goo-as], *f. pl.* Under-petticoat. *V.* ENAGUAS.

naife [nah'-ee-fay], *m.* A rough, unwrought diamond.

naipe [nah'-ee-pay], *m.* Playing card. **Naipes españoles**, Spanish playing cards.

naire [nah'-e-ray], *m.* Elephant-keeper.

nalga [nahl'-gah], *f.* Buttock, hip, rump.

nalgada [nal-gah'-dah], *f.* 1. Ham, the cured thigh of a hog. 2. Blow on the rump.

nalgado, da [nal-gah'-do, dah], *a.* Having round and fleshy posteriors.

nalgatorio [nal-gah-to'-re-o), *m. (coll.)* Seat, posteriors, nates.

nalguear [nal-gay-ar'], *vn.* To shake the posteriors in walking.

nalguilla [nal-geel'-lyah], *f.* The thick part of the hub of a wheel.

nana [nah'-nah], *f. (Mex. Coll.)* 1. A child's nurse. 2. A slumber song.

nancito [nan-thee'-to], *m.* A yellow berry of Nicaragua.

nandú [nan-doo'], *m.* The American ostrich.

nanquín [nan-keen'], *m.* Nankeen. *V.* MAHÓN.

nansa [nahn'-sah], *f.* Fish-pond.

nao [nah'-o], *f.* Ship, vessel. *V.* NAVE.

naonato, ta [nah-o-nah'-to, tah], *a.* Born on board ship.

napa [nah'-pah], *f.* 1. A cord for drawing in the tuna-nets. 2. *(Low.)* Backside.

napea [nah-pay'-ah], *f.* Wood-nymph.

napelo [nah-pay'-lo], *m. (Bot.)* Monk's-hood, wolf's-bane.

napia [nah'-pe-ah], *f.* Snout, nose.

napoleón [nah-po-lay-on'], *m.* A French silver five-franc piece.

Nápoles [nah'-po-lays], Naples.

napolitano, na [nah-po-le-tah'-no, nah], *a.* Neapolitan, relating to Naples.

naque [nah'-kay], *m.* Ancient company of two comedians.

naranja [nah-rahn'-hah], *f.* 1. Orange, the fruit of the orange-tree. **Media naranja**, *(Arch.)* cupola. 2. A cannon-ball of the size of an orange. *-a.* Orange.

naranjada [nah-ran-hah'-dah], *f.* 1. Conserve of oranges. 2. Orange-water, orangeade. 3. A rude saying or deed.

naranjado, da [nah-ran-hah'-do, dah], *a.* Orange-colored.

naranjal [nah-ran-hahl'], *m.* Orangery, grove or plantation of orange trees.

naranjazo [nah-ran-hah'-tho], *m.* Blow with an orange.

naranjero, ra [nah-ran-hay'-ro, rah], *m. & f.* 1. One who sells oranges. 2. *(Prov.)* Orange-tree.

naranjero, ra [nah-ran-hay'-ro, rah], *a.* 1. Applied to pieces of artillery which carry balls of the size of oranges. 2. Applied to a blunderbuss with a mouth of the size of an orange.

naranjilla [nah-ran-heel'-lyah], *f.* Small green orange used in making a conserve.

naranjo [nah-rahn'-ho], *m. (Bot.)* 1. Orange-tree. 2. *(coll.)* A booby, a noodle, an ignorant fellow.

narciso [nar-thee'-so], *m.* 1. *(Bot.)* Daffodil. **Narciso poético**, poet's narcissus. 2. Narcissus flower. 3. A precious stone of the color of daffodil. 4. Fop, coxcomb.

narcosis [nar-co'-sis], *f.* 1. Narcosis. 2. Narcotization.

narcótico, ca [nar-co'-te-co, cah], *a.* Narcotic, narcotical, producing stupor.

narcotina [nar-co-tee'-nah], *f.* Narcotine, an inodorous, insipid alkaloid of opium.

narcotismo [nar-co-tees'-mo], *m.* Narcotism, a state of stupor produced by narcotics.

narcotráfico [nar-co-trah'-fe-co], *m.* Drugs traffic.

nardino [nar-dee'-no], *a.* Made of spikenard.

nardo [nar'-do], *m. (Bot.)* Spikenard, nard, a plant of India, bulbous-rooted; and the ointment or confection prepared from it.

narguile [nar-gee'-lay], *m.* Narghile, hookah, an oriental pipe for smoking tobacco in which the smoke passes through perfumed water.

narigón [nah-re-gone'], *m. aug.* A large nose, a large-nosed person.

narigón, na, narigudo, da [nah-re-gone', nah], *a.* Having a large and long nose.

narigueta, nariguita [nah-re-gay'-tah, nah-re-gee'-tah], *f. dim.* A small nose.

nariz [nah-reeth'], *f.* 1. The nose. 2. The nostril. **Nariz chata**, flat or pugnose. **Dar en las narices**, *(coll.)* to smell or perceive a thing at a distance. *(Met.)* To find out what another person is about. **Meter la nariz en todas partes**, to be a busybody. **En mis propias narices**, under my very nose. **Tocarse las narices**, to be idle. 3. Sense of smell (olfato). 4. The projecting point of a bridge or pier which breaks the violence of the current. 5. The tubs or pipe of an alembic or other similar thing. 6. *(Naut.)* Cut-water, break of a ship's head. **Narices or ventanas de la nariz**, nostrils. **Hinchar las narices**, to be excessively irritated. **No ver (uno) más allá de sus narices**, not to see beyond one's nose, to be half-witted.

narizado, da [nah-re-thah'-do, dah], *a.* Having a large nose.

narra [nar'-rah], *f.* A tree of the Philippines whose wood is employed in boat-building; it tinges water a blue color and exhales an agreeable smell.

narración [nar-rah-the-on'], *f.* Narration, account, relation, legend.

narrador [nar-rah-dor'], *a.* Narrator. Also used as a noun.

narrar [nar-rar'], *va.* To narrate, to relate, to recite, to tell.

narrativa [nar-rah-tee'-vah], *f.* 1. Narrative (narración), relation, history, account. 2. Art or talent of relating things past (arte, talento).

narrativo, va, narratorio, ria [nar-rah-tee'-vo, vah], *a.* Narrative, narratory.

narria [nar'-re-ah], *f.* 1. Sledge, a carriage without wheels. 2. A fat, heavy, bulky woman.

narval [nar-vahl'], *m. (Zool.)* Narwhal, sea-unicorn.

nasa [nah'-sah], *f.* 1. Fyke, a fish-trap (trampa) (used in the Mediterranean) with a conical mouth; a bag-net. 2. Round, narrow-mouthed net; bow-net. 3. A wicker basket for holding fish (cesta); a kipe (provincial name). 4. *(Acad.)* Basket or jar for keeping bread, flour or such things.

nasal [nah-sahl'], *a.* Nasal, relating to the nose.

nasardo [nah-sar'-do], *m.* Nasard, one of the registers of an organ.

nasturcio [nas-toor'-the-o], *m.* (*Bot.*) Nasturtium.

nata [nah'-tah], *f.* 1. Cream. **Nata batida**, whipped cream. 2. The most esteemed or principal part of a thing; the cream. 3. *pl.* Whipped cream with sugar. 4. *V.* NATILLA.

natación [nah-tah-the-on'], *f.* 1. The art of swimming. 2. The act of swimming. **Natación a braza**, breaststroke. **Natación submarina**, underwater swimming.

natal [nah-tahl'], *a.* Natal, native.-*m.* Birth, birthday.

natalicio, cia [nah-tah-lee'-the-o, ah], *a. & m. & f.* Natal; nativity, birthday.

natalidad [nah-tah-le-dahd'], *f.* Birth rate.

natatorio, a [nah-tah-to'-re-o, ah], *a.* Natatory, relating to swimming.

naterón [nah-tay-rone'], *m.* Second curds after the first cheese is made. *V.* REQUESÓN.

natillas [nah-tee'-lyas], *f. pl.* Custard, a composition of milk, eggs, and sugar boiled together; it may be thickened with flour or starch, making a batter.

natío [nah-tee'-o], *m.* (*Prov.*) Birth; sprouting: used of plants. - *a.* Native.

natividad [nah-te-ve-dahd'], *f.* Nativity.

nativo, va [nah-tee'-vo, vah], *a.* 1. Native (país), produced by nature, natal; not artificial. 2. Fit, proper, apt. 3. Vernacular.

nato [nah'-to]. *a.* 1. Born. **Un actor nato**, a born actor. **Un criminal nato**, a hardened criminal. 2. Ex officio (por derecho).

natrón [nah-trone'], *m.* 1. Natron, native carbonate of soda. 2. A saline substance which separates from crucibles in glass-works.

natura [nah-too'-rah], *f.* 1. (*Ant.*) Nature. 2. The genital parts. 3. In music, a major scale.

natural [nah-too-rahl'], *m.* 1. Temper, genius, natural disposition (temperamento). 2. Instinct of brutes. 3. Native of a place or country.-*a.* 1. Natural, according to nature. 2. Natural, native, not artificial. 3. Native, pertaining to the place of birth. 4. Common, usual, regular, resembling nature. 5. Natural, ingenuous, without art or craft, unaffected. 6. Natural, not performed by industry or art. 7. Natural, that which imitates nature, and treats of her secrets and operations. 8. Natural, produced by the sole power of nature. **Al natural**, without art or affectation. **Buen natural**, good nature. **Fruta al natural**, fruit in its own juice. **Está muy guapa al natural**, she is very pretty just as she is.

naturaleza [nah-too-rah-lay'-thah], *f.* 1. Nature, aggregate, order, and disposition of all created beings; often personified. 2. Nature, the native state or property of things. 3. Nature, constitution of an animated body; complexion, constitution. 4. Nature, the property, virtue, or quality of things. 5. Nature, the regular course of things, the quality, order, and disposition of affairs. 6. Nature, instinct, property, or inclination. 7. Sex, genitals, especially the female. 8. Species, kind. 9. The state of a native with respect to the place where he was born. 10. Naturalization. 11. Nature, genius, temperament. **El joven es suizo de naturaleza**, the young man is Swiss by nationality.

naturalidad [nah-too-rah-le-dahd'], *f.* 1. State of being born in a certain place or country; birthright. 2. Naturalness, conformity to nature and truth. Ingenuity, candor. **Con la mayor naturalidad**, as if nothing had happened.

naturalismo [nah-too-rah-lees'-mo], *m.* 1. Naturalism, mere state of nature. 2. Realism, in a literary and artistic sense, strict copying of nature, without concealing its deformities.

naturalista [nah-too-rah-lees'-tah], *m.* Naturalist, one versed in the knowledge of nature, or natural philosophy, more especially of natural history.

naturalización [nah-too-rah-le-thah-the-on'], *f.* Naturalization, the act of investing aliens with the rights of native subjects.

naturalizar [nah-too-rah-le-thar'], *va.* To naturalize, to invest with the rights of native subjects.-*vr.* To be accustomed, to grow fit for any purpose.

naturalmente [nah-too-rahl'-men-tay], *adv.* Naturally (de modo natural), natively, by nature; humanly; plainly, without fiction, ingenuously, frankly.

naufragar [nah-oo-frah-gar'], *vn.* 1. To be stranded or shipwrecked (persona), to suffer shipwreck (barco). 2. To suffer wreck or ruin in one's affairs, to fail in one's purposes.

naufragio [nah-oo-frah'-he-o], *m.* 1. Shipwreck. 2. Miscarriage, disappointment, calamity, heavy loss.

náufrago, ga [nah'-oo-frah-go, gah], *a.* Relating to shipwreck, wrecked.

naumaquia [nah-oo-mah'-ke-ah], *f.* Naumachy, a mock seafight.

náusea [nah'-oo-say-ah], *f.* Nauseousness, squeamishness, nausea, disposition to vomit. (Most used in the plural.) **Tener náuseas**, to feel nauseated.

nauseabundo [nah-oo-say-ah-boon'-do], *a.* Nauseous, loathsome, exciting nausea.

nausear [nah-oo-say-ar'], *vn.* To nauseate, to loathe, to become squeamish: to suffer nausea.

nauseativo, va [nah-oo-say-ah-tee'-vo, vah], *a.* Nauseous.

nauseoso, sa [nah-oo-say-o'-so, sah], *a. V.* NAUSEABUNDO.

nauta [nah'-oo-tah], *m.* Mariner, a seafaring man.

náutica [nah'-oo-te-cah], *f.* Navigation, the art of conducting ships over the ocean.

náutico, ca [nah'-oo-te-co, cah], *a.* Nautical.

nautilo [nah-oo-tee'-lo], *m.* Nautilus, a cephalopod mollusk.

nava [nah'-vah], *f.* A plain or level piece of ground.

navaja [nah-vah'-hah], *f.* 1. Clasp knife (cuchillo), folding-knife. 2. Razor. 3. Tusk of a wild boar. 4. Tongue of backbites. **Navaja de muelle**, flick knife.

navajada [nah-vah-hah'-dah], *f.* A thrust or gash with a knife.

navajazo [nah-vah-hah'-tho], *m. V.* NAVAJADA.

navajero [nah-vah-hay'-ro], *m.* 1. Razor-case. 2. A piece of linen on which a barber cleans his razor. 3. Criminal who carries a knife.

navajita [nah-vah-hee'-tah], *f. dim.* A small clasp-knife.

navajo [nah-vah'-ho], *m. V.* NAVAZO.

navajón [nah-vah-hone'], *m. aug.* A large knife.

navajonazo [nah-vah-ho-nah'-tho], *m.* Gash or wound made with a large knife.

naval [nah-vahl'], *a.* Naval, consisting of ships; belonging to ships. **Armada naval**, royal navy, royal fleet.

navarro, rra [nah-var'-ro, rah], *a.* Belonging to or native of Navarre.

navazo [nah-vah'-tho], *m.* 1. Kitchen-garden in Sanlúcar upon a sandy shore. 2. Level piece of ground where the rains make a pool.

nave [nah'-vay], *f.* 1. Ship, a vessel with decks and sails. 2. Nave, the middle part or body of a church. 3. (*Mex.*) Car (coche). **Nave de San Pedro**, the Roman Catholic church. **Nave espacial**, spacecraft, space ship.

navecilla [nah-ve-theel'-yah], *f.* A vessel for incense.

navegable [nah-vay-gah, blay], *a.* Navigable (río), seaworthy (barco).

navegación [nah-vay-gah-the-on'], *f.* 1. Navigation, the act or practice of passing by water. 2. Passage, time which a ship takes in going from one place to another (barcos). 3. Navigation, art of navigating.

navegador, ra [nah-vay-gah-dor', rah], *a.* Navigating. -*m.* Navigator.

navegante [nah-vay-gahn'-tay], *pa. & m.* Navigator; navigating.

navegar [nah-vay-gar'], *vn.* 1. To navigate, to sail (barco), to pass by water. 2. To go from place to place for the purpose of trade. 3. (*Ant.*) To carry wares by sea from one part to another for trade.-*va.* To sail, to go, to travel (e. g. ten knots per hour).

naveta [nah-vay'-tah], *f.* 1. Vessel for incense in the church. 2. Small drawer.

navichuelo, la [nah-ve-choo-ay'-lo, lah], *m. & f. (Naut.)* A small vessel.

navicular [nah-ve-coo-lar'], *a.* Applied to the middle bone of the foot; the scaphoid.

navidad [nah-ve-dahd'], *f.* 1. Nativity. 2. Christmas day. **Por Navidades**, at Christmas.

navideño, ña [nah-ve-day'-nyo, nyah], *a.* Belonging to the time of nativity.

naviero, ra [nah-ve-ay'-ro, rah], *a.* Shipping. **Empresa naviera**, steamship concern.

navío [nah-vee'-o], *m.* A ship, especially a large ship, or a ship-of-war. **Navío de guerra**, a ship of war, a man of war. **Navío de línea or de alto bordo**, ship of the line. **Navío mercante**, merchant ship. **Navío de transporte**, transport. **Navío guardacosta**, guard-ship. **Navío de carga**, ship of burden. **Navío pesado**, a bad sailor.

náyade [nah'-yah-day], *f.* Naïad, water-nymph.

naylón [nah'-e-lone], *m.* Nylon.

nazareno, na [nah-thah-ray'-no, nah], *a.* 1. Nazarene, native of Nazareth. 2. Nazarite, one who neither shaved the beard, cut the hair, nor drank strong drink. *-m.* He who goes in processions in Passion Week, dressed in a long brown robe.

nazareo, ea [nah-thah-ray'-o, ah], *a.* Nazarite, among the Jews.

nazi [nah'-the], *m. & f. & a.* Nazi. **Partido Nazi**, Nazi Party. V. NACIONALSOCIALISMO, PARTIDO

nazismo [nah-thees'-mo], *m.* Nazism.

nébeda [nay'-bah-dah], *f.* Catmint, an aromatic herb.

nebladura [nay-blah-doo'-rah], *f.* Damage which crops receive from mist.

neblí [nay-blee'], *m. (Zool.)* Falcon gentle.

neblina [nay-blee'-nah], *f.* 1. Mist, small rain. 2. Confusion, obscurity.

nebrina [nay-bree'-nah], *f.* Juniper-berry.

nebuloso, sa [nay-boo-lo'-so, sah], *a.* Misty (aire), cloudy (cielo), nebulous, foggy, hazy.

necear [nay-thay-ar'], *vn.* To talk nonsense, to play the fool.

necedad [nay-thay-dahd'], *f.* Gross ignorance, stupidity; imprudence; foolishness (cualidad), folly, foppery, idiocy.

necesaria [nay-thay-sah'-re-ah], *f.* Privy, necessary, water-closet.

necesariamente [may-thay-sah'-re-ah-men-tay], *adv.* Necessarily, indispensably, consequently, needfully.

necesario, ria [nay-thay-sah'-re-o, ah], *a.* Necessary, requisite, needful. **Si fuere necesario**, if need be. **Lo necesario**, what is needful.

neceser [nay-thay-serr'], *m.* A case of necessary articles, as for the dressing-table. **Neceser de costura**, work-box, sewing box. **Bolsa de aseo**, toilet case. **Neceser de afeitar**, shaving kit.

necesidad [nay-they-se-dahd'], *f.* Necessity (apuro), need (miseria), want; cogency, extremity, constraint. **La necesidad carece de ley**, necessity has no law. **Esto es de primera necesidad**, this is absolutely essential. **Encontrarse en una necesidad**, to be in a difficult situation. **Pasar necesidades**, to suffer hardships.

necesitado, da [nay-thay-se-tah'-do, dah], *a.* Necessitous, poor, needy.-*pp.* of NECESITAR.

necesitado, da [nay-thay-se-tah'-do, dah], *m. & f.* A poor person, a needy man or woman.

necesitar [nay-they-se-tar'], *va.* To necessitate, to constrain, to compel. **Necesitamos 2 más**, we need 2 more. *-vn.* To want, to need, to lack. *-vr.* To be needed, to be wanted.

neciamente [nay'-the-ah-men-tay], *adv.* Ignorantly, stupidly, foolishly.

necio, cia [nay'-the-o, ah], *a.* 1. Ignorant, stupid, idiotic foolish (tonto). 2. Imprudent, injudicious. 3. *(And.)* Peevish (displicente). 4. *(And. Carib. Cono Sur)* Touchy, hypersensitive (quisquilloso). 5. *(CAm.)* Stubborn (enfermedad). *-m. & f.* Fool.

nécora [nay'-co-rah], *f.* Small crab.

necróforo [nay-cro'-fo-ro], *m.* Necrophorus, the sexton or burying beetle, noted for its keenness of smell.

necrolatría [nay-cro-lah-tree'-ah], *f.* Worship of the dead.

necrología [nay-cro-lo-hee'-ah], *f.* Necrology, a register of persons deceased.

necrológico, ca [nay-cro-lo'-he-co, cak], *a.* Necrological, belonging to necrology.

necrologio [nay-cro-lo'-he-o], *m.* Necrology, mortuary, register of bishops.

necrópolis [nay-cro'-po-les], *f.* Necropolis.

necropsia, or **necroscopia** [nay-crop'-se-ah], *f.* Necrosis, autopsy, post-mortem examination.

necrosis [nay-cro'-sis], *f.* Necrosis, mortification of the bones.

nectar [nec'-tar], *m.* 1. Nectar, the supposed drink of the gods. 2. Any very pleasant drink. 3. Nectar, the honey of plants.

nectáreo, rea [nec-tah'-ray-o, ah], *a.* Nectareal, noctarean, sweet as nectar.

nectarífero, ra [nec-tah-ree'-fay-ro, rah], *a.* Nectar-bealing.

nectarino, na [nec-tah-ree'-no, nah], *a.* V. NECTÁREO.

nectario [nec-tah'-re-o], *m. (Bot.)* Nectary, the part of a plant which secretes nectar or honey.

neerlandés, sa [nay-er-lan-days', sah], *a.* Netherlandish, Flemish, Dutch.

nefandamente [nay-fahn'-dah-men-tay], *adv.* Basely, nefariously, abominably.

nefando, da [nay-fahn'-do, dah], *a.* Base, nefarious, abominable, heinous.

nefario, ria [nay-fah'-re-o, ah], *a.* Nefarious, abominable, extremely wicked.

nefas [nay'-fas], *adv.* **Por fas o por nefas**, right or wrong.

nefasto [nay-fahs'-to], *a.* Pernicious (influencia); harmful; unlucky (viaje), ill-fated; *(LAm.)* Dreadful (atroz).

nefrítico, ca [nay-free'-te-co, cah], *a.* 1. Nephritic, belonging to the kidneys; troubled with the gravel. 2. Applied to a kind of jasper.

nefritis [nay-free'-tis], *f. (Med.)* Nephritis, Bright's disease.

negable [nay-gah'-blay], *a.* That which may be denied.

negación [nay-gah-the-on'], *f.* 1. Negation, the act of denying, denial (negativa). 2. Want or total privation of anything. 3. Negative particle.

negado, da [nay-gah'-do, dah], *a.* Incapable, inapt, unfit. *-pp.* of NEGAR.

negador, ra [nay-gah-dor', rah], *m. & f.* Denier, disclaimer.

negar [nay-gar'], *va.* 1. To deny (hecho, verdad), to contradict. 2. To deny, to refuse, not to grant, to gainsay. 3. To forbid, to prohibit, to hinder, to oppose. 4. To deny, to contradict an accusation (acusación). 5. To deny, to disown, to disclaim (relación, responsabilidad). 6. To deny, to disregard, to forget what one has previously held in esteem, to withdraw from a company frequented before. 7. To hide, to conceal. 8. To dissemble. 9. To refuse to acknowledge the obligations a person has contracted. **Negar la mano a uno**, to refuse to shake hands with somebody. *-vr.* 1. To decline doing something. 2. To desire to be denied to persons who call to see one. **Negarse con la cabeza**, to shake one's head. **Negarse a una visita**, to refuse to see a visitor. *(Yo niego, yo niegue, from Negar.* V. ACERTAR.)

negativa [nay-gah-tee'-vah], *f.* Negation; repulse; negative, refusal. **Negativa rotunda**, flat refusal.

negativamente [nay-gah-tee'-vah-men-tay], *adv.* Negatively.

negativo, va [nay-gah-tee'-vo, vah], *a.* Negative, implying negation or denial, negatory.-*f.* Negative, a developed photographic plate or film, showing reversed lights and shadows.

negligencia [nay-gle-gen'-the-ah], *f.* Negligence, neglect, heedlessness, forgetfulness, habit of acting carelessly.

negligente [nay-gle-hen'-tay], *a.* Negligent, careless, heedless, absent, thoughtless, listless.

negligentemente [nay-gle-hen'-tay-men-tay], *adv.* Negligently, neglectfully, giddily, loosely, listlessly, heedlessly.

negociabilidad [nay-go-the-ah-be-le-dahd'], *f. (Neol. Com.)* Negotiability, particularly of bills of exchange.

negociable [nay-go-the-ah'-blay], *a.* Negotiable.

negociación [nay-go-the-ah-the-on'], *f.* Negotiation, management; commerce. **Negociación colectiva**, collective bargaining.

negociado [nay-go-the-ah'-do], *m.* 1. Each separate division or section in the official departments (sección). 2. *V.* NEGOCIO. 3. *(Cono Sur)* Shop, store. 4. *(And. Cono Sur)* Illegal transaction. *-pp.* of NEGOCIAR.

negociador [nay-go-the-ah-dor'], *m.* 1. A man of business. 2. Negotiator, one employed to deal with others.

negociante [nay-go-the-ahn'-tay], *pa. & m.* Trader, dealer; negotiating, trading.

negociar [nay-go-the-ar'], *vn.* 1. To trade, to buy and sell goods. 2. To negotiate bills of exchange; to negotiate political affairs.

negocio [nay-go'-the-o], *m.* 1. Occupation, employment, management, business (empresa). 2. Affair (asunto), pretension, treaty, agency, concern. 3. Negotiation, trade, commerce. 4. *(And. Cono Sur)* Firm (firma), company. 5. *(And, Carib.)* **El negocio**, the fact. 6. *(And.)* Tale, piece of gossip. **Fingir negocios**, to affect the man of business. 4. Utility or interest in trading. **Eso es negocio tuyo**, that's your affair. **El negocio del espectáculo**, show business. **Buen negocio**, profitable deal. *-pl.* Business, commercial transactions. **El mundo de los negocios**, the business world.

negocioso, sa [nay-go-the-o'-so, sah], *a.* Diligent, prompt, careful.

negozuelo [nay-go-thoo-ay'-lo], *m. dim.* Any insignificant affair or business.

negra [nay'-grah], *f.* 1. A foil for fencing. 2. Negress, black woman. 3. Black piece (ajedrez). 4. *(CAm.)* Black mark. 5. Bad luck (mala suerte). **Tener la negra**, to be out of luck.

negrada [negrah'-dah], *f.* Black slaves (conjunto de negros).

negrear [nay-gray-ar'], *vn.* To grow black, to appear black (volverse negro).

negrecer [nay-gray-therr'], *vn.* To blacken, to become black. *(Yo negrezco, yo negrezca*, from *Negrecer. V.* CONOCER.)

negrero [nay-gray'-ro], *m.* 1. Trafficker in slaves. **Negrero** or **barco negrero**, a slaver. 2. *(Cuba)* The white man who is fond of Negresses.

negreta [nay-gray'-tah], *f. (Orn.)* Coot, a kind of duck of a blackish color.

negrilla [nay-greel'-lyah], *f.* 1. *(typ.)* Boldface type. 2. *(Zool.)* Conner eel.

negrillera [nay-gril-lyay'-rah], *f.* Plantation of black poplar.

negrillo [nay-greel'-lyo], *m.* 1. *(dim.)* A young Negro. 2. Black silver ore, stephanite. 3. *(Bot.) V.* OLMO.

negrito, ta [nay-gree'-to, tah], *a. (Mox.) V.* NEGRO, 6th def. *-f. (Tip.)* Bold face. **En negrita**, in bold type.

negro, gra [nay'-gro, grah], *a.* 1. Black, dark. **Un coche negro**, a black car. 2. Brown or gray; not well bleached. 3. Blackish; of a dark-brown color (oscuro). 4. Gloomy, black (estado, humor), dismal, melancholy. 5. Unfortunate, wretched. 6. *(Coll. Amer.)* An endearing expression, equivalent to my dove, my dear. 7. Cross, peeved (enfadado). **Más negro que el azabache**, as black as ink. **La cosa se pone negra**, it's not going well. **Estoy negro con esto**, I'm getting desperate about it.

negro, gra, *m. & f.* Negro, a blackamoor; Negress. **Negro de humo**, lamp-black. **Negro de plomo**, ochre-black. **Negro de carbón**, blue-black. 2. *(Met.* The least of anything). 3. *(Carib.)* Black coffee.

negrura [nay-groo'-rah], *f.* Blackness.

negruzco, ca [nay-grooth'-co, cah], *a.* Blackish, nigrescent, dark brown.

neguijón [nay-gee-hone'], *m.* Caries, rottenness of the teeth.

neguilla [nay-geel'-lyah], *f.* 1. *(Bot.)* Fennel-flower, love-in-a-mist. 2. Obstinate denial.

nema [nay'-mah], *f.* Seal or sealing of a letter.

nematócero, ra [nay-mah-to'-thay-ro, rah], *a.* Nematocerous, nemocerous, of thread-like antennae.

nemeo, mea [nay-may'-o, ah], *a.* Nemaean: applied to some ancient games.

némine discrepante [nay'-me-nay dis-cray-pahn'-tay], *(Lat.)* Unanimously: no one dissenting.

nemoroso, sa [nay-mo-ro'-so, sah], *a.* Woody, nemorous, consisting of wood; relating to wood.

nene, nena [nay'-nay, nay'-nah], *m. & f. (coll.)* An infant, a baby.

nenúfar [nay-noo'-far], *m. (Bot.)* White water-lily.

neoclasicismo [nay-o-clah-se-thees'-mo], *m.* Neoclassicism.

neoclásico [nay-o-clah'-se-co], *a.* Neoclassical.

neofascismo [nay-o-fas-thees'-mo], *m.* Neofascism.

neofascista [nay-o-fas-thees'-tah], *a. m & f.* Neofascist.

neófito [nay-o'-fe-to], *m.* 1. Neophyte, one regenerated; a convert. 2. Novice, beginner.

neografía [nay-o-grah-fee'-ah], *f.* Neography, a new system of writing.

neografismo [nay-o-grah-fees'-mo], *m.* Neography, new method of writing; contrary to the received custom.

neógrafo, fa [nay-o'-grah-fo, fah], *a.* Applied to one who uses a new and peculiar mode of writing.

neolatino, na [nay-o-lah-tee'-no, nah], *a.* Neo-Latin, Romanic: used of the languages derived from Latin.

neología [nay-o-lo-hee'-ah], *f.* Neology, introduction or use of new words and phrases.

neológico, ca [nay-o-lo'-he-co, cah], *a.* Neological, employing new words and phrases.

neologismo [nay-o-lo-hees'-mo], *m.* Neologism, a new and yet unsanctioned expression.

neólogo [nay-o'-lo-go], *m.* Neologist, a coiner of words.

neomenia [nay-o-may'-ne-ah], *f.* Neomenina, first day of new moon.

neón [nay-on'], *m. & a.* Neon. **Luces de Neón**, neon lights.

neoplasma [nay-o-plahs'-mah], *m. (Med.)* Neoplasm, a new growth due to morbid action.

neorama [nay-o-rah'-mah], *m.* Panorama upon a cylindrical surface, the observer being placed at the center.

neoyorquino, na [nay-o-yor-kee'-no, nah], *a.* From New York. *-m. & f.* New Yorker.

nepente [nay-pen'-tay], *m.* Nepenthe, a drug supposed to drive away all pain.

nepote [nay-po'-tay], *m. V.* SOBRINO. A privileged relative of the Pope.

nepotismo [nay-po-tees'-mo], *m.* Nepotism; favoritism exercised towards nephews or other relatives.

Neptuno [nep-too'-no], *m.* 1. The planet Neptune. 2. *(Poet.)* The sea.

nequicia [nay-kee'-the-ah], *f.* Perversity.

nereida [nay-ray'-e-dah], *f.* Nereid, a sea-nymph.

nervado, da [ner-vah'-do, dah], *a. (Bot.)* Nervate, nerved.

nervadura [ner-vah-doo-rah], *f.* Nervation or nervature of leaves; arrangement of nerves.

nervino, na [ner-vee'-no, nah], *a.* Calming and fortifying the nerves; nervine.

nervio [nerr'-ve-o], *m.* 1. A nerve. 2. The main and most powerful part of anything. 3. String of a musical instrument. 4. *(Naut.)* A small rope, the middle of which is fixed to a stay. 5. Nerve, energy, vigor (vigor); moral fiber (moral). 6. In botany, the perfect and unbranched vessels extending from the base towards the tip; nerve. 7. Tendon, or aponeurosis. 8. *(Anat.)* Tendon (tendón). 9. *(Fig.)* Soul, leading light (persona). **Crispar los nervios a uno**, to get on somebody's nerves. **Tener nervios de acero**, to have nerves of steel. **Un hombre sin nervio**, a weak man.

nerviosidad [ner-ve-o-se-dahd'], *f. V.* NERVOSIDAD.

nervioso, sa [ner-ve-o'-so, sah], *a.* 1. Nervous, relating to the nerves. 2. Nervous (estado temporal), vigorous (palabra, frase). 3. *(Bot.)* Nerved. **Sistema nervioso**, nervous system. **Poner nervioso a uno**, to make somebody nervous.

nervosamente [ner-vo-sah-men-tay], *adv.* Nervously.

nervosidad [ner-vor-se-dahd'], *f.* 1. Strength, nervousness. 2. Efficacy, vigor. 3. Flexibility.

nervoso, sa [ner-vo'-so, sah], *a.* 1 Nervous, relating to the nerves. 2 Nervous, strong, vigorous, robust.

nervudo, da [ner-voo'-do, dah], *a.* Nervous, well strung, strong, vigorous.

nesciencia [nes-the-en'-the-ah], *f.* Ignorance, nescience, want of knowledge.

nesciente [nes-the-en'-tay], *a.* Ignorant, foolish.

nesga [nes'-gah]. *f.* Gore, a triangular piece of linen or stuff sewn upon cloth.

nestorianismo [nes-to-re-ah-nees'-mo], *m.* Nestorianism, a heresy of the fifth century.

nestoriano [nes-to-re-ah'-no], *m.* Nestorian, one of the followers of Nestorius.

netezuelo, la [nay-tay-thoo-ay'-lo, lah], *m. & f. dim.* A little grandchild.

neto, ta [nay'-to, tah], *a.* Neat, pure, clean (puro), unadulterated; net, clear, genuine; without foreign mixture. **Producto neto**, net produce. **En neto**, purely. **Peso neto**, net weight.

neto [nay'-to], *m. (Arch.)* Naked pedestal of a column.

neuma [nay-oo'-mah], *m.* Expression by signs of what one wishes or thinks.

neumático, ca [nay-mah'-te-co, cah], *a.* Pneumatic, **Perforación neumática**, Pneumatic drilling.-*m.* Automobile tire. **Neumático de repuesto**, spare tire.

neumococo [nay-oo-mo-co'-co], *m.* Pneumococcus.

neumonía [nay-oo-mo-nee'-ah], *f.* Pneumonia, lung fever, inflammation of the lungs.

neumónico, ca [nay-oo-mo'-ne-co, cah], *a.* Pneumonic, relating to the lungs, or to pneumonia.

neuralgia [nay-oo-rahl'-he-ah], *f.* Neuralgia, pain along a nerve, without fever.

neurálgico, ca [nay-oo-rahl'-he-co, cah], *a.* Neuralgic, relating to neuralgia.

neurastenia [nay-oo-ras-tay'-ne-ah], *f. (Med.)* Neurasthenia.

neurasténico, ca [nay-oo-ras-tay'-ne-co, cah], *a.* Neurasthenic, suffering from nervous exhaustion. *(Neol.)*

neurítico, ca [nay-oo-ree'-te-co, cah], *a. (Med.)* Neurotic. -*pl.* Neurotica: applied to medicines supposed to strengthen the nerves.

neuritis [nay-oo-ree'-tis],. *(Med.)* Neuritis.

neurocirugía [nay-oo-ro-the-roo-he'-ah], *f.* Neurosurgery.

neurología [nay-oo-ro-lo-hee'-ah], *f.* Neurology, a description of the nerves.

neurólogo, ga [nay-oo-ro'-lo-go], *m & f.* Neurologist.

neuroma [nay-oo-ro'-mah], *m.* Neuroma, a tumor of a nerve.

neurona [nay-oo-ro'-nah], *f. (Anat.)* Neuron, neurone.

neuropatía [nay-oo-ro-pah-tee'-ah], *f.* A nervous disorder; neuropathy.

neuróptero, ra [nay-oo-rop'-tay-ro, rah], *a.* Neuropterous.

neurosis [nay-oo-ro'-sis], *f.* Neurosis, functional nervous disease.

neurotomía [nay-oo-ro-to-mee'-ah], *f. (Med.)* 1. Neurotomy, dissection of nerves. 2. Section or division of a nerve.

neutral [nay-oo-trahl'], *a.* Neutral, neuter, indifferent; it has been used.

neutralidad [nay-oo-trah-le-dahd'], *f.* Neutrality.

neutrino [nay-oo-tree'-no], *m. (Phy. & Chem.)* Neutrino, as a substantive, especially in the plural.

neutralidad [nay-oo-trah-le-dahd'], *f.* 1. Neutrality, a state of indifference. 2. Neutrality, state of peace with belligerent nations.

neutralizar [nay-oo-trah-le-thar'], *va. (Chem.)* To neutralize.

neutralmente [nay-oo-trahl'-men-tay], *adv.* Neutrally, indifferently.

neutro, tra [nay'-oo-tro, trah], *a.* 1. Neutral, neuter, not engaged on either side. 2. *(Gram.)* Neuter, a noun that implies

no sex; a verb that is neither active nor passive, intransitive. **Verbo neutro**, intransitive verb.

neutrón [nay-oo-trone], *m. (Phy. & Chem.)* Neutron.

nevada [nay-vah'-dah], *f.* 1. Snowfall, descent of snow. 2. Snowfall, the quantity of snow which falls at one time, a heavy fall of snow. 3. *(Bot.)* V. NEVADILLA.

nevadilla [nay-vah-deel'-lyah], *f. (Bot.)* Whitlow-wort, any species of Paronychia with dry silvery stippler and clustered flowers.

nevado, da [nay-vah'-do, dah], *a.* White as snow. -*pp.* of NEVAR.

nevar [nay-var'], *vn.* To snow; to fall in snow. **Nevar mucho**, to snow heavily. -*va.* To make white as snow. *(Nieva, nieve, from Nevar. V.* ACERTAR.)

nevasca [nay-vahs'-cah], *f.* 1. Fall of snow; snow and wind. 2. Snowstorm.

nevatilla [nay-vah-teel'-yah], *f. (Zool.)* Wag-tail. *V.* AGUZANIEVE.

nevera [nay-vey'-rah], *f.* 1. Ice-house. 2. Applied to any very cold room or place. 3. Icebox, refrigerator.

nevereta [nay-vay-ray'-tah], *f. V.* AGUZANIEVE.

nevería [nay-vay-ree'-ah], *f.* Ice-house, a place where ice is sold.

nevero, ra [nay-vay'-ro, rah], *m. & f.* One who sells ice. -*m.* Place of perpetual snow.

nevisca [nay-vees'-cah], *f. V.* NEVASCA.

neviscar [nay-vis-car'], *vn.* To snow lightly.

nevoso, sa [nay-vo'-so, sah], *a.* 1. Snowy, abounding with snow, nival, niveous. 2. Snowy: applied to weather indicating snow.

nexo [nek'-so], *m.* Knot, string, union.

nexo [nek'-so], *adv.* (Cant or low) No. *(Cf.* nix and Ger. nights.)

ni [nee], *conj.* Neither, nor. **Ni fui, ni tengo intención de ir**, I did not go, nor do I intend to go. **Ni le amo, ni le temo, I** neither love nor fear him. **Ni siquiera**, not even. **Ni usted lo sabe**, even you do not know it. **No dice ni si ni no**, he is neither *pro* nor *con*. **No quiere ni sal ni mostaza**, he doesn't want either salt or mustard. **Ni a ti te lo dirá**, he won't tell even you. **Ni que fueses su mujer**, not even if you were his wife. **Ni come ni duerme**, he neither eats, nor sleeps. **Ni más ni menos**, no more, no less. **Ni tú ni yo le podemos ayudar ahora**, neither you nor I can help him now. **Ni siquiera**, not even. **No quiero ni vino ni cerveza**, I don't want either wine or beer. **Se fue sin comer ni beber**, he left without eating or drinking.

niacina [ne-ah-thee'-nah], *f.* Niacine.

nícalo [nee'-cah-lo], *m. V.* NISCALO.

nicaragüense [ne-cah-rah-goo-en'-say], *m. & f. & a.* Nicaraguan.

nicerobino [ne-thay-ro-bee'-no], *a.* Applied to a precious ointment used by the ancients.

nicho [nee'-cho], *m.* 1. Niche, a recess in a wall to place a statue in. 2. Any hole or corner to put something in. 3. Any employment or destination in which a person ought to be placed according to his merits.

nicotina [ne-co-tee'-nah], *f.* Nicotine, a highly poisonous alkaloid of tobacco.

nictálope [nic-tah'-lo-pay], *m.* Nyctalops, one who sees best at night.

nictalopia [nic-tah-lo'-pe-ah], *f.* Nyctalopy, a disease of the eye; day-blindness.

nidada [ne-dah'-dah], *f.* Nestful of eggs, on which a hen sits; brood, covey.

nidal [ne-dahl'], *m.* 1. A nest, place where a hen or other bird lays her eggs. 2. Nest-egg (dinero). 3. Basis, foundation, motive. 4. Haunt.

nidificar [ne-de-fe-car'], *vn.* To nest, to build nests.

nidito [ne-dee'-to], *m. dim.* A small nest.

nido [nee'-do], *m.* 1. Nest, the bed formed by the bird for incubation. 2. Nest, any place where animals are produced (criadero). 3. Nest, habitation, abode, residence. 4. Hiding place (escondite). 5. *(Fig.)* Hiding place (guarida). **Nido de ladrones**, nest of thieves. **Nido de amor**, love nest. **Nido de víboras**, nest of vipers.

niebla [ne-ay'-blah], *f.* 1. Fog (densa), mist (neblina), haze, damp. 2. Disease of the eyes, which dims, the sight. 3. Mildew (hongo parásito). 4. Mental obscurity, confusion of ideas.

niego [ne-ay'-go], *a.* New-born (halcón). *V.* HALCÓN.

niel [ne-el'], *m.* Embossment, relief; raised work.

nielar [ne-ay-lar'], *va.* To form with a protuberance, to carve in relief, or raised work on plate; to engrave, to enamel.

nieta [ne-ay'-tah], *f.* Grand-daughter, grandchild.

nieto [ne-ay'-to], *m.* 1. Grand-son, grandchild. 2. Descendant.

nieve [ne-ay'-vay], *f.* 1. Snow. 2. Snowy weather: commonly used in the plural. 3. Fall of snow. 4. Extreme whiteness. 5. *(LAm.)* Ice cream (helado). 6. Snow (cocaína). **Las primeras nieves**, the first snows.

nigromancia [ne-gro-mahn'-the-ah], *f.* Necromancy; black art.

nigromante [ne-gro-mahn'-tay], *m.* Necromancer, conjurer, magician.

nigromántico, ca [ne-gro-mahn'-te-co, cah], *a.* Necromancer. -*m. & f. V.* NIGROMANTE.

nigua [nee'-goo-ah], *f.* Chigoe, jigger flea, an insect found in tropical America, which burrows under the nails.

nihilismo [ne-he-lees'-mo], *m.* 1. Nihilism, denial of all belief. 2. Russian anarchism, antagonism to religion, society, and government.

nihilista [ne-he-lees'-tah], *m.* Nihilist, anarchist.

niki [nee'-ke], *m.* T-shirt.

nimiamente [nee'me-ah-men-tay], *adv.* Excessively.

nilad [ne-lahd'], *m.* A shrub of about six feet high which grows in the Philippine archipelago.

nilíaco, ca [ne-lee'-ah-co, cah], *a.* Belonging to the Nile.

nilómetro [ne-lo'-may-tro], *m.* Nilometer, a column or gauge for measuring the height of water in the Nile.

nilón [ne-lone'], *m.* Nylon.

nimiedad [ne-me-ay-dahd'], *f.* 1. Superfluity, excess, nimiety. 2. Niceness, extravagant nicety. 3. *(coll.)* A rediculous sparingness, or frugality.

nimio, mia [nee'-me-o, ah], *a.* Excessive (excesivo), too much, prolix.

ninfa [neen'-fah], *f.* 1. Nymph. 2. Young lady. 3. Pupa, the chrysalis of a caterpillar.

ninfea [nin-fay'-ah], *f. (Bot.)* Water-lily. **Ninfea blanca**, white water-lily.

ninfo [neen'-fo], *m.* A beau, a young effeminate fop, a dude.

ninfómana [nen-fo'-mah-nah], *f.* Nymphomaniac.

ninfomanía [nin-fo-mah-nee'-ah], *f.* Nymphomania, morbid, insane sexual desire in women.

ningún [nin-goon'], *a.* None, not one: used before masculine nouns. **De ningún modo**, in no manner, by no means.

ninguno, na [nin-goo'-no, nah], *a.* None, not one, no, neither. **De ninguna manera**, by no means, in no manner. **Ninguna cosa**, nothing. **Ninguna belleza**, no beauty. -*pron.* Nobody, no-one; none; neither. **No lo sabe ninguno**, nobody knows. **Ninguno de los dos**, neither of them.

niña [nee'-nyah], *f.* 1. Pupil of the eye. 2. Little girl, a female child. 3. Tart, whore (prostituta). 4. *(LAm.)* Miss, mistress. **La niña bonita**, number fifteen. **Ser las niñas de los ojos de uno**, to be the apple of somebody's eye.

niñada [ne-nyah'-dah], *f.* Puerility, childishness, a childish speech or action.

niñato [ne-nyah'-to], *m.* Calf found in the belly of a cow which has been killed.

niñear [ne-nyay-ar'], *vn.* To act like a child, to behave in a childish manner.

niñera [ne-nyay'-rah], *f.* Nursemaid, servant employed to take care of children. 2. Baby-sitter.

niñería [ne-nyay-ree'-ah], *f.* 1. Puerility, childish action (acto). 2. Bauble, gewgaw, plaything. 3. Trifle, thing of no importance.

niñero, ra [ne-nyay'-ro, rah], *a. & m. & f.* One who is fond of children, or who delights in childish tricks; a dandler.

niñeta [ne-nyay'-tah], *f.* The small pupil of the eye.

niñez [ne-nyeth'], *f.* 1. Childhood, infancy. 2. Infancy, the first age of anything: beginning, commencement.

niñita [ne-nyee'-tah], *f. dim.* Babe, infant.

niño, ña [nee'-nyo, nyah], *a.* Childish, child-like, puerile (infantil).

niño [nee'-nyo], *m.* 1. Child, infant. 2. Person of little experience or prudence. 3. *(LAm.)* Master, sir. 4. *(Cono Sur)* undesirable. **Desde niño**, from infancy, from a child. **No es niño**, he is no more a child. **Niño prodigio**, child prodigy. **Ser el niño mimado de uno**, to be somebody's pet. **Cuando nazca el niño**, when the baby is born.

nioto [ne-o'-to], *m. V.* CAZÓN.

nipa [nee'-pah], *f.* A kind of palm-tree in the Philippine Islands; from the leaves thatches for roofs are made, and from the roots a spirituous drink.

nipe, or **nipis** [nee'-pay, nee'-pis], *m. (Com.)* A fabric made from the fibers of the *nipa* in the Philippines and in Madagascar.

nipón, na [ne-pone', nah], *m. & f. & a.* Nipponese, Japanese.

niquel [nee'-kel], *m.* Nickel, a silvery white metal.

niquelado [ne-kay-lah'-do], *a.* (Ore) Holding nickel; also nickel-plated.

niquelar [ne-kay-lar'], *va.* To nickel-plate.

niqui [nee'-ke], *m.* T-shirt.

niquiscocio [ne-kis-co'-the-o], *m.* Trifle, a thing of little importance.

níscalo [nees'-cah-lo], *m.* A non-poisonous mushroom.

níspera [nees'-pay-rah], *f.* A Nicaraguan timber-tree. *V.* ZAPOTE.

níspero [nees'-pay-ro], *m. (Bot.)* Medlar-tree.

níspola [nees'-po-lah], *f.* Fruit of the medlar-tree.

nitidez [ne-te-dayth'], *f.* 1. Brightness; spotlessness (limpieza); clarity, sharpness. 2. *(Fig.)* Unblemished nature.

nítido, da [nee'-te-do, dah], *a. (Poet.)* Bright, shining, lustrous, nitid, neat, spotless (limpio).

nito [nee'-to], *m.* A brake found in the Philippine Islands, from the petioles of which is obtained a fiber used in making hats and cigar-cases.

nitos [nee'-tos], *m.* Insignificant word, meaning nothing, in reply to an impertinent question, or to conceal anything.

nitral [ne-trahl'], *m.* Place where niter is formed; nitre-bed.

nitrato [ne-trah'-to], *m. (Chem.)* Nitrate.

nitrería [ne-tray-ree'-ah], *f.* Saltpeter-works, where saltpeter is prepared and refined.

nítrico [nee'-tre-co], *a.* Nitric, applied to an acid; consisting of niter.

nitrito [ne-tree'-to], *m.* Nitrite, a compound of nitrous acid.

nitro [nee'-tro], *m.* Niter, saltpeter; nitrate of potassium.

nitrobencina [ne-tro-ben-thee'-nah], *f. (Chem.)* Nitrobenzene.

nitrocelulosa [ne-tro-thay-loo-lo'-sah], *f.* Nitrocellulose, nitrated cellulose.

nitrógeno [ne-tro'-hay-no], *m. (Chem.)* Nitrogen, azote.

nitroglicerina [ne-tro-gle-thay-ree'-nah], *f.* Nitro-glycerine, a powerful explosive, basis of dynamite.

nitroso, sa [ne-tro'-so, sah], *a.* Nitrous, nitry, impregnated with nitre.

nivel [ne-vel'], *m.* 1. Level, instrument for ascertaining the level of a surface. 2. Level, a plane or surface without inequalities, levelness. 3. Level, standard. **A nivel**, perfectly level, in a line or row. **Nivel del agua**, water level. **Alto nivel de trabajo**, high level of employment. **No está al nivel de los demás**, he is not up to the standard of the others.

nivelación [ne-vay-lah-the-on'], *f.* 1. Act of levelling. 2. Levelling, the operation of obtaining comparative elevations in surveying.

nivelador [ne-vay-lah-dor'], *m.* One who ascertains the level of a surface, leveller.

niveladora [ne-vay-lah-do'-rah], *f.* (*Mech.*) Bulldozer.

nivelar [ne-vay-lar], *va.* 1. To ascertain the level of a surface. 2. To make even, to level. 3. To observe equity and justice.

níveo, ea [nee'-vay-o, ah], *a.* (*Poet.*) Snowy, like snow.

nizardo, da [ne-thar'-do, dah], *a.* Native of or belonging to Nice.

no [no], *adv.* No or not, nay. **No importa nada**, it signifies nothing. **No vale nada**, it is worth nothing. **Decir que no**, to give a flat denial. **Pues no**, but no, not so. **No sé qué, I** know not what, an inexplicable something. **Por si o por no**, at any rate. **Sin faltar un sí ni un no**, without an iota wanting. **No sea que**, lest. **No tengo nada**, I have nothing. **Cosa no esencial**, non-essential thing.

nobiliario [no-be-le-ah'-re-o], *m.* A genealogical account of the peerage of a country, nobiliary.

noble [no'-blay], *a.* 1. Noble, of noble extraction, high-born. 2. Illustrious, eminent, conspicuous, magnific, magnifical, generous. 3. Honorable, respectable. **Estado noble**, nobility. -*m.* Nobleman.

noblemente [no-blay-men-tay], *adv.* Nobly, generously, magnanimously.

nobleza [no-blay'-thah], *f.* 1. Nobleness, nobility (cualidad), antiquity of family with luster of pedigree. 2. Nobility, the body of noblemen (personas). 3. Gentility, elegance of behavior. 4. Nobleness, nobility, dignity, greatness, generousness, magnanimity, worth; stateliness. 5. Fine damask silk.

nocedal [no-thay-dahd'], *m.* V. NOGUERAL.

noche [no'-chay], *f.* 1. Night. 2. (*Poet.*) Night, death. 3. Night, state of obscurity, confusion, or ignorance. **Anoche** or **ayer noche**, last night. **Noche y día**, night and day, always, constantly. **De la noche a la mañana**, overnight. **Hasta muy entrada la noche**, until late at night. **Hacer noche en un sitio**, to spend the night in a place.

Nochebuena [no-chay-boo-ay'-nah], *f.* Christmas eve.

nochecita [no-chay-thee'-tah], *f.* (*Amer.*) Twilight.

nochizo [no-chee'-tho], *m.* (*Bot.*) Wild common hazelnut tree.

noción [no-the-on'], *f.* 1. Notion, idea. 2. Acceptation, meaning of a word. **No tener la menor noción de algo**, not to have the faintest idea about something.

nocional [no-the-o-nahl'], *a.* Notional.

nocivamente [no-the-vah-men'-tay], *adv.* Mischievously, hurtfully, harmfully.

nocivo, va [no-thee'-vo, vah], *a.* Noxious, hurtful, mischievous, malignant.

noctambulismo [noc-tam-boo-lees'-mo], *m.* The act of walking in sleep. *V.* SOMNAMBULISMO.

noctámbulo, la [noc-tahm'-boo-lo, lah], *m. & f.* Somnambulist, one who walks in his sleep; sleep-walker (sonámbulo); night-bird (nocheriego); roister (jaranero).

noctíluca [noc-tee'-loo-cah], *f.* Glow worm, noctiluca.

noctíluco [noc-tee'-loo-co], *m.* Noctiluca, a microscopic infusorian, a usual cause of phosphorescence in the ocean.

noctuinos [noc-too-ee'-nose], *m. pl.* Moths, nocturnal lepidoptera.

nocturlabio [noc-toor-lah'-be-o], *m.* Nocturnal, an antiquated instrument for measuring the altitude of the pole by night.

nocturnal [noc-toor-nahl'], *a.* Nocturned, nightly; done or doing by night.

nocturno, na [noc-toor'-no, nah], *a.* 1. Nocturna, nightly. 2. Lonely, melancholy, mournful. **Ave nocturna**, night-bird, such as owls.

nocturno [noc-toor'-no], *m.* 1. Nocturn, one of the three parts into which matins are divided. 2. (*Mus.*) Nocturn, a serenade; a dreamy sentimental composition appropriate to the evening or night.

nodal [no-dahl'], *a.* Nodal, referring to the nodes of a vibrating surface.

nodo [no'-do], *m.* 1. Node, a morbid shelling on the bone. 2. (*Ast.*) Node, the point where the orbit of a heavenly body intersects the ecliptic.

nodriza [no-dree'-thah], *f.* Nurse, a woman that has the care of another's child.

nódulo [no'-doo-lo], *m.* Nodule, a concretion formed in bodies; a small node.

nogada [no-gah'-dah], *f.* Sauce made of pounded walnuts and spice.

nogal [no-gahl'], *m.* (*Bot.*) 1. Common walnut-tree (árbol). Juglans. 2. The wood of the common walnut-tree.

noguera [no-gay'-rah], *f.* (*Bot.*) Walnut-tree.

noguerado, da [no-gay-rah'-do, dah], *a.* Of a walnut color.

nogueral [no-gay-rahl'], *m.* Plantation of walnut-trees.

nolición [no-lae-the-on'], *f.* Nolition, unwillingness; opposed to *volition*. (Theology.)

noli me tángere [no-le may tahn'-hay-ray], *m.* Nolimetangere, a malignant ulcer on the face or nose.

nómada, or **nómade** [no'-mah-dah, day], *a.* Nomad, nomadic, having no fixed abode.

nombradamente [nom-brah'-dah-men-tay], *adv.* Namely, expressly.

nombradía [nom-brah-dee'-ah], *f.* Fame, reputation, conspicuousness, credit.

nombrado [nom-brah'-do], *m.* Nominee, a person nominated to a place or office. -*a.* 1. Afore-mentioned (susodicho). 2. (*Fig.*) Famous, renowned.

nombrador [nom-brah-dor'], *m.* Nominator, appointer.

nombramiento [nom-brah-me-en'-to], *m.* 1. Nomination, naming (denominación), or mentioning by name. 2. Appointment, creation, commission.

nombrar [nom-brar'], *va.* 1. To name (dar nombre a), to mention by name (mencionar). 2. To nominate (para un puesto), to appoint. **Nombrar a uno embajador**, to nominate somebody as ambassador.

nombre [nom'-bray], *m.* 1. Name, the discriminative appellation of an individual; title. **Nombre de pila**, christian name. 2. Fame, reputation, credit. 3. Nickname. **Poner nombres a uno**, to call one names. 4. Power by which someone acts for another. 5. (*Gram.*) Noun. 6. (*Mil.*) Countersign watch-word. **Nombre apelativo**, (a) surname. (b) generic name. **Nombre colectivo**, collective noun. **Poner nombre**, to fix a price. **Nombre propio**, proper name. **Bajo el nombre**, under the name of. **Sin nombre**, nameless. **Su conducta no tiene nombre**, his conduct is unspeakable.

nomenclador [no-men-clah-dor'], *m.* 1. Nomenclature, a list of names; glossary; vocabulary of terms. 2. Nomenclator, one who assigns names in a science.

nomenclátor [no-men-clah'-tor], *m.* Nomenclator.

nomenclatura [no-men-clah-doo'-rah], *f.* 1. catalogue. 2. Nomenclature, technical glossary.

nomeolvides [no-may-ol-vee'-des], *f.* (*Bot.*) Forget-me-not.

nómina [no'-me-nah], *f.* 1. Catalogue, an alphabetical list of things or persons. 2. Payroll.

nominación [no-me-nah-the-on'], *f.* 1. Nomination, the act of mentioning by name. 2. Power of presenting to a benefice.

nominador, ra [no-me-nah-dor', rah], *m. & f.* Nominator, appointing power; one who appoints another to a position.

nominal [no-me-nahl'], *a.* Nominal, belonging to a name; relating to names rather than things; titular.

nominal [no-me-nahl'], *m.* Nominal, nominalist, one of a sect of scholastical philosophers.

nominalmente [no-me-nahl'-men-tay], *adv.* Nominally.

nominar [no-me-nar'], *va.* To name. *V.* NOMBRAR.

nominativo [no-me-nah-tee'-vo], *m.* (*Gram.*) Nominative: applied to the first case of nouns. -*a.* 1. Nominative. 2. (*Com. Fin.*) Bearing a person's name. **El cheque será nominativo a favor de X**, the check should be made out to X.

nominilla [no-me-neel'-lyah], f. A warrant or a certificate enabling a pensioner of an office to draw his dues.

nómino [no'-me-no], m. Nominee, a person appointed or nominated to any office or employment.

nomocanon [no-mo-cah'-none], m. Nomocanon, collection of imperial constitutions and canons.

nomografía [no-mo-grah-fee'-ah], f. Nomography, a treatise on laws.

nomógrafo [no-mo'-grah-fo], m. Nomographer, a writer on laws.

nomología [no-mo-lo-hee'-ah], f. Nomology, the science of laws and their interpretation.

nomológico, ca [no-mo-lo'-he-co, cah], a. Nomological.

nomparell [nom-pah-rayl'], f. (typ.) Nonpareil, a size of type; six-point.

non [none], a. Odd (número), uneven.

non [none], m. An odd number. **Andar de nones**, to be idle, to have nothing to do. **Estar de nones**, to serve for nothing. (coll.) **Pares y nones**, even or odd.

nona [no'-nah], f. 1. None, last of the minor canonical hours, answering to three o'clock P. M. 2. (Cono Sur) Grandma, granny.

nonada [no-nah'-dah], f. Trifle, little or nothing, nothingness.

nonadilla [no-nah-deel'-lyah], f. dim. of NONADA.

nonagenario, ria [no-nah-hay-nah'-re-oh, ah], a. Ninety years old, nonagenarian.

nonagésimo, ma [no-nah-hes'-se-mo, mah], a. Ninetieth, nonagesimal.

nonagonal [no-nah-go-nahl'], a. Enneagonal, nine-sided.

nonágono [no-nah'-go-no], m. Nonagon.

nonato, ta [no-nah'-to, tah], a. Not naturally born, but extracted from the mother's womb by Cesarean section.

nono [no-no], a. Ninth. V. NOVENO.

No obstante [no obs-tahn'-tay], conj. Nevertheless, notwithstanding, however.

nopal [no-pahl'], m. (Bot.) Nopal, cochineal fig-tree, prickly Indian pear-tree. It is vulgarly called in Castile, higuera chumba.

nopalera [no-pah-lay'-rah], f. (Amer.) Cochineal planation.

noque [no'-kay], m. 1. A tan-pit or vat in which the ooze is kept for tanning hides. 2. Heap or basket of bruised olives.

noquero [no-kay'-ro], m. Currier, leather-dresser.

norabuena [no-rah-boo-ay'-nah], f. Congratulation. V. ENHORABUENA.

noramala [no-rah-mah'-lah], f. A term of contempt or displeasure. Also adv. V. ENHORAMALA.

nord [nord], m. (Naut.) North wind.

nordest, nordeste [nor-dest', nor-des'-tay], m. North-east. **Nordest cuarto al norte**, north-east-by-north. Nordeste cuarto al este, north-east-by-east.

nordestear [nor-des-tay-ar'], vn. (Naut.) To be north easting.

nórdico, ca [nor'-de-co, cah], m. & f. & a. Nordic. **Es la ciudad más nórdica de Europa**, it is the most northerly city in Europe.

nordoveste [nor-do-vest'], m. North-west.

nordovestear [nor-do-ves-tay-ahr'], vn. (Naut.) To decline to north-west.

noreste [no-rays'-tay], m. North-east.

noria [no'-re-ah], f. 1. An irrigating wheel. 2. Wheel for drawing water from a well; a chain-pump. 3. Draw-well, a deep well.

norial [no-re-ahl'], a. Relating to the well called noria.

norma [nor'-mah], f. 1. Square, a rule or instrument by which workmen form or measure their angles. 2. Model, a standard or rule to guide and govern all operations. **Norma de vida**, principle. **Está sujeto a ciertas normas**, it is subject to certain rules.

normal [nor-mahl'], a. 1. Normal, according to an established law. 2. Model, serving as a standard. **Escuela normal**, normal school. -f. Normal, a perpendicular. -**mente**, adv.

normalidad [nor-mah-le-dahd'], f. Normality, normally (con normalidad); (Pol.) calm, normal conditions. **La situación**

ha vuelto a la normalidad, the situation has returned to normal.

normalización [nor-mah-le-thah-the-on'], f. Normalization.

normalizar [nor-mah-le-thar'], va. To normalize, to restore to normal; (Tec.) to standardize. -vr. To return to normal.

normalmente [nor-mahl'-men-tay], adv. Normally; usually.

normando, da [nor-mahn'-do, dah], a. Norman, relating to Normandy.

normativa [nor-mah-te-vah], f. Rules, regulations; guideline.

normativo [nor-mah-tee'-vo], a. 1. Normative (prescrito). 2. Regular (regular), standard. **Español normativo**, standard Spanish.

nornodeste [nor-no-des'-tay], m. (Naut.) North-north-east.

nornorueste [nor-no-roo-es'-tay], m. North-north-west.

noroeste [no-ro-ess'-tay], m. North-west.

nortada [nor-tah'-dah], f. Strong, continued north wind.

norte [nor'-tay], m. 1. North, the arctic pole. 2. North, the northern part of the sphere. 3. North or north wind (viento). 4. Rule, law, guide(guía), clew, direction. 5. (Carib.) United States. 6. (Carib.) Drizzle (llovizna). **En la parte del norte**, in the northern part. **Pregunta sin norte**, aimless question.

norteamericano, na [nor-tay-ah-may-re-cah'-no, nah], m. & f. & a. North American (generally from U.S.)

nortear [nor-tay-ar'], va. (Naut.) To steer or stand to the northward.

noruego, ga [no-roo-ay'-go, gah], m. & f. & a. Norwegian.

norueste [no-roo-es'-tay], m. North-west.

noruestear [no-roo-es-tay-ar'], vn. To decline to the north-west.

nos, pron.pers. 1. Us. **Nos lo dará**, he will give it to us. 2. Ourselves (reflexivo); to each other (recíproco). **No nos hablamos**, we don't speak to each other.

nosabo (Hacer el). (Prov. Coll.) To make believe, to feign ignorance.

nosografía [no-so-grah-fee'-ah], f. (Med.) Nosography, description of diseases.

nosología [no-so-lo-hee'-ah], f. (Med.) Nosology, classification of diseases.

nosotros, tras [no-so os, tras], pron. We, ourselves. **No irán sin nosotros**, they won't go without us.

nostalgia [nos-tahl'-he-ah], f. Nostalgia, inordinate homesickness.

nostálgico [nos-tahl'-he-co], a. Nostalgic, homesick.

nota [no'-tah], f. 1. Note, mark, or token put upon anything to make it known; schedule. 2. Note, explanatory annotation in a book or writing. 3. Censure, notice, remark upon one's actions, critique. **Incurrir en la nota**, to incur the imputation. 4. Style, manner of writing (estilo). 5. Memorandum or note taken down to help the memory; (Com.) account, statement. 6. Official communication of a government or a foreign minister. 7. Note, reproach, stigma. **Buena** or **mala nota**, good or bad standing or reputation in society. 8. (Mus.) Musical character, a single sound. 9. (LAm.) Effects of drugs. **Nota de gastos**, expense account. **Obtener buenas notas**, to get good marks. **Dar la nota**, to set the tone. **Tomar nota**, to take note. -pl. The collection of minutes of proceedings taken by a notary.

notabilidad [no-tah-be-le-dahd'], f. 1. Notability. (Neol.) 2. Notable (persona).

notabilísimo, ma [no-tah-be-lee'-se-mo mah], a. Super, of Notable.

notable [no-tah'-blay], a. 1. Notable, remarkable, noteworthy, conspicuous. 2. Very great.

notable [no-tah'-blay], m. Introductory observation.

notablemente [no-tah'-blay-men-tay], adv. Notably, observably, notedly.

notación [no-tah-the-on'] f. 1. An algebraic sign. 2. Notation, the art of representing the written sign in music. 3. Part of prosody which treats of the accentuation of syllables.

notar [no-tar'], va. 1. To note, to mark. 2. To remark, to observe, to note (observar), to heed, to notice, to take notice of, to mind. 3. To take short notes on a subject (apuntar). 4.

To comment, to expound. 5. To annotate a writing or book. 6. To dictate what another may write. 7. To find fault, to censure, to criticize (criticar): to reprehend. **No lo había notado,** I hadn't noticed it. **Te noto muy cambiado,** I find you very changed. *-vr.* To show, to be apparent, to be obvious. **La combinación no se te nota,** your slip doesn't show.

notaría [no-tah-ree'-ah], *f.* 1. Employment or profession of a notary (profesión). 2. A notary's office (despacho).

notariado [no-tah-re-ah'-do], *m.* Profession of a notary.

notarial [no-tah-re-ahl'], *a.* Notarial; legal (estilo), lawyer's.

notariato [no-tah-re-ah'-to], *m.* Title of a notary.

notario [no-tah'-re-o], *m.* 1. Notary, an officer whose business is to take notes of protests and other transactions, to draw and pass public instruments, and to attest and legalize private dealings and writings: it is now commonly applied to those officers who transact ecclesiastical affairs. 2. Amanuensis. **Entre dos amigos un notario y dos testigos,** *(Prov.)* ever among friends legal vouchers and warranties should not be omitted.

notho, tha [no'-to, tah], *a.* Bastard, illegitimate.

noticia [no-tee'-the-ah], *f.* 1. Notice, knowledge (conocimientos), information, note, light. 2. News, intelligence. **Noticias alegres,** glad tidings. **Poner en la noticia de,** to bring to one's knowledge, to advise, inform. **Tener noticias de uno,** to have news of somebody. **No tener la menor noticia de algo,** to know nothing at all about a matter.

noticiar [no-te-the-ar'], *va.* To give notice, to communicate intelligence.

noticiario [no-te-the-ah'-re-oh], *m.* 1. Newsreel. 2. Newscast.

noticiero [no-te-the-ay'-ro], *m. (Mex.)* 1. Newsreel. 2. Newscast. 3. *(Mex.)* News bulletin. *-a.* 1. News (noticias). 2. News-bearing (que da noticias).

noticioso, sa [no-te-the-o'-so, sah], *a.* Informed; knowing, learned, instructed.

notificación [no-te-fe-cah-the-on'], *f.* Notification, judicial intimation.

notificado, da [no-te-he-cah'-do, dah], *a. & pp.* of NOTIFICAR. Notified: applied to a person who has received a judicial notification.

notificar [no-te-fe-car'], *va.* To notify, to make known, to intimate: to inform.

notilla, ita [no-teel'-lyah], *f. dim.* A short note, memorandum, etc.

noto, ta [no'-to, tah], *a.* 1. Known, notorious. 2. Illegitimate, not born in wedlock.

noto [no'-to], *m.* South wind, notus.

notoriamente [no-to-re-ah'-men-tay], *adv.* Notoriously, manifestly, glaringly.

notoriedad [no-to-re-ay-dahd'], *f.* Notoriety, notoriousness, public knowledge. **Hechos de amplia notoriedad,** widely-known facts.

notorio, ria [no-to'-re-o, ah], *a.* Notorious, publicly known, glaring, flagrant, famous (famoso), well-known (conocido). **Un hecho notorio,** a well-known fact.

noumeno [no-oo-may'-no], *m. (Phil.)* Being or essence which every phenomenon declares or reveals; noumenon, "the thing in itself."

novación [no-vah-the-on'], *f. (Law.)* Renovation of an obligation formerly contracted.

noval [no-vahl'], *a.* Applied to land newly broken up and converted into arable ground, and to the fruits it produces.

novar [no-var'], *va. (Law.)* To renew an obligation formerly contracted.

novatada [no-vah-tah'-dah], *f.* 1. Rag (broma), ragging, hazing. 2. Beginner's mistake (error).

novato, ta [no-vah'-to, tah], *a. (Colt.)* New, commencing in anything. *-m.* Beginner (principiante).

novator [no-vah-tor'], *m.* Innovator, an introducer of novelties; novator.

novecientos, tas [no-vay-the-en'-tos, tas], *s. & a.* Nine hundred.

novedad [no-vay-dahd'], *f.* 1. Novelty, a new state of things, newness (cualidad), modernness. 2. Admiration excited by novelties or any extraordinary thing. 3. *(Coil.)* Remarkable occurrence, danger, trouble. 4. New feature (innovación), new development. **Los negocios continúan sin novedad,** Business goes on as usual. **Sin novedad en el frente,** all quiet on the front. **El enfermo sigue sin novedad,** the patient's condition is unchanged.

novedoso [no-vay-doh'-so], *a.* 1. Original, novel (idea, método). 2. *(Cono Sur, Mex.)* V. NOVELESCO.

novel [no-vel'], *a.* New (nuevo), inexperienced. *-m.* Beginner (principiante).

novela [no-vay'-lah], *f.* 1. Novel, a fictitious story, a tale. 2. Falsehood, fiction. 3. *(Law.)* Novel, any new law added to the Justinian codes. **Novela de amor,** love story. **Novela por entregas,** serial.

novelador [no-vay-lah-dor'], *m.* Novelist, a writer of novels.

novelar [no-vay-lar'], *va.* 1. To compose, to write, or to publish novels. 2. To relate stories.

novelería [no-vay-lay-ree'-ah], *f.* 1. Narration of fictitious stories. 2. Taste for novels and novelties.

novelero, ra [no-vay-lay'-ro, rah], *a.* 1. Fond of novels and fictitious tales (aficionado). 2. Fond of hearing and telling news. **Un novelero,** a newsmonger. 3. Newfangled. 4. Inconstant, wavering, unsteady. 5. Gossipy (chismoso). 6. Romantic (cuento).

novelesco, ca [no-vay-les'-co, cah], *a.* 1. Novelistic, pertaining to novels. 2. Romantic (romántico), fantastic; storybook (aventura).

novelista [no-vay-lees'-tah], *m. & f.* Novelist, a writer of novels.

novena [no-vay'-nah], *f.* 1. Term of nine days appropriated to some special worship. 2. Offering for the dead.

novenario [no-vay-nah'-re-o], *m.* Novenary, nine days' condolence for the deceased, or nine days of public worship offered to some saint.

novendial [no-ven-de-ahl'], *a.* Applied to any day of the novenary, or worship offered for the souls of the faithful.

noveno, na [no-vay'-no, nah], *a.* Ninth, the ordinal number of nine; ninthly.

noveno [no-vay'-no], *m.* One of the nine parts into which tithes are divided.

noventa [no-ven'-tah], *m. & a.* Ninety.

noventón, na [no-ven-tone', nah], *a.* Ninety years old. *-m.* A nonagenarian.

novia [no'-ve-ah], *f.* 1. Bride, a woman newly married (recién casada). 2. Woman betrothed. 3. Sweetheart (amiga); fiancée (prometida); bride (en boda). **Echarse una novia,** to get oneself a girl.

noviaje [no-ve-ah'-hay], *m.* Term of betrothal.

noviazgo [no-ve-ath'-go], *m.* Engagement, betrothal.

noviciado [no-ve-the-ah'-do], *m.* 1. Novitiate, the time spent in a religious house by way of trial before the vow is taken. 2. House or apartment in which novices live. 3. Novitiate, the time in which the rudiments of a science or art are learned; noviceship.

novicio [no-vee'-the-o], *m.* 1. Novice, one who has entered a religious house, but not yet taken the vow; a probationer. 2. Novice, a freshman, one in the rudiments of any knowledge.

novicio, cia [no-vee'-the-o, ah], *a.* Probationary: applied to a novice or probationer.

noviembre [no-ve-em'-bray], *m.* November.

novilunio [no-ve-loo'-ne-o], *m.* New moon conjunction of the moon.

novilla [no-veel'-lyah], *f.* Cow between three and six years of age; heifer.

novillada [no-veel-lyah'-dah], *f.* 1. Drove of young bulls or bullocks. 2. Fight of young bulls or bullocks.

novillejo, eja [no-veel-lyay'-do, dah], *m. & f. dim.* A young bull, a heifer.

novillero [no-veel-lyay'-ro], *m.* 1. Stable in which young cattle are kept 2. Herdsman who attends young cattle. 3. Piece of pasture ground where calves are put, separate from other cattle, to be weaned. 4. Truant, idler. 5. *(Taur.)* Novice, young bullfighter.

novillo [no-veel'-lyo], *m.* 1. A young bull or ox, particularly one not trained to the yoke. 2. *(Low.)* Cuckold. **Hacer novillos,** *(coll.)* to play truant.

novio [no'-ve-o], *m.* 1. Bridegroom (en boda). 2. A man betrothed to a woman. 3. One new to some dignity or state. 4. Sweetheart, boyfriend (amigo). **Los novios,** the engaged couple (prometidos). **Viaje de novios,** honeymoon.

novísimo, ma [no-vee'-se-mo, mah], *a.* Newest, most recent; last in the order of things.-*m.* Each of the four last incidents of mankind: death, judgment, heaven, and hell.

novocaína [no-vo-cah-ee'-nah], *f.* Novocaine.

nubada, nubarrada [noo-bab'-dah], *f.* 1. Shower of rain (chaparrón). 2. Plenty, abundance.

nubado, da, nubarrado, da [noo-bah'-do, dah], *a.* Clouded, figured like clouds.

nubarrón [noo-bar-rone'], *m.* A heavy shower of rain, a large cloud.

nube [noo'-bay], *f.* 1. A cloud. 2. Cloud, a crowd, a multitude, anything that spreads wide so as to interrupt the view (humo, insectos). 3. Film which obstructs the sight (en ojo). 4. Cloud or shade in precious stones. **Andar** or **estar por las nubes,** (1) *V.* **Subir a las nubes.** (2) To run mountain high: said of waves. (3) To be extremely annoyed. **Subir a las nubes,** to raise or increase prices very much.

nubífero, ra [noo-bee'-fay-ro, rah], *a. (Poet.)* Cloud-bringing.

nubiloso [noo-be-lo'-so] *a. V.* NUBLOSO.

núbil [noo'-beel], *a.* Nubile, marriageable.

nublado [noo-blah'-do], *m.* 1. A large cloud. 2. Perturbation of the mind, gloominess. 3. Dread or fear of impending danger. 4. Anger, black mood (enfado).

nublado, da [noo-blah'-do, dah], *a & pp.* of NUBLAR. Cloudy, misty, nebulous.

nublar, nublarse [noo-blar'], *va. & vr.* 1. To darken, to obscure. 2. To cloud, to disturb (vista); to affect (razón).

nubloso, sa [noo-blo'-so, sah], *a.* 1. Cloudy, dark, overcast. 2. Gloomy, ill-fated.

nubosidad [noo-bo-see-dahd'], *f.* Cloudiness, clouds.

nuboso [noo-bo'-so], *a.* Cloudy.

nubus [noo-boos]. *(Inform.)* Nubus.

nuca [noo'-cah], *f.* Nape of the neck, nucha.

nuclear [noo-clay-ar'], *a.* Nuclear. **Energía nuclear,** nuclear energy. **Física nuclear,** nuclear physics.

nucleico, ca [noo-clay'-co, cah], *a.* Nucleic.

núcleo [noo'-clay-o], *m.* 1. Kernel of a nut, nucleus. 2. Nucleus, a center of union or of development.

nudifloro, ra [noo-de-flo'-ro, rah], *a.* Nudiflorous, having naked flowers.

nudifoliado, da [noo-de-fo-le-ah'-do, dah], *a.* Having smooth or bare leaves; nudifolious.

nudillo [noo-deel'-lyo], *m.* 1. Knuckle, the joint of the fingers. 2. *(Arch.)* Wooden abutment to roofing-timbers. 3. Small knot in stockings. 4. Nodule.

nudismo [noo-dees'-mo], *m.* Nudism.

nudista [noo-dees'-tah], *m. & f.* Nudist.

nudo [noo'-do], *m.* 1. Knot, complication of a cord or string. 2. Knoll, node, articulation or joint of plants. 3. Joint in animal bodies. 4. The principal difficulty or doubt in certain matters (problema). 5. Tie, union, bond of association (vínculo). 6. Node, a swelling on nerves or bones. 7. Knot, intricacy, difficulty. 8. The crisis of a drama. **Echamos doce nudos por hora,** we ran twelve knots an hour. **Atravesársele a uno un nudo en la garganta,** to have a lump in one's throat, to be speechless on account of violent emotion. **Nudo corredizo,** slipknot.

nudoso, sa [noo-do'-so, sah], *a.* Knotty (madera), nodous, knotted, knaggy.

nuégados [noo-ay'-gah-dose], *m. pl.* A sort of paste of flour, honey, and nuts.

nuera [noo-ay'-rah], *f.* Daughter-in-law.

nuestramo [noo-es-trah'-mo], *f.* Our master, contracted from *nuestro amo.*

nuestro, tra [noo-es'-tro, trah], *a.* Our, pertaining to us. **Los nuestros,** the persons of the same party or profession as the speaker. **Un barco nuestro,** a boat of ours. **Es el nuestro,** it is ours.

nueva [noo-ay'-vah], *f.* News, fresh amount of anything.

nuevamente [noo-ay-vah-men-tay], *adv.* Newly, recently, freshly.

nueve [noo-ay'-vay], *m. & a.* 1. Nine, an arithmetical character by which the number nine is denoted. 2. A card with nine marks. 3. Ninth. **El nueve de Enero,** the ninth of January. **El libro nueve,** the ninth book.

nuevecito [noo-ay-vay-thee'-to], *a. dim.* Quite new, fresh, very lately made.

nuevo, va [noo-ay'-vo, vah], *a.* 1. New, not old; novel, modern, fresh. 2. New, having the effect of novelty, not known before. 3. New, renovated, repaired. 4. New, not being before. 5. Recently arrived in a country or place. 6. Inexperienced, not habituated, not familiar. 7. Beginning. **De nuevo,** again, a new, recently, of late. **¿Qué hay de nuevo?** what is the news? Is there any news? **Es nuevo en el oficio,** he's new to the trade. **Somos nuevos aquí,** we're new here. **La casa es nueva,** the house is new.

nuez [noo-eth'], *f.* 1. Walnut, the fruit of the walnut-tree; *(Mex.)* pecan nut. 2. Fruit of some trees in the shape of a nut. 3. Adam's apple, the prominent part of the throat. 4. Plummet. 5. **Nuez moscada** or **de especia,** *(Bot.)* nutmeg. **Nuez del país** or **nuez chiquita,** butter-nut. **Nuez grande,** hickory-nut. **Nuez dura,** hickory-nut.

nueza [noo-ay'-thah], *f. (Bot.)* Briony. **Nueza blanca,** white-berried briony. **Nueza negra,** Common black briony.

núfar [noo'-far], *f.* The spatterdock, or yellow water-lily.

nugatorio, rig [noo-gah-to'-re-o, ah], *a.* Nugatory, futile, deceitful.

nulamente [noo-lah-men'-tay], *adv.* Invalidly, ineffectually.

nulidad [noo-le-dahd'], *f.* 1. Nullity, want of force or efficacy. 2. Defeasance, a condition annexed to an act or deed, which, when performed by the obligee, renders the act or deed void. 3. *(coll.)* Insignificance.

nulo, la [noo'-lo, lah], *a.* 1. Null, void of effect, of no force. 2. Useless (persona). **Es nulo para la música,** he's useless at music.

numen [noo'-men], *m.* 1. Divinity, deity. 2. Genius, talent: commonly applied to poetical genius.

numerable [noo-may-rah'-blay], *a.* Numerable.

numeración [noo-may-rah-the-on'], *f.* Numeration, the art of numbering: first part of arithmetic.

numerador [noo-may-rah-dor'], *m.* 1. Numerator, numberer, he who numbers. 2. Numerator, the upper term of a common fraction.

numeral [noo-may-rahl'], *a.* Numeral, relating to numbers.

numerar [noo-may-rar'], *va.* 1. To number, to enumerate, to numerate, to calculate, to cipher. 2. To page, to mark the pages of a book. 3. To number, to reckon as one of the same kind. **Páginas sin numerar,** unnumbered pages.

numerario, ria [noo-may-rah'-re-o, ah], *a.* Numerary, belonging to a certain number. -*m.* Hard cash, coin.

numéricamente [noo-may'-re-cah-men-tay], *adv.* Individually, numerically.

numérico, ca [noo-may'-re-co, cah], *a.* Numerical, individual, numeral; denoting number.

número [noo'-may-ro], *m.* 1. Number, an aggregate of units. 2. Character, cipher, or figure which denotes the number. 3. Number, comparative multitude. 4. Number, harmony, proportional measure or cadence in music or poetry. 5. *(Gram.)* Number; singular or plural. 6. Determinate number of persons of any company or society. 7. Verse. 8. Size (de zapato). 9. Number, issue (periódico). 10. Item, number (de programa). *-pl.* Numbers, one of the five books of the Pentateuch. **Número uno**, number one, one's own selfish interests. **Sin número**, numberless, innumerable. **Número entero**, whole number. **Número primo**, prime number. **Número de referencia**, reference number. **Hacer el número**, to go over the top.

número Mach [noo'-may-ro mask], *m.* Mach number, ratio of the velocity of a moving body to the speed of sound.

numerosamente [noo-may-ro'-sah-men-tay], *adv.* Numerously.

numerosidad [noo-may-ro-se-dahd'], *f.* Numerosity, numerousness.

numeroso, sa [noo-may-ro'-so, sah], *a.* 1. Numerous, containing many. 2. Harmonious, melodious; consisting of parts rightly numbered, rhythmical, harmonical.

númida [noo'-me-dah], *a.* Numidian, of Numidia.

numídico, ca [noo-mee'-de-co, cah], *a.* V. NÚMIDA.

numisma [noo-mees'-mah], *m.* Coin.

numismática [noo-mis-mah'-te-cah], *f.* Numismatics, science of medals and coins.

numismático, ca [noo-mis-mah'-te-co, cah], *a.* Numismatical.

numismatografía [noo-mis-mah-to-grah-fee'-ah], *f.* Numismatography, description of ancient medals.

numo [noo'-mo], *m.* Money, coin.

numularia [noo-moo-lah'-re-ah], *f.* (*Bot.*) Money-wort.

numulario [noo-moo-lah'-re-o], *m.* A banker.

nunca [noon'-cah], *adv.* Never, at no time. **Nunca jamás**, never, never more. **No viene nunca**, he never comes.

nunciatura [noon-the-ah-too'-rah], *f.* Nunciature, the office or house of a nuncio.

nuncio [noon'-the-o], *m.* 1. Messenger. 2. Nuncio, envoy or ambassador from the Pope to Roman Catholic princes. 3. **El Nuncio** or **la casa del Nuncio**, the mad-house in Toledo.

nuncupativo, va [noon-coo-pah-tee'-vo, vah], *a.* 1. Nuncupative, nominal; verbally pronounced. 2. (Of a will) Declared orally by the testator and later written down.

nuncupatorio, ria [noon-coo-pah-to'-re-o, ah], *a.* Nuncupatory.

nupcial [noop-the-ahl'], *a.* Nuptial, pertaining to marriage, hymeneal.

nupcias [noop'-the-as], *f. pl.* Nuptials, wedding, marriage. **Casarse en segundas nupcias**, to marry again.

nutación [noo-tah-the-on'], *f.* 1. Direction of plants towards the sun. 2. (*Ast.*) Nutation, movement of the earth's axis, by which it inclines more or less to the plane of the ecliptic.

nutante [noo-tahn'-tay], *a.* (*Bot.*) Nodding.

nutra, nutria [noo'-trah, noo'-tre-ah], *f.* 1. Otter. 2. A kind of small sea-otter, the fur of which is so called.

nutricio, cia [noo-tree'-the-o, ah], *a.* Nutritious, nourishing, nutritive.

nutrición [noo-tre-the-on'], *f.* 1. Nutrition, the act or quality of nourishing. 2. (*Pharm.*) A certain preparation of medicines.

nutrido [noo-tree'-do], *a.* 1. Bien nutrido, well-nourished. 2. (*Fig.*) Large (grande), considerable; numerous (numeroso); abundant (abundante). **Abundante de**, full of.

nutrimental [noo-tre-men-tahl'], *a.* Nutrimental, having the quality of food.

nutrimento [noo-tre-men'-to], *m.* 1. Nutriment, food, aliment, nourishment. 2. Nutrition.

nutrir [noo-treer'], *va.* 1. To nourish, to fatten, to feed. 2. To nourish, to encourage, to foment, to support.

nutritivo, va [noo-tre-tee'-vo, vah], *a.* Nutritive, nourishing.

nutriz [noo-treeth'], *f.* Nurse.

nutual [noo-too-ahl'], *a.* Irremovable: said of chaplains and other ministers not removable at pleasure of the grantor.

ny [nee], *f.* Nu, thirteenth letter of the Greek alphabet, corresponding to N.

nylon [ny-lon], *m.* Nylon.

Ñ

ñ [ay'-nyay] is the fifteenth letter in the Spanish alphabet. The ancient Spanish writers used *nn* in words derived from the Latin having *gn*, as from *lignum was* written *lenno*, and now *leño*, the *n* with a *tilde*, or circumflex, being substituted in their place. Ñ has a strong nasal sound, resembling that of *n* in the English word *poniard*, and exactly similar to that of *gn* in the French word *poignard*.

ñagaza [nyah-gah'-thah], *f.* Bird-call, a decoy. V. AÑAGAZA.

ñame [nyah'-may], *m.* Yam.

ñandú [nyan-doo'], *m.* An Argentine variety of the American ostrich. V. NANDÚ.

ñapa [nyah'-pah], *f.* (*Amer.*) That which is thrown in for, at the end of a bargain. **Dar de ñapa**, to give a thing free. V. CONTRA and PILÓN.

ñaque [nyah'-kay], *m.* Heap of useless trifles.

ñigua [nyee'-goo-ah], *f.* V. NIGUA.

ñiquiñaque [nye-kee-nyah'-kay], *m.* An expression used by the vulgar to depreciate something.

ñoclo [nyo'-clo], *m.* A kind of macaroon, or round sweetmeat.

ñoña [nyo'-nyah], *f.* (*coll.*) Excrement.

ñoñería [nyo-nyay-ree'-ah], *f.* 1. Decrepitude, second childhood. 2. Insipidness (sosería); spinelessness (falta de carácter). 3. (*Cono Sur*) Senility (vejez). 4. (*Carib.*) Inanity (estupidez). 5. (*Carib.*) Endearment (cariñoso).

ñoño, ña [nyo'-nyo, nyah], *a.* (*coll.*) 1. Delicate, plaintive, timid (tímido). 2. Decrepit, impaired by age (viejo). 3. (*And, Carib.*) Vain, that likes to be flattered (vanidoso). 4. (*Mex.*) Thick (bruto).

ñorbo [nyor'-bo], *m.* A certain flower of Peru.

ñurumé [nyoo-roo-may'], *m.* (*Zool.*) An ant-eater of Paraguay.

O

o [oh], the sixteenth letter in the Spanish alphabet is pronounced like the English *o* in cone. *O*, in arithmetic, serves for naught or cipher; it is also used as a circle, of which there is no end, and therefore emblematic of eternity. *O*, in sea-charts, signifies west; Oeste. The seven anthema sung in the church, the seven days before the nativity of our Lord, are called *OO*, because they all commence with this letter.

o, *conj.* Or, either. **O rico o pobre**, either rich or poor. When followed by another *o*, the conjunction *u* is used instead of *o*, to avoid cacophony; as, *Siete u ocho*, seven or eight.

¡o! *int.* V. ¡Oh!

O conectado, *x.* (*Inform.*) Wired OR.

oasis [o-ah'-sis], *m.* Oasis, a fertile spot in a desert.

obcecación [ob-thay-cah-the-on'], *f.* Obduracy, blindness.

obcecado, da [ob-thay-cah'-do, dah], *a.* Blind (ciego); stubborn (terco); disturbed (trastornado).-*pp.* of OBCECAR.

obcecar [ob-thay-car'], *va.* To blind, to darken or obscure.

obduración [ob-doo-rah-the-on], *f.* Hardness of heart, obstinacy, obduracy.

obedecedor, ra [o-bay-dar-thay-dor', rah], *m.* ·&*f.* Obeyer, one who obeys or submits.

obedecer [o-bay-day-therr'], *va.* To obey, to yield to. **Obedecer a**, to be due to. (*Yo obedezco, yo obedezca*, from *Obedecer.* V. CONOCER.)

obedecimiento [o-bay-day-the-me-en'-to], *m.* Obedience, obsequiousness.

obediencia [o-bay-de-en'-the-ah], *f.* 1. Obedience, submission. 2. Obsequiousness, pliancy, flexibility; docility in animals. **A la obediencia**, at your service, your most obedient.

obediencial [o-bay-de-en-the-ahl'], *a.* Obediential, according to the rules of obedience.

obediente [o-bay-de-en'-tay], *a.* Obedient, obsequious, compliant, submissive.

obedientemente, *adv.* Obediently.

obelisco [o-bay-lees'-co], *m.* Obelisk, a slender stone pyramid. 2. Dagger, mark for reference.

obelo [o-bay'-lo], *m.* Obelisk. *V.* OBELISCO.

obencadura [o-ben-cah-doo'-rah], *f. (Naut.)* A complete set of shrouds in general.

obenques [o-ben'-kes], *m. pl (Naut.)* Shrouds. **Obenques mayores**, the main shrouds.

obertura [o-ber-too'-rah], *f. (Mus.)* Overture.

obesidad [o-bay-se-dahd'], *f.* Obesity, corpulence.

obeso, sa [o-bay'-so, sah], *a.* Obese, fat, corpulent.

óbice [o'-be-thay], *m.* Obstacle, impediment, hindrance, opposition.

obispado [o-bis-pah'-do], *m.* 1. Bishopric, the diocese of a bishop. 2. Episcopate, the office and dignity of a bishop.

obispal [o-bis-pahl'], *a.* Episcopal belonging to a bishhop; bishopric, diocese.

obispar [o-bis-par'], *vn.* 1. To be made bishop, to obtain a bishopric. 2. *(coll.)* To die, to expire.

obispillo [o-bis-peel'-lyo], *m. dim.* 1. Boy-bishop, a chorister boy dressed like a bishop, and allowed to imitate a bishop. 2. A large black pudding; a pork or beef sausage. 3. Rump or croup of a fowl.

obispo [o-bees'-po], *m.* 1. Bishop. **Obispo de anillo** or **de título**, bishop in partibus. **Obispo auxiliar**, assistant bishop. 2. A large black pudding.

óbito [o'-be-to], *m.* Death of a person (religión y ley).

obituario [o-be-too-ah'-re-o], *m.* 1. Obituary, a register of burials (necrología). 2. Decease (muerte).

objeción [ob-hay-the-on'], *f.* Objection, opposition, exception. **Objeción de conciencia**, conscientious objection.

objetar [ob-hay-tar'], *va.* To object, to oppose, to remonstrate, to resent (argumento).

objetivamente [ob-hay-tee'-vah-men-tay], *adv.* Objectively.

objetivar [ob-hay-te-var'], *va.* To make objective.

objetividad [ob-hay-te-ve-dahd'], *f.* Objectivity.

objetivismo [ob-hay-te-vees'-mo], *m.* 1. Objectivity. 2. Objectivism.

objetivo, va [ob-hay-tee'-vo, vah], *a.* Objective (no subjetivo). *-m.* 1. Lens. 2. Objective (meta). 3. Objective, target. 4. *(Fot.)* Lens; object lens. **Objetivo del juego**, trick.

objeto [ob-hay'-to], *m.* 1. Object (artículo). 2. Subject (tema). 3. Object, aim, end, purpose (meta). **Al objeto de**, with the object of. **Fue el objeto de un asalto**, he was the target of an attack.

objetor [ob-hay-tor'], *m.* Objector. **Objetor de conciencia**, conscientious objector.

oblación [o-blah-the-on'], *f.* Oblation, offering, gift.

voblada [o-blah'-dah], *f.* Funeral offering of bread for the souls of the deceased.

oblata [o-blah'-tah], *f.* 1. Host and chalice offered before being consecrated in the celebration of the mass. 2. Sum of money given to the church to defray the expense of bread, wine, candles, etc., for celebrating mass.

oblato, ta [o-blah'-to, tah], *a. & n.* 1. One who, on becoming a monk, donated his property to the community. 2. Anciently, a child offered to God to make him embrace the clerical profession. 3. A lay monk of certain orders. 4. A certain tax anciently paid. 5. An invalided soldier; who had a right of receiving a living and clothing from some abbey or priory.

oblea [o-blay'-ah], *f.* 1. Wafer, paste made to close letters. 2. *(Cono Sur)* Stamp (Correos).

obleero [o-blay-ay'-ro], *m.* 1. One who sells wafers about the streets.

oblicuángulo [o-ble-coo-ahn'-goo-lo], *a.* Oblique-angled.

oblicuidad [o-ble-coo-e-dahd'], *f.* Obliquity, deviation from physical rectitude.

oblicuo, cua [o-blee'-coo-o, ah], *a.* Oblique, not direct, not perpendicular, not parallel, crooked.

obligación [o-ble-cah-the-on'], *f.* 1. Obligation, the binding power of an oath, vow or duty; contract. 2. *(For.)* Obligation, bond; written security for the carrying out of something. 3. Obligation, duty of acknowledging a benefit received. 4. Obligation, bond, of a public debt or of a company, bearing interest. 5. *(Acad.)* Provision office, the place where provisions are sold, pursuant to a previous contract. *-pl.* 1. Character and integrity which a man must possess to be worthy of esteem. **Es hombre de obligaciones**, he is a man of integrity and honor. 2. Family which one is obliged to maintain. 3. Engagements. **Faltar a sus obligaciones**, to fall in one's duty. **Primero es la obligación que la devoción**, business before pleasure.

obligado [o-ble-gah'-do], *m.* 1. Contractor who engages to supply a city with some kind of provisions. 2. *(Law.)* Obligee, one bound by a contract. 3. Obligato, properly obligato, an accompaniment indispensable to the proper performance of a piece of music.

obligante [o-ble-gahn'-tay], *pa.* Obligating, imposing.

obligar [o-ble-gar'], *va.* 1. To oblige, to compel, to bind, to constrain, to necessitate. 2. To oblige, to confer favors, to lay obligations of gratitude. **Obligar a uno a hacer algo**, to force somebody to do something. *-vr.* To oblige or bind oneself.

obligatorio, ria [o-ble-gah-to'-re-o, ah], *a.* Obligatory, binding, coercive, compulsory.

obliteración [o-ble-tay-rah-the-on'], *f.* Obliteration.

obliterar [o-ble-tay-rar'], *va.* 1. *(LAm.)* To blot out, to obliterate, to make disappear. 2. *(Med.)* To obstruct or close some channel of the body.

oblongo, ga [o-blon'-go, gah], *a.* Oblong, greater in length than in breadth.

obnoxia, xia [ob-nok'-se-o, ah], *a.* Obnoxious, hurtful.

oboe [o-bo'-ay], *m.* 1. Oboe or haut-boy, a musical wind-instrument with a double reed. 2. Player on the oboe.

óbolo [o'-bo-lo], *m.* 1. Obolus, Athenian money. 2. Obole, a weight of twelve grains. 3. A small gift for charity.

obra [o'-brah], *f.* 1. Work, anything made. 2. Work, writings of an author. 3. Work, a new building on which men are at work (en construcción). 4. The repairs made in a house. 5. Work, every moral action. 6. Means, virtue, power. 7. Toil, work, labor, employment. 8. Workmanship (hechura). 9. *(Cono Sur)* Brick-works. **Obra de arte mayor**, masterly piece of work. **Obra piadosa**, charity. **Por obra de**, thanks to. **Obra literaria**, literary work. **Cerrado por obras**, closed for repairs.

obrada [o-brah'-dah], *f.* As much ground as two mules or oxen can plough in a day.

obrador, ra [o-brah-dor', rah], *m. & f.* 1. Workman or workwoman, artificer, mechanic. 2. Workshop. **Obradores**, *(Naut.)* workshop or working-places in a dock-yard.

obradura [o-brah-doo'-rah], *f.* That which is expressed at every pressful in oil-mills.

obraje [o-brah'-hay], *m.* 1. Manufacture (fabricación), anything made by art. 2. Manufactory, workshop (taller). *(Amer.)* A manufactory of coarse cloth baize, and other woollen stuffs. 3. *(And. Cono Sur)* Sawmill, timber yard (aserradero). 4. *(And.)* Textile plant (textil).

obrajero [o-brah-bay'-ro], *m.* 1. Foreman (capataz), overseer, superintendent. 2. *(Cono Sur)* Lumberman (maderero). 3. *(And.)* Craftsman (artesano).

obrar [o-brar'], *va.* 1. To work, to manufacture. 2. To operate, to produce effects; to act. 3. To operate, to produce the desired effect (medicinas). 4. To put into practice, to execute; to construct, to build (construir). 5. To ease nature. 6. To work, to bring about (milagro). -*vn. 1.* To act (actuar); to proceed. 2. To work, to have an effect (medicina). 3. To relieve nature. **Su carta obra en mi poder,** I have received your letter.

obrepción [o-brep-the-on'], *f.* Obreption, false narration to obtain some end.

obrepticiamente [o-brep-tee'-the-ah-men-tay], *adv.* Falsely, deceitfully.

obrepticio, cia [o-brep-tee'-the-o, ah], *a.* Obreptitious, obtained by a false statement of matters or fact, by deceit or surprise.

obreria [o-bray-ree'-ah], *f.* 1. Task of a workman. 2. Money destined for the repairs of a church.

obrero, ra [o-bray'-ro, rah], *m. & f.* 1. Worker, workman, day-laborer. 2. Missionary. 3. Prebendary who superintends the repairs of church buildings. 4. Person who collects money for the building of churches. -*a.* Working (clase); labor (sindicato).

obreropatronal [o-bray-ro-pah-tro-nahl'], *a.* Relating to capital and labor. **Relaciones obreropatronales,** capital and labor relations.

obrita [o-bree'-tah], *f. dim.* Small or little work.

obrizo, za [o-bree'-tho, thah], *a.* Pure, refined (oro).

obscenidad [obs-thay-ne-dahd'], *f.* Obscenity, impurity, unchastity, lewdness.

obsceno, na [os-thay'-no, nah], *a.* Obscene, impure, lewd, lustful.

obscuramente, *adv.* 1. Obscurely, darkly, faintly, abstrusely. 2. Obscurely, privately. 3. Obscurely, confusedly, not plainly.

obscurantismo [obs-coo-ran-tees'-mo], *m.* Obscurantism.

obscuras (a) [obs-coo'-ras, ah], *adv.* Obscurely, darkly.

obscurecer [obs-coo-ray-therr'], *va.* V. OSCURECER. 1. To obscure, to darken. 2. To cloud over. 3. To fill with gloom or darkness. 4. To cloud, to confuse the reason. 5. To render a subject less intelligible. 6. *(Pict.)* To use deep shades. -*v. impers.* To grow dark. -*vr.* 1. To cloud over. 2. To disappear.

obscurecimiento [obs-coo-ray-the-me-en'-to], *m.* 1. Obscuration, act of darkening. 2. Blackout (durante la guerra).

obscuridad [obs-coo-re-dahd], *f.* V. OSCURIDAD. 1. Obscurity, darkness. 2. Cloudiness, gloominess, opacity, density. 3. Obscurity, darkness of meaning, abstruseness, confusedness. 4. The humbleness of a stock whence a family or any other thing proceeds. 5. Retired, private life.

obscuro, ra [obs-coo'-ro, rah], *a.* V. OSCURO. 1. Obscure, dark, gloomy. 2. Obscure, unintelligible, confused, abstruse. 3. Obscure, little known, unknown. 4. *(Pict.)* Dark, deep, heavy. **Andar a obscuras,** *(Met.)* to grope in the dark, to proceed in a business without understanding its nature or principles.

obsecración [ob-say-crah-the-on'], *f.* Obsecration, entreaty, supplication.

obsecuente [ob-say-coo-en'-tay], *a.* Obsequious, obedient.

obsequiante [ob-say-ke-ahn'-tay], *pa. & n.* Obsequious; courtier, gallant.

obsequiar [ob-say-ke-ar'], *va.* To court, to wait upon, to serve, to obey. **Le obsequiaron con un reloj,** they presented him with a clock.

obsequio [ob-say'-ke-o], *m.* Obsequiousness, complaisance, civility, desire of pleasing, present (regalo). **Por obsequio de,** for the sake of, out of respect to.

obsequioso, sa [ob-say-ke-o'-so, sah], *a.* 1. Obsequious, obedient, compliant, obliging (servicial), attentive. 2. *(Mex.)* Fond of giving presents.

observación [ob-ser-vah-the-on'], *f.* 1. Observation, the act of observing (acto); remark (comentario), note. **Observaciones sueltas,** desultory remarks. 2. Observance, careful obedience. **Estar en observación,** to be under observation. **Hacer una observación,** to make a remark.

observador, ra [ob-ser-vah-dor', rah], *m. & f.* 1. Observer, remarker. 2. Observer, one who keeps any law, custom, or practice. -*m.* An astronomer.

observancia [ob-ser-vahn'-the-ah], *f.* 1. Observance, respect, reverence, regard. 2. Attentive practice, obedience, observation, ritual practice. 3. The original state of some religious orders, in contradistinction to their reformed condition. **Poner en observancia,** to execute punctually whatever is ordered.

observante [ob-ser-vahn'-tay], *pa. & a.* Observant, respectfully obedient; observing. -*m.* Monk of certain branches of the order of St. Francis.

observar [ob-ser-var'], *va.* 1. To observe (mirar), to regard attentively. 2. To observe, to notice, to mind, to heed. 3. To observe, to keep religiously or ritually, to follow. 4. To obey, to execute with punctuality and exactness. 5. **Observar algo a uno,** *(LAm.)* to point something out to somebody.

observatorio [ob-ser-vah-to'-re-o], *m.* Observatory, a place for astronomical or meteorological observations.

obsesión [ob-say-se-on'], *f.* Obsession.

obsesionar [ob-say-se-o-nar'], *va. & vr.* To obsess, to be obsessed (idea.) **Estar obsesionado con algo,** to be obsessed by something.

obsesivo [ob-say-see'-vo], *a.* Obsessive.

obseso, sa [ob-say'-so, sah], *a.* Beset, tempted, as with evil spirits.

obsidiana [ob-se-de-ah'-nah], *f.* Obsidian, a glassy, volcanic rock.

obsoleto [ob-so-lay'-to], *a.* Obsolete.

obstáculo [obs-tah'-coo-lo], *m.* Obstacle, impediment, obstruction, clog, hindrance. **No es obstáculo para que yo…,** it is no obstacle to my…

obstante (no) [obs-tahn'-tay], *pa.* Notwithstanding, nevertheless, however.

obstar [ob-star'], *vn.* To oppose, to obstruct, to hinder, to withstand.

obstetrical [obs-tay-tre-cahl'], *a.* Obstetrical.

obstetricia [obs-tay-tre'-the-ah], *f.* Obstetrics, midwifery.

obstétrico, ca [obs-tay'-tre-co, cah], *a.* Obstetrical, relating to childbirth. -*f.*

obstinación [obs-te-nah-the-on'], *f.* Obstinacy, stubbornness, obduracy.

obstinadamente [obs-te-nah'-dah-men-tay], *adv.* Obstinately, stubbornly.

obstinado, da [obs-te-nah'-do, dah], *a.* Obstinate, obdurate, headstrong, opinionated. -*pp.* of OBSTINARSE.

obstinarse [obs-te-nar'-say], *vr.* To be obstinate.

obstrucción [obs-trooc-the-on'], *f.* 1. *(Med.)* Obstruction in the vessels of the body. 2. Obstruction, closure of any passage.

obstructivo, va [obs-trooc-tee'-vo, vah], *a.* Obstructive, obstruent.

obstruir [obs-troo-eer'], *va.* To obstruct or block up the natural passages of the body (bloquear). -*vr.* To be obstructed or choked (abertura).

obtemperar [ob-tem-pay-rar'], *va. (Ant.)* To obey, to assent (used with prep. *a).*

obtención [ob-ten-the-on'], *f.* Attainment, obtainment, the act of attaining or obtaining.

obtener [ob-tay-nerr'], *va.* 1. To attain, to obtain, to procure. 2. To preserve, to maintain. *(Yo obtengo, obtenga, obtuve, obtuviera;* from *Obtener V.* TENER.)

obtento [ob-ten'-to], *m.* 1. Benefice, prebend, living. 2. Attainment.

obtentor [ob-ten-tor'], *m.* One who obtains a living on being ordained priest.

obtestación [ob-tes-tah-the-on'], *f.* Obtestation, protestation, a rhetorical figure in which the speaker calls to witness God, nature, men, or inanimate things.

obturador, triz [ob-too-rah-dor', treeth'], *a.* Serving to stop up or plug. -*m.* 1. Plug, stopper; breechblock. 2. Obturator, a surgical plate for closing a fissure. 3. Gas-check, a circular plate of glass placed over the mouth of vessels filled with gas, for carrying them. 4. A photographic shutter.

obturar [ob-too-rar'], *va.* To stop up, to plug, to obturate.

obtusángulo [ob-too-sahn'-goo-lo], *m. & a.* Obtuse angle; obtusangular.

obtuso, sa [ob-too'-so, sah], *a.* 1. Obtuse, blunt, not pointed; not shrill. 2. Obtuse, dull.

obué [o-boo-ay'], *m.* Oboe and oboe-player. *V.* OBOE.

obús [o-boos'], *m.* 1. Howitzer, a kind of mortar used for firing shells and grapeshot (cañón). 2. *(Neol.)* A conical shell.

obusero, ra [o-boo-say'-ro, rah], *a. (Mil.)* Shell-throwing: used of cannons and of a vessel provided with howitzers.

obvención [ob-ven-the-on'], *f.* A casual profit, obvention.

obviamente [ob'-ve-ah-men-tay], *adv.* Obviously.

obviar [ob-ve-ar'], *va.* To obviate (evitar), to prevent. -*vn.* To oppose, to stand in the way (estorbar).

obvio, via [ob'-ve-o, ah], *a.* Obvious, evident.

obyecto, ta [ob-yec'-to, tah], *m. (Met.)* Interposed.

oca [o'-cah], *f.* 1. *(Orn.)* Goose. 2. *(Bot.)* Oca oxalic, with yellow flowers. 3. Kind of game called *Royal goose.*

ocal [o-cahl'], *m.* 1. Cocoon of silk formed by two silkworms together, and the silk made from it.-*a.* Applied to very delicate sweet pears and apples.

ocalear [o-cah-lay-ar'], *vn.* To make *ocals* (gusanos de seda).

ocarina [o-cah-ree'-nah], *f. (Mus.)* Ocarina.

ocasión [o-cah-se-on'], *f.* 1. Occasion (vez), opportunity, chance (oportunidad), juncture, convenience. 2. Occasion, accidental cause or motive (motivo). 3. Danger, risk. 4. Cause (motivo). **Por ocasión**, by chance. **En algunas ocasiones**, sometimes. **Aprovechar la ocasión**, to take one's chance.

ocasionado, da [o-cah-se-o-nah'-do, dah], *a.* Provoking, vexatious, insolent; perilous. -*pp.* of OCASIONAR.

ocasionador, ra [o-cah-se-o-nah-dor', rah], *m. & f.* Occasioner, one that causes or promotes.

ocasional [o-cah-se-o-nahl'], *a.* 1. Occasional (composición), extemporaneous. 2. Chance (fortuito), accidental.

ocasionalmente, *adv.* Occassionally.

ocasionar [o-cah-se-o-nar'], *va.* 1. To cause, to occasion; to move, to excite. 2. To endanger.

ocasioncilla, ita [o-cah-se-on-theel'-lyah, thee'-tah], *f. dim.* of OCASIÓN.

ocaso [o-cah'-so], *m.* 1. The setting of the sun or any heavenly body. 2. Occident, the west. 3. Death.

occidental [oc-the-den-tahl'], *a.* Occidental, western.

occidente [oc-the-den'-tay], *m.* 1. Occident, the west. 2. Europe, in contrast to Asia or the Orient. 3. *(Met.)* Age, decadence.

occiduo, dua [oc-thee'-doo-o, ah], *a.* Occidental.

occipital [oc-the-pe-tahl'], *a.* Occipital, a bone in the hinder part of the head.

occipucio [oc-the-poo'-the-o], *m.* Occiput, the back part of the head, where it joins the spine.

occiso, sa [oc-thee'-so, sah], *a.* Murdered, killed.

oceánico, ca [o-thay-ah'-ne-co, cah], *a.* 1. Oceanic, belonging to the ocean. 2. Living or grooving in the ocean.

océano [o-thay'-ah-no], *m.* 1. The ocean. 2. Any vast expanse. **Océano Ártico**, Artic Ocean.

oceanografía [o-thay-ah-no-grah-fee'-ah], *f.* Oceanography, oceanic geography.

ocelotl (or **ocelote**), *m.* Ocelot, a leopard-like cat of Mexico and South America.

ochava [o-chah'-vah], *f.* The eighth part of something. *Ochavas del molinete, (Naut.)* the whelps of the windlass.

ochavado, da [o-chah-vah'-do, dah], *a.* Octagonal, eight-sided. -*pp.* of OCHAVAR.

ochavar [o-chah-var'], *va.* To forth an octagon.

ochavear [o-chah-vay-ar'], *va.* To be divided into eighths.

ochavo [o-chah'-vo], *m.* 1. An old small Spanish brass coin, valued at two maravedies. 2. Something octagonal.

ochenta [o-chen'-tah], *a. & m.* Eighty.

ochentavo, va [o-chen-tah'-vo, vah], *a.* The one-eightieth part.

ochentón, na [o-chen-tone', nah], *a.* Eighty years old.

ochete [o-chay'-tay], *m.* Bore or empty part of hollow projectiles.

ocho [o'-cho], *a. & m.* 1. Eight. 2. Eight, the figure 8.3. A card with eight marks. **El ocho de Marzo**, the eighth of March.

ochocientos [o-cho-the-en'-tos], *a. & m.* Eight hundred.

ochosén [o-cho-sen'], *m.* The smallest coin among the ancient Spaniards.

ocio [o'-the-o], *m.* 1. Leisure (tiempo libre), freedom from business; vacancy of mind. 2. Pastime (pasatiempo), diversion. **Ratos de ocio**, leisure.

ociosamente, *adv.* Idly, uselessly.

ociosidad [o-the-o-se-dahd'], *f.* Idleness, laziness, sluggishness, leisure.

ocioso, sa [o-the-o'-so, sah], *a.* Idle (inactivo), lazy, fruitless, unprofitable; foppish, useless (acto, palabras).

oclocracia [o-clo-crah'-the-ah], *f.* Ochlocracy, government by the multitude.

oclusión [o-cloo-se-on'], *f.* Occlusion, obliteration.

ocote [o-co'-tay], *m.* A very resinous pine-tree of Mexico; pitch-pine.

ocozoal [o-co-tho-ahl'], *m.* Mexican serpent, like a viper.

ocre [o'-cray], *m.* Ochre, a brown or yellow earth.

ocropira [o-cro-pee'-rah], *f.* Yellow fever.

ocroso, sa [o-cro'-so, sah], *a.* Ochreous, of the nature or color of ochre.

octaedro [oc-tah-ay'-dro], *m. (Geom.)* Octahedron, a solid bounded by eight plane triangles.

octagonal [oc-tah-go-nahl'], *a.* Octagonal.

octágono, na [oc-tah'-go-no, nah], *a.* Having eight sides and angles.

octágono [oc-tah'-go-no], *m.* An octagon.

octal [oc-tahl], *m.(Comput.)* Octal.

octangular [oc-tan-goo-lar'], *a.* Octangular.

octano [oc-tah'-no], *m. (Chem.)* Octane.

octante [oc-tahn'-tay], *m.* Octant, an instrument containing the eighth part of a circle.

octava [oc-tah'-vah], *f.* 1. Octave, a space of eight days comprising a church festival. 2. A poetical composition of eight lines of eleven syllables, rhyming thus: 1, 3, 5; 2, 4, 6; 7 and 8. 3. *(Mus.)* Octave. 4. *V.* OCTAVARIO.

octavar [oc-tah-var'], *vn.* 1. To form octaves on stringed instruments. 2. To deduct the eighth part.

octavario [oc-tah-vah'-re-o], *m.* 1. Book which contains the office for an octave festival. 2. Festival lasting a week.

octavilla [oc-tah-veel'-lyah], *f.* 1. Half-pint for excise taken on the retail of vinegar, oil, and wine. 2. *(Mus.)* Octave.

octavín [oc-tah-veen'], *m.* 1. A piccolo flutes. 2. Flageolet.

octavo [oc-th'-vo], *m.* 1. An eighth. 2. In America, an octoroon.

octavo, va, *a.* 1. Eighth; octave, octonary. 2. Octavos de final, *(Dep.)* quarter-finals.

octeto [oc-tay'-to], *m. (Mus.)* Octet.

octogenario, ria [oc-to-hay-nah'-re-o, ah], *a.* Octogenary, eighty years old.

octogentésimo [oc-to-hen-tay'-se-mo], *a.* Eight hundredth.

octogésimo [oc-to-hay'-se-mo], *a.* Eightieth.

octógono, na [oc-toh'-go-no, nah], *a. V.* OCTÁGONO.

octopétala [oc-to-pay'-tah-lah], *a. (Bot.)* Octopetalous, of eight petals.

octosilábico, ca, octosílabo, ba [oc-to-se-lah'-be-co, cah], *a.* Octosyllabic.

octubre [oc-too'-bray], *m.* October.

octuplicar [oc-too-ple-car'], *va.* To multiply by eight, to increase eight-fold.

óctuplo, pla [oc'-too-plo, plah], *a.* Octuple, eight-fold.

ocular [o-coo-lar'], *a.* Ocular. **Testigo ocular**, eyewitness. -*m.* Eyeglass, ocular, eye-piece.

oculista [o-coo-lees'-tah], *m. & f.* Oculist; eye specialist.

ocultación [o-cool-tah-the-on'], *f.* 1. Concealment, hiding. 2. *(Ast.)* Occultation of a star or planet. 3. Wrongful silence.

ocultador, ra [o-cool-tah-dor', rah], *m. & f.* Hider, concealer.

ocultamente [o-cool'-tah-men-tay], *adv.* Secretly, hiddenly.

ocultar [o-cool-tar'], *va.* 1. To hide (esconder), to conceal, to disguise (disfrazar), to secrete, to mask, to hoodwink, to cloak. 2. To keep back, to keep secret what ought to be said. *-vr.* To hide oneself. **Ocultarse a la vista**, to keep out of sight. **Ocultarse tras**, to hide behind.

ocultismo [o-cool-tees'-mo], *m.* Occultism.

oculto, ta [o-cool'-to, tah], *a.* Hidden (escondite), concealed, occult (ciencia), secret (pensamiento), clandestine. **De oculto**, incognito. **En oculto**, secretly, in secret.

ocupación [o-coo-pah-the-on'], *f.* 1. Occupation; business, concern; employment, office, pursuit; action. 2. Prolepsis. a rhetorical figure.

ocupado, da [o-coo-pah'-do, dah], *a.* Busy (persona), occupied (plaza), engaged. **La línea está ocupada**, *(Telec.)* the line is engaged. **Estoy muy ocupado**, I'm very busy.

ocupador [o-coo-pah-dor'], *m.* Occupier, possessor, occupant.

ocupante [o-coo-pahn'-tay], *pa. & n.* Occupant; an actual possessor of lands.

ocupar [o-coo-par'], *va.* 1. To occupy, to take possession of (espacio, silla). 2. To hold an employ (puesto), to fill a public station. 3. To occupy, to busy, to employ (obreros), to give employment. 4. To disturb, to interrupt, to obstruct. 5. To inhabit a house. 6. *(Met.)* To occupy or gain the attention. 7. *(Mex.)* To use (emplear). **Ocupa sus ratos libres pintando**, he uses his spare time to paint. **Las obras ocupan más de 1000 hombres**, the work keeps more than 1000 men busy. *-vr.* To occupy, to follow business. **Ocuparse de**, to concern oneself with. **Me ocuparé de ello mañana**, I will deal with it tomorrow.

ocurrencia [o-coor-ren'-the-ah], *f.* 1. Occurrence (suceso), accident, incident, occasion. 2. Bright thought or original idea which occurs to the mind (idea). **Me dio la ocurrencia de**, it occurred to me to.

ocurrente [o-coor-ren'-tay], *a.* Off hand, original, bright (listo), wity (chistoso). *-pa.* of OCURRIR.

ocurrir [o-coor-reer'], *vn.* 1. To meet, to go to meet, to anticipate. 2. To occur, to happen, to fall on the same day: applied to two feasts of different solemnities. 3. To obviate, to make opposition to. 4. To repair to proceed. **Se me ocurre una idea**, *(coll.)* a thought strikes me. *-v. impers.* To occur, to be presented to the memory or attention. **Nunca se me había ocurrido**, it had never crossed my mind.

oda [o'dah], *f.* 1. Ode, a lyric poem. 2. Ode, a poem written to be set to music.

odalisca [o-dah-lees'-cah], *f.* Odalisk, a woman of the harem of the Sultan of Turkey; a servant of his sisters, daughters, and wives, and often a concubine.

odiar [o-be-ar'], *va.* 1. To hate, to abhor, to detest. 2. *(Cono Sur)* To irk (fastidiar), to bore (aburrir). *-vr.* To hate one another.

odio [o'-de-o], *m.* Hatred, abhorrence, detestation, malevolence. **Tener odios**, to hate.

odiosamente [o-de-o'-sah-men-tay], *adv.* Odiously, hatefully.

odiosidad [o-de-o-se-dahd'], *f.* 1. Hatefulness, odiousness, odium. 2. *(And. Carib. Cono Sur)* Irksome, annoyance.

odioso, sa [o-de-oh'-so, sah], *a.* odious, hateful, detestable. 2. *(And. Cono Sur)* Irksome (molesto), annoying.

odisea [o-de-say'-ah], *f.* 1. The Odyssey, a poem written by Homer. 2. Adventure, ordeal.

odómetro [o-do'-may-tro], *m.* Instrument for measuring the road passed over; odometer.

odontalgia [o-don-tahl'-he-ah], *f.* Odontalgia, toothache.

odontálgico [o-don-tahl'-he-co], *m.* Odontalgic, remedy for toothache.

odontecnia [o-don-tec'-ne-ah], *f.* Dental surgery.

odontina [o-don-tee'-nah], *f.* 1. A remedy for curing toothache. 2. A dentifrice.

odontología [o-don-to-lo-hee'-ah], *f.* Odontology, the science of dentistry.

odontólogo [o-don-to'-lo-go], *m.* Odontologist, dentist.

odontotecnia [o-don-to-tec'-ne-ah], *f.* Practical art of dentistry.

odorífero, ra [o-do-ree'-fay-ro, rah], *a.* Odoriferous, fragrant, perfumed.

odorífico, ca [o-do-ree'-fe-co, cah], *a.* Odor-producing. **Órgano odorífico**, the organ which, in the hemiptera, secretes the smell which they emit at will.

odre [o'-dray], *m.* 1. Bag generally used for wine, oil, and other liquids, commonly made of a dreseed goatskin; a leather bottle lined with pitch. 2. Drunkard (borracho).

odrería [o-dray-ree'-ah], *f.* Shop where leather bottles are made or sold.

odrero [o-dray'-ro], *m.* One who makes or deals in leather bottles.

odrina [o-dree'-nah], *f.* Ox-skin bag.

oenas [o-ay'-nah], *f.* Stock-dove, wood-pigeon.

oenate [o-ay-nah'-tay], *f. (Orn.)* Fallow-finch, stone-chatter.

oesnorueste [o-es-no-roo-es'-tay], *m.* West-north-west.

oessudueste [o-es-soo-doo-es'-tay], *m.* West-south-west.

oeste [o-es'-tay], *m.* 1. West (región). 2. The west wind (viento). **En la parte del oeste**, in the western part. *-a.* West (parte), western; westerly (dirección); west (viento).

ofendedor, ra [o-fen-day-dor', rah], *m. & f.* V. OFENSOR.

ofender [o-fen-derr'], *va.* 1. To offend, to harm, to indure, to make angry. **Por temor a ofenderle**, for fear of offending him. 2. *(Mex.)* To touch up (mujer). *-vr.* To be vexed or displeased; to take offence.

ofendido [o-fen-dee'-do], *a.* Offended. **Darse por ofendido**, to take offence.

ofensa [o-fen'-sah], *f.* 1. Offence, injury, transgression, crime. 2. Offence; attack. 3. Offence, breaking the law of God.

ofensiva [o-fen-see'-vah], *f.* Offensive. **Ofensiva de paz**, peace offensive.

ofensivamente [o-fen-see'-vah-men-tay], *adv.* Offensively, injuriously.

ofensivo, va [o-fen-see'-vo, vah], *a.* 1. Offensive, displeasing, disgusting (asqueroso). 2. Assailant, not defensive. *-f.* **Tomar la ofensiva**, to take the offensive; to prepare for attack, and to attack in fact.

ofensivo [o-fen-see'-vo], *m.* Anything which serves as a defence or remedy.

ofensor, ra [o-fen-sor', rah], *m. & f.* Offender.

oferente [o-fay-ren'-tay], *m.* Offerer, one who offers.

oferta [o-ferr'-tah], *f.* 1. Offer, promise, offering. 2. Supply. **La ley de la oferta y la demanda**, the law of supply and demand.

ofertorio [o-fer-too'-re-o], *m.* 1. Offertory, the act of offering; the thing offered; the part of the mass where the priest offers up the host and wine. 2. The anthem belonging to this service.

oficial, la [o-fe-the-ahl', lah], *m. & f.* 1. Workman, workwoman, artificer, tradesman; journeyman. **Buen oficial**, a first-rate hand, a good operative. 2. Officer who holds a commission in the army or navy. 3. Clerk in a public office. **Oficial mayor de la secretaría de estado**, first under secretary of the state department. **Oficial mayor**, chief clerk (oficina). 4. Hangman, executioner. 5. *(Prov.)* Butcher, one who cuts up and retails meat. 6. Municipal magistrate. 7. Craftsman (artesano). **Es buen oficial**, he is a clever workman; he is a good officer. **Oficial médico**, medical officer. **Oficial de seguridad**, security officer. **Oficial técnico**, technical officer.

oficial [o-fe-the-ahl'], *a.* Official, pertaining to a public charge.

oficialazo [o-fe-the-ah-lah'-tho], *m. aug.* A skilful workman.

oficialejo [o-fe-the-ah-lay'-ho], *m. dim.* A petty workman.

oficialía [o-fe-the-ah-lee'-ah], *f.* 1. Clerk's place in a public office. **Oficialía mayor**, chief clerkship. 2. Artist's working-room.

oficialidad [o-fe-the-ah-le-dahd'], *f.* Body of officers of an army or regiment.

oficialmente [o-fe-the-al-men'-tay], *adv.* Officially, in an official manner.

oficiar [o-fe-the-ar'], *va.* To officiate, commonly in worship, to minister.

oficina [o-fe-thee'-nah], *f.* 1. Workshop. 2. Office, counting-house 3. (*Cono Sur*) Nitrate house. **oficinas**, offices, the lower apartments in houses, such as cellars. **Horas de oficina**, business hours.

oficinal [o-fe-the-nahl'], *a.* Officinal: applied to the drugs prepared by apothecaries.

oficinesco, ca [o-fe-the-nes'-co, cah], *a.* Departmental, relating to the offices of state, in a derogatory sense; «redtape.»

oficinista [o-fe-the-nees'-tah], *m.* Anyone employed in a public or a secretary's office.

oficio [o-fee'-the-o], *m.* 1. Office, employ, job (profesión), work, occupation, ministry. 2. Function, operation. 3. Official letter. 4. Trade, business, craft. 5. Notary's office. 6. Benefit, service. 7. (*Ec.*) Service; mass. **Oficio de difuntos**, office for the dead. **De oficio**, officially, by duty, not by request. **Mozo de oficio**, an under-servant in the king's palace. **Tomarlo por oficio**, to do a thing frequently. **Oficios**, solemn church service or divine service. **Los deberes del oficio**, the duties of the post. **Sabe su oficio**, he knows his job. **Estos son los gajes del oficio**, these are the occupational hazards or drawbacks.

oficiosamente [o-fe-the-o'-sah-men-tay], *adv.* Officiously.

oficiosidad [o-fe-the-o-se-dahd'], *f.* 1. Diligence, application to business. 2. Officiousness.

oficioso, sa [o-fe-the-o'-so, sah], *a.* 1. Officious, diligent, attentive to business, compliant, accommodating. 2. Officious, meddling, forward. **De fuente oficiosa**, from a semiofficial source.

oficleido [o-fe-clay'-e-do], *m.* Ophicleide, a brass wind-instrument, deeptoned, of open mouth-piece, and nine (or cleven) keys.

ofidios [o-fee'-de-ose], *m. pl.* Ophidia, the serpents or snakes.

ofiólatra [o-fe-o'-lah-trah], *a.* Ophiolatrous, relating to serpent-worship.

ofita [o-fee'-tah], *f.* Ophite, a kind of greenish porphyry.

ofrecedor [o-fray-thay-dor'], *m.* Offerer.

ofrecer [o-fray-therr'], *va.* 1. To offer, to make an offer, to hold out. 2. To present (presentar). 3. To manifest. 4. To dedicate, to consecrate. -*vr.* To offer (persona), to occur (suceder), to present itself. **Ofrecerse en sacrificio**, to offer oneself in sacrifice. **Ofrecerse de ayudante**, to offer one's services as an assistant. **Ofrecerse con la boca chica**, to make a complimentary offer without intending fulfilment. **¿Se le ofrece a usted algo?** at your service, what can I do for you? (*Yo ofrezco, yo ofrezca, from Ofrecer. V.* CONOCER.)

ofrecimiento [o-fray-the-me-en'-to], *m.* 1. Offer, promise, offering. 2. Occurrence, incident. 3. Extemporary discourse.

ofrenda [o-fren'-dah], *f.* Offering, oblation, gift.

ofrendar [o-fren-dar'], *va.* 1. To present offerings to God. 2. To contribute toward some end or purpose.

oftalmía [of-tal-mee'-ah], *f.* Ophthalmia, an inflammation of the eye.

oftálmico [of-tahl'-me-co], *a.* Ophthalmic.

oftalmografía [of-tal'-mo-grah-fee'-ah], *f.* Ophthalmography, a minute description of the eye.

oftalmología [of-tal-mo-lo-hee'-ah], *f.* Ophthalmology, the branch of medicine concerned with the eye and its diseases.

oftalmólogo [of-tal-mo'-lo-go], *m.* Ophthalmologist, oculist.

oftalmómetro [of-tal-mo'-may-tro], *m.* Ophthalmometer, an instrument for examining the refraction of the eye.

oftalmoscopia [of-tal-mos-co'-pe-ah], *f.* Ophthalmoscopy, examination of the eye.

oftalmoscopio [of-tal-mos-co'-pe-o], *m.* Ophthalmoscope, a mirror with a central aperture for viewing the interior of the eye.

ofuscación, *f.* **ofuscamiento**, *m.* [o-foos-cah-the-on', o-foos-cah-me-en'-to]. Obfuscation, dimness of the sight; confused reason.

ofuscar [o-foos-car'], *va.* To obfuscate, to darken, to render obscure. **Ofuscar la razón or el entendimiento**, to disturb the mind, to confuse the judgment. (*Met.*) To dazzle (deslumbrar).

ogro [o'-gro], *m.* Ogre, a fabulous monster.

¡oh! *int.* O! Oh! ¡Oh, quiera Dios!** God grant! **¡Oh, qué hermosa casa!** oh, what a fine house! (*Naut.*) Ho! **¡Oh, el barco!** ho! ship ahoy!

ohmio [o'-me-o], *m.* (*Elec.*) Ohm.

oíble [o-ee'-blay], *a.* Audible, that can be heard.

oída [o-ee'-dah], *f.* Act and effect of hearing.

oído, da [o-ee'-do, dah], *pp.* of OÍR. Heard. - *m.* 1. The sense of hearing (sentido). 2. Ear, organ of hearing. 3. Ear, power of judging of harmony. 4. Touch-hole of a gun. **Está sordo de un oído**, he is deaf in one ear. **Hablar al oído**, to whisper in one's ear. **Dolor de oídos**, earache. **Tener buen oído**, to have a quick ear. **Llegar a oídos**, or **a sus oídos**, to come to one's ears or knowledge. **Tocar de oído**, to play by ear. **Entra por un oído y sale por otro**, it goes in one ear and out of the other. **Ser todo oídos**, to be all ears.

oidor, ra [o-e-dor', rah], *m. & f.* Hearer, one who hears. -*a.* Hearing.

oidoría [o-e-do-ree'-ah], *f.* Office or dignity of an *oidor.*

oír [o-eer'], *va.* 1. To hear, to listen. **Has oído campanas y no sabes dónde**, you don't really know what you're talking about. 2. To understand, to comprehend. 3. To attend the lectures on some science or art, in order to study it. 4. To go to mass (misa); to hear (consejo). 5. To hear, to heed, to answer (súplica). 6. (*Jur.*) To hear (causa). **Oír misa**, to attend at or hear mass. **No haber oído la campana**, to be unobservant or ignorant of common things. **¿Oyes?** or **¿oye Vd.?** I say, do you hear? **Oiga or oigan**, exclamation of surprise. **Oye, oye**, hear! hear! **Oír, ver, y callar**, mind your own business. **Oír hablar de**, to hear it said that. **Le oí abrir la puerta**, I heard him open the door. (*Yo oigo, oiga, oyera; él oyó. V.* OÍR.)

oíslo [o-ees'-lo], *m.* Person beloved, wife (or husband). Very ancient word.

ojal [o-hahl'], *m.* 1. Button-hole. 2. Hole through anything.

ojalá [o-hah-lah'], *int.* Would to God! God grant! I hope so! **¡Ojalá que él viva!** may he live! **Ojalá que vaya**, I wish he may go, I wish he went. -*conj.* (*LAm.*) Even though.

ojaladera [o-hah-lah-day'-rah], *f.* A woman who works button-holes.

ojaladura [o-hah-lah-doo'-rah], *f.* The set of button-holes in a garment.

ojalar [o-hah-lar'], *va.* To make button holes.

ojazo [o-hah'-tho], *m. aug.* A large eye.

ojeada [o-hay-ah'-dah], *f.* Glance, glimpse, ogle.

ojeador [o-hay-ah-dor'], *m.* One who starts game for the chase.

ojeadura [o-hay-ah-doo'-rah], *f.* Act of glazing clothes.

ojear [o-hay-ar'], *va.* 1. To eye, to view with attention, to glance at (mirar). 2. To start game by hallooing. 3. To startle something. 3. (*Cono Sur*) To put the evil eye on (hechizar).

ojeo [o-hay'-o], *m.* The act of starting game for the chase by hallooing. **Echar un ojeo**, to start and drive game toward the sportsmen.

ojera [o-hay'-rah], *f.* 1. Bluish circle under the lower eye-lid, indicative of indisposition (sombra). 2. An eye-bath or eye-cup, a glass vessel for bathing the eye.

ojeriza [o-hay-ree'-thah], *f.* Spite, grudge, ill-will.

ojeroso, sa, ojerudo, da [o-hay-ro'-so, sah], *a.* Applied to persons with blackish circles under the eyes.

ojete [o-hay'-tay], *m.* 1. Eyelet-hole in clothes. 2. (*coll.*) Anus.

ojetear [o-hay-tay-ar'], *va.* To make eyelet-holes in clothes.

ojetera [o-hay-tay'-rah], *f.* 1. Piece of whalebone sewed near the eyelet-holes in clothes. 2. A woman or a machine which makes eyelet-holes.

ojialegre [o-he-ah-lay'-gray], *a.* Having lively, sparkling eyes.

ojiazul [o-he-ah-thool'], *a.* Blue-eyed. (*Neol. Amer.*)

ojito [o-hee'-to], *m. dim.* A small eye.

ojienjuto, ta [o-he-en-hoo'-to, tah], *a.* Dry-eyed.

ojillos [o-hel'-lyos], *m. pl.* Bright eyes; lovely eyes; roguish eyes.

ojimiel, ojimel [o-he-me-el', *m.* Oxymel, a mixture of honey and vinegar.

ojimoreno, na [o-he-mo-ray'-no, nah], *a.* Brown-eyed.

ojinegro, gra [o-he-nay'-gro, grah], *a.* Black-eyed.

ojiva [o-hee'-vah], *f.* 1. Diagonal rib of a vaulted arch. 2. Ogive, a pointed arch.

ojival [o-he-vahl'], *a.* Ogival, belonging to an ogive.

ojizaino, na [o-he-thah-ee'-no, nah], *a.* Squint-eyed, moon-eyed.

ojizarco, ca [o-he-thar'-co, cah], *a.* Blue or gray-eyed.

ojo [o'-ho], *m.* 1. The eye. 2. Eye, sight, ocular knowledge. 3. Eye of a needle (aguja). 4. Eye, any small perforation. 5. Head formed on liquors; drop of oil or grease which swims on liquors. 6. Arch of a bridge (puente). 7. Eye or socket, for receiving a handle. 8. Attention, cure, notice. 9. Keyhole. 10. Lather, formed from soap. 11. *(typ.)* Face of a priming type. 13. Mesh of a net. 14. Eye or hollow in bread or cheese (pan, queso). 15. Expression of ardent affection or endearment, or the object of it. 16. **Ojo de pollo**, *(LAm.)* corn, callus. **A cierra ojos** or **a ojos cerrados**, without hesitation; at all events. **En un abrir y cerrar de ojos**, in the twinkling of an eye. **A ojo**, (1) by the bulk or lump. (2) At the discretion of another. **A ojo, a los ojos de alguno** or **a sus ojos**, face to face, in presence of anyone. **Al ojo**, at sight, at hand. **Ojo alerta**, look sharp. **Ojos que no ven, corazón que no siente**, *(Prov.)* out of sight, out of mind. **Mal de ojo**, fascination, enchantment. **Mal de ojos**, sore eyes. **Niñas de los ojos**, apple of one's eye; darling, treasure. **Ojo de buey**, (1) *(Bot.)* oxeye. (2) *(coll.)* Doubloon of eight dollars. **Dichosos los ojos que ven a usted**, delighted to see you again! (expression used on meeting another after a considerable interval). **Entrarle (a uno) una cosa por el ojo** or **por los ojos**, to delight, to charm one. **Ojo eléctrico**, electric eye.

ojoso, sa [o-ho'-so, sah], *a.* Full of eyes.

ojota [o-ho'-tah], *f.* 1. A kind of shoe worn by Indian women. *(Peru.)* 2. *(And. Cono Sur)* Tanned llama leather (piel de llama).

ojuelo [o-hoo-ay'-lo], *m. dim.* A small eye. *-pl.* 1. Sparkling eyes, smiling eyes. 2. *(Prov.)* Spectacles.

ola [o'-lah], *f.* 1. A wave. 2. A sudden, violent commotion. **Ola de calor**, heat wave. **La nueva ola**, the latest fashion.

olaje [o-lah'-hay], *m.* Succession of waves, surge.

olán [o-lahn'], *m.* Holland, Dutch linen, batiste.

olé [o'-lay], *m.* Andalusian dance. **¡Olé!** *int.* Bravo!

oleáceo, cea [o-lay-ah'-thay-o, ah], *a.* Of the olive family (ash, etc.).

oleada [o-lay-ah'-dah], *f.* 1. Surge, swell of the sea. 2. A plentiful produce of oil. 3. Surging of crowded people. **Una gran oleada de gente**, a great surge of people.

oleaginosidad [o-lay-ah-he-no-se-dahd'], *f.* Oleaginousness, oiliness.

oleaginoso, sa [o-lay-ah-he-no'-so, sah], *a.* Oleaginous, oily.

oleaje [o-lay-ah'-hay], *m. V.* OLAJE.

olear [o-lay-ar'], *va.* To administer extreme unction.

oleario, ri [o-lay-ah'-re-o, ah], *a.* Oily.

oleato [o-lay-ah'-to], *m.* Oleate, a compound of oleic acid.

oleaza [o-lay-ah'-thah], *f. (Prov.)* The watery dregs which remain in the mill after the oil has been extracted.

oledero, ra [o-lay-day'-ro, rah], *a.* Odorous, fragrant.

oledor, ra [o-lay-dor', rah], *m. & f.* Smeller, one who smells.

oleico, ca [o-lay'-e-co, cah], *a.* Oleic, pertaining to oil.

oleína [o-lay-ee'-nah], *f.* Olein, a colorless oily substance, the base of fatty oils.

óleo [o'-lay-o], *m.* 1. Oil. *V.* ACEITE. **Al óleo**, in oil colors. 2. Extreme unction, the holy oil; act of anointing.

oleoducto [o-lay-o-dooc'-to], *m.* Pipeline.

oleolato [o-lay-o-lah'-to], *m.* Essential oils.

oleomargarina [o-lay-o-mar-gah-ree'-nah], *f.* Oleomargarine.

oleosidad [o-lay-o-se-dahd'], *f.* Oiliness.

oleoso, sa [o-lay-o'-so, sah], *a.* Oily, oleaginous.

oler [o-lerr'], *va.* 1. To smell, to scent, to snort (cocaína). 2. To smell, to find out, to search, to scent, to discover (descubrir). 3. To pry, to inspect curiously. *-vn.* 1. To smell, to strike the nostrils. 2. To smell, to have a particular tincture or smack of any quality. **Oler a chamusquina**, to come from hot words to hard blows. **No oler bien alguna cosa**, *(Met.)* to be a suspicious thing. *(Yo huelo, huela; olí. V.* OLER.)

olfacción [ol-fac-the-on'], *f. (Med.)* Olfaction, the act or the sense of smell.

olfatear [ol-fah-tay-ar'], *va.* To smell, to scent.

olfato [ol-fah'-to], *m.* Scent, the sense or organ of smell.

olfatorio, ria [ol-fah-to'-re-o, ah], *a.* Olfactory.

olíbano [o-lee'-bah-no], *m. (Bot.)* Incense, a gum-resin produced by the Lycian juniper.

oliente [o-le-en'-tay], *pa.* Smelling, odorous.

oliera [o-le-ay'-rah], *f.* Vessel in which holy oil is kept.

oligarca [o-le-gar'-cah], *m.* Oligarch, a member of an oligarchy.

oligarquía [o-le-gar-kee'-ah], *f.* Oligarchy, a form of government by the few.

oligárquico, ca [o-le-gar'-ke-co, cah], *a.* Oligarchical.

olimpiada [o-lim-pe-ah'-dah], *f.* Olympiad, period of four years, olympic games.

olímpico, ca [o-leem'-pe-co, cah], *a.* Olympic.

olimpo [o-leem'-po], *m.* 1. Height, eminence. 2. *(Poet.)* Heaven.

oliscar [o-lis-car'], *va.* 1. To smell, to scent. 2. To investigate, to ascertain. *-vn.* To stink.

olisquear [o-lis-kay-ar'], *va. V.* OLISCAR.

oliva [o-lee'-vah], *f.* 1. Olive-tree (árbol). *V.* OLIVO. 2. The olive itself (aceituna).

olivar [o-le-var'], *m.* Plantation of olive-trees, olive-grove, olive-yard.

olivarse [o-le-var'-say], *vr.* To form bubbles (pan).

olivastro de Rodas [o-le-vahs'-tro], *m. (Bot.) V.* LINÁLOE.

olivera [o-le-vay'-rah], *f.* Olive-tree. *V.* OLIVO.

olivífero, ra [o-le-vee'-fay-ro, rah], *a. (Poet.)* Producing olives, olive-bearing.

olivo [o-lee'-vo], *m. (Bot.)* Olive-tree.

olla [ol-lyal'], *f.* 1. A round earthen pot, or wide-mouthed jar (recipiente). 2. Olla, an olio, a dish made of boiled meat and vegetables. 3. Any gulf in which are whirlpools; a whirlpool (de río). 4. Chimney (alpinismo). 5. *(Cono Sur)* **Olla común**, canteen.

olla a presión [ol'-lyah ah pray-se-on'], *f.* Pressure cooker.

olla express [ol'-lyah ex-press'], *f. (Mex.)* Pressure cooker.

ollao [ol-lyah'-o], *m. (Naut.)* Eyelet-hole, round hole in sails.

ollar [ol-lyar'], *a.* Soft, readily workable (piedra).

ollaza [ol-lyah'-thah], *f. aug.* A large pot or boiler.

ollazo [ol-lyah'-tho], *m.* Blow with an earthen pot or jar.

ollería [ol-lyay-ree'-ah], *f.* Pottery; a shop where earthenware is sold.

ollero [ol-lyay'-ro], *m.* 1. Potter. 2. Dealer in earthenware.

ollita [ol-lyee'-tah], *f. dim.* Pipkin, a small pot.

olluela [ol-lyoo-ay'-lah], *f.* Pit or hollow under the Adam's apple.

olmeda [ol-may'-dah], *f.* **Olmedo**, *m.* Elm-grove.

olmo [ol'-mo], *m. (Bot.)* Elm-tree.

ológrafo [o-lo'-grah-fo], *a.* Holographic, written in the hand of the testator.

olor [o-lor'], *m.* 1. Odor (aroma), scent. 2. Stink, stench. 3. Cause or motive of suspicion. 4. *(Met.)* Fame, reputation. 5. *(Cono Sur, Mex.)* Spices. **Agua de olor**, sweet-scented water. **Buen olor**, nice smell. **Tiene mal olor**, it smells bad.

oloroso, sa [o-lo-ro'-so, sah], *a.* Odoriferous, fragrant, perfumed.

olote [o-lo'-tay], *m. (Amer.)* Corn-cob.

olvidadizo, za [ol-ve-dah-dee'-tho, thah], *a.* Short of memory, forgetful, oblivious.

olvidado, da [ol-ve-dah'-do, dah], *a. & pp.* of OLVIDAR. 1. Forgotten, forsaken, forlorn. 2. Forgetful (persona). 3. Ungrateful (ingrato). 4. *(And. Cono Sur) V.* OLVIDADIZO.

olvidar [ol-ve-dar'], *va.* To forget, to neglect, to omit. **Olvidar hacer algo**, to forget to do something.

olvido [ol-ve'-do], *m.* Forgetfulness (cualidad), carelessness, heedlessness, neglect, oblivion (estado). **Echar al olvido or en olvido**, to forget designedly, to cast in oblivion.

ombligada [om-ble-gah'-dah], *f.* Part corresponding to the navel, in skins of animals.

ombligo [om-blee'-go], *m.* 1. The navel, umbilicus. 2. Navelstring, the umbilical cord. 3. Center or middle of a thing. **Ombligo do Venus**, Venus navelwort, or pennywort.

ombliguero [om-ble-gay'-ro], *f. (Bot.) V.* OREJA DEABAD, or MONJE.

ombliguero [om-ble-gay'-ro], *m.* Bandage put upon the navel of new-born children.

ombría [om-bree'-ah], *f.* Shade, place secluded from the sun.

ombú [om-boo'], *m. (Argen. Cuba)* Tree with a wood so spongy that it burns at once to ashes.

omega [o-may'-gah], *f.* Omega, last letter in the Greek alphabet: long O.

omental [o-men-tahl'], *a.* Belonging to the omentum; omental.

omento [o-men'-to], *m.* Omentum, the caul or covering of the bowels.

omicron [o'-me-crone], Name of the Greek short O, fifteenth of their alphabet.

ominosamente [o-me-no'-sah-men-tay], *adv.* Ominously, with good or bad omen.

ominoso, sa [o-me-no'-so, sah], *a.* Ominous (de mal agüero), foreboding ill.

omisión [o-me-se-on'], *f.* Omission, carelessness, neglect, negligence, heedlessness.

omiso, sa [o-mee'-so, sah], *a.* Neglectful, remiss, heedless, careless.

omitir [o-me-teer'], *va.* To omit, to neglect.

ómnibus [om'-ne-boos], *m.* Omnibus, a public carriage for a number of persons.

omnímodamente [om-ne'-mo-dah-men-tay], *adv.* Entirely, by all means.

omnímodo, da [om-nee'-mo-do, dah], *a.* Entire, total.

omnipotencia [om-ne-po-ten'-the-ah], *f.* Omnipotence.

omnipotente [om-ne-po-ten'-tay], *a.* Omnipotent, almighty.

omnipotentemente [om-ne-po-ten'-tay-men-tay], *adv.* Omnipotently.

omnipresencia [om-ne-pray-sen'-the-ah], *f.* Omnipresence.

omniscencia [om-nis-then'-the-ah], *f.* Omniscience.

omniscio, ia [om-nees'-the-o, ah], *a.* Omniscient.

omnívoro, ra [om-nee'-vo-ro, rah], *a.* Omnivorous, living upon foods of all kinds.

omoplato [o-mo-plah'-to], *m. (Anat.)* Omoplate, the shoulderblade, scapula.

onagra [o-nah'-grah], *f. (Bot.)* A genus of the evening-primrose family, now referred to Enothera.

onagro [o-nah'-gro], *m.* Wild ass.

once [on'-thay], *a. & m.* Eleven; figure eleven. **El once de enero**, the eleventh of January. **El libro once**, the eleventh book.

oncear [on-thay-ar'], *va.* To weigh out by ounces.

oncejera, oncijera [on-thay-hay'-rah], *f.* A small snare for catching birds.

oncejo [on-thay'-ho], *m. (Prov.)* String, band, tie.

onceno, na [on-thay'-no, nah], *a.* Eleventh.

onda [on'-dah], *f.* 1. A wave. 2. Fluctuation, agitation. **Radio de onda corta**, short-wave radio. **Onda de choque**, shock wave. **Onda marina**, ocean wave. **Onda sonora**, sound wave. **Agarrar la onda**, *(LAm.)* to get it (entender). **Estar en la onda**, to be in (moda).

ondeado [on-day-ah'-do], *m. & a.* Anything in waves.

ondear [on-day-ar'], *vn.* 1. To undulate. 2. To fluctuate. 3. To ripple (agua), to fly (bandera); to stream (flotar al viento).

La bandera ondea a media asta, the flag is flying at half mast. *-vr.* To float backward and forward.

ondina [on-dee'-nah], *f.* Undine, water-sprite.

ondulación [on-doo-lah-the-on'], *f.* Waving, undulation.

ondulado, da [on-doo-lah'-do, dah], *a.* Waved, wavy (pelo), Undulations (superficie), undulating (terreno), corrugated (papel). **Ondulado permanente**, permanent wave. **Cabello ondulado**, wavy hair.

ondular [on-doo-lar'], *vn.* To ripple, to wave, to undulate.

oneiromancía [o-nay-ee-ro-mahn'-the-ah], *f.* Oneiromancy, divination by means of dreams.

oneroso, sa [o-nay-ro'-so, sah], *a.* Burdensome, troublesome, onerous (pesado).

onfacino, na [on-fah-thee'-no, nah], *a.* Extracted from green olives (aceite).

onice *f.* ónix, *m.* [o'-ne-thay, o'-ne-kay]. Onyx, a precious stone.

onomatopéyico, ca [o-no-mah-to-pay'-ye-co, cah], *a.* Onomatopeic, imitative in sound.

onomatopeya [o-no-mah-to-pay'-yah], *f.* Onomatopoeia, the selection of words to imitate natural sounds.

onoquiles [o-no-kee'-les], *f. (Bot.)* Dyer's bugloss, alkanet.

ontología [on-to-lo-hee'-ah], *f.* Ontology, metaphysics.

ontologista [on-to-lo-hees'tah], *m.* Ontologist, metaphysician.

onza [on'-thah], *f.* 1. Ounce, the twelfth part of a pound, troy weight, or nineteenth of a Castilian pound. 2. Ounce, lynx.

onzavo, va [on-thah'-vo, vah], *a.* Eleventh. *-m.* Eleventh part.

opa [o'-pah], *f.* A hole left in a newly-built wall on removing the scaffold. *-a. (Amer.)* 1. Dumb, silent. 2. Silly, foolish.

opacamente [o-pah-cah-men-tay], *adv.* Obscurely, darkly.

opacidad [o-pah-the-dahd'], *f.* 1. Opacity, cloudiness, darkness. 2. *(Fig.)* Dullness, lifelessness (oscuridad). 3. *(Fig.)* Gloominess (melancolía).

opaco, ca [o-pah'-co, cah], *a.* 1. Opacous, opaque. 2. Melancholy, gloomy. 3. *(Fig.)* Dull, lustreless, lifeless (oscuro).

opalino, na [o-pah-lee'-no, nah], *a.* Opaline, opalescent.

ópalo [o'-pah-lo], *m.* Opal, a precious stone.

opción [op-the-on'], *f.* 1. Option, choice (elección). 2. Right to an office or dignity (derecho). 3. Chance, likelihood (posibilidad). **No hay opción**, there is no choice. **Con opción a 8 más**, with an option on 8 more.

opcional [op-the-o-nahl'], *a.* Optional.

ópera [o'-pay-rah], *f.* Opera, a musical drama.

operable [o-pay-rah'-blay], *a.* 1. Capable of operating. 2. Operable, practicable.

operación [o-pay-rah-the-on'], *f.* 1. Operation, the act of exercising some power or faculty. 2. Operation, agency, effect or action produced. 3. *(Surg.)* Operation. *(Com.)* Transaction, venture. **Operaciones de banco**, banking business. **Operaciones marítimas**, shipping trade or business. 4. A chemical process. *-pl.* 1. Operations of an army. 2. Works, deeds, actions. **Operaciones de rescate**, rescue operations. **Operaciones en bolsa**, stock-exchange transactions.

operador, ra [o-pay-rah-dor'], *m & f.* 1. Surgical operator. 2. *(Min.)* Prospector. 3. Cameraman (rodaje); projectionist (proyección). 3. *(Comput.)* Operator. **Operador de equipos informáticos**, computer (equipment) operator. **Operador de introducción de datos**, data-entry operator. **Operador de procesadores de texto**, word processing operator.

operante [o-pay-rahn'-tay], *pa. & n.* Operator; operating.

operar [o-pay-rar'], *va.* 1. To produce, to bring about (cambio, cura). 2. *(Med.)* To operate. 3. *(LAm.)* To use, to operate (máquina); to manage (negocio). **Operar a uno de apendicitis**, to operate on somebody for appendicitis. *-vn.* 1. To operate, to act. 2. *(Com.)* To operate, to deal. *-vr.* 1. To occur (ocurrir). 2. *(Med.)* To have an operation.

operario [o-pay-rah'-re-o], *m.* 1. Operator, laborer. 2. Friar who assists sick or dying persons.

operativo, va [o-pay-rah-tee'-vo, vah], *a.* Operative. *-m.* (*LAm.*) Operation. **Operativo policial**, police operation.

operculado, da [o-per-coo-lah'-do, dah], *a.* Operculate, covered with a lid.

opercular [o-per-coo-lar'], *a.* Opercular, serving as a lid.

opérculo [o-perr'-coo-lo], *m.* Operculum, lid, cover of a pore or cell.

opereta [o-pay-ray'-tah], *f.* Operetta, a light opera.

operista [o-pay-rees'-tah], *com.* Opera singer.

operoso, sa [o-pay-ro'-so, sah], *a.* Laborious, operose.

opiado, da [o-pe-ah'-do, dah], *a.* Opiate, narcotic.

opiata [o-pe-ah'-tah], *f.* Opiate.

opiate, ta [o-pe-ah-to, tah], *a. & a.* Opiate narcotic.

opilación [o-pe-lah-the-on'], *f.* 1. Oppilation, obstruction of the vessels of the body. 2. (*coll.*) Amenorrhoea, abnormally scanty or obstructed menstruation.

opilar [o-pe-lar'], *va.* To oppilate, to obstruct.

opilativo, va [o-pe-lah-tee'-vo, vah], *a.* Obstructive, oppilative.

opimo, ma [o-pe'-mo, mah], *a.* Rich, fruitful, abundant.

opinable [o-pe-nah'-blay], *a.* Disputable, problematical.

opinante [o-pe-nahn'-tay], *pa. & a.* Arguing; opinionated.

opinante [o-pe-nahn'-tay], *m.* Arguer.

opinar [o-pe-nar'], *vn.* To argue, to judge, to form one opinion, to opine (dar opinión). **Opinar que...**, to think that. **Fueron opinando uno tras otro**, they gave their opinions in turn.

opinativo, va [o-ge-nah-tee'-vo, vah], *a.* Opinionative, opinative.

opinión [o-pe-ne-on'], *f.* 1. Opinion, persuasion of the mind, judgment. 2. Reputation, character. **Hacer opinión**, to form an opinion, to be a man whose opinion is an authority. **Cambiar de opinión**, to change one's mind.

opinioncilla, ita [o-pe-ne-on-theel'-lyah], *f. dim.* Opinion founded on slight grounds.

opio [o'-pe-o], *m.* Opium.

opíparo, ra [o-pee'-pah-ro, rah], *a.* Opiparous, sumptuous (comida).

oploteca [o-plo-tay'-cah], *f.* Museum of ancient, rare, or valuable weapons.

ópol [o'-pol], *m.* Juice, sap of a plant, in general. (*Gr.*)

oponente [o-po-nayn'-tay], *a.* Opposing (contrario), contrary. *-m & f.* Opponent (adversario).

oponer [o-po-nerr'], *va.* 1. To oppose, to go against, to contradict. 2. To oppose, to object in a disputation. *-vr.* 1. To oppose, to be adverse, to act against, to be contrary. 2. To front, to be opposite to. 3. To steed in competition with another. **Oponerse la razón a la pasión**, to use reason against passion. **Yo no me opongo**, I don't oppose it. (*Yo opongo, oponga; opuse, opusiera; opondré; from Oponer.* V. PONER.)

opopónaca, opopónace [o-po-po'-nah-cah, o-po-po'-nah-thay], *f.* (*Bot.*) Rough parsnip.

opopónaco, opopónax [o-po-po'-nah-co], *m.* Opoponax, a gum resin obtained from the rough parsnip.

oportunamente [o-por-too'-nah-men-tay], *adv.* Opportunely, conveniently.

oportunidad [o-por-too-ne-dahd'], *f.* 1. Opportunity, convenience, appropriateness of time or circumstances. 2. Opportuneness (cualidad); timeliness; appropriateness. **Igualdad de oportunidades**, equality of opportunity. **En dos oportunidades**, on two occasions.

oportunismo [o-por-too-nees'-mo], *m.* Opportunism.

oportunista [o-por-too-nees'-tah], *m. & f.* Opportunist.

oportuno, na [o-por-too'-no, nah], *a.* Convenient (adecuado), seasonable, opportune (buena hora), appropriate (apropiado), expedient (aconsejable). **Una respuesta oportuna**, a suitable reply.

oposición [o-po-se-the-on'], *f.* 1. Opposition, situation so as to face something opposed, counterview. 2. Opposition, contrariety of affection, of interest, of party, of measures, of meaning, etc. 3. Opposition, the members of a legislative house who oppose the measures of the ministry. 4. (Fine arts) Contrast. 5. Competition among competitors for a prebend, professorship, etc. 6. (*Ast.*) Opposition between two heavenly bodies. **Hacer oposiciones**, to be a candidate for.

opositar [o-po-se-tar'], *vn.* To go in for a public competition.

opositor, ra [o-po-se-tor', rah], *m. & f.* Opposer, opponent. *-a.* Opposing (contrario). **El líder opositor**, the leader of the opposition.

opresión [o-pray-se-on'], *f.* 1. Oppression, cruelty, severity, coercion, hardship. 2. Oppression, pressure.

opresivamente [o-pray-se-vah-men-tay], *adv.* Oppressively, overwhelmingly.

opresivo, va [o-pray-see'-vo, vah], *a.* 1. Oppressive, cruel. 2. Oppressive, heavy, overwhelming.

opresor [o-pray-sor'], *m.* Oppressor; extortioner. *-a.* Oppressive, tyrannical.

oprimir [o-pre-meer'], *va.* 1. To oppress by hardship or severity. 2. To overpower, to overwhelm, to subdue. 3. To crush, to press, to squeeze (presionar). 4. To be too tight for (ropa).

oprobio [o-pro-be-o], *m.* Opprobrium, ignominy, shame, injury.

oprobioso, sa [o-pro-be-o'-so, sah], *a.* Opprobrious, reproachful.

optar [op-tar'], *va.* To choose, to select. **Optar entre, to** choose between. **Poder optar**, to apply for.

optativo [op-tah-tee'-vo], *m.* (*Gram.*) Optative, one of the modes of verbs. *-a.* Optional (opcional).

óptica [op'-te-cah], *f.* 1. Optics, the science of light and vision (ciencia). 2. Optician's (tienda).

óptico, ca [op'-te-co, cah], *a.* Optic, optical, visual. *-m.* Optician.

óptimamente [op'-te-mah-men-tay], *adv.* In the best way, perfectly.

optimismo [op-te-mees'-mo], *m.* Optimism.

optimista [op-te-mees'-tah], *com.* Optimist.

óptimo, ma [op'-te-mo, mah], *a.* Best, the best, optimum, eminently good.

optómetra [op-to'-may-trah], *m.* Optometrist.

optomotría [op-to-may-tree'-ah], *f.* Optometry.

opuestamente [o-poo-ays'-tah-men-tay], *adv.* Oppositely.

opuesto, ta [o-poo-es'-to, tah], *a.* Opposite (ángulo, lado), contrary (opinión), adverse. *-pp. irr.* of OPONER.

opugnación [o-poog-nah-the-on'], *f.* Oppugnancy, opposition.

opugnador [o-poog-nah-dor'], *m.* Oppugner, opposer.

opugnar [o-poog-nar'], *va.* To oppugn; to impugn, to attack, to resist, to contradict.

opulencia [o-poo-len'-the-ah], *f.* Opulence, wealth, affluence.

opulentamente [o-poo-len-tay], *adv.* Opulently.

opulento, ta [o-poo-len'-to, tah], *a.* Opulent, wealthy, rich, affluent.

opuncia [o-poon'-the-ah], *f.* Prickly pear cactus.

opúsculo [o-poos'-coo-lo], *m.* A short, compendious treatise.

oquedal [o-kay-dahl'], *m.* Plantation of lofty trees.

ora [o'-rah], *adv.* At present. V. AHORA. Whether.

oración [o-rah-the-on'], *f.* 1. Oration (discurso), harangue, declamation. 2. Prayer, supplication. 3. Sentence: in grammar, an expression composed of one or more words which makes perfect sense. **Partes de la oración**, the parts of speech. 4. Position, a proposition which denies or affirms a thing. 5. A part of the mass. 6. (*LAm.*) Pagan invocation, magic charm. **Las oraciones**, sun-setting, the angelus, when the angel's salutation to the Virgin is repeated by the people; also, the bell which calls to this prayer. **Oración compuesta**, complex sentence. **Pronunciar una oración**, to make a speech.

oracional [o-rah-the-o-nahl'], *m.* Prayerbook.

oracionero [o-rah-the-o-nay'-ro], *m.* He who goes praying from door to door.

oráculo [o-rah'-coo-lo], *m.* 1. Oracle, something delivered by supernatural wisdom. 2. Oracle, the place where, the determinations of heaven are inquired. 3. Oracle, person famed for wisdom.

orada [o-rah'-dah], *f* V. DORADA.

orador, ra [o-rah-dor', rah], *m. & f.* 1. Orator, a public speaker. 2. Panegyrist, encomiast, preacher.

oral [o-rahl'], *a.* Oral, delivered by the mouth.

oralmente [o-ral-men'-tay], *adv.* Orally, by mouth.

orangután [o-ran-goo-tahn'], *m.* Orang-utan (orang-outang), an anthropoid ape of Borneo.

orar [o-rar'], *vn. & a.* 1. To harangue. 2. To pray. 3. To ask, to demand.

orate [o-rah'-tay], *com.* Lunatic, madman. **Casa de orates**, a mad-house.

oratoria [o-rah-to'-re-ah], *f.* Oratory, eloquence.

oratoriamente [o-rah-to-re-ah-men-tay], *adv.* Oratorically.

oratorio [o-rah-to'-re-o], *m.* 1. Oratory, a private place for prayer. 2. Oratorio, a dramatic musical composition upon a sacred subject. It receives its name from the Oratory in Rome. 3. A congregation of presbyters.

oratorio, ria [o-rah-to'-re-o, ah], *a.* Oratorial, rhetorical, oratorical.

orbe [or'-bay], *m.* 1. Orb, sphere. 2. Orb, terrestrial sphere, celestial body. 3. Orb, circle described by any of the mundane spheres. 4. Globe-fish.

orbicular [or-be-coo-lar'], *a.* Orbicular, circular.

órbita [or'-be-tah], *f.* 1. Orbit, the path of a planet. 2. Cavity in which the eye is placed, orbit. 3. *(Mex.)* Socket.

orbitales [or-be-tah'-les], *a. & m. pl.* Orbital: used of the bones which form the orbit of the eye.

orca [or'-cah], *f.* Grampus, orca.

orcaneta [or-cah-nay'-tah], *f. (Bot.)* Dyer's bugloss, alkanet.

orchilla [or-cheel'-lyah], *f. (Bot.)* Archil, roccella, true dyer's orchil.

orco [or'-co], *m.* 1. *(Zool.)* Grampus. V. ORCA. 2. Hell.

orcotomía [or-co-to-mee'-ah], *f.* Orchotomy, castration.

órdago [or'-dah-go], **De órdago**, first class.

ordalía [or-dah-lee'-ah], *f.* Ordeal, a trial by fire or water.

ordeata [or-day-ah'-tah], *a.* 1. Peeled barley. 2. Ptisan, a medical drink.

orden [or'-den], *com.* 1. Order, regularity, settled mode. 2. Order, method, course, rule, regulation. 3. Order, class. 4. Order, a society of dignified persons. 5. Order a religious fraternity. 6. The sixth sacrament of the Roman Catholic church. 7. Arrangement of chords in a musical instrument. 8. Order, mandate, precept-command. 9. Relation of one thing to another. 11. *(Mex.)* Order (pedido). 12. *(Mex.)* Portion (porción). **Por su orden**, in its turn, successively. **No haber orden de conseguir algo**, *(coll.)* to have no means or possibility of obtaining a thing. **De primer orden**, first-rate. **Fuera de orden**, out of order. **Orden público**, public order. **Orden del día**, order of the day. **Dar una orden**, to give an order. **Orden religiosa**, religious order.

ordenación [or-day-nah-the-on'], *f.* 1. Methodical arrangement; disposition, ordination. 2. Edict, ordinance. 3. Clerical ordination. 4. Part of architecture which treats of the capacity which every room should have. 5. Part of the composition of a picture.

ordenada [or-day-nah'-dah], *f. (Math.)* Ordinate, a line drawn perpendicular to the axis of a curve.

ordenadamente [or-day-nah'-dah-men-tay], *adv.* Orderly.

ordenado, da [or-day-nah'-do, dah], *a.* Ordained, ordinate, orderly (en orden), just. *-pp.* of ORDENAR.

ordenador, ra [or-day-nah-dor', rah], *m. & f.* One who ordains, ordainer; orderer. V. COMISARIO. *-m.* Computer. **Ordenador central**, mainframe computer. **Ordenador de gestión**, business computer. **Ordenador para juegos**, game computer. **Ordenador para jugar al ajedrez**, chess computer.

ordenamiento [or-day-nah-me-en'-to], *m.* 1. The act and effect of ordaining, regulating, or putting in order. 2. Law, edict, ordinance.

ordenando, ordenante [or-day-nahn'-do, or-day-nahn'-tay], *m.* He who is ready to receive holy orders.

ordenanza [or-day-nahn'-thah], *f.* 1. Method, order. 2. Law, statute, ordinance (decreto); command; ordination. 3. *m.* Orderly man, a corporal or soldier who attends a commanding officer. **Estar de ordenanza**, to be on duty, to be in waiting.

ordenar [or-day-nar'], *va.* 1. To arrange (poner en prueba), to put in order, to class, to dispose. 2. To order (mandar), to command, to enact. 3. To ordain, to regulate; to direct. 4. To order, to confer holy orders. **Ordenar sus asuntos**, to put one's affairs in order. *-vr.* To be ordained, to receive holy orders.

ordeñadero [or-day-nyah-day'-ro], *m.* Milk-pail.

ordeñador, ra [or-day-nyah-dor', rah], *m. & f.* Milker, one who milks animals. *-f.* Milking machine.

ordeñar [or-day-nyar'], *va.* 1. To milk animals. 2. To pick olives by hand.

ordinal [or-de-nahl'], *a.* Ordinal, noting order. *-m.* Ordinal, ritual; a book containing orders.

ordinariamente [or-de-nah'-re-ah-men-tay], *adv.* Frequently; ordinarily; customarily; rudely.

ordinariez [or-de-nah-re-eth'], *f.* 1. *(coll.)* Low rank of a person; common stock. 2. Rough manners, rude behavior.

ordinario, ria [or-de-nah'-re-o, ah], *a.* 1. Ordinary (normal), common, usual, customary, familiar. 2. Coarse, mean, of low rank, vulgar, rude (grosero). **Decreto, provisión** or **auto ordinario**, decree given by a judge at the instance of one of the contending parties. **Son gente muy ordinaria**, they're very common people.

ordinario [or-de-nah'-re-o], *m.* 1. Ordinary, settled establishment of daily expense: commonly applied to the expenses of the table. 2. Ordinary, established judge of ecclesiastical causes. 3. Ordinary, a bishop. 4. Mail, post, or courier, who goes and arrives at stated times (recadero). 5. The carrier, muleteer, or driver of beasts of burden, who usually goes and comes from one place to another. 6. Ordinary, a book containing the prayers of the mass. **De ordinario**, regularly, commonly.

orear [o-ray-ar'], *va.* 1. To cool, to refresh (viento). 2. To dry, to air, to expose to the air. *-vr.* To take the air, to take an airing, to air (ropa).

orégano [o-ray'-gah-no], *m. (Bot.)* Wild marjoram; *(Mex.)* grass.

oreja [o-ray'-hah], *f.* 1. Auricle, the external ear. 2. Ear, the organ of hearing. 3. Flap of a shoe for adjusting to the instep (zapato). 4. Flatterer, tale-bearer. 5. *(Mech.)* Lug, flange, ear, a projecting piece of certain instruments, as the claw of a hammer, the barb of an arrow, the head of a nail. 6. *(LAm.)* Curiosity. 7. *(LAm.)* Grass (soplón). **Con las orejas caídas**, crestfallen, down in the mouth; dejected. **Bajar las orejas**, to yield; to humble oneself. **Poner las orejas coloradas**, to make one blush to the ears. **Verle las orejas al lobo**, to escape from great danger.

orejano, na [o-ray-hah'-no, nah], *a.* 1. *(Amer.)* Ownerless, unbranded: said of animals. In Spain, motherless: said of a calf. 2. *(Carib.)* Cautious (cauteloso). 3. *(CAm. Carib.)* Peasant, countryman.

orejeado, da [o-ray-hay-ah'-do, dah], *a.* Informed, advised, instructed. *-pp.* of OREJEAR.

orejear [o-ray-hay-ar'], *vn.* 1. To shake the ears (caballos). 2. To act with reluctance. 3. *(Prov.)* To whisper in the ear. 4. *(Cono Sur)* To uncover one's cards one by one. 5. *(And. Carib. Cono Sur)* To suspect (recelar).

orejera [o-ray-hay'-rah], *f.* Earmuff.

orejeta [o-ray-hay'-tah], *f.* Each of the two wooden languets which the scabbard of a sword carries within.

orejita [o-ray-hee'-tah], *f. dim.* A small auricle or external ear.

orejón [o-ray-hone'], *m.* 1. Slice of dried apple or other fruit as **Orejones de durazno**, dried peaches. 2. Pull by the ear. 3. A young nobleman of Peru, educated for public employments. 4. *(And. Mex.)* Goitre. 5. *(And.)* Herdsman (vaquero); plainsman (llanero). 6. *(Mex.)* Cuckold. -*a.* 1. *(And.)* Absent-minded (distraído). 2. *(And. CAm. Mex.)* Rough, coarse.

orejudo, da [o-ray-hoo'-do, dah], *a.* Flap-eared, long-eared.

orellana [o-rel-lyah'-nah], *f. (Bot.)* Arnatto or arnotto, a drug of dyestuff; prepared from the seeds of the arnotta.

oreo [o-ray'-o], *m.* Breeze, fresh air.

orfandad, orfanidad [or-fan-dahd'], *f.* 1. Orphanage, state of orphans: want of friends or support. 2. *(Fig.)* Forlornness, scarcity (escasez), paucity.

orfebrería [or-fay-bray-ree'-ah], *f.* Gold or silver twist or braid.

orfeón [or-fay-on'], *m.* Glee club, choral society.

órfico, ca [or'-fe-co, cah], *a.* Orphean, relating to Orpheus.

organdí [or-gan-dee'], *m.* Organdy.

organero [or-gah-nay'-ro], *m.* Organ-maker, organ-builder.

orgánicamente [or-gah'-ne-cah-men-tay], *adv.* Organically.

orgánico, ca [or-gah'-ne-co, cah], *a.* 1. Organic, organical, consisting of various parts. 2. Organic, relating to the organs. 3. Harmonious.

organigrama [or-gah-ne-grah'-mah], *m.* Flow chart; organization chart.

organillero [or-gah-nil-lyay'-ro], *m.* Organ grinder.

organillo [or-gah-neel'-lyo], *m. dim.* Barrel-organ, hand-organ.

organismo [or-gah-nes'-mo], *m.* 1. Organism, an organized or living being. 2. Social organization. **Organismos de gobierno**, organs of government.

organista [or-gah-nees'-tah], *com. (Mus.)* Organist.

organizable [or-gah-ne-thah'-blay], *a.* Organizable, capable of organization.

organización [or-gah-ne-thah-the-on'], *f.* 1. Organization, construction. 2. Order, arrangement. **Organización de las Naciones Unidas**, United Nations Organization.

organizador, ra [or-gah-ne-thah-dor', rah] *a.* Organizing. **Comité organizador**, organizing committee. -*m. & f.* Organizer.

organizar [or-gah-ne-thar'], *va.* 1. To tune an organ. 2. To organize, to form organically.

órgano [or'-gah-no], *m.* 1. Organ, a musical wind instrument, a pipe organ. 2. Organ, natural instrument, as the tongue is the organ of speech. 3. Machine for cooling liquors. 4. *(Amer.)* The high round fluted cactus, called so because it resembles an organ-pipe. 5. *(Met.)* Organ or medium by which a thing is communicated.

organografía [or-gah-no-grah-fee'-ah], *f.* Description of organs; organography.

orgasmo [or-gahs'-mo], *m. (Med.)* Orgasm.

orgía [or-hee'-ah], *f.* Frantic revel.

orgullo [or-gool'-lyo], *m.* 1. Pride, haughtiness, loftiness. 2. Activity, briskness.

orgullosamente [or-gool-lyo'-sah-men-tay], *adv.* Haughtily.

orgulloso, sa [or-gool-lyo'-so, sah], *a.* 1. Proud, haughty, lofty, lordly. 2. Brisk, active. **Estar orgulloso de**, to be proud to.

orientación [o-re-en-tah-the-on'], *f.* 1. Orientation, position, exposure. 2. Bearings. 3. Orientation, guidance. **Orientación profesional**, vocational guidance. **Una casa con orientación norte**, a house with a northely orientation. **Lo hizo para mi orientación**, he did it for my guidance.

oriental [o-re-en-tahl'], *a.* 1. Oriental, eastern. 2. *(Cono Sur)* Uruguayan; *(Cuba)* Oriente province. -*m.* An oriental.

orientar [o-re-en-tar'], *va.* 1. To turn a thing to the eastward. 2. To orientate, to orient, to find the petition of with regard to the cardinal points. **Orientar una vela**, *(Naut.)* to trim a sail. 3. To guide (guiar), to direct. **Me ha orientado en la materia**, he has guided me through the subject. -*vr.* 1. To know the place which is occupied, to find one's bearings (persona). 2. To confide the course to be taken.

orientativo [o-re-ayn-tah-tee'-vo], *a.* Guiding, illustrative.

oriente [o-re-en'-tay], *m.* 1. Orient, the east; the Levant. 2. Source, origin. 3. Youth, juvenile age. 4. East wind (viento). 5. Orient; Asia, and the contiguous regions of Europe and Africa.

orificación [o-re-fe-cah-the-on'], *f.* Filling of a tooth (con oro, plata.)

orificar [o-re-fe-car'], *va.* To fill a tooth (con oro, plata.)

orífice [o-ree'-fe-thay], *m.* Goldsmith.

orificia [o-re-fee'-the-ah], *f.* Art and profession of a goldsmith.

orificio [o-re-fee'-the-o], *m.* Orifice, mouth, aperture. 2. **Orificio de centrado** *(Comput.)*, hub.

origen [o-ree'-hen], *m.* 1. Origin, source, motive, fountain, original. 2. Natal country; family, lineage, extraction. 3. Beginning or moral cause of things. **País de origen**, country of origin.

original [o-re-he-nahl'], *a.* 1. Original, primitive. 2. *(coll.)* Extravagant.

original [o-re-he-nahl'], *m.* 1. Original, first copy, archetype. 2. Source, fountain.

originalidad [o-re-he-nah-le-dahd'], *f. (coll.)* Originality.

originalmente [o-re-he-nahl'-men-tay], *adv.* Originally, radically.

originar [o-re-he-nar'], *va.* To originate, to bring into existence. -*vr.* To originate, to take existence, to descend, to derive existence from, to cause, to occasion.

originariamente [o-re-he-nah'-re-ah-men-tay], *adv.* Radically, originally.

originario, ria [o-re-he-nah'-re-o, ah] *a.* Original (original), primary, primitive. **Ser originario de**, to originate from. **País originario**, country of origin.

originario [o-re-he-nah'-re-o], *m.* Native, descendent.

orilla [o-reel'-lyah], *f.* 1. Limit, extent, border, margin. 2. Edge of stuff or cloth. 3. Bank of a river, shore of the sea. 4. Extent, limit of something not material. 5. *(Ant.)* Footpath in a street, avoiding mud. 6. *(LAm.)* Pavement (acera). **A la orilla**, near a place, on the brink. **Orilla del mar**, seashore.

orilla [o-rel-lyah], *f.* A brisk wind or fresh breeze. **Hacer buena** or **mala orilla**, andalusian expressions for good or bad weather.

orillar [o-reel-lyar'], *va.* 1. To arrange, to conclude, to expedite, to put in order. 2. To leave a selvage on cloth. 3. To adorn the border of some fabric or garment. -*vr. & vn.* To approach or reach the shore.

orillo [o-reel'-lyo], *m.* Selvage or list of cloth.

orín [o-reen'], *m.* 1. Rust, the red oxide of iron. 2. Stain, taint of guilt; defect. 3. *pl.* V. ORINA.

orina [o-ree'-nah], *f.* Urine.

orinal [o-re-nahl'], *m.* Urinal, chamber-vessel, chamber-pot.

orinar [o-re-nar'], *vn.* To urinate, to make water.

oriniento, ta [o-re-ne-en'-to, tah], *a.* Rusty, moldy.

orinque [o-reen'-kay], *m. (Naut.)* Buoyrope.

oriol [o-re-ole'], *m.* Golden oriole or thrush.

orión [o-re-on'], *m. (Ast.)* Orion, a conspicuous constellation.

oriundo, da [o-re-oon'-do, dah], *a.* Originated, derived from.

orla [or'-lah], *f.* 1. List, selvage, border, fringe, trimming. 2. *(Her.)* Orle. 3. *(typ.)* An ornamental border.

orlador, ra [or-lah-dor', rah], *m. & f.* Borderer, one who makes borders.

orladura [or-lah-doo'-rah], *f.* Border, edging, list.

orlar [or-lar'], *va.* To border, to garnish with an edging.

orlo [or'-lo], *m.* An organ-stop, named after an ancient reed-instrument.

orlón [or-lone'], *m.* Orlon.

ormesi [or-may-see'], *m.* A kind of silk stuff.

ornadamente [or-nah'-dah-men-tay], *adv.* Ornamentally.

ornado, da [or-nah'-do, dah], *a. & pp.* of **Ornar.** Ornamented, ornate.

ornamentar [or-nah-men-tar'], *va.* To adorn, to embellish, to ornament, to bedeck.

ornamento [or-nah-men'-to], *m.* Ornament, embellishment, decoration. -*pl.* 1. Sacred vestments. 2. Frets, mouldings, etc., in architectural works. 3. The moral qualities of any person.

ornar [or-nar'], *va.* To adorn, to embellish, to garnish.

ornato [or-nah'-to], *m.* Dress, apparel; ornament, decoration.

ornis [or'-nees], *m.* A sort of muslin from India.

ornitolito [or-ne-to-lee'-to], *m.* Part of a bird petrified.

ornitología [or-ne-to-lo-hee'-ah], *f.* Ornithology.

ornitológico, ca [or-ne-to-lo'-he-co, cah], *a.* Ornithological.

ornitólogo [or-ne-to'-lo-go], *m.* Ornithologist.

ornitomancia [or-ne-to-mahn'-the-ah], *f.* Ornithomancy, divination by the flight of birds.

ornitorrinco [or-ne-tor-ren'-co], *m.* Platypus.

oro [o'-ro], *m.* 1. Gold. 2. Gold color (pelo de mujer). 3. Ornaments, or trinkets made of gold. 4. Gold, money, wealth, riches. 5. *pl.*-Diamonds, a suit at cards. **A peso de oro,** to succeed by means of money. **Como oro en paño,** we show our values of things by the care we take of them. **Oro en pasta, bruto o virgen,** bullion. **Oro en libritos, libritos de oro fino,** gold-leaf. **Oro en polvo,** gold-dust. **Oro mate,** gold-size. **Como un oro, como mil oros,** as clean and beautiful as gold. **No es oro todo lo que reluce,** *(Prov.)* all is not gold that glitters. **Oro es lo que oro vale,** gold is worth what it will buy; other things than money have value.

orobanquia [o-ro-bahn'-ke-ah], *f.* Broom-rape; a parasitic, gamopetalous plant which sometimes destroys a whole crop, especially of beans.

orografía [o-ro-grah-fee'-ah], *f.* Orography, description of mountains.

orología [o-ro-lo-hee'-ah], *f.* Orology, a treatise on mountains.

orondo, da [o-ron'-do, dah], *a.* 1. Pompous, showy: hollow. 2. *(LAm.)* Calm, serene.

oropel [o-ro-pel'], *m.* 1. A thin plate of brass, latten-brass. 2. Tinsel, anything showy and of little value.

oropelero [o-ro-pay-lay'-ro], *m.* Brass-worker.

oropéndola [o-ro-pen'-do-lah], *f.* Loriot, golden oriole.

oropimente [o-ro-pe-men'-tay], *m.* Orpiment, a sulphide of arsenic.

oroya [o-ro'-yah], *f. (Amer. Peru)* Hanging basket or sling for carrying passengers and goods over rope bridges; it is generally made of leather.

orozuz [o-ro-thooth'], *m. (Bot.)* Licorice or liquorice.

orquesta [or-kes'-tah], *f.* 1. Orchestra, a body of musicians using stringed and wind-instruments. 2. Orchestra, place in a playhouse for musicians.

orquestación [or-kes-tah-the-on'], *f.* Orchestration.

órquide [or'-ke-day], *f. (Bot.)* Orchid.

orquídeo, dea [or-kee'-day-o, ah], *a.* Orchidaceous.

orquitis [or-kee'-tis], *f.* Orchitis, inflummation of the testicle.

orraca [or-rah'-cah], *f.* A kind of spirit distilled from the coconut.

ortega [or-tay'-gah], *f.* Hazel-grouse.

ortiga [or-tee'-gah], *f. (Bot.)* Nettle.

ortigaje [or-te-gah'-hay], *m.* A disease of grape-vines marked by the yellow color of the leaves.

ortivo, va [or-tee'-vo, vah], *a. (Ast.)* Oriental, eastern, ortive.

orto [or'-to], *m.* Rising of a star.

ortodoncia [o-to-don-the-ah], *f.* Orthodontics.

ortodóntico [or-to-don'-te-co], *m. (Med.)* Orthodontist.

ortodoxia [or-to-dok'-se-ah], *f.* Orthodoxy: (Catholicism).

ortodoxo, xa [or-to-dok'-so, sah], Orthodox, not heretical.

ortografía [or-to-grah-fee'-ah], *f.* Orthography.

ortográficamente [or-to-grah'-fe-cah-men-tay], *adv.* Orthographically.

ortográfico, ca [or-to-grah'-fe-co, cah], *a.* Orthographical.

ortógrafo [or-to'-grah-fo], *m.* Orthographer.

ortología [or-to-lo-hee'-ah], *f.* Orthoepy, art of pronunciation.

ortopedia [or-to-pay-de-ah], *f.* Orthopaedia, orthopaedics, art of correcting deformities in the human body, especially in children.

ortopédico, ca [or-to-pay'-de-co, cah], *a.* Orthopaedic, relating to orthopaedia.

ortopedista [or-to-pay-dees'-tah], *m. (Med.)* Orthopaedist.

ortóptero [or-top'-tay-ro], *a.* Orthopeterous. *-m. pl.* The orthoptera, an order of insects, having wings folded lengthwise, as the common locust.

oruga [o-roo'-gah], *f.* 1. *(Bot.)* Rocket, an herb of the mustard family. 2. Caterpillar.

orujo [o-roo'-ho], *m.* Skin or peel of pressed grapes.

orvalle [or-vahl'-lyay], *m. (Bot.)* V. GALLOCRESTA.

orza [or'-thah], *f.* 1. Gallipot, a jar for sweetmeats, small earthen pot, crock. 2. *(Naut.)* Luff.

orzaderas [or-thah-day'-ras], *f. pl. (Naut.)* Lee-boards.

orzaga [or-thah'-gah], *f. (Bot.)* Orach.

orzar [or-thar'], *vn. (Naut.)* To luff, to steer closer to the wind.

orzuelo [or-thoo-ay'-lo], *m.* 1. Stye, a small inflamed swelling on the eyelid; a hordeolum. 2. Snare to catch birds; a trap for catching wild beasts.

os [ose], *pron.* You or ye. It is placed before and after verbs, and used instead of *vosotros.* **Os digo,** I tell you. **Os bendigo,** I bless you. **Vosotros os vestís,** you dress yourselves. 2. Each other (recíproco). **Os escribís,** you write each other.

osa [o'-sah], *f.* She-bear. **Osa mayor,** ursa major.

osadamente [osah'-dah-men-tay], *adv.* Boldly, daringly.

osadía [o-sah-dee'-ah], *f.* 1. Courage, boldness, intrepidity, hardiness. 2. Zeal, fervor, ardor.

osado, da [o-sah'-do, dah], *a.* Daring, bold, high-spirited, high-mettled. *-pp.* of OSAR.

osambre [o-sahm'-bray], *m.* **Osamenta** [o-sah-men'-tah], *f.* A skeleton.

osar [o-sar'], *vn.* 1. To dare, to venture, to outdare. 2. To imagine, to fancy.

osario [o-sah'-re-o], *m.* 1. Charnel-house. 2. Any place where there are bones.

oscilación [os-the-lah-the-on'], *f.* Oscillation, vibration of a pendulum, swing (vaivén); winding (luz); fluctuation (precios).

oscilador [os-the-lah-dor], *m.* Oscillator.

oscilar [os-the-lar'], *vn.* 1. To oscillate, to vibrate as a pendulum (péndulo), to rock (mecerse). 2. To fluctuate. 3. To hesitate (persona). **Los precios oscilan mucho,** prices are fluctuating a lot.

oscilatorio, ria [os-the-lah-to'-re-o, ah], *a.* Oscillatory, vibratory.

oscitante [os-the-tahn'-tay], *a. (Med.)* Oscitant, gaping, yawning.

osco, ca [os'-co, cah], *a.* Oscan, belonging to this ancient region of Italy.

osculación [os-coo-lah-the-on'], *f. (Geom.)* Osculation.

osculatorio, ria [os-coo-lah-to'-re-o, ah], *a. (Geom.)* Osculatory.

ósculo [os'-coo-lo], *m.* Kiss. V. BESO.

oscuramente [os-coo'-rah-men-tay], *adv.* V. OBSCURAMENTE.

oscurantismo [os-coo-ran-tees'-mo], *m.* Antiquated ideas; "old fogyism."

oscuras (A) [ah os-coo'-ras], *adv.* V. A OBSCURAS.

oscurecer [os-coo-ray-therr'], *va.* V. OBSCURECER.

oscurecimiento [os-coo-ray-the-me-en'-to], *m.* V. OBSCURECIMIENTO.

oscuridad [os-coo-re-dahd'], *f.* V. OBSCURIDAD.

oscuro, ra [os-coo'-ro, rah], *a.* V. OBSCURO.

osecico, illo, osezuelo [o-say-thee'-co], *m. dim.* Small bone.

óseo, a [oh'-say-o, ah], *a.* Osseous, bony.

osera [o-say'-rah], *f.* Den of bears.

osezno [o-seth'-no], *m.* Whelp or cub of a bear.

osfresia [os-fray'-se-ah], *f.* The sense of smell.

osfrésico, ca [os-fray'-se-co, cah], *a.* Olfactory, relating to the sense of smell.

osículo [o-see'-coo-lo], *m. dim.* Ossicle, a diminutive bone.

osificación [o-se-fe-cah-the-on'], *f.* Ossification.

osificarse [o-se-fe-car'-say], *vr.* To ossify.

osífico, ca [o-see'-fe-co, cah], *a.* Ossific.

osmazoma [os-mah-tho'-mah], *f.* or **Osmazomo**, *m.* Osmazome, a substance contained in meat, imparting taste and odor to broths.

ósmico [os'-me-co], *a.* Osmic, relating to osmium.

osmio [os'-me-o], *m. (Min.)* Osmium.

oso [o'-so], *m.* 1. Bear. **Oso hormiguero**, ant-eater. **Oso colmenero**, bear that robs beehives. **Piel de oso**, bear-skin. **Oso de peluche**, teddy bear. 2. *(Carib.)* Braggart; bully.

ososo, sa [o-soh'-so, sah], *f.* Osseous, bony.

ostaga [os-tah'-gah], *f. (Naut.)* Tie, runner.

oste [os'-tay], *int. (Ant.) V.* OXTE.

ostealgia [os-tay-ahl'-he-ah], *f.* Boneache, ostalgia.

osteítis [os-tay-ee'-tis], *f.* Osteitis, inflammation of bone.

ostensible [os-ten-see'-blay], *a.* Ostensible, apparent.

ostensiblemente [os-ten-see'-blay-men-tay], *adv.* Ostensibly.

ostensión [os-ten-se-on'], *f.* Show, manifestation.

ostensivo, va [os-ten-see'-vo, vah], *a.* Ostensive, showing, betokening.

ostentación [os-ten-tah-the-on'], *f.* 1. Ostentation, appearance. 2. Ambitious display, vain show, flourish parade.

ostentador, ra [os-ten-tah-dor', ran], *m & f.* Boaster, ostentator.

ostentar [os-ten-tar'], *va.* 1. To show (mostrar), to demonstrate. 2. To have (tener). 3. To have, to possess (poderes legales). **Ostentar el título en el deporte**, to hold the title in sport. -*vn.* To boast, to brag; to be fond of vain shows.

ostentativo, va [os-ten-tah-tee'-vo, vah], *a.* Ostentatious.

ostento [os-ten'-to], *m.* Portent, prodigy.

ostentosamente [os-ten-to'-sah-men-tay], *adv.* Ostentatiously, boastfully; gaudily.

ostentoso, sa [os-ten-to'-so, sah], *a.* Sumptuous, ostentatious, boastful, jaunty, gaudy, garish.

osteócopo [os-tay-o'-co-po], *a. (Med.)* Osteocopic, bone-breaking (dolor).

osteografía [os-tay-o-grah-fee'-ah], *f.* Osteography, description of the bones.

osteolita [os-tay-o-lee'-tah], *f.* Osteolite, fossil bone.

osteología [os-tay-o-lo-hee'-ah], *f.* Osteology, that part of anatomy which deals with the bones.

osteólogo [os-tay-o'-lo-go], *m.* Osteologer, a describer of the bones.

osteópata [os-tay-o'-pah-tah], *m.* Osteopath.

osteopatía [os-tay-o-pah-tee'-ah], *f.* Osteopathy.

ostiario [os-te-ah'-re-o], *m.* Ostiary, door-keeper, one of the minor orders of the Roman Catholic church.

ostiatim [os-te-ah'-tim], *adv.* From door to door.

ostión [os-te-on'], *m. (Prov. Andal.)* An oyster larger and coarser than the common one.

ostra [os'-trah], *f.* 1. Oyster. 2. *(Fig.)* Dull person (pesado); retiring individual (huraño); regular (permanente).

ostracismo [os-trah-thees'-mo], *m.* Ostracism, a method of banishment practiced by the Athenians.

ostracita [os-trah-thee'-tah], *f.* Ostracite, the common oyster in its fossil state.

ostral [os-trahl'], *m.* Oyster-bed.

ostrera [os-tray'-rah], *f.* 1. *V.* OSTRAL. 2. Oyster-wench, oyster-woman. 3. Oyster-plover.

ostrero [os-tray'-ro], *m.* Dealer in oysters.

ostrífero, ra [os-tree'-fay-ro, rah], *a.* Producing oysters, ostriferous.

ostro [os'-tro], *m.* 1. Oyster; large oysters are denominated in the masculine gender; they are also called *Ostrones.* 2. South wind. 3. Purple anciently obtained from a mollusk: Tyrian purple.

ostrogodo, da [os-tro-go'-o, dah], *a.* Ostrogothic.

ostugo [os-too'-go], *m.* Piece, part.

osudo, da [o-soo'-do, dah], *a.* Bony.

osuno, na [o-soo'-no, nah], *a.* Bear-like, bearish.

otacústico [o-tah-coos'-te-co], *a.* Otacoustic, assisting the sense of hearing. -*m.* Otacousticon, instrument to assist hearing.

otalgia [o-tahl'-he-ah], *f.* Otalgia, earache.

otálgico, ca [o-tahl'-he-co, cah], *a.* Otalgic, suitable for allaying earache.

otáñez [o-tah'-nyeth], *m. (hum.)* An old squire who courts or attends a lady; an old beau.

oteador, ra [o-tay-ah-dor', rah], *m. & f.* Spy, sly, observer.

otear [o-tay-ar'], *va.* To observe, to examine, to pry into, to discover by artifice; to inspect, to descry (alcanzar a ver), to look down on (mirar desde arriba).

otero [o-tay'-ro], *m.* Hill, eminence, height, in a plain.

ótico, ca [oh'-te-co, cah], *a. (Med.)* Otic, aural, employed in treating the ear.

otitis [o-tee'-tes], *f.* Otitis, inflammation of the ear.

oto [o'-to], *m. (Zool.)* Bustard, otis. *V.* AVUTARDA.

otología [o-to-lo-hee'-ah], *f. (Med.)* Otology, study of ear diseases.

otólogo, [o-to'-lo-go], *m.* Otologist, ear specialist.

otomana [o-to-mah'-nah], *f.* Ottoman, a cushioned seat, like a sofa.

otomano, na [o-to-mah'-no, nah], *a.* Ottoman, relating to the Turkish empire.

otona [o-to'-nah], *f. (Bot.)* Ragwort.

otoñada [o-to-nyah'-dah], *f.* Fall season, autumn season.

otoñal [o-to-nyahl'], *a.* Fall, autumnal.

otoñar [o-to-nyar'], *vn.* 1. To spend the fall season. 2. To grow in fall (plantas). -*vr.* To be seasoned, to be tempered.

otoño [o-to'-nyo], *m.* 1. Fall, autumn. 2. Aftermath, second crop of grass.

otorgador, ra [o-tor-gah-dor', rah], *m. & f.* Consenter, granter, stipulator.

otorgamiento [o-tor-gah-me-en'-to], *m.* 1. Grant, license. 2. The act of making an instrument in writing (acto).

otorgancia [o-tor-gahn'-the-ah], *f. (Law.)* Authorization. **Auto de otorgancia**, act of empowering or authorizing.

otorgante [o-tor-gahn'-tay], *pa. & m. & f.* 1. Granter; authorizing. 2. The party that signs and executes any public instrument.

otorgar [o-tor-gar'], *va.* 1. To consent, to agree to (consentir en), to condescend. 2. To covenant, to stipulate. 3. *(Law.)* To declare, to execute, to do. **Quien calla otorga**, silence gives consent.

otorrea [o-tor-ray'-ah], *f.* Otorrhoea, a discharge from the ear.

otorrino (laringólogo) [o-tor-ree'-no], *m & f. (Med.)* Ear, nose and throat specialist.

otoscopio [o-tos-co'-pe-oh], *m. (Med.)* Otoscope.

otro, tra [o'-tro, trah], *a.* Another, other. **Otra taza de café**, another cup of coffee. **Otra cosa**, something else. **Con otras 8 personas**, with another 8 people. -*pron.* Another one, others. **El otro**, the other one. **Tomar el sombrero de otro**, to take somebody else's hat. -*int.* Again! exclamation of disgust.

otrosí [o-tro-see'], *adv.* Besides, moreover. -*m. (Law.)* Every petition made after the principal.

ova [o'-vah], *f. (Bot.)* Sea-lettuce, laver. -*pl. (Prov.)* Eggs. *V.* HUEVAS.

ovación [o-vah-the-on'], *f.* Ovation, a lesser triumph among the Romans.

ovacionar [o-vah-the-o-nahr'], *va.* To acclaim.

ovado, da [o-vah'-do, dah], *a. & pp.* of OVAR. 1. Oval. 2. Fecundated by the male bird.

oval [o-vahl'], *a.* Oval, oblong; *(Mex. Med.)* pessary.

ovalado, da [o-vah-lah'-do, dah], *a.* Egg-shaped, oval-formed.

óvalo [o'-vah-lo], *m.* Oval, a body or figure in the shape of an egg.

ovar [o-var'], *vn.* To lay eggs.

ovárico, ca [o-vah'-re-co, cah], *a.* Ovarian.

ovario [o-vah'-re-o], *m.* 1. Ovary, the organ in a female by which impregnation is performed. 2. *(Bot.)* Ovarium, ovary, the seed-vessel of plants, the lowest part of the pistil. 3. Ornament in architecture in the form of an egg.

ovecico [o-vay-thee'-co], *m. dim.* A small egg.

oveja [o-vay'-hah], *f.* 1. Ewe, a female sheep. **Cada oveja con su pareja**, like seeks like. **Encomendar las ovejas al lobo**, to set the wolf to guard the sheep. **Oveja negra**, black sheep. 2. *(Cono Sur)* Whore.

ovejero [o-vay-hay'-ro], *m.* Shepherd.

ovejuela [o-vay-hoo-ay'-lah], *f. dim.* A young ewe.

ovejuno, na [o-vay-hoo'-no, nah], *a.* Relating to ewes.

overa [o-vay'-rah], *f.* Ovary of oviparous animals.

overo, ra [o-vay'-ro, rah], *a.* Dappled: applied to animals speckled, or trout-colored. *-pl. (coll.)* Eyes which look quite white, as if without a pupil.

ovezuelo [o-vay-thoo-ay'-lo], *m. dim.* A small egg.

oviforme [o-ve-for'-may], *a.* Egg-shaped.

ovil [o-vel'], *m.* Sheep-cot. *V.* REDIL.

ovillar [o-vil-lyar'], *vn.* To wind into a clew (lana), to hank. *-vr.* To shrug or contract oneself into a ball or clew.

ovillejo [o-vil-lyay'-ho], *m.* 1. *(dim.)* A small clew or ball. 2. A kind of metrical composition.

ovillo [o-veel'-lyo], *m.* 1. Clew, thread wound upon a bottom. 2. Any confused heap or multitude of things.

ovino, na [o-vee'-no, nah], *a.* Ovine, pertaining to sheep. **Ganado ovino**, sheep.

ovíparo, ra [o-vee'-pah-ro, rah], *a.* Oviparous, bringing forth eggs.

ovoide [o-vo'-e-day], *a.* Ovoid, egg-shaped. *-m.* 1. Ovoid. 2. *(LAm. Dep.)* Rugby ball.

óvolo [o'-vo-lo], *m. (Arch.)* Ovolo, a quarter-round; a convex moulding.

ovoso, sa [o-vo'-so, sah], *a.* Full of sea-weeds.

ovulación [o-voo-lah-the-on'], *f.* Ovulation.

óvulo [o'-voo-lo], *m.* Ovule, germ contained in an ovary before impregnation.

oxalato [ok-sah-lah'-to], *m. (Chem.)* Oxalate, salt formed with oxalic acid.

oxálico [ok-sah'-le-co], *a.* Oxalic: applied to acid made from sorrel.

oxálide [ok-sah'-le-day], *f. (Bot.)* Oxalis.

oxalme [ok-sahl'-may], *m.* Acid brine.

oxear [ok-say-ahr'] *va.* To shoo or scare away fowls.

oxidación [ok-se-dah-the-on'], *f. (Chem.)* Oxidation.

oxidar [ok-se-dar'], *va.* To oxidate, to oxidize, to rust. *-vr.* To absorb oxygen.

óxido [ok'-se-do], *m.* Oxide. **Óxido de zinc**, zinc oxide.

oxigenable [ok-se-hay-nah'-blay], *a. (Chem.)* Oxygenazable.

oxigenación [ok-se-hay-nah-the-on'], *f.* Oxygenation, combining with oxygen.

oxigenado, da [ok-se-hay-nah'-do, dah], *a.* 1. Oxygenated. 2. Peroxided (pelo). **Rubia oxignada**, peroxide blond. *-pp.* of OXIGENAR.

oxigenar [ok-se-hay-nar'], *va.* To oxygenate, to saturate with oxygen. *-vr.* To oxygenate, to be oxygenated.

oxígeno [ok-see'-hay-no], *m. (Chem.)* Oxygen. **Oxíogeno líquido**, liquid oxygen.

oxigonio [ok-se-go'-ne-o], *a.* Acute-angled.

oxígono, na [ok-see'-go-no, nah], *a.* Acute-angled; having all the angles acute.

oximaco [ok-se-mah'-co], *m.* A bird of prey with a curved black bill.

¡oxte! [ox'-tay], *int.* Keep off, clear off, begone. **¡Oxte puto!** exclamation on touching anything very hot or burning.

oyamel [o-yah-mel'], *m.* Mexican fir.

oyente [o-yen'-tay], *pa.* Hearing. *m. & f.* Auditor, hearer.

ozena [o-thay'-nah], *f. (Med.)* Ozaena, an ulceration of the nostrils, producing a fetid pus.

ozono [o-tho'-no], *m.* Ozone, considered an allotropic form of oxygen, generally produced by electricity.

ozonómetro [o-tho-no'-may-tro], *m.* Ozonometer, an instrument for measuring the amount of ozone in the air.

P

p [pay], seventeenth letter of the alphabet, is pronounced in the Spanish as in the English language.

pabellón [pah-bel-lyone'], *m.* 1. Pavilion, a kind of tent (tienda); field-bed. 2. Curtain hanging in the form of a tent. 3. **Pabellón de armas**, *(Mil.)* bell tent. 4. *(Naut.)* National colors, flag (bandera). 5. Summer house in the shape of a pavilion (en jardín). 6. Mouth (de trompeta). **Pabellón de música**, bandstand. **Pabellón de convivencia**, flag of convenience.

pábilo [pah'-be-lo], *m.* 1. Wick, as of a torch or candle. 2. Snuff of a candle.

pablar [pah-blar'], *va. (coll.)* Word used for consonance, as **Ni hablar, ni pablar**, not to speak.

pábulo [pah'-boo-lo], *m.* Pabulum, nourishment, food, provender, support, nutriment.

paca [pah'-cah], *f.* 1. The spotted cavy. 2. Bale of goods, bundle, package.

pacal [pah-cahl'], *m.* Bundle, parcel.

pacana [pah-cah'-nah], *f.* Pecan, an American tree like a walnut-tree, with an olive-shaped nut.

pacato, ta [pah-cah'-to, tah], *a.* Pacific, quiet, timid (tímido), tranquil, mild, gentle (modesto).

pacedero, ra [pah-thay-day'-ro, rah], *a.* Pasturable, fit for pasture (tierra).

pacedura [pah-thay-doo'-rah], *f.* Pasture-ground.

pacer [pah-therr'], *vn.* 1. To pasture, to graze. 2. To gnaw, to corrode, to feed. *-va.* 1. To eat, to graze (hierba). 2. To graze, to pasture (ganado).

pachamanca [pah-chah-mahn'-cah], *f.* (Peru) Barbecue, meat roasted out-of-doors, by covering with hot stones; barbecue feast.

pachanga [pah-chan'-gah], *f.* 1. Party (fiesta); binge (juerga), booze-up. 2. *(Carib.)* Mix-up (lío).

pachón [pah-chone'], *m.* 1. A peaceful, phlegmatic man. 2. Pointer, pointer-dog.

pachona [pah-cho'-nah], *f.* Pointer-bitch.

pachorra [pah-chor'-rah], *f.* Sluggishness, a slow and phlegmatic disposition.

pachorrudo, da [pah-chor-roo'-do, dah], *a.* Sluggish, tardy, phlegmatic.

pachulí [pah-choo-lee'], *m.* 1. *(Bot.)* Patchouli (perfume). 2. *(Esp.)* Bloke (tío).

paciencia [pah-the-en'-the-ah], *f.* 1. Patience, endurance. 2. Patience, the quality of expecting long without rage or discontent. 3. Patience, forbearance, long-suffering. 4. Slowness, tardiness in action. 5. Exhortatory exclamation to have patience. **Perder la paciencia**, to loose one's temper.

paciente [pah-the-en'-tay], *a.* 1. Patient, calm under affliction or pain, forbearing. 2. Consenting, accommodating: spoken of a contented cuckold.

paciente [pah-the-en'-tay], *m & f.* 1. Patient, sufferer, that which receives impressions from external agents. 2. *(coll.)* Patient; a sick person.

pacientemente [pah-the-ayn'-tay-men-tay], *adv.* Patiently, tolerantly.

pacienzudo, da [pah-the-en-thoo'-do, dah], *a. (coll.)* Patient, tolerant.

pacificación [pah-the-fe-cah-the-on'], *f.* Pacification, the act of making peace; quietness, peace of mind.

pacificador, ra [pah-the-fe-cah-dor', rah], *m. & f.* Pacificator pacifier, peace-maker, reconciler.

pacíficamente [pah-thee'-fe-cah-men-tay], *adv.* Pacifically.

pacificar [pah-the-fe-car'], *va.* To pacify, to appease (apaciguar); to calm (calmar). *-vn.* To treat for peace.

pacífico, ca [pah-thee'-fe-co, cah], *a.* Pacific, peaceful, desirous of peace; tranquil, undisturbed; mild, gentle. -*m.* Pacific (Océano).

pacifista [pah-the-fees'-tah], *m. & f.* Pacifist.

paco [pah'-co], *m.* 1. Paco, a kind of vicuña: alpaca. 2. (Chile) Police force. 3. Diminutive of *Francisco.* 4. *pl.* Silver ores containing chlorides, etc., and iron. 5. (*LAm.*) Cop, policeman.

pacotilla [pah-co-teel'-lyah], *f.* 1. Venture, goods embarked in a ship on the private account of an individual. **Ser de pacotilla**, of poor quality. (*Acad.*) 2. (*And. CAm. Cono Sur*) Rabble, crowd, mob.

pactar [pac-tar'], *va.* To covenant, to contract, to stipulate. -*vn.* To come to an agreement.

pacto [pahc'-to], *m.* Pact, covenant, agreement. **Pacto de caballeros**, gentleman's agreement. **Pacto social**, social contract. **Pacto de Varsovia**, Warsaw Pact.

pácul [pah'-cool], *m.* A wild plantain of the Philippines which yields a textile fiber not so good as the abacá.

padecer [pah-day-therr'], *va.* 1. To suffer corporal affliction. 2. To sustain an injury. 3. To be liable to 4. To endure (aguantar). -*vn.* **Padecer de**, to suffer from. **Padece del corazón**, he suffers with his heart. (*Yo padezco, yo padezca, from Padecer. V.* CONOCER.)

padecimiento [pah-day-the-me-en'-to], *m.* Suffering, sufferance.

padilla [pah-deel'-lyah], *f.* 1. A small frying-pan. 2. A small oven.

padrastro [pah-drahs'-tro], *m.* 1. Stepfather. 2. Obstacle, impediment. 3. Height, eminence which commands a tower or other place 4. Hangnail.

padrazo [pah-drah'-tho], *m. aug.* of PADRE. An indulgent parent.

padre [pah'-dray], *m.* 1. Father. 2. Father, the appellation of the first person of the Trinity. 3. Male of all animals. 4. Father, ancestor (antepasado). 5. Source, origin, principal author. 6. Father, one who acts with paternal care. 7. Father an ecclesiastical writer of the first centuries. 8. Father, the appellation of a religious man. 9. Father, the title of a confessor. **Padre de familia**, householder, housekeeper. **Padre Santo**, the Pope. **Padre nuestro**, the Lord's prayer; the large bead in the rosary over which the Lord's prayer is to be said. **Padre espiritual**, confessor. **Padre político**, father-in-law. -*pl.* 1. Parents, the father and mother. 2. Ancestors. 3. The members of a religious congregation taken as a body. **¡Mi padre!** no, indeed! never! **¡Que lo haga su padre!**, get someone else to do it! **Se llevó un susto padre**, he was frightened out of his wits. **Se pega la vida padre**, he lives like a king. **Tiene un éxito padre**, he's a big hit.

padrear [pah-dray-ar'], *vn.* 1. To resemble the father in features or habits. 2. To be kept for procreation (ganado).

padrinazgo [pah-dre-nath'-go], *m.* Compaternity, act of assisting at baptism, title or charge of a god-father.

padrino [pah-dree'-no], *m.* 1. Godfather (de un niño). 2. Second in duel. 3. Protector, assistant. **Padrino de boda**, best man. 4. Sponsor (que patrocina). **El que no tiene padrinos no se bautiza**, you can't get anywhere without connections.

padrón [pah-drone'], *m.* 1. Poll, a register of persons in a place who pay taxes (censo). 2. A kind of public monument among the Romans. 3. Mark or note of infamy. 4. An indulgent parent. 5. (*LAm.*) Stallion (caballo); (*And.*) breeding bull (toro).

paella [pah-el'-lyah], *f.* Rice dish originated in Valencia, Spain.

pafio, fia [pah'-fe-o, ah], *a.* Paphian, of Paphos.

paflón [pa-flone'], *m.* (*Arch.*) Soffit, the under side of a cornice or archway. *Cf.* PLAFÓN.

paga [pah'-gah], *f.* 1. Payment, fee (honorarios), salary. 2. Satisfaction for a fault or error committed. 3. Sum or fine paid. 4. Monthly pay of a soldier. 5. Friendly intercourse, mutual friendship. **Entrega contra paga**, cash on delivery.

pagadero, ra [pah-gah-day'-ro, rah], *a.* Payable, due. **Pagadero a plazos**, payable in instalments.

pagadero [pah-gah-day'-ro], *m.* Time and place of payment.

pagado, da [pah-gah'-do, dah], *a.* Paid. **Pagado por adelantado**, paid in advance. -*pp.* of PAGAR.

pagador, ra [pah-gah-dor', rah], *m. & f.* 1. Payer, one who pays. 2. Paymaster. **Mal pagador**, bad payer.

pagaduría [pah-gah-doo-ree'-ah], *f.* Paymaster's office.

pagamento [pah-gah-men'-to], *m.* Payment.

paganismo [pah-gah-nees'-mo], *m.* Paganism, heathenism.

pagano [pah-gah'-no], *m.* 1. Heathen, pagan. 2. Peasant, rustic. 3. (*coll.*) One who pays his share.

pagano, na [pah-gah'-no, nah], *a.* Heathenish, unchristian, paganish.

pagar [pah-gar'], *va.* 1. To pay, to discharge a debt (deuda), to acquit. 2. To be liable to customs duties; *used of* merchandise. 3. To pay (crimen, ofensa), to atone, to make amends. 4. To please, to give pleasure. 5. To pay, to reward, to requite (amor), to fee. -*vn.* 1. (*LAm.*) To pay. 2. (*Cono Sur*) To take bets (tomar apuestas). -*vr.* To be pleased (with oneself); to be fond of (another). **Pagar la visita**, to return a visit. **Pagar el pato**, (*coll.*) to receive unmerited punishment, or to pay for another man's misconduct. **Su tío le paga los estudios**, his uncle is paying for his education. **Paga 20 dólares de habitación**, he pays 20 dollars for his room. **Lo pagó con la vida**, he paid for it with his life.

pagaré [pah-gah-ray'], *m.* A note of hand, a promissory note.

pagaya [pa-gah'-yah], *f.* A Philippine oar, tied about with a twining stem.

página [pah'-he-nah], *f.* Page of a book.

paginar [pah-he-nahr'], *va.* To paginate; to number the pages.

pago [pah'-go], *m.* 1. Payment, discharge of a debt. 2. Payment, reward, the thing given in discharge of a debt or promise. **Suspender el pago**, to stop payment. 3. Lot of land; especially of vineyards. **Pronto pago**, prompt payment. **Dar cuenta con pago**, to close or balance an account. **En pago**, in payment, as a recompense, in return. **Pago en especie**, payment in kind. **Efectuar un pago**, to make a payment. **En pago de**, in return for. -*a.* (*coll.*) Paid.

pagoda [pah-go'-dah], *f.* Pagoda, Chinese temple.

pagodita [pa-go-dee'-tah], *f.* An earth which the Chinese employ in making figures.

pagote [pah-goh'-tay], *m.* (*coll.*) One who is charged with the faults of others, and pays or suffers for them all, scapegoat.

pagua [pah'-goo-ah], *f.* 1. (*Mex.*) Avocado, alligator pear. 2. (*Cono Sur*) Hernia (hernia); large swelling (hinchazón).

paguro [pah-goo'-ro], *m.* Small crab.

paila [pah'-e-lah], *f.* 1. A large pan of copper, brass, or iron. 2. A boiler.

pailón [pah-e-lone'], *m.* A large copper.

pairar [pah-e-rar'], *vn.* (*Taut.*) To bring to, to lie to. *V.* CAPEAR.

pairo [pah'-e-ro], *m.* (*Naut.*) Act of lying to with all sail set.

país [pah-ees'], *m.* 1. Country (nación), land (tierra), region, ground. 2. In painting, landscape (paisaje). 3. (*Met.*) Field, subject: applied to scientific researches. **País natal**, native land. **Vino del país**, local wine.

paisaje [pah-e-sah'-hay], *m.* Landscape, countryside, scenery.

paisana [pah-e-sah'-nah], *f.* 1. Country-woman, a woman of the same country as another person. 2. A kind of country dance.

paisanaje [pah-e-sah-nah'-hay], *m.* 1. The lay inhabitants of a country, in contradistinction to the military men and clergy: the peasantry. 2. Quality of being of the same country.

paisano, na [pah-e-sah'-no, nah], *a.* Of the same country.

paisano [pah-e-sah'-no], *m.* 1. Fellow-countryman, one of the same country as another. 2. Countryman: appellation given by soldiers to those who are not military men; a civilian. 3. Compatriot (compatriota). 4. (*Cono Sur*) Foreigner (extranjero); (*Cono Sur*) Arab (árabe); (*Mex.*) Spaniard; (*And. Cono Sur*) Chinaman, Chinese woman.

paja [pah'-hah], *f.* 1. Straw, the stalk on which corn grows; haum. 2. Straw, the stalk of corn after being thrashed. 3.

pajada

Beard of grain, blade of grass. 4. Straw, chaff, anything proverbially worthless, froth. 5. *(CAm.)* Lie (mentira). 6. *(Cono Sur)* Dope (droga). 7. *(And. CAm.)* Tap (grifo); canal (canal). **Paja trigaza**, wheat straw. **Techo de paja**, thatched roof.

pajada [pah-hah'-dah], *f.* Straw boiled with bran.

pajado, da [pah-hah'-do, dah], *a.* Pale, straw-colored.

pajar [pah-har'], *m.* Place where straw is kept.

pájara [pah'-hah-rah], *f.* 1. The female of any bird, henbird. 2. *(Prov.)* Paper kite (cometa). 3. Loose woman (putilla); thieving woman (ladrona). **Pájara pinta**, a game of forfeits. **Dar pájara a uno**, *(And. CAm.)* to swindle somebody. **Sufrir una pájara**, to suffer a fainting (en el deporte).

pajarear [pah-hah-ray-ar'], *va.* 1. To go bird-catching. 2. To loiter about. 3. *(Mex.)* To be skittish: speaking of horses.

pajarel [pah-hah-rel'], *m. V.* JILGUERO.

pajarera [pah-hah-ray'-rah], *f.* Aviary.

pajarería [pah-hah-ray-ree'-ah], *f.* 1. Abundance of sparrows or little birds. 2. Place where straw is sold. 3. Pet shop (tienda). 4. *(Carib.)* Vanity (vanidad).

pajarero [pah-hah-ray'-ro], *m.* 1. Bird catcher (cazador). 2. One who idles about. 3. Bird fancier (criador). 4. *(And. CAm.)* Bird-scarer.

pajarero, ra [pah-hah-ray'-ro, rah], *a.* 1. Merry, cheerful, gay. 2. Shy (caballos). 3. Gaudy, ill-matched (colores). 4. *(Carib.)* meddlesome (entrometido).

pajaril [pah-hah-reel'], *m. (Naut.)* Passaree or passarado, a rope fastened to the corner of a sail.

pajarilla [pah-hah-reel'-lyah], *f.* 1. *(dim.)* A small bird, hen or female of a bird. 2. Milt of a hog. 3. *(Prov.) V.* PALOMILLA (as insect). **Se abrasan las pajarillas**, it's intolerably hot.

pajarito, ta [pah-hah-ree'-to, tah], *m. & f. dim.* A small bird. *-f.* Bow tie; *V.* CUELLO.

pájaro [pah'-hah-ro], *m.* 1. Bird, a general name for the feathered kind: used generally for the smaller birds. 2. Sparrow. **Adiestrar pájaros**, to teach birds to sing. 3. *(Met.)* A conspicuous person; a sly fellow. 4. *(Carib.)* Queer (homosexual). **Pájaro solitario**, man who shuns company. *-pl.* The song-birds. **Más vale pájaro en mano que ciento volando**, a bird in the hand is worth two in the bush. **Pájaro carpintero**, woodpecker. **Tener pájaros en la cabeza**, to be featherbrained. *-a.* 1. *(Cono Sur)* Scatty (atolondrado), feather-brained; shady (sospechoso); loud (chillón). 2. *(Carib.)* Poofy, queer (afeminado). 3. *(Cono Sur)* Vague, distracted. **Es un pájaro de cuidado**, he's a nasty piece of work, a nasty customer.

pajarota [pah-hah-ro'-tah], *f.* A false, idle report, a hoax.

pajarraco [pah-har-rah'-co], *m.* 1. A large bird. 2. *(coll.)* A low, cunning fellow.

pajaza [pah-hah'-thah], *f.* Refuse of straw left by horses in the manager.

pajazo [pah-hah'-tho], *m.* Prick of stubbles received in a horse's face when feeding among them.

paje [pah'-hay], *m.* 1. Page, a young boy attending on a great personage. 2. *(Naut.)* Cabin-boy.

pajear [pah-hay-ar'], *vn. (coll.)* To behave, to conduct oneself.

pajel [pah-hel'], *m. (Zool.)* Red sea bream.

pajera [pah-hay'-rah], *f.* A place where straw is kept.

pajero [pah-hay'-ro], *m.* One who deals in straw, and carries it about for sale.

pajica, pajilla [pah-hee'-cah, pah-heel'-lyah], *f.* Cigar made of a maize-leaf: *(CAm. Carib. Mex.)* Straw hat.

pajita [pah-hee'-tah], *f.* 1. Drinking straw. 2. **Quedarse mascando pajita**, *(Carib.)* to be left feeling foolish.

pajizo, za [pah-hee'-tho, thah], *a.* 1. Made of straw, thatched with straw. 2. Straw-color.

pajón [pah-hone'], *m.* 1. Coarse straw. 2. *(coll.)* An unpolished, ill-bred man. *-a. (Mex.)* Lank (pelo).

pajoso, sa [pah-ho'-so, sah], *a.* Made of straw.

pajote [pah-ho'-tay], *m.* Straw interwoven with a bulrush, with which gardeners cover fruit-trees and plants.

pajuela [pah-hoo-ay'-lah], *f.* 1. Short, light straw. 2. Match for lighting.

pajuelero [pah-hoo-ay-lay'-ro], *m.* Match-maker.

pajujero [pah-hoo-hay'-ro], *m. (Prov.)* Place where straw is deposited to rot and become manure.

pajuncio [pah-hoon'-the-o], *m. (Prov.)* 1. Booby, ninny, fool. 2. In contempt, rush, worthless thing.

pajuz [pah-hooth'], *m. (Prov.)* Refuse of straw in the manger or stable.

pajuzo [pah-hoo'-tho], *m. (Prov.)* Bad straw, designed for manure.

pala [pah'-lah], *f.* 1. A wooden shovel for grain; shovel. **Palas con mango**, shovels with handles. 2. Peel used by bakers. 3. Blade of an oar. 4. Upper-leather of a shoe (zapato). 5. The breadth or flat surface of the teeth. 6. Craft, cunning, artifice. 7. Dexterity, cleverness. 8. *(Bot.)* Common Dante of a spathe. 9. Leaf of the prickly pear. 10. Smooth part of an epaulet from which the fringe hangs. **Pala mecánica**, power shovel. **Pala para el pescado**, fish slice. **Pala matamoscas**, fly swat.

palabra [pah-lah'-brah], *f.* 1. Word (vocablo), a single part of speech. 2. Word, affirmation, confirmation. 3. Word, promise (promesa), offer. 4. *(Div.)* The Word, or only-begotten Son. 5. **Palabra clave**, *(Comput.)* keyword. **Palabra de matrimonio**, promise of marriage. **Se han dado palabra**, they are engaged. **Palabras mayores**, offensive or insulting words; also, things that require great expense. **Soltar la palabra**, not to oblige a person to keep his word. **Dejar a uno con la palabra en la boca**, to turn away without listening to one who is speaking. **Decir a uno cuatro palabritas al oído**, *(coll.)* to intimidate a person by informing him that his character is known; also, to obtain a thing by secret flattery. **De palabra**, by word of mouth. **Pedir la palabra**, to ask for the floor. **Tomar la palabra**, to take a man at his word, to speak first. **A la primera palabra**, at the first word (meaning quick apprehension). **En una palabra**, in a word. **Sin chistar palabra**, without a word. **Ceder la palabra a uno**, to yield to somebody. **Es hombre de palabra**, he is a man of his word. **Palabra de código**, *(Comput.)* code word.

¡palabra! [pah-lah'-brah], *int.* I say, a word with you.

palabrada [pah-lah-brah'-dah], *f* Low, scurrilous language.

palabrería [pah-lah-bray-ree'-ah], *f.* Wordiness, much talk, emptiness of meaning.

palabrero, ra [pah-lah-bray'-ro, rah], *a.* Talkative, loquacious.

palabrista [pah-lah-brees'-tah], *com.* One who is full of idle talk, a loquacious person.

palabrita [pah-lah-bree'-tah], *f.* 1. *(dim.)* A short word: it is commonly used for an endearing expression. 2. Word full of meaning.

palabrota [pah-lah-bro'-tah], *f. aug.* A course expression, rude word.

palaciego, ga [pah-lah-the-ay'-go, gah], *a.* Pertaining to the palace. *-m.* Courtier (persona).

palacio [pah-lah'-the-o], *m.* 1. Palace, a royal residence; a house eminently splendid. 2. Castle, the mansion of the ancient nobility. **Palacio episcopal**, bishop's palace. **Palacio real**, royal palace.

palacra, palacrana [pah-lah'-crah, pah-lah-crah'-nah], *f.* A piece of native gold: ingot of pure gold.

palada [pah-lah'-dah], *f.* 1. A shovelful. 2. *(Naut.)* Every stroke of an oar.

paladar [pah-lah-dar'], *m.* 1. Palate, the roof of the mouth. 2. Palate, the instrument of taste and the taste itself. 3. Taste, relish; longing desire. **A medida or a sabor de su paladar**, according to the taste of anyone.

paladear [pah-lah-day-ar'], *va.* 1. To rub the palate of a newborn child with any sweet substance. 2. To amuse, to divert. 3. To clean the mouth or palate of animals. *-vn.* To manifest a desire of sucking (recién nacido). *-vr.* To get the taste of a thing by little and little; to relish.

paladeo [pah-lah-day'-o], *m.* The act of tasting or relishing.

paladial [pah-lah-de-ahl'], *a.* Palatal, pronounced by the palate, as **y, r.**

paladín [pah-lah-deen'], *m.* Paladin, a knight.

paladinamente [pah-lah-de'-nah-men-tay], *adv.* Publicly, clearly.

paladino, na [pah-lah-dee'-no, nah], *a.* Manifest, clear, apparent, public.

paladio [pah-lah'-de-o], *m. (Min.)* Palladium, a metal.

paladión [pah-lah-de-on'], *m.* Palladium, safeguard.

palafrén [pah-lah-frén], *m.* Palfrey, a small horse for ladies; a servant's horse.

palafrenero [pah-lah-fray-nay'-ro], *m.* Groom, hostler.

palahierro [pah-lah-e-er'-ro], *m.* Bushing for the spindle of the upper millstone.

pala mecánica [pah'-lah may-cah'-ne-cah], *f.* Power shovel, steam shovel.

palamenia [pah-lah-may'-ne-ah], *f.* The oars of a row-galley.

palanca [pah-lahn'-cah], *f.* 1. Lever. 2. A staff or pole by which a burden is supported between two men. 3. Exterior fortification with stakes. 4. *(Fig.)* Lever; pull, influence. 5. *(And. Mex.)* Punting pole (barca). **Palanca de impulsión**, operating lever. **Palanca de mano**, hand lever. **Palanca de retroceso**, return lever. **Mecanisno de palanca**, lever system.

palancada [pah-lan-cah'-dah], *f.* Stroke with a lever.

palancana, palangana [pah-lan-gah'-nah], *f.* 1. A basin. 2. *(And. CAm.)* Platter, serving dish. *-m & f. (Cono Sur)* Intruder (intruso); *(LAm.)* Shallow person (frívolo).

palanganero [pah-lahn'-gah-nay'-ro], *m.* Wash-stand, usually resting on three feet.

palangre [pah-lahn'-gray], *m.* A line from which several fish-hooks are suspended.

palanquera [pah-lan-kay'-rah], *f.* Inclosure with stakes or poles.

palanquero [pa-lahn-kay'-ro], *m.* Driver of stakes, pile-driver.

palanqueta [pah-lan-kay'-tah], *f.* 1. *(Mil.)* Bar-shot or cross-bar-shot, two balls joined by a bar. 2. *(dim.)* A small lever.

palanquín [pah-lan-keen'], *m.* 1. Porter who carries burdens. 2. *(Naut.)* Double-tackle, clew garnet. 3. Palanquin, a covered carriage or litter used in the east.

palastro [pah-lahs'-tro], *m.* Iron plate, sheet of hammered iron.

palatina [pah-lah-tee'-nah], *f.* Tippet, neckcloth for women in winter.

palatinado [pah-lah-te-nah'-do], *m.* 1. Palatinate; dignity of a palatine. 2. A county palatine.

palatino, na [pah-lah-tee'-no, nah], *a.* Palatial, belonging to the palace or the courtiers.

palay [pah-lah'-ee], *m. (Phil. Is.)* Rice with its husk.

palazo [pah-lah'-tho], *m.* Blow with a shovel or stick.

palazón [pah-lah-thone'], *m. (Naut.)* Masting, the masts of vessels.

palco [pahl'-co], *m.* 1. *(Th.)* Box, box seat. 2. Scaffold raised for spectators. **Palco de la presidencia**, *(Taur.)* president's box.

paleador [pah-lay-ah-dor'], *m.* Man who works with a shovel.

palear, ra [pah-lay-ahr']. *V.* APALEAR.

palenque [pah-len'-kay], *m.* 1. Palisade, enclosure made with piles; paling. 2. Passage from the pit to the stage in a playhouse. 3. *(And. Cono Sur)* Tethering post (caballos). 4. *(Cono Sur)* Din, racket (alboroto).

paleografía [pah-lay-o-grah-fee'-ah], *f.* Paleography, art of reading ancient MSS.

paleolítico [pah-lay-o-lee'-te-co], *a.* Paleolithic.

paleología [pah-lay-o-lo-hee'-ah], *f.* Paleology, the study of ancient languages.

paleontología [pah-lay-on-to-lo-hee'-ah], *f.* Paleontology, the science which treats of organic fossil remains and of the ancient life of the globe.

paleontólogo, ga [pah-lay-on-to'-lo-go], *m & f.* Paleontologist.

paleozoico [pah-lay-o-tho'-e-co], *a. (Geol.)* Paleozoic.

palería [pah-lay-ree'-ah], *f.* Art and business of draining low wet lands.

palero [pah-lay'-ro], *m.* 1. One who makes or sells shovels. 2. Ditcher, drainer; pioneer. *-a. (And.)* Big-headed (fanfarrón).

palestina [pah-les-tee'-nah], *f.* Two-line small pica; type of 22 points.

palestra [pah-les'-trah], *f.* 1. A place for wrestling and other athletic exercises: a palaestra. 2. A place for disputations or debates. 3. *(Poop)* Art of wrestling.

paléstrico, ca [pah-lees'-tre-co, cah], *a.* Relating to a place for wrestling or other exercises; palestric, palestrical, belonging to the exercise of wrestling.

palestrita [pah-les-tree'-tah], *m.* One versed in athletic or logical exercises.

paleta [pah-lay'-tah], *f.* 1. Fire-shovel. 2. Palette, a painter's tablet. 3. Iron ladle, used in public kitchens to distribute viands. 4. *(dim.)* A small shovel. 5. Blade-bone of the shoulder. 6. Trowel, a mason's tool. 7. *pl.* Chopsticks to eat with. 8. *(LAm.)* Lollipop (pirulí). 9. *(LAm.)* Topside of beef.

paletada [pah-lay-tah'-dah], *f.* Trowelful of mortar.

paletilla [pah-lay-teel'-lyah], *f.* 1. *(dim.)* A little fire-shovel. 2. A shoulder-blade. 3. *V.* PALMATORIA. 4. A cartilage under the pit of the stomach.

paleto [pah-lay'-to], *m.* 1. Fallow-deer. *V.* GAMO. 2. Clown, rustic (palurdo).

paletón [pah-lay-tone'], *m.* Bit, the part of a key in which the wards are formed.

paletoque [pah-lay-to'-kay], *m.* Kind of dress like a scapulary which hangs to the knees.

pali [pah'-le], *a. & m.* An ancient language of India, derived from the Sanscrit.

palia [pah'-le-ah], *f.* 1. Altar-cloth. 2. Veil which hangs before the tabernacle; square piece of linen put over the chalice.

paliación [pah-le-ah-the-on'], *f.* Palliation, extenuation.

paliadamente [pah-le-ah'-dah-men-tay], *adv.* Dissemblingly, in a palliative manner.

paliar [pah-le-ar'], *va.* 1. To palliate, to extenuate, to excuse, to relieve (dolor), to lessen (efecto); to diminish (importancia). 2. To mitigate, to excuse (ofensa). 3. To conceal, to gloss over (defecto).

paliativo, va [pah-le-ah-tee'-vo, vah], **paliatorio, ria**, *a.* Palliative, mitigating, that may be palliated.

palidecer [pah-le-day-ther'], *m.* To grow pale.

palidez [pah-le-deth'], *f.* Paleness, wanness, pallor, ghastliness.

pálido, da [pah'-le-do, dah], *a.* Pallid, pale, ghastly, sickly (enfermo).

palillero [pah-leel-lyay'-ro], *m.* 1. One who makes or sells toothpicks. 2. Toothpick case.

palillo [pah-leel'-lyo], *m.* 1. *(dim.)* A small stick. 2. Knittingneedle case, a utensil which women carry fastened to the waist by the apron-strings. 3. Toothpick (mondadientes). 4. Bobbin, a wooden implement for making net-work or laces. 5. Drum-stick. 6. Peruvian plant similar to the guava-tree. *-pl* 1. After-dinner table-talk. 2. Small pins put on the billiard-table in certain games. 3. *(coll.)* Trifles, things of no moment. **Palillos chinos**, chopsticks. **Estar hecho un palillo**, to be as thin as a rake.

palimpsesto [pa-limp-ses'-to], *m.* Palimpsest, an ancient parchment twice written upon, the first writing more or less erased.

palíndromo [pah-lin-dro'-mo], *m.* Palindrome, a word, line, or sentence, which, read either from left to right, or viceversa, has the same meaning.

palio [pah'-le-o], *m.* 1. Cloak, short mantle (manto). 2. Pallium, a pontifical ornament, worn by patriarchs and archbishops. 3. Anything in the form of a canopy (dosel). 4. Premium or plate given as a reward in racing. **Recibir con palio**, to receive under a pall, as kings, etc.

palique [pah-lee'-kay], *m. (coll.)* Trifling conversation, chitchat, small talk.

palito [pah-lee'-to], *m. dim.* A little stick.

palitroque, palitoque [pah-le-tro'-kay], *m.* 1. A rough, illshaped stick. 2. *(Cono Sur)* Skittles (juego); skittle alley (local), bowling alley.

paliza [pah-lee'-thah], *f.* Cudgelling, caning, cowhiding, beating, thrashing, drubbing. **Dar una paliza a uno**, to give somebody a beating. **El viaje fue una paliza**, the journey was ghastly.

palizada [pah-le-thah'-dah], *f.* 1. Palisade or palisado. 2. Paling, *V.* ESTACADA.

palma [pahl'-mah], *f.* 1. *(Bot.)* Date palm-tree. **Palma indiana**, coconut-tree. 2. Leaf of a palm-tree. 3. Palm of the hand. 4. Quick sole of a horse's hoof. 5. Insignia of victory. 6. Insignia of virginity. 7. *(Fig.)* Clapping, applause. **Llevarse la palma**, to carry the day. **Andar en palmas**, to be universally applauded. **Conocer como la palma de la mano**, to know like the back of one's hand.

palmacristi [pal-mah-crees'-te], *f.* Palma Christi, the castor-oil plant.

palmada [pal-mah'-dah], *f.* Slap with the palm of the hand. -*pl.* Clapping of hands, applause. **Dar palmadas**, to clap.

palmadilla [pal-mah-deel'-yah], *f.* A kind of dance.

palmar [pal-mar'], *a.* 1. Measuring a palm, or three inches. 2. Relating to palms. 3. Clear, obvious, evident.

palmar [pal-mar'], *m.* 1. Plantation or grove of palm-trees. 2. Fuller's thistle. -*pl. (Amer.)* Woods of dwarf palms, a kind of palmetto.

palmar [pal-mar'], *vn.* 1. To peg out (morir). 2. To loose (en juego). **Hemos palmado**, we've lost.

palmario, ria [pal-mah'-re-o, ah], *a.* Clear, obvious, evident.

palmatoria [pal-mah-to'-re-ah], *f.* 1. A rod with which boys at school were beaten on the hand (castigo). 2. A small candlestick with a handle (de vela).

palmeado, da [pal-may-ah'-do, dah], *a.* 1. Palmiped, webfooted, palmated (aves). 2. *(Bot.)* Palmate: applied to the leaves and roots of plants. -*pp.* of PALMEAR.

palmear [pal-may-ar'], *va.* To slap with the open hand.

palmejar [pal-may-har'], *m. (Naut.)* Thick stuff, thick plank nailed to the inner sides of ships.

palmera [pal-may'-rah], *f.* Palm-tree. *V.* PALMA.

palmero [pal-may'-ro], *m.* Palmer, a pilgrim, a crusader who bore a palm in his hand.

palmeta [pal-may'-tah], *f.* 1. Ferule. *V.* PALMATORIA. 2. Slap on the palm of the hand. **Palmeta matamoscas**, fly swater.

palmífero, ra [pal-mee'-fay-ro, rah], *a. (Poet.)* Palmiferous.

palmípedo, da [pal-mee'-pay-do, dah], *a.* Web-footed, palmiped.

palmitieso [pal-me-te-ay'-so], *a.* Hard-hoofed horse.

palmito [pal-mee'-to], *m.* 1. Dwarf, fan-palm; palmetto. 2. Its root. 3. Little face (cara de mujer). **Buen palmito**, a pretty face. 4. *(Cuba)* Top of a palm-tree containing a bud which is palatable and nutritious.

palmo [pahl'-mo], *m.* 1. Palm, a measure of length from the thumb to the end of the little finger extended; hand, handbreadth. **En un palmo de tierra**, in a short space of ground. 2. Game, commonly called span-farthing. **Palmo a palmo**, inch by inch. **Medir a palmos**, *(Met.)* to have complete knowledge of something. **Dejar a uno con un palmo de narices**, to disappoint one in an affair in which he expected to succeed. **Quedarse con un palmo de narices**, to be out of luck. 3. *(CAm.)* Cunt (vagina). **Con un palmo de lengua fuera**, panting.

palmotear [pal-mo-tay-ar'], *va.* To slap with the hand. *V.* PALMEAR.

palmoteo [pal-mo-tay'-o], *m.* Clapping of hands, clap.

palo [pah'-lo], *m.* 1. Stick, cudgel. 2. Timber, log. 3. Wood of some American trees which serves for medicine or dyes.

4. Blow given with a stick; whack. 5. Execution on the gallows. 6. Suit at cards (cartas). 7. Stalk of fruit, pedicle. 8. In writing, a line which projects above or below. 9. *(Her.)* Pale, a vertical band one-third the width of the shield. 10. Club (porra), banderilla (banderilla), spear (garrocha). 11. *(LAm.)* Swig, draught of liquor. 12. **Dar un palo**, to do a job (robo). 13. *(LAm.)* **Un palo de casa**, a splendid house. **Dar palo**, to turn out contrary to one's expectations. **Palo de escoba**, broomstick. **Cuchara de palo**, wooden spoon. **Andar a palos**, to be always squabbing. **A palo seco**, bare.

palo dulce [pah'-lo dool'-thay], *m. (Bot.)* Licorice. *V.* OROZUZ.

palo santo [pah'-lo sahn'-to], *m. (Bot.)* Lignum-vitae.

paloma [pah-lo'-mah], *f.* 1. Pigeon, dove. **Paloma mensajera**, homing pigeon. **Paloma torcaz**, ring-dove. 2. A meek, mild, dove-like person. 3. *(Ast.)* Columba, one of the southern constellations. 4. Handstand (ejercicio). 5. *(CAm. Carib. Mex.)* Kite (cometa).

palomaduras [pah-lo-mah-doo'-ras], *f. pl. (Naut.)* Seams of the sails, where the bolt-rope is sewed to them.

palomar [pah-lo-mar'], *a.* Applied to hard-twisted linen or thread. -*m.* Pigeon-house, dove-cot.

palomariego, ga [pah-lo-mah-re-ay'-go, gah], *a.* Applied to domestic pigeons in the fields.

palomear [pah-lo-may-ar'], *vn.* 1. To shoot pigeons. 2. To care for them.

palomera [pah-lo-may'-rah], *f.* 1. A bleak place. 2. Small dove-cot.

palomería [pah-lo-may-ree'-ah], *f.* Pigeon-shooting.

palomero [pah-lo-may'-ro], *m.* One who deals in doves or pigeons.

palomero [pah-lo-may-ro], *a.* Applied to arrows with long iron points.

palomilla [pah-lo-meel'-lyah], *f.* 1. *(dim.)* A young pigeon. 2. A sort of ashy moth reared in barley. 3. Backbone of a horse. 4. Peak of a packsaddle. 5. Horse of a milk-white color. 6. A wall-bracket; a galley-rack. 7. Brass box of the axis of a wheel. 8. Chrysalis or pupa. 9. *(Bot.)* Common fumitory. 10. *(And. Cono Sur)* Urchin (travieso); *(CAm. Cono Sur, Mex.)* Mob of kids (niños).

palomina [pah-lo-mee'-nah], *f.* 1. Pigeon-dung. 2. *(Bot.)* Fumitory. 3. A kind of black grape.

palomino [pah-lo-mee'-no], *m.* 1. A young pigeon. 2. *(coll.)* Stain of excrements upon the shirt. 3. *(And. Cono Sur, Mex.)* Palomino (caballo); white horse (caballo). 4. Pigeon droppings (excremento).

palomita [pah-lo-mee'-tah], *f.* 1. Squab, pigeon. **Palomitas de maíz**, popcorn.

palomo [pah-lo'-mo], *m.* Cock-pigeon.

palón [pah-lone'], *m. (Her.)* Guidon, an ensign resembling a flag.

palotada [pah-lo-tah'-dah], *f.* Stroke with a battledoor. **No dar palotada**, not to have hit on the right thing in all that is said or done; not to have begun a line or title of what was undertaken or ordered; not to answer anything to the purpose.

palote [pah-lo'-tay], *m.* 1. Stick of a middling size, drumstick. 2. Rule or line used by scholars in writing. 3. *(Carib. Cono Sur)* Rolling pin; *(Cono Sur)* beanpole (persona). -*pl.* The first lines formed by boys in writing.

paloteado [pah-lo-tay-ah'-do], *m.* 1. Rustic dance performed with sticks. 2. Noisy scuffle or dispute, in which they come to blows.-**Paloteado, da**, *pp.* of PALOTEAR.

palotear [pah-lo-tay-ar'], *vn.* To scuffle, to clash, to strike sticks against one another; to contend or dispute loudly.

paloteo [pah-lo-tay'-o], *m.* Fight with sticks.

palpable [pal-pah'-blay], *a.* 1. Palpable, perceptible to the touch. 2. Palpable, plain, evident, clear.

palpablemente [pal-pah'-blay-men-tay], *adv.* Palpably, evidently.

palpadura [pal-pah-doo'-rah], *f.* or **palpamiento** [pal-pah-me-en'-to], *m.* Palpation, the act of feeling, touching, palpableness.

palpar [pal-par'], *va.* 1. To feel, to touch. 2. To grope in the dark. 3. To know positively, as if one had felt it. *4.* To appreciate, to understand. *-vr.* To be felt. **Es una enemistad que se palpa**, it's a hostility which one can feel.

pálpebra [pahl'-pay-brah], *f.* Eyelid. *V.* PÁRPADO.

palpebral [pal-pay-brabl'], *a.* Palpebral, belonging to the eyelid.

palpitación [pal-pe-tah-the-on'], *f.* Palpitation, as of the heart: panting, heaving.

palpitante [pal-pe-tahn'-tay], *pa.* Vibrating, palpitating, throbbing (corazón).

palpitar [pal-pe-tar'], *vn.* 1. To palpitate, to pant, to flutter, to heave. 2. *(And. Cono Sur)* **Me palpita**, I have a hunch.

palpo [pahl'-po], *m.* Palpus, an organ of touch in insects, accessory to the mouth.

palta [pahl'-tah], *f. (Bot. Peru.)* Alligator-pear. *V.* AGUACATE.

palto [pahl'-to], *m. (Bot.)* Alligator-pear tree.

palude [pah-loo'-day], *f.* Lake, pool. *V.* LAGUNA.

palúdico, ca [pah-loo'-de-co, cah], *a.* 1. Malarial, afflicted with malaria. 2. Paludal, marshy.

paludismo [pah-loo-dees'-mo], *m. (Med.)* Malaria.

paludoso, sa [pah-loo-do'-so, sah], *a.* Marshy, swampy.

palumbario [pah-loom-bah'-re-o], *a.* Dove-hunting (azor).

palurdo [pah-loor'-do], *m.* A clown, a churl, a rustic.

palurdo, da [pah-loor'-do, dah], *a.* Rustic, clownish, rude.

palustre [pah-loos'-tray], *a.* Marshy, fenny, boggy. *-m.* Trowel.

palustrillo [pah-loos-treel'-lyo], *a.* Angle-float, a plasterer's trowel.

pallaco [pal-lyah'-co], *m. (Amer.)* Piece of ore of good quality found in a waste-heap.

pallaquear [pal-lyah-kay-ar'], *va.* (Peru) *V.* PALLAR.

pallar [pal-lyar'], *va.* To extract the richest metallic part of minerals.

pallete [pal-lyay'-tay], *m. (Naut.)* Fender, paunch-mat.

pallón [pal-lyone'], *m.* 1. The quantity of gold or silver resulting from an assay. 2. Assay of gold when incorporated with silver.

pamandabuán [pah-man-dah-boo-ahn'], *m.* A Philippine craft like a dugout, but larger; it carries oars and sometimes a mast, with a sail of matting.

pamela [pah-may'-lah], *f.* Picture hat, sun hat.

pamema [pa-may'-mah], *f.* 1. Trifle, bagatelle to which it was desired to give importance; folderol (bagatela). 2. Flattery (halagos). 3. Fuss (quejas).

pampa [pahm'-pah], *f.* 1. *(S. Amer.)* An extensive plain. 2. *(Cono Sur)* Region of nitrate deposits; open area on the outskirts of a town (descampado). *m.* A tree of the Philippine Islands. The wood is used for making chests and for sheathing boats.

pámpana [pahm'-pah-nah], *f.* Vine-leaf (hoja). **Tocar or zurrar la pámpana**, *(coll.)* to threaten, to chastise.

pampanada [pam-pah-nah'-dah], *f.* Juice of tendrils or vine-shoots.

pampanaje [pam-pah-nah'-hay], *m.* 1. Abundance of vine-shoots. 2. Vain parade.

pampanilla [pam-pah-neel'-lyah], *f.* A covering of foliage, used by Indians to screen their nakedness.

pámpano [pahm'-pah-no], *m.* 1. Young vine-branch or tendril. 2. *(Zool.)* *V.* SALPA. 3. *(Amer.)* A delicious steelblue harvest-fish.

pampanoso, sa [pam-pah-no'-so, sah], *a.* Abounding with foliage, tendrils, and clusters of grapes.

pampero [pam-pay'-ro], *m.* 1. *(Arg.)* A violent wind from the south-west; so called because it blows from the pampas. 2. Inhabitant of the pampas (persona).

pampero, ra [pam-pay'-ro, rah], *m. & f. & a.* A dweller on the pampas.

pampirolada [pam-pe-ro-lah'-dah], *f.* 1. Sauce made of garlic, bread, and water, pounded in a mortar. 2. *(coll.)* A silly thing without substance.

pamplemusa [pam-play-moo'-sah], *f. (Bot.)* The shaddock and its fruit; grape-fruit.

pamplina [pam-plee'-nah], *f.* 1. *(Bot.)* Duck-weed. 2. *(Bot.)* Mouse-ear. 3. A plant yielding food to canary birds. 4. *(coll.)* Futility, trifle, a worthless thing. 5. Soft soap (jabón). 6. Nonsense (disparates). **Sin más pamplinas**, without any more beating about the bush.

pamporcino [pam-por-thee'-no], *m. (Bot.)* Cyclamen.

pamposado, da [pam-po-sah'-do, dah], *a.* Lazy, idle, cowardly.

pampringada [pam-prin-gah'-dah], *f.* 1. *V.* PRINGADA. 2. *(Met. Coll.)* 1. Frivolous, futile thing.

pan [pahn], *m.* 1. Bread, a loaf. 2. Pie-crust. 3. Mass of figs, salt, sugar, etc., in the shape of a loaf. 4. Food in general. 5. Wheat. **Este año hay mucho pan**, this year there is plenty of wheat. 6. A wafer or bread for the Eucharist, baked with baking-irons. 7. Leaf of gold or silver. 8. Greek prefix, signifying "all." 9. All grains, except wheat, of which bread is made. **Pan casero o bazo**, household bread. **Pan por pan, vino por vino**, the plain unvarnished truth. **Pan de centeno**, rye bread. **Pan moreno**, brown bread. **Es el pan nuestro de cada día**, *(fig.)* our daily bread. **Eso es pan comido**, it's a cinch. **Contigo pan y cebolla**, with you I'd gladly have love in a cottage. **Estar a pan y agua**, to be on bread and water. **Por un mendrugo de pan**, for a bite to eat. **Es más bueno que el pan**, he is kindness itself. **Se venden como pan bendito**, they sell like hot cakes. **Quitarle a uno el pan de la boca**, to take the bread out of somebody's mouth.

pana [pah'-nah], *f.* 1. Velveteen (paño), corduroy. 2. *pl. (Naut.)* Limber-boards, which form part of the lining of the ship's floor. *-m & f. (Carib.)* Pal, buddy.

panacea [pah-nah-thay'-ah], *f.* Panacea, universal medicine.

panada [pah-nah'-dah], *f.* Panada or panado.

panadear [pah-nah-day-ar'], *va.* To make bread for sale.

panadeo [pah-nah-day'-o], *m.* Baking bread.

panadería [pah-nah-day-ree'-ah], *f.* 1. Trade or profession of a baker. 2. Baker's shop (tienda), bake-house.

panadero, ra [pah-nah-day'-ro, rah], *m. & f.* Baker, maker or seller of bread, kneader. *-f.* Baker's wife.

panadizo, panarizo [pah-nah'-dee'-tho], *m.* 1. Whitlow, felon 2. *(coll.)* Pale-faced, sickly person.

panado, da [pah-nah'-do, dah], *a.* Applied to bread macerated in water for sick persons. *-m.* Panada or panado.

panal [pah-nahl'], *m.* 1. Honey-comb. 2. Anything pleasing to the taste.

panameño, ña [pah-nah-may'-nyo, nyah], *m. & f. & a.* Panamanian, from Panama.

panamericanismo [pah-nah-may-re-cah-nees'-mo], *m.* Pan Americanism.

panamericano, na [pahn-ah-may-re-cah'-no, nah], *a.* Pan-American, of both Americas.

panarra [pah-nar'-rah], *m.* Dolt, simpleton.

panática [pah-nah'-te-cah], *f.* Provision of bread.

panca [pahn'-cah], *f.* 1. The husk of an ear of maize. 2. A Philippine fishing-boat. It is provided with outriggers and with paddles, and is steered by a *papaya.*

pancarpia [pan-car'-pe-ah], *f.* A garland.

pancarta [pan-car'-tah], *f.* Placard, banner.

pancera [pan-thay'-rah], *f.* Armor which covers the belly.

páncreas [pahn'-cray-as], *m. (Anat.)* Pancreas, sweetbread.

pancromático, ca [pan-cro-mah'-te-co, cah], *a. (Photog.)* Panchromatic.

panda [pahn'-dah], *m. (Zool.)* Panda.

panda [pahn'-dah], *f.* 1. Gallery in a cloister. 2. *V.* PANDILLA.

pandear [pan-day-ar'], *vn.* To bend, to be inclined, to belly, to bulge out.

pandeo [pan-day'-o], *m.* Bulge, anything that bulges out in the middle.

panderada [pan-day-rah'-dah], *f.* 1. Number of timbrels joined in concert. 2. Stroke with a timbrel. 3. *(coll.)* A silly, untimely, or unreasonable proposition.

panderazo

panderazo [pan-day-rah'-tho], *m.* Blow with a timbrel.

pandereta [pan-day-ray'-tah], *f.* Tambourine.

panderetear [pan-day-ray-tay-ar'], *vn.* To play on the timbrel.

pandereteo [pan-day-ray-tay'-o], *m.* The act of beating the timbrel.

panderetero, ra [pan-day-ray-tay'-ro, rah], *m. & f.* 1. One who beats the timbrel. 2. A maker or seller of timbrels.

panderillo [pan-day-reel'-lyo], *m. dim.* A small timbrel.

pandero [an-day'-ro], *m.* 1. Timbrel, a musical instrument. 2. *(coll.)* Silly person who talks at random (tonto). 3. *(Prov.)* Paper kite (cometa).

pandilla [pan-deel'-lyah], *f.* 1. Plot, league, party, faction. 2. Party of persons joined together for recreation in the country or for mischief.

pandillador, pandillero, pandillista [pan-dil-lyah-dor' lyay'-ro, lyis'-tah], *m.* Gangster, member of a rowdy gang.

pando, da [pahn'-do, dah], *a.* 1. Bulged. 2. Slow of motion (aguas profundas). 3. Heavy, bulky (personas). 4. *(CAm.)* Oppressed (oprimido); full (saciado). 5. *(CAm. Mex.)* Round-shouldered (de hombros).

pandorga [pan-dor'-gah], *f.* 1. Concert of musical instruments. 2. *(coll.)* Fat, bulky woman (gorda). 3. *(Prov.)* Kite (cometa). 4. *(And.)* Bother (molestia). 5. *(Mex.)* Practical joke (broma).

panecico, illo, ita [pan-nay-thee'-co], *m.* A small loaf of bread, a roll of bread.

panegírico, ca [pah-nay-hee'-re-co, cah], *a.* Panegyrical.

panegírico [pah-nay-hee'-re-co], *m.* Panegyric, eulogy.

panegirista [pah-nay-he-rees'-tah], *m.* Panegyrist, encomiast, eulogist.

panel [pah-nayl'], *m.* 1. Panel (madera). 2. **Paneles de instrumentos**, dashboard. **Panel de control (área de estado)**, *(Comput.)* control panel (status area).

panela [pah-nay'-lah], *f.* 1. *(Col.)* Brown sugar. 2. *(Her.)* A heart-shaped shield.

panera [pah-nay'-rah], *f.* 1. Granary. 2. Pannier, a bread-basket.

panes [pah'-nees], *m. pl.* 1. Corn or grain in the field. 2. Fauns, satyrs.

panetela [pah-nay-tay'-lah], *f.* 1. Panada, soup made by boiling bread and water. 2. *(Amer.)* Sponge-cake. 3. A long and slender cigar of Havana.

panetería [pah-nay-tay-ree'-ah], *f.* Room or office in the palace of the Spanish monarch, where bread and table-linen are kept for use; pantry.

panetero [pah-nay-tay'-ro], *m.* Pantler, the officer in the palace who keeps the bread.

pánfilo [pahn'-fe-lo], *m.* 1. A slow, sluggish, heavy person. 2. A jesting game, extinguishing a small candle in pronouncing this word.

panfleto [pan-flay'-to], *m.* Pamphlet; *(LAm.)* satire, lampoon, scandal sheet.

pangelín [pan-hay-leen'], *m.* Angelin-tree, forty or fifty feet high, with leaves like the walnut and a nut with a bitter and sourish taste.

pangolín [pan-go-leen'], *m.* Pangolin, the scaly ant-eater.

paniaguado [pah-ne-ah-goo-ah'-do], *m.* 1. Table-fellow, one who receives board and lodging from a friend. 2. Comrade, an intimate friend.

pánico, ca [pah'-ne-co, cah], *a.* Panic, struck with groundless fear. Also *m.*

paniculo [pah-nee'-coo-lo], *m.* Panicle, pellicle, a membrane.

paniego, ga [pah-ne-ay'-go, gah], *a.* Eating or yielding much bread.

paniego [pah-ne-ay'-go], *m.* Bag of coarse cloth, in which charcoal is carried and sold.

panificar [pan-ne-fe-car'], *va.* To convert pasture-land into arable ground or corn-fields.

panilla [pah-neel'-lyah], *f.* A small measure of oil (1/4 lb.).

panizal [pah-ne-thahl'], *m.* A maize-field.

panizo [pah-nee'-tho], *m.* 1. *(Bot.)* Panic-grass. 2. *(Prov.)* Maize, Indian-corn.

panocha [pah-no'-chah], *f.* 1. Corncob, ear of maize. 2. *(Mex.)* Unrefined brown sugar (azúcar). 3. *(And. CAm. Cono Sur)* Large pancake of maize and cheese. 4. Brass, money (dinero). 5. *(Mex.)* cunt.

panoja [pah-no'-hah], *f.* *(Bot.)* Panicle, a species of inflorescence, consisting of a branched raceme or corymb. Grasses present spikes arranged in panicles.

panorama [pah-no-rah'-mah], *m.* Panorama; vista, view, scene; outlook (perspectiva), prospect.

panorámica [pah-no'-rah-me-cah], *f.* General view.

panorámico [pah-no-rah'-me-co], *a.* Panoramic.

pansofía [pan-so-fee'-ah], *f.* Universal science.

pantaletas [pan-tah-lay'-tahs], *f. pl.* Panties.

pantalla [pan-tahl'-lyah], *f.* 1. Lamp-shade (de lámpara). 2. Any screen or shelter (biombo). **Pantalla de chimenea**, fire-screen. 3. A person who puts himself before a thing to shelter and conceal it. 4. Screen (cine). **Pantalla de televisión**, television screen. **Los personajes de la pantalla**, screen personalities. 5. *(Cono Sur)* Fan (abanico). 6. *(Fig.)* Blind, pretext; decoy. 7. *(LAm.)* Henchman (esbirro). 8. *(CAm.)* Large mirror. 9. *(Comput.)* Display. **Pantalla de cristal líquido**, liquid cristal display. **Pantalla de mapa de bits**, bitmap display. **Pantalla táctil**, touch sensitive screen. **Pantalla de radar**, radar screen.

pantalón [pan-tah-lone'], *m.* V. PANTALONES.

pantalones [pan-tah-lo'-ness], *m. pl.* 1. Pants, slacks. **Ponerse los pantalones**, *(Coll.)* to show who is the boss (generally applied to the man of the house). **Llevar los pantalones**, *(Coll.)* to wear the pants, to be the head of a household. 2. *(And.)* Man, male. 3. *(Carib.)* Guts, courage.

pantano [pan-tah'-no], *m.* 1. Pool of stagnant water, fen, moor, marsh (natural), morass 2. A reservoir or lake for the purpose of irrigation (artificial). 3. Hindrance, obstacle, difficulty.

pantanoso, sa [pan-tah-no'-so, sah], *a.* 1. Marshy, fenny, boggy. 2. Full of difficulties, obstacles, and obstructions.

panteísmo [pan-tay-ees'-mo], *m.* Pantheism, belief that the universe is God.

panteísta [pan-tay-ees'-tah], *com.* Pantheist.

panteología [pan-tay-o-lo-hee'-ah], *f.* Pantheology.

panteón [pan-tay-on'], *m.* Pantheon, a temple of ancient Rome, now consecrated to the Holy Virgin under the title of Our Blessed Lady of the Rotunda. Hence, a splendid mausoleum for kings and other celebrities.

pantera [pan-tay'-rah], *f.* 1. Panther. 2. A mineral crystal enclosing foreign bodies.

panti [pahn'-te], *m.* Tights.

pantógrafo [pan-to'-grah-fo], *m.* Pantograph, a mathematical instrument for copying a drawing.

pantómetro [pan-to'-may-tro], *m.* Pantometer; proportional compasses for measuring heights and angles.

pantomima [pan-to-mee'-mah], *f.* Pantomime, a dumb show.

pantomímico, ca [pan-to-mee'-me-co, cah], *a.* Pantomimic, pantomimical.

pantomimo [pan-to-mee'-mo], *m.* Pantomime, a mimic, one who expresses his meaning by signs.

pantoque [pan-to'-kay], *m.* *(Naut.)* Bilge or fiat of the ship.

pantorrilla [pan-tor-reel'-lyah], *f.* Calf of the leg.

pantorrillera [pan-tor-reel-lyay'-rah], *f.* A stocking used to make the calf look big.

pantorrilludo, da [pan-tor-reel-lyoo'-do, dah], *a.* Having large or thick calves.

pantuflazo [pan-too-flah'-tho], *m.* Blow given with a slipper.

pantuflo [pan-too'-flo], *m.* Slipper.

panza [pahn'-thah], *f.* 1. Belly (abultado), paunch. 2. The projecting part of certain artificial bodies.

panzada [pan-thah'-dah], *f.* 1. Bellyful (hartazgo). 2. Push with the belly.

panzón [pan-thone'], *m.* Large-bellied person.

panzudo, da [pan-thoo'-do, dah], *a.* Big-bellied.

pañal [pah-nyahl'], *m.* 1. Swaddling-clout or cloth. 2. Cloth in which anything is wrapped up. 3. Tail of a shirt. -*pl.* 1.

Swaddling-clothes. 2. *(Met.)* The elements of education and instruction. **Estar en pañales**, to have little knowledge of anything. 3. Childhood, infancy. 4. Diaper. **Criarse en buenos pañales**, to be born with a silver spoon.

pañalico, illo, ito [pah-nyah-lee'-co], *m. dim.* A small swaddling-cloth.

pañalón [pah-nyah-lone'], *m.* One who has part of his clothes always falling off.

pañero [pah-nyay'-ro], *m.* Woollen draper, clothier.

pañete [pah-nyay'-tay], *m.* 1. *dim.* of PAÑO. 2. Cloth of inferior quality or light body (tela). *-pl.* 1. A kind of pants worn by fishermen and tanners. 2. Linen attached to the crucifix below the waist. 3. *(Cono Sur)* Horse blanket.

pañito, pañizuelo [pah-nyee'-to], *m. dim.* A small cloth. *(Mex.)* Small handkerchief; also, a Madras pocket-handkerchief.

paño [pah'-nyo], *m.* 1. Cloth, woollen stuff. 2. Any woven stuff, whether of silk, flax, hemp, wool or cotton. **Paño de seda negro**, strong black silk serge. 3. The breadth of any stuff made of wool, silk, etc. 4. **Paños de corte**, very fine pieces of Flemish tapestry. 5. The red color of a bloodshot eye; livid spot on the face; a ring-worm. 6. Spot in looking glasses, crystals, or precious stones. 7. *(Naut.)* Canvas, sail-cloth. 8. *(Arquit.)* Stretch, length. 9. Mist, cloud, cloudiness (en cristal); flaw (en diamantes). 10. *(Carib.)* Fishing net (red). 11. *(And.)* Plot of land (tierra). **Paños**, clothes, garments. **Paños menores**, small clothes, undergarments; dishabille. **Paño de sol**, *(Mex.)* a large square handkerchief embroidered with colored silk thrown over the head and shoulders as a protection from the sun, when traveling. **Paño de cocina**, dishcloth. **Paño higiénico**, sanitary towel. **Paños de secar**, tea towel.

pañol [pah-nyole'], *m. (Naut.)* Room in a ship where stores are kept. **Pañol de pólvora**, *(Naut.)* magazine. **Pañol del agua**, water store.

pañolero de Santa Bárbara [pah-nyo-lay'-ro], *m. (Naut.)* The gunner's yeoman. **Pañolero del pañol de proa**, *(Naut.)* the boatswain's yeoman.

pañolón [pah-nyo-lone'], *m.* A long square shawl.

pañoso, sa [pah-nyo'-so, sah], *a.* Ragged, dressed in rags.

pañuelo [pah-nyoo-ay'-lo], *m.* Handkerchief, kerchief, hand-cloth, scarf (de cabeza). **Pañuelos estampados**, printed handkerchiefs.

papa [pah'-pah], *m.* 1. The Pope. 2. *f. (Prov. and Amer.)* Potato. 3. *(Peru.)* A piece of silver found where there are no mines of this metal. 4. *(Zool.)* The yellow-bird, American goldfinch or yellow wabbler. 5. *pl.* Pap, a soup for infants; any sort of pap; any kind of food. *V.* PUCHAS. 6. Not a blind thing. **No entiendo ni papa**, I don't understand a word. 7. *(Cono Sur)* Bash, blow. 8. *(Carib.)* Soft job, plum. 9. *(Mex.)* Porridge (sopa).

papá [pah-pah'], *m. (coll.)* Papa, a fond name for father.

papada [pa'-pah'-dah], *f.* Double-chin; gill. **Papada de buey** or **toro**, dewlap of oxen. **Papada de puerco**, neck of a hog or pig.

papadilla [pah-pah-deel'-lyah], *f.* The fleshy part under the chin.

papado [pah-pah'-do], *m.* Popedom, pontificate, papacy.

papafigo [pah-pah-fee'-go], *m.* The fig-pecker, beccafico, the European garden-warbler.

papagaya [pah-pah-gah'-yah], *f.* Female parrot.

papagayo [pah-pah-gah'-yo], *m.* 1. Parrot. 2. Red fish full of venomous prickles. **Hierba del papagayo**, three-colored amaranth. 3. *(Carib. Mex.)* Large kite (cometa). 4. *(And.)* Bedpan (bacinilla).

papahigo [pah-pah-ee'-go], *m.* 1. Cap, headgear covering the face and neck. 2. *V.* PAPAFIGO. 3. *(Naut.)* Course, the lower sail.

papahuevos [pah-pah-oo-ay'-vos], *m.* Simpleton, clodpoll.

papal [pah-pahl'], *a.* Papal, papistical.

papalina [pah-pah-lee'-nah], *f.* 1. Cap with flaps which cover the ears (gorra). 2. Binge (juerga). 3. *(CAm.)* Potato chips.

papalote [pah-pah-lo'-tay], *m. (Cuba)* Kite. *V.* COMETA.

papalmente, *adv.* In a papal manner.

papamoscas [pah-pah-mos'-cas], *m.* 1. *(Orn.) V.* MOSCARETA. 2. Ninny.

papanatas [pah-pah-nah'-tas], *m.* Oaf, simpleton, ninny.

papandujo, ja [pah-pan-doo'-ho, hah], *a. (coll.)* Too soft: applied to over-ripe fruit.

papar [pah-par'], *va.* 1. To swallow soft food without chewing (tragar). 2. *(coll.)* To eat. 3. To pay little attention to things which claim much notice. *-vr.* **Paparse algo**, to eat up, to scoff.

páparo [pah'-pah-ro], *m.* Gawk, gump a rustic who stares stupidly.

paparrabias [pah-par-rah'-be-as], *m. & f. (coll.)* A testy, fretful person.

paparrasolla [pah-par-rah-sol'-lyah], *f.* Hobgoblin, a bugbear for children.

paparrucha [pah-par-roo'-chah], *f. (coll.)* 1. Silliness, folly, impertinence (disparate). 2. Hoax, humbug. 3. *V.* PATRAÑA. **Contar grandes paparruchas**, to tell incredible tales.

papasal [pah-pah-sahl'], *m.* Game among boys; any trifling amusement.

papaya [pah-pah'-yah], *f.* Papaw, the fruit of the *Papayo*.

papayo [pah-pah'-yo], *m. (Bot.)* Papaw tree.

pápaz [pah'-path], *m.* Christian priest, so called in Africa.

papazgo [pah-path'-go], *m.* Popedom, pontificate.

papear [pah-pay-ahr'], *vn.* To eat, to scoff.

papel [pah-pel'], *m.* 1. Paper. 2. Paper, writing, treatise, discourse. 3. Part acted in a play; actor, actress. 4. Anything written or printed which does not form a book. 5. A figure; a person of importance. 6. *(Com.)* Document; obligation (oficial). 7. *(Fin.)* **Papel moneda**, paper money (billetes). 8. Stocks, shares (valores). 9. *(And.)* One-peso note. 10. *(LAm.)* Bag. *-pl.* 1. Manuscripts. 2. Wry faces, gesticulations. **Hacer papel**, to cut a figure, to play a part, to personate. **Papel jaspeado**, marbled paper. **Papel sellado**, stamped paper, stamp. **Papel pintado**, stained paper. **Papel de seda**, tissue-paper. **Papel viejo**, waste paper. **Papel de lija**, sand-paper. **Hoja de papel**, leaf of paper. **Pliego de papel**, sheet of paper. **Papel de entapizar**, wall-paper, paper-hanging. **Papel de cartas**, notepaper. **Papel de fumar**, cigarette paper. **Papel para máquinas de escribir**, typing paper. **Papel prensa**, newsprint. **Sobre el papel**, on paper. **Los papeles, por favor**, your papers, please. **Desempeñar un papel**, *(fig.)* to play a part. **Hacer el papel de**, to act as.

papeleador [pah-pay-lay-ah-dor'], *m.* Searcher of papers; scribbler.

papelear [pah-pay-lay-ar'], *vn.* 1. To run over papers. 2. *(coll.)* To figure, or make a figure.

papeleo [pah-pay-lay'-o], *m. (Coll.)* Red tape.

papelera [pah-pay-lay'-rah], *f.* 1. A number of written papers placed together. 2. Writing-desk, scrutoire, papercase (mesa).

papelería [pah-pay-lay-ree'-ah], *f.* 1. Heap of papers without order (montón). 2. A stationery shop (tienda).

papelero [pah-pay-lay'-ro], *m.* Paper maker (fabricante).

papeleta [pah-pay-lay'-tah], *f.* 1. Slip of paper on which something is written (trozo de papel). 2. Case of paper in which money or sweetmeats are kept. 3. *(CAm.)* Visiting card.

papelillo [pah-pay-leel'-lyo], *m. dim. V.* PAPELEJO.

papelina [pah-pay-lee'-nah], *f.* 1. A small wine-glass with a foot. 2. A very thin sort of cloth; poplin.

papelista [pah-pay-lees'-tah], *m.* One who is always employed about papers and writings.

papelito [pah-pay-lee'-to], *m. dim.* A small paper, paper for a hair-curl.

papelón [pah-pay-lone'], *m.* 1. *(Aug.)* A large piece of paper posted up, such as edicts and proclamations; prolix writing. 2. Pamphlet. 3. Boaster. 4. *(And. Carib.)* Sugar loaf. **Escritor de papelones sueltos**, pamphleteer.

papelonear [pah-pay-lo-nay-ar'], *vn.* To be boastful or presumptuous.

papera [pah-pay'-rah], *f.* 1. Wen on the throat. 2. Mumps.

papero [pah-pay'-ro], *m.* 1. Pot in which a child's pap is made. 2. Potato grower; potato dealer.

papialbillo [pah-pe-ahl-beel'-lyo], *m.* Weasel.

papila [pah-pee'-lah], *f. (Med.)* Papilla, the fine termination of nerves in some organs.

papilar [pah-pe-lar'], *a.* Papillary, papillous, very small eminences on the skin.

papilla [pah-peel'-lyah], *f.* 1. Pap, food for infants. 2. Guile, deceit, artifice. **Dar papilla**, to deceive by insidious caresses.

papilonáceo, a [pah-pe-lo-nah'-thay-o, ah], *a.* Papilionaceous, butterfly-like.

papión [pah-pe-on'], *m.* A kind of large monkey. *V.* CEFO.

papiráceo, cea [pah-pe-rah'-thay-o, ah], *a.* Papyraceous, papery, dry and thin.

papiro [pah-pee'-ro], *m. (Bot.)* Egyptian papyrus or paper-tree.

papirolada [pah-pe-ro-lah'-dah], *f.* Sauce made of garlic and bread. *V.* PAMPIROLADA.

papirotada [pah-pe-ro-tah'-dah], *f.* Fillip on the neck or face; rap at the nose.

papirote [pah-pe-ro'-tay], *m. (coll.)* Fillip.

papista [pah-pees'-tah], *a.* Papist, Roman Catholic. **Más papista que el papa**, more papist than the Pope, more royalist than the king.

papo [pah'-po], *m.* 1. The fleshy part which hangs from the chin. 2. Quantity of food given to a bird of prey at once. 3. Down of thistles. **Papos**, furbelow.

papudo, da [pah-poo'-do, dah], *a.* Double-chinned.

papujado, da [pah-poo-hah'-do, dah], *a.* 1. Full gorged (pájaros). 2. Swollen, thick, elevated.

pápula [pah'-poo-lah], *f.* Papula, a scrofulous tumor on the throat.

paquebote [pah-kay-bo'-tay], *m.* Packet or packet-boat, a vessel appointed to carry the mail.

paquete [pah-kay'-tay], *m.* 1. A small packet, a little bale, a parcel (correos). 2. Bundle of letters sealed or tied up together. 3. A packet-boat. 4. Dandy (majo). 5. **Meter un paquete a uno**, to put somebody on a charge. 6. *(Comput.)* **Paquete integrado**, integrated package. **Paquete de hojas de cálculo electrónicas**, electronic spreadsheet. **Paquete exclusivo**, dedicated package. **Paquete de aplicaciones**, application package. 7. *(Med.)* Dose. 8. *(LAm.)* Nuisance (cosa pesada). 9. *(Mex.)* Tough job (asunto). 10. *(Cono Sur)* Queer. 11. *(LAm.)* Package holiday (vacaciones).

paquidermo, ma [pah-ke-derr'-mo, mah], *a.* Thick-skinned, pachydermatous. *m. pl. (Zool.)* The pachydermata.

par [pahr], *a.* 1. Equal, alike, on a par, even. **Sin par**, matchless. -*adv.* Near. *V.* CERCA or JUNTO.

par [pahr], *m.* 1. Pair, couple. 2. Peer of the realm. 3. Handle of a bell. 4. Equal (igual). 5. (Golf) Par. **Pares y nones**, odd or even: a play. **A la par**, jointly, equally; at par, without discount. **A pares**, by pairs, two and two. **De par en par**, broad, open (puerta). **Ir a la par**, to go halves, to have an equal share in the business. **A par de**, near, joining, like. **A pares**, by pairs. **Números pares**, round or even numbers. **Caminar al par de**, to walk abreast of. **Estar abierto de par en par**, to be wide open. **Estar por debajo de la par**, to be under par. -*f.* **Las pares**, the placenta or after-birth.

para [pah'-rah], *prep.* For, to, in order to (finalidad), toward, wherefore, to the end that. **Ese hombre es para todo** or **es para nada**, that man is fit for everything or he is fit for nothing. **Para entre los dos**, between us both. **Para evitar**, to avoid. **¿Para qué?** why?, what for? **Leer para sí**, to read to oneself. **Para siempre**, for ever. **Para eso**, for that, for so much: used in contempt. **Lo traje para ti**, I brought it for you. **Ir para casa**, to go home. **Tengo bastante para vivir**, I have enough to live on. **Lo traje para que lo veas**, I brought it so that you could see it. **Para mañana**, for tomorrow. **Tan amable para todos**, so kind to everybody.

parabás [pah-rah-bahs'], *m.* Thick border of a palm mat on the step of an altar.

parabién [pah-rah-be-en'], *m.* Compliment of congratulation, felicitation. **Dar el parabién**, to congratulate, to compliment.

parabienero [pah-rah-be-ay-nay'-ro], *m. (coll.)* One who congratulates; a person full of compliments.

parábola [pah-rah'-bo-lah], *f.* 1. Parable. 2. *(Geom.)* Parabola.

parabólico, ca [pah-rah-bo'-le-co, cah], *a.* Parabolical, parabolic, relating to parables or parabolas.

parabrisas [pah-rah-bree'-sahs], *m.* Windshield.

paracaídas [pah-rah-cah-e'-das], *m.* Parachute. **Paracaídas de frenado**, *(Aer.)* drag chute.

paracaidista [pah-rah-cah-ee-dees'-tah], *m & f.* Parachutist, parachute jumper. *(Mex. Coll.)* Squatter.

paracéntrico, ca [pah-rah-then'-tre-co, cah], *a.* Paracentric, deviating from circularity.

parachoques [pah-rah-cho'-kes], *m.* Bumper, fender; *(Ferro.)* buffer.

paracleto, paráclito [pah-rah-clay'-to, pah-rah'-cle-to], *m.* Paraclete, name given to the Holy Ghost.

paracronismo [pah-rah-cro-nees'-mo], *m.* Parachronism.

parachoques [pah-rah-cho'-kays], *m.* Fender (automóvil.)

parada [pah-rah'-dah], *f.* 1. Halt, halting, the place where one halts. 2. The end of the motion of anything. 3. Stop, suspension, pause. 4. Fold for cattle. 5. Relay of mules or horses. 6. Dam (presa), bank. 7. Stakes (apuestas), set, bet; anything staked. 8. Parade, a place of parade for troops. 9. *(CAm. Mex.)* Clip of cartridges (cartuchos). 10. *(LAm.)* Vanity (vanidad), pride, presumption. 11. *(And.)* Crafty trick. 12. *(And.)* Farmer's market. **Parada de autobús**, bus stop. **Parada de taxis**, taxi stand.

paradera [pah-rah-day'-rah], *f.* 1. Sluice, flood-gate. 2. A kind of fish-net.

paradero [pah-rah-day'-ro], *m.* 1. Halting-place. 2. Term or end of anything. **No saber el paradero de alguno**, not to know the whereabouts of a person; not to know what has become of him.

paradigma [pah-rah-deeg'-mah], *m.* Example, instance, paradigm.

paradisíaco, ca [pah-rah-de-see'-ah-co, cah], *a.* Paradisiacal, relating to paradise.

paradislero [pah-rah-dis-lay'-ro], *m.* 1. Sportsman waiting for his game. 2. Newsmonger.

parado, da [pah-rah'-do, dah], *a.* 1. Stationary, still, stopped, motionless. 2. Remiss, careless, indolent, cold, inactive. 3. Unemployed, without business or employment (obrero). 4. **Estuve parado durante 2 horas,** *(LAm.)* I was standing for 2 hours. 4. *(And. Carib.)* To be unlucky. 5. *(LAm.)* Still (pelo), straight. 6. *(Carib. Cono Sur)* Vain (vanidoso). **Me quedé parado**, I was completely confused. **Salir bien parado**, to come off well.

paradoja [pah-rah-do'-hah], *f.* Paradox.

paradójico, ca [pah-rah-do'-he-co, cah], *a.* Paradoxical.

paradojo, ja [pah-rah-do'-ho, hah], *a.* Paradoxical, extravagant.

parador [pah-rah-dor'], *m.* 1. Sojourner, lodger. 2. Inn, hostelry. **Parador para turistas**, tourist court, motel.

parafernales (Bienes), [pah-rah-fer-nah'-les], *a. & m. pl.* Paraphernalia, goods which a wife brings, independent of her portion, and which are at her disposal.

parafernalia [pah-rah-fer-nah'-le-ah], *f.* Paraphernalia.

parafina [pah-rah-fee'-nah], *f.* Paraffin, a translucent solid mixture of hydrocarbons, used in candles, and in other industrial applications.

parafrasear [pah-rah-frah-say-ar'], *va.* To paraphrase.

paráfrasis [pah-rah'-frah-sis], *f.* Paraphrase, explanation in more intelligible terms.

parafraste [pah-rah-frahs'-tay], *m.* Paraphrast, expounder.

parafrástico, ca [pah-rah-frahs'-te-co, cah], *a.* Paraphrastic, paraphrastical.

paragoge [pah-rah-go'-gay], *f. (Gram.)* Addition of a letter or syllable at the end of a word.

paragonar [pah-rah-go-nar'], *va.* To paragon, to compare, to equal.

paraguas [pah-rah'-goo-as], *m.* 1. Umbrella. 2. *(And. Carib. Mex.)* Mushroom (seta comestible); toadstool (no comestible).

paraguay [pah-rah-goo-ah'-ee], *m.* A species of parrot.

paraguayano, na [pah-rah-goo-ah-yah'-no, nah], *a.* Of Paraguay.

paraíso [pah-rah-ee'-so], *m.* 1. The garden of Eden. 2. Paradise, any delightful place. 3. Paradise, heaven.

paraje [pah-rah'-hay], *m.* 1. Place, residence. 2. Condition, disposition.

paral [pah-rahl'], *m.* 1. Wooden trough in which the keel of a ship runs in launching. 2. A scaffolding-pole.

paraláctico, ca [pah-rah-lahc'-te-co, cah], *a.* Parallactic.

paralaje [pah-rah-lah'-hay], *f. (Ast.)* Parallax. So, too, **Paralaxi.**

paralelepípedo [pah-rah-lay-lay-pee'-pay-do], *m. (Geom.)* Parallelopiped.

paralelismo [pah-rah-lay-lees'-mo], *m.* Parallelism.

paralelizar [pah-rah-lay-le-thar'], *va.* To parallel, to compare.

paralelo, la [pah-rah-lay'-lo, lah], *a.* Parallel, similar, correspondent.

paralelo [pah-rah-lay'-lo], *m.* Parallel, resemblance, comparison.

paralelogramo, ma [pah-rah-lay-lo-grah'-mo, mah], *a.* Parallelogramical.

paralelogramo [pah-rah-lay-lo-grah'-mo], *m.* Parallelogram.

paralipómenos [pah-rah-le-po'-may-nos], *m.* Two books of the Bible, 1st and 2nd Chronicles.

parálisis [pah-rah'-le-sis], *f.* Paralysis. **Parálisis cerebral**, cerebral palsy. **Parálisis infantil**, infantile paralysis, poliomyelitis.

paralítico, ca [pah-rah-lee'-te-co, cah], *a.* V. PERLÁTICO.

paralizar [pah-rah-le-thar'], *ra.* 1. To paralyze, to palsy. 2. To impede moral action. 3. To stop (tráfico). **Estar paralizado de un brazo**, to be paralyzed in one arm. *-vr.* To become paralyzed.

paralogismo [pah-rah-lo-hees'-mo], *m.* Paralogism, false reasoning.

paralogizar [pah-rah-lo-he-thar'], *vn.* To paralogize, to reason sophistically.

paramentar [pah-rah-men-tar'], *va.* To adorn, to embellish.

paramento [pah-rah-men'-to], *m.* 1. Ornament (adorno), embellishment, facing. 2. Cloth, with which anything is covered.

paramera [pah-rah-may'-rah], *f.* A great extent of territory where bleak deserts abound.

paramilitar [pah-rah-me-le-tar], *a.* Paramilitary.

parámetro [pah-rah'-may-tro], *m. (Geom.)* Parameter.

páramo [pah-rah'-mo], *m.* 1. Paramo, an Alpine plain open to the winds. 2. Any place extremely cold. 3. Waste land (descampado). 4. *(And.)* Drizzle (llovizna).

parancero [pah-ran-thay'-ro], *m.* Bird-catcher.

parangón [pah-ran-gone'], *m.* Paragon, model, comparison.

parangona [pah-ran-go'-nah], *f. (Print.)* Paragon type; about 20-point.

parangonar, parangonizar [pah-ran-go-nar'], *va.* To paragon, to match, to compare.

paranínfico [pah-rah-neen'-fe-co], *a. (Arch.)* Applied to a style of building having statues of nymphs instead of columns.

paraninfo [pah-rah-neen'-fo], *m. (Archaic.)* Paranymph: a bridesmaid or best man.

paranoia [pah-rah-noy'-ah], *f.* Paranoia.

paranoico, ca [pah-rah-noy'-co, cah], *m. & f. & a.* Paranoiac.

paranormal [pah-rah-nor-mal'], *a.* Paranormal.

paranza [pah-rahn'-thah], *f.* Hut in which sportsmen lie in ambush for game (caza).

parao [pah-rah'-o], *m.* Large vessel in the Philippines, carrying a high cabin at the poop.

parapeto [pah-rah-pay'-to], *m.* 1. *(Mil.)* Parapet, breast-work. 2. Rails or battlements on bridges and quays. **Parapetos de combate**, *(Naut.)* netting, parapets in the waist of the ship.

paraplejia [pah-rah-play'-he-ah], *f.* Paraplegia.

parapléjico, ca [pah-rah-play'-he-co, cah], *a.* Paraplegic.

parapoco [pah-rah-po'-co], *com.* A numskull, a blockhead.

parapsicología [pah-rah-pse-co-lo-hee'-ah], *f.* Parapsychology.

parar [pah-rar'], *vn.* 1. To stop, to halt, to desist, to give over. 2. **Parar en**, to end up as (proyecto). 3. To point (caza). **El coche ha parado**, the car has stopped. **Parar en seco**, to stop dead. **No para de quejarse**, he never stops complaining. **Fueron a parar en la comisaría**, they finished up at the police station. *-va.* 1. To stop, to detain, to put an end to the motion or action of a thing (coche, motor, respiración). 2. To get ready, to prepare (arreglar). 3. To end, to bring to a close. 4. To treat or use ill. 5. To stake at cards (naipes). 6. To point out the game. 7. To devolve, to come to the possession of. 8. To happen, to fall out. 9. To come to an end, to finish (acabar). 10. To change one thing into another. 11. **Pararla con uno**, *(And.)* to take it out on somebody (vengarse). **Ir a parar**, to come to, to end this or that way. **No poder parar**, not to rest; to be uneasy. **Sin parar**, non-stop, instantly, without delay. *-vr.* 1. To stop, to halt (proceso). 2. To assume another character. 3. **Pararse en algo**, to pay attention to something: 4. *(LAm.)* To stand up (levantarse), to straighten up (enderezarse); to stand on end (pelo). 5. *(LAm. Fig.)* To prosper, to become wealthy.

pararrayo [pah-rar-rah'-yo], *vn.* A lightning-rod or conductor.

parasca [pah-rahs'-cah], *f.* A portion of the Scriptures assigned to be read in the synagogue.

paraselene [pah-rah-say-lay'-nay], *f. (Met.)* Mock-moon.

parasema [pah-rah-say'-mah], *f.* Figure-head of a vessel.

parasismo [pah-rah-sees'-mo], *m.* Paroxysm, a fit.

parasítico, ca [pah-rah-see'-te-co, cah], *a.* Parasitic, living upon another.

parásito, ta [pah-rah'-se-to, tah], *a.* Parasitic. *-m.* Parasite. **Ruidos parásitos**, interference, static.

parasitología [pah-rah-se-to-lo-hee'-ah], *f.* Parasitology.

parasol [pah-rah-sole'], *m.* Parasol. V. QUITASOL.

paratesis [pah-rah-tay'-sis], *f.* Prayer which the Greek bishop makes at the ceremony of confirmation.

paratifoidea [pah-rah-tee-foy-day'-ah], *f. (Med.)* Paratyphoid, paratyphoid fever.

parauso [pah-rah'-oo-so], *m.* Drill for metals; a mandrel.

parazonio [pah-rah-tho'-ne-o], *m.* Broad-sword without a point.

parca [par'-cah], *f.* Fate, death.

parcamente, *adv.* Sparingly, parsimoniously.

parce [par'-thay], *m.* Written excuse or pardon given to grammar scholars.

parcela [par-thay'-lah], *f.* 1. Plot (solar), piece of ground. 2. *(Fig.)* Part, portion; area.

parcero [par-thay'-ro], *m.* Partner, copartner.

parchazo [par-chah'-tho], *m.* 1. *(Augm.)* A large plaster. 2. *(Met. Coll.)* Deception, jest.

parche [par'-chay], *m.* 1. A plaster for a wound or sore. 2. Parchment with which a drum is covered. 3. *(Poet.)* Drum. 4. Patch on the face.

parcial [par-the-ahl'], *a.* 1. Partial, inclined to favor without reason. 2. Partial, partisan (partidista), inclined to favor a party or side of the question. 3. Partial (incompleto), affecting only one part; subsisting only in a part. 4. Partial, friendly, familiar. 5. Sociable, communicable.

parcialidad [par-the-ah-le-dahd'], *f.* 1. Partiality (cualidad), prejudice against or in favor of a person. 2. Friendship, familiar intercourse, sociability. 3. Party (grupo), faction.

parcializar [par-the-ah-le-thar'], *va.* To partialize, to render partial.

parcialmente [par-the-ahl'-men-tay], *adv.* Partially, familiarly, friendly.

parcidad [par-the-dahd'], *f.* Parsimony, frugality.

parcionero [par-the-o-nay'-ro], *m.* Partner in a business.

parco, ca [par'-co, cah], *a.* 1. Sparing, scanty. 2. Sober, moderate. -*m. (Prov.)* **Muy parco en elogios**, sparing in one's praises. *V.* PARCÉ.

pardal [par-dahl'], *a.* Clownish, rustic; cunning. -*m.* 1. *(Orn.)* A sparrow. 2. A leopard. 3. A crafty fellow. 4. PARDILLO. 5. *(Bot.)* Aconite, wolf's-bane.

pardear [par-day-ar'], *vn.* To grow gray or brownish; to become dusky.

par diez [par de-eth']. Kind of jocular oath. *V.* PAR DIOS.

pardillo [par-deel'-lyo], *m.* 1. Greater redpoll, linnet. 2. Robin-redbreast. 3. A kind of grape, and the wine made from it. 4. Yokel, rustic (persona: rústico). -*a.* Grayish, brown (paño).

pardo, da [par'-do, dah], *a.* 1. Gray, drab, brown; a mixture of black and white containing some yellow or red (color). 2. Cloudy (nube). **Oso pardo**, brown bear. **De noche todos los gatos son pardos**, all cats are gray after dark; dim light favors the concealment of blemishes.

pardo [par'-do], *m.* Leopard.

pardusco, ca [par-doos'-co, cah], *a.* Light brown, grayish, grizzly.

parear [pah-ray-ar'], *va.* To match (formar pares), to pair, to couple. -*vn. (Carib.)* To skive.

parecer [pah-ray-therr'], *m.* 1. Opinion (opinión), advice, counsel. 2. Countenance, air, mien: look (aspecto). **A mi parecer**, in my opinion.

parecer [pah-ray-therr'], *vn.* 1. To appear, to be visible. 2. To seem. 3. To form a judgment of a thing, to seem. 4. To appear, to be found (objeto perdido). 5. To judge, to approve or disapprove. 6. To look like (semejar). **Al parecer**, seemingly, to all appearance. **Parece muy difícil**, it seems very difficult. **Parece que va a llover**, it looks as though it's going to rain. **Me parece bien que vayas**, I think you should go. **Pareció el sol entre las nubes**, the sun showed through the clouds. -*vr.* To present oneself to view; to assimilate or conform to; to be like, to resemble. **Se parecen mucho**, they look very much alike. **Se parece al abuelo**, he takes after his grandfather. (*Yo parezco, yo parezca*, from *Parecer. V.* CONOCER.)

pareciente [pah-ray-the-en'-tay], *a.* Similar, apparent.

parecido, da [pah-ray-thee'-do, dah], *a. & pp.* of PARECER. 1. Appeared, found. 2. Resembling, like (semejante). 3. Good or ugly-looking, well or ill-favored, with the adverbs *bien* or *mal.* **Son muy parecidos**, they are very similar. **Bien parecido**, good-looking.

pared [pah-red'], *f.* 1. Wall of bricks or stones. 2. Surface of a field of barley which is close and even. **Entre cuatro paredes**, confined, retired: imprisoned. **Darse contra las paredes**, to butt against the wall, to struggle ineffectively. **Las paredes oyen**, walls have ears. **Pegado a la pared**, to be broke. **Se sube por las paredes**, he's hopping mad. **Es como si hablara a una pared**, it's like talking to a brick wall. **Estaba blanco como la pared**, he was as white as a sheet/ghost.

paredaño, ña [pah-ray-dah'-nyo, nyah], *a.* Having a wall between.

paredilla [pah-ray-deel'-lyah], *f. dim.* A slight wall.

paredón [pah-ray-done'], *m. aug.* 1. A thick wall (muro): standing wall (de ruina). 2. Wall of rock (de roca). 3. **Llevar a uno al paredón**, to put somebody up against a wall.

paregórico [pah-ray-go'-re-co], *a.* Paregoric, anodyne.

pareja [pah-ray'-hah], *f.* 1. Pair (par), couple (esposos), brace; match; coupling. 2. Boyfriend (amigo), girlfriend (amiga); lover (amante); other half (cónyuge). 3. *(LAm.)* Pair of horses (caballos); team of draught animals (de tiro). **Pareja de baile**, dancing partner. **No encuentro la pareja de este guante**, I can't find the glove that goes with this one.

parejo, ja [pah-ray'-ho, hah], *a.* Equal (igual), similar (semejante). **Por parejo** or **por un parejo**, on equal terms, on a par.

parejura [pah-ray-hoo'-rah], *f.* Equality, similitude, uniformity.

parénesis [pah-ray'-nay-sis], *f.* Admonition, precept, instruction.

parental [pa-ren-tahl'], *a.* Parental.

parentela [pah-ren-tay'-lah], *f.* Parentage, kindred, kinsfolk, relations.

parentesco [pah-ren-tes'-co], *m.* 1. Cognation, kindred, relationship. 2. Union, chain, link.

paréntesis [pah-ren'-tay-sis], *m.* 1. Parenthesis, a short digression included in a sentence. 2. Interruption or suspension of things. **Entre** or **por paréntesis**, parenthetically, by parenthesis. **Entre paréntesis**, *(coll.)* by-the-bye. 3. Parenthesis, the character ().

pareo [pah-ray'-o], *m.* The act of pairing (unión), couplin, or matching.

parergone [pah-rer-gone'], *m.* Additional ornament.

pares [pah'-res], *f. pl. V.* SECUNDINAS.

paresia [pah-ray'-se-ah], *f. (Med.)* Paresis, slight paralysis.

parhelia [pah-ay'-le-ah], *f.* **Parhelio,** *m.* Parhelion, a mock sun.

parhilera [par-e-lay'-rah], *f. (Arch.)* Ridge-pole, ridge-piece.

paria [pah'-re-ah], *m.* Pariah, a Hindu outcast: one of the lowest caste.

parias [pah'-re-as], *f.* 1. Tribute paid by one prince to another. 2. Placenta.

parición [pah-re-the-on'], *f.* Child-bearing, parturition; season of bringing forth young.

parida [pah-ree'-dah], *f.* 1. Woman lately delivered (mujer). *V.* PARIDO. 2. Silly thing, stupid remark (dicho).

paridad [pah-ree-dahd'], *f.* 1. Parity, the act of comparing; equality (igualdad). 2. Comparison (comparación).

paridera [pah-re-day'-rah], *a.* Fruitful, prolific (hembras). -*f.* 1. Place where cattle bring forth their young. 2. Act of bringing forth young.

parido, da [pah-ree'-do, dah], *a. & pp.* Of PARIR. *Parida*, 1. Delivered, brought to bed. 2. Lately delivered.

parienta [pah-re-ayn'-tah], *f.* 1. Relative, relation. 2. **La parienta**, the wife.

pariente, ta [pah-re-en'-tay, tah], *m. & f.* 1. Relation, by birth or marriage; kinsman, kinswoman. 2. Anything resembling another. 3. *(coll.)* Appellation given by husband and wife to each other. **Pariente político**, relative by marriage. **Los parientes políticos**, the in-laws.

parietal [pah-re-ay-tahl'], *a.* Relating to a wall. *(Anat.)* Parietal (hueso).

parietaria [pah-re-ay-tah'-re-ah], *f. (Bot.)* Pellitory.

parificar [pah-re-fe-car'], *va.* To exemplify.

parihuela [pah-re-oo-ay'-lah], *f.* Handbarrow, litter; **parihuelas**, stretcher.

pario (mármol) [pah'-re-o], *a.* Parian marble.

parir [pah-reer'], *va.* 1. To bring forth a foetus, to give birth. 2. To lay eggs, to spawn. 3. To produce, to cause. 4. To explain, to clear up, to publish. **Poner a parir**, to oblige one to perform a thing against his will; to put one to his trumps.

parisién, siense [pah-re-se-en', se-en'-say], *m. & f. & a.* Parisian.

parking [pahr'-keen], *m.* Car park.

parla [pahr'-lah], *f.* Easy delivery, loquacity, gossip.

parladillo [par-lah-deel'-lyo], *m.* An affected style.

parlador, ra [par-lah-dor', rah], *m. & f.* A chattering person.

parladuría [par-lah-doo-ree'-ah], *f.* An impertinent speech; loquacity.

parlamental [par-lah-men-tahl'], *a.* Parliamentary.

parlamentar, parlamentear [par-lah-men-tar'], *vn.* 1. To talk, to converse. 2. To parley (enemigos), to treat for the surrender of a place.

parlamentario [par-lah-men-tah'-re-o], *m.* 1. Member of parliament. 2. A person who goes to parley with an enemy.

3. A flag of truce, a cartel. 4. Parliamentarian, one who adhered to the English parliament in the time of Charles I.

parlamentario, ria [par-lah-men-tah'-re-o, ah], a. Parliamentary, parliamentarian.

parlamento [par-lah-men'-to], m. 1. Speech or harangue in a public assembly. 2. Parliament, the legislative assembly of Great Britain. 3. Parley (entre enemigos). 4. A flag of truce.

parlanchín, na [par-lan-cheen', nah], a. & a. Chatterer, jabberer.

parlante [par-lahn'-tay], pa. Speaking; a talker.

parlar [par-lar'], va. 1. To chatter. 2. To disclose what ought to be kept secret. **Parlar en balde**, to talk nonsense.

parlatorio [par-lah-to'-re-o], m. 1. Converse, parley. 2. Parlor, the place in convents where nuns are allowed to converse with their friends.

parlera, parlantina [par-lay'-rah, par-lan-tee'-nah], f (coll.) A talkative little woman.

parlería [par-lay-ree'-ah], f. 1. Loquacity, garrulity, gossip: tale, jest. 2. Singing or chirping of birds: purling of brooks and rivers.

parlerito, ita [par-lay-ree'-to, tah], a. dim. (coll.) Talkative, garrulous.

parlero, ra [par-lay'-ro, rah], a. 1. Loquacious, talkative (hablador). 2. Talking (pájaro): singing, song; expressive (ojos). -m. 1. Tale-bearer, tattler. 2. Bird that chirps and chatters. 3. Purling brook or rill. 4. Interesting conversation.

parleta [par-lay'-tah], f. Conversation on the weather, or on trifling subjects.

parlón, na [par-lone', nah], a. Loquacious, garrulous.

parlotear [par-lo-tay-ar'], vn. To prattle, to prate, to chatter, to gossip.

parloteo [par-lo-tay'-o], m. Prattle, talk.

parmesano, na [par-may-sah'-no, nah], a. Parmesan, of Parma.

parnaso [par-nah'-so], m. 1. (Poet.) Parnassus, Helicon. 2. A collection of selected poems. 3. Assemblage of poets.

paro [pah'-ro], m. 1. Lockout, suspension of work. **Paro forzoso**, layoff (en una fábrica.), unemployment (desempleo), stoppage, standstill, (suspensión en el trabajo). 2. (Orn.) Titmouse. 3. (And. Carib.) Throw (de dados).

parodia [pah-ro'-de-ah], f. Parody.

parodiar [pah-ro-de-ar'], va. To parody.

paródico, ca [pah-ro'-de-co, cah], a. Parodical.

parola [pah-ro'-lah], f. 1. (coll.) Eloquence, fluency (soltura), volubility. 2. Chat (charla), idle talk.

pároli [pah'-ro-lee], m. Double of what was laid in stakes at the game of bank.

parolina [pah-ro-lee'-nah], f. V. PAROLA.

parón [pah-rone'], m. Sudden halt.

parónimo, ma [pah-ro'-ne-mo, mah], a. Paronymous; words cognate or alike.

paronomasia [pah-ro-no-mah'-se-ah], f. Paronomasia, a rhetorical figure.

parótida [pah-ro'-te-dah], f. 1. A parotid gland. 2. Swelling of the parotid glands, mumps.

paroxismal [pah-rok-sis-mahl'], m. Paroxysmal.

paroxismo [pah-rok-sees'-mo], m. Paroxysm. V. PARASISMO.

parpadear [par-pah-day-ar'], vn. 1. To wink, to open and shut the eyes by turns. 2. To blink (ojo); to blink (luz).

parpadeo [par-pah-day'-o], m. Blinking, winking; flickering; twinkling.

párpado [par'-pah-do], m. The eyelid.

parpalla [par-pahl'-lyah], f. A milled copper piece.

parpar [par-par'], m. Quacking, the cry of a duck.

parque [par'-ka], m. 1. Park, an enclosed wood or ornamental grounds. 2. Park of artillery, park of provisions. **Parque de automóviles**, car park. **Parque nacional**, national park. 3. (LAm. Mil.) Equipment (equipo); ammunition (munición); ammunition dump (depósito).

parquedad [par-kay-dahd'], f. Parsimony.

parra [par'-rah], f. 1. Vine raised on stakes or nailed to a wall. 2. Earthen jar or pot, broad and low, with handles.

párrafo [par'-rah-fo], m. Paragraph, a distinct part of a discourse. **Párrafo aparte**, new paragraph (punto y aparte), to change the subject (cambio de conversación).

parragón [par-rah-gone'], m. Standard silver for assayers.

parral [par-rahl'], m. 1. Vine abounding with shoots for want of dressing, and the place where there are such vines. 2. A large earthen jar for honey.

parranda [pahr-rhan'-dah], f. 1. Spree party (juerga). 2. (And. Cono Sur, Mex.) Lot, group, heap.

parrar [par-rar'], vn. To extend, to spread out in branches and bowers.

parricida [par-re-thee'-dah], com. Parricide, one who kills his father or mother, or any other person to whom he owes reverence.

parricidio [par-re-thee'-de-o], m. Parricide, murder of a father or mother, or of any person to whom reverence is due.

parrilla [par-reel'-lyah], f. 1. An earthen jug with broad base and narrow neck. -pl. Gridiron, broiler, toaster; grate, furnace grating (objeto). 2. (Aut.) Radiator grille (de radiador); (Cono Sur) roof rack.

parriza [par-ree'-thah], f. Wild vine.

párroco [par'-ro-co], m. Rector or incumbent of a parish; a parson.

parrón [par-rone'], m. V. PARRIZA.

parroquia [par-ro'-ke-ah], f. 1. Parish, the parochial church (iglesia). 2. Parish, the precinct or territory of a parochial church (zona). 3. The spiritual jurisdiction of a rector or parson in his parish. 4. The clergy of a parish.

parroquial [par-ro-ke-ahl'], a. Parochial. -f. Parochial church.

parroquialidad [par-ro-ke-ah-le-dahd'], f. Parochial right, the right of a parishioner.

parroquiano, na [par-ro-ke-ah'-no], m & f. 1. Parishioner. 2. Customer, an accustomed buyer or patron.

parroquiano, na [par-ro-ke-ah'-no, nah], a. Belonging to a parishioner. V. PARROQUIAL.

parsi [par'-se], a. & m. 1. Parsee, a Zoroastrian. 2. The sacred language of Persia (before being mixed with Arabic).

parsimonia [par-se-mo'-ne-ah], f. Economy, frugality (frugalidad), husbandry, temperance.

parte [par'-tay], f. 1. Part, a portion of some whole (sección). 2. Part, a determinate quantity of some aggregate number. 3. Part, portion, share (participación, porción), lot. 4. District, territory, place (región). 5. Part, the right or left side. 6. Part, side (lado), every one of two or more things opposite to each other. 7. Part, the sense given to words or acts. 8. Party, a person concerned in a business with others (persona). 9. (Law.) Party, one of two litigants. 10. It is used for the time present with reference to the past. **De ocho días a esta parte**, within these last eight days. 11. Part, character in a play. 12. Partes, parts (cualidades), talents. 13. (Anat.) Partes, parts. 14. (Mex. Mec.) Spare part. **Tercera parte**, third. **Parte del mundo**, part of the world. **En gran parte**, to a large extend. **Formar parte de**, to form a part of. **Llevar la mejor parte**, to come off best. **Mirar a otra parte**, to look the other way. **Por todas partes se va a Roma**, all roads lead to Rome. **Por parte de madre**, on the mother's side. **Parte contraria**, opposing party. -m. 1. Royal or official communication. 2. Receiving-house for the post office. 3. Official notice of mails. 4. Dispatch, telegram, urgent message. **Parte por parte**, part by part, distinctly. **A partes** or **en partes**, by parts, or in parts. **De parte a parte**, from side to side, through. **De parte**, by orders, by command. **En parte**, partly, in part. -f. pl. 1. Parts, talents, endowments. 2. Privy parts. 3. Party, faction. **Por todas partes**, on all hands, on all sides. -adv. In part, partly.

partear [par-tay-ar'], va. To deliver or assist women in childbirth.

partenópeo, pea [par-tay-no'-pay-o, ah], a. Parthenopean, Neapolitan.

partenueces [par-tay-noo-ay'-thes], m. Nut-cracker.

partera [par-tay'-rah], *f.* Midwife.

partería [par-tay-ree'-ah], *f.* Midwifery, obstetrics.

partero [par-tay'-ro], *m.* Obstetrician, man-midwife, accoucheur.

partesana [par-tay-sah'-nah], *f.* Partizan; a kind of halberd.

partesanero [par-tay-sah-nay'-ro], *m.* Pikeman.

partible [par-tee'-blay], *a.* Divisible, separable, partible.

partición [par-te-the-on'], *f.* Partition, division, distribution, lot.

particionero, ra [par-te-the-o-nay'-ro, rah], *a.* Participant, having a part in a business.

participación [par-tee-the-pah-the-on'], *f.* 1. Parcipation, sharing in common. *(Com.)* Copartnership. **Cuenta en participación**, joint account. 2. Participation, communication, conversation. 3. *(Dep.)* Entry. 4. Lottery ticket (de lotería). 5. Notice (aviso).

participante [par-te-the-pahnt'-tay], *pa.* Sharing, participant.

participar [par-te-the-par'], *va. & vn.* 1. To give notice, to inform of, to announce (noticia). 2. To participate, to partake, to share. 3. To partake, to take part, to participate, to have something of the property, nature, claim, right, etc. **Participar en una carrera**, to enter in a race. **Participar de una cualidad**, to share a quality.

partícipe [par-tee'-the-pay], *a.* Participant, sharing.

participial [par-te-the-pe-ahl'], *a. (Gram.)* Participial.

participio [par-te-thee'-pe-o], *m. (Gram.)* Participle.

partícula [par-tee'-coo-lah], *f.* 1. Particle, small part. 2. *(Gram.)* Particle. 3. Molecule. **Partícula beta**, beta particle.

particular [par-te-coo-lar'], *a.* 1. Particular (especial), peculiar (propio), special. 2. Particular, odd, distinguished from others. 3. Particular, individual, single, not general. private (personal). 4. Applied to a play represented in a private theater. **En particular**, particularly, in particular. **Nada de particular**, nothing special. **Secretario particular**, private secretary.

particular [par-te-coo-lar'], *m.* 1. A private gentleman (persona). 2. A peculiar matter or subject treated upon; topic (asunto). **No dijo mucho sobre el particular**, he didn't say much about the matter.

particularidad [par-te-coo-lah-re-dahd'], *f.* 1. Particularity (propiedad), peculiarity. 2. Friendship, intimacy (amistad).

particulariza [par-te-coo-lah-re-thar'], *va.* To particularize (especificar), to detail (dar detalles), to distinguish (distinguir). -*vr.* To singularize, to be particular.

particularmente [par-te-coo-lar-men-tay], *adv.* Particularly, especially, namely.

partida [par-tee'-dah], *f.* 1. Departure, going away from a place (salida). 2. Death, decease. 3. Party of soldier. 4. Item in an account, charge, entry (entrada), record, annotation. 5. Parcel, lot. 6. Game at play (ajedrez, naipes). 7. *(Naut.)* Crew of a ship, gang. 8. Consignment (envío). 9. Stake (apuesta), wager, bet. **¡Buena partida!**, excellent conduct! **Partida doble**, *(Com.)* double entry. **Partida simple**, single entry (in book-keeping). **Partida de defunción**, death certificate. **Partida de nacimiento**, birth certificate. **Echar una partida**, to have a game. -*pl.* Parts, talents, accomplishments.

partidamente [par-tee'-dah-men-tay], *adv.* Separately, distinctly.

partidario [par-te-dah'-re-o], *m.* 1. Partisan, the commander of a party of troops. 2. Party-man, adherent to a faction.-*a.* 1. Having the care of a certain district. 2. Partisan. **Soy muy partidario de**, I'm in favor of.

partido, da [par-tee'-do, dah], *a.* 1. Divided, split. 2. Free, liberal, munificent. 3. *(Her.)* Party, parted. -*pp.* OfPARTIR.

partido [par-tee'-do], *m.* 1. Party, a number of persons confederated. 2. Advantage, profit, utility (provecho). 3. Favor, protection, interest. 4. A game, a contest, a match (equipo). 5. Odds given to one in a game: party engaged to play a game. 6. Treaty, agreement; terms proposed for adjusting a difference. 7. Proper means for the performance

of what is to be done. 8. Interest or one's own convenience. 9. *(Cono Sur)* Hand (naipes). 12. *(And. Carib.)* **Al partido**, share and share alike. **Tomar partido**, (a) to embrace a resolution, to resolve. (b) to engage or enlist in a party. **Partido político**, political party. **Partido de fútbol**, football match. **Sacar partido de**, to profit from, to take advantage of.

partidor [par-te-dor'], *m.* 1. Parter, divider. **Partidor de leña**, cleaver, the instrument and the workman employed in cleaving wood. 2. Bodkin to divide the hair. 3. *(Arith.)* V. DIVISOR.

partija [par-tee'-hah], *f.* V. PARTICIÓN.

partil [par-teel'], *a.* Applied to the astrological aspects.

partimento, partimiento [par-te-men'-to], *m.* V. PARTICIÓN.

partir [par-teer'], *va.* 1. To part, to divide, to sever, to disunite, to separate, to cut, to cleave. 2. To break by violence (abrir). 3. To part, to share (repartir), to divide, to distribute. 4. To crack the stones of fruit (nuez). 5. To attack in combat or battle. 6. To resolve. 7. *(Arith.)* To divide. 8. To divide a beehive in two, at the proper season. **Partir la cabeza a uno**, to split somebody's head open. -*vn.* 1. To part, to depart, to march, to set out on a journey (ponerse en camino). 2. To start (comenzar). **A partir del lunes**, from Monday. -*vr.* To be divided in opinion. **Partir la diferencia**, to split the difference. **Partir por entero**, to carry off the whole: to divide a number. **Partir mano**, to desist, to abandon. **Partirse el alma**, to make a tremendous effort, to die; to die broken-hearted.

partitivo, va [par-te-tee'-vo, vah], *a. (Gram.)* Partitive.

partitura [par-te-too'-rah], *f.* The musical score. **Partitura de una ópera**, the full score of an opera.

parto [par-to], *m.* 1. Childbirth, parturition. 2. Newborn child. 3. Any natural production. 4. Any literary composition. 5. Any particular thing that may happen, and is hoped to be of importance. **Tener un parto difícil**, to have a difficult labor.

parturiente [par-too-re-en'-tay], *a.* Parturient.

párulis [pah'-roo-lis], *m.* Gumboil, an abscess of the gums.

parva [par'-vah], *f.* 1. Unthrashed corn laid in heaps to be thrashed. 2. Multitude, large quantity. 3. V. PARVEDAD, 2d def.

parvada [par-vah'-dah], *f. (Prov.)* Place for unthrashed corn.

parvedad, parvidad [par-vay-dahd'], *f.* 1. Littleness, minuteness. 2. Snack, bite of food taken in the morning of a fast day.

parvo, va [par'-vo, vah], *a.* Small, little.

parvulario [par-voo-lah'-re-o], *m.* Nursery school, kindergarden.

parvulez [par-voo-leth'], *f.* Smallness, small size.

parvulico, ica, illo, illa, ito, ita [par voo-lee'-co], *a. dim.* Very little.

párvulo, la [par'-voo-lo, lah], *a.* Very small; innocent; humble, low.-*n.* A child.

pasa [pah'-sah], *f.* 1. Raisin, dried grape. 2. Passage of birds. -*pl.* The curled hair of negroes.

pasabalas [pah-sah-bah'-las], *m. (Mil.)* Ball calibre-gauge.

pasable [pah-sah'-blay], *a.* 1. Passable (tolerable). 2. *(LAm.)* Fordable (arroyo). 3. *(Cono Sur)* Saleable.

pasacalle [pah-sah-cahl'-lyay], *m.* Music played on the guitar and other instruments in the streets. An ancient dance.

pasacampana [pah-sah-cam-pah'-nah], *f. (Vet.)* A tumor which forms on the calcaneum of horses.

pasada [pah-sah'-dah], *f.* 1. Passage, the act of passing (acto). 2. Pace, step; measure of five feet. 3. A malicious action to someone's hurt. 4. *(Ant.)* Competency, sufficiency. **De pasada**, on the way, in passing, hastily, cursorily. 5. *(CAm. Cono Sur)* Telling-off (reprimenda). 6. *(And.)* Shame (vergüenza).

pasadera [pah-sah-day'-rah], *f.* 1. A stepping-stone. 2. Sieve, strainer. 3. *(Naut.)* Furling-line of spun-yarn.

pasaderamente [pah-sah-day'-rah-men-tay], *adv.* passably.

pasadero, ra [pah-sah-day'-ro, rah], *a.* 1. Supportable, sufferable. 2. Passable, tolerably good (tolerable). -*m.* V. PASADERA.

pasadillo [pah-sah-deel'-lyo], *m.* A small embroidery on both sides of a piece of stuff.

pasadizo [pah-sah-dee'-tho], *m.* A narrow passage or covered way.

pasado, da [pah-sah'-do, dah], *pp.* of PASAR. **1. Lo pasado pasado**, what is past is forgotten and forgiven. **El mes pasado**, last month. 2. Stale (comida); overripe (fruta); overdone (muy hecho); stale (cuento, noticia); antiquated (idea); old (ropa); faded (belleza). **La carne está pasada**, the meat is off. -*m.* 1. Past time (tiempo). 2. A (military) deserter. -*pl.* Ancestors. V. ASCENDIENTES and ANTEPASADOS.

pasador [pah-sah-dor'], *m.* 1. One who carries a thing from one place to another. 2. A smuggler, one who deals in contraband goods (persona). 3. Bolt of a lock (pestillo). 4. A woman's brooch (de pelo). 5. Cylinder which founded use for making tubes without soldering. 6. A clock peg. 7. Bolt-pin, linch-pin, cotter. 8. A shoemaker's tool for smoothing the inside of a shoe. 9. A sieve. 10. A piece of a loom. -*pl.* 11. Irons placed between the tympanum and the brisket. 12. Cord straps. 13. *(Naut.)* Marline-spike.

pasagonzalo [pah-sah-gon-thal'-lo], *vn. (Colt.)* Flip, a slight blow, briskly given.

pasahilo [pah-sah-ee'-lo], *m.* Thread-guide.

pasaje [pah-sah'-hay], *m.* 1. Passage, the act of passing (acto). 2. Road, way, the place of passing. 3. Passage-money. 4. *(coll.)* Event, accident, a piece of business. 5. Transition or change of voice. 6. Passage of a book or writing. 7. *(Carib. Cono Sur, Mex.)* Cul-de-sac (sin salida). 8. *(Liter. Mus.)* Passage. 9. *(And. Carib.)* Story (cuento). 10. *(And.)* Tenement building (pisos).

pasajeramente [pah-sah-hay'-rah-men-tay], *adv.* Transiently, going along, without detention.

pasajero, ra [pah-sah-hay'-ro, rah], *a.* 1. Applied to a common thoroughfare. 2. Transient, transitory, fugitive. 3. Applied to birds of passage.

pasajero, ra [pah-sah-hay'-ro, rah], *m. & f.* Traveler, passenger. **Pasajero de cámara**, cabin passenger:

pasamanar [pah-sah-mah-nar'], *va.* To make ribbons, trimmings, lace. etc.

pasamanera [pa-sah-mah-nay'-rah], *f.* Lace-woman, lace-maker.

pasamanería [pah-sah-mah-nay-ree'-ah], *f.* The trade of a lace-man; the profession of a fancy-trimming maker, twister; or ribbon-weaver, and the place where those things are sold; passementerie work.

pasamanero [pah-sah-mah-nay'-ro], *m.* Lace-maker, lace-man, a fancy-trimming maker, a twister, a ribbon-maker.

pasamanillo [pah-sah-mah-neel'-lyo], *m. dim.* A narrow lace; a small twist for the edge of a coat.

pasamano [pah-sah-mah'-no], *m.* 1. Balustrade, banister (de escalera), rail (barra). 2. Kind of lace or edging for clothes; passementerie. 3. *(Naut.)* Gangway.

pasamontañas [pah-sah-mon-tah'-nyahs], *m.* Balaclava (casco), ski mask.

pasante [pah-sahn'-tay], *m.* 1. Assistant or student of a physician or lawyer. 2. A student who acts the teacher or lecturer to beginners. 3. *(Her.)* Passant: applied to animals in a shield appearing to walk. 4. Game of cards.

pasantía [pah-san-tee'-ah], *f.* Profession of a student of the law or medicine, who practices under the direction of another.

pasapán [pah-sah-pahn'], *m. (coll.)* V GARGUERO.

pasapasa [pah-sah-pah'-sah], *m.* Legerdemain, slight of hand, hocus-pocus.

pasaporte [pah-sah-por'-tay], *m.* 1. Passport. 2. *(Mil.)* Furlough. 3. A free license to do anything.

pasapuré [pah-sah-pooh'-ray], *m.* Grinder, mincer.

pasar [pah-sar'], *vn.* 1. To pass, to move from place to place. 2. To go or pass in any manner or to any end, to go through.

3. To go to any determinate place. 4. To make way for a person, inviting him to come forward. 5. To be in motion, or to steer from one place to another: speaking of immaterial things. 6. With the preposition *a* and some infinitives, to proceed to. 7. To ascend, to be promoted to a higher post. 8. To pass away, to elapse (tiempo). 9. To travel through a place or country. 10. To die. 11. To pass, to become current, as money. 12. To be marketable (mercancías). 13. To pass, to be in a certain state, speaking of health, conveniences of life, etc. 14. To pass, to be spent, to go away progressively. 15. To be executed before a notary. -*va.* 1. To convey from one place to another. 2. To send or carry a thing from one part to another (enviar). 3. To pierce, to penetrate, to go through (armadura). 4. To pass beyond the limit of the place of destination (frontera, límite). 5. To change for better or worse, from one thing to another. 6. To pass or advance from one class to another. 7. To exceed in number, quantity, quality, or abilities. 8. To depart, to decease. 9. To suffer, to bear, to undergo (penas). 10. To strain or percolate liquor, to clarify it. 11. Not to censure or find fault with anything. 12. To pass over in silence, to omit (omitir). 13. To dissemble, to overlook. 14. To stop, to terminate. 15. To run over one's lesson, to rehearse; to run over a book. 16. To carry one thing above another, so as to touch it lightly. 17. To teach privately; to study privately with some professor. 18. To present an act, charter, or privilege to be confirmed. 19. To handle an affair with judgment and prudence (asunto). 20. To draw up an instrument. 21. To dry by the sun or in an oven. -*v. imp.* To pass, to happen (suceder), to turn out. -*vr.* 1. To go over to another party. 2. To cease, to finish; to lose its force (efecto). 3. Not to shut well. 4. To be spoiled (fruta). 5. To pass unimproved: applied to a favorable opportunity. 6. To go too far (excederse). 7. To fade (belleza); to go bad (comida). **Pasar de largo**, (a) to pass by without stopping; (b) *(Met.)* not to reflect upon what one reads. **Pasa al frente**, *(coll.)* this sum is carried forward. **Pasar el tiempo**, to loiter, to pass away time. **Pasar por alto**, to overlook, to overpass, not to take notice. **Pasar en claro alguna cosa**, to omit any mention of a thing. **Pasar por encima**, to overcome difficulties. **Ir pasando**, to be about the same, neither better nor worse.**¿Cómo lo pasa Vd.?** how do you do? **Pasarse de bueno**, to be too good. **Pasarse de cortés**, to be over polite. **Nos hicieron pasar a otra habitación**, they showed us into another room. **El médico pasará visita**, the doctor will call. **El túnel pasa la montaña**, the tunnel goes right through the mountain. **Hemos pasado el aniversario**, we are past the anniversary. **Pasarlo bien**, to have a good time. **El hilo pasa por el agujero**, the thread goes through the hole. **El río pasa por la ciudad**, the river flows through the city. **Pasaré por tu casa**, I'll call on you. **Pasar de los límites**, to exceed the limits. **Pasa por buen pintor**, he is considered to be a good painter. **Han pasado 4 años**, 4 years have gone by. **Lo que pasa es que…**, what's happening is that… **Siempre me pasa lo mismo**, I'm always having the same trouble. **Se me pasó el turno**, I missed my turn. **Se ha pasado todo el día leyendo**, he has spent the whole day reading.

pasarela [pah-sah-ray'-lah], *f.* Footbridge (puente); *(Teat. etc.)* Walkway, catwalk.

pasatiempo [pah-sah-te-em'-po], *m.* Pastime, diversion, amusement, game.

pasavante [pah-sah-vahn'-tay], *m.* 1. Safe-conduct furnished to a ship by the commander of the enemy's forces. 2. A permit for articles of commerce.

pasavolante [pah-sah-vo-lahn'-tay], *m.* An inconsiderate speech or action.

pasavoleo [pah-sah-vo-lay'-o], *m.* Ball which passes the line in bowling.

pascua [pahs'-coo-ah], *f.* 1. Passover, a feast among the Jews. 2. Easter, the day on which the Savior's resurrection is commemorated. 3. *(Met.)* Christmas. 4. *(coll.)* Any festival of the church which lasts three days. **Hacer pascua**, to begin to eat meat after Lent. **Santas pascuas**, be it so. **Pascua de Navidad**, Christmas. **Estar como unas pascuas**, to be as happy as a sandboy.

pascual [pas-coo-ahl'], a. Paschal, relating to Easter.

pascuilla [pas-coo-eel'-lyah], f. The first Sunday after Easter.

pase [pah'-say], m. 1. An act of a court of justice which orders a decree to be expedited and carried into effect. 2. A written permission to sell or carry goods freely from place to place. 3. A kind of passport. 4. (Cine) Showing. 5. (LAm.) Dose (drogas). **Pase de impresión**, (Comput.) print pass.

paseadero [pah-say-ah-day'-ro], m. Walk, avenue, public walk.

paseador, ra [pah-say-ah-dor', rah], m. & f. A walker: applied to one who walks much, or to a horse.

paseante [pah-say-ahn'-tay], m. & f. 1. Walker (que pasea), one who goes for a walk. 2. Idler, lazy vagabond.

pasear [pah-say-ar'], va. & vn. 1. To walk, to take the air, to exercise. 2. To be at the walk, to be in the field. 3. To move at the slowest pace (caballo). 4. To walk about, to bring out to walk (niño, perro). 5. To take the air or exercise on horseback or in a coach. 6. (CAm.) To squander (dinero). - vr. 1. To walk for exercise or amusement. 2. To loiter, to wander idly, to gape about. 3. (Mex.) To take a day off. **Pasearse en bicicleta**, to go for a ride. **Pasearse en coche**, to go for a drive. **Pasearse a caballo**, to ride.

paseata [pah-say-ah'-tah], f. (coll.) A walk, airing drive.

paseo [pah-say'-o], m. 1. Ride, drive. 2. Walk, outing (excursión). 3. Short walk (distancia). 4. Parade (avenida). **Paseo al aire libre**, outdoor walk. **Paseo campestre**, picnic. **Ir de paseo**, to go walking, to go on an outing. **Paseo marítimo**, promenade. **Enviar a uno a paseo**, to tell somebody to go to blazes.

pasera [pah-say'-rah], f. (Prov.) Place where raisins are dried, and the act of drying them.

pasibilidad [pah-se-be-le-dahd'], f. Passibleness, susceptibility to impressions from external agents.

pasible [pah-see'-blay], a. Able to endure, long-suffering.

pasicorto, ta [pah-se-cor'-to, tah], a. Short-stepped (caballos).

pasiego, ga [pah-se-ay'-go, gah], m. & f A highlander of Santander, celebrated for his sturdiness, and the women as the best wet-nurses.

pasiflora [pah-se-flo'-rah], f. The botanical name of the passion-flower.

pasilargo, ga [pah-se-lar'-go, gah], a. Long-stepped (caballos).

pasillo [pah-seel'-lyo], m. 1. (dim.) A short step. 2. A small, narrow passage. 3. Basting-stitch.

pasión [pah-se-on'], f. 1. Passion, any effect caused by external agency; susceptibility of effect from external action; the act of suffering torments. 2. Passion, the last suffering of the Redeemer. 3. Passion, affection or violent emotion of the mind, anger. 4. Passion, ardent inclination, fondness. **Pasión de ánimo**, a passion or emotion of the soul; a broken heart. **Con pasión**, passionately.

pasionaria [pah-se-o-nah'-re-ah], f. (Bot.) Passion-flower: a climbing vine, native of Peru, where it is more often called *ñorbo*.

pasionario [pah-se-o-nah'-re-o], m. pl. Passion-book, from which the passion is sung in Holy Week.

pasionero [pah-se-o-nay'-ro], m. One who sings the passion.

pasito [pah-see'-to], adv. Gently, softly. **Pasito a pasito**, very leisurely or gently.

pasito [pah-see'-to], m. dim. A short step.

pasitrote [pah-se-tro'-tay], m. Short trot of horses alone.

pasiva [pah-see'-vah], f. (dram.) Passive voice of the verb.

pasivamente [pah-see-vah-men-tay], adv. Passively.

pasivo, va [pah-see'-vo, vah], a. 1. Passive, receiving impression from some external agent. 2. Passive, unresisting, not acting. 3. (Gram.) Passive. **Voz pasiva**, passive voice; capable of being elected.

pasivo [pah-see'-vo], m. (Com.) Liabilities.

pasmado [pas-mah-do], a. 1. Astonished, amazed. **Dejar pasmado a uno**, to amaze somebody. 2. Bewildered (atontado). **Estar pasmado**, to stand gaping. 3. (LAm.) Infected (herida); unhealthy-looking (persona). 4. (CAm. Mex.) Thick (tonto). 5. (LAm.) Overripe (fruta).

pasmar [pas-mar'], va. 1. To cause a spasm, or a suspension or loss of the senses (atontar). 2. To benumb, to make torpid: to stupefy, to stun. 3. To chill (enfriar), to deaden. - vn. To marvel, to wonder. -vr. 1. To wonder, to be astonished (asombrarse). 2. To suffer from lockjaw. 3. (LAm.) To become infected (infectarse); to fall ill (enfermar); to catch a fever (con fiebre). 4. (Carib. Mec.) To dry up (fruta). 5. To fade (color).

pasmarota, pasmarotada [pas-mah-ro'-tah], f. 1. A feigned spasm, often used by beggars. 2. Admiration or astonishment without cause or motive.

pasmazón [pas-mah-thone'], f. (Mex.) Swelling upon the loins of horses, caused by the saddle or harness.

pasmo [pahs'-mo], m. 1. Spasm, convulsion; violent and involuntary contraction. 2 (Med.) Lockjaw, tetanus. 3. Astonishment, amazement (asombro), admiration. 4. Object of admiration or astonishment. **De pasmo**, V. PASMOSAMENTE. 5. (Med.) Chill (enfriamiento). 6. (LAm.) Fever (fiebre).

pasmosamente [pas-mo'-sah-men-tay], adv. Wonderfully, astonishingly.

pasmoso, sa [pas-mo'-so, sah], a. Marvellous, wonderful.

paso, sa [pah'-so, sah], a. & pp. irr. of PASAR. Dried (fruta).

paso [pah'-so], m. 1. Pace, step (de pie), a measure of space. 2. Passage, the act of passing. 3. Pace, gait, manner of walking (modo de andar). 4. Pace, pacing, a motion of mules and horses. 5. Flight of steps. 6. Passage, lobby, passage for a room; pass, a narrow entrance. 7. Step, measure or diligence in the pursuit of an affair: commonly used in the plural. 8. Step, instance of conduct, mode of life. 9. Footstep (sonido). 10. Passport, license, pass. 11. Explanation given by a master or usher. 12. Passage in a book; or writing (episodio). 13. Progress, advance, improvement. 14. Death, decease. 15. Image carried about during Holy Week. 16. (Elec. Tec.) Pitch. 17. Difficulty, awkward situation, crisis (apuro). (LAm.) Ford (vado). -pl. 1. Running stitches with which clothes are basted. 2. Conduct, proceedings, steps.- adv. Softly, gently. **Paso a paso**, step by step; slowly. **A buen paso**, at a good rate, step, or gait. **A cada paso**, at every step, frequently. **A ese paso**, at that rate. **Al paso**, without delay, instantly; going along; in the manner of, like. **Andar en malos pasos**, to follow evil paths. **Salir del paso** or **del vado**, to get out of a difficulty. **A pocos pasos**, at a short distance; with little care. **Dar paso**, to clear the way; to promote, to facilitate. **De paso**, passing by; lightly, briefly, by the way; at the same time, at once. **Vista de paso**, a cursory view. **Al paso que**, at he same time that, whilst. **Paso de cebra**, zebra crossing. **Paso a nivel**, level crossing. **Abrirse paso**, to make one's way. **Paso atrás**, step backwards. **A paso de tortuga**, at a snail's pace. **Romper el paso**, to break step. **Dar un mal paso**, to take a false step.

paspié [pas-pe-ay'], m. A kind of dance.

pasquín [pas-keen'], m. Pasquinade, lampoon.

pasquinada [pas-kee-nah'-dah], f. Pasquinade.

pasquinar [pas-ke-nar'], va. To ridicule, to lampoon, to satirize.

pasta [pahs'-tah], f. 1. Paste, any viscous or tenacious mixture. 2. Paste, flour and water boiled; the mass from which vermicelli and other things are made for soup. 3. Pie-crust. 4. Bullion, mass of gold or silver for coining. 5. In book-binding, pasteboard covered with leather burnished or mottled; roan leather (libros). 6. Pulp from which paper or cardboard is made. 7. V. EMPASTE. 8. **Pasta** or **buena pasta**, excessive meekness or mildness. 9. (Culin.) Dough; pastry (para pastel); pastries (pasteles), cakes; noodles (fideos), spaghetti. 10. Dough (dinero), money. **Pasta de carne**, meat paste. **Pasta gansa**, big money.

pasta de dientes [pahs'-tah day de-ayn'-tes], *f.* Toothpaste.

pasta dentífrica [pahs'-tah den-tee'-fre-cah], *f.* Toothpaste.

pastar [pas-tar], *m.* To pasture, to graze. *-va.* To lead cattle to graze, to feed cattle.

pasteca [pas-tay'-cah], *f. (Naut.)* Snatch-block.

pastel [pas-tel], *m.* 1. Pie, pastry. **Pastel de carne** or **de picadillo**, mince pie. **Pastel de manzana**, *etc.*, apple pie, etc. 2. *(Bot.)* Woad. 3. Trick in the dealing of cards. 4. Meeting, assembly for some secret design. 5. *(Print.)* Mass of types to be recast; words too black, having too much ink. 6. *(Art.)* Pastel (pintura).

pastelada [pas-tay-lah'-dah], *f.* Plot, snare.

pastelear [pas-tay-lay-ar'], *vn.* To trim politically; to try to secure popularity by time-serving.

pastelera [pas-tay-lay'-rah], *f.* Pastrycook's wife; she who makes and sells pastry.

pastelería [pas-tay-lay-ree'-ah], *f.* 1. Pastrycook's shop (tienda), confectionery (dulces), confectioner's cake shop (tienda). 2. Pastry, pies or baked paste (pasteles).

pastelero [pes-tay-lay'-ro], *m.* 1. Pastrycook. 2. A political trimmer.

pastelillo, ito [pas-tay-leel'-lyo], *m. dim.* A little pie, a patty. **Pastelillo**, Tart: a kind of pastry.

pastelón [pas-tay-lone'], *m. aug.* A large pie.

pasterización [pas-tay-re-tha-the-on'], *f.* Pasteurization.

pasterizar [pas-tay-re-thar'], *va.* Pasteurize.

pasteurizado [pas-tay-oo-re-thah'-do], *a.* Pasteurized.

pasteurizar [pas-tay-oo-re-thar'], *va.* To pasteurize.

pastilla [pas-teel'-lyah], *f.* 1. Tablet, lozenge. 2. Drop, candy. **Pastilla de menta**, peppermint drop. **Pastilla para la tos**, cough drop.

pastinaca [pas-te-sah'-cah], *f.* 1. *(Bot.)* Parsnip. 2. *(Cool.)* Stingray.

pasto [pahs'-to], *m.* 1. Pasture, the act of grazing. 2. Pasture, the grass which serves for the feeding of cattle (hierba). 3. A pasture-ground (campo). 4. Any pabulum, food, aliment, or nourishment (comida). **Pasto espiritual**, Spiritual nourishment. **A pasto**, abundantly, plentifully, at meals, as ordinary meat or drink. **Echar el pasto al ganado**, to put animals out to pasture. **Vino de pasto**, ordinary wine.

pastor, ra [pas-tor', rah], *m. & f.* 1. Shepherd, shepherdess, one who tends sheep (de ovejas). 2. Pastor, shepherd, a clergyman. 3. An American freshwater fish.

pastoral [pas-to-rahl'], *a.* Pastoral, rural, rustic. *-f.* Pastoral, a poem in which the speakers assume the character of shepherds; an idyll.

pastoralmente [pas-to-rahl'-men-tay], *adv.* Pastorally, rustically, shepherd-like.

pastorcico, illo, ito [pastor-thee'-co], *m. dim.* A little shepherd.

pastorear [pas-to-ray-ar'], *va.* 1. To graze, to pasture (rebaño); to bring cattle to pasture. 2. To feed souls with sound doctrine. 3. *(CAm. Cono Sur)* To lie in wait for (acechar). 4. *(CAm.)* To spoil (mimar).

pastorela [pas-to-ray'-lah], *f.* Pastoral, an ample melody in rustic style.

pastoreo [pas-to'-ray-o], *m.* Pasturing, act of tending flocks.

pastoría [pas-to-re'-ah], *f.* A pastoral or rural life, pastors.

pastoril [pas-to-reel'], *a.* Pastoral.

pastorilmente [pas-to-reel-men-tay], *adv.* V. PASTORALMENTE.

pastosidad [pas-to-se-dahd'], *f.* Mellowness, softness.

pastoso, sa [pas-toh'-so, sah], *a.* 1. Soft, mellow, doughy (material), clammy. 2. Painted or drawn with a colored crayon or pencil. 3. *(Cono Sur)* Grassy. 4. *(And.)* Lazy (vago).

pastura [pas-too'-rah], *f.* 1. Pasture, the grass on which animals feed (campo). 2. Fodder, dry food for cattle (comida).

pasturaje [pas-too-rah'-hay], *m.* 1. Pasturage, a common ground on which cattle graze. 2. Duty paid for the right of grazing cattle on a certain ground.

pasudo, da [pah-soo'-do, dah], *a. (Amer.)* Kinky, woolly, curly, as a Negro's hair.

pata [pah'-tah], *f.* 1. Foot and leg of beasts. 2. Duck, the female of the drake. 3. A barilla-producing plant of the benches of the Canary Islands. 4. Leg (de mueble). **Pata de cabra**, (a) a crowbar, a nailpuller; (b) a shomaker's heel-burnisher. **Pata de gallina**, a radial crack in trees; the beginning of rot. **Pata de gallo**, (a) a ridiculous saying, a bull (used generally with *salir con*); (b) crow's-foot, a wrinkle near the eye. (3) Stupidity, silliness. **A la pata coja**, hopscotch, a game played by hopping on one foot over a diagram upon the ground. **A pata**, on foot. **Patas arriba**, reversed, topsyturvy, heels-over-head; upside down, in disorder. **Estirar la pata**, to peg out. **Tener mala pata**, to be unlucky.

pataca [pah-tah'-cah], *f.* 1. *(Bot.)* Jerusalem artichoke. 2. Copper coin.

pataco, ca [pah-tah'-co, cah], *a.* V. PATÁN.

patacón [pah-tah-cone'], *m.* Dollar or patacoon, a silver coin weighing an ounce; cut with shears.

patache [pah-tah-'chay], *m. (F. Naut.)* Tender, a vessel attending a squadron.

patada [pah-tah'-dah], *f.* 1. Kick (coz), a blow with the foot. 2. *(coll.)* Step, pace. 3. Track, murk left by the foot of an animal. *A* **patadas**, in abundance. **Echar a uno a patadas**, to kick somebody out. **Tratar a uno a patadas**, to push somebody around.

patagalana [pah-ta-ga-lah'-nah], *f. (coll.)* Limping; having a short leg.

patagón [pah-tah-gone'], *m* 1. A large clumsy foot. 2. A Patagonian.

patagónico, ca [pah-tah-go'-ne-co, cah], *a.* Patagonian.

patagorcillo, lla [pah-tah-gor-theel'-lyo], *m. & f.* Fricassee made of the livers and lights of animals.

patagua [pah-tah'-goo-ah], *f.* 1. Patagua, a stout tree of America, of the linden family, which grows in miry places and has a white light wood. 2. A nearly cylindrical vessel on which mate is spread.

patalear [pah-tah-lay-ar'], *vn.* 1. To kick about violently. 2. To stamp the foot (en el suelo). 3. To putter.

pataleo [pah-tah-lay'-o], *m.* 1. The act of stamping the foot (en el suelo). 2. Noise made by the feet. 3. *(Fig.)* Protest; scene (lío), fuss.

pataleta [pah-tah-lay'-tah], *f.* 1. *(coll.)* A fainting-fit. 2. A ridiculous speech or action; an absurd enterprise.

pataletilla [pah-tah-lay-teel'-lyah], *f.* A kind of dance.

patán, na [pat-tahn', nah], *a.* Clownish, churlish, rustic. *-m. & f.* Clown, a churl, a countryman or women.

patanería [pah-tah-nay-ree'-ah], *f.* Clownishness, churlishness, rusticity, rudeness.

patarata [pah-ta-rah'-tah], *f.* 1. Fiction, idle story. 2. Affected concern or affectation (afectación), kickshaw.

patarraez [pah-tar-rah-eth'], *m. (Naut.)* Preventer shroud. **Patarraez de una máquina de arbolar**, *(Naut.)* the shroud of a sheer-hulk for masting ships.

patata [pah-tah'-tah], *f. (Bot.)* Potato. **Patata de siembra**, seed potato. **Patatas fritas**, French fries, chips, crisps. **No entendió una patata**, he didn't understand a word of it.

patatal [pah-tah-tahl'], *m.* Potato field.

patatero, ra [pah-tah-tay'-ro, rah], *m. & f.* 1. A potato-seller. 2. One who is fond of potatoes.

patatús [pah-tah-toos'], *m. (coll.)* Swoon, a fainting-fit.

patax [pah-tahx'], *m.* V. PATACHE.

pateadura [pah-tay-ah-doo'-rah], *f.* Kicking, stamping (acto).

patear [pah-tay-ar'], *va. & vn.* 1. To kick (dar patadas). 2. To stamp the foot (pisotear). 3. To drive about to obtain some end. 4. To be extremely irritated or vexed. 5. *(Carib.)* To abuse. **Tuve que patear toda la ciudad**, I had to tramp round the whole town.

patena [pah-tay'-nah], *f.* 1. Paten, a dish for the eucharistic bread. **Limpio como una patena**, as clean as a whistle, as a new pin.

patentado [pah-ten-tah'-do], *a.* Patent, patented; proprietary. -*m.* patentee.

patentar [pah-ten-tahr'], *va.* To patent.

patente [pah-ten'-tay], *a.* 1. Patent, manifest, evident, clear, palpable. 2. *(Cono Sur)* Superb (excelente). -*f.* 1. Patent, a writ conferring exclusive right or privilege; warrant, commission. 2. Letters of marque. 3. Letter of obedience expedited by prelates and addressed to their religious subjects. 4. Money paid by newcomers to the members of a company or office. 5. *(LAm. Aut.)* Number plate (placa); driving licence (carnet). **Patente de sanidad**, bill ol health. **Patente de invención**, patent.

patentemente [pah-ten'-tay-men-tay], *adv.* Openly, clearly, visibly, obviously.

patentizar [pah-ten-te-thar'], *va.* To make a thing evident.

patera [pah-tay'-rah], *f.* Goblet, patera.

paternal [pah-ter-nahl'], *a.* Paternal, fatherly.

paternalmente [pah-ter-nahl'-men-tay], *adv.* Paternally, fatherly.

paternidad [pah-ter-ne-dahd'], *f.* 1. Paternity (de hijo), fathership. 2. A title of respect given to religious men.

paterno, na [pah-terr'-no, nah], *a.* Paternal, fatherly.

paternóster [pah-ter-nos'-ter], *m.* 1. The Lord's prayer; paternoster. 2. A big tight knot.

patesca [pah-tes'-cah], *f. (Naut.)* A large block.

pateta [pah-tay'-tah], *m.* 1. A nickname given to a lame person. 2. *(coll.)* Devil, old Nick.

patéticamente [], *adv.* Pathetically.

patético, ca [pah-tay'-te-co, cah], *a.* 1. Pathetic, passionate, moving. 2. Plaintive. 3. *(Cono Sur)* Clear, evident.

patiabierto, ta [pah-te-ah-be-err'-to, tah], *a.* Straddling, club-footed, crooked-legged.

patialbillo [pah-te-al-beel'-lyo], *m.* Weasel. V. PAPIALBILLO.

patiblanco, ca [pah-te-blan'-co, cah], *a.* White-footed.

patibulario, ria [pah-te-boo-lah'-re-o, ah], *a.* Horror-producing (horroroso), sinister. **Rostro patibulario**, sinister expression.

patíbulo [pah-tee'-boo-lo], *m.* Gibbet, gallows.

patico, ito [pah-tee'-co, ee'-to], *m. dim.* A young goose, a gosling.

paticojo, ja [pah-te-co'-ho, hah], *a. (coll.)* Lame, crippled.

patiestevado, da [pah-te-es-tay-vah'-do, dah], *a.* Bow-legged.

patihendido, da [pah-te-en-dee'-do, dah], *a.* Cloven-footed.

patilla [pah-teel'-lyah], *f.* 1. *(Naut.)* Spike nailed to the stern post, on which the rudder moves. 2. Chape of a buckle. 3. Trigger. 4. *(Cono Sur)* Bench. 5. *(And. Carib.)* Watermelon (sandía). 6. *(Cono Sur. Bot.)* Layer. 7. Sidepiece (de gafas). 8. *(Comput.)* Pin. -*s. pl.* 1. Whiskers, sideburns. 2. *(Coll.)* Demon.

patimuleño, ña [pah-te-moo-lay'-nyo, nyah], *a.* Mule-footed: applied to horses with narrow hoofs.

patín [pah-teen'], *m.* 1. Skate. **Patines de rueda**, roller skates. **Patines de hielo**, ice skates. 2. *(Orn.)* Goosander. 3. Small courtyard.

pátina [pah'-te-nah], *f.* Patina.

patinador, ra [pah-te-nah-dor', rah], *m. & f.* Skater.

patinaje [pah-te-nah'-hay], *m.* 1. Skating. 2. Skidding.

patinar [pah-te-nar'], *vn.* 1. To skate (persona). 2. To skid (coche). 3. To screw-up (meter la pata).

patinazo [pah-te-nah'-tho], *m.* 1. *(Aut.)* Skid. 2. Screw-up (error), blunder. **Dar un patinazo**, to make a boob.

patineta [pah-te-nay'-tah], *f.* or **patinete** [pah-te-nay'-tay], *m.* Skate-board.

patio [pah'-te-o], *m.* 1. Court, an open space in front of a house or behind it. 2. Pit in playhouses. 3. Hall in universities, academies, or colleges. **Patio de recreo**, playground.

patita [pah-tee'-tah], *f.* A small foot or leg of beasts. **Poner de patitas en la calle**, to put a person in the street, to discharge him.

patitieso, sa [pah-te-te-ay'-so, sah], *a.* 1. Deprived by sudden accident of sense and feeling (paralizado). 2. Stiff, stately, starchy: applied to a proud, pesumptuous person of an affected gait. 3. Benumbed, stupefied, surprised.

patito [pah-tee'-to], *m.* Duckling.

patituerto, ta [pah-te-too-err'-to, tah], *a.* 1. Crook-legged, having crooked legs or feet. 2. Ill-disposed, perverse.

patizambo, ba [pah-te-thahm'-bo, bah], *a.* Knock-kneed, bandy-legged.

pato, ta [pah'-to, tah], *a.* Equal, similar.

pato [pah'-to], *m.* 1. Drake, duck. 2. *(Esp.)* Bore, dull person (pesado). 3. Boredom (aburrimiento). 4. To be clumsy (torpe). 5. *(And.)* Sponger (gorrón). 6. *(And.)* Sucker (inocentón). 7. *(Cono Sur)* **Ser un pato**, to be broke. V. ÁNADE. **Estar hecho un pato**, to get a ducking. **Pagar el pato**, to suffer undeserved punishment. V. PAGAR. **Pato real**, mallard. **Pato de reclamo**, decoy duck.

patochada [pah-to-chah'-dah], *f.* Blunder, nonsense, folly.

patógeno, na [pah-to'-hay-no, nah], *a.* Pathogenic.

patognómico, ca [pah-tog-no'-me-co, cah], *a.* Pathognomonic: applied to those signs of a disease which are characteristic, or inseparable from it.

patojear [pah-to-hay-ar'], *vn. (Cuba)* To waddle in walking.

patojo, ja [pah-to'-ho, hah], *a.* Waddling, like a duck.

patología [pah-to-lo-hee'-ah], *f. (Med.)* Pathology, the branch of medicine concerned with the cause, origin and nature of disease, including the changes occurring as a result of disease.

patológico, ca [pah-to-lo'-he-co, cah], *a.* Pathologic.

patologista [pah-to-lo-hees'-tah], or **Patólogo**, *m. (Med.)* Pathologist.

patón, na [pah-tone', nah], *a.* Large-footed, clumsy-footed.

patón [pah-tone'], *m.* Clumsy foot.

patoso [pah-to'-so], *a.* 1. Boring (aburrido). 2. Troublesome (molesto). 3. Clumsy (torpe). -*m.* Bore (pelmazo). 2. Trouble-maker (agitador).

patraña [pah-trah'-nyah], *f.* A fabulous story (cuento), a fictitious account.

patrañuela [pah-trah-nyoo-ay'-lah], *f. dim.* An insignificant tale.

patria [pah'-tre-ah], *f.* 1. Native country, place of birth, home. 2. The native or proper place for anything. 3. *(Met.)* Heaven. **Madre patria**, mother country. **Luchar por la patria**, to fight for one's country.

patriarca [pah-tre-ar'-cah], *m.* 1. Patriarch, a father and head of a numerous progeny in primitive ages. 2. Founder of a religious order. 3. Patriarch, a bishop of the highest rank. 4. Patriarch, an honorary title conferred by the Pope. **Vive como un patriarca**, he enjoys all the conveniences of life.

patriarcado [pah-tre-ar-cah'-do], *m.* Patriarchate, the dignity and jurisdiction of a patriarch.

patriarcal [pah-tre-ar-cahl'], *a.* Patriarchal.

patriciado [pah-tre-the-ah'-do], *m.* Dignity of a patrician.

patricio, cia [pah-tree'-the-o, ah], *a.* Native, national; patrician.

patricio [pah-tree'-the-o], *m.* Patrician, noble.

patrimonial [pah-tre-mo-ne-ahl'], *a.* 1. Patrimonial, claimed by right of birth. 2. Patrimonial, relating to a patrimony.

patrimonialidad [pah-tre-mo-ne-ah-le-dahd'], *f.* Birthright, privilege conferred by birth of obtaining eclesiastical benefices.

patrimonio [pah-tre-mo'-ne-o], *m.* 1. Patrimony. 2. Possessions acquired by oneself. 3. *(Com.)* Net worth. **El patrimonio artístico de la nación**, our national art heritage. **Patrimonio nacional**, national wealth.

patrio, tria [pah'-tre-o, ah], *a.* 1. Native, belonging to a native place or country. 2. Paternal.

patriota [pah-tre-oh'-tah], *m. & f.* Patriot.

patriótico, ca [pah-tre-oh'-te-co, cah], *a.* Patriotic, beneficent.

patriotismo [pah-tre-o-tes'-mo], *m.* Patriotism.

patrocinar [pah-tro-the-nar'], *va.* To favor, to patronize, to protect, to countenance, to sponsor. **Un movimiento patrocindo por...**, a movement under the auspices of...

patrocinio [pa'-tro-thee'-ne-o], *m.* Protection, patronage, favor.

patrón, ona [pah-trone', nah], *m. & f.* 1. Patron (protector), patroness. 2. Master (de esclavo), boss, mistress. *-m.*.1. Standard, model. 3. Pattern (costura). *4. (Agr.)* Prop (puntal). 5. *(Agr.)* Stock (de árbol).

patrona [pah-tro'-nah], *f.* 1. Patroness, a female patron. 2. Patroness; tutelar salut of a church, protectress of a province, town, etc. 3. Galley which follows immediately that of the commodore.

patronado, da [pah-tro-nah'-do, dah], *a.* Having a patron: applied to churches and prebends. *-m. (Prov.)* V. PATRONATO.

patronal [pah-tro-nahl'], *a.* **Organización patronal**, employer's organization. **La clase patronal**, management. **Cierre patronal**, lockout.

patronato, patronazgo [pah-tro-nah'-to], *m.* 1. Patronage, patronship, the right of presenting to a benefice. 2. Foundation of a charitable or pious establishment. **Bajo el patronato de**, under the auspices of.

patronear [pah-tro-nay-ar'], *va.* To be a commander of a trading vessel.

patronía [pah-tro-nee'-ah], *f.* Mastership of a vessel.

patronímico [pah-tro-nee'-me-co], *m. & a* 1. Patronimic, family name. 2. A surname formed from the father's name; as from Sancho, Sánchez, from Pedro, Pérez.

patrono [pah-tro'-no], *m.* 1 Lord of the manor. 2. V. PATRÓN.

patrulla [pah-trool-lyah], *f.* 1. Patrol, a small detachment of soldiers to secure the safety or peace of a place. 2. A crowd of people going about the streets.

patrullar [pah-troo'-lyar'], *va.* To patrol, to go the rounds in a camp or garrison.

patrullera [pah-trool-lyay-rah], *f.* Patrol boat.

patudo, da [pah-too'-do, dah], *a. (coll.)* Having large feet or paws.

patulea [pah-too-lay'-ah], *f. (coll.)* Soldiery or disorderly folks.

patullar [pah-tool-lyar'], *vn.* 1. To trample (pisar), to run through thick and thin. 2. To labor hard in the pursuit of something.

paúl [pah-ool'], *m.* A low, damp place, a bog.

paulatinamente [pah-oo-lah-tee'-nah-men-tay], *adv.* Gently, slowly, by little and little.

paulatino, na [pah-oo-lah-tee'-no, nah], *a.* Slowly, by degrees.

paulina [pah-oo-lee'-nah], *f.* 1. Decree of excommunication, interdict. 2. *(coll.)* Reproof, chiding, objurgation. 3. An anonymous, offensive letter (carta).

paulinia [pah-oo-lee'-ne-ah], *f.* Paullinia, or guarana, a shrub of Brazil. The seeds yield a stimulating beverage, and are used medicinally for headaches.

paulonia [pah-oo-lo'-ne-ah], *f. (Bot.)* Paulownia, a tree of Japan with large heart-shaped leaves and pale-violet flowers.

pauperismo [pah-oo-pay-rees'-mo], *m.* Pauperism, abject poverty.

paupérrimo, ma [pah-oo-perr'-re-mo, mah], *a. sup.* Very poor.

pausa [pah'-oo-sah], *f.* 1. Pause, stop, intermission. 2. Pause, suspense, delay. 3. Rest, repose. 4. *(Mus.)* Pause, rest, a stop in music, and the character which marks it. **A pausas**, at leisure, by pauses.

pausadamente [pah-oo-sah'-dah-men-tay], *adv.* Slowly, deliberately.

pausado, da [pah-oo-sah'-do, dah], *a.* 1. Slow, deliberate. 2. Calm, quiet, paused. *-pp.* of PAUSAR.

pausar [pah-oo-sar'], *vn.* To pause, to cease, to hesitate, to forbear from motion or action.

pauta [pah'-oo-tah], *f.* 1. Ruled paper, and the apparatus by which the lines are ruled upon it (línea). 2. Rule, guide, pattern, example, model. 3. Ruler (regla). **Marcar la pauta**, to set a standard.

pautada [pah-oo-tah'-dah], *f.* The ruled staff on which music is written.

pautador [pah-oo-tah-dor'], *m.* One who marks lines on paper with a ruling-machine.

pautar [pah-oo-tar'], *va.* 1. To rule lines on paper. 2. To give rules, to prescribe the manner of performing an action.

pava [pah'-vah], *f* 1. Turkey-hen, the female of the turkey. **Pelar la pava**, to talk, to court. 2. Peahen, the female of the peacock. 3. *(LAm.)* Kettle (para hervir). 4. *(And. Carib.)* Broad-brimmed straw hat (sombrero). 5. *(And. CAm.)* Fringe (fleco). 6. *(Cono Sur, Mex.)* Chamber pot (orinal). 7. *(And. Cono Sur)* Coarse banter (guasa); tasteless joke (chiste). *-a. (coll.)* Applied to any woman very inactive or indolent.

pavada [pah-vah'-dah], *f.* 1. A flock of turkeys. 2. A childish game.

pavana [pah-vah'-nah], *f.* 1. Pavan (danza). **Pasos de pavana**, a grave, solemn step; a stately gait. 2. Kind of neckcloth, formerly worn by women.

pavería [pah-vay-ree'-ah], *f.* 1. Place for rearing turkeys. 2. *(Cono Sur)* silliness, stupidity.

pavero, ra [pah-vay'-ro, rah], *a.* Rearing or feeding turkeys. *-m. & f.* 1. One who feeds or sells turkeys. 2. *(And. Cono Sur)* Practical joker.

pavés [pah-bes'], *m.* Kind of large, oblong shield.

pavesa [pah-vay'-sah], *f.* 1. Embers, hot cinders; snuff of the candle. 2. Remains, relic. **Estar hecho una pavesa**, *(coll.)* to be very weak or debilitated. **Ser una pavesa**, *(coll.)* to be very mild or gentle.

pavesada [pah-vay-sah'-dah], *f.* V. EMPAVESADA.

pavesear [pah-vay-say-ar'], *vn.* To flicker, to flutter.

pavía [pah-vee'-ah], *f.* A clingstone peach.

paviano, na [pah-ve-ah'-no, nah], *a.* Pavian, belonging to Pavia, in Italy.

pávido, da [pah'-ve-do, dah], *a.* Timid, fearful.

pavilla, ita [pah-veel'-lyah, ee'-tah], *f. dim.* A little turkey-hen.

pavillo, ito [pah-veel'-lyo, ee'-to], *m. dim.* A small turkey.

pavimentación [pah-ve-men-tah-theon'], *f.* Paving.

pavimentar [], *va.* To pave.

pavimento [pah-ve-men'-to], *m.* Pavement, a floor of stone, tiles, or other materials.

paviota [pah-ve-o'-tah], *f. (Orn.)* Mew, sea-gull. V. GAVIOTA.

pavipollo [pah-ve-pol'-lyo], *m.* A young turkey.

pavito real [pah-vee'-to ray-ahl'], *m.* Pea-chick or pea-chicken.

pavo [pah'-vo], *m.* 1. *(Orn.)* Turkey. 2. Peacock-fish. **Pavo silvestre**, *(Orn.)* wood-grouse. **Pavo real**, *(Orn.)* peacock. V. PAVÓN. 3. Idiot (necio); sucker (víctima). 4. **Ponerse hecho un pavo**, to blush like a lobster. 5. *(And.)* Large kite (cometa). 6. *(And.)* Big shot (espadón); evil-looking person (sospechoso). 7. **Ir de pavo**, *(LAm.)* to travel free. 8. *(Carib.)* youngster (joven).

pavo [pah'-vo], *a. (coll.)* Peacock-like.

pavón [pah-vone'], *m.* 1. *(Orn.)* Peacock. 2. A piece of wood with which gunpowder is glazed. 3. *(Ast.)* A northern constellation.

pavonada [pah-vo-nah'-dah], *f.* 1. Short walk 2. Strut, an affected stateliness in walking.

pavonar [pah-vo-nar'], *va.* To give iron or steel a bluish color.

pavonazo [pah-vo-nah'-tho], *m. (Pict.)* Crimson or purple color.

pavoncillo, ito [pah-von-theel'-lyo], *m. dim.* A little peacock.

pavonear [pah-vo-nay-ar'], *vn.* 1. To strut, to flaunt about the streets, to flutter. 2. *(coll.)* To amuse with false hopes.

pavor [pah-vor'], *m.* Fear, dread, terror.

pavordear [pah-vor-day-ar'], *va.* To swarm (abejas).

pavorido, da [pah-vo-ree'-do, dah], *a.* Intimidated, struck with terror.

pavorosamente [pah-vo-ro-sah-men-tay], *adv.* Awfully, fearfully.

pavoroso, sa [pah-vo-roh'-so, sah], *a.* Awful, formidable, dreadful.

pavura [pah-voo'-rah], *f.* Fear, dread, terror. *V. PAVOR.*

paya [pah'-yah], *f.* Hoyden or hoiden: a wild, boisterous girl; a tomboy.

payasada [pah-yah-sah-dah], *f.* Clownish trick, stunt; ridiculous thing.

payaso [pah-yah'-so], *m.* A clown

payo [pah'-yo], *m.* 1. Clown, churl. 2. Non-gipsy (entre gitanos).

payuelas [pah-yoo-ay'-lahs], *f. pl. (Med.)* Chicken pox.

paz [pat], *f.* 1. Peace, tranquility, ease. 2. Peace, respite from war; truce, armistice, an agreement between belligerents to end a war. 3. Peace, rest from commotions, quiet from disturbances, and reconciliation from differences. 4. Peace, the quiet and good correspondence of one with the others. 5. A pleasant, peaceful disposition. 6. Equality of luck among card-players. 7. Clear or even accounts. 8. A salute or kiss on the meeting of absent friends. 9. A ceremony of the mass. **A la paz de Dios**, God be with you. **Bandera de paz**, a flag of truce. **En paz**, quit, clear. **Gente de paz**, a friend: a familiar way of answering to one who asks, who is there? or, who knocks at the door? **Descansar en paz**, to rest in peace. **Mantener la paz**, to keep the peace. **Hacer las paces**, to make peace.

¡paz! [path], *int.* Peace! hush! **Paz sea en esta casa**, peace be in this house, a salute on entering.

pazán [path-thahn'], *m.* Egyptian antelope.

pazguato, ta [path-goo-ah'-to, tah], *m. & f.* Dolt, a simple, stupid person.

pazpuerco, ca [path-poo-err'-co, cah], *a.* Dirty, slovenly.

pe [pay], *f.* Name of the letter **P**. **De pe a pa**, entirely, from beginning to end.

peaje, pedaje [pay-dah'-hay, pay-dah-hay], *m.* Bridge-toll, ferriage.

peajero [pay-ah-hay'-ro], *m.* Toll-gatherer.

peal [pay-ahl'], *m.* 1. Sock. 2. Worthless person. 3. Lasso.

peal [pay-ahl'], *a.* Heavy, dull, stupid, sickly.

peana [pay-ah'-nah], *f.* 1. Pedestal, the basis of a statue. 2. Frame at the foot of an altar to tread upon.

peatón, ona [pay-ah-ton', nah], *m. & f.* Pedestrian. *-m.* Rural postman.

peatonal [pay-ah-to-nahl'], *a.* Pedestrian. **Calle peatonal**, pedestrianized street.

peazgo [pay-ath'-go], *m.* Bridge-toll. *V. PEAJE.*

pebete [pay-bay'-tay], *m.* 1. An aromatic composition used as a perfume. 2. Stench. an unpleasant smell. 3. Tube filled with gunpowder and other ingredients, and used to convey fire to rockets and other artificial fireworks; fuse (de cohete). 4. *(Cono Sur)* Roll (panecillo).

pebetero [pay-bay-tay'-ro], *m.* Censer, a vessel in which perfumes are burnt.

pebrada [pay-brah'-dah], *f. V. PEBRE.*

pebre [pay-bray], *m.* 1. A kind of sauce made of garlic, cloves, and other spices. 2. Pepper. *V. PIMIENTA.*

peca [pay'-cah], *f.* Freckle, a speck, a spot.

pecable [pay-cah'-blay], *a.* Peccable, liable to sin.

pecadazo [pay-cah-dah'-tho], *m. aug.* A heinous or atrocious sin.

pecadillo [pay-cah-deel'-lyo], *m. dim* Peccadillo, a slight fault.

pecado [pay-cah'-do], *m.* 1. Sin. **Pecado mortal**, deadly sin. **Pecado venial**, venial sin. **Pecado original** original sin. 2. Extravagance, excess. 3. *(coll.)* Devil, the instigator of sin. **Por mis pecados**, for my sins. 4. Defect (defecto). **Más feo que un pecado**, as ugly as sin. **Estar en pecado**, to be in sin. **Los siete pecados capitales**, the seven deadly sins. **Pecado, da**, *pp.* of PECAR.

pecador [pay-cah-dor'], *m.* 1. Sinner, a person who has committed a sin. 2. Sinner, any individual capable of sinning.

3. *(Met.)* A sinner, an offender, a delinquent: one who neglects totally that which he ought to do. **Pecador de mí!** poor me, sinner as I am! 4. An ignorant, stupid person.

pecadora [pay-cah-do'-rah], *f* 1. *V. PECADOR.* 2. A prostitute.

pecadorazo, za [pay-cah-do-rah'-tho, thah], *m. & f. aug.* A great sinner.

pecadorcillo, illa, ito, ita [pay-cah-dor-theel'-lyo], *m. & f. dim.* Little sinner.

pecaminosamente [pay-cah-me-no'-sah-men-tay], *adv.* Sinfully, wickedly.

pecaminoso, sa [pay-cah-me-no'-so, sah], *a.* Sinful.

pecante [pay-cahn'-tay], *a.* Peccant, vicious, abundant.

pecar [pay-car'], *vn.* 1. To sin, to violate the laws of God. 2. To sin, to offend against right, to be wanting in what is right and just, or in the rules of art. 3. To commit excesses of any description. 4. To boast, to brag. 5. To have a strong propensity. 6. To occasion or to merit punishment. **Peca de generoso**, he is too generous. **Nunca se peca por demasiado cuidado**, one can't be too careful.

pecarí [pay-cah-ree'], *m. (Zool.)* Peccary, a wild hog of Mexico and South America.

peccata minuta [pec-cah'-tah me-noo'-tah]. *(coll.)* Slight offense, trivial vice or sin.

pece [pay'-thay], *m.* 1. Clay wetted for making mud walls. 2. Ridge of land between two furrows. 3. *(Obs.)* Fidel. *V. PEZ.*

pececico, illo, ito [pay-thay-thee'-co], *m. dim.* A small fish.

peceño, ña [pay-thay'-nyo, nyah], *a.* 1. Of the color of pitch: applied to the hair of horses. 2. Applied to things which have a pitchy taste.

pecera [pay-thay'-rah], *f.* Glass globe for gold-fish.

pecezuela [pay-thay-thoo-ay'-lah], *f. dim.* A small piece.

pecezuelo [pay-thay-thoo-ay'-lo], *m. dim.* 1. Small foot. 2. Small fish.

pecha [pay'-chah], *f.* Tax, impost, tribute.

pechada [pay-chah'-dah], *f. (Amer.)* A blow upon the chest.

pechar [pay-char'], *m.* To pay taxes.

pechera [pay-chay'-rah], *f.* 1. Stomacher. 2. The bosom of a shirt (camisa). 3. A breast collar for horses and mules. 4. *(Cono Sur. Tec.)* Apron.

pechería [pay-chay-ree'-ah], *f.* Paying tax, toll, or duty.

pechero, ra [pay-chay'-ro, rah], *a.* Liable to pay duty or taxes; commoner, in contraposition to nobleman.

pechero [pay-chay'-ro], *m.* Bib, a piece of linen put on the breast of children.

pechiblanco, ca [pay-che-blahn'-co, cah], *a.* White-breasted.

pechicatería [pay-che-cah-tay-ree'-ah], *f. (Cuba)* Meanness, parsimony.

pechico, illo [pay-chee'-co], *m. dim.* A small breast, teat, etc.

pechicolorado [pay-che-co-lo-rah'-do], *m.* Robin-redbreast, a kind of gold-finch.

pechigonga [pay-che-gon'-gah], *f.* A game at cards.

pechina [pay-chee'-nah], *f.* 1. A kind of shell which pilgrims carry on their hats and shoulders. 2. Curvilineal triangle, formed by the arches, where they meet, to receive the annulet of the cupola.

pechirrojo [pay-cheer-ro'-ho], *m.* *(Orn.)* *V.* PECHICOLORADO.

pechisacado, da [pay-che-sah-cah'-do, dah], *a. (Met. Coll.)* Haughty, arrogant.

pechito [pay-chee'-to], *m. dim. V.* PECHITO.

pecho [pay'-cho], *m.* 1. The breast. 2. The internal part of the breast, especially in men; chest. 3. Breast, the mammary gland (de mujer). 4. Bosom, breast, as the seat of the passions, the seat of tenderness, or the receptacle of secrets. 5. Regard, esteem, confidence. 6. Courage, valor, fortitude. 7. Quality and strength of the voice to sing, preach, etc. 8. Breast, heart, conscience. 9. Tax formerly paid to the government by those who did not belong to the nobility. 10. Any contribution paid to anyone besides the king. **Dar el pecho**, to suckle. **Hombre de pelo en pecho**, a brave, daring man. **Tomar a pecho**, to take to heart. **A pecho descubierto**, unarmed, without defence.

pechuelo [pay-choo-ay'-lo], *m. dim.* A small or little breast.

pechuga [pay-choo'-gah], *f.* 1. Breast of a fowl. 2. Bosom of man or woman. 3. *(Geog.)* Slope, hill. 4. *(LAm.)* Nerve, gall, cheek. 5. *(And. CAm.)* Abuse of trust (abuso de confianza). 6. *(CAm.)* Trouble, annoyance (molestia).

pechugón [pay-choo-gone'], *m.* Blow on the breast. *-a.* 1. Busty, big-bosomed (de mucho pecho). 2. *(LAm.)* Forward (descarado); outspoken (franco); sponging, parasitical; on the make (egoísta). 3. *(Cono Sur)* Bold, single-minded (resuelto).

pechuguera [pay-choo-gay'-rah], *f.* Cough, hoarseness (ronquera).

pechuguica, illa [pay-choo-gee'-cah], *f. dim.* A small breast of a fowl.

peciento, ta [pay-the-en'-to, tah], *a.* Of a pitchy color.

peciluengo, ga [pay-the-loo-en'-go, gah], *a.* Long-stalked: applied to fruit with stalks on trees.

pecina [pay-thee'-nah], *f.* 1. Fish-pond. 2. *V.* LODAZAL.

pecinal [pay-ce-nahl'], *m.* Pool of standing or muddy water.

pecio [pay'-the-o], *m.* Fragment of a ship which has been ship-wrecked.

pecíolo [pay-thee'-o-lo], *m. (Bot.)* Petiole, leaf-stalk or flower-stalk.

pécora [pay'-co-rah], *f.* 1. A sheep, head of sheep. 2. A cunning fellow, knave; a gay, merry person. 3. Bitch (lagarta). 4. Harpy (arpía). 5. Loose woman, whore (puta).

pecorea [pay-co-ray'-ah], *f.* 1. Robbery committed by straggling soldiers; marauding. 2. Idle, strolling and loitering about the streets.

pecoso, sa [pay-co'-so, sah], *a.* Full of freckles, freckled.

pectina [pec-tee'-nah], *f.* Pectin, vegetable jelly, a substance obtained from pears and used in confectionery.

pectoral [pec-to-rahl'], *a.* Pectoral, belonging to the breast. *-m.* Cross worn by bishops on the breast; a breast-plate.

peculado [pay-coo-lah'-do], *m.* Peculation, theft, embezzlement of public money.

peculiar [pay-coo-le-ar'], *a.* Peculiar, its own, or one's own, special.

peculiaridad [pay-coo-le-ah-re-ay-dahd'], *f.* Peculiarity; special feature.

peculiarmente [pay-coo-le-ahr'-men-tay], *adv.* Peculiarly.

peculio [pay-coo'-le-o], *m.* Stock or capital which the father permits a son to hold for his own use and benefit.

pecunia [pay-coo'-ne-ah], *f. (coll.)* Hard cash, specie.

pecuniariamente [pay-coo-ne-ah'-re-ah-men-tay], *adv.* In ready money.

pecuniario, ria [pay-coo-ne-ah'-re-o, ah], *a.* Pecuniary, relating to money.

pedacico, illo ito [pay-dah-thee'-co], *m.* Small piece or bit, a gobbet. **A pedacicos**, piecemeal.

pedagogía [pay-dah-go-hee'-ah], *f.* Pedagogy, the science and art of teaching.

pedagógico, ca [pay-dah-go'-he-co, cah], *a.* Pedagogical.

pedagogo [pay-dah-go'-go], *m.* 1. Pedagogue, schoolmaster, pedant. 2. A prompter, ruler, or director to another.

pedaje [pay-dah'-hay], *m.* Bridge-toll. *V.* PEAJE.

pedal [pe-dahl'], *m.* Pedal (bicicleta). 1. The pedal pipes of an organ, and the keys, played by the feet, which control them. 2. The pedal of a pianoforte or harp. 3. The treadle of a sewing-machine, etc. 4. A pedal-base holding-note.

pedalear [pe-dah-lay-ahr'], *vn.* To pedal.

padáneo [pay-dah'-nay-o], *a.* Petty, puisne, inferior: applied to the members of inferior courts of justice.

pedante [pay-dahn'-tay], *m.* Pedant, a schoolmaster, a vain man of low knowledge.

pedantear [pay-dan-tay-ar'], *m.* To pedantize, to play the pedant, to use pedantical expressions.

pedantería [pay-dan-tay-ree'-ah], *f.* Pedantry, awkward ostentation of needless learning.

pedantesco, ca [pay-dan-tes'-co, cah], *a.* Pedantic, awkwardly ostentatious of learning.

pedantismo [pay-dan-tees'-mo], *m.* Pedantry.

pedazo [pay-dah'-tho], *m.* Piece, bit; a part of a whole, a lump. **Pedazo del alma**, my dear, my love. **A pedazos** or **en pedazos**, in bits, in fragments. **Estar hecho pedazos**, (a) to be broken in pieces; (b) *(Met.)* to be very fatigued.

pedazuelo [pay-dah-thoo-ay'-lo], *m. dim.* A small piece or bit.

pedenial [pay-dey-nahl'], *m.* 1. Flint. 2. Silex.

pedestal [pay-des-tahl'], *m.* 1. Pedestal, the basis of a column or statue. 2. *V.* PEANA. 3. Foundation, the fundamental part of a thing.

pedestre [pay-des'-tray], *a.* Pedestrious, pedaneous, going on foot (viajero).

pediatra [pay-de-ah'-trah], *m. & f.* Pediatrician, child specialist.

pediatría [pay-de-ah-tree'-ah], *f.* Pediatrics.

pedicoj [pay-de-coh'], *m.* Jump on one foot.

pedicular [pay-de-coo-lar'], *a.* Pedicular, lousy.

pedículo [pay-dee'-coo-lo], *m.* 1. *(Bot.)* Peduncle of a flower. 2. *(Med.)* The pedicle of a tumor.

pedicuro [pay-de-coo'-ro], *m.* Chiropodist.

pedida [pay-dee'-dah], *f.* **Pedida de mano**, engagement.

pedido [pay-dee'-do], *m.* 1. A voluntary contribution, which is called for by government in urgent necessities of the state. 2. *V.* PETICIÓN. 3. *(Com.)* An order of goods or merchandise.- **Pedido, da**, *pp.* of PEDIR. **A pedido de**, at the request of.

pedidor, ra [pay-de-dor', rah], *m. & f.* Petitioner, craver.

pedidura [pay-de-doo'-rah], *f.* Begging, petitioning.

pedigón [pay-de-gone'], *m. (coll.)* Craver, an insatiable asker.

pedigree [pay-de-gree'], *m.* Pedigree.

pedigüeño, ña [pay-de-goo-ay'-nyo, nyah], *a.* Craving, demanding frequently and importunately.

pediluvio [pay-de-loo'-ve-o], *m. (Med.)* Pediluvium, a bath for the feet.

pedimento [pay-de-men'-to], *m.* Petition. *V.* PETICIÓN.

pedir [pay-deer'], *va.* 1. To ask for, to request, to supplicate, to solicit. 2. To ask, to demand or require information. 3. To crave, to manifest a desire of obtaining something from another. 4. To demand and fix a price on goods set for sale (precio). 5. To demand, to inquire after, to wish for. 6. To ask for a woman in marriage (matrimonio). **Pedir limosna**, to beg, to ask alms. **Pedir justicia** or **pedir en juicio**, to claim, to bring an action or claim against a person before a judge. **Pedir cuentas**, to call for the accounts. **Pedir cuenta**, to bring a person to account. **A pedir de boca**, according to desire; adequately. **Pedírselo a uno el cuerpo**, to long anxiously. **Pedir la paz**, to sue for peace. **La casa está pidiendo una mano de pintura**, the house is crying out for a dab of paint. *(Yo pido, pida: el pidió or pidiera. V. PEDIR.)*

pedo [pay'-do], *m.* 1. Wind from the bowels; flatulence, fart. **Tirarse un pedo**, to let off a fart. 2. *(Cono Sur)* **Agarrarse un pedo**, to get sloshed. **Andar pedo**, to be sloshed (borracho).

pedorrear [pay-dor-ray-ar'], *va.* 1. To discharge wind. 2. *(Met.)* To sing or play badly.

pedorreras [pay-dor-ray'-ras], *f. pl.* 1. A kind of very tight breeches. 2. Flatulences.

pedorrero, ra, pedorro, rra [pay-dor-ray'-ro, rah], *a.* Discharging much wind, flatulent.

pedorreta [pay-dor-ray'-tah], *f.* Noise made by children with the mouth.

pedrada [pay-dah'-dah], *f.* 1. Throw or cast of a stone; lapidation (acto). **Matar a uno a pedradas**, to stone somebody to death. 2. A blow from a stone or the mark left by it. 3. A smart repartee, taunt, sneer. **Pedrada** or **pedradas**, an exclamation in denouncing a crime, you should be stoned. 2. A sneer at one who shows his teeth.

pedrea [pay-dray'-ah], *f.* 1. Throwing stones (combate). 2. Falling of stones. 3. Conflict of boys fighting with stones: lapidation. 4. Small prizes in the lottery (premios).

pedrecita [pay-dray-thee'-tah], *f. dim.* A small stone.

pedregal [pay-dray-gahl'], *m*. Place full of stones.

pedregoso, sa [pay-dray-go'-so, sah], *a*. 1. Stony, abounding with stones. 2. Afflicted with the gravel.

pedrejón [pay-dray-hone'], *m*. Large loose stone.

pedreñal [pay-dray-nyahl'], *m*. Kind of small firelock.

pedrera [pay-dray'-rah], *f*. Quarry, a stone-pit.

pedrería [pah-dray-ree'-ah], *f*. A collection of precious stones; jewels.

pedrero [pay-dray'-ro], *m*. 1. Stone-cutter (persona). 2. A swivel-gun. 3. Slinger, one who throws with a sling. 4. Lapidary, one who deals in precious stones.

pedrezuela [pay-dray-thoo-ay'-lah], *f. dim*. A small stone.

pedriscal [pay-dres-cahl'], *m*. V. PEDREGAL.

pedrisco [pay-drees'-co], *m*. 1. Hailstone (lluvia de piedras). 2. Heap of stones (montón).

pedrisquero [pay-dris-kay'-ro], *m*. A heap, hailstone.

pedriza [pay-dree'-thah], *f*. 1. Quarry. V. PEDRERA. 2. Heap of loose stones.

pedrusco [pay-droos'-co], *m*. Rough piece of marble.

pedunculado, da [pay-doon-coo-lah'-do dah], *a*. (*Bot*.) Peduncled.

pedunculillo [pay-doon-coo-lee'-lyo], *m. dim*. (*Bot*.) Pedicle or pedicel.

pedúnculo [pay-doon'-coo-lo], *m*. 1. (*Bot*.) Peduncle, flower-stalk. 2. Name of certain cerebral appendages.

peer [pay-err'], *vn*. To break wind.

pega [pay'-gah], *f*. 1. The art of joining or cementing things. 2. Varnish of pitch put on earthen vessels. 3. Act of firing a blast. 4. (*coll*.) A jest, a joke (chasco), a trick, hoax (truco). 5. (*Orn*.) Magpie. 6. Snag, difficulty (dificultad). 7. Searching question (pregunta). 8. (*Carib. Cono Sur. Mex.*) Job (trabajo). 9. (*Carib*.) Birdlime (liga). **Todo son pegas**, there's nothing but problems. **De pega**, false.

pegadillo [pay-gah-deel'-lyo], *m*. 1. (*dim*.) A little patch; a sticking-plaster. 2. Man who is introduced into a house or conversation, and remains, to the general annoyance.

pegadizo, za [pay-gah-dee'-tho, thah], *a*. 1. Clammy, glutinous, viscous. 2. Catching, contagious. 3. Adhering selfishly: applied to one who sticks to another from base motives. 4. Sticky (pegajoso). 5. Sham, imitation (postizo). 6. Parasitic (persona).

pegado [pay-gah'-do], *m*. Patch, sticking-plaster, cataplasm. **Pegado, da**, *pp*. of PEGAR.

pegador [pay-gah-dor'], *m*. Paper-hanger, one who applies wallpaper. **Pegador de carteles**, bill-poster, bill-sticker.

pegadura [pay-gah-doo'-rah], *f*. 1. Pitching, daubing with pitch. 2. The sticking of one thing to another.

pegajoso, sa [pay-gah-ho'-so, sah], *a*. 1. Sticky, viscous, glutinous, dauby, mucous. 2. Catching, contagious. 3. Attractive, alluring; adhesive.

pegamento [pay-gah-men'-to], *m*. Glue, adhesive; glue (droga). **Pegamento de caucho**, rubber solution.

pegamiento [pay-gah-me-en'-to], *m*. The act and effect of conglutinating or cementing.

pegante [pay-gahn'-tay], *a*. Viscous, glutinous.

pegar [pay-gar'], *va*. 1. To join one thing to another with cement or viscous matter. 2. To join, to unite, to sew one thing with another. 3. To close or apply closely two things. 4. To dash things violently together, to clap. 5. To chastise, to punish, to beat. 6. To infect (enfermedad), to communicate a distemper. 7. To hit (pelota), to give, to hit, to deal (golpe). 8. (*LAm*.) To be lucky; to manage it (lograrlo); to make a hit (caer en gracia). 9. (*Mex*.) To tie, to fasten; to hitch up (caballo). 10. (*Carib*.) To start (trabajo). -*vn*. 1. To root or take root (plantas). 2. To make an impression on the mind; to communicate vices, manners, etc. 3. To assault, to attack. 4. To join, to be contiguous, to cleave, to cling. 5. To begin to take effect. 6. To fall asleep. 7. To say or do something disagreeable or displeasing. **Pegarla**, to betray one's confidence. 8. To hit, to beat (dar golpes). 9. To strike hot (sol). 10. (*Carib. Mex*.) To work hard. -*vr*. 1. To intrude, to enter without invitation or permission. 2. To stick, to adhere;

to unite itself by its tenacity or penetrating power, to cohere, to grow. 3. To insinuate itself, to steal upon the mind. 4. To be taken with, to be strongly affected with a passion. 5. To spend one's fortune on things which belong to others. **No pegar ojo**, not to sleep a wink. **Pegársele (a uno)**, (a) to stick to one, to derive advantage from something; (b) to be prejudiced in the management of other's interests. **Pegar una silla a una pared**, to move a chair up against a wall. **Dicen que pega a su mujer**, they say he knocks his wife about. **Pegar un grito**, to let out a yell. **El piano pega en la pared**, the piano is touchng the wall. **Pega con**, to match. **La flecha pegó en el blanco**, the arrow hit the target. **A estas horas el sol pega fuerte**, the sun strikes very hot at this time.

pega reborda [pay'-gah-ray-bor'-dah], *f*. (*Zool*.) Shrike, butcher-bird.

pegaseo, sea [pay-gah'-say-o, ah], *a*. (*Poet*.) Belonging to Pegasus.

pegásides [pay-gah'-se-days], *f. pl*. The Muses.

pegaso [pay-gah'-so], *m*. 1. Pegasus, a winged horse. 2. A northern constellation west of Andromeda.

pegata [pay-gah'-tah], *f*. (*coll*.) Trick, fraud, imposition.

pegatina [pay-gah-tee'-nah], *f*. Sticker.

pegatista [pay-gah-tees'-tah], *m*. An indigent wretch, who lives upon the offals of other men's tables; a sponger.

pego [pay'-go], *m*. (*Esp*.) 1. **Dar el pego**, it looks great. 2. **Me ha dado el pego**, he's done me down.

pegote [pay-go'-tay], *m*. 1. Kind of sticking-plaster. 2. Fricassee with a thick, clammy sauce. 3. A sponger, a toad-eater, a sycophant. 4. Botch (chapuza). 5. **Tirarse el pego**, to show off.

peguera [pay-gay'-rah], *f*. 1. Pile of pine-wood, burnt for the purpose of making pitch. 2. Place where sheep are marked with pitch.

peguero [pay-gay'-ro], *m*. One who makes or deals in pitch.

pegujal, pegujar [pay-goo-hahl'], *m*. 1. Stock or capital which a son holds by permission of his father, for his own use and benefit. 2. A small dead or live stock on a farm.

pegujalero, pegujarero [pay-goo-hah-lay'-ro], *m*. A small farmer, grazier who keeps but a small flock of sheep.

pegujón [pay-goo-hone'], *m*. Pellet or little ball of wool or hair.

pegunta [pay-goon'-tah], *f*. Mark of pitch on wool, cattle, etc.

peguntar [pay-goon-tar'], *va*. To mark cattle, etc., with melted pitch.

peinada [pay-e-nah'-dah], *f*. Combing, the act of combing and dressing hair.

peinado [pay-e-nah'-do], *m*. 1. Hairdressing, coiffure. 2. Hair style.

peinado, da [pay-e-nah'-do, dah], *a. & pp*. of PEINAR. 1. Combed, curled, dressed (pelo). 2. Applied to a man very effeminate in dress.

peinador, ra [pay-e-nah-dor', rah], *m. & f*. 1. One who dresses or combs hair (persona). 2. Hairdresser. -*m*. 3. Cloth put about the neck while the hair is combed. 4. (*LAm*.) Dressing table (tocador).

peinadura [pay-e-nah-doo'-rah], *f*. 1. The act of combing or dressing the hair. 2. Hair pulled out with a comb.

peinar [pay-e-nar'], *va*. 1. To comb or dress the hair (pelo). 2. To comb wool. 3. To touch or rub slightly. 4. To excavate or eat away part of a rock or earth. 5. (*Poet*.) To move or divide anything gently. **Las aves peinan las olas**, the birds skim the waves. **Peinar el estilo**, to correct, to chastise, or to purify the style. -*vr*. To comb one's hair; to do one's hair.

peinazo [pay-e-nah'-tho], *m*. Cross-piece of a door or window-frame.

peine [pay'-ee-nay], *m*. 1. Comb, an instrument for the hair. 2. Card, an instrument to card wool. 3. Rack, an engine of torture. 4. Weaver's reed. 5. Hemp-comb. 6. Instep of the foot; hoof. **¡Se va a enterar lo que vale un peine!**, now he'll find out what's what!

peinería [pay-e-nay-ree'-ah], *f.* Shop where combs are made and sold.

peinero, ra [pay-e-nay'-ro, ah], *m. & f.* Comb-maker, comb-seller.

peineta [pay-ee-nay'-tah], *f.* An ornamental convex dressing-comb for the hair which women use.

peje [pay'-hay], *m.* 1. Fish. 2. Cunning, crafty fellow.

pejemuller [pay-hay-mool'-lyerr'], *f.* Mermaid, a sea-woman.

pejepalo [pay-hay-pah'-lo], *m.* An inferior kind of codfish, by reason of being tough and dry.

pejiguera [pay-he-gay'-rah], *f.* Difficulty, embarrassment, disgust.

pel [payl], *f.* Skill, hide, pelt. *V.* PIEL.

pela [pay'-lah], *m.* 1. Peeling (peladura). 2. Peseta. **Doscientas pelas,** two hundred pesetas. 2. *(Mex.)* A whipping in school. 3. *(Met.)* A reprimand.

pelada [pay-lah'-dah], *f.* 1. Pelt, the skin of a sheep stripped of the wool. 2. *(LAm.)* Haircut (corte de pelo). 3. *(Cono Sur)* Bald head (calva). 4. *(And. CAm. Carib.)* Blunder (error).

peladera [pay-lah-day'-rah], *f.* Shedding of the hair, alopecia.

peladero [pay-lah-day'-ro], *m.* Place where birds and hogs are scalded for stripping them.

peladilla [pay-lah-deel'-lyah], *f.* 1. Sugar-almond. 2. Small pebble; round whitish stone.

peladillo [pay-lah-deel'-lyo], *m.* A variety of clingstone peach of smooth purplish skin and firm flesh.

peladillos [pay-lah-deel'-lyos], *m. pl.* The wool stripped from the skin of a sheep.

peladiza [pay-lah-dee'-thah], *f.* In tanneries the wool which is removed from sheep-skins.

pelado, da [pay-lah'-do, dah], *a. & pp.* of PELAR. 1. Plucked; bared, decorticated. 2. Hairless, without hair (cabeza). 3. Applied to fields or mountains without shrubs or plants; bare, bald. 4. *(LAm.)* Broke (sin dinero), penniless. 5. *(Mex.)* Coarse, crude (grosero). 6. *(CAm. Carib.)* Impudent (descarado). **Estar pelado** or **ser un pelado,** *(coll.)* to be penniless, to be nobody. **Cobra el sueldo pelado,** he gets just the bare salary. **El cinco mil pelado,** exactly five thousand.

pelador [pay-lah-dor'], *m.* Plucker, one, who plucks or decorticates.

peladura [pay-lah-doo'-rah], *f.* 1. Plucking, decortication. 2. Peeling (acción). 3. Bare patch (calva).

pelafustán [pay-lah-foos-tahn'], *m.* Ragamuffin, vagabond, vagrant.

pelagallos [pay-lah-gahl-lyos], *m. (coll.)* Nickname applied to persons of the lowest rank who have no known occupation.

pelagatos [pay-lah-gah'-tos], *m.* 1. Vagrant. 2. Ragamuffin.

pelagiano, na [pay-lah-he-ah'-no, nah], *a.* Pelagian, denying original sin.

pelagóscopo [pay-lah-gos'-co-po], *m.* An optical instrument for seeing objects below the water.

pelagra [pay-lah'-grah], *f. (Med.)* An endemic disease of southern Europe, characterized by scaly inflammation of the skin.

pelaire [pay-lah'-e-ray], *m.* Wool-dresser.

pelairía [pay-lah-ee-ree'-ah], *f.* Trade of a wool-comber.

pelaje [pay-lah'-hay], *m.* 1. Nature and quality of the hair and of wool. 2. Quality, and external appearance, especially of clothes.

pelambrar [pay-lam-brar'], *va.* To steep hides in lime-pits to take off the hair. *V.* APELAMBRAR.

pelambre [pay-lahm'-bray], *m.* 1. The quantity of hides put into lime-pits. 2. The mixture of lime and water with which tanners strip off hair from hides. 3. Hair of the body in general, particularly that which comes off. 4. Want of hair. 5. Bare patch (calva). 6. *(Cono Sur)* Gossip, slander (murmullos).

pelambrera [pay-lam-bray'-rah], *f.* 1. Quantity of hair in one place. 2. Want or shedding of hair. 3. The place where hides are macerated in limepits.

pelambrero [pay-lan-bray'-ro], *m.* The workman who steeps hides in limepits.

pelambrón, na [pay-lam-brone'], *a. (coll.) V.* POBRETÓN.

pelamen [pay-lah'-men], *m. (coll.) V.* PELAMBRE.

pelamesa [pay-lah-may'-sah], *f.* 1. Scuffle in which the hair is torn off. 2. A bushy head of hair.

pelámide [pay-lah'-me-day], *f.* Young brood of tunny-fish.

pelandusca [pay-lan-doos'-cah], *f. (coll.)* A strumpet.

pelantrín [pay-lan-treen'], *m. (Prov.)* A petty farmer.

pelar [pay-lar'], *va.* 1. To cut or pull out the hair; to pluck the feathers. 2. To divest of the bark or husk, to blanch, to shell (guisantes). 3. To trick, to cheat, to rob. 4. To boil, to scald. 5. To fleece, to clean out (naipes). 6. To do in (matar). 7. *(LAm.)* To beat up. **Esta agua está pelando,** this water is boiling. *-vr.* 1. To cast the hair. 2. **Pelárselas por algo,** to crave. 3. **Corre que se las pela,** he runs like nobody's business.

pelarruecas [pay-lar-roo-ay'-cas], *f.* A poor woman who lives by spinning.

pelaza [pay-lah'-thah], *f.* 1. Quarrel, affray, scuffle. 2. A caterwauling of cats.

pelaza [pay-lah'-thah], *a.* Applied to chopped or beaten straw of the stalks of barley.

pelazga [pay-lahth'-gah], *f. (coll.)* Quarrel, scuffle.

peldaño [pel-dah'-nyo], *m.* Every step of a flight of stairs (de escalera).

pelde [pel-day], *m. V.* APELDE.

peldefebre [pel-day-fay'-bray], *m.* Camlet, barracan, a stuff made of wool and goat's hair; camel's hair.

pelea [pay-lay'-ah], *f.* 1. Battle, action, engagement, combat, fight. 2. Quarrel (riña), dispute, conflict. 3. Struggle, toil, fatigue. **Pelea de gallos,** cock-fight. **Armar una pelea,** to kick up a row.

peleador [pay-lay-ah-dor'], *m.* Fighter, combatant.

peleante [pay-lay-ahn'-tay], *pa.* Combating, fighting.

pelear [pay-lay-ar'], *va.* 1. To fight, to combat. 2. To quarrel, to contend, to dispute. 3. To toil, to labor hard. **Pelear con todas sus fuerzas,** *(coll.)* to fight tooth and nail, might and main. *-vr.* To scuffle, to come to blows.

pelechar [pay-lay-char'], *va.* 1. To get hair. 2. To chance the coat (caballos). 3. To fledge, to shed feathers. 4. *(coll.)* To improve one's fortune (enriquecerse), to recover health (salud).

pelele [par-lay'-lay], *m.* 1. A man of straw; insignificant fellow. 2. Rompers (traje de niño).

pelendengue [pay-len-den'-gay], *m.* Frivolous coppery, extreme nicety in dress.

peleón [pay-lay-on'], *a. & m.* 1. Very ordinary wine. 2. Pugnacious (persona), aggressive; quarrelsome.

peleona [pay-lay-oh'-nah], *f.* Scuffle, quarrel, dispute.

pelete [pay-lay'-tay], *m.* 1. He who punts at certain card games. 2. *(coll.)* A poor man. 3. Rag doll, puppet (muñeco). **Era un pelele en sus manos,** he was a puppet in his hands.

peletería [pay-lay-tay-ree'-ah], *f.* 1. Trade of a furrier or skinner. 2. Fellmonger's shop, where fine skins and furs are sold.

peletero [pay-lay-tay'-ro], *m.* Furrier, one who dresses fine skins or deals in furs.

pelgar [pel-gar'], *m.* A ragamuffin, a blackguard.

peliagudo, da [pay-le-ah-goo'-do, dah], *a.* 1. Downy, furry, having long fine hair or fur (animales). 2. *(coll.)* Arduous, difficult. 3. Ingenious, skilful, dexterous.

peliblanco, ca [pay-le-blahn'-co, cah], *a.* Having white hair.

peliblando, da [pay-le-blahn'-do, dah], *a.* Having fine soft hair.

pelicabra [pay-le-cah'-brah], *f.* Satyr, a fabulous animal.

pelícano [pay-lee'-cah-no], *m. (Orn.)* Pelican.

pelicano, na [pay-le-cah'-no, nah], *a.* Having gray hair; hoary.

pelicorto, ta [pay-le-cor'-to, tah], *a.* Having short hair.

película [pay-lee'-coo-lah], *f.* Film, a thin membrane, thin layer. **Película cinematográfica,** motion-picture film.

Película de largo metraje, full-length film. **Película sonora** or **película hablada**, talking picture. **Rollo de películas**, film roll. **Tira de película**, filmstrip.

peliculero [pay-le-coo-lay'-ro], *m.* Scenario writer.

peligrar [pay-le-grar'], *vn.* To be in danger; to be in peril, to risk, to peril.

peligro [pay-lee'-gro'], *m.* Danger, risk (riesgo), peril, hazard, jeopardy, menace (amenaza). **Correr peligro, tener peligro,** or **estar en peligro,** to be in peril or danger.

peligrosamente [pay-le-gro'-sah-men-tay], *adv.* Perilously, dangerously, hazardously, jeopardously.

peligrosidad [pay-le-gro-se-dahd'], *f.* Danger; riskiness.

peligroso, sa [pay-le-groh'-so, sah], *a.* Dangerous, perilous; hazardous.

pelilargo, ga [pay-le-lar'-go, gah], *a.* Having long hair.

pelillo [pay-leel'-lyo], *m.* 1. (*dim.*) Short, tender hair. 2. Trifle, a slight cause of disgust or displeasure. **Echar pelillos a la mar,** not to bear malice; to become reconciled. **No tener pelillos en la lengua,** to speak one's mind openly. **No reparar en pelillos,** not to bother with details.

pelinegro, gra [pay-le-nay'-gro, grah], *a.* Having black hair.

pelirrojo; ja [pay-leer-ro'-ho, hah], *a.* Red-haired.

pelirrubio, bia [pay-leer-roo'-be-o, ah], *a.* Having fair, light, or flaxen hair.

pelitieso, sa [pay-le-te-ay'-so, sah], *a.* Having strong, bushy hair.

pelito [pay-lee-to], *m.* Short, tender hair.

pelitre [pay-lee'-tray], *m.* (*Bot.*) Pellitory of Spain.

pelitrique [pay-le-tree'-kay], *m.* Fiddle-faddle, trifle.

pella [pel'-lyah], *f.* 1. Ball, anything in a round form. 2. Mass of metal in its crude state. 3. Lard in the state in which it is taken from hogs. 4. A sum of money borrowed and not paid, or of money taken under false pretences. 5. (*Orn.*) Heron. 6. Head of cauliflower.

pellada [pel-lyah'-dah], *f.* 1. Gentle blow, dab. 2. A trowelful of mortar or slaked lime.

pelleja [pel-lyay'-hah], *f.* 1. Skin or hide stripped from an animal (piel). 2. (*Low.*) A strumpet. 3. Whore (puta).

pellejería [pel-lyay-hay-ree'-ah], *f.* 1. Shop where skins are dressed and sold. 2. (*Cono Sur*) Difficulty, jam.

pellejero [pel-lyay-hay'-ro], *m.* Furrier, he whose trade is to dress and sell skins, leather-dresser, pelt-monger.

pellejina [pel-lyay-hee'-nah], *f.* A small skin.

pellejo [pel-lyay'-ho], *m.* 1. Skin, hide, felt, pelt (de animal). 2. A skin dressed and pitched, in which liquors are carried. 3. Peel, skin (fruta). 4. (*Joc.*) Tippler, drunkard (borracho). **No quisiera estar en su pellejo,** (*coll.*) I would not stand in his shoes. **Arriesgarse el pellejo,** to risk one's neck. **Salvar el pellejo,** to save one's skin.

pellejudo, da [pel-lyay-hoo'-do, dah], *a.* Having a great quantity of skin.

pellejuela [pel-lyay-hoo-ay'-lah], *f. dim.* A small skin or hide, stripped from an animal.

pellejuelo [pel-lyay-hoo-ay'-lo], *m. dim.* A small skin.

pellica [pel-lee'-cah], *f.* 1. Coverlet of fine furs. 2. A robe of fine furs. 3. A small dressed skin.

pellico [pel-lyee'-co], *m.* 1. Dress made of skins or furs. 2. (*Prov.*) Offensive language.

pelliquero [pel-lye-kay'-ro], *m.* A maker of coverlets of fine fur.

pelliza [pel-lyee'-thah], *f.* Pelisse, fur cloak, dregs formed of skins.

pellizcar [pel-lyeeth-car'], *va.* 1. To pinch, to squeeze between the fingers and thumb; to pluck or wound artfully, to gripe. 2. To pilfer. 3. To take but little food; to take only a bit or pinch. *-vr.* (*Met.*) To long for anything.

pellizco [pel-lyeeth'-co], *m.* 1. Pinch, the act of pinching. 2. A nip. 3. A small bit or portion. 4. (*Met.*) Remorse, disquietude. **Un pellizco de sal,** a pinch of salt.

pellón, pellote [pel-lyone', pel-lyo'-tay], *m.* 1. A long robe made of skins or furs. 2. (*Amer.*) A skin, checkered in colors, placed on a riding-saddle.

pelluzgón [pel-lyooth-gone'], *m.* Lock of hair, wool, or tow.

pelma [pel'-mah], *f. V.* PELMAZO.

pelmacería [pel-mah-thay-ree'-ah], *f.* Heaviness, slowness.

pelmazo [pel-mah'-tho], *m.* 1. What is crushed or flattened. 2. Heavy paste or cake: food which lies heavy on the stomach. 3. A slow, heavy person; a procrastinator.

pelo [pay'-lo], *m.* 1. Hair. 2. Down, the tender feathers of birds (pájaros). 3. A down or bloom which grows on the skins or husks of fruit (de fruta). 4. Soft fibers of plants. 5. Any slender thread of wool, silk, etc. 6. Pile, the hair or bur on the right side of cloth. 7. Hair spring in watches (de reloj). 8. Flaw in precious stones or crystals (en joyas); split in metals, horses' hoofs, etc. 9. Abscess in a woman's breast. 10. A hair or splinter; trifle, anything of little value. 11. (*Com.*) Raw silk. 12. Color of animals' skins. *V.* PELAJE. 13. The grain of wood. **Venir a pelo,** to come to the purpose. **Pelo arriba** or **a contrapelo,** against the grain. **Gente de pelo,** rich people. **No tener pelo de tonto,** to be bright, quick, clever. **En pelo,** bare-backed, naked. **Ha quedado al pelo,** it fits like a glove. **Dar a uno para el pelo,** to knock somebody silly. **No se mueve un pelo de aire,** there isn't a breath of air stirring. **Soltarse el pelo,** to burst out, to drop all restraint. **No tiene pelo de tonto,** he's no fool.

pelón, na [pay-lone', nah], *a.* (*coll.*) Hairless (calvo), bald. *- m. & f.* 1. Poor, indigent man. 2. In Peru, a caressing term applied to children.

pelona, pelonia [pay-lo'-nah, pay-lo-nee'-ah], *f.* Baldness (calvicie).

pelonería [pay-lo-nay-ree'-ah], *f.* (*coll.*) Poverty, want, indigence.

pelosilla [pay-lo-seel'-lyah], *f.* (*Bot.*) Mouse-ear; hawkweed.

peloso, sa [pay-lo'-so, sah], *a.* Hairy.

pelota [pay-lo'-tah], *f.* 1. Ball, a round plaything. 2. Ball of soft material. 3. Cannon or musket ball. 4. Ball game or play performed with balls. 5. Balls (testículos). 6. **En pelotas,** stark naked. 7. (*LAm.*) Bunch, gang (de amigos). 8. (*CAm. Carib. Mex.*) Passion (pasión). 9. (*CAm. Carib. Mex.*) Passion (pasión). **Juego de pelota,** ball-game in general; also tennis and the tennis court. **Devolver la pelota a uno,** to turn the tables on somebody. **Coger a uno en pelotas,** to catch somebody on the hop.

pelotari [pay-lo-tah'-re], *m.* Professional player of jai alai.

pelota vasca [pay-lo'-tah vahs'-cah], *f.* Jai alai, Basque ball game.

pelotazo [pay-lo-tah'-tho], *m.* 1. Blow or stroke with a ball. 2. (*Esp.*) Drink.

pelote [pay-lo'-tay], *m.* Goat's hair.

pelotear [pay-lo-tay-ar'], *vn.* 1. To play at ball. 2. To argue, to dispute (discutir); to contend. 3. To throw from one part to another. *-va.* To examine the items of an account, and compare them with the parcels received. *-vr.* To throw snowballs at each other; to quarrel, to dispute.

pelotera [pay-lo-tay'-rah], *f.* Battle, quarrel, dispute, contention: applied in general to women's quarrels.

pelotería [pay-lo-tay-ree'-ah], *f.* 1. Heap of balls. 2. Heap of goat's hair.

pelotero [pay-lo-tay'-ro], *m.* 1. Ball-maker. 2. (*LAm.*) Ball player, sportsman, footballer, baseball player.

pelotilla [pay-lo-teel'-lyah], *f.* 1. (*dim.*) A small ball. 2. Small bell of wax, stuck with small pieces of glass, and fastened to a cat-o'-nine-tails, with which penitent persons once lashed themselves.

peloto [pay-lo'-to], *a.* (*Prov.*) *V.* CHAMORRO.

pelotón [pay-lo-tone'], *m.* 1. (*Aug.*) A large ball (pelota). 2. Bundle or ball of hair closely pressed together. 3. (*Mil.*) Platoon, a small body of foot-soldiers. 4. A crowd of persons close together without order (de personas). **Cabeza de pelotón,** leading group.

peltre [pel'-tray], *m.* Pewter, an alloy of tin and lead.

peltrero pel-tray'-ro], *m.* Pewterer, pewter-worker.

peluca [pay-loo'-cah], *f.* Wig; periwig, peruke. 2. The person who wears a wig. 3. A very severe reproof from a superior to an inferior.

pelucón [pay-loo-cone'], *m.* One who struts about in a large bushy wig; any fantastical fellow.

peludo, da [pay-loo'-do, dah], *a.* Hairy, hirsute, covered with hair.

peludo [pay-loo'-do], *m.* A bass mat of mat oval shape.

peluquera [pay-loo-kay'-rah], *f.* 1. Hairdresser. 2. A haircutter's or peruke-maker's wife.

peluquería [pay-loo-kay-ree'-ah], *f.* 1. Shop where wigs are made and sold. 2. Hairdresser's, barber's; barbershop.

peluquero [pay-loo-kay'-ro], *m.* Hairdresser, hair-cutter, wig-maker.

peluquilla, ita [pay-loo-keel'-lyah], *f. dim.* A small wig.

peluquín [pay-loo-keen'], *m.* A small bag-wig, peruke.

pelusa [pay-loo'-sah], *f.* 1. Down which covers plants or fruit. 2. Villous substance falling from clothes. 3. *(Joc.)* Cash, riches.

pelusilla [pay-loo-seel'-lyah], *f. dim.* 1. The down of plants or fruit when it is very short. 2. Envy (envidia).

pelvímetro [pel-vee'-may-tro], *m.* Pelvimeter.

pelvis [pel'-vis], *f. (Anat.)* Pelvis, pelvic cavity.

pena [pay'-nah], *f.* 1. Punishment, pain (dolor), penalty; chastisement, correction. 2. Pain, painfulness, affliction, sorrow, grief (tristeza), uneasiness of mind, anxiety (molestar); a violent emotion of the mind. 3. Pain, labor, hardship, difficulty (dificultad), toil. 4. Necklace. 5. *(LAm.)* Bashfulness (timidez), shyness, timidity; embarrassment (vergüenza). **Pena capital, de muerte** or **ordinaria**, capital punishment or penalty. **A duras penas**, with great difficulty or trouble; scarcely; hardly. **Ni pena ni gloria**, without pain or pleasure. **Da pena verlos así**, it grieves me to see them like that. **Tener una pena**, to have a pain. **Alma en pena**, soul in torment. **Pena de muerte**, death penalty.

pena, *adv. V.* SOPENA.

penachera, *f. V.* PENACHO.

penacho [pay-nah'-cho], *m.* 1. Tuft of feathers on the heads of birds. 2. Plumes, feathers worn as an ornament. 3. Loftiness, haughtiness, presumption. 4. Anything that rises in the form of a tuft or crest of feathers.

penachudo, da [pay-nah-choo'-do, dah], *a.* Crested, tufted, plumed.

penadamente, *adv. V.* PENOSAMENTE.

penadilla [pay-nah-deel'-lyah], *f.* A kind of blister or small pustule.

penado, da [pay-nah'-do, dah], *a. & pp.* Of PENAR. 1. Punished, chastised; suffered. 2. Painful. 3. Narrow-mouthed (vasijas).

penal [pay-nahl'], *a.* Penal, concerning punishment; judicial.

penalidad [pay-nah-le-dahd'], *f.* 1. Act of suffering punishment. 2. Suffering, calamity, trouble (trabajos), hardship; penalty.

penalización [pay-nah-le-thah-the-on'], *f.* Penalty; penalization. **Recorrido sin penalizaciónes**, clear round.

penalizar [pay-nah-le-thar'], *va.* To penalize.

penalti [pay'-nahl-te], *m.* penalty.

penante [pay-nahn'-tay], *pa. & a.* 1. Suffering pain or affliction; love lorn, love-sick. 2. Narrow-mouthed (vasijas). *-m. (Prov.)* Lover, gallant.

penar [pay-nar'], *vn.* 1. To suffer pain, to agonize; to be tormented in a future life (alma). 2. To crave, to desire anxiously. 3. To linger. *-va.* To chastise, to inflict punishment. *-vr.* 1. To grieve, to mourn.

penates [pay-nah'-tes], *m. pl.* Penates, the house-gods of the ancient heathens.

penatígero [pay-nab-tee'-hay-ro], *m. (Poet.)* He who carried the household gods or penates.

penca [pen'-cah], *f.* 1. Pricking leaf of a cactus or other similar plant (hoja). 2. A leather strap with which convicts were whipped by the hangman. 3. *(And.)* **Penca de hombre**,

a fine looking man. 4. **Agarrar una penca,** *(LAm.)* to get drunk.

pencar [pen-cahr'], *vn.* To slog away.

pencazo [pen-cah'-tho], *m.* Lash with the hangman's strap.

penco [pen'co], *m. (Mex. and Cuba)* An raw-boned, hardtrotting horse.

pencudo, da [pen-coo'-do, dah], *a.* Acuminated.

pendanga [pen-dahn'gah], *f. (coll.)* A common prostitute.

pendejo [pen-day' -ho], *m.* 1. Hair over the pubis and groin. 2. Coward (cobarde), poltroon. 3. *(Cono Sur)* Kid (muchacho). *-a.* 1. *(LAm.)* silly (necio), stupid; irresponsible (irresponsable). 2. *(And.)* Smart (listo). 3. *(Carib. Mex.)* Ham-fisted (torpe).

pendencia [pen-den'-the-ah], *f.* Quarrel, affray, dispute, feud, jangling contention.

pendenciar [pen-den-the-ar'], *vn.* To wrangle, to quarrel.

pendenciero, ra [pen-den'-the-ay'-ro, rah], *a.* Quarrelsome.

pender [pen-derr'], *vn.* 1. To impend, to hang over (amenaza). 2. To depend. 3. To be irresolute, to leave a thing undecided. **Cuenta pendiente**, an unsettled account. **Deuda pendiente**, a balance unpaid.

pendiente [pen-de-en'-tay], *a.* 1. Pendant (asunto), hanging (colgado). 2. *(Fig.)* **Estamos pendientes de lo que él decida**, we are dependent on what he may decide. **Tener una asignatura pendiente**, to have an outstanding subject. **Pendiente de**, pending, in abeyance.

pendiente [pen-de-en-tay], *f.* Slope, declivity: grade, gradient, of a road or railway; dip or pitch. *-m.* Earring, a pendant.

pendil [pen-deel'], *m.* A mantle worn by women. **Tomar el pendil**, to elope unexpectedly.

pendingue (tomar el). To take French leave.

péndol [pen'-do-le], *m. (Naut.)* Boot topping.

péndola [pen'-do-lah], *f.* 1. A pen. *V.* PLUMA. 2. Pendulum.

pendolaje [pen-do-lah'-hay], *m.* The plunder of a captured vessel.

pendolario [pen-do-lah'-re-o], *m. V.* PENDOLISTA.

pendolero, ra [pen-do-lay'-ro, rah], *a.* Hanging, pendant.

pendolista [pen-do-lees'-tah], *m.* 1. Penman. 2. *(coll.)* Cheat, swindler, impostor.

pendolita [pen-do-lee'-tah], *f.* The spiral spring of the balance of a watch.

pendón [pen-done'], *m.* 1. Standard, the colors of a country (estandarte). 2. Banner carried in processions. 3. Standard, a shoot or principal branch of a stock, preserved at the felling of woods. 4. *(Her.)* Pennon, a family banner, borne in coats of arms. 5. *(coll.)* Nickname of a tall, awkward woman. 6. *pl.* Reins of the leading mule. 7. Whore (prostituta).

pendona [pen-do'-nah], *f.* Whore.

pendoncito [pen-don-thee'-to], *m. dim.* Pennon, a small flag.

pendonear [pen-do-nay-ahr'], *vn.* To loaf around the streets.

péndulo, la [pen'-doo-lo, lah], *a.* Pendant, hanging, pendulous. *-m.* 1. Pendulum. 2. An instrument for measuring the action of gravity. **Péndulo sideral**, an astronomical clock.

pene [pay'-nay], *m.* Penis, male organ of reproduction.

peneque [pay-nay'-kay], *a. (coll.)* Intoxicated, drunken.

penetrabilidad [pay-nay-trah-be-le-dahd'], *f.* Penetrability.

penetrable [pay-nay-trah'-blay], *a.* 1. Penetrable. 2. That can be understood.

penetración [pay-nay-trah-the-on'], *f.* 1. Penetration, the act of piercing or penetrating (acto). 2. Penetration, mental discernment, intelligence. 3. Penetration, acuteness, sagacity, clear-sightedness (cualidad).

penetrador, ra [pay-nay-trah-dor', rah]. *m. & f.* Discerner, he who penetrates or distinguishes. *-a. V.* PENETRANTE.

penetral [pay-nay-trahl'], *m. (Poet.)* The interior or most retired part.

penetrante [pay-nay-trahn'-tay], *pa. & a.* 1. Penetrating, piercing. 2. Heart-rending. 3. Clear-sighted, keen. 4. Applied to a deep wound.

penetrar [pay-nay-trar'], *va.* To penetrate, to pierce; to pass through; to force in. 2. To penetrate, to affect the mind. 3. To penetrate, to fathom, to comprehend. 4. To permeate; to pervade. -*vn.* 1. To penetrate, to go in. **El cuchillo penetró en la carne**, the knife went into the flesh. 2. To enter (persona). 3. To pierce (emoción). **La ingratitud penetró hondamente en su corazón**, the ingratitude pierced him to the heart. -*vr.* **Penetrarse de.** 1. To become imbued (absorber). 2. To understand fully.

penetrativo, va [pay-nay-trah-tee'-vo, vah], *a.* Penetrative, penetrant.

penicilina [pay-ne-the-lee'-nah], *f. (Med.)* Penicillin.

península [pay-neen'-soo-lah], *f.* Peninsula.

peninsular [pay-neen-soo-lahr'], *a.* Peninsular.

penique [pay-nee'-kay], *m.* Penny, an English copper coin.

penisla [pay-nees'-lah], *f. V.* PENÍNSULA.

penitencia [pay-ne-ten'-the-ah], *f.* 1. Penitence, penance (condición). 2. Repentance. 3. Any act of mortification (acto). 4. Public punishment which the Inquisition inflicted upon some culprits. **Imponer una penitencia a uno**, to give somebody a penance. **Hacer penitencia**, to do penance.

penitenciado, da [pay-ne-ten-the-ah'-do, daha], *a. & n.* One who was punished by the Inquisition. -*pp.* of PENITENCIAR.

penitencial [pay-ne-ten-the-ahl'], *a.* Penitential.

penitenciar [pay-ne-ten-the-ar'], *va.* To impose penance for a fault.

penitenciaría [pay-ne-ten-the-ah-ree'-ah], *f.* 1. An ecclesiastical court at Rome. 2. Office of a penitentiary canon. 3. Penitentiary, a reformatory prison.

penitenciario [pay-ne-ten-the-ah'-re-o], *m.* 1. Penitentiary, a dignitary canon who has the power of absolving in certain cases. 2. Penitentiary, the president of an ecclesiatical court at Rome.

penitente [pay-ne-ten'-tay], *a.* Penitent, repentant, contrite.

penitente [pay-ne-ten'-tay], *com.* 1. Penitent, one who does penance. 2. Penitent, one who confesses to a confessor. 3. Associate in a party of pleasure or debauchery.

pennado, da [pen-nah'-do, dah], *a. (Bot.)* Pinnate.

penol [pay-nol'], *m. (Naut.)* Yard-arm.

penología [pay-no-lo-hee'-ah], *f.* Penology.

penosamente [pay-no-sah-men-tay], *adv.* Painfully (dolorosamente), grievously

penoso, sa [pay-no'-so, sah], *a.* 1. Painful (doloroso), grievous, laborious (difícil), distressing, tormenting. 2. *(And. Carib. Mex.)* Bashful, timid (timido).

penoso [pay-no'-so], *m.* An affected fop, a buck or dude.

pensado, da [pen-sah'-do, dah], *a. & pp.* Of PENSAR. Deliberate, premeditated. **De caso pensado**, on purpose, designedly. **Lo tengo bien pensado**, I have thought it over.

pensador, ra [pen-sah-dor', rah], *a.* Thoughtful, meditative, contemplative.-*m. & f.* Thinker, profound student.

pensamiento [pen-sah-me-en'-to], *m.* 1. Thought (facultad), idea (propósito), meditation, contemplation. 2. Thought, resolution, design. **Ni por pensamiento**, not even the thought of it. **En un pensamiento**, in a jiffy, in a moment. **Venir al pensamiento**, to come to somebody's mind. **Mi pensamiento es**, my idea is to. 3. *(Bot.)* Pansy.

pensar [pen-sar'], *vn.* 1. To think, to consider, to reflect, to cogitate, to meditate. 2. To think, to imagine, to fancy, to muse. 3. To think, to intend, to mean. 4. To take into serious consideration; to weigh maturely. 5. To feed cattle. **Sin pensar**, unexpectedly, thoughtlessly. **Pensar en**, to think of. **Pensar para sí**, to think to oneself. -va. 1. To think. 2. To think over (problemas). 3. **Pensar 1** infin, to intend to. 4. To think up (idea). **Lo pensó mejor**, she thought better of it. **Esto es para pensarlo**, this needs thinking about.

pensativamente [pen-sah-te-vah-men-tay], *adv.* Moodily, thoughtfully.

pensativo, va [pen-sah-tee'-vo, vah], *a.* Pensive, thoughtful, cogitative.

pensil [pen-seel'], *a.* Pensile, hanging supported. -*m.* A beautiful garden.

pensilvano, na [pen-seel-vah'-no, nah], *a.* Pennsylvanian.

pensión [pen-se-on'], *f.* 1. Pension, an annual charge laid upon anything. 2. Pension, a fixed sum paid annually by government. 3. Toil, labor attending an enterprise or office, trouble, encumbrance, painful duty. 4. Boarding house (casa de huéspedes). 5. Board and lodging (precio). 6. *(Fig.)* Drawback, snag. 7. *(And. Cono Sur)* Worry (preocupado). **Pensión completa**, full board. **Pensión vitalicia**, annuity.

pensionado, da [pen-se-o-nah'-do, dah], *m. & f.* Pensioner, pensionary one who receives a pension. -*pp.* of PENSIONAR.

pensionar [pen-se-o-nar'], *va.* 1. To impose annual charges, pensions, or other burdens. 2. To give a grant (estudiante). 3. *(And. Cono Sur)* To bother (molestar).

pensionario [pen-se-o-nah'-re-o], *m.* 1. One who pays a pension. 2. Pensionary, the recorder of a city.

pensionista [pen-se-o-nees-tah], *com.* 1. Pensioner (jubilado), pensionery, one who receives a pension. 2. Boarder in a boarding-house (huésped). 3. *(LAm.)* Subscriber. 4. Boarder, in a boarding school (interno).

Penta. A Greek word signifying five.

pentacórdeo [pen-tah-cor'-day-o], *m.* Pentachord, five-stringed harp.

pentadáctilo, la [pen-tah-dac-te-lo, lah], *a.* Five fingered or toed; having five finger-like processes or radial arms.

pentaedro [pen-tah-ay'-dro], *m.* Pentahedron, a solid of five faces.

pentagloto [pen-tah-glo'-to], *a.* Pentaglottical, written in five languages.

pentágono [pen-tah'-go-no], *m.* Pentagon.

pentágrafo [pen-tah'-grah-fo], *m.* Pentagraph.

pentagrama [pen-tah-grah'-mah], *m.* The musical staff.

pentámetro [pen-tah'-may-tro], *m.* Petameter.

pentángulo [pen-tahn'-goo-lo], *m.* Pentangle.

pentapétalo, la [pen-tah-pay'-tah-lo, lah], *a. (Bot.)* Pentapetlous.

pentasílabo, ba [pen-tah-see'-lah-bo, bah], *a.* Of five syllables.

pentástilo [pen-tahs'-te-lo], *m. (Arch.)* Pentastyle.

pentateuco [pen-tah-tay'oo-co], *m.* The Pentateuch.

pentecostés [pen-tay-cos-tays'], *m.* Pentecost, Whitsuntide.

penúltimo, ma [pay-nool'-te-mo, mah], *a.* Penultimate.

penumbra [pay-noom'-brah], *f.* Penumbra.

penuria [pay-noo're-ah], *f.* Penury, indigence.

peña [pay'-nyah], *f.* 1. Rock, large stone. 2. Group (grupo), circle. **Peña deportiva**, supporter's club. **Forma parte de la peña**, he's a member of the circle. 3. *(And. CAm. Carib.)* V. SORDO. 4. *(Cono Sur)* Pawnshop (montepío).

peñado [pay-nyah'-do], *m. V.* PEÑASCO.

peñascal [pay-nyas-cahl'], *m.* Rocky hill or mountain.

peñasco, peñedo [pay-nyahs'-co], *m.* 1. A large rock (piedra). 2. A strong silk stuff.

peñascoso, sa [pay-nyas-co'-so, sah], *a.* Rocky, mountainous.

peñol [pay-nyole'], *m.* A large rock, rocky mountain.

péñola [pay'-nyo-lah], *f. (Poet.)* A pen.

peñón [pay-nyone'], *m.* A large rock, rocky mountain.

peón [pay-on'], *m.* 1. Pedestrian. 2. Day-laborer. **Peón de albañil**, hodman. 3. Foot-soldier. 4. Top, spinning-top (peonza), humming-top. 5. In prosody, a foot of four syllables, three short and one long. 6. Pawn in chess (ajedrez); man, in draughts.

peonada [pay-o-nah'-dah], *f.* Day-work of a laborer.

peonaje [pay-o-nah'-hay], *m.* 1. Multitude of people on foot. 2. The body of *peones* who work at once in the same place.

peonería [pay-o-nay-ree'-ah], *f.* As much land as can be ploughed in a day.

peonía [pay-o-nee'-ah], *f.* 1. *(Bot.)* Peony. 2. Quantity of land given to a soldier in a conquered country.

peonza [pay-on'-thah], *f.* 1. Top, whipping top, gig. 2. A noisy, little fellow.

peor [pay-ore'], *a.* Worse (comparativo); worst (superlativo). **Tu ejercicio es peor que el mío**, your exercise is worse than mine. **Tu ejercicio es el peor de todos**, your exercise is the worst of all.-*adv.* Worse. **Peor que nunca**, worse than ever. **Lo peor es que…**, the worst of it is that… **En el peor de los casos**, if the worst comes to the worst.

peoría [pay-o-ree'-ah], *f.* Deterioration, detriment.

peormente [pay-or'-men-tay], *adv.* Worse.

pepián [pay-pe-ahn'], *m. V.* PIPIÁN.

pepinar [pay-pe-nar'], *m.* Cucumber field.

pepinillos [pay-pe-neel'-lyos], *m. pl. (dim.).* Gherkins, pickled cucumbers.

pepino [pay-pee'-no], *m. (Bot.)* Cucumber.

pepita [pay-pee'-tah], *f.* 1. Seed of some fruits, such as melons, apples, etc: kernel. 2. Pip, a distemper in fowls. 3. Nugget, piece of pure native gold. -*pr.* 4. Josie. See JOSEFA in Appendix.

pepitaña [pay-pe-tah'-nyah], *f. (Prov.)* A pipe made of cornstalk.

pepitoria [pay-pe-to'-re-ah], *f.* 1. Fricassee made of giblets, livers, and lights. 2. Medley of things. 8. *(Mex.)* Peanut or almond candy.

pepitoso, sa [pay-pe-to'-so, sah], *a.* 1. Abounding in grains or seeds. 2. Applied to fowls with the pip.

peplo [pay'-plo], *m.* Peplum, a loose gown of the ancient Greek women.

pepón [pay-pone'], *m. (Bot.)* Watermelon. *V.* SANDÍA. -*a. (And.)* Good-looking, dishy.

pepsina [pep-see'-nah], *f.* Pepsin, the digestive ferment.

péptico, ca [pep'-te-co, cah], *a.* Peptic.

peptona [pep-to'-nah], *f.* Peptone.

pequeñamente [pay-kay'-nyah-men-tay], *adv.* Little, in a small degree or quantity, not much.

pequeñez [pay-kay-nyeth'], *f.* 1. Smallness of size (tamaño); littleness, minuteness. 2. Youth, tender age. 3. Lowness of mind, pusillanimity. **Preocuparse por pequeñeces**, to worry about trifles.

pequeñito, ta [pay-kay-nyee'-to, tah], *a. dim. V.* PEQUEÑUELO.

pequeño, ña [pay-kay'-nyo, nyah], *a.* 1. Little or small of size, minute. 2. Young, of a tender age. 3. Low-spirited, humble, abject.

pequín [pay-keen'], *m.* Silk stuff manufactured in Pekin.

per [per], *prep.* Used in Spanish in composition only, as *perdonable*, pardonable.

pera [pay'-rah], *f.* 1. Pear, the fruit of the pear-tree. 2. A small tuft of hair left to grow on the chin (barba, barbilla). 3. *(coll.)* A sinecure. 4. Bulb (bocina). 5. Bulb (bombilla). 6. Cushy job (empleo). 7. *(LAm. Dep.)* Punchball. **Pedir peras al olmo**, to look for pears on elm-trees. **Tocarse la pera**, to sit on one's backside.

perada [pay-rah'-dah], *f.* Conserve made of the juice of pears.

peraile [pay-rah'-e-lay], *m.* Woolcomber. *V.* PELAIRE.

peral [pay-rahl'], *m. (Bot.)* Pear-tree.

peraleda [pay-rah-lay'-dah], *f.* Orchard of pear-trees.

peraltar [pay-ral-tar'], *va.* To raise the arch of a vault or dome above a semicircle to the figure of a parabola.

peralte [pay-rahl'-tay], *m.* Height of an arch above a right angle.

perantón [pay-ran-tone'], *m.* 1. *(Bot.)* Marvel-plant. 2. A very tall person.

peraza [pay-rah'-thah], *f.* Fruit of an ingrafted pear-tree.

perca [perr'-cah], *f. (Zool.)* Perch.

percal [per-cahl'], *m. (Com.)* Percale, a dress material. *(Per.)*

percalina [per-cah-lee'-nah], *f.* Percaline, a lining material of one color; book muslin.

percance [per-cahn'-thay], *m.* 1. Perquisite, something above the settled salary: generally used in the plural. 2. Mischance, misfortune. **Percance, del oficio**, *V.* GAJES DEL OFICIO.

percarburo [per-car-boo'-ro], *m. (Chem.)* Percarbid(e).

percatar [per-cah-tar'], *vn.* 1. To think, to consider maturely. 2. To take care; to be on one's guard. -*vr.* **Percatarse de**, to notice (observar); to heed (hacer caso de); to guard against (guardarse de).

percebe [per-thay'-bay], *m.* A mollusk having five crusty plates and a fleshy foot. It is common on the coast of Galicia, and eaten cooked without any seasoning.

percebimiento [per-thay-be-me-en'-to], *m.* Prevention, warning. *V.* APERCIBIMIENTO.

percepción [per-thep-the-on'], *f.* Perception, notion (idea), idea, feeling.

perceptibilidad [per-thep-te-be-le-dahd'], *f.* Perceptibility, faculty of perception.

perceptible [per-thep-tee'-blay], *a.* Perceptible (visible), perceivable.

perceptiblemente [per-thep-tee'-blay-men-tay], *adv.* Perceivably, perceptibly.

perceptivo, va [per-thep-tee'-vo, vah], *a.* Perceptive.

percha [per'-chah], *f.* 1. Perch, a piece of timber to support anything. 2. Clothes-rack (perchero). 3. Snare for catching partridges. 4. String on which fowlers hang their game. 5. *(Zool.)* Perch. 6. *(Cono Sur)* Pile (montón). 7. *(Mex.)* Gang (grupo). 8. Build, physique (tipo); figure (de mujer). **Percha de herramientas**, toolrack. **Tener percha**, to be smart.

perchador, ra [per-chah-dor', rah], *m. & f.* Napper, one who raises the nap on cloth.

perchar [per-char'], *va.* To raise the nap on cloth.

perchero [per-chay'-ro], *m.* Clothes rack, hallstand.

percherón [per-chay-rone'], *m.* Percheron, Percheron Norman horse.

perchonar [per-cho-nar'], *vn.* 1. To leave on a vine-stock several long shoots. 2. To lay snares for catching game.

percibir [per-the-beer'], *va.* 1. To receive, to collect. 2. To perceive (notar), to comprehend.

percibo [per-thee'-bo], *m.* Act of receiving or perceiving.

perclórico [per-clo'-re-co], *a.* Perchloric.

percloruro [per-clo-roo'-ro], *m. (Chem.)* Perchloride.

percocería [per-co-thay-ree'-ah], *f.* Small work of silver or spangles; filagree, etc.

percuciente [per-coo-the-en'-tay], *a.* Percutient, striking.

percudir [per-coo-deer'], *va.* To tarnish the lustre of things (deslumbrar).

percusión [per-coo-se-on'], *f.* Percussion, collision.

percusor [per-coo-sor'], *m.* One who strikes.

percutir [per-coo-teer'], *va. (Med.)* To percuss.

perdedero [per-day-day'-ro], *m.* Occasion or motive of losing.

perdedor, ra [per-day-dor', rah], *m. & f.* Loser.

perder [per-derr'], *va.* 1. To lose, to be deprived of something. 2. To lose, to forfeit, to suffer diminution of. 3. To lose, to squander away, to lavish, to misspend. 4. To lose, to miss, not to find. 5. To lose, to ruin (arruinar), to send, to perdition. 6. To lose, to be disappointed, not to obtain what has been wished (decaer). 7. To spoil, to mar, to damage. 8. To bet, to lay a wager. **Perder la ocasión or el lance**, to let an opportunity slip. **Perder terreno**, to lose ground. **Perder tiempo**, (a) to lose time, or not to profit of it; (b) to labor in vain. **He perdido la costumbre**, I have got out of the habit. **No pierde nada**, he doesn't miss a thing. -*vr.* (1.) To go astray, to miss one's way. 2. To be lost (desaparecer), to be confounded, to be bewildered. 3. To forget or lose the thread of one's subject or discourse. 4. To be spoiled (arruinarse), to be lost or given up to vice. 5. To fall into disuse, to be out of fashion. 6. To cease to be perceived by sight or hearing. 7. To run risk of losing life. 8. To love excessively. 9. *(Naut.)* To be shipwrecked. 10. To sustain a loss. 11. To congeal itself: applied to rivers which disappear under the earth and rise again. 12. *(LAm.)* To go on the streets (prostituirse). **Tener que perder**, to be a person of credit, to have much to lose. **Perder los estribos**, to lose patience. **Salir perdiendo**, to lose. **Ha perdido mucho en mi estimación**, he has gone down a lot in my estimation. **Echar a perder**, to spoil. **Nada se pierde con intentar**, there's no harm in trying.

perdición [per-de-the-on'], *f.* 1. Losing or the act of losing anything. 2. Perdition, destruction, ruin, loss. 3. Unbridled, excessive love. 4. Prodigality, extravagance. 5. Perdition, hell.

pérdida [perr'-de-dah], *f.* 1. Loss, privation of what was possessed. 2. Loss, detriment, damage; waste (de tiempo). 3. Quantity or thing lost. 4. Wastage (de líquido). **Pérdida contable**, book loss. **Vender algo con pérdida**, to sell something at a loss. **Pérdida de datos**, *(Comput.)* data leakage.

perdidamente [per-de'-dah-men-tay], *adv.* Desperately, furiously; uselessly.

perdidizo, za [per-de-dee'-tho, thah], *a.* Lost designedly or on purpose. **Hacerse perdidizo**, to lose designedly at cards, as gamesters do at times.

perdido, da [per-dee'-do, dah], *a. & pp.* Of PERDER. 1. Lost, strayed, misguided; profligate, dissolute. **Gente perdida**, Vagrants, vagabonds. **Mujer perdida**, prostitute. 2. **Estar perdido por**, to be mad about. 3. **Ponerse perdido de barro**, to get covered in mud. 4. *(LAm.)* Idle (vago); down and out (pobre).

perdidoso, sa [per-de-do'-so, sah], *a.* Sustaining loss.

perdigana [per-de-gah'-nah], *f. (Prov.)* A young partridge.

perdigar [per-de-gar'], *va.* 1. To broil partridges slightly before they are roasted. 2. To stew larded meat in an earthen pan. 3. To dispose, to prepare.

perdigón [per-de-gone'], *m.* 1. A young partridge. 2. Partridge trained to decoy others. 3. *(Prov.)* Squanderer, lavisher of money at the gaming-table. **Perdigones**, hail-shot, small shot, bird-shot.

perdiguero, ra [per-de-gay'-ro, rah], *a.* Setter, retriever: applied to a dog used by fowlers who pursue partridges.

perdiguero [per-de-gay'-ro], *m.* Poulterer, dealer in partridges or any other kind of game.

perdimiento [per-de-me-en'-to], *m.* V. PERDICIÓN and PÉRDIDA.

perdiz [per-deeth'], *f. (Orn.)* Partridge. **Perdiz real**, common partridge.

perdón [per-done'], *m.* 1. Pardon, forgiveness, absolution; mercy (indulto), grace remission of a debt. 2. Drop of oil wax, etc., which falls burning. **Con perdón**, under favor; with your leave. **Pedir perdón a uno**, to ask somebody's forgiveness. **¡Perdón!**, sorry!

perdonable [per-do-nah'-blay], *a.* Pardonable, forgivable.

perdonador, ra [per-do-nah-dor', rah], *m. & f.* Pardoner, excuser.

perdonanza [per-do-nahn'-thah], *f. V.* DISIMULO and PERDÓN.

perdonar [per-do-nar'], *va.* 1. To pardon (ofensa, persona), to forgive; to remit a debt. 2. To exempt anyone from doing what he should execute (de obligación); to spare, to excuse. 3. To beg leave or permission: an expression of civil denial or light apology. **¡Perdone!**, *(coll.)* sorry! *-vr.* To decline doing anything; to excuse oneself from doing anything. **Perdónanos nuestras deudas**, forgive us our trespasses. **No perdona nada**, he is wholly unforgiving. **Perdonar la vida a uno**, to spare somebody's life. **No perdonar ocasión**, to miss no chance.

perdonavidas [per-do-nah-vee'-das], *m. (coll.)* Bully, hector.

perdulario, ria [per-doo-lah'-re-o, ah], *a.* Extremely careless of one's own interest or person.

perdurable [per-doo-rah-blay], *a.* Perpetual, everlasting, continual.

perdurablemente [per-doo-rah'-blay-men-tay], *adv.* Eternally, perpetually.

perdurar [per-doo-rahr'], *vn.* To last, to endure, to survive; to stand.

perecear [pay-ray-thay-ar'], *va.* To protract, to delay, to put off.

perecedero, ra [pay-ray-thay-day'-ro, rah], *a.* Perishable, decaying, fading.

perecedero [pay-ray-thay-day'-ro], *m.* Misery, extreme want.

perecer [pay-ray-therr'], *vn.* 1. To perish, to die, to be destroyed. 2. To perish, to suffer or undergo damage, toil,

or fatigue. 3. To be extremely poor, to perish for want of the necessaries of life. *-vr.* 1. To crave, to desire anxiously. 2. To be violently agitated, to die with love. **Perecer de hambre**, to perish with hunger. **Perecer de risa**, to be convulsed with laughter. **Perecer ahogado**, to drown. *(Yo perezco, yo perezca, from Perecer. V.* CONOCER.*)*

perecido, da [pay-ray-thee'-do, dah], *a & pp.* of PERECER. Dying with anxiety, lost, undone.

pereciente [pay-ray-the-en'-tay], *pa.* Perishing.

perecimiento [pay-ray-the-me-en'-to], *m.* Loss, decay, decline; wreck of a ship.

peregrinación [pay-ray-gre-nah-the-on'], *f.* 1. Peregrination, traveling in foreign countries (viajes). 2. Pilgrimage. 3. The course of this life.

peregrinamente [pay-ray-gree'-nah-men-tay], *adv.* Rarely, curiously.

peregrinante [pay-ray-gre-nahn'-tay], *pa.* Sojourner; traveling; he who peregrinates.

peregrinar [pay-ray-gre-nar'], *m.* 1. To peregrinate, to travel in foreign countries (viajar). 2. To go on a pilgrimage. 3. To exist in this mortal life.

peregrinidad [pay-ray-gre-ne-dahd'], *f.* Strangeness, wonderfulness.

peregrino, na [pay-ray-gree'-no, nah], *a.* 1. Peregrine, foreign (persona). 2. Traveling or sojourning in foreign countries. 3. Going on a pilgrimage; migratory (pájaros). 4. Strange, wonderful, seldom seen (raro). 5. Very handsome or perfect.

peregrino [pay-ray-gree'-no], *a.* A pilgrim, a palmer.

perejil [pay-ray-heel'], *m.* 1. *(Bot.)* Parsley. 2. Showy dress or apparel. *-pl.* Honorary titles attached to offices.

perejilón [pay-ray-he-lone'], *m. (Prov.)* Creeping crow-foot.

perendeca [pay-ren-day'-cah], *f. (coll.)* Whore, hussy, trull.

perendengue [pay-ren-den'-gay], *m.* 1. Pendant of the ears, ear crop. 2. Any cheap or tawdry feminine ornament (adorno). 3. **Perendengues**, snags (pegas). 4. Standing, importance (categoría).

perene [pay-ray'-nay], *a. V.* PERENNE.

perengano, na [pay-ren-gah'-no, nah], *m. & f.* So-and-so: used after other names, as **fulano, mengano, zutano, y perengano**. In America the word *parencejo* is commonly used.

perennal [pay-ren-nahl'], *a.* 1. *V.* PERENNE. 2. Continually mad, without lucid intervals.

perennalmente [pay-ray-nahl'-men-tay], *adv. V.* PERENNEMENTE.

perenne [pay-ren'-nay], *a.* Perennial, perpetual. **De hoja perenne**, evergreen.

perennemente [pay-ray'-nay-men-tay], *adv.* Continually, perpetually.

perennidad [pay-ren-ne-dahd'], *f.* Perennity, continuity.

perentoriamente [pay—ren-to'-re-ah-men-tay], *adv.* Peremptorily.

perentoriedad [pay-ren-to-re-ay-dahd'], *f.* Peremptoriness, great urgency.

perentorio, ria [pay-ren-to'-re-o, ah], *a.* Peremptory (orden), absolute, decisive.

perero [pay-ray'-ro], *m.* Instrument formerly used to pare fruit.

pereza [pay-ray'-thah], *f.* 1. Laziness, tardiness, negligence, idleness, carelessness, sloth. 2. Slowness in movements. 3. Difficulty in rising from bed or from a seat.

perezosamente [pay-ray-tho-sah-men-tay], *adv.* Lazily, slothfully, negligently, idly.

perezoso, sa [pay-ray-tho'-so, sah], *a.* Lazy, careless, indolent, slothful, negligent, idle; sometimes used as a noun, for a lazy person or a lubber. *-m. (Zool.)* The sloth.

perfección [per-fec-the-on'], *f.* Perfection, superior excellence, faultlessness, completeness; beauty, grace; high degree of virtue. *-pl.* Accomplishments.

perfeccionador [per-fec-the-o-nah-dor'], *m.* Perfecter.

perfeccionamiento [per-fec-the-o-nah-me-en'-to], *m.* The act of perfecting, finishing, completion.

perfeccionar [per-fec-the-o-nar'], *va.* To perfect (hacer perfecto), to complete (proceso), to finish, to heighten.

perfectamente [per-fec'-tah-men-tay], *adv.* Perfectly, completely.

perfectible [per-fec-tee'-blay], *a.* Perfectible, capable of being made perfect.

perfectivo, va [per-fec-tee'-vo, vah], *a.* Perfective.

perfecto, ta [per-fec'-to, tah], *a.* 1. Perfect, complete (completo), accomplished. 2. Faultless, consumate, accurate. 3. Beautiful, fair, handsome. 4. Excellent, of the highest grade. 5. *(Gram.)* Perfect (tense). *-m.* Improvements made in an inheritance.

perficiente [per-fe-the-en'-tay], *a.* That which perfects.

pérfidamente [perr'-fe-dah-men-tay], *adv.* Perfidiously.

perfidia [per-fee'-de-ah], *f.* Perfidy, treachery.

pérfido, da [perr'-fe-do, dah], *a.* Perfidious, treacherous, disloyal.

perfil [per-feel'], *m.* 1. Profile, contour, outline. **Tomar perfiles**, to place oiled paper over a painting, in order to draw its outlines. 2. Light architectural ornament; hair. 3. Stroke of certain letters. 4. Profile, side-view. 5. Features (rasgos). 6. Social courtesies (cortesías).

perfilado, da [per-fe-lah'-do, dah], *a.* Applied to a wellformed face (rostro), nose (rariz, etc. *-pp.* of PERFILAR.

perfiladura [per-fe-lah-doo'-rah], *f.* Art of drawing profiles; the sketching of outlines.

perfilar [per-fe-lar'], *va.* 1. To draw profiles, to sketch outlines. 2. *(Fig.)* To put the finishing touches (rematar). *-vr.* 1. To incline, to be bent to one side. 2. To show one's profile (persona). 3. *(Fig.)* To take shape. **El proyecto se va perfilando**, the plan is taking shape. 4. *(LAm.)* To slim. 5. *(Cono Sur. Dep.)* To dribble and shoot.

perfoliada, or **perfoliata** [per-fo-le-ah'-tah], *f. (Bot.)* Hare's-ear. *V.* CORAZONCILLO. St. John's wort.

perfoliado, da [per-fo-le-ah'-do, dah], *a. (Bot.)* Perfoliate.

perforación [per-fo-rah-the-on'], *f.* Perforation; piercing (proceso); drilling, boring; punching.

perforador, ra [per-fo-rah-dor', rah], *a.* Perforating. *-f.* 1. Jackhammer. 2. Punch; drill.

perforar [per-fo-rar'], *va.* To perforate; to puncture (pinchar); to make (agujero); to sink (pozo).

perfumadero [per-foo-mah-day'-ro], *m. V.* PERFUMADOR, 2d def.

perfumado, da [per-foo-mah'-do, dah], *a. & pp.* of PERFUMAR. Odoriferous, perfumated.

perfumador [per-foo-mah-dor'], *m.* 1. Perfumer. 2. Vessel in which perfumes are kept. 3. Perfuming-pan.

perfumar [per-foo-mar'] or **perfumear** [per-foo-may-ar'], *va.* To perfume, to fumigate.

perfume [per-foo'-may], *m.* Perfume; odor, fragrance; good or bad smell or flavor.

perfumería [per-foo-may-ree'-ah], *f.* A perfumer's shop.

perfumero, ra [per-foo-may'-ro, rah], *m. & f.* Perfumer.

perfumista [per-foo-mees'-tah], *m.* Perfumer, dealer in perfumes.

perfunctoriamente [per-foonc-to'-re-ah-men-tay], *adv.* Perfunctorily, superficially.

perfunctorio, ria [per-foonc-to'-re-o, ah], *a.* Perfunctory.

perfusión [per-foo-se-on'], *f.* Affusion, sprinkling water on the head.

pergaminero [per-gah-me-nay'-ro], *m.* Parchment-maker.

pergamino [per-gah-mee'-no], *m.* 1. Parchment, vellum; skin dressed for writing. 2. Parchment, diploma, a formal writing on parchment.

pergenio [per-hay-ne-o], *m. V.* PERGEÑO.

pergeño [per-hay'-nyo], *m. (coll.)* Skill, dexterity.

pérgola [per'-go-lah], *f.* Pergola.

peri [pay'-re], *f.* 1. A beautiful and beneficent fairy in Persian mythology. 2. *(Gram.)* An inseparable prefix derived from the Greek, and meaning around.

periancio, periantio [pay-re-ahn'-the-o], *m. (Bot.)* Perianth.

períbolo [per-ree'-bo-lo], *m. (Arch.)* Peribolos, the inclosed court of an edifice.

pericardio [pay-re-ar'-de-o], *m.* Pericardium.

pericarpio [pay-re-car'-pe-o], *m.* Pericarp, covering of any fruit.

pericia [pay-ree'-the-ah], *f.* Skill, knowledge, practical experience.

perico [pay-ree'-co], *m.* 1. Curls formerly worn by women. 2. A kind ot small parrot, parakeet, indigenous to Cuba and South America. 3. Dim. of PEDRO. 4. Wig, toupé (peluca). 5. Chamberpot (orinal). 6. *(And.)* Coffee with a dash of milk.

pericón [pay-re-cone'], *m.* 1. Knave of clubs in the game of *Quínolas.* 2. A large fan.

pericón, na [pay-re-cone, nah], *a.* Fit for all things: generally, applied to horses fit for draught or saddle.

pericona [pay-re-co'-nah], *f.* Shaft mule; a mule fit for the coach as well as the saddle.

pericráneo [pay-re-crah'-nay-o], *m.* Pericranium.

peridromo [pay-re-dro'-mo], *m. (Arch.)* Peridrome, a covered gallery around a building.

periecos [pay-re-ay'-cose], *m. pl.* Perioeci, people on the opposite side of the globe, in the same latitude.

periferia [pay-re-fay'-re-ah], *f.* Periphery. *V.* CIRCUNFERENCIA.

periférico [pay-re-fay'-re-co], *a.* Peripherical; marginal; outlying (barrio).

perifollo [pay-re-fol'-lyo], *m. (Bot.)* Common chervil. **Perifollos**, ribbons and other ornaments of women, particularly if excessive or tawdry.

perifonear [pay-ro-fo-nay-ar'], *va.* To broadcast by radio.

perifrasear [pay-re-frash-say-ar'], *va.* To periphrase, to use circumlocutions.

perífrasis, perífrasis [pay-ree'-frah-ses], *f.* (Rhet.) Periphrasis, circumlocution.

perifrástico, ca [pay-re-frahs'-te-co, cah], *a.* Periphrastic, round about, circumlocutory.

perigallo [pay-re-gahl'-lyo], *m.* 1. Skin hanging from the chin of lean persons. 2. Kind of glossy ribbon worn by women. 3. *(coll.)* A tall, lean man. 4. Kind of slender sling. 5. *(Naut.)* Line, a thin rope; navel-line; topping-lift.

perigeo [pay-re-hay'-o], *m. (Astron.)* Perigee, perigeum.

perigonio [pay-re-go'-ne-o], *m. (Bot.)* Perigynium, perianth.

perihelio [pay-re-ay'-le-o], *m. (Astron.)* Perihelion.

perilla [pay-reel'-lyah], *f.* 1. *(dim.)* A small pear. 2. Ornament in form of a pear. 3. Pommel of a saddle-bow, a knob. 4. A small tuft of hair growing on the chin. *V.* PERA, 2d def. **De perilla**, to the purpose, at a proper time.

perillán, na [pay-reel-lyan', nah], *a. (coll.)* Artful, knavish, vagrant.

perillán, na [pay-reel-lyahn', nah], *m. & f.* 1. Huckster, sly, crafty fellow. 2. *(coll.)* A clever fellow.

perillo [pay-reel'-lyo], *m.* Ginger-bread nut.

perilustre [per-e-loos'-tray], *a. (Ant.)* Very illustrious.

perímetro [pay-ree'-may-tro], *m.* Perimeter. *V.* ÁMBITO.

perínclito, ta [pay-reen'-cle-to, tay], *a.* Famous, renowned, grand.

perineal [pay-re-nay-ahl'], *a.* Perineal.

perineo [pay-re-nay'-o], *m. (Anat.)* Perineum.

perineumonía [pay-re-nay-mo-ne'-ah], *f.* Pneumonia, inflammation of the lungs. *V.* PULMONÍA.

perinola [pay-re-no'-lah], *f.* 1. A handtop with four faces; a teetotum. 2. A neat little woman.

períoca [pay-ree'-o-cah], *f.* Synopsis, plot of a book.

periódicamente [pay-re-o'-de-cah-men-tay], *adv.* Periodically.

periódico, ca [pay-re-o'-de-co, cah], *a.* Periodical, periodic.

periódico [pay-re-o'-de-co], *m.* Newspaper, periodical. **Periódico de la tarde**, evening newspaper.

periodismo [pay-re-o-dees'-mo], *m.* Journalism.

periodista [pay-re-o-dees'-tah], *m & f.* 1. Journalist, newspaperman (hombre), newspaperwoman (mujer), reporter, pressman (hombre), presswoman (mujer). 2.

Author or publisher of a periodical. **Periodista de televisión**, television journalist.

periodístico, ca [pay-re-o-dees'-te-co, cah], a. Journalistic. **Informe periodístico**, newspaper report.

período [pay-ree'-o-do], m. 1. Period, a determinate space of time. 2. Period, clause, a complete sentence. 3. Period, the time of revolution of a planet. 4. (Mus.) Period, phase.

periostio [pay-re-os'-te-o], m. Periosteum, the nutritive membrane which covers a bone.

peripatético [pay-re-pah-tay'-te-co], m. Peripatetic, a follower of Aristotle.

peripatético, ca [pay-re-pah-tay'-te-co, cah], a. 1. Belonging to the Peripatetics. 2. Applied colloquially to any person of ridiculous or extravagant opinions.

peripecia [pay-re-pay'-the-ah], f. (Poet.) Peripetia, sudden change of condition in the persons of a drama, or in fortune.

periplo [pay-ree'-plo], m. Diary of a voyage; voyage around a coast.

peripuesto, ta [pay-re-poo-es'-to, tah], a. Very gay, very fine, very spruce in dress. **Tan peripuesto**, all dressed up.

periquete [pay-re-kay'-tay], m. (coll.) Jiffy, instant. **En un periquete**, in a jiffy.

periquillo [pay-re-keel'-lyo], m. A small sweetmeat made of sugar alone.

periquito [pay-re-kee'-to], m. 1. (Orn.) Parakeet, small parrot. 2. (Naut.) Sky-sail, skyscraper.

periscios [pay-rees'-the-ose], m. pl. Periscii, inhabitants of the polar circles.

periscopio [pay-ris-co'-pe-o], m. Periscope.

peristáltico, ca [pay-ris-tahl'-te-co, cah], a. Peristaltic: applied to the motion of the intestines.

peristilo [pay-ris-tee'-lo], m (Arch.) Peristyle, colonnade.

perita [pay-ree'-tah], f. dim. A small pear.

peritaje [pay-re-tah'-he], m. 1. Expert work (trabajo); expertise (pericia); report of an expert (informe).

perito, ta [pay-ree'-to, tah], a. Skillful, able, experienced. -m. 1. Connoisseur. 2. Appraiser of goods. 3. A critical person, a skilful workman. **Perito agrónomo**, agronomist. **Perito forense**, legal expert.

peritoneo [pay-re-to-nay-o], m. (Anat.) Peritoneum, the serous membrane of the abdomen.

peritonitis [pay-re-to-nee'-tis], f (Med.) Peritonitis.

perjudicador, ra [per-hoo-de-cah-dor', rah], m. & f. One who prejudices, injures, or causes damage.

perjudicar [per-hoo-de-car'], va. 1. To prejudice, to cause damage to another, to injure, to harm (salud, fama). 2. To wrong (en lo moral). 3. To spoil the appearance of, not to suit (desfavorecer). **Perjudicar los intereses de alguien**, to prejudice someone's interests.

perjudicial [per-hoo-de-the-ahl'], a. Prejudicial, hurtful, mischievous, pernicious.

perjudicialmente [per-hoo-de-the-ahl'-men-tay], adv. Prejudicially, mischievously.

perjuicio [per-hoo-ee'-the-o], m. Prejudice, mischief, injury, detriment, damage, grievance, harm. **En perjuicio de**, to the detriment of. **Sufrir grandes perjuicios**, to suffer great damage.

perjurador, ra [per-hoo-rah-dor', rah], m. & f. Perjurer, forswearer.

perjurar [per-hoo-rar'], vn. To swear falsely; to commit perjury. -vr. To perjure oneself.

perjurio [per-hoo'-re-o], m. Perjury, false oath.

perjuro, ra [per-hoo'-ro, rah], a. Perjured, forsworn.

perjuro, ra [per-hoo'-ro, rah], m. &f. 1. Forswearer, perjurer. 2. V. PERJURIO.

perla [perr'-lah], f. Pearl, margarite: anything precious, clear, or bright. **Perlas**, fine teeth. **De perlas**, much, to the purpose; excellently, eminently fine. **Ser una perla**, to be a treasure.

perlático, ca [per-lah'-te-co, cah], a. Paralytic, palsied.

perlería [per-lay-ree'-ah], f. Collection of pearls.

perlesía [per-lay-see'-ah], f. Paralysis, palsy.

perlino, na [per-lee'-no, nah], a. Pearl-colored.

perlita [per-lee'-tah], f. dim. A small pearl.

perlongar [per-lon-gar'], vn. (Naut.) To coast, to sail along the coast.

permanecer [per-mah-nay-therr'], vn. To persist, to endure, to last. **Permanecer dormido**, to go on sleeping.

permaneciente [per-mah-nay-the-en', tay], pa. & a. Permanent; persisting.

permanencia [per-mah-nen'-the-ah], f. Duration, permanency, perseverance, constancy, consistency, permanence (cualidad), stay (estancia).

permanente [per-mah-nen'-tay], a. Permanent, durable, lasting. -f. Permanent, permanent wave.

permanentemente [per-mah-nen'-tay-men-tay], adv. Permanently.

permanganato [per-man-gah-nah'-to], m. (Chem.) Permanganate.

permeabilidad [per-may-ah-be-le-dahd'], f. Permeability, previous nature.

permisible [per-me-see'-blay], a. Permissible.

permisión [per-me-se-on'], f. 1. Permission, leave. 2. Confession, grant; the thing yielded.

permisivamente [per-me-see'-vah-men-tay], adv. Permissively.

permisivo, va [per-me-see'-vo, vah], a. Permissive.

permiso [per-mee'-soo], m. Permission, leave, licence (documento), allowance, liberty, excuse me (queriendo entrar, pasar). **Dar su permiso**, to give one's permission. **Permiso de entrada**, entry permit.

permisor [per-me-sor'], m. Granter. V. PERMITIDOR.

permistión [per-mis-te-on'], f. Permixtion, the act of mixing.

permitente [per-me-ten'-tay], pa. He that grants or permits.

permitidero, ra [per-me-te-day'-ro, rah], a. What may be permitted.

permitidor [per-me-te-dor'], m. Permitter, granter, he who allows or permits.

permitir [per-me-teer'], va. 1. To permit, to consent, to agree to, to give leave. 2. To permit, to suffer without authorizing or approving. 3. To permit, to give time or place to execute a thing. 4. To permit, not to hinder what one could and ought to avoid. To show oneself, to appear benign, generous, and liberal. **Permitir a uno hacer algo**, to allow somebody to do something. -vr. To be permitted, to be allowed. **Eso no se permite**, that is not allowed.

permuta [per-moo'-tah], f. Exchange of one thing for another, barter.

permutable [per-moo-tah'-blay], a. Permutable, capable of being permuted.

permutación [per-moo-tah-the-on'], f. 1. V. PERMUTA. 2. (Math.) Permutation, alteration of the order of elements or numbers.

permutante [per-moo-tahn'-tay], pa. & a. Permutant; exchanging.

permutar [per-moo-tar'], va. To exchange (cambiar), to barter, to commute, to permute. -vn. **Permutar con uno**, to exchange with somebody.

perna [perr'-nah], f. Flat shellfish.

pernada [per-nah'-dah], f. Blow with the leg; a violent movement of the leg.

pernaza [per-nah'-thah], f. (Aug.) A thick or big leg.

pernear [per-nay-ar'], vn. 1. To kick, to shake the legs (agitar las piernas). 2. To drive about in pursuit of an affair. 3. To be vexed, to fret. -va. To drive pigs to market and sell them by retail.

perneo [per-nay'-o], m. (Prov.) Public sale of hogs.

pernería [per-nay-ree'-ah], f. Collection of pins or bolts.

pernetas (En) [per-nay'-tas], adv. Bare-legged.

pernete [per-nay'-tay], m. (Naut.) Small pin, peg, or bolt.

perniabierto, ta [per-ne-ah-be-err'-to, tah], a. Bandy-legged.

perniciosamente [per-ne-the-o'-sah-men-tay], adv. Perniciously, noxiously, hurtfully.

pernicioso, sa [per-ne-the-oh'-so, sah], a. Pernicious, mischievous, destructive.

pernil [per-neel'], *m.* 1. Ham, shoulder of an animal, especially of pork. 2. Thigh of breeches; pantalets.

pernio [perr'-ne-o], *m.* A kind of hinges for doors and windows.

perniquebrar [per-ne-kay-brar'], *va.* To break the legs.

pernituerto, ta [per-ne-too-err'-to, tah], *a.* Crook-legged.

perno [perr'-no], *m.* 1. A round-headed pin; a large nail, a spike. 2. Hook of a hinge for doors and windows. 3. *(Mech.)* Joint pin, crank pin. 4. *(Naut.)* A bolt. **Perno de ojo**, eye-bolt. **Estar hasta el perno**, *(And.)* to be at the end of one's tether.

pernoctar [per-noc-tar'], *vn.* To pass the night: to be awake, to watch, or to sit up the whole night.

pero [pay'-ro], *m.* 1. A kind of apple. 2. Apple-tree.

pero, *conj.* But, except, yet (sin embargo). **Hizo muy mal, pero muy mal**, he was wrong, a thousand times wrong. **pero vamos a ver**, well, let's see. -*m.* Fault, defect. **He encontrado un pero**, I have found a snag.

perogrullada, or **verdad de perogrullo** [pay-ro-grool-lyah'-dah], *f.* Platitude, truism, truth of no moment and universally known.

perojimenez [pay-ro-he-may'-neth], *m.* A variety of grape and the wine made from it.

perol [pay-role'], *m.* Boiler, kettle, copper, *(Carib.)* Saucepan (cacerola); *(Cono Sur, Mex.)* Metal casserole dish; *(Carib.)* Kitchen utensil (útil).

perón [pay-rone'], *m. (Mex. Bot.)* V. PERO.

peroné [pay-ro-nay'], *m. (Anat.)* Fibula, perone, the lesser bone of the leg.

peroración [pay-ro-rah-the-on'], *f.* Peroration (discurso), he conclusion of an oration (conclusión).

perorar [pay-ro-rar'], *vn.* 1. To conclude a speech or oration. 2. To make an harangue or speech, to declaim. 3. To solicit effectually.

perorata [pay-ro-rah'-tah], *f. (coll.)* An harangue, a speech.

peróxido [pay-rok'-se-do], *m.* Peroxide, highest grade of oxide.

perpendicular [per-pen-de-coo-lar'], *a.* 1. Perpendicular. 2. At right angles (en ángulo recto). -*f.* Perpendicular; vertical.

perpendicularmente [per-pen-de-coo-lahr'-men-tay], *adv.* Perpendicularly.

perpendículo [per-pen-dee'-coo-lo], *m.* 1. Plumb, plummet: an instrument by which perpendicularity is discerned. 2. Pendulum.

perpetración [per-pay-trah-the-on'], *f.* Perpetration, the act of committing a crime.

perpetrador, ra [per-pay-trah-dor', rah], *m. & f.* Perpetrator, aggressor.

perpetrar [per-pay-trar'], *va.* To perpetrate, to commit a crime.

perpetua [per-pay'-too-ah], *f. (Bot.)* Eternal flower, everlasting, the blossom of goldilocks. **Perpetua encarnada**, *(Bot.)* globe amaranth.

perpetuación [per-pay-too-ah-the-on'], *f.* Perpetuation.

perpetuamente [per-pay'-too-ah-men-tay], *adv.* Perpetually, for ever.

perpetuán [per-pay-too-ahn'], *m.* Everlasting, a kind of woollen stuff.

perpetuar [per-pay-too-ar'], *va.* 1. To perpetuate. 2. To continue without cessation or intermission.

perpetuidad [per-pay-too-e-dahd'], *f.* 1. Perpetuity, duration. 2. Perpetuity, exemption from intermission or cessation. **Condena a perpetuidad**, life sentence.

perpetuo, tua [per-pay'-too-o, ah], *a.* Perpetual; everlasting; ceaseless.

perpiaño [per-po-ah'-nyo], *m.* Perpender, a front binding-stone in a wall.

perplejamente [per-play'-hah-men-tay], *adv.* Perplexedly, confusedly.

perplejidad [per-play-he-dahd'], *f.* Perplexity, irresolution, embarrassment.

perplejo, ja [per-play'-ho, hah], *a.* Doubtful, uncertain, perplexed. **Me miró perplejo**, he looked at me in perplexity.

perpunte [per-poon'-tay], *m.* A quilted under-waistcoat to protect the body from cutting weapons.

perquirir [per-ke-reer'], *va.* To seek diligently.

perra [perr'-rah], *f.* 1. A female dog; bitch, slut. **Perra salida**, a bitch in heat. 2. Drunkenness. 3. Slothfulness, laziness. 4. Tantrum, pet (rabieta). **El niño cogió una perra**, the child had a tantrum. 5. Mania (manía), crazy idea. **Le cogió la perra de ir a Eslobodia**, he got an obsession about going to Slobodia. 6. *(Cono Sur)* Old hat (sombrer∂); leather water bottle (cantimplora).

perrada [per-rah'-dah], *f.* 1. Pack of dogs (perros). 2. A false compliment. 3. Dirty trick (mala jugada).

perramente [per'-rah-men-tay], *adv.* Very ill; badly.

perrazo [per-rah'-tho], *m. aug.* A large dog.

perrengue [per-ren'-gay], *m. (coll.)* 1. One who is peevish; a snarler. 2. Negro.

perrera [per-ray'-rah], *f.* 1. Kennel, doghouse (de perros). 2. Drag, grind, fag, employment attended with much fatigue and little profit (trabajo). 3. *com.* A bad payer (mal pagador). 4. Mule or horse spent with age and cast off. 5. *(Carib.)* Row, shindy.

perrería [per-ray-ree'-ah], *f.* 1. Pack of dogs (perros). 2. Set or nest of rogues. 2. Expression or demonstration of vexation or wrath.

perrero [per-ray'-ro], *m.* 1. Dog-catcher (que recoge perros vagabundos). 2. Houndman, person whose business is to take care of hounds or dogs used in the chase. 3. One who is very fond of hounds and dogs. 4. Impostor, cheat.

perrezno, na [per-reth'-no, nah], *m. & f.* Whelp, puppy.

perrico [per-ree'-co], *m. dim.* A little dog.

perrillo [per-reel'-lyo], *m.* 1. *(dim.)* A little dog. **¡Perrillo de falda!**, lap-dog. 2. Trigger of a gun. 3. A semi-lunar piece of a hollers bridle.

perrito [per-ree'-to], *m. dim.* A little dog.

perro [per'-ro], *m.* 1. Dog. **Perro de aguas**, water-dog. **Perro de presa**, bull dog. **Perro de ayuda**, newfoundland dog, a large dog kept to defend his master. 2. One who obstinately asserts an opinion or perseveres in an undertaking. 3. Damage, loss, deception. 4. *(Met.)* Dog, name of contempt or ignominy pivot to a person. 5. *(And.)* Drowsiness. 6. *(Cono Sur)* Clothes peg. **Ponerse como un perro** or **hecho un perro**, to get into a vehement passion. **¡A otro perro con ese hueso!** tell that to the marines! **Perro viejo** (an old dog), a clever, experienced man. **Perro esquimal**, husky. **Perro lobo**, alsatian. **Perro del hortelano**, dog in the manger. **Tiempo de perros**, dirty weather. **Se llevan como perros y gatos**, they're always squabling, they fight like cat and dog. **Perro ladrador, poco mordedor**, his bark is worse than his bite. **Llevar una vida de perros**, to lead a dog's life. **Es un perro viejo**, he's an old fox. **A perro flaco todos on pulgas**, misfortunes rain upon the wretched. **A otro perro con ese hueso**, pull the other one. **Morir como un perro**, to die a forgotten man. **Perro sarnoso**, mangy cur. **Allí no atan los perros con longanizas**, money does not grow on trees there.

perroquete [per-ro-kay'-tay], *m. (Naut.)* Top-mast.

perruna [per-roo'-nah], *f.* Dog-bread, coarse bread for dogs.

perruno, na [per-roo'-no, nah], *a.* Doggish, canine; currish.

persa [perr'-sah], *a. & n.* Persian.

persecución [per-say-coo-the-on'], *f.* 1. Persecution. 2. Toils, troubles, fatigue, molestation.

perseguidor, ra [per-say-gee-dor', rah], *m. & f.* Persecutor; one who harasses or molests; a foe.

perseguimiento [per-say-gee-me-en'-to], *m.* Persecution; hunt.

perseguir [per-say-geer'], *va.* 1. To pursue a fugitive (fugitivo). 2. To dun, to importune, to beset. 3. To persecute, to pursue with malignity (propósito). 4. To persecute, to pursue, to importune much. **La persiguió durante 2 años**, he was after her for 2 years. **Le persigue la mala suerte**, he is dogged by ill luck. *(Yo persigo, persiga; él persiguió, persiguiera;* from *Perseguir. V.* PEDIR.

perseo [per-say'-o], *m. (Ast.)* Perscus, a northern constellation.

persevante [per-say-vahn'-tay], *m.* Pursuivant at arms.

perseverancia [per-say-vay-rahn'-the-ah], *f.* Perseverance, constancy.

perseverante [per-say-vay-rahn'-tay], *a.* Perseverant, persistent.

perseverantemente [per-say-vay-rahn'-tay-men-tay], *adv.* Constantly, perseverantly.

perseverar [per-say-vay-rar'], *vn.* To persevere, to persist, to abide.

persiana [per-se-ah'-nah], *f.* 1. Persienne, slatted shutter (postigo). 2. Blind (enrollable). **Persianas,** Venetian blinds.

persiano, na [per-se-ah'-no, nah], *a. & n.* Persian.

pérsico, ca [per'-se-co, cah], *a.* Persianan. Peach-tree and its fruit.

persignarse [per-sig-nar'-say], *vr.* 1. To make the sign of the cross. 2. To admire, to be surprised at a thing. 3. To handsel, to begin to sell; to make the first act of sale.

pérsigo [perr'-se-go], *m. (Bot.)* Peach.

persistencia [per-sis-ten'-the-ah], *f.* Persistence, steadiness, perseverance, obstinacy.

persistente [per-sis-ten'-tay], *pa. & a.* Permanent, firm, persistent.

persistir [per-sis-teer'], *vn.* To persist, to continue firm, to persevere.

persona [per-so'-nah], *f.* 1. Person, individual, or particular man or woman. 2. Person, the exterior appearance. 3. Personage, a distinguished character; a man of merit or talents. 4. *(Gram.)* Person, the quality of the noun that modifies the verb. 5. Person, man or Roman in a fictitious dialogue. **De persona a persona,** from person to person, from man to man. **En persona** or **por su persona,** personally, in person. **Es buena persona,** he's a good sort. **Tercera persona,** third party. **Pagaron 2 dólares por persona,** they paid 2 dollars a head.

personado [per-so-nah'-do], *m.* Benefice which confers a prerogative on the incumbent, yet without jurisdiction.

personaje [per-so-nah'-hay], *m.* 1. Personage, a man or woman of eminence. 2. Personage, character assumed, a disguised person, a stranger. 3. A kind of ecclesiastical benefice.

personal [per-so-nahl'], *a.* Personal, particular. *-m.* 1. Personnel (plantilla), staff; establishment (total); crew, complement. **2. El personal,** the people, the public. **Personal de una a oficina,** office personnel. **Estar falto de personal,** to be short-handed. **Había exceso de personal en el cine,** there were too many people in the cinema.

personalidad [per-so-nah-le-dahd'], *f.* 1. Personality, the personal existence of anyone. 2. Personality, reflection upon private actions or character. 3. Legal capacity for intervening in some business.

personalizar [per-so-nah-le-thar'], *va.* To fall into personalities in writing or talking. *-vr.* To show oneself a party at law. *-vn.* To make a personal reference.

personalmente [per-so-nahl-men-tay], *adv.* Personally, in person; hypostatically.

personarse [per-so-nar'-say], *vr.* 1. *V.* AVISTARSE. 2. To appear in person, to go personally. **El juez se personó en el lugar del accidente,** the judge went to the scene of the accident.

personaza [per-so-nah'-thah], *f. aug.* Huge personage.

personería [per-so-nay-ree'-ah], *f.* Charge or employment of an agent, deputy, or attorney.

personero, ra [per-so-nay'-ro, rah], *m. & f.* Deputy, agent, attorney, trustee, receiver.

personificación [per-so-ne-fe-cah-the-on'], *f.* Personification.

personificar [per-so-ne-fe-car'], *va.* To personify (encarnar), to personalize.

personilla [per-so-neel'-lyah], *f.* Mannikin, a ridiculous little fellow.

perspectiva [pers-pec-tee'-vah], *f.* 1. *(Art.)* Perspective, the science of perspective. 2. Work executed according to the rules of perspective. 3. View (vista), vista. 4. A deceitful appearance. **Buenas perspectivas de mejora,** good prospects. **Encontrarse ante la perspectiva de,** to be faced with the prospect of.

perspectivo [pers-pec-tee'-vo], *m.* Professor of perspective.

perspicacia, perspicacidad [pers-pe-cah'-the-ah], *f.* 1. Perspicaciousness, perspicacity, quickness of sight. 2. Perspicacity, clear-sightedness (agudeza de vista), keenness.

perspicaz [pers-pe-cath'], *a.* 1. Perspicacious, quick-sighted. 2. Acute, sagacious, clear-sighted.

perspicuamente [pers-pe-coo-ah-men'-tay] *adv.* Perspicuously.

perspicuidad [pers-pe-coo-e-dahd'], *f.* 1. Perspicuity, clearness, transparency. 2. Perspicuity, clearness to the mind, neatness of style.

perspicuo, cua [pers-pee'-coo-o, ah], *a.* 1. Perspicuous, clear, transparent. 2. Perspicuous, clear to the understanding: it is applied to him who writes with clearness and elegance, and to his style.

perspiración [pers-pe-rah-the-on'], *f.* Perspiration (sudor).

perspirar [pers-pe-rar'], *vn.* To perspire (sudar).

perspiratorio, ria [pers-pe-rah-to'-re-o' ah], *a.* Perspiratory.

persuadidor, ra [per-soo-ah-de-dor', rah], *m. & f.* Persuader.

persuadir [per-soo-ah-deer'], *va.* To persuade, to influence by argument or expostulation, to induce. **Dejarse persuadir,** to allow oneself to be persuaded. *-vr.* To be persuaded, to form a judgment or opinion; to be convinced.

persuasible [per-soo-ah-see'-blay], *a.* Persuasible, persuadable.

persuasión [per-soo-ah-se-on'], *f.* Persuasion, the act or state of being persuaded; opinion, judgment.

persuasiva [per-soo-ah-see'-vah], *f.* Persuasiveness, persuasive.

persuasivo, va [per-soo-ah-see'-vo, vah], *a.* Persuasive, moving.

persuasor, ra [per-soo-ah-sor', rah], *m. & f.* Persuader.

pertenecer [per-tay-nay-therr'], *vn.* 1. To belong to, to appertain, to concern. 2. To behoove, to become, to pertain; to relate to. **Pertenecer a,** to concern. *(Yo pertenezco, yo pertenezca,* from *Pertenecer. V.* ABORRECER.

pertenecido [per-tay-nay-thee'-do], *m. V.* PERTENENCIA. **Pertenecido, da,** *pp.* of PERTENECER.

perteneciente [per-tay-nay-the-en'-tay], *pa. & a.* 1. Belonging, appertaining. 2. Apt, fit, ready.

pertenencia [per-tay-nen'-the-ah], *f.* 1. Right of property; place or territory belonging to anyone. 2. Appurtenance, dependence; an accessory or appendage.

pértica [perr'-te-cah], *f.* Perch, a measure of 10 geometric feet (9.70 feet).

pértiga [perr'-te-gah], *f.* 1. A long pole or rod. 2. A tall, slender woman. 3. Hook on which a door or window is hung. 4. *V.* PÉRTICA.

pertigal [perr-te-gahl'], *m.* Pole. *V.* PÉRTIGA.

pértigo [perr'-te-go], *m.* Pole of a wagon or cart.

pertiguear [per-te-gay-ar'], *va.* To beat a tree with a pole to gather the fruit.

pertiguería [per-te-gah-ree'-ah], *f.* Office or employment of a verger.

pertiguero [per-te-gay'-ro], *m.* Verger, he that carries the mace before the dean.

pertinacia [per-te-nah'-the-ah], *f.* Pertinancy (obstinación), obstinacy, stubbornness, doggedness.

pertinaz [per-te-nath'], *a.* Pertinacious (persona), obstinate, opinionated, persistent (tos), pertinacy (obstinación).

pertinazmente [per-te-nath'-men-tay], *adv.* Pertinaciously, contumaciously.

pertinente [per-te-nen'-tay], *a.* Pertinent, related to the matter at hand; to the purpose. **No es pertinente hacerlo ahora**, this is not the appropriate time to do it.

pertinentemente [per-te-nen'-tay-men-tay], *adv.* Pertinently, opportunely, congruously.

pertrechar [per-tray-char'], *va.* 1. To supply a place with ammunition and warlike stores. 2. To dispose, to arrange, to prepare. *-vr.* To be provided with the necessary stores and tools for defense.

pertrechos [per-tray'-chos], *m. pl.* 1. Ammunition, arms, and other warlike stores. 2. Tools, instruments.

perturbable [per-toor-bah'-blay], *a.* Capable of being perturbed.

perturbación [per-toor-bah-the-on'], *f.* Perturbation (mental), disquiet of mind; confusion.

perturbadamente [per-toor-bah'-dah-men-tay], *adv.* Confusedly.

perturbado [per-toor-b-ah'-do], *a.* Mentally unbalanced. *-m. f.* Mentally unbalanced person.

perturbador, ra [per-toor-bah-dor', rah], *m. & f.* Perturbator, perturber, disturber, perturbatrix. *a.* 1. Perturning (noticia). 2. Unruly (conducta), subversive (movimiento).

perturbar [per-toor-bar'], *va.* 1. To perturb, to disturb (orden, calma); to interrupt, to harrow. 2. *(Med.)* To upset, to disturb; to perturb (mentalmente).

peruano, na [pay-roo-ah'-no, nah], *a.* Peruvian, of Peru.

peruétano [pay-roo-ay'-tah-no], *m.* 1. *(Bot.)* Wild or choke pear-tree. 2. Anything that overtops or rises above the rest. *-a. (And. Carib. Mex.)* Boring, tedious; stupid.

perulero, ra [pay-roo-lay'-ro, rah], *a.* 1. One who has come from Peru to Spain. 2. *m.* A wealthy man. *(Cf.* INDIANO.) 4. A narrow-bottomed and strait-mouthed pitcher.

peruviano [pay-roo-ve-ah'-no], *m.* Peruvian balsam.

perversamente [per-ver'-sah-men-tay], *adv.* Perversely, malevolently.

perversidad [per-ver-se-dahd'], *f.* Perversity (cualidad), obstinate wickedness, malignity.

perversión [per-ver-se-on'], *f.* 1. Perversion, the act of perverting. 2. Perversion, perverseness, depravation, corruption.

perverso, sa [per-verr'-so, sah], *a.* Perverse, extremely wicked, mischievous.

pervertido, da [per-ver-tee'-do], *a. m & f.* Perverted, deviant.

pervertidor, ra [per-ver-te-dor', rah], *m. & f.* Perverter, corrupter.

pervertimiento [per-ver-te-me-en'-to], *m.* Perversion, act of perverting.

pervertir [per-ver-teer'], *va.* 1. To pervert, to distort from the true end (texto). 2. To pervert, to corrupt, to turn from the right. 3. To seduce from the true doctrine and faith. *-vr.* To become corrupted or depraved. *(Yo pervierto, yo pervierta; él pervirtió, pervirtiera,* from *Pervertir. V.* ADHERIR.)

pervigilio [per-ve-lee'-he-o], *m. (Med.)* Vigilance, pervigilium, watching, want of sleep, restlessness.

pervulgar [per-vool-gar'], *va.* 1. To divulge, to make public. 2. *(Acad.)* To promulgate.

peryodato [per-yo-dah'-to], *m. (Chem.)* Periodate.

peryoduro [per-yo-doo'-ro], *m.* Periodide, an iodide containing more iodine than a protoiodide.

pesa [pay-sah], *f.* 1. Weight, a piece of a determined weight. 2. Piece of metal suspended from clocks. 3. A counterweight. **Pesa de una romana**, weight or drop-ball of a steel yard.

pesada [pay-sah'-dah], *f. (Com.)* Quantity weighed at once.

pesadamente [pay-sah'-dah-men-tay], *adv.* 1. Heavily, weightily, ponderously, cumbrously. 2. Sorrowfully, grievously. 3. Slowly (lentamente), tardily, lazily.

pesadez [pay-sah-deth'], *f.* 1. Heaviness, the quality of being heavy (peso). 2. Gravity, weight tendency to the center. 3. Slowness (lentitud), sluggishness, drowsiness. 4. Peevishness, fretfulness. 5. Excess, abundance. 6. Trouble,

pain, fatigue (fatiga). 7. Obesity, corpulence. **Es una pesadez tener que…**, it's a bore having to…

pesadilla [pay-sah-deel'-lyah], *f.* 1. Nightmare. 2. *(Fig.)* Worry, obsession, bogey. **Ese equipo es nuestra pesadilla**, that is our bogey team.

pesado, da [pay-sah'-do, dah], *a.* 1. Heavy, ponderous, massive. 2. Deep, profound (used of sleep). 3. Peevish, fretful, troublesome, violent; cumbersome, cumbrous. 4. Tedious (persona), wearisome, tiresome, dull, fastidious. 5. Offensive, causing pain, injurious; oppressive. 6. Lazy, clumsy, tardy, sluggish. 7. Fat, gross, corpulent. 8. Hard, insufferable, mischievous. **Día pesado**, a cloudy, gloomy day. **Tener el estómago pesado**, to feel full up. **Esto se hace pesado**, this is becoming tedious. *-pp.* of PESAR. *-m & f.* 1. Boring person (aburrido), bore; loud mouth (fanfarrón). 2. *(Carib. Fig.)* Big shot.

pesador, ra [pay-sah-dor', rah], *m.* 1. Weigher, one who weighs. 2. *(And. CAm. Carib.)* Butcher.

pesadumbre [pay-sah-doom'-bray], *f.* 1. Heaviness, weightiness, gravity. 2. Quarrel, dispute, contest. 3. Grief, trouble, displeasure, affliction, pain, disgust.

pesalicores [pay-sah-le-co'-res], *m.* Hydrometer, areometer.

pésame [pay'-sah-may], *m.* Compliment of condolence.

pesamentero, ra [pay-sah-men-tay'-ro, rah], *m. & f. (Mex.)* One who under pretext of condolence gets into a house to sponge for meals.

pesante [pay-sahn'-tay], *m.* A weight of half a drachm.

pesantez [pay-san-teth'], *f.* Gravity, the force of gravity.

pesar [pay-sar'], *m.* 1. Sorrow, grief (tristeza), concern, repentance. 2. The saying or deed which causes sorrow or displeasure. **Con gran pesar mío**, much to my sorrow. **pesar (A)** [ah-pay-sar'], *adv.* In spite of, notwithstanding. **A pesar de**, in spite of.

pesar [pay-sar'], *vn.* 1. To weigh, to be of weight (tener peso). 2. To weigh, to be considered as important, to be valuable. 3. To repent, to be sorry for (arrepentirse). 4. To prevail, to preponderate. 5. To weigh heavily (resultar pesado). 6. To count for a lot (opinión). 7. *(And. CAm.)* To sell meat. *-va.* 1. To weigh (peso), to ascertain the weight of a thing. 2. To weigh (examinar), to examine, to consider. 3. *(Naut.)* To use the lead for establishing the exact position which any piece of the ship should have. **Mal que le pese**, *(coll.)* in spite of him. **Me pesa el abrigo**, the coat weighs me down. **Pesar las responsabilidades**, to weigh up one's chances. **Pese a las dificultades**, in spite of the difficulties. **Pesa 5 kilos**, it weighs 5 kilos. **Ese paquete no pesa**, that parcel isn't heavy.

pesario [pay-sah'-re-o], *m.* Pessary, an instrument worn in the vagina to correct a displacement of the womb.

pesaroso, sa [pay-sah-ro'-so, sah], *a.* 1. Sorrowful, full of repentance. 2. Restless, uneasy.

pesca [pes'-cah], *f.* 1. Fishing, angling. 2. Fish, in the natural state in the water. **Pesca con arpón**, spear fishing. **Pesca de altura**, deep-sea fishing. **Allí la pesca es muy buena**, the fishing is very good there.

pescadazo [pes-cah-dah'-tho], *m. aug.* Great fish.

pescadera [pes-cah-day'-rah], *f.* Fish woman.

pescadería [pes-cah-day-ree'-ah], *f.* Fish-market (mercado); fish shop (tienda).

pescadero, ra [pes-cah-day'-ro], *m & f.* Fishmonger (by retail).

pescadilla [pes-cah-deel'-lah], *f.* Whiting; small hake.

pescadillo [pes-cah-deel'-lyo], *m. dim.* A little flab.

pescado [pes-cah'-do], *m.* 1. Fish, chiefly that which is fit for food. *(Pescado* is a fish when caught; in the water, uncaptured, it is a *pez.)* 2. Codfish when salted. 3. Foodfishes. 4. *(And. Cono Sur)* Secret police. **Día** or **comida de pescado**, a fish-day, or fasting fare, though not of fish. **Pescado, da**, *pp.* of PESCAR.

pescador [pes-cah-dor'], *m.* 1. Fisherman, fisher, angler (de caña). 2. Fish having a pouch under the jaws to catch others. **Pescador, ra**, is used also adjectively.

pescadora [pes-cah-do'-rah], *f.* Fish-wife, fish-woman, a woman that sells fish; the wife of a fisher.

pescante [pes-cahn'-tay], *m.* 1. Crane, an instrument for raising heavy weights. 2. Coach-box (de carruaje). 3. Machine used in shifting the decorations on the stage. **Pescante de bote**, *(Naut.)* a davit. **Pescante de ancla**, fish-davit.

pescar [pes-car'], *va.* 1. To fish, to angle, to catch fish (coger). 2. To pick up anything. 3. To take one at his word, to catch in the act. 4. To obtain one's end. 5. To land, to get (lograr), to manage; to grasp (significado). 6. To catch (persona). -*vn.* 1. To fish, to go fishing. 2. **La chica viene a ver si pesca**, the girl is coming to see if she can get hitched. 3. *(And. Cono Sur)* To nod, to doze. **Viene a pescar un marido**, she's come to get herself a husband. **Logró pescar unos cuantos datos**, he managed to bring up a few facts.

péscola [pes'-co-lah], *f.* The beginning of a furrow in a ploughed field.

pescozada [pes-co-thah'-dah], *f. V.* PESCOZÓN.

pescozón [pes-co-thone'], *m.* Blow on the neck or head with the hand.

pescozudo, da [pes-co-thoo'-do, dah], *a.* Having a thick neck.

pescuezo [pes-coo-ay'-tho], *m.* 1. The neck. 2. Stiff-necked haughtiness, loftiness, or pride. **Sacar el pescuezo**, to be haughty, to be elated. **Poner a uno el pie sobre el pescuezo**, to humiliate one.

pescuño [pes-coo'-nyo], *m.* Large wedge for fastening the coulter of a plough.

pesebre [pay-say'-bray], *m.* Crib, rack, or manager (cuadra).

pesebrejo [per-say-bray'-ho], *m.* Cavity in which horses' teeth are fixed.

pesebrera [pay-say-bray'-rah], *f.* Range of mangers in a stable.

pesebrón [pay-say-brone'], *m.* Boot of a coach.

peseta [pay-say'-tah], *f.* Peseta (moneda española). **Arrojar la peseta**, to be sick, to vomit.

pesetero [pay-say-tay'-ro], *a.* 1. Money-grubbing (avaro), mercenary. 2. *(Mex.)* Small-time (comerciante). 3. *(Carib.)* Mean (tacaño).

pesga [pes'-gah], *f.* Weight. *V.* PESA and PESO.

pesiar [pay-se-ar'], *vn.* To utter curses or execrations.

pesillo [pay-seel'-lyo], *m.* Small scales for weighing gold or silver coin.

pésimamente [pay'-se-mah-men-tay], *adv. super.* Very badly.

pesimismo [pay-se-mees'-mo], *m.* 1. Pessimism, condition of a pessimist. 2. A system of German philosophy which considers existence as an evil.

pesimista [pay-se-mees'-tah], *m & f.* Pessimist, one who looks at the dark side of things.

pésimo, ma [pay'-se-mo, mah], *a. super.* Very bad. **Lo hiciste pésimo**, *(Mex.)* you did it terribly.

pesita [pay-see'-tah], *f. dim.* A small.

peso [pay'-so], *m.* 1. Weight, gravity, heaviness. 2. Weight, importance. 3. Weight or power of reason. 4. Peso, monetary currency of many South American countries (moneda). 5. Burden. 6. Judgment, good sense. 7. Weighty object (objeto). 8. Weight (boxeo). 9. Heavy feeling (modorra). 10. Scales, balance, weghing machine. **Caerse de su peso**, to go without saying. **Peso ligero**, lightweight. **Peso medio**, middleweight. **Peso pluma**, featherweight. **El peso de los años**, the weight of the years. **Razones de peso**, good reasons. **Vender a peso**, to sell by weight. **Pesos y medidas**, weights and measures.

pésol [pay'-sole], *m.* French bean. *V.* FRISOL.

pespuntador, ra [pes-poon-tah-dor', rah], *m. & f.* Back-stitcher.

pespuntar [pes-poon-tar'], *va.* To back-stitch, to sew with a back seam.

pespunte [pes-poon'-tay], *m.* Back-stitching, back seam.

pesquera [pes-kay'-rah], *f.* Fishery, a place for catching fish.

pesquería [pes-kay-ree'-ah], *f.* 1. Trade or calling of a fisherman. 2. Act of fishing. 3. Fishery.

pesquero [pes-kay'-ro], *a.* Fishing. -*m.* Fishing boat.

pesquisa [pes-kee'-sah], *f.* Investigation (indagación), inquiry, examination. -*m.* Policeman.

pesquisante [pes-ke-sahn'-tay], *pa.* Investigating; inquirer.

pesquisar [pes-ke-sar'], *va.* To inquire, to examine, to investigate.

pesquisador, ra [pes-ke-sa-dor', rah], *m. & f.* Examiner, searcher, inquirer. **Juez pesquisador**, a magistrate appointed to inquire into the circumstances of a violent death.

pestaña [pes-tah'-nyah], *f.* 1. Eye-lash (de ojo). 2. Fag-end of a piece of linen. 3. Fringe, edging. **No pegué pestaña**, I didn't get a wink of sleep. **Pestaña de protección contra grabación**, *(Comput.)* write-protect notch.

pestañear [pes-tah-nyay-ar'], *va.* To wink, to blink. **No pestañear** or **sin pestañear**, to look with the eyes fixed, not to wink.

pestañeo [pes-tah-nyay'-o], *m.* Winking, blinking.

peste [pes'-tay], *f.* 1. Pest, plague, pestilence. 2. Pest, anything troublesome, vexatious or mischievous. 3. Corruption of manners. 4. Foul smell. 5. *(coll.)* Great plenty or abundance. 6. *(And. Carib.)* Bubonic plague. 7. *(Cono Sur)* Smallpox (viruela). 8. *(And.)* Cold (resfrío). 9. *(Cono Sur)* Infectious disease (enfermedad). **Peste negra**, black Death. **Una peste de ratones**, a plague of mice. -*pl.* Words of menace.

pesticida [pes-te-thee'-dah], *m.* Pesticide.

pestíferamente [pes-tee'-fay-rah-men-tay], *adv.* Pestiferously, pestilently.

pestífero, ra [pes-tee'-fay-ro, rah], *a.* 1. Pestiferous (dañino), causing much damage. 2. Applied to anything extremely bad or mischievous. 3. Foul smelling.

pestilencia [pes-te-len'-the-ah], *f.* Pest, plague, pestilence (plaga).

pestilencial [pes-te-len-the-ahl'], *a.* Pestiferous, pestilential, infectious, contagious, destructive.

pestilencioso, sa [pes-te-len-the-o'-so, sah], *a.* Pestilential.

pestilente [pes-te-len'-tay], *a.* Pestilent (dañino), pernicious. *V.* PESTIFERO.

pestillo [pes-teel'-lyo], *m.* 1. Bolt, for a door. 2. Bolt of a look.

pestiño [pes-tee'-nyo], *m.* Fritter or pancake.

pestorejazo [pes-to-ray-hah'-tho], *m. V.* PESCOZÓN.

pestorejo [pes-to-ray'-ho], *m.* The posterior fleshy part of the neck.

pestorejón [pes-to-ray-hone'], *m.* Blow on the back of the neck.

pesuña [pes-soo'-nyah], *f.* Solid hoof of graminivorous animals.

pesuño [pes-soo'-nyo], *m.* Hoof of cloven-footed animals.

petaca [pe-tah'-cah], *f.* 1. A trunk or chest covered with hides or leather; a covered hamper. 2. A case for keeping cigars or fine-cut tobacco (de cigarrillos). 3. *(CAm. Mex. Anat.)* Hump. -*m & f.* 1. *(LAm.)* Short squat person (rechoncho). 2. Lazy person (vago).

petaláceo, cea [pay-tah-lah'-thay-o, ah], *a. (Bot.)* Petalaceous, petalous.

petalismo [pay-tah-lees'-mo], *m.* Petalism, banishment in Syracuse, by writing the name on a leaf.

pétalo [pay'-tah-lo], *m. (Bot.)* Petal, flower-leaf.

petaquilla [pay-tah-keel'-lyah], *f.* Hamper covered with hides or leather; a small trunk.

petar [pay-tar'], *va. (coll.)* To please, to gratify, to content.

petardear [pay-tar-day-ar'], *va.* 1. To bend down a gate or door with petards. 2. To cheat (estafar), to deceive, to gull, by borrowing and not paying.

petardero [pay-tar-day'-ro], *m.* 1. A gunner whose duty consists in landing, fixing, and firing petards. 2. Impostor, cheat, swindler.

petardista [pay-tar-dees'-tah], *com.* 1. Deceiver, defrauder, a cheat, an impostor. 2. Swindler.

petardo [pay-tar'-do], *m.* 1. Petard, a warlike engine. 2. Cheat, fraud, imposition, gull, hoax, scurvy trick, disappointment. **Ser un petardo**, to be dead boring.

petate [pay-tah'-tay], *m.* 1. Fine sort of mat made of palm; used for a sleeping-mat by the natives in South America and the Philippines (para dormir). 2. Impostor, swindler, extorter (estafador). 3. *(Prov.)* A good for-nothing fellow, a despicable person, poor devil (pobre hombre). **Liar el petate**, *(coll.)* to pack up one's duds, to move away or be dismissed.

petequia [pay-tay-ke'-ah], *f. (Med.)* Petechia, spot on the skin in malignant fevers.

petequial [pay-tay-ke-ahl'], *a.* Petechial, pestilentially spotted.

petición [pay-te-the-on'], *f.* 1. Petition, the act of asking. 2. Petition, single branch or article of a prayer. 3. Demand, claim, request. 4. *(Law.)* Petition, the writing with which one juridically demands before the judge; prayer annexed to a judicial declaration produced in court. **Petición de aumento de salarios**, demand for higher wages. **Petición de divorcio**, petition for divorce. **"Petición de emisión" (RTS)**, *(Comput.)* "request to send" (RTS).

peticionario, ria [pay-tee-the-on-ah'-re-o, ah], *m. & f.* Petitioner. (Used also as an adjective.)

petillo [pay-teel'-lo], *m. dim.* A small stomacher; a breast jewel.

petimetra [pay-te-may'-trah], *f.* A belle, a smart lady.

petimetre [pay-te-may'-tray], *m.* Fop, coxcomb, beau.

petirrojo [pay-teer-ro'-ho], *m. (Orn.)* Robin-redbreast.

petitoria [pay-te-to'-re-ah], *f. V.* PETICIÓN.

petitorio, ria [pay-te-to'-re-o, ah], *a.* Petitory, petitionary.

petitorio [pay-te-to'-re-o], *a.* Impertinent and repeated petition.

peto [pay'-to], *m.* 1. Breastplate. 2. Plastron used by fencers. 3. Dickey, false shirt or blouse front.

petraria [pay-trah'-re-ah], *f.* Ancient machine for throwing stones.

petrarquista [pay-trar-kees'-tah], *a. & m.* Follower of Petrarch.

pétreo, a [pay'-tray-o, ah], *a.* 1. Rooky. 2. Stony, of stone, hard, inflexible.

petrera [pay-tray'-rah], *f. (Prov.)* Battle fought with stones.

petricación [pay-tre-fe-cah-the-on'], *f.* Petrification.

petrificado [pay-tre-fe-cah'-do], *a.* Petrified.

petrificante [pay-tre-fe-cahn'-tay], *pa.* Petrifying.

petrificar [pay-tre-fe-car'], *va.* To petrify, to change to stone. -*vr.* To petrify, to become stone.

petróleo [pay-tro'-lay-o], *m.* Petroleum, oil.

petrolero, ra [pay-tro-lay'-ro, rah], *a.* Petroleum. **Flota petrolera**, tanker fleet. -*m.* 1. Arsonist. 2. Oil tanker. -*m. & f.* Dealer in oil.

petrolífero, ra [pay-tro-lee'-fay-ro, rah], *a.* Oil-bearing.

petroquímica [pay-tro-kee'-me-cah], *f.* Petrochemistry.

petroso, sa [pay-tro'-so, sah], *a.* Rocky.

petulancia [pay-too-lahn'-the-ah], *f.* Petulance, insolence, flippancy, pertness.

petulante [pay-too-lahn'-tay], *a.* Petulant, insolent, flippant, pert.

petunia [pay-too'-ne-ah], *f. (Bot.)* Petunia.

peucédano [pay-oo-thay'-dah-no], *m. (Bot.)* Sulphur-wort.

peyorativo, va [pay-yo-rah-tee'-vo, vah], *a.* Depreciatory, disparaging (mostly as regards morals).

pez [peth], *f.* Pitch, tar. **Pez griega**, rosin, colophony. **Pez naval**, a mixture of pitch, rosin, tallow, etc., melted for applying to ships.

pez [peth], *m.* 1. Fish: a generic term; the zoological class of fishes among vertebrate animals. *Cf.* PESCADO. 2. Fish, a name common to all fresh-water fishes when they are small and eatable. **Pez colorado**, or **de color**, the goldfish, golden carp. **Pez espada**, swordfish. **Pez martillo**, the hammer-headed shark. **Pez sapo**, the toad-fish. **Pez sierra**, the saw-fish. **Pez volador**, the flying fish. 3. *(Acad.)* Catch, haul; anything advantageous which has cost toil or solicitude.

Picar el pez, to be entrapped or deceived. **Salga pez o salga rana**, hit or miss.

pezolada [pay-tho-lah'-dah], *f.* Threads at the fag-end of cloth.

pezón [pay-thone'], *m.* 1. *(Bot.)* Stem of fruits, leaf-stalk or flower-stalk. 2. Nipple, teat, dug. 3. Arm of an axle-tree; end of a vertical beam in paper mills.

pezonera [pay-tho-nay'-rah], *f.* 1. Nipple-shield. 2. Linch-pin.

pezpita *f.* **pezpítalo**, *m.* [peth-pee'-tah, peth-pee'-tah-lo], *(Orn.)* Wagtail.

pezuelo [pay-thoo-ay'-lo], *m.* The beginning of cloth where the warp is knotted, in order to commence the weaving.

pezuña [pay-thoo'-nyah], *f.* 1. Nose-worm, a disease incident to sheep. 2. *V.* PESUÑA. 3. *(And. Mex.)* Dirt hardened on the feet.

pez vela [peth vay'-lah], *m.* Sailfish.

piache, or **tarde piache** [pe-ah'-chay]. Too late, act of coming or being late.

piada [pe-ah'-dah], *f.* 1. Chirping of birds, puling of chickens. 2. Mimicking of another's voice.

piador, ra [pe-ah-dor', rah], *m. & f.* One who pules like a chicken or chirps like a bird.

piadosamente [pe-ah-do'-sah-men-tay], *adv.* Piously, holily, clemently, mercifully, faithfully.

piadoso, sa [pe-ah-do'-so, sah], *a.* 1. Pious, godly, mild, merciful, clement. 2. Reasonable, moderate.

piafar, [pe-ah-far'], *vn.* To paw, to stump (caballos).

piale [pe-ah'-lay], *m. (Amer.)* A cast of the lasso about the legs of the animal to be caught.

piamáter [pe-ah-mah'-ter], *f.* Piamater, membrane covering the brain.

piamente [pee'-ah-men-tay], *adv.* In a mild manner, piously.

pián, pián [pe-ahn', pe-ahn'], *adv.* One foot after another rising and falling; with precaution.

pian piano [pe-ahn' pe-ah'-no], *adv.* Gently, softly.

pianista [pe-ah-nees'-tah], *com.* Pianist, a performer upon the pianoforte. -*m.* 1. A pianoforte-maker. 2. One who sell pianos.

piano, or **pianoforte** [pe-ah'-no, pe-ah-no-for'-tay], *m.* Piano, pianoforte. **Piano de cola**, a grand piano. **Tocar el piano**, to play the piano. **Piano mécanico**, pianola.

pianola [pe-ah-no'-lah], *f.* Pianola, player piano.

piante [pe-ahn'-tay], *pa.* Peeping.

piar [pe-ar'], *vn.* 1. To peep, to pule, to cry like a chicken, to chirp as a bird. 2. To call, to whine, to cry or wish for anything with anxiety. **Piar por**, to cry for.

piara [pe-ah'-rah], *f.* 1. Herd of swine. 2. Drove of mares or mules. 3. *(Prov.)* Flock of ewes.

piariego, ga [pe-ah-re-ay'-go, gah], *a.* Applied to a person who has a herd of mares, mules, or swine.

pica [pee'-cah], *f.* 1. Pike, a long lance. 2. A bullfighter's javelin. 3. *(Med.)* Pica, a depraved appetite for things unfit for food, as chalk, etc. **A pica seca**, with great labor and without utility. 4. Spades (naipes). -*m.* Inspector (de autobús).

picacero, ra [pe-cah-thay'-ro, rah], *a.* Applied to birds of prey that chase magpies.

picacureba [pa-cah-co-ray'-bah], *f.* Brazilian pigeon.

picacho [pe-cah'—cho], *m.* Top, summit; sharp point of any thing.

picada [pe-cah'-dah], *f.* Puncture, incision made by pricking. *Picadas, (Her.)* birds whose beak is of a different enamelling.

picadero [pe-cah-day'-ro], *m.* 1. Riding-house (escuela), riding-school. 2. Block, boat skid; *(Naut.)* stock-block. 3. Stamping-ground of a buck in rutting time.

picadillo [pe-cah-deel'-lyo], *m.* Minced meat, hash.

picado, da [pe-cah'-do, dah], *a. & pp.* of PICAR. 1. Pricked (material). 2. Minced (carne). 3. Choppy (mar). 4. **Estar picado**, to be offended (enojado).

picado [pe-cah'-do], *m.* Minced meet, hash.

picador [pe-cah-dor'], *m.* 1. Horse-breaker (caballos). 2. "Picador" (toros), horseman armed with a spear to fight the bull. 3. Pricker. 4. Block on which meat is chopped.

picadura [pe-cah-doo'-rah], *f.* 1. The act of pricking. 2. Puncture, a wound made by pricking (pinchazo). 3. Ornamental gusset in clothes. 4. Bite of on animal or bird.

picaflor [pi-cab-flor'], *m. (Orn.)* Humming-bird. This bird is known also by the names of *Colibrí, Pájaro mosca,* and (in Mexico) *Chupa mirtos. V.* CHUPA FLORES.

picamaderos [pe-cah-mah-day'-ros], *m.* Woodpecker.

picante [pe-cahn'-tay], *pa. & a.* Pricking, piercing, stinging, sharp (comentario); piquant, high-seasoned, acrid, hot (comida, sabor).

picante [pe-cahn'-tay], *m.* 1. Piquancy, pungency, acrimony; keen satire. 2. *(Amer.)* Dish with red-pepper sauce.

picantemente [pe-cahn'-tay-men-tay], *adv.* Piquantly.

picapedrero [pe-cah-pay-dray'-ro], *m.* Stone-cutter.

picapleitos [pe-cah-play'-tos], *m. (coll.)* A litigious person: a pettifogging lawyer.

picaporte [pe-cah-por'-tay], *m.* A kind of picklock or latchkey (pestillo).

picaposte [pe-cah-pos'-tay], *m. V.* PICAMADEROS.

picapuerco [pe-cah-poo-err'-co], *m. (Orn.)* Bird of the woodpecker kind.

picar [pe-car'], *va.* 1. To prick with a pointed instrument (perforar). 2. To prick, to pierce with a small puncture. 3. To sting (insecto), pierce, or wound with a point darted out, as that of wasps or scorpions. 4. To mince or chop anything fine, to break into small pieces. 5. To peck like birds. 6. To nibble, to pick up or bite a little at a time: to eat squeamishly. 7. To nibble at the bait, as fish (pez). 8. To begin to get customers and thrive in business. 9. To pursue or harass an enemy. 10. To itch, to smart. 11. To burn or irritate the palate (paladar). 12. To prick, to spur (caballo), to goad, to incite, to stimulate. 13. To spur a hole. 14. To pique, to vex, to provoke with words or actions (provocar). 15. To tame a horse. 16. Joined with *en,* to begin to operate, or have effect. 17. To burn, to scorch. *-vr.* 1. To be offended or vexed, to be piqued (persona). 2. To be moth-eaten, to be damaged. 3. To begin to rot (fruta). 4. To be elated with pride. 5. *(Met.)* To be deceived. 6. To be in heat (animales). 7. To fret, to be angry, to be peevish. **Picar el anzuelo,** to bite the hook. **Picar la carne,** to chop meat. **El sol pica,** the sun scorches. **Picar muy alto,** to aim too high. **Le pican los celos,** he is feeling pangs of jealousy. **Picar en,** to peck at. **Yo no pico en esas cosas,** I don't dabble in such things. **Ha picado mucha gente,** lots of people have fallen for it. **Me pican los ojos,** my eyes hurt. **El que se pica, ajos come,** if the cap fits, wear it. **Le pica la conciencia,** his conscience pricks him.

pícaramente [pee-cah-rah-men-tay], *adv.* Knavishly, roguishly,

picarazo, za [pe-cah-rah'-tho, thah], *a.* Great rogue.

picardear [pe-car-day-ar'], *vn.* To play the knave.

picardía [pe-car-dee'-ah], *f.* 1. Knavery, roguery: deceit, malice, foulness, a wanton trick, wantoness. 2. Lewdness. 3. Meeting of rogues. **Le gusta decir picardías a la gente,** he likes saying naughty things to people.

picardihuela [pe-car-de-oo-ay'-lah], *f.* A prank, a roguish trick.

picaresca [pe-cah-res'-cah], *f.* A nest of rougues, meeting of knaves.

picaresco, ca, picaril [pe-cah-res'-co, cah, pe-cah-reel'], *a.* Roguish (travieso), knavish.

picarillo [pe-cah-reel'-lyo], *m. dim.* A little rogue.

pícaro, ra [pee'-cah-ro, rah], *a.* 1. Knavish, roguish, vile, low. 2. Mischievous, malicious, crafty, sly (taimado), naughty (travieso). 3. Merry, guy. *-m. & f.* Rogue, knave, villain (granuja), loafer.

picaros [pee'-cah-ros], *m. pl.* Scullions, kitchen-boys.

picarón [pe-cah-rone'], *a. & m. aug.* 1. Great rogue (granuja), villain. 2. *(And. Cono Sur, Mex.)* Fritter.

picaronazo, za [pe-cah-ro-nah'-tho, thah], *a. aug.* Very roguish, villainous.

picarote [pe-cah-ro'-tay], *a. aug.* Subtle, crafty; notorious villain.

picarrelincho [pe-car-ray-leen'-cho], *m. (Orn.) V.* AGUZANIEVE.

picatoste [pe-cah-tos'-tay], *m.* Toast of bread fried with slices of ham.

picaza [pe-cah'-thah], *f.* 1. *(Orn.)* Magpie, commonly called *urraca.* 2. *(Prov.)* Hoe for clearing the ground of weeds.

picazo [pe-cah'-tho], *m.* 1. Blow with a pike. 2. Sting of an insect, stroke with the beak of a bird. 3. Young magpie.

picazón [pe-cah-thone'], *m.* 1. Itching, prurience, itch. 2. Peevishness, fretfulness. 3. *(Fig.)* Annoyance (disgusto), pique; uneasy feeling (remordimiento).

pícea [pee'-thay-ah], *f. (Bot.)* Silver fir.

pichel [pe-chel'], *m.* Pewter tankard, a mug. *(Mex.)* Pitcher.

pichelería [pe-chay-lay-ree'-ah], *f.* Factory of tankards or tin pots.

pichelero [pe-chay-lay'-ro], *m.* Maker of pewter pots or tankards.

pichelete [pe-chay-lay'-tay], *m. dim.* A small tankard or mug.

pichiciago [pe-che-the-ab'-go], *m. (Zool.)* A burrowing animal of Chile, having the back covered with curious defensive plates, called also CLAMIFORO.

pichón [pe-chone'], *m.* 1. A young pigeon. 2. *(Coll.)* Darling (hombre). 3. *(Mex. Coll.)* Pushover. 4. *(LAm.)* Novice (novato), greenhorn. **Tiro de pichón,** trapshooting.

picnic [peek'-neek], *m.* 1. Picnic (excursión). 2. Picnic basket (cesta).

picnostilo [pec-nos-tee'-lo], *m. (Arch.)* Too little space between columns.

pico [pee'-co], *m.* 1. Beak of a bird, bill, bib. 2. A sharp point of any kind. 3. A pickle. 4. Twibill, an iron tool used by paviers. 5. Dock-spade, a spade with a long crooked bill. 6. Spout of a jar or any similar vessel (de jarra). 7. The beak iron of an anvil. 8. Peak, top, or summit of a hill. 9. Balance of an account, small odds. 10. Mouth. 11. Loquacity, garrulity. 12. *(Orn.)* Woodpecker (especie). 13. A weight of 137 1/2 pounds used in the Philippine Islands. 14. Talkativeness (labia). 15. Spade (naipes). 16. *(And. CAm. Mex.)* Kiss (beso). 17. Fix, shot (droga). **Pico de oro,** a man of great eloquence. **Tener mucho pico,** to talk too much and divulge secrets. **Perder por el pico,** to lose by too much chattering. **Lo tengo en el pico de la lengua,** I have it on the tip of my tongue. **Darse el pico,** to kiss (besar). **Son las 3 y pico,** it's just after 3. **Irse del pico,** to talk too much.

picolete [pe-co-lay'-tay], *m.* Staple for the bolt of a lock.

picón, na [pe-cone', nah], *a.* 1. Applied to animals with the upper teeth projecting over the under ones; or to cattle nipping the grass the contrary way for want of teeth. 2. *(And. Carib.)* Cheeky (respondón). 3. *(And. Carib.)* Touchy (quisquilloso). 4. *(Carib.)* Mocking.

picón [pe-cone'], *m.* 1. Lampoon or nipping jest employed to induce another to do or perform something. 2. A sort of very small charcoal used in braziers. 3. Small fresh-water fish. 4. *(Prov.)* Broken rice.

piconero [pe-co-nay'-ro], *m.* Maker of small charcoal for braziers.

picor [pe-cor'], *m.* 1. The pungent taste left by anything which is hot or piquant. 2. Itching in a part of the body.

picoso, sa [pe-co'-so, sah], *a.* Pitted with the small-pox.

picota [pe-so'-tah], *f.* 1. A kind of pillar or gibbet on which the heads of those who have been hanged are exposed. 2. A kind of pillory. 3. *(Naut.)* Cheek of a pump. 4. Top or peak of a mountain. 5. Point of a turret or steeple.

picotada [pe-co-tah'-dah], *f. V.* PICOTAZA.

picotazo [pe-co-tah'-tho], *m.* Stroke with the beak of a bird.

picote [pe-co'-tay], *m.* 1. Coarse stuff made of goat's hair. 2. A glossy silk stuff.

picoteado, da [pe-co-tay-ah'-do, dah], *a.* Peaked, having many points or angles. *-pp.* of PICOTEAR.

picotear [pe-co-tay-ar'], *va.* To strike with the beak. *-vn.* 1. To gossip. 2. To toss the head (caballo). 3. To nibble, to pick (comer). *-vr.* To wrangle or quarrel (mujeres).

picotería [pe-co-tay-ree'-ah], *f.* Loquacity, volubility, gossip.

picotero, ra [pe-co-tay'-ro, rah], *a.* Wrangling, chattering, prattling.

picotillo [pe-co-teel'-lyo], *m.* Interior cloth of goat's hair.

picrato [pe-crah'-to], *m.* Picrate, a salt of picric acid.

pícrico [pee'-cre-co], *a.* Picric, of an exceedingly bitter taste. **Ácido pícrico**, picric acid, a yellow crystalline body.

pictografía [pic-to-grah-fee'-ah], *f.* Pictography, picture writing.

pictórico, ca [pic-to'-re-co, cah], *a.* 1. Pictorial. 2. Worth painting (escena). 3. Artistic (talento).

picudilla [pe-coo-deel'-lyah], *f.* 1. Kind of pointed olive. 2. An insectivorous bird.

picudo, da [pe-coo'-do, dah], *a.* 1. Beaked, pointed (puntiagudo). 2. Prattling, babbling, chattering. 3. *(Carib.)* Over-the-top (cursi). 4. *(Mex.)* Crafty, clever (astuto). *-m.* Boll weevil.

pido [pee'-do], *m. (coll.)* Demand, request, petition.

pidón, na [pee'-done´, nah], *a. (coll.)* V. PEDIGÜEÑO.

pie [pe-ay'], *m.* 1. The foot. 2. Foot leg, that by which anything is supported. 3. Foot, the base. 4. Trunk of trees and plants. 5. Lees, sediment. 6. Last hand or player in a game of cards. 7. The last word pronounced by an actor. 8. Foot, a measure of length. 9. Motive (causa), occasion. 10. Footing, basis, foundation, groundwork. 11. Footing, rule, use, custom. 12. Foot, verse, a certain number of syllables. 13. End or conclusion of a writing. 14. First color given in dyeing. 15. Foot of a stocking. 16. Foothold (seguridad). 17. *(Cono Sur)* Deposit (enganche). **No creas a pie juntillas todo lo que te digan**, don't believe all they tell you. **Al pie de la hora**, instantly, without delay. **A sus pies, señora**, at your service, madam. **Pie ante pie**, step by step. **A pie**, on foot. **Al pie**, near, close to, at the foot of. **A pie firme**, without stirring, steadfastly. **En pie**, constantly, firmly; uprightly, erect. **Estar con un pie en la sepultura**, to have one foot in the grave. **De pies a cabeza**, from head to foot. **Echar el pie atrás a alguno**, to outdo someone. **Echar el pie atrás**, to flinch, to desist. **Soldados de a pie**, foot soldiers, infantry. **Pie de atleta**, athlete's foot. **A pie firme**, steadfastly. **Levantarse con el pie izquierdo**, to get up on the wrong side of the bed. **Estar de pie**, to be standing. **Parar los pies a uno**, to curb somebody. **A los pies de la cama**, at the foot of the bed. **Estar al pie del cañón**, to be ready to act. **En pie de guerra**, on a war footing. **Dar pie a**, to give cause for.

piececito [pe-ay-thay-the'-to], *m. dim.* A little foot.

piedad [pe-ay-dahd'], *f.* 1. Piety, godliness: mercy, pity (compasión), compassion. 2. Charity. **Tener piedad de**, to take pity on.

pie de imprenta [pe-ay day im-pren'-tah], *m.* Printer's mark.

piedra [pe-ay'-drah], *f.* 1. A stone. 2. Gravel in the kidneys. 3. Hail. 4. Place where foundlings are exposed. 5. Gun-flint. 6. Hardness of things. **Piedra de amolar** or **afilar**, whetstone, grinding stone. **Piedra imán**, magnet. **Piedra lipis**, copper sulphate. **Piedra sepulcral**, a gravestone, a headstone. **No dejar piedra por mover**, not to leave a stone unturned. **Quedarse de piedra**, to be thunderstruck. **Tener el corazón de piedra**, to be hardhearted.

piedrecica, illa, ita, piedrezuela [pe-ay-dray-thee'-cah], *f. dim.* A little stone.

piel [pe-el'], *f.* 1. The skin. 2. Hide of an animal cured and dressed, pelt. 3. Peel or skin of fruits. **Piel de gallina**, goose-flesh, the skin roughened by cold. **Piel de cabra**, goatskin. **Piel de cerdo**, pigskin. **Abrigo de pieles**, fur coat.

piélago [pe-ay'-lah-go], *m.* 1. The high sea. 2. Great plenty or abundance. V. TARQUÍN.

pielecita [pe-ay-lay-thee'-tah], *f. dim.* A small hide.

pienso [pe-en'-so], *m.* Fodder, feed. **Piensos compuestos**, mixed feed. **Dar un pienso**, to bait or give food to an animal. **¡Ni por pienso!**, I wouldn't dream of it!

pierna [pe-err'-nah], *f.* 1. The leg. 2. Leg of butcher's meat or of fowls. 3. Down stroke of letters. 4. Check of a printing-press. 5. *(Cono Sur)* Player. **En piernas**, bare-legged. **A pierna suelta** or **a pierna tendida**, at one's ease; without care; soundly. **Estirar las piernas**, to take a walk, to stretch one's legs. **Cortar las piernas**, to render a thing impossible.

piernitendido, da [pe-er-ne-ten-dee'-do, dah], *a.* With extended legs.

pieza [pe-ay'-thah], *f.* 1. Piece, part of a whole; a fragment. 2. Coin, piece of money. 3. Piece of cloth woven at one time. 4. Piece of furniture. 5. Room in a house. 6. Piece of ordnance. 7. Buffoon, wag, jester. 8. Any bird or animal of the chase. 9. Any manufactured article and each of the parts which compose it. 10. Piece or man in the games of draughts, chess, etc. 11. *(Her.)* Each of the parts into which the coat of arms or shield is divided. **Quedarse de una pieza** or **hecho una pieza**, *(coll.)* to be stunned, to remain astonished. **Hacer piezas**, to take anything to pieces. **Pieza arqueológica**, object. **Juan es una pieza**, *(LAm.)* Juan is as honest as the day is long. **Pieza de oro**, gold coin. **Buena pieza**, rogue, villain. **Me he quedado de una pieza**, I was speechless. **Pieza de artillery**, piece of artillery. **Pieza de ajedrez**, chess piece.

piezgo [pe-eth'-go], *m.* 1. Neck of a leather bottle; the hind or fore foot of an animal. 2. A dressed skin for wine or other liquors.

pífano, pífaro [pee'-fah-no, pee'-fah-ro], *m.* 1. Fife, a musical instrument. 2 Fifer.

pifia [pee'-fe-ah], *f.* 1. A failure to properly strike the billiard ball with the cue, a miss. 2. Error, blunder (error). 3. *(And. Cono Sur)* Joke (chiste); mockery (burla). 4. *(And.)* Hissing, booing (rechifla).

pifiar [pe-fe-ar'], *vn.* 1. To suffer the breath to be too audible in playing the flute. 2. To miss the billiard ball. 3. *(Cono Sur)* To fail (fracasar), to come to cropper. 4. *(And. CAm.)* To be disappointed, to suffer a setback.

pigargo [pe-gar-go], *m.* Ring-tail hawk.

pigmentación [peeg-men-tah-the-on'], *f.* Pigmentation.

pigmento [pig-men'-to], *m.* Pigment, coloring matter of the skin.

pigmeo, mea [pig-may'-o, ah], *a.* Dwarfish. *-m. & f.* A dwarf.

pignorar [pig-no-rar'], *va.* To pledge, to hypothecate.

pigre [pee'-gray], *a.* Slothful, lazy, indolent.

pigricia [pe-gree'-the-ah], *f.* 1. Laziness (pereza), idleness. 2. Place in schools for lazy boys. 3. *(And. Cono Sur)* Trifle, bagatelle; small bit, pinch.

pigro, gra [pee'-gro, grah], *a.* Negligent, careless, lazy.

pihuela [pe-hoo-ay'-lah], *f.* 1. Leash, a leather strap tied to a hawk's leg. 2. Obstruction, hindrance, impediment. **Pihuelas**, fetters, shackles.

pijama [pe-hah'-mah] or **piyama** [pe-yah'-mah], *m.* (Used mostly in the plural.) Pajamas or pyjamas.

pijo [pee'-ho], *a.* 1. Stuck-up (engreído). 2. Fussy (quisquilloso). 3. Thick (tonto). *-m.* Spoiled brat (mimado).

pijota [pe-ho'-tah], *f. (Zool.)* Hake, coaling. V. MERLUZA.

pijote [pe-ho'-tay], *m. (Naut.)* Swivel-gun loaded with small grape-shot

pijotería [pe-ho-tay-ree'-ah], *f.* 1. Nuisance (molestia), small annoyance. 2. *(LAm.)* Insignificant sum (pequeña cantidad). 3. *(LAm.)* Meanness (tacañería).

pila [pee'-lah], *f.* 1. A large (stone) trough containing water for cattle. 2. Baptismal font. 3. Pile, heap of things thrown together (montón). **Una pila de**, a heap of. 4. Pile of shorn wool belonging to one owner. 5. Parish. 6. A holy-water basin. **Nombre de pila**, Christian name. 7. *(Arch.)* Buttress of an arch of a bridge. 8. Galvanic or voltaic pile. **Pila de agua bendita**, holy water stoup. 9. Battery; cell. **Aparato a pilas**, battery-run apparatus.

pilada [pe-lah'-dah], *f.* Quantity of mortar made at once; pile, heap.

pilar [pe-lar'], *m.* 1. The large water basin of a fountain. 2. Pillar, a column of stone; post. 3. Pillar, a person who supports something. 4. Stone or mound for a landmark on roads. **Pilar de una cama,** bed-post.

pilarejo, pilarito [pe-lah-ray'-ho, pe-lah-ree'-to], *m. dim.* A small pillar.

pila seca [pe'-lah say'-cah], *f.* Dry cell or dry battery.

pilastra [pe-lahs'-trah], *f.* Pilaster, a square column.

pilatero [pe-lah-tay'-ro], *m.* In woollen factories, fuller who assists at fulling the cloth.

pilche [peel-chay], *m.* (Peru) Cup or bowl of wood. (*Acad.*)

píldora [peel'-do-rah], *f.* 1. Pill, a medicine. 2. Affliction, bad news. **Píldora antifatiga,** anti-fatigue pill.

pildorera [peel-do-ray'-rah], *f.* Pill box.

píleo [pee'-lay-o], *m.* 1. A hat or cap worn by the ancient Romans. 2. Red hat worn by cardinals.

pileta, pilica [pe-lay'-tah, pe-lee'-cah], *f. dim.* of PILA.

pillada [pil-lyah'-dah], *f.* A knavish trick (trampa), a sham, an unworthy action.

pillador [pil-lyah-dor'], *m.* Pillager, plunderer, swindler.

pillaje [pil-lyah'-hay], *m.* Pillage, plunder, marauding, foray.

pillar [pil-lyar'], *va.* 1. To pillage, to plunder, to foray. 2. To lay hold of (atrapar), to chop at. 3. To catch (coger); to catch (sorprender). 4. To get (ganga, puesto). 5. To grasp (significación). 6. To knock down (coche). **Quien pillapilla,** he who plunders most has most. **Pillar una mona,** to become intoxicated. **Por fin le pilló la policía,** the police nabbed him eventually.

pillastre, pillastrón [pil-lyahs'-tray, pil-lyas-trone'], *m.* A roguish fellow, an impudent man.

pillería [pil-lyay-ree'-ah], *f.* 1. A number of vagabonds or rogues going together (banda). 2. A knavish trick or sham.

pillo, lla [peel'-lyo, lyah], *a.* Applied to a loafer, or blackguard. -*m.* 1. A vagabond, a rascal. 2. A petty thief.

pilluelo [pe-lyoo-ay'-lo], *m.* Rascal, vagabond, hoodlum.

pilocarpo [pi-lo-car'-po], *m.* Jaborandi, a Brazilian plant, which yields the medicinal lkaloid pilocarpin.

pilón [pe-lone'], *m.* 1. A large watering trough for cattle, the basin of a fountain (abrevadero). 2. Drop or ball of a steelyard. 3. Great stone or counterpoise in an olive-press. 4. Heap of grapes ready to be pressed. 5. Heap of mortar (mortero). 6. (*Mex.*) Drinking fountain. 7. (*Mex.*) Tip (propina). **Pilón de azúcar,** a loaf of refined sugar formed in; mould. **Beber del pilón,** to believe current rumors.

piloncillo [pi-lon-theel'-lyo], *m.* (*Amer.*) The crust of sugar that remains in the boiler.

pilonero, ra [pe-lo-nay'-ro, rah], *m. & f.* Newsmonger.

pilongo, ga [pe-lon'-go, gah], *a.* 1. Peeled and dried (castaño). 2. Thin, lean, meagre.

pilórico, ca [pe-lo'-re-co, cah], *a.* Pyloric, relating to the pyloric orifice.

píloro [pee'-lo-ro], *m.* Musk-rat. 2. (*Anat.*) Pylorus, inferior part of the stomach.

piloso, sa [e-lo'-so, sah], *a.* Pilous, hairy.

pilotaje [pe-lo-tah'-hay], *m.* 1. Piloting. 2. Pilotage, pilot's fee. 3. Pilots. 4. Steering, driving. 5. Piling, piles.

pilotar, pilotear [pe-lo-tar', pe-lo-tay-ar'], *va.* 1. To pilot. 2. To steer, to drive. 3. (*LAm.*) To guide (persona).

pilote [pe-lo'-tay], *m.* Pile.

pilotín [pe-lo-teen'], *m.* Pilot's apprentice, or second pilot.

piloto [pe-lo'-to], *m.* 1. Pilot of a ship or aircraft. 2. The pilot fish. 3. (*Naut.*) First mate. 4. (*Cono Sur*) Raincoat. 5. (*Aut.*) Driver. **Piloto automático,** (*Aer.*) Autopilot. **Piloto de prueba,** test pilot. -*a.* **Casa piloto,** model home.

piltraca, piltrafa [peel-trah'-cah], *f.* Piece of flesh which is almost nothing but skin.

pimentada [pe-men-tah'-dah], *f.* Sauce, the principal ingredient of which is Cayenne paper.

pimental [pe-men-tahl'], *m.* Ground bearing pepper; pepper patch.

pimentero [pe-men-tay'-ro], *m.* 1. Pepper box. 2. (*Bot.*) The plant which produces pepper.

pimentón [pe-men-tone], *m.* Ground red pepper, paprika.

pimienta [pe-me-en'-tah], *f.* (*Bot.*) Pepper (black pepper). **Pimienta de Tabasco or malagueta,** myrtle.

pimiento [pe-me-en'-to], *m.* 1. (*Bot.*) Capsicum, red or Cayenne pepper. 2. The plant of every species of capsicum. 3. The fruit of all the species of capsicum. **Pimiento dulce,** the sweet fruit of the common capsicum. **Pimiento picante,** the fruit of shrubby and bird-pepper capsicum. 4. Mildew, blight in plants, as wheat, barley, etc. 5. Chaste-tree. *V.* SAUZGATILLO.

pímpido [peem'-pe-do], *m.* Kind of dog-fish, resembling the *mielga.*

pimpinela [pim-pe-nay'-lah], *f.* (*Bot.*) Burnet, pimpinel, a rossaceous plant.

pimpleo, a [pim-play'-o, ah], *a.* Belonging to the muses.

pimplón [pim-plone'], *m.* (*Prov. Sant.*) Waterfall, cascade.

pimpollar [pim-pol-lyar'], *m.* Nursery of young plants and trees.

pimpollecer [pim-pol-lyay-therr'], *vn.* To sprout, to bud.

pimpollejo, ico, ito [pim-pol-lyar'-ho], *m. dim.* A small sprout, sucker, or shoot.

pimpollo [pim-pol'-lyo], *m.* 1. Sucker, sprout, shoot. 2. Rosebud not yet opened (capullo). 3. A spruce, lively lad. 4. Anything perfect of its kind. 5. To look very smart (elegante).

pimpollón [pim-pol-lyone'], *m. aug.* A large sucker, sprout, or shoot.

pimpolludo, da [pim-pol-lyoo'-do, dah], *a.* Full of buds or sprouts.

pina [pee'-nah], *f.* 1. A mound of earth in the form of a cone. 2. Jaunt, felloe, any piece of the circumference of a coach or cart wheel.

pinabete [pe-nah-bay'-tay], *m.* (*Bot.*) Spruce fir-tree.

pinacoteca [pe-nah-co-tay'-cah], *f.* Gallery, or museum, of paintings.

pináculo [pe-nah'-coo-lo], *m.* Pinnacle, the highest part of a magnificent building.

pinado, da [pe-nah-do, dah], *a.* (*Bot.*) Pinnate, pinnate.

pinal, pinar [pe-nahl', pe-nar'], *m.* Grove of pines.

pinariego, ga [pe-nah-re-ay'-go, gah], *a.* Belonging to pines.

pinastro [pe-nahs'-tro], *m.* Wild pine.

pinaza [pe-nah-thah], *f.* (*Naut.*) Pinance, a small vessel.

pincel [pin-thel'], *m.* 1. Pencil, a small brush used by painters. 2. Painter. **Es un gran pincel,** he is a great painter. 3. The work painted. 4. Mode of painting. 5. Second feather in a martin's wing.

pincelada [pin-thay-lah'-dah], *f.* Stroke with a pencil. **Dar la última pincelada,** to give the finishing stroke.

pincelero [pin-thay-lay'-ro], *m.* Pencil-maker, one who makes and sells hair pencils or small brushes.

pincelillo, ito [pin-thay-leel'-lyo], *m. dim* A small pencil.

pincerna [pin-therr'-nah], *com.* One who serves drinks at feasts.

pinchadura [pin-chah-doo'-rah], *f.* (*coll.*) Puncture, act of pricking.

pinchar [pin-char'], *va.* 1. (*coll.*) To prick, to wound. 2. To prod (estimular). **Le pinchan para que se case,** they keep prodding him to get married. -*vr.* To prick oneself (droga).

pinchazo [pin-chah'-tho], *m.* A prick, a stab; jab (de droga).

pinche [peen'-chay], *m.* 1. Scullion, kitchen-boy (de cocina); any ragged boy. 2. (*Cono Sur*) Minor office clerk (oficinista). 3. (*And.*) Bad horse, nag. 4. (*Cono Sur*) Hatpin. -*a.* 1. (*Mex.*) Bloody (maldito). 2. (*CAm.*) Stingy (tacaño).

pincho [peen'-cho], *m.* 1. Thorn, prickle of plants, pointed stick (aguijón); (*Cono Sur*) spike, prickle. 2. (*Culin.*) **Un pincho de tortilla,** a portion of omelette.

pindárico, ca [pin-dah'-re-co, cah], *a.* Pindaric, after the style of Pindar.

pindonga [pin-don'-gah], *f.* A gad-about (mujer).

pindonguear [pin-don-gay-ar'], *vn.* (*coll.*) To gad about (mujeres).

pineda [pe-nah'-dah], *f.* 1. A kind of linen garters. 2. (*Prov.*) *V.* PINAL.

pingajo [pin-gah'-ho], *m.* A rat or patch hanging from clothes.

pinganello [pin-gah-nayl'-lyo], *m. V.* CALAMOCO.

pinganilla [pin-gah-neel'-lyah], *a. (Amer. Peru, coll.)* Bedecked, fashionably attired. **En pinganillas,** *(Mex.)* on tiptoe. *V.* DE PUNTILLLAS.

pinganitos [pin-gah-nee'-tos], *m.* **En pinganitos,** in a prosperous or elevated state.

pingo [peen'-go], *m.* 1. Rag (harapo). 2. *pl.* Worthless clothes (ropa), duds, whether ragged or in good repair. 3. *(Amer.)* A fine saddle horse. **Andar, estar** or **ir de pingo,** to gad about and neglect home duties (mujer). 4. Slut (marrana). 5. *(Mex.)* Scamp (niño). 6. *(Cono Sur)* Lively child (niño).

pingorote [pin-go-ro'-tay], *m. V.* PERUÉTANO, 2d def.

pingorotudo, da [pin-go-ro-too'-do, dah], *a. (Prov.)* High, lofty, elevated.

ping-pong [ping-pong], *m.* Ping-pong.

pingüe [peen'-goo-ay], *m. (Naut.)* Pink, a vessel with a very narrow stern; a pink-stern.

pingüe [pin-goo-ay], *a.* 1. Fat, greasy, oily, pinguid. 2. Rich, plentiful, abundant.

pingüedinoso, sa [pin-goo-ay-de-noh'-so, sah], *a.* Fatty, oleaginous, pinguid.

pingüino [pin-goo-ee'-no], *m.* Penguin.

pingüísimo, ma [pin-goo-ee'-se-mo, mah], *a. sup.* Excessively fat.

pinguosidad [pin-goo-o-se-dahd'], *f.* Fatness.

pinico [pe-nee'-co], *m. dim.* 1. Small step. 2. Small pine.

pinífero, ra [pe-nee'-fay-ro, rah], *a. (Poet.)* Piniferous.

pinillo [pe-neel'-lyo], *m. (Bot.)* Groundpine, germander.

pinito [pe-nee'-to], *m. dim.* First step. **Hacer pinitos,** to take the first steps (as of a little child or a convalescent).

pinjante [pin-hahn'-tay], *m. (Arch.)* Moulding at the caves of buildings.

pino, na [pee'-no, nah], *a.* Very perpendicular, as the sides of a mountain. *-m. (coll.)* The first step of a child or of a convalescent beginning to walk. **A pino,** erect, upright: applied to bells turned half-round in ringing.

pino [pee'-no], *m.* 1. *(Bot.)* Pine. **Pino albar,** Scotch pine. **Pino de comer,** stone pine. **Pino real,** clustian pine. **Pino rodeno** or **rodezno,** cluster pine. **Pino uñal,** Siberian pine. 2. Ship constructed of pine. **Hacer el pino,** stand on one's head.

pinocha [pe-no'-chah], *f.* Pine loaf.

pínola [pee'-no-lah], *f.* 1. Detent of a repeating watch. 2. Spindle.

pínole [pee'-no-lay] *(Acad.),* or **Pinole** [pe-no'-lay], *m.* 1. An aromatic powder used in making chocolate. 2. *(Mex.)* Parched corn, ground and mixed with sugar and water for a drink.

pinoso, sa [pe-no'-so, sah], *a.* Producing or belonging to pines.

pinta [peen'-tah], *f.* 1. Spot (punto), blemish, scar. 2. Any mark by which the qualities of a thing are known. 3. Trump (triunfo en cartas). **¿Qué pinta?,** ¿what's trump? 4. Drop (gota). 5. Pint, a liquid measure. 6. Appearance (aspecto), look. 7. Worthless creature (persona inútil). 8. *(And. Carib. Cono Sur)* Coloring, coloration; *(LAm.)* birthmark (señal). **Una tela a pinta azules,** a cloth with blue spots. **Tener buena pinta,** to look good (persona). *-pl.* 1. Spots on the skin in malignant fevers. 2. Basset, a game of cards.

pintacilgo, pintadillo [pin-tah-theel'-go, pin-tah-deel'-lyo], *m. (Orn.)* Goldfinch.

pintada [pin-tah'-dah], *f.* The Guinea fowl.

pintadera [pin-tah-day'-rah], *f.* Instrument for ornamenting bread.

pintado, da [pin-tah'-do, dah], *a. & pp.* of PINTAR. 1. Painted, mottled. **Venir pintado,** to fit exactly. 2. *(LAm.)* Like, identical. **El niño salió pintado al padre,** the boy looked exactly like his father.

pintamonas [pin-tah-mo'-nas], *m. (coll.)* Nickname for a bad painter, a dauber.

pintar [pin-tar'], *va.* 1. To paint, to picture, to represent by delineation and colors. 2. To paint, to describe, to delineate, to represent something by writing or words. 3. To fancy, to imagine, to feign according to fancy. 4. To exaggerate, to heighten by representation. 5. To pay, to discharge, to satisfy. **Pintar algo azul,** to paint something blue. **No pinta nada,** he cuts no ice. *-vn.* 1. To begin to ripen (fruta). 2. To show, to give signs of. *-vr.* 1. To paint one's face (maquillarse). 2. *(LAm.)* To scarper (escaparse).

pintarrajar, pintarrajear [pin-tar-rah-jar'], *va. (coll.) V.* PINTORREAR.

pintarrajo [pin-tar-rah'-ho], *m. (Col.)* A bungling piece of painting.

pintarrojo [pin-tar-ro'-ho], *m. (Prov. Gal.)* Robin. *V.* PARDILLO.

pintarroia, *f. V.* LIJA.

pintica, illa, ita [pin-tee'-cah], *f. dim.* A little spot or dot.

pintiparado, da [pin-te-pah-rah'-do, dah], *a.* Perfectly like, closely resembling; apposite, fit. *-pp.* of PINTIPANAR.

pintiparar [pin-te-pah-rar'], *va.* To compare, to estimate the relative quality.

pintojo, ja [pin-toh'-ho, hah], *a.* Spotted, stained, mottled.

pintor [pin-tor'], *m.* Painter. **Pintor de brocha gorda,** house painter.

pintora [pin-to'-rah], *f.* Paintress; a painter's wife.

pintorcillo [pin-tor-theel'-lyo], *m. dim.* Applied to a wretched painter or dauber.

pintoresco, ca [pin-to-res'-co, cah], *a.* Picturesque.

pintorreador [pin-tor-ray-ah-dor'], *m.* Dauber, miserable painter.

pintorrear [pin-tor-ray-ar'], *va.* To daub, to paint without skill.

pintura [pin-too'-rah], *f.* 1. Painting, the art of representing objects by delineation and colors. 2. Picture, painting, a painted resemblance. **Pintura al temple;** size painting. 3. Forming letters with the pen. 4. *(Met.)* Picture, written description of anything. **Pintura embutida,** painting in mosaic, etc. 5. Paint (material).

pinturero, ra [pin-too-ray'-ro, rah], *a. & n.* Exaggerating, buffoon-like.

pinul, pinullo [pe-nool'-lyo], *m.* An Indian drink made from maize. *Cf.* PINOLE.

pínula [pee'-noo-lah], *f.* 1. Detent of a repeating watch. 2. Sight of an optical instrument.

pinzas [peen'-thas], *f. pl.* 1. Pincers (tenazas). 2. Forceps, tweezers. 3. Clothes pin (de ropa), peg. **Pinza de pelo,** *(Carib.)* hair grip.

pinzón [pin-thone'], *m. (Orn.)* Chaffinch.

pinzote [pin-tho'-tay], *m. (Naut.)* Whip-staff, formerly fastened to the rudder.

piña [pee'-nyah], *f.* 1. Cone or nut (del pino). 2. Pineapple. 3. Virgin silver treated with mercury. 4. A white, matt, transparent, and very fine fabric, made in the Philippines from the leaves of the pineapple, and which serves for handkerchief bands, towels, and garments of women and children. 5. *(Carib. Mex.)* Hub. 6. Punch (golpe). 7. *(Mex.)* Chamber (revólver).

piñata [pe-nayh'-tah], *f.* 1. Pitcher, pot. 2. Jar or pot ornamented with fancy paper and filled with sweetmeats, which is hung from the ceiling so that the merrymakers, one by one and blindfolded, try to break it with a stick. It is very popular at Christmas festivities and at children's parties.

piño [pe-nyo], *m.* Ivory, tooth.

piñón [pe-nyone'], *m.* 1. The pine-nut seed or kernel. 2. Pinion, the joint of the wing remotest from the body. 3. Pinion, the tooth of a wheel. 4. Spring-nut of a gun. **Comer los piñones,** to celebrate Christmas eve.

piñonata [pe-nyoh-nah'-tah], *f.* Conserve of pine-nut kernels.

piñonate [pe-nyoh-nah'-tay], *m.* Paste made of the kernels of pine-nuts and sugar.

piñoncico, illo, ito [pe-nyon-thee'-co], *m. dim.* 1. A small pinenut kernel. 2. Pinion, the joint of the wing remotest from the body.

piñuela [pe-nyoo-ay'-lah], *f.* 1. Figured silk. 2. Nut or fruit of cypress. 3. (Nicaragua) The American agave, from which the *cabuya* is made.

pío, a [pee'-o, ah], *a.* 1. Pious, devout, religious, holy. 2. Mild, merciful. 3. Pied, piebald (caballo).

pío [pee'-o], *m.* 1. Puling of chickens. 2. Anxious desire. **No decir ni pío**, not to breathe a word.

piocha [pe-o'-chah], *f.* Trinket for women's headdresses.

piojento, ta [pe-o-hen'-to, tah], *a.* Lousy.

piojería [pe-o-hay-ree'-ah], *f.* 1. Lousiness. 2. Misery (miseria), poverty.

piojicida [pe-o-he-thee'-dah], *com.* In jocular style, a lousekiller.

piojillo [pe-o-heel'-lyo], *m.* 1. *(dim.)* A small louse (bichos en plantas, pájaros). 2. A white spot in leather which is not well dressed.

piojo [pe-o'-ho], *m.* 1. A louse. 2. Disease in hawks and other birds of prey. **Piojo pegadizo**, Crablouse; a troublesome hanger-on.

piojoso, sa [pe-o-hoh'-so, sah], *a.* 1. Lousy, mean, contemptible. 2. Miserable, stingy.

piojuelo [pe-o-hoo-ay'-lo], *m. dim.* A small louse.

piola [pe-o'-lah], *f.* 1. *(Naut.)* Housing house-line, a line of three strands. 2. *(LAm.)* Rope (soga), tether. 3. *(And. Carib.)* Cord (cuerda). 4. *(Cono Sur)* Cock (pene).

pionero [pe-o-nay'-ro], *a.* Pioneering. -*m & f.* Pioneer.

pionía [pe-o-nee'-ah], *f.* A hard, red, bean-shaped seed used in Venezuela among the country people for making collars and bracelets. V. BUCARE.

piorno [pe-or'-no], *m. (Bot.)* Spanish broom.

piorrea [pe-or-ray'-ah], *f. (Med.)* Pyorrhea.

pipa [pee'-pah], *f.* 1. A cask for wine and other liquors. 2. Pipe, a liquid measure of two hogsheads. 3. V. PEPITA. 4. Pipe (para fumar). **Fumar una pipa**, to smoke a pipe. 5. Pipe which children make of corn-stalks; reed of a clarion. 6. *(LAm.)* Belly (barriga). 7. Rod (pistola). 8. **Pasarlo pipa**, to have a great time.

pipar [pe-par'], *vn.* To smoke a tobacco-pipe.

pipería [po-pay-ree'-ah], *f.* Collection of pipes.

piperina [pe-pay-ree'-nah], *f.* Piperin, an alkaloidal principle obtained from white pepper.

pipero [pe-pay'-ro], *m.* Cooper, pipe or butt maker.

pipí [pe-pee'], *m.* 1. *(Orn.)* Pitpit, a bird known also as honey-creeper. 2. Pee, piss, wee-wee (entre niños).

pipián [pe-pe-ahn'], *m.* A kind of Indian fricassee.

pipiar [pe-pe-ar'], To pule, to chirp, to peep.

pípila [pee'-pe-lah], *f. (Mex. Amer.)* Hen-turkey.

pipiolo [pe-pe-o'-lo], *m. (coll.)* Novice (novato), raw; hand, beginner; recruit.

pipirigallo [pe-pe-re-gahl'-lyo], *m. (Bot.)* Sainfoin, a forage plant.

pipiripao [pe-pe-re-pah'-o], *m. (coll.)* A splendid feast.

pipiritaña [pe-pe-re-tah'-nyah], *vr.* **Pipitaña** [pe-pe-tah'-nyah], *f.* Flute made of green cane.

pipo [pee'-po, *m.* 1. Small bird that eats flies. 2. *(Carib.)* Child (niño). 3. *(And. Carib.)* Crooked employee (empleado). 4. *(And.)* Contraband liquor (licor).

pipote [pe-po'-tay], *m.* A keg.

pipotillo [pe-po-teel'-lyo], *m. dim.* A small keg.

pique [pee'-kay], *m.* 1. Pique (resentimiento), offence taken. 2. A beau, gallant, lover. 3. A term in a game. 4. Bottom, ground. 5. *(LAm.)* Bounce (rebote). 6. *(CAm. Cono Sur. Min.)* Mineshaft. 7. *(And.)* Jigger flea (insecto). **Irse a pique**, *(Naut.)* to founder. **A pique**, in danger, on the point of. **Estar a pique**, to be about or on the point of: *Piques (Naut.)* crotches. V. HORQUILLAS.

pique [pe-kay'], *m.* Pique, a heavy cotton fabric having a corded or lozenge-shaped pattern.

piquera [pe-kay'-rah], *f.* 1. A hole in a hive, through which bees fly in and out (de colmena). 2. Cock-hole in a barrel. 3. *(Mex.)* Dive (taberna).

piquería [pe-kay-ree'-ah], *f.* Body of pikemen.

piquero [pe-kay'-ro], *m. (Mil.)* Pikeman.

piqueta [pe-kay'-tah], *f.* Pick-axe, mattock, pitcher.

piquete [pe-kay'-tay], *m.* 1. Sore or wound of little importance. 2. Small hole made in clothes with a pinking iron (agujero). 3. A pointed stake shod with iron. 4. Picket or piquet, a small detachment of soldiers. 5. Picket (de huelguistas). 6. *(Cono Sur)* Yard, small corral. 7. *(Carib.)* Street band. **Piquete avanzado**, picket-guard.

piquetero [pe-kay-tay'-ro], *m.* In mines, the boy who carries the picks or mattocks to the workmen.

piquetilla [pe-kay-teel'-lyah], *f. dim.* A small pick-axe.

piquillo [pe-keel'-lyo], *m. dim.* A small beak or bill.

piquituerto [pe-ke-too-err'-to], *m. (Orn.)* Cross-bill, picarin.

pira [pee'-rah], *f.* 1. A funeral pyre, on which the dead are burnt. 2. **Hacer pira**, to clear off; *(Escol.)* to cut class.

pirado [pe-rah'-do], *a.* Crazy (tonto); high (drogado).

piragón [pe-rah-gon'], *m.* V. PIRAUSTA.

piragua [pe-rah'-goo-ah], *f. (Naut.)* Pirogue, a small vessel, canoe.

piragüismo [pe-rah'-goo-ah], *m.* Canoeing.

piragüista [pe-rah-goo-ees'-tah], *m & f.* Canoeist.

piramidal [pe-rah-me-dahl'], *a.* Pyramidal.

piramidalmente [pe-rah-me-dahl'-men-tay], *adv.* Pyramidally.

pirámide [pe-rah'-me-day], *f.* Pyramid.

piramista [pe-rah-mees'-tah], *f.* A kind of butterfly.

pirata [pe-rah'-tah], *m.* 1. Pirate, corsair. 2. A cruel wretch. -*a.* **Disco pirata**, bootleg record. **Pirata informático**, *(Comput.)* hacker.

piratear [pe-rah-tay-ar'], *vn.* 1. To pirate; to rob at sea, to cruise, to steal. 2. *(Comput.)* Hacking.

piratería [pe-rah-tay-ree'-ah], *f.* 1. Piracy on the sea 2. Piracy, any robbery; bootlegging (de disco). **Pirateo de software**, software piracy.

pirático, ca [pe-rah'-te-co, cah], *a.* Piratical, piratic.

pirausta [pe-rah-oos'-tah], *f.* Large firefly; an insect formerly fabled to live in fire, and to die apart from it.

pirenaico, ca [pe-ray-nah'-e-co, cah], *a.* Pyrenean, of the Pyrenees.

pirexia [pe-rek'-se-ah], *f.* Pyrexia, essential, fever.

pírico, c [pee'-re-co, cah], *a.* Relating to fire, particularly to fireworks.

pirita [pe-ree'-tah], *f.* 1. Pyrites, an obsolescent name for the sulphurets of iron, copper, and other metals. 2. Marcasite, a fossil. V. MARCASITA.

piritoso, sa [pe-re-to'-so, sah], *a.* Pyritous.

pirofilacio [pe-ro-fe-lah'-the-o], *m.* Subterraneous fire.

piróforo [pe-ro'-fo-ro], *m.* 1. Pyrophore, a composition which will ignite in contact with air. 2. A tropical firefly.

piromancia [pe-ro-mahn'-the-ah], *f.* Pyromancy, divination by fire.

piromanía [pe-ro-mah-nee'-ah], *f.* Pyromania, a morbid desire to start fires.

pirómano, na [pe-ro'-mah-no], *m & f.* Arsonist, fire raiser.

piromántico, ca [pe-ro-mahn'-te-co, cah], *a.* Belonging to pyromancy.

pirómetro [pe-ro'-may-tro], *m.* Pyrometer, an instrument for measuring heat and its effects.

pironomia [pe-ro-no'-me-ah], *f.* Pyronomy, the art of regulating fire for chemical processes.

piropear [pe-ro-pay-ar'], *va.* To pay an amorous compliment to.

piropo [pe-ro'-po], *m.* 1. Precious stone. V. CARBUNCLO. 2. Compliment, flattery, endearing expression.

piróscapo [pe-ros'-cah-po], *m.* A steam ship.

piróscopo [pe-ros'-co-po], *m.* Pyroscope, an instrument for measuring radiant heat.

piroseno [pe-ro-say'-no], *m.* Pyroxene, a bisilicato mineral.

pirosis [pe-ro'-sis], *f.* Pyrosis, a burning sensation in the stomach.

pirotecnia [pe-ro-tec'-ne-ah], *f.* Pyrotechnics or pyrotechny, the art of making fire-works and of the use of explosive substances.

pirotécnico, ca [pe-ro-tec'-ne-co, cah], *a.* Pyrotechnical.

piroxilina [pee-roc-se-lee'-nah], *f.* Gun cotton.

pirriquio [pir-ree'-ke-o], *m.* Foot of Latin verse.

pirrónico, ca [pir-ro'-ne-co, cah], *a. V.* ESCÉPTICO.

pirueta [pe-roo-ay'-tah], *f.* Pirouette, circumvolution, twirling round on the toe, dancing, gyration.

pis [pees], *m. V.* PIPÍ.

pisa [pee'-sah], *f.* 1. Tread, the act of treading. 2. Kick, a blow with the foot. 3. Portion of olives or grapes pressed at once.

pisada [pe-sah'-dah], *f.* 1. Footstep, footprint (huella). **Seguir las pisadas**, to follow one's example. 2. Kick with the foot.

pisador [pe-sah-dor'], *m.* 1. Treader of grapes. 2. Horse that prances in walking.

pisadura [pe-sah-doo'-rah], *f.* Act of treading.

pisafalto, pisasfalto [pe-sah-fahl'-to], *m.* Mixture of bitumen and pitch.

pisapapeles [pe-sah-pah-pay'-les], *m.* Paper weight.

pisar [pe-sar'], *va.* 1. To tread, to trample (atropellar); to stamp on the ground, to step on (casualidad); to flatten (dañando). 2. To beat down stones and earth with a mallet. 3. To touch upon, to be close to. 4. To despise, to abandon. 5. To tread, to copulate (pájaros). 6. To pinch, to steal (robar). 7. *(And.)* To cover (hembra); *(CAm.)* To fuck. **Pisar el acelerador**, to step on the accelerator. **No se deja pisar por nadie**, he doesn't let anybody trample over him. -*vn.* 1. To tread, to step, to walk (andar). 2. *(Fig.)* **Pisar fuerte**, to act determinedly.

pisaúvas [pe-sah-oo'-vas], *m.* Treader of grapes.

pisaverde [pe-sah-verr'-day], *m. (coll.)* Fop, coxcomb, popinjay.

piscator [pis-cah-tor'], *m.* A universal almanac.

piscatorio, ria [pis-cah-to'-re-o, ah], *a.* Piscatory.

piscicultura [pis-the-cool-too'-rah], *f.* Pisciculture, fish culture.

pisciforme [pis-the-for'-may], *a.* Fish-shaped.

piscina [pis-the'-nah], *f.* 1. Fish pond (tanque). 2. Swimming pool. 3. Piscina, basin with a drain for water disposal in connection with sacred rites.

piscis [pees'-this], *m. (Ast.)* Pisces, a zodiacal sign.

piso [pee'-so], *m.* 1. Tread, trampling, footing. 2. Floor (suelo), pavement, flooring, surface: foundation of a house. 3. Story or floor, as first floor, second floor, etc.: loft. **Piso bajo**, ground floor. **A un piso**, on the same floor. 4. Money paid for board and lodging in a lodging-house, inn, etc. 5. Sole (de zapato). 6. *(Cono Sur)* Stool (tablero). 7. Mat (estera); *(Cono Sur, Mex.)* Table runner (tapete).

pisón [pe-sone'], *m.* Rammer, an instrument for driving earth, stones, or piles (herramienta). **A pison**, by blows of a rammer.

pisonear [pe-so-nay-ar'], *va.* To ram, to drive down.

pisotear [pe-so-tay-ar'], *va.* To trample, to tread underfoot.

pisoteo [pe-so-tay'-o], *m.* The act of treading underfoot.

pisotón [pe-so-ton'], *m.* 1. Stamp on the foot. 2. Newspaper scoop (periodismo).

pista [pees'-tah], *f.* 1. Trace, track, spoor of an animal. 2. Footprint. 3. Track for foot or horse racing. 4. *(Aer.)* Airstrip. 5. Clue (de indicio). 6. Tack (de cinta). 7. *(Dep.)* Track, course; court (cancha). **Pista de aterrizaje**, landing strip, landing field. **Pista de despegue**, runway. **Seguir la pista de uno**, to be on somebody's track. **Pista de hielo**, ice rink.

pistacho [pis-tah'-cho], *m.* Pistachio, pistachio nut.

pistadero [pis-tah-day'-ro], *m.* Pestle, for pounding.

pistar [pis-tar'], *va.* To pound with a pestle; to extract the juice of a thing.

pistero [pis-tay'-ro], *m.* A round jug with a spout, used to give broth, medicines, etc.

pistilo [pis-tee'-lo], *m. (Bot.)* Pistil, the central female part of a flower, which contains the ovule.

pisto [pees'-to], *m.* 1. A kind of thick broth given to the sick. 2. *(Prov.)* Dish of tomatoes and red pepper fried with oil. 3. *(And. CAm.)* Dough. 4. *(And.)* Barrel (de revólver). 5. *(Mex.)* Shot of liquor. **A pistos**, by little and little, by driblets.

pistola [pes-to'-lah], *f.* Pistol, small hand-gun. **Un par de pistolas**, a brace of pistols. **Pistola de agua**, water pistol.

pistolera [pis-to-lay'-rah], *f.* Holster.

pistolero [pis-to-lay'-ro], *m.* Gunman.

pistoletazo [pis-to-lay-tah'-tho], *m.* Pistol-shot; the wound of a pistol; the report of a pistol.

pistolete [pis-to-lay'-tay], *m.* Pistolet, pocket pistol.

pistón [pis-tone'], *m.* 1. Piston, embolus, as the sucker of a pump. 2. A percussion-cap, primer. 3. The piston of a brass wind-instrument.

pistonera [pis-to-nay'-rah], *f.* A box or case for carrying percussion-caps.

pistoresa [pis-to-ray'-sah], *f.* Short dagger.

pistraje, pistraque [pis-trah'-hay], *m.* Broth or sauce of an unpleasant taste.

pistura [pis-too'-rah], *f.* Act of pounding.

pita [pee'-tah], *f.* 1. *(Bot.)* American agave or century-plant. 2. Kind of thread made of the agave (fibra). 3. Term used to call hens. 4. Game among boys.

pitaco [pe-tah'-co], *m.* Stem or stalk of the aloe-plant.

pitágoras [pe-tah'-go-rahs], *m.* Pythagoras.

pitagórico, ca [pe-tah-go'-re-co, cah], *a. & n.* Pythagorean.

pitancería [pe-tan-thay-ree'-ah], *f.* 1. Place where allowances of meat and other things are distributed. 8. Distribution or office of distributor of allowances.

pitancero [pe-tan-thay'-ro], *m.* 1. Person appointed to distribute allowances of meat or other things. 2. Friar who is not ordained, but lives upon charity. 3. Steward or purveyor to a convent. 4. Superintendent of a choir in cathedrals.

pitancica, illa, ita [pe-tan-thee'-cah], *f. dim.* Small pittance.

pitanza [pe-tahn'-thah], *f.* 1. Pittance, daily allowance; alms. 2. *(coll.)* Price of something; salary given for any work. 3. *(Cono Sur)* Bargain.

pitaña [pe-tah'-nyah], *f. V.* LEGAÑA.

pitañoso, sa [pe-tah-nyo'-so, sah], *a. V.* LEGAÑOSO.

pitar [pe-tar'], *vn.* 1. To pipe, to play on a pipe. 2. *(LAm.)* To smoke. 3. To work (funcionar). **Pitó el árbitro**, the referee blew his whistle. **Salir pitando**, to beat it. -*va.* 1. To discharge a debt. 2. To distribute allowances of meat or other things. 3. To blow (silbato); to referee (partido). 4. To whistle at (árbitro).

pitarra [pe-tar'-rah], *f.* Distemper of the eyes. *V.* LEGAÑA.

pitillera [pe-tel-lyay'-rah], *f.* Cigarette case.

pitillo [pe-teel'-lyo], *m.* Cigarette.

pítima [pee'-te-mah], *f.* 1. *(Med.)* Plaster placed over the heart to quiet it. 2. *(coll.)* Drunkenness.

pitío [pe-tee'-o], *m.* Whistling of a pipe or of birds.

pitipié [pe-te-pe-ay'], *m. V.* ESCALA.

pito [pee'-to], *m.* 1. Whistle (instrumento, tren). 2. Hooter (de un coche). 3. Pipe, a small flute; boy's whistle (silbato). 4. *(Orn.)* Magpie, woodpecker (pájaro), tick (insecto). 5. A species of bug in India. 6. Play among boys. 7. *(Prov.)* Cocoon of a silkworm open at one end. 8. *(coll.)* Miembro viril. **No tocar pito**, not to have a share in a thing. **No vale un pito**, it (he) is not worth a straw. **Tener voz de pito**, to have a squeaky voice. **No me importa un pito**, I couldn't care less. **Entre pitos y flautas**, what with one thing and another.

pitoflero, ra [pe-to-flay'-ro, rah], *m. & f. (coll.)* A musician of little skill.

pitométrica [pe-to-may'-tre'-cah], *f.* Gauge, the art of gauging vessels.

pitón [pe-tone'], *m.* 1. Tenderling, the top of an animal's horn when it begins to shoot forth. 2. Protuberance, prominence. 3. Sprig or shoot of a tree; sprout of the agave. 4. *(Zool.)* Python.

pitonisa [pe-to-ne'-sah], *f.* 1. Pythia, pythoness, the priestess of Apollo. 2. Witch (bruja), sorceress, enchantress.

pitorra [pe-tor'-rah], *f.* *(Orn.)* Woodcock. *V.* CHOCHAPERDIZ.

pitorreo [pe-toe-ray'-o], *m.* *V.* CHOTEO.

pitpit [peet'-peet], *m.* Pitpit, guitguit, a small American bird. *Cf.* PIPI.

pituita [pe-too-ee'-tah], *f.* Pituita, mucus.

pituitario, ria [pe-too-e-tah-re-o, ah], *a.* *(Anat.)* Pituitary. **Glándula pituitaria**, pituitary gland.

pituitoso, sa [pe-too-e-to'-so, sah], *a.* Pituitous, pituitary, mucous.

piulco [pe-ool'-co], *m.* Surgical aspirator, syringe-shaped.

pivote [pe-vo'-tay], *m.* 1. Pivot (gorrón). 2. Pivot (baloncesto).

píxide [peek'-se-day], *f.* 1. A small box of wood or metal. 2. Pyx, box in which the consecrated host is kept.

pizarra [pe-thar'-rah], *f.* 1. Slate, a gray mineral (piedra). 2. Slate, for writing or figuring. 3. Blackboard (en colegios).

pizarral [pe-tha-rahl'], *m.* Slate quarry.

pizarreño, ña [pe-thar-ray'-nyo, nyah], *a.* Slate-colored, slaty, slatey.

pizarrero [pe-thar-ray'-ro], *m.* Slater, one who polishes slates.

pizarrín [pe-that-reen'], *m.* Slate-pencil.

pizarrón [pe-thar-rone'], *m.* Blackboard.

pizca [peeth'-cah], *f.* *(coll.)* Mite, whit, jot, anything proverbially small. **Ni pizca**, nothing at all, not an iota. **Una pizca de sal**, a pinch of salt.

pizcar [peeth-car'], *va.* *(coll.)* 1. To pinch. *V.* PELLIZCAR. 2. *(Mex.)* To harvest or glean (maíz).

pizpereta, pizpireta [pith-pe-ray'-tah], *a.* Sharp, brisk, lively (mujeres).

pizpita [pith-pee'-tah], *f.* *(Orn.)* Wagtail *V.* PEZPITA.

placa [plah'-cah], *f.* 1. Star, insignia of an order of knighthood. 2. A photographic plate. 3. *(Mex.)* Check for baggage (para equipaje). 4. *(LAm. Mus.)* Gramophone record. **Placas de transparencias**, transparency (or lantern) plates. **Placa de matrícula**, number plate. **Placa madre**, *(Comput.)* motherboard.

placabilidad [plah-cah-be-le-dahd'], *f.* Placability.

placable [plah-cab'-blay], *a.* Placable.

placear [plah-thay-ar'], *va.* To publish, to proclaim, to post up.

placebo [plah-thay'-bo], *m.* *(Med.)* Placebo.

placel [plah-thel'], *m.* *(Naut.)* Banks of sand or rocks in the sea.

pláceme [plah'-thay-may], *m.* Compliment of congratulation.

placenta [plah-then'-tah], *f.* 1. *(Anat.)* Placenta, after-birth. 2. *(Bot.)* Placenta.

placenteramente [plah-then-tay-rah-men-tay], *adv.* Joyfully.

placentero, ra [plah-then-tay'-ro, rah], *a.* Joyful, merry, pleasant, mirthful, humorous.

placer [plah-therr'], *m.* 1. Pleasure (deleite), content, rejoicing, amusement, complacence. 2. Will, consent. 3. The place near the bane of a river where gold-dust is found. 4. *V.* PLACEL. **A placer**. (a) with the greatest pleasure; (b gently, commodiously. **Por hacer placer**, to oblige or please a person. **Los placeres del ocio**, the pleasures of idleness.

placer [plah-thay'-res], *v. impers.* To please, to gratify, to humor, to content. **Que me place**, it pleases me; I approve of it.

placero, ra [plah-thay'-ro, rah], *a.* 1. Belonging to a market or other public place. 2. Roving idly about.

placeta [plah-thay'-tah], *f. dim.* A small square or public place.

placetilla, placetuela [plah-thay-teel'-lyah], *f. dim. V.* PLACETA.

placible [plah-thee'-blay], *a.* Placid, agreeable.

plácido [plah'-the-do, dah], *a.* Placid, easy, quiet.

placiente [plah-theen'-tay], *a.* Pleasing, mild; acceptable.

placilla, ita [plah-theel'-lyah], *f. dim. V.* PLACETA.

plafón [plah-fone'], *m.* *(Arch.)* Soffit of an architrave.

plaga [plah'-gah], *f.* 1. Plague, pest, any public calamity, as pestilence, scarcity, etc. 2. Scourge (de un pueblo). 3. Disaster, catastrophe, anything vexatious. 4. Plenty, abundance of a harmful thing. 5. Climate, country; zone. 6. *(Naut.)* Each of the cardinal points of the compass. **Plaga del jardín**, garden plague.

plagar [plah-gar'], *va.* To plague, to torment. **Han plagado la ciudad de carteles**, they have covered the town with posters. **Esta sección está plagada de minas**, this part has mines everywhere. -*vr.* To be overrun with.

plagiar [plah-he-ar'], *va.* 1. To plagiarize, or commit literary thefts (libros). 2. Among the ancient Romans, to buy and enslave a free man. 3. *(LAm.)* Kidnapping (secuestro).

plagiario, ria [plah-he-ah'-re-o, ah], *a. & m. & f.* Plagiari, plagiarist, copier.

plagiato [plah-he-ah'-to], *m.* 1. Abduction. 2. *V.* PLAGIO.

plagio [plah'-he-o], *m.* Plagiarism (copia), a literary theft.

plagoso, sa [plah-goh'-so, sah], *a.* Wounding, making wounds.

plaguear [plah-gay-ar'], *vn.* To beg alms piteously.

plan [plahn], *m.* 1. Plan (proyecto), design, draft of a building, town, etc. 2. Plan, the delineation of the horizontal posture of something. 3. Plan, writing in which a thing is described minutely (idea). 4. Slab, *(Naut.)* floor-timber. 5. Date (aventura); date (persona); boyfriend, girlfriend. 6. Programme (programa). 7. *(Med.)* Régime. 8. Level; height. 9. Set-up, system (sistema). 10. *(Cono Sur, Mex.)* Flat bottom (barco). 11. *(LAm.)* Level ground (llano). 12. *(And. CAm. Carib.)* Flat (de espada). **Plan de combate**, *(Naut.)* quarterbill. **Plan de vuelo**, *(Aer.)* flight plan. **Plan de desarrollo**, development plan. **Ha sido un plan muy pesado**, it turned out to be a very tedious kind of amusement. **Ponerse en plan**, to get in the mood. **En ese plan**, in that way. **Lo hicieron en plan de broma**, they did it for a laugh.

plana [plah'-nah], *f.* 1. Page of a book or writing. 2. A level, fruitful piece of ground. 3. Trowel, a bricklayer's tool. 4. Copy or page written by scholars during school-hours. **A plana renglón**, copied word for word; arriving or happening at the nick of time. **Plana de anuncios**, advertisement page.

planada [plah-nah'-dah], *f.* Plain, level ground.

plancha [plahn'-chah], *f.* 1. Flatiron. 2. Plate (lámina), a thin piece of metal, slab (losa). 3. Iron (utensilio); ironing (acto); ironed clothes (ropa planchada). 4. Press-up (ejercito). **Plancha de acero**, steel plate. **Plancha de cobre**, copper plate. **Plancha eléctrica**, electric iron.

planchada [plan-chah'-dah], *f.* *(Naut.)* Framing or apron of a gun.

planchador, ra [plan-chah-dor', rah], *m. & f.* Ironer. **Planchadora eléctrica**, ironer, electric ironer.

planchar [plan-char'], *va.* 1. To iron linen. 2. *(LAm.)* To flatter. 3. *(Mex.)* To stand up (dejar plantado). *V.* APLANCHAR.

planchear [plan-chay-ar'], *va.* To plate, to sheath, to cover with metal.

plancheta [plan-chay'-tah], *f.* Circumferentor, instrument used to measure distances and take heights.

planchica, illa, ita [plan-chee'-cah], *f. dim.* A small plate.

planchón [plan-chone'], *m. aug.* A large plate.

planeador [plah-nay-ah-dor'], *m.* *(Aer.)* Glider.

planear [plah-nay-ar'], *va.* 1. To plan (proyectar). 2. To organize. -*vn.* *(Aer.)* To glide.

planeo [plah-nay'-o], *m.* *(Aer.)* Gliding.

planeta [plah-nay'-tah], *m.* Planet, a heavenly body.

planetario [plah-nay-tah'-re-o], *m.* 1. Planetarium, orrery, an astronomical instrument. 2. Astronomer.

planetario, ria [plah-nay-tay'-re-o, ah], *a.* Planetary.

planga [plahn'-gah], *f.* Kind of eagle, with black and white feathers.

planicie [plah-nee'-the-ay], *f. V.* LLANO and LLANURA.

planificación [plah-ne-fe-cah-the-on'], *f.* City planning.

planificar [plah-ne-fe-cahr'], *va.* To plan.

planilla [plah-neel'-lyah], *f.* 1. List, blank form. 2. List of candidates for office.

planipedia [plan-ne-pay'-de-ah], *f.* A mean play, acted by strollers.

planisferio [plah-ni-fay'-re-o], *m.* Planisphere, a sphere projected on a plane.

plano, na [plah'-no, nah], *a.* Plain, level, smooth, flat. **Caer de plano**, to fall flat. **Rechazar algo de plano**, to turn something down flat.

plano [plah'-no], *m.* 1. Plan, design, draft, groundplot, delineation. 2. *(Geom.)* Plane, a level surface. 3. *(Cine, Fot.)* Shot. 4. Flat (de espada). **De plano**, openly, clearly. **De distinto plano social**, of a different social level. **Primer plano**, foreground. **Estar en primer plano**, to be in the limelight. **Levantar un plano**, to make a survey (topografía). **Plano inclinado**, chute. **Poner en primer plano**, to bring to the fore. (Cine) **Primer plano**, close-up shot.

planocóncavo, va [plabh-no-con'-cah-vo, vah], *a.* Plano-concave.

planocónico, ca [plah-no-co'-ne-co, cah], *a.* Plano-conical.

planoconvexo, xa [plah-no-con-vec'-so, sah], *a* Plano-convex.

planometría [plah-no-may-tree'-ah], *f.* Planometry, the mensuration of plane surfaces.

planoplano [plah-no-plah'-no], *m.* *(Alg.)* Biquadrate.

planta [plahn'-tah], *f.* 1. Sole of the foot. 2. Plant, any vegetable production. 3. Plantation, the act of planting. 4. A planation or nursery of young plants. 5. Plan of a building. 6. Position of the feet in dancing or fencing. 7. Project: disposition; point of view. 8. Plant or site of a building. **Planta baja**, ground floor. **De buena planta**, well-built (hombre). **Planta de embalaje**, assembly plant.

plantación [plan-tah-the-on'], *f.* Plantation, planting, act of planting.

plantado [plan-tah-do], *a.* **Dejar plantado a uno**, to leave somebody suddenly.

plantador, ra [plan-tah-dor', rah], *m. & f.* Planter, one who plants; an instrument used for planting.

plantaje [plan-tah'-hay], *m.* Collection of plants.

plantaminas [plan-tah-mee'-nahs], *m.* Minelayer.

plantar [plan-tar'], *va.* 1. To plant (terreno, plantas). 2. To set up (monumento), to fix upright. 3. To strike a blow (golpe). 4. To put into a place: to place or introduce somewhere. **Plantar en la cárcel**, to throw into jail. 5. To plant, to found, to establish. 6. *(coll.)* To leave in the lurch, to disappoint. 7. To jilt. **Plantar a uno en la calle**, to pitch somebody into the street. **Plantar a uno**, to curb somebody. -*vr.* 1. To stand upright, to stop. 2. To arrive soon. 3. To stop, to halt, to be unwilling to go (animal). 4. In some games not to wish more cards than are held. 5. *(And. CAm. Mex.)* To doll someone up.

plantaria [plan-tah'-re-ah], *f.* V. ESPARGANIO.

plantario [plan-tah'-re-o], *m.* Plot of ground where young plants are grown or reared.

plante [plahn'-tay], *m.* 1. Stoppage, strike (huelga). 2. Mutiny (motín).

planteamiento [plan-tay-ah-me-ayn-to] *m.* 1. Exposition (exposición). 2. Raising (de un problema). 3. Laying out, layout, setting out (enfoque de un problema).

plantear [plan-tay-ar'], *va.* To set forth, to state (exponer), plan (proponer), to trace, to try, to attempt, to create (problema), to raise, to bring up (cuestión, dificultad), to start (pleito). **Nos ha planteado muchos problemas**, it has created a lot of problems for us. -*vr.* To think (pensar).

plantel [plan-tel'], *m.* 1. Nursery or nursery-garden, a plantation of young trees. 2. Seminary or training school.

plantífero, ra [plan-tee'-fay-ro, rah], *a.* Rearing plants.

plantificar [plan-te-fe-car'], *va.* 1. To plant. V. PLANTAR. 2. *(coll.)* To beat, to box, or kick.

plantígrado, da [plan-te-grah'-do, dah], *a.* Plantigrade, walking on the sole of the foot. Also PLANTÍOGRADO, DA.

plantilla [plan-teel'-lyah], *f.* 1. *(dim.)* A young plant. 2. The insole, the inner sole of a shoe (de zapato). *(coll.)* Mustard or other draughts applied to the feet. 3. Vamp, a sole of linen, put to the feet of stockings. 4. Model, pattern, foundry pattern. 5. Plate of a gun-lock. 6. Celestial configuration. 7. Establishment (personas), personnel; list, roster; *(Dep.)* team, squad. **Plantilla de personal**, staff. 8. *(Comput.)* Template.

plantillar [plan-teel-lyar'], *va.* To vamp or sole shoes or stocking.

plantío, ia [plan-tee'-o, ah], *a.* Planted, ready to be planted (tierra).

plantío [plan-tee'-o], *m.* 1. Plantation, the act of planting. 2. Nursery, a plantation of young trees.

plantista [plan-tees'-tah], *s.* 1. Bully, hector, bravado. 2. In gardens, royal parks, etc., a planter of trees and shrubbery.

plantón [plan-tone'], *m.* 1. Scion, a sprout or shoot from a plant; a shoot ingrafted on a stock. 2. *(Mil.)* Sentry who performs duty as punishment. **Estar de plantón**, to stand waiting for someone for a long time. **Dar plantón a uno**, to stand somebody up.

planudo, da [plah-noo'-do, dah], *a.* *(Naut.)* Applied to a vessel which draws little water, as being too flat.

plañidera [plah-nye-day'-rah], *f.* Mourner woman paid for weeping at funerals.

plañido [plah-nye'-do], *m.* Moan, lamentation, crying. **Plañido, da** *pp.* of PLAÑIR.

plañir [plah-nyeer'], *vn.* To lament, to grieve, to bewail, to sob; to whimper and whine.

plaqué [plah-kay'], *m.* Plaque, an object of metal, covered with a thin layer of gold or silver.

plaqueta [plah-kay'-tah], *f.* Small plate, tag. **Plaqueta sanguínea**, blood platelet.

plasma [plash'-mah], *f.* Prase, a precious stone. -*m.* Plasma (sangre).

plasmador, ra [plas-mah-dor', rah], *m. & f.* Moulder, former.

plasmante [plas-mahn'-tay], *pa.* Moulding; moulder.

plasmar [plas-mar'], *va.* To mould, to form of clay, to make moulds.

plasmo [plahs'-mo], *m.* (Sculpture) Model, type.

plasta [plahs'-tah], *f.* 1. Thick paste, soft clay, anything soft. 2. *(Met. Coll.)* Botch (chapuza), something done without rule or order. -*m & f.* Bore (pelmazo).

plaste [plahs'-tay], *m.* Size, of glue and lime.

plastecer [plas-tay-thar'], *va.* To size, to besmear with size.

plastecido [plas-tay-thee'-do], *m.* Act of sizing. —**Plastecido, da**, *pp.* of PLASTECER.

plástica [plahs'-te-cah], *f.* Art of moulding in clay.

plasticidad [plas-te-the-dahd'], *f.* 1. Plasticity. 2. *(Fig.)* Expressiveness, descriptiveness.

plástico, ca [plahs'-te-co, cah], *a.* Plastic.

plastificado [plas-te-fe-cah'-do], *a.* Treated with plastic.

plastografía [plas-to-grah-fee'-ah], *f.* Plastography.

plata [plah'-tah], *f.* 1. Silver (metal). 2. Plate, wrought silver. 3. *(LAm.)* money (dinero). 4. *(Her.)* Plate; white. **Plata virgen or bruta**, crude mass of silver. **Plata labrada**, (a) wrought silver; (b) payment made in articles equivalent to money. **Valer tanto como la plata**, to be worth its weight in gold. **En plata**, briefly, without turnings or windings.

platabanda [plah-tah-bahn'-dah], *f.* Band or bar of flat iron.

plataforma [plah-tah-for'-mah], *f.* 1. *(Mil.)* Platform, an elevation of earth raised on ramparts; temporary platform. 2. A machine for making pieces of watches. 3. The platform of a street-car or tramway. 4. The stage of a microscope. **Plataforma de lanzamiento**, *(Aer.)* launching pad. **Plataforma de seguridad**, safety island. **Plataforma giratoria**, (r.w.) turntable. **Plataforma subterránea de lanzamiento**, *(Aer.)* silo.

platal [plah'-tahl], *(coll.)* Great wealth. V. DINERAL.

platanal

platanal, platanar [plah-tah-nal', plah-tah-nar'], *m.* Banana grove.

plátano [plah'-tah-no], *m.* 1. Banana. 2. Plantain. 3. Banana tree. 4. Plane tree.

platea [plah-tay'-ah], *f.* Parquet, orchestra.

platear [plah-tay-ar'], *f.* To silver.

plateresco, ca [plah-tay-res'-co, cah], *a.* Applied to fanciful ornaments in architecture; over-florid, plateresque.

platería [plah-tay-ree'-ah], *f.* 1. Silver-smith's shop (tienda). 2. Trade of a silversmith.

platero [plah-tay'-ro], *m.* Silversmith, plate-worker. **Platero de oro,** goldsmith.

plática [plah'-te-cah], *f.* 1. Talk, chat (charla), conversation: colloquy, converse. 2. Sermon (religioso), speech delivered on some public occasion, address, lecture. 3. Pratic or pratique, permission to a ship's crew to come on shore to buy and traffic. 4. *V.* PRÁCTICA. **Tomar pláctica,** to obtain practice. **Estar de plática,** to be chatting. **Se pasaron la mañana de plática,** they spent the morning chatting.

platicar [plah-te-car'], *va.* 1. To chat, to converse, to talk, to speak, to commune (charlar). 2. To practice a profession.

platija [plah-tee'-hah], *f.* (*Zool.*) Plaice, flounder.

platilla [plah-teel'-lya], *f.* Silesian linen.

platillo [plah-teel'-lyo], *m.* 1. (*dim.*) A small dish, saucer. 2. A side dish, as opposed to the entree or main course. 3. (*Mus.*) Cymbal, a percussion instrument. 4. Valve of a pump. **Platillo volador,** (*Aer.*) flying saucer.

platina [plah-tee'-nah], *f.* 1. An ore of platinum. 2. An exterior metallic ornament of carriages. 3. Platen, bedplate; also imposing-table, in printing. 4. Supports of any machine and lids which inclose the works of watches.

platino [plah-tee'-no], *m.* Platinum, the heaviest of metals.

platirrostro, tra [plah-teer-ros'-tro, trah], *a.* Platyrhine, having a broad nose, snout, or beak. *-m. V.* TODI.

plato [plah'-to], *m.* 1. Dish, plate (utensilio), a vessel to eat on. 2. Dish, mess, food served in a dish. 3. Daily fare. 4. Ornament in the frieze of Doric, architecture. 5. Chuck in which are made the teeth of wheels for watches. **Platos lisos, llanos or trincheros,** dining-plates. **Plato de segunda mesa,** makeshift, person or thing which has belonged to another, and whose possession is not flattering. **Plato frutero,** fruit dish. **Pagar los platos rotos,** to pay for the damage. **Un plato de arroz,** a dish of rice. **Plato fuerte,** main course.

platón [plah-tone'], *m.* (*Aug.*) Platter, a large dish.

platónicamente [plah-to-ne-cah-men-tay], *adv.* Platonically.

platónico, ca [plah-to'-ne-co, cah], *a.* Platonic, relating to Plato. **Amor platónico,** platonic love.

plato tocadiscos [plah'-to to-ca-dees'-cos], *m.* Turntable.

plato volador [plah'-to voh-lah-dor'], *m.* Flying saucer.

platuja [plah-too-hah], *f.* (*Prov.*) *V.* PLATIJA.

plausibilidad [plah-oo-se-be-le-dahd'], *f.* Plausibility, speciousness.

plausible [plah-oo-see'-blay], *a.* Plausible, specious.

plausiblemente [plah-oo-see'-blay-men-tay], *adv.* Plausibly, colorably.

plauso [plah'-oo-so], *m.* Applause by the clapping of hands.

plaustro [plah'-oos'-tro], *m.* (*Poet.*) Cart, wagon, carriage. *V.* CARRO.

playa [plah'-yah], *f.* Beach, shore (orilla), strand, sea coast. **En la playa,** on the beach, at the seaside.

playado, da [plah-yah'-do, dah], *a.* Applied to a river or sea with a shore.

playazo [plah-yah'-ro], *m.* Wide or extended shore.

playeras [plah-yay'-rahs], *f. pl.* Sneakers (zapatillas de lona).

playero [plah-yay'-ro], *a.* Beach (de playa).

playón [plah-yone'], *m. aug.* A large shore or beach.

playuela [plah-yoo-ay'-lah], *f.* Dim. of PLAYA.

plaza [plah'-thah], *f.* 1. Square, place, or market-place (mercado). 2. Place, a fortified town. 3. Room, space (espacio); stall. 4. Place, office, public employment. 5. Enlisting or enrolling of soldiers in the king's service. 6. Reputation, character, fame. **Plaza de armas,** military department, garrison, military parade-ground. (*Naut.*) The waist. **De dos plazas,** two-seater.

plazo [plah'-tho], *m.* 1. Time (término), limit. 2. Installment (pago), payment. 3. Terms. 4. Due date. **A plazo,** on time, on credit. **De largo plazo,** long-term. **Nos dan plazo de 8 días,** they allow us a week. **Se ha cumplido el plazo,** time is up.

plazuela [plah-thoo-ay'-lah], *f. dim.* A small square or place.

ple [play], *m.* (*Mex.*) *V.* BLE.

pleamar [play-ah-mar'], *f.* (*Naut.*) High water, high tide.

plebe [play'-bay], *f.* Common people, populace.

plebeyo, ya [play-bay'-yo, yah], *a.* Plebeian. *-m. & f.* Commoner.

plebiscito [play-bes-thee'-to], *m.* 1. Plebiscitum, a Roman law voted by the plebe at the instance of their tribune. 2. Plebiscite, an expression by vote of the will of the people.

pleca [play'-cah], *f.* (*Print.*) A straight line, a rule.

plectro [plec'-tro], *m.* 1. Plectrum, a small staff or tool for plucking the strings of a lyre, etc. 2. (*Poet.*) Plectrum, poesy.

plegable [play-gah'-blay], *a.* Pliable, capable of being folded.

plegadamente [play-gah-dah-men-tay], *adv.* Confusedly.

plegadera [play-gah-day'-rah], *f.* Folder, used by book binders.

plegadizo, za [play-gah-dee'-tho, thah], *a.* Pliable, folding.

plegado [play-gah-do], *m.* Folding; bending.

plegador [play-gah-dor'], *m.* 1. An instrument for folding or plaiting. 2. Plaiter, he that plaits. 3. (*coll.*) Collector of alms for religious communities. 4. Beam of a silk-loom.

plegadura [play-gah-doo'-rah], *f.* 1. Fold, double, complication. 2. Plaiting, folding, doubling. 3. Cream made by doubling.

plegamiento [play-gah-me-ayn-to], *m.* Jacknifing (de camión).

plegar [play-gar'], *va.* 1. To fold, to plait, to double. 2. To corrugate, to crimple, to purse up. 3. To turn the warp on the yarn-beam. 4. Among bookbinders, to fold the sheets of a book that is to be bound. (*Yo pliego, yo pliegue, from Plegar. V.* ACERTAR.)

plegaria [play-gah'-re-ah], *f.* 1. Public prayer, supplication. 2. Bell rung at noon for prayer.

pleguería [plah-gay-ree'-ah], *f.* Fold, crumple.

pleita [play'-ee-tah], *f.* A piloted strand of bass.

pleiteador, ra [play-e-tay-ah-dor', rah], *m. & f.* **Pleader, a litigious person, a** wrangler.

pleiteante [play-e-tay-ahn'-tay], *pa. & n.* Litigating; pleader, litigant.

pleitear [play-e-tay-ar'], *va.* 1. To plead, to litigate, to contend. 2. (*LAm.*) Brawler.

pleitesía [play-tay-see'-ah], *f.* Tribute. **Rendir pleitesía,** to render tribute, to pay homage (to some one).

pleitista [play-e-tees'-tah], *m.* Pettifogger, an encorager of lawsuits.

pleito [play'-e-to], *m.* 1. Convenant, contract, bargain. 2. Dispute, contest, controversy. 3. Debate, contention, strife. 4. Litigation, judicial contest, lawsuit. 5. (*LAm.*) Quarrel (discusión). **Pleito de acreedores,** proceedings under a commission of bankruptcy. **Ganar el pleito,** to win one's case.

plenamar [play-ah-mahr'], *f. V.* PLEAMAR.

plenamente [play-nah-men'-tay], *adv.* Fully, completely.

plenariamente [play-nah-re-ah-men'-tay], *adv.* Completely, fully, plenarily.

plenario, ria [play-nah'-re-o, ah], *a.* Complete, full, plenary.

plenilunio [play-ne-loo'-ne-o], *m.* Full moon.

plenipotencia [play-ne-po-ten'-the-ah], *f.* Plenipotence, fulness of power.

plenipotenciario [play-ne-po-ten-the-ah'-re-o], *m.* Plenipotentiary.

plenitud [play-nee-tood'], *f.* Plenitude, fulness, abundance.

pleno, na [play'-no, nah], *a.* Full. *V.* LLENO. **En pleno verano**, at the height of summer. **Le dio en plena cara**, it hit him full in the face.

pleonasmo [play-o-nahs'-mo], *m.* Pleonasm, a figure of speech.

pleonástico, ca [play-o-nahs'-te-co, cah], *a.* Pleonastic, involving pleoneasm.

plepa [play'-pah], *f.* 1. A charge; a person who has many defects, physically or morally. 2. Pain (molesto).

plétora [play'-to-rah], *f.* Plethora (abundancia), fulness of blood.

pletórico, ca [play-to'-re-co, cah], *a.* Plethoric.

pleural [play-oo-rahl'], *a.* Pleural, relating to the pleura.

pleuresía [play-oo-ray-see'-ah], *f.* Pleurisy, a disease. **Pleuresía falsa**, pleurodynia.

pleurítico, ca [play-oo-ree'-te-co, cah], *a.* Pleuritical, pleuritic.

pleuritis [play-oo-ree'-tis], *f.* Inflammation of the pleura, pleurisy.

pleurodinia [play-oo-ro-dee'-ne-ah], *f.* Pleurodynia, stitch in the side; pain in the intercostal muscles.

plexímetro [plec-see'-may-tro], *m.* Pleximeter, a medical instrument for practicing percussion.

plexo [plec'-so], *m. (Anat. and Bot.)* Plexus; network.

pléyadas, pléyades [play'-yah-dahs], *f. pl. (Ast.)* The Pleiades.

plica [plee'-cah], *f.* 1. Sealed parcel containing a will or document to be published in due time; escrow. 2. *(Med.)* Matted hair; plica.

pliego [ple-ay'-go], *m.* 1. Sheet of paper (hoja). 2. Parcel of letters enclosed in one cover. 3. A tender or proposal by persons who wish to contract with the government. 4. *V.* PLEGADURA and PLIEGUE.

pliegue [ple-ay'-gay], *m.* 1. Fold or pleat in clothes, crease; gather. 2. Ruff anciently worn.

plinto [pleen'-to], *m. (Arch.)* Plinth of a pillar.

plisado [ple-sah-do], *m.* Pleating.

plomada [plo-mah'-ah], *f.* 1. Artificer's lead-pencil. 2. Plumb, plummet. 3. *(Naut.)* Lead used by seamen for sounding the depth of water. 4. All the weights attached to fishing-nets; sinkers.

plomar [plo-mar'], *va.* To put a leaden seal, hanging by a thread to some instrument, privilege, etc.

plomazón [plo-mah-thone'], *f.* Gilding cushion.

plombagina [plom-bah-hee'-nah], *f.* Plumbago, graphite.

plomería [plo-may-ree'-ah], *f.* 1. Covering of lead on roofs. 2. Storehouse of lead ware (taller).

plomero [plo-may'-ro], *m.* Plumber, a worker in lead.

plomizo, za [plo-mee'-tho, thah], *a.* Leaden, made of lead; having the qualities of lead.

plomo [plo'-mo], *m.* 1. Lead, a very heavy metal (metal). 2. Any piece of lead. **Plomo en plancha**, lead in sheets. 3. Ball of lead. **Andar con pies de plomo**, to proceed with the utmost circumspection. **A plomo**, perpendicularity, plumb. **Caer a plomo**, to fall flat down. 4. Plumb, a plummet. 5. *(LAm.)* Bullet. 6. *(Mex.)* Gunfight.

plomoso [plo-mo'-so], **sa**, *a.* Leaden. *V.* PLOMIZO.

plóter [plo-tayr]. *(Comput.)* Printer plotter.

pluma [ploo'-mah], *f.* 1. Feather, the plume of birds. 2. Pen, for writing (de escribir). **Pluma estilográfica**, fountain pen. 3. Art of writing, penmanship (caligrafía). 4. Writer, author. **Buena pluma**, a good penman, a skiful writer. **Golpe de pluma**, dash with the pen. 5. *(coll.)* Wealth, opulence. 6. *(coll.)* Air expelled from the bowels. 7. *(CAm.)* Fib, tale (mentira). 7. *(Cono Sur)* Prostitute (puta). 8. *(Cono Sur)* Crane (grúa).

plumada [ploo-mah'-dah], *f.* 1. Act of writing something short. 2. Dash with a pen, a line with a crayon. 3. Feathers which falcons have eaten, and have still in the crop.

plumado, da [ploo-mah'-do, dah], *a.* Feathered, feathery, plumy.

plumaje [ploo-mah'-hay], *m.* 1. Plumage of a fowl or bird. 2. Plume, an ornament of feathers (adorno).

plumajería [ploo-mah-hay-ree'-ah], *f.* Heap of leathers.

plumajero [ploo-mah-hay'-pro], *m.* One who dresses feathers and makes plumes.

plumazo [ploo-mah'-tho], *m.* 1. A mattress or pillow stuffed with feathers (colchón, almohada). 2. Stroke (de una pluma). **Abolir de un plumazo**, to abolish by a stroke of the pen (denoting rapidity of action).

plumazón [ploo-mah-thone'], *f.* Collection of feathers.

plúmbeo, bea [ploom'-bay-o, ah], *a.* Leaden, made of lead, having the qualities of lead.

plumeado [ploo-may-ah'-do], *m. (Pict.)* Series of lines similar to those made with a pen in a miniature.

plumear [ploo-may-ar'], *va. (Pict.)* To draw lines with a pen or pencil, to shade a drawing.

plúmeo, mea [ploo'-may-o, ah], *a.* Plumigerous, having feathers, plumous.

plumería [ploo-may-ree'-ah], *f. V.* PLUMAJERÍA.

plumero [ploo-may'-ro], *m.* 1. Bunch of feathers, feather-duster (para limpiar). 2. Box in which feathers or plumes are preserved (portaplumas). 3. Plume (adorno). 4. Plumage.

plumífero, ra [ploo-mee'-fay-ro, rah], *a. (Poet.)* Plumigerous.

plumilla [ploo-meel'-lyah], *f.* Script type.

plumión [ploo-me-on'], *m. V.* PLUMON.

plumista [ploo-mees'-tah], *m.* 1. One who lives by writing, a petty notary. 2. A worker in feather, plume-maker.

plumita [ploo-mee'-tah], *f. dim.* A small feather of pen.

plumón [ploo-mone'], *m.* 1. Soft, downy feathers. 2. Feather-bed (cama), flock-bed.

plumoso, da [ploo-mo'-so, sah], *a.* Covered with feathers, plumigerous, plumy.

plúmula [ploo'-moo-lah], *f. (Bot.)* Plumule.

plural [ploo-rahl'], *a. (Gram.)* Plural.

pluralidad [ploo-lah-le-dahd'], *f.* Plurality, multitude; majority. **A pluralidad de votos**, by the majority of voices.

pluriempleado [ploo-re-aym-play'-ah-do], *a.* Having more than one job.

pluriempleo [ploo-re-aym-play'-o], *m.* Having more than one job.

plus [ploos], *m.* Extra pay, bonus.

pluscuamperfecto [ploos-kwam-per-fec'-to], *m.* The pluperfect tense or past perfect.

plusmarca [ploos-mahr'-cah], *f.* Record.

plusmarquista [ploos-mahr-kees'-tah], *m & f.* Record holder.

pluspetición [ploos-pay-te-the-on'], *f.* Asking for more than what is due.

plus ultra [ploos ool'-trah]. **Ser el non plus ultra**, *(coll.)* to be transcendent.

plusvalía [ploos-vah-lee'-ah], *f.* Appreciation, added value.

plúteo [ploo'-tay-o], *m.* Each compartment of book-shelves in a library.

plutocracia [ploo-to-crah'-the-ah], *f.* Plutocracy.

plutocrático, ca [ploo-to-crah'-te-co, cah], *a.* Plutocratic.

plutonio [ploo-to'-ne-o], *m.* Plutonium.

pluvial [ploo-ve-ahl'], *m. (Orn.)* Golden plover.

pluvial, pluvioso, sa [ploo-ve-ahl'], *a.* Rainy. **Capa pluvial**, a priest's cope, worn at the celebration of mass.

pluviatil [ploo-ve-ah'-teel], *a.* Softened or mellowed by rain (temperatura).

pluvímetro *(Acad.)* [ploo-vee'-may-tro], or **Pluviómetro**, *m.* Rain-gauge.

pneumático [nay-oo-mah'-te-co], **ca**, *a. V.* NEUMÁTICO.

poa [po'-ah], *f. (Naut.)* Bow-line, bridle.

pobeda [po-bay'-dah], *f.* Plantation of poplars.

población [po-blah-the-on'], *f.* 1, Population, the act of populating. 2. Population, the state of a city, town, or country with regard to the number of its inhabitants. 3. *V.* POBLADO.

poblacho [po-blah'-cho], *m.* 1. A mean and ugly village. 2. Populace, rabble, mob.

poblachón [po-blah-chone'], *m. aug.* 1. *V.* POBLACHO, 1st def. 2. A large collection of houses, more than a village and less than a town.

poblado [po-blah'-do], *m.* Town, village, or place inhabited (habitado).—**Poblado, da,** *pp.* of POBLAR. **La ciudad más poblada del país,** the most populous city in the country.

poblador, ra [po-blah-dor', rah], *m. & f.* Populator, founder (fundador).

poblar [po-blar'], *va. & vn.* 1. To found a town, to populate a district, to people (habitar). 2. To fill, to occupy. 3. To breed, to procreate fast. 4. To bud, to get leaves. **Las estrellas que pueblan el espacio,** the stars that fill space.

poblazo [po-blah'-tho], *m.* V. POPULACHO.

poblezuelo [po-blay-thoo-ay'-lo], *m. dim.* A small village.

pobo [po'-bo], *m. (Bot.)* White poplar. V. ÁLAMO BLANCO.

pobre [po'-bray], *a.* 1. Poor, necessitous, indigent, needy. 2. Poor, barren, dry. 3. Humble, modest. 4. Poor, unhappy, pitiable, wretched. 5. Poor, trifling, paltry, unimportant. **Pobre y soberbio,** proud pauper. **¡Pobre de mí!,** poor old me!

pobre [po'-bray], *m.* 1. A poor person (necesitado), a beggar (mendigo). 2. A man of very pacific and quiet temper.

pobrecico, ica, illo, illa, ito, ita [po-bray-thee'-co], *a. dim.* A poor little thing.

pobremente [po'-bray-men-tay], *adv.* Poorly, miserably, needily.

pobrería [po-bray-ree'-ah], *f.* Poor people, beggars.

pobrero [po-bray'-ro], *m.* One who is appointed by a religious community to distribute charities.

pobreta [po-bray'-tah], *f. (coll.)* Strumpet, prostitute.

pobrete, pobreto [po-bray'-tay], *m.* 1. A poor, unfortunate man. 2. A useless person, of mean abilities and sentiments.

pobretería [po-bray-tay-ree'-ah], *f.* 1. Poor people, beggars. 2. Poverty, indigence.

pobretón, na [po-bray-tone', nah], *a.* Very poor.

pobreza [po-bray'-thah], *f.* 1. Poverty, indigence, necessity, want, need. 2. Poorness, sterility, barrenness. 3. Heap of worthless trifles. 4. Voluntary vow of poverty. 5. Poorness, lowness or littleness of spirit. **Pobreza de espíritu,** poorness of spirit.

pobrezuelo [po-bray-thoo-ay'-lo], *m. dim.* A poor man.

pobrismo [po-brees'-mo], *m.* Poor people, beggars.

pocero [po-thay'-ro], *m.* 1. One who digs pits and wells. 2. Nightman, one who cleanses wells, pits, or common sewer's.

pocho, cha [po'-cho, chah], *a.* 1. *(coll.)* Discolored, that has lost the color. 2. *(Fig.)* Depressed, gloomy. 3. *(Cono Sur)* Chubby (gordito).

pochola [po-cho'-lah], *f.* Nice girl.

pocholada [po-cho-lah'-dah], *f.* Nice thing.

pocico [po-thee'-co], *m. dim.* A small well.

pocilga [po-theel'-gah], *f.* 1. Hogsty, a place for swine. 2. Any nasty, dirty place.

pocillo [po-theel'-lyo], *m.* 1. *(dim.)* Small well. 2. Vessel for collecting any liquor or fluid. 3. *(Prov.)* Chocolate-cup.

pócima [po'-the-mah], *f.* Potion, a draught of physic.

poción [po-the-on'], *f.* Drink, liquor; potion. V. BEBIDA.

poco, ca [po'-co, cah], *a.* Little, scanty (escaso), limited, small in quantity, small in extent (pequeño), not much, few, some. **De poco interés,** of small interest. **Todas las medidas son pocas,** any measure will be inadequate. *-adv.* Little (no mucho), in a small degree or quantity, in a scanty manner, shortly, briefly, in a short time. **Poco antes** or **poco después,** a little before or after. **Poco a poco,** gently, softly; stop! by little and little. **De poco tiempo acá,** latterly. **Tener en poco,** to set little value on a thing. **A poco, por poco, en poco,** to be very near a thing. **Qué poco,** how little: indicating the difficulty or impossibility of anything. **Ahora trabaja muy poco,** he only works a little now. **Poco amable,** unkind. **Por poco,** almost. *-m.* Little, a small part or proportion. **Un poco,** a little.

pocoyán [po-co-yahn'], *m.* A bee of the Philippine Islands, somewhat larger than the European.

póculo [po'-coo-lo], *m.* 1. Drinking cup. 2. *(Obs.)* Drink.

poda [po'-dah], *f.* Pruning of trees, pruning season (temporada).

podadera [po-dah-day'-rah], *f.* Pruning-knife, pruning-hook, hedging-bill.

podador, ra [po-dah-dor', rah], *m. & f.* Pruner of trees or vines.

podadura [po-dah-doo'-rah], *f. (Prov.)* V. PODA.

podagra [po-dah'-grah], *f.* Gout in the feet.

podar [po-dar'], *va.* To prune trees; to head, to lop (mondar).

podazón [po-dah-thone'], *f.* The pruning season.

podenco [po-den'-co], *m.* Hound.

podenquillo [po-den-keel'-lyo], *m. dim.* A young or small bound.

poder [po-derr'], *m.* 1. Power (fuerza), faculty, authority (autoridad), dominion, command, influence, mastery, force. 2. Military strength of a state. 3. Power or letter of attorney. 4. Power, possession (posesión). 5. Power, ability, force, vigor, capacity, possibility. **A poder de,** by force. **Poder esmerado** or **supremo,** supreme power. **El dinero es poder,** money is power. **Tiene poder para arruinarnos,** he has the power to ruin us. **Poder ejecutivo,** executive power.

poder [po-derr'], *va.* 1. To be able, may or can, to possess the power of doing anything (capacidad). 2. To be invested with authority or power. 3. To have force or energy to act or resist. 4. In geometry, to value, to produce. **A más no poder,** able to resist no longer. **No poder más,** not to be able to do more; to be exhausted; not to help to do a thing. *-v. imp.* To be possible or contingent. *-vn.* 1. May (posibilidad). 2. Can (absoluto). 3. **Puede que vaya,** I may go. **Puede no venir,** he may not come. **Los que pueden,** those who can. 4. *(CAm. Mex.)* To annoy, to upset.

poderdante [po-der-dahn'-tay], *com.* The constituent, the person who authorizes another.

poderhabiente [po-der-ah-be-en'-tay], *m.* Attorney, one authorized or empowered to transact another's business.

poderío [po-day-ree'-o], *m.* 1. Power, authority (señorío), dominion, jurisdiction. 2. Wealth, riches.

poderosamente [po-day-ro'-sah-men-tay], *adv.* Powerfully, mightily.

poderoso, sa [po-day-ro'-so, sah], *a.* 1. Powerful, mighty, potent. 2. Rich, wealthy. 3. Eminent, excellent. 4. Powerful, efficacious. 5. Powerful, able, forcible.

podio [po'-de-o], *m.* A long pedestal on which several columns are supported.

podofilina [po-do-fe-lee'-nah], *f.* Podophyllin, a purgative principle obtained from the may-apple or podophyllum.

podologo, ga [po-do'-lo-go], *m & f.* Chiropodist.

podómetro [po-do'-may-tro], *m.* Pedometer, instrument for measuring a person's steps or the circumvolutions of a wheel.

podón [po-done'], *m.* Mattock, hoe, an instrument for pulling up weeds.

podre [po'-dray], *f.* Pus, corrupted blood.

podrecer [po-dray-therr'], *va. & vn.* V. PUDRIR. *-vr.* To be putrid, rotten, or corrupt.

podrecimiento [po-dray-the-me-en'-to], *m.* 1. Rottenness, putrefaction. 2. Pain, grief.

podredumbre [po-dray-doom'-bray], *f.* 1. Pus, putrid matter, corruption (corrupción). 2. Grief, internal pain (tristeza).

podredura [po-dray-doo'-rah], *f.* Putrefaction, corruption.

podrición [po-dre-the-on'], *f.* V. PODREDURA.

podridero [po-dre-day'-ro], *m.* V. PUDRIDERO.

podrido [po-dre'-do], *a.* 1. Rotten, bad; putrid (putrefacto). 2. *(Cono Sur)* Fed-up (harto).

podrimiento [po-dre-me-ayn'-to], *m.* V. PODRIMIENTO.

podrir [po-drer'], *va.* V. PUDRIR.

poema [po-ay'-mah], *m.* Poem, a metrical composition.

poesía [po-ay-see'-ah], *f.* 1. Poetry. **Poesías,** poetical works. 2. Poetical composition.

poeta [po-ay'-tah], *m.* A poet.

poetastro [po-ay-tahs'-tro], *m* Poetaster.

poética [po-ay'-te-cah], *f.* Poetry; poetics, the art or practice of writing poems.

poéticamente [po-ay'-te-cah-men-tay], *adv.* Poetically.

poético, ca [po-ay'-te-co, cah], *a.* Poetic, poetical.

poetilla [po-ay-teel'-lyah], *m. dim.* Poetaster.

poetisa [po-ay-tee'-sah], *f.* Poetess, a female poet.

poetizar [po-ay-te-thar'], *vn.* To poetize, to write like a poet.

poetón [po-ay-tone'], *m.* Poetaster, a vile poet.

pogrom [po-grom'], *m.* Pogrom, organized massacre of helpless people.

poíno [po-ee'-no], *m.* A wooden frame, on which barrels of wine or beer are laid.

polaca [po-lah'-cah], *f.* Polonaise, a Polish song and dance.

polaco, ca [po-lah'-co, cah], *a.* Polish, relating to Poland. -*m.* The Polish language. -*m. & f.* A native of Poland.

polacra [po-lah'-crah], *f. (Naut.)* Polacre, a vessel with three pole-masts, used in the Mediterranean.

polaina [po-lah'-e-nah], *f.* Legging gaiter, puttee. -*pl.* Spats.

polar [po-lar'], *a.* Polar.

polaridad [po-lah-re-dahd'], *f.* Polarity.

polarización [po-lah-re-thah-the-on'], *f.* Polarization, a modification of light by refraction or by reflection at 35°.

polarizar [po-lah-re-thar'], *va.* To polarize.

polca [pol'-cah], *f.* 1. Polka, a well known dance originally from Poland. 2. *(And.)* Blouse; *(And. Cono Sur)* Long jacket.

polcar [pol-car'], *vn.* To dance the polka.

polea [po-lay'-ah], *f.* 1. Pulley. 2. *(Naut.)* Tackle-block, or the double block of a tackle.

poleadas [po-lay-ah'-das], *f. pl.* V. GACHAS or PUCHAS.

poleame [po-lay-ah'-may], *m.* Collection of masts for vessels.

poleita [po-lay-ee'-tah], *f. (Naut.)* A small block.

polémica [po-lay'-me-cah], *f.* 1. Polemics, dogmatical divinity. 2. *(Mil.)* The science of fortification. 3. Literary or political controversy.

polémico, ca [po-lay'-me-co, cah], *a.* Polemical, polemic.

polemizar [po-lay-me-thar'], *vn.* To indulge a polemic. **No quiero polemizar**, I don't want to get involved in an argument.

polemonio [po-lay-moh'-ne-o], *m. (Bot.)* Jacob's-ladder, Greek valerian.

polemoscopio [po-lay-mos-co'-pe-o], *m. (Opt.)* Polemoscope, telescope used by military commanders.

polen [po'-len], *m. (Bot.)* Pollen.

polenta [po-len'-ah], *f.* Porridge, a kind of batter or hasty pudding.

poleo [po-lay'-o], *m.* 1. *(Bot.)* Penny royal. 2. A strutting gait; a pompous style. 3. Stiff, cold wind.

poleví [po-lay-vee'], *m.* A high wooden heel formerly worn by women.

poliandria [po-le-ahn-dre'-ah], *f. (Bot.)* Polyandria.

poliantea [po-le-an-tay'-ah], *f.* Polyanthea, a literary collection.

poliantes tuberosa [po-le-ahn'-tes too-bay-ro'-sah], *f. (Bot.)* Common tuberose.

poliarquía [po-le-ar-kee'-ah], *f.* Polygarchy, government of many persons.

poliárquico, ca [po-le-ar'-ke-ko, cah], *a.* Relating to polygarchy.

policán, or **pelicán** [pay-le-cahn'], *m.* Pelican, instrument for drawing teeth.

policarpo [po-le-car'-po], *a. (Bot.)* Polycarpous.

pólice [pos'-le-thay], *m.* The thumb.

policía [po-le-thee'-ah], *f.* 1. Police, a branch of the executive government of a country, which watches over the preservation of public order (organización). 2. Politeness, good-breeding (cortesía). 3. Cleanliness, neatness (limpieza). **Policía de barrio**, neighborhood police. **Policía militar**, military police.

policíaco, ca [po-le-thee'-ah-co, cah], *a.* Police, relative to the police. **Novela policíaca**, detective novel, mystery story. **Vigilancia policíaca**, police watch.

policial [po-le-the-ahl'], *a.* Police. -*m. (CAm.)* Policeman.

policromo, ma [po-le-cro'-mo, mah], *a.* Polychrome, varicolored.

polideportivo [po-le-day-por-te'-vo], *m.* Sports center.

poliéster [po-le-ays'-tayr], *m.* Polyester.

polietileno [po-le-ay-te-lay'-no], *m.* Polyethylene.

polifacético [po-le-fah-thay'-te-co], *a.* Many-sided, versatile.

polifónico, ca [po-le-fo'-ne-co, cah], *a.* Polyphonic.

polífono, na [po-lee'-fo-no, nah], *a.* V. POLIFÓNICO.

polígala [po-lee'-gah-lah], *f. (Bot.)* Milkwort. **Polígala vulgar**, common milkwort.

poligamia [po-le-gah'-me-ah], *f.* 1. Polygamy. 2. *(Bot.)* Polygamia, the name of a class in the Linnaean system.

polígamo, ma [po-lee'-gah-mo, mah], *m. & f.* 1. Polygamist. 2. One who has several wives or husbands.

poligarquía [po-le-gahr'-ke-ah], *f.* V. POLIARQUÍA.

políglota [po-le'-glo-tah], *f.* A polyglot, or a Bible in many languages.

polígloto, ta [po-le'-glo-to, tah], *a.* Polyglot, written in various languages. -*m. & f.* One who knows many languages.

polígono [po-lee'-go-no], *m.* 1. Polygon, a multilateral figure. 2. *(Bot.)* Polygon, a small evergreen plant, a species of germander. 3. Face of a fortification for instructing pupils how to attack a place. 4. Practical school of artillery. 5. *(Esp.)* Site (solar), building lot, area (zona); housing estate (viviendas).

polígono, na [po-lee'-go-no, nah], *a.* Polygonal, multangular.

poligrafía [po-le-grah-fee'-ah], *f.* Polygraphy, the art of writing in ciphers.

polihedro [po-le-ay'-dro], *m. (Geom.)* Polyhedron.

polilla [po-leel'-lyah], *f.* 1. Moth, clothes-moth. 2. Consumer, waster.

polimatía [po-le-mah-tee'-ah], *f.* Polymathy, the knowledge of many arts and sciences.

polimerización [po-le-may-re-tha-the-on'], *f.* Polymerization.

polímero [po-lee'-may-ro], *m.* Polymer.

polimorfismo [po-le-mor-fees'-mo], *m.* Polymorphism.

polimorfo, fa [po-le-mor'-fo, fah], *a.* Polymorphous, of several forms.

polín [po-leen'], *m. (Naut.)* Wooden roller, for moving great guns or any other heavy object.

polinización [po-le-ne-thah-the-on'], *f.* Pollination.

polinomio [po-le-no'-me-o], *m. (Math.)* Polynomial, an expression of more than two terms.

poliomielitis [po-le-o-me-ay-lee'-tis], *f.* Infantile paralysis, poliomyelitis, polio.

polipétalo, la [po-le-pay'-tah-lo, lah], *a.* Polypetalous.

poliorima [po-le-o-rah'-mah], *m.* Polyorama, an apparatus presenting a view of many objects.

pólipo [po'-le-po], *m.* 1. Polypus, a genus of zoophytes. 2. Polypus, a fleshy or gelatinous tumor. 3. V. PULPO.

poliscopio [po-les-co'-pe-o], *m. (Opt.)* Polyscope.

polisílabo, ba [po-le-see'-lah-bo, bah], *a.* Polysyllabic, polysyllabical.

polisílabo [po-le-see'-lah-bo], *m.* Polysyllable.

polisón [po-le-sone'], *m.* Bustle, pad formerly worn beneath a woman's skirt.

polispermático, ca [po-lis-per-mah'-te-co, cah], or **polispermo, ma**, *a. (Bot.)* Polyspemous, many seeded.

politécnico, ca [po-le-tek'-ne-co, cah], *a.* Polytechnico, embracing many arts.

politeísmo [po-le-tay-ees'-mo], *m.* Polytheism.

politeísta [po-le-tay-ees'-tah], *com. & a* Polytheist.

política [po-lee'-te-cah], *f.* 1. Policy, politics; the art or science of government. 2. Politeness, civility. **Mezclarse en la política**, to go in for politics. **Política económica**, economic policy.

políticamente [po-lee'-te-cah-men-tay], *adv.* Politically, civilly.

politicastro [po-le-te-cahs'-troh], *m.* Politicaster: used in contempt.

político, ca [po-lee'-te-co, cah], *a.* 1. Political, politic (diplomático). 2. Polite, courteous (cortés). 3. In-law (pariente). **Padre político**, father-in-law.

político [po-lee'-te-co], *m.* Politician.

politiquear [po-le-te-kay-ar'], *vn.* To affect the politician.

politizar [po-le-te-thar'], *va.* To politicize.

poliuretano [po-le-oo-ray-tah'-no], *m.* Polyurethane.

póliza [po'-le-thah], *f.* 1. Check, draft, an order for the payment of money. 2. **Póliza de seguro**, policy of insurance. 3. A permit for the custom-house. 4. Entrance-ticket for some ceremony. 5. Tax stamp (impuesto). 6. Insurance certificate (de seguro).

polizón [po-le-thone'], *m.* 1. Bum, tramp (vago) 2. Stowaway.

polla [pol'-lyah], *f.* 1. Pullet, young hen, chicken. 2. *(coll.)* A comely young lass. 3. Money staked in games at carafe by all the players; pool. 4. *(Cono Sur)* Lottery. 5. *(Esp.)* Prick (pene).

pollada [po-lyah'-dah], *f.* Flock of young fowls; hatch, covey.

pollagallina [pol-lyah-gal-lyee'-nah], *f.* Hen-chicken.

pollastro, ra [pol-lyahs'-tro, trah], *m. & f.* A large chicken. 1. *(coll.)* A cunning fellow: a knowing person. 2. A fine stout lad.

pollazón [pol-lyah-thone'], *m.* Hatching and rearing fowls; hatch.

pollera [po-lyay'-rah], *f.* 1. A narrow-mouthed basket or net (cesto), in which pullets are kept; a hen-coop (criadero). 2. A go-cart, in which children learn to walk. 3. A short, trooped petticoat.

pollería [pol-lyay-ree'-ah], *f.* Shop or market where poultry is sold.

pollero [pol-lyay'-ro], *m.* 1. One who keeps or rears fowls. 2. Place or yard where fowls are kept. 3. One who keeps or feeds fowls for sale; a poulterer. 4. *(LAm.)* Gambler.

pollico, ica, illo, illa, ito, ita [pol-lyee'-co], *n.* A small chicken.

pollina [pol-lyee'-nah], *f.* Young she-ass.

pollino [pol-lyee'-no], *m.* 1. Properly, a young, untamed ass, but now applied to any ass or jument. 2. *(Met.)* Ass, a stupid fellow.

pollito, ta [pol-lyee'-to, tah], *m. & f.* Chickens: applied to boys and girls of tender age.

pollo [pol'-lyo], *m.* 1. Chicken just hatched, nestling. 2. Young bee. 3. *(coll.)* Artful, clever man. 4. A bird which has not yet changed its feathers.

polluelo, la [pol-loo-ay'-lo, lah], *m. & f. dim.* A small chicken.

polo [po'-lo], *m.* 1. Pole, the extremity of the axis of the earth. 2. Pole of the magnetic needle. 3. Support, foundation. 4. Personal service of forty days in the year by the natives of the Philippine Islands. 5. Pole; focus, centre. **Polo de atracción**, focus of interest. **Polo negativo**, negative pole.

polo [po'-lo], *m.* Polo, polo game.

polonés, sa [po-lo-nays', sah], *a.* Polish. *V.* POLACO.

polonesa [po-lo-nay'-sah], *f.* 1. Polonaise. *V.* POLACA. 2. A fur-trimmed jacket, girded at the waist.

poltrón, na [pol-trone', nah], *a.* 1. Idle, lazy, lubberly. 2. Commodious, easy. **Silla poltrona**, elbow-chair.

poltrón [pol-trone'], *m. (coll.)* Poltroon.

poltronería [pol-tro-nay-ree'-ah], *f.* Idleness, laziness, indolence, sluggishness.

poltronizarse [pol-tro-ne-thar'-say], *vr.* To become lazy.

polución [po-loo-the-on'], *f.* 1. Pollution, stain; bodily deformity. 2. A voluntary or involuntary emission of semen.

poluto, ta [po-loo'-to, tah], *a.* Polluted, contaminated, defiled; unclean. filthy.

polvareda [pol-vah-ray'-dah], *f.* 1. Cloud of dust (polvo). 2. Altercation, dispute, debate.

polvera [pol-vay'-rah], *f.* Compact, vanity case.

polvificar [pol-ve-fe-car'], *va. (coll.)* To pulverize, to reduce to powder or dust.

polvillo, ito [pol-veel'-lyo], *m. dim.* 1. Fine dust. 2. *(And. Cono Sur. Agr.)* Blight. 3. *(And. Cono Sur)* Tobacco refuse.

polvo [pol'-vo], *m.* 1. Dust, earth reduced to dust. 2. Powder, dust, the state of solid bodies comminuted. 3. Powder for the hair: in the two last senses it is commonly used in the plural. 4. A pinch (porción), so much as can be taken between the ends of the fingers. **Polvo de patata** or **patata en polvo**, a confectioned potato. **Sacudir el polvo**, to bent out the dust with a stick: to whip severely. **Quitar el polvo de un mueble**, to dust a piece of furniture. **Hacer algo polvo**, to smash something. **Ponerse polvos**, to powder one's face.

polvo de hornear [pol'-vo day or-nay-ar'], *m.* Baking powder.

polvo de talco [pol'-vo day tahl'-co], *m.* Talcum powder.

pólvora [pol'-vo-rah], *f.* 1. Powder, gunpowder. 2. Artificial fireworks (fuegos artificiales). 3. Provocation, cause of anger (mal genio). 4. Vivacity (viveza), liveliness, briskness. **5.** Powder, dust. **Es una pólvora**, he is as hot as pepper. **Mojar la pólvora**, to appease, to allay the rage of an angry person. **Propagarse como la pólvora**, to spread like wildfire.

polvorear [pol-vo-ray-ar'], *va.* To powder, to sprinkle as with dust.

polvoriento, ta [pol-vo-re-en'-to, tah], *a.* Dusty, full of dust; covered with dust.

polvorín [pol-vo-reen'], *m.* 1. Powder reduced to the finest dust. 2. Powder-flask, priming-horn. 3. Powder-magazine. 4. *(Cono Sur)* Gnat (insecto). 5. *(And. Carib.)* Cloud of dust (polvareda).

polvorista [pol-vo-rees'-tah], *m.* 1. Manufacturer of gunpowder. 2. Maker of fire-works.

polvorizable [pol-vo-re-thah'-blay], *a.* Pulverizable.

polvorización [pol-vo-re-thah-the-on'], *f.* Pulverization.

polvorizar [pol-vo-re-thar'], *va.* 1. To pulverize. 2. *V.* POLVOREAR.

polvorón [pol-vo-rone'], *m. (LAm. Culin.)* Cake.

polvoroso, sa [pol-vo-ro'-so, sah], *a.* Dusty, covered with dust.

poma [po'-mah], *f.* 1. Apple. *V.* MANZANA. 2. Perfume-box, a bottle containing perfumes (frasco). 3. Metallic vessel with different perfumes, having small apertures to admit their escape when set on a fire to perfume rooms.

pomada [po-mah'-dah], *f.* 1. Ointment (medicina). 2. Pomatum, pomade (cosmético). **Pomada para los labios**, lip-salve. 2. **Hacer algo pomada**, *(Cono Sur)* to break something to bits.

pomar [po-mar'], *m.* Orchard, a garden of fruit-trees, particularly of apple-trees.

pomelo [po-may'-lo], *m. (Esp.)* Grapefruit.

pómez [po'-meth], *f.* Pumice-stone.

pomífero, ra [po-mee'-fay-ro, rah], *a. (Poet.)* Pomiferous, having apples.

pomo [po'-mo], *m.* 1. Fruit in general, but in particular the fruit of the apple-tree. 2. Glass bull in the shape of an apple, used to hold perfumes (frasco). 3. Pommel of sword (espada). 4. *(Prov.)* Nosegay, a bunch of flowers. 5. A glass bottle.

pomología [po-mo-lo-hee'-ah], *f.* Pomology, science and practice of fruit-growing.

pompa [pom'-pah], *f.* 1. Pomp, ostentation in feasts or funerals, pageantry. 2. Pomp, splendor, parade, grandeur. 3. Pomp, a procession of splendor and ostentation. 4. Bubble. 5. Fold in clothes raised by the wind. 6. The expanded tail of a turkey or peacock. 7. *(Naut.)* Pump. *V.* BOMBA.

pompas fúnebres [pom'-pahs foo'-nay-brays], *f. pl.* Funeral, burial, funeral services.

pompearse, pomponearse [pom-pay-ar'-say], *vr.* To appear with pomp and ostentation.

pompeyano, na [pom-pay-yah'-no, nah], *a.* Pompeian, of Pompeii.

pomposamente [pom-po'-sah-men-tay], *adv.* Pompously, magnificently, loftily, flourishingly.

pomposo, sa [pom-po'-so, sah], *a.* Pompous, ostentatious, magnificent, splendid, majestic, inflated, swelled.

pómulo [po'-moo-lo], *m.* Prominence of the cheek-bone (hueso); cheek (mejilla).

ponchada [pon-chah'-dah], *f.* The quantity of punch made at one time.

ponche [pon'-chay], *m.* Punch, a liquor.

ponchera [pon-chay'-rah], *f.* 1. Punch bowl (para ponche). 2. *(And. Carib. Mex.)* Washbasin (palangana); *(And.)* Bath (bañera). 3. *(Cono Sur)* Paunch (barriga).

poncho [pon'-cho], *m.* Poncho (manta), man's jacket; blanket (frazada).

poncho, cha [pon'-cho, chah], *a.* Lazy (vago), indolent, heedless.

ponchón, na [pon-chone', nah], *a.* Extremely careless, excessively lazy.

ponderable [pon-day-rah'-blay], *a.* 1. Ponderable, capable of being weighed; measurable by scales. 2. Wonderful, important.

ponderación [pon-day-rah-the-on'], *f.* 1. Weighing mentally, pondering or considering. 2. Exaggeration, heightening.

ponderado, ta [pon-day-rah'-do, dah], *a. & pp.* of PONDERAR. 1. Presumptuous, arrogant, insolent. 2. Exaggerated.

ponderador, ra [pon-day-rah-dor', rah], *m. & f.* 1. Ponderer; he who exaggerates. 2. One who weighs or examines.

ponderal [pon-day-rahl'], *a.* Ponderal, relating to weight.

ponderar [pon-day-rar'], *va.* 1. To weigh (estadística). 2. To ponder, to consider, to attend (considerar). 3. To exaggerate, to heighten; to cry up. **Ponderar algo a uno**, to speak warmly of something to somebody.

ponderativo, va [pon-day-ray-tee'-vo, vah], *a.* Exaggerating, hyperbolical.

ponderosamente [pon-day-ro-sah-men-tay], *adv.* Attentively, carefully: with great attention.

ponderosidad [pon-day-ro-se-dahd'], *f.* Ponderousness, ponderosity, weightiness. V. PESADEZ.

ponderoso, sa [pon-day-ro'-so, sah], *a.* 1. Heavy, ponderous, weighty. 2. Grave, circumspect, cautious.

ponedero, ra [po-nay-day'-ro, rah], *a.* 1. Laying eggs. 2. Capable of being laid or placed.

ponedero [po-nay-day'-ro], *m.* 1. Nest, hen's nest. 2. Nest-egg.

ponedor, ra [po-nay-dor', rah], *m. & f.* 1. One who puts, sets, or places. 2. Better, wagerer; outbidder. 3. In paper-mills, the maker who delivers the sheet to the coucher. *-a.* Applied to horses trained to rear on their hind legs, and to fowls laying eggs.

ponencia [po-nen'-the-ah], *f.* Charge, post, or office of a chairman of a committee, or of a final judge or arbiter: and the exercise of such office.

ponente [po-nen'-tay], *a.* Who has the casting vote: arbitrator, final judge: said of a judge or the chairman of a committee.

ponentino, na, ponentisco, ca [po-nen-tee'-no, nah], *a.* Occidental, western, belonging to the west.

poner [po-nerr'], *va.* 1. To put, to place (colocar), to set, to lay a thing in a place. 2. To establish and determine distances. 3. To dispose, to arrange (escaparate). 4. To suppose (suponer), to believe. 5. To impose (impuesto, multa), to enjoin. 6. To oblige, to compel. 7. To wager, to bet, to stake (en el juego). 8. To appoint, to invest with office. 9. To bring an example or comparison in confirmation. 10. To leave, to permit without interposition. **Yo lo pongo en Vd.,** I leave it to you. 11. To write, to set down what another dictates. 12. To lay eggs; to bring forth. 13. To employ; to apply one to some employment or office (en colocación). **Poner toda su fuerza**, to act with all one's might. 14. To labor for an end. 15. To add (añadir), to join. 16. To contribute, to bear apart. 17. To enforce; to adduce, to concert, to agree. 18. To treat one badly. 19. To cause (emoción, miedo). 20. To give (nombre). To switch on, to turn on, to put on (radio). **Poner algo a secar al sol**, to put something to dry in the sun. **Ponlo más fuerte**, turn it up. **Al niño le pusieron Luis**, they called the child Louis. **Pongamos 120**, let's say 120. **La has puesto colorada**, now you've made her blush. *-vr.* 1. To apply oneself to, to set about. 2. To object, to oppose. 3. To undergo a change; to become. **Ponerse pálido**, to grow pale. 4. To set: applied to the luminous heavenly bodies. 5. To arrive in a short time at a determined place (lugar). 6. To dress, to deck out, or adorn oneself. 7. Joined with *de, por, cual, como*, to treat as the words express; sometimes in the true sense, sometimes ironically. E. g. **Poner por escrito**, to put in writing. **Al poner del sol**, at sunset. **Poner al sol**, to expose to the sun, to sun. **Poner a asar**, to spit, to roast. **Eso no quita ni pone**, that neither adds nor diminishes. **Poner en duda**, to question, to doubt. **Poner nombre**, to rate or appraise goods. **Ponerse bien**, to get on in the world; to obtain full information of an affair. **Ponerse colorado**, to flush, to blush. **¿Quién se pone a ello?** who dares to do it? **Ponerse a bien con Dios**, to make one's peace with God. **Ponerse a razones**, to enter into a dispute. **Ponérsele a uno**, to take a whim, a fancy. **Ponerse en ocasión**, to expose oneself to danger. **Ponerse los zapatos, el sombrero**, to put on one's shoes, one's hat. **Ponerse moreno**, to become sunburned. **Póngase Vd. en la razón**, be moderate in your demands. **Ponerse a escribir**, to set about, or devote oneself, to writing. **Poner en relieve**, to carve in relief, to describe graphically. **Nada se pone por delante**, nothing stops him, to inflict public punishment. **Poner como un Cristo a alguno**, to flog a person severely. **Poner de vuelta y media**, to humiliate a person, by word or action. **Poner delante**, to remind, to suggest. **Poner coto**, to stop an abuse; to put a bound. **Se puso serio**, he became serious. **Se pusieron a gritar**, they started to shout. **Poner una escucha telefónica**, to tap. **Poner una trampa**, to trap. **Poner en funcionamiento**, entry into service. (*Yo pongo, yo puse, pusiera; ponga. V.* PONER.)

pongo [pon'-go], *m.* (*Peru, Ec.*) A narrow and dangerous pass of a river. (*Peru and Bol.*) An Indian servant. (*Zool.*) A kind of anthropomorphous ape.

poni [po'-ne], *m.* Pony.

poniente [po-ne-en'-tay], *m.* 1. The west (oeste). 2. (*Naut.*) West wind (viento).

ponleví [pon-lay-vee'], *m.* High wooden heel, formerly worn by women.

pontazgo, pontaje [pon-tath'-go, pon-tah'-hay], *m.* Bridge-toll, portage.

pontear [pon-tay-ar'], *va.* To erect bridges.

pontezuelo, la [pon-tay-thoo-ay'-lo, lah], *m.·& f. dim.* Small bridge.

pontificado [pon-te-fe-cah'-do], *m.* Pontificate, the government of the Pope; papacy, popedom.

pontifical [pon-te-fe-cahl'], *a.* Pontifical, papal, belonging to the Pope, or to an arch-bishop or bishop.

pontifical [pon-te-fe-cahl'], *m.* 1. A pontifical robe worn by bishops when they officiate at the mass. 2. Pontifical, a book containing the rites and ceromonies of the Roman Catholic church. 3. Parochial tithes.

pontificalmente [pon-te-fe-cahl'-men-tay], *adv.* Pontifically.

pontificar [pon-te-fe-car'], *vn.* 1. To govern as high pontiff. 2. To celebrate the solemn mass pontifically.

pontífice [pon-tee'-fe-thay], *m.* 1. Pope, pontiff. 2. Archbishop or bishop of a diocese.

pontificio, cia [pon-te-fee'-the-o, ·ah], *a.* Pontifical.

pontil [pon-teel'], *m.* 1. Pontil or ponty, an iron rod for handling hot bottles in glass-making. 2. Glass over which emery is spread.

pontín [pon-teen'], *m.* A vessel for coasting trade in the Philippines.

ponto [pon'-to], *m.* 1. (*Nat.*) Starting-pole. 2. (*Poet.*) The sea.

pontón [pon-tone'], *m.* 1. Ponton or pontoon (de puente), a floating bridge to cross a river. 2. Hulk, an old ship serving as store-ship, hospital, or prison-ship. 3. (*Naut.*) Mud-scow, a kind of flat-bottomed boat, furnished with pulleys, tackles, etc., to clean harbors. 4. Timber above nineteen feet long. 5. A log bridge.

pony [po'-ne], *m.* Pony.

ponzoña [pon-tho'-nyah], *f.* 1. Poison, venom, toxine. 2. Anything infectious or malignant.

ponzoñosamente [pon-tho-nyo'-sah-men-tay], *adv.* Poisonously.

ponzoñoso, sa [pon-tho-nyo'-so, sah], *a.* 1. Poisonous, venomous, toxic. 2. Prejudicial to sound morals.

popa [po'-pah], *f. (Naut.)* Poop, stern. **Navío de popa llana,** *(Naut.)* A square sterned vessel. **Velas de popa,** *(Naut.)* aftersails. **De popa a proa,** *(Naut.)* from stem to stern. **A popa, en popa, de popa,** *(Naut.)* aft, abaft. **Viento en popa** *(Naut.),* before the wind. *(Met.)* Prosperity.

popamiento [po-pah-me-en'-to], *m.* Act of despising or cajoling.

popar [po-par'], *vn.* 1. To depreciate, to contemn. 2. To cajole, to flatter, to fawn; to caress, to soothe, to wheedle.

popero [po-pay'-ro], *m.* Helmsman, steersman.

popeses [po-pay'-ses], *m. pl. (Naut.)* Stays of the mizzenmast: aftermost, sternmost.

poplíteo, tea [po-plee'-tay-o, ah], *a.* Popliteal, belonging to the space behind the knees.

popote [po-po'-tay], *m.* A kind of Indian straw, of which brooms are made.

populacho [po-poo-lah'-cho], *m.* Populace, mob, rabble, crowd.

población [po-poo-lah-the-on'], *f.* Population. V. POBLACIÓN.

popular [po-poo-lar'], *a.* 1. Popular, relating to the people (del pueblo). 2. Popular, pleasing to the people (ampliamente aceptado). 3. Popular. 4. Vulgar, current. *m. & f.* Plebeian.

popularidad [po-poo-lah-re-dahd'], *f.* Popularity.

popularizar [po-poo-lah-re-thar'], *va.* To popularize, to make popular. *-vr.* To become popular.

popularmente [po-poo-lahr-men-tay'], *adv.* Popularly.

populazo [po-poo-lah'-tho], *m.* Populace, mob, rabble.

populeón [po-poo-lay-on'], *m.* White popular ointment.

populoso, sa [po-poo-lo'-so-sah], *a.* Populous, numerous, full of people.

popurrí [po-poor-ree'], *m.* Potpourri.

poquedad [po-kay-dahd'], *f.* 1. Parvity, paucity, littleness. 2. Cowardice, pusillanimity. 3. Trifle, thing of no value. **Poquedad de ánimo,** imbecility. 4. Mite, very small portion of a thing (poca cantidad).

póquer [po'-kayr], *m.* Poker.

poquillo, lla [po-keel'-lyo, lyah], *a. dim.* 1. Small, little. 2. Trifling.

poquillo [po-keel'-lo], *adv. dim.* Very little time.

poquísimo, ma [po-kee'-se-mo, mah], *a. sup.* Very little, excessively small.

poquitico, ica, illo, illa, ito, ita [po-ke-tee'-co], *a. dim.* Almost nothing.

poquito, ta [po-kee'-to, tah], *a.* 1. *(dim.)* Very little. 2. Weak of body and mind, diminutive. **Poquita cosa,** a trifling thing. **A poquitos,** in minute portions. **De poquito,** pusillanimous. **poquito a poco,** gently.

por [por], *prep.* 1. For, on account of. **Por** refers to the source or to the reason or motive for an action. **Por miedo de las consecuencias,** for fear of consequences. 2. By, through: indicating in passive expressions the agent by whom an action is performed. **Esta carta fue escrita por el general al rey,** this letter was written *by* the general to the king. 3. Indicates multiplication or unit of number or measure. **Seis por ocho,** six (multiplied) by eight. **Por docenas,** by the dozen. **Diez por ciento,** ten per cent. 4. For the sake of, in behalf of, in favor of. **Hablo por el señor A.,** I speak for Mr. A. **¡Una limosna por Dios!** an alms for God's sake! *(Cf.* PORDIOSERO.) 5. After the verbs, *to go, to send,* and the like, it shows the immediate object of the errand. **Ir por leña,** to go for fire-wood. **Por ahí,** about that, a little more or less. **Por tanto** or **por ende,** for so much, for that. 6. Through (a través de), between; to. **¿Por qué calle vino Vd?** through what street did you come? 7. As, by, on account of. **Recibir por esposo,** to take as a husband. 8. By means of, indicating the future action of the verb. **Está por venir, por ver, por saber,** it is to come, to be seen, to be known. 9. Indicates exchange or offset of a thing against another. **Quiere vender su casa por $80,000,** he wants to sell his house for $80,000. **Ojo por ojo, y diente por diente,** an eye for an eye and a tooth for a tooth. 10. It is sometimes redundant,

as, **Fernando está por alcalde,** Ferdinand is Mayor. **Uno vale por muchos,** one is worth many. **La casa está por acabar,** the house is not yet finished. **Por ahora,** for the present. **Por San Juan,** about Saint John's or midsummer. **Por bien o por mal,** well or ill. **Por encima,** slightly, superficially; over, upon. **Por acá o por allá,** here or there. **Por más que** or **por mucho que,** however much; in vain. **Por si acaso,** if by chance. **Sin qué ni por qué** or **sin qué ni para qué,** without rhyme or reason. **¡Sí, por cierto!** yes, indeed. **De por sí,** by itself. **El niño corría por toda la casa,** the child ran all over the house. **Por más que Vd. diga,** you may say what you will, it is in vain. **Por cuanto,** whereas. **Por lo tanto,** therefore. **Por supuesto,** of course. **Hablar por hablar,** to talk just for talking's sake. **Fue por necesidad,** it was from necessity. **Por lo que dicen,** from what they say. **Por centenares,** by the hundred. **Llevar periódicos por las casas,** to deliver papers round the houses. **Por la mañana,** in the morning. **Hablo por todos,** I speak on behalf of everybody. **Por difícil que sea,** however hard it is.

porca [por'-cah], *f.* A ridge of land between two furrows.

porcal [por-cahl'], *a.* Applied to a kind of large plumes.

porcaso [por-cah'-so], *m.* The hogtapir.

porcelana [por-thay-lah'-nah], *f.* 1. Porcelain, chinaware (loza). 2. Enamel, used by goldsmiths and jewellers. 3. Porcelain-color, a mixture of white and blue. 4. Kind of wide china cup.

porcentaje [por-then-tah'-hay], *m.* Percentage; proportion, ratio; rate. **Un elevado porcentaje de,** a high percentage of.

porchada [por-chah'-dah], *f.* Paper holder (stretcher) in paper-factories.

porche [por'-chay], *m.* 1. Porch (de casa), portico. 2. Arcade (de tiendas).

porcino [pr-thee'-no], *m.* 1. A young pig (lechón). **Pan porcino,** *(Bot.)* sow-bread V. ARTANITA. 2. Bruise, a swelling caused by a blow on the head.

porcino, na [por-thee'-no, nah], *a.* Hoggish, porcine.

porción [por-the-on'], *f.* 1. Part, portion. 2. Lot, parcel of goods. 3. Pittance, daily allowance of food. **Una porción de,** a number of.

porcionero, ra [por-the-o-nay'-ro, rah], *a.* Apportioning; participant.

porcionista [por-the-o-nees'-tah], *com.* 1. Holder of a share or portion. 2. Boarder in a college, or one who pays for his portion and assistance in a college.

porcipelo [por-the-pay'-lo], *m. (coll.)* Bristle.

porco [por'-co], *m. (Prov.)* V. PUERCO.

porcuno, na [por-coo'-no, nah], *a.* Hoggish.

pordiosear [por-de-o-say-ar'], *va.* To beg, to ask charity.

pordiosería [por-de-o-say-ree'-ah], *f.* Beggary, asking charity.

pordiosero, ra [por-de-o-say'-ro, rah], *m. & f.* Beggar.

porfía [por-fee'-ah], *f.* 1. An obstinate dispute or quarrel (disputa). 2. Obstinacy (terquedad), stubbornness; conceitedness. 3. Repetition; importunity. **A porfía,** in an obstinate manner.

porfiadamente [por-fe-ah-dah-men-tay], *adv.* Obstinately, pertinaciously, contentiously.

porfiado, da [por-fe-ah'-do, dah], *a.* Obstinate (terco), stubborn, opinionated, conceited. *-pp.* of PORFIAR.

porfiador, ra [por-fe-ah-dor', rah], *m. & f.* Contender, wrangler, brawler, pleader.

porfiar [por-fe-ar'], *va.* 1. To contend. 2. To wrangle. 3. To importune by repetition. 4. To persist in a pursuit (persistir).

porfídico, ca [por-fee'-de-co, cah], *a.* Porphyritic, containing porphyry, or like it.

pórfido, pórfiro [por'-fe-do, por'-fe-ro], *m.* Porphyry, jasper.

porisma [po-rees'-mah], *f. (Geom.)* Porism.

pormenor [por-may-nor'], *m.* Detail, minute account.

porno [por'-no], *a.* Porno, pornographic.

pornografía [por-no-grah-fee'-ah], *f.* Pornography, obscenity.

pornográfico, ca [por-no-grah'-fe-co, cah], *a.* Pornographic, obscene.

poro [po'-ro], *m.* 1. Pore, as of the skin. 2. Pore, interstice.

porongo [po-ron'-go], *m. (Peru and Bol.)* An earthenware jug or pitcher.

pororoca [po-ro-ro'-cah], *f.* Brazilian name for the extraordinary collision of the waters of the river Amazons with the ocean at the great equinoctial tides.

porosidad [po-ro-se-dahd'], *f.* 1. Porosity. 2. That which is exhaled through the pores.

poroso, sa [po-ro'-so, sah], *a.* Porous.

porque [por'-kay], *com.* 1. Because, for the reason that, on this or that account. 2. Why, for which or what reason: relatively.

por qué [por-kay'], *conj.* Why? for what reason? interrogatively.

porqué [por-kay'], *m. (coll.)* 1. Cause, reason (motivo), motive. 2. Allowance, pittance, pension. **El porqué de la revolución**, the factors that underlie the revolution.

porquecilla [por-kay-thel-lyah], *f. dim.* A small sow.

porquera [por-kay'-rah], *f.* Lair, the conch of a wild boar.

porquería [por-kay-ree'-ah], *f.* 1. Nastiness, uncleanliness, filth (sustancia). 2. Hoggishness, brutishness, rudeness (cualidad). 3. Trifle thing of little value (objeto). 4. A dirty, ungenteel action. 5. Nuisance, dirty trick (acto). 6. Rubbish (basura). **Porquerías**, *(coll.)* small dishes made of the entrails of swine. **Estar hecho una porquería**, to be covered in muck. **La novela es una porquería**, the novel is just rubbish.

porqueriza [por-kay-ree'-thah], *f.* Hogsty.

porquerizo, porquero [por-kay-ree'-tho], *m.* Swineherd.

porquerón [por-kay-rone'], *m.* Catchpoll, bumbailiff.

porqueta [porkay'-tah], *f. V.* CUCARACHA.

porquezuela [por-kay-thoo-ay'-lah], *f. dim.* 1. A small sow. 2. A slut or dirty woman.

porquezuelo [por-kay-thoo-ay'-lo], *m. dim.* 1. A young pig. 2. A nasty, dirty man.

porra [por'-rah], *f.* 1. Stick with a large head or thick knob at the end (palo); club. 2. The last player in certain games. 3. *(coll.)* Vanity, boast, presumption. 4. *(coll.)* A stupid, heavy, ignorant person. 5. *(And. Cono Sur)* Curl (mechón). 6. *(CAm. Mex.)* Political gang (pandilla). 7. *(Mex.) (Dep.)* Fans. 8. *(CAm.)* Metal cooking pot (olla). **Mandar a uno a la porra**, to chuck somebody out. **¡Vete a la porra!**, go to blazes!

porráceo, cea [por-rah'-thay-o, ah], *a.* Of a dark or leek-green color.

porrada [por-rah'-dah], *f.* 1. Blow with a club-headed stick. 2. *(coll.)* Foolishness, nonsense.

porrazo [por-rah'-tho], *m.* Blow with any instrument, or that occasioned by a fall.

porrear [por-ray-ar'], *vn. (coll.)* To persist importunely, to dwell long upon.

porrería [por-ray-ree'-ah], *f. (coll.)* Obstinacy, stupidity (necedad), folly, silliness, tediousness.

porreta [por-ray'-tah], *f.* The green leaf of leeks, garlic, or onions. **En porreta**, *(coll.)* stark naked.

porrilla [por-reel'-lyah], *f.* 1. A small hammer used by smiths. 2. *(dim.)* A small club-headed stick. 3. *(Vet.)* Osseous tumor in horses' joints.

porrillo (A) [por-reel'-lyo], *adv. (coll.)* Copiously, abundantly.

porrina [por-ree'-nah], *f.* State of crops when small and green.

porrino [por-ree'-no], *m.* The tender plant of a leek.

porrizo [por-ree'-tho], *m.* Bed or plot of leeks.

porro, rra [por'-ro, rah], *a.* 1. *(coll.)* Dull, stupid, ignorant. 2. *(Esp.)* Joint. 3. *(And. Carib.)* Folk dance.

porrón [por-rone'], *m.* 1. An earthen pitcher for water. 2. A kind of flask. **Un porrón de**, a lot of.

porrón, na [por-rone', nah], *a.* Heavy, sluggish (torpe), slow (lerdo).

porrudo [por-roo'-do], *m. (Prov.)* Shepherd's crook.

porta [por'-tah], *f.* 1. Door, gate. 2. *(Naut.)* Gun-port, embrasure of a battery. **Portas de las miras de proa**, *(Naut.)* head chaseports. **Portas de guardatimón**, *(Naut.)* stern-ports.

portaaguja [por-tah-ah-goo'-hah], *f.* A surgical needle-holder.

portaanimálcules [por-tah-ah-ne-mahl'-coo-los], *m.* Live box, animalcule cage. (Microscopy.)

portaaviones [por-tah-ah-ve-o'-nees], *m.* Aircraft carrier.

portabandera [por-tah-ban-day'-rah], *f.* Pocket in the girdle which supports the staff of the colors.

portacaja [por-tah-cah'-hah], *f.* The carrier of a silk loom.

portacarabina [por-tah-ca-rah-bee'-nah], *f.* Leather bag in which the muzzle of a horseman's carabine rests.

portacartas [por-tah-car'-tas], *m.* Mailbag for letters.

portada [por-tah'-dah], *f.* 1. Portal, porch (pórtico). 2. Frontispiece, the principal front of a building; facade (fachada). 3. Title-page of a book. 4. Division of a certain number of threads to form the warp.

portadera [por-tah-day'-rah], *f.* A chest in which provisions are carried on a horse or mule: commonly used in the plural.

portador, ra [por-tah-dor', rah], *m. & f.* 1. Bearer, carrier, porter. 2. Tray or board on which bread or meat is carried. **Páguese al portador**, pay the bearer.

portaestandarte [por-tah-es-tan-dar'-tay], *m. (Mil.)* Standard-bearer cornet.

portafolio [por-tah-fo'-le-o], *m.* Briefcase.

portafusil [por-tah-foo-seel'], *m. (Mil.)* Sling of a musket.

portaguión [por-tah-gee-on'], *m.* Standard-bearer of cavalry.

portaje [por-tah'-hay], *m. V.* PORTAZGO.

portal [por-tahl'], *m.* 1. Porch (pórtico), entry, entrance. 2. Portico, piazza. 3. *(Prov.)* Gate of a town (de ciudad).

portalazo [por-tah-lah'-tho], *m. aug.* A large door or porch.

portalejo [por-tah-lay'-ho], *m. dim.* Little porch or portico.

portaleña [por-tah-lay'-nyah], *f.* 1. Embrasure, for cannon. *V.* CAÑONERA. 2. Planks of which doors are made.

portalero [por-tah-lay'-ro], *m.* An officer who has the charge of preventing smuggling, receiving the duties, etc., at the gates of a town.

portalico, illo, ito [por-tah-lee'-co], *m. dim.* A small vestibule or porch.

portalón [por-tah-loone'], *m. (Naut.)* Gangway.

portamanteo [por-tah-man-tay'-o], *m.* Portmanteau, cloak-bag.

portamonedas [por-tah-mo-nay'-das], *m.* A small purse, porte-monnaie.

portanario [por-tah-nah'-re-o], *m. (Anat.)* Pylorus.

portante [por-tahn'-tay], *m.* Quick pace of a horse.

portantillo [por-tan-teel'-lyo], *m. dim.* A gentle amble, an easy pace.

portanuevas [por-tah-noo-ay'-vas], *com.* Newsmonger.

portañola [por-tah-nyo'-lah], *f. (Naut.)* Port-hole. **Portañolas de la luz de los camarotes**, *(Naut.)* light-ports. **Portañolas de los remos**, *(Naut.)* row-ports.

portañuela [por-tah-nyoo-ay'-lah], *f.* 1. Lining of the fall of breeches. 2. Fly (de pantalón).

portaobjetos [por-tah-ob-hay'-tos], *m.* Object-holder of a microscope, stage; glass slip.

portaollas [por-tah-ol'-lyas], *m.* Pot-holder.

portapaz [por-tah-path'], *com.* The plate on which the pax or image is presented to be kissed by the pious at mass.

portaparaguas [por-tah-pah-rah'-goo-as], *m.* Umbrella-stand.

portaplacas, portaplanchas [por-tah-plahn'-chas], *m.* Dark slide, photographic plate-holder.

portar [por-tar'], *va.* To carry, to bring. *-vr.* 1. To behave (conducirse), to comport, to act. 2. To show up well (distinguirse). 3. *(LAm.)* To behave well. **Se ha portado como un cochino**, he has behaved like a pig.

porta-rollo [por-tah-rohl'-lyo], *m.* A photographic roll-holder.

portaronzal [por-tah-ron-thahl'], *m.* A strap fixed at the left holster to which the halter is fastened.

portátil [por-tah'-teel], *a.* Portable, easily carried.

portaventanero [por-tah-ven-tah-nay'-ro], *m.* Carpenter who makes windows and doors.

portaviento [por-tah-ve-en'-to], *m.* Airblast of a furnace.

portavoz [por-tah-voth'], *m.* 1. Loudspeaker, megaphone (altoparlante). 2. Spokesman (persona), mouthpiece.

portaz [por-tath], *m.* (*Zool.*) The nylghau.

portazgo [por-tath'-go], *m.* Toll, turn-pike-duty.

portazguero [por-tah-gay'-ro], *m.* Toll-gatherer, collector.

portazo [por-tah'-tho], *m.* 1. A loud slam with a door. 2. Act of slamming door in one's face. **Dar un portazo**, to slam the door.

porte [por'-tay], *m.* 1. Cost of carriage (gasto); freight, portage, porterage: postage (Correos). 2. Deportment, demeanor, conduct (conducta). 3. Nobility: illustrious descent. 4. Size or capacity of a thing. 5. (*Naut.*) Burden or tonnage of a ship. **Porte franco**, frank, free of postage. **Navío de mil toneladas de porte**, a ship of one thousand tons burden.

porteador, ra [por-tay-ah-dor', rah], *a.* Carrying, transporting.

portear [por-tay-ar'], *va.* To carry or convey for a price. *-vr.* To pass from one place to another.

portento [por-ten'-to], *m.* Prodigy, wonder; portent.

portentosamente [por-ten-to'-sah-men-tay], *adv.* Prodigiously.

portentoso, sa [por-ten-to'-so, sah], *a.* Prodigious, marvelous, portentous.

porteo [por-tay'-o], *m.* Transportation, portage. **Gastos de porteo**, transportation or portage costs.

portería [por-tay-ree'-ah], *f.* 1. The principal door of a large building: a porter's lodge (conserjería). 2. Employment or office of a porter. 3. (*Naut.*) All the ports in a ship.

portero, ra [por-tay'-ro, rah], *m. & f.* Porter (conserje), gate-keeper. **Portero automático**, answering device.

portezuela [por-tay-thoo-ay'-lah], *f.* 1. (*dim.*) A little door. 2. Flap, pocket-flap. 3. (*Mex.*) A pass between hills.

pórtico [por'-te-co], *m.* Portico (portal), piazza; porch; hall; lobby.

portillo [por-teel'-lyo], *m.* 1. Aperture in a wall. 2. Opening, passage, gap (abertura), breach (brecha). 3. Wicket (postigo), gate, a small door in another larger. 4. Means to an end. 5. Cavity in anything broken. 6. Small gate of a town, through which nothing is allowed to pass that is liable to pay duty.

portón [por-tone'], *m.* The inner or second door of a house.

portorriqueño, ña [or-tor-re-kay'-nyo, nya], *a.* Puerto Rican. *V.* PUERTORRIQUEÑO.

portuario, ria [por-too-ah'-re-o, ah], *a.* Relative to a seaport. **Ciudad portuaria**, seaport city.

portugués [por-too-ghes'], *m.* The Portuguese language.

portugués, sa [por-too-ghes', sah], *a.* Portuguese. **A la Portuguesa**, in the Portuguese fashion.

portuláceas [por-too-lah'-thay-as], *a. & f. pl.* Of the purslane or portulaca family; portulacas.

porvenir [por-vay-neer'], *m.* Future, time to come. **En el porvenir**, in the future. **Un hombre sin porvenir**, a man with no future.

pos (**En**) [pos], *adv.* After, behind; in pursuit of.

posa [po'-sah], *f.* 1. Passing bell; the ringing of bells for persons deceased. 2. Stops made by the clergy who conduct a funeral, to sing a response. 3. *pl.* (*coll.*) Breech, seat; buttocks.

posada [po-sah'-dah], *f.* 1. Home, dwelling-house. 2. Longing or lodging house (hospedaje). **Posada con asistencia**, board and lodging, inn, tavern, hotel. 3. Pocket-case, containing a knife, spoon, and fork. 4. (*CAm. Mex.*) Typical party held at Christmas.

posadera [po-sah-day'-rah], *f.* Hostess.

posaderas [po-sah-day'-ras], *f. pl.* Buttocks. *V.* ASENTADERAS.

posadería [po-sah-day-ree'-ah], *f.* Inn, tavern, lodging-house.

posadero [po-sah-day'-ro], *m.* 1. Inn-keeper, the keeper of a lodging or boarding-house, or tavern. 2. Seat made of flags or bass-ropes. 3. Breech, seat, buttocks.

posado, da [po-sah'-do, dah], *a. & pp.* of POSAR. Lodged, rested, lined, reclined, landed (avión).

posante [po-sahn'-tay], *pa.* Reposing: used at sea for smooth sailing.

posar [po-sar'], *vn.* 1. To lodge, to board. 2. To sit down, to repose, to rest. 3. To perch, to light or sit upon. *-va.* To lay down a burden (carga). *-vr.* 1. To alight (ave, insecto). 2. To settle (líquido). 3. To land (avión). **El avión se encontraba posado**, the aircraft was on the ground.

posca [pos'-cah], *f.* Mixture of vinegar and water, formerly given by way of refreshment.

posdata [pos-dah'-tah], *f.* Postscript.

pose [po'-say], *m.* A kind of hook for fishing upon sandbanks. *-f.* 1. Pose. 2. Attitude (actitud). 3. Composure (aplomo). 4. Pose (afectación); affectedness; affected posture (postura afectada).

poseedor, ra [po-say-ay-dor', rah], *m. & f.* Possessor, holder, owner.

poseer [po-say-err'], *va.* 1. To hold, to possess, to have, to own (ventaja). 2. To be master of a language or other thing.

poseído, da [po-say-ee'-do, dah], *a. & pp.* of POSEER. 1. Possessed. 2. Applied to one who executes desperate actions (enloquecido).

poseído [po-say-ee'-do], *m.* (*Prov.*) Arable land belonging to a private person, as distinguished from commons.

posesión [po-say-se-on'], *f.* 1. Possession, the act of possessing, dominion. 2. Possession, the thing possessed. 3. Possession by evil spirits. 4. (*Met.*) Reputation, good or bad. *-pl.* Lands, real estates (propiedades). **Las cartas están en posesión de su padre**, the letters are in the possession of his father.

posesional [po-say-se-o-nahl'], *a.* Including or relating to possession.

posesionarse [po-say-se-o-nar'-say], *vr.* To take possession of.

posesionero [po-say-se-o-nay'-ro], *m.* Cattle-keeper who has acquired possession of pasturace.

posesivo, va [po-say-see'-vo, vah], *a.* (*Gram.*) Possessive, denoting possession.

poseso, sa [po-say'-so, sah], *a. & pp. irr.* of POSEER. Possessed; possessed by evil spirits.

posesor, ra [po-say-sor', rah], *m. & f. V.* POSEEDOR.

posesorio, ria [po-say'-re-o, ah], *a.* Possessory.

poseyente [po-say-yen'-tay], *pa.* Possessing, possessive.

posfecha [pos-fay'-chah], *f.* Post-date.

posfechar [pos-fay-char'], *va.* To post-date.

posibilidad [po-si-be-le-dahd'], *f.* 1. Possibility, the state or condition of being possible. 2. Possibility, the state of being possible: feasibility; likelihood. 3. Wealth, riches. **No existe posibilidad alguna de que venga**, there is no possibility of his coming. **Estar en la posibilidad de**, to be in a position to.

posibilitar [po-se-be-le-tar'], *va.* To render possible, to facilitate.

posible [po-see'-blay], *a.* Possible. **Posibles**, wealth, income, capital, means. **Serviré a Vd. con mis posibles**, I will serve you with all my might. **¿Es posible?** is it possible? **Lo antes posible**, as soon as possible. **Hacer posible una cosa**, to make something possible.

posiblemente [po-se'-blay-men-tay], *adv.* Possibly.

posición [po-se-the-on'], *f.* 1. Position, the art of placing. 2. Position, posture, situation. 3. Question and answers of an interrogatory. 4. Position, rule in arithmetic. 5. (*LAm.*) Position, post, job (puesto).

posicionar [po-se-the-o-nar'], *va.* To position. *-vr.* to adopt an attitude.

positivamente [po-se-te-vah-men-tay], *adv.* Positively, absolutely, certainly, by all means.

positividad [po-se-te-ve-dahd'], *f.* State of positive electricity.

positivismo [po-se-te-vees'-mo], *m.* 1. Positiveness, holding to what is positive. 2. Positivism, a system of philosophy receiving only proved facts, rejecting a priori notions. 3. Agnosticism, chiefly in England. 4. Utilitarianism.

positivo, va [po-se-tee'-vo, vah], *a.* 1. Positive, sure, certain, indubitable, true. 2. Positive: applied to laws settled by arbitrary appointment. 3. Positive, absolute, real. 4. *(Gram.)* Positive, a degree of comparison. **De positivo,** certainly, without doubt.

pósito [po'-se-to], *m.* A public granary (granero). **Pósito pío,** granary which lends grain to widows or poor laborers without charging interest.

positón, positrón [po-se-tone', po-se-trone'], *m.* Positron.

positura [po-se-too'-rah], *f.* 1. Posture, state, disposition. 2. *V.* POSTURA.

posma [pos'-mah], *f. (coll.)* Sluggishness, sloth, dulness. *-com.* A dull, sluggish, dronish person. Also *a.*

poso [po'-so], *m.* 1. Sediment, dregs, lees, feculence. 2. Rest, repose.

posoperativo [pos-o-pay-rah-to-re-o], *a.* Post-operative.

posparto [pos-pahr-to], *m. V.* POSTPARTO.

pospelo (A) [pos-pay'-lo], *adv.* Against the grain; reluctantly.

pospierna [pos-pe-err'-nah], *f.* The thigh of an animal.

posponer [pos-po-ner'], *va.* 1. To place one thing after another. 2. To postpone, to put off, to delay (aplazar). 3. To postpone, to set in value below something else.

pospuesto, ta [pos-poo-es'-to, tah], *pp. irr.* of POSPONER.

posta [pos'-tah], *f.* 1. Post-horses. 2. Post-house, post-office; post stage, where post-horses are stationed. 3. Post, distance from one relay or, post-house to another. 4. Chop of meat or fish. 5. Slug of lead, mould-shot. 6. Night-sentry. 7. Stake in cards. *-m.* Person who travels post. **Correr la posta, or ir en posta,** to post or travel post. **A posta,** designedly, on purpose.

postal [pos-tahl'], *a.* Postal. **Giro postal,** money order. **Paquete postal,** parcel post. **Tarjeta postal,** postal card. *-f.* Postcard.

postdata [pos-dah-tah], *f. V.* POSDATA.

poste [pos'-tay], *m.* 1. Post-pillar (columna). 2. Kind of punishment. **Poste indicador,** signpost. **Poste de llegada,** winning post.

postelero [pos-tay-lay'-ro], *m. (Naut.)* Skid or skeed, knee of the quarterdeck of a ship.

postema [pos-tay'-mah], *f.* 1. An abscess tumor. 2. Dull, troublesome person (pelmazo).

postemero [post-tay-may'-ro], *m.* Large lancet.

póster [pos'-tayr], *m.* Poster.

postergación [pos-ter-gah-the-on'], *f.* Act of leaving behind.

postergar [pos-ter-gar'], *va.* To leave behind.

posteridad [pos-tay-re-dahd'], *f.* Posterity.

posterior [pos-tay-re-or'], *a.* 1. Posterior, following. 2. Later (en orden). 3. Later, subsequent (tiempo). **Ser posterior a,** to be later than.

posterioridad [pos-tay-re-o-re-dahd'], *f.* Posteriority.

posteriormente [pos-tay-re-or'-men-tay], *adv.* Lastly, afterward, hereafter.

posteta [pos-tay'-tah], *f. (Print.)* Number of printed sheets stitched together; a quantity of sheets for packing books.

postgraduado [pos-grah-doo-ah'-do], *a.* Postgraduate. *-m. & f.* Postgraduate.

postigo [pos-tee'-go], *m.* 1. Wicket (puerta pequeña), small door. 2. Sally-port, postern (portillo). 3. A door of one leaf. 4. Any of the divisions of a door or widow. 5. *V.* PORTILLO for a small gate of a town.

postiguillo [pos-te-geel'-lyo], *m. dim.* A small wicket or back-door.

postila [pos-tee'-lyah], *f.* Postil, marginal notes.

postilación [pos-te-lah-the-on'], *f.* Act of making marginal notes.

postilador [pos-te-lah-dor'], *m.* Annotator, postiler.

postilar [pos-te-lar'], *va.* To write marginal notes upon, to gloss, to comment.

postilla [pos-teel'-lyah], *f.* Scab or crust on wounds.

postillón [pos-teel-lyone'], *m.* 1. Postilion driver. 2. Hack.

postilloso, sa [pos-teel-lyo'-so, sah], *a.* Scabby, pustulous.

postín [pos-teen'], *m.* 1. Elegance (lujo); tone (entono). 2. Side (fachenca), swank.

postitis [pos-tee'-tis], *f.* Posthitis, inflammation of the prepuce.

postiza [pos-tee'-thah], *f.* 1. *(Naut.)* Dead work on galleys for guiding the oar. 2. *V.* CASTAÑUELA.

postizo, za [pos-tee'-tho, thah], *a.* Artificial, not natural; false (dientes); dummy (exterior). **Dientes postizos,** false teeth. **Pelo postizo,** false hair.

postizo [pos-tee'-tho], *m.* With wigmakers, hair to supply the front or back of the head.

postliminio [post-le-mee'-ne-o], *m.* Postliminy, among the Romans, reinstatement of one taken by the enemy to his possessions.

postmeridiano, na [post-may-re-de-ah'-no, nah], *a.* Postmeridian, afternoon.

postor [pos-tor'], *m.* Bidder at a public sale; bettor.

postparto [post-par'-to], *m.* The latest young of animals in the season: applied chiefly to ewes.

postración [pos-trah-the-on'], *f.* 1. Prostration, kneeling. 2. Prostration, dejection, depression.

postrado, da [pos-trah'-do, dah], *a. & pp.* of POSTRAR. Prostrate, prostrated.

postrador, ra [pos-trah-dor', rah], *m. & f.* 1. One who prostrates himself. 2. Foot-stool in the choir, on which the chorister kneels.

postrar [pos-trar'], *va.* 1. To prostrate, to humble (humillar). 2. To debilitate (debilitar), to exhaust. *-vr.* 1. To prostrate oneself, to kneel to the ground. 2. To be extremely debilitated.

postre [pos'-tray], *a.* Last in order. *V.* POSTRERO.

postre [pos'-tray], *m.* Dessert, the last course at table. **¿Qué hay de postre?,** what is there for dessert?

postremo, ma [pos-tray'-mo, mah], *a. V.* POSTRERO and ÚLTIMO.

postrer [pos-trayr'], *a. V.* POSTRERO. (Used before a noun.)

postreramente [pos-tray-rah-men-tay], *adv.* Ultimately, lastly.

postrero, ra [pos-tray'-ro, rah], *a.* Last in order, hindermost.

postrero [pos-tray'-ro], *m. V.* TRASERO.

postrimeramente [pos-tre-may'-rah-men-tay], *adv.* Finally, at last.

postrimería [pos-tre-may-ree'-ah], *f.* 1. Death. *V.* NOVÍSIMO. 2. The last years of life.

postrimero, ra [pos-tre-may'-ro, rah], *a. V.* POSTRERO and TRASERO.

póstula [pos'-too-lah], *f.* Solicitation, petition.

postulación [pos-too-lah-the-on'], *f.* 1. Postulation (proposición); petition. 2. Nomination for prelate of some church, made by the chapter, of a person who requires dispensation.

postulado [pos-too-lah'-do], *m.* Postulate, position assumed without proof; axiom.

postulador [pos-too-lah-dor'], *m.* 1. Member of a chapter who votes for an unqualified prelate. 2. One who solicits the canonization of a saint.

postulanta [pos-too-lahn'-tah], *f.* Postulant, female candidate for admission to a religious order.

postulante [pos-too-lahn'-tay], *m. f.* Aspirant to a position.

postular [pos-too-lar'], *va.* 1. To seek for (pedir), to solicit, to postulate (proponer). 2. To elect a prelate laboring under a canonical impediment. 3. *(CAm. Mex.)* To nominate (candidato).

póstumo, ma [pos'-too-mo, mah], *a.* Posthumous.

postura [pos-too'-rah], *f.* 1. Posture, position, situation. 2. Posture, collocation of the parts of the body with respect to each other (del cuerpo). 3. Act of planting trees or plants; the tree or plant transplanted. 4. Assize of provisions. 5. Bid (en subasta), price fixed by a bidder or buy-out. 6. Bet, wager. 7. Paint which women put on their faces. 8. Egg of a fowl or bird, and the act of laying it (acto). 9. Agreement, contract.

potable [po-tah'-blay], *a.* 1. Potable, drinkable. 2. Good enough (acceptable).

potador [po-tah-dor'], *m.* He who examines and marks weights and measures.

potaje [po-tah'-hay], *m.* 1. Pottage, boiled food. 2. Vegetables dressed for food in days of abstinence. 3. Drink made of several ingredients. 4. Medley of useless things.

potajería [po-tah-hay-ree'-ah], *f.* 1. Heap of dry pulse. 2. Place where dry pulse or vegetables are preserved for use.

potala [po-tah'-lah], *f.* 1. Stone which serves to moor boats. 2. A small, slow-going vessel.

potanza [po-tahn'-thah], *f.* Cook, in clockwork; a bearing for the pallets.

potar [po-tar'], *va.* To equalize and mark weights and measures.

potasa [po-tah'-sah], *f.* Potash.

potásico [po-tah'-se-co], *a.* 1. *(Chem.)* Potassio, relating to potassium in its higher valence. **Yodo potásico**, potassio or potassium iodide.

potasio [po-tah'-se-o], *m.* Potassium, a metallic element lighter than water, upon which it burns with a violet flame.

pote [po'-tay], *m.* 1. A jug for keeping liquids (jarra). 2. Pot, jar (tarro); flower-pot. 3. Standard measure or weight. 4. Pout, sulky look (puchero).

potecillo, ito [po-tay-theel'-lyo], *m. dim.* A little pot or jar.

potencia [po-ten'-the-ah], *f.* 1. Power, the faculty of performing. 2. Power, authority, dominion. 3. Power, ability, potency. 4. Possibility. 5. Power of generation; productive virtue. 6. Power, kingdom, state. 7. *(Math.)* Power, product of a quantity multiplied by itself. 8. A tool for ironing the brim of a hat. (*Cf.* «potence» in heraldry.)-*pl.* The nine rays of light which encircle the head of the infant Jesus, designed to express his universal power over everything created. **Potencias beligerantes**, belligerent powers. **Potencias del alma**, the memory, understanding, and will. **Potencia muscular**, muscular power. **Las grandes potencias**, the great powers. **Es una guerra civil en potencia**, it is a civil war in the making.

potencial [po-ten-the-ahl'], *a.* 1. Potential, possessing a power. 2. Potential, having the effect, without the external properties. 3. *(Gram.)* Potential mode.

potencialidad [po-ten-the-ah-le-dahd'], *f.* Potentiality, equivalence.

potencialmente [po-ten-the-ahl'-men-tay], *adv.* Potentially: equivalently.

potenciar [po-ten-the-ahr'], *va.* To favor (promover); to develop (desarrollar); to strengthen (fortalecer).

potentado [po-ten-tah'-do], *m.* Potentate, sovereign, monarch.

potente [po-ten'-tay], *a.* 1. Potent, powerful (poderoso), mighty. 2. Potent, strong, vigorous. 3. *(coll.)* Great, bulky.

potentemente [po-ten'-tay-men-tay], *adv.* Powerfully, potently.

potentísimo, ma [po-ten-tee'-se-mo], *a. sup.* Most powerful.

potenza [po-ten'-thah], *f.* A potent cross (heráldica).

poteo [po-tay'-o], *m.* Drinks, drinking.

poterna [po-terr'-nah], *f.* *(Mil.)* Postern, sally-port.

potestad [po-tes-tahd'], *f.* 1. Pointer, dominion, command, jurisdiction. *V.* POTENTADO. 2. *(Arith.)* Power, the product of multiplying a number by itself. **Patria potestad**, paternal authority.

potestativo, va [po-tes-tah-tee'-vo, vah], *a.* *(For.)* That which is in the faculty or power of anyone: facultative.

potista [po-tees'-tah], *com.* *(Vul.)* Tippler, drunkard.

potito [po-tee'-to], *m.* 1. Small jar. 2. *(LAm.)* Backside.

potra [po'-trah], *f.* 1. *(coll.)* (a) Rupture, scrotal hernia; (b) suerte). 2. Fily. *V.* POTRO.

potrada [po-trah'-dah], *f.* Troop of young mares at pasture.

potranca [po-trahn'-cah], *f.* Filly, young mare (no más de tres años).

potrear [po-tray-ar'], *va.* 1. *(coll.)* To vex, to molest, to annoy. 2. *(And. CAm.)* To beat. 3. *(Carib. Mex.)* To break, to tame (caballo).

potrera [po-tray'-rah], *a.* Applied to a hempen head-stall for horses.

potrero [po-tray'-ro], *m.* 1. Surgeon who cures ruptures. 2. Herder, herdsman of colts. 3. Pasture ground. 4. *(Amer.)* A farm for rearing horses. 5. *(Cono Sur)* Playground (parque). 6. *(Mex.)* Open grassland (llanura).

potrico, illo [po-tree'-co], *m. dim.* 1. A small colt. 2. *(Cono Sur)* Tall glass (vaso). 3. *(And.)* Small canoe (canoa).

potril [po-treel'], *m. & a.* Pasture for young horses.

potrilla [po-treel'-lyah], *f.* Nickname given to old persons affecting rakish youth.

potro, tra [po'-tro, trah], *m. & f.* 1. Colt, foal, a young horse up to the time when it changes its milk teeth, or about four and a half years of age. -*m.* 2. A wooden horse; rack (de tormento), a kind of torture. 3. A wooden frame for shoeing unruly horses (de herrar). 4. Anything which molests or torments. 5. An earthen chamber-pot. 6. Bubo, a venereal tumor. 7. Pit in the ground in which beekeepers divide a beehive into two portions, giving a queen-bee to each. 8. A kind of stand where they card wool a second time. **Potro de madera**, vaulting horse.

potroso [po-tro'-so], *sa. a.* 1. Afflicted with a rupture. 2. *(coll.)* Fortunate, lucky.

poyal [po-yahl'], *m.* 1. A sort of striped stuff with which benches are covered. 2. *V.* POYO.

poyata [po-yah'-tah], *f.* Shelf, cupboard.

poyatilla [po-yah-teel'-lyah], *f. dim.* A little shelf.

poyato [po-yah'-to], *m.* Terrace, in landscape gardening.

poyo [po'-yo], *m.* 1. Bench, a seat made of stone and mortar against a wall. 2. Fee given to judges.

poza [po'-thah], *f.* 1. Puddle. 2. *(Agr.)* A pool for macerating hemp. 3. Hole made in children's bread, and filled with must or honey.

pozal [po-thahl'], *m.* 1. Bucket, pail. 2. Coping of a well. 3. Vessel sunk in the earth to catch any fluid.

pozanco [po-thahn'-co], *m.* Pond of stagnant water.

pozero [po-thay'-ro], *m.* Well-digger.

pozo [po'-tho], *m.* 1. Well (de agua). 2. A deep hole in a river; a whirlpool. 3. Anything complete in its line. **Es un pozo de ciencia**, he is deeply learned. **Pozo de petróleo**, oil well. **Pozo de ventilación**, ventilation shaft.

pozol, pozole [po-thohl'], *m.* Boiled barley and beans. (Aztec.)

pozuela [po-thoo-ay'-lah], *f. dim.* A small puddle or pond.

pozuelo [po-thoo-ay'-lo], *m.* 1. *(dim.)* A small well or pit. 2. Vessel sunk in the ground to collect oil, etc., in mills.

práctica [prahc'-te-cah], *f.* 1. Practice, constant habit. 2. Practice, customary use; exercise. 3. Practice, manner, mode, method (método). 4. Practice of any profession. 5. The act of learning a profession under a master. **En la práctica**, in practice. **Prácticas profesionales**, professional training. **Aprender con la práctica**, to learn by practice.

practicable [prac-te-cah'-blay], *a.* Practicable, feasible.

practicador, ra [prac-te-cah-dor', rah], *m. & f.* Practicer, practitioner.

prácticamente [prahc'-te-cah-men-tay], *adv.* Practically. **Está prácticamente terminado**, it's practically finished.

practicante [prac-te-cahn'-tay], *m.* Practitioner in surgery and medicine under a master. -*pa.* Practising.

practicar [prac-te-car'], *va.* 1. To practise (habilidad, virtud), to perform (ejecutar), to do, to put in execution. 2 To practice, to do habitually. 3. To learn the practice of a profession under a master. **Practicar el francés con su profesor**, to practice one's French with one's teacher.

práctico, ca [prahc'-te-co, cah], *a.* 1. Practical (estudio, formación). 2. Skillful, experienced, expert (persona). 3. Practical; handy (herramienta); convenient (casa). -*m.* A skilful pilot.

practicón, na [prac-te-cone', nah], *m. & f.* One of great practical knowledge and experience.

paradal [prah-dahl'], *m.* Extent of country abounding in meadows and pasture-lands.

pradecillo [prah-day-theel'-lyo], *m.* A small meadow

pradeño, ña [prah-day'-nyo, nyah], *a.* Relating to meadows or fields.

pradera, pradería [prah-day'-rah, prah-day-ree'-ah], *f.* 1. Country abounding in meadows and pasture-grounds (prado). 2. Mead, meadow, rich pasture-ground.

praderoso, sa [prah-day-ro' -so, sah], *a.* Relating to meadows.

pradico, illo [prah-dee'-co], *m. dim.* A small meadow.

prado [prah'-do], *m.* 1. Lawn, field, meadow; a piece of pasture-ground. 2. Prado, a public walk in Madrid. **Prado de guadaña**, meadow mowed annually.

pragmática [prag-mah'-te-cah], *f.* 1. Royal ordinance. 2. Rescript of a sovereign to an application made to him in a particular case.

pragmático, ca [prag-mah'-te-co, cah], *a.* Pragmatic, pragmatical. *-m.* Commentator upon national laws.

prasio [prah'-se-o], *m.* Prase, quartz of a leek-green color, usually cryptocrystalline.

prasma [prahs'-mah], *m.* Dark green agate.

prática [prha'-te-cah], *f.* V. PRÁCTICA.

pravedad [prah-vay-dahd'], *f.* Perversity, iniquity, depravity.

pravo, va [prah'-vo, vah], *a.* Depraved, perverse, knavish, lewd.

praxis [prahk'-sis], *f.* Practice. V. PRÁCTICA

pre [pray], Daily pay allowed to soldiers.

pre, A preposition used in the composition of nouns and verbs, either to augment the signification or to mark priority of time and rank.

preadamita [pray-ah-dah-mee'-tah], *a. & n.* Preadamite, existing before Adam.

preámbulo [pray-ahm'-boo-lo], *m.* 1. Preamble (de libro, discurso), exordium, preface. 2. *(coll.)* Evasion, circumlocution. **Sin más preámbulos**, without further ado.

prebenda [pray-ben'-dah], *f.* 1. Prebend, the right of enjoying any temporal fruits by reason of employment office, etc. 2. Prebend, ecclesiastical benefice: commonly used to express a canonry. 3. Sinecure. 4. *(Acad.)* Portion, piously given to a woman, to enable her to marry or to become a nun; or to a student as a foundation scholarship. **Prebenda de oficio**, any of the four prebends, doctoral, magisterial, lectural, or penitentiary.

prebendado [pray-ben-dah'-do], *m.* Prebendary, a dignitary who enjoys a prebend in a cathedral or collegiate church. **Prebendado, da**, *pp.* of PREBENDAR.

prebendar [pray-ben-dar'], *va.* To confer an ecclesiastical benefice or prebend.

prebostal [pray-bos-tahl'], *a.* Provostal.

prebostazgo [pray-bos-tath'-go], *m.* Provostship.

preboste [pray-bos'-tay], *m.* 1. Provost, one who governs a college or community. 2. *(Mil.)* Provost marshal, the officer in charge of military police and thus responsible for military discipline.

precariamente [pre-cah'-re-ah-men-tay], *adv. (For.)* Precariously.

precariedad [pre-cah'-re-dahd], *f.* Precariousness.

precario, ria [pre-cah'-re-o, ah], *a.* 1. Precarious, held only as a loan, and at the will of the owner. 2. Precarious, uncertain (dudoso). 3. Unpredictable (impredecible). *-m.* Precarious state. **Dejar a uno en precario**, to leave somebody in a difficult situation.

precaución [pray-cah-oo-the-on'], *f.* Precaution, guard, vigilance. **Tomar precauciones**, to take precautions.

precaucionado, da [pray-cah-oo-the-o-nah'-do, dah], *a.* Sagacious, cautious, clear-sighted.

precaucionarse [pray-cah-oo-the-o-nar'-say], *vr.* To be cautious.

precautelar [pray-cah-oo-tay-lar'], *va.* To caution, to forewarn.

precaver [pray-cah-verr'], *va.* To prevent or obviate, to stave off (evitar); to forestall (anticipar). *-vr.* To guard against, to be on one's guard.

precavido, da [pray-cah-vee'-do, dah], *a.* Cautious, farsighted, on one's guard. *-pp.* of PRECAVER.

precedencia [pray-thay-den'-the-ah], *f.* 1. Precedence, priority (prioridad). 2. Pre-eminence, preference. 3. Superiority (preeminencia), primacy.

precedente [pray-thay-den'-tay], *a.* Preceding (anterior), foregoing. *-m.* Precedent. **Sin precedente**, all-time; without exception.

preceder [pray-thay-der'], *va.* To precede (anteceder), to go before; to be superior in rank or order, to excel. **Le precedía un coche**, he was preceded by a car.

preceptista [pray-thep-tees'-tah], *m. & a.* Preceptist, theorist.

preceptivamente [pre-thep-tee'-vah-men-tay], *adv.* Preceptively.

preceptivo, va [pray-thep-tee'-vo, vah], *a.* Preceptive, mandatory, directory.

precepto [pray-thep'-to], *m.* Precept, order injunction, mandate, rule.

preceptor, ra [pray-thep-tor'], *m. & f.* Master, teacher, preceptor.

preces [pray'-thes], *f. pl.* 1. Prayers; public or private devotion. 2. Supplication for a bull or commission from the Vatican.

precesión [pray-thay-se-on'], *f.* 1. V. RETICENCIA. 2. *(Ast.)* Precession.

preciado, da [pray-the-ah'-do, dah], *a.* 1. Valued, appraised; esteemed (estimado). 2. Valuable, precious, excellent. 3. Proud, elated. presumptuous (presuntuoso). *-pp.* of PRECIAR.

preciador, ra [pray-the-ah-dor', rah], *m. & f.* Appraiser.

preciar [pray-the-ar'], *va.* To value, to appraise. *-vr.* To boast, to brag; to take pride in, to glory. **Preciarse de algo**, to pride oneself on something.

precinta [pray-theen'-tah], *f.* 1. Strap of wood, iron, tin, or leather, to secure the corners of boxes. 2. *(Naut.)* Parcelling, narrow pieces of tarred canvas, with which the seams of ships are covered, and which are also put around cables and ropes.

precintado [pre-thin-tah'-do], *a.* Sealed.

precintar [pray-thin-tar'], *va.* 1. To strap the corners of boxes with leather to prevent their opening. 2. To cross boxes of goods, as a mark that they are not to be opened.

precinto [pray-theen'-to], *m.* 1. The act of strapping. 2. A sealed strap with which trunks, parcels, etc., are bound lengthwise and crosswise, so that they may be opened only by the proper individuals.

precio [pray'-the-o], *m.* 1. Price, cost (costo), value (valor). 2. Price, reward; premium. 3. Price, value; estimation, esteem, consideration; character, credit. **Precio al contado**, cash price. Precio **de coste**, at cost price. **Precio neto**, net price. **Precio de venta**, sale price. **No tener precio**, to be priceless.

preciosamente [pre-the-o'-sah-men-tay], *adv.* Preciously, richly.

preciosidad [pray-the-o-se-dahd'], *f.* Worth (valor), excellence, preciousness (excelencia), beautiful thing (objeto). **Es una preciosidad**, it's lovely.

precioso, sa [pray-the-o'-so, sah], *a.* 1. Precious (excelente), valuable (valioso), excellent, 2. Pleasant, gay, merry.

precipicio [pray-the-pee'-the-o], *m.* 1. Precipice. 2. A sudden fall. 3. Ruin, destruction (ruina).

precipitación [pre-the-pe-tah-the-on'], *f.* 1. Precipitation, haste (prisa), precipitancy. 2. *(Chem.)* Precipitation, the fall of solid particles to the bottom of a liquid.

precipitadamente [pre-the-pe-tah'-dah-men-tay], *adv.* Precipitately, hastily, in a hurry.

precipitadero [pray-the-pe-tah-day'-ro], *m.* V. PRECIPICIO.

precipitado

precipitado, da [pray-the-pe-tah'-do, dah], *a. & pp.* of PRECIPITAR. Precipitate, hasty (partida), abrupt; sudden. -*m. (Chem.)* Precipitate.

precipitante [pray-the-pe-tahn'-tay], *m. (Chem.)* Precipitater.

precipitar [pray-the-pe-tar'], *va.* 1. To precipitate, to cast headlong. 2. To expose, to ruin. 3. To perform the chemical process of precipitation. -*vr.* To act in a precipitate manner (lanzarse); to run headlong to destruction; to haste, to hurry (correr). **Precipitarse a hacer algo**, to rush to do something. **Precipitarse sobre uno**, to rush at somebody.

precípite [pray-thee'-pe-tay], *a.* In danger, on the verge of falling.

precipitoso, sa [pray-the-pe-to' -so, sah], *a.* 1. Steep, slippery, precipitous (lugar). 2. Precipitous, rash, inconsiderate.

precipuo, pua [pray-thee' -poo-o, ah], *a.* Chief, principal.

precisamente [pray-the-sah-men'-tay], *adv.* 1. Precisely (con precisión), exactly, nicely. 2. Inevitably, indispensably, necessarily. 3. Just at the moment. **Precisamente por eso**, for that very reason. **Llegó precisamente cuando nos íbamos**, he arrived just as we were leaving.

precisar [pray-the-sar'], *va.* To compel, to oblige, to necessitate (necesitar), to determine exactly (determinar). **No precisa lavado**, it needs no washing. **Hay alguna rareza que no puedo precisar**, there is some oddity which I cannot pin down.

precisión [pray-the-se-on'], *f.* 1. Necessity (necesidad), obligation. 2. Compulsion, the state of being compelled. 3. Preciseness, exactness. 4. Precision (exactitud), exact limitation. **Tener precisión de hacer alguna cosa**, to be obliged or under the necessity of doing a certain thing. 5. *(Mex.)* Urgency.

precisivo, va [pray-the-see'-vo, vah], *a.* That which prescinds or abstracts, precisive.

preciso, sa [pray-thee' -so, sah], *a.* 1. Necessary (necesario), requisite, needful. 2. Precise (exacto), exact, punctual. 3. Distinct, clear. 4. Severed, cut off; abstracted. **Una descripción precisa**, a precise description. **Las cualidades precisas**, the essential qualities. 5. *(Carib.)* Conceited.

precitado, da [pray-the-tah'-do, dah], *a.* Forecited, quoted before.

precito, ta [pray-thee'-to, tah], *a.* Damned, condemned to hell.

preclaramente [pray-clah'-rah-men-tay], *adv.* Illustriously, distinctly.

preclaro, ra [pray-clah' -ro, rah], *a.* Illustrious, famous, eminent.

precocidad [pray-co-the-dahd'], *f.* Precocity, untimely ripeness of fruit, forwardness.

precocinado [pray-co-the-nah'-do], *a.* Precooked.

precocinar [pray-co-the-nahr'], *va.* To precook.

precognición [pray-cog-ne-the-on'], *f.* Precognition.

preconización [pray-co-ne-thah-the-on'], *f.* Preconization.

preconizador [pray-co-ne-thah-dor'], *m.* One who proclaims the elected prelates in the Roman consistory.

preconizar [prey-co-ne-thar'], *va.* To patronize, to proclaim, to publish in the Roman consistory, to praise (elogiar), to recommend (recomendar), to suggest (proponer).

preconocedor, ra [pray-co-no-thay-dor', rah], *m. & f.* One who foresees or anticipates a future event.

preconocer [pray-co-no-therr'], *va.* To foreknow, to foretell.

precordial [pray-cor-de-ahl'], *a.* Praecordial, relating to the diaphragm.

precoz [pray-coth'], *a,* Precocious, ripe before the usual time, forward.

precursor, ra [pray-coor-sor', rah], *a.* Preceding, going before. -*m.* Precursor, harbinger, forerunner, herald.

predecesor, ra [pray-day-thay-sor', rah], *m. & f.* Predecessor, antecessor, forerunner.

predecir [pray-day-theer'], *va.* To foretell, to anticipate, to predict. *(Yo predigo, prediga, predije, from Predecir. V. DECIR.)*

predefinición [pray-day-fe-ne-the-on'], *f.* Predetermination of the Divine Providence.

predefinir [pray-day-fe-ner'], *va.* To predetermine.

predestinación [pray-des-te-nah-the-on'], *f.* Predestination, preordination.

predestinado [pray-des-te-nah'-do], *m.* Foreordained to eternal glory. -**Predestinado, da**, *pp.* of PREDESTINAR.

predestinar [pray-des-te-nar'], *va.* To predestine, to destine beforehand, to foredoom, to predestinate.

predeterminación [pray-day-ter-me-nah-the-on'], *f.* Predetermination, foreordination.

predeterminar [pray-day-ter-me-nar'], *va.* To predetermine, to anticipate a resolution, to foredoom.

predial [pray-de-ahl'], *a.* Predial, consisting of or relating to landed property, or farms.

prédica [pray'-de-cah], *f.* Preachment, sermon, discourse by a non-Catholic preacher.

predicable [pray-de-cah'-blay], *a.* 1. Fit to be preached. 2. Commendable, praiseworthy. 3. Predicable.

predicable [pray-de-cah'-blay], *m.* Predicable, a logical term.

predicación [pray-de-cah-the-on'], *f..* Preaching, sermon.

predicadera [pray-de-cah-day'-rah], *f. (Prov.)* Pulpit. **Predicaderas** *(coll.)* style of the pulpit, facility of preaching or praying.

predicado [pray-de-cah'-do], *m. (Log.)* Predicate.

predicador, ra [pray-de-cah-dor', rah], *m. & f.* Preacher, orator, homilist, eulogist.

predicamental [pray-de-cah-men-tahl'], *a.* Predicamental.

predicamento [pray-de-cah-men'-to], *m.* 1. Predicament, degree of estimation in which a person is held. 2. Category, class or kind described by any definitive marks.

predicante [pray-de-cahn'-tay], *m.* Sectarian or heretical preacher.

predicar [pray-de-car'], *va.* 1. To render clear and evident, to publish. 2. To preach. 3. To praise to excess. 4. to reprehend vice. -*vr.* To predicate, to comprise an affirmation.

predicatorio [pray-de-cah-to'-re-o], *m.* V. PÚLPITO.

predicción [pray-dic-the-on'], *f.* Prediction. **Predicción del tiempo**, weather forecast.

predicho, cha [pray-dee'-cho, chah], *pp. irr.* of PREDECIR.

predilección [pray-de-lec-the-on'], *f.* Predilection. **Tener predilección por**, to have a predilection for.

predilecto, ta [pray-de-lec' -to, tah], *a.* Beloved in preference to others; darling, favorite.

predio [pray'-de-o], *m.* Landed property, farm, real property. **Predio rústico**, piece of arable ground. **Previo urbano**, dwelling-house in town or country.

prediolo [pray-de-o'-lo], *m.* A small farm.

predisponer [pray-dis-po-nerr'], *va.* 1. To predispose, to prearrange. 2. *(Not Acad.)* To predispose towards, to contract disease readily.

predisposición [pray-dis-po-se-the-on'], *f.* 1. Predisposition. 2. Inclination, propensity.

predispuesto, ta [pray-dis-poo-es' -to, tah], *a. & pp. irr.* of PREDISPONER. Predisponent, predisposed.

predominación [pray-do-me-nah-the-on'], *f. V.* PREDOMINIO.

predominante [pray-do-me-nahn'-tay], *pa.* Predominant, prevailing.

predominar [pray-do-me-nar'], *va.* 1. To predominate, to overrule, to overpower, to control, to compel. 2. To exceed in height, to overlook, to command; to prevail (prevalecer).

predominio [pray-do-mee'-ne-o], *m.* Predominance (dominio), superiority (superioridad).

preelección [pray-ay-lec-the-on'], *f.* Predestination.

preeminencia [pray-ay-me-nen'-the-ah], *f.* Pre-eminence, mastery.

preeminente [pray-ay-me-nen'-tay], *a.* Pre-eminent, superior.

preestablecer [pray-es-tah-blay-therr,], *va.* To pre-establish.

preexcelso, sa [pray-ex-thel'-so, sah], *a.* Illustrious, great, eminent.

preexistencia [pray-ek-sis-ten'-the-ah], *f.* Pre-existence.

preexistente [pray-ek-sis-ten-tay], *pa.* Pre-existent.

preexistir [pray-ek-sis-teer'], *vn.* To pre-exist.

prefabricado, da [pray-fah-bre-cah'-do dah], *a.* Prefabricated.

prefabricar [pre-fah-bre-cahr'], *va.* To prefabricate.

prefacio [pray-fah'-the-o], *m.* 1. Part of the mass which immediately precedes the canon. 2. Preface.

prefación [pray-fah-the-on'], *f.* Preface, introduction.

prefacioncilla [pray-fah-the-on-theel-lyah], *f. dim.* A short preface.

prefecto [pray-fec'-to], *m.* 1. Prefect, head of a county or municipality. 2. Master or principal of a college. 3. Prefect, a magistrate in ancient Rome.

prefectura [pray-fec-too'-rah], *f.* Prefecture.

preferencia [pray-fay-ren'-the-ah], *f.* Preference, choice, preeminence. **Mostrar preferencia por**, to show preference to.

preferente [pray-fay-ren'-tay], *pa. & a.* Pre-eminent: preferring.

preferible [pray-fay-ree'-blay], *a.* Preferable.

preferiblemente [pre-fay-ree'-blay-men-tay], *adv.* Preferably.

preferido [pre-fay-ree'-do], *a.* Favorite. **Es mi cantante preferido**, he is my favorite singer.

preferir [pray-fay-reer'], *va.* To prefer. **Preferir té a café**, to prefer tea to coffee. *-vr.* To proffer, to offer spontaneously to do anything. (*Yo prefiero, prefiera; él prefirió*; from *Preferir* V. ADHERIR.)

prefiguración [pray-fe-goo-rah-the-on'], *f.* Prefiguration.

prefigurar [pray-fe-goo-rar'], *va.* To prefigure, to foretoken, to model a statue, to sketch a painting.

prefijar [pray-fe-har'], *va.* To prefix, to determine.

prefijo, ja [pray-fee'-ho, hah], *pp. irr.* Of PREFIJAR. Prefixed.

prefijo [pray-fee'-ho], *m.* (*Gram.*) Prefix.

prefinición [pray-fe-ne-the-on'], *f.* Act of prefining or fixing a term.

prefinir [pray-fe-neer'], *va.* To determine.

prefoliación [pray-fo-le-ah-the-on'], *f.* (*Bot.*) Vernation, prefoliation, arrangement of leaves within the bud.

prefulgente [pray-fool-hen'-tay], *a.* Resplendent, lucid, shining.

pregaria [pre-gah'-re-ah], *f.* V. PLEGARIA.

pregón [pray-gone'], *m.* Publication by the common crier, cry.

pregonador, ra [pray-go-na-dor', rah], *m. & f.* Hawker, huckster, street-vender.

pregonar [pray-go-nar'], *va.* 1. To proclaim in public places (proclamar). 2. To cry goods or provisions about the streets (mercancía). 3. To render public, to make known; to applaud publicly.

pregoneo [pray-go-nay'-o], *m.* Hawking, crying goods on the streets.

pregonería [pray-go-nay-ree'-ah], *f.* 1. Office of common crier. 2. A kind of tax or tribute.

pregonero [pray-go-nay'-ro], *m.* 1. Common crier, town crier (municipal). 2. One who renders public or divulges a secret. 3. One who proclaims the biddings at public sales.

pregonero, ra [pray-go-nay'-ro, rah], *a.* Publishing, praising, proclaiming.

preguerra [pray-gayr'-rah], *f.* Prewar.

pregunta [pray-goon'-tah], *f.* Question, query, inquiry. **Absolver las preguntas**, (*For.*) to answer under oath. **Estar a la cuarta pregunta**, (*coll.*) to be hard up or penniless. **Contestar a una pregunta**, to answer a question. **A preguntas necias, oídos sordos**, ask a silly question and you will get a silly answer. **Hacer una pregunta**, to ask a question. *-vn.* To ask, to inquire. *-vr.* To wonder.

preguntador, ra [pray-goon-tah-dor', rah], *m. & f.* Questioner, examiner, interrogator.

preguntante [pray-goon-tahn'-tay], *pa.* Inquiring.

preguntar [pray-goon-tar'], *va.* To ask, to question, to demand, to inquire. **Preguntar algo a uno**, to ask somebody something. *-vr.* To wonder.

preguntón, na [pray-goon-tone', nah], *m. & f.* An inquisitive person, a busy inquirer.

prehistoria [pray-is-to'-re-ah], *f.* Prehistoric or legendary times.

prehistórico, ca [pray-is-to'-re-co, cah], *a.* Prehistoric, legendary; previous to the beginning of history.

preinserto, ta [pray-in-serr'-to, tah], *a.* That which is previously inserted.

prejudicial [pray-hoo-de-the-ahl'], *a.* (*Law.*) Pre-judicial, requiring a previous judicial decision before the final sentence.

prejuicio [pray-hoo-ee'-the-o], *m.* Prejudice, bias, prejudgment.

prejuzgar [pray-hooth-gar'], *va.* To judge or decide things before the right time, to prejudge.

prelacía [pray-lah-thee'-ah], *f.* Prelacy, prelature.

prelación [pray-lah-the-on'], *f.* Preference, preferment.

prelada [pray-lah'-dah], *f.* A female prelate, the abbess or superior of a convent or nunnery.

prelado [pray-lah'-do], *m.* Prelate, an ecclesiastic of the highest order and dignity; the superior of a convent or religious house.

prelativo, va [pray-lah-tee'-vo, vah], *a.* Deserving preferment.

prelatura [pray-lah-too'-rah], *f.* 1. Prelacy, prelature. 2. The whole body of prelates.

preliminar [pray-le-me-nar'], *a.* Preliminary, proemial, exordial. *-m.* A preliminary sketch; protocol.

prelucir [pray-loo-theer'], *vn.* To sparkle or shine forth.

preludiar [pray-loo-de-a'], *vn.* 1. To attempt, to essay. 2. (*Mus.*) To make a flourish or introduction to the main piece. *-va.* To announce (anunciar), to herald.

preludio [pray-loo'-dee-o], *m.* Prelude; flourish.

prelusión [pray-loo-se-on'], *f.* Prelude, prologue, preface.

premática [pray-mah'-te-cah], *f.* (*Old.*) V. PRAGMÁTICA.

prematrimonial [pray-mah-tre-mo-ne-ahl'], *a.* Premarital.

prematuramente [pray-mah-too-rah-men-tay], *adv.* Prematurely.

prematuro, ra [pray-mah-too'-ro, rah], *a.* Premature, precocious; unseasonable. **Bebé prematuro**, premature baby.

premeditación [pray-may-de-tah-the-on'], *f.* Premeditation, forethought, precogitation.

premeditado, da [pray-may-de-tah'-do, dah], *a. & pp.* of PREMEDITAR. Premeditated, prepense, pre-conceived.

premeditar [pray-may-de-tar'], *va.* 1. To consider or meditate carefully, to weigh maturely. 2. To premeditate.

premiado [pray-me-ah'-do], *a.* Prize (novela); prize winning. *-m & f.* Prizewinner.

premiador, ra [pray-me-ah-dor', rah], *m. & f.* Rewarder.

premiar [pray-me-ar'], *va.* To reward (recompensar), to remunerate, to give or award a prize.

premio [pray'-me-o], *m.* 1. Reward (recompensa), recompense, remuneration. 2. Premium, interest. **Premio de seguro**, rate or premium of insurance. 3. Premium, increase in value of money or securities. 4. Prize, award (en concurso). **Premio de consolación**, consolation prize.

premiosamente [pre-me-o'-sah-men-tay], *adv.* Tightly, compressedly; by force.

premiosidad [pray-me-o-se-dahd'], *f.* Want of ease and readiness in the manner of speaking or of writing.

premioso, sa [pray-me-o'-so, sah], *a.* 1. Tight (vestido), close, pinching. 2. Troublesome, tiresome, burdensome. 3. Unready in speech (al hablar), expressing oneself with difficulty.

premisa [pray-mee'-sah], *f.* 1. Premise, in logic; an antecedent proposition. 2. Mark, indication.

premiso, sa [pray-mee'-so, sah], *a.* 1. Premised. V. PREVENIDO. 2. (*Law.*) Precedent, former, going before.

premoción [pray-mo-the-on'], *f.* Previous movement or motion.

premonición

premonición [pray-mo-ne-the-on'], *f.* Premonition.

premonitorio [pray-mo-ne-to'-re-o], *a.* Indicative, warning, premonitory.

premonstratense, premostratense [pray-mons-trah-ten-say], *a.* Premonstratensian: applied to an order of regular canons founded by St. Norbert.

premorir [pray-mo-reer'], *va. (Law.)* To die before another.

premura [pray-moo'-rah], *f. (coll.)* Narrowness, pressure (presión), haste, hurry. **Con premura de tiempo**, under pressure.

prenatal [pray-nah-tahl'], *a.* Antenatal, prenatal.

prenda [pren'-dah], *f.* 1. Pledge (garantía), security for the fulfilment of an obligation. 2. Pledge, any household ornament or furniture, especially when pawned or sold. 3. Pledge, earnest, security. 4. A garment or ornament. 5. Any object dearly loved, as wife or children; jewel (joya), pledge of affection. 6. Talents, gifts (cualidades). 7. Forfeits (juegos). **Dejar algo en prenda**, to pawn something. **No soltar prenda**, to give nothing away.

prendado [pren-dah'-do], *pp.* of PRENDAR.

prendador, ra [pren-dah-dor', rah], *m. & f.* Pledger, pawner; one who redeems a pledge.

prendamiento [pren-dah-me-en'-to], *m.* Act of pledging or pawning.

prendar [pren-dar'], *va.* 1. To take pledges, to lend on pledges. 2. To please, to ingratiate oneself. *-vr.* To take a fancy to something: used with the preposition *de.*

prendedero [pren-day-day'-ro], *m.* 1. Hook, fillet, brooch. 2. Fillet, a band tied round the head, which serves to keep the hair up.

prendedor [pren-day-dor'], *m.* 1. Catcher 2. Breast-pin.

prender [pren-derr'], *va.* 1. To seize, to grasp, to catch (persona), to pin. 2. To imprison. 3. *(coll.)* To detain for the purpose of entertaining in a friendly manner. 1. To take root (plantas). 2. To cover: applied to the act of brutish procreation. 3. To catch or take fire (fuego, horno). 4. To adorn, to embellish (mujeres). *-vn.* 1. To catch, to stick (engancharse). 2. To catch (fuego), to take (inyección); to take, to take root (planta).

prendería [pren-day-ree'-ah], *f.* Shop in which old clothes and furniture are sold; pawnbroker's shop; frippery.

prendero, ra [pren-day'-ro, rah], *m. & f.* 1. Broker, one who sells old furniture and clothes; fripper. 2. Pawnbroker (prestamista).

prendido [pren-dee'-do], *m.* 1. Dress of women. 2. Pattern for bone-lace.—**Prendido, da**, *pp.* of PRENDAR.

prendimiento [pren-de-me-en'-to], *m.* 1. Seizure, capture (captura). 2. *(Cono Sur, Med.)* Constipation.

prenoción [pray-no-the-on'], *f.* Prenotion or first knowledge of things.

prenombre [pray-nom'-bray], *m.* Prenomen, name prefixed to the family name among the Romans.

prenotar [pray-no-tar'], *va.* To note by anticipation.

prensa [pren'-sah], *f.* 1. Press, an instrument with which something is pressed. 2. Press, a machine for printing. 3. Press. *V.* IMPRENTA. **Dar a la prensa**, to publish. **Aprobar un libro para la prensa**, to pass a book for the press. **Tener mala prensa**, to have a bad press.

prensado [pren-sah'-do], *m.* Luster, which remains on stuff. **Prensado, da**, *pp.* of PRENSAR.

prensador, ra [pren-sah-dor', rah], *m. & f.* Presser, one who presses clothes and stuff, pressing machine.

prensadura [pren-sah-doo'-rah], *f.* The act of pressing, pressure.

prensapapeles [pren-sah-pah-pay'-les], *m.* A paper weight.

prensar [pren-sar'], *va.* To press. *V.* APRENSAR.

prensista [pren-sees'-tah], *m.* Pressman in a printing-office.

prenunciar [pray-noon-the-ar'], *va.* To foretell, to prognosticate.

prenuncio [pray-noon'-the-o], *m.* Prediction, prognostication.

preñada [pray-nye-dah'-dah], *a.* Pregnant (animales).

preñadilla [pray-nah-deel'-lyah], *f.* A delicate fish of the rivers of Ecuador, olive-green, with black spots and about four inches long; called **imba** by the Indians.

preñado, da [pray-nyah'-do, dah], *a.* 1. Full, pregnant. 2. Big with child, pregnant. 3. Enclosing within itself something undiscovered. *-m.* Pregnancy (embarazo), gestation. **Palabras preñadas de amenaza**, words charged with menace.

preñar [pray-nyar'], *va.* To get pregnant, to impregnate, to fertilize.

preñez [pray-nyeth'], *f.* 1. Pregnancy, gestation. *V.* PREÑADO. 2. Conception 3. The state of a thing that is impending or hanging over. 4. Confusion, difficulty, obscurity.

preocupación [pray-o-coo-pah-the-on'], *f.* 1. Preoccupation, anticipation in taking possession. 2. Prepossession, bias, prejudice (prejuicio); preconception (ofuscación). **Tiene la preocupación de que su mujer le es infiel**, he has an obsession that his wife is unfaithful to him.

preocupadamente [pray-o-coo-pah'-dah-men-tay], *adv.* Prejudicedly.

preocupado [pray-o-coo-pah'-do], *a.* Worried, anxious, concerned.

preocupar [pray-o-coo-par'], *va.* Preoccupy (inquietar). 2. To prejudice (influir), to prepossess the mind. **Esto me preocupa muchísimo**, this worries me greatly. *-vr.* To worry (inquietarse), to care; to concern (ocuparse). **No te preocupes por eso**, don't worry about that.

preordinación [pray-or-de-nah-the-on'], *f.* Preordination.

preordinadamente [pray-or-de-nah'-dah-men-tay], *adv.* In a manner preordained.

preordinar [pray-or-de-nar'], *va.* To preordain, to foreordain.

preparación [pray-pah-rah-the-on'], *f.* 1. Preparation (acto). 2. Preparedness (estado), readiness. 3. Training (formación). 4. Competence (competencia). 5. *(Cono Sur)* Appetizer (bocadito). **Estar en preparación**, to be in preparation.

preparado [pray-pah-rah'-do], *a.* 1. Prepared (dispuesto); *(Culin.)* ready to serve. 2. Competent (competente), able. **"Preparado para transmitir"**, *(Comput.)* "clear to send" (CTS).

preparamento, preparamiento [pray-pa-rah-men'-to], *m.* Preparation.

preparar [pray-pah-rar'], *va.* To prepare (disponer), to make ready. *-vr.* To be prepared, to be in readiness. **Prepararse para**, to prepare to.

preparativo, va [pray-pah-rah-tee'-vo, vah], *a.* Preparative, qualifying.

preparativo [pray-pah-rah-tee'-vo], *m.* Thing prepared, preparative.

preparatoriamente [pray-pah-rah-to'-re-ah-men-tay], *adv.* Preparatorily.

preparatorio, ria [pray-pah-rah-to'-re-o, ah], *a.* Preparatory, previous, introductory.

preponderancia [pray-pon-day-rahn'-the-ah], *f.* Preponderance, overbalancing.

preponderante [pray-pon-day-rahn'-tay], *a.* Preponderant, that which turns the scale.

preponderar [pray-pon-day-rar'], *vn.* 1 To preponderate, to outweigh, to overbalance. 2. To prevail. 3. To overpower.

preponer [pray-po-nerr'], *va.* To put before, to prefer.

preposición [pray-po-se-the-on'], *f. (Gram.)* Preposition, a part of speech.

prepositivo, va [pray-po-se-tee'-vo, vah], *a.* Prepositive, prefixed.

prepósito [pray-po'-se-to], *m.* 1. President, chairman. 2. Provost.

prepositura [pray-po-se-too'-rah], *f.* Dignity of a provost.

preposteración [pray-pos-tay-rah-the-on'], *f.* Inversion of the regular order of things.

prepósteramente [pray-pos'-tay-rah-men-tay], *adv.* Preposterously.

preposterar [pray-pos-tay-rar'], *va.* To render preposterous, to transpose.

prepóstero, ra [pray-pos'-tay-ro, rah], *a.* Preposterous, absurd.

prepotencia [pray-po-ten'-the-ah], *f.* Preponderance, superiority, prepotency.

prepotente [pray-po-ten'-tay], *a.* 1 Very powerful. 2. Abusive of power over one's inferiors.

prepucial [pray-poo-the-ahl'], *a.* Preputial, relating to the prepuce.

prepucio [pray-poo'-the-o], *m.* Prepuce, foreskin.

prepuesto, ta [pray-poo-es'-to, tah], *pp. irr.* of PREPONER. Preferred.

prerrogativa [pray-ro-gah-tee'-vah], *f.* Prerogative, privilege; liberty.

presa [pray'-sah], *f.* 1. Capture (acto), seizure. 2. Prize (cosa apresada, barco), spoils or booty taken from an enemy. 3. Dike (dique), dam, mole, bank, drain, trench (trinchera), conduit. 4. Slice of meat, a bit of any other kind of eatables. 5. Tusks, fangs (colmillos). 6. Claw (ave de rapiña). 7. Carcass of a fowl or bird killed by a hawk or other bird of prey. 8. Among fishermen, fish weir (represa), stake work. **Hacer presa**, to catch and tie something so that it cannot escape. 9. Clutch (asimiento).

presada [pray-sah'-dah], *f.* Color of a leek; a pale green color.

presagiar [pray-sah-he-ar'], *va.* To presage, to forebode, to foretell.

presagio [pray-sah'-he-o], *m.* Presage, an omen, a token.

presagioso, sa, présago, ga [pray-sah-he-oh'- so, sah, pray' -sah-go, gah], *a.* Ominous, presaging, divining, guessing.

presbicia [pres-bee'-the-ah], *f.* Farsightedness, presbyopia.

présbite, ta [pres'-be-tay, tah], *a. & m. & f.* Presbyopic, seeing objects better at a distance; a presbyope.

presbiterado, presbiterato [pres-be-tay-rah'-do, pres-be-tay-rah'-to], *m.* Priesthood, the dignity or order of priest.

presbiteral [pres-be-tay-rahl'], *a.* Sacerdotal, relating to a presbyter.

presbiterianismo [pres-be-tay-re-ah-nees'-mo], *m.* Presbyterianism.

presbiteriano, na [pres-be-tay-re-ah'-no, nah], *a. & m. & f.* Presbyterian

presbiteriato [pres-be-tay-re-ah'-to], *m.* Dignity of a presbyter or elder among the Presbyterians.

presbiterio [pres-be-tay'-re-o], *m.* Presbyterium, chancel, the part in a church where the high altar stands.

presbítero [pres-bee'-tay-ro], *m.* A priest.

presciencia [pres-the-en'-the-ah], *f.* Prescience, foreknowledge, forethought.

prescindible [pres-thin-dee'-blay], *a.* Capable of being prescinded or abstracted.

prescindir [pres-thin-deer'], *va.* 1. To prescind, to cut off to abstract. **Prescindiendo de eso**, laying that aside. 2. To cease from doing something. *-vn.* 1. To do without (pasarse sin). 2. To dispense with (deshacer de); to disregard (desatender). **Han prescindido del coche**, they've given up their car. **No podemos prescindir de él**, we can't manage without him.

prescito, ta [pres-thee'-to, tah], *a. V* PRECITO.

prescribir [pres-cre-beer'], *va.* 1. To prescribe, to determine. 2. To acquire a right by uninterrupted possession 3. To despair of success; to stand in need of. *-vn.* To prescribe, to form a custom which has the force of law.

prescripción [pres-crip-the-on'], *f.* 1 Prescription, the act of prescribing. 2. Introduction, anything proemial. 3. *(Law.)* Prescription, right or title acquired by peaceful possession. **Prescripción médica**, medical prescription.

prescriptible [pres-crip-tee'-blay], *a.* Prescriptible, that may be prescribed

prescripto, ta [pres-creep'-to, tah], *pp. irr.* of PRESCRIBIR. Prescribed, prescript, accurately laid down in a precept.

presea [pray-say'-ah], *f.* Jewel, any ornament of great value.

preselección [pray-say-leclthe-on'], *f.* Seeding; short listing (de candidatos).

preseleccionar [pray-say-layc-the-o-nahr'], *va.* To seed; to shortlist (candidatos).

presencia [pray-sen'-the-ah], *f.* 1. Presence, coexistence. 2. Presence figure, port, air, mien, demeanor. 3. *(Met.)* Memory or representation of a thing. **Presencia de ánimo**, serenity, coolness, presence of mind. **En presencia de**, in the presence of.

presencial [pray-sen-the-ahl'], *a.* Presential, relating to actual presence.

presencialmente [pray-sen-the-ahl'-men-tay], *adv.* Presentially.

presenciar [pray-sen-the-ar'], *vn.* To be present, to witness, to assist at.

presentable [pray-sen-tah'-blay], *a.* Presentable, producible.

presentación [pray-sen-tah-the-on'], *f.* 1. Presentation, presentment, exhibition. 2. A church festival in memory of the Virgin's presentation in the temple, celebrated on the 21st of November. 3. The act of offering or presenting an ecclesiastical benefice. 4. Introduction. **Presentación en sociedad**, coming-out, début.

presentado [pray-sen-tah'-do], *m. & a.* 1. Teacher of divinity, who expects soon to be ranked as master. 2. Presentee, person presented.—**Presentado, da**, *pp.* of PRESENTAR.

presentador, ra [pray-sen-tah-dor'-rah], *m. & f.* Presenter, one that presents, one who offers a benefice.

presentalla [pray-sen-tahl'-lyah], *f.* Gift offered by the faithful to the saints.

presentar [pray-sen-tar'], *va.* 1. To present, to exhibit, to view. 2. To present, to favor with a gift, to offer openly and freely. 3. To present or prefer to ecclesiastical benefices. 4. To perform (obra); to show (película); to present (estrella). 5. To introduce (persona). **El coche presenta ciertas modificaciones**, the car has certain modifications. **Ser presentada en la sociedad**, to come out, to make one's début. *-vr.* 1. To appear in a court of justice; to present oneself before anyone. 2. To run, to stand (candidato). 3. To show (mostrarse). **Presentarse a la policía**, to report to the police. **El día se presenta muy hermoso**, it looks like being a lovely day.

presente [pray-sen'-tay], *a.* 1. Present, being face to face (persona). 2. *(Gram.)* Present, one of the tenses of verbs; in this last sense it is also used as a substantive. 3. Present: applied to the time now passing, or what is now in its course. 4. *(LAm.)* By hand (en sobre). **Estar presente en**, to present at. **La presente carta**, this letter. *-m.* Present, gift, keepsake. **Al presente or de presente**, at present, now. **Tener presente**, to bear in mind. **Hacer presente**, (a) to state, to set forth, to inform; (b) to consider one as present (for emoluments, etc.). **La presente**, the present letter.

presentemente [pray-sen-tay-men-tay], *adv.* Presently, at present, now.

presentero [prey-sen-tay'-ro], *m.* Presenter; one who offers a benefice.

presentillo [pray-sen-teel'-lyo], *m. dim.* A small gift.

presentimiento [pray-sen-te-me-en'-to], *m.* Presentiment, foreboding, misgiving.

presentir [pray-sen-teer'], *va.* To have a presentiment of a future event, to foresee, to forebode. *(Yo presiento, yo presienta; él presintió* from *Presentir. V.* ADHERIR.)

presera [pray-say'-rah], *f. (Bot.)* Goosegrass, cleavers. *V.* AMOR DE HORTELANO.

presero [pray-say'-ro], *m.* The person who has the care of a dam or dike.

preservación [pray-ser-vah-the-on'], *f.* Preservation, conservation.

preservador, ra [pray-ser-vah-dor', rah], *m. & f.* Preserver.

preservar [pray-ser-var'], *va.* To preserve, to defend from evil; to save.

preservativamente [pray-ser-vah-tee'-vah-men-tay], *adv.* Preservatively.

preservativo [pray-ser-vah-tee'-vo], *m.* Preservative, preventive.

preservativo, va [pray-ser-vah-tee'-vo, vah], *a.* Preservative, having the power of preserving.

presidencia [pray-se-den'-the-ah], *f.* 1. Presidency. 2. Chairmanship.

presidenta [pray-se-den'-tah], *f.* President's wife; moderatrix.

presidente [pray-se-den'-tay], *m.* 1. President, one placed at the head of others; chairman (de comité, de reunión); speaker; judge. 2. President, the chief executive officer of a republic.

presidiar [pray-se-de-ar'], *va.* To garrison a place.

presidiario [pray-se-de-ah'-re-o], *m.* A criminal condemned to hard labor or banishment in a garrison.

presidio [pray-see'-de-o], *m.* 1. Garrison of soldiers. 2. Fortress garrisoned by soldiers. 3. Assistance, aid, help, protection. 4. Place destined for punishing criminals by hard labor; bridewell, house of correction; penitentiary (cárcel). 5. Punishment by hard labor.

presidir [pray-se-deer'], *va.* To preside in an assembly, community, meeting, etc.

presilla [pray-seel'-lyah], *f.* 1. A small string with which something is tied or fastened. 2. Loop in clothes (lazo), which serves as a button-hole. 3. Sort of linen. **Presilla de un sombrero**, loop for a hat.

presión [pray-se-on'], *f.* Pressure. **Presión arterial**, blood pressure. **Hacer presión**, to pressure, to try to influence.

preso, sa [pray-so, sah], *m. & f.* Prisoner. **Preso político**, political prisoner.

preso, sa [pray'-so, sah], *pp. irr.* of PRENDER. Taken. **Estar preso de pánico**, to be panic-stricken.

prespiración [pres-pe-rah-the-on'], *f.* Penetration of water into the earth.

prest [prest], *m. V.* PRE.

presta [pres'-tah], *f.* (*Bot. Prov.*) *V.* HIERBABUENA or MENTA.

prestación [pres-tah-the-on'], *f.* 1. (*Law.*) Act of lending or granting. 2. (*Aut. Mec.*) Feature, detail. 3. (*Comput.*) Capability. 4. (*Mex. Com.*) Fringe benefit. **Prestación comercial**, obligatory service.

prestadizo, za [pres-tah-dee'-tho, thah], *a.* That may be lent or borrowed.

prestado, da [pres-tah'-do, dah], *a. & pp.* of PRESTAR. Lent. **Tomar prestado**, to borrow. **Dar prestado**, to lend. **De prestado**, for a short time; improperly.

prestador, ra [pres-tah-dor', rah], *m. & f.* Lender; one who lends money at usurious interest.

prestamente [pres'-tah-men-tay], *adv.* Speedily, promptly, quickly.

prestamista [pres-tah-mees'-tah], *com.* Money-lender.

préstamo [pres'-tah-mo], *m.* Loan. *V.* EMPRÉSTITO. **Préstamo hipotecario**, mortgage.

prestancia [pres-tahn'-the-ah], *f.* Excellence. *V.* EXCELENCIA.

prestante [pres-tahn'-tay], *a. V.* EXCELENTE.

prestar [pres-tar'], *va.* 1. To lend, to grant the use of something. 2. To credit, to give credit. 3. To aid, to assist. 4. To give, to communicate. 5. (*Prov.*) To extend, to expand. 6. (*Law.*) To pay the interest, duty, etc., which is ordered. **Prestar paciencia**, to bear something with patience. 7. To take, to swear (juramento). 8. (*LAm.*) To borrow (pedir prestado). 9. (*Carib. Cono Sur*) To do good to, to be good for. *-vn.* 1. To be useful, to contribute to the attainment of something. 2. To guard, to preserve: applied to God, who lends all things. *-vr.* To offer oneself, to agree to anything. **La situación se presta a muchas interpretaciones**, the situation lends itself to many interpretations. **Prestar servicio de asistencia** (*Comput.*), to provide assistance.

preste [pres'-tay], *m.* Priest who celebrates the high mass. **Preste Juan**, prester John, title of the Abyssinian monarchs, because anciently the king was a priest.

préster [pres'-ter], *m.* 1. Hurricane. 2. Meteor like lightning.

presteza [pres-tay'-thah], *f.* Quickness, promptitude, haste, speed, nimbleness.

prestidigitación [pres-te-de-he-tah-the-on'], *f.* Legerdemain, sleight of hand, jugglery.

prestidigitador [pres-te-de-he-tah-dor'], *m.* Juggler, prestidigitator.

prestidigitar [pres-te-de-he-tar'], *va.* To juggle, to perform feats of sleight of hand.

prestigiador [pres-te-he-ah-dor'], *m.* Cheat, juggler, impostor.

prestigiar [pres-te-he-ar'], *va.* To give prestige to; to make famous (dar fama); to honor (honrar).

prestigio [pres-tee'-he-o], *m.* 1. Conjuring, juggling, imposture. 2. Sleight of hand, legerdemain. 3. Prestige (fama), fame, favorable reputation (reputación). **Tener buen** or **mal prestigio de una persona**, (*coll.*) to be well or ill inclined to a person. **Tener una cosa buen** or **mal prestigio**, to forebode good or evil from an affair.

prestigioso, sa [pres-te-he-o'-so, sah], *a.* Deceitful, illusory, prestigious.

prestito [pres-tee'-to], *adv.* Quickly, promptly.

presto, ta [pres'-to, tah], *a.* 1. Quick (rápido), prompt, ready (listo), diligent. 2. Ready, prepared, disposed.

presto [pres'-to], *adv.* Soon, quickly (rápidamente), speedily. **De presto**, promptly, swiftly.

presumible [pray-soo-mee'-blay], *a.* Presumable, supposable.

presumidico, ica, illo, illa, ito, ita [pray-soo-me-dee'-co], *a. dim.* Confident, a little presumptuous.

presumido, da [pray-soo-mee'-do, dah], *a.* Presumptuous, arrogant, insolent, forward. *-pp.* of PRESUMIR.

presumir [pray-soo-meer'], *va.* 1. To presume (suponer), to suppose, to suspect, to conjecture. 2. (*And. Cono Sur*) To court (pretender); to flirt with (coquetear con). *-vn.* To show off (chulearse), to presume, to boast, to form confident opinions, to make arrogant attempts. **Para presumir ante las amistades**, in order to show off before one's friends. **Presumir de experto**, to pride oneself on being an expert.

presunción [pray-soon-the-on'], *f.* 1. Presumption, supposition, conjecture (conjetura). 2. Presumptuousness, blind and arrogant confidence; vanity, conceitedness (cualidad). 3. Suspicion (sospecha).

presuntamente [pray-soon-tah-men-tay], *adv.* Presumptively.

presuntivamente [pray-soon-tee'-vah-men-tay], *adv.* Conjecturally.

presuntivo, va [pray-soon-tee'-vo, vah], *a.* 1. Presumptive, taken by previous supposition. 2. Presumptive, supposed.

presunto, ta [pray-soon'-to, tah], *pp. irr.* Of PRESUMIR. Presumed. **El presunto asesino**, the alleged murderer.

presuntuosamente [pray-soon-too-oh'-sah-men-tay], *adv.* Presumptuously, arrogantly.

presuntuoso, sa [pray-soon-too-oh'-so, sah], *a.* Presumptuous, vain, arrogant, insolent.

presuponer [pray-soo-po-nerr'], *va.* To presuppose, to take for granted.

presuposición [pray-soo-po-se-the-on'], *f.* Presupposition, presupposal, pretext.

presupuesto [pray-soo-poo-es'-to], *m.* 1. Motive, pretext, pretence. 2. An estimate, calculation; budget of state (de obras, proyecto). 3. Supposition.

presupuesto, ta [pray-soo-poo-es'-to, tah], *pp. irr.* of PRESUPONER.

presura [pray-soo'-rah], *f.* 1. Hurry, haste, promptitude. 2. Oppression, pressure, anxiety. 3. Eagerness, importunity.

presurosamente [pray-soo-roh'-sah-men-tay], *adv.* Hastily, promptly.

presuroso, sa [pray-soo-ro'-so, sah], *a.* Hasty (apresurado), prompt, quick (rápido); light, nimble.

pretal [pray-tahl'], *m.* Poitrel, breast-plate, or breast-leather of a home.

pretencioso [pray-ten-the-oh'-so], *a.* 1. Pretentious (vanidoso), presumptuous; showy. 2. (*LAm.*) Conceited (presumido).

pretender [pray-ten-derr'], *va.* 1. To pretend, to claim (afirmar), to solicit. 2. To try (aspirar), to attempt. 3. To woo, to court (mujer). **Han pretendido robarme**, they have attempted to rob me. **El libro pretende ser importante**, the book tries to look important. **Pretende llegar a ser médico**, she hopes to become a doctor.

pretendiente, ta [pray-ten-de-en'-tay, tah], *m. & f.* Pretender, candidate, office-hunter, solicitor.

pretensión [pray-ten-se-on'], *f.* 1. Pretension, solicitation for obtaining something. 2. Pretension, claim (reclamación, afirmación). 3. Aim, object (objetivo). **Tener pretensiones de**, to have pretensions to. **Tener pocas pretensiones**, to be undemanding.

pretenso, sa [pray-ten'-so, sah], *pp. irr.* Of PRETENDER.

pretensor, ra [pray-ten-sor', rah], *m. & f.* Pretender, claimant.

pretera [pray-tay'-rah], *f.* Backgammon.

preterición [pray-tay-re-the-on'], *f.* 1. Preterition, the act of going past, the state of being past. 2. (*Law.*) Preterition, the act of omitting lawful children in a last will.

preterir [pray-tay-reer'], *va.* (*Law.*) To omit lawful children in a last will.

pretérito, ta [pray-tay'-re-to, tah], *a.* 1. Preterite, past. 2. (*Gram.*) Preterite: applied to past tenses of verbs.

pretermisión [pray-ter-me-se-on'], *f.* Preterition, pretermission.

pretermitir [pray-ter-me-teer'], *va.* To omit, to pretermit, to pass by.

preternatural [pray-ter-nah-too-rahl'], *a.* Preternatural.

preternaturalizar [pray-ter-nah-to-rah-le-thar'], *va.* To pervert, to render preternatural.

preternaturalmente [pray-ter-nah-too-rahl'-men-tay], *adv.* Preternaturally.

pretexta [pray-tex'-tah], *f.* A long gown worn by magistrates of ancient Rome.

pretextar [pray-tex-tar'], *va.* To make use of a pretext, to feign an excuse.

pretexto [pray-tex'-to], *m.* Pretext, excuse (disculpa), pretence, mask, cover.

pretil [pray-teel'], *m.* Parapet (puente, balcón), battlement, breastwork.

pretina [pray-tee'-nah], *f.* 1. Girdle, waistband; belt. 2. Waist, everything which girds or surrounds. 3. (*Carib.*) Flies (bragueta).

pretinazo [prey-tee-nah'-tho], *m.* Blow given with a girdle.

pretinero [pray-tee-nay'-ro], *m.* One who makes girdles.

pretinilla [pray-te-neel'-lyah], *f. dim.* A small belt or girdle.

pretor [pray-tor'], *m.* 1. Pretor, a magistrate in ancient Rome. 2. Blackness of the waters where tunny-fish abound.

pretoría [pray-to-re'-ah], *f.* Dignity of a pretor. *V.* PRETURA.

pretorial, pretoriano, na [pray-to-re-ahl'], *a.* Pretorian.

pretoriense [pray-to-re-en'-say], *a.* Belonging to the pretor's palace.

pretorio [pray-to'-re-o], *m.* Place in ancient Rome where the pretor resided and administered justice.

pretorio, ria [pray-to'-re-o, ah], *a. V.* PRETORIAL.

pretura [pray-too'-rah], *f.* Pretorship.

prevalecer [pray-vah-lay-therr'], *vn.* 1. To prevail (imponerse), to predominate (dominar), to outshine. 2. To take root (plantas). 3. To grow and increase (used of things not material). (*Yo prevalezco, yo prevalezca*, from *Prevalecer. V.* CONOCER.)

prevaleciente [pray-vah-lay-the-en'-tay], *pa. & a.* Prevalent; prevailing.

prevalente [pray-vah-len'-tay], *a.* Prevalent.

prevalerse [pray-vah-lerr'-say], *vr.* To use anything, or to avail oneself of it; to prevail.

prevaricación [pray-vah-re-cah-the-on'], *f.* Prevarication.

prevaricador, ra [pray-vah-re-cah-dor', rah], *m. & f.* 1. Prevaricator. 2. Turn-coat.

prevaricar [pray-vah-re-car'], *vn.* 1. To fail in one's word, duty, or judgment. 2. (*coll.*) To turn the coat, to change sides.

prevaricato [pray-vah-re-cah'-to], *m.* (*Law.*) Prevarication in a solicitor or advocate.

prevención [pray-ven-the-on'], *f.* 1. Disposition, preparation (preparativo). 2. Supply of provisions; sustenance, subsistence. 3. Foresight, forecast, forethought (cualidad). 4. Advice, intimation, warning instruction, monition. 5. Prevention, preoccupation. 6. (*Mil.*) Police guard. **A prevención** or **de prevención**, by way of precaution. (*Met.*) Prejudice, pro or contra. **Medidas de prevención**, emergency measures.

prevenidamente [pray-v-ay-nee'-dah-men-tay], *adv.* Beforehand, previously.

prevenido, da [pray-vay-nee'-do, dah], *a. & pp.* of PREVENIR. 1. Prepared, provided; plentiful, abundant. 2 Provident, careful, cautions. **Hombre prevenido vale por dos**, forewarned is forearmed.

preveniente [pray-vay-ve-en'-tay], *pa.* Predisposing, prevenient.

prevenir [pray-vay-neer'], *va.* 1. To prepare (disponer), to arrange beforehand. 2. To foresee (preveer), to foreknow. 3. To prevent or anticipate, to forestall (anticipar). 4. To advise, to caution, to give notice. 5. To prevent (impedir), to impede, to hinder. 6. To prevent, to preoccupy. 7. To ingratiate oneself. 8. (*Acad.*) To come upon, to surprise. **Prevenir a uno de algo**, to provide somebody with something. **Prevenir a uno**, to warn somebody. **Más vale prevenir que curar**, prevention is better than cure. -vr. To be prepared; to be predisposed (disponerse); to guard or be in a state of defence. (*Yo prevengo, yo prevenga, previene*, from *Prevenir. V.* VENIR.)

preventivamente [pray-ven-tee'-vah-men-tay], *adv.* Preventively.

preventivo, va [pray-ven-te'-vo, vah], *a.* Preventive; previously prepared or arranged.

prever [pray-verr'], *va.* 1. To foresee (antever), to foreknow. 2. To anticipate, to envisage (anticipar); to plan (proyectar); to make allowances (tener en cuenta). **No teníamos previsto nada para eso**, we had not made any allowance for that. **Ya lo preveía.** I expected as much. (*Yo preveo, yo prevea, él previó*, from *Prever. V.* VER.)

previamente [pray'-ve-ah-men-tay], *adv.* Previously.

previo, via [pray'-ve-o, ah], *a.* Previous, antecedent, prior. **Autorización previa**, prior authorization.

previsible [pray-ve-see'-blay], *a.* Foreseeable; predictable.

previsión [pray-ve-se-on'], *f.* Foresight (clarividencia), foreknowledge, prescience, forecast (pronóstico). **Previsión del tiempo**, weather forecast.

previsor, ra [pray-ve-sor', rah], *m. & f.* One who foresees; prudent (precavido).

previsto, ta [pray-vees'-to, tah], *pp. irr.* Of PREVER.

prez [preth'], *m.* 1. Honor or glory gained by a meritorious act. 2. Notoriety.

priapismo [pre-ah-pees'-mo], *m.* (*Med.*) Priapism, a disease.

priesa [pre-ay'-sah], *f. V.* PRISA.

prietamente [pre-ay'-tah-men-tay], *adv. V.* APRETADAMENTE.

prieto, ta [pre-ay'-to, tah], *a.* 1. Blackish (oscuro), of a very dark color. 2. Narrow-minded, illiberal. 3. Close-fisted, mean (tacaño). 4. Tight (apretado), compressed.

prima [pree'-mah], *f.* 1. Female cousin (pariente). 2. Morning, the first three hours of the day. 3. Prime, one of the seven canonical hours. 4. Tonsure. 5. (*Mil.*) The first quarter of the night, from eight to eleven o'clock. 6. Treble, the most slender string of stringed instruments. 7. (*Com.*) Premium given for insurance. 8. Premium, the price in excess beyond the face value of a paper. 9. The obligation of paying the agreed rate per cent if a paper is not taken up or a purchase completed. 10. Bonus, extra payment (de sueldo). 11. (*Cono Sur*) **Bajar la prima**, to moderate one's language.

primacía [pre-mah-thee'-ah], *f.* 1. Priority, precedence in time or place (prioridad). 2. Primateship, primacy (primer lugar), mastership.

primacial [pre-mah-the-ahl'], *a.* Relating to primacy.

primada [pre-mah'-dah], *f. (coll.)* Trick, of which someone is the object as being slow-witted.

primado [pre-mah'-do], *m.* 1. Primeness, the state of being first. 2. Primate, the chief ecclesiastic of a country.

primado, da [pre-mah'-do, dah], *a.* Primary, first in intention; first in dignity. **Iglesia primada**, primacial church.

primal, la [pre-mahl', lah], *a.* Yearling.

primal [pre-mahl'], *m.* Lace, a plaited cord of silk.

primariamente [pre-mah'-re-ah-men-tay], *adv.* Principally, chiefly, primarily.

primario, ria [pre-mah'-re-o, ah], *a.* Principal, primary.

primario [pre-mah'-re-o], *m.* Professor who lectures at the hour of prime.

primate [pre-mah'-tay], *f.* Most important. *-m.* 1. *(Zool.)* Primate. 2. Important person (prócer).

primavera [pre-mah-vay'-rah], *f.* 1. The spring season (estación). 2. Kind of flowered silk. 3. *(Bot.)* Primrose. 4. *(Met.)* Season of beauty, health and vigor: prime.

primaveral [pre-mah-vay-rahl'], *a.* Spring-like.

primazgo [pre-math'-go], *m.* Cousinship, relation of consanguinity among cousins.

primearse [pre-may-ar'-say], *vr.* To treat each other as cousins.

primer [pre-merr'], *a.* First; used before nouns. *V.* PRIMERO.

primera [pre-may'-rah], *f.* 1. Kind of card game. 2. *(Ferr.)* First class. 3. **De primera**, first-class. **Comer de primera**, to eat really well. 4. **A la primera de cambio**, as soon as I turned my back.

primeramente [pre-may'-rah-men-tay], *adv.* First; in the first place, mainly, primely.

primerizo, za [pre-may-ree'-tho, thah], *a.* 1. First, that antecedes or is preferred to other persons or things. 2. Firstling, first produced or brought forth; primiparous.

primeriza [pre-may-ree'-thah], *f.* Woman who has born her first child; primipara.

primero, ra [pre-may'-ro, rah], *a.* 1. First, the ordinal number of one. 2. Chief, principal (principal), leading. 3. Superior, most excellent. 4. Prior, former. 5. Basic (fundamental); urgent (urgente); raw (materia). **De buenas a primeras**, all at once, rashly, without reflection. **A primeros de siglo**, at the start of the century. **Lo primero es que...**, the fundamental thing is that...

primero [pre-may-ro], *adv.* First (primeramente), rather (antes), sooner. **Primero pediría limosna que prestado**, he would rather beg than borrow. **De primero**, at the beginning, before.

primeros auxilios. [pre-may'-ros ah-ooc-see' -lee-os], *. pl.* First aid, assistance.

primevo, va [pre-may'-vo, vah], *a.* Primeval, original.

primichón [pre-me-chone'], *m.* Skein of fine, soft silk, for embroidering.

primicia [pre-mee'-the-ah], *f.* 1. First-fruits of anything. 2. Offering of the first-fruits. 3. **Primicia informativa**, scoop.

primicial [pre-me-the-ahl'], *a.* Primital, relating to first-fruits.

primigenio, nia [pre-me-hay'-ne-o, ah], *a.* Primogenial, first-born.

primilla [pre-meel'-lyah], *f.* 1. *(coll.)* Pardon of the first fault committed. 2. *(dim.)* A little female cousin.

primísimo, ma [pre-mee'-se-mo, mah], *a. sup.* Uncommonly neat, extremely spruce.

primitivamente [pre-me-tee'-vah-men-tay], *adv.* Originally.

primitivo, va [pre-me-tee'-vo, vah], *a.* 1. Primitive, original (original), primeval. 2. Primary (color). 3. Ordinary (acción). 4. *(Hist.)* Primitive; uncivilized. **Es una obra primitiva**, it is an early work. **En condiciones primitivas**, in primitive conditions.

primo, ma [pree'-mo, mah], *a.* 1. First, the ordinal number of one. 2. Of the first rank, excellent. **Hilo primo**, fine waxed thread, used by shoemakers.

primo [pree'-mo], *m.* 1. Cousin (pariente). **Primo hermano**, first cousin, cousin german. 2. *(coll.)* Simpleton, one easily

deceived. **Hacer el primo**, to be easily taken in. *-adv.* First, in the first place.

primogénito, ta [pre-mo-hay'-ne-to, tah], *a.* First-born, eldest, firstling, primogenitive.

primogenitura [pre-mo-hay-ne-too'-rah], *f.* Primogeniture, seniority, the right of the first-born.

primoprimus [pre-mo-pree'-moos], *m.* The first impulse or emotion of the mind.

primor [pre-mor'], *m.* 1. Beauty (belleza); dexterity, ability, accuracy, exquisiteness, excellence, delicacy (delicadeza). 2. Nicety, neatness of workmanship. 3. Care, skill (maestría). 4. Fine thing, lovely thing (objeto). **Hecho con primor**, done most skillfully. **Hace primores con la aguja**, she makes lovely things with her needlework.

primordial [pre-mor-de-ahl'], *a.* Primordial, original.

primorear [pre-mo-ray-ar'], *vn.* To perform with elegance and neatness.

primorosamente [pre-mo-roh'-sah-men-tay], *adv.* Finely, nicely, neatly, handsomely, excellently.

primoroso, sa [pre-mo-ro'-so, sah], *a.* Neat, elegant, excellent, fine, curious, handsome; graceful, dexterous. **Artesano de manos primorosas**, a neat, able workman.

prímula [pree'-moo-lah], *f. (Bot.)* Primrose, cowslip.

princesa [prin-thay'say], *f.* 1. Princess, the consort or daughter of a prince, or the heiress to a principality. 2. Princess; in Spain, the apparent heiress to the crown.

principada [prin-the-pah'-dah], *f.* Act of authority or superiority performed by him who has no right to execute it.

principado [prin-the-pah'-do], *m.* 1. Princedom, the rank, estate, or power of a prince. 2. Principality, the territory of a prince. 3. Pre-eminence, superior excellence.

principal [prin-the-pahl'], *a.* 1. Principal (más importante), chief, capital, essential. 2. Illustrious, renowned, celebrated. 3. Foremost, first, chief: **Casa principal**, capital house, hotel. **Cuarto principal**, apartments on the first floor or story.

principal [prin-the-pahl'], *m.* 1. In a garrison, the main guard. 2. Principal, capital, stock. 3. Principal, head of a commercial establishment (persona).

principalidad [prin-the-pah-le-dahd'], *f.* Principalness, the state of being principal; nobility.

principalmente [prin-the-pahl'-men-tay], *adv.* Principally, mainly, chiefly.

príncipe [preen'-the-pay], *m.* 1. Prince, a sovereign or chief ruler. 2. Prince, a sovereign of rank next to a king. 3. Prince, son of a king, kinsman of a sovereign: popularly, the eldest son of his that reigns under any denomination is called a prince. 4. Prince, the most eminent, chief, or principal of anybody of men. 5. Prince, appellation of honor granted by kings. 6. With bee-masters, the young queen bees not yet in a state to breed. **Como un príncipe**, princely, or in a prince like manner. **Príncipe consorte**, prince consort. **Príncipe heredero**, crown prince.

principela [prin-the-pay'-lah], *f.* A sort of light camlet.

principiador, ra [prin-the-pe-ah-dor', rah], *m. & f.* Beginner.

principiante [prin-the-pe-ahn'-tay], *m.* Beginner, a learner.

principiar [prin-the-pe-ar'], *va.* To commence, to begin.

principiera [prin-the-pe-ay'-rah], *f. (Prov.)* A small metal saucepan in which broth is warmed.

principillo, principito [prin-the-peel'-lyo], *m. dim.* A petty prince.

principio [prin-thee'-pe-o], *m.* 1. Beginning (comienzo), commencement. 2. Principle, element, constituent part. 3. Principle, original cause; ground of action, motive; origin (origen), fountain. 4. Principle, first position, fundamental truth. 5. Principle, first on which morality is founded (moral). 6. Any of the courses served up at table besides the boiled meat. 7. *(Chem.)* An element or body not decomposable by means now at command. **Principios**, the preliminaries to a volume, as license, approbation, dedication, etc. **Al principio** or **a los principios**, at the beginning. **Del principio al fin**, from beginning to end. **Bajo el mismo principio**, on the same ground. **A principios del mes**, early in the month.

principote [prin-the-po'-tay], *m. (coll.)* He who assumes a lofty air and importance; a petty prince.

pringada [prin-gah'-dah], *f.* Toasted bread steeped in gravy.

pringar [prin-gar'], *va.* 1. To baste meat which is roasting. 2. To stain with grease, to scald with boiling fat; to tar a person: this formerly was the punishment of slaves. 3. To wound (herir), to ill-treat. 4. To meddle, to interfere; to take a share in. 5. *(Cono Sur)* To give (enfermedad). 6. *(Cono Sur)* To put in the family way (mujer). 7. To drop a brick (meter la pata). **Pringar el pan en la sopa**, to dip one's bread in the soup. **Pringar a uno en un asunto**, to involve somebody in a matter. *-vn.* 1. To take a beating (perder). 2. *(Mil.)* To sweat one's guts out (trabajar). 3. To peg out (morir). 4. *(CAm. Carib. Mex.)* To drizzle (lloviznar). *-vr.* To draw unlawful advantage from a thing intrusted to one's care. **O nos pringamos todos, o ninguno**, either we all carry the can or none of us do.

pringón, na [prin-gone', nah], *a.* Nasty, dirty (sucio), greasy (mancha). *-m.* 1. The act of begreasing oneself. 2. Stain of grease.

pringoso, sa [prin-go'-so, sah], *a.* Greasy, fat.

pringue [preen'-gay], *com.* 1. Grease, lard. 2. Greasiness, oiliness, fatness. 3. The act of begreasing or staining with grease.

pringuera [preen-gay'-rah], Dripping.

prior [pre-or'], *m.* 1. Prior, the superior of convents or religious houses. 2. *(Prov.)* Rector, curate. 3. Prior in some cathedrals. 4. President of the *Consulado* in Andalusia, a court appointed to try and decide causes concerning trade and navigation.*-a.* Prior, precedent.

priora [pre-o'-rah], *f,* Prioress.

prioral [pre-o-rahl'], *a.* Belonging to a prior or prioress.

priorato [pre-o-rah'-to], *m.* 1. Priorship, dignity of a prior or prioress. 2. District of the jurisdiction of a prior. 3. Priory of Benedictines.

priorazgo [pre-o-rath'-go], *m.* Priorship. V. PRIORATO.

prioridad [pre-o-re-dahd'], *f.* Priority (precedencia); precedence in time or place; seniority (antigüedad), greater age. **Tener prioridad**, to have priority.

prioste [pre-os'-tay], *m.* Steward of a brotherhood or confraternity.

prisa [pree'-sah], *f.* 1. Urgency, celerity, promptness in executing. 2. Haste, hurry (apresuramiento). 3. Speed (velocidad). **A toda prisa**, with the greatest promptitude. **Darse prisa**. To hurry up. **Estar de prisa**, to be in a hurry. **Andar de prisa**, to be very busy, to be driven for time. **Vivir de prisa**, to live fast, to abuse body and mind. **Voy con mucha prisa.** I'm in a great hurry. **Tener prisa**, to be in a hurry.

prisco [press'-co], *m.* A kind of peach.

prisión [pre-se-on'], *f.* 1. Seizure, capture, apprehension. 2. Prison (cárcel), jail. 3. Anything which binds or holds physically. 4. Bond, union; cement or cause of union. *-pl.* Chains, shackles, fetters.

prisioncilla, ita [pre-se-on-theel'-lyah], *f. dim.* A small prison or jail.

prisionero, ra [pre-se-o-nay'-ro], *m & f.* 1. Prisoner, a soldier taken by an enemy. 2. Captivated by affection or passion.

prisma [press'-mah], *m.* 1. *(Geom.)* Prism. 2. A triangular prism of glass.

prismático, ca [pris-mah'-te-co, cah], *a.* Prismatic.

prismatizar [pris-mah-te-thar'], *va.* To decompose light by a prism.

priste [press'-tay], *m.* Saw-fish.

prístino, na [press'-te-no, nah], *a.* Pristine, first, original.

prisuelo [pre-soo-ay'-lo], *m.* Muzzle, which serves to keep the mouths of ferrets shut.

pritaneo [pre-tah-nay'-o], *m.* Prytaneum, senate-house in Athens.

privación [pre-vah-the-on'], *f.* 1. Privation (acto), want. 2. Privation the act of degrading from rank or office. 3. *(Met.)* Deprivation of anything desired, loss. **Sufrir privación de libertad**, to suffer loss of liberty.

privada [pre-vah'-dah], *f.* 1. Privy, water-closet. 2. Filth thrown into the street.

privadamente [pre-vah-dah-men-tay], *adv.* Privately, privily; separately.

privadero [pre-vah-day'-ro], *m.* One who cleans wells or cesspools.

privado, da [pre-vah'-do, dah], *a. & pp.* of PRIVAR. 1. Privy, private (particular), performed in presence of a few. 2. Private, particular, personal, not relating to the public.

privado [pre-vah'-do], *m.* Favorite, minion, court minion.

privanza [pre-vahn'-thah], *f.* Favor, protection; familiar intercourse between a prince or great personage and a person of inferior rank.

privar [pre-var'], *va.* 1. To deprive, to despoil; to dispossess of a public place or employment. 2. To prohibit (prohibir), to interdict. 3. To suspend sensation. 4. To delight (extasiar). 5. To drink (beber). **Privar a uno de algo**, to deprive somebody of something. **No me prives de verte**, don't keep me from seeing you. *-vn.* 1. To enjoy the peculiar protection of a prince or great personage. 2. To obtain (existir), to be present; to prevail (predominar). **En ese período privaba la minifalda**, at that time miniskirts were in. *-vr.* 1. To deprive oneself (abstenerse de). 2. To get tanked up (emborracharse).

privativamente [pre-vah-tee'-vah-men-tay], *adv.* Conclusively, solely, privatively.

privativo, va [pre-vah-tee'-vo, vah], *a.* 1. Privative, causing privation. 2. Special, singular, particular, peculiar; exclusive.

privatización [pre-vah-te-thah-the-on'], *f.* Privatization.

privatizar [pre-vah-te-thar'], *va.* To privatize.

privilegiadamente [pre-ve-lay-he-ah'-dah-men-tay], *adv.* In a privileged manner.

privilegiar [pre-ve-lay-he-ar'], *va.* To privilege, to grant a privilege.

privilegiativo [pre-ve-lay-he-ah-tee'-vo], *va, a.* Containing a privilege.

privilegio [pre-ve-lay'-he-o], *m.* 1. Privilege, immunity; grant, concession, grace: liberty, franchise, faculty. 2. Patent, copyright. **Privilegio del fuero**, exemption from secular jurisdiction, enjoyed by ecclesiastics.

pro [pro], *com.* Profit (provecho), benefit, advantage. V. PROVECHO. **Buena pro**, much good may it do you. **En pro**, in favor of, for the benefit of: **Hombre de pro**, a worthy men.

proa [pro'-ah], *f.* Prow of a ship, foreship, bow. **Por nuestra proa**, *(Naut.)* ahead of us. **Llevar la proa hacia la mar**, *(Naut.)* to stand off, to stand out to sea. **Poner la proa al rumbo**, *(Naut.)* to stand on the course.

proal [pro-ahl'], *a.* Relating to the prow; forward.

probabilidad [pro-bah-be-le-dahd'], *f.* Probability, likelihood, credibility, chance (perspectiva), prospect. **Probabilidades de vida**, expectation of life.

probabilísimo, ma [pro-bah-be-lee'-se-mo, mah], *a. sup.* Most probable.

probabilismo [pro-bah-be-lees'-mo], *m.* Probability, doctrine of probable opinions.

probabilista [pro-bah-be-lees'-tah], *m.* Probabilist, one who acts upon probabilities.

probable [pro-bah'-blay], *a.* Probable, likely, credible, capable of proof. **Es probable que**, it is probable that…

probablemente [pro-bah'-blay-men-tay], *adv.* Probably, credibly, likely.

probación [pro-bah-the-on'], *f.* Proof, probation, trial, examination.

probado, da [pro-bah'-do, dah], *a.* Proved, tried. *-pp.* of PROBAR.

probador, ra [pro-bah-dor', rah], *m. & f.* 1. Taster (persona), one who tries or proves anything. 2. Defender, advocate. 3. Fitting-room (tienda).

probadura [pro-bah-doo'-rah], *f.* Trial, the act of tasting or trying anything.

probanza [pro-bahn'-thah], *f.* Proof, evidence.

probar [pro-bar'], *va.* 1. To try, to examine the quality of a thing. 2. To prove (hecho, teoría), to give evidence, to justify, to make good. 3. To taste, to try by the mouth (comida). 4. With the preposition **a** and an infinitive mode, it signifies to attempt, to endeavor. **Probó a levantarse y no pudo**, he attempted to rise and could not. **Prueba un poco de esto**, try a bit of this. *-vn.* To suit (sentar), to fit, to agree. (*Yo pruebo, yo prueba*, from *Probar. V.* ACORDAR.)

probativo, va, probatorio, ria [pro bah-tee'-vo, vah], *a.* Probatory, probationary.

probatoria [pro-bah-toh'-re-ah], *f.* Legal investigation: preliminary examination.

probatura [pro-bah-too'-rah], *f.* (*coll.*) *V.* PROBADURA.

probeta [pro-bay'-tah], *f.* 1. A kind of barometer. 2. Powder-prover, a device for testing the explosive force of powder. 3. (*Chem.*) A test tube.

probidad [pro-be-dahd'], *f.* Probity, honesty, sincerity, veracity.

problema [pro-blay'-mah], *m.* 1. Problem, a doubtful question proposed. 2. (*Geom.*) Problem, practical proposition.

problematicamente [pro-blay-mah'-te-cah-men-tay], *adv.* Problematically.

problemático, ca [pro-blay-mah'-te-co, cah], *a.* Problematical, disputable, unsettled.

probo, ba [pro'-bo, bah], *a.* Upright, honest.

probóscide [pro-bos'-the-day], *f.* (Non-Acad.) 1. Proboscis, the trunk of an elephant. 2. Proboscis, the projecting sucking mouth-parts of certain insects. *V.* TROMPA.

procacidad [pro-cah-the-dahd'], *f.* Procacity, petulance, insolence (desvergüenza), forwardness, brazenness (descaro), indecency (indecoro).

procaína [pro-cah-ee'-nah], *f.* Novocaine.

procaz [pro-cath'], *a.* Procacious, petulant, forward, insolent (atrevido), indecent (indecoro).

procedencia [pro-thay-den'-the-ah], *f.* 1. Derivation: the act of proceeding. 2. The place from which persons or articles come.

procedente [pro-thay-den'-tay], *pa.* 1. Coming from, proceeding from. 2. According to legal rules, according to law.

proceder [pro-thay-derr'], *m.* Procedure, manner of proceeding, conduct, demeanor, management.

proceder [pro-thay-derr'], *vn.* 1. To proceed (pasar), to go on. 2. To issue, to proceed from (conducirse). 3. To behave, to conduct oneself. 4. To proceed, to prosecute a design. 5. (*Law.*) To proceed against, to carry on a judicial process. 6. To proceed by generation. **Todo esto procede de su negativa**, all this springs from his refusal. **Conviene proceder con cuidado**, it is best to go carefully.

procedimiento [pro-thay-de-me-en'-to], *m.* 1. Procceding, procedure, transaction. 2. Proceeding or legal procedure. **Por un procedimiento deductivo**, by a deductive process. 3. Link control protocol, procedure.

procela [pro-thay'-lah], *a.* (*Poet.*) Storm, tempest.

proceloso, sa [pro-thay-lo'-so, sah], *a.* Tempestuous, stormy.

prócer [pro'-ther], *a.* Tall, lofty, elevated. *-m.* Person who occupies an exalted station or is high in office; the grandees and high-titled nobility of Spain.

procerato [pro-thay-rah'-to], *m.* Exalted station.

proceridad [pro-thay-re-dahd'], *f.* 1 Procerity, tallness, height or stature. 2. Elevation, eminence.

procero, prócero [pro-thay'-ro], *a. V.* PRÓCER.

procesado [pro-thay-sah'-do], *a.* 1. Applied to the writings in a process. 2. Comprised in a criminal suit. *-pp.* of PROCESAR.

procesador [pro-thay-sah-dor'], *m.* Processor. **Procesador de textos**, word processor. **Procesador de equipos**, hardware processor. **Procesador de matrices**, array processor.

procesal [pro-thay-sahl'], *a.* Belonging to a process or lawsuit.

procesamiento [pro-thay-saha-me-ayn'-to], *m.* 1. Processing. 2. (*Comput.*) **Procesamiento de datos**, data processing. **Procesamiento de textos**, word processing.

procesar [pro-thay-sar'], *va.* (*Law.*) 1. To indict, to accuse, to inform against, to sue criminally (demandar). 2. To institute a suit.

procesión [pro-thay-se-on'], *f.* 1. Procession, proceeding from another. 2. Procession, train marching in ceremonious solemnity; parade. **La procesión va por dentro**, still waters run deep.

procesional [pro-thay-se-o-nahl'], *a.* Processional or processionary; relating to processions.

procesionalmente [pro-thay-se-o-nahl'-men-tay], *adv.* Processionally.

procesionario [pro-thay-se-o-nah'-re-o], *m.* Book carried about in processions.

proceso [pro-thay'-so], *m.* 1. Process, lawsuit. 2. Judicial records concerning a lawsuit. **Error de proceso**, (*Law. Prov.*) one who by ability, although convicted, evades the fine. 3. Progress. *V.* PROGRESO. 4. (*Comput.*) **Proceso prioritario**, foreground processing. **Proceso algorítmico**, algorithmic process.

procidencia [pro-the-den'-the-ah], *f.* (*Med.*) Procidence.

procinto [pro-theen'-to], *m.* Procinct, complete preparation.

proción [pro-the-on'], *m.* (*Ast.*) Procyon, a star; the most conspicuous in the constellation Canis minor, famous for its variable proper motion.

proclama [pro-clah'-mah], *f.* Proclamation, publication, banns of marriage.

proclamación [pro-clah-mah-the-on'], *f.* 1. Proclamation, the publication of a decree by superior order. 2. Acclamation, public applause.

proclamar [pro-clah-mar'], *va.* 1. To proclaim (publicar), to give public notice. 2. To bestow public praise, to shout. *-vr.* **Proclamarse campeón**, to become champion.

proclítico, ca [pro-clee'-te-co, cah], *a.* (*Gram.*) Proclitic, attached to a following word.

proclive [pro-clee'-vay], *a.* Proclivous, inclining; disposed.

proclividad [pro-cle-ve-dahd'], *f.* Proclivity, propensity to evil.

procomún, procomunal [pro-co-moon'], *m.* A public utility.

procónsul [pro-con'-sool], *m.* Proconsul.

proconsulado [pro-con-soo-lah'-do], *m.* Proconsulship, office of proconsul or vice-consul.

proconsular [pro-con-soo-lar'], *a.* Proconsular, vice-consular.

procreación [pro-cray-ah-the-on'], *f.* Procreation, generation.

procreador, ra [pro-cray-ah-dor', rah], *m. & f.* Procreator, generator, getter.

procreante [pro-cray-ahn'-tay], *pa.* Procreating.

procrear [pro-cray-ar'], *va.* To procreate, to generate, to produce.

procronismo [pro-cro-nees'-mo], *m.* Prochronism, anachronism.

procumbente [pro-coom-ben'-tay], *a.* (*Bot.*) Procumbent.

procura [pro-coo'-rah], *f.* 1. Power of attorney. *V.* PROCURACIÓN. 2. (*Prov.*) *V.* PROCURADURÍA.

procuración [pro-coo-rah-the-on'], *f.* 1. Care, diligence, careful management. 2. Power or letter of attorney. 3. Procurement, the act of procuring. 4. Place and office of an attorney or administrator. 5. *V.* PROCURADURÍA.

procurador, ra [pro-coo-rah-dor', rah], *m. & f.* Procurer, obtainer, one that solicits.

procurador [pro-coo-rah-dor'], *m & f.* 1. Attorney, procurator, lawyer (abogado), one who takes upon himself the charge of other people's business. 2. Proctor, attorney at law.

procuradora [pro-coo-rah-do'-rah], *f.* She who manages the affairs of a nunnery.

procuraduría [pro-coo-rah-do-ree'-ah], *f.* Attorney's office; the employment of an attorney; procurement; proctorship.

procurante [pro-coo-rahn'-tay], *pa.* Solicitor, intendant.

procurar [pro-coo-rar'], *va.* 1. To solicit, to adopt measures for attaining an end, to try (intentar). 2. To procure, to manage (lograr), to transact for another. 3. To act as an attorney. 4. To get, to obtain (conseguir). **Procura conservar la calma**, try to keep calm. **Por fin procuró dominarse**, eventually he managed to control himself.

procurrente [pro-coor-ren'-tay], *m.* Peninsula, a great mass of earth reaching into the sea: as all Italy.

prodición [pro-de-the-on'], *f.* Treason, treachery.

prodigalidad [pro-de-gah-le-dahd'], *f.* 1. Prodigality (derroche), profusion, waste, extravagance (despilfarro), lavishness (liberalidad). 2. Plenty, abundance.

pródigamente [pro'-de-gah-men-tay], *adv.* Prodigally (con prodigalidad), lavishly (generosamente), wastefully, profusely.

prodigar [pro-de-gar'], *va.* To waste, to lavish (disipar), to misspend, to fling away. -*vr.* To be generous with what one has; to show off (dejarse ver).

prodigiador [pro-de-he-ah-dor'], *m.* Prognosticator, foreteller.

prodigio [pro-dee'-he-o], *m.* Prodigy, portent, monster; marvel.

prodigiosamente, *adv.* Prodigiously, miraculously, marvellously, amazingly; monstrously, enormously, beautifully. **Ella cantó prodigiosamente**, she sung charmingly.

prodigiosidad [pro-de-he-o-se-dahd'], *f.* Prodigiousness, portentousness.

prodigioso, sa [pro-de-he-oh'-so, sah], *a.* 1. Prodigious, marvellous, extraordinary; monstrous. 2. Fine, exquisite, excellent.

pródigo, ga [pro'-de-go, gah], *a.* Prodigal (derrochador), wasteful, lavish (liberal); liberal, generous, munificent. **La pródiga naturaleza**, bountiful nature. **Ser pródigo de sus talentos**, to be generous in offering one's talents.

prodrómico, ca [pro-dro'-me-co, cah], *a.* (*Med.*) Prodromic, relating to a prodrome.

pródromo [pro'-dro-mo], *m.* (*Ned.*) Prodrome, a sign of approaching disease.

producción [pro-dooc-the-on'], *f.* 1. Production, growth, product (objeto). 2. Enunciation, mode of expressing oneself, enouncement.

producibilidad [pro-doo-the-be-le-dahd'], *f.* Producibleness, productiveness.

producible [pro-doo-thee'-blay], *a.* Producible.

producidor, ra [pro-doo-the-dor', rah], *m. & f.* Producer, procreator.

producir [pro-doo-theer'], *va.* 1. To produce, to bring forth, to engender, to generate (motivar). 2. (*Law.*) To produce, to bring as evidence, to allege, to maintain, to exhibit. 3. To produce, to bear (vegetal). 4. To produce (países). 5. To produce, to cause, to occasion. 6. To yield revenue. 7. To quote, to cite. **Le produjo gran tristeza**, it caused her much sadness. **Producir en serie**, to mass-produce. -*vr.* 1. To enounce or explain oneself. 2. To become manifest, to be published. 3. To come about (cambio); to arise (dificultad, crisis); to happen (accidente); to break out (disturbio). **En ese momento se produjo una explosión**, at that moment there was an explosion. (*Yo produzco, yo produzca; produje*; from PRODUCIR. *V.* CONDUCIR.)

productible [pro-dooc-tee'-blay], *a.* Capable of yielding some product; productible.

productivo, va [pro-dooc-tee'-vo, vah], *a.* Productive, constitutive, originary.

producto [pro-dooc'-to], *m.* 1. Product, something produced, as grain, fruit, metals; production. 2. Proceed (ingreso), produce, fruit, growth. 3. (*Math.*) Product, quantity produced by multiplication. 4. Product, the final result of a chemical operation. —**Producto, ta**, *pp. irr.* of PRODUCIR. **Productos agrícolas**, agricultural produce. **Productos de consumo**, consumer goods.

productor [pro-dooc-tor'], *a.* 1. Productive, producing. **Clase productora**, those who produce. -*m.* **productora**. 1. Producer. 2. Workman (obrero). 3. (Cine, Tv.) Producer.

proejar [pro-ay-har'], *vn.* 1. To row against the wind or current. 2. To resist, to bear up under misfortunes.

proel [pro-el], *m.* (*Naut.*) Seaman stationed at the prow.

proemial [pro-ay-me-ahl'], *a.* Proemial, preliminary, introductory.

proemio [pro-ay'-me-o], *m.* Proem, preface, introduction.

proeza [pro-ay'-thah], *f.* Prowess, valor, bravery.

profanación [pro-fah-nah-the-on'], *f.* Profanation, profaneness, irreverence.

profanador, ra [pro-fah-nah-dor', rah], *m. & f.* Profaner, polluter, violator.

profanamente [pro-fah'-nah-men-tay], *adv.* Profanely.

profanamiento [pro-fah-nah-me-en'-to], *m.* *V.* PROFANACIÓN.

profanar [pro-fah-nar'], *va.* 1. To profane, to violate, to desecrate (violar). 2. To defile, to disgrace, to dishonor, to abuse.

profanidad [pro-fah-ne-dahd'], *f.* 1. Indecency, immodesty, or excess in dress and outward show. 2. Want of competence or knowledge for handling a matter.

profano, na [pro-fah'-no, nah], *a.* 1. Profane, irreverent (irrespetuoso). 2. Worldly, irreligious. 3. Extravagant, flashy, loud, immodest or unchaste in dress and outward show. 4. Wanting in knowledge or authority upon a subject.

profecía [pro-fay-thee'-ah], *f.* 1. Prophecy, supernatural knowledge and prediction of future events. 2. Conjecture, surmise.

profecticio [pro-fec-tee'-the-o], *a.* Acquired by a son who lives under his father's direction; derived from one's fathers.

proferir [pro-fay-rer'], *va.* To pronounce, to utter (palabra, sonido), to express, to name. (*Yo profiero, yo profiera; él profirió*; from *Proferir. V.* ADHERIR.)

profesante [pro-fay-san' -tay], *pa. & m. & f.* Professor; professing.

profesar [pro-fay-sar'], *va.* 1. To profess (admiración, creencia), to declare openly, to teach publicly (materia). 2. To be admitted into a religious order by making the vows. 3. To profess, to exercise, to evince.

profesión [pro-fay-se-on'], *f.* 1. Profession, calling, vocation, occupation (en formulario). 2. Declaration, assurance. 3. Custom, hábit. **Abogado de profesión**, a lawyer by profession.

profesional [pro-fay-se-o-nahl'], *a.* Professional; relating to or in accordance with a protection.

profesionalmente [pro-fay-se-o-nahl'-men-tay], *adv.* Professionally.

profeso, sa [pro-fay' -so, sah], *a.* Professed: applied to those who have taken vows.

profesor, ra [pro-fay-sor', rah], *m. & f.* Professor, teacher. **Profesor de gimnasia**, gym instructor. **Es profesora de griego**, she is professor of Greek.

profesorado [Pro-fay-so-rah' -do], *m.* 1. Faculty, body of teachers. 2. Teaching profession (profesión).

profeta [pro-fay'-tah], *m.* 1. Prophet, foreteller. 2. Title given to Mohammed by the Moslems.

profetal [pro-fay-tahl'], *a.* Relating to prophecy.

proféticamente [pro-fay'-te-cah-men-tay], *adv.* Prophetically.

profético, ca [pro-fay' -te-co, cah], *a.* Prophetic, prophetical.

profetisa [pro-fay-tee'-sah], *f.* Prophetess.

profetizar [pro-fay-te-thar'], *va.* 1. To prophesy; to predict. 2. To conjecture, to surmise.

proficiente [pro-fe-the-en' -tay], *a.* Proficient, making progress in any business.

proficuo, cua [pro-fee' -coo-o, ah], *a.* Profitable, useful, advantageous.

profiláctica

profiláctica [pro-fe-lahc'-te-cah], *f.* *(Med.)* Hygiene, prophylactia medicine.

profiláctico [pro-fe-lahc'-te-co], *a.* prophylactic, preventive preservative.

profilaxis [pro-fe-lahk'-sis], *f.* Prophylaxis, preventive treatment of disease in an individual.

prófugo, ga [pro'-foo-go, gah], *a.* Fugitive, vagabond.

profundamente [pro-foon-dah-men-tay], *adv.* Profoundly, deeply, highly, acutely, high.

profundidad [pro-foon-de-dahd'], *f.* 1. Profundity, depth (hondura), concavity. 2. Height, excellence, grandeur; impenetrability; intensity. **Tener una profundidad de 30 cm**, to be 30 cm deep.

profundizar [pro-foon-de-thar'], *va.* 1. To make deep (ahondar), to dig deep, to deepen. 2. To penetrate, to dive into a matter; to fathom, to explore.

profundo, da [pro-foon'-do, dah], *a.* 1. Profound, deep (hondo); descending far below the surface; low with respect to the neighboring places. 2. Profound (misterio, pensador), intellectually deep, recondite. 3. Intense, dense; at full extents. **Tener 20 cm de profundo**, to be 20 cm deep.

profundo [pro-foon'-do], *m.* 1. *(Poet.)* Profound, the sea, the deep. 2. *(Poet.)* Hell.

profusamente [pro-foo'-sah-men-tay], *adv.* Profusely, lavishly, prodigally, extravagantly.

profusión [pro-foo-se-on'], *f.* Profusion, lavishness, profuseness, extravagance, prodigality.

prufuso, sa [pro-foo'-so, sah], *a.* 1. Profuse (abundante), plentiful. 2. Lavish (extravagante), prodigal: extravagant.

progenie [pro-hay'-ne-ay], *f.* Progeny (hijos), race, offspring, issue.

progenitor [pro-hay-ne-tor'], *m.* Progenitor (antepasado), ancestor, forefather.

progenitura [pro-hay-ne-too'-rah], *f. V.* PROGENIE and PRIMOGENITURA.

progimnasma [pro-him-nahs'-mah], *m.* Essay, attempt; a preparatory exercise.

progne [pro-nayl'], *f. (Poet.)* The swallow.

programa [pro-grah'-mah], *m.* 1. Proclamation, public notice. 2. Theme, subject of a discourse, design, or picture. 3. Prospectus, program, prearranged plan or course of proceedings; scheme of lectures by a professor; or order of exercises. 4. Specification according to which a certain procedure must be carried out, program. **Programa de estudios**, curriculum. 5. *(Cono Sur)* Love affair (amorío). 6. *(Comput.)* **Programas de aprendizaje**, training software. **Programas de ayuda**, help software. **Programas de communicaciones**, communication software. **Programas de contabilidad**, accounting software. **Programas de dominio público**, public domain software. **Programas de entretenimiento**, entertainment software. **Programas de redes**, networking software. **Programas de utilidades**, utility software. **Programas educativos**, educational software. **Programas gratuitos**, freeware. **Programas para diagramas**, flowcharting software. **Programas para estadísticas**, statistical software. **Programas para gráficos**, graphics software. **Programas para la recuperación de datos**, data recovery software. **Programas para la empresa**, business software. **Programa de ajuste**, retrofit software.

programación [pro-grah-mah-the-on'], *f.* Programing. **Programación fija**, *(Comput.)* firmware.

programado [pro-grah-mah'-do], *a.* Programed; planned (visita).

programador, ra [pro-grah-mah-dor'], *m & f.* Programer. *(Comput.)* **Programador de aplicaciones**, applications programer. **Programador de sistemas**, systems programmer.

programar [pro-grah-mar'], *va.* To plan; to draw up a program for (detalladamente); *(Comput.)* to program.

progresar [pro-gray-sar'], *vn.* To progress, make progress; to improve, better.

progresión [pro-gray-se-on'], *f.* Progression, process; progressiveness.

progresista [pro-gray-sees'-tah], *a. & com.* Progressive.

progresivamente [pro-gray-see'-vah-men-tay], *adv.* Progressively, onward, forward.

progresivo, va [pro-gray-see'-vo, vah], *a.* Progressive (que avanza), advancing.

progreso [pro-gray'-so], *m.* Progress, advancement, growth; forwardness. **Hacer progresos**, to progress.

prohibente [pro-e-ben'-te], *pa.* Prohibiting.

prohibición [pro-e-be-the-on'], *f.* Prohibition, interdict. **Levantar la prohibición de**, to remove the ban on.

prohibicionista [pro-e-be-the-o-nes'-tah] *m & f.* Prohibitionist.

prohibir [pro-e-beer'], *va.* To prohibit, to forbid, to restrain. **Prohibir una droga**, to prohibit a drug. **Queda terminantemente prohibido**, it is strictly forbidden to.

prohibitivo, va [pro-e-be-tee'-vo, vah], *a.* Prohibitory, forbidding.

prohibitorio, ria [pro-e-be-to'-re-o, ah], *a.* Prohibitory.

prohijador, ra [pro-e-ha-dor', rah], *m. & f.* Adopter, he that adopts a son.

prohijamiento [pro-e-hah-me-en'-to], *m.* Adoption.

prohijar [pro-e-har'], *va.* 1. To adopt, to make him a son who is not so by birth. 2. To ascribe, to attribute, to impute.

prohombre [pro-om'-bray], *m.* 1. In trades-unions the officer who governs the union. 2. One who enjoys special consideration among those of his class.

pro indiviso [pro in-de-vee'-so], *adv. (For.)* Undivided, undistributed: sold of legacies.

prójimo [pro'-he-mo], *m.* Fellow creature (semejante); neighbor (vecino). **No tener prójimo**, to be unfeeling or cruel, to be hard-hearted.

prolabio [pro-lah'-be-o], *m. (Med.)* Prolabium, the red external part of a lip.

prolapso [pro-lahp'-so], *m. (Med.)* Prolapse, descent of a viscus.

prole [pro'-lay], *f.* Issue, offspring, progeny, race; fruit.

prolegómeno [pro-lay-go'-may-no], *m.* Prolegomena, introductory discourse.

prolepsis [pro-lep'-sis], *f. (Rhet.)* Prolepsis, anticipation and answering of objections or counter-arguments.

proletariado [pro-lay-tah-re-ah'-do], *m.* 1. Proletarianism, the condition of the poorest classes. 2. The class of proletarians, the proletariat.

proletario, ria [pro-lay-tah'-re-o, ah], *a.* Proletarian, without property, very poor; plebeian.

prolífero, ra [pro-lee'-fay-ro, rah], *a. (Biol.)* Proliferous, reproducing freely; in botany, marked by excessive development of parts.

proliferar [pro-le-fay-rahr'], *vn.* To proliferate.

prolífico, ca [pro-lee'-fe-co, cah], *a.* Prolific, fruitful, productive.

prolijamente [pro-lee'-hah-men-tay], *adv.* Prolixly, tediously.

prolijidad [pro-la-he-dahd'], *f.* 1. Prolixity, tediousness. 2. Minute attention to trifles: trifling nicety.

prolijo, ja [pro-lee'-ho, hah], *a.* 1. Prolix (extenso), tedious (pesado), particular. 2. Over careful, triflingly nice. 3. Troublesome, impertinent, long-winded.

prólogo [pro'-lo-go], *m.* 1. Prologue, preface (preámbulo); introduction. 2. Prologue to a play.

prologuista [pro-lo-gees'-tah], *m.* Writer of prologues.

prolonga [pro-lon'-gah], *f. (Mil.)* Rope which ties the carriage of a cannon when passing difficult places.

prolongación [pro-lon-gah-the-on'], *f.* Prolongation (acto), lengthening, lingering, extension (de carretera).

prolongadamente [pro-lon-gah'-dah-men-tay], *adv.* Tardily.

prolongado, da [pro-lon-gah'-do, dah], *a.* Prolonged, extended. *-pp.* of PROLONGAR.

prolongador, ra [pro-lon-gah-dor', rah], *m. & f.* One who prolongs or delays anything.

prolongamiento [pro-lon-gah-me-en'-to] *m.* Delay. V. PROLONGACIÓN.

prolongar [pro-lon-gar'], *va.* 1. To prolong (alargar), to protract, to lengthen out, to continue. 2. (*Com.*) To allow to stand over. **Prolongar un plazo**, To grant an extension of time. -*vr.* (*Naut.*) To go alongside. **Prolongarse a la costa**, (*Naut.*) to range along the shore. **La sesión se prolongó bastante**, the meeting went on long enough.

proloquio [pro-lo'-ke-o], *m.* Maxim, moral, apothegm.

prolusión [pro-loo-se-on'], *f.* Prolusion, prelude. V. PRELUSIÓN.

promediar [pro-may-de-ar'], *va.* To divide into two equal parts (objeto), to shank equally. -*vn.* To mediate (mediar), to form by mediation; to interpose in a friendly manner.

promedio [pro-may'-de-o], *m.* 1. Middle, the part equally distant from the two extremities (de distancia). 2. An average. **El promedio de asistencia diaria**, the average daily attendance.

promesa [pro-may'-sah], *f.* Promise (ofrecimiento), offer; pious offering. **Simple promesa**, a promise not confirmed by a vow or oath. **Faltar a una promesa**, to break a promise.

prometedor, ra [pro-may-tay-dor', rah], *a.* Promising, full of promise.

prometer [pro-may-terr'], *va.* 1. To promise (ofrecer), to bid fair. 2. To assever, to assure, to insure: often used menacingly. **Prometer hacer algo**, to promise to do something. **Esto promete ser interesante**, this promises to be interesting. -*vr.* 1. To flatter oneself, to expect with confidence (esperar). 2. To devote oneself to the service or worship of God. 3. To give a promise of marriage. **Prometerse algo bueno**, to promise oneself a treat. -*vn.* To promise, to show signs of forwardness (tener porvenir). **Es un jugador que promete**, he's a promising player.

prometida [pro-may-tee'-dah], *f.* Fiancée.

prometido [pro-may-tee'-do], *m.* 1. Promise (promesa), offer. 2. Outbidding, overbidding. 3. Fiancé (persona). **Prometido, da**, *pp.* of PROMETER.

prometimiento [pro-may-te-me-en'-to], *m.* Promise, offer.

prominencia [pro-me-nen'-the-ah], *f.* Prominence, protuberance (elevación), process, knob, elevation of a thing, above its surroundings.

prominente [pro-me-nen'-tay], *a.* Prominent (protuberante), protuberant; jutting out.

promiscuamente [pro-mes'-coo-ah-men-tay], *adv.* Promiscuously.

promiscuo, cua [pro-mees'-coo-o, ah], *a.* Promiscuous, confusedly mingled (revuelto); ambiguous (sentido).

promisorio, ria [pro-me-so'-re-o, ah], *a.* Promissory.

promoción [pro-mo-the-on'], *f.* Promotion (ascenso), advancement, encouragement, preferment. **Promoción de ventas**, sales promotion. **Fue de mi promoción**, he belonged to the same class/regiment as I did.

promocionar [pro-mo-the-o-nahr'], *va.* To promote; to give rapid promotion (persona). -*vr.* To improve oneself.

promontorio [pro-mon-to'-re-o], *m*, 1. A considerable elevation of ground. 2. Anything bulky and unwieldy; an impediment, obstruction. 3. Promontory, headland, forehand, cape.

promotor, ra [pro-mo-tor'], *m & f.* 1. Promoter, advancer, forwarder, furtherer. 2. **Promotor fiscal**, (*Law.*) a secular or ecclesiastical attorney-general. **Promotor de ventas**, sales promoter.

promovedor, ra [pro-mo-vay-dor', rah], *m. & f.* Promotor.

promovendo [pro-mo-ven'-do], *m.* A person who aspires to promotion.

promover [pro-mo-verr'], *va.* 1. To promote (proceso), to advance, to further, to forward, to help. 2. To promote (intereses), to raise to a higher dignity or employment (ascender).

promulgación [pro-mool-ga-the-on'], *f.* Promulgation.

promulgador, ra [pro-mool-gah-dor', rah], *m. & f.* Publisher, promulgator.

promulgar [pro-mool-gar'], *va.* To promulgate, to publish.

pronación [pro-nah-the-on'], *f.* Pronation, the act of turning the hand (or fore limb) downward; also the position of a limb so turned.

proneidad [pro-nay-dahd'], *f.* Proneness, inclination, propensity.

prono, na [pro'-no, nah], *a.* 1. Prone, bending downward. 2. Prone, inclined, disposed.

pronombre [pro-nom'-bray], *m.* (*Gram.*). Pronoun. **Pronombre personal**, personal pronoun.

pronominal [pro-no-me-nahl'], *a.* Pronominal.

pronosticación [pro-nos-te-cah-the-on'], *f.* Prognostication, foreboding, forecasting.

pronosticador, ra [pro-nos-te-cah-dor', rah], *m. & f.* 1. Foreteller, prognosticator, foreboder, forecaster.

pronosticar [pro-nos-te-car'], *va.* To prognosticate, to predict, to foretell, to conjecture, to augur.

pronóstico, ca [pro-nos'-te-co, cah], *a.* Prognostic, foreshowing.

pronóstico [pro-nos'-te-co], *m.* 1. Prognostic, prediction, divination, omen (presagio), forerunner. 2. Almanac or calendar published by astrologers. **Pronóstico del tiempo**, weather forecast. 3. (*Med.*) Prognosis. **De pronóstico reservado**, of uncertain gravity.

prontamente [pron'-tah-men-tay], *adv.* Promptly, lightly, nimbly.

prontitud [pron-te-tood'], *f.* 1. Promptitude, promptness. 2. Readiness or liveliness of, with quickness of fancy; activity.

pronto, ta [pron'-to, tah], *a.* 1. Prompt (respuesta), quick (servicio), rapid, ready, hasty, fast, forward, expedient. **De pronto**, without premeditation, unintentionally; for the present; to suit the occasion. 2. (*Cono Sur*) Ready (dispuesto); tight (borracho).

pronto [pron'-to], *adv.* 1. Promptly, quickly (rápidamente), expeditiously; at once (enseguida); soon (dentro de poco). 2. Early (temprano). **Lo más pronto posible**, as soon as possible. **Por lo pronto**, meanwhile. **Levantarse pronto**, to get up early. **Iremos a comer un poco pronto**, we'll go and have lunch a bit early.

pronto [pron'-to], *m.* A sudden emotion of the mind, a quick motion. **Por el pronto**, provisionally, temporarily. **Primer pronto**, first movement. **Un pronto**, a sally.

prontuario [pron-too-ah'-re-o], *m.* 1. Memorandum-book. 2. Compendium of rules of some science or art.

pronuba [pro'-noo-bah], *f.* (*Poet.*) Bridesmaid; goddess of wedlock.

pronunciación [pro-noon-the-ah-the-on '], *f.* 1. Pronunciation, utterance; enunciation; articulation. 2. (*Law.*) Publication.

pronunciador, ra [pro-noon-the-ah-dor', rah], *m. & f.* Publisher, pronouncer.

pronunciamiento [pro-noon-the-ah-me-en'-to], *m.* 1. (*Law.*) Publication. 2. Insurrection, uprising.

pronunciar [pro-noon-the-ar'], *va.* 1. To pronounce, to utter, to articulate (articular), to enunciate. 2. To pronounce judgment, to issue by authority. 3. To pass upon, or deliberate on, while the principal point is decided. (*Acad.*) **Pronunció unas palabras en las que...**, she said that.... -*vr.* 1. To rise in insurrection, to declare oneself (declararse). **Pronunciarse a favor de**, to pronounce in favor of. 2. (*Pol.*) To revolt, to rise, to rebel. 3. (*Fig.*) To become pronounced (hacerse más marcado). 4. To cough up (soltar la pasta).

propagación [pro-pah-gah-the-on'], *f.* Propagation, successive production, offspring; extension.

propagador, ra [pro-pah-gah-dor', rah], *m. & f.* Propagator.

propaganda [pro-pah-gahn'-dah], *f.* 1. Propaganda. 2. Advertising.

propagantista [pro-pah-gahn-dees'-tah], *m. & f. & a.* Propagandist.

propagar [pro-pah-gar'], *va.* 1. To propagate, to generate, to multiply the species. 2. To propagate, to diffuse, to extend. 3. To propagate, to enlarge, to increase, to promote.

propagativo, va [pro-pah-gah-tee'-vo, vah], *a.* That which propagates.

propaladia [pro-pah-lah'-de-a], *f.* Title of a play.

propalar [pro-pah-lar'], *va.* To publish, to divulge (divulgar), to disseminate (diseminar).

propano [pro-pah'-no], *m.* Propane.

propao [pro-pah'-o], *m. (Naut.)* Breast work, bulkhead

propartida [pro-par-tee'-dah], *f.* Time approaching that of departing.

propasar [pro-pah-sar'], *va.* To go beyond, to transgress, to exceed. *-vr.* To be deficient in good-breeding.

propender [pro-pen-derr'], *vn.* To tend towards, to incline to by nature.

propensamente [pro-pen'-sah-men-tay], *adv.* In a propense manner, with inclination or propension.

propensión [pro-pen-se-on'], *f.* Propension, propensity, tendency, inclination, liability.

propenso, sa [pro-pen'-so, sah], *a.* Inclined, disposed, minded, apt to, prone, open to. **Propenso a accidentes**, accident-prone.

propiamente [pro'-pe-ah-men-tay], *adv.* Properly, with propriety; fittingly.

propiciación [pro-pe-the-ah-the-on'], *f.* 1. Propitiation, atonement. 2. Act of making propitious.

propiciador, ra [pro-pe-the-ah-dor', rah], *m. & f.* Propitiator.

propiciamente [pro-pee'-the-ah-men-tay], *adv.* Propitiously.

propiciar [pro-pe-the-ar'], *va.* 1. To propitiate (atraer), to conciliate. 2. To favor (favorecer); to create a favorable atmosphere for; to cause (provocar); to aid (ayudar).

propiciatorio, ria [pro-pe-the-ah-to'-re-o, ah], *a.* Propitiatory.

propiciatorio [pro-pe-the-ah-to'-re-o], *m.* Propitiatory, mercy-seat; the covering of the ark of the covenant.

propicio, cia [pro-pee'-the-o, ah], *a.* Propitious, kind, favorable (momento).

propiedad [pro-pe-ay-dahd'], *f.* 1. *(For.)* Dominion, possession (pertenencia), eminent domain; exclusive right of possession. *V.* DOMINIO. 2. Landed estate or property (objeto, tierras). 3. Property, particular quality which is peculiar to a thing. 4. Propriety (lo apropiado), appropriateness, aptness, expedience. 5. *(Gram.)* Exact signification of a term. 6. Propensity, inclination. 7. Close imitation. 8. *(Phil.)* V. PROPIO. **Ser de la propiedad de**, to be the property of. **Propiedad particular**, private property. **Propiedad industrial**, patent rights.

propienda [pro-pe-en'-dah], *f.* Listing nailed to the sides of a quilting or embroidering frame.

propietaria [pro-pe-ay-tah'-re-ah], *f.* Proprietress, a temple possessor in her own right.

propietariamente [pro-pe-ay-tah'-re-ah-men-tay], *adv.* With the right of property.

propietario, ria [pro-pe-ay-tah'-re-o, ah], *a.* Proprietary, invested with the right of property; belonging with full right of property.

propietario [pro-pe-ay-tah'-re-o], *m.* 1. Proprietary, proprietor, owner, landlord. 2. **Propietario de una finca**, freeholder. 3. Proprietary, a religious who sins against the vow of poverty.

propíleo [pro-pee'-lay-o], *m.* Propyleum, vestibule of a temple; a peristyle of columns.

propina [pro-pee'-nah], *f.* Present, pay beyond the agreed price, gratuity, tip. **Dar algo de propina**, to give something extra.

propinación [pro-pe-nah-the-on'], *f.* Treat, invitation to drink.

propinar [pro-pe-nar'], *va.* 1. To invite, to drink, to present a glass of wine or liquor. 2. *(coll.)* To prescribe medicines. 3. To deal (golpe), to hit; to give (paliza).

propincuidad [pro-pin-coo-e-dahd'], *f.* Propinquity, proximity, nearness.

propincuo, cua [pro-peen'-coo-o, ah], *a.* Near, contiguous.

propio, pia [pro'-pe-o, ah], *a.* 1. Proper, one's own, belonging to anyone. 2. Proper, suitable, becoming accommodated, adapted, fit, convenient. 3. Proper (apropiado), peculiar (particular) to anyone. 4. Proper (sentido), natural, original, genuine. 5. Exact, precise in speaking or writing. 6. *V.* MISMO. 7. Resembling, like, similar. **Con su propia mano**, with his own hand. **Tienen casa propia**, they have a house of their own. **Una bebida propia del país**, a typical drink of the country.

propio [pro'-pe-o], *m.* 1. *(Phil.)* Proper, peculiar or distinctive quality: characteristic property of a class, genus, or species. 2. Special delivery for letters of importance: messenger. *-pl.* Lands, estates, etc., belonging to a city or civic corporation.

propóleos [pro-po'-lay-os], *m.* Propolis, bee-glue.

proponedor, ra [pro-po-nay-dor', rah], *m. & f.* Proposer, offerer, proponent.

proponer [pro-po-nerr'], *va.* 1. To propose (idea, proyecto), to offer for consideration, to hold out, to represent. 2. To resolve, to determine, to mean. 3. To resent; to propose the means. **Le propuse que fuéramos juntos**, I proposed to him that we should go together. *-vr.* 1. **Proponerse hacer algo**, to propose to do something. 2. **Te has propuesto hacerme perder el tren**, you set out deliberately to make me miss the train.

proporción [pro-por-the-on'], *f.* 1. Proportion, portion, comparative relation of one thing to another. 2. Symmetry, adaptation of one thing to another: aptitude, fitness. 3. Similarity of arguments and reasons. 4. Opportunity, occasion, chance (oportunidad). 5. Relationship (relación); rate (porcentaje). 6. *(Mex.)* Proporciones, wealth. **A proporción**, conformably, proportionally; as fast as. **Estar fuera de proporción**, to be out of proportion. **Esto no guarda proporción con lo otro**, this is out of proportion with the rest.

proporcionable [pro-por-the-o-nah'-blay], *a.* Proportionable. *V.* PROPORCIONADO.

proporcionablemente, proporcionadamente, *adv.* Proportionally, proportionally.

proporcionado, da [pro-por-the-o-nah'-do, dah], *a.* Proportionate, regular, competent, commensurate, conformable, harmonious. *-pp.* of PROPORCIONAR.

proporcional [pro-por-the-o-nahl'], *a.* Proportional.

proporcionalidad [pro-por-the-onah-le-dahd'], *f.* Proportionableness, proportionality.

proporcionalmente [pro-por-the-o-nahl'-men-tay], *adv.* Proportionally, proportionally.

proporcionar [pro-por-the-o-nar'], *va.* 1. To proportion, to form symmetrically. 2. To adjust (adaptar), to adapt. 3. To afford, to furnish. **Proporcionar dinero a uno**, to give somebody money. *-vr.* To prepare oneself for any design.

proposición [pro-po-se-the-on'], *f.* 1. Proposition, the act of proposing. 2. Proposal, scheme, overture. 3. Proposition, assertion of affirmation or denial. 4. *(Math.)* Proposition, an established truth required to be demonstrated.

propósito [pro-poh'-se-to], *m.* 1. Purpose, aim, object, design, intention (intención). 2. Subject matter (tema). **A propósito**, for the purpose; fit for; apropos; by-the-bye. **De propósito**, on purpose, purposely. **Fuera de propósito**, untimely, not to the purpose, foreign to the subject, out of the question. **Volvamos al propósito**, let us return to the point in question.

propretor [pro-pray-tor'], *m.* Roman magistrate.

proptosis [prop-to'-ses], *f. (Med.)* Ptosis, falling of an organ.

popuesta [pro-poo-es'-tah], *f.* 1. Proposal, proposition, offer, overture. 2. Representation, declaration. 3. Proposal for employment.

propuesto, ta [pro-poo-es'-to, tah], *pp. irr.* of PROPONER. Proposed.

propugnación [pro-poog-nah-the-on'], *f.* Advocacy.

propugnáculo [pro-poog-nah'-coo'-lo], *m.* 1. A fortress. 2. *(Met.)* Bulwark, defence, support.

propugnar [pro-poog-nahr'], *va.* To advocate (proponer), to propose; to defend (apoyar).

propulsión [pro-pool-see-ohn'], *f.* Propulsion. **Propulsión a chorro**, jet propulsion. **Avión de propulsión**, jet plane.

propulsar [pro-pool-sar'], *va.* To repel *V.* REPULSAR.

propulsiva [pro-pool-see'-vah], *f.* PROPULSA.

propulsor [pro-pool-sor'], *m.* Propeller, propellant: a mechanism driven by a motive power within a vessel, and which acts upon the water, as oars, wheels, screw.

prora [pro'-rah], *f. (Poet.)* Prow of a ship.

prorrata [pror-rah'-tah], *f.* 1. Quota, a portion assigned to each contribuent. 2. Apportionment.

prorratear [pror-rah-tay-ar'], *va.* 1. To divide a quantity into certain shares. -*vn.* 2. To apportion.

prorrateo [pror-rah-tay'-o], *m.* Division into shares, distribution, average.

prórroga, prorrogación [pror'-ro-gah], *f.* 1. Prorogation, lengthening out to a distant time; prolongation. 2. *(For.)* Amplification of powers to cases and persons which they did not comprise.

prorrogable [pror-ro-gah'-blay], *a.* Capable of being prorogued.

prorrogación [pror-ro-gah-the-on'], *f.* Deferment, prorogation.

prorrogar [pror-ro-gar'], *va.* To prorogue (sesión), to put off, to adjourn.

prorrumpir [pror-room-peer'], *vn.* 1. To break forth, to burst out with violence, to issue. 2. To burst forth, to burst out into cries and lamentations.

prosa [pro'-sah], *f.* 1. Prose. 2. Tedious conversation, dull, absurd speech. 3. Prose chanted after mass. 4. *(Cono Sur)* Vanity (vanidad). 5. *(And. CAm.)* Pomposity.

prosador [pro-sah-dor'], *m. (coll.)* A sarcastic speaker, a malicious babbler.

prosaico, ca [pro-sah'-e-co, cah], *a.* 1. Prosaic, written in prose; belonging to prose. 2. Prosy, dull, tedious (monótono).

prosaísmo [pro-sah-ees'-mo], *m.* 1. Defect of verses which lack rhythm. 2. Prosiness, dulness.

prosapia [pro-sah'-pe-ah], *f.* Race, ancestry, lineage (linaje), a generation of people.

proscenio [pros-thay'-ne-o], *m.* Proscenium, place on the stage.

proscribir [pros-cre-beer'], *va.* To proscribe (partido), to outlaw (criminal), to censure capitally; to doom to destruction.

proscripción [pros-crip-the-on'], *f.* Prescription, banishment, outlawry.

proscripto [pros-creep'-to], *m.* Outlaw (bandido).

proscripto, ta, proscrito, to [pros-creep'-to, pros-cree'-to, tah], *pp. rr.* of PROSCRIBIR. Proscribed.

prosecución [pro-say-coo-the-on'], *f.* 1. Prosecution, pursuit, endeavor to carry on anything. 2. Pursuit, the act of following another.

proseguible [pro-say-gee'-blay], *a.* Pursuable.

proseguimiento [pro-say-gee-me-en'-to], *m.* V. PROSECUCIÓN.

proseguir [pro-say-geer'], *va.* To pursue (estudio), to prosecute, to follow, to continue anything already begun (continuar). -*vn.* 1. **Continuar en una actitud,** to continue in one's attitude. 2. To continue (condición). **Prosiguió con el cuento,** he went on with the story.

proselitismo [pro-say-le-tees'-mo], *m.* Proselytism, zeal for making proselytes.

prosélito [pro-say'-le-to], *m.* Proselyte, convert.

prosista [pro-sees'-tah], *m. & f.* 1. Author who writes in prose. 2. *(coll.)* Prattler, babbler, idle talker, proper.

prosita [pro-see'-tah], *f. dim.* A short discourse in prose.

prosodia [pro-so'-de-ah], *f.* 1. Orthoepy, the science or art of correct pronunciation. 2. Loquacity, idle talk. 3. Prosody, the science of metrical forms; formerly a division of grammar. 4. Regular mode of pronouncing each syllable of a word when singing.

prosódico, ca [pro-so'-de-co, cah], *a.* Orthoepic, relating to pronunciation; or prosodic.

prosopografía [pro-so-po-grah-fee'-ah], *f.* Prosopography, description of the physiognomy of a person or animal

prosopopeya [pro-so-po-pay'-yah], *f.* 1. Prosopopoeia, personification, a figure of speech. 2. *(coll.)* Splendor, pageantry.

prospecto [pros-pec'-to], *m.* Prospectus; leaflet, sheet of instructions.

prósperamente [pros'-pay-rah-men-tay], *adv.* Prosperously, luckily.

prosperar [pros-pay-rar'], *va.* To prosper, to make happy; to favor. -*vn.* To prosper, to be prosperous, to thrive.

prosperidad [pros-pay-re-dahd'], *f.* Prosperity, good fortune, success.

próspero, ra [pros'-pay-ro, rah], *a.* Prosperous (rico), successful (venturoso), fortunate, fair.

prostaféresis [pros-tah-fay'-ray-sis], *f. (Ast.)* Prosthaphaeresis, correction to be applied to the mean place of a heavenly body to obtain the true place or movement.

próstata [pros'-ta-tah], *f.* The prostate gland.

prostático, ca [pros-tah'-te-co, cah], *a.* Prostatic, pertaining to the prostate.

prostatitis [pros-ta-tee'-tis], *f.* Prostatitis, inflammation of the prostate.

prosternación [pros-ter-nah-the-on'], *f.* Profound reverence and humiliation, falling down.

prosternarse [pros-ter-nar'-say], *vr.* To fall down, to prostrate oneself in adoration (postrarse), to bend as a suppliant.

prostíbulo [pros-tee'-boo-lo], *m.* House of prostitution, disorderly place.

prostilo [pros-tee'-lo], *a. (Arch.)* Prostyle, having only pillars in front.

prostitución [pros-te-too-the-on'], *f.* 1. Prostitution, the act of setting or being set to sale for vile purposes. 2. Prostitution, the life of a strumpet.

prostituir [pros-te-too-eer'], *va.* To prostitute (mujer), to expose to crimes for a reward; to expose on vile terms. -*vr.* To hack, to turn hackney or prostitute.

prostituta [pros-te-too'-tah], *f.* Prostitute, woman of the town, whore.

prostituto, ta [pros-te-too'-to, tah], *pp. irr.* of PROSTITUIR. Prostituted.

protagonismo [pro-tah-go-nees'-mo], *m.* Defense (defensa); support (apoyo); initiative (iniciativa); leadership (liderazgo); leading role (papel).

protagonista [pro-tah-go-nees'-tah], *m & f.* Protagonist, principal personage of a dramatic story.

protagonizar [pro-tah-go-ne-thahr'] *va.* 1. To take the chief role in, to play the leading part. 2. To lead (rebelión, proceso); to stage (manifestación); to figure in (accidente). **Una entrevista protagonizada por X,** an interview whose subject was X.

prótasis [pro'-tah-sis], *f.* 1. Protasis, the first piece of a dramatic poem. 2. *(Gram.)* Protasis, the first part of a compound period.

protección [pro-tec-the-on'], *f.* Protection, support, favor, countenance.

proteccionismo [pro-tec-the-o-nees'-mo], *m.* The economic doctrine of protection or protectionism: opposite of free trade.

proteccionista [pro-tec-the-o-nees'-tah], *m.* Protectionist, a partisan of protectionism.

protector [pro-tec-tor'], *m.* 1. Protector, defender, guardian, conservator. 2. Steward of a community, charged with maintaining its interest.

protectora [pro-tec-to'-rah], *f.* Protectress, a woman who protects.

protectorado [pro-tec-to-rah'-do], *m.* Protectorate, the dignity of a protector and the time during which it lasts.

protectoría [pro-tec-to-ree'-ah], *f.* Protectorship, protectorate.

protectorio, ria [pro-tec-to'-re-o, ah], *a.* Relating to a protector.

protectriz [pro-tec-treeth'], *f.* Protectress.

proteger [pro-tay-herr'], *va.* To protect (resguardar), to defend (defender), to favor, to countenance.

protegido da [pro-tay-hee'-do, dah], *m. & f.* Protege, protegee, favorite.-*a. & pp.* of PROTEGER. Protected, sheltered.

proteína [pro-tay-ee'-nah], *f.* Protein.

protervamente [pro-tayr'-vah-men-tay], *adv.* Frowardly, stubbornly, perversely.

protervia, protervidad [pro-terr'-ve-ah], *f.* Obstinacy, protervity, peevishness, stubbornness.

protervo, va [pro-terr'-vo, vah], *a.* Stubborn, peevish, obstinate, perverse.

prótesis [pro'-tay-sis], *f. (Gram.)* Prosthesis or prothesis, addition of letters at the beginning of a word, for the sake of euphony; as *aqueste* for *este*.

protesta [pro-tes'-tah], *f.* 1. *(Law.)* Protest (queja), a solemn declaration. 2. A solemn promise, asseveration, or assurance. **Hacer protestas de lealtad,** to protest one's loyalty.

protestación [pro-tes-tah-the-on'], *f.* 1. Protestation, profession, a solemn declaration 2. Threat, menace.

protestante [pro-tes-tahn'-tay], *com.* A Protestant.

protestante [pro-tes-tahn'-tay], *a.* Protestant, belonging to protestants. -*pa.* Protesting.

protestantismo [pro-tes-tan-tees'-mo], *m.* Protestantism.

protestar [pro-tes-tar'], *va.* 1. To protest, to give a solemn declaration. 2. To assure, to assever. 3. To threaten, to menace. 4. To make a public declaration of faith and belief. 5. *(Law.)* To make a solemn declaration for the purpose of preserving one's right. **Protestar una letra,** to protest a bill of exchange. -*vn.* 1. To protest (quejarse); to object (objetar); to remonstrate. 2. To protest (inocencia). **Protestar contra una demora,** to protest about a delay.

protestativo, va [pro-tes-tah-tee'-vo, vah], *a.* That which protests.

protesto [pro-tes'-to], *m.* 1. *(Com.)* Protest of a bill. 2. *V.* PROTESTA.

protético, ca [pro-tay'-te-co, cah], *a.* Prothetic, prefixed.

protocolar, protocolizar [pro-to-co-lar'], *va.* To place in the protocol, to record, to register.

protocolario [pro-to-co-lah-re-o], *a.* 1. Established by protocol (exigido por el protocolo). 2. *(Fig.)* Formal (ceremonial).

protocolo [pro-to-co'-lo], *m.* Protocol, registry, a judicial record. **Protocolo de control de enlace,** link control protocol, procedure.

protomedicato [pro-to-may-de-cah'-to], *m.* 1. Tribunal or college of king's physicians, where student of medicine are examined and licensed. 2. Office of a first or royal physician.

protomédico [pro-to-may'-de-co], *m.* First physician, one of the three physicians to the king.

protón [pro-tone'], *m. (Phy.)* Proton.

protonotario [pro-to-no-tah'-re-o], *m.* Prothonotary, chief clerk or chief notary.

protoplasma [pro-to-plahs'-mah], *m.* Protoplasm.

protosulfuro [pro-to-sool-foo'-ro], *m.* Protosulphide.

prototípico, ca [pro-to-tee -pe-co, cah], *a.* Prototypal, belonging to a prototype.

prototipo [pro-to-tee'-po], *m.* Prototype, origins.

protóxido [pro-tok'-se-do], *m.* Protoxide.

protozoario, ria [pro-to-tho-ah'-re-o, ah], *a.* Protozoic.

protozoo [pro-to-tho'-o], *m.* Protozoan, protozoon, one-celled organism.

protuberancia [pro-too-bar-rahn'-the-ah], *f.* Protuberance, prominence.

provecto, ta [pro-vec'-to, tah], *a.* Advanced in years, learning, or experience.

provecho [pro-vay'-cho], *m.* 1. Profit, benefit, advantage, utility, gain. 2. Profit, improvement, proficiency, progress; advancement. **Hombre de provecho,** a useful man. **Ser de provecho,** to be useful or profitable. **Buen provecho,** good appetite. **En provecho propio,** to one's own advantage.

provechosamente [pro-vay-cho'-sah-men-tay], *adv.* Profitably, gainfully, advantageously, usefully.

provechoso, sa [pro-vay-cho'-so, sah], *a.* Profitable, beneficial, gainful, lucrative, useful, advantgeous.

proveedor, ra [pro-vay-ay-dor', rah], *m. & f.* Purveyor, contractor, furnisher.

proveeduría [pro-vay-ay-doo-ree'-ah], *f.* 1. Store-house for provisions. 2. Employment and office of purveyor.

proveer [pro-vay-err'], *va.* 1. To provide (disponer), to procure beforehand, to get ready, to furnish, to fit, to accommodate. 2. To supply with provisions to provide provisions for an army (suministrar). 3. To dispose, to adjust. 4. To confer a dignity or employment. 5. To decree, to doom by a decree, to despatch a suit at law. 6. To minister, to supply with the necessaries of life, to maintain. -*vr. (coll.)* To ease the body.

proveído [pro-vey-ee'-do], *m.* Judgment, sentence, decree. **Proveído, da,** *pp.* of PROVEER.

proveimiento [pro-vay-e-me-en'-to], *m.* Supply, the act of providing or supplying with provisions.

proveniente [pro-vay-ne-en'-tay], *pa.* Proceeding, originating in.

provenir [pro-vay-neer'], *vn.* To arise, to proceed; to take rise or origin from, to originate in. **Provenir de,** to come from.

provenzal [pro-ven-thahl'], *a.* Provencal, relating to Provence, and its language; Languedocian.

proverbiador [pro-ver-be-ah-dor'], *m.* Collection of proverbs.

proverbial [pro-ver-be-ahl'], *a.* Proverbial.

proverbialmente [pro-ver-be-ahl-men-tay], *adv.* Proverbially.

proverbiar [pro-ver-be-ar'], *vn. (coll.)* To use proverbs.

proverbio [pro-vayr'-be-o], *m.* 1. A proverb. 2. Prophecy, prediction from certain words. **Proverbios,** Book of Proverbs, a canonical book of the Old Testament.

proverbista [pro-ver-bees'-tah], *m. (coll.)* One attached to the use of proverbs.

próvidamente [pro' -ve-dah-men-tay], *adv.* Providently, carefully.

providencia [pro-ve-den'-the-ah], *f.* 1. Providence, foresight (cualidad), forecast, forethought (prevención). 2. Providence, the act of providing disposition or measures taken to obtain some end. 3. Divine Providence. 4. State or order of things. **Dictar providencia,** to take steps to.

providencial [pro-ve-den-the-ahl'], *a.* Providential.

providencialmente [pro-ve-den-the-ahl'-men-tay], *adv.* Providentially, provisionally.

providenciar [pro-ve-den-the-ar'], *va.* To ordain, to command.

providente [pro-ve-den-tay], *a.* Provident, prudent, careful.

provido, da [pro'-ve-do, dah], *a.* Provident, careful, diligent.

provincia [pro-veen'-the-ah], *f.* 1. Province, one of the divisions of a kingdom. 2. A certain number of convents under the direction of a provincial. 3. Provincial court appointed to try and decide civil causes. 4. Province, an important business which is to be treated upon.

provincial [pro-vin-the-ahl'], *a.* Provincial.

provincialismo [pro-vin-the-ah-lees'-mo], *m.* Provincialism.

provinciano, na [pro-vin-the-ah'-no, nah], *a. m & f.* Provincial; country (rural).

provisión [pro-ve-se-on'], *f.* 1. Store of provisions collected for use (suministro); provender. 2. Writ, decree, or sentence issued by Spanish tribunals in the king's name. 3. Title or instrument, by virtue whereof an incumbent holds his benefice. 4. Act of conferring an employment or office (acto). 5. *(Com.)* A remittance of funds by the drawer of a bill of exchange to the drawee so that he may accept it.

provisional [pro-ve-se-oh-nahl'], *a.* Provisional.

provisionalmente [pro-ve-se-o-nahl'-men-tay], *adv.* Provisionally.

proviso, or **al proviso** [pro-vee'-so], *adv.* Upon the spot, immediately, instantly.

provisor, ra [pro-ve-sor', rah], *m. & f.* 1. Provider. *V.* PROVEEDOR. 2. Vicar-general, an ecclesiastical judge.

provisoría [pro-ve-so-ree'-ah], *f.* 1. In some convents and colleges, the store-room, where provisions are kept; pantry. 2. Place or office of a provisor or vicar-general.

provisorio, ria [pro-ve-so'-re-o, ah], *a.* (*LAm.*) Provisional, temporarily established.

provisto, ta [pro-vees'-to, tah], *a.* 1. Provided with a benefice. 2. (*Cono Sur*) Provisions, supplies. -*pp. irr.* of PROVEER.

provocación [pro-vo-cah-the-on'], *f.* 1. Provocation, displeasure, irritation. 2. Cause or motive of anger.

provocador, ra [pro-vo-cah-dor', rah], *m. & f.* Provoker; causer, promoter.

provocar [pro-vo-car'], *va.* 1. To provoke (persona), to rouse (enojar), to excite, to nettle. 2. To anger, to enrage, to offend. 3. To vomit. 4. To facilitate, to promote. 5. To move, to excite. 6. To bring about (cambio); to promote (proceso); to cause (explosión, protesta, guerra). 7. (*LAm.*) **¿Te provoca un café?**, would you like some coffee? (gustar, apetecer).

provocativo, va [pro-vo-cah-tee'-vo, vah], *a.* 1. Provocative, exciting, inducing. 2. Quarrelsome, provoking.

próximamente [proc'-se-mah-men-tay], *adv.* Soon, nearly, immediately, in the near future.

proximidad [proc-se-me-dahd'], *f.* 1. Proximity, nearness, vicinity. 2. Relation, kindred by birth.

próximo, ma [proc'-se-mo, mah], *a.* Next (anterior, siguiente), nearest (cercano), neighbor, proximate. **En fecha próxima**, soon. **El mes próximo**, next month.

proyección [pro-yec-the-on'], *f.* 1. Projection, shooting forward (acto). 2. (*Arch.*) Corbel, jetty, projecture. 3. (*Math.*) Apparent representation of an object upon a plane; graphic representation. 4. Movement impressed upon a projectile. **La proyección de los periódicos sobre la sociedad**, the hold of newspapers over society.

proyectar [pro-yec-tar'], *va.* 1. To project, to scheme, to contrive. 2. To throw into the air, to project. 3. To draw a figure in the vertical and horizontal planes of projection. -*vr.* 1. To strike against a bottom. 2. To throw itself forward, as a shadow. 3. (*Naut.*) To be ranged along the same line. **Está proyectado para**, it is designed to.

proyectil [pro-yec-teel'], *m.* Missile, projectile. **Proyectil balístico**, ballistic missile. **Proyectil cohete**, rocket missile; space rocket. **Proyectil de alcance intermedio**, intermediate range ballistic missile. **Proyectil de sondeo**, probe rocket. **Proyectil dirigido**, guided missile. **Proyectil irterceptor**, interceptor missile. **Proyectil antiproyectil**, anti-missile missile.

proyectista [pro-yec-tees'-tah], *m.* Projector, schemer.

proyecto [pro-yec'-to], *m.* Project, scheme, plan, design. **Cambiar de proyecto**, to change one's plans. **Tener proyectos para**, to have plans for.

proyecto, ta [pro-yec'-to, tah], *a.* Projected, expanded, dilated.

proyector [pro-yec-tor'], *m.* 1. Projector. 2. Searchlight. 3. Spotlight.

proyectura [pro-yec-too'-rah], *f.* Projecture, part of a building which juts beyond the wall. *V.* VUELO.

prudencia [proo-den'-the-ah], *f.* 1. Prudence, counsel, management, circumspection. 2. Temperance, moderation.

prudencial [proo-den-the-ahl'], *a.* Prudential (adecuado); sensible (razonable). **Tras un intervalo prudencial**, after a decent interval.

prudencialmente [proo-den-the-ahl'-men-tay], *adv.* Prudentially.

prudente [proo-den'-tay], *a.* Prudent, circumspect, judicious (decisión), considerate.

prudentemente [proo-den-tay-men-tay], *adv.* Prudently.

prueba [proo-ay'-bah], *f.* 1. Proof, reason, argument, evidence. 2. Sign, token (indicio), indication, mark. 3. Experiment, essay, attempt; a test-portion, a test, trial. 4. (*Print.*) Proof, proof-sheet. 5. In photography, proof, the first print from a negative. 6. (*Dep.*) Event; race. 7. (*LAm.*) Circus act. **A prueba de** with a noun is to be rendered by «proof» connected by hyphen with the equivalent of the

noun. Thus; **A prueba de luz**, light-proof. **A prueba de bomba**, bomb-proof; satisfactorily. **Tomar una cosa a prueba**, to take a thing on trial. **Prueba de acceso**, entrance test. **A prueba de balas**, bullet-proof. **Sala de pruebas**, fitting room. **Prueba de Turing**, (*Comput.*) Turing test.

prurito [proo-ree'-to], *m.* 1. Prurience, itching. 2. Great desire or appetite.

prusiato [proo-se-ah'-to], *m.* (*Chem.*) Prussiate.

prúsico [proo'-se-co], *a.* Prussic, hydrocyanic. **Ácido prúsico**, Prussic, hydrocyanic acid.

psicoanálisis [se-co-ah-nah'-le-sis], *f.* Psychoanalysis.

psicoanalista [se-co-ah-nah-lees'-tah], *m & f.* Psychoanalyst.

psicodélico [se-co-day'-le-co], *a.* Phychedelic. -*m.* Light show.

psicofísica [se-co-fee'-se-ca], *f.* Psychophysics.

psicología [se-co-lo-hee'-ah], *f.* Psychology, study of the subconscious. **Psicología industrial**, industrial psychology.

psicológico, ca [se-co'-lo'-he-co, cah], *a.* Psychological.

psicólogo, ga [se-co'-lo-go, gah], *m. & f.* Psychologist.

psiconeurótico, ca [se-co-nay-oo-roh'-te-co, cah], *a.* Psychoneurotic.

psicópata [se-co'-pah-tah], *m.* Psychopath.

psicopatía [se-co-pah-tee'-ah], *f.* Psychopathy.

psicopático, ca [se-co-pah'-te-co, cah], *a.* Psychopathic.

psicopatología [se-co-pah-to-lo-hee'-ah], *f.* Psychopathology.

psicosis [se-co'-sis], *f.* Psychosis.

psicosomático, ca [se-co-so-mah'-te-co-cah], *a.* Psychosomatic, referring to illnesses not organic in origin.

psicotecnia [se-co-tec'-ne-ah], *f.* Psychological testing.

psicotécnico, ca [se-co-tec'-ne-co, cah], *a.* Psychotechnological.

psicoterapia [se-co-tay-rah'-pe-ah], *f.* Psychotherapy.

psique [see'-kay], *f.* Psyche.

psiquiatra [se-ke-ah'-trah], *m.* Psychiatrist.

psiquiatría [se-ke-ah-tree'-ah], *f.* Psychiatry.

psíquico, ca [see'-ke-co, cah], *a.* Psychic.

púa [poo'-ah], *f.* 1. Sharp point (punta), barb (de gancho, alambre). 2. (*Bot.*) Graft. 3. Tooth (de un peine). 4. Prick. 5. (*Zool.*) Spine. 6. (*Mus.*) Plectrum. 7. (*coll.*) Sharpie. **Alambre de púas**, barbed wire.

púber [poo'-ber], *a.* Pubescent.

púbero, ra [poo'-bay-ro, rah], *a.* Pubescent, arrived at puberty.

pubertad [poo-ber-tahd'], *f.* Puberty, pubescence.

pubes [poo'-bes], *m.* (*Anat.*) Pubes, the pubic region.

pubescencia [poo-bes-then'-the-ah], *f.* Pubescence, puberty.

pubescer [poo-bes-therr'], *vn.* To attain the age of puberty.

púbico [poo'-be-co], *a.* Pubic.

pubis [poo'-bes], *m.* Pubis.

pública [poo'-ble-cah], *f.* In universities, a lecture before the examination for the degree of licentiate.

publicación [poo-ble-cah-the-on'], *f.* Publication, proclamation.

publicador, ra [poo-ble-cah-dor', rah], *m. & f.* Publisher, proclaimer.

públicamento [poo-ble-cah-men-tay], *adv.* Publicly, openly.

publicano [poo-ble-cah'-no], *m.* Publican, toll-gatherer.

publicar [po-ble-car'], *va.* 1. To publish, to proclaim, to make known. 2. To publish, to print a book.

publicata [poo-ble-cah'-tah], *f.* 1. Certificate of publication. 2. Each of the three announcements of the banns of marriage.

publicidad [poo-ble-the-dahd'], *f.* 1. Publicity, notoriety. **En publicidad**, publicicly. 2. (*Com.*) Advertising. **Publicidad de lanzamiento**, advance publicity.

publicista [poo-ble-thees'-tah], *m.* Publicist, a writer on public law or on topics of public interest.

publicitario [poo-ble-the-tah'-re-o], *a.* Advertising; publicity. -*m.* Advertising man.

público, ca [poo'-ble-co, cah], *a.* 1. Public, notorious, known by all. 2. Vulgar, common, general. **En público**, publicly.

público [poo'-ble-co], *m.* Public, the general body of a nation. **Hay poco público**, there aren't many people.

pucha [poo'-chah], *f.* (*Cuba*) A small bouquet of flowers, nosegay.

puchada [poo-chah'-dah], *f.* 1. A cataplasm, chiefly of flour. 2. Watered mortar, used by stone masons.

puchecilla [poo-chay-theel'-lyah], *f.* A thin batter of flour and water.

pucherito [poo-chay-ree'-to], *m.* (*coll.*) Crying grimaces of children.

puchero [poo-chay'-ro], *m.* 1. A glazed earthen pot (olla). 2. Olla, a dish composed of beef or lamb, ham or bacon, Spanish peas, and vegetables: a standing dish in Spanish countries. 3. Daily food, regular aliment. 4. Grimace or distortion of the face which precedes crying (mueca). **Hacer pucheros**, (*coll.*) to snivel.

puches [poo'-ches], *com. pl.* Sort of pap. *V.* GACHAS.

pucho [poo'-cho], *m.* (*Amer.*) 1. Tip or end of a cigar (colilla). 2. A small quantity or sum; driblet. 3. (*LAm.*) Scrap (resto); (*fig.*) trifle (minimedad).

pucuna [poo-coo'-nah], *f.* A blow-gun in Peru. (*Indian.*)

pudendas [poo-dayn-dahs] *a. & f. pl.* The pudenda.

pudendo, da [poo-den'-do, dah], *a.* Shameful, obscene, immodest.

pudendo [poo-dayn-do], *m.* The male organ.

pudibundo, da [poo-de-boon'-do, dah], *a.* Shamefaced, modest.

pudicicia [poo-de-thee'-the-ah], *f.* Pudicity, chastity, modesty.

púdico, ca [poo'-de-co, cah], *a.* Chaste, modest, maidenly.

pudiente [poo-de-en'-tay], *a. & m.* Powerful (poderoso), rich, opulent.

pudín [poo-deen'], *m.* Pudding.

pudor [poo-dor'], *m.* Bashfulness, modesty (recato), shyness (timidez), shamefacedness.

pudoroso, sa [poo-do-ro'-so, sah], *a.* Modest (recatado), shamefaced, bashful, shy.

pudrición [poo-dre-the-on'], *f.* Rottenness, the act of rotting (proceso).

pudridero [poo-dre-day'-ro], *m.* 1. Rotting-place, where something is put to rot, fermenting pit. 2. Royal vault in the monastery at Escorial.

pudridor [poo-dre-dor'], *m.* Vessel in which rags are steeped for making paper.

pudrimiento [poo-dre-me-en'-to], *m.* Rottenness, putrefaction. *V.* PUDRICIÓN.

pudrir [poo-dreer'], *va.* 1. To rot (descomponer), to make putrid, to bring to corruption. 2. To molest, to consume, to cause extreme impatience. -*vn.* To have died (haber muerto), to be buried, to rot. -*vr.* 1. To corrupt, to become rotten, to decay. 2. To be broken-hearted, to die of grief. **Mientras se pudría en la cácel**, while he was languishing in jail.

puebla [poo-ay'-blah], *f.* Seed which a gardener sows.

pueblecico, ito [poo-ay-blay-thee'-co], *m. dim.* Any small town.

pueblerino [poo-ay-blay-ree'-no], *a.* Rustic, countrified (lugareño), small-town, village. -*f.* Villager (aldeano).

pueblo [poo-ay'-blo], *m.* 1. Town, village (aldea); any inhabited place. 2. Population, inhabitants of a place. 3. Common people (plebe), populace. 4. Nation, people. **Pueblo elegido**, chosen people. **Pueblo de mala muerte**, dregs of society.

puente [poo-en'-tay], *com.* 1. A bridge. **Puente volante**, flying-bridge. **Puente levadizo**, draw-bridge. 2. (*Naut.*) Deck of a ship. 3. (*Mus.*) Bridge in stringed instruments. 4. Transom, lintel, crossbeam. **Hacer puente**, to take a long weekend. **Puente aéreo**, airlift. **Cabeza de puente**, bridgehead. **Puente colgante**, suspension bridge. **Puente de mando**, bridge. **A enemigo que huye puente de plata**, let the enemy escape.

puentecico, illo, ito [poo-en-tay-thee'-co], *m. dim.* A small bridge.

puentecilla [poo-en-tay-theel'-lyah], *f. dim.* A small bridge of a stringed instrument.

puerca [poo-err'-cah], *f.* 1. A sow (cerda). 2. Sow-bug, slater, woodlouse (cochinilla), a crustacean commonly found in damp spots. 3. Scrofulous swelling, glandulous tumor. 4. Slut, slatternly woman.

puercamente [poo-err'-cah-men-tay], *adv.* 1. Dirtily, filthily, hoggishly, nastily. 2. Rudely, coarsely, vulgarly, meanly.

puerco, ca [poo-err'-co, cah], *a.* 1. Nasty (asqueroso), filthy, dirty, foul, abominable, coarse (grosero). 2. Rude, coarse, mean.

puerco [poo-err'-co], *m.* 1. Hog (cerdo). 2. Wild-boar (jabalí). **Puerco montés**, *V.* JABALÍ. 3. A brutish, ill-bred man.

puericia [poo-ay-ree'-the-ah], *f.* Boyhood.

puericultor, ora [poo-ay-re-cool-tor'], *m & f.* Specialist in puericulture.

puericultura [poo-ay-re-cool-too'-rah], *f.* Puericulture, child care, prenatal and infant welfare.

pueril [poo-ay-reel'], *a.* 1. Boyish, childish, puerile. 2. Belonging to the first quadrant of the celestial map.

puerilidad [poo-ay-re-le-dahd'], *f.* Puerility, boyishness, childishness, silliness; trifle.

puerilmente [poo-ay-reel'-men-tay], *adv.* Puerilely, childishly, boyishly.

puérpera [poo-err'-pay-rah], *f.* A lying-in woman.

puerperal [poo-er-pay-rahl'], *a.* Puerperal, relating to childbirth.

puerperio [poo-er-pay'-re-o], *m.* 1. Child birth, travail, labor. 2. The puerperal condition; the time immediately following labor.

puerquezuela [poo-er-kay-thoo-ay'-lo], *m. dim.* Little pig.

puerro [poo-err'-ro], *m.* (*Bot.*) Leek.

puerta [poo-err'-tah], *f.* 1. Door or doorway, gateway. 2. Beginning of an undertaking. 3. Door, gate, that which serves to stop any passage. 4. Duty paid at the entrance of the gates in towns. 5. The Turkish government, the Porte. **Puerta de dos hojas**, folding-door. **Puerta trasera**, back door. **Llamar a la puerta**, to knock at the door. **A puerta cerrada**, secretly. **Dar con la puerta en los hocicos**, to slam the door in one's face. **Puerta corredera**, sliding door. **A las puertas de la muerte**, at death's door. **Estar en puertas**, to be imminent. **De puerta en puerta**, from door to door. **Puerta O**, (*Comput.*) OR gate. **Puerta Y**, (*Comput.*) AND gate.

puertaventana [poo-er-tah-ven-tah'-nah], *f.* Door with a window in it.

puertecita [poo-er-tay-thee'-tah], *f. dim.* A small door.

puertecillo [poo-er-tay-theel'-lyo], *m. dim.* A small port.

puertezuela [poo-er-toy-thoo-ay'-lah], *f. dim. V.* PUERTECITA.

puertezuelo [poo-er-tay-thoo-ay'-lo], *m. dim. V.* PERTECILLO.

puerto [poo-err'-to], *m.* 1. Port, harbor, haven for ships. **Puerto habilitado**, a port of entry. **Puerto franco**, free port. 2. Pass, through mountains. 3. Asylum, shelter, refuge (refugio). **Llegar a puerto**, to solve a problem. 4. (*Prov.*) Dam in a river.

puerto aéreo or **aeropuerto** [poo-err'-to ah-ay'-ray-o, ah-ay-ro-poo-err'-to], *m.* Airport.

puertorriqueño, ña [poo-err-tor-re-kay' -nyo, nyah], *a. & m. & f.* Puerto Rican, from Puerto Rico.

pues [poo-es'], *adv., conj.* 1. Then (entonces), therefore. 2. Inasmuch as; since. 3. Sure, surely; certainly. **¡Pues no faltaba más!** surely, of course.

Pues, *int.* Well, then; therefore. **¿Y pues?** well, and what of that? **Pues sí**, (*Iron.*) Yes, indeed! **¿Pues y qué?** why not? what else? what then? **Pues no le tenía yo por rico**, indeed I did not think him rich. **Pues ese es mi rival**, well, that is my rival.

puesta [poo-es'-tah], *f.* 1. Putting, placing (acto). 2. (*Astron.*) Setting. 3. Egg-laying. 4. Resigning a hand of cards. **Puesta del sol**, sunset. **A puesta** or **puestas de sol**, at sunset. **Puesta en libertad**, freeing. **Puesta a punto**, final preparation, setup.

puesto [poo-es'-to], *m.* 1. Place or space occupied (lugar); particular spot, an assigned post. 2. Shop or place where anything is sold by retail; stall, booth. 3. Post (trabajo), employment, dignity, office. 4. House in which stallions are kept and let to mares. 5. *(Mil.)* Barrack for soldiers. 6. Place covered with bushes to conceal sportsmen. 7. *(Cono Sur)* Small farm. **Puesto de trabajo**, work station. **Puesto de control**, checkpoint. **Puesto de socorro**, first-aid post.

puesto, ta [poo-es'-to, tah], *pp. irr.* of PONER. Put. **Con el sombrero puesto**, with one's hat on. **Tenerlos bien puestos**, to be a real man.

puesto [poo-es'-to], *adv.* Because, for this reason that, on this account that. **Puesto que**, although. *V.* AUNQUE.

¡puf! [poof]. *int.* A word expressive of the unpleasant sensation of a bad smell.

pufo [poo'-fo], *m.* 1. Trick (trampa). 2. Debt (deuda).

púgil [poo'-heel], *m.* Prize-fighter, boxer, bruiser, pugilist.

pugilar [poo-he-lar'], *m.* Hebrew manual of the Scriptures used in synagogues.

pugilato [poo-he-lah'-to], *m.* Pugilism, boxing or fighting.

pugna [poog'-nah], *f.* Combat, conflict, battle. **Estar en pugna con**, to clash with.

pugnacidad [poog-nah-the-dahd'], *f.* Pugnacity, quarrelsomeness.

pugnante [poog-nahn'-tay], *pa.* Fighting, opposing.

pugnar [poog-nar'], *vn.* To fight (luchar), to combat, to contend; to rival; to solicit; to importune. **Pugnar por**, to fight for.

pugnaz [poog-nath'], *a.* Pugnacious, quarrelsome.

puja [poo'-hah], *f.* 1. Outbidding or overbidding at a public sale (en subasta). 2. *(And.)* Ticking-off.

pujadero, ra [poo-hah-day'-ro, rah], *a.* That which might be outbid, or enhanced.

pujador, ra [poo-hah-dor', rah], *m. & f.* Outbidder, overbidder, highest bidder.

pujame, pujamen [pooh-hah'-may], *m. (Naut.)* Under part of the sails.

pujamiento [poo-hah-me-en'-to], *m.* Flow or violent agitation of the blood.

pujante [poo-hahn'-tay], *a.* Powerful (potente), puissant, strong (fuerte), predominant, forcible.

pujanza [poo-hahn'-thah], *f.* Power, might, strength, puissance.

pujar [poo-har'], *va.* 1. To outbid. 2. To labor under an impediment of speech, to falter. 3. To be eager in the pursuit of a thing, to endevor earnestly. 4. *(coll.)* To make a face as if to cry. -*vn.* 1. To bid (en subasta) 2. To struggle (esforzarse). **Pujar para hacer algo**, to struggle to do something. 3. To falter (vacilar). 4. To struggle for words (no encontrar palabras). 5. To be on the verge of tears (hacer pucheros). 6. *(CAm.)* To moan (quejarse).

pujavante [poo-hah-vahn'-tay], *m.* Butteris, an instrument for paring a horse's foot.

pujo [poo'-ho], *m.* 1. Tenesmus (medicina). 2. Violent desire, eagerness, longing (ansia); anxiety. **Sentir pujo de llorar**, to be on the verge of tears.

pulcritud [pool-cre-tood'], *f.* Pulchritude, beauty, grace, gentility.

pulcro, cra [pool'-cro, crah], *a.* 1. Beautiful, graceful. 2. Affectedly nice in dress (elegante). 3. Exquisite (exquisito); dainty (delicado).

pulga [pool'-gah], *f.* 1. Flea. 2. Playing tops for children (de juego). 3. *(LAm. Comput.)* Bug. **Tener malas pulgas**, to be easily piqued or fretted, to be ill-tempered. **Buscar las pulgas a uno**, to tease somebody.

pulgada [pool-gah'-dah], *f.* Inch, the twelfth part of a foot.

pulgar [pool-gar'], *m.* 1. The thumb. **Dedo pulgar del pie**, the great toe. 2. Shoots left on vines.

pulgarada [pool-gah-rah'-dah], *f.* 1. Fillip, flick (papirote). 2. Pinch, quantity taken between the thumb and forefinger. 3. *V.* PULGADA.

pulgón [pool-gone'], *m.* Vine-fretter, plant louse, aphis.

pulgoso, sa [pool-goh'-so, sah], *a.* Pulicose, abounding with fleas.

pulguera [pool-gay'-rah], *f.* 1. Place abounding with fleas. 2. *(Bot.)* Pulic, flea-wort.

pulguita [pool-gee'-tah], *f.dim.* A little flea.

pulguilla [pool-geel'-lya], *f.dim.* A little flea.

pulicán [poo-le-cahn'], *m.* Pelican, instrument for drawing teeth.

pulicaria [poo-le-cah'-re-ah], *f.* Flea-wort. *V.* ZARAGATONA.

pulidamente [poo-lee'-dah-men-tay], *adv.* Neatly (con pulcritud), sprucely, cleancy, nicely, compactly.

pulidero [poo-le-day'-ro], *m.* 3. Polisher, glosser. 2. Polisher, an instrument for polishing or burnishing.

pulidez, pulideza [poo-le-deth'], *f.* Neatness, cleanliness.

pulido, da [poo-lee'-do, dah], *a.* Neat (pulcro), cleanly (limpio), nice. -*pp.* of PULIR.

pulidor, ra [poo-le-dor'], *m & f.* 1. Polisher, furbisher. 2. Instrument for polishing and burnishing.

pulimentable [poo-le-men-tah'-blay], *a.* Susceptible of polish.

pulimentar [poo-le-men-tar'], *va.* 1. To gloss (dar lustre), to polish very bright (pulir). 2. *(coll.)* To finish.

pulimento [poo-le-men'-to], *m.* 3. Polish, glossiness, artificial gloss (brillo). 2. *(coll.)* Finishing.

pulir [poo-leer'], *va.* 1. To polish, to burnish, to furbish. 2. To adorn, to beautify. 3. To pinch (robar); to sell (vender). -*vr.* 1. To be polished: to adorn, beautify, embellish, or deck oneself. 2. To become polished or elegant in dress or manners.

pulmón [pool-mone'], *m.* Lung. **Pulmón de hierro**, *(Med.)* iron lung.

pulmonaria [pool-mo-nah'-re-ah], *f. (Pot.)* Lungwort. **Pulmonaria oficinal**, common lungwort.

pulmonía [pool-mo-nee'-ah], *f.* Pneumonia, lung fever.

pulmoníaco ca, pulmonario, ria [pool-mo-nee'-ah-co, cah], *a.* Affected with inflammation of the lungs; pulmonary, pulmonic.

pulpa [pool'-pah], *f.* 1. Pulp, the most solid part of the flesh. 2. Pulp of fruit (de fruta). 3. *(Cono Sur)* Boneless meat.

pulpejo [pool-pay'-ho], *m.* The fleshy prominence of some organs of the body, especially the bell of the thumb or lobe of the ear.

pulpería [pool-pay-ree'-ah], *f.* In America, a grocery store (tienda), where all sorts of provisions and liquors are retailed. In Cuba, and some parts of South America, it is called *Bodega*.

pulpero [pool-pay'-ro], *m.* 1. In America, grocer. 2. Catcher of cuttle-fish.

pulpeta [pool-pay'-tah], *f.* Slice of stuffed meat.

pulpetón [pool-pay-tone'], *m. aug.* Large slice of stuffed meat.

púlpito [pool'-pe-to], *m.* 1. Pulpit. 2. The dignity or office of a preacher. **Paño de púlpito**, pulpit-cloth.

pulpo [pool'-po], *m.* Cuttle-fish, poulp, octopus.

pulposo, sa [pool-po'-so, sah], *a.* Pulpous, fleshy.

pulque [pool'-kay], *m.* Liquor prepared in America from the maguey or Agave Americana. **Pulque curado**, *(Coll. Mex.)* the same liquor, prepared with pineapple and sugar; a common beverage in that country.

pulquería [pool-kay-ree'-ah], *f.* The Place where the liquor *pulque* is sold.

pulsación [pool-sah-the-on'], *f.* 1. Pulsation. 2. Pulse, the beating of an artery (latido). 3. Tap (en máquina de escribir). 4. *(Comput.)* **Pulsación doble**, strike over.

pulsada [pool-sah'-dah], *f.* Any pulse beat.

pulsador, ra [pool-sah-dor', rah], *m. & f.* One who examines the pulse.

pulsar [pool-sar'], *va.* 1. To touch. *V.* TOCAR. 2. To feel the pulse. 3. To explore, to try, to sound or examine an affair. -*vn.* To pulsate, to beat as the pulse.

pulsátil [pool-sah'-teel], *a.* 1. Sounding when struck, as bells. 2. *V.* PULSATIVO.

pulsativo, va [pool-sah-tee'-vo, vah], *a.* Pulsing, beating.

pulsatorio, ria [pool-sah-to'-re-o, ah], *a.* Relating to the pulse.

pulsear [pool-say-ar'], *vn.* To test who has most strength in the wrists by grasping hands and resting the elbows on a table (entre dos personas).

pulsera [pool-say'-rah], *f.* 1. Bandage-applied to a vein or artery. 2. Bracelet for the wrists. **Pulsera para reloj**, watch strap.

pulsímetro [poo-see'-may-tro]. *m.* 1. Pulsimeter, an instrument for learning the readiness with which evaporation is effected in a vacuum. 2. Pulsimeter, an instrument for measuring the rapidity of the pulse.

pulsión [pool-se-on'], *f.* Propulsion, propagation of undulatory motion in an elastic fluid.

pulsista [pool-sees'-tah], *m. & a.* Applied to a medical man well skilled in the doctrine of the pulse.

pulso [pool'-so], *m.* 1. Pulse, the beating of an artery, perceived by the touch. 2. Part of the wrist where the pulse is felt (muñeca). **Echar un pulso a**, to have a trial of strengh with. **Levantar una silla a pulso**, to lift a chair with one hand. 3. Steadiness of the hand (firmeza). **A pulso**, with the strength of the hand. 4. Attention, care, circumspection. **Obra con gran pulso**, he acts with a great deal of circumspection. **Tomar el pulso**, (1) to feel the pulse. (2) To feel one's pulse, to try or know one's mind artfully. 5. *(And.)* V. PULSERA.

pultáceo, cea [pool-tah'-thay-o, ah], *a.* Pultaceous, semifluid.

pululante [poo-loo-lahn'-tay], *pa.* Pullulating.

pulular [poo-loo-lar'], *vn.* 1. To pullulate, to germ, to bud. 2. To multiply with great rapidity, as bacteria or insects. 3. To swarm (estar plagado), to be lively.

pulverizable [pool-vay-re-thah'-blay], *a.* Reducible to powder; pulverable, pulverizable.

pulverización [pool-vay-re-thah-the-on'], *f.* Pulverization (de sólidos), comminution, spray (de perfume, insecticida).

pulverizador de átomos [pool-vah-ree-thah-dore' day ah'-to-mos], *m.* Atom smasher.

pulverizar [pool-vay-re-thar'], *va.* To pulverize (sustancia), to grind, to comminute, to powder (reducir a polvo), to spray (plantas).

pulverulento, ta [pool-vay-roo-len'-to, tah], *a.* Pulverulent, dusty (superficie), in the storm of powder.

pulzol, puzol, punzó [pool-thole', poon-the'], *m. & a.* A bright scarlet color.

pulla [pool'-layah], *f.* 1. Loose, obscene expression. 2. Repartee, witty saying. 3. Eagle that dwells in the trunks of trees.

pullista [pool-lyees'-tah], *com.* One fond of witty sayings, or who says loose expressions.

pum! [poom], *int.* Bang! exclamation expressing a noise, explosion, or knock.

puma [poo'-mah], *m. (Zool.)* Puma, the American panther or cougar.

pumarada [poo-ma-rah'-dah], *f.* An Asturian name for an apple-orchard.

puna [poo'-nah], *f. (Peru and Bol.)* 1. A lofty, bleak region, uninhabitable through cold. 2. Difficulty of breathing from rarefied air. *Cf.* VETA.

punción [poon-the-on'], *f.* Puncture of a swelling to evacuate it.

puncha [poon'-chah], *f.* Thorn, prick, anything that pricks the flesh.

pundonor [poon-do-nor'], *m.* Point of honor (honra); punctiliousness.

pundonorcillo [poon-do-nor-theel'-lyo], *m.* Punctilio.

pundonorosamente [poon-do-no-ro-sah-men-tay], *adv.* Punctiliously.

pundonoroso, sa [poon-do-no-ro'-so, sah], *a.* Having a nice sense of honor (honrado), punctilious (escrupuloso).

punganos [poon-gah'-nos], *m. pl.* Instruments to open cockles, oysters, etc.

pungente [poon-gen'-tay], *pa.* Pungent.

pungimiento [poon-he-me-en'-to], *m.* Act of punching or pricking.

pungir [poon-heer'], *va.* 1. To punch, to prick (punzar). 2. To stimulate the passions, the spirit, the heart.

pungitivo, va [poon-he-tee'-vo, vah], *a.* Punching, pricking.

punible [poo-nee'-blay], *a. (Law.)* Punishable, actionable.

punición [poo-ne-the-on'], *f.* Punishment, chastisement.

púnico, ca [poo'-ne-co, cah], *a.* Punic, relating to the Carthaginians.

punki [poon'-ke], *a.* Punk. *-m & f.* Punk.

punta [poon'-tah], *f.* 1. Point, the sharp end of an instrument (extremo puntiagudo). 2. Extremity of anything which terminates in an angle; top, head, summit; point, prong, nib, tip. 3. Point, headland, promontory. 4. Prong of an antler. 5. Tartness, sour taste. 6. Point-lace. 7. *(typ.)* A bodkin for picking type from a form. 8. Somewhat, some good points: implying a high grade of intellectual or moral qualities (used with *tener.*) 9. Tracing-point, style, graver. 10. The end of a log, after beams, etc., have been sawed from it. 11. The pointing out of game by a dog. **De puntas**, on tiptoe, softly. **Puntas**, scallops (vestido). **Tener algo en la punta de la lengua**, to have something on the tip of one's tongue. **Se le pusieron los pelos de punta**, her hair stood on end. **Horas punta**, rush hours. **Sacar punta a**, to sharpen, to find fault with. **Ir de punta en blanco**, to get all dressed up. 12. Small nail (clavo). 13. *(Carib.)* Best quality tobacco (tabaco). 14. *(LAm.)* Group (grupo). 15. **En punta**, *(CAm.)* wholesome.

puntación [poon-tah-the-on'], *f.* Punctuation. V. PUNTUACIÓN.

puntada [poon-tah'-dah], *f.* 1. Stitch with a needle and thread. **Puntada cruzada**, cross-stitch. 2. Word carelessly dropped in conversation (indirecta). 3. *(LAm. Med.)* Stitch; sharp pain (dolor agudo). 4. *(Mex.)* Witty remark, witticism.

punta de combate [poon'-tah day com-bah-tay], *f. (Mil.)* Warhead.

puntal [poon-tahl'], *m.* 1. Prop to support a wall or building; fulcrum. 2. The stay in the bed of a plough-share. 3. *(Naut.)* Stanchion. **Puntal de la bodega**, *(Naut.)* depth of the hold.

puntapié [poon-tah-pe-ay'], *m.* A kick. **Mandar (a alguno) a puntapié**, to have complete ascendency over one.

puntar [poon-tar'], *va.* To mark with small dots or points.

punteado [poon-tay-ah-do], *a.* Dotted (moteado), covered with dots; stippled (grabado con puntos). *-m.* Series of dots; stippling.

punteadura [poon-tay-ah-doo'-rah], *f.* Teeth of a wheel.

puntear [poon-tay-ar'], *va.* 1. To play upon the guitar. 2. To punctuate, to mark, to point out. 3. To sew, to stitch. 4. *(Cono Sur)* To fork over (tierra). 5. *(Cono Sur)* To head (marcha). *-vn. (Naut.)* To go obliquely, catching the wind when it is slack.

puntel [poon-tel'], *m.* Pontil or pontee, a glass-blower's iron rod.

puntera [poon-tay'-rah], *f.* 1. *(Bot.)* Common houseleek. 2. A patch over the tip of a shoe (de zapato). 3. Tip, a re-enforcing piece put over the toe of a shoe. 4. *(coll.)* A kick (puntapié).

puntería [poon-tay-ree'-ah], *f.* 1. The act of levelling or pointing firearms. 2. Aim, the direction of a weapon (el apuntar). 3. Teeth of a wheel. **Tener mala puntería**, to be a bad shot.

punterico, illo, ito [poon-tay-ree'-co], *m. dim.* A little fescue.

puntero [poon-tay'-ro], *m.* 1. Fescue, a pointer to point out letters to children (palo). 2. A pointed instrument for marking anything, puncheon (herrero). 3. Chisel used by stone-cutters. 4. Graver, style. 5. *(LAm. Dep.)* Leading team, team which is ahead. 5. *(LAm.)* Hand (de reloj). **Puntero de celda (resaltar)**, cell pointer (highlight).

puntero, ra [poon-tay'-ro, rah], *a.* Taking good aim with firearms.

punterola [poon-tay-ro'-lah], *f. (Min.)* Poll-pick, a bar of iron with a steel point.

puntiagudo, da [poon-te-ah-goo'-do, dah], *a.* Sharp-pointed, mucronated.

puntica, ita [poon-tee'-cah], *f. dim.* A small point or sharp end of an instrument.

puntico, ito [poon-tee'-co], *m. dim.* of PUNTO.

puntilla [poon-teel'-lyah], *f.* 1. A small point. 2. A narrow lace edging. **De puntillas**, softly, gently; on tiptoe. **Ponerse de puntillas**, to persist obstinately in one's opinion. 3. *(Mech.)* Brad, joiner'snail; a carpenter's tracing-point. 4. V. CACHETE.

puntillazo [poon-til-lyah'-tho], *m.* Kick.

puntillo [poon-teel'-lyo], *m.* 1. Punctilio, trifling, despicable thing, in which a punctilious person places honor. 2. *(dim.)* A small point.

puntillón [poon-til-lyone'], *m.* Kick. V. PUNTILLAZO.

puntilloso, sa [poon-til-lyo'-so, sah], *a.* Ticklish, difficult, litigious, punctilious.

puntizón [poon-te-thone'], *m.* Holes pricked in the paper sheet by the frisket.

punto [poon'-to], *m.* 1. Dot, point (señal). 2. Point, subject under consideration (en discusión). 3. End or design. 4. Degree, state. 5. Nice point of ceremony: point of honor; punctilio. 6. Opportunity, fit place or time (lugar, tiempo). **Al punto**, instantly. 7. Point, period in writing. 8. Aim, sight. 9. Stitch, in sewing or surgery. 10. Point, gist, substance of a matter. 11. Actual state of any business matter. 12. Turn, finished state of something prepared by the fire. 13. Part or question of a science. 14. The smallest part of a thing. 15. Tumbler of a gun-lock. 16. Hole in stockings; mesh of a net; vacancy in lace. 17. Right sound of musical instruments. 18. Part of the bell where the clapper strikes. 19. Weight used in passementerie to keep the narrow linens stretched. 20. In straps, a hole for receiving the tongue of a buckle. 21. Speckle, dot upon the face of a silk fabric which bears no special design. 22. Each nib of a pen. 23. A fine cloth of thread cotton, or silk (material). 24. In schools, each mistake of a scholar in reciting a lesson from memory. 25. Dot, spot, on dice or cords. 26. End of the course in universities, recess, intermission in business in courts, when the time of vacation arrives. 27. Highest point or pitch. 28. Cab-stand, fixed place for public vehicles for hire. 29. Point object of destination or action. 30. Twelfth part of a line. 31. *(Comput.)* Spot. **Poner los puntos muy altos**, to soar very high; to make extravagant pretensions. **Punto de malla**, mesh of a net. **Punto de media**, stocking-net. **Punto de tul**, tulle. **En su último punto**, in the highest pitch. **Punto crudo**, the moment in which something happens. **A punto fijo**, exactly, with certainty. **Punto de apoyo**, point of support, fulcrum. **Bajar de punto**, to decay, to decline. **Punto**, or **punto final**, period. **Punto y coma**, semicolon. **Dos puntos**, Colon. **Vencer por puntos**, to win on points. **Punto del revés**, purl. **Punto de parada**, breakpoint. **Punto de arranque**, starting point. **Hemos llegado a un punto muerto**, we have reached deadlock. **Llegar a punto**, to come just at the right moment. **Estar en su punto**, *(Culin.)* to be done to a turn.

puntoso, sa [poon-to'-so, sah], *a.* 1 Acuminated, having many points. 2. Spirited, lively, courageous. 3. Too punctilious in etiquette.

puntuación [poon-too-ah-the-on'], *f.* 1. Punctuation. 2. Marking (escuela).

puntual [poon-too-ahl'], *a.* 1. Punctual (llegada), exact (cálculo), accurate. 2. Certain, sure. 3. Convenient, adequate.

puntualidad [poon-too-ah-le-dahd'], *f.* 1. Punctuality (exactitud), exactness (precisión). 2. Certitude, preciseness.

puntualizar [poon-too-ah-le-thar'], *va.* 1. To imprint on the mind or memory (recordar). 2. To finish, to accomplish, to complete. 3. To give a detailed account (precisar).

puntualmente [poon-too-ahl'-men-tay] *adv.* Punctually, exactly, faithfully, accurately.

puntuar [poon-too-ar'], *va.* To punctuate, to point, to evaluate (valorar): to mark (examen).

puntuoso, sa [poon-too-o'-so, sah], *adv.* V. PUNTOSO and PUNDOROSO.

puntura [poon-too'-rah], *f.* 1. Puncture. 2. Point which holds the sheet in a printing-press.

punzada [poon-thah'-dah], *f.* 1. Prick, push. 2. Sting, pain; compunction.

punzador, ra [poon-thah-dor', rah], *m. & f.* Pricker, wounder.

punzadura [poon-thah-doo'-rah], *f.* Puncture, prick.

punzante [poon-than'-tay], *a.* 1. Shooting (dolor). 2. Sharp (herramienta). 3. *(Fig.)* Biting (comentario).

punzar [poon-thar'], *va.* 1. To punch, to bore or perforate. 2. To prick (pinchar), to wound. 3. To sting, to cause pain (dolor). 4. To sting or afflict the mind.

punzó, or **punzón** [poon-tho'], *a.* Deep scarlet red.

punzón [poon-thone'], *m.* 1. Punch, an instrument used by artists and workmen; puncheon, puncher; typefounder's punch. 2. Young horn of a deer.

punzonar [poon-tho-nar'], *va.* To punch.

punzoncico, illo, ito [poon-thon-thee'-co], *m. dim.* A small punch.

punzonería [poon-tho-nay-ree'-ah], *f.* Collection of moulds for making a fount of types.

puñada [pooh-nyah'-dah], *f.* Cuff, blow with the fist. *-pl.* Fisticuffs.

puñado [pooh-nyah'-do], *m.* Handful; a few. **A puñados**, plentifully, abundantly. **¡Gran puñado**! or; **¡qué puñado!** *(coll.)* expression of contempt for the quantity or the quality of a thing offered.

puñal [pooh-nyahl'], *m.* Poniard, dagger.

puñalada [pooh-nyay-lah'-dah], *f.* 1. Stab with a dagger, knife. 2. A sudden blow or shock of grief or pain. **Dar** or **tirar una puñalada a uno**, to make a pass at a person. **Murió de una puñalada**, he was stabbed to death.

puñalejo [pooh-nyah-lay'-ho], *m. dim.* Small poniard.

puñalero [pooh-nyah-lay'-ro], *m.* Maker or seller of poniards.

puñeta [pooh-nyay'-tah], *f.* 1. Silly thing (bobada); silly complaint (queja); stupid remark (dicho). 2. **Hacer la puñeta a uno**, to muck somebody around. **Tengo un catarro de la puñeta**, I've got a bloody awful cold.

puñetazo [pooh-nyay-tah'-tho], *m.* Punch, blow with the fist shut. **Dar puñetazos en**, to hammer on.

puñete [pooh-nyay'-tay], *m.* Blow with the fist. **Puñetes**, bracelets for the wrists.

puño [pooh'-nyo], *m.* 1. The fist, 2. Handful (cantidad), grasp. 3. Scantiness, narrowness. 4. Wristband. 5. Handruffle; cuff, mittens. 6. Hilt (de espada), guard of a sword; handle (de herramienta); head of a staff or cane. 7. *(Naut.)* Each of the lower points of a sail in which the tacks are fastened. **Apretar los puños**, to exert the utmost efforts. **Pegar a puño cerrado**, to strike with might and main. **Hombre de puños**, a strong, valiant man. **Ser como un puño**, to be miserable; close-fisted. **De propio puño**, in one's own handwriting.

puones [poo-oh'-nes], *m. pl.* The large, uneven teeth of cards.

pupa [poo'-pah], *f.* 1. Pustule, pimple, blister (ampolla); lip sore (úlcera). 2. The plaintive sound of children to express uneasiness.

pupila [poo-pee'-lah],*f.* 1. Pupil of the eye. 2. Orphan girl, ward.

pupilaje [poo-pe-lah'hay], *m.* 1. Pupilage, wardship. 2. Board, the state of one who boards with another. 3. Boarding-house.

pupilar [poo-pe-lar'], *a.* Pupillary, belonging to a pupil or ward, or to the pupil of the eye.

pupilero, ra [poo-pe-lay'-ro, rah], *m. & f.* Master or mistress of a boarding house or boarding-school.

pupilo [poo-pee'-lo], *m.* 1. Pupil, ward. 2. Pupil, scholar; student.

pupitre [poo-pee'-tray], *m.* A writing-desk.

puposo, sa [poo-po'-so, sah], *a.* Pustulous, pustulate.

puramente [poo-rah-men'-tay], *adv.* Purely, chastely; entirely, merely: genuinely.

puré [poo-ray'], *m.* Puree, thick soup. **Puré de patatas**, mashed potatoes. **Puré de manzanas**, apple sauce.

pureza [poo-ray'-thah], *f.* Purity, innocence, integrity; chastity; purity of diction; fineness, genuineness; cleanness, excellence.

purga [poor'-gah], *f.* 1. Purge, a cathartic medicine. 2. *(Amer.)* Refining, especially of sugar.

purgable [poor-gah'-blay], *a.* That may be purged.

purgación [poor-gah'-the-on'], *f.* 1. Purgation. 2. Catamenia. 3. Gonorrhoea, gleet: commonly used in the plural. 4. Act of clearing from imputation of guilt.

purgador, ra [poor-gah-dor', rah], *m. & f.* One who purges, purger.

purgante [poor-gahn'-tay], *a. & m.* Purgative, laxative, cleanser.

purgar [poor-gar'], *va.* 1. To purge, to purify, to cleanse. 2. To atone, to expiate (pecado). 3. To purify (purificar), to refine. 4. To suffer the penalties of purgatory. 5. To purge, to evacuate the body. 6. To clear from guilt or imputation of guilt. -*vr.* To rid or clear oneself from guilt.

purgativo, va [poor-gah-tee'-vo, vah], *a.* Purgative, cathartic, purging.

purgatorio [poor-gah-to'-re-o], *m.* 1. Purgatory. 2. Any place where life is imbittered by painful drudgery and troubles.

purificación [poo-re-fe-cah-the-on'], *f.* 1. Purification, making pure, cleansing, expurgation. 2. Purification, a festival of the Christian church, on 2nd February. 3. The ancient act of churching women. 4. Cleansing the chalice after the wine is drunk at mass.

purificadero, ra [poo-re-fe-cah-day'-ro, rah], *a.* Cleansing, purifying.

purificador, ra [poo-re-fe-cah-dor', rah], *m. & f.* 1. Purifier, purger. 2. Purificator, the cloth with which the priest wipes the chalice.

purificar [poo-re-fe-car'], *va.* To purify, to clean, to cleanse, to clear, to fine. -*vr.* 1. To be purified, to be cleansed. 2. To be churched.

purificatorio, ria [poo-re-fe-cah-to'-re-o, ah], *a.* Purificatory, purificative.

puriforme [poo-re-for-may], *a.* Puriform, presenting the appearance of pus.

purísima (La) [lah poo-ree'-se-mah], *f.* Epithet of the Virgin Mary in the mystery of her immaculate conception.

purismo [poo-rees'-mo], *m.* The act of affecting too much purity of diction, purism.

purista [poo-rees'-tah], *m.* 1. Purist, one over-particular as to purity of literary style. 2. One who writes or speaks in a pure style.

puritanismo [poo-re-tah-nees'-mo], *m.* Puritanism.

puritano, na [poo-re-tah'-no, nah], *a.* Puritan (iglesia, tradición), puritanical (actitud), puritanic.

puritano, na [], *m. dim.* A Puritan.

puro, ra [poo'-ro, rah], *a.* 1. Pure (color, lengua, sustancia), free, unmingled. 2. Pure, clear (cielo), clean, neat, genuine, net, fine. 3. Pure (moralmente), chaste, modest. 4. Pure, guiltless, innocent, just. 5. Pure, incorrupt, not vitiated, exempt from imperfections. 6. *(Mex.)* Only, just. 7. *(And. Carib. Mex.)* Identical. -*m.* Cigar, a little roll of tobacco for smoking, to distinguish it from *cigarro* and *cigarrillo*, a small roll of paper filled with fine-chopped tobacco. **De puro aburrimiento**, out of sheer boredom. **Por pura casualidad**, by sheer chance.

púrpura [poor'-poo-rah], *f.* 1. Rockshell, purple-shell, royal purple. 2. Cloth dyed with purple. 3. Dignity of a king or cardinal. 4. *(Poet.)* Blood.

purpurante [poor-poo-rahn'-tay], *pa.* Giving a purple color.

purpurar [poor-poo-rar'], *va.* 1. To purple, to make red. 2. To dress in purple. 3. To take or show a purple color.

purpúreo, rea [poor-poo'-ray-o, ah], *a.* 1. Purple. 2. Belonging to a cardinal or to the cardinalate.

purpúrico [poor-poo'-re-co], *a.* **Ácido purpúrico**, purpuric acid, obtained by treating uric acid with nitric acid; murexide.

purpurina [poor-poo-ree'-nah], *f.* 1. Bronze ground for painting. 2. Purpurin, a coloring matter obtained from madder.

purpurino, na [poor-poo-re'-no, nah], *a.* Pùrple.

purrela [poor-ray'-lah], *f.* Wine of the most inferior quality.

purriela [poor-re-ay'-lah], *f.* Anything despicable or of little value.

purulencia [poo-roo-len'-the-ah], *f.* Purulence, purulency.

purulento, ta [poo-roo-len'-to, tah], *a.* Purulent.

pus [poos], *m.* Pus.

pusilánime [poo-se-lah'-ne-may], *a.* Pusillanimous, mean-spirited, dastardly, timorous, faint-hearted.

pusilanimemente [poo-se-lah'-ne-may-men-tay]; *adv.* Heartlessly.

pusilanimidad [poo-se-lah-ne-me-dahd'], *f.* Pusillanimity, cowardliness, timorousness.

pústula [poos'-too-lah], *f.* Pustule, pimple.

pustoloso, sa [poos-to-lo'-so, sah], *a.* Pustulous, pustular.

puta [poo'-tah], *f.* Whore, prostitute, harlot. **Casa de putas**, brothel. -*a.* Bloody; bloody awful. **De puta madre**, terrific.

putada [poo-tah'-dah], *f.* Dirty trick.

putaísmo, putanismo [poo-tah-ees'-mo], *m.* Whoredom, harlotry.

putañear [poo-tah-nyay-ar'], *vn.* *(Low.)* To whore, to go whoring.

putañero [poo-tah-nyay'-ro], *a.* *(Low.)* Whorish, given to lewdness. -*m.* Whoremaster, whoremonger.

putativo, va [poo-tah-tee'-vo, vah], *a.* Putative, reputed.

puteado [poo-tay-ah'-do], *a.* 1. Corrupted (maleado), perverted. 2. Fed up (harto).

puteal [poo-tay-ahl'], *m.* Stone used as the cover of a well on which soothsayers prophesied.

putear [poo-tay-ar'], *va.* 1. To corrupt malear), to pervert. 2. To mess around (fastidiar). 3. To kick around (maltratar). 4. To upset (enfadar). 4. *(LAm.)* To swear at (insultar). -*vn.* 1. To go whoring (ir de putas). 2. To have a rough time of it (padecer).

putería [poo-tay-ree'-ah], *f.* *(Low.)* 1. The manner of living and trade of a prostitute. 2. Brothel. 3. Meretricious arts of lewd women.

putero [poo-tay'-ro], *m.* *(Low.)* Whoremaster, whoremonger.

putesco, ca [poo-tes'-co, cah], *a.* *(coll.)* Relating to whores.

putilla, ita [poo-teel'-lyah], *f. dim.* *(coll.)* Young prostitute.

puto [poo'-to], *m.* *(Low.)* Catamite, sodomite. -*a.* Bloody, bloody awful.

putput [poot'-poot], *m.* *(Orn.)* Hoopoe. *V.* ABUBILLA.

putredinal [poo-tray-de-nahl'], *a.* Putrefying, corrupting.

putrefacción [poo-tray-fac-the-on'], *f.* Putrefaction, corruptness.

putrefactivo, va [poo-tray-fac-tee'-vo, vah], *a.* Putrefactive.

putrefacto [poo-tray-fahc'-to], *a.* Rotten, putrid; decayed.

putridez [poo-tre-deth'], *f.* Putridity.

pútrido, da [poo'-tre-do, dah], *a.* Putrid, rotten.

puya [poo'-yah], *f.* Pointed rod.

puyero, ra [poo-yay'-ro, rah], *m. & f.* *(Cuba)* 1. *V.* PULLISTA. 2. One who is knock-kneed.

puzol, *m.* **puzolana**, *f.* [poo-thole', pool-tho-lah'-nah]. Puzzolana, a porous volcanic production.

Q

q [koo], eighteenth letter of the Spanish alphabet, which is always followed by *u*; it sounds as the English *k*.

Qbus [o-boos]. *(Inform.)* Qbus.

que [kay], *pron. rel.* 1. That. 2. Who (persona, sujeto), speaking of persons. 3. Which (cosa), speaking of things. 4. What, a particle expressive of admiration. **¡Qué desgracia!** what a misfortune! 5. What as an interrogative. **¿Qué es eso?** or **¿qué cosa es esa?** what is that? **¿Qué es eso?** or **¿qué hay?** what is the matter, or what is the matter there? 6. Than, as, a comparative particle: **más qué** or **más de**, more than, **tanto que**, as much as. **Algo que** something that. 7. Whether. **Que venga o que no venga**, whether he comes or not. **Más bien tarde que temprano**, rather sooner than later. 8. Because, why. 9. *conj.* Used after a verb it is a particle, which governs and determines another verb. **Le mandó que viniese**, he ordered him to come. 10. Where, in what place? **¿Qué es del libro?** Where is the book? 11. **Lo que**, that which. **Sea lo que fuere**, let it be what it may. **Hay en eso algo más de lo que se presume.** There is in that affair more than what is imagined. **No hay para qué**, there is no occasion for it. **No hay de qué**, don't mention it; you are welcome. **Sin qué ni para qué**, without cause or motive. Note.—*Que* in interrogatory or exclamatory use receives the accent to distinguish it from the relative and the conjunction. See the examples.

-Conj. Not translated. **Quiero que vayas**, I want you to go. **Te dije que lo hicieras**, I told you to do it. **me apuesto a que no lo haces**, I bet you don't do it. **¡Que to diviertas!**, enjoy yourself!

-Adj. interr. What. **¿Qué hora es?**, What time is it? **¿Qué quieres?**, what do you want? **¡Qué de gente!**, what a lot of people! **¿Qué te parece?**, what do you think of it?

quebrable [kay-brah'-blay], *a.* Breakable.

quebrada [kay-brah'-dah], *f.* 1. Ravine. 2. A deep pass (puerto). 3. A commercial failure.

quebradero [kay-brah-day'-ro], *m.* Breaker. **Quebradero de cabeza**, 1. That which molests, importunes, or occupies the mind. 2. Object of amorous care.

quebradillo [kay-brah-deel'-lyo], *m.* 1. Wooden shoe-heel. 2. Flexure of the body in dancing.

quebradizo, za [kay-brah-dee'-tho, thah], *a.* 1. Brittle, fragile. 2. Infirm, sickly. 3. Flexible (voz). 4. *(Met.) V.* FRÁGIL.

quebrado, da [kay-brah'-do, dah], *a.* Broken (terreno); debilitated, enervated. *-pp.* of QUEBRAR.

quebrado [kay-brah'-do], *m.* 1. *(Arith.)* Fraction, broken number. 2. *(Poet.)* Verse consisting of two, three, or four syllables, left so on purpose after a stanza of verses of eight or more syllables. 3. Bankrupt. 4. *(coll.)* A ruptured person.

quebrador, ra [kay-brah-dor', rah], *m. & f.* 1. Breaker. 2. One who violates a law.

quebradura [kay-brah-doo'-rah], *f.* 1. The act of breaking or splitting. 2. A cleaving or chopping, a gap, a fissure, a slit, a fracture. 3. Rupture, hernia.

quebraja [kay-brah'-hah], *f.* Crack, flaw, split in wood or iron.

quebrajar [kay-brah-har'], *va. V.* RESQUEBRAJAR.

quebrajoso, sa [kay-brah-ho'-so, sah], *a.* Brittle, fragile.

quebramiento [kay-brah-me-en'-to], *m. V.* QUEBRANTAMIENTO.

quebrantable [kay-brah-tah'-blay], *a.* Frangible, brittle.

quebrantador, ra [kay-bran-tah-dor', rah], *m. & f.* 1. Breaker; debilitator. 2. *(Met.)* Violator, transgressor of any law.

quebrantadura [kay-bran-tah-doo'-rah], *f.* Fracture, rupture, a bursting.

quebrantahuesos [kay-bran-tah-oo-ay'-sos], *m.* 1. *(Orn.)* Osprey. 2. A troublesome person, bore (pesado).

quebrantamiento [kay-bran-tah-me-en'-to], *m.* 1. Fracture, rupture; breaking a prison. 2. Weariness, fatigue. 3. Violation of the law; e. g. (a) *(Law.)* Act of breaking a will. (b) **quebrantamiento** or **robo de una casa**, burglary. (c) **Quebrantamiento de sepultura**, desecration of a grave.

quebrantanueces [kay-bran-tah-noo-ay'-thes], *m.* *(Orn.)* Nutcracker.

quebrantaolas [kay-bran-tah-o'-las], *m.* Breakwater.

quebrantar [kay-bran-tar'], *va.* 1. To break (romper), to crack, to burst open, to crash. 2. To pound, to grind. 3. To persuade, to induce. 4. To move to pity. 5. To transgress a law, to violate a contract. 6. To vex, to molest, to fatigue. 7. To weaken, to debilitate (resistencia). 8. To diminish, to temper the excess of anything. 9. To annul, to revoke; to break a will. 10. To shatter (posición). 11. To tone down (color). 12. *(LAm.)* To break in (caballo). *-vr.* To be shattered (persona).

quebrantaterrones [kay-brahn-tah-ter ro'-nes], *m. (coll.)* Clodhopper, rustic.

quebranto [kay-brahn'-to], *m.* 1. The act of breaking. 2. Weakness, debility, lassitude. 3. Commiseration, pity, compassion. 4. Object worthy of pity. 5. Great loss (pérdida), severe damage (daño). 6. *(Naut.)* Cambering of a ship's deck or keel. 7. Depression (depresión). 8. Sorrow (aflicción).

quebrar [kay-brar'], *va.* 1. To break (romper), to burst open; to cast asunder. 2. To double, to twist (torcer). 3. To interrupt, to intercept. 4. To transgress a law, to violate a contract. 5. To temper, to moderate. 6. To spoil the bloom of the countenance. 7. To overcome, to conquer. 8. To diminish friendship, to dissolve a connection, or abandon a correspondence. 9. To tone down. *-vn.* To fail, to be insolvent, to become bankrupt. *-vr.* 1. To be ruptured, to labor under a rupture. 2. To interrupt the continuity of hills or banks. **Quebrar amistad**, to cut acquaintance. **Quebrar el corazón**, to break one's heart. **Quebrarse la cabeza**, to be oversolicitous in the pursuit of anything. *(Yo quiebro, quiebre,* from *Quebrar. V.* ALENTAR.)

queche [kay'-chay], *f. (Naut.)* Smack, a Dutch-built vessel; ketch.

quechemarín [kay-chay-mah-reen'], *m.* Coasting lugger.

quechua [kay'-choo-ah], *a. & m.* Kechuan, the official language of the Peruvian empire at the time of the conquest.

queda [kay'-dah], *f.* The time of retirement marked by the sound of a bell or the beat of a drum; curfew.

quedada [kay-dah'-dah], *f.* Stay, residence, sojourn.

quedar [kay-dar'], *vn.* 1. To stay, to stop in a place. 2. To continue, to tarry, to remain (en un estado). 3. To be wanting. 4. To hold, to last, to subsist. 5. To knock down a thing to the last bidder. 6. To behave, to conduct oneself, to acquire a reputation or to be reputed. **Quedar por andar**, to have to walk farther. **Quedar por cobarde**, to shrink back as a coward. **Quedar por valiente**, to enjoy the reputation of a brave man. **Quedar limpio**, *(coll.)* to remain with an empty purse, to be square. **Quedar con uno**, to agree, to arrange or compound with anyone. 7. With a past participle it is often employed in place of *estar*, to be. **Quedar armado**, to be armed. **Quedar bien** or **mal**, to behave or come off well or ill in an affair: to fail or succeed in an attempt. **Quedar ciego**, to go blind. **Ha quedado como un canalla**, he showed himself a swine. **Nos queda poco dinero**, we haven't much money left. **Quedan pocos días para la fiesta**, only a few days remain till the party. **Quedar en**, to turn out to be. *-va. (Prov.)* To leave. *-vr.* 1. To remain, to continue; to retain, to possess, to keep. 2. To falter, to lose the thread of a speech or argument; to stop short. 3. *(Cono Sur)* To become paralysed (miembro). **Quedarse helado**, to be astonished, to be thunderstruck. **Quedarse en ayunas de alguna cosa**, not to understand a word of the matter. **Quedarse a obscuras** or **en blanco**, to be left in the dark (literally or figuratively); to be left in the lurch. **Quedársele a uno en el tintero**, to forget a thing entirely. **Quedarse con unos amigos**, to stay with some friends. **Se quedó con mi pluma**, he kept my pen. **Quedarse con uno**, to bore the pants off somebody (aburrir).

quedito, ta [kay-dee'-to, tah], *a. dim.* Soft, gentle; easy. This diminutive is more energetic than its primitive, *quedo.*

quedito [kay-dee'-to], *adv. V.* QUEDO.

quedo [kay'-do], *adv.* Softly, gently; in a low voice.

Q-Z

quedo, da [kay'-do, dah], *a.* Quiet (voz), still (inmóvil), noiseless; easy, gentle.

quehacer [kay-ah-therr '] *m.* Occupation, domestic business (chore). **Cada uno tiene sus quehaceres.** Every one has his own affairs. **Tener mucho que hacer,** to have a lot to do.

queirópteros [kay-rop'-tay-ros], *a. & m. pl.* Cheiropterous; the cheiroptera, the bats.

queja [kay'-hah], *f.* 1. Complaint, expostulation, murmur, grumbling, moan (quejido). 2. Resentment of an injury or insult. 3. Quarrel, dispute. **Tener una queja de alguno,** *(coll.)* to have a bone to pick with one. **Presentar queja de uno,** to make a complaint about somebody.

quejarse [kay-har'-say], *vr.* To complain of, to expostulate, to murmur, to grumble (refunfuñar). **quejarse de,** to clamor against; to mention with sorrow, to lament. **Quejarse de vicio,** to complain without cause. *V.* QUERELLARSE.

quejicoso, sa [kay-he-co'-so, sah], *a.* Plaintful, querulous, always complaining.

quejidito [kay-he-dee'-to], *m. dim.* Slight complaint, a low moan.

quejido [kay-hee'-do], *m.* Groan, moan, lament.

quejigal [kay-he-gahl'], *m.* Plantation of muricated oaks.

quejigo [kay-hee'-go], *m. (Bot.)* Muricated oak.

quejita [kay-hee'-tah], *f. dim.* Murmur; resenting; slight complaint.

quejosamente [kay-ho-sah-men-tay], *adv.* Querulously.

quejoso, sa [kay-ho'-so, sah], *a.* Plaintful, querulous (tono).

quejumbre [key-hoom'-bray], *f. (Prov.) V.* QUEJA.

quejumbroso, sa [kay-hoom-bro'-so, sah]. *a.* Complaining, plaintive.

quelidón [kay-le-done'], *m.* Martin, a bird of the swallow family.

quelidonia [kay-le-do'-ne-ah], *f. (Bot.)* Celandine, an herb of the poppy family.

quelónidos [kay-lo'-ne-dos], or **quelonios,** *a. & m. pl.* Chelonieus: turtles and tortoises.

quema [kay'-mah], *m.* 1. Burn, the act of burning (acto), combustion, fire, conflagration. 2. *(Met.)* Oven, furnace.

quemado [kay-mah-do], *a.* 1. Burned, burnt. **Aquí huele a quemado,** I smell something burning in here. 2. Burned out (agotado). 3. Discredited (moralmente).

quemador, ra [kay-mah-dor', rah], *m. & f.* Incendiary; burner.

quemadura [kay-ma-doo'-rah], *f.* 1. Mark or hurt by fire, burn. 2. *(Agr.)* Brand, smut upon plants.

quemajoso, sa [kay-mah-ho'-so, sah], *a.* Smarting, burning.

quemar [kay-mar'], *va.* 1. To burn, to consume by fire. 2. To fire, to set on fire, to kindle. 3. To burn, to parch, to dry, or scorch. 4. To dispose of a tiling at a low price. 5. To scorch (líquido). 6. To cut (plantas). 7. To burn up (fortuna). 8. *(Fig.)* To annoy, to upset (molestar). 9. *(CAm. Mex.)* To denounce (denunciar). 10. *(Carib. Mex.)* To swindle (estafar). 11. *(Carib.)* To shoot (con arma de fuego). **Estar quemado con algo,** to be sick and tired of something. *-vn.* To be too hot. **Esto está que quema,** it's burning hot. *-vr.* 1. To be very hot, to be parched with heat; to heat oneself. 2. To fret, to be impatient, to be offended. 3. *(coll.)* To be near, to almost attain or touch a thing desired. 4. To burn oneself out (agotarse). 5. To fret (inquietarse). 6. *(Carib. Cono Sur)* To get depressed (deprimirse). 7. To be discredited (moralmente, políticamente). Quemaropa, (1) immediate, very near, quite close, contiguous. (2) *(Met.)* Unawares, unexpectedly: applied to an unanswerable argument, or to an action unobjectionable either from its promptitude or justice. **Quemarse la sangre,** to be subject to constant vexations. **¡Que te quemas!,** you're getting warm.

quemazón [kay-mah-thone'], *f.* 1. Burn, hurt by fire; combustion, conflagration. 2. The act of burning. 3. Excessive heat (calor). 4. Eagerness, covetousness. 5. *(coll.)* Pert language, smart repartee. 6. *(Cuba)* Auction where goods are sold very cheap.

quencho [ken'-cho], *m. (Orn.)* Gull.

quequisque [kay-kees'-kay], *m. (Bot.)* An arum.

queratitis [kay-rah-tee'-tis], *f.* Keratitis, inflammation of the cornea.

querella [kay-rayl'-lyah], *f. 1.* Complaint (queja), expression of pain or grief. 2. A complaint before a judge against anyone. 3. Petition or libel exhibited to a court of justice by children, praying that the last will of their parents be set aside.

querellador, ra [kay-rayl-lyah-dor', rah], *m. & f.* Lamenter; complainant.

querellante [kay-rayl-lyahn'-tay], *pa.* Murmuring, complaining. *-m. & f.* Complainant.

querellarse [kay-rayl-lyar'-say], *vr.* 1. To lament, to bewail one's own sorrow; to complain of another (quejarse), to be querulous. 2. To complain or prefer a complaint in a court of justice.

querellosamente [kay-rayl-lyo'-sah-men-tay], *adv.* Plaintively, querulously.

querelloso, sa [key-rayl-lyo'-so, sah], *a.* Querulous.

querencia [kay-ren'-the-ah], *f.* 1. Haunt of wild hearts. 2. Favorite and frequent place of resort.

querencioso, sa [kay-ren-the-o'-so, sah], *a.* Frequented by wild beasts.

querer [kay-rerr'], *va.* 1. To wish, to desire (desear), to list. **Quiero comer,** I have an appetite. 2. To love (amar), to cherish, to like. 3. To will, to resolve, to determine. 4. To attempt, to procure, to require (requerir). 5. To conform, to agree. 6. To accept a challenge at a game of hazard. 7. To suit, to fit. 8. To cause, to occasion. *-vn.* To be near being, to verify anything. **Sin querer,** unwillingly. **Querer más,** to have rather. **¿Qué quiere decir eso?** what does that mean? **¿Qué más quiere?** what more does he wish? what more is necessary? **Como Vd. quiera,** as you will it, let it be so. **Como quiera,** anyhow, in anyway. **Quien todo lo quiere, todo lo pierde,** *(Prov.)* all covet, all lose. **No quiero más,** I don't want any more. **Querer es poder,** where there's a will there's a way. **Pero no quiso,** but he refused. **Querer bien a uno,** to be fond of somebody. *-m.* Will, desire, study.

queresa [kay-ray'-sah], *f. V.* CRESA.

querido, da [kay-ree'-do, dah], *a. & pp* of QUERER. Wished, desired, dear, beloved (persona amada). *-m. & f.* Darling, fondling lover, sweetheart. **Querido, querida** or **querido mío,** my dear, my love, honey, my pet, my darling.

quermes [kayr'-mes], *m.* Kermes, an insect used as a scarlet dye. **Quermes mineral,** kermes mineral, a preparation of antimony.

querocha [kay-roh'-chah], *f. V.* CRESA.

querochar [kay-ro-char'], *m.* To emit the semen of bees.

querosina [kay-ro-see'-nah], *f.* Kerosene, coal oil.

querub, querube [kay'-roob]. *(Poet.) V.* QUERBÍN. *(Heb.)*

querúbico, ca [kay-roo'-be-co, cah], *a.* Cherubic, relating to cherubs.

querubín [kay-roo-been'], *m.* Cherub, a celestial spirit.

quesadilla [kay-sah-deel'-lyah], *f.* 1. A sort of cheese-cake (tarta). 2. A sweetmeat; a fritter.

quesear [kay-say-ar'], *vn.* To make cheese.

quesera [kay-say'-rah], *f.* 1. Dairy. 2. Cheese-board, cheese-mould, cheese-vat.

quesería [kay-say-ree'-ah], *f.* 1. Season for making cheese. 2. Dairy (tienda).

quesero [kay-say'-ro], *m.* Cheesemonger, cheesemaker.

quesero, ra [kay-say'-ro, rah], *a.* Caseous, cheesy.

quesillo, ito [kay-seel'-lyo], *m. dim.* A small cheese.

queso [kay'-so], *m.* 1. Cheese. 2. **Quesos** (pies), plates. **Queso de bola,** Dutch cheese.

quetzal [kee-thahl'], *m.* 1. *(Orn.)* Quetzal. 2. Quetzal, Guatemalan monetary unit.

¡quiá! [ke-ah']. Interjection denoting incredulity or denial. Come now! No, indeed!

quiasmo [ke-ahs'-mo], *m.* 1. Chiasm, junction of two things which form a cross. 2. *(Anat.)* Decussation of the optic nerves.

quibey [ke-bay'-e], *m. (Bot.)* Dog's bane, an herb which grows in the island of Puerto Rico, very poisonous to animals which eat it. The flower resembles a violet, but is white.

quiquicial, *m.* **quicialera,** *f* [ke-the-ahl'] [ke-the-ah-lay'-rah]. 1. Sidepost, or jamb of a door or window; a jamb. 2. *V.* QUICIO.

quicio [kee'-the-o], *m.* 1. Hinge of a door; a but-hinge. 2. Prop, support. **Fuera de quicio,** violently, unnaturally. **Sacar una cosa de quicio,** to unhinge, to overturn, to violate or pervert.

quid [kid], *m.* Essence, gist. **El quid del asunto,** the gist of the matter.

quídam [kee'-dam], *m. (coll.)* A certain person.

quiebra [ke-ay'-brah], *f.* 1. Crack (grieta), fracture. 2. Gaping or opening of the ground. 3. Loss, damage. 4. Failure, bankruptcy. 5. **Quiebras del terreno** or **de la tierra,** undulations of the ground or surface.

quiebrahacha [ke-ay-brah-ah'-chah], *m. (Cuba)* A tree much esteemed for the solidity and firmness of its wood; a kind of fir.

quiebro [ke-ay'-bro], *m.* 1. *(Mus.)* Trill. 2. Movement or inclination of the body.

quien [ke-en'], *pron. rel.* 1. Who, which. 2. One or the other. *V.* CUAL and QUE. When interrogative it is accented; as. **¿Quién ha venido?** who has come? **La señorita con quien hablaba,** the young lady to whom I was talking. **No hay quien lo aguante,** nobody can stand him.

quienquiera [ke-en-ke-ay'-rah], *pron.* Whosoever, whatever.

quietador, ra [ke-ay-tah-dor', rah], *m. & f.* Quieter.

quietamente [ke-ay'-tah-men-tay], *adv.* Quietly, calmly.

quietar [ke-ay-tar'], *va.* To appease. *V.* AQUIETAR.

quiete [ke-ay'-tay], *f.* Rest, repose, quiet.

quietismo [ke-ay-tees'-mo], *m.* Quietism, sect of mystics.

quietista [ke-ay-tees'-tah], *a. & m.* Quietist.

quieto, ta [ke-ay'-to, tah], *a.* 1. Quiet, still (inmóvil); undisturbed. 2. Quiet, peaceable, pacific (carácter). 3. Orderly, virtuous, moderate. **Estar quieto como un poste,** to stand stock-still.

quietud [ke-ay-tood'], *f.* Quietude, quietness, quiet, want of motion, rest, repose; tranquility.

quijada [ke-hah'-dah], *f.* Jaw or jawbone.

quijal, quijar [ke-hahl', ke-har'], *m.* Grinder, a back tooth; jaw.

quijarudo, da [ke-hah-roo'-do, dah], *a.* Large-jawed.

quijera [ke-hay'-rah], *f.* 1. Cheeks of a cross-bow. 2. Piece of leather on the headstall of a horse. 3. Among carpenters, a strengthening piece put on each side.

quijo [kee'-ho], *m.* A hard rock found in several mines as the matrix of ore.

quijones [ke-ho'-nes], *m. pl.* Dill, an aromatic herb resembling anise.

quijotada [ke-ho-tah'-dah], *f.* A quijotic enterprise, an action ridiculously extravagant.

quijote [ke-hoh'-tay], *m.* 1. Armor for the thigh. 2. A man who engages in quixotic enterprises. 3. Fleshy part over the hoofs of horses or asses.

quijotería [ke-ho-tay-ree'-ah], *f.* Quixotry, quixotism.

quijotesco, ca [ke-ho-tes'-co, cah], *a.* Quixotic.

quilatador [ke-lah-tah-dor'], *m.* Assayer of gold and silver.

quilatar [ke-lah-tar'], *va.* To assay gold and silver.

quilate [ke-lah'-tay], *m.* 1. Degree of purity of gold or precious stones. 2. A carat, the twenty-fourth part in weight and value of gold. 3. Weight of four grams. 4. An ancient coin. 5. Decree of perfection.

quilatera [ke-lah-tay'-rah], *f.* Instrument for ascertaining the carats of pearls.

quilo [ke-lo], *V.* KILO.

quilómetro [ke-loh'-may-tro], *m. V.* KILÓMETRO.

quiloso, sa [ke-lo'-so, sah], *a.* Chylous, chylaceous.

quilla [keel'-lyah], *f. (Naut.)* Keel of a ship. **Descubrir la quilla,** to heave down a ship. **Dar de quilla** or **tumbar a la quilla,** to careen, to overhaul a vessel.

quillaje [keel-lyah'-hay], *m.* Harbor dues which used to be paid in France.

quillotro, tra [kil-lyo'-tro, trah], *a. (coll.)* This or that other.

quimbámbulas [kim-bam'-boo-las], *f. pl. (Cuba)* Rough, craggy spots.

quimera [ke-may'-rah], *f.* 1. Dispute, quarrel (riña), scuffle, feud. 2. Chimera, wild fancy. 3. Hallucination (alucinación). 4. Unfounded suspicion (sospecha).

quimérico, ca, quimerino, na [ke-may'-re co, cah], *a.* Chimerical, fantastic, unreal.

quimerista [ke-may-rees'-tah], *m.* 1. Wrangler, brawler. 2. One who indulges in chimeras.

quimerizar [ke-may-re-thar'], *vn.* To fill the head with fantastic ideas.

química [kee'-me-cah], *f.* Chemistry. **Química de polímeros,** polymer chemistry.

químicamente [kee'-me-cah-men-tay], *adv.* Chemically.

químico [kee'-me-co], *m.* Chemist.

químico, ca [kee'-me-co, cah], *a.* Chemical.

quimificar [ke-me-fe-car'], *va.* To convert into chyme.

quimista [ke-mees'-tah], *m. V.* ALQUIMISTA.

quimo [kee'-mo], *m. (Med.)* Chyme.

quimón [ke-mone'], *m.* Fine printed cotton, chintz.

quimono [ke-mo'-no], *m.* Kimono, Japanese garb.

quimosina [kee-mo-see'-nah], *f.* Rennin.

quina, quinaquina [kee'-nah], *f.* Peruvian or Jesuits' bark.

quinal [ke-nahl'], *m.* (Peru) The cinchona-tree and a group of such trees.

quinario, ria [ke-nah'-re-o, ah], *a.* Consisting of five.

quinario [ke-nah'-re-o], *m.* A Roman coin of five units.

quinas [kee'-nas], *f. pi.* 1. Arms of Portugal, consisting of five scutcheons, in memory of the five wounds of Christ. 2. Fives, on dice.

quincalla [kin-cahl'-lyah], *f.* Hardware, notions, trinkets.

quincallería [kin-cal-lyay-ree'-ah], *f.* 1. Notions store. 2. Hardware store. 3. Trinket manufacturing.

quince [keen'-thay], *a. & m.* 1. Fifteen. 2. Fifteenth (fecha). 3. A game at cards. **Quince días,** fortnight.

quincena [kin-thay'-nah], *f.* 1. Fortnight, two weeks (quince días). 2. Semi-monthly pay (pago). 3. *(Mus.)* Interval comprising fifteen successive notes of two octaves. 4. Fifteenth, a register in the pipes of an organ.

quincenal [kin-thay-nahl'], *a.* Biweekly, fortnightly.

quincenalmente [kin-thay-nahl-men'-tay] *adv.* Every two weeks, fortnightly.

quinceno, na [kin-thay'-no, nah], *a.* Fifteenth.

quincha [keen'-chah], *f.* (Peru) A wall of clay and canes.

quincuagenario, ria [kin-coo-ah-hay-nah'-re-o, ah], *a.* Fiftieth.

quincuagésima [kin-coo-ah-hay'-se-mah], *f.* Quinquagesima Sunday.

quincuagésimo, ma [kin-coo-ah-hay'-see-mo, mah], *a.* Fiftieth.

quincuatro [kin-coo-ah'-tro], *m.* Roman festival of five days in honor of Minerva.

quincunce [kin-coon'-thay], *m.* Quincunx.

quincurión [kin-coo-re-on'], *m.* A chief or corporal of five soldiers.

quindecágono, na [kin-day-cah'-go-no, nah], *a.* Quindecagon.

quindécima [kin-day'-the-mah], *f.* The fifteenth part.

quindejas [kin-day'-has], *f. (Prov.)* Rope of three strands, made of bass or *esparto.*

quindenio [kin-day'-ne-o], *m.* Space or period of fifteen years.

quinete [ke-nay'-tay], *m.* Kind of camlet.

quingentésimo, ma [kin-hen-tay'-se-mo, mah], *a.* The five hundredth.

quiniela [ke-ne-ay'-lah], *f.* Pools coupon.

quinientos, tas [ke-ne-en'-tos, tas], *a.* Five hundred.

quinina [ke-nee'-nah], *f.* Quinine, the principal alkaloid of cinchona.

quino [kee'-no], *m.* 1. The cinchona-tree, an evergreen of the madder family. 2. A juice like opium extracted from various African vegetables in the banks of the Gambia.

quinoidina [ke-noi-dee'-nah], *f.* Quinoidine, a resinous substance of yellow and red cinchona barks.

quínolas, quinolillas [kee'-no-las], *f. pl.* Reversis, a game at cards.

quinque [keen-kay'], *m.* An Argand lamp (lámpara).

quinquefolio [kin-kay-fo'-le-o], *m.* (*Bot.*) Common cinquefoil.

quinquenio [kin-kay'-ne-o], *m.* Space or period of five years; lustrum.

quinquercio [kin-kerr'-the-o], *m.* Five Grecian games of wrestling, jumping, rumling, quoits, etc.

quinquenal [kin-kay-nahl'], *a.* Quinquennial.

quinqui [kin'-ke], *m.* Bandit (bandido); delinquent (delincuente); small-time dealer (vendedor).

quinquillería [kin-keel-lyay-ree'-ah], *f.* Hardware. *V.* QUINCALLERÍA and BUHONERÍA.

quinquillero [kin-keel-lyay'-ro], *m.* Hawker, peddler, hardwareman. *V.* BUHONERO.

quinta [keen'-tah], *f.* 1. Country-seat, a country-house (casa). 2. The act of choosing one out of five. 3. The act of drawing lots for men to serve in the army. 4. Quint, the sequence at five cards in the game of piques. 5. (*Mus.*) Fifth, an interval of three tones and a semitone major.

quinta columna [keen'-tah co-loom'-nah], *f.* Fifth column.

quintacolumnista [kin-tah-co-loom-nees'-tah], *m. & f.* Fifth columnist.

quintador, ra [kin-tah-dor', rah], *m.* 1. One who draws lots in fives.

quintaesencia [kin-tah-ay-sen'-the-ah], *f.* Quintessence.

quintal [kin-tahl'], *m.* 1. Quintal, a hundred-weight. 2. Fifth part of one hundred. **Quintal métrico**, weight of one hundred kilograms, ton.

quintalada [kin-tah-lah'-dah], *f.* The sum of 2,5 per cent on the freights paid to masters of vessels.

quintaleño, ña, quintalero, ra [kin-tah-lay'-nyo, nyah], *a.* Capable of containing a quintal.

quintana [kin-tah'-nah], *f.* A country house.

quintanar [kin-tah-nar'], *m.* Quintain, ancient tilting-post.

quintante [kin-tahn'-tay], *m.* An astronomical instrument larger than the sextant.

quintañón, na [kin-tah-nyone', nah], *a.* A hundred years old; much advanced in years.

quintar [kin-tar'], *va.* 1. To draw one out of five. 2. To draw lots for soldiers. 3. To come to the number of five. 4. To pay to govermment the duty of 20 per cent on gold or silver. 5. To plough ground the fifth time.-*vn.* To attain the fifth: applied to the moon on the fifth day.

quintería [kin-tay-ree'-ah], *f.* Farm; grange.

quinterillo [kin-tay-reel'-lyo], *m. dim.* A farmer who rents a small farm.

quinterno [kin-terr'-no], *m.* 1. Number of five sheets of paper. 2. Lot, or row, of five numbers in the ancient lottery.

quintero [kin-tay'-ro], *m.* 1. Farmer, one who rents a farm (dueño). 2. Overseer of a farm; servant who takes care of a farm.

quinteto [kin-tay'-to], *m.* Quintet, a musical composition for five performers.

quintil [kin-teel'], *m.* The month of July, according to the ancient Roman calendar.

quintilla [kin-teel'-lyah], *f.* A metrical composition of five verses.

quintillizos [kin-tel-lye-thos], *m. & pl.* Quintuplets.

quintillón [kin-teel-lyon'], *m.* Quintillon

quintín [kin-teen'], *m.* Sort of fine cloth of a loose texture.

quinto [keen'-to], *m.* 1. One-fifth. 2. Fifth, a duty of 20 per cent on prizes, etc., paid to the Spanish government. 3. Share of pasture land. 4. One called up for military service, draft, conscription, draftee.

quinto, ta [keen'-to, tah], *a.* Fifth, the ordinal number of five.

quintuplicar [kin-too-ple-car'], *va.* To multiply by five.

quíntuplo, pla [keen'-too-plo, plah], *a.* Quintuple, five-fold.

quiñón [ke-nyone'], *m.* Share of profit arising from an enterprise undertaken with another person.

quiosco [ke-os'-co], *m.* Kiosk, pavillion, stand. **Quiosco de periódicos**, newstand.

quipos [kee'-pos], *m. pl.* Ropes of various colors, and with different knots, used by the ancient inhabitant of Peru to record memorable events and keep accounts.

quiquiriquí [ke-ke-re-kee'], *m.* Imitation of cock-crowing; cock-a-doodle-doo.

quiragra [ke-rah'-grah], *f.* Gout in the hand.

quirieleisón [ke-re-ay-lay-re-sone'], *m.* Lord, have mercy upon us! the responses chanted in the funeral service. *V.* KIRIELEISÓN.

quirinal [ke-re-nahl'], *a.* Relating to the feast of Romulus, and to one of the seven hills of Rome.

quirite [ke-ree'-tay], *m.* Roman citizen or knight.

quirivel [ke-re-vel'], *m.* (*Bot.*) *V.* PERDIGUERA.

quirófano [ke-ro'-fah-no], *m.* Operating room.

quirografía [ke-ro-grah-fee'-ah], *f.* Chirography, the art of writing.

quiromancia [ke-ro-mahn'-the-ah], *f.* Chiromancy, palmistry.

quiromántico [ke-ro-mahn'-te-co], *m.* Palmister, chiromancer.

quirópteros [ke-rop'-tay-ros], *m. pl.* Bats: the cheiroptera.

quiroteca [ke-ro-tay'-kah], *f.* (*coll.*) Glove.

quirúrgico, ca [ke-roor'-he-co, cah], *a.* Surgical.

quirurgo [ke-roor'-go], *m.* (*coll.*) Surgeon.

quisicosa [ke-se-co'-sah], *f.* (*coll.*) Enigma, riddle, obscure question.

quisling [kees'-lin], *m.* Quisling, traitor of his country.

quisquilla [kis-keel'-lyah], *f.* 1. A ridiculous nicety; bickering, trifling dispute (bagatela). 2. (*Zool.*) Shrimp.

quisquilloso, sa [kis-kil-lyo'-so, sah], *a.* Fastidious, precise, morose; touchy (sensible), quibbling (sofístico).

quiste [kees'-tay], *m.* (*Acad.*) Cyst, a tumor with fluid contents.

quita [kee'-tah], *f.* Acquittance, or discharge from a debt, or a part of it (deuda); (*LAm.*) rebate (descuento).

¡quita! *int.* God forbid! **¡Quita de ahí!** away with you! out of my sight!

quitación [ke-tah-the-on'], *f.* 1. Salary, wages, pay, income. 2. *V.* QUITA.

quitador, ra [ke-tah-dor', rah], *m. & f.* One who takes away, remover.

quitaguas [ke-tah'-goo-ahs], *m. V.* PARAGUAS.

quitaipón [ke-tah-e-pone'], *m. V.* QUITAPÓN. **De quita y pon**, adjustable, removable: used of mechanical contrivances.

quitamanchas [ke-tah-mahn'-chas], *m.* A clothes-cleaner.

quitameriendas [ke-tah-may-re-en'-das], *f.* (*Bot.*) Common meadow saffron.

quitamiento [ke-tah-me-en'-to], *m. V.* QUITA.

quitamotas [ke-tah-mo'-tas], *m. & f.* A servile flatterer.

quitante [ke-tahn'-tay], *pa.* Taking away, removing.

quitanza [ke-tahn'-thah], *f.* (*Com.*) Receipt, discharge.

quitapelillos [ke-tah-pay-leel'-lyos], *com.* (*coll.*) Flatterer, fawner, wheedler.

quitapenas [ke-tah-pay'-nahs], *m.* Pistol (pistola); knife (navaja).

quitapesares [ke-tah-pay-sah'-res], *com.* (*coll.*) Comfort, consolation.

quitapón [ke-tah-pone'], *m.* Ornament of the headstall of draught horses and mules.

quitar [ke-tar'], *va.* 1. To take away, to remove; to separate, to extract. 2. To release or redeem a pledge. 3. To hinder, to disturb. 4. To forbid, to prohibit. 5. To abrogate, to annul. 6. To free from an obligation. 7. To unsurp, to rob (robar). 8. To strip or deprive of anything. 9. To suppress an office. 10. To parry a thrust. **No quita nada de su valor**, it does not detract at all from its value. **Le van a quitar ese privilegio**, they are going to take that privilege away from him. **Quitar a uno de hacer algo**, to stop somebody from doing something. -vr. 1. To abstain, to refrain. 2. To retire, or withdraw. 3. To get rid of. **Quitarse de la vista de uno**, to remove oneself from somebody's side. **Quitarse la ropa**, to take off one's clothing.

quitasol [ke-tah-sole'], *m*. Parasol, sunshade.

quitasueño [ke-tah-soo-ay'-nyo], *m. (Coll.)* Anxiety or worry causing sleeplessness.

quite [kee'-tay], *m.* 1. Obstacle, impediment, hindrance; the act of taking away. 2. Parade, parry, in fencing. **No tiene quite**, it is unavoidable, there is no help for it.

quiteño, ña [ke-tay'-nyo, nyah], *a.* Native of or belonging to Quito.

quito, ta [kee'-to, tah], *a. & pp. irr. obs.* of QUITAR. Free from an obligation, clear from a charge, quite. -*m.* A dyewood (yielding black) of the Napo region in South America.

quitrín [ke-treen'], *m. (Cuba)* Gig, a light chaise.

quiyá [kee-yah'], *f.* Name of an otter of the Argentine Republic.

quizá, quizás [ke-thah', ke-thahs'], *adv.* Perhaps. *V.* ACASO.

quórum [kwo'-room], *m.* Quorum (de una asamblea), a term from Latin.

R

r [er'-ray, er'-ah], *f.* This letter at the beginning of a word, after *l, n, s*, and in compound words, the primitive of which begins with *r*, has a hard and rough sound, as, *rata, malrotar, enriquecer, cariredondo*. When *ab* and *ob* are not prepositions, as in *abrogar, obrepción*, the *r* becomes liquid; as in *abrojo, obrero*. —*R* in the middle of a word, or between two vowels, has a very smooth sound; as in *morosidad peregrinar*. The harsh and rough sound of *r* between two vowels, in the middle of simple words, is always expressed by double *rr*; thus, barraca, correcto. *R* is used as a contraction of *reprobar*, like *A* for *aprobar*, in voting for degrees in universities; it is also used as a contraction for **real**, royal, and for *reverendo*, reverend.

raba [rah'-bah], *f.* Bait used in the pilchard-fishery.

rabada [rah-bah'-dah], *f.* Hind quarter of mutton.

rabadán [rah-bah-dahn'], *m.* The principal shepherd of a sheep-walk.

rabadilla [rah-bah-deel'-lyah], *f.* Rump, croup, the extremity of the backbone.

rabanal [rah-bah-nahl'], *m.* Ground sown with radishes.

rabanero, ra [rah-bah-nay'-ro, rah], *a.* 1. Very short: applied to the garments of women. 2. *f. (Coll.)* A shameless and insolent woman.-*m. & f.* Seller of radishes.

rabanete [rah-bah-nay'-tay], *m dim.* A small radish.

rabanillo [rah-bah-neely o], *m*.1. *(dim.)* Small radish. 2. The tart sharp taste of wine which is on the turn. 3. *(Coll.)* Ardent desire, longing. 4. Acrimony, asperity, rudeness.

rabaniza [rah-bah-nee'-thah], *f.* Radish seed.

rábano [rah'-bah-no], *m. (Bot.)* Radish. **Rábano picante or rusticano**, horse radish. **Tomar el rábano por las hojas**, to get hold of the wrong end of the stick.

rabazuz [rah-ba-thooth'], *m.* Inspissated juice of licorice.

rabear [rah-bay-ar'], *vn.* To wag the tail.

rabel [rah-bel'], *m.* 1. Rebeck, an ancient musical instrument with three strings, played with a bow. 3. *(Coll.)* Breech, backside.

rabelejo, ico, illo, ito [rah-bay-lay'-ho], *m. dim.* of RABEL.

rabera [rah-bay'-rah], *f.* 1. Tail, the hind or back part of anything. 2. Handle of a cross-bow. 3. Remains of uncleaned grain or seeds.

raberón [rah-bay-rone'], *m.* The tops of a felled tree, cut for fire wood.

rabí [rah-bee'], *m.* Rabbi, rabbin.

rabia [rah'-be-ah], *f.* 1. Hydrophobia, rabies. 2. Rage, fury. **Me da rabia**, it maddens me. **Tomar rabia a**, to take a dislike to. 3. *(LAm.)* **Con rabia**, extremely, terribly.

rabiar [rah-be-ar'], *vn.* 1. To labor under hydrophobia. 2. To rage (enfadarse), to be furious. 3. To labor under racking pain. 4. To flush, to be agitated and hurried to excess. **Rabiar por**, to wish or long for a thing with itching desire or anxiety. **Rabiar de hambre**, to be furiously hungry. **Quema que rabia**, it is as hot as hell.

rabiatar [rah-be-ah-tar'], *va.* To tie by the tail.

rabiazorras [rah-be-ah-thor'-ras], *m. (Prov.)* Among shepherds, the east wind.

rabicán, rabicano [rah-be-cahn'], *a.* White-tailed, having white hairs in the tail (caballos).

rabicorto, ta [rah-be-cor'-to, tah], *a.* Short-tailed.

rábido, da [rah'-be-do, dah], *a. (Poet.) V.* RABIOSO.

rabieta [ra-be-ay'-tah], *f. (Coll.)* Violent, fretting impatience.

rabihorcado [rah-be-or-cah'-do], *m. (Orn.)* Frigate bird, or frigate pelican.

rabilargo, ga [rah-be-lar'-go, gah], *a.* Long-tailed; having a long train.

rabilargo [rah-be-lar'-go], *m. (Orn.)* Blue crow.

rabillo [rah-beel'-lyo], *m.* 1. Mildew on the stalk of corn. 2. *(dim.)* Little tail. 3. Tip (punta); corner (ángulo); thin part (parte delgada). **Mirar con el rabillo del ojo**, to look out of the corner of one's eyes.

rabinegro, gra [rah-be-nay'-gro, grah], *a.* Black-tailed.

rabínico, ca [rah-bee'-ne-co, cah], *a.* Rabbinical.

rabinismo [rah-be-nees'-mo], *m.* Rabbinism.

rabinista [rah-be-nees'-tah], *com* Rabbinist.

rabino [rah-bee'-no], *m.* Rabbi, a teacher of the Hebrew law. **Gran rabino**, the chief of a synagogue.

rabiosamente [rah-be-o-sah-men-tay], *adv.* Furiously, outrageously, madly, ragingly.

rabioso, sa [rah-be-o'-so, sah], *a.* 1. Rabid, mad: applied to dogs and other brutes. 2. Furious (enfado), outrageous, choleric, raging, fierce. **Poner rabioso a uno**, to enrage somebody.

rabisalsera [rah-be-sal-say'-rah], *m. (Coll.)* Pert, smart, forward, saucy, impudent (mujeres).

rabiseco, ca [rah-be-say'-co, cah], *a.* 1. Dry-tailed, poor, lean, starving. *(Met.)* Snappish, peevish.

rabito [rah-bee'-to], *m. (dim.)* A small tail.

rabiza [rah-bee'-thah], *f.* 1. Point of a fishing-rod, to which the line is fastened. 2. *(Naut.)* End, tip of anything, particularly the tapering end of a rope.

rabizar [rah-be-thar'], *va.* To point the end of a rope.

rable [rah'-blay], *m.* Ferret, an instrument to skim melted glass.

rabo [rah'-bo], *m.* 1. Tail of animals: applied to certain animals, as pigs. etc. instead of *cola*. 2. Tail, the lower, back, or hind part of anything; train. 3. All instruments to cut velvet in the loom. 4. In paper-mills, the tail which supports the hammer that beats the pulp. **Rabo de puerco**, *(Bot.)* hog's fennel, sea-sulphur wort. **Rabo de junco**, *(Orn.)* tropic bird. **Rabo entre piernas**, *(Coll.)* crestfallen, dejected. *V.* RABERA. **Mirar con el rabo del ojo**, to look askance.

rabón, na [rah-bohn', nah], *a.* 1. Docked, bob-tailed, short-tailed. 2. *(LAm.)* Short (pequeño). 3. *(Cono Sur)* Stark naked (desnudo). 3. *(Carib. Cono Sur)* Damaged (cuchillo). 4. *(Mex.)* Down on one's luck (desgraciado).

rabona [rah-bo'-nah], *f. (Peru)* A canteen woman, or wife of a soldier.

rabosear [rah-bo-say-ar'], *va.* To spatter with dirt.

raboso, sa [rah-bo'-so, sah], *a.* Ragged, tattered.

rabotada [bah-bo-tah'-dah], *f.* 1. A gruff and insolent reply with rude gestures. *(Acad.)* 2. A hit with a tail.

rabotear [rah-bo-tay-ar'], *va.* To crop the tail.

rabudo, da [rah-boo'-do, dah], *a.* Long-tailed.

rábula [rah'-boo-lah], *m.* An ignorant, vociferous lawyer.

racahut [rah-cah-oot'], *m.* Raccahout, a farinaceous preparation from potatoes, edible acorns, etc.

rácano [rah'-cah-no], *a.* 1. Bone-idle. 2. Stingy (tacaño). 3. Sly (artero).

racha [rah'-chah], *f.* 1. Gust of wind. 2. Short period of good luck. **Buena racha**, piece of luck.

racial [rah-the-ahl'], *a.* Racial, race.

racimado, da [rah-the-mah'-do, dah], *a.* Clustered, in racemes.

racimar [rah-the-mar'], *va. (Prov.) V.* REBUSCAR. *-vr. V.* ARRACIMARSE.

racimo [rah-thee'-mo], *m.* 1. Bunch of grapes. 2. Cluster of small things disposed in order; raceme. 3. *(Coll.)* Criminal hanging on the gallows.

racimoso, sa [rah-the-mo'-so, sah], *a.* Full of grapes, racemose, racemiferous.

racimudo, da [rah-the-moo'-do, dah], *a.* In large bunches or racemes.

raciocinación [rah-the-o-the-nah-the-on'], *f.* Ratiocination, the art of reasoning.

raciocinar [rah-the-o-the-nar'], *va.* To reason, to ratiocinate.

raciocinio [rah-the-o-thee'-ne-o], *m.* Reasoning, argument.

ración [rah-the-on'], *f.* Ration, food for one meal. 2. Boardwages; allowance for soldiers or sailors, pittance. **Ración de hambre**, scanty allowance. **Raciones**, rations. 3. A prebend in Spanish cathedrals.

racionabilidad [rah-the-o-nah-be-le-ahd'], *f.* Rationality, the power of reasoning.

racional [rah-the-o-nahl'], *a.* 1. Rational, reasonable. 2. *(Ast.)* Rational: applied to the horizon where plane is conceived to pass through the center of the earth. 3. Rational, the essential predicate that constitutes the difference between man and beast. 4. *(Math.)* Rational. *-m.* Rational, pectoral, or breast plate, one of the sacred vestments of the chief priest among the Jews.

racionalidad [rah-the-o-nah-le-dahd'], *f.* 1. Rationality, reasonableness. 2. Fitness, agreement with right. 3. Faculty of reasoning.

racionalizar [rah-the-o-nah-le-thar'], *va.* To rationalize.

racionalmente [rah-the-o-nahl'-men-tay], *adv.* Rationally.

racionamiento [rah-the-o-nah-me-en'-to], *m.* Rationing.

racionar [rah-the-o-nar'], *va.* To ration.

racionista [rah-the-o-nees'-tah], *va.* 1. Person on an allowance. 2. Second-rate actor.

racismo [rah-thees'-mo], *m.* Racism.

racista [rah-thees'-tah], *com.* Racist.

rada [rah'-dah], *f.* Road, roadstead, anchoring-ground for ships.

radar [rah'-dahr], *m.* (Radio) Radar.

radiación [rah-de-ah-the-on'], *f.* Radiation.

radiactividad [rah-de-o-ahc-te-ve-dahd'], *f.* Radioactivity.

radiactivo [rah-de-o-ahc-tee'-vo], *a.* Radioactive.

radiado, da [rab-de-ah'-do, dah], *a. pp.* of RADIAR. Radiated.

radiador [rah-de-ah-dor'], *m.* 1. Radiator. 2. Radiator, steam heater.

radial [rah-de-ahl'], *a.* Radial.

radiante [rah-de-ahn'-tay], *a.* Radiant.

radiar [rah-de-ar'], *va.* 1. To radiate. 2. To broadcast, to radio.

radicación [rah-de-ca-the-on'], *f.* Taking root.

radical [rah-de-cahl'], *a.* Radical.-*com.* Radical. *-m.* Radical.

radicalmente [rah-de-cahl'-men-tay], *adv.* Radically.

radicar [rah-de-car'], *vn.* 1. To take root. 2. To be located. *-vr.* To establish oneself, to take up residence.

radícula [rah-dee'-coo-lah], *f. (Bot.)* Radicle, radicule.

radio [rah'-de-o], *m.* 1. Radius. 2. Spoke (de rueda). 3. Radium. **Radio de acción**, sphere of jurisdiction. *-f.* Radio.

radioactividad [rah-de-o-ac-te-ve-dahd'], *f.* Radioactivity. **Radioactividad atmosférica**, *(Mil.)* fallout.

radioactivo, va [rah-de-o-ac-tee'-vo, vah], *a.* Radioactive.

radioaficionado, da [rah-de-o-ah-fe-the-o-nah'-do, dah], *m. & f.* Radio amateur.

radioastronomía [rah-de-o-as-tro-no-mee'-ah], *f.* Radio astronomy.

radioaviación [rah-de-o-ah-ve-ah-the-on'], *f. (Aer.)* Radio navigation.

radiobaliza [rah-de-o-bah-lee'-tha], *f.* Radio beacon.

radiobiología [rah-de-o-be-o-lo-hee'-ah], *f.* Radiobiology.

radiocompás [rah-de-o-com-pahs'], *m.* Radio compass, radio direction finder.

radiocomunicación [rah-de-o-co-moo-ne-cah-the-on'], *f.* Radio communication.

radiodifundir [rah-de-o-de-foon-deer'], *va.* To broadcast via radio.

radiodifusora [rah-de-o-de-foo-so'-rah], *f.* Broadcasting station, radio station.

radioelemento [rah-de-o-ay-lay-men'-to], *m.* Radioelement.

radioemisora [rah-de-o-ay-me-so'-rah], *f.* Radio station.

radioescucha [rah-de-o-es-coo'-chah], *com.* Radio listener.

radiofaro [rah-de-o-fah'-ro], *m.* Radio beacon.

radiofoto [rah-de-o-fo'-to], *f.* Radiophoto.

radiofrecuencia [rah-de-o-fray-coo-en'-the-ah], *f.* Radio frequency.

radiografía [run-de-o-grah-fee'-ah], *f.* 1. Radiograph, X-ray film. 2. Radiography.

radiógrafo [rah-de-o'-grah-fo], *m.* Radiographer, X-ray specialist.

radiograma [rah-de-o-grah'-ma], *m.* Radiogram.

radioisótopo [rah-de-o-so'-to-po], *m.* Radioisotope.

radiología [rah-de-o-lo-hee'-ah], *f.* Radiology.

radiólogo [rah-de-o'-lo-go], *m.* Radiologist.

radiómetro [rah-de-o'-may-tro], *m.* Radiometer.

radionavegación [rah-de-o-nah-vay-gah-the-on'], *f.* Radio navigation.

radionavegante [rah-de-o-nah-vay-gahn'-tay], *m.* Radio navigator.

radioquímica [rah-de-o-kee'-me-cah], *f.* Radiochemistry.

radiorreceptor [rah-de-o-or-ray-thep-tor'], *m.* Radio receiver.

radioscopia [rah-de-os-co'-pe-ah], *f.* Radioscopy.

radiosensitivo, va [rah-de-o-sen-se-tee'-vo, vah], *a.* Radiosensitive.

radioso, sa [rah-de-o'-so, sah], *a.* Radiant.

radiosonda [rah-de-o-son'-dah], *f.* Radiosonde.

radiotecnia [rah-de-o-tec'-ne-ah], *f.* Radiotechnology.

radiotelefonía [rah-de-o-tay-lay-fo-nee'-ah], *f.* Wireless, radiotelephony.

radioteléfono [rah-de-o-tay-lay'-fo-no], *m.* Radiotelephone. **Radio teléfono, emisor-receptor portátil**, walkie-talkie.

radiotelegrafista [rah-de-o-tay-lay-grah-fees'-tah], *com.* Wireless operator.

radiotelégrafo [rah-de-o-tay-lay'-grah-fo], *m.* Radiotelegraph.

radiotelegrama [rah-de-o-tay-lay-grah'-mah], *m.* Radiotelegram.

radiotelescopio [rah-de-o-tay-les-co'-pe-o], *m.* Radio telescope.

radioterapia [rah-de-o-tay-rah'-pe-ah], *f.* Radiotherapy.

radiotransmisor [rah-de-o-trans-me-sor'], *m.* Radio transmitter.

radioyente [rah-de-o-yen'-tay], *m. & f. V.* RADIOESCUCHA.

raedera [rah-ay-day'-rah], *f.* 1. Scraper, raker. 2. Roller or cylinder for reducing lead into sheets.

raedor, ra [rah-ay-dor', rah], *a.* Scraper, eraser. *V.* RASERO.

raedura [rah-ay-doo'-rah], *f.* 1. Rasure, crasure. 2. Scrapings, filings, parings.

raer [rah-err'], *va.* 1. To scrape, to grate: to rub off, to abrade, to fret. 2. To rase or blot out, to erase. 3. To lay aside entirely, to efface (vicio, mala costumbre).

rafa [rah'-fah], *f.* 1. Buttress to support mud walls. 2. A small cut or opening in a canal.

ráfaga [rah'-fah-gah], *f.* 1. A violent gust of wind. 2. Any cloud of small density which appears at a distance. 3. Instantaneous flash or gleam of light.

raído, da [rah-ee'-do, dah], *a. & pp.* of RAER. 1. Scraped. 2. Worn out. 3. Impudent, shameless: free, undisguised.

raigal [rah-e-gahl'], *a.* Relating to the root.

raigambre [rah-e-grahm'-bray], *f.* Collection of roots of different trees united.

raigón [rah-e-gon'], *m.* 1. Large root. 2. Root (de un diente).

raimiento [rah-e-me-en'-to], *m.* 1. Scraping. 2. Effrontery.

raíz [rah-eeth'], *f.* 1. Root. 2. Foundation. **Raíz cuadrada**, square root. **Raíz cúbica**, cube root. **A raíz de**, (a) level with: (b) right after. 3. As a result of. **De raíz**, completely, from the ground up.

raja [rah'-hah], *f.* 1. Splinter, chip. 2. Slice. 3. Crack (grieta), fissure. 4. Sliver (pedacito). 5. Cunt (vajina).

rajá [rah-hah'], *m.* Rajah.

rajable [rah-hah'-blay], **rajadizo, za** [rah-hah-dee'-tho, tha], *a.* Easily split, easily splintered.

rajadura [rah-hah-doo'-rah], *f.* Crack, cleft.

rajar [rah-har'], *va.* 1. To split (hender), to crack; to cleave; to slit; to slice (fruta). 2. *(LAm.)* To slander (difamar). 3. *(LAm.)* To flunk. 4. *(And. Carib.)* To crush (aplastar). 5. *(Cono Sur.)* To fire (obrero). 6. *(Carib.)* To pester (fastidiar). -*vn.* To chatter (hablar); to brag (jactarse). -*vr.* 1. To split (henderse). 2. To back out (desistir). 3. *(And. Carib. Cono Sur)* To run away (huir). 4. *(And. Cono Sur)* To be mistaken (equivocarse). To break off or break open, to chip, to break into chinks, to cleave. 5. To split *(Coll.)* To crack, to boast, to tell falsehoods.

rajeta [rah-hay'-tah], *f.* Sort of coarse cloth of mixed colors.

rajica, illa, ita [rah-hee'-cah], *f. dim.* 1. A small chink, crack, or fissure. 2. A small splinter or chip of wood.

rajuela [rah-hoo-ay'-lah], *f. dim. V.* RAJICA.

ralea [rah-lay'-ah], *f.* 1. Race, breed, stock. 2. Genus, species, quality.

ralear [rah-lay-ar'], *vn.* 1. To thin, to make thin, or rare. 2. *(Prov.)* To manifest or discover the bad inclination of breed or anything. 3. *(Agr.)* To make thin racemes or bunches of grapes.

ralentí [rah-len-tee'], *m.* 1. Slow motion (cine). 2. Neutral. **Funcionar al ralentí**, to be ticking over.

raleón, na [rah-lay-on', nah], *a.* Applied to a bird of prey which takes the game pursued by another.

raleza [rah-lay'-thah], *f.* Thinness, want of compactness; rarity; liquidity.

ralillo, illa, ito, ita [rah-leel'-lyo], *a.* Somewhat thin or rare.

ralladera [ral-lyah-day'-rah], *f.* Grater, an instrument for grating.

rallado [rahl-lyah'-do], *a.* Grated (queso).

ralladura [ral-lyah-doo'-rah], *f.* Mark left by the grater; the small particles taken off by grating.

rallar [ral-yar'], *va.* 1. To grate, to reduce to powder. 2. To vex, to molest.

rallo [rahl'-lyo], *m.* Grater, an instrument for grating.

rallón [ral-lyone'], *m.* Arrow or dart.

rallye [rah-le], *m.* Rally.

ralo, la [rah'-lo, lah], *a.* 1. Thin (pelo), rare, not compact. 2. *V.* RARO.

rama [rah'-mah], *f.* 1. Shoot or sprig of a plant, bough, limb, of a tree. 2. Branch of a family. 3. Rack used in manufactories, to bring cloth to its proper length and breadth. 4. *(Print.)* Chase for enclosing types. **En rama**, raw material, crude stuff. **Tabaco en rama**, leaf tobacco. **Seda en rama**, raw silk. **Andarse por las ramas**, to go about the bush, not to come to the point.

ramada [rah-mah'-dah], *f. (Prov.) V.* ENRAMADA.

ramadán [rah-mah-dahn'], *m.* Ramadan, the Mohammedan month of fasting, their ninth lunar month.

ramaje [rah-mah'-hay], *m.* 1. Branch age, collection of branches. 2. Flowering branchs designed in cloth.

ramal [rah-mahl'], *m.* 1. A strand of a rope. 2. Anything springing from another, as a staircase. 3. Halter, of a horse or mule. 4. Principal passage in mines; branch, division. 5. A thin, dependent upon something else; offset, branch, etc.

ramalazo [rah-mah-lah'-tho], *m.* 1. Lash (azote), a stroke with a cord or rope. 2. Marks left by lasher. 3. A sudden and acute pain or grief (dolor). Spot in the face. 5. Result or consequence of injuring another.

ramalito [rah-mah-lee'-to], *m. dim.* A small halter, small brands, a lash or cord of a cat-o'-nine-tails.

rambla [rahm'-blah], *f.* 1. A sandy place, ground covered with sand after a flood. 2. A ravine or water-course which carries off the water of heavy rains (arroyo).

ramblazo [ram-blah'-tho], *m.* Gravelly bed of a current or rivulet.

ramblizo [ram-blee'-tho], *m. (Prov.) V.* RAMBLAZO.

ramera [rah-may'-rah], *f.* Whore, prostitute.

ramería [rah-may-ree'-ah], *f.* Brothel, bawdy-house, formerly the residence of licensed prostitutes in Spanish towns.

ramerita, rameruela [rah-may-ree'-tah], *f. dim.* A little whore.

ramero [rah-may'-ro], *m.* A young hawk hopping from branch to branch.

ramial [rah-me-ahl'], *m.* Ramie-patch, ground planted in ramie.

ramificación [rah-me-fe-cah-the-on'], *f.* 1. Ramification, the production of branches. 2. Ramification, division or separation into branches.

ramificarse [rah-me-fe-car'-say], *vr.* To ramify, to be divided into branches.

ramilla, ita [rah-meel'-lyah], *f. dim.* 1. Small shoot or sprig, twig. 2. *(Met.)* Any light trifling thing.

ramillete [rah-mel-lay'-tay], *m.* 1. Bouquet (flores), bunch of flowers. 2. *(Fig.)* Collection.

ramilleto [rah-meel-lyay'-to], *m.* 1. Nosegay, tuft. 2. Cluster of single-pedicelled flowers, umbel. 3. Pyramid of sweetmeats and fruits served at table. 4. Collection of flowers or beauties of literature.

ramilletero, ra [rah-mil-lyay-tay' -ro, rah], *m. & f.* One who makes and sells nosegays.

ramilletero [rah-mil-lyay-tay'-ro], *m.* Vase with artificial flowers put on altars.

ramillo, ito [rah-meel'-lyo], *m.* 1. *(dim.)* A small branch. 2. *(Prov.) V.* DINERILLO.

ramina [rah-mee'-nah], *f.* Ramie yarn.

ramio [rah'-me-o], *m.* Ramie, a plant belonging to the nettle family yielding a fine textile fibre.

ramiza [rah-mee'-thah], *f.* Collection of lopped branches.

rámneo, nea [rahm'-nay-o, ah], *a. (Bot.)* Rhamnaceous, of the buckthorn family.

ramo [rah'-mo], *m.* 1. Branch of a bough or limb (de árbol); branchlet; also a limb cut off from a tree. 2. Any part separated from a whole. 3. A string of onions. 4. Branch of trade. 5. Concern, business. 6. Branch or special part of an art or science. 7. Branch, outgrowth of something not material. **Domingo de Ramos**, Palm Sunday.

ramojo [rah-mo'-ho], *m.* Small branch lopped from a tree, small wood.

ramón [rah-mone'], *m.* Top of branches cut off for the feed of sheep in snowy weather.

ramonear [rah-mo-nay-ar'], *vn.* 1. To cut off the branches of trees. 2. To nibble the tops of branches (ganado).

ramoneo [rah-mo-nay' -o], *m.* Act of cutting or lopping branches.

ramoso, sa [rah-mo'-so, sah], *a.* Branchy, ramous.

rampa [rahm'-pah], *f.* 1. *(Prov.)* Cramp. 2. *(Mil.)* Slope of a glacis. 3. Aclivity.

rampante [ram-pahn'-tay], *a. (Her.)* Rampant.

rampiñete [ram-pe-nyay'-tay], *m.* Bar of iron with a curved point used by artillery men.

ramplón, na [ram-plone', nah], *a.* Applied to a large coarse shoe, rude, unpolished. *-m. (Vet.)* The calk of a shoe.

ramplón [ram-plone'], *m.* Calk of horses, shoes.

rampojo [ram-po'-ho], *m.* 1. Rape, the stalk of a cluster of crepes when freed from the fruit. 2. *(Mil.)* Caltrop, an iron with three spikes, thrown into the rond, to annoy the enemy's horse. V. ABROJO.

rampollo [ram-poy-lyo], *m.* Branch cut from a tree to be planted.

ramujos [rah-moo'-hose], *m. pl.* Twin, small wood.

rana [rah'-nah], *f.* 1. A frog. 2. *(Vet.)* Ranula. V. ALEVOSA. **Rana marina or pescadora**, *(Zool.)* frogfish, fishing-frog, or angler. **Pero salió rana**, but he turned out badly.

ranacuajo [rah-nah-coo-ah' -ho], *m.* 1. Spawn of frogs. V. RENACUAJO. 2. A little, insignificant man.

rancajada [ran-cah-hah'-dah], *f.* Wound in plants or sprouts.

rancajado, da [ran-cah-hah'-do, dah], *a.* Wounded with a splinter of wood.

rancajo [ran-cah'-ho], *m.* Splinter in the flesh.

rancanca [ran-cahn'-cah], *m.* South American bird of prey: its plumage is chiefly black, but the cheeks and throat are bare and of a bright carmine color.

ranciadura [ran-the-ah-doo'-rah], *f.* V. RANCIDEZ.

ranciarse [ran-the-ar'-say], *vr.* V. ENRANCIARSE.

rancidez [ran-the-deth'], *f.* Rancidity, rancidness, rankness.

rancio, cia [rahn'-the-o, ah], *a.* Rank (comestible), rancid, stale, strong-scented, long kept, old (vino).

rancio [rahn-the-o], *m.* Rancidity, rankness, fulsomeness.

rancioso, sa [ran-the-o'-so, sah], *a.* 1. V. RANCIO. 2. Having the taste of oil.

rancheadero [ran-chay-ah-day'-ro], *m.* Place containing huts.

ranchear [ran-chay-ar'], *va.* To build huts, to form a mess.

ranchera [ran-chay'-rah], *f. (Mex.)* Typical Mexican song.

ranchería [ran-chay-ree'-ah], *f.* 1. Hut or cottage where laborers meet to mess together: horde. 2. *(Amer.)* A collection of huts, like a hamlet.

ranchero [ran-chay'-ro], *m.* 1. Steward of a mess. 2. An owner of a small farm. 3. *(Mex.)* Countryman, farm-dweller, rancher.

rancho [rahn'-cho], *m.* 1. Food given dully to a set of persons, as soldiers or convicts. 2. Mess, a set of persons who eat and drink together. 3. A free clear passage. **Hacer rancho**, to make room. 4. A friendly meeting of persons to discuss a question. 5. *(Naut.)* Restroom; mess. **Rancho de enfermería**, mess-room for the sick. 6. Each of the divisions of the crew. 7. Provision of food for a voyage. 8. Hut in which peasants are sheltered overnight (cobertizo). 9. *(Mex.)* A stock-farm; a small farm (granja), a ranch. 10. *(Amer.)* A place consisting of a few huts, where travelers may find provisions.

randa [rahn'-dah], *f.* Lace, trimming, netting, network.

randado, da [ran-dah-do, dah], *a.* Laced, adorned with lace.

randaje [ran-dah'-hay], *m.* Network, lace-work.

randal [ran-dahl'], *m.* Sort of stuff made into lace or net fashion.

randera [ran-day'-rah], *f.* Lace-worker.

ranear [rah-nay-ar'], *vn.* To croak as frogs.

raneta [rah-nay'-tah], *f.* Rennet, a kind of apple.

rangífero [ran-hee'-fay-ro], *m.* Reindeer.

rango [rahn'-go], *m.* Rank (categoría), quality.

rangua [rahn'-goo-ah], *f.* An iron box in which the spindles of machines move, pivot collar, shaft socket.

ranilla [rah-neel'-lyah], *f.* 1. *(dim.)* A small frog. 2. Frog of the hoof of horse or mule. 3. Cracks in the hood of horses. 4. Disease in the bowels of cattle.

raninas [rah-nee'-nas], *f. pl.* Ranulary veins, two veins under the tongue.

raniz [rah-neeth'], *m. & f.* A kind of linen.

ránula [rah'-noo-lah], *f.* Tumor under the tongue of a horse.

ranunculáceo, cea [rah-noon-coo-lah' -thay-o, ah], *a.* Ranunculaceous, of the crowfoot or buttercup family.

ranúnculo [rah-noon' -coo-lo], *m. (Bot.)* Crow-foot, buttercup.

ranura [rah-noo' -nah], *f.* 1. Groove, rabbet. 2. *(Comput.)* Slot

raña [rah'-nyah], *f.* A device which fishermen use for catching cuttle-fishes on rocky bottoms.

rapa [rah'-pah], *f. (Prov.)* Flower of the olive-tree.

rapacejo [rah-pah-thay'-ho], *m.* Border, edging.

rapacería [rah-pah-thay-ree'-ah], *f.* Puerility; a childish, boyish speech or action.

rapacidad [rah-pah-the-dahd'], *f.* Rapacity, robbery.

rapecillo, lla [rah-pah-theel'-lyo, lyah], *m. & f. dim.* A little boy or girl.

rapador, ra [rah-pah-dor', rah], *m. & f.* 1. One who scrapes or plunders. 2. *(Coll.)* Barber.

rapadura [rah-pah-doo'-rah], *f.* 1. Shaving, the act of shaving; the state of being shaved; rasure; plundering. 2. *(LAm.)* Brown sugar (azúcar). V. RASPADURA.

rapagón [rah-pah-gone'], *m.* A beardless young man.

rapamiento [rah-pah-me-en'-to], *m.* Act of shaving or erasing.

rapante [rah-pahn'-tay], *a.* 1. Snatching, robbing, or tearing off. 2. *(Her.)* Rampant.

rapapiés [rah-pah-pe-ays'], *m.* Squib that runs along the ground; chaser.

rapapolvo [rah-pah-pol'-vo], *m. (Coll.)* A sharp reproof.

rapar [rah-par'], *va.* 1. To shave (barba), as with a razor. 2. *(Coll.)* V. AFEITAR. 3. To plunder, to carry off with violence; to skin, to peel. *-vr. (Mex.)* To pass, bring, or hold.

rapasa [rah-pah'-sah], *f. (Min.)* A stone very soft and easy to work.

rapaz [rah-path'], *a.* Rapacious (ávido); ferocious, thieving (ladrón); predatory.

rapaz, za [rah-path', thah], *m. & f.* A young boy or girl.

rapazada [rah-pah-thah'-dah], *f.* Childish action or speech.

rapazuela [rah-pah-thoo-ay'-lah], *f. dim.* V. RAPACILLO.

rapazuelo, la, *m. & f. dim.* V. RAPACILLO.

rapazuelo, ela [rah-pah-thoo-ay'-lo, lah], *a. dim.* Rapacious, greedy.

rape [rah' -pay], *m. (Coll.)* Shaving, cutting off hair or beard carelessly (afeitado).

rapé [rah-pay'], *m.* Rappee, a kind of snuff. **Rapé francés**, French snuff.

rapeta [rah-pay'-tah], *f.* **rapetón** [rah-pay-tone'], *m. (Prov.)* A net for sardine-fishing on the Cantabrian coast.

rápidamente [rah'-pe-dah-men-tay], *adv.* Rapidly.

rapidez [rah-pe-deth'], *f.* Rapidity, velocity, celerity.

rápido, da [rah'-pe-do, dah], *a.* 1. Rapid, quick, swift. 2. *(And. Carib. Cono Sur)* Fallow (campo). 3. *(Carib.)* Clear (tiempo).

rapidura [ray-pe-doo'-rah], *f.* Crude sugar. V. RASPADURA, 3d def.

rapiego, ga [rah-pe-ay'-go, gah], *a.* Ravenous (pájaros).

rapiña [rah-pee'-nyah], *f.* Rapine, robbery. **Ave de rapiña**, bird of prey. **Vivir de rapiña**, to live off the catch.

rapiñador, ra [rah-pe-nyah-dor', rah], *m. & f.* Plunderer, robber.

rapiñar [rah-pe-nyar'], *va. (Coll.)* To plunder, to rob.

rapista [rah-pees'-tah], *m. (Coll.)* Barber, shaver.

rapo [rah' -po], *m.* A round-rooted turnip.

rapónchigo [rah-pon'-che-go], *m. (Bot.)* Esculent bellflower, rampion.

rapóntico [rah-pon'-te-co], *m. (Bot.)* V. RUIBARBO RAPÓNTICO.

raposa [rah-po'-sah], *f.* 1. Female fox. V. ZORRA. Canis vulpes. 2. *(Met.)* Cunning, deceitful person.

raposear [rah-po-say-ar'], *m.* To use artifices like a fox, to be foxy.

raposera [rah-po-say'-rah], *f.* Fox-hole, fox-den.

raposería [rah-po-say-ree'-ah], *f.* Cunning of a fox; artful kindness.

raposilla, ita [rah-po-seel'-lyah], *f. dim.* Artful wench.

raposino, na [rah-po-see'-no, nah], *a.* Foxy. *V.* RAPOSUNO.

raposo [rah-po'-so], *m.* Male fox. **Raposo ferrero,** ironcolored fox, whose skin is used for furs.

raposuno, no [rah-po-soo'-no, nah], *a.* Vulpine, foxy.

rapsoda [rap-so'-dah], *a.* Rhapsodic, rapt.

rapsodia [rap-so'-de-ah], *f.* Rhapsody, incoherent composition.

rapta [rahp'-tah], *a.* Applied to a woman who is snatched by a man by force or artifice; abducted.

rapto [rahp'-to], *m.* 1. Rapine, robbery, kipnapping (secuestro). 2. Ecstasy (éxtasis), rapture, exultance. 3. Abduction of a woman by force or deceit. 4. Outburst, fit. 5. (*Ast.*) *V.* MOVIMIENTO.

raptor, ra [rap-tor'], *m & f.* Abductor, kipnapper.

raque [rah'-kay], *m.* (*Naut.*) Salvage, beach-combing.

raquear [rah-kay-ar'], *vn.* To beach-comb, to salvage shipwrecks.

raqueta [rah-kay'-tah], *f.* 1. Racket. 2. (*Bot.*) Wall rocket. 3. Croupier's rake. **Raqueta de nieve,** snowshoe.

raquetero [rah-kay-tay'-ro], *m.* Racket-maker, racket-seller.

raquialgia [rah-ke-ahl'-he-ah], *f.* 1. Rachialgia, pain in the spinal column. 2. Progressive decay of the spinal column.

raquis [rah'-kees], *m.* Backbone.

raquítico, ca [rah-kee'-te-co-cah], *a.* Rickety, diseased with the rickets.

raquitis [rah-kee'-tis], *f.* Rickets, a disease.

raramente [rah-rah-men'-tay], *adv.* Rarely, seldom: ridiculously, oddly.

rarefacción [rah-ray-fac-the-one'], *f.* Rarefaction (aire).

rarefacer [rah-ray-fah-therr'], *va. V.* RARIFICAR. -*vn.* To rarefy.

rarefacto, ta [rah-ray-fac'-to, tah], *pp. irr.* of RAREFACER.

rareza [rah-ray'-thah], *f.* 1. Rarity (cualidad), rareness, uncommonness, infrequency. 2. Rarity, a thing valued for its scarcity; a curiosity, oddity.

raridad [rah-re-dahd'], *f.* 1. Rarity, uncommonness, infrequency. 2. Rarity, thinness, subtility. 3. Oddity.

rarificar [rah-re-fe-car'], *va.* To rarefy, to make thin, to dilate. -*vr.* To rarefy, to become thin.

rarificativo, va [rah-re-fe-cah-tee'-vo, vah], *a.* That which has the power of rarefying.

raro, ra [rah'-ro, rah], *a.* 1. Rare (poco frecuente), porous, having little density. 2. Rare, scarce, uncommon, odd (extraño). 3. Renowned, famous, excellent. 4. Extravagant, odd. **Rara vez,** seldom. **Son raros los que saben hacerlo,** very few people know how to do it. **De rara perfección,** of rare perfection. -*adv.* Rarely.

ras [rahs], *m.* Level, an even surface. **Ras en ras, ras con ras,** on an equal footing upon a par.

rasadura [rah-sah-doo'-rah], *f.* The act of measuring salt, and other dry articles, with a strickle.

rasamente [rah-sah-men-tay], *adv.* Publicly, openly, clearly.

rasante [rah-sahn'-tay], *a.* Low. **Tiro rasante,** low shot. -*m.* Slope. **Cambio de rasante,** brow of a hill.

rasar [rah-sar'], *va.* 1. To strike, to level corn with a strickle. 2. To graze, to skim (casi tocar), to touch lightly.

rascacielos [ras-cah-the-ay'-los], *m.* Skyscraper.

rascadera [ras-cah-day'-rah], *f. V.* RASCADOR and ALMOHAZA.

rascador [ras-cah-dor'], *m.* 1. Scraper, to scrape and clean bones, metal, etc.; scratcher; rasp. 2. Hat-pin, bodkin.

rascadura [ras-cah-doo'-rah], *f.* 1. The act of scratching, scraping, or rasping. 2. Scratch, made by scraping.

rascalino [rash-cah-lee'-no], *m. V.* TIÑUELA.

rascamiento [ras-cah-me-en'-to], *m.* Act of scraping or scratching.

rascamoño [ras-cah-mo'-nyo], *m.* Women's hat-pin, bodkin.

rascar [ras-car'], *va.* 1. To scratch (cabeza), to scrape (raer). 2. To sniff out (descubrir), to smell out. -*vr.* 1. To scratch. 2. (*LAm.*) To get drunk (emborracharse).

rascazón [ras-cah-thone'], *f.* Pricking, tickling, or itching sensation which induces scratching.

rasclo [rahs'-clo], *m.* An instrument used in coral-fishing.

rasco [rahs'-co], *m. V.* RASCADURA.

rascón, na [ras-cone', nah], *a.* Sour, sharp (amargo), acrid. -*m.* (*Orn.*) Rail, a wading bird; marsh-hen, mud-hen, sora.

rascuñar [ras-coo-nyar'], *va. V.* RASGUÑAR.

rascuño [ras-coo'-nyo], *m. V.* RASGUNO.

rasel [rah-sel'], *m.* (*Naut.*) Narrow part of a ship towards the head and stern.

rasero [rah-say'-ro], *m.* Strickle, strike, an instrument for levelling the contents of a dry measure. **Medir por un rasero,** to apply the same measure or standard to everything.

rasete [rah-say'-tay], *m.* Satinet, a sort of light fabric with a satiny gloss; sixteen for lining.

rasgado, da [ras-gah'-do, dah], *a,* & *pp.* of RASGAR. 1. Rent, open. 2. Applied to a wide balcony or large window (balcón, ventana). **Ojos rasgados,** large or full eyes. **Boca rasgada,** wide mouth.

rasgado [ras-gah'-do], *m. V.* RASGÓN.

rasgador, ra [ras-gah-dor', rah], *m.* & *f.* Tearer, cleaver, one who scratches, tears, or lacerates.

rasgadura [ras-gah-doo'-rah], *f.* Rent, tatter, strip torn from a fabric.

rasgar [ras-gar'], *va.* 1. To tear or cut asunder, to rend, to claw, to lacerate. 2. *V.* RASGUEAR.

rasgo [rahs'-go], *m.* 1. Dash (raya), stroke, line elegantly drawn (de pluma). **Rasgo de pluma,** dash of a pen. 2. A grand, magnanimous action. **Rasgo de generosidad,** stroke of generosity. 3. Feature (característica), trait. **Rasgo fisonómico,** facial feature.

rasgón [ras-gone'], *m.* Rent, rag, tatter, laceration.

rasqueado [ras-gay-ah'-do], *m.* Act of making flourishes. -**Rasqueado, da,** *pp.* of RASQUEAR.

rasguear [ras-gay-ar'], *vn.* To flourish, to form figures by lines. -*va.* To play a dash or arpeggio on the guitar.

rasguillo [ras-geel'-lyo], *m. dim.* A small dash of a pen.

rasgueo [ras-gay'-o], *m.* 1. The act of forming into fine strokes by a pen. 2. Lines elegantly drawn.

rasgueta [ras-gay'-tah], *f.* (*Mex.*) A currycomb.

rasguñar [ras-goon-nyar'], *va.* 1. To scratch, to scrape. 2. To sketch the outlines of a drawing or picture.

rasguñito, ñuelo [ras-goon-nyee'-to], *m. dim.* Slight scratch or sketch.

rasguño [ras-goo'-nyo], *m.* 1. Scratch, scar; nip. 2. Sketch, the dotted outlines of a drawing or picture.

rasilla [rah-seel'-lyah], *f.* 1. Serge, a kind of woollen stuff. 2. A fine tile for flooring.

raso [rah'-so], *m.* Satin. **Rasos franceses dobles lisos,** double French plain satin. **Rasos franceses labrados,** French figured silk. -*a.* 1. Clear of obstructions or impediments. 2. Clear (despejado). 3. Plain: flat (llano). 4. Having no title or mark of distinction. **Tiempo raso,** fine weather. **Cielo raso,** clear sky. **Soldado raso,** a private, a common soldier. **Al raso,** by the open air.

raspa [rahs'-pah], *f.* 1. Board of an ear of corn. 2. Spine, finray of fish. 3. Grape stalk (de uva). 4. Rasp, a coarse file. 5. Rind of certain fruits. 6. (*LAm.*) Scolding (reprimenda). 7. (*Carib. Mex.*) Brown sugar. 8. (*Cono Sur*) Rasp (herramienta).

raspadera [ras-pah-day'-rah], *f.* (*Prov.*) Raker.

raspadillo [ras-pah-deel'-lyo], *m.* Fraud or imposition practiced by gamblers.

raspador [ras-pah-dor'], *m.* Rasp, coarse file.

raspadura [ras-pah-doo'-rah], *f.* 1. The act of filing, rasping, or scraping; erasure (borradura). 2. Filings, raspings, scrapings, shavings. 3. (Cuba) Pan sugar, crude sugar. *V.* CHANCACA. 4. Certain cakes made with crude sugar.

raspajo [ras-pah'-ho], *m.* (*Prov.*) Stalk of a bunch of grapes.

raspamiento [ras-pah-me-en'-to], *m.* Act of rasping or filing.

raspante [ras-pahn'-tay], *pa.* & *a.* Rasping, rough: applied to wine which grates the palate.

raspar [ras-par'], *va.* 1. To scrape, to rasp (limar), to pure off. 2. To prick, to have a sourish taste (vino). 3. To steal, carry off. 4. *(Mex.)* To scold (regañar). 5. *(Mex.)* To say unkind things to (maltratar).

raspear [ras-pay-ar'], *vn.* To have a hair in the pen, which occasions blots.

raspinegro, gra [ras-pe-nay'-gro, grah], *a. (Prov.) V.* ARISPRIETO.

raspón (De) [ras-pone', day], *adv.* Scrapingly, thievishly. *-m.* 1. Scratch (rasguño), graze. 2. *(LAm.)* Scolding (regaño). 3. *(Mex.)* Cutting remark (dicho). 4. *(And.)* Straw hat (somebrero).

rasqueta [ras-kay'-tah], *f. (Naut.)* Scraper, an instrument for scraping the planks of a ship.

rastel [ras-tel'], *m.* Bar or lattice of wood or iron.

rastillador, ra [ras-tel-lyah-dor'], *m. dim. f. V.* RASTRILLADOR.

rastillar [ras-til-lyar'], *va.* To hackle flax. *V.* RASTRILLAR.

rastillero [ras-til-lyay'-ro], *m. (Low.)* Shoplifter, robber who steals and flies.

rastra [rahs'-trah], *f.* 1. Sled or sledge (de transporte), a carriage without wheels. 2. The act of dragging along. 3. Anything hanging and dragging about a person. 4. A track or mark left on the ground. *V.* RASTRO. 5. String of dried fruit. 6. Train, the result of some action which brings damage or inconvenience (consecuencia). 7. Trawl (de pesca). 8. *(Mex.)* Prostitute (puta). **Andar a rastras,** to have a difficult time of it.

rastrallar [ras-tral-lyar'], *vn.* To crack with a whip.

rastrallido [ras-tral-lyee'-do], *m.* The crack of a whip.

rastreador, ra [ras-tray-a-dor', rah], *m. & f.* Tracker, smeller, follower.

rastrear [ras-tray-ar'], *va.* 1. To trace, to follow by the footsteps (seguir). 2. To harrow or rake on the farm, or drag in fishing (sacar a la superficie). 3. To inquire into, to investigate, to fathom. 4. To sell carcasses by wholesale in a slaughterhouse. *-vn.* To skim the ground, to fly very low.

rastreo [ras-tray'-o], *m. (Prov.)* Fringe or small pieces of stuff hanging round.

rastrero, ra [ras-tray'-ro, rah], *a.* 1. Creeping, dragging. 2. Applied to a dog that runs by a trail. 3. Low, humble (disculpa), cringing. 4. Applied to things floating in the air or to birds flying near the ground. *-m.* Inspector of a slaughterhouse; a workman employed there.

rastrillada [ras-tree'-lyah'-dah], *f.* A rakeful.

rastrillador, ra [ras-treel-lyah-dor, rah], *m. & f.* Heckler; flax-dresser, hatcheller; raker.

rastrillaje [ras-treel-lyah'-hay], *m.* Raking; batchelling; handling with a rake or hatchel.

rastrillar [ras-treel-lyar'], *va.* 1. To hackle, to dress flax, to comb, to hatcher. 2. To separate the straw from the corn with a rake; to rake (recoger).

rastrilleo [ras-treel-lyay'-o], *m.* The act of hackling or raking.

rastrillo [ras-treel'-lyo], *m.* 1. Hackle, an instrument to dress flax and hemp; flax-comb. 2. Portcullis. 3. Hammer of a gun-lock. 4. Ward of a key (de cerradura, llave). 5. Ward of a lock. 6. Gateway of a palisade.

rastro [rahs'-tro], *m.* 1. Track on the ground; trail (huella). 2. Rake, harrow (grada). 3. Slaughterhouse (matadero); place where meat is sold by the carcass. 4. Sign, token, vestige, relic. 5. Grapple for gathering oysters. **Seguir el rastro de uno,** to follow somebody's trail. **Desaparecer sin dejar rastro,** to vanish without trace.

rastrojera [ras-tro-hay'-rah], *f.* Stubble ground and the time which the stubble lasts.

rastrojo [ras-tro'-ho], *m.* Stubble (de campo). **Sacar (a uno) de los rastrojos,** to raise one from a humble position.

rasura [rah-soo'-rah], *f.* 1. Shaving as with a razor (afeitado). 2. Scraping, filing. *-pl.* Boiled lees of wine, which serve to clean plate, etc.

rasurada [rah-soo-rah'-dah], *f.* Shave.

rasurar [rah-soo-rar'], *va.* To shave with a razor (afeitar).

rata [rah'-tah], *f.* 1. Rat. 2. She-mouse. *-m.* Mean devil (tacaño).

rata almizclada or **almizclera** [rah'-tah al-mith-clah'-dah, al-mith-clay'-rah], *f. (Zool.)* Muskrat.

ratafía [ra-tah-fee'-ah], *f.* Ratafia, a spirituous liquor. *V.* ROSOLI.

ratania [ra-tah'-ne-ah], *f. (Bot.)* Ratany or ratanhy, a Peruvian shrub of astringent properties.

ratear [rah-tay-ar'], *va.* 1. To lesson or abate in proportion. 2. To distribute or divide proportionally. 3. To filch, to commit petty thefts. *-vn.* To trail along the ground, to creep.

rateo [rah-tay'-o], *m.* Distribution made at a certain rate or proportion.

rateramente [rah-tay-rah-men-tay], *adv.* Meanly, vilely.

ratería [rah-tay-ree'-ah], *f.* 1. Larceny, petty theft. 2. Vile conduct in things of little value.

ratero, ra [rah-tay'-ro, rah], *a.* 1. Creeping on the ground. 2. Skimming on the ground, flying low; spoken of birds. 3. Committing petty thefts (ladrón); pilfering. 4. Mean, vile.

rateruelo, ela [rah-tay-roo-ay'-lo, lah], *m. & f. dim.* Little pilferer.

ratificación [rah-te-fe-cah-the-on'], *f* Ratification, the act of ratifying; confirmation, approbation.

ratificar [rah-te-fe-car'], *va.* To ratify (tratado), to approve.

ratificatorio, ria [rah-te-fe-cah-to'-re-o, ah], *a.* Ratificatory, confirming.

ratigar [rah-te-gahr'], *va. (Prov.)* To secure any loads on carts with a rope.

rátigo [rah'-te-go], *m. (Prov.)* Articles carried in carts.

ratihabición [rah-te-ah-be-the-on'], *f. (Law.)* Ratification, making valid.

ratina [rah-tee'-nah], *f.* Petersham, ratteen, woollen cloth woven like serge.

ratito [rah-tee'-to], *m. dim.* A little while, a short time.

rato [rah'-to], *m.* 1. *(Prov.)* He-mouse. *V.* RATÓN. 2. Short space of time. **Al cabo de rato,** it turned out ill after thinking so long about it. **Buen rato,** a pretty time, a good while; many: a great quantity. **A ratos perdidos,** in leisure hours. **De rato en rato, a ratos,** from time to time occasionally. **Hace rato que se fue,** he's been gone a while. **Pasar el rato,** to kill time. **Hay para rato,** there's still a long way to go.

rato, ta [rah'-to, tah], *a. (For.)* Firm, valid, conclusive.

ratón [rah-tone'], *m.* 1. He-mouse. 2. *(Naut.)* Hidden rock which frets cables. 3. *(Mil.)* Mechanism serving to fire off mines. 4. *(Carib.)* Hangover (resaca). 5. *(Carib.)* Squib, cracker (petardo).

ratona [rah-toh'-nah], *f.* Female mouse or rat.

ratonar [rah-to-nar'], *va.* To gnaw like mice or rats. *-vr.* 1. To become sick as cats from eating rats. 2. (For hidden rocks) To fret or wear any cables.

ratoncito [rah-ton-thee'-to], *m. dim.* A little mouse.

ratonera [rah-to-nay'-rah], *f.* 1. Mouse trap (trampa). **Caer en la ratonera,** to fall into a snare. **Ratonera, gato de agua.** Rat-trap, placed on water. 2. Hole where rats breed. 3. *(And. Cono Sur)* Hovel (barrio bajo).

ratonero, ra [rah-to-nay'-ro, rah], **Ratonesco, ca** [rah-to-nes'-co, cah], *a.* Belonging to mice, mousy.

raudal [rah-oo-dahl'], *m.* 1. Torrent (torrente), rapid stream. 2. Plenty, abundance. **Entrar a raudales,** to pour in.

raudamente [rah'-oo-dah-men-tay], *adv.* Rapidly.

raudo, da [rah'-oo-do, dah], *a.* Rapid, precipitate.

rauta [rah'-oo-tah], *f (Coll.)* Road, way, route.

raya [rah'-yah], *f.* 1. Stroke, dash, or line drawn with a pen. 2. A line or limit between two provinces or countries (límite); frontier. 3. The term line, or boundary put to anything. 4. Stripe, streak. **Tener a raya,** to keep within bounds. **Tener a uno a raya,** to keep one at bay. 5. Part in the hair. 6. Strip of ground cleared of combustible matter. *(Acad.)* **Tres en raya,** a boyish play. **A raya,** correctly, within just limits. 7. *m. (Zool.)* Ray.

rayado, da [rah-yah'-do, dah], *a.* 1. Striped (tela, diseño). 2. Ruled (papel), fined. 3. Streaked, variegated. 4. *(And. Cono Sur)* Cracked (loco). 5. *(Carib.)* No parking area.

rayano, na [rah-yah'-no, nah], *a.* Neighboring, contiguous.

rayar [rah-yar'], *va.* 1. To form strokes, to draw lines (papel). 2. To mark with lines or strokes, to streak (como diseño), to variegate in hues. 3. To rifle or striate the interior of firearms. 4. To expunge. 5. *(LAm.)* To spur on (caballo). *-vn.* 1. To excel, to surpass. 2. *(Met.)* To approximate, to touch. *-vr.* 1. To get scratched (objeto). 2. *(And)* To see one's wishes fulfilled. 3. *(And. Cono Sur)* To get angry (enojarse).

rayo [rah'-yo], *m.* 1. A right line. 2. Ray of light (de luz). 3. Radius of a circle; spoke of a wheel. 4. Thunderbolt; flash of lightning. 5. Firearms, *(Met.)* Sudden havoc, misfortune (desgracia), or chastisement. 6. A lively, ready genius; great power or efficacy of action (persona). **Rayo directo, incidente, reflejo,** and **refracto,** direct, incidental, reflected, and refracted light. **Rayo equis,** X ray. **Rayo visual,** field of vision. **Echar rayos,** to show great anger or wrath. **La noticia cayó como un rayo,** the news was a bombshell. **Pasar como un rayo,** to rush past. **Sabe a rayos,** it tastes awful.

rayón [rah-yone'], *m.* Rayon.

rayoso, sa [rah-yo'-so, sah], *a.* Full of lines.

rayuela [rah-yoo-ay'-lah], *f.* 1. *(dim.)* A small line. 2. Game of drawing lines.

rayuelo [rah-yoo-ay'-lo], *m. (Orn.)* Small kind of snipe.

raza [rah'-thah], *f.* 1. Race, generation, lineage, family, clan: branch of a family. 2. Quality of cloth and other things. 3. Each of the races of mankind. 4. Ray of light. 5. Cleft in a horse's hoof. **Raza blanca,** white race.

razado [rah-thah'-do], *a.* Applied to coarse woollen cloth of unequal color.

rázago [rah'-thah-go], *m.* Coarse cloth made of tow.

razón [rah-thone'], *f.* 1. Reason (facultad), the rational faculty. 2. Ratiocination. Reason (motivo), clearness of faculty. 4. Reasonableness, moderation. **Póngase Vd. en la razón,** be moderate in your demand. 5. Reason, cause, motive, principle. 6. Reason, argument, ground of persuasion; consideration, occasion. 7. Account, calculation. 8. Order, mode, method. 9. Reason, reasonableness, right, justice. 10. Expression or word which explains the idea; term. 11. Ratio, a relation between two mathematical quantities. 12. Firm, partnership, name of a commercial establishment. **A razón de,** at the rate of. **En razón,** with regard to. **Tener razón,** to be right. **Dar la razón a uno,** to agree that somebody is right. **Razón de más,** all the more reason. **Dar razón de sí,** to give an account of oneself.

razonable [rah-tho-nah'-blay], *a.* Reasonable; moderate; fair; just.

razonablejo, ja [rah-tho-nah-blay'-ho, hah], *a. (Coll.)* Moderate, rational.

razonablemente [rah-tho-nah'-blay-men-tay], *adv.* Reasonably; moderately.

razonado, da [rah-tho-nah'-do, dah], *a.* Rational, prudent, judicious. *-pp.* of RAZONAR.

razonador, ra [rah-tho-nah-dor', rah], *m. & f.* Reasoner.

razonamiento [rah-tho-nah-me-en'-to], *m.* Reasoning, argument, discourse, oration.

razonante [rah-tho-nahn'-tay], *pa.* Reasoning; reasoner.

razonar [rah-tho-nar'], *va.* 1. To reason, to discourse. 2. To talk (hablar), to converse. *-va.* 1. To name, to call. 2. To advocate, to allege. 3. To take a memorandum of things, to place to account. 4. To compute, to regulate.

razoncita [rah-thon-thee'-tah], *f. dim.* A short memorandum or account.

re [ray], *prep.* Always used in composition, signifying repetition. Also as an intensive, signifying *very*; as, *rebueno,* very good. *-m. (Mus.)* Re, the second note of the musical scale.

reacción [ray-ac-the-on'], *f.* 1. Reaction, revulsion. 2. Rebound. 3. *(Met.)* Resistance, opposition. 4. An alliance of efforts to overthrow a political power or to replace it by another. 5. *(Med.)* Reaction, a period of feverishness succeeding a chill.

reaccionar [ray-ac-the-o-nar'], *va.* To react, to respond.

reaccionario, ria [ray-ac-the-o-nah'-re-o, ah], *a.* 1. Reactionary; revulsive. 2. Reactionary, revolutionary. 3. Conservative, absolutist.

reacción en cadena [ray-ac-the-on' en cah-day'-nah], *f.* Chain reaction.

reacio, cia [ray-ah'-the-o, ah], *a.* Obstinate, intractable, reluctant.

reactividad [ray-ac-te-ve-dahd'], *f.* Reactivity.

reactivo [ray-ac-tee'-vo], *m.* Reagent, an agent employed to determine the composition of other bodies. Used also as adjective.

reactor [ray-ac-tor'], *m.* Reactor. **Reactor nuclear,** nuclear reactor.

readmisión [ray-ad-me-se-on'], *f.* Readmission.

readmitir [ray-ad-me-teer'], *va.* To readmit.

reafirmación [ray-ah-feer-mah-the-on'], *f.* Reaffirmation.

reafirmar [ray-ah-feer-mahr'], *va.* To reaffirm.

reagradecer [ray-ah-grah-day-therr'], *va.* To estimate highly.

reagradecimiento [ray-ah-grah-day-the-me-en'-to], *m.* Act of esteeming, estimation.

reagravación [ray-ah-grah-vah-the-on'], *f.* Reaggravation.

reagravar [ray-ah-grah-var'], *va.* To aggravate anew.

reagrupación [ray-ah-groo-pah-the-on'], *f.* Regrouping.

reagrupar [raygroo-pahr'], *va.* To regroup.

reagudo, da [ray-ah-goo'-do, dah], *a.* Very acute.

reajustar [ray-ah-hoos-tahr'], *va.* To readjust.

reajuste [ray-ah-hoos'-tay], *m.* Readjustment.

real [ray-ahl'], *a.* 1. Real (verdadero), actual. 2. Royal, kingly, king-like. 3. Grand, magnificent, splendid. 4. Real, true, certain. 5. Open, fair, ingenuous, candid; generous, noble. *-m.* 1. Camp, the king's tent. 2. Main body of an army. **Real de plata,** silver real, or two reals vellón. **Está sin un real,** he hasn't a bean.

reala [ray-ah'-lah], *f.* Herd which a shepherd forms of his own flock, and of other owners.

realce [ray-ahl'-thay], *m.* 1. Raised work, embossment. 2. Brightness of colors, reflection of light; high light. 3. Lustre, splendor (esplendor).

realdad [ray-al-dahd'], *f.* Royal power, and its exercise; sovereignty.

realegrarse [ray-ah-lay-grar'-say], *vr.* To be very joyful.

realeza [ray-ah-lay'-thah], *f.* Royalty, regal dignity.

realidad [ray-ah-le-dahd'], *f.* Reality, fact; truth and sincerity (verdad). **En realidad, en realidad de verdad,** truly, really, effectually.

realimentación [ray-ah-le-men-tah-the-on'], *f. (Elec.)* Feedback.

realismo [ray-ah-lees' -mo], *m.* 1. Royalism, support of a monarchy. 2. Absolutism in political government. 3. *(Neol.)* Realism in art, or literature.

realista [ray-ah-lees'-tah], *m.* 1. Royalist, loyalist, one who a supports monarch or monarchy: used as an adjective. 2. Realist, a partisan of realism in art or literature.

realizable [ray-ah-le-thah'-blay], *a.* Realizable.

realización [ray-ah-le-thah-the-on'], *f.* 1. Realization, accomplishment, fulfillment. 2. Sale, reduction of merchandise for sale.

realizar [ray-ah-le-thar'], *va.* 1. To realize (bienes), to bring into being or action. 2. *(Com.)* To realize upon, to convert into money. 3. To make (viaje). 4. To fulfil (promesa). *-vr.* 1. To come true (sueño). 2. To fulfil oneself (persona).

realmente [ray-ahl'-men-tay], *adv.* Really (en efecto), effectually; formally, actually; royally.

realzar [ray-al-thar'], *va.* 1. To raise, to elevate; to emboss. 2. To heighten the colors in a painting, to emboss. 3. To illustrate, to aggrandize.

reamar [ray-ah-mar'], *pa.* To love in return; to love much.

reanimar [ray-ah-ne-mar'], *va.* To cheer, to reanimate.

reanudar [ray-ah-noo-dar'], *va* To renew, to resume.
Reanudar las esperanzas, to renew one's hopes.
Reanudar el trabajo, to resume work.

reañejo, ja [ray-ah-nyay'-ho, hah], *a*. Oldish, growing old.

reaparecer [ray-ah-pah-ray-therr'], *vn*. To reappear.

reaparición [ray-ah-pah-re-the-on'], *f*. Reappearing, reappearance.

reapertura [ray-ah-per-too'-rah], *f*. Reopening.

reapreciar [ray-ah-pray-the-ar'], *va*. To revalue, to reestimate.

reapretar [ray-ah-pray-tar'], *va*. To press again, to squeeze.

rearar [ray-ah-rar'], *va*. To plough again.

reasegurar [ray-ah-say-goo-rar'], *va*. (*Com.*) To reinsure.

reaseguro [ray-ah-say-goo'-ro], *m*. (*Com.*) Reinsurance.

reasignar [ray-ah-sig-nar'], *va*. To assign anew.

reasumir [ray-ah-soo-meer'], *va*. To retake, to resume, to reassume.

reasunción [ray-ah-soon-the-on'], *f*. The act of resuming, reassumption.

reata [ray-ah'-tah], *f*. 1. Rope which ties one horse or mule to another, to make them go in a straight line (caballos). 2. (*Met.*) Blind submission to the opinion of others. **Reatas**, (*Naut.*) Woolding, ropes tied round a mast to strengthen it. 3. (*And. Carib. Mex.*) Flowerbed, border (de flores). 4. (*Mex.*) Bamboo screen (enrejado).

reatadura [ray-ah-tah-doo'-rah], *f*. The act of tying one beast after another with a rope.

reatar [ray-ah-tar'], *va*. 1. To tie one beast to another with a rope; to retie or tie tightly. 2. (*Naut.*) To woold, to tie ropes round masts or yards in order to strengthen them.

reato [ray-ah'-to], *m*. The obligation of atonement for a sin after absolution.

reaventar [ray-ah-ven-tar'], *va*. To winnow corn a second time.

rebaba [ray-bah'-bah], *f*. 1. Seam of a cussing in plaster or metal; burr or flash. 2. Projecting piece of stone in a wall, etc. 3. Mortar crowded out between stones and bricks. 4. The chipped edge of sawed timbers and planks.

rebaja [ray-bah'-hah], *f*. 1. Abatement, deduction, diminution. 2. (*Com.*) Drawback, a return of duties on exportation, rebate.

rebajamiento [ray-bah-hah-me-en'-to], *m*. 1. Curtailment, abatement. 2. Abasement.

rebajar [ray-bah-har'], *va*. 1. To abate, to lessen, to diminish (intensidad). 2. To lower the price (precio), to dock a bill or account, to allow a discount, to curtail the quantity. 3. To weaken the light and give a deeper shade to the tints of a painting. 4. (*Mil.*) To dismiss from service, to muster out. **Rebajar el precio a uno en un 5 por 100**, to give somebody a discount of 5 %. *-vr*. 1. To humble oneself, to be humbled. 2. To commit low actions.

rebajo [ray-bah'-ho], *m*. Groove in timber or stone.

rebalaje [ray-bah-lah'-hay], *m*. Crooks or windings in a river.

rebalsa [ray-bahl'-sah], *f*. Stagnant water, a pool or puddle.

rebalsar [ray-bal-sar'], *va*. 1. To dam water to form a pool. 2. To stop, to detain.

rebanada [ray-bah-nah'-dah], *f*. Slice of bread and other things.

rebanadilla [ray-bah-nah-deel'-lyah], *f*. *dim*. A small slice.

rebanador, ra [ray-bah-nah-dor', rah], *a*. Slicing. *-m. & f.* Slicer. *-f.* Slicing machine.

rebanar [ray-bah-nar'], *va*. 1. To slice, to cut into slices. 2. To slice, to cut, to divide.

rebanco [ray-bahn'-co], *m*. (*Arch.*) The second bench or seat.

rebanadera [ray-bah-nyah-day'-rah], *f*. Drag, a hooked instrument for taking things out of a well.

rebanadura [ray-bah-nyah-doo'-rah], *f*. *V.* ARREBAÑADURA.

rebañar [ray-bah-nyar'], *va. V.* ARREBAÑAR.

rebañego, ga [ray-bah-nyay'-go, gah], *a*. Gregarious.

rebaño [ray-bah'-nyo], *m*. 1. Flocks of sheep, herd of cattle. 2. Crowd, heap. 3. Flock, assembly of the faithful.

rebañuelo [ray-bah-nyoo-ay'-lo], *m. dim*. Small flock or heap.

rebaptizando, da [ray-bap-te-thahn'-do, dah], *a*. A person who is to be rebaptized.

rebaptizar [ray-bap-te-thar'], *va. V.* REBAUTIZAR.

rebasadero [ray-bah-sah-day'-ro], *m*. (*Naut.*) Difficult place to pass.

rebasar [ray-bah-sar'], *va*. 1. (*Naut.*) To sail past any point or difficult place. 2. (*Met.*) To exceed (en calidad, número), to go beyond, to pass from a line or given point. **Han rebasado ya los límites razonables**, they have already gone beyond all reasonable limits.

rebastar [ray-bas-tar'], *vn*. To be more than enough.

rebatar [ray-bah-tar'], *va. V.* ARREBATAR.

rebate [ray-bah'-tay], *m*. Dispute, disagreement.

rebatible [ray-bah-tee'-blay], *a*. That can be refuted or rebutted.

rebatimiento [ray-bah-te-me-en'-to], *m*. Repulsion, refutation.

rebatir [ray-hah-teer'], *va*. 1. To rebate, to curb, to resist (tentación); to repel (ataque). 2. To parry, to ward off (golpe). 3. To object, to refute; to rebut. 4. (*Arith.*) To allow from a sum a quantity which ought not to have been comprised in it. 5. To repress the passions of the soul.

rebato [ray-bah'-to], *m*. 1. An unexpected attack (ataque), a surprise; an unexpected event; alarm, a fit, a transport. 2. A sudden fit of passion. **De rebato**, suddenly. 3. Summons of the people by a bell in case of danger.

rebautizar [ray-bah-oo-te-thar'], *va*. To rebaptize.

rebeber [ray-bay-berr'], *va*. 1. To drink often. 2. *V.* EMBEBER.

rebeca [ray-bay'-kah], *f*. Cardigan.

rebeco, ca [ray-bay'-co, cah], *a*. Cross-grained, intractable, harsh.

rebelar [ray-bay-lar'], *va*. To excite rebellion. *-vr*. 1. To revolt; to rebel, to mutiny. 2. To get at variance, to break off friendly intercourse. 3. To resist, to oppose; to excite the passions irrationally.

rebelde [ray-bel'-day], *m*. Rebel. *-a*. 1. Rebellious. 2. Stubborn, ill-tractable, perverse. 3. (*Law.*) Not attending the summons of a judge, non-appearance in court. 4. Rebellious (pasiones, afecciones).

rebeldía [ray-bel-dee'-ah], *f*. 1. Rebelliousness, contumacy, disobedience. 2. Obstinacy, stubbornness. 3. (*Law.*) Default, non-appearance in court. **En rebeldía**, by default.

rebelión [ray-bay-le-on'], *f*. Rebellion, revolt, insurrection.

rebelón, na [ray-bay-lone', nah], *a*. Restive (caballo).

rebellín [ray-bayl-lyeen'], *m*. (*Mil.*) Ravelin.

rebencazo [ray-ben-cah'-tho], *m*. Blow with a port-rope.

rebendecir [ray-ben-day-theer'], *va*. To bless or consecrate anew.

rebenque [ray-ben'-key], *m*. 1. Rope for flogging galley slaves. 2. (*Naut.*) Ratline, or ratlin, a short cross-rope.

rebeza [ray-bay'-thah], *f*. (*Naut.*) Change in the course of tides or currents.

rebién [ray-be-en'], *adv*. (*Coll.*) Very well.

rebina [ray-bee'-nah], or **rebinadura** [ray-be-nah-doo'-rah], *f*. (*Agr.*) Ploughing a third time.

rebinar [ray-be-nar'], *va*. (*Agr.*) *V.* TERCIAR.

rebisabuela [ray-be-sah-boo-ay'-lah], *f*. The great-great-grandmother.

rebisabuelo [ray-be-sah-boo-ay'-lo], *m*. The great-great-grandfather.

rebisnieta, rebiznieta [ray-beeth-ne-ay'-tah], *f*. The great-great-granddaughter

rebisnieto, rebiznieto [ray-beeth-ne-ay'-to], *m*. The great-great-grandson.

reblandecer [ray-blan-day-therr'], *va*. To make tender.

reblandecimiento [ray-blan-day-the-me-en'-to], *m*. (*Med.*) Softening of organic tissues. **Reblandecimiento cerebral**, softening of the brain.

rebobinar [ray-bo-be-nahr'], *va*. To rewind.

rebociño [ray-bo-thee'-nyo], *m.* *(Prov.)* A short cloak or mantle for women.

rebolisco [ray-bo-less'-co], *m.* (Cuba) Tumult of people without a real occasion.

rebolla [ray-bol'-lyah], *f.* Local name of a kind of oak-tree.

rebollar [ray-bol-lyar'], *m.* Thicket of oak saplings.

rebollidura [ray-bol-lye-doo'-rah], *f.* *(Mil.)* Honey-comb, a flaw in the bore of ordance.

rebollo [ray-bol'-lyoh], *m.* 1. *(Bot.)* The Turkey oak. 2. *(Prov.)* Boll or trunk of a tree.

rebolludo, da [ray-bol-lyoo'-do, dah], *a.* 1. *V.* REHECHO and DOBLE. 2. Applied to a rude, hard diamond.

reboñar [ray-bo-nyar'], *vn.* *(Prov.)* To stop on account of too much water (molino de agua).

reborda [ray-bor'-dah], *f.* A certain mode of fishing along the Levant coasts.

reborde [ray-bor'-day], *m.* Ledge.

rebosadero [ray-bo-sah-day'-ro], *m.* Place where anything overflows.

rebosadura [ray-bo-sah-doo'-rah], *f.* **rebosamiento**, *m.* Overflow, as of liquor in a vessel.

rebosante [ray-bo-sahn'-tay], *a.* Brimming with, overflowing with.

rebosar [ray-bo-sar'], *vn.* 1. To run over, to overflow (líquido, recipiente). 2. To abound (abundar), to be plenty. 3. To evince, to display, to be unable to hide an affection or passion of the spirit.

rebotadera [ray-bo-tah-day'-rah], *f.* Iron plate which raises the nap on cloth to be shorn.

rebotador, ra [ray-bo-tah-dor', rah], *m. & f.* One who rebounds; clincher.

rebotadura [ray-bo-tah-doo'-rah], *f.* The act of rebounding.

rebotallero, ra [ray-bo-tah-lyay'-ro, rah], *a.* *(Min.)* Searcher, working on a percentage.

rebotar [ray-bo-tar'], *va.* 1. To rebound (pelota). 2. To change color, to turn (vino, licores). -*va* 1. To clinch a spike or nail (clavo), to turn the point of something sharp. 2. To raise the nap of cloth to be shorn. 3. To repel. -*vr.* To change one's opinion, to retract.

rebote [ray-bo'-tay], *m.* Rebound, rebounding, resilience. **De rebote**, on a second mission.

rebotica [ray-bo-tee'-cah], *f.* Back room behind an apothecary's shop.

rebotiga [ray-bo-tee'-gah], *f.* *(Prov.)* *V.* TRASTIENDA.

rebotín [ray-bo-teen'], *m.* The second growth of mulberry leaves.

rebozado [ray-bo-thah'-do], *a.* Fried in batter.

rebozar [ray-bo-thar'], *va.* 1. To overlay or baste meat. 2. *V.* EMBOZAR. -*vr.* To be muffled up in a cloak.

rebozo [ray-bo'-tho], *m.* 1. The act of muffling oneself up. *V.* EMBOZO. 2. Muffler for the face. *V.* REBOCIÑO. **De rebozo**, secretly, hiddenly.

rebramar [ray-brah-mar'], *vn.* To low and bellow repeatedly; to answer one noise by another.

rebramo [ray-brah'-mo], *m.* Noise with which deer respond to each other.

rebrote [ray-bro'-tay], *m.* New outbreak.

rebrotín [ray-bro-teen'], *m.* The second growth of clover which has been cut.

rebudiar [ray-boo-de-ar'], *vn.* To snuffle and grunt.

rebueno, na [ray-boo-ay'-no, nah], *a.* *(Coll.)* Very good, excellent.

rebufar [ray-boo-far'], *vn.* To blow or snort repeatedly, like animals.

rebufo [ray-boo'-fo], *m.* The recoil of a fire-arm; expansion of air at the muzzle on firing a shot. (Literally, snorting.)

rebujal [ray-boo-hahl'], *m.* 1. Number of cattle in a flock below even fifties. (For instance, in a flock of 430 sheep the 30 are *rebujal.*) 2. A small piece of amble lable.

rebujalero [ray-boo-hah-lay'-ro], *m.* A petty farmer.

rebujar [ray-boo-har'], *va.* To wrap up linen and other cloth in an awkward manner.

rebujo [ray-boo'-ho], *m.* 1. Muffler, a part of female dress. 2. *(Prov.)* A portion of tithe paid in money. 3. Wrapper for any common article.

rebullicio [ray-bool-lyee'-the-o], *m.* Great clamor or tumult.

rebullir [ray-bool-lyeer'], *vn.* To stir, to begin to move.

reburujar [ray-boo-roo-har'], *va.* *(Coll.)* To wrap up, to pack in bundles.

reburujón [ray-boo-roo-hone'], *m.* Bundle wrapped up carelessly.

rebusca [ray-boos'-cah], *f.* 1. Research, searching. 2. Gleaning fruit and grain. 3. Refuse, remains (restos), relic. 4. *(And. Cono Sur)* Small business (negocio).

rebuscador, ra [ray-boos-cah-dor', rah], *m. & f.* Gleaner, researcher.

rebuscar [ray-boos-car'], *va.* 1. To glean grapes left by the vintagers. 2. To search (objeto), to inquire with great curiosity and attention. -*vn.* To search carefully.

rebusco [ray-boos'-co], *m.* Research; gleaning. *V.* REBUSCA.

rebutir [ray-boo-teer'], *va.* *(Prov.)* To stud; to fill up.

rebuznador, ra [ray-booth-nah-dor', rah], *m. & f.* One who brays like an ass.

rebuznar [ray-booth-nar'], *va.* To bray, as an ass.

rebuzno [ray-booth'-no], *m.* Braying of an ass.

recabar [ray-cah-bar'], *va.* 1. To obtain by entreaty. 2. To claim as a right (reclamar). 3. *(LAm.)* To ask for (solicitar).

recadero [ray-cah-day'-ro], *m.* *(Prov.)* Porter, messenger (mensajero).

recado [ray-cah'-do], *m.* 1. Message (mensaje), errand. 2. Present, gift sent to an absent person (regalo). 3. Compliments sent to the absent. 4. Provision of things necessary for some purpose (compras). 5. Outfit, all needed implements for doing certain things. 6. Precaution, security. 7. Instrument, record. 8. *(Amer.)* Saddle and trappings of a horse (montura). 9. *(Carib.)* Greetings (saludos). **Recado de escribir**, escritoire, writing-desk. **A recado, a buen recado**, with great care and attention. **Hacer un recado**, to go out on an errand.

recaer [ray-cah-err'], *vn.* 1. To fall back, to relapse. 2. To devolve. 3. To fall under another's power. **Las sospechas recayeron sobre el conserje**, suspicion fell on the porter. *(Yo recaigo, yo recaiga, from Recaer. V.* CAER.

recaída [ray-cah-ee'-dah], *f.* 1. Relapse, in sickness. 2. A second fall, a second offence.

recalada [ray-cah-lah'-dah], *f.* *(Naut.)* The act of descrying the land; landfall.

recalar [ray-cah-lar'], *va.* 1. To soak, to impregnate with liquor. 2. *(Naut.)* To descry a known point, after a cruise. 3. To bring another vessel to port. 4. To penetrate a calm (corriente de aire).

recalcadamente [ray-cahl-cah'-dah-men-tay], *adv.* Closely, contiguously; vehemently.

recalcar [ray-cal-car'], *va.* 1. To squeeze. 2. To accent words or phrased with marked design. **Recalcar algo a uno**, to insist on something to somebody. -*vr.* To inculcate, to repeat often.

recalcitrante [ray-cal-the-trahn'-tay], *a.* Recalcitrant, perverse, obstinate.

recalcitrar [ray-cal-the-trar'], *vn.* 1. To kick or strike with the heel. 2. To wince, to kick as unwilling of the rider (caballos). 3. To oppose, to make resistance where obedience is due (resistir).

recalentamiento [ray-cah-len-tah-me-en'-to], *m.* Rekindling: heat.

recalentar [ray-cah-len-tar'], *va.* 1. To heat again, to rekindle. 2. To excite (apetito sexual). -*vr.* To become scorched or injured through heat: applied to farm products.

recalmón [ray-cal-mohn'], *m.* A sudden decrease in the force of the wind.

recalvastro, tra [ray-cal-vahs'-tro, trah], *a.* Bald from forehead to crown.

recalzar [ray-cal-thar'], *va.* 1. To prick the outlines of a design on paper. 2. To mould up plants; to prepare mortar or cement.

recalzo [ray-cahl'-tho], *m.* 1. The act of repairing a decayed wall. 2. Outside felloe of a cart-wheel.

recalzón [ray-cal-thone'], *m.* Outer felloe of a wheel.

recamado [ray-cah-mah'-do], *m. (Com.)* Embroidery of raised work.

recamador, ra [ray-cah-mah-dor', rah], *m. & f.* Embroiderer.

recamar [ray-cah-mar'], *va.* To embroider with raised work, to fret.

recámara [ray-cah'-mah-rah], *f.* 1. Bedroom (dormitorio). 2. Chamber, breech (de cañón).

recamarera [ray-cah-mah-ray'-rah], *f. (Mex.)* Upstairs maid.

recamarilla [ray-cah-mah-reel'-lyah], *f.* **dim.** A small wardrobe; a small chamber of a firearm.

recambiar [ray-cam-be-ar'], *va.* 1. To recharge, to cleanse a second time. 2. To add the re-exchange on a protested bill. 3 *(Com.)* To draw again upon the drawer or indorser of a bill of exchange not paid when mature.

recambio [ray-cahm'-be-o], *m.* 1. A new exchange or barter. 2. Re-exchange. 3. Retribution, reward. **Recambio de piezas,** *(Comput.)* parts replacement.

recamo [ray-cah'-mo], *m.* 1. Embroidery of raised work. 2. Button hole, bordered with lace, and garnished at the end with a tassel.

recanación [ray-cah-nah-the-on'], *f.* Act of measuring by canal, a measure of about two ells.

recancanilla [ray-can-cah-neel'-lyah], *f.* 1. Affectation of limping, by boys, for amusement. 2. Tergiversation; an affected tone of talking.

recantación [ray-can-tah-the-on'], *f.* Recantation, public retractation.

recantón [ray-can-tone'], *m.* Cornerstone, set upright at the corners of houses and streets.

recapacitar [ray-cah-pah-the-tar'], *vn.* To recall, to recollect, to think over (sobre).

recapitulación [ray-cah-pe-too-lah-the-on'], *f.* Recapitulation, summary.

recapitular [ray-cah-pe-too-lar'], *va.* To recapitulate, to sum up a charge or discourse; to draw to a head.

recarga [ray-car'-gah], *f.* 1. Additional tax or duty. 2. Second charge of firearms.

recargado, da [ray-car-gah'-do, dah], *a.* Overdone, excessive. **Recargado de adornos,** overly ornamented.

recargar [ray-car-gar'], *va.* 1. To reload, to load again. 2. To remand to prison on a new charge. 3. To make a new charge or accusation (sentencia); to recharge. 4. *(For.)* To increase the sentence of a culprit. **Recargar el café de azúcar,** to put too much sugar in the coffee.

recargo [ray-car'-go], *m.* 1. A new charge or accusation. 2. Increase of a fever. 3. A new burden (nueva carga). 4. Extra charge.

recata [ray-cah'-tah], *f.* The act of tasting or trying again.

recatadamente [ray-kah-tah'-dah-men-tay], *adv.* Cautiously, prudently; modestly; cunningly.

recatado, da [ray-cah-tah'-do, dah], *a.* 1. Prudent, circumspect; shy, coy. 2. Honest, candid, modest. *-pp.* of RECATAR.

recatamiento [ray-cah-tah-me-en'-to], *m. V.* RECATO.

recatar [ray-cah-tar'], *va.* 1. To secrete. 2. To try or taste again. *-vr.* To take care, to proceed with prudence (ser prudente); to be cautious. **Recatarse de algo,** to fight shy of something.

recatear [ray-cah-tay-ar'], *vn.* 1. To give sparingly, to hold back. 2. *V.* RECATEAR.

recatería [ray-cah-tay-ree'-ah], *f. V.* RECATONERÍA.

recato [ray-cah'-to], *m.* 1. Prudence, circumspection, caution. 2. Modesty (modestia), honor; bashfulness, coyness.

recatón [ray-cah-tone'], *m.* Metal socket of a lance or pike. *V.* REGATÓN.

recatonazo [ray-cah-to-nah'-tho], *m.* Stroke with a pike or lance.

recatonear [ray-cah-to-nay-ar'], *va.* To buy by wholesale, in order to retail again.

recatonería, recatonía [ray-cah-to-nay-ree'-ah], *f. V.* REGATONERÍA.

recaudación [ray-cah-oo-dah-the-on'], *f.* 1. The act of collecting rents or taxes; recovery of debts. 2. Collector's office.

recaudador [ray-cah-oo-dah-dor'], *m.* Tax-gatherer, collector of rents.

recaudamiento [ray-cah-oo-dah-me-en'-to], *m.* 1. Collection of rents or taxes. 2. Office or district of a collector.

recaudar [ray-cah-oo-dar'], *va.* 1. To gather, to collect rents or taxes (impuestos). 2. To put or hold in custody.

recaudo [ray-cah'-oo-do], *m* 1. Collection of rents or taxes. 2. Provision, supply. 3. Caution, security for or against. 4. *V.* RECADO. 5. *(CAm. Cono Sur, Mex.)* Spices (especias). 6. *(CAm. Cono Sur, Mex.)* Daily supply of fresh vegetables.

recavar [ray-cah-var'], *va.* To dig the ground a second time.

recazar [ray-cah-thar'], *va.* To seize prey in the air or on the ground, like a hawk.

recazo [ray-cah'-tho], *m.* 1. Guard, part of the hilt of a sword. 2. Back part of the blade of a knife.

recebar [ray-thay-bar'], *va* To spread gravel.

recebo [ray-thay'-bo], *m.* Sand or fine gravel spread over the bed of a highway to even it and make it firm.

recel [ray-thel'], *m.* A sort of striped tapestry.

recelar [ray-thay-lar'], *va. & vr.* 1. To fear, to distrust, to suspect. 2. To excite a mare sexually towards receiving the jackass (caballos).

recelo [ray-thay'-lo], *m.* Misgiving, imagination of something ill without proof, suspicion (suspicacia).

receloso, sa [ray-thay-lo'-so, sah], *a.* Distrustful, suspicious.

recentadura [ray-then-tah-doo'-rah], *f.* Leaven preserved for raising bread.

recental [ray-then-tahl'], *a.* Applied to a sucking lamb.

recentar [ray-then-tar'], *va.* To put sufficient leaven into dough to raise it. *-vr. V.* RENOVARSE.

receñir [ray-thay-nyeer'], *va.* To regird, to gird tight.

recepción [ray-thep-the-on'], *f.* 1. Reception, receiving, acceptation. 2. Reception (ceremonia). 3. Drawing room (cuarto).

recepcionista [ray-thep-the-o-nees'-tah], *m & f.* Receptionist (hotel), desk clerk.

receptación [ray-thep-tah-the-on'], *f.* Reception of stolen goods.

receptacular [ray-thep-tah-coo-lar'], *a. (Bot.)* Contained in the receptacle.

receptáculo [ray-thep-tah'-coo-lo], *m.* 1. Receptacle, vessel for liquids. 2. Refuge, asylum. 3. Gutter for the eaves of buildings.

receptador [ray-thep-tah-dor'], *m.* Receiver of stolen goods; abettor of crimes.

receptar [ray-thep-tar'], *va.* To receive stolen goods, to abet any crime. *-vr.* To take refuge.

recepticios, as [ray-thep-tee'-the-os, as], *a. (For.)* Property under the sole control of a married woman.

receptividad [ray-thep-te-ve-dahd'], *f.* Receptivity, receptiveness.

receptivo, va [ray-thep-tee'-vo, vah], *a.* Receptive.

recepto [ray-thep'-to], *m.* Asylum, place of refuge.

receptor, ra [ray-thep-tor', rah], *a.* Applied to one who receives anything, especially stolen goods.

receptor [ray-thep'-tor], *m.* 1. Receiver, treasurer. 2. Investigating official. 3. Radio receiver. **Receptor de control,** monitor. **Descolgar el receptor,** television receiver.

receptoría [ray-thep-to-ree'-ah], *f.* 1. Receiver's or treasurer's office. 2. Place of a receiver or treasurer. 3. Power of a delegate judge.

recercador, ra [ray-ther-cah-dor', rah], *a.* Girding, hemming in, investing.

recésit [ray-thay'-sit], *m.* Vacation. *V.* RECLE.

receso [ray-thay'-so], *m.* 1. Recess, remote apartment; recession. 2. *(Mex.)* Recess, the time when the legislature is not in session. **Receso del sol**, the apparent motion of the sun away from the equator.

receta [ray-thay'-tah], *f.* 1. Prescription, recipe of a physician or surgeon. 2. *(Coll.)* Memorandum of orders received; order for goods. 3. Account of parcels sent from one office to another.

recetador [ray-thay-tah-dor'], *m.* Prescriber of medicines.

recetar [ray-thay-tar'], *va.* 1. To prescribe, medicines. 2. *(Met.)* To make extravagant charges or unreasonable demands.

recetario [ray-thay-tah'-re-o], *m.* 1. Memorandum or register of the prescriptions made by a physician. 2. Apothecary's file of prescriptions not paid for by his customers. 3. Pharmacopoeia.

recetor [ray-thay-tor'], *m.* Receiver, treasurer. V. RECEPTOR

recetoria [ray-thay-to-ree'-ah], *f.* Treasury, place for keeping money.

rechazador, ra [ray-chah-thah-dor', rah], *m. & f.* Repelled contradictor.

rechazamiento [ray-chah-thah-me-en'-to], *m.* 1. Repulsion. 2. Repelling (ataque).

rechazar [ray-chah-thar'], *va.* 1. To repel (ataque), to repulse, to drive back (enemigo), to impel in an opposite direction, to force back. 2. To contradict, to impugn.

rechazo [ray-chah'-tho], *m.* 1. Rejection. 2. Recoil (de cañón), rebound. **De rechazo**, incidentally, casually, by rebounds.

rechifla [ray-chee'-flah], *f.* Whistle (silbido), whistling of the winds.

rechiflar [ray-che-flar'], *va.* 1. To mock, to make fun of, to ridicule. 2. To whistle insistently, to make cat-call. 3. *(Cono Sur)* To get cross (enojarse).

rechinador, ra [ray-che-nah-dor', rah], *a.* Creaking, grating.

rechinamiento [ray-che-nah-me-en'-to], *m.* Creaking of a machine, gnashing of teeth.

rechinante [ray-che-nahn'-tay], *pa.* Creaking; gnashing.

rechinar [ray-che-nar'], *vn.* 1. To creak (madera, puerta), to clash; to hurtle; to grate (piezas sin lubricar, dientes). **Rechinar los dientes**, to gnash the teeth. 2. To engage in anything with reluctance. 3. *(And. Cono Sur, Mex.)* To rage (rabiar).

rechinido [ray-che-nee'-do], *m.* V. RECHINO.

rechino [ray-chee'-no], *m.* Creaking, clang, clangor, clash.

rechoncho, cha [ray-chon'-cho, chah], *a. (Coll.)* Chubby (persona).

rechupete (De) [ray-choo-pay'-tay], *(Coll.)* Exquisite, highly agreeable. **Me ha salido de rechupete**, it turned out marvelously for me.

recial [ray-the-ahl'], *m.* Rapid, rapids in rivers.

reciamente [ray'-the-ah-men-tay], *adv.* Strongly, forcibly, stoutly.

recibí [ray-the-bee'], *m.* Received payment.

recibidero, ra [ray-the-be-day'-ro, rah], *a.* Receivable.

recibidor [ray-the-be-dor'], *m.* 1. Receiver 2. Entrance hall.

recibimiento [ray-the-be-me-en'-to], *m.* 1. Reception, receipt. 2. Entertainment to one from abroad. 3. Antechamber (antecámara). 4. General reception of company.

recibir [ray-the-beer'], *va.* 1. To accept, to receive, to let in. 2. To take charge of. 3. To sustain, to support. 4. To imbibe, to drink in, to draw in. 5. To super, to receive, to admit. 6. To receive company or visits. 7. To receive, to go and meet a person. 8. To fasten, to secure with mortar. 9. To experience an injury; to receive an attack. -*vr.* To be admitted to practice a profession **Recibir a cuenta**, to receive on account. **Recibir a prueba**, to receive on trial. **Recibir a uno con los brazos abiertos**, to welcome somebody with open arms. **La oferta fue mal recibida**, the offer was badly received.

recibo [ray-thee'-bo], *m.* 1. Reception. 2. Receipt, discharge, acquittance. **Acusar recibo**, *(Com.)* to acknowledge receipt. 3. Visit, entertainment or reception of friends.

reciclado [ray-the-clah'-do], *a.* Recycled. -*m.* Recycling.

reciclaje [ray-the-clah'-hay], *m.* Recycling; retraining.

reciclar [ray-the-clahr'], *va.* To recycle; to retrain (persona); to modify (plan).

recidiva [ray-the-dee'-vah], *f.* 1. Relapse of a disease when convalescence was progressing. 2. *(For.)* V: REINCIDENCIA.

recién [ray-the-en'], *adv.* Recently, lately (used before participles instead of *reciente*). **Recién casado**, newly-wed. **Recién muerto**, recently deceased. **Recién hecho**, newly-made.

reciente [ray-the-en'-tay], *adv.* Recent, new, fresh; just made, modern.

recientemente [ray-the-en'-tay-men-tay], *adv.* Recently, newly, freshly, just now, latterly, lately.

recinchar [ray-thin-char'], *va.* To bind round one thing to another with a girdle.

recinto [ray-theen'-to], *m.* Precinct, district. **Recinto amurallado**, walled enclosure.

recio, cia [ray'-the-o, ah], *a.* 1. Stout, strong, robust, vigorous. 2. Coarse, thick (grueso), clumsy. 3. Rude, uncouth, intractable. 4. Arduous, grievous, hard to bear. 5. Severe, rigorous (tiempo). 6. Swift, impetuous. **Recio de complexión**, of a strong constitution. **En lo más recio del invierno**, in the depths of winter.

recio, *adv.* Strongly, stoutly: rapidly; vehemently, vigorously. **Hablar recio**, to talk loud. **De recio**, strongly, violently, precipitately, rapidly.

récipe [ray'-the-pay], *m. (Coll.)* 1. Prescription of a physician. 2. Displeasure, disgust; ungenteel or bad usage.

recipiente [ray-the-pe-en'-tay], *m. (Chem.)* 1. Recipient (persona), receiver. 2. Receiver, bell-glass, of an air-pump. 3. Bowl, pot (utensilio de cocina).

reciprocación [ray-the-pro-cah-he-on'], *f.* Reciprocation, mutuality.

recíprocamente [ray-the'-pro-cah-men-tay], *adv.* Reciprocally, mutually, conversely.

reciprocar [ray-the-pro-car'], *va.* To reciprocate. -*vr.* To correspond mutually.

recíproco, ca [ray-thee'-pro-co, cah], *a.* Reciprocal, mutual (mutuo). **Verbo recíproco**, reciprocal verb, as **reciprocarse.**

recisión [ray-the-se-on'], *f.* Recision, abrogation.

recísimo, ma [ray-thee'-se-mo, mah], *a. sup.* Most vehement.

recitación [ray-the-tah-the-on'], *f.* Recitation, reciting.

recitado [ray-the-tah'-do], *m. (Mus.)* Recitative, tuneful pronunciation.- **Recitado, da**, *pp.* of RECITAR.

recitador, ra [ray-the-tah-dor', rah], *m. & f.* Reciter.

recital [ray-the-tahl'], *m. (Mus.)* Recital; *(Liter.)* reading.

recitar [ray-the-tar'], *va.* To recite, to rehearse.

recitativo, va [ray-the-tah-tee'-vo, vah], *a.* Recitative.

recizalla [ray-the-thahl'-lyah], *f.* Second filings or fragments.

reclamación [ray-clah-mah-te-on'], *f.* 1. Reclamation. 2. Objection (objeción), remonstrance. 3. *(Com.)* Complaint, claim (reivindicación). **Reclamación salarial**, wage claim.

reclamante [ray-clah-mahn'-tay], *m. & f.* Claimant.

reclamar [ray-clah-mar'], *va.* 1. To decoy birds with a call or whistle. 2. To reclaim, to demand; to cry unto. 3. *(Naut.)* To hoist or lower a yard by means of a block. -*vn.* To contradict, to oppose.

reclame [ray-clah'-may], *m. (Naut.)* Sheave-hole in a top-mast-head.

reclamo [ray-clah'-mo], *m.* 1. Decoy-bird (caza). 2. Call, an instrument to call birds. 3. Allurement, inducement (aliciente), enticement. 4. *(Naut.)* Tie-block. 5. Reclamation. 6. *(Print.)* Catch-word. **Acudir al reclamo**, *(Coll.)* to answer, to go where there is a thing suitable to one's purpose.

reclinable [ray-cle-nah'-blay], *a.* Capable of being reclined.

reclinación [ray-cle-nah-the-on'], *f.* Reclining.

reclinado, da [ray-cle-nah'-do, dah], *a. pp.* of RECLINAR. Reclined, recumbent.

reclinar [ray-cle-nar'], *va. & vn.* To recline, to lean back. **Reclinarse en, sobre**, to lean on or upon.

reclinatorio [ray-cle-nah-to'-re-o], *m.* 1. Couch, thing to lean on. 2. A stool for kneeling on at prayers.

recluir [ray-cloo-eer'], *va.* To shut up, to seclude.

reclusión [ray-cloo-se-on'], *f.* 1. Reclusion, shutting up. 2. Recess, place of retirement; closeness. **Reclusión mayor**, imprisonment in condition of maximum security.

recluso, sa [ray-cloo'-so, sah], *a. & m. & f.* Recluse. *-pp. irr.* of RECLUIR.

reclusorio [ray-cloo-so'-re-o], *m.* Recess, place of retirement.

recluta [ray-cloo'-tah], *f.* Recruiting (ejército): supply. *-m.* Recruit, a new soldier who enlists voluntarily.

reclutador [ray-cloo-tah-dor'], *m.* Any person employed in recruiting or raising new soldiers.

reclutamiento [ray-cloo-tah-me-en'-to], *m.* Recruiting of soldiers.

reclutar [rar-cloo-tar'], *va.* 1. To recruit, to supply an army with new men. 2. To repair anything wasted by new supplies. 3. *(Cono Sur)* To round up (ganado). 4. *(Cono Sur)* To contract (obrero).

recobrar [ray-co-brar'], *va.* 1. To recover, to get back what was lost. 2. *(Naut.)* To rouse in, to take up the end of a rope which hangs loose. *-vr.* To recover from sickness, to regain vigor of body or mind; to recollect.

recobro [ray-co'-bro], *m.* Recovery, restoration of thing lost.

recocer [ray-co-therr'], *va.* To boil again, to boil too much. *-vr.* To consume oneself with rage and indignation.

recocho, cha [ray-co'-cho, chah], *a.* Boiled too much, over-done.

recocido, da [ray-co-thee'-do, dath], *a.* 1. Over boiled. 2. Skilful, clever. 3. Over-ripe, dried up. *-m.* The operation of annealing metals. *-f.* The act of boiling again. *-pp.* of RECODER.

recodadero [ray-co-dah-day'-ro], *m.* Place for leaning on one's elbow.

recodar [ray-co-dar'], *vn. & vr.* To lean with the elbow upon anything.

rocodo [ray-co'-do], *m.* 1. A turn in a road or street; the bend of a river. 2. A corner or angle jutting out.

recogedero [ray-co-hay-day'-ro], *m.* 1. Place where things are gathered or collected. 2. Instrument with which things are gathered.

recogedor [ray-co-hay-dor'], *m.* 1. One who shelters or harbors. 2. Gatherer, gleaner.

recoger [ray-co-herr'], *va.* 1. To retake, to take back. 2. To gather (objetos), to collect, to hoard; to pick out; to contract. 3. To gather the fruits. 4. To receive, to protect, to shelter (necesitado). 5. To lock up in a mad-house. 6. To suspend the use, or stop the course of anything. 7. To extract intelligence from books. **Recoger un vale**, to take up a note. **Van a recoger las monedas antiguas**, they are going to call in the old coins. **Te vendremos a recoger a las 8**, we'll come for you at 8 o'clock. *-vr.* 1. To take shelter (refugiarse); to withdraw into retirement (retirarse). 2. To reform, or retrench one's expenses. 3. To go home, to retire, to rest. 4. To abstract oneself from worldly thoughts.

recogida [ray-co-hee'-dah], *f.* 1. The act of taking back anything which circulates. 2. A woman shut up in a house of correction. 3. *(Agr.)* Harvest. 4. *(Mex. Agr.)* Roundup.

recogidamente [ray-co-he-dah-men-tay], *adv.* Retiredly.

recogido, da [ray-co-hee'-do, dah], *a.* Retired, secluded (lugar); contracted, *-pp.* of RECOGER.

recogimiento [ray-co-he-me-en'-to], *m.* 1. Collection, assemblage. 2. Retreat, shelter. V. RECLUSIÓN. 3. House where women are confined, or live in retirement. 4. Abstraction from worldly concerns; preparation for spiritual exercises. 5. Absorption (estado); seclusion. 6. Devotion (cualidad).

recolar [ray-co-lar'], *va.* To strain a second time.

recolección [ray-co-lec-the-on'], *f.* 1. Summary, abridgment. 2. Harvest of grain or fruit. 3. Collection of money or taxes. 4. Convent where a strict observance of the rules prevails. 5. Retirement, abstraction from worldly affairs.

recolectar [ray-co-lec-tar'], *pa.* 1. To gather the harvest. 2. To collect many things, to hoard. 3. To collect from different litigants.

recoleto, ta [ray-co-lay'-to, tah], *a.* Belonging to a convent where strict order is maintained. *-m. & f.* Devotee who lives retired; a recollect.

recolorado, da [ray-co-lo-rah'-do, dah], *a.* Copper-nosed, red-faced, red-nosed.

recombinar [ray-com-be-nar'], *va.* To recombine.

recomendable [ray-co-men-dah'-blay], *a.* Commendable, laudable.

recomendablemente [ray-co-men-dah-blay-men-tay], *adv.* Laudably.

recomendación [ray-co-men-dah-the-on'], *f.* 1. Recommendation (indicación). 2. Injunction, application. 3. Praise, eulogy (elogio). 4. Dignity, authority. **Carta de recomendación**, letter of introduction. **Recomendación del alma**, prayers for the dying.

recomendar [ray-co-men-dar'], *va.* 1. To charge, to enjoin. 2. To recommend (indicar), to commend. 3. To entrust (confiar). 4. To advise (aconsejar). **Recomendar a uno que haga algo**, to recommend somebody to do something. *(Yo recomiendo, yo recomiende, from Recomendar. V.* ACRECENTAR.)

recomendaticio, cia [ray-co-men-dah-tee'-the-o, ah], *a.* Commendatory.

recomendatorio, ria [ray-co-me-dah-to'-re-o, ah], *a.* Recommendatory.

recompensa [ray-com-pen'-sah], *f.* 1. Compensation, satisfaction. 2. Recompense, reward, remuneration, fee, gratuity. **En recompensa**, in return.

recompensable [ray-com-pen-sah'-blay], *a.* Capable of being rewarded.

recompensación [ray-com-pen-sah-the-on'], *f.* Compensation, reward, recompense.

recompensar [ray-com-pen-sar'], *va.* To recompense, to reward, to gratify, to fee.

recomponer [ray-com-po-nerr'], *va.* To recompose, to mend, to repair.

recomposición [ray-com-po-se-the-on'], *f. (Chem.)* Recomposition.

recompostura [ray-com-pos-too-rah], *f.* V. RECOMPOSICIÓN.

recomprar [ray-com-prar'], *va.* To buy again, to buy back.

recompuesto, ta [ray-com-poo-es'-to, tah], *pp. irr.* from RECOMPONER.

reconcentramiento [ray-con-then-trah-me-en'-to], *m.* Act of introducing or establishing in the center.

reconcentrar [ray-con-then-trar'], *va.* 1. To introduce, to enter into something else, to concentre (atención). 2. To dissemble. 3. To make more concentrated (solución). *-vr.* To root, to take root: applied to sentiments and affections.

reconciliable [ray-con-the-le-ah'-blay], *a.* Reconcilable.

reconciliación [ray-con-the-le-ah-the-on'], *f.* 1. Reconciliation, reconcilement, renewal of friendship; agreement of things seemingly opposite. 2. Short confession detailing things previously omitted.

reconciliador, ra [ray-con-the-le-ah-dor', rah], *m. & f.* Reconciliator, reconciler.

reconciliar [ray-con-the-le-ar'], *va.* 1. To reconcile; to make friends with one; to accommodate. 2. To hear a short confession. 3. To consecrate anew any sacred place which has been polluted or defiled. *-vr.* 1. To confess offences. 2. To renew friendship.

reconciliatorio, ria [ray-con-the-le-ah-to'-re-o, ah], *a.* Conciliatory.

reconcomerse [ray-con-com-err'-say], *vr.* To scratch frequently from continual itching.

reconcomio [ray-con-co'-me-o], *m. (Coll.)* 1. Shrugging the shoulders with satisfaction or resignation, or from itching or stinging. 2. Fear, apprehension. 3. Craving, violent desire.

recóndito, ta [ray-con'-de-to, tah], *a.* Recondite, secret, hidden, concealed, latent, abstruse. **En lo más recóndito de**, in the depths of.

reconducción [ray-con-dooc-the-on'], *f.* Renewal of a lease.

reconducir [ray-con-doo-theer'], *va.* 1. To conduct back. 2. *(For.)* To renew a lease or contract.

reconfesar [ray-con-fay-sar'], *va.* To confess again.

reconfortante [ray-con-for-tahn-tay], *a.* Comforting; cheering; heart-warming. -*m.* *(LAm.)* Tonic.

reconfortar [ray-con-for-tahr'], *va.* To confort (confortar); to cheer (animar).

reconocedor, ra [ray-co-no-thay-dor', rah], *m. & f.* Examiner; one who recognizes.

reconocer [ray-con-no-therr'], *va.* 1. To try, to examine closely, to find out, to ascertain. 2. To summit to the command or jurisdiction of others. 3. To own, to confess. 4. To acknowledge favors received. 5. To consider, to contemplate. 6. To comprehend, to conceive. 7. To acknowledge the right of property of others; to recognize (aceptar). 8. To reconnoitre, to scout. 9. To recognize the official existence of a country, or to sanction acts done in another land. -*vr.* 1. To repent. 2. To confess oneself culpable (admitir). 3. To judge justly of one's own self. **Se le reconoce por el pelo**, you can recognize him by his hair. **Le reconocen por inteligente**, they agree that he is intelligent. **Por fin reconocieron abiertamente que era falso**, eventually they openly admitted that it was untrue. *(Yo reconozco, yo reconozca, from Reconocer. V. CONOCER.)*

reconocidamente [ray-co-no-the'-dah-men-tay], *adv.* Gratefully, confessedly.

reconocido, da [ray-co-no-thee'-do, dah], *a.* 1. Acknowledged, confessed. 2. Grateful, obliged. 3. *n.* Recognizee; one in whose favor a bond is given. -*pp.* OF RECONOCER.

reconociente [ray-co-no-the-en'-tay], *pa.* Recognizing.

reconocimiento [ray-co-no-the-me-en'-to], *m.* 1. Recognition. 2. Acknowledgment, gratitude; owning, confession. 3. Recognizance, subjection, submission. 4. Examination, inquiry. 5. Recognizance, acknowledgment of a bond or other writing in court. 6. Survey, inspection.

reconquista [ray-con-kees'-tah], *f.* Reconquest, a place reconquered.

reconquistar [ray-con-kis-tar'], *pa.* To reconquer (territorio).

reconsideración [ray-con-se-day-rah-the-on'], *f.* Reconsideration.

reconsiderar [ray-con-se-day-rahr'], *va.* To reconsider.

reconstituir [ray-cons-te-too-eer'], *va. & vr.* To reconstitute, to reconstruct.

reconstituyente [ray-cons-te-too-yen'-tay], *m. (Med.)* Tonic.

reconstrucción [ray-cons-trooc-the-on'], *f.* V. REEDIFICACIÓN.

reconstruir [ray-cons-troo-eer'], *va.* To reconstruct.

recontar [ray-con-tar'], *va.* To recount (cantidad), to relate distinctly.

recontento [ray-con-ten'-to], *m.* Contentment, deep satisfaction.

recontento, ta [ray-con-ten'-to, tah], *a.* Very content.

reconvalecer [ray-con-vah-lay-therr'], *vn.* To recover from sickness. *(Yo reconvalezco, yo reconvalezca, from Reconvalecer. V. CONOCER.)*

reconvención [ray-con-ven-the-on'], *f.* Charge, accusation; recrimination, expostulation; reproach (reproches).

reconvenir [ray-con-vay-neer'], *va.* 1. To charge, to accuse. 2. To retort, to recriminate, to accuse the prosecutor; to convert the plaintiff into the defendant; to expostulate. 3. To call to saccount, to reproach, to reprimand (reprender), to remonstrate.

reconvertir [re-con-ver-teer'], *va.* To reconvert; to rationalize (industria).

recopilación [ray-co-pe-lah-the-on'], *f.* 1. Summary, abridgment. 2. Collection of things taken from books. **Recopilación de las leyes**, abridgment or collection of the statutes.

recopilador [ray-co-pe-lah-dor'], *m.* Compiler, collector, abridger.

recopilar [ray-co-pe-lar'], *va.* To abridge, to collect.

record, récord [ray'-cord], *a.* Record. **En un tiempo record**, in a record time.

recordable [ray-cor-dah'-blay], *a.* Worthy of being recorded.

recordación [ray-cor-dah-the-on'], *f.* 1. Remembrance, calling to recollection. 2. V. RECUERDO.

recordador, ra [ray-cor-dah-dor', rah], *m. & f.* One who remembers; or that which serves to remind one of something.

recordar [ray-cor-dar'], *va.* To remind; to call to recollection (traer a la memoria). **Recordar algo a uno**, to remind somebody of something. -*vn.* 1. To awaken from sleep. 2. To remember. **No recuerdo**, I don't remember. -*vr.* To hit upon, to remember. *(Yo recuerdo, yo recuerde, from Recordar. V. ACORDAR.)*

recordativo, va [ray-cor-dah-tee'-vo, vah], *a.* That which reminds or may be reminded.

recordatorio, ria [ray-cor-dah-to'-re-o, ah], *a. (For.)* 1. Said of the official writing or order by which the fulfilment of a requisition or obligation is recalled. 2. Recollection.

recorrer [ray-cor-rerr'], *va.* 1. To run over, to examine, to survey (registrar). 2. To read over, to peruse. 3. To mend, to repair. -*vn.* 1. To recur, to have recourse to. 2. To rearrange a paragraph or page in printing. **Recorrer la memoria**, to call to recollection. **Recorrer una provincia a pie**, to go over a province on foot. **Recorrer un escrito**, to run one's eye over a document.

recorrido [ray-cor-ree'-do], *m.* 1. Route (ruta.) 2. Distance traveled (distancia). 3. Repair. 4. Scolding. **El recorrido del primer día fue de 450 km**, the first day's run was 450 kms. **Tren de largo recorrido**, long-distance train.

recortada [ray-cor-tah'-dah], *f.* In painting, a shadow as strong at the beginning as at the end.

recortado [ray-cor-tah'-do], *m.* Figure cut out of paper.

recortado, da [ray-cor-tah'-do], *a. (Bot.)* Notched, incised, cut irregularly. -*p.p.* of RECORTAR.

recortadura [ray-cor-tah-doo'-rah], *f.* V. RECORTE.

recortar [ray-cor-tar'], *va.* 1. To cut away (exceso), to shorten, to pare off. 2. To cut figures in paper. 3. To delineate a figure in profile. -*vr.* To stand out, to be outlined.

recorte [ray-cor'-tay], *m.* Outline, profile. -*pl.* Cuttings, trimmings, projecting pieces trimmed away by a cutting instrument; clippings. **Recortes de periódico**, newspaper cuttings. **El libro está hecho de recortes**, the book is a scissors-and-paste job.

recorvar [ray-cor-var'], *va.* V. ENCORVAR.

recorvo, va [ray-cor'-vo, vah], *a.* V. CORVO.

recoser [ray-co-serr'], *va.* To sew again a rip or rent.

recostadero [ray-cos-tah-day'-ro], *m.* Reclining or restingplace.

recostado, da [ray-cos-tah'-do, dah], *a. & pp.* of RECOSTAR. Recumbent, reclined.

recostar [ray-cos-tar'], *va.* To lean against, to recline. -*vr.* To go to rest; to repose or recline (reclinar). *(Yo me recuesto, yo me recueste, from Recostarse. V. ACORDAR.)*

recova [ray-co'-vah], *f.* 1. Purchasing eggs in the country (negocio), butter, or poultry, to retail in town. 2. A poultry market (mercado). 3. (Peru, Chile) Market-place. 4. Pack of hounds.

recovar [ray-co-var'], *va.* To buy fowls, eggs, etc., to sell again.

recoveco [ray-co-vay'-co], *m.* 1. Turning, winding. 2. Simulation, artifice.

recovero [ray-co-vay'-ro], *m.* Huckster, in eggs, butter, or poultry.

recre [ray'-cray], *m.* Vacation of choristers V. RECLE.

recreación [ray-cray-ah-the-on'], *f.* Recreation, relief, diversion, amusement.

recrear [ray-cray-ar'], *va.* To amuse, to delight, to gratify, to glad or gladden, to recreate (crear de nuevo). -*vr.* To divert oneself.

recreativo, va [ray-cray-ah-tee'-vo, vah], *a.* Recreative, diverting.

recrecer [ray-cray-therr'], *va. & vn.* 1. To grow again. 2. To augment, to increase (crecer). 8. To occur, to happen. -*vr.* To grow big, to be overgrown. 2. To recover one's spirits.

recrecimiento [ray-cray-the-me-en'-to], *m.* Growth, increase, augmentation.

recreído, da [ray-cray-ee'-do, dah], *a.* Intractable, returned to liberty (halcón).

recremento [ray-cray-men'-to], *m.* Recrement, spume, dregs, dross, scoria, residuum.

recreo [ray-cray'-o], *m.* 1. Recreation, amusement (diversión). 2. Recess. **Hora de recreo,** recess hour. **Sala de recreo,** recreation room. **Patio de recreo,** play-ground. **Viaje de recreo,** pleasure trip.

recría [ray-cree'-ah], *f.* Repasturing of colts.

recriar [ray-cre-ar'], *va.* To favor by good feeding and care, the development of colts and mules reared in another region.

recriminación [ray-cre-me-nah-the-on'], *f.* Recrimination, counter-charge.

recriminar [ray-cre-me-nar'], *va.* To recriminate, to make a counter-charge.

recrudecer [ray-croo-day-ther'], *vn, vr.* To recrudesce.

recrudecimiento [ray-croo-day-the-me-ayn'-to], *m.* Recrudescence.

recta [rec-tah], *f.* Straight line. **Recta de llegada,** home straight.

rectamente [rec-tah-men-tay], *adv.* Rightly, justly, justifiably, honestly, fairly, good.

rectangular [rec-tan-goo-lar'], *a.* Right-angled.

rectángulo, la [rec-tahn'-goo-lo, lah], *a.* Rectangular: rectangled. -*m.* Rectangle.

rectificable [rec-te-fe-cah'-blay], *a.* Rectifiable, which may be rectified.

rectificación [rec-te-fe-cah-the-on'], *f.* Rectification.

rectificador, ra [rec-te-fe-cah-dor', rah], *a.* Rectifying, verifying. -*m. & f.* Rectifier, verifier.

rectificar [rec-te-fe-car'], *va.* 1. To rectify, to make right. 2. To verify, to confirm. 3. To rectify (cálculo), to clarify, to redistil.

rectificativo, va [rec-te-fe-cah-tee'-vo, vah], *a.* That which rectifies or corrects.

rectilíneo, nea [rec-te-lee'-nay-o, ah], *a.* Rectilinear, rectilineous, rectilineal.

rectitud [rec-te-tood'], *f.* 1. Straightness, the shortest distance between two points. 2. Rectitude, uprightness, honor, honesty; exactitude.

recto, ta [rec'-to, tah], *a.* 1. Straight (línea), erect; right (ángulo). 2. Just (juez), upright, honest (persona), faithful, fair. **La flecha fue recta al blanco,** the arrow went straight to the target. 1. *(Anat.)* Rectum. 2. Superior of a community or establishment. **Rector de una universidad,** rector of a university. 3. Curate, rector.

rectorado [rec-to-rah'-do], *m.* Rectorship.

rectoral [rec-to-rahl'], *a.* Rectorial. -*f.* Rectory, a rector's dwelling.

rectorar [rec-to-rar'], *vn.* To attain the office of rector.

rectoría [rec-to-ree'-ah], *f.* 1. Rectory, curacy. 2. Office and dignity of a rector.

recua [ray'-coo-ah], *f.* 1. Drove of beasts of burden. 2. Multitude of things in succession.

recuadrar [ray-coo-ah-drahr'], *va. V.* CUADRICULAR.

recuadro [ray-coo-ah'-dro], *m. (Arch.)* Square compartment.

recuarta [ray-coo-ar'-tah], *f.* One of the chords of a guitar: the second string put in the place of the fourth when the strings are doubled.

recudimento, recudimiento [ray-coo-de-men'-to], *m.* Power vested in a person to gather rents or taxes.

recudir [ray-coo-deer'], *va.* To pay money in part of wages or other dues. -*vn.* To rebound, to rebound, to set out again to revert to the original place or state.

recuelo [ray-coo-ay'-lo], *m.* The lye which is caught in a vat after passing through a strainer.

recuenco [ray-coo-en'-co], *m.* Ground which forms an inclosed space or corner.

recuento [ray-coo-en'-to], *m.* 1. Inventory (inventario). *V.* INVENTARIO. 2. Recension, muster.

recuentro [ray-coo-en'-tro], *m. V.* RENCUENTRO.

recuerdo [ray-coo-err'-do], *m.* 1. Remembrance, hint given of what has passed, memento, memory; recognition (memoria). 2. Souvenir (regalo). 3. Jewel (joya). 4. Regards (saludos). **Guardar un feliz recuerdo de uno,** to have happy memories of somebody.

recuero [ray-coo-ay'-ro], *m.* Muleteer, mule-driver.

recuesta [ray-coo-es'-tah], *f.* 1. Request, intimation. *V.* REQUERIMIENTO. 2. Duel.

recuesto [ray-coo-es'-to], *m.* Declivity, a gradual descent.

recula [ray-coo'-lah], *f. (Prov.)* Recoil, retrocession.

reculada [ray-coo-lah'-dah], *f.* 1. *(Naut.)* The falling of a ship astern. 2. The action of falling back or retrograding; recoil.

recular [ray-coo-lar'], *vn.* 1. To fall back, to retrograde, to recoil. 2. *(Coll.)* To give up, to yield.

reculo, la [ray-coo'-lo, lah], *a.* Having no tail (pollos, gallinas). -*m. V.* RECULADA.

reculones (A) [ray-coo-lo'-nes], *adv. (Coll.)* Retrogradely.

recuperable [ray-coo-pay-rah'-blay], *a.* Recoverable.

recuperación [ray-coo-pay-rah-the-on'], *f.* Recovery, the act of recovering or rescuing, recuperative. **Recuperación de datos,** data retrieval.

recuperador, ra [ray-coo-pay-rah-dor', rah], *m. & f.* Rescuer, redeemer.

recuperar [ray-coo-pay-rar'], *va.* To recover (recobrar), to rescue, to regain. -*vr.* To recover from sickness, to gather strength.

recuperativo, va [ray-coo-pay-rah-tee'-vo, vah], *a.* That which recovers or has the power of recovering.

recura [ray-coo'-rah], *f.* Comb-saw, used by comb-makers.

recurar [ray-coo-rar'], *va.* To make or open the teeth of combs.

recurrente [ray-coor-ren'-tay], *a. (Anat.)* Recurrent: used of certain arteries which turn back towards their origin. -*pa.* of RECURRIR.

recurrir [ray-coo-reer'], *va.* To recur, to have recourse to. -*vn.* To revert.

recurso [ray-coor'-so], *m.* 1. Recourse, application for help or protection. 2. Recourse, return to the same place. 3. Appeal, recourse to a higher court of justice. **Sin recurso,** definitively, without appeal. 4. *(Comput.)* **Recurso de distribución de datos,** data distribution facility. **Recurso de gestión de datos,** data management facility.

recusable [ray-coo-sah'-blay], *a.* Refusable, exceptionable.

recusación [ray-coo-sah-the-on'], *f.* Refusal, exception; recusation.

recusante [ray-coo-sahn'-tay], *pa.* Refusing, recusant.

recusar [ray-coo-sar'], *va.* 1. To refuse (rechazar), to admit, to decline admission. 2. To recuse or challenge a judge. **Recular los testigos,** to object to, to challenge, witnesses.

red [red], *f.* 1. Net (pesca), particularly for fishing and fowling. 2. Grate of the parlour in nunneries. 3. Grate through which fish or bread is sold. 4. Prison with a strong grate (cerca). 5. Snare, trap, fraud (trampa). 6. Silk coif or headdress. 6. *(Fig.)* Network, system; mains supply system. **Red barrederal,** drag net. **Red de araña,** cobweb. **Red de combate.** *(Naut.)* netting. **Red de pájaros,** a thin, clear stuff. **Caer en la red,** to fall into the snare. **Red de espionaje,** spy network. **Red vascular,** vascular system. **Red de ventas,** *(Comput.)* dealers network.

redacción [ray-dac-the-on'], *f.* 1. Compilement: the act of editing a newspaper or other publication. 2. The office where it is published (oficina). 3. The editorial staff. 4. Composition (escuela).

redactar [ray-dac-tar'], *va.* To compile, to write (escribir), to compose, to edit a work or a periodical.

redactor [ray-dac-tor'], *m.* Compiler, editor (director).

redada [ray-dah'-dah], *f.* 1. Casting a net, a netful of fish. 2. Multitude, crowd.

redaño [ray-dah'-nyo], *m. (Anat.)* Caul, kell, the omentum.

redar [ray-dar'], *va.* To cast a net.

redargución [ray-dar-goo-the-on'], *f.* Retort, refutation.

redargüir [ray-dar-goo-eer'], *va.* 1. To retort, to reply. 2. *(For.)* To impugn a writing as suffering from some defect.

redaza [ray-dah'-thah], *f.* A certain fishing-net.

redazo [ray-dah'-tho], *m.* In artillery, a kind of fire-pillow.

redear [ray-day-ar'], *va. V.* MAJADEAR.

redecilla [ray-day-theel'-lyah], *f.* 1. A head-dress formerly used in Spain. 2. *(dim.) V.* REDECICA.

redecita [ray-day-thee'-tah], *f. dim.* A small net.

rededor [ray-day-dor'], *m.* Environs. *V.* CONTORNO. **Alrededor**, round about, thereabout, little more or less.

redel [ray-del'], *m. (Naut.)* Loof-frame.

redención [ray-den-the-on'], *f.* 1. Redemption, the act of redeeming. 2. Recovery of lost liberty, ransom. 3. Salvation, refuge.

redentor, ra [ray-den-tor', rah], *m. & f.* Redeemer, one who rescues, redeems, or ransoms. **Nuestro redentor**, our Redeemer, Jesus Christ.

redero [ray-day'-ro], *m.* Net-marker; one who catches birds or fish with nets.

redero, ra [ray-day'-ro, rah], *a.* Reticular, retiform, reticulated.

redhibición [red-e-be-the-on'], *f.* Redhibition, the rescinding of a sale through hiding a defect in the thing sold.

redhibir [red-e-beer'], *va.* To rescind a sale (by the buyer), on account of the concealment by the seller of some defect or vice in the thing sold.

redhibitorio, ria [red-e-be-to'-re-o, ah], *a.* Redhibitory, relating to redhibition; giving the right to redhibition.

redición [rayt-de-the-on'], *f.* Repetition of what had been said.

redicho, cha [ray-dee'-cho, chah], *a.* Speaking with affected precision.

rediezmar [ray-de-eth-mar'], *va.* To decimate again, to tithe a second time.

rediezmo [ray-de-eth'-mo], *m.* The ninth part of crops already tithed.

redil [ray-deel'], *m.* Sheep-fold, sheep cot, fold-coop.

redimible [ray-de-mee'-blay], *a.* Redeemable.

redimir [ray-de-meer'], *va.* 1. To redeem, to rescue, to ransom (cautivo). 2. To redeem a pledge. 3. To succor, to relieve, to extricate or liberate. **Redimirse de algún trabajo**, to extricate oneself from trouble and difficulties.

redina [ray-dee'-nah], *f.* Weigh wheel, a wheel of velvet looms.

redingote [ray-din-go'-tay], *m.* Riding-coat, a kind of great-coat.

redistribución [ray-dis-tre-boo-the-on'], *f.* A new or second distribution.

rédito [ray'-de-to], *m.* Revenue, rent, proceeds.

redituable, reditual [ray-de-too-ah'-blay], *a.* Producing rent, benefit, or profit; rentable.

redituar [ray-de-too-ar'], *va.* To yield or produce any benefit or profit; to rent.

redivivo, va [ray-de-vee'-vo, vah], *a.* Redivivus, revived, restored.

redoblado, da [ray-do-blah'-do, dah], *a. & pp.* of REDOBLAR. 1. Redoubled (celo). 2. Stout and thick. 3. *(Mil.)* Quick step.

redoblamiento [ray-do-blah-me-en'-to], *m.* Reduplication.

redoblar [ray-do-blar'], *va.* 1. To double (esfuerzo, celo), to increase by as much again. 2. To clinch (clavo), to rivet. 3. To touch the same chord twice. *(Mil.)* To play double beats on the drum.

redoble [ray-do'-blay], *m.* 1. Repeated touching of the same chord; double beat on the drum. 2. Amplification of a discourse by putting forward new arguments.

redoblegar [ray-do-blay-gar'], *va. V.* REDOBLAR and DOBLEGAR.

redoblón [ray-do-blone'], *m.* Rivet, clinch-nail.

redoler [ray-do-lerr'], *vn. (Coll.)* To suffer pain silently and continually.

redolino [ray-do-lee'-no], *m. (Prov.)* Wheel for drawing lots.

redolor [ray-do-lor'], *m.* A dull ache remaining after some acute suffering.

redoma [ray-do'-mah], *f.* 1. A broad-bottomed bottle; a flask (frasco). 2. *(Cono Sur)* Fishbowl (pez).

redomadazo, za [ray-do-ma-dah'-tho, thah], *a. aug.* Very artful or sly.

redomado, da [ray-do-mah'-do, dah], *a.* Artful, sly, crafty, cunning.

redomazo [ray-do-mah'-tho], *m.* Stroke or blow in the face with a bottle.

redonda [ray-don'-dah], *a.* Applied to a round ball or capsule of silk. *-f.* 1. Circle, neighborhood. *V.* COMARCA. 2. Pasture-ground. 3. *(Mus.)* Semibreve, whole note. **A la redonda**, round about. **En muchas millas a la redonda**, for many miles round or about.

redondamente [ray-don-dah-men-tay], *adv.* 1. In circumference, in a circle, around. 2. Roundly, clearly, plainly.

redondeador [ray-don-day-ah-dor'], *m.* Rounding-tool, used for trimming the brims of hats.

redondear [ray-don-day-ar'], *va.* 1. To round, to make round. 2. To give to soles of shoes the same form as the last has on its sole. *. -vr.* 1. To extricate oneself from difficulties; to clear oneself of debts. 2. To acquire property or revenues so as to live in comfortable circumstances. *(Coll.)*

redondel [ray-don-del'], *m.* 1. *(Coll.)* A circle. 2. A round cloak, a circular.

redondela [ray-dn-day'-lah], *f.* Table stand.

redondeo [ray-don-day'-o], *m. (Com.)* One free of all indebtedness.

redondete [ray-don-day'-tay], *a. dim.* Roundish, circular.

redondez [ray-don-deth'], *f.* Roundness, circular form, globosity.

redondilla [ray-don-deel'-lyah], *f.* Roundel or roundelay a stanza of four verses, of eight syllables each.

redondo, da [ray-don'-do, dah], *a.* 1. Round (forma), circular, spherical: orbed, orbicular. 2. Round. 3. Free from debts; unencumbered, in easy circumstances (negocio). 4. Applied to land turned to pasture. 5. Applied to persons whose grandparents were of equal rank by birth. 6. Clear, manifest, straight. 7. Just; exact, entire. **Girar en redondo**, to turn right round. **En números redondos**, in round numbers. **Será un negocio redondo**, it will be a really good deal. 8. *(Mex.)* Dense, thick (lerdo).

redondo [ray-don'-do], *m.* 1. Specie, hard cash. 2. Globe, orb, anything found.

redondón [ray-don-done'], *m.* A large circle or orbicular figure.

redopelo [ray-do-pay'-lo], *m.* 1. Rubbing cloth against the grain. 2. Scuffle, affray. **Al redopelo**, against the natural lay of the hair: hence, against all rule and reason. **Traer al redopelo**, to vex, to drag about contemptuously.

redor [ray-dor'], *m.* 1. A round mat. 2. *(Poet.) V.* REDEDOR.

redro [ray'-dro], *adv. (Coll.)* Behind, backwards. *-m.* Each of the rings upon the horns of goats.

redrojo, redruejo [ray-dro'-ho], *m.* 1. A small bunch of grapes remaining after the vintage. 2. After-fruit or blossom. 3. A puny child, slow of growth. 4. *(Cono Sur)* Rest (exceso). 5. *(Mex.)* Rags (harapos).

redrojuelo [ray-dro-hoo-ay'-lo], *m. (Coll.)* Languid boy who does not thrive.

redruña [ray-droo'-nyah], *f.* Left-hand or side in hunting.

reducción [ray-dooc-the-on'], *f.* 1. Reduction, the act of reducing. 2. Mutation, alteration, exchange for an equivalent.

3. Reduction of a place or country by force of arms. 4. Conversion of infidels to the true religion; Indian people converted. 5. *(Chem.)* Resolution of compounds. 6. Reduction, an operation in algebra. 7. Solution, liquefaction.

reducible [ray-do-the'-blay], *a.* Reducible, convertible.

reducidamente [ray-doo-the-dah-men'-tay], *adv.* Sparingly.

reducido, da [ray-doo-thee'-do, dah], *a. & pp.* of REDUCIR. Reduced, diminished, narrow, close, limited (limitado), confined (espacio).

reducimiento [ray-doo-the-me-en'-to], *m.* Reduction, reducement.

reducir [ray-doo-theer'], *va.* 1. To reduce a thing to its former state (tamaño). 2. To exchange, to barter; to convert, to commute; to resolve. 3. To diminish, to lessen (número); to contract, to abridge. 4. To divide into small parts. 5. To convert a solid body into a liquid. 6. To comprehend, to contain, to include, to confine. 7. To reclaim, to bring back to obedience. 8. To persuade, to convert. 9. *(Pict.)* To reduce a figure or picture to smaller dimensions. 10. *(Chem.)* To decompose. a body. **Reducir algo al absurdo**, to make something seem ridiculous. **Reducir una cosa a escombros**, to reduce a house to rubble. *-vr.* To confine oneself to a moderate way of life; to resolve on punctuality. *(Yo reduzco, yo reduzca, from Reducir. V. CONDUCIR.)*

reductillo [ray-dooc-teel'-lyo], *m. dim.* A small redoubt.

reductivo, va [rar-dooc-tee'-vo, va], *a.* Reductive.

reducto [ray-dooc'-to], *m. (Mil.)* Redoubt.

redundancia [ray-doon-dahn'-the-ah], *f.* Superfluity, redundance, overflowing; excess, copiousness.

redundante [ray-doon-dahn'-tay], *pa. & a.* Redundant, superfluous.

redundantemente [ray-doon-dahn'-tay], *adv.* Redundantly.

redundar [ray-doon-dar'], *vn.* 1. To overflow, to be redundant. 2. To redound, to conduce, to contribute.

reduplicación [ray-doo-ple-cah-the-on'], *f.* Reduplication.

reduplicado, da [ray-doo-ple-cah'-do], *a. & pp.* of REDUPLICAR, Reduplicate, reduplicative.

reduplicar [ray-doo-ple-car'], *va.* To reduplicate, to double, to redouble; to repeat the same thing.

reedificable [ray-ay-de-fe-cah'-blay], *a.* Capable of being rebuilt.

reedificación [ray-ay-de-fe-cah-the-on'], *f.* Rebuilding.

reedificador, ra [ray-ay-de-fe-cah-dor', rah], *m. & f.* Rebuilder, re-edifier.

reedificar [ray-ay-de-fe-car'], *va.* To rebuild; to restore, to re-edify.

reelección [ray-ay-lec-the-on'], *f.* Re-election.

reelecto, ta [ray-ay-lec'-to, tah], *pp. irr.* Of REELEGIR.

reelegir [ray-ay-lay-heer'], *va.* To re-elect.

reembarcar [ray-em-bar-car'], *va.* To reship, to re-embark. *-vr.* To re-embark, to take shipping again.

reembarco [ray-em-bar'-co], *m.* Reembarkation, reshipment.

reembargar [ray-em-bar-gar'], *va* To seize or to embargo a second time.

reembolsable [ray-em-bol-sah'-blay], *a.* Capable of reimbursing; payable.

reembolsar [ray-em-bol-sar'], *va.* To recover money advanced; to reimburse (persona), to repay (dinero).

reembolso [ray-em-bol'-so], *m.* Recovery, of money advanced.

reempacar [ray-an-pah-car'], *va.* To repack, to pack anew.

reemplazable [ray-em-plah-thah'-blay], *a.* Replaceable.

reemplazar [ray-em-pla-thar'], *va.* To substitute, to replace.

reemplazo [ray-em-plah'-tho], *m.* Replacement, substitution, substitute.

reemplear [ray-em-play-ar'], *va.* To re-employ; to repurchase.

reencargar [ray-en-car-gar'], *va.* To recommend again; to recharge.

reencarnación [ray-en-car-nah-the-on'], *f.* Reincarnation.

reencarnar [ray-en-car-nar'], *vn. & vr.* to reincarnate.

reencomendar [ray-en-co-men-dar'], To commend again, to recommend eagerly.

reencuentro [ray-en-coo-en'-tro], *m.* 1. Reencounter, collision a slight combat, a skirmish. 2. Affray.

reenganchar [ray-en-gan-char'], *va.* 1. *(Mech.)* To couple again. 2. *(Mil.)* To re-enlist. *-vr.* To enlist oneself again, to be crimped or drafted.

reenganchamiento, reenganche [ray-en-gan-chah-me-en'-to], *m. (Mil.)* Act of re-enlisting or being crimped or drafted again into the army: money given to a soldier who enlists again.

reengendrador [rar-en-han-drah-dor'], *m.* One who regenerates or restores; regenerator.

reengendramiento [ray-en-hen-drah-me-en'-to], *m.* Regeneration.

reengendrante [ray-en-hen-drahn'-tay], *pa.* Regenerating; one who regenerates or restores.

reengendrar [ray-en-hen-drar'], *va.* 1. To regenerate, to reproduce, to produce anew. 2. To renew, to revive.

reenrumbar [ray-en-room-bar'], *va.* To re-route, to redirect.

reensayar [ray-en-sah-yar'], *va.* To re-examine, to prove again.

reensaye [ray-en-sah'-yay], *m.* Re-examination; second assay.

reensayo [ray-en-sah'-yo], *m.* Second essay, or rehearsal, of a comedy or other thing.

reestrenar [ray-ays-tray-nahr'], *va.* To revive, to put on again.

reestreno [ray-ays-tray-no], *m. (Teat.)* Revival; (Cine) Reissue.

reestructuración [ray-ays-trooc-too-rah-the-on'], *f.* Restructuring, reorganizing.

reestructurar [ray-ays-trooc-too-rahr'], *va.* To restructure.

reexaminación [ray-ek-sah-me-nah-the-on'], *f.* Re-examination.

reexaminar [ray-ek-sah-me-nar'], *va.* To re-examine.

reexportación [ray-ex-por-tah-the-on'], *f. (Com.)* Re-exportation.

reexportar [ray-ex-por-tar'], *va.* To re-export, to export imported commodities.

refacción [ray-fac-the-on'], *f.* 1. Refection, refreshment. 2. Restitution, reparation.

refajo [ray-fah'-ho], *m.* 1. A kind of short petticoat used by mountaineers or highlanders; kilt. 2. An inner petticoat of baize or other strong material.

refalsado, da [ray-fal-sah'-do, dah], *a.* False, deceitful.

refección [ray-fec-the-on'], *f.* Refection, refreshment; reparation.

refectolero [ray-fec-to-lay-ro], *m.* V. REFITOLERO.

refectorio [ray-fec-to'-re-o], *m.* Refectory, the eating-room in convents.

referencia [ray-fay-ren'-the-ah], *f.* Reference, relation to narration. **Con referencia a**, with reference to.

referente [ray-fay-ren'-tay], *pa.* Referring, relating. **Referente a**, relating to, referring to.

referendo [ray-fay-ren'-do], *m.* Referendum.

referéndum [ray-fay-ren-doom], *m.* Referendum.

referible [ray-fay-ree'-blay], *a.* Referrible.

referir [ray-fay-reer'], *va.* 1. To refer (relacionar), to relate, to report. 2. To direct, to mark out a certain course. 3. To mark weights and measures. **Referir que**, to say that... **Todo lo refiere a su teoría favorita**, he refers everything to his favorite theory. *-vr.* 1. To refer, to have relation to; to respect. 2. To refer to some former remark. **Referirse al parecer de otro**, to refer to another's opinion. *(Yo refiero, yo refiera, from Referir. V. ADHERIR.)*

refigurar [ray-fe-goo-rar'], *va.* To retrace an image formerly seen or conceived.

refilón (De) [ray-fe-lone', day], *adv.* Obliquely. V. DESOSLAYO. **Mirar a uno de refilón**, to take a sideways glance at.

refina [ray-fee'-nah], *f.* A kind of superfine wool.

refinación [ray-fe-nah-the-on'], *f.* Purification, the act of refining.

refinadera [ray-fe-nah-day'-rah], *f.* Refiner, a long cylindrical stone used to work chocolate.

refinado, da [ray-fe-nah'-do, dah], *a.* Refined: subtle, artful; fine, nice. -*pp.* of REFINAR.

refinador [ray-fe-nah-dor'], *f.* Refiner.

refinadura [ray-fe-nah-doo'-rah], *f.* Refining, purifying liquors or metals; refinement.

refinamiento [ray-fe-nah-me-en'-to], *m.* 1. Refining. 2. Nicety, exactness. 3. (*Neol.*) Exaggeration in drawing distinctions.

refinar [ray-fe-nar'], *va.* 1. To refine (sistema), to purify, to fine. 2. To refine, to make elegant; to bring to perfection; to render more dexterous or useful.

refinería [ray-fe-nay-ree'-ah], *f.* Refinery.

refino, na [ray-fee'-no, nah], *a.* Extra fine, refined.

refirmar [ray-feer-mar'], *va.* To strengthen, to secure, to ratify.

refitolero, ra [ray-fe-to-lay'-ro, rah], *m. & f.* 1. One who has the care of the refectory. 2. (*Coll.*) Busybody, intermeddler. 3. (Cuba) *a.* Obsequious, with affectation.

refitor [ray-fe-tor'], *m.* In bishoprics, the portion of tithe received by the cathedral chapter.

refitorio [ray-fe-to'-re-o], *m.* Refectory. *V.* REFECTORIO.

reflectar [ray-flec-tar'], *vn.* (*Opt.*) To reflect, to cast back.

reflector [ray-flec-tor'], *m.* 1. Reflector of light, heat, or sound. 2. Searchlight. 3. Spotlight.

refleja [ray-flay'-hah], *f.* Reflection, observation, remark.

reflejar [ray-flay-har'], *vn.* 1. To reflect the rays of light. 2. To reflect, to meditate upon. *V.* REFLEXIONAR.

reflejo [ray-flay'-ho], *m.* 1. Reflex. 2. Reflection (imagen), glare. 3. Streaks (de pelo). **Mirar su reflejo en el agua,** to look at one's reflection in the water.

reflejo, ja [ray-flay-ho], *a.* 1. Reflected, reflective, reflex (movimiento). 2. Meditative.

reflexibilidad [ray-flek-se-be-le-dahd'], *f.* Reflexibility.

reflexible [ray-flek-see'-blay], *a.* Reflective, reflexible.

reflexión [ray-flek-se-on'], *f.* 1. Reflection: applied to the reflection of light. 2. (*Art.*) A reflected or secondary light. 3. Meditation, attentive consideration, reflection, cogitation. **Con reflexión,** on reflection. **Hacer reflexiones,** to meditate.

reflexionar [ray-flek-se-o-nar'], *vn.* To reflect, to meditate, to consider.

reflexivamente [ray-flek-see'-vah-men-tay], *adv.* Reflexively.

reflexivo, va [ray-flek-see'-vo, vah], *a.* Reflexive, reflective (persona): considerate, cogitative. **Verbo reflexivo,** a reflexive verb.

reflorecer [ray-flor-ray-therr'], *vn.* 1. To reflourish, to blossom again. 2. To return to former splendor. (*Yo reflorezco, yo reflorezca,* from *Reflorecer. V.* CONOCER.)

refluente [ray-floo-en'-tay], *pa. & a.* Refluent; flowing back.

refluir [ray-floo-eer'], *vn.* To flow back, to reflow.

reflujo [ray-floo'-ho], *m.* Reflux, ebb. **Reflujo de la marea,** (*Naut.*) ebb or ebb-tide.

refocilación [ray-fo-the-lah-the-on'], *f.* Reinvigoration, restoration of strength by refreshment: refection.

refocilar [ray-fo-the-lar'], *va.* To strengthen, to revive, to reinvigorate, to refect, to amuse (divertir), to cheer up (alegrar). -*vr.* 1. To be strengthened or revived. 2. To cheer up no end (alegrarse).

refocilo [ray-fo-thee'-lo], *m.* Reinvigoration, pleasure.

reforestación [ray-fo-res-ah-the-on'], *f.* Reforestation.

reforjar [ray-for-har'], *va.* To reforge, to execute again.

reforma [ray-for'-mah], *f.* 1. Reform, correction, amendment. 2. Dismissal from an office or employment. 3. Reformation, the act of reforming. 4. Reformation, change from worse to better reform. 5. Renovated discipline in religious houses.

reformable [ray-for-mah'-blay], *a.* Reformable.

reformación [ray-for-mah-the-on'], *f.* Reformation, reform. *V.* REFORMA.

reformado [ray-for-mah'-do], *m.* A reformed officer, an officer on halfpay; disbanded. -*pp.* of REFORMAR.

reformador, ra [ray-for-mah-dor', rah], *m. & f.* Reformer, corrector, mender.

reformar [ray-for-mar'], *va.* 1. To reform, to restore a thing to its primitive form (modificar). 2. To reform, to correct, to mend. 3. To lessen, to reduce, to diminish. 4. To dispossess of a place or employment, to discharge, to dismiss. 5. To clear up, to explain: speaking of the meaning of words or phrases. -*vr.* 1. To reform, to change from worse to better, to mend, to have one's manners reformed. 2. To use prudence and moderation in speech and conduct.

reformativo, va [ray-for-mah-tee'-vo, vah], *a.* That which reforms.

reformatorio, ria [ray-for-mah-to'-re-ah], *a.* Corrective. -*m.* House of correction, reformatory.

reformista [ray-for-mees'-tah], *com.* Reformer, reformist.

reforzada [ray-for-thah'-dah], *f.* 1. Sort of narrow tape, list, or fillet. 2. A small sausage. 3. The bass string of a stringed instrument.

reforzado, da [ray-for-thah'-do, dah], *a. & pp.* of REFORZAR. 1. Strengthened. 2. Applied to a re-enforced gun, which has more metal than usual at the breech, to make it stronger.

reforzado [ray-for-thah'-do], *m. V.* REFORZADA for a kind of tape.

reforzamiento [ray-for-thah-me-ayn-to], *m.* Reinforcement.

reforzar [ray-for-thar'], *va.* To strengthen, to fortify: to animate. -*vr.* To be strengthened and recovered. (*Yo refuerzo, yo refuerce,* from *Reforzar. V.* ACORDAR.)

refoseto [ray-fo-say'-to], *m.* (*Mil.*) Cuvette in a fosse.

refracción [ray-frac-the-on'], *f.* Refraction, as of light.

refractar [ray-frac-tar'], *va.* To refract, to change the direction of a ray of light. -*vr.* To be refracted.

refractario, ria [ray-frac-tah'-re-o, ah], *a.* 1. Refractory, disobedient, rebellious, obstinate. 2. Not fulfilling one's promise. 3. Refractory, resisting fusion.

refracto, ta [ray-frahc'-to, tah], *a.* Refracted (rayos de luz).

refrán [ray-frahn'], *m.* Proverb, idiom, saying of common use. **Tener refranes,** (*Coll.*) to be versed in tricks and villainies.

refranero [ray-frah-nay'-ro], *m.* Collection of proverbs.

refrangibilidad [ray-fran-he-be-le-dahd'], *f.* Refrangibility, refrangibleness.

refrangible [ray-fran-hee'-blay], *a.* Refrangible.

refregadura [ray-fray-gah-doo-rah], *f. V.* REFREGÓN.

refregamiento [ray-fray-gah-me-en'-to], *m.* Rubbing, friction.

refregar [ray-fray-gar'], *va.* 1. To rub one thing against another (frotar), to fray. 2. (*Coll.*) To upbraid, to censure, to reprove, to be stained all over.

refregón [ray-fray-gone'], *m.* 1. Rubbing, friction. 2. Mark (senal) made or left by rubbing. 3. A brief conversation.

refreír [ray-fray-eer'], *va.* To fry well or excessively.

refrenamiento, *m.* **refrenación,** *f.* [ray-fray-nah-me-en'-to], *f.* Curb, the act of curbing or refraining; refrenation.

refrenar [ray-fray-nar'], *va.* 1. To curb a horse with a bridle (caballo). 2. To refrain, to coerce, to hold back, to rein.

refrendación [ray-fren-dah-the-on'], *f.* Legalizing by subscription.

refrendar [ray-fren-dar'], *va.* 1. To legalize a public act, to countersign (firmar); to mark weights, etc. 2. To vise passports and countersign them. 3. (*Coll.*) To repeat what had been done (repetir).

refrendario [ray-fren-dah'-re-o], *m.* Officer appointed to countersign edicts, ordinances, or other public acts.

refrendata [ray-fren-dah'-tah], *f.* Counter-signature, the act of countersigning; countersign.

refrescador, ra [ray-fres-cah-dor', rah], *a.* Refreshing, refrigerating.

refrescadura [ray-fres-cah-doo'-rah], *f.* Refreshing (act and effect).

refrescamiento [ray-fres-cah-me-ayn-to], *m. V.* REFRESCO.

refrescante [ray-fres-cahn'-tay], *pa.* Cooling, refreshing, refreshful.

refrescar [ray-fres-car'], *va.* 1. To refresh, to moderate the heat of anything, to cool (enfriar), to refrigerate. 2. To drink iced drinks. 3. To renew, to refresh; to awaken feeling. 4. To recover strength and vigor. 5. To rest after fatigue. -*vn.* To cool, to take the air. Used frequently also as a reflexive verb. -*vr.* 1. -vn. 2. (*And. Colombia*) To have a tea.

refrescativo, va [ray-fres-cah-tee'-vo, vah], *a.* Refrigerative, refreshing.

refresco [ray-fres'-co], *m.* 1. Refreshment: moderate food for gathering strength. 2. A cold beverage. 3. Entertainment of cool beverages, sweetmeats, and chocolate. **De refresco**, anew, once more.

refriega [ray-fre-ay'-gah], *f.* Affray, skirmish, encounter, scuffle, strife, fray.

refrigeración [ray-fre-hay-rah-the-on'], *f.* Refrigeration, cooling, refrigerating.

refrigerador [ray-fre-hay-rah-dor'], *m.* Refrigerator.

refrigerante [ray-fre-hay-rahn'-tay], *a.* Refrigerant, cooling, refrigerative. -*m.* 1. (*Chem.*) Refrigerator, cooling chamber. 2. (*Med.*) Cooler.

refrigerar [ray-fre-hay-rar'], *va.* To cool, to refresh, to comfort, to refrigerate.

refrigerativo, va [ray-fre-hay-rah-tee'-vo vah], *a.* Refrigerative, cooling, refrigerant.

refrigeratorio [ray-fre-hay-rah-to'-re-o], *m.* Refrigerator, part of a still employed to cool the condensing vapors.

refrigerio [ray-fre-hay'-re-o], *m.* 1. Refrigeration, comfort experienced through coolness. 2. Refreshment, refection, a light repast. 3. Consolation, comfort.

refringente [ray-frin-hen'-tay], *pa. & a.* Refracting; refractivo.

refringir [ray-frin-heer'], *va.* To refract, break, or intercept the rays of light. Also *vr.*

refrito [ray-free'-to], *pp. irr.* of REFREÍR.

refrotar [ray-fro-tar'], *va.* To rub.

refuelle [ray-foo-ayl'-lyay], *m.* A kind of net for catching fish.

refuerzo [ray-foo-err'-tho], *m.* 1. Reinforcement, increase of strength. 2. Backing, bracing, strengthening piece; welt of a shoe. 3. Succor, help, aid.

refugiado, da [ray-foo-he-ah'-do, dah], *a. & pp.* of REFUGIAR. Sheltered. It has been used as a substantive for a refugee or emigrant.

refugiar [ray-foo-he-ar'], *va.* To shelter, to refuge, to afford protection. -*vr.* To take refuge, to fly for shelter.

refugio [ray-foo'-he-o], *m.* 1. Refuge, retreat, shelter, asylum, safe harbor. 2. In Madrid, a brotherhood formed to alleviate the suffering of the poor. **Refugio antiaéreo**, bomb shelter. **Refugio de montaña**, mountain hut.

refulgencia [ray-fool-hen'-the-ah], *f.* Refulgence, splendor.

refulgente [ray-fool-hen'-tay], *a.* Refulgent.

refulgir [ray-fool-heer'], *vn.* To shine with splendor, to be resplendent.

refundición [ray-foon-de-the-on'], *f.* The act of casting metals anew.

refundir [ray-foon-deer'], *va.* 1. To melt or cast metals anew. 2. To contain, to include. 3. (*And. CAm. Mex.*) To lose (perder). 4. (*Cono Sur*) To ruin (arruinar). -*vn.* To redound. **Refundir infamia**, to defame, to dishonor.

refunfuñador, ra [ray-foon-foo-nyah-dor', rah], *m. & f.* Grumbler, growler, snarler.

refunfuñadura [ray-foon-foo-nyah-doo'-rah], *f.* Growling, grumbling. *V.* REFUNFUÑO.

refunfuñar [ray-foon-foo-nyar'], *va.* To snarl, to growl (gruñir), to snort; to grumble (quejarse), to mutter.

refunfuño [ray-foon-foo'-nyo], *m.* Grumbling, murmuring, growl, short.

refutación [ray-foo-tah-the-on'], *f.* Refutation, confutation.

refutable [ray-foo-tah'-blay], *a.* Refutable.

refutador, ra [ray-foo-ta-dor', rah], *m. & f.* Refuter.

refutar [ray-foo-tar'], *va.* To refute, to confute, to convict; to control. *V.* REHUSAR.

refutatorio, ria [ray-foo-tah-too'-re-o, ah], *a.* That which refutes.

regadera [ray-gah-day'-rah], *f.* 1. Shower. 3. Canal for irrigation.

regadío [ray-gah-dee'-o], *m.* Irrigated fund.

regadío, ía [ray-gah-dee'-o], *a.* Irrigated.

regadizo, za [ray-gah-de'-tho, thah], *a.* That which can be irrigated or watered.

regador [ray-gah-dor'], *m.* 1. One who waters or irrigates. 2. Instrument used by comb-makers.

regadura [ray-gah-doo'-rah], *f.* Irrigation.

regaifa [ray-gah'-e-fah], *f.* A stone in an oil-mill with a grooved channel along which the oil runs into the vat.

regajal, regajo [ray-gah-hahl', ray-gah'-ho], *m.* Puddle or pool of stagnant water; rill which makes it.

regala [ray-gah'-lah], *f.* (*Naut.*) Gunwale or gunnel.

ragalada [ray-ga-lah'-dah], *f.* 1. King's stables. 2. The number of horses belonging to the king's stables.

regaladamente [ray-gah-lah-dah-men-tay], *adv.* Delicately, pleasantly, daintily.

regalado, da [ray-gah-lah'-do, dah], *a.* Delicate (delicado), dainty, suave, lickerish. -*pp.* of REGALAR. **Me lo dio medio regalado**, he gave it to me for a song.

regalador, ra [ray-gah-lah-dor', rah], *m. & f.* 1. One fond of entertaining his friends; a person of a generous disposition. 2. Sort of stick used by wing-bag makers for cleaning the skins.

regalar [ray-gah-lar'], *va.* 1. To present, to favor with a gift. 2 To regale, to refresh, to entertain. 3. To caress, to cajole, to make much of. 4. To regale, to gratify, to make merry, to delight, to cherish. **Regalar algo a uno**, to give somebody something. -*vr.* 1. To regale, to feast; to fare sumptuously. 2. To entertain oneself, to take pleasure.

regalejo [ray-gah-lay'-ho], *m. dim.* A small gift.

regalía [ray-gah-lee'-ah], *f.* 1. The rights or prerogatives of the crown (del rey). 2. Privilege (privilegio), exemption. 3. (*And. CAm. Carib.*) Gift (regalo). 4. (*LAm.*) Royalty (derechos); advance payment (avance). -*pl.* Perquisites.

regalillo [ray-gah-leel'-lyo], *m.* 1. (*dim.*) A small present. 2. Muff, for the hands.

regaliolo [ray-gah-le-o'-lo], *m.* (*Orn.*) Golden-crested wren.

regalito [ray-gah-lee'-to], *m. dim.* A small present.

regaliz [ray-gah-leeth'], *m.* (*Bot.*) Licorice.

regalo [ray-gah'-lo], *m.* 1. Present, gift, largess. 2. Pleasure (placer), gratification. 3. Dainty, something nice and delicate; regalement. 4. Convenience, repose, comfort; luxury (comodidad). 5. Affliction dispensed by Providence. **Regalo de boda**, wedding present.

regalón, na [ray-gah-lone', nah], *a.* 1. Delicate, fond of convenience and ease. 2. Spoiled, pampered (niños). 3. (*LAm.*) **Es el regalón de su padre**, he's the apple of his father's eyes.

regantío, ía [ray-gan-tee'-o, ah], *a.* Applied to the land or its fruits, that are usually watered. *V.* REGADÍO.

reagañada [ray-gah-nyah'-dah], *f.* A kind of delicate cake.

regañado, da [ray-gah-nyah'-do, dah], *a.* 1. Given reluctantly, or with repugnance. 2. Applied to a kind of plum or bread which splits. 3. Frowning. -*pp.* of REGANAR.

regañador, ra [ray-gah-nyah-dor', rah], *m. & f.* Grumbler.

regañamiento [ray-gah-nyah-me-en'-to], *m.* Grumbling, snarling, growl.

regañar [ray-gah-nyar'], *vn.* 1. To snarl (perro), to growl, to murmur, to grumble (persona), to claw off. 2. To be peevish, to quarrel (2 personas). 3. To crack or open like ripe fruit. 4. To dispute familiarly at home, to have domestic broils. -*va.* (*Coll.*) To reprehend, to chide. **A regañadientes**, reluctantly, with reluctance.

regañir [ray-gah-nyeer'], *vn.* To yelp, to howl repeatedly.

regaño [ray-gah'-nyo], *m.* 1. A gesture of annoyance; sternness of look. 2. Threat, warning. 3. Scorched bread. 4. *(Coll.)* Reprimand.

regañón, na [ray-gah-nyone', nah], *a.* 1. Snarling, growling; a grumbler, murmurer, snarler. 2. Troublesome: generally applied to the north-east wind.

regar [ray-gar'], *va.* 1. To water (planta), to irrigate (tierra). 2. To sprinkle with water: to rain heavily. 3. To wash or water countries (ríos, nubes). 4. *(Fig.)* To sprinkle (esparcir). 5. *(And. CAm.)* To spill (derramar). 6. *(Carib.)* To hit (pegar). **Una costa regada por un mar tranquilo**, a coast washed by a calm sea. *-vn.* 1. *(Carib.)* To joke (bromear). 2. *(Carib.)* To act rashly (actuar sin pensar).

regata [ray-gah'-tah], *f.* 1. A small channel or conduit, through which water is conveyed to gardens. 2. Regatta, a race of boats or light craft.

regatar [ray-gah-tar'], *va. (Naut.)* To put a ferrule to a boathook. *-vn. V.* REGATEAR.

regate [ray-gah'-tay], *m.* 1. A quick motion of the body to avoid a blow. 2. Escape, evasion.

regatear [ray-gah-tay-ar'], *va.* 1. To haggle (objeto), to be tedious in a bargain. 2. To retail provisions bought by wholesale. 3. To refuse or decline the execution of a thing (negar); to avoid. **Aquí regatean el vino**, they are mean with their wine here. *-vn.* 1. To wriggle, to move sidewise; to use evasions. 2. *(Naut.)* To rival in sailing.

regateo [ray-gah-tay'-o], *m.* The act of haggling or bartering.

regatería [ray-gah-tay-ree'-ah], *f.* Huckste's shop. *V.* REGATONERÍA.

regatero, ra [ray-gah-tay'-ro, rah], *a. & m. & f.* Haggling; hawker. *V.* REGATÓN.

regatista [ray-gah-tees'-tah], *m & f.* Competitor (sailing).

regato [ray-gah'-to], *m.* A small rivulet.

regatón, na [ray-gah-tone', nah], *m. & f.* 1. Huckster, regrater. 2. Haggler. 3. Socket, ferrule. *-a.* Retailing.

regatonear [ray-gah-to-nay-ar'], *vn.* To huckster, to buy by wholesale and sell by retail.

regatonería [ray-gah-to-nay-ree'-ah], *f.* 1. Sale by retail. 2. Huckster's shop.

regazar [ray-gah-thar'], *pa.* To tuck up. *V.* ARREGAZAR.

regazo [ray-gah'-tho], *m.* 1. Lap of a woman; part of the dress. 2. Lap, part of the body from the waist to the knees. 3. Fond and endearing reception.

regencia [ray-hen'-the-ah], *f.* 1. Regency, ruling or governing. 2. Regency, administration of a regent; vicarious government. 3. Regency, the district governed by a regent. 4. Regency, those collectively to whom vicarious regality is entrusted. 5. Regentship.

regeneración [ray-hay-nay-rah-the-on'], *f.* 1. Regeneration. 2. *(Surg.)* Granulation in a wound.

regenerado, da [ray-hay-nay-rah'-do, dah], *a. & pp.* of REGENERAR. Regenerate, regenerated.

regenerar [ray-hay-nay-rar'], *va.* To regenerate, to reproduce.

regenerativo, va [ray-hay-nay-rah-tee'-vo, vah], *a.* That which regenerates.

regenta [ray-hen'-tah], *f.* Wife of a regent, regentess.

regentar [ray-hen-tar'], *va.* To rule; to govern; to exercise any business affecting superiority.

regente [ray-hen'-tay], *m.* 1. Regent, one invested with vicarious royalty (príncipe). 2. Regent, the president of a court of justice. 3. Master of a school in religious orders. 4. In Spanish universities, some supernumerary professors. 5. Manager, director: in printing-office. *-pa.* Ruling.

regentear [ray-hen-tay-ar'], *va.* 1. To domineer, to rule as master. 2. To be pedant.

regera [ray-hay'-rah], *f. (Naut.)* Sternfast, stern-moorings.

regiamente [ray'-he-ah-men-tay], *adv.* Royally, in a kingly manner.

regibado, da [ray-he-bah'-do, dah], *a.* Hump-backed, crook-backed, gibbous.

regicida [ray-he-thee'-dah], *com. & a.* Regicide, murderer of a king.

regicidio [ray-he-thee'-de-o], *m.* Murder of a king, regicide.

regidor [ray-he-dor'], *m.* 1. Alderman, a magistrate of a city. 2. Governor, director, prefect. *-a. V.* REGITIVO.

regidora [ray-he-do'-rah], *f.* An alderman's or governor's wife.

regidoría, regiduría [ray-he-do-ree'-ah], *f.* Governorship; the place, employment, or office of an alderman.

regilera [ray-he-lay'-rah], *f.* Windmill of paper, a child's plaything.

régimen [ray'-he-men], *m.* 1. Regimen, management, rule (regla), conduct, system. 2. *(Gram.)* Government of parts of speech. 3. *(Med.)* Regimen, a prescribed manner of living. **Bajo el régimen del dictador**, under the dictator's régime. **Estar a régimen**, to be on a diet. **Prisión de régimen abierto**, open prison.

regimentar [ray-he-men-tar'], *va.* To organize a regiment.

regimiento [ray-he-me-en'-to], *m.* 1. Administration, government. 2. Magistracy of a city; office of employment of an alderman or a city magistrate; municipality. 3. Regiment of soldiers; a corps.

regio, gia [ray'-he-o, ah], *a.* 1. Royal, regal, kingly. 2. Stately, sumptuous, magnificent. **Agua regia**, aqua regia, nitrohydrochloric acid.

regiomontano, na [ray-he-o-mon-tah'-no, nah], *a. & m. & f.* Name applied to persons and things from Monterrey, Mexico.

región [ray-he-on'], *f.* 1. Region, kingdom, tract of land, ground. 2. Space occupied by an element. 3. Region, a cavity of the body.

regional [ray-he-o-nahl'], *a.* 1. Belonging to a region or district. 2. *(Mex.)* Peculiar to the country, native.

regionalismo [ray-he-o-nah-lees'-mo], *m.* 1. Regionalism, localism. 2. Local idiom.

regir [ray-heer'], *va.* 1. To rule (país), to govern, to direct. 2. To rule, to conduct, to manage (empresa), to lead, to command. 3. To govern as verbs or prepositions. 4. To have the bowels in good order. **Los factores que rigen los cambios de mercado**, the factors which govern changes in the market. *-vn.* 1. *(Naut.)* To obey the helm. 2. To be in force. **Regirse por**, to be ruled by.

registrado, da [ray-his-trah'-do, dah], *a.* Registered, *-pp.* of REGISTRAR.

registrador [ray-his-trah-dor'], *m.* 1. Register, registrar, recorder (persona), master or clerk of records. 2. Searcher. 3. Toll gatherer, who enters all imported goods in the toll-register. 4. Controller.

registrador, ra [ray-his-trah-dor', rah], *a.* Registering, recording. **Registradora or Caja registradora**, cash register.

registrar [ray-his-trar'], *va.* 1. To inspect, to search (equipaje, lugar, persona). 2. To investigate, to examine, to control. 3. To register (anotar), to record. 4. To put slips of paper between the leaves of a book. *-vr.* To be registered or matriculated. **No se ha registrado nunca nada parecido**, nothing of the kind has ever been recorded.

registro [ray-hees'-tro], *m.* 1. The act of searching or examining. 2. Place or spot where anything can be surveyed. 3. Entry of goods or merchandise (entrada). 4. Enrolling office, where registers or records are kept; census. *V.* PROTOCOLO. 5. Register (libro), in which entries are made; a certificate of entry. 6. Register of a stove or grate. 7. *(Print.)* Catchword; register or correspondence of the pages. 8. Prier, one who inquires too closely. 9. Regulator of a watch or clock. 10. Mark put in breviaries or missals at certain places. 11. Register in an organ or harpsichord. 12. Direction to book-binders at the end of a volume. 13. Search (búsqueda). **Registro de defunciones**, register of deaths. **Registro mercantil**, business register. **Firmar el registro**, to sign the register. 14. Bookmark (de libro). 15. *(And. Cono Sur)* Wholesale textiles store (tienda). 16. *(Comput.)* Record.

regitivo, va [ray-he-tee'-vo, vah], *a.* Ruling, governing.

regizgar [ray-reeth-gar'], *vn. (Prov.)* To shudder with cold.

regla [ray'-glah], *f.* 1. Rule (instrumento), ruler, for drawing a straight line; rule in arithmetic, 2. Rule of religious orders. 3. Rule, maxim, precept; law, statute, precept, canon, fundamental principle. 4. Instrument by which paper is ruled for musical compositions. 5. Manner of making or casting up accounts. 6. Moderation (moderación), measure, order, rule, management. 7. Order of nature. 8. Menstruation. **A regla**, regularly, prudently. **Regla fija**, standard. **Reglas del juego**, rules of the game. **Todo está en regla**, everything is in order.

regladamente [ray-glah'-dah-men-tay], *adv.* Regularly, orderly.

reglado, da [ray-glah'-do, dah], *a.* Regulated, temperate. *-pp.* of REGLAR.

reglamentación [ray-glah-men-tah-the-on'], *f.* 1. Regulation (acto). 2. Rules (reglas).

reglamentar [ray-glah-men-tahr'], *va.* To regulate; to make rules for; to establish regulations for.

reglamentario [ray-glah-men-tah-re-o], *a.* Regulation, obligatory, set; statutory (estatuario); proper (apropiado), due. **En el traje reglamentario**, in the regulation dress.

reglamento [ray-glah-men'-to], *m.* Regulation (reglas), order, ordinance, by-law. **Reglamento de aduana**, customs regulations.

reglar [ray-glar'], *a.* Regular. **Puerta reglar**, the regular door for entering nunneries.

reglar [ray-glar'], *va.* 1. To rule (línea, papel), to draw lines with a rule. 2. To rule, to regulate, to measure. *-vr.* To mend, to reform. **Reglarse a lo justo** to be right.

reglero [ray-glay'-ro], *m.* Ruler, for drawing lines.

regleta [ray-glay'-tah], *f.* (*Print.*) Lead, piece of mental put between lines of types. Reglet.

reglón [ray-glone'], *m.* Level, used by masons.

regnícola [ray-nee'-co-lah], *a. & m. & f.* Native of a kingdom.

regocijadamente [ray-go-the-hah'-dah-men-tay], *adv.* Merrily, joyfully.

regocijado, da [ray-go-the-hah'-do, dah], *a.* Merry, joyful, rejoicing, festive. *-pp.* of REGOCIJAR.

regocijador, ra [ray-go-the-hah-dor', rah], *m. & f.* Rejoicer, cheerer, gladder.

regocijar [ray-go-the-har'], *va.* To gladden, to cheer, to delight, to exult, to rejoice, to exhilarate. **La noticia regocijó a la familia**, the news delighted the family. *-vr.* To rejoice (alegrarse), to be merry (pasarlo bien).

regocijo [ray-go-thee'-ho], *m.* 1. Joy (alegría), pleasure, satisfaction, mirth, merriment, hilarity, exhilaration. 2. Rejoicing, demonstration of joy. 3. Bull-feast in the morning.

regodearse [ray-go-day-ar'-say], *vr.* (*Coll.*) 1. To be merry, to rejoice; to be delighted. 2. To dally, to trifle, to play the fool. 3. To assume an air of reluctance, to cloak some ardent desire. 4. To joke, to jest. 5. (*LAm.*) To be fussy (ser exigente).

regodeo [ray-go-day'-o], *m.* 1. Joy, mirth, merriment. 2. A feigned refusal of a thing earnestly desired. 3. Joke, jest, diversion, dalliance.

regojo [ray-go'-ho], *m.* 1. Crumb or piece of bread left on the table after meals. 2. A puny boy.

regojuelo [ray-go-hoo-ay'-lo], (*dim.*) A very small morsel of bread.

regolar [ray-go-lar'], *m.* (*Prov.*) Scholar, student.

regoldano, na [ray-gol-dah'-no, nah], *a.* Applied to the wild chestnut.

regoldar [ray-gol-dar'], *vn.* 1. To belch, to cruet. 2. To boast, to brag.

regolfar [ray-gol-far'], *va. & vr.* To flow back.

regolfo [ray-gol'-fo], *m.* 1. Reflux, the act of flowing back against the current; whirlpool. 2. Gulf, bay; an arm of the sea.

regomello [ray-go-mayl'-lyo], *m.* (*Prov.*) Remorse, compunction.

regona [ray-go'-nah], *f.* Large canal for irrigating lands.

regordete, ta [ray-gor-day'-tay, tah], *a.* Chubby (persona), plump, short and stout.

regostarse [ray-gos-tar'-say], *vr.* To delight, to take pleasure, to dally.

regosto [ray-gos'-to], *m.* Delight, pleasure.

regraciación [ray-grah-the-ah-the-on'], *f.* Act of thanking, gratitude.

regraciar [ray-grah-the-ar'], *va.* To testify gratitude, to thank.

regresar [ray-gray-sar'], *vn.* 1. To return to a place, to regress. 2. To retain or recover possession of an ecclesiastical benefice. *-va.* To resign a benefice in favor of another.

regresión [ray-gray-se-on'], *f.* Regression, return, regress.

regreso [ray-gray'-so], *m.* 1. Return, regression, regress. 2. Reversion, devolution. 3. The act of resigning a benefice in favor of another. 4. The act of retaking possession of a benefice or property resigned or ceded.

regruñir [ray-groo-nyeer'], *vn.* To snarl, to growl.

reguardarse [ray-goo-ar-dar'-say], *vr.* To take care of oneself.

regüeldo [ray-goo-el'-do], *m.* 1. Eructation, belch. 2. Boast, brag.

reguera [ray-gay'-rah], *f.* 1. Canal for watering lands or plank. 2. Stern of a ship or tail of a greyhound.

reguero [ray-gay'-ro], *m.* 1. A small rivulet. 2. Mark, spot left from any liquid being spilt (señal). 3. *V.* REGUERA.

reguerón [ray-gay-rone'], *m.* The principal canal of irrigation.

reguilete [ray-gee-lay'-tay], *m.* *V.* REHILETE.

regulable [ray-goo-lah-blay], *a.* Adjustable.

regulación [ray-goo-lah-the-on'], *f.* Regulation, adjustment; comparison, computation. **Regulación del tráfico**, traffic control.

regulado, da [ray-goo-lah'-do, dah], *a. & pp.* of REGULAR. Regulated; orderly, regular.

regulador, ra [ray-goo-lah-dor', rah], *m. & f.* 1. Regulator, governor, as of a machine, particularly a steam engine. 2. A standard clock for the regulation of others.

regulador de humedad [ray-goo-lah-dor' day oo-may-dahd'], *m.* (*Mech.*) Humidistat.

regular [ray-goo-lar'], *pa.* To regulate, to adjust; to put in order, to methodize, to compare. *-a.* 1. Regular, orderly. 2. Moderate sober, formal. 3. Common, ordinary, frequent; likely, probable, convenient. 4. Regular: applied to a religious order. **Por lo regular**, commonly. **Tiene un latido regular**, it has a regular beat.

regular [ray-goo-lar'], *m.* Regular, in the Catholic church; person who belongs to a religious order.

regularidad [ray-goo-lah-re-dahd'], *f.* 1. Regularity, order, orderliness. 2. Common usage, custom. 3. Exact discipline.

regularizar [ray-goo-lah-re-thar'], *va.* To systemize, to subject to rules.

regularmente [ray-goo-lahr'-men-tay], *adv.* Orderly in manner: ordinarily, generally, naturally.

régulo [ray'-goo-lo], *m.* 1. Chief of a petty state. 2. Basilisk. 3. (*Chem.*) Regulus, the purest part of metals. 4. (*Ast.*) Regulus, a star of the first magnitude in the constellation Leo. 5. (*Orn.*) Golden-crested kinglet. *V.* ABADEJO.

regurgitación [ray-goor-ge-tah-the-on'], *f.* (*Med.*) Regurgitation.

regurgitar [ray-goor-he-tar'], *vn.* To regurgitate, to overflow.

rehabilitación [ray-ah-be-le-tah-the-on'], *f.* Rehabilitation.

rehabilitar [ray-ah-be-le-tar'], *va.* 1. To rehabilitate; to reinstate one in his rights and privileges. 2. To refit, to repair, to restore.

rehabituarse [ray-ah-be-too-ar'-say], *vr.* To return to vicious habits.

rehacer [ray-ah-therr'], *va.* 1. To mend, to repair, to make again. 2. To add new strength and vigor. 3. To increase the weight or quantity of something. *-vr.* 1. To regain strength and vigor (reponerse). 2. (*Mil.*) To rally, to form anew; to resume the former position. (*Yo rehago, yo rehaga, yo rehice*, from *Rehacer. V.* HACER.)

rehacimiento [ray-ah-the-me-en'-to], *m.* Renovation, renewal; recuperation.

rehacio, cia [ray-ah'-the-o, ah], *a.* Obstinate, stubborn.

reharto, ta [ray-ar'-to, tah], *pp. irr.* of REHARTAR. Supersaturated.

rehartar [ray-ar-tar'], *va.* To satiate again.

rehecho, cha [ray-ay'-cho, chah], *a. & pp. irr.* of REHACER. 1. Renewed, renovated; done over again. 2. Squat, broad shouldered.

rehelear [ray-hay-lay-ar'], *vn.* To be bitter. Note.-The h is aspirated in this word. *(Acad.)*

reheleo [ay-hay-lay'-o], *m.* Bitterness.

rehén [ray-en'], *m.* Hostage: generally used in the plural.

rehenchimiento [ray-en-che-me-en'-to], *m.* Act of stuffing or refilling.

rehenchir [ray-en'-cheer'], *va.* To fill again, to stuff anew.

rehendija, rehendrija [ray-en-dee'-hah], *f.* Crevice, cleft.

reherimiento [ray-ay-re-me-en'-to], *m.* Repulsion.

reherir [ray-ay-reer'], *va.* To repel, to repulse.

reherrar [ray-er-rar'], *va.* To reshoe a horse.

rehenrir [ray-en-reer'], *vn.* 1. To boil again. 2. To be inflamed with love, to be blinded by passion. -*vr.* To ferment, to grow sour.

rehiladillo [ray-e-lah-deel'-lyo], *m.* Ribbon. *V.* HILADILLO.

rehilandera [ray-e-lan-day'-rah], *f.* Wind-mill made of paper. *V.* REGILERA.

rehilar [ray-e-lar'], *va.* To twist or contract too much. -*vn.* 1. To stagger, to reel. 2. To whiz, to whir, as a missile in flight.

rehilete, rehilero [ray-e-lay'-tay], *m.* 1. A kind of shuttlecock played with battledores. 2. A small arrow bearded with paper or feathers. 3. A malicious saying, smart speech.

rehilo [ray-ee'-lo], *m.* Shaking, shivering.

rehinchimiento [ray-in-che-me-en'-to], *m.* The act of filling or stuffing again.

rehogar [ray-o-gar'], *va.* To dress meat with a slow fire, basting it with butter or oil.

rehollar [ray-ol-lyar'], *va.* **To trample under foot, to tread upon.** *V.* PISOTEAR.

rehoya [ray-o'-yah], *f. V.* REHOYO.

rehoyar [ray-o-yar'], *va.* To dig holes again for planting trees.

rehoyo [ray-o'-yo], *m.* A deep hole or pit.

rehuída [ray-oo-ee'-dah], *f.* A second flight, running away again; rapid turn of hunted game.

rehuir [ray-oo-eer'], *vn.* 1. To withdraw, to retire. 2. To return to the place where it was roused. 3. To reject, to condemn. -*va.* To deny or reduce.

rehumedecer [ray-oo-may-day-therr'], *va. & vr.* To dampen well.

rehundido [ray-oon-dee'-do], *m. (Arch.)* Part which serves as a seat for a projection. *V.* VACIADO.

rehundir [ray-oon-deer'], *va.* 1. To sink. 2. To melt metals. 3. To waste, to dissipate, to lavish. -*vn.* To increase perceptibly.

rehurtado, da [ray-oor-tah'-do, dah], *a.* 1. Making windings to make dogs lose the scent (caza). 2. Artfully evasive, delusive, furtive. -*pp.* of REHURTARSE.

rehurtar [ray-oor-tar'], *va.* To steal or cheat again. -*vr.* To take a different route whence it rose (caza).

rehurto [ray-oor'-to], *m.* A movement of the body to avoid impending danger; a shrug.

rehusar [ray-oo-sar'], *va.* To refuse, to decline, to deny what is solicited or required, to abnegate.

reidero [ray-e-day'-ro], *m.* Immoderate laughter.-*a.* Ready to laugh.

reidor, ra [ray-e-dor', rah], *m. & f.* Laugher.

reimpresión [ray-im-pray-se-on'], *f.* . Reimpression of a book, etc., reprint. 2. Number of copies reprinted at once.

reimpreso, sa [ray-im-pray'-so, sah], *pp. irr.* of REIMPRIMIR.

reimprimir [ray-im-pre-meer'], *va.* To reprint, to print a new edition.

reina [ray'-e-nah], *f.* 1. Queen. 2. *(Coll.)* Any woman admired and loved. 3. Queen-bee. 4. Queen at chess. **Reina mora**, *V.* INFERNÁCULO. **Reina de la fiesta**, carnival queen.

reinado [ray-e-nah'-do], *m.* Reign, time of a sovereign's rule.

reinante [ray-nahn'-tay], *pa.* Reigning, excelling; prevailing.

reinar [rar-e-nar'], *va.* 1. To reign, to govern, to command. 2. To reign (prevalecer), to prevail, to predominate. 3. To reign, to obtain power or dominion. **Reina una confusión total**, total confusion reigns.

reincidencia [ray-in-the-den'-the-ah], *f.* Backsliding, falling in again, relapse into vice or error.

reincidente [ray-in-the-den'-tay], *pa.* Relapsing, falling away.

reincidir [ray-in-the-deer'], *m.* To relapse back into vice or error; to backslide.

reincorporación [ray-in-cor-po-rah-the-on'], *f.* Reincorporation, renewing.

reincorporar [ray-in-cor-po-rar'], *va.* To re-incorporate a second time. -*vr.* To re-embody.

reino [ray'-e-no], *m.* 1. Kingdom, reign, dominion of king. 2. Kingdom, name given to districts which, although only a part of the territories subject to a monarch, had before a king. 3. Kingdom, a class or order of beings, as vegetable or animal kingdom. 4. Kingdom of heaven.

reinserción [ray-en-ser-the-on'], *f.* **Reinserción social**, social rehabilitation.

reintegración [ray-in-tay-grah-the-on'], *f.* Reintegration or redintegration; the act of restoring

reintegrar [ray-in-tay-grar'], *va.* 1. To reintegrate (completar), to restore. 2. To be reinstated or restored. 3. To pay back (suma). 4. To attach a fiscal stamp to (documento). **Reintegrar una cantidad**, to refund. -*vr.* To return to.

reintegro [ray-in-tay'-gro], *m.* 1. Reimbursement, refund, repayment. 2. Return of one's stake (lotería).

reír [ray-eer'], *vn.* 1. To laugh; to smile. **Reír a carcajadas**, to laugh excessively and loudly. 2. To laugh at or sneer. 3. *(Med.)* To have convulsions resembling laughter. 4. To smile: applied to agreeable landscapes, arbors, lakes, and meads. **Sólo para hacer reír**, just to make people laugh. -*vr.* 1. To begin to tear or rend. 2. To scoff, to make jest of. **Reírse de nada**, to giggle or titter idly, to laugh at a feather. **Reírse de**, to laugh at.

reiteración [ray-e-tay-rah-the-on'], *f.* 1. Repetition, reiteration. 2. *(Comput.)* Replication. **Reiteración absoluta**, absolute replication. **Reiteración mixta**, mixed replication. **Reiteración relative**, relative replication.

reiteradamente [ray-e-tay-rah-dah-men-tay], *adv.* Repeatedly.

reiterar [ray-e-tay-rar'], *va.* To reiterate, to repeat, to reaffirm.

reiterativo, va [ray-e-tay-rah-tee'-vo, vah], *a.* Reiterative, expressing repeated action.

reivindicación [ray-e-vin-de-cah-the-on'], *f. (For.)* Recovery, claim (reclamación), grievance (queja). **Reivindicación salarial**, wage claim.

reivindicar [ray-e-vin-de-car'], *va.* 1. To recover, to claim (reclamar); to assert one's claim to. 2. To vindicate (reputación). 3. *(Jur.)* To recover (derecho). 4. *(LAm.)* To demand (exigir).

reja [ray'-hah], *f.* 1. Plough sharer, cotter or courter. 2. Ploughing, turning over ground with a plough; tillage. 3. Iron grate of a window or fence. 4. *(LAm.)* Prison (cárcel). 5. *(Cono Sur)* Cattle truck. **Estar entre rejas**, to be behind bars.

rejado [ray-hah'-do], *m.* Grate of a door or window.

rejalcar [ray-hal-car'], *va.* To plough.

rejalgar [ray-hal-gar'], *m.* Realgar, red sulphide of arsenic, *(Arab.)*

rejazo [ray-hah'-tho], *m.* Stroke or blow with a plough share.

rejería [ray-hay-ree'-ah], *f.* Manufactory of the iron-work of grates, doors, or windows.

rejero [ray-hay-ro], *m.* Maker of bars, lattices, and grates.

rejilla [ray-heel'-lyah], *f.* 1. A small lattice in confessionals, to hear women's confessions; or a grating in a door in order to see who knocks. 2. Cane, for the backs and seats of chairs. etc. 3. *V.* REJUELA, 2d def. 4. Small stove (brasero). 5. *(Cono Sur)* Meat (fresquera). 6. *(Mex.)* Luggage ruck.

rejo [ray'-ho], *m.* 1. A pointed iron bar or spike (punta). 2. Sting of a bee or other insect. 3. Nail or round iron with which quoits are played. 4. Rim of iron put around the frame of a door to strengthen it. 5. Strength, vigor. 6. In seeds, the radicle, the organ from which the root is formed. 7. *(LAm.)* Whip (látigo). 8. *(Carib.)* Stick (porra). 9. *(Carib.)* Stick (porra). 10. *(And.)* Milking (ordeño).

rejón [ray-hone'], *m.* 1. Dagger, poniard. 2. A kind of lance or spear used by bullfighters. 3. A short broad knife with a sharp point.

rejonazo [ray-ho-nah'-tho], *m.* Thrust with a dagger.

rejoneador [ray-ho-nay-ah-dor'], *m.* Bull-fighter who throws the spear called *rejón.*

rejonear [ray-ho-nay-ar'], *va.* To wound bulls with the spear used by bullfighters.

rejoneo [ray-ho-nay'-o], *m.* The act of fighting bulls with a spear.

rejuela [ray-hoo-ay'-lah], *f.* 1. *(dim.)* A small grate. 2. A small brasier of wood covered with brass used for a stove.

rejurar [ray-hoo-rar'], *vn* To swear again.

rejuvenecer [ray-hoo-vay-nay-therr'], *vn.* To grow young again.

relación [ray-lah-the-on'], *f.* 1. Relation, report, narration, memoir, account (narración). 2. A brief report to a judge, of the state and merits of a cause. 3. Prologue, a long piece in a dramatic poem which an individual recites. 4. Relation, correspondence, analogy, coherence, concurrence. **Relación jurada**, deposition upon oath. **Entrar en relaciones**, *(Com.)* to connect oneself. **Buenas relaciones**, good relations. **Relaciones amorosas**, courting. **Llevan varios meses de relaciones**, they've been going out for some months.

relacionado, da [ray-lah-the-o-nah'-do, dah], *a.* Relative, related, connected. **Relacionado con**, related to, in connection with.

relacionar [ray-lah-the-o-nar'], *va.* To relate, to report, to narrate. *-vr.* 1. **Es hombre que se relaciona**, he's a man with connections. 2. To make contacts (formar amistades).

relacionero [ray-lah-the-o-nay'-ro], *m.* Reporter, narrator; ballad-singer.

relajación [ray-lah-hah-the-on'], *f.* 1. Relaxation (sosiego), extension, dilatation: relenting. 2. *(For.)* Remission or diminution of a penalty imposed upon a delinquent. 3. Commutation of a vow, release from an oath. 4. Delivery of an offender by the ecclesiastical judge to a criminal court of justice, in cases of murder. 5. *V.* QUEBRADURA. 6. Relaxation of discipline or good order, laxity of conduct; relaxation, intermission from a task or work.

relajadamente [ray-lah-hah'-dah-men-tay], *adv.* Dissolutely, licentiously.

relajado [ray-lah-hah'-do], *a. (Coll.)* Dissolute, dissipated. *-pp.* of RELAJAR.

relajador, ra [ray-lah-hah-dor', rah], *a.* Relaxing, remitting.

relajamiento [ray-lah-hah-me-en'-to], *m.* Relaxation, laxity, slackness.

relajante [ray-lah-hahn'-tay], *a.* 1. Relaxing (ejercicio). 2. *(Cono Sur)* Sickly (comida). 3. Revolting (repugnante).

relajar [ray-lah-har'], *va.* 1. To relax (sosegar), to slacken (aflojar), to make less tense. 2. To relax, to remit, to render less rigorous. 3. To annul a vow, to release from an oath or obligation. 4. To deliver a capital offender from an ecclesiastical to the criminal tribunal. 5. To relax, to ease, to amuse, to divert. 6. *(For.)* To lighten a penalty. 7. *(LAm.)* To cloy (comida). 8. *(Carib.)* To mock (hacer mofa). *-vr.* 1. To be relaxed, loosened, or diluted: applied to a member of the animal body. 2. To grow vicious; to be corrupted by evil customs. 3. *V.* QUEBRASE. 4. To become dissolute (moralmente).

relamer [ray-lah-merr'], *va.* To relick, to lick again. *-vr.* 1. To lick one's lips (persona); to relish. 2. To be extravagantly fond of dress; to paint (maquillarse). 3. To boast, to rag.

relamido, da [ray-lah-mee'-do, dah], *a.* Affected, too fine or nice in dress. *-pp.* of RELAMER.

relámpago [ray-lahm'-pah-go], *m.* 1. Flash of lightning, meteor. 2. Anything passing as suddenly as a flash of lightning. 3. Thought or idea flashing upon the mind; ingenious witticism. 4. Blemish in the eyes of horses.

relampagueante [ray-lam-pah-gay-ahn'-tay], *pa.* Lightening.

relampaguear [ray-lam-pah-gay-ar'], *vn.* 1. To lighten, to emit flashes of lightning. 2. To flash, to sparkle, to gleam. 3. *(Carib.)* To twinkle (parpadear).

relampagueo [ray-lam-pah-gay'-o], *m.* Lightening, flashing or darting light.

relance [ray-lahn'-thay], *m.* 1. Repeated casting of a net, a second chance or lot. 2. A fortuitous event. 3. A repeated attempt. 4. Series of lucky or unlucky chances. **De relance**, fortuitously, by chance.

relanzar [ray-lan-thar'], *va.* 1. To repel, to repulse. 2. To cast in again the tickets or lots to be drawn.

relapso, sa [ray-lahp'-so, sah], *a.* Relapsed, falling back into criminal conduct.

relatador, ra [ray-lah-tah-dor', rah], *m & f.* Relater, narrator.

relatante [ray-lah-tahn'-tay], *pa.* Reporting, narrating.

relatar [ray-lah-tar'], *va.* 1. To relate, to report, to narrate, to give out. 2. *(For.)* To make a report of a lawsuit.

relativamente [ray-lah-tee'-vah-men-tay], *adv.* Relatively, comparatively.

relatividad [ray-lah-te-ve-dahd], *f.* Relativity.

relativo, va [ray-lah-tee'-vo, vah], *a.* 1. Relative, comparative. 2. *(Gram.)* Relative, relating to an antecedent. 3. *(Music.)* Relative major or minor key.

relato [ray-lah'-to], *m.* Statement, narration.

relator, ra [ray-lah-tor'], *m. & f.* 1. Relater, teller, narrator. 2. Reporter, a counsellor at law appointed by the supreme courts to make the briefs of the causes that are to be tried: he reads them before the court, they having first been examined and approved by both the parties concerned.

relatora [ray-lah-to'-rah], *f.* The wife of the reporter of a court of justice.

relatoría [ray-lah-to-ree'-ah], *f.* Office of a reporter of judicial causes in a court of justice.

relevadura [ray-lay-vah-doo'-rah], *f.* A second washing.

relavajo [ray-lah-vah'-hay], *m.* Washing-place for things or clothes.

relavar [ray-lah-var'], *va.* To wash again.

relave [ray-lah'-vay], *m.* Second washing of metals.

relavillo [ray-lah-veel'-lyo], *m. dim.* Slight rewashing.

relax [ray-lacs], *m.* 1. Relaxation (sosiego); rest (descanso). **Hacer relax**, to relax.

releer [ray-lay-err'], *va.* To read over again, to revise.

relegación [ray-lay-gah-the-on'], *f.* Relegation, judicial banishment; exile.

relegar [ray-lay-gar'], *va.* To relegate, to banish; to exile.

relejar [ray-lay-har'], *vn.* To diminish in thickness in proportion to the height (muro).

releje [ray-lay'-hay], or **relej** [ray-lay'], *m.* 1. *(Mil.)* Raised work in the chamber of a piece of ordinance where the powder is placed, in order to economize. 2. Tapering of a wall or talus from below upward. 3. A clammy moisture sticking to the lips or mouth.

relente [ray-len'-tay], *m.* 1. Night dew, softness occasioned by the falling of dew. 2. *(Coll. and met.)* Slowness, deliberation in speech or action.

relentecer [ray-len-tay-therr'], *vn. & vr.* To be softened, to relent and soften by the falling of dew.

relevación [ray-lay-vah-the-on'], *f.* 1. Relevation, the act of raising or lifting up, liberation. 2. Alleviation, relief from a burden or obligation. 3. Remission, forgiveness, pardon.

relevante [ray-lay-vahn'-tay], *a.* Excellent, great, eminent.

relevar [ray-lay-var'], *va.* 1. To emboss. 2. To exonerate, to disburden; to relieve from a burden or charge. 3. To forgive, to pardon. 4. To exalt, to aggrandize. 5. To relieve or substitute a sentinel or body of troops by another. **Relevar a uno de una obligación**, to relieve somebody of a duty. **Relevar a uno de un cargo**, to relieve somebody of his post. *-vn. (Art.)* To raise an object so as to appear like raised work.

relevo [ray-lay'-vo], *m. (Mil.)* Relief. **Relevo de la guardia**, changing of the guard.

reliar [ray-le-ahr'], *va.* To roll (cigarrillo).

relicario [ray-le-cah'-re-o], *m.* 1. Shrine, a place where relics are collected and guarded. 2. Reliquary, a casket in which relics are kept.

relictos [ray-leek'-tos], *m. pl. (For.)* Possessions which one leaves at his death.

relief [ray-le-ef'], *m. (Mil.)* Warrant for an officer to receive either rank or pay that fell to him during his absence.

relieve [ray-le-ay'-vay], *m.* 1. Relief, relievo, raised work, embossment. **Alto relieve, todo relieve**, alto-relievo. **Bajo relieve**, bas-relief. **Medio relieve**, demi-relief. 2. Offals, scrapes, or remnants on the table after meals; leavings; broken victuals. 3. The thread of the arbor of a screw.

religa [ray-lee'-gah], *f.* The second portion of alloy put to a metal to fit it for working.

religación [ray-le-gah-the-on'], *f.* Binding, tying.

religar [ray-le-gar'], *va.* To bind, to solder.

religión [ray-le-he-on'], *f.* 1. Religion; piety, worship. 2. A community with regulations approved by the Church. 3. Belief in any divinity. **Entrar en religión**, *(Coll.)* to take the habit of a religious order.

religionario, religionista [ray-le-he-o-nah'-re-o], *com.* Religionist; sectary: Protestant.

religiosamente [ray-le-he-o-sah-men-tay], *adv.* 1. Religiously, piously. 2. Religiously, exactly, punctually. 3. Moderately.

religiosidad [ray-le-he-o-se-dahd'], *f.* Religiousness; piety, sanctity; punctuality.

religioso, sa [ray-le-he-o'-so, sah], *a.* 1. Religious, godly, pious. 2. Religious, teaching or professing religion. 3. Religious, exact, strict in observance of holy duties. 4. Moderate.

relimar [ray-le-mar'], *va.* To file again.

relimpiar [ray-lim-pe-ar'], *va.* To clean a second time.

relimpio, ia [ray-leem'-pe-o, ah], *a. (Coll.)* Very neat, clean.

relinchador, ra [ray-lin-chah-dor', rah], *a.* Neighing or whinnying often.

relinchante [ray-lin-chahn'-tay], *pa.* Neighing, whinnying.

relinchar [ray-lin-char'], *vn.* To whinny, to neigh, as a horse.

relincho, relinchido [ray-leen'-cho], *m.* Neigh, neighing, whinny of a horse.

relindo, da [ray-leen'-do, dah], *a.* Very neat and fine.

relinga [ray-leen'-gah], *f. (Naut.)* Bolt-rope.

relingar [ray-lin-gar'], *va. (Naut.)* To sew bolt-ropes to sails. *-vn.* To rustle: said of bolt-ropes and sails moved by the wind.

reliquia [ray-lee'-ke-ah], *f.* 1. Relic (tesoro), residue, remains. 2. Relics of saints. 3. Footstep, tract, vestige (vestigio). 4. Habitual complaint. **Reliquia de familia**, heirloom.

reliz [ray-leeth'], *m. (Mex.)* A landslide.

rellanar [rayl-lyah-nar'], *va.* To relevel. *-vr.* To stretch oneself at full length.

rellano [rayl-lyah'-no], *m.* Landing-place of a stair.

rellenar [rayl-lyay-nar'], *va.* 1. To fill again. 2. To stuff with victuals, to feed plentifully. 3. *(Coll.)* To stuff a fowl or gut with forced meat. *-vr.* To stuff oneself.

relleno [ray-lyay'-no], *m.* 1. Stuffing. 2. Repletion, act of refilling. **Relleno de pavo**, turkey stuffing.

relleno, na [rayl-lyay'-no, nah], *a. & pp.* of RELLENAR. 1. Cropful, crop-sick, satiated. 2. Packed, stuffed.

reloco, ca [ray-lo'-co, cah], *a. (Coll.)* Raving and, furiously insane.

reloj ray-lo'], *m.* Clock (de pared), watch (de muñeca). **Reloj de agua**, clepsydra. **Reloj de arena**, sand-glass, hour-glass.

Reloj de bolsillo, pocket-watch. **Reloj de sol** or **reloj solar**, sun-dial. **Reloj lunar**, lunar dial. **Reloj de longitudes**, chronometer. **Reloj de despertador**, alarm-clock. **Estar como un reloj**, *(Coll.)* to be regular and well-disposed.

relojera [ray-lo-hay'-rah], *f.* 1. Clockcase. 2. Watchmaker's wife.

relojería [ray-lo-hay-ree'-ah], *f.* 1. The art of making clocks and watches. 2. Watchmaker's shop.

relojero [ray-lo-hay'-ro], *m.* Watchmaker, clockmaker.

reluciente [ray-loo-the-en'-tay], *a.* Resplendent, glittering, brilliant, shining (brillante).

relucir [ray-loo-theer'], *vn.* To shine (brillar), to glow, to glisten; to excel, to be brilliant.

reluchar [ray-loo-char'], *m.* To struggle, to wrestle, to strive, to labor, to debate.

relumbrante [ray-loom-brahn'-tay], *pa.* Resplendent.

relumbrar [ray-loom-brar'], *vn.* To sparkle, to shine, to glisten, to glitter, to glare.

relumbrera [ray-loom-bray'-rah], *f. V.* LUMBRERA.

relumbrón [ray-loom-brone'], *m.* 1. Luster, dazzling brightness; fleeting idea or sound. 2. Tinsel: any expression or phrase striking but of false showiness.

remachado, da [ray-mah-chah'-do, dah], *a.* 1. Clinched, riveted. 2. Flat-nosed. *-pp.* of REMACHAR.

remachador [ray-mah-chah-dor'], *m.* Riveter, rivet gun. **Remachador de tipo pistola**, zipgun.

remachar [ray-mah-char'], *va.* To flatten; to clinch (clavo), to rivet (metales); to secure, to affirm.

remache [ray-mah'-chay], *m.* Flattening, clinching, securing; rivet.

remachón [ray-mah-chone'], *m.* Buttress. *V.* MACHÓN.

remador, ra [ray-mah-dor'], *m & f.* Rower. *V.* REMERO.

remadura [ray-mah-doo'-rah], *f.* Rowing.

remaldecir [ray-mal-day-theer'], *f.* To curse the cursers.

remallar [ray-mal-lyar'], *va.* To mend the meshes of a net or coat of mail.

remanadera [ray-mah-nah-day'-rah], *f.* In tanneries, graining-board, on which hides are pounded.

remandar [ray-man-dar'], *va.* To order several times.

remanecer [ray-mah-nay-therr'], *vn.* 1. To appear, to occur. 2. To remain, to be left. *(Yo remanezco, yo ramanezca, from Remanecer. V.* ABORRECER.)

remaneciente [ray-mah-nay-the-en'-tay], *pa. & a.* Remaining, remanent, left out.

remanente [ray-mah-nen'-tay], *m.* Remainder, residue; remanent, remnant.

remangadura [ray-man-gah-doo'-rah], *f. (Prov.)* The act of tucking up.

remangar [ray-man-gar'], *va.* To tuck up. *V.* ARREMANGAR.

remango [ray-mahn'-go], *m.* Plaits of the petticoat at the waist.

remansarse [ray-man-sar'-say], *vr.* To obstruct the course of a fluid.

remanso [ray-mahn'-so], *m.* 1. Smooth, stagnant water. 2. Tardiness, sluggishness (pachorra).

remante [ray-mahn'-tay], *m.* Rower.

remar [ray-mar'], *m.* 1. To row, to paddle. 2. To toil, to struggle.

remarcar [ray-mar-car'], *va.* To mark again.

rematadamente [ray-mah-tah'-dah-men-tay], *adv.* Entirely, totally.

rematado, da [ray-mah-tah'-do, dah], *a.* 1. Ended, terminated. 2. Totally lost, utterly ruined. **Es loco rematado**, he is stark mad. *-pp.* of REMATAR.

rematamiento [ray-mah-tah-me-en'-to], *m. V.* REMATE.

rematar [ray-mah-tar'], *va.* 1. To close, to terminate, to finish (proceso), to abut, to end at. 2. To adjudge to the best bidder. 3. To kill game with one shot (animal). 4. To finish a seam. 5. *(Arquit.)* To top, to be at the very top of. 6. *(Com.)* To sell off cheaply (vender). 7. *(LAm.)* To buy at an auction (en subasta, comprar). *-vn.* To terminate, to be at an end (terminar). **Rematar al mejor postor**, to knock down to the highest bidder. **Fue una situation que remató en tragedia**, it was a situation which ended in tragedy. *-vr.* To be utterly ruined or destroyed.

remate [ray-mah'-tay], *m.* 1. End, conclusion, expiration. **Remate de cuentas**, closing of accounts. 2. An edge, a border, a limb. 3. The last or best bidding. 4. Artificial flowers put at the corners of altars. 5. Vignette, in a book. 6. (*Arch.*) Finial, the top or finishing of a pinnacle or gable; also, the entire pinnacle; abutment. **De remate**, utterly, irremediably, without hope. 7. (*Com.*) Sale (venta); (*LAm.*) auction (subasta).

rembalso [rem-bahl'-so], *m.* Rabbeting of a window-shutter, which makes it close with the frame.

remecedor [ray-may-thay-dor'], *m.* A persons who knocks down olives with a pole or long rod.

remecer [ray-may-therr'], *va.* To rock; to swing, to move to and fro.

remedable [ray-may-dah'-blay], *a.* Imitable.

remedador, ra [ray-may-dah-dor', rah], *m. & f.* Imitator, mimic.

remedar [ray-may-dar'], *va.* 1. To copy, to imitate, to mimic: to gesticulate, to mock. 2. To follow the track and footsteps of others. 3. To adopt the dress and manners of another.

remediable [ray-may-de-ah'-blay], *a.* Remediable.

remediador, ra [ray-may-de-ah-dor', rah], *m. & f.* Protector, comforter, helper, curer.

remediar [ray-may-de-ar'], *va.* 1. To remedy (poner remedio a), to mend, to repair. 2. To assist, to support, to help (necesitado). 3. To free from danger, to liberate, to repair mischief. 4. To avoid executing anything that may cause damage (evitar), or to do it contrary to the will of another. **Lo que no se puede remediar, se ha de aguantar**, what cannot be cured must be endured.

remedición [ray-may-de-the-on'], *f.* Act of measuring a second time.

remedio [ray-may'-de-o], *m.* 1. Remedy, reparation, help. **No tener remedio**, to be irremediable or unavoidable. **Como último remedio**, as a last resort. **No hay más remedio que**, the only thing is to. **Esto no tiene remedio**, it is unavoidable. **No tener remedio**, there is no help for it. **Sin remedio**, without fail. 2. Amendment, correction. 3. Remedy, curative medicine. 4. Resource, refuge. 5. Action at law. **No tener un remedio**, to be destitute of aid or assistance.

remedión [ray-may-de-on'], *m. aug.* A performance at a theater in place of one previously announced, when the last cannot be presented for some unlooked-for reason.

remedir [ray-may-deer'], *va.* To remeasure.

remedo [ray-may'-do], *m.* Imitation, copy; mockery.

remellado, remellón [ray-mel-lyah'-do, ray-mel-lyone'], *a.* Unnaturally everted, ectropic.

remellar [ray-mel-lyar'], *va.* To unhair hides in a tannery.

rememorar [ray-may-mo-rar'], *va.* To remember, to recall.

rememorativo, va [ray-may-mo-ray-tee'-vo, vah], *a.* That which remembers or recalls.

remendado, da [ray-men-dah'-do, dah], *a.* 1. Patched: mended. 2. Spotted, tabby (caballos, perros). *-pp.* of REMENDAR.

remendar [ray-men-dar'], *va.* 1. To patch, to mend; to correct. 2. To adjust one thing to another. (*Yo remiendo, yo remiende*, from *Remendar*. V. ACERTAR.)

remendón [ray-men-done'], *m.* Botcher, patcher, one who mends old clothes; a cobbler, a fripper.

rementir [ray-men-teer'], *vn.* To lie frequently.

remera [ray-may'-rah], *f.* Flight-feather, each of the large feathers with which the wings of birds terminate.

remero [ray-may'-ro], *m.* Rower, paddler. V. RIMERO.

remesa [ray-may'-sah], *f.* Sending of goods; remittance of money.

remesar [ray-may-sar'], *va.* 1. To pluck out the hair. 2. (*Com.*) To remit (dinero), to send money or goods.

remesón [ray-may-sone'], *m.* 1. Plucking out of hair; hair plucked out. 2. Stopping a horse in full gallop. 3. A skillful thrust in fencing.

remeter [ray-may-terr'], *va.* To put back, to put in; to put a clean cloth on children.

remiel [ray-me-el'], *m.* The second extract of soft sugar taken from cane.

remiendo [ray-me-en'-do], *m.* 1. Batch, clout. 2. Amendment, addition. 3. Reparation, repair. 4. Brindle, the state of being spotted or tabby. 5. (*Coll.*) Badge of military orders worn by the knights. 6. (*Print.*) Short work of which few copies are printed. **A remiendos**, by patchwork, by piecemeal. **Echar un remiendo a**, to patch.

remilgadamente [ray-meel-gah'-dah-men-tay], *adv.* With affected nicety or gravity; with prudery, squeamishly.

remilgado, da [ray-meel-gah'-do, dah], *a. & pp.* of REMILGARSE. Applied to persons affectedly nice, grave, or prudish: used as a substantive, especially in the feminine.

remilgarse [ray-meel-gar'-say], *vr.* To be affectedly nice or grave.

remilgo [ray-meel'-go], *m.* 1. Affected nicety or gravity; prudery (gazmoñería), squeamishness (sensibilidad). 2. Prim look (mueca). **Hacer remilgos a**, to react in a prudish way to.

reminiscencia [ray-me-nis-then'-the-ah], *f.* Reminiscence, recollection, memory.

remirado, da [ray-me-rah'-do, dah], *a.* Prudent (prudente), cautious. *-pp.* of REMIRAR.

remirar [ray-me-rar'], *va.* To revise; to review. *-vr.* 1. To do or finish a thing with great care. 2. To inspect or consider with pleasure. 3. To reflect on or examine oneself.

remisamente [ray-me'-sah-men-tay], *adv.* Remissly, carelessly.

remisible [ray-me-see'-blay], *a.* Remissible.

remisión [ray-me-se-on'], *f.* 1. The act of sending (envío). 2. Remission, sending back, remitting, remitment. 3. Remission, forgiveness, grace. 4. Remissness, indolence. 5. Remission, abatement, cessation of intenseness. 6. The act of referring to another book or work (referencia).

remisivamente [ray-me-see'-vah-men-tay], *adv.* With remision.

remisivo, va [ray-me-see'-vo, vah], *a.* Remitting, serving to remit.

remiso, sa [ray-mee'-so, sah], *a.* 1. Remiss, careless, indolent. 2. Remiss, not rigorous.

remisoria [ray-me-so'-re-ah], *f.* Order of a superior judge to refer a cause to another tribunal: generally used in the plural.

remisorio, ria [ray-me-so'-re-o, ah], *a.* Having power to forgive or pardon. **Letras remisorias**, judge's orders, transferring a cause to another court.

remite [ray-me-tay], *m.* Name and address of sender.

remitente [ray-me-ten'-tay], *m. & f.* Remitter, sender. **Devuélvase al remitente**, return to sender.

remitir [ray-me-teer'], *va.* 1. To remit, to transmit. 2. To remit, to pardon, to forgive. 3. To remit, to give up, to suspend, to defer, to put off. 4. To return a cause to an inferior court. 5. To remit, to relax, to make less tense. 6. To refer (usuario). 7. To postpone (aplazar). **Remitir una dirección a uno**, to leave a decision to somebody. *-vn.* To remit, to slacken (disminuir), to grow less tense. *-vr.* 1. To refer or submit to the judgment and opinion of another. 2. To quote, to cite.

remo [ray'-mo], *m.* 1. (*Naut.*) An oar. **Pala de un remo**, (*Naut.*) blade or wash of an oar. **Manual de un remo**, (*Naut.*) handle of an oar. 2. Long and hard labor. 3. Rowing. **Practicar el remo**, to row. *-pl.* (*Coll.*) 1. The arms and legs of a person; the hind and fore legs of a horse. 2. The wings of a bird.

remoción [ray-mo-the-on'], *f.* Removal, act of removing.

remodelación [ray-mo-day-lah-the-on'], *f.* Remodelling; (*Aut.*) Restyling.

remodelar [ray-mo-day-lalr'], *va.* To remodel; (*Aut.*) to restyle.

remojadero [ray-mo-hah-day'-ro], *m.* Steeping-tub.

remojar [ray-mo-har'], *va.* 1. To steep, to imbrue, to wet much or long, to soak again (sin querer). 2. To celebrate with a drink (suceso). 3. *(Mex.)* To bribe (sobornar).

remojo [ray-mo'-ho], *m.* The act of steeping or soaking. **Dejar la ropa en remojo,** to leave clothes to soak.

remojón [ray-mo-hon'], *m.* 1. Soaking, drenching. **Darse un remojón,** to go in for a dip. 2. *(Culin.)* Piece of bread soaked in milk.

remolacha [ray-mo-lah'-chah], *f. (Bot.)* Beetroot. The red beet.

remolar [ray-mo-lar'], *m.* The master carpenter who makes oars, or the shop where oars are made.

remolcador [ray-mol-cah-dor'], *m.* 1. Towboat, tug. 2. Towcar.

remolcar [ray-mol-car'], *va.* To tow, to take in tow (coche, bote.)

remoler [ray-mo-lerr'], *va.* 1. To regrind, to grind excessively (moler). 2. *(And. CAm.)* To annoy (fastidiar). *-vn. (Cono Sur, And.)* To live it up.

remolimiento [ray-mo-le-me-en'-to], *m.* Act of regrinding.

remolinante [ray-mo-le-nahn'-tay], *pa.* Whirling, making gyrations.

remolinar [ray-mo-le-nar'], *vn.* To make gyrations. *-vr.* 1. To whirl oneself round. 2. To be surrounded by a multitude; to be confounded with the crowd.

remolinear [ray-mo-le-nay-ar'], *va.* To whirl anything about. *-vn.* V. REMOLINAR.

remolino [ray-mo-lee'-no], *m.* 1. Whirlwind (viento). 2. Whirlpool (en río). 3. Cow-lick, or twisted tuft of hair upon some part of an animal (pelo). 4. Crowd (de gente), throng. 5. Disturbance, commotion.

remolón, na [ray-mo-lone', nah], *a.* 1. Soft, indolent, lazy: applied to those who shun labor with art and study. 2. Applied to the upper tusk of a wild boar.

remolón [ray-mo-lon'], *m.* The upper tusk of a wild boar. sharp tooth in horses.

remolonear [ray-mo-lo-nay-ar'], *vn.* To lag, to loiter in doing what ought to be done. *-vr.* To be idle, to refuse stirring, from sloth and indolence.

remolque [ray-mol'-kay], *m.* 1. Towing (de un coche, bote.) 2. Towrope (cable). **Llevar un coche a remolque,** to tow a car.

remondar [Ray-mon-dar'], *va.* To clean a second time; to take away what is useless.

remono, na [ray-mo'-no, nah], *a.* Very neat, very pretty.

remonta [ray-mone'-tah], *f.* 1. Repair of the feet of shoes or boots. 2. The act of supplying the cavalry with fresh horses; collection of cavalry horses; remounting cavalry.

remontamiento [ray-mon-tah-me-en'-to], *m.* Act of soaring or towering.

remontar [ray-mon-tar'], *va.* 1. To frighten away (animales), to oblige one to withdraw. 2. To remount the cavalry; to supply them with fresh horses. 3. To repair the saddles of mules and horses. 4. To put new soles or feet to boots. *-vr.* 1. To tower (edificio), to soar (pájaros). 2. To conceive great and sublime ideas; to form sublime conceptions. 3. To go back (recuerdos), go up stream (río). **Sus recuerdos se remontan en el siglo pasado,** her memories go back to the last century. **Remontaron el río,** they went up the stream.

remonte [ray-mon'-tay], *m.* Soar, a towring flight; elevation or sublimity of ideas.

remontista [ray-mon-tees'-tah], *m.* Commissioner for the purchase of cavalry horses.

remoquete [ray-mo-kay'-tay], *m.* 1. Thump with the fist. 2. A witty expression (comentario). 3. Gallantry, courtship.

rémora [ray'-mo-rah], *f.* 1. Sucking fish, remora. 2. Hindrance, obstacle; cause of delay.

remordedor, ra [ray-mor-day-dor', rah], *a.* Causing remorse.

remorder [ray-mor-derr'], *va.* 1. To bite repeatedly. 2. To cause remorse, to sting, to make uneasy. *-vr.* To manifest concern, to suffer remorse.

remordimiento [ray-mor-de-me-en'-to], *m.* Remorse, uneasiness, compunction.

remosquear [ray-mos-kay-ar'], *va. & vr.* To blur: said of ink in printing when it spreads beyond the face of the types.

remostar [ray-mos-tar'], *va.* To put must into old wine. *-vr.* To grow sweet and assume the flavor of must (vino).

remostecerse [ray-mos-tay-ther'-say], *vr.* V. REMOSTARSE.

remosto [ray-mos'-to], *m.* The act of putting must into old wine.

remotamente [ray-mo'-tah-men-tay], *adv.* 1. Remotely, at a distance. 2. Without chance of happening or of succeeding. 3. Confusedly. 4. Unlikely.

remoto, ta [ray-mo'-to, tah], *a.* Remote, distant, far off; foreign, alien; unlike.

removedor [ray-mo-vay-dor'], *m.* A mover.

remover [ray-mo-verr'], *va.* 1. To remove (objetos), to shift from place to place. 2. To remove an obstacle (quitar). 3. To alter. 4. To dismiss. **Remover el pasado,** to stir up the past. *(Yo remuevo, yo remueva,* from *Remover.* V. MOVER.)

removimiento [ray-mo-ve-me-en'-to], *m.* 1. Removal. 2. Revulsion.

remozadura, *f.* **remozamiento,** *m.* [ray-mo-thah-doo'-rah], Act of appearing or becoming young.

remozar [ray-mo-thar'], *va.* To endeavor, to appear young; to make one appear younger than he is (persona); to give a new look (organización), *-vr.* To be rejuvenated.

remplazar [rem-pla-thar'], *va.* V. REEMPLAZAR.

remplazo [rem-plah'-tho], *m.* V. REEMPLAZO.

rempujar [rem-poo-har'], *va.* 1. To push a person out of his place. 2. To jostle. 3. To impel, to carry away. 4. To beat game, so as to drive it to a determined place.

rempujo [rem-poo'-ho], *m.* 1. Impulse, push, thrust. 2. Pressure of an arch upon its supporters. V. EMPUJE.

rempujón [rem-poo-hone'] *m.* Impulse, push, thrust.

remuda [ray-moo'-dah], *f.* 1. Exchange, re-exchange. 2. **Remuda de caballos,** relay of horses.

remedamiento [ray-moo-dah-me-en'-to], *m.* 1. Removal, exchange. 2. Change of clothing.

remudar [ray-moo-dar'], *va.* 1. To move or change again. 2. To exchange one thing for another.

remugar [ray-moo-gar'], *va. (Prov.)* V. RUMIAR.

remullir [ray-mool-lyeer'], *va.* To beat up again, to mollify.

remunerable [ray-moo-nay-rah'-blay], *a.* Remunerable, rewardable.

remuneración [ray-moo-nay-rah-the-on'], *f.* Remuneration, recompense, reward: gratuity, consideration.

remunerador, ra [ray-moo-nay-rah-dor', rah], *m. & f.* Remunerator.

remunerar [ray-moo-nay-rar'], *va.* To reward, to remunerate

remuneratorio, ria [ray-moo-nay-rah-to'-re-o, ah], *a.* Remunerative.

remusgo [ray-moos'-go], *m.* Too cool an atmosphere or situation.

remusguillo [ray-moos-geel'-lyo], *m. dim.* Coolish place, chilly situation.

renacentista [ray-nah-then-tees'-tah], *a.* Renaissance.

renacer [ray-nah-therr'], *vn.* 1. To be born again, to spring up again, to grow again. 2. To acquire grace by baptism. **Hoy me siento como renacio,** today I feel renewed. (*Yo renazco, yo renazca,* from *Renacer.* V. CONOCER.)

renaciente [ray-nah-the-en'-tay], *pa. & a.* Renascent, springing anew.

renacimiento [ray-nah-the-men-en'-to], *m.* 1. Regeneration: new birth. 2. The Renaissance in architecture and literature.

renacuajo [ray-nah-coo-ah'-ho], *m.* 1. Spawn of frogs or young tadpoles. 2. Little, shapeless man.

renadío [ray-nah-dee'-o], *m.* Crop which, after having been reaped in the blade, sprouts again.

renal [ray-nahl'], *a.* Renal, belonging to the kidneys.

rencilla [ren-theel'-lyah], *f.* A grudge remaining after a quarrel.

rencilloso, sa [ren-theel-lyo'-so, sah], *a.* Peevish, quarrelsome, touchy.

renco, ca [ren'-co, cah], *a.* Hipshot, having the hip dislocated, lame.

rencor [ren-cor'], *m.* Rancor, animosity, grudge. **Guardar rencor**, to bear malice.

rencorosamente [ren-co-ro'-sah-men-tay], *adv.* Rancorously.

rencoroso, sa [ren-co-ro'-so, sah], *a.* 1. Rancorous, spiteful (malicioso). 2. Resentful (resentido); bitter (amargado).

rencoso [ren-co'-so], *a.* Applied to a ram with one testicle concealed.

renda [ren'-dah], *f. (Prov.)* The second dressing of vines.

rendaje [ren-dah'-hay], *m.* Reins of the bridle of horses or mules.

rendejo [ren-dah'-ho], *m.* Mimic. *V.* ARRENDAJO.

rendar [ren-dar'], *va. (Prov.)* To dress vines a second time.

rendición [ren-de-the-on'], *f.* 1. Rendition, surrendering, yielding. 2. Product, profit accruing. 3. *(Cono Sur)* Trading balance; *(Fin.)* balance.

rendidamente [ren-dee'-dah-men-tay], *adv.* Humbly, submissively, compliantly.

rendido, da [ren-dee'-do, dah], *a.* Tired out, fatigued, submissive (sumiso), humble (admirador).

rendija [ren-dee'-hah], *f.* Crevice, crack, cleft.

rendimiento [ren-de-me-en'-to], *m.* 1. Rendition, delivery into the hands of another. 2. Weariness, faintness. 3. Humiliation, submission; obsequiousness (servilismo); humbling, compliance. 4. Rent, income; yearly produce. **El rendimiento del motor**, the performance of the engine. **Rendimiento del capital**, return on capital.

rendir [ren-deer'], *va.* 1. To subject (voluntad), to subdue (país), to conquer (vencer), to overcome. 2. To render, to surrender, to yield, to give up, to deliver up. **Rendir el puesto**, *(Mil.)* to give up a post, to commit it to another. 3. To render, to give back (devolver), to return, to restore, to produce. 4. To vomit, to throw up from the stomach. **Rendir gracias** *V.* AGRADECER. **Rendir obsequios.** *V.* OBSEQUIAR. *-vn.* 1. To yield (producir). **El negocio no rinde**, the business doesn't give good results. **Este año he rendido poco**, it has done poorly this year. *-vr.* 1. To be tired, to be worn out with fatigue (cansarse). 2. To yield (ceder), to submit to another, to give way. 3. *(Naut.)* To spring (mástil). **Rendir la guardia**, to set the watch.

renegado [ray-nay-gah'-do], *m.* 1. Renegade, apostate. 2. A malicious, wicked person. 3. Ombre, a sort of card game. **Renegado, da**, *pp.* of RENEGAR.

renegador, ra [ray-nay-gah-dor', rah], *m. & f.* Shearer, blasphemer; apostate.

renegar [ray-nay-gar'], *va.* 1. To deny (negar), to disown, to abnegate. 2. To detest (odiar), to abhor. *-vn.* 1. To apostatize. 2. To blaspheme, to curse. 3. To abhor, to detest (odiar). 4. To curse, to swear (jurar). 5. To grumble (quejarse). 6. *(And. Mex.)* To get angry (enojarse). 7. *(And. Conso Sur, Mex.)* To protest (protestar). **Renegar de su familia**, to disown one's family. **Renegar de**, to detest.

rengífero [ren-hee'-fay-ro], *m.* The reindeer.

renglón [ran-glone'], *m.* 1. Line written or printed from one margin to another (línea). **A renglón seguido**, in the very next line. 2. Part of one's revenue or income. 3. *(LAm.)* Line of goods (género). 4. *(LAm.)* Area, department.

renglonadura [ren-glo-nah-doo'-rah], *f.* Ruling of paper: ruled lines.

rengo, ga [ren'-go, gah], *a.* Hurt in the reins, back, or hip.

rengue [ren'-gay], *m.* Train.

reniego [ray-ne-ay'-go], *m.* 1. A kind of execration or blasphemy. 2. Curse (juramento). 3. grumble (queja). *(Yo reniego, yo reniegue, from Renegar. V. ACRECENTAR.)*

reniforme [ray-ne-for'-may], *a.* Reniform, kidney-shaped.

renil [ray-neel'], *a.* Barren, a barren ewe.

renitencia [ray-ne-ten'-the-ah], *f.* Resistance, opposition.

renitente [ray-ne-ten'-tay], *a.* Renitent, repugnant.

reno [ray'-no], *m.* Reindeer.

renombrado, da [ray-nom-brah'-do, dah], *a.* Renowned, celebrated, famous, *-pp.* of RENOMBRAR.

renombre [ray-no'-bray], *m.* 1. Surname (apellido), family name. 2. Renown, glory, fame.

renovable [ray-no-vah'-blay], *a.* Renewable, replaceable.

renovación [ray-no-vah-the-on'], *f.* 1. Renovation, renewal. 2. Change, reform. 3. Act of consuming old bread designed for the host, and of consecrating new. **Renovación de la suscripción**, renewal of one's subscription.

renovador, ra [ray-no-vah-dor', rah], *m. & f.* Renovator, reformer.

renovante [ray-no-vahn'-tay], *va.* Renovating, renewing.

renovar [ray-no-var'], *va.* 1. To renew (aviso), to renovate. 2. To change, to reform. 3. To polish. 4. To barter. 5. To reiterate, to republish. 6. To consume old wafers designed for the host, and consecrate new bread. **Renovar la memoria**, to bring to recollection. *-vr.* To recollect oneself, to reform. *(Yo renuevo, yo renueve, from Renovar. V. ACORDAR.*

renquear [ren-kay-ar'], *m.* To limp (cojear), to halt, to claudicate.

renta [ren'-tah], *f.* 1. Rent, profit, income (ingresos). 2. Rent, money paid for anything held of another. 3. Tax, contribution' revenue. 4. Public debt (deuda). 5. *(LAm.)* Rent. **A renta**, let at a rent. **Renta nacional**, national income. **Vivir de sus rentas**, to live on one's private income.

rentabilidad [ren-tah-be-le-dahd'], *f.* Return, yield, profitability.

rentable [ren-tah'-blay], *a.* Profitable, income-yielding. **La línea ya no es rentable**, the line is no longer economic.

renter [ren-tar'], *va.* To yield.

rentería [ren-tay-ree'-ah], *f.* Productive land or property.

rentero, ra [ren-tay'-ro], *m. & f.* 1. Renter, farmer. 2. One who farms out land.

rentilla [ren-teel'-lyah], *f.* 1. *(dim.)* A small rent. 2. A card game. 3. A dice game.

rentista [ren-tees'-tah], *m.* 1. Financier: a modern word. 2. One who possess an income irrespective of its source. 3. Bondholder, one who lives upon interest paid from the public treasury.

rentístico, ca [ren-tees'-te-co, cah], *a.* Belonging to public revenues.

rento [ren'-to], *m. (Prov.)* 1. Country residence with farmyard. 2. Annual rent paid by a laborer or colonist.

rentoso, sa [ren-to'-so, sah], *a.* Yielding income, rent-producing.

renuencia [ray-noo-en'-tha-ah], *f.* Contradiction, reluctance.

renuente [ray-noo-en'-tay], *a.* Indocile, intractable, remiss.

renuevo [ray-noo-ay'-vo], *m.* 1. Sprout, shoot; a young plant to be transplanted. 2. Nursery of young trees and plants. 3. Renovation, renewal. V. REMUDA.

renuncia [ray-noon'-the-ah], *f.* Renunciation, resignation, renouncement, adjurement.

renunciable [ray-noon-the-ah'-blay], *a.* That can be renounced or resigned: transferable.

renunciación [ray-noon-the-ah-the-on'], *f.* Renunciation. *V.* RENUNCIA.

renunciamiento [ray-noon-the-ah-me-en'-to], *m.* Renouncement. *V.* RENUNCIA.

renunciante [ray-noon-the-ah'-tay], *pa. & m. & f.* Renouncer, renouncing, abjurer.

renuncíar [ray-noon-the-ar'], *va.* 1. To renounce (derecho), to resign (puesto, responsabilidad). 2. To renounce, to disown; to abnegate. 3. To renounce, to leave, to forego, to give up (hábito, proyecto), to lay to; to fall from; to refuse, to reject; to depreciate, to abandon. *-vn.* To revoke, to renege at cards.

renunciatario [ray-noon-the-ah-tah'-re-o], *m.* A person to whom something has relinquished.

renuncio [ray-noon'-the-o], *m.* 1. Revoke, the fault committed in playing cards, by not furnishing a card of the same suit which was played by another. 2. *(Met. Coll.)* Error, mistake.

renvalsar [ren-val-sar'], *va.* To shave off doors or windows so that they may fit well.

reñidamente [ray-nyee-dah-men'-tay], *adv.* Quarrelsomely, in a wrangling manner.

reñidero [ray-nyee-day'-ro], *m.* Cockpit; fighting-pit; a place for fighting animals.

reñido, da [ray-nyee'-do, dah], *a.* At variance with another. *-pp.* of REÑIR. **Un partido reñido,** a hard-fought game. **Está reñeida con su familia,** she has fallen out with his family.

reñidor, ra [ray-nye-dor', rah], *m. & f.* Quarreler, wrangler.

reñir [ray-nyeer'], *va. & vn.* 1. To wrangle, to quarrel (disputar), to dispute, to fight (pelear), to fall out. 2. To scold (regañar), to reprimand, to chide, to reproach. 3. To argue, to discuss. **He reñido con su novio,** she's fallen out with her boyfriend. **Se pasan la vida riñendo,** they spend their whole time quarrelling. *(Yo riño, yo riña; el riñó, riñera; from Reñir. V.* PEDIR.)

reo [ray'-o], *com.* 1. Offender, criminal, culprit (delincuente). 2. Defendant in a suit at law. 3. Series, continuity. 4. *(Cono Sur)* Tramp (vagabundo).

reoctava [ray-oc-tah'-vah], *f.* V. OCTAVILLA.

reojar [ray-o-har'], *va.* To bleach wax.

reojo [ray-o'-ho], *m.* **Mirar de reojo,** to look obliquely, to dissemble the looks by directing the view above a person; to look contemptuously or angrily.

reordenar [ray-ro-day-nahr'], *va.* To realign.

reorganización [ray-or-gah-ne-thah-the-on'], *f.* Reorganization.

reorganizar [ray-or-gah-ne-thar'], *va.* To reorganize, to organize anew.

reóstato [ray-os'-tah-to], *m.* Rheostat.

repacer [ray-pah-therr'], *va.* To consume the entire grass of pasture-ground.

repadecer [ray-pah-day-therr'], *va. & vn.* To suffer extremely.

repagar [ray-pah-gar'], *va.* To pay a high or excessive price.

repajo [ray-pah'-ho], *m.* Inclosure for the pasture of cattle.

repantingarse [ray-pan-te-gar'-say], **repanchingarse,** *vr.* To lean back in a chair with the legs stretched out.

repapilarse [ray-pah-pe-lar'-say], *vn.* To eat to excess, to lick one's lips, to smack with reilsh.

reparable [ray-pah-rah'-blay], *a.* 1. Reparable, remediable: objectionable. 2. Worthy of attention.

reparación [ray-pah-rah-the-on'], *f.* 1. Reparation (acto), repair. 2. Repeating a lesson among scholars. 3. Compensation, pay. **Efectuar reparaciones en,** to carry out repairs to.

reparada [ray-pah-rah-dah], *f.* Sudden bound of a horse.

reparador, ra [ray-pah-rah-dor', ah], *m. & f.* 1. Repairer. 2. Observer, one who makes remarks.

reparamiento [ray-pah-rah-me-en'-to], *m. V.* REPARO and REPARACIÓN.

reparar [ray-pah-rar'], *va.* 1. To repair, to restore. 2. To observe with careful attention (observar). 3. To consider (considerar), to reflect, to give heed. 4. To repair, to amend an injury by an equivalent (ofensa), to make up, to compensate, to expiate, to make amends, to correct. 5. To suspend, to detain. 6. To guard, to defend, to protect, to help. 7. To give the final touch to moulds. *-vn.* 1. To regain strength; to recover from illness. 2. To stop or halt in any part. 3. *(CAm. Mex.)* To rear (caballo). **Reparar en,** to observe. **Sin reparar en los gastos,** heedless of expense. *-vr.* 1. To refrain, to forbear. 2. *(Mex.)* To rear on the hind legs, as a horse.

reparativo, va [ray-pah-rah-tee'-vo, vah], *a.* Reparative.

reparo [ray-pah'-ro], *m.* 1. Repair, reparation, supply of loss, restoration. 2. Restoration, repair of an edifice. 3. Careful inspection and investigation, notice. 4. Inconveniency, difficulty, doubt (duda), objection (objeción). 5. Strengthening cataplasm for the stomach. 6. Anything to support, assist, or defend. 7. Provisional anchorage for repairing damages. 8. Parry or guard, in fencing. 9. *(CAm. Mex.)* Bucking, rearing (caballo).

reparón [ray-pah-ron'], *m. (Coll.)* Great doubt or difficulty.

reparón, na [ray-pah-ron', nah], *a.* Too cautious, too circumspect.

repartible [ray-per-tee'-blay], *a.* Distributable.

repartición [ray-par-te-the-on'], *f.* 1. Partition, distribution (distribución). 2. *(Cono Sur)* Government department, administrative section. 3. *(LAm. Pol.)* Redistribution (de tierras).

repartidamente [ray-par-tee'-dah-men-tay], *adv.* In several portions or partitions.

repartidero, ra [ray-par-te-day'-ro, rah], *a.* Distributing, parting.

repartidor, ra [ray-par-te-dor', rah], *m. & f.* 1. Distributer; delivery man. 2. Assessor of taxes.

repartimiento [ray-pay-te-me-en'-to], *m.* 1. Partition, division, distribution, apportionment. 2. Portion of territory which was given as a fief to the conquerors of Spanish America. 3. Assessment of taxes.

repartir [ray-par-tee'], *va.* 1. To divide, to distribute (distribuir), to apportion, to share out. 2. To scatter, to sow. 3. To assess taxes. 4. To allot (trabajos), to give out (premios), to serve out (comida), to deliver (cartas, leche, pan). **Las guarniciones están repartidas por toda la costa,** the garrisons are distributed all round the coast. *-vr.* To be distributed.

reparto [ray-par'-to], *m.* 1. Distribution (distribución). 2. *(Correos)* Delivery. 3. *(Teat.)* Casting; cast (lista), cast list. 4. *(CAm. Carib. Mex.)* Building sie (solar).

repasadera [ray-pah-sah-day'-rah], *f.* Planes, a carpenter's tool.

repasadora [ray-pah-sah-do'-rah], *f.* Woman occupied in carding wool.

repasar [ray-pah-sar'], *va.* 1. To repass, to pursue the same course (used also intransitively). 2. To re-examine, to revise (texto), to review and correct or polish work already done (notas). 3. To glance rapidly over something written. 4. To explain again, to run over the results of one's former studies. 5. To clean dyed wool for carding. 6. To sew again, to mend clothes. 7. To air clothes at the fire. 8. To remix mercury with metal to purify it.

repasata [ray-pah-sah'-tah], *f. (Coll.)* Reprehension, censure, chiding.

repas agent on the patient.

repaso [ray-pah'-so], *m.* 1. The act and effect of running over a thing that one has already studied. 2. Revision, the act of re-examining and revising: examining a thing after it is finished. 3. The act and effect of repealing or remixing quicksilver with metal. 4. Reprimand, chastisement. *-pl.* A number of flaws or porosities in the body of an organ. **Repaso general,** general overhaul. **Dar un repaso a una lección,** to revise a lesson.

repastar [ray-pas-tar'], *va.* To feed a second time.

repasto [ray-pahs'-to], *m.* Increase of food; an additional meal.

repatriación [ray-pah-tre-ah-the-on'], *f.* Repatriation.

repatriar [ray-pah-tre-ar'], *vn. (mer.)* To return to one's country, to repatriate. *-va.* To repatriate; to deport (criminal); to send home, to send back to one's country of origin.

repechar [ray-pay-char'], *va. & vn.* To mount a declivity or slope.

repecho [ray-pay'-cho], *m.* Declivity, slope (vertiente). *a.* To repel (enemigo); to refute, to reject (idea, oferta). **Este material repele el agua,** this material is water-repellent.

repeliente [ray-pay-le-en'-tay], *pa.* Repellent.

repellar [ray-pel-lyar'], *va.* To run a trowel over the plaster thrown on a wall.

repelo [ray-pay'-lo], *m.* 1. A small part or share of anything that rises against the grain, or has transverse fibres. 2. Anything which goes against the grain, crooked grain. 3. A slight scuffle or dispute (riña). 4. Repugnance, aversion. 5. *(And. Mex.)* Junk (baratijas).

repelón [ray-pay-lone'], *m.* 1. The action of pulling out the hair. 2. A small part torn from anything; a thread loose in stockings. 3. A short gallop. **A repelones**, by degrees, by little and little.

repeloso, sa [ray-pay-lo'-so, sah], *a.* 1. Of a bad grain, having transverse timbres (madera). 2. Touchy, peevish.

repelús [ray-pay-loos'], *m.* Inexplicable fear. **Me da repelús**, it gives me the willies.

repensar [ray-pen-sar'], *va.* To consider, to reflect, to contemplate; to think deeply.

repente [ray-pen'-tay], *m.* A sudden movement (movimiento), an unexpected event. **De repente**, suddenly, all of a sudden.

repentinamente [ray-pen-tee'-nah-men-tay], *adv.* Suddenly.

repentino, na [ray-pen-tee'-no, nah], *a.* Sudden (súbito), unforeseen, unexpected (imprevisto), abrupt, extemporaneous, unpremeditated.

repentirse [ray-pen-tee'-no], *vr.* V. ARREPENTIRSE.

repentista [ray-pen-tees'-tah], *m.* Maker of extemporary verses.

repentizar [ray-pen-te-thar'], *va.* To improvise (en discurso), to compose verses off hand.

repentón [ray-pen-tone'], *m.* 1. An unexpected event or incident. 2. A sudden movement.

repeor [ray-pay-or'], *a.* Much worse.

repercudida [ray-per-coo-dee'-dah], *f.* Repercussion, rebound.

repercudir [ray-per-coo-deer'], *vn.* To rebound. V. REPERCUTIR.

repercusión [ray-per-coo-se-on'], *f.* Repercussion (sonido), reverberation (reverberación), Repercussion (consecuencia). **Repercusiones**, repercussions.

repercusivo, va [ray-per-coo-see'-vo, vah], *a.* Repercussive; repellent.

repercutir [ray-per-coo-teer'], *vn.* 1. To cause repercussion, to repercuss, to drive back, to rebound (objeto); to retrograde, to reverberate. 2. *(Mex.)* To smell bad (oler mal). *-va.* To repel.

repertorio [ray-per-to'-re-o], *m.* 1. Repertory, index of noteworthy matters (lista). 2. Repertory, repertoire, a list of plays, especially such as are presented in a theater by a stock company.

repesar [ray-pay-sar'], *va.* To reweigh, to weigh again.

repeso [ray-pay'-so], *m.* 1. Weighing a second time. 2. Weight-office, whither articles may be carried to be weighed a second time. 3. Charge of reweighing. **De repeso**, with the whole weight of a body; with the whole force of authority and persuasion.

repetición [ray-pay-te-the-on'], *f.* 1. Repetition, reiteration; iteration. 2. Repeater, a repeating clock or watch. 3. Collegial dissertation or discourse; a thesis. 4. *(For.)* An action for an accounting.

repetidamente [ray-pay-tee'-dah-men-tay], *adv.* Repeatedly.

repetidor, ra [ray-pay-te-dor', rah], *m. & f.* Repeater, a teacher or student who repeats with another his lessons, and explains them.

repetir [ray-pay-teer'], *va.* 1. To demand or claim repeatedly and urgently. 2. To repeat, to reiterate, to use again, to do again, to try again (volver a hacer). 3. To repeat, to recite, to rehearse. **Le repito que es imposible**, I repeat that it is impossible. *-vn.* 1. To have the taste of what was eaten or drunk in the mouth. 2. To deliver a public discourse previous to the examination for the higher degrees in the universities. *-vr.* 1. To repeat oneself (artista). 2. To recur (suceso). *(Yo repito, yo repita; él repitió; from* REPETIR. V. PEDIR.)

repetitivo, va [ray-pay-te-tee'-vo, vah], *a.* That which contains a repetition.

repicado, da [ray-pe-cah'-do, dah], *a.* 1. Chopped. 2. Starched, stiff; affectedly nice. *-pp.* of REPICAR.

repicapunto [ray-pe-cah-poon'-to], *adv.* **De repicapunto**, nicely, delicately, excellently.

repicar [ray-pe-car'], *va.* 1. To chop (carne). 2. To chime, to ring a merry peal. 3 To reprick (picar otra vez). 4. In the game of piquet; to count ninety before the adverse party counts one. *-vr.* To glory, to boast, to pique oneself on.

repilogar [ray-pe-lo-gar'], *va.* To recapitulate, to epitomize, to repeat the sum of a former discourse.

repinarse [ray-pe-nar'-say], *va.* To soar, to elevate.

repintar [ray-pin-tar'], *va.* To repaint (volver a pintar), to paint again. *-vr.* 1. To paint oneself. 2. *(Print.)* To set off, to make a double impression.

repique [ray-pee'-kay], *m.* 1. Act of chopping or cutting. 2. Chime, a merry peal on festive occasions; the peal of bells. **El último repique** or **llamada**, the last peal. 3. Dispute, altercation, a slight scuffle. 4. In piquet, counting ninety before the other player can count one.

repiquete [ray-pe-kay'-tay], *m.* 1. A merry peal rung on festive occasions. 2. Chance, opportunity. 3. *(Cono Sur)* Trill, song. 4. *(And.)* Pique, resentment (resentimiento).

repiquetear [ray-pe-kay-tay-ar'], *va.* 1. To ring a merry peal on festive occasions. 2. To tap, to beat (mesa, tambor). *-vr.* To bicker, to wrangle, to quarrel.

repiqueteo [ray-pe-kay-tay'-o], *m.* A continued peal of bells.

repisa [ray-pee'-sah], *f.* 1. Pedestal of abutment for a bust of vase. 2. A bracket.

repiso [ray-pee'-so], *m.* Weak, vapid wine.

repiso, sa [ray-pee'-so, sah], *a.* Sorrowful, repentant. *(Acad.)*

repitiente [ray-pe-te-en'-tay], *pa.* Repeating, he who repeats and defends a thesis.

repizcar [ray-peeth-car'], *va.* To pinch. V. PELLIZCAR.

repizco [ray-peeth'-co], *m.* The act of pinching. V. PELLIZCO.

replantar [ray-plan-tar'], *va.* To replant ground.

replantear [ray-plan-tay-ar'], *va.* 1. To mark out the ground plan of an edifice again. 2. To raise again (cuestión).

replanteo [ray-plan-tay'-o], *m.* 1. The act of replanting. 2. Second description of the ground plan of a building.

repleción [ray-play-the-on'], *f.* 1. Fullness due to overeating. 2. Satisfaction of a need or desire.

replegable [ray-play-gah'-blay], *a.* Capable of being folded back.

replegar [ray-play-gar'], *va.* 1. To redouble, to fold often (doblar). 2. *(Mil.)* To fall back or to double the wing of an army, regiment, etc., upon its center or any other part, as the evolution may be necessary. *-vr.* To withdraw, to fall back.

repleto, ta [ray-play'-to, tah], *a.* Replete (lleno), very full. **Repleto de**, fillled with. **La plaza estaba repleta de gente**, the square was solid with people.

réplica [ray'-ple-cah], *f.* 1. Reply, answer (respuesta); repartee; objection. 2. *(Art.)* Replica, copy.

replicación [ray-ple-cah-the-on'], *f.* *(Law.)* V. RÉPLICA.

replicador, ra [ray-ple-cah-dor', rah], *m. & f.* Replier, disputant.

replicante [ray-ple-cahn'-tay], *pa. & n* Replier, respondent; replying.

replicar [ray-ple-car'], *vn.* 1. To reply, to make return to an answer. 2. To reply, to impugn the arguments of the adverse party; to contradict. *-va. (Law.)* To respond; to repeat.

replicón, na [ray-ple-cone', nah], *a. (Coll.)* Replica, frequent disputer.

repliegue [ray-ple-ay'-gay], *m.* 1. The act of doubling or folding often (pliegue). 2. A fold, crease, convolution.

repoblación [ray-po-blah-the-on'], *f.* Repopulation (gente), act of repeopling.

repoblar [ray-po-blar'], *va.* To repeople; to repopulate (zona, país); to afforest.

repoda [ray-poh'-dah], *f.* The act of pruning a second time.

repodar [ray-po-dar'], *va.* To prune again.

repodrir [ray-po-dreer'], *va. & vr.* V. REPUDRIR.

repollar [ray-pol-lyar'], *vn.* To form round heads of leaves, like cabbage.

repollo [ray-pol'-lyo], *m.* 1. *(Bot.)* White cabbage. 2. Round head formed by the leaves of plants.

repolludo, da [ray-pol-lyoo'-do, dah], *a.* Cabbage-headed; round-head.

reponche [ray-pon'-chay], *m. V.* RUIPONCE.

reponer [ray-po-nerr'], *va.* 1. To replace (devolver a su lugar); to collocate. 2. To restore a suit at law to its primitive state. 3 To oppose anew, to reply. *-vr.* To recover lost health or property. **Reponerse de**, to recover from. (*Yo repongo, yo reponga; yo repuse, repondré;* from *Reponer. V.* PONER.)

reportación [ray-por-tah-the-on'], *f.* Moderation, forbearance.

reportado, da [ray-por-tah'-do, dah], *a.* Moderate, temperate, forbearing. *-pp.* of REPORTAR.

reportaje [ray-por-tah'-hay], *m.* Report, article, news item. **Reportaje gráfico**, illustrated report.

reportamiento [ray-por-tah-me-en'-to], *m.* Forbearance.

reportar [ray-por-tar'], *va.* 1. To moderate or repress one's passions, to refrain, to forbear: 2. To obtain (beneficio), to reach; to attain. 3. To carry or bring (traer). 4. To return an instrument with the certificate of its execution. 5. (*Fig.*) To check (moderar). 6. (*LAm.*) To report (informar); to denounce (denunciar). **Esto le habrá reportado algún beneficio**, this will have brought him some benefit. *-vr.* 1. To forbear. 2. (*CAm. Mex.*) To present oneself.

reporteril [ray-por-tay-reel'], *a.* (*Neol.*) Reportorial, relating to reporters. (Note.—The noun is *Reporter*, taken from the English.)

reportorio [ray-por-to'-re-o], *m.* Almanac, calendar.

reposadamente [ray-po-sah'-dah-men-tay], *adv.* Peaceably, quietly.

reposadero [ray-po-sah-day'-ro], *m.* 1. A vat in which indigo is prepared. 2. A trough for receiving melted metal.

reposado, da [ray-po-sah'-do, dah], *a.* Quiet (tranquilo), peaceful, gentle (descansado). *-pp.* of REPOSAR.

reposar [ray-po-sar'], *vn.* 1. To rest (descansar), to repose; to take a nap (dormir), to lie by, to lie to. 2. To rest in the grave; to rest in peace. *-va.* **Reposar la comida**, to let one's meal go down. *-vr.* To settle (líquido).

reposición [ray-po-se-the-on'], *f.* 1. The act of restoring a suit a law to its primitive state. 2. (*Chem.*) Preservation of liquids in proper vessels. 3. Reposition.

reposo [ray-poh'-so], *m.* Rest, repose, tranquility.

repostar [ray-pos-tar'], *va.* To restock, to resupply with. *-vr.* To lay in a fresh supply. **Repostar combustible**, to refuel.

repostería [ray-pos-tay-ree'-ah], *f.* 1. Office or shop for preparing confectionery and beverages (tienda). 2. All the provisions, instruments, and persons employed in this office.

repostero, ra [ray-pos-tay'-ro], *m. & f.* 1. Pastrycook (pastelero). 2. Covering ornamented with a coat of arms. 3. (*And.*) Kitchen shelf unit. 4. Butler to the king (palaciego).

repregunta [ray-pray-goon'-tah], *f.* 1. A second demand or question on the same subject. 2. (*Law.*) A cross-examination.

repreguntar [ray-pray-goon-tar'], *va.* To question repeatedly about the same subject.

reprenda [ray-pren'-dah], *f.* Pledge taken a second time.

reprender [ray-pren-derr'], *va.* To reprehend, to reprimand, to blame, to censure, to reprove, to chide; to correct.

reprendiente [ray-pren-de-en'-tay], *pa.* Censuring, reprimanding.

reprensible [ray-pren-see'-blay], *a.* Reprehensible.

reprensión [raypren-se-on'], *f.* Reprehension, blame, censure. reprimand, reproof, lesson. **Sujeto sin represión**, an irreprehensible person.

represor, ra [ray-pren-sor', rah], *m. & f.* Reprehender, censurer, reprover.

represa [ray-pray'-sah], *f.* 1. Water collected for working a mill; dam (presa). 2. The act of stopping or retaining; restriction. 3. Pool. lake (estanque).

represalia, represaria [ray-pray-sah'-le-ah, ray-pray-sah'-re-ah], *f.* Reprisal, reprise.

represar [ray-pray-sar'], *va.* 1. To recapture or retake from the enemy. 2 To stop (parar), to detain, to retain. 3. To repress, to moderate one's passions.

representable [ray-pray-sen-tah'-blay], *a.* That which may be represented.

representación [ray-pray-sen-tah-the-on'], *f.* 1. Representation, the act of representing. 2. Power, authority. 3. Dramatic poem. 4. Figure, image, idea. 5. Remonstrance, memorial, address. 6. Authority, dignity, character of a person. 7. (*Law.*) Right of succession to an inheritance in the person of another. **Hacer representaciones a**, to make representations to. **Representación visual**, (*Comput.*) visual display. **Representación simbólica**, (*Comput.*) symbolic representation.

representador, ra [ray-pray-sen-tah-dor', rah], *m. & f.* 1. Representative. 2. Player, actor.

representante [ray-pray-sen-tahn'-tay], *pa.* Representing another.

representante, ta [ray-pray-sen-tahn'-tay, tah], *m. & f.* 1. Player, comedian. 2. Representer, representative.

representar [ray-pray-sen-tar'], *va.* 1. To represent, to make appear, to set forth; to manifest; to refer; to express (expresar). 2. To play on the stage, to perform, to act (papel). 3. To represent another, as his agent, deputy, or attorney. 4. To be the symbol or image of anything. 5. To look (edad). 6. To mean (significar). **Representa unos 55 años**, he looks about 55. **Representar una dificultad a uno**, to represent a difficulty to somebody. *-vr.* To offer, to occur; to present itself. **Representarse una escena**, to imagine a scene.

representativo, va [ray-pray-sen-tah-tee'-vo, vah], *a.* Representative.

represión [ray-pray-se-on'], *f.* Repression.

represivo, va [ray-pray-see'-vo, vah], *a.* Repressive, restrictive.

reprimenda [ray-pre-men'-dah], *f.* Reprimand.

reprimido [raypre-mee'-do], *a.* Repressed.

reprimir [ray-pre-meer'], *va.* To repress, to refrain, to contain, to control, to curb (refrenar), to suppress (bostezo, risa). *-vr.* **Reprimirse de**, to stop oneself from.

reprobable [ray-pro-bah'-blay], *a.* Reprehensible.

reprobación [ray-pro-bah-the-on'], *f.* Reprobation, reproof.

reprobado, da [ray-pro-bah'-do, dah], *a.* 1. Flunked, not passed (en un examen). 2. *V.* RÉPROBO.

reprobador, ra [ray-pro-bah-dor', rah], *m. & f.* Reprover, condemner.

reprobar [ray-pro-bar'], *va.* To reject, to condemn (censurar), to contradict, to exclude, to upbraid, to reprobate, to damn (condenar). (*Yo repruebo, yo repruebe*, from *Reprobar. V.* ACORDAR.)

reprobatorio, ria [ray-pro-bah-to'-re-o, ah], *a.* That which reprobates or reproves; objurgatory.

réprobo, ba [ray'-pro-bo, bah], *m. & f. & a.* Reprobate, graceless, wicked.

reprochar [rayprochar'], *va.* 1. To reproach, to impute blame to. 2. To reject, to dismiss, to exclude.

reproche [ray-pro'-chay], *m.* 1. Reproach, reproof. 2. Fault which may be reproved. 3. Repulse, rebuff, displeasure.

reproducción [ray-pro-dooc-the-on'], *f.* 1. Reproduction. 2. Reproduction of a summons, or any other judicial precpt or decree.

reproducir [ray-pro-doo-theer'], *va.* To reproduce.

reproductible [ray-pro-dooc-tee'-blay], *a.* That can be reproduced or reproduced anew.

reproductividad [ray-pro-dooc-tee-ve-dahd'], *f.* Reproductiveness.

reproductivo [ray-pro-dooc-tee'-vo], *a.* Reproductive, producing anew.

reproductor, ra [ray-pro-dooc-tor'], *a. & n.* Serving for reproduction.

repromisión [ray-pro-me-se-on'], *f.* Repeated promise.

repropiarse [ray-pro-pe-ahr'-say], *vr.* To be unwilling to obey, to be restive (caballos).

repropio [ray-pro-pe-o], *a.* Restive (caballos).

reprueba [ray-proo-ay-bah], *f.* New proof in addition to a preceding one.

reptil [rep-teel'], *a. & m.* Reptile; crawler, creeper.

reptilívoro, ra [rep-te-lee'-vo-ro, rah], *a.* Devouring reptiles, reptilivorous.

república [ray-poo'-ble-cah], *f.* 1. Republic, commonwealth. 2. Republic, public welfare; political government. **República bananera**, banana republic. **Segunda República**, Second Spanish Republic.

republicanismo [ray-poo-ble-cah-nees'-mo], *m.* Republicanism.

republicano, na [ray-poo-ble-cah'-no, nah], *a.* 1. Republican, inhabitant of a republic. 2. Republican, approving republican government, democratic.

republicano, na [ray-poo-ble-cah'-no, nah], *m. & f.* Republican, democrat, common-wealthsman. *V.* REPÚBLICA.

repúblico [ray-poo'-ble-co], *m.* A man greatly attached to the welfare of the public, a patriot; a man capable of holding public offices, a statesman.

repudiación [ray-poo-de-ah-the-on'], *f.* Repudiation, divorce.

repudiar [ray-poo-de-ar'], *va.* 1. To repudiate (mujer, violencia), to divorce a wife. 2. To renounce (herencia), to relinquish.

repudio [ray-poo'-de-o], *m.* Repudiation, divorce.

repudrir [ray-poo-dreer'], *va.* To rot (pudrir). *-vr.* To pine away.

repuesta [ray-poo-es'-tah], *f.* Money staked in the game of ombre.

repuesto [ray-poo-ess'-to], *m.* 1. Refill (de pluma). 2. Extra, spare. 3. Replacement (reemplazo). 4. Stock (provisión). **De repuesto**, as a substitute, extra, as a spare. **Rueda de repuesto**, spare wheel.

repuesto, ta [ray-poo-es'-to, tah], *p. irr.* of REPONER.

repugnancia [ray-poog-nahn'-the-ah], *f.* 1. Reluctance (desgana), repugnance, resistance. 2. Repugnance, aversion, loathing (asco). 3. Opposition, contradiction, contrariety. **Con repugnancia**, in a reluctant manner.

repugnante [ray-poog-nahn'-tay], *a.* Repugnant, repulsive, loathsome.

repugnar [ray-poog-nar'], *va.* 1. To oppose, to contradict (contradecir), to repugn, to withstand. 2. To act with reluctance, to implicate. 3. To disgust, to revolt (dar asco a). *-vr.* To conflict, to be in opposition.

repujado, da [ray-poo-ha'-do, dah], *a.* Repoussé, formed in relief.

repulgado [ray-pool-gah'-do], *a. V.* AFECTADO. *-pp.* of REPULGAR.

repulgar [ray-pool-gar'], *va.* 1. To hem, to double in the border of cloth with a seam; to border, to double the edge. 2. To put an edging upon pastry.

repulgo [ray-pool'-go], *m.* 1. Hem, the border of cloth doubled in with a seam. 2. The external ornament of a pie. 3. Vain and ridiculous scruple. **Detenerse en repulgos de empanada**, to waste time over trifles.

repulido, da [ray-poo-lee'-do, dah], *a.* Prim, neat, spruce. *-pp.* of REPULIR.

repulir [ray-poo-leer'], *va.* 1. To repolish (objeto). 2. To dress affectedly (persona). Used also as reflexive.

repulsa [ray-pool'-sah], *f.* 1. Refusal, counter-check, repulse. 2. (*Fig.*) Strong condemnation (censura); severe reprimand (reprimenda).

repulsar [ray-pool-sar'], *va.* To reject, to decline, to refuse.

repulsión [ray-pool-se-on'], *f.* 1. *V.* REPULSA. 2. Repulsion.

repulsivo, va [ray-pool-see'-vo, vah], *a.* Repulsive, repulsory.

repulso, sa [ray-pool'-so, sah], *pp. .rr.* of REPELER.

repulular [ray-poo-loo-lar'], *va.* To repullulate.

repullo [ray-pool'-lyo], *m.* 1. Jerk, leap; a sudden violent motion of the body. 2. A small arrow or dart. 3. An external mark of pain or grief.

repunta [ray-poon'-tah], *f.* 1. Point, headland. 2. Sign of displeasure (indicio); disagreement, dispute, scuffle. 3. Very short thing, very small portion.

repuntar [ray-poon-tar'], *vn.* (*Naut.*) To begin to ebb. 2. (*LAm.*) To make itself felt (manifestarse). 3. (*Cono Sur*) To rise to previous levels. *-vr.* 1. To be on the turn (vino). 2. To be soured, to be displeased with one another.

repurgar [ray-poor-gar'], *va.* 1. To glean or purity again. 2. To administer a second purging draught.

reputación [ray-poo-tah-the-on'], *f.* Reputation, repute, character, credit, fame, renown.

reputante [ray-poo-tahn'-tay], *pa.* One who estimates.

reputar [ray-poo-tar'], *va.* To repute, to estimate (estimar), to appreciate, to deem (considerar). **Reputar a uno de inteligente**, to consider somebody intelligent.

requebrado, da [ray-kay-brah'-do, dah], *a. & pp.* of REQUEBRAR. Enamored, using tender expressions. *-m. & f.* Lover, loving expression.

requebrador [ray-kay-brah-dor'], *m.* Wooer, suitor.

requebrar [ray-kay-brar'], *va.* To woo, to court, to make love, to dally. (*Yo requiebro, yo requiebre*, from *Requebrar.* V. ACRECENTAR.)

requejada, *f.* **requejal**, *m.* [ray-kay- hah'-dah, ray-kay-hahl'], (*Prov.*) *V.* REQUEJO.

requejo [ray-kay'-ho], *m.* (*Prov.*) Ground ending in a hill before entering upon a plain.

requemado, da [ray-kay-mah'-do, dah], *a.* 1. Brown-colored, sun-burnt (piel). 2. Thin silk for veils, black and lustreless. *-pp.* of REQUEMAR.

requemadura [ray-kay-mah-doo'-rah], *f.* A burn upon a burn.

requemamiento [ray-kay-mah-me-ayn'-to], *m. V.* RESQUEMO.

requemar [ray-kay-mar'], *va.* 1. To burn a second time. 2. To roast to excess (comida). 3. To extract the juice of plants. 4. To inflame the blood. 5. To scorch (fuego). 6. (*Fig.*) To inflame (sangre). *V.* RESQUEMAR. *-vr.* 1. To burn with passion, to be deeply in love. 2. To scorch; to parch, to get parched.

requemazón [ray-kay-mah-thone'], *f. V.* RESQUEMO.

requeridor [ray-kay-re-dor'], *f.* A person who requests, advises, or intimates.

requerimiento [ray-kay-re-me-en'-to], *m.* 1. Request (petición), requisition. 2. Intimation, injunction, summons (llamada).

requerir [ray-kay-reer'], *va.* 1. To require, to need (necesitar). 2. To summon. 3. To intimate, to notify. 4. To investigate. 5. To request (pedir). 6. To court, to woo a woman. 7. To induce, to persuade. **Esto requiere cierto cuidado**, this requires some care. **El ministro requirió sus gafas**, the minister sent for his glasses. (*Yo requiero, yo requiera; él requirió, requiriera;* from *Requerir. V.* ASENTIR.)

requesón [ray-kay-sone'], *m.* Cottage cheese.

requesonarse [ray-kay-so-nar'-say], *vr.* To become curds a second time.

requiebro [ray-ke-ay'-bro], *m.* 1. Endearing expressions, the language of love; love-tale. 2. Quiver, trill of the voice.

requiebro [ray-ke-ay'-bro]. *m.* Crushed ore.

réquiem [ray'-key-aym], *m.* Requiem.

requilorio [ray-ke-lo'-re-o], *m. & pl.* (*Coll.*) Useless ceremony, or circumlocution, before doing a simple thing.

requintador, ra [ray-kin-tah-dor', rah], *m. & f.* Outbidder, in the letting of lands or tenements.

requintar [ray-kin-tar'], *va.* 1. To outbid a fifth part, in tenements, after an agreement is made. 2. To exceed, to surpass, to superadd. 3. (*Mus.*) To raise or lower the tone five points. 4. (*And.*) To abuse (insultar), *-vn.* (*Carib.*) To resemble each other (parecerse).

requinto [ray-keen'-to], *m.* 1. The second fifth taken from a quantity from which one-fifth had before been taken. 2. An advance of a fifth in rent. 3. Extraordinary imposed levied on the Peruvians in the time of Philip II. 4. A very small and high-pitched flute, and the one who plays it.

requirir [ray-ke-reer'], *va. V.* REQUERIR.

requisa [ray-kee'-sah], *f.* 1. Night and morning visit of a jailer to his prisoners. 2. Survey, inspection (inspección). 3. *(LAm.)* Seizure (confiscación).

requisar [ray-ke-sar'], *va.* 1. To inspect, to review. 2. To make a levy of horses for army use. 3. *(LAm.)* To seize, to confiscate (confiscar).

requisición [ray-ke-se-the-on'], *f.* 1. A levy of horses for military service. 2. *(Cono Sur, Mex.)* Search (registrar).

requisito [ray-ke-see'-to], *m.* Requisite, necessary condition.

requisito, ta [ray-ke-see'-to, tah], *pp. irr.* of REQUERIR. **Requisito previo**, pre-requisite.

requisitorio, ria [ray-ke-se-to'-re-o, ah], *a.* Requisitory: applied to a warrant from one judge to another, requiring compliance with his orders: used as a substantive in the feminine termination.

requive [ray-kee'-vay], *m. V.* ARREQUIVE.

res [res], *f.* Head of cattle or sheep; an animal (doméstico, salvaje); a creature.

resaber [ray-sah-berr'], *va.* To know very well. *-vn.* To affect too much the learned man.

resabiar [ray-sah-be-ar'], *va.* To cause one to become vicious or contract evil habits. *-vr.* 1. To get vices, to become vicious. 2. To be discontented or dissatisfied, to fall into a pit. 3. *V.* SABOREARSE.

resabido, da [ray-sah-bee'-do, dah], *a.* Very learned; affecting learning. *-pp.* of RESABER.

resabio [ray-sah'-be-o], *m.* 1. An unpleasant taste left on the palate. 2. Vicious habit, bad custom.

resabioso, sa [ray-sah-be-oh'-so, sah], *a.* (Peru) Crafty, artful.

resaca [ray-sah'-cah], *f.* 1. *(Naut.)* Surge, surf, the undertow. 2. *(Com.)* A redraw, a draft against the indorser of a protested bill. 3. Hangover (después de beber). 4. *(And. CAm. Mex.)* Strong liquor (aguardiente). 5. *(Cono Sur)* The dregs of society (personas). 6. *(Carib.)* Beating (paliza).

resacar [ray-sah-car'], *va. (Com.)* To redraw.

resalado, da [ray-sah-lah'-do, dah], *a.* Very graceful, charming: commonly said of women only.

resalir [ray-sah-leer'], *vn.* To jut out, to project.

resaltar [ray-sal-tar'], *vn.* 1. To rebound (rebotar), to fly back. 2. To crack, to burst in pieces. 3. To jut out (salir), to project. 4. To appear, to be evident. **Hacer resaltar algo**, to throw something into relief.

resalte [ray-sahl'-tay], *m.* Prominence, protuberance; any striking point.

resalto [ray-sahl'-to], *m.* Rebound (rebote), resilience, prominence; act of shooting boars when rising from their bed.

resaludar [ray-sah-loo-dar'], *vn.* To return a salute, to salute again.

resalutación [ray-sah-loo-tah-the-on'], *f.* Return of a salute, act of resaluting.

resalvia [ray-sahl'-ve-ah], *f. (Agr.)* A count of the staddles which must be left in felling trees.

resalvo [ray-sahl'-vo], *m.* Staddle, sapling, or branch of a tree left for new growth in forestry.

resallar [ray-sal-lyar'], *va.* To weed again.

resallo [ray-sahl'-lyo], *m.* A re-weeding.

resanar [ray-sah-nar'], *va.* To regild defective spots.

resangría [ray-san-gree'-ah], *f.* Bleeding again.

resarcible [ray-sar-thee'-blay], *a.* Indemnifiable.

resarcidor, ra [ray-sar-the-dor', rah], *m. & f.* Indemnifier.

resarcimiento [ray-sar-the-me-en'-to], *m.* Compensation, reparation of damage, indemnity.

resarcir [ray-sar-theer'], *va.* To compensate (compensar), to recompense, to reward, to make amends, to repair, to indemnify. **Resarcirse de lo perdido**, to make up one's loss.

resbaladero [res-bah-lah-day'-ro], *m.* A slippery place or road; anything dangerous.

resbaladero, ra [res-bah-lah-day'-ro, rah], *a.* Applied to a slippery place or road.

resbaladizo, za [res-bah-lah-dee'-tho, thah], *a.* 1. Slippery, glib. 2. *V.* RESBALADERO. 3. Exposed to temptation.

resbalador, ra [res-bah-lah-dor', rah], *m. & f.* Slider; backslider.

resbaladura [res-bah-lah-doo'-rah], *f.* Slippery track; backsliding.

resbalante [res-bah-lahn'-tay], *pa.* Slider; slipping.

resbalar [res-bah-lar'], *vn. & vr.* 1. To slip (sin querer), to slide; not to tread firm. 2. To tail in the performance of engagements. 3. To slide (deslizarse). 4. To slip up (fallar). **El embrague resbala**, the clutch is slipping. **Me resbala**, it leaves me cold.

resbalo [res-bah'-lo], *m. (Anger. Ec.)* A very precipitous hill.

resbalón [res-bah-lone'], *m.* 1. Slip, the act of slipping. 2. Slip, fault, error, offence. **De resbalón**, erroneously; unsteadily.

resbaloso, sa [res-bah-lo'-so, sah], *a.* Slippery. *V.* RESBALADIZO.

rescaldar [res-cal-dar'], *va.* To heat, to scorch.

rescatador, ra [res-cah-tah-dor', rah], *m. & f.* Redeemer, ransomer.

rescatar [res-cah-tar'], *va.* 1. To ransom (cautivo), to redeem (delitos), to extricate. 2. To exchange, to barter, to commute. 3. *(Amer.)* To buy ore in mines. 4. To save, to resuce (salvar). 5. To get back (dinero).

rescate [res-cah'-tay], *m.* 1. Ransom, redemption by purchase. 2. Ransom money paid for the redemption of slaves. 3. Exchange, permutation, barter. **Operaciones de rescate**, rescue operations.

rescatín [res-cah-teen'], *m. (Amer.)* One who buys from Indians their small collections of ore.

rescaza [res-cah'-thah], *f. V.* ESCORPINA.

rescindente [res-the-den'-tay], *pa. & a.* Rescinding.

rescindir [res-thin-deer'], *va.* To rescind (contrato), to annul, to cut back (puestos de trabajo).

rescisión [res-the-se-on'], *f.* Rescission.

rescisorio, ria [res-the-so'-re-o, ah], *a.* Rescissory.

rescoldera [res-col-day'-rah], *f.* Pyrosis, heartburn.

rescoldo [res-col'-do], *m.* 1. Embers, hot ashes, cinders. 2. *(Met.)* Scruple, doubt, apprehension.

rescontrar [res-con-trar'], *va.* To balance in accounts, to compensate.

rescribir [res-cre-beer'], *va.* To reply, to write an answer to a letter.

rescripto [res-creep'-to], *m.* Rescript order, mandate.

rescriptorio, ria [res-crip-to'-re-o, ah], *a.* Belonging to a rescript. *(Yo rescuentro, yo rescuentre*, from *Rescontrar. V.* ACORDAR.)

rescuentro [res-coo-en'-tro], *m.* Balance of accounts, compensation.

resecación [rar-say-cah-the-on'], *f.* Drying up, drying out, thoroughly drying.

resecar [ray-say-car'], *vn.* To dry again, to dry thoroughly.

reseco, ca [ray-say'-co, cah], *a.* Too dry; very lean.

reseco [ray-say'-co], *m.* Drying out of trees or shrubs; dry part of a honeycomb.

reseda [ray-say'-dah], *f. (Bot.)* 1. Mignonette. 2. Woad. *V.* GUALDA.

resegar [ray-say-gar'], *va.* To reap again, to cut or mow a second time.

resellante [ray-say-lyahn'-tay], *pa.* Recoining, restamping.

resellar [ray-sel-lyar'], *va.* 1. To recoin, to coin again. 2. To limp in one's ideas, so as to accept others less advanced.

resello [ray-say'-lyo], *m.* Recoinage.

resembrar [ray-sem-brar'], *va.* To resow.

resentido, da [ray-sen-tee'-do, dah], *a.* Angry, resentful, displeased. *-pp.* of RESENTIRSE.

resentimiento [ray-sen-te-me-en'-to], *m.* 1. Flaw, crack, cleft. 2. Resentment, grudge.

resentirse [ray-sen-teer'-say], *vr.* 1. To begin to give way, to fail, to be out of order. 2. To resent, to express displeasure.

3. To remain weak (debilitarse). **Resentirse por algo**, to resent something. **Me resiento todavía del golpe**, I can still feel the effects of the injury.

reseña [ray-say'-nyah], *f.* 1. A distinguishing mark on the human or animal body. 2. Signal. 3. Description (descripción), succinct narration, or review of historical events. 4. *(Mil.)* Review of soldiers; muster. 5. (Cono Sur: esp Chile) Procession held on Passion Sunday.

reseñar [ray-say-nyar'], *va.* 1. To summarize, to review, to outline 2. To review (tropas). 3. To describe (describir); to write up (narrar). 4. To book (delincuente).

resequido, da [ray-say-kee'-do], *a.* V. RESECO.

reserva [ray-serr'-vah], *f.* 1. Reserve (provisión, surtido), something kept in store. 2. Reserve, secret (secreto). 3. Discretion, caution (cualidad). **Andar con reservas**, to proceed cautiously. **Llanta** or **neumático de reserva**, spare tire. **Reserva natural**, nature reserve. **Con ciertas reservas**, with certain reservations.

reservación [ray-ser-vah-the-on'], *f.* Reservation.

reservadamente [ray-ser-vah-dah-men-tay], *adv.* Secretly, reservedly.

reservado, da [ray-ser-vah'-do, dah], *a. & pp.* of RESERVAR. Reserved, cautious (actitud), circumspect, close, reserved (asiento), private (asunto). **Caso reservado**, a great crime, which none but a superior can absolve. *(Coll.)* Confidential.

reservado [ray-ser-vah'-do], *m.* 2. The Host kept in the ciborium. 2. Reserved or private room (restaurante). 3. Reserved compartment (tren).

reservar [ray-ser-var'], *va.* 1. To reserve, to keep in store (guardar). 2. To defer, to postpone. 3. To privilege, to exempt. 4. To separate, to set aside, to lay aside, to keep back. 5. To restrain, to limit, to confine. 6. To conceal (ocultar), to hide; to shut up (callar). 7. V. JUBILAR.- . **Lo reserva para el final**, he's keeping it till last. **Prefiero reservar los detalles**, I prefer to keep the details to myself. *vr.* 1. To preserve oneself. 2. To act with circumspection or caution.

resfriado [res-fre-ah'-do], *m.* Cold, a disease caused by cold; the obstruction of respiration.—**Resfriado, da**, *pp.* of RESFRIAR.

resfriador [res-fre-ah-dor'], *m.* Refrigerator.

resfriadura [res-fre-ah-doo'-rah], *f.* Cold in horses.

resfriamiento [res-fre-ah-me-en'-to], *m.* Refrigeration, V. ENFRIAMIENTO.

resfriar [res-fre-ar'], *va.* 1. To cool, to make cold. 2. To moderate ardor or fervor. *-vn.* To begin to be cold. *-vr.* 1. To catch a cold. 2. To proceed with coolness, not to pursue a business with the activity it requires.

resfriecer [res-fre-ay-ther'], *vn. (Brov.)* To begin to grow cold (tiempo).

resfrío [res-free'-o], *m.* Cold. V. RESFRIADO.

resguardar [res-goo-ar-dar'], *va.* To preserve, to defend; to protect, to harbor. *-vr.* To be guarded against, to be on one's guard (cautela).

resguardo [res-goo-ar'-do], *m.* 1. Guard, preservation, security, safety. 2. Defence (protección), shelter, protection. 3. Security for the performance of a contract or agreement. 4. Watchfulness to prevent smuggling. 5. Body of custom house officers. 6. Preventive-service. 6. Voucher (vale), certificate; guarantee (garantía); slip (recibo). **Resguardo de consigna**, cloakroom check.

residencia [ray-se-den'-the-ah], *f.* 1. Residence, mansion, lodging, home. 2. Residence, the time appointed for clergymen to reside at a benefice. 3. Account demanded of a person who holds a public station; instrument or account rendered. 4. Place and function of a resident at foreign courts. 5. Among the Jesuits, a house of residence not yet formed into a college. **Residencia para ancianos**, old people's home.

residencial [ray-se-den-the-ahl'], *a.* Residentiary.

residenciar [ray-se-den-the-ar'], *va.* To call a public officer to account for his administration.

residenciado, da [ray-se-den-the-ah'-do, dah], *a. & pp.* of RESIDENCIAR. Resident, residentiary.

residente [ray-se-den'-tay], *pa. & a.* Residing or resident in a place, residentiary.

residente [ray-se-den'-tay], *m.* Resident, a minister at foreign courts, of lower rank than a plenipotentiary.

residentemente [], *adv.* Constantly, assiduously,

residir [ray-se-deer'], *vn.* 1. To reside, to dwell, to lodge. 2. To be present, to assist personally by reason of one's position. 3. To be lodged or inherent in, as a faculty or right. **Residir en**, to reside in. **La dificultad reside en que…**, the difficulty lies in the fact that…

residuo [ray-see'-doo-o], *m.* 1. Residue, remainder. **Residuos de una mesa**, leavings, fragments. 2. *(Chem.)* Residuum. 3. Refuse (basura), waste; left-overs (sobras). **Residuos nucleares**, nuclear waste.

resiembra [ray-se-em'-brah], *f.* Seed thrown on ground without letting it remain.

resigna [ray-seeg'-nah], *f.* Resignation of a benefice.

resignación [ray-sig-nah-the-on'], *f.* 1. Resignation, submission to the will of another, abnegation. 2. Resignation of a public place or employment.

resignadamente [ray-sig-nah'-dah-men-tay], *adv.* Resignedly.

resignante [ray-sig-nahn'-tay], *pa. & m.* Resigner; resigning.

resignar [ray-sig-nar'], *va.* To resign, to give up, to yield up, to abrogate. *-vr.* To resign, to submit to the will of another.

resignatorio [ray-sig-nah-to'-re-o], *m.* Resignee.

resina [ray-see'-nah], *f.* Resin, rosin.

resinero, ra [ray-se-nay'-ro, rah], *a.* Relating to resins.

resinífero, ra [ray-se-nee'-fay-ro, rah], *a.* Resin-boaring, resiniferous.

resinita [ray-se-nee'-tah], *f.* Mineral resin, a stone looking like pitch.

resinócero [ray-se-no'-thay-ro], *m.* A compound of rosin and wax; resinointment.

resinoso, sa [ray-se-no'-so, sah], *a.* Resinous.

resina [ray-see'-sah], *f.* The eighth part formerly taken as duty on wine vinegar, or oil.

resisar [ray-se-sar'], *va.* To diminish any measures or things which have already been taxed.

resistencia [ray-sis-ten'-the-ah], *f.* Resistance, opposition (oposición), defense, endurance (del cuerpo), strength (fuerza); toughness (dureza). **Oponer resistencia a**, to resist. **El maratón es una prueba de resistencia**, the marathon is a test of endurance.

resistente [ray-sis-ten'-tay], *pa.* Resisting, repelling.

resistero [ray-sis-tay'-ro], *m.* 1. The hottest part of the day, from twelve to two o'clock in the summer season. 2. Heat produced by the reflection of the sun's rays and the place where it is perceived.

resistible [ray-sis-tee'-blay], *a.* Resistible, endurable, supportable.

resistidero [ray-sis-te-day'-ro], *m.* The hottest part of the day. V. RESISTERO.

resistidor, ra [ray-sis-te-dor', rah], *m. & f.* Resister, opponent.

resistir [ray-sis-teer'], *vn. & va.* 1. To resist (enemigo), to oppose. 2. To contradict, to repel. 3. To endure (durar), to tolerate. 4. To reject, to oppugn. 5. To put up with (agotamiento, decepción). 6. To resist; to struggle (luchar); to put up a fight (combatir). **No puedo resistir este frío**, I can't bear this cold. **El coche resiste todavía**, the car is still going. *-vr.* To struggle, to contend. **Me resisto a creerlo**, I refuse to believe it.

resma [res'-mah], *f.* Ream of paper; *i. e.* long ream of 500 sheets.

resmilla [res-meel'-lyah], *f.* Parcel of one hundred sheets of letter-paper.

resobado, da [ray-so-bah'-do, dah], *a.* Hackneyed, commonplace.

resobrar [ray-so-brar'], *vn.* To be much over and above.

resobrino, na [ray-so-bree'-no, nah], *m. & f.* Son or daughter of a nephew or niece.

resol [ray-sole'], *m.* Reverberation of the sun's rays.

resolana [ray-so-lah'-nah], *f. (Prov.) V.* RESOLANO.

resolano [ray-so-lah'-no], *m.* Place sheltered from the wind for taking the sun.

resolar [ray-so-lar'], *va.* To repave (pavimento); to resole (zapatos).

resoluble [ray-so-loo'-blay], *a.* Resolvable, resoluble.

resolución [ray-so-loo-the-on'], *f.* 1. Resolution, deliberation, resoluteness. 2. Determination, courage boldness, firmness. 3. Decision (decisión), solution of a doubt (respuesta); conclusiveness; determination of a difference. **Tomar una resolución**, to take a decision. 4. Easiness of address, freedom from constraint. **En resolución**, in short, in a word. 5. Dissolution; analysis or resolution. 6. Activity, promptitude; mind. 7. *(Med.)* Resolution, ordinary termination of an inflammation. 8. *(Cono Sur)* Finishing (terminación).

resolutivamente [ray-so-loo-tee'-vah-men-tay], *adv.* Resolutely, determinately.

resolutivo, va [ray-so-loo-tee'-vo, vah], *a.* 1. *(Med.)* Resolutive, having the power to dissolve: in this sense it used as a substantive. 2. Analytical.

resoluto, ta [ray-so-loo'-to, tah], *a. & pp. irr.* 1. Resolute, bold, audacious. 2. Compendious, brief. 3. Prompt, dexterous.

resolutoriamente [ray-so-loo-to'-re-ah-men-tay], *adv.* Resolutely.

resolutorio ria [ray-so-loo-to'-re-o, ah], *a.* Resolute, prompt.

resolvente [ray-sol-ven'-tay], *pa. & a.* Resolvent, resolving.

resolver [ray-sol-ver'], *va.* 1. To resolve (problema), to determine, to decide (asunto). 2. To sum up, to reduce to a small compass. 3. To decide, to decree. 4. To solve a difficulty, to unriddle; to find out. 5. To dissolve, to analyze (cuerpo de materiales); to dissipate. 6. To undo, to destroy. 7. To divide a whole into its parts. *-vr.* 1. To resolve (problema), to determine. 2. To be included or comprised. **Todo se resolvió en una riña más**, in the end it came down to one more quarrel.

resolladero [ray-so-lyah-day'-ro], *m.* Vent, air-hole; breathing-hole.

resollar [ray-sol-lyar'], *vn.* 1. To respire, to breathe audibly (respirar). 2. To talk; commonly used with a negative. **No resolló**, he did not utter a word. 3. To rest, to take breath. **Hace tiempo que no resuella**, he has given no sign of life for some time. *(Yo resuello, yo resuelle, from Resollar. V.* ACORDAR.)

resonación [ray-so-nah-the-on'], *f.* Resounding, noise of repercusion.

resonancia [ray-so-nahn'-the-ah], *f.* 1. Resonance (repercusión), repercussion of sound. 2. *(Poet.)* Consonance, harmony.

resonante [ray-so-nahn'-tay], *pa. & a.* Resonant, resounding.

resonar [ray-so-nar'], *vn.* To resound, to be echoed back, to chink, to clatter.

resoplar [ray-so-plar'], *vn.* 1. To breathe audibly and with force. 2. To snort, as a high-mettled horse or a bull.

resoplido, resoplo [ray-so-plee'-do], *m.* 1. Continued audible breathing; a continual blowing through the nose (respiración). 2. Snorting as of a horse or bull. **Dar resoplidos**, to breath heavily.

resorber [ray-sor-berr'], *va.* To sip again, to reabsorb.

resorte [ray-sor'-tay], *m.* 1. Spring (muelle), an elastic body; an elastic piece of tempered steel. 2. Cause, medium, means (medio). 3. *(LAm.)* Elastic band (gomita). 4. *(LAm.)* Responsibility (responsabilidad).

respailar [res-pah-e-lar'], *va. (Coll.)* To show by gestures vexation over doing something.

respaldar [res-pal-dar'], *m.* Leaning-stock. *V.* RESPALDO.

respaldar [res-pal-dar'], *va.* 1. To endorse (documento), as on the back of a writing. 2. *(Fig.)* To back, to support. 3. *(LAm.)* To ensure (asegurar); to guarantee. *-vr.* 1. To lean, as against a chair or bench. 2. To dislocate the backbone (caballo).

respaldo [res-pahl'-do], *m.* 1. Back or fore part of anything. 2. Endorsement (firma). 3. Leaning-stock, back of a seat (silla).

respectivamente, respective, *adv.* Respectively, proportionally.

respectivo, va [res-pec-tee'-vo, vah], *a.* Respective, relative, comparative. **En lo respectivo a**, as regards.

respecto [res-pec'-to], *m.* Relation, proportion; relativeness; respect. **Respecto a** or **respecto de**, in consideration of. *- adv.* With respect to, with regard to. **Al respecto**, relatively, respectively.

respetable [res-pay-tah'-blay], *a.* Respectable, considerable.

respetador, ra [res-pay-tah-dor', rah], *m. & f.* Respector, venerator.

respetar [res-pay-tar'], *va.* To respect, to venerate, to revere, to honor. **Hacerse respetar**, to win respect.

respeto [res-pay'-to], *m.* Respect (consideración), regard, consideration, veneration; attention; observance. **Respeto a** or **respeto de**, with regard to. **Respeto de sí mismo**, self-respect. **Faltar al respeto**, to be disrespectful.

respetuosamente [res-pec-too-o'-sah-men-tay], *adv.* Respectfully.

respetuoso, sa [res-pay-too-o'-so, sah], *a.* 1. Respectable. 2. Respectful, ceremonious; obsequious, dutiful.

réspice [res'-pe-thay], *m.* 1. *(Coll.)* Short, brusque reply (respuesta). 2. A short, but sharp reproof.

respigador, ra [res-pe-gah-dor', rah], *m. & f.* Gleaner.

respigar [res-pe-gar'], *m.* To glean, as after reapers.

respigón [res-pe-gone'], *m.* 1. Hangnail. 2. Sore upon the fleshy part of the hoof of horses.

respingar [res-pin-gar'], *vn.* 1. To kick, to wince. 2. To obey reluctantly.

respingo [res-peen'-go], *m.* 1. Kick, jerk. 2. Reluctance, unwillingness, peevishness.

respingoso, sa [res-pin-go'-so, sah], *a.* 1. Kicking, wincing (animales). 2. Growing, tetchy.

respirable [res-pe-rah'-blay], *a.* Respirable, capable of respiration.

respiración [res-pe-rah-the-on'], *f.* Respiration, breathing; expiration; vent. **Quedarse sin respiración**, to be out of breath.

respiradero [res-pe-rah-day'-ro], *m.* 1. Vent, breathing-hole. 2. *(Arch.)* Air-passage, louver. 3. Cupping-glass. 4. Rest, repose. 5. An organ of respiration.

respirante [res-pe-rahn'-tay], *pa.* Respiring, breathing, exhaling.

respirar [res-pe-rar'], *vn.* 1. To respire, to breathe. (Sometimes used as transitive.) 2. To rest, to respire, to take rest from toil. 3. To exhale scents or odors. 4. To speak: in this sense it is frequently used with a negative. **No respiró**, he did not open his lips. 5. To get breath. 6. To exhale; to animate. **Sin respirar**, without drawing breath. **No tener por donde respirar**, *(Coll.)* to have no valid answer to a charge.

respiratorio, ria [res-pe-rah-to'-re-o, ah], *a.* Respiratory, serving for breathing or related to it.

respiro [res-pee'-ro], *m.* 1. Act of breathing. 2. Moment of rest (descanso). 3. *(Met.)* Longer time for making payment.

resplandecencia [res-plan-day-then'-the-ah], *f.* Resplendency, splendor, lustre; fame, glory.

resplandecer [res-plan-day-therr'], *vn.* 1. To emit rays of light. 2. To glitter, to glisten, to gleam, to be brilliant, to glow. 3. To shine (relucir), to outshine, to be eminent or conspicuous.

resplandeciente [res-plan-day-the-en'-tay], *pa. & a.* Resplendent, shining (brillante), glittering; luminous, light.

resplandina

resplandina [res-plan-dee'-nah], *V. (Coll.)* Sternness of countenance, sharp reproof.

resplandor [res-plan-dor'], *m.* 1. Splendor, brightness, brilliancy (brillantez), luminousness. 2. A kind of shining paint for women. 3. *(Mex.)* Sunlight (luz del sol). 4. Glare (brillo).

responder [res-pon-derr'], *va. & vn.* 1. To answer; to resolve a doubt, to respond. 2. To re-echo. 3. To acknowledge, to own a benefit received; to be grateful. 4. To yield, to produce. 5. To answer, to have the desired effect. 6. To correspond (corresponder); to be situated; to answer to. 7. To show oneself pleased. 8. To be, or to make oneself responsible for something. 9. To reply to a letter (contestar). 10. To answer back (replicar). 11. To obey (mandos), to respond to (situación, tratamiento). **Responder a una pregunta**, to answer a question. **Responder a una descripción**, to fit a description. **Responder de**, to be responsible for. **Responder al nombre de**, to be called, to go by the name of.

respondiente [res-pon-de-en'-tay], *pa. & a.* Respondent; answering.

respondón, na [res-pon-done', nah], *a.* Giving answers constantly; ever ready to reply.

responsabilidad [res-pon-sah-be-le-dahd'], *f.* Responsibility, liability, accountableness. **Responsabilidad solidaria**, joint responsibility.

responsabilizar [res-pon-sah-be-le-thar'], *va.* **Responsabilizar a uno**, to make somebody responsible. *-vr.* To make oneself responsible.

responsable [res-pon-sah'-blay], *a.* Responsible, liable, accountable, answerable. **Hacerse responsable de algo**, to assume responsibility for something.

responsar, responsear [res-pon-sar'], *vn.* To repeat the responses.

responsión [res-pon-se-on'], *f.* Sum which the members of the Order of St. John, who enjoy an income, contribute to the treasury of the order.

responsivo, va [res-pon-see'-vo, vah], *a. (For.)* Responsive, pertinent to the question, relevant in reply.

responso [res-pon'-so], *m.* Responsary, separate from the divine office for the dead.

responsorio [res-pon-so'-re-o], *m.* Response.

respuesta [res-poo-es'-tah], *f.* 1. Answer, reply; response. 2. Report of firearms. 3. Sound echoed back 4. Refutation.

resquebradura, resquebrajadura [res-kay-brah-ha-doo'-rah], *f.* Crack, cleft, flaw, split.

resquebrajar [res-kay-brah-har'], *vn.* To crack, to split. *-vr.* To crack, to split.

resquebrajo [res-kay-brah'-ho], *m.* Crack, cleft.

resquebrajoso, sa [res-kay-brah-ho'-so, sah], *a.* Brittle, fragile.

resquebrar [res-kay-brar'], *vn.* To crack, to begin to open; to burst.

resquemar [res-kay-mar'], *va. & vn.* To burn or sting the tongue (comida).

resquemo [res-kay'-mo], *m.* **resquemazón** [res-kay-mah-thone'], *f.* 1. Pungency of any food. 2. A disagreeable taste and odor which eatables acquire from being burned by too much fire.

resquicio [res-kee'-the-o], *m.* 1. Chink between the jamb and leaf of a door (abertura); crack, cleft. 2. Subterfuge, evasion. 3. *(Met.)* Faint hope. 4. Chance (posibilidad). 5. *(And. Carib.)* Vestige (vestigio). 6. *(Carib.)* Little bit (pedacito).

resta [res'-tah], *f.* Rest, residue, remainder (residuo). *V.* RESTO.

restablecer [res-tah-blay-therr'], *va.* To restore, to re-establish. to reinstate. *-vr.* To recover from a disease, to mend.

restablecimiento [res-tah-blay-the-me-en'-to], *m.* Re-establishment, restoration, resettlement.

restador [res-tah-dor'], *m. (Arith.)* Remainder.

restallar [res-tal-lyar'], *vn.* 1. To crack, as a whip. 2. To crackle, to creak.

restante [res-tahn'-tay], *pa. & m.* Remainder, residue; remaining. **Lo restante**, the rest.

restañadura [res-tah-nyah-doo'-rah], *f.* The act of recovering with tin; retinning.

restañar [res-tah-nyar'], *va.* 1. To retin, to cover with tin a second time. 2. To stanch, to stop blood. 3. *V.* RESTALLAR. *-vr.* To restagnate, to stand without flow.

restaño [res-tah'-nyo], *m.* 1. Kind of glazed silk, interwoven with gold or silver. 2. *V.* ESTANCACIÓN.

restar [res-tar'], *va.* 1. To subtract, to find the residue of anything. 2. In tennis, to return a ball, to strike it back (pelota). **Restar autoridad a uno**, to take away authority. *-vn.* To be left, to remain due.

restauración [res-tah-oo-rah-the-on'], *f.* 1. Restoration, redintegration, restoring. 2. Restoration, liberty recovered by an oppressed or subjugated people.

restaurador, ra [res-tah-oo-rah-dor', rah], *m. & f.* Restorer.

restaurante [res-tah-oo-rahn'-tay], *m.* 1. Restorer, re-establisher. 2. (Gallicism) Restaurant. *V.* FONDA. *-pa.* Restoring.

restaurar [res-tah-oo-rar'], *va.* To restore, to retrieve; to repair, to renew.

restaurativo, va [res-tah-oo-rah-tee'-vo, vah], *a.* Restorative.

restinga [res-teen'-gah], *f.* Ridge of rocks in the sea; sandbank.

restingar [res-teen-gar'], *m.* Place containing ridges of rocks or sands banks.

restitución [res-te-too-the-on'], *f.* Restitution, restoring.

restituible [res-te-too-ee'-blay], *a.* That which may be restored.

restituidor, ra [res-te-too-e-dor', rah], *m. & f.* Restorer, re-establisher.

restituir [res-te-too-eer'], *vn.* 1. To restore, to give up, to give back, to lay down. 2. To re-establish. 3. To reanimate. *-vr.* To return to the place of departure.

restitutivo, va [res-te-too-tee'-vo, vah], **Restitutorio, ria** [res-te-too-to'-re-o, ah], *a.* Relating to restitution.

resto [res'-to], *m.* 1. Remainder, residue, balance, rest (lo que queda). 2. Sum staked at play. 3. Rebound of the ball in the game of tennis. 4. Stake (apuesta). 5. *(Fig.)* Without limit. 6. Arrest, attachment. **Restos humanos**, human remains.

restregar [res-tray-gar'], *va.* 1. To rub (frotar), to scrub (fregar). 2. *(Coll.)* To rub it in, to rub sarcastically.

restregón [res-tray-gone'], *m.* Scrubbing.

restreñimiento [res-tray-nye-me-ayn'-to], *m. (Prov.) V.* RESTRIÑIMIENTO.

restribar [res-tre-bar'], *vn.* To lean upon strongly.

restricción [res-trec-the-on'], *f.* Restriction, limitation, modification. **Restricciones eléctricas**, electricity cuts. **Sin restricción de**, without restrictions as to.

restrictivamente [res-trec-tee'-vah-men-tay], *adv.* Restrictively.

restrictivo, va [res-trec-tee'-vo, vah], *a.* Restrictive, restringent.

restricto, ta [res-treec'-to, tah], *a.* Limited, confined; restrictive.

restringa [res-treen'-gah], *f. V.* RESTINGA.

restringente [res-trin-hen'-tay], *m.* Restrainer; restringent. *-pa.* Restraining.

restringible [res-trin-hee'-blay], *a.* Restrainable, limitable.

restringido [res-trin-hee'-do], *a.* Restricted, limited.

restringir [res-trin-heer'], *va.* To restrain, to restrict, to restringe, to confine, to control, to constrain, to limit.

restriñente [res-tre-nyen'-tay], *pa. & a.* Restringent; binding.

restriñidor, ra [res-tre-nye-dor', rah], *m. & f.* Restrainer, binder.

restriñimiento [res-tre-nye-me-en'-to], *m.* Restriction, making costive.

restriñir [res-tre-nyeer'], *va.* To bind, to make costive, to restrain.

restrojera [res-tro-hay'-rah], *f. (Prov.)* Female servant taken to attend reapers at harvest-time.

restrojo [res-tro'-ho], *m.* V. RASTROJO.

resucitado, da [ray-soo-the-tah'-do, dah], *a. & pp.* of RESUCITAR. **Pájaro resucitado**, little humming-bird; it is dormant in winter, hence its name.

resucitador, ra [ray-soo-the-tah-dor', rah], *m. & f.* Restorer, reviver.

resucitar [ray-soo-the-tar'], *va.* 1. To resuscitate, to revive. 2. To renew, to renovate, to modernize. *-vn.* 1. To revive, to return to life. 2. To recover from a dangerous disease.

resucha [ray-soo'-chah], *f.* A worthless animal (vaca, buey).

resudación [ray-soo-dah-the-on'], *f.* Perspiration, transudation.

resudar [ray-soo-dar'], *m.* To transude, to perspire, to transpire.

resudor [ray-soo-dor'], *m.* Slight perspiration.

resuello [ray-soo-ay'-lyo], *m.* 1. Breath (aliento), breathing (respiración), respiration. 2. Pursiness, shortness of breath.

resueltamente [ray-soo-el-tah-men'-tay], *adv.* Resolutely, resolvedly, confidently, boldly.

resuelto, ta [ray-soo-el'-to, tah], *a. & pp. irr.* of RESOLVER. 1. Resolute (decidido), audacious, bold, determined, steady, constant, confident. 2. Prompt, quick, diligent. **Estar resuelto a algo**, to be set on something.

resulta [ray-sool'-tah], *f.* 1. Rebound, resilience. 2. Result, effect, consequence. 3. Vacancy, a post or employment unoccupied. 4. Success. **De resultas**, in consequence.

resultado [ray-sool-tah'-do], *m.* Result, issue, consequence. -**Resultado, da**, *pp.* of RESULTAR.

resultancia [ray-sool-tahn'-the-ah], *f.* Result, resultance.

resultante [ray-sool-tahn'-tay], *pa.* Resulting, following, proceeding from.

resultar [ray-sool-tar'], *vn.* 1. To rebound. 2. To result, as a consequence or effect, to follow; to proceed from. 3. To remain, to be done or provided for. 4. To prove (Illegar a ser). 5. To stem from (derivarse de). 6. To ensue (seguir). 7. To turn out well (salir bien). 8. To look well (parecer bien). **El conductor resultó muerto**, the driver was killed. **Ahora resulta que no vamos**, now it turns out that we're not going. **Resultó de lo mejor**, it worked out very well. **Esa corbata no resulta con ese traje**, that tie doesn't go with the suit.

resumbruno, na [ray-soom-broo'-no, nah], *a.* Brown, of the color of a hawk's feathers, between red and black.

resumen [ray-soo'-men], *m.* 1. Abridgment, summary, extract, compendium. 2. Recapitulation, detail repeated. 3. *(Law.)* Brief. **En resumen**, briefly, in short; lastly.

resumidamente ray-soo-mee'-dah-men-tay], *adv.* Briefly, compendiously, summarily.

resumido, da [ray-soo-mee'-do, dah], *a. & pp.* of RESUMIR. Abridged. **En resumidas cuentas**, in short, briefly.

resumir [ray-soo-meer'], *va.* 1. To abridge (reducir). 2. To reassume, to resume; to repeat, as the propounder of a thesis, the syllogism of an opponent. 3. To summarize (condensar). *vr.* To include; to convert. **Resumirse en**, to be reduced to.

resunción [ray-soon-the-on'], *f.* Summary, abridgment. 2. Repetition of several words inserted in a speech.

resuntivo, va [ray-soon-tee'-vo, vah], *a.* That which restores or resumes.

resupinado, da [ray-soo-pe-nah-do, dah], *a. (Cabot.)* Resupinate, inverse in position.

resurgir [ray-soor-her'], *vn.* 1. To reappear (reaparecer), to revive; to be resurrected (resucitar). 2. *(Fig.)* To acquire a new spirit.

resurrección [ray-soor-rec-the-on'], *f.* Resurrection, revival, resuscitation.

resurtida [ray-soor-tee'-dah], *f.* Rebound, repercussion.

resurtir [ray-soor-teer'], *vn.* To rebound, to fly back.

retablo [ray-tah'-blo], *m.* 1. Picture drawn on a board. 2. Splendid ornament of altars.

retacar [ray-tah-car'], *va.* To hit the ball twice on a truck-table. *-vr. (Cono Sur)* To dig one's heels in.

retacería [ray-tah-thay-ree'-ah], *f.* Collection of remnants.

retaco [ray-tah'-co], *m.* 1. A short, light fowling-piece. 2. A short tack or stick of a truck-table. 3. A short thick person.

retador [ray-tah-dor'], *m.* Challenger.

retaguardia [ray-tah-goo-ar'-de-ah], *f.* Rear-guard. **A retaguardia**, in the rear.

retahíla [ray-tah-ee'-lah], *f.* File, range, or series of many things following one another.

retajar [ray-tah-har'], *va.* 1. To cut round (cortar). 2. To cut again and again the nib of a pen. 3. To circumcise. 4. *(LAm.)* To castrate (castrar).

retal [ray-tahl'], *m.* Remnant of cloth or lace; clipping.

retallar [ray-tal-lyar'], *vn.* To shoot or sprout anew. *-va.* To regrave, to retouch a graving. V. RETALECER.

retallecer [ray-tal-lyay-therr'], To resprout, to put forth new shoots from the root-stock.

retallo [ray-tah'-lyo], *m.* A new sprout of a plant sprung from the root-stock.

retama [ray-tah'-mah], *f. (Bot.)* 1. Broom. **Retama de flor blanca**, white single seed broom. **Retama blanca**, Spanish genista, furze, green-weed.

retamal, retamar [ray-tah-mahr'], *m.* **Retamera**, *f.* Place where furze or broom grows, and is gathered.

retamilla [ray-tah-meel'-lyah], *f. (Bot.)* Jointed genista or furze.

retamón [ray-tah-mone'], *m. (Bot.)* 1. Purging broom. 2. V. RETAMA DE ESCOBAS.

retapar [ray-tah-par'], *va.* To cover again.

retar [ray-tar'], *va.* 1. To impeach or charge one with a criminal offense before the king. 2. To challenge (desafiar), to combat; to reprehend. 3. *(Cono Sur)* To insult (insultar).

retardación [ray-tar-dah-the-on'], *f.* Retardation, delay, detention, loitering.

retardar [ray-tar-dar'], *va.* To retard, to defer, to delay, to obstruct.

retardilla [ray-tar-deel-lyah], *f.* A slight difference or dispute.

retardo [ray-tar'-do], *m.* Cunctation, delay, procrastination, retardment.

retasa [ray-tah'-sah], *f.* Second valuation or assessment.

retasar [ray-tah-sar'], *va.* To value or assess a second time.

retazar [ray-tah-thar'], *va.* To tear in pieces; to divide up (dividir); to chop (leña).

retazo [ray-tah'-tho], *m.* 1. Remaining piece, remnant, cuttings. 2. Fragment or portion of some discourse or reasoning.

retejador [ray-tay-hah-dor'], *m. & a.* Repairer of a tile-roof; mending, reparative.

retejar [ray-tay-har'], *va.* 1. To repair the roof of a building, to tile anew. 2. To mend, to patch; to risk.

retejer [ray-tay-herr'], *va.* To weave closely.

retejo [ray-tay'-ho], *m.* Repairing of a roof, retiling.

retemblar [ray-tem-blar'], *vn.* To tremble or shake repeatedly: to vibrate. *(Yo retiemblo, yo retiemble*, from *Retemblar.* V. ACRECENTAR.)

retemblor [ray-tem-blor'], *m.* A second vibration, repeated shaking.

retén [ray-tayn'], *m.* 1. Store, stock, reserve. 2. Military reserve corps. 3. Detent, ratchet, catch.

retención [ray-ten-the-on'], *f.* 1. Retention, keeping back. 2. Retention of an office which was held before advancing to another. 3. Stagnation, retention within the body of an excretion which ought to be expelled.

retendor, ra [ray-tay-nay-dor', rah], *m. & f.* Retainer.

retener [ray-tay-nerr'], *va.* 1. To retain, to withhold; to keep back from its owner. 2. To guard, to preserve. 3. To maintain and enjoy a position after being advanced to another. 4. To suspend, as by a king, the use of an ecclesiastical rescript. **Retener a uno preso**, to keep somebody in detention. *(Yo* *retengo, yo retenga; él retuvo, retuviera;* from *Retener. V.* TENER.)

retenida [ray-tay-nee'-dah], *f. (Naut.)* Guy. **Retenida de proa,** *(Naut.)* headfast, a rope to fasten the head of a ship.

retenidamente [ray-tay-nee'-dah-men-tay], *adv.* Retentively.

retentar [ray-ten-tar'], *va.* To threaten with a relapse of a former disorder.

retentiva [ray-ten-tee'-vah], *f.* 1. Retentiveness. 2. Memory.

retentivo, va [ray-ten-tee'-vo, vah], *a.* Retentive, retaining.

retentriz [ray-ten-treeth'], *a. (Med.)* Retentive.

reteñir [ray-tay-nyeer'], *va.* To dye over again, to tinge a second time. -*vn.* To tingle, to sound, to resound. V. RETINIR.

retesamiento [ray-tay-sah-me-en'-to], *m.* Coagulation, hardness.

retesarse [ray-tay-sar'-say], *vr.* To become hard, to be stiff, as teats with milk.

reteso [ray-tay'-so], *m.* 1. Stiffness or distention of teats with milk. 2. *V.* TESO.

reticencia [ray-te-then'-the-ah], *f.* 1. Reticence (reserva), concealment by silence. 2. Insinuation (sugerencia), suggestion; implication (transcendencia).

reticulado, da [ray-te-coo-lah'-do, dah], *a. V.* RETICULAR.

reticular [ray-te-coo-lar'], *a.* Reticular, resembling network.

retículo [ray-tee'-coo-lo], *m.* 1. Network, reticular tissue: used generally of plant structure. 2. Cobweb, micrometer of a telescope or microscope.

retín [ray-teen'], *m. V.* RETINTÍN.

retina [ray-tee'-nah], *f.* Retina of the eye.

retinte [ray-teen'-tay], *m.* 1. Second dye given to anything. 2. *V.* RETINTÍN.

retintín [ray-tin-teen'], *m.* 1. A tinkling sound (tilín); jingle (tintineo); clink. 2. An affected tone of voice usually satirical. **Decir algo con retintín,** to say something sarcastically.

retinto [ray-teen'-to], *a.* Dark, obscure, almost black. -*pp. irr.* of RETEÑIR.

retiñir [ray-te-nyeer'], *vn.* To tinkle, to resound, to click.

retiración [ray-te-rah-the-on'], *f. (Typ.)* Second form put in a press in order to print the back of a sheet.

retirada [ray-te-rah'-dah], *f.* 1. *(Mil.)* Retreat. **Tocar retirada,** to sound a retreat. 2. Retreat, retirement, place of security. 3. Place of retirement, closet.

retiradamente [ray-te-rah'-dah-men-tay], *adv.* Secretly, retiredly.

retirado, da [ray-te-rah'-do, dah], *a. & pp.* of RETIRAR. Retired, solitary, cloistered; close; remote (lugar), distant; retired (oficial), pensioned. **Hombre retirado,** a man fond of retirement. **Oficial retirado,** half pay officer.

retiramiento [ray-te-rah-me-en'-to], *m.* Retirement. *V.* RETIRO.

retirar [ray-te-rar'], *va.* 1. To withdraw, to retire, to lay aside (mover), to reserve, to hide away (quitar). 2. To repel, to force the enemy to retire or retreat. 3. To print the back of a sheet. 4. To revoke; to retreat. 5. To take out (pieza). 6. To withdraw (moneda, sello). 7. To retire, to pension off (jubilar). 8. To withdraw (acusación, palabras). -*vr.* 1. To retire, to retreat, to cease to pursue; to recede, to go back. 2. To retire from intercourse with the world; to retire from trade. 3. To retire from a public station. 4. To retire from company. 5. To take refuge; to retire to one's house or department. 6. *(Mil.)* To raise a siege or blockade; to abandon a post (jubilarse). 7. To retire or retreat from danger. 8. To retire (después de cenar). **Retirarse ante un peligro,** to retreat. **Cuando me retire de los negocios,** when I retire from business.

retiro [ray-tee'-ro], *m.* 1. Retreat, the act of retiring (acto): recess: act of declining any business. 2. Retreat, retirement, place of retirement (lugar). 3. Concealedness, privacy, obscurity, retirement, private life. **Retiro prematuro,** early retirement.

retirona [ray-te-ro'-nah], *f. (Coll.) V.* RETIRADA.

reto [ray'-to], *m.* 1. Challenge to combat (desafío). 2. Threat (amenaza), menace. 3. *(Cono Sur)* Telling off (reprimenda).

retobado, da [ray-to-bah'-do, dah], *a.* 1. *(Peru. Met. and coll.)* Artful, crafty. 2. *(LAm.)* Wild (animal); wild (persona), unruly; rebellious (rebelde). 3. *(And. CAm. Mex.)* Grumbling (gruñón). 4. *(And. Cono Sur)* Cunning (taimado).

retobar [ray-to-bar'], *va. (Amer. Com.)* To cover parcels of goods with hides for transportation.

retobo [ray-to'-bo], *m.* 1. A covering of hides. 2. *(LAm.)* Stubbornness (terquedad); grumble (protesta). 3. *(LAm.)* Aftertaste (resabio).

retocamiento [ray-to-cah-me-en'-to], *m.* Action of retouching.

retocar [ray-to-car'], *va.* 1. To uptouch a painting, to mend. 2. To finish any work completely. 3. To play back (grabación).

retomar [ray-to-mar'], *va.* To take up again.

retoñar, retoñecer [ray-to-nyar', ray-to-nyay-therr'], *vn.* 1. To sprout or shoot again: applied to a plant which has been cut. 2. To appear again: applied to cutaneous distempers.

retoño [ray-toh'-nyo], *m.* Sprout or shoot from a plant which has been cut above the neck of the root.

retoque [ray-toh'-kay], *m.* 1. Repeated and frequent pulsation. 2. Finishing stroke, to render a work perfect. 3. Symptom, threatening, of some disease.

retorcedura [ray-tor-thay-doo'-rah], *f.* Twisting, wreathing.

retorcer [ray-tor-therr'], *va.* 1. To twist (brazo), to contort, to convolve. 2. To retort, to convince by returning an argument. 3. *(Met.)* To interpret perversely. -*vr.* 1. To get into knots (cuerda). 2. To writhe (persona); to squirm. **Restorcerse de dolor,** to writhe in pain. *(Yo retuerzo, yo retuerza,* from *Retorcer. V.* COCER.)

retorcido [ray-tor-thee'-do], *m.* A kind of twisted sweetmeat. **Retorcido, da,** *pp.* of RETORCER.

retorcijo [ray-tor-thee'-ho], *m.V.* RETORCIMIENTO.

retorcimiento [ray-tor-the-me-en'-to], *m.* Twisting (brazo), wreathing (cuerpo entero), contortion.

retórica [ray-to'-re-cah], *f.* Rhetoric. *pl. (Coll.)* Sophistries or reasons not fitted to the case.

retóricamente [ray-to-ree'-cah-men-tay], *adv.* Rhetorically.

retórico, ca [ray-toh'-re-co, cah], *a.* Rhetorical, oratorical. -*m.* Rhetorician, one who speaks with eloquence; one who teaches rhetoric.

retornable [ray-tor-nah-blay], *a.* **Envase no retornable,** non-returnable empty.

retornamiento [ray-tor-nah-me-en'-to], *m.* Return.

retornante [ray-tor-nahn'-tay], *pa.* Returning.

retornar [ray-tor-nar'], *vn.* To return, to come back, to retrocede or retrograde. -*va.* 1. To return (devolver), to restore, to give back. 2. To turn, to twist, to contort, to cause to go back. 3. To replace (devolver a su lugar).

retornelo [ray-tor-nay'-lo], *m.* 1. Ritornello, the burden of a song. 2. *(Poet.)* The final strophe of a song.

retorno [ray-tor'-no], *m.* 1. Return (vuelta), coming back; return chaise or horse. 2. Repayment (pago), return of a favor. 3. Barter, exchange (cambio), traffic. 4. *(Mex. Aut.)* Turning place.

retorsión [ray-tor-se-on'], *f.* 1. Retortion, bending back. 2. Retortion, retorsion, act of replying sharply.

retorsivo, va [ray-tor-see'-vo, vah], *a.* That which retorts.

retorta [ray-tor'-tah], *f.* 1. Retort, a chemical vessel. 2. A sort of linen of medium fineness.

retortero [ray-tor-tay'-ro], *m.* Twirl, rotation. **Andar al retortero,** To hover about. **Traer al retortero,** (1) *(Coll.)* to bring one from one side almost to the other. (2) *(Met. and coll.)* To keep one on the go (with peremptory occupations). (3) *(Met. and coll.)* To twist one around, to decieve with false promises and dissembled flatteries.

retortijar [ray-tor-te-har'], *va.* To twist, to form into a ring. *V.* ENSORTIJAR.

retortijón [ray-tor-te-hone'], *m.* The act of twisting, contortion. **Retortijón de tripas,** griping.

retostado, da [ray-tos-tah'-d, dah], *a. & pp.* of RETOSTAR. Brown-colored.

retostar [ray-tos-tar'], *va.* To toast again, to toast brown.

retozador, ra [ray-to-thah-dor', rah], *m. & f.* Frisker, one not constant, a wanton.

retozadura [ray-to-thah-doo'-rah], *f.* V. RETOZO.

retozar [ray-to-thar'], *vn.* 1. To frisk and skip about, to romp, to frolic, to dally with, to sport, to play. 2. To hoiden, to romp immodestly. 3. Of passions, to sport within us. *-va.* To tickle, to invite laughter and merriment; to titillate amorously. **Retozar la risa**, to be moved to laughter.

retozo [ray-to'-tho], *m.* Friskiness, romping (holgorio), wantonness, lascivious gaiety, frisk, a frolic, dalliance. **Retozo de la risa**, suppressed laugh.

retozón, na [ray-to-thone', nah], *a.* Wanton, rompish, frolicsome, playful (juguetón), gamesome, coltish.

retozona [ray-to-tho'-nah], *f.* Romp, a rude, noisy girl.

retrabar [ray-trah-bar'], *pa.* To revive a quarrel.

retracción [ray-trac-the-on'], *f.* Retraction, drawing back.

retractable [ray-trac-tah'-blay], *a.* Retractable, which may be or should be retracted or recanted.

retractación [ray-trac-tah-the-on'], *f.* Retractation, recantation.

retractar [ray-trac-tar'], *va.* To retract. *-vr.* To go back on one's word. **Me retracto de la acusación hecha**, I withdraw the accusation.

retráctil [ray-trahc'-teel], *a.* (*Zool.*) Retractile, hidden in repose.

retractilidad [ray-trac-te-le-dahd'], *f.* Retractility.

retracto [ray-trahc'-to], *m.* (*Law.*) Retrieval, the act or right of retrieving or recovering a thing sold to another.

retractor [ray-trac-tor'], *m.* Retractor, a surgical instrument for holding apart the edges of an incision.

retraer [ray-trah-err'], *va.* 1. To reclaim, to dissuade. 2. To retrieve, to recover a thing sold. *-vr.* 1. To take refuge, to flee. 2. To withdraw from (retirarse de), to retire, to live a retired life. 3. In politics, to retire, to abandon all participation in public matters. (*Yo retraigo, yo retraiga, retraje, from Retraer. V.* TRAER.)

retraído [ray-trah-ee'-do], *m.* 1. Fugitive, one who has taken sanctuary in a sacred place. 2. A lover of solitude. **Retraído, da**, *pp.* of RETRAER.

retraimiento [ray-trah-e-me-en'-to], *m.* 1. Retreat, refuge (lugar), asylum. 2. Inner apartment or room. 3. Retirement from public political life.

retranca [ray-trahn'-cah], *f.* 1. A kind of large cropper for mules and lethal beasts of burden. 2. (*Amer.*) Brake of a wagon or railway car.

retranquear [ray-tran-kay-ar'], *va.* (*Arch.*) To model pillars.

retranqueo [ray-tran-kay'-o], *m.* (*Arch.*) Position given to bodies outside of their square.

retransmisión [ray-trans-me-se-on'], *f.* Repeat, rebroadcast.

retransmitir [ray-trans-me-teer'], *va.* To relay (mensaje), to pass on; to repeat; to broadcast live (en vivo).

retrasado, da [ray-trah-sah'-do, dah], *a.* 1. Late, retarded. **Retrasado mental**, moron, person mentally retarded. 2. To be slow (reloj). **Tengo el reloj retrasado 8 minutos**, my watch is 8 minutes slow. 3. Backward, underdeveloped (país). 4. Unused (comida).

retrasar [ray-trah-sar'], *va.* To defer, to put off, to dally, to delay. *-vn. & vr.* To retrograde, to decline (producción), to be slow (reloj), to be late (persona, tren).

retraso [ray-trah'-so], *m.* 1. Delay (demora), putting off, time lag (intervalo), slowness (tardanza). **Llegar con retraso**, to be late. 2. Backwardness (de país). 3. **Retraso mental**, mental deficiency.

retratable [ray-trah-tah'-blay], *a.* Retractable, retractible.

retratación [ray-trah-tah-the-on'], *f.* Retractation, recantation.

retratador, ra [ray-trah-tah-dor', rah], *m. & f.* Limner, portrait-painter.

retratar [ray-trah-tar'], *va.* 1. To portray, to draw portraits, to limn. 2. To imitate, to copy. 3. To paint, to describe. 4. To photograph. 5. To retract, to gainsay, to disavow. 6. To retrieve, to get back a thing sold. *-vr.* 1. To recant; see 5th

def. (with these significations the spelling *retractar* is quite to be preferred.) 2. To have one's picture painted. 3. To pay (dinero).

retratillo [ray-trah-teel'-lyo], *m. dim.* A small portrait.

retratista [ray-trah-tees'-tah], *m.* 1. Portrait-painter, limner. 2. (*Amer.*) Portrait photographer.

retrato [ray-trah'-to], *m.* 1. Portrait, effigy. 2. Copy, resemblance, imitation. 3. Metrical description, poetical portrait. 4. (*Law.*) V. RETRACTO. 5. (*Fig.*) Portrayal (descripción), depiction. 6. (*Fig.*) Likeness (semejanza). **Ser el vivo retrato de**, to be the very image of.

retrayente [ray-trah-yen'-tay], *pa. & m. & f.* Retractor, recanter; retrieving.

retrechería [ray-tray-chay-ree'-ah], *f.* 1. Cunning or craft for eluding the confession of the truth or the fulfilment of what was offered. 2. (*Coll.*) Flattery, sycophancy.

retrechero, ra [ray-tray-chay'-ro, rah], *a. & n.* (*Coll.*) 1. Flattering; a flatterer. 2. dissimulating, concealing the truth; eluding the fulfilment of what was offered. 3. (*LAm.*) Mean (tracaño); unreliable (tramposo), deceitful; suspicious (sospechoso).

retrepado, da [ray-tray-pah'-do, dah], *a.* Leaning backward in a natural or affected manner (orgullo); reclining (silla).

retreparse [ray-tray-par'-say], *vr.* To lean back, to recline in a chair.

retreta [ray-tray'-tah], *f.* (*Mil.*) 1. Retreat, to withdraw, or go back to their quarters for the night (soldados). 2. Open-air band concert.

retrete [ray-tray'-tay], *m.* 1. Closet, a small room for privacy. 2. Water-closet.

retretico, illo, ito [ray-tray-tee'-co], *m. dim.* Little water-closet, close-stool.

retribución [ray-tre-boo-the-on'], *f.* Retribution, recompense, reward (recompensa); damage.

retribuir [rar-tre-boo-eer'], *m.* To pay back (pagar), to recompense (compensar).

retribuyente [ray-tray-boo-yen'-tay], *pa. & a.* Retributive, retributory; retributing.

retroacción [ray-tro-ac-the-on'], *f.* Retroaction.

retroactivo, va [ray-tro-ac-te'-vo, vah], *a.* Retroactive: spoken of a law which is applied to past transactions. **Ley de efecto retroactivo**, retrospective law.

retrocarga [ray-tro-car'-gah], (used in the expression **De retrocarga**), breech loading.

retroceder [ray-tro-they-derr'], *vn.* 1. To retrograde, to go backward (volver atrás), to retrocede, to fail back: to grow worse. 2. To recede from, to draw back from an opinion or judgment. **Retrocedió unos pasos**, he went back a few steps.

retrocesión [ray-tro-thay-se-on'], *f.* Retrocession, returning or receding.

retroceso [ray-tro-thay'-so], *m.* 1. Retrocession. 2. (*Fig.*) Backing down. 3. (*Med.*) Renewed attack.

retrocohete [ray-tro-co-ay'-tay], *m.* (*Aer.*) Retro-rocket.

retrogradación [re-tro-grah-dah-the-one'], *f.* Retrogradation, retrogression.

retrogradar [ray-tro-grah-dar'], *vn.* 1. To retrograde. 2. To incline to reaction, to oppose progress (política). *V.* RETROCEDER.

retrógrado, da [ray-tro'-gah-do, dah], *a.* Retrograde.

retronar [ray-tro-nar'], *vn.* To thunder again, to continue thundering after a storm is nearly over.

retropilastra [ray-tro-pe-lahs'-trah], *f.* Pilaster behind column.

retropropulsión [ray-tro-pro-pool-se-on'], *f.* Jet propulsion.

retrospectiva [ray-tros-payc-tee'-vah], *f.* 1. Retrospective (exhibición). 2. **En retrospectiva**, with hindsight.

retrospectivamente [ray-tros-payc-tee'-vah-men-tay], *adv.* Retrospectively; in retrospect.

retrotracción [ray-tro-trac-the-on'], *f.* (*Law.*) Antedating anything.

retrotraer [ray-tro-trah-err'], *va.* To apply to the present time what happened before. *(Yo retrotraigo, yo retrotraiga, yo retrotraje,* from *Retrotraer.* V. TRAER.)

retrovender [ray-tro-ven-derr'], *va. (Law.)* To sell back to the first vender for the same price.

retroversión [ray-tro-ver-se-on'], *f. (Med.)* Retroversion, backward displacement.

retrovisión [ray-tro-ve-se-on'], *f.* Rear view. **Espejo de retrovisión**, rear-view mirror.

retrovisor [ray-tro-ve-sor'], *a.* **Espejo retrovisor**, driving mirror.

retrucar [ray-troo-car'], *vn.* To hit again, like a ball rebounding; to kiss (billar).

retruco [ray-troo'-co], *vn.* Repercussion of a ball.

retruécano [ray-troo-ay'-cah-no], *m.* A pun, a quibble, a play upon words.

retruque [ray-troo'-kay], *m.* 1. Betting, a higher wager on a card. 2. A kiss (billar). 3. *(And. Cono Sur)* Sharp retort (réplica). 4. *(Cono Sur, Mex.)* On the rebound; as a consequence.

retuerto, ta [ray-too-err'-to, tah], *pp. irr.* of RETORCER. Retwisted. *-a.* Very bad, sterile.

retumbante [ray-toom-bahn'-tay], *pa. & a.* Resonant, pompous, sonorous, bombastic, ridiculously tumid.

retumbar [ray-toom-bar'], *vn.* To resound, to make a great noise, to jingle, to boom, to clink. **La cascada retumbaba a lo lejos**, the waterfall boomed in the distance.

retumbo [ray-toom'-bo], *m.* Resonance, echo.

retundir [ray-toon-deer'], *va.* 1. To equal or hew stones in a building. 2. *(Met.)* To repel, to discuss.

reuma [ray'-oo-mah]. 1. *f.* Rheum defluxion. 2. *m.* Rheumatism.

reumático, ca [ray-oo-mah'-te-co, cah], *a.* Rheumatic.

reumatismo [ray-oo-mah-tees'-mo], *m.* Rheumatism.

reunión [ray-oo-ne-on'], *f.* 1. Meeting (asamblea), conference. 2. Gathering. 3. Joining, reuniting (reunión). 4. Bringing together. **Reunión en la cima**, Summit, conference.

reunir [ray-oo-neer'], *va.* 1. To join, to reunite (juntar). 2. To bring together, to assemble (datos), to pool (recursos), to save (ahorrar). 3. To combine (cualidades), to have, to possess (condiciones). **Los 4 reunidos no valen lo que él**, the 4 of them together are not as good as he is. **Reunió a sus amigos para discutirlo**, he assembled his friends to talk it over. *-vr.* 1. To meet (personas). 2. To gather, **Reunirse para**, to get together to.

revacunar [ray-vah-coo-nar'], *va.* To revaccinate.

reválida [ray-vah'-le-dah], *f.* 1. Passing one's final exams. 2. Final exams (para un título).

revalidar [ray-vah-le-dar'], *va.* To revalidate. *-vr.* To pass one's final exams (para un título).

revalorar [ray-vah-lo-rahr'], *va.* To revalue.

revalorizar [ray-vah-lo-re-thar'], *m.* To reevaluate.

revancha [ray-vahn'-chah], *f.* 1. Revenge, compensation for loss in gaming; return match. (A Gallicism used instead of **desquite**) 2. V. DESQUITE. **Tomarse la revancha**, to take revenge.

revecero ra [ray-vay-thay'-ro, rah], *a.* Changeable, mutable.

reveedor [ray-vay-ay-dor'], *m.* V. REVISOR.

revejecer [ray-vay-hay-therr'], *vn.* To grow prematurely old.

revejecido, da [ray-vay-hay-thee'-do, dah], *a. & pp.* of REVEJECER. Prematurely old, antiquated.

revejido, da [ray-vay-hee'-do, dah], *a.* Become old prematurely.

revelación [ray-vay-lah-the-on'], *f.* 1. Revelation, the act and effect of revealing. 2. Revelation from heaven; revealed religion. **Fue una revelación para mí**, it was a revelation to me.

revelado [ray-vay-lah'-do], *m.* Developing.

revelador, ra [ray-vay-la-dor', rah], *m. & f.* 1. Revealer. 2. Developer, in photography.

revelamiento [ray-vay-lah-me-en'-to], *m.* 1. V. REVELACIÓN. 2. Photographic development.

revelante [ray-vay-lahn'-tay], *pa.* Revealing.

revelar [ray-vay-lar'], *va.* 1. To reveal, to manifest, to communicate, to disclose (secreto). 2. To impart from heaven, to show the future. 3. To develop a photographic plate. 4. To betray (mostrar); to give away (delatar).

reveler [ray-vey-lerr'], *va. (Med.)* To redirect the cause of on illness in any important organ towards a less important organ.

revellín [ray-vel-lyeen'], *m. (Mil.)* Ravelin.

revendedera [ray-ven-day-day'-dah], *f. V.* REVENDEDORA.

revendedor [ray-ven-day-dor'], *m.* Retailer (al por menor), hawker (de calle), huckster, peddler.

revendedora [ray-ven-day-do'-rah], *f.* Huckstress, a female peddler.

revender [ray-ven-derr'], *va.* To retail (al por menor), to sell by retail, to peddle, to hawk (por la calle).

revenirse [ray-vay-neer'-say], *vr.* 1. To be consumed by degrees. 2. To be pricked, to grow sore, to ferment (vino, conservas). 3. To relinquish a preconceived opinion, to give up a point obstinately contested. 4. To discharge moisture. *(Yo me revengo, yo me revenga; él se revino, revendrá* from *Revenirse.* V. VENIR.)

reventa [ray-ven'-tah], *f.* Retail; second sale. **Precio de reventa**, resale price.

reventación [ray-ven-tah-the-on'], *m.* Disruption, rupture; vanishing in spray.

reventadero [ray-ven-tah-day'-ro], *m.* 1. A rough, uneven ground, of difficult access (terreno áspero). 2. Any painful and laborious work (trabajo). 3. *(And. Cono Sur, Mex.)* Bubbling spring (hervidero).

reventar [ray-ven-tar'], *vn.* 1. To burst, to break in pieces, to crack; of waves, to break into foam. 2. To toil, to drudge. 3. To burst forth, to break loose; applied to a violent passion. 4. To sprout, to shoot; to grow. 5. To long for, to crave. **Casi reventaba de ira**, he almost exploded with anger. *-va.* 1. To molest, to harass, to violate. 2. To burst (globo), to brake (barrera). 3. To flog (caballo), to work to death (persona). 4. To sink, to ruin (proyecto). 5. To do down (perjudicar). **Reventar de risa**, to burst into laughter. **Tengo una cubierta reventada**, I have a puncture. *(Yo reviento, yo reviente,* from *Reventar.* V. ACRECENTAR.)

reventazón [ray-ven-tah-thone'], *f.* 1. Disruption, rupture. 2. *(Naut.)* Breaker, the breaking of waves into foam.

reventón [ray-ven-tone'], *m.* 1. Bursting or cracking. **Reventón de neumático** or **de llanta**, tire blowout. 2. Great difficulty and distress (apuro). 3. Steep, declivity. 4. Toil, drudgery, severe labor and fatigue. 5. Death (muerte). 6. *(Cono Sur)* Outcrop of ore. 7. *(Cono Sur. Fig.)* Explosion (estallido).

rever [ray-verr'], *va.* To review (sentencia), to revise, to overlook, to resurvey.

reverberación [ray-ver-bay-rah-the-on'], *f.* Reverberation, the reflection of light. 2. Calcination in a reverberatory furnace.

reverberar [ray-ver-bay-rar'], *vn.* To reverberate (sonido), to reflect upon a polished surface (superficie), to play (luz).

reverbero [ray-ver-bay'-ro], *m.* 1. V. REVERBERACIÓN. 2. Reflector for the light of a light-house. 3. Reflector of polished glass or metal. **Horno de reverbero**, a reverberatory furnace, a smelting furnace.

reverdecer [ray-ver-day-therr'], *vn.* 1. To grow green again (tierra, planta). 2. To sprout again, to acquire new vigor and strength. *(Yo reverdezco, yo reverdezca,* from *Reverdecer.* V. CONOCER.)

reverencia [ray-vay-ren'-the-ah], *f.* 1. Reverence, respect, veneration, homage, honor, observance. 2. Bow of reverence (inclinación); obeisance. 3. Reverence, title given in Spain to members of religious orders. **Hacer una reverencia**, to bow.

reverenciable [ray-vay-ren-the-ah'-blay], *a.* Reverend.

reverenciador, ra [ray-vey-ren-the-ah-dor', rah], *m. & f.* Reverencer.

reverencial [ray-vay-ren-the-ahl'], *a.* Reverential.

reverencialmente [ray-vay-ren-the-al'-men-tay], *adv.* Reverentially, reverently.

reverenciar [ray-vay-ren-the-ar'], *va.* To venerate, to revere, to respect; to hallow; to reverence.

reverendamente [ray-vay-ren-dah-men'-tay], *adv.* Repectfully, reverentially.

reverendísimo, ma [ray-vay-ren-dee'-se-mo, mah], *a. sup.* Most reverend, right reverend.

reverendo, da [ray-vay-ren'-do, dah], *a.* 1. Reverend, the honorary epithet of prelates and distinguished members of religious orders; worthy of reverence. 2. Extremely circumspect and cautious. 3. Solemn (solemne). 4. (*LAm.*) Big (inmenso).

reverente [ray-vey-ren'-tay], *a.* Respectful, reverent; low.

reversible [ray-ver-see'-blay], *a.* (*Law.*) Returnable, revertible.

reversión [ray-ver-se-on'], *f.* Reversion, return.

reverse [ray-verr'-se], *m.* 1. Reverse side of coins. 2. Back part of anything.

reverso [ray-ver'-so], *m.* Back, other side; wrong side; reverse (de moneda). **El reverso de la medalla**, the other side of the coin.

reverter [ray-ver-terr'], *vn.* To overflow. *V.* REBOSAR. (*Yo reviento, yo reviena, from Reverter. V.* ATENDER.)

revés [ray-ves'], *m.* 1. Back part (dorso), back side, wrong side, underside (lado inferior). 2. Stroke with the back of the hand (golpe). 3. Disappointment, cross, misadventure. 4. Change of temper and disposition. 5. Reverse. *V.* REVERSO. **De revés**, diagonally, from left to right. **Al revés or del revés**, on the contrary, contrariwise (in slang. Over the left). **Todo nos salió al revés**, it all turned out wrong for us. **Llevar algo del revés**, to wear something the wrong way round.

revesado, da [ray-vay-sah'-do, dah], *a.* 1. Intractable, stubborn, obstinate. 2. Difficult entangled, perplexed, obscure. *-pp.* of REVESAR.

revesar [ray-vay-sar'], *va.* To vomit.

revestimiento [ray-ves-te-me-en'-to], *m.* Revestment, a coating or covering of a surface for strengthening or beautifying it.

revestir [ray-ves-teer'], *va.* 1. To dress, to put on clerical robes, to revest, to wear (vestir) 2. To repair or fortify a wall; to line (forrar); to crust. 3. (*Fig.*) To cloak (encubrir). 4. To have, to possess (cualidad). *-vr.* 1. To be swayed or carried along by some power or other to be invested with. 2. To be haughty, lofty, or elated with pride. **Los árboles se revisten de hojas**, the trees put on their leaves again.

revezar [ray-vay-thar'], *vn.* To alternate, to come in by turn, to relieve one after another, to work in rotation.

revezero [ray-vay-thay'-ro], *m.* One who alternates.

revezo [ray-vay'-tho], *m.* Alternacy, the act of relieving one another; reciprocal succession.

revidar [ray-ve-dar'], *va.* (*Prov.*) To reinvite.

reviejo, ja [ray-ve-ay'-ho, hah], *a.* Very old. *-m.* Withered branch of a tree.

reviernes [ray-ve-err'-nes], *m.* Each of the first seven Fridays after Easter.

revindicar [ray-van-de-car'], *va.* To claim.

revirado, da [ray-ve-rah'-do, dah], *a.* (*Bot.*) Twisted: applied to fibers of trees.

revirar [ray-ve-rar'], *va.* (*Naut.*) To veer again, to tuck again.

reviro [ray-vee'-ro], *m.* (*Naut.*) Canting or flaring, the curvature given to a timber in a ship.

revirón [ray-ve-rone'], *m.* Piece of sole leather put between the solepieces to make then even. *-a.* 1. (*CAm. Carib.*) Disobedient, rebellious.

revisar [ray-ve-sar'], *va.* To revise (texto, apuntes), to review, to examine (teoría), to review (tropas), to check. **Revisar las cuentas**, to audit accounts.

revisión [ray-ve-se-on'], *f.* Revision (repaso), reviewing, re-examination (reexaminación).

revisita [ray-ve-see'-tah], *f.* Revision, second examination.

revisor, ra [ray-ve-sor'], *m & f.* Reviser, censor, corrector, reviewer.

revisoria [ray-ve-so-ree'-ah], *f.* Office of censor or reviser:

revista [ray-vees'-tah], *f.* 1. Review (examen), revision. 2. (*Mil.*) Review (de tropas). 3. Magazine, review (periódico), publication. 4. Section (sección), page. 5. (*Teat.*) Revue: variety show. 6. (*And.*) Trim (de pelo). **Revista musical**, musical comedy, musical review. **Revista del corazón**, magazine of real life romance stories. **Revista de modas**, fashion paper.

revistar [ray-vis-tar'], *va.* To revise a suit at law, to try a cause a second time: to review troops.

revisto, ta [ray-vees'-to, tah], *pp. irr.* of REVER.

revitalizar [ray-ve-tah-le-thar'], *va.* To revitalize.

revite [ray-vee'-tay], *m.* Invitation to play in games.

revividero [ray-ve-ve-day'-ro], *m.* Place for rearing silkworms.

revivificar [ray-ve-ve-fe-car'], *va.* To revivificate, to vivify.

revivir [ray-ve-veer'], *vn.* To revive (suceso), to return to life, to acquire new life: to resuscitate (vivir de nuevo).

revocable [ray-vo-cah'-blay], *a.* Revocable, reversible.

revocablemente [ray-vo-cah'-blay-men-tay], *adv.* In a revocable manner.

revocación [ray-vo-cah-the-on'], *f.* Revocation: abrogation; act of recalling. **Revocación de una sentencia**, (*Law.*) reversal.

revocador, ra [ray-vo-cah-dor', rah], *m. & f.* 1. One who revokes abrogates or recalls. 2. Plasterer, white washer.

revocadura [ray-vo-cah-doo'-rah], *f.* 1. *V.* REVOQUE. 2. (*Pict.*) Painted borders of canvas.

revocante [ray-vo-cahn'-tay], *pa.* Revoker, recalling, abrogating.

revocar [ray-vo-car'], *va.* 1. To revoke (decisión), to repeal, to annul, to abrogate, to abolish; to countermand. (*Law.*) To reverse. 2. To dissuade from (persona), to induce one to desist. 3. To plaster (enlucir), to whitewash (enlacar), or to freshen paintings. 4. To yield to an impulse, to retrocede. 5. To recall, to call one from one place to another.

revocatorio, ria [ray-vo-cah-to'-re-o, ah], *a.* That which revokes or annuls; reversal.

revoco [ray-vo'-co], *m.* 1. Plaster, Whitewash. *V.* REVOQUE. 2. Cover of broom of furze laid on charcoal baskets.

revolar [ray-vo-lar'], *vn.* To fly again, to take a second flight. *V.* REVOLOTEAR.

revolcadero [ray-vol-cah-day'-ro], *m.* A weltering or wallowing place for wild boars and other beasts.

revolcadura [ray-vol-cah-doo'-rah], *f.* Action of wallowing.

revolcar [ray-vol-car'], *va.* 1. To knock down (derribar), to tread upon. 2. To overcome, to outshine in a controversy. 3. To floor (adversario). *-vr.* 1. To wallow in mire or anything filthy (animal). 2. To be obstinately bent upon an idea or design. (*Yo revuelco, yo revuelque, from Revolcar. V.* ACORDAR.)

revolcón [ray-vol-cone'], *m.* (*Coll.*) *V.* REVUELCO.

revolear [ray-vo-lay-ar'], *vn.* To flutter, to take short flights; to fly precipitately. *-va.* (*Cono Sur, Mex.*) To whirl (lazo).

revolotear [ray-vo-lo-tay-ar'], *vn.* To flutter, to fly round, to hover.

revoloteo [ray-vo-lo-tay'-o], *m.* Fluttering; a short flight; a quick motion with the wings.

revoltijo [ray-vol-tee'-ho], *m. V.* REVOLTILLO.

revoltillo [ray-vol-teel'-lyo], *m.* 1. Parcel of things jumbled together. 2. Tripes of a sheep. 3. Medley, confusion, disorder; mash; jumble (confusión). 4. Fricassee. 5. (*CAm. Cono Sur, Mex.*) Bundle.

revoltón [ray-vol-tone'], *m.* Vine-fretter, vine-grub. (used also adjectively.)

revoltoso, sa [ray-vol-toh'-so, sah], *a.* Turbulent, seditious, naughty (niño),

revoltura [ray-vol-too'-rah], *f.* (*Mex.*), A mixture of fluxes added to silver one.

revolución [ray-vo-loo-the-on'], *f.* 1. Revolution, the act of revolving. 2. Revolution of a planet. 3. Revolution, change in the state of a government; disturbance; sedition, commotion.

revolucionador, ra [ray-vo-loo-the-o-nah-dor, rah], *n. & a.* Revolutionist; revolutionary.

revolucionar [ray-vo-loo-the-o-nar'], *va.* To disturb or agitate a country, to produce a revolution. *-vr.* To rise or break into a commotion: it is a neologism.

revolucionario, ria [ray-vo-loo-the-o-nah'-re-o, ah], *a.* Revolutionary. *-m. & f.* Revolutionist, revolutioner, socialist.

revolvedero [ray-vol-vay-day'-ro], *m.* Coursing-place.

revolvedor, ra [ray-vol-vay-dor', rah], *m. & f.* Revolter, disturber; a turbulent, seditious, or rebellious person.

revolver [ray-vol'-ver], *m.* Revolver, a pistol containing five or more revolving chambers.

revolver [ray-vol-verr'], *va.* 1. To move a thing up and down (mover); to stir (líquido), to shift, to return; to revert; to retrace or go back again. 2. To revolve, to wrap up (envolver); to convolve. 3. To stir up disturbances, to excite commotions. 4. To revolve in the mind, to hesitate. 5. To face an enemy in order to attack him. 6. To evolve, to separate. 7. To turn short swiftly (caballos). 8. To go into, to investigate (indagar). **Han revuelto toda la casa**, they've messed up the whole house. *-vn.* **Revolver en una maleta**, to rummage in a case. *-vr.* 1. To move to and fro. 2. To change, as the weather. 3. To turn round (volverse); to writhe (con dolor). 4. To be stirred up (sedimento). 5. *(And.)* To get a lucky break (prosperar). **Se revolvía en su silla**, he was fidgeting about on his chair.

revolvimiento [ray-vol-ve-me-en'-to], *m.* Commotion, perturbation, revolution.

revoque [ray-vo'-kay], *m.* 1. Act of whitewashing (acto). 2. Plaster, whitewash (cal), rough-cast laid on houses or walls.

revotarse [ray-vo-tar'-say], *vr.* To vote contrary to a previous vote; to reconsider a ballot.

revuelco [ray-voo-el'-co], *m.* Wallowing, rolling.

revuelo [ray-voo-ay'-lo], *m.* 1. Flying to and fro of a bird. 2. Irregular motion; disturbance. **De revuelo**, by the way, speedily, promptly. **Armar un gran revuelo**, to cause a great stir. *(Yo revuelo, yo revuele, from Revolar. V. ACORDAR.)*

revuelta [ray-voo-el'-tah], *f.* 1. Second turn (vuelta), return. **Dar vueltas y revueltas a algo**, to go on turning something over and over. 2. Revolution, revolt (motín), sedition; contention, dissension, commotion (commoción), fuss (jaleo). 3. Delay, tardiness. 4. Meditation, reflection. 5. Commutation, change. 6. Point from which a thing commences a tortuous or oblique direction.

revuelto, ta [ray-voo-ell'-to, tah], *a. &: pp. irr.* of REVOLVER. 1. Mixed up (objetos), in a turmoil, in confusion. 2. Perverse, dissatisfied. 3. Unruly (revoltoso), restless (inquieto), mischievous (niño); rebellious (población). **Huevos revueltos**, scrambled eggs. **Todo estaba revuelto**, everything was in disorder.

revulsión [ray-vool-se-on'], *f.* Revulsion.

revulsivo, va, revulsorio, ria [ray vool-see'-vo, vah], *a.* Revulsory, revulsive.

rey [ray'-e], *m.* 1. King. **Rey de armas**, *(Her.)* the king at arms. **Los reyes**, epiphany, twelfth-night. **Dios guarde al rey** God save the king. 2. A Spanish dance. 3. Queen-bee; chief among animals. 4. King in cards or chess. **Rey de bastos** or **de copas**, (a) king of clubs or hearts. (b) A wooden king, a king without authority.

reyecico, illo, ito [ray-yay-thee'-co], *m. dim.* A petty king, the king of a small kingdom.

reyerta [ray-yerr'-tah], *f.* Dispute, difference, quarrel.

reyezuelo [ray-yay-thoo-ay'-lo], *m.* 1. A petty king. 2. *(Orn.)* Kinglet.

rezadero, ra [ray-thah-day'-ro, rah], *a.* Praying often.

rezado [ray-thah'-do], *m.* Prayer, divine service. *V.* REZO. **Rezado, da**, *pp.* of REZAR.

rezador, ra [ray-thah-dor', rah], *m. & f.* One who prays often.

rezagado [ray-thah-gah'-do], *m.* Straggler, one who is left behind on a march; tramp, one too indolent to work.

rezagante [ray-thah-gahn'-tay], *pa.* Delayer; leaving behind.

rezagar [ray-thah-gar'], *va.* 1. To leave behind (dejar atrás); to outstrip; more commonly reflexive. 2. To suspend action, to put off, to defer, to postpone (aplazar). *-vr.* To stay behind (quedar atrás); to loiter (ir despacio).

rezago [ray-thah'-go], *m.* 1. Remainder, residue. 2. Group of straggling cattle (ganado). 3. *(And. Mex.)* Unclaimed letters (Correos).

rezar [ray-thar'], *va.* 1. To pray, to say or rend prayers (oración). 2. To quote, to recite. 3. *(Vulg.)* To announce, to say in writing. *-vn.* To growl, to mutter, to pray, to read (texto), to grumble (quejarse). **Eso no reza conmigo**, that has nothing to do with me.

rezelar, *va.* **rezelo**, *m.* (and derivatives). *V.* RECELAR, REZELO.

rezno [reth'-no], *m.* 1. Tick, bot, bott (larva), sheep-tick, dog-tick. 2. *V.* RICINO.

rezo [ray'-tho], *m.* 1. Prayer, the act of praying. 2. Divine office, formulary of devotion.

rezón [ray-thone'], *m. (Naut.)* Grappling.

rezongador, ra [ray-thon-gah-dor', rah], *m. & f.* Grumbler, growler, mutterer.

rezongar [ray-tho-gar'], *vn.* To grumble, to mutter, to murmur, to growl.

rezonglón, na, rezongón, na [ray-thon-glon', nah], *a. & m.* Grumbler; grumbling.

rezumadero [ray-thoo-mah-day'-ro], *m.* Dripping-place; dripping.

rezumarse [ray-thoo-mar'-say], *vr.* 1. To ooze, to flow by stealth; to run gently, to leak. 2. To transpire, to escape from secrecy, to notice.

rho [ro], *f.* Rho *(r)*, seventeenth letter of the Greek alphabet, corresponding to *r*.

ría [ree'-ah], *f.* Mouth of a river.

riachuelo, riatillo [re-ah-choo-ay'-lo, re-ah-teel'-lyo], *m.* Rivulet, streamlet; small river.

riada [re-ah'-dah], *f.* Freshet, overflow, flood.

riba [ree'-bah], *f. (Prov.)* Bank between a higher and lower field.

ribadoquín [re-bah-do-keen'], *m.* Small gun now disused.

ribaldería [re-bal-day-ree'-ah], *f.* Ribaldry; wickedness; coarse abuse.

ribaldo, da [re-bahl'-do, dah], *a. & n.* Ribaldous; ribald; wicked, obscene. *V.* RUFIÁN.

ribazo [re-bah'-tho], *m.* A sloping bank; mound, hillock.

ribecillo [re-bay-theel'-lyo], *m.* Narrow silk or worsted galloon.

ribera [re-bay'-rah], *f.* 1. Shore of the sea, bank of a river; strand, verge of any water. 2. Irrigated plain. 3. *(Cono Sur; Mex.)* Riverside community (de campo); shanty town (chabolas). **Ser de monte y ribera**, to be fit for everything.

ribereño, ña [re-bay-ray'-nyo, nyah], *a.* Belonging to the seashore or bank of a river.

riberiego, ga [re-bay-re-ay'-go, gah], *a.* Grazing on the banks of rivers: applied to such flocks as are not removed to other sheep-walks, or are not *trashumantes*, as opposed to *estantes*. Grazier of sheep on the banks of rivers.

ribero [re-bay'-ro], *m.* Bank or parapet of a dam of water.

ribes [ree'-bes], *f. (Bot.)* Currant-bush.

ribete [re-bay'-tay], *m.* 1. Ribbon or tape sewed to the edge of cloth; seam, border, fringe, binding. 2. Cantle, the small quantity given above the precise measure or weight. 3. Additions to a tale, for embellishment.

ribetear [re-bay-tay-ar'], *va.* To edge, to border.

riboflavina [re-bo-flah-vee'-nah], *f.* Riboflavin.

ricacho, cha [re-cah'-cho, chah], *a. (Coll.)* Very rich.

ricadueña [re-cah-doo-ay'-nyah], *f.* Lady, daughter or wife of a noble.

ricafembra, ricahembra [re-cah-fem'-brah], *f.* Lady, daughter or wife of a noble.

ricahombría [re-cah-om-bree'-ah], *f.* Dignity of the *ricos hombres*, ancient nobility of Castile.

ricamente [re'-cah-men-tay], *adv.* 1. Richly, opulently. 2. Excellently, splendidly. **Muy ricamente**, very well. **He dormido tan ricamente**, I've slept splendidly.

ricazo, za [re-cah'-tho, thah], *a. aug.* Very rich, opulent.

ricial [re-the-ahl'], *a.* Growing again: applied to the aftercrop of corn, cut green for the feed of cattle.

ricino [re-thee'-no], *m. (Bot.)* PalmaChristi, the castoroil plant.

rico, ca [ree'-co, cah], *a.* 1. Noble, of an ancient and illustrious family. 2. Rich, wealthy, opulent. 3. Pleasing to the taste, delicious (sabroso). **Estos pasteles son riquísimos**, these cakes are very good. 4. Choice, select; able. 5. Valuable (joya), precious; luxurious (muebles). 6. Bonny (niño); cute, lovely. **¡Oye, rico!**, hey, man!

ricohombre, ricohome [re-co-om'-bray, re-co-o'-may], *m.* Grandee, a peer of the flint rank in Spain, a nobleman of the ancient nobility of Castile.

rictus [reek'-toos], *m.* Rictus, gaping of the mouth, grimace, grin (de burla), sneer (de desprecio).

ricura [re-koo'-rah], *f.* 1. Tastiness (lo sabroso), delicious quality. 2. Smashing girl (chica).

ridículamente [re-dee'-coo-lah-men-tay], *adv.* Ridiculously, contemptibly.

ridiculez [re-de-coo-leth'], *f.* 1. A ridiculous speech or action. 2. Ridicule, folly, extravagance, oddity, eccentricity. 3. Extreme nicety or sensibility.

ridiculizar [re-de-coo-le-thar'], *va.* To ridicule, to burlesque, to laugh at.

ridículo, la [re-dee'-coo-lo, lah], *a.* 1. Ridiculous, odd, eccentric, laughable, ludicrous. 2. Strange, contemptible; despicable; absurd. 3. Excessively nice and sentimental. **Hacer el ridículo**, to make oneself ridiculous.

ridículo [re-dee'-coo-lo], *m.* 1. Ridicule, mockery. 2. Handbag, reticule.

ridiculoso, sa [re-de-coo-lo'-so, sah], *a.* Ridiculous, extravagant.

riego [re-ay'-go], *m.* Irrigation; watering (aspersión). **Riego por aspersión**, watering by spray.

riel [re-el'], *m.* 1. A small ingot of unrefined gold or silver, lingot. 2. Rail of a railway whether for locomotives or for street use. In this sense it is also spelled **rail**, as in English.

rielado, da [re-ay-lah'-do, dah], *a.* Reduced to ingots (oro, plata).

rielar [re-ay-lar'], *vn. (Poet.)* 1. To glisten, to be reflected upon the waters: used of moonlight. 2. To shine with a tremulous light.

rielera [re-ay-lay'-rah], *f.* Mould in which ingots of gold or silver are cast.

rienda [re-en'-dah], *f.* 1. Rein of a bridle. 2. Moderation, restraint in speech and action. -*pl.* 1. *(Met.)* Government, direction. 2. Reins of the feuding horse. **A rienda suelta**, loose-reined, violently, swiftly. **Soltar la rienda**, to give way to vices or passions. **Tener las riendas**, to bolts the reins, to hold back a horse. **Tirar las riendas**, to draw back, to restrain.

riente [re-en'-tay], *pa.* Smiling, laughing (risueño).

riesgo [re-es'-go], *m.* Danger, risk, hazard, peril, jeopardy. **Con riesgo de**, at the risk of.

riesgoso, sa [re-es-go'-so, sah], *a.* Risk.

rifa [ree'-fah], *f.* 1. Scuffle, dispute, contest. 2. Raffle, a species of gums or lottery.

rifador [re-fah-dor'], *m.* Raffler; disputer.

rifadura [re-fah-doo'-rah], *f. (Naut.)* Act of splitting a sail.

rifar [re-far'], *va.* 1. To raffle, to cast dice for a prize. 2. *(Naut.)* To split a sail, in a storm. -*vn.* To quarrel, to dispute.

-*vr.* 1. **Rifarse algo**, to quarrel over something. 2. *(CAm.)* To take a risk (arriesgarse).

rifirrafe [re-fe-rah'-fay], *m. (Coll.)* A short quarrel, hasty words.

rígidamente [ree'-he-dah-men-tay], *adv.* Rigidly.

rigidez [re-he-deth'], *f.* Rigidity, asperity.

rígido, da [ree'-he-do, dah], *a.* Rigid (tieso), rigorous, severe, inflexible, harsh, to get stiff (aterirse), strict (moralmente). **Quedarse rígido**, to go rigid.

rigodón [re-go-done'], *m.* Rigadoon, a country dance.

rigor [re-gor'], *m.* 1. Rigor, a convulsive shuddering with a sense of cold. 2. Rigidity of the nerves. 3. Rigor (severidad), sternness, severity, harshness of temper. 4. Rigour, strictness, exactness, precision (precisión). 5. Power, intensity, keenness, hardness, vehemence. 6. Cruelty or excess of chastisement. 7. The last push or extremity. **A todo rigor**, if the worst comes to the worst. **En rigor**, at most. **Una edición hecha con el mayor rigor crítico**, an edition produced with absolute meticulousness.

rigorismo [re-go-rees'-mo], *m.* Rigorousness, severity.

rigorista [re-go-rees'-tah], *a. & com.* Applied to one very rigid, severe, or inflexible in moral opinions.

rigorosamente, rigurosamente [re-go-ro-sah-men'-tay], *adv.* Rigorously (con precisión); severely (severamente), scrupulously. **Eso no es rigurosamente exacto**, that is not strictly accurate.

riguroso, sa [re-goo-ro'-so, sah], *a.* Rigorous (estudio, método), strict (aplicación), austere, rigid, severe (medida), harsh; scrupulously nice. **Su tratamiento riguroso de los empleados**, his harsh treatment of the employees.

rija [ree'-hah], *f.* 1. A kind of lachrymal fistula. 2. Quarrel, scuffle, dispute.

rijador, ra [re-hah-dor', rah], *a.* Quarrelsome, litigious.

rijente [re-hen'-tay], *a.* Rough, cruel, horrid.

rijo [ree'-ho], *m.* Concupiscence, lust, sensuality.

rijoso, sa [re-ho'-so, sah], *a.* 1. Quarrelsome (peleador). 2. Restless at the sight of the female (caballos). 3. Lustful (cachondo), sensual.

rima [ree'-mah], *f.* 1. Rhyme, complete or incomplete, known as assonance. 2. Arrangement of things in a regular series. **Octava rima**, ottava rima.

rimado, da [re-mah'-do, dah], *a. & pp.* Of RIMAR. Versified.

rimar [re-mar'], *va. & vn.* 1. To inquire after, to investigate. 2. To rhyme, to make verses.

rimbombante [rim-bom-bahn'-tay], *pa.* 1. Resounding (resonante). 2. Pompous, bombastic. 3. *(Fig.)* Showiness (ostentación).

rimbombar [rim-bom-bar'], *vn.* To resound, to echo.

rimbombe, rimbombo [rim-bom'-bay], *m.* Repercussion of sound.

rimel [ree'-mayl], *m.* Eye shadow.

rimero [re-may'-ro], *m.* Collection of things placed regularly one over another in a pile.

rincón [rin-cone *m.* 1. Inside corner, an angle formed by the meeting of two walls; a coin. 2. Place of privacy, a lurking-place. 3. House, dwelling. 4. Small district or country. *Cf.* ESQUINA.

rinconada [rin-co-nah'-dah], *f.* Corner, formed by two houses, streets, or roads.

rinconcillo [rin-con-theel'-lyo], *m. dim.* A small corner.

rinconera [rin-co-nay'-rah], *f.* 1. Small triangular table in a corner. 2. *(Arquit.)* Wall between corner and window.

rinconero, ra [rin-co-nay'-ro, rah], *a.* Transverse, athwart.

ringle [reen'-glay], *m.* **Ringla** [reen'-glah], *f. V.* RINGLERA.

ringlera [rin-glay'-rah], *f. (Coll.)* Row, file.

ringlero [rin-glay'-ro], *m.* Line drawn with a pencil, for writing straight.

ringorrango [rin-go-rahn'-go], *m. (Coll.)* 1. Flourish with a pen (en escritura). 2. Extravagant nicety in dress.

rinoceronte [re-no-thay-ron'-tay], *m.* Rhinoceros.

rinoscopia [re-nos-co'-pe-ah], *f. (Med.)* Rhinoscopy, examination of the nasal cavities.

riña [ree'-nyah], *f.* Quarrel (disputa), scuffle, dispute, fray, brawl, fight.

riñón [ree-nyohn'], *m.* 1. Kidney. **Tener cubierto el riñón,** to be rich. 2. Central point of a country.

riñonada [ree-nyo-nah'-dah], *f.* 1. Coat of fat about the kidneys. 2. Dish of kidneys.

río [re'-o], *m.* 1. River, stream. 2. Any large quantity of fluids. **Río de lágrimas,** flood of tears. **Río abajo,** downstream. **Cuando el río suena, agua lleva,** there's no smoke without fire.

riolada [re-o-lah'-dah], *f.* The assemblage of many things at one time.

riostra [re-os'-trah], *f.* Post placed obliquely to strengthen an upright post, spur, strut.

riostrar [re-os-trar'], *va.* To strengthen by means of oblique posts.

ripia [ree'-pe-ah], *f.* Shingle, for roofing houses.

ripiar [re-pe-ar'], *va.* To fill up the chinks of a wall with small stones and mortar.

ripio [ree'-pe-o], *m.* 1. Remainder, residue, rubble (basura). 2. Word used to fill up a verse. **No perder ripio,** not to miss the least occasion.

riponce [re-pon'-thay], *m. (Bot.)* V. RAPÓNCHIGO.

riqueza [re-kay'-thah], *f.* 1. Riches, wealth (bienes), opulence. 2. Fertility, fruitfulness. 3. Ornament, embellishment. **Vivir en la riqueza,** to live in luxury.

risa [ree'-sah], *f.* 1. Laugh, laughter. 2. Cause or object of laughter; pleasing emotion. 3. Derisory smile or laugh. **Caerse de risa,** to shake with laughter: **Comerse de risa,** to suppress a desire to laugh (through respect). **Destornillarse de risa,** to laugh excessively. **Tentado a,** or **de, la risa,** (1) prone to laugh immoderately. (2) Amorous, lascivious. **Tomar algo a risa,** to take something as a joke. **Ser la risa (el hazmerreír) de todos,** to be the laughing stock of everyone. **Llorar de risa,** to cry laughing. **Tener un ataque de risa,** to have a fit of laughter.

risada [re-sah'-dah], *f.* Horse-laugh; immoderate laughter.

risco [rees'-co], *m.* A steep rock (inclinado), crag.

riscoso, sa [ris-co'-so, sah], *a.* Steep and rocky.

risibilidad [re-se-be-le-dahd'], *f.* Risibility.

risible [re-see'-blay], *a.* Risible, laughable, ludicrous.

risica, ita [re-see'-cah, ee'-tah], *f. dim.* 1. Feigned laugh. 2. Smile.

risotada [re-so-tah'-dah], *f.* Loud laugh, horse-laugh.

ríspido, da [rees'-pe-do, dah], *a.* V. ÁSPERO.

ristra [rees'-trah], *f.* 1. String of onions or garlic. 2. Row, file, series of things.

ristre [rees'-tray], *m.* Rest or socket for a lance, used to couch the lance in the posture of attack.

risueño, ña [re-soo-ay'-nyo, nyah], *a.* Smiling; pleasing, agreeable.

rítmico, ca [reet'-me-co, cah], *a.* Rhythmical.

ritmo [reet'-mo], *m.* Rhyme, rhythm. *V.* RIMA. **Ritmo de crecimiento,** rate of growth. **Trabajar a ritmo lento,** to go slow (lento).

rito [ree'-to], *m.* Rite, ceremony.

ritual [re-too-ahl'], *m.* Ritual, a book of religious rites and observances; ceremonial. *-a.* Ritual, according to some religious institution.

rival [re-vahl'], *m.* Rival, competion.

rivalidad [re-vah-le-dahd'], *f.* 1. Rivlary. 2. Competition, emulation.

rivalizar [re-vah-le-thar'], *va.* To corrival, to vie with.

rivera [re-vay'-rah], *f. (Prov.)* Brook, river, stream.

riza [ree'-thah], *f.* 1. Green stubble of grain cut for food. 2. Desolation, ravage, destruction.

rizado [re-thah'-do], *m.* Fluting, crimp, frizzle. *-a.* Curly (pelo); ridged (superficie); undulating (terreno).

rizador [re-thah-dor'], *m.* 1. Curling iron, for hair. 2. Hairdresser's frizzler.

rizagra [re-thah'-grah], *f.* An instrument for extracting the roots of teeth.

rizal [re-thahl'], *a. V.* RICIAL.

rizar [re-thar'], *va.* 1. To curl hair. 2. To crimple craps with a crimping iron; to plait.

rizo, za [ree'-tho, thah], *a.* Naturally curled or frizzled.

rizo [ree'-tho], *m.* 1. Curling or frizzling the hair; curl, frizzle, ringlet: crimpling of cloth. 2. Cut velvet. **Rizos,** *(Naut.)* points, used to reef the courses and top-sails of a ship. **Rizar el rizo,** to loop the loop.

ro [ro], *int.* Word used to lull children.

roa [ro'-ah], *f. (Naut.)* Stem. *V.* RODA.

roano, na [ro-ah'-no, nah], *a.* Sorrel, roan (caballo).

rob [rob], *m.* Rob, the inspissated juice of ripe fruit, mixed with honey or sugar to the consistency of a conserve; fruit jelly.

roba [ro'-bah], *f. (Prov.) V.* ARROBA.

robada [ro-bah'-dah], *f. (Prov.)* Space of ground of 400 square yards in extent.

robado, da [ro-bah'-do, dah], *a. & pp.* of ROBAR. Robbed, stolen; naked, without ornament.

robador, ra [ro-bah-dor', rah], *m. & f.* Robber.

robaliza [ro-bah-lee'-thah], *f.* Kind of fish, perch.

róbalo [ro'-bah-lo], *m.* Sea-bass, labrax; a fish like bream.

robamiento [ro-bah-me-en'-to], *m. V.* ARROBAMIENTO.

robar [ro-bar'], *va.* 1. To rob (dueño), to plunder, to steal (objeto). 2. To abduct, to kidnap (persona). 3. To sweep away part of its banks (río). 4. To overcharge, to overreach in the sale of goods. 5. To gain another's affections, to ingratiate oneself. 6. To diminish the color, to weaken or lower the coloring. 7. With bee-masters, to take the heed from a divided hive and put them into an empty one, by removing the honey-comb. **Robar algo a uno,** to steal something from somebody. **Robar el corazón a uno,** to steal somebody's heart.

robda [rob'-dah], *f.* Kind of ancient tribute.

robezo [ro-bay'-tho], *m.* A wild-goat. *V.* BICERRA.

robí [ro-been'], *m.* Rust of metal.

robinia [ro-bee'-ne-ah], *f.* The locust tree.

robladero, ra [ro-blah-day'-ro, rah], *a.* Clinched; recurvate, recurvous.

robladura [ro-blah-doo'-rah], *f.* Riveting, clinching.

roblar [ro-blar'], *va.* 1. To strengthen, to make strong. 2. To clinch a nail, to rivet.

roble [ro'-blay], *m.* Oak, oak-tree. *(Fam.)* Robust, strong person (persona). *(Met.)* Anything very strong and hard. **Más fuerte que un roble,** as strong as an ox.

roblecillo, ito [ro-blay-theel'-lyo], *m. dim.* A small oak-tree.

robleda [ro-blay'-dah], *f.* Oak-grove.

robledal, robledo [ro-blay-dahl', ro-blay'-do], *m.* Plantation of oak-trees, oak-grove.

roblizo, za [ro-blee'-tho, thah], *a.* Oaken, strong, hard.

roblón [ro-blone'], *m.* A rivet.

robo [ro'-bo], *m.* Robbery, theft; the thing robbed or stolen. **Robo en la vía pública,** highway robbery. **Robo a mano armada,** armed robbery. **Robo de ciclo,** *(Comput.)* cycle stealing.

roboración [ro-bo-rah-the-on'], *f.* Corroboration, strengthening.

roborante [ro-bo-rahn'-tay], *pa. & a.* Corroborant: applied to strengthening medicines; corroborating.

roborar [ro-bo-rar'], *va.* To confirm, to corroborate, to give strength.

roborativo, va [ro-bo-rah-tee'-vo, vah], *a.* Corroborative.

robot [ro'-bot], *m.* Robot.

robótica [ro-boh'-te-cah], *f.* Robotics.

robradura [ro-brah-doo'-rah], *f.* Clinching, riveting.

robrecillo, ito [ro-bray-thel'-lyo], *m. dim. V.* ROBLECILLO.

robredo [ro-bray'-do], *m. V.* ROBLEDAL.

robustamente [ro-boos'-tah-men-tay], *adv.* Robustly.

robustez [ro-boos-teth'], *f.* Robustness, hardiness, lustiness, force.

robusto, ta [ro-boos'-to, tah], *a.* Strong, robust, vigorous, hale.

roca [ro'-cah], *f.* 1. Rock, precipice; vein or bed of hard stone. 2. Cliff, rocky height on land or in the sea. 3. *(Geol.)* Rock, a simple or compound mineral mess, which, by its extent, forms an important part of the earthy crust. 4. Anything very firm and hard. 5. Stone. **Corazón de roca**, heart of stone. **Firme como una roca**, as solid as a rock.

rocada [ro-cah'-dah], *f.* Portion of wool or flax for the distaff.

rocadero [ro-cah-day'-ro], *m.* 1. Knob or head of a distaff. 2. Piece of paper formed like a cone, and put round the flux or wool on a distaff. 3. Rock of a distaff or spinning-wheel.

rocador [ro-cah-dor'], *m.* Head of a rock or distaff.

rocalla [ro-cahl'-lyah], *f.* 1. Drift of pebbles washed together by floods or torrents; talus of rocks. 2. Chippings of stone made in working it. 3. Flint glass, of which beads and rosaries are made.

rocambolesco [ro-cahm-bo-les'-co], *a.* Odd (raro), bizarre; ornate (estilo), baroque.

roce [ro'-thay], *m.* 1. Friction, rub (acto), attrition. 2. Familiarity (familiaridad), frequent conversation. **Tener roce con**, to be in close contact with.

rocha [ro'-chah], *f. V.* ROZA, 2d def.

rocho [ro'-cho], *m.* Roc, a fabulous bird of extraordinary size and strength.

rociada [ro-the-ah'-dah], *f.* 1. The act of sprinkling or irrigating gently; aspersion (aspersión); a sprinkling. 2. *(Naut.)* Spray. 3. Drops of dew on plants; herbs with dew on them, given to animals as medicine. 4. Shower of stones or balls: scattering (de insultos). 5. Slander, aspersion. 6. Roughness, asperity used with a person in discharging him.

rociadera [ro-the-ah-day'-rah], *f. V.* REGADERA.

rociado [ro-the-ah'-do], **da**, *a.* Dewy; bedewed. *-pp.* of ROCIAR.

rociador [ro-the-ah-dor'], *m.* Sprinkler. **Rociador de aire**, airbrush.

rociamiento [ro-the-ah-me-en'-to], *m.* Sprinkling or bedewing.

rociar [ro-the-ar'], *vn.* To be bedewed or sprinkled with dew; to fall in dew. *-va.* 1. To sprinkle with wine, water, or other fluids. 2. To strew about. 3. To plunder several persons at the same time.

rocín [ro-theen'], *m.* 1. Hack (caballo), jade working horse; a horse of little value. 2. A heavy, ignorant clown.

rocinal [ro-the-nahl'], *a.* Belonging to a hack horse.

rocinante [ro-the-nahn'-tay], *m. V.* ROCÍN: applied to a miserable hack.

rocinazo [ro-the-nah'-tho], *m. aug.* 1. A large hack. 2. A very ignorant person.

rocinillo [ro-the-neel'-lyoh], *m. dim.* A very small truck.

rocío [ro-thee'-o], *m.* 1. Dew (de noche). 2. Slight shower of rain (llovizna), sprinkling. 3. Divine inspiration, holy thoughts. **Rocío de la mar**, *(Naut.)* spoon-drift, the foam of the sea in a storm.

rockero [ro-kay'-ro], *a.* Rock; **música rockera**, rock music. **Es muy rockero**, (aficionado) he's a real rock fan.

rococó [ro-ko-ko'], *a.* Rococo.

rocoso, sa [ro-co'-so, sah], *a.* Rocky, craggy.

roda [ro'-dah], *f.* 1. *(Naut.)* Stem. 2. Duty or impost on sheep-flocks.

rodaballo [ro-dah-bahl'-lyo], *m.* Turbot, flounder.

rodada [ro-dah'-dah], *f.* Rut (de rueda), the track of a wheel.

rodadero, ra [ro-dah-day'-ro, rah], *a.* Rolling or wheeling easily.

rodadizo, za [ro-dah-dee'-tho, thah], *a.* Easily rolled round.

rodado, da [ro-dah'-do, dah], *a.* 1. Dapple, dappled, roan (caballos). 2. *V.* PRIVILEGIO. 3. Round, fluent (frases). 4. Experienced (experimentado). 5. Rounded (piedra). **Venir rodado**, to attain an object accidentally. *-pp.* of RODAR.

rodado [ro-dah'-do], *m. (Min.) V.* SUELTO.

rodador [ro-dah-dor'], *m.* 1. Roller, anything that rolls or falls rolling down. 2. Vagabond, vagrant. 3. A kind of mosquito.

rodadura [ro-dah-doo'-rah], *f.* 1. Rolling, the act of rolling. 2. Rut (rodada), the truck of a wheel.

rodaja [ro-day'-hah], *f.* 1. A small wheel (ruedecilla). 2. Rowel of a spur. 3. Jagging-iron used by pastry-cooks: bookbinder's tool. 4. *(And.)* Vehicle tax (impuesto).

rodaje [ro-dah'-hay], *m.* 1. Wheel-works, as of a watch. 2. *(And.)* Vehicle tax (impuesto).

rodajilla [ro-dah-heel'-lyah], *f. dim.* A very small wheel or circular body.

rodal [ro-dahl'], *m.* Place, spot, seat.

rodamiento [ro-dah-me-ayn-to], *m.* **Rodamiento a bolas**, ball bearing.

rodante [ro-dahn'-tay], *pa.* Rolling.

rodapelo [ro-dah-pay'-lo], *m.* Rubbing against the grain. *V.* REDOPELO.

rodapié [ro-dah-pe-ay'], *m.* 1. Fringe of silk or other stuff found at the feet of a bedstead, table, or balcony, to hide the feet. 2. The stained or painted lower part of white-washed walls, about from the ground, a socle. 3. A board or low shutter put on balconies.

rodaplancha [ro-dah-plahn'-chah], *f.* The main ward of a key.

rodar [ro-dar'], *vn.* 1. To roll, to revolve on an axis. 2. To roll, to run on wheels (sobre ruedas). 3. To roll, to move along on the surface, to roll down a hill. 4. *V.* RODEAR. 5. To abound, to be in great plenty. 6. To wander about in vain in quest of business; to be tossed about; to go about, to go up and down. 7. To lose an employment, station, dignity, or esteem. 8. To happen accidentally. **Rodar por la escalera**, to fall downstairs. **Ir rodando**, to move about. *-va.* 1. To drive, to impel, to give an impulse. 2. To travel (viajar). 3. To race, to drive (en carreteras). 3. To shoot, to film (cine). 4. *(Carib.)* To seize (agarrar); to imprison (encarcelar). 5. *(LAm.)* To round up (ganado). **Ha rodado medio mundo**, he's been over half the world.

rodeado, da [ro-day-ah'-do, dah], *a. & pp.* of RODEAR. Surrounded. **Rodeado de negocios**, overwhelmed with business.

rodeador, ra [ro-day-ah-dor', rah], *m. & f.* Roller, wrapper.

rodear [ro-day-ar'], *vn.* 1. To go round a place or object; to encompass. 2. To go a round-about way, to come about. 3. To make use of circumlocutions; to use circuitous language or indirect expressions. *-va.* 1. To wrap up, to put one thing around another; to circle, to compass, to girdle. 2. To whirl about. 3. To dispose, to arrange. **Los soldados rodearon el edificio**, the soldiers surrounded the building. *-vr.* 1. **Rodearse de**, to surround oneself with. 2. To turn round (volverse).

rodela [ro-day'-lah], *f.* Shield, a round buckler or target.

rodelero [ro-day-lay'-ro], *m.* Soldier armed with a shield or target.

rodenal [ro-day-nahl'], *m.* A clump of rodello pines.

rodeno [ro-day'-no], *m.* A kind of pine.

rodeno, na [ro-day'-no, nah], *a.* Red (rocas, pines).

rodeo [ro-day'-o], *m.* 1. Detour, the act of going round; a circuitous way or road; turn to elude another (desvío). 2. Place in a fair or market where horned cattle are exposed to sale. 3. Delay, protraction, tedious method. 4. Evasion (evasión), subterfuge. 5. *(Coll. Mex.)* Enclosing cattle for the purpose of counting and marking them. 6. *(LAm.)* Roundup, rodeo. **Dar un rodeo**, to make a detour. **Dejarse de rodeos**, to talk straight.

rodeón [ro-day-on'], *m.* A complete rolling or winding round.

rodera [ro-day'-rah], *f.* Rut, cart track.

rodero, ra [ro-day'-ro, rah], *a.* Relating to wheels.

rodero [ro-day'-ro], *m.* Collector of the duty on sheep.

rodete [ro-day'-tay], *m.* 1. A small wooden wheel for moving a millwheel. 2. Bolster, a horizontal circle at the fore axle-tree of a carriage for turning it. 3. A kind of ward in a lock. 4. A rower of platted hair which women tie on the top of their heads for ornament. 5. A kind of pad or bolster put on the head of women (de pelo), to carry vessels with greater ease, or for ornament. 6. Border round the sleeves of gowns. 7. Roll (de grasa). 8. Pad (para llevar carga). 9. Ward (de cerradura).

rodezno [ro-deth'-no], *m.* 1. A large wheel, consisting of many pieces. 2. A toothed wheel in grist-mills.

ródico, ca [ro'-de-co, cah], *a.* Relating to rhodium.

rodilla [ro-deel'-lyah], *f.* 1. The knee. 2. Shoulder in a lock to fit the lizard of a key. *V.* RODETE, 3d def. 3. Dusting cloth, cloth for cleaning (paño). **De rodillas,** on one's knees. **Doblar las rodillas,** to bend the knees; to kneel down. **Pedir algo de rodillas,** to ask for something on bended knees.

rodillada [ro-dil-lyah'-dah], *f.* Push with the knee, a kneeling position.

rodillazo [rod-dil-lyah'-zo], *m.* Push with the knee.

rodillera [ro-dil-lyay'-rah], *f.* 1. Anything put for comfort or protection over the knees (protección). 2. Patch, or reenforcing piece, added to the knees of pants or long underwear; knee cap. 3. Damage upon the knees of horses from kneeling. 4. Bulging of pantaloons over the knee. 5. Pad (para llevar carga).

rodillero, ra [ro-dil-lyay'-ro, rah], *a.* Belonging to the knees.

rodillo [ro-deel'-lyo], *m.* 1. Roller, a cylinder of wood for moving heavy things. 2. Roller or rolling-stone, to level walks or roads. 3. Roller for distributing printing ink; brass roller, used to form plate-glass. 4. Rolling-pin used by pastry-cooks. **Rodillo pintor,** paint roller.

rodilludo, da [ro-dil-lyoo'-do, dah], *a.* Having large knees.

rodio [roh'-de-o], *m.* Rhodium, a metal.

rodio, dia, rodiota [roh'-de-o, ah, ro-de-o'-tah], *a.* Rhodian, belonging to Rhodes or its inhabitants.

rododendro [bo-do-den'-dro], *m.* Rhododendron, a shrub of the heath family.

rodomiel [ro-do-me-el'], *m.* The juice of roses mixed with honey.

rodrigar [ro-dre-gar'], *va.* To prop up vines.

rodrigazón [ro-dre-gah-thone'], *f.* Time for putting props to vines.

rodrigón [ro-dre-gone'], *m.* 1. Stay or prop for vines. 2. *(Coll.)* Page or servant who waits upon women.

roedero [ro-ay-day'-ro], *m.* Place frequently gnawed.

roedor, ra [ro-ay-dor', rah], *m. & f.* Gnawer; detractor. **Gusano roedor,** a gnawing worm: remorse.

roedores [ro-ay-do'-rays], *m. pl.* *(Zool.)* The rodents.

roedura [ro-ay-doo'-rah], *f.* 1. Gnawing, corroding. 2. The part gnawed off and the mark left behind.

roel [ro-el'], *m.* *(Her.)* Bezant, a roundel or upon a shied.

roela [ro-ay'-lah], *f.* Round piece of crude silver or gold.

roer [ro-err'], *va.* 1. To gnaw (comida), to corrode, to consume by degrees (metal); to destroy gradually. 2. To molest, to harass. **Roer el anzuelo,** to free oneself from peril. 3. To gnaw bones.

roete [ro-ay'-tay], *m.* A medicinal wine prepared from pomegranates.

rogación [ro-gah-the-on'], *f.* Request, petition, supplication. -*pl.* Rogation.

rogador, ra [ro-gah-dor', rah], *m. & f.* Supplicant, petitioner.

rogar [ro-gar'], *va.* 1. To implore, to entreat; to crave, to court: to obtest. 2. To pray, to say prayers. **Rogar a uno,** to ask somebody to. **Rogar que,** to ask that. -*vn.* 1. To beg (pedir). **Hacerse de rogar,** to play hard to get, to have to be coaxed. 2. To pray. -*vr.* **"Se ruega la mayor puntualidad",** "Please be punctual".

rogativa [ro-gah-tee'-vah], *f.* Supplication, prayer.

rogativo, va [ro-gah-tee'-vo, vah], *a.* Supplicatory.

rogatorio, ria [ro-gah-toh'-re-o, re-ah], *a.* Rogatory, pertaining to investigation.

rogo [ro'-go], *m.* *(Poct.)* Fire, funeral pyre.

roído [ro-ee'-do], *a. & pp.* of ROER. 1. Gnawed, corroded. 2. Penurious, despicable.

rojeante [ro-hay-an'-tay], *pa.* Rubific, rubifying.

rojear [ro-hay-ar'], *vn.* 1. To redden (volverse rojo), to be ruddy; to blush. 2. To be reddish (tirar a rojo); to show red (mostrarse rojo).

rojete [ro-hay'-tay], *m.* Rouge for the face.

rojez, rojeza [ro-heth'], *f.* Reddish.

rojizo, za [ro-hee'-tho, thah], *a.* Reddish.

rojo, ja [roh'-ho, hah], *a.* 1. Red, ruby. 2. Ruddy, reddish, of high gold color. **Poner rojo a uno,** to make somebody blush. -*m.* 1. Red, red color. 2. **Rojo de labios,** rouge, lipstick. 3. Red, Republican.

rojura [ro-hoo'-rah], *f.* Redness.

rol [rol], *m.* 1. List (lista), roll, catalogue (catálogo). 2. Muster-roll of a merchant ship.

roldana [rol-dah'-nah], *f.* *(Naut.)* Sheave, pulley-wheel.

rolde [rol'-day], *m.* Circle formed by persons or things.

roleo [ro-lay'-o], *m.* Volute. *V.* VOLUTA.

rolla [rol'-lyah], *f.* Collar of a draught-horse.

rollar [rol-lyar'], *va. V.* ARROLLAR.

rollete [rol-lyay'-tay], *m. dim.* A small roll.

rollizo, za [rol-lyee'-tho, thah], *a.* Plump (persona), round (objeto), robust, strapping.

rollo [rol'-lyo], *m.* 1. A roll, anything of a cylindrical form; roll of cloth (paño): rouleau. 2. *V.* ROLLA. 3. A column of cloth, an insignia of jurisdiction. 4. Gallows erected in a cylindrical form. 5. Acts or records rolled up, that they may be carried with greater case. 6. Long round stone. 7. *(Culin.)* Rolling pin. 8. *(Culin.)* Roll (empanada). 9. *(Esp.)* Bore (cosa pesada); boring speech (discurso); tedious explanation (explicación); lecture (conferencia); tale (cuento). **La conferencia fue un rollo,** the lecture was an awful bore. **Cortar el rollo,** to stop the flow. 10. *(Esp.)* Alternative culture (contracultura), alternative life-style. **Montarse el rollo,** to organize one's life-style. 11. *(Esp.)* Ambience (ambiente), atmosphere. **Me va el rollo,** I like this scene. 12. **Largar el rollo,** *(And. Cono Sur)* to be sick (vomitar).

rollón [rol-lyone'], *m. V.* ACEMITE.

rollona [rol-lyo'-nah], *a.* *(Coll.)* Fat, plump, and robust: applied to a short, lusty woman.

romadizarse [ro-mah-de-thar'-say], *vr. V.* ARROMADIZARSE.

romadizo [ro-mah-dee'-tho], *m.* Nasal catarrh (permanente), cold in the head (resfriado).

romaico, ca [ro-mah'-e-co, cah], *a. & n.* Romaic, belonging to modern Greece.

romana [ro-mah'-nah], *f.* Steelyard, a balance or lever. **Hacer romana,** to balance, to equipoise.

romanador [ro-mah-nah-dor'], *m.* Weighmaster in a slaughterhouse.

romanar [ro-mah-nar'], *va.* To weigh with a steel-yard.

romance [ro-mahn'-thay], *m.* 1. The common or vernacular Spanish language (castellano), as derived from the Roman or Latín. 2. Romance (amorío), a species of poetry, a tale of wild adventures in war or love, a ballad. **Hablar en romance,** to speak out, to speak plainly. -*pl.* *(Coll.)* Wiles, stratagems, deceitful tricks.

romancear [ro-man-thay-ar'], *va.* 1. To translate into Spanish or into the vulgar language. 2. *(Gram.)* To periphrase, to express by circumlocution.

romancero, ra [ro-man-thay'-ro, rah], *a.* 1. Singing or composing romances or ballads. 2. Using evasions and subterfuges.

romancero [ro-man-thay'-ro], *m.* 1. Collection of romances or ballads; legendary tales. 2. Romancer.

romancesco [ro-man-thes'-co], *a.* Proper to a novel or romance; novelistic, romantic.

romancista [ro-man-thees'-tah], *m.* Author who writes in the vulgar or native language, on subjects generally discussed in the Latin tongue. -*a.* A surgeon who did not study Latin; (a charlatan).

romancito [ro-man-thée'-to], *m. dim.* A short romance.

romanear [ro-mah-nay-ar'], *va.* To weigh with a steelyard. - *vn.* To outweigh, to preponderate.

romaneo [ro-mah-nay'-o], *m.* Weighing with a steelyard.

romanesco [ro-mah-nes'-co], *a.* 1. Roman, belonging to the Roman arts and customs. 2. *V.* ROMANCESCO.

romanía (De), *adv.* Crestfallen.

románico [ro-mah'-ne-co], *a.* Romanic, Romanesquo (en arquitectura).

romanilla, ita [ro-mah-neel'-lyah], *f. dim.* A small steelyard.

romanista [ro-mah-nees'-tah], *a. & n.* Romanist, versed in Roman law or Romance philology.

romanizar [ro-mah-ne-thar'], *va.* To Romanize, to follow the manners, customs, and fashions of Rome.

romano, na [ro-mah'-no, nah], *a.* 1. Roman relating to Rome. 2. Tubby, variegated with gray and black (gato). 3. *(Typ.)* A type of about great primer size, 16-point. Bourgeois or 9-point. **A la Romana**, in the Roman fashion.

romanticismo [ro-man-te-thees'-mo], *m.* 1. The spirit of Christian civilization in literature, as contrasted with that of Greco-Roman paganism. 2. Romanticism, romantic literary style as opposed to the classic.

romántico, ca [ro-man-tee-co'-cah], *a.* 1. Not bound by the literary rules of classic authors. 2. Romantic, proper to novels. 3. Romantic, sentimental in excess.

romanza [ro-mahn'-thah], *f. (Music.)* Romance, romanza, a simple rhythmical melody.

romanzado, da [ro-man-thah'-do, dah], *a.* Turned or translated into Spanish. *-pp.* of ROMANZAR.

romanzar [ro-man-thar'], *va. V.* ROMANCEAR.

romanzón [ro-man-thone'], *m.* A long and tedious romance.

romaza [ro-mah'-thah], *f. (Bot.)* Dock. **Romaza aguda**, sharp-pointed dock.

rombo [rom'-bo], *m.* Rhomb, a quadrangular figure, having its four sides equal, with unequal angles.

romboidal [rom-bo-e-dahl'], *a.* Rhomboidal, like a rhomb.

romboide [rom-bo'-e-day], *m. (Geom.)* Rhomboid.

romera [ro-may'-rah], *f. (Bot.)* Rosemary-leaved sun-rose.

romeraje [ro-may-rah'-hay], *m. V.* ROMERÍA.

romeral [ro-may-rah'], *m.* Place abounding with rosemary.

romería [ro-may-ree'-ah], *f.* 1. Pilgrimage. **Ir de romería**, to go on a pilgrimage. 2. Trip, excursion.

romero [ro-may'-ro], *m.* 1. *(Bot.)* Rosemary. 2. Pilgrim, palmer.

romero, ra [ro-may'-ro, rah], *a.* Traveling on religious account.

romí, romín [ro-mee', ro-meen'], *m.* Bastard saffron. *V.* AZAFRÁN ROMIN.

romo, ma [roh'-mo, mah], *a.* 1. Obtuse, blunt. 2. Flat-nosed: in this sense it is used as a substantive. *-n.* Hinny, mule begotten by a horse and a she-ass.

rompecabezas [rom-pay-cah-bay'-thas], *m.* 1. Puzzle, riddle (acertijo), jigsaw (juego), puzzle. 2. An offensive weapon, a slingshot.

rompecoches [rom-pay-co'-ches], *m.* Everlasting, a strong cloth.

rompedera [rom-pay-day'-rah], *f.* Chisel for cutting hot iron.

rompedero, ra [rom-pay-day'-ro, rah], *a.* Brittle, fit to be broken.

rompedor, ra [rom-pay-dor', rah], *m. & f.* Breaker, destroyer, crusher; one who wears out his clothes very soon.

rompedura [rom-pay-doo'-rah], *f. V.* ROTURA.

rompeesquinas [rom-pay-es-kee'-nas], *m.* A hector or braggart who hangs about street corners.

rompehuelgas [rom-pay-oo-ell'-gahs], *m.* Strike-breaker.

rompeolas [rom-pay-oh'-lahs], *m.* Breakwater.

romper [rom-perr'], *va. & vn.* 1. To break, to force asunder; to break in pieces, to dash, to fracture, to crash; to cut asunder. 2. To wear out clothes soon (gastar). 3. To defeat, to rout. 4. To break up land, to plough it for the first time. 5. To pierce, to penetrate. 6. To break off; to fall out, to quarrel. 7. To dawn, to begin. 8. To interrupt; a speech or conversation. 9. To deliberate, to resolve. 10. To break out (guerra), to spring up, to dissipate clouds. 11. To violate, to infringe; to transgress. 12. To exceed, to go beyond the limits. 13. To prune vine-stalks of their useless green branches. 14. To

snap (cuerda), to tear (papel). 15. To break (ayuno, continuidad, silencio). 16. To break (contrato, pacto). 17. To break (olas). 18. **Romper en llanto**, to burst into tears. 19. **Quien rompe paga**, one must pay the consequences. *-vr.* 1. To become free and easy in one's deportment. 2. To break, to smash; to tear, to rip. **No te vayas a romper**, don't be so fussy.

rompiente [rom-pe-en'-tay], *m.* Surf breakers; shoreline or submerged rock on which the sea breaks.

rompimiento [rom-pe-me-en'-to], *m.* 1. Rupture, the act of breaking (acto). 2. Aperture in a solid body (abertura), crack (grieta); cleft, fracture. 3. Funeral dues paid by such as have their own tomb. 4. An apparent depth of a piece of painting which seems to break its superficies. 5. First ploughing of land. 6. *(Met.)* Rupture, dispute among persons.

rompope [rom-po'-pay], *m. (Mex. & C. A.)* Kind of eggnog.

ron [ron], *m.* Rum, spirit made from molasses or cane-juice.

ronca [ron'-cah], *f.* 1. Threat, menace; boast, brag. 2. Cry of a buck in rutting-time. 3. A kind of halberd. **Echar roncas**, *(Coll.)* (1) to threaten, to menace. (2) To be hoarse.

roncador, ra [ron-cah-dor', rah], *m. & f.* Snorer. *-m.* 1. Snoring-fish. 2. The little buss, roncador, a food-fish of California. 3. *V.* SOBRESTANTE. *-f. (Peru, Eg.)* A large spur which makes noise.

roncamente [ron-cah-men-tay], *adv.* Hoarsely, with a harsh voice; in a coarse, vulgar manner.

roncar [ron-car'], *vn.* 1. To snore (estando dormido), to make a harsh noise; to roar (ciervo, mar, tiempo). 2. *(Coll.)* To threaten (amenazar), to boast, to brag. 3. To cry like a buck in rutting-time. 4. *(And. Cono Sur)* To be bossy.

ronce [ron'-thay], *m.* Flattery.

roncear [ron-thay-ar'], *vn.* 1. To defer, to protract, to use evasions, to lag. 2. To wheedle. 3. *(Naut.)* To sail badly or slowly.

roncería [ron-thay-ree'-ah], *f.* 1. Sloth, laziness, tardiness. 2. Flattery, soothing expressions. 3. *(Naut.)* Bad sailing.

roncero, ra [ron-thay'-ro, rah], *a.* 1. Slothful, tardy. 2. Snarling, growling. 3. Flattering, wheedling, melliloquent. 4. Slow, tardy. 5. Unwilling (desganado); slack (gandul), slow. 6. Grumpy (gruñón). 7. *(And. CAm. Cono Sur)* Sly (taimado), sharp; nosey (entrometido).

roncha [ron'-chah], *f.* 1. Weal, hives; a bean-like swelling. 2. Bruise (cardenal), ecchymosis. 3. Loss of money by fraud or imposition. 4. *(Prov. Ar.)* Slice of anything cut round.

ronchar [ron-char'], *va.* To chow anything crisp or hard. *V.* RONZAR. *-vn.* To make wheals.

ronchón [ron-chone'], *m. aug.* A large swelling.

ronco, ca [ron'-co, cah], *a.* Hoarse (persona), husky, having a rough voice.

ronco [ron'-co], *m. (Coll.)* Snore. *V.* RONQUIDO.

roncón [ron-cone'], *m.* Drone of a bagpipe.

ronda [ron'-dah], *f.* 1. Rounds, the act of going about at night. 2. Night;. patrol; rounds performed by a night watch; a beat. **Ir de ronda**, to go the rounds. 3. Space between the houses and the inside of the wall of a fortress. 4. Three first cards in a hand to play (naipes). 5. Round (bebidas, negociaciones). 6. *(Cono Sur)* Ring-a-ring-a-roses.

rondador [ron-dah-dor'], *m.* 1. Watchman, night guard. 2. One who is going about at night, one who is hovering about one place.

rondalla [ron-dahl'-lyah], *f.* Fable, story.

rondar [ron-dar'], *va. & vn.* 1. To go round by night in order to prevent disorders (inspeccionar). 2. To take walks by night about the streets, to serenade. 3. To go round, to follow anything continually, to haunt, to harass (acosar). 4. To hover about one place, to move round a thing. 5. To threaten to relapse, to impend. 6. To flutter (mariposa). **Me está rondando un catarro**, I've got a cold hanging about.

rondel [ron-del'], *m.* Roundelay, kind of poetry little used.

rondeña [ron-day'-nyah], *f.* Music or song peculiar to Ronda and like that of the fandango.

rondín [ron-deen'], *m.* 1. Rounds of a corporal on the walls to visit the sentinels. 2. Watchman in naval arsenals.

rondí, or **rondiz** [ron-dee', ron-deeth'], *m.* Base or fierce of a precious stone.

rondó [ron-doh'], *m.* (*Mus.*) Rondeau, a kind of jig or lively tune, which ends with the first strain repeated.

rondón [ron-done'], A word merely used adverbially. **De rondón**, rashly, abruptly, intrepidly.

ronfeo [ron-fay'-o], *f.* A long, broad sword.

rongigata [ron-ge-hah'-tah], *f.* V. REHILANDERA.

ronquear [ron-kay-ar'], *vn.* To be hoarse with cold.

ronquedad [ron-kay-dahd'], *f.* Hoarseness, roughness of voice.

ronquera [ron-kay'-rah], *f.* Hoarseness, occasioned by catching cold.

ronquido [ron-kee'-do], *m.* 1. Snore. 2. Any rough, harsh sound.

ronquillo, illa, ito, ita [ron-keel'-lyo], *a. dim.* of RONCO. Slightly hoarse.

ronronear [ron-ro-nay-ar'], *vn.* To purr.

ronza [ron'-thah], *f.* (*Naut.*) The state of a vessel adrift.

ronzal [ron-thahl'], *m.* 1. Halter, a fastening for a beast. 2. (*Naut.*) V. PALANCA.

ronzar [ron-thar'], *va.* 1. (*Naut.*) To rouse, to haul without the aid of a tackle. 2. To chew hard things.

roña [ro'-nyah], *f.* 1. Scab (de oveja), mange in sheep, manginess. 2. (*Coll.*) Craft, fraud, cunning. 3. (*Met.*) Nastiness, dirt, filth (mugre). 4. (*Met.*) Moral infection or hurt. 5. Moral danger (peligro moral). 6. Meanness (tacañeía). 7. (*Carib. Mex.*) Envy (envidia); grudge (inquina), ill will. 8. (*And. Med.*) Feigned illness. 9. Rust (óxido).

roñada [ro-nyah'-dah], *f.* (*Naut.*) Garland.

roñeía [ro-nyay-ree'-ah], *f.* 1. Craft, cunning, deceitfulness. 2. Sordid parsimony.

roñoso, sa [ro-nyo'-so, sah], *a.* 1. Scabby, diseased with a scab, leprous. 2. Dirty (sucio), nasty, filthy. 3. Wily, sly, crafty. 4. Mean, sordidly parsimonious. 5. (*And.*) Unpolished, coarse (tosco). 6. (*And.*) Tricky (tramposo). 7. (*Carib. Mex.*) Bitter (rencoroso).

ropa [ro'-pah], *f.* 1. Cloth; all kinds of silk, woollen, or linen, used for domestic purposes. 2. Wearing apparel, clothes. 3. Robe, gown (vestiduras). **Ropa blanca**, linen. **Poca ropa**, ill-clothed: poor. 4. Dress of particular authority for the bar, senate, etc. 5. Anything put between or under others for a seat. **Ropa usada or ropa vieja**, cast-off wearing apparel. **A quemaropa**, (1) point blank. (2) Off one's guard.

ropaje [ro-pah'-hay], *m.* 1. Wearing apparel. 2. Drapery in pictures and statues. 3. Apparel, generally elegant, proper to some authority. 4. Odd garb (raro); heavy clothing (excesivo).

ropálico, ca [ro-pah'-le-co, cah], *a.* Applied to verses with the first word a monosyllable, and all the others increasing progressively.

ropavejería [ro-pah-vay-hay-ree'-ah], *f.* Frippery, old-clothes shop.

ropaverejero [ro-pah-vay-ray-hay'-ro], *m.* Flipper, oldclothes man.

ropería [ro-pay-ree'-ah], *f.* 1. Trade of dealers in old clothes (negocio). 2. Store for ready-made clothing (tienda). 3. Wardrobe of a community or clothes-room of a hospital. 4. Office or keeper of a wardrobe.

ropero [ro-pay'-ro], *m.* 1. Salesman who deals in clothes. 2. Sleeper of the wardrobe or vestiary in a religious community. 3. Head shepherd, who superintends the making of cheeses, and has the care of them. 4. Boy who guards the clothes of herdsman.

ropeta [ro-pay'-tah], *f. dim.* A short garment.

ropetilla [ro-pay-teel'-lyah], *f.* 1. A wretched, short garment. 2. Jacket with loose hanging sleeves.

ropilla [ro-peel'-lyah], *f.* 1. Kind of short jacket with double sleeves, the outer ones hanging loose. 2. (*dim.*) A short garment.

ropita [ro-pee'-tah], *f. dim.* V. ROPETA.

ropón [ro-pone'], *m.* A wide, loose gown, worn over the clothes (bata).

roque [ro'-kay], *m.* Rook, castle, a man at Chess. V. TORRE.

roqueda [ro-kay'-dah], *f.* Rocky place.

roquedo [ro-kay'-do], *m.* Rock, stony precipice.

roqueño, ña [ro-kay'-nyo, nyah], *a.* Rocky, full of rocks (rocoso). **Montañas Roqueñas**, the Rocky Mountains.

roquero, ra [ro-kay'-ro, rah], *a.* 1. Rocky, abounding with rocks; situated on rocks. 2. V. Rockero. 3. Person who sings Rock & Roll.

roqués [ro-kes'], *a.* Applied to a kind of falcon.

roqueta [ro-kay'-tah], *f.* Ancient kind of tower in a fortress.

roquete [ro-kay'-tay], *m.* 1. A garment worn by bishops and abbots. 2 Rocket. V. ATACADOR.

rorro [ror'-ro], *m.* A sucking child.

rosa [ro'-sah], *f.* 1. (*Bot.*) Rose. 2. Red spot in any part of the body. 3. Rose diamond. 4. Bunch of ribbons or like things in the form of a rose: rosette. 5. Rosy or florid aspect; rosecolor. 6. Flower of saffron; artificial rose. **Rosas**, flowers, delights, pleasures; amenity. **Agua de rosas**, rose water. **Palo de rosa**, rosewood. **Estar como una rosa**, to be fresh and clean. **Color de rosa**, pink.

rosáceo, cea [ro-sah'-thay-o, ah], *a.* Rosaceous, rose colored. *-f. pi.* The rose family of plants.

rosacruz [ro-sah-crooth'], *m.* Rosicrucian, a name given to a sect of philosophers.

rosada [ro-sah', dah], *f.* V. ESCARCHA.

rosado, da [ro-sah'-do, dah], *a. & pp.* of ROSARSE. 1. Rose, crimsoned, flushed. 2. Rosy, relating to roses. 3. Made up with roses. **Agua rosada**, rosewater. *-m.* Rosé (vino).

rosal [ro-sahl'], *m.* (*Bot.*) Rose-bush (planta). **Rosal amarillo**, single yellow rose. **Rosal blanco**, single white rose. **Rosal japonés**, japanese rose.

rosariero [ro-sah-re-ay'-ro], *m.* Maker and seller of rosaries.

rosario [ro-sah'-re-o], *m.* 1. Rosary, a string of beads for praying. 2. The collection of *avemarías* and *padrenuestros* said at once, and counted by the beads of a rosary. 3. An assemblage of people who sing the prayers of the rosary in procession. 4. Chain-pump. 5. (*Coll.*) Backbone. 6. Feminine proper name.

rosarse [ro-sahr'-say], *vr.* V. SONROSEARSE.

rosbif [ros-beef'], *m.* Roast beef. (*Eng.*)

rosca [ros'-cah], *f.* 1. Screw, a mechanical power. 2. Anything round and spiral; spiral motion. 3. A distinctive badge of the scholars in some colleges in Spain. 4. (*Cono Sur*) Pad (para llevar carga). 5. (*Cono Sur*) Card players (naipes). 6. (*Cono Sur*) Noisy argument (discusión). **Rosca de pan**, a round twisted loaf of bread. **Comerse una rosca**, to make it. **Hacer la rosca a uno**, to suck up to somebody.

rosco [ros'-co], *m.* (*Culin.*) Doughnut.

roscón [ros-cone'], *m. aug.* 1. A large screw. 2. A twisted loaf of bread.

rosega [ro-say'-gah], *f.* (*Naut.*) Creeper, grapnel, to recover things fallen into the water.

róseo, sea [ro'-so-o, ah], *a.* Rosy, roseate.

roséola [ro-say'-o-lah], *f.* Roseola, an exanthem commonly without fever, of small rosy spots; false measles, rötheln.

rosero, ra [ro-say'-ro, rah], *m. & f.* Collector of saffron flowers.

roseta [ro-say'-tah], *f.* 1. V. COROLA. Small rose (rosa pequeña. 2. Rowel (de espuela). 3. Rosette (cinta de colores).

rosetón [ro-say-tone'], *m.* 1. A large rose on pieces of architecture and sculpture. 3. (*Aug.*) A large rose. (*Mex.*) Free, gratis.

rosicler [ro-se-clerr'], *m.* 1. Roset, a bright rose color. 2. Rich silver ore, ruby silver.

rosillo, illa [ro-seel'-lyo], *a.* Clear red.

rosita [ro-see'-tah], *f. 1. dim.* A small rose. 2. (*Cono Sur*) earring (pendiente).

rosmaro [ros-mah'-ro], *m.* Walrus, morse, rosmarine.

roso, sa [ro'-so, sah], *a.* Red, rosy. V. ROJO.

rosoli [ro-so'-le], *m.* Rossolis, sundew, a pleasant, sweet spirituous liquor, composed of brandy, sugar, cinnamon, anise, etc.

rosquete [ros-kay'-tay], *m. (Prov.)* A small cake made in a spiral shape.

rosquilla [ros-keel'-lyah], *f.* 1. A kind of very sweet cake made in a spiral shape. 2. Vine fretter.

rostral [ros-trahl'], *a.* 1. V. ROSTRATA. 2. *(Arch.)* Rostral column.

rostrado, da [ros-trah'-do, dah], *a.* Rostral, resembling the beak of a ship.

rostrico, rostrillo [ros-tree'-co, ros-treel'-lyo], *m.* 1. Veil or headdress on images. 2. Small seed pearl.

rostrituerto, ta [ros-tre-too-err'-to, tah], *a.* Showing anger or displeasure in the countenance.

rostro [ros'-tro], *m.* 1. Rostrum, the beak of a ship, and the bill or beak of a bird. 2. Countenance, human face. 3. Aspect of affairs. **A rostro firme**, resolutely, in front of. **Rostro a rostro**, face to face.

rota [ro'-tah], *f.* 1. Rout, defeat. 2. *(Naut.)* Course. 3. Rota, an ecclesiastical court in Catholic countries. 4. V. NUNCIATURA. 5. Rattan, a kind of Indian cane.

rotación [ro-tah-the-on'], *f.* 1. Rotation, circular motion; circumrotation. 2. Revolution of planets.

rotador, ra [ro-tah-dor', rah], *a.* Serving for rotation. *-m. pl.* The rotifera or so-called wheel-animalcules.

rotamente [ro-tah-men-tay], *adv.* Impudently, barefacedly.

rotante [ro-tahn'-tay], *pa.* Rolling, vagrant.

rotar [ro-tar'], *vn.* V. RODAR.

rotativo, va [ro-tah-te'-vo, vah], *a.* Rotating. *-m.* 1. Rotary press. 2. Newspaper (periódico). 3. Revolving light.

roto, ta [ro'-to, tah], *a. & pp. irr.* of ROMPER. 1. Broken, destroyed. 2. Leaky, battered, or pierced. 3. Debauched, lewd, intemperate, ragged. *-m.* Hole (en vestido), torn piece, worn part. **Nunca falta un roto para un descosido**, you can always find a companion in misfortune.

rotograbado [ro-to-grah-bah'-do], *m.* Rotogravure.

rotonda [ro-ton'-dah], *f.* 1. The hindmost of the three parts of a diligence. 2. Rotunda, a circular temple or meeting-room.

rotor [ro-tor'], *m.* Rotor.

rótula [ro'-too-lah], *f.* 1. Kneecap. 2. Lozenge. 3. *(Mech.)* Swivel.

rotulación [ro-too-lah-the-on'], *f.* Labeling.

rotulado [ro-too-lah'-do], *m.* 1. Label. 2. Poster, sign.

rotulador, ra [ro-too-lah-dor', rah], *a.* Labeling, lettering. *-m. & f.* Labeler, letterer.

rotular [ro-too-lar'], *va.* 1. To label (objeto). 2. To self-address.

rotulista [ro-too-lees'-tah], *m.* 1. Poster artist. 2. Sign painter.

rótulo [ro'-too-lo], *m.* 1. Inscription on books and papers, title. 2. Printed bill posted up; show-bill, poster. 3. Certificate of the virtues of one for beatification. 4. List, manifest, of the contents of a chest, of a boat, etc.

rotunda [ro-toon'-dah], *f.* 1. Rotunda, a round building. 2. Round-house for locomotives.

rotundamente [ro-toon-dah-men'-tay], *adv.* 1. Spherically. 2. Explicitly.

rotundidad [ro-toon-de-dahd'], *f.* Roundness, rotundity, sphericity.

rotundo, da [ro-toon'-do, dah], *a.* 1. Round (redondo), circular, round, spherical. 2. Flat (negativa); clear (victoria), convincing.

rotura [ro-too'-rah], *f.* 1. Rupture, fracture, crack (grieta), breakage. 2. *(Agr.)* Breaking up of ground which has never been tilled. 3. Hernia in beasts. 4. Dissoluteness, libertinism.

roturación [ro-too-rah-the-on'], *f.* Plowing of new ground, breaking up ground for tilling.

roya [ro'-yah], *f.* Rust, a disease of corn; mildew red blight.

royal [ro-yah'], *m.* Kind of French linen.

royo, ya [ro'-yo, yah], *a. (Prov.)* Red. V. ROJO.

roza [ro'-thah], *f.* 1. Stubbing, clearing the ground of brambles and bushes. 2. Ground cleared of brambles and bushes.

rozadero [ro-thah-day'-ro], *m.* Stubbing-place; ground cleared of trees.

rozado, da [ro-thah'-do, dah], *a. & pp.* of ROZAR. 1. Stubbed, cleared of brambles and bushes. 2. *(Naut.)* Fretted, galled.

rozador, ra [ro-thah-dor', rah], *m. & f.* Stubber, weeder.

rozadura [ro-thah-doo'-rah], *f.* 1. Friction; rubbing. 2. Gall, a slight wound by fretting off the skin. 3. Clashing, clash.

rozagante [ro-thah-gahn'-tay], *a.* 1. Pompous, showy, trailing on the ground (túnica, vestido). 2. Haughty, lofty, arrogant.

rozamiento [ro-thh-me-en'-to], *m.* Friction; rubbing.

rozar [ro-thar'], *va.* 1. To stub up, to clear the ground of brambles and bushes. 2. To nibble the grabs (ganado). 3. To scrape. 4. To graze (hierba), to touch slightly. 5. To remove the bulging or curvature of a wall. 6. To gall, to hurt by fretting the skin. **Rozar a uno al pasar**, to brush past somebody. *-vn.* To touch slightly against each other. *-vr.* 1. To strike or cut each other (pies). 2. To treat or discourse familiarly. 3. To falter, to stammer. 4. *(Naut.)* To fret, to gall: applied to cables or things which rub against one another. 5. To have a resemblance or connection with something else.

roznar [roth-nar'], *m.* 1. To grind hard things with the teeth (animales). 2. To bray, as an ass.

roznido [roth-nee'-do], *m.* 1. Noise made by the teeth in eating hard things. 2. Braying of an ass.

rozno [roth'-no], *m.* A little ass.

rozo [ro'-tho], *m.* 1. Chip of wood. 2. Stubbing, wooding; rubbing; fretting.

rua [roo'-ah], *f.* 1. Village street. 2. High road.

ruán [roo-ahn'], *m.* 1. V. RUANO. 2. Sort of linen manufactured at Rouen.

ruana [roo-ah'-nah], *f. (Amer. Col.)* V. PONCHO.

ruanete [roo-ah-nay'-tah], *m.* Kind of foreign linen.

ruano, na [roo-ah'-no, nah], *a.* 1. Prancing about the streets (caballos). 2. Sorrel-colored, roan (caballos). 3. Round, of a circular form.

ruante [roo-an'-tay], *a.* 1. Prancing or strutting through the streets; rider. 2. *(Her.)* Spreading the tail (pavos).

ruar [roo-ar'], *m.* 1. To roll through the streets (coche). 2. To strut about the streets, to court the ladies. 3. To ride.

rúbeo, oa [roo'-bay-o, ah], *a.* Ruby, reddish.

rubéola [roo-bay'-o-lah], *f.* Measles.

rubeta [roo-bay'-tah], *f.* Toad.

rubí [roo-bee'], *m.* 1. Ruby, a precious stone of a red color. 2. Red color, redness of the lips. **Rubí de Bohemia**, rosy quartz. **Rubí del Brasil**, red topaz. **Rubí espinela**, spinel ruby, tinged with chromium oxide.

rubia [roo'-be-ah], *f.* 1. *(Bot.)* Madder, a root used by dyers and in medicine. 2. Small red-colored river fish. 3. Blonde, **Rubia de bote**, peroxide blonde. **Rubia platino**, platinum blonde.

rubiáceas [roo-be-ah'-thay-as], *f. pl.* The madder family of plants; rubiceae.

rubial [roo-be-ahl'], *m.* 1. Field planted with madder. 2. District or soil having a red color.

rubicán [roo-be-cahn'], *a.* Rubican, of a bay or sorrel color with white hairs (caballo).

rubicela [roo-be-thay'-lah], *f.* Rubicelle, a red dish-yellow topaz.

rubicundez [roo-be-coon-deth'], *f.* 1. Flush, red color. 2. Ruby color.

rubicundo, da [roo-be-coon'-do, dah], *a.* 1. Golden-red; blonde. 2. Rosy with health. 3. Reddish, rubicund (cara).

rubificar [roo-be-fe-car'], *vn.* To rubify, to make red.

rubín [roo-been'], *m.* Ruby. V. RUBÍ.

rubio, bia [roo'-be-o, ah], *a.* Golden, fair, ruddy.

rubio [roo'-be-o], *m.* Red gurnard.

rubión [roo-be-on'], *a.* Of a slight reddish color: applied to a kind of wheat.

rublo

rublo [roo'-blo], *m.* Rouble, a Russian coin.

rubor [roo-bor'], *m.* 1. Blush, red color of the cheeks, flush. 2. Shame, bashfulness. **Causar rubor a una**, to make somebody blush.

ruborizarse [roo-bo-re-thar'-say], *vr.* To blush, to flush with embarrassment.

ruboroso, sa [roo-bo-roo'-so, sah], *a.* Shameful. *V.* VERGONZOSO.

rúbrica [roo'-bre-cah], *f.* 1. Red mark (señal). 2. Rubric, a peculiar mark or flourish added to one's signature. 3. Rubric, in law and prayer books. 4. *(Met.)* Blood used to attest a truth. **Bajo la rúbrica de**, under the heading of.

rubricante [roo-bre-cahn'-tay], *pa. & a.* Rubifying; rubific.

rubricante [roo-bre-cahn'-tay], *m.* Junior counsel appointed to sign the divisions of the acts or proceedings of the council.

rubricar [roo-bre-car'], *va.* 1. To mark with a red color. 2. To sign with one's peculiar mark or flourish without writing the name. 3. To subscribe, sign, and seal a writing. 4. *(Met.)* To sign anything with one's blood.

rubriquista [roo-bre-kees'-tah], *m.* A person versed in the ceremonies of the church.

rubro, bra [roo'-bro, brah], *a.* Red, reddish; rubric. -*m.* 1. *(LAm.)* Heading title. 2. *(LAm.)* Book-keeping (de cuenta). 3. *(LAm.)* Section, department (sección).

ruc [rooc], *m.* Very large fabulous bird. *V.* ROCHO.

rucio, cia [roo'-the-o, ah], *a.* 1. Bright silver gray (caballos, asnos). 2. *(Coll.)* Light gray (pelo).

ruda [roo'-dah], *f. (Bot.)* Rue.

rudamente [roo'-dah-mén-tay], *adv.* Rudely, roughly, churlishly, loutishly, abruptly, ruggedly.

rudera [roo-day'-rah], *f.* Rubbish, ruins of demolished buildings.

rudeza [roo-day'-thah], *f.* 1. Roughness, asperity or unevenness of surface. 2. Roughness of temper, rudeness, coarseness of behavior and address, churlishness, grossness. 3. Stupidity, dullness.

rudimentario, ria [roo-de-men-tah'-re-o, ah], *a. (Biol.)* Rudimentary, undeveloped.

rudimento [roo-de-men'-to], *m.* 1. *V.* PRINCIPIO. 2. Rudiment, first trace of an organ. -*pl.* Rudiments of a science or art.

rudo, da [roo'-do, dah], *a.* 1. Rude, rough, unpolished (sin labrar), coarse, churlish, clownish. 2. Hard, rigorous, severe. 3. Stupid (estúpido), dull. 4. Simple (sencillo), uncultured; plain (llano).

rueca [roo-ay'-cah], *f.* 1. Distaff for flax. 2. Winding, twisting. 3. *(Naut.)* Fish of a mast or yard.

rueda [roo-ay'-dah], *f.* 1. A wheel. 2. Circle formed by a number of persons (círculo); crown. 3. A round slice of eatables. 4. Short sun-fish. 5. *(For.)* The placing of one prisoner among others in order to obtain recognition. 6. Breaking on the wheel, a torture anciently used. 7. A kind of hoops for feminine attire. 8. The semicircular spread of a peacock's tail (pavo). 9. Turn, time, succession. **Rueda de prensa**, press conference.

ruedecica [roo-ay-day-thee'-cah], **cilla, zuela**, *f. dim.* A small wheel.

ruedo [roo-ay'-do], *m.* 1. Rotation, turning or going around; circuit. 2. Border (borde), selvage, fringe. 3. Plat, mat (esterilla), or rug made of base, and formed into round or square mats. 4. A plush mat. 5. Circumference of anything (contorno). 6. *(Cono Sur)* Luck (suerte). 7. Arena, bullfighting ring.

ruego [roo-ay'-go], *m.* Request, prayer, petition, entreaty, supplication. **A ruego de**, at the request of.

ruejo de Molina [roo-ay'-ho], *m. (Prov.)* Mill-wheel.

ruequecilla [roo-ay-kay-theel'-lyah], *f.* A small distaff.

rufalandaina [roo-fah-lan-dah'-e-nah], *f.* Noisy mirth.

rufalandario, ria [roo-fah-lan-dah'-re-o, ah], *a.* Slovenly, negligent in dress; not clean.

rufián [roo-fe-ahn'], *m.* Ruffian, pimp (chulo), pander, the bully of a brothel.

rufiana [roo-fe-ah'-nah], *f.* Bawd, procuress.

rufianar [roo-fe-ah-nar'], *va.* To pimp, to pander.

rufiancete, cillo [roo-fe-an-thay'-tay], *m. dim.* Little ruffian or pimp.

rufianejo [roo-fe-ah-nay'-ho], *m. dim. V.* RUFIANCETE.

rufianería [roo-fe-ah-nay-ree'-ah], *f.* Pimping. *V.* ALCAHUETERÍA.

rufianesco, ca [roo-fe-ah-nes'-co, cah], *a.* Pimp-like, relating to bawds and pimps.

rufo, fa [roo'-fo, fah], *a.* 1. Carroty, red-haired (pelirrojo). 2. Frizzed, curled.

ruga [roo'-hah], *f.* 1. Wrinkle, corrugation. *V.* ARRUGA. 2. A slight fault.

rugar [roo-gar'], *va.* To wrinkle, to corrugate. *V.* ARRUGAR.

rugby [roog'-be], *m.* Rugby.

rugible [roo-hee'-blay], *a.* Capable of bellowing or roaring.

rugido [roo-hee'-do], *m.* 1. Reprint of a lion. 2. Rumbling in the bowels. **Rugido de tripas**, intestinal rumblings.

rugiente [roo-he-en'-tay], *a.* Bellowing, roaring.

rugimiento [roo-he-me-ayn'-to], *m. V.* RUGIDO.

ruginoso, sa [roo-he-no'-so, sah], *a.* Covered with rust, rusty.

rugir [roo-heer'], *vn.* 1. To roar (león), to bellow (toro); to halloo. 2. To make a noise, to creek, to rustle. -*vr.* To be whispered about.

rugosidad [roo-go-se-dahd'], *f.* The state of being wrinkled or corrugated, rugosity.

rugoso, sa [roo-go'-so, sah], *a.* Rugose, full of wrinkles (arrugado); ridged (desigual).

ruibarbo [roo-e-bar'-bo], *m. (Bot.)* Rhubarb. **Ruibarbo compacto**, thick leaved rhubarb. **Ruibarbo mutante**, nodding rhubarb.

ruido [roo-ee'-do], *m.* 1. Noise, clamor, din (alboroto), clatter; murmur, outcry (grito). 2. Dispute, difference, lawsuit. 3. Rumor, report, empty sound or show. 4. Sound made purposely and for some individual end. **Ser más el ruido que las nueces**, great cry and little wool (more noise than nuts). **Ruido de fondo**, background noise. **No hagas tanto ruido**, don't make so much noise.

ruidosamente [roo-e-do'-sah-men-tay], *adv.* Noisily, loudly.

ruidoso, sa [roo-e-do'-so, sah], *a.* Noisy (estrepitoso), clamorous, obstreperous.

ruin [roo-een'], *a.* 1. Mean (vil), vile, low, despicable, churlish, forlorn; little. 2. Humble, decayed; wicked, malicious. 3. Covetous, avaricious, insidious, treacherous, infamous. 4. Applied to a vicious animal. -*m.* A wicked, infamous person. -*f.* Small nerve in the tail of cats. -*pl.* *(Coll.)* Braid.

ruina [roo-ee'-nah], *f.* 1. Ruin, decline, downfall, destruction (de esperanzas), confusion, overthrow, fall (del imperio). **Será mi ruina**, it will be the ruin of me. -*pl.* Ruins of an edifice. **Ir en ruina**, to be destroyed, to go to ruin. 2. Cause of ruin, decadence.

ruinar [roo-e-nar'], *va.* To ruin, to destroy. *V.* ARRUINAR.

ruindad [roo-in-dahd'], *f.* 1. Meanness (cualidad), baseness, malice. 2. Humility, poverty. 3. Covetousness, avariciousness.

ruinmente [roo-in'-men-tay], *adv.* Basely, meanly.

ruinoso, sa [roo-e-no'-so, sah], *a.* Worthless, ruinous, baneful, destructive.

ruiponce [roo-e-pon'-thay], *m. (Bot.) V.* RAPÓNCHIGO.

ruipóntico [roo-e-pon'-te-co], *m. (Bot.)* Rhubarb, pie-plant, an herb the leaf stalks of which are used in cooking.

ruiseñor [roo-e-say-nyor'], *m. (Orn.)* Nightingale.

rujada [roo-hah'-dah], *f. (Prov. Ar.)* Heavy shower of rain.

rujar [roo-har'], *va. (Prov.)* To irrigate, to bath.

rular [roo-lar'], *vn. (Vulg.)* To roll. *V.* RODAR.

ruleta [roo-lay'-tah], *f.* Roulette, a game of chance.

rulo [roo'-lo], *m.* 1. Ball (pelota), bowl. 2. A conical stone which turns in oil-mills. 3. Roller (rodillo). 4. Hair-curler (del pelo).

ruló [roo-lo'], *m.* A printer's ink-roller.

rumano, na [roo-mah'-no, nah], *a.* Rumanian, belonging to Rumania. -*m.* Rumanian, the Romance tongue of this country.

rumba [room'-bah], *f.* Rumba or rhumba.

rumbadas [room-bah'-dahs], *f. pl. V.* ARRUMBADAS.

rumbo [room'-bo], *m.* 1. Rhumb, a point of the compass. 2. Road (camino), route, way. 3. Course of a ship. 4. Pomp, ostentation, pageantry. 5. Course of events (tendencia); line of conduct (conducta). 6. Generosity (liberalidad); lavish display (boato). 7. *(CAm.)* Party (fiesta). 8. *(Cono Sur)* Cut (herida). **Ir con rumbo a**, to be heading for. **Viajar con rumbo**, to travel in style.

rumbosamente [room-bo'-sah-men-tay], *adv.* Pompously, magnificently, liberally.

rumboso, sa [room-bo'-so, sah], *a.* Pompous, magnificent, splendid, liberal.

rumia [roo'-me-ah], *f.* Rumination, chewing the cud.

rumiador, ra [roo-me-ah-dor', rah], *m. & f. & a.* Ruminator; mediator; ruminant.

rumiadura [roo-me-ah-doo'-rah], *f.* Rumination.

rumiante [roo-me-ahn'-tay], *pa. & a.* Ruminant; musing.

rumiar [roo-me-ar'], *va.* 1. To ruminate, to chew the cud. 2. To brood upon a subject (asunto); to muse, to meditate.

rumión, na [roo-me-on', nah], *a.* Ruminating much.

rumo [roo'-mo], *m.* The first hoop of the head of a cask.

rumor [roo-mor'], *m.* 1. Rumor, report, hearsay. 2. A gentle sound, murmur (murmullo).

rumorcico, illo, ito [roo-mor-thee'-co], *m. dim.* A flying report.

rumorearse [roo-mo-ray-ar'-say], *vr.* **Se rumorea que...**, it is rumored that...

rumoreo [roo-mo-ray'-o], *m.* Murmuring, rumoring.

rumoroso, sa [roo-mo-ro'-so, sah], *a.* Causing rumor.

runas [roo'-nas], *f. pl.* Runes, alphabetical characters employed by the ancient Scandinavians.

runcho [roon'-cho], *m. (Ec. Colom.)* Opossum.

runfla [roon'-flah], *f.* Series, multitude (multitud), number of things, gang (pandilla).

rúnico, ca [roo'-ne, co, cah], *a.* Runic, relating to the Goths, Scandinavians, and other nations of ancient Europe, or their language.

runrún [roon-roon'], *m. (Coll.)* Rumor (rumor), report. *V.* RUMOR.

ruñar [roo-nyar'], *va.* To groove the ends of staves for the heads and bottoms of burrels, to fit.

rupia [roo'-pe-ah], *f.* 1. Rupee, the standard monetary unit of India, Pakistan, Bhutan, Sri Lanka, the Maldive, the Seychelles and Nepal. 2. A skin disease characterized by the formation of large crusts.

rupicabra [roo-pe-cah'-brah], *f.* Chamois-goat.

ruptil [roop-teel'], *a. (Bot.)* Ruptile.

ruptura [roop-too'-rah], *f.* Rupture. *V.* ROTURA.

ruqueta [roo-kay'-tah], *f. (Bot.) V.* JARAMAGO.

rural [roo-rahl'], *a.* Rural, country. -*m. (Cono Sur)* Estate car, station wagon.

ruralmente [roo-rahl'-men-tay], *adv.* Rurally.

rus [roos], *m. V.* ZUMAQUE.

rusco, ca [roos'-co, cah], *a.* Rude, peevish, forward. *V.* BRUSCO.

rusiente [roo-se-en'-tay], *a.* Turning red by the action of fire.

ruso, sa [roo'-so, sah], *a.* Russian. -*m.* The Slavic tongue spoken in Russia.

rustical [roos-te-cahl'], *a.* Rustical, rural, wild.

rústicamente [roos'-te-cah-men-tay], *adv.* Rustically, rudely, boisterously.

rusticano, na [roos-te-cah'-no, nah], *a.* 1. Wild: said of the radish and other plants. 2. Rural.

rusticar [roos-te-car'], *vn.* To go to the country, to pass time there; to rusticate.

rusticidad [roos-te-the-dahd'], *f.* Rusticity, simplicity; rudeness, clownishness, clumsiness, crudity (grosería), coarseness (ordinariez).

rústico, ca [roos'-te-co, cah], *a.* 1. Rustic belonging to the country (del campo). 2. Rustic, unmannerly (sin educación), clownish. **En rústica**, in paper covers, unbound.

r'stico [roos'-te-co], *m.* Rustic, peasant, country clown.

rustiquez, rustiqueza [roos-te-keth'], *f.* Rusticity. *V.* RUSTICIDAD.

rustro [roos'-tro], *m. V.* RUMBO.

ruta [roo'-tah], *f.* Route, itinerary.

rutilante [roo-te-lahn'-tay], *a.* Brilliant, fleshing.

rutilar [roo-te-lar'], *vn. (Poet.)* To radiate, to shine, to be splendid.

rútilo, la [roo'-te-lo, lah], *a.* Of a bright yellow or orange color.

rutina [roo-tee'-nah], *f.* Routine, custom, habit.

rutinario, ria [roo-te-nah'-re-o, ah], *a.* Done by routine, routinary.

rutinero, ra [roo-te-nay'-ro, rate], *a.* Found of routine, routinist.

ruzafa [roo-thah'-tah], *f.* Garden, park.

S

s [sy'-say] is the twentieth letter in the order of the Spanish alphabet. It has always a harsh, hissing sound, like *ss* in English as *dispossess*. No Spanish word begins with *s* followed by a consonant: in all words derived from other languages, the *s* is either omitted or preceded by *e*, as, **ciencia**, science; **espíritu**, spirit; **Escipión**, Scipio. *S* is never doubled. **-S.** is a contraction for **Señor**, Mr. or Sir; **Santo.** Saint, **Su, sus**, his, her, their, or your; **Sud** or **Sur**, south; **S. O.**, south-west, **S. E.** south-east; **S. M., Su Majestad, SS. AA., sus Altezas;** S. S. S.; **Smo.** stands for **Santísimo**, very holy. In commerce s/c stands for **Su cuenta** (your account).

sábado [sah'-bah-do], *m.* 1. Saturday. 2. Sabbath, among the Jews. **Sábado de Gloria**, Easter Saturday.

sabalera [sah-bah-lay'-rah], *f.* Kind of fire-grate in furnaces.

sabalero [sah-bah-lay'-ro], *m.* Shad-fisher.

sábalo [sah'-bah-lo], *m.* Shad.

sábana [sah'-bah-nah], *f.* 1. Sheet for a bed (de cama). 2. Altar-cloth. **Pegársele a uno las sábanas**, to rise late (to lie abed) from laziness.

sabana [sah'-bah-nah], *f. (Amer. Cuba)* Savannah, an extended plain.

sabandija [sah-ban-dee'-hah], *f.* Any disgusting insect or reptile (insecto, reptil).

sabanear [sah-bah-nay-ar'], *va.* 1. To scour the savannah in order to find an animal or to collect the herd. 2. *(CAm.)* To flatter (halagar). 3. *(CAm. Carib.)* To pursue, to chase (perseguir).

sabanero, ra [sah-bah-nay'-ro, rah], *a.* 1. Dwelling in a savannah. 2. Relative to a savannah.

sabanero [sah-bah-nay'-ro], *m.* The man on horseback who takes care of the cattle grazing on the plains.

sabanilla [sah-bah-neel'-lyah], *f.* 1. *(Dim.)* A small sheet. 2. A short piece of linen. 3. Altar-cloth; napkin.

sabañón [sah-bah-nyone'], *m.* Chilblain.

sabatario [sah-bah-tah'-re-o], *a.* Applied to the Jews who keep Saturday for their Sabbath; Sabbatarian.

sabático, ca [sah-bah'-te-co, cah], *a.* 1. Sabbatical, belonging to Saturday, or the Jewish Sabbath. 2. Every seventh year among the Jews.

sabatina [sah-bah-tee'-nah], *f.* 1. Divine service performed on Saturday. 2. A literary exercise performed by students on Saturday evening.

sabatino, na [sah-bah-tee'-no, nah], *a.* Performed on Saturday or belonging to it.

sabedor

sabedor, ra [sah-bay-dor', rah], *m. & f.* One who knows or is informed of something.

sabeísmo [sah-bay-ees'-mo], *m.* Ancient fire-worship.

sabeliano, na [sah-bay-le-ah'-no, nah], *a. & n.* Sabellian, relating to Sabellius or Sabellianism. **sabeo, bea** [sah-bay'-o, ah], *a.* Sabaean, Arabian, of Sheba.

saber [sah-berr'], *va.* 1. To know, to have knowledge of. 2. To experience, to know by experience. 3. To be able, to be possessed of talents or abilities: to be learned or knowing. **Saber mucho latín**, to be very sagacious and prudent. 4. To subject, to submit. 5. To fit, to suit, 6. To relish, to savor, to taste. 7. To use, to practice customarily; to be in the habit. 8. To resemble, to appear like. 9. *V.* PODER. **El dice que no sabe escribir**, he says that he cannot write. -*v. imp.* To have a taste of. **Hacer saber**, to make known, to communicate. **Sabérselo todo**, in an ironical sense, to know everything: applied to assuming, intolerant persons. **No se sabe**, it is not known. **No sabe en dónde tiene la cara**, he does not know his duty. **No saber de sí**, to be overwhelmed with occupation. **No sé que**, I don't know what; an indefinable something. **Sabe que rabia**, it has a sharp taste. **Cuando lo supe**, when I heard about it. **Vete a saber**, your guess is as good as mine. **Tiene que saber contenerse**, he must control himself. -*vn.* **Saber a**, to taste of. **Esto sabe a queso**, this tastes of cheese. -*vr.* **Se sabe que…**, it is known that… **Por fin se supo el secreto**, finally the secret was revealed.

saber [sah-berr'], *m.* 1. Learning, knowledge, lore. *V.* SABIDURÍA. 2. Science, faculty.

sabiamente [sah'-be-ah-men-tay], *adv.* Wisely (prudentemente), knowingly, learnedly, sagely.

sabicú [sah-be-coo'], *m. (Amer. Cuba)* A handsome tree of Cuba, belonging to the pulse family, having white fragrant flowers and a hard wood.

sabidillo, lla [sah-be-deel'-lyo, lyah], *a. dim.* of SABIDO. Commonly applied to persons who have pretensions to learning and wisdom.

sabido, da [sah-bee'-do, dah], *a. & pp.* Of SABER. Learned, well-informed.

sabiduría [sah-be-doo-ree'-ah], *f.* 1. Learning, knowledge, wisdom, sapience. 2. *V.* NOTICIA.

sabiendas (A) [sah sah-be-en'-das], *adv.* Knowingly (sabiendo) and prudently, consciously (con intención). **A sabiendas de que…**, knowing full well that….

sabiente [sah-be-en'-tay], *pa.* Sapient, knowing.

sabihondez [sah-be-on-deth'], *f.* Assumption of being wise, without being really so.

sabihondo, da [sah-be-on'-do, dah], *a.* Presuming to decide difficult questions without sufficient knowledge.

sabina [sah-bee'-nah], *f. (Bot.)* Savin or sabine.

sabinar [sa-be-nar'], *m.* A clump of sabines.

sabino, na [sah-bee'-no, nah], *a.* 1. Applied to horses or mules of a mixed white and chestnut color. 2. Sabine, of the Sabines, neighbors of the ancient Romans.

sabio, bia [sah'-be-o, ah], *a.* Sage, wise (juicioso), learned (docto), sapient, knowing; cunning.

sabio, bia [sah'-be-o], *m. & f.* A sage, a wise person.

sablazo [sah-blah'-tho], *m.* 1. Stroke with a sabre. 2. Sponging (gorronería). **Dar un sablazo a uno**, to touch somebody for a loan.

sable [sah'-blay], *m.* 1. Sabre, cutlass. 2. *(Her.)* Sable, black.

sablear [sah-blay-ahr'], *va.* **Sablear algo a uno**, to scrounge something from somebody.

sablón [sah-blone'], *m.* Coarse sand, gravel.

saboca, *f. (Prov.) V.* SABOGA.

saboga [sah-bo'-gah], *f.* A species of shad.

sabogal [sah-bo-gahl], *a.* Applied to the net for catching shad.

saboneta [sah-bo-nay'-tah], *f.* A hunting-case watch.

sabor [sah-bor'], *m.* 1. Relish, taste, savor. 2. Pleasure; desire. **A sabor**, at pleasure; to the taste; according to one's wish. **Sin sabor**, tasteless.

saborear [sah-bo-ray-ar'], *va.* 1. To give a relish: to give a zest. 2. To engage one's affections; to make one embrace our opinion. 3. To flavor, to add a flavor to. **Saborear el triunfo**, to enjoy one's triumph. -*vr.* 1. To enjoy eating and drinking with peculiar pleasure. 2. To be pleased or delighted.

saboreo [sah-bo-ray'-o], *m. V.* PALADERO.

sabotaje [sah-bo-tah'-hay], *m.* Sabotage.

sabotear [sah-bo-tay-ar'], *va.* To sabotage.

saboyana [sah-bo-yah'-nah], *f.* 1. A kind of wide petticoat. 2. A delicious paste of a particular composition.

saboyano, na [sah-bo-yah'-no, nah], *a.* Of Savoy, Savoyard.

sabrosamente [sah-bro-sah-men'-tay], *adv.* Pleasantly, tastefully.

sabrosico, ica, illo, illa, ito, ita [sah-bro-see'-co], *a. dim.* A little savory.

sabroso, sa [sah-bro'-so, sah], *a.* 1. Savory, palatable, salted, saltish. 2. Delightful, pleasurable to the mind. 3. Solid (libro). 4. Salty, daring (cuento, chiste). 5. *(And. Carib.)* Lovely, nice, pleasant (agradable). 6. *(And. Carib. Mex.)* Talkative (parlanchín). 7. *(Mex.)* Big-headed (fanfarrón).

sabucal [sah-boo-cahl'], *m.* Clump of willows.

sabuco [sah-boo'-co], *m. V.* SAÚCO.

sabuesa [sah-boo-ay'-sah], *f.* Bitch, of a hound or bangle.

sabueso [sah-boo-ay'-so], *m.* Hound, bloodhound, beagle, harehound, foxhound.

sábula [sah'-boo-la], *m.* Gravel, coarse sand.

sabuloso, sa [sah-boo-lo'-so, sah], *a.* Sabulous, gritty, sandy, gravelly.

saburra [sah-boor'-rah], *f.* Accumulation of matters in the stomach, in consequence of bad digestion, saburra.

saburral [sah-boor-rahl'], *a.* Saburral, relating to foulness of the stomach.

saca [sah'-cah], *f.* 1. Exportation, extraction; the net of extracting or exporting. 2. Suck, a large bag made of coarse stuff. 3. First authorized register of a sale. 4. *(Prov.)* Valuation, computation; agreement. **Estar de saca**, (a) to be on sale; (b) to be marriageable: spoken of women.

sacabala [sah-ca-bah'-lah], *f. (Surg.)* A kind of bullet-extracting forceps.

sacabalas [sah-cah-bah'-las], *m.* A kind of forceps for drawing a ball from a great gun.

sacabocado, sacabocados [sah-ca-bo-cah'-do], *m.* 1. A hollow punch. 2. Anything that cuts out a round piece. 3. Anything that effects one's purpose.

sacabotas [sah-cah-bo'-tas], *m.* Bootjack.

sacabrocas [sah-cah-bro'-cas], *m.* Pincers used by shoemakers.

sacabuche [sah-cah-boo'-chas], *m.* 1. *(Naut.)* A tube or pipe which scribes as a pump. 2. Sackbut, a musical wind-instrument. 3. Player on the sackbut. 4. Nickname of a despicable person.

sacacorchos [sah-cah-cor'-chos], *m.* Corkscrew.

sacacuartos [sah-cah-coo-ahr'-tos], *m. V.* SACADINERO.

sacada [sah-cah'-dah], *f.* District separated from a province.

sacadilla [sah-cah-deel'-lyah], *f.* Noise made to rouse game.

sacadinero, sacadineros [sah-cah-de-nay'-ro], *m. (Coll.)* Catchpenny; expensive toys or baubles.

sacador, ra [sah-cah-do', rah], *m. & f.* Extracter, exporter.

sacadura [sah-cah-doo'-rah], *f.* 1. A sloping cut, by which tailors make clothes fit better. 2. *(And. Cono Sur)* Extraction.

sacafilásticas [sah-cah-fe-lahs'-te-cas], *f.* A kind of iron used by artillery-men to take the spikes out of guns.

sacafondo [sah-cah-fon'-do], *m.* A cooper's auger.

sacaliña [sah-cah-lee'-nyah], *f.* 1. An ancient kind of dart. 2. A knack of tricking a person out of something; a wheedle to get one's money. *V.* SOCALIÑA.

sacamanchas [sah-cah-mahn'-chas], *m.* 1. He who takes out spots or stains from clothes. 2. *(Coll.)* He who publishes another's faults. 3. Cleaning material.

sacamiento [sah-cah-me-en'-to], *m.* Taking a thing from the place where it is; taking or drawing out.

sacamolero [sah-cah-mo-lay-ro], *m. V.* SACAMUELAS.

sacamuelas [sah-cah-moo-ay'-las], *m.* 1. Tooth-drawer, dentist (dentista). 2. Anything which causes a shedding of teeth. 3. Chatterer (parlanchín).

sacanabo [sah-cah-nah'-bo], *m. (Naut.)* Pump-hook.

sacanete [sah-cah-nay'-tay], *m.* Lansquenet, a game at cards.

sacapelotas [sah-cah-pay-lo'-tas], *m.* 1. Nickname given to common people. 2. Ancient instrument for extracting balls.

sacapotras [sah-cah-po'-tras], *m.* Nickname of a bad surgeon.

sacapuntas [sah-cah-poon'-tahs], *m.* Pencil sharpener.

sacar [sah-car'], *va.* 1. To extract, to get out, to draw out, to remove, to take out, to put out of place. 2. To dispossess of an employment or office, to except or exclude. 3. To manufacture (producto), to produce. 4. To imitate, to copy (copia). 5. To clear, to free; to place in safety. 6. To find out, to resolve, to know; to dissolve; to discover, to insert. 7. To pull out, to eradicate, to take, to extort, to sack. 8. To brood, to hatch eggs (huevos). 9. To compel to bring forth what was hidden; to show (cualidad), to manifest. 10. To excite passion or anger. **Esa pasión lo saca de sí,** this passion carries him beside himself. 11. To deduce, to infer; to deride (deducir). 12. To ballot, to draw lots. 13. To procure, to obtain (conseguir); to gain at play. 14. To throw a ball, making it bounce on the ground. 15. To produce (obra), to create, to invent. 16. To extend, to enlarge. 17. To buy in a shop. 18. To transcribe, to copy. 19. To appear or go out with anything new. 20. To carry corn to be thrashed. 21. To draw a sword, bayonet, etc. 22. It is used instead of *salir con;* as, **Hemos sacado buen tiempo,** we set out with fine weather. *V.* TRAER. 23. To cite, to name, to quote. **Sacar a bailar,** *(Coll.)* to name or cite unnecessarily any person or thing not alluded to in conversation. 24. To injure, to impair: applied to things which affect the beauty, health, etc. 25. To obtain by cunning and craft. 26. To put on (lustre). 27. To mention (en periódico). 28. *(And. CAm.)* To flatter (lisonjear). 29. *(And. Mex.)* **Sacar algo a uno,** to reproach somebody for something. **Sacar agua,** to draw water. **Sacar a bailar a una señora,** to invite a lady to dance. **Sacar en claro** or **en limpio,** to clear up all doubts, to come to a conclusion. **Sacar fruto,** to reap the fruit of one's labor. **Sacar a luz,** to print, to publish; to develop, to exhibit. **Sacar apodos,** to call nicknames. **Sacar el pecho,** to come up to the breast. *(Met.)* To stand up in defence of a person. **Sacar la cara,** to present oneself by proxy. **Sacar la espina,** to eradicate an evil. **Sacar mal la cuenta,** to turn out unfavorably. **Sacar las uñas,** to avail oneself of every means in an emergency. **Sacar una información a uno,** to get information out of somebody. **Sacar la lengua,** to stick one's tongue out. **Sacan 200 coches diarios,** they make 200 cars a day. **Nos quiso sacar una foto,** he wanted to take a photo of us. **Han sacado 35 diputados,** they have got 35 members. **Sacar faltas a uno,** to point out somebody's defects. **Sacar adelante,** to bring up (niño).

sacarífero, ra [sah-cah-ree'-fay-ro, rah], *a.* Sugar-producing.

sacarificación [sah-cah-re-fe-cah-the-on'], *f.* Conversion into sugar.

sacarina Mexah-cah-ree'-nah], *f.* Saccharin, artificial sweetener.

sacarino, na [sah-cah-ree'-no, nah], *a.* Saccharine.

sacaroideo, ea [sah-cah-roi-day'-o, ah], *a.* Like sugar.

sacarol [sah-cah-rohl'], *m.* Sugar as an excipient.

sacarímetro, sacarómetro [sah-cah-ree'-mah-tro], *m.* Saccharimeter.

sacatapón [sah-cah-tah-pone'], *m.* Corkscrew; bung-drawer.

sacate [sah-cah'-tay], *m. (Mex.)* Grass, herb; hay.

sacatrapos [sah-cah-trah'-pos], *m.* 1. Worm for drawing the wad of a firelock. 2. One who obtains what he wants by artifice.

sacelación [sah-thay-lah-the-on'], *f. (Med.)* Application of small bags of heating materials to a diseased part.

sacelo [sah-thay'-lo], *m.* Chapel or hermitage among the Romans.

sacerdocio [sah-ther-do'-the-o], *m.* Priesthood, ministry.

sacerdotal [sah-ther-do-tahl'], *a.* Sacerdotal, ministerial.

sacerdote [sah-ther-do'-tay], *m.* Priest, clergyman, minister.

sacerdotisa [sah-ther-do-tee'-sah], *f.* Priestess.

saciable [sah-the-ah'-blay], *a.* Satiable, that may be satiated.

saciar [sah-the-ar'], *va.* 1. To satiate, to cloy. 2. To gratify desire (deseo). 3. To satisfy (anhelo). *-vr.* To satiate oneself.

saciedad [sah-the-ay-dahd'], *f.* Satiety. **Demostrar algo hasta la saciedad,** to prove something up to the hilt.

saciña [sah-thee'-nyah], *f. (Bot.)* A kind of willow.

saco [sah'-co], *m.* 1. Sack, bag (bolso). **Sacos vacíos,** readymade bags. 2. A coarse stuff worn by country people. 3. Coarse cloth worn as penance. 4. Anything which includes within itself many other things. 5. Pillage, sack, plunder; heap. *V.* SAQUEO. 6. Long coat (prenda). 7. Nick (cárcel). **A saco,** sacking, plundering. **No echar una cosa en saco roto,** not to be heedless of advice, not to waste an opportunity. 6. Sagum, short, round jacket worn by Roman soldiers. (Note. —The fourth acceptation is commonly taken in an unfavorable sense.) **Saco de arena,** sandbag. **Saco de viaje,** traveling bag.

sacra [sah'-crah], *f.* Each of the three tablets on the altar, which the priest, in saying mass, may read without opening the missal.

sacramental [sah-crah-men-tahl'], *a.* Sacramental. *-m. & f.* Individual or confraternity destined to the worship of the sacrament of the altar.

sacramentalmente [sah-crah-men-tahl'-men-tay], *adv.* Sacramentally; in confession.

sacramentar [sah-crah-men-tar'], *va.* To administer the sacraments. *-vn. V.* JURAMENTAR. *-vr.* To transubstantiate Christ into the eucharist.

sacramentario [sah-crah-men-tah'-re-o], *a.* Applied to heretics who deny the real presence in the eucharist.

sacramente [sah'-crah-men-tay], *adv. V.* SAGRADAMENTE.

sacramento [sah-crah-men'-to], *m.* 1. Sacrament. 2. *V.* MISTERIO. 3. Sacrament, Christ transubstantiated in the host. **Sacramento del altar,** the eucharist.

sacratísimo, ma [sah-crah-tee'-se-mo, mah], *a. sup.* of SAGRADO.

sacre [sah'-cray], *m.* 1. *(Orn.)* Saker, a large lanner falcon. 2. Small cannon.

sacrificadero [sah-cre-fe-cah-day'-ro], *m.* Place where a sacrifice is performed.

sacrificador [sah-cre-fe-cah-dor'], *m.* Sacrificer, sacrificator.

sacrificante [sah-cre-fe-cahn'-tay], *pa. & a.* Sacrificing, hazarding, sacrificial, sacrificatory.

sacrificar [sah-cre-fe-car'], *va.* 1. To sacrifice, to offer or perform a sacrifice. 2. To pay homage. 3. To sacrifice, to destroy or give up for the sake of something else. 4. To sacrifice, to expose to hazard and danger. *-vr.* 1. To devote oneself to God. 2. To submit, to conform oneself to.

sacrificio [sah-cre-fee'-the-o], *m.* 1. Sacrifice, the act of offering to heaven; offering. 2. Sacrifice, submission, obsequiousness; obedience, compliance. 3. Sacrifice, anything destroyed or quitted for the sake of something else. **Sacrificio del altar,** sacrifice of the mass. 4. Any dangerous surgical operation.

sacrílegamente [sah-cree'-lay-gah-men-tay], *m.* Sacrilegiously.

sacrilegio [sah-cre-lay'-he-o], *m.* Sacrilege; church-robbing, pecuniary punishment for sacrilege.

sacrílego, ga [sah-cree'-lay-go, gah], *a.* Sacrilegious.

sacrismoche, cho [sah-cris-mo'-chay, cho], *m.* In jocular style, a man in a ragged black coat.

sacristán [sah-cris-tahn'], *m.* 1. Sacristan, sexton, clerk. 2. Hoop formerly worn by women.

sacristana [sah-cris-tah'-nah], *f.* 1. Sacristan or sexton's wife. 2. Nun, or lay woman who provides things necessary for church service.

sacristancillo, ito [sah-cris-tahn-thel'-lyo], *m. dim.* A little sexton or clerk.

sacristanía [sah-cris-tah-nee'-ah], f. Office of a sexton.

sacristía [sah-cris-tee'-ah], f. 1. Sacristy, vestry. 2. Office and employment of a sacristan or sexton. 3. *(Coll.)* Stomach.

sacro, cra [sah'-cro, crah], a. Holy, sacred. V. SAGRADO. **Fuego sacro**, St. Anthony's fire. **Hueso sacro**, the sacrum.

sacrosanto, ta [sah-cro-sahn'-to, tah], a. Sacred, consecrated, very holy.

sacudida [sah-coo-dee'-dah], f. 1. The act of shaking off or rejecting anything, jerk (tirón), shock (de terremoto), blast (de explosión), jolt (choque). **Sacudida eléctrica**, electric shock. **Dar una sacudida a una alfombra**, to beat a carpet. 2. *(Fig.)* Violent change; sudden jolt.

sacudidamente [sah-coo-dee'-dah-men-tay], adv. Rejectingly.

sacudido, da [sah-coo-dee'-do, dah], a. & pp. of SACUDIR. 1. Harsh, indocile, intractable. 2. Unembarrassed, resolved.

sacudido [sah-coo-dee'-do], m. Spanish step in dancing.

sacudidor [sah-coo-de-dor'], m. 1. Shaker, one who shakes off. 2. Instrument for beating or cleansing.

sacudidura [sah-coo-de-doo'-rah], f. Dusting, cleansing.

sacudimiento [sah-coo-de-me-en'-to], m. Act of shaking off or rejecting.

sacudir [sah-coo-deer'], va. 1. To shake (árbol, edificio, persona, tierra), to jerk (cuerda), to hustle. 2. To dart, to throw, to discharge; to beat (como castigo), to chastise with blows. 3. To remove, to separate. 4. *(Naut.)* To flap in the wind. 5. To shake (conmover). **Una tremenda emoción sacudió a la multitud**, a great wave of excitement ran through the crowd. **Sacudir a uno**, to beat somebody up. *-vr.* To reject with disdain, to turn away in a harsh and violent manner.

sacha [sah'-chah], f. A garden hoe.

sachadura [sah-chah-doo'-rah], f. Hoeing or turning up the ground with a hoe or dibble.

sachar [sah-char'], va. To turn the ground with a hoe or dibble.

sacho [sah'-cho], m. A hoe.

sadismo [sah-dees'-mo], m. Sadism.

saduceísmo [sah-doo-thay-ees'-mo], m. Sadduceeism, Sadducism.

saduceo, ea [sah-doo-thay'-o, ah], a. Sadducean.

saeta [sah-ay'-tah], f. 1. Arrow, dart. 2. Cock of a sundial, gnomon; hand of a watch or clock (de reloj). 3. Magnetic needle. 4. Bud of a vine. 5. *(Ast.)* A northern constellation. 6. *pl.* Moral sentence or couplet of missionaries; pious ejaculations. 7. *(Mus.)* Sacred song in flamenco style sung during Holy Week processions.

saetada [sah-ay-tah'-dah], f. **saetazo** [sah-ay-tah'-tho], m. Arrow-wound.

saetear [sah-ay-tay-ahr'], va. V. ASAETEAR.

saetera [sah-ay-tay'-rah], f. 1. Loop-hole in turrets and old walls, through which fire-arms are discharged. 2. A small grated window in prisons.

saetero, ra [sah-ay-tay'-ro, rah], a. 1. Relating to arrows. 2. Applied to a honey-comb made in a right line.

saetero [sah-ay-tay'-ro], m. Archer, bowman.

saetía [sah-ay-tee'-ah], f. 1. *(Naut.)* Settee, a vessel with lateen sails, used in the Mediterranean. 2. Loophole. V. SAETERA.

saetilla [sah-ay-teel'-lyah], f. dim. 1. Small arrow or dart. 2. Small magnetic needle. 3. Hand of a watch. 4. Moral sentence.

saetín [sah-ay-teen'], m. 1. Mill-race through which water runs from the dam to the wheel of a mill (molino). 2. Peg, pin, tack. 3. *(Com.)* Sateen, a variety of plain satin.

saetón [sah-ay-tone'], m. Dart, a sharp-pointed weapon from a crossbow.

sáfico, ca [sah'-fe-co, cah], a. Sapphic: applied to a kind of verse of five feet.

safio [sah'-fe-o], m. *(Prov.)* V. CONGRIO.

safra [sah'-frah], f. *(Cuba)* The season for cutting the sugarcane, and boiling its juice for sugar. V. ZAFRA.

safre [sah'-fray], m. Saffre, cobalt blue. V. ZAFRE.

saga [sah'-gah], f. 1. Witch. 2. Saga, a primitive mythological tradition or legend of Scandinavia.

sagacidad [sah-gah-the-dahd'], f. 1. Sagacity, quickness of scent in dogs. 2. Sagaciousness, penetration.

sagapeno [sah-gah-pay'-no], m. Sagapenum or gum sagapen, a resinous juice.

sagatí [sah-gah-tee'], **saetí**, m. Sagathee, a kind of woollen cloth like serge.

sagaz [sah-gath'], a. 1. Sagacious, quick of scent (perros). 2. Sagacious, discerning, far-sighted, farseeing, prescient, keen-witted.

sagazmente [sah-gath-men-tay], adv. Sagaciously.

sagita [sah-hee'-tah], f. 1. The versed sine of an arc, sagitta. 2. The height of an arch.

sagital [sah-he-tahl'], a. 1. Sagittal belonging to an arrow, sagittated. 2. *(Anat.)* Sagittal: applied to a suture of the skull.

sagitario [sah-he-tah'-re-o], m. 1. Archer. 2. Sagittarius, sign in the zodiac.

sagma [sahg'-mah], f. *(Arch.)* Measure taken of many members, as of a cornice.

sago [sah'-go], m. A loose, wide greatcoat. V. SAYO.

sagradamente [sah-grah-dah'-men-tay], adv. Sacredly, inviolably, religiously.

sagrado, da [sah-grah'-do, dah], a. 1. Sacred, consecrated; venerable, holy. 2. Cursed, execrable.

sagrado [sah-grah'-do], m. 1. Asylum, a sacred place where debtors or malefactors take refuge. 2. Asylum, haven or refuge, even though not sacred.

sagrariero [sah-grah-re-ay'-ro], m. Keeper of relics.

sagrario [sah-grah'-re-o], m. 1. Place in a church wherein consecrated things are deposited. 2. Cibary, the place where the consecrated host is kept.

sagú, or **sagui** [sah-goo', sah'-gee], m. Sago, a farinaceous food obtained from various Asiatic palms.

ságula [sah'-goo-lah], f. *(Prov.)* A small frock. V. SAYUELO.

saguntino, na [sah-goon-tee'-no, nah], a. Native of or belonging to Saguntum.

sahina [sah-ee'-nah], f. V. ZAHINA.

sahornarse [sah-or-nar'-say], vr. To be excoriated.

sahorno [sah-or'-no], m. Excoriation.

sahumado, da [sah-oo-mah'-do, dah], a. & pp. of SAHUMAR. Fumigated; select apposite, proper.

sahumador [sah-oo-mah-dor'], m. 1. Perfumer. 2. A perfuming-pot, used to impregnate something with a sweet scent.

sahumadura [sah-oo-mah-doo'-rah], f. 1. The act of perfuming with a sweet scent. 2. *(Naut.)* Fumigation in ships.

sahumar [sah-oo-mar'], va. 1. To perfume (incensar). 2. To fumigate, to smoke (fumigar), to fume.

sahumerio [sah-oo-may'-re-o], m. 1. Smoke, vapor, steam, fumigation. 2. The medical application of fumes to parts of the body. 3. Aromatics burnt for perfumes.

sahumo [sah-oo'-mo], m. Smoke, steam, vapor. V. SAHUMERIO.

saíca [sah-ee'-cah], f. Saick, a kind of Turkish vessel.

saín [sah-een'], m. Grease or fat of an animal; dirt on clothes.

saína [sah-ee'-nah], f. V. ALCANDÍA.

sainar [sah-e-nar'], va. To fatten animals.

sainete [sah-e-nay'-tay], m. 1. A kind of farce or short dramatic composition. 2. Flavor, relish, zest. 3. A high-flavored sauce. 4. Any delicate bit of a fine taste. 5. Anything pleasing or engaging. 6. Taste or elegance in dress.

sainetear [sah-e-nay-tay-ar'], vn. To act farces.

sainetillo [sah-e-nay-teel'-lyo], m. dim. A slight relish or flavor.

saíno [sah-ee'-no], m. A kind of West Indian hog.

saja, sajadura [sah'-hah, sah-hah-doo'-rah], f. Scarification.

sajar [sah-har'], va. To scarify.

sajelar [sah-hay-lar'], va. Among potters, to sift and to clean the clay.

sajón, na [sah-hone', nah], a. Saxon.

sal [sahl], *f.* 1. Salt, common salt. 2. *(Chem.)* Salt, a compound of a base and an acid. 3. Wit, facetiousness. 4. Grace, charm, pep. 5. *(Fig. LAm.)* Misfortune, piece of bad luck. **Sal gema**, rock salt. **Sal y pimienta**, salt and pepper. **Sal gorda**, kitchen salt. **Sal de fruta**, fruit salts.

sala [sah'-lah], *f.* 1. Hall, the first large room in a house (cuarto grande). 2. Hall where judges meet to try and decide causes (de edificio público). 3. Board of commissioners. 4. A public meeting, a public entertainment. **Sala de muestras**, showroom. **Sala de estrados**, hall or court of justice. **Sala de espectáculos**, concert room. **Sala de fiestas**, dance hall. **Sala de pruebas**, fitting room.

salacidad [sah-lah-the-dahd'], *f.* Salacity, lechery.

salacot [sah-lah-cot'], *m.* A Philippine hat in the shape of a parasol, and with many trimmings.

saladamente [sah-lah-dah-men-tay], *adv.* Wittily, facetiously; saltly.

saladar [sah-lah-dar'], *m.* Salt-marsh.

saladero [sah-lah-day'-ro], *m.* Salting-place, salting-tub.

saladillo [sah-lah-deel'-lyo], *m. dim.* of SALADO. Fresh bacon half-salted.

salado, da [sal'-lah'-do, dah], *a. & pp.* of SALAR. 1. Salted, salty. 2. Witty (gracioso), facetious. 3. *(Bot.)* Applied to plants growing on the seashore from which soda is obtained by burning. 4. *(LAm.)* Unlucky (desgraciado). 5. *(Cono Sur)* Dear (artículo). **Es un tipo muy salado**, he's a very amusing chap. *-m.* 1. Sea. 2. Land rendered barren by too large a portion of saline particles.

salador, ra [sah-lah-dor', rah], *m. & f.* Salter; salting-place for meat.

saladura [sah-lah-doo'-rah], *f.* Salting, seasoning with salt.

salamandra [sah-lah-mahn'-drah], *f.* 1. Salamander, a kind of lizard. 2. *(Met.)* That which exists in the ardor of love or affection.

salamanqués, sa [sah-lah-man-kays', key-sah], *a.* V. SALAMANTINO.

salamanquesa [sah-lah-man-kay'-sah], *f.* Star-lizard.

salamí [sah-lah-me'], *m.* Salami.

salángana [sah-lahn'-gah-nah], *f.* An Asiatic swift which makes the edible nests of which the Chinese are fond.

salar [sah-lar'], *va. 1.* To salt (plato), to season with salt; to preserve with salt, to cure, to corn. 2. *(And.)* To feed salt to (para conservar). 3. *(LAm.)* To ruin (arruinar), to spoil.

salariar [sah-lah-re-ar'], *va.* To give a salary or wages.

salario [sah-lah'-re-o], *m.* Wages, salary, hire; a temporary stipend; military pay.

salaz [sah-lath'], *a.* 1. Salty. 2. Salacious, lustful.

salazón [sah-lah-thon'], *f.* Seasoning, salting.

salce [sahl'-thay], *m. (Bot.)* Willow. Salix. V. SAUCE.

salceda [sal-thay'-dah], *f.* Plantation of willows.

salcedo [sal-thay'-do], *m.* A damp spot naturally overgrown with trees.

salcereta [sal-thay-ray'-tah], *f.* Dicebox.

salcochar [sal-co-char'], *va.* To dress meat, leaving it half raw and without salt.

salchicha [sal-chee'-chah], *f.* 1. Kind of small sausage. 2. *(Mil.)* Saucisse a long narrow bag of pitched cloth filled with powder, serving to set fire to mines.

salchichería [sal-che-chay-ree'-ah], *f.* Shop in which sausages are sold.

salchichero, ra [sal-che-chay.'-ro, rah], *m. & f.* Maker or seller of sausages.

salchichón [sal-che-chone'], *m. aug.* A large sausage.

saldar [sal-dar'], *va.* To liquidate a debt (deuda), to settle an account, to sell off (existencias).

saldo [sahl'-do], *m.* 1. Balance (balance). 2. Amount left. 3. Clearance sale (liquidación). 4. Remnants (restos). **Saldo acreedor**, credit balance. **Saldo deudor**, debit balance.

salebrosidad [sah-lay-bro-se-dahd'], *f.* Saltness.

saledizo [sah-lay-dee'-tho], *m.* Jutting; corbel, jetty, coving.

saledizo, za [sah-lay-dee'-tho], *a.* Salient.

salegar [sah-lay-gar'], *m.* Salt-lick, a spot where salt is fed to cattle.

salera [sah-lay'-rah], *f.* One of the stones of which the saltlick (salegar) is composed.

salero [sah-lay'-ro], *m.* 1. Salt-cellar, for the table (de mesa). 2. Salt-pan: magazine of salt. 3. *(Coll.)* Witty saying; gracefulness, wit.

saleroso, sa [sah-lay-ro'-so, sah], *a.* Facetious, witty, humorous; graceful.

saleta [sah-lay'-tah], *f. dim.* A small hall.

salgada, salgadera [sal-gah'-dah, sal-gah-day'-rah], *f. (Bot.)* V. ORZAGA.

salguera [sal-gay'-rah], *f.* V. MIMBRERA.

salguero [sal-gay'-ro], *m.* Osier, willow.

salicilato [sah-le-the-lah'-to], *m. (Chem.)* Salicylate.

sálico, ca [sah'-le-co, cah], *a.* Salic, of the Salian Franks.

salicor [sah-le-cor'], *f. (Bot.)* Long, fleshy-leaved salwart.

salicornia [sah-le-cor'-ne-ah], *f.* Glasswort.

salida [sah-lee'-dah], *f.* 1. Start, setting or going out, departure, exit (lugar). 2. Outlet, outgate. 3. Environs of a town. 4. Issue, result (resultado), conclusion. 5. Projection, prominence (saliente). 6. Salableness. 7. Expenditure, outlay. 8. *(Mil.)* Sally, sortie. **Puerta de salida**, sally-port. 9. Subterfuge, pretext. 10. Means or reasons by which an argument, difficulty or peril is overcome 11. *(Naut.)* Headway. **Estar de salida**, to be ready for sailing. **La salida fue triste**, leaving was sad. **Salida de emergencia**, emergency exit. **Es sólo una salida**, it's only a pretext.

salidizo, za [sah-le-dee'-tho, thah], *f. & a.* V. SALEDIZO.

salido, da [sah-lee'-do, dah], *a. & pp.* of SALAR. Gone out, departed. **salido**, projecting, prominent. **Salida**, in heat, eager for the male.

saliente [sah-le-en'-tay], *a. & pa. 1.* Outjutting, salient, projecting. 2. *(Fig.)* Salient; outstanding. 3. Outgoing (miembro).

salífero, ra [sah-lee'-fay-ro, rah], *a.* Salt-bearing.

salificable [sah-le-fe-cah'-blay], *a.* Salifiable.

salín [sah-leen'], *m.* Salt magazine. V. SALERO.

salina [sah-lee'-nah], *f.* Salt-pit, salt-pan (depresión), salt-work, salt-mine (mina).

salinero [sah-le-nay'-ro], *m.* Salter, dealer in salt; salt-man, salt-maker.

salino, na [sah-lee'-no, nah], *a.* Saline.

salir [sah-leer'], *vn. irr.* 1. To go out of a place, to leave (persona). 2. To depart (autobús, tren), to set out, to march out, to come out, to go forth, to go away or to go abroad, to come forth. 3. To get out of a narrow place or crowd. 4. To appear to show itself. **Salió entonces una nueva moda**, at that time a new fashion appeared. 5. To shoot, to spring; to grow. 6. To proceed, to issue from. 7. To get over difficulties, to escape from danger; to extricate oneself from errors or doubts. 8. *(Naut.)* To exceed, to excel, to pass another vessel in sailing. 9. To happen, to occur (suceder). 10. To cost (costar). **El caballo me salió en sesenta guineas**, the horse stood me in sixty guineas. **Salen caros en Méjico los géneros ingleses**, English goods are dear in Mexico. 11. To finish well or ill; to correspond or imply; to complete a calculation. 12. *(Mil.)* To sally, to issue out. 13. To acquire; to become; to grow common or vulgar. 14. To dismiss, to dispose of. 15. To say or do a thing unexpectedly or unseasonably. 16. To resemble, to appear like (parecerse). 17. To separate, to retire, to desist; to be chosen or elected. **Salir al cabo or salir con**, to go through. **Salir a luz**, to leave the press, to be published or printed; to be produced, to be developed. **Salir con algo**, to obtain something. **Salir de sus casillas**, to step out of one's line or usual way of acting; to be off the hinges; to be out of oneself; to lose one's temper. **El salió herido**, he came out wounded. **Salir de la dificultad**, to extricate oneself from a difficulty. **Salir los colores al rostro**, to blush. *-vr.* 1. To violate a contract; not to fulfil one's engagements. 2. To drop, to leak (líquido). 3. To support or maintain an opinion. **Salirse de la religión**, to quit a religious order. **Salirse con**

la suya, to accomplish one's end, to have one's way. **Salir a nado**, to save oneself by swimming, to do something very difficult. **Salir a su padre**, to resemble one's father. **Salir de una empresa**, to relinquish an enterprise. **Salir del vado, del paso**, to get out of a difficulty. **Salir calabazas**, to be plucked, to fail in an examination. **Salir pitando**, (1) to run away hastily and in confusion. (2) *(Coll.)* To get hot quickly in debate. **Salir del coma**, to emerge from a coma.

salitrado, da [sah-le-trah'-do, dah], *a.* Impregnated with or composed of saltpetre.

salitral [sah-le-trahl'], *a.* Nitrous. -*m.* Saltpetre bed or works.

salitre [sah-lee'-tray], *m.* Saltpetre, nitre.

salitrería [sah-le-tray-ree'-ah], *f.* Saltpetre-work.

salitrero, ra [sah-le-tray'-ro, rah], *a.* Saltpetre refiner, dealer in saltpetre.

salitroso, sa [sah-le-tro'-so, sah], *a.* Nitrous, salinitrous.

saliva [sah-lee'-vah], *f.* Saliva. **Gastar saliva**, to waste one's breath.

salivación [sah-le-vah-the-on'], *f.* Salivation, spitting out.

salival [sah-le-vahl'], *a.* Salivous, salivary.

salivar [sah-le-var'], *vn.* To spit, to salivate. -*a.* Salivary.

salivera [sah-le-vay'-rah], *f.* Round knob on the bits of a bridle.

salivoso, sa [sah-le-vo'-so, sah], *a.* Salivous. V. SALIVAL.

sallador [sal-lyah-dor'], *m.* Weeder, weeding-hook, hoe.

sallar [sal-lyar'], *va.* To weed.

sallo [sah'-lyo], *m. (Prov.)* Hoe.

salma [sahl'-mah], *f.* Ton, twenty hundred-weight.

salmantino, na [sal-man-tee'-no, nah], *a.* Salamancan, relating to Salamanca.

salmear, salmodiar [sal-may-ar'], *va.* To sing psalms.

salmer [sal-merr'], *m. (Arch.)* Plane or impost from which an arch springs.

salmerón [sal-may-rone'], *a.* Which has a large ear (trigo).

salmista [sal-mees'-tah], *m* Psalmist; chanter of psalms.

salmo [sahl'-mo], *m.* Psalm.

salmodia [sal-mo'-de-ah], *f.* 1. Psalmody. 2. The Psalter.

salmógrafo [sal-mo'-grah-fo], *m.* Writer of psalms.

salmón [sal-mone'], *m. (Zool.)* Salmon. **Salmón pequeño**, salmonet.

salmonado, da [sal-mo-nah'-do, dah], *a.* Tasting like salmon.

salmoncillo, ito [sal-mon-theel'-lyo], *m. dim.* A small salmon.

salmonera [sal-mo-nay'-rah], *f.* A net for fishing salmon.

salmonete [sal-mo-nay'-tay], *m.* Redmullet, or surmullet.

salmorejo [sal-mo-ray'-ho], *m.* Sauce for rabbits.

salmuera [sal-moo-ay'-rah], *f.* 1. Brine. 2. Pickle made of salt and water.

salmuerarse [sal-moo-ay-rar'-say], *vr.* To be diseased by eating too much salt (ganado).

salobral [sah-lo-brahl'], *a.* Salty, briny. -*m.* Brine.

salobre [sah-lo'-bray], *a.* Brackish, saltish.

salobreño, ña [sah-lo-bray'-nyo, nyah], *a.* Saltish, containing salt (tierra).

saloma [sah-lo'-mah], *f. (Naut.)* Singing out of sailors, chantey.

salomar [sah-lo-mar'], *vn. (Naut.)* To sing out.

salón [sah-lone'], *m.* 1. *(Aug.)* Saloon, a large hall (sala). 2. Meat salted and smoked. **Salón de actos**, assembly room. **Salón de belleza**, beauty parlor. **Salón de sesiones**, assembly hall.

salpa [sahl'-pah], *f. (Zool.)* Gilt-head, salon, bighead.

salpicadera [sahl-pe-cah-day'-rah], *f.* Fender.

salpicadero [sahl-pe-cah-d-ay-ro], *m. (Aut.)* Dashboard.

salpicadura [sal-pe-cah-doo'-rah], *f.* The act of spattering, and the stain made by it; dab, dash of dirt.

salpicar [sal-pe-car'], *va.* 1. To splatter, to splash, to dab, to dash. 2. To work without continuity or order, to fly from one subject to another. 3. To sprinkle (conversación, oración). 4. *(And. Cono Sur)* Raw vegetable salad. **Salpicar un coche de barro**, to splash a car with mud. **Este asunto salpica al gobierno**, the government has got egg on its face over this affair.

salpicón [sal-pe-cone'], *m.* 1. Salmagundi, a mixed dish. 2. Anything else in small pieces. 3. Bespattering.

salpimentar [sal-pe-men-tar'], *va.* To season with pepper and salt.

salpimentón [sal-pe-men-tone'], *m.* Salmagundi. *V.* SALPICÓN.

salpimienta [sal-pe-me-en'-tah], *f.* Mixture of salt and pepper.

salpinga [sal-peen'-gah], *f.* African serpent.

salpresar [sal-pray-sar'], *va.* To season with salt.

salpreso, sa [ ], *pp. irr.* of SALPRESAR.

salpuga [sal-poo'-ah], *f.* A poisonous kind of ant.

salpullido or **sarpullido** [sal-pool-lyee'-do, sar-pool-lyee'-do], *m.* Prickly heat, skin rash.

salpullir [sal-pool-lyeer'], *va.* To break out in pustules or pimples.

salsa [sahl'-sah], *f.* 1. Sauce, condiment. 2. Ornaments, decorations. 3. Seasoning, spice. 4. Scene (ambiente). **Salsa mayonesa**, mayonnaise. **salsa de tomate**, tomato sauce. **Estar en su salsa**, to be in one's element.

salsedumbre [sal-say-doom'-bray], *f.* Salineness, saltness.

salsera [sal-say'-rah], *f.* 1. Saucer, a pan for sauce. 2. *V.* SASERILLA.

salsereta [sal-say-ray'-tah], *f. dim.* A small saucer; a dice-box.

salserilla [sal-say-reel'-lyah], *f. dim.* A small saucer, in which colors are mixed.

salsero [sal-say'-ro], *m. (Bot.)* Spanish thyme.

salserón [sal-say-rone'], *m. (Prov.)* Measure of grain, containing about a peck.

salseruelo [sal-say-roo-ay'-lo], *m. V.* SALSERILLA.

salsifí [sal-se-fee'], *m.* Salsify, oysterplant.

salsilla, ita [sal-seel'-lyah], *f. dim.* Sauce of little flavor or taste.

saltabanco, saltabancos, saltaembanco or **saltaembancos** [sal-tah-bahn'-co], *m.* Saltimbanco, mountebank, quack.

saltabardales [sal-tah-bar-dah'-les], *m.* Romp, a wild youth.

saltabarrancos [sal-tah-bar-rahn'-cos], *m. (Coll.)* A noisy, turbulent fellow.

saltación [sal-tah-the-on'], *f.* 1. Saltation, leaping or hopping. 2. Dancing, dance.

saltadero [sal-tah-day'-ro], *m.* 1. Leaping-place, high ground from which leaps can be taken. 2. An artificial fountain, a jet.

saltado, da [sal-tah'-do, dah], *a.* Prominent, jutting over. - *pp.* of SALTAR.

saltador, ra [sal-tah-dor', rah], *m. & f.* Jumper, leaper; hopper.

saltadura [sal-tah-doo'-rah], *f.* Hollow made in the surface of a stone when heaving it.

saltambarca [sal-tam-bar'-cah], *f.* A rustic dress, open behind.

saltamontes [sal-tah-mon'-tes], *m.* Locust, grasshopper.

saltante [sal-tahn'-tay], *pa.* Salient, leaping, jumping.

saltaojos [sal-tah-oh'-hos], *m.* Kind of peony.

saltaperico [sal-tah-pay-ree'-co], *m. (Prov.) V.* SALTAMONTES.

saltar [sal-tar'], *vn.* 1. To leap, to jump (muro, obstáculo), to hop; to frisk, to skip (omitir); to rebound, to dash. **Saltar a tierra**, to land, to disembark. 2. To burst (explosivo), to break in pieces; to fly asunder, to crack (madera), to flash. 3. To be clear and obvious, to occur to the memory; to excel, to surpass. 4. To be irritated, to be agitated, to betray emotion. 5. To speak incoherently and irrelevantly. 6. *(Naut.)* To chop about, to change suddenly (viento). **Saltar de gozo**, to be highly delighted. **Andar a la que salta**, to give oneself up to a vagabond life. **Saltar en paracaídas**, to jump. **Saltar por una ventana**, to jump out of a window. **Hacer saltar un edificio**, to blow a building up. -*va.* 1. To leap, to pass over or into by leaping. 2. To cover the female (animales). -*vr.* 1. **Saltarse un párrafo**, to skip a paragraph. 2. **Saltarse todas las reglas**, to break all the rules.

saltarelo [sal-tah-ray'-lo], *m.* Ancient Spanish dance.

saltarén [sal-tah-ren'], *m.* 1. Certain tune on the guitar. 2. Grasshopper.

saltarín, na [sal-tah-reen', nah], *m. & f.* 1. Dancer, dancing master. 2. A restless young rake.

saltarregla [sal-tar-ray'-glah], *f.* Bevelsquare, sliding-rule.

saltaterandate [sal-tah-tay-ran-dah'-tay], *m.* A kind of embroidery.

saltatriz [sal-tah-treeth'], *f.* A female rope-dancer: ballet-girl; danseuse, a professional dancing woman.

salteador [sal-tay-ah-dor'], *m.* Highway man, footpad.

salteamiento [sal-tay-ah-me-en'-to], *m.* Assault, highway robbery.

saltear [sal-tay-ar'], *va.* 1. To assault, to attack, to invade; to rob on the highway (robar); to hold up (atracar). 2. To fly from one work to another without continuity. 3. To anticipate maliciously in the purchase of anything; to surprise, to take by surprise (sorprender). 4. To circumvent or gain ascendency over another's feelings.

salteo [sal-tay'-o], *m.* Assault on the high road; highway robbery.

salterio [sal-tay'-re-o], *m.* 1. Psalter psalm-book. 2. Psaltery, a kind of harp. 3. Rosary, made of 150 Hail Marys. 4. A kind of flute.

saltero, ra [sal-tay'-ro, rah], *a.* Living on mountains, highlander.

saltico, ito [sal-tee'-co, ee'-to], *m. dim.* A little hop or leap.

saltillo [sal-teel'-lyo], *m.* 1. A little hop or leap. **A saltillos**, leaping, hopping. 2. *(Naut.)* Beak, bulk-head.

saltimbanco, saltimbanqui [sal-tim-bahn'-co], *m.* V. SALTABANCO.

salto [sahl'-to], *m.* 1. Leap, bound; distance leaped; leaping, jerk, jump (al agua). 2. Leaping-place, ground from which leaps can be taken. 3. Irregular transition from one thing to another. 4. Assault, plunder, robbery. 5. Skip, omission of clauses, lines, or leaves in reading or writing. 6. Ascent to a higher post without passing through the intervening. 7. *(Amer. Colom. Argen.)* Cataract, falls. **Salto mortal**, somerset. **Salto de viento**, *(Naut.)* the sudden shifting of the wind. **A saltos**, leaping by hops. **De un salto**, at one jump. **Salto en el vacío**, leap in the dark. **Dar un salto**, to jump. **Salto de altura**, high jump. **Triple salto**, hop. **Aquí hay un salto de 50 versos**, there is a gap here of 50 lines. **Salto de agua**, waterfall.

saltón [sal-tohn'], *m.* Grasshopper.

saltón, na [sal-tohn', nah], *a.* Hopping or leaping much. **Ojos saltones**, goggle-eyes.

salubérrimo, ma [sah-loo-ber'-re-mo, mah], *a. sup.* Most salubrious.

salubre [sah-loo'-bray], *a.* Healthful. V. SALUDABLE.

salubridad [sah-loo-bre-dahd'], *f.* Healthfulness (sanidad), salubrity, salutariness, wholesomeness.

salud [sah-lood'], *f.* 1. Health. 2. Welfare, prosperity. 3. Salvation. 4. *(LAm.)* Bless you! (al estornudar). **En sana salud**, in good health. **Estar bien de salud**, to be in good health. **Devolver la salud a uno**, to give somebody back his health.

saludable [sah-loo-dah'-blay], *a.* Salutary, healthful, salubrious, wholesome for soul or body.

saludablemente [sah-loo-dah-blay-men-tay], *adv.* Salubriously, healthfully, healthily.

saludación [sah-loo-dah-the-on'], *f.* V. SALUTACIÓN.

saludador [sah-loo-dah-dor'], *m.* 1. Greeter, saluter. 2. Quack, who cures distempers by the breath, the saliva, etc.

saludar [sah-loo-dar'], *va.* 1. To greet, to salute, to hail, to accost. 2. To express content or joy by words or actions. 3. To proclaim a king or emperor. 4. To fire a salute. 5. To apply delusive remedies to cure diseases, like quacks. **Saludar a uno**, to go and say hello to somebody. **Le saluda atentamente**, yours faithfully.

saludo [sah-loo'-do], *m.* 1. Salute with a volley of firearms. 2. Salute, salutation, greeting. **Volver el saludo**, to return the salute or bow. **Atentos saludos**, best wishes. **Saludo completo**, full handshake.

salumbre [sah-loom'-bray], *f.* Flower of salt, red spume which forms on salt.

salutación [sah-loo-tah-the-on'], *f.* 1. Salutation, greeting, salute. 2. Exordium of a sermon.

salutíferamente [sah-loo-tee'-fay-rah-men-tay], *adv.* Salubriously.

salutífero, ra [sah-loo-tee'-fay-ro, rah], *a.* Salutiferous, healthful, salubrious.

salva [sahl'-vah], *f.* 1. Pregustation, the tasting of viands before they are served up to royalty. 2. Salute of firearms, salvo. **Hacer la salva**, to drink to one's health, to beg leave to speak. 3. Rash proof of innocence, given by running a great risk. 4. Oath, solemn promise (promesa), assurance.

salvación [sal-vah-the-on'], *f.* 1. Salvation. 2. Preservation from great danger. **Ejército de Salvación**, the Salvation Army.

salvachía [sal-vah-chee'-ah], *f. (Naut.)* Salvage, a strap formed by braided cords, used to fasten shrouds and stays.

salvadera [sal-vah-day'-rah], *f.* Sandbox for writing.

salvado [sal-vah'-do], *m.* Bran. **Salvado, da**, *pp.* of SALVAR.

salvador, ra [sal-vah-dor', rah], *m. & f.* Saviour, rescuer, redeemer. **El Salvador, el Salvador del mundo**, our Savior, our Redeemer.

salvaguardar [sal-vah-goo-ahr-dar'], *va.* To safeguard; *(Comput.)* to backup.

salvaguardia [sal-vah-goo-ar'-de-ah], *m.* 1. Safeguard, security, protection, shield of friendship, palladium. 2. Guard, watchman. *-f.* Safe conduct, a kind of passport.

salvajada [sal-va-hah'-dah], *f.* Rude, unmannerly behavior.

salvaje [sal-vah'-hay], *a.* 1. Savage, wild, barbarous, ferocious, ignorant, foolish, undomesticated. 2. Wild, rough, mountainous.

salvaje [sal-vah'-hay], *m.* A savage, born and brought up in the wilderness.

salvajemente [sal-vah'-hay-men-tay], *adv.* Savagely, wildly.

salvajería [sal-vah-hay-ree'-ah], *f.* Rusticity; clownish, uncouth conduct, savageness.

salvajez [sal-vah-heth'], *f.* Savageness, rustic indocility.

salvajina [sal-vah-hee'-nah], *f.* 1. A wild beast. 2. A multitude of wild animals. 3. Collection of skins of wild beasts.

salvajino, na [sal-vah-hee'-no, nah], *a.* 1. Savage, wild, untamed. 2. Having the taste of game (carne).

salvajismo [sal-vah-hees'-mo], *m.* Barbarism, savagery.

salvamente [sal-vah-hees'-mo], *adv.* Securely, safely.

salvamento, salvamiento [sal-vah-men'-to], *m.* Safety, the act of saving, place of safety; salvation. **Operaciones de salvamento**, rescue operations.

salvante [sal-vahn'-tay], *pa.* Saving, excepting. *-adv. (Coll.)* Save.

salvar [sal-var'], *va.* 1. To save (persona), to free from danger; to receive into eternal happiness. 2. To save, to help or save by an excuse or reservation. 3. To remove impediments or difficulties. 4. To mention and correct errors of the pen in a notarial instrument, at the foot thereof. 5. To pass over or near a thing. 6. To taste, to prove the food or drink of nobles. 7. To prove judicially the innocence of a person. 8. To except, to exclude (excluir). 9. To rise above (árbol, edificio). 10. *(Cono Sur)* To pass (exam). *-vr.* To escape from danger, to get over difficulties, to attain salvation. **Me salvó la vida**, he saved my life. **El agua salvaba el peldaño más alto**, the water came up to the top-most step.

salvavidas [sal-vah-vee'-das], *m.* 1. Life-preserver. 2. Life-boat made unsinkable by the help of cork.

¡salve! [sahl'-vay], *v. defective.* God bless *you!-f.* Salutation or prayer to the Virgin Mary.

salvedad [sal-vay-dahd'], *f.* License, security, safe-conduct, excuse.

salvia [sahl'-ve-ah], *f. (Bot.)* Sage Salvia. **Salvia oficinal**, garden sage.

salviado, da [sal-ve-ah'-do, dah], *a.* Containing sage.

salvilla [sal-veel'-lyah], *f.* 1. Salver (bandeja), a glass stand. 2. A tray, a waiter, a plate on which something is presented.

salvo, va [sahl'-vo, vah], *pp. irr.* of SALVAR. Saved, proved, corrected.

salvo [sahl'-vo], *adv.* Saving, excepting, barring. **Poner algo a salvo**, to put something in a safe place. **A salvo**, without injury or diminution. **Dejar algo a salvo**, to make an exception of something.

salvoconducto [sal-vo-con-dooc'-to], *m.* Pass, safe-conduct or letters of safeconduct; passport; license or permission.

salvohonor [sal-vo-o-nor'], *m. (Coll.)* Breech posteriors.

salz [salth'], *m. V.* SAUCE.

salza [salh'-thah], *f.* A mud-volcano.

sama [sah'-thah], *f.* A kind of seabream.

sámago [sah'-mah-go], *m.* A defective, useless piece of building wood.

samaritano, na [sah-mah-re-tah'-no, nah], *a.* Samaritan.

samba [sam'-ba], *f.* Samba, popular dance and musical rhythm of Brazil.

sambenitar [san-bay-ne-tar'], *va.* To make infamous, to dishonor publicly.

sambenito [sam-bay-nee'-to], *m.* 1. Garment worn by a penitent convict of the Inquisition. 2. An inscription in churches, contain the name, punishment, and signs of the chastisement of those doing penance; note of infamy. 3. Evil report due to an act. **Echar el sambenito a otro**, to pin the blame on somebody else.

sambeque [sam-bay'-kay], *m. (Cuba) V.* ZAMBRA.

samblaje [sam-blah'-ha], *m..* Joinery. *V.* ENSAMBLADURA.

sambuca [sam-boo'-cah], *f.* 1. Ancient triangular musical stringed instrument. 2. Ancient warlike machine, a sort of huge bridge for storming walls.

sambumbia [sam-boom'-be-ah], *f.* 1. *(Cuba)* A fermented drink made from cane-juice, water, and peppers. 2. *(Peru)* Hubbub, confusion.

samnítico, ca [sam-nee'-te-co, cah], *a.* Belonging to the Samnites or to the ancient gladiators.

san [sahn], *a.* Saint: used always in the masculine gender, and before the name. *V.* SANTO.

sanable [sah-nah'-blay], *a.* Curable, healable.

sanador, ra [sah-nah-dor', rah], *m. & f.* Curer, healer.

sanalotodo [sah-nah-lo-to'-do], *m.* Panacea, remedy or plaster for all distempers and sores, a general remedy.

sanamente [sah-nah-men-tay], *adv.* Naturally, agreeably.

sanar [sah-nar'], *va.* 1. To heal, to cure, to restore to health. 2. To reclaim from vice. *-vn.* To heal (herida), to recover from sickness (persona).

sanate [sa-nah'-tay], *m.* A Nicaragua bird like the magpie.

sanativo, va [sah-nah-tee'-vo, vah], *a.* Sanative, curative.

sanatorio [sah-nah-to'-re-o], *m.* Sanatorium, sanitarium.

sanción [san-the-on'], *f.* 1. Sanction, law. 2. Solemn authorization. **Imponer sanciones**, to impose sanctions.

sancionar [san-the-o-nar'], *va.* To sanction (castigar), to authorize.

sancochar [san-co-char'], *f.* To parboil.

sancocho [san-co'-cho], *m. (Amer. Ec.)* A dish composed of yucca, meat, plantains, cocoa, the chief breakfast dish through all South America.

sanctasanctórum [sanc-tah-sanc-to'-room], *m.* Sanctuary.

sanctus [sahnc'-toos], *m.* A part of the mass. **Tocan a sanctus** or **santus**, they ring the bell at mass before the canon.

sandalia [san-dah'-le-ah], *f.* Sandal, a kind of slippers.

sandalina [san-dah-lee'-nah], *f.* A stuff manufactured in Venice.

sandalino, na [san-dah-lee'-no, nah], *a.* Tinctured with sanders.

sándalo [sahn'-dah-lo], *m. (Bot.)* 1. Bergamot mint. 2. True sandal-wood or sanders. 3. *(Bot.)* Sanders, sandal-wood.

sandáraca [san-dah'-ra-cah], *f.* 1. Sandarach, a red sulphuret of arsenic. 2. Sandarac, a white resin exuded by the juniper-tree.

sandez [san-deth'], *f.* Folly, simplicity: want of understanding. **Decir sandeces**, to talk nonsense.

sandía [san-dee'-ah], *f. (Bot.)* Water melon.

sandiar [san-de-ar'], *m.* Water melon-patch.

sandio, dia [sahn'-de-o, ah], *a.* Foolish, nonsensical.

sandix [san-dix'], *m.* Minium, red lead.

sandunga [san-doon'-gah], *f. (Coll.)* Gracefulness, elegance; cajoling, wheedling; flattering, allurement, fascination.

sandunguero, ra [san-doon-gay'-ro, rah], *a.* Alluring, wheedling, fascinating; elegant.

sandwich [sand-wich], *m.* Sandwich.

saneable [sah-nay-ah'-blay], *a.* Reparable.

saneado, da [sah-nay-ah'-do, dah], *a.* 1. Drained. 2. Beat of its kind.

saneamiento [sah-nay-ah-me-en'-to], *m.* 1. Surety, bail, guarantee; indemnification (compensación), reparation. 2. Drainage (alcantarillado).

sanear [sah-nay-ar'], *va.* 1. To give security, to give bail. 2. To indemnify, to repair (daño). 3. To clean, disinfect (edificio). 4. To drain. 5. To compensate (comprador). 6. To restructure (capital, compañía).

sanedrín [sah-nay-dreen'], *m.* Sanhedrim, the supreme council of the Jewish nation.

sanes [sah'-nes]. **Por vida de sanes**, a minced oath.

sangley [san-glay'-e], *m.* Chinese trader in the Philippine Islands.

sangradera [san-grah-day'-rah], *f.* 1. Lancet for blood-letting. 2. An earthen basin. 3. Lock, sluice (desagüe), drain.

sangrador [san-grah-dor'], *m.* 1. Phlebotomist, blood-letter. 2. Fissure, opening.

sangradura [san-grah-doo'-rah], *f.* 1 *(Surg.)* Bleeding; part of the arm usually bled. 2. Draining of a canal or river. 3. *(Cono Sur)* Outlet.

sangrante [san-grahn'-tay], *a.* 1. Bleeding (herida, persona). 2. *(Fig.)* Crying (injusticia).

sangrar [san-grar'], *vn.* 1. To bleed, to let blood; to open a vein. 2. To drain, to draw water from a canal or river. 3. *(Print.)* To indent the first line of a paragraph. *-va.* To bleed. *-vr.* To be bled.

sangraza [san-grah'-thah], *f.* Corrupt or filthy blood.

sangre [sahn'-gray], *f.* 1. Blood; gore. 2. Blood, race, family, kindred. **Ser de la sangre azul**, *(Coll.)* to belong to the nobility. 3. Substance, fortune. 4. Wound from which blood issues. **A sangre fría**, in cold blood. **La sangre se me hiela en las venas**, my blood curdles in my veins. **Bullir la sangre**, to be vigorous and healthy as in youth. **querer beber la sangre a otro**, to hate a person mortally. **No creo que llegue la sangre al río, I** don't think it will be too disastrous.

sangría [san-gree'-ah], *f.* 1. *(Surg.)* Bleeding, blood-letting. 2. Any incision which emits blood. 3. Present made to a person who bleeds. 4. An extraction or stealing of something to small parcels. 5. *(Print.)* Indenting a line. 6. Inside of the arm, where a vein is usually opened. 7. *V.* SANGRADURA. 8. A beverage of red wine, lemon, and water; sangaree. 9. Irrigation (acequia). 10. *(Culin.)* Fruit cup.

sangrientamente [san-gre-en-tah-men'-tay], *adv.* Bloodily, cruelly.

sangriento, ta [san-gre-en'-to, tah], *a.* 1. Bloody (batalla), bloodstained, gory. 2. Bloody, cruel (chiste), sanguinary, bloodthirsty.

sangual [san-goo-ahl'], *m. (Orn.)* Osprey.

sanguaza [san-goo-ah'-thah], *f.* 1. Serpous blood. 2. Reddish fluid of vegetables.

sangüeso [san-goo-ay'-so], *m. (Bot.)* Raspberry-bush.

sanguífero, ra [san-gee'-fay-ro, rah], *a.* Sanguiferous.

sanguificación [san-gee-fe-cah-the-on'], *f. (Med.)* Sanguification.

sanguificar [san-gee-fe-car'], *va.* To sanguify, to make blood.

sanguificativo, va [san-gee-fe-cah-tee'-vo, vah], *a.* Producing blood.

sanguijuela [san-gee-hoo-ay'-lah], *f.* 1. Leech. 2. Sharper, a cheat. **Sanguijeulas del Estado,** sinecure officials (drawing pay, but doing nothing for it).

sanguinaria [san-gee-nah'-re-ah], *f.* 1. *(Bot.)* Blood-root, a medicinal herb. 2. Bloodstone, of a dark green color, variegated by red spots; hematite; an amulet to prevent bleeding from the nose.

sanguinariamente [san-gee-nah'-re-ah-men-tay], *adv.* Sanguinarily.

sanguinario, ria [san-gee-nah'-re-o, ah], *a.* Sanguinary, cruel, bloody.

sanguíneo, nea, sanguino, na [san-gee'-nay-o, ah], *a.* 1. Sanguine, red, the color of blood. 2. Sanguineous.

sanguinolencia [san-gee-no-len'-the-ah], *f.* Bloodiness, blood-thirstiness.

sanguinolento [san-gee-no-len'-to], **ta,** *a.* V. SANGRIENTO.

sanguinoso, sa [san-gee-no'-so, sah], *a.* 1. Sanguine, sanguinous. 2. Bloody, sanguinary, cruel.

sanguiñol [san-gee-nyol'], *m.* *(Bot.)* V. SANGUEÑO.

sanícula [sah-nee'-coo-lah], *f.* *(Bot.)* Sanicle. **Sanicula europea,** Wood sanicle.

sanidad [sah-ne-dahd'], *f.* 1. Soundness, health, vigor, sanity. **En sanidad,** in health. **Carta de sanidad,** bill of health. **Casa de sanidad,** health-office. **Juez de sanidad,** commissioner of the board of health. 2. Candor, ingenuousness.

sanie, sanies [sah'-ne-ay, sah'-ne-es], *f.* *(Med.)* Sanies.

sanioso, sa [sah-ne-o'-so, sah], *a.* *(Med.)* Sanious.

sanitario, ria [sah-ne-tah'-re-o, ah], *a.* Sanitary, promotive of health.

sanjuanero, ra [san-hoo-ah-nay'-ro, rah], *a.* Applied to fruits ripe on St. John's day.

sanjuanista [san-hoo-ah-nees'-tah], *a. & m.* A knight of St. John of Jerusalem.

sanmiguelada [san-me-gay-lah'-dah], *f.* *(Prov.)* Michaelmas.

sanmigueleño [san-me-gay-lay-nyo], **ña,** *a.* Applied to fruits ripe at Michaelmas.

sano, na [sah'-no, nah], *a.* 1. Sound (madera, órgano), healthy (clima), wholesome, hale, hearty; salutary; sane; secure. 2. Sincere, well-disposed, discreet, wise, steady. 3. Safe, free from fault, harmless. 4. Entire, complete: **Sano y salvo,** safe and sound. **No ha quedado plato sano en toda la casa,** there wasn's a plate left whole in the house.

sánscrito [sahns'-cre-to], *m.* Sanskrit, the sacred language of Hindustan.

santa [sahn'-tah], *f.* Female saint. *-m.* V. SANTUARIO.

Santa Bárbara [san'-tah bar'-ba-rah], *f.* 1. *(Naut.)* Magazine, powder-room. 2. St. Barbara.

santamente [san'-tah-men-tay], *adv.* 1. Reverently, piously, religiously; simply. 2. Briskly, freely.

santasantórum [san-tah-san-to'-room], *m.* 1. Sanctuary, sanctum-sanctorum, holy of holies. 2. Sanctum: something especially valued by anyone. 3. The mysterious or occult.

santazo, za [san-tah'-tho, thah], *a. aug.* A great saint.

santelmo [san-tel'-mo], *m.* *(Naut.)* St. Elmo's light, a fiery meteor on the masts of ships in stormy weather.

santero, ra [san-tay'-ro, rah], *m. & f.* Caretaker of a sanctuary.

santiago [san-te-ah'-go], *m.* 1. St. James, the war-whoop of the Spaniards on engaging with Moors and other infidels. 2. A middling sort of linen manufactured in Santiago.

santiagués, sa [san-te-ah-ghes', sah], *a.* Belonging to Santiago de Galicia.

santiaguiño, ña [san-te-ah-ghes'-no, nah], *a.* Belonging to Santiago de Chile.

santiaguista [san-te-ah-gees'-tah], *a.* Belonging to the order of Santiago. *-m.* A knight of Santiago or St. James.

santiamén [san-te-ah-men'], *m.* *(Coll.)* Moment, twinkling of an eye.

santico, ca [san-tee'-co, cah], *m. & f.* 1. *(Dim.)* Little image of a saint. 2. In familiar language, a good child.

santidad [san-te-dahd'], *f.* 1. Sanctity, sanctitude, piety, holiness, godliness. 2. Holiness, a title given to the Pope.

santificable [san-te-fe-cah'-blay], *a.* Sanctifiable.

santificación [san-te-fe-cah-the-on'], *f.* Sanctification, making holy. **Santificación de las fiestas,** Keeping holidays.

santificador [san-te-fe-cah-dor'], *m.* Sanctifier.

santificante [san-te-fe-cahn'-tay], *pa.* Blessing, sanctifying.

santificar [san-te-fe-car'], *pa.* 1. To sanctify, to hallow. 2. To dedicate to God. 3. To bless, to praise. 4. To honor and serve as a saint. 5. *(Met.)* To justify, to exculpate. *-vr.* 1. To employ oneself in pious works. 2. To justify, to clear from guilt.

santiguada [san-te-goo-ah'-dah], *f.* Blessing, the act of making the sign of the cross.

santiguador, ra [san-te-goo-ah-dor', rah], *m. & f.* One who cures by the sign of the cross.

santiguamiento [san-te-goo-ah-me-en'-to], *m.* Act of crossing or curing with the sign of the cross.

santiguar [san-te-goo-ar'], *va.* 1. To bless (persignar), to make the sign of the cross over a sick person. 2. To chastise, to punish. *-vr.* 1. To make the sign of the cross over oneself; to cross oneself. 2. To make a great fuss (exagerar).

santiguo [san-tee'-goo-o], *m.* The act of making the cross over oneself.

santimonia [san-te-mo'-ne-ah], *f.* 1. Sanctity, sanctimony, holiness. 2 *(Bot.)* Corn marigold, garden chrysanthemum.

santiscario [san-tis-cah'-re-o], *m.* *(Coll.)* Caprice, whim: used only in the colloquial and rather uncommon phrase. **De mi santiscario.**

santísimo, ma [san-tee'-se-mo, mah], *a. sup.* Most holy. **El Santísimo,** the holy sacrament.

santo, ta [sahn'-to, tah], *a. & n.* 1. Saintly, holy, virtuous, ghostly. 2. Saint, a person eminent for piety (persona). 3. *(Coll.)* Simple, plain, artless. 4. Sacred, dedicated to God; inviolable. 5. Grateful, delightful, pleasant. 6. Just, upright, pious. 7. Holy: applied to the Roman Catholic and apostolic church. **Santo y bueno,** well and good. **Santo día,** the whole day. **Todas los Santos,** all Saints' day. **Santo varón,** a holy man: a harmless idiot or simpleton; a great hypocrite.

santo [sahn'-to], *m.* 1. Saint, the image of a saint. 2. *(Mil.)* Watchword. **Santo Tomás,** St. Thomas. **Llegar y besar el santo,** to pull it off at the first attempt. **Se le fue el santo al cielo,** he forgot what he was about to say. **Santo y seña,** password. **No es santo de mi devoción,** I'm not very keen on him. **Desnudar a un santo para vestir a otro,** to rob Peter to pay Paul.

santolina [san-to-lee'-nah], *f.* *(Bot.)* Lavender-cotton.

santón [san-tone'], *m.* 1. *(Aug.)* A pretended saint, a hypocrite. 2. A kind of recluse among the Moors.

santoral [san-to-rahl'], *m.* A collection of sermons or lives of the saints; church-choir book.

santuario [san-too-ah'-re-o], *m.* 1. Sanctuary; temples and sacred things. 2. *(And. Carib.)* Native idol (ídolo).

santucho, cha [san-too'-cho, chah], *m. & f.* *(Coll.)* Hypocrite.

santurrón [san-toor-rohn', nah], *m. & f. & a.* *(Coll.)* Hypocrite, canter, zealot.

santurronería [san-toor-ro-nay-ree'-ah], *f.* Hypocrisy. V. BEATERÍA.

santus [san-toos], *m.* V. SANCTUS.

saña [sah'-nyah], *f.* Anger (furor), passion, rage and its effects.

sañosamente [sah-nyo-sah-men-tay], *adv.* Furiously.

sañoso, sa [sah-nyo'-so, sah], *a.* Furious.

sañudo, da [sah-nyoo'-do, dah], *a.* Furious, enraged.

sapa [sah'-path], *f.* Woody residue left after chewing *buyo,* a compound of areca and betel-nuts with lime. *Cf.* BUYO, 3d def.

sapajú [sah-pa-hoo'], *m.* Sapajou, ospuchin, a South American monkey, often seen in captivity.

sapán [sah-pahn'], *m.* *(Bot.)* Sapan wood, a brownish-red dye-wood; sapan-tree.

sapera [sah-pay'-rah], *f.* *(Bot.)* Sea-heath.

sápido, da [sah'-pe-do, dah], *a.* High-flavored, of an exquisite taste.

sapiencia [sah-pe-en'-the-ah], *f.* Wisdom.

sapienciales [sah-pe-en-the-ah'-les], *m. pl.* Books of wisdom, works on morals: used in the singular as an adjective.

sapiente [sah-pe-en'-tay], *a.* Wise. V. SABIO.

sapientísimamente [aah-pe-en-**tee'**-se-mah-men-tay], *adv.* Most wisely.

sapillo [sah-peel'-lyo], *m.* 1. (*Dim.*) A little toad. 2. A small tumor under the tongue.

sapina [sah-pee'-nah], *f.* A glasswort, or plant yielding barilla, which grows in the Levant and in southern Spain.

sapino [sah-pee'-no], *m.* (*Bot.*) Savin, sabin, a small tree of the pine family.

sapo [sah'-po], *m.* 1. A large toad. V. ESCUERZO. **Echar sapos y culebras**, (*Coll.*) to be beside oneself; to be extremely angry. 2. (*LAm.*) Game of throwing coins into the mouth of an iron toad. 3. (*CAm. Carib.*) Informer (soplón).

saponáceo, cea [sah-po-nah'-thay-o, ah], *a.* Saponaceous, soapy.

saponaria [sah-po-nah'-re-ah], *f.* (*Bot.*) Common soapwort.

saponificable [sah-po-ne-fe-cah'-blay], *a.* Saponifiable.

saponificación [sah-po-ne-fe-cah-the-on'], *f.* Saponification, the process or result of making soap.

saponificar [sah-po-ne-fe-car'], *va.* To saponify, to convert fat or oil into soap by the action of an alkali. -*vr.* To become saponified.

saporífero, ra [sah-po-ree'-fay-ro, rah], *a.* Imparting savor.

saprino [sah-pree'-no], *m.* (*Ent.*) A diminutive beetle of the silpha family, about one-tenth of an inch in length; of most brilliant coloring, punctated with black. Found all over the world.

saque [sah'-kay], *m.* 1. The act of tossing a ball. 2. He that tosses the ball. 3. A line or base from which a ball is tossed. **Saque inicial**, kick-off. **Saque de portería**, goal-kick.

saqueador, ra [sah-kay-ah-dor', rah], *m. & f.* Depopulator, ransacker, free hooter.

saquear [sah-kay-ar'], *va.* 1. To ransack, to plunder, to foray, to pillage. 2. To take away unlawfully.

saqueo [sah-kay'-o], *m.* Pillage, plunder, foray.

saquera [sah-kay'-rah], *f.* (*Prov.*) Needle for sewing sacks, a packing needle.

saquería [sah-kay-ree'-ah], *f.* Place for or collection of sacks.

saquete, saqueto [sah-kay'-tay], *m. dim.* Little sack.

saquilada [sah-ke-lah'-dah], *f.* A small quantity of grain put into a sack to be ground.

saquillo, ito [sah-keel'-lyo, ee'-to], *m. dim.* A small bag.

saraguete [sah-rah-gay'-tay], *m.* Hop, a family dance.

sarampión [sa-ram-pe-on'], *m.* Measles, an eruptive disease.

sarangosti [sa-ran-gos'-te], *m.* (*Naut.*) Saragosti, a gum used in the East Indies, instead of pitch and tar, to caulk ships.

sarao [sah-rah'-o], *m.* Ball. an entertaiment of dancing.

sarape [sa-rah'-pay], *m.* Serape, Mexican blanket.

sarcasmo [sar-cahs'-mo], *m.* Sarcasm, keen and bitter irony.

sarcástico, ca [sar-cahs'-te-co, cah], *a.* Sarcastic, taunting.

sarcia [sar'-the-ah], *f.* Load, burden. V. CARGA.

sarcillo [sar-theel'-lyo], *m.* (*Prov.*) Hoe.

sarcócola [sar-co'-co-lah], *f.* Sarcocolla, a resinous gum from Ethiopia.

sarcófago [sar-co'-fah-go], *m.* 1. Tomb, grave. 2. Sarcophagus.

sarcología [sar-co-lo'-he-ah], *f.* (*Anat.*) Sarcology, that part of anatomy which treats the fleshy parts of the body.

sarcótico, ca [sar-co'-te-co, cah], *a.* Sarcotic, promotive of healing wounds by generating new flesh.

sarda [sar'-dah], *f.* A kind of mackerel.

sardesco, ca [sar-des'-co, cah], *a.* 1. Belonging to small ass or horse. 2. (*Coll.*) Rude. stubborn.

sardesco [sar-des'-co], *m.* A small ass.

sardina [sar-dee'-nah], *f.* Sardine; anchovy.

sardinel [sar-de-nel'], *m.* Work of bricks placed on edge.

sardinero, ra [sar-de-nay'-ro, rah], *a.* Belonging to anchovies. -*m. & f.* Dealer in anchoviesor or pilchards.

sardineta [sar-de-nay'-tah], *f.* 1. A small anchovy or pilchard. 2. Part of cheese which overtops the cheesevat. 3. (*Naut.*) Knittle, a small line for various purposes on shipboard. 4. *pl.* Loops of galloon ending in a point placed on certain military uniforms.

sardio, sardo [sar'-de-o], *m.* Sard, sardine, a precious stone.

sardo, da [sar'-do, dah], *a.* Sardinian.

sardonia [sar-do'-ne-ah], *f.* (*Bot.*) Crow-foot, spearwort.

sardónice [sar-do'-ne-thay], *f.* Sardonyx. a precious stone.

sardónico, ca [sar-do'-ne-co, cah], *a.* 1. Sardonic, relating to the herb sardonia. 2. Insincere, affected (risa).

sardonio, sardónique, sardónix [sar-do'-ne-o], *m.* V. SARDÓNICE.

sarga [sar'-gah], *f.* 1. Serge, a silk stuff; also, a kind of woollens. 2. (*Art.*) Fabric painted in distemper or oil, like tapestry, used for decorating rooms. 3. A kind of osier or willow.

sargadilla [sar-gah-deel'-lyah], *f.* A soda-ash plant common in Spain and in the south of France.

sargado, da [sar-gah'-do, dah], *a.* Sergelike. V. ASARGADO.

sargal [sar-gahl'], *m* A clump of osiers.

sargatillo [sar-gah-teel'-lyo], *m.* A kind of willow of Spain.

sargazo [sar-gah'-tho], *m.* (*Bot.*). Sealentils, gulf-weed, sargasso, Sargassum.

sargenta [sar-hen'-tah], *f.* 1. Sergeant's halberd. 2. Sergeant's wife.

sargentear [sar-hen-tay-ar'], *va.* 1. To perform the duty of a sergeant. 2. to take the command. 3. To act in an overbearing manner.

sargentería [sar-hen-tay-ree'-ah], *f.* Place or duty of a sergeant.

sargentía [sar-hen-tee'-ah], *f.* Office of a sergeant.

sargento [sar-hen'-to], *m.* Sergeant. **Sargento primero** Sergeant-major. **Sargento mayor de un regimiento**, (*Mil.*) a mayor.

sargentón [sar-hen-tone'], *m.* 1. (*Aug.*) A tall sergeant. 1. (*Coll.*) A strong, masculine woman.

sargo [sar'-go], **m.** (*Zool.*) A kind of sea-roach or sea-bream.

sarguero [sar-gay'-ro], *m.* Painter of sarga.

sargueta [sar-gay'-tah], *f.* A thin, light serge.

sarilla [sah-reel-lyah], *f.* (*Bot.*) Marjoram.

sarjía [sar-hee'-ah], *f.* Sacrification. V. SAJA.

sármata [sar'-ma-tah], *a.* V. SARMÁTICO.

sarmático, ca [sar-mah'-te-co, cah], *a.* Sarmatian.

sarmentador, ra [sar-men-tah-dor', rah], *m. & f.* One who gathers pruned vine-shoots.

sarmentar [sar-men-tar'], *va.* To gather pruned vine-shoots.

sarmenticio, cia [sar-men-tee'-the-o, ah], *a.* Applied to Christians in derision, because they suffered themselves to be burned with the slow fire of vine-shoots.

sarmentillo [sar-men-teel'-lyo], *m. dim* Of SARMIENTO.

sarmentoso, sa [sar-men-to'-so, sah], *a.* 1. Full of vine-shoots. 2. Creeping, twining, leaning on other bodies for support; used of plants.

sarmiento [sar-me-en'-to], *m.* Vine-shoot, the branch on which grapes grow.

sarna [sar'-nah], *f.* 1. Itch, a cutaneous disease. 2. Mange, the itch or scab in cattle.

sarnazo [sar-nah'-tho], *m.* A malignant itch.

sarnoso, sa [sar-no'-so, sah], *a.* Itchy, affected with itch, scabbed, scaly; mangy. -*m.* Scab, a nickname for a paltry fellow.

sarpullido or **salpullido** [sar-pool-lyee'-do, sal-pool-lyee'-do], *m.* Prickly heat, skin rash.

sarpullir, *vn.* To be flea-bitten. -*vn.* To be full of flea-bites.

saracénico, ca [sar-rah-thay'-ne-co, cah], *a.* Saracenic, belonging to the Saracens.

sarraceno, na [sar-rah-thay'-no, nah], *m. & f.* Saracen, Moor: a name of the middle ages for the Arabs and their descendants.

sarracín [sahr-rah'-theen'], *a. V.* SARRACENO.

sarracina [sar-rah-thee'-nah], *f.* A tumultuous contest between a number of persons.

sarria [sar'-re-ah], *f.* 1. A wide net made of ropes. 2. *(Prov.)* Large basket.

sarrillo [sar-reel'-lyo], *m.* 1. A rattling in the throat of a dying person. 2. *(Bot.) V.* YARO.

sarrio [sar'-re-o], *a.* A kind of wild goat, with the horns bent forward.

sarro [sar'-ro], *m.* 1. A hard, strong bitumen. 2. Sediment which adheres to vessels. 3. Incrustation of the tongue in fevers; sordes: tartar of the teeth. 4. A tumor which grows in the tongue and roughens it.

sarroso, sa [sa-rro'-so, sah], *a.* Incrusted, covered with sediment.

sarta [dar'-tah], *f.* String of bends or pearls; any set of things filed on a line: series. **Una sarta de mentiras**, a pack of lies.

sartal [sar-tahl'], *a.* Stringed. *-m.* String of breads, etc.

sartalejo [sar-tah-lay'-ho], *m. dim.* A small string of pearls or precious stones.

sartén [sar-tayn'], *f.* Frying-pan. **Tener la sartén por el mango**, to have the command or advantage in a situation. **Saltar de la sartén y caer en las brasas**, to jump out of the frying-pan into the fire.

sartenada [sar-tay-nab'-dah], *f.* As much meat or fish as a frying-pan can hold.

sartenazo [sar-tay-nah'-tho], *m.* 1. Blow with a frying-pan. 2. *(Coll.)* A weighty blow with something. 3. *(Met. Coll.)* Trick played off: jest, joke.

sarteneja [sar-tay-nay'-hah], *f. dim.* A small frying-pan. *(Mex.)* Dried out pool, parched soil, cracked soil.

sartenica, illa, ita [sar-tay-nee'-cah], *f. dim.* A small frying-pan.

sartorio [sar-to'-re-o], *m.* Sartorius, the tailor's muscle.

sasafrás [sah-sa-frahs'], *m. (Bot.)* Sassafras.

sastra [sahs'-trah], *f.* Wife of a tailor, tailoress.

sastre [sahs'-tray], *m.* Tailor. **Es un cajón de sastre**, he is a superficial scribbler. **Es un buen sastre**, *(Coll.)* he is a cunning blade.

sastrecillo [sas-tray-theel'-lyo], *m. dim.* A petty tailor.

sastrería [sas-tray-ree'-ah], *f.* 1. Tailor's trade; tailoring. 2. A tailor's shop (tienda).

Satán, Satanás [sah-tahn', sah-tah-nahs'], *m.* Satan.

satánicamente [sah-tah-ne-cah-men-tay], *adv.* Satanically.

satánico, ca [sah-tah'-ne-co, cah], *a.* Satanic, devilish.

satélite [sah-tay'-le-tay], *m.* 1. *(Ast.)* Satellite. **Satélite artificial**, artificial satellite, man-made satellite. 2. Satellite, obsequious follower, subordinate associate. 3. *(Coll.)* Bailiff, constable.

saterión [sah-tay-re-on'], *m. (Bot.) V.* SATIRIÓN.

satín [sah-teen'], *m. (Neol.)* Satin. *V.* RASO.

satinador, ra [sah-te-nah-dor', rah], *m. & f.* Glazing apparatus, rolling press (aparato); one who glosses (persona).

satinar [sah-te-nar'], *va.* To gloss, to make glossy, to calender, to glaze.

sátira [sah'-te-rah], *f.* 1. Satire, a poem in which wickedness or folly is censured. 2. A lively, bitter, and witty woman. 3. A biting joke.

satíricamente [sah-tee'-re-cah-men-tay], *adv.* Satirically.

satírico [sah-tee'-re-co], *m.* Satirist, one who writes satires.

satírico, ca [sah-tee'-re-co, cah], *a.* Satirical, censorious.

satirilla [sah-te-reel'-lyah], *f. dim.* A sharp, sneering insinuation.

satirillo [sah-te-reel'-lyo], *m. dim.* A little satyr.

satirio [sah-tee'-re-o], *m.* Kind of water rat.

satirión [sah-te-re-on'], *m. (Bot.)* The orchis which yields salep.

satirizante [sah-te-re-thahn'-tay], *pa.* Satirizing, writing satires.

satirizar [sah-te-re-thar'], *va.* To satirize, to write satires, to lampoon, to libel.

sátiro [sah'-te-ro], *m.* Satyr, a sylvan god.

satisdación [sah-tis-dah-the-on'], *f. (Law.) V.* FIANZA.

satisfacción [sah-tis-fac-the-on'], *f.* 1 Satisfaction, amends, atonement, recompense, apology (disculpa), excuse. 2. Gratification (de ofensa), the act of pleasing, content, complacence, satisfaction, the state of being pleased. 3. Presumption; confidence, security. 4. Satisfaction, one of the three parts of the sacrament of penance. **A satisfacción**, fully, according to one's wishes. **Con satisfacción**, *(Coll.)* without ceremony, in a friendly manner. **Tomar satisfacción**, to satisfy oneself, to vindicate oneself, to revenge.

satisfacer [sah-tis-fah-therr'], *va.* 1. To satisfy, to pay fully what is due (deuda, paga). 2. To satisfy, to content, to gratify (éxito), to humor. 3. To satisfy, to expiate, to atone; to reward. 4. To satisfy, to give a solution. 5. To allay the passions; to indulge; to satiate. 6. To free from debt, perplexity, or suspense. *-vr.* 1. To satisfy oneself; to take satisfaction; to be revenged (vengarse). 2. To be satisfied, to vindicate oneself. 3. To be convinced, to be undeceived or disabused. **Satisfacer una letra**, to honor a draft. **satisfacerse con muy poco**, to be content with very little. *(Yo satisfago, yo satisfice, yo satisfaga, from Satisfacer. V.* HACER.)

satisfactoriamente [sah-tes-fac-to'-re-ah-men-tay], *adv.* Satisfactorily.

satisfactorio, ria [sah-tis-fac-to'-re-o-ah], *a.* Satisfactory.

satisfecho, cha [sah-tis-fay'-cho, chah], *a. & pp. irr.* of SATISFACER. Satisfied, confident, content; arrogant. **Satisfecho consigo mismo**, self-satisfied.

sativo, va [sah-tee'-vo, vah], *a.* Sown, that which is cultivated, as opposed to what grows wild.

sátrapa [sah'-trah-pah], *m.* 1. Satrap, a Persian governor. 2. *(Met. Coll.)* A sly, crafty fellow.

satrapía [sah-trah-pee'-ah], *f.* Dignity of a Persian satrap.

saturable [sah-too-rah'-blay], *a.* Saturable.

saturación [sah-too-rah-the-on'], *f.* 1. Saturity, filling one thing with another. 2. Saturation; the solution in a liquid of all the solid which it can hold; the impregnation of an acid with alkali.

saturar [sah-too-rar'], *va.* 1. To saturate, to imbibe, to impregnate. 2. To fill, to glut.

saturativo, va [sah-too-rah-tee'-vo, vah], *a.* Possessing the power of saturating, saturant.

saturnal [sah-toor-nahl'], *a.* Saturnalian. **Saturnales**, saturnalia.

saturnino, na [sah-toor-nee'-no, nah], *a.* Saturnine, melancholy, grave, gloomy.

saturno [sah-toor'-no], *m.* 1. *(Ast.)* Saturn. 2. Lead.

sauce [sah'-oo-thay], *m.* (Boy) Willow.

saucedal, *m.* **saucera**, *f.* [sah-oo-thar-dahl', sah-oo-thay'-rah], Plantation of willows, *V.* SALCEDA.

saúco [sah-oo'-co], *f.* 1. *(Bot.)* Elder or alder-tree. 2. Second hoof of horses.

sauna [sah-oo-nah], *f.* Sauna.

sauquillo [sah-oo-keel'-lyo], *m. (Bot.)* Dwarf elder.

saurios [sah'-oo-re-os], *m. pl.* Saurians, a division of reptiles; lizards.

sausería [sah-oo-say-re'-ah], *f.* Larder in a palace.

sasier [sah-oo-se-err'], *m.* Chief of the larder in a palace.

sauz [sah'-ooth], *m. (Bot.) V.* SUCE.

sauzal [sau-oo-thahl'], *m. V.* SAUCEDAL and SALCEDA.

sauzgatillo [sah-ooth-gah-teel'-lyo], *m. (Bot.)* Agnus castus tree, chase tree.

savia [sah'-ve-ah], *f.* The sap of plants, the nutrient fluid.

saxafrax [sak-sah-frahx'], *f. (Bot.) V.* SAXIFRAGA.

saxátil [sak-sah'-teel], *a.* Growing among or adhering to rocks: said of animals and plants; saxicolous.

sáxeo, ea [sak'-say-o, ah], *a.* Stony.

saxícola [sak-see'-co-lah], *f. (Zool.)* A genus of birds of the family Turdidae.

saxífraga, saxifragua [sak-see'-frah-gah, sak-se-frah'-goo-ah], *f. (Bot.)* The saxifrage plant; mountain saxifrage.

saxo [sak-so], *m. (Mus.)* Sax.

saxofón, saxófono [sax-o-fone', sax-o'-fo-no], *m.* Saxophone.

saya [sah'-yah], *f.* 1. Dress skirt (falda), outer skirt, of a woman; petticoat (enaguas) 2. Ancient tunic or gown worn by men.

sayal [sah-yahl'], *m.* A coarse woollen stuff, sackcloth.

sayalería [sah-yah-lay-ree'-ah], *f.* Shop for weaving coarse cloth.

sayalero [sah-yah-lay'-ro], *m.* Weaver of coarse stuff.

sayalesco, ca [sah-yah-les'-co, cah], *a.* Made of sackcloth or other coarse stuff.

sayalete [sah-yah-lay'-tay], *m. dim.* A thin or light stuff used for undergarments.

sayaza [sah-yah'-thah], *f. aug.* A coarse petticoat.

sayete, sayito [sah-yay'-tay], *m. dim.* A small frock, a short dress.

sayo [sah'-yo], *m.* A large wide coat without buttons, any loose coat or dress; small frock. **Sayo vaquero,** a loose jacket worn by cowboys. **A su sayo,** of one's own accord, in one's own mind. **Cortar (a uno) un sayo,** to blame or censure anyone in his absence.

sayón [sa-yon'], *m.* 1. A corpulent, ill-looking fellow. 2. Aug. of SAYO.

sayonazo [sah-yo-nah'-tho], *m. aug.* of SAYÓN.

sayuela [sah-yoo-ay'-lah], *f.* Woollen shift worn by some religious. 2. Kind of fig-tree.

sayuelo [sah-yoo-ay'-lo], *m. dim.* Little frock, small kind of jacket.

sazón [sah-thone'], *f.* 1. Maturity, state of perfection. 2. Season, taste, relish, flavor, seasoning. 3. Occasion, opportunity, season, conjunction. **A la sazón,** then, at that time. **En sazón,** seasonably, opportunely.

sazonadamante [sah-tho-nah'-dah-men-tay], *adv.* Maturely, seasonably.

sazonado, da [sah-tho-nah'-do, dah], *a. & pp.* of SAZONAR. 1. Seasoned, mature, mellow. 2. Applied to a witty saying, or to a word to the purpose.

sazonador, ra [sah-tho-nah-dor', rah], *m. & f.* Seasoner.

sazonar [sah-tho-nar'], *va.* 1. To season, to give a relish. 2. To mature, to bring to maturity. *-vr.* To ripen, to mature.

scooter [scoo'-tayr], *m.* Motor scooter.

se [say]. *The reflexive pronoun,* himself, herself, itself. **Él se lava,** he washes himself. **Ella se peina,** she combs herself. **Él se cortó,** he cut himself. Possessive to the person or thing that governs the verb used before the pronouns *me, te, le,* it reflects the action of the verb on the object which they represent. *Se* is used instead of the other cases of the pronouns of the third person, as **¿Le entregó Vd. la carta?** did you deliver him or her the letter? **Sí, se la entregué,** yes, I delivered it *to him,* or *to her.*

Passive voice. Se represents frequently the passive form of a verb, as **Se dice,** it is said. **Se cree,** it is thought. **Se hace,** it is done.

Reciprocal. Each other, one another. **Se ayudan mutuamente,** they help each other. **Los jugadores se pasan el balón,** the players pass the ball to one another.

sea que [say'-ah kay], *adv.* Whether.

sebáceo, cea [say-bah'-thay-o, ah], Sebaceous, tallowy.

sebastián [say-bas-te-ah'-no], *m. V.* SEBESTÉN.

sebato [say-bah'-to], *m. (Chem.)* Sebate.

sebe [say'-bay], *f.* Stockade, wattle of high pales interwoven with long branches.

sebesta [say-bes'-tah], *f.* Sebesten-fruit, sebestine.

sebestén [say-bes-ten'], *m. (Bot.)* Sebesten-tree, a tree of India and western Asia resembling the sloe.

sebillo [say-beel'-lyo], *m.* Paste made with suet, to soften the bands; kind of soap.

sebo [say'-bo], *m.* 1. Tallow (para velas), candlegrease, suet; any kind of grease or fat. **Sebo en rama** or **en bruto,** rough tallow. 2. *(Met. Coll.)* A large capital, a great fortune. 3. *(Naut.)* Animal grease, with which the bottoms of ships, the masts, etc., are besmeared.

seboso, sa [say-bo'-so, sah], *a.* Tallowy (de vela), fat, greasy (mugriento), unctuous; greased.

seca [say'-cah], *f.* 1. Drought, dry weather. 2. Inflammation and swelling in the glands. 3. *V.* SECANO, 3d def. **A secas,** alone, singly.

secacul [say-cah-cool'], *m. (Bot.)* A plant like a parsnip, and having a very aromatic root.

secadal [say-cah-dahl'], *m.* A dry, barren ground.

secadero [say-cah-day'-ro], *m.* Place where something is dried (lugar); drying shed, room, or floor; drier; fruit drier.

secadero, ra *a.* Capable of being dried (fruta).

secadillo [say-cah-deel'-lyo], *m.* A sort of dry, round biscuit: commonly used in the plural.

secador [say-cah-dor'], *m.* 1. Place where clothes are hung to dry. 2. **Secador de cabello,** hair-drier.

secadora [say-cah-do-rah], *f.* Drier, clothes drier.

secamente [say-cah-men-tay], *adv.* 1. Dryly, morosely; crabbedly, peevishly. 2. Coldly, frigidly.

secano [say-cah'-no], *m.* 1. Dry, unirrigated, arable land. 2. Dryness. 3. Sandbank uncovered by water (banco de arena).

secante [say-cahn'-tay], *m.* Drier, a drying oil used for painting. *-f. (Geom.)* Secant.

secar [say-car'], *va.* To dry out, to dry off, to dry (lágrimas), to wipe (superficie), to blot (tinta). *-vr.* 1. To dry (ropa lavada), to be dried up (planta), to grow dry. 2. To become lank, lean, or meager, to decay. 3. To grow cool in intercourse with a friend. 4. To be extremely thirsty. 5. To feel repugnance to do anything, however necessary.

secaral [say-cah-rahl'], *m.* Dryness, drought. *V.* SEQUERAL

secatura [say-cah-too'-rah], *f.* 1. Insipidity; want of spirit or life, flatness, want of understanding. 2. Coolness, indifference.

sección [sec-the-on'], *f.* 1. Act of cutting. 2. Section, a division of a book. 3. *(Geom.)* Section, the cutting of lines, figures, and solid bodies. 4. *(Arch.)* Section of a building; delineation of its height and depth. 5. Topographical division, section: in hydraulics, section, capacity of the bed of a river, its width and depth.

seccionar [sec-the-o-nar'], *va.* To section, to divide into sections (dividir).

seccionario, ria [sec-the-o-nah'-re-o, ah], *a.* Sectional, relating to a section.

secesión [say-thay-se-on'], *f.* Secession.

seceso [say-thay'-so], *m.* Excrement, stool.

seco, ca [say'-co, cah], *a.* 1. Dry, not wet, not moist. 2. Dry, not rainy (clima). 3. Dry, not succulent. 4. Barren, arid, sapless, withered. 5. Lean, lank, meager. 6. Bare (estilo), only, mere. **A secas,** solely. 7. Barren, without ornament or embellishment. 8. Rude, dry, ill-mannered. **Es un hombre seco,** he is a man of few words, he is not sociable. 9. Lukewarm, cold, without affection. **Pan seco,** stale, dry bread. **En seco,** (1) without cause or motive. (2) In a dry place. 10. *(LAm.)* Slap, smack (golpe).

secor [say-cor'], *m. V.* SEQUEDAD.

secreción [say-cray-the-on'], *f.* 1. *(Med.)* Secretion, act of separating the fluids of the body. 2. *V.* APARTAMIENTO.

secreta [say-cray'-tah], *f.* 1. Secret police, plain-clothes police. 2. Secret policeman, plain-clothes policeman. 3. Privy, water-closet. 4. Secret inquiry or verbal investigation.

secretamante [say-cray-tah-men-tay], *adv.* Secretly, clandestinely.

secretar [say-cray-tar'], *va.* 1. *(Med.)* To secrete, to secern, to separate. 2. To prepare skins, the hair of which is to be taken off and prepared for making felt hats.

secretaría [say-cray-tah-ree'-ah], *f.* 1. Secretary's office. 2. Secretaryship.

secretario, a [say-cray-tah'-re-ah], *a, f*. 1. Secretary. **Secretario general**, general secretary. **Secretaria particular**, personal secretary. 2. Minister of State *(Mex.)*; Secretary of State (USA). 3. A scribe, a notary. 4. Clerk, amanuensis, one who writes for another. **Secretario de Estado**, etc., *V*. MINISTRO. **Secretario general**, general secretary. **Secretario de prensa**, press secretary.

secretear [say-cray-tay-ar'], *vn. (Coll.)* To speak in private (conversar), to whisper (cuchicher).

secretico, illo, ito [say-cray-tee'-co], *m. dim*. A trifling secret. **Secretillos**, private conversation between friends.

secretista [say-cray-tes'-tah], *m*. 1. Author who writes on the secrets of nature: naturalist. 2. Secretist, a dealer in secrets.

secreto, ta [say-cray'-to, tah], *a*. 1. Secret, hidden (escondido), obscure, occult; dark; clandestine. 2. *(Coll.)* Confidential.

secreto [say-cray'-to], *m*. 1. Secrecy, careful silence. 2. Secret, the thing hidden or concealed, arcanum (escondido); nostrum. 2. Caution, silence, dissimulation, concealment; darkness. 4. Scrutoire, a case or hidden drawer for papers; a secret drawer in a desk or trunk. **Secreto a voces**, open secret. **Observar el secreto**, to maintain secrecy. **Secreto de Estado**, state secret. **Secreto profesional**, professional confidence. **De secreto**, secretly. **De secreto inviolable**, top secret. **En secreto**, in secret, in private, informally. **Tener una cosa secreta**, to keep something to oneself. 5. Secrecy (cualidad). 6. Secret drawer (cajón). 7. Combination (de cerradura).

secretón [say-cray-tone'], *m*. Fine dimity.

secretorio, ria [say-cray-to'-re-o, ah], *a. (Med.)* Secretory.

secta [sec'-tah], *f*. 1. A sect. 2. Doctrine or opinion of a sect.

sectador, ra [sec-tah-dor', rah], *m. & f*. Sectarist.

sectario, ria [sec-tah'-re-o, ah], *a. & n*. Sectarian; sectary.

sector [sec-tor'], *m. (Geom.)* Sector. **Sectores simples / de doble cara**, *(Comput.)* single / double side sectors.

secuaz [say-coo-ath'], *a. & m. & f*. Following the opinions of others, sectary of the school of; sequacious; attendant.

secuela [say-coo-ay'-lah], *f*. 1. Sequel, continuation. 2. Sequence, the act of following a party or doctrine. 3. Consequence (consecuencia), induction.

secuencia [say-coo-en'-the-ah], *f*. Sequence (cine).

secuestrable [say-coo-es-trah'-blay], *a*. Sequestrable, legally forfeitable.

secuestración [say-coo-es-trah-the-on'], *f*. Sequestration, the setting aside of property from the possession and control of persons, pending judicial proceedings. *V*. SECUESTRO.

secuestrador, ra [say-coo-es-trah-dor'], *m*. Sequestrator.

secuestrar [say-coo-es-trar'], *va*. To sequestrate, to sequester, to distress, to kidnap, to abduct (persona); to confiscate, to seize (artículos); to hijack (avión).

secuestrario, ria [say-coo-es-trah'-re-o, ah], *a*. Belonging to sequestration.

secuestro [say-coo-es'-tro], *m*. 1. Sequestration. 2. The person in whose hands sequestered property is trusted as a deposit. 3. Seizure of a person by robbers, demanding money for ransom. 4. Sequestrum, a piece of dead bone separated from the living. **Depositario de un secuestro**, garnishee, he in whose hands money is attached.

secular [say-coo-lar'], *a*. 1. Secular, happening or coming once in a century. 2. Secular, not spiritual or ecclesiastical. 3. Not bound by monastic rules. 4. Lay, laical.

secularidad [say-coo-lah-re-dahd'], *f*. Secularity.

secularizable [say-coo-la-re-thah'-blay], *a*. Secularizale, capable of being secularized.

secularización [say-coo-lah-re-thah-the-on'], *f*. Secularization.

secularizar [say-coo-lah-re-thar'], *va*. To secularize.

secundar [say-coon-dar'], *va*. 1. To aid another in some toil. 2. To favor the purposes of another, to second. 3. To repeat a second time.

secundariamente [say-coon-dah'-re-ah-men-tay], *adv*. Secondarily.

secundario, ria [say-coon-dah'-re-o, ah], *a*. 1. Secondary, second in order; subordinate. 2. Accessory.

secundinas [say-coon-dee'-nas], *f. pl*. After-birth and secundines.

secura [say-coo'-rah], *f*. 1. Dryness, droughtiness. 2. Coolness, indifference.

sed [sayd], *f*. 1. Thirst. 2. Drought. 3. Eagerness, anxiety, violent desire. **Tener mucha sed**, to be very thirsty.

seda [say'-dah], *f*. 1. Silk, the thread of the silkworm. 2. Stuff formed of silken threads. 3. Sewing-silk. **Seda en rama** or **cruda**, raw silk. **Seda de coser**, sewing-silk. 4. Wild boar's bristles. **Ser una seda, como una seda**, to be of a sweet temper. **Tejedor de seda**, silk-weaver.

sedadera [say-dah-day'-rah], *f*. Hackle for dressing flax.

sedal [say-dahl'], *m*. 1. Angling-line fixed to a fishing-hook. 2. Seton, an artificial ulcer: by farriers it is called a rowel. 3. **Sedal de zapatero**, shoemaker's thread.

sedante [say-dahn'-tay], *a. (Med.)* Sedative. -*m*. Sedative.

sedar [say-dar'], *va*. To allay, to quiet.

sedativo, va [say-dah-tee'-vo, vah], *a. (Med.)* Sedative.

sede [say'-day], *f*. See, seat (de gobierno). **La Santa Sede**, the holy see, or the papal dignity. **Sede plena**, actual occupation of a chair or dignity. **Sede vacante**, vacant bishopric.

sedear [say-day-ar'], *va*. To clean jewels, gold, or silver with a brush.

sedentario, ria [say-den-tah'-re-o, ah], *a*. Sedentary.

sedeña [say-day'-nyah], *f*. Fine tow of flax, produced by the second hackling; cloth made of such tow.

sedeño, ña [say-day'-nyo, nyah], *a*. 1. Silky, silken (sedoso); silk-like. 2. Made or consisting of hair.

sedera [say-day'-rah], *f*. 1. A brush made of bristles. 2. *(Prov.)* Weaver's seat.

sedería [say-day-ree'-ah], *f*. 1. Silks, silk stuff. 2. Shop of a silk-mercer (tienda).

sedero [say-day'-ro], *m*. Silk-mercer.

sedición [say-de-the-on'], *f*. Sedition, popular commotion; an insurrection, mutiny.

sediciosamente [say-de-the-o-sah-men-tay], *adv*. Seditiously, factiously, mutinously.

sedicioso, sa [say-de-the-o'-so, sah], *a*. Seditious, factious, mutinous.

sediento, ta [say-de-en'-to, tah], *a*. 1. Thirsty, dry. 2. Eagerly, desirous, anxious.

sedimentación [say-de-men-tah-the-on'], *f*. Sedimentation.

sedimentar [say-de-men-tar'], *va. & vr*. To settle, deposit (depositar).

sedimento [say-de-men'-to], *m*. Sediment, feculence, lees.

sedoso, sa [say-do'-so, sah], *a*. Silky, like silk, silk-like, silken.

seducción [say-dooc-the-on'], *f*. Seduction (acto), deceiving; abuse.

seducir [say-doo-theer'], *va*. To seduce (mujer), to corrupt, to abuse, to lead on (moralmente), to charm (cautivar). **Seduce a todos con su simpatía**, she captivates everyone with her charm.

seductivo, va [say-dooc-tee'-vo, vah], *a*. Seductive, apt to mislead; corruptful.

seductor, ra [say-dooc-tor', rah], *a*. Seductive, fascinating, charming (encantador). -*m. & f*. 1. Seducer, corrupter, deceiver. 2. Seducer, charmer.

segable [say-gah'-blay], *a*. Fit to be reaped.

segadera [sah-gah-day'-rah], *f*. Reaping hook, sickle.

segadero, ra [say-gah-day'-ro, rah], *a*. Fit to be reaped.

segador ra [say-gah-dor', rah], *m. & f*. Reaper, harvester: sickle man. -*f*. A reaping or harvesting-machine.

segar [say-gar'], *va*. 1. To reap (trigo), to cut down with a reaping-hook, to crop; to moor. 2. To cut off, to abscind anything grown higher than the rest. *(Yo siego, yo siegue, from Segar. V*. ACRECENTAR.)

segazón [say-gah-thone'], *f*. Harvest season, reaping.

seglar [say-glar'], *a.* 1. Worldly. 2. Secular, laical, lay: in this last sense it is used as a substantive.

seglarmente [say-glar'-men-tay], *adv.* Secularly.

segmento [seg-men'-to], *m.* 1. Segment, part cut off. 2. *(Geom.)* Segment, the part of a circle comprised between an arc and its chord. 3. Segment, each ring or articulation of articulated animals.

segregación [say-gray-gah-the-on'], *f.* Segregation, separation.

segregar [say-gray-gar'], *va.* 1. To segregate, to set apart. 2. To disunite, to unfasten. 3. *(Med.)* To secrete. 4. To excommunicate.

segregativo, va [say-gray-gah-tee'-vo, vah], *a.* That which separates.

segueta [say-gay'-tah], *f.* A very slender fine saw for jewellers or marquetry.

seguida [say-gee'-dah], *f.* The act of following or state of being followed; procession: continuation. **De seguida**, successively, without interruption. **En seguida**, forthwith, immediately.

seguidero [say-gee-day'-ro], *m.* Guide rule, ruled lines to follow in writing.

seguidilla [say-gee-deel'-lyah], *f.* A merry Spanish tune and dance.

seguidillera [say-gee-deeh-lyay'-rah], *f.* Person fond of singing and dancing *seguidillas.*

seguido, da [say-gee'-do, dah], *a.* Continued, successive, straight, directed. *-pp.* of SEGUIR. **5 días seguidos**, 5 days running. **Una enfermedad muy seguida**, a very lengthy illness.

seguido [say-gee'-do], *m.* Narrowing a stocking at the foot.

seguidor, ra [say-gee-dor', rah], *m. & f.* 1. Follower 2. A leaf of ruled paper to guide boys in writing straight.

seguimiento [say-gee-me-en'-to], *m.* Pursuit, the act of following another, hunt: continuation of a lawsuit.

seguir [say-geer'], *va.* 1. To follow, to pursue (carrera, rumbo). 2. To follow, to prosecute, to be in pursuit of one. 3. To follow, to accompany, to attend; to come after; to make at; to march in. 4. To follow, to profess, or exercise any science or art. 5. To manage a suit at law or any other business. 6. To agree or conform to. 7. To copy, to imitate. 8. To direct to the proper road or method. **Seguir los acontecimientos de cerca**, to monitor events closely. *-vn.* To follow (venir después). 2. To continue (continuar). **Y los que siguen**, and the next ones. *-vr.* 1. To ensue, to follow as a consequence (venir después). 2. To succeed, to follow in order. 3. To issue, to spring from. 4. To go on.

segullo [say-gool'-lyo], *m.* The first stratum of a gold-mine.

según [say-goon'], *prep.* According to. **Según Vd. me dice**, according to what you tell me. **Según y como**, just as. **Vuelvo la caja, según y como la recibí**, I return the box just as I received it.

segunda [say-goon'-dah], *f.* 1. Second in music. 2. Double wards of a lock or key. 3. *V.* INTENCIÓN. *V.* SEGUNDO DA.

segundar [say-goon-dar'], *vn.* 1. To repeat over again (repetir). 2. To be second.

segundero, ra [say-goon-day'-ro, rah], *a. (Agr.)* Second crop from some plants in the same year. *-m. (Naut.)* Second hand upon a chronometer and other time-pieces.

segundilla [say-goon-deel'-lyah], *f.* 1. Small bell used for certain acts of devotion. 2. *(Peru)* The end of some ceremony which may be seen without paying.

segundillo [say-goon-deel'-lyo], *m. (Mus.)* Semitone, one of them which are called accidentals.

segundo, da [say-goon'-do, dah], *a.* Second, immediately following the first; favorable. **De segunda mano, por segunda mano**, at second hand. **En segundo lugar**, secondly. **Segunda intención**, duplicity, falsity.

segundo [say-goon'-do], *m.* Second of time or of a degree.

segundogénito, ta [say-goon-do-hay'-ne-to, tah], *a.* Secondborn (niños).

segundón [say-goon-don'], *m.* The second son of a family or any of the brothers after the eldest.

segur [say-goor'], *f.* 1. Axe (hacha). 2. Axe or emblem of the law. 3. Sickle, a reaping-hook.

segurador [say-goo-rah-dor'], *a.* Securer, asserter, security, bondsman.

seguramente [say-goo-rah-men-tay], *adv.* Securely, probably, certainly; fastly; safely. **Seguramente tendrá otro**, they'll probably have another.

segurar [say-goo-rar'], *va. V.* ASEGURAR.

segureja [say-goo-ray'-hah], *f. dim.* A small hatchet, a hollow drawing-knife for cleaning the inside of staves.

seguridad [say-goo-re-dahd'], *f.* 1. Security, surety, certainty, safety (lo salvo), confidence. 2. Fastness; custody; corroboration. 3. Pledge-bail. **Seguridad en carretera**, road safety. **Para mayor seguridad**, to be on the safe side. **En la seguridad de su victoria**, in the certainty of winning.

seguro, ra [say-goo'-ro, rah], *a.* 1. Secure, free from danger; easy, assured, confident, confiding. 2. Secure, sure, certain. 3. Firm, constant. **Estar seguro de una cosa**, *(Coll.)* to depend upon a thing. **A segura le llevan preso**, that which is most secure is not beyond danger. **Está más seguro en el banco**, it's safer in the bank. **Es seguro que...**, it is certain that.....

seguro [say-goo'-ro], *m.* 1. Permission, leave, license. 2. Insurance of goods on sea or land. 3. *(Mech.)* Click, stop, detent, pawl, ratchet; tumbler of a lock. **Compañía de seguros**, insurance company. **Cámara u oficina de seguros**, insurance office. **Póliza de seguro**, policy of insurance. **Premio de seguro**, premium of insurance. **A buen seguro**, certainly, indubitably. **De seguro**, assuredly. **Sobre seguro**, confidently. **Hacer el seguro**, to insure.

seguro colectivo [say-goo'-ro co-lec-tee'-vo], *m.* Group insurance.

seguro de enfermedad [say-goo'-ro day en-fer-may-dahd'], *m.* Health insurance.

seguro sobre la vida [say-goo'-ro so'-bray lah vee'-dah], *m.* Life insurance.

seguro social [say-goo'-ro so-the-ahl'], *m.* Social security.

seis [say-ees], *a.* Six, sixth. *V.* SEXTO. *-m.* 1. The figure 6.2. Six, upon cards or dice. **Seis por ocho**, *(Mus.)* 6/8, six-eight measure; six eighth notes to a measure.

seisavado, da [say-sah-vah'-do, dah], *a.* That which has six sides and six angles.

seisavo [say-sah'-vo], *m.* 1. *V.* HEXÁGONO. 2. The sixth part of a number.

seiscientos, tas [say-ces-the-en'-tos, tas], *a.* Six hundred.

seiseno, na [say-e-say-no, nah], *a.* Sixth. *V.* SEXTO.

seisillo [say-e-seel'-lyo], *m. (Mus.)* Union of six equal notes.

seísmo [say-ee'-mo], *m.* Tremor, shock, earthquake.

seismógrafo [say-ees-mo-grah-fo], *m.* Seismograph, an instrument for recording the direction and force of earthquakes.

seismología [say-ees-mo-lo-hee'-ah], *f.* Seismology, the study of earthquakes.

seismológico, ca [say-ees-mo-lo'-he-co, cah], *a.* Seismological.

seismómetro [say-ees-mo'-may-tro], *m.* Seismometer. *V.* SEISMÓGRAFO.

selección [say-lec-the-on'], *f.* Selection, choice, exception. **Selección múltiple**, multiple choice.

seleccionar [say-lec-the-o-nar'], *va.* To pick, to choose, to select.

selectividad [say-lec-te-ve-dahd'], *f.* Selectivity, selectiveness.

selecto, ta [say-lec'-to, tah], *a.* Select (en calidad), choice, excellent.

selene [say-lay'-nay], *f.* The moon.

selenio [say-lay'-ne-o], *m.* Selenium, a chemical element, related to sulphur.

selenita [say-lay-nee'-tah], *com.* Inhabitant of the moon.

selenites [say-lay-nee'-tes], *f.* Selenite, crystallized gypsum.

selenografía [say-lay-no-grah-fee'-ah], *f.* Selenography, description of the moon.

sellado [sayl-lyah'-do], *a.* Sealed; stamped, franked. -*m.* 1. Sealing (acto). 2. (*Cono Sur*) Stamps, stamp duty.

sellador [sel-lya-dor'], *m.* Sealer.

selladura [sel-lyah-doo'-rah], *f.* Sealing.

sellar [sel-lyar'], *va.* 1. To seal (documento, carta), to put on a seal. 2. To seal, to stamp (pasaporte). 3. To conclude, to finish a thing. 4. To cover, to close up. 5. To obligate as by benefits. **Sellar los labios**, to silence.

sello [sel'-lyo], *m.* 1. Stamp. 2. Signet. 3. Seal. 4. (*Fig.*) Seal stamp, impression. **Sello fiscal**, revenue stamp. **Sello postal, Sello de correo**, postage stamp. **Sellos de premio**, trading stamps. **Sello aéreo**, airmail stamp.

selva [sel'-vah], *f.* Forest (bosque), jungle (jungla). **Selva espesa**, thicket.

selvático, ca [sel-vah'-te-co, cah], *a.* Forest-born, reared in a forest, belonging to a forest.

selvatiquez [sel-vah-te-keth'], *f.* Rusticity, savageness, wildness.

selvicultura [sel-ve-cool-too'-rah], *f.* Forest culture, forestry.

selvoso, sa [sel-vo'-so, sah], *a.* 1. Belonging to forests. 2. Well-wooded.

semafórico, ca [say-ma-fo'-re-co, cah], *a.* Semaphoric, telegraphic.

semáforo [say-mah'-fo-ro], *m.* 1. Traffic light, stoplight. 2. Semaphore, marine signal telegraph, railroad traffic sign.

semana [say-mah'-nah], *f.* 1. A week. **Semana Santa**, Passion-week, Holy week, Easter. **Día entre semana**, working day. 2. Any septenary period of time; hebdomad.

semanal [say-mah-nahl'], *a.* Hebdomadal, weekly.

semanalmente [say-mah-nahl'-men-tay], *adv.* Weekly.

semanario, ria [say-mah-nah'-re-o, ah], *a. & m. & f.* Weekly publication.

semanería [say-mah-nay-ree'-ah], *f.* Functions performed, or work done in the course of a week.

semanero [say-mah-nay'-ro], *m.* One who enters upon weekly functions in his turn.

semanero, ra [say-mah-nay'-ro, rah], *a.* Applied to persons engaged by the week.

semántica [say-man'-te-cah], *f.* Semantics.

semblante [sem-blahn'-tay], *m.* 1. Expression in the face of some emotion; look, mien, feature. 2. Face, countenance. 3. Aspect, looks, phase of things, on which we base a contempt of them; feature. **Las cosas han tomado otro semblante** or **cambiado de semblante**, (*Coll.*) things have taken a different aspect. **Tener buen semblante**, to look well (salud).

semblanza [sem-blahn'-thah], *f.* In literature, biographical sketch.

sembradera [sem-brah-day'-rah], *f.* Anything used for sowing seed; seeder.

sembradío, día [sem-brah-dee'-o, ah], *a.* Fit or prepared for sowing of seed.

sembrado [sem-brah'-do], *m.* Corn-field; ground sown with grain.

sembrador, ra [sem-brah-dor', rah], *a.* Sowing seed. -*m. & f.* Sower (persona). -*f.* (*Amer.*) Seeder, a machine for sowing seeds.

sembradura [sem-brah-doo'-rah], *f.* Insemination, sowing or scattering seed.

sembrar [sem-brar'], *va..* 1. To sow, to scatter seed. 2. To scatter (objetos), to spread, to propagate, to divulge. 3. To give a cause or beginning. 4. To perform a useful undertaking. 5. To collect without order. **Sembrar de sal**, to sow the land with salt (a punishment for treason). **El que siembra recoge**, one reaps what one has sown.

semeja [say-may'-hah], *f.* 1. Resemblance, likeness. 2. Mark, sign. **No es él, ni su semeja**, it is not he, nor anything like him.

semejable [say-may-hah'-blay], *a.* Like, resembling, similar.

semejablemente [say-may-hah'-blah-men-tay], *adv.* Likely.

semejado, da [say-may-hah'-do, dah], *a.* Like. *V.* PARECIDO. -*pp* of SEMEJAR.

semejante [say-may-hahn'-tay], *a.* Similar (parecido), like, conformable. -*m. V.* SEMEJANZA. **Nuestros semejantes**, our fellow-creatures. **Son muy semejantes**, they are very much alike.

semejantemente [say-men-han'-tay-men-tay], *adv.* Likewise, in the same manner, similarly.

semejanza [say-may-hahn'-thah], *f.* Resemblance, conformity, semblance, similitude; likeness, likelihood. **Tener semejanza con**, to look like.

semejar [say-may-har'], *vn.* To be like, to resemble; to liken. -*vr.* To resemble.

semen [say'-men], *m.* 1. Semen, sperm, the fertilizing fluid of animals. 2. (*Bot.*) Seed.

semencera [say-men-thay'-rah], *f.* Sowing scattering seed for growth. *V.* SEMENTERA.

semental [say-men-tahl'], *a.* Seminal.

sementar [say-men-tar'], *va.* To sow, to scatter seed.

sementera [say-men-tay'-rah], *f.* 1. Sowing seed. 2. Land sown with seed (tierra). 3. The seed sown. 4. Seedtime. 5. Origin, cause, beginning.

sementero [say-men-tay'-ro], *m.* 1. Seedlip or seedlop, a vessel in which the sower carries his seed; hopper. 2. Sowing, scattering seed.

sementilla [say-men-teel'-lyah], *f. dim.* of SIMIENTE.

sementino, na [say-men-tee'-no, nah], *a.* Belonging to seed or seed-time.

semestral [say-mes-trahl'], *a.* Semi-yearly, semi-annually. **Informe semestral**, semiannual report. **Cuota semestral**, semiannual fee.

semestre [say-mes'-tray], *a.* Lasting six months. -*m.* Space of six months, semester; leave of absence for six months.

semi [say'-me], *prefix.* Semi, a word which, in composition, signifies *half*; sometimes it is equivalent to *casi*, almost.

semianual [say-me-ah-noo-ahl'], *a.* Semi-annual, half-yearly.

semibreve [say-me-bray'-vay], *f.* (*Mus.*) Semibreve, whole note *(0)*.

semicabrón, semicapro [say-me-car-brone'], *m.* Satyr.

semicircular [say-me-theer-coo-lar'], *a.* Semicircular, semiangular.

semicírculo [say-me-theer'-coo-lo], *m.* Semicircle.

semiconsciente [say-me-cons-thé-ayn'-tay], *a.* Semiconscious.

semicorchea [say-me-cor-chay'-ah], *f.* (*Mus.*) Semiquaver; sixteenth note.

semicircunferencia [say-me-theer-coon-fay-ren'-the-ah], *f.* Semicircumference.

semicopado [say-me-co-pah'-do], *m.* A note which joins the second part of a measure with the first of that which follows it; a syncopated note.

semicromático, ca [say-me-cro-mah'-te-co, cah], *a.* (*Mus.*) Semichromatic.

semidea [say-me-day'-ah], *f.* (*Poet.*) Demigoddess.

semidiáfano, na [say-me-de-ah'-fah-no, nah], *a.* Semidiaphanous.

semidiametro [say-me-de-ah'-may-tro], *m.* Semidiameter, radius.

semidiapasón [say-me-de-ah-pah-sone'], *m.* (*Mus.*) Semidiapason, defective octave.

semidiapente [say-me-de-ah-pen'-tay], *m.* (*Mus.*) Semidiapente, defective fifth.

semidiatesarón [say-me-de-ah-tay-sah-rone'], *m.* (*Mus.*) Semidiatessaron, defective fourth.

semidifunto, ta [say-me-de-foon'-to, tah], *a.* Half-dead, almost dead.

semidiós [say-me-de-os'], *m.* **Semidiosa** [say-me-de-oh'-sah], *f.* Demi-god; demi-goddess.

semidítono [say-me-dee'-to-no], *m.* (*Mus.*) Semiditone, minor third.

semidoble [say-me-do'-blay], *a.* Semidouble: applied in the Catholic church to feasts.

semidocto [say-me-doc'-to], *m.* Sciolist, a half-learned man, half scholar. *-a.* Half-learned.

semidormido, da [say-me-dor-mee'-do, dah], *a.* Half asleep, sleepy.

semidragón [say-me-drah-gone'], *m.* Semidragon.

semiesfera [say-me-es-fay'-rah], *f.* Hemisphere.

semiesférico, ca [say-me-es-fay'-re-co, ah], *a.* Semiglobular, hemispherical.

semifinal [say-me-fe-nahl'], *a.* Semifinal, **Semifinales**, semifinals.

semiflósculo [say-me-flos'-coo-lo], *m. (Bot.)* Semifloret.

semiflosculoso, sa [ay-me-flos-coo-lo'-so, sah], *a. (Bot.)* Semifloscular, semiflosculous.

semifluido, da [say-me-floo'-e-do, dah], *a.* Semi-fluid.

semifusa [say-me-foo'-sah], *f. (Mus.)* Double demisemiquaver, a sixtyfourth note.

semigola [say-me-go'-lah], *f. (Mil.)* Demigorge, half the entrance into a bastion.

semihombre [say-me-om'-bray], *m.* Half-man.

semilla [say-meel'-lyah], *f.* 1. Seed, from which plants are produced. 2. Origin, abuse. **Semillas**, all sorts of seed and grain, wheat and barley excepted; quantity of seed sown.

semillatero [say-mee-lyah-tay'-ro], *m. (Prov.)* V. SEMILLERO.

semillero [say-meel-lyay'-ro], *m.* 1. Seedplot, ground on which plants are sown to be afterwards transplanted; nursery. 2. *(Fig.)* Hotbed; breeding ground. **Un semillero de delincuencia**, a hotbed of crime.

semilunar [say-me-loo-nar'], *a.* Semilunar, semilunery.

semilunio [say-me-loo'-ne-o], *m.* Half the time in which the moon performs its course; half-moon.

semimetal [say-me-may-tahl'], *m.* Semimetal, imperfect metal.

seminal [say-me-nahl'], *a.* 1. Seminal, radical. 2. Spermatic.

seminario [say-me-nah'-re-o], *m.* 1. Seed-plot, nursery, ground in which plants are sown to be afterwards transplanted. 2. Seminary, a school. 3. Musical school for children. 4. Beginning, root, origin, source.

seminarista [say-me-nah-rees'-tah], *m.* A scholar who boards and is instructed in a seminary.

semínima [say-mee'-ne-mah], *f.* 1. *(Mus.)* Crotchet, quarter note. 2. Trifle, thing of no moment.

semioctava [say-mè-oc-tah'-vah], *f.* Poetical composition of four verses in alternate rhymes.

semiordenada [say-me-or-day-nah'-dah], *f. (Math.)* Semiordinate.

semipedal [say-me-pay-dahl'], *a.* Measuring half a foot in length.

semipelagiano, na [say-me-pay-lah-he-ah'-no, nah], *m. & f.* Semi-Pelagian, one who adopts part of the errors of Pelagius.

semiplena [say-me-play'-nah], *f. (For.)* Imperfect proof, half proof.

semiplenamente [say-me-play'-nah-men-tay], *adv.* Half proved.

semipoeta [say-me-po-ay'-tah], *m.* Poetaster.

semiprobanza [say-me-pro-bahn'-thah], *f.* A half proof; imperfect evidence.

semiprueba [say-me-prooo-ay'-bah], *f. (Law.)* Semiproof.

semipútrido, da [say-me-poo'-tre-do, dah], *a.* Half putrid.

semiracional [say-me-rah-the-o-nahl'], *a.* Stupid, ignorant.

semirrecto [say-mir-rec'-to], *a.* Of forty-five degrees: half a right angle.

semirrubio, bia [say-mir-roo'-be-o, ah], *a.* Nearly blonde.

semisalvaje [say-me-sal-vah'-hay], *m.* Semisavage, half savage.

semisestil [say-me-ses-teel'], *m. (Ast.)* Semisextile.

semisumador [say-me-soo-mah-dor], . *(Comput.)* Half-adder.

semita [say-mee'-tah], *m.* Semite, a descendant of Shem.

semiterciana [say-me-ter-the-ah'-nah], *f.* Semitertian.

semítico, ca [say-mee'-te-co, cah], *a.* Semitic, relating to Shem. **Lengua semítica**, semitic tongue, one of a great family of languages, of which hebrew, Arabic, Ethiopic, and Assyrian are types.

semitono [say-me-toh'-no], *m.* (plus.) Semitone.

semitransparente [say-me-trans-pah-ren'-tay], *a.* Almost transparent.

semivibración [say-me-ve-brah-the-on'], *f.* Vibration of the pendulum that ascends or descends.

semivivo, va [say-me-vee'-vo, vah], *a.* Half alive.

semivocal [say-me-vo-cahl'], *a.* Semivowel, as *f, l, m, n, r, s.*

semivulpa [say-me-vool'-pah], *f.* Animal like a wolf.

sémola [say'-mo-lah], *f.* 1. Groats or grits, made of decorticated wheat; wheat ground coarse. 2. An Italian paste of the quality of vermicelli, in the form of very small grain, for the use of the sick.

semoviente [say-mo-ve-en'-tay], *a.* Moving of itself.

sempiterna [sem-pe-terr'-nah], *f.* Sort of serge, everlasting.

sempiternamente [sem-pe-ter'-nah-men-tay], *adv.* Eternally.

sempiterno, na [sem-pe-terr'-no, nah], *a.* Eternal, everlasting, sempiternal.

sen, *m.* **sena** *f.* [sen, say'-nah], 1. *(Bot.)* Senna, a purgative shrub. 2. *f.* Six marks on dice. *-pl.* **Senas**, double sixes.

Sena [say'-nah], *m.* The river Seine. See Appendix.

Senado [say-nah'-do], *m.* 1. Senate, a council of senators. 2. Any meeting of grave persons. 3. Senate-house, town-hall.

senadoconsulto [say-nah-do-con-sool'-to], *m.* Senatusconsultum, degree of a senate.

senador [say-nah-dor'], *m.* Senator.

senaduría [say-nah-doo-ree'-ah], *f.* Senatorship, a senator's dignity.

senara [say-nah'-rah], *f.* A piece of sown ground, assigned to servants as part of their wages.

senarero [say-nah-ray'-ro], *m.* Servant who enjoys a piece of sown ground as part of his wages.

senario [say-nah'-re-o], *m.* A senary number; a verse consisting of six iambic feet.

senatorio, ria [say-nah-to'-re-o, ah], *a.* Senatorial.

senciente [sen-the-en'-tay], *pa. & a.* Sentient, perceiving.

sencillamente [sen-thel'-lya-men-tay], *adv.* Ingenuously, plainly, abstractedly.

sencillez [sen-theel-lyeth'], *f.* 1. Slightness, slenderness. 2. Simplicity, plainness, artlessness, harmlessness. 3. Silliness, weakness, ignorance.

sencillo, lla [sen-theel'-lyo, lyah], *a.* 1. Simple, unmixed, uncompounded. 2. Light, slight, thin, of light body (fabrics). 3. Silly, weak, easily imposed upon. 4. Ingenuous, plain, artless, harmless. 5. Simple, not ornate in style, expressing ideas naturally. 6. Single: applied to coin of less value than another of the same name. **Es muy sencillo**, it's very simple.

senda [sen'-dah], *f.* 1. Path, foot-path. 2. Means for attaining an end.

senderar [sen-day-rar'], *va.* To make a path. *-vn.* To walk on a path or footpath.

senderear [sen-day-ray-ar'], *va.* 1. To guide or conduct on a footpath. 2. To adopt extraordinary means to obtain an end. 3. To make a path.

sendero [sen-day'-ro], *m.* Path, footpath. *V.* SENDA.

sendica, illa, ita [sen-dee'-cah], *f. dim.* Little pathway.

sendos, das [sen'-dos, das], *a.* 1. Each of two, either, one each, each. 2. Great; abundant. **Les dio sendos libros**, she gave them a book each. **Con sendas peculiaridades**, each with its own peculiarity.

senectud [say-nec-tood'], *f.* Old age, senescence.

senescal [say-nees-cahl'], *m.* 1. Seneschal, lord high chamberlain or high steward. 2. Chief commander of a town, especially in time of war. 3. Lord chief of justice. It is used only in speaking of foreign countries.

senescalía [say-nes-cah-lee'-ah], *f.* Place, dignity, or employment of a seneschal.

senil [say-neel'], *a.* 1. Senile. 2. *(Ast.)* Fourth quadrant of the celestial map.

seno [say-no]. *m.* 1. Chest, thoracic cavity; bosom. 2. Womb. **Seno materno**, womb. 3. Lap of a woman. 4. Circular space formed by moving round. 5. Hole, cavity, sinus. 6. Gulf, bay. 7. Any cavity in the interior of the human body. 8. Security, support; asylum, refuge. 9. *(Geom.)* The sine of an arc. 10. Sinus, cavity of a wound. 11. Center, middle part. 12. *(Naut.)* Curvature of a sail. **Seno recto**, sine. **Seno segundo**, cosine. **Seno todo** or **total**, total sine or radius. **Seno verso**, versed sine.

sensación [sen-sah-the-on'], *f.* Sensation, feeling. **Una sensación de placer**, a feeling of pleasure.

sensacional [sen-sah-the-o-nahl'], *a.* Sensational.

sensacionalismo [sen-sah-the-o-nah-lees'-mo], *m.* Sensationalism.

sensatez [sen-sah-teth'], *f.* Judiciousness, reasonableness, prudence, good sense.

sensato, ta [sen-sah'-to, tah], *a.* Sensible, judicious, prudent, reasonable, wise.

sensibilidad [sen-se-be-le-dahd'], *f.* Sensibility, quickness of perception, sensitiveness.

sensible [sen-see'-blay], *a.* 1. Sensitive. 2. Sensible, having the power of perceiving by the senses (que siente). 3. Sensitive, having sense or perception, but not reason. 4. Perceived by the mind. 5. Causing grief or pain. 6. Sensible, having quick intellectual feeling, easily moved or affected. 7. Regrettable (lamentable). 8. Perceptible (cambio), tangible (diferencia); heavy (golpe). **Un aparato muy sensible**, a very sensitive device. **Una sensible mejoría**, a noticeable improvement.

sensiblemente [sen-see'-blay-men-tay], *adv.* Sensibly, with grief or pain.

sensitiva [sen-se-tee'-vah], *f.* *(Bot.)* Sensitive plant.

sensitivo, va [sen-se-tee'-vo, vah], *a.* Sensitive; sensual; sensible.

sensorio [son-so'-re-o], *m.* Sensorium or sensory, the seat of sensation.

sensorio, ria [sen-so'-re-o, ah], *a.* Belonging to the sensorium.

sensual [sen-soo-ahl'], *a.* 1. Sensitive, having sense or perception. 2. Sensual (sexual), lewd, lustful. 3. Belonging to the carnal appetites.

sensualidad [sen-soo-ah-le-dahd'], *f.* Sensuality, lust, lewdness.

sensualismo [sen-soo-ah-lees'-mo], *m.* 1. Sensationalism, a doctrine opposed to idealism, which places the origin of ideas in the senses. 2. Sensuality.

sensualista [sen-soo-ah-lees'-tah], *a.* Sensualistic.

sensualmente [sen-soo-ahl'-men-tay], *adv.* Sensually, carnally.

sentada [sen-tah'-dah], *f.* Stone put in its proper place. V. ASENTADA.

sentadillas (A) [sen-tah-deel'-lyas], *adv.* With both legs on one side; side-saddlewise; as women ride horseback.

sentado, da [sn-tah'-do, dah], *a.* Sedate, judicious, grave, prudent. **Estar sentado**, to sit. **Dar algo por sentado**, to take something for granted.

sentamiento [sen-tah-me-ayn'-to], *m.* *(Arch.)* V. ASIENTO.

sentar [sen-tar'], *vn.* 1. To fit, to become, to suit (ropa). **Esta chaqueta no me sienta bien**, this coat does not fit me well. **Ese color le sienta bien a su cara**, that color suits her complexion well. **Sentar bien**, to down well. **A mí me sienta como un tiro**, it suits me like a hole in the head. *-va.* 2. To set up, to establish (cimientos). To seat (persona). V. ASENTAR. 4. To press down the seams of clothes, as tailors, with a goose. 5. To please, to be agreeable. 6. *(And. Carib.)* To crush (persona). 7. *(And.)* To rein in (caballo). **No le sentó bien la conversación**, the conversation did not please him. **Sentar las bases**, to lay the fundations. *-vr.* 1. To sink, to subside. V. ASENTARSE. 2. To sit down (persona), to squat, to seat oneself. 3. *(Coll.)* To fall plump upon one's breech. 4. To occupy the seat which belongs to one's plans or employment, to seat oneself in an office or dignity.

sentencia [sen-ten'-the-ah], *f.* 1. Sentence, the judicial decision of a suit at law, judgment; the penalty in a criminal case. 2. Opinion, persuasion of the mind. 3. Sentence, a maxim. 4. Sentence, a period in writing. **Decir sentencias a alguno**, to scold, to abuse one. **Fulminar la sentencia**, to pass judgment. **Sentencia de muerte**, death sentence.

sentenciar [sen-ten-the-ar'], *va.* 1. To sentence, to pass judgment; to condemn. 2. To oppress one's opinion. 3. To determine, to decide.

sentenciario [sen-ten-the-ah'-re-o], *m.* Collection of sentences.

sentención [sen-ten-the-on'], *f.* A severe, rigorous sentence.

sentenciosamente [sen-ten-the-o-sah'-men-tay], *adv.* Sententiously.

sentencioso, sa [sen-ten-the-o'-so, sah], *a.* Sententious (personas), pithy (dicho), axiomatic.

sentenzuela [sen-ten-thoo-ay'-lah], *f. dim.* Slight sentence.

sentidamente [sen-tee'-dah-men-tay], *adv.* Feelingly, painfully.

sentido, da [sen-tee'-do, dah], *a.* 1. Sensible, fooling, expressive of sensibility. 2. Split, cloven, relaxed. 3. Putrefying. 4. *(Mex.)* Having good hearing (de buen oído). **Darse por sentido**, to show resentment. *-pp.* of SENTIR.

sentido [sen-tee'-do], *m.* 1. Sense (del cuerpo), the faculty of perceiving objects: any of the five senses. 2. Sense (juicio), understanding, reason. 3. Acceptation, signification, import, sense, meaning, construction. 4. Mode of understanding something, or the judgment made of it. 5. Intelligence or knowledge by which certain things are executed. 6. *(Mex.)* Ear (oreja). **Sentido común**, common sense. **Estar sentido**, *(Coll.)* to be miffed, to be a little offended. **Los cinco sentidos**, the five senses. **Perder el sentido**, to lose consciousness. **Sentido común**, common sense. **Iban en sentido inverso al nuestro**, they were traveling in the opposite direction to us.

sentimental [sen-te-men-tahl'], *a.* 1. Sentimental, affecting, pathetic. 2. Emotional, easily affected. 3. Sentimental, ridiculously affected.

sentimentalismo [sen-te-men-tah-lees'-mo], Sentimentalism, sentimentality.

sentir [sen-teer'], *va.* 1. To feel, to perceive by the senses (percibir). 2. To hear (oír). **Sin sentir**, without being seen, felt, or known. 3. To endure, to suffer (enfermedad). 4. To grieve, to regret (lamentar), to mourn, to be sorry for. **Sentir el ruido de un coche**, to hear the noise of a car. **Sin sentir frío**, without feeling the cold. *-vn.* 1. To judge, to form an opinion. 2. To foresee, to foreknow. 3. To accommodate the action to the expression, to exhibit a suitable feeling. *-vr.* 1. To be moved, to be affected, to complain. 2. To crack or flaw (vasos, campanas). 3. To be in a ruinous state. 4. To be sensible of, to feel pain in any part of the body; to acknowledge the obligation or necessity. 5. To resent. 6. *(Naut.)* To spring (mástil). **Sentirse como en su casa**, to feel at home. **Sentirse actor**, to feel oneself to be an actor. 7. *(LAm.)* To get cross (enfadarse).

sentir [sen-teer'], *m.* 1. Feeling, opinion, judgement. 2. V. SENTIMIENTO.

seña [say'-nyah], *f.* 1. Sign, mark (del cuerpo), token or note given without words, nod, dumb motion. 2. Signal, notice given by a sign. 3. Sign, a token of something. 4. *(Mil.)* Password, watchword. **Por señas, por más señas**, as a stronger proof of it. **Señas particulares**, identifying marks. **Hacer señas a uno**, to make a sign to somebody. **Hablar por señas**, to talk by signs.

señal [say-nyahl'], *f.* 1. Sign, mark, signature, token (indicio); mark or note of distinction. 2. Landmark to mark a boundary. 3. Sign, indication, symptom, **Señales claras o evidentes**, open marks. 4. Vestige, stamp, impression, footstep; scar. 5. Representation, image. 6. Earnest, handsel, pledge; earnest money given in token that a bargain is ratified. 7. *(Mil.)* Standard, banner. 8. Sign, wonder, prodigy, prognostic. 9. Signal, a sign to give notice. 10. A diagnostic or prognostic symptom. -*pl.* (*Naut.*) Signals. 11. (*LAm.*) Earmark. **Señales de bruma**, fog-signals. **Señales de peligro**, signals of distress. **En señal**, in proof of. **Ni señal**, not a trace. **Es buena señal**, it's a good sign. **Hacer una señal grosera**, to make a rude sign. **Señal de peligro**, danger signal. **Señal de ocupado**, danger signal.

señaladamente [say-nyah-lah-dah'-men-tay]. *Adv.* Especially (especialmente), remarkably, namely; signally.

señalado, da [say-nyah-lah'-do, dah], *a. & pp.* of SEÑALAR. Famous, celebrated, noble. **Dejar señalado a uno**, to scar somebody permanently.

señalamiento [say-nyah-lah-me-en'-to], *m.* Assignation, determining or appointing a certain time or place.

señalar [say-nyah-lar'], *va.* 1. To stamp, to mark out (significar). 2. To sign decrees or despatches. 3. To signalize, to point out, to make known. 4. To speak positively, to say expressly. 5. To name, to nominate, to constitute; to fix; to determine. 6. To mark with a wound, especially in the face. 7. To make signals, to indicate. **Señalar con el dedo**, to point with the finger. **Señalan la llegada de la primavera**, they announce the arrival of spring. **Tuve que señalarle varios errores**, I had to point out several mistakes to him. - *vr.* 1. To distinguish oneself, to excel. 2. To mark the game at piquet. **Señalar los motivos de**, to account for.

señaleja [say-nyah-lay'-hah], *f. dim.* A little sign or mark.

señalero [say-nayh-lay'-ro], *m.* A person who formerly bore the royal ensign; king's ensign.

señas [say'-nyahs], *f. pl.* Address, residence of someone.

señolear [say-nyo-lay-ar'], *m.* To catch birds with a lure.

señor [say-nyor'], *m.* 1. Lord, master, owner of a thing (de bienes). 2. Sir, a title given to an equal or inferior; mister. 3. God, the lord and master of all things. 4. Master; governor. **Quiere parecer un señor**, he tries to look like a gentleman. **El señor de la casa**, the master of the household. **El señor presidente**, the president. **Señor director**, the manager, the headmaster. **Muy señor mío**, Dear Sir.

señora [say-nyo'-rah], *f.* 1. Lady, a word of complaisance used of women. 2. Lady, mistress or owner of a thing (de bienes). 3. Madam: used in address to ladies of every degree. 4. Dame, gentlewoman. 5. Mother-in-law. 6. Mistress of a house or school. **Nuestra señora**, the Virgin Mary. **Muy señora mía**, Dear Madam.

señoreaje [say-nyo-ray-ah'-hay], *m.* 1. Seigniorage, acknowledgment of power. 2. Duty belonging to the king for the coining of money.

señoreante [say-nyo-ray-ahn'-tay], *pa.* Domineering.

señorear [say-nyo-ray-ar'], *va.* 1. To master, to domineer (dominar), to lord, to rule despotically. 2. To excel, to occupy a higher station. 3. To treat another repeatedly with the title of lord. 4. To govern one's passions. -*vr.* To affect peculiar gravity in one's deportment; to assume an air of importance (darse humos).

señoría [say-nyo-ree'-ah], *f.* 1. Lordship, a title given to persons of a certain rank and distinction (título). 2. Person to whom this title is given. 3. Government of a particular state; senate; prince. 4. Seigniory, a lordship.

señorial [say-nyo-re-ahl'], *a.* Manorial, manerial.

señoril [say-nyo-reel'], *a.* Lordly, belonging to a lord, genteel.

señorilmente [say-nyo-ril'-men-tay], *adv.* Nobly, grandly, majestically, lordly.

señorío [say-nyo-ree'-o], *m.* 1. Seigniory, dominion, command. 2. Imperiousness, arrogance of command. 3. Lordship, manor or territory belonging to a lord. 4. Gravity or stateliness of deportment. 5. Freedom and selfcontrol in action.

señorita [say-nyo-ree'-tah], *f. dim.* 1. Miss: a title of honor given to young ladies; a little, pretty, or amiable young lady. 2. Madam, a term of compliment used in addressing young ladies. 3. (*LAm.*) Schoolteacher (profesora).

señorito [say-nyo-ree'-to], *m. dim.* 1. Master: a title of honor given to young gentlemen, a little, pretty, or amiable young

lord. 2. Lordling, one who assumes an air of dignity and importance.

señorón, na [say-nyo-rone', nah], *m. & f. aug.* Great seignior or lady.

señuelo [say-nyoo-ay'-lo], *m.* Lure, enticement, attachment.

sépalo [say'-pah-lo], (*Both.*) Sepal, each division of the calyx.

separable [se-pah-rah'-blay], *a.* Separable.

separación [say-pah-rah-the-on'], *f.* 1. Separation. 2. Resignation, withdrawal. 3. Parting. **Separación de poderes**, separation of powers. **Separación racial**, racial segregation. **Separación entre registros**, (*Comput.*) interrecord gap, record gap. **Separación entre los caracteres (puntos)**, character pitch.

separadamente [say-pah-rah'-dah-men-tay], *adv.* Separately, severally.

separado, da [say-pah-rah'-do, data], *a. & pp.* of SEPARAR. Separate, separated. **Vive separado de su mujer**, he is separated from his wife.

separador, ra [say-pah-rah-dor', rah], *m. & f.* Separator, divider.

separar [say-pah-rar'], *va.* 1. To separate (objeto), to part, to divide, to cut, to chop, to hackle. 2. To separate, to set sports, to lay aside; to repose; to divorce. 3. To anatomize; to dissect in order to show or study the structure of animal bodies. **Los negocios le separan de su familia**, business keeps him away from his family. -*vr.* To separate, to part (componentes), to be disunited; to come off, to go off, to fly off; to withdraw, to drop all communication and intercourse to retire, to sequester. **Separarse de un grupo**, to leave a group. **Se ha separado de su mujer**, he has left his wife.

separatista [say-pah-rah-tees'-tah], *a. & n.* Separatist, laboring to part a territory or colony from the capital.

separativo, va, separatorio, ria [say pa-rah-tee'-vo, vah], *a.* That which separates, separators.

sepedón [say-pay-done'], *m.* Seps, a kind of serpent.

sepelio [say-pay'-le-o], *m.* Burial by the church of the faithful.

sepia [say'-pe-ah], *f.* 1. (*Zool.*) Cuttlefish. V. JIBIA. 2. Sepia, a coloring matter obtained from the cuttle-fish, and used in water-colors.

sepsis [sep'-sis], *f.* (*Med.*) Sepsis.

septenario [sep-tay-nah'-re-o], *m.* 1. Septenary, septenarious, of seven figures. 2. Of seven elements. -*m.* Space of seven days, seven years, etc.

septenio [sep-tay'-ne-o], *m.* Space of seven years.

septentrión [sep-ten-tre-on'], *m.* 1. Septentrion, the north; that part of the sphere which extends from the equator to the arctic pole. 2. (*Naut.*) North wind. 3. (*Ast.*) The Great Bear.

septentrional [sep-ten-tre-o-nahl'], *a.* Septentrional, northern, north, northerly.

septicemia [sep-te-thay'-me-ah], *f.* (*Med.*) Septicemia, blood poisoning.

séptico, ca [sep'-te-co, cah], *a.* Septic, septical, productive of putrefaction.

septiembre [sep-te-em'-bray], *m.* September.

séptima [sep'-te-mah], *f.* 1. Sequence of seven cards, in the game of piquet. 2. (*Mus.*) The interval of a seventh.

séptimo, ma [sep'-te-mo, mah], *a.* Seventh, the ordinal number of seven; one of the seven parts into which a whole is divided.

septo [sep'-to], *m.* (*Anat.*) Septum.

septuagenario, ria [sep-tooth-hay-nah'-re-o, ah], *a.* Septuagenary, seventy years old.

septuagésima [sep-too-ah-hay'-se-mah], *f.* The third Sunday before the first Sunday in Lent.

septuagésimo, ma [sep-too-ah-hay'-se-mo, mah], *a.* 1. Seventieth, the ordinal number of seventy. 2. Septuagesimal, consisting or seventy.

septuplicación [sep-too-ple-cah-the-on'], *f.* Multiplying by seven.

septuplicar [sep-too-ple-car'], *va.* To make seven-fold; to multiply by seven.

séptuplo, pla [sep'-too-plo, plah], *a.* Septuple, seven-fold.

sepulcral [say-pool-crahl'], *a.* Sepulchral, monumental.

sepulcro [say-pool'-cro], *m.* 1. Sepulcher, grave, tomb. 2. A small chest in which the sacred host is preserved in Roman Catholic churches. 3. *(Met.)* An unhealthy country.

sepultación [say-pool-tah-the-on'], *f.* Sepulture: Interment.

sepultador [say-pool-tah-dor'], *m.* Burier, grave-digger.

sepultar [say-pol-tar'], *va* 1. To bury (enterrar), to inter, to entomb. 2. To hide (esconder), to conceal.

sepultura [say-pool-too'-rah], *f.* 1. Sepulture, interment. 2. Tomb, grave (tumba).

sepulturero [say-pool-too-ray'-ro], *m.* Grave-digger, sexton.

sequedad [say-kay-dahd'], *f.* 1. Aridity, dryness. 2. Barrenness, sterility, scarcity of provisions in a country. 3. Defect in nutrition of a member. 4. Asperity of intercourse, sourness of temper, abruptness: dryness of style. 5. Want of devotion and fervor in spiritual matters.

sequedad, sequeral [say-kay-dahd', say-kay-rahl'], *m.* A dry, barren soil.

sequero [say-kay'-ro], *m.* 1. Dry, unirrigated arable ground. 2. *V.* SECADERO.

sequeroso, sa [say-kay-ro'-so, sah], *a.* Dry, wanting moisture.

sequete [say-kay'-tay], *m.* 1. Piece of hard, dry bread. 2. Harshness and asperity of address or intercourse. 3. A violent shock.

sequía [say-kee'-ah], *f.* Dryness; thirst, drought (falta de lluvias). *V.* SEQUEDAD.

sequillo [say-keel'-lyo], *m.* Biscuit made of flour and sugar.

sequío [say-kee'-o], *m.* Dry, unirrigated arable ground.

séquito [say-ke-to], *m.* 1. Retinue (comitiva), suite. 2. Popularity, public applause.

sequizo, za [say-kee'-tho, thah], *a.* Dry: applied to fruits and other eatables that are not juicy.

ser [serr], *vn.* 1. To be: an auxiliary verb, by which the passive is formed. 2. To be in some place or situation. 3. To be or to exist really. 4. To be, to happen, to occur, to fall out. **¿Cómo fue eso?** how did that happen? 5. To be worth. **¿A cómo es eso?** what is the price of that? 6. To be born in a place; to originate in (origen). **¿De dónde es usted? - Soy de Sevilla**, where are you from? - I am from Seville. 7. To affirm or deny. 8. To be the property of one, to belong to, to pertain (posesión). 9. To be useful, to serve, to contribute to anything. 10. Joined to nouns which signify employment or occupation, it means to be occupied in them. **Ya sea de este modo o de otro**, whether it be this way or the other. **Sea lo que fuere**, be that as it may. **En ser**, in being, in existence. **Ser uno de tantos**, to be one of the number. **Es quien es**, or **se porta como quien es**, he is what he ought to be, or he behaves as he should. **Ser cómplice de**, to have a hand in. **Ser para todo**, to be fit for everything; to be up to everything. **¿Qué es del libro?** where is the book? **Mañana será otro día**, tomorrow may bring better luck. **Ser uña y carne**, to be hand and glove, to be close friends. **Eso no es de la incumbencia de Vd.**, that does not concern you; it is none of your business. **Es difícil**, it's difficult. **Ese coche no es para correr mucho**, that car isn't made to go very fast. **Somos seis**, there are six of us. **Fue construido**, it was built. **Ser o no ser**, to be or not to be. **Es de desear que**, it is to be wished that...**Está siendo estudiado, it's being examined**.

ser [serr], *m.* Being, the entity, essense, or nature of things; vague; point or burden of a piece.

sera [say'-rah], *f.* A large pannier or basket.

serado [say-rah'-do], *m.* A parcel of panniers or baskets.

seráfico, ca [say-rah'-fe-co, cah], *a.* Seraphic, angelic (angélico): applied especially to St. Francis and his religionists.

serafín [say-rah-feen'], *m.* 1. Seraph, seraphim, angel. 2. An extreme beauty.

serafina [say-rah-fee'-nah], *f.* A Port of swan-skill, resembling fine baize.

seraje [say-rah'-hay], *m.* Panniers or baskets, especially of charcoal.

serape [say-ra'-pay], *m. (Mex.)* A narrow blanket, worn by men, or thrown over the saddle. *V.* MANGA.

serapino [say-rah-pee'-no], *m.* A sort of gum, obtained by incision from the fennel-giant.

serasa [say-rah'-sah], *f.* Chintz. *V.* ZARAZA.

serasquier [say-ras-ke-err'], *m.* Seraskier, a Turkish generalissimo.

serba [serr'-bah], *f.* Service, a kind of wild pear, the fruit of the service-tree.

serbal, serbo [ser-bahl', serr'-boh], *m. (Bot.)* Service-tree. **Serbal de cazadores**, mountain-ash service-tree.

serena [say-ray'-nah], *f.* Evening dew. **A la serena**, *V.* AL SERENO.

serenamente [say-ray'-nah-men-tay], *adv.* Serenely, composedly, coolly, quietly.

serenar [say-ray-nar'], *va. & vn.* 1. To clear up, to grow fair, to become serene (tiempo). 2. To settle, to grow clear. 3. To pacify, to tranquilize (tranquilizar), to moderate, to compose; to be serene.

serenata [say-ray-nah'-tah], *f.* Serenade, concert, nightmusic.

serenero [say-ray-nay'-ro], *m.* Night-wrap, a loose cover which ladies used to throw over the head at night.

sereni [say-ray-nee'], *m.* A light boat on board large vessels, used for greater despatch. 2. A yawl.

serenidad [say-ray-ne-dahd'], *f.* 1. Serenity, the clearness of mild and temperate weather. 2. Serene highness, a title given to princes. 3. Serenity, meekness, mildness, sereneness, serenitude. 4. *V.* DESVERGÜENZA.

serenísimo, ma [say-ray-nee'-se-mo, mah], *a. sup.* 1. Most serene, honorary title of princes, or kings' children. 2. Extremely serene, calm, or quiet.

sereno [say-ray'-no], *m.* 1. Evening dew, night dew (rocío). 2. Night-watch, watchman (persona). 3. Settled (tiempo); cloudless (cielo). **Estar sereno**, to be sober. **Dormir al sereno**, to sleep out in the open.

serial [say-re-ahl'], *m.* Serial.

seriamente [say'-re-ah-men-tay]. *adv.* Seriously, gravely, solemnly, in earnest, for good and all.

sericícola [say-re-thee'-co-lah], *a.* Sero-cultural, relating to silk culture.

sericicultura [say-re-the-cool-too'-rah], *f.* Silk-culture, sericulture.

sérico, ca [say'-re-co, cah], *a.* Silken.

serie [say'-re-ay], *f.* Series, order, gradation, sequence, suite. **Fabricar en serie**, to mass-produce. **Artículos fuera de serie**, goods left over.

seriedad [say-re-ay-dahd'], *f.* 1. Seriousness, gravity (gravedad). 2. Sternness of mien, rudeness of address. 3. Simplicity, plainness, sincerity. 4. Dignity (dignidad). **Falta de seriedad**, frivolity.

serigrafía [say-re-gah-fee'-ah], *f.* Silk-screen process.

serijo, serillo [say-ree'-ho, say reel'-lyo], *m.* A small basket made of palm-leaves.

serio, ria [say'-re-o, ah], *a.* 1. Serious (actitud, expresión), grave, dignified. 2. Serious, important, weighty. 3. Grand, majestic, solemn. 4. Uncouth, rude, severe, gold. 5. Plain, true, sincere. **Ponerse serio**, to look serious. **Un traje serio**, a formal suit. **Es una persona poco seria**, he's a very irresponsible sort.

sermocinal [ser-mo-the-nahl'], *a.* Oratorical, relating to a public speech.

sermón [ser-mon'], *m.* 1. Sermon, homily. 2. Censure, reprehension.

sermonario, ria [ser-mo-nah'-re-o, ah], *a.* Relating to a sermon.

sermonario [ser-mo-nah'-re-o], *m.* Collection of sermons.

sermonear [ser-mo-nay-ar'], *va. (Coll.)* To lecture, to censure, to reprimand; to sermonize.

sermonización [ser-mo-ne-thah-the-on'], *f.* Speaking in public; colloquy, conversation.

seroja. *f.* **serojo,** *m.* [say-ro'-hah, ho]. A withered leaf, fallen from a tree. **serojas,** small trees left on a piece of woodland, after the large trees have been cut down.

serón [say-rone'], *m.* 1. A large frail or pannier used to carry figs, raisins, etc.; seroon. 2. Hamper, crate.

seronero [say-ro-nay'-ro], *m.* The maker of trails or panniers called *serones.*

serosidad [say-ro-se-dahd'], *f.* Serosity, serousness, thin or watery blood.

seroso, sa [say-ro'-so, sah], *a.* Serous, thin, watery.

serotino, na [say-ro-tee'-no, nah], *a.* Serotinous, produced late in the season.

serpa [serr'-pah], *f.* Layer, a long twig or spray of vine planted in the ground, without being separated from the mother plant, in order to rage another stock.

serpear [ser-pay-ar'], *vn.* To wind like a serpent, to move in undulations, to crawl, to creep; to meander, to serpentize.

serpentaria [ser-pen-tah'-re-ah], *vn. (Bot.)* Snake-root, a medicine root.

serpentario [ser-pen-tah'-re-o], *m.* A northern constellation: the constellation Ophiuchus.

serpentear [ser-pen-tay-ar'], *vn.* To move like a serpent, to serpentine.

serpenticida [ser-pen-te-thee'-dah], *com.* Serpent-killer.

serpentígero, ra [ser-pen-tee'-hay-ro, rah], *a. (Poet.)* Serpentigerous, bearing serpents.

serpentín [ser-pen-ten'], *m.* 1. *(Min.)* Serpentine, a speckled green stone resembling the serpent's skin. 2. Cock, hammer of a gun or musketlock. 3. *(Chem.)* Worm for distilling liquors. 4. Serpent, a musical instrument; a wind-instrument of low pitch, now disused. 5. Ancient piece of ordnance.

serpentina [ser-pen-tee'-nah], *f.* 1. Cock, hammer of a gunrock. 2. Culverin, missile weapon. 3. *(Chem.)* Serpentine, or worm for distilling liquors.

serpentinamente [ser-pen-tee'-nah-men-tay], *adv.* In a serpentine manner.

serpentino, na [ser-pen-tee'-no, nah], *a.* 1. Serpentine, winding like a serpent; resembling a serpent; belonging to the oil of serpents. 2. Applied to a slanderous tongue. 3. Serpentine: applied to a kind of marble.

serpentón [ser-pen-tohn'], *m.* 1. *(Aug.)* A large serpent. 2. A musical instrument. *V.* SERPENTÍN.

serpia [serr'-pe-ah], *f. (Prov.)* Gummy or viscous matter of a vine-stock.

serpiente [ser-pe-en'-tay], *f.* 1. Serpent (culebra). **Serpiente de cascabel,** rattle-snake. 2. Serpent, devil, Satan.

serpiginoso, sa [ser-pe-he-no'-so, sah], *a. (Med.)* Serpiginous.

serpigo [ser-pee'-go], *m. (Med.)* Tetter, ring-worm, serpigo.

serpol [ser-pole'], *m. (Bot.)* Wild thyme.

serpollo [ser-pol'-lyo], *m.* Shoot, sprout especially of a tree which has been pruned.

serradizo, za [ser-rah-dee'-tho, thah], *a.* Fit to be sawed.

serrado, da [ser-rah'-do, dah], *a.* Serrate, toothed like a saw, laciniate. *-pp.* of SERRAR.

serrador [ser-rah-dor'], *m.* Sawer or sawyer. *V.* ASERRADOR.

serradoras [ser-rah-do'-ras], *f. pl.* Sawdust. *V.* SERRÍN.

serrallo [ser-rahl'-lyo], *m.* 1. Seraglio, the palace of the grand signior. 2. Place of obscenity. *(Per.)*

serranía [ser-ah-nee'-ah], *f.* Ridge of mountains, a moutainous country.

serraniego, ga [ser-rah-ne-ar'-go, gah], *a. V.* SERRANO.

serranil [ser-rah-neel'], *m.* Kind of knife.

serrano, na [ser-rah'-no, nah], *a. & m. & f.* Mountaineer. highlander, inhabiting mountains.

serrar [ser-rar'], *va.* To saw. *V.* ASERRAR. *(Yo sierro, yo sierre,* from *Serrar. V.* ACERTAR.)

serreta [ser-ray'-tah], *f.* 1. Dim. of SIERRA. 2. Piece of a cavesson or nose-band, used in breaking a horse.

serrato, ta [ser-rah'-to, tah], *a. (Anat.)* Denticulated, serrated.

serrezuela [ser-ray-thoo-ay'-lah], *f. dim.* A small saw.

serrijón [ser-re-hone'], *m.* Short chain of mountains.

serrín [ser-reen'], *m.* Sawdust. *V.* ASERRADURAS.

serrino, na [ser-ree'-no, nah], *a.* 1. Belonging to chains of mountains. 2. Applied to a quick, irregular pulse.

serrucho [ser-roo'-cho], *m.* Hand-saw with a small handle. **Serrucho braguero,** pit-saw.

servador [ser-vah-dor'], *m.* Preserver: applied by poets to Jupiter..

serventesio [ser-ven-tay'-se-o], *m. (Poet.)* Quartetto, like the first four verses of an octave.

servible [ser-vee'-blay], *a.* Fit for service, serviceable, adaptable.

servicial [ser-ve-the-ahl'], *a.* Obsequious, diligent, obliging, compliant, friendly, accommodating, serviceable. *m. (Coll.)* Clyster.

servicialmente [ser-ve-the-ahl'-men-tay], *adv.* Obsequiously, serviceably.

serviciar [ser-ve-the-ar'], *va.* To collect the sheep-walk dues, donations to the state, etc.

servicio [ser-vee'-the-o], *m.* 1. Service, the act of serving; the state of a servant. 2. Service, favor, kind office; good turn. 3. Divine service. 4. Utility, benefit, advantage. 5. Closestool, privy-chair. 6. Service, cover, course. **Servicio de mesa,** service for the table. 7. Personal service or residence of beneficed clergy. 8. Toilet. 9. Service (en hotel). 12. Serve, service (tenis). 13. Job, case (de policía). **Estar al servicio de,** to be in the service of. **Hacer un servicio para uno,** to do somebody a service. **Servicio a domicilio,** delivery service. **Servicio incluido,** service charge included. 14. *(Comput.)* **Servicio de asistencia en materia de software,** software support service. **Servicio de asistencia telefónica,** phone assistance. **Servicio y apoyo,** service and support.

servidero, ra [ser-ve-day'-ro, rah], *a.* 1. Fit for service, utilizable. 2. Requiring personal attendance.

servido, da [ser-vee'-do, dah], *a. & pp.* of SERVIR. 1. Served, pleased. 2. Second-hand, used.

servidor [ser-ve-dor'], *m.* 1. Servant (criado), waiter. 2. One who politely tenders his services to another. **Servidor de Vd.,** your servant; at your service. 4. Pan of a close-stool.

servidora [ser-ve-do'-rah], *f.* 1. Maid, female servant. 2. A term of courtesy used by women.

servidumbre [ser-ve-doom'-bray], *f.* 1 Attendance, servitude (estado); whole establishment of servants. 2. Slavery, mancipation, state of a slave. 3. Mighty or inevitable obligation to do anything. 4. Servitude, service, the act of serving or attending at command. 5. *(Law.)* Right which one has over another person or thing, as the liberty of passing through a house or garden; right of way. 6. Subjection of the passions.

servil [ser-veel'], *a. & m.* 1. Servile (actitud), slavish (imitación), fawning; sneaking. 2. Servile, peculiar to servants, dependent, menial. 3. Servile, low, mean, abject; mechanical.

servilidad [ser-ve-le-dahd'], *f. (Prov.)* Servility, meanness, baseness, submision from fear.

servilismo [ser-ve-lees'-mo], *m.* Servilism, blind adhesion to authority.

servilmente [ser-veel'-men-tay], *adv.* Servilely, slavishly; basely; indecently.

servilla [ser-veel'-lyah], *f.* A kind of thin-soled shoe.

servilleta [ser-veel-lyay'-tah], *f.* Napkin used at table.

servilletero, ra [ser-veel-lyay-tah'-ro, rah], *a.* Relating to table-linen.

servio, via [serr'-ve-o, ah], *a.* Servian, native of or relating to Servia.

serviola [ser-ve-o'-lah], *f. (Naut.)* Cathead, anchor beam.

servir [ser-veer'], *va.* 1. To serve, to perform menial services. **Servir de mayordomo,** to serve as steward. 2. To serve, to do a favor or kind office. To serve (en restaurante), to hold an employment, to occupy a public station. 4. To court a lady. 5. To serve, to perform somebody else's functions; to act as a substitute. 6. To serve (comida), to wait at table. 9. To heat the oven. 10. To dress victuals for the table. 11. To administer. **Para servir a Vd.**, at your service. **Servir de**, to serve for. **Servir a la patria**, to serve one's country. **Servir patatas a uno**, to serve somebody with potatoes. -vn. 1. To serve, to be in the services of another (criado), to be subject to another. 2. To correspond, to agree. 3. To serve, to answer the purpose; to conduce; to be useful or convenient (ser útil). 4. To serve, to be a soldier. 5. To be employed at anything by another's orders. **Sirvió 10 años**, he served 10 years. **No sirve para nada**, it's no use at all. -vr. 1. To deign, to vouchsafe, to condescend, to please. **Sirva de aviso**, let this be a warning. 2. To make use of; to employ for some purpose. **Sírvase usted darme su dirección**, please give me your address. **Yo no serviría para futbolista**, I'd be no good as a footballer. **Si el señor se sirve pasar por aquí**, if the gentleman would care to come this way.

servo [ser-vo], *m.* Servo.

servoasistido [ser-vo-ah-sees-tee'-do], *m.* Servo-assisted.

servodirección [ser-vo de-rayc-the-on'], *m.* *f.* Power steering.

servofreno [ser-vo-fray'-no], *m.* Power brake.

servomotor [ser-vo-mo-tor'], *m.* Servomotor.

sesada [say-sah'-dah], *f.* Fried brains.

sésamo [say'-sah-mo], *m.* Sesame, gingili, an annual herb the seeds of which yield a bland oil.

sesalpil [say-sah-peel'], *m.* Sex-appeal.

sesear [say-say-ar'], *vn.* To pronounce the *c* (before *e* and *i*) and *z* as *s*, (a feature of the Andalusian and South American countries).

seseli [say-say'-le], *m.* *(Bot.)* Wild spicknel, seseli.

sesenta [say-sen'-tah], *m.* Sixty, figures of 60.-*a.* Sixty, sixtieth.

sesentavo, va [say-sen-tah'-vo, vah], *a. &: n.* One-sixtieth; a sixtieth part.

sesentón, na [say-sen-tone', nah], *m. & f. & a.* One turned of sixty, sexagenalian, sixty years old.

sesera [sary-say'-rah], *f.* 1. Brain-pan. 2. The entire brain.

sesga [ses'-gah], *f.* Gore or goring.

sesgadamente [see-gah-dah-men-tay], *adv.* Slantwise, slopwise, slopingly. *V.* SESGAMENTE.

sesgado, da [ses-gah'-do, dah], *a. & pp.* of SESGAR. Sloped, oblique, slanting.

sesgadura [ses-gah-doo'-rah], *f.* Slope, the act of sloping.

sesgamente [ses'-gah-men-tay], *adv.* Obliquely, slopingly; mildly.

sesgar [ses-gar'], *va.* To slope (inclinar), to cut slantwise, to take or give an oblique direction.

sesgo, ga [ses'-go, gah], *a.* 1. Sloped, oblique, turned or twisted obliquely. 2. Serene, tranquil, unruffled. 3. Severe of aspect, grave, uncouth. **Al sesgo**, slopingly, obliquely.

sesgo [ses-go]. *m.* 1. Slope, obliqueness, oblique direction. 2. Mean medium.

sesil [say-seel'], *a. (Bot.)* Sessile, joined to the stem without any stalk.

sesión [say-se-on'], *f.* 1. Session, sitting, meeting of a council or congress. 2. Conference, consultation. **Abrir la sesión**, to open the meeting. **Celebrar una sesión**, to hold a meeting.

sesma [ses'-mah], *f.* 1. The sixth part of a yard or any other thing. 2. A division of territory. 3. *V.* SEXMA.

sesmero [ses-may'-ro], *m.* A person appointed to manage the public affairs, belonging to the district called *sesma* or *sesmo*. *V.* SEXMERO.

sesmo [ses'-mo], *m.* 1. A division of territory in some Spanish provinces. 2. *V.* LINDE.

seso [say'-so], *m.* 1. The brain: generally used in the plural. 2. Brain. understanding, prudence, wisdom. 3. Stone put under a pot to keep it steady on the fire. **No tener seso**, not to have common sense. **Tener los sesos de un mosquito, de un chorlito**, not to have the brains of a sparrow.

sesqui [ses'-ke]. *(Lat.)* Used in composition, and implying one and a half, as *sesquihora*, an hour and a half.

sesquiáltero, ra [ses-ke-ahl'-tay-ro, rah], *a.* Sesqualter, one and a half.

sesquidoble [ses-ke-do'-blay], *a.* Two and a half times.

sesquimodio [ses-ke-mo'-de-o], *m.* A bucket and a half.

sesquióxido [ses-ke-ok'-se-do], *m.* Sesquioxide.

sesquipedal [ses-ke-pay-dahl'], *a.* Sesquipedal, sesquipedalian, a foot and a half in length.

sesquiplicado, da [ses-ke-ple-cah'-do, dah], *a.* Sesquiplicate.

sesteadero [ses-tay-ah-day'-ro], *m.* A proper place for taking a nap after dinner; resting-place for cattle.

sestear [ses-tay-ar'], *vn.* To take a nap or rest after dinner.

sestero [ses-tay'-ro], *m. V.* SESTEADERO.

sesudamente [say-soo'-dah-men-tay], *adv.* Maturely, wisely, prudently.

sesudo, da [say-soo'-do, dah], *a.* Judicious, discreet, prudent, wise.

seta [say'-tah], *f.* 1. Bristle, the stiff hair of swine. 2. *(Bot.)* A general name for all the species of mushroom (hongo): it is given particularly to the field agaric, agaricus campestris: called also in Spanish *seta de cardo*. 3. Blobber-lip. *V.* JETA. 4. Snuff of a candle.

sete [say'-tay], *m.* Mint, or office where money is struck with a die.

setecientos, tas [say-tay-the-en'-tos, tas], *a. & n.* Seven hundred.

setena [say-tay'-nah], *f.* Seven things of a kind. -*pl.* A punishment by which, anciently, seven-fold payment was obligated.

setenta [say-ten'-tah], *a.* Seventy.

setentavo, va [say-ten-tah'-vo, vah], *a. & n.* One-seventieth; a seventieth part.

setentón, na [say-ten-tone', nah], *a. & n.* Seventy years old; turned of seventy.

setentrión [say-ten-tre-on'], *m.* Septentrion, the north; the north wind.

setentrional [say-ten-tre-o-nahl'], *a.* Septentrional, northern, northerly.

setero, ra [say-tay'-ro, rah], *a.* Bristly, hairy.

setiembre [say-te-em'-bray], *m. V.* SEPTIEMBRE.

sétima [say'-te-mah], *f. V.* SÉPTIMA.

sétimo, ma [say'-te-mo, mah], *a.* Seventh. *V.* SÉPTIMO, MA.

seto [say'-to], *m.* Fence (cercado), defence, inclosure. **Seto vivo**, hedge, quickset.

setuagenario, ria [say-too-ah-hay-nah'-re-o]. *V.* SEPTUAGENARIO.

setuagésimo, ma [say-too-ah-hay'-se-mo], *a. V.* SEPTUAGÉSIMO.

setuplicar [say-too-ple-car'], *va. V.* SETUPLICAR.

sétuplo, pla [say-too-plo], *a. V.* SÉPTUPLO.

seudo [say-oo'-do], *a.* Pseudo, false.

seudomédico [say-oo-do-may'-do-co], *m.* Charlatan, quack.

seudomorfo, fa [say-oo-do-mor'-fo, fah], *a.* Pseudomorphous.

seudónimo, ma [say-oo-do'-ne-mo, mah], *a.* Pseudonymous, fictitious. -*m.* Pseudonym, pen name.

severamente [say-vay'-rah-men-tay], *adv.* Severely.

severidad [say-vay-re-dahd'], *f.* 1. Severity, rigor, harshness, austerity, acerbity. 2. Severity, strictness, punctuality, exactness. 3. Gravity, seriousness.

severizarse [say-vay-re-thar'-say], *vr.* To become serious or grave.

severo ra [say-vay'-ro, rah], *a.* 1. Severe (carácter), rigorous, rigid, harsh (invierno). 2. Grave, serious. 3. Severe, punctual, exact, strict.

sevillano, na [say-veel-lyah'-no, nah], *a.* Of Seville, Sevillan.

sexagenario, ria [sek-sah-hay-nah'-re-o, ah], *a.* Sexagenary, sixty years old.

sesagésima [sek-sah-hay'-se-mah], *f.* Sexagesima, second Sunday before Lent.

sexagésimo

sexagésimo, ma [sek-sah-hay'-se-mo, mah], *a*. Sexagesimal, sixtieth.

sexagonal [sek-sah-go-nahl'], *a*. Sexagonal.

sexángulo, la [sek-sahn'-goo-lo, lah], *a*. Sexangular. *-m.* Sexangle.

sexenio [sek-say'-ne-o], *m*. Space of six years.

sexo [sek'-so], *m*. 1. Sex, the organic difference between male and female. 2. Womankind, by way of emphasis. **El sexo débil**, the gentle sex. **El sexo masculino**, the male sex.

sexología [sek-so-lo-hee'-ah], *f*. Sexology.

sexólogo, ga [sek-so'-lo-go], *m & f*. Sexologist.

sexta [sex'-tah], *f*. 1. One of the hours into which the Hebrews, and Romans divided the artificial day, and including three of the hours now used. 2. A sequence of six cards at the game of piquet. 3. Sixth, one of the minor canonical hours after tierce.

sextante [sex-tahn'-tay], *m*. 1. Coin weighing two ounces. 2. Sextant, an astronomical instrument.

sextario [sex-tah'-re-o], *m*. Ancient measure.

sextercio [sex-ter'-the-o], *m*. V. SESTERCIO.

sextil [sex-teel'], *a*. (*Astro*.) Sextile.

sextilla [sex-teel'-lyah], *f*. Sextain, a Spanish metrical composition of six feet.

sextina [sex-tee'-nah], *f*. A kind of Spanish metrical composition.

sexto, ta [sex'-to, tah], *a*. Sixth, the ordinal number of six. *-m.* Book containing canonical decrees.

sexual [sex-soo-ahl'], *a*. Sexual.

sexualidad [sec-soo-ah-le-dahd'], *f*. 1. Sexuality. 2. Sex (sexo). **Determinar la sexualidad**, to determine the sex of.

si [see], *conj*. If, although; in case that, provided that, unless, when. **Si bien**, although. V. AUNQUE. **Si acaso, por si acaso**, if by chance. **Si no**, if not, otherwise.

sí [see], *adv*. Yes, yea; without doubt indeed. *-m.* 1. Assent, consent, permission. 2. (*Mus*.) Si, the seventh note of the scale. **Dar el sí**, to say yes: to promise to marry. **Creo que sí**, I think so. **Porque sí**, because that's the way it is.

sí, *pronoun*. Reflexive form of the personal pronoun of the third person, in both genders and numbers; employed in oblique cases and always with a preposition. Himself, herself themselves. **De por sí**, apart, separately. **De sí**, of itself; spontaneously. **Lo quieren todo para sí**, they want the whole lot for themselves. **No lo tiene en sí misma**, she doesn't have it in her. **Ella lo quiere para sí** she wants it for herself.

siampán [se-am-pam'], *m*. Dye-stuff produced in the province of this name.

sibarita [se-bah-ree'-tah], *com*. Sybarite, a native of Sybaris. *-a.* Given to pleasures, luxurious, sensuous.

sibarítico, ca [se-ba-ree'-te-co, cah], *a*. 1. Sybaritical, luxurious. 2. Sensual.

sibil [se-beel'], *m*. A small cellar under ground (sótano), where wine, water, or other things are kept fresh.

sibila [se-bee'-lah], *f*. Prophetess; sibyl.

sibilante [se-be-lahn'-tay], *a*. (*Poet*.) Sibilant, hissing.

sibilino, na [se-be-lee'-no, nah], *a*. Sibylline.

sibucao [se-boo-cah'-o], *m*. Sapan-tree which furnishes a dye-wood: it belongs to the leguminosae. Cf. SAPÁN.

sicamor [se-cah-mor'], *m*. (*Bot*.) European Judas-tree.

sicario [se-cah'-re-o], *m*. A paid assassin. Cf. SEIDE.

siciliano, na [se-the-le-ah'-no, nah], Sicilian, relating to Sicily.

siclo [see'-clo], *m*. Shekel, an ancient Jewish coin.

sicoanálisis [se-co-ah-nah'-le-sis], *f*. V. PSICOANÁLISIS.

sicofanta [se-co-fahn'-tay], *m*. Sycophant, flatterer, parasite.

sicología [se-co-lo-hee'-ah], *f*. V. PSICOLOGÍA.

sicológico, ca [se-co-lo'-he-co, cah], *a*. V. PSICOLÓGICO.

sicólogo, ga [se-co'-lo-go, gah], *m. & f*. V. PSICÓLOGO.

sicomoro [se-co'-mo-ro], *m*. (*Bot*.) Sycamore, the mulberry-leaved fig-tree.

siconeurótico, ca [se-coh-nay-oo-roh'-te-co, cah], *a*. V. PSICONEURÓTICO.

sicópata [se-co'-pah-tah], *m*. V. PSICÓPATA.

sicopático, ca [se-co-pah'-te-co, cah], *a*. V. PSICOPÁTICO.

sicosis [se-co'-sis], *f*. V. PSICOSIS.

sicoterapia [se-co-tay-rah'-pe-ah], *f*. V. PSICOTERAPIA.

SIDA [see'-dah], *m*. abr. de **síndrome de inmuno-deficiencia adquirida** (acquired immuno-deficiency syndrome, AIDS).

sideral [see-day-rahl'], *a*. Sidereal, astral, space. **Viajes siderales**, space travel.

sidéreo, rea [se-day'-ray-o, ah], *a*. Sidereal, starry.

siderismo [se-day-rees'-mo], *m*. (*Neol*.) Worship of the stars. V. SABEÍSMO.

sideritis [se-day-ree'-tis], *f*. Siderites, a mineral. **Sidelitis** or **Sideritide**, (*Bot*.) iron-wort.

siderografía [se-day-ro-grah-fee'-ah], *f*. The art of engraving on steel.

siderotecnia [se-day-ro-tek'-ne-ah], Siderotechny, the art of working iron.

siderurgia [se-day-roor'-he-ah], *f*. Siderurgy.

siderúrgico, ca [se-day-roor'-he-co'-cah], *a*. Pertaining to iron and steel. **Industria siderúrgica**, iron and steel industry.

sidra [see'-drah], *f*. Cider.

sidrería [se-dray-ree'-ah], *f*. Cider bar.

siega [se-ay'-gah], *f*. Harvest (época), reaping time, mowing, fruits gathered.

siembra [se-em'-brah], *f*. 1. Seed-time. 2. Corn-field.

siempre [se-em'-pray], *adv*. 1. Always, at all times. 2. (*LAm.*) Certainly (seguramente). **Siempre jamás**, for ever and ever. **Como siempre**, as usual.

siempreviva [se-em-pray-vee'-vah], *f*. (*Bot*.) House-leek.

sien [se-ayn'], *f*. Temple, the upper part of the side of the head.

sierpe [se-err'-pay], *f*. 1. Serpent. V. SERPIENTE. 2. A shrew, peevish, clamorous, spiteful woman. 3. Anything which moves by undulation in a serpentine shape. 4. A peevish, fretful person. 5. (*Bot*.) Sucker.

sierra [se-er'-rah], *f*. 1. Saw. **Sierra de mano**, a panel-saw or hand-saw. **Sierra para metales**, hacksaw. **Sierra circular**, circular saw. **Sierra mecánica**, power saw. 2. Ridge of mountains and craggy rocks. 3. Waves rising mountain high in a storm. 4. (*Zool*.) Saw-fish. **Van a la sierra a pasar el fin de semana**, they're off to the mountains for the weekend.

sierrecilla [se-er-ray-theel'-lyah], *f. dim*. Small saw.

siervo, va [se-err'-vo, vah], *m. & f*. 1. Serf, slave, servant. 2. Servant by courtesy.

sieso [se-ay'-so], *m*. Fundament, anus.

siesta [se-es'-tah], *f*. 1. The hottest part of the day; the time for a nap after lunch; siesta, nap (sueñecito). 2. Sleep taken after lunch. **Echarse una siesta**, to have a siesta, nap, doze.

siete [se-ay'-tay], *a. & m*. 1. Seven. 2. Seventh. 3. Seven, the figure 7. 4. Card with seven figures. **De siete en siete**, by seven and seven. **Más que siete**, (*Coll.*) very much, in excess, too much. **Hablar más que siete**, to talk too much.

sieteañal [se-ay-tay-ah-nyahl'], *a*. Septennial.

sietedurmientes [se-ay-tay-door-me-en'-tes], *m. pl*. Seven sleepers, great sleeper.

sieteenrama [se-ay'-tay-en-rah'-mah], *f*. (*Bot*.) V. TORMENTILLA.

sietemesino, na [se-ay-tay-may-see'-no, nah], *a*. Born seven months after conception.

sietenal [se-ay-tay-nyahl'], *a*. Seven years old, septennial.

sífilis [see-fe-lis], *f*. Syphilis, a specific venerial disease; vulgarly, the pox.

sifilítico, ca [se-fe-lee'-te-co, cah], *a*. Syphilitic, relating to syphilis or affected by it.

sifón [se-fone'], *m*. 1. Siphon, a bent tube with unequal arms, for drawing liquids over the side of a cask or other vessel. 2. (*And.*) Beer (cerveza).

sigilación [se-he-lah-the-on'], *f*. Impression, mark.

sigilado, da [se-he-lah'-do, dah], *a*. Marked with some defect or affected by some disease. *-pp.* of SIGILAR.

sigilar [se-he-lar'], *va*. 1. To keep a thing secret. 2. To seal.

sigilo [se-hee'-lo], *m.* 1. Seal. *V.* SELLO. 2. Secret, secrecy, discretion. **Sigilo sacramental**, inviolable secrecy of the confession.

sigilosamente [se-he-lo'-sah-men-tay], *adv.* Silently, secretly.

sigiloso, sa [se-he-lo'-so, sah], *a.* Silent, reserved; keeping a secret.

sigla [see'-glah], *f.* Initial letter, employed as an abbreviation (in inscriptions, etc.).

siglo [see'-glo], *m.* 1. Century, a hundred years. 2. Age (época), duration of anything. 3. A very long time (largo tiempo). **Un siglo que no te veo**, I have not seen you for ages. **Por los siglos de los siglos**, for ever and ever. **Siglo de cobre**, the brazen age. **Siglo de hierro**, the iron age. **Siglo de plata**, the silver age. **Siglo de oro**, the golden age (Spain, about 1492-1660).

sigma [seeg'-mah], *f.* Sigma, eighteenth letter of the Greek alphabet, corresponding to *s.*

signáculo [sig-nah'-coo-lo], *m.* Seal, signet.

signar [sig-nar'], *va.* To sign (firmar), to mark with a signet. *-vr.* To make the sign of the cross.

signatario, ria [sig-nah-tah'-re-o, ah], *a.* Signatory, signing. **Poderes signatarios**, authority to sign. *-m. & f.* Signatory, signer.

signatura [sig-nah-too'-rah], *f.* Sign, mark; signature in printing; a Roman tribunal.

significación [sig-ne-fe-cah-the-on'], *f.* 1. Signification, meaning expressed by a sign or word. 2. Signification, the act of making known by signs; significance. 3. *V.* SIGNIFICATIVO.

significado [sig-ne-fe-cah'-do], *m.* Signification, object signified by means of words. —**Significado, da**, *pp.* of SIGNIFICAR.

significador, ra [sig-ne-fe-cah-dor', rah], *m. & f.* One who signifies.

significante [sig-ne-fe-cahn'-tay], *a.* Significant, expressive.

significantemente [sig-ne-fe-cahn'-tay-men-tay], *adv. V.* SIGNIFICATIVAMENTE.

significar [sig-ne-fe-car'], *va.* 1. To signify, to denote, to mean (palabra). 2. To declare, to make known (expresar). 3. To import, to be worth. *-vr.* To become known (distinguirse).

significativamente [sig-ne-fe-cah-tee'-vah-men-tay], *adv.* Significatively.

significativo, va [sig-ne-fe-cah-tee'-vo, vah], *a.* Significative, expressive.

signo [seeg'-no], *m.* 1. Sign, mark. 2. *(Coll.)* Fate, destiny. 3. Benediction with the sign of the cross. 4. *(Ast.)* Sign of the zodiac. 5. Type, emblem. 6. Any of the characters in which music is written. **Signo de admiración**, exclamation mark. **Signo del zodíaco**, sign of the zodiac.

siguiente [se-gee-en'-tay], *a.* Following, successive, sequent.

sílaba [see'-la-bah], *f.* 1. Syllable. 2. *(Mus.)* Two or three sounds which correspond with every letter of the gamut.

silabar [se-la-bar'], *vn. V* SILABEAR.

silabario [se-la-bah'-re-o], *m.* A book which contains and explains syllables; syllabary.

silabear [se-lah-bay-ar'], *an.* To pronounce by syllables.

silabeo [se-la-bay'-o], *m.* Syllabication, the act of forming syllables.

silábico, ca [se-lah'-be-co, cah], *a.* Syllabical, syllabic.

silba [seel'-bah], *f.* Whistling, catcall, hissing (in public derision).

sílabus, or **silabo**, *m.* Syllabus, a brief statement by the Pope of errors condemned (in 1864).

silbador, ra [sil-bah-dor', rah], *m. & f.* Whistler; exploder, a hisser.

silbar [sil-bar'], *vn.* 1. To whistle. 2. To whiz (bullets) *-va.* To hiss, to express disapprobation (en público), to catcall.

silbático, illo, ito [sil-bah-tee'-co], *m. dim.* A small whistle.

silbato [sil-bah'-to], *m.* 1. Whistle, a wind instrument. 2. A small chink or crack, through which passes any liquid or air that whizzes.

silbido [sil-bee'-do], *m.* Whistle, whistling hiss; sibilation. **Silbido de oídos**, whizzing or humming in the ear.

silbo [seel'-bo], *m.* Whistle, hiss, whistling.

silboso, sa [sil-bo'-so, sah], *a. (Poet.)* Whistling, hissing.

silenciario, ria [se-len-the-ah'-re-o, ah], *a.* Observing profound silence.

silenciario [se-len-the-ah'-re-o], *m.* Silentiary, officer appointed to preserve silence in a place or assembly; silent place.

silenciero, ra [se-len-the-ay'-ro, rah], *a.* Charged with preserving silence; which preserves peace.

silencio [se-len'-the-o], *m.* 1. Silence; habitual taciturnity; secrecy. 2. State of holding the peace. 3. Reservedness, prudence. 4. Stillness, repose. *-int.* Silence! hush. **En silencio**, in silence. **Reducir al silencio**, to silence.

silenciosamente [se-len-the-o'-sah-men-tay], *adv.* Silently, softly, gently.

silencioso, sa [se-len-the-oh'-so, sah], *a.* Silent; solitary, mute.

sileno [se-lay'-no], *m.* Silenus, a demigod.

siler montano [se-lerr' mon-tah'-no], *m. (Bot.)* Mountain lasserwort.

silería [se-lay-ree'-ah], *f.* Place where subterraneous granaries are made.

silero [se-lay'-ro], *m.* A subterraneous granary for wheat, a silo.

sílex [se'-lex], *m.* Silex.

sílfide [sil-fe-day], *f.* **Silfo**, *m.* Sylph.

silguero [sil-gay'-ro], *m. (Orn. Prov.)* Linnet. *V.* JILGUERO.

silibo [se-lee'-bo], *m. (Bot.)* Silybum, a genus of plants.

silicato [se-le-cah'-to], *m.* Silicate, a compound of silicic acid.

sílice [see'-le-thay], *m.* Silica, silicon dioxide (occurring as quartz or as opal).

silíceo, ea [se-lee'-thay-o, ah], *a.* Siliceous, flinty.

silicio [se-lee'-the-o], *m.* 1. Silicon, a non-metallic element, next in abundance to oxygen. 2. *V.* CILICIO.

silicona [se-le-co'-nah], *f.* Silicone.

silicua [se-lee'-coo-ah], *f.* 1. Siliqua carat, a former weight of four grains. 2. Silique, a seed-vessel, husk, pod; or shell of leguminous plants.

silícula [se-lee'-coo-lah], *f. (Bot.)* Silicle, a short silique.

silicuoso, sa [se-le-coo-o'-so]. *a.* Siliquose, having a pod or capsule.

siligo [se-lee'-go], *m. V.* NEGUILLA.

silla [seel'-lyah], *f.* 1. Chair, movable seat (asiento). 2. See, the seat of episcopal power, the diocese of a bishop. 3. **Silla** or **silla de montar**. Saddle. 4. Seat. 5. Seat, anus. **Silla de rejilla, de junco**, cane or bamboo-bottomed chair. **Silla de columpio**, rocking-chair. **Silla giratoria**, pivot chair. **Silla plegadiza**, folding-chair, camp-stool. **Pegársele (a uno) la silla**, to make a very long call, to be a stayer. **Silla de cubierta**, deck chair. **Silla eléctrica** electric chair. **Le movieron la silla para que se cayese**, they pulled the rug out from under him.

sillar [sil-lyar'], *m.* 1. A square hewn stone. 2. Back of a horse where the saddle is placed.

sillarejo [sil-lyah-ray'-ho], *m.* A small hewn stone.

sillera [sil-lyay'-rah], *f.* Place where sedan-chairs are shut up.

sillería [sil-lyay-ree'-ah], *f.* 1. Sent, set or parcel of chairs. 2. Shop where chairs are made or sold. 3. Stalls about the choir of a church. 4. Building of hewn stone.

sillero [sil-lyay'-ro], *m.* Saddler, chairmaker (artesano).

silleta [sil-lyay'-tah], *f.* 1. *(Dim.)* A small chair. 2. Hollow stone on which, chocolate is ground. 3. Close stool (taburete), privy-chair. 4. Side-saddle.

silletero [sil-lyay-tay'-ro], *m.* 1. Chair man, one employed in carrying sedan-chairs. 2. Chair-maker, one who makes or sells chairs.

sillico [sil-lyee'-co], *m.* Basin of close-stool.

sillín [sil-lyeen'], *m.* 1. A seat, saddle. 2. A small saddle for a driving-horse or a bicycle.

sillita [sil-lyee'-tah], *f. dim.* A small chair.

sillón [sil-lyone'], *m.* 1. A large armchair. 2. Side-saddle for ladies (de montar).

silo [see'-lo], *m.* 1. A subterraneous granary for wheat, a silo. 2. Any cavern or dark place.

silogismo [se-lo-hees'-mo], *m.* Syllogism.

silogístico, ca [se-lo-hees'-te-co, cah], *a.* Syllogistic, syllogistical.

silogizar [se-lo-he-thar'], *vn.* To syllogize, to reason, to argue.

silueta [se-loo-ay'-tah], *f.* Silhouette, a profile in shadow, outline (de edificio), skyline (de ciudad).

siluro [se-loo'-ro], *m.* Catfish, sheatfish, silurus.

silva [seel'-vah], *f.* 1. A miscellany 2. A kind of Spanish metrical composition.

silvamar [sil-vah-nar'], *m.* Sarsaparilla.

silvano [sil-vah'-no], *m.* 1. Sylvan, a wood-god or satyr. 2. Tellurium.

silvático, ca [sil-vah'-te-co, cah], *a. V.* SELVÁTICO.

silvestre [sil-ves'-tray], *a.* Wild, uncultivated; rustic, savage.

silvoso, sa [sil-vo'-so, sah], *a. V.* SELVOSO.

sima [see'-mah], *f.* 1. Deep and dark cavern; abyss; chasm; pit; deep fissure, pothole.

simarruba [se-mar-roo'-bah], *f. (Bot.)* Bitter-wood, quassia.

simbólicamente [sem-bo'-le-cah-men-tay], *adv.* Symbolically, typically, hieroglyphically.

simbólico, ca [sim-bo'-le-co, cah], *a.* 1. Symbolical, representative, expressing by signs. 2. Analogous, resembling.

simbolización [sim-bo-le-thah-the-on'], *f.* Symbolization.

simbolizar [sim-bo-le-thar'], *vn.* To symbolize, to resemble, to figure.

símbolo [seem'-bo-lo], *m.* 1. Symbol mark, sign, device. 2. *(Mil.)* Watch word. 3. Symbol, a badge to know one by. 4. Symbol, type, representation, figure. 5. Creed, belief, articles of faith.

símbolo, la [seem'-bo-lo], *a. V.* SIMBÓLICO.

simetría [se-may-tree'-ah], *f.* Symmetry, proportion, shapeliness, harmony.

simétricamente [se-may'-tre-cah-men-tay], *adv.* Symmetrically.

simétrico, ca [se-may'-tre-co, cah], *a.* Symmetrical, proportionate.

simia [see'-me-ah], *f.* A female ape. *V.* MONA.

simiente [se-me-en'-tay], *f.* 1. Seed. *V.* SEMILLA. 2. *V.* SEMEN. 3. Source origin.

simienza [se-me-en'-thah], *f. (Prov.)* Seed-time. *V.* SEMENTERA.

simil [see'-mil], *m.* 1. Resemblance, similarity. *V.* SEMEJANZA. 2. Simile, comparison, similitude.-*a.* Similar; like. *V.* SEMEJANTE.

similar [se-me-lar'], *a.* 1. Similar, homogeneous. 2. Resembling.

similitud [se-me-le-tood'], *f.* Similitude, resemblance.

similitudinariamente [se-me-le-too-de-nah'-re-ah-men-tay], *adv.* Similarly.

similitudinario, ria [se-me-le-too-de-nah'-re-o, ah], *a.* Similar, similitudinary.

simio [see'-me-o], *m..* Male ape. *V.* MONO.

simonía [se-mo-nee'-ah], *f.* Simony.

simoniaco, ca, simoniático, ca [se-mo-nee'-ah-co, cah], *a.* Simoniac or simoniacal.

simpatía [sim-pah-tee'-ah], *f.* 1. Sympathy (compasión), fellow-feeling (solidaridad), congeniality. 2. Charm (de lugar, persona), personality. **Tener simpatía por alguien**, to find someone charming and congenial. **Ganarse la simpatía de todos**, to win everybody's affection. **Mostrar su simpatía por**, to show one's support for.

simpáticamente [sim-pah-te-cah-men-tay], *adv.* Sympathetically. *V.* CONFORMEMENTE.

simpático, ca [sim-pah'-te-co, cah], *a.* Sympathetic, sympathetical, analogous, nice (persona), kind (bondadoso), charming (encantador). **No le hemos caído muy simpáticos**, she didn't much take to us.

simpatizar [sim-pah-te-thar'], *vn.* (used with the prep. *con*). To be congenial, to have a liking for someone. **Simpatizo mucho con él**, I like him, he and I get along well.

simplazo, za [sim-plah'-tho, thah], *aug.* A great simpleton, a stupid person.

simple [seem'-play], *a.* 1. Single, simple, pure, mere, naked, unsigned; unconditional. 2. Silly, foolish, simple, crazy, idiotical. 3. Simple, undesigning, artless. 4. Simple, plain, mild, gentle, ingenuous (persona). 5. Insipid, tasteless. 6. Single, brief. 7. Informal, extra-judicial. **Es cosa de una simple plumada**, it's a matter of a mere stroke of the pen. **Somos simples aficionados**, we are just amateurs. **Un simple abogado**, a solicitor of little importance. **Es un simple soldado** he's just an ordinary soldier. -*m.* 1. Simple, an herb or plant which alone serves for medicine. 2. Simpleton (persona).

simplecillo, illa, ito ita [sim-play-theel'-lyo], *m. & f.* A little simpleton.

simplemente, *adv.* Simply, with simplicity and plainness, sillily; absolutely, merely.

simpleza [sim-play'-thah], *f.* 1. Simpleness (cualidad), silliness, fatuity. 2. Rusticity, rudeness. 3. Simplicity, sincerity. **Se enojó por una simpleza**, he got annoyed over nothing.

simplicidad [sim-ple-the-dahd'], *f.* 1. Simplicity, plainness, artlessness, homeliness. 2. Simpleness, silliness, fatuity.

simplicista [sim-ple-thees'-tah], *m.* Simplist, simpler, herbalist.

simplificar [sim-ple-fe-car'], *va.* To simplify, to make simple.

simplísimo, ma [im-plee'-se-mo, mah], *a. sup.* Extremely silly or foolish.

simplista [sim-plees'-tah], *m.* Simplist, herbalist.

simplón, na [sim-plone', nah], *m. & f. aug.* of SIMPLE. Great simpleton.

simplonazo, za [sim-plo-nah'-tho, thah], *a. aug.* of SIMPLÓN. Extremely simple or silly.

simulación [se-moo-lah-the-on'], *f.* 1. Simulation, feigning, hollowness. 2. Subterfuge, evasion.

simulacro [se-moo-lah'-cro], *m.* 1. Simulachre, image, idol. 2. Ghost, phantom. **Un simulacro de ataque**, a mock attack.

simuladamente [se-moo-lah'-dah-men-tay], *adv.* In a dissembling or hypocritical manner.

simulador, ra [se-moo-lah-dor', rah], *m. & f.* Simulator, dissembler.

simular [se-moo-lar'], *va.* To simulate, to practise simulation.

simulcadencia [se-mool-cah-den'-the-ah], *f. (Rhet.)* Figure of rhetoric repeating a consonant in a word forming a cadence.

simulcadente [se-mool-cah-den'-tay], *a.* Applied to words or sentences having a cadence.

simultáneamente [se-mool-tah'-ne-ah-men-tay], *adv.* Simultaneously.

simultaneidad [se-mool-tah-nay-dahd'], *f.* Simultaneity.

simultáneo, nea [se-mool-tah'-nay-o, ah], *a.* Simultaneous.

simún [se-moon'], *m.* Simoom (viento), a hot wind of the desert in Africa and Arabia.

sin [seen], *prep.* Without, besides. Joined to a verb it is a negative or privative. **Sin embargo**, notwithstanding, nevertheless, however. **Sin pies ni cabeza**, without head or tail, without order. **Almendras sin cáscara**, shelled almonds. **Salió sin abrigo**, he went out without a coat. **Sin qué ni por qué**, without cause or motive. **Sin afeitar**, unshaven. **Sin lavar**, unwashed. **Sin saberlo ella**, without her knowing it.

sinabafa [se-nah-bah'-fah], *f.* Cloth or stuff of the natural color of wool.

sinagoga [se-nah-go'-gah], *f.* Synagogue, a Jewish congregation, and the place where they meet for worship and religious instruction.

sinalefa [se-nah-lay'-fah], *f.* (*Gram.*) Synalepha, the union or blending into a single syllable of two successive vowels of different syllables.

sinamay [se-nah-mah'-e], *m.* A very light fabric made in the Philippines from the filaments of *abacá*.

sinantéreas [se-nan-tay'-ray-ahs], *a. & f. pl.* (*Bot.*) Synantherge, a former order of plants now called *Compositae*.

sinapismo [se-nah-pees'-mo], *m.* Sinapism, mustardpoultice.

sincategoremático, ca [sin-cah-tay-go-ray-mah'-te-co, cah], *a.* Syncategorematic.

sincerador, ra [sin-thay-rah-dor', rah], *m. & f.* Exculpator, excuser.

sinceramente [sin-thay'-rah-men-tay], *adv.* Sinecerely, frankly, heartily, cordially.

sincerar [sin-thay-rar'], *va.* To exculpate. *-vr.* To excuse, justify, or vindicate oneself. **Sincerarse ante el juez,** to justify one's conduct to the judge.

sinceridad [sin-thay-re-dahd'], *f.* Sincerity, purity of mind, frankness, cordiality, good-will.

sincero, ra [sin-thay'-ro, rah], *a.* Sincere, ingenuous, honest; pure.

sincipucio [sin-the-poo'-the-o], *m.* Sinciput.

sincondrosis [sin-con-dro'-sees], . (*Anat.*) Synchondrosis, union of two bones by means of a cartilage.

síncopa [seen'-coo-pah], *f.* 1. Syncopa, a contraction of words, by cutting off a part. 2. (*Mus.*) Syncopation, the beginning of a tone upon an unaccented beat, and its continuation through the following accented beat.

sincopado, da [sin-co-pah'-do, dah], *a.* Syncopated.

sincopal [sin-co-pahl'], *m. V.* SÍNCOPE.

sincopal [sin-co-pahl'], *a.* Applied to malignant fevers.

sincopar [sin-co-par'], *m.* 1. To syncopate, to contract, words. 2. To abridge.

síncope [seen'-co-pay], *f.* (*Med.*) Syncope, a fainting-fit.

sincopizar [sin-co-pe-thar'], *va. & vr.* To swoon, to faint.

sincresis [sin-cray'-sis], *f.* Fusion, mixture.

sincretismo [sin-cray-tees'-mo], *m.* 1. Syncretism, a philosophical system allied to electicism. 2. Conciliation of different religious doctrines.

sincrónico [sin-cro'-ne-co], *a.* Synchronous; synchronized.

sincronismo [sin-cro-nees'-mo], *m.* Synchronism, coincidence in time of different events; simultaneousness.

sincronizar [sin-cro-ne-thar'], *va.* To synchronize.

sindéresis [sin-day'-ray-sis], *f.* Discretion, natural capacity for judging rightly.

sindicación [sin-de-cah-the-on'], *f.* The act of informing against.

sindicado [sin-de-cah'-do], *m.* A body of trustees; a syndicate, **-Sindicado. da,** *pp.* of SINDICAR.

sindicador, ra [sin-de-cah-dor', rah], *m. & f.* Informer, prosecutor.

sindicadura [sin-de-cah-doo'-rah], *f.* Office and dignity of a syndic.

sindical [sin-de-cahl'], *m.* Syndical, relating to a syndic or syndicate.

sindicalismo [sin-de-cah-lees'-mo], *m.* Unionism.

sindicar [sin-de-car'], *va.* To inform, to lodge an information; to accuse.

sindicatura [sin-de-ca-too'-rah], *f.* Trusteeship.

síndico [sin'-de-co], *m.* 1. Syndic; recorder. 2. One whose office is to collect the fines imposed by a court. 3. Treasurer of the alms of religious houses. **Síndico or procurador general,** the attorney-general of a town or corporation.

síndrome [sin'-dro-may], *m.* Syndrome. **Síndrome tóxico,** poisoning.

sinécdoque, sinédoque [se-nec'-do-kay], *f.* (*Rhet.*) Synecdoche, a trope which puts a part for the whole, or the whole for a part.

sinecura [se-nay-coo'-rah], *f.* Sinecure, an office having emoluments with few or no duties.

sinedra [se-nay'-drah], *f.* Seats for the audience in a public hall.

sinedrio [se-nay'-dre-o], *m. V.* SANEDRÍN.

sinéresis [se-nay'-ray-sis], *f.* Syneresis, a figure whereby two syllables are united into one.

sínfisis [seen'-fe-sis], *f.* (*Anat.*) Symphysis, union of bones by means of an intervening body.

sínfito [seen'-fe-to], *m.* (*Bot.*) Comfrey.

sinfonía [sin-fo-nee'-ah], *f.* 1. Symphony, concert of concordant sounds; composition of instrumental music. 2. Symphony, a concerted instrumental piece for many instruments. 3. *V.* GAITA.

sinfonista [sin-fo-nees'-tah], *com.* 1. Symphonist, one who composes a symphony. 2. A player in an orchestra.

sinfonola [sin-fo-no'-lah], *f.* Jukebox.

singladura [sin-glah-doo'-rah], *f.* (*Naut.*) A day's run (recorrido); the distance traversed by a ship in 24 hours.

singlar [sin-glar'], *vn.* (*Naut.*) To sail daily with a favorable wind on a direct course.

singlón [sin-glone'], *m.* (*Naut.*) Any of the timbers placed over the keel.

singular [sin-goo-lar'], *a.* 1. Singular, single, not common to others; unique. 2. Singular, individual, particular. 3. Singular, extraordinary, extravagant, strange. 4. Singular, excellent. 5. (*Gram.*) Singular. **En singular,** in the singular. **Se refiere a él en singular,** it refers to him in particular.

singularidad [sin-goo-lah-re-dahd'], *f.* Singularity, notability, oddity.

singularizar [sin-goo-lah-re-thar'], *va.* To distinguish (distinguir), to particularize, to singularize. *-vr.* To distinguish oneself (distinguirse); to be singular.

singularmente [sin-goo-lahr'-men-tay], *adv.* Singularly,

singulto [sin-gool'-to], *m.* Hiccough, singultus.

siniestra [se-ne-es'-trah], *f.* The left hand. *V.* IZQUIERDA.

siniestramente [se-ne-es'-trah-men-tay], *adv.* Sinistrously, perversely.

siniestro, tra [se-ne-es'-tro, trah], *a.* 1. Sinister, left, on the left side. 2. Sinistrous, vicious. 3. Sinister, unhappy, unlucky.

siniestro [se-ne-es-tro], *m.* 1. Perverseness, depravity, evil habit. 2. (*Com.*) Shipwreck, or great damage.

Sinnúmero [sin-noo'-may-ro], *m.* A numberless quanity. **Un sinnúmero de personas,** an endless number of persons.

sino [see'-no], *conj.* But: used in contrasting an affirmative idea with a negative. **No es blanco, sino negro,** it is not white, but black. 2. Except, besides (salvo). **Nadie lo sabe sino Juan,** nobody knows it except John. 3. Solely, only: always proceded by a negative proposition. **No sino,** not only so.

sino [see'-no], *m.* Fate, destiny.

sinoble [se-no'blay] *a* (*Her.*) *V.* SINOPLE.

sinoca [se-no'-cah], *f.* (*Med.*) Synocha, inflammatory continued fever.

sinocal [se-no-cahl'], *a.* Synochal, pertaining to the synocha fever.

sinodal [se-no-dahl'], *a.* Synodic, synodical. *-m.* Examiner of curates and confessors.

sinodático [se-no-dah'-te-co], *m.* Pecuniary contribution paid by the clergy to the bishops.

sinódico, ca [se-no'-de-co, cah], *a.* 1. Synodal, synodical. 2. Synodic, reckoned from one conjunction of the moon with the sun until another.

sínodo [see'-no-do], *m.* 1. Synod, an ecclesiastical assembly. 2. Conjunction of the heavenly bodies. 3. Stipend allowed to missionaries in America.

sinólogo, ga [se-no'-lo-go, gah], *m. & f.* Sinologue, versed in the Chinese language and literature.

sinónimo, ma [se-no'-ne-mo, mah], *a.* Synonymous. *-pl.* Synonima.

sinónimo [se-no'-ne-mo], *m.* Synonym.

sinónomo, ma [se-no'-no-mo, mah], *a. V.* SINÓNIMO.

sinople [se-no'-play], *a.* (*Her.*) Sinople, green.

sinopsis [se-nop'-sis], *f.* Synopsis, compendium, epitome.

sinóptico, ca [se-nop'-te-co, cah], *a.* Synoptic, synoptical, compendious.

sinovia [se-noo'-ve-ah], *f.* Synovia, the fluid of the joints.

sinovial [se-no-ve-ahl'], *a.* Synovial, secreting synovia.

sinrazón [sin-rah-thone'], *f.* Wrong, injury, injustice.

sinsabor [sin-sah-bor'], *m.* Displeasure, disgust, pain, uneasiness (inquietud), offensiveness.

sinsonte [sin-son'-tay], *m.* The mocking-bird.

sintáctico, ca [sin-tahc'-te-co, cah], *a.* (*Gram.*) Syntactic, belonging to syntax.

sintagma [sin-tahg'-mah], *m.* Orderly method, system.

sintaxis [sin-tahk'ses], *f.* 1. (*Gram.*) Syntax. 2. Coordination of things among themselves.

síntesis [seen'-tay-ses], *f.* Synthesis opposed to analysis.

sintético, ca [sin-tay'-te-co, cah], *a.* Synthetical.

sintetizador [sin-tay-te-thah-dor'], *m.* Synthesizer. **Sintetizador de la voz**, voice synthesizer.

sintetizar [sin-tay-te-thar'], *va.* To synthesize or synthetize: to unite by synthesis.

síntoma [sin'-to-mah], *m.* 1. Med. Symptom. 2. Sign. token.

sintomáticamente [sin-to-mah'-te-cah-men-tay], *adv.* Symptomatically.

sintomático, ca [sin-to-mah'-te-co, cah], *a.* Symptomatic, symptomatical.

sintomatología [sin-to-mah-to-lo-hee'-ah], *f.* (*Med.*) Symptomatology, a part of pathology.

sintonía [sin-to-nee'-ah], *f.* Syntony (acto); tunning.

sintonizar [sin-to-ne-thar'], *va.* (Radio) To syntonize.

sinuosidad [se-noo-o-se-dahd'], *f.* Sinuosity, sinuousness.

sinuoso, sa [se-noo-oh'-so, sah], *a.* Sinuous (camino), wavy (línea).

sinusitis [se-noo-see'-tees], *f.* Sinusitis.

sinvergüenza [sin-ver-goo-ayn'-thah], *m & f.* 1. Scoundrel (pillo), villain, rascal; rotter (canalla). 2. Shameless person (descarado).

sipia [see'-pe-ah], *f.* Refuse of olives, which remains in oil-mills.

siquiatra [se-ke-ah'-trah], *m. & f.* V. PSIQUIATRA.

siquiatría [se-ke-ah-tree'-ah], *f.* V. PSIQUIATRÍA.

síquico, ca [see'-ke-co, cah], *a.* V PSÍQUICO.

siquier, siquiera [se-ke-err', se-ke-ay-rah], *conj.* At least (por lo menos): though, although; or; scarcely; otherwise. **Dame siquiera un poquito**, give me at least a little of it. **Ni siquiera quiso escucharlo**, he would not even listen to him. **Dame un abrazo siquiera**, at least give me a hug. **Come un poco siquiera**, at least eat a little bit.

sirena [se-ray'-nah], *f.* 1. Syren, a sea-nymph. 2. A woman who sings charmingly. 3. (*Zool.*) Siren, a batrachian.

sirga [seer'-gah], *f.* 1. (*Naut.*) Towrope, tow-line. 2. Line used in draging nets. **A la sirga**, sailing with a dragging line.

sirgadura [seer-gah-doo'-rah], *f.* (*Naut.*) Towing or hauling a barge or vessel along a canal, or by the banks of a river.

sirgar [seer-gar'], *va.* (*Naut.*) To tow a vessel with a line.

sirgo [seer'-go], *m.* Twisted silk; stuff made of silk.

siriaco, ca [se-re-ah'-co, cah], *a.* Syrian, of Syria. *-m.* Syriac, the language of ancient Syria.

sirio [see'-re-o], *m.* (*Ast.*) Sirius or dog-star.

sirle [seer'-lay], *m.* Sheep-dung or goat's dung.

siro, ra [see'-ro, rah], *a.* V. SIRIACO.

siroco [se-ro'-co], *m.* Sirocco, a south-east wind on the Mediterranean.

sirte [seer'-tay], *f.* 1. Syrte, hidden rock, quicksand, moving sandbunk. 2. Peril, danger.

sirvienta [seer-ve-en'-tah], *f.* Female servant, serving-maid.

sirviente [seer-ve-en'-tay], *pa. & com.* Serving, being a servant, menial, serving-man. *V.* SIRVIENTA.

sisa [see'-sah], *f.* 1. Petty theft (robo). 2. Any pilfering trifle clipped from the whole. 3. Clippings, tailors' cabbage. 4. Size. linseed oil boiled with ochre used by gilders. 5. Assize. 6. Excise on eatables or liquors.

sisador, ra [se-sah-dor', rah], *m. & f.* Filcher, petty thief; one that exacts more than is due; sizer; cutter.

sisar [se-sar'], *va.* 1. To pilfer, to filch; to steal small quantities of a thing (artículos); to curtail, to lessen. 2. To cut clothes. 3. To size, to prepare with size, for gilding.

sisca [sees'-cah], *f.* (*Bot. Prov.*) Cylindrical sugar-cane.

sisear [se-say-ar'], *vn.* To hiss, to sound *s* inarticulately, in order to express disapproval.

siseo [se-say'-o], *m.* Hissing.

sisero [se-say'-ro], *m.* Excise collector.

sisimbrio [se-seem'-bre-o], *m.* (*Bot.*) Water-radish, radish water-cress.

sísmico, ca [sees'-me-co, cah], *a. a.* Seismic. **Movimiento sísmico**, earthquake.

sismógrafo [sis-mo'-grah-fo], *m.* Seismograph, apparatus to register the motions of an earthquake.

sisón [se-sone'], *m.* 1. Filcher, pilferer, petty thief. 2. (*Orn.*) Godart or moor-cock.

sistema [sis-tay'-mah], *m.* 1. System, a combination of things acting together. 2. System, a scheme which reduces many things to a regular dependence or corporation. 3. Hypothesis, supposition. 4. Gold or silver lace of one pattern. **Sistema de calefacción**, heating system. **Sistema montañoso**, mountain range. 5. **Sistema de apoyo ejecutivo**, executive support system. **Sistema de ayuda en la toma de decisiones**, decision support system. **Sistema de control del inventario**, inventory control system. **Sistema de correo oral**, voice mail system. **Sistema de diseño y fabricación**, design and manufacturing system. **Sistema de gestión de nóminas**, payroll system. **Sistema de información de gestión**, management information system (MIS). **Sistema de informes informáticos**, information reporting system. **Sistema de procesamiento de transacciones**, transaction processing system. **Sistema de registro de las cuentas por pagar**, accounts payable system. **Sistema de registro de pedidos**, order-entry system. **Sistema de registro de las cuentas por cobrar**, accounts receivable system. **Sistema integrado para la oficina**, integrated office system. **Sistema "libro mayor"**, general ledger system. **Sistema de fabricación asistida por ordenador**, computer-aided manufacturing system. **Sistema de inteligencia artificial**, artificial intelligence system. **Sistema experto**, expert sistem, knowledge processing system. **Sistema de gestor de datos**, expert system, knowledge processing system. **Sistema visual**, vision system.

sistemar [sis-tay-mar'], *va.* (*Amer.*) To systematize, to order.

sistemáticamente [sis-tay-mah'-te-cah-men-te], *adv.* Systematically.

sistemático, ca [sis-tay-mah'-te-co, cah], *a.* Systematic.

sistematizar [sis-tay-mah-te-thar'], *va.* To reduce to system, to systematize.

sistilo [sis-tee'-lo], *m.* (*Arch.*) Systyle.

sístole [sees'-to-lay], *f.* 1. (*Anat.*) Systole, contraction of the heart. 2. (*Rhet.*) Shortening of a long syllable.

sistro [sees'-tro], *m.* Sistrum, an ancient musical stringed instrument; a curved metal band crossed by many wires or rods.

sitácidos [se-tah'-the-dos], *m. pl.* The psittacid birds, the gray parrots.

sitiador [se-te-ah-dor'], *m.* Besieger.

sitial [se-te-ahl'], *m.* 1. Seat of honor for princes and prelates in a public assembly. 2. Stool, form, seat without a back.

sitiar [se-te-ar'], *va.* 1. To besiege, to lay siege to a place. 2. To surround, to hem in, to compass. 3. To deprive of the means of effecting something. **Sitiar por hambre**, (*Met.*) to compel one by necessity to submit.

sitibundo, da [se-te-boon'-do, dah], *a.* (*Poet.*) V. SEDIENTO.

sitio [see'-te-o], *m.* 1. Room (espacio), place (lugar, space taken up by a body or object. 2. Situation, location of a town, city, or building. 3. (*Mil.*) Siege, blockade. 4. Country house, country residence. 5. (*CAm. Cono Sur*) Building site (solar). 6. *(Carib. Mex.)* Small farm. 7. *(LAm.)* Taxi rank (parada). **Sitio de inspección**, checkpoint. **En cualquier sitio**, anywhere. **Dejar a uno en el sitio**, to kill somebody.

sito, ta [see'-to, tah], *a.* Situated, placed, located, lying, assigned. *V.* SITUADO.

sitófago, ga [se-toh'-fah-go, gah], *a.* Living upon wheat.

situación [se-too-ah-the-on'], *f.* 1. Situation, position. 2. Situation, condition of affairs. 3. Assignation, appointment, assignment. **Situación económica**, financial position.

situado [se-too-ah'-do], *m.* 1. Allowance, pay, or salary assigned upon certain goods or effects. 2. Post, position.

situado, da [se-too-ah'-do], *a. & pp.* of SITUAR. Situate, situated, placed, located, lying.

situar [se-too-ar'], *va.* 1. To put a thing in a certain place, to situate. 2. To assign a fund, out of which a salary, rent, or interest is to be paid. *-vn.* To be established in any place or business: to station oneself. **Esto se sitúa entre los dos mejores**, this places him among the best.

slalom [slah-lom], *m.* Slalom.

slogan [slo'-gan], *m.* Slogan.

smoking [smo'-kin], *m.* Tuxedo, dinner-jacket.

snob or **esnob** [es-nob'], *m.* Snob.

snobismo [sno-bees'-mo], *m. V.* ESNOBISMO.

so [so], *prep.* Under; below. Used in composition, it occasionally diminishes the import of the verb, as in *soasar*, to underdo meat; in other cases it augments it, as *sojuzgar*, to subjugate; and it sometimes retains its signification, as in *soterrar*, to put underground, to inter. **So color**, under color; on pretence. **¡So burro!** you, idiot!

soasar [so-ah-sar'], *va.* To half roost, to parboil, to underdo meat.

soata [so-ah'-tah], *f. (Amer.)* Dish composed of maize and uyama, a kind of squash, served for breakfast in Guayana, Venezuela.

soba [so'-bah], *f.* 1. The act and effect of making something soft and limber; rumpling, contusion; beating. 2. Kneading (amasado).

sobacal [so-bah-cahl'], *a.* Axillary, relating to the armpit or to an axil.

sobaco [so-bah'-co], *m.* 1. Armpit, armhole, axilla. 2. *(Bot.)* Axil.

sobadero, ra [so-bah-day'-ro, rah], *a.* That may be handled.

sobado [so-bah'-do], *m.* 1. The repeated and violent handling of something. 2. *V.* SOBADURA. **Sobados**, loaves of bread made in La Mancha. 3. *a.* worn, shabby (desgastado), dogeared (manoseado). *-Sobado, da. pp.* of SOBAR.

sobadura [so-bah-doo'-rah], *f.* Kneading, rubbing.

sobajadura [so-bah-hah-doo'-rah], *f.* Scrubbing, rubbing.

sobajamiento [so-bah-hah-me-en'-to], *m.* Friction, rubbing, scrubbing.

sobajanero [so-bah-hah-nay'-ro], *m. (Coll.)* Errand-boy.

sobajar [so-bah-har'], *va.* To scrub, to rub hard.

sobanda [so-bahn'-dah], *f.* Bottom or end of a cask.

sobaquera [so-bah-kay'-rah], *f.* 1. Opening left in clothes under the armpit; arm-hole. 2. *(CAm. Carib.)* Underarm odor. **Coger a alguien las sobaqueras**, to gain ascendency over a person. **Funda sobaquera**, shoulder holster.

sobaquina [so-bah-kee'-nah], *f.* Smell of the armpit.

sobar [so-bar'], *va.* 1. To handle (tela), to soften. 2. To pummel, to chastise with blows. 3. To handle with too much familiarity and frequency. 4. To fondle, to feel (personas); to finger, to paw, to lay hands on (persona). 5. *(LAm.)* To set (hueso). 6. *(And.)* To skin (despellejar). 7. To pester (molestar). 8. *(And. Carib. Mex.)* To flatter (lisonjear).

sobarba [so-bar'-bah], *f.* Nose-band of a bridle.

sobarbada [so-bar-bah'-dah], *f.* 1. A check given a horse by pulling the reins with violence. 2. Chuck under the chin; jerk. 3. *(Met.)* Reprimand, scolding.

sobarbo [so-bar'-bo], *m.* Lever or pallet for raising the pestles in a fulling-mill.

sobarcar [so-bar-car'], *va..* 1. To carry something heavy under the arm. 2. To draw clothes up to the armholes.

sobeo [so-bay'-o], *m.* Caresses, love-play, fondling.

soberanamente [so-bay-rah'-nah-men-tay], *adv.* Sovereignly, supremely.

soberanear [so-bay-rah-nay-ar'], *m.* To lord it, to domineer like a sovereign.

soberanía [so-bay-rah-nee'-ah], *f.* 1. Sovereignty, supreme power over others, majesty. 2. Pride, haughtiness, arrogance, loftiness.

soberano, na [so-bay-rah'-no, nah], *a.* 1. Sovereign, supreme, kingly. 2. Sovereign, superior, predominant. **Una soberana paliza**, a real walloping.

soberano [so-bay-rah'-no], *m.* Sovereign; lord, paramount; king; liege.

soberbia [so-berr'-be-ah], *f.* 1. Pride (orgullo), haughtiness (altanería), an inordinate desire to be preferred to others; presumption; arrogance; loftiness. 2. Pomp, pageantry, 3. Anger, passion. 4. Insulting word or action.

soberbiamente [so-ber-be-ah-men-tay], *adv.* Haughtily, arrogantly, proudly, superbly.

soberbio, bia [so-berr'-be-o, ah], *a.* 1. Proud (orgulloso), arrogant, elated, haughty, passionate. 2. Losty, sublime, eminent, superb. 3. Fiery, mettlesome (caballos).

sobina [so-bee'-nah], *f.* A wooden pin or peg.

sobo [so'-bo], *m.* Frequent working of a thing to make it soft and limber.

sobón, na [so-bone', nah], *a.* 1. One who makes himself too familiar by half; too free with his hands. 2. A sly, lazy fellow (gandul). 3. *(And.)* Soapy (adulón). **¡No seas sobón!**, get your hands off me!

sobordo [so-bor'-do], *m.* Manifest, freight-list; the statement of a cargo taken on board of a vessel; a memorandum of the articles daily received while a vessel is lading.

sobornación [so-bor-nah-the-on'], *f. V.* SOBORNO.

sobornado [so-bor-nah'-do], *m.* Mishaped loaf of bread in the oven.-**Sobornado, da**, *pp.* of SOBORNAR.

sobornador, ra [so-bor-na-dor', rah], *m. & f.* Suborner, corrupter, one who is guilty of subornation.

sobornal [so-bor-nahl'], *a.* Added to the load which a vessel carries. *-m.* A small bale; a seroon.

sobornar [so-bor-nar'], *va.* To suborn, to bribe, to procure by secret collusion, to corrupt, to buy off.

soborno [so-bor'-no], *m.* 1. Subornation. 2. Bribe, gift or money offered for doing a bad action; the act of buying someone off. 3. Incitement, inducement. 4. In Peru, used for *Sobornal*.

sobra [so'-brah], *f.* 1. Overplus, surplus (excedente), excess. **Sobras de la comida**, offals, leaving, broken victuals. 2. Grievous offence, injury. **De sobra**, over and above; superfluously. **Estar de sobra**, *(Coll.)* to be one too many.

sobradamente [so-brah-dah-men-tay], *adv.* Abundantly: superabundantly; excessively.

sobradar [so-brah-dar'], *va.* To erect edifices with lofts or granaries.

sobradillo [so-brah-deel'-lyo], *m.* 1. *(Dim.)* A cock-loft. 2. Penthouse; a shelter over a balcony or window.

sobrado [so-brah'-do], *m.* 1. *V.* DESVÁN and GUARDILLA. 2. *(Prov.)* Granary.

sobrado, da [so-brah'-do, dah], *a.* 1. Hold, audacious, licentious. 2. Rich, wealthy (rico). 3. Bold (atrevido). 4. *(Cono Sur)* Colossal (enorme). *-adv. V.* SOBRADAMENTE.

sobrancero, ra [so-bran-thay'-ro, rah], *a.* 1. Disengaged, unemployed. 2. A supernumerary ploughman, who supplies the place of another.

sobrante [so-brahn'-tay], *m.* 1. Residue, superfluity, overplus. 2. Rich, wealthy, *-pa.* of SOBRAR.

sobrar [so-brar'], *vn.* 1. To have more than is necessary or required. 2. To be over and above: to be more than enough (ser más que suficiente), to be intrusive. 3. To remain (quedar de más), to be left. **Más vale que sobre que no que falte,**

(Prov.) it is better to have too much of a thing than to be in want of it.

sobrasada [so-brah-sah'-dah], *f. V.* SOBREASADA.

sobrasar [so-brah-sar'], *va.* To add fire under a pot to make it boil sooner or better; to surround with coals.

sobre [so'-bray], *prep.* 1. Above (encima de), over (cantidad). *V.* ENCIMA. 2. Super, over: used in composition, as *sobrecargar*, to overchange or overload. **Tiene mucha ventaja sobre todos los demás,** he possesses great advantages over the rest. 3. Moreover, besides. 4. A little more; a few more. 5. Above, higher; with power or superiority. 6. *(Naut.)* Off. 7. To, towards, near. 8. On, upon. 9. After, since. 10. Before or around. **Está sobre la mesa,** it's on the table. **Estar sobre uno,** to keep on at somebody. **Un préstamo sobre una propiedad,** a loan on a property.

sobre [so'-bray], *m.* 1. Envelope of a letter. 2. Address, superscription.

sobreabundancia [so-bray-ahn-boon-dahn'-the-ah], *f.* Superabundance.

sobreabundante [so-bray-ah-boon-dahn'-tay], *a.* Superabundant, more than enough; luxuriant.

sobreabundantemente [so-bray-ah-bon-dahn'-tay-men-tay], *adv.* Superabundantly.

sobreabundar [so-bray-ah-boon-dar'], *vn.* To superabound; to be exuberant.

sobreaguar [so-bray-ah-goo-ar'], *vn.* To be on the surface of water, to float on water.

sobreaguda [so-bray-ah-goo'-dah], *f.* One of the seven small letters in music.

sobreagudo [so-bray-ah-goo'-do], *m. (Mus.)* Highest treble in music.

sobrealiento [so-bray-ah-le-en'-to], *m.* Difficult respiration.

sobrealimentar [so-bray-ah-le-men-tar'], *va.* 1. Supercharge. 2. To give extra nourishment.

sobrealzar [so-bray-al-thar'], *va.* To praise, to extol.

sobreañadir [so-bray-ah-nyah-deer'], *va.* To superadd, to superinduce.

sobrañal [so-brey-ah-nyahl'], *a.* Applied to animals more than a year old.

sobreasada [so-bray-ah-sah'-dah], *f.* In Mallorca, a kind of sausage half roasted, and done over again when it is to be eaten.

sobreasar [so-bray-ah-sar'], *va.* To roast again what was half roasted before.

sobrebásico, ca [ro-bray-bah'-se-co, cah], *a. (Chem.)* Having an excess of base; a basic salt.

sobreboya [so-bray-bo'-yah], *f. (Naut.)* Marking buoy, a small buoy fastened to a large one in the water, to show its position.

sobrebrazal [so-bray-brah-thahl'], *m. (Naut.)* False rail.

sobrecaja [so-bray-cah'-hah], *f.* Outer case.

sobrecalza [so-bray-cahl'-thah], *f. V.* POLAINA.

sobrecama [so-bray-cah'-mah], *f.* Coverlet, quilt.

sobrecaña [so-bray-cah'-nyah], *f. (Vet.)* Tumor on a horse's leg.

sobrecarga [so-bray-car'-gah], *f.* 1. An additional bundle thrown over a load. 2. Additional trouble or vexation. 3. Surcharge (correos), overburden. 4. Rope thrown over a load to make it fast (cuerda). **Sobrecarga de importación,** import surcharge.

sobrecargado, da [so-bray-car-gah'-do, dah], *a. & pp.* of SOBRECARGAR. Overloaded.

sobrecargar [so-bray-car-gar'], *va.* 1. To overload (camión), to surcharge, to overburden. 2. To make one seam over another.

sobrecargo [so-bray-car'-go], *m.* 1. Ship's purser (barco). 2. Plane stewardess (avión).

sobrecarta [so-bray-car'-tah], *f.* 1. Cover, envelope, of a letter. 2. The second injunction; decree or warrant, repenting a former order.

sobrecartar [so-bray-car-tar'], *va.* To repeat a former injunction.

sobrecebadera [so-bray-thay-bah-day'-rah], *f. (Naut.)* Sprit top-sail.

sobrecédula [so-bray-thay'-doo-lah], *f.* Second royal order or despatch.

sobreceja [so-bray-thay'-hah], *f.* The part of the forehead over the eyebrows.

sobrecejo [so-bray-thay'-ho], *m.* Frown (ceño); supercilious aspect, cloudiness of look.

sobrecelestial [so-bray-thay-les-te-ahl'], *a.* Supercelestial.

sobreceño [so-bray-thay'-nyo], *m.* Frown. *V.* SOBRECEJO.

sobrecerco [so-bray-therr'-co], *m.* Ornament or fringe placed round another to strengthen it.

sobrecincha [so-bray-theen'-chah], *f.* One of the girths of a saddle; a surcingle.

sobrecincho [so-bray-theen'-cho], *m.* Surcingle, an additional girth, put over the common girth.

sobreclaustro [so-bray-clah'-oos-tro], *m.* Apartment over a cloister.

sobrecoger [so-bray-co-herr'], *vn.* To surprise, to overtake. *-m.* To become apprehensive.

sobrecogimiento [so-bray-co-he-me-en'-to], *m.* Fearfulness, apprehension.

sobrecomida [so-bray-co-mee'-dah], *f.* Dessert. *V.* POSTRE.

sobrecomprimir [so-bray-com-pre-meer'], *va. (Aer.)* To pressurize.

sobrecopa [so-bray-co'-pah], *f.* Cover or lid of a cup.

sobrecrecer [so-bray-cray-therr'], *vn.* To outgrow, to overgrow.

sobrecreciente [so-bray-cray-the-en'-tay], *pa.* Outgrowing, overgrowing.

sobrecruces [so-bray-croo'-thes], *m. pl.* Cross-joints to strengthen a wheel.

sobrecubierta [so-bray-coo-be-err'-tah], *f.* 1. Double cover. 2. Coverlet, quilt. 3. *(Naut.)* Upper deck.

sobredezmero [so-bray-deth-may'-ro], *m.* Assistant in collecting duties.

sobredicho, cha [so-bray-dee'-cho, chah], *a.* Above-mentioned.

sobrediente [so-bray-de-en'-tay], *m.* Gag-tooth which grows over another.

sobredorar [so-bray-do-rar'], *va.* 1. To gild anew, to overgild. 2. To palliate, to extenuate, to exculpate.

sobredosis [so-bray-do'-sees], *f.* Overdose.

sobreedificar [so-bray-ay-de-fe-car'], *va.* To build over something.

sobreempeine [so-bray-em-pay'-e-nayh], *m.* That part of spatterdashes or gaiters which covers the instep.

sobreentender [so-bray-en-ten-derr'], *va. & va. V.* SOBRENTENDER.

sobreescrito [so-bray-es-cree'-to], *m.* 1. Superscription, inscription, direction, address. 2. Mien, aspect; pretext.

sobreesdrújulo, la [so-bray-es-droo'-hoo-lo, lah], *a. V.* SOBRESDRÚJULO.

sobreestadía [so-bray-es'-tah-dee'-ah], *f. (Com.)* One of the extra lay days: an allowance of time made in loading or unloading a vessel and the sum paid.

sobreexceder [so-bray-ex-thay-derr'], *va. V.* SOBREXCEDER.

sobrefaz [so-bray-fath'], *f.* 1. Superficies, surface, outside. 2. *(Mil.)* Face prolonged, the distance between the angle of the shoulder of a bastion and the curtain.

sobrefino, na [so-bray-fee'-no, nah], *a.* Superfine, overfine.

sobreguarda [so-bray-goo-ar'-dah], *m.* Second guard placed for greater security.

sobreguardilla [so-bray-goo-ar-deel'-lyah], *f.* Penthouse, shelter, shed.

sobrehaz [so-bray-ath'], *f.* 1. Surface, outside. 2. Outside cover of something.

sobrehueso [so-bray-oo-ay'-so], *m.* 1. Morbid swelling on the bones or joints. 2. Trouble, encumbrance, burden.

sobrehumano, na [so-bray-oo-mah'-no, nah], *a.* Superhuman.

sobrehusa [so-bray-oo'-sah], *f.* A stew made in Andalusia from fried fish.

sobreimpresión [so-bray-em-pray-se-on'], *f.* Overprint (correos).

sobreimprimir [so-bray-em-pre-meer'], *va.* To overprint.

sobrejalma [so-bray-hahl'-mah], *f.* Woollen cover for a packsaddle.

sobrelecho [so-bray-lay'-cho], *m.* That side of a stone which lies on a bed of mortar.

sobrellave [so-brel-lyah'-vay], *f.* Double key, a large key. -*m.* In royal palaces, an officer who keeps a second key of every door.

sobrellenar [so-bray-lyay-nar'], *va.* To overfill, to overflow, to glut.

sobrelleno, na [so-brel-lyay'-no, nah], *a.* Overfull, superabundant.

sobrellevar [so-brel-lyay-var'], *adv.* 1. To ease another's burden; to carry (peso). 2. To inure to hardships by degrees, to undergo. 3. To overlook the failings of interiors or subjects.

sobremallero [so-bray-mal-lyay'-ro], *m.* One of the four kinds of net used in the sardine-fishery off the Cantabrian coast.

sobremanera [so-bray-mah-nay'-rah], *adv.* Beyond measure; excessively.

sobremano [so-bray-mah'-no], *f.* (*Vet.*) Osseous tumor on the hoofs of horses' fore feet.

sobremesa [so-bray-may'-sah], *f.* 1. Table-carpet, tablecloth (mantel). 2. Dessert (del postre). 3. Sitting on after a meal. **Charla de sobremesa**, after-dinner talk, table talk. **Un cigarro de sobremesa**, an after dinner cigar. V. POSTRE. **De sobremesa**, immediately after dinner.

sobremesana [so-bray-may-sah'-nah], *f.* (*Naut.*) Mizzen top-sail.

sobrenadar [so-bray-nah-dar'], *va.* To swim on the surface of any fluid, to overfloat.

sobrenatural [so-bray-nah-too-rahl'], *a.* Supernatural, preternatural, metaphysical.

sobrenombre [so-bray-nom'-bray], *m.* 1. Surname, the family name. 2. Nickname; a name given in contempt.

sobrentender [so-bren-ten-derr'], *va. & vr.* To understand something not expressed, but which must be supposed from what has gone before; to be understood.

sobreojo [so-bray-o'-ho], *m.* A supercilious aspect; a look of envy, hatred, or contempt.

sobrepaga [so-bray-pah'-gah], *f.* Increase of pay; extra pay.

sobrepaño [so-bray-pah'-nyo], *m.* Upper cloth, put over others; wrapper.

sobreparto [so-bray-par'-to], *m.* 1. Time of lying-in, which follows the delivery. 2. Delicate state of health which follows confinement.

sobrepasar [so-bray-pah-sar'], *va.* 1. To excel, to surpass. 2. To exceed (límite).

sobrepeine [so-bray-pay'-nay], *m.* The act of cutting the hair but slightly.-*adv.* (*Coll.*) Slightly, briefly.

sobrepelliz [so-bray-pel-lyeth'], *f.* Surplice.

sobrepeso [so-bray-pay'-so], *m.* Over-weight.

sobrepié [so-bray-pee-ay'], *m.* (*Vet.*) Osseous tumor at the top of horses' hoofs.

sobreplán [so-bray-plahn'], *m.* (*Naut.*) Rider.

sobreponer [so-bray-po-nerr'], *va.* To add one thing to another; to put one over another. -*vr.* To exalt oneself above other things; to wise oneself, to overcome, to overpower. **Sobreponerse a una enfermedad**, to pull through an illness. (*Yo sobrepongo, yo sobreponga; yo sobrepuse; from Sobreponer.* V. PONER.)

sobreprecio [so-bray-pray'-the-o], *m.* 1. Surcharge. 2. Markup.

sobreprima [so-bray-pree'-ma], *f.* Increased premium (en seguros).

sobreproducción [so-bray-pro-dooc-the-on'], *f.* Overproduction.

sobrepuerta [so-bray-poo-err'-tah], *f.* 1. Cornice, a kind of louver-board put over interior doors, from which curtains are hung. 2. In a general sense, any painting, woven stuff, carved work, etc., put over doors for ornament.

sobrepuesto, ta [so-bray-poo-es'-to, tah], *a. & pp. irr.* of SOBREPONER. Counterfeit, fictitious.

sobrepuesto [so-bray-poo-es'-to], *m.* 1. Honeycomb formed by bees after the hive is full. 2. Earthen vessel added to beehives when they are too full.

sobrepuja [so-bray-poo'-hah], *f.* Outbidding, bidding more than another.

sobrepujamiento [so-bray-poo-hah-me-en'-to], *m.* The act and effect of surpassing, excelling.

sobrepujante [so-bray-poo-hahn'-tay], *pa.* Surpassing, excelling.

sobrepujanza [so-bray-poo-hahn'-thah], *f.* Great strength and vigor.

sobrepujar [so-bray-poo-har'], *va.* To exceed, to surpass, to excel, to foil, to overturn.

sobrequilla [so-bray-keel'-lyah], *f.* (*Naut.*) Keelson.

sobrerronda [so-brer-ron'-dah], *f.* (*Mil.*) Counter-round.

sobrerropa [so-brer-ro'-pah], *f.* A sort of long robe worn over other clothes.

sobresal [so-bry-sahl'], *f.* (*Chem.*) An acid salt.

sobresalario [so-bray-sah-lah'-re-o], *m.* Perquisites: what is added to a salary.

sobresalido, da [ro-bray-sah-lee'-do, dah], *a. & pp.* of SOBRESALIR. Elated, inflated, haughty.

sobresaliente [so-bray-sah-le-en-tay], *a.* Excelling, surpassing, excellent.

sobresaliente [so-bray-sah-le-en'-tay], *m.* 1. (*Mil.*) Officer who commands a small body of troops always ready for an emergency. 2. Substitute. 3. An actor or actress (*sobresaliente*), ready to perform the part of one absent or sick.

sobresalir [so-bray-sah-leer'], *vn.* To exceed in height, to overtop, to overreach, to surpass, to outvie. (*Yo sobresalgo, yo sobresalga, from Sobresalir.* V. SALIR.)

sobresaltadamente [so-bray-sal-tah'-dah-men-tay], *adv.* Suddenly, unexpectedly.

sobresaltado, da [so-bray-sal-tah'-do, dah], *a.* Startled, frightened.

sobresaltar [so-bray-sal-tar'], *va.* 1. To rush violently upon, to assail, to surprise or to fall upon unexpectedly. 2. To frighten, to terrify, to startle. -*vn.* To fly in one's face, to be striking (cuadros). -*vr.* To be startled at, to be surprised, confused, or perplexed.

sobresalto [so-bray-sahl'-to], *m.* A sudden assault, a surprise (sorpresa); a sudden dread or fear. **De sobresalto**, unexpectedly, unawares.

sobresanar [so-bray-sah-nar'], *va.* 1. To heal superficially. 2. To screen, to palliate.

sobresanos [so-bray-sah-'nos], *m. pl.* (*Naut.*) Tabling, a broad hem on sails, to strengthen that part which is fastened to the bolt-rope.

sobrescribir [so-bres-cre-berr'], *va.* To superscribe, to inscribe, to address or direct a letter.

sobrescrito [so-bres-cree'-to], *m.* Superscription, address or direction of a letter.-**Sobrescrito, ta**, *pp.* of SOBRESCRIBIR.

sobresdrújulo, la [so-bres-droo'-hoo-lo, lah], *a.* Accented upon the syllable preceding the antepenult; as, *devuélvemelo*.

sobreseer [so-bray-say-err'], *vn.* 1. To desist from a design; to supersede; to relinquish a claim or pretension; to overrule. 2. (*Law.*) To discontinue an action.

sobreseguro [so-bray-say-goo'-ro], *adv.* In a safe manner, without risk.

sobreseimiento [so-bray-say-e-me-en'-to], *m.* Omission, suspension; discontinuance.

sobresello [so-bray-sel'-lyo], *m.* A double seal.

sobresembrar [so-bray-sem-brar'], *va.* 1. To sow over again. 2. To diffuse erroneous doctrines; to sow discord.

sobreseñal [so-bray-say-nyahl'], *f.* Ensign or standard arbitrarily adopted by the ancient knights.

sobresolar [so-bray-so-lar'], *va.* 1. To pave anew. 2. To newsole boots or shoes.

sobrestadías [so-brays-tah-dee'-ahs], *f.* V. SOBREESTADÍA.

sobrestante [so-bres-tahn'-tay], *m.* Overseer; foreman; comptroller; overlooker.

sobrestante [so-bres-tahn'-tay], *a.* Immediate, near.

sobresueldo [so-bray-soo-el'-do], *m.* Addition to one's pay or allowance.

sobresuelo [so-bray-soo-ay'-lo], *m.* A second floor or pavement laid over another.

sobretarde [so-bray-tar'-day], *f.* Close of the evening.

sobretejer [so-bray-tay-herr'], *va..* To work a stuff on both sides.

sobretodo [so-bray-to'-do], *m.* Overcoat, surtout, a greatcoat.

sobretodo [so-bray-to'-do], *adv.* Above all; before all things.

sobreedor [so-bray-ah-dor'], *m.* Supervisor, overseer.

sobrevalorar [so-bray-va-lo-rahr'], *va.* To overvalue.

sobrevenda [so-bray-ven'-dah], *f. (Med.)* Surband, bandage placed over others.

sobrevenida, [so-bray-vay-nee'-dah], *f.* Supervention.

sobrevenir [so-bray-vay-neer'], *m.* To happen (ocurrir); to fall out, to come unexpectedly; to come between; to come in the way; to supervene.

sobreventar [so-bray-ven-tar'], *m. (Naut.)* To gain the weather-gauge of another ship.

sobreverterse [so-bray-ver-terr'-say], *vr.* To run over, to overflow.

sobrevestir [so-bray-ves-teer'], *va.* To put on a great coat.

sobrevidriera [so-bray-ve-dre-ay'-rah], *f.* Wire net before a glass window.

sobreviento [so-bray-ve-en'-to], *m.* Gust of wind; impetuous fury, surprise.

sobreviniente [so-bray-ve-ne-en'-tay], *pa.* Happening, falling out, coming in the way.

sobreviviente [so-bray-ve-ve-en'-tay], *va. pa. & m. & f.* Survivor, surviving. *V.* SUPERVIVIENTE.

sobrevivir [so-bray-ve-veer'], *vn.* To survive (accidente, desastre), to outlive. **Sobrevivir a alguno,** to outlive or survive a person.

sobrevolar [so-bray-vo-lahr'], *va.* To fly over.

sobrexceder [so-brex-thay-derr'], *va.* To surpass, to excel another, to exceed.

sobrexcitación [so-brex-the-tah-the-on'], *f.* Over-stimulation of vital organs.

sobriamente [so-bre-ah-men-tay], *adv.* Soberly, frugally, abstemiously.

sobriedad [so-bre-ay-dahd'], *f.* Sobriety, abstemiousness, abstinence.

sobrina [so-bree'-nah], *f.* Niece.

sobrinazgo [so-bre-nath'-go], 1. The relationship of a nephew or niece. 2. Nepotism.

sobrino [so-bree'-no], *m.* Nephew.

sobrio, ria [so'-bre-o, ah], *a.* Sober (templado), temperate, frugal, abstemious.

soca, or **soca de planta** [so'-cah], *f. (Amer.)* The sugar-cane which is cut down to be planted for the new crop.

socaire [so-cah'-e-ray], *m.* 1. *(Naut.)* Slatch, slack of a rope or cable. 2. Shelter, lee, lee gauge.

socairero [so-cah-e-ray'-ro], *m.* Skulker, lurker, one who hides himself from his business or duty.

socaliña [so-cah-lee'-nyah], *f.* Cunning or artifice to gain a thing from one who is not obliged to give it.

socaliñar [so-ca-lee-nyar'], *va.* To extort by cunning or stratagem.

socaliñero, ra [so-cah-le-nyay'-ro, rah], *m. & f.* Artful exacter, a cheat.

socalzar [so-cal-thar'], *va.* To strengthen the lower part of a building or wall which threatens ruin.

socamarero [so-cah-may-ray'-ro], *m.* 1. The second steward, or man-servant of a great house. 2. The second lord chamberlain.

socapa [so-cah'-pah], *f.* Pretext, pretence. **A socapa,** on presence, under color.

socaspicol [so-cah-pis-cole'], *m.* V. SOCHANTRE.

socar [so-car'], *va. (Naut.)* To set taut a rope, shroud, or stay.

socarra [so-car'-rah], *f.* 1. The act of half roasting meat, or leaving it half rare. 2. Craft, cunning.

socarrar [so-car-rar'], *va.* To half roast or dress meat.

socarrén [so-car-rayn'], *m.* Eave, the edge of the roof, gable end.

socarrena [so-car-ray'-nah], *f.* Hollow, cavity, interval.

socarrina [so-car-ree'-nah], *f. (Coll.)* Scorching, singeing.

socarrón, na [so-car-rone', nah], *a.* Cunning (taimado), sly (humor), crafty.

socarronería [so-car-ro-nay-ree'-ah], *f.* Craft (astucia), cunning, artfulness.

socava [so-cah'-vah], *f.* 1. The act of mining or undermining. 2. The act of opening the ground around trees.

socavar [so-cah-var'], *va.* To excavate, to undermine (excavar). **Socavar la tierra,** to turn up the ground.

socavón [so-cah-vone'], *m.* 1. Cave, cavern (cueva); a passage under ground. 2. Adit, the entrance to a mine. **Socavones,** pits or shafts in mines.

sociabilidad [so-the-ah-be-le-dahd'], *f.* Sociableness, sociability, civility.

sociable [so-the-ah'-blay], *a.* 1. Sociable (persona), ready to unite in a general interest. 2. Sociable, inclined to company, companionable. 3. Sociable, familiar, friendly, courteous.

sociablemente [so-the-ah'-blay-men-tay], *adv.* Sociably, companionably.

social [so-the-ahl'], *a.* 1. Social, relating to society, or to a general or public interest. 2. Social, companionable, relating to company or friendly intercourse.

socialismo [so-the-ah-lees'-mo], *m.* Socialism, a political doctrine proposing a reconstruction of society.

socialista [so-the-ah-lees'-tah], *m & f.* Socialist, one professing socialism.

socialmente [so-the-ahl'-men-tay], *adv.* Socially.

sociedad [so-the-ai-dahd'], *f.* 1. Society, the company and converse of persons of sense and information. 2. Friendship, familiar intercourse. 3. Society, union of many in one general interest; corporation, consociation, fraternity, fellowship. 4. Society (asociación), partnership. **Sociedad inmobiliaria,** building society. **Notas de sociedad,** gossip column.

sociedad anónima [ah-no'-ne-mah], *f.* (Abbreviated S.A.) Incorporated company *(Inc.)*

socio [so'-the-o], *m.* 1. Partner, associate. 2. Member (de un club). **Se ruega a los señores socios….,** members are asked to…

sociología [so-the-o-lo-hee'-ah], *f.* Sociology, the study of the evolution and organization of society.

sociológico, ca [so-the-o-lo'-he-co, cah], *a.* Sociological.

sociólogo, ga [so-the-o'-lo-go, gah], *m. & f.* Sociologist.

socolor [so-co-lor'], *m.* Pretext, pretence, color.

socollada [so-col-lyah'-dah], *f. (Naut.)* Jerk, the violent straining of the ropes, cables, and shrouds, caused by the rolling and pitching of a ship.

soconusco [so-co-noos'-co], *m.* The cocoa from the province of that name in Chiapas (Mexico) and in N. W. Guatemala, considered to be of the best quality.

socorredor, ra [so-cor-ray-dor', rah], *m. & f.* Succourer, assister; administering relief, helper.

socorrer [so-cor-rerr'], *pa.* 1. To succour, to aid, to help (persona). 2. To pay a part of what is due.

socorrido, da [so-cor-ree'-do, dah], *a & pp.* of SOCORRER. Furnished, well supplied. **La plaza de Acapulco es muy socorrida,** the market of Acapulco is well supplied. *(Coll.)* Handy, useful.

socorrismo [so-cor-rees'-mo], *m.* Life-saving.

socorrista [so-cor-rees'-tah], *m & f.* Lifeguard, life-saver.

socorro [so-cor'-ro], *m.* 1. Succor, support, assistance, help (ayuda). 2. Part of a salary or allowance paid beforehand. 3. Succor, a fresh supply of men or provisions thrown into a besieged place. **Trabajos de socorro**, relief work.

socrático, ca [so-crah'-te-co, cah], *a.* Socratic, relating to the doctrines of Socrates.

socucho [so-coo'-cho], *m. (Mex.)* 1. A large and narrow room in the lower story of a house. 2. Hiding-place, cave.

socrocio [so-cro'-the-o], *m.* 1. Poultice or cataplasm of a saffron color. 2. Pleasure, delight, satisfaction.

sochantre [so-chahn'-tray], *m.* Subchanter, the deputy of the preceptor in a cathedral.

soda [so'-dah], *f.* 1. *(Bot.)* V. SOSA. 2. Soda water (bebida).

sodio [so'-de-o], *m. (Chem.)* Sodium, a silver-white, alkaline, metallic element.

sodomía [so-do-mee'-ah], *f.* Sodomy, an unnatural crime.

sodomita [so-do-mee'-tah], *m. & a.* Sodomite, one who commits sodomy.

sodomítico, ca [so-do-mee'-te-co, cah], *a.* Belonging to sodomy.

soez [so-eth'], *a.* Mean, vile, base, worthless, shameful.

soezmonte [so-eth'-men-tay], *adv.* Meanly, basely, vilely, shamefuly.

sofá [so-fah'], *m.* Sofa.

sofá cama [so-fah' cah'-mah], *m.* Studio couch.

sofaldar [so-fal-dar'], *va.* To truss up; to raise up; to tuck up; to lift up anything in order to discover it.

sofaldo so-fahl'-do], *m.* The act of trussing or tucking up clothes.

sofí [so-fee'], *m.* 1. Sufi, sofi, the Emperor or Shah of Persia. 2. A sect of mystics of that country. *V.* SUFÍ.

sofión [so-fe-one'], *m.* Hoot, shout in scorn or contempt; reprimand (reprimenda), censure.

sofisma [so-fees'-mah], *m.* Sophism, a fallacious argument.

sofismo [so-fees'-mo], *m. V.* SUFISMO.

sofista [so-fees'-tah], *m.* Sophister, a disputant; an artful but insidious logician; a caviller, a sophist.

sofistería [so-fis-tay-ree'-ah], *f.* Sophistry, fallacy.

sofisticación [so-fis-te-cah-the-on'], *f.* Sophistication, adulteration.

sofisticado [so-fis-te-cah'-do], *a.* Sophisticated; affected, over-refined.

sofísticamente [so-fees'-te-cah-men-tay], *adv.* Sophistically, fallaciously.

sofisticar [so-fis-te-car'], *va.* To cavil, to falsify; to sophisticate.

sofístico, ca [so-fees'-te-co, cah], *a.* Sophistical, fallacious.

sófito [so'-fee-to], *m. (Arch.)* Soffit, under side of the cornice ornamented with panels, etc.

soflama [so-flah'-mah], *f.* 1. A subtile flame; the reverberation of fire (fuego). 2. Glow, blush. 3. Deceitful language.

soflamar [so-flah-mar'], *va.* 1. To use deceitful language, to impose upon, to deceive (engañar). 2. To rise a blush.

soflanero [so-flah-nay'-ro], *m.* Sophister, one that makes use of captious or deceitful language.

sofocación [so-fo-cah-the-on'], *f.* 1. Suffocation, strangling. 2. *(Med.)* Suffocation, apnea, loss of breath.

sofocado [so-fo-cah'-do], *a.* **Estar sofocado**, to be out of breath.

sofocante [so-fo-cahn'-tay], *m.* Ribbon with a tassel, worn by ladies round the neck. *-pa.* of SOFOCAR.

sofocar [so-fo-car'], *va.* 1. To choke, to impede respiration, to suffocate (persona). 2. To quench, to smother (incendio). 3. To oppress, to harass. 4. To importune, to molest. 5. To provoke by abusive language. *-vr.* 1. To suffocate (ahogarse). 2. *(Fig.)* To blush. **No vale la pena de que te sofoques**, it's not worth upsetting yourself about it.

sofoco [so-fo'-co], *m.* 1. Suffocation. 2. Great aversion given or received, loathing.

sofocón [so-fo-cone'], *m.* Displeasure, provocation. **Llevarse un sofocón**, to have a sudden shock.

sófora [so'-fo-rah], *f. (Bot.)* A tree of Japan cultivated for ornament in European gardens.

sofreír [so-fray-eer'], *vn.* To fry slightly.

sofrenada [so-fray-nah'-dah], *f.* 1. A sudden check given to a horse with the bridle (caballo). 2. A rude reprehension; a severe reprimand (bronca). 3. A fit of sickness, or any other accident that forewarns us of our frailties.

sofrenar [so-fray-nar'], *va.* 1. To check a horse by a violent pull of the bridle. 2. To reprehend rudely; to reprimand severely (bronca).

sofrenazo [so-fray-nah-tho], *m.* A violent pull of the bridle.

sofrito, ta [so-free'-to, tah], *pp. irr.* of SOFREIR.

software [soft-oo-ah-ray], *m. (Comput.)* Software. **Software del ratón**, mouse software. **Software para presentaciones gráficas**, presentation graphics software.

soga [so'-gah], *f.* 1. Rope; halter (de animal), cord. 2. *(Coll.)* A sly, cunning fellow. 3. Measure of land which varies in different provinces; measure of rope. **Sopa de un pozo**, bucket-rope for a a well. *-int.* A term expressing astonishment and aversion. **Siempre se rompe la soga por lo más delgado**, the rope always breaks at the thinnest part. **Estar con la soga al cuello la garganta**, *(Met.* to be in imminent danger.

soguear [so-gay-ar'], *va.* 1. To measure with a rope. 2. *(And. CAm. Cono Sur)* To tie with a rope (atar). 3. *(Carib.)* To tame (domesticar).

soguería [so-gay-ree'-ah], *f.* Ropewalk, rope-yard; collection of ropes.

soguero [so-gay'-ro], *m.* A rope-maker, a cord-maker.

soguica, illa, ita [so-gee'-cah], *f. dim.* A small rope.

soguilla [so-geel'-lyah], *f. (Prov.)* A small band of braid or plaited hair.

soja [so-hah], *f.* Soya.

sojuzgador [so-hooth-gah-dor'], *m.* Conqueror, subduer.

sojuzgar [so-hooth-gar'], *va.* To conquer, to subjugate.

sol [sole], *m.* 1. Sun, sunshine, sunlight. 2. *(Met.)* The light, warmth or influence of the sun. 3. A kind of face of ancient make. 4. *(Mus.)* G, sol, the fifth note of the scale. **Sol mayor**, G major. 5. Sol, a Perovian currency." **Rayo de sol**, sunbeam. **Quemadura del sol**, sunburn. **Reloj del sol**, sundial. **La luz del sol**, sunlight. **El sol sale**, the sun rises. **El sol se pone**, the sun sets. **Al sol puesto**, at nightfall. **A la puesta del sol**, at sunset. **Al salir del sol**, at sunrise. **El sol pica**, the sun scorches. **No dejar ni a sol ni a sombra**, to molest or pursue a person constantly. **Tomar el sol**, to bask in the sun. **Soles**, sparkling, dazzling eyes. **Este niño es un sol**, this is a lovely child.

solada [so-lah'-dah], *f.* Floor, site; seat.

solado [so-lah'-do], *m.* Floor, covered with tiles or flags: pavement.-**Solado, da**, *pp.* of SOLAR.

solador [so-la-dor'], *m.* Tiler, pavier.

soladura [so-lah-doo'-rah], *f.* Act of paving; materials used for paving or flooring.

solamente [so-lah-men-tay], *adv.* Only, solely.

solana [so-lah'-nah], *f.* Sunparlor, sunporch, a place warmed by the sun, open gallery for taking the sun, solarium, sunroom.

solanáceas [so-lah-nah'-thay-as], *f. pl.* The solanaceae, the nightshade family.

solanar [so-lah-nar'], *m. (Prov.)* V. SOLANA for a gallery.

solanazo [so-lah-nah'-tho], *m. aug.* A violent, hot, and troublesome easterly wind.

solano [so-lah'-no], *m.* 1. Easterly winds. 2. *(Bot.)* Nightshade.

solapa [so-lah'-pah], *f.* 1. Lapel (de chaqueta), a double breast on clothes. 2. Color, presence, pretext. 3. *(Vet.)* Cavity of a small wound in animals.

solapadamente [so-lah-pah'-dah-men-tay], *adv.* In a dissembling manner; deceitfully.

solapado, da [so-lah-pah'-do, dah], *a.* Cunning, crafty, artful, evasive (evasivo). *-pp.* of SOLAPAR.

solapadura (Obra de) [so-lah-pah-doo'-rah], *f. (Naut.)* Clincher-work, clinching.

solapamiento [so-lah-pah-me-en'-to], *m. (Vet.)* Cavity of a wound in animals.

solapar [so-lah-par'], *va..* 1. To button one breast-part of clothes over another. 2. To cloak, to hide under a false pretence.

solape, solapo [so-lah'-pay], *m.* Lapel; pretense. *V.* SOLAPA. **A solapo,** in a hidden or furtive manner.

solar [so-lar'], *m.* 1. Ground on which a house is built, ground-plot. 2. Spot on which stands the original mansion of a noble family. 3. *(CAm. Carib.)* Patio (corral). 4. *(And. Carib.)* Tenement house (tugurio). *-a.* Solar, solary, belonging to the sun.

solar [so-lahr'], *va.* 1. To floor a room; to pave a stable or coach-yard. 2. To sole shoes or boots.

solariego, ga [so-lah-re-ay'-go, gah], *a.* 1. Belonging to the ancient mansion of a noble family. 2. Relating to free hold and other estates, which appertain with full and unlimited right of property to the owner. 3. Descending from an ancient noble family.

solas (A) [so'-lahs], *adv.* All alone by myself, yourself, himself, herself, themselves. *V.* SOLO. **Ella estaba a solas,** she was alone. **Los niños estaban a solas,** the children were by themselves.

solaz [so-lath'], *m.* Solace (consuelo), consolation, relaxation, comfort. **A solaz,** pleasantly, agreeably.

solazar [so-lah-thar'], *va.* To solace, to comfort (alegrar), to cheer, to amuse. *-vr.* To be comforted, to be joyful, to relax.

solazo [so-lah'-tho], *m. aug. (Coll.)* A scorching sun.

solazoso, sa [so-lah-tho'-so, sah], *a.* Comfortable, delectable.

soldada [sol-dah'-dah], *f.* Wages, pay given for service.

soldadero, ra [sol-dah-day'-ro, rah], *a.* Stipendiary, receiving wages or hire.

soldadesca [sol-dah-des'-cah], *f.* 1. Soldiery, the profession of a soldier (profesión); military art or science, soldiership (used in a depreciative sense). 2. Sham-fight. **A la soldadesca,** in a soldierly manner, for the use of soldiers.

soldadesco, ca [sol-dah-des'-co, cah], *a.* Soldierly, soldierlike, military.

soldado [sol-dah'-do], *m.* 1. Soldier. **Soldado raso,** a common soldier, a private. **Soldado de infantería,** infantryman. **Soldado de a caballo,** trooper. horse-soldier, cavalryman. 2. **Soldado, da,** *pp.* of SOLDAR.

soldador [sol-dah-dor'], *m.* 1. Solderer. 2. Soldering-iron.

soldadura [sol-dah-doo'-rah], *f.* 1. The act of soldering by means of a metallic cement, welding. 2. Solder (sustancia). 3. Correction or mending of something. **Soldadura autógena,** welding.

soldán [sol-dahn'], *m.* Sultan, Mohammedan title. *V.* SULTÁN.

soldar [sol-dar'], *va.* To solder (estañar), to weld (autógena), to mend, to correct, to join (unir), to cement (cementar); to patch up (disputa). *-vr.* To knit (huesos).

soleado [so-lay-ah'-do], *a.* Sunny.

solear [so-lay-ahr'], *va.* To put in the sun (dejar al sol), to bleach (blanquear).

solecismo [so-lay-thees'-mo], *m.* Solecism, violation of purity of style. *V.* SOLES in Appendix.

solecito [so-lay-thee'-to], *m. (Coll.)* A scorching sun.

soledad [so-lay-dahd'], *f.* 1. Solitude (estado), loneliness (aislamiento), solitariness. 2. Solitude, a lonely place, a desert (lugar). 3. The state of an orphan, orphanage. 4. Grieving, mourning.

soledoso, sa [so-lay'-do-so, sah], *a.* Solitary.

solejar [so-lay-har'], *m.* A place exposed to the sun.

solemne [so-lem'-nay], *a.* 1. Yearly, anniversary, performed once a year at the revolution of the sun. 2. Celebrated, famous. 3. Grand, solemn, high. 4. Festive, joyous, gay, cheerful. **Es un solemne bobo,** *(Coll.)* he is a downright booby.

solemnemente [so-lem'-nay-men-tay], *adv.* Solemnly, in a festive manner.

solemnidad [so-lem-ne-dahd'], *f.* 1. Solemnity (cualidad), solemnness. 2. Solemnity, a religious festival, and the pomp or magnificence of a feast or festival. 3. *pl.* Formalities prescribed by law. **Pobre de solemnidad,** a poor man in real distress.

solemnizador, ra [so-lem-ne-thah-dor', rah], *m. & f.* One who solemnizes; a panegyrist.

solemnizar [so-lem-ne-thar'], *va.* 1. To solemnize, to praise, to applaud. 2. To solemnize, to perform in a festive manner; to keep or cerebrate joyously.

sóleo [so'-lay-o], *m.* Soleus, a muscle of the calf of the leg.

soler [so-lerr'], *vn. irr. & defect.* 1. To accustom or be accustomed; to be used to; to be apt to, to be wont; to keep. 2. *(Cono Sur)* To occur (ocurrir). **Suele pasar por aquí,** he usually comes this way. **Suele ocurrir,** it sometimes happens. **Suele dar buenas propinas,** he usually gives good tips. **Solíamos venir todos los años,** we used to come every year. *-m. (Naut.)* Under flooring of a ship.

solera [so-lay'-rah], *f.* 1. Entablature, the uppermost row of stones of a wall, on which the beams rest; stringpiece, cross-beam, rib. 2. A flat stone, which serves as a foundation to the base of a pillar; a plinth (plinto). 3. Lower millstone (piedra de molino). 4. *(Prov.)* Lees (delvino). 5. *(Mex.)* Flagstone (baldosa). 6. *(Cono Sur)* Kerb (de acera).

solercia [so-lerr'-the-ah], *f.* Industry; abilities, talents; artfulness.

solería [so-lay-ree'-ah], *f.* 1. Floor or pavement of a room. 2. Parcel of skins used for soles. *V.* SOLADO.

solero [so-lay'-ro], *m. (Prov.)* Lower millstone.

solerte [so-lerr'-tay], *a.* Cunning, sagacious.

soleta [so-lay'-tah], *f.* 1. A linen sole put into stockings. 2. *(Mex.)* A biscuit covered with sugar icing. 3. Ladies' fingers; a cake.

soletar, soletear [so-lay-tar', so-lay-tay-ar'] *va.* To vamp a pair of stockings with a linen sole.

soletoro, ra [so-lay-tay'-ro, rah], *m. & f.* Vamper, one who soles and pieces old things with something new.

solevantado, da [so-lay-van-tah'-do, dah], *a. & pp.* of SOLEVANTAR. In quiet, agitated, perturbed.

solevantamiento [so-lay-van-tah-me-en'-to], *m.* The act of rising in rebellion. *V.* SUBLEVACIÓN.

solevantar. [so-lay-van-tar'], *va.* 1. To raise something and put something else under it (objeto). 2. To induce one to leave his habitation, home, or employment. 3. To agitate, to excite commotion.

solevar [so-lay-var'], *va.* To raise, to lift up. *V.* SOLEVANTAR.

solfa [sol'-fah], *f.* 1. The art of uniting the various sounds of music, solfa, musical notations (signos). 2. Accordance, harmony; concord. 3. *(Coll.)* A sound beating or flogging. **Estar en solfa,** to be arranged (or to arrange) with art and judgment. **Poner a uno en solfa,** to make someone look ridiculous

solfatara [sol-ta-tah'-rah], *f. (Geol.)* Solfatara, a volcanic area emitting vapors and sublimates.

solfeador [sol-ta-tah-dor'], *m.* 1. Songster, one who sings according to the rules of melody and measure. 2. Musicmaster. 3. *(Coll.)* One who deals out blows.

solfear [sol-fay-ar'], *m.* 1. To sing according to the rules of melody and measure. 2. *(Coll.)* To cudgel, to flog. 3. *(Cono Sur)* To nick, to swipe (hurtar).

solfeo [sol-fay'-o], *m.* 1. Solfa (música), singing of scales, voice practice, melodious song. 2. *(Coll.)* Beating, flogging, drubbing (paliza).

solfista [sol-fes'-tah], *com.* Musician.

solicitación [so-le-the-tah-the-on'], *f.* Solicitation, importunity, temptation, inducement.

solicitado, da [so-le-the-tah'-do, dah], *a. (Com.)* In good request or demand.

solicitador, ra [so-le-the-tah-dor', rah], *m. & f.* Solicitor, agent; one who solicits for another.

solícitamente [so-lee'-the-tah-men-tay], *adv.* Solicitiously, diligently.

solicitante [so-le-the-tahn'-tay], *pa. V.* SOLICITADOR.

solicitar [so-le-the-tar'], *va.* To solicit, to importune, to entreat; to urge; to court, to ask for (permiso), to attract (atención, interés), to pursue (persona).

solícito, ta [so-lee'-the-to, tah], *a.* Solicitous, anxious, careful, nice.

solicitud [so-le-the-tood'], *f.* Solicitude, anxiety, importunity. **Solicitud de bus,** *(Comput.)* bus request.

sólidamente [so'-le-dah-men-tay], *adv.* Solidly, anally, with true reasons.

solidar [so-le-dar'], *va.* 1. To harden, to render firm and solid. 2. To consolidate, to establish.

solidariamente [so-le-dah'-re-ah-men-tay], *adv.* Jointly, mutually.

solidaridad [so-le-dah-re-dahd'], *f.* Solidarity, community, equal participation.

solidario, ria [so-le-dah'-re-o, ah], *a.* 1. Solidary, equal in participation, one in interests. 2. Individually and collectively responsible. **Hacerse solidario de una opinión,** to echo an opinion.

solidez [so-le-deth'], *f.* 1. Solidity, firmness, strength. 2. Integrity, firmness of mind.

solidificar [so-le-de-fe-cahr'], *va.* To solidify, to harden.

sólido, da [so'-le-do, dah], *a.* 1. Solid, firm, compact, consistent. 2. Built on sound reasons. *-m.* 1. A solid, compact body. 2. *(Med.)* Solid, the part containing the fluids of the animal body.

soliloquiar [so-le-lo-ke-ar'], *vn.* To discourse or reason with oneself; to talk to oneself, to soliloquize.

soliloquio [so-le-lo'-ke-o], *m.* Soliloquy, monologue.

solimán [so-le-mahn'], *m. (Chem.)* Corrosive sublimate.

solio [so'-le-o], *m.* Throne with a canopy.

solípedo, da [so-lee'-pay-do, dah], *a.* Solipede, solidungulous, whole-hoofed.

solitaria [so-le-tah-re-ah], *f.* Tapeworm. *V.* TENIA.

solitariamente [so-le-tah'-re-ah-men-tay], *adv.* Solitarily, lonesomely.

solitario, ria [so-le-tah'-re-o, ah], *a.* 1. Solitary, lonely (vida, persona); lonely, bleak, lonesome, isolated (lugar). 2. Cloistered, retired. *-m.* 1. Solitary, lonely, recluse, a hermit. **Vivir solitario,** to live alone. 2. Solitaire, a card game played by one person alone. 3. Solitaire, a single rich diamond.

sólito, ta [so'-le-to, tah], *a.* Accustomed.

soliviadura [so-le-ve-ah-doo'-rah], *f.* The act of raising a little.

soliviantar [so-le-ve-an-tar'], *va.* To induce to novelties or changes.

soliviar [so-le-ve-ar'], *va.* 1. To raise or lift up in order to take anything from underneath. 2. To rob, to steal. *-vr.* To rise, to get up a little.

solivio [so-lee'-ve-o], *m.* The act of rising or raising a little.

solivión [so-le-ve-on'], *m. aug.* A sudden and violent lifting up.

solla [sol'-lyah], *f.* Plaice.

sollado [sol-lyah'-do], *m. (Naut.)* Orlop.

sollamar [sol-lyah-mar'], *va.* To scorch, to singe, to burn slightly.

sollar [sol-lyar'], *va. (Met.)* To blow, to blow with bellows.

sollastre [sol-lyahs'-tray], *m.* 1. Scullion, kitchen-boy. 2. *(Coll.)* A skillful rogue.

sollastría [sol-lyas-tree'-ah], *f.* Scullery; the business of a scullion.

sollastrón [sol-lyas-trone'], *m. aug.* 1. A very crafty, subtle, sly fellow. 2. A loafer. 3. A designing, low fellow.

sollo [sol'-lyo], *m.* Common pike.

sollozar [sol-lyo-thar'], *vn.* To sob.

sollozo [sol-lyo'-tho], *m.* 1. Sob. 2. *(Cal. and Mex.)* Huckleberry.

solo [so'-lo], *m.* 1. Solo, musical composition for one voice; a tune played by a single instrument. 2. A game at cards. 3.

A play in certain games of cards, a lone hand. 3. *(Cono Sur)* Tedious conversation (lata).

solo, la [so'-lo], *a.* 1. Alone, single, solitary. 2. Alone, only, lonely, without company, bereft of favor and protection. **A solas,** alone, unaided. **Venir solo,** to come alone. **Tendremos que comer pan solo,** we shall have to eat plain bread.

sólo [so'-lo], *adv.* Only. *V.* SOLAMENTE.

solomillo, solomo [so-lo-meel'-lyo, so-lo'-mo], *vn.* Loin, the fleshy and boneless part on the spine; chine.

solsticial [sols-te-the-ahl'], *a.* Solstitial.

solsticio [sols-tee'-the-o], *m.* Solstice, the tropical point.

soltar [sol-tar'], *va.* 1. To untie, to loosen. 2. To set at liberty, to discharge. 3. To burst out into laughter or crying (risa). 4. To explain, to decipher, to solve. 5. To drop (dejar caer), to cast off (amarra), to release (freno), to set free (animales), to let go of (riendas). **Soltar la carga,** to throw down a burden. **Soltar la palabra,** to absolve one from an obligation or promise; to pledge one's word for anything. **Soltó una par de palabrotas,** he came out with a couple of rude words. *-vr.* 1. To get loose. 2. To grow expeditious and handy in the performance of a thing. 3. To forego all decency and modesty. 4. To lose control (perder el control). 5. To become expert (adquirir pericia). **No se vaya a soltar el perro,** don't let the dog get out. **Soltarse de las manos de uno,** to escape from somebody's clutches. **Soltarse del estómago,** to have diarrhoea.

soltera [sol-tay'-rah], *f.* A spinster, an unmarried woman. *V.* SOLTERO, RA.

soltería [sol-tay-ree'-ah], *f.* Celibacy.

soltero [sol-tay'-ro], *m.* Bachelor, an unmarried man.

soltero, ra [sol-tay'-ro, rah], *a.* Single (persona no casada), unmarried. **Madre soltera,** unmarried mother.

solterón [sol-tay-rone'], *m.* An old bachelor.

solterona [sol-tay-ro'-nah], *f.* An old maid.

soltura [sol-too'-rah], *f.* 1. The act of discharging or setting at liberty. 2. Release from confinement. 3. Agility, activity. 4. Laxity, looseness, licentiousness.

solubilidad [so-loo-be-le-dahd'], *f.* Solubility, solubleness.

soluble [so-loo'-blay], *a.* 1. Soluble, that can be loosened or untied. 2. Resoluble, that may be resolved (problema). 3. Solvable.

solución [so-loo-the-on'], *f.* 1. Solution, the act of loosening or untying. 2. Resolution of a doubt, removal of an intellectual difficulty. 3. Solution, the reduction of a solid body into a fluid state. 4. The climax or catastrophe in a drama or epic poem. 5. Lean, satisfaction. **Dar solución a una duda,** to solve or explain a doubt.

solucionar [so-loo-the-o-nahr'], *va.* To solve.

solutivo, va [so-loo-tee'-vo, vah], *a.* Solutive, having the power of loosening, untying, or dissolving.

solvabilidad [sol-vah-be-le-dahd'], *f. (Com.)* Solvency, abilit to pay one's debts.

solvencia [sol-ven'-the-ah], *f.* 1. Solvency, ability to pay debts contracted. 2. Solid reputation (reputación). 3. *(Cono Sur)* Ability (aptitud). **Fuentes de toda solvencia,** completely reliable sources.

solventar [sol-ven-tar'], *va.* To pay debts (cuenta, deuda).

solvente [sol-ven'-tay], *pa. & a.* 1. Solvent, unbinding, dissolvent, having power to cause dissolution. 2. Solvent, able to pay debts contracted.

solver [sol-verr'], *va.* To loosen, to untie; to solve, to find out.

solviente [sol-ve-en'-tay], *va.* Solving, loosening, having power to cause solution.

soma [so'-mah], *f.* 1. The coarse sort of flour. 2. *(Prov.)* Load, burdensomeness. **Bestia de soma,** a beast of burden.

somanta [so-mahn'-tah], *f. (Coll.)* Beating, severe chastisement.

somatén [so-mah-ten'], *m.* 1. Alarm (alarma), uproar, confusion (jaleo). **Tocar a somatén,** sonar la alarma. 2. Mob, an unexpected attack.

somatología [so-mah-to-lo-hee'-ah], *f.* Somatology, the doctrine of organic bodies, especially of the human body; embracing anatomy and physiology.

sombra [som'-brah], *f.* 1. Shade (protección), interception of light. 2. Shadow (proyectora por objeto), shade, the representation of a body by which the light is intercepted. 3. Shade, shadow, spirit, ghost (fantasma), manes. 4. *(Met.)* Shade, shadow, shelter, favor, protection. 5. Resemblance, appearance. 6. Sign, vestige. 7. Shadow, dark part of a picture. 8. Shade, parts of a picture not brightly colored. 9. Umber, a brown color. 8. *(CAm. Cono Sur)* Parasol (quitasol). 9. *(CAm. Cono Sur)* Guide lines (para escribir). **Andar a sombra de tejado**, to abscond. **Hacer sombra**, to protect; to impede; to obscure, to outshine. **No ser ni su sombra**, to be but the shadow of one's former self. **No se fía ni de su sombra**, he doesn't even trust his own shadow. **Tener buena sombra**, to be likeable. **Hacer sombra a uno**, to put someone in the shade. **Gobierno en la sombra**, shadow cabinet. **Sombras chinescas**, shadow play, shadow pantomime. **Dirigente en la sombra**, shadow leader.

sombras *(Coll.)* darkness, obscurity (oscuridad); ignorance (ignorancia).

sombraje [som-brah'-hay], *m.* Hut covered with branches.

sombrajo [som-brah'-ho], *m.* 1. Shadow or figure corresponding to the body by which the light is intercepted. 2. A shed or hut in vineyards.

sombrar [som-brar'], *va.* To frighten to astonish. *V.* ASOMBRAR.

sombreado [som-bray-ah'-do], *m.* Shading, the act of marking with different gradations of colors. —**Sombreado, da**, *pp.* of SOMBREAR.

sombrear [som-bray-ar'], *va.* To shade, to mark with different gradations of colors; to paint in obscure colors.

sombrerazo [som-bray-rah'-tho], *m.* 1. *(Aug.)* A large hat. 2. A flap or blow with a hat.

sombrerera [som-bray-ray'-rah], *f.* 1. Hat-box, hat-case. 2. Hatter's wife. milliner. 3. *(Cono Sur)* Hatstand.

sombrerería [som-bray-ray-ree'-ah], *f.* 1. Manufactory of hats. 2. Shop where hats are sold.

sombrerero [som-bray-ray'-ro], *m.* Hatter, hat-maker.

sobrerete [som-bray-ray'-tay], *m. dim.* 1. A small hat. 2. Bonnet, cap (cubo, hongo). 3. Spark-arrester, spark-catcher (locomotora); cowl (chimenea)

sombrerillo, ito [som-bray-reel'-lyo, ee'-to], *m.* 1. *(Dim.)* A small or little hat. **Sombrerillo de señora**, lady's hat. 2. *(Bot.)* Navelwort.

sombrero [som-bray'-ro], *m.* Hat. **Sombrero apuntado** or **de tres picos**, a cocked hat. **Sombrero jarano**, broad brimmed Mexican hat. **Sombrero de copa**, top hat. **Sombrero de paja**, straw hat. **Sombrero safari**, safari hat. **Sombrero tejano**, stetson. **Sombrero apuntado**, cocked hat. **Sombrero hongo**, bowler hat. **Sombrero de jipijapa**, Panama hat.

sombría [som-bree'-ah], *f.* Shady place.

sombrilla [som-breel'-lyah], *f.* 1. Parasol. 2. Slight shade.

sombrita [som-bree'-tah], *f. dim.* A slight shade.

sombrío, bría [som-bree'-o, ah], *a.* 1. Shady, gloomy (persona), sombre (lugar). 2. Hazy, murky, thick (del tiempo). 3. Taciturn.

sombrío [som-bree'-o], *m.* 1. Part of a piece of painting, which is to be shaded or painted in darker colors than the rest. 2. A dull, heavy color. 3. A shady place.

sombroso, sa [som-bro'-so, sah], *a.* Shady.

someramente [so-may-rah-men-tay], *adv.* Superficially.

somero, ra [so-may'-ro, rah], *a.* Superficial, shallow; making but a slight impression on the mind.

someter [so-may-terr'], *va.* To subject (persona), to submit, to subdue, to reduce to submission. —*vr.* To humble oneself; to submit, to acquiesce, to comply. **Someterse a una operación**, to undergo an operation.

sometimiento [so-may-te-me-en'-to], *m.* Submission (estado), subjection, subduing.

somnambulismo [som-nam-boo-lees'-mo], *m.* Somnanbulism, walking in sleep. **Somnambulismo artificial**, hypnotism.

somnámbulo, la [som-nahm'-boo-lo, lah], *m. & f. & a.* 1. Somnambule, somnambulist. 2. Medium, a person habitually submitted to the influence of hypnotism.

somnífero, ra [som-nee'-fay-ro, rah], *a.* Somniferous, soporiferous.

somnílocuo, cua [som-nee'-lo-cwo, cwah], *a.* Somniloquous, given to talking in sleep.

somnolencia [som-no-len'-the-ah], *f.* Sleepiness, drowsiness, somnolency.

somonte [so-mon'-tay], *a.* Coarse, rough, shaggy.

somorgujador [so-mor-goo-hah-dor'], *m.* Diver, one that goes under water to search for anything.

somorgujar [so-mor-goo-har'], *va & vr.* o dip, to plunge, to duck.

somorgujo, somorgujón, somormujo [so-mor-moo'-ho], *m.* *(Orn.)* Dun-diver, diver, merganser, grebe. **A lo somurjo, a lo lomormujo**, under water.

sompesar [som-pay-sar'], *va.* To take up a thing in order to guess its weight; to heft.

son [sohn], *m.* 1. Sound, noise, report, tale, reason, mode. **En son**, in such a manner, apparently. **Sin ton ni son**, without rhyme or reason. **A son de qué**, for what reason. **A son**, at or to the sound of. **Bailar a cualquier son**, to be easily moved by affection or passion. **Al son de la marcha nupcial**, to the sounds of the wedding march. **Bailar uno al son que le tocan**, to adapt oneself to circumstances. **Bailar sin son**, to be exceedingly eager. **¿A qué son?** with what motive? 2. *(Carib.)* Cuban folk song and dance. 3. Style, manner.

sonable [so-nah'-blay], *a.* 1. Sonorous, loud, sounding. 2. Celebrated, famous.

sosada [so-sah'-dah], *f. V.* SONATA.

sonadera [so-nah-day'-rah], *f.* The act of blowing the nose.

sonado, da [so-nah'-do, dah], *a.* 1. Celebrated, famous (famoso). 2. Generally reported. 3. **Estar sonado**, to be crazy. -*pp.* of SONAR.

sonador, ra [se-nah-dor'-rah], *m. & f.* 1. One who makes a noise. 2. Handkerchief.

sonaja [so-nah'-hah], *f.* Timbrel, a musical instrument.

sonajero [so-nah-hay'-ro], *m.* 1. A small timbrel. 2. A rattle.

sonajica, illa, ita, uela [so-nah-hee'-cah], *f. dim.* Small timbrel.

sonambulismo [so-nahm-boo-lees'-mo], *m. V.* SONAMBULISM. *(Acad.)*

sonámbulo, la [so-nahm'-boo-lo', lah], *m. & f. & a.* Somnambule, somnambulist.

sonante [so-nahn'-tay], *a.* Sounding, sonorous. **Dinero contante y sonante**, ready cash.

sonar [so-nar'], *va.* 1. To sound, to play upon a musical instrument. 2. To like or dislike. **Bien me sonó lo que dijo**, I was much pleased with what he said. 3. To sound, to pronounce. 4. To allude, to refer to a thing without any direct mention. -*vn.* 1. To sound or make a noise. 2. To be pronouced. 3. To be talked of (ser mencionado). 4. To sound familiar (ser conocido). 5. *(Cono Sur)* To come a cropper (fracasar). **Han sonado las 10**, it has struck 10. **Esas palabras suenan extrañas**, those words sound strange. **No me suena el nombre**, the name doesn't ring a bell with me. -*v. imp.* To raise or propagate rumours, to be reported, to be whispered. -*vr.* To blow one's nose.

sonata [so-nah'-tah], *f.* Sonata, a musical composition in three or four movements.

sonda [son'-dah], *f.* 1. *(Naut.)* Sounding, heaving the lead. 2. Sound, load, a cord with a heavy weight attached for sounding. 3. Borer, any instrument for examining the strata of the earth. 4. *(Med.)* Sound; probe. 5. In artillery, searcher, proof stick.

sondable [son-dah'-blay], *a.* That may be sounded.

sondalesa [son-dah-lay'-sah], *f. (Naut.)* Lead-line, the log sounding-line. **Sondalesa de mano**, *(Naut.)* hand-lead. **Sondalesa de la bomba**, *(Naut.)* gauge-rod of the pump.

sondar, sondear [son-dar', son-day-ar'], *va.* 1. *(Naut.)* To sound, to heave the lead. **Sondar la bomba**, *(Naut.)* to sound the pump. 2. To try, to sift, to sound another's intentions; to explore, to fathom.

sondeo [son-day'-o], *m.* The act and effect of sounding; exploring, fathoming.

sonecillo [so-nay-theel'-lyo], *m dim.* 1. A sound scarcely perceptible. 2. A short little tune.

sonetico [so-nay-tee'-co], *m.* 1. *(Dim.)* V. SONTÍN. 2. A merry little song.

sonetín [so-nay-teen'], *m.* An insignificant sonnet.

sonetista [so-nay-tees'-tah], *m.* One who writes sonnets.

soneto [so-nay'-to], *m.* Sonnet.

songuita [son-gee'-tah], *f. (Cuba)* Jest, irony.

sónico, ca [soh'-ne-co, cah], *a.* Sonic. **Barrera sónica**, sonic barrier.

sonido [so-nee'-do], *m.* 1. Sound, noise. 2. Fame, report, rumor. 3. Sound, pronunciation. 4. Literal signification. **Sonido agudo**, acute sound.

sonochada [so-no-chah'-dah], *f.* 1. The beginning of night. 2. Watching in the early hours of night.

sonochar [so-no-char'], *vn.* To watch the first hours of the night.

sonómetro [so-no'-may-tro], *m.* Sonometer, an instrument for testing the vibration of strings.

sonora [so-no'-rah], *f.* Cithern, a musical instrument.

sonoramente [so-no'-rah-men-tay], *adv.* Sonorously; harmoniously.

sonoridad [so-no-re-dahd'], *f.* Sonorousness.

sonoro, ra, sonoroso, sa [so-no'-ro, rah], *a.* 1. Sonorous, soniferous. 2. Pleasing, agreeable, harmonious. **Efectos sonoros**, sound effects.

sonreír, sonreírse [son-ray-eer', eer-say], *vn. & vr.* To smile. (*Yo sonrío, yo sonría; él sonrió, sonriera; from Sonreír. V. REIR.*)

sonrisa [son-ree'-sah], *f.* **Sonriso**, *m.* Smile.

sonrodadura [son-ro-dah-doo'-rah], *f.* The act of sticking in the mud.

sonrodarse [son-ro-dar'-say], *vn.* To stick in the mud.

sonrojar, sonrojear [son-ro-har'], *va.* To make one blush with shame, to flush.

sonrojo [son-ro'-ho], *m.* 1. Blush (rubor). 2. Offensive word which causes a blush (dicho).

sonrosado, da [son-ro-sah'-do, dah], *a.* Pink, blushing pink.

sonrosar, sonrosear [son-ro-sar'], *va.* To dye a rose color. **Sonrosearse**-*vr.* To blush.

sonroseo [son-ro-say'-o], *m.* Blush.

sonsaca [son-sah'-cah], *f.* Wheedling; petty theft.

sonsacador, ra [son-sah-cah-dor', rah], *m. & f.* 1. Wheedler, prier, shooter, coaxer. 2. A petty thief.

sonsacamiento [son-sah-cah-me-en'-to], *m.* Wheedling, extortion, petty theft.

sonsacar [son-sah-car'], *va.* 1. To steal privately out of a bag (obtener). 2. To obtain by gunning and craft. *(Met.)* To entice, to allure. 3. To pump a secret out of a person (engatusar).

sonsaque [son-sah'-kay], *m.* Wheedling; petty theft.

sonsonete [son-so-nay'-tay], *m.* 1. Noise arising from repeated gentle beats imitating some musical sound. 2. Singsong voice. 3. Tap (golpecitos). 4. Monotonous delivery (voz). 5. Jingle (copla).

soñador, ra [so-nyah-dor', rah], *m. & f.* Dreamer; one who relates dreams and idle stories.

soñante [so-nyahn'-tay], *pa.* Dreaming.

soñar [so-nyar'], *va.* 1. To dream, to have dreams. 2. To dream, to think idly, to entertain fantastical ideas. **Ni soñarlo**, not even dreamed of. **Soñar con algo**, to dream of something. **Soñar en voz alta**, to talk in one's sleep. **Soñé contigo ayer noche**, I dreamt about you last night. (*Yo sueño, yo sueñe, from Soñar. V. ACORDAR.*)

soñarrera [so-nyar-ray'-rah], *f.* 1. *(Prov.)* Dreaming, heavy sleep. 2. Drowsiness, propensity to sleep long.

soñera [so-nyay'-rah], *f.* Sleepiness, wish to sleep.

soñlencia [so-nyo-len'-the-ah], *f.* Sleepiness, drowsiness, somnolence.

soñolientamente [so-nyo-le-ayn'-tay], *adv.* Sleepily, heavily.

soñoliento, ta [so-nyo-le-en'-to, tah], *a.* 1. Heavy, sleepy, drowsy. 2. Sleepy, soporiferous, causing sleep. 3. Sleepy, dull, lazy.

sopa [so'-pah], *f.* 1. Soup (caldo, pan mojado). 2. Soup, broth. 3. Bread cut or broken to be thrown into soup; generally in plural. **Sopa de ajo, de gato**, meager soup, made of bread, oil, salt, garlic and water. **Sopa de leche**, milk porridge or milk soup. **Sopa de guisantes**, pea-soup. **Sopa borracha**, soup made with wine, biscuit, sugar and cinnamon. **Sopa de fideos**, noodle soup. **Los encontramos hasta en la sopa**, they're everywhere. **Estoy hecho una sopa**, I'm soaking wet. **Estar como una sopa**, to be tight. **Dar sopas con honda a uno**, to be streets ahead of one.

sopaipa [so-pah'-ee-pah], *f.* A sort of fritter steeped in honey.

sopalancar [so-pah-lan-car'], *va.* To put a lever under something to lift it.

sopanda [so-pahn'-dah], *f.* 1. Brace, any of the leather thongs which support the body of a coach. 2. Joist, crossbeam, a stout timber placed horizontally.

sopapeadura [so-pah-pay-ah-doo'-rah], *f.* 1. Buffet or slap with the hand under the chin; a chuck. 2. *(Coll.)* A number of slaps or chucks.

sopapear [so-pah-pay-ar'], *va.* 1. *(Coll.)* To chuck under the chin, to slap. 2. *(Coll. Met.)* To vilify, to abuse.

sopapo [so-pah'-po], *m.* 1. Box, blow, or slap with the hand. 2. Sucker, a movable valve in hydraulic vessels or pumps.

sopar [so-par'], *va.* To sop bread. V. ENSOPAR.

sopear [so-pay-ar'], *va.* 1. To sop, to steep breed. V. ENSOPAR. 2. To tread, to trample, to domineer. 3. To maltreat.

sopeña [so-pay'-nyah], *f.* Cavity formed by a rock at its foot.

sopera [so-pay'-rah], *f.* Tureen.

sopero [so-pay'ro], *m.* 1. Soup-plate (plato sopero); lover of soups (persona). 2. *(And.)* Nosey (curioso).

sopesar [so-pay-sar'], *va.* 1. To try the weight of, try to lift (levantar) 2. To weigh, to consider (palabras). 3. To weigh up (situación).

sopetear [so-pay-tay-ar'], *va.* 1. To sop, to steep bread in sauce, broth, or other liquors. 2. To abuse with foul language.

sopeteo [s-pay-tay'-o], *m.* The act of dipping breed in broth, etc.

sopetón [so-pay-tone'], *m.* 1. Plentiful soup. 2. A heavy box or slap with the hand (golpe). **De sopetón**, suddenly.

sopica, illa, ita [so-pee'-cah], *f. dim.* Sippet, a light soup.

sopilote [so-pe-lo'-tay], *m. (Mex.)* A vulture.

sopista [so-pees'-tah], *m.* Person living upon charity.

¡sopla! [so'-plah], *int.* An expression of admiration.

sopladero [so-plah-day'-ro], *m.* Draught or air-hole to subterraneous passages.

soplado, da [so-plah'-do, dah], *a. & pp.* of SOPLAR. Blown; overnice and spruce.

soplador, ra [so-plah-dor', rah], *m. & f.* 1. Blower, that which blows. 2. That which excites or inflames. 3. *(Fig.)* Troublemaker. 4. *(And. CAm.)* Prompter.

soplamocos [so-plah-mo'-cos], *m. (Coll.)* Box or slap on the nose (puñetazo).

soplar [so-plar'], *vn. & va.* 1. To blow, to emit wind at the mouth. 2. To blow with bellows. 3. To blow, to make a current of air. 4. To be blown away by the wind (vela). 5. To blow, to drive by the wind, to separate with wind. 6. To rob or steal in an artful manner (robar). 7. To suggest notions or ideas, to inspire. 8. In the game of draughts to huff a man. 9. To tipple, to drink much. 10. To split on (delatar). 11. To charge (cobrar). **Soplar a uno**, to whisper to somebody. -*vr.* To eat or drink a great deal. **Soplarse una docena de pasteles**, to wolf a dozen cakes.

soplete [so-play'-tay], *m.* In glasshouses, a blow pipe; a soldering pipe.

soplico [so-plee'-co], *m. dim.* A slight puff or blast.

soplido [so-plee'-do], *m.* V. SOPLO.

soplillo [so-pleel'-lyo], *m.* 1. Crape, a thin stuff. 2. Anything extremely thin and light. 3. (*Dim.*) V. SOPLICO.

soplo [so'-plo], *m.* 1. Blow, puff, gust (viento), blowing, act of blowing (con la boca). 2. Instant, moment, short space of time. 3. Blast. 4. Tip, tip off, advice given secretly, and with caution; generally malicious advice or information (chismoso). **La semana pasó como un soplo**, the week sped by.

soplón, na [so-plone', nah], *a. & n.* 1. Informer. 2. (*Mex.*) Cop. 3. (*CAm.*) Prompter (teatro).

soploncillo, illa [so-plon-theel'-lyo, lyah], *m. & f. & a. dim.* Little tattler.

sopón [so-pone'], *m.* Person living upon charity soup. Aug. of SOPA.

soponcio [so-pon'-the-o], *m.* Grief or fit arising from disappointment.

sopor [so-por'], *m.* Heaviness, drowsiness, sleepiness.

soporífero, ra [so-po-ree'-fay-ro, rah], *a.* Soporific, soporiferous. V. SOPORÍFICO.

soporífico, ca [so-po-ree'-fe-co, cah], *a.* Opiate, narcotical, soporific, somniferous.

soporoso, sa [so-po-ro'-so, sah], *a.* Soporiferous.

soportable [so-por-tah'-blay], *a.* Tolerable, supportable.

soportador, ra [so-por-tah-dor', rah], *m. & f.* Supporter.

soportal [so-por-tahl'], *m.* Portico.

soportar [so-por-tar'], *va.* To suffer, to tolerate, to support, to abide.

soprano [so-prah'-no], *m.* V. TIPLE.

so protesta [so-pro-tes'-tah], *adv.* (*Com.*) Under protest.

sopuntar [so-poon-tar'], **va.** To place marks under a superfluous or erroneous word.

sor [sore], *f.* Sister. V. HERMANA. **Sor María**, sister Mary (monjas).

sora [so'-rah], *f.* Peruvian drink made of a decoction of maize.

sorba [sor'-bah], *f.* Sorb-apple. V. SERBA.

sorbedor [sor-bay-dor'], *m.* Sipper, one who sips.

sorber [sor-berr'], *va.* 1. To sip (con los labios), to suck (mar); to sup. 2. To imbibe, to soak as a sponge, to absorb. **Sorber por una paja**, to drink through a straw. **Sorber por las narices**, to sniff.

sorbete [sor-bay'-tay], *m.* 1. Sherbet, a beverage of fruitjuice, sugar, etc., chilled; water ice. 2. (*Carib. Cono Sur*) Drinking straw (pajita). 3. (*Mex.*) Top hat (sombrero de copa). 4. (*CAm.*) Ice-cream (helado).

sorbetón [sor-bay-tone'], *m. aug.* A large draught of liquor.

sorbible [sor-bee'-blay], *a.* Which may be sipped.

sorbición [sor-be-the-on'], *f.* (*Men.*) Absorption.

sorbillo, ito [sor-beel'-lyo], *m. dim.* Sup, a small draught.

sorbo [sor'-bo], *m.* 1. Imbibition, drinking or sipping; absorption. 2. Sup, draught. 3. Anything comparatively small. **Beber a sorbos**, to sip.

sorce [sor'-thay], *m.* Field-mouse.

sorda [sor'-dah], *f.* 1. Woodcock. V. CHOCHA. 2. (*Naut.*) Stream-cable employed in launching a ship.

sordamente [sor-dah-men-tay], *adv.* Secretly, silently.

sordastro, tra [sor-dahs'-tro, trah], *a.* Deaf.

sordera, sordez [sor-day'-rah, sor-deth'], *f.* Deafness.

sódidamente [sor-de-dah-men-tay], *adv.* Sordidly, dirtily.

sordidez [sor-de-deth'], *f.* 1. Sordidness, nastiness. 2. Covetousness, avarice.

sórdido, da [sor'-de-do, dah], *a.* 1. Sordid, dirty (sucio), filthy. 2. Licentious, impure, indecent, scandalous.

sordina [sor-dee'-nah], *f.* 1. Kit, a small fiddle. 2. Mute, a piece put on the bridge of a fiddle, to weaken the sound. 3. Muffler, damper,, a mute for a trumpet.

sordo, da [sor'-do, dah], *a.* 1. Deaf, unable to hear. 2. Silent, still, quiet (máquina). 3. Deafening. **Quedarse sordo**, to go deaf. **Permanecer sordo a**, to remain deaf to. **Sordo como una tapia**, deaf as a stone.

sordomudo, da [sor-do-moo'-do], *a. m & f.* Deaf and dumb.

sorgo [sor'-go], *m.* V. ZAHINA.

soriasis [so-re-ah'-sis], *f.* Psoriasis, a squamous disease of the skin, of remarkable chronicity.

sórico [so'-re-co], *a.* Belonging to psoriasis.

sorites [so-ree'-tes], *m.* (*Log.*) Sorites, proposition or argument accumulated on another.

sorna [sor'-nah], *f.* 1. Sluggishness, laziness, slowness (lentitud). 2. A feigned sloth in doing or saying anything.

sornavirón [sor-nah-ve-rone'], *m.* (*Coll.*) Sudden stroke with the back of the open hand.

soro [so'-ro], *m.* Year-old hawk.

soroche [so-ro'-chay], *m.* (*Peru and Ec.*) 1. Disease caused by rarefaction of the air at great altitudes in men and beasts. 2. A friable, shining silver ore.

soroque [so-ro'-kay], *f.* (*Min.*) Matrix of ores.

sóror, *f.* Sister. V. SOR.

sorprendente [sor-pren-den'-tay], *a.* 1. Surprising. 2. Rare, extraordinary, Strange. *-pa.* of SORPRENDER.

sorprender [sor-pren-derr'], *va.* 1. To surprise, to fall upon unexpectedly, to take by surprise; to come upon; to overtake. 2. To execute something silently and with caution. 3. To surprise, to astonish by something wonderful or sudden. - *vr.* To be surprised, to be amazed. **No me sorprendería de que fuera así**, I wouldn't be surprised if it were like that.

sorpresa [sor-pray'-sah], *f.* 1. Surprise (emoción); taking by surprise; deceit, imposition. 2. Surprise, sudden confusion or perplexity. 3. Amazement, astonishment, consternation. **Tomar por sorpresa**, to surprise, to take unawares. **Con gran sorpresa**, much to my surprise.

sorra [sor'-rah], *f.* 1. (*Naut.*) Ballast of stones or coarse gravel. 2. Side of a tunny-fish.

sorregar [sor-ray-gar'], *va.* To water in another course: applied to rivulets which casually change their channels.

sorrero, ra [sor-ray'-ro, rah], *a.* (*Prov.*) V. ZORRERO.

sorriego [sor-re-ay'-go], *m.* Water which passes occasionally from one channel to another.

sorrostrada [sor-ros-trah'-dah], *f.* Great face or beak.

sorteador [sor-tay-ah-dor'], *m.* One who casts lots.

sorteamiento [sor-tay-ah-me-en'-to], *m.* V. SORTEO.

sortear [sor-tay-ar'], *va.* 1. To draw or cast lots. 2. To fight bulls with skill and dexterity. 3. To cleverly elude or shun a conflict, risk, or difficulty. 4. To dodge (obstáculo). **El torero sorteó al toro**, the bullfighter eluded the bull. **Sorteamos el tráfico**, we dodged the traffic.

sorteo [sor-tay'-o], *m.* Act of casting or drawing lots.

sortero [sor-ta'-ro], *m.* Fortune-teller. V. AGORERO.

sortiaria [sor-te-ah'-re-ah], *f.* Superstitious divination by letters, schedules, or playing-cards.

sortija [sor-tee'-hah], *f.* 1. Ring (anillo), finger-ring. 2. Ring, a circle of metal, used for a variety of purposes: hoop. 3. A curl of hair, naturally or artifically made.

sortijita, sortijuela [sor-te-hee'-lah], *f. dim.* Little ring, ringlet.

sortijón [sor-te-hone'], *m. aug.* A large ring.

sortilegio [sor-te-lay'-he-o], *m.* Sortilege, sorcery (brujería), magical prediction (vaticinio).

sortílego, ga [sor-tee'-lay-go, gah], *m. & f. & a.* Sorcerer, conjurer, fortune-teller.

sos (*Arg.*) Sois.

sosa [so'-sah], *f.* 1. (*Bot.*) A name given to various marine plants which, on being burned, afford soda or miller or mineral alkali; glasswort, kelp. 2. Soda-ash, barilla; sal soda. 3. Soda, sodium oxide, a strong alkali.

sosacar [so-sah-cahr'], *va.* V. SONSACAR.

sosamente [so-sah-men'-tay], *adv.* Insipidly, tastelessly.

sosaño [so-sah'-nyo], *m.* Derision, mockery.

sosegadamente [so-say-gah-dah-men-tay], *adv.* Quietly, calmly.

sosegado, da [so-say-gah'-do, dah], *a.* Quiet (tranquilo), peaceful, pacific, calm (persona), -*pp.* of SOSEGAR.

sosegador, ra [so-say-gah-dor', rah], *m. & f.* Pacifier, appeaser.

sosegar [so-say-gar'], *va.* 1. To appease, to calm (calmar), to pacify, to silence, to quiet. 2. To lull (arrullar), to put to sleep. -*vn.* 1. To rest, to repose. 2. To be calm or composed. **Soségese Vd.**, compose yourself.

sosería [so-say-ree'-ah], *f.* Insipidity (insipidez), tastelessness; insipid expression.

sosez [so-seth'], *f. (Prov.)* Insipidness, silliness. **Decir soseces**, to use silly jokes.

sosiego [so-se-ay'-go], *m.* Tranquillity, calmness.

sosio [so'-se-o], *m. (Chem.) V.* SODIO.

soslayar [sos-lah-yar'], *va.* To do or place a thing obliquely (ladear).

soslayo [sos-lah'-yo], *m.* Slant, obliquity. **Al soslayo** or **de soslayo**, askew, sidewise.

soso, sa [soh'-so, sah], *a.* 1. Insipid, unsalted, tasteless (ìnsípido). 2. Cold, coy, silly, senseless.

sospecha [sos-pay'-chah], *f.* Suspicion, mistrust, jealousy.

sospechar [sos-pay-char'], *va.* To suspect; to mistrust; to conjecture.

sospechilla [sos-pay-cheel'-lyah], *f. dim.* Slight suspicion.

sospechosamente [sos-pay-cho'-sah-men-tay], *adv.* Suspiciously, doubtfully, jealously.

sospechoso, sa [sos-pay-cho'-so, sah], *a.* Suspicious, liable to suspicion; inclined to suspect: suspected, mistrustful. **Todos son sospechosos**, everybody is under suspicion. **Tiene amistades sospechosas**, some of his acquaintances are suspect.

sospesar [sos-pay-sar'], *va.* To suspend, to raise above the ground.

sosquín [sos-keen'], *m.* Slap or blow treacherously given.

sostén [sos-ten'], *m.* 1. Support, the act of sustaining or supporting. 2. *(Naut.)* Firmness or steadiness of a ship in pursuing her course. 3. Brassière, bra (prenda). 4. Sustenance (alimento). **El principal sostén del gobierno**, the mainstay of the government.

sostenedor, ra [sos-tay-nay-dor', rah], *m. & f.* Supporter.

sostener [sos-tay-nerr'], *va.* 1. To sustain, to support, to maintain, to hold out, to countenance. 2. To sustain, to bear, to endure, to suffer, to tolerate. 3. To sustain, to maintain, to supply with the necessaries of life (con alimentos). 4. To maintain (acusación); to stand by (opinión); to stand by (promesa); to keep up (presión). **Los dos sosteníamos la cuerda**, we were both holding the rope. **Su partido le sostiene en el poder**, his party keeps him in power. -*vr.* 1. To support or maintain oneself. 2. *(Naut.)* To bear up. 3. To continue (continuar). **Apenas podía sostenerse de puro cansancio**, he was so utterly tired he could hardly stand. **El mercado se sostiene firme**, the market remains firm. *(Yo sostengo, sostenga, sostuve, sostendré,* from *Sostener. V.* TENER.)

sostenido, da [sos-tay-nee'-do, dah], *a. & pp.* of SOSTENER. Supported, supportful, sustained. -*m. (Music.)* Sharp, a note raised a semitone; also the character which denotes it.

sostenimiento [sos-tay-ne-me-en'-to], *m.* Sustenance, the act of sustaining; support.

sostituir [sos-te-too-eer'], *va.* To substitute. *V.* SUBSTITUIR.

sostituto [sos-te-too'-to], *m.* Substitute. *V.* SUBSTITUTO.

sota [so'-tah], *f.* 1. Knave, at cards 2. Deputy, substitute: used in composition to express the last meaning. 3. Helper.

sotabanco [so-tah-bahn'-co], *m. (Arch.)* Pediment of an arch over a cornice.

sotabraga [so-tah-brah'-gah], *f. (Mil.)* Axle-tree band, yoke hoop.

sotacaballerizo [so-tah-cah-bal-lyay-ree'-tho], *m.* Deputy equerry.

sotacochero [so-tah-co-chay'-ro], *m.* Postilion.

sotacola [so-tah-co'-lah], *f.* Crupper. *V.* ATAHARRE.

sotacómitre [so-tah-co'-me-tray], *m. (Naut.)* Boatswain's mate.

sotacoro [so-tah-co'-ro], *m.* Place under the upper choir.

sotalcaide [so-tal-cah'-e-day], *m.* Subwarden.

sotamaestro [so-tah-mah-es'-tro], *m.* Usher at a school.

sotaministro [so-tah-me-nees'-tro], *m. V.* SOTOMINISTRO.

sotamontero [so-tah-me-mon-tay'-ro], *m.* Under-huntsman, deputy forester.

sotana [so-tah'-nah], *f.* 1. Cassock, of a priest or scholar. 2. *(Coll.)* Flogging, drubbing.

sotanado, da [so-tah-nah'-do, dah], *a.* Vaulted, arched, groined.

sotanear [so-tah-nay-ar'], *va. (Coll.)* To boat, to chastise or reprehend severely.

sotaní [so-tah-nee'], *m.* Short round under petticoat without plaits.

sotanilla [so-tah-neel'-lyah], *f.* 1. *(Dim.)* A small cassock. 2. The dress of collegians.

sótano [so'-tah-no], *m.* Cellar under ground (bodega).

sotaventado, da [so-tah-ven-tah'-do, dah], *a. (Naut.)* Driven to leeward, lee. -*pp.* of SOTAVENTAR.

sotaventar [so-tah-ven-tahr'], *va. (Naut.)* To fall to leeward, to lose the weather-gauge.

sotavento [so-tah-ven'-to], *m.* Leeward, lee. **Tener buen sotavento**, *(Naut.)* to have sea-room. **Costa de sotavento**, *(Naut.)* lee-shore. **A sotavento**, under the lee.

sotayuda [so-tah-yoo'-dah], *m.* Under-assistant to officers at court.

sotechado [so-tay-chah'-do], *m.* A roofed or covered place.

soteño, ña [so-tay'-nyo, nyah], *a.* Produced in groves or forests.

soterráneo, nea [so-ter-rah'-nay-o, ah], *a.* Subterraneous.

soterrar [so-ter-rar'], *va.* 1. To bury, to put under ground. 2. To hide, to conceal, to overwhelm. *(Yo sotierro, yo sotierre,* from *Soterrar. V.* ACRECENTAR.)

sotillo [so-teel'-lyo], *f. dim.* Little grove.

soto [so'-to], *m.* Grove (arboleda), thicket (matorral), forest.

sotrozo [so-tro'-tho], *m.* Linch-pin, axlepin. *(Mech.),* key.

soviet [so-ve-et'], *m.* Soviet.

soviético, ca [so-ve-ay'-te-co, cah], *a.* Soviet.

soy *V.* ser, I am.

soya [so'-yah], *f.* Soya bean.

sprinter [es-prin'-teyr], *m & f.* Sprinter.

sputnik [es-poot'-nik], *m.* Sputnik, Russian satellite.

standard [es-tand'-ard], *m.* Standard. **Standard de vida**, standard of living.

status [es-tah-toos], *m.* Status.

stress [es-trays'], *m.* Stress.

stressante [es-tray-sahn'-tay], *a.* Stressful.

su [soo], *pron. poss.* His, her, its, their, one's. **Se alaba a un soldado por su valor, una mujer por su hermosura, a una casa por su situación y a los libros por su mérito**, a soldier is praised by *his* courage, a woman by *her* beauty, a house by *its* situation and books by *their* merit. **Fui en su busca**, I went in search of him, of her, or of them.

suarda [soo-ar'-dah], *f.* 1. Grease which clings to the clothes. 2. The greasy matter which sweat brings on the skin of animals.

suasivo, va [soo-ah-see'-vo, vah], *a. V.* PERSUASIVO.

suasorio, ria [soo-ah-so'-re-o, ah], *a.* Suasory, suasive.

suave [soo-ah'-vay], *a.* 1. Smooth (superficie), soft (aire), delicate, mellow. 2. Easy, tranquil, quiet. 3. Gentle (movimiento, reprimenda, curva, color), tractable, docile (persona), mild, meek. 4. *(Cono Sur, Mex.)* Vast, huge (enorme). 5. *(Mex.)* Good-looking (atractivo). **Tabaco suave**, mild tobacco.

suavecico, illo, ito [soo-ah-vay-thee'-co], *a. dim.* of SUAVE.

suavemente [soo-ah-vay-men-tay], *adv.* Gently, sweetly, softly, mildly, kindly.

suavidad [soo-ah-ve-dahd'], *f.* 1. Softness, delicacy, sweetness. 2. Suavity, meekness; tranquillity, gentleness, lenity, forbearance.

suavizador [soo-ah-ve-thah-dor'], *m.* Softner.

suavizar [soo-ah-ve-thar'], *va.* 1. To soften. 2. To mollify (persona), to mitigate. 3. To render metals pliable or ductile.

sub [soob], A Latin preposition signifying *under, below.*—It is used only in composition, and then it means under, less, or in a subordinate degree; also a deputy; as, **Sub-lunar,** under the moon. **Sub-inspector,** the deputy inspector.

subacetato [soob-ah-thay-tah'-to], *m. (Chem.)* Subacetate.

subácido, da [soob-ah'-the-do, dah], Subacid.

subalcaide [soob-al-cah'-e-day], *m.* Deputy or sub-governor or jailer.

subalternar [soob-al-ter-nar'], *va.* To subject, to subdue.

subalterno, na [soob-al-terr'-no, nah], *a.* Subaltern, inferior, subject. -*m.* Subaltern, a subaltern officer.

subarrendador, ra [soob-ar-ren-dah-dor', rah], *m. & f.* Undertenant, sub-renter.

subarrendamiento [soob-ar-ren-dah-me-en'-to], *m.* Farming or renting under another renter.

subarrendar [soob-ar-ren-dar'], *va.* To sublet, to sublease. *(Yo subarriendo, yo subarriende,* from *Subarrendar. V.* ACRECENTAR.)

subarrendatario, ria [soob-ar-ren-dah-tah'-re-o, ah], *m. & f.* One who takes a sub-lease: a sub-renter.

subasta, subastación [soob-bahs'-tah], *f* Auction, juridical sale of goods by public auction.

subastar [soob-bas-tar'], *m.* To sell by auction.

subcampeón, ona [soob-cam-pay-on'], *m & f.* Runner-up.

subcarbonato [soob-car-bo-nah'-to], *m. (Chem.)* Subcarbonate, a salt in which the base is in excess of the carbonic acid.

subcolector [soob-co-lec-tor'], *m.* Subcollector.

subcomendador [soob-co-men-dah-dor'], *m.* Deputy-commander of a military order.

subconsciencia [soob-cons-the-en'-the-ah], *f.* Subconsciousness.

subconsciente [soob-cons-the-en'-tay], *a.* Subconscious.

subcutáneo, nea [soob-coo-tah'-nayo, ah], *a.* Subcutaneous; below the skin.

subdecano [soob-day-cah'-no], *m.* Subdean.

subdécuplo, pla [soob-day'-coo-plo, plah], *a.* Subdecuple, containing one part of ten.

subdelegable [soob-day-lay-gah'-blay], *a.* That which may be subdelegated.

subdelegación [soob-day-lay-gah-the-on'], *f.* Subdelegation, substitution.

subdelegado [soob-day-lay-gah'-do], *m.* Subdelegate.

subdelegar [soob-day-lay-gar'], *va.* To subdelegate, to commit to another one's jurisdiction or power.

subdesarrollado, da [soob-day-sah-rol-lyah'-do, dah], *a.* Under-developed.

subdesarrollo [soob-day-sah-rol'-lyo], *m.* Underdevelopment.

subdiaconado, subdiaconato [soob-dee-ah-co-nah'-do], *m.* Subdeaconship.

subdiácono [soob-de-ah'-co-no], *m.* Subdeacon.

subdirección [soob-de-rayc-the-on'], *f.* Section, subdepartment.

subdirector, ra [soob-de-rayc-tor'], *m & f.* Subdirector, assistant manager.

subdirectorio [soob-de-rayc-to'-re-o], *m. (Comput.)* Subdirectory.

subdistinción [soob-dis-tin-the-on'], *f.* Subdistinction.

subdistinguir [soob-dis-tin-geer'], *va.* To distinguish that which has already been distinguished.

súbdito, ta [soob'-de-to, tah], *a.* Subject, inferior.

subdividir [soob-de-ve-deer'], *va.* To subdivide.

subdivisible [soob-de-ve-see'-blay], *a.* Subdivisible.

subdivisión [soob-de-ve-se-on'], *f.* Subdivision, subsection.

subduplo, pla [soob-doo'-plo, plah], *a.* Subduple, containing one part of two.

subejecutor [soob-ay-hay-coo-tor'], *m.* Deputy executor.

subentender [soob-en-ten-derr'], *va.* To understand what is tacitly meant.

subérico [soo-bay'-re-co], *a.* Suberic, extracted from cork.

suberina [soo-bay-ree'-nah], *f.* Suberine, a modification of cellulose found in cork.

suberoso, sa [soo-bay-ro'-so, sah], *a.* Suberose, corky.

subestimación [soo-bays-te-mah-the-on'], *f.* Substation.

subestimar [soo-bays-te-mahr'], *va.* To underestimate (capacidad, enemigo), to undervalue (objeto, propiedad).

subfletar [soob-flay-tar'], *va. (Naut.)* To hire a ship of another freighter.

subgerente [soob-hay-ren'-tay], *m.* Assistant manager.

subida [soo-bee'-dah], *f.* 1. Ascension, going up; mounting. 2. Ascent, acclivity, rise (cantidad, precio). 3. Attack of a disease. 4. Enhancement, rise, augmentation of value or price; amelioration of things. **En la subida había muchas flores,** there were a lot of flowers on the way up.

subidero, ra [soo-be-day'-ro, rah], *a.* Mounting, rising.

subidero [soo-be-day-ro]. *m.* Ladder, mounting-block.

subido, da [soo-bee'-do, dah], *a. & pp.* OF SUBIR. 1. Raised on high, mounted. 2. Strong, having a deep tinge of color: strong-scented. 3. Finest, most excellent.

subidor [soo-be-dor'], *m.* Porter, one who carries things from lower to higher places.

subiente [soo-be-en'-tay], *m. (Arch.)* Ornaments of foliage ascending on columns or pilasters.

subílla [soo-beel'-lyah], *f. Awl. V.* ALESNA.

subíndice [soo-een'-de-thay], *m. (Comput.)* subscript.

subinquilino [soo-in-ke-lee'-no], *m.* Undertenant, one who rents a house of another tenant.

subintración [soob-in-trah-the-on'], *f.* 1. Immediate succession of things. 2. *(Med.)* Subingression.

subintrar [soob-in-trar'], *va.* To enter successively one after another.

subir [soo-beer'], *vr.* 1. To mount, to ascend, to come up, to go up (calle, cuesta), to climb. 2. To increase (precio, sueldo), to swell, as rivers, etc. 3. Of numbers, to amount to. 4. To enter leaves, as silkworms on commencing their cocoons. 5. To rise in dignity, fortune, etc. 6. *(Mus.)* To raise the voice gradually. -*va.* 1. To enhance, to increase the value. **Subir el color,** to raise a color, to render it brighter. 2. To raise, to lift up: to build up, to erect. 3. To set up, to straighten from an inclined position. **Subir a caballo,** to mount a horse. **Subirse el vino, licor a la cabeza,** to become tipsy. **Subir una pared,** to build a wall. **Le subieron los colores a la cara,** she blushed. **Seguíamos subiendo,** we went on climbing. **Sigue subiendo la bolsa,** the market is still rising. **Subirse al tren,** to get on the train.

súbitamente [soo'-be-tah-men-tay], *adv.* Suddenly, on a sudden.

súbito, ta [soo'-be-to, tah], *a.* Sudden (repentino), hasty (precipitado), unforeseen, unexpected (imprevisto). **Súbito, de súbito,** *adv.* Suddenly, unexpectdly.

subjección [soob-hay-the-on'], *f. (Rhet.)* A figure used in debating and answering within ourselves.

subjetivo, va [soob-hay-tee'-vo, vah], *a.* Subjective.

subjuntivo [soob-hoon-tee'-vo], *m. (Gram.)* Subjunctive.

sublevación [soo-blay-vah-the-on'], *f.* **Sublevamiento.** *m.* Insurrection, sedition, revolt.

sublevar [soo-blay-var'], *va.* To excite a rebellion. -*vr.* To rise in rebellion.

sublimación [soo-ble-mah-the-on'], *f.* Sublimation, act of sublimating.

sublimado [soo-ble-mah'-do] **Sublimado corrosivo.** *m. (Chem.)* Corrosive sublimate.-**Sublimado, da,** *pp.* of SUBLIMAR.

sublimar [soo-ble-mar'], *m.* 1. To heighten, to elevate, to sublime, to exalt. 2. *(Chem.)* To sublimate.

sublimatorio, ria [soo-ble-mah-too'-re-o, ah], *a.* Sublimatory.

sublime [soo-blee'-may], *a.* Sublime, exalted, eminent, heroic, majestic.

sublimemente [soo-blee'-may-men-tay], *adv.* Sublimely, loftily.

sublimidad [soo-ble-me-dahd'], *f.* Sublimity, loftiness, grandeur.

sublujación [soo-bloo-hah-the-on'], *f.* An imperfect luxation of a joint.

sublunar [soob-loo-nar'], *a.* Sublunar, sublunary: terrestial, earthly.

submarinista [soob-mah-re-nees-tah], *a.* **Exploración submarinista**, underwater exploration. *-m. & f.* Underwater fisherman.

submarino, na [soob-mah-ree'-no, nah], *a.* Submarine. *-m.* Submarine torpedo boat.

subministrar [soob-me-nes-trahr'], *m.* V. SUMINISTRAR.

subnormal [soob-nor-mahl'], *a.* Subnormal. *-m & f.* Subnormal person.

subordinación [soob-or-de-nah-the-on'], *f.* Subordination, subjection, subordinacy.

subordinadamente [soo-bor-de-nah-dah-men-tay], *adv.* Subordinately, subserviently.

subordinado, da [soob-or-de-nah'-do, dah], *a. & pp.* of SUBORDINAR. Subordinate, subservient; subordinated.

subordinar [soob-or-de-nar'], *m.* To subordinate, to subject.

subpolar [soob-po-lar'], *a.* Under the pole.

subprecio [soob-pray'-the-o], *m. (Com.)* Mark-down.

subprefecto [soob-pray-fec'-to], *m.* Subperfect, deputy prefect.

subprefectura [soob-pray-fec-too'-rah], *f.* 1. In France and America, subprefecture, a division of a prefecture. 2. The office of subprefect, and time of its duration. 3. Town in which the subprefect lives and the place where he has his offices.

subproducto [soob-pro-dooc'-to], *m.* By-product.

subrayar [soob-rah-yar'], *va.* To underscore, to underline.

subrepción [soob-rep-the-on'], *f.* 1. A hidden action, an underhand business. 2. Subreption, obtaining a favor by false representation; surreption.

subrepticiamente [soob-rayc-tee'-the-ah-men-tay], *adv.* Surreptitiously.

subrepticio, cia [soob-rep-tee'-the-o, ah], *a.* 1. Surreptitious, fraudulently obtained. 2. Surreptitious, done in a clandestine manner.

subrigadier [soo-bre-gah-de-err'], *m.* Sub-brigadier, an officer who discharged the duties of second sergeant in the Royal Guards.

subrogación [soob-ro-gah-the-on'], *f.* Surrogation or subrogation, the act of putting in another's place.

subrogar [soob-ro-gar'], *m.* To surrogate or to subrogate, to substitute.

subsanar [soob-sah-nar'], *m.* 1. To exculpate, to excuse (falta). 2. To med, to repair.

subscribir [soobs-cre-beer'], *m.* 1. To subscribe, to put a signature at the end of a writing. 2. To subscribe to, to accede, to agree to. *-vr.* To subscribe, to promise to pay a stipulated sum for the aid of some undertaking.

subscripción, *f.* 1. Subscription, signature. 2. Subscription, contribution to an enterprise.

subscripto, ta, subscrito, ta [soobs-creep'-to, tah], *pp. irr.* of SUBSCRIBIR.

subscriptor, ra [soobs-creep-tor'], *m. & f.* Subscriber.

subsecretario [soob-say-cray-tah'-re-o], *m.* The assistant secretary.

subsecuencia [soob-say-coo-en'-the-ah], *f.* Subsequence.

subsecuente [soob-say-coo-en'-tay], *a.* Subsequent. V. SUBSIGUIENTE.

subsecuentemente [soob-say-coo-ayn-tay-men-tay], *adv.* V. SUBSIGUIENTEMENTE.

subseguirse [soob-say-geer'-say], *vr.* To follow next.

subséxtuplo, pla [soob-sex'-too-plo, plah], *a.* Subsextuple, containing one part of sex.

subsidiariamente [soob-se-de-ah'-re-ah-men-tay], *adv.* In a subsidiary manner.

subsidiario, ria [soob-se-de-ah'-re-o, ah], *a.* Subsidiary, auxiliary.

subsidio [soob-see'-de-o], *m.* 1. Subsidy (subvención), aid (ayuda): commonly of money. 2. Subsidy war-tax. **Subsidio de enfermedad**, sick benefit. **Subsidio de paro**, unemployment benefit. *(And.)* Anxiety (inquietud).

subsiguiente [soob-se-gee-en'-tay], *a.* Subsequent, succeeding.

subsiguientemente [soob-se-ge-ayn'-tay-men-tay], *adv.* Subsequenty.

subsistencia [soob-sis-ten-the-ah], *f.* 1. Subsistence, permanence, stability. 2. Subsistence, competence, livelihood, living.

subsistente [soob-sis-ten'-tay], *pa. & a.* Subsistent, subsisting.

subsistir [soob-sis-teer'], *vn.* 1. To subsist (malvivir), to last. 2. To subsist, to have the means of living. 3. *(And.)* To live together (vivir juntos). **Todavía subsiste el edificio**, the building still stands.

subsolano [soob-so-lah'-no], *m.* Northeast wind.

substancia [soobs-tahn'-the-ah], *f.* 1. Nutriment, sustenance, aliment, pabulum; whatever nourishes. 2. Sap which nourishes. 3. Substance, essence, being, nature of things. 4. Substance, property, wealth. **En substancia**, (1) *(Med.)* in substance. (2) V. SUBTANCIA.

substancial [soobs-tan-the-ahl'], *a.* 1. Substantial, real, material. 2. Nutritive, nutritious. 3. Essential, of prime importance.

substancialmente [soobs-tan-the-ahl'-men-tay], *adv.* Substantially.

substanciar [soobs-tan-the-ar'], *va.* 1. To extract the substance, to abridge. 2. To substantiate, to prove fully. 3. To pursue the proceedings in a cause until its final determination.

substancioso [soobs-tan-the-o'-so], *a.* 1. Nutritive, nutritious. 2. Substantial.

substantivar [soobs-tan-te-var'], *va..* To use adjectives as substantives. V. SUSTANTIVAR.

substantivo [soobs-tan-tee'-vo], *m. (Gram.)* V. SUSTANTIVO.

substitución [soobs-te-too-the-on'], *f.* Substitution. V. SUBTITUCIÓN.

substituir [soobs-te-too-eer'], *va.* To substitute. V. SUSTITUIR.

substituyente [soobs-te-too-yen'-tay], *pa.* Substituting. V. SUSTITUYENTE.

substituto [soobs-te-too'-to], *m.* Substitute. V. SUSTITUTO.

substracción [soobs-trac-the-on'], *f.* 1. Subtraction, taking part from a whole. 2. Privation, concealment.

substraendo [soobs-trah-en'-do], *m.* The subtrahend.

substraer [soob's-trah-err'], *va.* To subtract, to remove. *-vr.* To withdraw oneself, to elude.

subtangente [soob-tan-hen'-tay], *f. (Geom.)* Subtangent.

subtender [soob-ten-derr'], *va.* 1. To sustain, to bear up. 2. *(Geom.)* To subtend.

subteniente [soob-tay-ne-en'-tay], *m.* V. ALFÉREZ.

subtensa [soob-ten'-sah], *f. (Geom.)* Subtense; chord.

subtenso, sa [soob-ten'-so, sah], *pp. irr.* of SUBTENDER.

subterfugio [soob-ter-foo'-he-o], *m.* Subterfuge, evasion, trick.

subterráneamente [soob-tayr-rah'-nay-ah-men-tay], *adv.* Subterraneously.

subterráneo, nea [soob-ter-rah'-nay-o, ah], *a.* Subterraneous, subterranean. *-m.* 1. Subway. 2. Subterraneous structure. 3. Underground cave or vault.

subtitulado [soob-te-too-lah-do], *m.* Subtitling.

subtitular [soob-te-too-lahr'], *va.* To subtitle.

subtítulo [soob-tee'-too-lo], *m.* Subtitle.

subtropical [soob-tro-pe-cahl'], *a.* Subtropical.

suburbano, na [soo-boor-bah'-no, nah], *a.* Suburban, relating to a suburb.-*a.* Suburban resident.

suburbio [soo-boor'-be-o], *m.* Suburb (afueras), outskirt.

subvención [soob-ven-the-on'], *f.* Help, assistance, grant, subsidy.

subvencionar [soob-vayn-the-o-nar'], *va.* To subsidize, to aid.

subvenir [soob-vay-neer'], *va.* 1. To aid, to assist, to succor. 2. To provide (necesidades), to supply, to furnish, to defray (gastos).

subversión [soob-ver-se-on'], *f.* Subversion.

subversivo, va [soob-ver-see'-vo, vah], *a.* Subversive, destructive.

subversor [soob-ver-sor'], *m.* Subverter, overturner.

subvertir [soob-ver-teer'], *va.* To subvert (minar), to destroy, to ruin.

subyugar [soob-yoo-gar'], *va.* To subdue (país), to subjugate, to overcome.

succino [sooc-thee'-no], *m.* Succinite, amber.

succión [sooc-the-on'], *f.* 1. Suction, drawing in with the breath. 2. Suck.

suceder [soo-thay-derr'], *vn.* 1. To succeed, to come after one, to follow in order. 2. To inherit, to succeed by inheritance, to come into an estate. 3. (*For.*) To come into the place of one who has quitted or died.-*a. impers.* To happen (pasar), to come to pass, to come about, to fall out. **Sucedió así**, it happened so. **Suceda lo que suceda**, happen what may. **Lo que sucede es que....**, the fact is that.....**Suceder a una fortuna**, to inherit a fortune.

sucesible [soo-thay-see'-blay], *a.* Capable of success.

sucesión [soo-thay-se-on'], *f.* 1. Succession, series, concatenation. 2. Issue (hijos), offspring, children. 3. Inheritance (herencia).

sucesivamente [soo-thay-see'-vah-men-tay], *adv.* Successively.

sucesivo, va [soo-thay-see'-vo, vah], *a.* Successive, following in order, consecutive (consecutivo). **En lo sucesivo**, in time, in process of time; hereafter.

suceso [soo-thay'-so], *m.* 1. Event (acontecimiento), incident. 2. Issue, result, outcome; sucess. 3. *V.* TRANSCURSO.

sucesor, ra [soo-thay-sor', rah], *m.* Successor, succeeder.

suche [soo'-chay], *m.* 1. A fragrant yellow flower esteemed in Peru. 2. A fish of Lake Titicaca, held in high esteem.

suchicopal [soo-che-co-pahl'], *m.* kind of copol or styrax.

suciamente [soo'-the-ah-men-tay], *adv.* Nastily, filthily, foully.

suciedad [soo-the-ay-dahd'], *f.* Nastiness, filthiness (cualidad), obscenity.

sucino [soo-thee'-no], *m.* Amber. *V.* SUCCINO.

sucintamente [soo-then-tah-men-tay], *adv.* Succinctly, briefly

sucintarse [soo-then-tahr'-say], *vr. V.* CEÑIRSE.

sucinto, ta [soo-theen'-to, tah], *a.* 1. Girded, tucked up. 2. Brief, succinct, compendious, concise (declaración).

sucio, cia [soo'-the-o, ah], *a.* 1. Dirty, nasty, filthy (mugriento). 2. Stained with sin, tainted with guilt and imperfections. 3. Obscene (palabra), unchaste, smutty. 4. Uncivil, unpolished. 5. (*Naut.*) Foul; applied to a ship's bottom, to the sky or weather; to rowing out of rhythm; and to a rocky shore, or a bottom where there are reefs.

suco [soo'-co], *m.* Juice; sap.-*a.* (*Amer.*) Orange-colored.

sucoso, sa [soo-co'-so, sah], *a.* Juicy, succulent. *V.* JUGOSO.

sucotrino [soo-co-tree'-no], *a.* Socotrine.

súcubo [soo'-coo-bo], *m.* Succubus, a pretended demon, which, in intercourse with men, took the form of a woman.

sucucho [soo-coo'-cho], *m.* Storeroom of a ship.

súcula [soo'-coo-lah], *f.* Cylinder. *V.* CABRIA.

suculencia [soo-coo-len'-the-ah], *f.* Juiciness, succulence.

suculento, ta [soo-coo-len'-to, tah], *a.* Succulent (jugoso), juicy. *V.* JUGOSO.

sucumbir [soo-coom-beer'], *vn.* 1. (*Law.*) To lose a suit at law. 2. To succumb, to yield, to sink under a difficulty. 3. (*Met.*) To die.

sucursal [soo-coor-sahl'], *a. & f.* Branch, subsidiary (filial), succursal used primarily of a minor church, thence of other establishments; branch of a commercial house.

sud [good], *m.* 1. The south. 2. South, the south wind.

sudadero [soo-dah-day'-ro], *m.* 1. Handkerchief, for wiping off the sweat. 2. Bath, sweating-room, sudatory. 3. Moist ground, a place where water oozes out by drops. 4. Sweating-place for sheep previous to their being shorn.

sudamericano, na [soo-dah-may-re-cah'-no, nah], *a.* South American.

sudador, ra [soo-dah-dor', rah], *a. & n.* That which sweats or exudes.

sudante [soo-dahn'-tay], *pa.* Sweating.

sudar [soo-dar'], *va.* 1. To sweat, to perspire, to exude. Sometimes used transitively. 2. To give with repugnance. 3. To toil, to labor. 4. To ooze (recipiente), to distil. 5. To cough up (dinero). **Hacer sudar la prensa**, to print much. **Sudar la gota gorda**, to sweat blood.

sudario [soo-dah'-re-o], *m.* 1. Handkerchief or cloth for wiping off the sweat. 2. Cloth put on the face of the dead.

sudatorio, ria [soo-dah-to'-re-o, ah], *a.* Sudorific, causing sweat.

sudeste [soo-des'-tay], *m.* South east.

sudoeste [soo-do-es'-tay], *m.* 1. Southwest. **Sudoeste cuarto al oeste**, south-west by west. **Sudoeste cuarto al sur**, south-west by south. 2. South-west wind; (*Naut.*) south-wester.

sudor [soo-dor'], *m.* 1. Sweat, perspiration. 2. Sweat, labor, toil drudgery. 3. Viscous matter or gum that distils from trees. **Cubrirse de sudor**, to sweat profusely.

sudoriento, ta [soo-do-re-en'-to, tah], *a.* Sweated, moistened with sweet.

sudorífero, ra [soo-do-ree'-fay-ro, rah], *a.* Sudorific, causing sweat.

sudorífico, ca [soo-do-ree'-fe-co, cah], *a.* Sudorific, promoting sweat.

sudorífico [soo-do-ree'-fe-co], *m.* Sudorific, a medicine promoting sweat.

sudoso, sa [soo-do'-so, sah], *a.* Sweaty, moist with sweat.

sudsudeste [sood-soo-des'-tay], *m.* South-south-east.

sudsudoeste [sood-soo-do-es'-tay], *m.* South-south-west.

sudueste [soo-doo-es'-tay], *m.* South west. *V.* ÁFRICO and SUDOESTE.

sueco, ca [soo-ay'-co, cah], *a.* Swedish. **Hacerse uno el sueco**, (*Coll.*) to wink at a thing, to pretend not to have taken notice.

suegra [soo-ay'-grah], *f.* 1. Mother in-law. 2. A hard crust of bread.

suegrecita [soo-ay-gray-thee'-tah], *f. dim.* (*Coll.*) Little mother-in-law.

suegro [soo-ay'-gro], *m.* Father-in-law.

suela [soo-ay'-lah], *f.* 1. Sole of the shoe (zapato). 2. Sole-leather (trozo de cuero). 3. (*Zool.*) Sole. 4. A horizontal rafter, laid as the foundation for partition-walls. 5. Leather tip of a billiard cue. **Media suela**, half sole. **Duro como la suela de un zapato**, tough as leather, tough as old boots.

sueldo [soo-el'-do], *m.* 1. Old Spanish coin. 2. An ancient Roman coin. 3. Sou or sol, a French penny. 4. Pay given to soldiers. 5. Wages, salary, stipend (mensual). **Sueldo atrasado**, back pay. **Asesino a sueldo**, hired assasin.

suelo [soo-ay'-lo], *m.* 1. Ground (tierra), soil, surface of the earth (superficie). 2. Earth, terra firma, the principal part of the world; hence the earth. 3. Pavement, ground-floor. 4. Floor (de cuarto), flooring, story. 5. The bottom or lower part of various things, as of a well, a vase, of a jar of wine; sole of anything that touches the ground. 6. Dregs, legs, settlings of any liquid. 7. Ground-plot, ground on which a building stands. 8. End; bottom. -*pl.* 1. (*Vulg. Vet.*) Sole, planter files of a horse's hoof. 2. Scatterings or leavings of grain. **Echarse por los suelos**, (a) to stretch oneself on the ground, (b) to humble oneself too much. **Venirse al suelo**, to fall to the ground. **Dar consigo en el suelo**, to fall down. **Por los suelos**, cast down, in a state of depreciation; prostrate.

suelta [soo-el'-tah], *f.* 1. Act of loosening or letting loose; solution. 2. Fetters, with which the feet of a beast are tied when grazing. **Dar suelta a las palomas**, to release pigeons.

sueltamente [soo-el-tah-men-tay], *adv.* Loosely, lightly, expeditiously: licentiously; spontaneously; laxly.

suelto, ta [soo-el'-to, tah], *a. & pp. irr.* Of SOLTAR. 1. Loose (no envasado), light (ágil), expeditious, swift, able. 2. Free (en movimiento), bold, afaring. 3. Easy, disengaged. 4. Voluble, fluent. 5. Blank (versos sin rima). 6. *(Coll.) V.* SOLTERO. 7. Small change (dinero). **Suelto de lengua**, audacious, shameless, ill-tongued, free to speak. **Arena suelta**, loose sand. **Comprar cosas sueltas, al suelto**, to buy things by the lump or bulk. **El libro tiene dos hojas sueltas**, the book has two pages loose. **Lo dejamos suelto**, we leave it untied. **Son tres poesías sueltas**, these are 3 separate poems.

suelto [soo-el'-to], *m.* Loose piece of metal or mineral found near mines.

sueño [soo-ay'-nyo], *m.* 1. Sleep (dormir), the act of sleeping. 2. Vision, dream, the fancies of a sleeping person. 3. Drowsiness, heaviness, inclination to sleep (somnolencia). **Tengo sueño, I** am sleepy. 4. Any fantastical idea without foundation. 5. Shortness, lightness, or swiftness with which something appears or passes. **Caerse de sueño**, to be overcome with drowsiness. **Conciliar el sueño**, to woo sleep. **Espantar el sueño**, to scare away sleep, to prevent sleeping. **En sueños** or **entre sueños**, dreaming, sleeping. **A sueño pesado**, in a profound sleep; deep sleep; difficult to dispel. **Tener el sueño ligero**, to be a light sleeper. **Se me ha quitado el sueño**, I'm not sleepy any more.

suero [soo-ay'-ro], *m.* 1. Whey. 2. Serum.

sueroso, sa [soo-ay-ro'-so, sah], *a. V.* SEROSO.

suerte [soo-er'-tay], *f.* 1. Chance (azar), fortuitous event; lot (elección), fortune, luck (fortuna), fate (destino), doom, good-luck, haphazard. 2. Rind, sort: species. 3. Manner, mode, way. 4. Skillful movements of a bullfighter. 5. Piece of ground separated from the rest by bounds or landmarks. 6. Original, stock, lineage. 7. Sort, kind (especie). **La suerte está echada**, the die is cast. **De suerte que no debe nada**, so that he owes nothing. **Echar suertes**, to cast or draw lots. **Dejar a uno a su suerte**, to abandon somebody. **Lo echaron a suertes**, they drew lots for it. **Estar de suerte**, to be in luck. **Tuvo la suerte de que hacía buen tiempo**, he was luckly that it was fine.-*pl.* **Suertes**, feats, tricks; legerdemain.

suestar [soo-es-tar'], *vn. (Naut.)* To veer towards the south east.

sueste [soo-es'-tay], *m.* South east. **Sueste cuarto al este**, *(Naut.)* south east by east. **Sueste cuarto al sur**, *(Naut.)* south east by south.

suficiencia [so-fe-the-en'-the-a], *f.* Sufficiency. **A suficiencia**, sufficiently, enough.

suficiente [soo-fe-the-en'-tay], *a.* 1. Sufficient, enough (bastante). 2. Qualified, apt, fit (idóneo), capable (capaz), competent.

suficientemente [soo-fe-the-ayn'-tay-men-tay], *adv.* Sufficiently, competently.

sufijo, ja [soo-fee'-ho, hah], *a.* Suffixed, affixed. -*m.* Suffix, affix.

sufismo [soo-fees'-mo], *m.* Sufism, A mystical doctrine among Mohammedans, chiefly in Persia.

sufocación [soo-fo-cah-the-on'], *f.* Suffocation. *V.* SOFOCACIÓN.

sufocador, ra [soo-fo-cah-dor', rah], *m. & f.* Suffocator, choker.

sufocante [soo-fo-cahn'-tay], *pa. & a.* Suffocating, suffocative.

sufocar [soo-fo-car'], *va.* 1. To suffocate, to choke, to smother. 2. To quench or put out fire. 3. To molest, to harass, to oppress. *V.* SOFOCAR.

sufoco [soo-fo'-co], *m. (Prov.)* Suffocation, fumigation.

sufra [soo'-frah], *f.* A stout strap which receives the shafts of a carriages; ridge-band.

sufragáneo, sufragano [soo-frah-gah'-nay-o], *m.* Suffragan, a bishop subject to a metropolitan. -*a.* Belonging to a suffragan.

sufragar [soo-frah-gar'], *va.* 1. To favor, to aid (ayudar), to assist. 2. To suffice, to be sufficient. 3. To defray (proyecto); to make up.

sufragio [soo-frah'-he-o], *m.* 1. Vote suffrage (voto), voice. 2. Favor, support, aid (apoyo), assistance. 3. Suffrage, any work appropriated to the souls of the deceased in purgatory.

sufragista [soo-frah-hees'-tah], *f.* Suffragist.

sufrible [soo-free'-blay], *a.* Sufferable, tolerable, bearable.

sufridera [soo-fhe-day'-rah], *f.* Smith's tool for punching holes on an anvil.

sufridero, ra [soo-fre-day'-ro, rah], *a.* Supportable, tolerable.

sufrido, da [soo-free'-do, dah], *a. & pp.* of SUFRIR. 1. Bearing up under adversities, long-suffering (paciente). 2. Consenting, accommodating: spoken of a contented cuckold. **Mal sufrido**, impatient, rude, severe.

sufridor, ra [soo-fre-dor', rah], *m. & f.* Sufferer (persona), one who suffers patiently.

sufriente [soo-fre-en'-tay], *pa.* Tolerating, bearing.

sufrimiento [soo-fre-me-en'-to], *m.* Sufferance, patience, tolerance.

sufrir [soo-freer'], *va.* 1. To suffer, to bear with patience, to undergo. 2. To bear or carry a load; to sustain an attack. 3. To clinch a nail. 4. To permit, to tolerate. 5. To pay and suffer. 6. To abide; to comport; to go under. **No sufre la menor descortesía**, he won't tolerate the slightest rudeness. -*vn.* To suffer. **Sufrir de**, to suffer from. **Sufre de reumatismo**, she suffers from rheumatism. **Es menester sufrir y consufrir**, we must bear and forbear.

sufumigación [soo-foo-me-gah-the-on'], *f.* Suffumigation, operation of fumes, administered as a remedy or cure.

sufusión [soo-foo-se-on'], *f.* Suffusion, kind of cataract in the eyes.

sugerencia [soo-hay-ren'-the-ah], *f.* Suggestion.

sugerente [soo-hay-ren'-tay], *pa.* Suggesting.

sugerir [soo-hay-reer'], *va.* 1. To hint (insinua), to suggest, to intimate. 2. To suggest, to prompt.

sugestión [soo-hes-te-on'], *f.* 1. Suggestion (sugerencia), intimation, hint (insinuación). 2. Temptation by the devil. 3. **Sugestión magnética, hipnótica**, hypnotic suggestion, control of the will of the person hypnotized.

sugestionar [soo-hes-te-o-nar'], *va. & vr.* To influence by suggestion.

sugestivo [soo-hays-tee'-vo], *a.* 1. Stimulating (estimulante), evocative (evocador). 2. Attractive (atractivo).

sugo [soo'-go], *m. (Prov.) V.* JUGO.

suicida [soo-e-thee'-dah], *com.* Suicide, a self-murderer.

suicidarse [soo-e-the-dar'-say], *vr.* To commit suicide.

suicidio [soo-e-thee'-de-o], *m.* Suicide, self-murder.

suite [soo-ee'-tay], *m.* A Central American dwarf palm used for thatching. Geonoma (species).

Suiza [soo-ee'-thah], *f.* Switzerland.

suizo, za [soo-ee'-tho, thah], *a.* Swiss.

sujeción [soo-hay-the-on'], *f.* 1. Subjection, the act of subduing; coersion, control, obedience; the act of submitting or surrendering; connection. 2. Objection, argument.

sujetador [soo-hay-tha-dor'], *m.* Fastener; clip (para pelo), clip (para papeles), bra (prenda).

sujetar [soo-hay-tar'], *va.* 1. To subdue (dominar), to reduce to submission. 2. To subject, to put under, to keep down (persona), to overcome, to conquer, to make liable, to nail down (clavo), to fasten together (papeles).-*vr.* To be inherent, to adhere.

sujeto, ta [soo-hay'-to, tah], *a. & pp. irr.* of SUJETAR. 1. Subject, liable (propenso a), exposed, chargeable. 2. Amenable before a court of justice. **Estar sujeto a cambios inesperados**, to be liable to sudden changes.

sujeto [soo-hay'-to], *m*. 1. Subject, topic, theme, matter in discussion. 2. *(Gram.)* Subject, that of which something is affirmed (or denied). 3. A person: commonly used to express any undefined person or individual. **Es un buen sujeto**, *(Coll.)* he is a clever fellow also, he is an honest man. **Un sujeto sospechoso**, a suspicious character. **Buen sujeto**, good chap.

sulfanilamida [sool-fah-ne-lah-mee'-dah], *f*. Sulfanilamide, sulfa.

sulfapiridina [sool-fah-pe-re-dee'-nah], *f*. Sulfapyridine.

sulfatiazol [sool-fah-te-ah-thole'], *m*. Sulfathiazole.

sulfato [sool-fah'-to], *m*. Sulphate. **Sulfato de cobre**, copper sulphate.

solfido [sool-fee'-do], *m*. Sulphid, sulfid or sulphide.

sulfhídrico [soolf-ee'-dre-co], *a*. Sulphydric, hydrosulphuric (acid).

sulfito [sool-fee'-to], *m*. Sulphite, a salt of sulphurous acid.

sulfonamida [sool-fo-nah-mee'-dah], *f*. Sulfonamide.

sulfonamidas [sool-fo-nah-me'-dahs], *f. pl*. Sulfa drugs.

súlfur [sool'-foor], *m*. Brimstone, sulphur. *V*. AZUFRE.

sulfurar [sool-foo-rar'], *va*. To irritate, to anger, to enrage.

sulfúreo, rea [sool-foo'-ray-o, ah], *a*. Sulphureous, sulphurous.

sulfúrico [sool-foo'-re-co], *a*. 1. Sulphuric (ácido). 2. Sulphuric, consisting of sulphur.

sulfuro [sool-foo'-ro], *m*. Sulphid, sulphide, sulfid: a combination of sulphur with a metal.

sulfuroso, sa [sool-foo-ro'-so, sah], *a*. 1. Sulphurous, containing sulphur. 2. Sulphurous acid, containing one molecule of sulphur to two of oxygen.

sultán [sool-tahn'], *m*. 1. Sultan, an appellation which the Turks give to their emperor. 2. Mohammedan prince or governor.

sultana [sool-tah'-nah], *f*. Sultana or sultaness, the queen of a Turkish emperor.

suma [soo'-mah], *f*. 1. Sum, the whole of anything. 2. Sum, many particulars aggregated to a total; a sum of money. 3. Substance, heads of anything. 4. Sum, amount or result of reasoning or computation, act of summing up, conclusion. 5. Sum, compendium, abridgment. **En suma**, in short; finally. **Hacer sumas**, to add up. **Suma global**, lump sum.

sumaca [soo-mah'-cah], *f*. A small schooner used in the coasting trade along the Atlantic coast of South America.

sumador [soo-mah-dor], . *(Comput.)* Adder. **Sumador de un dígito**, one digit-adder.

sumadora mecánica [soo-mah-do'-rah may-cah'-ne-cah], *f*. Adding machine.

sumamente [soo'-mah-men-tay], *adv*. Chiefly; extremely, mightily, highly.

sumando [soo-mahn'-do], *m. (Math.)* Each of the quantities which are added together.

sumar [soo-mar'], *va*.. 1. To sum, to collect particulars into a total; to add. 2. To collect into a narrow compass (recoger); to sum up, to recapitulate. **La cuenta suma 6 dólares**, the bill adds up to $6. -*vn*. To cast up accounts; to result.

sumaria [soo-mah'-re-ah], *f*. The preparatory proceeding in a suit at law; verbal process.

sumariamente [soo-mah'-re-ah-men-tay], *adv*. Summarily; in a plain manner.

sumario, ria [soo-mah'-re-o, ah], *a*. Summary, compendious; plain, without formalities.

sumario [soo-mah'-re-o], *m*. Compendium, abridgment, summary; abstract, compend; result of computation.

sumergible [soo-mer-hee'-blay], *a*. Submergible, submersible, sinkable. -*m*. Submersible, submarine.

sumergimiento [soo-mer-he-me-en'-to], *m. V*. SUMERSIÓN.

sumergir [soo-mer-heer'], *va*. 1. To submerge, to drown, to immerse (bañar). 2. To embarass, to involve in difficulties.

sumersión [soo-mer-se-on'], *f*. Submersion, immersion.

sumidad [soo-me-dahd'], *f*. Top, summit.

sumidero [soo-me-day'-ro], *m*. 1. Sewer, drain (cloaca), sink (fregadero). 2. *(Carib.)* Quagmire (tremedal). 3. *(Fig.)* Drain.

sumido, da [soo-mee'-do, dah], *a. & pp* of SUMIR. Drowned; overflowed, plunged into vice.

sumillería [soo-mil-lyay-ree'-ah], *f*. Lord chamberlain's office.

suministración [soo-me-nis-trah-the-on'], *f*. Supply, the act of furnishing or supplying, subministration.

suministrador, ra [soo-me-nis-trah-dor', rah], *m. & f*. Provider, one who subministers.

suministrar [soo-mee-nis-trar'], *va*. To subminister, to supply (artículos, información), to furnish, to minister.

sumir [soo-meer'], *va*. To take; to receive. in this sense it is confined to the receiving of the chalice in the celebration of the mass. -*vr*. 1. To sink under ground (objeto), to be swallowed up. 2. To be sunk (boca, pecho). **Sumir un barco**, *(Naut.)*, to stave a vessel. **El desastre le sumió en la tristeza**, the disaster plunged him into sadness. 3. *(LAm.)* To cower (encogerse).

sumisamente [soo-mee'-sah-men-tay], *adv*. Submissively low.

sumisión [soo-me-se-on'], *f*. 1. Submission, obsequiousness, compliance, acquiescence, obedience. 2. *(Law.)* Renunciation.

sumiso, sa [soo-mee'-so, sah], *a*. Submissive, humble, resigned, compliant, meek.

sumista [soo-mees'-tah], *m*. Abridger writer of compendiums or summaries computer; young student in morality.

sumo, ma [soo'-mo, mah], *a*. Highest, loftiest, greatest; most elevated; excessive. **A lo sumo**, at most; to the highest pitch.

suncho [soon'-cho], *m. (Naut.)* Clamp. **Sunchos de la bomba**, Pump-clamps.

sunción [soon-the-on'], *f*. Receiving the chalice at mass.

sunsún [soon-soon'], *m*. (Cuban) A humming-bird.

suntuario, ria [soon-too-ah'-re-o, ah], *a*. Sumptuary: applied to laws relating to expense or regulating the cost of living.

suntuosamente [soon-too-o'-sah-men-tay], *adv*. Sumptuous.

suntuosidad [soon-too-o-se-dahd'], *f*. Sumptuosity, costliness, sumptuousness.

suntuoso, sa [soon-too-oh'-so, sah], *a*. Sumptuous, expensive; new-fangled.

supedáneo [soo-pay-dah'-nay-o], *m*. Species of pedestal to a crucifix.

supeditación [soo-pay-de-tah-the-on'], *f*. The act of subduing or trampling under foot.

supeditado, da [soo-pay-de-tah'-do, dah], *pp*. of SUPEDITAR. Trampled under foot. **Supedito de los contrarios**, suppressed by enemies.

supeditar [soo-pay-de-tar'], *adv. To* subdue, to trample under foot, to overpower.

súper. A Latin preposition, used in composition, denoting (a) over, above: (b) pre-eminence.

superable [soo-pay-rah'-blay], *a*. Surmountable, conquerable.

superabundancia [soo-per-ah-boon-dahn'-the-ah], *f*. Superabundance, overflow.

superabundante [soo-per-ah-boon-dahn'-tay], *pa. & a*. Superabundant, luxuriant.

superabundantemente [soo-per-ah-boon-dahn-tay], *adv*. Superabundantly, overflowingly.

superabundar [soo-per-ah-boon-dar'], *vn*. To superabound.

superación [soo-pay-rah-the-on'], *f*. 1. Overcoming (acto). 2. Improvement (mejora).

superano [soo-pay-rah'-no], *m. (Mus.) V*. TIPLE.

superante [soo-pay-rahn'-tay], *pa*. Surpassing, surmounting.

superar [soo-pay-rar'], *va*. To overcome (adversario), to conquer, to surpass (rival), to excel, to overpower, to exceed (esperanzas). **Las escenas superan a toda imaginación**, the scenes are more extraordinary than anyone could imagine.

superavit [soo-pay-rah'-vit], *m*. Overplus, residue.

supercarburante [soo-per-car-boo-rahn'-tay], *m*. High-grade fuel.

superchería [soo-per-chay-ree'-ah], *f.* Artful fallacy, fraud, deceit, or cozenage; foul dealing.

superchero, ra [soo-per-chay'-ro, rah], *a.* Wily, deceitful, insidious.

superciliar [soo-per-the-le-ar'], *a.* Superciliary, above the eyebrows.

supereminencia [soo-per-ay-me-nen'-the-ah], *f.* Supereminence.

supereminente [soo-per-ay-me-nen'-tay], *a.* Supereminent.

supererogación [soo-per-ay-ro-gah-the-on'], *f.* Supererogation.

supererogatorio, ria [soo-per-ay-ro-gah-to'-re-o, ah], *a.* Supererogatory.

supererestructura [soo-per-es-trooc-too'-rah], *f.* Superstructure.

superfetación [soo-per-fay-tah-the-on'], *f.* Superfetation, superimpregnation.

superficial [soo-per-fe-the-ahl'], *a.* 1. Superficial, on the surface. 2. Superficial, shallow, smattering.

superficialidad [soo-per-fe-the-ah-le-dahd'], *f.* Superficiality.

superficialmente [soo-per-fe-the-al'-men-tay], *adv.* Superficially, flashily, on the surface.

superficiario, ria [soo-per-fe-the-ah'-re-o, ah], *a.* V. SUPERFICIONARIO.

superficie [soo-per-fee'-the-ay], *f.* Superficies, surface, area. **Superficie inferior**, lower surface. **El submarino salió a la superficie**, the submarine surfaced.

superficionario, ria [soo-per-fe-the-o-nah'-re-o, rah], *a.* (*Law.*) Applied to those who occupy the property of others by paying rent.

superfino, na [soo-per-fee'-no, nah], *a.* Superfine.

superfluamente [soo-per-floo-ah-men'-tay], *adv.* Superfluously.

superfluidad [soo-per-floo-e-dahd'], *f.* Superfluity.

superfluo, ua [soo-per'-floo-o, ah], *a.* Superfluous, exuberant.

superfosfato [soo-per-fos-fah'-to], *m.* Superphosphate.

superhombre [su-per-om'-bray], *m.* Superman.

superhumeral [soo-per-oo-may-rahl'], *m.* Ephod, scapulary: band for the cover of a reliquary.

superíndice [soo-per-een'-de-thay], *m.* (*Comput.*) Superscript.

superintendencia [soo-per-in-ten-den'-the-ah], *f.* 1. Superintendence, supervision. 2. Charge and jurisdiction of superintendent; superintendency.

superintendente [soo-per-in-ten-den'-tay], *com.* 1. Superintendent, intendent; an officer of high rank, who oversees any allotment of public business. **Superintendente de la casa de moneda**, warden of the mint. 2. Comptroller, overseer, supervisor.

superior [soo-pay-re-or'], *a.* Superior, paramount, higher, greater. **Ser superior**, to be superior to. **Vive en el piso superior**, he lives on the upper floor. **Un estudio de nivel superior a los existentes**, a study on a higher plane than the present ones.

superior, ra [soo-pay-re-or', rah], *m. & f.* Superior

superiorato [soo-pay-re-o-rah'-to], *m.* Office of a superior and the term of such office.

superioridad [soo-pay-re-o-re-dahd'], *f.* Superiority, pre-eminence.

superiormente [soo-pay-re-or-men'-tay], *adv.* Masterly, in a superior manner.

superlativar [soo-per-lah-te-var'], *va.* To make a term superlative.

superlativo, va [soo-per-lah-tee'-vo, vah], *a.* Superlative. **En grado superlativo**, superlatively.

supermercado [soo-per-mer-cah'-do], *m.* Supermarket.

superno, na [soo-per'-no, nah], *a.* Supreme, highest, supernal.

supernumerario, ria [soo-per-noo-may-rah'-re-o, ah], *a.* Supernumerary.

superpoblado, da [soo-per-po-blah'-do, dah], *a.* Overpopulated (país, región).

superposición [soo-per-po-se-the-on'], *f.* 1. Addition. 2. Placing above. 3. Superposition.

superpotencia [soo-per-po-ten'-the-ah], *f.* (*Pol.*) Superpower.

superproducción [soo-per-pro-dooc-the-on'], *f.* Overproduction.

supersaturar [soo-per-sah-too-rar'], *va.* To supersaturate.

supersónico, ca [soo-per-so'-ne-co, cah], *a.* Supersonic.

superstición [soo-pers-te-the-on'], *f.* Superstition.

supersticiosamente [soo-pers-te-the-o'-sah-men-tay], *adv.* Superstitiously.

supersticioso, sa [soo-pers-te-the-o'-so, sah], *a.* Superstitious; scrupulous beyond need.

supersubstancial [soo-per-soobs-tahn-the-ahl'], *a.* Supersubstantial (eucaristía).

supervalente [soo-per-vah-len'-tay], *a.* Prevalent, exceeding in value.

supervalorar [soo-per-va-lo-rahr'], *va.* To overvalue, to overstate.

supervención [soo-per-ven-the-on'], *f.* (*For.*) The taking effect of a new law.

superveniencia [soo-per-vay-ne-en'-the-ah], *f.* Supervention, the act of supervening.

superveniente [soo-per-ve-ne-en'-tay], *pa. & a.* Supervenient, supervening.

supervenir [soo-per-ve-neer'], *m.* To supervence; to come as an extraneous addition. V. SOBREVENIR.

supervisor, ra [soo-per-ve-sor'], *m & f.* Supervisor.

supervivencia [soo-per-ve-ven'-the-ah], *f.* 1. Survivorship. 2. Money or annuity, stipulated in marriage settlements in favor of the surviving consort.

superviviente [soo-per-ve-ve-ayn'-tay], *a.* Surviving. -*m & f.* Survivor.

supinación [soo-pe-nah-the-on'], *f.* Supination, lying with the face upward.

supinador [soo-pe-nah-dor'], *a.* Supinator, a muscle turning the hand palm upward.

supino, na [soo-pee'-no, nah], *a.* 1. Supine, indolent, lying with the face upward. 2. Ignorant from negligence.

supino [soo-pe-no], *m.* (*Gram.*) Supine.

suplantación [soo-plan-tah-the-on'], *f.* Supplanting, the act of supplanting.

suplantador, ra [soo-plan-tah-dor', rah], *m. & f.* Supplanter.

suplantar [soo-plan-tar'], *va.* 1. To falsify a writing by blotting out words, and putting others in their place. 2. (*Coll.*) To supplant, to displace by stratagem.

suplefaltas [soo-play-fahl'-tas], *m.* (*Coll.*) Substitute.

suplemento [soo-play-men'-to], *m.* 1. Supply, the act of supplying. Supplement.

supletorio, ria [soo-play-to'-re-o, ah], *a.* Suppletory, supplemental, that which fills up deficiencies.

súplica [soo'-ple-cah], *f.* Petition, request, supplication, memorial. (*Coll.*) A favor asked.

suplicación [soo-ple-cah-the-on'], *f.* 1. Request, petition, supplication. 2. (*For.*) Appeal from the decision of a court. 3. Conical tube of thin and light paste; a kind of pastry. V. BARQUILLO. **A suplicación**, by petition, memorializing.

suplicante [soo-ple-cahn'-tay], *pa. & f.* Supplicant, petitioning; memorialist, petitioner, suitor; suitress.

suplicar [soo-ple-car'], *va.* 1. To entreat, to implore, to supplicate, to crave. 2. To make a humble reply to a superior. **Suplicar de la sentencia**, to petition against the sentence; to appeal to a higher court.

suplicatorio [soo-ple-cah-to'-re-oh], *f.* (*Law.*) Letter supplicatory, rogatory, a writ or any legal instrument sent in by a tribunal or judge to another of equal authority, that they may attend to what is solicited (inmunidad parlamentaria).

suplicio [soo-plee'-the-o], *m.* 1. Punishment (castigo), torture (tortura). **Es un suplico tener que escuchar eso**, it's torture to have to listen to that. 2. Place of execution. 3. *(Met.)* Bodily or mental suffering, anguish.

suplidor, ra [soo-ple-dor', rah], *m. & f.* Substitute, deputy.

supliente [soo-ple-en'-tay], *pa. & a.* Substitute, supplying.

suplimiento [soo-ple-me-en'-to], *m. V.* SUPLEMENTE.

suplir [soo-pleer'], *va.* 1. To supply (necesidad), to fill up as deficiencies happen, to furnish. 2. To supply, to serve instead of. 3. To excuse, to overlook, to disguise.

suponedor, ra [soo-po-ne-dor', rah], *m. & f.* Supposer.

suponer [soo-po-nerr'], *va.* 1. To suppose, to surmise. **Supongamos, supóngase,** let us suppose. 2. To suppose, to fancy, to imagine (imaginar). 3. To attribute (atribuir). *-vn.* To possess weight or authority. **Con las dificultades que son de suponer,** with all the difficulties that one might expect. **Es un suponer, I** was only thinking about. **El traslado le supone grandes gastos,** the move involves a lot of expense for him. *(Yo supongo, suponga, súpuse, supondré, from Suponer. V.* PONER.*)*

suportar [soo-por-tar'], *va. V.* SOBRELLEVAR.

suposición [soo-po-se-the-on'], *f.* 1. Supposition (supuesto), surmise. 2. Authority (autoridad), distinction (distinción), eminence in point of talents. 3. Imposition, falsehood. 4. (Logic) Acceptance of one term in piece of another.

supositar [soo-po-se-tar'], *va. (Divin.)* To exist under both divine and human nature in one person.

supositicio, cia [soo-po-se-tee'-the-o, ah], *a.* Supposititious. *V.* FINGIDO.

supositivo, va [soo-po-se-tee'-vo, vah], *a.* Suppositive, implying supposition.

supositorio [soo-po-se-to'-re-o], *m. (Med.)* Suppository. *V.* CALA.

suprarrenal [soo-pra-ray-nahl'], *a.* Suprarenal. **Glándula suprarrenal,** suprarenal gland.

supraspina [soo-pras-pee'-nah], *f. (Anat.)* Cavity at the top of the shoulder, the supra-spinal fosea of the scapula.

supraspinato [soo-pras-pe-nah'-to], *m. (Anat.)* Supraspinatus, muscle which raises the arm.

suprema [soo-pray'-mah], *f.* The supreme council of the Inquisition.

supremacía [soo-pray-mah-thee'-ah], *f.* Supremacy.

supremamente [soo-pray-mah-men-tay], *adv.* Ultimately, supremely.

supremo, ma [soo-pray'-mo, mah], *a.* Supreme; highest, most excellent, paramount; excessive.

supresión [soo-pray-se-on'], *f.* Suppression: obstruction; extinction.

supresivo, va [soo-pray-see'-vo, vah], *a.* Suppressive, tending to suppress.

supreso, sa [soo-pray'-so, sah], *pp. irr.* of SUPRIMIR. Suppressed.

suprimir [soo-pre-meer'], *va.* 1. To suppress (rebelión, crítica), to impede, to obstruct. 2. To abolish a place or employment, to extinguish (derecho, institución). 3. To suppress (libro), to keep in, to omit, to conceal.

suprior, ra [soo-pre-or', rah], *m. & f.* Sub-prior, sub-prioress.

supriorato [soo-pre-o-rah'-to], *m* Office of sub-prior or prioress.

supuesto [soo-poo-es'-to], *m.* 1. Supposition. 2. *(Phil.)* Individuality of a complete and incommunicable substance.

supuesto, ta, *a. & pp. irr.* of SUPONER. Suppositious, suppositive, supposed. **Por supuesto,** of course. **Supuesto que,** allowing that; granting that; since.

supuración [soo-poo-rah-the-on'], *f.* Suppuration.

supurante [soo-poo-rahn'-tay], *pa.* Suppurating, generating pus.

supurar [soo-poo-rar'], *va.* To waste or consume moisture by heat. *-m. (Med.)* To suppurate, to form pus.

supurativo, va [soo-poo-rah-tee'-vo, vah], *a.* Suppurative.

supuratorio, ria [soo-poo-rah-to'-re-o, ah], *a.* That which suppurates.

suputación [soo-poo-tah-the-on'], *f.* Computation, calculation, supputation.

suputar [soo-poo-tar'], *va.* To compute, to calculate, to suppute.

sur [soor], *m.* South: south wind. **Navegar al sur,** *(Naut.)* to steer a southerly course; to stand to the southward.

sura [soo'-rah], **surata** [soo-rah'-tah], *f.* A chapter or section of the Koran.

surada [soo-rah'-dah], *f. (Naut.)* A strong south wind.

sural [soo-rahl'], *a.* Sural: applied to the veins that run down the leg.

surcador, ra [soor-cah-dor', ra], *m. & f.* Ploughman, plowman, plougher.

surcar [soor-car'], *va.* 1. To furrow, to make furrows with a plough (tierra). 2. *(Met.)* To furrow, to flute (agua, olas). 3. To pass through a liquid. **Surcar los mares,** *(Naut.)* to plough the seas.

surco [soor'-co], *m.* 1. Furrow, hollow track. 2. Line, wrinkle. **A surco,** applied to pieces of ground furrowed in the middle.

surculado, da [soor-coo-lah'-do, dah], *a.* Applied to plants of one stem without branches.

súrculo [soor'-coo-lo], *m.* Single stem of a tree or plant without branches.

surculoso, sa [soor-coo-lo'-so, sah], *a.* Applied to a plant which has only one stem.

sureste [soo-rays'-tay], *m.* South-east.

surf [soorf], *m.* **Surf a vela,** windsurfing; surfboarding.

surgente [soor-hen'-tay], *pa.* Surging, salient.

surgidero [soor-he-day'-ro], *m.* Road, port, anchoring-place.

surgidor [soor-he-dor'], *m.* A person who anchors.

surgir [soor-heer'], *vn.* 1. To spout (líquido), to spurt (agua). *V.* SURTIR. 2. To appear, to present itself, to sprout. **Han surgido varios problemas,** several problems have arisen. 3. *(Naut.)* To anchor.

surirela [soo-re-ray'-lah], *f.* Surirella, a genus of diatoms, mostly freshwater.

suroeste [soo-ro-ess'-tay], *m.* South-west.

surrealismo [soor-re-ah-lees'-mo], *m.* Surrealism.

surrealista [soor-ray-ah-lees'-tah], *a.* Surrealist(ic).

sursueste [soor-soo-es'-tay], *m.* South-south-east.

surtida [soor-tee'-dah], *f.* 1. *(Mil.)* Sallyport. 2. Sally, sortie. 3. Backdoor.

surtidero [soor-te-day'-ro], *m.* Conduit. *V.* BUZÓN. **Surtidero de agua,** reservoir, basin.

surtido [soor-tee'-do], *m.* 1. Assortment, supply (existencias). **De surtido,** in common use. 2. Selection (selección), range. *-***Surtido, da,** *pp.* of SURTIR.

surtidor, ra [soor-te-dor', rah], *m. & f.* Purveyor, caterer. **Surtidor,** jet, spout, or shoot of water.

surtimiento [soor-te-me-en'-to], *m.* Supply, the act of supplying; assortment.

surtir [soor-teer'], *vn.* To spout, to spurt with violence (agua). *-va.* To supply (suministrar), to furnish, to provide, to accommodate, to fit out. **Surtir efecto,** to have the desired effect. **Surtir un pedido,** to fill an order.

surto, ta [soor'-to, tah], *pp.* Anchored: it is the old irregular participle of *Surgir.*

susamiel [soo-sah-me-el'], *f.* Paste, made of almonds, sugars and spice.

suscepción [soos-thep-the-on'], *f.* The act of receiving sacred orders.

susceptibilidad [soos-thep-te-be-le-dahd'], *f.* 1. Susceptibility to influences, aptitude for receiving an action. 2. Delicacy, susceptibility of emotions; sensibility.

susceptible [soos-thep-tee'-blay], *a.* Susceptible. **susceptible de sufrir daño,** liable to suffer damage.

susceptivo, va [soos-thep-tee'-vo, vah], *a.* Susceptible, susceptive.

suscitación [soos-the-tah-the-on'], *f.* Excitation; an excited state.

suscitar [soos-the-tar'], *va.* 1. To excite, to stir up (rebelión). 2. To rouse, to promote vigor, to suscitate, to provoke (conflicto, escándalo), to arouse (sospecha).

suscribir [soos-cre-beer'], *va. V.* SUBSCRIBIR. Still a popular spelling.

suscripción [soos-crip-the-on'], *f. V.* SUBSCRIPCIÓN.

suscriptor, ra [soos-creep-tor', rah], *m. & f.* Subscriber. *V.* SUBSCRIPTOR.

suscrito, ta [soos-cree'-to, tah], *a. & pp. irr.* of SUSCRIBIR.

suscritor, ra [soos-cre-tor', rah], *m. & f. V.* SUSCRIPTOR.

susidio [soo-see'-de-o], *m. (Amer.)* Inquietude, restlessness, sudden dread.

susodicho, cha [soo-so-dee'-cho, chah], *a.* Forementioned, aforesaid.

suspendedor, ra [soos-pen-day-dor', rah], *m. &f.* Suspender.

suspender [soos-pen-derr'], *va.* 1. To suspend, to keep suspended (objeto); to hang. 2. To suspend, to stop (trabajo, pago), to delay, to dally. 3. To surprise, to amaze (pasmar). **Suspender los pagos**, to stop payment. **Suspender hasta más tarde**, to put off till later.

suspensión [soos-pen-se-on'], *f.* 1. Suspension, detention, pause. 2. Hesitation, suspense, uncertainty, indetermination. 3. Admiration, amazement. 4. Suspension, privation, an ecclesiastical censure. **Suspensión de hostilidades**, cessation of hostilities.

suspensivo, va [soos-pen-see'-vo, vah], *a.* That which has the power of suspending. *-pl. (Gram.)* Dotted lines showing that something has been omitted; thus …

suspenso, sa [soos-pen'-so, sah], *pp. irr.* of SUSPENDER. Hung; suspended, suspense (colgado). *-m.* 1. *(Univ.)* Fail, failure. 2. *(LAm.)* Suspense. **Estar en suspenso**, to be in suspense.

suspensorio, ria [soos-pen-so'-re-o, ah], *a.* Suspensory.

suspensorio [soos-pen-so'-re-o], *m.* Suspensory bandage.

suspicacia [soos-pe-cah'-the-ah], *f.* Suspiciousness, jealousy.

suspicaz [soos-pe-cath'], *a.* Suspicious, jealous.

suspicazmente [soos-pe-cath'-men-tay], *adv.* Suspiciously.

suspirador, ra [soos-pee-rah-dor', rah], *m. & f.* One who continually sighs or suspires; one who breathes with difficulty.

suspirar [soos-pe-rar'], *vn.* 1. To sigh, to suspire, to groan. 2. To crave, to desire anxiously. **Suspirar por el mando**, to aspire after command.

suspiro [soos-pee'-ro], *m.* 1. Sigh, suspiration: breath. 2. Hissing of the wind, sharp sound of a piece of glass. 3. *pl.* Lady's-fingers, a variety of cake. 4. *(Bot.) V.* TRINITARIA. **El último suspiro**, the end of a thing; the last gasp or breath.

sustancia [soos-tahn'-the-ah], *f. V.* SUBSTANCIA. **Sustancia** is the more conversational form. **En sustancia**, briefly, summarily. **Sin sustancia**, lacking in substance.

sustancial [soos-tan-the-ahl'], *a. V.* SUBSTANCIAL.

sustancialmente [soos-tan-the-ahl'-men-tay], *adv. V.* SUBSTANCIALMENTE.

sustanciar [soos-tan-the-ahr'], *va. V.* SUBSTANCIAR.

sustancioso, sa [soos-tan-the-oh'-so, sah], *a. V.* SUBSTANCIOSO.

sustantivadamente [soos-tan-te-vah'-dah-men-tay], *adv.* Substantively, as a substantive.

sustantivar [soos-tan-te-var'], *va.* To use adjectives or any other part of speech as substantives.

sustantivo [soos-tan-tee'-vo], *m. (Gram.)* Substantive, noun.

sustantivo, va [soos-tan-tee'-vo], *a.* Substantive, betokening existence.

sustenido [soos-tay-nee'-do], *m.* 1. Spanish step in dancing. 2. *(Mus.) V.* SOSTENIDO.

sustenido, da [soos-tay-nee'-do], *a. (Mus.)* Sharp, a semitone higher.

sustentable [soos-ten-tah'-blay], *a.* Defensible, sustainable.

sustentación [soos-ten-tah-the-on'], *f.* Sustentation, support.

sustentáculo [soos-ten-tah'-coo-lo], *f.* Prop, stay, support.

sustentador, ra [soos-ten-tah-dor', rah], *m. & f.* Sustainer.

sustentamiento [soos-ten-tah-me-en', to], *m.* Sustenance, necessaries of life.

sustentante [soos-ten-tahn'-tay], *pa.* Sustaining.

sustentante [soos-ten-tahn'-tay], *m.* Defender, supporter; he who sustains conclusions in a faculty.

sustentar [soos-ten-tar'], *va.* 1. To sustain, to bear up: to feed or support, to nourish (alimento). 2. To sustain, to assert, to maintain. **Sustentarse del aire**, to live on vain hopes; to live upon the air; to be extravagant.

sustento [sus-ten'-to], *m.* 1. Food, sustenance; maintenance (mantenimiento). 2. Support, the act of supporting, sustaining, or maintaining.

sustillo [soos-teel'-lyo], *m. dim.* A slight fright.

sustitución [soos-te-too-the-on'], *f.* Substitution, surrogation.

sustituidor, ra [soos-te-too-e-dor', rah], *m. & f.* One that substitutes.

sustituir [soos-te-too-eer'], *va.* 1. To substitute, to surrogate. 2. To substitute, to put one thing instead of another. **Tendremos que sustituir al profesor enfermo**, we'll have to substitute the teacher who is ill. *-vn.* To substitute; to deputize. **Sustituir a**, to replace.

sustituto [soos-te-too'-to], *m.* Substitute, one acting with delegated power.

sustituto, ta [soos-te-too'-to], *a. & pp. irr.* of SUSTITUIR. Substitute, surrogate, delegate.

sustituyente [soos-te-too-yen'-tay], *pa.* Substituting.

susto [soos'-to], *m.* Fright, sudden terror. **Caerse del susto**, to be frightened to death.

sustracción [soos-trac-the-on'], *f. V.* SUBSTRACCIÓN.

sustraendo [soos-trac-en'-do], *m.* Subtrahend. *V.* SUBSTRAENDO.

sustraer [soos-trah-err'], *va. V.* SUSTRAER. *(Yo sustraigo, yo sustraiga, sustraje*, from *Sustraer. V.* TRAER.)

sustrato [soos-trah'-to], *m.* Substratum.

susurración [soos-soor-rah-the-on'], *f.* Susurration, a whisper.

susurrador, ra [soo-soor-rah-dor', rahl, *m. & f.* Whisperer.

susurrante [soo-soor-rahn'-tay], *a.* Whispering (viento), murmuring (arroyo), rustling (follaje).

susurrar [soo-soor-rar'], *vn.* 1. To whisper (persona), to divulge a secret. 2. To purl, as a stream: to hum gently, as the air, to murmur (arroyo). *-vr.* To be whispered about, to begin to be divulged.

susurro [soo-soor'-ro], *m.* Whisper (cuchicheo), humming, murmur.

susurrón, na [soo-soor-rone', nah], *a.* Murmuring or whispering secretly. *-m..* Grumbler, malcontent.

sutil [soo-teel'], *a.* 1. Subtle, thin (aire), slender. 2. Subtle (observación), acute, cunning, keen (persona, mente). 3. Light, volatile.

sutileza [soo-te-lay'-thah], *f.* 1. Subtility, thinness, slenderness, fineness (cualidad). 2. Subtlety, cunning, artifice, sagacity: acumen, perspicacity; nicety. 3. One of the four qualities of the glorified body. **Sutileza de manos**, address in handling or operating, sleight of hand: light-fingeredness or nimbleness of a thief.

sutilidad [soo-te-le-dahd'], *f. V.* SUTILEZA.

sutilización [soo-te-le-tha-the-on'], *f.* Subtilization, the act of subtilizing; subtilation.

sutilizador, ra [soo-te-le-thah-dor', rah], *m. & f.* One who subtilizes or attenuates.

sutilizar [soo-te-le-thar'], *va.* 1. To subtilize, to make thin and subtile (reducir). 2. To subtilize, to file, to polish (pulir). 3. To subtilize, to discuss in a profound and ingenious manner.

sutilmente [soo-teel'-men-tay], *adv.* Subtlely, pointedly; nicely, finely, delicately.

sutorio, ria [soo-to'-re-o, ah], *a.* Belonging to the shoemakers trade; sutorial.

sutura [soo-too'-rah], *f.* 1. Seam, suture. *V.* COSTURA. 2. *(Anat.)* Sutura, the close connection of two bones.

suversión [soo-ver-se-on'], *f.* Subversion, ruin, destruction. *V.* SUBVERSIÓN.

suversivo, va [soo-ver-see'-vo, vah], *a.* Subversive. *V.* SUBVERSIVO.

suvertir [soo-ver-teer], *va. V.* SUBVERTIR.

suyo, ya [soo'-yo, yah], *pron. poss.* His (de él), hers (de ella), theirs (de ellos, de ellas), one's; his, her, or its own, one's own or their own. **Es el suyo,** it is his. **Lo suyo,** his. **No es amigo suyo,** he is no friend of hers. *-a & pron.* **Eso es muy suyo,** that's just like him. **Aguantar lo suyo,** to shoulder one's burden. **Cada cual a lo suyo,** it's best to mind one's own business.

suya [soo'-yah], *f.* View, intention, design. **Salirse con la suya,** to put one's wished for end in execution. **Él hizo una de las suyas,** he played one of his pranks.

suyos [soo'-yos], *m. pl.* Their own, near friends, relations, acquaintances, servants.

svástica [es-vahs'-te-cah], *f.* Swastika or swastica.

T

t [tay], twenty-first letter of the alphabet, is pronounced in Spanish as in the English words *tap, true.* It never undergoes the variations it does in English, in *creature, nation,* etc.; consequently, **criatura, patio, tía,** etc., must be pronounced *cre-ah-too'-rah, pah'-te-o, tee'-ah.* **T** is never written double.

taba [tah'-bah], *f.* 1. Ankle-bone, astragalus. 2. Knuckle-bones, a vulgar game with sheep's shanks (juego). **Menear las tabas,** to move about nimbly.

tabacal [tah-bah-cahl'], *m.* Tobacco-field (plantación).

tabacalero, ra [tah-bah-ca-lay'-ro, rah], *a. (Phil. Islands)* Relating to the culture, manufacture, or sale of tobacco; tobacco, as adjective. *-m.* Tobacconist (en tienda), tobacco grower (cultivador), tobacco merchant (comerciante).

tabaco [tah-bah'-co], *m.* 1. *(Bot.)* Tobacco. **Tabaco en polvo,** snuff. **Tabaco en rama** or **de hoja,** Leaf-tobacco. **Tabaco fruticoso,** shrubby tobacco. **Tabaco de pipa,** pipe tobacco. **Tabaco negro,** dark tobacco. 2. Mildew on plants, as wheat, barley, etc. *V.* ROYA. 3. Cigar. 4. *(LAm.)* Reefer, joint (droga). 5. *(Carib.)* Slap (golpe).

tabacoso, sa [tah-bah-coo'-so, sah], *a. (Coll.)* Using much tobacco, snuffy.

tabalada [tah-bah-lah'-dah], *f.* 1. A heavy fall upon the breech. 2. *(Coll.) V.* TABANAZO.

tabalario [tah-bah-lah'-re-o], *m. (Coll.)* The breech, posteriors.

tabalear [tah-bay-lay-ar'], *va.* To rock to and fro. *-vn.* To drum with the finger on a table.

tabaleo [tah-bah-lay'-o], *m.* 1. Drumming of the fingers on the table. 2. *(Coll.)* A spanking.

tabalete [tah-bah-lay'-tay], *m.* A kind of woollen stuff finer than drugget.

tabanazo [ta-bah-nah'-tho], *m. (Coll.)* Blow with the hand.

tabanco [tah-bahn'-co], *m.* 1. Stall for selling eatables to the poor. 2. *(Mex.)* A floor dividing a room into upper and lower apartments. *V.* TAPANCO.

tabanera [tah-bah-nay'-rah], *f.* A place where there are many horse-flies.

tábano [tah'-bah-no], *m. (Ent.)* Gadfly, horse-fly, breeze-fly.

tabanque [tah-bahn'-kay], *m.* Treadle, which serves for putting a potter's wheel in motion.

tabaola [tab-bah-o'-lah], *f.* Confused noise of a crowd. *V.* BATAHOLA.

tabaque [tah-bah'-kay], *m.* 1. A small work-basket. 2. A kind of nail somewhat larger than tacks.

tabaquera [tah-bah-kay'-rah], *f.* 1. A kind of round snuffbox used by common people (para tabaco). 2. Case for a tobacco-pipe (de pipa). 3. Bowl of a tobacco-pipe.

tabaquería [tah-bah-kay-ree'-ah], *f.* 1. Tobacco and snuff shop (tienda). 2. *(Carib.)* Cigar factory (fábrica).

tabaquero [tah-bay-kay'-ro], *m.* Tobacconist (en tienda), tobacco grower (cultivador), tobacco merchant (comerciante).

tabaquillo [tah-bah-keel'-lyo], *m. (Dim.)* 1. A weak sort of tobacco. 2. A small work-basket.

tabaquista [tah-bah-kees'-tah], *com.* One who takes much snuff, or professes to be a judge of tobacco.

tabardete [tah-bar-day'-tay], *m. V.* TABARDILLO.

tabardillo [tah-bar-deel'-lyo], *m.* A burning fever.

tabardina [tah-bar-dee'-nah], *f.* A coarse coat like the *tabardo,* but shorter.

tabardo [tah-bar'-do], *m.* Wide, loose coat of coarse cloth with hanging sleeves, worn by laborers in bad weather, tabard.

tabarra [tah-bahr'-rah], *f.* Nuisance, bore. **Dar la tabarra,** to be a nuisance.

tabasco [tah-bahs'-co], *m.* Tabasco pepper or sauce.

tabaxir [tah-bak-seer'], *m. (Bot.)* Tabasheer, a silicious concretion formed in the joints of the bamboo, opal-like, and used in the East Indies as a medicine.

tábega [tah'-bay-gah], *f.* A small kind of sailing craft.

tabelario, ria [tah-bay-lah'-re-o, ah], *a.* Tabellary, relating to secret balloting by tablets, among the ancient Romans.

tabelión [tah-bay-le-on'], *m.* (Roman history.) *V.* ESCRIBANO.

tabellar [tah-bel-lyar'], *va.* 1. To fold cloth in woollen manufactures, leaving the ends free so that the purchaser may easily mark them. 2. To mark with the maker's name or seal.

taberna [tah-berr'-nah], *f.* 1. A tavern, always applied to a house where wine is retailed. 2. *(Cuba)* Trading on the highways.

tabernáculo [tah-ber-nah'-coo-lo], *m.* 1. Tabernacle; a movable chapel, where the Jews kept the ark of the Testament. 2. Tabernacle, the place where the host is kept.

tabernario, ria [tah-ber-nah'-re-o, ah], *a. (Coll.)* Relating to a tavern.

tabernera [tah-ber-nay'-rah], *f.* Tavern-keeper's wife: woman who keeps a tavern.

tabernería [tah-ber-nay-ree'-ah], *f.* Business of a tavernkeeper.

tabernero [tah-ber-nay'-ro], *m.* Tavern-keeper, one who keeps a liquor shop.

tabernil [tah-ber-neel'], *a. (Coll.)* TABERNARIO.

tabernilla [tah-ber-neel'-lyah], *f. dim.* A small tavern: very often applied to the house where the best wine is retailed.

tabes [tah'-bes], *f. (Med.)* Consumption, tabes.

tabí [tah-bee'], *m.* Tabby, an ancient kind of silken stuff like a heavy taffeta.

tabica [tah-bee'-cah], *f. (Arch.)* Lintel or cross-board put over a vacancy in a wall.

tabicar [tah-be-car'], *va.* 1. To shut up with a wall; to wall up (puerta). 2. To close, to shut up something which ought to be open or free.

tabicón [tah-be-cone'], *m.* A thick wall. *V.* TABIQUE MAESTRO.

tábido, da [tah'-be-do, dah], *a. (Med.)* 1. Tabid, wasted by disease, consumptive. 2. Putrid, corrupted.

tabífico, ca [tah-bee'-fe-co, cah], *a.* Wasting, causing consumption.

tabillas [tah-beel'-lyas], *f. pl.* Husks of clover-seed; husks of radish-seed.

tabinete [tah-bay-nay'-tay], *m.* A silk and cotton stuff much used for making women's footwear.

tabique [tah-bee'-kay], *m.* A thin wall (pared), a partition-wall made of bricks or tiles placed on edge. **Tabique colgado,** a partition raised on a beam. **Tabique maestro,** the chief partition-wall.

tabiteña [tah-be-tay'-nyah], *f. (Prov.)* A kind of pipe or small flute, made of a stalk of wheat.

tabla [tah'-blah], *f.* 1. A board (madera). 2. A similar piece of other material, as of marble or copper. 3. Plain space on clothes. 4. Table, for eating and other purposes. 5. *V.* ARANCEL. 6. *V.* TABLILLA, 4th def. 7. Table of contents prefixed to a book. 8. List, catalogue. 9. A piece of painting on boards or stones. 10. The broadest and most fleshy part of any of the members of the body. 11. Bed or plot of earth in a garden. 12. House where merchandise is registered as sold at market, in order to collect the duty. 13. Plank or board of a ship to escape drowning in shipwreck. 14. Place where meat is weighed and sold: butcher's block. *-pl.* 1. Stages on which actors perform. 2. An equal or drawn game at chess or drafts. 3. Astronomical tables. 4. Tables containing the decalogue. **Tabla de juego,** gambling-house. **Tabla de dibujo,** drawing board. **Tabla de planchar,** ironing board. **Tabla de multiplicar,** multiplication table. **Tabla de tiempos,** *(Comput.)* timing chart.

tablachina [tah-blah-chee'-nah], *f.* Kind of wooden shield or buckler.

tablacho [tah-blah'-cho], *m.* Sluice or flood-gate.

tabladillo [tah-blah-deel'-lyo], *m. dim.* A small stage.

tablado [tah-blah'-do], *m.* 1. Stage, flooring (plataforma). 2. Stage of a theater. 3. Boards or bottom of a bedstead. 4. *(Met.)* Scaffold.

tablaje [tah-blah'-hay], 1. Pile of boards. 2. Gambling or gaming-house; perquisites of the keeper of a gaming-table.

tablajear [tah-blah-hay-ar'], *vn.* To gamble; to be a gambler by profession.

tablajería [tah-blah-hay-ree'-ah], *f.* Gaming, gambling; hire of the gaming-table.

tablajero [tah-blah-hay'-ro], *m.* 1. Scaffold-maker; a carpenter, who builds scaffolds and stages. 2. Keeper of a gaming-house; gambler. 3. Butcher. *V.* CORTADOR. 4. *(Prov.)* Young surgeon walking the hospital.

tablar [tah-blar'], *m.* Division of gardens into plots or beds.

tablazo [tah-blah'-tho], *m.* 1. Blow or stroke with a board. 2. Arm of the sea or of a river.

tablazón [tah-blah-thone'], *f.* 1. Boards or planks put together, so as to form a platform or other piece of construction; lumber. 2. Decks and sheathing of a ship. **Tablazón exterior,** *(Naut.)* outside planks or planking.

tablear [tah-blay-ar'], *va.* 1. To divide a garden into beds or plots (tierra). 2. To make the ground even with a thick board. 3. To hammer bars of iron into plates.

tablero [tah-blay'-ro], *m.* 1. Board planed and fashioned for some purpose. 2. Timber fit for sawing into boards. 3. Dog-nail, a sort of nails used in flooring houses. 4. Stock of a crossbow. 5. **Tablero de ajedrez** or **de damas,** chess or checker-board, draft-board. **Tablero de chaquete** or **tablas reales** or **pretera,** *(Mex.)* backgammon-board, tables. 6. Gambling-house, gaming-table. 7. *(Arch.)* Any plane level part of a building surrounded with a moulding. *V.* ABACO. 8. Shop counter; money-table. **Tablero de conmutadores,** a switch-board.

tableta [tah-blay'-tah], *f.* 1. *(Dim.)* Tablet, a small piece of board (de madera). 2. A tablet or memorandum. 3. Cracknel, a kind of paste hard baked, a sweet mass. 4. *(Med.)* Tablet, pill. 5. Bar (de chocolate), stick. **Tableta para escribir,** tablet, writing-pad.

tableteado [tah-blay-tay-ah'-do], *m.* The crackling sound of boards trod upon.-**Tableteado, da,** *pp.* of TABLETEAR.

tabletear [tah-blay-tay-ar'], *vn.* To move tables or boards, making a noise with them.

tabletera [tah-blay-tay'-rah], *f. & a. V.* TABLERA.

tabletica, [tah-blay-tee'-cah], *f. dim.* 1. A small tablet. 2. Kind of hard pastry cakes.

tablica, ita [tah-blee'-cah, ee'-tah], *f. dim.* A small board or table.

tablilla [tah-bleel'-lyah], *f.* 1. *(Dim.) V.* TABLICA. 2. Kind of sweet cakes; in pharmacy, a tablet or troche. 3. Bands on a billiard or truck table.

tablón [tah-blone'], *m. aug.* 1. Plank, a thick board; beam; stroke. **Tablón de anuncios,** notice board. 2. *(LAm.)* Plot, bed.

tabloncillo [tah-blon-theel'-lyo], *m.* Flooring-board; in some bull-rings, a row of seats at the foot of the guardrail.

tabloza [tah-blo'-thah], *f.* Painter's palette. *V.* PALETA.

tabú [tah-boo'], *a.* Taboo. **Varias palabras tabús,** several taboo words.

tabuco [tah-boo'-co], *m.* Hut, small apartment.

tabuquillo, tabuquito [tah-boo-keel'-lyo], *m. dim.* A small, miserable hut or cottage.

tabulación [tah-boo-lah-the-on'], *f.* Tabbing.

tabulador [tah-boo-lah-dor'], *m.* Tab.

tabular [tah-boo-lar'], *va.* To tabulate.

taburacura [tah-boo-rah-coo'-rah], *f.* A kind of yellow rosin.

taburete [tah-boo-ray'-tay], *m.* Chair without arms. **Taburetes,** forms with backs in the pit of a playhouse.

taburetillo [tah-boo-ray-teel'-lyo], *m. dim.* Drawing room chair for ladies.

taca [tah-cah], *f.* 1. Cupboard, small closet. 2. Each plate of the crucible of a forge.

tacada [tah-cah'-dah], *f.* 1. Act of striking the ball with the cue. 2. *(Prov.) V.* MANCHA.

tacamaca, tacamahaca [tah-cah-ma-ha cah], *f.* 1. Tacamahac, kind of medicinal gum resin from various tropical trees. 2. The balsam-poplar of the United States.

tacañamente [tah-cah-nyah-men'-tay], *a.* Sordidly, meanly.

tacañear [tah-cah-nyay-ar'], *m.* To act the miser; to behave in a wicked or malicious manner.

tacañería [tah-cah-nyay-ree'-ah], *f.* 1. Malicious cunning; low craft. 2. Narrowness of mind; sordid parsimony, closeness, meanness.

tacaño, ña [tah-cah'-nyo, nyah], *a.* 1. Malicious, artful, knavish. 2. Stingy, sordid, close, mean.

tacazo [tah-cah'-tho], *m.* A smart stroke with a cue.

taceta [ta-thay'-tah], *f.* A copper basin or bowl, used in oil-mills.

tacha [tah'-chah], *f.* 1. Fault, defect, imperfection, macula. 2. Crack, fissure, flaw. 3. A sort of small nails, somewhat larger than tasks. **Sano y sin tacha,** sound and without blemish. *V.* TACHO. **Poner tacha,** to make objections.

tachable [tah-chah'-blay], *a.* Exceptionable, liable to objection, censurable.

tachar [tah-char'], *va.* 1. To censure, to tax, to find fault with (criticar); to charge with a fault; to reprehend. **Tachar a alguno de ligero,** to accuse one of levity. 2. To blot, to efface, to scratch out, to dash. 3. To blame, to reprehend. *(Law.)* To impeach. **Tachar testigos,** to object, to refuse, or challenge a witness. 4. To cross out (borrar).

tachero [tah-chay'-ro], *m. (Cuba)* One who works at molasses boilers.

tacho [tah'-cho], *m.* 1. *(Cuba)* A boiler in which molasses is brought to the consistency necessary to convert it into sugar (para azúcar). 2. *(Peru, Bol.)* A narrow-mouthed earthen jar used for heating water.

tachón [tah-chone'], *m.* 1. Stroke or line drawn through a writing to blot it out. 2. Tacks used as an ornament for chairs; lace trimming. 3. A sort of large tacks with gilt or plated heads.

tachonar [tah-cho-nar'], *va.* 1. To adorn with lace trimming. 2. To garnish with tacks or nails with gilt heads. 3. To spot, to sprinkle.

tachonería [tah-cho-nay-ree'-ah], *f.* Ornamental work with gilt-headed tacks.

tachoso, sa [tah-cho'-so, sah], *a.* Faulty, defective, blemished.

tachuela [tah-choo-ay'-lah], *f.* 1. Tack (clavito), a small nail. 2. *(And. Carib.)* Metal pan (recipiente); *(Carib. Mex.)* metal cup. 3. *(CAm. Cono Sur, Mex.)* Short stocky person.

tacica, illa, ita [tah-thee'-cah], *f. dim.* A small cup.

tácitamente [tah'-the-tah-men-tay], *adv.* Silently, secretly; tacitly, informally.

tácito, ta [tah'-the-to, tah], *a.* 1. Tacit, silent. 2. Implied, inferred.

taciturnidad [tah-the-toor-ne-dahd'], *f.* 1. Taciturnity, silence. 2. Melancholy, deep sadness.

taciturno, na [tah-the-toor'-no, nah], *a.* Tacit, silent, reserved; melancholy.

taco [tah'-co], *m.* 1. Stopper (tapón), stopple. 2. Wad (de fusil), wedding. 3. Rammer. 4. Pop-gun (fusil de juguete). 5. *(Coll.)* Volley of oaths. 6. Cue (billar). **Echar tacos**, *(Coll.)* to swear or speak in a great rage. 7. **Tener 16 tacos**, to be 16 (years old). 8. *(Cono Sur, Mex.)* Obstruction, blockage (obstáculo). 9. *(Mex.)* Rolled tortilla, taco. 10. (Cono Sur) Short stocky person (chaparro). 11. *(CAm. Carib.)* Worry (preocupación).

tacómetro [tah-co'-may-tro], *m.* Tachometer.

tacón [tah-cone'], *m.* Heel-piece of a shoe, heel. **Tacones altos**, high heels.

taconazo [tah-co-nah'-tho], *m.* Blow with a shoe-heel.

taconear [tah-co-nay-ar'], *vn. (Coll.)* To make a noise with the heel-piece, to heel; to walk or strut loftily on the heels.

taconeo [tah-co-nay'-o], *m.* Noise made with the heels in dancing steps or in walking.

taconero [tah-co-nay'-ro], *m.* Heelmaker, one who makes wooden heels.

táctica [tahc'-te-cah], *f.* 1. The art of orderly array. 2. *(Mil.)* Tactics. **Táctica naval**, naval tactics.

táctico [tahc'-te-co], *m.* Tactician.

táctil [tak'-till], *a.* Tactual.

tacto [tahc'-to], *m.* 1. Touch, the sense of feeling (sentido). 2. The act of touching or feeling (acto). 3. Handiness, dexterity, certainty, tact. **Ser áspero al tacto**, to feel rough.

tacuacha [tah-coo-ah'-chah], *f. (Cuba)* A trick skillfully done. **Ocular una tacuacha**, to play a very pretty trick.

tadorno [tah-dor'-no], *m. (Orn.)* Shell-drake.

tafallo [ta-fahl'-lyo], *m. (Prov.)* V. CHAFALLO.

tafanario [tah-fa-nah'-re-o], *m. (Coll.)* Breech, notes.

tafetán [tah-fay-tahn'], *m.* Taffeta, a thin silk. **Tafetanes**, flags, colors, standard, ensign. **Tafetán inglés**, court-plaster; sticking plaster.

tafetanillo [tah-fay-ta-neel'-lyo], *m. dim.* A very thin taffeta.

tafia [tah'-fe-ah], *f. (Van.)* Rum.

tafilete [tah-fe-lay'-tay], *m.* Morocco leather.

tafiletear [tah-fe-lay-tay-ar'], *va.* To adorn with morocco leather.

tafiletería [tah-fe-lay-tay-ree'-ah], *f.* Art of dressing morocco leather, and the place where it is dressed.

tafurea [tah-foo-ray'-ah], *f. (Naut.)* A flat-bottomed boat for carrying horses.

tagalo, la [tah-gah'-lo, lah], *a.* Tagal, belonging to the Tagala, the aboriginal Malay race of the Philippine Islands. *-m.* Their language, which has a written form. *-pl.* The Tagala.

tagarino [tay-ga-ree'-no], *m.* Moor who lived among the Christians, and by speaking their language well could scarcely be known.

tagarnillera [tah-gar-neel-lyay'-rah], *f.* An artful, deceitful person.

tagarnina [tah-gar-nee'-nah], *f.* 1. V. CARDILLO. 2. *(Coll.)* A bad cigar. 3. *(And. CAm. Mex.)* Drunkenness.

tagarote [tah-ga-ro'-tay], *m.* 1. *(Orn.)* Hobby. 2. Scribe, clerk, pen-pusher, a writer in an office. 3. A gentleman sponger (hidalgo que vive a expensas de los demás). 4. A tall, ill-shaped person.

tagarotear [tah-ga-ro-tay-ar'], *va. (Coll.)* To write a bold, free, and running hand.

tahalí [tah-ah-lee'], *m.* Shoulder-belt.

taharal [tah-ah-rahl'], *m.* Plantation of tamarisk-trees.

taheño [tah-ay'-nyo], *a.* Having a red beard.

tahona [tah-oh'-nah], *f.* 1. Horse-mill; a corn-mill, worked by mules or horses; crushing-mill. 2. Baker's shop (panadería), where bread is baked and sold: generally applied to places where fine bread is baked.

tahonero [tah-o-nay'-ro], *m.* Miller who directs or manages a horse-mill.

tahulla [tah-ool'-lyah], *m. (Prov.)* A piece of ground, near forty square yards, sown with about two pecks of grain.

tahur [tah-oor'] *m.* Gambler, gamester, cogger.

tahur, ra [tah-oor', rah], *a.* Belonging to gambling or to gamblers.

tahurería [tah-oo-ray-ree'-ah], *f.* Gambling; gaming-house; fraudulent gambling.

taifa [tah'-e-fah], *f.* 1. Faction, party. 2. *(Coll.)* Assemblage of evil life or little sense.

taimado, da [tah-e-mah'-do, dah], *a.* Sly (astuto), cunning, crafty, lazy (perezoso).

taimería [tah-e-may-ree'-ah], *f.* Rascality, viciousness, shameless craftiness.

taita [tah'-e-tah], *f.* A fondling name with which a child calls its father. *-m.* 1. *(Cono Sur)* In direct address, term of respect used before a name. 2. *(Cono Sur)* Tough (matón), bully; quarrelsome person (pendenciero). 3. Pimp (coime).

taja [tah'-hah], *f.* 1. *(Prov.)* A kind of saddle-tree put over packsaddles for carrying burdens. 2. Cut, incision; dissection. 3. Tally, a stick notched in conformity with another stick.

tajada [tah-hah'-dah], *f.* 1. Slice, a cut, a fritter. 2. *(Coll.)* Hoarseness. 3. **Coger una tajada**, to get tight (emborracharse).

tajadera [tah-hah-day'-rah], *f.* 1. Chopping-knife (hacha), chopping-block (tajadero). 2. *(Prov.)* Sluice of a mill-dam. 3. V. CORTAFRÍO. 4. *(Mech.)* Round chisel (cincel), gouge.

tajadero [tah-hah-day'-ro], *m.* Chopping-block for meat; trencher.

tajadilla [tah-hah-deel'-lyah], *f.* 1. A small slice of anything. 2. A small slice of liver, etc., in low chop-houses. 3. *(Prov.)* Bit of confected orange or lemon, sold as a relish by retailers of brandy.

tajado, da [tah-hah'-do, dah], *pp.* of TAJAR. 1. Cut, notched. 2. *(Her.)* Applied to a diagonal bar of a shield.

tajador, ra [tah-hah-dor', rah], *m. &. f.* One who cuts or chops. V. TAJADERO.

tajadura [tah-hah-doo'-rah], *f.* 1. Cut, notch; section. 2. Act and effect of cutting.

tajalápices [tah-ha-lah'-pe-thess], *m.* Pencil sharpener.

tajamanil [tah-hah-mah-neel'], *m. & f.* V. TEJAMANIL.

tajamar [tah-hah-mar'], *m.* 1. *(Naut.)* Cutwater (de puente), stem. 2. Cutwater, edge on the up-stream side of a bridgepier. **Escoras del tajamar**, props of the cutwater.

tajamiento [ta-hah-me-en'-to], *m.* V. TAJADURA.

tajamoco [tah-hah-mo'-co], *m. (Ent.)* Goatchafer.

tajante [tah-hahn'-tay], *m. (Prov.)* Butcher. *-pa.* 1. Cutting. 2. *(Fig.)* Incisive, sharp, emphatic; sharp (distinción). **Es una persona tajante**, he's an incisive person.

tajantemente [tah-han'-tay-men-tay], *adv. (Fig.)* Incisively, sharply, emphatically.

tajaplumas [tah-hah-ploo'-mas], *m.* Penknife. V. CORTAPLUMAS.

tajar [tah-har'], *va.* 1. To cut, to chop, to cut off, to cut out, to hew. 2. To cut a pen.

tajea [tah-hay'-ah], *f.* 1. Furrow or small channel for the irrigation of lands. V. ATARJEA. 2. Culvert, drain under a road.

tajero [tah-hay'-ro], *m.* V. TARJERO.

tajo [tah'-ho], *m.* 1. Cut (acto herida), incision. 2. Cutting of a quill with a penknife. 3. Chopping-block or board. 4. Cutting, reaping, or digging of laborers in a line; cut or opening in a mountain. 5. Cutting edge (filo). 6. As name of a river, see Appendix. **Darse un tajo en el brazo**, to cut one's arm. **Largarse al tajo**, to get off to work.

tajón [tah-hone'], *m.* 1. *(Aug.)* A large block. 2. Chopping-block. 3. A vein of earth or soft stone in a lime-stone quarry.

tajoncillo [tah-hon-theel'-lyo], *m. dim.* A small block.

tajuela, *f.* **tajuelo**, *m.* [tah-hoo-ay'-lah]. A low stool with four feet.

tal [tahl'], *a.* 1. Such, so, as. 2. Equal, similar, of the same form or figure. 3. As much, so great. 4. Used before the names of persons not known, and to determine what is not specified. **Estaba allí un tal Ramirez**, one Ramirez was there. **Tal cual**, middling, so-so; so as it is. **El tal** or **la tal** that person, such a one: generally used contemptuously. **Tal para cual**, every one with his like; also, tit for tat: a Roland for an Oliver. **Tal por cual**, worthless, of no importance; good and bad. **No hay tal**, there is no such thing. **A tal**, with such a condition, under the circumstances. **Con tal que**, provided that. **Otro que tal**, similar, very like, equally worthless. **¿Qué tal?** how's that? how goes it? what do you say? what do you think? **Tal cosa**, such a thing. **Y como tal**, and as such. **Como tal**, just as. **Ella sigue tal cual**, she's so-so.

tala [tah'-lah], *f.* 1. Felling of trees (acto). 2. Destruction, ruin, desolation, havoc. 3. *(Carib.)* Axe (hacha). 4. *(Carib.)* Vegetable garden (huerto). 5. *(Cono Sur)* Grazing (pasto).

talabartero [tah-lah-bar-tay'-ro], *m.* Belt-maker.

talabarto [tah-lah-bar'-to], *m.* Swored-belt.

talabricense [tah-lah-bre-then'-say], *a.* Of Talavera. -*n.* A Talaveran.

talador, ra [tah-lah-dor', rah], *m & f.* Destroyer, one who lays waste.

taladrador, ra [tah-lah-drah-dor', rah], *m. & f.* Borer, piercer, penetrater. -*f.* Drill.

taladrar [tah-lah-drar'], *va.* 1. To bore, to perforate. 2. To pierce, to penetrate the ear. 3. To penetrate into or comprehend a difficult point. **Un ruido que taladra los oídos**, an ear-splitting noise.

taladrillo [tah-lah-dreel'-lyo], *m. dim.* A small borer, little bore.

taladro [tah-lah'-dro], *m.* 1. Drill (herramienta). 2. Auger. 3. Drill hole (agujero).

talaje [tah-lah'-hay], *m. (Sp. Am.)* 1. Pasturage. 2. Grazing.

talamera [tah-lah-may'-rah], *f.* Tree used for ensnaring birds.

talamite [tah-lah-mee'-tay], *m.* A galley rower.

tálamo [tah'-lah-mo], *m.* 1. Pre-eminent place where brides celebrated their weddings and received congratulations. 2. Bride-chamber, bridal bed.

talanquera [tah-lan-kay'-rah], *f.* 1. Parapet, breast-work of pales. 2. Defence, a spot which defends from danger.

talante [tah-lahn'-tay], *m.* 1. Mode or manner of performing anything. 2. Appearance, aspect (aspecto). 3. Will (humor), pleasure, disposition. **Eastar de buen talante**, to be ready or in a good dispotion to do anything. **Hacer algo de buen talante**, to do something willingly.

talar [tah-lar'], *va.* 1. To fell trees (árboles). 2. To desolate, to lay waste a country.

talar [tah-lar'], *a.* Applied to long robes reaching to the heels.

talares [tah-lah-rays]. *m. pl.* The wings on the heels of Mercury; talaria.

talavera [tah-lah-vay'-rah], *f.* Earthenware manufactured in Talavera.

talaveran, na [tah-lah-vay-rah'-no, nah], *a.* Of Talavera.

talco [tahl'-co], *m.* 1. Mica, a laminated translucent mineral. 2. A class of silicates. 3. Talcum powder.

talcualillo, lla [tal-coo-ah-leel'-lyo, lyah], *a. (Coll.)* 1. Somewhat beyond mediocrity. 2. Somewhat improved in health: said of the sick.

tálea [tah'-lay-ah], *f.* Stockade or palisade which the Romans made use of in their camps.

taled [tah-led'], *m.* A kind of woollen amice with which the Jews cover their heads and necks in their religious ceremonies.

talega [tah-lay'-gah], *f.* 1. Bag, a wide short sack (bolsa). 2. Sack containing 1,000 dollars in silver. **Una** or **dos talegas**, *(Met.)* one or two thousand dollars. 3. A bagful. 4. *(Coll.)* Sins which a penitent sinner is going to confess. 5. Bag for the hair. 6. *(Coll.)* Knowledge which one has acquired

previous to attending a public school. **talegazo** [tah-lay-gah'-tho], *m.* Stroke or blow with a full bag.

talego [tah-lay'-go], *m.* 1. Bag or sack made of coarse sackcloth (bolsa grande). **Tener talego**, to have money. 2. A clumsy, awkward fellow.

talegón [tah-lay-gone'], *m. aug.* of TALEGA or TALEGO.

taleguilla [tah-lay-geel'-lyah], *f.* 1. A small bag. **Taleguilla de la sal**, *(Coll.)* daily expenditure, money spent each day. 2. The breeches that bullfighters wear.

taleguito [tah-lay-gee'-to], *m. dim.* of TALEGO.

talentada [tah-len-tah'-dah], *f. (Prov.)* Will, propensity, inclination

talento [tah-len'-to], *m.* 1. Talent, ancient weight or money of different value. 3. Talent, abilities, endowments, or gifts of nature; ingenuity, genius, accomplishments: in the sense of abilities it is commonly used in the plural.

talentoso, sa [tah-len-to'-so, sah], *a.* Able, ingenious, talented.

talero [tah-lay'-ro], *m.* Short whip.

talidad [tah-le-dahd'], *f.* That which determines a thing to be included generically or specifically in another.

talión [tah-le-on'], *m.* Retaliation, requital.

talionar [tah-le-o-nar'], *va.* To retaliate, to require.

talismán [tah-lis-mahn'], *m.* 1. Talisman, a magical character. 2. Doctor of the Mohammedan law.

talla [tahl'-lyah], *f.* 1. Raised work, cut in wood or stone, sculpture (escultura). **Obra de talla**, carved work. 2. Dues paid by vessels to the lord of the manor. 3. Hansom, or reward for the capture of some noted criminal. 4. *(Prov.)* Jug with water put into the air to cool, or suspended in a draught. 5. Stature, size. 6. Operation of cutting for the stone. 7. *(Mil.)* A wooden instrument for measuring a man's height. **Poner talla**, to offer a reward for the apprehension of a criminal. **Camisas de todas las tallas**, shirts in all sizes. **No dio la talla**, he didn't measure up, he wasn't up to it.

tallado, da [tal-lyah'-do, dah], *a. & pp.* of TALLAR. Cut, chopped, carved, engraved. **Bien** or **mal tallado**, of a good or bad figure. -*m.* Carving; sculpting; engraving. **Tallado en madera**, woodcarving.

tallador [tal-lyah-dor'], *m.* 1. Engraver. 2. Carver. 3. Diesinker.

talladura [tal-lyah-doo'-rah], *f.* Engraving.

tallar [tal-lyar'], *m.* Grove or forest of fire-wood fit for cutting.

tallar [tal-lyar'], *a.* Applied to wood fit for cutting or for fuel.

tallar [tal-lyar'], *va.* 1. To cut, to chop. 2. To carve in wood, to engrave on copper-plate. 3. To charge with dues or imposts. 4. To show all the cards in one's hand at basset. -*vn. (Cono Sur)* To chat (chismear); to gossip.

tallarín [tal-lyah-reen'], *m.* A kind of thin paste.

tallarola [tal-lyah-ro'-lah], *f.* Iron plate used for cutting the silk in velvet looms.

tallazo [tal-lyah'-tho], *m. aug.* of TALLE and TALLO.

talle [tahl'-lyay], *m.* 1. Shape, form, figure, proportion of the human body. 2. Waist, the middle of the body. 3. Mode or manner of performing a thing. 4. Fit of clothes (número). 5. Genus, species, class. **Largo de talle**, *(Coll.)* long drawn out. 6. Look, appearance (aspecto).

tallecer [tal-lyay-therr'], *vn.* To shoot, to sprout.

taller [tal-lyerr'], *m.* 1. Workshop, office, laboratory. 2. School, academy, a seminary of arts and sciences. 3. Ancient coin. **Taller de máquinas**, machine shop. **Taller de reparaciones**, repair shop.

talleta [tal-lyay'-tah], *f. (Amer.)* A paste of almonds, nuts, and honey. V. ALFAJOR.

tallista [tah-lyees'-tah], *m.* Carver in wood, engraver.

tallo [tahl'-lyo], *m.* 1. Shoot, sprout, stem which bears leaves, etc. 2. *(And.)* Cabbage (repollo). 3. *(LAm.)* Vegetables, greens. 4. *(Culin.)* Crystallized fruit.

talludo, da [tal-lyoo'-do, dah], *a.* 1. Grown into long stalks. 2. Tall, slender. 3. Callous, hardened in vicious habits. 4.

Overgrown, grown to seed. 5. *(CAm. Mex.)* **Es un viejo talludo**, he's old but there's life in him yet.

talluelo [tal-lyoo-ay'-lo], *m. dim.* of TALLO.

talmente [tahl'-men-tay], *adv. (Coll.)* In the same manner.

talmud [tal-mood'], *m.* Talmud, a book which contains the doctrines and ceremonies of the law of Moses.

talmúdico, ca [tal-moo'-de-co, cah], *a.* Talmudic, relating to the Talmud.

talmudista [tal-moo-dees'-tah], *m.* Professor or interpreter of the Talmud.

talo [tah'-lo], *m.* A kind of cake of maize flour.

talón [tah-lone'], *m.* 1. The heel. 2. Heel-piece of a shoe (de zapato). 3. *(Arch.)* Cymatium, ogee fluting. 4. *(Com.)* Check (cheque), sight draft, voucher. 5. The stub of such a draft. 7. A coupon or check for baggage (en Amér. contraseña). **Levantar los talones**, to take to one's heels. **Dar con el talón en el fondo**, *(Naut.)* to touch ground with the stern-post.

talonario [tah-lo-nah'-re-o], *m.* Stubs, coupons. **Talonario de cheques**, check book.

talonear [tah-lo-nay-ar'], *vn.* To be nimble, to walk fast. *-va. (LAm.)* To dig one's heels into (caballo).

talonesco [tah-lo-nes'-co], *a. (Coll.)* Relating to the heels.

talpa, talparia [tahl'-pah], *f. (Coll.)* Abscess in the pericranium, tumor in the head.

talque [tahl'-kay], *m.* A kind of argillaceous earth, of which crucibles are made.

talus, talud [tah'-loos, tah-lood'], *m.* Talus, a slope on the outside part of a wall or rampart.

talvina [tal-vee'-nah], *f.* A kind of milk, extracted from several seeds, of which porridge and dumplings are made.

tamal [tah-mahl'], *m.* 1. *(Amer.)* A kind of small dumpling, made of Indian meal, stuffed with minced meat or other eatables, and boiled in the husk of the Indian corn. 2. (Honduras) A bundle of sarsaparilla. 3. *(LAm.)* Fraud (trampa), trick, set a trap.

tamalero, ra [tah-mah-lay'-ro, rah], *m & f. (Mex.)* Tamalseller.

tamándoa [tah-mahn'-do-ah], *f.* Ant-eater of Peru.

tamañamente [ta-mah-nyah-men'-tay], *adv.* As great as, tantamount.

tamañico, ica, illo, illa, ito, ita [tah mah-nyee'-co], *a.* Very small.

tamañito, ta [tah-mah-nyee'-to, tah], *m.* 1. Fearful, intimidated. 2. Abashed, ashamed.

tamaño [tah-mah'-nyo], *m.* Size, shape, bulk, stature, magnitude. **Tamaño de bolsillo**, pocket-size. **Tener el mismo tamaño**, to be the same size.

tamaño, ña [tah-mah'-nyo, nyah], *a.* 1. Showing the size, shape, or bulk or anything. 2. Very little.

tamañuelo, la [tah-mah-nyoo-ay'-lo, lah], *a. dim.* Small, slender, little.

támaras [tah'-ma-ras], *f. pl.* 1. Clusters of dates. 2. Chips, faggots of brush-wood.

tamarindo [tah-ma-reen'-do], *m. (Bot.)* Tamarind-tree and fruit.

tamarisco, tamariz [tah-ma-rees'-co, tah-mah-reeth'], *m. (Bot.)* Tamarisk-shrub.

tamarizquito, tamarrusquito, ta [tah-ma-rith-kee'-to, tah-mar-roos-kee'-to, tah], *a. (Coll.)* Very small.

tamba [tahm'-bah], *f. (Low.)* Blanket of a bed.

tambalear, tambalearse [tam-bah-lay-ar'], *vn. & vr.* To stagger, to waver.

tambaleo [tam-bah-lay'-o], *m.* Reeling, staggering.

tambanillo [tam-bah-neel'-lyo], *m.* A raised ornament on the angles of buildings.

tambarillo [tam-bah-reel'-lyo], *m.* Chest or trunk with an arched cover.

tambero, ra [tam-bay'-ro, rah], *m. & f. (Peru)* Inn-keeper (fondista); dairy farmer (granjero).

también [tam-be-en'], *conj. & adv.* Also, too, likewise; as well, moreover. **Y bebe también**, and he drinks as well.

tambo [tahm'-bo], *m. (Peru, Amer.)* Inn.

tambor [tam-bor'], *m.* 1. A drum. 2. Drummer (persona). **Baquetas del tambor**, drumsticks. **Tambor mayor**, drummajor. 3. *(Mil.)* Small inclosure as a screen to the gates of a fortress. 4. A small room, made in another room by partition-walls, tambor or wooden screen at the doors of churches. 5. *(Arch.)* Tambor, tholus, keystone of a vaulted roof or cupola. 6. Barrel, arbor, of a watch or clock any cylindrical part of machinery. Hence further: rolling-pin, band-pulley, tumbler, wheel-house, paddle-box. 7. Tambor-frame for embroidering silk, muslin, or linen. **Tambor del oído**, ear drum. 8. *(Carib. Mex.)* Burlap (tela).

tambora [tam-bo'-rah], *f.* Bass drum.

tamborete [tam-bo-ray'-tay], *m. dim.* 1. Timbrel. 2. *(Naut.)* Cap of the mast-head, moorshead.

tamboril [tam-bo-reel'], *m.* Tambourine, tabor, tabret, a kind of drum beaten in villages on festive occasions.

tamborilada [tam-bo-re-lah'-dah], *f. (Coll.)* Fall on the breech; a slap on the face or shoulders (espaldarazo).

tamborilazo [tam-bo-re-lah'-tho], *m.* Blow or fal on the breech.

tamborilear [tam-bo-re-lay-ar'], *vn.* 1. To drum (con los dedos); to beat (el tamboril). 2. To cry up, to be loud in one's praise. 3. *(Print.)* To plane or level types.

tamborilero [tam-bo-re-lay'-ro], *m.* Drummer.

tamborilete [tam-bo-re-lay'-tay], *m. (Typ.)* Planer, a smooth wooden block used for levelling a form of type.

tamborilillo [tam-bo-re-leel'-lyo], *m.* A small tambourine.

tamborinero [tam-bo-re-nay'-ro], *m. V.* TAMBORILERO.

tamboritear [tam-bo-re-tay-ar'], *pa. V.* TAMBORILEAR.

tamboritero [tam-bo-re-tay'-ro], *m. V.* TAMBORILERO.

tamborito [tam-bo-ree'-to], *m.* National dance and musical rhythm of Panama.

tamborón [tam-bo-rone'], *m.* A large drum.

tamén, tamene [tah-mayn', tah-may'-nay], *m. (Mex.)* Indian porter or carrier.

tamerlán [tah-mer-lahn'], *m.* Emperor of the Tartars.

tamiz [tah-meeth'], *m.* A fine sieve, made of silk or hair.

tamo [tah'-mo], *m.* 1. Down which falls from woollen or line in weaving. 2. Dust in corn. 3. Mould under beds on dusty floors.

tamojo [tah-mo'-ho], *m. (Bot.) V.* BARBILLA TAMOJO.

tampoco [tam-po'-co], *adv.* Neither, nor, not either. **Yo tampoco lo compré**, I didn't buy one either. **Ni yo tampoco**, nor did I. '**Yo no fui**' '**Yo tampoco**', 'I didn't go', 'neither did I'.

tamujo [tah-moo'-ho], *m. (Bot.)* Buckthorn, box-thorn.

tan [tahn'], *m.* Sound of the tamborine, or of anything like that.

tan [tahn'], *adv.* So, so much, as well, as much. **Tan grande**, so great, very much. **Tan rápido**, so fast. **A es tan feo como B**, A is as ugly as B. **No te esperaba tan pronto**, I wasn't expecting you so soon. *V.* TANTO.

tanate [tah-nah'-tay], *m. (Mex.)* A seron made of hide, to transport articles; in some parts a basket of particular form, and also a *pita* bag.

tanatero [tah-nah-tay'-ro], *m. (Mex.)* The miner who takes out the ore, and carries it in the *tanate*.

tanato [tah-nah'-to], *m. (Chem.)* Tannate, a salt of tannic acid.

tanca [tahn'-cah], *f.* A viscous matter with which bees daub their hives before they begin to work at the honey-comb; bee-glue.

tanda [tanh'-dah], *f.* 1. Turn, rotation. 2. Task, something to be done imposed by another. 3. Certain number of persons or cattle employed in a work (turno). 4. Any undetermined number or quantity: generally applied to a number of stripes and lashes. 5. Series (serie). 6. Game (billar); innings (béisbol). 7. *(LAm. Teat.)* Show, performance; *(Cono Sur)* farce (farsa); *(Cono Sur)* musical (comedia musical).

tanga [tanh'-gah], *f.* Tanga, G-string.

tanganillas (En) [tan-gah-neel'-lyas], *adv.* Waveringly, in danger of falling.

tanganillo [tan-gah-neel'-lyo], *m. dim.* A small prop or stay.

tángano [tahn'-gah-noo], *m.* Hob, a boys game; bone or stone used in this game.

tangencia [tan-hen'-the-ah], *f.* Tangency, the state of touching

tangente [tan-hen'-tay], *a. (Geom.)* Tangent. **Salirse por la tangente**, to go off at a tangent.

tangerina [tan-hay-ree'-nah], *f.* Tangerine.

tangibilidad [tan-he-be-le-dahd'], *f.* Tangibility.

tangible [tan-hee'-blay], *a.* Tactile, susceptible of touch.

tangidera [tan-he-day'-rah], *f. (Naut.)* Cable.

tango [tahn'-go], *m.* Tango, Argentine musical rhythm and dance.

tanino [tah-nee'-no], *m. (Chem.)* Tannin, tannic acid, gallotannic acid.

tanor, ra [tah-nor', rah], *a.* A Philippine Malay who served as domestic to the Spaniards.

tanoría [tah-no-ree'-ah], *f.* Domestic service by the Philippines to the Spaniards.

tanque [tahn'-kay], *m.* 1. Vat, large trough, tank. 2. A small pool, a pond. 3. *(Mil.)* Tank. 4. Beeswax.

tanqueta [tan-kee'-tah], *f.* Small tank.

tanquía [tan-kee'-ah], *f.* An ointment for making hair fall off.

tantalato [tan-ta-lah'-to], *m. (Chem.)* Tantalate, a salt of tantalic acid.

tantálico [tan-tah'-le-co], *a.* Tantalic, an acid from tantalium.

tantalita, *f.* **tantalito**, *m.* [tan-ta-lee'-tah, to], *f.* Tantalite, a mineral composed chiefly of ferrous tantalate.

tántalo [tahn'-tah-lo], *m. (Min.)* Tantalum, a metal.

tantarantán [tan-tah-rah-tahn'], *m.* 1. Rub-a-dub-dub, redoubled beat of a drum (tambor).

tanteador [tan-tay-ah-dor'], *m.* Measurer, calculator, marker.

tantear [tan-tay-ar'], *va.* 1. To measure, to proportion. 2. To mark the game with counters. 3. To consider carefully, to scrutinize. 4. *(Art.)* To sketch the outlines of a design. 5. To keep the score of. 6. *(CAm. Mex.)* To lie in wait for (acechar). 7. *(Mex.)* To swindle (estafar); to make a fool of (burlarse). **Tantear si la superficie está bien segura**, to test the surface to see if it is safe.

tanteo [tan-tay'-o], *m.* 1. Computation, calculation, average. 2. Number of counters for marking a game. 3. Prudent judgment of an affair. 4. Outlines of a picture.

tantico, tantillo [tan-tee'-co, tan-teel'-lyo], *m.* Small sum or quantity.

tanto [tahn'-to], *m.* 1. A certain sum or quantity. 2. Copy of a writing. 3. Counter, mark of a game. **Tanto por ciento**, percentage. **Por un tanto alzado**, for a lump sum.

tanto, ta [tahn'-to], *a.* 1. So much, as much; very great. 2. Odd, something over a determined number. **Veinte y tantos**, twenty and upwards. **Tiene tanto dinero como yo**, he has as much money as I have. **Es uno de tantos**, it's one of many.

tanto [tahn'-to], *adv.* 1. So, in such a manner. 2. A long time. **Tanto más o menos**, so much more or less. **Tanto que**, as much as. **Tanto mejor**, so much the better. **Tanto peor**, so much the worse. **Tanto monta**, it is as good as the other; it is all the same. **Tanto más cuanto**, thereabouts, more or less. **En tanto** or **entre tanto**, in the mean time. **Tanto por tanto**, at the same price; upon a par. **Tantos a tantos**, equal numbers. **Por el tanto** or **por lo tanto**, (1) for that same reason; on that ground. (2) For the same price. **Por tanto** or **por lo tanto**, therefore, for the reasons expressed. **La mitad y otro tanto**, the half and as much more. **Tanto uno como otro**, both one and the other; both of them.

tañedor, ra [tah-nyay-dor', rah], *m. & f.* Player on a musical instrument.

tañer [tah-nyerr'], *va.* To play an instrument harmoniously.

tañido, da [tah-nyee'-do, dah], *pp.* of TAÑER. Played; touched.

tañido [tah-nyee'-do], *m.* Tune: sound: clink.

tao [tah'-o], *m.* Badge worn by officers of the orders of St. Anthony and St. John.

tapa [tah'-pah], *f.* 1. Lid (de caja, olla), cover, cap (de botella). 2. Horny part of a hoof. 3. Heel-piece of a shoe (de zapato). 4. Sluicegate (de canal). 5. *(Mex. Aut.)* Hubcap. 6. *(Carib.)* Commission (comisión). **Tapa de los sesos**, top of the skull. **Tapa de bomba**, *(Naut.)* the hood of the pump.

tapaagujeros [tah-pa-ah-goo-hay'-ros], *m. (Coll.)* 1. A clumsy mason. 2. One who supplants another in any matter; a makeshift.

tapabalazo [tah-pah-bah-lah'-tho], *m. (Naut.)* Shot-plug.

tapaboca [tah-pah-bo'-cah], *m. (Coll.)* 1. Slap on the mouth (manotada). 2. Any action or observation which interrupts the conversation, and cuts one short. 3. Choke-pear; any sarcasm by which another is put to silence. 4. *(Mil.)* Tampion, tamkin.

tapacubos [tah-pah-coo'-bos], *m.* Hubcap (de automovil.)

tapaculo [tah-pah-coo'-lo], *m.* Fruit of the dog-rose.

tapada [tah-pah'-dah], *f.* A woman concealing her face under a thick veil or Spanish mantilla to avoid being known.

tapadera [tah-pah-day'-rah], *f.* 1. A loose lid or movable cover of a pot or other vessel (tapa); covercle. 2. The leather cover of the stirrup of a Mexican saddle.

tapadero [tah-pah-day'-ro], *m.* A large stopper or stopple.

tapadijo [tah-pah-dee'-ho], *m.* Evasion, subterfuge, blind term. *(Neol.)*

tapadillo [tah-pah-deel'-lyo], *m.* 1. The act of a woman's covering herself with her veil or mantle, that she may not be seen. 2. *(Prov.) V.* COBERTIZO. 3. A certain flute-stop of an organ.

tapadizo [tah-pah-dee'-tho], *m.* 1. Action of women hiding the face with a mantle. 2. *(Prov.) V.* COBERTIZO.

tapado [tah-pah'-do], *m. (Arg., Ch.)* 1. Spotless horse or mare. 2. *(Col. & Hond.)* Indian barbecue 3. Ladies' wrap or cape. 4. *(And. Cono Sur)* Buried treasure (tesoro). *-a.* 1. *(Cono Sur)* Animal of one color. 2. *(And.)* Lazy (vago).

tapador, ra [tah-pah-dor', rah], *m. & f.* 1. One who stops or shuts up, coverer. 2. Plug, stopper, stopple.

tapadura [tah-pah-doo'-rah], *f.* Act of stopping, covering, or hiding.

tapafogón [tah-pah-fo-gone'], *m.* Cap of a gun, which covers the venthole.

tapafunda [tah-pah-foon'-dah], *f.* Holster-cover of pistols.

tapajuntas [tah-pah-hoon'-tahs], *m.* 1. Flashing joint (en construcción). 2. Molding on window or doorframe.

tápalo [tah'-pah-lo], *m. (Mex.)* Shawl. *V.* CHAL.

tapamiento [tah-pah-me-en'-to], *m.* Act of stopping or covering.

tapaojos [tah-pah-o'-hos], *m. (Amer.)* A bandage for the eyes of horses or mules (venda).

tapar [tah-par'], *va.* 1. To stop up, to cover, to put under cover, to choke up, to obstruct, to occlude. 2. To conceal (derrota), to hide, to cover up (cara), to mantle, to hoodwink, to dissemble. 3. *(And.)* To crush (aplastar); to rumple (chafar). 4. *(And.)* To abuse (insultar). **Tapar la boca**, to stop one's mouth. **Tapar una abertura de agua**, *(Naut.)* to stop or fother a leak. **El árbol tapa el sol a la ventana**, the tree keeps the sunlight off the window.

tapara [tah-pah'-rah], *f. (Sp. Am.)* Calabash.

tapara [tah'-pah-rah], *f.* Caper.

taparo [tah-pah'-ro], *m.* 1. *(Sp. Am.)* Calabash tree. 2. Oneeyed person (tuerto).

taparrabo [tah-par-rah'-bo], *m.* 1. Breechclout, loincloth. 2. Swim trunks.

tapatío, tía [tah-pah-tee'-o, ah], *a. & m. & f* Name applied to persons and things from Guadalajara, Mexico.

tapeo [tah-pay'-o], *m.* **Ir de tapeo**, *(Esp.)* to go round the bars.

tapetado, da [tah-pay-tah'-do, dah], *a.* Of a dark-brown or blackish color.

tapete [tah-pay'-tay], *m.* 1. A small floor-carpet or rug. 2. A cover for a table or chest. **Estar sobre el tapete**, to be on the tapis (discusión).

tapia [tah'-pe-ah], *f.* 1. Mud-wall. 2. Massive wall. **Sordo como una tapia**, stone-deaf.

tapiador [tah-pe-ah-dor'], *m.* Builder of mud-walls.

tapial [tah-pe-ahl'], *m.* Mould for making mud-walls.

tapiar [tah-pe-ar'], *va.* 1. To stop up with a mud-wall. 2. To stop a passage, to obstruct a view.

tapicería [tah-pe-thay-ree'-ah], *f.* 1. Tapestry (arte). 2. Office in the royal palace where the tapestry and carpets are kept. 3. Shop where tapestries are sold (tienda).

tapicero [tah-pe-thay'-ro], *m.* One who makes tapestry. **Tapicero mayor**, Tapestry-keeper in a palace.

tapiería [tah-pe-ay-ree'-ah], *f.* Series of mud-walls.

tapines, tapinos [tah-pee'-nes, tah-pee'-nos], *m. pl. (Naut.)* Stoppers for ventholes.

tapinosis [tah-pe-no'-sis], *f. (Rhet.)* Figure where, with words and low phrases, any great thing is explained.

tapioca [tah-pe-o'-cah], *f.* Tapioca, the prepared starch of the cassava.

tapir [tah-peer'], *m.* Tapir, a pachydermatous mammal, having a sort of proboscis. It lives in forests and by rivers. Found in Malaysia and in South America. Syn. DANTA, ANTA, GRAN BESTIA.

tapirujarse [tah-pe-roo-har'-say], *vr.* V. TAPERUJARSE.

tapisote [tah-pe-so'-tay], *m. (Bot.)* Yellow-flowered pea.

tapiz [tah-peeth'], *m.* 1. Tapestry (de pared). 2. Grass-plot adorned with flowers.

tapizar [tah-pe-thar'], *va.* To hang with tapestry (pared); to upholster (mueble), to cover; to upholster (coche); to carpet (suelo).

tapizar [tah-pe-thar'], *m.* Cork, plug, bung.

tapón [tah-pon'], *a. (CAm. Cono Sur)* Tailless. -*m.* 1. Stopper (de botella), cap, top; cork (corcho); plug, bung, wad; *(Med.)* tampon; *(Mex. Elec.)* Fuse. 2. Chubby person (persona). 3. Obstacle (estorbo). 4. Traffic jam.

taponar [tah-po-nahr'], *va.* To stopper (botella), to put the cup on; to plug (tubo); to block; *(Med.)* to tampon.

tapsia [tap'-se-ah], *f. (Bot.)* Deadly carrot.

tapujarse [tah-poo-har'-say], *vr.* To muffle oneself in a cloak or veil.

tapujo [tah-poo'-ho], *m.* 1. Muffle, a cover for the face. 2. False pretext, subterfuge (subterfugio), feigned excuse, secrecy (secreto). **Andar con tapujos**, to behave deceitfully.

taque [tah'-kay], *m.* 1. Noise made by a door on being locked. 2. Bang or rap given to it in order to call someone.

taquera [tah-kay'-rah], *f.* Rack or stand for billiard-cues.

taquigrafía [tah-ke-grah-fee'-ah], *f.* Tachygraphy, shorthand, the art of quick writing. Syn. ESTENOGRAFÍA.

taquigráfico, ca [tah-ke-grah'-fe-co, cah], *a.* Tachygraphic, shorthand.

taquígrafo [tah-keeh-grah'-fo], *m.* Short-hand writer.

taquilla [tah-keel'-lyah], *f.* 1. Ticket office, box office. **Éxito de taquilla**, box-office hit, dramatic success. 2. Letter file or cabinet for documents in offices. 3. *(CAm.)* Bar; liquor store (tienda). 4. *(And. CAm. Cono Sur)* Tack (clavo).

taquillero, ra [tah-keel-lyay'-ro, rah], *a. (Th.)* Relating to box office. **Éxito taquillero**, box-office hit. -*m. & f.* Ticket seller.

taquímetro [tah-kee'-may-tro], *m.* Tachymeter, kind of theodolite for surveying.

taquín [tah-keen'], *m.* V. CARNICOL.

taquinero [tah-ke-nay'-ro], *m. (Prov.)* A person who plays a game of knuckle-bones.

tara [tah'-rah], *f.* 1. *(Com.)* Tare, an allowance made to a purchaser of the weight of the box, cask, sack, etc., in which goods are packed. 2. Tally, a stick on which the weight is marked.

tarabita [tah-rah-bee'-tah], *f. (S. A.)* Rope bridge. V. PUENTE DE CIMBRIA. Called *oroya* in Peru.

taracea [tah-rah-thay'-ah], *f.* 1. Marquetry, checkered work, inlaid work. 2. *(Coll.)* Patchwork of cloth or linen.

taracear [tah-rah-thay-ar'], *va.* To inlay, to make inlaid work.

tarado [tah-rah'-do], *a.* 1. Damaged, defective, imperfect; maimed (animal). 2. *(Cono Sur)* Physically impaired (mutilado), crippled; odd (raro), eccentric. 3. *(LAm.)* Stupid (idiota); crazy (loco).

tarafes [tah-rah'-fes], *m. pl. (Cant.)* Dice.

taragallo [tah-rah-gahl'-lyo], *m.* Clog, suspended from the necks of beasts, to prevent them from running away.

taraja [tah-rah'-hah], *f. (S. A.)* Screw plate.

tarambana [tah-ram-bah'-nah], *com.* Giddy, unstable person; madcap.

tarando [tah-rahn'-do], *m.* Reindeer.

tarángana [tah-rahn'-gah-nah], *f.* V. MORCILLA.

tarantela [tah-ran-tay'-lah], *f.* A powerful, impressive tune, such as is played for the bite of the tarantula.

tarántula [ta-rahn'-too-lah], *f.* Tarantula, a kind of venomous spider.

tarantulado, da [tah-ran-too-lah'-do, dah], *a.* V. ATARANTADO.

tarará [tah-ra-rah'], *f.* Sound of a trumpet, as a signal for action.

tararear [tah-rah-ray-ar'], *va. & vn.* 1. To sound the trumpet. 2. To chuck under the chin. 3. *(Coll.)* To sing a song using the word *tarara* instead of the proper words.

tararira [tah-rah-ree'-rah], *f. (Coll.)* Noisy mirth. -*com.* Noisy person.

tarasca [tah-rahs'-cah], *f.* 1. Figure of a serpent formerly borne in the procession of Corpus Christi day, indicating the triumph of Christ over the devil. 2. Crooked, ugly, ill-natured, licentious, and impudent woman. 3. Carnival dragon (monstruo). 4. *(And. CAm. Cono Sur)* Big mouth (boca).

tarascada [tah-ras-cah'-dah], *f.* 1. Bite (mordisco), a wound with the teeth. 2. *(Coll.)* A pert, harsh answer (réplica).

tarascar [tah-ras-car'], *va.* To bite.

tarascón [tah-ras-cone'], *m. aug.* of TARASCA.

taratántara [tah-ra-tahn'-tah-rah], *f.* A word imitative of the sound of a trumpet. *(Latin.)*

taravilla [tah-ra-veel'-lyah], *f.* 1. A mill-clack. 2. A kind of wooden latch for doors or windows; sneck. 3. A person who prattles much and fast.

taray [tah-rah'-e], *m. (Bot.)* Tamarisk, an evergreen shrub.

tarazar [tah-ra-thar'], *va.* 1. To bite. 2. To molest, to harass, to mortify.

tarazón [tah-ra-thone'], *m.* A large slice, especially of fish.

tarazoncillo [tah-ra-thon-theel'-lyo], *m. dim.* A small slice.

tarbea [tar-bay'-ah], *f.* A large hall.

tardador, ra [tar-dah-dor', rah], *m. & f.* Delayer, deferrer, tarrier.

tardanza [tar-dahn'-thah], *f.* Slowness (lentitud), delay (demora), tardiness, detention; dalliance, lingering.

tardar [tar-dar'], *vn. & vr.* To delay (retardarse), to put off, to take, to dally. **A más tardar**, at the latest, no later than. **Aquí tardan mucho**, they are very slow here. **Escribiré sin tardar**, I'll write without delay. **Tardará dos horas**, he'll take two hours.

tarde [tar'-day], *f.* 1. Afternoon; the time from noon till night. 2. Evening, the close of the day. **A la tarde**, in the evening. **Por la tarde**, in the afternoon. -*adv.* Late; past the time. **De tarde en tarde**, now and then, occasionally: seldom. **Tarde, mal y nunca**, slow and unpunctual. **Hacerse tarde**, to grow late. **Más vale tarde que nunca**, better late than never. **Para luego es tarde**, by-and-bye is too late; don't put off. **Algo tarde**, backward, latish. **Tarde o temprano**, sooner or later.

tardecer [tar-day-therr'], *vn.* To verge upon evening; to grow late.

tardecica, ita [tar-day-thee'-cah], *f. dim.* The close of the evening.

tardecillo [tar-day-theel'-lyo], *adv.* A little late; slowly.

tarde piache [tar-day pe-ah'-chay], *a. (Coll.)* Very late, the opportune time past.

tardíamente [tar-dee'-ah-men-tay], *adv.* Too late, out of time.

tardío, día [tar-dee'-o, ah], *a.* 1. Late, too late. 2. Slow, tardy, dilatory.

tardo, da [tar'-do, dah], *a.* 1. Slow (lento), sluggish, tardy. 2. Dull, inactive, lazy.

tardón, na [tar-don', nah], *a. aug.* Very tardy, phlegmatic.

tarea [ta-ray'-ah], *f.* 1. Task, work imposed by another (trabajo asignado); shift, 2. Care, toil, drudgery; exercise. **Ahora disfruta sus tareas**, he now enjoys the fruits of his labor. **Tarea del colegio**, schoolwork, homework. **Es una tarea poco grata**, it's not a very satisfying job.

targum [tar-goom'], *m.* Targum, Chaldaic version of the Bible.

tarida [tah-ree'-dah], *f.* Ancient vessel used in the Mediterranean for carrying implements of war.

tarifa [tah-ree'-fah], *f.* Tariff (precio), a list of the prices of goods or merchandise, book of rates or duties; rate (tasa); price list (lista de precios); fare (en vehículos). **Tarifa de suscripción**, subscription rate.

tarima [tah-ree'-mah], *f.* 1. A movable platform on a floor or pavement (plataforma); low bench (banquillo), table, footstool. 2. Bedstead.

tarimilla [tah-re-meel'-lyah], *f. dim.* A small bedstead.

tarimón [tah-re-mone'], *m. aug.* A large bedstead; a foot-stool.

tarina [tah-ree'-nah], *f.* Middle-sized dish for meat.

tarja [tar'-hah], *f.* 1. An ancient Spanish copper coin worth about one-fourth of a real. 2. Tally. 3. Target, shield, buckler. 4. Sign-board. **Beber sobre tarja**, *(Coll.)* to get drink on tick.

tarjador, ra [tar-hah-dor', rah], *m. & f.* One who keeps a tally.

tarjar [tar-har'], *va.* 1. To tally, to mark on a tally what has been sold on credit. 2. *(And. Cono Sur)* To cross out (tachar).

tarjea [tar-hay'-ah], *f.* 1. A canal for watering lands or plants. 2. Sewer.

tarjero [tar-hay'-ro], *m.* Tally-keeper. V. TARJADOR.

tarjeta [tar-hay'-tah], *f. dim.* of TARJA. 1. Sign-board, sign. 2. Card, used in messages of civility or business. **Tarjeta de visita**, a visiting card. **Tarjeta de correos** or **postal**, postal card. **Tarjeta de negocios**, business card. **Tarjeta de gráficos**, graphics card. **Tarjeta de visita**, visiting card. **Tarjeta procesador**, *(Inform.)* processor card. **Tarjeta de vídeo**, *(Inform.)* video card.

tarjeta de crédito [tar-hay'-tah day cray'-de-to], *f.* Credit card. **Tarjeta Visa**, Visa card.

tarjeteo [tar-hay-tay'-o], *m.* Exchange of cards.

tarjetero [tar-hay-tay'-ro], *m.* 1. Cardcase. 2. Card index.

tarjetón [tar-hay-tone'], *m. aug.* A large buckler or target.

tarlatana [tar-lah-tah'-nah], *f.* A sort of thin linen or thread crape.

tarpón [tar-pon'], *m.* Tarpon.

tarquín [tar-keen'], *m.* Mire, mud.

tarquinada [tar-kee'-nah-dah], *f. (Coll.)* Rape.

tarraja [tar-rah'-hah], *f. (Arch.)* Metal instrument for cutting ornamental mouldings in gypsum.

tarro [tar'-ro], *m.* 1. Earthenware or glass vessel. 2. *(And. Cono Sur)* Tin (lata), can. 3. *(Carib. Cono Sur, Mex.)* Horn (cuerno). 4. *(Cono Sur)* Stroke of luck (chiripa). 4. *(Carib.)* Cuckolding (del marido). 5. *(Carib.)* Difficult matter (asunto).

tarso [tar'-so], *m. (Anat.)* Tarsus, the ankle.

tarta [tar'-tah], *f.* 1. Tart (torta), a delicate pastry. 2. Pan for baking tarts. **Tarta nupcial**, wedding cake.

tártago [tar'-tah-go], *m.* 1. *(Bot.)* Spurge. 2. Misfortune (desgracia), unfortunate event. 3. A severe jest, galling satire or lash.

tartajear [tar-tah-hay-ar'], *m.* To stutter, to stammer.

tartajoso, sa [tar-tah-ho'-so, sah], *a.* Stammering, stuttoring.

tartalear [tar-tah-lay-ar'], *vn. (Coll.)* 1. To reel, to stagger. 2. To be perplexed; not to be able to talk (al hablar).

tartaleta [tar-tah-lay'-tah], *f.* A kind of light paste for covering tarts. **tartaletas**, fruit-pies.

tartamudear [tar-tah-moo-day-ar'], *vn.* To stutter, to stammer, to falter, to lisp, to fumble, to halt.

tartamudeo, *m.* **tartamudez**, *f.* [tar-tah-moo-day'-o, tar-tah-moo-deth'], Lisp, stuttering, stammering.

tartamudo, da [tar-tah-moo'-do, dah], *a. & m.* Stuttering, stammering; stutterer.

tartán [tar-tahn'], *m. (Com.)* Tartan, a Scotch plaid.

tartana [tar-tah'-nah], *f.* 1. *(Naut.)* Tartan, a small coasting vessel in the Mediterranean. 2. Long covered wagon for passengers with two wheels.

tartanero [tar-tah-nay'-ro], *m.* The driver of a *tartana*.

tartáreo rea [tar-tah'-ray-o, ah], *a. (Poet.)* Tartarean, hellish.

tartárico [tar-tah'-re-co], *a.* Tartaric, relating to tartar of wine. V. TÁRTRICO.

tartarizar [tar-tah-re-thar'], *va.* To tartarize, to impregnate with tartar, to refine with the salt of tartar.

tártaro [tar'-tah-ro], *m.* 1. Argol, tartar, the lees of wine. 2. Dental tartar.

tártaro, ra [tar'-tah-ro, rah], *a.* Tartarian, of Tartary.

tartera [tar-tay'-rah], *f.* 1. Baking-pan for tarts and other pastry. 2. Dripping-pan.

tartrato [tar-trah'-to], *m. (Chem.)* Tartrate, a salt of tartaric acid.

tártrico [tar'-tre-co], *a.* Tartaric. **Ácido tártrico**, tartaric acid.

tarugo [tar-roo'-go], *m.* 1. A wooden peg or pin; stopper, plug (tapón), bung. 2. *(Carib.)* Fright (susto). 3. *(LAm.)* Chump (imbécil). 4. *(Mex.)* Fear (miedo).

taruguillo [tah-roo-geel'-lyo], *m. dim.* Of TARUGO.

tarumba [tah-room'-bah], *a.* **Volver a uno tarumba**, *(Coll.* phrase) to confuse one, to get him mixed. **Volverse tarumba**, to become rattled. *(Amer. Turumba.)*

tas [tahs], *m.* Kind of anvil used by silversmiths.

tasa [tah'-sah], *f.* 1. Rate, price of provisions fixed by magistrates, assize. 2. Measure, rule (medida, norma). 3. Valuation or appraisement of valuables. **Tasa de crecimiento**, growth-rate. **Tasa de nacimiento**, birth rate.

tasación [tah-sah-the-on'], *f.* Valuation, appraisement. V. TASA.

tasadamente [tah-sah-dah-men'-tay], *adv.* Barely, scantily, scarcely.

tasado, da [tah-sah'-do, dah], *a.* Limited, restricted. **Tiempo tasado**, limited amount of time.

tasador [tah-sah-dor'], *m.* 1. Appraiser, valuator, valuer. 2. *(Law.)* Taxing judge.

tasajear [tah-sah-hay-ar'], *va. (Amer.)* To cut meat for making jerked beef, to jerk (carne).

tasajo [tah-sah'-ho], *m.* Jerked beef, hung-beef.

tasar [tah-sar'], *va.* 1. To appraise, to value, to estimate. 2. To observe method and rule; to regulate. 3. **Tasar judicialmente**, to tax, to rate at. 4. To give scantily of what one is obliged to give.

tascador [tas-cah-dor'], *m.* Brake, for dressing flax or hemp.

tascar [tas-car'], *va.* 1. To brake, to scutch or dress flax or hemp. 2. To nibble the grass (animales). 3. To swingle (lino), to beat.

tascina [tas-thee'-nah], *f. (Min.)* Silver selenide.

tasco [tahs'-co], *m.* 1. Refuse of flax or hemp. 2. *(Naut.)* Toppings of hemp.

tasconio [tas-co'-ne-o], *m.* V. TALQUE.

tasquera [tas-kay'-rah], *f.* Dispute, scuffle, contest.

tasquil [tas-keel'], Chip which flies from a stone on working it.

tástara [tas-tar'-rah], *f. (Prov.)* Coarse bran.

tastaz [tas-tath'], *m.* Polishing powder made of old crucibles.

tata [tah'-tath], *m.* Word by which little children begin to call their parents. Used in Mexico vulgarly at all ages. -*a.* 1. Nanny (niñera), nursemaid; maid (chacha). 2. *(LAm.)* Younger sister (hermana menor).

tatarabuela [tah-tah-ra-boo-ay'-lah], *f.* The great-great grandmother.

tatarabuelo [tah-tah-rah-boo-ay'-lo], *m.* The great-great-grandfather.

tataradeudo, da [tah-tah-rah-day'-oo-do, dah], *m. & f.* Very old and distant relation.

tataranieta [tah-tah-rah-ne-ay'-tah], *f.* A great-great-granddaughter.

tataranieto [tah-tah-rah-nee-ay'-to], *m.* A great-great-grandson.

tatas [tah'-tas], *adv. (Prov.)* **Andar a tatas**, to walk timidly; to go on all fours.

¡tate! [tah'-tay], *int.* Take care, beware; stay, so it is. **Tate, tate,** little by little.

tato [tah'-to], *m.* 1. *(Coll. Prov.)* A younger brother. 2. Hog-headed armadillo.

tato, ta [tah'-to, tah], *a. & n.* Stammering; stutterer who converts *c* and *s* into *t*.

tatuaje [tah-too-ah'-hay], *m.* Tattooing (acto), tattoo (dibujo).

tatuar [tah-too-ar'], *a.* To tattoo.

tau [tah'-oo], *m. V.* TAO. *-f.* 1. The Greek t, nineteenth letter of the Greek alphabet. 2. Tau cross, tau (cruz).

taumaturgo [tah-oo-mah-toor'-go], *m.* The author of great and stupendous things, miracle worker; thaumaturge.

taurina [tah-oo-ree'-nah], *f.* Taurin, a crystallizable substance found in the bile of various animals.

taurino, na [tah-oo-ree'-no, nah], *a.* Relating to a bull; taurine. **El negocio taurino**, the bullfighting business.

tauro [tah'-oo-ro], *m. (Ast.)* Taurus, a sign of the zodiac.

taurómaco [tah-oo-ro'-mah-co], *m.* One fond of bullfighting.

tauromaquia [tah-oo-ro-mah'-ke-ah], *f.* The art of bullfighting.

tautología [tah-oo-to-lo-hee'-ah], *f.* Tautology.

tautológico, ca [tah-oo-to-lo'-he-co, cah], *a.* Tautological.

tautologista [tah-oo-to-lo-hees'-tah], *com.* Tautologist.

tautometría [tah-oo-to-may-tree'-ah], *f.* Repetition of the same measure.

tauxia [tah'-ooc-se'-ah], *f. V.* ATAUXIA.

taxativamente [tac-sah-tee'-vah-men-tay], *adv.* Limitedly.

taxativo, va [tak-sah-tee'-vo, vah], *a. (Law.)* Limited to circumstances (restringido).

taxi [tak'-se], *m.* Taxi, taxicab.

taxidermia [tak-se-derr'-me-ah], *f.* Taxidermy, the art of preserving dead animals so as to present a life-like appearance.

taxidermista [tak-se-dayr-mees'-tah], *m. & f.* Taxidermist.

taxímetro [tak-see'-may-tro], *m.* 1. Taximeter. 2. Taxi, taxicab.

taxista [tak-sees'-tah], *m & f.* Taxidriver, cabby.

taz a taz, or **taz por taz** [tath ah tath], *adv. (Coll.)* This for that; tit for tat.

taza [tah'-thah], *f.* 1. Cup. 2. Cup, the liquor contained in a cup (contenido). 3. Basin of a fountain (de fuente). 4. A large wooden bowl. 5. *(Coll.)* Buttocks, breech. 6. Bowl (de retrete). 7. *(Cono Sur)* Washbasin (palangana). 8. **Taza de noche,** *(Cono Sur)* Chamberpot.

tazaña [tah-thah'-nyah], *f.* Serpent. *V.* TARASCA.

tazmía [tath-mee'-ah], *f.* Share of tithes.

tazón [tah-thone'], *m. aug.* A large bowl or basin; pitcher.

te [tay], *pron.pers.* 1. You; thee (a Dios). 2. You (dativo). **Te he traído esto,** I've brought you this. 3. Yourself (reflexivo). **Te vas a caer,** You'll fall.

té [tay], *m.* 1. *(Bot.)* Tea; a plant (planta). 2. Tea, decoction of tea leaves-*f.* Name of the letter T. -*pron.* Thee, the oblique case of Thou.

tea [tay'-ah], *f.* Candlewood, a piece of resinous wood, which burns like a torch.

teame, teamide [tay-ah'-may, tay-ah-mee'-day], *f.* A stone repelling iron.

teatino [tay-ah-tee'-no], *m.* 1. A delicate sort of paste. 2. Theatin, one of a religious order founded by Pope Paul IV.

teatral [tay-ah-trahl'], *a.* Theatrical, belonging to a theater.

teatralmente [tay-ah-tral-men'-tay], *adv.* Theatrically.

teatro [tay-ah'-tro], *m.* 1. Stage, on which any show is exhibited. 2. Theater, stage, playhouse. 3. The people

attending at a playhouse. 4. Theater, collection of plays belonging to a nation. 5. The profession or practice of dramatic art. 6. Stage, place where anything is exposed to the applause or censure of the world. **Teatro de aficionados**, amateur theater. **Escribir para el teatro**, to write for the stage. **El teatro de Cervantes**, Cervantes' plays. **Hacer teatro**, to exaggerate.

tebaico, ca [tay-bah'-e-co, cah], *a.* Thebaic, belonging to Egyptian Thebes.

tebano, na [tay-bah'-no, nah], *a.* Theban, of Thebes.

teca [tay'-cah], *f.* Teak, a large East-Indian tree, and its hard, elastic wood valued for ship-building.

tecale, tecali [tay-cah'-lay], *m. (Mex.)* A very white, transparent marble: in many of the windows of convents it is used instead of glass.

techado [tay-chah'-do], *m. V.* TECHO. **Techado, da,** *pp.* of TECHAR.

techar [tay-char'], *va.* To roof; to cover with a roof.

techo [tay'-cho], *m.* 1. Roof (exterior), ceiling (interior), the inner roof of a building. 2. *(Met.)* Dwelling-house, habitation, place of abode: native soil; cover. **Bajo techo,** under cover. **Ha tocado techo,** it has reached its ceiling.

techumbre [tay-choom'-bray], *f.* Upper roof, ceiling; a lofty roof; as of a church.

tecla [tay'-clah], *f.* 1. Key (máquina de escribir). 2. *(Fig.)* Touchy subject. **Dar en la tecla,** *(Coll.)* 1. To catch on, to get the knack. 2. To get into the habit. **Techa de borrado,** delete key. **Tecla del cursor,** cursor key. **Tecla de edición,** edit key.

teclado [tay-clah'-do], *m.* Keyboard (Mús, máquina de escribir); manual (de órgano).

teclear [tay-clay-ar'], *vn.* 1. To finger. 2. *(Fig.)* To drum, to rap one's fingers (con dedos). 3. *(Cono Sur)* To be weak (estar enfermo). 4. *(Cono Sur)* To be very poor (ser pobre). 5. *(And. Cono Sur)* To be going very badly (negocio). -*va.* To feel out, to try out, to experiment with.

tecleo [tay-clay'-o], *m.* 1. Fingering. 2. Drumming (condedos), tapping.

tecnecio [tec-nay'-the-o], *m.* Technetium.

técnica [tec'-ne-cah], *f.* Technique; method (método); craft (destreza), skill. **Técnica de E/S,** *(Inform.)* I/O technique.

técnicamente [tec'-ne-cah-men-tay], *adv.* Technically.

tecnicidad [tec-ne-the-dahd'], *f.* Technicality.

tecnicismo [tec-ne-thees'-mo], *m.* 1. Technical vocabulary. 2. Technical term.

técnico, ca [tec'-ne-co, cah], *a.* Technical. -*m.* Technician. -*f.* Technique. **Es un técnico en la materia,** he's an expert on the subject.

tecnicolor [tec-ne-co-lor'], *m.* Technicolor.

tecnocracia [tec-no-crah'-the-ah], *f.* Technocracy.

tecnología [tec-no-lo-hee'-ah], *f.* Technology, language proper and exclusive to the arts and sciences. **Tecnología de la Información.** Information Technology, **Tecnología magneto-óptica,** *(Inform.)* magneto-optical technology.

tecnológico, ca [tec-no-lo'-he-co, cah], *a.* Technological, technical.

tecomate [tay-co-mah'-tay], *m. (Mex.)* A cup made of a gourd.

tedero [tay-day'-ro], *m.* Iron candlestick for holding burning fir or a torch.

tedéum [tay-day'-oom], *m.* Te Deum, a hymn of the church.

tediar [tay-de-ar'], *va.* To loathe, to hate, to abhor.

tedio [tay'-de-o], *m.* Disgust, dislike, abhorrence, tediousness.

tedioso, sa [tay-de-oh'-so, sah], *a.* Tedious, loathful, fastidious, tiresome, disgusting, nauseous to the taste or mind.

tegual [tay-goo-ahl'], *m.* Tax or duty paid to the king.

tegumento [tay-goo-men'-to], *m.* Tegument, covering.

teína [tay-ee'-nah], *f. (Chem.)* Thein the alkaloid of the tea-plant.

teinada [tay-e-nah'-dah], *f. V.* TINADA.

teísmo [tay-ees'-mo], *m.* Theism, deism.

teísta [tay-ees'-tah], *com.* Theist, deist.

teja [tay'-hah], *f*. Roof-tile, for covering buildings. **De tejas abajo**, in a natural order, without supernatural interference; in this world.

tejadillo [tay-hah-deel'-lyo], *m*. Roof of a coach.

tejado [tay-hah'-do], *m*. Roof covered with tiles; shed. **Tiene el tejado de vidrio**, he himself is open to the same charge. -**Tejado, da**, *pp*. of TEJAR.

tejamanil [tay-hah-mah-neel'], *m*. *(Mex.)* Shingles. V. TAJAMANIL.

tejano, na [tay-hah'-no, nah], *m*. & *f*. & *a*. Texan.

tejar [tay-har'], *m*. Tile-works, tile-kiln.

tejar [tay-har'], *va*. To tile, to cover with tiles.

tejaroz [tay-hah-roth'], *m*. Penthouse, a shed covered with tiles.

tejavan [tay-hah-vah'-nah], *f*. Shed (civertizo); shed roof (tejado).

tejazo [tay-hah'-tho], *m*. Blow with a tile.

tejedera [tay-hay-day'-rah], *f*. 1. V. TEJEDORA. 2. Water-spider.

tejedor [tay-hay-dor'], *m*. 1. Weaver (artesano). 2. Cloth manufacturer. 3. *(Orn.)* Weaver-bird.

tejedora [tay-hay-do'-rah], *f*. Female weaver.

tejedura [tay-hay-doo'-rah], *f*. 1. Texture (textura), weaving, the act of weaving (acto). 2. Anything woven.

tejeduría [tay-hay-doo-ree'-ah], *f*. 1. The art of weaving (arte). 2. Mill, a factory for weaving (fábrica).

tejemaneje [tay'-hay-mah-nay'-hay], *m*. *(Coll.)* Doing things in an artful way. **Se trae un tremendo tejemaneje con sus papeles**, he's making a tremendous to-do with his papers.

tejer [tay-herr'], *va*. 1. To weave cloth. 2. To regulate, to adjust. 3. To discuss, to devise; to entangle. 4. To cross and mix according to rule, as in dancing.

tejera, tejería [tay-hay'-rah, tay-hay-ree'-ah], *f*. Tile-kiln. V. TEJAR.

tejero [tay-hay'-ro], *m*. Tile-maker.

tejido [tay-hee'-do], *m*. 1. Texture (textura), weaving, the act of weaving. 2. Texture, fabric, web, a thing woven. V. TELA. 3. Tissue of an organized body. **Tejido celular**, cellular tissue *(Bot.)*, connective tissue *(Anat.)*. **Tejido de punto**, knitting; knitted fabric. -**Tejido, da**. *pp*. of TEJER.

tejillo [tay-heel'-lyo], *m*. 1. A band used by women as a girdle. 2. *(Dim.)* A small quoit.

tejo [tay'-ho], *m*. 1. Quoit, round tile with which boys play; also the game. 2. *(Bot.)* Yew-tree. 3. A round metal plate.

tejocote [tay-ho-co'-tay], *m*. *(Bot. Mex.)* A fruit resembling a sloe.

tejoleta [tay-ho-lay'-tah], *f*. 1. Piece of burnt clay; tile. 2. A shuffle-board.

tejolote [tay-ho-lo'-tay], *m*. *(Mex.)* Stone pestle for a culinary mortar.

tejón [tay-hone'], *m*. 1. A wedge or plate of gold. 2. *(Zool.)* Badger.

tejuelo [tay-hoo-ay'-lo], *m*. 1. Space between the bands on the back of a book for the title. 2. *(Mech.)* Bush, pillow block, socket, sole-plate.

tela [tay'-lah], *f*. 1. Cloth, fabric, any stuff woven in a loom. **Tela de cebolla**, onion skin. **Tela de saco**, sackcloth. 2. Gold or silver lace. 3. Chain or warp of cloth which is put at one time in a loom. 4. Pellicle, the thin interior skin of the animal body or of fruits; membrane. 5. Film or pellicle on the surface of liquors. 6. Quibble, quirk. 7. Cobweb of a spider, web of some other insects. **Tela de araña**, spider's web. 8. Argument; matter (materia); thread of a discourse. **El asunto trae mucha tela**, it's a complicated matter. 9. Membrane or opacity in the eye. 10. *(And.)* Thin maize pancake (tortilla).

telabrejo [tay-lah-bray'-ho], *m*. *(Mex.)* 1. A thing of small account. 2. A person of small account.

telamón [tay-lah-mon'], *m*. *(Arch.)* V. ATLANTE.

telar [tay-lar'], *m*. 1. Loom, in which cloth is woven; a frame in which other things are made. 2. Upper part of the scene-work in a theater, out of sight of the public, where the curtains are raised and lowered.

telaraña [tay-lah-rah'-nyah], *f*. 1. Cobweb. 2. A small cloud. 3. Anything trifling and of little weight. **Mirar las telarañas**, *(Coll.)* To be absentminded.

telecomunicación [tay-lay-co-moo-ne-cah-the-on'], *f*. 1. Telecommunication. 2. *(Comput.)* Telecommuting

telecopiadora [tay-lay-co-pe-ah-do'-rah], *f*. Fax copier.

telediario [tay-lay-de-ah'-re-o], *m*. Television news bulletin.

teledirección [tay-lay-de-rec-the-on'], *f*. Remote control.

teledirigido, da [tay-lay-de-re-hee'-do, dah], *a*. Remote-control.

teledirigir [tay-lay-de-re-heer'], *va*. To operate by remote control.

teleférico [tay-lay-fay'-re-co], *m*. Cable car

telefio [tay-lay'-fe-o], *m*. Orpine.

telefonazo [tay-lay-fo-nah'-tho], *(Coll.)* Phone call.

telefonear [tay-lay-fo-nay-ar'], *va*. *vn*. To telephone, to phone.

telefonema [tay-lay-fo-nay'-mah], *m*. Telephone message.

telefonía [tay-lay-fo-nee'-ah], *f*. Telephony.

telefónico, ca [tay-lay-fo'-ne-co, cah], *a*. Telephonic, telephone.

telefonista [tay-lay-fo-nees'-tah], *f*. Telephone operator. -*m*. Telephone service man.

teléfono [tay-lay'-fo-no], *m*. Telephone, phone. **Teléfono automático**, dial phone. **Teléfono rojo**, the hot line. **Está hablando por teléfono**, he's on the phone.

telefoto, *m*. **telefotografía**, *f*. [tay-lay-fo'-to, tay-lay-fo-to-grah-fee'-ah]. Telephotography.

telegrafía [tay-lay-grah-fee'-ah], *f*. Telegraphy.

telegrafiar [tay-lay-grah-fe-ar'], *va*. *vn*. To telegraph.

telegráficamente [tay-lay-grah'-fe-cah-men-tay], *adv*. Telegraphically.

telegráfico, ca [tay-lay-grah'-fe-co, cah], *a*. Telegraphic, telegraph.

telegrafista [tay-lay-grah-fees'-tah], *com*. Telegrapher, telegraphist.

telégrafo [tay-lay'-grah-fo], *m*. Telegraph.

telegrama [tay-lay-grah'-mah], *m*. Telegram.

teleguiar [tay-lay-gee-ar'], *va*. To operate by remote control.

teleimpresor [tay-lay-im-pray-sor'], *m*. Teleprinter.

telemando [tay-lay-mahn'-do], *m*. Remote control.

telemecánico, ca [tay-lay-may-cah'-ne-co, cah], *a*. Telemechanic. -*f*. Telemechanics.

telemedición [tay-lay-may-de-the-on'], *f*. Telemetering.

telemetría [tay-lay-may-tree'-ah], *f*. Telemetry.

telemétrico, ca [tay-lay-may'-tre-co, cah], *a*. Telemetric.

telémetro [tay-lay'-may-tro], *m*. 1. Range finder. 2. Telemeter.

telenovela [tay-lay-no-vay'-lah], *f*. Soap opera.

teleobjectivo [tay-lay-ob-hay-tee'-vo], *m*. Telephoto lens.

teleología [tay-lay-o-lo-hee'-ah], *f*. Teleology.

telepatía [tay-lay-pah-tee'-ah], *f*. Telepathy.

telepático, ca [tay-lay-pah'-te-co, cah], *a*. Telepathic.

telequinesia [tay-lay-ke-nay'-se-ah], *f*. Telekinesis.

telera [tay-lay'-rah], *f*. 1. Plough pin. 2. Pen (para ganado). 3. Jaw (of a vise).

telerán [tay-lay-ran'], *m*. Teleran.

telerreceptor [tay-ler-ray-thep-tor'], *m*. Television set.

telescópico, ca [tay-les-co'-pe-co, cah], *a*. Telescopic.

telescopio [tay-les-co'-pe-o], *m*. Telescope.

telesilla [tay-lay-seel'-lya], *m*. Chair lift.

telespectador, ra [tay-les-pec-tah-dor', rah], *m*. & *f*. Televiewer.

telesquí [tay-les-kee'], *m*. Ski lift.

telestesia [tay-les-tay'-se-ah], *f*. Telesthesia.

telestudio [tay-les-too'-de-o], *m*. Television studio.

teleta [tay-lay'-tah], *f*. Blotting paper.

teletipo [ta-lay-tee'-po], *m*. Teletype.

teletubo [tay-lay-too'-bo], *m*. Television picture tube.

televidente [tay-lay-ve-den'-tay], *m*. Television viewer, televiewer.

televisar [tay-lay-ve-sar'], *m*. To televise.

televisión [tay-lay-ve-se-on'], *f.* Television. **Televisión por cable**, cable television. **Mirar la televisión**, to watch television.

televisivo [tay-lay-ve-see'-vo], *a.* Television. **Serie televisiva**, television series.

televisor [tay-lay-ve-sor'], *m.* Television set.

tellina [tel-lyee'-nah], *f.* Bivalve shellfish: mussel.

telliz [tel-lyeeth'], *m.* Cloth thrown oer the saddle of a horse for ornament.

telliza [tel-lyee'-thah], *f.* Coverlet of a bed.

telón [tay-lon'], *m.* (*Theat.*) Drop curtain. **Telón de boca**, front curtain. **Telón de hierro**, iron curtain.

telúrico, ca [tay-loo'-re-co, cah], *a.* Telluric.

telurio [tay-loo'-re-o], **Teluro**, *m.* (*Min.*) Tellulium, a metallic element.

tema [tay'-mah], *m.* Text, proposition, theme, subject, composition. **Tema de actualidad**, current issue. **Pasar del tema**, to dodge the issue. *-f.* 1. Topic of madmen's discourses. 2. Dispute, contention; obstinacy in asserting a controverted point. 3. Animosity, passionate malignity, capricious opposition. **A tema**, emulously, obstinately. **Cada uno tiene su tema**, (*Coll.*) every man has his hobby. **Tener tema**, to be stubborn.

temario [tay-mah'-re-o], *m.* 1. Schedule. 2. List of topics. 3. Program (programa). 4. Agenda (de junta).

temático, ca [tay-mah'-te-co, cah], *a.* 1. Relating to a theme or subject, thematic. 2. *V.* TEMOSO.

tembladal [tem-blah'-dah], *m. V.* TREMEDAL.

tembladera [tem-blah-day'-rah], *f.* 1. Tankard, a wide-mouthed vessel with two handles. 2. Diamond-pin, or other similar ornament of the headdress of ladies. 3. (*Zool.*) Torpedo electric ray.

tembladero [tem-blah-day'-ro], *m. V.* TREMEDAL.

temblador, ra [tem-blah-dor', rah], *m. & f.* Quaker, shaker, trembler.

temblante [tem-blahn'-tay], *m.* Kind of loose bracelet worn by women. *-pa.* Trembling quavering.

temblar [tem-blar'], *vn.* To tremble (persona), to shake with fear, to move with violent agitation; to quake, to shiver (de frío). **Temblar las carnes**, (*Coll.*) to have a horror of a thing. **Temblar de miedo**, to tremble with fright. **Tiemblo de pensar en lo que pueda ocurrir, I** tremble to think what may happen.

tembleque [tem-blay'-kay], *m.* 1. Diamond-pin or plume or other similar ornament of the headdress of ladies. 2. *V.* LENTEJUELA. 3. Violent shaking. 4. (*LAm.*) Weakling (persona). **Le entró un tembleque**, he began to shake violently.

temblequear, templetear [tem-blay-kay-ar'], *vn.* To tremble, to shake with fear; to move with violent agitation.

temblón, na [tem-blone', nah], *a.* Tremulous. **Hacer la temblona**, to affect timidity.

temblón [tem-blone'], *m.* (*Bot.*) Aspen or asp tree.

temblor [tem-blor'], *m.* Trembling, involuntary motion proceeding from fear or weakness. **Temblor de tierra**, earthquake. **Le entró un temblor violento**, he began to shake volently.

temblorcillo [tem-blor-theel'-lyo], *m. dim.* A slight shivering.

tembloroso, sa [tem-blo-ro'-so, sah], *a.* Trembling, trembly, tremulous, quivering, shaking. **Con voz temblorosa**, in a shaky voice.

tembloso, so [tem-blo'-so, sah], *a.* Tremulous.

temedero, ra [tay-may-day'-ro, rah], *a.* Awful, dreadful.

temedor, ra [tay-may-dor', rah], *a.* 1. Applied to a trembler. 2. Awful, dreadful.

temedor, ra [tay-may-dor'], *m. & f.* Trembler.

temer [tay-merr'], *va.* 1. To apprehend, to fear, to dread; to reverence, to respect. 2. To suspect, to misdoubt. **Temo que lo ha perdido**, I'm afraid he has lost it. *-vn.* To be afraid. **No temas**, don't be afraid.

temerariamente [tay-may-rah'-re-ah-men-tay], *adv.* Rashly, hastily, inconsiderately.

temerario, ria [tay-may-rah'-re-o, ah], *a.* Rash (persona), inconsiderate, imprudent, daring, overbold, hasty (juicio), headlong.

temeridad [tay-may-re-dahd'], *f.* Temerity, rashness (cualidad), imprudence; fool-hardiness. **Ser una temeridad**, (1) said of imprudence or rashness. (2) (*Coll.*) To be excessive.

temerón, na [tay-may-rone', nah], *a.* Affecting noise, authority, or bullying.

temerosamente [tay-may-ro'-sah-men-tay], *adv.* Timorously.

temeroso, sa [tay-may-ro'-so, sah], *a.* 1. Awe-inspiring; exciting fear or suspicion, dreadful (espantoso). 2. Timid, timorous; fearful (miedoso); cowardly.

temible [tay-mee'-blay], *a.* Dreadful, terrible, awful.

temiente [tay-me-en'-tay], *pa.* One who dreads or apprehends.

temor [tay-mor'], *m.* Dread, fear (miedo), apprehension, suspicion (recelo). **Sin temor a**, fearless of.

temoso, sa [tay-mo'-so, sah], *a.* Obstinate, stubborn.

tempanador [tem-pa-nah-dor'], *m.* Instrument for cutting off the tops of beehives.

tempanar [tem-pa-nar'], *pa.* To furnish staves; to cover the tops of beehives

témpano [tem'-pah-no], *m.* 1. Floe (de hielo). 2. *V.* TÍMPANO. 3. Tympan, stretched skin or other thing: open, plain space. 4. Large cork put in the top of beehives. 5. (*Arch.*) Tympan of an arch. **Témpano de hielo**, a piece of ice.

temperación [tem-pay-rah-the-on'], *f. V.* TEMPERAMENTO.

temperadamente [tem-pay-ra-dah-men'-tay], *adv. V.* TEMPLADAMENTE.

temperamental [tem-pay-rah-men-tahl'], *a.* 1. Temperamental. 2. Vigorous, forceful (fuerte).

temperamento [tem-pay-rah-men'-to], *m.* 1. Temperature, climate (clima). 2. Arbitration, compromise, means for ending disputes or dissensions. 3. Temperament (genio), constitution (constitución); as nervous, lymphatic, etc. 4. (*LAm.*) Climate (clima), summer (verano).

temperancia, temperanza [tem-pay-rahn'-the-ah], *f. V.* TEMPLANZA.

temperante [tem-pay-rahn'-tay], *pa.* (*Med.*) That which tempers.

temperar [tem-pay-rar'], *va.* 1. *V.* ATEMPERAR. 2. (*Amer.*) *V.* VERANEAR.

temperatura [tem-pay-rah-too'-rah], *f.* Temperature, the degree of cold or warmth, measured by the thermometer.

temperie [tem-pay'-re-ay], *f.* Temperature of the air; its constitution as produced by different degrees of heat and cold, dryness and dampness.

tempero [tem-pay'-ro], *m.* Seasonableness, fitness of the soil for the growth of seeds.

tempestad [tem-pes-tahd'], *f.* 1. Tempest, storm. 2. Violent perturbation of the mind. **Tempestades**, violent, abusive language.

tempestar [tem-pes-tar'], *vn.* To be a tempest, to screech out.

tempestivamente [tem-pes-tee'-vah-men-tay], *adv.* Seasonably, opportunely.

tempestivo, va [tem-pes-tee'-vo, vah], *a.* Seasonable, opportune.

tempestuosamente [tem-pes-too-oh'-sah-men-tay], *adv.* Tempestuously, turbulently.

tempestuoso, sa [tem-pes-too-oh'-so, sah], *a.* Tempestuous, stormy, turbulent.

templa [tem'-plah], *f.* (*Art.*) Distemper, size for painting.

templadamente [tem-plah-dah-men'-tay], *adv.* Temperately, moderately, abstemiously, freshly; calmly.

templadera [tem-plah-day'-rah], *J.* (*Prov.*) Sluice put into a channel to let a certain quantity of water pass.

templadico, ca [tem-plah-dee'-co, cah], *a. dim.* Somewhat temperate.

templado, da [tem-plah'-do, dah], *a.* 1. Temperate, tempered, moderate (moderado), abstemious (en beber), frugal, lukewarm. 2. Well-tuned. 3. Bold, forthright (franco); courageous (valiente). 4. Bright (listo); *(CAm. Mex.)* able (hábil), competent. 5. *(And.).* Severe (severo). 6. *(And. Carib.)* Tipsy (borracho). *-pp.* of TEMPLAR.

templador, ra [tem-plah-dor', rah], *m. & f.* Tuner; one who tempers. *-m.* 1. Tuning key for musical instruments. 2. *(Peru)* Circular stockade in the midst of the arena for refuge of bullfighters.

templadura [tem-plah-doo'-rah], *f.* Temper, the act of tempering.

templanza [tem-plahn'-thah], *f.* 1. Temperance, moderation (cualidad), abstinence, abstemiousness. 2. Sobriety. 3. Disposition of the air or climate of a country: degree of heat or cold. 4. *(Art.)* Due proportion and good disposition of colors.

templar [tem-plar'], *va.* 1. To temper, to soften, to moderate, to cool. 2. To temper steel; to anneal glass. 3. To tune musical instruments. 4. To observe a due proportion of parts in a painting. 5. *(Naut.)* To trim the sails to the wind. 6. To mix, to assuage, to soften. 7. To prepare, to dispose. 8. To train a hawk. 9. *(And.)* To knock down (derribar); *(CAm.)* to hit (golpear); to beat (pegar). *-vr.* 1. To be moderate (persona); to refrain from excess. 2. To warm up (agua). 3. *(And.CAm.)* To die (morir). 4. *(Carib.)* To flee (huir). 5. *(And. Carib.)* To get drunk (emborracharse). 6. *(Cono Sur)* To fall in love (enamorarse). 7. *(Cono Sur)* To go too far (excederse).

templario [tem-plah'-re-o], *m.* Templar, one of the order of Templars.

temple [tem'-play], *m.* 1. Temperature of the season or climate. 2. Temper given to metals. 3. Temperament, medium, due mixture of opposites. 4. Frame or disposition of the mind (espíritu). 5. The concordance of musical instruments. 6. Religion of the Templars; a temple or church. **Al temple**, painted in distemper. 7. *(LAm.)* Infatuation (enamoramiento).

templecillo [tem-play-theel'-lyo], *m. dim.* A small temple.

templete [tem-play'-tay], *m. dim.* V. TEMPLECILLO. Applied to architectural ornaments in form of a temple.

templista [tem-plees'-tah], *m.* Painter in distemper.

templo [tem'-plo], *m.* 1. Temple, church for the worship of God. 2. Blessed soul. 3. Temple dedicated to the false gods of the Gentiles. **Templo metodista**, Methodist chapel. **Como un templo**, huge (grande).

témpora [tem'-po-rah], *f.* Ember week, days of fast prescribed by the Roman Catholic church, in the four seasons of the year: generally used in the plural.

temporada [tem-po-rah'-dah], *f.* A certain space of time. **La temporada de la ópera** or **del teatro**, the opera or play season. **Temporada alta**, high season. **En plena temporada**, at the height of the season.

temporal [tem-po-rahl'], *a.* 1. Temporary, temporal. 2. Secular, temporal, pertaining to the civil power. 3. Temporal, belonging to the temples of the head. *-m.* 1. Season, whether good or bad. 2. Tempest, storm (tormenta). 3. *(Prov.)* Temporary laborer. 4. *(Carib.)* Shady character (persona).

temporalidad [tem-po-rah-le-dahd'], *f.* 1. Temporality, the secular revenues of the clergy. 2. Temporal concerns, affairs of this life.

temporalizar [tem-po-rah-le-thar'], *va.* To make temporary what might or should be everlasting.

temporalmente [tem-po-ral-men'-tay], *adv.* Temporarily, with respect to this life; for some time, or for a certain time.

temporáneo, nea [tem-po-rah'-nay-o, ah], *a.* Temporary, unstable.

temporario, ria [tem-po-rah'-re-o, ah], *a.* Temporary, not lasting.

temporero, temporil [tem-po-ray'-ro], *m.* Temporary laborer, one who works only for a season.

temporizador, ra [tem-po-re-thah-dor', rah], *m. & f.* Temporizer, trimmer.

temporizar [tem-po-re-thar'], *vn.* 1. To pass the time in any place or thing. 2. To comply with the times, to temporize. V. CONTEMPORIZAR.

tempranal [tem-prah-nahl'], *a.* Producing early fruits (tierra).

tempranamente [tem-prah-nah-men'-tah], *adv.* Early, prematurely.

tempranero, ra [tem-prah-nah'-ro, rah], *a.* V. TEMPRANO.

tempranilla [tem-prah-neel'-lyah], *f.* *(Prov.)* Sort of early grape.

temprano, na [tem-prah'-no, nah], *a.* Early, soon, anticipated, forehanded.

temprano [tem-prah'-no], *adv.* Very early, prematurely, soon.

temulento, ta [tay-moo-len'-to, tah], *a.* Intoxicated, inebriated.

tena [tay'-nah], *f. (Agr.)* A flock of sheep or goats, not over sixty head.

tenacerar [tay-nah-thay-ar'], *va.* To tear with pincers, *-vn.* To insist obstinately and pertinaciously.

tenacero [tay-nah-thay'-ro], *m.* He who makes or uses pincers.

tenacicas [tay-nah-thee'-cas], *f. pl.* 1. *(Dim.)* Small tongs. 2. Pincers; snuffers.

tenacidad [tay-nah-the-dahd'], *f.* 1. Toughness. 2. Tenacity. 3. Ingrained nature; persistence; stubborness.

tenacilla [tay-nah-teel'-lyah], *f. pl. dim.* Small tongs. **Tenacillas de boca**, float-pointed pliers. **Tenacillas de punta**, sharp-pointed pliers.

tenáculo [tay-nah'-coo'-lo], *m. (Med.)* Tenaculum, a curved sharp hook for holding an artery which is to be tied.

tenada [tay-nah'-dah], *f. (Prov.)* Sheep-fold, sheep-cot.

tenallón [tay-nah'-dah], *m. (Mil.)* Tenaillon, outwork on the flanks of a fortification: commonly used in the plural in both languages.

tenante [tay-nahn'-tay], *m. (Her.)* Supporter; figure of a man, angel, etc. supporting a shield.

tenate [tay-nah'-tay], *m. (Mex.)* V. TANATE.

tenaz [tay-nath'], *a.* 1. Tenacious, sticking. 2. Firm, stubborn, obstinate, persevering (persona). 3. Avaricious, covetous. 4. Hard to remove, (mancha).

tenaza [tay-nah'-thah], *f.* 1. Tenaille, a kind of outwork of a fortress. 2. Claws or talons of animals. *-pl.* 3. Tongs. 4. Pincers, forceps. **Unas tenazas**, a pair of pliers.

tenazada [tay-nah-thah'-dah], *f.* 1. The act of griping with pincers or tongs. 2. The act of biting strongly.

tenazmente [tay-nah-thah'-dah], *adv.* Tenaciously.

tenazón [tay-nah-thone'], *f.* **A tenazón**, point-blank, without taking aim. **Parar de tenazón**, to stop a horse short in his course.

tenazuelas [tay-nah-thoo-ay'-las], *f. pl. dim.* Tweezers.

tenca [ten'-cah], *f. (Zool.)* Tench.

tención [ten-the-on'], *f.* Holding, retaining.

tencón [ten-cone'], *f. (Zool.)* A large tench.

ten con ten [ten con ten'], *m.* Moderation, temperance.

tendajo [ten-dah'-ho], *m.* V. TENDEJÓN.

tendal [ten-dahl'], *m.* 1. Tilt, canvas cover (toldo). 2. A long and broad piece of canvas placed under olive-trees when picking the fruit. 3. V. TENDEDERO. 4. *(LAm.)* Heap (montón). 5. *(Cono Sur)* Shearing shed; *(And. Carib.)* Brickworks (fábrica).

tendalera [ten-dah-lay'-rah], *f. (Coll.)* Confusion and disorder of things lying about on the floor.

tendalero [ten-dah-lay'-ro], *m.* Place where washed wool is dried.

tendedero [tan-day-day'-ro], *m.* 1. Clothes-line. 2. Place for hanging clothes.

tendedura [ten-day-doo'-rah], *f.* Tension, stretching or extending.

tendejón [ten-day-hone'], *m.* Sutler's tent in a camp.

tendel [ten-del'], *m.* Line by which masons raise a wall; plumb-line.

tendencia [ten-den'-the-ah], *f.* Tendency, inclination, direction towards a place, inference or result. **Tendencia del mercadeo**, run of the market. **Tener tendencia a**, to have a tendency to.

tendencioso, sa [ten-den-the-o'-so, sah], *a*. Tentdentious. **Literatura tendenciosa**, Propaganda literature.

tendente [ten-den'-tay], *a*. Tending, lending, directing.

tender [ten-derr'], *va*. To stretch or stretch out (estirar), to unfold, to expand, to spread out (extender, desplegar); to distend. -*vn*. To direct, to tend, to refer a thing to some end or object. **Las plantas tienden a la luz**, plants grow towards the light. **Ella tiende al pesimismo**, she has a tendency to be pessimistic. -*vr*. 1. To stretch oneself at full length (echarse). 2. In card-playing, to throw all the cards upon the table (naipes).

tenderete [ten-day-ray'-tay], *m*. 1. Kind of game at cards. 2. *V*. TENDALERA. 3. (*Mex.*) A second-hand clothing, shop. 4. *V*. TENDEDERO. 5. Stall (puesto mercado).

tendería [ten-day-ree'-ah], *f*. Place full of shops.

tendero, ra [ten-day'-ro, rah], *m. & f*. Shopkeeper; haberdasher; grocer.

tendezuela [ten-day-thoo-ay'-lah], *f. dim*. of TIENDA.

tendidamente [ten-dee'-dah-men-tay], *adv*. Diffusely, diffusively.

tendido [ten-dee'-do], *m*. 1. A row of seats for spectators at a bullfight. 2. Quantity of clothes dried by a laundress at once. 3. Roof of a house from the ridge to the eaves. 4. (*Amer.*) Riffle, among miners. 5. (*And. Mex.*) Stall (puesto mercado). 6. (*CAm. Carib.*) Long tether. 7. (*And. Mex.*) Bedclothes (ropa de cama). —**Tendido, da**, *pp*. of TENDER.

tendiente [ten-de-en'-tay], *pa*. Tending, expanding.

tendón [ten-done'], *m*. Tendon. **Tendón de Aquiles**, (*Anat.*) Achilles' tendon.

tenducha, tenducho [ten-doo-chah, cho], *f. & m*. A wretched shop.

tenebrario [tay-nay-brah'-re-o], *m*. A large candlestick or girandole, used in Roman Catholic churches in Holy week.

tenebrosidad [tay-nay-bro-se-dahd'], *f*. Darkness, obscurity, gloom.

tenebroso, sa [tay-nay-bro'-so, sah], *a*. Tenebrous, dark (oscuro), gloomy (sombrío); obscure in style, horrid.

tenedero [tay-nay-day'-ro], *m*. (*Naut.*) Bottom of the sea where the anchor catches. Gripe of an anchor. **Fondo de buen tenedero**, good anchoring ground.

tenedor [tay-nay-dor'], *m*. 1. Holder, keeper, tenant; guardian. **Tenedor de libros**, book-keeper. **Tenedor de póliza**, policy-holder. 2. Fork to eat with. 3. He who detains balls at play.

teneduría [tay-nay-doo-ree'-ah], *f*. 1. The position of book-keeper. 2. The art of book-keeping.

tenencia [tay-nen'-the-ah], *f*. 1. Possession (de propiedad), holding, the act of holding or possessing. 2. Lieutenancy, lieutenantship. **Tenencia ilícita de armas**, illegal possession of weapons.

tener [tay-nerr'], *va*. 1. To have, to contain, to comprise, to comprehend, to have within. 2. To take, to gripe, to hold last (agarrar). 3. To hold, to possess, to enjoy, to have (sentimiento). 4. To be rich and opulent in ready money. 5. To hold, to maintain, to support. 6. To subject, to domineer, to hold in subjection. 7. To hold an opinion, to keep (promesa), to retain. 8. To hold, to estimate, to judge, to take, to set a value upon. In this sense it is followed by the preposition **en** and the adjectives **poco, mucho**, etc. 9. To lodge, to receive in one's house. 10. To be obliged, to have to do; to be at the expense of anything. 11. To be adorned or favored with anything. 12. To detain, to stop. 13. To keep or fulfil. 14. With nouns of time, it signifies duration or age; when united with **que** and followed by an infinitive verb, it implies necessity or obligation. **Tener que hacer**, to have something to do. **Tener que ir**, to be obliged to go. 15. To have: used as an auxiliary verb. 16. With some nouns it means to suffer what the noun signifies. **Tener hambre**, to be hungry. **Tener sueño**, to be sleepy. **Tener miedo**, to be afraid. **Tener verguenza**, to be ashamed. **Tener celos de uno**, to be jealous of one. **Tener para sí**, to maintain a particular or singular opinion, liable to objections. **Hemos**

tenido muchas dificultades, we have had a lot of difficulties. **Lo tenía en la mano**, he was holding it in his hand. **Tener gran admiración a uno**, to have a great admiration for somebody. **Lo tengo por poco honrado, I** consider him to be rather dishonest. -*vr*. 1. To take care not to fall (estar de pie). 2. To stop, to halt. 3. To resist, to oppose. 4. To adhere, to stand to. **Tenerse en pie**, to keep on foot; to stand. **Tenga Vd. la bondad de decirme**, please tell me. **Tener razón**, to be right. **Tener consigo**, to have with or about one. **No tenerlas todas consigo**, to be not easy in mind, to be suspicious. **Tener correa para rato**, to have stamina. **Tener** forms numerous other phrases, many of which will be found under the respective nouns or adjectives with which it is associated. (*Yo tengo, tuve, tenga, tendré. V*. TENER.)

tenería [tay-nay-ree'-ah], *f*. Tan-yard, tannery.

tenesmo [tay-nes'-mo], *m*. Tenesmus.

tengua [ten'-goo-ah], *a. & n*. (*Amer. Mex.*) Hare-lipped.

tenia [tay'-ne-ah], *f*. Tape-worm.

teniente [tay-ne-en'-tay], *a*. 1. Immature, unripe. 2. Deaf. 3. Miserly, mean.

teniente [tay-ne-en'-tay], *m*. 1. Deputy, substitute. 2. Lieutenant. **Teniente de una compañía**, lieutenant of a company. **Teniente general**, lieutenant-general. 3. Miser.

tenis [tay'-nis], *m*. Tennis. **Cancha de tenis**, tennis court.

tenista [tay-nees'-tah], *m. & f*. Tennis player.

tenor [tay-nor'], *m*. 1. Permanent establishment or order of something; continuity of state. 2. Tenor, contents, sense contained. 3. Tenor, one of the four voices in music; tenorist, who sings tenor. 4. Tenor, a nautical instrument of this pitch. **A tenor de**, on the lines of. **El tenor de esta declaración**, the sense of this statement.

tenorio [tay-no-re-o], *m*. Ladykiller, Don Juan.

tensar [ten-sahr'], *va*. To tauten; to draw (arco).

tensión [ten-se-on'], *f*. 1. Tension, the act of stretching. 2. Tension, the state of being extended. 3. (*Elec.*) Voltage; tension. (*Anat.*) **Tensión arterial**, blood presure. 4. (*Med.*) Tension; strain (estrés). **Tensión nerviosa**, nervous strain.

tenso, sa [ten'-so, sah], *a*. Tense (estirado), tight, extended, stiff. **Es una situación muy tensa**, it is a very tense situation.

tentación [ten-tah-the-on'], *f*. 1. Temptation, enticement. 2. That which is offered to the mind. **Resistir la tentación**, to resist temptation.

tentacioncilla [ten-tah-the-on-theel'-lyah], *f. dim*. A slight temptation.

tentaculado, da [ten-tah-coo-lah'-do, dah], *a*. (*Zool.*) Tentaculate, having tentacles.

tentáculo [ten-tah'-coo-lo], *m*. Tentacle, a flexible process generally about the head.

tentadero [ten-tah-day'-ro], *m*. Corral or enclosed place for fuming calves.

tentador, ra [ten-tah-dor', rah], *m. & f*. Tempter.

tentadura [ten-tah-doo'-rah], *f*. (*Min.*) Test for finding out the metal incorporated with mercury.

tentalear [ten-tah-lay-ar'], *va*. (*Prov.*) To try, to feel to examine.

tentar [ten-tar'], *va*. 1. To touch (tocar); to try (probar), to examine or prove by touch, to feel. 2. To grope. 3. To tempt (atraer), to instigate, to incite, to stimulate. 4. To attempt, to procure. 5. To hesitate. 6. To probe a wound; to tent. 7. To experiment; to try; to prove. Andar tentando, to make essays or trials; to grope or feel where one cannot see. Me tentó con una copita de anís, she tempted me with a glass of anise. Tentar a uno a hacer algo, to tempt somebody to do something. (*Yo tiento, yo tiente*, from *Tentar. V*. ACRECENTAR.)

tentativa [ten-tah-tee'-vah], *f*. Attempt (intento), trial, first examination, effort (esfuerzo).

tentativo, va [ten-tah-tee'-vo, vah], *a*. Tentative.

tente bonete [ten'-tay bo-nay'-tay], *adv*. Abundantly, excessively. **Tente en el aire**, (*com.*) the child of a quadroon and a mulatto, on either nice. **Tente en pie**, *m. (Coll.)* a light repast taken between meals.

tentemozo [ten-tay-mo'-tho], *m.* Prop to a house, to prevent its falling.

tentempié [ten-tem-pe-ay'], *m.* Snack, hasty repast.

tentón [ten-tone'], *m. (Coll.)* Touch, act of touching: especially applied to touching anything suddenly.

tenudo, da [tay-noo'-do, dah], *pp. irr. obs.* of TENER. Held. It was generally joined with the verb *ser*, when it signified, to be obliged, to be necessitated.

tenue [tay'-noo-ay], *a.* 1. Thin (palo), tenuous, delicate. 2. Worthless, of little value or importance. 3. Applied to soft consonants (sonido).

tenuemente [tay-noo-ay-men'-tay], *adv.* Slightly.

tenuidad [tay-noo-e-dahd'], *f.* 1. Tenuity, weakness. 2. Trifle, thing of little value or importance.

tenuta [tay-noo'-tah], *f.* Provisional possession of an estate during a lawsuit.

tenutario, ria [tay-noo-tah'-re-o, ah], *a.* Provisional tenant.

teñidura [tay-nye-doo'-rah], *f.* Art of dyeing or tingeing.

teñir [tay-nyeer'], *va.* 1. To tinge (colorar), to dye (con tinte); to stain: to paint the trace. 2. *(Met.)* To give another color to things, to dissemble or misrepresent. 3. *(Pict.)* To darken, to sadden a color. **Teñir una prenda de azul**, to dye a garment blue. *(Yo tiño, él tiñó, yo tiña*, from Teñir. *V.* PEDIR.)

teocalli [tay-o-cahl'-lyee], *m. (Mex.)* Teocalli, a pyramidal mound on which the Aztecs celebrated their sacrifices.

teocracia [tay-o-crah'-the-ah], *f.* Theocracy, government by priests.

teocrático, ca [tay-o-crah'-te-co, cah], *a.* Theocratic, theocratical.

teodolito [tay-o-do-lee'-to], *m.* Theodolite.

teologal [tay-o-lo-gahl'], *a.* Theological.

teología [tay-o-lo-hee'-ah], *f.* Theology, divinity. **Teología moral**, casuistry. **No meterse en teologías**, *(Coll.)* not to involve oneself in subtleties.

teológicamente [tay-o-loh'-he-cah-men-tay], *adv.* Theologically.

teológico, ca [tay-o-loh'-he-co, cah], *a. V.* TEOLOGAL.

teologizar [tay-o-lo-he-thar'], *vn.* To treat or discourse upon the principles of theology, to theologize.

teólogo [tay-o'-lo-go], *m.* 1. A divine, a clergyman. 2. A professor or student of theology.

teólogo [tay-oh'-lo-go], **ga**. *a.* Theological.

teorema [tay-o-ray'-mah], *m.* Theorem.

teorético, ca [tay-o-ray'-te-co, cah], *a.* Theoretic.

teoría, teórioca [tay-o-ree'-ah, tay-o'-re-cah], *f.* Theory, speculation. **Teoría atómica**, atomic theory.

teóricamente [tay-oh'-re-cah-men-tay], *adv.* Theoretically.

teórico, ca [tay-oh'-re-co, cah], *a.* Theoretically, speculative.

teoso, sa [tay-oh'-so, sah], *a.* Resinous.

teosofía [tay-o-so-fee'-ah], *f.* Theosophy, a philosophy of the universe, universal religion, a mystical speculation.

teosófico, ca [tay-o-so'-fe-co, cah], *a.* Theosophical, pertaining to theosophy.

teósofo [tay-oh'-so-fo], *m.* Theosophist.

teotl, teutl [tay-otl'], *m.* The supreme being among the Aztecs.

tepalcate [tay-pal-cah'-tay], *m. (Mex.)* Small pieces of broken earthenware (vasija).

tepe [tay'-pay], *m.* Green sod.

tepeguaje [tay-pay-goo-ah'-hay], *m.* A very hard and compact Mexican wood. -*a. (Met. Mex.)* Set, obstinate.

tepeizquinte [tay-pay-eeth-keen'-tay], *m.* South American animal, resembling a sucking pig.

tepetate [tay-pay-tah'-tay], *m.* 1. A layer of soil used for building houses in Mexico. 2. All mining ground which holds no ore.

tequila [tay-kee'-lah], *m.* Tequila, Mexican liquor distilled from the century plant.

tequío [tay-kee'-o], *m.* In Mexico, charm, tax. *V.* CARGA CONCEJIL.

terapéutica [tay-rah-pay'-oo-te-cah], *f.* Therapeutics, the branch of medicine, which treats of remedies.

terapéutico, ca [tay-rah-pay'-oo-te-co, cah], *a.* Therapeutic, remedial, curative.

terapia [tay'-rah-pe], *f.* Therapy. **Terapia de grupo**, group therapy.

tercamente [ter-cah-men'-tay], *adv.* Opinionately, opinionatively, obstinately.

tercena [ter-thay'-nah], *f.* 1. Wholesale tobacco warehouse. 2. *(And.)* Butcher's (tienda).

tercenal [ter-thay-nahl'], *m. (Prov.)* Heap containing thirty sheaves of corn.

tercenista [ter-thay-nees'-tah], *m.* Keeper of a wholesale tobacco warehouse.

tercer [ter-therr'], *m.* Third. -*a.* Third: used before a substantive.

tercera [ter-thay'-rah], *f.* 1. *(Mus.)* Third, a consonance comprehending an interval of two tones. 2. One of the strings of a guitar. 3. Series of three cords in order at play. 4. Procuress, bawd.

terceramente [ter-thay'-rah-men-tay], *adv.* Thirdly.

tercería [ter-thay-ree'-ah], *f.* 1. Mediation (arbitración), arbitration. 2. Arbitration dues or fees. 2. Depository. 4. Temporary occupation of a castle, fortress, etc.

tercerilla [ter-thay-reel'-lyah], *f.* Triplet, metrical composition.

tercermundista [ter-thayr-moon-dees'-tah], *a.* Third-world.

tercero, ra [ter-thay'-ro, rah], *a.* Third.

tercero [ter-thay'-ro], *m.* 1. Third (persona, piso). 2. Mediator (árbitro), arbitrator. 3. Collector of tithes. 4. Religious of the third order of St. Francis. 5. Pimp, procurer, bawd.

tercerol [ter-thay-role'], *m. (Naut.)* Main-sail; third pair of oars.

tercerola [ter-thay-ro'-lah], *f.* 1. Short kind of carbine. 2. Tierce, small cask.

tercerón, na [ter-thay-rone', nah], *m. & f. (Amer.)* A yellow man or woman, the offspring of a white and amulatto woman.

terceto [ter-thay'-to], *m.* 1. A kind of metrical composition; a tiercet, terzet, or terza-rima. 2. *(Mus.)* Terzetto, trio, a composition for three voices. 3. *V.* TERCERILLA.

tercia [terr'-the-ah], *f.* 1. Third, the third part. 2. Store-house or barn, where tithes are deposited. 3. One of the hours into which the Romans divided the day. 4. Canonical hour which follows immediately the first so called from falling at three o'clock.

terciación [ter-the-ah-the-on'], *f.* Act of ploughing a third time.

terciado [ter-the-ah'-do], *m.* 1. Cutlass, a short and broad sword. 2. Kind of ribbon somewhat broader than tape. -*a.* **Azúcar terciado**, brown sugar. **terciado, da** [ter-the-ah-do], -*pp.* of TERCIAR.

terciana [ter-the-ah'-nah], *f.* Tertian. **Fiebre terciana**, tertian fever.

tercianario, ria [ter-the-ah-nah'-re-o, ah], *m. & f.* 1. A person suffering from malaria. 2. A country where malaria is common.

tercianela [ter-the-ah-nay'-lah], *f.* Sort of silk, resembling taffeta.

tercianiento, ta [ter-the-ah-ne-en'-to, tah], *a. (Amer. Peru) V.* TERCIANARIO.

terciano, na [ter-the-ah'-no, nah], *a.* Tertian, occurring with a regular intermission between two or more things.

terciar [ter-the-ar'], *va.* 1. To sling anything diagonally. 2. To divide a thing into three parts. 3. To tertiate, to plough the third time. 4. To slant, to slope (inclinar). 5. *(And. Cono Sur, Mex.)* To hoist on to one's shoulder. 6. *(LAm.)* To water down (vino). -*vn.* 1. To make up the number of three. 2. To mediate, to arbitrate, to go between. 3. To join, to share, to make one of a party. **Terciar la carga**, to divide a burden into three equal parts. **Terciar entre dos rivales**, to mediate between two rivals. -*vr.* 1. **Si se tercia una buena oportunidad**, if a good chance presents itself. 2. **Si se tercia**

alguna vez que yo pase por allí, if I should happen to go that way.

terciario, ria [ter-the-ah'-re-o, ah], *a.* 1. Third in order or degree. 2. Tertiary, belonging to a geological period following the Mesozoic. *-m.* *(Arch.)* Rib in the vaulting of Gothic arches.

terciazón [ter-the-ah-thone'], *m.* Third ploughing.

tercio, cia [terr'-the-o, ah], *a.* Third.

tercio [terr'-the-o], *m.* 1. The third part (tercera parte). 2. Half a load. 3. Regiment of infantry in ancient Spanish warfare. 4. Third part of a horse-course. 5. Third part of the rosary; third part of a sword. 6. *(LAm.)* Pack, package, bale. 7. *(Carib.)* Fellow (hombre). **Hacer buen tercio,** to do good to a person. **Hacer tercio,** to join an association. **Hacer mal tercio,** to do a bad turn, to serve ill. *-pl.* 1. Height of horses, measured by hands. 2. Robust or strong limbs of a man.

terciodécuplo, pla [ter-the-o-day'-coo-plo, plah], *a.* Product of any quantity multiplied by thirteen.

terciopelado [ter-the-o-pay-lah'-do], *m.* Stuff resembling velvet.

terciopelado, da [ter-the-o-pay-lah'-do, dah], *a.* Velvet-like.

terciopelero [ter-the-o-pay-lah'-ro], *m.* Velvet-weaver.

terciopelo [ter-the-o-pay'-lo], *m.* Velvet.

terco, ca [terr'-co, cah], *a.* 1. Pertinacious, obstinate (obstinado), opinionative, contumacious. 2. Firm or hard as marble (material). **Terco como una mula,** as stubborn as a mule.

terebinto [tay-ray-been'-to], *m.* *(Bot.)* Turpentine or mastich-tree.

terebrante [tay-ray-brahn'-tay], *a.* *(Med.)* Boring, piercing (dolor).

tereniabín [tay-ray-ne-ah-been], *m.* White, sweetish, purgative matter, resembling mastich, which adheres to the leaves of plants; liquid manna.

térete [tay'-ray-tay], *a.* Round, plump, robust.

tergiversación [ter-he-ver-sah-the-on'], *f.* Tergiversation, evasion, subterfuge.

tergiversar [ter-he-ver-sar'], *va.* To distort (torcer), to boggle, to shift. *-vn.* To prevaricate (no resolverse); to chop and change (vacilar).

terliz [ter-leeth'], *m.* Tick, ticking, bed-ticking; tent-cloth.

termal [ter-mahl'], *a.* Thermal.

termas [ter-mas], *f. pl.* Hot baths.

térmico [ter'-me-co], *a.* Thermic, heat.

terminable [ter-me-nah'-blay], *a.* Terminable.

terminacho [ter-me-nah'-cho], *m.* *(Coll.)* Rude word or phrase (de palabra) (fea).

terminación [ter-me-nah-the-on'], *f.* 1. Termination, conclusion. 2. *(Gram.)* Termination, or last syllable of a word.

terminado [ter-me-nah'-do], *m.* Story, door, or flight of rooms.-**Terminado, da,** *pp.* of TERMINAR.

terminador, ra [ter-me-nah-dor', rah], *m. & f.* One who terminates.

terminal [ter-me-nahl'], *a.* Final, ultimate, terminal. *-m.* *(Elec. Comput.)* Terminal. *-f.* *(Aer. Ferro.)* Terminal; *(LAm. Ferro.)* Terminus.

terminante [ter-me-nahn'-tay], *pa.* Ending, closing, terminating. *-a.* Conclusive or decisive with regard to a point in question; definite. **En términos terminantes,** in definite terms, with propriety or punctuality, in point.

terminantemente [ter-me-nan-tay-men'-tay], *adv.* Absolutely, conclusively, by all means. **Queda terminantemente prohibido,** it is strictly forbidden to.

terminar [ter-me-nar'], *va. & vn.* 1. To end (forma, objeto), to close, to terminate. 2. To finish (acabar), to consummate; to end at, to abut. 3. *(Med.)* To come to a crisis. 4. *(Gram.)* To end a word. **Esto va a terminar en tragedia,** this will end in tragedy. **Cuando termine de hablar,** when he finishes speaking. *-vr.* To end, to come to an end.

terminativo, va [ter-me-nah-tee'-vo, vah], *a.* Terminative, respective, relative to a term.

término [terr'-me-no], *m.* 1. The end of anything. 2. Term, boundary, landmark (de tierra); limit, goal. 3. Manner, behavior, conduct. 4. District of a town or city. 5. Aim, object. 6. Term, the word by which a thing is expressed. 7. Term, the appointed time or determined place (plazo). 8. Crisis of a disease. 9. Determinate object of an operation. 10. Period including the beginning and end of something. 11. The precise moment to do anything. 12. Term or word of any language, a technical word, diction; conception. 13. Condition, constitution, state. 14. *(Arch.)* Stay, resembling the support which the ancients gave the head of their god Terminus. 15. Compartment in a painting. 16. *(Mus.)* Tone, pitch. **Primer término,** foreground of a picture. **En términos hábiles,** on reasonable terms, so as not to prejudice another. **Términos,** terms of an argument, syllogism, or arithmetical question. **¿En qué términos?** upon what terms? **Poner término a,** to put an end to. **Término medio** middle term. **Según los términos del contrato,** according to the terms of the contract. **En otros términos,** in other words.

terminología [ter-me-no-lo-hee'-ah], *f.* *(Neol.)* Terminology, the technical terms of a science or an art.

terminote [ter-me-no'-tay], *m. aug.* of TÉRMINO. A vulgar or affected expression.

termite [ter-mee'-tay], *m.* Termite, a white ant.

termodinámica [ter-mo-de-nah'-me-cah], *f.* Thermodynamics. **termodinámica aérea,** aerothermodynamics.

termoelétrico, ca [ter-mo-ay-lec'-tre-co, cah], *a.* Thermoelectric.

termófilo, la [ter-mo'-fe-lo, lah], *a.* Fond of living in warm countries.

termología [ter-mo-lo-hee'-ah], *f.* A treatise on heat.

termómetro [ter-mo'-may-tro], *m.* Thermometer.

termos [ter'-mos], *m.* Thermos or vacuum bottle.

termostato [ter-mos-tah'-to], *m.* Thermostat.

terna [terr' nah], *f.* 1. A ternary number. 2. A kind of stuff of a fine appearance after the fur or pile is fallen off. 3. Game at dice.

ternario, ria [ter-nah'-re-o, ah], *a.* Ternary, ternarious, containing three unities.

ternario [ter-nah'-re-o], *m.* 1. Three days' devotion or religious offices. 2. *(Mus.)* A measure of three equal parts.

terne [terr'-nay], *a.* *(Coll.)* V. VALENTÓN.

ternecio, ica, ito, ita [ter-nay-thee'-co], *a.* Very tender.

ternejal [ter-nay-hahl'], *a.* V. TERNE.

ternejón, na [ter-nay-hone', nah], *a.* V. TERNEJÓN.

ternecico, ica, illo, illa, ito, ita [ter-nay-ree'-co, cah, el'-lyo, eel'-lyah, ee'-to, ee'-tah], *m. & f.* A young calf.

ternero, ra [ter-nay'-ro, rah], *m. & f.* Calf; veal; heifer.

ternerón, na [ter-nay-rone', nah], *a.* 1. Easily moved, weeping at will. 2. *(Cono Sur, Mex.)* Overgrown, big (mozo).

terneruela [ter-nay-roo-ay'-lah], *f. & m.* A sucking calf.

terneza [ter-nay'-thah], *f.* 1. Softness, delicacy, pliantness. 2. Tenderness (cualidad), affection, endearment, fondness. 3. Suavity. 4. Readiness to shed tears.

ternilla [ter-neel'-lyah], *f.* Gristle, the cartilaginous part of the body.

ternilloso, sa [ter-neel-lyo'-so, sah], *a.* Gristly, cartilaginous, webbed, finfooted.

ternísimo, ma [ter-nee'-se-mo, mah], *a. super.* of TIERNO.

terno [terr'-no], *m.* 1. Ternary number (grupo de tres). 2. *(Coll.)* Wearing apparel, dress, rich clothes (traje). **Un terno de diamantes,** a set of diamonds. 3. Ornaments for celebrating high-mass. 4. Oath. V. VOTO. **Echar ternos** or **tacos,** to swear excessively, to speak in a great rage. 5. *(Print.)* Union of three sheets one within another. 6. In the game of lotto, the lot of obtaining three numbers in the row of five.

ternura [ter-noo'-rah], *f.* Tenderness (cualidad), delicacy, humanity, fondness. V. TERNEZA.

terquedad [ter-kay-dahd'], *f.* Stubbornness, obstinacy (obstinación), pertinacity, contumacy, inflexibility.

terracota [ter-rah-co'-tah], *f.* Terracotta.

terrácueo, cuea [ter-rah'-coo-ay-o, ah], *a*. Terraqueous.

terrada [ter-rah'-dah], *f*. Kind of bitumen made with ochre and glue.

terradillo [ter-rah-deel'-lyo], *m. dim*. A small terrace.

terrado [ter-rah'-do], *m*. Terrace, flat roof of a house. *V*. AZOTEA.

terraja [ter-rah'-hay], *f*. 1. A screwplate, screw-stock, or die-stock. 2. *V*. TARRAJA.

terraje [ter-rah'-hay], *m*. Rent paid to the owner of land.

terrajero [ter-rah-hay'-ro], *m. V*. TERRAZGUERO.

terral [ter-rahl'], *m. & a*. Applied to a land breeze.

terrapene [ter-rah-pay'-nay], *m*. *(Zool.)* Terrapin.

terraplén, terrapleno [ter-rah-playn'], *m*. *(Mil.)* The horizontal surface of a rampart terrace, mound; hence the graded road-bed of a railway.

terraplenar [ter-rah-play-nar'], *va*. To raise a rampart; to make a platform or terrace.

terraplenador [ter-rah-play-nah-dor'], *m*. One who makes a terrace or platform.

terráqueo, quea [ter-rah'-kay-o, ah], *a*. Terraqueous, containing both land and water.

terrateniente [ter-rah-tay-ne-en'-tay], *m*. Master or possessor of land or property.

terraza [ter-rah'-thah], *f*. 1. A glazed jar with two handles. 2. Terrace, a space somewhat raised and separated from the surface which is prolonged along the wall of a garden or courtyard (terraza). 3. Pavement café (café). 4. Nut (cabeza).

terrazgo [ter-rath'-go], *m*. 1. Arable land. 2. Land-tax or rent of arable land paid to the landlord.

terrazguero [ter-rath-gay'-ro], *m*. Laborer who pays rent to the lord of the manor for the land which he occupies.

terrazo [ter-rah'-tho], *m. (Art.)* Ground of a painting.

terrazuel [ter-rah-thoo-ay'-lah], *f. dim*. of TERRAZA.

terrear [ter-ray-ar'], *m*. To show the ground: speaking of crops which stand very thin.

terregoso, sa [ter-ray-go'-so, sah], *a*. Cloddy, full of clods.

terremoto [ter-ray-mo'-to], *m*. Earthquake.

terrenal [ter-ray-nahl'], *a*. Terrestrial. earthly, mundane.

terrenidad [ter-ray-ne-dahd'], *f*. Quality of the soil or ground.

terreno, na [ter-ray'-no, nah], *a*. 1. Terrene, earthly, terrestrial. 2. Worldly, terrestrial, perishable.

terreno [ter-ray'-no], *m*. 1. Land, ground (tierra, suelo), a field. 2. Field, sphere of action. 3. *(Geol.)* A group of several formations which have a certain analogy by their antiquity, form, or composition. **Terreno abierto**, *(Mil.)* open ground: that is, free of rocks, mountains, or other formidable obstacles and of fortified posts. **Los accidentes del terreno**, the characteristics of the terrain. **Ganar terreno**, to gain ground. **Terreno de fútbol**, football ground. **Eso no es mi terreno**, that's not my field.

térreo, rea [ter'-ray-o, ah], *a*. Terreous, earthy.

terrera [ter-ray'-rah], *f*. 1. A steep piece of ground. 2. *(Orn.)* Kind of lark.

terrero [ter-ray'-ro], *m*. 1. Terrace, platform. 2. Heap of earth. 3. Mark, to shoot at. 4. Terrace, or other part of the palace, where court is paid to the ladies. **Hacer terrero**, to court a lady. 5. In the Canary Islands, an open, clear spot where an athletic contest, common in the country, takes place. 6. *(Mil.)* An artificial wall of earth.

terrero, ra [ter-ray'-ro, rah], *a*. 1. Earthly (de la tierra), terreous. 2. Abject, humble. 3. Skimming the ground (pájaros).

terrestre [ter-res'-tray], *a*. Terrestrial; earthly (de la tierra), land; land (ruta), overland; *(Mil.)* ground (fuerzas).

terrestridad [ter-res-tre-dahd'], *f*. Earthiness.

terrezuela [ter-ray-thoo-ay'-lah], *f*. 1. *(Dim.)* A small piece of ground. 2. Light and poor soil.

terribilidad [ter-re-be-le-dahd'], *f*. Terribleness, roughness, asperity, ferocity.

terrible [ter-ree'-blay], *a*. 1. Terrible, dreadful, ferocious, horrible. 2. Rude, unmannerly. 3. Immense, very large.

terriblemente [ter-ree'-blay-men-tay], *adv*. Terribly, frightfully.

terrícola [tar-ree'-co-lah], *com*. Inhabitant of the earth.

terrífico, ca [ter-ree'-fe-co, cah], *a*. Terrific, frightful.

terrígeno, na [ter-ree'-hay-no, nah], *a*. Terrigenous, earth-born.

terrino, na [ter-ree'-no, nah], *a*. Terrene, earthy.

territorial [ter-re-to-re-ahl'], *a*. Territorial.

territorio [ter-re-toh'-re-o], *m*. 1. Territory, district; ground; land. 2. Territory, a district still under provisional or colonial government.

terrizo, za [ter-ree'-tho, thah], *a*. 1. Earthy, earthen. 2. Unglazed.

terrojo [ter-ro'-ho], *m*. 1. Red earth. 2. *V*. TERRAZGO.

terromontero [ter-ro-mon-tay'-ro], *m*. Hill, hillock.

terrón [ter-rone'], *m*. 1. A flat clod of earth, globe. 2. Lump of anything. **Terrón de azú**, lump sugar. 3. Heap, collection of things. 4. Dregs of olives which remain in the mill. *-pl*. Landed property.

terronazo [ter-ro-nah'-tho], *m*. 1. *(Aug.)* A large clod of earth. 2. Blow with a clod.

terroncillo [ter-ron-theel'-lyo], *m. dim*. A small cold.

terrontera [ter-ron-tay'-rah], *f*. Break in a mountain.

terror [ter-ror'], *m*. Terror, dread, consternation.

terrorífico, ca [ter-ro-ree'-fe-co, cah], *a. V*. TERRÍFICO.

terrorismo [ter-ro-rees'-mo], *m*. The act of terrifying: applied to unlawful violence.

terrorista [ter-ro-rees'-tah], *m*. A person who employs authority to commit unlawful violence.

terrosidad [ter-ro-se-dahd'], *f*. Earthiness.

terroso, sa [ter-ro'-so, sah], *a*. Terreous, earthy.

terruca [ter-roo'-cah], *f*. 1. *(Dim.) V*. TERREZUELA. 2. *(Neol. Coll.)* Native country.

terruño [te-roo'-cah], *m*. 1. A piece of land (parcela). 2. One's native soil.

tersar [ter-sar'], *va*. To smooth, to polish, to clean, to make smooth and clean.

tersícore [ter-se'-co-ray], *f*. Terpsichore, the muse of the dance.

tersidad [ter-se-dahd'], *f*. Smoothness, terseness.

terso, sa [terr'-so, sah], *a*. 1. Smooth (liso), polished, glossy (brillante). 2. Pure, elegant, correct, terse (estilo). **Piel tersa**, smooth skin.

tersura [ter-soo'-rah], *f*. Smoothness, cleanliness, purity; elegance, terseness.

tertulia [ter-too'-le-ah], *f*. 1. Club, assembly, circle, coterie, evening party (reunión informal). 2. Part of the boxes in a play-house reserved for women only. **Estar de tertulia**, to talk, to sit around talking.

tertuliano, na [ter-too-te-ah'-no, nah], *a*. Member of a club, assembly, or circle of friends.

tertulio, a, [ter-too'-le-o, ah], *a*. Relating to a meeting of friends or party.

teruelo [tay-roo-ay'-lo], *m. (Prov.)* Bowl or box in which lots are put to be cast.

teruncio [ter-roo'-the-o], *m*. A Roman coin, the fourth part of an as.

terutero [tay-roo-tay'-ro], *m*. A bird which lives by the banks of rivers and whose note resembles the sound of its name.

terzón, na [ter-thone', -nah], *a. & n*. Heifer, a three-year-old ox.

terzuelo, la [ter-thoo-ay'-lo-lah], *a*. Applied to the third bird which leaves the nest.

terzuelo [ter-thoo-ay'-lo], *m*. Third part of anything.

tesaliense, tesalio, lia, tésalo, la [tay-sah-le-en'-say, tay-sah'-le-o, ah, tay'-sah-lo, lah], *a*. Thessalonian, of Thessaly.

tesalónico, ca [tay-sah-lo'-ne-co, cah], *a*. Thessalonian, of Thessalonica.

tesar [tay-sar'], *va*. 1. *(Naut.)* To haul (cuerda) taut, to tauten. 2. *(Prov.)* As applied to yoked oxen, to back, to pull back.

tesauro [tay-sah'-oo-ro], *m*. Dictionary, vocabulary, index.

tesela [tay-say'-lah], *f.* Tessella, each of the small cubes or squares for making mosaic pavements.

teselato, tao [tay-say-lah'-to, tah], *a.* Tessellate, tessellated, inlaid, mosaic.

tésera [tay'-say-rah], *f.* Sign or counter sign; a cubical piece of wood or bone used by the Romans as a pledge of hospitality, etc.

tesis [tay'-sis], *f.* 1. Thesis. 2. *V.* CONCLUSIÓN.

teso, sa [tay'-so, sah], *a. V.* TIESO.

teso [tay'-so], *m.* Brow of a hill.

tesón [tay-sone'], *m.* Tenacity, firmness, inflexibility.

tesorería [tay-so-ray-ree'-ah], *f.* Treasury, treasurers office, exchequer: treasurership, office or dignity of a treasurer.

tesorero, ra [tay-so-ray'-ro, rah], *m. & f.* 1. Treasurer. 2. Canon who keeps the relics.

tesoro [tay-so'-ro], *m.* 1. Treasure (dineral), wealth, riches. 2. Treasury exchequer. 3. Anything valuable and precious. 4. Treasure, a complete abridgment of useful knowledge. **Tesoro escondido**, buried treasure. **El libro es un tesoro de datos**, the book is a mine of memories.

test [test], *m.* Test.

testa [tes'-tah], *f.* 1. Forehead, front, face. 2. Front, face, of material things.

testáceo, cea [tes-tah'-thay-o, ah], *a.* Testaceous, provided with a hard constinuous shell, as a mollusk. -*m.* Testacean, a shell-bearing invertebrate especially a mollusk.

testación [tes-tah-the-on'], *f.* 1. Leaving by will. 2. Obliteration.

testada [tes-tah'-dah], *f. V.* TESTARADA.

testado, da [tes-tah'-do dah], *a. & pp.* of TESTAR. Dying testate.

testador [tes-tah-dor'], *m.* Testator.

testadora [tes-tah-do'-rah], *f.* Testatrix.

testadura [tes-tah-doo'-rah], *f.* Obliteration, lineal erasure of written letters.

testaférrea [tes-tah-fayr'-ray-ah], *m. V.* TESTAFERRO.

testaferro [tes-tah-fer'-ro], *m.* One who lends his name on a contract or business belonging to another, used in a depreciative sense.

testamentaria [tes-tah-men-tah-ree'-ah], *f.* Testamentary, execution.

testamentaria [tes-tah-men-tah'-re-ah], *f.* Executrix.

testamentario [tes-tah-men-tah'-re-o], *m.* Executor.

testamentario, ria [tes-tah-men-tah'-re-o, ah], *a.* Testamentary.

testamento [tes-tah-men'-to], *m.* 1. Last will, testament. **Testamento cerrado**, a sealed testament. **Testamento abierto**, a will made viva voce before three witnesses and a notary, before five witnesses, citizens of the place in which it is executed. Or before seven, even though nonresident, and without a notary. 2. Part of the Holy Scriptures.

testar [tes-tar'] *va. & n.* 1. To will, to make a last will or testament, to leave, to bequeath. 2. To blot, to scratch out.

testarada [tes-tah-rah'-dah], *f.* 1. A stroke or blow with the head. 2. Stubbornness, obstinacy.

testarrón, na [tes-tah-rone'], *a. V.* TESTARUDO.

testarronería [tes-tar-ro-nay-ree'-ah], *f.* Stubborness, obstinacy, tenacity.

testarudo, da [tes-tah-roo'-do, dah], *a.* Obstinate, stubborn.

teste [tes'-tay], *m.* Testis, testicle.

testera [tes-tay'-rah], *f.* 1. Front or fore part of anything; forehead of an animal. 2. Head-stall of the bridle of a horse, or head-piece of a bridle.

testerada [tes-tay-rah'-dah], *f. V.* TESTARADA.

testero [tes-tay'-ro], *m. V.* TESTERA.

testicular [tes-te-coo-lar'], *a.* Testicular, pertaining to the testicles.

testículo [tes-tee'-coo-lo], *m.* A testicle.

testificación [tes-te-fe-cah-the-on'], *f.* Attestation, testification.

testificante [tes-te-fe-cahn'-tay], *pa.* witnessing, attesting.

testificar [tes-te-fe-car'], *va.* To attest (atestiguar). to witness, to certify, to testify (dar testimonio).

testificata [tes-te-fe-cah'-tah], *f. (Law.)* Legal testimony.

testificativo, va [tes-te-fe-cah-tee'-vo, vah], *a.* That which testifies.

testigo [tes-tee'-go], *m. & f.* 1. Witness, one who gives testimony. 2. Inanimate witness, evidence. **Testigo de vista** or **ocular**, an eye-witness. **Testigo de cargo**, witness for the prosecution.

testimonial [tes-te-mo-ne-ahl'], *a.* That which bears a true testimony: applied to a testimonial or writing produced as an evidence.

testimoniales [tes-te-mo-ne-ah'-les], *f. pl.* Testimonials, an authentic writing verifying what is contained in it; a certificate: in particular, a certificate of good character given by a bishop to a parishioner who moves to another diocese.

testimoniar [tes-te-mo-ne-ar'], *va.* To testify, to attest, to bear witness, to aver; to avouch.

testimoniero, ra [tes-te-mo-ne-ay'-ro, rah], *a.* 1. Bearing false witness. 2. Dissembling, hypocritical.

testimonio [tes-te-mo'-ne-o], *m.* 1. Testimony, deposition of a witness, proof by witness. 2. Testimony, open attestation, attestation. 3. An instrument legalized by notary. **Testimonio** or **falso testimonio**, false accusation or testimony; imposture.

testimoñero, ra [tes-te-mo-nyay'-ro, rah], *a.* Hypocritical. *V.* TESTIMONIERO.

testón [tes-tone'], *m.* A coin having a head.

testudo [tes-too'-do], *m.* Machine for covering soldiers in an attack on a fortification.

testuz, testuzo [tes-tooth', tes-too'-tho], *m. (Vet.)* Hind part of the head, nape; in some animals, crown of the head. *(Acad.)*

tesura [tay-soo'-rah], *f.* 1. Stiffness, firmness. 2. Starched and affected gravity.

teta [tay'-tah], *f.* 1. Mammary gland, breast. 2. Nipple (pezón), teat (de biberón); dug of animals. **Teta de vaca**, teat or dug of a cow; kind of large grapes. **Niño de teta**, a child at the breast; a suckling.

tetánico, ca [tay-tah'-ne-co, cah], *a.* Tetanic, tetanical.

tétano [tay'-tah-no], **tétanos**, *m. (Med.)* Tetanus, lockjaw; tonic spasm.

tetar [tay-tar'], *va.* To suckle, to give suck. *V.* ATETAR.

tetaza [tay-tah'-thah], *f. aug.* Flabby, ugly dugs.

tetera [tay-tay'-rah], *f.* Tea-pot, tea kettle, with strainer.

tetero [tay-tay'-ro], *m. (Amer.)* Nursing bottle. *V.* BIBERÓN.

tetica, ita [tay-tee'-cah], *f. dim.* A small dug or teat.

tetilla [tay-tee'-lyah], *f.* 1. *(Dim.)* A small nipple or teat (de hombre). 2. Kind of paste in the figure of a teat.

tetina [tay-tee'-nah], *f.* Teat (de biberón).

tetona [tay-to'-nah], *a.* Having large teats.

tetracordio [tay-trah-cor'-de-o], *m. (Mus.)* Tetrachord, fourth.

tetraédrico, ca [tay-trah-ay'-dre-co, cah], *a.* Tetrahedral.

tetraedro [tay-trah-ay'-dro], *m. (Geom.)* Tetrahedron.

tetragínico, ca [tay-trah-hee'-ne-co, cah], *a. (Bot.)* Having four pistils.

tetrágono [tay-trah'-go-no], *m. (Geom.)* Tetragon.

tetrágono, na [ ], *a. (Geom.)* Tetragonal.

tetragrámatron [tay-trah-grah'-mah-trone], *m.* Word composed of four letters, particularly the name of *Dios*.

tetrámetro [tay-trah'-may-tro], *m.* Iambic verse of eight feet or four measures. -*pl. (Zool.)* A section of coleoptera, having four joints upon the tarsi.

tetrapétalo [tay-trah-pay'-tah-lo] *(Bot.)* Tetrapetalous: fourpetalled.

tetrarca [tay-trar'-cah], *vn.* Tetrarch.

tetrarquía [tay-trah-kee'-ah], *f.* Tetrarchate, tetrarchy.

tetrástilo [tay-trahs'-te-lo], *m.* Building sustained by four columns or pilasters.

tetrasílabo, ba [tay-trah-see'-lah-bo, bah], *a. V.* CUATRISÍLABO.

tétricamente [tay'-tre-cah-men-tay], *adv.* Gloomily.

tétrico, ca [tay'-tre-co, cah], *a.* Crabbed, grave, gloomy (pensamiento, humor), sullen.

tetuda [tay-too'-dah], *a.* 1. Having large nipples. 2. *(Prov.)* Applied to a kind of oblong olives.

teucalí [tay-oo-cah-lee'], *m. V.* TEOCALLA.

teucrio [tay'-oo-cre-o], *m. (Bot.)* Germander.

teucro, cra [tay'-oo-cro, crah], *a. & a.* Trojan.

teurgia [tay-oor'-he-ah], *f.* Theurgy, black magic, superstitious art of calling on beneficent genii.

teutón [tay-oo-tone'], *m. (& pl.).* Teuton, especially the ancient Germanic tribes or language.

teutónico, ca [tay-oo-toh'-ne-co, cah], *a.* 1. Teutonic, of a German military order. 2. German, Teutonic.

textil [tex-teel'], *a.* Textile, capable of being made into threads and woven.

texto [tex'-to], *m.* 1. Text, the original words of an author. 2. Text of Scripture. 3. *(Print.)* Name of a size of types: great primer.

textorio, ria [tex-to'-re-o, ah], *a.* Textrine, textorial, belonging to weaving.

textual [tex-too-ahl'], *a. 1.* Textual (de texto), agreeing with the text. 2. *(Fig.)* Exact; literal. **Son sus palabras textuales**, those are his exact words.

textualista [tex-too-ah-lees'-tah], *m.* 1. Textualist, he who adheres to the text. 2. Texturist, one ready in quotation of texts.

textualmente [tex-too-ahl'-men-tay], *adv. 1.* According to the text; textually. 2. *(Fig.)* Exactly; literally.

textura [tex-too'-rah], *f.* 1. Texture, as of stuff or cloth. 2. Succession and order of things.

tez [teth], *f.* 1. Grain; shining surface. 2. Bloom of the complexion, hue.

tezado, da [tay-thah'-do, dah], *a.* Very black. *V.* ATEZADO.

tezcucano, na [teth-coo-cah'-no, nah], *a.* Tezcucan, belonging to Tezcuco, a city of Mexico.

tezontle [tay-thon'-tlay], *m. (Mex.)* A porous stone esteemed for building in Mexico.

theta [thay'-tah], *f.* Eighth letter of the Greek alphabet, represented in Latin by *th*, in modern Spanish by *t* alone.

ti [tee]. The oblique case of **tú**, thou. When preceded by the preposition **con**, it takes the termination **go**, as **contigo**, with you. **Ti mismo**, yourself, thyself.

ti [tee], *pron.* You; yourself. **Esto no se refiere a ti**, this doesn't refer to you.

tía [tee'-ah], *f.* 1. Aunt (pariente). 2. *(Coll.)* A good old woman (mujer). 3. *(Coll.)* Used in Spain to express colloquially a common woman. **Cuéntaselo a tu tía**, *(Coll.)* tell it to your grandmother. **Tía**, a name given to decent old persons in low condition, in stead of *Doña*; as, **da esto a la tía Isabel**, give this to aunt Elizabeth. **Tía buena**, smashing girl.

tialismo [te-ah-lees'-mo], *m.* Ptyalism, abnormal discharge of saliva.

tiangui [te-ahn'-gee], **Tiangue** [te-ahn'-gay] (in the Philippine Islands), *m.* The market, and market-days, in the small towns of the Mexican republic and in the Philippine Islands.

tiara [te-ah'-rah], *f.* 1. Tiara, miter worn by the Pope. 2. Pontificate, papal dignity. 3. Diadem of the ancient kings of Persia.

tibetano, na [te-bay-tah'-no], *a. m & f.* Tibetan.

tibia [tee'-be-ah], *f.* 1. Shinbone. 2. A flute.

tibial [te-be-ahl'], *a. (Anant.)* Tibial, relating to the tibia.

tibiamente [tee'-be-ah-men-tay], *adv.* Tepidly, carelessly, lukewarmly.

tibieza [te-be-ay'-thah], *f.* 1. Tepidity, lukewarmness (desustancia); coldness. 2. Coolness, frigidity, jejuneness. 3. Carelessness, negligence.

tibio, bia [tee'-be-o, ah], *a. 1.* Tepid, lukewarm (agua), careless, remiss. 2. *(CAm. Carib.)* Cross, angry.

tibir [te-beer'], *m.* Name of gold-dust on the African coast.

tibor [te-bor'], *m.* 1. A large china jar. 2. *(Amer. Cuba)* A chamber pot.

tiburón [te-boo-ron'], *m.* 1. Shark. 2. *(Fig.)* Gogetter, unscrupulous person; *(Cono Sur)* wolf, Don Juan.

tictac [tic-tac'], *m.* Tick tock (de reloj); beat (de corazón); tapping (de máquina de escribir).

tiempecillo, tiempecito [te-em-pay-theel'-lyo, thee'-to], *m. dim.* A little time.

tiempo [te-em'-po], *m.* 1. Time. 2. Term, a limited space of time (específico, limitado). 3. Any of the four seasons. 4. Time, opportunity, occasion; tide, season; leisure. 5. Weather, temperature, climate. 6. State, condition. 7. Draft, portion. 8. *(Gram.)* Time, tense. 9. Age. 10. Time, space, duration of an action. 11. Time, musical measure. **Tiempo borrascoso**, stormy weather. **Tiempo variable**, unsettled weather. **Tiempo apacible**, moderate weather. **Haga buen o mal tiempo**, rain or shine. **A tiempo**, timely, in time, just in time (en el momento oportuno); on time. **Nunca llega a la oficina a tiempo**, he never arrives at the office on time. **A un tiempo**, at once; at the same time. **Con tiempo**, timely, beforehand. **De tiempo en tiempo**, from time to time. **Por tiempo**, for some time, undetermined time. **La carta llegó a su tiempo**, the letter was duly received. **A tiempo que**, just as. **Abrir el tiempo**, the weather clears up. **Dar tiempo al tiempo**, to await the right occasion to do something. **Tomarse tiempo**, to take time, to defer. **En tiempo hábil**, in the appointed time. **Cada cierto tiempo**, every so often. **Todo el tiempo**, all the time. **El tiempo apremia**, time presses. **El tiempo dirá**, time will tell. **Ganar tiempo**, to save time. **En los tiempos que corremos**, in these dreadful times. **Primer tiempo**, first half. **En mis tiempos**, in my time, when I was young. **Malgastar el tiempo**, to waste time. **¿Qué tiempo tiene ese niño?**, how old is that child? **Tiempo de declinación**, *(Comput.)* decay time. **Tiempo de desplazamiento de caracteres**, *(Comput.)* skew time. **Tiempo de formación**, *(Comput.)* rise time. **Tiempo de subida**, *(Comput.)* rise time.

tienda [te-en'-dah], *f.* 1. *(Mil.)* Tent. 2. *(Naut.)* Awning over vessels. 3. Tilt for carts or wagons. 4. Shop or stall. **Poner or abrir tienda**, to open a shop. **Tienda de informática**, *(Comput.)* computer store.

tienta [te-en'-tah], *f.* 1. *(Med.)* Probe. 2. Craft, cunning, artful industry. **A tientas**, doubtfully uncertainly in the dark, at random. **Andar a tientas**, to crope in the dark, to fumble.

tientaaguja [te-en-tah-ah-goo'-hah], *f.* An auger for testing the ground on which it is proposed to build.

tiento [te-en'-to], *m.* 1. Touch, the act of feeling (sensación física). 2. A blind man's stick. 3. Circumspection, prudent consideration (prudencia). 4. Poy, a rope-dancer's pole. 5. Sureness of the hand, a steady band. 6. Stroke. *V.* GOLPE. 7. Mahlstick, maulstick, a painter's staff. 8. *(Mus.)* Prelude, flourish. 9. *(Zool.)* Tentacle. **Dar un tiento**, to make a trial. **Por el tiento**, by the touch. **Al tiento**, obscurely, doubtfully.

tiernamente [te-er-nah-men'-tay], *adv.* Tenderly, compassionately.

tiernecico, ica, illo, illa, ito, ita [te-er-nay-thee'-co], *a. dim.* of TIERNO.

tierno, na [te-err'-no, nah], *a.* 1. Tender, soft, docile: delicate: lady-like. 2. Affectionate, fond, amiable, mild, easily moved to tears. 3. Recent, modern. young; tender; applied to age.

tierra [te-er'-rah], *f.* 1. Earth, the solid part of our globe, land (superficie), soil, ground, mould. 2. Native country. 3. Earth, the terraqueous globe. 4. Arable land. 5. Land, country, region, a distinct part of the globe: as **Tierra Santa**, the Holy Land. 6. *(LAm.)* Dust (polvo). **Tierra de los duendes**, fairy-land. **Tierra adentro**, *(Naut.)* in land. **Correr hacia la tierra**, *(Naut.)* to stand inshore. **Tomar tierra**, *(Naut.)* to anchor in a port. **Tierra firme**, continent. **Besar la tierra**, *(Coll.)* to fall with one's mouth against the ground. **Besar la tierra que otro pisa**, to kiss the ground another treads on (excessive respect). **Echar tierra a alguna cosa**, to bury an affair in oblivion. **Echarse por tierra**, to be humiliated. **Poner tierra en**, or **por medio**, to absent oneself.

tiesamente [te-ay'-sah-men-tay], *adv.* Firmly, stiffly, strongly.

tieso, sa [te-ay'-so, sah], *a.* 1. Stiff (rígido), hard, firm, solid. 2. Robust, strong; valiant, animated. 3. Stubborn (terco), obstinate, inflexible. 4. Tight, rigid (rígido): too grave or circumspect. **Con las orejas tiesas**, with its ears pricked. **Me recibió muy tieso**, he received me very stiffly. **Ponerse tieso con uno**, to stand one's ground. **Estar tieso**, to be broke.

tieso [te-ay'-so], *adv.* V. TIESAMENTE.

tieso [te-ay'-so], *m.* Firmness, inflexibility: hardness.

tiesta [te-es'-tah], *f.* Edge of the staves which serve for the ends of casks.

tiesto [te-es'-to], *m.* 1. Potsherd. 2. A large earthen pot.

tiesura [te-ay-soo'-rah], *f.* 1. Stiffness (rigidez), rigidity. 2. Stiffness, harshness in behavior.

tifo [tee'-fo], *m.* (*Med.*) Typhus, a malignant fever. **Tifo de Ameérica**, yellow fever. **Tifo asiático**, asiatic cholera. **Tifo de Oriente**, the plague.

tifoideo, dea [te-foi-day'-o, ah], *a.* Typhoid, typhus-like.—*f.* Typhoid fever.

tifón [te-fone'], *m.* 1. Whirlwind. V. TORBELLINO. 2. Typhoon (huracán). 3. (*Mex. Min.*) Outcrop of ore.

tifus [tee'-foos], *m.* Typhus fever. **Tifus icteroides**, yellow fever.

tignaria [tig-nah'-re-ah], *f.* Knowledge of the fittest timber for building.

tigre [tee'-gray], *m.* 1. Tiger. 2. (*And.*) Black coffee with a dash of milk; (*And.*) Cocktail (combinado).

tigresa [te-gray-sah], *f.* Tigress.

tigridia [te-gree'-de-ah], *f.* (*Bot.*) Tigridia, tiger-flower, a plant of the iris family, native of Mexico, cultivated for the beauty of its flowers.

tija [tee'-hah], *f.* The shaft of a key.

tijera, or **tijeras** [te-hay'-rah], *f.* 1. Scissors. 2. Carpenter's horse, cooper's mare, for holding the wood while dressing, any instrument in the form of an X. 3. Sheep-shearer. 4. A small channel or drain. 5. Detractor, murmurer. **Meter la tijera en**, to cut into. **Silla de tijera**, folding chair.

tijerada [te-hay-rah'-dah], *f.* V. TIJERETADA.

tijereta [te-hay-ray'-tah], *f.* 1. (*Dim.*) Small scissors. 2. Small tendril of vines. 3. A common insect, the earwig. 4. A South American bird.

tijeretada [te-hay-ray-tah'-dah], *f.* A cut with scissors, a clip.

tijeretazo [te-hay-ray-tah'-tho], *m.* A cut with scissors.

tijeretear [te-hay-ray-tay-ar'], *va.* 1. To cut with scissors. 2. To dispose of other people's affairs at one's pleasure. 3. (*CAm. Cono Sur, Mex.*) To gossip (chismear).

tijerica, ita [te-hay-ree'-cah], *f. dim* A small pair of scissors.

tijerilla [te-hay-reel'-lyah], *f. dim.* V. TIJERETA.

tijeruela [te-hay-roo-ay'-lah], *f.* Small tendril of vines.

tila [tee'-lah], *f.* (*Bot.*) 1. Lime-tree, linden-tree. 2. The flower of this tree. 3. Infusion, tea, of linden flowers.

tilar [te-lar'], *m.* Grove or plantation of lime or linden trees.

tildar [tel-dar'], *va.* 1. To blot, to scratch out. 2. To brand, to stigmatize. 3. To mark letters with a dash, as the ñ, to put an accent.

tilde [teel'-day], *f.* 1. Tilde (sobre la ñ). 2. Accent (acento). 3. Dot or dash over a letter. 3. Iota, a tittle (cosa insignificante).

tildón [til-done'], *m.* (*Aug.*). A long dash or stroke.

tilia [tee'-le-ah], *f.* (*Bot.*) V. TILO.

tilichero [te-le-chay'-ro], *m.* (*Amer.*) Peddler, a vender of small articles.

tiliches [te-lee'-ches], *m. pl.* (*Amer.*) Small fancy articles.

tilín [te-leen'], *m.* A word imitating the sound of a bell. **Hacer tilín**, to please, to become a favorite.

tilla [teel'-lyah], *f.* (*Naut.*) Midship, gangway.

tillado [teel-lyah'-do], *m.* A wooden floor.

tillar [teel-lyar'], *va.* To floor. V. ENTARIMAR.

tilma [teel'-mah], *f.* (*Mex.*). A cloak fastened at the shoulder by a knot.

tilo [tee'-lo], *m.* 1. (*Bot.*) Linden-tree, lime-tree. 2. (*Cono Sur*) V. TILA.

tilosis [te-lo'-sis], *f.* Falling out of the eyelashes.

timador, ra [te-mah-dor'], *m & f.* Swindler, trickster.

tímalo [tee'-mah-lo], *m.* Grayling (pez).

timar [te-mar'], *va.* 1. To steal (propiedad); to swindle somebody out of. 2. To swindle (persona). *-vr.* To make eyes at each other.

timba [teem'-bah], *f.* 1. (*Coll.*) Hand in a game of chance; also a low gambling-house (en juego de azar). 2. (*Phil.Is.*) bucket for water. 3. (*CAm. Carib. Mex.*) Pot-belly.

timbal [tim-bahl'], *m.* Kettle drum. V. ATABAL.

timbalear [tim-bah-lay-ar'], *vn.* To beat the kettle-drum.

timbaleo [tim-bah-lay'-o], *m.* Beat of the kettle-drum.

timbalero [tim-bah-lay'-ro], *m.* Kettle drummer.

timbirimba [tim-bah-reem'-bah], *f.* (*Coll.*) V. TIMBA.

timbra [teem'-brah], *f.* (*Bot.*) Mountain hyssop.

timbrar [tim-brar'], *va.* 1. To put the crest to the shield in a coat of arms. 2. To stamp a seal or device upon paper (estampillar).

timbre [teem'-bray], *m.* 1. (*Her.*) Timbre or simmer, crest of a coat of arms. 2. Seal, device, stamped upon paper, indicating a person's name, etc. 3. A bell provided with a spring. 4. Tone color, clang-tint, peculiar harmonious sound of the voice or instruments. 5. Any glorious deed or achievement. **Timbre de alarma**, alarm bell. **Tocar el timbre**, to ring the bell. **Timbre nasal**, nasal timbre.

timiama [te-me-ah'-mah], *f.* Sweet perfume. V. ALMEA.

tímidamente [tee'-me-dah-men-tay], *adv.* Timidly, fearfully, timorously.

timidez [te-me-deth'], *f.* Timid, Cowardly, dastardly.

tímido, da [tee'-me-do, dah], *a.* Timid, cowardly, dastardly.

timo [tee'-mo], *m.* Swindle (estafa), confidence trick, confidence game; gag (broma). **Dar un timo a uno**, to swindle somebody.

timón [te-mone'], *m.* 1. Beam of a plough (arado); pole of a coach (carruaje). 2. (*Naut.*) Helm, rudder. 3. Part which governs the movement of various machines. **Timón de dirección**, direction. **Coger el timón**, to take the helm.

timonear [te-mo-nay-ar'], *va.* (*Naut.*) To govern the helm; to steer.

timonel [te-mo-nel'], *m.* (*Naut.*) Timoneer, helmsman.

timonera [te-mo-nay'-rah], *f.* 1. (*Naut.*) The helmsman's post before the bittacle. 2. Each of the large tail-feathers of a bird.

timonero [te-mo-nay'-ro], *m.* Timoneer, helmsman.

timorato, to [te-mo-rah'-to, tah], *a.* 1. Full of the fear of God. 2. Timorous (tímido). 3. Prudish (mojigato).

timpa [teem'-pah], *f.* Bar of iron in a furnace hearth.

timpánico, ca [tim-pah'-ne-co, cah], *a.* (*Anat.*) Tympanic, relating to the eardrum.

timpanillo [tim-pah-neel'-lyo], *m. dim.* 1. A small kettle drum, a small tympanum or tympan. 2. (*Print.*) Inner tympan of a printing-press. 3. (*Arch.*) Gablet, a small ornamental gable or gabled canopy.

timpanítico, ca [tim-pah-nee'-te-so, cah], *a.* Affected with tympanites or wind-dropsy.

timpanitis [tim-pah-nee'-tis], *f.* (*Med.*) 1. Tympanites, distension of the abdomen by gases. 2. Myringitis, inflammation of the eardrum.

tímpano [teem'-pah-no], *m.* 1. Kettledrum. 2. (*Anat.*) Tympanum, the drum of the ear. 3. Tympan of a printing-press. 4. Cylinder. 5. (*Arch.*) Tympanum.

tina [tee'-nah], *f.* 1. A large earthern jar. 2. Vat, dyer's cooper (recipiente). 3. Bathing-tub.

tinaco [te-nah'-co], *m.* 1. Wooden trough, tub, or vat. 2. (*Mex.*) Water tank (cisterna).

tinada [te-nah'-dah], *f.* 1. Pile of wood or timber. 2. Shed for cattle.

tindado, tinador [te-nah'-do, te-nah-dor'], *m.* Shed for sheltering cattle.

tinaja [te-nah'-hah], *f.* A large earthen jar.

tinajería [te-nah-hay-ree'-ah], *f.* (*Prov.*) The place where large earthen jars are kept.

tinajero [te-nah-hay'-ro], *m.* 1. One who makes or sells water-jars. 2. *(Mex.)* Kitchen dresser. 3. *V.* TINAJERÍA.

tinajica, illa, ita [te-nah-hee'-cah], *f. dim.* A small earthen wide-mouthed jar.

tinajón [te-nah-hone'], *m.* 1. A large wide-mouthed jar for catching rain. 2. A fat and lusty person.

tinero [te-nay'-ro], *m.* Dyer who takes care of the copper in woollen manufactories.

tineta [te-nay'-tah], *f. dim.* of TINA. Kit, small tub.

tinge [teen'-hay], *m. (Orn.)* Kind of black owl.

tingladillo [tin-glah-deel'-lyo], *m. (Naut.)* Clinker-work, lappointed work having the edges overlapping and riveted together.

tinglato [tin-glah'-to], *m.* 1. A small roof jutting out from the wall to shelter people from the rain. 2. A hovel, a covered passage. 3. Workshop, shed.

tinglar [tin-glar'], *vn. (Naut.)* To make lap-jointed work.

tingle [teen'-glay], *f.* Instrument used by glaziers for opening the lead and flatting it on the glass.

tinica, illa, ita [te-nee'-cah], *m. dim.* A small vat.

tinicla [te-nee'-clah], *f. (Mil. Antiq.)* Large coat of arms.

tiniebla [te-ne-ay'-blah], *f.* Darkness (oscuridad), obscurity, privation of light. **Estamos en tinieblas sobre sus proyectos,** we are in the dark about his plans. *-pl.* 1. Utter darkness, hell; the night; gross ignorance; matins sung the last three days of Holy week.

tinillo [te-neel'-lyo], *m.* A tank for collecting must as it flows from the wine-press.

tino [tee'-no], *m.* 1. Skill in discovering things by the act of feeling (habilidad). 2. A steady hand to hit the mark. 3. Judgment, prudence, circumspection. 4. Knack, dexterity. 5. *(Zool.)* A wood-boring beetle. 6. Tact (tacto), good judgement (juicio). 7. Moderation (moderación). **Salir de tino,** to be out of one's senses. **Sacar de tino,** (a) to astound, to confound. (b) to make one angry; to act inconsiderately.

tinta [teen'-tah], *f.* 1. Tint, hue, color. 2. Ink. 3. Dye (de pulpo), ink. 3. Act, process of dyeing. 4. *pl.* Colors prepared for pointing. **De buena tinta,** *(Coll.)* Efficaciously, ably. **Saber algo de buena tinta,** to know from good authority. **Tinta de imprenta,** printing-ink. **Con tinta,** in ink. **Medias tintas,** half measures (medidas).

tintar [tin-tar'], *va.* To tinge, to dye. *V.* TEÑIR.

tinte [teen'-tay], *m.* 1. Act and effect of dyeing or staining (acto). 2. Tint, paint, color, stain: dye. 3. A dyer's shop. 4. Palliation, cloak, color.

tintero [tin-tay'-ro], *m.* 1. Ink-well, inkstand. 2. A printer's ink-fountain or ink-table. **Dejar or dejarse en el tintero,** *(Coll.)* to forget or omit designedly. **Quedársele a uno en el tintero,** *(Coll.)* to forget a thing entirely.

tintillo [tin-teel'-lyo], *m. (Dim.)* A light-colored wine.

tintín [tin-teen'], *m.* Clink, a sharp sound of metals, or of glasses striking together.

tintinear [tin-te-nay-ar'], *vn.* To tinkle (de campanilla), to jingle (de cadena).

tintineo [tin-te-nay'-o], *m.* Tinkling (de una campanilla)

tintirintín [tin-te-ren-teen'], *m.* Echo or sound of a trumpet, or other sharp-sounding instrument.

tinto, ta [teen'-to, tah], *a. 1.* Deep-colored. 2. Dyed (teñido); stained (manchado). *V.* TEÑIDO. **Vino tinto,** red wine.

tintóreo, rea [tin-toh'-ray-o, ah], *a.* Tinctoreal, affording color, or pertaining to hues.

tintorera [tin-to-ray'-rah], *f. (Zool. Amer.)* The female of the shark.

tintorería [tin-to-ray-ree'-ah], *f.* 1. Dry cleaning and dyeing. 2. Dry cleaning shop (tienda). 3. *(Tec.)* Dyeworks (fábrica).

tintorero, ra [tin-to-ray'-ro, rah], *m. & f.* Dyer.

tintura [tin-to-ray'-ro, rah], *f.* 1. Dyeing or staining (acto). 2. Tincture, color or taste superadded by something. 3. Tint, color, stain, spot. 4. Paint for ladies. 5. Superficial knowledge, smattering. 6. Tincture, extract of drugs. **Tintura de yodo,** iodine.

tinturar [tin-too-rar'], *va.* 1. To tingle, to dye, to imbue or impregnate with color or taste. 2. To tincture, to imbue the mind, to teach superficially.

tiña [tee'-nyah], *f.* 1. Scalled-head, ring-worm of the scalp, favus. It forms yellow crusts. 2. *(Coll.)* Want, indigence, wretchedness. 3. Meanness (tacañería), close-fistedness. 4. Small spider which injures beehives.

tiñería [te-nyay-ree'-ah], *f.* Poverty, indigence, misery. *(Vulg.)* Meanness.

tiñoso, sa [te-nyo'-so, sah], *m.* 1. Scabby, scurvy. 2. Penurious, niggardly, miserable (miserable); sordid, mean.

tiñuela [te-nyoo-ay'-lah], *f. V.* CUSCUTA.

tío [tee'-o], *m.* 1. Uncle. 2. *(Coll.)* Good old man: used colloquially for a peasant. *V.* TÍA. **Tío abuelo,** great-uncle. **Ese tío del sombrero alto,** that guy with the tall hat. **Es un tío grande,** he's a great guy.

tiorba [te-or'-bah], *f.* Theorbo, a large lute.

tiovivo [tee-oh-vee'-vo], *m.* Merry-go-round, carrousel.

tipa [tee'-pah], *f. (Amer.)* 1. A basket made of hide. 2. A great tree of Peru the wood of which is prized for the cubing of ships.

tipazo [te-pah'-tho], *m.* Tall guy (hombre grande), big guy; arrogant fellow (arrogante); *(And.)* Big wig (persona importante.)

típico, ca [tee'-pe-co, cah], *a.* 1. Typical (característico), characteristic. 2. Quaint (pintoresco), picturesque; full of local color (lleno de color local); rich in folklore (folklórico); traditional (tradicional). **Baile típico,** regional dance. **Unas jóvenes con su típico peinado,** some girls with their hair done in the traditional fashion.

tiple [tee'-play], *m.* 1. Treble, the highest musical register of instruments or voices; soprano (voz). 2. *(com.)* One who sings treble. 3. A small guitar. 4. *m.* (Slang) Tipple, wine. 5. *(Naut.)* Mast of a single piece.

tiplisonante [te-ple-so-nahn'-tay], *a. (Coll.)* Treble-toned.

tipo [tee'-po], *m.* 1. Type (clase), sort, kind, pattern, model, figure. 2. Printing type. 3. Rate. 4. Fellow, chap (hombre). 5. Build, physique (de hombre). **Tipo de cambio,** rate of exchange. **Tipo de interés,** rate of interest. **Un tip nuevo de bicicleta,** a new king f bicycle. **Dos tipos sospechosos,** two suspicious characters. **Tipo gótico,** Gothic type.

tipografía [te-po-grah-fee'-ah], *f.* 1. Printing. *V.* IMPRENTA. 2. Typography, type-setting.

tipográfico, ca [te-po-grah'-fe-co, cah], *a.* Typographical.

tipógrafo [te-po'-grah-fo], *m.* Printer.

tipolita, [te-po-lee'-tah], *f.* Typolite, a stone or fossil which preserves the impression of an animal or plant.

típula [tee'-poo-lah], *f.* Tipula, crane fly, daddy-long-legs; an insect looking like a huge mosquito.

tiquín [te-keen'], *m.* A long cane used in place of oars by Philippine Indians.

tira [tee'-rah], *f.* 1. A long narrow stripe; list. 2. A light dart or arrow. 3. *(Naut.)* Fall. 4. Strip; slip of paper. **Tira de un aparejo,** fall of a tackle. **Tira de películas,** film strip.

tirabala [te-rah-bah'-lah], *m.* Pop-gun.

tirabeque [te-rah-bay'-kay], *m. (Agr.)* Tender peas.

tirabotas [te-rah-bo'-tas], *f.* Boot-hook for pulling on boots.

tirabraguero [te-rah-brah-gay'-ro], *m. (Surg.)* Truss.

tirabuzón [te-rah-boo-thone'], *a.* 1. Cork-screw (sacacorchos). 2. *(Met.)* Curl (rizo), ringlet of hair.

tiracabeza [te-rah-cah-bay'-thah], *f.* Obstetric forceps.

tirachinas [te-rah-che'-nahs], *m.* Catapult.

tiracol [te-rah-cole'], *m. V* TIRACUELLO.

tiracuello [te-rah-coo-ay'-lyo], *m.* A sword-belt worn by officers.

tirada [te-rah'-dah], *f.* 1. Cast, throw, the act of throwing (acto). 2. Distance of one place from another (distancia). 3. Process, or space of time. 4. *(LAm.)* Boring speech (discurso). 5. *(Cono Sur)* Hint (indirecta). 6. *(Carib.)* Dirty trick (mala pasada). **De una tirada** or **en una tirada,** at one stretch. 7. Act of printing or stamping. 8. Edition, total number of copies printed. **Tirada aparte,** offprint, reprint.

tiradera [te-rah-day'-rah], *f.* 1. Strap. 2. Indian arrow. 3. *(CAm. Carib. Cono Sur)* Sash (faja); belt (correa); *(Carib.)* harness, strap (de caballo).

tiradero [te-rah-day'-ro], *m.* 1. Post, where a hunter stations himself to shoot game. 2. *(Mex.)* Mess.

tirado, da [te-rah'-do, dah], *a.* As applied to a ship, long and low. -*m.* 1. Wire-drawing. 2. Act of printing press-work.

tirador, ra [te-rah-dor', rah], *m. & f.* 1. Thrower (persona); drawer (cajón). 2. Sharp-shooter, good marksman (persona). 3. An iron button fixed to a door, window, etc., whereby it is opened or shut. 4. *(Print.)* Pressman. 5. Catapult (tirachinas). 6. *(And. Cono Sur)* Wide gaucho belt (cinturón). **Tirador de oro,** gold-wire drawer. *(Prov.)* Rifleman.

tirafondo [te-rah-fon'-do], *m. (Med.)* A ball extractor; extractor for foreign bodies in a wound.

tiralíneas [te-rah-lee'-nay-as], *m.* Instrument for drawing lines; ruling pen, ruler.

tiramiento [te-rabh-me-en'-to], *m.* Tension, act of stretching or making tense.

tiramira [te-rah-mee'-rah], *f.* A long narrow path; a long ridge of mountains.

tiramollar [te-rah-mol-lyar'], *va. (Naut.)* To ease off, to slacken. **Tiramollar un aparejo,** to overhaul a tackle.

tiranamente [te-rah-nah-men'-tay], *adv* Tyrannically. V. TIRÁNICAMENTE.

tiranía [te-rah-nee'-ah], *f.* 1. Tyranny, despotic government. 2. Tyranny, severity, inclemency, rigorous command. 3. Exorbitant price of merchandise. 4. Ascendency of some passion.

tiránicamente [te-rah'-ne-cah-men-tay], *adv.* Tyrannically, violently, imperiously.

tiranicida [te-rah-ne-thee'-dah], *a. & m* Tyrannicide, one who kills a tyrant.

tiranicidio [te-rah-ne-thee'-de-o], *m.* Tyrannicide, the killing of a tyrant.

tiránico, ca [te-rah'-ne-co, cah], *a.* Tyrannical, despotic, imperious.

tiranización [te-rah-ne-thah-the-on'], *f.* Tyranny, despotism.

tiranizadamente [te-rah-ne-thah-dah-men'-tay], *adv.* Tyrannically.

tiranizar [te-rah-ne-thar'], *va.* 1. To tyrannize, to domineer, to oppress. 2. To usurp. 3. To extort high prices.

tirano, na [te-rah'-no, nah], *a. & n.* 1. Tyrannical, despotic, arbitrary. 2. Applied to a merchant who sells goods at an exorbitant price. 3. Tyrannical (pasiones).

tirano [te-rah'-no], *m.* 1. Tyrant, a despotic ruler, severe master. 2. Merchant who sells goods at an exorbitant price. 3. Ruling passion. 4. *(Zool.)* Tyrant fly-catcher.

tirante [te-rahn'-tay], *m.* 1. Joist which runs across a beam. 2. Trace part of a harness; gear. 3. *(Mech.)* Brace, collarpiece, beam; stay rod, tie rod. 4. Suspenders, braces. 5. *(Arch.)* Anchor, truss-rod, a special apparatus employed in certain constructions. -*a.* 1. Tight (cuerda), extended, drawn; tightly bound. 2. Tense, strained (relaciones, situación). **Traer or tener la cuerda tirante,** to use too much rigor. **Las cosas andan algo tirantes,** things are rather strained.

tirantez [te-ran-teth'], *f.* 1. Length of a thing which runs in a straight line. 2. Tenseness, tightness (tensión). **Ha disminuido la tirantez,** the tension has lessened.

tirapié [te-rah-pay'], *m.* Stirrups or strap, with which shoemakers make their work fast.

tirar [te-rar'], *va. & vn.* 1. To throw (lanzar), to cast, to dart, to fling; to toss. 2. To imitate, to resemble. 3. To attract (imán), to draw towards one. 4. To incline to, to tend (tender). 5. To hurt, to injure, to thwart. 6. To tug, to pull (objeto); to draw. 7. To discharge firearms, to fire, to let off. 8. To persuade, to induce, or lend by compulsion. 9. To earn, to acquire, to gain, or become entitled to. 10. To continue in the same state without declining from it. **El enfermo va tirando,** the invalid is pulling through. 11. To enlarge, to extend. 12. To lavish. 13. *(Print.)* To print sheets. 14. To draw metal into slender threads. 15. V. QUITAR. 16. To receive or take an allotted part. 17. To direct one's course, to take the road. **Tire Vd. por este camino,** take this way. **Tire Vd. a la derecha,** turn to the right. 18. To tend, to aim at (proponerse); to make use of means and direct them to some end. **Tirar a la mar,** *(Naut.)* To throw overboard; to stand out to sent. **A todo tirar,** to the utmost, to the greatest extent. **Tira y afloja,** (1) a boyish game. (2) *(Met.)* last and loose, blowing hot and cold, ordering and counter-ordering. **Tirarlas de guapo or de rico,** to claim (presume on being) to be pretty, or rich. **El viento ha tirado la valla,** the wind has knocked the fence down. **Has tirado el dinero comprando eso,** you've thrown your money away buying that. **Este vestido tira un poco de aquí,** this dress is a bit tight here. **No le tira el estudio,** study does not attract him. **Tirar a su padre,** to take after one's father. **Tira tú ahora,** it's your go now. -*vr.* To throw oneself (lanzarse). **Tirarse por la ventana,** to throw oneself out of the window.

tirela [te-ray'-lah], *f.* A striped stuff.

tireta [te-ray'-tah], *f. (Prov.)* Ribbon or thong of leather.

tirica, ita [te-ree'-cah], *f. dim.* A small stripe of linen.

tiricia [te-ree'-the-ah], *f.* Jaundice. V. ICTERICIA.

tirilla [te-reel'-lyah], *f.* 1. A piece of backstitched linen used for a neck-band of a shirt. 2. *(Cono Sur)* Shabby dress.

tirio, ria [tee'-re-o, ah], *a.* Tyrian, of Tyre.

tirita [te-ree'-tah], *f. (Cos.)* Tag, tape; *(Med.)* plaster.

tiritaña [te-re-tah'-nyah], *f.* 1. A sort of thin silk; thin woollen cloth. 2. A thing of little value.

tiritar [te-re-tar'], *vn.* To shiver, to shake from cold. **Tiritar de risa,** to titter. **Dejaron el pastel tiritanto,** they almost finished the cake off.

tiritón [te-re-tone'], *m. (Coll.)* Shivering, shaking from cold.

tiritona [te-re-to'-nah], *f. (Coll.)* Shivering, especially affected.

tiro [tee'-ro], *m.* 1. Cast, throw (lanzamiento), shot, fling. 2. Shot, range, the distance traversed by a projectile. 3. Mark made by a throw (señal). 4. Charge, shot; gun which is discharged. 6. Theft. 6. Prank, imposition. 7. Serious physical or moral injury. 8. Set of coach-horses or mules. 9. Trace of coach-harness. 10. Rope which pulls up the materials used in building. 11. Landing-place of a stairway. 12. The report of firearms. 13. **Tiro de un mina,** the shaft of a mine. 14. *(Arquit.)* Flight of stairs. 15. Draught (de chimenea). 16. Veiled attack (ataque). 17. *(And. Cono Sur, Mex.)* Marble (canica). 18. *(Cono Sur)* Distance, course (carreras). 19. *(Mex.)* Issue (número). 20. *(Cono Sur)* Hint (indirecta). 21. *(Carib.)* Craftiness (astucia). **Una pistola de tres o cuatro tiros,** a three or four barrelled pistol or revolver. **Tiro al blanco,** target practice. **Le pegó un tiro a su amante,** she shot her lover. **Matar a uno a tiros.** to shoot somebody. **Estar a tiro,** to be within range.

tirocinio [te-ro-thee'-ne-o], *m.* 1. First attempt, essay, or trial. 2. Novitiate, in the religious sense.

tiroideo, dea [te-ro'-e-day-o-ah], *a.* Thyroid.

tiroides [te-ro'-e-des], *f.* Thyroid, thyroid gland.

tirolés, sa [te-ro-les', sah], *a.* Tyrolian, of the Tyrol. -*m.* Peddler, trader in toys and tinware.

tirón [te-ron'], *m.* 1. Tyro, beginner, novice, apprentice. 2. Pull (acción brusca), haul, tug. 3. V. ETIRÓN. 4. Time. V. VEZ. **De un tirón,** at once, at a stroke. **Le dieron un tirón a su bolso,** they snatched her bag. **Se lo bebió de un tirón,** he drank it down in one go.

tiroriro [te-ro-ree'-ro], *m. (Coll.)* Sound of a musical wind instrument; the instrument itself.

tirotear [te-ro-tay-ar'], *vn.* To shoot at random.

tiroteo [te-ro-tay'-o], *m.* Shooting at random (tiros), sharpshooting; irregular discharge of musketry; gunfight (batalla); skirmish (escaramuza).

tirreno, na [tir-ray'-no, nah], *a.* Tyrrhene, relating to ancient Tuscany.

tirria [teer'-re-ah], *f. (Coll.)* Aversion, antipathy, dislike. **Tener tirria a,** to dislike.

tirso [teer'-so], *m.* Wand, used in sacrifices to Bacchus. *V.* TALLO.

tisana [te-sah'-nah], *f.* A medical drink.

tisanuro, ra [te-sah-noo'-ro, rah], *m.* Thysanuran: applied to a division of wingless insects; spring-tails, bristletails.

tísica [tee'-se-cah], *f.* Phthisis. *V.* TISIS.

tísico, ca [tee'-se-co, cah], *a. & n.* 1. Phthisical. 2. Applied to a person troubled with phthisis or consumption. **Estar tísico**, to be phthisical, consumptive.

tisis [tee'-sis], *f.* Phthisis, phthisie, pulmonary consumption.

tisú [te-soo'], *m.* Tissue, a silk stuff interwoven with gold and silver.

titanato [te-tah-nah'-to], *m. (Chem.)* Titanate, a salt of titanic acid.

titánico, ca [te-tah'-ne-co, cah], *a.* 1. Titanic, relating to the Titans. 2. Huge, colossal. 3. *(Chem.)* Pertaining to the metal titanium.

titanio [te-tah'-ne-o], *m.* Titanium.

titano [te-tah'-no], *m. (Chem.)* Titanium, a dark-gray metallic element.

títere [tee'-tay-ray], *m.* 1. Puppet marionette. 2. Dwarf, a ridiculous little fellow. **No dejar títere con cabeza**, to turn everything upside down.

titerero, ra [te-tay-ray'-ro, rah], *a. V.* TITIRITERO.

tití [te-tee'], *m.* A very small monkey.

titicana [te-te-cah'-nah], *f. (Bot.)* A sour cane of America.

titilación [te-te-lah-the-on'], *f.* Titillation, tickling slight pleasure.

titilar [te-te-lar'], *va.* 1. To titillate, to tickle. 2. To please by slight gratification.

titímalo [te-tee'-mah-lo], *m. (Bot.)* Spurge, a plant with a milky acrid juice. *V.* LECHETREZNA.

titiritaina [te-te-re-tah'-e-nah], *f. (Coll.)* Confused noise of flutes or festive amusements.

titiritero [te-te-re-tay'-ro], *f & m.* Puppet player, a puppet-show man.

tito [tee'-to], *m. (Bot.)* A land of chick-peas.

titubear [te-too-bay-ar'], *vn.* 1. To totter (al andar), to stagger. 2. To stutter, to stammer. 3. To waver, to hesitate (vacilar). **Titubear en**, to hesitate to.

titubeo [te-too-bay'-o], *m.* Vacillation, wavering; making trials or essays.

titulado [te-too-lah'-do], *m.* Person having a title of nobility. *-a* To be entitled (libro). 3. *(Univ.)* Having a degree (persona). **—Titulado, da**, *pp.* of TITULAR.

titular [te-too-lar'], *a.* Titular, distinguished by a title; titulary.

titular [te-too-lahr'], *va.* To title, to give a title or name. *-vn.* To obtain a title from a sovereign. *-vr.* 1. To be given some title. 2. To hold such and such a title, to be entitled (llamarse).

titulillo [te-too-leel'-lyo], *m. dim.* 1. A petty title. 2. In typography, the caption or motto put at the top of the page above the text.

titulizado, da [te-too-le-thah'-do, dah], *a.* Titled, distinguished.

título [tee'-too-lo], *m.* 1. Title, an inscription on the exterior of something. 2. Title, heading, a division of the contents of a literary work. 3. Title, an appellation of honor: in Spain it designates the dignity of duke, marquis, count, viscount, or baron (noble). 4. Title, foundation of a claim or right: legal title to property. 5. A diploma, a patent, a title, given to empower anyone to exercise a profession (cualificación profesional). 6. Cause, reason, pretext. 7. *(Com.)* Claim, a name given to diverse documents which represent public debt. **A título**, on presence, under pretext. **A título de**, by way of. **Título universitario**, university degree. **Título de propiedad**, title deed. **Le sobran títulos para hacerlo**, he has every right to do it.

tiza [tee'-thah], *f.* 1. Calcined stag's horn. 2. Whiting, a kind of chalk or pipeclay, used by silversmiths. 3. Chalk for blackboards or for billiard cues.

tizna [teeth'-nah], *f.* Matter for staining or blackening.

tiznajo [teeth-nah'-ho], *m. (Coll.) V.* TIZNÓN.

tiznar [teeth-nar'], *va.* 1. To smut, to stain (manchar). 2. To tarnish, to blot. *-vr.* 1. To get smudged, to get soiled (mancharse). 2. *(CAm. Cono Sur, Mex.)* To get drunk (emborracharse).

tizne [teeth'-nay], *com.* Soot which sticks to frying-pans or kettles (mugre); the smut of coal.

tiznón [teeth-none'], *m.* A large spot, soil, or stain.

tizo [tee'-tho], *m.* Half-burnt charcoal.

tizón [tee-thon'], *m.* 1. Half-burnt wood. 2. Smut in wheat and other grains. 3. *(Met.)* Spot, stain (mancha), disgrace. 4. That part of a hewn stone which is concealed in the wall.

tizona [tee-tho'-nah], *f. (Coll.)* Name of El Cid's famous sword.

tizonada [te-tho-nah'-dah], *f.* Stroke with a half-burnt stick.

tizonazo [te-tho-nah'-tho], *m.* 1. Stroke with burning charred wood. 2. In Jocular style, hell fire.

tizoncillo [te-thon-theel'-lyo], *m.* 1. *(Dim.)* A small burning coal. 2. Mildew, a little smut in corn.

tizonear [te-tho-nay-ar'], *vn.* To stir up a fire; to arrange wood or coals for lighting a fire.

tizonera [te-tho-nay'-rah], *f.* Heap of ill-burnt charcoal.

tizonero [te-tho-nay'-ro], *m.* Poker, for stirring the fire.

tlascalteca [tlas-cal-tay'-cah], *a.* Of Tlascala, a state in Mexico.

tlazole [tlah-tho'-lay], *m. (Mex.)* Maize tops serving as forage to beasts.

tmesis [may-sis], *f. (Gram.)* Figure in poetry which divides a compound word into two.

TNT, Abbreviation of **Trinitrotolueno**, *m.* TNT, Trinitrotoluene.

toa [to'-ah], *f.* In some parts of America rope, hawser.

toalla [to-ah-lyah], *f.* 1. Towel. 2. Pillow-sham. **Toalla afelpada**, turkish towel.

toallero [to-ahl-lyay'-ro], *m.* Towel rail.

toalleta [to-al-lyay'-tah], *f. dim.* Napkin; small towel.

toba [to'-bah], *f.* 1. *(Bot.)* Cotton thistle. 2. *(Prov.)* Stalk of a thistle given to asset. 3. Calcareous matter on the teeth. 4. Tophus, a spongy stone; a calcareous tufa; sinter.

tobera [to-bay'-rah], *f.* Towel, tubers, an iron pipe, through which the nozzle of bellows is thrust in a forge.

tobillera [to-be-lyay'-rah], *f.* 1. Anklet. 2. *(Coll.)* Bobby-soxer, adolescent girl (adolescente).

tobillo [to-beel-lyo], *m.* The ankle.

tobogán [to-bo-gahn'], *m.* 1. Toboggan (trineo). 2. Switchback (de feria). 3. Children slide (para niños).

toca [to'-cah], *f.* A hood; a thin stuff: toque, a kind of headdress (sombrero).

tocadiscos [to-cah-dees'-cos], *m. (Coll.)* Phonograph, record player.

tocado [to-cah'-do], *m.* Ornament, dress; coiffure, headdress (sombrero), head-gear a set of ribbons for garnishing a dress. **Tocado de mujer**, commode, the head-dress.

tocado, da [to-cah'-do], *a. & pp.* of TOCAR. Touched, felt; contaminated; infected. **Estar tocada alguna cosa**, to have begun to rot or putrefy.

tocador, ra [to-cah-dor', rah], *m. & f.* 1. One who beats or touches. *-m.* 2. Handkerchief round the head. 3. Toilet, a lady's dressing-case or table (neceser, mueble). 4. Dressing room (cuarto). 5. *(Prov.)* Key for tuning musical instruments.

tocadorcito [to-cah-dor-thee'-to], *m. dim.* of TOCADOR.

tocamiento [to-cah-me-en'-to], *m.* 1. Touch, contact. 2. Supernatural inspiration.

tocante [to-cahn'-tay], *a.* Respecting, relative.

tocante, or **tocante a**, *prep.* Concerning, relating to; in order to.

tocar [to-car'], *va.* 1. To touch. 2. Touch a thing lightly; to reach with the hand. 3. To play on a musical instrument. 4. To toll or ring a bell. 5. To try metals on a touch stone, to touch, to magnetize; to examine, to prove. 6. To touch, to bent of, to discuss a matter lightly (tema). 7. To know a thing certainly. 8. To touch (conmover), to inspire, to move, to persuade. 9. To strike slightly, to sound anything. 10. To hit, to strike (obstáculo). 11. To suffer, to undergo (consecuencias). 12. To touch, to communicate or infect; to chastise. 13. To comb and dress the hair with ribbons. -vn. 1. To appertain, to belong. 2. To interest, to concern; to be a duty or obligation; to import. 3. To fall to one's share or lot. 4. To touch, to be contiguous to; to arrive in passing. 5. To be allied or related. **Tocar de cerca alguna cosa**, to have an interest, to be concerned. **Tocar de cerca algún asunto**, to have complete knowledge of a subject or matter. **Tocar a la puerta**, to rap at the door. **Tocar la diana**, *(All.)* to bent the reveille. **A toca teja**, *(Coll.)* ready money. **Tocarle a uno**, to fall to somebody. **Te toca jugar**, it's your turn. **Ahora toca torcer a la derecha**, now you have to turn right. -vr. 1. *(Coll.)* To be covered, to put on the hat. 2. To comb and arrange the hair.

tocasalva [to-cah-sahl'-vah], *f. V.* SALVILLA.

tocata [to-cah'-tah], *f.* A musical composition of brief extend for some instrument: toccata.

tocayo, ya [to-cah'-yo, yah], *a.* Having the same name, namesake.

tochedad [to-chey-dahd'], *f.* Clownishness, rusticity, ignorance.

tocho [toh'-cho], *m.* 1. *(Prov.)* Pole. 2. Bar of iron.

tocho, cha [toh'-cho, chah], *a.* Clownish, unpolished, homespun.

tochura [to-choo'-rah], *f.* *(Prov.)* Waggishness, sarcastic gaiety.

tocinero, ra [to-the-nay'-ro, rah], *m. & f.* Porkman, one who sells pork or bacon.

tocino [to-thee'-no], *m.* 1. Bacon, salt pork. 2. Hog's lard. **Tocino rancio**, rank pork.

tocología [to-co-lo-hee'-ah], *f.* Tocology, the art of obstetrics.

tocólogo [to-co'-lo-go], *m.* Tocologist, obstetrician.

tocón [to-cone'], *m.* Stump of a tree; stump of an arm or leg.

toconal [to-co-nahl'], *m.* An olive-yard plumed with stumps.

tocororo [to-co-ro'-ro], *m.* *(Zool.)* A Cuban trogon, with lively colors.

tocuyo [to-coo'-yo], *m.* *(Ven.Peru)* A plain home-spun cotton stuff.

todabuena, todasana [to-dah-boo-ay'-nah, to-dah-sah'-nah], *f.* *(Bot.)* A medicinal species of St. John's-wort.

todavía [to-dah-vee'-ah], *adv.* 1. Notwithstanding, nevertheless. 2. Yet, still. **Todavía no**, not yet. **Todavía no lo ha encontrado**, he still has not found it.

todi [to'-de], *m.* *(Zool.)* Tody, a West Indian insectivorous bird, having the head and neck of brilliant green.

todo, da [toh'-do, dah], *a. y pron.* All, whole (entero), entire, every. **Me gusta todo**, I like everything. **Toda la casa ardió**, the whole house burnt. **Con todo eso**, not withstanding, nevertheless, however. **A todo**, at most. **Del todo**, entirely, quite. **En todo y por todo**, wholly, absolutely. **Ser el todo**, to be the principal or chief. **Hacer a todo**, to be fit for anything. **Me gusta todo**, I like everything. **Todos los días**, every day.-*adv.* Entirely, totally, completely, all. **A todo riesgo**, fully comprehensive. **Con todas mis fuerzas**, with all my might. **Todo el mundo**, everybody, everyone. **Todo lo que sé**, all that I know. **En todo el día no lo he visto**, I haven't seen him all day. **Todos ustedes**, all of you. **Todo eran quejas**, it was all complaints.

todo [toh'-do], *m.* 1. Whole composition of integral parts. 2. *(Geom.)* A greater quantity compared with a less. 3. All, everything. **Todos**, everybody. **Lo han vendido todo**, they've sold it all. **Tienen un coche nuevo y todo**, they have a new car and everything. **Ir a todo**, to go forward resolutely. **A pesar de todo**, even so. **Para todo**, all-purpose.

todopoderoso, sa [to-do-po-day-ro'-so, sah], *a.* All-powerful, almighty; properly applied to God only. -*m.* The Almighty.

toesa [to-ay'-sah], *f.* Toise, fathom; a French measure.

tofana [to-fah'-nah], *f. & a.* A very active poison.

tofo [to'-fo], *m.* Tumor in the belly of cattle.

toga [to'-gah], *f.* 1. Toga, loose cloak (worn by professors, judges graduates, etc.). 2. Dignity of a superior judge. **Tomar la toga**, to qualify as a lawyer.

togado, da [to-gah'-do, dah], *a.* Gowned: applied to those who have a right to wear a toga.

toisón [to-e-son'], *m.* The name of the highest order of Spanish knighthood; the Golden Fleece. *V.* TUSÓN.

tojal [to-hahl'], *m.* Clump of furze or whin.

tojines [to-hee'-nes], *m. pl.* *(Naut.)* Belaying cleats.

tojino [to-hee'-no], *m.* *(Naut.)* Notch or knob to secure anything from moving in a ship; pieces of wood on the sides of a vessel used as steps.

tojo [to'-ho], *m.* *(Bot.)* Whin, furze.

tola [to'-lah], *f.* An Indian mound (S.America.)

tolano [to-lah'-no], *m.* Tumor in horses' gums. -*pl.* *(Coll.)* Short hair on the neck.

tolda [tol'-dah], *f.* 1. *(Naut.)* Awning. 2. *(Carib.)* Large sack (bolsa grande). 3. *(And.)* Tent (tienda).

toldadura [tol-dah-doo'-rah], *f.* Hanging of stuff to moderate the light or heat.

toldar [tol-dar'], *va. V.* ENTOLDAR.

toldero [tol-day'-ro], *m.* *(Prov.)* Retailer of salt.

toldilla [tol-deel'-lyah], *f.* *(Naut.)* Bound-house.

toldillo [tol-deel'-lyo], *m.* 1. Covered sedan-chair. 2. *(Dim.)* Small awning.

toldo [tol'-do], *m.* 1. Awning (de playa). 2. *(Prov.)* Shop where salt is retailed. 3. Ostentation, pomp. 4. *(And. Cono Sur)* Indian hut. 5. *(Mex.)* Hood, top. 6. *(Fig.)* pride.

tole tole [to'-lay to'-lay], *m.* Confused noise of the populace. *(Coll.)* **Tomar el tole**, to run off, to flee.

toledano, na [to-lay-dah'-no, nah], *a.* Toledan, of Toledo.

toledo [to-lay'-do], *m.* A song-bird of Central America.

tolerable [to-lay-rah'-blay], *a.* Tolerable, supportable.

tolerablemente [to-lay-rah'-blay-men-tay], *adv.* Tolerably, middlingly.

tolerancia [to-lay-rahn'-the-ah], *f.* Toleration, permission; tolerance, indulgence.

tolerante [to-lay-rahn'-tay], *a.* Tolerant: applied to a government which tolerates freedom of worship, and to persons who tolerate what they cannot approve.

tolerantismo [to-lay-ran-tees'-mo], *m.* Free exercise of all worship and religious opinions.

tolerar [to-lay-rar'], *va.* To tolerate, to suffer, to permit; to indulge, to overlook, to comport. **No se puede tolerar esto**, this cannot be tolerated. **Su madre le tolera demasiado**, his mother spoils him.

tolete [to-ray'-tay], *m.* 1. *(Naut.)* Thole, thole-pin. 2. *(Amer.)* A small club for catching alligators. 3. *(Cuba)* A stick.

tolla [tol'-lyah], *f.* 1. Bog, commonly covered with moss. *V.* TOLLADAR. 2. *(Cuba)* A canoe-shaped trough for watering horses.

tolladar [tol-lyah-dar'], *m. V.* ATOLLADERO.

tollina [tol-lyee'-nah], *f.* *(Coll.)* Cudgelling, cowhiding.

tollo [tol'-lyo], *m.* 1. *(Zool.)* Spotted dog-fish. 2. Cave or hollow for concealing sportsmen in wait for game. 3. Bog. *V.* ATOLLADERO.

tolondro, tolondrón [to-lon'-dro], *m.* 1. Contusion on the head arising from a blow 2. A giddy, hare-brained fellow.

tolondrón, na [to-lon-drone', nah], *a.* Giddy, hare-brained; foolish. **A tolondrones**, precipitately, giddily, inconsiderately, interruptedly; with contusions or bruises.

tolú [to-loo'], *m.* A balsam which owes its name to a town in Colombia.

tolva [tol'-vah], *f.* Hopper (recipiente), in a mill.

tolvanera [tol-vah-nay'-rah], *f.* Cloud of dust raised by whirlwinds.

toma [to'-mah], *f.* 1. Taking, receiving, hold, gripe, grasp. 2. Capture, conquest, seizure. 3. Portion of anything taken at once (cantidad). 4. Opening into a canal or drain. 5. Inlet (entrada); outlet (salida); plug (enchufe). 6. *(Cine, TV)* Take, shot. 7. *(LAm.)* Irrigation channel (acequia). **Toma de conciencia**, awareness. **Toma de antena**, aerial socket.

Toma directa, live shot. *-int.* There, well, what. **Toma de circuito integrado**, *(Comput.)* IC socket.

tomata [to-mah'-dah], *f.* 1. Conquest, capture, seizure. 2. Take, the quantity of copy taken at one time by a compositor for setting up; the same in type.

tomadero [to-mah-day'-ro], *m.* 1. Handle (asidero), haft. 2. Opening into a drain.

tomado [to-mah'-do], *m.* Ornamental plait in cloths. **-Tomado, da**, *pp.* of TOMAR.

tomador, ra [to-mah-dor', rah], *m. & f.* 1. Taker, receiver. 2. Retriever, a dog that finds or fetches the game. 3. *(Coll.)* Pickpocket, pilferer.

tomadura [to-mah-doo'-rah], *f.* Catch, seizure, gripe, hold, grasp, capture: commonly, the portion of a thing taken at once.

tomajón, na [to-mah-hone', nah], *a.* Taking or accepting easily or frequently.

tomar [to-mar'], *va.* 1. To take (aire, baño, curva, decisión, medida, paso, ruta), to catch, to seize, to grasp (agarrar), to recover. 2. To receive in any mode; to get. 3. To occupy, to capture, to take possession of. 4. To eat or drink. 5. To understand, to apprehend; to interpret, to perceive. 6. To contract, to acquire (afecto, asco). 7. To take into service, to employ. 8. To intercept or block roads or paths. 9. To take by stealth, to rob. 10. To buy, to purchase. 11. To undertake, to apply oneself to a business. 12. To imitate, to copy, 13. To take, to choose, to select. 14. To surprise, to overtake. 15. To surprise, to overwhelm. 16. To cover the female. 17. To take a trick in cards. 18. *(Naut.)* To arrive in port or at an anchoringplace. 19. To take into one's company. 20. With names of instruments, to set about, or execute the action implied. **Tomar la pluma**, to write. 21. In playing ball, to call a halt, because the players are not in their proper places, or some, other reason. *-vn.* 1. To take, to take root. 2. *(LAm.)* To drink (beber). 3. **Toma y daca**, give and take. *-vr.* To get covered with rust (metales). **Tomar calor**, to get warm, to push an affair warmly. **Tomar frío**, to catch cold. **Tomar el fresco**, to take the air. **Tomar el sol**, to take the sun, or expose oneself to the sun. **Tomar fuerzas**, to gather strength. **Tomar resolución**, to resolve. **Tomar por su cuenta**, to take upon one's account. **Tomar puerto**, *(Naut.)* to get into a port. **Tomarse con alguno** or **tomarla con alguno**, to pick a quarrel with one. **Tomar la puerta**, to go out of the house, to be off. **Tomar a pecho**, to take to heart; to undertake a thing with too much zeal. **Tomar a uno entre cejas** or **entre dientes**, to take a dislike to a person. **Tomar el trabajo** (or **tanto trabajo**), to take trouble for the sake of helping another. **Tomar la delantera**, to excel another. **Tomar el rábano por las hojas**, to put the cart before the horse. **Tomamos unas cervezas**, we had a few beers. **Tomarse la venganza por su mano**, to take vengeance with one's own hands. **Se lo sabe tomar bien**, he knows how to take it.

tomate [to-mah'-tay], *m. (Bot.)* Tomato, a nutritious vegetable, the fruit of the tomato-plant.

tomatera [to-mah-tay'-rah], *f.* 1. Tomato plant (planta). 2. *(Cono Sur)* Drunk spree (juerga).

tomavistas [to-mah-vees'-tas], *m.* 1. Motion picture camera. 2. Television camera.

tómbola [tom'-bo-lah], *f.* Raffle.

tomento, tomionto [to-may'-to], *m.* Coarse tow.

tomentoso, sa [to-men-to'-so, sah], *m. (Bot.)* Tomentose, tomentous; coated with downy wool-like hairs.

tomillar [to-mil-lyar'], *m.* Bed of thyme.

tomillo [to-meel'-lyo], *m. (Bot.)* Thyme.

tominejo, ja [to-me-nay'-ho, hah], *m. & f.* Genus of small bright-plumaged birds, of which the humming-bird is the smallest.

tomiza [to-mee'-thah], *f.* Bass rope.

tomo [to'-mo], *m.* Bulk or body of a thing (bulto). 2. Importance, value, consequence. **Es cosa de mucho tomo**, it is a matter of great consequence. 3. Tome, volume. **De tomo y lomo**, of weight and bulk; of importance.

tomón, na [to-mon'], *a.* Accepting. V. TOMAJÓN.

ton [ton], *m.* V. TONO. Used only in the phrase, **sin ton ni son**, without motive or cause, without rhyme or reason; unreasonably, inordinately.

tona [to'-nah], *f. (Prov.)* Surface of a liquid.

tonada [to-nah'-dah], *f.* 1. Tune, a metrical composition suited for singing and the music set to it. 2. *(LAm.)* Accent (acento). 3. *(Carib.)* Fib (embuste); pun (juego de palabras).

tonadica [to-nah-dee'-cah], *f. dim.* A short tune or song.

tonadilla [to-nah-deel'-lyah], *f.* 1. *(Dim.)* V. TONADICA. 2. An interlude of music formerly used in comedies; now seldom employed, and then only at the end.

tonalidad [to-nah-le-dahd'], *f.* 1. *(Mus.)* Key; tonality; tone. 2. (Arte) Shade; color scheme. **Una bella tonalidad de verde**, a beautiful shade of green.

tonante [to-nahn'-tay], *pa. (Poet.)* Thundering (Jupiter).

tonar [to-nar'], *vn. (Post.)* To thunder, to emit a thundering noise.

tonca, tonga [ton'-cah], *f. (Bot.)* The tonka bean, employed in flavoring tobacco (vainilla adulterada.). In Peru called *Pucherí*.

tondino [ton-dee'-no], *m. (Arch.)* Moulding on the astragal of a column.

tonel [to-nel'], *m.* 1. Cask, barrel. 2. *(Naut.)* An ancient measure of ships; ten **toneles** make twelve **toneladas**.

tonelada [to-nay-lah'-dah], *f.* 1. Ton (medida), a measure or weight of twenty hundred-weight. 2. Ton, tonnage (capacidad de un barco). 3. Collection of casks in a ship. **Bajel de quinientas toneladas**, *(Naut.)* a ship of five hundred tons burden. 4. Tonnage duty.

tonelaje [to-nay-lah'-hay], *m.* Tonnage.

tonelería [to-nay-lay-ree'-ah], *f.* 1. Trade of a cooper; workshop of a cooper. 2. Quantity of wafer casks for a ship.

tonelero [to-nay-lay'-ro], *m.* Cooper, trooper.

tonelete [to-nay-lay'-tay], *m.* 1. Ancient armor pasting from the waist to the knees. 2. *(Dim.)* Little butt or barrel.

tonga, tongada [ton'-gah], *f.* 1. Couch; a layer or stratum; lay, row, ledge, flake. 2. *(And. Cono Sur)* Job, task (tarea). 3. *(And.)* Nap (siesta).

tónica [toh'-ne-cah], *f. (Mus.)* Keynote, tonic.

tónico, ca [toh'-ne-co, cah], *a.* Tonic, strengthening.

tónico [toh'-ne-co], *m. (Med.)* Tonic, a medicine.

tonificar [to-ne-fe-cahr'], *va.* To tone up; to invigorate.

tonillo [to-neel'-lyo], *m.* Disagreeable, monotonous tone in reading or speaking.

tonina [to-nee'-nah], *f. (Com.)* Fresh tunny.

tonismo [to-nees'-mo], *m.* Tetanus, according to some writers.

tono [toh'-no], *m.* 1. Tone, modulation of the voice. 2. The manner of doing a thing. 3. Tune. 4. *(Med.)* Tone. 5. A small spiral of motel, which, placed in horns or trumpets, modifies their tone. 6. Tuning-fork (diapason). 7. Deportment, manner, social address. 8. Shade (de color). **Estar a tono**, to be in key. **Bajar el tono**, to lower one's voice. **Fuera de tono**, inappropriate.

tonsila [ton-see'-lah], *f.* Tonsil.

tonsilar [ton-se-lar'], *a.* Tonsillar, belonging to the tonsils.

tonsilitis [ton-se-le'-tis], *f. (Med.)* Tonsilitis.

tonsura [ton-soo'-rah], *f.* 1. Tonsure, the first clerical degree of the Roman Catholic church. 2. The act of cutting hair or wool.

tonsurar [ton-soo-rar'], *va.* 1. To tonsure (un clérigo) to give the first clerical degree. 2. To cut the hair, to cut off wool.

tontada [ton-tah'-dah], *f.* Nonsense; a foolish speech or action.

tontaina [ton-tah'-e-nah], *com. & a.* Stupid, fool; foolish.

tontamente [ton-tah-men-tay], *adv.* Foolishly, stupidly.

tontazo, za [ton-tah'-tho, thah], *a. aug.* Doltish, very stupid.

tontear [ton-tay-ar'], *vn.* To talk nonsense (hacer el tonto), to act foolishly; to fool.

tontedad, tontera [ton-tay-dhd', ton-tay'-rah], *f. V.* TONTERÍA.

tontería [ton-tay-ree'-ah], *f.* 1. Foolishness (cualidad), foolery, folly, foppery, ignorance; nonsense. 2. Silly thing (cosa); foolish act (acto). 3. Triviality (bagatela). 4. Silly scruple (escrúpulo). **Hacer una tontería**, to do a silly thing. **Lo vendió por una tontería**, he sold it for a song.

tontico [ton-tee'-co], *m. dim.* A little dolt.

tontillo [ton-teel'-lyo], *m.* 1. (*Dim.*) *V.* TONTICO. 2. Hoop skirt, a part of a lady's dress.

tontina [ton-tee'-nah], *f.* Tontine, a division of a sum of money among various persons, to be divided at a fixed epoch, with the interest, among the survivors.

tonto, ta [ton'-to, tah], *a.* Stupid, foolish, ignorant, fatuous. **Hacerse el tonto**, to play the fool. **Tonto de capirote**, great fool, idiot. **A tontas y a locas**, sillily and madly, without rhyme or reason, inordinately. -*m.* 1. Clown, funny man. 2. (*And. CAm. Cono Sur*) Jemmy (palanca).

¡top! (*Naut.*) Hold! stop! a word of command.

topacio [to-pah'-the-o], *m.* Topaz, a precious stone.

topada [to-pah'-dah], *f. V.* TOPETADA.

topadizo, za [to-pah-dee'-tho, thah], *a.* (*Coll.*) *V.* ENCONTRADIZO.

topador [to-pah-dor'], *m.* Encounterer, one who butts or strikes against another. Said properly of rams and other horned animals.

topar [to-par'], *va.* 1. To run or strike against. 2. To meet with by chance (persona). 3. To depend upon, to consist in. **La dificultad topa en esto**, (*Coll.*) the difficulty consists in this. 4. To accept a bet at cards. -*vn.* 1. To butt or strike with the head. 2. (*Met.*) To abut or lean against. 3. (*Mex.*) To quarrel (reñir).

toparca [to-par'-cah], *m.* Toparch, a ruler of a small state, composed of very few places.

toparquía [toh'-par-kee'-ah], *f.* Toparchy, seigniory, jurisdiction or lordship.

tope [toh'-pay], *m.* 1. Top, the highest point or part. 2. Butt (con cabeza), the striking of one thing against another. 3. Rub, the point of difficulty. 4. Obstacle, impediment (pega). 5. Scuffle (pelea), quarrel (riña). 6. The highest point of a mast. **A tope o al tope**, juncture, union, or incorporation of the extremities of things. **Al tope**, conjointly, contiguously. **Hasta el tope**, up to the top, or the brim.

tope [toh'-pay], *a.* Maximum. **Edad tope para un puesto**, maximum age for a job.

topera [to-pay'-rah], *f.* Mole-hole.

topetada [to-pay-tah'-dah], *f.* Butt, by a horned animal.

topetar [to-pay-tar'], *va.* To butt (golpear); to offend, to encounter.

topetón [to-pay-ton'], *m.* Collision, encounter, blow.

topetudo, da [to-pay-too'-do, dah], *a.* Applied to animals accustomed to butt.

tópico, ca [toh'-pe-co, cah], *a.* Topical, belonging to a particular place. -*m.* (*Med.*) Topical application.

topil [to-peel'], *m.* (*Mex.*) *V.* ALGUACIL.

topinaria [to-pe-nah'-re-ah], *f. V.* TARPARIA.

topinera [to-pe-nay'-rah], *f. V.* TOPERA.

topo [toh'-po], *m.* 1. (*Zool.*) Mole. 2. Stumbler. 3. (*Coll.*) A numbskull, a dolt. 4. A league and a half among the Indians.

topografía [to-po-grah-fee'-ah], *f.* Topography.

topográficamente [to-po-grah'-fe-cah-men-tay], *adv.* Topographically.

topográfico, ca [to-po-grah'-fe-co, cah], *m.* Topographer.

topógrafo [to-pó-grah-fo], *m.* Topographer.

toque [toh'-kay], *m.* 1. Touch (acto). 2. Ringing of bells. 3. A military call by drum or bugle. 4. Essay, trial, test. 5. Touch-stone. 6. Experience, proof. 7. Aid, assistance, or inspiration by God. 8. (*Coll.*) Blow given to anything. **Toque de luz**, light in a picture. **Dar un toque**, to give one a trial in any business. **El primero** or **el segundo toque (de un tambor)**, the first or second beat of a drum.

El último toque (de una campana), the last peal of a bell. 9. (*And.*) Turn (vuelta).

toqueado [to-kay-ah'-do], *m.* Sound of a stroke with the hands or feet.

toquería [to-kay-ree'-ah], *f.* 1. Collection of women's headdresses. 2. Business of making women's veils.

toquero [to-kay'-ro], *m.* Veil-maker for nuns, headdress maker.

toquetear [to-kay-tay-ar'], *va.* 1. To touch repeatedly (manosear). 2. (*Mus.*) To mess about on.

toquilla [to-kee'-lyah], *f.* 1. (*Dim.*) Small headdress of gauze, small veil. 2. Ribbon or lace round the crown of a hat. 3. A small triangular kerchief used by women for the neck or on the head. 4. The plant from which Panama hats are made.

tora [toh'-rah], *f.* 1. Tribute paid by Jewish families. 2. Book of the Jewish law; Pentateuch, torah (or thorah). (*Heb.*) 3. A herb.

tora [toh'-rah], *f.* Frame of figure of a bull in artificial fireworks.

torácico, ca [to-rah'-the-co, cah], *a.* (*Anat.*) Thoracic.

torada [to-rah'-dah], *f.* Drove of bulls.

toral [to-rahl'], *a*: 1. Main, principal. 2. Mold (molde).

tórax [to'-rax], *m.* Chest, breast, thorax.

torazo [to-rah'-tho], *m. aug.* Large bull.

torbellino [tor-bel-lyee'-no], *m.* 1. Whirlwind (viento), cyclone. 2. A lively, boisterous, restless person. 3. A concurrence or multitude of things that present themselves at the same time.

torca [tor'-cah], *f.* Cavern in mountains.

torcal [tor-cahl'], *m.* Place where there are caves.

torcaz [tor-cath'], *a.* Applied to gray wild pigeons with white necks.

torce [tor'-thay], *f.* Link of a chain or collar.

torcecuello [tor-thay-coo-ayl'-lyo], *m.* (*Orn.*) Wry-neck.

torcedero [tor-thay-day'-ro], *m.* Twisting-mill, an engine for twisting.

torcedero, ra [tor-thay-day'-ro, rah], *a. V.* TORCIDO.

torcedor, ra [tor-thay-day'-ro, rah], *m. & f.* 1. Twister, a spindle for twisting thread. 2. Anything which causes displeasure or grief.

torcedura [tor-thay-doo'-rah], *f.* 1. Twisting. 2. A light, paltry wine.

torcer [tor-therr'], *va.* 1. To twist (miembro), to double, to curve, to distort (sentido). 2. To warp (madera). 3. To turn, to deviate from the right road, to deflect, to turn aside. 3. To crook, to pervert from rectitude; to leave the paths of virtue. (Used intransitively in this sense.) 4. To put a wrong construction on anything. 5. To pervert (justicia), as judges do justice. 6. To dissuade, to induce to change an opinion. 7. To impugn, to retort, to refute an argument. -*vn.* 1. To turn (camino, vehículo, viajero). 2. To spin (pelota). **El coche torció a la izquierda**, the car turned left. -*vr.* 1. To be dislocated, to be spruced; to go crooked. 2. To turn sour (vino). 3. To deceive at gaming. **Torcerse un pie**, to twist one's foot.

torcho [tor'-cho], *a.* Said of iron forged into very thin wire.

torcida [tor-thee'-dah], *f.* Wick for lamps and candles.

torcidamente [tor-the'-dah-men-tay], *adv.* Obliquely, tortuously, crookedly.

torcidillo [tor-the-deel'-lyo], *m.* A kind of twisted silk.

torcido, da [tor-thee'-do, dah], *a. & pp.* of TORCER. 1. Oblique, tortuous, crooked (camino). 2. (*And. CAm. Carib.*) Unlucky (desgraciado).

torcido [tor-thee'-do], *m.* 1. A kind of twisted sweetmeat. 2. (*Prov.*) Light, bad wine.

torcijón [tor-the-hone'], *m.* 1. Gripes, pains in the bowels. 2. *V.* TOROZÓN.

torcimiento [tor-the-me-en'-to], *m.* 1. Turning or bending of what was straight. 2. Deflection, deviation from the paths of virtue. 3. Circumlocution or periphrasis.

torculado [tor-coo-lah'-do], *m.* Female screw.

tórculo [tor'-coo-lo], *m.* A small press; a rolling press for prime.

tordella [tor-day'-lyah], *f.* Large kind of thrush.

tórdiga [tor'-de-gah], *f.* Neat's leather for coarse shoes.

tordillo, lla [tor-deel'-lyo, lyah], *a.* Of a thrush-color, grayish, grizzled.

tordo [tor'-do], *m. (Orn.)* Thrush.

tordo, da [tor'-do, dah], *a.* Speckled black and white (caballos).

toreador [to-ray-ah-dor'], *m.* Bullfighter: commonly applied to bullfighters on foot.

torear [to-ray-ar'], *va.* 1. To fight in the ring (toro). 2. To let a bull to cows. 3. To dodge (esquivar). 4. *(Fig.)* To keep at bay (mantener a raya). 5. *(Fig.)* To plague (acosar). 6. *(CAm. Cono Sur)* To provoke (animal), to enrage. 7. *(And. Cono Sur)* To bark furiously at (perro). -*vn.* 1. *(Taur.)* To fight, to be a bullfighter. **No volverá a torear**, he will never fight again. 2. *(And. Cono Sur)* To bark furiously.

toreo [to-ray'-o], *m.* Art or practice of fighting bulls.

torería [to-ray-ree'-ah], *f. (Cuba, Peru, etc.)* 1. Pranks of young folks. 2. The office of bullfighter.

torero, ra [to-ray'-ro], *m & f.* Bullfighter.

torés [to-res'], *m. (Arch.)* Torus, large ring or round moulding at the base of a column.

torete [to-ray-tay], *m.* 1. *(Dim.)* A small bull (animal). 2. *(Colt.)* A difficult point, an intricate business.

torga [tor'-gah], *f.* Yoke put on the necks of hogs.

toril [to-reel'], *m.* Place where bulls are shut up until they are brought out.

torillo [to-ray'-lyo], *m.* 1. *(Dim.)* Little bull. 2. Dowel, a pin for fastening timber. 3. *(Anat.)* Peritoneum.

torio [to'-ree-o], *m. (Chem.)* Thorium.

toriondez [to-re-on-deth'], *f. (Prov.)* The cow's desire for the bull.

toriondo, da [to-re-on'-do, dh], *a.* Applied to cattle rutting.

torloroto [tor-lo-ro'-to], *m.* A shepherd's pipe or flute.

tormellera [tor-may-lyay'-rah], *f.* Craggy, covered with high rocks.

tormenta [tor-men'-tah], *f.* 1. Perturbation of the waters of the ocean through the violence of winds. 2. Storm (tempestad), tempest; hurricane. 3. Storm, adversity, misfortune (desgracia). **Sufrió una tormenta de celos**, she suffered a great pang of jealously.

tormentador, ra [tor-men-tah-dor', rah], *m. & f.* V. ATORMENTADOR.

tormentar [tor-men-tar'], *vn.* To be violently agitated; to suffer a storm.

tormentario, ria [tor-men-tah'-re-o, ah], *a.* Projectile (artillería).

tormentila [tor-men-tee'-lah], *f. (Bot.)* Tormentil, septfoil, a slender trailing Old World herb with yellow flowers; its root is a powerful astringent, and has been used in diarrhoea.

tormentín [tor-men-teen'], *m. (Naut.)* A small mast on the bowsprit.

tormento [tor-men'-to], *m.* 1. Torment, pain, anguish, torture, pang, affliction. 2. Rack, torture. 3. *(Mil.)* Battering ordnance. **Dar tormento**, to torture, to put to the rack. **Estos zapatos son un tormento**, these shoes are agony.

tormentoso, sa [tor-men-to'-so, sah], *a.* 1. Stormy, boisterous, turbulent. 2. *(Naut.)* Easily dismasted (barco).

tormo [tor'-mo], *m.* Tor, a high, pointed, isolated rock.

torna [tor'-nah], *f.* 1. Restitution. 2. Return (vuelta). V. TORNADA. 3. Drain of water for irrigation. -*pl.* 1. Return, recompense, restitution.

tornaboda [tor-nah-bo'-dah], *f.* Day after a wedding.

tornachile [tor-nah-chee'-lay], *m. (Mex.)* A thick pepper.

tornada [tor-nah'-dah], *f.* Return from a journey.

tornadera [tor-nay-day'-rah], *f.* A two-pronged winnowing fork used in Castile.

tornadizo, za [tor-nah-dee'-tho, thah], *a. & m. & f.* Turncoat, deserter.

tornado [tor-nah'-do], *m.* Hurricane in the Gulf of Guinea off western Africa: tornado.

tornadura [tor-nah-doo'-rah], *f.* 1. Return: recompense. 2. Land measure of ten feet.

tornaguía [tor-nah-gee'-ah], *f.* Return of a receipt issued by the custom-house, showing that the goods have arrived at their destination.

tornajo [tor-nah'-ho], *m.* Trough.

tornapunta [tor-nah-poon'-tah], *f. (Arch.)* Stay, prop. V. PUNTUAL.

tornar [tor-nar'], *va. & vn.* 1. To return, to restore, to make restitution. 2. To return, to come back again (volver). 3. To repeat, to do again. 4. To change (transformar). **Tornar cabeza a alguna cosa**, *(Coll.)* to attend to anything, to consider, to be attentive.

tornasol [tor-nah-sole'], *m.* 1. *(Bot.)* Turnsole, sunflower. V. GIRASOL. 2. Changeable color of stuff.

tornasolar [tor-nah-so-lar'], *va.* To cause changes in color.

tornátil [tor-nah'-teel], *a.* Turned, made by a turner or with a wheel.

tornaviaje [tor-nah-ve-ah'-hay], *m.* Return-trip.

tornavirada [tor-nah-ve-rah'-dah], *f.* A roundabout way; a round trip.

tornavoz [tor-nah-voth'], *m.* Sound-board (de púlpito), or sounding-board.

torneador [tor-nay-ah-dor'], *m.* 1. Turner, one who works on a lathe. V. TORNERO, 1st def. 2. Tilter at tournaments.

torneante [tor-nay-ahn'-tay], *pa.* Tilting at tournaments, turning, revolving.

tornear [tor-nay-ar'], *va. & vn.* 1. To shape by turning on a lathe. 2. To turn, to wind round about, to put into a circular motion. 3. To tilt at tournaments. 4. To meditate.

torneo [tor-nay'-o], *m.* 1. Tournament; public festival of knights. 2. Dance in imitation of tournaments. **Torneo por equipos**, team tournament.

tornera [tor-nay'-rah], *f.* Doorkeeper of a nunnery.

tornería [tor-nay-ree'-ash], *f.* Turning, the act of forming on a lathe.

tornero, ra [tor-nay'-ro], *m & f.* 1. Turner, one who turns on a lathe. 2. The maker of lathes. 3. *(Prov.)* Messenger or servant of a nunnery.

tornillero [tor-nil-lyay'-ro], *m. (Coll.)* Deserter.

tornillo [tor-neel'-lyo], *m.* 1. Bolt (perno, pasador). 2. Screw. 3. *(Mil.)* Desertion. 4. Small vise. **Faltar un tornillo**, *(Coll.)* to have a screw loose. **Apretar los tornillos a**, *(Coll.)* to put the screws on.

torniquete [tor-ne-kay'-tay], *m.* 1. Turnstile. 2. Tourniquet.

torniscón [tor-nis-con'], *m. (Coll.)* 1. Crack on the head. 2. Slap in the face (manotada). 3. *(Sp. Am.)* Sharp pinch (apretón).

torno [tor'-no], *m.* 1. Winch. 2. Lathe (de tornear). 3. Potter's wheel. 4. Vise. 5. Revolution, turn. 6. Turn, bend (en un río). **Torno de hilar**, spinning wheel. **Torno de mano**, clomp. **En torno a**, around. 7. Brake (freno). **En torno a este tema**, on this theme.

toro [toh'-ro], *m.* 1. Bull. **Toro mejicano**, bison. V. BISONTE. **Correr toros**, to fight bulls. 2. *(Arch.)* Ogee moulding. 3. Moulding of the breech of a cannon. **Pillar el toro a uno**, to get somebody into a corner. **Este año no habrá toros**, there will be no bullfight this year.

torondo, torondón [to-ron'-do, done'], *m.* V. TOLONDRO.

toronja [to-ron'-hah], *f. (Bot.)* Grapefruit, shaddock.

toronjil [to-ron-heel'], *m.* **Toronjina**, *f.* [tor-ron-heel']. *(Bot.)* Balm-gentle.

toronjo [to-ron'-ho], *m. (Bot.)* Grapefruit tree.

toroso, sa [to-ro'-so, sah], *a.* Strong, robust.

torozón [to-ro-thone'], *m.* Gripes, pains in the bowels (animales).

torpe [tor'-pay], *a.* 1. Awkward, clumsy, slow (poco ágil), dull, heavy, torpid, having a slow motion. 2. Dull, stupid, rude. 3. Lascivious, unchaste, obscene. 4. Indecorous, disgraceful, infamous. 5. Dull, slow of comprehension.

torpedero [tor-pay-day'-ro], *m.* Torpedo-boat, a small fighting craft, very swift, designed for discharging torpedoes.

torpedo [tor-pay'-do], *m.* 1. (*Zool.*) Torpedo, electric ray, camp-fish, numbfish. 2. Torpedo, an explosive weapon of naval warfare.

torpemente [tor'-pay-mentay], *adv.* 1. Awkwardly, clumsily. 2. Obscenely, basely; slowly. 3. Stiffly. 4. Slow-wittedly. 5. (*Fig.*) Vilely, dishonestly. 6. (*Fig.*) Crudely.

torpeza [tor-pay'-thah], *f.* 1. Heaviness, dulness, rudeness. 2. Torpidness, torpor; slowness. 3. Impurity, unchastity, lewdness, obscenity. 4. Want of ornament or culture. 5. Rudeness, ugliness. **Fue una torpeza mía,** it was tactless of me.

torpor [tor-por'], *m.* Torpor, numbness, want of motion.

torrar [tor-rar'], *va. V.* TOSTAR.

torre [tor'-rah], *f.* 1. A tower; turret, embattled tower. 2. Steeple of a church, in which bells are hung. 3. (*Prov.*) Country-house with a garden. 4. Castle, rook (en ajedrez). 5. (*Naut.*) Turret. **Torre de control, torre de mando,** (*Aer.*) control tower. **Torre de perforación,** derrick. **Torre de conducción eléctrica,** electricity pylon. 6. (*Carib. Mex.*) Factory chimney.

torrear [tor-ray-ar'], *va.* To fortify with towers or turrets.

torrecilla [tor-ray-theel'-lyah], *f.* Turret.

torrefacción [tor-ray-fac-the-on'], *f.* Torrefaction, roasting.

torrefacto [tor-ray-fahc'-to], *a.* High roast.

torreja [tor-ray'-hah], *f.* (*Mex.*) Fritter.

torrejón [tor-ray-hone'], *m.* Ill-shaped turret.

torrencial [tor-ren-the-ahl'], *a.* Torrential; overpowering.

torrentada [tor-ren-tah'-dah], *f.* Sweep of a torrent, impetuous current.

torrente [tor-ren'-tay], *m.* 1. Torrent (de río), a rapid stream; an impetuous current. 2. Abundance, plenty. 3. Strong, coarse voice.

torrentera [tor-ren-tay'-rah], *f.* Gully washed out by a freshet.

torreón [tor-ray-one'], *m.* A great tower in fortresses for defense.

torrero [tor-ray'-ro], *m.* 1. Bailiff or steward of a country house and garden. 2. A lighthouse-keeper.

torreta [tor-ray'-tah], *f.* 1. (*Aer., Mil., Naut.*) Turret; conning tower (de submarino). 2. (*Elec.*) Pylon, mast.

torreznada [tor-reth-nah'-dah], *f.* Plentiful dish of rashers.

torreznero [tor-reth-nay'-ro], *a.* (*Coll.*) A lazy fellow, who sits over the fire.

torrezno [tor-reth'-no], *m.* 1. Rasher of bacon. 2. A voluminous book.

tórrido, da [tor'-re-do, dah], *a.* Torrid, parched, hot.

torrija [tor-ree'-hah], *f.* Slice of bread, fried in white wine, eggs, and butter or oil.

torrontés [tor-ron-tes'], *a.* Applied to a kind of white grapes.

torsión [tor-se-on'], *f.* 1. Torsion, act and effect of twisting. 2. State of being twisted.

torso [tor'-so], *m.* Trunk or body of a statue.

torta [tor'-tah], *f.* 1. A round cake made of various ingredients (pastel). 2. (*Coll.*) **Torta** or **torta de pan,** a loaf of bread. 3. Font, or portion of type fresh from the casting. 4. (*CAm. Mex.*) Omelette. 5. (*Tip.*) Fount. 6. Punch (puñetazo). **Agarrar una torta,** to get pissed.

tortada [tor-tah'-dah], *f.* A kind of large pie.

tortedad [tor-tay-dahd'], *f.* Condition of twist (*Acad.*)

tortera [tor-tay'-rah], *f.* 1. Pan for baking tarts or pies. 2. Knob at the end of a twisting spindle.

tortero [tor-tay'-ro], *m.* Knob of spindle for twisting.

torticoli [tor-te-co'-le], *m.* (*Med.*) Torticollis, the wry neck.

tortilla [tor-teel'-lyah], *f.* 1. Omelet, beaten eggs cooked in a frying pan. 2. (*Mex.*) A pancake made of mashed Indian corn. 3. **Tortilla de huevos,** omelet. **Hacerse tortilla,** to break into small pieces, to cake. **Volverse la tortilla,** (*Met.*) to turn the scale, to take a course contrary to that expected.

tortillera [tor-tel-lyay'-rah], *f.* 1. (*CAm. Mex.*) Tortilla seller. 2. Lesbian (lesbiana).

tortis [tor'-tis]. Used only in the phrase. **Letra de tortis,** a kind of Gothic printing letter.

tortita [tor-tee'-tah], *f. dim.* Small loaf or cake.

tórtola [tor'-to-lah], *f.* (*Orn.*) Turtle dove.

tortolico [tor-to-lee'-co], *a.* 1. Innocent, candid, inexperienced. 2. *V.* TORTOLILLO.

tortolillo, ito [tor-to-leel'-lyo], *m. dim.* A small cook turtle-dove.

tórtolo [tor'-to-lo], *m.* 1. (*Orn.*) Male turtle-dove. 2. Lovebird (amante).

tortor [tor-tor'], *m. pl.* (*Naut.*) Fraps.

tortozón [tor-to-thone'], *m.* Kind of large grapes.

tortuga [tor-too'-gah], *f.* Tortoise. **Paso de tortuga,** snail-gallop. **Concha de tortuga,** tortoise-shell. **Tortuga gráfica,** (*Comput.*) Graphics turtle

tortuosamente [tor-too-o'-sah-men-tay], *adv.* Tortuously, circuitously.

tortuosidad [tor-too-o-se-dahd'], *f.* Tortuosity, flexure, tortuousness.

tortuoso, sa [tor-too-o'-so, sah], *a.* Tortuous, winding.

tortura [tor-too'-rah], *f.* 1. Tortuosity, flexure. 2. Rack, torture.

torturar [tor-too-rahr'], *va.* To torture.

torvo [tor'-vo], **va,** *a.* Fierce, stern, severe, grim.

torzadillo [tor-thah-deel'-lyo], *m.* A kind of twisted cord, less thick than common.

torzal [tor-thahl'], *m.* Cord, twist, twisted or plaited lace, torsel, intertexture.

torzón [tor-thone'], *m.* (*Vet.*) *V.* TOROZÓN.

torzonado, da [tor-tho-nah'-do, dah], *a.* Contracted or twisted: applied to animals diseased in the bowels.

torzuelo [tor-thoo-ay'-lo], *a.* **Halcón torzuelo,** the third hawk which leaves the nest.

tos [tos], *f.* Cough. **Tos ferina** or **sofocante,** whooping cough.

tosa [toh'-sah], *f. V.* TOZA.

toscamente [tos'-cah-men-tay], *adv.* Coarsely, rudely, grossly, clownishly, lubbarly, fatly.

toscano, na [tos-cah'-no, nah], *a.* 1. Tuscan: applied to an architectural order. 2. Native of Tuscany.

tosco, ca [tos'-co, cah], *a.* 1. Coarse, rough, unpolished. 2. Ill-bred, uninstructed, clownish, clumsy, crabbed.

tosecilla [to-say-theel'-lyah], *f. dim.* Slight cough.

toser [to-serr'], *vn.* To cough: to feign a cough. -*va.* 1. (*Fig.*) **No le tose nadie,** nobody can compete with him. **2. A mí no me tose nadie,** I'll not stand for that.

tosidura [to-see'-doo-rah], *f.* The act of coughing.

tosigar [to-se-gar'], *va. V.* ATOSIGAR.

tósigo [toh'-se-go], *m.* 1. Poison, especially that from the yew-tree. 2. Grief, pain, anguish, vexation.

tosigoso, sa [to-se-go'-so, sah], *a.* 1. Poisonous, venomous. 2. Coughing, having a cough.

tosquedad [tos-kay-dahd'], *f.* Roughness, coarseness; rudeness; clumsiness.

tostada [tos-tah'-dah], *f.* 1. Toast, slice of toasted bread. 2. Disappointment. 3. (*Cono Sur*) Long boring conversation (conversación). **Pegar una tostada a alguno,** (*Coll.*) (1) to play a serious trick upon one; to disappoint him. (2) To put one to the blush.

tostadera [tos-tah-day'-rah], *f.* Toaster, an instrument for toasting.

tostado, da [tos-tah'-do, dah], *a. & pp.* of TOSTAR. 1. Torrid, parched, dried with heat; toasted. 2. Applied to a lively light-brown color.

tostador, ra [tos-tah-dor', rah], *m. & f.* 1. Toaster, one who toasts. 2. Toaster, a toasting instrument.

tostadura [tos-tah-doo'-rah], *f.* Act and effect of toasting.

tostar [tos-tar'], *va.* 1. To toast (pan), to torrefy, to roast. **Tostar café,** to roast coffee. 2. To tan (piel). 3. (*Carib. Cono Sur*) to continue vigorously what one has begun. 4. (*Mex.*) To offend (ofender). -*vr.* To tan.

tostón [tos-tone'], *m.* 1. Soup, made of toasted bread and oil; toasted chick-pea (torrado). 2. Roast sucking pig (cochinillo).

3. Testoon, silver coin (moneda). 4. *(Culin.)* Small cube of toast (cubito). 6. Bore (lata), boring thing. 7. Bad play (comedia).

total [to-tahl'], *m.* 1. Whole (totalidad), total, complement. 2. *(Com.)* Total. **Total debe**, debit total. *-a.* General, universal, total; entire, all-out. **Una revisión total de su teoría**, a complete revision of his theory.

totalitario, ria [to-tah-le-tah'-re-o, ah], *a. & m. & f.* Totalitarian.

totalidad [to-tah-le-dahd'], *f.* Totality, whole quantity. **La totalidad de los obreros**, all the workers. **La totalidad de la población**, the whole population.

totalizar [to-tah-le-thar'], *va.* To total, to add up. *-vn.* To add up to.

totalmente [to-tal-men'-tay], *adv.* Totally, wholly, completely.

totem [to-tem'], *m.* Totem.

totémico, ca [to-tay'-me-co, cah], *a.* Totem. **Poste totémico**, totem pole.

totemismo [to-tay-mees'-mo], *m.* Totemiam.

totilimundi [to-te-le-moon'-de], *m.* Cosmorama. *(Fam.)* Everybody. *V.* MUNDINOVI.

totoloque [to-to-lo'-kay], *m.* A game of the ancient Mexicans.

totoposte [to-to-pos'-tay], *m. (Amer.)* Corn-bread of Indian meal.

totora [to-toh'-rah], *f. (Amer.)* A cat-tail or reed-mace of Peru and Bolivia.

totovía [to-to-vee'-ah], *f. (Orn.)* Woodlark.

totuma, *f.* **totumo**, *m.* [to-too'-mah, mo]. *(Amer.)* 1. A large dish made from a gourd. 2. Chocolate cup, in some parts of America. 3. *(Amer.* and Canary Islands.) A massive head.

toucán [to-oo-cahn'], *m. (Orn.)* Toucan.

toxemia [tok-say'-me-ah], *f.* Toxemia, blood poisoning.

toxicar [toc-se-car'], *va.* To poison. *V.* ATOSIGAR.

tóxico, ca [toc'-se-co, cah], *a.* Toxic, poisonous. *-m.* Poison.

toxicohemia [toc-se-co-ay-me-ah], *f. (Med.)* Toxicohaemia, toxaemia a poisoned condition of the blood.

toxicología [toc-se-co-lo-hee'-ah], *f.* Toxicology.

toxicológico, ca [toc-se-co-lo'-he-co, cah], *a.* Toxicological, relating to poisons and their effects.

toxicomanía [toc-se-co-mah-nee'-ah], *f.* Drug addiction.

toxicómano [toc-se-coh'-mah-no], *a.* Addicted to drugs. *-m & f.* Drug addict.

toxina [tok-see'-nah], *f. (Med.)* Toxin.

toza [to'-thah], *f.* 1. *(Prov.)* Piece of the bark of a tree. 2. *(Amer.)* Log, a bulky piece of wood.

tozo, za [too'-tho, thah], *a. (Art.)* Low in stature, dwarf.

tozolada [to-tho-lah'-dah]. *f.* **Tozolón**, *m.* Stroke or blow on the neck.

tozudo, da [to-thoo'-do, dah], *a.* Stubborn. *V.* OBSTINADO and TERCO.

tozuelo [to-thoo-ay'-lo], *m.* Fat part of the neck.

traba [trah'-bah], *f.* 1. Ligament, ligature. 2. Hobble (de caballo), cord with which the feet of cattle are tied. 3. Obstacle, impediment, hindrance; trammel, fetter, shackle; anything which hinders the easy execution of something else. 4. Piece of cloth uniting the two parts of the scapulary of certain monastic habits. **Poner trabas a**, to shackle.

trabacuenta [trah-bah-coo-en'-tah], *f.* 1. Error, mistake. 2. Difference, dispute, controversy.

trabadero [trah-bah-day'-ro], *m.* The small part of animals' feet.

trabado, da [trah-bah'-do, dah], *a. & pp.* of TRABAR. 1. Connected, joined (unido); thickened, inspissated. 2. Robust, strong. 3. Having two white fore feet, or two white feet on one side (caballo).

trabador [trah-bah-dor'], *m.* A carpenter's saw-set.

trabadura [trah-bah-doo'-rah], *f.* Union, junction.

trabajadamente [traah-bah-hah'-dah-men-tay], *adv. V.* TRABAJOSAMENTE.

trabajado, da [trah-bah-hah'-do, dah], *a. & pp.* of TRABAJAR. 1. Labored. 2. Tired, weary; exhausted with fatigue. 3. Wrought (metales).

trabajador, ra [trah-bah-hah-dor', rah], *m. & f.* 1. Laborer, an assiduous or industrious person, painstaker. 2. A daylaborer.

trabajar [trah-bah-har'], *va. & vn.* 1. To work, to labor, to manufacture, to form by labor. 2. To work, to travail, to toil. 3. To work, to be in action, to be diligent. 4. To work, to act, to execute. 5. To work, to endeavor, to contend for. 6. To solicit, to procure. 7. To support, to sustain: applied to building or machinery. 8. To nourish and produce (tierra). 9. To work the ground, to till the soil. 10. To molest, to vex, to harass. 11. To bear, to produce (árbol, suelo). 12. To trouble (mente). **Trabajar atrozmente**, to work to excess. **Estoy trabajando el latín**, I am working away at Latin. **Trabajar mucho**, to work hard. **Trabajar por horas**, to be paid by the hour. **Trabajar por**, to strive to.

trabajillo [trah-bah-heel', lyo], *m. dim.* Slight work, toil, labor, trouble, or hardship.

trabajo [trah-bah'ho], *m.* 1. Work, labor, toil, occupation. 2. Obstacle, impediment, hindrance, difficulty. 3. Trouble, hardship, ill-success. 4. Work, a writing on any subject; thing wrought. *-pl.* Poverty, indigence, need, want. **Trabajo de manos**, manual or handiwork. **Trabajo de punto**, knitting, knitting-work. **Día de trabajo**, working-day. **Mucho trabajo para nada**, much ado about nothing. **No hay atajo sin trabajo**, *(Prov.)* no gains without pains. **Trabajo de chinos**, hard slog. **Trabajos forzados**, hard labor. **Tomarse el trabajo de**, to take the trouble to.

trabajosamente [trah-bah-ho'-sah-men-tay], *adv.* Laboriously, with difficulty, painfully.

trabajoso, sa [trah-bah-ho'-so, sah], *a.* 1. Laborious, elaborate. 2. Imperfect, defective. 3. Painful (doloroso), hard. 4. *(Med.)* Pale, sickly. 5. *(And.)* Unhelpful (poco amable); bad-tempered (malhumorado).

trabal [trah-bahl'], *a.* Applied to clash nails.

trabalenguas [trah-bah-len'-goo-ahs], *m.* Tongue twister.

trabamiento [trah-bah-me-en'-to], *m.* Act of joining or uniting.

trabanco [trah-bahn'-co], *m.* Piece of wood attached to a dog's collar, to prevent him from putting down his head.

trabar [trah-bar'], *va.* 1. To join (unir), to unite, to connect. 2. To join, to bring into harmony or concord. 3. To fetter, to shackle (encadenar). 4. To thicken, to inspissate. 5. To fetter, to dispute, to qua rel, to scuffle. **Trabarse de palabras**, to become angry in a dispute. 6. To set the teeth of a saw. 7. To seize, to take hold of (agarrar). 8. *(CAm. Carib.)* To deceive (engañar). **Trabarse la lengua**, to stammer, to speak with unnatural hesitation. **Trabar conversación**, to enter upon or keep up a long conversation.

trabazón [trah-bah-thone'], *f.* Juncture, union; connection; coalescence.

trabe [trah'-bay], *f.* Beam.

trábea [trah'-bay-ah], *f.* A long gown.

trabilla [trah-beel'-lyah], *f.* 1. *(Dim.)* A small clasp or tie. 2. In knitting a dropped stitch (puntada).

trabón [trah-bone'], *m.* 1. Fetter for a horse's foot. 2. Crossplanks in oil-mills.

trabuca [trah-boo'-cah], *f.* Cracker, a fire-work.

trabucación [trah-boo-cah-the-on'], *f.* Confusion, mistake.

trabucador, ra [trah-boo-cah-dor', rah], *m. & f.* Disturber.

trabucante [trah-boo-cahn'-tay], *pa.* Preponderating; causing mistakes.

trabucar [trah-boo-car'], *va.* 1. To derange, to throw into confusion, to perturbate. 2. To interrupt a conversation, to cut the thread of a discourse. *-vn.* To stumble, to tumble. *-vr.* To equivocate, to mistake.

trabucazo [trah-boo-cah'-tho], *m.* 1. Shot with a blunderbuss. 2. The report of a blunderbuss. 3. *(Coll.)* A sudden fright.

trabuco [trah-boo'-co], *m.* 1. Catapult, ancient battering engine. 2. Blunderbuss.

trabuquete [trah-boo-kay'-tay], *m.* Ancient machine used to throw large stones.

traca [trah'-cah], *f.* 1. *(Naut.)* Strake, the uniform range of the planks of a ship. 2. String of fireworks.

trácala [trah'-cah-lah], *f.* 1. *(Men.)* Artifice scheme, trick. 2. *(And.)* Crowd (gentío). 3. *(Mex.)* Trickster (tramposo).

tracalero, ra [trah-cah-lay'-ro, rah], *a. (Mex.)* Tricky, artful.

tracamundana [trah-cah-moon-dah'-nah], *f. (Coll.)* 1. A ridiculous exchange of trifles. 2. Commotion, confusion, mess (lio).

tracción [trac-the-on'], *f.* 1. Act and effect of drawing. 2. Traction, pulling a load, as on railways. **Tracción delanter**, front-wheel drive.

tracias [trah'-the-as], *m.* North-north-west wind.

tracio, cia [trah'-the-o, ah], *a.* Thracian, of Thrace.

tracista [trah-thees'-tah], *m.* Projector, schemer, intriguer.

tracoma [trah-co'-mah], *f. (Med.)* Trachoma.

tractor [trac-tor'], *m.* Tractor. **Tractor blindado**, armored tractor. **Tractor de oruga**, caterpillar tractor.

tradición [trah-de-the-on'], *f.* 1. Tradition. 2. *(Law.)* V. ENTREGA.

tradicional [trah-de-the-on'], *a.* Traditional.

tradicionalmente [trah-de-the-o-nahl'-men-tays], *adv.* Traditionally.

traducción [trah-dooc-the-on'], *f.* 1. Translation, version, interpretation. 2. A rhetorical figure, by which a word is used in different senses.

traducir [trah-doo-theer'], *va.* 1. To translate, to interpret in another language, 2. To change, to truck. *(Yo traduzco, traduzca; traduje, tradujera; from Traducir. V. CONDUCIR.)*

traductor, ra [trah-dooc-tor', rah], *m & f.* Translator.

traedizo, za [trah-ay-dee'-tho, thah], *a.* That which may be drawn; tractable.

traedor, ra [trah-ay-dor', rah], *m. & f.* Carrier.

traedura [trah'-ay-doo'-rah], *f.* The act of carrying, bringing, or conducting.

traer [trah-err'], *va.* To fetch, to bring, to carry, to conduct any way. 2. To bring, to carry, to attract (imán), to draw towards oneself. 3. To bring about (causar), to cause, to occasion. 4. To come, to handle, to manage. 5. To assign reasons or authorities to prove a thing (autoridad). 6. To bring to, to oblige, to compel to do something. 7. To bring over, to reduce, to bind, to prevail upon, to persuade. 8. To be engaged in, to carry on, to have. 9. To use, to wear. **Traer medias de seda**, to wear silk stockings. **Traer y llevar cuentos**, to carry tales backwards and forwards. **Traer en bocas** or **lenguas**, to traduce one's reputation, to censure or speak ill of one's actions. **Traer perdido a alguno**, to be deeply in love; to be the ruin of a person. **Traer a consecuencia**, to place a thing in a situation which enhances or diminishes its value; to say something pertinent. **Traer un pleito con alguno**, to be engaged in a lawsuit against someone. **Traer a uno entre ojos**, *(Met.)* to be suspicious of a person. **Traer consigo**, to carry along. **Traer a la mano**, to fetch or carry. **Traer al ojo alguna cosa**, to keep a thing carefully in sight; to impress a thing upon one's mind. **Traer a cuento**, to turn the conversation to a desired point. *-vr.* 1. To be dressed well or poorly. 2. To have a graceful or ungainly deportment. As a reflexive verb used always with the adverbs *bien* or *mal.* **Traerlas**, to be annoying (molestar). **Tiene un padre que se las trae**, she has an excessively severe father.

trafagador [tra-fah-gah-dor'], *m.* Trafficker, dealer.

trafagante [trah-fah-gahn'-tay], *pa.* Trafficking, trading.

trafagar [trah-fah-gar'], *vn.* 1. To traffic, to carry on trade. V. TRAFICAR 2. *(Prov.)* To travel, to journey.

tráfago [trah'-fah-go], *m.* 1. Traffic, commerce, trade. 2. A careful management of affairs.

trafagón, na [trah-fah-gone', nah], *a.* Active, industrious, deeply engaged in trade and commerce.

trafalmejo, ja [trah-fal'-may'-ho, hah], *a.* Bold, intrepid, audacious.

traficación [trah-fe-cah-the-on'], *f.* Traffic, trade, commerce; shopping. V. TRÁFICO.

traficante [trah-fe-cahn'-tay], *pa. & m.* Merchant, trader; trading.

traficar [trah-fe-car'], *vn.* 1. To traffic, to carry on trade and commerce, to trade. 2. To travel, to journey.

tráfico [trah'-fe-co], *m.* Commerce, traffic, trade, negotiation. **Tráfico de mercancías**, goods traffic.

trafulla [trah-fool-lyah], *f. (Coll.)* Cheating, defrauding, swindling in gaming.

tragacanta [trah-gah-cahn'-tah], *f.* 1. *(Bot.)* Goat's-thorn, milk-vetch. 2. Tragacanth, a gum.

tragacanto [trah-gah-cahn'-to], *a.* Tragacanth: applied to the gum obtained from various species of astragalus.

tragacete [trah-gah-thay'-tay], *m.* Javelin, a Moorish missive weapon.

tragadero [trah-gah-day'-ro], *m.* 1. Esophagus, gullet. 2. Pit, gulf, abyss. **Tragadero de un puerto**, *(Naut.)* mouth of a harbor.

tragadieces [trah-gah-de-eth'-ess], **Tragaveintes** [trah-gah-veyn'-tess], *m. (Mex.)* Jukebox.

tragador, ra [trah-gah-dor', rah], *m. & f.* Glutton, gobbler.

tragahombres [trah-gah-om'-bres], *m. (Coll.)* Bully, hector.

trágala [trah'-gah-lah], *m.* A song of the liberals against the absolutism which began with this word. **Cantarle a uno el trágala**, to crow over one who has to accept what he detested.

tragaldabas [trah-gah-dah'-bas], *m. (Coll.)* Glutton.

tragaleguas [trah-gah-lay'-goo-as'], *m. (Coll.)* A brisk walker.

tragaluz [trah-gah-looth'], *f.* Skylight.

tragamallas [trah-gah-mahl-lyas], *m. (Coll.)* 1. Impostor, cheat, swindler. 2. Glutton, gormandizer.

tragantada [trah-gan-tah'-dah], *f.* A large draught of liquor.

tragantón, na [trah-gan-tone', nah], *m. & f. (Coll.)* A glutton. *-a.* Gluttonous, voracious.

tragantona [trah-gan-to'-nah], *f.* 1. A plentiful repast. 2. The act of swallowing or forcing down the throat. 3. *(Met.)* Difficulty of believing an extraordinary thing.

tragaperras [trah-gah-payr-rahs], *m.* Slot machine.

tragar [trah-gar'], *va.* 1. To swallow. 2. To devor, to eat voraciously, to glut. 3. To swallow up, to ingulf. 4. To swallow, to receive or believe without examination. **Hacer tragar algo a uno**, to force somebody to listen to something. *-vr.* To dissemble, to play the hypocrite; to pocket an affront. **Tragar el anzuelo**, *(Met.)* to allow oneself to be deceived. **No poder tragar a alguno**, to abhor or dislike one.

tragavirotes [trah-gah-ve-ro'-tess], *m. (Coll.)* A man who without cause is rude and puffed with pride.

tragazo [tra-gah'-tho], *m. aug.* A large draught.

tragazón [tra-gah-thone'], *f.* Voracity, gluttony.

tragedia [trah-hay'-de-ah], *f.* 1. Tragedy, a dramatic representation which has a mournful end. 2. Tragedy, any mournful event. **Parar en tragedia**, to have a disastrous issue. 3. Among the pagans a song in praise of Bacchus.

tragélafo [trah-hay-lah-fo], *m.* A fabulous animal between a goat and deer.

trágicamente [trah-he-cah-men-tay], *adv.* Tragically.

trágico, ca [trah'-he-co, cah], *a.* 1. Tragic, relating to tragedy. 2. Tragic, calamitous, disastrous.

tragicomedia [trah-he-co-may'-de-ah], *f.* Tragi-comedy.

tragicómico, ca [trah-he-co'-me-co, cah], *a.* Tragi-comical.

trago [trah'-go], *m.* 1. Draught of liquid (cantidad), swallowed at one time; swallow. 2. Calamity, adversity, misfortune (desgracia). **A tragos**, by degrees, slowly, gently. **Echar un trago**, to take a dram. **Un trago de agua**, a drink of water. **No vendría mal un trago de vino**, a drop of wine would not come amiss.

tragón, na [trah-gone, ah], *a.* Gluttonous, voracious, ravenous.

tragón [trah-gone], *m.* Glutton.

tragonazo, za [trah-go-nah'-tho, thah], *a. aug.* Applied to a great glutton.

tragonería, tragonía [trah-go-nay-ree'-ah], *f.* Gluttony.

traguillo, ito [trah-geel'-lyo], *m. dim.* of TRAGO.

traición [trah-e-the-on'], *f.* Treason, disloyalty; faithlessness; falsehood. **Matar a uno a traición**, to kill somebody treacherously. **A traición**, treacherously, treasonably.

traicionar [tra-he-the-o-nar'], *va.* To do treason.

traicionero, ra [trah-e-the-o-nay'-ro, rah], *a.* Treasonous, treasonable. *V.* TRAIDOR.

traída [trah-ee'-dah], *f.* Carriage, the act of fetching or carrying from place to place.

traído, da [trah-ee'-do, dah], *a. & pp.* of TRAER. 1. Brought, fetched, carried. 2. Used, worn (usado), second-hand.

traidor, ra [trah-e-dor', rah], *a.* 1. Treacherous (persona), faithless, disloyal, perfidious, false, traitorous. 2. Insidious, deceitful (animales). -*m.* Traitor, betrayer.

traidora [trah-e-do'-rah], *f.* Traitress.

traidoramente [trah-ee-do-rah-men-tay], *adv.* Treacherously, treasonably, traitorously, perfidiously.

tráiler [trah-ee-layr], *m.* 1. (Cine) Trailer. 2. *(Aut.)* Caravan.

traílla [trah-eel'-lyah], *f.* 1. Leash, lash (de perro), a cord or leather thong, by which a dog is led. 2. Pack-thread. 3. Instrument for levelling ground; a roadscraper.

traillar [trah-eel-lyar'], *va.* To level ground.

traíña [trah-ee'-nyah], *f.* 1. Net for deep-sea fishing. 2. Jack, a small bowl. *V.* BOLICHE.

trainera [trah-ee-nay-rah], *f.* Small fishing boat.

traja [trah'-hah], *f. (Amer.)* A load which vessels carry on deck.

trajano, na [trah-hah'-no, nah], *a.* Trajan; relating to the Emperor Truman.

traje [trah'-hay], *m.* 1. Suit, dress, habit, guise, apparel, clothes. 2. A complete dress of a woman, wardrobe; attire. 3. Mask, a dress used for disguise. **Traje de etiqueta**, dress suit. **Traje para la nieve**, snowsuit. **Traje para vuelos espaciales**, space suit. **Traje sastre**, tailored suit. **Traje de luces**, bullfighter's costume. **Traje de novia**, wedding dress.

trajear [trah-hay-ar'], *va.* To dress a person in a manner suited to his or her rank or condition.

traje de etiqueta [trah'-hay day ay-te-kay'-tah], *m.* Dress suit.

trajilla [trah-hee'-lyah], *f.* A harrow without teeth for levelling ground.

trajín [trah-heen'], *m.* 1. Carriage (acarreo). *V.* TRAJINO and TRÁFAGO. 2. Coming and going (ir y venir). 3. **Trajines**, affairs.

trajinante [trah-he-nahn'-tay], *m.* Carrier.

trajinar [tra-he-nar'], *va.* 1. To transport goods from place to place (acarrear). 2. To travel. 3. *(Coll.)* To fidget about. 4. *(Cono Sur)* To swindle (estafar). 5. *(Cono Sur)* To search (registrar). -*vn.* To bustle about (ajetrearse); to travel (viajar).

trajinería [trah-he-nay-ree'-ah], *f.* Carrying trade.

trajinero [trah-he-nay'-ro], *m.* Carrier.

trajino [trah-hee'-no], *m.* Carriage, the act of transporting merchandise.

tralla [trahl'-lyah], *f.* 1. Cord, bassweed rope. 2. Lash, snapper of a whip. 3. *(Mil.)* Pontoons for forming bridges.

trama [trah'-mah], *f.* 1. Weft or proof of cloth. 3. Kind of weaving silk. 3. Deceit, imposition, fraud, plot (complot), machination. 3. *(Comput.)* Raster.

tramador, ra [trah-mah-dor', rah], *m.* 1. Weaver. 2. Plotter; artful contriver, hatcher.

tramar [trah-mar'], *m.* 1. To weave. 2. To plot, to form crafty designs, to hatch, to scheme. 3. **Está tramando algo**, they're up to something.

tramilla [trah-meel'-lyah], *f. (Amer.)* Twine.

tramitación [trah-me-ta-the-on'], *f. (For.)* Progressive forwarding of a judicial proceeding according to prescribed procedure.

tramitar [trah-me-tahr'], *va.* To transact (despachar); to negotiate (negociar); to proceed with (proseguir).

trámite [trah'-me-tay], *m.* 1. Step (etapa), requirement, each step in transaction (negocio). 2. *(For.)* Procedure or course of a judicial process (procedimiento). **Trámites oficials**, official channels. **Hacer los trámites para un viaje**, to make the arrangements for a journey.

tramo [trah'-mo], *m.* 1. Piece, morsel. 2. Piece of ground separated from another. 3. Flight of stairs (escalera).

tramojo [trah-mo'-ho], *m.* 1. Part of grain, which the reaper holds in his hand. 2. Band for tying the sheaf. 3. Trouble, affliction.

tramón [trah-mone'], *m.* The shortest wool which remains in the comb during the combing.

tramontana [trah-mon-tah'-nah], *f.* 1. The north wind (viento). 2. Vanity (vanidad), pride, haughtiness. **Perder la tramontana**, *(Met.)* to become mad with passion.

tramontano, na [trah-mon-tah'-no, nah], *a.* Transmontane, beyond the mountains.

tramontar [trah-mon-tar'], *vn.* To pass to the other side of the mountains. -*va.* To assist, to relieve. -*vr.* To flee, to escape.

tramoya [trah-mo'-yah], *f.* 1. Machinery used in theaters to represent sudden disappearance, wonderful feats, etc. 2. Craft, artifice.

tramoyista [trah-mo-yees'-tah], *m.* 1. The machinist of a theater. 2. The scene shifter. 3. Impostor, swindler (estafador), deceiver.

trampa [trahm'-pah], *f.* 1. Trapsnare. 2. Trap-door (escotilla). 3. Movable part of a counter fitted with hinges for raising and lowering. **Caer en la trampa**, to fall into the snare, to be deceived by artifice. **Este juego no tiene trampa ni cartón**, this is the real thing. 4. Fraud (estafa), deceit, stratagem, malpractice. **Hacer trampas**, to cheat. 5. Debt fraudulently contracted.

trampal [tram-pahl'], *m.* Quagmire; a dirty or muddy place.

trampantojo [tram-pan-to'-ho], *m.* Trick played before one's eyes in order to deceive (juego de manos).

trampazo [tram-pah'-tho], *m.* The last twist of the cord employed to torture an offender.

trampeador, ra [tran-pay-ah-dor', rah], *m. & f.* Borrower, swindler cheat sharper.

trampear [tram-pay-ar'], *vn. & va.* 1. To stain money on false presences, to swindle one out of his money, to lurch, to shift, to play tricks, to cog. 2. To impose upon, to deceive.

trampilla [tram-peel'-lyah], *fr.* 1. Floor peephole (mirilla). 2. Coal bin door. 3. Pants fly (bragueta).

trampista [tram-pees'-tah], *a.* Cheating, deceitful. -*com.* Cheat, swindler.

trampolín [tram-po-leen'], 1. Springboard (de píscina). 2. Diving board. 3. Trampoline. 4. *(Fig.)* Stepping stone, springboard.

tramposo, sa [tram-po'-so, sah], *a.* Deceitful, swindling. -*m.* Cheater, swindler.

tranca [trahn'-cah], *f.* 1. Bar across a door or window, to prevent entrance. 2. *(Naut.)* Cross-bar. 3. Beam (viga). 4. *(Cono Sur)* Safety catch (de escopeta). 5. *(Carib. Aut.)* Traffic jam.

trancada [tran-cah'-dah], *f. V.* TRANCO and TRANCAZO.

trancado [tran-cah'-do], *vn.* A small harpoon for catching eels. -*pp.* of TRANCAR.

trancahilo [tran-cah-ee'-lo], *m.* Knot in thread or ropes.

trancanil [tran-cah-neel'], *m.* *(Naut.)* Water-way, for carrying off the water from the deck through the scupper holes; stringer plate.

trancar [tran-car'], *va.* 1. To barricade. *V.* ATRANCAR. 2. To bar (ventana).

trancazo [tran-cah-zoh], *m.* 1. Blow (golpe). 2. *(Med.)* Flu.

trance [tranh'-thay], *m.* Blow with a bar; influenza, grippe, moment (momento difícil), hypnotic state (estado hipnótico), drugged condition (estado drogado). **Trance mortal**, last moment of peril. **Estar en el trance de**, to be on the point of.

trancenil, [tran-thay-neel'], *m.* A gold or silver husband, garnished with jewels.

tranchete [trahn-chay'-tay], *m.* A broad, curvated knife, used for pruning, etc., shoemaker's heel-knife.

trancho [trahn'-cho], *m.* (*Prov.*) V. ALACHA.

tranco [trahn'-co], *m.* 1. A long step or stride (paso). 2. Threshold of a door. **A trancos**, in haste, in a trice.

trangallo [tran-gahl'-lyo], *m.* Yoke fixed on shepherds' dogs' necks, during the brooding-time of game.

tranquera [tran-kay'-rah], *f.* 1. Palisade (cercado). 2. (*LAm.*) Cattle gate.

tranquero [tran-kay'-ro], *m.* Jamb or lintel of a door or window, made of stone.

tranquilamente [tran-kee-lah-mehn-tay], *adv.* Quietly, peacefully, tranquilly, composedly.

tranquilidad [tran-kee-lee-dahd], *f.* Tranquility, tranquilness, rest, peace, repose, composure. **Perder la tranquilidad**, to lose patience.

tranquilizante [tran-ke-le-thahn'-tay], *m.* Tranquilizer.

tranquilizar [tran-ke-le-thar'], *va.* To calm, to appease, to tranquillize, to pacify. -*vr.* To calm down.

tranquilo, la [tran-kee'-lo, lah], *a.* Tranquil, calm (mar, mente, estado), quiet, pacific, gentle, contented. **Dejar a uno tranquilo**, to leave somebody along.

tranquilla [tran-keel'-lyah], *f.* 1. (*Dim.*) A small bar. 2. Trap, snare, stratagem.

tranquillón [tran-keel-lyone'], *m.* Mashlin, maslin, mixed grain.

transacción [tran-sac-the-on'], *f.* Composition of a difference, accommodation, adjustment. **Transacción comercial**, business deal.

transalpino, na [trans-al-pee'-no, nah], *a.* Transalpine.

transatlántico or **trasatlántico** [tran-sah-tlan'-te-co, trah-sah-tlan'-te-co], *m.* Transatlantic, ocean liner.

transar, *va.* (Canary Islands and *Amer.*) V. TRANSIGIR. Much used reflexively.

transbordador [trans-bor-dah-dor], *m.* Ferry; shuttle. **Transbordador para coches**, car ferry.

transbordar [trans-bor-dar'], *va.* (*Naut.*) To transship (a través de un río).

transbordo [trans-bor'-do], *m.* 1. Transshipment. 2. Transfer (traslado).

transcendencia [trans-then-den'-the-ah], *f.* V. TRASCENDENCIA.
transcendental [trans-then-den-tahl'], *a.* V. TRACENDENTAL.
transcendente [trans-then-den'-tay], *pa.* V. TRASCENDENTE.
transcender [trans-then-derr'], *va.* & *vn.* V. TRASCENDER.
transceptor [trans-thep-tor], Transceiver. (*Comput.*)
transcontinental [trans-con-te-nen-tahl'], *a.* Transcontinental, crossing the continent.

transcribir [trans-cre-beer'], *va.* To transcribe.

transcripción [trans-crip-the-on'], *f.* Transcription, the process and result of transcribing.

transcripto, ta, transcrito, ta [trans-creep'-to, tah, cree'- to, tah], *pp. irreg.* of TRANSCRIBIR.

transcurrir [trans-coor-reer'], *vn.* 1. To pass away (tiempo), to elapse. **Han transcurrido 7 años**, 7 years have passed. 2. To be, to turn out (suceso). **La tarde transcurrió aburrida**, the evening was boring.

transcurso [trans-coor'-so], *m.* Course or process of time.

transeúnte [tran-say-oon'-tay], *a.* Transient; transitory. -*com.* 1. Sojourner. 2. Passer-by.

transexual [trans-sayc-soo-ahl'], *a.* Transsexual. -*m.* & *f.* Transsexual.

transferencia [trans-fay-ren'-the-ah], *f.* Transfer, transference. **Transferencia bancaria**, banker's order.

transferible [trans-fay-ree'-blay], *a.* Transferable, capable of being transferred.

transferidor, ra [trans-fay-re-dor', rah], *m.* & *f.* V. TRASFERIDOR.

transferir [trans-fay-reer'], *va.* 1. To move, to remove, to transport. 2. (*LAm.*) To transfer (trasladar), to convey, to make over. 3. To employ a word figuratively.

transfigurable [trans-fe-goo-rah'-blay], *a.* Changeable, that can he transformed.

transfiguración [trans-fe-goo-rah-the-on'], *f.* Transformation, transfiguration.

transfigurar [trans-fe-goo-rar'], *va.* To transfigure, to transform. To be transfigured; to lose form or figure. (Used particularly as a reflexive verb.)

transfijo, ja [trans-fee'-ho, hah], *a.* Transfixed.

transfixión [trans-fik-se-on'], *f.* Transfixion, piercing through.

transflorar [trans-flo-rar'], *va.* To copy a picture or drawing by holding it against the light.

transflorear [trans'-flo-ray-ar'], *va.* To enamel, to inlay, to variegate with colors.

transfojar [trans-fo-har'], *va.* V. TRASHOJAR.

transfollado, da [trans-fol-lyah'-do, dah]. *a.* (*Vet.*) Applied to tumours round a horse's legs.

transformación [trans-for-mah-the-on'], *f.* Transformation, metamorphosis.

transformador, ra [trans-for-mah-dor', rah], *a.* Transforming. -*m* & *f.* Transformer, one who transforms. (*Phy.* & *elec.*) Transformer.

transformamiento [trans-for-mah-me-en'-to], *m.* Transformation.

transformar [trans-for-mar'], *va* 1. To conform, to transmute; to transfigure, to metamorphose. 2. To gain such an ascendency in another's affections, that it almost changes his or her character. -*vr.* To assume different sentiments or manners.

transformativo, va [trans-for-mah-tee'-vo, vah], That possesses power to transform.

transformismo [trans-for-mees-mo], *m.* Evolution, transmutation.

transformista [trans-for-mees-tah], *m* & *f.* Quick-change artist.

transfretar [trans-fray-gar'], *va.* To rub.

transfregar [trans-fray-tar'], *va.* To cross an arm of the sea.

tránsfuga, tránsfugo [trans'-foo-gah], *m.* Deserter, fugitive.

transfundición [trans-foon-de-the-on'], *f.* V. TRANSFUSIÓN.

transfundir [trans-foon-deer'], *va.* 1. To transfuse (sangre). 2. To communicate (noticia).

transfusión [trans-foo-se-on'], *f.* Transfusion: communication. **Transfusión de sangre**, blood transfusion.

transgangético, ca [trans-gah-hay'-te-co, cah], *a.* Beyond the Ganges.

transgredir [trans-gray-deer'], *va.* To transgress.

transgresión [trans-gray-se-on'], *f.* Transgression, crime, fault, sin.

transgresor, ra [trans-gray-sor', rah], *m.* & *f.* Transgressor, offender.

transición [tran-se-the-on'], *f.* Transition, change, removal.

transido, da [tran-see'-do, dah], *a.* 1. Worn out with anguish or grief. 2. Avaricious.

transigencia [trans-see-hen-the-ah], *f.* 1. Compromise (acto). 2. Accommodating attitude (actitud).

transigir [tran-se-heer'], *va.* To accommodate differences; to settle dial putts; to compound.

transistor [tran-ses-tor'], *m.* Transistor.

transitable [tran-se-tah'-blay], *a.* That may be passed through; passable (camino), practicable.

transitar [tran-se-tar'], *vn.* To travel, to go on a journey; to pass by a place.

transitivo, va [tran-see-tee'-vo, vah], *a.* Transitive.

tránsito [trahn'-se-to], *m.* 1. Passage, transition. 2. Inn, for travelers. 3. Road, way. 4. Change, removal. 5. Death of holy persons. 6. (*Ast.*) Transit. **Calle de mucho tránsito**, busy street. **Hacer tránsito**, to make a stop.

transitoriamente [trans-see-to-re-ah-men-tay], *adv.* Transitorily.

transitorio, ria [tran-se-to'-re-o, ah], *a.* Transitory (pasajero), perishable.

translación [trans-lah-the-on'], *f.* Translation. V. TRASLACIÓN.

translaticiamente [trans-lah-te-the-ah-men-tay], *adv.* Metaphorically. *V.* TRASLATICIAMENTE.

translaticio, cia [trans-lah-tee'-the-o, ah]. *V.* TRASLATICIO.

translativo, va [trans-lah-tee'-vo, vah*]*, *a. V.* TRASLATIVO.

translimitación [trans-le-me-tah-the-on'], *f.* Sending of troops to the territory of a neighboring state with the purpose of intervening in favor of one of two contending parties.

translimitar [trans-le-me-tar'], *m.* To pass unexpectedly, or by previous authorization, beyond the boundary of a state, for a military operation, without the purpose of violating the territory.

translucidez [trans-loo-the-deth'], *f.* Translucence.

translúcido [trans-loo'-the-do, dah], *a.* Translucent, semitransparent.

transmarino, na [trans-ma-ree'-no, nah], *a.* Transmarine.

transmigración [trans-me-grah-the-on'], *f.* Transmigration, the removal of families from one country to another.

transmigrar [trans-me-grar'], *vn.* To transmigrate, or pass from one country to another.

transminar [trans-me-nar'], *va.* To undermine.

transmisibilidad [trans-me-se-be-le-dahd'], *f.* Transmissibility.

transmisible [trans-me-see'-blay], *a.* Transmissible, capable of transmission.

transmisión [trans-me-se-on'], *f.* 1. Transmission, transmittal. 2. *(Elec.)* Transmission. **Transmisión en circuito**, hookup. **Transmisión exterior**, outside broadcast. 3. *(Comput.)* **Transmisión de datos en paralelo**, parallel data transmission. **Transmisión de datos en serie**, serial data transmission. **Transmisión asíncrona**, asynchronous transmission. **Transmisión bidireccional alternativa**, half duplex transmission. **Transmisión bidireccional simultánea**, full duplex transmission. **Transmisión en dúplex**, full duplex transmission. **Transmisión en semidúplex**, half-duplex transmission. **Transmisión "simplex"**, simplex transmission. **Transmisión síncrona**, synchronous transmission. **Transmisión unidireccional**, symplex transmission.

transmisor, ra [trans-me-sor', rah], *a.* Transmitting. *-m.* *(Elec.)* Transmitter.

transmitir [trans-me-teer'], *va.* To transfer, to transmit, to make over, to convey.

transmontar [trans-mon-tar'], *va. V.* TRAMONTAR.

transmutable [trans-moo-tah'-blay], *a.* Transmutable, convertible.

transmutación [trans-moo-tah-the-on'], *f.* Transmutation.

transmutar [trans-moo-tar'], *va.* To transmute.

transmutativo, va [trans-moo-tah-tee'-vo, vah], **Transmutatorio, ria** [trans-moo-tah-to'-re-o, ah], *a.* Transmutative, that which transmutes.

transparencia [trans-pa-ren'-the-ah], *f.* Transparency, clearness, diaphaneity.

transparentarse [trans-pa-ren-tar'-say], *vr.* 1. To be transparent (vidrio). 2. To shine through: used sometimes as an active verb. **Se transparentaba su verdadera intención**, his real intention became plain.

transparente [trans-pa-ren-tay], *a.* Transparent, lucid, fine, clear, limpid.

transparante [trans-pah-ren-tay], *m.* 1. Window-shade. 2. A glass window in churches behind the altar

transpirable [trans-pe-rah'-blay], *a.* Perspirable, transpirable.

transpiración [trans-pe-rah-the-on'], *f.* Transpiration, insensible perspiration.

transpirar [trans-pe-rar'], *vn.* To transpire, to perspire insensibly (sudar), To seep through (líquido).

transpirenaico, ca [trans-pe-ray-nah'-e-co, cah], *a.* Beyond the Pyrenees.

transplantación [trans-plan-tah-the-on'], *f. (Prov.) V.* TRASPLANTE.

transplante [trans-plahn'-tay], *m. V.* TRASPLANTE.

transponedor, ra [trans-po-nay-dor', rah], *m. & f.* Transponer, transplanter.

transponer [trans-po-nerr'], *va.* 1. To remove, to transport, to transpose. 2. To hide, to conceal craftily. 3. To transplant (trasplantar). *-vr.* 1. To be rather drowsy. 2. To set below the horizon. 3. To hide (esconderse). 4. To doze (dormirse).

transportación [trans-por-tah-the-on'], *f.* Transportation, conveyance, carriage.

transportador, ra [trans-por-tah-dor,' rah], *a.* Transporting, conveying. *-m.* Transporter, conveyor, carrier.

transportamiento [trans-por-tah-me-en'-to], *m.* 1. Transportation, carriage. 2. Transport, ecstasy, perturbation which impedes freedom of action.

transportar [trans-por-tar'], *va.* 1. To transport (acarrear), to convey, to remove. 2. *(Mus.)* To change the key. **El avión podrá transportar 400 pasajeros**, the plane will be able to carry 400 passengers. *-vr.* To be in a transport, to be out of one's senses.

transpote [trans-por'-tay], *m.* 1. Transport (acto), transportation, conveyance. **Bajel de transporte**, *(Naut.)* transport or transport-ship, to carry stores and soldiers. 2. Transport, fury, fit of passion. 3. To transfer (de diseño).

transportín [trans-por-teen'], *m. V.* TRANSPORTÍN.

transportista [trans-por-tees-tah], *m.* Carrier.

transposición [trans-po-se-the-on'], *f.* Transposition, transposal.

transpositivo, va [trans-po-se-tee'-vo, vah], *a.* Transpositional, transpositive, consisting in transposition.

transterminante [trans-ter-me-nahn'-tay], *pa.* Transgressing the limits.

transterminar [trans-ter-me-nar'], *va.* To pass from the limits of one jurisdiction to another; to trespass.

transtiberino, na [trans-te-bay-ree'-no, nah], *a.* Across the Tiber.

transubstanciación [tran-soobs-tan-the-ah-the-on'], *f.* Transubstantiation.

transubstancial [tran-soobs-tan-the-ahl'], *a.* Converted into another substance.

transubstanciar [trans-soobs-tan-the-ar'], *va.* To transubstantiate.

transversal [trans-verr-sahl'], *a.* Transversal.

transversalmente [trans-ver-sahl-men-tay], *adv.* Transversally, collaterally.

transverso, sa [trans-verr'-so, sah], *a.* Transverse.

tranvía [tran-vee'-ah], *m.* Tram (vehículo), tramcar, streetcar.

tranza [trahn'-thah], *f. (Prov.)* Sale of a debtor's property to satisfy his creditors.

tranzadera [tran-thah-day'-rah], *f.* Knot of plaited cords or ribbons.

tranzar [tran-thar'], *ra.* 1. To plait or weave cords or ribbons; to braid. 2. To cut, to truncate. 3. *V.* REMATAR.

tranzón [tran-thone'], *m.* Part of a forest which has been cut or cleared for fuel.

trapa [trah'-pah], *f.* Noise made by stamping with the feet, or bawling.

trapacear [trah-pa-thay-ar'], *vn.* To deceive by falsehoods and artful contrivances.

trapacería [trah-pah-thay-ree'-ah], *f.* Fraud, deceit, counterfeit. *V.* TRAPAZA.

trapacero, ra [trah-pa-thay'-ro, rah], *f. & m. & f.* Cheating, deceitful. *V.* TRAPACISTA.

trapacete [trah-pa-thay'-tay], *m. (Com.)*

trapacista [trah-pa-thees'-tah], *m. & a.* Impostor, cheat, sharper, swindler; deceiver; fraudulent, false.

trapajo [tah-pah'-ho], *m.* Rag, tatter.

trapajoso, sa [trah-pah-ho'-so, sah], *a.* Ragged, tattered.

trápala [trah'-pah-lah], *f.* 1. A violent noise by stamping with the feet, or bawling. 2. Deceit, cheat by false representations. *-com.* Garrulous, loquacious babbler. *-m.* Garrulity, loquacity, talkativeness.

trapalear [trah-pah-lay-ar'], *vn.* To be loquacious or garrulous; to babble.

trapalón, na [trah-pah-lone', nah], *a. & m. & f.* Loquacious; babbler, prater. Deceitful, bombastic fellow.

trapaza

trapaza [trah-pah'-thah], /. Fraud, A deceitful trick upon a buyer.

trapazar [trah-pa-thar'], *vn. V.* TRAPALEAR.

trapazo [trah-pah'-tho], *m.* A large rag.

trapa [trah'-pay], *m.* Buckram.

trapeado [trah-pay-ah'-do], *m.* (Art term) The drapery of a figure

trapear [trah-pay-ar'], *va. (Art.)* To drape the figure.

trapecio [trah-pay'-the-o], *m.* 1. *(Goom.)* Trapezium. 2. Trapeze for gymnastic exercises.

trapería [trah-pay-ree'-ah], *f.* 1. Street inhabited by woollendrapers. 2. Frippery, rag-fair. 3. Woollen draper's shop (tienda).

trapero, ra [trah-pay'-ro, rah], *m. & f. & a.* Dealing in rags or frippery.

trapezoide [trah-pay-tho'-e-day], *m.* 1. Trapezoid, a geometrical figure of unequal sides, none parallel. 2. Trapezoid, a bone of the wrist.

trapico [trah-pee'-co], *m. dim.* Little rag.

trapiche [trah-pee'-chay], *m.* 1. A sugar- mill (de azúcar), or engine for preparing the sugar-cane. **Trapiche de vapor**, steam sugar-mill. 2. *(Cuba)* A small sugar plantation. 3. *(Mex.)* Both the machinery and plantation.

trapichear [trah-pe-chay-ar'], *vn. (Coll.)* 1. To trade in a small way. 2. *(Coll.)* To contrive, to seek artifices not always permissible for the attainment of some object. 3. *(Cono Sur)* To scrape a living by buying and selling (comerciar). *-va.* To deal in, to trade in.

trapicheo [trah-pe-chay'-o], *m.* Small trading; a dodge.

trapichero [trah-pe-chay'-rō], *m.* 1. A worker in a sugarmill. 2. *(And. Carib.)* Busybody. (entromedito). 3. *(Cono Sur)* Small-time dealer.

trapiento, ta [trah-pe-en'-to, tah], *a.* Ragged, tattered.

trapillo [trah-peel'-lyo], *m.* 1. Courtier of a vulgar woman. 2. Little rag.**Estar, andar** or **salir de trapillo**, to be in an undress, to be in dishabille, to have a loose or negligent dress.

trapío [trah-pee'-o], *m.* 1. Sprightly manner, graceful gestures, whether respectable or vulgar and loose, which some women have. 2. Liveliness and smartness in a fighting bull.

trapisonda [trah-pe-son'-dah], *f. (Coll.)* Bustle, noise, confusion, clatter; clatter, deception, *(Vul.)* Carousing.

trapito [trah-pee'-to], *m. dim. V.* TRAPICO.

trapo [trah'-po], *m.* 1. Cloth. 2. Rag (paño), tatter. 3. Sails of a ship. 4. Clothes (vestidos de mujer). **Poner como un trapo**, to reprimand severely. **Trapo de fregar**, dishcloth. **Gasta una barbaridad en trapos**, she spends an awful lot on clothes. **Sacar los trapos a relucir**, to let fly.

traque [trah'-kay], *m.* Crack, the noise made by a bursting rocket, or the priming of a gun.

tráquea [trah'-kay-ah], *f.* 1. Windpipe, trachea. 2. Tracheae of insects.

traqueal [trah'-kay-ahl'], *a.* 1. Tracheal, of or pertaining to a trachea. 2. Breathing by means of tracheae.

traquear [trah-kay-ar'], *vn.* 1. To crack, to make a loud noise. 2.*(Carib.)* To drink. *-va.* 1. To frequent, to handle a thing much. 2. To shake, to agitate, to move to and fro.

traqueartería [trah-kay-ar-tay-ree'-ah], *f.* Traehea, windpipe.

traqueo [trah-kay'-o], *m.* 1. Noise of artificial fireworks. 2. The act of shaking or moving to and fro.

traqueotomía [trah-kay-o-to-mee'-ah], *f.* Tracheotomy.

traquescote [trah-kes-co'-tay], *(Naut.)* Trackscout.

traquetear [trah-kay-tay-ar'], *va.* To shake (recipiente), to agitate, to move to and fro, to handle too much. *-vn.* 1. To crackle (cohete), to bang; to rattle (vehículo); to rattle (ametrallador). 2. *(Cono Sur, Mex.)* To bustle about (apresurarse).

traqueteo [trah-kay-tay'-o], *m.* Shaking, shake, concussion.

traquiarteria [trah-ke-ar-tay'-re-ah], *f. V.* TRAQUEARTERIA.

traquido [trah-kee'-do], *m.* Report of fire-arms.

traquítico, ca [trah-kee'-te-co, cah], *a.* Trachytic, like trachyte.

traquito [trah-kee'-to], *m.* Trachyte, a dull grayish volcanic rock of granite-like aspect.

tras [trahs], *prep.* After, behind (lugar), besides. **Tras una puerta**, behind a door. **Tras de venir tarde**, besides coming late. In composition it is equivalent to *trans*, as *traspasar*. Usage authorizes its employment in nearly all cases in place of *trans. (Acad.)* **Ir or andar tras alguno**, to go in pursuit after one, to seek diligently; to follow after one.

tras [trahs], *m.(Coll.)* 1. Breech, bottom. *V.* TRASERO. 2. Blow or stroke attended with noise; crash dash. (Onomatopoetic.) **Tras, tras**, repeated strokes or noise.

trasalcoba [trah-al-co'-bah], *f.* Alcove behind the principal recess.

trasalpino, na [trahs-al-pee'-no, nah], *a. V.* TRANSALPINO.

trasanteayer [trahs-an-tay-ah-yerr'], *adv. V.* ANTEANTEAYER.

trasañejo, ja [trahs-ah-nyey'-ho, hah], *a.* Three years old (vino).

trasatlántico, ca [trahs-at-lahn'-te-co, cah], *a. V.* TRANSATLÁNTICO.

trasbisnieto, ta [trahs-bis-ne-ay'-to, tah], *m. & f. V.* TATARANIETO.

trasbordar and trasbordo [trahs-bor-dahr], *V.* sub TRANS.

trasca [trahs'-cah], *f. (Prov.)* Leather thong.

trascabo [trahs-cah'-bo], *m.* Trip, a trick by which a wrestler throws his antagonist.

trascantón [trahs-can-tone'], *m.* Stone placed at the corner of a street; curb-stone. **Dar trascantón or trascantonada**, to hide oneself behind a corner.

trascantonada [trahs-can-to-nah'-dah], *f.* 1. *V.* TRASCANTÓN. 2. Action of waiting beside a corner.

trascartarse [trahs-car-tar'-say], *vr.* To remain behind: applied to a card which, had it come sooner, would have won the game.

trascartón [trahs-car-tone'], *m.* Drawing of a winning card after the game is lost.

trascendencia [trahs-then-den'-the-ah], *f.* 1. Transcendence, perspicacity of things. 2. Result, consequence. **Encuentro sin trascendenica**, causal meeting.

trascendental [trahs-then-den-tahl'], *a.* 1. Transcendental, far-reaching (consecuencias), extending to other things, transcendent. 2. Trascendental, of very high degree, of great importance by reason of its probable consequences (importancia). 3. (Philosophy) Investigating the nature of our faculties, the value of ideas, etc. 4. *(Math.)* Trascendental, into whose calculation the infinite enters.

transcendentalismo [trahs-then-den-tah-less'-mo], *m.* Transcendentalism, every philosophical system transcending observation and experience and rising into abstract investigations.

trascendentalista [trahs-then-den-tah-lees'-tahl], *m. & a.* Transcendentalism, one who holds the doctrine of transcendentalism.

transcendente [trans-then-den-tay], *pa. & a.* Transcendent.

trascender [tras-then-derr'], *vn.* 1. To be transcendent, to extend itself. 2. To emit a good, strong odor; to be pervasive, to penetrate. 3. To penetrate, to perceive quickly and clearly. 4. To transcend, to go beyond (not recognised by the Academy in this sense). 5. To come out (saberse). 6. To spread (propagarse). **En esta novela todo trasciende a romanticismo**, everything in this novel smacks of romanticism. *Por fin ha trascendido la triste noticia*, the sad news had come out at last. *(Yo trasciendo, trascienda*, from *Trascender. V.* ENTENDER.)

trascendido, da [trahs-then-dee'-do, dah], *a & pp.* of TRASCEBDER. Acute, endowed with great penetration.

trascocina [trahs-co-thee'-nah], *f.* Back-kitchen.

trascolar [trahs-co-lar'], *va. (Med.)* 1. To strain, to percolate. 2. *(Coll.)* To pass over a mountain. *(Yo trascuelo, trascuele*, from *Trascolar. V.* ACORDAR.)

trasconejarse [trahs-co-ne-har'-say], *vn.*1. To squat: applied to game pursued by dogs. 2. To sheer off, to escape. 3. *(Coll.)* To be missing or mislaid: said of papers, documents, or small articles. *(Yo me trascuerdo, trascuerde, from Trascordarse. V. ACORDAR.)*

trascordarse [trahs-cor-dar'-say], *vr.* To forget.

trascoro [trahs'-co'-ro], *m.* Space in a church at the back of the choir.

trascorral [trahs-cor-rahl'], *m.* 1. Back court or back yard. 2. *(Coll.)* Breech, buttocks.

trascribir [trahs-cre-beer']. *va. V.* TRANSCRIBIR.

trascripción [trahs-crep-the-on], *f. V.* TRANSCRIPCIÓN.

trascuarto [trahs-coo-ar'-to], *m.* Back room.

trascurso [trahs-coor'-so], *m.* Course or process of time. *V.* TRANSCURSO.

trasdobladura [trahs-do-blah-doo'-rah], *f.* Treble, triple.

trasdoblar [trahs-do-blar'], *m.* To treble, to multiply by three.

trasdoblo [trahs-do'-blo], *m.* Treble, triple. *V.* TRIPLE.

trasdós [trash-dose'], *m. (Arch.)* Extrados, the back or outer surface of an arch: opposed to soffit.

trasdosear [trahs-do-say-ar'], *m.* To strengthen upon the back.

trasechador [trahs-ay-chah-dor'], *m.* Fighter, contestant.

trasegador [trah-say-gah-dor'], *m.* One who racks wine.

trasegar [trah-say-gar'], *va.* 1. To overset, to turn topsyturvy. 2. To decant, to rack wine. 3. To mix up (trastornar). *(Yo trasiego, yo trasiegue, trasegué. from Trasegar. V. ACERTAR.)*

traseñalador, ra [trah-say-nyah-lah-dor', rah], *m. & f.* One who alters marks.

traseñalar [trah-say-nay-lar'], *m.* To alter or blot out a mark and make a new one.

trasera [trah-say'-rah], *f.* Back or posterior part; croup.

trasero, ra [trah-say'-ro, rah], *a.* Remaining behind, coming after, hinder.

trasero [trah-say-ro]. *m.* 1. Buttock, rump of animals. **Traseros**, in jocular style, our ancestors, or predecessors. 2. *(Anat.)* Bottom.

trasferencia [trans-fay-ren-the-ah], *f. V.* TRANSFERENCIA.

trasferible [trans-fay-re-blay], *a. V.* TRANSFERIBLE.

trasferidor [trahs-fay-re-dor'], *m.* Transferrer. *V.* TRANSFERIDOR.

trasferir [trahs-fay-reer'], *m. V.* TRANSFERIR.

transfigurable, *a.* **transfiguración** and **trasfigurar** [transfe-goo-rah-blay], *va. V.* TRANSFIGURABLE, TRANSFIGURACIÓN, and TRANSFIGURAR.

trasfijo, ja, *a.* and **trasfixión** [trans-fe-ho], *f. V.* TRANSFIJO and TRANSFIXIÓN.

trasflorar and **trasflorear** [trans-flo-rahr], *va. V.* TRANSFLORAR and TRANSFLOREAR.

trasfojar [trahs-fo-har'], *va.* To run over the leaves of a book. *V.* TRASHOJAR.

trasfollado, da [trahs-fol-lyah'-do, dah], *a. V.* TRANSFOLLADO.

trasformación [trahs-for-mah-the-on'], *f.* Transformation. *V.* TRANSFORMACIÓN.

trasformador [trahs-for-mah-dor], *m. V.* TRANSFORMADOR.

trasformamiento [trahs-for-ma-me-ayn-to], *m. V.* TRANSFORMACIÓN.

trasformar [trahs-for-mar], *va. V.* TRANSFORMAR.

trasformativo, va [trahs-for-mah-te-vo], *a. V.* TRANSFORMATIVO.

trasfregar [trahs-fray-gar'], *va.* To rub.

trasfretano, na [trash-fray-tah'-no, nah], *a.* Transmarine.

trásfuga, trásfugo [trahs'-foo-gah, trahs'-foo-go], *m.* Deserter, fugitive. *V.* TRÁNSFUGA.

trasfusión or **transfusión** [trahs-foo-see-on'], *f.* Transfusion. **Trasfusión de sangre**, blood transfusion.

trasgo [trahs'-go], *m.* 1. Goblin (duende), hobgoblin, sprite. *V.* DUENDE. 2. A lively, restless, noisy boy.

trasgredir [trahs-gray-deer'], *va.* To transgress.

trasgresión [trahs-gray-se-on'], *f. V.* TRANSGRESIÓN.

trasgresor, ra [tahs-gray-sor', rah], *m. &f.* Transgressor. *V.* TRANSGRESOR.

trasguear [trahs-gray-ar'], *vn.* To play the hobgoblin.

trasguero [trahs-gay'-ro], *m.* One who imitates the tricks of hobgoblins.

trashogar [trahs-o-gar'], *m.* 1. Front of a chimney. 2. *V.* TRASHOGUERO, 1st def.

trashoguero [trahs-o-gay'-ro], *m.* 1. Iron plate, placed at the back part of a fireplace. 2. Block of wood placed against the wall to keep in the fire.

trashoguero, ra [trahs-o-gay'-ro, rah], *a.* Idling, loitering the whole day near the fire-place.

trashojar [trahes-o-har'], *va.* To run over the leaves of a book.

trashumante [trahs-oo-mahn'-tay], *pa. & a.* Applied to flocks of sheep which pasture in the north of Spain in summer and in the south in winter. **trashumantes**, traveling or merino sheep.

trashumar [trahs-oo-mar'], *va.* To drive sheep to or from the common pasture grounds in spring and autumn.

trasiego [trah-se-ay'-go], *m.* 1. Removal, the act of moving things. 2. The act of decanting liquors.

trasijado, da [trah-se-hah'-do, dah], *a.* Lank, meager: thinflanked.

trasijar [trah-se-har'], *vn. & vr.* To grow thin or meager.

traslación [trahs-lah-the-on'], *f.* 1. Translation, removal. 2. Translation, version, rendering into another language, and the subject-matter so translated.

trasladante [trahs-lah-dahn'-tay], *pa.* Translating, transcribing.

trasladar [trahs-lah-dar'], *va.* 1. To move (mudar), to remove (quitar), to transport. 2. To translate (pensamiento, sentimiento). 3. To transcribe. **Trasladar su pensamiento al papel**, to put one's thoughts on paper. *-vr.* To go, to move. **Trasladarse a otro puesto**, to move to a new job.

traslado [trahs-lah'-do], *m.* 1. A copy (copia). 2. Imitation, resemblance, likeness, counterpart. 3. *(Law.)* The reference or act of delivering written judicial proceedings to the other party, in order that on examination of them he may prepare the answer. **Dar traslado a uno de una orden**, to give somebody a copy of an order.

traslapar [trahs-lah-par'], *m. V.* SOLAPAR.

traslaticiamente [trahs'-lah-te-the-ah-men'-tay], *adv.* Metaphorically, figuratively.

traslaticio, cia, traslato, ta [trahs-lah-tee'-the-o, ah], *a.* Metaphorical, figurative.

traslativo, va [trahs-lah-tee'-vo, vah], *a.* Metaphorical, figurative.

traslúcido, da [trahs-loo'-the-do, dah], *a.* Transparent, clear, pellucid.

traslucido, da [trahs-loo-thee'-do, dah], *pp.* of TRASLUCIRSE.

trasluciente [trahs-loo-the-en'-tay], *a.* Translucent, transparent, translucid.

traslucirse [trahs-loo-theer'-say], *vr.* 1. To be transparent (ser transparente); to shine through (ser visible). 2. To conjecture, to infer. 3. *(Fig.)* To leak out (saberse). 4. *(Fig.)* To reveal one's inmost thoughts (persona).

traslumbramiento [trahs-loom-brah-me-en'-to], *m.* The state of being dazzled by excessive light.

traslumbrarse [trahs-loom-brar'-say], *vr.* 1. To be dazzled with excessive light (ser deslumbrado). 2. To vanish, to disappear.

trasluz [trahs-looth'], *m.* 1. Light which passes through a transparent body. 2. *(Art.)* Transverse light. 3. *(Carib.)* Resemblance (semblanza).

trasmallo [trahs-mahl'-lyo], *m.* 1. Trammel-net, drag-net, a coarse-meshed net, having a smaller one behind it. 2. Iron handle of a hammer.

trasmano [trahs-mah'-no], *m.* Second player at a game of cards.

trasmañana [trahs-mah-nyah'-nah], *f.* The day after tomorrow.

trasmarino, na [trahs-mah-ree'-no, nah], *a. V.* TRANSMARINO.

trasmatar [trahs-mah-tar'], *va. (Coll.)* To persuade oneself of having longer to enjoy life than another; to outlive.

trasmigración [trahs-me-grah-the-on'], *f. V.* TRANSMIGRACIÓN.

trasmigrar [trahs-me-grar'], *va. V.* TRANSMIGRAR.

trasminar [trahs-me-nar'], *va.* To undermine, to excavate, to dig under ground. *-vn.* To emit a strong scent. *-vr.* To pierce, to penetrate.

trasmisible trahs-me-see'-blay], *a. V.* TRANSMISIBLE.

trasmisión [trahs-me-se-on'], *f. V.* TRANSMISIÓN.

trasmisor, ra [trahs-me-sor', rah], *a. V.* TRANSMISOR.

transmitido, da [trahs-me-tee'-do, dah], *a. & pp.* of TRASMITIR. Transmitted, traditive.

trasmitir [trahs-me-teer'], *va. (Law.) V.* TRANSMITIR.

trasmochadero [trahs-mo-chah-day'-ro], *m.* A thicket of firewood. *-a.* Serving for fuel.

trasmochar [trahs-mo-char'], *va.* To cut branches of trees for fuel.

trasmontar [trahs-mon-tar'], *va.* To pass to the other side of the mountain. *V.* TRAMONTAR.

trasmota [trahs-mo'-tah], *f. (Prov.)* After wine, made by water poured on the pressed grapes.

trasmudar [trahs-moo-dar'], *va. V.* TRANSMUDAR.

trasmutable [trahs-moo-tah'-blay], *a. V.* TRANSMUTABLE.

trasmutación [trahs-moo-tah-the-on'], *f. V.* TRANSMUTACIÓN.

trasmutar [trahs-moo-tar'], *va.* To alter, to transmute, to convert. *V.* TRANSMUTAR.

trasmutativo, va [trahs-moo-tah-tee'-vo, vah], *a. V.* TRANSMUTATIVO.

Trasmutatorio, ria, *a. V.* TRANSMUTATIVO.

trasnochada [trahs-no-chah'-dah], *f.* 1. Last night (noche anterior). 2. Watch, the act of watching a whole night (noche sin dormir).

trasnochado, da [trahs-no-chah'-do, dah], *a. & pp.* of TRASNOCHAR. Having watched the whole night; fatigued from night-watching.

trasnochador, ra [trahs-no-chah-dor', rah], *m & f.* Night-watcher.

trasnochar [trahs-no-char'], *vn.* To watch, to sit up a whole night, to have a night out (ir de juerga).

trasnombrar [trahs-nom-brar'], *va.* To change or confound names.

trasnominación [trahs-no-me-nah-the-on'], *f. V.* METONIMIA.

trasoír [trahs-o-eer'], *va.* To mistake, to misunderstand, to hear the wrong thing.

trasojado, da [trahs-o-hah'-do, dah], *a.* Having sunken eyes, emaciated, worn out.

trasoñar [trah-so-nyar'], *vn.* To dream, to fancy erroneously.

traspágina [trash-pah'-he-nah], *f.* Back page.

traspalar [trahs-pah-lar'], *va.* 1. To shovel, to remove with a shovel. 2. To move, to remove. 3. *(Prov.)* To dig under a vine; to clear the ground of grass.

traspapelarse [trahs-pah-pay-lar'-say], *vn.* To be mislaid among other papers (escritura).

trasparencia [trahs-pe-ren'-the-ah], *f.* Transparency. *V.* TRANSPARENCIA.

trasparentarse [trahs-pah-ren-tahr'-say], *vn. V.* TRANSPARENTARSE.

trasparente [trahs-pah-ren'-tay], *a. V.* TRANSPARENTE.

traspasación [trahs-pah-sah-the-on'], *f. (Law.)* Conveyance, transfer. *V.* TRASPASO.

traspasamiento [trahs-pah-sah-me-en'-to], *m.* 1. Transgression, trespass. 2. Transfer, the act of conveying. 3. Grief, anguish.

traspasar [trahs-pah-sar'], *va.* 1. To pass over, to go beyond (límite); to cross (calle). 2. To remove, to transport. 3. To transfix, to transpierce; to introduce with great force. 4. To cross a river. 5. To return, to repass. 6. To transgress, to violate a law. 7. To exceed proper bounds; to trespass. 8. To transfer, to make over. **La bala le traspasó el pulmón,** the bullet pierced his lung. **La escena me traspasó el corazón,** the scene pierced me to the core. *-vn.* To be touched with compasion, to be afflicted.

traspaso [trahs-pah'-so], *m.* 1. Conveyance, transfer (venta). 2. Grief, anguish (pena). 3. Trespass, violation of a law; treachery. 4. Infringement (de ley). 5. Property transferred (propiedad, bienes).

traspeinar [trahs-pay-nar'], *va.* To comb again.

traspellar [trahs-pel-lyar'], *va. V.* CERRAR.

traspié [trahs-pe-ay'], *m.* 1. Slip (tropiezo), stumble. **Dar traspiés,** (1) to stumble without falling. (2) *(Met.)* To stumble, to dip, to commit errors or faults. 2. Trip, a wrestler's trick with his antagonist.

traspilastra [trahs-pe-lahs'-trah], *f. (Arch.) V.* CONTRAPILASTRA.

traspillarse [trahs-peel-lyar'-say], *vr.* To grow thin, to be emaciated.

traspintar [trahs-pin-tar'], *va.* To know from the cards drawn those that are to follow. *-vr.* To be disappointed: to turn out contrary to one's expectation.

traspirable [trahs-pe-rah'-blay], Transpirable. *V.* TRANSPIRABLE.

traspiración [trahs-pe-rah-the-on'], *f. V.* TRANSPIRACIÓN.

traspirar [trahs-pe-rar'], *va. V.* TRANSPIRAR.

trasplantación [trahs-plan-tah-the-on'], *f. (Prov.) V.* TRASPLANTE.

trasplantar [trahs-plan-tar'], *va.* 1. To transplant, to remove plants. 2. To migrate.

trasplante [trash-plahn'-tay], *m.* Transplantation. **Trasplante de corazón,** heart transplant.

trasponedor, ra [trahs-po-nay-dor', rah], *m. & f. V.* TRANSPONEDOR.

trasponer [trahs-po-nerr'], *m. V.* TRANSPONER. *(Yo traspongo, trasponga; traspuse, traspondré, traspusiera; from Trasponer. V.* PONER.)

traspontín [trahs-pon-teen'], *m. (Coll.) V.* TRASERO.

trasporarse [trahs-po-rar'-say], *vr. V.* TRANSPORARSE.

trasportación [trahs-por-tah-the-on'], *f.* Transportation. *V.* TRANSPORTACIÓN

trasportador, ra [trahs-por-tah-dor', rah], *V.* TRANSPORTADOR.

trasportamiento [trahs-por-tah-me-en'-to], *m. V.* TRANSPORTAMIENTO.

trasportar [trahs-por-tar'], *va. V.* TRANSPORTAR.

trasporte [trahs-por'-tay], *m. V.* TRANSPORTE.

trasportín [trahs-por-teen'], *m.* A thin and small mattress, put between other mattresses.

trasposición [trahs-po-se-the-on'], *f.* Transposition, transposal. *V.* TRANSPOSICIÓN.

transpositivo, va [trahs-po-se-tee'-vo, vah], *a. V.* TRANSPOSITIVO.

traspuesta [trahs-poo-es'-tah], *f.* 1. Transport, removal. 2. Corner or turning of a mountain, which serves for a lurking-place. 3. Flight (huida), disappearance. 4. Backyard (patio) or court; back door; out offices of a dwelling-house.

traspuesto, ta [trahs-poo-es'-to, tah], *pp. irr.* of TRASPONER. Transported.

traspunte [trahs-poon'-tay], *m.* A prompter in a theater (apuntador). *V.* APUNTADOR.

trasquero [trahs-kay'-ro], *m* Leather cutter, one who cuts out leather thongs.

trasquiladero [trash-ke-lay-day'-ro], *m.* Place where sheep are shorn.

trasquilador [trahs-ke-lah-dor'], *m.* Shearer.

trasquiladura [trahs-ke-lah-doo'-rah], *f* The act of shearing.

trasquilar [trahs-ke-lar'], *va.* 1. To shear sheep (oveja); to cut the bar in an irregular manner (cortar). 2. To clip, to curtail, to diminish.

trasquilimocho, cha [trahs-ke-le-mo'-cho, chah], *a. (Coll.)* Close shorn or cropped.

trasquilón [trahs-ke-lone'], *m.* 1. Cut of the shears: as much wool or hair as is cut off by one snip of the shears. **A trasquilones,** irregularly, rudely 2. *(Coll.)* Part of one's fortune, which has been clipped or lost through the fraud of others.

trastada [trahs-tah'-dah], *f.* *(Coll.)* A bad act, or one ill-judged and ill-advised, practical joke (broma pesada), piece of bad behavior (grosería).

trastazo [trahs-tah'-tho], *m.* *(Coll.)* A whack, thump, blow.

traste [trahs'-tay], *m.* 1. Fret, a sort or slender strip of metal fastened at intervals in the neck of a guitar, or like instrument, to determine the intervals of the scale. 2. *(Prov.)* A small glass or cup, kept in wine-cellars for the use of wine-tasters. 3. *(Prov.)* V. TRASTO. **Sin trastes**, without head or tail; in a disorderly manner. **Dar al traste con los negocios**, *(Coll.)* to fail, to be unfortunate in business. **Ir al traste**, to fail.

trasteado [trahs-tay-ah'-do], *m.* Number of frets upon the neck of a lute or guitar.—**Trasteado, da**, *pp.* of TRASTEAR.

trasteador, ra [trahs-tay-ah-dor', rah], *m. & f.* A noisy fellow, who throws everything into disorder and confusion.

trasteante [trahs-tay-ahn'-tay], *pa. & a.* Applied to a dexterous performer on the guitar.

trastear [trahs-tay-ar'], *va.* 1. To put frets upon the neck of a guitar. 2. To remove furniture from one part of a house to another (mover). 3. To play well on the guitar. 4. To talk upon a subject in a lively manner (entretener). 5. *(Mex.)* To feel up (acariciar). *-vn.* 1. To move things around (mover objetos). 2. *(And. CAm.)* To move house (mudar de casa). 3. To make bright conversation (conversar).

trastejadura [trahs-tay-hay-doo'-rah], *f.* V. TRASTEJO.

trastejar [trahs-tay-har'], *va.* 1. To tile; to cover with tiles. 2. To go over, to examine something in order to repair it.

trastejo [trahs-tay'-ho], *m.* 1. Tiling, covering houses with tiles. 2. Any uninterrupted and disorderly motion.

trastera [tras-tay'-rah], *f.* 1. Lumber room (habitación). 2. *(Mex.)* Cupboard (armario). 3. *(Carib.)* Heap of junk.

trastería [trahs-tay-ree'-ah], *f.* 1. Heap of lumber (trastos). 2. A ridiculous or foolish action.

trasterminante [trahs-ter-me-nahn'-tay], *pa. & m.* V. TRANSTERMINANTE.

trasterminar [trahs-ter-me-nar'], *va.* V. TRANSTERMINAR.

trastero [trahs-tay'-ro], *m.* 1. Lumber room (habitación); storage room. 2. *(Mex.)* Cupboard, closet. 3. *(Mex.)* Bum (culo). 4. *(CAm. Mex.)* Dish-rack (para platos).

trastiberino, na [trahs-te-bay-ree'-no], *a.* V. TRANSTIBERINO.

trastienda [trahs-te-en'-dah], *f.* 1. Back-room behind a shop (habitación). 2. Prudence, precaution, forecast. 3. *(Cono Sur, Mex.)* Bum (culo).

trasto [trahs'-to], *m.* 1. Furniture, movables or goods put in a house or use or ornament; luggage. **Trastos de cocina**, kitchen utensils. 2. Useless person, puppy. 3. Scenery (decorado); stage furniture (accesorios). 4. Gear (avíos). **Tirarse los trastos a la cabeza**, to have a blazing row. **Trastos de pescar**, fishing tackle.

trastornable [trahs-tor-nah'-blay], *a.* 1. Movable; easily turned, topsy-turvy. 2. Fickle, restless.

trastornadamente [trahs-tor-nah'-dah-men'-tay], *adv.* Upside down. in confusion.

trastornado, da [trahs-tor-nah'-do, dah], *a.* 1. Mentally unbalanced (persona). 2. Overthrown, in disorder, in confusion.

trastornador, ra [trahs-tor-nah-dor'-rah], *m. & f.* Disturber, a turbulent person; subverter.

trastornadora [trahs-tor-nah-doo'-rah], *f.* Overturning, inversion, perversion.

trastornamiento [tras-tor-nah-me-en'-to], *m.* Overturning, inverting.

trastomar [trahs-tor-nah'], *va.* 1. To overthrow, to reverse, to overturn (volcar). 2. To confuse (ideas), to perplex the mind (volver loco). *-vr.* 1. To delight (encantar). *-vr.* 1. To go crazy (persona), to become mentally unbalanced. 2. To fall through (proyecto). **Esa chica le ha trastornado**. that girl has bowled him over.

trastorno [trahs-tor'-no], *m.* 1. Overthrow, overturn, confusion (perturbación). 2. Calamity, misfortune. 3. Mental disorder.

trastrabado, da [trahs-trah-bah'-do, dah], *a.* Applied to a horse with the far hind foot and the near fore foot white.

trastrás [trahs-trahs'], *m.* The last in some children's games.

trastrigo [trahs-tree'-go], *m.* *(Prov.)* Wheat of the best quality.

trastrocamiento [trahs-tro-cah-me-en'-to], *m.* Transposition, inversion.

trastrocar [trahs-tro-car'], *va.* To invert or change the order of things.

trastrueco, trastrueque [trahs-troo-ay'-co], *m.* Inversion, transposition.

trastuelo [trahs-too-ay'-lo], *m. dim.* Little, useless person.

trastumbar [trahs-toom-bar'], *va.* To throw down, to overturn, to overset.

trasudadamente [trah-soo-dah-dah-men'-tay], *adv.* With sweat and fatigue.

trasudar [trah-soo-dar'], *va. & vn.* 1. To sweat, to perspire. 2. To apply oneself to a business with assiduity and care.

trasudor [trah-soo-dor'], *m.* A gentle sweat; transudation.

trasuntar [trah-soon-tar'], *va.* 1. To copy (copiar), to transcribe. 2. To abridge.

trasuntivamente [trah-soon-te-vah-men'-tay], *adv.* Compendiously.

trasunto [trah-soon'-to], *m.* 1. Copy (copia), transcript. 2. Likeness, close resemblance (semejanza). **Ese chico es un trasunto de su padre**, that boy is the picture of his father.

trasvanarse [trah-svah-nar'-say], *vr.* 1. To be forced out of the arteries or veins (sangre). 2. To be spilled.

trasvase [trah-svah'-say], *m.* Pouring, decanting; diversion.

trasverberación [trahs-ver-bay-rah-the-on'], *f.* V. TRANSFIXIÓN.

trasversal [trahs-ver-sahl'], *a.* Transversal. V. TRANSVERSAL.

trasversalmente [trahs-ver-sahl'-men-tay], *adv.* V. TRANSVERSALMENTE.

trasverso [trahs-ver'-so], sa, *a.* Transverse.

trasverter [trahs-ver-tayr'], *vn.* To overflow, to run over.

trasvinarse [trahs-ve-nar'-say], *vr.* 1. To leak out (vino). 2. To be guessed, surmised, or supposed.

trasvolar [trahs-vo-lar'], *va.* To fly across.

trata [trah'-tah], *f.* The African slavetrade formerly carried. on. *(Acad.)*

tratable [trab-tah'-blay], *a.* 1. Tractable, ductile, flexible. 2. Tractable, complaint, kindly (amable).

tratadico, illo, ito [trah-tah-dee'-co], *m. dim.* A brief tract or treatise.

tratadista [trah-tah-dees'-tah], *com.* Author of treatises.

tratado [trah-tah'-do], *m.* 1. Treaty, convention, compact, relating to public affairs. 2. Treatise, tractate. **Tratado de paz**, peace treaty. *-***Tratado, da**, *pp.* of TRATAR.

tratador, ra [trah-tah-dor', rah], *m. & f* Mediator, arbitrator, umpire.

tratamiento [trah-tah-me-en'-to], *m.* 1. Treatment (de persona, problema), usage. 2. Compellation, style of address, title of courtesy. **Tratamiento de tú**, familiar address.

tratante [trah-tahn'-tay], *m.* Dealer, merchant. **Tratante en víveres**, dealer in provisions, who buys by wholesale and sells by retail. **Tratante en caballos**, dealer in horses, horses Jockey. *-pa.* Treating, handling.

tratar [trah-tar'], *va.* 1. To treat on a subject, to discuss; to confer, to consult. 2. To touch, to handle, to manage. 3. To baffle, to trade. 4. To manage to conduct. 5. To use, to treat; (and *Med.*) to treat, to employ curative measures. 6. *(Met.)* To study or be careful to attain an object. 7. To have illicit. relations with a person (tener relaciones). 8. To give a person the title of courtesy to which he is entitled. *-vn.* 1. **Tratar de**, to deal with. 2. **Tratar con**, to have to do with *-vn.* 1. To entertain a friendly intercourse. 2. To be on terms of intimacy. 3. To live well or ill. **Tratar de hacer alguna cosa**, *(Coll.)* to be resolved upon doing a thing. **Tener tratada alguna cosa**, to have spoken for or engaged a thing. **La trata muy bien en esa pensión**, they treat her well in that boarding house. **Le trato desde hace 6 meses**, I have known him for

6 months. **No tratamos con traidores**, we don't treat with traitors. **Se tratan de usted**, they address each other as «usted».

tratillo [trah-teel'-lyo], *m. dim.* A peddling trade.

trato [trah'-to], *m.* 1. Treatment, manner of using; behavior (conducta), conduct. 2. Manner (manera de ser), address. 3. Concernment; pact, agreement. 4. Treat. 5. Trade, traffic, commerce. 6. Friendly intercourse, conversation, communication. 7. Gallantry. Sexual intercourse between man and woman. 8. Treachery, infidelity. 9. Religious meditation, prayer. 10. Compellation, title of courtesy. 11. (*Mex.*) Market stall (puesto). 12. (*Mex.*) Small business (negocio). **Mal trato**, (*Met.*) bad conduct with anyone, ill usage. **Tener buen trato**, (*Coll.*) to be affable and polite. **Tener trato de gentes**, to be accustomed to good society. **Ese no es el trato**, that was not the agreement.

trauma [trah'-oo-mah], *f.* (*Med.*) Trauma.

traumático, ca [trah-oo-mah'-te-co, cah], *a.* Traumatic, relating to wounds.

traumatismo [trah-oo-mah-tees'-mo], *m.* 1. Traumatism, wound. 2. State in which a grave wound puts the system.

traumatizar [trah-oo-mah-te-thar'], *va.* To traumatize; (*Fig.*) to shock, to affect profoundly.

traumatología [trah-oo-mah-to-lo-he'-ah], *f.* Orthopedic surgery.

traumatólogo, ga [trah-oo-mah-to'-lo-go], *m. & f.* Orthopedic surgeon.

travata [trah-vah'-tah], *f.* Tornado, hurricane in the Gulf of Guinea.

traversa [trah-verr'-sah], *f.* 1. (*Naut.*) Back-stay. 2. (*Gil.*) Traverse, a ditch with one or two parapets of planks loaded with earth.

traverso [trah-verr'-so], *m.* A kind of net made of esparto used in tuna fishing.

travertino [trah-ver-tee'-no], *m.* Travertine, a calcareous tufa, which, on exposure, acquires a reddish color.

través [trah-ves'], *m.* 1. Inclination to one side, bias. 2. Misfortune, calamity, adversity. 3. V. FLANCO. **De través** or **al través**, across, athwart. -*adv.* 1. Across, crossways. **Mirar de través**, to squint. 2. **Al través**, across, over. **Lo sé a través de un amigo**, I know about it through a friend.

travesaño [trah-vay-sah'-nyo], *m.* 1. Cross-timber; transom. 2. Long holster of a bed. 3. (*CAm. Carib. Mex.*) Sleeper.

travesear [trah-vay-say'-ar'], *m.* 1. To be uneasy, to run to and fro in a restless manner; to be flighty. 2. To jest, to joke. 3. To lead a debauched life: to behave improperly. 4. To talk wittily (hablar). 5. (*Mex.*) To show off one's horsemanship (jinete).

travesero [trah-vay-say'-ro], *m.* Bolster of a bed; transom.

travesero, ra [trah-vay-say'-ro, rah], *a.* Transverse, across.

travesía [trah-vay-see'-ah], *f.* 1. Oblique or transverse position or manner. 2. Distance, road (de pueblo), passage; traject, cross road. **Hacer buena travesía**, (*Naut.*) to have a fine passage. 3. Fortification with traverses. 4. Money won or lost at gambling (en el juego). 5. (*Naut.*) Side wind (viento). 6. (*And. Cono Sur*) Arid plain (desierto).

travesío, ía [trah-vay-see'-o, ah], *a.* 1. Traversing: applied to cattle that traverse the limits of their pasture. 2. Transverse, oblique, or lateral wind.

travesío [trah-vay-see'-o], *m.* Crossing, place where persons or things cross.

travestido, da [trah-ves-tee'-do, dah], *a.* (*Antiq.*) Disguised.

travestismo [trah-ves-tees'-mo], *m.* Transvestism.

travesura [trah-vay-soo'-rah], *f.* 1. Prank (broma), ludicrous or jocose trick to amuse (gracia). 2. Penetration, lively fancy; sprightly conversation. 3. Mischief, trick, a culpable action, and worthy of reproof or punishment (mala pasada). **Son travesuras de niño**, they're just childish pranks.

traviesa [trah-ve-ay'-sah], *f.* 1. Oblique petition, passage. V. TRAVESÍA. 2. Wager laid by bystanders at card-tables.

travieso, sa [trah-ve-ay'-so, sah], *a.* 1. Transverse, oblique. 2. Restless (inquieto), uneasy, flighty, knavish, turbulent, noisy; mischievous (niños). 3. Subtle, shrewd.

tráxito, ta [trak'-se-to, tah], *m.* (*Biol.*) Rough.

traxitofito [trak-se-to-fee'-to], *m.* (*Bot.*) A plant with leaves rough to the touch.

trayecto [trah-yec'-to], *m.* 1. Journey (de persona), run (de vehículo). 2. Trisecting, act of casting over it. 3. Road (camino), route, way; stretch (tramo). **Recorrer un trayecto**, to cover a distance. 4. Trajection, space cast across.

trayectoria [trah-yec-toh'-re-ah], *f.* Trajectory (camino), the curved path described by a projectile.

trayente [trah-yen'-tay], *pa.* Bringing, carrying, conducting.

traza [trah'-thah], *f.* 1. First sketch or draught, trace, outline. 2. Plan, scheme, project, contrivance, a plot, an artifice; manner, means (medio). 3. Appearance, aspect, prospect (aspecto). 4. Skill (habilidad). 5. (*Cono Sur*) Track (huella). **Tiene trazas de ser un pícaro**, he has the looks of a rogue. **Tener traza para hacer algo**, to be skillful at doing something.

trazado, da [trah-thah'-do, dah], *a. & pp.* TRAZAR. Traced, outlined. **Bien or mal trazado**, person of a good or bad disposition or figure.

trazador, ra [trah-thah-dor', rah], *m. & f.* 1. Planner (persona), sketcher, contriver, inventor, schemer. 2. Tracer. 3. (*Comput.*) Plotter.

trazar [trah-thar'], *va.* 1. To contrive, to devise, to plan out (planificar), to scheme, to project. 2. To trace (en discurso), to mark out. 3. To draw the first sketch or plan. 4. To contrive (medios), to devise.

trazo [trah'-tho], *m.* 1. Sketch (esbozo), plan, design, project. 2. Moulding. V. LÍNEA. 3. (*Painting*) Fold of the drapery. **Trazo de lápiz**, pencil stroke. **Trazo discontinuo**, broken line.

trazumarse [trah-thoo-mar'-say], *vr.* To leak, to ooze. V. REZUMARSE.

treballa [tray-bahl', lyah], *f.* Sauce for goose, consisting of almonds, garlic, bread, eggs, spices, sugar, etc.

trébedes [tray'-bay-des], *f. pl.* Trivet, a tripod used in kitchens.

trebejo [tray-bay'-ho], *m.* 1. Top, play-thing. 2. Fun, jest, joke. -*pl.* 1. The pieces of a chess-board. 2. Implements of an art or trade.

trebeliánica, or **cuarta trebeliánica** [tray-bay-le-ah'-ne-cah], *f.* The fourth part of an estate, to be deducted by the fiduciary heir, who holds it in trust for another.

trébol [tray'-bol], *m.* (*Bot.*) Trefoil, clover. **Trébol real**, (*Bot.*) Melilot. **Trébol silvestre**, shamrock.

trece [tray'-thay], *a.* 1. Thirteen. **Estarse en sus trece**, to persist, to execute with perseverance. 2. Thirteenth. V. DECIMITERCIO. -*m.* The figure 13.

trecemesino, na [tray-thay-may-see'-no, nah], *a.* Of thirteen months.

trecenario [tray-thay-nah'-re-o], *m.* Space of thirteen days.

tracenato, trecenazgo [tray-thay-nah'-to], *m.* Office in the order of Santiago for which thirteen knights are chosen.

treceno, na [tray-thay'-no, nah], *a.* Thirteenth, completing thirteen.

trecésimo, ma [tray-thay'-ee-mo, mah], *a.* Thirtieth, completing thirty.

trechel [tray-chel'], *m.* (*Bot.*) A somewhat brown variety of wheat.

trecheo [tray-chay'-o], *a.* Passing of ores and soil in basked, which the workmen in a row pass from one to another.

trecho [tray'-cho], *m.* Space, distance of time or place. **A trechos**, by intervals. **De trecho en trecho**, at certain distances.

trecientos, tas [tray-the-en'-tos, tas], *a.* Three hundred.

tredécimo, ma [tray-day'-the-mah], *a.* Thirteenth.

trefe [tray'-fay], *a.* 1. Lean, thin, meagre. 2. Spurious, adulterated.

tregua [tray'-goo-ah], *f.* 1. Truce, cessation of hostilities. 2. Rest, repose. **No dar treguas**, to give no respite.

treílla [tray-eel'-lyah], *f. V.* TRAÍLLA.

treinta [tray'-in-tah], *a. & n.* Thirty, thirtieth.

treintaidoseno, na [trary-in-tah-e-do-say'-no-nah], *a.* 1. Thirty-second. 2. Applied to the cloth the warp of which consists of thirty-two hundreds of threads.

treintanario, treintonario [tray-in-tah-nah'-re-o], *m.* Space of thirty days; thirty masses said for a person deceased; a trental.

treintañal [tray-in-tah-nyahl'], *a.* Containing thirty years.

treintañera [tray-en-tah-nyay'-rah], *f.* Woman of about thirty.

treintena [tray-in-tay'-nah], *f.* 1. Thirty. 2. The thirtieth part.

treinteno, na [tray-in-tay'-no, nah], *a.* Thirtieth.

treja [tray'-hah], *f.* Mode of playing at billiards.

tremadal [tray-mah-dahl'], *m. V.* TREMADAL.

tremebundo, da [tray-may-boon'-do, dah], *a.* Dreadful, frightful, fearful.

tremedal [tray-may-dahl'], *m.* Quagmire, marsh, morass.

tremendo, da [tray-men'-do, dah], *a.* 1. Tremendous, dreadful, terrible (terrible). 2. Awful, grand; worthy of respect. 3. Huge or executive in its line. **Le dio una tremenda paliza**, he gave him a tremendous beating. 4. Inventive, witty, entertaining (persona).

tremente [tray-men'-tay], *pa.* Trembling.

trementina [tray-men-tee'-nah], *f.* Turpentine.

tremer [tray-merr'], *vn.* To tremble.

tremés, tremesino, na [tray-mes'], *a.* Three months old.

tremielga [tray-me-el'-gah], *f. (Zool.)* Electric-ray, crampfish, torpedo.

tremís [tray-mees'], *m.* Ancient gold coin.

tremó [tray-mo'], *m.* A pier-glass.

tramolante [tray-mo-lahn'-tay], *pa.* Waving in the air.

tremolar [tray-mo-lar'], *m. dim.* 1. *(Naut.)* To hoist the colors, jacks, or pendants. 2. To wave, to move or scatter through the air.

tremolina [tray-mo-lee'-nah], *f.* 1. Rustling of the wind. 2. Bustle, noise. **Levantar una tremolina**, *(Coll.)* (a) to raise a rumpus. (b) To excite a quarrel.

tremor [tray-mor'], *m.* Trembling, tremor.

trémulamente [tray'-moo-lah-men-tay], *adv.* Tremblingly, tremulously.

tremulante, tremulento, ta [tray-moo-lahn'-tay], *a. V.* TRÉMULO.

trémulo, la [tray'-moo-lo, lah], *a.* Tremulous, quivering, shaking.

tren [trayn], *m.* 1. Traveling equipage, train, retinue. 2. Show, pomp, ostentation. 3. Railroad train. 4. *(Mil.)* Convoy. 5. **Tren de vida**, life style. 6. Speed (velocidad). 7. *(LAm.)* En tren de, in the process of. 8. *(Carib.)* Workshop (taller). 9. *(CAm. Mex.)* Coming and going (trajín). 10. *(Cono Sur, Mex.)* Tram (tranvía). 11. *(Carib.)* Cheeky remark (majadería). **Tren de correo**, mail train. **Tren de recreo**, excursion train. **Tren de elevado**, elevated train. **Tren expreso**, fast train. **Cambiar de tren**, to change train. **Tomar un tren**, to catch a train. **Perder el tren**, to miss the train.

trena [tray'-nah], *f.* 1. Scarf, sash. 2. Garland of flowery. 3. *(Call.)* Prison, jail. 4. Burnt silver.

trenado, da [tray-nah'-do, dah], *a.* Reticulated, formed of network.

trenca [tren'-cah], *f.* Each of two pieces of wood put across in a beehive.

trencellín [tren-thel-lyeen'], *m. V.* TRENCILLO.

trencha [tren'-chah], *f. (Naut.)* A ripping chisel.

trencica, ita [tren-thee'-cah], *f. dim.* o TRENZA.

trencilla [tren-theel'-lyah], *f.* Braid. **Trencilla de oro, de plata, de seda, de algodón**, gold, silver, silk, or cotton braid.

trencillar [tren-theel-lyar'], *va.* To garnish with a band of gold or silver lace and jewels.

trencillo [tren-theel'-lyo], *m.* 1. *(Com.) V.* TRENCILLA. 2. Hat-band of gold or silver, garnished with jewels.

treno [tray'-no], *m.* 1. A kind of sledge. 2. *pl.* Lamentations.

trenque [tren'-kay], *m. (Prov.)* Mole or bank to turn off the current of a river.

trenza [tren'-thah], *f.* 1. Braid of three strands. 2. All a woman's hair though not braided; tress.

trenzadera [tren-thah-day'-rah], *f.* Tape. *V.* TRANZADERA.

trenzado [tren-thah'-do], *m.* 1. Braided hair. 2. A step in dancing. **-Trenzado, da**, *pp.* of TRENZAR.

trenzar [tren-thar'], *va.* To braid the hair. *-vn.* To weave in and out (bailadores). *-vr. (LAm.)* **Trenzarse en una discusión**, to get involved in an argument.

treo [tray'-o], *m. (Naut.)* Square-sail, cross-jack sail.

trepa [tray'-pah], *f.* 1. Climbing (subida). 2. Edging sewed to clothes for ornament. 3. *(Coll.)* Flogging, lashing, beating (paliza). 4. Artful trick; malice; subtlety.

trepado, da [tray-pah'-do], *a.* Strong, robust (animales). *-pp.* of TREPAR.

trepado [tray-pah'-do], *m.* Edging sewed on clothes.

trepador, ra [tray-pah-dor', rah], *a.* Climber, climbing. *-m.* 1. A climbing-place. 2. *(Zool.)* A sea-wolf, wolf-fish. *-f.* 1. *(Bot.)* Climber, a climbing-plant. 2. *pl. (Zool.)* Climbers.

trepanar [tray-pa-nar'], *va.* To Trepan, to trephine.

trépano [tray'-pah-no], *m. (Surg.)* Trepan, trephine, an instrument for perforating the skull.

trepante [tray-pahn'-tay], *pa.* Wily, artful, crafty.

trepar [tray-par'], *vn.* 1. To climb, to clamber, to crawl. 2. To creep upon supports (hiedra). *-va.* To ornament with edging.

trepe [tray'-pay], *m. (Coll.)* Scolding. **Echar un trepe**, to tell off.

trepidación [tray-pe-dah-the-on'], *f.* 1. Tremor, quaking of the earth. 2. An apparent vibration which ancient astronomers attributed to the firmament.

trepidante [tray-pe-dahn'-tay], *a. V.* TEMEROSO and TRÉMULO.

trepidar [tray-pe-dar'], *vn.* 1. To quiver, to tremble. 2. *(Met. Amer.)* To waver, to vacillate.

trépido, da [tray'-pe-do, dah], *a.* Tremulous.

tres [trays], *a. & n.* 1. Three. 2. Third. *V.* TERCERO. 3. The figure. **Capítulo tres**, third chapter. **Tres veces**, Three times. **Ni a la de tres**, on no account.

tresalbo, ba [tray-sahl'-bo, bah], *a.* Having three white feet (caballo).

tresañal [tray-sah-nyahl'], *a. V.* TRESAÑEJO.

tresañejo, ja [tray-sah-nyay'-ho, hah], *a.* Three years old: done three years ago.

tresbolillo (Al) [trays-bo-leel'-lyo], *adv. exp.* Quincunx, a mode of planting trees and grapevines, so that each four form a square with a fifth in the middle, like the five-spot on a die.

trescientos, tas [trays-the-en'-tose, tas], *a. & a.* Three hundred.

tresdoblar [tres-do-blar'], *va.* To triple. *V.* TRIPLICAR.

tresdoble [tres-do'-blay], *m.* The state or quality of being three-fold.

tresillo [tray-seel'-lyo], *m.* Ombre, a game played by three. 2. Three-piece suite (muebles).

tresmesino, na [tres-may-see'-no, nah], *a. V.* TRESMESINO.

tresnl [tres-nahl'], *m. (Prov.)* Collection of triangular plots of ground disposed for irrigation.

trestanto [tres-tahn'-to], *m. V.* TRIPLO. *-adv.* Three times as much.

treta [tray'-tah], *f.* 1. Thrust in fencing. 2. Trick, wile, artifice, craft, finesse.

treudo [tray'-oo-do], *m. (Prov.) V.* CATASTRO.

trezavo, va [tray-thah'-vo, vah], *a.* Thirteenth, any of thirteen equal parts.

treznar [treth-nar'], *va. (Prov.) V.* ATRESNALAR.

tría [tree'-ah], *f.* Frequent entering and going out of bees in a hive.

triaca [tre-ah'-cah], *f.* 1. Theriaca, treacle. 2. An antidote, preservative, or preventive.

triacal [tre-ah-cahl'], *a.* Made of treacle, theriacal.

triache [tre-ah'-chay], *m.* (*Amer. Cuba*) Coffee of inferior quality.

triangulación [tre-an-goo-lah-the-on'], *f.* Triangulation, laying out triangles on the earth; trigonometrical survey.

triangulado, da [tre-an-goo-lah'-do, dah], *a.* In the shape of a triangle.

triangular [tre-an-goo-lar'], *a.* Triangular.

triagularmente [tre-ahn-goo-lahr-men-tay], *adv.* Triangularly.

triángulo [tre-ahn'-goo-lo], *m.* Triangle. **Triángulo cuadrantal**, spheric triangle having one or more sides quadrants.

trianular [tre-ah-noo-lar'], *a.* (*Zool.*) Presenting three rings; three-ringed.

triquera [tre-ah-kay'-rah], *f.* Vessel for theriaca or other medicine.

triar [tre-ar'], *vn.* To go out and in frequently, as bees in a beehive; to work, as bees.

triario [tre-ah'-re-o], *m.* Veteran Roman soldier forming a reserve corps in rear.

tribal [tre-bahl'], *a.* Tribal.

tribón [tre-bon'], *m.* V. TRIGÓN.

tribu [tree'-boo], *f.* Tribe.

tribuir [tre-boo-eer'], *va.* To attribute. V. ATRIBUTE.

tribulación [tre-boo-lah-the-on'], *f.* Tribulation, affliction.

tribulante [tre-boo-lahn'-tay], *pa.* Afflicting.

tríbulo [tree'-boo-lo], *m.* (*Bot.*) Caltrop thistle: generic name of several prickly plants. V. ABROJO.

tribuna [tre-boo'-nah], *f.* 1. Rostrum or pulpit among the ancients, tribune (de orador). 2. A raised stand from which to address an assembly. 3. Tribunal, a gallery or raised place in a church where persons of distinction assist at the divine offices. 4. Gallery for spectators in assemblies. **Tribuna del acusado**, dock.

tribunado [tre-boo-nah'-do], *m.* Tribuneship, the office and dignity of tribune.

tribunal [tre-boo-nahl'], *m.* 1. Hall, where judges meet to administer justice. 2. Tribunal, court of justice; judicature. 3. (*Univ.*) Board of examiners (examinadores). 4. (*Fig.*) Tribunal; forum. 5. (*Cono Sur. Mil.*) Court martial. **Tribunal de menores**, juvenile court. **Llevar a uno ante los tribunales**, to take somebody to court.

tribunali (Pro) [tre-boo-nah'-le], *adv.* **Pro tribunali**, 1. Applied to the sentence or decision of a judge, sitting in a court of justice, with the solemnities required by the laws. 2. (*Met.*) In a decisive tone, decisively.

tribunicio, cia [tre-boo-nee'-the-o, ah], *a.* V TRIBÚNICO.

tribúnico, ca [tre-boo'-ne-co, cah], *a.* Tribunitial.

tribuno [tre-boo'-no], *m.* 1. Tribune, a magistrate of ancient Rome. 2. Tribune, one who defends the rights of the people. 3. An agitator, public haranguer.

tributación [tre-boo-tah-the-on'], *f.* Tribute, contribution. V. TRIBUTO.

tributar [tre-boo-tar'], *va.* 1. To pay taxes or contributions. 2. To pay homage and respect.

tributario, ria [tre-boo-tah'-re-o, ah], *a.* Liable to pay taxes. or contributions, tributary.

tributo [tre-boo'-to], *m.* 1. Tax, contribution; tribute. 2. Toil, trouble, difficulty.

trica, tricas [tree'-cah], *f.* (*Prov.*) Quibbles, sophisms.

tricenal [tre-thay-nahl'], *a.* 1. Which is repeated every thirty years. 2. Which lasts thirty years.

tricentésimo, ma [tre-then-tay'-se-mo, mah], *a.* Containing three hundred: three hundredth.

tricésimo, ma [tre-thay'-se-mo, mah], *a.* Thirtieth.

triciclo [tre-thee'-clo], *m.* 1. A three wheeled carriage among the ancients. 2. A tricycle.

tricípete [tre-thee'-pay-tay], *a.* Three headed.

triclinio [tre-clee'-ne-o], *m.* 1. A table with three benches about it. 2. Couch, commonly for three persons, on which the ancient Greeks and Romans reclined to eat. 3. Dining-room of the ancient Romans.

tricolor [tre-co-lor'], *a.* Tri-colored.

tricoma [tre-co'-mah], *f.* (*Med.*) Plica Polonica, a Polish disease of the hair.

tricordiano, na [tre-cor-de-ah'-no, nah], *a.* Three-stringed, consisting of three cords.

tricorne [tre-cor'-nay], *a.* Three-horned.

tricornio [tre-cor'-ne-o], *a. & n.* 1. Three-horned. 2. A three cornered hat.

tricotar [tre-co-tahr'], *va. vn.* To knit.

tridente [tre-den'-tay], *a.* Trident, having three teeth. -*m.* Trident, Neptune's three-pointed scepter.

tridentífero, ra [tre-den-tee'-fay-ro, rah], *a.* Tridentiferous, bearing a trident.

tridentino, na [tre-den-tee'-no, nah], *a.* Of Trent, in the Tyrol: especially of the church council held there.

tridimensional [tre-de-men-se-o-nahl'], *a.* Tridimensional.

triduano, na [tre-doo-ah'-no, nah], *a.* Tertian.

triduo [tree'-doo-o], *m.* Space of three days.

triedro [tre-ay'-dro], **Ángulo triedro**. The meeting of three plane angles at one point.

trienal [tre-ay-nahl'], *a.* Triennial.

trienio [tre-ay'-ne-o], *m.* Space of three years.

trieñal [tre-ay-nyahl'], *a.* Triennial.

trífido, da [tree'-fe-do, dah], *a.* (*Poet.*) Trifid, three-cleft.

trifilo, lla [tre-feel'-lyo, lyah], *a.* (*Bot.*) 1. Three-leaved. 2. Three-lobed, or disposed in three leaflets. 3. (*Zool.*) A beetle.

trifolio [tre-fo'-le-o], *m.* Trefoil. V. TRÉBOL.

triforme [tre-for'-may], *a.* Triform.

trifulca [tre-fool'-cah], *f.* 1. (*Coll.*) Quarrel and confusion among various persons. 2. (*Min.*) A combination of levers for moving the bellows.

trifurcar [tre-foor-car'], *va. & vr.* To trifurcate, to divide into three parts, or branches.

trigal [tre-gahl'], *m.* Wheat-field.

trigamia [tre-gah'-mee-ah], *f.* 1. Trigamy, the state of having been married three times. 2. The state of having three husbands or three wives at one time.

trígamo, ma [tree'-gah-mo, mah], *m. & f.* 1. Trigamous, thrice married. 2. (*Bot.*) Applied to plants containing three sorts of flowers on the same flower-head.

trigaza [tre-gah'-thah], *f.* Short straw of wheat.

trigésimo, ma [tre-hay'-se-mo, mah], *a.* Thirtieth.

trigla [tree'-glah], *f.* (*Zool.*) Red surmullet, garnet.

triglifo [tre-glee'-fo], *m.* (*Arch.*) Triglyph.

trigo [tree'-go], *m.* Wheat. -*pl.* Crops; grain-fields. **Trigo candeal**, white wheat. **Trigo marzal**, spring wheat. **Trigo mocho**, summer or beardless wheat. **Trigo sarraceno**, buckwheat. **No es trigo limpio**, he's a shady character. **Meterse en trigo ajeno**, to meddle in someone else's affairs.

trigón [tre-gone'], *m.* A triangular musical instrument, having wire strings.

trígono [tree'-go-no], *m.* 1. (*Ast.*) Three celestial signs. 2. (*Geom.*) Triangle.

trigonometría [tre-go-no-may-tree'-ah], *f.* Trigonometry.

trigonométrico, ca [tre-go-no-may'-tre-co, cah], *a.* Trigonometrical.

trigrama [tre-grah'-mah], *m.* A word of three letters: trigram.

trigueño, ña [tri-gay'-nyo, nyah], *a.* Swarthy, brownish.

triguera [tre-gay'-rah], *f.* 1. (*Bot.*) Common wheat-grass. 2. Canary-seed.

triguero, ra [tre-gay'-ro, rah], *a.* Growing among wheat.

triguero [tre-gay'-ro], *m.* 1. Sieve for corn. 2. Corn-merchant, grain-dealer (comerciante).

trilátero, ra [tre-lah'-tay-ro, rah], *a.* Trilateral, having three sides.

triling̈e [tre-leen'-goo-ay], *a.* 1. Trilingual, talking or relating to three languages. 2. Trilingual, recorded in three languages.

trilio [tree'-le-o], *m.* (*Bot.*) Trillium.

891

trilítero, ra [tre-lee'-tay-ro, rah], *a.* Triliteral, employing or consisting of three letters. A characteristic of Semitic languages.

trilla [treel'-lyah], *f.* 1. *(Zool.)* Red surmullet, gurnard. 2. A sort of harrow for separating corn from chaff. 3. The act and time of thrashing. 4. *(Carib.)* Short cut (atajo). 5. *(Mex.)* Track (senda).

trilladera [treel-lyah-day'-rah], *f.* A harrow used to separate corn from chaff.

trillado, da [treel-lyah'-do, dah], *a. & pp.* of TRILLAR. 1. Thrashed, beaten (camino). 2. Trite (gastado), stale, hackneyed. **Camino trillado**, beaten track, common routine.

trillador, ra [treel-lyah-dor', rah], *a.* Thrashing, threshing. **Máquina trilladora**, threshing machine. *-m. & f.* Thresher.

trilladura [treel-lyah-doo'-rah], *f.* Act of thrashing.

trillar [treel-lyar'], *va.* 1. To thrash, to separate corn from the chaff, to tread out corn. 2. To beat, to abuse. 3. To frequent, to visit often; to repent.

trillís [treel-lyees'], *m.* A song-bird of Chili, a species of thrush.

trillizos [treel-lyee'-thos], *m. pl.* Triplets.

trillo [treel'-lyo], *m.* 1. A harrow, used in Spain for thrashing, or separating corn from the chaff. 2. *(Amer.)* Foot-path, pathway, trail little used.

trillón [treel-lyone'], *m.* Trillion, a million billions.

trilogía [tree-lo-hee'-ah], *f.* Trilogy.

trimembre [tre-mem'-bray], *a.* Consisting of three members or parts.

trimestral [tre-mes-trahl'], *a.* 1. Trimestrial, belonging to a trimester or period of three months. 2. Lasting three months.

trimestralmente [te-mays-trahl'-men-tay], *adv.* Quarterly, three monthly.

trimestre [tre-mes'-tray], *m.* Space of three months.

trimielga [tre-me-ayl'-gah], *f.* V. TORPEDO, 1st def.

trinacrio, ia [tre-nah'-cre-o, ah], *a. (Port.)* Sicilian, Trinacrian.

trinado [tre-nah'-do], *m.* 1. Trill, shake, quiver, tremulous sound. 2. Twittering of birds.

trinar [tre-nar'], *vn.* 1. To trill, to quaver, to shake the voice; to speak in a tremulous voice (enfadarse). 2. *(Met. Coll.)* To get vexed or furious. **Está que trina**, he's hopping mad.

trinca [treen'-cah], *f.* 1. Assemblage of three things or persons of the same class or description. 2. *(Naut.)* Any cord used for making fast. **A la trinca**, *(Naut.)* close-hauled. 3. *(And. Cono Sur)* Band (pandilla), gang. 4. *(Carib. Mex.)* Drunkenness (embriaguez). 5. *(Cono Sur)* Marbles (canicas).

trincadura [trin-cah-doo'-rah], *f.* A barge of very large size with two masts and leg-of-mutton sails.

trincafía [trin-cah-fee'-ah], *f. (Naut.)* Clove-hitch, a kind of turn or knot.

trincafiar [trin-cah-fe-ar'], *va. (Naut.)* To marl.

trincar [trin-car'], *va.* 1. To break, to chop, to divide into small pieces. 2. *(Naut.)* To fasten the rope-ends. **Trincar las puertas**, *(Naut.)* to bar in the port-lids. 3. *(Peru. Coll.)* To tie strongly, to secure. 4. *vn. (Coll.)* To drink wine or liquor in company with others.

trincha [treen'-chah], *f.* 1. A belt for securing the outer clothes to the body. 2. *(Amer.)* Socket chisel, cutting gouge.

trinchante [trin-chahn'-tay], *m.* 1. Carver at table. 2. Carvingknife (cuchillo).

trinchar [trin-char'], *va.* 1. To carve (cortar), to divide meat. 2. To dispose or decide with an air of authority.

trinchera [trin-chay'-rah], *f.* 1. *(Mil.)* Trench (zanja), entrenchment, ditch to cover the troops from the enemy's fire. 2. Trench coat (prenda). 3. *(Naut.)* Parapet upon the gunwales of the quarter-deck. 4. *(LAm.)* Fence (cercado).

trinchero [trin-chay'-ro], *m.* Any plate on which meat is eaten at table; trencher.

trincherón [trin-chay-rone'], *m. aug.* A large plate or platter.

trinchete [trin-chay'-tay], *m.* Shoemaker's paring-knife; stone cutter's chisel. V. TRANCHETE.

trincos [treen'-cose], *m. (Orn.)* Kind of stork like a swam.

trineo [tre-nay'-o], *m.* Sledge, sled.

trinidad [tre-ne-dahd'], *f.* The Trinity.

trinitaria [tre-ne-tah'-re-ah], *f. (Bot.)* Three-colored violet, pansy, heart's-ease, forget me-not.

trinitario, ria [tre-ne-tah'-re-o, ah], *a. & n.* 1. Trinitarian. 2. *(Mex.)* A member of a society hired to carry the corpse and accompany the funeral procession.

trinitrotolueno [tre-ne-tro-to-loo-ay'-no], *m. (Chem.)* Trinitrotoluene, high explosive. It is used more in the abbreviation TNT.

trino, na [tree'-no, nah], *a.* Containing three distinct things; ternary.

trino [tree'-no], *m. (Ast.)* 1. Trine, the aspect of two planets when 120° apart. 2. Triune, three in one. V. TRINADO.

trinomio [tre-no'-me-o], *m. (Alg.)* Trinomial, an algebraic quantity of three terms.

trinquetada [trin-kay-tah'-dah], *f. (Naut.)* Sailing under the foresail.

trinquete [trin-kay'-tay], *m.* 1. *(Naut.)* Foremast, foresail. 2. Tennis, a game.

trinquetilla [trin-kay-teel'-lyah], *f. (Naut.)* Fore stay-sail.

trinquis [treen'-kis], *m. (Coll.)* A draught of wine or liquor. *(Acad.)*

trío [tree'-o], *m.* 1. Working of bees in a hive. 2. *(Mus.)* Trio.

triones [tre-o'-nes], *m. (Ast.)* Stars, called Charles's Wain, the Great Dipper.

triorque [tre-or'-kay], *m. (Orn.)* Triorchis, a kind of falcon.

tripa [tree'-pah], *f.* 1. Gut, intestine, bowel. **Tripas para longanizas**, hogs' casings for sausages. 2. Belly (vientre), especially of the pregnant woman. 3. Belly or wide part of vessels (vasijas). *-pl.* 1. Core, the inner part of fruit (fruta). 2. The interior of something. **Hacer de tripas corazón**, to hide one's dissatisfaction or disappointment; also to pluck up heart.

tripartido, da [tre-par-tee'-do, dah], *a. & pp.* of TRIPARTIR. Tripartite, divided into three parts.

tripartir [tre-par-teer'], *va.* To divide into three parts.

tripartito, ta [tre-par-tee'-to, tah], *a.* Tripartite.

tripastos [tre-pahs'-tos], *m.* Pulley with three sheaves.

tripe [tree'-pay], *m.* Shag, a kind of woollen cloth.

tripería [tre-pay-ree'-ah], *f.* Shop where tripe is sold; a heap of tripe.

tripero, ra [tre-pay'-ro, rah], *m. & f.* 1. One who sells tripe. 2. Woollen belt to keep the belly warm; cummerbund.

tripétalo, la [tre-pay'-ta'-lo, lah], *a. (Bot.)* Tripetalous.

tripilla [tre-peel'-lyah], *f. dim.* A small gut.

tripitrape [tre-pe-trah'-pay], *m.* 1. *(Coll.)* Heap of old furniture and lumber. 2. Confusion of thoughts or ideas.

triple [tree'-play], *a.* Triple, treble. *-m.* Triple. **Es el triple de lo que era**, it is three times what it was. *-adv.* **Esta cuerda es triple gruesa que ésa**, this string is three times thicker than that bit.

tríplica [tree'-ple-cah], *f. (Law.)* Rejoinder.

triplicación [tre-ple-cah-the-on'], *f.* Multiplication by three.

triplicado, da [tre-ple-cah'-do, dah], *a. & pp.* of TRIPLICAR. Triplicate.

triplicar [tre-ple-car'], *va.* 1. To treble, to triple. 2. *(Law. Prov.)* To rejoin.

tríplice [tree'-ple-thay], *a.* Treble, triple.

triplicidad [tre-ple-the-dahd'], *f.* Triplicity, trebleness.

triplito [tre-plee'-to], *m. (Min.)* Triplite, a ferrous manganese phosphate.

triplo, pla [tree'-plo, plah], *a.* Treble, triplicate, triple: used as a substantive.

trípode [tree'-po-day], *com.* Tripod, trivet.

trípol, trípoli [tree'-pol, tree'-po-le], *m.* Tripoli, rottenstone, tripolite, a polishing powder.

tripón, na [tre-pone', nah], *a.* Pot-bellied, big-bellied.

triptongo [trip-ton'-go], *m.* Triphthong.

tripudio [tre-poo'-de-o], *m.* Dance, ball.

tripudo, da [tre-poo'-do, dah], *a.* Pot-bellied, big-bellied.

tripulación [tre-poo-lah-the-on'], *f.* Crew (de barco, avión).

tripulante [tre-poo-lahn'-tay], *m.* Crew member.

tripular [tre-poo-lar'], *va. (Naut.)* To man ships; to fit out, to equip.

triquina [tre-kee'-nah], *f.* Trichina, a worm, parasitic in muscles in the larval stage and in the intestines when mature. The cause of the disease trichinosis.

triquinosis [tre-ke-no'-sis], *f.* Trichinosis, a serious disease produced by trichinosis in the muscles and intestines of the body.

triquiñuela [tre-ke-nyoo-ay'-lah], *f. (Coll.)* Cheat, fraud.

triquitraque [tre-ke-trah'-kay], *m.* 1. Crack, clack, clattering, clashing. 2. Fire-cracker, pulling-cracker. 3. Rocket, serpent.

trirreme [trir-ray'-may], *m. (Naut.)* Trireme.

tris [trees], *m.* 1. Noise made by the breaking of glass (estallido). 2. Trice, an instant. **Venir en un tris**, to come in an instant. 3. *(LAm.)* Noughts and crosses (juego).

trisa [tree'-sah], *f. (Zool.)* Shad. *V.* SÁBALO.

trisagio [tre-sah'-he-o], *m.* Trisagion, angelic chorus of Holy, holy, holy; any festivity repeated three days.

trisarquía [tre-sar-kee'-ah], *f.* Triumvirate.

trisca [tris'-cah], *f.* 1. Noise made by treading on something which breaks under the feet; any noise. 2. *(Carib.)* Mockery (mofa); private joke (chiste).

triscador, ra [tris-cah-dor', rah], *m. & f.* 1. A noisy, rattling person. 2. *m. (Tech.)* Saw-set, an instrument for setting the teeth of a saw.

triscar [tris-car'], *vn.* 1. To stamp, to make a noise with the feet. 2. To caper, to frisk about, to frolic. *-va.* Among carpenters to set the teeth of a saw; to bend these alternately to the one side or the other. *V.* also TRABAR.

trisecar [tre-say-car'], *va.* To divide into three equal parts, to trisect.

trisección [tre-sec-the-on'], *f.* Trisection, division into three parts.

trisílabo, ba [tre-see'-lah-bo, bah], *a.* Trisyllabic, containing three syllables.

tristacho, cho [tris-tah'-cho, chah], *a. (Prov.)* Sorrowful, melancholy.

triste [trees'-tay], *a.* 1. Sorrowful, sad (estado), mournful (canción). 2. Gloomy (cuarto), dismal (paisaje), heavy, morose. 3. Abject, mean, low. 4. Dull, gloomy, sombre, murky. 5. *(Fig.)* Sorry, sad. 6. *(LAm.)* Poor (pobre). 7. *(And.)* Shy (tímido). **Poner triste a uno**, to make somebody sad. **Hizo un triste papel**, he cut a sorry figure. **Su padre es un triste vigilante**, his father is just a poor old watchman.

tristecico, ica, illo, illa, ito, ita [], *a. dim.* of TRISTE.

tristemente [trees-tay-men'-tay], *adv.* Mournfully, heavily, grievously.

tristeza [tris-tay'-thah], *f.* 1. Grief, sorrow, affliction, melancholy, gloom. 2. Lowness or depression of spirits. **Morirse de tristeza**, *(Met.)* to be broken-hearted; also, to die broken-hearted.

trisulco, ca [tre-sool'-co, cah], *a.* 1. Three pronged, having three points. 2. Of three furrows, or channels.

trísulo [tree'-soo-lo], *m. (Chem.)* A salt produced by two neutral salts, both with the same acid, but with different bases.

tritíceo, ea [tri-tee'-thay-o, ah], *a.* Triticean, belonging to wheat, wheaten.

tritón [tre-tone'], *m.* 1. *(Myth.)* Triton. 2. *(Zool.)* Triton, newt.

trítono [tree'-to-no], *m. (Mus.)* Tritone, an interval of three tones: the ratio of 45 to 32.

trituración [tre-too-rah-the-on'], *f.* Trituration, pulverization.

triturador, ra [tre-too-rah-dor', rah], *a.* Crushing. *-f.* Crusher, crushing machine.

triturar [tre-too-rar'], *vn.* To triturate, to comminute, to crush.

triunfada [tre-oon-fah'-dah], *f.* Trumping at cards.

triunfador, ra [tre-oon-fah-dor', ah], *m. & f.* Conqueror, victor, triumpher.

triunfal [tre-oon-fahl'], *a.* Triumphal.

triunfalmente [tre-oon-fahl'-men-tay], *adv.* Triumphally.

triunfante [tre-oon-fahn'-tay], *a. & pa.* Triumphant (ganador), magnificent, conquering.

triunfantemente [tre-oon-fahn'-teh-men-tay], *adv.* Triumphantly.

triunfar [tre-oon-far'], *vn.* 1. To conquer. 2. To triumph, to celebrate a victory (salir victorioso), to exult, to conquer the passions. 3. To make an idle show of grandeur and wealth. 4. To trump at cards. **Triunfar en la vida**, to succeed in life. **Triunfar en un concurso**, to win a competition.

triunfo [tre-oon'-fo], *m.* 1. Triumph, victory (victoria); conquest; exultation. 2. Slap with the back of the band. 3. Trump card. **Ha sido un verdadero triunfo**, it has been a real triumph.

triunviral [tre-oon-ve-rahl'], *a.* Triumviral, pertaining to the triumvirs.

triunvirato [tre-oon-ve-rah'-to], *m.* Triumvirate.

triunviro [tre-oon-vee'-ro], *m.* Triumvir.

trivial [tre-ve-ahl'], *a.* 1. Frequented, beaten (carretera, camino). 2. Trivial, vulgar, common, known by all.

trivialidad [tre-ve-ah-le-dahd'], *f.* Trivialness, triteness; vulgarity; idleness.

trivialmente [tre-ve-ahl'-men-tay], *adv.* Trivially.

trivio [tree'-ve-o], *m.* Crossroad, point where three roads meet.

triza [tree'-thah], *f.* 1. Mite, a small particle. 2. *(Naut.)* Cord, rope. **Hacer algo trizas**, to smash something to bits.

tro [tro], *m.* A musical instrument, after the fashion of a violin, used in Siam.

trocable [tro-cah'-blay], *a.* Changeable.

trocadamente [tro-cah-dah-men-tay], *adv.* Contrarily, false.

trocado [tro-cah'-do], *m.* Change, small coin.

trocado, da [tro-cah'-do, dah], *a. & pp.* Of TROCAR. Changeful, permuted.

trocador, ra [tro-cah-dor', rah], *m. dim.* One who exchanges or permutes.

trocaico [tro-cah'-e-co], *a.* Trochaic.

trocar [tro-car'], *va.* 1. To exchange, to barter; to change (cambiar), to commute; to equivocate (confundir). 2. To vomit (comida). 3. *(Cono Sur)* To sell (vender); *(And.)* to buy (comprar). *-vr.* 1. To be changed or reformed. 2. To exchange seats with another. **Trocar la alegría en tristeza**, to change gaiety into sadness.

trocar [tro-car'], *m. (Surg.)* Trocar.

trocatinta [tro-cah-teen'-tah], *f. (Coll.)* 1. A sad or unintentional mistake, in taking one thing for another 2. A ridiculous barter or exchange.

trocatinte [tro-cah-teen'-tay], *m.* Mixed color, changing color.

trocear [tro-thay-ar'], To divide into pieces.

troceo [tro-thay'-o], *m. (Naut.)* Parrel, a thick rope for securing the yards.

trocha [troh'-chah], *f.* 1. A narrow path across a high road. 2. *(LAm.)* Gauge. 3. *(Cono Sur)* Lane. 4. *(And.)* Trot (trote). 5. *(And.)* Portion (porción).

trochemoche (A) [tro-chay-mo'-chay], *adv.* Helter-skelter, pell-mell, in confusion and hurry.

trochoela [tro-choo-ay'-lah], *f. dim.* Little path.

trociscar [tro-thees-car'], *pa.* To make troches or lozenges.

trocisco [tro-thees'-co], *m.* Troche, lozenge, a medicine prepared as a cake.

trocla [tro'-clah], *f. V.* POLEA.

troco [tro'-co], *m. (Zool.) V.* RUEDA.

trofeo [tro-fay'-o], *m.* Trophy (objeto), colors, things taken from an enemy; emblem of triumph; victory; pageant. Trophies, military insignia.

trófico, ca [tro'-fe-co, cah], *a.* Trophic, relating to nutrition.

trofología [tro-fo-lo-hee'-ah], *f.* Dietetic regimen, or a treatise concerning it.

trofológico, ca [tro-fo-lo'-he-co, cah], *a.* Dietetic.

troglodita [tro-glo-dee'-tah], *con. & a.* 1. Troglodyte, a cave-dweller. 2. Name given by the Greeks to certain barbarous peoples of Africa who lived in caverns. 3. A barbarous, cruel man. 4. A great eater. 5. A chimpanzee. 6. A wren.

troglodítico, ca [tro-glo-dee'-te-co, cah], *a.* Troglodytic.

trogón [tro-gone'], *m.* Trogon. V. TROGÓNIDOS.

trogonidos [tro-go'-ne-dose], *m. pl.* Trogons, a family of climbing birds, of warm climates, having brilliant plumage.

troj [troh], *f.* V. TROJE.

trojado, da [tro-hah'-do, dah], *a.* Contained in a knapsack.

troje, troj [tro'-hay], *f.* Granary, mow.

trojero [tro-hay'-ro], *m.* Store-keeper, guard of a granary.

trola [tro-lah], *f.* Fib, lie.

trolebús [tro-lay-boos'], *m.* Trolley bus.

trolero [tro-lay'-ro], *m.* Fibber, liar.

tromba [trom'-bah], *f.* A water-spout.

trombón [trom-bone'], *m.* Trombone, a brass windinstrument. V. SACABUCHE.

trombosis [trom-bo'-sis], *f. (Med.)* Thrombosis.

trompa [trom'-pah], *f.* 1. Trumpet, horn (instrumento) 2. Proboscis or trunk of an elephant. 3. A large top. 4. *(CAm. Mex.)* Shut your trap. 5. *(Anat.)* Tube, duct. 6. Drunkenness (borrachera). *-m.* Trumpeter. **Trompa de Eustaquio**, Eustachian tube connecting the middle ear with the pharynx.

trompada [trom-pah'-dah], *f.* 1. *(Coll.)* Blow with a top. 2. Encounter of two persons face to face. 3. *(Andal. and Amer.)* A blow with a fist.

trompar [trom-par'], *vn.* To whip a top.

trompazo [trom-pah'-tho], *m.* 1. Blow with a top, trumpet, or fist. 2. Misfortune, accident.

trompear [trom-pay-ar'], *vn.* A top, to play at chess.

trompero [trom-pa'-ro], *m.* Top maker. 2. Cheat, impostor.

trompero, ra [trom-pay'-ro, rah], *a.* Deceptive, false, deceiving.

trompeta [trom-pay'-tah], *f.* 1. Trumpet (instrumento). 2. Trumpet-shell. 3. Reefer (droga). 4. *(Cono Sur)* Daffodil *-m.* Trumpeter.

trompetada [trom-pay-tah'-dah], *f. (Coll.)* V. CLARINADA.

trompetazo [trom-pay-tah'-tho], *m.* 1. Stroke with a trumpet. 2. Trumpet-blast.

trompetear [trom-pay-tay-ar'], *(Coll.)* To sound the trumpet.

trompetería [trom-pay-tay-ree'-ah], *f.* Pipes of an organ.

trompetero [trom-pay-tay'-ro], *m.* Trumpeter (de orquesta), horn-blower; trumpet-maker.

trompetilla [trom-pay-teel'-lyah], *f.* 1. *(Dim.)* A small trumpet. 2. Hearing-trumpet. 3. Proboscis, lancet of gnats and other insects. 4. A Philippine cigar of conical shape.

trompetista [trom-pay-tis'-tah], *m & f.* Trumpet player.

trompicar [trom-pe-car'], *vn.* To stumble frequently; to falter. *-va.* 1. *(Coll.)* To appoint one irregularly to an employment which belonged to another. 2. To trip, to make stumble.

trompicón [trom-pe-cone'], *m.* Stumbling. V. TROPEZÓN.

trompilla [trom-peel'-lyah], *f. dim.* A small trumpet or horn.

trompillar [trom-pil-lyar'], *vn.* To stumble, to falter. V. TROMPICAR.

trompis [trom'-pis], *vn.* In colloquial phrase, **andar a trompis**, to come to fisticuffs.

trompo [trom'-po], *m.* 1. Man at chess. 2. Whipping-top (juguete). 3. *(LAm.)* Clumsy person (desmañado); rotten dancer (bailador). **Ponerse como un trompo**, *(Met.)* to be as full as a top; to cut or drink to satiety.

trompón [trom-pone'], *m.* A big whipping-top. **A trompón** or **de trompón**, in a disorderly manner.

tron [tron], *m. (Coll.)* Report of firearms.

tronada [tro-nah'-dah], *f.* Thunderstorm.

tronado [tro-nah'-do], *f.* 1. Old (viejo), broken-down. 2. **Estar tronado**, to be potty (loco); to be ruined (arruinado). 3. *(LAm.)* To be high (drogas).

tronador, ra [tro-nah-dor', rah], *m. & f.* 1. Thunderer, thundering. 2. Squib, cracker, rocket.

tronar [tro-nar'], *v. imper.* To thunder. *-vn.* 1. To thunder, to make a noise like thunder or the discharge of guns, to fulminate. 2. To break relations with anyone. 3. Among gamblers, to lose all one's money. **Por lo que pueda** or **por lo que pudiere tronar**, for what may happen. *(Yo trueno, truene, from Tronar. V. ACORDAR.)*

troncal [tron-cahl'], *a.* Relating to the trunk or stock.

troncar [tron-car'], *va.* 1. To truncate, to mutilate, to cut off. 2. To interrupt a conversation, to cut the thread of a discourse.

tronchado [tron-chah'-do], *a. (Her.)* Applied to a shield having a diagonal bar. **Tronchado, da**, *pp.* of TRONCHAR.

tronchante [tron-chahn'-tay], *a.* Killingly funny.

tronchar [tron-char'], *va.* 1. To cut by the trunk or root (cortar), to chop down (talar); to break with violence. 2. *(Fig.)* To cut off (vida); to shatter (esperanza). *-vr.* 1. To fall down (árbol). 2. To tire oneself out (cansarse). 3. **Troncharse de risa**, to split one's sides laughing.

tronchazo [tron-chah'-tho], *m.* 1. *(Aug.)* A large stalk. 2. A blow with a stalk or stem.

troncho [tron'-cho], *m.* 1. Sprig, stem, or stalk of garden plants. 2. *(Cono Sur)* Piece (trozo). 3. *(And.)* Knot (enredo).

tronchudo, da [tron-choo'-do, dah], *a.* Having a long stem or stalk.

tronco [tron'-co, *m.* 1. Trunk of a tree; a log of wood. 2. Stock, the origin of a family. 3. Trunk of an animal without the trend and limbs. 4. An illiterate, despicable, useless person. 5. Hind pair of horses in a coach. **Estar hecho un tronco**, to be bereft of feeling and sensation: literally, to be like a log of wood.

troncón [tron-cone'], *m. aug.* A large stalk or trunk; a large log of wood.

tronera [tro-nay'-rah], *f.* 1. *(Mil.)* Embrasure of a battery. 2. *(Naut.)* Loophole. 3. Louver. 4. Dormer, a small sky-light. 5. A harum-scarum fellow, a hare-brained, foolish person (tarambana). 6. Paper cracker; squib. *-pl.* 1. Holes and pockets of truck and billiard-tables. 2. Openings.

tronerar [tro-nay-rar'], *va.* V. ATRONERAR.

tronerilla [tro-nay-reel'-lyah], *f. dim.* of TRONERA.

tronga [tron'-gah], *f.* (Slang or low) Kept mistress, concubine.

tronido [tro-nee'-do], *m.* Thunder. V. TRUENO.

tronitoso, sa [tro-ne-to'-so, sah], *a. (Coll.)* Resounding, thundering.

trono [tro'-no], *m.* Throne; royal dignity; seat of the image of a saint. *-pl.* Thrones, seventy choirs of angels. **Heredar el trono**, to inherit the crown.

tronquillo [tron-keel'-lyo], *m.* Ornamental metal-work for applying to the covers of books.

tronquista [tron-kees'-tah], *m.* Coachman that drives a pair of horses.

tronquito [tron-kee'-to], *m. dim.* of TRONCO.

tronzar [tron-thar'], *va.* 1. To shatter, to break into pieces. 2. To plait, to fold. 3. To cut up (cortar). 4. To tire out (persona).

tronzo, za [tron'-tho, thah], *a.* Having one or both ears cut off (caballos).

tropa [tro'-pah], *f.* 1. Troop (multitud), a body of soldiers. 2. Troop, a small body of calvary. 3. A number of people collected together; crowd, multitude; troop, herd. 4. Beat to arms. 5. *(Cono Sur)* Convoy of carts (vehículos). 6. *(Mex.)* Rude person (maleducado). **En tropa**, in crowds, without order. **Tropas de asalto**, storm troops.

tropel [tro-pel'], *m.* 1. Noise made by a quick movement of the feet. 2. Hurry (prisa), bustle, confusion, huddle. 3. Heap of things, confusedly tumbled together; crowd. **De tropel**, tumultuously, in a throng.

tropelía [tro-pay-lee'-ah], *f.* 1. Precipitation, hurry, confusion. 2. Vexation, oppression, injustice, outrage (atropello).

tropellar [tro-pel-lyar'], *va. (Prov.)* To trample.

tropezadero [tro-pay-thah-day'-ro], *m.* Any stumbling or slippery place; a bad, uneven road or path.

tropezado, da [tro-pay-thah'-do, dah], *a. & pp.* of TROPEZAR. Stumbled, obstructed.

tropezador, ra [tro-pay-thah-dor', rah], *m. & f.* Tripper, stumbler.

tropezadura [tro-pay-thah-doo'-rah], *f.* Stumbling, obstructing, entangling.

tropezar [tro-pay-thar'], *vn.* 1. To stumble in walking. 2. To be detained or obstructed. 3. To slip into crimes or blunders. 4. To wrangle, to dispute (reñir). 5. To discover a fault or defect. 6. To meet accidentally (topar). 7. To light on, to happen, to find. 8. To slip up (cometer un error). -*vr.* To stumble, to cut the feet in walking (caballos). **Tropezar con uno**, to turn into somebody. **Tropezar con dificultad**, *(Fig.)* to run into a difficulty. *(Yo tropiezo, tropiece, from Tropezar. V. ACRECENTAR.)*

tropezón, na [tro-pay-thone', nah], *a.* Stumbling, tripping frequently. **A tropezones**, with a variety of obstructions.

tropezón [tro-pay-thone'], *m.* 1. V. TROPIEZO. 2. Act of tripping.

tropezoncico, illo, ito [tro-pay-thon-thee'-co], *m. dim.* of TROPEZÓN.

tropezoso, sa [tro-pay-tho'-so, sah], *a.* Apt to stumble or trip.

tropical [tro-pe-cahl'], *a.* 1. Tropical, belonging to the tropics. 2. *(Cono Sur)* Rhetorical, melodramatic.

trópico [tro'-pe-co], *m. (Ast.)* Tropic, either of two parallels at a distance from the equator N. and S. of 23° 28' and corresponding to the solstitial points.

trópico, ca [tro-pe-co, cah], *a.* 1. *(Ast.)* Tropical. 2. *(Rhet.)* Tropical, containing tropes.

tropiezo [tro-pe-ay'-tho], *m.* 1. Stumble, trip. 2. Obstacle (obstáculo), obstruction, impediment. 3. Slip (error), fault, error. 4. Difficulty, embarrassment. 5. Quarrel, dispute (riña).

tropilla [tro-peel'-lyah], *f. dim.* A small bray or detachment of troops.

tropo [tro'-po], *m. (Rhet.)* Trope, figurative sense.

tropología [tro-po-lo-hee'-ah], *f.* 1. Figurative language, allegorical sense, tropology. 2. Mingling of morality and doctrine in a discourse; tropology.

tropológico, ca [tro-po-lo'-he-co, cah], *a.* 1. Topological, expressed by tropes. 2. Doctrinal, moral, relative to reform in customs.

troposfera [tro-pos-fay'-rah], *f.* Troposphere.

troque [tro'-kay], *m.* A kind of bunch formed in cloths when dyeing them.

troquel [tro-kel'], *m.* Die, in which a hollow figure is engraved.

troquillo [tro-keel'-lyo], *m. (Arch.)* Trochilus, concave moulding next the torus.

trotamundos [tro-tah-moon'-dos], *m. & f.* Globetrotter.

trotaconventos [tro-tah-con-ven'-tose], *f. (Vulg.)* Procuress. V. ALCAHUETA.

trotador, ra [tro-tah-dor', rah], *m. & f.* Trotter.

trotar [tro-tar'], *vn.* To trot: to move swiftly, to be in haste. -*va.* To make a horse trot.

trote [tro'-tay], *m.* 1. Trot. **Al trote**, in a trot: in haste or hastily. **Tomar al trote**, to run away. 2. Traveling (viajes); bustle (ajetreo). 3. **De mucho trote**, tough (ropa). 4. **Trotes**, shady affair (asunto turbio). 5. **Trotes**, hardships (apuros). **Yo ya no estoy para esos trotes**, I can't go chasing around like that any more.

trotillo [tro-teel'-lyo], *m. dim.* A light trot.

trotón, na [tro-tone', nah], *a.* Trotting, whose ordinary pace is a trot (caballo).

trotón [tro-tone'], *m.* A trotter.

trotonería [tro-to-nay-ree'-ah], *f.* A continual trot.

trovador, ra [tro-vah-dor', rah], *m. & f.* 1. Troubador, versifier, poet. 2. Finder. -*a.* Versifying; parodic.

trovar [tro-var'], *va.* 1. To versify. 2. To imitate a metrical composition by turning it to another subject, to parody. 3. To invert or pervert the sense of a thing.

trovero [tro-vay'-ro], *m.* Trouvère.

trovista [tro-vees'-tah], *m.* Finder; versifier.

Troya [tro'-yah], *f.* Troy. **Aquí fue Troya**, here was Troy applied to the site of a memorable place. **¡Arda Troya!** let happen what will: proceed with the disorder! (ironical).

troyano, na [tro-yah'-no, nah], *a.* Trojan.

troza [tro'-thah], *f.* Trunk of a tree to be sawn into boards.

trozo [tro'-tho], *m.* 1. Piece or part of a thing cut off. 2. *(Naut.)* Junk for making oakum. 3. *(Gil.)* Division of a column, forming the van or rear guard. 4. Throstle, a species of spindle. **Trozo de madera**, a log. **Trozos escogidos**, selections, selected passages.

trucar [troo-car'], *m.* To play the first card.

trucha [troo'-chah], *f.* 1 Trout. 2. Crane. V. CABRIA. **Ayunar, o comer trucha**, either to fast or eat trout; the best or nothing.

truchero [troo-chay'-ro], *m.* A fisherman who catches and sells trout.

truchimán, na [troo-che-mahn', nah], *a. (Coll.)* Fond of business, or of making agreements. -*m. &f.* A go-between. V. TRUJAMÁN.

truchimanear [troo-che-mah-nay-ar'], *vn.* To act as a go-between.

truchuela [troo-choo-ay'-lah], *f.* Small codfish. V. ABADEJO.

truco [troo'-co], *m.* 1. A skillful push at trucks. **Trucos**, trucks, a game resembling billiards. 2. *(And. Cono Sur)* Punch (puñetazo). 3. *(Cono Sur)* Popular card game.

truculento, ta [troo-coo-len'-to, tah], *a.* Truculent, fierce.

trueco [troo-ay'-co], *m.* Exchange, barter. V. TRUEQUE. **A trueco**, in exchange.

trueno [troo-ay'-no], *m.* 1. Thunderclap. 2. Report of firearms; a noise like thunder (de cañón). 3. Wild youth (tarambana). 4. *(Carib.)* Binge (juerga). 5. *(And.)* Gun.

trueque [troo-ay'-kay], *m.* Exchange (cambio), truck, barter, commutation. V. TRUECO.

trufa [troo'-fah], *f.* 1. Imposition, fraud, deceit. 2. *(Bot.)* Truffle.

trufador, ra [troo-fah-dor', rah], *m. & f.* Fabulist, storyteller, liar.

trufar [troo-far'], *va.* To stuff or cook with truffles. -*vn.* To tell stories, to deceive. V. MENTIR.

trufeta [troo-fay'-tah], *f.* A sort of linen.

truhán, na [troo-ahn', nah], *m. &f.* 1. A scoundrel, a knave. 2. Buffoon, jester, juggler, mountebank.

truhanada [troo-ah-nah'-dah], *f.* V. TRUHANERÍA.

truhanamente [troo-ah-nah-men'-tay], *adv.* Jestingly, buffoon-like.

truhanear [troo-ah-nay-ar'], *vn.* 1. To deceive, to swindle. 2. To banter, to jest, to play the buffoon.

truhanería [troo-ah-nay-ree'-ah], *f.* 1. Imposture, swindle. 2. Buffoonery, low jest.

truhanesco, ca [troo-ah-nes'-co, cah], *a.* Belonging to a buffoon.

tuhanillo, illa [troo-ah-neel'-lyo], *m. &f. dim.* A mean, petty buffoon.

truja [troo'-hah], *f. (Prov.)* Place where olives are kept before being pressed in the mill.

trujal [troo-hahl'], *m.* 1. *(Prov.)* Oilmill. 2. Copper, in which the materials for manufacturing soap are prepared. 3. *(Prov.)* V. LAGAR.

trujaleta [troo-hah-lay'-tah], *f. (Prov.)* Vessel in which the juice of olives falls from the mill.

trujamán [troo-hah-mahn'], *m.* 1. Dragoman, interpreter. 2. Broker, factor.

trujamanear [troo-hah-mah-nay-ar'], *vn.* 1. To act as an interpreter. 2. To exchange, to barter, to buy, or sell goods for others; to act as a broker or factor. 3. To play the buffoon.

trujamanía [troo-hah-mah-nee'-ah], *f.* Brokering, brokerage.

trujillano, na [troo-heel-lyah'-no, nah], *a.* Of Trujillo.

trujimán, na [troo-he-mahn', nah], *a.* V. TRUJAMÁN.

trulla [trool'-lyah], *f.* 1. Noise, bustle (bullicio); multitude. 2. Trowel, mason's level.

trullo [trool-lyo], *m.* 1. *(Orn.)* Teal. 2. *(Prov.)* Kind of vat for pressed grapes. 3. Nick, jail.

truncadamente [troon-cah'-dah-men-tay], *adv.* In a truncated manner.

truncado, da [troon-cah'-do, dah], *a. & pp.* of TRUNCAR. Truncate.

truncar [troon-car'], *va.* 1. To truncate (acordar), to maim; to mutilate a discourse. 2. *(Fig.)* To cut short (carrera, vida).

trunco, ca [troon'-co, cah], *a.* V. TRONCHADO, TRUNCADO.

trupial [troo-pe-ahl'], *m. (Orn.)* Troupial. V. TURUPIAL.

truque [troo'-kay], *m.* A game of cards.

truquero [troo-kay'-ro], *m.* Keeper or owner of a trucktable.

truquiflor [troo-ke-floor'], *m.* A game at cards.

trusas [troo'-sas], *f. pl. 1.* Trunk-hose, wide slashed breeches, in Greek fashion, which reached to the middle of the thigh. 2. *(Carib.)* Bathing trunks (bañador). 3. *(And. Mex.)* Panties, knickers (de mujer).

truyada [troo-yah'-dah, troo-jah'-dah in Cuba], *f. (Amer.)* Crowd multitude.

tsar [sahr], *m.* (Russian spelling) Czar, tsar. V. ZAR.

tsetse [tset-say'], *f.* Tsetse fly, a blood-sucking fly of southern Africa; its bite is deadly to cattle and horses, but not harmful to man, to the ass, and the goat.

tú [too], *pron. pers.* Thou: used in the familiar style of friendship. **Hoy por ti y mañana por mí,** *(Coll.)* turn about is fair play.

tu [too]. Possessive pronoun. Thy, thine. Plural *tus.* Apocopated from *tuyo, tuya.*

tuáutem [too-ah'-oo-tem], *m. (Coll.)* Principal person, leader, mover, author; essential point.

tuba [too'-bah], *f.* 1. *(Mus.)* Tuba. 2. Liquor obtained from the Nipa and other palms of the Philippine Islands.

tuberculífero, ra [too-ber-coo-lee'-fay-ro, rah], *a.* Tuberculous, affected by tuberculosis; tubercular, characterized by the presence of tubercles.

tuberculiforme [too-ber-coo-le-for'-may], *a.* Tubercular, tuberculiform.

tuberculina [too-ber-coo-lee'-nah], *f. (Med.)* Tuberculin (used in the diagnosis and treatment of tuberculosis).

tuberculización [too-ber-coo-le-thah-the-on'], *f.* Tuberculosis, tuberculization.

tubérculo [too-berr'-coo-lo], *m.* 1. *(Bot.)* Tuber, a thick underground stem like the potato. 2. *(Med.)* Tubercle in the lungs, etc.

tuberculosis [too-ber-coo-lo'-sees], *f.* Tuberculosis.

tuberculoso, sa [too-ber-coo-lo'-so, sah], *a.* Tuberculous, affected with tuberculosis.

tubería [too-bay-ree'-ah], *f.* Tubing a series of tubes or pipes.

tuberossa [too-bay-ro'-sah], *f. (Bot.)* Tuberose, oriental hyacinth.

tuberosidad [too-bay-ro-se-dahd'], *f.* Tuberosity; swelling.

tuberoso, sa [too-bay-ro'-o, sah], *a.* Tuberous.

tubífero, ra [too-bee'-fay-ro, rah], *a. (Biol.)* Provided with tubes.

tubiforme [too-be-for'-may], *a.* Tubiform, tubular, tube shaped.

tubo [too'-bo], *m.* Tube. V. CAÑÓN. **Tubo de radio,** radio tube. **Tubo lanzatorpedos,** torpedo tube. **Tubo digestivo,** alimentary canal. **Tubo de imagen,** television picture tube. **Tubo de respiración,** breathing-tube.

tubular [too-boo-lar'], *a.* 1. Tubular; tube-shaped. 2. Fitted to receive a tube.

tubuliforme [too-boo-le-for'-may], *a.* Tubuliform, like a tubule.

tubuloso, sa [too-boo-lo'-so, sah], *a.* Tubulose, tubulous; tubular. *-f. (Chem.)* A special arrangement of vessels to which a tube may be adapted, crossing through a cork or plug.

tucán [too-cahn'], *m.* 1. Toucan, a climbing bird of South America, noted for its great and long beak. 2. Constellation near the Antarctic pole.

tucía [too-thee'-ah], *f.* Tutty. V. ATUTÍA.

tuciorista [too-the-o-rees'-tah], *com.* One who follows the safest doctrine.

tudel [too-del'], *m.* A metal pipe with a reed put into a bassoon.

tudesco [too-des'-co], *m.* 1. A kind of wide cloak. V. CAPOTE. 2. German, native of Germany.

tueca, tueco [too-ay'-cah], *f. & m.* Cavity made by woodlice in timber.

tuera [too-ay'-rah], *f. (Bot.)* Colocynth, bitter apple.

tuerca [too-err'-cah], *f.* Nut or female screw.

tuerce [too-err'-thay], *m.* V. TORCEDURA.

tuero [too-ay'-ro], *m.* 1. Dry wood cut for fuel. 2. *(Bot.)* Spicknel, a European aromatic perennial.

tuerto, ta [too-err'-to, tah], *a. & pp. irr.* of TORCER. One-eyed (mutilado), blind of one eye; squint-eyed. **A tuertas,** contrariwise, on the contrary. **A tuertas o a derechas, a tuerto o a derecho,** right or wrong; inconsiderately.

tuerto [too-err'-to], *m.* Wrong, injury.

tuétano [too-ay'-tah-no], *m.* Marrow; pith of trees. **Hasta los tuétanos,** with all vigor and activity; to the quick.

tufarada [too-fah-rah'-dah], *f.* A strong accent or smell.

tufillo [too-feel'-lyo], *m. (Fig.)* Slight smell.

tufo [too'-fo], *m.* 1. A warm exhalation from the earth or from chimneys or lamps which do not burn well. 2. A strong and offensive smell (olor). 3. Locks of hair which fall over the ear. 4. High notion, lofty idea, vanity. 5. V. TOBA.

tugurio [too-goo'-re-o], *m. (Coll.)* Hut, cottage, hovel (chavola); poky little room (cuartucho); den (cafetucho).

tuición [too-e-the-on'], *f. (Law.)* Tuition; protection.

tuína [too-ee'-nah], *f.* A long, full jacket. (In Peru, *tuín,* masculine.)

tuitivo, va [too-e-tee'-vo, vah], *a. (Law.)* Defensive, that which shelters or protects.

tul [tool], *m.* Tulle, an open-meshed fabric of silk or cotton used for veils, mantillas, etc.

tulipán [too-le-pahn'], *m. (Bot.)* Tulip.

tulipero [too-le-pay'-ro], *m. (Bet.)* Tulip-tree.

tullidura [tool-lyo-doo'-rah], *f.* Dung of birds of prey.

tullimiento [tool-lye-me-en'-to], *m.* Contraction of the tendons.

tullir [tool-lyeer'], *vn.* 1. To void, to omit dung (pájaros). 2. To ill-treat (maltratar). 3. To cripple (listar). *-vr.* To be cripled.

tumba [toom'-bah], *f.* 1. Tomb (sepultura), sepulchral monument, vault. 2. Roof of a coach. 3. Tumble. V. TUMBO. **Llevar a uno a la tumba,** to carry somebody off.

tumbacuartillos [toom-bah-coo-ar-teel'-lyose], *m.* Sot, a vicious frequenter of taverns.

tumbadero, ra [toom-bah-day'-ro, rah], *a.* Tumbler; falling. **Redes tumbaderas,** drop-nets for catching wild animals.

tumbado, da [toom-bah'-do, dah], *a. pp.* of TUMBAR. 1. Tumbled. 2. Vaulted, arched.

tumbaga [toom-bah'-gah], *f.* Pinchbeck; ring or toy of pinchbeck.

tumbagón [toom-bah-gone'], *m. aug.* Any large piece made of pinchbeck; bracelet set with stones.

tumbar [toom-bar'], *va.* 1. To tumble, to throw down. 2. To overwhelm (olor), to deprive of sensation. 3. To knock down (derribar). 4. *(LAm.)* To fell (árboles). *-vn.* 1. To tumble. 2. *(Naut.)* To heel, to lie along, to have a false list. 3. **Un olor que tumba,** a smell which knocks you back. *-vr.* 1. *(Coll.)* To lie down, to sleep (acostarse). 2. To go flat (trigo). 3. *(Fig.)* To give up to, to decide, to take it easy.

tumbilla [toom-beel'-lyah], *f.* Horse for airing bed-linen.

tumbo [toom'-bo], *m.* 1. Tumble, fall. 2. A matter of consequence. 3. Book containing the privileges and title deeds of monasteries, etc. **Dando tumbos,** with all sort of difficulties.

tumbón [toom-bone'], *m.* 1. Coach; trunk with an arched roof or lid. *(Coll.)* V. TUNO.

tumbona [toom-bo'-nah], *f.* Easy chair (butaca); deckchair (de playa).

tumbonear [toom-bo-nay-ar'], *vn.* 1. To vault, to make arches. 2. V. TUNAR.

tumefacción [too-may-fac-the-on'], *f.* Tumefaction, swelling.

tumefacerse [too-may-fah-therr'-say], *vr.* To tumefy, to swell.

tumefacto, ta [too-may-fac'-to, tah], *a.* Tumescent.

tumescencia [too-mes-then'-the-ah], *f.* Tumescence, swelling from a tumor.

tumescente [too-mes-then'-tay], *a.* Tumescent, slightly swollen.

túmido, da [too'-me-do, dah], *m.* 1. Swollen, tumid, inflated. 2. Pompous, tumid, elevated (estilo).

tumor [too-more'], *m.* Tumor, exuberance.

tumorcico, illo, ito [too-mor-thee'-co], *m dim.* A small tumor.

túmulo [too'-moo-lo], *m.* Tomb, sepulchral monument; funeral pile.

tumulto [too-mool'-to], *m.* 1. Tumult, uproar, commotion. 2. Faction, mob.

tumultuar [too-mool-too-ar'], *m.* To raise a tumult, to stir up disturbances, to mob. *-vr.* To rise, to make a tumult.

tumultuariamente [too-mool-too-ah'-re-ah-men-tay], *adv.* Tumultuously, outrageously.

tumultuario, ria [too-mool-too-ah'-re-o, ah], *a.* Tumultuary, tumultuous.

tumultuosamente [too-mool-too-oh'-sah-men-tay], *adv.* Tumultuously. *V.* TUMULTUARIAMENTE.

tumultuoso, sa [too-mool-too-oh'-so, sah], *a.* Tumultuous, glamorous, mobish.

tuna [too'-nah], *m.* 1. *(Bot.)* The prickly pear or fly, the fig of the *Cactus opuntia.* 2. An idle and licentious life; truantship. **Andar a la tuna,** *(Coll.)* to play the truant; to wander idly about, to loiter. *-f.* Student music group.

tunal [too-noahl'], *m.* *(Bot.)* The prickly pear cactus.

tunantada [too-nan-tah'-dah], *f.* Rascality, wickedness, debauchery.

tunante [too-nahn'-tay], *pa.* Leading a licentious life. *-m.* Truant, idler, rake, a lazy loiterer. *-a.* Truant, lacy, loitering, sly, cunning, crafty.

tunantería [too-nan-tay-ree'-ah], *f.* *(Coll.)* 1. Debauchery, idleness, vagrancy, libertinism. 2. Truantship.

tunar [too-nar'], *vn.* To lead a licentious, vagrant life, to loiter.

tunda [toon'-dah], *f.* 1. The soft of shearing cloth. 2. A severe chastisement.

tundente [toon-den'-tay], *a.* Doing injury to a part of the body without drawing blood; raising a tumor.

tundición [toon-de-the-on'], *f.* Shearing of cloth.

tundidor [toon-de-dor'], *m.* Shearer of cloth.

tundidura [toon-de-doo'-rah], *f.* The act of shearing.

tundir [toon-deer'], *va.* 1. To shear cloth (paño). 2. *(Coll.)* To cudgel, to flog. 3. To beat (pegar).

tundizno [toon-deeth'-no], *m.* Shearings cut from cloth.

tundra [toon'-drah], *f.* Tundra, treeless plain of Arctic regions.

túnel [too'-nel], *m.* Tunnel. **Túnel de lavado,** car wash. **Túnel aerodinámico,** wind-tunnel.

tungstato [toongs-tah'-to], *m.* *(Chem.)* Tungstate, a salt of tungstic acid.

tungsteno [toongs-tay-to], *m.* Tungsten, wolfram, a steelgray, heavy metallic element.

túngstico, ca [toongs'-te-co, cah], *a.* Tungstic, an oxide and an acid derived from tungsten; tungstenic.

túnica [too'-ne-cah], *f.* 1. Tunic, a garment worn by the ancients. 2. Tunic, a woollen shirt worn by religious persons. 3. Tunicle, pollicle, or integument which covers the shell of fruit. 4. Tunic, tunicle, integument of parts of the body. 5. A long wide gown.

tunicela [too-ne-thay'-lah], *f.* 1. Tunic. 2. Garment worn by bishops; wide gown.

tuno [too'-no], *m.* Truant, rake, cunning rogue, a lazy loiterer. *-a.* Truant, lazy, loitering; sly, cunning.

tun tun (al), *phrase. (Coll.)* At random, heedlessly, come what will, impulsively.

tupa [too'-pah], *f.* 1. *(Coll.)* Satiety, repletion. 2. The act of pressing close.

tupé [too-pay'], *m.* 1. Toupée (peluca), foretop. 2. *(Met.)* Effrontary, insolence.

tupí [too-pee'], *a. & m,* Name of the principal race of Indians in Brazil and their language which is in general use in the Amazonian regions.

tupido, da [too-pee'-do, dah], *a & pp.* Of TUPIR. 1. Dense, thick (denso), close-woven (tela). 2. *(Met.)* Dense, overgrown, rank. 3. *(LAm.)* Blocked (obstruido). 4. *(Mex.)* Common (frecuente).

tupir [too-peer'], *va.* 1. To press close, to squeeze, closing the pores or interstices. 2. *(LAm.)* To block (obstruir). *-vr.* To stuff or glut oneself (comer mucho); to overeat.

turaní [too-rah-nee'], **turaniense** [too-rah-ne-en'-say], *a.* Turanian, a family of agglutinative languages.

turba [toor'-bah], *f.* 1. Crowd, confused multitude, heap. 2. Turf, sod, peat, used for fuel.

turbación [toor-bah-the-on'], *f.* Perturbation (alarma), confusion (confusión), disorder; light headedness; the act of exciting disturbances.

turbadamente [toor-bah-dah-men'-tay], *adv.* In a disorderly manner.

turbado [toor-bah'-do], *a.* Disturbed, worried, upset; embarrassed; bewildered.

turbador, ra [toor-bah-dor', rah], *f.* Disturber, perturbator.

turbal [toor-bahl'], *m.* Turf-bog, peat-moss; collection of peat or fuel.

turbamulta [toor-bah-mool-tah], *f.* Crowd, multitude.

turbante [toor-bahn'-tay], *m.* 1. Turban worn by the Turks (sombrero). 2. Disturber.

turbar [toor-bar'], *va.* To disturb (orden, paz, razón), to alarm, to surprise, to disturb (persona), to disconcert (desconcertar); to upset (alterar). *-vr.* To be uneasy, alarmed, discomposed.

turbativo, va [toor-bah-tee'-vo, vah], *a.* Troublesome, alarming.

turbiamente [toor-be-ha-men'-tay], *adv.* Obscurely, confusedly.

turbiedad [toor-be-ay-dahd'], *f.* Muddiness, turbidness; obscurity.

turbina [toor-bee'-nah], *f.* A turbine water-wheel placed horizontally.

turbinado, da [toor-be-nah'-do, dah], *a.* Turbinated, twisted, spiral-framed.

turbinista [toor-be-nees'-tah], *f. (Conch.)* Wreath shell, spiral shell. Turbo.

turbino [toor-bee'-no], *m.* Powder made of the root of turbith.

turbio, bia [toor'-be-o, ah], *a.* 1. Muddy (agua), turbid, disturbed (vista), troubled. 2. Unhappy, unfortunate. 3. Dark, obscure (idioma).

turbión [toor-be-on'], *m.* 1. A heavy shower of rain. 2. Hurricane; violent concussion of things.

turbit [toor-beet'], *m. (Bot.)* Turpeth, turbith, the root of an East Indian plant allied to jalap.

turbohélice [toor-bo-ay'-le-thay], *m.* Turbo-propeller engine.

turbopropulsor [toor-bo-pro-pool-sor'], *m.* Turboprop.

turborreactor [toor-bor-ray-ac-tor'], *m. (Aer.)* Turbojet.

turborretropropulsión [toor-bor-ray-tro-pro-pool-se-on'], *f.* Turbo-jet propulsion.

turbulencia [toor-boo-len'-the-ah], *f.* 1. Turbidness, muddiness. 2. Turbulence, confusion, disorder.

turbulentamente [toor-boo-len-tah-men-tay], *adv.* Turbulently.

turbulento, ta [toor-boo-len'-to, tah], *a.* 1. Turbid, thick, muddy. 2. Turbulent (elementos, río), disorderly, tumultuous.

turca [toor'-cah], *f. (Coll.)* Tipsiness. **Vestirse una turca** or **coger una turca,** to get drunk.

turco, ca [toor'-co, cah], *adj.* Turkish. *-m. & f.* A Turk; a Turkish woman. *-m. (Slang.)* Wine.

turcomano, na [toor-co-mah'-no, nah], *a.* Turkoman, a Tartar inhabitant of Turkestan, of Turkish origin.

túrdiga [toor'-de-gah], *f.* 1. Piece of new leather, of which coarse shoes, called *abarcas* are made. 2. Strip of hide.

turdión [toor-de-on'], *m.* Ancient Spanish dance.

turgencia [toor-han'-the-ah], *f.* 1. Swelling, turgescence. 2. Ostentation, vanity, pride.

turgente [toor-hen'-tay], *a.* 1. Turgescent, tumid, protuberant. 2. (*Poet.*) Massive, lofty.

túrgido, da [toor'-he-do, dah], *a.* (*Poet.*) Lofty, bulky.

turicha [too-ree'-chah], *f.* V. TURUPIAL.

turífero, ra [too-ree'-fay-ro, rah], *a.* Incense-producing or bearing.

turismo [too-rees'-mo], *m.* Tourism, touring (excursionismo), traveling. **Hacer turismo**, to go touring. **Ahora se hace más turismo que nunca**, numbers of tourists are greater now than ever.

turista [too-rees'-tah], *m. & f.* Tourist, traveler.

turma [toor'-mah], *f.* Testicle. **Turma de tierra**, (*Bot.*) truffle.

turmalina [toor-mah-lee'-nah], *f.* (*Miner.*) Tourmaline, a translucent mineral of various colors, generally blackish: schorl. It is a complex aluminum-boron silicate: used in polariscopes.

turmera [toor-may'-rah], *f.* (*Bot.*) Ledum-leaved rock-rose.

turmeruela [toor-may-roo-ay'-lah], *f.* (*Blot.*) Umbel-flowered rock-rose.

turnar [toor-nar'], *vn.* To alternate, to go or work by turns.

turnio, nia [toor'-ne-o, ah], *a.* 1. Squint-eyed: in this sense it is used as a substantive. 2. Torvous, of a stern countenance.

turno [toor'-no], *m.* 1. Turn (vez, oportunidad), successive or alternate order (orden); change, vicissitude. 2. (*Naut.*) Time in which sailors are employed in some particular business. **Al turno**, by turns. **Por su turno**, in one turn. **Turno de día**, day shift. **Trabajo de turnos**, shift working. **Estuvo con la querida de turno**, he was with his girlfriend of the moment.

turón [too-rone'], *m.* A kind of fieldmouse.

turpial [toor-pe-ahl'], *m.* Troopial. V. TURUPIAL.

turquesa [toor-kay'-sah], *f.* 1. Turquoise or turkois, a precious stone. 2. Mould for making pellets or balls to be thrown from a crossbow.

turquesado, da [toor-kay-sah'-do, dah], *a.* Of the turquoise color.

turquesco, ca [toor-kes'-co, cah], *a.* Turkish. **A la turquesa**, in the Turkish manner.

turquí, turquino, na [toor-kee'], *a.* Of a deep blue color.

turrar [toor-rar'], *va.* To toast, to roast.

turrón [toor-rone'], *m.* Nougat, paste made of almonds, pinekernels, nuts, and honey.

turronero [toor-ro-nay'-ro], *m.* One who makes or retails the sweetmeat called *turrón*.

tursión [toor-se-on'], *m.* Fish resembling a dolphin.

turulato, ta [too-roo-lah'-to, tah], *a.* (*Coll.*) Billy, stupefied, confounded, startled.

turulés [too-roo-lays'], *a.* Said of a kind of strong grapes.

turumbón [too-room-bone'], *m.* Contusion on the head.

turupial [too-roo-pe-ahl'], *m.* Troopial, a bird of Venezuela, of the size of a thrush, with black and gold plumage, a great songster and easy to tame. V. TURICHA.

tus [toos], *int.* A word used in calling dogs.

tusa [too'-sah], *f.* (*Amer.*) 1. The corn-cob (mazorca). 2. (*Cuba*) Cigarette covered with the finest husk of the corn. 3. (*Cono Sur*) Horse's name. 4. (*Cono Sur*) Clipping (esquileo). 5. (*And.*) Pockmark (hoyo). 6. (*CAm. Carib.*) Whore (puta).

tusco, ca [toos'-co, cah], *a.* Tuscan, Etruscan.

tusílago [too-see'-lah-go], *m.* (*Bot.*) Coltsfoot.

tuso, sa [too'-so, sah], *m. & f.* (*Coll.*) Name given to dogs.

tusón [too-sone'], *m.* 1. Fleece of a sheep. 2. (*Prov.*) Colt not two years old.

tusona [too-so'-nah], *f.* 1. Strumpet, having her head and eyebrows either shaved, as a punishment, or lost from disease. 2. (*Andal.*) Filly not two years old.

tute [too'-tay], *m.* A special card game.

tuteamiento [too-tay-ah-me-en'-to], *m.* V. TUTERO.

tutear [too-tay-ar'], *m.* To treat with familiarity. **Tutear a uno**, to address somebody as *tú.*

tutela [too-tay'-lah], *f.* Guardianship, tutelage, tutorage, protection (protección). **Tutela dativa**, (*Law.*) guardianship appointed by a court. **Bajo tutela**, in ward.

tutelar [too-tay-lar'], *a.* Tutelar, tutelary.

tuteo [too-tay'-o], *m.* Addressing persons by the pronoun *Tú* (thou).

tutía [too-tee'-ah], *f.* Tutty. V. ATUTÍA.

tutilimundi [too-te-le-moon'-de], *m.* V. MUNDINOVI.

tutiplén [too-te-plen'], *adv.* Only used in the colloquial phrase, **a tutiplén**, abundantly to satiety.

tutor [too-tor'], *m.* 1. Tutor, instructor. 2. Guardian of the person and estate of a minor. 3. Defender, protector.

tutora [too-to'-rah], *f.* Tutorees, guardian; governess.

tutoría [too-to-ree'-ah], *f.* Tutelage, guardianship. V. TUTELA.

tutriz [too-treeth'], *f.* Tutoress, governess. V. TUTORA.

tuya [too'-yah], *f.* Thuya, white cedar or red cedar. One species yields sandarac.

tuyo, ya [too'-yo, yah], *pron. poss.* Thine, yours. **Ese sombrero es tuyo**, that is yours. **Los tuyos**, the friends and relatives of the party addressed.

U

u [oo] is the twenty-second letter in the spanish alphabet and fifth of the vowels; it loses its sound after *q* and *g*, and becomes a liquid, except where it is followed by an *a*, as in *gauarismo*, or when marked with a diaresis, as in *agüero*, when it retains its proper sound. The letters *b, v*, and *u* were formerly used as equivalent to each other in writing or printing.

u [oo]. A disjunctive conjunction used in the place of *o*, to avoid cacophony (before *o* or *ho*), as, *plata u oro*, silver or gold; *víctima u holocausto*, a victim or a holocaust.

ualita [oo-ah-lee'-tah], *f.* A mineral substance occurring in the aspect of raw cotton.

ubérrimo, ma [oo-berr'-re-mo, mah], *a.* Very fruitful; extremely abundant.

ubicación [oo-be-cah-the-on'], *f.* Situation in a determined place, position.

ubicar [oo-be-car'], *vn. & vr.* 1. To locate or situate, to be located (edificio). 2. To find (encontrar). 3. To classify (clasificar). 4. (*LAm.*) To get a job (en un puesto); to settle in (establecerse).

ubicuidad [oo-be-coo-e-dahd'], *f.* Ubiquity, presence everywhere at once.

ubicuo, cua [oo-bee'-kwo, kwah], *a.* Ubiquitous, omnipresent.

ubiquidad [oo-be-ke-dahd'], *f.* V. UBICUIDAD.

ubiquitario, ria [oo-be-ke-tah'-re-o, ah], *a. & n.* Ubiquitarian, one of a sect which denies transubstantiation, affirming that the body of Jesus Christ in virtue of his divinity is present in the eucharist.

ubio [oo'-be-o], *m.* (*Prov.*) V. YUGO.

ubre [oo'-bray], *f.* Dug or teat of female animals, udder.

ubrera [oo-bray'-rah], *f.* Thrush, ulcerations in the mouth of sucking children.

ucencia [oo-then'-the-ah], *com.* Your excellency. V. VUECELENCIA.

udómetro [oo-doh'-me-tro], *m.* Udometer, a rain-gauge.

uesnorueste [oo-es-no-roo-es'-tay], *m.* V. OESNORUESTE.

uessudueste [oo-es-soo-doo-es'-tay], *a.* V. OESSUDUESTE.

uesto [oo-es'-tay], *m.* 1. West. 2. Zephyr, west wind.

¡uf! *int.* Exclamation denoting weariness or annoyance.

ufanamente [], *adv.* Ostentatiously, boastfully.

ufanarse [oo-fah-nar'-say], *vr.* To boast, to be haughty, or elated.

ufanía [oo-fah-nee'-ah], f. 1. Pride (orgullo), haughtiness. 2. Joy, gaiety, pleasure, satisfaction.

ufano, na [oo-fah'-no, nah], a. 1. Proud (orgulloso), haughty, arrogant. 2. Gay (alegre), cheerful, content; masterly.

ufo (A) [oo'-fo], adv. In a sponging manner; parasitically.

ujier [oo-he-err'], m. Usher, an employee in the king's palace, corresponding to a porter.

úlcera [ool'-thay-rah], f. Ulcer. **Úlcera duodenal**, (Med.) duodenal ulcer.

ulceración [ool-thay-rah-or'], f. Ulceration.

ulcerado, da [ool-thay-rah'-do, dah], a. & pp. of ULCERAR. Ulcered, ulcerated.

ulcerar [ool-thay-rar'], va. To ulcerate. -vr. To exulcerate.

ulcerativo, va [ool-thay-rah-tee'-vo, vah], a. Causing ulcera.

ulceroso, sa [ool-thay-ro'-so, sah], a. Ulcerous.

ule [oo'-lay], m. The caoutchouc, or rubber-tree. V. HULE.

ulema [oo-lay'-mah], m. Doctor of the law among the Turks.

ulmáceas [ool-mah'-thay-as], f pl. Ulmaceae, the elm family.

ulmaria [ool-ma'-re-ah], f. Meadow sweet, meadow-wort, queen of the meadows.

ulterior [ool-tay-re-or'], m. Ulterior, posterior, farther (lugar).

ulteriormente [ool-tay-re-or-men-tay], adv. Farther, beyond, any more or longer.

ultimado, da [ool-te-mah'-do, dah], a. & pp. of ULTIMAR. Ended, finished, ultimate.

últimamente [ool'-te-mah-men-tay], adv. Lastly (por último), finally, just now, ultimately.

ultimar [ool-te-mar'], vn. 1. To end, to finish (terminar). 2. (LAm.) To finish off (rematar a persona); to kill (matar).

ultimato [ool-te-mah-to], m. Ultimatum.

ultimátum [ool-te-mah'-toom], m. 1. Ultimatum: used in diplomacy. 2. (Coll.) A final resolution.

ultimidad [ool-te-me-dahd'], f. The last stage.

último, ma [ool'-te-mo, mah], m. 1. Last (final), latest (másreciente), hindomost; late, latter. 2. Highly finished, most valuable. 3. Remote; extreme (extremo). 4. Final, conclusive, ultimate. **Estar a lo último** to understand completely. **Estar a lo último or en las últimas**, to be expiring. **Porúltimo**, lastly, finally, **Último entre todos**, last of all, last among them all. **A últimos de mes, semana, etc.**, at the end of the month, week, etc. **Vestido en el último piso**, they live on the top floor. **Vestido a la última**, dressed in the latest style. **Pedirme eso encima ya es lo último**, for him to ask that of me as well really is the limit.

últimas [ool'-te-mas], f. pl. Last or end syllables.

ultra [ool'-trah], adv. Besides, moreover; beyond.

ultracatólico, ca [ool-trah-cah-to'-le-co, cah], a. Ultramontane.

ultracongelado [ool-trah-con-he-lah-do], a. (Esp.) Deep-frozen.

ultraderecha [ool-trah-day-ray-chah], f. Extreme right.

ultrajador, ra [ool-trah-hah-dor', rah], a & f. One who outrages or insults.

ultrajamiento [ool-trah-hah-me-en'-to], m. Outrage, affront, injury.

ultrajar [ool-trah-har'], va. 1. To outrage, to offend (ofender), to treat injuriously. 2. To despise, to depreciate; to abuse.

ultraje [ool-trah'-hay], m. Outrage, contempt, injurious language, abuse.

ultrajosamente [ool-trah-jo-sah-men-tay], adv. Outrageously.

ultrajoso, sa [ool-trah-ho'-so, sah], a. Outrageous, overbearing.

ultramar [ool-trah-mar'], a. Ultramarine, foreign. -m. (Art.) V. ULTRAMARINO.

ultramarino, na [ool-trah-mah-ree'-no, nah], a. Ultramarine, from overseas. -m. pl. Fancy, imported groceries.

ultramarino [ool-trah-mah-ree'-no], m. Ultramarine, the finest blue, from the lapis lazuli.

ultramaro [ool-trah-mah'-ro], m Ultramarine blue.

ultramicroscopio [ool-trah-me-cros-co'-pe-ol], m. Dark-field microscope.

ultramoderno, na [ool-trah-mo-der'-no, nah], a. Ultramodern.

ultramontaismo [ool-trah-mon-tah-nees'-mo], m. Ultramontenism, the policy of the authority of the Pope over any national church.

ultramontano, na [ool-trah-mon-tah'-no, nah], a. Ultramontane, supporting the policy of the widest power of the Pope over all ecclesiastical matters.

ultrasónico, ca [ool-tra-so'-ne-co, cah], a. Ultrasonic.

ultrasonido [ool-trah-so-nee'-do], m. Ultrasonic, ultrasound.

ultratumba [ool-trah-toom'-bah], f. Beyond the grave, other world.

ultravioleta [ool-trah-ve-o-lay'-tah], a. Ultraviolet.

úlula [oo'-loo-lah], f. (Orn.) Owl. V. AUTILLO.

ulular [oo-loo-lar'], vn. (Prov.) To howl (animal, viento); to cry aloud, to ululate.

ululato [oo-loo-lah'-to], m. Howl, screech, hue and cry.

umbela [oom-bay'-lah], f. Umbel, inflorescence resembling a parasol.

umbelífero, ra [oom-bay-loo'-fay-ro, rah], a. Umbelliferous, in the form of a parasol. -f. pl. The parsley family.

umbilicado, da [oom-be-le-cah'-do, dah], m. Navel-shaped; umbilicated.

umbilical [oom-be-le-cahl'], a. Umbilical.

umbla [oom'-blah], f. Umber, fish of the salmon family.

umbral [oom-brahl'], m. 1. Threshold (de entrada): lintel, architrave. 2. Begenning, commencement, rudiment. 3. **Umbrales**, (S. Am.) timber for thresholds. **Estar en los umbrales de**, to be on the threshold of.

umbralar [oom-brah-lar'], va. To lay down the ground-timber of a door or gate; to place an architrave.

umbrátil [oom-brah'-teel], a. Umbratile; resembling.

umbría [oom-bree'-ah], f. Umbrosity, umbrageousness; a shady place.

umbrío, a [oom-bree'-o, ah], a. Umbrageous.

umbroso, sa [oom-bro'-so, sah], a. Shady.

un [oon], a. One, a used for uno, but always before words: it is also used occasionally before verbs, to give force to an expression. **Un hombre**, a man.

una [oo'-nah], a. V. UNO. **A una**, with one accord.

unánime [oo-nah'-ne-may], a. Unanimous.

unanimente [oo-nah-ne-mah-men-tay], adv. Unanimously.

unanimidad [oo-nah-ne-me-dahd'], f. Unanimity.

uncia [oon'-the-ah], f. An ancient coin.

uncial [oon-the-ahl'], a. Uncial, said of a form of (capital) letters used in a manuscripts from the fourth to the eighth century.

unciforme [oon-the-for'-may], a. Unciform, shaped like a hook. m. Unciform, a bone of the wrist.

unción [oon-the-on'], f. 1. Unction, anointing. 2. Extreme unction. 3. Unction, anything that excites piety and devotion. -pl. Course of salivation, practiced in venereal cases.

uncionario, ria [oon-the-o-nah'-re-o, ah], a. Being under salivation. -m. Place of salivating.

uncir [oon-theer'], va. To yoke oxen or mules for labor.

undante [oon-dahn'-tay], a. (Poet.)V. UNDOSO.

undecágono [oon-day-cah'-go-no], m. (Math.) Undecagon, a figure having eleven angles and eleven sides.

undécimo, ma [oon-day'-the-mo, mah], a. Eleventh.

undécuplo, pla, [oon-day'-coo-plo, plah], a. Eleven times as much.

undísono, na [oon-dee'-so, nah], a. Billowy, sounding like waves.

undívago, ga [oon-dee'-vah-go, gah], a. Wavy, moving like the waves.

undoso, sa [oon-do'-so, sah], a. Wavy, undulary, undulatory.

undulación [oon-doo-lah-the-on'], f. Undulation.

undular [oon-doo-lar'], vn. To rise or play in waves, to undulate.

undulatorio, ria [oon-doo-lah-to'-re-o, ah], a, Undulatory.

ungarina [oon-gah-ree'-nah], f. V. ANGUARINA.

ungido [oon-hee'-do], *m.* Anointed of the Lord, king, sovereign. —**Ungido, da**, *pp.* of UNGIR.

ungimiento [oon-he-me-en'-to], *m.* Unction, the act of anointing.

ungir [oon-heer'], *va.* To anoint, to consecrate.

ungüentario, ria [oon-goo-en-tah'-re-o, ah], *a.* Preparing sweet-scented ointment or perfumes. *m.* Perfume-box, in which sweet-scented ointments are kept; anointer.

ungüento [oon-goo-en'-to], *m.* 1. Unguent, ointment, liniment. 2. Perfume, balsam.

unguiculado, da [oon-ge-coo-lah'-do, dah], *a.* (*Zool.*) Unguiculate, having claws.

unguífero ra [oon-gee'-fay-ro, rah], *a.* Unguiferous, bearing a nail or a claw.

ungüis [oon'-goo-ees], *m.* The lachrymal bone of the nose, thin like a nail.

ungulado, da [un-goo-lah'-do, dah], *a.* Ungulate, having hoofs.

uniarticulado, da [oo-ne-ar-te-coo-lah'-do, dah], *a.* (*Biol.*) Uniarticulate, single-jointed.

unible [oo-nee'-blay], *a.* That which may be united.

unibus [oo-nee-boos], Unibus (*Comput.*)

únicamente [oo'-ne-cah-men-tay], *adv.* Only, simply.

unicario [oo-ne-cah'-re-o], *m.* A tree of India, the leaves of which the Malays boil and mix with the betel, which they constantly chew.

unicaule [oo-ne-cah'-oo-lay], *a.* Having but one stalk (plantas).

unicelular [oo-ne-the-loo-loor], *a.* Unicellular, single-cell.

unicidad [oo-ne-the-dahd'], *f.* (*Phil.*) Singularity, distinctive quality.

único, ca [oo'-ne-co, cah], *a.* Singular, alone, that of which there is but one; single; unique, sole; only (solo); rare, unmatched, unparalleled. **La única dificultad es que…**, the only difficulty is that…. **Es lo único que nos hacía falta**, that's all we needed.

unicoloro, ra [oo-ne-co-lo'-ro, rah], *a.* Unicolor, of one color.

unicornio [oo-necor'-ne-o], *m.* 1. Unicorn. 2. A northern constellation. Monoceros. 3. (*Zool.*) Narwhal. 4. A mineral rock, yellow, ashy, or gray.

unidad [oo-ne-dahd'], *f.* 1. Unity (cualidad). 2. Unit, the root of numbers. 3. (*Arith.*) A number less than ten. 4. Principle of dramatic unity. 5. Conformity, union. **Unidad termal británica**, (*Phy.*) BTU. British thermal unit. **Unidad de lugar**, unity of place. **Unidad de información**, bit of information. **Unidad central de procesamiento**, central processing unit.

unidamente [oo-ne-dah-men'-tay], *adv.* Jointly, unanimously, conjunctively, compactly, unitedly.

unido [oo-nee-do], *a.* 1. Joined (juntado), linked. 2. (*Fig.*) United. **Una familia muy unida**, a very united family.

unifamiliar [oo-nee-fah-me-le-ar], *a.* Single-family.

unificar [oo-ne-fe-car'], *va.* To unite into one.

uniflorígero, ra [oo-ne-flo-hay'-ro, rah], **unifloro, ra** [oo-ne-flo'-ro, rah], *a.* One-flowered, uniflorous.

unifoliado, da [oo-ne-fo-le-ah-do, dah], *a.* UNifoliate, Unifoliar', one leaved.

uniformar [oo-ne-for-mar'], *va.* 1. To make uniform (igualar). 2. To put into uniform (persona).

uniforme [oo-ne-for'-may], *a.* Uniform.

uniforme [oo-ne-for-may], *m.* (*Mil.*) Uniform regimentals.

uniformemente [oo-ne-for-may-men-tay], *adv.* Uniformly.

uniformidad [oo-ne-for-me-dahd'], *f.* Uniformity, resemblance, hormony.

unigénito [oo-ne-hay'-ne-to], *a.* Only-begotten.

unilateral [oo-ne-lah-tay-rahl'], *m.* (*For.*) Unilateral, binding on one party only.

unión [oo-ne-on'], *f.* 1. Union, conjunction. 2. Conformity, resemblance. 3. Concord, unity (cualidad). 4. Union, marriage. 5. Composition of ingredient. 6. Combination, physical or chemical union. 7. Consolidation of the lips of a wound. 8. Alliance, confederacy. coalition, consociation. 9.

Contiguity; continuity. 10. Incorporation, coherence; sameness, similarity. 11. Hoop, ring. 12. Among jewellers match, likeness in form and size of one pearl with another. **La unión hace la fuerza**, united we stand. **En unión con**, together with.

unípara [oo-nee'-pa-rah], *a.* Uniparous, bringing one at a birth.

unípede [oo-nee'-pe-day], *a.* Uniped, having only one foot.

unipersonal [oo-ne-per-so-nahl'], *a.* Unipersonal, consisting of one person only.

unipolar [oo-ne-po-lar'], *a.* Unipolar, having one pole only.

unipolaridad [oo-ne-po-lah-re-dahd'], *f.* A. State of a unipolar body; unipolarity.

unir [oo-neer'], *va.* 1. To join (objectos, piezas), to unite, to conjoin, to couple, to knit. 2. To join, to mix (líquidos), to incorporate, to combine, to coalesce. 3. To bind, to tie (atar), to consociate; to confederate. 4. To approach, to bring near; to close. 5. To collect, to aggregate. 6. To conform. 7. To consolidate. *-vr.* 1. To join (personas), to unite, to associate, to be united; to adhere, to concur. 2. To be contiguous. 3. To be united; to be married. **Les une una fuerte simpatía**, they are bound by a strong affection. **Unirse en matrimonio**, to marry.

unisexual [oo-ne-sec-soo-ahl'], *a.* (*Bot.*) Unisexual, having flowers of one sex only.

unison [oo-nee'-son], *vn.* Unison, musical consonance.

unisonancia [oo-ne-so-nahn'-the-ah], *f.* Uniformity of sound, unison; monotony.

unísono [oo-nee'-so-no], *a.* 1. Unison, sounding alone. 2. Having the same sound.

unísono [oo-ne-so-no], *m.* Unison, a single unvaried note.

unitario [oo-ne-tah'-re-o], *m.* Unitarian, one who rejects the doctrine of the Trinity. *-a.* Advocating political centralization.

unitarismo [oo-ne-tah-rees'-mo], *m.* 1. The doctrine of those who deny the Trinity. 2. Political centralization.

unitivo, va [oo-ne-tee'-vo, vah], *a.* Unitive.

univalvo, va [oo-ne-vahl'-vo, vah], *a.* Univalve (conchas).

universal [oo-ne-ver-sahl'], *a.* Universal, world (mundial), general, oecumenical; learned, well-informed. **De fama universal**, known all over the world. **Historia universal**, world history.

universalidad [oo-ne-ver-sah-le-dahd'], *f.* 1. Universality. 2. Generality of information.

universalismo [oo-ne-ver-sah-lees'-mo], *m.* Opinion founded on the authority of universal consent.

universalista [oo-ne-ver-sah-lees'-tah], *com.* One who holds the foregoing opinion.

universalmente [oo-ne-ver-sal-men'-tay], *adv.* Universally, generally.

universidad [oo-ne-ver-se-dahd'], *f.* 1. Universality, generality. 2. University. 3. Corporation, community. 4. The whole circle of nature; the vegetable, animal, or mineral kingdom. **Universidad laboral**. technical college.

universitario [oo-ne-ver-se-tah-re-o], *a.* University; academic. *-m.* **Universitaria**, *f.* University.

universo [oo-ne-verr'-so], *m.* The universe.

universo, sa [oo-ne-verr'-so, sah], *a.* Universal.

univocación [oo-ne-vo-cah-the-on'], *f.* Univocation.

unívocamente [oo-nee'-vo-cah-men-tay], *adv.* Univocally, unanimously.

univocarse [oo-ne-vo-car'-say], *vr.* To have the same meaning.

unívoco, ca [oo-nee'-vo-co, cah], *a.* 1. Univocal: used as a substantive. 2. Unanimous; resembling.

uno [oo'-no], *m.* 1. One. 2. One, any individual, intimate friend, another, self. 3. (*Math.*) Radical, or root of a number.

uno, na [oo'-no, nah], *a.* 1. One; closely resembling the same (idéntico); sole, only. 2. It is used relatively or to supply a name, as **Uno dijo**, it was said, or one said. **Uno a otro**, one another, reciprocally. **Todo es uno**, it is all the same; it is foreign to the point. **Uno a uno**, one by one. **Uno por uno**, one and then another: used to mark the distinction more forcibly. **Váyase uno por otro**, let one go for the other. **Una cosa**, a thing undetermined. **Una y no más**, never, no more. **Ser para en una**, to be well matched: applied to a married couple. **Ir a una**, to act of the same accord, or to the same end. **Cada uno a la suyo**, everyone should mind his own business. **Uno nunca sabe qué hacer**, one never knows what to do.

untador, ra [oon-tah-dor', rah], *m. & f.* Anointer, surgeon who administers or performs mercurial frictions.

untadura [oon-tah-doo'-rah], *f.* 1. Unction, the act of anointing (acto). 2. Unction, ointment.

untamiento [oon-tah-me-en'-to], *m.* Unction, the act of anointing.

untar [oon-tar'], *va.* 1. To rub, to anoint, to grease, to oint. 2. To suborn, to bribe. **Untar las manos**, to grease the hands, y. e. To bribe. 3. To varnish a piece of painting. **Untar los dedos en tinta**, to smear one's finger with ink. *-vr.* 1. To be greased with unctuous matter. 2. To embezzle.

untaza [oon-tah'-thah], *f.* Grease. *V.* ENJUNDIA.

unto [oon'-to], *m.* 1. Grease, fat of animals. 2. Unguent, ointment. **Unto de oso**, bear's grease. **Unto de puerco**, hog's lard.

untoso, sa [oon-to'-so, sah], *a. (Prov.) V.* UNTUOSO.

untuosidad [oon-too-o-se-dahd'], *f.* Unctuosity, greasiness.

untuoso, sa [oon-too-o'-so, sah], *a.* Unctuous, greasy.

untura [oon-too'-rah], *f.* 1. Unction, act of anointing. 2. Unction, ointment, matter used in anointing.

uña [oo'-nyah], *f.* 1. Nail of the fingers and toes (de la mano, del pie). 2. Hoof (pezuña) claw, or talon of beasts; fang. 3. Painted hook of instruments. 4. Part of the trunk of a felled tree, which sticks to the root. 5. Crust on sores or wounds. 6. Excrescence or hard tumor on the eyelids. 7. Dexterity in stealing or filching. 8. Curved beak of a scorpion. **Uña de la gran bestia**, elk's hoove. **Uñnas de cangrejo**, crab's claws. **Hincar** or **meter la uña**, to overcharge, to be sell at an exorbitant price. **Mostrar las uñas**, to be inexorable. **Mostrar la uña**, to show one's teeth, to discover one's foibles. **Comerse las uñas**, to bite one's nails. **Uña encarnada**, ingrowing nail. **Estar de uñas con uno**, to be at daggers drawn with somebody.

uñada [oo-nyah'-dah], *f.* Impression made with the nail, scratch, nip.

uñarada [oo-nyah-rah'-dah] *f.* Scratch with the nail.

uñate [oo-nyah'-thah], *m* 1. (Coll.) Pinching with the nail. 2. *V.* UÑETA.

uñero [oo-nyah'-thah], *f. aug.* Large nail.

uñero [oo-nyay'-ro], *m.* 1. A callous excrescence at the root of a nail. 2. An in-growing nail.

uñidura [oo-nay-doo'-rah], *f.* The act of yoking oxen or mules for labor.

uñir [oo-nyeer'], *va. (Prov.)* To yoke. *V.* UNCIR.

uñita [oo-nyee'-tah], *f. dim.* Little nail.

uñoso, sa [oo-nyo'-so, sah], *a.* Having long nails or claws.

¡upa! [oo'-path], *int.* Up. up: a term used to make children get up from the ground. *V.* AUPA.

upar [oo-par'], *vn. (Coll.)* To endeavor to get up.

uracho [oo-rah'-cho], *m. (Anat.)* Urachus, a ligamentous cord that terminates in the naval-string.

Urania [oo-rah'-ne-ah], *f. (Myth.)* Urania, the muse of astronomy.

uranio [oo-rah'-ne-o], *m (Chem.)* Uranite, a rare, heavy metallic element.

uranita [oo-rah-nee'-tah], *f (Chem.)* Uranite, autunite; phosphate of uranium and calcium.

uranografía [oo-rah-no-grah-fee'-ah], *f.* Uranography, ouranography, description of the heavens.

uranometría [oo-rah-no-may-tree'-ah], *f.* Uranometry, the measurement of the heavens.

uranómetro [oo-rah-no'-may-tro], *m.* An instrument for measuring heavenly bodies and their movements.

uranoscopio [oo-rah-nos-co'-pe-o], *m.* Star-gazor, a fish with eyes on the top of the head.

uraño, ña [oo-rah'-nyo, nyah], *a.* Coy, reserved, timid; wild, untamed. *V.* HURAÑO.

urari [oo-rah'-re], *m.* Woorare, curare, arrow-poison of South America.

urato [oo-rah'-to], *m.* 1. (Chem.) Urate, a salt of uric acid. 2. *(Agr.)* A manure of urine and plaster or earth.

urbanamente [oor-bah-nah-men'-tay], *adv.* Courteously, politely, complacently.

urbanidad [oor-bah-ne-dahd'], *f.* Urbanity, civility, politeness, courteousness, gentleness, complaisance.

urbanismo [oor-bah-nees-mo], *m.* 1. Town planning (planificació). 2. *(Carib.)* Real-estate development.

urbanización [oor-bah-ne-thah-the-on], *f.* City planning.

urbanizar [oor-bah-ne-thar'], *va.* To urbanize (tierra).

urbano, na [or-bahn'-no, nah], *a.* 1. Urban (de la ciudad), peculiar to towns or cities. 2. Urbane, courteous (cortés), polite, well-bred.

urca [oor'-cah], *f.* 1. (Naut.) Hooker, dogger; a pink-built and sloop-rigged vessel. 2. *(Naut.)* Storeship. 3. *(Zool.)* Species of whale *V.* ORCA.

urce [oor'-thay], *m. (Bot.)* Health. *V.* BREZO.

urceiforme [oor-thay-e-for'-may], *a. (Bot.)* Urceolate, swolen below and contracted at the orifice.

urchilla [oor-cheel-lyah], *f.* Archil or orchil, a violet color, used by dyers.

urdidera [oor-de-dor', rah], *f.* 1. Woman who warps. 2. A warping frame

urdidor, ra [oor-de-dor', rah], *m. & f.* 1. Warper. 2. *m.* Warping-frame warping mill.

urdidura [oor-de-doo'-rah], *f.* The act of warping.

urdimbre [oor-deem'-bray], *f.* Chain, warp, as opposed to woof.

urdir [oor-deer'], *va.* 1. To warp (tela), to dispose threads for the loom. 2. To contrive, to scheme.

urea [oo-ray'-ah], *f.* Urea, a crystallizable substance excreted in the urine.

urente [oo-ren'-tay], *a.* Hot, burning, parching. *(Acad.)*

uremia [oo-ray'-me-ah], *f. (Ned.)* Uraemia, a morbid state occasioned by presence of urea in the blood.

urémico, ca [oo-ray'-me-co, cah], *a.* Uremic, relatin to or affected by uremia.

urétera [oo-ray'-tay-rah], *f. (Anat.) V.* URETRA.

urétere [oo-ray'-tay-ray], *m. (Anat.)* Ureter, the duct by which the urine passes from the kidney to the bladder or cloaca.

urético, ca [oo-ray'-te-co, cah], *a.* Belonging to the urethra.

uretra [oo-ray'-trah], *f. (Anat.)* Urethra, the canal by which urine is expelled from the bladder.

uretritis [oo-ray-tree'-tis], *f.* 1. Urethritis, inflammation of the urethra. 2. Gonorrhoea.

uretrorrea [oo-ray-tror-ray'-ah], *f. (Med.)* Gleet; flux from the urethra.

uretrótomo [oo-ray-tro'-to-mo], *m.* Urethrotome.

urgencia [oor-hen'-the-ah], *f* Urgency, exigence; obligation. **En caso de urgencia**, in case of necessity.

urgente [oor-hen'-tay], *a.* Urgent, pressing, cogent. **Carta urgente**, express letter.

urgentemente [oor-hen'-tay-men-tay], *adv.* Urgently.

urgir [oor-heer'], *m.* To be urgent, to require speedy cure or immediate execution; to be actually obliged; to turbo, to press forward. **Me urge la respuesta**, the reply presses. **Me urge terminarlo**, I must finish it as soon as I can.

úrico, ca,[oo'-re-co, cah], *a.* Uric, relating to urine. **Ácido úrico**, uric acid.

urinálisis [oo-re-nah'-le-sis], *m.* Urinalysis, urine analysis.

urinario, ria [oo-re-nah'-re-o, ah], *a.* Urinary.

urna [oor'-nah], *f.* 1. Urn, in which the ashes of the dead were formerly put. 2. Glass case (de cristal), in which small statues or images are kept. 3. Urn used by painters and sculpters to represent rivers.

urnición [oor-ne-the-on'], *f. (Naut.)* Top-timbers. *V.* BARRAGANETE.

uro [oo'-ro], *m.* A kind of wild ox.

urogallo [oo-ro-gahl'-lyo], *m. (Orn.)* Bird like a cock.

urología [oo-ro-lo-he'-ah], *f.* Urology.

urólogo, ga [oo-ro'-lo-go], *m & f.* Urologist.

uromancia [oo-ro-mahn'-the-ah], *f.* Uromancy, pretended divination by the examination of urine.

uroscopia [oo-ros-co'-pe-ah], *f.* Uroscopy, methodical inspection of urine for medical diagnosis.

urraca [oor-rah'-cah], *f.* 1. *(Orn.)* Magpie. 2. Chatterbox (habladora).

ursa [oor'-sah], *f.* She-bear. V. OSA.

ursulina [oor-soo-lee'-nah], *f.* Nun of the order of St. Ursula.

urticáceas [oor-te-cah'-thay-as], *f. pl. & a.* Urticaceae, the nettle family, including elms, mulberries, hops, etc; urticaceous.

urticaria [oor-te-cah'-re-ah], *f.* Urticaria, nettlerash, hives; an eruptive skin disease provoking great itching.

uruca [oo-roo'-cah], *f. (Bot.)* Arnotto. V. ACHIOTE.

uruguayo, ya [oo-roo-goo-ah'-yo, yah], *a. & n.* Belonging to, or native of Uruguay.

usación [oo-sah-the-on'], *f.* Use the act of using.

usadamente [oo-sah'-dah-men-tay], *adv.* According to custom.

usado, da [oo-sah'-do, dah], *a. & pp.* of USAR. 1. Used (sello), employed. 2. Used, worn out (ropa). 3. Experienced, skillful, fashionably frequent. 4. Second hand articles. **Libros usados**, second hand books. **Ropa usada**, second hand wearing apparel; cast-off clothing.

usagre [oo-sah'-gray], *m.* A breaking out in the faces of teething children, scald-head, infantile eczema.

usaje [oo-sah'-hay], *f.* Usage, custom. V. LAO.

usanza [oo-sahn'-thah], *f.* Usage, custom.

usar [oo-sar'], *va.* 1. To use (utilizar), to make use of; to wear. 2. To use, to accustom (soler), to habituate, to practice. 3. To exorcise an employment or office. 4. To enjoy a thing. 5. To communicate, to treat or use familiarly. **Sin usar**, unused. *-vn.* To use, to make use. *-vr.* To use, to be in use or fashion, to be wont. **La chistera ya no se usa**, top hats are not worn nowadays.

usencia [oo-sen'-the-ah], *com.* You reverence, a contraction of *vuestra reverencia*: an appellation of honor among friars.

usía [oo-see'-ah], *com.* Your lordship or your ladyship, a contraction of *vuestra señoría*.

usier [oo-se-err'], *m.* Usher, porter. V. UJIER.

usiría [oo-se-ree'-ah], *com.* V. USÍA.

usitado, da [oo-se-tah'-do, dah], *a. (Prov.)* Frequently used.

uso [oo'-so], *m.* 1. Use (empleo), employment, service. 2. Usufruct; enjoyment. 3. Use, custom (costumbre), style, fashion (estilo, moda), mode. 4. *(Com. Law.)* Usance, a time fixed for the payment of bills of exchange. 5. Office, exercise; wearing, wear. 6. Frequent continuation, constant use, experience; assiduousness. 7. Wear; wear and tear. **De uso corriente**, in everyday use. **Estar fuera de uso**, to be out of use. **Hacer uso de**, to make use of. **Es un uso muy antiguo**, it is a very ancient custom.

ustaga [oos-tah'-gah], *f. (Naut.)* Tie.

usted [oos-ted'], *com.* You (your worship, your honor), a contraction of *vuestra merced (vuesarced, usted)*, a pronoun used in polite style to address all persons of respectability, either orally or by letter. **Usted** and **ustedes** used to be written in abbreviation, thus: *Vm., Vms., Vmd., Vmds.* At present *usted* is represented by *Ud.* or *Vd.*, and *ustedes (pl.)* by *Vds.*, and often printed in full. The loose articulating of the *d* frequently causes it to become inaudible, particularly in Spanish America; so that **usted** sounds as *usté.* **El coche de usted**, your car. **Sin usted**, without you.

ustión [oos-te-on'], *f.* Ustion, the act of making medical preparation by burning; exustion.

ustorio [oos-to'-re-o], *a.* Burning. V. ESPEJO USTORIO.

usual [oo-soo-ahl'], *a.* 1. Usual, customary, ordinary, general. 2. Tractable, social. **Año usual**, current year.

usualmente [oo-soo-ahl-men-tay], *adv.* Usually.

usuario, ria [oo-soo-ah'-re-o, a], *a. (Law.)* Having the sole use of a thing.

usucapión [oo-soo-cah-pe-on'], *f. (Law.)* Usucapion or usucaption.

usucapir [oo-soo-cah-peer'], *va. (Law.)* To acquire a right of property in anything, by possession for a specified time.

usufructo [oo-soo-frooc-to], *m.* Usufruct, profit, advantage; enjoyment.

usufructuar [oo-soo-frooc-too-ar'], *va.* 1. To enjoy the usufruct of anything. 2. To render productive or fruitful.

usufructuario, ria [oo-soo-frooc-too-ah'-re-o, ah], *a.* Possessing the usufruct of a thing.

usura [oo-soo'-rah], *f.* 1. Interest, payment for the use of money lent. 2. Gain, profit. 3. Usury.

usurar [oo-soo-rar'], *vn.* V. USUREAR.

usurariamente [oo-soo-rah-re-ah-men-tay], *adv.* Usuriously, interestedly.

usuario, ria [oo-soo-ah'-re-o, ah], *a.* Usurious, practising usury.

usurear [oo-soo-ray-ar'], *vn.* To practise usury, to lend or to borrow money on interest. 2. To reap great benefit or advantage.

usurero, ra [oo-soo-ray'-ro, rah], *m. & f.* Usurer, money-lender, griper.

usurpación [oo-soor-pah-the-on'], *f.* Usurpation.

usurpador, ra [oo-soor-pah-dor', rah], *m. & f.* Usurper.

usurpar [oo-soor-par'], *va.* 1. To usurp (corona, derechos); to assume another's once, dignity, or employment; to grasp. 2. To make use of a word instead of another, or in another sense.

utensilio [oo-ten-see'-le-o], *m.* Utensil; tool, device, contrivance. **Utensilios para escribir**, writing materials. **Utensilios para pescar**, fishing tackle.

uterino, na [oo-tay-ree'-no, nah], *a.* 1. Uterine, belonging to the womb. 2. Uterine, born of the same mother.

útero [oo'-tay-ro], *m.* Uterus, womb.

uteromanía [oo-tay-ro-mah-nee'-ah], *f.* Nymphomania.

útil [oo'-teel], *a.* Useful, profitable; commodious. **Es muy útil tenerlo aquí cerca**, it's very handy having it here close by.

útil [oo'-teel], *m.* V. UTILIDAD. *-pl.* Utensils.

utilidad [oo-te-le-dahd'], *f.* 1. Usefulness (cualidad de útil), utility. 2. Profit. **utilidad neta**, net profit.

utilitario, ria [oo-te-le-tah'-re-o, ah], *a.* Utilitarian.

utilitarismo [oo-te-le-tah-rees'-mo], *m.* Utilitarianism.

utilizable [oo-te-le-thah'-blay], *a.* Usable, practicable for use.

utilizar [oo-te-te-thar'], *m.* To be useful. *-va.* To reap benefit or profit: to take advantage of or profit by. *-vr.* To interest oneself in a business.

útilmente [oo'-teel-men-tay], *adv.* Usefully.

utopia [oo-to'-pe-ah], *f.* V. UTOPÍA.

utopía [oo-to-pee'-ah], *f.* 1. Utopia, an imaginary island having a perfect social and political system. 2. Plan or system which is charming in theory, but unrealizable in practice.

utópico, ca [oo-to'-pe-co, cah], *a.* Utopian, chimerically good, ideal.

utopista [oo-to-pees'-tah], *m.* 1. A dreamer. 2. Utópian schemer.

utrero, ra [oo-tray'-ro, rah], *m. & f.* Bull or heifer between two and three years old.

utretro [oo-tray'-tro], *adv.* As above.

uva [oo'-vah], *f.* 1. Grape. 2. Tippler. 3. Wart on the eyelid. 4. Fruit of the barberry-bush. 5. Tumor on the epiglottis. **Uva de Corinto**, *(Bot.)* currants. **Uva pasa**, raisin. **Uva espín, espina** or **crespa**, goose-berry. *-pl.* Bunch of grapes. **Estar de mala uva**, to be in a bad mood.

uvada [oo-va'-dah], *f.* 1. Abundance of grapes. 2. *(Prov.)* Kind of land measure.

uval [oo-vahl'], *a.* Belonging to grapes.

uvate [oo-vah'-tay], *m.* Conserve of grapes.

uvayema [oo-vah-yay'-mah], *f.* Species of wild vine.

úvea [oo'-vay-ah], *f.* Uvea, the outermost coat of the eye.

uvero, ra [oo-vay'-ro, rah], *m. & f.* Retailer of grapes.

uviforme [oo-ve-for'-may], *a.* Shaped like a bunch of grapes.

úvula [oo'-voo-lah], *f. (Anat.)* Uvula.

uxoricida [ook-so-re-thee'-dah], *m.* Uxoricide, wife-murderer.

uzas [oo'-thas], *f.* Kind of Brazilian crab.

uyama [oo-yah'-mah], *f.* A species of calabash of Guayana, a province of Venezuela.

V

v [vay], *f.* In the Spanish alphabet *V* is the twenty-third letter in order, and should be pronounced as in English. As the Spaniards press very lightly their lower lips against the upper teeth in pronouncing this letter, it frequently sounds like *b* especially at the start of words. *V.* was very often used in manuscript instead of the capital *U*; as, *Vn día* for **Un día**. *V.*, or *Vd.*, stance as a contraction for **Usted**, *(sing.)* you, and VV., or Vds., for Ustedes, *(pl.)* you (formerly Vm. Vmd., Vms. Vmds.); also for vuestra, vuestras; as V. M, vuestra majestad, your majesty; V. S. Usía (vuestra señoría), your lordship or ladyship, etc. V in Roman numerals stands for five, for verb in grammar, for wind (viento) in meteorology, and volume in mathematical calculations.

vaca [vah'-cah], *f.* 1. Cow. **Vaca lechera**, milk-cow. 2. Beef. 3. *(Prov.)* Joint stock of two partners in gambling. 4. Tanned leather, cowhide. **Vaca marina**, sea-cow. *V.* MANATÍ. **Vaca sagrada**, sacred cow. **Pasar las vacas gordas**, to have a grand time of it. 5. *(LAm.)* Enterprise with profits on and pro rata basis.

vacación [vah-cah-the-on'], *f.* Vacation, intermission; recess of courts of law and public boards. *-pl.* Holidays. **Vacaciones**, vacation, holiday. **Estar de vacaciones**, to be on vacation.

vacada [vah-cah'-dah], *f.* Drove of cows.

vacancia [vah-can'-the-ah], *f.* Vacancy.

vacante [vah-cahn'-tay], *a.* Vacant, disengaged. *-f.* 1. Vacancy of a post or employment. 2. Vacation, time unengaged. 3. Rent fallen due during the vacancy of a benefice. **Proveer una vacante**, to fill a post.

vacar [vah-car'], *vn.* 1. To cease, to stop; to be vacant. 2. To devote oneself to a particular thing; to follow a business. *-va.* To vacate an office.

vacarí [vah-cah-ree'], *a.* Leathern: said of a leather shield, etc.

vaciadero [vah-the-ah-day'-ro], *m.* Drain, sink (desaguadero).

vaciadizo, za [vah-the-ah-dee'-tho, thah], *a.* Cast, moulded.

vaciado [vah-the-ah'-do], *m.* 1. Form or image, moulded or cast in plaster of Paris or wax; excavation. 2. *(Arch.)* Cavity in a pedestal below its ornamental mouldings. 3. *(Mex.)* Great (estupendo). 4. Hollowing out (acto). —**Vaciado, da**, *pp.* of VACIAR.

vaciador [vah-the-ah-dor'], *m.* Moulder, one who casts or moulds; one who evacuates, hollows, or makes empty.

vaciamiento [vah-the-ah-me-en'-to], *m.* 1. Casting, moulding; evacuating, hollowing. 2. *V.* VACÍO.

vaciar [vah-the-ar'], *va.* 1. To empty (recipiente, contenido), to evacuate, to exhaust, to clear. 2. To mould, to form, to model. 3. To fail into, to discharge itself (río). 4. *(Arch.)* To excavate. 5. To explain at large. **Vació la leche en un vaso**, he poured the milk into a glass. **Vació los bolsillos en la mesa**, he emptied out his pockets on the table. *-vn.* 1. To fall, to decrease (aguas). 2. Not to make good use of one's time. 3. To fade, to lose color or luster. *-vr.* 1. To be spilt (líquidos). 2. To divulge what should be kept secret. 3. To be empty or vacant.

vaciedad [va-the-ay-dahd'], *f.* 1. Emptiness, vacuity. 2. Emptiness, frothiness. 3. An inconsiderate or arrogant speech; obscene language.

vaciero [vah-the-ay'-ro], *m.* Shepherd whose sheep are all dry or barren.

vacilación [vah-the-lah-the-on'], *f.* 1. Hesitation, vacillation, reeling, staggering. 2. Perplexity, irresolution.

vacilante [vah-the-lahn'-tay], *pa. & a.* Vacillating; irresolute; unstable.

vacilar [vah-the-lar'], *vn.* 1. To vacillate, to waver, to fluctuate; to be perplexed; to wander or be confused; to reel, to stagger (persona). 2. To flicker (luz). 3. To hesitate. **Vacilar entre dos posibilidades**, to hesitate between two possibilities. 4. **Vacilar con uno**, to tease somebody. 5. *(CAm, Carib, Mex.)* To get plastered (emborracharse).

vacile [vah-the-lay], *m.* 1. Hesitation (duda). 2. Teasing (guasa). **Estar de vacile**, to chat.

vacío, cía [vah-thee'-o, ah], *a.* 1. Void, empty, vacuous. 2. Unoccupied, disengaged; idle (charla); fruitless. 3. Concave, hollow. 4. Defective, deficient. 5. Vain (vanidoso), arrogant, presumptuous. 6. Not with young (ganado). 7. Unloaded or empty (caballos, mulas). 8. Uninhabited. 9. Unoccupied by people. **El teatro estaba medio vacío**, the theater was half empty.

vacío [vah-thee'-o], *m.* 1. Void, empty space, vacuum, aperture. 2. Mould for casting metal. 3. Vacancy, place or employment unfilled. 4. Concavity, hollowness. 5. Blank space in a book or writing. 6. *(Com.)* Ullage of a cask or other vessel: wantage. 7. Animal not with young. 8. Vacuity, cavity. 9. Flank of animals. **De vacío**, empty: unemployed. **Se nota ahora un gran vacío en la familia**, one is conscious now of a big gap in the family. **Tener un vacío en el estómago**, to feel hungry.

vacisco [vah-thees'-co], *m.* Fragment in quicksilver mines.

vaco, ca [vah'-co, cah], *a.* Vacant.

vacuidad [vah-coo-e-dahd'], *f.* Vacuity, emptiness.

vacuista [vah-coo-ees'-tah], *m.* Vacuist, a philosopher that holds a vacuum.

vacuna [vah-coo'-nah], *f.* 1. Vaccine (sustancia). 2. Vaccination (acto), shot. **Vacuna antidiftérica**, diphtheria shot. **Vacuna contra la viruela**, smallpox shot.

vacunación [vah-coo-nah-the-on'], *f.* Vaccination (acto de vacunar).

vacunador [vah-coo-nah-dor'], *m.* Vaccinator.

vacunar [vah-coo-nar'], *va.* 1. To vaccinate. 2. To prepare (preparar), to inure (habituar); to forearm (prevenir).

vacuno, na [vah-coo'-no, nah], *a.* Belonging to cattle, vaccine, bovine.

vacuo, a [vah'-coo-o, ah], *a.* Unoccupied. *V.* VACÍO and VACANTE.

vacuo [vah-coo-o], Vacuum.

vade [vah'-day], *m. V.* VADEMÉCUM.

vadeable [vah-day-ah'-blay], *a.* 1. Fordable. 2. *(Met.)* Conquerable, superable.

vadeador, ra [vah-day-ah-dor', rah], *a.* Wading.

vadeamiento [vah-day-ah-me-en'-to], *m.* Act of fording.

vadear [vah-day-ar'], *va.* 1. To wade, to ford (río). 2. To conquer, to surmount (dificultad). 3. To sound, to try to examine. *-vr.* To conduct oneself.

vademécum [vah'-day-may'-coom], *m.* 1. A book, a case, or other portable and useful thing, which is habitually carried on the person. 2. Portfolio in which school children keep their papers.

vadera [vah-day'-rah], *f.* Ford, a shallow part of a river.

¡vade retro! [vah'-day ray'-tro], *adv. exrpres.* Get away! go away!

vadiano, na [vah-de-ah'-no, nah], *a. & n.* Anthropomorphite, ascribing human attributes to a deity.

vado [vah'-do], *m.* 1. Ford (de río), a broad, shallow, level part of a river. 2. Expedient; resource, way out (salida). **No hallar vado**, to see no way out.

vadoso, sa [vah-do'-so, sah], *a.* Shoaly, shallow.

vafe [vah'-fay], *m. (Prov.)* Bold stroke or undertaking.

vagabundear [vah-gah-boon-day-ar'], *vn. (Coll.)* To rove or loiter about, to act the vagrant.

vagabundo, da [vah-gah-boon'-do, dah], *a. & m. & f.* Vagabond, idle vagrant, loitering about: having no fixed abode.

vagamente [vah-gah-men-tay], *adv*. In a vague, unsettled manner.

vagamundear [vah-gah-moon-day-ar'], *vn. V.* VAGABUNDEAR.

vagamundo, da [vah-gah-moon-do], *a. V.* VAGABUNDO.

vagancia [vah-gahn'-the-ah], *f.* Vagrancy.

vagante [vah-gahn'-tay], *pa.* Vagrant (errante).

vagar [vah-gar'], *vn.* 1. To rove or loiter about (entretenerse); to wander (errar), to range. 2. To be at leisure, to be idle (gandulear). 3. To revolve in the mind. 4. To be loose and irregular.

vagar [vah-gar'], *m.* 1. Leisure (tiempo libre). 2. Slowness, indolence.

vagarosamente [vah-gah-ro'-sah-men-tay], *adv.* Vagrantly.

vagaroso, sa [vah-gah-ro'-so, sah], *a.* Errant, vagrant.

vagido [vah-hee-do], *m.* Cry of a child: a convulsive sob.

vagina [vah-hee'-nah], *f. (Anat.)* Vagina.

vaginal [vah-he-nahl'], *a.* Vaginal, relating to the vagina.

vaginante [vah-he-nahn'-tay], *a. (Zool.)* Sheathing, used of the upper wings of coleoptora and orthoptera.

vaginitis [vah-he-nee'-tis], *f.* Vaginitis, inflammation of the vagina.

vago, ga [vah'-go, gah], *a.* 1. Errant, vagrant, 2. Restless, uneasy. 3. Vague, wavering, fluctuating, unsettled; lax, loose. 4. *V.* VACO. **Voz vaga**, a vague report.

vago [vah'-go], *m.* 1. *(Prov.)* Uncultivated plot of ground. 2. Vagabond (vagabundo).

vagón [vah-gone'], *m.* A railway coach or car for passengers or merchandise. (Eng. wagon.) **Vagón-cama**, sleeping-car. **Vagón cisterna**, tanker. **Vagón de mercancías**, goods van.

vagón-comedor [vah-gone'-co-may-dor'], *m.* Dining car (trenes).

vagón-dormitorio [vah-gone'-dor-e-toh'-re-o], *m.* Pullman, sleeping car (trenes).

vagoneta [vah-go-nay'-tah], *f.* A small open car for transportation.

vagón-salón [vah-gone'-sah-lone'], *m.* (r.w.) Parlor car.

vaguada [vah-goo-ah'-dah], *f.* 1. Water way. 2. Line of the channel; a line which marks the course of the water in rivers.

vagueación [vah-gay-ah-the-on'], *f.* Restlessness, levity, unsteadiness; flight of fancy.

vaguedad [vah-gay-dahd'], *f.* Levity, inconstancy.

vaguido [vah-gee'-do], *m.* Giddiness, the state of being giddy.

vahar [vah-ar'], *vn.* To exhale, to emit steam or vapor.

vaharada [vah-ah-rah'-dah], *f.* The act of emitting steam, vapor, or breath.

vaharera [vah-ah-ray'-rah], *f.* 1. *(Med.)* Thrush, a disease of sucking children. 2. *(Brov.)* All unripe melon.

vaharina [vah-ah-ree'-nah], *f. (Coll.)* Steam, vapor, mist.

vahear [vah-ay-ar'], *m.* To exhale, to emit steam or vapor.

vahído [vah-ee'-do], *m.* Vertigo, giddiness.

vaho [vah'-o], *m.* 1. Steam, vapor (vapor). 2. Breath (aliento), whiff (olor). 3. *(Med.)* Inhalation.

vaída [vah-ee'-dah], *f. (Arch.)* Vault or arch, cut into four vertical planes.

vaina [vah'-e-nah], *f.* 1. Scabbard of a sword. 2. Knife or scissors case. 3. Pod (de guisante), capsule, husk (de nuez), hull, cod. 4. *(Naut.)* Bolt-rope tabling, to which the bolt-rope is fastened. 5. *(And.)* Fluke (chiripa). 6. *(Cono Sur)* Swindle (estafa). **Vaina abierta**, scabbard of a large sword formerly used, which covered only one-third of it, in order to be easily drawn.

vainazas [vah-e-nah'-thas], *m. (Coll.)* A humdrum, dull, or dronish person.

vainero [vah-e-nay'-ro], *m.* Scabbard-maker.

vainica [vah-e-nee'-cah], *f.* 1. *(Dim.)* A small pod or husk. 2. Hemstitch.

vainilla [vah-e-neel'-lyah], *f.* 1. *(Dim.)* A small pod or husk. 2. *(Bot.)* Vanilla. 3. Fruit of this plant. 4. A heliotrope which grows in America.

vaivén [vah-e-ven'], *m.* 1. Fluctuation vibration. *(Mech.)* Alternating movement. 2. Unsteadiness, inconstancy, vacilla-

tion. 3. Giddiness. 4. Risk, danger. 5. *(Naut.)* Line, cord, or rope, of different thickness.

vajilla [vah-heel'-lyah], *f.* Table-service of dishes, plates, etc. **Vajilla de porcelana**, Chinaware. **Lavar la vajilla**, to wash up.

val [vahl], *m.* 1. Vale, dale, valley: a contraction of *valle*. 2. *(Brov.)* Sew or drain, sink. 3. Ancient contraction of *vale*, from *valer*.

valaco, ca [vah-lah'-co, cah], *a.* 1. Wallachian. 2. The language spoken in Wallachia, a Romance tongue.

valais [vah-lah'-ees], *m.* Lumber.

valar [vah-lar'], *a.* Relating to a rampart, inclosure, or hedge.

vale [vah'-lay], *m.* 1. Farewell, adieu; valediction. 2. Bond or promissory note. 3. Note of pardon given to schoolboys by the master. 4. First or single hand at cards. 5. Voucher, coupon (cupón); *(LAm.)* Bill (cuenta). **Vale de correo**, money order.

valedero, ra [vah-lay-day'-ro, rah], *a.* Valid, efficacious, binding.

valedor, ra [vah-lay-dor', rah], *m. & f.* Protector (protector), defender.

valencia [vah-len'-the-ah], *f. (Chem.)* Valence.

valenciano, pa [vah-len-the-ah'-no, nah], *a.* Valencian, of Valencia.

valentacho [vah-len-tah'-cho], *m.* Hector, bully, braggadocio.

valentía [vah-len-tee'-ah], *f.* 1. Valor, courage, gallantry, bravery (valor), manliness. 2. Feat, heroic exploit (acto). 3. Brag, boast (dicho). 4. Fire of imagination. 5. *(Art.)* Uncommon dexterity in imitating nature. 6. An extraordinary or vigorous effort.

valentísimo, ma [vah-len-tee'-se-mo, mah], *a. sup.* Most valiant; perfect in an art or science.

valentón [vah-len-tone'], *m.* Braggadocio, hector.

valentón, na [vah-len-tone', nah], *a.* Arrogant, vainglorious.

valentonada, valentona [vah-len-to-nah'-dah], *f.* Brag (dicho), boast.

valentonazo [vah-len-to-nah'-tho], *m. aug.* Bully, boaster. *V.* VALENTÓN.

valentoncillo, lla [vah-len-ton-theel'-lyo, lyah], *a. dim.* A little vain or presumptuous.

valeo [vah-lay'-o], *m.* 1. Round mat; shaggy mat. 2. Rug or plat of bass.

valer [vah-lerr'], *va.* 1. To protect, to defend, to favor, to patronize. 2. To yield, to produce fruits or rent. 3. To equal (serigual), to be equivalent to. 4. To amount to (contar). 5. To bear a certain price, to be worth. -*vn.* 1. To be valuable, meritorious, deserving. 2. To prevail, to avail. 3. To serve as an asylum or refuge. 4. To be valid or binding; to be a head or have authority; to have power, to be able; to hold. 5. To have course, to be current; also to be worth (monedas). 6. To be in favor, to have influence or interest. -*vr.* 1. To employ, to make use of. 2. To avail oneself of, to have recourse to. **¡Válgate Dios!**, heaven bless or pardon you! exclamation of surprise or disapprobation, according to circumstances. **¡Vágame Dios!**, good God! Bless me! expression of surprise or disgust. **Más vale** or **más valiera**, it is better, it would be better. **Más vale algo que nada**, something is better than nothing. **Más vale tarde que nunca**, better later than never. **Vale lo que pesa**, he is worth his weight in gold. **Más vale maña que fuerza**, *(Prov.)* wiles often do what force cannot. **No poderse valer con alguno**, not to be able to manage a person. **Vale la pena de**, it is worth while; worth the trouble of. **Hacer valer**, to give authority or support. **No poderse valer**, to be incapable; not to know how to help oneself. **El asunto le valió muchos disgustos**, the affair caused him lots of trouble. **No vale nada**, it's worthless. **Más vale que vayas tú**, it would be better for you to go. **Es viejo pero todavía vale**, it's old but it still serves. *(Yo valgo, yo valga, valdré V.* VALER.)

valer [vah-lerr'], *m.* Value.

valeriana [vah-lay-re-ah'-nah], *f. (Bot.)* Valerian. **Valeriana griega**, Jacob's-ladder or Greek valerian.

valerosamente [vah-lay-ro-sah-men'-tay], *adv.* Valiantly, courageously.

valeroso, sa [vah-lay-ro'-so, sah], *a.* I. Valiant, brave, courageous, gallant, heroic. 2. Strong, active; powerful.

valetudinario, ria [vah-lay-too-de-nah'-re-o, ah], *a.* Valetudinarian, valetudinary, infirm of health.

valhala [val-hah'-lah], *f.* Walhalla, the paradise of Odin, in Scandinavian mythology.

valí [va-lee'], *m.* Governor of a Moslem province or territory.

valía [ah-lee'-ah], *f.* Appraisement, valuation. 2. Credit, favor, use. 3. Party, faction. **A las valías**, at the highest price which a commodity fetches in the course of a year.

validable [vah-le-dah'-blay], *a.* Justifiable, ratifiable.

validación [vah-le-dah-the-on'], *f.* Validity of an act.

válidamente [vah'-le-dah-men'-tay], *adv.* In a solid or binding manner.

validar [vah-le-dar'], *va.* To give validity, to render firm or binding.

validez [vah-le-deth'], *f.* Validity, stability.

válido, da [vah'-le-do, dah], *a.* 1. Valid, firm, prevalent, weighty, conclusive. 2. Binding, obligatory.

valido, da [vah-lee'-do, dah], *a. & pp.* Of VALER. 1. Availing of, relying upon, confident of. 2. Favored regarded with peculiar kindness; accepted, esteemed. 3. Universally respected. 4. Strong, powerful.

valido [vah-lee'-o], *m.* A favorite of a sovereign; a court minion.

valiente [vah-le-en'-tay], *a.* 1. Strong, robust, vigorous, powerful. 2. Valiant, spirited, brave (valeroso), courageous, active, strenuous; efficacious, valid. 3. Eminent, excellent. 4. *(Coll.)* Glint, excessive.

valiente [vah-le-en'-tay], *m.* 1. Bully, hector, braggadocio. 2. Gallant.

valientemente [vah-le-ayn'-tay-men-tay], *adv.* 1. Vigorously, strongly. 2. Valiantly, courageously, strenuously, manfully. 3. Superabundantly, excessively. 4. Elegantly, with propriety.

valija [vah-lee'-hah], *f.* 1. Valise (portamantas), grip sack. 2. Mail-bag. 3. The post, mail. 4. Satchel (cartera).

valijero [vah-le-hay'-ro], *m.* Postal clerk who distributes mail to towns along a route.

valimiento [vah-le-me-en'-to], *m.* 1. Use, the act of using or employing. 2. Utility, benefit, advantage. 3. A temporary or gratuitous contribution. 4. Interest, favor, protection, support; good graces.

valioso, sa [vah-le-o'-so, sah], *a.* 1. Very valuable (de valor), highly esteemed, of great influence. 2. Rich, wealthy.

valiza [vah-lee'-thah], *f. (Naut.)* Beacon, buoy, pointing out sandbanks. or shoals. **Valiza terrestre**, land-mark.

valizaje [vah-le-thah'-hay], *m.* Duties paid by the shipping in some ports, towards keeping in repair the beacons and buoys.

valla [vahl'-lyah], *f.* 1. Intrenchment; ground surrounded with palisades. 2. Barrier (barrera), barricade. *3. (And. Carib. Mex.)* Cockpit (de gallos). 4. *(And.)* Ditch (zanja).

valladar [val-lyah-dar'], *m.* 1. *(Prov.)* V. VALLADO. 2. Obstacle.

valladear [val-lyah-day-ar'], *va.* To enclose with stakes, pales, or palisades. V. VALLAR.

vallado [val-lyah'-do], *m.* Inclosure with stakes or palisades, paling, fence, lock.-**Vallada, do**, *pp.* of VALLAR.

vallar [val-lyar'], *va.* To fence, to hedge, to inclose with pales or states.

valle [vah'-lyay], *m.* 1. Vale, dale, valley. 2. The whole number of villages, places, and cottages situated within a district or jurisdiction. **Hasta el valle de Josafat**, unto the valley of Jehoshaphat, or until the day of judgment.

vallejo [val-lyay'-ho], *m. dim.* A small valley.

vallejuelo [val-lyay-hoo-ay'-lo], *m. dim.* of VALLEJO.

vallico [val-lyee'-co], *m. (Bot.)* Raygrass.

valón, na [vah-lone', nah], *a.* Walloon, belonging to southern provinces of Belgium.

valones [vah-lo'-nes], *m. pl.* A sort of pants or wide breeches, formerly worn in Spain.

valor [vah-lor'], *m.* 1. Value, price (precio); equivalency. 2. Validity, forge. 3. Activity, power. 4. Valor (valentía), fortitude, courage, manliness. 5. Income, revenue. 6. Surety, firmness of an act. **Este contrato será entonces sin ningún valor ni efecto**, *(Law.)* this agreement will then be void and null. **Relaciones de valores**, account of rates. **Sin valor**, worthless. **Valor añadido**, mark-up. **Valores en cartera**, investments. **Tuvo el valor de pedírmelo**, he had the nerve to ask me for it.

valoración [vah-lo-rah-the-on'], *f. V.* VALUACIÓN.

valorar [vah-lo-rar'], *v.* To value, to evaluate, to appraise. **Valorar poco**, to attach a little value to.

valoría [vah-lo-ree'-ah], *f.* Value, price, worth.

valorización [vah-lo-rah-the-on'], *f.* Valuation; appraisal.

valorizar [vah-lo-re-thar'], *va. (Mex.) V.* VALORAR.

vals [vahls], *m.* Waltz.

valsar [val-sar'], *vn.* To waltz.

valación [vah-loo-ah-the-on'], *f.* Appraisement, valuation.

valuador, ra [vah-loo-ah-dor', rah], *m. & f.* Valuer, appraiser.

valva [vahl'-vah], *f.* 1. *(Zool.)* Valve, shell of mollusks. 2. *(Bot.)* Valve, a portion of the pericarp of plank.

valuar [vah-loo-ar'], *va.* To rate, to value, to appraise.

valvasor [val-vah-sor'], *m.* Gentleman, nobleman, hidalgo.

válvula [vahl'-voo-lah], *f.* 1. Valve, as in the piston of a pump. 2. An aperture, opening. **Válvula de radio**, radio tube. **Válvula de seguridad**, Safety valve.

valvulado, da [val-voo-lah'-do, dah], *a. (Bot.)* Valvate, provided with a valve.

valvular [val-voo-lar'], *a.* Valvular, having many valves.

valvulilla [val-voo-leel'-lyah], *f. dim.* Valvule.

¡vamos! [vah'-mose], *int. (Coll.)* Well, come! Well, go on! come on!

vampiro [vam-pee'-ro], *m.* 1. Ghoul. 2. Vampire bat. 3. Usurer, miser, skinflint.

vanadiato [vah-nah-de-ah'-to], *m. (Chem.)* Vanadate, a salt of vanadic acid.

vanádico, ca [vah-nah'-de-co, cah], *a.* Vanadic, of or derived from vanadium.

vanadio [vah-nah'-de-o], *m.* Vanadium, a white metal, not ductile, soluble in nitric acid, but resisting sulphuric and hydrochloric acids.

vanagloria [vah-nah-glo'-re-ah], *f.* Vaingloriousness, ostentatiousness, boast.

vanagloriarse [vah-nah-glo-re-ar'-say], *vr.* To be vainglorious, to boast of, to flourish.

vanaglorioso, sa [vah-nah-glo-re-o'-so, sah], *a.* Vainglorious, conceited, ostentatious.

vanamente [vah-nah-men'-tay], *adv.* 1. Vainly, uselessly. 2. Superstitiously. 3. Without foundation. 4. Arrogantly, presumptuously, proudly; frivolously, idly.

vandalismo [van-dah-lees'-mo], *m.* Vandalism.

vándalo, la [vahn'-dah-lo, lah], *m. & f.* Vandal.

vandálico, ca [van-dah'-le-co, cah], *a.* Vandalic.

vandola [van-do'-lah], *f. (Naut.)* Jurymast.

vanear [vah-nay-ar'], *vn.* To talk nonsense.

vanesa [vah-nay'-sah], *f.* Vanessa, a genus of butterflies.

vaneta [vah-nay'-tah], *f. (Her.)* Scallop.

vanguardia [van-goo-ar'-de-ah], *f.* Vanguard, clan. **Estar en la vanguardia del progreso**, to be in the van of progress.

vanguardismo [van-goo-ar-dees'-mo], *m.* Ultramodern manner.

vanidad [vah-ne-dahd'], *f.* 1. Vanity. 2. Ostentation, vain parade. 3. Nonsense, unmeaning speech. 4. Inanity (necedad), levity, conceit; foppishness; flirtation. 5. Illusion, phantom. **Hacer vanidad**, to boast of anything.

vanidoso, sa [vah-ne-do'-so, sah], *a.* Vain, showy, foppish, haughty.

vanilocuencia [vah-ne-lo-coo-en'-the-ah], *f.* Verbosity, pomposity.

vanílocuo, cua [vah-nee'-lo-coo-o, ah], *a.* Talking foolishly.

vaniloquio [vah-ne-lo'-ke-o], *m.* Useless talk.

vanistorio [vah-nis-to'-re-o], *m.* (*Coll.*) Ridiculous or affected vanity.

vano, na [vah'-no, nah], *a.* 1. Vain (inútil), wanting solidity. 2. Inane, empty, fallacious. 3. Useless, frivolous (frívolo). 4. Arrogant, haughty, presumptuous, conceited, foppish. 5. Insubstantial, groundless, futile. **En vano**, in vain, unnecessarily, uselessly, wantonly.

vano [vah'-no], *m.* (*Arch.*) Vacuum in a troll, as the windows, doors, etc.

vapor [vah-pore'], *m.* 1. Vapor, steam, breath. 2. Exhalation, mat. 3. Vertigo, faintness. 4. A steamboat, steamer. *-pl.* Vapors, a hysterical attack. **Vapor de agua**, water vapor. **Echar vapor**, to give off steam.

vaporable [vah-po-rah'-blay], *a.* Vaporous, fumy, exhalable.

vaporación [vah-po-rah-the-on'], *f.* Evaporation.

vaporar, vaporear, vaporizar [vah-po-rar', ray-r', vah-pore-thar'], *va. V.* EVAPORAR

vaporización [vah-po-re-thah-the-on'], *f.* Vaporization.

vaporizador [vah-po-re-thah-dor], *m.* Vaporizer, sprayer.

vaporoso, sa [vah-po-ro'-so, sah], *a.* Vaporous (de vapor), fumy, vaporish.

vapolación [vah-poo-lah-the-on'], *f.* (*Coll.*) Whipping, flogging.

vapulamiento [vah-poo-lah-me-en'-to], *m. V.* VAPULACIÓN.

vapular [vah-poo-lar'], *va.* (*Coll.*) To whip, to flog.

vapuleo [vah-poo-lay'-o], *m.* (*Call.*) Whipping, flogging, beating (paliza).

vaquear [vah-kay-ar'], *f.* To cover cows with the bull.

vaquería [vah-kay-ree'-ah], *f.* 1. Herd or drove of black cattle. 2. A barns for grazing cattle; milk-dairy. 3. (*LAm.*) Cattle farming (cuidado de ganado). 4. (*Carib.*) Hunting with a lasso.

vaqueriles [vah-kay-ree'-les], *m. pl.* Winter pasture for cows

vaquerillo [vah-kay-reel'-lyo], *m. dim.* Boy who attends cows.

vaqueriza [vah-kay-ree'-thah], *f.* Stable for cattle in winter.

vaquerizo, za [vah-kay-ree'-tho, thah], *a.* Relating to cows.

vaquero [vah-kay'-ro], *m.* 1. Cowherd, cowboy, cow-keeper (que cuida ganado). 2. Jacket or loose dress worn by women and children. 3. (*LAm.*) Milkman (lechero). 4. (*And.*) Truant (ausente). **Vaqueros**, jeans (pantalones).

vaquero, ra [vah-kay'-ro, rah], *a.* Belonging to cowherds.

vaqueta [vah-kay'-tah], *f.* Sole-leather, tanned cowhide (cuero).

vaquetear [vah-kay-tay-ar'], *va.* To flog with leather thongs.

vaqueteo [vah-kay-tay'-o], *m.* Flogging with leather thongs.

vaquilla, vaquita [vah-keel'-lyah], *f. dim.* A small cow, a young cow, a heifer.

vara [vah'-rah], *f.* 1. Rod (barra), slender twig. 2. Pole, staff. 3. Verge, a rod, a wand, an emblem of authority: a cross is fixed to its upper end, on which oaths are administered. **Vara de alguacil**, the appointment, commission, or office of a constable. 4. Verge: it is commonly taken for the very jurisdiction of which it is an emblem. 5. Yard-stick, for measuring. 6. Yard, a measure of three feet, 33 British inches, or 8.36 decimeters; a yard of sloth, of this length. 7. Herd of forty or fifty head of swine. 8. Chastisement, rigor. 9. Shaft of a carriage. **Vara alta**, sway, high hand. **Vara de pescar**, fishingrod. **Vara** or **varilla de cortina**, a curtain-rod. **Dar la vara**, to annoy, to pester.

varada [vah-rah'-dah], *f.* (*Naut.*) The act of a vessel running aground or stranding (encalladura).

varadera [vah-rah-day'-rah], *f.* Skid, or skeed.

varadero [vah-rah-day'-ro], *m.* A ship yard; a place for repairing vessels.

varadura [vah-rah-doo'-rah], *f.* The grounding of a vessel.

varal [vah-rahl'], *m.* 1. A long pole or perch (palo). 2. (*Coll.*) A tall, slender person (persona).

varapalo [vah-rah-pah'-lo], *m.* 1. A long pole or perch (palo); switch. 2. Blow with a stick or pore (golpe). 3. (*Coll.*) Grief, trouble, vexation.

varar [vah-rar'], *va.* 1. To run aground. 2. To launch a new-built ship. *-vn.* 1. (*Naut.*) To ground, to be stranded. 2. To be stopped.

varaseto [vah-rah-say'-to], *m.* Treillage a contexture of poles used in gardens.

varazo [vah-rah'-tho], *m.* Stroke with a pole or stick.

varbasco [varh'-bahs'-co], *m. V.* VERBASCO.

varchilla [var-cheel'-lyah], *f.* Measure of grain, which contains the third part of a *fanega*.

vardasca [var-das'-cah], *f.* A thin twin.

vardascazo [var-das-cah'-tho], *m.* Stroke with a stick.

vareador [vah-ray-ah-dor'], *vn.* One who beats down with a pole or staff.

vareaje [vah-ray-ah'-hay], *m.* 1. Retail trade, selling by the yard; measuring by the yard. 2. The act of beating down the fruit of trees.

varear [vah-ray-ar'], *va.* 1. To beat down the fruit of trees with a pole or rod. 2. To cudgel, to beat. 3. To wound bulls or oxen with a goad. 4. To measure or sell by the yard. *-vr.* To grow thin or lean.

varejón [vah-ray-hone'], *m.* A thick pole or staff.

varendaje [vah-ren-dah'-hay], *m.* (*Naut.*) Collection of floor-timbers.

varenga [vah-ren'-gah], *f.* (*Naut.*) Floor-timber.

vareo [vah-ray'-o], *m.* 1. Measurement, measuring. 2. The set of beating down the fruit of trees.

vareta [vah-ray'-tah], *f.* 1. (*Dim.*) A small rod or twig (ramita). 2. Lime twig for catching birds. 3. Stripe in a stuff different in color from the ground. 4. A piquant expression. 5. A circuitous manner of speech (indirecta).

varetazo [vah-ray-tah'-tho], *m.* A stroke with a stick.

varetear [vah-ray-tay-ar'], *va.* To variegate stuffs with stripes of different colors.

varga [var'-gah], *f.* The steepest part of an eminence.

várgano [var'-gah-no], *m.* (*Prov.*) Fence of a rural farm.

variable [vah-re-ah'-blay], *a.* Variable, changeable; fickle.

variablemente [vah-re-ah-blay-men-tay], *adv.* Variably, fast and loose.

variación [vah-re-ah-the-on'], *f.* 1. Variation varying. 2. Change, mutation. **Variación de la aguja**, (*Naut.*) variation of the compass.

variado, da [vah-re-ah'-do, dah], *a.* Variegated, colored. *-pp.* of VARIAR.

variamente [vah-re-ah-men'-tay], *adv.* Variously, differently.

variante [vah-re-ahn'-tay], *pa.* Varying, deviating. *-f.* Difference or discrepancy, deviation. *-m.* (*Esp.*) Pickled vegetables. 2. (*And.*) Path (senda), short cut (atajo).

variar [vah-re-ar'], *va.* To change (cambiar), to alter: to shift; to variegate to diversify. *-vn.* 1. To vary, to differ from. 2. (*Naut.*) To cease a deviation of the magnetic needle. **Variar de opinión**, to change one's mind. **Para variar**, for a change.

várice [vah'-re-thay], *f.* (*Med.*) Varix, a dilated vein.

varicela [vah-re-thay'-lah], *f.* (*Med.*) Varicella, chicken-pox, an eruptive disease.

várices [vah'-re-thays], *f. pl.* Varicose veins.

varicocele [vah-re-co-thay'-lah], *m.* (*Med.*) Varicocele, a swelling formed by dilated veins of the scrotum.

varicoso, sa [vah-re-co'-so, sah], *a.* (*Surg.*) Varicose.

variedad [vah-re-ay-dahd'], *f.* Variety (diversidad), particular distinction; change, variation.

varilarguero [vah-re-lar-gay'-ro], *m.* In bullfighting, the horseman or *picador* armed with a spear to resist the attack of the bull.

varilla [vah-reel'-lyah], *f.* 1. (*Dim.*) A small rod. 2. A curtainrod. 3. Spindle, pivot. 4. Switch. 5. Rib or stick of a fan. **Un abanico con varillas de márfil**, a fan with ivory ribs. 6. (*Mex.*) Cheap fares. 7. (*Carib.*) Nuisance (vaina).

varillaje [vah-ril-layah'-hay], *m.* Collection of ribs of a fan, umbrella, or parasol.

vario, ria [vah'-re-o, ah], *a.* 1. Various, divers, different. 2. Inconstant, variable, unsteady. 3. Vague, undetermined. 4. Variegated (color). **Hay varias posibilidades**, there are several possibilities. -*pl.* Some, several.

vario [vah-ree'-o], *m.* Pink, minnow.

varioloide [vah-re-o-lo'-e-day], *f. (Med.)* Varioloid, modified small-pox.

varioloso, sa [vah-re-o-lo'-so, sah], *a.* Variolous, variolar, relating to small-pox.

variopinto [vah-re-o-pin-to], *a.* Many-colored, colorful; of diverse colors.

variz [vah-reeth'], *m. (Surg.)* V. VÁRICE.

varón [vah-ron'], *m.* 1. Man, a human being of the male sex. 2. A male human being, grown to manhood, which is considered from 30 to 45 years (hombre). 3. Man of respectability. 4. *(Cono Sur, Mex.)* Beams (vigas). **Buen varón**, (1) a wise and learned man. (2) *(Iron.)* A plain, artless being. **Hijo varón**, male child. **Tuvo 4 hijos, todos varones**, she had 4 children, all boys.

varonesa [vah-ro-nay'-sah], *f.* A woman.

varonía [vah-ro-nee'-ah], *f.* Male issue; male descendants.

varonil [vah-ro-neel'], *a.* Male, manly (viril), of the male kind; masculine; vigorous (enérgetico), spirited.

varonilmente [vah-ro-neel'-men-tay], *adv.* Manfully, valiantly, courageously.

varraco [var-rah'-co], *m.* V. VERRACO.

vasallaje [vah-say-lyah'-hay], *m.* 1. Vassalage, dependence, servitude. 2. Liege-money, a tax paid by vassals to their lord. 3. Surrender, yielding to another.

vasallo, lla [vas-sahl'-lyo, lyah], *m. & f.* 1. Vassal, subject; one who acknowledges a superior lord. 2. Feudatory.

vasallo, lla [vas-sahl'-lyo, lyah], *a.* Subject relating to a vassal.

vasar [vah-sar'], *m.* Buffet on which glasses or vessels are put.

vasco, ca [vas'-co, cah], *a.* V. VASCONGADO.

vascongado, da [vas-con-gah'-do, dah], *a. & m. & f.* The native of the provinces of Álava, Guipúzcoa, and Biscay, and the things belonging to them.

vascuence [vahs-coo-en'-thay], *m.* 1. Basque, Biscay dialect, which is considered the primitive language of Spain, called also *Lengua Euscara*, or *Euskera*.

vascular [vas-coo-lar'], *a.* Vascular.

vasculoso, sa [vas-coo-lo'-so, sah], *a.* Vascular, vasculiferous.

vase [vah'-say], *vr.* Third person singular of the present indicative of *Ir*, to go. In plays, *Exit*.

vasectomía [vah-sayc-to-mee'-ah], *f.* Vasectomy.

vaselina [vah-say-lee'-nah], *f.* Vaseline, trademark for petroleum jelly.

vasera [vah-say'-rah], *f.* Buffet, a kind of cupboard.

vásico [vah'-se'-co], *m. dim.* A small glass, cup, or vessel.

vasija [vah-se'-hah], *f.* 1. Vessel in which liquors or foodstuffs are kept; any butt, pipe, or cask. 2. Collection of vessels in a cellar for keeping liquors.

vasillo, ito [vah-seel'-lyo], *m. dim.* A small glass or cup.

vaso [vah'-so], *m.* 1. Vessel in which anything, but particularly liquids, is put; vase. 2. Tumbler, glass, drinking vessel of any kind; the quantity of liquid contained in it. 3. Vessel, any vehicle in which men or goods are carried on the water; and the burden or capacity of a vessel. 4. The capacity (cantidad), room, or extent of a thing. 5. *(Ast.)* Crater, a southern constellation. 6. Horse's hoof. 7. Vessel, vein, or artery. 8. Receptacle, capacity of one vessel to contain another. **Vaso de barro**, the human body; an earthen vessel. **Vaso de agua**, glass of water.

vasos sanguíneos [vah'-sos san-gee'-nay-os], *m. pl.* Blood vessels.

vástago [vahs'-tah-go], *m.* 1. Stem, bud, shoot. 2. *(Met.)* Descendant, the offspring of an ancestor (hijo, descendiente). 3. *(CAm. And. Carib)* Trunk of the banana tree (tronco).

vastamente [vas'-tah-men-tay], *adv.* Vastly, extensively.

vastedad [vas-tay-dahd'], *f.* Vastness, immensity.

vasto, ta [vahs'-to, tah], *a.* Vast, huge, immense.

vate [vah'-tay], *m. (Poet.)* Bard, Druid.

Vaticano [vah-te-cah'-no], *m.* 1. Vatican, a hill of Rome, west of the Tiber, containing the basilica of St. Peter and the Pope's palace. 2. *(Met.)* Papal authority, or the pontifical court.

vaticinador, ra [vah-te-the-nah-dor', rah], *m. & f.* Prophet, diviner.

vaticinar [vah-te-the-nar'], *va.* To divine, to foretell.

vaticinio [vah-te-thee'-ne-o], *m.* Divination, vaticination.

vatídico, ca [vah-tee'-de-co, cah], *a. (Poet.)* Prophetical.

vatio [vah'-te-o], *m.* Watt, an electrical unit of the rate of work, being the rate when the electro-motive force is one volt and the volume of current one ampere; equal to ten ergs per second.

vaya [vah'-yah], *f.* Scoff, jest.-*int.* Go; go to; come! indeed! certainly!

ve [vay], *f.* Name of the letter V.

véase [vay'-ah-say]. See; a direction of reference.

vecera [vay-thay'-rah], *f. (Prov.)* Drove of swine and other animals.

vecería [vay-ther-ree'-ah], *f.* Herd of swine, or animals belonging to a neighborhood.

vecero, ra [vay-thay'-ro, rah], *a. & m. & f.* 1. One who performs alternately, or by turns. 2. Applied to trees which yield fruit one year every two.

vecinal [vay-the-nahl'], *a.* Belonging to the neighborhood.

vecinamente [vay-the-nah-men'-tay], *adv.* Near, contiguously.

vecindad [vay-theen-dahd'], *f.* 1. Population, inhabitants of a place. 2. Vicinity, contiguity, vicinage (vecindad). 3. Right of an inhabitant, acquired by residence in a town for a time determined by law (habitantes). 4. Affinity, similarity, proximity (proximidad). **Hacer mala vecindad**, to be a troublesome neighbor.

vecindario [vay-theen-dahy'-re-o], *m.* 1. Number of inhabitants of a place. 2. Roll or list of the inhabitants of a place. 3. Neighborhood, vicinity; right acquired by residence.

vecino, na [vay-thee'-no, nah], *a.* 1. Neighboring, living in the neighborhood. 2. Neighbor, near to another, adjoining, next, near (cercano). 3. Like, resembling, coincident. **Las dos fincas son vecinas**, the two estates adjoin.

vecino [vay-thee'-no], *m.* 1. Neighbor, inhabitant, housekeeper. 2. Denizen, citizen, freeman. **Un pueblo de 800 vecinos**, a village of 800 inhabitants.

vectación [vec-tah-the-on'], *f.* Action of carrying in a vehicle; passive exercise.

vector [vec-tor'], *m.* 1. *(Aer.)* Vector. 2.*(Geom.)* Radius vector. Vector interrupción, *(Comput.)* interrupt vector.

vectorizar [vec-to-re-thar'], *va.* To vector.

veda [vay'-dah], *f.* Prohibition, interdiction by law.

vedado [vay-dah'-do], *m.* Warren, park, inclosure for game. - **Vedado, da**, *pp.* Of VEDAR.

vedamiento [vay-dah-me-en'-to], *m.* Prohibition.

vedar [vay-dar'], *va.* 1. To prohibit (prohibir), to forbid. 2. To obstruct, to impede (impedir); to suspend or deprive.

vedas [vay'-das], *m. pl.* The Vedas, four sacred books, collections of hymns, the most ancient Sanscrit literature.

vedegambre [vay-day-gahm'-bray], *m. (Bot.)* Hellebore. **Vedegambre** or **verdegambre blanco**, white hellebore or white veratrum.

vedeja [vay-day'-hah], *f. V.* GUEDEJA.

vedijudo, d [vay-day-hoo'-do, dah], *a. (Prov.)* V. VEDIJUDO.

védico, ca [vay'-de-co, cah], *a. (Neol.)* Vedaic, derived from or pertaining to the Vedas.

vedija [vay-dee'-hah], *f.* 1. Entangled lock of wool (lana); flake. 2. Tuft of entangled hair; matted hair (greña).

vedijero, ra [vay-de-hay'-ro, rah], *m. & f.* Collector of loose locks of wool at shearing.

vedijudo, da [vay-de-hoo'-do, dah], **vedijoso, of** [vay-de-ho'-so, sah], *a.* Having entangled or matted hair.

vedijuela [vay-de-hoo-ay'-lah], *f. dim.* Small lock of wool.

veduño [vay-doo'-nyo], *m.* 1. Quality, variety, strain of vines or grapes. 2. *V.* VIDEÑO.

veedor, ra [vay-ay-dor', rah], *m. & f.* 1. Spy, watcher, busybody. 2. Overseer, inspector. 3. Caterer, provider of provisions.

veeduría [vay-ay-doo-ree'-ah], *f.* Place or employment of an overseer or inspector; the inspector's office; controllership.

vega [vay'-gah], *f.* 1. A fertile plain or valley; a tract of level and fruitful ground; a mead or a meadow. 2. *(Cuba)* A tobacco field generally by the bank of a river.

vegetabilidad [vay-hay-tah-be-le-dahd'], *f.* Vegetability.

vegetable [vay-hay-tah'-blay], *a. & m. V.* VEGETAL.

vegetación [vay-hay-tah-the-on'], *f.* Vegetation (plantas), growing or growth of plants.

vegetal [vay-hay-tahl'], *a. & m.* Vegetable, vegetal, plant.

vegetante [vay-hay-tahn'-tay], *pa.* Vegetating.

vegetar [vay-hay-tar'], *vn.* To vegetate, to shoot out.

vegetariano, na [vay-hay-tah-re-ah'-no, nah], *m. & f. & a.* Vegetarian.

vegetativo, va [vay-hay-tah-tee'-vo, vah], *a.* Vegetative.

veguero, ra [vay-gay'-ro, rah], *a.* Belonging to an open plain. *-m.* 1. *(Cuba)* The steward who takes care of a *vega.* 2. A cigar rudely made of a single leaf.

vehemencia [vay-ay-men'-the-ah], *f.* 1. Vehemence, violence, impetuosity. 2. Efficacy, force. 3. Fervor, heat.

vehemente [vay-ay-men'-tay], *a.* Vehement (insistente), impetuous; persuasive, vivid; fervent (partido), fiery; keen.

vehementemente [vay-ay-men-tay-men-tay], *adv.* Vehemently, fervently, forcibly, urgently, hotly.

vehículo [vay-ee'-coo-lo], *m.* 1. Vehicle, carriage, means of transporting. 2. Vehicle, conductor as of sound or of electricity.

vehme (La Santa) [vay'-may], *f.* Name of a kind of German inquisition during the middle ages. Charles V. abolished it.

veigelia [vay-e-hay'-le-ah], *f. (Bot.)* Weigelia, an ornamental plant from China Diervilla, formerly Weigelia roses.

veintavo [vay-in-tah'-vo], *m.* The twentieth part of a thing.

veinte [vay'-in-tay], *a. & m.* 1. Twenty. 2. *V.* VIGÉSIMO. 3. Number or figure 20.

veintena [vay-in-tay'-nah], *f.* 1. A score. 2. The twentieth part.

veintenar [vay-in-tay-nar'], *m. V.* VEINTENA.

veintenario, ria [vay-in-tay-nah'-re-o, ah], *a.* Containing twenty years.

veinteno, na [vay-in-tay'-no, nah], **Veintésimo, ma**, *a. (Ant.)* Twentieth **veinteno**, applied to cloth containing two thousand threads in the warp.

veinteñal [vay-in-tay-nyahl'], *a.* Lasting twenty years.

veinticinco [vay-in-te-theen'-co], *a. & m.* Twenty-five.

veinticuatreno, na [vay-in-te-coo-ah-tray'-no, nah], *a.* Twenty-fourth.

veinticuatría [vay-in-te-coo-ah-tree'-ah], *f.* Aldermanry, the office and dignity of a *veinticuatro* (alderman) in some towns of Andalusia, such as Seville.

veinticuatro [vay-in-te-coo-ah'-tro], *a.* Twenty-four (cardinal). *-m.* 1. Alderman of Seville and other towns of Andalusia, the corporation of which consists of twenty-four members. 2. Twenty-fourmo (24mo), a book or pamphlet containing twenty-four leaves to the sheet. 3. The twenty-fourth (ordinal). 4. The figure 24.

veintidós [vay-in-te-dose'], *a. & m.* Twenty-two.

veintidoseno, na [vay-in-te-do-say'-no, nah], **Veintedoseno, na**, *a.* 1. Applied to cloth the warp of which contains 2,200 threads. 2. Twenty-second.

veintinueve [vay-in-te-noo-ay'-vay], *a. & m.* Twenty-nine.

veintiocheno, na [vay-in-te-o-chay'-no, nah], *a. V.* VEINTEOCHENO.

veintiocheno, na [vay-in-te-o-chay'-no, nah], *a.* Applied to a warp of 2,800 threads.

veintiocho [vey-in-te-o'-cho], *a. & m.* Twenty-eight.

veintiséis [vay-in-te-sa-ees], *a. & m.* Twenty-six.

veintiseiseno, na [vay-in-te-say-e-say'-no, nah], *a.* Twenty-sixth.

veintiseiseno, na [vay-in-te-say-e-say'-no, nah], *a.* Applied to the warp of cloth having 2,600 threads.

veintisiete [vay-in-te-se-ay'-tay], *a. & m.* Twenty-seven.

veintitantos, tas [vayn-te-tahn'-tos, tahs], *a. pl.* Twenty-odd, over twenty.

veintitrés [vay-in-te-trays'], *a. & m.* Twenty-three.

veintiún [vay-in-te-oon'], *a.* Abbrev. of **Veintiuno.** Only before nouns.

veintiuna [vay-in-te-oo'-nah], *f.* The game of twenty-one.

veintiuno, na [vay-in-te-oo'-no, nah], *a. & n.* Twenty-one.

vejación [vay-hah-the-on'], *f.* Vexation, molestation, oppression.

vejador, ra [vay-hah-dor', rah], *m. & f.* Scoffer, molester, teaser.

vejamen [vay-hah'-men], *m.* Taunt, scurrilous criticism.

vejaminista [vay-hah-me-nees'-tah], *m.* Censor, critic.

vejancón, na [vay-han-cone', nah], *a. & n. aug. (Coll.)* Decrepit; peevish from old age.

vejar [vay-har'], *va.* 1. To vex (molestar), to molest, to harass (acosar). 2. To scoff, to censure. 3. To tease.

vejarrón, na [vay-har-rone', nah], *a. & n. aug. (Coll.)* Very old.

vejecito, ta [vay-hay-thee'-to, tah], *a. & m. & f. dim. V.* VIEJECITO.

vejestorio [vay-hes-to'-re-o], *m. (Coll.)* Old trumpery; a petulant old man.

vejazo, za vay-hah'-tho, thah], *a. aug.* Of VIEJO. (Also noun.)

vejeta [vay-hay'-tah], *f.* The crested lark. *V.* COGUJADA.

vejete [vay-hay'-tay], *m. (Coll.)* 1. A ridiculous old man. 2. Actor who impersonates an old man.

vejez [vay-heth'], *f.* 1. Old age. 2. Decay, the state of being worn out. 3. Imbecility and peevishness of old age. 4. A trite story (cuento).

vejezuela [vay-hay-thoo-ay'-lah], *f. dim.* An old hag.

vejezuelo [vay-hay-thoo-ay'-lo], *m. dim.* A little old man.

vejiga [vay-hee'-gah], *f.* 1. Bladder; urinary bladder, gallbladder. 2. Blister; any slight elevation on a plain surface. *-pl.* 1. Pustules of small-box. 2. Wind-galls in horses. **Vejiga natatoria de los peces**, the swimming bladder of a fish.

vejigación [vay-he-gah-the-on'], Vesication, blistering.

vejigatorio, ria [vay-he-gah-to'-re-o, ah], *a.* Blistering, raising blisters. *-m.* A blistering plaster, vesicatory.

vejigazo [vay-he-gah'-tho], *m.* Blow with a bladder full of wind.

vejigón [vay-he-gone'], *m. aug.* Large bladder or blister.

vejigüela, or **vejiguica, illa, ita** [vay-he-goo-ay'-lah, vay-he-gee'-cah], *f. dim.* Small bladder.

vejón, na [vay-hone', nah], *m. & f.* Very old person.

vela [vay'-lah], *f.* 1. Watch, attendance without sleep, vigil (vigilia). 2. Watchfulness (despierto), vigilance. 3. Watchman, night-guard. 4. Pilgrimage. *V.* ROMERÍA. 5. Candle (candela). **Velas de molde**, mould candles. **Velas de cera**, wax candles. **Velas de sebo**, tallow candles. 6. Night-work in offices (trabajo nocturno). 7. Awning. 8. Sail (deporte), ship. 9. Erect ear of a horse or other animal. 10. *(Naut.)* Sail, sheet. 11. Wing or arm of a windmill. 12. Devout waiting by order, hours, or turn before the most sacred sacrament. 13. *(CAm. Carib.)* Wake (velorio). 14. *(Cono Sur)* Nuisance (molestia). 15. *(Carib. Mex.)* Telling off (bronca). **Vela mayor**, main-sail. **Vela de gavia**, main-top sail. **Vela de sobremesana**, mizzen-top-sail. **Vela de juanete mayor**, main-top-gallant-sail. **Vela de juanete de proa**, fore-top-gallant-sail. **Vela de estay**, stay sail. **Velas de proa**, head-sails. **Velas de popa**, after sails. **Velas mayores**, courses. **Vela de cruz**, a square-sail. **Vela de lustrar**, port-sail. **Caída de una vela**, drop or depth of a sail. **Gratil de una vela**, head of a sail. **Vela caza-da**, trimmed sail. **Vela larga** or **desaferrada**, unfurled sail. **Vela cargada arriba** or **sobre las candelizas**, a sail hauled up in the brails. **Vela tendida**, taut or full sail. **Vela que fla-mea**, sail which shivers in the wind. **Vela cuadrada**, square-sail. **Marear una vela**, to set a sail. **Hacerse a la vela**, to set a sail. **En vela**, vigilantly, without sleep. **Alzar velas**, (a) to raise sail, to make ready to sail; (b) *(Met.)* to disappear carrying off one's effects. **Apocar las velas**, to take in sail, to shorten sail.

velacho [vay-lah'-cho], *m. (Naut.)* Foretop-sail.

velación [vay-lah-the-on'], *f.* Watch act of watching. **Velaciones**, nuptial benedictions.

velada [vay-lah'-dah], *f.* 1. Watch. *V.* VELACIÓN. 2. Evening party, evening gathering. **Velada musical**, musicale.

velado [vay-lah'-do], *m. (Coll.)* Husband, married man.

velador, ra [vay-lah-dor', rah], *m. & f.* 1. Watchman (vigilante), night-guard. 2. Careful observer, vigilant keeper, spy. 3. A large wooden candlestick (candelero), used by tradesmen to work at night; table or bench on which a night-light is placed. 4. *(Cono Sur)* Night light (lámpara). 5. *(Mex.)* Lamp-shade (pantalla).

veladura [vay-lah-doo'-rah], *f. (Art.)* A mellow and transparent tint employed to alter the tone of what has been painted.

velaje [vay-lah'-hay], *m. (Naut.)* Sails in general. *V.* VELAMEN.

velamen [vay-lah'-men], *m. (Naut.)* Sails in general; set of sails; trim of sails. **Arreglar el velamen**, *(Naut.)* to trim the sails.

velar [vay-lar'], *vn.* 1. To watch (vigilar), to be watchful, to wake. 2. To watch, to keep guard by night. 3. To watch, to be attentive, to be vigilant. 4. *(Naut.)* To appear above the water, as rocks. 5. To assist by turns before the holy sacrament when it is manifested. *-va.* 1. To guard, to watch, to keep. 2. To throw a piece of white gauze over a married couple, after the nuptial benediction has been given. 3. To observe attentively. 4. *(Poet.)* To cover, to hide. 5. To watch with the sick or deceased at night.

velarte [vay-lar'-tay], *m.* Sort of fine broadcloth.

velatorio [vay-lah-to'-re-o], *m.* Funeral wake.

veleidad [vay-lay-e-dahd'], *f.* 1. Velleity, the lowest degree of desire; feeble will. 2. Levity, inconstancy, fickleness, versatility (cualidad).

veleidoso, sa [vay-lay-e-do'-so, sah], *a.* Fickle, inconstant, feeble-willed, giddy, fast and loose.

velejar [vay-lay-har'], *vn. (Naut.)* To make use of sails.

velería [vay-lay-ree'-ah], *f.* A tallow-chandler's shop.

velero [vay-lay'-ro], *m.* 1. Tallow-chandler. 2. Pilgrim.

velero, ra [vay-lay'-ro, rah], *a.* Swift-sailing (barco).

velesa [vay-lay'-sah], *f. (Bot.)* Lendwort.

veleta [vay-lay'-tah], *f.* 1. Weather cock. 2. The float or cork of a fishing-line (pesca). 3. *(Met.)* A fickle person (persona).

velete [vay-lay'-tay], *m.* A light, thin veil.

velfalla [vel-fahl'-lyah], *f.* A sort of linen.

velicación [vay-le-cah-the-on'], *f. (Med.)* Vellication, stimulation.

velicar [vay-le-car'], *va.* To vellicate, to twitch.

velico, illo, ito [vay-lee'-co, ca, eel'-lyo, ee'-to] *m.* 1. *(Dim.)* A small veil. 2. Embroidered gauze.

velilla, ita [vay-leel'-lyah], *f. dim.* A small candle.

vellecillo [vel-lyay-theel'-lyo], *f. dim.* Very short, soft hair.

vellido, da [vel-lyee'-do, dah], *a.* Downy, villous.

vello [vayl'-lyo], *m.* 1. Down, soft hair on parts of the skin; nap. 2. The downy matter which envelops seeds or fruit, gossamer. 3. Short, downy hair of brutes.

vellón [vel-lyone'], *m.* 1. Fleece, wool of one sheep; lock of wool (lana). 2. Old copper coin.

vellonero [vel-lyo-nay'-ro], *m.* Collector of fleeces at shearing.

vellora [vel-lyo'-rah], *f. (Prov.)* Knot taken from woollen cloth.

vellorita [vel-lyo-ree'-tah], *f. (Bot.)* Cowslip.

vellosa [vel-lyo'-sah], *f. (Prov.)* Coarse cloth or rug worn by mariners.

vellosidad [veyl-lyo-se-dahd'], *f.* Downiness, hirsuteness.

vellosilla [vel-lyo-seel'-lyah], *f. (Bot.)* Creeping mouse-ear, mouse ear hawk-weed.

velloso, sa [vel-lyo'-so, sah], *m.* Downy, hairy, cottony.

velludillo [vel-lyoo-deel'-lyo], *m.* Velveteen.

velludo, da [vel-lyoo'-do, dah], *a.* Downy, hairy, shaggy, woolly.

velludo [vel-lyoo'-do], *m.* Shag, velvet.

vellutero [vel-lyoo-tay'-ro], *m. (Prov.)* Velvet worker.

velo [vay'-lo], *m.* 1. Veil, curtain. 2. Veil, a part of female dress. 3. Veil, a part of the dress of nuns. 4. Piece of white gauze thrown over a couple at marriage. 5. Feast at the profession of a nun or at taking the veil. 6. Veil, cover, disguise. 7. Pretence, pretext (pretexto), cover, mask. 8. Confusion, obscurity, perplexity, of the sight or intellect (falta de claridad). **Correr el velo**, to pull off the mask; to disclose something before unknown. **Tomar el velo**, to become a nun.

velocidad [vay-lo-the-dahd'], *f.* Speed, velocity, rapidity. **Velocidad aérea**, air speed. **Velocidad de crucero**, cruising speed. **A toda velocidad**, at full speed. **Disminuir velocidad**, to slow down.

velocímetro [vay-lo-thee'-may-tro], *m.* Speedometer.

velocípedo [vay-lo-thee'-pay-do], *m.* Velocipede; bicycle or tricycle.

velódromo [vay-lo'-dro-mo], *m.* Velodrome.

velón [vay-lone'], *m.* 1. Lamp in which oil is burnt (lámpara). 2. *(And. Cono Sur, Mex.)* Thick tallow candle. 3. *(CAm.)* Sponger (parásito). 4. *(And. Carib.)* Person who casts covetous glances.

velonera [vay-lo-nay'-rah], *f.* Wooden lamp-stand or bracket.

velonero [vay-lo-nay'-ro], *m.* Lamp-maker.

veloz [vay-loth'], *a.* Swift, nimble, active, fleet.

velozmente [vay-loth-men-tay], *adv.* Swiftly, fleetly, nimbly.

vena [vay'-nah], *f.* 1. Vein, a blood vessel. 2. Fiber of plants. 3. Hollow, cavity. 4. Vein of metal in a mine. 5. Tendency of mind or genius (talento). **Vena poética**, a poetical vein. 6. Diverse quality or color of earth or stones. 7. Vein or stripe in stones; mineral water found under ground. **Coger** or **hallar a alguno de vena**, to find one in a favorable disposition.

venablo [vay-nah'-blo], *m.* Javelin, formerly used in hunting wild boars. **Echar venablos**, to break out into violent expressions of anger.

venadero [vay-nah-day'-ro], *m.* Place much frequented by deer.

venadico, illo, ito [vay-nah-dee'-co], *m.* A small deer.

venado [vay-nah'-do], *m.* 1. Deer, venison. **Pintar venados**, *(Coll.)* to play hooky. 2. *(Carib.)* Deerskin (piel). 3. *(Carib.)* Whore (puta). 4. *(And.)* Contraband (contrabanda).

venaje [vay-nah'-hay], *m.* Current of a stream.

venal [vay-nahl'], *a.* 1. Venal, relating to the veins. 2. Marketable, salable. 3. Venal, mercenary.

venalidad [vay-nah-le-dahd'], *f.* Venality, mercenariness.

venalogía [vay-nah-lo-hee'-ah], *f.* Treatise on the veins.

venate [vay-nah'-tay], *m.* A small bird.

venático, ca [vay-nah'-te-co, cah], *a.* Rather crazy, a bit mad.

vanatorio, ria [vay-nah-to'-re-o, ah], *a.* Venatic, used in hunting.

vencedor, ra [ven-thay-dor', rah], *m. & f.* Conqueror, victor.

vencejo [ven-thay'-ho], *m.* 1. String, band. 2. *(Orn.)* Swift, black-martin, martlet, martinet.

vencer [ven-therr'], *va.* 1. To conquer, to subdue, to defeat (derrota), to vanquish, to overpower, to master, to foil. 2. To conquer, to surpass, to excel. 3. To surmount, to overcome (dificultad, obstáculo), to clear. 4. To gain a lawsuit. 5. To bend, to turn down. 6. To prevail upon, to persuade. 7. To suffer, to tolerate or bear with patience. 8. To incline, to twist a thing. *-vn.* 1. To fall due. 2. To conquer, to gain, to succeed. *-vr.* To govern one's passions or desires. **Por fin le venció el sueño**, finally sleep overcame him. **Se venció el plazo**, the time's up.

vencible [ven-thee'-blay], *a.* Vincible, conquerable; superable.

vencida [ven-thee'-dah], *f.* Action of conquering or being conquered.

vencido, da [ven-thee'-do, dah], *a. & pp.* Of VENCER. 1. Conquered, subdued. 2. Due; payable. **Darse por vencido**, to give up. **Con los intereses vencidos**, with the interest which is due. 3. *(LAm.)* Out of date (billete, permiso).

vencimiento [ven-the-me-en'-to], *m.* 1. Victory, conquest. 2. Bent, the act of bending or turning down. 3. **Vencimiento de plazo**, *(Com.)* maturity of a bill of exchange, period of falling due. **Al vencimiento del plazo**, at the expiration of the time that a bill comes due.

venda [ven'-dah], *f.* 1. Bandage, roller. 2. *(Ant.)* Fillet, a band tied round the head or other part; a diadem.

vendaje [ven-dah'-hay], *m.* 1. Commission or the sale of goods by a factor or agent. 2. Ligature with a fillet, bandage, or roller.

vendar [ven-dar'], *va.* 1. To tie with a band, inlet, bandage, or roller; to filet. 2. To hoodwink, to darken the understanding. **Vendar los ojos**, to hoodwink.

vendaval [ven-dah-vahl'], *m.* A strong wind south by west.

vendavalada [ven-dah-vah-lah'-dah], *f.* A storm of southerly wind.

vendedor, ra [ven-day-dor', rah], *m. & f.* Seller, trader, retailer, huckster, vender.

vendehúmos [ven-day-oo'-mos], *m.* A person who claims intimacy with people in power in order to sell favors.

vendeja [ven-day'-hah], *f.* 1. A public sale (venta). 2. Collection of goods offered for sale (géneros).

vender [ven-derr'], *va.* 1. To sell, to vend. 2. To expose for sale. 3. To soil, to betray for money, to prostitute, to devote to crimes for a reward. 4. To render dear or difficult. 5. To persuade, to delude with false pretences. 6. *(Met.)* To betray faith, confidence, or friendship. **Vender salud.** *(Coll.)* to be or appear very robust. **Vender por mayor**, to sell in the lump, or by wholesale. **Vender al por menor** or **a destajo**, to sell at retail. -*vr.* 1. To boast of talents or merits one does not possess. 2. To devote oneself to the service of another. **Venderse caro**, to be of difficult access. **Venderse barato**, to make oneself cheap. **Vender cara la vida**, to fight desperately. **Vender al contado**, to sell for cash. **Vender a plazo**, to sell on credit. **Vender gato por liebre**, to sell a cat for a hare (to deceive in the quality of things sold).

vendible [ven-dee'-blay], *a.* Salable, marketable.

vendica, illa, ita [ven-dee'-cah], *f. dim.* Small fillet or bandage; a small diadem.

vendición [ven-de-the-on'], *f.* Sale, selling, rendition.

vendido, da [ven-dee'-do, dah], *a. & pp.* of VENDER. Sold. **Estar vendido**, to be duped, to be exposed to great risks.

vendimia [ven-dee'-me-ah], *f.* 1. Vintage. 2. Large gain or profit. **La vendimia de 1998**, the 1998 vintage.

vendimiado, da [ven-de-me-ah'-do, dah], *a. & pp.* of VENDIMIAR. Gathered vintage.

vendimiador, ra [ven-de-me-ah-dor', rah], *m. & f.* Vintager.

vendimiar [ven-de-me-ar'], *va.* 1. To gather the vintage. 2. To enjoy unlawful perquisites; to reap benefits or profit unjustly. 3. *(Coll.)* To kill, to murder (matar).

venduta [ven-doo-tah], *f.* 1. *(Amer.)* Auction (subasta), vendue. 2. *(Carib.)* Greengrocer's shop (frutería). 3. *(Carib.)* Swindle (estafa).

vendutero [ven-doo-tay'-ro], *m.* 1. Auctioneer. 2. *(Carib.)* Greengrocer.

veneciano, no [vay-nay-the-ah'-no, nah], *a.* Venetian, relating to Venice.

veneficiar [vay-nay-fe-the-ar'], *va.* To bewitch, to injure by witchcraft.

venencia [vay-nen'-the-ah], *f.* A small vessel, like a piece of reed, at the end of a long rod, which is used in Xerez for testing wines.

venenífero, ra [vay-nay-nee'-fay-ro, rah], *a. (Poet.)* V. VENENOSO.

veneno [vay-nay'-no], *m.* 1. Poison, venom, anything injurious to health: venenation. 2. Poisonous mineral, ingredients in paints or dye-stuffs. 3. Wrath, fury, passion. 4. Bad, insipid taste. 5. *(Met.)* Poison, something pernicious to morals and religion.

venenosamente [vay-nay-no-sah-men'-tay], *adv.* Venomously.

venenosidad [vay-nay-no-se-dahd'], *f.* Poisonousness, venomousness.

venenoso, sa [vay-nay-no'-so, sah], *a.* Venomous, poisonous.

venera [vay-nay'-rah], *f.* 1. Porcelain shell, or Mediterranean scallop, worn by pilgrims who return from St. Jago or Santiago in Galicia. 2. Badge, jewel, or star worn by the knights of military orders. 3. Vein of metal in a mine; spring of water.

venerable [vay-nay-rah'-blay], *a.* 1. Venerable. 2. Epithet of respect to ancient ecclesiastics and prelates.

venerablemente [vay-nay-rah-blay-men-tay], *adv.* Venerably; with respect or veneration.

veneración [vay-nay-rah-the-on'], *f.* 1. Veneration. 2. Worship; honor.

venerador, ra [vay-nay-rah-dor', rah], *m. & f.* Venerator, worshipper.

venerando, da [vay-nay-rahn'-do, dah], *a.* Venerable.

venerante [vay-nay-rahn'-tay], *va.* Venerating, worshipping.

venerar [vay-nay-rar'], *va.* To venerate, to respect, to worship, to honor.

venéreo, rea [vay-nay'-ray-o, ah], *a.* Venereal, sensual.

venero [vay-nay'-ro], *m.* 1. A vein of metal in a mine. 2. A spring of water. 3. Radius or horary line of sun-dials 4. Origin, root, source.

veneruela [vay-ne-roo-ay'-lah], *f.* 1. A small porcelain shell. 2. Dim of VENERA.

venezolana [vay-nay-tho-lah'-no, nah], *a.* Venezuelan, of Venezuela.

vengable [ven-gah'-blay], *a.* Worthy of revenge, that may be revenged.

vengador, ra [ven-gah-dor', rah], *m. & f.* Avenger, revenger.

vengancilla [ven-gan-theel'-lyah], *f. dim.* A slight revenge.

venganza [ven-gahn'-thah], *f.* Revenge, vengeance. **Tomar venganza de uno**, to take vengeance on somebody.

vengar [ven-gar'], *va.* To revenge, avenge. -*vr.* To be revenged.

vengativamente [ven-gah-tee'-vah-men-tay], *adv.* Revengefully.

vengativo, va [ven-gah-tee'-vo, vah], *a.* Revengeful, vindictive (espíritu, persona).

venia [vay'-ne-ah], *f.* 1. Pardon (perdón), forgiveness. 2. Leave, permission (permiso). 3. Royal license to minors to manage their own estates. 4. Bow with the head.

venial [vay-ne-ahl'], *a.* Venial, pardonable; excusable.

venialidad [vay-ne-ah-le-dahd'], *f.* Veniality.

venialmente [vay-ne-al-men'-tay], *adv.* Venially.

venida [vay-nee'-dah], *f.* 1. Arrival (llegada); return (vuelta), regress, coming. 2. Overflow of a river. 3. Attack in fencing. 4. Impetuosity, rashness.

venidero, ra [vay-ne-day'-ro, rah], *a.* Future, coming. **En lo venidero**, henceforth. -*pl.* Posterity, successors.

venido, da [vay-nee'-do, dah], *a. & pp.* of VENIR. Come, arrived. **Venido del cielo**, come from heaven: expressing the excellence of a thing. **Bienvenido** or **bienvenida**, welcome.

venimécum [vay-ne-may'-coom], *m.* Vademecum.

venir [vay-neer'], *vn.* 1. To come, to draw near, to advance towards. 2. To come, to move towards another. **Ven acá**, *(Coll.)* come hither: used to call the attention and to advise anyone. 3. To come, to happen (suceder), to come to pass. 4. To follow, to succeed. 5. To come, to proceed from, to originate in, to be occasioned by; to be inferred, to be deduced. 6. To appear before a judge; to come into court. 7. To assent, to submit, to yield. 8. To answer, to fit, to suit. **Esta chaqueta no me viene**, that jacket does not fit me. 9. To grow, to shoot up. 10. To make an application, to ask. 11. To occur, to be presented in the memory or attention. 12. To resolve, to determine. 13. To attack, to assault. 14. *(Arith.)* To result. 15. To be of one's party or opinion; to accompany. 16. To fall, to be overset. 17. Used impersonally, come here take this. 18. To succeed finally. **Vino a conseguir la plaza**, he obtained the place. **Venir a cuentas**, to calculate, to count. 19. To change the state or quality. 20. To be transferred; to pass from one to another. 21. To adduce; to produce. 22. To excite, to effect; to attain a degree of excellence or perfection. 23. Used to express politely satisfaction or pleasure at the arrival of anyone; to welcome. **Venir de perilla**, to come in the nick of time; to fit or to answer perfectly well. **Cosas que van y vienen**, things which wax and wane. **No hay mal que por bien no venga**, *(Prov.)* there is no evil which may not be turned to good. **¿A qué viene eso?** to what purpose is that? What does it amount to? **Él se mete en lo que no le va, ni le viene**, he meddles in business that does not concern him. **Venirle a la mano alguna cosa**, to get something without exertion. **Venir muy ancho**, to be in abundance; to be beyond the desert of the receiver. **Venir rodado**, to attain an object accidentally. **Venir a las manos**, to come to blows. **No me vengas con historias**, don't come telling tales to me. **Se puede ver venir la noche**, one can face the evening ahead. **Viene de**, to come from. **Viene a llenar un gran vacío**, it serves to fill a large gap. **El tapón viene justo a la botella**, the stopper fits the bottle exactly. **Venían andando desde mediodía**, they had been walking since midday. *-vr.* To ferment (vino), to attain perfection by fermentation, as bread or wine. It is often used the same as the neuter verb *venir*. **Venirse a buenas**, to yield, to submit, to comply with things required or enforced. **Venirse a casa**, to come home. **Venirse durmiendo**, to be falling asleep. **Venirse abajo**, to fall, to collapse. **Venirse a los ojos**, to show in one's eyes; to betray by one's glances. **Venirse al suelo**, to fall to the ground. **Venirse a la boca**, to taste unpleasantly. **Venirse el cielo abajo**, to rain very heavily. **Como se viene, se va**, easy come, easy go. *(Yo vengo, yo venga, from Venir. V. VENIR.)*

venora [vay-no'-rah], *f. (Prov.)* Range of stones or bricks in a drain or trench.

venoso, sa [vay-no'-so, sah], *a.* 1. Venous, belonging to veins. 2. Veiny, veined, full of veins.

venta [ven'-tah], *f.* 1. Sale, act of selling, market; custom. **Venta confidencial**, a trust sale. 2. A poor inn on roads far from towns or villages (posada). **Estar de venta** or **estar en venta**, to be on sale. *(Coll.)* Applied to a woman who stands much at a window, to see and be seen. 3. *(Met.)* Open place exposed to the weather. 4. *(Carib. Mex.)* Small shop, stall.

ventada [ven-tah'-dah], *f.* A gust of wind.

ventaja [ven-tah'-hah], *f.* 1. Advantage, preference; grain, good; commodity, commodiousness; hand; additional pay. 2. Odds given in a game. **Es un plan que tiene muchas ventajas**, it is a plan that has many advantages. **Dejar buena ventaja**, to bring in a good profit.

ventajosamente, *adv.* Advantageously, gainfully.

ventajoso, sa [ven-tah-ho'-so, sah], *a.* Advantageous, comparatively superior; profitable, lucrative, fruitful, good.

ventalla [ven-tahl'-lyah], *f.* Valve. V. VÁLVULA.

ventalle [ven-tahl'-lya], *m.* Fan. V. ABANICO.

ventana [ven-tah'-nah], *f.* 1. Window. 2. Window-shutter. 3. Nostril. 4. Either of the senses of seeing or hearing. 5. *(And.)* Forest clearing (claro de bosque). **Ventana de guillotina**, sash window. **Tirar algo por la ventana**, to throw something out of the window.

ventanaje [ven-tah-nah'-hay], *m.* Number or series of windows in a building.

ventanazo [ven-tah-nah'-tho], *m.* Slap of a window.

ventanear [ven-tah-nay-ar'], *vn.* To frequent the window, to gaze repeatedly from the window.

ventanera [ven-tah-nay'-rah], *a.* Window-gazer: applied to women who are constantly at the window.

ventanero [ven-tah-nay'-ro], *m.* Window-maker.

ventanica, illa [ven-tah-nee'-cah], *f. dim.* 1. A small window. 2. Window (de sobre, taquilla).

ventanico, illo [ven-tah-nee'-co, neel'-lyo], *m. dim.* A small window-shutter.

ventar [ven-tar'], *va. & vn.* V. VENTEAR.

ventarrón [ven-tar-rone'], *m.* Violent wind.

venteadura [ven-tay-ah-doo'-rah], *f.* Split made in timber by the wind.

ventear [ven-tay-ar'], *vn. & a.* 1. To blow. **Ventea muy fresco del N. O.**, it blows very fresh from the N. W. 2. To smell, to scent. 3. To investigate, to examine. 4. To dry, to expose to the air. 5. *(CAm. Mex.)* To brand (animal). 6. *(Cono Sur)* To get far ahead of (adversario). 7. *(And. Carib.)* To fan (abanicar). *-vr.* 1. To be filled with wind or air. 2. To break wind. 3. *(And. Carib. Cono Sur)* To be outdoors a great deal (estar mucho afuera). 4. *(And. Carib.)* To get conceited (engreírse).

venteo [ven-tay'-o], *m.* Vent-hole in a cask.

venteril [ven-tay-reel'], *a.* Suited to a poor inn.

ventero, ra [ven-tay'-ro, rah], *m. & f.* Keeper of a small inn on roads.

ventilación [ven-te-lah-the-on'], *f.* Ventilation; discussion.

ventilado [ven-te-lah'-do], *a.* Draughty, breezy.

ventilador [ven-te-lah-dor'], *m.* Ventilator.

ventilar [ven-te-lar'], *va.* 1. To ventilate (cuarto); to winnow, to fan. 2. To examine, to discuss. 3. To air (asunto). 4. *(Fig.)* To make public (asunto privado). *-vr.* To move with a current of air (cuarto), to circulate (aire).

ventilla [ven-teel'-lyah], *f.* Pallet, valve-pallet of an organ.

ventisca [ven-tees'-cah], *f.* Storm, attended with a heavy fall of snow.

ventiscar [ven-tis-car'], *vn.* To blow hard, attended with snow, to drift, to be drifted by the wind, as snow.

ventisco [ven-tees'-co], *m.* V. VENTISCA.

ventiscoso, sa [ven-tis-co'-so, sah], *a.* Windy, stormy, tempestuous.

ventisquear [ven-tis-kay-ar'], *v. imp.* To snow hard.

ventisquero [ven-tis-kay'-ro], *m.* 1. Snow-drift (montón); glacier. 2. Mountain height most exposed to snow-storms. 3. Snow-storm (tormenta).

ventola [ven-to'-lah], *f. (Naut.)* Tophamper, resistance of the upper works to the wind.

ventolera [ven-to-lay'-rah], *f.* 1. Gust, a sudden blast of wind (ráfaga). 2. Vanity (vanidad); pride, loftiness; fancy. 3. V. REHILANDERA. 4. Whim (capricho), unexpected and extravagant thought or resolution. 5. *(Mex.)* Fart (pedo).

ventolina [ven-to-lee'-nah], *f. (Naut.)* Light, variable wind; cats-paw.

ventor [ven-tor'], *m.* Pointer, pointerdog; fox-hound.

ventorrillo, ventorro [ven-tor-reel'-lyo, ven-tor'-ro], *m.* A petty inn or tavern near a town.

ventosa [ven-to'-sah], *f.* 1. *(Med.)* Cupping-glass. 2. Vent (agujero), air-hole, spiracle. 3. *(Zool.)* Sucker, a muscular organ of certain aquatic creatures for sucking, catching prey, or clinging to rocks. **Pegar una ventosa**, to swindle one out of his money.

ventosear, ventosearse [ven-to-say-ar', ar'-say], *vn. & vr.* To break wind.

ventosero, ra [ven-to-say'-ro, rah], *a.* Fond of cupping.

ventosidad [ven-to-se-dahd'], *f.* Flatulency, windiness.

ventoso, sa [ven-to'-so, sah], *a.* 1. Windy; flatulent. 2. Pointing. 3. Vain, inflated. 4. Windy, tempestuous.

ventral [ven-trahl'], *a.* Ventral: applied to anything used to encircle the belly.

ventrecha [ven-tray'-chah], *f.* Belly of fishes.

ventregada [ven-tray-gah'-dah], *f.* 1. Brood, litter. 2. Abundance.

ventrera [ven-tray'-rah], *f.* Roller or girdle for the belly; sash, cummerbund.

ventricular [ven-tre-coo-lar'], *a.* Ventricular; belonging to the ventricles of the heart.

ventrículo [ven-tree'-coo-lo], *m.* 1. Ventricle, the stomach. 2. Any of the cavities of the heart or brain.

ventril [ven-treel'], *m.* 1. A piece of wood which serves to counterpoise the movement of the beam in oil-mills. 2. Bellyband of a harness.

ventrílocuo [ven-tree'-lo-coo-o], *m.* Ventriloquist.

ventriloquia [ven-tre-lo'-ke-ah], *f.* Ventriloquism, the art or practice of the ventriloquist.

ventrón [ven-trone'], *m. aug.* of VIENTRE.

ventrosidad [ven-tro-se-dahd'], *f. (Med.)* Excessive development of the belly; ventrosity.

ventroso, sa. [ven-tro'-so, sah], **ventrudo, da** [ven-troo'-do, dah], *a.* Big-bellied.

ventura [ven-too'-rah], *f.* 1. Luck (suerte), fortune. 2. Contingency, casualty, hazard, hap, venture. **Buena ventura**, good fortune told by gipsies and vagrants. **Probar ventura**, to try one's fortune, to venture at, on, or upon. 3. Risk, danger. **A ventura** or **a la ventura**, at a venture, at hazard. **Ir a la aventura**, to live in a disorganized way.

venturero, ra [ven-too-ray'-ro, rah], *a.* 1. Casual, incidental. 2. Lucky, fortunate. 3. Vagrant, idle, adventurous.

venturero [ven-too-ray'-ro], *m.* Fortune-hunter, adventurer, land-loper.

venturilla [ven-too-reel'-lyah], *f.* Good luck.

venturina [ven-too-ree'-nah], *f.* Goldstone, a precious stone of a brown color spotted with gold.

venturo, ra [ven-too'-ro, rah], *a.* Future; that which is to come.

venturón [ven-too-rone'], *m. aug.* Great luck.

venturosamente [ven-too-ro-sah-men-tay], *adv.* Luckily, fortunately.

venturoso, sa [ven-too-ro'-so, sah], *a.* Lucky (afortunado), fortunate, successful, happy, prosperous.

venus [vay'-noos], *f.* 1. Venus, the goddess of beauty and love. 2. A beautiful woman. 3. Venery, sensual pleasure. 4. *(Chem.)* Copper. -*m. (Acad.)* Venus; Hesper; the evening star, the planet nearest the earth.

venusio [vay-noo'-se-o], *m.* Copper in the highest grade of perfection, inalterable in the free air, and hence highly useful in the industrial arts.

venustidad [vay-noos-te-dahd'], *f.* Beauty, gracefulness.

venusto, ta [vay-noos'-to, tah], *a.* Beautiful, graceful.

venza [ven'-thah], *f.* Scarf-skin, used by gold-beaters.

ver [verr], *va.* 1. To see, to look into (indagar). 2. To see, to observe, to consider, to reflect. 3. To see, to visit. 4. To foresee, to forecast. 5. To fancy, to imagine; to judge. 6. To see, to find out, to discover; to explore. 7. To be present at the report of a lawsuit. 8. To experience. 9. To examine. 10. To see at a future time. 11. Used with the particle *ya*, it is generally a voice; as, **ya verá**, he shall see. **Ver venir**, to see what one is driving at; to await the resolution or determination of another person. **Es de ver, es para ver**, or **es digno de ser visto**, it is worth notice, it is worthy of being observed. **Estar de ver**, to be worth seeing. **Estar por ver**, to be yet to come to pass; to be doubtful. **No poder ver a alguno**, to abhor or detest one, not to suffer or endure him. **Al ver**, on seeing a thing. **¿A ver?** is it not so? let us see (for «vamos a ver»). **A ver** or **veamoslo**, let us see it. **A más ver** or **hasta más ver**, *(Coll.)* farewell, until we meet again. **Hacer ver**, to show or to make appear. **Si te vi (ya) no me acuerdo**, out of sight, out of mind. **Ver tierras** or **mundo**, to travel. **Tener que ver una persona con otra**, to have relation or connection; to have carnal communication. **Eso nada tiene que ver con esto**, that has nothing to do with this. **Ojos que no ven, corazón que no siente**, *(Prov.)* out of sight, out of mind. **Ver las orejas del lobo**, to see the ears of the wolf, to be in great danger. **Ver visiones**, to build castles in the air. **Ver el cielo abierto**, to see a great opportunity. -*vr.* To be seen; to be in a place proper to be seen; to be conspicuous. 2. To find oneself in a state or situation. **Verse pobre**, to be reduced to poverty. **Verse negro**, to be in great want or affliction; to be greatly embarrassed. 3. To be obvious or evident. 4. To concur, to agree. 5. To represent the image or likeness, to see oneself in a glass. 6. To know the cards, at play. **Ver si**, to try to, to attempt. **Verse en ello**, to consider, to weigh in the mind. **Ya**

se ve, (a) it is undeniable; it is evident; it is as you say, it is easily to be seen certainly, to be sure. (b) *(Iron.)* Likely, indeed, that such a thing should happen. **Verse** or **irse viendo**, to discover, to view what should be concealed. **Verse y desearse**, to have very great care, anxiety, and fatigue in executing a thing. **No tes verás en ese espejo**, you will not succeed. **Verse las caras** (lit. to see each other face to face), there'll be the mischief to pay. **Hacer ver a uno las estrellas**, to make one feel a quick, lively pain; to make him see stars. *(Yo veo, yo vi, yo vea. V.* VER.)

ver [verr], *m.* 1. Sense of sight, seeing. 2. Light, view, aspect, appearance.

vera [vay'-rah], *f.* 1. *(Prov.)* Edge, border. V. ORILLA. 2. An American tree of very hard wood. **A la vera del camino**, beside the road.

veracidad [vay-rah-the-dahd'], *f.* Veracity, fidelity.

veranada [vay-rah-nah'-dah], *f.* Summer season.

veranadero [vay-rah-nah-day'-ro], *m.* Place where cattle pasture in summer.

veranal [vay-rah-nahl'], *a.* Summer, relating to summer.

veranar, veranear [vay-rah-nar', vay rah-nay-ar'], *vn.* To spend or pass the summer. **Veranean en Miami**, they go to Miami for the summer.

veraneante [vay-rah-nay-ahn'-tay], *m & f.* Holidaymaker, vacationer.

veraneo [vay-rah-nay'-o], *m.* 1. The act of passing the summer, or part of it, in some particular way or place. 2. *V.* VERANERO. **Lugar de veraneo**, summer resort. **Estar de veraneo**, to be away on one's summer holiday.

veranero [vay-rah-nay'-ro], *m.* Place where cattle graze in summer.

veranico, illo, ito [vay-rah-nee'-co], *m. dim.* of VERANO.

veraniego, ga [vay-rah-ne-ay'-go, gah], *a.* 1. Relating to the summer season. 2. Thin or sickly in summer. 3. Imperfect, defective.

verano [vay-rah'-no], *m.* 1. Summer, summer season. 2. In Ecuador, the dry season (época seca).

veras [vay'-ras], *f. pl.* 1. Reality, truth (verdad). 2. Earnestness, fervor, and activity with which things are done or desired. **De veras**, in truth, really; joking apart. **Lo siento de veras**, I am truly sorry. **Ahora va de veras que lo hago**, now I really am going to do it.

veratrina [vay-ra-tree'-nah], *f.* Veratrine, alkaloid of hellebore.

veratro [vay-rah-tro], *m. V.* ELÉBORO.

veraz [vay-rath'], *a.* Veracious.

verbal [ver-bahl'], *a.* Verbal; oral; nuncupative. **Copia verbal**, a literal copy.

verbalmente [ver-bahl-men-tay], *adv.* Verbally, orally.

verbasco [ver-bahs'-co], *m. (Bot.)* Great mullein.

verbásculo [ver-bahs'-coo-lo], *m. (Bot.)* Mullein.

verbena [ver-bay'-nah], *f.* 1. *(Bot.)* Vervain, verbena. 2. In Madrid, the evening given to diversions, before some celebrated saint's day (de santo).

verbenáceas [ver-bay-nah'-thay-as], *f. pl.* The verbena or vervain family of plants.

verberación [ver-bay-rah-the-on'], *f.* Verberation; the act of the wind or water striking against something.

verberar [ver-bay-rar'], *va.* To verberate, to bed, to strike; to dart against (viento, agua).

verbigracia [ver-be-grah'-the-h], *adv.* For example, for instance: in abbreviation. *v. g.* or *v. gr.*, corresponding to *e. g.* in English.

verbo [verr'-bo], *m. (Gram.)* Verb. 2. Word, second person of the holy Trinity. **Verbos**, swearing, angry expressions; abusive language. **Verbo activo o transitivo**, transitive or active verb. **Verbo neutro o intransitivo**, intransitive or neuter verb. **Verbo substantivo**, the verb *ser*, as indicating essence or substance. **Verbo unipersonal o impersonal**, an impersonal verb, one used only in the third person.

verbosidad [ver-bo-se-dahd'], *f.* Verbosity, wordiness.

verboso, sa [ver-bo'-so, sah], *a.* Verbose, prolix.

verdacho [ver-dah'-cho], *m.* A kind of gritty green earth, used by painters.

verdad [ver-dahd'], *f.* 1. Truth, veracity, reality. 2. Truth, verity, clear expression; certain existence of things. 3. A sort of delicate paste. 4. Axiom, maxim, truism. 5. Virtue of veracity or truth. **Verdad es que** or **es verdad que**, it is true that. **Tratar de verdad**, to love truth. **A la verdad** or **de verdad**, truly, in fact, in truth. **Es verdad**, it is true. **Decir cuatro verdades a uno**, to tell somebody a few home truths. **Faltar a la verdad**, to lie. **En verdad**, *V.* VERDADERAMENTE.

verdaderamente [ver-dah-day-rah-men-tay], *adv.* Truly, in fact, verily, indeed, legitimately.

verdadero, ra [ver-dah-day'-ro, rah], *a.* True, real, sincere, ingenuous, good, veritable; truthful.

verdal [ver-dahl'], *a.* 1. **Ciruela verdal**, green gage, a plum. 2. *(Calif.)* **Una verdal, o verdeja**, an early white grape of sweet flavor.

verdasca [ver-dahs'-cah], *f. V.* VARDASCA.

verde [verr'-day], *m.* 1. Green, verdure. 2. Verdigris. 3. Youth. 4. Person in the bloom of age. 5. Green barley or grass, given to horses or mules as a purge (hierba). **Verde limón**, bright green. **Verde botella**, bottle green. **Verde pardo**, brown green. 6. *(And.)* Plantain. 7. *(Carib. Mex.)* Country (campo). 8. *(Carib.)* Policeman (policía). **Sentarse en el verde**, to sit on the grass. *-a.* 1. Green, of the color of plants. 2. Unripe (fruta), immature, not perfectly fresh (legumbres). 3. Young, blooming verdant. **Viejo verde**, a dirty old man. 4. Loose, immodest, smutty, savoring of obscenity. 5. **Poner verde a uno**, to give somebody a dressing-down (regañar.)

verdea [ver-day'-ah], *f.* A sort of Florence white wine.

verdear [ver-day-ar'], *vn.* 1. To grow green (volverse verde), to get a greenish color. 2. *(Cono Sur)* To drink maté. 3. *(Cono Sur. Agr.)* To graze. *-va.* To collect grapes and olives to sell.

verdeceledón [ver-day-thay-la-done'], *m.* Sea-green, a color made of light blue and straw color.

verdecer [ver-day-therr'], *vn.* To grow green.

verdecico, ica, ito, ita, [ver-day-thee'-co], *a. dim.* of VERDE.

verdecillo [ver-day-theel'-lyo], *m. (Orn.)* Greenfinch.

verdecillo, illa [ver-day-theel'-lyo], *a. dim.* Greenish.

verdeesmeralda [ver-day-es-may-rahl'-dah], *a.* Emerald green.

verdegay [ver-day-gah'-e], *m. & a.* Verditer: applied to a light bright green.

verdeguear [ver-day-gay-ar'], *m.* To grow green.

verdemar [ver-day-mar'], *m. & a.* Sea-green, used by painters.

verdemontaña [ver-day-mon-tah'-nyah], *f.* Mountain-green, a mineral imported from Hungary, and a green paint prepared from it.

verdeoscuro, ra [ver-day-os-coo'-ro, rah], *a. & m. (Prov.)* Dark green, greenish.

verderol [ver-day-role'], *m.* 1. *(Orn.)* The yellow-hammer. 2. Kind of green shellfish.

verderón [ver-day-ron'], *m.* 1. *(Zone.)* A shellfish about two inches long with deep grooves. 2. *(Prov.) V.* VERDEROL, the bird.

verdete [ver-day'-tay], *m.* Verditer, copper acetate. *V.* CARDE-NILLO.

verdevejiga [ver-day'-hay-hee'-hah], *f.* Sap-green, deepcolored green.

verdezuelo [ver-day-thoo-ay'-lo], *m. V.* VERDEROL.

verdín [ver-deen'], *m.* 1. *V.* VERDINA. 2. Green scum on still water or damp walls (capa). 3. Oxide of copper. 4. Green stain (en la ropa).

verdina [ver-dee'-nah], *f.* The green color of fruits when not ripe.

verdinegro, gra [ver-de-nay'-gro, grah], *a.* Of a deep green color.

verdino, na [ver-dee'-no, nah], *a.* Of a bright green color.

verdiseco, ca [ver-de-say'-co, cah], *a.* Pale green.

verdolaga [ver-do-lah'-gah], *pl. (Bot.)* Purslane.

verdón [ver-done'], *m. (Orn.)* Greenfinch.

verdor [ver-dor'], *m.* 1. Verdure, herbage, green color of plants. 2. Acerbity or unplesant taste of unripe fruit. 3. Vigor and strength of the animal body.

verdoso, sa [ver-do'-so, sah], *a.* Greenish.

verdoyo [ver-do'-yo], *m.* A green mould growing on walls.

verdugado [ver-doo-gah'-do], *m.* Under petticoat formerly worn.

verdugal [ver-doo-gahl'], *m.* Young shoots growing in wood after outting.

verdugo [ver-doo'-go], *m.* 1. The young shoot of a tree. 2. Rapier, a long, narrow sword. 3. Welt, mark of a lash on the skin (látigo). 4. Hangman, executioner, herdsman. 5. Things which afflict the mind (tormento). 6. Very cruel person. 7. *(Arch.)* Row of bricks in a stone or mud wall. 8. Small rings for the cars, hoop. 9. *(Mil.)* Leathern whip.

verdugón [ver-doo-gone'], *m.* 1. A long shoot of a tree. 2. *(Aug.)* A large mark of a lash.

verduguillo [ver-doo-geel'-lyo], *m.* 1. *(Dim.)* A small shoot of a tree. 2. A small, narrow razor. 3. A long, narrow sword.

verdulera [ver-doo-lay'-rah], *f.* 1. Market woman, who sells vegetables and herbs (comerciante). 2. A mean, low woman; a word of contempt.

verdulería [ver-doo-lay-ree'-ah], *f.* Vegetable stand, vegetable shop.

verdulero [ver-doo-lay'-ro], *m.* Greengrocer.

verdura [ver-doo'-rah], *f.* 1. Verdure. 2. Greens, culinary vegetables, garden stuff. 3. Foliage in landscape and tapestry. 4. Vigor, luxuriance.

verdurita [ver-doo-ree'-tah], *f.* Slight heritage or vegetation.

verdusco, ca [ver-doos'-co, cah], *a.* Greenish, verging upon green.

verecundo, da [vay-ray-coon'-do, dah], *a.* Bashful, diffident. *V.* VERGONZOSO.

vereda [vay-ray'-dah], **f.** 1. Path, footpath. 2. Circular order or notice sent to several towns or places. 3. Route of traveling preachers. 4. *(Peru.)* Sidewalk (acera). 5. *(And.)* Village (pueblo), settlement. 6. *(Mex.)* Parting (raya). **Entrar en vereda**, to toe the line. **Ir por la vereda**, to do the right thing.

veredario, ria [vay-ray-dah'-re-o, ah], *a.* Hired, on hire (caballos).

veredero [vay-ray-day'-ro], *m.* Messenger sent with orders or despatches.

veredicto [vay-ray-deec'-to], *m.* 1. *(For.)* Verdict, the decision of a trial. 2. Sentence, degree, opinion.

verga [ver'-gah], *f. (Naut.)* Yard. 2. The organ of generation in male animals, penis. 3. Nerve or cord of the crossbow.

vergajo [ver-gah'-ho], *m.* Cord of the penis of the bull and other quadrupeds, especially when separated from them (pizzle).

vergajón [ver-gah-hone'], *a.* **Hierro vergajón**, round iron.

vergarzoso [ver-gar-tho'-so], *m. (Zool.)* A species of American armadillo.

vergel [ver-hel'], *m.* 1. Fruit and flower garden (jardín). 2. Luxuriant vegetation.

vegeta [ver-hay'-tah], *f.* A small twig.

vergeteado, da [ver-hay-tay-ah'-do, dah], *a. (Her.)* Vergette, paley, having the field divided by several small pales.

vergonzante [ver-gon-thahn'-tay], *a.* Bashful, shame-faced (avergonzado). *-com.* An honest, decent, needy person.

vergonzosamente [ver-gon-tho-sah-men-tay], *adv.* Shamefully, bashfully; confoundedly.

vergonzoso, sa [ver-gon-tho'-so, sah], *a.* 1. Bashful (persona), modest, shamefaced; diffident. 2. Shameful; contumelious. **Partes vergonzosas**, privy parts.

verguear [ver-gay-ar'], *va.* To beat with a rod.

vergüenza [ver-goo-en'-thah], *f.* 1. Shame (sentimiento). 2. Bashfulness (timidez), confusion; modesty; diffidence, honor. 3. A base action. 4. Regard of one's own character; dignity, honor. 5. Disgrace (escándalo). **Perder la vergüen-**

za, to become abandoned. **Tener vergüenza**, to be ashamed. **Es una vergüenza**, it is a shameful thing. **Vergüenzas**, privy parts.

vergueta [ver-gay'-tah], *f.* A small switch or rod.

verguilla [ver-geel'-lyah], *f.* Gold or silver wire without silk.

vericueto [vay-re-coo-ay'-to], *m.* A rough and pathless place. **Vericuetos**, strange or ridiculous ideas.

verídico, ca [vay-ree'-de-co, cah], *a.* Veridical, telling the truth.

verificación [vay-re-fe-cah-the-on'], *f.* Inquiry, examen, verification, by argument or evidence.

verificador, ra [vay-re-fe-cah-dor', rah], *a.* Verifying, checking. *-m. & f.* Checker, tester, verifier.

verificar [vay-re-fe-car'], *va.* 1. To verify (hechos), to prove what was doubted. 1. To verify, to confirm, to prove by evidence; to examine the truth of a thing. *-vr.* To be verified, to prove true.

verificativo, va [vay-re-fe-cah-tee'-vo, vah], *a.* Tending to prove; verificative.

verija [vay-ree'-hah], *f.* Region of the genitals.

veril [vay-reel'], *m. (Naut.)* The shore of a bay, of a sound, etc.

verilear [vay-re-lay-ar'], *vn. (Naut.)* To sail along the shore.

verino [vay-ree'-no], *m.* A fine sort of South American tobacco, grown in a locality of the same Caste. *(Prov.)* Pimple, small pustule.

verisímil [vay-re-see'-meel], *a.* Probable, likely, credible.

verisimilitud [vay-re-se-me-le-tood'], *f.* Verisimilitude, probability, likelihood.

verisímilmente [vay-re-see'-meel-men-tay], *adv.* Probably, likely.

verja [ver'-hah], *f.* Grate of a door or window; a grate with cross-bars (reja).

verjel [ver-hel'], *m.* 1. Flower-garden; beautiful orchard. 2. Anything pleasing to the sight.

vermes [verr'-mes], *m. pl.* Intestinal worms.

vermicular [ver-me-coo-lar'], *a.* Vermiculous, full of grubs; vermicular.

vermicular [ver-me-coo-lar'], *va. (Arch.)* To vermiculate, to ornament an edifice with worm-like figures.

vermiforme [ver-me-for'may], *a.* Vermiform, worm-like.

vermífugo [ver-mee'-foo-go], *a. & m. (Med.)* Vermifuge, anthelmintic.

verminoso, sa [ver-me-no'-so, sah], *a.* Full of grubs, verminous.

vermíparo, ra [ver-mee'-pa-ro, rah], *a.* Vermiparous, producing worms.

vermívoro, ra [ver-mee'-vo-ro, rah], *a.* Vermivorous, eating worms or grubs.

vermú [ver-moo'], *m.* Vermouth.

vernáculo, la [ver-nah'-coo-lo, lah], *a.* Vernacular, native, of one's own country. **Lengua vernácula**, vernacular language.

vernal [ver-nahl'], *m.* Vernal, belonging to spring.

vernerita [ver-ne-ree'-tah], *f. (Min.)* Wernerite, a translucent sodium-calcium silicate.

vernier [ver-ne-err'], *m. (Opt.)* Vernier.

vero [vay'-ro], *m. (Her.)* Cup or bellformed vase on a shield.

verónica [vay-ro'-ne-cah], *f.* 1. Image of the face of our Lord Jesus Christ. 2. *(Bot.)* Speedwell.

verosímil [vay-ro-see'-meel], *a.* Verisimilar. *V* VERISÍMIL.

verosimilitud [vay-ro-se-me-le-tood'], *f.* Verisimility. *V.* VERISIMILITUD.

verraca [ver-rah'-cah], *f. (Naut.)* A tent pitched on shore by sailors for sheltering stores or utensils.

verraco [ver-rah'-co], *m.* Boar, male swine.

verraquear [ver-rah-kay-ar'], *vn.* 1. To grunt like a boar (gruñir. 2. *(Met. Coll)* To cry angrily and long (niños).

verriondez [ver-re-on-deth'], *f.* 1. Rutting-time of boars and other animals. 2. Withering state of herbs.

verriondo, da [ver-re-on'-do, dah], *a.* 1. Foaming like a boar at rutting-time. 2. Witherlag, flaccid.

verrón [ver-rone'], *m.* V.VERRACO. *(Acad.)*

verrucaria [ver-roo-cah'-re-ah], *f. (Bot)* Wartwort.

verruga [ver-roo'-gah], *f.* Wart, pimple.

verrugoso, sa [ver-roo-go'-so, sah], *a.* Warty.

verruguera [ver-roo-gay'-rah], *f. (Bot.)* European turnsole.

verruguica, illa, ita [], *f. dim* A small wart or pimple.

verruguiento, ta [ver-roo-gee-en'-to, tah], *a.* Full of warts, warty.

versado, da [ver-sah'-do, dah], *a. & pp.* Of VERSAR. Versed, conversant. **Versado en diferentes lenguas**, conversant in different languages.

versal [ver-sahl'], *a. (Print.) V.* MAYÚSCULA.

versalilla, versalita [ver-sah-leel'-lyah, ee'-tah], *f. & a. (Print.)* Small capital letter.

versar [ver-sar'], *vn. & vr.* 1. To be versed or conversant; to grow skillful in the management of a business. With the preposition *sobre*, to treat of, to write upon, to discuss. 2. *(Carib.)* To versify (versificar). 3. *(Carib).* To chat (charlar). 4. *(Mex.)* To tease (guasear).

versátil [ver-sah'-teel], *a.* 1. Versatile, which may be turned readily. 2. Changeable, variable.

versatilidad [ver-sah-te-le-dahd'], *f.* Variability, inconstancy.

versecillo [ver-say-theel'-lyo], *m. dim. V.* VERSILLO.

versería [ver-say-ree'-ah], *f.* A collection of verses; poetry.

versico [ver-see'-co], *m. dim. V.* VERSILLO.

versícula [ver-see'-coo-lah], *f.* Place where the choir-books are placed.

versiculario [ver-se-coo-lah'-re-o], *m.* One who takes care of the choir books.

versículo [ver-see'-coo-lo], *m.* 1. Versicle, a small part of the responsory which is said in the canonical hours. 2. Verse of a chapter.

versificación [ver-se-fe-cah-the-on'], *f.* Versification.

versificador, ra [ver-se-fe-cah-dor', rah], *m. & f.* Versifier, versificator.

versificar [ver-se-fe-car'], *va.* To versify, to make verses.

versiforme [ver-se-for'-may], *a.* Subject to change of form.

versillo [ver-seel'-lyo], *m. dim.* A little verse.

versión [ver-se-on'], *f.* 1. Translation, version. 2. Version, manner of relation. 3.*(Med.)* Version, turning of a child for facilitating delivery.

versista [ver-sees'-tah], *m. (Coll.)* Versifier, verseman, versificator, one who writes blank verse.

verso [verr'-so], *m.* 1. Verse, a line consisting of a certain succession of sounds and number of syllables; metre. 2. Culverin of a small bore, now disused. **Verso libre**, free verse. **Teatro en verso**, verse drama. *-pl.* Lines.

vértebra [verr'-tay-brah], *f.* Vertebra, a joint in the back-bone.

vertebrado, da [ver-tay-brah'-do, dah], *a.* Vertebrate, having vertebrae. *-m. pl. (Zool.)* Vertebrate animals.

vertebral [ver-tay-brahl'], *a.* Vertebral.

vertedera [ver-tay-day'-rah], *f. (Agr.)* The mould-board of a plough.

vertedero [ver-tay-day'-ro], *m.* Sewer, drain, rubbish dump (de basura).

vertedor, ra [ver-tay-dor', rah], *m. & f.* 1. Nightman, who empties the common sewer. 2. Conduit, sewer. 3. *(Naut.)* scoop (cuchara), made of wood, for throwing out water (botes, barcos).

vertello [ver-tayl'-lyo], *m. (Naut.)* Track to form the parrels.

verter [ver-terr'], *va.* 1. To spill (contenido, líquido), to shed. 2. To empty vessels (recipiente). 3. To translate writings. 4. To divulge, to publish, to reveal a secret. 5. To exceed, to abound. *-vn.* To flow (río), to run; to fall (pendiente).

vertibilidad [ver-te-be-le-dahd'], *f.* Versatility, versatileness.

vertible [ver-tee'-blay], *a.* Movable, changeable, variable.

vertical [ver-te-cahl'], *a.* Vertical, perpendicular to the horizon. *-m.* The plane which intersects the horizon in the points of the true east and west.

verticalmente [ver-te-cahl'-men-tay], *adv.* Vertically.

vértice [ver'-te-thay], *m.* Vertex, zenith; crown of the head.

verticidad [ver-te-the-dahd'], *f.* The power of turning, verticity; rotation.

verticilado, da [ver-te-the-lah'-do, dah], *a.* (*Bot.*) Verticillate.

verticilo [ver-te-thee'-lo], *m.* (*Bot.*) Verticil, a whorl.

vertiente [ver-te-en'-tay], *com.* 1. Waterfall, cascade. 2. Spring, source. 3. Slope (declive). 4. Side (lado).

vertiginoso, sa [ver-te-he-no'-so, sah], *a.* Giddy, vertiginous.

vértigo [verr'-te-go], *m.* 1. Giddiness, vertigo. 2. Transient disturbance of the judgment. 3. Sudden frenzy (frenesí). **Puede provocar vértigos**, it may cause giddiness. **Con una velocidad de vértigo**, at a giddy speed.

vertimiento [ver-te-me-ayn'-to], *m.* Effusion, shedding.

vesana [vay-sah'-nah], *f.* (*Agr.*) A straight furrow.

vesania [vay-sah'-ne-ah], *f.* Incipient insanity, craziness

vesical [vay-se-cahl'], *a.* 1. (*Zool.*) Vesical, relating to the bladder. 2. Forming bubbles on escaping from an orifice.

vesícula [vay-see'-coo-lah], *f.* 1. (*Anat.*) Vesicle, a membranous sac like a bladder. 2. (*Bot.*) Vesicle, a little air-sac of some aquatic plant. **Vesícula biliar**, the gall-bladder. **Vesícula elemental** or **orgánica**, elementary mass of bioplasm, cell.

vesicular [vay-se-coo-lar'], *a* **Vesicular**, like a little bladder or vesicle.

vesiculoso, sa [vay-se-coo-lo'-so, sah], *a.* Vesiculate, full of vesicles.

veso [vay'-so], *m.* (*Zool.*) Weasel, a carnivorous animal.

véspero [ves'-pay-ro], *m.* Vesper, the evening star.

vespertillo [ves-per-teel'-lyo], *m.* Bat. V. MURCIÉLAGO.

vespertina [ves-per-tee'-nah], *f.* Evening discourse in universities.

vespertino, na [ves-per-tee'-no, nah], *a.* Vespertine, happening in the evening.

vespertino [ves-per-tee'-no], *m.* Doctrinal sermon preached in the evening.

vesta [ves'-tah], *f.* 1. Vesta, goddess of the domestic hearth. 2. One of the asteroids.

vestal [ves-tahl'], *f. & a.* Vestal virgin, a priestess of the temple of Vesta.

veste [ves'-tay], *f.* (*Poet.*) Clothes, garments, V. VESTIDO.

vestfaliano, na [vest-fah-le-ah'-no, nah], *a.* Westphalian, of Westphalia.

vestíbulo [ves-tee'-boo-lo], *m.* 1. Vestibule, portal, hall, lobby. 2. Vestibule, a cavity of the internal ear.

vestido [ves-tee'-do], *m.* 1. Dress, wearing apparel, clothes, garments, clothing, garb, habiliments. 2. Ornament, embellishment. 3. (*And. CAm. Cono Sur*) Suit (de hombre). **Vestidos usados**, second-hand clothes. **Vestido de noche**, evening-gown. **Vestido y calzado**, without labor. **Vestido de seda**, silk dress.-**Vestido, da**, *pp.* of VESTIR.

vestidura [ves-te-doo'-rah], *f.* 1. Vesture, robe of distinction. 2. Vestment for divine worship.

vestidurilla, ita [ves-te-doo-ree'-lyah], *f. dim.* of VESTIDURA.

vestigio [ves-tee'-he-o], *m.* 1. Vestige, footstep; ruins, remains of buildings. 2. Memorial, mark, sign, index.

vestimenta [ves-te-men'- tah], *f.* Clothes (ropa), garments, -*pl.* Ecclesiastical robes.

vestir [ves-teer'], *va.* 1. To clothe, to dress (cuerpo, persona), to accoutre. 2. To deck, to adorn. 3. To make clothes for others (sastre). 4. To cloak, to disguise, to palliate. 5. To instruct, to inform, to advise, 6. To rough-cast the walls of a building. 7. To affect a passion or emotion. 8. To give liberally, to make liberal presents. 9. (*Met.*) To embellish a discourse. 10. Used of animals and plants in respect to their coverings. -*vn.* To dress in a special color or fashion. **Vestir de uniforme**, to dress in uniform. -*vr.* 1. To be covered; to be clothed. **La primavera viste los campos**, spring clothes the fields. 2. To dress oneself on rising after sickness. **Le viste un buen sastre**, he has his clothes made at a good tailor's. **Vestir bien**, to dress well. **Le gusta vestirse en**

París, he likes to buy his clothes in Paris. **El que de lo ajeno se viste en la calle lo desnudan**, he who wears borrowed plumes risks public exposure. (*Yo visto, él vistió; yo vista, vistiera;* from *Vestir.* V. PEDIR.)

vestuario [ves-too-ah'-re-o], *m.* 1. Vesture, all the necessaries of dress; clothes; uniform; equipment, habiliment for the troop. 2. Tax for the equipment of the troop. 3. Vestry, place where clergymen dress. 4. Money given to ecclesiastics for dress, and stipends to assistants. 5. Green-room, dressing-room in a theatre; vestiary. **Vestuarios**, deacon and subdeacon who attend the priest at the altar.

vestugo [ves-too'-go], *m.* Stem or bud of an olive.

veta [vay'-tah], *f.* 1. Vein of ore, metal, or coal in mines. Vein in wood or marble, grain. 3. Strip of a different color in cloth or stuff. **Descubrir la veta**, to discover one's sentiments or designs. 4. (*Ecuador* Sickness, nausea, and headache from great elevations in the Andes. *Cf.* ZAROCHE.

vetado, da [vay-tah'-do, dah], *a. & pp.* Of VETEAR. V. VETEADO.

vetar [vay-tar'], *va.* To veto.

veteado, da [vay-tay-ah'-do, dah], *a.* Striped, veined, streaky, cross-grained.

vetear [vay-tay-ar'], *va.* To variegate, to form veins of different colors, to grain.

veteranía [vay-tay-rah-nee'-ah], *f* Status of being a veteran; long service (servicio).

veterano, na [vay-tay-rah'-no, nah], *a.* Experienced, veteran, long practiced (soldados). -*m.* Veteran, an old soldier.

veterinaria [vay-tay-re-nah'-re-ah], *f.* Veterinary medicine or surgery.

veterinario, ria [vay-tay-re-nah'-re-o], *m & f.* Veterinary surgeon.

vetica, illa [vay-tee' -cah, eel'-lyah], *f. dim.* A small vein; a narrow stripe.

veto [vay'-to], *m.* Veto, official disapproval of a law.

vetustamente [vay-toos-tah-men'-tay], *adv.* Anciently.

vetustez [vay-toos-teth'], *f.* A venerable antiquity, notable old age.

vetusto, ta [vay-toos'-to, tah], *a.* Very ancient.

vez [veth], *f.* 1. Turn, the alternative of things in successive progression. 2. Time, or the determinate time or occasion on which something is performed. 3. Epoch. 4. Return, act or performance of anything that bears a successive progression. 5. Draught, the quantity of liquor drunk at once. 6. Herd of swine belonging to the inhabitants of a place. 7. United with *cada*, it intimates repetition. **Cada vez**, each time. -*pl.* Power or authority committed to a substitute. **A la vez or por vez**, successively, by turns, by order or series. **Una vez**, once. **Dos veces**, twice. **Tres veces**, thrice or three times. **De una vez**, at once. **Más de una vez**, more than once. **En vez**, instead of. **Tal vez**, perhaps. **Rara vez**, seldom, once, in a while. **Llegará mi vez**, my turn will come. **Hacer las veces de otro**, to supply one's place. **A veces**, sometimes, by turns, on some occasions. **Todas las veces que**, whenever, as often as. **Muchas veces**, often. **Pocas veces**, seldom. **Varias veces**, several times. **Habíase una vez una princesa**, once upon a time there was a princess.

veza [vay'-thah], *f.* (*Bot.*) Vetch.

vezar [vay-thar'], *va.* To accustom, to habituate. V. AVEZAR.

vía [vee'-ah], *f.* 1. Way, road (calle), route (ruta). V. CAMINO. 2. Carriage track, mark of wheels. 3. Grade, track, permanent way, line, of a railway; also rail. 4. Way, mode, manner, method, procedure, gait. 5. Profession, calling, trade. 6. Post-road. 7. Passage, gut in the animal body. 8. Spiritual life. **Vía férrea**, railroad, railway. **Vía láctea**, (*Ast.*) the Milky Way. **Vía pública**, the streets of a town. **Vía terrestre**, overland route. **Vía ancha**, broad gauge. **Vías respiratorias**, respiratory track. **Un país en vías de desarrollo**, a developing country.

viabilidad [ve-ah-be-le-dahd'], *f.* (*Med.*) Viability, probability of life of the foetus.

viable [ve-ah'-blay], *a.* Viable, capable of living.

viadera [ve-ah-day'-rah], *f.* Part of a loom near the treadles.

viador [ve-ah-dor'], *m.* Passenger, traveler.

viaducto [ve-ah-dooc'-to], *m.* 1. Viaduct. 2. *(Mex.)* Expressway for rapid transit.

viajador, ra [ve-ah-hah-dor', rah], *m. & f.* V. VIAJERO.

viajante [ve-ah-hahn'-tay] *com. & pa.* 1. Traveler, voyager; traveling. 2. Commercial traveler.

viajar [ve-ah-har'], *vn.* To travel, to perform a journey or voyage, to itinerate. **Viajar en coche**, to go in a car.

viajata [ve-ah-hah'-tah], *f.* A short journey, especially one for a few days of diversion.

viaje [ve-ah'-hay], *m.* 1. Journey, tour (largo), voyage (pormar), travel, drive (coche). 2. Way, road. 3. *(Arch.)* Deviation from a right line. 4. Gait. 5. Excursion; errand. 6. Load carried at once. 7. Quantity of water from the general reservoir, to be divided into particular channels or conduits. 8. *(Carib.)* Time (vez). 9. Trip (viaje corto, excursión). **Hacer un viaje por toda Europa**, to tour Europe. **Viaje en coche**, a drive. **Viaje de recreo**, pleasure trip. **Agencia de viajes**, travel agency. **Viaje de ida**, outward journey. **Viaje de ida y vuelta**, return trip. **Viaje de novios**, honeymoon. **Viajes espaciales**, space travel. **Viaje en barco**, boat trip (corto), voyage (largo).

viajero, ra, [ve-ah-hay'-ro, rah], *m. & f.* Traveler, passenger.

vial [ve-ahl'], *a.* Wayfaring; belonging to a journey: used in a mystical sense. -*m.* Avenue, a road formed by two parallel rows of trees or shrubbery. *(Acad.)* **Seguridad vial**, road safety. **Circulación vial**, road traffic.

vianda [ve-ahn'-dah], *f.* 1. Food, viands, meat, victuals, fare. 2. A meal served at table.

viandante [ve-an-dahn'-tay], *m. & f.* Traveler (viajero), passenger, especially a tramp.

viandista [ve-an-dees'-tah] *m.* Waiter, who serves viands or puts them on the table.

viaraza [ve-ah-rah'-thah], *f.* Loose, diarrhea (animales).

viático [ve-ah'-te-co], *m.* 1. Viaticum, provision for a journey. 2. Viaticum, the sacrament administered to the sick.

víbora [vee'-bo-rah], *f.* 1. Viper. 2. *(Met.)* Viper, a malicious and perfidious person.

viborera [ve-bo-ray'-rah], *f. (Bot.)* Viper's bugloss. **Viborera común**, common viper's bugloss.

viborezno, na [ve-bo-reth'-no, nah], *a.* Viperine, viperous. -*m.* Young, small viper.

viborillo, illa [ve-bo-reel'-lyo, lyah], *m. & f. dim.* V. VIBOREZNO.

vibración [ve-brah-the-on'], *f.* Vibration (temblor), oscillation, fluttering.

vibrante [ve-brahn'-tay], *pa.* 1. Vibrating, undulating. 2. Bounding (pulso). 3. Ringing (voz, slogan), exciting (reunión).

vibrar [ve-brar'], *va.* 1. To vibrate, to oscillate, to brandish. 2. To throw, to dart. -*vn.* To vibrate, to play and down or to and fro.

vibrátil [ve-brah'-teel], *a.* 1. Vibratile, capable of vibration. 2. *(Med.)* Vibratory, used of a pain in which the nerves of the patient vibrate like drawing cords.

vibratilidad [ve-brah-te-le-dahd'], *f.* Faculty of producing vibrations.

vibratorio, ria [ve-brah-to're-o, ah], *a.* Vibratory.

vibrión [ve-bre-on'], *m. (Biol.)* Vibrio, a microbe endowed with an oscillating movement.

viburno [ve-boor'-no], *m. (Bot.).* Viburnum.

vicaría [ve-cah'-ree-ah], *f.* Vicarship; vicarage. **Vicaría perpetua**, perpetual curacy.

vicaria [ve-cah'-re-ah], *f.* Vicar, the second superior in a convent of nuns.

vicarial [ve-cah-re-ahl'], *a.* Vicarial, relating to a vicar, held by a vicar.

vicariato [ve-cah-re-ah'-to], *m.* Vicarial, the dignity of a vicar; the district subjected to a vicar; vicarship.

vicario [ve-cah'-re-o], *m.* 1. Vicar, deputy in ecclesiastical affairs. -*a.* Vicar, he who exercises the authority of the supe-

rior of a convent in his absence; one who transacts all ecclesiastical affairs as substitute for a bishop or archbishop. **Vicario apostólico**, missionary bishop in non-Catholic countries. **Vicario de coro**, choral-vicar, superintendent of the choir. **Vicario general**, vicar-general, an ecclesiastical judge appointed to exercise jurisdiction over a whole territory, in opposition to a **vicario pedáneo**, who has authority over a district only.

vicario, ria [ve-cah'-re-o, ah], *a.* Vicarial, vicarious; vicariate.

vice [vee'-thay], Vice, used in composition to signify deputy, or one of the second rank.

vicealmiranta [ve-thay-al-me-rahn'-tah], *f.* The galley next in order to the admiral's.

vicealmirantazgo [ve-thay-al-me-ran-tath'-go], *m.* 1. Office or rank of viceadmiral. 2. Vice-admiralty.

vicealmirante [ve-thay-al-me-rahn'-tay], *m.* Vice-admiral.

vicecamarero [ve-thay-cah-ma-ray'-ro], *m.* Vice-chamberlain.

vicecancelario [ve-thay-can-thay-lah'-re-o], *m.* V. VICE-CANCILLER.

vicecanciller [ve-thay-can-theel-lyerr'], *m.* Vice-counsellor.

viceconsiliario [ve-thay-con-se-le-ah'-re-o], *m.* Vice-counsellor.

vicecónsul [ve-thay-con'-sool], *m.* Vice-consul.

viceconsulado [ve-thay-con-soo-lah'-do], *m.* Vice-consulate.

vicegerente [ve-thay-hay-ren'-tay], *a.* Vicegerent.

vicelegado [ve-thay-lay-gah'-do], *m.* Vice-legate.

vicelegatura [ve-thay-lay-gah-too'-rah], *f.* Office and jurisdiction of a vicelegate.

vicemaestro [ve-thay-mah-es'-tro], *m.* Vice-principal.

vicenal [ve-thay-nahl'], *a.* Arrived at the age of twenty years.

vicepatrono [ve-thay-pah-tro'-no], *m.* vice-patron.

vicepresidencia [ve-thay-pray-se-den'-the-ah], *f.* Vice-presidency.

vicepresidente [ve-thay-pray-se-den'-tay], *m.* Vicepresident.

viceprovincial [ve-thay-pro-veen'-the-ahl], *m. & a.* Vice-provincial.

vicerrector, ra, [ve-ther-rec'-tor, rah], *m. & f.* Vice-rector.

vicerrectorado, *m.* **vicerrectoría**, *f.* [ve-ther-rec-to-rah'-do]. Vicerectorship.

vicesenescal [ve-thay-say-nes-cah'], *m.* Vice-seneschal or steward.

vicesimario, ria [ve-thay-see-mah'-re-o, ah], *a.* Vicenary, belonging to the number twenty: twentieth.

vicésimo, ma [ve-thay'-se-mo, mah], *a.* Twentieth. V. VIGÉSIMO.

viceversa [vee-thay-ver'-sah], *adv.* On the contrary; to the contrary; vice versa.

viciar [ve-the-ar'], *va.* 1. To vitiate, to mar, to spoil or corrupt (costumbres). 2. To counterfeit, to adulterate (sustancia). 3. To forge, to falsify. 4. To annul, to make void. 5. To deprave, to pervert. 6. To put a false construction on a passage or expression. -*vr.* To deliver oneself up to vices (persona); to become too much attached or addicted to anything.

vicio [vee'-the-o], *m.* 1. Defect, imperfection of body, of soul, or of things; viciousness, faultiness, depravation, folly. 2. Vice, moral corruption, depravity. 3. Artifice, fraud. 4. Excessive appetite, extravagant desire. 5. Deviation from rectitude, defect or excess (defecto). 6. Luxuriant growth. **Los sembrados llenan mucho vicio**, the cornfields are luxuriant. 7. Forwardness or caprice of children. **De vicio**, by habit or custom. 8. Vices of horses or mules. 9. **Estar de vicio**, *(LAm.)* To be idle. **Quejarse de vicio**, to complain without cause, or make ado about trifles. **No le podemos quitar el vicio**, we can't get him out of the habit.

viciosamente [ve-the-o-sah-men'-tay], *adv.* Viciously; falsely; corruptly.

vicioso, sa [ve-the-o'-so, sah], *a.* 1. Vicious. 2. Luxuriant, overgrown, vigorous. 3. Abundant; provided; delightful. 4. *(Prov.)* Spoiled (niños).

vicisitud [ve-the-se-tood'], *f.* Vicissitude, accident (desgracia), upset, sudden change (cambio).

vicisitudinario, ria [ve-the-se-too-de-nah'-re-o, ah], *a.* Changeable, variable.

víctima [veec'-te-mah], *f.* Victim; sacrifice. **Fue víctima de una estafa**, she was the victim of a swindle. **No hay que lamentar víctimas del accidente**, there were no casualties in the accident.

victimario [vec-te-mah'-re-o], *m.* Servant who attends the sacrificing priest.

víctor, vítor [veec'-tor, vee'-tor], *m.* 1. Shout, cry of acclamation. Long live! 2. Public rejoicing in honor of the achiever of some glorious deed. 3. Tablet containing a eulogy of the hero of a festival.

victorear [vic-to-ray-ar'], *va.* To shout, to acclaim, to cheer, to applaud. V. VITOREAR.

victoria [vic-to'-re-ah], *f.* Victory, triumph, conquest, palm. - *int.* Victory. **Cantar victoria**, or *la* **Victoria**, to triumph, to obtain victory or to rejoice for victory.

victorial [vic-to-re-ahl'], *a.* Relating to victory.

victoriosamente [vic-to-re-o'-sah-men-tay], *adv.* Victoriously.

victorioso, sa [vic-to-re-oh'-so, sah], *a.* 1. Victorious, conquering. 2. Title given to warriors.

vicuña [ve-coo'-nyah], *f.* Vicuña or vicugna, a South American wool-bearing quadruped, allied to the *Alpaca*, celebrated for its wool.

vid [veed], *f.* (*Bot.*) Vine, grapevine.

vida [vee'-dah], *f.* 1. Life. 2. Living, continuance in life. 3. Life, the duration of it. 4. Livelihood (profesión). 5. Life, conducts behavior, deportment; state, condition. 6. Life history of one's actions during life. 7. Aliment necessary to preserve life. 8. (*Met.*) Life, anything animating and agreeable, liveliness (de ojos, mirada). **Vida mía or mi vida**, my life: expression of endearment. 9. State of grace, eternal life. 10. Principle of nutrition, vital motions or functions. 11. (*Law.*) The determined number of ten years. **Buscar la vida**, to earn an honest livelihood; to scrutinize the life of another. **Dar mala vida**, to treat very ill. **Darse buena vida**, to give oneself up to the pleasures of life; to conform oneself to reason and law. **De por vida**, for life, during life. **En mi vida** or **en la vida**, never. **Hacer vida**, to live together as husband and wife. **Personas de mala vida**, profligate libertines. **Pasar la vida**, to live very frugally, on necessaries only. **Saber las vidas ajenas**, to spy into other people's affairs. **Tener siete vidas**, to have escaped many perils. **Un amigo de toda la vida**, a lifelong friend. **Vida perra**, dog's life. **Escapar con vida**, to escape live. **Vender cara la vida**, to sell one's life dearly.

vidalita [ve-da-lee'-tah], *f.* A special form of Argentine folk poem.

vida media [vee'-dah may'-de-ah], *f.* (*Chem.*) Half life.

vide [vee'-day] (*imp.* of Lat. videre). See: a direction, in books, to the reader. Commonly abbreviated to V. V. VÉASE.

vidente [ve-den'-tay], *pa.* He who sees, seeing.

video [vee'-day-o], *m.* Video; video (aparato). **Película de video**, videofilm.

videocámara [vee'-day-o-cah'-mah-rah], *f.* Video camera.

videoclub [vee'-day-o cloob], *m.* Videoclub.

videograbadora [vee'-day-o grah-bah-do'-dah], *f.* Video recorder.

videoteca [vee'-day-o-tay-cah], *f.* Video library.

videojuego [vee'-day-o-hoo-ay'-go], *m.* Video game.

¡vidita! [ve-dee'-tah], *f.* My life. Used in South America as an expression of tenderness.

vidorra [ve-dor'-rah], *f.* Gay life, easy life.

vidriado [ve-dre-ah'-do], *m.* Glazed earthenware, crockery.

vidriado, da [ve-dre-ah'-do, dah], *a.* Fretful, peevish, cross. -*pp.* of VIDRIAR.

vidriar [ve-dre-ar'], *va.* To varnish, to glaze earthenware.

vidriera [ve-dre-ay'-rah], *f.* 1. A glass window. 2. A glass case or cover. 3. (*LAm.*) Shop window (escaparate). 4. (*Carib.*) Tobacco stall.

vidriería [ve-dre-ay-ree'-ah], *f.* Glazier's shop, a shop where glasswares are sold: glasshouse, glass-shop, glass ware.

vidriero [ve-dre-ay'-ro], *m.* Glazier, a dealer in glass, glassmaker.

vidrio [vee'-dre-o], *m.* 1. Glass. **Vidrio colorado** or **teñido de color**, stained glass. **Vidrio plano** or **de vidresera**, Window glass. 2. Vessel or other thing made of glass. 3. Anything very nice and brittle. 4. A very touchy person. 5. (*Poet.*) Water. **Pagar los vidrios rotos**, to receive undeserved punishment, to carry the can. 6. (*Cono Sur*) Bottle of liquor.

vidrioso, sa [ve-dre-o'-so, sah], *a.* 1. Vitreous, brittle (frágil), glassy. 2. Slippery, as from ice or sleet (superficie). 3. Peevish, touchy, irascible. 4. Very delicate (asunto).

vidual [ve-doo-ahl'], *a.* Belonging to widowhood.

viduño, vidueño [ve-doo'-nyo], *m.* Peculiar quality of grapes or vines. V. VEDUÑO.

viejarrón, na [ve-ay-har-rone', nah], *m.* (*Coll.*) An old codger: it implies contempt.

viejazo [ve-ay-hah'-tho], *m.* (*Coll.*) An old man worn out with age.

viejecito, ita, viejezuelo, ela [ve-ay-hay-thee'-to], *a.* somewhat old.

viejo, ja [ve-ah'-oh, hah], *a.* 1. Old, stricken in years. 2. Ancient, antiquated. 3. Applied to a youth of judgment and knowledge beyond his years. **Cuentos de viejas**, old woman's stories. **Perro viejo**, (*Coll.*) a keen, clever, experienced person; old dog. **Viejo como el mundo**, as old as the hills. **Hacerse viejo**, to grow old. -*m & f.* 1. Old person. 2. **Mi viejo**, my dad.

vienés, sa [ve-ay-nes', sah], *a.* Viennese of Vienna (Austria).

vientecillo [ve-en-tay-theel'-lyo], *m. dim.* A light wind.

viento [ve-en'-to], *a.* 1. Wind (corriente de aire). 2. The air, and the space it occupies. 3. Wind, its direction from a particular point. 4. Wind, anything insignificant or light as wind; vanity, petty pride. 5. Windage of a gun. 6. Scent of dogs (de perros). 7. Nape-bone of a dog, between the ears. 8. Rope or cord, by which a thing is suspended. 9. Anything that violently agitates the mind. 10. That which contributes to an end. 11. Conceit (vanidad). 12. (*And.*) Strings of a kite (cometa). 13. (*CAm. Carib. Med.*) Rheumatism. **Viento galerno**, a fresh gale. **Viento en popa**, wind right aft. **Viento terral** or **de tierra**, a land breeze. **El viento refresca**, (*Naut.*) the wind freshens. **Hace mucho viento**, it is windy. **Echar a uno con viento fresco**, to chuck somebody out. **Contra viento y marea**, come hell or high water.

vientre [ve-en'-tray], *m.* 1. Belly (estómago) abdomen. 2. Fetus in the womb (matriz), pregnancy. 3. The belly or widest part of vessels (de vasija). 4. The body, or essential part of an instrument or act. 5. Stomach, when speaking of a great eater. **Desde el vientre de su madre**, from his birth. **Vientre flojo**, looseness of the bowels.

vientrecillo [ve-en-tra-theel'-lyo], *m. dim.* Ventricle.

viernes [ve-err'-nes], *m.* 1. Friday. 2. Fast day, when meat is not to be eaten. **Cara de viernes**, a wan, thin face. **Viernes Santo**, Good Friday.

viga [vee'-gah], *f.* Beam, balk (de madera). **Viga trasversal**, crossbeam.

vigente [ve-hen'-tay], *a.* In force (leyes, regulaciones).

vigésimo, ma [ve-hay'-se-mo, mah], *a.* Twentieth.

vigía [ve-hee'-ah], *f.* 1. (*Naut.*) Rock which projects but slightly from the sea. 2. V. ATALAYA. 3. Act of watching. 3. Lookout, watch.

vigiar [ve-he-ar'], *vn.* (*Naut.*) To look out, to watch.

vigilancia [ve-he-lahn'-the-ah], *f.* Vigilance, watchfulness, heedfulness. **Burlar la vigilancia de uno**, to escape somebody's vigilance.

vigilante [ve-he-lahn'-tay], *a.* Watchful, vigilant, careful. -*m.* 1. Watchman (guardián), guard. 2. *(Cono Sur)* Policeman (policía).

vigilantemente [ve-he-lahn'-tay-men-tay], *adv.* Vigilantly, heedfully.

vigilar [ve-he-lar'], *vn.* To watch over (velar por), to keep guard, to look after (cuidar), to tend (máquina); to guard (frontera). **Vigilar a los niños para que no se hagan daño**, to see that children come to no harm.

vigilativo, va [ve-he-lah-tee'-vo, vah], *a.* That which makes watchful.

vigilia [ve-hee'-le-ah], *f.* 1. The act of being awake (estar sin dormir), or on the watch. 2. Lucubration, nocturnal study (estudio). 3. Vigil, a fast kept before a holiday; service used on the night before a holiday. 4. Watchfulness, want of sleep. 5. Watch, limited time for keeping guard. 6. Office of the dead, to be sung in churches. **Pasar la noche de vigilia**, to spend a night without sleep.

vigor [ve-gor'], *m.* Vigor (fuerza), strength, force, energy, drive (empuje).

vigorar [ve-go-rar'], *va.* To strengthen, To invigorate.

vigorizar [ve-go-re-thar'], *va.* 1. to invigorate. 2. *(Met.)* To animate, to inspirit.

vigorosamente [ve-go-ro'-sah-men-tay], *adv.* Vigorously, lustily.

vigorosidad [ve-go-ro-se-dahd'], *f.* Vigorous, strength.

vigoroso, sa [ve-go-ro'-so, sah], *a.* Vigorous, strong, active; generous.

vigota [ve-go'-tah], *f. (Naut.)* Dead-eye, chain plate.

viguería [ve-gay-ree'-ah], *f. (Naut.)* The timber-work of a vessel.

vigués, sa [ve-gays', sah], *a. & n.* Native of Vigo.

vigueta [ve-gay'-tah], *f. dim.* A small beam.

vihuela [ve-oo-ay'-lah], *f.* Guitar.

vihuelista [ve-oo-ay-lees'-tah], *com.* Guitar-player.

vil [veel], *a.* 1. Mean, despicable (conducta), sordid, servile. 2. Worthless, infamous, ungrateful, vile. 3. Contemptible, abject, paltry.

vilano [ve-lah'-no], *m.* Burr or down of the thistle.

vileza [ve-lay'-thah], *f.* 1. Meanness, vileness, depravity. 2. Contemptibleness, abjectness. 3. A disgraceful action, an infamous deed; turpitude, paltriness. 4. Rabble, mob.

vilipendiador, ra [ve-le-pen-de-ah-dor', rah], *a. & n.* Reviling; reviler.

vilipendiar [ve-le-pen-de-ar'], *pa.* To contemn, to revile.

vilipendio [ve-le-pen'-de-o], *m.* Contempt (desprecio), disdain.

vilipendioso, sa [ve-le-pen-de-oh'-so, sah], *a.* Contemptible, causing contempt.

villa [veel'-lyah], *f.* 1. Town which enjoys by charter peculiar privileges. 2. Corporation of magistrates of a **villa**.

villadiego [vil-lyah-de-ay'-go], *m.* **Coger** or **tomar las de Villadiego**, to run away, to pack off bag and baggage.

villaje [vil-lyah'-hay], *m.* Village; hamlet.

villanaje [vil-lyah-nah'-hay], *m.* Villanage, the middling class in villages; peasantry.

villanamente [vil-lyah'-nah-men-tay], *adv.* Rudely, boorishly.

villancejo, villancete [vil-lyan-thay'-ho], *m. V.* VILLANCICO.

villancico [vil-lyan-thee'-co], *m.* Christmas carol: a metric composition sung in churches on certain festivals.

villanciquero [vil-lan-the-kay'-ro], *m.* One who composes small metric compositions, to be sung in churches.

villanchón, na [vil-lyan-chone', nah], *a.* Clownish, rustic, rude.

villanería [vil-lyah-nay-ree'-ah], *f.* 1. Lowness of birth, meanness. *V.* VILLANÍA. 2. Middling classes of society. *V.* VILLANAJE.

villanesco, ca [vil-lyah-nes'-co, cah], *a.* Rustic, rude, boorish.

villanía [vil-lyah-nee'-ah], *f.* 1. Lowness of birth, meanness. 2. Villainy (cualidad), villainousness, rusticity: indecorous word or act.

villano, na [vil-lyah'-no, nah], *a.* 1. Belonging to the lowest class of country people. 2. Rustic, clownish. 3. Worthless, unworthy. 4. Villainous, wicked.

villano [vil-lyah'-no], *m.* 1. A kind of Spanish dance. 2. A vicious horse. 3. Villain, a rustic; an unsociable villager.

villanote [vil-lyah-no'-tay], *a. aug.* of VILLANO. Highly rude.

villazgo [vil-lyath'-go], *m.* 1. Charter of a town. 2. Tax laid upon towns.

villeta [vil-lyay'-tah], *f. dim.* A small town or borough.

villica, ita [vil-lyee'-cah], *f. dim.* Small town.

villivina [vil-lye-vee'-nah], *f.* A kind of linen.

villoría [vil-lyo-ree'-ah], *f.* Farm-house.

villorín [vil-lyo-reen'], *m.* A sort of coarse cloth.

villorrio [vil-lyor'-re-o], *m.* A small village; a miserable little place or hamlet.

vilmente [veel-men'-tay], *adv.* Vilely; abjectly, contemptibly, villainously.

vilo [vee'-lo], *adv.* A word only used adverbially, as, **en vilo**, (1) in the air. (2.) *(Met.)* Insecurely.

vilordo, da [ve-lor'-do, dah], *a.* Slothful, lazy, heavy.

vilorta [ve-lor'-tah], *f.* 1. Ring of twisted willow. 2. A kind of cricket, played in Old Castile.

vilorto [ve-lor'-to], *m.* 1. A certain reed which grows in the north of Spain. 2. Snare of this reed.

vimbre [veem'-bray], *m. (Bot.)* Osier. *V.* MIMBRE.

vimbrera [veem-bray'-rah], *f. V.* MIMBRERA.

vinagre [ve-nah'-gray], *m.* 1. Vinegar. 2. Acidity, sourness. 3. *(Met. Coll.)* A person of a peevish temper.

vinagrera [ve-nah-gray'-rah], *f.* 1. Vinegar cruet. 2. Caster, with both vinegar and oil-cruets. 3. *(Peru and Colombia) V.* ACEDÍA.

vinagrero [ve-nah-gray'-ro], *m.* Vinegar-merchant.

vinagreta [ve-nah-gray-tah], *f. (Culin.)* Vinaigrette (salsa).

vinagrillo [ve-nah-greel'-lyo], *m.* 1. *(Dim.)* Weak vinegar. 2. A cosmetic lotion, used by women. 3. Rose-vinegar; snuff prepared with rose-vinegar.

vinagroso, sa [ve-nah-gro'-so, sah], *a.* 1. flourish, peevish, fretful. 2. *(Coll.)* In bad condition.

vinajera [ve-nah-hay'-rah], *f.* Vessel in which wine and water are served at the altar for the mass.

vinariego [ve-nah-re-ay'-go], *m.* Vintager, one who possesses and cultivates a vineyard.

vinario, ria [ve-nah'-re-o, ah], *a.* Belonging to wine.

vinatería [ve-nah-tay-ree'-ah], *f.* 1. Wine-trade (comercio). 2. Wine-shop (tienda).

vinatero [ve-nah-tay'-ro], *m.* Vintner, wine-merchant.

vinaza [ve-nah'-thah], *f.* Last wine drawn from the lees.

vinazo [ve-nah'-tho], *m.* Very strong wine.

vinculable [vin-coo-lah'-blay], *a.* That may be entailed.

vinculación [vin-coo-lah-the-on'], *f.* Entail, act of entailing.

vincular [vin-coo-lar'], *va.* 1. To entail an estate. 2. To ground or toured upon: to assure. 3. To continue, to perpetuate. 4. To secure with chains. **Vincular su suerte a la de otro**, to make one's fate depend on somebody else's.

vínculo [veen'-coo-lo], *m.* 1. Tie, link, chain. 2. Entail, an estate entailed. 3. Charge or encumbrance laid upon a foundation. **Vínculo de parentesco**, family ties.

vindicación [vin-de-cah-the-on'], *f.* 1. Vindication, just venegeance or satisfaction for a grievance (venganza). 2. The act of giving every one his due.

vindicar [vin-de-car'], *va.* 1. To vindicate, to revenge, to avenge (vengar). 2. To vindicate (justificar), to claim, to reclaim, to assert. 3. To vindicate, to justify, to defend, to support.

vindicativo, va [vin-de-cah-tee'-vo, vah], *a.* 1. Vindictive, revengeful. 2. Defensive, vindicatory.

vindicta [vin-deec'-tah], *f.* Vengeance, revenge.

vínico, ca [vee'-ne-co, cah], *a.* Vinic, belonging to wine.

vinícola [ve-nee'-co-lah], *a.* Relating to production of wine, wine-growing. *-m.* V. VINARIEGO.

vinicultor, ra [ve-ne-cool-tor'], *m. & f.* Wine grower.

viniente [ve-ne-en'-tay], *pa.* Coming.

vinificación [ve-ne-fe-cah-the-on'], *f.* Vivification, fermentation of must and its conversion into wine.

vinílico, ca [ve-nee'-le-co, cah], *a.* Vinyl.

vinilo [ve-nee'-lo], *m. (Chem.)* Vinyl.

vino [vee'-no], *m.* 1. Wine. **Vino clarete**, claret or pale red wine. **Vino de agujas**, sharp, rough wine. **Vino de cuerpo**, a strong-bodied wine. **Vino dulce**, sweet, clear wine. **Vino tinto**, red wine. **Una buena cosecha de vino**, a good vintage. 2. Preparation of fruit or vegetables by fermentation, called by the general name of *wine*. 3. Anything which intoxicates. **Vino de Jerez**, sherry wine. **Vino de Borgoña**, Burgundy wine. **Vino de Champaña**, Champagne wine. **Vino de Oporto**, Port wine. **Vino de frambuesa**, raspberry wine. **Vino de grosella**, currant wine. **Vino de consagrar**, communion wine. **Ahogar las penas en vino**, to drown one's sorrows. **Bautizar el vino**, to water down the wine.

vinolencia [ve-no-len'-the-ah], *f.* Intoxication, inebriation, excess in drinking wine.

vinolento, ta [ve-no-len'-to, tah], *a.* Intoxicated, inebriated.

vinosidad [ve-no-se-dahd'], *f.* Quality of being vinous, vinosity.

vinoso, sa [ve-no'-so, sah], *a.* 1. Vinous, vinose. 2. Intoxicated, inebriated.

vinote [ve-no'-tay], *m.* The liquid remaining in the boiler after the wine is distilled and the brandy made.

vinterana [vin-tay-rah'-nah], *f. (Bot.)* A tree of South America, the bark of which, is known by the name of "white cinnamon" in Ecuador, and used as a substitute for cinnamon.

viña [vee'-nyah], *f.* Vineyard (viñedo). **La viña del Señor**, the church.

viñadero [ve-nyah-day'-ro], *m.* Keeper of a vineyard.

viñador [ve-nyah-dor'], *m.* Cultivator of vines; husbandman.

viñedo [ve-nyay'-do], *m.* Country or district abounding in vineyards.

viñero [ve-nyay'-ro], *m.* Vintager who owns and cultivates vineyards.

viñeta [ve-nyay'-tah], *f.* 1. Vignette, an ornament at the beginning or end of chapters in books. 2. *(Not. Acad.)* Vignette, a photograph, engraving, etc., having a border gradually shaded off.

viñetero [ve-nyay-tay'-ro], *m. (Typ.)* A font-case for ornamental letters and vignettes.

viola [ve-o'-lah], *f.* 1. Viola, a tenor violin or alto. 2. *(Bot.)* Violet. V. ALHELÍ.

violáceo, ea [ve-o-lah'-thay-o, ah], *a.* Violaceous, violet-colored.

violación [ve-o-lah-the-on'], *f.* Violation.

violado, da [ve-o-lah'-do, dah], *a. & pp.* of VIOLAR. 1. Having the color of violets; made or confectioned with violets. 2. Violated.

violador, ra [ve-o-lah-dor', rah], *m. & f.* Violator, profaner, raper.

violar [ve-o-lar'], *va.* 1. To violate a law, to offend (ley). 2. To ravish, to rape, to violate a woman. 3. To spoil, to tarnish. 4. To profane or pollute the church.

violencia [ve-o-len'-the-ah], *f.* 1. Violence, impetuousness, compulsion, force. 2. Wrong construction, erroneous interpretation. 3. Rape. 4. Excessiveness, intenseness of cold, etc. **Apelar a la violencia**, to resort to violence. **No violencia**, non-violence.

violentamente, *adv.* 1. Violently, forcibly. 2. Unnaturally. 3. Embarrassingly. 4. Distortedly (interpretación).

violentar [ve-o-len-tar'], *va.* 1. To enforce by violent means, to violate. 2. To put a wrong construction on a passage or writing. 3. *(Met.)* To open or break a thing by force (puerta),

to enter a place against the will of its proprietor. *-vr.* To be violent.

violento, ta [ve-o-len'-to, tah], *a.* 1. Violent, impetuous, boisterous, furious. 2. Violent, forced, unnatural (postura). 3. Strained, absurd, erroneous. 4. Embarrassed, awkward (estado de persona). 5. *(LAm.)* Quick, sudden. **Mostrarse violento**, to turn violent. **Para mí todo esto es un poco violento**, this is all a bit awkward.

violero [ve-o-lay'-ro], *m.* A player upon the viola.

violeta [ve-o-lay'-tah], *f. (Bot.)* Violet.

violeto [ve-o-lay'-to], *m.* A clingstone peach. V. PELADILLO.

violín [ve-o-leen'], *m.* 1. Violin (instrumento), fiddle. 2. Fiddler, violinist.

violinete [ve-o-le-nay'-tay], *m.* Kit, a pocket-violin, used by dancing-masters.

violinista [ve-o-le-nees'-tah], *m.* Violinist.

violón [ve-o-lone'], *m.* 1. Bass-viol, double bass (instrumento). 2. Player on the bass-viol.

violoncelo [ve-o-lon-thay'-lo], *m.* Violoncello.

violoncillo [ve-o-lon-theel'-lyo], *m.* Small bass-viol or player on it.

violonchelo [ve-o-lon-chay'-lo], *m.* V. VIOLONCELO.

vipéreo, rea [ve-pay'-ray-o, ah], *a.* V. VIPERINO

viperino, na [ve-pay-ree'-no, nah], *a.* Viperine, viperous.

viquitortes [ve-ke-tor'-tes], *m. pl. (Naut.)* Quarter-gallery knees.

vira [vee'-rah], *f.* 1. A kind of light dart or arrow of ancient warfare. 2. Stuffing between the upper leather and inner sole. 3. Welt of a shoe.

viracocha [ve-rah-co'-chah], *m. (Peru)* Name of the Creator among the Incas, and which the Indians later applied to their white conquerors.

virada [ve-rah'-dah], *f. (Naut.)* Tacking, tack. **Virada de bordo**, tack putting the ship about.

virador [ve-ra-dor'], *m.* 1. *(Naut.)* Top rope; viol. 2. Liquid used in photography to tone.

virar [ve-rar'], *vn* 1. *(Naut.)* To tack, to put about. 2. *(And. Cono Sur)* To turn round (volver); to turn over (invertir). *-va.* To wind, to twist. **Virar el cable**, to heave taut. **Virar de bordo**, to tack or go about.

viratón [ve-rah-tone'], *m.* A kind of large daft or arrow.

virazón [ve-rah-thone'], *f. (Naut.)* Sea-breeze.

víreo [vee'-ray-o], *m.* V. VIRIO.

virgen [veer'-hen], *com.* Virgin, maid. Man who has not had carnal connection with a woman. *-a.* Anything in its pure and primitive state. **Cera virgen**, virgin wax. **Plata virgen**, native silver. *-f.* 1. One of the upright posts, between which the beam of an oil-mill moves. 2. The Holy Virgin Mary; image of the Virgin. 3. A nun. **Vírgenes**, nuns vowed to chastity.

virgiliano, na [veer-he-le-ah'-no, nah], *a.* Virgilian, characteristic of Virgil.

virginal [veer-he-nahl'], *a.* Virginal, maiden, virgin.

virgíneo, nea [veer-hee'-nay-o, ah], *a.* V. VIRGINAL.

virginia [veer-hee'-ne-ah], *f. (Bot.)* Virginia tobacco.

virginidad [veer-he-ne-dahd'], *f.* Virginity, maidenhood.

virgo [veer'-go], *m.* 1. *(Ast.)* Virgin, a sign of the zodiac. 2. Virginity. 3. *(Anat.)* Hymen.

virguería [veer-gay-ree'-ah], *f.* Silly adornment (adorno), frill; pretty thing (objeto). **Hacer virguerías con algo**, to be clever enough to handle something well.

vírgula [veer'-goo-lah], *f.* 1. A small rod. 2. Slight line.

virgulilla [veer-goo-leel'-lyah], *f.* 1. Comma: it is called *coma* in printing and *tilde* in writing. 2. Any fine stroke or light line.

virgulto [veer-gool'-to], *m.* Shrub, bush, small tree.

viril [ve-reel'], *m.* 1. A clear and transparent glass. 2. A small locket or round case in the center of the monstrance, with two plates of glass, between which the host is placed, to expose it to the congregation in Catholic churches.

viril [ve-reel'], *a*. Virile, manly.

virilidad [ve-re-le-dahd'], *f*. 1. Virility (cualidad), manhood (estado). 2. Vigor, strength.

virilla, ita [ve-ree'-lyah], *f. dim.* of VIRA. **Virilla**, ornament of gold or silver formerly worn in shoes.

virilmente [ve-reel'-men-tay], *adv*. In a manly manner.

virio [vee'-re-o], *m. (Orn.)* Vireo, a green and yellow bird of the United States.

viripotente [ve-re-po-ten'-tay], *a*. Marriageable, nubile (mujeres).

virol [ve-role'], *m. (Her.) V.* PERFIL.

virola [ve-ro'-lah], *f*. Collar, hoop, ferrule, ring put upon canes, pocket-knives, etc.

virolento, ta [ve-ro-len'-to, tah], *a*. Diseased with small-pox, pock-marked.

virología [ve-ro-lo-hee'-ah], *f*. Virology.

virotazo [ve-ro-tah'-tho], *m*. 1. *(Aug.) V.* VIROTÓN. 2. Wound with a dart or arrow.

virote [ve-ro'-tay], *m*. 1. Shaft, dart, arrow. 2. Dude, fop, a showy, vain young man; inflated person. 3. A long iron rod fastened to a collar on the neck of a slave, who showed an intention of running away. 4. *(Prov.)* Vine three years old. 5. A puffed-up man, too serious and erratic. 6. A carnival trick. **Mirar por el virote**, *(Met.)* to be attentive to one's own concerns or convenience.

virotón [ve-ro-tone'], *m. aug.* Large dart or arrow.

virreina [vir-ray'-e-nah], *f*. Lady of a viceroy.

virreinato, virreino [vir-ray-e-nah'-to], *m*. Viceroyship; duration of this office; the district governed by a viceroy.

virrey [vir-ray'-e], *m*. Viceroy.

virtual [veer-too-ahl'], *a. 1*. Virtual (real). 2. Potential (potencial).

virtualidad [veer-too-ah-le-dahd'], *f*. Virtuality, efficacy.

virtualmente [veer-too-ahl'-men-tay], *adv*. Virtually, in effect.

virtud [veer-tood'], *f*. 1. Virtue (capacidad), efficacy (eficacia), power, force. 2. Virtue, acting power. 3. Virtue, efficacy without visible action. 4. Virtue, medicinal efficacy. 5. Virtue, moral goodness, integrity, rectitude. 6. Habit, disposition, virtuous life. 7. Vigor, courage. 8. In mechanics, the moving power. 9. In the sacraments, their efficacy and value. **En virtud de**, in virtue of. **Hacer virtud**, to do well.

virtuosamente [veer-too-oh'-sah-men-tay], *adv*. Virtuously.

virtuoso, sa [veer-too-oh'-so, sah], *a*. 1. Virtuous, just. 2. Powerful, vigorous.

viruela [ve-roo-ay'-lah], *f*. 1. Pock, a pustule on the skin. 2. Small-pox. **Picado de viruelas**, pockmarked.

virulencia [ve-roo-len'-the-ah], *f*. 1. Virulence, virus. 2. Virulence, acrimony, malignance.

virulento, ta [ve-roo-len'-to, tah], *a*. 1. Virulent, malignant. 2. Purulent.

virus [vee'-roos], *m. (Med.)* Virus, poison, contagion.

viruta [ve-roo'-tah], *f*. Shaving, a thin slice of wood; chip, -*pl*. Cuttings.

visa [vee'-sah], *f*. Visa.

visado [ve-sah'-do], *m*. Visa; permit. **Visado de tránsito**, transit visa.

visaje [ve-sah'-hay], *m*. Grimace. **Hacer visajes**, to make wry faces.

visar [ve-sar'], *va*. To examine a document, to visé (pasaporte).

víscera [vees'-thay-rah], *f*. Viscus, any organ of the body which has an appropriate use. -*pl*. viscera. **Las víceras**, the viscera.

visceral [vis-thay-rahl'], *a*. Visceral, belonging to the viscera.

viscina [vis-thee'-nah], *f. (Chem.)* Viscin, a principle peculiar to birdlime.

viscosa [vis-co'-sah], *f. (Chem.)* Viscose (for making rayon and other synthetic fabrics).

viscosidad [vis-co-se-dahd'], *f*. Viscosity (cualidad), glutinousness, glutinous or viscous matter.

viscoso, sa [vis-co'-so, sah], *a*. Viscous, viscid, glutinous, mucilaginous.

visera [ve-say'-rah], *f*. 1. Eye protector, eye shade, visor, that part of the head-piece which covers the face. 2. Box with a spy-hole, through which a pigeon-keeper observes the pigeons. 3. *(Cuba)* Blind of a horse's bridle.

visibilad [ve-se-be-le-dahd'], *f*. Visibility. **La visibilidad queda reducida a cero**, visibility is down to nil.

visible [ve-see'-blay], *a*. 1. Visible, perceptible to the eye. 2. Visible, apparent, open, conspicuous.

visiblemente [ve-see'-blay-men-tay], *adv*. Visibly, clearly; evidently.

visicalc [ve-se-calc], *(Comput.)* Visicalc (visible calculator).

visigodo [ve-se-go'-do], *a*. Visigothic.

visillo [ve-seel'-lyo], *m*. Type of window, blind or curtain.

visión [ve-se-on'], *f*. 1. Sight, vision object of sight. 2. Vision, the act of seeing (vista). 3. *(Coll.)* A frightful, ugly, or ridiculous person. 4. Phamtom, apparition, freak. 5. Spiritual vision, revelation, prophecy; beautiful vision. **Ver visiones**, to be led by fancy, to build castles in the air. **Visión beatífica**, celestial bliss. **Su visión del problema**, his view of the problem.

visionario, ria [ve-se-o-nah'-re-o, ah], *a. & n*. Visionary; not real; fanatical.

visir [ve-seer'], *m*. Vizier, the Turkish prime minister.

visita [ve-see'-tah], *f*. 1. Visit. 2. Visitor (persona), visitant. 3. Visit to a temple to pray. 4. Visit of a doctor to a patient. 5. Visitation, inquisition. 6. Recognition, register, examination. 7. House in which the tribunal of ecclesiastical visitors is held. 8. Body of ministers who form a tribunal to inspect prisons; visit to prisons. **Derecho de visita**, right of search. **Visita de médico**, very short call. **Estar de visita en**, to be on a visit to. -*pl. (Coll.)* Frequent visits; haunts, places of resort.

visitación [ve-se-tah-the-on'], *f*. Visitation, visiting, visit.

visitador, ra [ve-se-tah-dor', rah], *m. & f*. visitor (visitante), visitant. 2. Visitor, an occasional judge, searcher, surveyor.

visitante [ve-se-tahn'-tay], *m. & f*. Visitor, guest.

visitar [ve-se-tar'], *va*. 1. To visit, to pay a visit; to visit a temple or church, to visit a patient as physician. 2. To make a judicial visit, search, or survey; to try weights and measures. 3. To search ships; to examine prisons. 4. To travel, to traverse many countries. 5. To inform oneself personally of anything. 6. To appear, as a celestial spirit. 7. To frequent a place. 8. To visit religious persons and establishments as an ecclesiastical judge. 9. *(Theol.)* To send a special counsel from heaven. 10. *(Law.)* To make an abstract of the charge against a prisoner at visitation. -*vr*. 1. To visit, to keep up the intercourse of ceremonial salutations at the houses of each other. 2. To absent oneself from the choir. **Visitar los altares**, to pray before each altar for some pious purpose.

visiteo [ve-se-tay'-o], *m*. Making or receiving of many visits.

visitero, ra [ve-se-tay'-ro, rah], *a. (Coll.)* Visitor, frequent caller.

visitón [ve-se-tone'], *m. (Aug.* of VISITA) *(Coll.)* A long and tedious visit.

visivo, va [ve-see'-vo, vah], *a*. Visive, having the power of seeing.

vislumbrar [vis-loom-brar'], *va*. 1. To have a glimmering sight of a thing: not to perceive it distinctly (entrever). 2. *(Met.)* To know imperfectly, to conjecture by indications. -*vr*. To glimmer, to appear faintly.

vislumbre [vis-loom'-bray], *f*. 1. A glimmering light. 2. Glimmer, glimmering, faint or imperfect view. 3. Conjecture, surmise. 4. Imperfect knowledge, confused perception. 5. Appearance, slight resemblance. 6. Projecting part of a thing which is scarcely discovered.

viso [vee'-so], *m*. 1. Prospect, an elevated spot, affording an extensive view. 2. Luster, the shining surface of things; brilliant reflection of light. 3. Color, cloak, presence, pretext. 4. Apparent likeness; aspect, appearance (aspecto). 5. Gleam (metal). **A dos visos**, with a double view or design. **Al viso de**, at the sight of.

visón [ve-son'], *m.* Mink.

visor [ve-sor'], *m.* Viewfinder (camara).

visorio, ria [ve-so'-re-o, ah], *a.* Belonging to the sight, visual.

víspera [ves'-pay-rah], *f.* 1. Evening before the day in question; the last evening before a festival. 2. Fore-runner, prelude. 3. Immediate nearness or succession. *-pl.* 1. vesper, one of the parts into which the Romans divided the day. 2. Vespers, the evening service. **En vísperas de**, at the eve of. **Vísperas Sicilianas**, Sicilian vespers: a threat of general punishment.

vista [vees'-tah], *f.* 1. Sight, vision, the sense of seeing. 2. Sight, the act of seeing, vision, view. 3. Sight, eye, eyesight, organ of sight. 4. Aspect, appearance (aspecto). 5. Prospect, view, landscape, vista. 6. Apparition, appearance. 7. Meeting, interview. 8. Clear knowledge or perception. 9. Relation, respective connection, comparison. 10. Intent, view, purpose (intención). 11. First stage of a suit at law. 12. Opinion, judgment. 13. Foresight (perspicacia). 14. View, scene (panorama). 15. Hearing, trial. *-m.* A surveyor in a customhouse. *-f. pl.* 1. Meeting, conference, interview. 2. Presents to a bride by a bridegroom, the day preceding the nuptials. 3. Lights, windows in a building, balconies, verandas. 4. Prospect, an extensive view. **Vista de un pleito**, or **día de la vista de un proceso**, or **una causa**, *(Law.)* the trial or the day of trial of a civil lawsuit, or a criminal prosecution. **A vista de**, in presence of; inconsideration of. **A la vista**, on sight, immediately: before, near, or in view, carefully observing, seeing, or following. **A primera vista**, at first view. **Aguzar la vista**, to sharpen the sigh or perception. **Dar una vista**, to give a passing glance. **Echar la vista**, to choose mentally. **¡Hasta la vista!** good-bye! **Perderse de vista**, *(Coll. and Met.)* to have great superiority in its line (slang, to be «Out of sight»). **Conocer de vista**, to know by sight. **Echar una vista**, to look after. **Tener vista**, to be showy; to be beautiful. **Hacer la vista gorda**, to wink, to connive. **En vista de**, in consequence of; in consideration of. **Comer y tragar con la vista**, *(Met.)* to have a fierce and terrible aspect. **No tenemos ningún cambio a la vista**, we do not have any change in view. **Con la vista puesta en**, with one's eyes fixed on. **Bajar la vista**, to look down. **A 5 años vista**, 5 years from then. **Con vistas a una solución del problema**, with a view to solving the problem.

vistazo [vees-tah'-tho], *m.* Glance. **Dar un vistazo**, to glance, to play the eye.

vistillas [vees-teel'-lyas], *f. pl.* Eminence, affording an extensive prospect, views.

visto, ta [vees'-to, tah], *a.* Obvious to the sight, clear. *-pp. irr.* of VER. **El está bien visto** or **mal visto**, he is respected, or not respected. **Eso es bien** or **mal visto**, that is proper, or approved; improper, or disapproved. **Visto bueno** (in manuscript, V⁰. B⁰.), set after a draft, order, permit, license, account, etc., in public offices, means. The preceding document has been examined and found to be correct; consequently it may signify. Pay the bearer; Let him or the merchandise pass, etc. **Visto es** or **vista está**, it is evident. **No visto**, extraordinary, prodigious. **Visto que**, considering that. **Está muy visto**, it is very common.

vistosamente [vees-to'-sah-men-tay], *adv.* Beautifully, delightfully.

vistoso, sa [vees-to'-so, ash], *a.* Beautiful, delightful, showy (ropa), spectacular (partido).

visual [ve-soo-ahl'], *a.* Visual. **Campo visual**, field of vision.

visualidad [ve-soo-ah-le-dahd'], *f.* Visuality, the agreeable effect which beautiful objects as a whole produce.

visualizar [ve-soo-ah-le-thar'], *va.* 1. *(LAm.)* To see (divisar), to make out. 2. *(Fig.)* To visualize (imaginarse).

visura [ve-soo'-rah], *f.* Minute inspection of anything.

vita [vee'-tah], *f. (Naut.)* Cross-beam on the forecastle, to which cables are fastened.

vital [ve-tahl'], *a.* Vital. **De importancia vital**, of vital importance.

vitalicio, cia [ve-tah-lee'-the-o, ah], *a.* Lasting for life; during life. **Pensión vitalicia**, annuity, life pension. **Empleo vitalicio**, employment or place for life.

vitalicista [ve-tah-le-thees'-tah], *com.* One who enjoys an annuity or income for life.

vitalidad [ve-tah-le-dahd'], *f.* Vitality.

vitalismo [ve-tah-lees'-mo], *m.* Vitalism, a doctrine that the phenomena of the organism are due to so-called vital forces, distinct from the general laws of matter.

vitalista [ve-tah-lees'-tah], *a. & n.* Vitalist, relating to vitalism; one who holds that doctrine.

vitalmente [ve-tahl'-men-tay], *adv.* Vitally.

vitamina [ve-tah-mee'-nah], *f.* Vitamin.

vitando, da [ve-tahn'-do, dah], *a.* 1. That ought to be shunned or avoided. 2. Odious, execrable.

vitela [ve-tay'-lah], *f.* 1. Calf. 2. Vellum, calf-skin.

viteline [ve-tay-lee'-nah], *a.* Of a dark yellow color.

vitícola [ve-tee'-co-lah], *a.* Viticultural, relating to cultivation of the grape. *-m.* Viticulturist, vine-grower.

viticultor, ra [ve-te-cool-tor'], *m & f.* Vine grower (cultivador); proprietor of a vineyard (dueño).

viticultura [ve-te-cool-too'-rah], *f.* Viticulture, culture of the vine.

vitiligo [ve-te-lee'-go], *m.* Vitiligo, a skin disease, characterized by spots showing loss of pigment.

vito [vee'-to], *m.* 1. A lively Andalusian dance. 2. *(Med.)* Chorea. **El baile de San Vito**, St. Vitus' dance.

vitola [ve-to'-lah], *f.* 1. *(Mil.)* Ball caliber, gauge for musket and cannon halls. 2. Measure, size for cigars. 3. *(Amer.Met.)* Appearance, mien, of a person (aspecto).

¡vitor! [vee'-tor], *int.* Shout of joy; Huzza! long live!

vítor [vee'-tor], *m.* 1. Triumphal exclamation; public rejoicing. 2. Tablet containing panegyrical epithets to a hero.

vitorear [ve-to-ray-ar'], *va.* To shout, to lheer, to address with acclamations of joy and praise, to clap.

vitoria [ve-to'-re-ah], *f. V.* VICTORIA.

vitorioso, sa [ve-to-re-oh'-so, sah], *a. V.* VICTORIOSO.

vitre [vee'-tray], *m.* Thin canvas.

vítreo, trea [vee'-tray-o, ah], *a.* Vitreous, glassy, resembling glass.

vitrificable [ve-tre-fe-cah'-blay], *a.* Vitrificable.

vitrificación [ve-tre-fe-cah-the-on'], *f.* Vitrification, vitrifaction.

vitrificar [ve-tre-fe-car'], *va.* To vitrify.

vitrina [ve-tree'-nah], *f.* Glass case (aparador), show case, display-window (escaparate).

vitriolado, da [ve-tre-o-lah'-do, dah], *a.* Vitriolate, vitriolated.

vitriólico, ca [ve-tre-o'-le-co, cah], *a.* Vitriolic.

vitriolo [ve-tre-o'-lo], *m.* Vitriol. **Vitriolo azul**, blue vitriol, copper sulphate. **Vitriolo verde**, green vitriol, ferrous sulphate. **Vitriolo blanco**, white vitriol, zinc sulphate.

vitualla [ve-too-ahl'-lyah], *f.* Victuals, viands, food, provisions: generally used in the plural.

vituallado, da [ve-too-al-lyah'-do, dah], *a.* Victualled, provided with victuals.

vitulino, na [ve-too-lee'-no, nah], *a.* Belonging to a calf.

vituperable [ve-too-pay-rah'-blay], *a.* Vituperable, blameworthy, condemnable.

vituperación [ve-too-pay-rah-the-on'], *f.* Vituperation.

vituperador, ra [ve-too-pay-rah-dor', rah], *m. & f.* A blamer, censurer.

vituperante [ve-too-pay-rahn'-tay], *pa.* Vituperating, censuring, decrying.

vituperar [ve-too-pay-rar'], *va.* To vituperate, to censure, to reproach, to decry, to condemn.

vituperio [ve-too-pay'-re-o], *m.* 1. Vituperation, reproach (reproche), blame, censure. 2. Infamy, disgrace.

vituperiosamente [ve-too-pay-re-o-sah-men'-tay], *adv.* Opprobriously, reproachfully.

vituperosamente [ve-too-pay-ro-sah-men'-tay], *adv.* Reproachfully.

vituperoso, sa [ve-too-pay-ro'-so, sah], *a.* Opprobrious, reproachful.

viuda [ve-oo'-dah], *f.* 1. Widow (persona). **Condesa viuda de**, countess widow of. 2. *(Zool.)* Viuda, a noteworthy bird of South America and Africa; a tyrant fly-catcher. 3. *(Bot.)* Mourning widow or mourning bride; scabious.

viudal [ve-oo-dahl'], *a.* Belonging to a widow or widower.

viudedad [ve-oo-day-dahd'], *f.* 1. Widowhood, viduity. 2. Dowry. 3. Usufruct enjoyed during widowhood of the property of a deceased person.

viudez [ve-oo-deth'], *f.* Widowhood.

viudita [ve-oo-dee'-tah], *f. dim.* 1. A spruce little widow. 2. *(Bot.)* Scabious, mourning bride.

viudo [ve-oo'-do], *m.* Widower. *-a.* Applied to birds that pair.

¡viva! [vee'-vah], *int.* Long live, hurrah, huzza, a shout of joy, triumph, applause, or encouragement. *-m.* Huzza, a shout, a cry of acclamation.

vivac [ve-vahc'], *m.* Town-guard to keep order at night; bivouac, nightguard, a small guard-house.

vivacidad [ve-vah-the-dahd'], *f.* Vivacity, liveliness (personalidad), brightness (inteligencia), vigor; brilliancy.

vivamente [ve-vah-men'-tay], *adv* Vividly, to the life, with a strong resemblance.

vivandero, ra [ve-van-day'-ro, rah], *m. & f. (Mil.)* Sutler.

vivaque [ve-vah'-kay], *m.* Bivouac, a small guard-house.

vivaquear [ve-vah'-kay-ar'], *vn.* To bivouac.

vivar [Ve'-var], *m.* 1. Warren for breeding rabbits or other animals; vivary. 2. Burrow of a rabbit. 3. Fishpond (estanque).

vivar [ve-var'], *va. (Peru, etc.)* V. VITOREAR.

vivaracho, cha [ve-vah-rah'-cho, cha], *a.* Lively (persona), smart, sprightly, frisky, superficially (atractivo), bright (ojos).

vivario [ve-vah'-re-o], *m.* Fish-pond.

vivaz [ve-vath'], *a.* 1. Lively (vivo), active, vigorous (vigoroso). 2. Ingenious, acute, witty. 3. As used of plants, perennial, evergreen.

vivencia [ve-vayn'-the-ah], *f.* Experience, knowledge gained from experience.

víveres [vee'-vay-res], *m. pl.* Provision for an army or fortress.

vivero [ve-vay'-ro], *m.* 1. *(Bot.)* The mastic-tree. 3. Warren; fish-pond; vivary (de peces). 4. Seedbed (semillero).

viveza [ve-vay'-thah], *f.* 1. Liveliness, vigor, activity, gaiety. 2. Celerity, briskness. 3. Ardor, energy, vehemence. 4. Acuteness, perspicacity, penetration. 5. Witticism. 6. Strong resemblance. 7. Luster, splendor. 8. Grace and brilliancy in the eyes. 9. Inconsiderate word or act. **La viveza de su inteligencia**, the sharpness of his mind. **Contestar con viveza**, to answer sharply.

vividero, ra [ve-ve-day'-ro, rah], *a.* Habitable.

vividor, ra [ve-ve-dor', rah], *m. & f.* A long liver.

vividor, ra [ve-ve-dor', rah], *a.* Frugal, economical, careful, in mode of life.

vivienda [ve-ve-en'-dah], *f.* 1. Dwelling-house, apartments, lodgings. 2. Dwelling, accomodation. **El problema de la vivienda**, the housing problem.

viviente [ve-ve-en'-tay], *a.* Living. **Todo ser viviente**, every living thing.

vivificación [ve-ve-fe-cah-the-on'], *f.* Vivification, enlivening.

vivificador, ra [ve-ve-fe-cah-dor', rah], *m. & f.* One who vivifies, animates, or enlivens.

vivificante [ve-ve-fe-cahn'-tay], *pa.* Vivifying, life-giving.

vivificar [ve-ve-fe-car'], *va.* 1. To vivify, to vivificate, to animate, to enliven. 2. To comfort, to refresh.

vivificativo, va [ve-ve-fe-cah-tee'-vo, vah], *a.* Vivificative, life-giving, animating, comforting.

vivífico, ca [ve-vee'-fe-co, cah], *a.* Vivific, springing from life.

vivíparo, ra [ve-vee'-pah-ro, rah], *a.* Viviparous; opposed to oviparous.

vivir [ve-veer'], *vn.* 1. To have life, to live; to enjoy life. 2. To live, to continue, to last, to keep. 3. To have the means of supporting life. 4. To live; emphatically, to enjoy happiness. 5. To live, to pass life in a certain manner. 6. To be remembered, to enjoy fame. 7. To be, to exist; to be present in memory. 8. To live, to inhabit, to reside, to lodge. 9. To temporize. 10. To guard life. 11. To have eternal life. **Alegría de vivir**, joy of living. **Como se vive se muere**, as we live so shall we die. **No me deja vivir**, he doesn't leave me alone. **¿Quién vive?** *(Mil.)* who is there? **Vivir para ver**, live and learn (or strange enough). **Ha vivido momentos de verdadera angustia**, she went through moments of real agony. **No dejar vivir a uno**, to give somebody no peace. **Vivir por encima de sus posibilidades**, to live beyond one's means. **Ganar lo justo para vivir**, to earn a bare living. **¡Viva el rey!**, long life to the king!, long live the king! **Y vivieron felices y comieron perdices**, and they lived happily ever after.

vivisección [vee-vee-sec-the-on'], *f.* Vivisection, dissection of a living animal for purpose of scientific inquiry.

vivo, va [vee'-vo, vah], *a.* 1. Living, enjoying life, active. 2. Lively (descripción), efficacious, intense (emoción). 3. Disencumbered, disengaged. 4. Alive, kindled. 5. Acute (dolor), ingenious; vivid, bright (color), smart. 6. Hasty, inconsiderate. 7. Diligent, nimble. 8. Pure, clean. 9. Constant, enduring. 10. Vivid, florid, excellent. 11. Very expressive or persuasive. 12. Blessed. 13. Sharp (listo), clever, lively (animado). 14. *(Cono Sur)* Naughty (travieso). **En vivo**, living. *Viva voz*, by word of mouth. **Cal viva**, quicklime. **Carne viva**, quick flesh in a wound. **Ojos vivos**, very bright, lively eyes.

vivo [veé-vo], *m.* 1. Edging, border of clothing, stone, wood, etc., after dressing and trimming, or polishing. 2. *(Arch.)* Jut, any prominent part of a building which juts out. Mange, the itch or scab in dogs.

vizcacha [veeth-cah'-chah], *f.* A large kind of hare, Peruvian hare.

vizcaíno, na [veeth-cah-ee'-no, nah], *a.* Biscayan, of Biscay.

vizcondado [veeh-con-dah'-do], *m.* Viscountship.

vizconde [veeth-con'-day], *m.* Viscount.

vizcondesa [veeth-con-day'-sah], *f.* Viscountess.

viznaga [veeth-nah'-gah], *f. (Bot.)* Carrot-like ammi.

vizvirindo, da [vith-ve-reen'-do, dah], *a. (Mex.)* V. VIVARACHO.

vocablo [vo-cah'-blo], *m.* Word, term, diction, vocable.

vocabulario [vo-cah-boo-lah'-re-o], *m.* 1. Vocabulary, dictionary, lexicon. 2. *(Coll.)* Person who announces or interprets the will of another.

vocación [vo-cah-the-on'], *f.* 1. Vocation, calling by the will of God. 2. Trade, employment, calling. 3. *V.* ADVOCACIÓN and CONVOCACIÓN.

vocal [vo-cahl'], *a.* Vocal, oral. *-f.* Vowel. *m.* Voter, in a congregation or assembly.

vocalista [vo-cah-lees'-tah], *m & f.* Vocalist, singer.

vocalización [vo-cah-le-thah-the-on'], *f.* Vocalization.

vocalizar [vo-cah-le-thar'], *vn.* To vocalize, to articulate.

vocalmente [vo-cahl'-men-tay], *adv.* Vocally, articulately.

vocativo [vo-cah-tee'-vo], *m. (Gram.)* Vocative, the fifth case of nouns.

voceador, ra [vo-thay-ah-dor', rah], *m. & f.* Vociferator.

vocear [vo-thay-ar'], *va. & vn.* 1. To cry (mercancías), to cry out, to glamor, to scream, to bawl, to halloo. 2. To cry, to publish, to proclaim; to call to: applied occasionally to inanimate things. 3. To shout, to huzza; to applaud by acclamation; to boast publicly (reivindicar).

vocería [vo-thay-reé-ah], *f.* Clamor (jaleo), outcry, hallooing.

vocero [vo-thay'-ro], *m.* (*LAm.*) Spokesman.

vociferación [vo-the-fay-rah-the-on'], *f.* Vociferation, clamor, outcry, boast.

vociferador, ra [vo-the-fay-rah-dor', rah], *m. & f.* Boaster, bragger.

vociferante [vo-the-fay-rahn'-tay], *pa. & n.* Vociferating, caller.

vociferar [vo-the-fay-rar'], *vn.* To vociferate, to bawl, to proclaim, to clamor. -*va.* To boast, to brag loudly or publicly (proclamar).

vocinglería [vo-thin-glay-ree'-ah], *f.* 1. Clamor (griterío), outcry, a confused noise of many voices. 2. Loquacity.

vocinglero, ra [vo-thin-glay'-ro, rah], *a.* Brawling, prattling, chattering, vociferous. -*m. & f.* Loud babbler.

vodka [vod-kah], *f.* Vodka.

vodu [vo-doo'] *m.* voodoo.

voladera [vo-lah-day'-rah], *f.* One of the float or pallets of a water-wheel.

voladero, ra [vo-lah-day'-ro, rah], *a.* Volatile, flying, fleeting. -*m.* Precipice, abyss.

voladizo, za [vo-lah-dee'-tho, ah], *a.* Projecting from a wall, jutting out.

voladizo, *m.* Any short cover projecting from a wall; corbel.

volado [vo-lah'-do], *m.* V. AZUCARILLO.

volado, da [vo-lah'-do, dah], *a.* 1. (*Typ.*) Superior. 2. (*Cono Sur*) Proyecting (voladizo); protuberant (abultado). -*m.* 1. (*CAm.*) Fib (mentira). 2. (*Carib. Cono Sur*) Flounce, ruffle. 3. (*Mex.*) Game of heads of tails (juego). 4. (*Mex.*) Adventure (aventura).

volador, ra [vo-lah-dor', rah], *a.* 1. Flying, running fast. 2. Hanging in the air. 3. Blowing up with gunpowder (fuegos artificiales). -*m.* 1. Rocket. 2. Flying-fish. -*f.* Fly-wheel of a steam-engine.

volandas, or **en volandas** [vo-lahn'-das], *adv.* 1. In the air, through the air, as if flying 2. (*Coll.*) Rapidly, in an instant.

volandera [vo-lan-day'-rah], *f.* 1. (In oil-mills) Runner, the stone which runs edgewise upon another stone. 2. (*Coll.*) A vague or flying report, lie. 3. Wash of an axle-tree, nave-box of a wheel. 4. (*Print.*) Ledge on a type galley.

volandero, ra [vo-lan-day'-ro, rah], *a.* 1. Suspended in the air, volatile. 2. Fortuitous, casual. 3. Unsettled, fleeting, variable, volatile.

volandillas (En) [en vo-lan-deel'-lyas], *adv.* V. VOL-ANDAS (EN).

volanta [vo-lahn'-tah], *f.* (*Cuba*) A two-wheel covered vehicle with very long shafts.

volante [vo-lahn'-tay], *pa. & a.* 1. Flying (que vuela), volant, fluttering, unsettled. 2. Applied to the pulsation of the arteries. 3. Applied to a kind of meteors. **Papel volante,** short writing or manuscript easily disseminated: it generally contains some satire or libel.

volante [vo-lahn'-tay], *m.* 1. An ornament of light gauze hanging from a woman's headdress. 2. Shuttle-cock. 3. Coining-mill, or that part of it which strikes the die. 4. Balance of a watch. 5. (*Mech.*) Fly-wheel, a heavy governing wheel. 6. Livery servant or foot-boy who runs before his master, or rides behind. 7. Lawn tennis. 8. Flier, a long narrow sheet of paper. 9. (*Cuba*) (1) V. VOLANTA. (2) A linen coat. (*Mex.*) A dress-coat.

volantín [vo-lan-teen'], *m.* 1. A certain apparatus for fishing. 2. (*LAm.*) Kite (cometa). 3. (*And.*) Rocket (cohete).

volantón [vo-lan-tone'], *m.* A fledged bird able to fly.

volapié [vo-lah-pe-ay'], *m.* A lot in bull-fighting which consists in wounding the beast while running, the latter standing. **A volapié, adv.** Half running, half flying.

volapuk [vo-lah-pook']. *m.* Volapük, a commercial universal language invented by the Swiss professor J. M. Schleyer.

volar [vo-lar'], *vn.* 1. To fy, as with wings. 2. To fly, to pass through the air. 3. To fly, to move swiftly. 4. To vanish, to

disappear all of a sudden. 5. To rise in the air like a steeple or pile. 6. To make rapid progress in studies; to subtilize, to refine sentiments; to move with rapidity or violence. 7. To project, to hang over. 8. To execute with great promptitude and facility; to extend, to publish anything rapidly. -*va.* 1. To rouse the game. 2. To fly, to attack by a bird of prey. 3. To blow up, to spring a mine; to blast rocks or mines. 4. (*Met.*) To irritate (irritar), to exasperate. 5. To ascend high. 6. (*LAm.*) To put to flight (ahuyentar). 7. (*Mex.*) To pinch (robar). 8. (*Mex.*) To swindle (estafar). **Echar a volar,** (*Met.*) to disseminate, to give to the public. **Echarse a volar,** to leave the parental nest. **Voy volando,** I'll go as quickly as I can.

volatería [vo-lah-tay-ree'-ah], *f.* 1. Fowling; sporting with hawks. 2. Fowls, a flock of birds. 3. A vague or desultory speech; idle or groundless ideas. -*adv.* Fortuitously, adventitiously.

volátil [vo-lah'-teel], *a.* 1. Volatile, flying through the air, or capable of flying; wafting. 2. Changeable, inconstant, fugitive. 3. (*Chem.*) Volatile, vaporizing slowly at ordinary temperatures.

volatilidad [vo-lah-te-le'-dadh], *f.* Volatility, quality of flying away by evaporation.

volatilización [vo-lah-te-le-thah-the-on'], *f.* Volatilization.

volatilizar [vo-lah-te-le-thar'], *va.* To volatilize, to vaporize, to transform into the gaseous state -*vr.* To be dissipated in vapor, to be exhaled or vaporized.

volatín [vo-lah-teen'], *m.* Rope-dancer, and each of his exercises (acrobacia).

volatinero [vo-lah-te-nay'-ro], *m.* Rope-walker; acrobat.

volatizar [vo-lah-te-thar'], *va.* (*Chem.*) To volatilize.

volcán [vol-cahn'], *m.* 1. Volcano. 2. Excessive ardor: violent passion. 3. (*And. Cono Sur*) Summer torrent (torrente). 4. (*CAm. Carib.*) Pile, heap (montón). 5. (*Carib.*) deafening noise (estrépito).

volcánico, ca [vol-cah'-ne-co, cah], *a.* Volcanic, relating to a volcano.

volcar [vol-car'], *va.* 1. To overset, to capsize, to turn one side upwards. 2. To make dizzy or giddy (marear). 3. To make one change his opinion. 4. To tire one's patience with buffoonery or scurrilous mirth. 5. (*Fig.*) Irritate (irritar). -*vn.* 1. To overturn, to upset. -*vr.* 1. To be upset (recipiente). 2. (*Fig.*) To go out of one's way. (*Yo vuelco, yo vuelque,* from *Volcar.* V. ACORDAR.)

volear [vo-lay-ar'], *va.* To throw anything up in the air so as to make it fly; particularly to bat a ball or serve it in tennis.

volea [vo-lay'-ah], *f.* 1. Swingle-tree, whipple-tree (carruajes). 2. Volley (en el juego de pelota); lob (en tenis).

voleo [vo-lay'-o], *m.* 1. Blow given to a ball in the air. 2. Step in a Spanish dance. 3. (*Coll.*) Scolding, harsh reproof. **De un voleo** or **del primer voleo,** at one blow; at the first blow; in an instant.

volframio [vol-frah'-me-o]. *m.* Wolfram, tungsten.

volibol [vo-le-bol'], *m.* Volley-ball.

volición [vo-le-the-on'], *f.* Volition, power of willing, act of will.

volitivo, va [vo-li-tee'-vo, vah], *a.* Having power to will.

volquearse [vol-kay-ar'-say], *vr.* To tumble, to wallow. V. REVOLCARSE.

volquete [vol-kay'-tay], *m.* Dumping truck.

voltaísmo [vol-tah-ees'-mo], *m.* Voltaism, electricity produced by the contact of dissimilar substances.

voltaje [vol-tah'-hay], *m.* (*Elec.*) Voltage.

voltamperio [vol-tam-pay'-re-o], *m.* (*Elec.*) Volt-ampere.

voltariedad [vol-tah-re-ay-dahd'], *f.* Fickleness, inconstancy, volatility.

voltario, ria [vol-tah-re-o, ah], *a.* Fickle (cambiable), inconstant, giddy.

volteador [vol-tay-ah-dor'], *m.* Tumbler, one who shows or teaches postures and feats of activity.

voltear [vol-tay-ar'], *va.* 1. To whirl, to revolve. 2. To overturn (recipiente), to over set. 3. To change the order or state of things. 4. To knock down, to throw down violently, to fell.

5. To throw an arch across, to construct it. 6. *(Carib.)* To search all over. *-vn.* To roll over (personas, cosas); to tumble, to exhibit feats of agility.

volteo [vol-tay'-o], *m.* 1. Whirl, whirling. 2. Overturning. 3. Tumbling, 4. Dumping.

voltereta [vol-tay-ray'-tah], *f.* Somersault.

volteranismo [vol-tay-re-ah-nees'-mo], *m.* Voltairianism, cynicism, scepticism.

volteriano, na [vol-tay-re-ah'-no, nah], *a.* Voltairian, of Voltaire.

voltímetro [vol-tee'-may-tro], *m. (Elec.)* Voltmeter.

voltio [vol'-te-o], *m.* Volt.

voltizo, za [vol-tee'-tho, thah], *a.* Inconstant, fickle.

volubilidad [vo-loo-be-le-dahd'], *f.* Volubility; inconstancy, fickleness, glibness, fluency.

voluble [vo-loo'-blay], *a.* 1. Easily moved about. 2. Voluble, inconstant, fickle (inconstante). 3. *(Bot.)* Twining, said of a stem which climbs in spirals.

volublemente [vo-loo'-blay-men-tay], *adv.* Volubly.

volumen [vo-loo'-men], *m.* 1. Volume, size, bulkiness (abultado); corpulence. 2. Volume, bound book. 3. *(Geom.)* Volume, space occupied by a body. **Volumen de ventas**, amount of business done. **Poner la radio a todo volumen**, to turn the radio up full.

voluminoso, sa [vo-loo-me-no'-so, sah], *a.* Voluminous; of large bulk.

voluntad [vo-loon-tahd'], *f.* 1. Will, choice, determination. 2. Divine determination. 3. Goodwill, benevolence, kindness. 4. Desire (deseo), pleasure; free will, volition (volición), election, choice. 5. Disposition, precept; intention (intención), resolution. **De voluntad** or **de buena voluntad**, with pleasure, gratefully. **Última voluntad**, one's last will. **Por causas ajenas a mi voluntad**, for reasons beyond my control. **No tiene voluntad para dejar de beber**, he hasn't the willpower to give up drinking.

voluntariamente [vo-loon-tah'-re-ah-men-tay], *adv.* Spontanously, voluntarily, fain.

voluntariedad [vo-loon-tah-re-ay-dahd'], *f* Free-will, spontaneousness.

voluntario, ria [vo-loon-tah'-re-o, ah], *a.* Voluntary, spontaneous, willing, gratuitous, free.

voluntario [vo-loon-tah'-re-o], *m.* Volunteer; a solider who serves of his own accord.

voluntariosamente [vo-loon-tah-re-oh'-sah-men-tay], *adv.* Spontaneously, selfishly.

voluntarioso, sa [vo-loon-tah-re-oh'-so, sah], *a.* 1. Selfish, humorous, one who merely follows the dictates of his own will; desirous. 2. Headstrong, wilful, willing, well-intentioned.

voluptuosamente [vo-loop-too-o-sah-men'-tay], *adv.* Voluptuously, sensuously; licentiously.

voloptuosidad [vo-loop-too-o-se-dahd'], *f.* Voluptuousness, licentiousness.

voluptuoso, sa [vo-loop-too-oh'-so, sah], *a.* Voluptuous, sensuous; licentious, sensual, lustful.

voluta [vo-loo'-tah], *f. (Arch.)* Volute, an ornament of the capitals of columns. 2. A mollusk having an oval shell of a short spiral.

volvedor [vol-vay-dor'], *m.* Screw-driver (destornillador), turn-screw.

volver [vol-verr'], *va. & vn.* 1. To turn, to give turns (objeto, viajero). 2. To return, to restore, to repay, to give back (devolver), to give up. 3. To come back (regresar), to return, to come again to the same place. 4. To return to the same state. 5. To turn from a straight line (carreteras). 6. To direct, to aim; to remit; to send back a present. 7. To translate languages. 8. To change the outward appearance (transformar); to invert, to change from one place to another. 9. To vomit, to throw up victuals. 10. To make one change his opinion; to convert, to incline. 11. To return a ball. 12. To reflect a sound. 13. To turn away, to discharge. 14. To regain,

to recover. 15. To repeat, to reiterate: in this sense it is accompanied by *a*. 16. To stand out for a person, or to undertake his defence; to defend: here it is used with **por**. 17. To re-establish, to replace in a former situation. 18. To plough land a second time. 19. To resume the thread of a discourse interrupted. 20. To reiterate, to repeat. **Volver la puerta**, to shut the door. **Hacer volver** or **mandar volver**, to recall. **Volver atrás**, to come back. **Volver a uno loco**, to confound one with arguments, so that he appears stupid. **Volver sobre sí**, to reflect on oneself with purpose of amendment, to make up one's losses; to recover serenity of mind. **Volver en sí**, to recover one's senses. **Volver la cara**, to face about. **Me volvió la espalda**, he turned his back on me. **Vuelve fieras a los hombres**, it turns men into wild beasts. **Han vuelto a pintar la casa**, they have painted, the house again. *-vr.* 1. To turn, to grow sour. 2. To turn towards one. 3. To retract an opinion (desdecirse), to change. **Volverse blanco**, to become white. **Volverse loco**, to be deranged, to become a fool. **Volverse atrás**, to flinch, to retract. **La burla se volvió contra él**, the jest rebounded on him. **Volverse la tortilla**, to turn the tables or scales. —N.B. **Volver**, followed by a verb in the infinitive preceded by the preposition *a*, is generally omitted in English, and the verb in the infinitive mood is translated in the corresponding tense and person, with the addition of the adverb *again*; as **Él volvió a hablar**, he spoke again. **Ellos lo volverán a negar**, they will deny it again. **Volver a la carga**, to return to the charge, to insist. **Volver lo de arriba abajo**, to turn upside down; to invert the order of things.

volvible [vol-vee'-blay], *a.* That may be turned.

volvimiento [vol-ve-me-en'-to], *m.* Act of turning.

volvo, vólvulo [vol'-vo, vol'-vo-lo], *m.* Volvulus, iliac passion.

vólvoce [vol'-vo-thay], *m.* Volvox, the so-called globe-animalcule, a minute green globe, of microscopic life, now referred to the vegetable kingdom.

vómer [vó-mer], *m.* Vomer, a bone dividing the nostrils vertically.

vómica [vo'-me-cah], *f. (Med.)* Vomica, a sac of pus in the lungs or other viscus.

vómico, ca [vo'-me-co, cah], *a.* Causing vomiting: applied to the nut called vomic, or *nux vomica*; it is not, however, *emetic*, as its name implies.

vomipurgante [vo-me-poor-gahn'-tay], *a.* Purgative and emetic at once.

vomitado, da [vo-me-tah'-do, dah], *a. & pp.* of VOMITAR. *(Coll.)* Meagre; pale-faced.

vomitador, ra [vo-me-tah-dor, rah], *m. & f.* One who vomits.

vomitar [vo-me-tar'], *va.* 1. To vomit (devolver). 2. To foam, to break out into injurious expressions. 3. *(Coll.)* To reveal a secret (secreto), to discover what was concealed. 4. *(Coll.)* To pay what was unduly retained. *-vn.* 1. To vomit (devolver). 2. **Eso me da ganas de vomitar**, that makes me sick.

vomitivo, va [vo-me-tee'-vo, vah], *a.* Emetic, vomitive. *-m. (Med.)* Emetic.

vómito [vo'-me-to], *m.* 1. The act of vomiting (acto). 2. Vomit, matter thrown from the stomach. **Provocar a vómito**, to nauseate, to loathe: used in censuring indecent expressions, or to condemn something. **Vómito negro**, a bilious disease; yellow fever.

vomitón, na [vo-me-tone', nah], *a.* Often throwing milk from the stomach: applied by nurses to a sucking child.

vomitona [vo-me-to'-nah], *f. (Coll.)* Violent vomiting after eating heartily.

vomitorio, ia [vo-me-to're-o, ah], *a.* Vomitive, emetic. *-m.* Passage or entrance in Roman theaters.

voracidad [vo-rah-the-dahd'], *f.* 1. Voracity, greedines. 2. *(Met.)* Destructiveness of fire etc.

vorágine [vo-rah'-he-nay], *f.* Vortex, whirlpool.

voraginoso sa [vo-rah-he-no'-so, sah], *a.* Engulfing; full of whirlpools.

voraz [vo-rath'], *a.* 1. Voracious (devorador), greedy to eat, ravenous. 2. Extremely irregular, excessively destructive, fierce.

vorazmente [vo-rath'-men-tay], *adv.* Voraciously, greedily, gluttonously.

vormela [vor-may' -lah], *f.* Kind of spotted weasel.

vórtice [vor'-te-thay], *m.* Whirlpool (agua), whirlwind (viento), hurricane. **Vórtice aéreo**, whirlwind, water-spout.

vorticela [vor-te-thay'-lah], *f.* Vorticella, a typical genus of infusorians.

vortiginoso, sa [vor-te-he-no'-so, sah], *a.* Vortical.

vos [vose], *pron.* You, ye. *V.* VOSOTROS. Used as respectful to persons of dignity.

vosearse [vo-say-ar' -say], *vr.* (*Prov.*) To address as *vos*.

vosotros, tras [vo-so' -tros, trahs], *Pron. Pers. pl.* You.

votación [vo-tah-the-on'], *f.* Voting. **Votación a mano alzada**, show of hands.

votado, da [vo-tah'-do, dah], *a. & pp.* of VOTAR. Devoted.

votador, ra [vo-tah-dor', rah], *m. & f.* 1. One who vows or swears. 2. Voter.

votante [vo-tahn' -tay], *a.* Voter in a corporation or assembly.

votar [vo-tar'], *vn.* 1. To vow. 2. To vote (candidato, partido). 3 To give an opinion. 4. To curse, to utter oaths.

votivo, va [vo-tee'-vo, vah], *a.* Votive, offered by a vow.

voto [vo'-to], *m.* 1. Vow (promesa). 2. Vote, suffrage. 3. Opinion, advice, voice: hence, also, voter. **Voto de calidad** or **decisivo**, casting vote. **A pluralidad de votos**, by a majority of votes. 4. A gift offered to saints by the faithful. 5. Supplication to God. 6. Angry oath or execration (juramento). 7. Wish (deseo), desire. **Voto a Dios**, (*Low.*) A menacing oath. **Voto de amén**, a vote blindly given in obedience to the will of another. **Ser** or **tener voto**. (a) to come to a vote; (b) to understand clearly the matter under consideration, or to be free from bias. **Voto de castidad**, vow of chastity. **Pronunciar sus votos**, to take vows. **Derecho al voto**, the right to vote. **Depositar un voto**, to cast a vote. **Por una mayoría de votos**, by a majority vote. **Voto de censura**, vote of censure. **Voto de gracias**, vote of thanks. **Voto de confianza**, vote of confidence. **Votos emitidos**, votes cast. **Voto solemne**, solemn vow. **No tienes ni voz ni voto**, you have no say in this matter.

voz [voth], *f.* 1. Voice. 2. Any sound made by breath (sonido). 3. Clamor, outcry. **Dar voces**, to cry, to call aloud. 4. Vocable, expression, word (vocablo), term. 5. Power or authority to speak in the name of another. 6. Voice, vote, suffrage: right of suffrage; opinion expressed. 7. Rumor (rumor), public opinion. 8. Motive, pretext. 9. Word, divine inspiration. 10. (*Gram.*) Voice, active or passive. 11. (*Mus.*) Vocal music; treble, tenor; tune corresponding to the voice of a singer. 12. Order, mandate of a superior. 13. (*Law.*) Life. **Voz activa**, right or power of voting. **Tomar voz**, to acquire knowledge, to reason: to confirm or support anything by the opinions of others. **A media voz**, with a slight hint; with a low voice; in a submissive tone. **A voces**, clamorous cry, loud voice. **En voz**, (a) verbally; (b) (*Mus.*) in voice. **Anudarse la voz**, to be unable to speak because of violent excitement. **Dar una voz**, to hail one from a distance. **Dar voces al viento**, to toil in vain. **La voz del pueblo**, the voice of the people. **Levantar la voz**, to raise one's voice. **Canción a cuatro voces**, song for four voices. **Voz común**, hearsay. **Tener voz y voto**, to be present as a full member.

vozarrón [vo-thar-rone'], *m.* A strong, heavy voice.

voznar [voth-nar'], *vn.* To cry like swans, to cackle like geese.

vudú [voo-doo'], *m.* Voodoo.

vuduísmo [voo-doo-ees'-mo], *m.* Voodooism.

vuecelencia, vuecencia [voo-ay-thay-len' -the-ah], *com.* A contraction of *vuestra excelencia*, your excellency.

vuelco [voo-el' -co], *m.* Eversion, overturning, upset. **Mi corazón dio un vuelco**, my heart missed a beat.

vuelo [voo-ay'-lo], *m.* 1. Flight, the act of flying. 2. Wing of a bird. 3. Part of a building which projects beyond the wall. 4. Width or fulness of clothes. 5. Ruffle, flounce, ornament set to the wristband of a shirt; frill. 6. Space flown through at once. 7. Elevation or loftiness in discoursing or working. 8. Leap or bound in pantomimes. **Coger al vuelo**, to catch in flight. **Vuelo en formación**, formation flying. **Vuelo libre**, free flight. **Vuelo sin motor**, gliding, glide. **Vuelo sin parar**, non-stop flight. **Vuelo tripulado** manned flight. **Vuelo en picado** dive. **Tocar las campanas a vuelo**, to peal the bells. **De altos vuelos**, grandiose. **Cortar los vuelos a uno**, to clip somebody's wings.

vuelta [voo-el'-tah], *f.* 1. Turn, the act of turning, gyration, twirl; turn of an arch; circumvolution; circuit. 2. Requital, recompense; regress. 3. Iteration, rehearsal. 4. Back side, wrong side (tela, papel). 5. Whipping, flogging, lashing on the back-side. 6. Turn-out, deviation from a line or straight road. 7. Return from a spot. 8. Turn, time of execution. 9. Turn, inclination, bent. 10. Ruffle. *V.* VUELO. 11. (*Naut.*) Turn, hitch, lashing, 12. Turn, change of things (cambio). 13. Trip, excursion, short voyage. 14. Reconsideration, recollection. 15. Land once, twice, or thrice labored. 16. Wards in a lock or key. 17. Order of stitches in stockings (de puntos). 18. Roll, envelope. 19. Unexpected sally or witticism. 20. Change, surplus money to be returned in dealing. 21. (*Mus.*) Number of verses repeated. 22. (*Mech.*) Rotation stroke; potter's wheel. 23. Stroll, walk (paseo). 24. Beating (paliza). **A vuelta de**, in the course of, within. **A la vuelta**, at your return; that laid aside; about the time; upon. **La vuelta de**, towards this or that way. **Dar una vuelta**, to make a short excursion; to clean something; to examine a thing properly. **Dar vueltas**, to walk to and fro on a public walk; to seek anything; to discuss repeatedly the same topic. **A vuelta** or **a vueltas**, Very near, almost; also, with another thing otherwise. **No tener vuelta de hoja**, to be unanswerable. **Tener vuelta**, (*Coll.*) an admonition to return a thing lent. *-int.* Return; let him return or go back the same way. **No hay que darle vueltas**, (*Met.*) no quibbling about it, it will prove to be the very thing. **Poner de vuelta y media**, to abuse a person by word or action. **Dar media vuelta**, to face about; to turn half somersault. **A la vuelta de la esquina**, round the corner. **De vuelta iremos a verlos**, we'll go and see them on the way back.

vuelto, ta [voo-el'-to, tah], *pp. irr.* of VOLVER.

vuesa [voo-ay'-sah], *a.* Contracted from *vuestra*, and used before *merced eminencia*, ete.

vuesamerced [voo-ay-sah-mer-thed'], *f.* You, sir; you, madam; your worship, your honor; a contraction of *vuestra merced*, a title of courtesy to a person who is not entitled to that of *vueseñoría* or *vuestra señoría*, your lordship.

vuesarced [voo-ay-sar-thed'], *f.* Contraction of *vuesamerced*.

vueseñoría [voo-ay-say-nyo-ree'-ah]. *f.* Contraction of *vuestra señoría*.

vuestro, tra [voo-es'-tro, trah], *a. pron.* Your, yours. It is used absolutely by subjects to a sovereign, or by a sovereign to a subject. **Muy vuestro**, entirely yours. **Vuestra señoría**, your lordship or ladyship.

vulcanita [vool-cah-nee'-tah], *f.* Vulcanite.

vulcanizar [vool-cah-ne-thar'], *va.* To vulcanize, to mix sulphur with rubber at a high temperature.

vulgacho [vool-gah'-cho], *m.* Mob, populace, dregs of the people.

vulgar [vool-gar'], *a.* 1. Vulgar (lengua), common (término), ordinary; vulgar or vernacular dialect, as opposed to the learned languages; without specific peculiarity. 2. Ordinary (persona), coarse (modales, rasgos).

vulgar [vool-gar'], The vulgar.

vulgaridad [vool-gah-re-dahd'], *f.* Vulgarity (acto); vulgarism, manners or speech of the lowest people; vulgar effusion.

vulgarismo [vool-gah-rees'-mo], *m.* Colloquialism, colloquial expression.

vulgarizar [vool-gah-re-thar'], *va.* 1. To make vulgar or common. 2. To translate from another idiom into the common language of the country. *-vr.* To become vulgar.

vulgarmente [vool-gar'-men-tay], *adv.* Vulgarly, commonly; among the common people.

vulgata [vool-gah'-tah], *f.* Vulgate, the Latin version of the Bible, approved by the Roman Church.

vulgo [vool'-go], *m.* 1. Multitude, populace, mob. 2. Way of thinking of the populace. 3. Universality or generality of people. *-adv.* V. VULGARMENTE.

vulnerable [vool-nay-rah'-blay], *a.* Vulnerable.

vulneración [vool-nay-rah-the-on'], *f.* The act of wounding.

vulnerar [vool-nay-rar'], *va.* 1. To wound. V. HERIR. 2. To injure the reputation.

vulneraria [vool-nay-rah'-re-ah], *f. (Bot.)* Kidney vetch.

vulnerario, ria [vool-nay-rah'-re-o, ahl, *a.* 1. Vulnerary, useful in healing wounds. 2. *(Law.)* Applied to an ecclesiastic who has wounded or killed anyone.

vulnerario [vool-nay-rah'-re-o], *m.* Clergyman guilty of killing or wounding.

vulpécula [vool-pay'-coo-lah], *f.* V. VULPEJA.

vulpeja [vool-pay'-hah], *f.* A bitch fox.

vulpinita [vool-pe-nee'-tah], *f.* Vulpinite.

vulpino, na [vool-pee'-no, nah], *a.* 1. Proper to a fox, foxy, vulpine. 2. *(Met.)* Foxy, crafty, deceitful.

vultúridos [vool-too'-re-dos], *m. pl.* A division of the birds of prey; the vultures.

vulva [vool'-vah], *f. (Anat.)* Vulva, the external orifice of the female genitals.

vulvaria [vool-vah'-re-ah], *f.* Vulvaria, the fetid orach, a common European plant.

vulvario, ria [vool-vah'-re-o, ah], *a. (Anat.)* Vulvar, pertaining to the vulva.

W

w This letter does not belong to the Spanish alphabet and is only used in terms, chiefly proper names, taken from languages of northern Europe. It is named *V doble* (double v). In chemistry W stands for Wolfram (tungsten).

wáter [vah'-tayr], *m.* Lavatory, water closet.

X

x [ay'-kis], *f.* The twenty-fourth letter of the alphabet. This letter is pronounced like cs or gs in English.

xantásilo [csan-tok'-se-lo], *m. (Bot.)* Xanthoxlum, prickly ash. V. ZANTÓXILO.

xapurcar [csah-poor-car'], *va. (Prov.)* To stir up dirty water.

xara [csah'-rah, properly shah'-rah], *f.* The law of the Moors.

xenofobia [csay-no-pho'-be-ah], *m.* Xenophobia.

xenófobo [csay-noh'-pho-bo], *a.* Xenophobic.

xerofagia [csay-ro-fah'-he-ah], *f.* Xerophagy.

xerófila [csay-ro'-fe-lah], *m. (Bot.)* Xerophyte

xi [csee], *f.* Fourteenth letter of the Greek alphabet, corresponding to X.

xifoideo, ea [cse-foi-day'-o, ah], *a.* Xiphoid, relating to the xiphoid cartilage.

xifoides [cse-foi'-days], *a. & m. (Zool.)* Xiphoid, swordshaped; the cartilage ending the sternum below.

xilófago, ga [cse-lo'-fah-go], *a.* Xylophagous, feeding on or boring in wood. *-m.* A dipterous insect living in elms.

xilofón, xilófono [se-lo-fone', se-lo'-fo-no], *m. (Mus.)* Xilophone.

xilografía [cse-lo-grah-fee'-ah], *f.* Xylography, wood-engraving.

xilográfico, ca [cse-lo-grah'-fe-co, cah], *a.* Xylographic, relating to engraving upon wood.

xo [cso], int. Whoa! V. JO and CHO.

Y

y [yay, ee gre-ay'-gah], *f.* The twenty-fifth letter of the Castilian alphabet, stands as a vowel and a consonant. **Y**, when alone, or after a vowel, or followed by a consonant, or at the end of a word, is a vowel, and sounds as *e* or *ee* in English: *Hoy y mañana* (today and tomorrow), *o'-ee ee mah-nyah'-nah*. **Y**, before a vowel in the same syllable, or between two vowels in the same word, is a consonant, and sounds like the English *y* in the words *yard, yell, you.*

y [ee], *conj.* And. It is frequently used in interrogatives, or by way of a reply; as **¿Y tú, no haces lo mismo?** and you, do you not do the same? **¿Y tú, dónde has estado?** and you, where have you been? **¿ Y bien?** and well then? **Alfonso, Fernando y Manuel**, Alphonsus, Ferdinand, and Emmanuel. When the conjunction *y* is followed by a word beginning with *i* or *hi*, the conjunction *e* is used instead; as, **Sabiduría e ignorancia**, wisdom and ignorance. **Padre e hijo**, father and son.

ya [yah], *adv.* 1. Already (pasado). 2. Presently, immediately, now (presente). 3. Finally, ultimately. 4. At another time, on another occasion. **Ya no es lo que ha sido**, it is not now what it has been. **Ya estamos en ello**, we've got it, we understand it. **Ya voy, I** am going, or **I** am going presently. *-part.* Now. **Ya esto, ya aquello**, now this, now that. **Ya que has venido**, since you are coming, or since you are here. *-int.* Used on being brought to recollect something. **¿No se acuerda Ud. de tal cosa? Ya, ya**, do you not remember such a thing? Yes, yes: **Ya se ve, yes**, you can see it! it is clear, it is so. **Ya estaba yo en eso, I** was already of that mind.

yaacabó [yah-ah-cah-bo'], *m.* A hawk or falcon of Venezuela, whose note sounds like *ya acabó.* (Imitative.)

yaca [yah'-cah], *f. (Bot.)* A large-leaved Indian tree.

yacaré [yah-cah-ray'], *m. (Zool. Amer.)* Crocodile.

yacedor [yah-thay-dor'], *m.* A lad who takes horses to graze by night.

yacente [yah-then'-tay], *pa. & a.* Jacent, vacant; lying.

yacer [yah-therr'], *vn.* 1. To lie, to lie down. 2. To lie down in the grave. 3. To be fixed or situated in a place; to exist. 4. To graze by night in the field. *(Yo yazgo* or *yago, yazga* or *yaga.* V. YACER.)

yaciente [yah-the-en'-tay], *a.* Extended, stretched.

yacija [yah-thee'-hah], *f.* 1. Bed (cama), couch. 2. Tomb, grave (sepultura). **Ser de mala yacija**, to be a vagrant; to be restless; to have a bad bed.

yacimiento [yah-the-me-ayn'-to], *m.* Bed, deposit; site (arqueológico).

yactura [yac-too'-rah], *f.* Loss, damage.

yáculo [yah'-coo-lo], *m.* 1. A serpent which darts from trees in order to attack. 2. *(Zool.)* Dace.

yacumana [yah-coo-mah'-nah], *f.* Name given to the boa in the Amazonian provinces.

yagre [yah'-gray], *m.* Sugar, extracted from the palm or cocoa tree. V. JACRA.

yagua [yah'-goo-ah], *f.* Bark of the royal palm.

yak [yahk], *m.* Yak, a bovine quadruped of central Asia.

yalotecnia [yah-lo-tec'-ne-ah], *f.* The art of working glass.

yámbico, ca [yahm'-be-co, cah], *a.* Iambic: applied to a Latin verse.

yambo [yahm'-bo], *m.* An iambic foot.

yanacona [yah-nah-co'-nah], **Yanacuna** [yah-nah-coo'-nah], *com. (Peru)* The Indian bound to personal service.

yankee [yahn'-kee], *com. & a.* 1. A person born or living in New England. 2. A native of the United States.

yanqui [yahn'-kee], *a.* A native of the United States.

yantar [yahn-tar'], *m.* 1. *(Prov.)* Viands, food. 2. A kind of king's taxes.

yapa [yah'-pah], *f.* A thing or quantity which the seller presents to the buyer. *V.* ÑAPA and CONTRA.

yarda [yar'-dah], *f.* An English yard, equal to 91 centimeters; a *vara*, the Spanish measure of 3 feet, is equivalent to 8.36 decimeters.

yarey [yah-ray'-e], *m. (Cuba)* A species of *guano* (palm-tree).

yaro [yah'-ro], *m. (Bot.)* Arum, an aquatic plant.

yareta [yah-ray'-tah], *f.* A kind of combustible; peat.

yatagán [yah-tah-gahn'], *m.* A kind of a sabre-dagger used by the orientals.

yate [yah'-tay], *m.* Yacht, a pleasure craft, sailing or propelled by steam.

yayero, ra [yah-yay'-ro, rah], *a. (Cuba)* Intermeddling, busybody.

yedra, or yedra arborácea [yay'-drah], *f. (Bot.)* Ivy. **yedra terrestre**, ground ivy.

yegua [yay'-goo-ah], *f.* 1. Mare. **Yegua madre**, A dam. 2. *(And. Cono Sur)* Old bag, whore. 3. *(And. CAm.)* Cigar stub.

yeguada, yegüería [yay-goo-ah'-dah, yay-goo-ay-ree'-ah], *f.* 1. Stud (caballeriza), a herd of breeding mares and stallions. 2. *(CAm. Carib.)* Piece of stupidity (estupidez).

yeguar [yay-goo-ar'], *a.* Belonging to mares.

yegüero, yegüerizo [yay-goo-ay'-ro, yay-goo-ay-ree'-tho], *m.* Keeper of breeding mares.

yegüezuela [yay-goo-ay-thoo-ay'-lahl, *f. dim.* Little mare.

yelmo [yel'-mo], *m.* Helmet, helm, a part of ancient armor.

yema [yay'-mah], *f.* 1. Bud, first shoot of trees. 2. Yolk of an egg. 3. Center, middle. **Dar en la yema**, *(Met.)* to hit the nail on the head. 4. The best or best placed in its line. 5. Fleshy tip of the finger. 6. *(Coll.)* Ace of diamonds in cards.

yente [yen'-tay], *pa. irr.* of IR. Going, one that goes.

yerba [yerr'-bah], *f. V.* HIERBA, which is the modern spelling of this word. 1. Herb, a generic name for all the smaller plants. 2. Flaw in the emerald which tarnishes its luster. 3. Grass (see plural). **Pisar buena** or **mala yerba**, to be of a good or bad temper. **Yerba carmín**, Virginian poke. **Yerba de cuajo**, *V.* ALCACHOFA. **Yerba doncella**, periwinkle. **Yerba piojera**, stavesacre. **Yerba de mar or marina**, Sea-weed. **Yerba del Paraguay**, Paraguay tea or maté. -*pl.* 1. Greens, vegetables; all kinds of garden stuff. 2. Grass of pasture land for cattle. 3. Poison given in food; poisonous plant. 4. Time when colts are born.

yerbabuena [yer-bah-boo-ay'-nah], *f.* Mint, peppermint. *V.* HIERBABUENA. Mentha.

yerbatear [yer-bah-tay-ar'], *vn. (Amer. Argen.)* To take *maté*, Paraguay tea.

yerbatero, ra [yer-bah-tay'-ro, rah], *a. & n.* 1. Using arrowpoison. 2. *(Peru)* One who sells or carries grass or fodder for horses.

yerbazal [yer-bah-thahl'], *m. V.* HERBAZAL.

yermar [yer-mar'], *va.* To dispeople, to lay waste.

yermo [yerr'-mo], *m.* Desert, wilderness, waste country.

yermo, ma [yerr'-mo, mah], *a.* Waste, desert, uninhabited; herbless. **Tierra yerma**, uncultivated ground.

yernar [yer-nar'], *va. (Coll. Prov.)* To make one a son-in-law by force.

yerno [yer'-no], *m.* Son-in-law. **Engaña yernos**, baubles, geegaws, trifles.

yero [yay'-ro], *m. (Bot.) V.* YERVO.

yerro [yer'-ro], *m.* Error, mistake, inadvertency, fault.

yerto [yerr'-to, tah], *a.* Stiff, motionless, inflexible; rigid, tight.

yervo [yerr'-vo], *m. (Bot.)* Tare, true bitter vetch. Ervum tetrapernum.

yesal, yesar [yay-sahl'], *m.* Gypsumpit, where gypsum is dug.

yesca [yes'-cah], *f.* 1. Spunk, tinder (materia inflamada). 2. Fuel (pábulo), incentive or aliment of passion. 3. Flint and tinder for making a light. -*pl. Yescas*, anything excessively dry or combustible.

yesera [yay-say'-rah], *f.* Kiln, where gypsum is calcined and prepared for use.

yesería [yay-say-ree'-ah], *f.* 1. *V.* YESERA. 2. Building constructed with gypsum.

yesero, ra [yay-say'-ro, rah], *a.* Belonging to gypsum.

yesero [yay-say'-ro], *m.* One that prepares or sells gypsum.

yesgo [yes'-go], *m. (Bot. Prov.)* Dwarf elder.

yeso [yay'-so], *m.* Gypsum, gypse, sulphate of lime. **Yeso mate**, plaster of Paris. **Yeso blanco**, whiting.

yesón [yay-sone'], *m.* Piece of rubbish or fragment of gypsum already used in building.

yesoso, sa [yay -so'-so, sah], *a.* Gypseous.

yesquero [yes-kay'-ro], *m.* Tinderbox.

yeyuno [yay-yoo'-no], *m.* Jejunum, the second portion of the small intestines between the duodenum and the ileum.

yezgo [yeth'-go], *m. (Bot.)* Dwarf elder.

y griega [ee gre-ay-gah], *f.* Name of the letter y. (Greek y, as contrasted to the Latin I.)

yo [yo], *prom. pers.* 1. **Yo mismo**, I myself. **Yo, el rey**, I the king. **Soy yo**, it is **I. Soy yo el que lo dice**, I am the one who says it. **Si yo fuera usted**, if I were you. -*m.* **El yo**, the I, the ego.

yodado (or ato) [yo-dah'-do, to], *a.* Iodic, containing iodine.

yodo [yo'-do], *m.* Iodine, a bluish black haloid element used in medicine and in photography.

yoduro [yo-doo'-ro], *m.* Iodid, iodide, a compound of iodine.

ýpsilon [eep'-se-lon], *f.* Twentieth letter of the Greek alphabet, corresponding to y.

yoga [yoh'-gah], *m.* Yoga.

yogur [yoh-goor'], *m.* Yoghurt.

yole [yo'-lay], *m. (Naut.)* Yawl.

yuca [yoo'-cah], *f. (Bot.)* Adam's needle; the root of this plant is farinaceous, and eaten like potatoes. Yucca.

yucateco, ca [yoo-cah-tay'-co, cah], *a.* Of Yucatan.

yugada [yoo-gah'-dah], *f.* Extent of ground which a yoke of oxen can plough in a day: a yoke of land.

yugo [yoo'-go], *m.* 1. Yoke, for draught-oxen. 2. Nuptial tie, with which a new-married couple is veiled; marriage ceremony. 3. Oppressive authority, absolute power. 4. Confinement, prison, yoke. 5. Kind of gallows under which the Romans passed their prisoners of war. 6. *(Naut.)* Transom, a beam across the sternpost. **Sacudir el yugo**, to throw off the yoke.

yuguero [yoo-gay'-ro], *m.* Ploughman, ploughboy.

yugular [yoo-goo-lar'], *a. (Anat.)* Jugular.

yumbo, ba [yoom'-b, bah], *m. & f. & a.* A savage Indian of eastern Ecuador.

yunga [yoo-gah], *f. (Peru, Bol.) a. & m. pl.* Name given in Bolivia to the hot region of the north-east where famous coffee is raised.

yunque [yoon'-kay], *m.* 1. Anvil (herramienta). 2. Constancy, fortitude. 3. *(Anat.)* Incus, a bone of the ear. 4. One of the blades of a cloth-shearer's shears. **Estar al yunque**, to bear up under the frowns of fortune; to bear impertinent or abusive language.

yunta [yoon'-tah], *f.* 1. Couple, pair, yoke. 2. *(Prov.) V.* YUGADA.

yuntería [yoon-tay-ree'-ah], *f.* Place where draught-oxen are fed.

yuntero [yoon-tay'-ro], *m. V.* YUGUERO.

yunto, ta [yoon-to, tah], *a.* Joined, united, close. *V.* JUNTO.

yuruma [yoo-roo'-mah], *f.* Starch obtained from a species of palm along the Orinoco.

yusera [yoo-say-rah], *f.* The horizontal stone in oil-mills which lies under the roller.

yusión [yoo-se-on'], *f.* Precepts, command.

yute [yoo'-tay], *m.* 1. Jute, a textile fiber obtained from an Asiatic herb of the linden family. 2. Jute fabric.

yuxtaponer [yoox-tah-po-nerr'], *va.* To juxtapose, to put side by side.

yuxtaposición [yoox-tah-po-se-the-on'], *f.* Juxtaposition.

yuyuba [yoo-yoo'-bah], *f.* V. AZUFAIFA.

Z

z [thay'-dah, thay'-tah], *f.* The twenty-sixth letter of the Spanish alphabet. Whether at the beginning, middle, or end of words, it sounds in Spanish like the English *th* in *thank, cathedral, tenth. Latin words terminating in x take z in* Spanish, as *lux, luz; velox, veloz.* In the plural and in compound words it is superseded by *c*, as *paz* makes *paces, pacífico, apaciguar.*

¡za! [thah], *int.* A word used to frighten dogs or other animals.

zábida, zábila [thah'-be-dah, thah'-be-lah], *f. (Bot.)* Common or yellow-flowered aloe.

zaborda, *f.* **zabordamiento**, *m.* [thah-bor'-dah, thah-bor-dah-me-en'-to], *(Naut.)* Stranting; the act of getting on shore.

zabordar [thah-bor-dar'], *vn. (Naut.)* To touch ground, to get on shore, to be stranded.

zabordo [thah-bor'-do], *m. (Naut.)* Stranding.

zaboyar [thah-bo-yar'], *va. (Prov.)* To join-bricks with mortar.

zabra [thah'-brah], *f. (Naut.)* A small vessel, used on the coast of Biscay.

zabucar [thah-boo-car'], *va.* 1. To revolve something. 2. To shake, to agitate. V. BAZUCAR.

zabullida [thah-bool-lyee'-dah], *f.* Dipping, ducking.

zabullidor, ra [thah-bool-lyee-dor', rah], *m. & f.* One who ducks or gets under water.

zabullidura [thah-bool-lyo-doo'-rah], *f.* Submersion, ducking.

zabullimiento [thah-bool-lyee-me-en'-to], *m.* V. ZAMBULLIDA.

zabullir [thah-bool'-lyeer'], *va.* To plunge, to immerse, to put under water, to immerge. *-vr.* 1. To plunge suddenly under water, to sink. 2. To lurk, to lie concealed.

zabuqueo [thah-boo-kay'-o], *m.* V. BAZUQUEO.

zacapela, zacapella [thah-cah-pay'-lah, par'-lyah], *f.* Uproar, yell, noisy bustle. *Cf.* GAZAPELA.

zacate [thah-cah'-tay], *m. (Mex. and Philip. Islands)* 1. Grass, herbage. 2. Hay, forage.

zacateca [thah-cah-tay'-cah], *m. (Cuba)* Undertaker, funeral director, sexton.

zacatín [thah-cah-teen'], *m.* A place where garments are sold.

zádiva [thah'-de-vah], *f. (Bot.)* A plant the leaves of which soften corns.

zafacoca [thah-fah-co'-cah], *com. (Amer. Coll.)* Noisy confusion, squabbling; rioting.

zafada [thah-fah]-dah], *f.* 1. Flight, escape. 2. *(Naut.)* The act of lightening the ship.

zafar [thah-far'], *va.* 1. To adorn, to embellish. 2. To disembarrass. 3. *(Naut.)* To lighten a ship. *-vr.* 1. To escape (huir), to avoid risk, to run away. 2. To avoid, to decline; to excuse, to free oneself from trouble, to get clear off. 3. To slip off the border of a wheel: applied to the belt of machinery.

zafareche [thah-fah-ray'-chay], *m. (Prov.)* V. ESTANQUE.

zafarí [thah-fah-ree'], *m.* A sort of pomegranate, with quadrangular seeds.

zafariche [thah-fah-ree'-chay], *m. (Prov.)* Shelf for holding water vessels or jars.

zafarrancho [thah-far-rahn'-cho], *m.* 1. *(Naut.)* The state of being clear for action. **Hacer zafarrancho**, *(Naut.)* to make ready for action. 2. *(Coll.)* Ravage, destruction, 3. Scuffle, wrangle, squabble.

zafería [thah-fay-ree'-ah], *f.* A small village, a farm-house.

zafiamente [thah-fe-ah-men'-tay], *adv.* Clownishly, lubberly, clumsily.

zafiedad [thah-fe-ay-dahd'], *f.* Clownishness, rusticity, clumsiness.

zafio, fia [thah'-fe-o, ah], *a.* Clownish, coarse, uncivil, ignorant.

zafío [thah-fee'-o], *m. (Zool.)* V. SAFÍO or CONGRIO.

zafir, zafiro [thah-feer', thah-fee'-ro], *m.* Sapphire, a precious stone.

zafíreo, ea [thah-fee'-ray-o, ah], *a.* Sapphire-colored.

zafirino, na [thah-fe-ree'-no, nah], *a.* Of the color of sapphire.

zafo, fa, [thah'-fo, fah], *a.* 1. Free, disentangled, empty. 2. *(Naut.)* Clear. 3. Free, exempt from danger or risk. 4. *(LAm.)* Free (libre).

zafón [thah-fone'], *m.* V. ZAHÓN.

zafra [thah'-frah], *f.* 1. Drip-jar, a large metal bowl, pierced at the bottom, placed over a jar for draining oil; or a dish in which oil is kept. 2. Crop of sugar-cane and the making of sugar. 3. A broad strap which holds the thills of a cart. 4. *(Min.)* Poor ore mingled with rubbish.

zafre [thah'-fray], *m. (Min.)* Zaffre or saffre, cobalt oxyd roasted with silica, and employed chiefly for giving a blue color to porcelain.

zafreño, ña [thah-fray'-nyo, nyah], *a.* Belonging to the town of Zafra.

zaga [thah'-gah], *f.* 1. Load packed on the back part or a carriage. 2. The extremity behind. 3. *(Mil.)* V. RETAGUARDIA. *-m.* The last player at a game of cards. *-adv.* V. DETRÁS. **A zaga** or **en zaga**, behind. **No ir** or **no quedarse en zaga**, *(Coll.)* not to be less than any other, or inferior to any man.

zagal [thah-gahl'], *m.* 1. A stout, spirited young man. 2. Swain, a young shepherd subordinate to the chief herd; subordinate coachman. 3. Under petticoat.

zagala [thah-gah'-lah], *f.* A shepherdess, lass, girl.

zagalejo, ja [thah-gah-lay'-ho, hah], *m. & f. dim.* A young shepherd or shepherdess.

zagalejo [thah-gah-lay'-ho], *m.* An under petticoat of close woven stuff worn over the white petticoat.

zagalico, illo, ito [thah-gah-lee'-co], *m. dim.* A little shepherd.

zagalón, na [thah-gah-lone', nah], *m. & f.* An overgrown lad or girl.

zagú [thah-goo'], *m.* The sago-plant. V. SAGÚ.

zagua [thah'-goo-ah], *f.* A shrub yielding barilla which grows in southern Europe and northern Africa.

zaguán [thah-goo-ahn'], *m.* Porch, entrance, hall, vestibule (entrada).

zaguanete [thah-goo-ah-nay'-tay], *m.* 1. *(Dim.)* Small entrance of a house. 2. A small party of the king's lifeguards.

zaguero, ra [thah-gay'-ro, rah], *a.* Going or remaining behind.

zahareño, ña [thah-ah-ray'-nyo, nyah], *a.* 1. Intractable, wild, haggard (pájaros). 2. *(Met.)* Sour, haughty, indocile.

zaharí [thah-ah-ree'], *a.* V. ZAFARÍ.

zahén [thah-ayn'], *a.* **Dobla zahén** or **zahena**, a Moorish gold coin.

zaherible [thah-ay-ree'-blay], *a.* Blamable, censurable, blameworthy.

zaheridor, ra [thah-ay-re-dor', rah], *m. & f.* Censurer, one who blames.

zaherimiento [thah-ay-re-me-en'-to], *m.* Censurer, blame.

zaherir [thah-ay-reer'], *va.* 1. To censure, to blame, to reproach; to upbraid (reprender). 2. To mortify one by criticising him with a bad intention (criticar).

zahina [thah-ee'-nah], *f.* Sorghum, a gruminuceous plant resembling broomcorn, cultivated in Spain for fodder.

zahinar [thah-e-nar'], *m.* Land sown with sorghum, sorghum-field.

zahinas [thah-hee'-nahs], *f. pl.* Light und soft fritters, puffcakes. **Zahinas de levadura**, froth of barm.

zahón [thah-on'], *m.* 1. A leather apron divided at the lower part and tied behind the thighs and at the waist; worn to protect the clothes. 2. *pl.* A kind of wide breeches, overalls.

zahonado, da [thah-oh-nah'-do, dah], *a.* Of a dark color, brownish.

zahondar [thah-on-dar'], *va.* To dig the ground, to penetrate. *V.* AHONDAR. *-vn.* To sink into the ground (pies).

zahora [thah-o'-rah], *f.* (*Prov.*) Luncheon among friends, with music.

zahorar [thah-o-rar'], *m.* To have a repast with music.

zahorí [thah-o-ree'], *m.* 1. Clairvoyant, seer (adivino). 2. Water diviner (manantiales). 3. Mind reader (que adivina los pensamientos). 4. Very perceptive person (perspicaz).

zahorra [thah-or'-rah], *f.* (*Naut.*) Ballast. *V.* LASTRE.

zahumerio [thah-oo-may'-re-o], *m.* (*Obs.*) *V.* SAHUMERIO.

zahurda [thah-oor'-dah], *f.* 1. Pigsty, hogsty. 2. A small, dirty, miserable house. 3. An ipterous insect of Europe.

zaida [thah-ee'-dah], *f.* (*Orn.*) A variety of the African heron.

zaino, na [thah'-e-no, nah], *a.* 1. Of a chestnut color (caballos). 2. Vicious (animales). 3. Treacherous, wicked, vicious.

zalá [thah-lah'], *f.* Religious adoration paid by the Moors to God; prayer with various ceremonies.

zalagarda [thah-lah-gar'-dah], *f.* 1. Ambuscade, ambush (emboscada). 2. Gin, trap, snare. 3. Sudden attack, surprise. *f.* Mockfight: vulgar noise. 5. (*Coll.*) Malicious cunning.

zalama, zalamería [thah-lah'-mah, thah-lah-may-ree'-ah], *f.* Flattery, adulation, wheedling.

zalamelé [thah-lah-may-lay'], *m. V.* ZALAMA.

zalameramente [thah-lah-may'-rah-men-tay], *adv.* Fawningly.

zalamero, ra [thah-lah-may'-ro, rah], *m. & f.* Wheedler, flatterer, Owner.

zalea [thah-lay'-ah], *f.* 1. An undressed sheep-skin. 2. Sheep-skin mats.

zalear [thah-lay-ar'], *va.* 1. To move a thing with care. 2. To frighten dogs. *V.* ZACEAR.

zalema [thah-lay'-mah], *f.* Bow, courtesy. (*Arab.*)

zaleo [thah-lay'-o], *m.* 1. Skin of a beast lacerated by the wolf, undressed sheep-skin. 2. The act of shaking or moving to and fro.

zalomar [thah-lo-mar'], *vn.* (*Naut.*) To sing out. *V.* SALOMAR.

zamacuco [thah-mah-coo'-co], *m.* (*Coll.*) 1. Dunce, dolt. 2. Intoxication, inebriation.

zamanca [thah-mahn'-cah], *f.* (*Coll.*) Drubbing, flogging, castigation.

zamarra [thah-mar'-rah], *f.* 1. Dress worn by shepherds, made of undressed sheep-skin (chaqueta). 2. The skin so used.

zamarrear [thah-mar-ray-ar'], *va.* 1. To shake (perro), to drag or pull to and fro. 2. To pin up close in a dispute (en discusión). 3. (*Met.*) To drag, to ill-treat.

zamarreo [thah-mar-ray'-o], *m.* Action of dragging or shaking from side to side.

zamarrico [thah-mar-ree'-co], *m. dim.* of ZAMARRO. A portmanteau or bag of sheepskin, having the wool inside.

zamarrilla [thah-mar-reel'-lyah], *f.* 1. (*Dim.*) A short loose coat of sheepskins. 2. (*Bot.*) Poly, mountain germander, a medicinal plant with yellow flowers which are very bitter.

zamarro [thah-mar'-ro], *m.* 1. A shepherd's coat of sheep-skins. 2. Sheep or lamb skin. 3. Dolt, stupid person. *-m. pl.* (*Amer. Colom.*) Leather leggings.

zamarrón [thah-mar-rone'], *m. aug.* of ZAMARRA and ZAMARRO. A large sheep-skin.

zamarruco [thah-mar-roo'-co], *m.* (*Orn.*) Titmouse.

zambaigo, ga [tham-bah'-e-go, gah], *a. & m. & f.* Son or daughter of an Indian by a Chinese woman, or of a Chinaman and Indian woman.

zambapalo [tham-bah-pah'-lo], *m.* Ancient dance.

zambarco [tham-bar'-co], *m.* A broad breast-harness for coach-horses and mules.

zámbigo, ga [thahm'-be-go, gah], *a.* Bandy-legged.

zambo, ba [thahm'-bo, bah], *a.* 1. Bandy-legged. 2. Applied to the son of an Indian by a Chinese woman, or of a Chinaman by an Indian woman. *-m.* An American wild monkey, resembling a dog, with the head of a horse.

zamboa [tham-bo'-ah], *f.* 1. (*Bot.*) A sweet kind of quincetree. 2. Citron-tree. *V.* AZAMBOA.

zambomba [tham-bom'-bah], *f.* A kind of rustic drum (tambor), consisting of a skin stretched over the mouth of a jar, with a reed fastened at the centre. This rubbed up and down with the moistened hand produces a strong, hoarse, monotonous sound. *-int.* Whew! interjection denoting surprise.

zambombo [tham-bom'-bo], *m.* Clown, rustic, ill-bred person.

zamborondón, na, zamborotudo, da [tham-bo-ron-done', nah, tham-bo-ro-too'-do, dah], *a.* Clownish, clumsy, ill-shaped.

zambra [thahm'-brah], *f.* 1. A Moorish festival or feast, attended with dancing and music. 2. Shout, noisy mirth (jaleo). 3. Kind of Moorish boat.

zambucar, zambucarse [tham-boo-car'], *vn. & vr.* To be hidden, to be concealed; to hide oneself.

zambuco [tham-boo'-co], *m.* Squatting, lying close to the ground, withdrawn from sight; hiding, concealing.

zambullida [tham-bool-lyee'-dah], *f.* 1. Dipping, ducking, submersion. 2. Infencing, thrust on the breast.

zambullidura [tham-bool-lyee-doo'-rah], *f.* **Zambullimiento** [tham-boo-lyee-me-en'-to], *m. V.* ZABULLIDURA.

zambullir [tham-bool-lyeer'], *va. & vr.* To plunge into water, to dip, to dive (debajo del agua).

zambullo [tham-bool'-lyo], *m.* (*Naut.*) A large bucket for the use of the sick.

zamorano, na [thah-mo-rah'-no, nah], *a.* Belonging to Zamora. **Gaita Zamorana**, kind of bagpipe.

zampabodigos, zampabollos [tham-pah-bo-dee'-gos, tham-pah-bol'-lyos], *m.* (*Coll.*) Glutton (glotón). *V.* ZAMPATORATAS.

zampada [tham-pah'-dah], *f.* (*Prov.*) Act of concealing or putting one thing within another.

zampadura [tham-pah-doo'-rah], *f. V.* ZAMPAMIENTO.

zampalimosnas [tham-pah-le-mos'-nas], *m.* A sturdy beggar.

zampamiento [tham-pah-me-en'-to], *m.* The act of concealing or reveling over a thing.

zampapalo [tham-pah-pah'-lo], *m.* (*Coll.*) *V.* ZAMPATORTAS.

zampar [tham-par'], *va.* 1. To conceal in a clever manner; to thrust one thing into another, so as to be covered by it and withdrawn from light (ocultar). 2. To devour eagerly (devorar). 3. To hurl (arrojar). 4. (*LAm.*) To fetch (golpe). *-vr.* 1. To thrust oneself suddenly into a place. 2. To bump (lanzarse).

zampatortas [tham-pah-tor'-tas], *m.* (*Coll.*) 1. A glutton. 2. Clown, rustic.

zampear [tham-pay-ar'], *vn.* To drive stakes in a ground to make it solid.

zampeado [tham-pay-ah'-do], *m.* (*Arch.*) Woodwork and masonry in marshy foundations.

zampoña [tham-po'-nyah], *f.* 1. A rustic instrument, a kind of bagpipe. *V.* PIPITAÑA. 2. A poetical vein, genius or talent for poetry. 3. (*Coll.*) Frivolous saying.

zampoñear [tham-po-nyay-ar'], *vn.* 1. To play the bagpipe. 2. (*Met.*) To be prolix and frivolous in conversation, to prose.

zampuzar [tham-poo-thar'], *va.* 1. To plunge, to dip, to dive. 2. To hide, to conceal.

zampuzo [tham-poo'-tho], *m.* Immersion, submersion, concealment.

zamuro [thah-moo'-ro], *m.* (*Orn.*) Carrion-vulture, vultur aura.

zanahoria [than-nah-o'-re-ah], *f.* 1. (*Bot.*) Carrot. 2. (*Cono Sur*) Idiot (imbécil); clumsy oaf (desmañado).

zanahoriate [thah-nah-o-re-ah'-tay], *m. V.* AZANORIATE.

zanca [thahn'-cah], *f.* 1. Shank, purl of the leg of a fowl or bird which extends from the claws to the thigh. 2. A long shank or leg. 3. Large pin. **Zancas de araña**, shifts, evasions, subterfuges. **Zancas largas**, *m.* (Long shanks) woodcock, a European bird of the snipe family.

zancada [than-cah'-dah], *f.* Long stride. **En dos zancadas,** *(Coll.)* expeditiously, speedily.

zancadilla [than-cah-dee'l-lyah], *f.* 1. Trip, a stroke or catch by which a wrestler supplants his antagonist. 2. Trick, deceit, craft; act of supplanting. 3. *(Naut.)* Elbow in the hawse. **Echar la zancadilla a uno,** to trip somebody up.

zancado, da [than-cah-do, dah], *a.* Insipid (salmón).

zancajear [than-cah-hay-ar'], *va.* To run about the streets bespattering the legs with dirt and mud.

zancajera [than-cah-hay'-rah], *f.* Coach step.

zancajiento, ta [than-cah-he-en'-to, tah], *a.* Bandy-legged. *V.* ZANCAJOSO.

zancajo [than-cah'-ho], *m.* 1. Heel-bone of the foot. 2. The part of a shoe or stocking which covers the heel. 3. A short, ill-shaped person. 4. An ignorant, stupid person. **No llegar al zancajo** or **a los zancajos,** not to come up or near one in any line.

zancajoso, sa [than-cah-ho'-so, sah], *a.* 1. Bandy-legged. 2. Wearing dirty stockings with holes at the heels. 3. Clumsy, awkward, unhandy.

zancarrón [than-car-rone'], *m.* 1. The bare heel-bone. 2. Any large bone without flesh. 3. A withered, old, ugly person. 4. An ignorant pretender at any art or science.

zanco [thahn'-co], *m.* 1. Stilt. 2. Dancer or walker on stilts. 3. *(Naut.)* Flag-staff. **Subirse en zancos,** to be haughty and elated with good fortune.

zancudo, da [than-coo'-do, dah], *a.* Long-shanked, having long, thin legs. -*m.* A long-beaked mosquito. -*pl. (Zool.)* Wading birds, such as the heron, the flamingo, the jacana, etc.

zandalia [than-dah'-le-ah], *f.* Sandal. *V.* SANDALIA.

zandunga [than-doon'-gah], *f. V.* SANDUNGA. *(Coll.)* Gracefulness, elegance; cajoling, wheedling; flattering, allurement, fascination.

zandunguero, ra [than-doon-gay'-ro, rah], *m. & f. V.* SANDUNGUERO.

zanefa [thah-nay'-fah], *f.* A printed border. *V.* CENEFA.

zanga [thahn'-gah], *f.* Ombre played by four.

zangada [than-gah'-dah], *f.* Raft or float made of cork.

zangala [than-gah'-lah], *f.* Buckram.

zangamanga [than-gah-mahn'-gah], *f.* Falsehood, tending to deceive or defraud person.

zanganada [than-gah-nah'-dah], *f.* 1. Dronish or duggardly act. 2. *(Coll.)* An impertinent saying or act.

zangandongo [than-gan-don'-go], *m.* 1. *(Coll.)* Idler, a lazy person, who affects ignorance and grant of abilities. 2. Dolt, an ignorant, stupid, awkward person.

zangandullo, zangandungo [than-gan-dool'-lyo], *m. (Col.) V.* ZANGANDONGO.

zanganear [than-gah-nay-ar'], *vn.* To drone, to live in idleness (gandulear).

zángano [thahn'-gah-no], *m.* 1. Drone, a bee which makes no honey; the male bee (gandul). 2. Sluggard, idler, sponger. 3. *(Coll.)* Sly, omening, or playful cunning person, taking it either in a good or bad meaning, according to the sense of the phrase.

zangarilla [than-gah-reel'-lyah], *f.* A small watermill for grinding wheat, on the banks of rivers in Estremadura.

zangarilleja [than-gah-re-lyay'-hah], *f.* Trollop, a dirty, lazy girl.

zangarrear [than-gar-ray-ar'], *vn.* To scrape a guitar.

zangarriana [than-gar-re-ah'-nah], *f.* 1. An infirmity of the head, incident to sheep. 2. *(Coll.)* Badness, melancholy. 3. *(Coll.)* Any periodical disease.

zangarullón [than-gah-rool-lyone'], *m.* A tall, sluggish, lazy lad.

zangolotear [than-go-lo-tay-ar'], *vn.* 1. To move in a violent yet ridiculous manner (agitar). 2. To slam, to move because the screws or nails which hold certain things are loose. 3. To fidget (persona).

zangoloteo [than-go-lo-tay'-o], *m.* A violent yet ridiculous waddling, a wagging motion or movement.

zangolotino, na [than-go-lo-tee'-no, nah], *a.* Said of the boy whom it is desired to pass for a child; childish.

zangón [than-gone'], *m. (Coll.) V.* ZANGARULÓN.

zangotear [than-go-tay-ar'], *m. V.* ZANGOLOTEAR.

zangoteo [than-go-tay'-o], *m. V.* ZANGOLOTEO.

zanguanga [than-goo-ahn'-gah], *f. (Coll.)* A feigned disease; a fictitious disorder.

zanguango [than-goo-ahn'-go], *m. (Coll.)* 1. Lazy fellow who always finds pretexts to avoid work. 2. A fool, a booby.

zanguayo [than-goo-ah'-lyo], *m. (Coll.)* Tall idler, that pretends to be ill, silly, or unable to work.

zanja [thahn'-hah], *f.* 1. Ditch (fosa), trench (foso), drain; a pit dug in the ground (hoyo). 2. *(LAm.)* Gully (barranco). 3. *(And.)* fence (límite).

zanjar [than-har'], *va.* 1. To open ditches or drains, to excavate. 2. To lay a foundation, to ground; to establish. 3. To terminate or settle a business amicably.

zanjica, illa, ita [than-hee'-cah], *f. dim.* Small drain; slender foundation.

zanjón [than-hone'], *a. aug.* 1. A deep ditch (zanja profunda); lard drain. 2. *(Carib. Cono Sur)* Cliff (risco).

zanjencillo [than-hen-theel'-lyo], *m. dim.* A small drain or trench.

zanqueador, ra [than-kay-ah-dor', rah], *m. & f.* 1. One who waddles in walking. 2. A great walker.

zanqueamiento [than-kay-ah-me-en'-to], *m.* The act of waddling in walking.

zanquear [than-ker-ar'], *vn.* To waddle (andar mal), to trot or run about; to walk much and fast (rápidamente).

zanquilargo, ga [than-ke-lar'-go, gah], *a.* Long shanked, long-legged.

zanquilla, zanquita [than-keel'-lyah, kee'-tah], *f. dim.* Thin, long shank or leg.

zanquituerto, ta [than-ke-too-err'-to, tah], *a.* Bandy-legged.

zanquivano, na [than-ke-vah'-no, nah], *a.* Spindle shanked.

zantoxíleo, ea [than-tok-see'-lay-o, ah], *a.* Like prickly ash.

zantóxilo [than-tok'-se-lo], *m.* Xanthoxylum, prickly ash.

zapa [thah'-pah], *f.* 1. Spade (pala). 2. A trench for military purposes. 3. Shagreen, a skin made rough in imitation of sealskin. 4. Kind of carving in silver.

zapador [than-pah-dor'], *m. (Mil.)* Sapper.

zapapico [thah-pah-pee'-co], *m.* Pickaxe.

zapar [thah-par'], *m.* To sap, to mine.

zaparrada [than-par-rah'-dah], *f.* A violent fall.

zaparrastrar [thah-par-ras-trar'], *vn.* To trail (ropa).

zaparrastroso, sa [thah-par-ras-tro'-so, sah], *a.* 1. Dirty from trailing on the ground. 2. Ill-made, badly done.

zaparrazo [thah-par-rah'-tho], *m.* 1. A violent fall, attended with great noise. 2. *(Coll.)* Sudden calamity, misfortune.

zapata [thah-pah'-tah], *f.* 1. A piece of sole leather put on the hinds of a door to prevent its creaking. 2. A kind of colored half-boots. 3. Bracket of a beam. 4. *(Naut.)* Shoe. **Zapata de la quilla,** *(Naut.)* the false keel.

zapatazo [thah-pah-tah'-tho], *m.* 1. *(Aug.)* Large shoe. 2. Blow with a shoe (golpe con zapato). 3. Fall; the noise attending a fall (caída, ruido). 4. Clapping noise of a horse's foot. **Mandar (a uno) a zapatazos,** to lead one by the nose, to have complete control over one. **Tratar (a uno) a zapatazos,** to treat one badly and with scorn.

zapateado [thah-pah-tay-ah'-do], *m.* A dance consisting of keeping time by beating the feet on the floor. —**Zapateado, da,** *pp.* of ZAPATEAR.

zapateador, ra [thah-pah-tay-ah-dor', rah], *m. & f.* Dancer, who beats time with the sole of his shoe.

zapatear [thah-pah-tay-ar'], *va.* 1. To kick or strike with the shoe (patear). 2. To lead by the nose. 3. To beat time with the sole of the shoe. 4. To hit frequently with the button of the foil. 5. To strike the ground with the feet: used of rabbits when chased. -*vr.* To oppose with spirit; not to give up a contested point; to resist in debating.

zapateo [thah-pah-tay'-o], *m.* Act of keeping time by beating the foot on the floor.

zapatera [thah-pah-tay'-rah], *f.* 1. A shoemaker's wife. 2. Olive spoiled in the pickle.

zapatería [thah-pah-tay-ree'-ah], *f.* 1. Trade of a shoemaker; a shoemaker's shop (tienda). 2. Place or street which contains number of shoemakers' shops. 3. Shoemaking business.

zapateril [thah-pah-tay-reel'], *a.* Belonging to a shoemaker.

zapaterillo, illa [thah-pah-tay-reel'-lyo], *m. & f. dim.* A petty shoemaker.

zapatero [thah-pah-tay'-ro], *m.* Shoe maker. **Zapatero de viejo**, cobbler.

zapateta [thah-pah-tay'-tah], *f.* 1. Slap on the sole of a shoe. 2. Caper, leap, Jump.-*int.* Oh!, an exclamation of admiration.

zapatico, illo, ito [thah-pah-tee'-co], *m. dim.* A nice little shoe.

zapatilla [thah-pah-teel'-lyah], *f.* 1. Slipper (para casa). 2. (*Dim.*) A little shoe. 3. Pump (de baile), any shoe with a thin sole neatly finished. 4. Piece of chamois or buckskin put behind the lock of a gun or pistol. 5. Button at the end of a foil. 6. Exterior hoof of animals.

zapatillero [thah-pah-teel-lyay'-ro], *m.* Shoemaker who makes slippers, pumps, and children's shoes.

zapato [thah-pah'-to], *m.* Shoe. **Zapatos abotinados para señoras**, ladies' gaiters. **Zapato de madera**, a wooden shoe. **Andar con zapatos de fieltro**, to proceed with great caution and silence. **Zapatos de tenis**, tennis shoes.

zapatón [thah-pah-tone'], *m.* 1. (*Aug.*) A large, clumsy shoe. 2. A wooden shoe.

zapatudo, da [thah-pah-too'-do, dah], *m.* 1. Wearing large or strong shoes. 2. Large hoofed or clamored (bestias).

¡zape! [thah'-pay], *int.* 1. Shooo! scat! A word used to frighten cats away. 2. An exclamation of aversion, or of negation at cards. 3. God forbid! far be it from me!

zapear [thah-pay-ar'], *va.* 1. To frighten cats away by crying zape. 2. (*And. CAm.*) To spy on (espiar).

zapito [thah-pee'-to], *m.* (*Prov.*) Milk pail.

zapote [thah-po'-tay], *m.* (*Bet.*) Sapota-tree, sapodilla, and its luscious apple-shaped fruit.

zapuzar [thah-poo-thar'], *va.* To duck. V. CHAPUZAR.

zaque [thah'-kay], *va.* 1. Bottle or urine bag made of leather (de vino). 2. (*Coll.*) Tippler, drunkard.

zaquear [thah-kay-ar'], *va.* To rack, to defecate: to draw off liquor from one vessel into another.

zaquizami [thah-ke-thah-mee'], *m.* 1. Garret (buhardilla), cockloft. 2. A small, dirty house.

zar [thar], *m.* Czar, the Emperor of all the Russias.

zara [thah'-rah], *f.* (*Bot.*) Indian corn, maize. V. MAÍZ.

zarabanda [thah-rah-bahn'-dah], *f.* 1. Saraband, a lively dance and tune. 2. Bustle, noise.

zarabandista [thah-rah-ban-dees'-tah], *com.* Dancer.

zarabutero, ra [thah-rah-boo-tay'-ro, rah], *a.* (Leroy.) V. EMBUSTERO.

zaradión, zaradique [thah-rah-de-on'], *m.* Medicine for dogs, especially for curing the mange.

zaragata [thah-rah-gah'-tah], *f.* Turnmoil, scuffle, quarrel.

zaragatada [thah-rah-gah-tah'-dah], *f.* A roguish or cunning trick.

zaragate, zarayate, or **saragate** [thah-rah-gah'-tay], *m.* (*Mex.*) Loafer. vagabond, rogue. This word, as well as zángano, is often used in an affectionate; jocular style, and answers to the English, little rogue, in the same sense.

zaragatona [thah-rah-gah-toh'-nah], *f.* (*Bot.*) Fleawort.

zaragocí [thah-rah-go-thee'], *m.* Kind of plum.

zaragozano, na [thah-rah-go-thah'-no, nah], *a.* Saragossan, of Saragossa.

zaragüelles [thah-rah-goo-el'-lyes], *m. pl.* 1. A sort of drawers or wide breeches; a large pair of breeches ill made. 2. Overalls. or overall pantaloons.

zaramago [thah-rah-mah'-go], *m.* (*Prov.*) V. JARAMAGO.

zaramagullón [thah-rah-mah-gool-lyone'], *m.* (*Orn.*) Didapper, minute merganser.

zarambeque [thah-ram-bay'-kay], *m.* A kind of merry tune and noisy dance.

zaramullo [tha-rah-mool'-lyo], *m.* Busybody, a vain, meddling person.

zaranda [thah-rahn'-dah], *f.* 1. Screen or frame for sifting earth or sand. 2. Riddle of esparto in oblong shape for screening stems of grapes, etc. 3. (*Carib.*) Spinning top (juguete).

zarandador [thah-ran-dah-dor'], *m.* Sifter of wheat.

zarandajas [thah-ran-dah'-has], *f. pl.* 1. Trifles, worthless scraps or remnants. 2. Odds given at the game of trucks.

zarandajillas [thah-ran-dah-heel'-lyas], *f. pl. dim.* Little trifles.

zarandalí [thah-ran-dah-lee'], *adv.* (*Prov.*) Applied to a blackspotted dove.

zarandar, zarandear [thah-ran-dar', thah-ran-day-ar'], *va.* 1. To winnow corn with a sieve. 2. To stir and move nimbly. 3. To separate the precious from the common. 4. To sift and toss about pins in a vessel (cribar). -*vr.* 1. To be in motion, to move to and fro (ir y venir). 2. (*LAm.*) To strut about (pavonearse).

zarandeo [thah-ran-day'-o], *m.* Act of sifting or winnowing.

zarandero [thah-ran-day'-ro], *m.* V. ZARANDADOR.

zarandija [thah-ran-dee'-hah], *f.* (*Zool.*) An insect which burrows in the ground and devastates gardens; the molecricket. (*Cf.* SABANDIJA.) V. GRILLOTALPA.

zarandillo [thah-ran-deel'-lyo], *m.* 1. (*Dim.*) A small sieve or riddle. 2. (*Coll.*) One who frisks nimbly about.

zarapallón [thah-rah-pal-lyone'], *m.* A shabby, dirty fellow.

zarapatel [thah-rah-pah-tel'], *m. & f.* A kind of salmagundi.

zarapeto [thah-rah-pay'-to], *m.* (*Coll.*) Intriguer, crafty person.

zarapito [thah-rah-pee'-to], *m.* (*Orn.*) Whimbrel, curlew-jack.

zaratán [thah-rah-tahn'], *m.* Cancer in the breast. (*Arab.*)

zaraza [thah-rah'-thah], *f.* Chintz, a delicate cotton stuff.

zarcear [thar-thay-ar'], *va.* To clean pipes or conduits with briers. -*vn.* To move to and fro.

zarcero, ra [thar-thay'-ro, rah], *a.* Fit to pursue the game among briers: applied to pointers.

zarceto, ta [thar-thay'-to, tah], *m. & f.* (*Orn.*) Widgeon. V. CERCETA.

zarcillo [thar-theel'-lyo], *m.* 1. Earring (pendiente). 2. Tendril of a vine or other climbing plant. 3. (*Prov.*) Hoop of a butt or barrel.

zarco, ca [thar'-co, cah], *a.* 1. Walleyed, of a light blue color (ojos). 2. Clear and pure (agua).

zarevitz [thah-ray-veeth'], *m.* Czarwitz, the first-born son of the Emperor of Russia, and heir-apparent to the throne. His wife is culled Zarevna.

zargatona [thar-gah-to'-nah], *f.* V. ZARAGATONA.

zariano, na [thah-re-ah'-no, nah], *a.* Belonging to the Czar.

zarina [thah-ree'-nah], *f.* Czarina, empress, the wife of the Emperor of Russia.

zarja [thar'-hah], *f.* Reel, for winding silk. V. AZARJA.

zaroche [thah-ro'-chay], *m.* (*Ecuador*) Mountain sickness from too rapid advance into rarefied air. V. TEJA.

zarpa [thar'-pah], *f.* 1. Weighing anchor. 2. Dirt or mud sticking to the skirts of clothes (salpicadura). 3. Superior thickness of foundation walls. 4. Claw of a beast or bird. **Echar la zarpa**, to gripe, to claw.

zarpada [thar-pah'-dah], *f.* Clawing, a strike or dig with claws.

zarpanel [thar-pah-nel'], *a.* (*Arch.*) V. CARPANEL.

zarpar [thar-par'], *va.* (*Naut.*) To weigh anchor. **El ancla está zarpada**, (*Naut.*) the anchor is atrip.

zarpazo [thar-pah'-tho], *m.* Sound of a body falling on the ground.

zarposo, sa [thar-po'-so, sah], *a.* Bespattered with mire or dirt.

zarracatería [thar-rah-cah-tay-ree'-ah], *f.* Deceitful flattery.

zarracatín [thar-rah-cah-teen'], *m.* Haggler. miser.

zarrampla [thar-rahm'-plah], *com. (Coll).* Blockhead; awkward.

zarramplín [thar-ram-pleen'], *m.* Bungler, botcher; an insignificant fellow.

zarramplinada [thar-ram-ple-nah'-dah], *f.* Work clumsily performed; thing of little moment.

zarrapastra [thar-rah-pahs'-trah], *f.* Dirt or mire sticking to the skirts of clothes.

zarrapastrón, na [thar-rah-pas-trone', nah], *a. & n.* Tatterdemalion, ragged fellow.

zarrapastrosamente [thar-rah-pahs-tro-sah-men-tay], *adv.* Raggedly.

zarrapastroso, sa [thar-rah-pas-tro'-so, sah], *a.* Ragged, dirty, uncleanly.

zarria [thar'-re-ah], *f.* 1. Dirt or mire sticking to clothes (salpicadura). 2. Leather thongs for tying on *abarcas.*

zarriento, ta [thar-re-en-to, tah], *a.* Bespattered with mud or mire.

zarrio [thar'-re-o], *m. V.* CHARRO.

zarza [thar'-thah], *f. (Bot.)* Common bramble, the European blackberry-bush. **Zarzas,** *(Met.)* thorns, difficulties.

zarzagán [thar-thah-gahn'], *m.* A cold north-east wind.

zarzaganete [thar-thah-gah-nay'-tay], *m. dim.* A light northeast wind.

zarzaganillo [thar-thah-gah-neel-lyo], *m.* A violent storm at north-east.

zarzahán [thar-thah-ahn'], *m.* A kind of striped silk.

zarzaidea [thar-thah-e-day'-ah], *f. (Bot.)* Raspherry-bush.

zarzal [thar-thahl'], *m.* Briery, a place where briers grow; place full of briers or brambles.

zarzamora [thar-thah-mo'-rah], *f. (Bot.)* Blackberry, berry of the bramble.

zarzaparrilla [thar-thah-par-reel'-lyah], *f (Bot.)* Sarsaparilla.

zarzaparrillar [thar-thah-par-reel-lyar'], *m.* Plantation of sarsaparilla.

zarzaperruna [thar-thah-per-roo'-nah], *f. (Bot.)* Dog-rose.

zazarrosa [thar-thar-ro'-sah], *f (Bot.)* Dog-rose. *V.* ZARZAPERRUNA.

zarzo [thar'-tho], *m.* Hurdle, a texture of canes, sticks, or twigs.

zarzoso, sa [thar-tho'-so, sah], *a.* Briery, full of brambles or briers.

zarzuela [thar-thoo-ay'-lah], *f.* Spanish operetta or musical comedy.

¡zas! [thahs]. Word used to express the sound of repeated blows: raps at a door.

zascandil [thas-can-deel], *m.* 1. *(Coll.)* A crafty impostor or swindler (poco fiable). 2. An upstart.

zata, zatara [thah'-tah, thah-tah -rah], *f.* Raft made by laying pieces of timber across each other.

zatico, illo [thah-tee'-co], *m.* A small bit of bread.

zato [thah'-to], *m (Prov).* Morsel of bread.

zayar [thah-yar'], *va. (Naut.)* To house, to haul a tackle.

zarahán [thah-thah-ahn'], *m.* Sort of flowered silk.

zazosito, ita [thah-tho-see'-to, tah], *a. dim.* of ZAZOSO.

zazoso, sa [tha-tho'-so, sah], *a.* Pronouncing a *c* or *z* instead of an *s. V.* CECEOSO.

zea [thay'-ah], *f.* 1. Hip-bone. *V.* CEA. 2. *(Bot.)* Spelt-corn.

zebra [thay'-brah], *f.* Zebra. *V.* CEBRA.

zebú [thay-boo'], *m.* Zebu, the Indian ox, having a hump on the shoulder, *(Geog.) V.* Appendix.

zeda [thay'-dah], *f.* Name of the letter *z* in Spanish.

zedilla [thay-deel'-lyah], *f.* Cedilla, the ancient letter which was formed of a *c* and a comma under it, thus, *ç*: and the mark, itself.

zedoaria [thay-do-ah'-re-ah], *f. (Bot.)* Zedoary.

zeé [thay-ay'], *a. V.* ZAHÉN.

zelandés, sa [thay-lan-days', sah], *a.* Zenlandian, of Zealand.

zend [thend], *m.* Zend, the ancient Persian language.

zendaveeta [then-dah-vee'-tah], *m.* The sacred books of the Persians, attributed to Zoroaster.

zenit [thay-neet'], *m. V.* CENIT.

zenzalino, na [then-thah-lee'-no, nah], *a.* Belonging to gnats.

zenzalo [then'-thah-lo], *m.* Gnat, mosquito. *V.* CÉNZALO.

zeppelín [thay-pay-leen'], *m.* Zeppelin.

zequí [thay'-kee], *m.* Zechin; an Arabic gold coin formerly used in Spain, worth about two dollars. *V* CEQUÍ.

zequia [thay'-ke-ah], *f.* Canal for irrigating lends. *V.* ACEQUIA.

zeta [thay'-tah], *f.* 1. Name of the letter *z. V.* ZEDA. 2. Sixth letter of Greek alphabet.

zeugma [thay-oog'-mah], *f. (Rhetoric)* Zeugma, a kind of ellipsis.

zigema [the-hay'-mah], *f. (Zool.)* 1. The hammer-headed shark. 2. Zygaena, a genus of moths typical of the zygenidae stoutbodied moths.

zigofilo [the-go-fee'-lo], *m. (Bot.)* Beancaper.

zigzag [theeg-thahg'], *m. V.* ZISZÁS *(Acad.)*

zilórgano [the-lor'-gah-no], *m.* A kind of musical instrument. *V.* XILÓRGANO.

zimología [the-mo-lo-hee'-ah], *f.* Zymology, the knowledge or study of the principles of fermentation, or a treatise on this subject.

zimosímetro [the-mo-see'-may-tro], *f.* Kind of thermometer.

zimotecnia [the-mo-tec''-ne-ah], *f. (Chem.)* Treatise on fermentation.

zinc [thinc], *m.* Zinc a metal. *V.* CINC.

zincografía [theen-co-grah-fee'-ah], *f.* Zincography, the art of preparing relief-plates for printing upon zinc instead of stone.

zinga [theen'-gah], *f. (Naut.) V.* SINGLADURA.

zinnia [thee'-ne-ah], *f. (Bot.)* Zinnia.

zipizape [the-pe-thah'-pay], *m. (Coll.)* A noisy scuffle with blows. **Armar un zipizape,** to cause a rumpus.

zirigaña [the-re-gah'-nyah], *f. (Prov.)* Adulation. *V.* CHASCO and FRIOLERA.

¡zis, zas! [this, thas]. *(Coll.)* Words expressing the sound of repeated blows or strokes.

ziszás [this-thahs'], *m:* Zigzag.

zizaña [the-thah'-nyah], *f.* 1. *(Bot.)* Darnel. 2. Discord, disagreement; anything injurious. 3. Vice mixed with good actions. **Sembrar zizaña,** to sow discord. This word is now written CIZAÑA.

zizañar [the-thah-nyar'], *va.* To sow discord or vice.

zizañero [the-thah-nyay'-ro], *f.* Makebate a breeder of quarrels, firebrand.

zizigia [the-thee'-he-ah], *f.* Syzygy, a point of opposition or conjunction of the moon. (Also spelt **Cicigia.**)

zoantropía [tho-an-tro-pee'-ah], *f.* Insanity in which the patient believes himself transformed into an animal.

zoca [tho'-cah], *f.* Square. *V.* PLAZA.

Zócalo [tho'-cah-lo], *m.* 1. *(Arch.)* Socle or zocle, a flat, square member under the base of a pedestal. 2. Skirting board (depared). 3. *(Mex.) (Mil.)* Parade ground; town square (plaza); walk (bulevar).

zocato, ta [tho-cah'-to, tah], *m.* 1. Overripe: applied to cucumbers or eggplants which grow yellow. 2. *V.* ZURDO.

zoclo [tho'-clo], *m. V.* ZUECO.

zoco, ca [tho'-co, cah], *m. (Coll.) V.* ZURDO. *-m.* 1. A wooden shoe. 2. Plinth.

zocoba [tho-co'-bah], *f.* 1. *(Bot.)* Herb in South America used as an antidote to poison. 2. Tree in New Spain yielding fine yellow wood.

zodiacal [tho-de-ah-cahl'], *a.* Zodiacal, relating to the zodiac.

zodíaco [tho-dee'-ah-co], *m. (Ast.)* The zodiac, an imaginary belt or zone about 8° each side of the ecliptic and parallel to it.

zofra [tho'-frah], *f.* A Moorish carpet.

zoilo [tho' -ee-loh], *m.* Zoilus, a malicious critic or censurer.

zolocho, cha [tho-lo'-cho, chah], *a. (Coll.)* Stupid, silly.

zollipar [thol-lye-par'], *vn.* To sob.

zollipo [thoh-lyee'-po], *m.* Sob, sigh.

zoma [tho' -mah], *f.* A coarse sort of flour. *V.* SOMA.

zombi [thom'-bee], *m*. Zombie.

zompo, pa [thom'-po, pah], *a*. Clumsy, awkward. *V*. ZOPO.

zona [tho'-nah], *f*. Zone. **Zona de batalla**, battle zone. **Zona fronteriza**, border area.

zoncería [thon-thay-ree'-ah], *f*. Insipidity, tastelessness.

zonote [tho-no'-tay], *m*. Deep deposit of water. *V*. CENOTE. (*Acad.*)

zonzamente [thon-thah-men-tay], *adv*. Insipidly.

zonzo, za [thon'-tho, thah], *a*. 1. Insipid, tasteless. 2. Stupid, thoughtless.

zonzorrión, na [thon-thor-re-on', nah], *m*. & *f*. A very dull and stupid person.

zoo [tho-o], *m*. Zoo.

zoófago, ga [tho-o'-fah-go, gah], *a*. Zoophagous, feeding upon animal substances.

zoófito [tho-o'-fe-to], *m*. (*Zool.*) Zoophyte, an animal which resembles a plant in form or growth, especially which grows in branching colonies.

zoofórica [thoo-fo'-re-cah], *a*. (*Arch.*) Zoophoric: applied to a column bearing the figure of an animal.

zoogloea [tho-o-glo-ay'-ah], *f*. (*Biol.*) Zoogloea, muciform masses of vibrios or other bacteria.

zoografía [thoo-grah-fee'-ah], *f*. Zoography, descriptive zoology.

zooide [tho-oi'-day], *a*. (*Miner.*) Resembling an animal or a part of one.

zoolatría [tho-o-lah-tree'-ah], *f*. Zoolatry, workship of animals.

zoología [tho-o-lo-hee'-ah], *f*. Zoology, the science or branch of biology which treats of animals.

zoológico, ca [tho-o-lo'-he-co, cah], *a*. Zoological, zoologic, pertaining to zoology.

zoólogo [tho-oh'-lo-go], *m* & *f*. Zoologist, a professor of zoology.

zoonomía [tho-o-no-mee'-ah], *f*. Zoonomia, laws of animal life.

zoonosis [tho-o-no'-sis], *m*. Zoonosis.

zoóporo [tho-os'-po-ro], *m*. (*Biol.*) Zoospore, name given to the spores of certain algae provided with cilia or vibratile fliaments.

zootecnia [tho-o-tec'-ne-ah], *f*. Zootechnics, the science relating to the breeding and domestication of animals.

zootomía [tho-o-to-mee'-ah], *f*. Zootomy, dissection of animals; comparative anatomy.

zootómico [tho-o-to'-me-co], *m*. Zootomist.

zoótropo [tho-oh'-tro-po], *m*. Zootrope, zoetrope, the wheel of life, a philosophical toy.

zopas, zopitas [tho'-pas, tho-pee'-tas], *m*. (*Coll.*) Nickname given to a person pronouncing *z* for *s*.

zopenco, ca [tho-pen'-co, cah], *a*. (*Coll.*) Doltish very dull.

zopenco [tho-pen'-co], *m*. (*Coll.*) Block, dolt, blockhead.

zopilote [tho-pen-lo'-tay], *m*. (*Orn. Mex.*) Buzzard, a species of hawk. N. B. In Mexico this word is generally written and pronounced *sopilÓte*.

zopisa [tho-pee'-sah], *f*. Pitch scraped from the bottom of ships; pitch mixed with wax.

zopo, pa [tho'-po, pah], *a*. 1. Lame, maimed, injured in hands or feet. 2. Clumsy, awkward.

zopo [tho'-po], *m*. A clumsy, stupid fellow.

zoquete [tho-kay'-tay], *m*. 1. Block, a short piece of timber (de madera). 2. Bit or morsel of bread. 3. A rude, thick, sluggish, ugly little person. 4. A dolt, a blookhead (zopenco). 5. Belfry. 6. A Short, thick stick, used in bending or twisting ropes. 7. (*LAm.*) Body dirt (suciedad). 8. (*Carib. Mex.*) Punch (puñetazo).

zoquetería [thoo-kea-tay-ree'-ah], *f*. Heap of blocks, plankcads, or short pieces of timber.

zoquetero, ra [tho-kay-tay'-ro, rah], *a*. Beggarly, poor, indigent, asking charity.

zoquetico, zoquetillo [tho-kay-tee'-co], *m*. *dim*. A small morsoel of bread.

zoquetudo, da [tho-kay-too'-do, dah], *a*. Rough, ill-finished.

zorcico [thor-thee'-co], *m*. 1. A musical composition in five-eight (5/8) time, popular in the Basque provinces. 2. Wards or dance set to this music.

zorita [tho-ree'-tah], *f*. (*Orn.*) Stook-dove, wood-pigeon.

zorollo [tho-rol'-lyo], *a*. Reaped while unripe (cereales).

zorongo [tho-ron'-go], *m*. 1. A handkerchief folded like a bandage which some people wear upon the head. 2. A broad flattened chignon which some women wear. 3. A lively Andalusian dance and its music.

zorra [thor'-rah], *f*. 1. Fox (animal). 2. Low strong cart for heavy goods. 3. (*Coll.*) Prostitute, strumpet (mujer). 4. Drunkenness, inebriation. 5. A sly, crafty person. 6. *V*. SORRA.

zorrastró, na [thor-ras-trone', nah], *m*. & *f*. (*Coll.*) Crafty, gunning, roguish person.

zorrazo [thor'-rah'-tho], *m. aug*. 1. A big fox. 2. A very artful fellow; a great knave.

zorrera [thor-ray'-rah], *f*. 1. Fox-hole (madriguera); kennel. 2. A smoking chimney, a smoky kitchen or room (habitación). 3. Heaviness of the head, drowsiness (modorra).

zorrería [thor-ray-ree'-ah], *f*. 1. Artfulness of a fox. 2. Cunning, craft knavery.

zorrero, ra [thor-ray'-ro, rah], *a*. 1. Slow, tardy, inactive; lagging. 2. (*Naut.*) Sailing heavily (barco). 3. Applied to large shot. 4. Cunning, capricious.

zorrero [thor-ray'-ro], *m*. 1. Terrier, a hunting dog. 2. Keeper of a royal forest.

zorrillo [thor-reel'-lyo], *m*. (*Zool.*) Skunk.

zorrita [thor-ree'-tah], *f. dim*. Little bitch fox.

zorro [thor'-ro], *m*. 1. A male fox. 2. Fox, a knave or cunning fellow. 3. *V*. ZORROCLOCO, 2d def. **Estar hecho un zorro**, to be extremely drowsy or heavy with sleep. *-pl*. Fox-skins; foxtails used in dusting furniture.

zorro, ra [thor'-ro, rah], *a*. *V*. ZORRERO.

zorrocloco [thor-ro-clo'-co], *m*. 1. (*Prov.*) A thin paste rolled up in a cylindric shape. 2. A dronish, humdrum heavy fellow; one who feigns weakness to avoid work. 3. (*Coll.*) Caress, demonstration of love or friendship. *V*. ARRUMACO.

zorronglón, na [thor-ron-glone', nah], *a*. Slow, heavy, lazy.

zorruela [thor-roo-ey'-lah], *f. dim*. A little bitch fox.

zorrullo [thor-rool'-lyo], *m*. A cylindrical piece of timber.

zorruno, na [thor-roo'-no, nah], *a*. Vulpine, foxy, foxlike.

zorzal [thor-thahl'], *m*. 1. (*Orn.*) Thrush. 2. Artful, cunning man (listo). 3. (*Cono Sur*) Simpleton (tonto).

zorzaleña [thor-thah-lay'-nyah], *f*. Applied to a small, round kind of olives.

zorzalico, illo, ito [thor-thah-lee'-co], *m. dim*. of ZORZAR.

zoster [thos-terr'], *f*. (*Med.*) Shingles, an eruptive disease.

zote [tho'-tay], *m*. Ignorant, stupid, lazy person.

zozobra [tho-tho'-brah], *f*. 1. Uneasiness, anguish, anxiety (inquietud). 2. (*Naut.*) A foul or contrary wind. 3. An unlucky cast of the die.

zozobrante [tho-tho-brahn'-tay], *pa*. & *a*. That which is in great danger; sinking.

zozobrar [tho-tho-brar'], *m*. 1. (*Naut.*) To be weather-beaten; to sink, to founder; to upset, to capsize. 2. To be in great danger (peligrar). 3. To grieve, to be in pain; to be afflicted (persona).

zua, zuda [thoo'-ah, thoo'-dah], *f*. Persian wheel. *V*. AZUDA.

zubia [thoo'-be-ah], *f*. Drain, channel for water.

zucarino, na [thoo-cah-ree'-no, nah], *a*. Sugary. *V*. SACARINO.

zúchil [thoo'-cheel], *m*. (*Mex.*) 1. A bouquet. 2. A marigold. N. B. In the U. S. of Mexico this word is pronounced and written *Súchil*.

zueca pella [thoo-ay'-cah payl'-lah]. (**Jugar con alguno a la**) (*Coll.*) To tease, to bore, to vex.

zueco [thoo-ay'-co], *m*. 1. A wooden shoe. 2. A sort of shoe with a wooden or cork sole. 3. Clog, galosh or galoche. 4. (*Bot.*) Lady's clipper. 5. (*Poet.*) A plain, simple style.

zuiza [thoo-ee'-thah], *f.* 1. A tournament. 2. A party of young men at a feast. 3. Quarrel, dispute.

zuizón [thoo-e-thone'], *m.* (*Naut.*) A half pike, used in boarding.

zulacar [thoo-lah-car'], *va.* To anoint or cover with bitumen.

zulaque [thoo-lah'-kay], *m.* 1. Bitumen. V. BETÚN. 2. (*Naut.*) Stuff, a composition of quicklime, fish-oil tar, and other ingredients, with which the bottom of a ship is painted.

zulú [thoo-loo'], *com. & a.* Zulu, a warlike tribe of southern Africa.

zulla [thool-lyah], *f.* 1. (*Bot.*) French honey-suckle. 2. (*Coll.*) Human excrements.

zullarse [thool-lyar'-say], *vr.* (*Coll.*) To go to stool, to break wind (ventosear).

zullenco, ca [thool-lyen'-co, cah]. **Zullón, na** (*Coll.*), *a.* Breaking wind behind; flatulent.

zullón [thool-lyone'], *m.* The act of breaking wind, flatulence.

zullonear [thool-lyo-nay-ar'], *va.* To expel wind.

zumacal, zumacar [thoo-mah-cahl'], *m.* Plantation of sumach.

zumacar [thoo-mah-car'], *va.* To dress or tan with sumach.

zumacaya [thoo-mah-cah'-yah], *f.* V. ZUMAYA.

zumaque [thoo-mah'-kay], *m.* 1. (*Bot.*) Sumach-tree. 2. (*Coll.*) Wine.

zumaya [thoo-mah-yah], *f.* (*Orn.*) The common owl, barn-owl.

zumba [thoom'-bah], *f.* 1. A large bell, used by curriers. 2. Joke, jest; facetious raillery.

zumbador, ra [thoom-bah-dor', rah], *a.* Humming, buzzing. -*m.* Buzzer.

zumbar [thoom-bar'], *vn.* 1. To resound, to emit a harsh sound; to buzz (insecto), to hum (máquina). 2. To be near a certain time or place (quedar cerca). Me zumban los oídos, I have a buzzing in my ears. -*va. & vr.* 1. To jest, to joke. **Hacer zumbar las orejas**, (*Coll.*) to make one feel by a smart reprehension. **Ir zumbando**, to go with great violence and celerity. 2. (*And. Carib.*) To clear off (marcharse). 3. (*Carib.*) To overstep the mark (pasarse).

zumbel [thoom-bel'], *m.* 1. (*Coll.*) Frown, an angry mien or aspect. 2. (*Prov.*) Cord with which boys spin tops.

zumbido, zumbo [thoom-bee'-do, thoom'-bo], *m.* 1. Humming, a continued buzzing sound. 2. (*Coll.*) A blow.

zumbilín [thoom-be-leen'], *m.* A dart, or javelin, used in the Philippine Islands.

zumbón, na [thoom-bone', nah], *a.* 1. Waggish (persona), casting jokes. 2. (*Prov. Andal.*) Applied to a kind of pigeon with a small maw: in this sense it is also used as a substantive.

zumiento, ta [thoo-me-en'-to, tah], *a.* Juicy, succulent.

zumillo [thoo-meel'-lyo], *m.* 1. (*Bot.*) Dragon arum, "Aaron's beard." 2. Deadly carrot.

zumo [thoo'-mo], *m.* 1. Sap, juice (bebida), liquor, moisture; properly, any expressed juice, in contradistinction to that obtained by boiling, which is called *jugo*. 2. (*Met.*) Profit, utility. **Zumo de naranja**, orange squash.

zumoso, sa [thoo-mo'-so, sah], *a.* Juicy, succulent.

zuncho [thoon'-cho], *m.* Band, hoop, collar, ferrule.

zuño [thoo'-nyo], *m.* Frown, angry mien or countenance. V. CEÑO.

zupia [thoo'-pe-ah], *f.* 1. Wine which is fumed (vino), and has a bad taste and color; any liquor of a bad taste and looks. 2. Refuse, useless remains, lees.

zura, zurana [thoo'-rah, thoo-rah'-nah], *f.* Stock-dove. V. ZORITA.

zurcidera [thoor-the-day'-rah], *f.* Bawd, pimp.

zurcido [thoor-thee'-do], *m.* Stitching, uniting, finedrawing.

zurcidor, ra [thoor-the-dor', rah], *m. & f.* 1. Finedrawer, one whose business is to sew up rents. 2. Pimp, procuress.

zurcidura [thoor-the-doo'-rah], *f.* Fine-drawing, sewing up rents, darning.

zurcir [thoor-theer'], *va.* 1. To darn, to sew up rents, to fine-draw. 2. To join, to unite. 3. To hatch lies. **¡Que las zurzan!**, to blazes with them!

zurdear [thoor-day-ar'], *vn.* To be left handed.

zurdillo, illa [thoor-deel'-lyo], *a. dim.* Applied to one who is somewhat left-handed.

zurdo, da [thoor'-do, dah], *a.* 1. Left: applied to one of the hands. 2. Belonging to the left hand. 3. Left-handed. **A zurdas**, the wrong way.

zurear [thoo-ray-ar'], *vn.* To bill and coo (paloma).

zureo [thoo-ray'-o], *m.* Billing and cooing.

zurita [thoo-ree'-tah], *f.* (*Orn.*) Stock-dove. V. ZORITA.

zuriza [thoo-ree'-thah], *f.* Quarrel, dispute. V. ZUIZA.

zuro, ra [thoo'-ro, rah], *a.* Belonging to a stock-dove.

zurra [thoor'-rah], *f.* 1. The act of tanning or currying leather. 2. Flogging, drubbing, castigation. 3. Quarrel, dispute (pelea). 4. A severe reprimand. 5. To lash into, to criticize (criticar).

zurra, *int.* A term expressive of displeasure or anger.

zurraco [thoor-rah'-co], *m.* (*Coll.*) Cash.

zurrado, da [thoor-rah'-do, dah], *a. & pp.* of ZURRAR. Curried, dressed. -*m.* (*Coll.*) Glove.

zurrador [thoor-rah-dor'], *m.* 1. Leather-dresser, currier, tanner. 2. One who flogs or chastises.

zurrapa [thoor-rah'-pah], *f.* 1. Lees, sediment, dregs. 2. Anything vile or despicable.

zurrapiento, ta [thoor-rah-pe-en'-to, tah], *a.* V. ZURRAPOSO.

zurrapilla [thoor-rah-peel'-lyah], *f.* Small lees in liquor.

zurraposo, sa [thoor-rah-po'-so, sah], *a.* Full of lees and dregs.

zurrar [thoor-rar'], *va.* 1. To curry, to dress leather. 2. To flog, to chastise with a whip (pegar). 3. To contest, to urge with vehemence. -*vr.* 1. To have a sudden call of nature; to dirty oneself. 2. To be possessed by a great dread or fear.

zurriaga [thoor-re-ah'-gah], *f.* 1. Thong, a long leather strap; a whip for tops. 2. (*Orn. Prov.*) Lark. V. CALANDRIA.

zurriagar [thoor-re-ah-gar'], *va.* To flog, to chastise with a whip.

zurriagazo [thoor-re-ah-gah'-tho], *m.* 1. A severe lash or stroke with a whip (azote). 2. Unexpected ill-treatment; unfortunate calamity.

zurriago [thoor-re-ah'-go], *m.* 1. Whip for inflicting punishment. 2. (*Mex. Vulg.*) A mean, despicable fellow.

zurriar [thoor-re-ar'], *vn.* 1. (*Prov.*) To hum, to buzz. 2. To speak in a harsh and violent tone.

zurribanda [thoor-re-bahn'-dah], *f.* 1. Repeated flogging or chastisement with a whip. 2. A noisy quarrel.

zurriburri [thoor-re-boor'-re], *m.* 1. (*Coll.*) Ragamuffin, despicable person, low fellow (persona). 2. Turmoil (confusión). 3. Gang (pandilla).

zurrido, zurrío [thoor-ree'-do, thoor-ree'-o], *m.* 1. Humming, buzzing. 2. Confused noise or bustle.

zurrir [thoor-reer'], *m.* To hum, to buzz, to sound gratingly or confusedly.

zurrón [thoor-rone'], *m.* 1. Bag or pouch in which shepherds carry their provisions; game-bag. 2. Rind of fruits; chaff, husks of grain. 3. Bag, rack, of cow-hide in which Peruvian bark and other merchandise is brought from America; seroon. 4. (*Anat.*) Placenta.

zurrona [thoor-ro'-nah], *f.* Prostitute who wine her gallants.

zurroncillo [thoor-ron-theel'-lyo], *m. dim.* A small bag.

zurronero [thoor-ro-nay'-ro], *m.* One who makes bags or sacks.

zurruscarse [thoor-roos-car'-say], *vr.* (*Coll.*) To experience a sudden call of nature; to dirty oneself.

zurrusco [thoor-roos'-co], *m.* (*Coll.*) A slice of bread which is overtoasted. V. CHURRUSCO.

zurullo [thoo-rool'-lyo], *m.* 1. (*Coll.*) A piece of something lone and round, as of dough. 2. Rolling-pin 3. Human excrement (hez).

zurumbet [thoo-room-bet'], *m.* (*Bot.*) A large East Indian tree.

zurupeto [thoo-roo-pay'-to], *m.* An intrusive money-broker. (*Acad.*)

zutanico, illo [thoo-tah-nee'-co], *m. dim.* of ZUTANO.

zutano, na [thoo-tah'-no, nah], *m. & f.* A word invented to supply the name of some one, when the latter is not known or not desired to be expressed. Such a one. It is used with *fulano* or *mengano*, or with both; but neither *mengano* nor *zutano* can be used alone. When these three words are combined, the phrase always begins with *fulano*. Thus: *Fulano, zutano y mengano,* such and such a one.

zuzar [thoo-thar'], *va.* To set on dogs. *V.* AZUZAR.

¡zuzo! [thoo'-tho], *int.* A word used to call or set on a dog. *V.* ¡CHUCHO!

¡zuzón! [thoo-thone'], *m.* (*Bot.*) Groundsel, ragwort. Senecio; so-called from the hoary pappus. *V.* HIERBA CANA.

APPENDIX

A Vocabulary of Geographical Terms

WHICH ARE NOT IDENTICAL IN THE ENGLISH AND SPANISH LANGUAGES.

NOTE.—Adjectives derived from proper names, geographical and other, are entered in the body of the dictionary and therefore not repeated here. Thus: Abisinio, a, Abyssinian; Cesariano, na, Caesarian, belonging to Julius Caesar.

A

Abisinia [ah-be-see'-ne-ah], Abyssinia, *V.* ETIOPÍA.
Acaya [ah-cah'-yah], Achaea (district of ancient Greece).
Addis Abeba [ah'-dees ah-bay'-bah], Addis Ababa (Ethiopia).
Adrianápolis [ah-dre-ah-no'-po-lees] or **Andrianópolis** [ahn-dre-ah-no'-po-lees], Adrianople or Edirne (Turkey).
Adriático, Mar [mar ah-dre-ah'-te-co], Adriatic Sea.
África Ecuatorial Francesa [ah'-free-cah ay-coo-ah-to-re-ahl' frahn-thay'-sah], French Equatorial Africa.
Alasca [ah-lahs'-cah], Alaska.
Alejandría [ah-lay-han-dree'-ah], Alexandria (Egypt).
Alemania [ah-lay-mah'-ne-ah], Germany.
Aleutianas, Islas [ees'-lahs ah-lay-oo-te-ah'-nas], Aleutian Islands.
Almirantazgo, Islas del [ees'-lahs del al-me-rahn-tath'-go], Admiralty Islands.
Alpes [ahl'-pays]. Alps (mountains in S. Central Europe).
Alsacia-Lorena [al-sah'-the-ah lo-ray'-nah], Alsace-Lorraine.
Amarillo, Mar [mar ah-mah-ree'-lyo], Yellow Sea or Hwang Hai.
Amarillo, Río [ree'-o ah-mah-ree'-lyo] or **Hoang Ho** [ho-ang'-ho]. Yellow River or Hwang Ho.
Amazonas, Río [ree'-o ah-mah-tho'-nas], Amazon River.
Amberes [am-bay'-rays], Antwerp (Belgium).
América Central, *V.* CENTRO AMÉRICA.
América Ibera [ah-may'-ree-cah e-bay'-rah], Latin America.
Amigos, Islas de los, *V.* TONGA.
Amistad, Islas de la, *V.* TONGA.
Andalucía [an-dah-loo-thee'-ah], Andalusia (Spain).
Antártico, Océano [o-thay'-ah-no ahn-tar'-tee-co], Antarctic Ocean.
Antillas, Mar de las, *V.* MAR CARIBE.
Antillas Mayores [ahn-tee'-lyas mah-yo'-rays], Greater Antilles.
Antillas Menores [ahn-tee'-lyas may-no'-rays], Lesser Antilles.
Antioquía [an-te-o-kee'-ah], Antioch (Turkey).
Apalaches, Montes [mon'-tess ah-pah-lah'-chays], Appalachian Mountains.

Apeninos [ah-pay-nee'-nos], Apennines (mountains of Italy).
Aquisgrán [ah-kees-grahn'], Aachen or Aix-la-Chapelle (Germany).
Arabia Saudita [ah-rah'-bee-ah sah-oo-dee'-tah], Saudi Arabia.
Arábigo, Mar [mar ah-rah'-be-go], Arabian Sea.
Ardenas, Sierra [see-ay'-rrah ar-day'-nahs], Ardennes Mountains.
Argel [ar-hel'], Algiers (Algeria).
Argelia [ar-hay'-le-ah], Algeria.
Ártico, Océano [o-thay'-ah-no ar'-tee-co], Arctic Ocean.
Asiria [ah-see'-re-ah], Assyria.
Asís [ah-sees'], Assisi (Italy).
Atenas [ah-tay'-nas], Athens (Greece).
Ática [ah'-te-cah], Attica (Greece).
Atlántico, Océano [o-thay'-ah-no ah-tlahn'-te-co], Atlantic Ocean.
Austria-Hungría [ah'-oos-tree-ah oon-gree'-ah], Austria-Hungary.
Aviñón [ah-ve-nyone'], Avignon (France).
Azincourt [ah-theen-coor'], Agincourt (France).
Azules, Montañas [mon-tah'-nyahs ah-thoo'-lays], Blue Mountains.

B

Babilonia [bah-be-lo'-ne-ah], Babylon.
Baja California [bah'-hah cah-lee-for'-nee-ah], Lower California (Mexico).
Balcanes [bahl-cah'-nays], Balkans.
Baleares, Islas [ees'-lahs bah-lay-ah'-rays], Balearic Islands.
Báltico, Mar [mar bahl'-te-co], Baltic sea.
Barlovento, Islas de [ees'-lahs day bar-lo-vayn'-to], Windward Islands.
Basilea [bah-say-lay'-ah], Basle or Basel (Switzerland).
Baviera [bah-ve-ay'-rah], Bavaria (Germany).
Bayona [bah-yo'-nah], Bayonne (France).
Beirut [bay-root'], Beirut or Beyrouth (Lebanon).
Belén [bay-layn'], Bethlehem (Jordan).
Bélgica [bel'-he-cah], Belgium.

Belgrado [bel-grah'-do], Belgrade or Beograd (Yugoslavia).
Belice [bay-lee'-thay] or **Honduras Británica** [ohn-doo'-rahs bree-tah'-nee-cah], British Honduras.
Bengala [ben-gah'-lah], Bengal.
Berbería [ber-bay-ree'-ah], Barbary Coast (Africa).
Berna [behr'-nah], Berne or Bern (Switzerland).
Birmania [beer-mah'-nee-ah], Burma.
Bizancio [be-than'-the-o], Byzantium. V. ISTAMBUL or CONSTANTINOPLA.
Bolonia [bo-lo'-ne-ah], Bologna (Italy).
Borgoña [bor-go'-nyah], Burgundy.
Bósforo, Estrecho del [es-tray'-cho del bos'-fo-ro], Strait of Bosporus or Bosphorus.
Brasil [brah-seel'], Brazil.
Bretaña, Gran [grahn bray-tah'-nyah], Great Britain.
Británicas, Islas [ees'-lahs bree-tah'-nee-cahs], British Isles.
Brujas [broo'-has], Bruges (Belgium).
Bruselas [broo-say'-lahs], Brussels (Belgium).
Bucarest [boo-cah-rest'], Bucharest (Rumania).
Buena Esperanza, Cabo de [cah'-bo day boo-ay'-nah espay-rahn'-thah], Cape of Good Hope.
Burdeos [boor-day'-ose], Bordeaux (France).

C

Cabo Bretón, Isla [ees'-lah cah'-bo bray-tone], Cape Breton Island (Nova Scotia, Canada).
Cabo, Ciudad del [thee-oo-dahd' del cah'-bo], Capetown (Union of South Africa).
Cabo de Hornos [cah'-bo day or'-nos], Cape Horn.
Cachemira [cah-chay-mee'-rah], Cashmere or Kashmir (state of the Himalayas).
Calcuta [cahl-coo'-tah], Calcutta (India).
Camboja [cahm-bo'-hah], Cambodia (Indochina).
Canal de la Mancha [cah-nahl' day lah mahn'-chah], English Channel.
Canal de Panama, Zona del. V. ZONA DEL CANAL DE PANAMÁ.
Canarias, Islas [ees'-lahs cah-nah'-re-ahs], Canary Islands.
Cantábrica, Cordillera [cor-dee-lyay'-rah cahn-tah'-bree-cah], Cantabrian Mountains.
Caribe, Mar [mar cah-ree'-bay], or **Mar de las Antillas** [mar day lahs ahn-tee'-lyahs], Caribbean Sea.
Cárpatos, Montes [mon'-tess car'-pah-tose], Carpathian Mountains.
Cartago [car-tah'-go], Carthage (ancient city of N. Africa. Also a city in Costa Rica, C.A.).
Caspio, Mar [mar cahs'-pe-o], Caspian Sea.
Castilla la Nueva [cas-teel'-lyah lah noo-ay'-vah], New Castile (Spain).
Castilla la Vieja [cas-teel'-lyah lah ve-ay'-hah], Old Castile (Spain).
Cataluña [cah-tah-loo'-nyah], Catalonia (Spain).
Cáucaso [cow'-cah-ao], Caucasus.
Cayena [cah-yay'-nah], Cayenne (French Guiana).
Cayo Hueso [cah'-yo oo-ay'-so], Key West (Florida, U.S.A.).
Ceilán [thay-lahn'], Ceylon.
Centro América [then'-tro ah-may'-ree-cah] or **América Central** [then-trahl'], Central America.
Cercano Oriente, V. ORIENTE, CERCANO.
Cerdeña [ther-day'-nyah], Sardinia or Sardegna (Italian island in the Mediterranean).
Champaña [cham-pah'-nyah], Champagne (France).
Checoslovaquia [chay-cohs-lo-vah'-kee-ah], Czechoslovakia.
Chipre [chee'-pray], Cyprus (island in the Mediterranean).
Ciudad del Vaticano [the-oo-dahd' del vah-tee-cah'-no], Vatican City.
Colombia [co-lom'-bee-ah], Colombia.
Colonia [co-lo'-ne-ah], Cologne (Germany).
Congo [cohn'-go], Congolese.

Conastantinopla [conas-tan-te-no'-plah], Constantinople, V. ISTAMBUL.
Copenhague [co-pen-ah'-gay], Copenhagen (Denmark).
Córcega [cor'-thay-gah], Corsica (island in the Mediterranean).
Corea [coh-ray'-ah], Korea.
Corinto [co-reen'-to], Corinth (Greece).
Costa de Oro [cos'-tah day o'-ro], Gold Coast (W. Africa).
Cracovia [crah-co'-ve-ah], Cracow (Poland).
Creta [cray'-tah], Crete or Krete (island in the Mediterranean).
Croacia [cro-ah-the-ah], Croatia.

D

Dalmacia [dal-mah'-the-ah], Dalmatia.
Damasco [dah-mahs'-co], Damascus (Syria).
Danubio [dah-noo'-be-o], Danube (river of Europe).
Dardanelos [dar-dah-nay'-los], Dardanelles (formerly Hellespont).
Dinamarca [de-nah-mar'-cah], Denmark.
Dordeña [dor-do'-nyah], Dordogne (a river of France).
Dresde [dres'-day], Dresden (Germany).
Duero [doo-ay'-ro], Douro or Duero (river of the Iberian Peninsula).
Dunquerque [doon-kerr'-kay], Dunkirk (France).

E

Edimburgo [ay-deem-boor'-go], Edinburgh (Scotland).
Éfeso [ay-fay'-so], Ephesus (ancient Greek city in Asia Minor).
Egeo, Mar [mar ay-hay'-o], Aegean Sea.
Egipto [ay-heep'-to], Egypt.
Elba [el'-bah], Elbe (river in Europe).
Epiro [ay-pee'-ro], Epirus (ancient Greece).
Escalda [es-cahl'-dah], Scheldt (river in Belgium).
Escocia [es-co'-thee-ah], Scotland.
Esmirna [es-meer'-nah], Smyrna (Turkey).
Eslovaquia [es-lo-vah-ke-ah], Slovakia.
Eslovenia [es-lo-vay-me-ah], Slovenia.
España [es-pah'-nyah], Spain.
Esparta [ea-par'-tah], Sparta (ancient city of Greece).
Estados Pontificios [es-tah'-doas pon-tee-fee'-the-oas], Papal States or States of the Church.
Estados Unidos de América [es-tah'-dos oo-nee'-dos day ah-may'-re-cah], United States of America.
Estocolmo [es-to-col'-mo], Stockholm (Sweden).
Estrómboli [es-trom'-bo-lee], Stromboli (volcano N. of Sicily).
Etiopía [ay-te-o-pee'-ah], Ethiopia (formerly Abyssinia).
Eufrates [ay-oo-frah'-tays], Euphrates (river in Asia).

F

Falkland or **Malvinas, Islas**, V. MALVINAS, ISLAS.
Fenicia [fay-nee'-the-ah], Phoenicia.
Filadelfia [fe-lah-del'-fe-ah], Philadelphia (U.S.A.)
Filipinas [fe-le-pee'-nas], Philippines.
Finlandia [fin-lahn'-de-ah], Finland.
Flandes [flahn'-des], Flanders.
Florencia [flo-ren'-the-ah], Florence (Italy).
Francia [fran'-the-ah], France.
Frisias, Islas [ees'-lahs free'-see-ahs], Frisian Islands.

G

Gales [gah'-less], Wales.
Galia [gah'-le-ah], Gaul.
Galilea [gah-le-lay'-ah], Galilee.
Gante [gahn'-tay], Ghent (Belgium).

Garona [gah-ro'-nah], Garonne (river of France).
Gascuña [gas-coo'-nyah], Gascony (France).
Génova [hay'-no-vah], Genoa (Italy).
Ginebra [he-nay'-brah], Geneva (Switzerland).
Gran Bretaña [grahn bray-tah'-nyah], Great Britain.
Grecia [gray'-thee-ah], Greece.
Groenlandia [gro-enn-lahn'-de-ah], Greenland.
Groninga [gro-neen'-gah], Groningen (Netherlands).
Guayana [goo-ah-yah'-nah] Guyanese.

H

Habana [ah-bah'-nah], Havana (Cuba).
Haitiano, Cabo [cah'-bo ah-te-ah'-no], Cap Haitien.
Haití [ah-ee-tee'] or **Santo Domingo** [sahn'-to do-meen'- go] Haiti Island.
Haití. República de [ray-poo'-blee-cah day ah-ee-tee'], Rep. of Haiti.
Hamburgo [am-boor'-go], Hamburg (Germany).
Hangcheú [ahn-chay-oo'] Hangchow (Chinese seaport).
Hankeú [ahn-kay-oo'], Hankow (Chinese city).
Havre, El [el-ah'-vr], Le Havre (port of France).
Hawaii, Islas [ees'-lahs ha-wa'-ee], Hawaiian Islands.
Haya, La [lah ah'-yah], The Hague (Netherlands).
Hébridas, Islas [ees'-lahs ay'-bree-dahs], Hebrides Islands.
Helesponto [ay-les-pone'-to], V. DARDALENOS.
Holanda [o-lahn'-dah] or **Países Bajos** [pah-ee'-ses bah'- hos], Holland or The Netherlands.
Hungría [oon-gree'-ah], Hungary.

I

Ibérica, Península [pay-neen'-soo-lah e-bay'-re-cah], Iberian Peninsula.
Indias Occidentales [in'-dee-ahs ok-thee-den-tah'-less], West Indies.
Indias Orientales [in'-dee-ahs o-ree-en-tah'-less], East Indies.
Índico, Océano [oh-thay'-ah-no in'-dee-co], Indian Ocean.
Indo [in'-do], Indus (river of India and Pakistan).
Inglaterra [in-glah-tay'-rrah], England.
Irak [e-rak'], Iraq.
Irlanda [eer-lahn'-dah], Ireland.
Islandia [ees-lahn'-de-ah], Iceland.
Istambul [ees-tam-bool'], Istanbul (formerly Constantinople).
Italia [e-tah'-le-ah], Italy.

J

Japón [hah-pone], Japan.
Jerusalén [hay-roo-sah-layn'], Jerusalem.
Jónico, Mar [mar-ho'-ne-co], Ionian Sea.
Jordania [hor-dah'-ne-ah], Jordan.
Jutlandia [hoot-lahn'-de-ah], Jutland.

K

Kioto [kee-o'-to], Kyoto (Japan).

L

Lagos, Grandes [grahn'-days lah'-gos], Great Lakes (U.S.A.)
Laponia [lah-po'-ne-ah], Lapland.
Lausana [lah-oo-sah'-nah], Lausanne (Switzerland).
Lejano Oriente, V. ORIENTE, LEJANO.
Leningrado [lay-neen-grah'-do], Leningrad (formerly San Petersburgo and Petrogrado, Russia).
Líbano [lee'-bah-no], Lebanon.
Libia [lee'-bee-ah], Libya.
Lieja [le-ay'-hah], Liege (Belgium).
Lila [lee'-lah], Lille (France).
Liorna [lee-or'-nah], Leghorn (Italy).
Lisboa [lis-bo'-ah], Lisbon (Portugal).
Lituania [lee-too-ah'-nee-ah], Lithuania.
Londres [lon'-dress], London (England).
Lorena [lo-ray'-nah], Lorraine. V. ALSACIA-LORENA.
Lovaina [lo-vah'-e-nah], Louvain (Belgium).
Lucerna [loo-ther'-nah], Lucerne or Luzern (Switzerland).
Luisiana [loo-e-se-ah'-nah], Louisiana (U.S.A.).

M

Magallanes, Estrecho de [es-tray'-cho day mah-gal-lyah'-ness], Strait of Magellan.
Maguncia [mah-goon'-the-ah], Mainz (Germany).
Malaca, Península de [pay-neen'-soo-lah day mah-lah'-cah], Malay Peninsula.
Maldivas, Islas [ees'-lahs mal-dee'-vahs], Maldive Islands.
Malvinas or **Falkland, Islas** [ees'-lahs mal-vee'-nahs, fok'-land], Falkland Islands.
Mallorca [mal-lyor'-cah], Majorca or Mallorca (island in the Mediterranean).
Mancha, Canal de la [cah-nahl' day lah mahn'-chah], English Channel.
Marfil, Costa de [cos'-tah day mar-feel], Ivory Coast.
Mármara, Mar de [mar day mar'-mah-rah], Sea of Marmora or Marmara.
Marruecos [mah-roo-ay'-cos], Morocco.
Marsella [mar-say'-lyah], Marseille or Marseilles (France).
Martinica [mar-te-nee'-cah], Martinique.
Mauricio [mah-oo-ree'-the-o], Mauritius or Ile de France (British island in Indian Ocean).
Mediterráneo, Mar [mar may-de-tay-rah'-nay-o], Mediterranean Sea.
Menfis [men'-fees], Memphis (cap. Of ancient Egypt).
Menorca [may-nor'-cah], Minorca or Menorca (island in the Mediterranean).
México or **Méjico** [may'-he-co], Mexico.
Misisipi, Río [ree'-o me-see-see'-pee], Mississippi River (U.S.A.).
Misuri [me-soo'-re], Missouri (river and state of U.S.A.).
Molucas, Islas [ees'-lahs mo-loo'-cahs] or **Islas de las Especias** [day lahs es-pay'-thee-ahs], Moluccas or Spice Islands.
Mosa [mo'-sah], Meuse (river of France and Belgium).
Moscú [mos-coo'], Moscow.
Mosela [mo-say'-lah], Moselle (river of France and Germany).
Muerto, Mar [mar moo-err'-to], Dead Sea.

N

Nápoles [nah'-po-less], Naples (Italy).
Negro, Mar [mar nay'-gro], Black Sea.
Niágara, Cataratas del [cah-tah-rah'-tahs del nee-ah'-gah-rah], Niagara Falls.

Nilo [nee'-lo], Nile (river of Africa).

Nínive [nee'-nee-vay], Nineveh (ancient city of Assyrian Empire).

Nipón [nee-pone'], Nippon. *V.* JAPÓN.

Niza [nee'-thah], Nice (France).

Normandía [nor-man-dee'-ah], Normandy (France).

Norte América [nor'-tay ah-may'-ree-cah] or **América del Norte** [del nor'-tay], North America.

Noruega [no-roo-ay'-gah], Norway.

Nueva Escocia [noo-ay'-vah es-co'-thee-ah], Nova Scotia (Canada).

Nueva Gales del Sur [noo-ay'-vah gah'-lea del soor], New South Wales.

Nueva Orleáns [noo-ay'-vah or-lay-ahns'], New Orleans (U.S.A.).

Nueva York [noo-ay'-vah york], New York (U.S.A.).

Nueva Zelanda [noo-ay'-vah thay-lahn'-dah], New Zealand.

O

Odesa [o-day'-sah], Odessa (Russian seaport on Black Sea).

Olimpo, Monte [mon'-tay o-leem'-po], Mount Olympus.

Oriente, Cercano [ther-cah'-no o-ree-en'-tay] Near East.

Oriente Lejano [lay-hah'-no o-ree-en'-tay], Far East.

Ostende [os-ten'-day], Ostend (Belgium).

P

Pacífico, Océano [o-thay'-ah-no pah-thee'-fee-co], Pacific Ocean.

Países Bajos, *V.* HOLANDA.

Palestina [pah-les-tee'-nah], Palestine.

Parnaso [par-nah'-so], Parnassus.

Peloponeso [pay-lo-po-nay'-so], Peloponnesus (Greece).

Pensilvania [pen-sil-vah'-ne-ah], Pennsylvania (U.S.A.).

Perusa [pay-roo'-sah], Perugia (Italy).

Pirineos [pe-re-nay'-ose], Pyrenees (range of mountains separating Spain and France).

Polaco, Corredor [cor-ray-dor' po-lah'-co], Polish Corridor.

Polonia [po-lo'-ne-ah], Poland.

Polo Norte [po'-lo nor'-tay], North Pole.

Polo Sur [po'-lo soor], South Pole.

Pompeya [pom-pay'-yah], Pompeii (Italy).

Praga [prah'-gah], Prague (Czechoslovakia).

Puerto Príncipe [poo-err'-to preen'-thee-pay], Port-au-Prince (Haiti).

Puerto Said [poo-err'-to sah-eed'], Port Said (Egypt).

R

Rangún [rahn-goon'], Rangoon (Burma).

Reino Unido [ray'-no oo-nee'-do], United Kingdom (Great Britain and N. Ireland).

Rin or **Rhin** [rin], Rhine (river in Europe).

Rocosas, Montañas [mon-tah'-nyahs ro-co'-sahs], Rocky Mountains.

Ródano [ro'-dah-no], Rhone (river of Europe).

Rodas [ro'-dahs], Rhodes (island in the Aegean Sea).

Rojo, Mar [mar ro'-ho], Red Sea.

Ruan [roo-ahn'], Rouen (France).

Rumania [roo-mah-ne-ah], Romania.

Rusia [roo'-see-ah], Russia.

S

Sajonia [sah-ho'-nee-ah], Saxony (old German kingdom).

Salónica [sah-loh'-nee-kah], Salonika or Thessalonike (Greece).

Selva Negra [sell'-vah nay'-grah], Black Forest.

Sena [say'-nah], Seine (river of France).

Siam [see-am], *V.* THAILANDIA.

Sicilia [see-thee'-le-ah], Sicily (island of the Mediterranean).

Siracusa [see-rah-coo'-ash], Syracuse (Italy).

Siria [see'-re-ah], Syria.

Somalia [so-mah'-lee-ah], Somalia.

Sud América [sood ah-may'-ree-cah] or **América del Sur** [del soor] South America.

Suecia [soo-ay'-thee-ah], Sweden.

Suiza [soo-ee'-thah], Switzerland.

Surinam, *V.* GUAYANA

T

Tajo [tah'-ho], Tagus, Tajo or Tejo (river of Spain and Portugal).

Támesis [tah'-may-sis], Thames (river of England).

Tánger [tahn'-her], Tangier (Morocco).

Tauro, Montañas [mon-tah'-nyahs tah'-oo-ro], Taurus Mountains (Turkey).

Tebas [tay'-bas], Thebes (ancient cities of Greece and Egypt).

Teherán [tay-rahn'], Tehran or Teheran (Iran).

Tejas [tay'-has], Texas (U.S.A.)

Termópilas [ter-mo'-pee-lahs], Thermopylae (Greek pass).

Terranova [ter-rah-no'-vah], Newfoundland.

Tesalia [tay-sah'-le-ah], Thessaly (Greece).

Thailandia [tah-ee-lahn'-dee-ah], or **Siam** [see-am], Thailand or Siam.

Tierra Santa [tee-ay'-rrah sahn'-tah], Holy Land.

Tiro [tee'-ro], Tyre (ancient Phoenician port, now a port of Lebanon).

Tirreno, Mar [mar te-rray'-no], Tyrrhenian Sea.

Tokio [to'-kyo], Tokyo (Japan).

Tolón [to-lone'], Toulon (France).

Tolosa [to-lo'-sah], Toulouse (France).

Tonga [tohn'-gah] or **Islas de los Amigos** [ees'-lahs day los ah-mee'-gos] or **Islas de la Amistad** [day lah ah-mees-tahd'], Tonga or Friendly Islands.

Toscana [tos-cah'-nah], Tuscany.

Tracia [trah'-thee-ah], Thrace.

Trento [tren'-to], Trent or Trento (Italy).

Troya [tro'-yah], Troy.

Túnez [too'-neth], Tunis.

Turquía [toor-kee'-ah], Turkey.

U

Ucrania [oo-crah-ne-ah], Ukraine.

Unión de los Emiratos Arabes [oo-ne-on day los ay-me-rah-tos ah-rah-bays], United Arab Emirates.

Unión Sudafricana [oo-ne-on' sood-ah-free-cah'-nah], Union of South Africa.

Urales, Montes [mon'-tess oo-rah'-lees], Ural Mountains.

V

Varsovia [var-so'-ve-ah], Warsaw (Poland).

Vaticano, Ciudad del [thee-oo-dahd' del vah-tee-cah'-no], Vatican City.

Venecia [vay-nah'-the-ah], Venice (Italy).

Versalles [ver-sahl'-lyes], Versailles (France).

Vesubio [vey-soo'-be-o], Vesuvius (mountain and volcano of Italy).

Viena [ve-ay'-nah], Vienna (Austria).

Vírgenes, Islas [ees'-lahs veer'-hay-nays] Virgin Islands.

Vizcaya [veeth-cah'-yah], Biscay (Spain).

Z

Zona del Canal de Panamá [tho'-nah del cah-nahl' day pahnah-mah'], Panama Canal Zone.

Alphabetical List

of the Most Usual Proper Names in Spanish,

INCLUDING BIBLICAL AND HISTORICAL NAMES,

WHICH ARE WRITTEN DIFFERENTLY IN ENGLISH.

Abrahán [ah-brah-ahn'], Abraham.
Adán [ah-dahn'], Adam.
Adela [ah-day'-lah], Adele.
Adalaida [ah-day-lah'-e-dah], Adelaide.
Adolfo [ah-dol'-fo], Adolphus.
Adrián, Adriano [ah-dre-ahn', ah-dre-ah'-no], Adrian, Hadrian.
Ágata [ah'-gah-tah], Agatha.
Agustín [ah-goos-teen'], Augustin, Austin.
Alberto [al-berr'-to], Albert.
Alejandra or **Alejandrina** [ah-lay-hahn'-drah, ah-lay-hahn-dree'-nah], Alexandra, Alexandrina.
Alejandro [ah-lay-hahn'-dro], Alexander.
Alejo [ah-lay'-ho], Alexis.
Alfonso [al-fon'-so], Alphonsus.
Alfredo [al-fray'-do], Alfred.
Alicia [ah-lee'-the-ah], Alice.
Alonso [ah-lon'-so], Alphonsus.
Amadeo [ah-mah-day'-o], Amadeus.
Ambrosio [am-bro'-se-o], Ambrose, Ambrosius.
Amelia [ah-may'-le-ah], Amelie.
Ana [ah'-nah], Ann, Anne, Hannah; *coll.* Nan or Nancy.
Anabel [ah-nah-bel], Annabel.
Andrés [an-drays], Andrew.
Ángela [ahn-hay-lah], Angela, Angie.
Anibal [ah-nee'-bal], Hannibal.
Anselmo [an-sel'-mo], Anselm.
Antonio [an-to'-ne-o], Anthony; *coll.* Tony.
Aristóteles [ah-ris-to'-tay-less], Aristotle.
Arnaldo [ar-nahl'-do], Arnold.
Arquímedes [ahr-kee'-may-days], Archimedes.
Arturo [ar-too'-ro], Arthur.
Atanasio [ah-tah-nah'-se-o], Athanasius.
Atila [ah-tee'-lah], Attila.
Augusto [ah-goos'-to], Augustus.
Aureliano, Aurelio [ah-oo-ray-le-ah'-no, ah-oo-ray'-le-o], Aurelius.

Balduino [bahl-doo-ee'-no], Baldwin.
Bárbara [bar'-bah-rah], Barbara.; *coll.* Bab.
Bartolo [bar-toh'-lo], Bartholomew; *coll.* Bart.
Bartolomé [bar-to-lo-may'], Bartholomew.
Basilio [bah-see'-le-o], Basil.
Beatriz [bay-ah-treeth'], Beatrix, Beatrice.

Beltrán [bel-trahn'], Bertram.
Benita [bay-nee'-tah], Benedicta.
Benito [bay-nee'-to], Benedict.
Bernabé [ber-nah-bay'], Barnabas, Barnaby.
Bernardo [ber-nar'-do], Bernard.
Bernardino [ber-nar-dee'-no], Bernardinus.
Berta [berr'-tah], Bertha.
Blas [blahs], Blase.
Bonifacio [bo-ne-fah'-the-o], Boniface.
Brígida [bree'-he-dah], Bridget.
Buenaventura [boo-ay'-nah-ven-too'-rah], Bonaventure. *V.* VENTURA

Camila [cah-mee'-lah], Camilla.
Camilo [cah-mee'-lo], Camillus.
Carlos [car'-los], Charles; *coll.* Charley.
Carlota [car-lo'-tah], Charlotte.
Carolina [cah-ro-lee'-nah], Caroline.
Casandra [cah-sahn'-drah], Cassandra.
Casimiro [cah-se-mee'-ro], Casimir.
Catalina or **Catarina** [cah-tah-lee'-nah, ree'-nah], Catharine; *coll.* Kate, Kitty.
Catón [cah-tone'], Cato.
Cayetano [cah-yay-tah'-no], Cajetan.
Cecilia [thay-thee'-le-ah], Cecile; *coll.* Cis.
Cecilio [thay-thee'-le-o], Cecil.
César [thay'-sar], Caesar.
Cipriano [the-pre-ah'-no], Cyprian.
Ciriaco [the-re-ah'-co], Cyriacus.
Cirilo [the-ree'-lo], Cyrilus.
Claudia, Claudina [clah'-oo-de-ah, clah-oo-dee'-nah], Claudia.
Claudio [clah'-oo-de-o], Claude, Claudius.
Clemente [clay-men'-tay], Clement.
Clotilde [clo-teel'-day], Clotilde.
Conrado [con-rah'-do], Conrad.
Constancia, Constancio [cons-tahn'-the-ah, cons-tahn'-the-o], Constance.
Constantino [cons-tan-tee'-no], Constantine.
Constanza [cons-tahn'-thah], Constance.
Cornelio [cor-nay'-le-o], Cornelius.
Cosme [cos'-may], Cosmas.
Cristián [cris-te-ahn'], Christian.
Cristina [cris-tee'-nah], Christina.

Cristobal [cris-to'-bal], Christopher.
Darío [dah-ree'-o], Darius.
Diego [de-ay'-go], James.
Dionisia [de-o-nee'-se-ah], Dionysia.
Dionisio [de-o-nee'-se-o], Dennis.
Domingo [do-meen'-go], Dominic.
Dori [do-re], Doris.
Dorotea [do-ro-tay'-ah], Dorothy.

Edmundo [ed-moon'-do], Edmund.
Eduardo [ay-doo-ar'-do], Edward; *coll.* Eddy, Ned, Neddy.
Elena [ay-lay'-nah], Ellen.
Eleonor [ay-lay-o-nor], Eleanor, Eleanora; Ellie.
Elisabet [ay-le-sah-bayt], Elizabeth.
Elisa [ay-lee'-sah], Eliza.
Eliseo [ay-le-say'-o], Elisha, Ellis.
Ema [ay'-mah], Emma.
Emilia [ay-mee'-le-ah], Emily.
Emilio [ay-mee'-le-o], Emil, Emile.
Engracia [en-grah'-the-ah], Grace.
Enrique [en-ree'-kay], Henry.
Enriqueta [en-re-kay'-tah], Henrietta, Harriet.
Ernesto [err-nays'-to], Ernest.
Esteban [es-tay'-ban], Stephen.
Estela [ays-tay-lah], Stella.
Ester [es-terr'], Esther, Hester.
Eugenio [ay-oo-hay'-ne-o], Eugene.
Eusebio [ay-say'-be-o], Eusebius.
Eustaquio [ay-oos-tah'-ke-o], Eustace.
Eva [ay'-vah], Eve.
Ezequías [ay-thay-kee'-as], Hezekiah.
Ezaquiel [ay-thay-ke-el'], Ezekiel.

Federico [fay-day-ree'-co], Frederic; *coll.* Fred.
Felipa [fay-lee'-pah], Philippa.
Felipe, Filipo [fay-lee'-pay, fe-lee'-po], Philip; *coll.* Phil.
Felisa, Felicia [fey-lee'-se-ah, fay-lee'-the-ah], Felicia.
Fernando [fer-nahn'-do], Ferdinand.
Filemón [fee-lay-mone'], Philemon.
Florancia, Florencio [flo-ren'-the-ah, flo-ren'-the-o], Florence.
Francisca [fran-thees'-cah], Frances; *coll.* Fan, Fanny.
Francisco [fran-thees'-co], Francis.

Gaspar [gas-par'], Jasper.
Gerardo [hay-rar'-do], Gerard.
Gertrudis [herr-troo'-dees], Gertrude.
Gil [heel], Giles.
Gilberto [heel-berr'-to], Gilbert.
Godofredo [go-do-fray'-do], Godfrey.
Gregorio [gray-go'-re-o], Gregory.
Guillermo [gheel-lyerr'-mo], William.
Gustavo [goos-tah'-vo], Gustavus.

Herbarto, Heriberto [er-ber'-to, ay-ree-ber'-to], Herbert.
Herón [ay-rone'], Hiero or Hieron.
Hilario [e-lah'-re-o], Hilary.
Horacio [o-rah'-the-o], Horace, Horatio.
Hugo [oo'-go], Hugh.
Humberto [oom-berr'-to], Humbert.

Ignacio [ig-nah'-the-o], Ignatius.
Ildefonso [il-day-fon'-so], Alphonsus.
Inés [ee-nes'], Agnes, Inez.
Isabel [e-sah-bel], Elizabeth; *coll.* Bess, Bet, Betsy, Betty.
Isidoro, Isidro [e-se-do'-ro, e-see'-dro], Isidor.

Jacobo, Jaime [hah-co'-bo, hah'-e-may], James; *coll.* Jim or Jimmy.
Javier [ha-vee-er'], Xavier.
Jeremías [hay-ray-mee'-as], Jeremy.
Jerónimo [hay-ro'-ne-mo], Jerome; *coll.* Jerry.
Jesucristo [hay-soo-crees'-to], Jesus Christ.
Jesús [hay-soos'], Jesus.
Joaquín [ho-ah-keen'], Joachim.
Jonás [ho-nahs'], Jonah.
Jorge [hor'-hay], George.
José [ho-say'], Joseph.
Josefa [ho-say'-fah], Josephine.
Josué [ho-soo-ay'], Joshua.
Juan [hoo-ahn], John; *coll.* Jack or Johnny.
Juana [hoo-ah'-nah], Jane, Jennie; Joan, Joanna, *coll.* Jinny.
Judit [hoo-deet'], Judith.
Julio [hoo'-le-o], Julius.

Ladislao [lah-dees-lah'-o], Ladislas.
Lamberto [lam-berr'-to], Lambert.
Lázaro [lah'-thah-ro], Lazarus.
Leandro [lay-ahn'-dro], Leander.
León [lay-on'], Leo, Leon.
Leonardo [lay-o-nar'-do], Leonard.
Leonor [lay-o-nor'], Eleanor.
Leopoldo [lay-o-pole'-do], Leopold.
Leticia [lay-tee'-the-ah], Laetitia, Lettice.
Lidia [le-de-ah], Lydia.
Lisandro [lee-sahn'-dro], Lysander.
Livio [lee'-ve-o], Livy.
Lorenzo [lo-renn'-tho], Lawrence.
Lucas [loo'-cas], Luke.
Lucía [loo-thee'-ah], Lucy.
Lucio [loo'-the-o], Lucius.
Lucrecia [loo-cray'-the-ah], Lucretia.
Luis [loo-ees'], Lewis, Louis.
Luisa [loo-ee'-sah], Louisa.
Lutero [loo-tay'-ro], Luther.

Magdalena [mag-dah-lay'-nah], Magdalen.
Mahoma [mah-o'-mah], Mahomet or Mohammed.
Malaquías [mah-lah-kee'-as], Malachy.
Manuel [mah-noo-el'], Emanuel.
Manuela [mah-noo-ay'-lah], Emma.
Marcelo [mar-thay'-lo], Marcel.
Marcos [mar'-cos], Mark.
Margarita [mar-gah-ree'-tah], Margaret, Margery; *coll.* Madge, Meg.
María [mah-ree'-ah], Mary, Maria; *coll.* Mol. Molly.
Mariana [mah-re-ah'-nah], Marian.
Marta [mar'-tah], Martha.
Mateo [mah-tay'-o], Matthew; *coll.* Mat.
Matías [mah-tee'-as], Mattias.
Matilde [mah-teel'-day], Matilda.
Mauricio [mah-oo-ree'-the-o], Maurice, Morice.
Maximiliano [mak-se-me-le-ah'-no], Maximilian.
Miguel [mee-ghel'], Michael; *coll.* Mike.
Moisés [moi-says'], Moses.

Natalia [nah-tah-le-ah], Natalie.
Nerón [nay-rone'], Nero.
Néstor [ness'-tore], Nestorius.
Nicolás [ne-co-lahs'], Nicholas; *coll.* Nick.
Noé [no-ay'], Noah.

Octavio [oc-tah'-ve-o], Octavius.
Oliverio [o-le-vay'-reo], Oliver; *coll.* Noll.

Pablo [pah'-blo], Paul.

Patricio [pah-tree'-the-o], Patrick.
Pedro [pay'-dro], Peter.
Pelayo [pay-lah'-yo], Pelajo.
Pío [pee'-o], Pius.
Platón [plah-tone'], Plato.
Pompeyo [pom-pay'-yo], Pompey.
Prudencia [proo-den'-the-ah], Prudence.

Quintín [keen-teen'], Quentin.

Rafael [rah-fah-el'], Raphael.
Raimundo, Ramón [rah-e-moon'-do rah-mone'], Raymond.
Raquel [rah-kel'], Rachel.
Rebeca [ray-bay'-cah], Rebecca.
Renato [ray-nah'-to], Rene.
Ricardo [re-car'-do], Richard; *coll.* Dick, Dicky.
Roberto [ro-berr'-to], Robert; *coll.* Bob, Rob.
Rodolfo [ro-dole'-fo], Rodolphus, Ralph, Rolph.
Rodrigo [ro-dree'-go], Roderic.
Roger, Rogerio [ro-herr', ro-hay'-re-o], Roger.
Rómulo [ro'-moo-lo], Romulus.
Ronaldo [ro-nahl-do], Ronald.
Rosa [ro'-sah], Rose.
Rosalia [ro-sah-le-ah], Rosalie.
Rosario [ro-sah'-ree-o], Rosary.
Rubén [roo-bayn'], Reuben.
Ruperto [roo-perr'-to], Rupert.
Rut [root], Ruth.

Salomón [sah-lo-mon'], Solomon.
Salustio [sah-loos'-tee-o], Sallust.
Samuel [sah-moo-el'], Samuel; *coll.* Sam.
Sansón [sahn-son'], Samson.
Santiago [sahn-te-ah'-go], *V.* JACOBO.
Sara [sah'-rah], Sarah; *coll.* Sal, Sally.
Severo [say-vay'-ro], Severus.
Sigismundo [se-his-moon'-do], Sigismund.
Silvano [sil-vah'-no], Silvan.
Silvestre [sil-ves'-tray], Silvester.
Silvia [sil-ve-ah], Sylvia.
Sofía [so-fee'-ah], Sophia.
Susana [soo-sah'-nah], Susan, Susanna.

Teodora, Teodoro [tay-o-do'-rah, do'-ro], Thodora, Theodore.
Teodorico [tay-o-do-ree'-co], Theodorick, Dorick.
Teófilo [tay-o'-fe-lo], Theophilus.
Teresa [tay-ray'-sah], Theresa; *coll.* Tracy.
Timoteo [te-mo-tay'-o], Timothy.
Tito [tee'-to], Titus.
Tobías [to-bee'-as], Toby.
Tomás [to-mahs'], Thomas.

Urbano [oor-bah'-no], Urban.

Valentín [vah-len-teen'], Valentine.
Valeria [vah-lay-re-ah], Valerie.
Ventura [ven-too'-rah], Bonaventure.
Vicente [ve-then'-tay], Vincent.

Zacarías [thah-cah-ree'-as], Zachary.

An Alphabetical List of the Abbreviations

MOST COMMONLY USED IN SPANISH.

á. área
(a) alias.
A. Alteza; aprobado (en examen); amperio.
ACTH. Hormona adrenocorticotropa.
a. de J. C. antes de Jesucristo.
admón. administración.
admor. administrador.
adv. adverbio.
afmo. afectísimo.
agr. agriculture.
a la v/. a la vista (bank draft).
alg. álgebra.
alt. altitud.
a.m. antemeridiano.
amb. ambiguo.
anat. anatomía.
ant. antiguo, anticuado.
arit. aritmética.
arq. arquitecto, arquitectura.
art. artículo.
arz. or **arzbpo**. arzobispo.
astr. astronomía.
atto. atento.

B. Beato; Bueno (en examen).
BCG Bacilo Calmette-Guérin, vacuna antituberculosa.
bot. botánica.
bto. bulto; bruto.
Br. or **br**. bachiller.

C. centígrado.
c. or **cap**. capítulo.
C. A. corriente alterna (elec.).
C/a. cuenta abierta.
Cap. capitán.
C. C. corriente continua (elec.).
C. D. corriente directa (elec.).
cénts. céntimos or centavos.
CEPAL Comisión Económica para América Latina (Naciones Unidas).
C. F. caballos de fuerza.
cg. centigramo, centigramos.
Cía. compañía.
cir. cirugía.
cl. centilitro, centilitros.
cm. centímetro, centímetros.
Cnel. coronel.
col. columna.
Com. comercio.
Const. Constitución.
C. P. T. Contador Público Titulado.
cs. centavos or céntimos.
cta. cuenta.

c/u. cada uno.

D. Don.
D. D. T. dicloro-difenil-tricloro-metil-metano.
der. derecha o derecho.
des. desusado.
dg. decigramo.
dic. diciembre.
dim. diminutivo.
div. división.
dl. decalitro.
Dls. or **$** dólares.
dm. decímetro.
D. M. Dios mediante.
dom. domingo.
d/p días plazo.
Dr. doctor.
Dres. doctores.

E. este, oriente.
econ. economía.
elac. or **elect**. electricidad.
E. M. Edad Media.
ENE. estenordeste.
F. P. D. En paz descanse.
esc. escudo; escultura, escultor.
ESE estesudeste.
etc. or **&** etcétera.
etim. etimología.
E. U. A. Estados Unidos de América.

f. femenino, femenina.
F. Fahrenheit.
FAB. franco a bordo.
fam. familia; familiar.
FAO. Organización de las Naciones Unidas para la Agricultura y la Alimentación.
farm. farmacia.
f. c. or **F. C**. ferrocarril.
Fco. Francisco.
feb. febrero.
fig. figurado.
fil. filosofía.
fis. física.
For. forense.
fotog fotografía.
fr. fences.
fut. futuro.

g. or **gm**. or **gr**. gramo.
gal. galicismo; galón.
geog. geografía.
geom. geometría.
ger. gerundio.

gob. gobernador, gobierno.
Gral. general.

h. hijo.
hect. or **ha**. hectárea.
Hg. or **hg**. hectogramo, hectogramos.
Hl. or **hl**. hectolitro, hectolitros.
Hm. or **hm**. hectómetro, hectómetros.
hna., hno. hermana, hermano.
hol. holandés.
hosp. hospital.

ib. *ibidem*.
Ilmo., Ilma. Ilustrísimo, Ilustrísima.
Impr. imprenta.
Ing. ingeniero, ingeniería.
ingl. inglés.
izq. izquierda.

J. C. Jesucristo.
jue. jueves.

kg. kilogramo.
kgm. kilográmetro.
Kl. kilolitro.
Km. kilómetro.
km². kilómetro cuadrado.
Kms./h. kilómetros por hora.
kv. kilovatio.

l. litro litros.
LAB. libre a bordo.
lb., lbs. libra, libras.
Lic. Licenciado, abogado.
lín. línea.
lit. literatura.
lits./seg. litros por segundo.
lun. lunes.

m. metro; masculino; murió; meridiano; mediodía; minuto.
m3/seg. metros cúbicos por segundo.
mar. martes.
mat. matemáticas.
mec. mecánica.
med. medicina.
meng. menguante.
m/f. mi favor.
mg. miligramo, miligramos.
mierc. miércoles.
Min. minería.
mit. mitología.
m/L. mi letra (bank draft).
MM. miriámetro, miriámetros.
mm. milímetro, milímetros.
Mons. Monseñor.
m. p. h. millas por hora.
m. s. n. m. metros sobre el nivel del mar.
mús. música.

n. noche.
n/. nuestro.
N. Norte.
nac. nacional.
N. B. *Nota Bene*.
NE. nordeste.
neol. neologismo.
NNE. nornordeste.
NO. Noroeste.
No. or **núm**. número. (1°., primero; 2°., segundo; 3°., tercero, etc.).
nov. noviembre.

N. U. Naciones Unidas.
núm., núms. número, números.
N. S. Nuestro Señor.
N. S. J. C. Nuestro Señor Jesucristo.

O. Oeste.
OACI. Organización de Aviación Civil International (N. U.).
ob. obpo. obispo.
Oct. octubre.
OIT. Organización Internacional del Trabajo (N. U.).
OMS. Organización Mundial de la Salud (N. U.).
ONO. oestenoroeste.
onz. onza.
OSO. oestesuroeste.
OTAN or **OTAS**. Organización del Atlántico del Norte o Septentrional (NATO).

P. Papa.
p. participio.
p. a. participio activo.
p. A. Por ausencia.
PBAI. Proyectil balístico da alcance intermedio.
PBI. Proyectil balístico intercontinental.
pá., págs. página, páginas.
P. D. or **P. S**. Posdata.
p. ej. por ejemplo.
p. esp. peso específico.
pl. plural.
p. m. pasado meridiano.
P. O. Por orden.
P. P. or **p. p**. porte pagado; por poder.
p. pdo. or **ppdo**. próximo pasado.
P. R. Puerto Rico.
prep. preposición; preparatorio.
pres. presente; presidente.
pret. pretérito.
prof. profesor; profeta.
pron. pronombre.
prov. provincia.
P. S. *post scriptum*, posdata.
ps. or **$** pesos.
S. San or Santo; sur.
S. A. sociedad anónima; Sud América.
sáb. sábado.
S. A. de C. V. sociedad anónima de capital variable.
S. A. R. Su Alteza Real.
s/c. su cuenta.
S. C. or **s. c**. su casa.
S. C. de R. L. sociedad cooperativa de responsabilidad limitada.
s/cta. su cuenta.
S. en C. sociedad en comandita.
SE. sudeste, sureste.
sept. septentrional; septiembre.
s. e. u. o. salvo error u omisión.
s/f. su favor; sin fecha.
sing. singular.
S. M. Su Majestad.
SO. sudoeste, surosate.
spre. siempre.
Sr. señor.
Sra., Sras. señora, señoras.
Sres. señores.
Sria. secretaria.
Sría. secretaría.
ptas. pesetas.
pza. pieza.

q. que, quintal.
Q. B. S. M. or **q. b. s. m**. quebesa su mano.
Q. D. G. que Dios guarde.
q. eg. e. que en gloria esté.

q. e. p. d. que en paz descanse.
qm. quintal métrico.
qq. quintales.
quím. química.

Rep. República.
ret. retórica.
R. P. Reverendo Padre.

r. p. m. revoluciones por minuto.
rs. reales (moneda).
Srio. secretario.
Srta. señorita.
S. S. Su Santidad; seguro servidor.
s. s. or **ss**. seguro servidor.
SSE. sudsudeste, sursureste.
SSO. sudsudoeste, sursuroeste.
S. S. S. Su seguro servidor.
Sta. Santa.
Sto. Santo.
subj. subjuntivo.

t. tonelada.
TNT. trinitrotolueno.
Tte. teniente.

Tte. Cnel. teniente coronel.

U. or **Ud**. usted.
UIT. Unión Internacional de Telecomunicaciones (N. U.).
UNESCO. Organización de las Naciones Unidas para la Educación, la Ciencia y la Cultura.
UNICEF. Fondo de las Naciones Unidas para la Infancia.
UPU. Unión Postal Universal.
U. R. S. S. Unión de Repúblicas Socialistas Soviéticas.

V. usted; venerable; véase.
v. verbo.
va. verbo activo.
Vd., Vds. Usted, Ustedes.
V. E. Vuestra Excelencia.
vg. or **v. gr**. verbigracia.
vier. viernes.
V. M. Vuestra Majestad.
vn. verbo neutro.
Vo. Bo. visto bueno.
vol. volumen; voluntad.
vulg. vulgarismo.
VV. Ustedes.

zool. zoología.

Weights and Measures

(Pesas y Medidas)

LINEAR
(Lineales)

Metric Measures (Medidas métricas)		**U. S. Measures** (Medidas de E.U.A.)	
Kilómetro	0.62137 millas.	Milla	1.6093 kms.
Metro	39.37 pulgadas.	Milla marina	1.853 kms,
Decímetro	3.937 pulgadas.	Yarda	0.9144 ms.
Centímetro	0.3937 pulgadas.	Pie	0.3048 ms.
Milímetro	0.03937 pulgadas.	Pulgada	2.54 cms.

SURFACE
(Superficie)

Kilómetro cuadrado	247.104 acres.	Acre	0.4453 hectáreas.
Hectárea	2.471 acres.	Milla cuadrada	259 hectáreas.
Metro cuadrado	1550 pulg^2.	Yarda cuadrada	0.8361 m^2.
Decímetro cuadrado	15.50 pulg^2.	Pie cuadrado	929.03 cms^2.
Centímetro	0.155 pulg^2.	Pulgada cuadrada	6.4516 cms^2.

CUBIC
(Volumen)

Metro cúbico	1.308 yardas^3.	Pulgada cúbica	16.387 cm^3.
Decímetro cúbico	61.023 pulgadas^3.	Pie cúbico	0.0283 m^3.
Centímetro cúbico	0.0610 pulgadas^3.	Yarda cúbica	0.7646 m^3.

CAPACITY
(Capacidad)

Hectolitro	2.838 bushels	Cuarto de gal. (líq.)	0.9463 litros.
	6 26.418 galones.	Cuarto de gal. (áridos)	1.101 litros
Litro	0.9081 cuarto de galón (áridos)	Galón	3.785 litros
	ó 1.0567 cuarto de galón (liq.).	Bushel	35.24 litros

WEIGHTS
(Pesas)

Tonelada	2204.6 lb.	Onza (avoirdupois)	28.35 gms.
Kilogramo	2.2046 lb.	Libra "	0.4536 kgs.
Gramo	15.432 granos.	Tonelada larga	1.0161 ton. met.
Centigramo	0.1543 granos.	Tonelada corta	0.9072 ton. met.
		Grano	0.0648 gms.

Monetary Units

of America and the Iberian Peninsula

(Monedas de América y de la Península Ibérica)

País	Moneda
ARGENTINA	—Peso
BOLIVIA	—Boliviano
BRASIL	—Real
CANADA	—Dólar Canadiense
CHILE	—Peso Chileno
COLOMBIA	—Peso Colombiano
COSTA RICA	—Colón
CUBA	—Peso Cubano
ECUADOR	—Sucre / Dólar
EL SALVADOR	—Colón / Dólar
ESPAÑA	—Euro
EST ADOS UNIDOS DE AMERICA	—Dólar
GUATEMALA	—Quetzal / Dólar
HAITÍ	—Gourde
HONDURAS	—Lempira
MEXICO	—Peso
NICARAGUA	—Córdoba
PANAMÁ	—Balboa / Dólar
PARAGUAY	—Guaraní
PERÚ	—Nuevo Sol
PORTUGAL	—Euro
REP. DOMINICANA	—Peso
URUGUAY	—Peso
VENEZUELA	—Bolívar

THE NEW
VELÁZQUEZ

Spanish and English

DICTIONARY

Part One *Spanish* to *English*

Part Two *English* to *Spanish*

THE NEW
VELÁZQUEZ

Spanish and English

DICTIONARY

Prepared by
Lexicon

by
Mariano Velazquez de la Cadena
Late Professor of Spanish, Columbia University

and
Edward Gray, A. B., M.D., F.R.M.S.

and
Juan L Iribas, A. B., L. L. D.

Newly Revised by
Ida Navarro Hinojosa,
Manuel Blanco-González, M.A.

and
R.J. Nelson, Ph.D.

Velázquez Press

Velázquez Press   An imprint of Academic Learning Company, LLC

Visita www.VelazquezPress.com o www.AskVelazquez.com

Library of Congress Cataloging-in-Publication Data

Velázquez de la Cadena, Marlano, 1778-1860.
    [Pronouncing dictionary of the Spanish and English languages]
    New revised Velazquez Spanish and English dictionary/by Mariano Velázquez de la Cadena, and Edward Gray, and Juan L. Iribas; newly revised by Ida Navarro Hinojosa, Manuel Blanco-González, and R.J. Nelson; prepared by Lexicon.
        p. cm.
    Published in 1852 under the title: A pronouncing dictionary of the Spanish and English languages.
ISBN 1-59495-000-8
1. Spanish language Dictionaries—English. 2. English language Dictionaries—Spanish.
I. Gray, Edward, 1849-1920. II. Iribas, Juan L. III. Navarro Hinojosa, Ida.
IV. Blanco-González, Manuel, 1932- . V. Nelson, R.J. (Richard John).
VI. Lexicon Publications.
(Firm). VII. Title.
PC4640.V55 1999
463'.21—dc21

99-34721
CIP

Indice

Prólogo

La humanidad avanza con ritmo cada vez más acelerado, y las obras de consulta destinadas a servirla, como este diccionario, deben mantenerse a tono con tal progreso si han de suministrar satisfactoriamente la información que en ellas se busca. Por eso el *Diccionario Velázquez,* reconocido mundialmente como el diccionario bilingüe español-inglés más autorizado, necesita estar al día con relación a todas las voces nuevas que va imponiendo el prodigioso progreso de nuestra época en el campo de las ciencias, de los inventos y los descubrimientos; así como en las voces que las costumbres, en constante evolución, y los acontecimientos, van introduciendo en ambos idiomas.

De este modo el NUEVO DICCIONARIO VELÁZQUEZ REVISADO, cuidadosamente revisado, sin sacrificar ninguna de las tradicionales características que han hecho de sus anteriores ediciones el prototipo de los diccionarios de su género, viene a ser, sin lugar a duda, la más moderna y completa de las ediciones de dicha obra publicadas hasta hoy.

Se han incluido en esta novísima edición miles de voces nuevas, y también modismos y locuciones de uso general, que reemplazan expresiones que han dejado de ser de uso común y que, en consecuencia, ya no tienen razón de ocupar lugar en una obra eminentemente práctica como ésta.

Esta última revisión del diccionario ha sido exhaustiva. Se ha tratado de conseguir que el *Diccionario Velázquez* responda cada día más eficazmente a las necesidades de quienes recurren a él como medio práctico para resolver sus problemas de traducción en el campo de los negocios, de la información cotidiana, de la tecnología, de las ciencias en general, de la literatura, etc. y se ha prestado particular atención a las voces y locuciones de uso común en la América Hispana y en los Estados Unidos, ya que diariamente crecen y se intensifican las relaciones comerciales y amistosas entre estas dos grandes e importantes regiones del mundo moderno.

La revisión de las listas de equivalentes de los nombres geográficos que se escriben de manera diferente en español y en inglés se ha realizado con cuidado meticuloso. Las listas que forman parte de la presente edición incluyen todos los cambios que en tales nombres han determinado los acontecimientos históricos recientes.

De similar estudio han sido objeto las listas de nombres propios y de gentilicios que forman parte de los apéndices de la obra, así como las tablas de pesas y medidas. La de abreviaturas ha sido puesta al día para que responda, asimismo, al carácter fundamental-mente práctico de la obra.

Con tales innovaciones se ha acrecentado poderosamente la utilidad de este diccionario, y sus directores y editores se atreven a esperar que resultará un instrumento más valioso aún que las anteriores ediciones para quienes lo consulten, ya se trate de estudiantes de un nuevo idioma, de doctos que realicen estudios literarios en cualquiera de las dos lenguas, o en ambas, o de traductores profesionales, de hecho, para todos y cada uno de cuantos necesiten un guía autorizado que los ayude a recorrer el siempre escabroso camino que entraña la traducción de ideas del inglés al español, y viceversa.

Sinopsis

de la Lengua Inglesa.

ALFABETO

Las letras que componen el alfabeto inglés son veintiséis, a saber:

a, b, c, d, e, f, g, h, i, j, k, l, m, n, o, p, q, r, s, t, u, v, w, x, y, z.

Las vocales son *a, e, i, o, u* y algunas veces *w, y.*

Las consonantes son todas las demás.

(Para los sonidos de las letras inglesas, véase la "Introducción", que sigue a esta Sinopsis).

PARTES DE LA ORACIÓN

Las partes de la oración son diez, a saber: *The Article* (el Artículo), *the Noun* o *Substantive* (el Nombre o Sustantivo), *the Adjective* (el Adjetivo), *the Pronoun* (el Pronombre), *the Verb* (el Verbo), *the Participle* (el Participio), *the Adverb* (el Adverbio), *the Preposition* (la Preposición), *the Conjunction* (la Conjunción), y *the Interjection* (la Interjección).

DE LOS ARTÍCULOS

Los Artículos son dos, *a* o *an* (un, una), y *the* (el, los; la, las; los).

A se usa delante de consonante; como, *a* man (*un* hombre); y *an* delante de vocal o *h* muda: como *an* age (*un* siglo), *an* hour (*una* hora).

The se usa delante de nombres en ambos números: como *the* man (*el* hombre), *the* men (*los* hombres).

A se llama artículo *indefinido,* porque no se refiere a ninguna persona o cosa en particular: como *a* president (*un* presidente). *The* se llama artículo *definido,* porque se refiere siempre a una persona o cosa en particular, como "*The* president of *the* United States" (*El* presidente de *los* Estados Unidos).

El artículo *a* se pone delante de los nombres de peso, medida, número; los de los oficios, empleos, dignidades, y en las admiraciones, aunque no se usa en español: como "Tea is sold at *a* dollar *a* pound" (El té se vende a dólar *la* libra). "He has *a* sister who is *a* widow, and *a* brother who is *a* captain" (Él tiene una hermana viuda y un hermano que es capitán). "He is *an* American" (Él es americano). "What *a* beautiful woman! (¡Qué hermosa mujer!).

El artículo definido castellano, delante de un nombre común tomado en toda la extensión de su significado, no se traduce en inglés: v.g., "Man is mortal" (*El* hombre es mortal); pero si el sustantivo sólo designa una especie, aunque tomado en un sentido general, se expresa: v.g., "*The* negro is our brother" (*El* negro es nuestro hermano").

Cuando un nombre propio va precedido del de la dignidad, cargo, etc., no admite el artículo en inglés: v.g., "General Washington" (*El* general Washington), "Judge Field" (*El* juez Field). El artículo se omite también a menudo en inglés cuando se repite delante de varios sustantivos seguidos: v.g., "The father, mother and children are sick" (El padre, *la* madre y *los* niños están enfermos). Tampoco se traduce cuando precede a los nombres *Señor* o *Señora (Mr.* o *Mrs.),* seguidos de un nombre propio: v.g., "Have you seen Mr. or Mrs. N.?" (¿Ha visto Ud. *al* Señor o a *la* Señora N.?).

DEL NOMBRE O SUSTANTIVO

El Nombre se divide en *común* y *propio.*

Nombre *común* es el que conviene a muchas personas o cosas: como *city* (ciudad), *man* (hombre).

Nombre *propio* es el que conviene a una sola cosa o persona: como *London* (Londres), *Peter* (Pedro).

DEL GÉNERO

Los géneros son tres: *masculino, femenino* y *neutro.*

Todo nombre de varón o animal macho, es masculino; todo nombre de mujer o animal hembra, es femenino; todos los nombres de cosas inanimadas son del género neutro.

Hay nombres que distinguen el género por una palabra diferente: v.g., *brother* (hermano), *sister* (hermana); otros lo expresan por medio de la terminación: v.g., *lion* (león), *lioness* (leona); y otros que lo distinguen por medio de las palabras *male* o *female:* como "A *male* child" (un niño), "A *female* child" (una niña); *man* o *maid:* como "A *man*-servant" (un criado), "A *maid*-servant" (una criada); *cock* o *hen:* como

"A *cock* sparrow" (un gorrión), "A *hen* sparrow" (un gorrión hembra); *he* o *she:* como "A *he*-bear" (un oso), "A *she*-bear" (una osa).

DEL NÚMERO

Los Números de los nombres son dos, *singular* y *plural.*

El *plural* se forma generalmente añadiendo una *s* al singular: v.g., *guide* (guía), *guides* (guías); *book* (libro), *books* (libros).

Los nombres acabados en *ch* (cuando suena como en castellano), o en *ss, x* u *o,* precedida de consonante, forman el plural añadiendo *es* al singular: v.g., *church* (iglesia), *churches* (iglesias); *kiss* (beso), *kisses* (besos); *fox* (zorro), *foxes* (zorros); *hero* (héroe), *heroes* (héroes); pero si la *ch* suena como *k,* añaden solamente *s:* v.g., *monarch* (monarca), *monarchs* (monarcas).

Los terminados en *y,* precedida de una vocal, siguen la regla general: v.g., *day* (día), *days* (días); pero si la precede una consonante, la mudan en *i* y añaden *es:* v.g., *fly* (mosca), *flies* (moscas); *lady* (señora), *ladies* (señoras).

Los nombres que acaban en *f* o *fe* mudan estas letras en *v* y añaden *es:* v.g., *leaf* (hoja), *leaves* (hojas); *life* (vida), *lives* (vidas). Se exceptúan *chief* (jefe), *dwarf* (enano), *handkerchief* (pañuelo de mano), etc., y también *muff* (manguito), que forman el plural añadiendo *s.*

Hay algunos nombres cuyos plurales son irregulares: v.g., *man* (hombre), *men* (hombres); *foot* (pie), *feet* (pies), etc.; *child* (hijo), *children* (hijos). Estos nombres corresponden generalmente a palabras semejantes del alemán.

DE LOS CASOS DE LOS NOMBRES

Los casos son tres: *The Nominative* (el Nominativo), *the Possessive* o *Genitive* (el Posesivo o Genitivo) y *the Objective* o *Accusative* (el Objetivo o Acusativo).

El *Nominativo* y el *Objetivo* se distinguen sólo por su colocación en la frase: v.g., "The *father* loves *the son*" (El *padre* ama *al hijo);* "The *son* loves *the father*" (El *hijo* ama *al padre*).

El *Posesivo* denota *posesión* y se forma invirtiendo el orden y poniendo primero en inglés el nombre que es último en español, después del cual se pone un apóstrofo y la letra *s:* v.g., "My *father's* house" (La casa de mi *padre*); "The *boy's* hat" (El sombrero del *muchacho*). Cuando los plurales terminan en *s,* el Posesivo se forma añadiendo solamente el apóstrofo: como, "My *brothers'* horse" (El caballo de mis *hermanos*). Viniendo más de dos sustantivos seguidos, el apóstrofo y la *s* se ponen a cada uno de ellos: v.g., "The captain's son's friend's horse" (El caballo del amigo del hijo del capitán). En tal caso sería mejor

cambiar la construcción. Con el apóstrofo y la *s* (*'s*) se indica también el lugar, sitio o casa en donde se ha hecho alguna cosa: v.g., "He supped last night at your *sister's*", (Él cenó anoche en casa *de tu hermana*).

DE LOS ADJETIVOS

Los Adjetivos en inglés no admiten variación de género ni número: v.g., "A *prudent* man", (Un hombre *prudente*); "*Prudent* men", (Hombres *prudentes*); "A *prudent* woman", (Una mujer *prudente*); "*Prudent* women", (Mujeres *prudentes*); y se colocan generalmente antes del sustantivo: v.g., "He wants *hot* water", (Él quiere agua *caliente*).

La sola variación que admiten es la de los grados de comparación. Estos son *Positivo, Comparativo* y *Superlativo.*

El *Comparativo de aumento* se forma por medio del adverbio *more* (más), seguido de *than* (que): v.g., *intelligent* (inteligente), "*more* intelligent *than* he" (*más* inteligente *que* él). También se forma añadiendo una *r* a los monosílabos que acaban en *e,* o *er* a los que terminan en otra letra: v.g., *wiser* (más sabio); *black* (negro), *blacker* (más negro).

El *Comparativo de inferioridad* o *disminución* se forma por medio del adverbio *less* (menos), o *less than* (menos que): v.g., "He is *less* rich *than* she", (Él es *menos* rico *que* ella).

El *Comparativo de igualdad* con los adjetivos se expresa con los adverbios *as … (tan …) as* (como); o *not less … (no menos …) than* (que): v.g., "He is *as* generous *as* she (Él es *tan* generoso *como* ella); "She is *not less* generous *than* he" (Ella *no es menos* generosa *que* él).

El *Comparativo de igualdad* con los sustantivos se expresa por *as* o *so much* (tanto, tanta), en singular; y por *as many* (tantos, tantas) en plural, y el *como* siguiente por *as:* v.g., "She has *as* much gold *as* silver" (Ella tiene *tanto* oro *como* plata); "He has *as* many dogs *as* horses" (Él tiene *tantos* perros *como* caballos).

El *Superlativo* se forma con los adverbios *very* (muy), *most* o *least,* y también añadiendo *st* a los acabados en *e,* o *est* a los terminados en otras letras.

Cuando el positivo acaba en *y* la muda en *i,* y a ésta añade las letras *er* para el comparativo, y *est* para el superlativo: v.g., *dry* (seco), *drier* o *more dry* (más seco), *driest* (sequísimo), *very dry* (muy seco).

COMPARATIVOS Y SUPERLATIVOS IRREGULARES

Pos.	Comp.		Superl.	
Good,	*better,*		*best,*	*very good.*
Bueno,	mejor,	el mejor,		buenísimo.
Bad,	*worse,*		*worst,*	*very bad.*
Malo,	peor,	el peor,		malísimo.
Little,	*less* o *lesser,*		*least,*	*very little.*
Pequeño,	menor,	mínimo,		pequeñísimo.

DEL PRONOMBRE

Los Pronombres son de cuatro especies, a saber: *Personales, Relativos, Interrogativos* y *Adjetivos.*

Pronombres Personales

Primera Persona

Género Masculino o Femenino.

Singular.

Nom.	I	yo.
Pos.	Mine	mío, el mío, la mía, etc.
Obj.	Me	me, a mí.

Plural.

Nom.	We	nosotros, nosotras.
Pos.	Ours	el nuestro, la nuestra, etc.
Obj.	Us	nos, a nosotros, a nosotras.

Segunda Persona

Género Masculino o Femenino.

Singular.

Nom.	You	tú.
Pos.	Yours	de ti, el tuyo, la tuya, etc.
Obj.	You	te, a ti.

Plural.

Nom.	You	vosotros, etc.; Ud., Uds., etc.
Pos.	Yours	el de Ud., Uds., etc.
Obj.	You	os, a vosotros, a Ud., Uds., etc.

Tercera Persona

Género Masculino.

Singular.

Nom.	He	él.
Pos.	His	de él, el suyo, la suya, etc.
Obj.	Him	le, a él.

Plural.

Nom.	They	ellos.
Pos.	Theirs	el de ellos, etc.
Obj.	Them	los, les, a ellos.

Género Femenino.

Singular.

Nom.	She	ella.
Pos.	Hers	de ella, el suyo, la suya, etc.
Obj.	Her	la, a ella.

Plural.

Nom.	They	ellas.
Pos.	Theirs	el de ellas, etc.
Obj.	Them	las, les, a ellas.

Género Neutro.

Singular.

Nom.	It	ello, etc.
Pos.	Its	el suyo, la suya, etc.
Obj.	It	lo, la.

Plural.

El plural en el pronombre neutro *It,* es lo mismo que el del género masculino o femenino.

PRONOMBRES RELATIVOS

Los Pronombres Relativos son *who* (que, quien), *which* (que, cual), *that* (lo que); los cuales son invariables en ambos números.

Nom.	Who	Que, quien.
Pos.	Whose	De quien, cuyo.
Obj.	Whom	A quien, etc.

Who se aplica a personas: como, "The boy *who*" (el muchacho *que*).

Which se aplica a animales irracionales y a cosas: como, "A dog *which* barks" (un perro *que* ladra); "the book *which* was lost" (el libro *que* se perdió).

That se emplea frecuentemente en vez de *who* o *which,* por preferencia, antes de una cláusula o frase: como, "The boy *that* reads constantly" (el muchacho *que* lee asiduamente); "The book *that* was lost" (el libro *que* se perdió).

What es un relativo compuesto que comprende tanto el relativo simple como el antecedente: como, "This is *what* I wanted"; es decir, *the thing which* I wanted (esto es *lo que* yo quería).

PRONOMBRES INTERROGATIVOS

Los Pronombres Interrogativos son *who* (quién), *whose* (de quién), *whom* (a quién); *which* (qué), y *what* (qué). Se usan en las interrogaciones: como, "*Who* said that?" (¿quién dijo eso?); "*Whose* is this book?" (¿De quién es este libro?); "*Whom* did you see? (¿A quién viste?); "*Which* book do you want?" (¿qué libro quiere Ud.?); "*What* did he do?" (¿qué hizo él?).

PRONOMBRES ADJETIVOS

Hay cuatro clases de Pronombres Adjetivos:

Los Posesivos: My (mi, mis); *your* (tu, tus); *his* (su, sus, de él); *her* (su, sus, de ella); *our* (nuestro, nuestra; nuestros, nuestras); *your* (su, sus; de Ud., de Uds.); *their* (su, sus; de ellos, de ellas); *its* (su, sus); *own* (propio).

Los Distributivos: Each (cada); *every* (todo, toda); *either* (uno u otro); *neither* (ni uno ni otro).

Los Demostrativos: This (éste, ésta, esto); *that* (ése, ésa, eso; aquél, aquélla, aquello); con sus plurales: *these* (éstos, éstas); *those* (ésos, ésas, etc.).

Los Indefinidos: None (ninguno, etc.); *any* (alguno, etc.); *all* (todos, etc.); *such* (tal, etc.); *whole* (todo, etc.); *some* (alguno, etc.); *both* (ambos); *one* (uno); *other* (otro, etc.); *another* (otro, etc.).

Los tres últimos se declinan como nombres.

OBSERVACIÓN: *His* y *her* son pronombres posesivos cuando preceden inmediatamente al nombre, pero cuando vienen solos, *his* es el caso posesivo del pronombre personal *he*, y *her* el objetivo de *she*.

DEL VERBO

Los *Verbos* son de tres clases: *Transitivos o Activos, Pasivos e Intransitivos o Neutros*.

Verbo activo o transitivo es aquel cuya acción recae sobre algún objeto: v.gr., "James *strikes* the table" (Jaime *golpea* la mesa).

Verbo pasivo es el que representa una acción como sufrida o recibida por el sujeto: v.gr., "The table *was struck*" (la mesa *fue golpeada*).

Verbo neutro o intransitivo es el que expresa la existencia o el estado de los seres, o una acción que no pasa del sujeto: v.gr., "I *am* here" (Yo *estoy* aquí); "He *sleeps*" (él *duerme*); "I *run*" (yo *corro*).

El verbo se divide por razón de su forma, en *Regular, Irregular y Defectivo*.

Verbo regular es el que forma su imperfecto y pretérito de indicativo (*Indicative Imperfect*) y su participio pasivo (*Past Participle*) agregando *d* o *ed* al presente (*Present*); como *love* (amo); *loved* (amaba, amé); *loved* amado; *hoist* (alzar), *hoisted* (alzaba, alcé alzado).

Verbo irregular es el que se separa de la regla establecida en el párrafo anterior; como, *write* (escribo); *wrote* (escribía, escribí); *written* (escrito).

Se llama *Verbo defectivo* el que carece de alguno de sus tiempos y personas; a esta clase pertenecen la mayor parte de los auxiliares y todos los impersonales.

DE LOS MODOS Y TIEMPOS DEL VERBO

Los verbos tienen cuatro *modos: Infinitivo, Indicativo, Imperativo y Subjuntivo*.

Los *tiempos* del verbo son seis: the present (*el Presente*); the past (*el Imperfecto y Pretérito*); the perfect (*el Perfecto Próximo*); the pluperfect (*el Pluscuamperfecto*); the future (*el Futuro*) y the future perfect (*el Futuro Anterior*).

FORMACIÓN DE LOS TIEMPOS DEL VERBO

El *Presente de Infinitivo* es como la raíz de que nacen y se forman los demás tiempos y personas, y se distingue por la preposición *to*: v.gr., *to* admire (admirar); *to* abandon (abandonar). Cuando el presente de infinitivo se usa solo, debe estar precedido siempre de dicha preposición.

El Gerundio, que en inglés es *Participio Presente*, se forma añadiendo la terminación *-ing* al presente del infinitivo, el cual, en este caso, omite la preposición *to*, y también la *e*, si acaba en esta letra: v.g., *to* admire (admirar), admir*ing* (admirando); *to* abandon (abandonar), abandon*ing* (abandonando).

El Participio Pasivo de los verbos regulares se forma añadiendo una *d* al infinitivo de los que terminan en *e*, y *ed* a los que acaban en otra letra: v.g., *to* admire (admirar), admir*ed* (admirado); *to* abandon (abandonar), abandon*ed* (abandonado). Si el infinitivo acaba en *y* precedida de una vocal, añade *ed*: v.g., *to* pray (suplicar), pray*ed* (suplicado); pero si es una consonante la que precede a la *y*, la convierte en *i* y añade *ed*: v.g., *to* satisfy (satisfacer), satisf*ied* (satisfecho).

Presente de Indicativo. La primera persona singular, y la primera, segunda y tercera persona plural del *Presente de Indicativo* son lo mismo que el presente de infinitivo, sin la preposición *to*; pero en su lugar deben expresar el pronombre correspondiente: v.g., *to* admire (admirar); *I* admire, *we* admire, *you* admire, *they* admire (yo admiro, nosotros admiramos, etc.). Se exceptúa de esta regla el verbo *to be* (ser).

La tercera persona singular del *Presente de Indicativo* se forma añadiendo una *s* al presente de infinitivo: v.g., *to* love (amar), *he* love*s* (él ama); *to* abandon (abandonar), *he* abandon*s* (él abandona).

-Excepciones: Cuando el infinitivo acaba en *o, ch, sh, ss, th, x* o *z*, se añade *es*: v.g., *to* go (ir), *he* goe*s*, (él va); *to* beseech (suplicar), *he* beseech*es* (él suplica), etc. Si el verbo acaba en *y* precedida de una consonante, la convierte en *i* y añada *es*; pero si viene después de vocal, añade *s* solamente: v.g., *to* reply (replicar), *he* repl*ies* (él replica); *to* pay (pagar), *he* pay*s* (él paga).

El Imperfecto y *Pretérito* (past tense) de indicativo de los verbos regulares es lo mismo que su participio pasivo: v.g., *to* promise (prometer), promis*ed* (prometido), *I* promis*ed* (yo prometía o prometí). Si el infinitivo acaba en *y* precedida de consonante, la cambia en *i* y añade *ed*; pero si no, la retiene y añade *ed*: v.g., *to* reply (replicar), *I* repl*ied* (yo replicaba o repliqué); *to* delay (dilatar), *I* delay*ed* (yo dilataba o dilaté).

El Futuro, cuando significa simplemente una acción por venir, se forma por medio del auxiliar *shall* prefijado al infinitivo, sin la partícula *to*, en las primeras personas, y *will* en las demás. Pero cuando indica promesa, deseo vehemente, mando o amenaza, se expresa por medio de *will* en las primeras personas y *shall* en las demás.

El Condicional se forma con *should* y *would*.

Should en las primeras personas y *would* en las demás, aunque en la práctica se usa *would* en todas.

El Presente del Modo Subjuntivo se forma por medio de los auxiliares *may* o *can*, o de las conjunciones *if, though* o *whether*, prefijados al infinitivo

961

Sinopsis de la Lengua Inglesa

sin la partícula *to:* "I *may* write" (puede que yo escriba, o no escriba). "*Whether* it prove true or not" (Sea que el caso resulte verdadero o no). "*Though* he slay me, yet will I trust in him" (Aun cuando me matare, en él confiaré).

El Imperfecto de Subjuntivo se forma por medio de los auxiliares *might, could, would* o *should,* según su respectiva significación, prefijados al infinitivo sin la partícula *to:* v.g., *to* sell (vender), "I *might* sell" (yo quizá vendiera).

Los Tiempos Compuestos se forman, como en castellano, por medio del auxiliar *to have,* seguido del participio pasivo del verbo principal: v.g., I *have* arrived (he llegado); I *had* arrived (yo había o hube llegado); I *shall have* arrived (yo habré llegado); I *may have* arrived (yo haya llegado); I *might, could, would* o *should have* arrived (yo hubiera o hubiese llegado).

CONJUGACIÓN DE UN VERBO REGULAR

Infinitivo

To *love,*	*amar.*

Participio Presente

Loving,	*amando.*

Participio Pasivo

Loved,	*amado.*

Indicativo

Presente

I love,	*yo amo.*
You love,	*tú amas.*
He loves,	*él ama.*
We love,	*nos. amamos.*
You love,	*vos. amáis.*
They love,	*ellos aman.*

Imperfecto y Pretérito (Past.)

I loved,	*yo amaba, amé.*
You loved,	*tú amabas, amaste.*
He loved,	*él amaba, amó.*
We loved,	*nos. amábamos, amamos.*
You loved,	*vos. amabais, amasteis.*
They loved,	*ellos amaban, amaron.*

Perfecto

I have loved,	*yo he amado.*
You have loved,	*tú has amado.*
He has loved,	*él ha amado.*
We have loved,	*nos. hemos amado.*
You have loved,	*vos. habéis amado.*
They have loved,	*ellos han amado.*

Pluscuamperfecto

I had loved,	*yo había amado.*
You had loved,	*tú habías amado.*
He had loved,	*él había amado.*
We had loved,	*nos. habíamos amado.*
You had loved,	*vos. habíais amado.*
They had loved,	*ellos habían amado.*

Futuro

I shall o will love,	*yo amaré.*
You shall o will love,	*tú amarás.*
He shall o will love,	*él amará.*
We shall o will love,	*nos. amaremos.*
You shall o will love,	*vos. amaréis.*
They shall o will love,	*ellos amarán.*

Futuro Anterior (Future Perfect.)

I shall o will have loved,	*yo habré amado.*
You shall o will have loved,	*tú habrás amado.*
He shall o will have loved,	*él habrá amado.*
We shall o will have loved,	*nos. habremos amado.*
You shall o will have loved,	*vos. habréis amado.*
They shall o will have loved,	*ellos habrán amado.*

Condicional Simple (Conditional)

I should o would love,	*yo amaría.*
You would love,	*tú amarías.*
He would love,	*él amaría.*
We should o would love,	*nos. amaríamos.*
You would love,	*vos. amaríais.*
They would love,	*ellos amarían.*

Condicional Compuesto (Conditional Perfect)

I should o would have loved,	*yo habría amado.*
You would have loved,	*tú habrías amado.*
He would have loved,	*él habría amado.*
We should o would have loved,	*nos. habríamos amado.*
You would have loved,	*vos. habríais amado.*
They would have loved,	*ellos habrían amado.*

Imperativo

Love (you)	*ama tú.*
Let him love	*ame él.*
Let us love	*amemos nosotros.*
Love (you)	*amad vosotros.*
Let them love,	*amen ellos.*

Subjuntivo

Presente

That I may love,	*que yo ame.*
That you may love,	*que tú ames.*
That he may love,	*que él ame.*
That we may love,	*que nos. amemos.*
That you may love,	*que vos. améis.*
That they may love,	*que ellos amen.*

Imperfecto

I might, could, love	yo amara, amase.
You might, could, love	tú amaras, amases.
He might, could, love	él amara, amase.
We might, could, love	nos, amáramos, amásemos.
You might, could, love	vos. amárais, amáseis.
They might, could, love	ellos amaran, amasen.

Perfecto

That I may have loved,	que yo haya amado.
That you may have loved,	que tú hayas amado.
That he may have loved,	que él haya amado.
That we may have loved,	que nos. hayamos amado.
That you may have loved,	que vos. hayáis amado.
That they may have loved,	que ellos hayan amado.

Pluscuamperfecto

I might, could, have loved

yo hubiera, hubiese amado.

You might, could, have loved

tú hubieras, hubieses amado.

He might, could, have loved

él hubiera, hubiese amado.

We might, could, have loved

nos. hubiéramos, hubiésemos amado.

You might, could, have loved

vos. hubiérais, hubiéseis amado.

They might, could, have loved

ellos hubieran, hubiesen amado.

CONJUGACIÓN DE LOS VERBOS AUXILIARES

To Have y To Be

TO HAVE

Infinitivo

To have,   haber, tener.

Participio Presente.

Having,   habiendo, teniendo.

Participio Pasivo.

Had,   habido, tenido.

Indicativo

Presente.

I have,	yo he o tengo.
You have,	tú has o tienes.
He has,	él ha o tiene.
We have,	nos. hemos o tenemos.
You have,	vos. habéis o tenéis.
They have,	ellos han o tienen.

Imperfecto y Pretérito.

I had,	yo había, hube; tenía, tuve.
You had,	tú habías, hubiste: tenías, tuviste.
He had,	él había, hubo; tenía, tuvo.
We had,	nos. habíamos, hubimos; teníamos, tuvimos.
You had,	vos. habíais, hubisteis; teníais, tuvisteis.
They had,	ellos habían, hubieron; tenían, tuvieron.

Los demás tiempos de este verbo son regulares, y se conjugan por consiguiente como los de *To Love.*

Como ya se ha visto, por medio de este auxiliar se forman los tiempos compuestos de los verbos.

TO BE

Infinitivo

To be,   ser, estar.

Participio Presente

Being,   siendo, estando.

Participio Pasivo

Been,   sido, estado.

Indicativo

Presente.

I am,	yo soy o estoy.
You are,	tú eres o estás.
He is,	él es o está.
We are,	nos. somos o estamos.
You are,	vos. sois o estáis.
They are,	ellos son o están.

Imperfecto y Pretérito.

I was,	yo era, fui; estaba, estuve.
Youwere,	tú eras, fuiste; estabas, estuviste.
He was,	él era, fue; estaba, estuvo.
We were,	nos. éramos, fuimos; estábamos, estuvimos.
You were,	vos. érais, fuisteis; estábais, estuvisteis.
They were,	ellos eran, fueron; estaban, estuvieron.

Subjuntivo

Presente.

That I may be,	que yo sea o esté.
That you may be,	que tú seas o estés.
That he may be,	que él sea o esté.
That we may be,	que nos. seamos o estemos.
That you may be,	que vos. seáis o estéis.
That they may be,	que ellos sean o estén.

Imperfecto.

I was,	yo fuera, fuese; estuviera, estuviese.
You were,	tú fueras, fueses; estuvieras, estuvieses.

He was,   *él fuera, fuese; estuviera, estuviese.*

We were,   *nos. fuéramos, fuésemos; estuviéramos, etc.*

You were,   *vos. fuérais, fuéseis; estuviérais, etc.*

They were, *ellos fueran, fuesen; estuvieran, estuviesen.*

Lo restante del verbo es regular y se conjuga como *To Love.*

La Voz Pasiva se forma agregando el Participio Pasivo del verbo que se quiere conjugar, al tiempo correspondiente del auxiliar *To Be*: v.g., "I am loved" (yo soy amado); "I *was loved*" (yo era amado); "I *have been loved*" (yo he sido amado).

EL VERBO TO DO

Frases interrogativas, negativas y enérgicas se forman generalmente por medio del auxiliar *To Do,* en el presente de indicativo y en el imperfecto y pretérito del mismo. *Ejemplos*: He buys (él compra); he *does not* buy (él no compra); *does* he buy? (¿compra él?; he bought (él compró); *he did not* buy (él no compró); *did* he buy? (¿compró él?). Cuando *To Do* se usa enérgicamente, equivale a una forma enfática.

VERBOS IRREGULARES

Son *Verbos Irregulares* en inglés los que no forman su participio pasivo ni su imperfecto o pretérito con la adición de las letras *d* o *ed*: v. g., to *see* (ver); I *saw* (yo veía o vi), I have *seen* (he visto). Todas estas irregularidades están incluidas en este Diccionario, en sus respectivos lugares; pero para facilitar a los principiantes el hallarlas, se pone la siguiente lista de todas ellas en inglés solamente, para no hacer muy difusa esta Sinopsis.

Presente	Imperf.	Partic. Pas.
Abide	abode	abode
Am	was	been
Arise	arose	arisen
Awake	awoke	awoked
Bear (*producir*)	bore	born
Bear (*llevar*)	bore	borne
Beat	beat	beaten
Begin	began	begun
Bend	bent	bent
Bereave	bereft	bereft
Beseech	besought	besought
Bid	bid, bade	bidden, bid
Bind	bound	bound
Bite	bit	bitten, bit
Bleed	bled	bled
Blow	blew	blown
Break	broke	broken
Breed	bred	bred
Bring	brought	brought
Build	built	built
Burst	burst	burst
Cast	cast	cast
Catch	caught	caught
Chide	chid	chidden, chid
Choose	chose	chosen
Cleave	clove, cleft	cleft, cloven
Cling	clung	clung
Clothe	clothed, clad	clad
Come	came	come
Creep	crept	crept
Crow	crew	crowd
Cut	cut	cut
Dare	durst	dared
Deal	dealt	dealt
Dig	dug	dug
Draw	drew	drawn
Drink	drank	drunk
Drive	drove	driven
Dwell	dwelt	dwelt
Eat	ate	eaten
Fall	fell	fallen
Feed	fed	fed
Feel	felt	felt
Fight	fought	fought
Find	found	found
Flee	fled	fled
Fling	flung	flung
Fly	flew	flown
Forget	forgot	forgotten
Forsake	forsook	forsaken
Freeze	froze	frozen
Get	got	got, gotten
Gild	gilt	gilt
Gird	girt	girt
Give	gave	given
Go	went	gone
Grave	graved	graven
Presente	*Imperf.*	*Partic. Pas.*
Grind	ground	ground

Grow	grew	grown	Shoot	shot	shot
Hang	hung	hung	Show	showed	shown
Have	had	had	Shrink	shrank	shrunk
Hear	heard	heard	Shut	shut	shut
Hew	hewed	hewn	Sing	sang	sung
Hide	hid	hidden	Sink	sank	sunk
Hit	hit	hit	Sit	sat	sat
Hold	held	held	Slay	slew	slain
Hurt	hurt	hurt	Sleep	slept	slept
Keep	kept	kept	Slit	slit	slitted
Knit	knit	knit	Smite	smote	smitten
Know	knew	known	*Presente*	*Imperf.*	*Partic. Pas.*
Lade	laded	laden	Sow	sowed	sown
Lay	laid	laid	Speak	spoke	spoken
Leave	left	left	Speed	sped	sped
Lend	lent	lent	Spend	spent	spent
Let	let	let	Spill	spilt	spilt
Lie *(yacer)*	lay	lain	Spin	span	spun
Lose	lost	lost	Spit	spat	spit
Make	made	made	Split	split	split
Meet	met	met	Spread	spread	spread
Mow	mowed	mown	Spring	sprang	sprung
Pay	paid	paid	Stand	stood	stood
Read	read	read	Steal	stole	stolen
Rend	rent	rent	Stick	stuck	stuck
Rid	rid	rid	Sting	stung	stung
Ride	rode	ridden	Strew	strewed	strewn
Ring	rang	rung	Stride	strode	stridden
Rise	rose	risen	Strike	struck	struck/stricken
Rive	rived	riven	Strive	strove	striven
Run	ran	run	Strow	strowed	strown
Saw	sawed	sawn	Swear	swore	sworn
Say	said	said	Sweat	sweat	sweat
See	saw	seen	Sweep	swept	swept
Seek	sought	sought	Swell	swelled	swollen
Sell	sold	sold	Swim	swam	swum
Send	sent	sent	Swing	swung	swung
Set	set	set	Take	took	taken
Shake	shook	shaken	Teach	taught	taught
Shape	shaped	shaped, shapen	Tear	tore	torn
Shave	shaved	shaven	Tell	told	told
Shear	sheared	shorn	Think	thought	thought
Shed	shed	shed	Thrive	throve	thriven
Shine	shone	shone	Throw	threw	thrown
Shoe	shod	shod	Thrust	thrust	thrust

Tread	trod	trodden
Wax	waxed	waxen
Wear	wore	worn
Weave	wove	woven
Weep	wept	wept
Wet	wet	wet
Win	won	won
Wind	wound	wound
Wring	wrung	wrunt
Write	wrote	written

DE LA CONJUNCIÓN

Las *Conjunciones* se dividen en inglés, como en español, en *copulativas* y *disyuntivas.*

Copulativas son las que enlazan simplemente unas palabras con otras, y las oraciones entre sí: v.g., "Peter *and* John will speak" (Pedro y Juan hablarán); "Wisdom *and* ignorance are opposites" (Sabiduría e ignorancia son cosas opuestas).

Disyuntivas son las que significan división o alternativa entre las cosas: v.g., "I speak *neither* English *nor* German" (Yo no hablo *ni* inglés *ni* alemán).

DEL ADVERBIO

Los *Adverbios de modo* o *calidad,* que en castellano se forman añadiendo la terminación *mente* al adjetivo, se expresan en inglés por medio de la sílaba *ly* añadida al mismo: v.g., *wise* (sabio), wise*ly* (sabiamente); *clear* (claro), clear*ly* (claramente).

Los *Adverbios* admiten los grados de comparación, y los expresan con las mismas letras que los adjetivos: v.g., *near* (cerca), *near*er (más cerca), the *near*est (lo más cerca).

En inglés no se puede usar más de una negación; y así, *No quiero nada* se traduce, "I want nothing".

DE LA INTERJECCIÓN O EXCLAMACIÓN

La *Interjección* es una palabra que sirve para expresar los varios afectos del ánimo, o para llamar la atención: como, "*Oh,* what a beautiful creature! (¡*Oh,* qué hermosa criatura!) "*See!* (¡*Mira!*).

DE LA PREPOSICIÓN

Hay gran número de verbos en inglés que van acompañados de ciertas preposiciones, las cuales son como parte de ellos, entran en su significación y la hacen variar, a manera de los verbos separables en alemán: v.g., *To bring,* traer, llevar. *To bring about,* poner por obra, efectuar. *To bring forth,* dar de sí, producir; parir, dar a luz; exhibir. *To bring in,* introducir, hacer entrar; alegar, declarar; producir, dejar utilidad o ganancia. *To bring over,* transportar, hacer atravesar; atraer, ganar a alguno en su partido. *To bring out,* sacar, extraer; hacer salir; poner en evidencia; mostrar; descubrir; publicar. *To bring up,* subir, hacer subir; presentar; servir a la mesa; educar, enseñar. Estas modificaciones van indicadas con mucho cuidado en el texto de este diccionario.

OBSERVACIONES SOBRE ALGUNAS REGLAS DE LA SINTAXIS

Cuando los poseedores de una misma cosa son dos o más, el apóstrofo y la *s* se ponen sólo después del último: v.g., "The father and son's house" (La casa del padre y del hijo); "John and Henry's book" (El libro de Juan y de Enrique).

Dos o más sustantivos singulares, regidos por las conjunciones *either.............or, neither.............nor,* rigen al verbo, al adjetivo y al pronombre en singular: v.g., *"Either* Peter *or* John *is* guilty" (o Pedro o Juan *son* culpables); *"Neither* time *nor* distance *is* able to diminish our friendship" (ni el tiempo *ni* la distancia *son* capaces de disminuir nuestra amistad).

La preposición *to,* que designa el infinitivo, se omite frecuentemente después de los verbos *to bid, dare, need, make, see, hear, let* y los auxiliares *may, can, will, shall, must,* y sus pretéritos: v.g., "I dare *say"* (Me atrevo *a decir).*

Los verbos que significan *esperar, mandar, desear,* etc., rigen al otro verbo en presente de infinitivo con preferencia al perfecto del mismo: v.g., "I found him better than I expected *to find him"* y no *"to have found him"* (le hallé mejor de lo que yo esperaba *hallarle,* y no *haberle hallado).*

El participio presente inglés (gerundio español) se traduce en el presente de infinitivo con la misma preposición, excepto cuando esta es *by,* pues en tal caso se omite, y el participio se traduce por el gerundio: v.g., "The *taking* from another what is his, without his permisison, is called *stealing"* (El *tomar* de otro lo que no es suyo, sin su permiso, se llama *robar).* En este caso el participio es un nombre. "John was sent to prepare the way *by preaching* repentance" (Juan fue enviado para preparar el camino *predicando* la penitencia).

Algunas conjunciones requieren el indicativo y otras el subjuntivo; en general, cuando el sentido es contingente o dudoso, se debe usar el último: v.g., "If I *were* to write, he *would* not *do* it" (Si yo le *escribiera,* él no *lo haría);* "He will not be pardoned unless he *repent"* (Él no será perdonado, a menos que *se arrepienta).*

EXPLICACIÓN DE LAS ABREVIATURAS USADAS EN ESTA OBRA

adj. ....adjetivo.

adv. ....adverbio.

Aerosp. ....Aeroespacial.

Agr. ....Agricultura.

Albañ. ....Albañilería.

Alem. ....Alemania.

Alg. ....Algebra.

Amer. ....América.

Anat. ....Anatomía.

Ant. ....Antiguo.

Argent. ....Argentina.

Arit. ....Aritmética.

Arq. ....Arqueología.

Art. ....Arte.

Astrol. ....Astrología.

Aut. ....Autómata.

Auto. ....Automóvil.

Biol. ....Biología.

Bot. ....Botánica.

Carp. ....Carpintería.

Cir. ....Cirugía.

Coloq. ....Coloquial.

Com. ....Comercio.

comp. ....Comparativo.

conj. ....Conjunción.

Corresp. ....Corresponsal o
Correspondencia.

Culin. ....Culinario.

Dep. ....Deporte.

Des. ....Desusado.

dial. ....diálogo.

dip. ....diptongo.

Dipl. ....Diplomado.

E.U. ....Estados Unidos.

Ecol. ....Ecología.

Econ. ....Economía.

Educ. ....Educación.

ej. ....ejemplo.

Elec. ....Electricidad.

Electron. ....Electrónica.

Ento. ....Entomología.

erratic. ....errático.

Esco. ....Escocia.

Escul. ....Escultura.

Esp. ....España.

f. ....femenino.

Fam. ....Familiar.

Fest. ....Festivo.

Fig. ....Figurado.

Fil. ....Filosofía.

Fin. ....Finanzas.

Fis. ....Física.

For. ....Foro; Forense.

fot. ....fotografía.

Fr. ....Francés.

Frenol. ....Frenología.

Geogr. ....Geografía.

Geol. ....Geología.

Geom. ....Geometría.

Ger. ....Germania; Alemania.

Gram. ....Gramática.

Her. ....Heráldica.

Hist. ....Historia.

Hort. ....Horticultura.

imp. ....imperfecto.

Impr. ....Imprenta.

Inform. ....Informática.

Ingl. ....Inglaterra.

inter. ....interrogación.

interj. ....interjección.

irreg. ....irregular.

Ital. ....Italia.

Jur. ....Jurídico.

Log. ....Logaritmo.

m. ....masculino.

Mar. ....Marina.

Mat. ....Matemáticas.

Mec. ....Mecánica.

Med. ....Medicina

Messrs. ....Sres.

Met. ....Metafórico.

Meteo. ....Meteorología.

Mex. ....México.

Mil. ....Militar.

Min. ....Mineralogía; Mineral.

Mit. ....Mítico.

Mitol. ....Mitológico.

Mrs. ....Sra.

Mús. ....Música.

n. ....neutro.

Naut. ....Náutica.

Neg. ....Negativo.

Neol. ....Neología.

Ofic. ....Oficial; Oficina.

Opt. ....Óptica

Orn. ....Ornitología

p. ....participio.

pa. ....participio activo

Pint. ....Pintura.

pl. ....plural.

Poét. ....Poético.

Pol. ....Polonia.

pp. ....participio pasivo.

prep. ....preposición.

Pret. ....Pretérito.

pron. ....pronombre.

Prov. ....Provincia.

Quím. ....Química.

Rel. ....Religión.

Ret. ....Retórica.

s. ....sustantivo.

s./a. ....sustantivo / adjetivo.

s.pl. ....sustantivo plural.

Sociol. ....Sociología.

Teat. ....Teatro.

Tec. ....Técnica; Tecnología.

Telec. ....Telecomunicaciones.

Teol. ....Teología.

Tip. ....Tipografía.

TV. ....Televisión.

U.S. ....Estados Unidos.

Ud. ....Usted.

v. ....verbo.

va. ....verbo activo (transitivo).

Vet. ....Veterinaria.

vn. .....verbo neutro (intransitivo).

vr. ....verbo pronominal.

Vulg. ....Vulgarismo.

Zool. ....Zoología.

PRONUNCIACIÓN INGLESA

Sistema de Signos

En este diccionario hemos empleado los signos del IPA (International Phonetic Association).

Acentuación

El signo ['] se coloca delante de la sílaba acentuada. El signo [ˌ] se pone delante de la sílaba que lleva el acento secundario en las palabras largas: v.g., *privatization* [ˌpraɪvətaɪˈzeɪʃən].

Signos impresos en cursiva

Los signos escritos en IPA que van en cursiva, p. ej. en la palabra *privatization* [ˌpraɪvətaɪˈzeɪʃən], la [ə] cursiva indica que el sonido se puede pronunciar o no, o que es un sonido que se hace notar en una forma de hablar más lenta y cuidada, pero que en el habla común no se hace notar.

CÓMO PRONUNCIAR LOS SIGNOS DE LA IPA UTILIZADOS EN ESTE DICCIONARIO

Vocales

[æ] sonido breve y abierto, como la *a* en *tarro*.

[ɑ:] sonido largo de la *a*, como *paro*.

[e] sonido breve y abierto de la e, como en *cerro*.

[ə] vocal neutra, no acentuada, similar a la *e* del artículo *le* en francés.

[ɜ:] vocal anterior, en su forma larga, similar al sonido *eu* en el artículo francés *leur*.

[ɪ] sonido breve y abierto de la i, como en *iris*.

[i:] sonido largo de la i, como en *tino*, *pino*, etc.

[ɒ] sonido breve y abierto de la o, como en *forro*.

[ɔ:] sonido largo y cerrado de la o, como en *coro*.

[ʊ] sonido muy breve y cerrado de la u, como en *susurro*.

[u:] sonido largo de la u, como en *Lupe*, *duro*, etc.

[ʌ] sonido abierto y breve, sin su correspondiente en español. Se pronuncia en la parte anterior de la boca.

Consonantes

En general, las consonantes se pronuncian de manera similar a las del Español, exceptuando:

[j] se pronuncia como la *y* en *suyo*.

[ŋ] se pronuncia como la *n* en *fango*, es decir, pronunciando *ng*.

[ʳ] signo que indica una *r* suave, utilizada en posición final de la palabra, normalmente cuando la palabra siguiente empieza por vocal.

[ʒ] signo pronunciado como una *j* suave, como en la palabra francesa *jour*.

[ʃ] signo pronunciado como una *ch* suave o *sh*.

[tʃ] grupo que se pronuncia como una *ch*.

[θ] signo pronunciado como una *z* o *la c* seguida de *i* (cima) o *e* (cena).

[ð] signo pronunciado de manera similar a una *d* suave.

ABECEDARIO INGLÉS

a...............[eɪ]
b ....[bi:]
c...............[si:]
d ....[di:]
e...............[i:]
f ....[ef]
g ....[dʒi:]
h ....[eɪtʃ]
i ....[aɪ]
j ....[dʒeɪ]
k ....[keɪ]
l ....[el]
m ....[em]
n.............[en]
o.............[əʊ]
p.............[pi:]
q.............[kju:]
r.............[ɑːʳ]
s.............[es]
t.............[ti:]
u.............[ju:]
v.............[vi:]
w.............[ˈdʌblju:]
x.............[eks]
y.............[waɪ]
z.............[zi:]

Vocales

all ....[ɔ]
at ....[æ]
metal ....[ə]
far.....................................[ɑː]
pet.....................................[e]
bit ....[ɪ]
beet...................................[iː]
on......................................[ɒ]
work ....[ɜː]
door ....[ɔː]
up ....[ʌ]
book..................................[ʊ]
goose ....[uː]

Diptongos

die ....[aɪ]
bowl ....[aʊ]
mate ....[eɪ]
vote ....[əʊ]
fair ....[ɛə]
here ....[ɪə]
point..................................[ɔɪ]
sure ....[ʊə]

Consonantes

boat ....[b]
date ....[d]
face ....[f]
gate ....[g]
gipsy ....[dʒ]
hate ....[h]
jet......................................[dʒ]
key ....[k]
look...................................[l]
man...................................[m]
needle ....[n]
ring ....[ŋ]
pet.....................................[p]
queen ....[q]
red ....[r]
floo^r ....[ʳ]
system...............................[s]
shoe ....[ʃ]
take ....[t]
thing ....[θ]
that ....[ð]
van ....[v]
text....................................[ks]
zoo ....[z]
vision ....[ʒ]

A

a [eɪ] [ei], primera letra del alfabeto y una de las cinco vocales, tiene cuatro sonidos distintos en inglés; el primero como la *e* en castellano, aunque prolongada de modo que se parece algo al diptongo *ei*, como en *fate, face, waste,* etc.; el segundo como la *a* larga en castellano, en *far*; el tercero participa del sonido de *o* y *a* indistinto, cual se oye en *fall, wall;* y el cuarto es como una *a* breve en *fat*. Tiene también dos sonidos indistintos, como queda explicado en la introducción, donde se indican los respectivos signos para todos estos sonidos.

a [eɪ] [ei], y cuando no tiene acento, [a], artículo indefinido singular, significa **un** o **una** en castellano, ej. **A man,** un hombre; pero cuando precede a una palabra que empieza con vocal o **h** no aspirada, se convierte en **an;** ej. **An ox,** un buey; **an hour,** una hora. Muchas veces se pospone a palabras que en castellano la preceden; ej. **Such a man,** semejante hombre. **A** es algunas veces nombre sustantivo. Como, **A capital A,** Una *A* mayúscula.

a [ɑ] [a], *prep.* se halla a veces delante del participio activo, para denotar la acción de un verbo; ej. **It was a hunting party,** era un grupo de caza. **A** muchas veces denota proporción, como: **Six thousand a year,** seis mil al año o cada año. **A** se usa también en lugar de **in;** ej. **To be abed,** estar en cama.

a se emplea en las abreviaturas: ej. A. B., **Bachelor of Arts,** Bachiller en Artes. **A. M., Master of Artes,** Maestro en Artes. **A. D., Anno Domini,** El año del Señor. **A. M., Ante Meridian,** (Antes del mediodía) por la mañana.

Aaron's-beard [ærəns'bɔːd] [árons-biad], *s.* (*Bot.*) 1. Barba de Aarón, arbusto perenne de unos dos pies de altura, con flores amarillas, que crece en terrenos elevados; es una especie de hipérico. 2. Hiedra de Kenilworth, planta de las escrofulariáceas. 3. Hierba china de flores blancas, especie de saxífraga. Saxífraga sarmentosa. Hay también otras plantas que se llaman **Aaron's-beard.**

aaronic [ərənɪk] [a-ró-nic], **aaronical** [aronical] [ərɑnɪkəl], *a.* Aarónico; lo perteneciente al sacerdocio de Aarón.

ab [ɑb] [ab], *prefijo.* Significa lo mismo que en castellano: lejos, a distancia; desde; separación.

abaca ['æbəkəs] [á-ba-ca], *s.* Abacá, plátano de las Islas Filipinas.

abacist ['æbəsɪst] [á-ba-sist], *s.* El que calcula con el ábaco.

aback [ə'bæk] [a-bák], *adv.* Detrás, atrás. (*Fig.*) **To be taken aback,** quedar muy sorprendido. (*Mar.*) En facha. **To lay flat aback,** poner las velas en facha. **To lay the top-sails aback,** poner las gavias en facha. -*s.* (*Des.*) Una superficie plana cuadrada. V. ABACUS, 3a *acep.*

abaction [ə'bæk'ʃən] [a-bák-shon], *s.* (*For.*) Abigeato, hurto de ganado o bestias.

abactor [ə'bæk'tər] [a-bák-tor], *s.* (*For.*) Abigeo, cuatrero, ladrón de ganado o bestias.

abacus ['æbəkəs] [á-ba-kus], *s.* 1. Ábaco, tabla aritmética, aparato para contar y calcular. 2. Ábaco, el tablero que corona el capitel de una columna. 3. Cualquier loseta o tablilla de forma rectangular. 4. Aparador. 5. Báculo.

abaft [ə'bɑːft] [a-báft], *adv.* (*Mar.*) A popa o en popa; atrás, hacia la popa.

abaisance [ə'bɑsəns] [a-béi-sans], *s.* V. OBEISANCE.

abalienate [ə'bɑliənət] [a-ba-lie-néit], *va.* Enajenar.

abalienation [ə'bɑliənəʃən] [a-ba-lie-néi-shon], *s.* Enajenación, traspaso.

abalone [æbə'ləʊnɪ] [a-ba-lóu-ni], *s.* Oreja marina, molusco gasterópodo, común en la costa de California. La concha se emplea para taracear y para hacer abalorios, etc.; y la carne se seca para alimento y para la exportación.

abandon [ə'bændən] [a-bán-don], *s.* 1. Abandono, entrega. 2. Cesión. 3. Desamparo.

abandon, *va.* Abandonar, dejar, desamparar, entregar; desertar.

abandoned [ə'bændənd] [a-bán-do-nid], *pp.* Abandonado. Dejado, desamparado, entregado a los vicios.

abandoner [ə'bændənər] [a-bán-do-ner], *s.* Abandonador, desamparador, el que abandona.

abandoning [ə'bændənɪŋ] [a-bán-do-nin], *s.* Abandono, desamparo, cesión.

abandonment [ə'bændənmənt] [a-bán-don-ment], *s.* Abandono, abandonamiento.

abarticulation [əbɑːtɪkjʊləʃən] [a-bar-ti-kiu-lei-shon], *s.* Articulación de huesos con movimiento. V. DIARTHROSIS.

abase [ə'beɪs] [a-béis], *va.* 1. Abatir, humillar, envilecer, degradar. 2. Rebajar, reducir.

abasement [ə'beɪsmənt] [a-béis-ment], *s.* Abatimiento, envilecimiento, humillación, degradación.

abash [ə'bæʃ] [a-bash], *va.* 1. Avergonzar, sonrojar, correr. 2. Consternar.

abashment [ə'bæʃmənt] [a-bash-ment], *s.* 1. Confusión, vergüenza, rubor. 2. Consternación.

abasing [ə'beɪsɪŋ] [a-béi-sin], *pa. y a.* Humillante, vergonzoso.

abassi [ə'bɑsɪ] [á-ba-si], *s.* Antigua moneda rusa de poco valor.

abatable [ə'bətəbl] [a-bé-ta-bol], *a.* Abolible.

abate [ə'beɪt] [a-béit], *va.* 1. Minorar, disminuir, bajar, rebajar (to reduce). 2. Abatir, contristar. 3. Abolir, hacer cesar (un abuso). -*vn.* Menguar, disminuirse o minorarse alguna cosa, ir a menos, ceder, anular, derribar, apoderarse de, irse disminuyendo, calmarse (storm); amainar (wind); bajar (flood); moderarse (violence). 4. (*For.*) Anular, revocar. 5. (*Met.*) Humillar. **The fever begins to abate,** la fiebre empieza a remitir.

abatement [ə'beɪtmənt] [a-béit-ment], *s.* Rebaja, descuento que se hace de alguna cosa; extenuación, disminución. (*Her.*) Brisadas.

abater [ə'beɪtər] [a-bei-tar], *s.* Lo que disminuye una cosa, o hace o causa una rebaja. Regateo. Demeritorio.

abatis, abattis [ə'bətɪs] [a-ba-tis], *s.* (*Mil.*) Estacas, árboles cortados para formar con ellos una obra defensiva.

abattoir ['æbətwɑːʳ] [a-ba-tuaʳ], *s.* Matadero, particularmente uno de mucha extensión.

abb [ɑb] [ab], *s.* 1. Urdiembre o urdimbre. 2. Lana en borra.

abba [ɑb'ɑ] [a-ba] *s.* 1. Voz hebrea que significa padre. 2. Superior (de un convento).

abbacy ['æbəsɪ] [á-ba-si], *s.* (*Rel.*) 1. Abadía. 2. La dignidad, jurisdicción, rentas y privilegios pertenecientes a un abad.

abbasids ['æbəsɪds] [á-ba-sids] *pl.* (*Hist.*) Abasidas.

abbatial [ə'bəʃəl] [a-bé-shal], *a.* Abacial, abadengo. **Abbatial lands,** tierras abadengas.

abbé ['æbeɪ] [a-béi], *s.* (*Rel.*) Abate. Voz francesa, lo mismo que *abbot.*

abbess ['æbɪs] [á-bis], *s.* (*Rel.*) Abadesa.

abbey ['æbɪ] [a-bi], *s.* (*Rel.*) Abadía, monasterio, convento de monjes o monjas; también, refugio, santuario. **Abbey-lubber,** monje gordo y holgazán; bigardo; santurrón.

abbot ['æbət] [á-bot], *s.* (*Rel.*) Abad.

abbotship ['æbətʃɪp] [á-bot-ship], *s.* (*Rel.*) La dignidad y oficio de abad; abadía.

abbreviate [ə'briːvɪeɪt] [a-bri-viéit], *va.* Abreviar, reducir, compendiar. (*Mat.*) Simplificar.

abbreviation [ə'briːvɪeɪʃən] [a-bri-viéi-shon], *s.* Abreviación; abreviatura (shortened form).: **table of abbreviations,** cuadro de abreviaturas.

abbreviator [ə'briːvɪeɪtəʳ] [a-bri-viéi-tor], *s.* Abreviador, compendiador.

abbreviatory [ə'briːvɪətərɪ] [a-bri-via-tó-ri], *a.* Abreviatorio.

abbreviature [əˈbriːvɪeɪtwɑːʳ] [a-brí-via-tchuaʳ], *s.* Abbreviatura, compendio, epítome.

A B C *s.* Abecé, alfabeto, abecedario (alphabet).

abdicant [ˈænfɪkənt] [áb-di-kant], *a.* Abdicante, renunciante.

abdicate [ˈæbdɪkeɪt] [áb-di-keit], *va.* Abdicar, renunciar, dejar, desprenderse; hacer dimisión. **To abdicate from the throne,** abdicar del trono.

abdication [ˌæbdɪˈkeɪʃən] [ab-di-kéi-shon], *s.* Abdicación. renuncia, dimisión (of a function).

abdicative [əbˈdikətɪv] [ab-dí-ka-tiv], *a.* Abdicativo, renunciativo.

abditory [æbdɪtərɪ] [ab-dí-to-ri], *s.* Escondrijo, lugar o sitio para esconder y guardar joyas, plata o dinero.

abdomen [ˈæbdəmen] [ab-dó-men], *s.* Abdomen.

abdominal, abdominus [æbˈdɒmɪnl] [ab-dó-mi-nal], *a.* Abdominal. **Abdominal muscles,** músculos abdominales.

abduce [æbˈdjuːs] [ab-diús], *va.* 1. Desviar, apartar, separar una cosa de otra. 2. (*Anat.*) Mover de un lado a otro.

abducent [æbˈdjuːsənt] [ab-diú-sent], *a.* V. ABDUCTOR.

abduct [æbˈdʌkt] [ab-dákt], *va.* 1. Arrebatar, tomar, llevarse por fuerza. 2. Cometer un rapto o secuestro (hablando de una mujer, de un menor, etc.

abduction [æbˈdʌkʃən] [ab-dák-shon], *s.* 1. (*Anat.*) Abducción, acción por la cual una parte del cuerpo se separa de la línea que lo divide en dos segmentos iguales. 2. Abducción, forma particular de argumento. 3. Abducción, la acción de sacar hacia fuera. 4. (*For.*) El acto de sacar por fuerza o engaño a alguna persona. 5. Rapto, secuestro.

abductor [æbˈdʌktəʳ] [ab-dák-taʳ], *s.* 1. Abductor, nombre que se da en anatomía a varios músculos que sirven para la abducción. 2. (*For.*) El que saca por fuerza o engaño a una mujer u otra persona; raptor, secuestrador.

abeam [əˈbɪm] [a-bím], *adv.* (*Mat.*) Por el través. (*Mar.*) De través.

abear [əˈbɛəʳ] [a-bíar], *va.* (*Prov.*) Sufrir; soportar.

abearance [əˈbɛərəns] [a-bía-rans], *s.* (*For.*) Conducta, porte. V. BEHAVIOUR.

abecedarian [əˈbɪsɪdərɪən] [-abi-si-dá-rian], *s.* 1. El que enseña o aprende el abecé o la cartilla. 2. Niño de escuela.

abecedary [əˈbɪsɪdərɪ] [a-bí-si-da-ri], *s.* Abecedario, alfabeto.

abed [əˈbed] [a-béd], *adv.* 1. En cama o en la cama. 2. Acostado.

abel [əˈbel] [a-bel] *s.* Abel.

abelmosk [əˈbelməsk] [á-bel-mosk] *s.* (*Bot.*) Algalia.

aberr [əˈbɔr] [a-bér], *vn.* Errar, extraviarse; apartarse.

aberrance, aberrancy [əˈberəns] [a-bé-rans], *s.* Error, descamino, extravío, equivocación.

aberrant [əˈberənt] [a-bé-rant], *a.* Errado, descaminado, equivocado, extraviado. (*Anat.*) Anómalo.

aberration [æbeˈreɪʃən] [a-be-réi-shon], *s.* 1. Error. 2. Aberración, desvío de los rayos de la luz. 3. Aberración, movimiento aparente de las estrellas fijas.

aberring [æˈberɪŋ] [a-bé-rin], *part.* Errante, descaminado, extraviado.

aberuncate [æˈberənkeɪt] [a-bé-ran-keit], *va.* 1. Desarraigar, arrancar de raíz. 2. Extirpar.

abet [əˈbet] [a-bét], *va.* Apoyar, favorecer, patrocinar, sostener, excitar, animar, inducir. (*Jur.*) **To aid and abet,** ser cómplice de.

abetment [əˈbetmənt] [a-bét-ment], *s.* 1. Apoyo, protección, auxilio o favor. 2. Incitación. (*Jur.*) Complicidad.

abetter o abettor [əˈbetəʳ] [a-bé-tor], *s.* 1. Cómplice, promovedor, fomentador, ayudador. 2. Partidario, instigador.

abeyance [əˈberəns] [a-béians], *s.* (*For.*) Expectación, espera, expectativa de una reversión. **To have in abeyance,** tener en expectativa, en reserva. **Lands in abeyance,** bienes mostrencos, sin dueño conocido. **Heritance in abeyance,** herencia yacente.

abeyant [əˈberənt] [a-béiant], *a.* En reposo, durmiendo.

abgregation [əbgrɪˈgeʃən] [a-bri-géi-shon], *s.* Separación de la manada.

abhor [əbˈhɔːʳ] [a-bór], *va.* Aborrecer, detestar, odiar; desdeñar.

abhorrence [əbˈhɒrəns] [a-bó-rens], *s.* Aborrecimiento, odio, detestación, horror, aversión, execración. **To hold in abhorrence,** odiar, aborrecer.

abhorrent [əbˈhɒrent] [a-bó-rent], *a.* 1. Horroroso, aborrecible, detestable, abominable. 2. Ajeno, lo que es impropio o no correspondiente, contrario, extraño.

abhorrently [əbˈhɒrəntlɪ] [a-bó-ren-tli], *adv.* Aborreciblemente.

abhorrer [əbˈhɒrəʳ] [a-bó-raʳ], *s.* Aborrecedor, enemigo jurado.

abhorring [əbˈhɒrɪŋ] [a-bó-rin], *s.* Hastío, náusea; objeto de aversión.

abidance [əˈbaɪdəns] [a-bái-dans], *s.* 1. Residencia, morada. 2. Acatamiento, respeto (of the law)

abide [əˈbaɪd] [a-báid], *vn.* 1. Habitar, morar, vivir o estar de asiento en algún paraje- (*to abide, pa. abiding; pp.,* **pret. imp y pret. perf.** *abode*). 2. Quedar, continuar. *-va.* 1. Soportar, sufrir, aguantar. 2. Defender, sostener. 3. Atenerse a alguna cosa. 4. Perseverar. **To abide by o in,** sostenerse en su opinión, mantenerse en lo dicho. Pasar por, consentir. **To abide by the rules,** acatar las reglas. **To abide by a promise,** cumplir una promesa.

abider [əˈbaɪdəʳ] [a-bái-der], *s.* Habitador, habitante, vecino, inquilino.

abiding [əˈbaɪdɪŋ] [a-bái-din], *s.* Continuación, perseverancia, estabilidad, permanencia. *-a.* Permanente. **Law abiding,** respetuoso con las leyes.

abigail [əˈbɪgeɪl] [a-bi-guéil], *s.* Criada confidente al servicio de una señora.

ability [əˈbɪlɪtɪ] [a-bí-li-ti], *s.* 1. Potencia, habilidad, capacidad, aptitud. En plural, talento, ingenio; ej. **A man of abilities,** hombre de talento. 2. Haber o bienes, medios.

abintestate [əˈbɪntəsteɪt] [a-bín-tes-teit], *a.* Abintestato, el que muere sin hacer testamento. **Heir abintestate,** heredero abintestato.

abiogenesis [əˌbaɪəʊˈdʒenɪsɪs] [a-bio-yé-ne-sis], *s.* Abiogénesis, generación espontánea; la de los organismos vivos cuyo supuesto origen es la materia inanimada.

abiological [əˌbaɪəˈlɒdʒɪkəl] [a-bio-ló-yi-kal], *a.* Perteneciente a sustancia inanimada; abiológico.

abject [ˈæbdʒekt] [ab-yékt], *s.* Hombre vil, bajo, abyecto; abatido, humillado, desesperanzado.

abject, *a.* Vil, despreciable, bajo, indecente, abatido, abyecto (despicable); desalmado, miserable (wretched).

abjectedness [ˈæbdʒektnɪs] [ab-yék-tid-nis], *s.* Abyección, desesperación, pérdida de la esperanza, humillación, envilecimiento.

abjection, abjectness [ˈæbdʒekʃən] [ab-yék-shon], *s.* 1. Abyección, bajeza, vileza, abatimiento de alma; servilismo, cobardía. 2. Envilecimiento, Ayección.

abjectly [ˈæbdʒektlɪ] [áb-yek-tli], *adv.* Vilmente, bajamente, abyectamente.

abjudicated [ˈæbdʒədɪkeɪtɪd] [ab-yu-di-kéi-tid], *a.* Abjudicado.

abjudication [ˈæbdʒədɪkeɪʃən] [ab-yu-di-kéi-shon], *s.* Abjudicación.

abjuration [əbˈdʒɔreɪʃən] [abyuaréishon], *s.* Abjuración, el acto de abjurar.

abjure [əbˈdʒʊəʳ] [ab-yuaʳ], *va.* 1. Jurar, hacer o prestar juramento de no hacer alguna cosa. 2. Abjurar de (one's faith), desdecirse o retractarse con juramento de algún error. 3. Desterrar.

abjurement [əbˈdʒuːmənt] [ab-yúr-ment], *s.* Renuncia, adjuración.

abjurer [əbˈdʒʊərəʳ] [ab-yúa-raʳ], *s.* El que abjura o renuncia; renunciante.

ablactate [əˈblakteɪt] [a-blak-téit], *va.* Destetar. Quitar el pecho a un niño.

ablactation [ə'blækteɪʃən] [a-blak-téi-shon], s. 1. Destete. 2. Manera de injertar los árboles.

ablaqueation [ə'blækweɪʃən] [a-bla-kuéi-shon], s. Excava de árboles.

ablation [əbʃbn] [abléishon], s. 1. Quite, la acción de quitar. 2. Extirpación; separación.

ablative ['æblətɪv] [á-bla-tif], a. Lo que quita. **The ablative case,** ablativo, el sexto caso de la declinación del nombre en algunas lenguas.

ablaut [ə'blaʊt] [a-bláut] *(Gram.)* Apofonía.

ablaze [əbʃ] [a-bléis], a. En llamas.

-able. Terminación, o sufijo, muy común en adjetivos ingleses, equivalente a apto, a propósito, conveniente.

able ['eɪbl] [éi-bol], a. Fuerte, poderoso, capaz, hábil, rico, opulento, experto, experimentado. **To be able** o **to be able for,** poder; tener poder.

able-bodied ['eɪbl'bɒdɪd] [ei-bol-bó-did], a. Forzudo, robusto, fornido.

able-bodied seaman [,eɪbl'bɒdɪd'si:mən] [ei-bol-bo-did-sí-man] s. Marinero de primera clase.

ablegate ['əblɪgeɪt] [á-bli-geit], va. Enviar o dar empleo a alguno en país extranjero; diputar.

ablegate, s. Representante del Papa, enviado con una misión determinada a un país extranjero.

ableness [eɪblnɪs] [éi-bol-nis], s. Fuerza, vigor; habilidad, poder.

ablepsy [əbʃɪ] [á-bleps-i], s. Ceguera, ceguedad; ablepsia.

ablest [əbʃ] [a-blest], a. Superlativo de **able.** Poderosísimo, riquísimo. Muy hábil, muy capaz.

abloom [ə'blu:m] [a-blúm], a. En flor; floreciente.

abluent [əbluent] [á-bluent], a. Detersivo, detergente, limpiante.

ablush [ə'blu:ʃ] [a-blúsh], a. y adv. Sonrojante, abochornado.

ablution [ə'blu:ʃən] [a-blú-shon], s. Ablución; acción; de lavar, limpiar.

ably ['eɪblɪ] [éi-bli], adv. Hábilmente, con habilidad, con maña.

-ably. Sufijo que convierte en adverbios los adjetivos terminados en **-able.**

abnegate ['æbnɪgeɪt] [áb-ni-geit], va. Negar, rehusar, resignar, renunciar, renegar (rights).

abnegation [,æbnɪ'geɪʃən] [ab-ni-géi-shon], s. 1. Abnegación. 2. Renuncia (rights). 3. Repudiación.

abnegator [,æbnɪ'geɪtər] [ab-ni-géi-tar], s. Negador; impugnador.

abnodation ['æbnɒdeɪʃən] [ab-no-déi-shon], s. *(Jardin.)* El acto de cortar los nudos de un árbol.

abnormal [æb'nɔ:məl] [ab-nór-mal], a. Irregular, mal formado, disforme.

abnormality [æbnɔ:'mælɪtɪ] [ab-nor-má-li-ti] o **abnormity** [æbnɔ:'mɪtɪ] [ab-nór-mi-ti], s. Irregularidad, deformidad; monstruosidad; producción contraria al orden de la naturaleza.

aboard [ə'bɔ:d] [a-bord], adv. *(Mar.)* A bordo. **Life aboard is pleasant,** la vida a bordo es agradable. **To take aboard,** embarcar, llevar a bordo. **To go aboard,** ir a bordo, embarcarse. -prep. A bordo de.

abode [ə'bɒɒd] [a-bóud], s. 1. Domicilio, residencia, habitación. 2. Mansión, morada o estancia de asiento en algún paraje. **Of no fixed abode,** sin domicilio fijo.

abode, pret. y pp. de ABIDE.

abolish [ə'bɒlɪʃ] [a-bó-lish], va. Abolir, anular; revocar.

abolishable [ə'bɒlɪʃeɪbl] [abólisheibol], a. Abolible.

abolisher [ə'bɒlɪʃər] [a-bó-li-sher], s. Abolidor, anulador, revocador.

abolition, abolishment [ə'bɒlɪʃən] [ə'bɒlɪʃmənt] [a-bo-lí-shon] [a-bó-lish-ment], s. Abolición.

abolitionism [,æbəʊ'lɪʃənsem] [a-bo-li-sho-ní-sem] s. Abolicionismo.

abolitionist [æbəʊ'lɪʃənɪst] [a-bo-lí-sho-nist], s. Abolicionista, el partidario de la abolición de alguna cosa, especialmente de la esclavitud.

abomasum [əbəmasʊm] [a-bo-má-sum], s. Abomaso, el cuarto estómago de un animal rumiante.

a-bomb ['eɪbɒm] [ei-bomb], s. Bomba atómica.

abominable [ə'bɒmɪnəbl] [a-bó-mi-na-bol], a. Abominable, execrable, detestable; inmundo.

abominableness [ə'bɒmɪnəblnɪs] [abominábolnis], s. La propiedad o calidad que hace a alguna cosa abominable.

abominably [ə'bɒmɪnəblɪ] [a-bo-mi-na-bli], adv. Abominablemente.

abominate [ə'bɒmɪneɪt] [a-bó-mi-neit], va. Abominar, detestar, aborrecer.

abomination [ə,bɒmɪ'neɪʃən] [a-bo-mi-néi-shon], s. 1. Abominación, odio, detestación. 2. Polución, maldad, corrupción.

aboral [ə'bɒrəl] [a-bó-ral], a. Opuesto a la boca, situado fuera de ella.

aboriginal [,æbə'rɪdzɪnl] [a-bo-rí-yi-nal], a. Primitivo; originario, aborigen.

aborigines [,æbə'rɪdzɪnɪs] [a-bo-rí-yi-nis], s. pl. Los primeros habitantes de algún país aborígenes, indígenas.

abort [ə'bɔ:t] [a-bort], vn. Abortar, malparir. -*(Aer.)* Fracaso en el lanzamiento de un cohete.

abortion [ə'bɔ:ʃən] [a-bór-shon], s. Aborto, malparto. 2. Aborto, lo nacido antes de tiempo. *(Fig.)* Aborto, proyecto detenido en su desarrollo (failure). 3. Engendro.

abortive [ə'bɔ:tɪv] [a-bór-tif], a. 1. Abortivo. 2. Infructuoso, inútil, intempestivo, malogrado, frustrado. -s. Aborto, engendro.

abortively [ə'bɔ:tɪvlɪ] [a-bór-tif-li], adv. 1. Abortivamente. 2. Intempestivamente. 3. Prematuramente.

abortiveness [ə'bɔ:tɪvnɪs] [a-bór-tif-nis], s. Aborto; mal éxito de algo.

abound [ə'baʊnd] [a-báund], vn. Abundar. **To abound with,** abundar en.

abounding [ə'baʊndɪŋ] [a-báun-din], a. y part. (in, with, en). Abundante (en).

about [ə'baʊt] [a-báut], prep. 1. Alrededor, cerca de, por ahí, hacia. 2. Acerca, tocante a. 3. Pendiente, colgante. **I know nothing about that matter,** no sé nada de aquel asunto. **He is about coming,** está a punto de venir. **I carry no money about me,** no traigo dinero. **There's something strange about that girl,** esa chica tiene algo raro. **To beat about the bush,** andarse por las ramas. –adv. En contorno, por rodeos; aquí y allá. **To go about;** rodear. **To bring about. To go about a thing,** efectuar alguna cosa. *(Mar.)* Virar. **Within about 60 yards,** a unas 60 yardas. -EXPRESIONES. **Look about you,** tenga usted cuidado. **What are you about?,** ¿qué va usted a hacer?, **send him about his business,** envíelo usted a paseo. **He was walking about,** andaba por aquí y por allá. **There's a lot of flu about,** hay mucha gripe por ahí. **He was here about two weeks ago,** estuvo por aquí hace unas dos semanas.

above [ə'bʌv] [a-bóuf], prep. Encima, sobre, superior, más alto en cuanto a situación, dignidad, poder, etc. -adv. Arriba, la parte alta o lugar en alto. **Above all,** sobre todo, principalmente. **Above-board,** abiertamente, públicamente, a vista de todos. **Above cited** o **above mentioned,** ya citado o ya mencionado, supracitado, susodicho. **Above ground,** vivo; expresión que denota que aún no ha muerto alguno. **From above,** de arriba, de lo alto, del cielo. **To be above a thing,** (a) Ser incapaz de una cosa, ser superior a, no usar de. (b) Más que, o de; ej. **He was not above three hours in doing it,** no empleó más de tres horas en hacerlo. **I value honor above life,** precio mi honra más que la vida.

abradant [ə'brædənt] [a-bré-dant], a. Que desgasta o raspa. -s. Sustancia raspante.

abrade [ə'breɪd] [a-bréid], va. Raer o gastar, quitar restregando.

Abraham ['ebrəhæm] [éi-bra-jam] n. Abrahám.

abrasion [ə'breɪʒən] [a-bréi-shon], s. 1. Raspadura, la acción de raspar. 2. Lo que se quita de la superficie raspando. 3. Abrasión. *(Geol.)*, Erosión.

abrasive [əˈbreɪzɪv] [á-bre-sif], *a.* Rayente, raspante; que produce la acción de raspar o raer. -*s.* Sustancia raspante. Abrasivo.

abreast [əˈbrest] [a-brést], *adv.* De frente. **Four abreast,** cuatro de frente, o en fila. De costado. **Abreast, (Mar.)** por el través. **Abreast the port,** por el través del puerto. **To keep abreast of,** mantenerse informado, estar al día.

abrenunciation [əˈbrenənsɪˈeɪʃən] [a-bre-nun-siéi-shon], *s.* Renuncia, renunciación.

abreption [əˈbrepʃən] [a-brép-shon], *s.* Abstracción; arrebatiña. Rapto.

abreuvoir [əbreˌwɑːˈr] [a-bre-vuáʳ], *s.* 1. Abrevadero, bebedero. 2. Degolladura, hueco entre los ladrillos o piedras para llenarlo de argamasa.

abridge [əˈbrɪdʒ] [a-brích], *va.* 1. Abreviar, compendiar. 2. Cercenar, acortar, disminuir. 3. Privar, despojar o quitar. *(Alg.)* Reducir.

abridged [əˈbrɪdʒd] [a-brí-chid], *pp.* Privado; acortado.

abridger [əˈbrɪdʒəʳ] [a-brí-chaʳ], *s.* 1. Abreviador. 2. Compendiador.

abridgment [əˈbrɪdʒmənt] [a-brích-ment], *s.* 1. Compendio, epítome, recopilación. 2. Contracción, limitación. *(Jur.)* Privación (of rights).

abroach [əˈbrəʊtʃ] [a-bróuch], *adv. (Ant.)* Para derramarse; en estado de difundirse o propagarse. **To set abroach,** horadar, barrenar.

abroad [əˈbrɔːd] [a-bróud], *adv.* Fuera de casa o del país; en países extranjeros, en todas partes o direcciones. **To walk abroad,** salir, ir a dar una vuelta. **The schoolmaster is abroad,** educación difundida. **To set aborad,** divulgar, publicar. *(Fig.)* **The rumor is abroad that,** corre el rumor de que.

abrogable [ˈæbrəʊˈgeɪbl] [a-bró-ge-bol], **abrogative** [ˈæbrəgətɪv], *a.* Abrogable; que tiende a revocar o abrogar, o tiene tal propósito.

abrogate [ˈæbrəʊgeɪt] [a-bro-geit], *va.* Abrogar, anular, revocar.

abrogation [æbrəʊˈgeɪʃən] [a-bro-géi-shon], *s.* Abrogación, anulación, revocación, abolición.

abrotanum [əˈbrɒtənʌm] [a-bró-ta-nom], *s. (Bot.)* Abrótano, artemisa.

abrupt [əˈbrʌpt] [a-brapt], *a.* 1. Quebrado, desigual. 2. Precipitado, repentino; desunido, bronco, rudo, fogoso. 3. Abrupto, escarpado, brusco. **An abrupt halt,** una parada brusca.

abruption [əˈbrʌʃən] [a-bráp-shon], *s.* Rotura o separación repentina y violenta de una cosa.

abruptly [əˈbrʌptlɪ] [a-bráp-tli], *adv.* Precipitadamente; rudamente, ásperamente, bruscamente, ex-abrupto.

abruptness [əˈbrʌptnɪs] [a-brápt-nis], *s.* Precipitación, inconsideración; prontitud; sequedad, claridad.

abscess [ˈæbsɪs] [a-bsés], *s.* Absceso, apostema.

abscind [ˈæbsɪnd] [ab-sínd], *va.* Cortar, tajar.

abscissa [ˈæbsɪsə] [ab-sí-sa], *s.* Abscisa, la línea coordenada de la cual se hacen depender los valores de las demás.

abscission [ˈæbsɪʃən] [ab-sí-shon], *s.* Cortadura; anulación.

abscond [æbˈskɒnd] [abs-kónd], *vn.* Esconderse, fugarse, huir. -*va.* Ocultar, tapar.

absconder [æbˈskɒndəʳ] [abs-kóndaʳ], *s.* 1. Fugitivo, que toma las de Villadiego. 2. *(For.)* Contumaz, prófugo, que se oculta.

absence [ˈæbsəns] [áb-sens], *s.* 1. Ausencia. 2. Abstracción de ánimo. **Absence of mind,** distracción. 3. Descuido, negligencia. **Leave of absence,** *(Mil.)* permiso para ausentarse, licencia temporal. *(Jur.)* Incomparecencia. **In the absence of,** en ausencia de, a falta de.

absent [ˈæbsənt] [áb-sent], *a.* 1. Ausente. 2. Enajenado o fuera de sí; descuidado, negligente. 3. Divertido, distraído, abstraído. **Absent-minded,** *a.* Fuera de sí; absorto, abstraído en meditación.

absent, *vr.* Ausentarse, retirarse de.

absentaneous [ˈæbsəntənəs] [ab-sen-tá-nos], *a.* Ausente, lo que se ausenta.

absentee [æbsənˈtiː] [áb-sen-ti], *s.* Ausente, el que lo está de su empleo, país o hacienda.

absenteeism [ˌæbsənˈtiːzəm] [áb-sen-te-ísem], *s.* Ausentismo.

absenter [æbsəntəʳ] [ab-sén-taʳ], *s.* El que abandona su obligación u oficio.

absinthe [ˈæbsɪnθ] [ab-sínz], *s.* Licor francés popular, hecho con ajenjo y otras hierbas.

absinthian [ˈæbsɪnθən] [ab-sínzian], *a.* Lo perteneciente al ajenjo; amargo.

absinthiated [ˈæbsɪnθətɪd] [ab-sinzi-éi-tid], *a.* Tinturado o mezclado con ajenjo.

absinthium [ˈæbsɪnθʊm] [ab-sín-zium], *s. (Bot.)* Ajenjo. Artemisa absinthium.

absolute [ˈæbsəluːt] [áb-so-lut], *a.* 1. Absoluto, libre, irresponsable. 2. Amplio, completo. 3. Perentorio. 4. Positivo, arbitrario. **Absolute altitude,** *(Aer.)* altitud absoluta. **Absolute zero,** *(Quím.)* Cero absoluto. *(Jur.),* Irrevocable.

absolutely [æbsəluːtlɪ] [ab-so-lút-li], *adv.* 1. Absolutamente, enteramente, sin reserva. 2. Positivamente, sin reserva.

absoluteness [æbsəluːtnɪs] [ab-so-lút-nis], *s.* 1. Amplitud, independencia. 2. Despotismo, poder absoluto.

absolution [æbsəˈluːʃən] [ab-so-lú-shon] *s.* Absolución; perdón. **To grant absolution,** dar la absolución.

absolutism [ˈæbsəluːtɪzəm] [ab-so-lu-tísem], *s.* 1. Absolutismo, despotismo. 2. La doctrina de la predestinación.

absolutist [ˈæbsəluːtɪst] [ab-so-lú-tist], *s.* Absolutista, partidario del absolutismo.

absolutor [ˈæbsəluːtəʳ] [ab-so-lú-taʳ], **absolvatory** [ˈæbsəlvətərɪ] [ab-sol-va-to-ri], *a.* Absolutorio.

absolve [əbˈzɒlv] [ab-sólv], *va.* 1. Absolver, dar por libre de una acusación. 2. Absolver de un convenio o promesa. 3. Absolver deun pecado. 4. Dispensar, exentar.

absolver [ebˈzɒlvəʳ] [ab,sel',ve7r], *s.* Absolvedor, dispensador.

absonant, absonous [əbˈsənənt] [áb-so-nant], *a.* 1. Absurdo, repugnante a la razón. 2. Disonante, ridículo.

absorb [əbˈzɔːb] [ab-sérb], *va.* 1. Absorber. 2. Empapar, embeber. 3. Amortiguar. 4. Asumir. **To be absorbed in,** estar absorto en.

absorbable [əbˈzɔːbəbl] [ab-sér-ba-bol], *a.* Que puede ser absorbido o chupado.

absorbability [əbˈzɔːbəbɪlɪtɪ] [ab-ser-ba-bí-li-ti], *s.* Propiedad de ser absorbido.

absorbent [əbˈzɔːbənt] [ab-sér-bent], *a.* Absorbente, una clase de medicina; se da el nombre de absorbentes a los vasos y glándulas que sirven en el cuerpo humano para efectuar la absorción. Se usa también como sustantivo. Capaz de absorber.

absorpt o absorbed [əbˈzɔːpt] [əbˈzɔːbd] *(Ant.)* [ab-sórpt] [ab-sórbd], *pp.* Absorbido, chupado, desecado; hablando de los humores del cuerpo. *(Met.)* Absorto, arrebatado, enajenado.

absorption [əbˈzɔːpʃən] [ab-sór-shon], *s.* 1. Absorción, el acto de absorber. 2. *(Aut.)* Amortiguamiento. 3. Preocupación.

absorptive [əbˈzɔːptɪv] [ab-sér-tif], *a.* Absorbente, capaz de absorber.

abstain [əbˈsteɪn] [abs-téin], *vn.* Abstenerse, privarse de algún gusto o placer. **To abstain from comment,** abstenerse de comentarios.

abstainer [əbˈsteɪnəʳ] [abs-téi-nar], *s.* Abstinente, sobrio.

abstaining [əbˈsteɪnɪŋ] [abs-téi-nin], *s.* Abstinencia.

abstemious [əbˈstiːmɪəs] [abs-tí-mios], *a.* Abstemio, sobrio, templado, moderado.

abstemiously [əbˈstiːmɪəslɪ] [abs-tí-mios-li], *adv.* Sobriamente, moderadamente, templadamente.

abstemiousness [əbˈstiːmɪəsnɪs] [abs-tí-mios-nis], *s.* Sobriedad, moderación, templanza.

abstention [əbˈstenʃən] [abs-tén-shon], *s.* 1. Detención, el acto de detener o impedir. 2. Abstinencia; privación. 3. Abstención (from voting).

absterge [əb'stɜ:dʒ] [abs-térch], *va*. Absterger, limpiar, enjugar.

abstergent [əb'stɜ:dʒənt] [abs-tér-chent], *a*. Abstergente, lo que sirve para purificar o limpiar.

abstersion [əb'stɜ:ʃən] [abs-tér-shon], *s*. Abstersión.

abstersive [əb'stɜ:sɪv] [abs-tér-sif], *a*. Abstergente. -*s*. Limpiador.

abstinence, abstinency ['æbstɪnəns] [ábs-ti-nens], *s*. 1. Abstinencia. 2. Sobriedad, templanza. **Day of abstinence,** día de ayuno.

abstinent ['æbstɪnənt] [ábs-ti-nent], *a*. Abstinente, mortificado, sobrio, moderado.

abstinently ['æbstɪnəntlɪ] [abs-ti-nen-tli], *adv*. Abstinentemente.

abstract ['æbstrækt] [abs-trákt], *va*. 1. Abstraer, sustraer. 2. Extractar, extraer o hacer un extracto. 3. Considerar separadamente. **Abstracting from,** Separado de, sin contar con.

abstract, *a*. Abstracto, separado; refinado. Ideal, puro. Opuesto a concreto.

abstract, *s*. 1. Extracto, cantidad pequeña de alguna cosa. 2. Extracto, resumen, compendio, sumario. 3. Abstracción. 4. Preparación particular de una droga en polvos.

abstracted [æb'stræktɪd] [abs-trák-tid], *pp*. 1. Separado. 2. Abstraído, distraído. 3. Abstruso, metafísico. 4. Extraído, puro, sin mezcla.

abstractedly [æb'stræktɪdlɪ] [abs-trák-tid-li], *adv*. Abstractivamente; sencillamente.

abstractedness ['æbstræktɪdnɪs] [abs-trák-tid-nis] *s*. Abstracción.

abstracter ['æbstræktəʳ] [abs-trák-tar], *s*. 1. Extractador, abreviador, el que extracta, abrevia o compendia. 2. Ratero, ladrón.

abstraction ['æbstrækʃən] [abs-trák-shon], *s*. 1. Abstracción, la acción y efecto de abstraer o abstraerse. 2. Abstracción, el retiro de la comunicación o trato con las gentes. 3. Concepto, idea; noción. 4. Concepción no real; alguna cosa imaginaria. 5. Desatención, descuido. Ratería, hurto.

abstractionism ['æbstrækʃənɪzm] [abs-trák-sho-nisem], *s*. Abstraccionismo.

abstractive ['æbstræktɪv] [ab-strac'-tiv], *a*. Abstractivo.

abstractly, abstractively ['æbstræktlɪ] [abs-trák-tli], *adv*. En abstracto, abstractivamente.

abstractness ['æbstræktnɪs] [abs-trákt-nis], *s*. Separación; abstracción, sin relación con ningún objeto.

abstruse [æb'stru:s] [abs-trús], *a*. Abstruso, recóndito de difícil inteligencia. Oculto, oscuro.

abstrusely [æb'stru:slɪ] [abs-trús-li], *adv*. Oscuramente, difícilmente.

abstruseness, abstrusity [æb'stru:snɪs] [abs-trús-nis], *s*. 1. Oscuridad, dificultad; arcano, misterio. 2. Carácter abstruso.

absurd [əb'sɜ:d] [ab-sérd], *a*. Absurdo, repugnante a la razón, irracional, ridículo, inconsistente, disparatado.

absurdity [əb'sɜ:dɪtɪ] [ab-sér-di-ti], *s*. Absurdo, dicho o hecho repugnante a la razón. **The height of absurdity,** el colmo de lo absurdo.

absurdly [əb'sɜ:dlɪ] [ab-sérd-li], *adv*. Absurdamente, irracionalmente.

absurdness [əb'sɜ:dnɪs] [ab-sérd-nis], *s*. Absurdo, irracionalidad, disparate.

abulia [ə'bu:lɪə] [a-bú-lia] *n*. abulia.

abulic [ə'bu:lɪk] [a-bú-lik] *adj*. abúlico.

abundance [ə'bʌdəns] [a-bán-dans], *s*. Abundancia, copia, o gran cantidad de alguna cosa; exuberancia.

abundant [ə'bʌndənt] [a-bán-dant], *a*. Abundante, copioso, rico; lleno.

abundantly [ə'bʌndəntlɪ] [a-bán-dan-tli], *adv*. Abundantemente.

abuse [ə'bju:s] [a-bíus], *va*. 1. Abusar. 2. Engañar, seducir; profanar, ultrajar, violar. 3. Maltratar de palabra, burlarse con desprecio; denostar. **He has been abused,** le han engañado.

abuse, *s*. 1. Abuso. **Abuse of confidence,** abuso de confianza. 2. Abuso, corruptela. 3. Seducción, engaño. 4. Contumelia, injuria u ofensa de palabra, afrenta, burla, ultraje.

abuser [ə'bju:zəʳ] [a-bíu-sar], *s*. 1. Abusador. 2. Seductor. 3. Denostador. 4. Embaucador, embaidor, engañador.

abusive [ə'bju:sɪv] [a-bíusif], *a*. 1. Abusivo, insultante, injurioso, vil. **Abusive language,** palabras injuriosas. 2. Corrompido; mal empleado o usado.

abusively [ə'bju:sɪvlɪ] [a-biu-síf-li], *adv*. 1. Abusivamente. 2. Impropiamente. Insolentemente.

abusiveness [ə'bju:sɪvnɪs] [a-biu-síf-nis], *s*. Vituperación; palabras injuriosas, vituperio, propensión a injuriar a otro, insulto; abuso, calidad de abusivo.

abut [ə'bʌt] [abát], *vn*. Terminar, confinar, lindar, parar, rematar. **To abut upon,** salir a, terminar en, confinar con, empalmarse con, sobre.

abutilon [ə'bʌtɪlən] [abátilon], *s*. Abutilón, malvavisco de Indias.

abutment [ə'bʌtmənt] [a-bát-ment], *s*. 1. Linde, confín 2. Refuerzo, estribo. Lindero; mojón. 3. (*Carp.*) Empalme; remate. 4. (*Arq.*) Contrafuerte.

abuttal [ə'bʌtəl] [a-bá-tal], *s*. Límite, linde.

abutting [ə'bʌtɪŋ] [a-bá-tin] *a*. Lindante con.

abysmal [ə'bɪzməl] [a-bís-mal], 1. *a*. Abismal; insondable. 2. (*Fig.*) Profundo.

abyss [ə'bɪs] [á-bis], **abysm** [ə'bɪzm] [a-bí-sem], *s*. 1. Abismo, profundidad a que no se halla fondo. 2. El infierno. 3. Sima (*Her.*) Abismo, el centro del escudo.

abyssal [ə'bɪsəl] [a-bí-sal], *a*. 1. Perteneciente a grandes profundidades del océano. 2. Abismal, insondable.

Abyssinia [æbɪ'sɪnɪə] [a-bi-sí-nia] *N*. (*Geogr.*) Abisinia.

Abyssinian [æbɪ'sɪnɪən] [a-bi-sí-nian], *a*. Abisinio, de Abisinia.

ac *Ac*, *prefijo*. Forma de AD cuando se halla delante de **c** y **q:** como en **accept.**

-ac, *sufijo*. Con relación a, que tiene, o es afectado por: como **cardiac,** lo que tiene relación al corazón, o lo afecta.

acacia [ə'keɪʃə] [a-kéi-sha], *s*. 1. Acacia, nombre de un árbol de Egipto, que da la goma arábica. 2. Acacia, arbolillo espinoso con flores en racimos colgantes. 3. Acacia, el zumo de las endrinas silvestres.

academian, academic [ækə'di:mɪən] [ækə'di:mɪk] [a-ka-dí-mian] [a-ca-dé-mik], *s*. Académico; cursante en alguna universidad, estudiante. Colegial. **Academic year,** curso escolar.

academic, academical [ækə'di:mɪk] [ækə'di:mɪkəl] [a-ca-dé-mik] [a-ca-dé-mi-kal], *a*. Académico, lo que pertenece a las universidades. **Academic freedom,** libertad académica.

academically [ækə'di:mɪkəlɪ] [a-ca-dé-mi-kli] *adv*. En estilo o en forma académica.

academician, academist [ə,kædə'mɪʃən] [əkæ'dəmɪstən] [a-cá-de-mist], *s*. Académico, el individuo de alguna academia.

academism [ə,kædə'mɪst] [a-ca-de-mí-sem] *N*. Academismo.

academy [ə'kædəmɪ] [a-cá-de-mi], *s*. 1. Academia, sitio o lugar ameno, cerca de Atenas, donde Platón y sus discípulos tenían sus conferencias filosóficas. 2. Academia, sociedad establecida para el cultivo y adelantamiento de las ciencias y artes. 3. Academia, la casa o paraje en que se enseñan las ciencias o se tienen academias; universidad. 4. Figura académica, figura diseñada por el modelo vivo. 5. Conservatorio (of music). 6. Instituto de enseñanza media (in Scotland).

acaleph [ə'kæf] [a-ca-léf], *s*. Uno de los acalefos.

acalephae [ə'kæf] [a-ca-le-fe], *s. pl*. Acalefos, grupo de zoófitos que comprende las medusas y los hidróides.

acanaceous [ə'kænəʒəs] [a-ca-ná-sias], *a*. (*Bot.*) Espinoso.

acanthine [ə'kænθɪn] [a-can-cin], *a*. Acantino/na; concerniente, relativo o análogo al acanto.

acanthopterygii [əˈkənθɒpˌterɪdʒɪ] [a-can-zop-te-ri-yi] *s. pl.* Acantopterigios.

acanthus [əˈkæntʌs] [a-can-zus], *s. (Bot.)* Acanto o branca ursina.

acaridae [əˈkærɪdæ] [a-ca-ri-de] *s. pl. (Zool.)* Acáridos.

acarus [əˈkərʌs] [á-ca-ras], *s.* ACARI, *pl.* ácaro.

acatalectic [əˈkætəlɪk] [a-ca-ta-lék-tik], *s.* Acataléctico.

acaulescent, acauline, acaulous [əˈkɔləsnt] [a-cá-le-sent], *a. (Bot.)* Acaule, sin renuevo o vástago; de tallo muy poco visible.

accede [ækˈsiːd] [ak-síd], *vn.* 1. Acceder, venir o convenir en alguna cosa; asentir, consentir. 2. Subir, llegar a, obtener posesión de, alcanzar.

accelerando [ækˈsələrəndɒ] [ak-se-le-rán-do], *a. (Mús.)* Acelerando gradualmente el tiempo.

accelerate [ækˈseləreɪtɒ] [ak-sé-le-reit], *va.* Acelerar. -*vn.* Despacharse, apresurarse, darse prisa.

accelerating [ækˈseləreɪtɪŋ] [ak-se-le-réi-tin] *a.* Acelerador. **Accelerating force,** fuerza aceleratriz.

acceleration [ækˈseləreɪʃən] [ak-se-le-réi-shon], *s.* Aceleración; prisa; despacho. **Acceleration of** or **due to gravity,** aceleración terrestre.

accelerative [ækˈseləreɪtɪv] [ak-se-le-ré-ra-tif], *a.* Lo que aumenta la velocidad. Impulsivo, acelerador.

accelerator [ækˈseləreɪtər] [ak-se-le-réi-ta], *s.* Acelerador.

accelerometer [ækˈseləromɪtər] [ak-se-le-ro-mí-ta], *s. (Aer.)* Acelerómetro.

accent [ˈæksənt] [ák-sent], *s.* 1. Acento, la señal o virgulilla que se pone sobre una vocal, para denotar su pronunciación. **Written accent,** acento gráfico. 2. Acento, la modulación de la voz, y el tono que se pronuncia una palabra. **In broken accent,** con voz entrecortada. 3. El modo peculiar de pronunciar de las diferentes provincias en una misma nación. 4. *(Poét.)* Lenguaje, palabras. **To put the accent on,** acentuar, señalar, hacer hincapié en, recalcar.

accent, *va.* 1. Acentuar, pronunciar con el respectivo acento prosódico. 2. Acentuar, colocar la nota o signo que indica el acento.

accentual [ækˈsentjʊəl] [ak-sén-tual], *a.* Rítmico, que pertenece al acento o ritmo.

accentuate [ækˈsentjʊeɪt] [ak-sén-tueit], *va.* Acentuar, colocar los acentos según regla.

accentuation [ækˌsentjʊˈeɪʃən] [ak-sen-tuéi-shon], *s.* Acentuación.

accept [əkˈsept] [ak-sépt], *va.* Aceptar, admitir lo que se da, ofrece o encarga; recibir cariñosamente. **To accept a bill of exchange,** aceptar una letra de cambio. **To accept of,** aceptar.

acceptability [əkˌseptəˈbɪlətɪ] [ak-sep-ta-bí-li-ti], *s.* Aceptabilidad; agrado, gracia.

acceptable [əkˈseptəbl] [ak-sép-ta-bol], *a.* 1. Aceptable, grato, digno de aceptación. 2. Admisible. 3. Bien recibido.

acceptableness [əkˈseptəblnɪs] [ak-sep-téi-bol-nis], *s.* V. ACCEPTABILITY.

acceptably [əkˈseptəblɪ] [ak-sép-ta-bli], *adv.* Gustosamente, agradablemente.

acceptance [əkˈseptəns] [ak-sép-tans], *s.* Aceptación; buena acogida. **Acceptance of a bill of exchange,** aceptación de una letra de cambio.

acceptation [əkˈsepteɪʃən] [ak-sep-téi-shon], *s.* 1. Aceptación, recepción, recibimiento o recibo bueno o malo. 2. Acepción, sentido o significado en que se toma una palabra. 3. Aprobación, aplauso.

accepted [əkˈseptɪd] [ak-sép-tid] *a.* 1. Aceptado. 2. Corriente, normal. 3. Reconocido (a quality).

accepter [əkˈseptər] [ak-sép-tar], *s.* Aceptador. **Accepter of persons,** aceptador de personas.

acception [əkˈsepʃən] [ak-sép-shon], *s.* Acepción, el sentido o significado en que se toma alguna cosa.

acceptive [əkˈseptɪv] [ak-sép-tif], *a.* Pronto a aceptar.

acceptor [əkˈseptər] [ak-sép-tar], *s. (Com.)* Aceptante, el que acepta una letra de cambio.

access [ˈækses] [ak-sés], *s.* 1. Acceso, entrada, camino. **To give access to,** dar entrada a. 2. Acceso, modo de llegar a las personas o cosas. **Easy of access,** de fácil acceso, muy abordable. 3. Aumento, acrecentamiento, añadidura. 4. Accesión o acceso periódico de alguna enfermedad.

access road [ˈæksesˌrəʊd] [ák-ses-roud], *s.* Camino de acceso.

accessarily [ˈæksesərɪlɪ] [ak-se-sá-ri-li], *adv.* Accesoriamente.

accessariness [ˈæksesərɪnɪs] [ak-se-sá-ri-nis], *s.* Complicidad, la calidad de cómplice.

accessar [ˈæksesər] [ak-sé-sar], *s.* Cómplice, persona o cosa que se une a otra con alguna dependencia. *V.* ACCESSORY.

accessary [ækˈsesərɪ] [ak-sé-sa-ri] *a.* Accesorio, lo que se une a otra cosa o se agrega a ella con alguna dependencia.

accessible [ækˈsesɪbl] [ak-sé-si-bol], *a.* Accesible, lo que es de fácil acceso, aquello a que se puede llegar. **Accessible to pity,** capaz de compasión.

accession [ækˈseʃən] [ak-sé-shon], *s.* 1. Aumento, acrecentamiento. 2. Advenimiento, accesión. **Since the king's accession to the throne,** desde el advenimiento del rey al trono. 3. Acceso.

accessory [ækˈsesərɪ] [ak-sé-so-ri], *a.* Accesorio, contribuyente, secundario; que depende de lo principal. -*s.* 1. Persona o cosa que ayuda con alguna dependencia. 2. *(For.)* Cómplice. **Accessory after the fact,** encubridor, cómplice. **Accessory before the fact,** cómplice instigador. **Toilet accessories,** artículos de tocador.

accidence [ˈæksɪdəns] [ák-si-dans], *s.* Libro de rudimentos de la gramática.

accidence [ˈæksɪdəns] [ák-si-dans], *s.* Accidente, lance, contratiempo.

accident [ˈæksɪdənt] [ák-si-dent], *s.* 1. Accidente. **Accident insurance,** seguro contra accidentes. **Aircraft accident,** accidente de aviación. 2. Accidente o propiedad de una voz. 3. Accidente, casualidad, suceso imprevisto, incidente, lance. **A sad accident,** lance funesto. **By accident,** accidentalmente, casualmente. *(Gram.)* Desinencia, modo, caso, etc.

accidental [æksɪˈdentl] [ak-si-dén-tal], *s.* 1. Accidente, propiedad no esencial. 2. *(Mús.)* Bemol o sostenido accidental.

accidental, *a.* 1. Accidental, lo que no es esencial. 2. Casual, contingente.

accidentally [æksɪˈdentəlɪ] [ak-si-dén-ta-li], *adv.* Accidentalmente, por casualidad. **We met quite accidentally,** nos encontramos por pura casualidad.

accident-prone [ˈæksɪˈdentˈprəʊn] [ák-si-den-pron], *a.* Propenso a accidentes.

accipient [æksɪˈpɪənt] [ák-si-piant], *s.* Recibidor o recipiente; receptor.

accite [ˈæksɪt] [ák-sit], *va.* Llamar, citar. Convocar, reunir.

acclaim [ˈæklh] [a-kléim], *va.* y *vn.* Aclamar, aplaudir, ovacionar. **To acclaim a minister,** aclamar a un ministro.

acclamation, acclaim [ækləˈmeɪʃən] [a-kla-méi-shon], *s.* Aclamación, griterío o voces de la multitud en honor y aplauso de alguna persona, ovación.

acclamatory [ˈækləmətərɪ] [a-klá-ma-to-ri], *a.* Laudatorio.

acclimate [əˈklaɪmət] [á-kli-meit], *va.* Aclimatar, connaturalizar (persons).

acclimated [əˈklaɪmətd] [-akli-méi-tid], *pp.* y *a.* Aclimatado.

acclimation, acclimatization [əˈklaɪməʃən] [a-kli-méi-shon] [əˌklaɪmətaɪˈzeɪʃən] [a-kli-ma-tai-séi-shon], *s.* Aclimatación.

acclimatize [əˈklaɪmətaɪz] [a-klái-ma-taiz], *va.* Aclimatar, acostumbrar a otro clima; se dice de animales y plantas con motivo de la agencia humana. -*vn.* Aclimatarse los animales y plantas.

acclivity [əˈklɪvɪtɪ] [a-klí-vi-ti], *s.* Cuesta, rampa, subida, ladera.

acclivous, acclive [əˈklɪvəs] [əˈkliːv] [a-klívos] [a-klíf], *a.* Pendiente, que sube formando cuesta.

accolade [ˈækɒld] [á-ko-leid], *s.* 1. *(Mús.)* Corchete. Abrazadera vertical o barra gruesa. 2. *(Arq.)* Moldura curva de adorno. 3. Acolada, espaldarazo, parte del antiguo rito para armar a uno caballero.

accommodable [əˈkɒmədeɪbl] [a-ko-mo-déi-bol], *a.* Acomodable, lo que se puede acomodar; componible, concordable.

accommodableness [əˈkɒmədeɪblnɪs] [a-ko-mo-déi-bol-nis], *s.* Capacidad de acomodarse.

accommodate [əˈkɒmədeɪt] [a-kó-mo-deit], *va.* 1. Surtir, proveer o hacer alguna cosa como gracia o favor; socorrer, amparar. 2. Hospedar, alojar. 3. Acomodar, ajustar. 4. Reconciliar, componer. 5. (*Com.*) Prestar dinero. *-vn.* Conformarse. **To accommodate oneself with,** componerse con, conformarse a. 6. Caber, haber sitio para. **The car accommodates three people,** en el coche caben tres personas.

accommodate, *a.* Acomodado, apto.

accommodateness [əˈkɒmədeɪtnɪs] [a-ko-mo-déit-nis], *s.* Aptitud, acomodo.

accommodating [əˈkɒmədeɪtɪŋ] [a-ko-mo-déi-tin], *a.* 1. Acomodadizo. 2. Obsequioso, oficioso, servicial, galante.

accommodation [ə͵kɒməˈdeɪʃən] [a-ko-mo-déi-shon], *s.* 1. Comodidad, conveniencia. 2. Ajuste, compostura o concierto de alguna disputa. 3. Adaptación, idoneidad, reconciliación. 4. Alojamiento, habitación. **Book accommodation at the hotel,** reservar habitación en el hotel. 5. Cabida, capacidad, sitio, espacio. **Accommodation bill o note,** letra de cambio, aceptada sin recibir su valor para ayudar a algún amigo y sostener su crédito mercantil. Letra pro forma. **Accommodation train,** tren de escala. Puede ser también tren ómnibus. **Accommodation ladder** (*Mar.*) Escala real.

accommodator [əˈkɒmədeɪtəʳ] [a-ko-modéi-tar], *s.* El que maneja, ajusta o acomoda.

accompanable [əˈkʌmpəneɪbl] [a-kom-pá-ne-bol], *a.* Sociable.

accompanier [əˈkʌmpənɛːʳ] [a-kom-pá-niaʳ], *s.* Acompañador o compañero.

accompaniment [əˈkʌmpənɪmənt] [a-kom-pá-ni-ment], *s.* Acompañamiento.

accompanist [əˈkʌmpənɪst] [a-kóm-pa-nist], *s.* (*Mús.*) Acompañador, acompañante.

accompany [əˈkʌmpənɪ] [a-kóm-pa-ni], *va.* Acompañar, estar o ir en compañía de otro. *vn.* Asociarse; cohabitar.

accomplice [əˈkʌmplɪs] [a-kóm-plis], *s.* Cómplice, compañero en el delito.

accomplish [əˈkʌmplɪʃ] [a-kóm-plish], *va.* 1. Efectuar, completar. 2. Concluir, llevar a cabo. Satisfacer, saciar. 3. Cumplir, verificar. 4. Adornar, hermosear física o moralmente. **An accomplished mathematician,** un matemático consumado.

accomplishable [əˈkʌmplɪʃəbl] [a-kóm-pli-sha-bol], *a.* Capaz de ser cumplido, cumplidero; realizable.

accomplished [əˈkʌmplɪʃt] [a-kóm-plisht], *a.* Perfecto, cabal, acabado, completo, elegante, consumado, ileno de perfecciones.

accomplisher [əˈkʌmplɪʃəʳ] [a-kóm-pli-shaʳ], *s.* Perfeccionador, el que completa alguna cosa. Ejecutor.

accomplishment [əˈkʌmplɪʃmənt] [a-kóm-plish-ment], *s.* 1. Consumación o cumplimiento entero de alguna cosa. 2. Complemento, perfección, adquisición. En plural, talentos, conocimientos, prendas.

accompt [əˈkɒmt] [a-kómpt] *s.* (*ant.*) Cuenta V. ACCOUNT.

accomptant [əˈkɒmtənt] [a-kómp-tant], *s.* Contador. V. ACCOUNTANT.

accord [əˈkɔːd] [a-kórd], *va.* Ajustar, igualar una cosa con otra, acomodar, otorgar, conciliar, poner de acuerdo. *vn.* Acordar, concordar, convenir una cosa con otra; conciliar, acomodarse.

accord, *s.* 1. Acuerdo, convenio. 2. Acuerdo, unión de ánimos. 3. Buena inteligencia o armonía. **Of one's own accord,** espontáneamente. 4. Simetría. **With one accord,** unánimemente.

accordable [əˈkɔːdəbl] [akórdebol], *a.* Agradable, conforme.

accordance, accordancy [əˈkɔːdəns] [a-kór-dans], *s.* Conformidad, correspondencia de una cosa con otra; acuerdo, convenio, buena inteligencia. **In accordance with,** de acuerdo con, según, conforme a, con arreglo a, de conformidad con.

accordant [əˈkɔːdənt] [a-kór-dant], *a.* Acorde, conforme, propio, conveniente.

accordantly [əˈkɔːdəntlɪ] [a-kór-dan-tli], *adv.* Acordemente.

accorder [əˈkɔːdəʳ] [a-kór-daʳ], *s.* Ayudador, favorecedor.

according [əˈkɔːdɪŋ] [a-kór-din], *part.* Según, conforme. **According to,** Según, conforme a, en cumplimiento de. **According as,** *conj.* Según que, como.

accordingly [əˈkɔːdɪŋlɪ] [a-kór-din-li], *adv.* En conformidad, en efecto, de consiguiente.

accordion [əˈkɔːdɪən] [a-kór-dion], *s.* Acordeón, instrumento músico de viento, con fuelle y llaves. **Accordion pleating,** plisado de acordeón.

accordionist [əˈkɔːdɪənɪst] [a-kór-dio-nist] *s.* (*Mús.*) Acordeonista.

accost [əˈkɒst] [a-kóst], *va.* Saludar a uno yendo hacia él; trabar conversación, acercarse.

accostable [əˈkɒstbl] [a-kós-te-bol], *a.* Accesible, familiar, de fácil acceso, tratable, sociable.

accosted [əˈkɒstɪd] [a-kós-tid], *a.* (*Her.*) Acostado, lado a lado.

accouchement [əˈkuːʃmənt] [acóuchment], *s.* Parto.

accoucheur [əˈkuːʃəʳ] [a-ku-cháʳ], *s.* Comadrón, partero. V. MAN-MIDWIFE u OBSTETRICIAN.

accoucheuse [əˈkuːʃəʒe] [a-cu-cheus], *s.* Partera.

account [əˈkaʊnt] [a-káunt], *s.* 1. Cuenta, cálculo. **To settle accounts,** ajustar cuentas. **To keep an account,** tener cuenta abierta. 2. Caso, estimación o aprecio; dignidad, rango, consideración, respeto. 3. Informe, declaración, información; relación o narrativa de alguna cosa; motivo, modo. **On many accounts,** por muchos motivos. 4. Cómputo, manera de contar el tiempo; período. **The Julian account,** el período Juliano. **On no account,** de ninguna manera, por ningún concepto. **On account of,** por motivo de, por cuenta de. **Upon your account o for your sake,** por amor de usted **To turn to account,** a cargo de usted **Current account,** cuenta corriente. **Deposit account,** cuenta a plazo fijo. **Joint account,** cuenta indistinta. **To pay an account,** saldar una cuenta. **To pay on account,** pagar a cuenta, a buena cuenta. **Profit and loss account,** cuenta de ganancias y pérdidas. **People of no account,** gente de poca importancia.

account, *va.* 1. Tener, reputar, estimar, juzgar, considerar. **I account him handsome,** lo considero guapo. 2. Contar, numerar, computar. 3. Dar cuenta o señalar los motivos de alguna cosa, explicar el porqué. *-vn.* Responder; hacer patente, explicar alguna cosa. **To account for,** dar razón de, responder de.

accountability, accountableness [ə͵kaʊntəˈbɪlɪtɪ] [ə͵kaʊntəblˈnɪs] [a-kaun-ta-bí-li-ti] [a-kaun-téi-bol-nis], *s.* Responsabilidad, obligación de dar cuenta.

accountable [əˈkaʊntəbl] [a-káun-ta-bol], *a.* 1. Responsable, que está obligado a responder o satisfacer algún cargo. 2. Aquello de que se ha de dar o se puede dar cuenta o razón. Explicable.

accountancy [əˈkaʊntənsɪ] [a-káun-tan-si] *s.* Contabilidad.

accountant [əˈkaʊntənt] [a-káun-tant], *s.* 1. Tenedor de libros. 2. Contador; aritmético. **Accountant's office,** contaduría.

account-book [əˈkaʊntbʊk] [a-káunt-buk], *s.* Libro de cuentas.

accounted [əˈkaʊntɪd] [a-káun-tid], *pp.* Estimado, considerado, reputado, tenido por. **Accounted for,** de que ya se ha dado cuenta, o razón; que ya se ha tenido presente.

accounting [əˈkaʊntɪŋ] [akáuntin], *s.* 1. Contabilidad, el acto de contar o hacer cuentas. 2. Arreglo de cuentas.

Accounting-day [əˈkaʊntɪŋˈdeɪ] [a-káun-tin-dei], *s.* El día de ajuste de cuentas.

accouple [əˈkʌpl] [a-kápol], *va*. Unir, juntar, encadenar, acoplar, aparear.

accouplement [əˈkʌplmənt] [a-ka-pel-ment], *s*. Unión, ayuntamiento, pareja.

accourt [əˈkuːʳ] [a-kért], *va*. Cortejar, hacer la corte, galantear; recibir con cortesía, tratar bien.

accouter [əˈkuːtrə] [a-kú-tre], *va*. Aviar, equipar, vestir, ataviar.

accoutrement [əˈkuːtrəmənt] [a-ku-tre-ment], *s*. Avío, prevención, apresto, atavío, vestido, vestidura, ornamento, equipaje.

accredit [əˈkredɪt] [a-kré-dit], *va*. Dar crédito, favorecer, patrocinar, fomentar, acreditar, abonar una cantidad.

acreditation [əˌkredɪˈteɪʃən] [a-kre-di-téi-shon], *s*. Credencial, crédito.

accredited [əˈkredɪtɪd] [a-kré-di-tid], *pp*. Acreditado, abonado de confianza, confidente. *(Dipl.)* Autorizado.

accrescent [əˈkresnt] [a-kré-sent], *a*. Creciente, lo que va en aumento.

accretion [əˈkriːʃən] [a-kré-shon], *s*. Acrecentamiento, aumento. *(For.)* Acrecencia (derecho de).

accretive [əˈkriːtɪv] [a-kré-tif], *a*. Aumentativo, lo que aumenta o acrecienta; acrecentado, aumentado.

accroach [əˈkrəʊtʃ] [a-króuch], *va*. 1. Usurpar, v.g. tratándose de prerrogativas regias. 2. *(Des.)* Enganchar, traer a sí alguna cosa como gancho, agarrar, atraer a uno con maña.

accrue [əˈkruː] [akrú], *vn*. 1. Acrecentar, tomar incremento. 2. Resultar, provenir. **What profit do thence accrue?,** ¿qué ganancias resultan de eso? **Accrued interest,** interés acumulado.

accrument [əˈkruːmənt] [akrúment], *s*. Reclinación, acrecencia, aumento, acrecentamiento.

accubation [əˈkjuːbeɪʃən] [a-kiu-béi-shon], *s*. Reclinación. Postura que usaba la gente de algunos países recostándose para comer.

accumb [əˈkʌmb] [a-kámb], *vn*. Reclinarse o echarse para comer.

accumbent [əˈkʌmbənt] [a-kám-bent], *s*. El que está reclinado. *-a*. Reclinado para comer; apoyado sobre el codo.

accumulate [əˈkjuːnɪtl] [a-kiú-mu-leit], *va*. Acumular, amontonar, atesorar. *-vn*. Crecer, aumentarse.

accumulate, *a*. Juntado, acumulado, amontonado.

accumulation [əˌkjuːmjʊˈleɪʃən] [a-kiu-mu-léi-shon], *s*. Acumulación o amontonamiento. *-pl*. Ahorros.

accumulative [əˈkjuːmjʊlətɪv] [a-kiu-mú-la-tif], *a*. 1. Acumulativo. 2. Acumulado, amontonado, añadido.

accumulatively [əˈkjuːmjʊlətɪvlɪ] [a-kiu-mu-la-tív-li], *adv*. Acumulativamente.

accumulator [əˈkjuːnɪtr̩b̩ʳ] [-akiu-mu-léi-taʳ], *s*. Acumulador, amontonador, especialmente la batería o celda de acumulación; condensador.

accuracy [ˈækjʊrəsɪ] [a-kiú-ra-si], *s*. Cuidado, exactitud, diligencia, primor, esmero.

accurate [ˈækjʊrɪt] [a-kiú-reit], *a*. 1. Exacto, puntual. 2. Cabal, perfecto, primoroso. 3. Limado, pulido, acabado. **Accurate sciences,** las ciencias exactas.

accurately [ˈækjʊrɪtlɪ] [á-kiu-ret-li], *adv*. Exactamente, con exactitud, puntualmente, correctamente.

accurateness [ˈækjʊrɪtnɪs] [a-kiu-ret-nis], *s*. Exactitud, primor, puntualidad, precisión.

accurse [əˈkɜːs] [a-kérs], *va*. Maldecir, anatematizar, excomulgar.

accursed [əˈkɜːs] [a-kér-sid], *pp*. Maldito, maldecido. *-a*. Detestable, execrable, excomulgado, desventurado, perverso, infausto, fatal. **Accursed be,** maldito sea.

accusable [əˈkjuːsəbl] [a-kiú-sa-bol], *a*. Culpable, que puede ser acusado.

accusant [əˈkjuːsənt] [a-kiú-sant], *s*. Acusador.

accusation [əˈkjuːzeɪʃən] [a-kiu-séi-shon], *s*. 1. Acusación. 2. Cargo.

accusative [əˈkjuːsətɪv] [a-kiú-sa-tif], *s*. Acusativo, el cuarto caso en la declinación de los nombres latinos.

accusatory [əkjuːsətɔːrɪ] [a-kiu-sa-tó-ri], *a*. Acusatorio, lo que contiene algún cargo o acusación.

accuse [əˈkjuːz] [a-kiús], *va*. 1. Acusar, delatar, denunciar o manifestar el delito de otro. 2. Culpar, notar, tachar. 3. Censurar.

accuser [əˈkjuːsəʳ] [a-kiúsar], *s*. Acusador; denunciador, delator.

accustom [əˈkʌstəm] [a-kás-tom], *va*. Acostumbrar. *-vn*. Soler.

accustomable [əˈkʌstəməbl] [a-kas-to-me-bol], *a*. Acostumbrado; común, ordinario, habitual.

accustomably [əˈkʌstəməblɪ] [a-kas-to-ma-bli], *adv*. Acostumbradamente, según costumbre, habitualmente, frecuentemente, a menudo.

accustomarily [əˈkʌstəmərɪlɪ] [a-kas-to-mea-ri-li], *adv*. Acostumbradamente, como de costumbre, comúnmente, ordinariamente, según el uso.

accustomary [əˈkʌstəmərɪ] [a-kás-toma-ri], *a*. Acostumbrado, usual, ordinario.

accustomed [əˈkʌstəmd] [a-kás-tomd], *a*. Frecuente, usual, acostumbrado.

ace [eɪs] [éis], *s*. 1. Unidad; as, un punto de naipe o dado. 2. Migaja, parte pequeña de alguna cosa, partícula, átomo.

acentric [əˈsentrɪk] [a-sén-trik], *a*. Sin centro; no situado en el centro; no dirigido desde un centro.

acephala [əˈsefələ] [asé-fa-la], *s. pl*. Acéfalos, clase de moluscos, como la ostra.

acephalous [əˈsefələs] [a-sé-fa-los], *a*. 1. Acéfalo, lo que no tiené cabeza. 2. Deficiente al principio, como una línea de poesía.

acer [əˈseʳ] [é-ser], *s*. Arce, árbol. *V*. MAPLE.

acerate, acerated [əˈsereɪt] [əˈsereɪtɪd] [aseréit] [a-se-réi-tid], *a*. Puntiagudo, como una aguja.

acerb [əˈsɜːb] [a-sérb], *d*. Acerbo, ácido, agrio, áspero.

acerbate [əˈsɜːbeɪt] [a-sér-beit], *va*. Agriar, exasperar.

acerbity [əˈsɜːbɪtɪ] [a-sér-bi-ti], *s*. 1. Acerbidad. 2. Amargura, rigor, severidad, aspereza, crueldad, dureza, agrura, desabrimiento.

acerose [əˈserəʊs] [a-se-rous], *a*. 1. *(Bot.)* Aciculado. 2. Lleno de zurrón; aristado.

acerous [əˈserəs] [a-se-ros], *a*. 1. Que no tiene antenas, o las tiene rudimentarias. 2. Sin astras.

acesceny [əsesˈsenɪ] [aséseni], *s*. Agrura, acedía.

acescent [əˈsesnt] [a-sé-sent], *a*. Reputando, lo que empieza a tener punta de agrio.

acetabulum [ˈæsɪtəbələm] [a-se-tá-bu-lom], *s*. *(Anat.)* Acetábulo, cavidad cotiloidea (de la cadera). 2. Medida antigua de quince dracmas.

acetanilid [ˈæsɪtənɪlɪd] [a-si-ta-nil-id], *s*. Acetanilada, medicamento usado para aliviar la fiebre.

acetate [ˈæsɪteɪt] [á-si-teit], *s*. Acetato, sal formada con alguna base y ácido acético. **Acetate of copper,** cardenillo, verdegris.

acetic [əˈsetɪk] [a-sét-ik], *a*. Acético. **Acetic acid,** ácido acético.

acetification [əˈsetɪfɪˈkeɪʃən] [a-se-ti-fi-kéi-shon], *s*. Acetificación.

acetify [əˈsetɪfɪ] [a-sé-ti-fai], *va*. Acetificar; convertir en ácido acético.

acetimeter [əˈsetɪmiːtəʳ] [a-se-tí-me-taʳ], *s*. Acetímetro, instrumento usado para conocer la calidad del vinagre.

acetone [ˈæsɪtəʊn] [á-si-toun], *s*. Acetona; C3H6O: espíritu privacético; líquido incoloro, límpio y muy inflamable, que se obtiene por la destilación de algunos acetatos.

acetosity [ˈæsɪtəsɪtɪ] [a-si-tó-si-ti], *s*. *V*. ACIDITY.

acetous, acetose [ˈæsɪtəs] [a-sí-tous], *a*. Agrio, acedo, acetoso. **Acetous acid,** *(Quím.)* vinagre; nombre antiguo y erróneo.

acetyl [ˈæsɪtɪl] [a-sí-til] *s*. *(Quím.)* Acetilo.

acetylene ['æsɪtɪliːn] [a-sí-ti-lin], *s*. Acetileno, compuesto gaseoso de carbono e hidrógeno, C2H2. Es gas incoloro con olor peculiar y desagradable. **Acetylene torch,** soplete oxiacetilénico.

ache [eɪk] [éik], *s*. Dolor continuo, mal. **Headache,** dolor de cabeza. **Toothache,** dolor de muelas. **Earache,** dolor de oídos. **Stomach ache,** dolor de estómago.

ache, *vn*. Doler. **My head aches,** me duele la cabeza. **To ache for, to be aching to,** anhelar ansiar.

achievable [əˈtʃiːvəbl] [a-chí-va-bol], *a*. Ejecutable, hacedero, factible.

achievance [əˈtʃiːvəns] [a-chí-vans], *s*. Ejecución; hazaña, hecho.

achieve [əˈʃiːv] [a-chíf], *va*. 1. Ejecutar, acabar o perfeccionar alguna cosa, 2. Ganar, obtener.

achievement [əˈtʃiːvmənt] [a-chíf-ment], *s*. 1. Ejecución, el acto de ejecutar alguna cosa; hazaña o acción heroica. 2. Timbre o insignia de un escudo de armas, que denota alguna proeza o acción heroica.

achiever [əˈtʃiːvəʳ] [a-chí-vaʳ], *s*. Ejecutor, hacedor. *(Met.)* Vencedor.

Achilles' tendon [əˈkɪliːzˌtendən] [a-kí-lis-ten-don], *s*. *(Anat.)* Tendón de Aquiles.

aching ['eɪkɪŋ] [éi-kin], *s*. Dolor, desasosiego, incomodidad.

achlamydeous [əklaˈmɪdəs] [a-kla-mí-dos], *a*. *(Bot.)* Desnudo; sin cáliz ni corola.

achor [eɪkəʳ] [éikar], *s*. Acores, especie de herpe. Tiña mucosa.

achromatic [ækrəʊˈmætɪk] [a-kro-má-tik], *a*. *(Opt.)* Acromático; se dice del lente preparado de manera que no deja ver colores del iris.

achromatize [ækrəʊˈmətaɪz] [akrómatais], *va*. Acromatizar; hacer acromático.

acicular [əˈsɪkələʳ] [a-sí-ka-laʳ], *a*. Aciculado, acicular, alesnado, en forma de pequeñas agujas.

acid ['æsɪd] [á-sid], *a*. ácido, agrio, acedo. *(Fig.)* Mordaz, agrio, áspero. **An acid remark,** una observación áspera.

acidic [əˈsɪdɪk] [a-sí-dik], *a*. *(Quím.)* ácido, agrio.

acidifiable [əˈsɪdɪfaɪəbl] [a-si-di-fi-éi-bol], *a*. Acidificable.

acidification [ˌəsɪdɪfɪˈkeɪʃən] [a-si-di-fi-kéi-shon], *s*. Acidificación.

acidify [əˈsɪdɪfaɪ] [a-sí-di-fai], *va*. 1. Acedar, hacer ácido, agriar. 2. *(Quím.)* Acidular.

acidimeter [əˈsɪdɪmiːtəʳ] [a-si-dí-me-taʳ], *s*. Acidímetro, aparato para determinar la fuerza de los ácidos.

acidity, acidness [əˈsɪdɪti] ['əsɪdɪnɪs] [a-sí-di-ti] [á-sid-nis], *s*. Agrura, agrio, acedía, acidez.

acidosis [əˈsɪdəʊsɪs] [a-si-dóu-sis], *s*. *(Med.)* Asecencia, acidez, acidismo.

acid-proof ['æsɪdpruːf] [á-sid-pruf] *a*. A prueba de ácidos.

acid test [əˈsɪdtest] [á-sid-test] *s*. *(Quím.)* Prueba del ácido. *(Fig.)* Prueba decisiva.

acidulae [əˈsɪdjʊlæ] [a-sí-du-la], *s.pl*. Aguas minerales que contienen una gran cantidad de gas ácido carbónico, llamadas aguas aciduladas.

acidulate [əˈsɪdjut] [a-sí-du-leit], *va*. 1. Acidular, poner ligeramente ácido. 2. Amargar, causar penas, poner de mal humor.

acidulous [əˈsɪdjʊləs] [a-sí-do-los], *a*. Agrio, de la naturaleza de los ácidos, acídulo.

acinus [əˈsɪnəs] [á-si-nos] *s*. *(Bot.) (Anat.)* Acino.

ack ack ['ækˈæk] [ak-ak], *s*. Defensa antiaérea o contra aviones. *V.* ANTIAIRCRAFT.

acknowledge [əkˈnɒlɪdʒ] [ak-nó-lich], *va*. 1. Reconocer o confesar la verdad de alguna cosa. **To acknowledge oneself beaten,** darse por vencido. 2. Confesar algún delito. 3. Confesar con agradecimiento algún beneficio recibido, ser agradecido. 4. Declarar confesando plenamente. 5. Acusar recibo. **Please acknowledge receipt of this letter,** Sírvase usted acusar recibo de esta carta.

acknowledging [əkˈnɒlɪdʒɪŋ] [ak-nó-li-chin], *a*. Reconocido, agradecido al beneficio que se ha recibido.

acknowledgment [əkˈnɒlɪdʒmənt] [ak-nó-lich-ment], *s*. 1. Reconocimiento, el acto de reconocer o conceder la verdad de alguna cosa. 2. Confesión de alguna culpa. 3. Gratitud, reconocimiento, agradecimiento. **In acknowledgment of,** en reconocimiento de. 4. Concesión, consentimiento.

aclinic [əˈlɪnɪk] [a-klí-nik], *a*. Aclínico, magnético.

acme ['ækmɪ] [ak-mí], *s*. Cima, colmo, cumbre, apogeo. **The acme of glory,** el apogeo de la gloria. *(Met.)* Cenit, complemento, último punto de una cosa.

acne ['æknɪ] [ak-ní], *s*. Acne, enfermedad cutánea, frecuente en la cara durante la adolescencia.

acolothist, acolyte ['ækələθɪst] ['əkəlaɪt] [a-kó-lo-zist] [á-ko-lait], *s*. Acólito; monaguillo.

aconite ['ækənaɪt] [á-ko-nait], *s*. *(Bot.)* Acónito, hierba venenosa; planta medicinal.

aconitine ['əkɒnɪtɪn] [a-kó-ni-tin] *s*. *(Quím.)* Aconitina.

acorn ['eɪkɔːn] [éi-korn], *s*. Bellota.

acorned ['eɪkɔːnd] [ei-kór-nid], *a*. 1. Que tiene bellotas, cargada de su fruto (la encina). 2. Alimentado con bellotas.

acotyledon [ækəˈtɪlədən] [a-ko-tí-le-don], *s*. Acotilédone; vegetal desprovisto de cotilédones u hojas seminales.

acoustic [əˈkʌstɪk] [a-kás-tik], *a*. Acústico, lo perteneciente al oído.

acoustics [əˈkʌstɪks] [a-kás-tiks], *s*. 1. Acústica, ciencia que trata del oído y de los sonidos en general. 2. Acústicos, los medicamentos que se aplican al oído.

acquaint [əˈkweɪnt] [a-kuéint], *va*. 1. Imponer, instruir de raíz, familiarizar. 2. Informar, dar parte o aviso, poner al corriente. 3. Advertir, comunicar, hacer saber, avisar. 4. Dar a conocer, instruir, **He will acquaint you,** él le informará a Ud.

acquaintance [əˈkweɪntəns] [a-kuéin-tans], *s*. 1. Conocimiento, familiaridad. **I have no acquaintance with him,** no tengo trato con él. 2. Conocido, la persona que tiene trato con otra, sin que llegue a verdadera amistad. **He is an old acquaintance of mine,** es antiguo conocido mío. 3. Inteligencia, conocimiento. **Further acquaintance,** mayor conocimiento. 4. Relaciones, amistades. **A wide acquaintance,** muchas relaciones.

acquaintanceship [əˈkweɪntənʃɪp] [a-kuéin-tan-ship], *s*. Conocimiento; trato de una persona con otra.

acquainted [əˈkweɪntɪd] [a-kuéin-ted], *a*. Conocido; impuesto, instruido, informado. **I am not acquainted with the circumstances of that affair,** yo no estoy al corriente de las circunstancias de ese asunto. **To make acquainted,** hacer saber, informar.

acquest [əˈkwest] [a-kuést], *s*. *(Des.)* 1. Adquisición, el acto de adquirir y la misma cosa adquirida. 2. *(Ant.)* Conquista.

acquiesce [ækwɪˈes] [a-kuis], *vn*. Allanarse o asentir a alguna cosa; someterse, consentir, conformarse, aceptar.

acquiescence [ækwɪˈesns] [a-kui-sens], *s*. Aquiescencia, asenso, consentimiento, conformidad; sumisión.

acquiescent [ækwɪˈesnt] [a-kui-sent], *a*. Condescendiente, cómodo, conforme, sumiso.

acquirable [əˈkwaɪəbl] [a-kuí-ra-bol], *a*. Adquirible; ganable.

acquire [əˈkwaɪəʳ] [a-kuáiaʳ], *va*. Adquirir, ganar, alcanzar, aprender; obtener algo, ya buscándolo, ya comprándolo, o por medio de la práctica o del propio esfuerzo. **To acquire a taste for,** tomar gusto a.

acquired [əˈkwaɪəd] [a-kuáiad], *pp*. Adquirido. **An acquired fortune,** bienes adquiridos o no heredados.

acquirement [əˈkwaɪəmənt] [a-kuáia-ment], *s*. Adquisición, -*pl*. Conocimientos, saber.

acquirer [əˈkwaɪəʳ] [a-kuáiaʳ], *s*. Adquiridor.

acquiring [əˈkwaɪrɪŋ] [a-kuái-rin], *s*. Adquisición, la acción y efecto de adquirir.

adquisition [ækwɪˈzɪʃən] [a-kui-sí-shon], *s*. Adquisición, la cosa adquirida.

acquisitive [ˌækwɪˈzɪtɪv] [a-kuí-si-tif], *a*. 1. Adquirido, logrado, ganado. 2. Codicioso.

acquisitively [ækwɪˈzɪtɪvlɪ] [a-kuí-si-ti-vli], *adv.* Por adquisición.

acquisitiveness [ækwɪˈzɪtɪvnɪs] [a-kuí-si-tif-nis], *s.* Adquisividad, disposición a adquirir.

acquit [əˈkwɪt] [a-kuít], *va.* 1. Liberar, poner en libertad. 2. Descargar, absolver, dar por libre al reo demandado civil o criminalmente. 3. Desempeñar, cumplir, exentar, pagar. **To acquit oneself well,** desempeñar bien su obligación o cometido. **To acquit a debt.** pagar una deuda.

acquitment [əˈkwɪtmənt] [a-kuít-ment], *s.* Absolución, descargo, pago, satisfacción (of a debt).

acquittal [əˈkwɪtl] [a-kuí-tal], *s.* Absolución, la acción de absolver de los cargos hechos a un acusado; descargo.

acquittance [əˈkwɪtəns] [a-kuí-tens], *s.* 1. Descargo de una deuda. 2. Carta de pago. Finiquito o instrumento en que el acreedor confiesa haber recibido del deudor la cantidad que le debía.

acre [ˈeɪkəʳ] [éi-kar], *s.* 1. Acre, medida de tierra. 2. Campo; en plural, terrenos, finca. **God's acre,** campo santo, cementerio.

acreage [ˈeɪkrɪdz] [éi-krich], *s.* Acres (o acras) colectivamente. Superficie en acres.

acred [əˈkrɪd] [éi-krid], *a.* Hacendado.

acrid [əˈkrɪd] [á-krid], *a.* Acre, mordaz, picante o áspero al paladar, irritante, corrosivo.

acridity, acridness [əˈkrɪdɪtɪ] [əˈkrɪdnɪʃ] [á-krid-nis], *s.* Acritud, acrimonia.

acrimonious [əˈkrɪməʊnɪəs] [a-kri-mó-nius], *a.* Acre, corrosivo; sarcástico, sañudo; mordaz.

acrimoniously [ækrɪˈməʊnɪəslɪ] [a-kri-mó-nius-li], *adv.* Con acrimonia, con aspereza.

acrimoniousness [ækrɪˈməʊnɪəsnɪs] [a-kri-mó-nius-nis], *s.* Aspereza de genio, acritud.

acrimony [ˈækrɪmənɪ] [a-krí-mo-ni], *s.* 1. Acrimonia, acritud. 2. Aspereza de genio.

acritical [əˈkrɪtɪkl] [a-krí-ti-kal], *a.* Acrítico, sin crisis.

acritude [əˈkrɪtjuːd] [á-kri-tiud], *s.* Acrimonia, amargura; aspereza de genio, mordacidad de palabras.

acroatic [əkrəʊˈətɪk] [a-krouá-tik], *a.* Acroático, recóndito; de difícil inteligencia.

acrobat [ˈækrəbæt] [a-kró-bat], *s.* Acróbata, volatín.

acrobatic [ˈækrəbætɪk] [a-kro-bá-tik], *a.* Acrobático.

acrobatics [ˈækrəbætɪks] [a-kro-bá-tiks] *s.* Acrobacia.

acrocephalic [ˈækrəsɪfəlɪk] [a-kro-si-fá-lik] **acrocephalous** [ˈækrəsɪfələs] [a-kro-sí-fa-lus] *a.* Acrocéfalo.

acrogen [ˈækrədzɪn] [a-kró-yin], *s.* Planta del orden superior de las criptógamas, como el helecho.

acrogenous [ˈækrədzɪnəs] [a-kró-yi-nos], *a.* que crece por el vértice o extremidad superior; se dice de ciertas plantas criptógamas y algunos zoófitos.

acromegalia [ˈækrəməgælɪə] [a-kro-me-gá-lia] **acromegaly** [ˈækrəməgælɪ] [akromégali] *s. Med.* Acromegalia.

acromion [ˈækrəmɪəm] [a-kró-miom], *s.* Acromio, apófisis que forma la parte más elevada del omoplato.

acronycal [ˈækrənɪkl] [a-kró-ni-kal], *a. (Astr.)* Acrónico, acronicto.

acronycally [ˈækrənɪklɪ] [a-kró-ni-kli], *adv.* Acrónicamente.

acronym [ˈækrənɪm] [a-kró-nim] *s.* Siglas.

acropired [ˈækrəpaɪəd] [a-kro-páiad], *pp.* y *a.* Espigado, germinado, brotado.

acropolis [ˈækrəpəlɪs] [a-kró-po-lis], *s.* Acrópolis, la ciudadela de un pueblo griego, especialmente la de Atenas.

across [əˈkrɒs] [a-krós], *adv.* De través o en postura atravesada, al través, de una parte a otra. *-prep.* De medio a medio, por medio de. Del otro lado de. **The house across the road,** la casa del otro lado de la calle. A través. **Across the fields,** a través de los campos. **To go across,** atravesar, cruzar.

across-the-board [əˈkrɒsθəˈbɔːd] [a-krós-de-bórd], *a.* 1. Perteneciente a todas las clases y categorías, sin excepción. 2. Puesto en combinación para ganar segundo puesto (races).

acrostic [əˈkrɒstɪk] [a-krós-tik], *s.* Poema acróstico. *-a.* Acróstico.

acroter [əˈkrɒtəʳ] [a-kró-taʳ], *s.* Acrotera, uno de los pedestales pequeños, que se ponen en medio o a los lados de un frontispicio y sobre los cuales se colocan las figuras.

acrylic [əˈkrɪlɪk] [a-krí-lik], *a.* Acrílico.

act [ækt] [ákt], *vn.* 1. Obrar, ejercer fuerza mecánica, producir movimiento o efecto. 2. Hacer, estar Qcupado en alguna cosa; ponerse en acción. 3. Conducirse, portarse. 4. Fingir, simular. **To act dead,** fingirse muerto. *-va.* 1. Hacer un papel, remedar, representar. **To act the buffoon,** hacer el bufón o gracioso. **Don't act the fool,** no hagas el tonto. 2. Obrar, causar algún efecto, mover, ejecutar. **To act upon,** (a) Obrar a impulso de. (b) Influir. (c) Ejercer, desempeñar. **To act the part of a judge,** ejercer las funciones de juez.

act, *s.* 1. Hecho, acción bien o mal ejecutada, efecto. 2. Acto o jornada de una comedia. 3. Acta, Ley, decreto. **Act on petition,** recurso de urgencia. **Act of oblivion,** amnistía. **Act of faith,** acto de fe. **Act of bankruptcy,** declaración de quiebra. **Caught in the act,** cogido in fraganti.

acting [ˈæktɪŋ] [ák-tin], *s.* 1. Acción; representación, obra. 2. Interino, en funciones, en ejercicio.

actina [ˈæktɪn] [ak-tin], *s.* Actina.

actinia [ˈæktɪnɪə] [ak-tí-nia], *a.* Clase de pólipos cuyos tentáculos se abren como los de las flores.

actinic or actinical [ˈæktɪnɪk] [ˈæktɪnɪkl] [ac-tí-nik] [ac-tí-ni-kal], *a.* Actínico, capaz de producir cambios químicos (sun rays).

actinism [ˈæktɪnɪzm] [ac-ti-nísm], *s.* Actinismo, calidad de actínico.

action [ˈækʃən] [ák-shon], *s.* 1. Acción, operación, ocupación. **Always in action,** siempre en movimiento, activo. 2. Hecho, acción. 3. Acción, la serie de sucesos relacionados entre sí que forman el argumento de un poema o drama. 4. Acción, gesticulación. 6. Proceso. 7. Influencia. **He died in action,** murió en acto de servicio. **To take action,** tomar medidas, intentar una acción judicial. **To put into action,** poner en práctica (un plan).

actionable [ˈækʃənəbl] [ák-sho-na-bol], *a.* Punible, criminal, procesable.

actionably [ˈækʃənəblɪ] [ak-shó-na-bli], *adv.* De un modo procesorio.

actionary, actionist [ˈækʃənərɪ] [ˈækʃənɪst] [ak-shó-na-ri] [ák-sho-nist], *s.* Accionista.

action-taking [ˈækʃənˈteɪkɪŋ] [ak-shon-téi-kin], *a.* Litigioso.

actitation [ˈæktɪˈteɪʃən] [ak-si-téi-shon], *s.* Acción rápida y frecuente.

activate [ˈæktɪveɪt] [ák-ti-veit], *va.* Activar, hacer activo. *(Quím.)* Activar.

activator [ˈæktɪveɪtəʳ] [ak-ti-véitaʳ], *s. (Quím.)* Activador.

active [ˈæktɪv] [ak-tíf], *a.* 1. Activo, lo que tiene actividad para obrar. 2. Activo, lo que obra. 3. Diligente, eficaz, ocupado. 4. ágil, pronto, ligero. **Active volcano,** volcán en actividad. **On active service,** en servicio activo.

active list [ˈæktɪvˈlɪst] [ák-tif-list] *s. (Mil.)* Escala activa.

actively [ˈæktɪvlɪ] [ak-tív-li], *adv.* Activamente, ágilmente, vivamente; eficazmente.

activeness [ˈæktɪvnɪs] [ák-tif-nis], *s.* Agilidad, soltura, actividad, prontitud.

activism [ˈæktɪvɪzm] [ák-ti-vi-sem] *s.* Activismo.

activist [ˈæktɪvɪst] [ák-ti-vist] *a./s.* Activista.

activity [ˈæktɪvɪtɪ] [ak-tí-vit-i], *s.* Actividad; agilidad, vivacidad, vigor. **Field of activity,** esfera de actividad.

actor [ˈæktəʳ] [ák-taʳ], *sm.* 1. Agente, la persona que obra. 2. Cómico; actor, el que representa o hace papel en los teatros. 3. Actor, Demandante en juicio. **Leading actor,** primer actor.

actress [ˈæktrɪs] [ák-tres], *sf.* Comedianta, actriz, cómica.

actual [ˈæktjʊəl] [ák-chual], *a.* 1. Actual, práctico. 2. Actual, lo que realmente existe o es efectivo; lo que no es meramente potencial. 3. Efectivo. **I'd like to have the actual figures,**

me gustaría tener las cifras mismas. **In actual fact,** en realidad.

actuality [æktjʊˈælɪtɪ] [ák-chuá-li-ti], s. Actualidad, el estado actual de alguna cosa.

actualization [ˈæktjʊəlaɪˈzeɪʃən] [ak-chua-lai-séi-shon] s. Realización, actualización.

actualize [ˈæktjʊəlaɪz] [ák-chua-lais] va. Realizar, actualizar, describir con realismo.

actually [ˈæktjʊəlɪ] [ák-chua-li], adv. De hecho, en efecto, realmente, en realidad, verdaderamente.

actualness [ˈæktjʊəlnɪs] [ák-chual-nis], s. Actualidad.

actuarial [ˌæktjʊˈɛərɪəl] [ak-chuá-rial] **actuarian** [æktjɛərɪən] [ak-chuá-rian] a. Actuarial.

actuary [ˈæktjʊərɪ] [ák-chua-ri], s. 1. El empleado que tiene a su cargo los cómputos y las tarifas en las compañías de seguros. 2. Actuario, escribano, secretario, registrador.

actuate [ˈæktjʊeɪt] [ák-tueit] va. Mover, excitar, animar, poner en acción. **Actuated by anger, he killed his enemy,** movido por la ira, mató a su enemigo.

actuation [ˈæktjʊeɪʃən] [ak-tuéi-shon], s. Operación.

acuity [əˈkjuːɪtɪ] [á-kui-ti], s. Agudeza, sutileza en el corte o punta de armas, instrumentos, etc.

aculeate [əˈkjuːlɪeɪt] [a-kiú-leit], a. 1. Punzante, puntiagudo. 2. Erizado, espinoso.

acumen [ˈækjʊmen] [a-kiú-men], s. 1. Punta aguzada. 2. Agudeza, penetración, ingenio, vivacidad, chispa, perspicacia.

acuminate [ˈækjʊmɪneɪt] [a-kiú-mi-neit], vn. Rematar en punta, terminar en cono. -va. Aguzar, afilar.

acuminate, a. (Biol.) Aguzado, que va disminuyendo en forma de punta; terminado en punta.

acuminated [ˈækjʊmɪneɪtɪd] [a-kiú-mi-nei-ted], a: Punzante, puntiagudo.

acumination [ˈækjʊmɪneɪʃən] [a-kiu-mi-néi-shon], s. Punta aguda.

acupuncture [ˈækjʊpʌŋktʃər] [a-kiu-púk-cha], s. Acupuntura; inserción de agujas en carne viva como medio curativo. Se emplea mucho y desde muy antiguo por los chinos y japoneses.

acute [əˈkjuːt] [a-kiút], a. 1. Agudo, delgado, sutil, penetrante. 2. Agudo, ingenioso, perspicaz, de vivo ingenio. 3. (Med.) Agudo, sutil.

acute, s. (Gram.) Acento agudo.

acute, va. Pronunciar algo con acento agudo.

acutely [əˈkjuːtlɪ] [a-kiút-li], adv. Agudamente, con agudeza.

acuteness [əˈkjuːtnɪs] [a-kiút-nis], s. 1. Agudeza, sutileza o delicadeza en los filos, cortes o puntas de las armas o instrumentos. 2. Perspicacia o viveza de ingenio, talento, penetración. 3. Violencia de una enfermedad.

acyclic [æˈsaɪklɪk] [a-sái-klik] a. Acíclico.

-ad, sufijo. Hacia, en la dirección de. **Centrad,** hacia el centro.

-ad (U.S. Fam.) anuncio.

adage [ˈædɪdʒ] [á-dich], s. Adagio o refrán.

adagial [əˈdaːdʒɪəl] [a-dá-yial], a. Proverbial.

adagio [əˈdaːdʒɪəʊ] [a-dá-yio], s. Adagio, término usado en la música para denotar lentitud. También composición músca en este tiempo. Es voz italiana y quiere decir lentamente.

Adam [ˈædəm] [á-dam], s. 1. Adán, el primer hombre; el género humano. 2. La naturaleza humana depravada, no regenerada. **Adam's ale,** (Fam.) Agua.

Adam's apple [ˈædəmsˈɛrpl] [á-dams-éi-pol] 1. Nuez de la garganta. 2. (Bot.) Especie de limón. 3. Especie de banana grande.

adamant [ˈædəmənt] [á-da-mant], s. 1. Mineral o metal muy duro, real o imaginario. 2. (Des.) Diamante. 3. (Des.) Piedra imán. 4. (Poét.) Dureza.

adamantine [ˌædəˈmæntaɪn] [a-da-man-táin], **adamantean** [ˌædəˈmæntiːn] [a-da-man-tín], a. 1. Diamantino, duro como el diamante. 2. (Poét.) Impenetrable, adamantino.

adapt [əˈdæpt] [a-dápt], va. Adapter, acomodar o aplicar una cosa a otra; ajustar, cuadrar. **To adapt a novel for the theater,** adaptar una novela al teatro.

adaptabilily [əˌdæptəˈbɪlɪtɪ] [a-dap-ta-bí-li-ti], s. Adaptabilidad.

adaptable [əˈdæptəbl] [a-dáp-te-bol], a. Adaptable, acomodable.

adaptation [ˌædæpˈteɪʃən] [a-dap-téi-shon], **adaption** [ædæpʃən] [adápshon], s. Adaptación; aplicación de una cosa a otra.

adapter [əˈdæptər] [a-dáp-ta'] **adaptor** [əˈdæptər] [adápta'] s. (Elect.) Enchufe múltiple, adaptador.

adaptive [əˈdæptɪv] [a-dáp-tif], a. Capaz de adaptación; perteneciente o a propósito de ella.

adays [əˈdeɪs] [a-déis], adv. Actualmente, ahora, al presente.

add [æd] [ad], va. Añadir, aumentar, acrecentar, juntar, contribuir. **To add up,** sumar. **His explanation does not add up,** su explicación no tiene sentido.

addend [əˈdɛnd] [á-dend] s. (Mat.) Sumando.

addendum [əˈdendəm] [a-dén-dom], s. Apéndice, adición o suplemento. **Addenda,** adiciones, añadiduras.

adder [ˈædər] [á-da'], s. Sierpe, serpiente, culebra.

adder's grass [ˈædeːˈgræs] [á-das-gras], **adder's wort** [á-das-uért], s. (Bot.) Escorzonera.

adder's tongue [ˈædeːˈtʌŋ] [ádas-tong], s. (Bot.) Lengua de sierpe. Ofioglosa.

addible [əˈdɪbl] [á-di-bol], a. Lo que se puede añadir o sumar.

addibility [ədɪˈbɪlɪtɪ] [a-di-bí-li-ti], s. La propiedad o posibilidad de ser añadido o sumado.

addict [ˈædɪkt] [á-dikt], s. 1. Adicto, enviciado. 2. Adepto, partidario. **Drug addict,** toxicómano.

addict, va. Dedicar, destinar, aplicar. **To addict oneself to vice,** Entregarse a los vicios.

addicted [əˈdɪktɪd] [a-dík-tid], a. y pp. Dado, entregado, afecto a, apasionado por, adicto.

addictedness [əˈdɪktɪdnɪs] [a-dík-tid-nis], s. Inclinación, propensión.

addiction [əˈdɪkʃən] [a-dík-shon], s. Dedicación, entrega, rendimiento, sacrificio. Disposición, gusto, vicio.

adding machine [ˈædɪŋməˈʃiːn] [á-dín-ma-chín], s. Calculadora, máquina de calcular, sumadora.

addition [əˈdɪʃən] [a-dí-shon], s. 1. Adición, agregación. 2. Añadidura, aditamiento. 3. (Arit.) Suma, adición. **In addition to,** además de. **In addition,** además. **In addition to which,** por lo demás.

additional [əˈdɪʃənl] [a-dí-sho-nal], a. Adicional. -s. Aditamento.

additionally [əˈdɪʃənlɪ] [a-dí-sho-na-li], adv. Adicionalmente, además.

additive [ˈædɪtɪv] ad'-i-tiv], a. Que ha de ser añadido; que sirve para aumentar. Casi lo mismo que additory.

additory [ədɪˈtərɪ] [a-dí-to-ri], a. Aumentativo.

addle [ˈædl] [á-dol], a. Huero, vacío, vano, sin sustancia, infecundo, estéril; podrido.

addle, va. Hacer huero o vacío; podrir; esterilizar, hacer estéril.

addle-pated [ˈædlˈpætɪd] [á-dol-péitid], **addle-headed** [ˈædlhedɪd] [a-del-jé-did], a. Negado, totalmente inepto para alguna cosa; cabeza hueca o vacía.

address [əˈdres] [á-dres], va. 1. Prepararse o disponerse para alguna cosa 2. Hablar, interceder o rogar; recurrir, hacer presente alguna cosa de palabra; dirigir la palabra, dirigirse a uno, arengar. 3. Obsequiar. 4. vn. Encararse, engestarse. **To address the king,** Hablar al rey o suplicarle. **To address a letter,** Dirigir una carta, poner el sobrescrito.

address, s. 1. Dirección, señas de una casa. 2. Discurso, plática. **Cable address,** dirección cablegráfica. **Change of address,** cambio de dirección.

addressee [əˈdresiː] [a-dre-sí], s. Destinatario (letter, goods, etc.).

addresser [əˈdresər] [a-dré-sa'], s. Suplicante, exponente.

addressing machine [əˈdresɪŋməˈʃiːn] [a-dré-sin-ma-shín], s. Máquina para dirigir sobres, tarjetas, etc.

adduce [əˈdjuːs] [a-diús], va. Traer, llevar o asignar alguna cosa para juntarla a otra; alegar, aducir, citar.

adducent [əˈdjuːsənt] [a-diú-sant], a. (Anat.) Aductores, músculos que sirven para recoger o conducir hacia dentro algunas partes del cuerpo.

adducible [əˈdjuːsɪbl] [a-diú-si-bol], a. Aducible, que se puede aducir o alegar.

adduct [əˈdʌkt] [a-dákt] va. (Med.) Efectuar la aducción.

adduction [əˈdʌkʃən] [a-dák-shon], s. 1. (Anat.) Aducción. 2. Alegación.

adductive [əˈdʌktɪv] [a-dák-tif], a. Aductivo.

adductor [əˈdʌktər] [a-dák-ta^r], s. Aductor (músculo). V. ADDUCENT.

addulce [əˈdjuːls] [a-diúls], va. (Des.) Dulcificar, endulzar.

adelphous [əˈdelfəs] [a-dél-fos], a. Adelfo; se dice de los estambres cuando están pegados por sus filamentos formando uno o varios grupos. Se usa comúnmente como sufijo, v.g. *diadelphous*, es decir, en dos grupos.

ademption [əˈdemʃən] [a-dém-shon], s. Privación, revocación, disminución.

adenitis [ədenˈaɪtɪs] [a-de-nái-tis], s. Inflamación de una glándula.

adenography [æˈdɪnəgræfɪ] [a-di-nó-gra-fi], s. Adenografía, parte de la anatomía que trata de las glándulas.

adenoid [æˈdɪmɔɪd] [á-di-noid], a. y s. Glandiforme. Como sustantivo, se usa en plural.

adept [ˈædept] [a-dép'], s. Adepto, el que está iniciado y el que es consumado en un arte. a. Versado, cursado; profundo, consumado; iniciado.

adequacy [ˈædɪkwəsɪ] [a-dí-kua-si] s. Adecuación, suficiencia, exactitud.

adequate [ˈædɪkwɪt] [á-di-kueit], va. Adecuar, asemejar, igualar.

adequate, a. Adecuado, proporcionado.

adequately [ˈædɪkwɪtlɪ] [á-di-kueit-li], adv. Adecuadamente, proporcionadamente.

adequateness [ˈædɪkwɪtnɪs] [a-di-kuéit-nis], **adequation** [a-di-kuéi-shon], s. Adecuación o proporción exacta, igualdad.

adhere [ədˈhɪər] [a-día^r], vn. 1. Adherirse, unirse, avenirse o allegarse al partido o dictamen de otro. 2. Pegarse. 3. Aficionarse.

adherence [ədˈhɪərəns] [a-día-rans], **adherency** [ədˈhɪərənsɪ][a-día-ran-si], s. 1. Adhesión, tenacidad, viscosidad; calidad de adhesivo o pegajoso. 2. Adhesión, adherencia.

adherent [ədˈhɪərənt] [a-día-rant], a. 1. Adherente, pegajoso, lo que se pega. 2. Adherente, el que adhiere.

adherent, s. Adherente, secuaz, partidario, parcial.

adherently [ədˈhɪərəntlɪ] [a-día-ran-tli], adv. Con adhesión, parcialmente.

adherer [ədˈhɪərə] [a-día-ra^r], s. El que adhiere, partidario, parcial.

adhesion [ədˈhiːʒən] [a-dí-shon], s. Adhesión. (Med.) Adherencia.

adhesive [ədˈhiːzɪv] [a-dí-sif], a. Adhesivo, adherente, pegajoso. **Adhesive plaster, tape,** esparadrapo, cinta adhesiva.

adhesively [ədˈhiːzɪvlɪ] [a-di-síf-li], adv. Tenazmente, en unión estrecha.

adhesiveness [ədˈhiːzɪvnɪs] [a-di-síf-nis], s. Tenacidad, viscosidad.

adiabatic [ədɪəˈbætɪk] [a-dia-bá-tik] a. Adiabático.

adipocere [ədɪpoˈsɪər] [a-di-po-sía^r], s. Adipocira; grasa de los cadáveres; jabón amoniacal producido por la descomposición de las materias animales enterradas o sumergidas.

adipose [ədˈɪpəs] [á-di-pos], a. Adiposo, seboso.

adiposity [ədˈɪpəsɪtɪ] [a-di-pó-si-ti] s. Adiposidad.

adit [ˈædɪt] [á-dit], s. Mina, conducto subterráneo; entrada casi horizontal de una mina. (Mex.) Socavón.

adjacency [əˈdʒeɪsənsɪ] [ad-ja-sen-si], s. Adyacencia, proximidad, contigüidad, vecindad.

adjacent [əˈdʒeɪsənt] [ad-já-sent], a. Adyacente, contiguo, vecino. -s. Alguna cosa contigua o adyacente.

adjection [əˈdʒeɪkʃən] [ad-jék-shon], s. Adición, añadidura.

adjectival [əˈdʒektɪvəl] [ad-jék-ti-val], a. Del adjetivo, como adjetivo.

adjective [əˈdʒektɪv] [ad-jéck-tif], s. Adjetivo.

adjectively [əˈdʒektɪvlɪ] [ad-jéck-tif-li], adv. Adjetivado.

adjoin [əˈdʒɔɪn] [ad-jóin], va. Juntar, asociar, unir. -vn. Lindar, estar contiguo o cercano.

adjoining [əˈdʒɔɪnɪŋ] [ad-jói-nin], a. Contiguo, inmediato.

adjourn [əˈdʒɜːn] [ad-jén], va. Diferir, alargar, retardar; citar, emplazar; remitir; levantar una sesión. -vn. Separarse para volverse a reunir en un día señalado, retirarse.

adjournment [əˈdʒɜːnmənt] [ad-jérn-ment], s. 1. Citación, llamamiento, emplazamiento, emplazo, comparendo. 2. Suspensión de una deliberación diferida hasta un día señalado.

adjudge [əˈdʒʌdz] [ad-chách], va. 1. Adjudicar; dar una recompensa; decidir, juzgar. 2. Sentenciar a una pena, condenar. 3. Juzgar, decretar. -vn. Pronunciar la sentencia.

adjudgment [əˈdʒʌdzmənt] [ad-chách-ment], s. Adjudicación.

adjudicate [əˈdʒuːdɪkeɪt] [ad-yú-di-keit], va. Determinar judicialmente; adjudicar, declarar a favor de alguno la pertenencia de alguna cosa. V. ADJUDGE. -vn. Ejercer las funciones de juez; llegar a una decisión judicial.

adjudication [əˈdʒuːdɪkeɪʃən] [ad-yu-di-kéi-shon], s. Adjudicación.

adjunct [ˈædʒʌŋkt] [ad-yánkt], s. Adjunto, lo que está unido con otra cosa; compañero, colega, asociado.

adjunct, a. Adjunto, unido o arrimado, junto, contiguo.

adjunction [ˈædʒʌŋkʃən] [ad-yánk-shon], s. 1. Unión. 2. Adición.

adjunctive [ˈædʒʌŋktɪv] [ad-yánk-tif], s. 1. El que junta o une. 2. Adjunto o agregado. -a. Lo que junta.

adjunctively [ˈædʒʌŋktɪvlɪ] [ad-yánk-tif-li], adv. Juntamente.

adjunctly [ˈædʒʌŋktlɪ] [ad-yánk-tli], adv. Consiguientemente.

adjuration [ədʒʊˈreɪʃən] [ad-yu-réi-shon], s. El acto y modo de juramentar la forma del juramento; conjuro.

adjure [əˈdʒʊər] [ad-yúar], va. Juramentar, tomar juramento a otro, proponiéndole la fórmula o términos en que ha de jurar; conjurar.

adjurer [əˈdʒʊər] [ad-yúrar], s. El que toma el juramento.

adjust [əˈdʒʌst] [ad-yást], va. Ajustar, arreglar, acomodar, acordar, terminar, componer.

adjuster [əˈdʒʌstər] [ad-yás-ta^r], s. El que arregla o ajusta; mediador; tasador.

adjustment [əˈdʒʌstmənt] [ad-yást-ment], s. Ajuste, ajustamiento, aliño, arreglo.

adjustor [əˈdʒʌstər] [ad-yás-ta^r], s. Músculo que une ciertas partes; por ejemplo, el de los braquiópodos.

adjutancy [ˈædʒətənsɪ] [ad-yás-tan-si], s. 1. Ayudantía, el oficio o empleo de ayudante. 2. Hábil manejo, dirección acertada de algún cargo o negocio.

adjutant [ˈædʒətənt] [ad-yú-tant], s. Ayudante.

adjuvant [ˈædʒʊvənt] [ad-yú-vant], a. Lo que ayuda, es útil o provechoso. -s. Ayudante. Auxiliar.

ad-lib [ædˈlɪb] [ád-lib], a. **Ad libitum,** a voluntad, improvisado. -va. Improvisar, decir a voluntad, sin atenerse a lo escrito. (actores, oradores.)

adman [ˈædmæn] [ád-man], s. (Com.) Agente publicitario, agente de publicidad.

admeasurement [æˈdmeʒəmənt] [ad-mé-se-ment], s. La medida, arte o práctica de medir según reglas.

admensuration [æˌdmenjʊəˈreɪʃən] [ad-men-siu-réi-shon], s. Mensura o medida, medición.

administer [ədˈmɪnɪstər] [ad-mí-nis-ta^r], va. 1. Administrar, suministrar, dar, surtir o proveer de lo que se necesita. **To administer justice,** administrar justicia. 2. Administrar, servir o ejercer algún ministerio o empleo. 3. Regir, manejar, gobernar, contribuir. **To administer an oath,** tomar juramento.

administerial [əd'mɪnɪstərɪəl] [ad-mi-nís-te-rial], *a.* Administrativo, perteneciente a la administración.

administrable [əd'mɪnɪsreɪbl] [admi-nis-tréi-bol], *a.* Lo que se puede administrar.

administrant [əd'mɪnɪstənt] [ad-mi-nís-trant], *a.y s.* Manejador, director de un negocio, jefe ejecutivo; administrador\ra.

administrate [əd'mɪnɪsreɪt] [ad-mí-nis-treit], *va.* Dar o administrar remedios.

administration [əd,mɪnɪs'reɪʃən] [ad-mi-nis-tréi-shon], administración pública.

administrative [əd'mɪnɪsrətɪv] [ad-mi-nís-tra-tif], *s.* 1. (*For.*) Tenedor de bienes, fidei-comisario abintestato. 2. Administrador, el que administra. 3. El que administra los sacramentos. 4. El que oficia en el rito divino. 5. Gobernante.

administratorship [əd,mɪnɪsreɪtə'ʃɪp] [ad-mi-nis-tréi-to-ship], *s.* Administración, el empleo de administrador.

administratrix [əd'mɪnɪstərɪks] [ad-mi-nís-tra-triks], *sf.* 1. Administradora, la que administra. 2. La que gobierna. 3. Tenedora de bienes, fidei-comisaria abintestato.

admirable ['ædmərəbl] [ád-mi-ra-bol], *a.* Admirable, digno de admiración.

admirableness ['ædmərəblnɪs] [ad-mi-réi-bol-nis], **admirability** ['ædmərəbɪlɪti] [ad-mi-ra-bí-li-ti], *n.* Excelencia de alguna cosa.

admirably ['ædmərəbli] [ád-mi-ra-bli], *adv.* Admirablemente.

admiral ['ædmərəl] [ád-mi-ral], *s.* 1. Almirante, el que manda una armada o escuadra. **Admiral of the red,** almirante de la escuadra roja; **admiral of the white,** almirante de la blanca; **admiral of the blue,** almirante de la azul: tres grados que antes existían en la escuadra inglesa, así llamados por los colores de sus banderas respectivas. **Vice-Admiral,** Vicealmirante. **Rear-Admiral,** Contraalmirante o jefe de escuadra. 2. Almiranta, la nave en la que va el almirante.

admiralship ['ædmərəlʃɪp] [ád-mi-ral-ship], almirantía.

admiralty ['ædmərəlti] [ád-mi-ral-ti], *s.* Almirantazgo, tribunal en que se determinan los asuntos de la marina. **The Lords Commissioners of the Admiralty,** El consejo o junta del almirantazgo.

admiration [ædmə'reɪʃən] [ad-mi-réi-shon], *s.* Admiración.

admire [əd'maɪər] [ad-maiaᵣ], *va.* 1. Admirar. 2. Amar, tener amor y afición a alguna persona o cosa. *-vn.* Admirarse de alguna cosa.

admirer [əd'maɪərər] [ad-mai-raᵣ], *s.* 1. Admirador. 2. Amante, apasionado. **He is a great admirer of painting,** es muy aficionado a la pintura.

admiringly [əd'maɪərɪŋli] [ad-mai-rin-li], *adv.* Estupendamente, admirablemente.

admissibility [əd,mɪsə'bɪlɪti] [ad-mi-si-bí-li-ti], *s.* Admisibilidad.

admissible [əd'mɪsəbl] [admí-si-bol], *a.* Admisible, aceptable; permitido, lícito.

admission [əd'mɪʃən] [ad-mí-shon], *s.* Admisión, entrada, ingreso. **Admission fee,** Cuota de inscripción, matrícula. **The management reserves the right to refuse admission,** reservado el derecho de admisión. **By his own admission,** por confesión.

admissive [əd'mɪsɪv] [ad-mí-sif], *a.* Lo que implica o concede admisión.

admit [əd'mɪt] [ad-mít], *va.* 1. Admitir, recibir o dar entrada. **This place admits five hundred people,** este local admite quinientas personas. 2. Admitir o recibir para algún empleo. 3. Conceder o asentir a alguna proposición. **Ticket which admits two,** entrada para dos personas. 4. Admitir, conceder o permitir. 5. Confesar, reconocer. **He admits (to) stealing the car,** reconoce haber robado el coche.

admittance [əd'mɪtəns] [ád-mi-tans], *s.* 1. Entrada, permiso. 2. Entrada, el derecho de entrar en alguna parte. 3. Derechos de entrada. 4. Concesión de una proposición. 5. Admisión. **No admittance,** prohibida la entrada.

admittedly [əd'mɪtɪdli] [ad-mí-tid-li] adv. Cierto es que.

admitter [əd'mɪtər] [ad-mí-taᵣ], *s.* Admitidor, el que admite, o concede alguna proposición.

admittible [əd'mɪtɪbl] [ad-mí-ti-bol], *a.* Admisible.

admix [əd'mɪks] [ad-miks], *va.* Mezclar, juntar, unir o incorporar una cosa con otra.

admixtion [əd'mɪksʃən] [ad-míkshon], *s.* Mezcla, incorporación de una cosa con otra.

admixture [əd'mɪkstʃər] [ad-míks-cha], *s.* Mezcla, el ingrediente mezclado con otro o incorporado a él.

admonish [əd'mɒnɪʃ] [ad-mó-nish], *va.* Amonestar, prevenir, advertir, reprender, exhortar.

admonisher [əd'mɒnɪʃər] [ad-mó-ni-shaᵣ], *s.* Amonestador.

admonishment [əd,mɒnɪʃ'mənt] [ad-mó-nish-ment], *s.* Advertencia, prevención, amonestación, represión.

admonition [,ædmɒ'nɪʃən] [ad-mo-ní-shon], *s.* 1. Consejo, aviso. 2. Represión, amonestación, admonición.

admonitioner [,ædmɒ'nɪʃənər] [ad-mo-ní-sho-naᵣ], *s.* Admonitor o monitor.

admonitor [əd'mɒnɪtər] [ad-mó-ni-taᵣ], *n.* Admonitor, censor.

admonitory, admonitive [əd'mɒnɪtəri] [əd'mɒnɪtɪv] [ad-mo-ní-to-ri] [ad-mó-ni-tif], *a.* Admonitorio.

admove [əd'muːv] [ad-múv], *va.* Arrimar o acercar una cosa a otra.

adnascence [ædnəsəns] [ad-ná-sens], *s.* Adhesión de partes entre sí por toda su superficie.

adnascent ['ædnəsənt] [ad-ná-sent], **adnate** ['ædneɪt] [ad-néit], *a.* 1. (*Bot.*) Adnato, íntimamente adherido. 2. Enterado.

adnoun [əd'nɑʊn] [ad-náun], *s.* (*Gram.*) Adjetivo.

ado [ə'duː] [a-dú], *n.* 1. Trabajo, dificultad. 2. Bullicio, baraúnda, tumulto, ruido. 3. Pena, fatiga. **Much ado about nothing,** nada entre dos platos, o, más es el ruido que las nueces; poco mal y bien quejado. **I had much ado to do it,** lo hice a duras penas. **Without more ado,** sin más preámbulos

adobe [ə'dəʊbi] [a-dóu-bi], *s.* Adobe, ladrillo sin cocer.

adolescence [ædeɬs] [a-dó-le-sens] o **adolescency** [ædeɬsi] [a-dó-le-sen-si], *s.* Adolescencia.

adolescent [ædeɬt] [a-dó-le-sent], *a.y s.* Adolescente.

Adolph ['ædɒlf] [á-dolf] N. Adolfo.

adonic [ə'dɒnɪk] [a-dó-nik], *a.* Verso adónico que consta de un dáctilo y un espondeo.

Adonis [ə'dəʊnɪs] [a-dó-nis] N. Adonis.

adoors [ə'dɔːs] [a-dórs], *adv.* A la puerta o a las puertas.

adopt [ə'dɒpt] [a-dópt], *va.* Adoptar, prohijar, ahijar. **To adopt a child,** adoptar a un niño.

adopter [ə'dɒptər] [a-dóp-taᵣ], *s.* Prohijador, padre adoptivo, o madre adoptiva.

adoption [ə'dɒpʃən] [a-dóp-shon], *s.* Adopción, aprobación. **Country of adoption,** patria adoptiva.

adoptive [a-dóp-tif], *a.* 1. Adoptivo. El que adopta o prohija. **He was her adopter** o **adoptive father,** él era su padre adoptivo. **She was his adoptive daughter,** ella era su hija adoptiva. 2. Adoptante, el que adopta.

adorable [ə'dɔːreɪbl] [a-dó-rei-bol], *a.* Adorable.

adorableness [ə'dɔːreɪblnɪs] [a-do-réi-bol-nes], *s.* Adoración, mérito.

adorably [ə'dɔːrəbli] [a-dó-ra-bli], *adv.* Adorablemente.

adoral [ə'dɔːrəl] [a-dó-ral], *a.* Perteneciente a la boca o situado cerca de ella. *V.* ABORAL.

adoration [,ædɔː'reɪʃən] [a-do-réi-shon], *s.* 1. Adoración. 2. Incienso, adoración política o séquito por adulación o interés. 3. Respeto.

adore [ə'dɔːr] [a-dóᵣ], *va.* 1. Adorar, honrar y reverenciar con culto externo religioso. 2. Adorar, amar con extremo, idolatrar.

adorer [ə'dɔːrər] [a-dó-raᵣ], *s.* 1. Adorador. 2. (*Coloq.*) Amante.

adorn [əˈdɔːrn] [a-dórn], *va.* Adornar, ornar, embellecer, ataviar.

adorn, *s.* Adorno, atavío, ornamento, ornato. -*a.* Adornado, ataviado.

adorning [əˈdɔːrnɪŋ] [a-dór-nin], *s.* Adorno, Decoración.

adornment [əˈdɔːrnmənt] [a-dórn-ment], *s.* Adorno, atavío, gala.

adown [əˈdaʊn] [a-dáun], *adv.* Bajo, abajo, en el suelo, en tierra.

adown, *prep.* Abajo, hacia abajo.

adragant [əˈdrəgænt] [a-drá-gant], *s.* Adraganto, tragacanto.

adrenal [əˈdriːnl] [a-drí-nal], *a. (Med.)* Suprarrenal.

adrenalin, adrenaline [əˈdrenəlɪn] [a-drí-na-lin], *s. (Med.)* Adrenalina.

Adrian [ˈeɪdrɪən] [éi-drian] Adrián.

Adriatic Sea [ˌeɪdrɪˈætɪkˈsiː] [ei-driá-tik-sí] Mar Adriático.

adrift [əˈdrɪft] [a-dríft], *adv.* Flotando, a merced de las olas; a la ventura, a la deriva. **To turn someone adrift,** abandonar a uno a su suerte. **To break adrift,** romper las amarras. **To be all adrift,** ir a la deriva, no saber por dónde se anda.

adrip [əˈdrɪp] [a-dríp], *a.* Que está goteando.

adroit [əˈdrɔɪt] [a-dróit], *a.* Diestro, hábil.

adroitly [əˈdrɔɪtlɪ] [a-dróit-li], *adv.* Hábilmente, diestramente.

adroitness [əˈdrɔɪtnɪs] [a-dróit-nes], *s.* Destreza, habilidad, prontitud.

adry [əˈdraɪ] [a-drái], *adv.* Sediento.

adscititious [ˌædsɪˈtɪʃəs] [ad-sí-ti-shos], *a.* Completivo, lo que sirve para completar otra cosa; aumentado, añadido, interpuesto.

adstriction [əˈdstrɪkʃən] [ads-trík-shon], *s.* Astricción. V. ASTRICTION.

adulate [ˈædjuːt] [á-diu-leit], *va.* Adular, lisonjear, servilmente.

adulation [ˌædjuˈfbn] [a-diu-léi-shon], *s.* Adulación, lisonja, servil; alabanza exagerada y no sincera.

adulator [ˈædjutbr] [a-diuléi-taʳ], *s.* Adulador; parásito, lisonjero.

adulatory [ˈædjutbrɪ] [a-diú-la-to-ri], *a.* Adulatorio, lisonjero, cumplimentero, adulador.

adulatress [ˈædjolətrɪs] [a-diú-la-tris], *s.* Aduladora, lisonjera.

adult [ˈædʌlt] [á-dalt], *a. y s.* 1. Adulto, el que ha llegado al término de la adolescencia, mayor de edad. 2. Llegado a su mayor crecimiento o desarrollo.

adulteness [ˈædʌltnɪs] [á-dalt-nes], *s.* Edad adulta.

adulterant [əˈdʌltərənt] [a-dál-te-rant], *s.* 1. Adulterador, la persona que adultera; falsificador. 2. Lo que se usa para falsificar.

adulterate [əˈdʌltəreɪt] [a-dál-te-reit], *vn.* Adulterar, cometer adulterio. -*va.* Adulterar, corromper o mezclar con alguna cosa heterogénea, falsificar, viciar; sofisticar.

adulterate, *a.* 1. Adulterado. 2. Adulterado, corrompido o mezclado con alguna cosa extraña; falsificado.

adulterately [əˈdʌltəreɪtlɪ] [a-dál-te-reit-li], *adv.* 1. Adulterinamente. 2. Adulteradamente.

adulterateness [əˈdʌltəreɪtnɪs] [a-dál-te-ret-nes], *s.* Corrupción, contaminación.

adulteration [əˌdʌltəˈreɪʃən] [a-dal-te-réi-shon], *s.* Adulteración, corrupción, falsificación.

adulterer [əˈdʌltərəʳ] [a-dál-te-raʳ], *sm.* Adúltero.

adulteress [əˈdʌltərɪs] [a-dál-te-res], *sf.* Adúltera.

adulterine [əˈdʌltəriːn] [a-dál-te-rin], *s.* Hijo adulterino. -*a.* Espurio.

adulterous [əˈdʌltərəs] [a-dál-te-ros], *a.* Adulterino, espurio.

adultery [əˈdʌltərɪ] [a-dál-te-ri], *s.* 1. Adulterio. 2. Corrupción.

adumbrant [əˈdʌmbrənt] [a-dám-brent], *a.* 1. Bosquejado, trazado; lo que representa o da una idea, aunque imperfecta de la semejanza de una cosa con otra. 2. Sombreado ligeramente.

adumbrate [əˈdʌmbreɪt] [a-dam-bréit], *va.* Esquiciar, formar un esquicio o diseño de alguna cosa; bosquejar, sombrear, delinear.

adumbration [ˌædʌmˈbreɪʃən] [a-dam-bréi-shon], *s.* Esquicio, esbozo, trazo, diseño, rasgo; bosquejo o borrón de un trabajo en la pintura o escritura.

aduncate [əˈdʌnkeɪt] [a-dan-keit], *vn.* Encorvarse como un garfio. -*a.* Encorvado, torcido a manera gancho o pico de halcón.

aduncity [ˈædʌnsɪtɪ] [a-dán-si-ti], *s.* Corvadura, curvadura, la propiedad de ser o estar corvo o encorvado; sinuosidad.

aduncous [ˈædʌnkəs] [a-dán-kos], *a.* Corvo, encorvado, torcido, ganchoso; sinuoso, adunco.

adusk [əˈdʌsk] [a-dásk], *adv.* A la hora del crepúsculo, o en la oscuridad.

adust [əˈdʌst] [a-dást], *a.* 1. Adusto; tostado o requemado, consumido. 2. Moreno, como tostado por el sol; curtido. -*adv.* En el polvo; polvoriento.

adusted [əˈdʌstɪd] [a-dás-tid], *a.* Quemado o tostado al fuego; caliente.

adustion [əˈdʌsʃən] [a-dá-shon], *s.* Adustión, quemadura, inflamación.

ad valorem [ˌædˈvæləɒrəm] [ad-va-ló-rem], *(Com.)* Por avalúo o valoración.

advance [ədˈvɑːns] [ad-váns], *va.* 1. Avanzar. 2. Adelantar, promover. **They advanced the wedding date,** adelantaron la fecha de la boda. 3. Adelantar, mejorar; elevar, poner a mayor altura, o en más alto rango. **They advanced him to general,** le ascendieron a general. 4. Acelerar, apresurar. 5. Adelantar o anticipar dinero, pagar adelantado. 6. Proponer, ofrecer, insinuar. 7. Encarecer, hacer subir el precio de una cosa. **He advanced his price by fifty per cent,** aumentó el precio en un cincuenta por ciento. -*vn.* 1. Adelantar, hacer progresos; ir adelante. 2. Subir de valor o precio.

advance, *s.* 1. Avance. 2. Adelanto, paga adelantada. 3. Adelantamiento, mejora, adelanto, aprovechamiento, progreso. 4. Suplemento, préstamo. 5. Requerimiento de amores; insinuación. **A technical advance,** un adelanto técnico. **To make the first advances to,** dar los primeros pasos hacia.

advanced [ədˈvɑːnst] [ad-vánsd] *a.* Avanzado, adelantado. **Advanced ideas,** ideas avanzadas. **Advanced in years,** entrado en años.

advancement [ədˈvɑːnsmənt] [ad-váns-ment], *s.* 1. Adelantamiento, progresión. 2. Progreso; promoción. 3. Subida, prosperidad. 4. Elevación, promoción, ascenso. **The advancement of science,** el avance de la ciencia.

advancer [ədˈvɑːnsəʳ] [ad-ván-saʳ], *s.* 1. Promotor, impulsor. 2. Protector; adelantador; el que avanza.

advantage [ədˈvɑːntɪdʒ] [ad-ván-tich], *s.* 1. Ventaja, superioridad, preponderancia. 2. Ganancia, provecho, aprovechamiento, beneficio, lucro. 3. Ocasión favorable. 4. Sobrepaga, provecho excesivo. 5. Prerrogativa, comodidad. 6. Ventaja (tenis).

advantage, *va.* 1. Adelantar, ganar. 2. Remunerar. 3. Promover. **To take advantage of,** aprovecharse de, valerse de; engañar.

advantageable [ədˈvɑːntɪdʒbl] [ad-ván-ti-cha-bol], *a.* Provechoso, ganancioso.

advantage ground [ədˌvɑːntɪdʒˈgraʊnd] [ad-ván-tich-graund], *s.* Puesto ventajoso; situación favorable.

avantaged [ədˈvɑːntɪdʒd] [ad-ván-ti-cht], *a.* Adelantado, ventajoso.

advantageous [ˌædvɑːnˈteɪdʒəs] [ad-van-tí-chos], *a.* Ventajoso, útil, provechoso.

advantageously [ˌædvɑːnˈteɪdʒəslɪ] [ad-van-tí-chos-li], *adv.* Ventajosamente, con ventaja o utilidad.

advantageousness [ˌædvɑːnˈteɪdʒəsnɪs] [ad-ván-ti-chosnes], *s.* Ventaja, utilidad, conveniencia.

advene [ædˈviːn] [ad-vín], *vn.* Venir, arrimarse o añadirse una cosa a otra; acceder.

advenient [ædˈviːnɪənt] [ad-ví-nient], *a.* Sobreañadido, accesorio, adviniente. *V.* ADVENTITIOUS.

advent [ˈædvənt] [ád-vent], *s.* Adviento, las cuatro semanas que preceden a la festividad del Nacimiento de Jesús. 2. Venida o llegada.

adventitious [ˌædvənˈtɪʃəs] [ad-van-tí-shos], *a.* 1. Adventicio, lo que sobreviene por casualidad; extraño, exterior. 2. *(Med.)* Adventicio, no hereditario. 3. *(Bot.)* Formado sin orden, o en lugar insólito (espontáneo). 4. *(Biol.)* Accidental, que se presenta fuera de la habitación o el terreno natural. *V.* ADVENTIVE.

adventitiously [ˌædvənˈtɪʃəslɪ] [ad-van-tí-shos-li], *adv.* Accidentalmente.

adventive [ædˈventɪv] [ad-ván-tif], *a.* 1. *(Biol.)* Advenedizo, es decir, sólo parcialmente naturalizado o aclimatado. 2. Accidental, casual.

adventual [ædˈventwəl] [ad-ván-chual], *a.* 1. Relativo al Adviento. 2. Casual.

adventure [ædˈventʃər] [ad-ván-chuaʳ], *s.* 1. Aventura, casualidad, contingencia; lance. 2. Expedición o empresa rodeada de peligros y contingencias, riesgo; designio. 3. Ancheta, pacotilla, porción corta de mercaderías que se lleva o envía de un lugar a otro para su venta o despacho. **The spirit of adventure,** el espíritu de la aventura. *va.* Aventurar. *vn.* Aventurarse.

adventurer [ædˈventʃərər] [ad-ván-chu-raʳ], *s.* 1. Aventurero, el que busca aventuras.

adventuresome [ædˈventʃəsʌm] [ad-vén-cha-som], *a.* V. ADVENTUROUS.

adventurous [ædˈventʃərəs] [ad-vén-chu-ros], *a.* 1. Animoso, valeroso, esforzado, intrépido, arriesgado. 2. Aventurado, peligroso. 3. Osado, atrevido.

adventurously [ædˈventʃərəslɪ] [ad-vén-chu-ros-li], *adv.* Arriesgadamente, arrojadamente.

adventurousness [ædˈventʃərəsnɪs] [ad-vén-chu-ros-nes], **adventuresomenes** [ædˈventʃərəˌsemnɪs] [ad-vén-chua-som-nes], *s.* Intrepidez, arrojo, temeridad, osadía.

adverb [ˈædvɜːb] [ad-vérb], *s.* Adverbio, una de las partes de la oración.

adverbial [ˈædvɜːbɪəl] [ad-vér-bial], *a.* Adverbial, lo perteneciente al adverbio.

adverbially [ˈædvɜːbɪəlɪ] [advérbiali], *adv.* Adverbialmente.

adversary [ˈædvɜːsərɪ] [ad-vér-sa-ri], *s.* Adversario, contrario, enemigo, antagonista.

adversative [ˈædvɜːsətɪv] [ad-vér-sa-tif], *a.* Adversativo.

adverse [ˈædvɜːs] [ad-vérs], *a.* 1. Adverso, contrario, opuesto. 2. Adverso, desgraciado.

adversely [ˈædvɜːslɪ] [ad-vérs-li], *adv.* Adversamente, desgraciadamente; al contrario.

adverseness [ˈædvɜːsnɪs] [ad-vérs-nes], *s.* Oposición, resistencia.

adversity [ˈædvɜːsɪtɪ] [ad-vér-si-ti], *s.* Adversidad, suceso adverso, desgracia, miseria, calamidad, infortunio.

advert [ˈædvɜːt] [ad-vért], *vn.* Atender, cuidar o tener cuidado, hacer referencia. **I advert to his discourse,** me estoy refiriendo a su discurso. *-va.* Cuidar, aconsejar, considerar atentamente, advertir, notar.

advertence [ˈædvɜːtəns] [ad-vér-tans], **advertency** [ˈædvɜːtənsɪ] [ad-vér-tan-si], *s.* Atención, cuidado, consideración.

advertent [ˈædvɜːtənt] [ad-vér-tant], *a.* Atento, vigilante.

advertize [ˈædvɜːtaɪz] (G. B. **advertise**) [ád-ver-tais], *va.* 1. Avisar, informar, advertir. 2. Dar aviso al público, noticiar, poner o publicar anuncios. *-vn.* Hacer publicidad o propaganda. Poner un anuncio. **To advertize for,** buscar por medio de anuncios.

advertizement [ˈædvɜːtaɪzmənt] (G. B. **advertisement**) [ad-vér-tis-ment], *s.* 1. Noticia, aviso, anuncio. 2. Aviso al público; advertencia o aviso en los periódicos. **Classified advertizements,** anuncios por palabras.

advertizer [ˈædvɜːtaɪzəʳ] (G.B. **advertiser**) [ad-ve-tái-saʳ], *s.* 1. Avisador. 2. Cartel, anuncio, papel o periódico por cuyo medio se da algún aviso al público.

advertizing [ˈædvɜːtaɪzɪŋ] (G.B. **advertising**) [ad-ver-tái-sin], *s.* 1. Publicidad. 2. Propaganda. **Advertizing media,** Medios de publicidad.

advice [ədˈvaɪs] [ad-váis], *s.* 1. Consejo, el dictamen que se da o toma; consultación, deliberación. 2. Aviso, noticia. 3. Consulta. 4. Conocimiento, reflexión. 5. Advertencia. **To take legal advice,** consultar a un abogado. **I took his advice,** seguí su consejo.

advisability [ədˌvaɪzəˈbɪlɪtɪ] [ad-vai-sa-bí-li-ti], *s.* Prudencia, cordura; conveniencia.

advisable [ədˈvaɪzəbl] [adváisebol], *a.* Prudente, conveniente, propio.

advisableness [ədˈvaɪzəblnɪs] [ad-vai-sa-bol-nis], *s.* Prudencia, cordura, conveniencia, propiedad.

advise [ədˈvaɪz] [ad-váis], *va.* 1. Aconsejar, dar consejo. 2. Avisar, informar, advertir, enterar, dar noticia. *-vn.* 1. Aconsejarse, pedir o tomar consejo. 2. Considerar, deliberar, examinar. **To advise with,** aconsejarse con o de, consultar.

advised [ədˈvaɪzd] [ad-váist], *a.* 1. Avisado, advertido, prudente. 2. Premeditado, deliberado, discurrido, considerado. **To keep advised,** tener al tanto o al corriente.

advisedly [ədˈvaɪzdlɪ] [ad-váis-li], *adv.* Deliberadamente, prudentemente.

advisedness [ədˈvaɪzdnɪs] [ad-váis-nes], *s.* Cordura, juicio, reflexión, prudencia, deliberación.

advisement [ədˈvaɪzmənt] [ad-váis-ment], *s.* 1. Consejo, parecer, dictamen. 2. Prudencia, circunspección. 3. Deliberación, consideración.

advisor [ədˈvaɪzəʳ] (G.B. **adviser**) [ad-vái-saʳ], *s.* Consejero, aconsejador. **Legal adviser,** asesor jurídico.

advising [ədˈvaɪzɪŋ] [ad-vái-sin], *s.* Consejo, aviso.

advisory [ədˈvaɪzərɪ] [ad-vái-so-ri], *a.* Consultor, autorizado para dar su parecer, que tiene consejo.

advocacy [ˈædvəkəsɪ] [ad-vó-ka-si], *s.* Vindicación, defensa, apología, abogacía.

advocate [ˈædvəkɪt] [ád-vo-keit], *va.* Abogar, defender, sostener, interceder, mediar.

advocate, *s.* 1. Abogado, letrado. 2. Intercesor, medianero, favorecedor, defensor, protector.

advocation [ˈædvəkeɪʃən] [ad-vo-kéi-shon], *s.* Vindicación; patronato, apelación.

advolution [ˈædvəljuʃən] [ad-vo-lú-shon], *s.* Desarrollo o crecimiento hacia alguna cosa o algún estado.

adynamia [ˈædɪnæmɪə] [a-di-ná-mia], *s.* Adinamia, debilidad de las fuerzas vitales.

adynamic [ˈædɪnæmɪk] [a-di-ná-mik], *a.* Débil, adinámico.

adytum [ˈædɪtəm] [a-dí-tum], *s.* Adiote o ádito, santuario de los antiguos.

adz, adze [ædz] [ads], *s.* Azuela, herramienta de carpintería.

aedile [ˈediːl] [é-dil], *s.* Edil, magistrado romano; oficial municipal.

Aegean [ˈedʒɪn] [é-yin] *a.* Egeo. **Aegean Sea,** mar Egeo.

aegilops [ˈedʒɪləps] [é-chi-lops], *s.* 1. Egílope, tumor o hinchazón en el ángulo mayor o interno del ojo. 2. *(Bot.)* Egílope, rompesacos o rompesacos, una especie de grama.

aegis [ˈedʒɪs] [í-yis], *s.* Escudo, broquel, égide o égida. **Under the aegis of,** bajo los auspicios de.

Aegisthus [ˈedʒɪsθəs] [e-chís-tos] *N. (Mit.)* Egipto.

aegyptiacum [ˈedʒɪpʃəkəm] [e-yip-sha-kom], *s.* Egipciaco, especie de un ungüento compuesto de cardenillo, miel y vinagre.

aeneas [ˈeniːs] [é-nis] *N. (Mit.)* Eneas.

aeneid [ˈeneɪd] [é-neid] *N. (Mit.)* Eneida.

aeolian ['ɛəlɪən] [ió-lian], *a. V.* EOLIAN.

aelotropic ['elətəpɪk] [elotrópik] a. Alotrópico

aeolus ['ɛləs] [é-los] *N. (Mit)* Eolo.

aequinoctial ['ekɪnəkʃəl] [ekinókshal], *a.* Equinoccial. *V.* EQUINOCTIAL.

aerate ['ereɪt] [é-reit], *va.* 1. Airear, ventilar, exponer a la acción del aire, proveer de aire, dar aire. 2. Impregnar, saturar un líquido de aire o de ácido carbónico. 3. Arterializar la sangre. 4. Hacer etéreo, espiritualizar. **Aerated waters,** aguas cargadas de ácido carbónico natural o artificialmente; aguas gaseosas.

aeration ['ereɪʃən] [e-réi-shon], *s.* Renovación del aire, acción y efecto de darlo; ventilación.

aerator ['ereɪtəʳ] [e-réi-taʳ], *s.* Aparato para airear o para saturar un líquido de aire o de gas; aireador.

aerial ['ɛərɪəl] [é-rial], *a.* 1. Aéreo. 2. Puesto en el aire; elevado. 3. Etéreo.

aerial, *s.* Antena (de radio o de televisión.) **Transmitting aerial,** antena transmisora.

aerial photography [ɛərɪəl'fəʊtəgræfɪ] [eá-rial-fo-to-gra-fi], *s.* Fotografía aérea.

aerialist ['ɛərɪəlɪst] [é-ria-list] *s.* Equilibrista, volatinero.

aerie ['ɛərɪ] [é-ri], *s.* Nido de ave de rapiña. *V.* EYRY.

aeriform ['ɛərɪfɔːm] [éa-ri-fom] *a.* Gaseoso, aeriforme, inmaterial.

aerify ['ɛərɪfaɪ] [éa-ri-fai], *va.* 1. Aerificar, reducir al estado de aire. 2. Aerificar, llenar de aire

aerobatics [ɛərəʊ'bætɪks] [ea-ro-bá-tiks] *s.* Acrobacia aérea.

aerobe [ɛə'rəbɪ] [éa-ro-bi] *s. (Biol.)* Aerobio.

aerobic [ɛə'rəbɪ] [ea-ró-bik] *adj.* Aerobio.

aerodrome ['ɛərədrəʊm] [ea-ró-droum] *s.* Aeródromo.

aerodynamics ['ɛərəʊdaɪ'næmɪks] [ea-ro-dai-ná-miks], *s.* Aerodinámica.

aerodyne [ɛərə'daɪn]'[éa-ro-dain] *s.* Aerodino.

aerofoil ['ɛərəfɔɪl] [ea-ro-foil] *s.* Superficie sustentadora.

aeroembolism [ɛərə'əmbɒlɪzəm] [ea-rom-bo-lí-sem], *s. (Med.)* Aeroembolismo.

aerogram ['ɛərəʊgræm] [éa-ro-gram] *s.* Aerograma, radiograma.

aerograph ['ɛərəʊgræf] [ea-ró-graf] *s.* Aerógrafo.

aerography ['ɛərəʊgræfɪ] [ea-ró-gra-fi], *s.* Aerografía, descripción o teoría del aire.

aerolite ['ɛərəlaɪt] [earolait], *s.* Aerolito; meteorito. *V.* METEORITE.

aerology ['ɛərəlɒdʒɪ] [ea-ró-lo-chi], *s.* Aerología, ciencia que trata de las leyes y fenómenos de la atmósfera.

aeromancy ['ɛərəmænsɪ] [ea-ro-man-si] *s.* Aeromancia.

aeromarine [ɛərəmə'riːn] [ea-ro-ma-rin] *adj.* Aeromarítimo.

aeromechanic [ɛərəmɪ'kænɪk] [ea-ro-mi-ká-nik] *s.* Mecánico de aviación.

aeromechanics [ɛərəmɪ'kænɪks] [ea-ro-mi-ká-niks], *s.* Aeromecánica.

aeromedicine ['ɛərəmedɪsɪn] [ea-ro-mé-di-sin], *s.* Aeromedicina.

aerometer [ɛərə'miːtəʳ] [ea-ro-mi-taʳ], *s.* Aerómetro.

aerometric [ɛərə'metrɪk] [ea-ro-mé-trik], *a.* Aerométrico, relativo a la aerometría.

aerometry [ɛərə'metrɪ] [ea-ró-me-tri], *s.* Aerometría, medición de la fuerza, condensación o rarefacción del aire.

aeromodelling ['ɛərəʊ'mɒdlɪŋ] [ea-ro-mó-de-lin] *s.* Aeromodelismo.

aeromotor [ɛərə'məʊtəʳ] [ea-ró-mo-taʳ] *s.* Aeromotor.

aeronaut ['ɛərənɔːt] [é-ro-not], *s.* Aeronauta, el que se remonta por los aires en un globo.

aeronautic ['ɛərənɔːtɪk] [ea-ro-nó-tik] o **aeronautical** ['ɛərəʊ:tɪkl] [ea-ro-náu-ti-kal] *adj.* Aeronáutico.

aeronautics ['ɛərənɔːtɪks] [ea-ro-nó-tiks] o **aerostation** [ɛərəs'teɪʃən] [ea-ros-téi-shon], *s.* Aerostación, el arte de viajar por el aire en globos llenos de gas. **Aerostation** se usa algunas veces para denotar la ciencia de pesar el aire.

aeronaval ['ɛərəneɪvəl] [e-ro-néi-val] *adj.* Aeronaval.

aerophagia ['ɛərəfædʒɪə] [e-ro-fá-chia] *s.* Aerofagia.

aerophyte ['ɛərəfaɪt] [é-ro-fait], *s.* Aerofita; planta que crece totalmente en el aire y se alimenta de él.

aeroplane ['ɛərəplɪ] [é-ro-plein], *s.* Aeroplano, avión.

aeroscopy ['ɛərəskɒpɪ] [ea-rós-ko-pi], *s.* Aeroscopia, observación del aire.

aerosol ['ɛərəsɒl] [é-ro-sol], *s.* 1. Aerosol, suspensión de partículas sólidas o líquidas en medio gaseoso. 2. Pulverizador, vaporizador.

aerospace ['ɛərəʊspeɪs] [é-ros-peis], *s.* Aerospacio, espacio aéreo.

aerostat ['ɛərəstæt] [é-ros-tat], *s.* 1. Globo aerostático. 2. Aeronauta.

aerostatic ['ɛərəstætɪk] [e-ros-tá-tik], *a.* Aerostático.

aerostatics, *s.* Aerostática, aeronáutica.

aerotechnical ['ɛərəteknɪkəl] [e-ros-tá-ti-kal] *s.* Aerotécnico.

aerotherapeutics [ɛərəθerə'pətɪks] [e-ro-zi-ra-péu-tiks] *s.* Aeroterapia.

aerotherapy ['ɛərəθ'rəpɪ] [e-ri-zé-ra-pi] *s.* Aeroterapia.

aerothermodynamics [ɛərə'θɜːmədaɪ'næmɪks] [e-ro-zer-mou-dai-ná-miks], *s.* Aerotermodinámica, termodinámica de gases o aérea.

aery ['ɛərɪ] [éa-ri] *s.* Aguilera.

Aesop ['iːsɒp] [í-sop] *N.* Esopo.

aesthete ['iːsθiːt] [is-zít], *s.* Esteta, admirador de la belleza natural o artística.

aesthetic ['iːsθiːtɪk] [is-zí-tik], *a.* Estético. *V.* ESTHETIC.

aesthetical ['iːsθiːtɪkəl] [is-zí-ti-kal] *adj.* Estético.

aesthetician ['iːsθiːtɪʃən] [is-zi-ti-shan] *adj.* Estético.

aestheticism ['iːsθiːtɪsɪzm] [is-zé-ti-sí-sem] *s.* Esteticismo.

aesthetics ['iːsθiːtɪks] [is-zí-tiks], *s.* Estética.

aestival ['iːstɪvəl] [ís-ti-val], *a.* 1. Estival, lo que pertenece al estío o verano. 2. Estivo, lo que dura todo el estío. *V.* ESTIVAL.

aestivate ['iːstɪveɪt] [ís-ti-veit] *vn. (Zool.)* Pasar el verano en estado de letargo.

aetiological ['iːtɪələdʒɪkəl] [i-tio-ló-chi-kal] *adj.* Etiológico.

aetiology ['iːtɪələdʒɪ] [i-tió-lo-chi] *s.* Etiología.

aetites ['iːtaɪts] [i-táits], *s.* Etites, piedra del águila.

aetna ['iːtnə] [ít-na] *N.* Etna.

afar [ə'fɑːʳ] [afáʳ], *adv.* Lejos, distante, a gran distancia. **From afar,** de lejos, desde lejos, a distancia. **Afar off,** distante, muy distante, remoto.

afeard [ə'fɪəd] [a-fíad], *a. (Vulg.)* Espantado, atemorizado, aterrado, temeroso.

afebrile [ə'febrɪl] [a-fe-bril], *a.* Exento de fiebre.

afer [ə'ɜːʳ] [a-faʳ], *s.* Áfrico, ábrego, el viento sudoeste.

affability [æfə'bɪlɪtɪ] [a-fa-bí-li-ti], *s.* Afabilidad, suavidad, dulzura, agrado, cortesía, urbanidad, atención.

affable ['æfəbl] [á-fe-bol], *a.* Afable, cortés, benigno, favorable; comedido; cariñoso.

affableness ['æfəblnɪs] [a-fé-bol-nes], *s.* Afabilidad, dulzura, cariño.

affably ['æfəblɪ] [á-fe-bli], *adv.* Afablemente, cariñosamente.

affair [ə'feəʳ] [a-féaʳ], *s.* 1. Asunto o negocio. **Affair of state,** asunto de Estado. 2. *(Mil.)* Acción, encuentro entre dos tropas. **Affair of honor,** lance de honor, duelo. 3. Cuestión, acontecimiento. **Family affairs,** cuestiones familiares. **Social affair,** acontecimiento social. **She had an affair with her boss,** tuvo una aventura con su jefe. **Foreign affairs,** relaciones exteriores.

affect [ə'fekt] [a-fék], *s.* 1. Afecto, cualquiera de las pasiones del ánimo. 2. Calidad, circunstancia. 3. Pasión, sensación, afición.

affect, *va.* 1. Obrar, causar efecto en el ánimo; afectar, enternecer. **His mother's dead affected him deeply,** la muerte de su madre le afectó profundamente. 2. Conmover, mover o excitar las pasiones del ánimo. 3. Aspirar, anhelar. 4. Amar, tener afición a alguna persona o cosa. 5. Afectar, aparentar, fingir, hacer ostentación de cualidades o vicios; poner demasiado estudio en las palabras, movimiento o adornos.

affectation [æfek'teɪʃən] [a-fek-téi-shon], *s.* Afectación, la acción y efecto de afectar. 2. Afectación, pretensión mal fundada.

affected [ə'fektɪd] [a-fék-ted], *part. a.* 1. Movido, impresionado, commovido. 2. Afectado, lleno de afectación. 3. Inclinado. 4. Sujeto a algún mal o enfermedad. 5. Enternecido, conmovido.

affectedly [ə'fektɪdlɪ] [a-fék-ted-li], *adv.* Afectadamente.

affectedness [ə'fektɪdnɪs] [a-fék-ted-nes], *s.* Afectación, la acción y efecto de afectar; fingimiento.

affecter [ə'fektər] [a-fék-tar], *s.* Afectador, fingidor, el que afecta o finge alguna cosa.

affecting [ə'fektɪŋ] [a-fék-tin], *a.* Sensible, tierno, interesante, lastimero, lastimosa.

affectingly [ə'fektɪŋlɪ] [a-fék-tin-li], *adv.* Con afecto.

affection [ə'fekʃən] [a-fék-shon], *s.* 1. Impresión, el efecto que causan las cosas en el ánimo. 2. Afecto, amor, benevolencia, afición, cariño, inclinación. 3. Estado del cuerpo o alma, cualidad, propiedad, afección. 4. (*Med.*) Enfermedad, dolencia.

affectionate [ə'fekʃənɪt] [a-fék-sho-net], *a.* Cariñoso, benévolo, afectuoso, prendado, aficionado.

affectionately [ə'fekʃənɪtlɪ] [a-fek-sho-né-ti-li], *adv.* Cariñosamente, afectuosamente. **Affectionately yours,** suyo afectuosamente (letters).

affectioned [ə'fekʃənd] [a-fék-shond], *a.* 1. (*Ant.*) Inclinado, dispuesto. 2. (*Des.*) Afectado, lleno de afectación.

affective [ə'fektɪv] [a-fék-tif], *a.* Afectivo, tierno, afectuoso, persuasivo.

affectively [ə'fektɪvlɪ] [a-fék-tiv-li], *adv.* Apasionadamente.

affector [ə'fektər] [a-fék-tar], *s.* Fingidor, imitador.

affeer [ə'fiːr] [a-fíir], *va.* 1. V. ASSESS. 2. Confirmar.

afferent [ə'ferənt] [á-fe-rent], *a.* Aferente, que trae, que conduce hacia dentro; opuesto a **efferent.**

affiance [ə'faɪəns] [a-fáians], *s.* 1. Esponsales o contrato matrimonial. 2. Confianza.

affiance, *va.* 1. Tomar los dichos, contraer esponsales. 2. Inspirar confianza.

affianced [ə'faɪənst] [a-fáianst], *a.* El que ha hecho un contrato matrimonial. **Affianced bride,** Novia desposada, prometida.

affiancer [ə'faɪənsər] [a-fáian-sar], *s.* El o la que ha contraído o celebrado esponsales. (*Coloq.*) El o la que ha dado la palabra. 2. El que toma los dichos a los que se van a casar.

affiant [ə'faɪənt] [a-fáiant], *s.* El que hace declaración jurada; deponente, declarante.

affidavit [æfɪ'deɪvɪt] [a-fi-dá-vit], *s.* Declaración jurada.

affied [ə'faɪd] [a-fáid], *a.* Desposado. *-pp.* El o la que ha contraído esponsales.

affiliate [ə'fɪlɪeɪt] [a-fí-lieit], *va.* 1. Prohijar, ahijar, adoptar. 2. Venir o quedar en íntimas relaciones: asociar (university, corporation).

affiliated [ə'fɪlɪeɪtɪd] [a-fi-liéi-ted], *a.* 1. Prohijado, afiliado. 2. Asociado.

affiliation [ə'fɪlɪeɪʃən] [a-fi-liéi-shon], *s.* 1. Adopción. 2. Asociación, conexión, relación amistosa.

affinage [ə'fɪneɪdʒ] [á-fi-nech], *s.* Ensaye de los metales.

affined [ə'faɪnd] [a-fáind], *a.* Emparentado por afinidad.

affinity [ə'fɪnɪtɪ] [a-fí-ni-ti], *s.* 1. Afinidad, parentesco contraído por matrimonio. 2. Afinidad, relación o conexión.

affirm [ə'fɜːm] [a-férm], *vn.* 1. Afirmarse en alguna cosa. 2. Declarar formalmente, en especial ante un juez o con su sanción. *-va.* Confirmar, ratificar o aprobar alguna ley o fallo anterior; afirmar, declarar.

affirmable [ə'fɜːməbl] [a-fér-ma-bol], *a.* Lo que se puede afirmar.

affirmably [ə'fɜːməblɪ] [a-fér-ma-bli], *adv.* Afirmativamente.

affirmance [ə'fɜːməns] [a-fér-mans], *s.* Confirmación de alguna cosa.

affirmant [ə'fɜːmənt] [a-fér-mant], *s.* Afirmante.

affirmation [æfə'meɪʃən] [a-fer-méi-shon], *s.* Afirmación, la acción de afirmar. 2. Afirmación, aserto. 3. Confirmación, ratificación.

affirmative [ə'fɜːmətɪv] [a-fír-ma-tif], *a.* Afirmativo. *-s.* Aserción, lo que contiene una afirmación.

affirmatively [ə'fɜːmətɪvlɪ] [a-fér-ma-tív-li], *adv.* Afirmativamente, con aseveración.

affirmed [ə'fɜːmd] [a-férmd], *a.* Afirmado, ratificado.

affirmer [ə'fɜːmər] [-afér-ma'], *s.* Afirmante, el que afirma.

affix ['æfɪks] [a-fíks], *va.* Anexar, unir al fin de otra cosa; añadir, fijar, pegar, atar, unir. **He affixed his tie with a pin,** se sujetó la corbata con un alfiler. **To affix one's signature to a document,** poner la firma a un documento.

affix, *s.* (*Gram.*) Afijo, partícula unida a una voz, particularmente un prefijo o sufijo.

affixion ['æfɪkʃən] [a-fí-kshon], *s.* Anexión, la unión de alguna partícula al fin de una voz; el acto de añadir.

afflation [æfbn] [a-fléi-shon], *s.* Resuello, inspiración.

afflatus [æfbs] [afléitos], *s.* 1. Inspiración divina. 2. (*Med.*) Exhalación, emanación.

afflict [ə'flɪkt] [a-flíkt], *va.* Afligir, causar dolor, pena o sentimiento, oprimir, inquietar, enfadar, desazonar, atormentar. *-vn.* Afligirse, desconsolarse, amohinarse. **To be afflicted with,** estar afligido, oprimido por o a causa de.

afflictedness [ə'flɪktɪdnɪs] [a-flík-ted-nes], *s.* Aflicción, pena, sentimiento.

afflicting [ə'flɪktɪŋ] [a-flík-tin], *a.* Penoso, devorador, atormentador.

afflictingly [ə'flɪktŋlɪ] [a-flík-tin-li], *adv.* Opresivamente, afligidamente.

affliction [ə'flɪkʃən] [aflík-shon], *s.* Aflicción, calamidad, miseria, dolor.

afflictive [ə'flɪktɪv] [a-flík-tif], *a.* Aflictivo, lastimoso, penoso, molesto.

afflictively [ə'flɪktɪvlɪ] [a-flík-tiv-li], *adv.* Penosamente, afligidamente.

affluence ['æfluəns] [á-fluens], **affluency** ['æfluənsɪ] [á-fluen-si], *s.* 1. Concurrencia, concurso o junta de muchas personas. 2. Copia o abundancia, opulencia.

affluent ['æfluənt] [á-fluent], *a.* Opulento, afluente, abundante, copioso. **To be in affluent circumstances,** estar en la opulencia. *-s.* Afluente, río que desemboca en otro.

affluently ['æfluəntlɪ] [á-fluen-tli], *adv.* Abundantemente, copiosamente.

affluentness ['æfluəntnɪʃ] [á-fluent-nes], *s.* Opulencia, abundancia de riquezas.

afflux ['æflʌks] [a-fláks], **affluxion** [aflákshon], *s.* Concurrencia o confluencia; montón. Flujo.

afford [ə'fɔːd] [a-fórd], *va.* 1. Dar, producir. 2. Dar o conceder alguna cosa. **These trees afford little shelter,** estos árboles dan poca protección 3. Abastecer, proveer, proporcionar, franquear. **I cannot afford to sell it for less,** no puedo venderlo por menos. **I cannot afford such expenses,** no me puedo permitir semejantes gastos. 4. Permitirse, costearse. **Can we afford a new car?,** ¿podemos costearnos un coche nuevo?

afforest [æ'fɒrest] [a-fó-rest], *va.* Plantar un bosque.

afforestation [æfɒrɪs'teɪʃən] [a-fo-res-téi-shon], *s.* La plantación de un bosque.

affranchise ['æfrəntʃaɪz] [á-fran-chais], *va.* Manumitir, dar libertad al esclavo. V. ENFRANCHISE.

affranchisement, [æfrəntʃaɪz'mənt] [a-frán-chis-ment] *s.* V. ENFRANCHISEMENT.

affray [ə'freɪ] [a-fréi], *s.* Asalto o sorpresa tumultuaria, riña, pendencia, combate, tumulto.

affreight [ə'freɪt] [a-fréit], *va.* Fletar, alquilar un buque.

affreightment [ə'freɪtmənt] [a-fréit-ment], *s.* Acción y efecto de fletar un buque.

affricate ['æfrɪkət] [á-fri-ket] *s.* Africada. (consonant)

affricative ['æfrɪkətɪv] [a-frí-ka-tif] *a.* (*Gram.*) Africado.

affriction ['æfrɪkʃən] [a-frík-shon], *s.* Fricción, el acto de estregar una cosa con otra; frotación.

affright [ə'fraɪt] [a-fráit], *va.* Aterrar, espantar, causar terror o espanto, atemorizar, asustar.

affright, *s.* Terror, espanto; lo que causa miedo.

affrightedly [əˈfraɪtɪdlɪ] [a-frái-ted-li], *adv.* Con espanto; espantosamente.

affrighter [əˈfraɪtəʳ] [a-frái-taʳ], *s.* Asombrador, espantador, el que mete miedo o asombra.

affront [əˈfrʌnt] [a-frónt], *vn.* Encararse, ponerse cara a cara con otro, engestarse. *-va.* 1. Afrentar, insultar, provocar, ultrajar, ajar. 2. Arrostrar, hacer frente.

affront, *s.* Afrenta, sonrojo, bochorno, provocación, insulto, ultraje, injuria.

affronter [əˈfrʌntəʳ] [a-frón-taʳ], *s.* Agresor, provocador.

affronting [əˈfrʌntɪŋ] [a-frón-tin], *part. a.* Injurioso, provocativo.

affrontive [əˈfrʌntɪv] [a-frón-tif], *a.* Afrentoso, injurioso.

affuse [əˈfjuːz] [a-fiús], *va.* Echar alguna cosa líquida sobre otra; verter; difundir.

affusion [əˈfjuːʃən] [a-fiú-shon], *s.* El acto de echar alguna cosa líquida sobre otra.

Afghan [ˈæfgæn] [af-gán], *a.* 1. Afghan, ana, de Afganistán. 2. *s.* Género de cobertura de estambre trabajado a punto de aguja o de crochet.

Afghanistan [æfˈgænɪstæn] [af-gá-nis-tan] Afganistán.

afield [əˈfiːld] [a-fíld], *adv.* Campo a través, fuera de camino, por el campo. **Far afield**, muy lejos.

afire [əˈfaɪəʳ] [a-fáiaʳ], *adv.* Encendidamente, inflamado. En fuego.

aflame [əˈfleɪm] [a-fléim], *a.* En llamas. *(Fig.)* Inflamado.

aflat [əˈflæt] [a-flát], *adv.* Al ras con la tierra, a nivel del suelo.

afloat [əˈfləʊt] [a-flóut], *adv. (Mar.)* Flotante sobre el agua, a flote. **The ship managed to keep afloat after the collision,** el barco consiguió mantenerse a flote tras el choque.

afoot [əˈfuːt] [a-flút], *adv.* 1. A pie. 2. En acción o movimiento. En preparación. **There is something afoot,** se está tramando algo.

afore [əˈfɔːʳ] [a-fóʳ], *prep.* 1. Antes, más cerca, hablando de lugar. 2. Antes, con anterioridad de tiempo. 3. Delante. *-adv.* 1. Antes, anticipadamente, en tiempo pasado. 2. Primero; en frente. 3. *(Mar.)* A proa.

aforegoing [əˈfɔːˈgəʊɪŋ] [a-fór-goin], *a.* Antecedente, precedente.

aforehand [əˈfɔːhænd] [a-fór-jand], *adv.* De antemano; con preparación.

aforementioned [əˈfɔːmenˈʃənd] [a-fór-men-shond], **aforenamed** [əˈfɔːneɪmd] [a-fór-neimd], **aforesaid** [əˈfɔːseɪd] [a-fór-seid], *a.* Susodicho, ya dicho, ya mencionado, sobredicho, antedicho, supracitado.

aforethought [əˈfɔːθɔːt] [a-fór-zot], *a.* Premeditado. **With malice aforethought,** con premeditación.

aforetime [əˈfɔːtaɪm] [a-fór-taim], *adv.* En otro tiempo, en tiempo pasado, antiguamente.

afoul [əˈfaʊl] [a-fóul], *adv. y a.* En colisión; enredado.

afraid [əˈfreɪd] [a-fréid], *part. a.* Amedrentado, atemorizado, intimidado, espantado, temeroso, tímido. **I am afraid,** temo, tengo miedo. **I am afraid he is out,** lo siento pero ha salido.

afresh [əˈfreʃ] [a-frésh], *adv.* De nuevo, otra vez.

Africa [ˈæfrɪkə] [a-fri-ka] *N.* África. **South Africa,** África del Sur.

African [ˈæfrɪkən] [á-fri-kan], **afric** [ˈæfrɪk] [á-frik], *a. y s.* Africano.

Africander [ˈæfrɪkəndəʳ] [a-fri-kán-daʳ], *s.* El que ha nacido en África, pero es de raza europea.

Afrikaner [ˌæfrɪˈkɑːnəʳ] [a-fri-ká-naʳ] *s.* Afrikánder.

Africanist [æfrɪˈkɑːnɪst] [a-fri-ka-nist] *s.* Africanista.

Africanization [æfrɪˈkɑːnɪseɪʃən] [a-fri-ka-ni-séi-shon] *s.* Africanización.

Africanize [æfrɪˈkɑːnaɪz] [a-frí-ka-nais] *va.* Africanizar.

Afrikaans [æfrɪˈkɑːns] [á-fri-kaans] *s.* Afrikaans.

Afro-american [æfrəʊəˈmerɪkən] [a-froa-mé-ri-kan] *a./s.* Afroamericano.

Afro-asian [ˈæfrəʊˈeɪʃən] [a-fro-éi-shan] *a./s.* Afroasiático.

Afro-Cuban [ˈæfrəʊˈkuːbən] [a-fro-kiú-ban] *a./s.* Afrocubano.

afront [əˈfrʌnt] [a-frónt], *adv.* Enfrente, al frente, de cara.

aft [ɑːft] [áft], *adv. (Mar.)* A popa o en popa. **To haul down the mizzen sheet aft,** cazar del todo la escota de mesana. **Fore and aft,** de proa a popa.

after [ˈɑːftəʳ] [áf-taʳ], *prep.* 1. Después. 2. Detrás, en seguimiento de. 3. Según. **After the manner,** según, a la manera de. *-adv.* Después, en seguida de. **Soon after,** poco después. **Day after tomorrow,** pasado mañana. **Day after day,** día tras día, cada día. **The day after,** el día siguiente. *-a.* Posterior, ulterior, subsiguiente. **After** se usa en muchas voces compuestas, pero casi siempre en el sentido de después. **After the example of,** a ejemplo de.

after-acceptation [ˌɑːftəˈæksepˈteɪʃən] [áf-taʳ-a-sep-téi-shon], *s.* Aceptación tardía.

after-account [ˌɑːftərəˈkaʊnt] [áf-taʳ-a-káunt], *s.* Cuenta nueva o venidera.

after-act [ˌɑːftəˈækt] [áf-taʳ-ákt], *s.* Acto subsiguiente.

after-age [ˌɑːftəˈeɪdʒ] [áf-ta-reich], *s.* Posteridad, tiempo venidero. **After-ages,** Tiempos o siglos venideros.

after all [ˌɑːftəˈɔːl] [áf-ta-ral], *adv.* Después de todo, bien pensado todo.

after-attack [ˌɑːftəˈatækt] [áf-taʳ-a-ták], *s.* Ataque o choque subsiguiente.

afterbirth [ˌɑːftəˈbɜːθ] [áf-taʳ-berz], *s.* Secundinas o parias. Placenta. Nacimiento póstumo.

afterburner [ˌɑːftəˈɜːnəʳ] [áf-tar-bér-naʳ], *s. (Aer.)* 1. Quemador auxiliar para motores de turborreacción. 2. Inyector del combustible.

aftercare [ˌɑːftəˈkeəʳ] [áf-taʳ-keaʳ] *s.* Vigilancia postoperatoria.

after-clap [ˌɑːftəˈklæp] [áf-ta-kláp], *s.* Accidente o lance repentino que sucede después de acabarse al parecer alguna cosa; repetición de una acción. Golpe inesperado, revés.

after-comer [ˌɑːftəˈkʌməʳ] [áf-taʳ-kó-maʳ], *s.* Sucesor, el que viene después.

after-conduct [ˌɑːftəˈkɒndʌkt] [áf-taʳ-kón-dakt], *s.* Conducta subsiguiente.

after-conviction [ˌɑːftəˈkɒnvɪkʃən] [áf-taʳ-kon-dí-shon], *s.* Convencimiento subsiguiente.

after-cost [ˌɑːftəˈkɒst] [áf-taʳ-kost], *s.* Gasto extraordinario.

after-course [ˌɑːftəˈkɔːs] [áf-taʳ-kors], *s.* Viaje futuro. Proceder o conducta subsiguiente.

after-crop [ˌɑːftəˈkrɒp] [áf-taʳ-krop], *s.* Segunda cosecha.

after-damp [ˌɑːftəˈdæmp] [áf-taʳ-damp], *s.* La mofeta que queda en las minas después de una explosión de fuego grisu.

after-days [ˌɑːftəˈdeɪs] [áf-taʳ-deis], *s.* Posterioridad, tiempos venideros.

afterdeck [ˌɑːftədek] [áf-taʳ-dek] *s.* Cubierta de popa.

after-dinner [ˌɑːftərˈdɪnəʳ] [af-taʳ-dí-naʳ], *a.* Período después de la comida y antes de dejar mesa. *-s.* El tiempo que sigue a la comida. **At table after dinner,** de sobremesa.

aftereffect [ˈɑːftərɪfekt] [af-taʳ-e-fékt] *s.* Consecuencia, efecto secundario.

after-endeavour [ˌɑːftərˈɪndevəʳ] [af-taʳ-en-dé-vaʳ], *s.* Nuevo esfuerzo.

after-game [ˌɑːftəˈgeɪm] [áf-taʳ-geim], *s.* Juego de desquite; medio o recurso de que se vale uno después de haberle salido mal lo que intentó.

after-gathering [ˌɑːftəˈgaθərɪŋ] [af-taʳ-gá-ze-rin], *s.* Rebusco, la acción de recoger después de otro; espigadura.

afterglow [ˈɑːftəglaʊ] [áf-taʳ-glau], *s.* Brillo, viveza de color hacia el ocaso, después de la puesta del sol.

after-help [ˌɑːftəhelp] [áf-taʳ-jelp], *s.* Socorro o auxilio subsiguiente.

after-hope [ˈɑːftəhəʊp] [áf-taʳ-joup], *s.* Esperanza renovada.

after-hours [ˈɑːftəˈaʊz] [af-taʳ-áuas], *s.* A horas extraordinarias; tarde.

after-inquiry [ˈɑːftəinkwaɪərɪ] [aftainkuáiari], *s.* Examen o investigación subsiguiente.

after-law [ˈɑːftəlɔː] [áf-taʳ-loa], *s.* Ley posterior.

after-life [ˈɑːftəlaɪf] [áf-taʳ-laif], *s.* 1. El resto de la vida. 2. Vida venidera.

after-liver [ˈɑːftəlɪvəˈr], [af-taˈr-lí-vaˈr]s. Sobreviviente, venidero, descendiente; posteridad.

after-living [ˈɑːftəlɪvɪŋ] [af-taˈr-li-vin], s. V. AFTER-DAYS.

after-love [ˈɑːftəlʌv] [af-taˈr-lof], s. Segunda pasión, nuevos amores.

aftermath [ˈɑːftəmæθ] [áf-taˈr-maz], s. 1. Segunda siega; la hierba que crece después de la primera cosecha de heno en la misma estación: 2. *(Fig.)* Las consecuencias de una acción o un acontecimiento.

after-meeting [ˈɑːftəˈmiːtɪŋ] [af-taˈr-mí-tin], s. Reunión o junta que sigue a otra.

aftermost [ˈɑːftəməʊst] [áf-taˈr-most], s. *(Mar.)* El postrero, el último. De popa.

afternoon [ˈɑːftənuːn] [áf-taˈr-nun], s. Tarde, el tiempo que media desde el mediodía hasta el anochecer.

after-pains [ˈɑːftəˌpeɪns] [áf-taˈr-peins], s. Dolores de sobreparto.

after-part [ˈɑːftpɑːt] [áf-taˈr-part], s. Parte posterior.

afterpiece [ˈɑːftəpiːs] [áf-taˈr-pis], s. Sainete, entremés.

after-proof [ˈɑːftəˈpruːf] [áf-taˈr-pruf], s. Prueba, evidencia posterior.

after-reckoning [ˈɑːftərekənɪŋ] [áf-taˈr-re-kó-nin], s. Cuenta futura; nueva cuenta.

after-repentance [ˈɑːftərɪˌpəntəns] [áf-taˈr-ri-pen-tans], s. Arrepentimiento tardío.

after-report [ˈɑːftərɪpɔːt] [áf-taˈr-re-pórt], s. Noticia o conocimiento posterior.

after-state [ˈɑːftərɪsteɪt] [áf-taˈr-es-téit], s. El estado o vida futura.

after-sting [ˈɑːftərəstɪŋ] [áf-taˈr-es-tín], s. Picadura subsiguiente a otra.

after-supper [ˈɑːftəsʌpəˈr] [áf-taˈr-sá-paˈr], s. El tiempo entre cenar y acostarse.

after-taste [ˈɑːftəteɪst] [áf-taˈr-téist], s. Resabio, el sabor que deja alguna cosa; dejo, gustillo.

after-thought [ˈɑːftəθɔːt] [áf-taˈr-zót] s. Nuevo pensamiento, reflexión o reparo. *(Fig.)* Expediente tardío. -*adv.* Con madura reflexión.

after-times [ˈɑːftətaɪmz] [áf-taˈr-taims], s. Tiempos venideros, porvenir.

after-tossing [ˈɑːftətɒsɪŋ] [áf-taˈr-tó-sin], s. Marejada, movimiento de las olas después de una borrasca.

after-touch [ˈɑːftətʌtʃ] [áf-taˈr-tach], s. *(Pint.)* Retoque.

afterward [ˈɑːftələwəd] [áf-taˈr-uards] o **afterwards** [ˈɑːftələwəd] [áf-tauads], *adv.* Después. **Long afterwards,** Mucho tiempo después. En prosa, **afterwards** es el más usado.

afterwise [ˈɑːftəwaɪz] [áf-taˈr-uais], *a.* Discreto o prudente pasada la ocasión.

after-wit [ˈɑːftəwɪt] [áf-taˈr-uit], s. Discurso o expediente fuera de sazón; entendimiento tardío.

afterwitness [ˈɑːftəwɪtnɪs] [áf-taˈr-uít-nes], s. Testigo subsiguiente al acto o suceso de que se trata.

after-wrath [ˈɑːftəwrɑːθ] [áf-taˈr-raz], s. Resentimiento, rencor.

afterwriters [ˈɑːftfɑːf-ta-rai-tas], s. Escritores sucesivos.

aftward [ˈɑːftwɑːd] [áf-tauad], *adv.* V. AFTERMOST.

afterworld [ˈɑːftəwɔːld] [áf-taˈr-ueld] s. El más allá, el otro mundo.

aga [ˈæɡɑ] [á-ga], s. Agá, título de honor en Turquía.

again [əˈɡeɪn] [e-géin], *adv.* 1. Otra vez, segunda vez, aun, de nuevo. 2. Por otra parte, además. 3. En recompensa. 4. Dos veces tanto. **Again and again,** muchas veces. **As much again,** otro tanto más. **To do again,** volver a hacer. **He wrote again,** él volvió a escribir. **I will not do so again,** no lo haré más. **Give it to me again,** devuélvamelo usted **Come again tomorrow,** vuelva usted mañana.

against [əˈɡenst] [a-géinst], *prep.* 1. Contra. 2. Enfrente. **Over against my house,** Enfrente de mi casa. 3. Para cuando. **Against Christmas,** para Navidad. 4. Junto, cerca. **To be against,** oponerse a, reprobar.

agami [ˈæɡæmɪ] [a-gá-mi] s. Agamí.

agamic [ˈæɡæmɪk] [a-gá-mik], *a.* 1. Agámico, no provisto de órganos visibles de reproducción; asexual. 2. Producido sin unión, v.g. huevos agámicos.

agamous [ˈæɡæməs] [a-gá-mos], *a.* Asexual, criptógamo.

agape [əˈɡeɪp] [a-géip], s. Ágape, comida de los primeros cristianos en las iglesias.

agape, *adv.* Con la boca abierta.

agapetae [ˈæɡəpɪtɪ] [a-gé-pi-te], s. Agapetas, doncellas que en la primitiva iglesia vivían en comunidad, pero sin hacer voto alguno.

agar-agar [ˌeɪɡəˈeɪɡəˈr] [éi-gaˈr-éi-gaˈr]s. Agar, especie de alga.

agaric [ˈæɡərɪk] [a-gé-rik], s. Agárico, género de hongos; droga medicinal que usan también los tintoreros.

agasp [əˈɡæsp] [a-gásp], *adv.* y *a.* En el último suspiro; con viva aspiración, anhelante, deseando ardientemente.

agate [ˈæɡət] [á-guet], s. 1. Ágata, piedra preciosa. 2. Ágata, carácter de letra de 5 1/2 puntos: se llama **rubi** en Inglaterra. 3. Canica. (marble)

Agatha [ˈəɡəθɑː] [á-ga-za] N. Águeda.

agaty [ˈæɡətɪ] [á-ga-ti], *a.* Lo que participa de la naturaleza. del ágata.

agave [əˈɡeɪvɪ] [a-guéi-vi], s. Pita, maguey; erróneamente llamada áloe.

age [eɪdʒ] [éich], s. 1. Edad. **Seventy years of age,** Setenta años de edad. 2. Edad o siglo, sucesión o generación de hombres. **The golden age,** el siglo de oro. 3. Siglo, centuria, el espacio de cien años. 4. Senectud, vejez. **Full age,** mayoría o mayor edad. **Under age,** minoridad. **He is under age,** aún es menor de edad. **Of age,** mayor de edad. **Tender age,** primera edad, la infancia. **Age of discretion,** la edad de la razón. **What is your age?,** ¿qué edad tiene Usted? -*vn.* Envejecer. **She hasn't aged a bit,** no ha envejecido nada.

aged [ˈeɪdʒɪd] [éi-chid], *a.* 1. Viejo, cargado de años, anciano. 2. De la edad de.

age group [ˈeɪdʒɡruːp] [éich-group] s. Grupo de personas de la misma edad. **To be of different age groups,** no tener la misma edad.

ageless [ˈeɪdʒlɪs][éi-ch-les] *a.* Eterno, siempre joven.

agency [ˈeɪdʒənsɪ] [éi-chen-si], s. 1. Acción, operación. 2. Agencia, diligencia hecha por agente; intervención. **In the human agency,** en lo humano. 3. Agencia, empleo o cargo de agente, de factor, etc. **Agency office,** oficina de negocios. **Agency house,** casa de comisión. 4. Influencia. **The agency of climate,** la influencia del clima.

agenda [əˈdʒendə] [a-yen-da], **agendum** [ayendom], s. Agenda, libro de memoria.

agent [ˈeɪdʒənt] [éi-chant], *a.* Operativo, lo que obra o causa efecto en otra cosa. -*s.* 1. Agente, el que solicita o gestiona en pro de negocios de otro. **Insurance agent,** agente de seguros. 2. Agente, lo que obra y tiene facultad de producir o causar algún efecto. 3. Factor, diputado, delegado. 4. Asistente, auxiliar. **Business agent,** agente de negocios. **Estate agent,** agente inmobiliario.

agent provocateur [æ̃n̩kpɑːtɜːr] [éi-chant-pro-vo-kéi-taˈr] *s.* Agente provocador.

agentship [ˈeɪdʒəntʃɪp] [éi-chan-ship], s. Agencia, factoría, el oficio de agente o factor.

age-old [eɪdʒəʊld] [éich-ould] *a.* Secular, antiguo.

agglomerate [əˈɡlɒməreɪt] [a-gló-me-reit], *va.* Aglomerar, hacer ovillos; juntar o reunir en pelotón. *vn.* Aglomerarse. *s.* Aglomeración. *a.* Aglomerado.

agglutinant [əˈɡluːtɪnənt] [a-glú-ti-nant], *a.* Conglutinativo, que sirve para unir y pegar.

agglutinate [əˈɡluːtɪneɪt] [a-glú-ti-neit], *va.* Conglutinar, trabar, unir, pegar.

agglutination [əˈɡluːtɪˈneɪʃən] [a-glu-ti-néishon], s. Conglutinación o trabazón de una cosa con otra, unión, ligazón.

agglutinative [əˈɡluːtɪnətɪv] [a-glu-tí-na-tif], *a.* Conglutinativo, adhesivo,

aggrandize [əˈgrændaɪz] [á-gran-dais], va. 1. Engrandecer, hacer una cosa mayor de lo que era. 2. Elevar, exaltar. -vn. Acrecentarse, aumentarse.

aggrandizement [əˈgrændɪzmənt] [a-gran-dáis-ment], s. Engrandecimiento, elevación, exaltación.

aggrandizer [əˈgrændaɪzər] [a-gran-dái-sar], s. Ensalzador, el que engrandece a otro.

aggravate [ˈægrəveɪt] [á-gra-veit], va. 1. Agravar, hacer alguna cosa más pesada o dolorosa. 2. Hacer alguna cosa más enorme, exagerar. 3. Irritar. (Jur.) **Aggravated theft,** robo con agravante.

aggravating [ˈægrəveɪtɪŋ] [a-gra-véi-tin], a. Agravante; irritante, que molesta.

agravatingly [ˈægrəveɪtɪŋlɪ] [a-gra-véi-ting-li], adv. Con agravación; de un modo irritante, que veja o impacienta.

aggravation [ˌægrəˈveɪʃən] [a-gra-véi-shon], s. 1. Agravación. 2. Circunstancia agravante, lo que agrava algún delito. 3. Provocación, enormidad, exageración. 4. Vegación, molestia.

aggregate [ˈægrɪgɪt] [á-gre-gueit], a. Agregado, juntado, unido. -s Colección, agregado, el conjunto de muchas o varias cosas.

aggregate, va. Agregar, añadir, uniendo o juntando unas personas o cosas con otras, reunir, incorporar; admitir.

aggregately [ˈægrɪgɪtlɪ] [a-gri-guéi-tli], adv. Colectivamente.

aggregation [ˈægrɪgeɪʃən] [a-gri-guéi-shon], s. 1. Agregación; agregado, colección. 2. Masa, conjunto, total. 3. Coherencia, agregado de cuerpos de distinta naturaleza.

aggregative [ˈægrɪgeɪtɪv] [a-gré-ga-tif], a. Colectivo, junto.

aggregator [ˈægrɪgeɪtər] [a-gri-géi-tar], s. Colector, recaudador.

aggress [əˈgresər] [a-grés], vn. Acometer, embestir, ofender, atacar.

aggresion [əˈgreʃən] [a-gré-shon], s. Agresión, acometimiento, ataque, asalto, ofensa sin motivo.

aggressive [əˈgresɪv] [a-gré-sif], a. Agresivo; que tiene el carácter de agresión.

aggressiveness [əˈgresɪvɪs] [a-grésif-nis], s. Carácter agresivo; agresión.

aggressor [əˈgresər] [a-gré-sar], s. Agresor, el que acomete, ofende o provoca a otro.

aggrievance [əˈgriːvəns] [a-grí-vans], s. Agravio, injuria, daño, perjuicio, pérdida.

aggrieve [əˈgriːv] [a-gríf], va. Apesadumbrar, dar pesadumbre, vejar, oprimir, gravar, dañar. -vn. Lamentar.

aggrieved [əˈgriːvd] [a-grívd] a. Agraviado.

aggroup [əˈgruːp] [a-grup], va. Agrupar.

aghast [əˈɡɑːst] [a-gást], a. Espantado, horrorizado, estupefacto, despavorido; fuera de sí; atolondrado de horror; azorado, alborotado. (Fam.) Con la boca abierta.

agile [əˈdʒaɪl] [á-chail], a. Ágil, ligero, pronto, vivo.

agility [əˈdʒɪlɪtɪ] [a-chí-li-ti], **agileness** [əˈdʒɪlnɪs] [a-chíl-nes], s. Agilidad, ligereza, expedición para hacer alguna cosa, prontitud.

agillochum [əˈdʒɪlɒkəm] [a-chi-ló-kum], s. (Bot.) Aioe, madera de árbol así llamado.

agio [əˈdʒə] [á-chio], s. (Com.) Agio, agiotaje, el lucro o interés que deja la negociación de billetes, células de banco, letras, vales reales o cualquier papel-moneda.

agist [əˈdʒɪst] [á-chist], va. (For.) Apacentar ganado por un precio convenido.

agistment [əˈdʒɪstmənt] [a-chíst-ment], s. (For.) 1. Modificación del diezmo. 2. Pasto, pasturaje. 3. Montón, terrón, gavilla. 4. Ajuste, composición.

agistor [əˈdʒɪstər] [a-chís-tar], s. (For.) Guardabosque.

agitable [əˈdʒɪteɪbl] [a-chí-ta-bol], a. Agitable.

agitate [ˈædʒɪteɪt] [á-chi-teit], va. 1. Agitar, mover, afectar. 2. Inquietar el ánimo. 3. Agitar una cuestión. 4. Maquinar, imaginar. 5. Debatir, disputar, discutir. **The narration greatly agitated her,** la narración la conmovió mucho.

agitation [ˌædʒɪˈteɪʃən] [a-chi-téi-shon], s. 1. Agitación, la acción y efecto de agitar. 2. Discusión, ventilación; deliberación; perturbación. **The project now in agitation,** el proyecto que actualmente se discute.

agitator [əˈdʒɪteɪtər] [a-chi-téi-tar], s. Agitador, el que o lo que agita; incitador, instigador político.

agleam [əˈɡliːm] [a-glím], a. (Poét.) Centelleant.

aglet [ˈæɡl] [á-glet], s. 1. Herrete de agujeta o cordón. 2. Lámina u hoja de metal. Aglets, (Bot.) Borlillas, las puntas o remates de los estambres de las flores.

aglow [əˈɡləʊ] [a-glóu], adv. y a. En llamas, en incandescencia; ardiente, brillante.

agnail [əˈɡneɪl] [ág-neil], s. Panadizo, uñero.

agnate, agnatic [əˈɡneɪt] [əˈɡnætɪk] [ág-neit] [ag-ná-tik], a. Agnaticio. (For.) Agnado.

agnathous [əˈɡnæθəs] [ág-nei-zos], a. Que no tiene quijadas, o que las tiene rudimentarias.

agnation [əˈɡneɪʃən] [ag-néi-shon], s. Agnación, descendencia de un mismo padre por línea masculina no interrumpida; alianza, conexión.

agnes [ˈæɡnɪs] [ág-nes] N. Inés.

agnomen [æɡˈnəmən] [ag-nó-men], s. Sobrenombre debido a algún acto o suceso determinado.

agnominate [æɡˈnɒmɪneɪt] [ag-nó-mi-neit], va. Nombrar.

agnomination [æɡˈnɒmɪneɪʃən] [agnomineíshon], s. 1. (Ret.) Agnominación o paronomasia. 2. Agnomento, cognomento, sobrenombre.

agnostic [æɡˈnɒstɪk] [ag-nós-tik], a. Agnóstico, relativo al agnosticismo o caracterizado por él; que aparenta ignorar. -s. Partidario de la teoría del agnosticismo.

agnosticism [æɡˈnɒstɪsɪzəm] [ag-nos-ti-sí-zem], s. Agnosticismo; doctrina que consiste en suponer que se ignora sistemáticamente todo lo que no cae bajo el dominio de los sentidos, Dios y el alma humana inclusive. (Palabra propuesta por Huxley en 1869.)

agnus castus [æɡnəsˈkæstəs] [agnus kástus], s. (Bot.) Agnocasto o sauzgatillo.

ago [əˈɡəʊ] [e-góu], adv. Largo tiempo, pasado, después. **Some time ago,** hace algún tiempo. **Long ago,** hace mucho tiempo. **How long ago?** ¿Cuánto tiempo? **A good while ago,** hace ya algún tiempo.

agog [əˈɡɒɡ] [a-góg], adv. Con deseo o antojo, con apresuramiento o ansia. **To be agog,** tener gana, desear. **To set agog,** dar gana, hacer, desear.

agometer [əˈɡəmiːtər] [a-gó-mi-tar], s. Instrumento para medir o regular la resistencia eléctrica.

agone [əˈɡəʊn] [a-góun], adv. V. AGO.

agonic [əˈɡənɪk] [a-gó-nik], a. Agono, lo que no tiene ángulos.

agonism [əˈɡənɪzm] [agonísem], s. Combate de atletas.

agonistes, agonist [əˈɡənɪstɪs] [a-go-nísts], s. Atleta o combatiente; rival.

agonistic, agonistical [əˈɡənɪstɪk] [əˈɡənɪstɪkl] [ag-o-nís-tik] [a-go-nís-ti-kal], a. Atlético.

agonistically [əˈɡənɪstɪkəlɪ] [a-go-nís-ti-ka-li], adv. Atléticamente.

agonize [ˈæɡənaɪz] [á-go-nais], vn. 1. Estar agonizando o en las agonías de la muerte, en las últimas. 2. Luchar desesperadamente.

agonizingly [ˈæɡənaɪzɪŋlɪ] [a-go-nái-sin-li], adv. En agonía.

agonothete [ˈæɡənɒθiːt] [a-go-no-zít], s. El que dirigía los juegos en la antigua Grecia.

agonothetic [ˈæɡənɒθiːtɪk] [a-go-no-zí-tik], a. Gímnico, lo que pertenece a los juegos o ejercicios públicos.

agony [ˈæɡənɪ] [á-go-ni], s. 1. Agonía. 2. Agonía, angustia o aflicción extrema; paroxismo. **To go through agonies,** pasarlas moradas.

agony column [ˈæɡənɪkɒləm] [á-go-ni-ko-lom] s. Anuncios personales relativos a personas u objetos perdidos.

agora [ˈæɡərə] [á-go-ra] s. Agora.

agoraphobia [ˌægərəˈfəʊbɪə] [a-go-ra-fó-bia] *s.* Agorafobia.

agouti [ˈægətɪ] [a-góu-ti], *s.* Agutí, roedor de la América tropical, del tamaño de un conejo.

agraffe [əˈgræf] [a-gráf], *s.* 1. Broche o gancho, que a veces sirve de adorno. 2. Grapa sobre una cuerda del pianoforte para evitar la vibración entre ciertas piezas (el perno y el puente).

agraphia [əˈgræfɪə] [a-grá-fia], *s.* Incapacidad de escribir por enfermedad del cerebro.

agrarian [əˈgrɛərɪən] [a-gréa-rian], *a.* 1. Agrario, lo que pertenece a los campos o tierras. **Agrarian law,** Ley agraria. Ley para la distribución de las tierras públicas entre los soldados y el pueblo. 2. Agreste, selvático. 3. Comunista.

agrarianism [əˈgrɛərɪənɪzəm] [a-gréa-ria-ni-sem], *s.* Agrarianismo. División igual de la propiedad raíz. Los principios o la práctica de los que favorecen la redistribución de las tierras.

agree [əˈgriː] [a-grí], *vn.* 1. Concordar, convenir, acordar. 2. Ceder, entenderse, ponerse de acuerdo. **I will never agree to it,** jamás cederé o jamás convendré en ello. 3. Estipular. 4. Ajustar el precio. 5. Convenir. **The authors do not agree in this,** los autores no convienen o no son del mismo parecer en esto. **To agree in opinion,** ser de la misma opinión. 6. Acomodar o acomodarse, venir bien una cosa con otra. **That climate does not agree with me,** aquel clima no me va. 7. Sentar bien. **Chocolate does not agree with me,** el chocolate no me sienta bien. -*va.* Adaptar, acomodar, reconciliar.

agreeability [əˌgriːəˈbɪlɪtɪ] [a-gria-bí-li-ti], *s.* Afabilidad, agrado.

agreeable [əˈgriːəbl] [a-gría-bol], *a.* 1. Conveniente, proporcionado. 2. Agradable, lo que agrada, conforme, amable.

agreeableness [əˈgriːəblnɪs] [a-gría-bol-nes], *s.* 1. Conformidad, proporción. 2. Agrado, afabilidad. 3. Semejanza. 4. Amabilidad, gracia.

agreeably [əˈgriːəblɪ] [a-gría-bli], *adv.* Según; agradablemente.

agreed [əˈgriːd] [a-gríid], *part. a.* 1. Convenido, establecido, ajustado, determinado, aprobado. 2. De acuerdo.

agreeingly [əˈgriːɪŋlɪ] [a-gríin-li], *adv.* Conforme.

agreeingness [əˈgriːɪŋnɪs] [a-grí-in-nes], *s.* Conformidad, conveniencia, proporción, aptitud.

agreement [əˈgriːmənt] [a-grí-ment], *s.* 1. Concordia, conformidad, unión, correlación, conveniencia. 2. Semejanza de una cosa con otra. 3. Ajuste, convenio. **To come to an agreement,** convenirse, ajustarse. 4. Contrato, transacción, tratado, acomodamiento. **Collective agreements,** convenios colectivos.

agrestial, agrestic, agrestical [əˈgrestɪəl] [əˈgrestɪk] [əˈgrestɪkəl] [a-gres-chal] [a-gres-tik] [a-gres-ti-kal], *a.* Agreste, rústico, tosco, campestre, grosero, descortés.

agricole [ˈægrɪkəʊl] [a-grí-koul], *s.* **agricultor** [əˈgrɪkələʳ] [a-gri-kol-char], *s.* Agricultor. V. AGRICULTURIST.

agricultural [ˌægrɪˈkʌltʃərəl] [a-gri-kál-chu-ral], *a.* Agricultural. **Agricultural college,** escuela de peritos agrícolas. **Agricultural engineer,** perito agrícola o agrónomo.

agriculturalist [ˌægrɪˈkʌltʃərəlɪst] [a-gri-kál-chu-ra-list] *s.* Agricultor, agrónomo. Ingeniero agrónomo.

agriculture [ˈægrɪˌkʌltʃəʳ] [a-gri-kál-char], *s.* Agricultura, el arte de cultivar la tierra.

agriculturist [ˌægrɪˈkʌltʃərɪst] [a-gri-kál-chu-rist], *s.* Labrador, agricultor, agrícola.

agriculturism [ˌægrɪˈkʌltʃərɪzm] [a-gri-kal-chu-rí-sem], *s.* La ciencia de la agricultura.

agrigento [ˌægrɪˈgentə] [a-gri-yen-to] *N. (Geogr.)* Agrigento.

agrimony [ˈægrɪmənɪ] [a-grí-mo-ni], *s. (Bot.)* Agrimonia.

agrin [ˈægrɪn] [agrín], *adv.* En el acto de hacer visajes, o de rechinar los dientes.

agrippina [ˌægrɪpɪnə] [a-gri-pí-na] *N.* Agripina.

agronomics [əˈgrɒnəmɪks], [a-gro-nó-miks], *s.* Agrografía, descripción de las cosas del campo relacionadas con la agricultura; ciencia que trata de la distribución y la administración de la tierra, especialmente considerada como fuente de riqueza.

agronomist [əˈgrɒnəmɪst] [a-gró-no-mist], *s.* Agrónomo.

agronomy [əˈgrɒnəmɪ] [a-gró-no-mi], *s.* Agronomía, arte y teoría de la agricultura.

agrope [əˈgrəʊp] [a-gróup], *adv.* En el acto de tentar; a tientas, a ciegas.

aground [əˈgraʊnd] [a-gráund], *adv.* 1. *(Mar.)* Varado, encallado. **The ship ran aground,** la embarcación varó o dio en un bajío, o en un banco. 2. Empantanado, embarazado, impedido en el progreso de algún asunto.

ague [ˈeɪgjuː] [éi-guiu], *s.* Fiebre o calentura intermitente; escalofrío. **Dumb ague,** Una forma de fiebre intermitente en la que los síntomas no se manifiestan, o aparecen de una manera vaga e indefinida.

ague, *va.* Acometer una calentura intermitente.

agued [ˈeɪgjuːd] [éi-guiud], *a.* Febricitante, tercianario, calenturiento.

ague-cake [ˈeɪgjuːkeɪk] [éi-guiu-kéik], *s.* Hinchazón del bazo resultante de la fiebre intermitente.

ague-fit [ˈeɪgjuːfɪt] [éi-gui-fit], *s.* Accesión o paroxismo de una calentura intermitente.

ague-proof [ˈeɪgjuːpruːf] [éi-guiu-prúf], *a.* Capaz de resistir las calenturas, a prueba de calenturas.

ague-spell [ˈeɪgjuːspel] [éi-guiu-espél], *s.* Encanto o hechizo para curar la calentura intermitente.

ague-struck [ˈeɪgjuːstrʌk] [éi-guiu-strak], *a.* Acometido de calentura.

ague-tree [ˈeɪgjuːtriː] [éi-guiu-trí], *s.* Sasafrás, árbol medicinal de la Virginia.

aguish [ˈeɪgwɪʃ] [éi-güish], *a.* Febricitante o calenturiento; que tiene escalofríos, friolento; atacado de paludismo.

aguishness [ˈeɪgwɪʃnɪs] [éi-güish-nis], *s.* Escalofríos o síntomas de fiebre intermitente.

ahead [əˈhed] [a-jéd], *adv.* 1. Más allá, delante de otro. 2. *(Mar.)* Por la proa, avante. 3. Temerariamente. **To be ahead,** ir a la cabeza, ir delante. **To get ahead,** adelantar o ganar la delantera; también, tener el riñón bien cubierto. **Go ahead!** ¡adelante! ¡avancen! **To forge ahead,** avanzar rápidamente como cuando un buque da fondo inmediatamente después de aferrar velas; también, avanzar lentamente. **To run ahead,** obrar sin reflexión. **To run ahead of one's reckoning,** perder la cuenta.

aheap [əˈhep] [a-jíp], *adv.* En montón, en medio de un montón.

aheight, ahigh [əˈhaɪt] [a-jáit], *adv. (Ant.)* Arriba, en lo alto.

ahem! [əˈhem] [a-jém] *(interj.)* ¡Ejem!

ahold [əˈhəʊld] [a-jóuld], *adv. (Mar.)* Al viento.

ahoy [əˈhɔɪ] [a-jói], *inter.* ¡Ah, del barco! ¡Ha! Voz para llamar a los de un buque o bote. **Ship ahoy!,** ¡barco a la vista!

aid [eɪd] [éid], *va.* Ayudar, auxiliar, socorrer, coadyuvar, apoyar.

aid, *s.* 1. Ayuda, auxilio. 2. Subsidio, socorro que se da al gobierno como tributo extraordinario. 3. Ayudante, la persona que ayuda o asiste. **First aid** primeros auxilios. **State aid,** ayuda estatal. **Medical aid,** ayuda médica. **He was a great aid to me,** fue una gran ayuda para mí.

aide-de-camp [eɪddəˈkæmp] [éid-de-kamp], *s.* Ayudante de campo.

aide-mémoire [ˈeɪdmeˈmwɑː] [éid-me-muáʳ] *s.* Memorándum.

aider [eɪdəʳ] [éidarʳ], *s.* Auxiliador, auxiliante.

aidless [ˈeɪldərən] [éid-les], *a.* Desvalido, dsamparado, dejado.

aidman [ˈeɪdmən] [éid-man] *s. (U.S.)* Enfermero militar.

aid station [ˈeɪdˌsteɪʃən] [éid-es-téi-shon] *s. (Mil.)* Puesto de socorro.

aigre [eɪˈgriː] [éi-gri], *s.* Flujo impetuoso del mar.

aigrette [eɪˈgret] [éi-gret], s. V. EGRET. Cresta, penacho; plumero. Diadema (gems)

aiguille [eɪˈgwiːl] [éi-güil] s. Picacho, barrena.

aiguillette [eɪˈgwtdʒ] [éi-güi-let], s. Herrete de agujeta o franja.

ail [eɪl] [éil], va. Afligir, molestar, causar alguna pena o dolor. **What ails you?**, ¿qué le duele a usted?, ¿qué tiene usted?, ¿qué hay?, **Nothing ails me,** nada me duele, nada tengo. Este verbo se usa siempre de un modo indefinido y para inquirir acerca de algún dolor o pena. -vn. Sufrir, estar indispuesto.

ailanthus, ailantus [eɪˈlæntəs] [ei-lán-tas], s. Ailanto, árbol del cielo, de China.

aileron [ˈeɪlərɒn] [éi-le-ron], s. (Aer.) Alerón.

ailing [ˈeɪlɪŋ] [éi-lin], a. Doliente, achacoso, enfermizo.

ailment [ˈeɪlmənt] [éil-ment], s. Dolencia, indisposición, dolor, incomodidad.

aim [eɪm] [éim], vn. 1. Apuntar, asestar el tiro de alguna arma de fuego o arrojadiza. 2. Tirar, poner los medios dirigiéndolos a algún fin, poner la mira en alguna cosa. 3. Adivinar. -va. Apuntar o dirigir el tiro con el ojo, aspirar a, pretender, intentar, maquinar. **I aim to become a doctor,** aspiro a ser médico.

aim, s. 1. Puntería. 2. Blanco, la señal fija a que se tira con alguna arma arrojadiza o de fuego. **To miss one's aim,** errar el tiro. **To take one's aim well,** tomar bien sus medidas. s. Designio, mira, fin u objeto.

aimless [ˈeɪmlɪs] [éim-les], a. Sin objeto, sin designio, a la ventura.

ain't [eɪnt] [éint], v. (Fam.) Contracción de **is not, are not, am not, has not, have not.**

air [ɛər] [éa], s. 1. Aire, la atmósfera, el fluido que respiramos. **To take the air,** Tomar el aire. 2. Zéfiro, viento ligero. 3. Tono, tonada, aire de música. 4. Cara, semblante, aire o disposición personal de alguno. Ademán, exterior, modo, porte de una persona. **To have the air of a gentleman,** tener aires de gran señor. 5. Olor; vapor. **Factitious airs o gases,** aire ficticio. **Open air,** al raso. **Foul air,** aire viciado. **By air,** en avión, por avión.

air, va. Airear, estar o poner al aire; secar. **To air a room,** airear o ventilar un cuarto. **To air a skirt,** secar una camisa a la lumbre o al fuego.

air age [ɛərˈeɪdʒ] [éar-eich], s. Edad o era de la aviación.

air attaché [ɛərəˈtæʃeɪ] [éa-a-ta-shé] s. Agregado aéreo.

air-balloon [ɛərbəˈluːn] [éa-ba-lún], s. Globo aerostático.

air base [ɛərˈbeɪs] [éa-béis], s. Base aérea.

air-bladder [ɛərˈblædər] [éa-blá-da], s. Vejiga llena de aire.

air blast [ɛərˈblɑːst] [éa-blast], s. Chorro de aire.

air-borne [ɛərˈbɔːn] [éa-born], a. (Mil.) Aéreo, transportado por el aire.

air-brake [ˈɛərbreɪk] [éa-bréik], s. Freno neumático, o de aire.

air brush [ˈɛərbrʌʃ] [éa-brásh], s. Aerógrafo.

air-chamber [ˈɛərˌtʃeɪmbər] [éa-chéim-ba], s. Cámara de aire.

airburst [ˈɛərbɑːrst] [éa-berst] s. Explosión en el aire.

airbus [ˈɛərbʌs] [éa-bas] s. Aerobús.

air-cook [ˈɛərkuːk] [éa-cúk], s. Espita para permitir la salida del aire.

air-condition [ˈɛərkənˌdɪʃən] [éa-kon-dí-shon], va. Acondicionar el aire.

air-conditioned [ˈɛərkənˌdɪʃənd] [éa-kon-dí-shond], a. Con aire acondicionado, con clima artificial.

air-conditioner [ˈɛərkənˌdɪʃənər], [ea-kon-di-sho-no] s. Acondicionador del aire, aparato para acondicionar el aire.

air-conditioning [ˈɛərkənˌdɪʃənɪŋ] [ea-kon-dí-sho-nin], s. Acondicionamiento del aire, clima artificial.

air-cooled [ˈɛərkuːld] [ea-kúld], a. Enfriado por aire.

air-cooling [ˈɛərkuːlɪŋ] [ea-kú-lin], s. Enfriamiento por aire.

air corridor [ˈɛərˈkɒrɪdɔːr] [ea-kó-ri-da], s. Pasillo aéreo.

aircraft [ˈɛərkrɑːft] [éa-kraf], s. Aeronave. **Aircraft carrier,** Portaaviones.

aircraftman [ˈɛərkrɑːftmən] [ea-kráf-man] **aircraftsman** [ˈɛərkrɑːftsmən] [eakráfsman] s. (Mil.) Cabo segundo.

aircrew [ˈɛərkruː] [éa-kru] s. Tripulación de un avión.

air cushion [ˈɛərkʊʃən] [ea-ká-shon] s. Colchón de aire.

air-drill [ˈɛərdrɪl] [éa-dril], s. Taladro neumático.

airdrome [ˈɛərdrəʊm] [éa-droum], s. Aeródromo.

air duct [ˈɛərdʌkt] [éa-dakt] s. Tubo de ventilación.

air-engine [ˈɛərˌendʒɪn] [ea-én-chin], s. Máquina de aire. El aire caliente reemplaza en ella al vapor.

airfield [ˈɛərfiːld] [éa-fild] s. Aeródromo, campo de aviación.

airfoil [ˈɛərfɔɪl] [éa-foil], s. (Aer.) Cualquier superficie, como las de las alas o el timón, que al cambiar de posición modifica la dirección del vuelo.

air force [ˈɛərfɔːs] [éa-fors], s. Fuerza aérea.

airframe [ˈɛərfreɪm] [éa-freim] s. Estructura de avión.

airfreight [ˈɛərfreɪt] [éa-freit] s. Flete por avión.

airfreighter [ˈɛərfreɪtər] [ea-fréi-ta] s. Avión de carga.

air gap [ˈɛərgæp] [éa-gap] s. (Electr.) Entrehierro.

air gun [ˈɛərgʌn] [éa-gan], s. Pistola de aire comprimido.

air hammer [ˈɛərˌhæmər] [ea-já-ma] s. Martillo neumático.

air-hole [ˈɛərhəʊl] [éa-joul], s. 1. Respiradero, lumbrera, la abertura por donde entra y sale el aire. 2. Paja (en el hierro, etc.).

air hostess [ˈɛərˌhəʊstɪs] [ea-jós-tes] s. Azafata.

airily [ˈɛərɪli] [éa-ri-li], adv. Ligeramente; vivamente, alegremente.

airiness [ˈɛərɪnɪs] [éa-ri-nes], s. 1. Ventilación. 2. Vivacidad, viveza. 3. Ligereza, actividad.

airing [ˈɛərɪŋ] [éa-rin], s. 1. Caminata, viaje corto que se hace por diversión; paseo para tomar el aire. 2. Ventilación.

air intake [ˈɛərˌɪnteɪk] [ea-ín-teik] s. Toma de aire.

air lane [ˈɛərleɪn] [éa-lein], a. Falto de ventilación, sofocado.

airletter [ˈɛərletər] [ea-lé-ta], s. Carta aérea o por avión.

airlift [ˈɛərlɪft] [éa-lif], s. Puente aéreo de transporte. va. Transportar por puente aéreo.

airline [ˈɛərlaɪn] [éa-lain], s. 1. Línea aérea. 2. Compañía de aviación.

airliner [ˈɛərlaɪnər] [ea-lái-na], s. Avión de pasajeros.

airlock [ˈɛərlɒk] [éa-lok], s. (Mec.) Cámara de presión intermedia.

airmail [ˈɛərmeɪl] [éa-meil], s. Vía aérea, correo aéreo.

airmail, a. Aeropostal, por avión.

airman [ˈɛərmən] [éa-man], s. Aviador.

airmarshal [ˈɛərˌmɑːʃəl] [ea-már-shall] s. (Mil.) Teniente general.

air-mattress [ˈɛərmætrɪs] [ea-má-tres], s. Colchón de aire.

air meet [ˈɛərmiːt] [éa-mit], s. Concurso aéreo; congreso de aeronáutica.

air-minded [ˈɛərmaɪndɪd] [ea-máin-ded], a. Interesado en la aviación.

air-pipe [ˈɛərpaɪp] [éa-paip], s. Cañería para extraer el aire viciado; tubo de goma para dar aire a los buzos.

airplane [ˈɛərpleɪn] [éa-plein], s. Avión, aeroplano. **Airplane carrier,** Portaaviones.

air-plant [ˈɛərplɑːnt] [éa-plant], s. Epifito.

air pocket [ˈɛərpɒkɪt] [ea-pó-ket], s. (Aer.) Bolsa de aire. Bache.

airport [ˈɛərpɔːt] [éa-port], s. Aeropuerto, aeródromo.

airproof [ˈɛərpruːf] [éa-pruf], a. Hermético.

air-pump [ˈɛərpʌmp] [éa-pamp], s. Bomba de aire; bomba neumática.

air raid [ˈɛərreɪd] [éa-reid], s. Incursión aérea, ataque o bombardeo aéreo.

air-raid-shelter [ˈɛərreɪdˌʃeltər] [ea-reid-shél-ta], s. Refugio contra aeroplanos.

air-sac [ˈɛərsæk] [éa-sak], s. Celda para aire, en las aves.

air route [ˈɛərruːt] [éa-rut] s. Aerovía, ruta aérea.

airscrew [ˈɛərskruː] [éa-skru] s. Hélice.

air-sea base [ˈɛərsiːˈbeɪs] [éa-si-béis] Base aeronaval.

air-shaft [ˈɛərʃɑːft] [éa-shaft], s. Respiradero de mina.

airship [ˈɛərʃɪp] [éa-ship], s. Aeronave.

air shuttle [ˈɛərʃʌtl] [eashátel] s. Puente aéreo.

airsick [ˈɛərsɪk] [éa-sek] a. Mareado.

air sickness ['ɛəsɪknɪs] [ea-sík-nes], *s.* Mareo en el aire.

air speed ['ɛəspiːd] [éa-spid], *s.* Velocidad aérea.

airspraying ['ɛəspreɪɪŋ] [ea-spréin] *s.* Fumigación aérea.

airstream ['ɛəstriːm] [éa-strim] *s.* Corriente de aire.

airstrip ['ɛəstrɪp] [éa-strip], *s.* Pista de despegue, pista de aterrizaje.

air-tight ['ɛətaɪt] [éa-tait], *a.* Herméticamente cerrado o tapado.

air valve ['ɛəvælv] [éa-valv] **air vent** ['ɛəvent] [éa-vent] *s.* Respiradero, orificio de aireación.

airway ['ɛəweɪ]éa-uei, *s.* Aerovía, vía aérea.

airwoman ['ɛəˌwʊmən] [ea-uó-man] *s.* Aviadora.

airworthiness ['ɛəˌwɔːðɪnɪs] [ea-uér-zi-nes] *s.* Navegabilidad.

airworthy ['ɛəˌwɔːðɪ] [ea-uér-zi] *a.* En condiciones de vuelo.

airy ['ɛərɪ] [éa-ri], *a.* 1. Aéreo, lo que es del aire o pertenece a él. 2. Aéreo, ligero, trivial, lo que no tiene solidez ni fundamento. 3. Vivaz, vivo, alegre. 4. Abierto, vano, sin sustancia. 5. Vano, orgulloso, altanero.

aisle [aɪl] [áil], *s.* Nave de una iglesia, ala, costado.

aitch [eɪtʃ] [éich] *s.* Hache (letter).

aitchbone [ertʃbəʊn] [éich-boun] *s.* Cadera (of animals).

ajar [əˈdʒɑːr] [á-yar], *adv.* y *a.* 1. Semiabierto, entreabierto. Entornado. 2. En desacuerdo.

akimbo [əˈkɪmbəʊ] [a-kím-bou], *a.* En jarras, o en asas.

akin [əˈkɪn] [a-kín], *a.* 1. Consanguíneo, emparentado. 2. Del mismo género, de cualidades conformes.

AL, *n.* 1. Alabama. 2. American League (Liga estadounidense de béisbol).

alabaster ['æləbɑːstər] [a-la-bás-tar], *s.* Alabastro, especie de mármol blanco lechoso, y a veces con tintas de color.

alabastrine [ˌæləbæstrə-lá-bas-train] *a.* Alabastrino, de alabastro.

alack [əˈlæk] [a-lak] *(interj.)* ¡Ay de mí! ¡Ay!

alacrity [əˈlækrɪtɪ] [a-lá-kri-ti], *s.* Alegría, buen humor; ardor, celo.

aladdin [əˈlædɪn] [a-la-din] *N.* Aladino.

alan [əˈlæn] [a-lán] *N.* Alano.

aland [əˈlænd] [a-land], *adv.* A tierra.

Alans [əˈlænz] [a-láns] **Alani** [aláni] *N.* Alanos.

alar [əˈləˈr] [á-lar] *a.* Del ala. *(Méd.)* Axilar.

alarm [əˈlɑːm] [a-lárm], *s.* 1. Alarma, toque para tomar las armas. 2. Sobresalto, grito o señal para advertir un peligro. 3. Reloj con despertador.

alarm, *va.* 1. Tocar alarma. 2. Alarmar, asustar, sorprender: perturbar, inquietar.

alarm-bell [əˈlɑːmbel] [á-larm-bel], *s.* Campana de rebato.

alarm-clock [əˈlɑːmklɒk] [á-larm-klok], *s.* Despertador; reloj despertador.

alarming [əˈlɑːmɪŋ] [a-lár-min], *a.* Alarmante, sorprendente.

alarmingly [əˈlɑːmɪŋlɪ] [a-lár-min-li], *adv.* Espantosamente; de modo alarmante.

alarmist [əˈlɑːmɪst] [á-lar-mist], *s.* Alarmista, el que alarma o asusta.

alarm-post [əˈlɑːmpɒst] [á-larm-post], *s.* Atalaya, puesto de aviso.

alarm-watch [əˈlɑːmˈwɑːtʃ] [á-larm-uoch], *s.* Reloj con despertador.

alarum [əˈlærəm] [a-lá-rom], *s.* V. ALARM.

alas [əˈlæs] [ál-as], *inter.* ¡Ay! *V.* ALACK!

alate [aˈtl] [a-léit], **alated** [a-léi-ted], *a.* Alado, con alas.

alb [ælb] [álb], *s.* Alba, vestidura de lienzo blanco que se ponen los sacerdotes para celebrar la misa y otros oficios divinos.

albacore [ælbəkɔːr] [ál-ba-kor] *s. (Zool.)* Albacora.

albania [ælˈbeɪnɪə] [al-béi-nia] *N. (Geogr.)* Albania.

albanian [ælˈbeɪnɪən] [al-béi-nian], *a.* Albanés.

albata [ælˈbətə] [ál-ba-ta] *s.* Metal blanco, alpaca, plata alemana.

albatross ['ælbətɒs] [al-bá-tros], *s.* Albatros.

albeit [ɔːlˈbiːɪt] [ál-beit], *adv.* Aunque, bien que, no obstante, sin embargo, con todo.

albert ['ælbət] [ál-bert] *N.* Alberto.

albescent ['ælbesnt] [al-be-sent], *a.* Blanquecino.

Albigenses ['ælbɪˈdʒensiːz] [al-bi-chen-sis], *s.* Albigenses, nombre de unos sectarios franceses.

Albigensian ['ælbɪˈdʒensɪən] [al-bi-chen-sian] *a.* Albigense. **Albigensian Crusade,** cruzada de los albigenses.

Albinism ['ælbɪnɪzəm] [al-bi-nis-em] *s.* albinismo.

Albino [ælˈbɪnəʊ] [al-bí-nou], *a.* Albino.

Albion ['ælbɪən] [álb-ion], *s.* Albión, nombre antiguo de Inglaterra.

albite ['ælbaɪt] [al-báit] *s.* Albita.

albugineous ['ælbɪˈdʒɪnəs] [al-bu-chí-nos], *a.* Albuginoso, lo que tiene apariencia de clara de huevo.

album ['ælbəm] [ál-bom], *s.* 1. Librito de memoria. 2. Album, libro en que los amigos o conocidos del dueño de él, escriben alguna máxima suya o de otros, o alguna composición orginal, para que se conserve como autógrafa. 3. Libro para conservar fotografias, sellos de correos, etc.

albumen o albumin ['ælbjʊmɪn] [al-biú-min], *s.* 1. *(Quím.)* Albúmina, clara de huevo. 2. *(Bot.)* Albumen, materia nutritiva que rodea la semilla en muchas plantas.

albumenize ['ælbjʊmɪnaɪz] [al-biú-mi-nais], *va.* Impregnar con albumen, como se hace con el papel para la fotografia.

albuminoid [ælˈbjuːmɪnɔɪd] [al-biú-mi-noid], *a.* Albuminiforme. -s. Albuminoide, principio albuminoso que forma gran parte de los tejidos animales.

albuminous ['ælbjuːmɪnəs] [al-biú-mi-nos], *a.* Albuminoso: que contiene albumen.

albuminuria [ˌælbjuːmɪˈnərɪə] [al-biu-mi-mú-ria], *s.* Albuminuria; albúmina en la orina.

alburnum ['ælbɔːnəm] [al-bér-nom], *s. (Bot.)* Alburno o albura, la materia blanca que se halla entre la corteza y la madera del árbol. V. SAPWOOD.

alcaic [ælkaɪk] [al-káik], *s.* Verso alcaico. -a. Alcaico.

alcaid [ælkaɪd] [ál-kaid], *s.* Alcaide de un castillo.

alcazar [ælˈkeɪzər] [al-kéi-sad rf]s. Alcázar.

alchemist ['ælkɪmɪst] [ál-ki-mist], *s.* Alquimista, el que profesa el arte de la alquimia.

alchemy ['ælkɪmɪ] [ál-ki-mi], *s.* 1. Alquimia, el arte quimérica de purificar y trasmutar los metales. 2. Metal trabajado con el arte de la alquimia.

alcohol ['ælkəhɒl] [al-ko-jol], *s.* Alcohol. **Denatured alcohol,** alcohol desnaturalizado. **Grain alcohol,** alcohol de granos. **Wood alcohol,** alcohol metílico.

alcoholate ['ælkəhɒl] [al-kó-jo-leit] *s.* Alcoholato.

alcoholic [ælkəˈhɒlɪk] [al-ko-jó-lik], *a.* Alcohólico, que tiene alcohol, o las cualidades de él; producido por alcohol; conservado en alcohol. -s.pl. Líquidos alcohólicos.

alcoholimeter [ˌælkəhɒˈlɪmiːtər] [al-ko-jo-lí-mi-tar], **alcoholmeter** [ˌælkəhɒˈmiːtər] [al-ko-jól-mi-ta r], *s.* Alcoholímetro, alcohólmetro, especie de areómetro para medir la fuerza del alcohol.

alcoholism ['ælkəhɒlɪzəm] [al-ko-jo-lí-sem], *s.* Alcoholismo, enfermedad causada por el uso desarreglado o prolongado de bebidas alcohólicas.

alcoholization [ælkəhɒlarˈzerʃən] [al-ko-jo-lai-séi-shon], *s.* Alcoholización, el acto de alcoholar o alcoholizar.

alcoholize ['ælkəhɒlaɪz] [al-kó-jo-lais], *va.* Alcoholar o alcoholizar, extraer y rectificar el espíritu de cualquier licor.

Alcoran ['ælkərən] [al-ko-ran], *s.* Alcorán, libro que contiene la ley de Mahoma con sus ritos y creencias. V. KORAN.

alcoranish ['lkərənɪ] [al-ko-ra-ni-sem], *a.* Lo que pertenece al alcorán.

alcove [ælkəʊv] [al-kouv], *s.* 1. Alcoba, pieza o aposento destinado para dormir. 2. Cenador, glorieta o emparrado de jardín.

alcyon ['ælsaɪən] [al-sáion], *a.y s.* Lo mismo que HALCYON.

alcyone ['ælsaɪən] [al-sáion] *N.* Alción.

aldebaran ['ældəbərən] [al-de-ba-rán], *s. (Astr.)* Aldebarán, estrella principal de la constelación Tauro.

aldehyde ['ældehaid] [al-de-jaid], *s. (Quím.)* Aldehido; líquido incoloro y muy volátil, obtenido por la oxidación del alcohol. (Abreviado de **alcohol dehyratum.**)

alder ['ɔ:ldəʳ] [ál-daʳ], *s. (Bot.)* Aliso, árbol que tiene las hojas algo parecidas a las del avellano. **Alder grove,** alisar, aliseda.

alderman ['ɔ:ldəmən] [ál-dar-man], *s.* Regidor. Concejal.

alderman-like [,ɔ:ldəmən'laɪk] [ál-dar-man-laik], *a.* Magisterial; a manera de regidor.

aldermanly ['ɔ:ldəmənlɪ] [ál-dar-man-li], *a.* Como un regidor, con gravedad.

aldern ['ɔ:ldɜ:n] [ál-dern], *a.* Hecho de aliso.

ale [eɪl] [éil], *s.* Cerveza fuerte.

aleak [ə'li:k] [a-lík], *adv. y a.* En el acto de verterse y estado de perderse un líquido, en avería; derramándose.

aleatory [æl'tɔrɪ] [a-lí-to-ri], *a.* 1. Aleatorio, dependiente de un suceso fortuito. 2. Relativo o perteneciente a tahúres y fulleros.

ale-bench [eɪl'bentʃ] [éil-bench], *s.* Mostrador que suele ponerse en frente de las tabernas o casas en que se vende cerveza.

aleberry [eɪlberɪ] [éil-be-ri], *s.* Bebida hecha de cerveza hervida con especias, azúcar y tostadas de pan.

ale-brewer [eɪl'bru:əʳ] [eil-brúaʳ], *s.* Cervecero, el que por oficio hace la cerveza llamada *ale.*

ale-conner ['eɪlkɒnəʳ] [eil-kó-naʳ], *s.* Oficial o inspector de las cervecerías de Londres.

alecost ['eɪlkɒst] [éil-kost], *s. (Bot.)* V. TANZY.

a-lee [er'li:] [eilf], *adv. (Mar.)* A sotavento.

ale-fed [eɪl'fed] [éil-fed], *a.* Alimentado con cerveza.

alegard [æ'lə-gaʳ] [á-le-gaʳ], *s. (Prov. Ingl.)* Cerveza agria, vinagre de cerveza.

alehoof [eɪl'hu:f] [éil-juf], *s.* Hiedra terrestre.

alehouse [eɪl,haʊs] [éil-jaus], *s.* Cervecería.

alehouse-keeper [eɪl'haʊs,ki:pəʳ] [eil-jaus-kí-paʳ], *s.* Cervecero.

alembic ['eɪləmbɪk] [ei-lám-bik], *s.* Alambique.

alert [ə'lɜ:t] [á-lert], *a.* 1. Alerta, cuidadoso, vigilante. 2. Vivo, activo, dispuesto. **To be on the alert,** estar alerta. -*va.* Alertar.

alertness [ə'lɜ:tnɪs] [a-lért-nis], *s.* Cuidado, vigilancia, viveza, actividad, diligencia, agilidad; alegría.

aleurone [ə'lu:rən] [áluron] *s. (Bot.)* Aleurona.

alcutian [ə'lu:ʃən] [a-lu-shan], *a.* Aleuta, aleutino.

ale-vat [eɪl'væt] [éil-vat], *s.* Cuba o tina en que fermenta la cerveza.

ale-washed [eɪl'wɑ:ʃt] [éil-uasht], *a. (Ant.)* Mojado en cerveza.

alewife [eɪl'wɑɪf] [éil-uaif], *s.* 1. Cervecera, la mujer del cervecero. 2. Pez norteamericano, parecido a un sábalo pequeño, que se emplea generalmente como abono.

Alexander [ælɪg'zɑ:ndəʳ] [a-lek-sán-daʳ] *N.* Alejandro. **Alexander the Great,** Alejandro Magno.

alexanders [ælɪg'zɑ:ndɒz] [a-lek-sán-dars], *s. (Bot.)* Esmirnio, o apio caballar.

Alexandria [ælɪg'zɑ:ndrɪə] [a-lek-sán-dria] *N. (Geogr.)* Alejandría.

alexandrine [ælɪg'zændrɪn] [a-lek-san-drin], *s.* Verso alejandrino.

alexia [ælɪksɪə] [a-lík-sia] *a. (Med.)* Alexia.

alexipharmic, alexiteric, ó alexiterical [ælɪksɪ'fɑ:mɪk] [ælɪksɪ'tərɪk] [ælɪksɪ'tərɪkəl] [a-leks-fá-mik] [a-leks-té-rik] [a-leks-té-ri-kal], *a.* Alexifármaco o alexitérico, medicamento que tiene virtud preservativa o correctiva de los malos efectos del veneno.

alfalfa [æl'fælfə] [al-fél-fa], *s.* Alfalfa.

alfilaria [æl'fɪlɑrɪə] [al-fi-lá-ria], *s.* Hierba de California que se emplea como forraje. V. ALFILERERA.

Alfred [ælfred] [ál-fred] *N.* Alfredo.

alfresco [æl'freskəʊ] [al-frés-kou], Al raso. *(Ital.)*

alga [ælgə] [ál-ga], *pl.* **algae,** *s. (Bot.)* Alga, planta que se cría en las aguas, particularmente en el mar.

algal [ælgəl] [ál-gal], *a.* Algáceo, perteneciente a las algas.

algaroth [ælgərɒθ] [ál-ga-roz], *s.* Régulo de antimonio.

algebra [ældʒɪbrə] [ál-che-bra], *s.* Algebra, parte de las matemáticas.

algebraic, algebraical [ældʒɪˌbreɪk] [ældʒɪˌbreɪkl] [al-che-bráik] [al-che-brái-kal], *a.* Algebraico, lo que pertenece al álgebra.

algebraist [ældʒɪˌbreɪst] [ál-che-breist], *s.* Algebrista.

algeria [æl'dʒɪərɪə] [al-ché-ria] *N. (Geogr.)* Argelia.

algerian [æl'dʒɪərɪən] [al-ché-rian], *a.* Argelino: de Argel.

algerine [æl'dʒɪrɪn] [ál-che-rain], *a. y s.* 1. Argelino, natural de Argel. 2. *s.* Tejido blando de lana o chal con franjas de color claro.

algid [æl'dʒɪd] [ál-chid], *a.* álgido; que hiela, o causa frío. **Algid fever,** fiebre álgida.

algidity [æl'dʒɪdɪtɪ] [al-chí-di-ti] *s.* Algidez, frialdad.

algiers [æl'dʒɪz] [ál-chiars] *N. (Geogr.)* Argel.

algoid [æl'gɒɪd] [ál-goid], *a.* Algáceo, algoide, que se parece a las algas.

algology [æl'dʒɒlədʒɪ] [al-gó-lo-chi], *s.* Estudio o ciencia que trata de las algas.

algous [ælgəs] [ál-gos], *a.* Algoso; que pertenece a las algas: o lleno de algas.

algorithm [ælgərɪθm] [al-go-rí-zem], *s.* Algoritmo, ciencia del cálculo aritmético y algebraico; teoría de los números.

alguazil [ælgəsɪl] [al-go-sil], *s.* Alguacil, corchete, esbirro.

alias [eɪlɪæs] [éi-lias], *adv.* Alias, voz latina que significa de otro modo, de otra manera, o por otro nombre.

alibi [ælɪbɑɪ] [á-li-bai], *s. (For.)* Voz latina que significa ausencia, esto es, no haber estado en un lugar al tiempo de que se trata; coartada. **To prove an alibi,** Probar la coartada.

alible [ælɪbl] [á-li-bol], *a.* Nutritivo.

Alice [ælɪs] [á-lis] *N.* Alicia. **Alice in wonderland,** Alicia en el país de las maravillas.

alidade [ælɪdeɪd] [a-li-deid], *s.* Alidada, regla movediza que gira alrededor del centro de un instrumento y sirve para medir los ángulos.

alien [eɪlɪən] [éi-lian], *a.* Ajeno, extraño; forastero, extranjero; discorde, contrario.

alien, *s.* Extranjero, forastero.

alien, *va.* V. ALIENATE.

alienable [eɪlɪənəbl] [éi-lia-na-bol], *a.* Enajenable, traspasable.

alienate [eɪlɪəneɪt] [éi-lia-neit], *va.* 1. Enajenar, transferir, ceder. 2. Enajenar, desviar o apartar el afecto o cariño que se tenía hacia alguna persona; indisponer.

alienate, *a.* Ajeno, enajenado. -*s.* Extranjero.

alienation [ˌeɪlɪəˈneɪʃən] [ei-lian-éis-shon], *s.* 1. Enajenamiento o enajenación, la acción y efecto de enajenar o traspasar el dominio. 2. Enajenamiento, el acto de entibiarse la amistad y correspondencia entre dos o más personas; desunión, frialdad, desavenencia, desvío. 3. Enajenación del ánimo, locura, desvarío.

alienator [eɪlɪəˈneɪtəʳ] [ei-lia-néi-taʳ], *s.* Enajenador, cesionista. El que enajena a otro.

alienee [eɪlɪəni] [ei-lia-ni], *s.* Aquel a quien pasa la propiedad de una cosa.

alienism [eɪlɪənɪzm] [éi-lia-nis-em], *s.* 1. El estado legal de un extranjero. 2. El tratamiento de las enfermedades mentales.

alienist [eɪlɪənɪst] [éi-lia-nist], *s. (Med.)* Alienista, especialista en enfermedades mentales.

alienor [eɪlɪənəʳ] [éi-lia-noʳ], *s.* Enajenante: el o la que enajena.

aliferous, aligerous [əlɪ'fərəs] [əlɪ'dʒərəs] [a-lí-fe-ros] [a-lí-ye-ros], *a.* Alado, lo que tiene alas. *(Pét.)* Alígero.

aliform [ælɪfɔ:m] [áli-form], *a.* Aliforme, en forma de alas.

alight [ə'lɑɪt] [a-láit], *vn.* 1. Descender, bajar de un coche, etc. **To alight from a horse,** apearse de un caballo. 2. Echarse sobre alguna cosa, caer, posarse. 3. Caer en cuenta de alguna cosa por casualidad. -*a. y adv.* Encendido, inflamado; en llamas.

align [ə'lɑɪn] [a-láin], *va.* Alinear, poner en línea. Lo mismo que ALINE.

alignment [ə'lɑɪnmənt] [a-láin-ment], *s.* Alineamiento, acción y efecto de alinear.

alike [ə'lɑɪk] [a-láik], *adv.* 1. Igualmente, del mismo modo. 2. A la vez. -*a.* Semejante, igual. **To look alike,** parecerse. **They are all alike,** todos son parecidos.

alike-minded [ə'lɑɪk'mɑɪndɪd] [a-láik-main-did], *a.* Del mismo ánimo, o modo de pensar.

aliment ['ælɪmənt] [á-li-ment] *s.* Alimento. *va.* Alimentar.

alimental ['ælɪməntl] [a-li-mén-tal], *a.* Nutritivo, lo que nutre o alimenta, alimenticio, alimentoso.

alimentally ['ælɪməntəlɪ] [a-li-mén-ta-li], *adv.* Nutritivamente.

alimentariness [,ælɪmən'tərɪnɪs] [a-li-men-tá-ri-nes], *s.* Alimentación, nutrición.

alimentary ['ælɪməntərɪ] [a-li-mén-ta-ri], *a.* 1. Alimenticio, lo que toca al alimento. 2. Alimentoso, lo que tiene virtud de alimentar, jugoso. **Alimentary canal,** tubo digestivo.

alimentation ['ælɪmən'teɪʃən] [a-li-men-téi-shon], *s.* Alimentación.

alimentiveness [,ælɪmən'tɪvnɪs] [a-li-mén-tif-nes], *s.* Apetito o deseo de tomar alimento.

alimonious ['æɪmənɪəs] [a-li-mó-nios], *a.* Alimenticio, alimentoso.

alimony ['ælɪmənɪ] [a-lí-mo-ni], *s.* Alimentos, existencias, la parte de los bienes del marido, que por sentencia judicial se señala a la mujer por causa de divorcio o separación.

aline [ə'lɑɪn] [a-láin], *va.* Poner en línea, alinear. -*vn.* Ponerse en línea.

aliped [ə'lɪpd] [a-lípd], *a.* Alípede, quiróptero.

aliquant ['ælɪkwənt] [a-lí-kuant], *a.* Alicuanta, la parte que no mide cabalmente a su todo; así, tres es alicuanta de diez.

aliquot ['ælɪkwɒt] [a-lí-kuot], *a.* Alícuota, la parte que mide cabalmente a su todo; *p.ej.* tres es la parte alícuota de doce.

alish ['ælɪʃ] [álish], *a.* Acervezado, parecido o semejante a la cerveza llamada *ale.*

alive [ə'lɑɪv] [a-láif], *a.* 1. Vivo o viviente, 2. Vivo, no apagado, ni destruido. 3. Activo, vivo, alegre. 4. Se usa muchas veces enfáticamente para ponderar: v.g. **The best man alive,** el mejor hombre que existe, o que hay entre los vivientes. **Alive and kicking,** vivito y coleando. **Dead or alive,** vivo o muerto.

alkahest, *s. V.* ALCAHEST.

alkalescence ['ælkələsns] [al-ká-le-sens], *s.* Alcalescencia.

alkalescent ['ælkələsnt] [al-ká-le-sent], *a.* Alcalescente, lo que tiene tendencia o propiedades alcalinas.

alkali ['ælkəlɑɪ] [ál-ka-li], *s.* álcali, cualquier sustancia que, mezclada con los ácidos, produce sales: base.

alkalify ['ælkəlɑɪfɪ] [al-ká-li-fai], *va.* Convertir en álcali.

alkaligenous [,ælkəlɑɪ'dʒɪnəs] [al-ka-lí-che-nos], *a.* Alcalígeno, generador de álcalis.

alkalimeter [,ælkəlɪ'mɪtəʳ] [al-ka-lí-mi-taʳ], *s.* Alcalímetro, instrumento para medir la cantidad de álcali que contiene una sustancia.

alkaline ['ælkəlɑɪn] [ál-ka-lain], *a.* Alcalino, lo que tiene propiedades de álcali.

alkaline earth [,ælkəlɑɪn'ɜ:θ] [ál-ka-lain-erz] *s. / adj.* Alcalinotérreo.

alkalinity [,ælkə'lɪnɪtɪ] [al-ka-lí-ni-ti], *s.* Alcalinidad, estado alcalino, efecto de los álcalis.

alkalization [,ælkəlɪ'zerʃən] [al-ka-li-zéi-shon], *s.* Alcalización.

alkalize ['ælkəlɑɪz] [ál-ka-lais], *va.* Alcalizar, hacer alcalino.

alkaloid ['ælkəlɔɪd] [ál-ka-loid], *s.* Alcaloide, álcali orgánico o vegetal; base orgánica.

alkalosis ['ælkələsɪs] [al-ka-ló-sis] *s.* Alcalosis.

alkanet ['ælkənet] [ál-ka-net], *s. (Bot.)* Búgula o melera; ancusa.

alkermes ['ælkɜ:mes] [ál-keʳ-mes], *s.* Alquermes, confección cuyo principal ingrediente es el quermes.

all [ɔ:l] [ol], *a.* 1. Todo, lo que se comprende entera y cabalmente en el número. **All hands aloft,** *(Mar.)* todo el mundo arriba. **All hands below,** *(Mar.)* todo el mundo abajo. 2. Todo, lo que se comprende entera y cabalmente en la cantidad. **All his money is spent,** todo su dinero se ha gastado.

all, *s.* Todo el compuesto de partes integrantes. **All in the wind,** *(Mar.)* en facha. **When all comes to all,** con todo eso, en fin. **It is all the same,** es absolutamente lo mismo. **For good and all,** enteramente, para siempre. **To be all in all with one,** ser el favorito de alguna persona. **Not at all,** no por cierto, nada de eso, de ninguna manera. **All along,** por todo el tiempo, siempre. **By all means,** sin duda, absolutamente, sea como fuere. **He is undone to all intents and purposes,** está enteramente arruinado o perdido. **For all,** *loc. prep.* a pesar de.

all, *adv.* Del todo, enteramente. **All on a sudden,** de golpe y porrazo, de repente, repentinamente. **All the better,** tanto mejor. **All the worse,** tanto peor. **All at once,** de repente, de golpe. **All,** muchas veces se une con adjetivos y participios, como se ve por los siguientes. En las voces **Almighty, Already,** etc., se suprime una 1. (*V.* estas palabras en su lugar alfabético.)

all-abandoned [ɔ:lə'bændənd] [ol-a-bán-dond], *a.* Desamparado por todos.

all-abhorred [ɔ:lə'bɔ:d] [ol-a-bórd], *a.* Aborrecido de todos.

all-admiring [ɔ:læd'mɑɪrɪŋ] [ol-ad-máirin], *a.* Admirador de todo.

all-advised [ɔ:ləd'vɑɪst] [ol-ad-váist], *a.* Aconsejado de todos.

allah ['ælə] [alá], *s.* Alá, voz árabe que significa Dios.

all-American [ɔ:lə'merɪkæn] [ol-a-mé-ri-kan] *a.* Típicamente americano. **The all-American team,** el mejor equipo americano.

Allan ['ælən] [á-lan] *N.* Alano.

allantois ['æləntɔɪs] [ol-an-tóis], *s.* Alantóides, saco membranoso situado entre el corion y el amnios en el feto.

all-approved [ɔ:lə'pru:vd] [ol-a-prufd], *a.* Aprobado por todos.

all-around [ɔ:lə'rɑʊnd] [ol-a-ráund] *a.* Completo.

all-atoning [ɔ:lə'tənɪŋ] [ol-a-tó-nin], *a.* Lo que compensa o lo expía todo.

allay [ə'leɪ] [á-lei], *va.* Aliviar, aquietar, apaciguar, reprimir, suavizar, mitigar, endulzar.

allayment [ə'leɪmənt] [á-lei-ment], *s.* Alivio, descanso o desahogo.

all-bearing [ɔ:l'beərɪŋ] [ol-béa-rin], *a.* Lo que produce o cría todas las cosas.

all-beauteous [ɔ:l'bɪu:təs] [ol-biú-tuos], *a.* Enteramente hermoso.

all-beholding [ɔ:l'bɪhəʊldɪŋ] [ol-bi-jól-din], *a.* Lo que ve todas las cosas.

all-blasting [ɔ:l'blæstɪŋ] [ol-blás-tin], *a.* Lo que difama o arruina a todas las personas o cosas.

all-clear [ɔ:l'klɪəʳ] [ol-kléa] *s.* Final de la alarma.

all-changing [ɔ:l'tʃændʒɪŋ] [ol-chán-yin], *a.* Lo que está cambiando perpetuamente.

all-cheering [ɔ:l'tʃɪrɪŋ] [ol-chia-rin], *a.* Lo que todo lo alegra.

all-commanding [ɔ:l'kəmændɪŋ] [ol-kó-man-din], *a.* Lo que manda en todas partes.

all-complying [ɔ:l'kɒmplɑɪŋ] [ol-kom-plái-in], *a.* El que se acomoda a todo.

all-composing [ɔ:l'kɒmpəʊsɪŋ] [ol-kom-pó-sin], *a.* El que sosiega y lo compone todo.

all-comprehensive [ɔ:lkɒmprɪ'hensɪv] [ol-kom-pri-jén-sif], *a.* Lo que lo comprende todo.

all-concealing [ɔ:l'kənsi:lɪŋ] [ol-kon-sí-lin], *a.* Lo que todo lo oculta.

all-conquering [ɔ:l'kɒŋkərɪŋ] [ol-kón-ke-rin], *a.* Lo. que todo lo vence.

all-constraining [ɔːlˈkʰɒnsteɪnɪŋ] [ol-kons-tréi-nin], *a*. Lo que todo lo refrena, reprime o retiene.

all-consuming [ɔːlˌkʰɒnˈsjuːmɪŋ] [ol-kon-siú-min], *a*. Lo que todo lo consume o gasta.

all-daring [ɔːlˈdɛərɪŋ] [ol-déa-rin], *a*. Lo que osa o se atreve a todo.

all-destroying [ɔːlˈdɪstrɔɪɪŋ] [ol-dis-trói-yin], *a*. Lo que todo lo arruina.

all-devastating [ɔːlˈdevəsteɪtɪŋ] [ol-de-vas-téi-tin], *a*. Lo que todo lo devasta.

all-devouring [ɔːlˈdɪvərɪŋ] [ol-di-vó-rin], *a*. Lo que todo lo consume o devora.

all-dimming [ɔːlˈdɪmɪŋ] [ol-dí-min], *a*. Lo que obscurece todas las cosas.

all-discovering [ɔːlˈdɪskʌvərɪŋ] [ol-dis-ká-ve-rin], *a*. Lo que todo lo descubre.

all-disgraced [ɔːlˈdɪsɡreɪsd] [ol-dis-gréist], *a*. Enteramente deshonrado.

all-dispensing [ɔːlˈdɪspensɪŋ] [ol-dis-pén-sin], *a*. El que dispensa de todo, o el que tiene facultad de permitirlo todo por sí mismo.

all-divine [ɔːlˈdɪvaɪn] [ol-di-váin], *a*. Divinísimo, divino en sumo grado.

all-divining [ɔːlˈdɪvaɪnɪŋ] [ol-di-vái-nin], *a*. El que lo adivina o pronostica todo.

all-dreaded [ɔːlˈdriːded] [ol-drí-ded], *a*. Temido de todos.

all-drowsy [ɔːlˈdraʊsɪ] [ol-dráu-si], *a*. Muy soñoliento.

allegation [ælɪˈɡeɪʃən] [a-le-géi-shon], *s*. 1. Alegación o alegato. 2. Alegación, excusa o disculpa; razón. 3. Alegato, cita.

allege [əˈledʒd] [a-léch], *va*. 1. Alegar, afirmar, declarar, sostener. 2. Alegar, sacar a su favor algún dicho u otra cosa que sirva de disculpa; citar, exponer.

allegeable [əˈledʒiːbl] [a-lé-cha-bol], *a*. Lo que se puede alegar.

allegement [əˈledʒɪdmənt] [a-léch-ment], *s*. V. ALLEGATION.

alleger [əˈledʒər] [al-lé-gar], *s*. Alegador, afirmante, declarante.

allegiance [əˈlidʒəns] [al-lí-gians], *s*. Lealtad, fidelidad, la obligacion que debe todo vasallo a su soberano; sumisión, fidelidad, obediencia, homenaje. **To swear allegiance,** jurar fidelidad; hacer pleito homenaje.

allegiant [əˈlidʒənt] [al-lí-giant], *a*. Leal, obediente, sumiso.

allegoric [ælɪˈɡɒrɪk] [a-li-gó-rik], **allegorical** [ælɪˈɡɒrɪkəl] [a-li-gí-ri-kal], *a*. Alegórico.

allegorically [ˌælɪˈɡɒrɪkəlɪ] [a-li-gí-ri-ka-li], *adv*. Alegóricamente, en sentido alegórico.

allegoricalness [ælɪˈɡɒrɪkəlnɪs] [a-li-gí-ri-kal-nis], *s*. La calidad de ser alegórico.

allegorist [ælɪˈɡɒrɪst] [a-li-gí-rist], *s*. El que alegoriza, el autor u orador que explica el sentido de las cosas por alegorias.

allegorize [ˈælɪˈɡɒraɪz] [a-lí-go-rais], *va*. Alegorizar, interpretar alegóricamente. *-vn*. Tratar o discurrir alegóricamente.

allegory [ˈælɪˈɡɒrɪ] [a-lí-go-ri], *s*. Alegoría, metáfora continuada, discurso figurado.

allegretto [ˌæleˈtəʊ] [al-lei-gré-tou] (*Ital.*), *a*. Más vivo que el andante, pero no tanto como el alegro. *-s*. Movimiento en este tiempo.

allegro [əˈleɪɡrəʊ] [al-lé-grou], *s*. (*Mús.*) Alegro, voz tomada de la lengua italiana, que significa un movimiento moderadamente vivo en la música.

all-eloquent [ɔːlˈeləkwənt] [ol-í-lo-kuant], *a*. Elocuentísimo, muy elocuente.

allelujah [ælɪˈluːjə] [a-li-lú-ya], *s*. Aleluya, voz hebrea que expresa júbilo espiritual y significa "Alabad a Dios, o al Señor." V. HALLELUJAH.

all-embracing [ɔːlˈɪmbreɪsɪŋ] [il-im-bréi-sin], *a*. Lo que lo comprende o abraza todo.

allen [ˈælən] [á-lan] *N*. Alano.

all-ending [ælˈendɪŋ] [ol-én-din], *a*. Lo que acaba todas las cosas.

all-enlightening [ælənˈlaɪtnɪŋ] [al-in-láit-nin], *a*. Lo que ilumina por todas partes.

all-enraged [ælənˈreɪdʒd] [ol-in-réicht], *a*. Muy enojado o enfurecido.

allergen [ˈæləˌdʒən] [al-lér-chen], *s*. Alergeno.

allergic [əˈlədʒɪk] [a-lér-chik], *a*. (*Med.*) Alérgico.

allergist [əˈlədʒɪst] [a-lér-chist] *s*. Médico especialista en alergias.

allergy [əˈlədʒɪ] [a-lér-chi], *s*. (*Med.*) Alergia.

alleviate [əˈliːvɪeɪt] [á-li-viéit], *va*. Aligerar, aliviar, mitigar, aplacar.

alleviation [əˌliːvɪˈeɪʃən] [á-li-viéi-shon], *s*. 1. Aligeramiento, la acción de aligerar. 2. Alivio, disminución de algún dolor, o circunstancia atenuante de algún delito; mitigación.

alleviative [əˈliːvɪətɪv] [al-lí-via-tif], *s*. Paliativo.

alleviatory [əˈliːvɪətərɪ] [a-li-ia-tó-ri] *a*. Aliviador.

alley [ˈælɪ] [á-li, *s*. 1. Calle o paseo de jardín. 2. Callejuela, calle mas angosta que las comunes en las ciudades y pueblos grandes. 3. Espacio largo y angosto para el juego de bolos. **Blind-alley,** callejón sin salida. **Alleyway,** callejuela, calle estrecha. **Alley cat** [] *s*. Gato callejero.

all-flaming [ɔːlˈflæmɪŋ] [ol-flé-min], *a*. Lo que echa llamas por todos lados.

all-fools' Day [ˈɔːlfuːlzdeɪ] [ól-fuls-déi], *s*. El día primero de abril; se le da el nombre de día de los tontos, por la costumbre de hacer inocentadas ese día; día de los Inocentes.

all-forgiving [ɔːlfɔːˈɡɪvɪŋ] [ol-for-gí-vin], *a*. Que todo lo perdona.

all-fours [ɔːlfɔːz] [ol-fórs], *s*. Los cuatro palos, juego de naipes. **To go on all-fours,** gatear, andar a gatas.

all-giver [ɔːlˈɡɪvər] [ol-guí-var], *s*. Dios, el dador de todas las cosas.

all-good [ɔːlˈɡuːd] [ól-gud], *s*. Dios, el ser infinitamente bueno. *-a*. Dios, la suprema bondad.

all-guiding [ɔːlˈɡaɪdɪŋ] [ol-gái-din], *a*. Lo que guia o conduce todas las cosas.

all-hail [ɔːlˈheɪl] [ol-jéil], *s*. Salud completa.

all-hail, *va*. Saludar, desear salud.

All-hallow, All-hallows [ˈɔːlˈhæləʊz] [ol-jálou], *s*. El día de Todos los Santos.

All-hallowe'en [ˈɔːlˈhæləʊwiːn] [ol-já-louin], *s*. La noche del 31 de Octubre; víspera del día de Todos los Santos.

all-heal [ˈɔːlˈhiːl] [ol-jíl], *s*. (*Bot.*) Panacea, planta.

all-healing [ɔːlˈhiːlɪŋ] [ol-jí-lin], *a*. Que lo cura o sana todo.

all-helping [ɔːlˈhelpɪŋ] [ol-jél-pin], *a*. Lo que a todos ayuda.

all-hiding [ˌɔːlˈhaɪdɪŋ] [ol-jái-din], *a*. Lo que todo oculta.

all-honored [ɔːlˈhɒnɔːd] [ol-jó-nod], *a*. Honrado por todos.

all-hurting [ɔːlˈhɜːtɪŋ] [ol-jér-tin], *a*. Lo que a todo hiere o lastima.

alliable [əˈlaɪəbl] [a-láia-bol], *a*. Capaz de aliarse.

alliaceous [əˈlaɪəsəs] [a-lái-a-sas], *a*. Aliáceo.

alliance [əˈlaɪəns] [a-lái-ans], *s*. 1. Alianza, unión, liga o confederación que forman entre sí los estados para defenderse mutuamente de sus enemigos o para ofenderlos. 2. Alianza, conexión o parentesco, contraído por casamiento. 3. Parentesco, sea por afinidad o por consanguinidad. 4. Parentela, el conjunto de todo género de parientes.

all-idolizing [əˈlaɪədəlɪsɪŋ] [ol-ai-dó-li-sin], *a*. El que lo adora, venera o idolatra todo.

allied [ˈælaɪd] [a-láid], *a*. Aliado, unido, confederado. **Allied** to, pariente de.

allies [ˈælaɪz] [a-láis], *s. pl*. Aliados, confederados. V. **ALLY.**

alligate [ˈælɪɡeɪt] [á-li-geit], *va*. Ligar, atar o afianzar una cosa a otra.

alligation [ˌælɪɡeɪˈʃən] [a-li-géi-shon], *s*. 1. Aligación, la acción de ligar o atar. 2. (*Arit.*) Aligación, la regla por la cual se computa y averigua el precio común de mezcla de especies de diferente valor. 3. Ligazón, atadura, unión.

alligator [ˈælɪɡeɪtər] [a-li-géi-tar], *s*. Caimán o aligador, especie de cocodrilo de América. Lacerta alligator. (*Mex.*) Lagarto. **Alligator-pear,** avocado, aguacate (Cuba) o agualate (en Perú, palta). **Alligator-tree,** liquidámbar común de

América. **Alligator-apple,** anona de los pantanos. Este árbol de las Antillas da un fruto que es manjar predilecto de los cocodrilos.

all-imitating [æl'ɪmɪteɪtɪŋ] [ol-i-mi-téi-tin], *a.* Lo que lo imita todo.

all-in ['ɔːlɪn] [ol-in] *a.* Global. **All-in charge,** precio todo incluido. **All-in wrestling,** lucha libre.

all-informing [ˌɔːlɪn'fɔːmɪŋ] [ol-in-fó-min], *a.* Lo que lo mueve o anima todo.

all-interpreting [ˌɔːlɪntɜːprɪtɪŋ] [ol-in-ter-prí-tin], *a.* El que todo lo explica.

allision ['əlɪʃən] [a-lí-shon], *s.* Choque, la acción de golpear o dar una cosa contra otra.

alliterate [ə'lɪtəreɪt] *vn.* Escribir o hablar usando aliteraciones.

alliteration [ə'lɪtəreɪʃən] [a-li-te-réi-shon], *s.* Aliteración, paronomasia.

alliterative [ə'lɪtərətɪv] [a-li-té-ra-tif], *a.* Lo que pertenece a las voces que empiezan con la misma letra.

all-judging [ɔːl'dʒʌdʒɪŋ] [ol-yá-chin], *a.* El que tiene el derecho soberano de juzgar.

all-knowing [ɔːl'nəʊɪŋ] [ol-nóuin], *a.* Omnisciente, que todo lo sabe.

all-licensed ['ɔːlaɪsəns] [ol-lai-sens], *a.* Con libertad para todo.

all-loving [ɔːl'lʌvɪŋ] [ol-lá-vin], *a.* Amantísimo.

all-making [ɔːl'meɪkɪŋ] [ol-méi-kin], *a.* El que lo crea o cría todo, el que todo lo hace.

all-murdering [ɔːl'mɜːdərɪŋ] [ol-már-derin], *a.* Sangrientísimo, aniquilador, destructor.

all-night [ɔːl'naɪt] [ol-nait] *a.* Abierto toda la noche. Que dura toda la noche.

all-obedient [ɔːlo'bɪdɪənt] [ol-o-bí-di-ent], *a.* Obediente en absoluto.

all-oblivious [ɔːl'əblɪvɪəs] [ol-o-blí-vios], *a.* Lo que causa olvido total.

all-obscuring [ɔːl'əskjʊrɪŋ] [ol-obs-kiú-rin], *a.* Lo que esconde u obscurece todas las cosas.

allocate ['æləʊkeɪt] [á-lo-keit], *va.* Colocar, señalar puesto. Distribuir.

allocation [æləʊ'keɪʃən] [a-lo-kéi-shon, *s.* 1. Distribución. colocación. 2. Asignación, fijación.

allocution [æləʊ'kjuːʃən] [a-lo-kiú-shon], *s.* Alocución, arenga, discurso.

allodial ['æləʊdɪəl] [a-ló-dial], *a.* Alodial, libre de toda carga, independiente.

allodium ['æləʊdɪəm] [a-ló-diom] *s.* Alodio, posesión absoluta e independiente de tierras o bienes, sin reconocimiento de ningún dominio soberano.

allonge ['ælɒndʒ] [a-lónch], *s.* 1. Bote, botonazo, estocada, el golpe que se tira de punta con la espada o estoque. 2. El ramal largo con que se enseña a los caballos en el picadero.

allopath ['æləpəθ] [a-ló-paz] ó **allopathist** ['æləpəθɪst] [a-ló-pa-zist], *s.* Alópata, médico que profesa los principios de la alopatía.

allopathic ['æləpəθɪk] [a-lo-pá-zik], *a.* Alopático relativo a la alopatía, o que la favorece y prefiere.

allopathy ['æləpəθɪ] [a-ló-pa-zi], *s.* Alopatía, sistema de medicina por el cual se trata de curar una enfermedad produciendo un estado y fenómenos incompatibles con la misma: la práctica ordinaria de la medicina como opuesta a la homeopatía.

allot [ə'lɒt] [á-lot], *va.* 1. Distribuir por suerte. 2. Conceder. 3. Repartir, asignar, adjudicar, destinar, dar a cada uno su parte o lo que le toca.

allotment [ə'lɒtmənt] [a-lót-ment], *s.* Lote, parte o porcion de cualquier cosa que se da a alguno en el reparto de ella: asignación, repartimiento. (U.S.) Parte del sueldo de un miembro de las fuerzas armadas, que se envía a una persona designada por él.

allotropic [ə'lɒtrəpɪk] [a-lo-tró-pik], *a.* Alotrópico; lo que pertenece al alotropismo.

allotropism [ə'lɒtrəpɪzm] [a-lo-tro-písem], **allotropy** [ə'lɒtrəpɪ] [a-ló-tro-pi], *s. (Quím.)* Alotropia, la diferencia o el cambio en las propiedades físicas de ciertas sustancias o sus compuestos, sin cambio correspondiente en su composición química.

allotted [ə'lɒtɪd] [a-ló-tid], *pp. y a.* 1. Repartido, dividido, distribuido en lotes o porciones. 2. Asignado, señalado.

all-out ['ɔːl'aʊt] [ol-aut], *a.* Total. completo. -*adv.* Totalmente, resueltamente.

all-over [ɔːl'əʊvəʳ] [ol-óuvar], *a.* De diseño repetido.

allow [ə'ləʊ] [a-láu], *va.* 1. Admitir, reconocer. **To allow sth, to be true,** reconocer que algo es verdad. 2. Conceder o ceder, consentir, confesar, aprobar. 3. Permitir. **Smoking is allowed,** se permite fumar. 4. Dar, pagar. 5. Abonar en cuenta. 6. Descontar, desfalcar. 7. Señalar, adjudicar. *vn.* **I allow of that,** Concedo eso. **To allow for,** tener en cuenta.

allowable [ə'ləʊvəbl] [a-láua-bol], *a.* 1. Admisible, lo que se puede admitir sin contradicción. 2. Lícito, permitido, legítimo, justo.

allowableness [ə'ləʊvəblnɪs] [a-láua-bol-nis], *s.* Legitimidad, legalidad; propiedad; exención; permiso.

allowably [ə'ləʊvəblɪ] [a-láua-bli], *adv.* Con permiso, legítimamente.

allowance [ə'ləʊəns] [a-láuans], *s.* 1. Permiso, concesión. 2. Indulgencia o disminución de rigor. 3. Ración, gajes, salurio. 4. Señalamiento, pensión, abono, alimentos, mesada. 5. Licencia, excusa, connivencia. 6. Carácter establecido. **To keep on allowance,** poner a ración; poner a dieta. **To make allowance for,** hacerse cargo de, ser indulgente. **To give allowance to one's inclinations,** ceder a las propias inclinaciones. **Family allowance,** subsidios familiares.

alloy ['ælɔɪ] [a-lói], *va.* 1. Ligar, mezclar un metal con otro para poderlo acuñar con más facilidad, alear los metales. 2. Ligar, juntar una cosa con otra, o mezclarla para rebajar sus calidades.

alloy, *s.* 1. Liga, el metal de baja ley que se mezcla con el oro o la plata en la acuñación de la moneda. 2. Liga, la cosa que, añadida o mezclada con otra, rebaja sus calidades predominantes; mezcla.

alloyage [æ'lɔɪadʒ] [a-lói-ach], *s.* Liga, mezcla de metales; acción de ligar los metales.

all-penetrating [ɔːlˌpenɪ'treɪtɪŋ] [ol-pe-ni-tréi-tin], *a.* Que todo lo penetra.

all-perfect [ɔːl'pɜːfekt] [ol-pér-fekt], *a.* Perfectísimo.

all-perfectness [ɔːl'pɜːfektnɪs] [ol-pér-fekt-nis], *s.* Perfección completa, conjunto de perfecciones.

all-piercing [ɔːl'liːsɪŋ] [ol-pir-sin], *a.* Lo que penetra por todo.

all-powerful ['ɔːl'paʊəfʊl] [ol-páua-ful] o **all-potent** [ɔːl'pɒtənt] [ol-pó-tent], *a.* Omnipotente, todopoderoso.

all-praised ['ɔːl'preɪzd] [ol-préist], *a.* Alabado por todos.

all-purpose ['ɔːl'pɜːpəs] [ol-pér-pos] *a.* Para todo uso, universal.

all-right [ɔːl'raɪt] [ól-rait], *adv.* Bien, bueno, perfectamente, está bien.

all-round [ˌɔːl'raʊnd] [ól-raund], *a.* Completo, en todas formas. **All-round athlete,** deportista o atleta completo o en todos los campos.

all-ruling [ɔːl'ruːlɪŋ] [ol-rú-lin], *a.* El que todo lo gobierna.

all-saints'day ['ɔːl'seɪntsdeɪ] [ol-séints-dei], *s.* El día o fiesta de Todos los Santos, Nov. 1.

all-sanctifying ['ɔːl'sæŋktɪfaɪŋ] [ol-sánk-ti-fai-yin], *a.* Que todo lo santifica.

all-saving [ɔːl'seɪvɪŋ] [ol-séi-vin], *a.* Salvador o conservador de todo.

all-searching [ɔːl'sɜːtʃɪŋ] [ol-sér-chin], *a.* Lo que lo examina o penetra todo.

all-seeing [ɔːl'siːɪŋ] [ol-sí-in], *a.* Que todo lo ve.

all-seer [ɔːl'sɪəʳ] [ol-síar], *s.* Veedor u observador de todo, el que ve todas las cosas.

all-shunned [ɔːl'ʃʌnd] [ol-shánd], *a.* Evitado o huido por todos.

All-souls'day ['ɔːl'sɔʊlzdeɪ] [ól-souls-dei], *s.* El día de las ánimas, o día de difuntos. *(Mex.)* El día de los muertos, Nov. 2.

allspice ['ɔːl'spaɪs] [óls-pais], *s.* Pimienta de Jamaica.

all-star ['ɔːl'stɑː] [ól-sta'] *a.* De primeras figuras.

all-sufficiency ['ɔːl'səfɪʃənsɪ] [ol-sa-fí-shan-si], *s.* Habilidad infinita.

all-sufficient ['ɔːl'səfɪʃənt] [ol-sa-fí-shant], *a.* Bastante o suficiente para todo. -*s.* Dios.

all-surveying ['ɔːl'sɜːveɪɪŋ] [ol-ser-véi-yin], *a.* Que todo lo mira.

all-sustaining ['ɔːl'səstaɪnɪŋ] [ol-sas-téi-nin], *a.* Sostenedor y mantenedor de todas las cosas.

all-telling ['ɔːl'telɪŋ] [ol-té-lin], *a.* Hablador, el que todo lo dice o divulga.

all-time ['ɔːl'taɪm] [ól-taim], *a.* Sin precedente, absoluto; de todos los tiempos. **All-time high,** Lo más alto hasta ahora.

all-triumphant ['ɔːl'rɪʊmfənt] [ol-triúm-fant], *a.* Triunfante en todas partes.

allude [ə'luːd] [a-liúd], *va.* Aludir, hacer relación a alguna cosa sin mencionarla directamente.

alluminate [ə'luːmɪneɪt] [a-liú-mi-neit], *va.* Iluminar dibujos.

alluminor [ə'luːmɪnə'] [a-lu-mí-nar], *s.* Iluminador.

allure [ə'ljʊə'] [a-liúar], *va.* 1. Halagar, atraer con halagos, alucinar. cebar. 2. Atraer, seducir. **That can allure none but fools,** eso no puede seducir más que a los necios. *s.* Atractivo.

allurement [ə'ljʊəmənt] [a-liúa-ment], *s.* Halago, engañifa; atractivo, cebo, lisonja, aliciente, seducción.

allurer [ə'ljʊə'] [a-liúar], *s.* Halagador, seductor, engañador.

alluring [ə'ljʊərɪŋ] [a-liúa-rin], *a.* Halagüeño, seductivo, atractivo.

alluringly [ə'ljʊərɪŋlɪ] [a-liúa-rin-li], *adv.* Halagüeñamente, seductoramente.

alluringness [ə'ljʊərɪŋnɪs] [a-liúa-rin-nis], *s.* Aliciente, atractivo, incentivo, agrado.

allusion [ə'ljuːzən] [a-liúa-shon], *s.* 1. Alusión. 2. Indirecta.

allusive [ə'ljuːsɪv] [a-liú-sif] *a.* Alusivo.

allusively [ə'ljuːsɪvlɪ] [a-liu-síf-li], *adv.* Alusivamente.

allusiveness [ə'ljuːsɪvnɪs] [a-liu-síf-nis], *s.* La calidad de ser alusivo.

alluvial [ə'ljuːvɪəl] [a-liú-vial], *a.* Aluvial; lo que pertenece al aluvión, está contenido en él. o es producido por él.

alluvion [ə'ljuːvɪən] [a-liú-vion], *s.* 1. Aluvión, aumento de tierras causado por las avenidas o corrientes de los ríos; terreno. 2. Avenida, inundación.

alluvious [ə'ljuːvɪəs] [a-liú-vios], *a.* (Poco us.) V. ALLUVIAL.

alluvium [ə'ljuːvɪəm] [a-liú-viom], *s.* Terreno de origen reciente formado por la acumulación de cieno, arenas, etc., debida a la acción de las aguas: aluvión, 1a acep.

all-watched [ɔːl'wɑːtʃ] [al-uácht], *a.* Vigilado por todos.

all-weather ['ɔːl'weðə'] [ol-uéa-za'] *a.* Para todo tiempo.

all-wise [ɔːl'waɪz] [ol-uáis]. *a.* Infinitamente sabio, sapientísimo.

all-witted [ɔːl'wɪtd] [ol-uít], *a.* Ingeniosísimo.

all-worshipped ['ɔːl'wɔːʃɪpt] [ol-uér-shipt], *a.* Adorado de todos.

ally ['ælɪ] [al-i], *va.* 1. Hacer alianza o unión por afinidad o confederación. 2. Concordar o poner en relación una cosa con otra. -*vn.* Confederarse, aliarse.

ally, *s.* Aliado, confederado, el que tjene alianza con otro por afinidad, amistad o confederación.

almagest ['ælməgest] [al-má-yest] *s.* Almagesto.

almagra ['ælməgrə] [al-má-gra], *s.* Almagre.

alma-mater ['ælmə'meɪtə'] [al-ma-méi-tar], *s.* La universidad en donde se ha estudiado y se han recibido los grados escolásticos.

almanac ['ɔːlmənæk] [ál-ma-nak], *s.* Almanaque, calendario. **Almanac-maker,** almanaquista, calendarista, el que hace los calendarios.

almandine ['ɑːlməndaɪn] [al-man-dain] o **almandite** ['ɑːlməndaɪt] [al-man-dait], *s.* Almandina, especie de rubí más basto y ligero que el oriental.

almemor [ɔːlmɪmə'] [ol-mí-ma'] *s.* *(Rel.)* Almimbar.

almightiness ['ɔːlmaɪtɪnɪs] [al-mái-ti-nis], *s.* Omnipotencia, poder supremo para todas las cosas; atributo sólo de Dios.

almighty ['ɔːlmaɪtɪ] [al-mái-ti], *a.* Omnipotente, todopoderoso.

almond ['ɑːmənd] [ál-mond], *s.* Almendra. **Almonds of the throat,** *(Anat.)* Las amígdalas, dos glándulas de la garganta. **Almond-oil,** aceite de almendras. **Almond-paste,** pasta de almendras. **Bitter almonds,** almendras amargas. **Burnt almonds,** almendras bañadas o garapiñadas. **Unshelled almonds,** almendras con cáscara.

almond-eyed ['ɑːmənd'aɪd] [ál-mon-áid] *a.* De ojos rasgados.

almond-tree ['ɑːmənd'triː] [al-mon-tri], *s.* *(Bot.)* Almendro, árbol que da por fruto las almendras.

almond-willow ['ɑːmənd'wɪlɔʊ] [al-mon-uí-lou], *s.* *(Bot.)* Una especie de sauce.

almoner ['ɑːmənə'] [ál-mo-nar], *s.* Limosnero, el que está encargado de distribuir las limosnas.

almonry ['ɑːmənrɪ] [ál-mon-ri], *s.* El sitio o paraje en que se distribuyen las limosnas.

almoravid o almoravide ['ɑːmərəvɪd] [al-mo-rá-vid] *a./s.* Almorávide.

almost ['ɔːmɔʊst] [ól-moust], *adv.* Casi, cerca de. **It is almost night,** es casi de noche, es casi noche.

alms [ɑːmz] [áms], *s.* Limosna, caridad.

alms-basket [ɑːmz'bɑːskɪt] [ams-bás-kit], *s.* Canasto o cesto en que se echa limosna para los pobres.

alms-box [ɑːmz'bɒks] [áms-boks], *s.* Cepillo o caja de limosna; alcancía.

almsdeed [ɑːmz'diːd] [áms-did], *s.* Caridad, limosna, obra de caridad.

alms-folk [ɑːmz'fɔʊk] [áms-fouk], *s.* Personas caritativas.

almsgiver [ɑːmz'gɪvə'] [ams-gí-var], *s.* Limosnero, el que da limosna.

almsgiving [ɑːmz'gɪvɪŋ] [ams-gí-vin], *s.* El acto de dar limosna. Caridad.

almshouse [ɑːmz'haʊs] [áms-jaus], *s.* 1 Hospicio de pobres o casa de misericordia. 2. Asilo.

almsman [ɑːmz'mən] [áms-man], *s.* 1. Pobre, mendigo, pordiosero. 2. Limosnero, el que da limosnas.

alms-people [ɑːmz'piːpl] [ams-pí-pol], *s.* Hospicianos, los asilados de la casa de misericordia.

almug-tree [ɑːmʌ'triː] [ámag-tri], *s.* árbol que produce la goma arábiga. Se escribe también y preferentemente, ALGUM.

alnagar [ɑːməgə'] [a-ná-gar], **alnager** [ɑːməgə'] [a-ná-gar], *s.* El que mide por anas.

alnage [ɑːneɪg] [á-neich], *s.* La medición por anas.

alodial ['ælədɪəl] [a-ló-dial] *a.* Alodial.

alodium ['æləed ɪə] [a-ló-diom] *s.* Alodio.

aloe ['ælɔʊ] [á-lou], *s.* 1. *(Des.)* Aloe o lináloe, madera preciosa que se usa para perfumes. 2. *(Bot.)* Aloe, árbol que cría en los países cálidos. 3. *pl.* aunque en sintaxis singular: Aloe o acíbar, zumo o jugo medicinal que se saca del árbol llamado áloe común. 4. Zábida o zábila, planta parecida a la pita. de la que se saca tambien el acíbar.

aloetic ['æləʊtɪk] [a-lo-é-tik], **aloetical** ['æləʊtɪkl] [a-lo-é-ti-kal], *a.* Aloético, cosa perteneciente al acíbar.

aloft [ə'lɒft] [a-lóft], *prep.* Arriba, sobre. **All hands aloft,** *(Mar.)* Todo el mundo arriba. **To set aloft,** elevar, subir. - *adv.* En alto.

aloin [ə'lɔɪn] [a-lóin], *s.* Principio amargo, purgante, que se extrae del áloe.

alone [ə'lɔʊn] [a-lóun], *a.* Solo, solitario, sin compañía. **I was alone,** estaba solo. **All alone,** completamente solo. **To let (o leave) alone,** no desarreglar, no tocar las cosas; no mezclarse en algo; no molestar, dejar en paz a las personas.

Let me alone, déjeme usted en paz. *adv.* Solamente. **That alone can help us,** sólo eso nos puede ayudar.

aloneness [ə'ləʊnɪs] [a-lóun-nis], *s.* El estado de ser solo y sin igual; se aplica a Dios.

along [ə'lɒŋ] [a-lóng], *adv.* 1. A lo largo o por lo largo, por medio de cualquier espacio medido a lo largo. 2. Adelante. 3. Con, en compañía de, junto con. **Come along with me,** Venga usted conmigo. 4. En consecuencia, en virtud de. **All along,** a lo largo, de un cabo a otro, desde el principio al fin. **He lies all along,** está echado a la larga. **Move along, please!,** ¡circulen, por favor! **To get along (well) with someone,** llevarse bien con alguien.

alongshore [ə'lɒŋʃɔːʳ] [a-lóng-shoʳ] *adv.* A lo largo de la costa.

alongside [ə'lɒŋˈsaɪd] [a-lóng-said], *adv.* A lo largo de, al lado, al costado. *(Mar.)* Al costado, o costado con costado. **To come alongside,** atracar.

aloof [ə'luːf] [a-lúf], *adv.* 1. Lejos. De lejos, a lo largo. **To keep aloof from a rock,** *(Mar.)* Mantenerse lejos de un escollo. 2. Prudentemente; cautelosamente. **To stand aloof from politics,** no mezclarse en la política.

aloofness [ə'luːfnɪs] [a-lúf-nis] *s.* Reserva.

alopecia [ˌæləʊˈpiːʃə] [a-lo-pí-sha], *s. (Med.)* Alopecia, especie de tiña, que hace caer el cabello. *(Vulg.)* Pelona.

aloud [ə'laʊd] [a-láud], *adv.* Alto, con voz fuerte, recio.

alow [ə'laʊ] [a-láu], *adv.* Abajo o bajo: lo opuesto a **aloft.** *(Ant. Mar.).*

alpaca [æl'pækə] [al-pá-ka], *s.* 1. Alpaca, una especie de llama; el camello del Perú. 2. Tela que se fabrica con el pelo de este animal.

alpenstock ['ælpɪnstɒk] [al-pins-tok], *s. (Alem.)* Palo con punta de hierro que se emplea en la ascensión de los Alpes.

alpha ['ælfə] [al-fa], *s.* 1. Alfa, nombre de la primera letra del alfabeto griego. 2. Sinónimo de principio. **Alpha and omega,** el primero y el último, el principio y el fin.

alpha ray ['ælfə'reɪ] [ál-fa-rei], *s.* Rayo alfa.

alphabet ['ælfəbet] [ál-fa-bet], *s.* Alfabeto, abecedario.

alphabet, *va.* Colocar por orden alfabético.

alphabetarian [ˌælfəˈbetərɪən] [al-fa-be-tá-rian], *s.* Alfabetista, el que sabe el a,b,c.

alphabetic [ˌælfəˈbetɪk] [al-fa-bé-tik], **alphabetical** ['ælfəbetɪkəl] [al-fa-bé-ti-kal], *a.* Alfabético.

alphabetically [ˌælfəˈbetɪkəlɪ], [al-fa-bé-ti-ka-li], *adv.* Alfabéticamente.

alphabetize ['ælfəbetaɪz] [al-fá-be-tais], *va.* 1. Colocar alfabéticamente. 2. Proveer de un alfabeto.

alphameric [ˌælfəˈmerɪk] [al-fa-mé-rik] o **alphanumeric** [ˌælfənjuːˈmerɪk] [al-fa-niu-mé-rik] *a.* Alfnumérico.

alphenic [ælˈfenɪk] [al-fé-nik], *s.* Alfeñique: azúcar candi.

alphonsin ['ælfɒnsɪn] [al-fón-sin], *s.* Sacabalas, instrumento quirúrgico para extraer las balas de las heridas.

alphonsine tables [ˈælfɒnsɪnˈteɪblz] [al-fón-sin-téi-bols] *a.* Tablas alfonsinas.

alpine ['ælpaɪn] [ál-pain], *a.* 1. Alpino, perteneciente a los Alpes. 2. Alto, elevado.

alpist ['ælpɪst] [ál-pist], *s.* Alpiste, semilla menuda que se da a los pájaros.

Alps [ælps] [álps] *N. (Geogr.)* Alpes.

alquifou ['ælkɪfuː] [al-kí-fu], *s.* Alquifol, mineral de plomo que se usa en las alfarerías. Sulfuro de plomo.

already [ɔːlˈredɪ] [ol-ré-di], *adv.* Ya, a la hora de ésta, antes de ahora.

Alsace ['ælses] [al-sás] *N. (Geogr.)* Alsacia.

Alsatian [ælˈseɪʃən] [al-sá-shan] *a.* Alsaciano (habitante de Alsacia). Pastor alemán (dog).

alsike [ɔːlˈsaɪk] [ól-saik], *s.* Especie de trébol sueco, planta valiosa empleada como forraje, de flores rojizas o blancas.

also ['ɔːlsəʊ] [ól-sou], *adv.* También, igualmente, del mismo modo, aun, además.

also-run ['ɔːlsəʊrʌn] [ol-so-ran] 1. Caballo que no se coloca en una carrera. 2. Candidato vencido en una elección. 3. Nulidad.

alt ['ɔːlt] [alt], *s.* La parte más alta de la gama musical. (Abrev. de alto.)

altaic ['ɔːlteɪk] [al-téik] *a.* Altaico.

altar ['ɒltəʳ] [ál-tar], *s.* Altar; ara. **Altar boy,** monaguillo. **High altar,** altar mayor. **On the altars of,** en aras de.

altarge ['ɒltədʒ] [ál-tarch], *s.* Pie de altar, los emolumentos que se dan a los sacerdotes por el ejercicio de su ministerio; ofrenda hecha sobre el altar.

altar-cloth ['ɒltəklɒθ] [ál-tar-cloz], *s.* Sabanilla, la cubierta exterior del altar. *(Mex.)* Mantel o manteles.

altarpiece [ɒltəˈpiːs] [ál-tar-pis], *s.* Retablo, el cuadro o pintura del altar. Retablo, el altar en conjunto.

altar-screen [ɒltəˈskriːn] [ál-tar-skrín], *s.* Contra-retablo.

altar stone [ɒltəˈstəʊn] [al-tar-stóun] *s.* ara.

altar-table [ɒltəˈteɪbl] [al-tar-teibol], *s.* Mesa del altar.

altarwise [ɒltəˈwaɪz] [ál-tar-uais], *adv.* En forma de altar.

alter ['ɒltəʳ] [ál-tar], *va.* Alterar, mudar. **To alter one's condition,** tomar estado, casarse, *-vn.* Mudarse o cambiarse, alterarse. *(Mar.)* **To alter course,** cambiar de rumbo. *vn.* Cambiar. **To alter for the worse,** ir cada vez peor, empeorar.

alterability [ɒltərəˈbɪlɪtɪ] [al-te-ra-bí-li-ti], *s.* Alterabilidad.

alterable ['ɒltərəbl] [al-te-réi-bol], *a.* Alterable; mudable.

alterableness ['ɒltərəblnɪs] [al-te-réi-bol-nis], *s.* Alterabilidad.

alterably ['ɒltərəblɪ] [al-te-ra-bli], *adv.* De una manera mudable.

alterant ['ɒltərənt] [ál-te-rant] *a.* Alterante, lo que se altera.

alteration [ˌɒltəˈreɪʃən] [al-te-réi-shon], *s.* Alteración; mudanza, innovación, cambio.

alterative ['ɒltərətɪv] [al-té-ra-tif], *a.* Alterativo. *-s.* Remedio alterativo, alterante.

altercate [ɒltəˈkeɪt] [ál-ter-keit], *vn.* Altercar, controvertir.

altercation [ˌɒltəˈkeɪʃən] [al-ter-kéi-shon], *s.* Altercación, debate, disputa, controversia.

alterer ['ɒltərəʳ] [ál-te-rar], *s.* Alterador, cambiador.

altern ['ɒltɜːn] [al-térn], *a.* Alterno o alternativo, lo que obra por turno.

alternant [ɒlˈtɜːnənt] [al-tér-nant], *a. (Geol.)* Compuesto de capas alternadas, como algunas rocas.

alternate [ɒlˈtɜːneɪt] [ál-ter-neit], *a.* Alternativo, recíproco, lo que se hace o ejecuta con alternación. **On alternate days,** en días alternos. *s.* Vicisitud.

alternate, *va.* 1. Alternar, hacer alguna cosa alternativamente. 2. Alternar, variar. *-vn.* Turnar.

alternately [ɒlˈtɜːneɪtlɪ] [al-ter-néit-li], *adv.* Alternativamente, recíprocamente, por turno.

alternateness [ɒlˈtɜːneɪtnɪs] [al-ter-néit-nis], *s.* Alternación, sucesión, recíproca.

alternating [ɒlˈtɜːneɪtɪŋ] [al-ter-néi-tin], *pa. y a.* Alternante, alterno. **Alternating current,** *(Elec.)* Corriente alterna.

alternation [ɒlˈtɜːneɪʃən] [al-ter-néi-shon], *s.* Alternación, vez, turno, vicisitud. **In alternation,** alternativamente.

alternative [ɒlˈtɜːnətɪv] [al-tér-na-tif], *s.* Alternativa. *-a.* Alternativo. **We have no alternative,** no tenemos más remedio.

alternatively [ɒlˈtɜːnətɪvlɪ] [al-ter-na-tíf-li], *adv.* Alternativamente, recíprocamente, por turno, en sucesión recíproca.

alternativeness [ɒlˈtɜːnətɪvnɪs] [al-ter-na-tíf-nis], **alternity** [ɒlˈtɜːnɪtɪ] [al-tér-ni-ti], *s.* El estado recíproco o alternativo de alguna cosa: vicisitud, reciprocidad; turno.

alternator [ɒlˈtɜːneɪtəʳ] [al-ter-néi-tar], *s. (Elec.)* Alternador.

althea [ɒlˈθɪə] [al-zía], *s. (Bot.)* Malvavisco. Altea.

although [ɔːlˈðəʊ] [ól-do], *conj.* Aunque, no obstante, bien que], aun cuando, sin embargo. **Although very old, he is still very active,** aunque muy viejo aún es muy activo. Se escribe algunas veces **altho,** especialmente hoy en día.

altiloquent [ɒlˈtɪɒwənt] [al-tí-lo-kuent], *a.* Altilocuente, pomposo.

altimeter [ˈæltɪmiːtəʳ] [al-tí-mi-tar], s. Altímetro, instrumento para medir las alturas.

altimetry [ˈæltɪmiːtrɪ] [al-tí-mi-tri], s. Altimetría, parte de la geometría práctica, que enseña a medir las alturas.

altisonant [ˈæltɪsɒnənt] [al-ti-so-nant], **altisonous** [ˈæltɪsɒnəs] [al-ti-so-nos], a. Altisonane; pomposo y retumbante. (Poét.) Altísono.

altitude [ˈæltɪtjuːd] [ˈsl-ti-tiud], s. 1. Altura o altitud. 2. Elevación, cumbre, cima.

alto [ˈæltəʊ] [al-tou], s. 1. Contralto (de la voz). 2. Violón. 3. Alto de las cornetas.

altogether [ˌɔːltəˈgeðəʳ] [al-to-gé-dar], adv. Enteramente, del todo, para siempre.

alto-relievo [ˈæltɪrɪliːvə] [al-to-ri-lí-va], s. (Escul.) Alto relieve.

altruism [ˈæltrʊɪzəm] [al-tru-ísem], s. Altruísmo, consideración por los intereses de los demás; benevolencia; lo contrario de egoísmo.

altruist [ˈæltrʊɪst] [ál-tru-ist], s. Partidario del altruísmo o el que lo profesa.

altruistic [ˈæltrʊɪstɪk] [al-tru-ís-tic], a. Altruístico, perteneciente al altruísmo.

aludel [ˈæljʊdəl] [al-iú-dal], s. Aludel, vasija para sublimar.

alum [ˈæləm] [a-lam], s. Alumbre, piedra minera salina de sabor ácido.

alum, va. Alumbrar, dar a los paños un baño de agua de alumbre.

alumed [ˈæləmd] [a-lamd], a. Aluminado, mezclado con alumbre.

alumina [ˈæləmɪnə] [a-lá-mi-na] o **alumine** [ˈæləmaɪn] [a-liu-min], s. (Quím.) Alúmina, arcilla pura y blanca.

aluminate [ˈæljʊmɪnɪt] [a-liú-mi-neit] va. Aluminar.

aluminium [ˌæljʊˈmɪnɪəm] [a-liu-mí-ni-om] o **aluminum** [ˈæljʊˈmɪnəm] [a-liú-mi-nom], s. Aluminio.

aluminous [ˈæljʊˈmɪnəs] [a-liú-mi-nos], a. 1. Aluminoso, lo que tiene calidad o mezcla de alúmina; arcilloso. 2. Alumbroso.

alumna, alumnus [ˈæljʊmnəs] [a-liúm-na], s. Alumna, alumno; el discípulo de un colegio o universidad.

alunite [ˈæljʊnaɪt] [a-lá-nait] s. (Min.) Alunita.

alumniate [ˈæləmnɪeɪt] [a-lám-nieit], s. El tiempo que dura la instrucción; en un establecimiento de enseñanza.

alum-stone [ˈæləmˈstəʊn] [a-lam-stóun], s. Piedra alumbre; alumbre calcinado.

alum-water [ˌæləmˈwɔːləʳ] [a-lam-uó-taʳ], s. Agua de alumbre.

alum-works [ˈæləmˈwɜːks] [a-lam-wuérks], s. Alumbrera, la mina de donde se saca, o la factoría en que se hace el alumbre.

alutation [ˈæljʊˈteɪʃən] [a-liu-téi-shon], s. Curtimiento, la acción de curtir la piel o el cuero.

alveary [ˈælvɛərɪ] [al-véa-ri], s. Colmena.

alveolar [ælˈvɪələʳ] [al-vía-laʳ], a. Lo perteneciente a los alvéolos.

alveolate [ælˈvɪələɪt] [al-vío-leit], a. Alveolado, excavado profundamente, como el panal.

alveolus [ælˈvɪələs] [al-vío-los], s. ALVEOLI, pl. 1. Alvéolo, la cavidad que ocupan los dientes en la encía. 2. Celdilla que hacen las abejas en los panales. 3. Alvéolo de las plantas.

alvine [ælˈvaɪn] [al-váin]. a. Alvino, lo que pertenece al vientre.

always [ˈɔːlweɪz] [ól-ueis], adv. 1. Siempre, en todo o cualquier tiempo. 2. Constantemente, invariablemente.

alyssum [əˈlɪsəm] [a-lísam], s. (Bot.) Alisón, planta de la familia de las crucíferas que produce racimos de flores amarillas o blancas. **Sweet alyssum**, alisón fragante, con pequeñas flores blancas. Alyssum maritimun.

a.m. (Lat.) 1. **Artium magister**, Maestro en Artes; este es el segundo grado en las universidades de Inglaterra y de los Estados Unidos de América; en Alemania y otros países es Doctor en Filosofía. 2. **Ante meridiem**, antes del mediodía. 3. **Anno mundi**, año del mundo.

am [æm] [am], 1ª pers. de indicat. del verbo TO BE. **I am,** yo soy o estoy.

amability [æməˈbɪlɪtɪ] [a-ma-bi-li-ti], s. Amabilidad, agrado. V. AMIABILITY.

amadetto [æməˈdetəʊ] [a-ma-de-to], **amadot,** [a-ma-dot], s. Especie de pera.

Amadeus [æməˈdɪəs] [a-ma-dios] N. Amadeo.

amadou [ˈæmədʊ] [a-ma-du], s. Yesca para encender.

amain [əˈmeɪn] [a-méin], adv. 1. Con vehemencia, fuerza o vigor, vigorosamente. 2. (Mar.) En banda.

amalgam [əˈmælgəm] [a-mal-gam], **amalgama** [əˈmælgəmə] [a-mal-ga-ma], s. 1. Amalgama, mezcla de diferentes metales incorporados unos con otros. 2. (Met.) Toda mezcla o combinación de diversas substancias, castas o cosas.

amalgamate [əˈmælgəmeɪt] [a-mal-ga-meit], va. y vn. Amalgamar, unir o mezclar el azogue con los metales.

amalgamation [əˈmælgəˈmeɪʃən] [a-mal-ga-méi-shon], s. Amalgamación, la acción de amalgamar los metales.

amalgamator [əˈmælgəmeɪtəʳ] [a-mal-ga-méi-tar], s. Máquina de amalgamar.

amanita [æməˈnaɪtə] [a-ma-nai-ta] s. Amanita.

amanuensis [əˌmænjʊˈensɪs] [a-ma-niu-en-sis], s. Amanuense, el que escribe lo que otro le dicta.

amaranth [æməˈrænθ] [a-ma-ranz], s. 1. (Bot.) Amaranto. 2. Planta del género Gomphrena de la misma familia. 3. (Poet.) Una flor imaginaria que nunca se marchita.

amaranthine [æməˈrænθiːn] [a-ma-ran-zin], a. 1. Compuesto de amaranto. 2. De color de amaranto. 3. Inmarcesible.

amaryllis [æməˈrɪlɪs] [a-ma-ri-lis], n. Amarilis, planta bulbosa originaria del áfrica del Sur, y su flor. Entre las especies de la familia de las plantas amarilídeas se cuentan los narcisos, el junquillo y la pita.

amass [əˈmæs] [a-mas], va. Acumular, amontonar. **To amass a fortune,** acumular riquezas.

amassment [əˈmæsmənt] [a-mas-ment], s. Cúmulo, montón, conjunto, agregado.

amateur [æˈmətəʳ] [a-ma-ter], s. Aficionado.

amateurish [ˈæmətərɪʃ] [a-ma-té-rish], a. A modo de aficionado; superficial.

amateurism [ˈæmətərɪzəm] [a-ma-te-rísem] s. Calidad de aficionado o de no profesional.

amative [æˈmətɪv] [á-ma-tif], a. Lleno de amor; amatorio; que se refiere al amor entre los sexos.

amativeness [æˈmətɪvnɪs] [a-ma-tíf-nis], s. Amorosidad, principio amatorio o propensión o tendencia a amar.

amatorial [æˈmətərɪəl] [a-ma-tó-rial], **amatorious** [æˈmətərɪəs] [a-ma-tó-rios], a. Amatorio, lo que pertenece al amor.

amatory [ˈæmətərɪ] [a-ma-to-ri], a. Amatorio, lo que trata de amor o lo inspira.

amaurosis [əˈmɔːrəsɪs] [a-mau-ro-sis], s. Pérdida de la vista por enfermedad del nervio óptico; amaurosis.

amaurotic [əˈmɔːrətɪk] [a-mau-ro-tik], a. 1. Amaurótico, que está relacionado con la amaurosis. 2. Que la padece.

amaze [əˈmeɪz] [a-méis], va. 1. Aterrar, espantar, aturdir. 2. Confundir, dejar perplejo o parado, sorprender, asombrar; usado con la preposición at; menos frecuentemente con by o with.

amaze, s. Espanto, pasmo, confusión causada por miedo o admiración; asombro, sorpresa. (Poét.)

amazedly [əˈmeɪzlɪ] [a-méis-li], adv. Atolondradamente, con atolondramiento o pasmo.

amazedness [əˈmeɪznɪs] [a-méis-nis], **amazement** [əˈmeɪzmənt] [a-méis-ment], s. Espanto, pasmo, confusión. **With amazement,** con mucha admiración.

amazing [əˈmeɪzɪŋ] [a-méi-sin], a. Pasmoso, asombroso, extraño.

amazingly [əˈmeɪzɪŋlɪ] [a-méi-sin-li], adv. Pasmosamente, asombrosamente.

Amazon ['æməzən] [a-má-son], *s.* 1. Amazona, mujer guerrera. 2. Marimacho. 3. Papagayo de la América del Sur. 4. *N. (Geogr.)* Amazonas.

amazonian [,æmə'zəʊnɪən] [a-ma-sóu-nian], *a.* 1. Guerrera. 2. Lo perteneciente a las amazonas. 3. Amazónico.

amazon-like ['æməzən,laɪk] [á-ma-son-laik], *a.* Semejante a una amazona o a un marimacho.

ambages [æm'beɪdʒs] [am-bei-ches], *s.* Ambages, circunloquios o rodeos de palabras; subterfugios.

ambassador [æm'bæsədəʳ] [am-bá-sa-dor], *s.* Embajador.

ambassadorship [æm'bæsədəʃɪp] [am-bá-sa-do-ship] *s.* Embajada.

ambassadress [æm'bæsədrɪs] [am-bá-sa-dris], *sf.* Embajadora, la esposa del embajador.

ambassage [æm'bæseɪdʒ] [am-bá-seich], **ambassy** ['əmbəsɪ][ám-ba-si], *s. (Ant.)* Embajada, la comisión o encargo que lleva el embajador el estado a que va enviado. *V.* EMBASSY.

amber ['æmbəʳ] [ám-bar], *s.* 1. Ambar, resina fósil de color amarillo claro u oscuro. 2. Especie de cerveza pálida. -*a.* Ambarino, lo que contiene o está hecho de ámbar. **Amber beads**, Rosario ambarino o de ámbar. **Yellow amber**, Succino.

amber, *va.* Perfumar con ámbar, que antiguamente se decía ambarar.

amber-colored [,æmbə'kʌləd] [ám-ba-ká-lod], *a.* Lo que es de color de ámbar. **Amber-colored hair**, Pelo castaño.

amber-drink [,æmbə'drɪŋk] [ám-ba-drink], *s.* Bebida de color de ámbar.

amber-dropping [,æmbə'drɒpɪŋ] [am-ba-dró-pin], *a.* Lo que destila ámbar; se dice de los rizos o bucles del cabello.

ambergris [,æmbə'grɪs] [ám-ba-gris], *s.* Ámbar gris, especie de droga que se derrite como la cera y se usa como perfume y cordial.

amber-seed [,æmbə'siːd] [ám-ba-sid], *s.* Ambarilla, la semilla del abelmoso o algalia, de color almizcleño.

amber-tree [,æmbə'triː] [ám-ba-tri], *s. (Bot.)* Árbol de ámbar.

amber-varnish [,æmbə'vɑːnɪʃ] [ám-ba-va-nish], *s.* Barniz de succino.

amber-weeping [,æmbə'wiːpɪŋ] [ám-ba-ui-pin], *a.* Lo que echa lágrimas como ámbar.

ambidexter [,æmbɪ'dekstəʳ] [am-bi-déks-tar], *s.* 1. Hombre ambidextro. 2. Hombre falso, engañoso. 3. *(Fam.)* El que come a dos carrillos. 4. Prevaricador.

ambidexterity [,æmbɪ'dekstərɪtɪ] [am-bi-desk-té-ri-ti], *s.* 1. Igual manejo de ambas manos. 2. Doblez, simulación.

ambidextrous [,æmbɪ'dekstrəs] [am-bi-déks-tros], *a.* 1. Ambidextro, el que usa igualmente la mano izquierda que la derecha. 2. El que procede con doblez.

ambidextrousness [,æmbɪ'dekstrəsnɪs] [am-bi-déks-tros-nis], *s. V.* AMBIDEXTERITY.

ambience ['æmbɪəns] [ám-bians] *s.* Ambiente.

ambient ['æmbɪənt] [am-biant], *a.* Ambiente, lo que rodea, lo que está o anda alrededor. **The ambient air,** el ambiente, el aire que nos rodea.

ambigu ['æmbɪgʊ] [ám-bi-gu], *s.* Ambigú, comida, por lo común nocturna, compuesta de manjares calientes y fiambres. *(Fig.)* Baturrillo; mezcolanza de cosas opuestas.

ambiguity [,æmbɪ'gjʊɪtɪ] [am-bí-güi-ti], *s.* Ambigüedad, duda, confusión, incertidumbre.

ambiguous [æm'bɪgjʊəs] [am-bí-guos], *s.* 1. Ambiguo, lo que tiene ambigüedad. 2. Ambiguo, el que usa de equívocos.

ambiguously [æm'bɪgjʊəslɪ] [am-bí-guos-li], *adv.* Ambiguamente, de un modo ambiguo, confusamente.

ambiguousness [æm'bɪgjʊəsnɪs] [am-bí-guos-nis], *s.* Ambigüedad, la calidad de ser ambiguo.

ambit ['æmbɪt] [am-bit], *s.* Ámbito, circuito o circunferencia de algún espacio o lugar; contorno.

ambition [æm'bɪʃən] [am-bí-shon], *s.* Ambición, deseo de conseguir fama, honras o dignidades. *va.* Ambicionar.

ambitious [æm'bɪʃəs] [am-bí-shos], *a.* Ambicioso, poseído de la ambición.

ambitiously [æm'bɪʃəslɪ] [am-bí-shos-li], *adv.* Ambiciosamente, con ambición.

ambitiousness [æm'bɪʃəsnɪs] [am-bí-shos-nis], *s.* Ambición, deseo ardiente de posición, de gloria, de renombre.

ambivalence [æm'bɪvələns] [am-bí-va-lans] *s.* Ambivalencia.

ambivalent [æm'bɪvələnt] [am-bí-va-lent] *a.* Ambivalente.

ambivert [æm'bɪvɜːt] [am-bi-vert], *s.* Ambivertido, tipo psicológico intermedio entre el extravertido y el introvertido.

amble ['æmbl] [am-bol], *vn.* Amblar, andar a paso de andadura.

amble, *s.* Paso de andadura del caballo, llamado también paso castellano.

ambler ['æmbləʳ] [am-blar], *s.* Caballo que marcha a paso de andadura.

amblingly ['æmblɪŋlɪ] [ám-blin-li], *adv.* A paso de andadura.

amblygon ['æmblɪgɒn] [ám-bli-gon], *s.* Ambligonio, obtusángulo.

amblyopia [æm'blɪɒfɪə] [am-bló-fia], *s.* Ambliopía, oscurecimiento y debilidad de la vista, sin defecto apreciable del ojo.

ambrosia [æm'brəʊzɪə] [am-bróu-sia], *s.* 1. Ambrosía, manjar o alimento de los dioses. 2. *(Bot.)* Ambrosía, un género de plantas de la familia de las compuestas.

ambrosial [æm'brəʊzɪəl] [am-bróu-sial], *a.* Delicioso, deleitable, celestial.

ambrosian [æm'brəʊzɪən] [am-bróu-sian] *a. (Rel.)* Ambrosiano.

ambry ['æmbrɪ] [ám-bri], **almery** [ál-me-ri], *s.* 1. Casa de beneficencia, limosnería. 2. Armario, despensa. 3. Sausería, oficina en que se guarda la plata y demás servicio de mesa. *V.* ALMONRY.

ambs-ace [æmbs'eɪs] [ams-éis], *s. (Ant.)* Ases: parejas de ases en algunos juegos.

ambulance ['æmbjʊləns] [ám-biu-lans], *s.* 1. Hospital de campaña, o de sangre. 2. Ambulancia, vagón cubierto para retirar los heridos del campo, o transportar los enfermos a un hospital.

ambulant ['æmbjʊlənt] [ám-biu-lant], *a.* Ambulante.

ambulate ['æmbjʊleɪt] [am-biu-léit], *vn.* Andar.

ambulation [,æmbjʊ'leɪʃən] [am-biu-léi-shon], *s.* Paseo, la acción de pasearse.

ambulative [æm'bjʊlətɪv] [am-biú-la-tif], *a.* Ambulativo.

ambulatory ['æmbjʊlətrɪ] [am-biu-la-tó-ri], *a.* Lo que anda o puede andar; ambulante, ambulativo, mudable, inconstante, ambulatorio. -*s.* Galería cubierta o descubierta, sitio para pasearse.

ambury ['æmbjʊrɪ] [ám-biu-ri], *s.* Verruga o tumor en el cuerpo de caballo. Lo mismo que ANBURY.

ambuscade, ambuscado ['æmbəskeɪd] [am-bius-keid], *s.* Emboscada, celada.

ambuscadoed ['æmbəskeɪdɪd] [am-bus-kéi-did], **ambushed** ['æmbʊʃt] [am-búsht], *a.* Emboscado.

ambush ['æmbʊʃ] [am-búsh], **ambushment** ['æmbʊʃmənt] [am-búsh-ment], *s.* 1. Emboscada, celada. 2. Sorpresa, acontecimiento repentino del que está emboscado. **To lie in ambush,** Estar emboscado.

ambustion ['æmbʊʃən] [am-bú-shon], *s. V.* AMOEBA.

ameba [ə'miːbə] [a-mí-ba] *s. (Zool.)* Ameba, amiba.

ameboid [ə'mɪbɔɪd] [a-mi-boid], *a. V.* AMOEBOID.

amel [ə'mel] [am-el], *s.* Esmalte, la materia con que se esmalta alguna cosa. *V.* ENAMEL. **Amel corn,** centeno blanco.

ameliorate [ə'miːlɪəreɪt] [a-mí-lio-reit], *va./vn.* Mejorar (to improve). *V.* MELIORATE.

amelioration [ə,miːlɪə'reɪʃən] [a-mi-lio-réi-shon], *s.* Mejoramiento, mejora; medro; adelanto; perfeccionamiento.

ameliorator [ə,miːlɪə'reɪtəʳ] [a-mi-lio-réi-tar], *s.* Mejorador, aumentador, perfeccionador.

amen ['ɑːˈmen] [a-men] o *(Mús.)* [a-men], *adv.* Amén, voz por la cual al fin de cada oración o petición se entiende, **así sea;** y al fin del credo, **así es.**

amenability [əˈmiːnəˈbɪlɪtɪ] [a-mi-na-bí-li-ti], o **amenableness** [əˈmiːnəˈbɪlnɪs] [a-mi-ná-bil-nes], *s.* Responsabilidad, obligación de reparar un daño.

amenable [əˈmiːneɪbl] [a-mí-na-bol], *a.* 1. Responsable, obligado a satisfacer por algún cargo. **Amenable to the law,** responsable ante la ley. 2. Tratable, dócil, sumiso, sujeto a. **Amenable to a fine,** sujeto a multa. **Amenable to advice,** sensible a los consejos. **Amenable to high temperaturas.** que se puede someter a temperaturas elevadas.

amend [əˈmend] [a-ménd], *va.* Enmendar, corregir el error, reparar. **To amend the constitution,** enmendar la constitución. -*vn.* Enmendarse, reformarse, restablecerse.

amendable [əˈmendeɪbl] [a-mén-da-bol], *a.* Reparable, reformable, corregible, componible.

amende [əˈmendə] [a-ménd], *s.* Enmienda, recompensa, castigo penal, multa. **Amende honorable,** reparación, satisfacción pública. *(For.)* Castigo con nota de infamia, que se imponía por ciertos crímenes contra la decencia o moral pública.

amender [əˈmendə^r] [a-mén-dar], *s.* Reformador, corrector.

amending [əˈmendɪŋ] [a-mén-da-rin], *s.* La acción de enmendar.

amendment [əˈmendmənt] [a-ménd-ment], *s.* Enmienda, mudanza de malo a mejor; reformación, reforma; restauración, corrección. **To propose an amendment,** proponer una enmienda.

amends [əˈmendz] [a-ménds], *s.* Recompensa, compensación, satisfacción, reparación. **He will never be able to make amends for the favors he has received,** jamás podrá él corresponder a los favores que ha recibido.

amenity [əˈmiːnɪtɪ] [a-mé-ni-ti], *s.* Amenidad, lo agradable de una situación o paraje. Afabilidad, dulzura. Comodidad. **Shower, telephone and other amenities,** ducha, teléfono y otras comodidades.

amenorrhea [eɪˈmenəˈrɪə] [ei-me-na-ría], *s.* Amenorrea, detención del flujo menstrual.

ament [əˈment] [a-ment], **amentum** [əˈmentəm] [a-mentum], *s. (Bot.)* Amento, espiga articulada por su base y compuesta de flores de un mismo sexo. V. CATKIN. *(Med.)* Débil mental, subnormal.

amentaceous [əˈmenˈteɪʃə] [a-men-téi-shos], *a.* Amentáceo, lo que tiene amentos o se refiere o pertenece a ellos.

amentia [əˈmenʃə] [a-mén-sha], *s.* Demencia, locura.

amentiferous [əˈmentɪfərəs] [a-men-tí-fo-ros] *a. (Bot.)* Amentífero.

amerce [əˈmɜːs] [a-mérs], *va.* Multar, imponer pena pecuniaria por algún delito.

amerceable [əˈmɜːsəbl] [a-mér-sa-bol], *a.* Digno de ser multado.

amercement [əˈmɜːsmənt] [a-mérs-ment], **amerciament** [əˈmɜːʃəmənt] [a-mér-sha-ment], *s.* Multa, pena pecuniaria que se impone por algún delito.

amercer [əˈmɜːsə^r] [a-mér-sar], *s.* Multador, el que multa.

America [əˈmerɪkə] [a-mé-ri-ka] *N. (Geogr.)* América. **North America,** América del Norte. **South America,** América del Sur.

American [əˈmerɪkən] [a-mé-ri-kan], *s.* y *a.* Americano.

Americanism [əˈmerɪkənɪzəm] [a-me-ri-ka-nísem], *s.* 1. Americanismo, palabra, frase o idioma peculiar de la América en general, o en particular de los Estados Unidos. 2. Ciudadanía americana; afición a las instituciones y costumbres americanas.

Americanize [əˈmerɪkənaɪz] [a-me-ri-ka-nais], *va.* Americanizar: asemejar a los americanos en costumbres o ideas.

Americium [əˈmerɪsɪəm] [a-me-rí-siam] *s.* Americio.

Amerind [æmərɪnd] [á-me-rin] *s.* Amerindio.

Amerindian [æməˈrɪndɪən] [a-me-rín-dian] *a.* Amerindio.

amethodical [æmeˈθɒdɪkəl] [a-me-zó-di-kal], *a.* Irregular, sin método.

amethyst [æmeˈθɪst] [a-mé-cist], *s.* Amatista, piedra preciosa de color violeta que tira a purpúreo.

ametropia [æmeˈtrəʊpɪə] [a-me-trou-pia] *s. (Med.)* Ametropía.

amiability [ˈeɪmɪəˈbɪlɪtɪ] [ei-mia-bí-li-ti], *s.* Amabilidad. V. AMABILITY.

amiable [ˈeɪmɪəbl] [ei-mi-abol], *a.* Amable, digno de ser amado, amigable, amistoso, agradable.

amiableness [ˈeɪmɪəblnɪs] [ei-mi-abol-nis], *s.* Amabilidad.

amiably [ˈeɪmɪəblɪ] [ei-mia-bli], *adv.* Amablemente, cariñosamente.

amianth [ˈeɪmɪənθ] [ei-mianz], **amianthus** ['eɪmɪənθəs] [ei-mian-zos], *s. (Min.)* Amianto, mineral parecido al asbesto que se deshace en hebras y astillas, y del cual se obtiene una tela incombustible.

amicability ['æmɪkəˈbɪlɪtɪ] [a-mi-ka-bí-li-ti], o **amicableness** ['æmɪkeɪblnɪs] [a-mi-kéi-bol-nis], *s.* Afecto, cariño, amistad.

amicable ['æmɪkəbl] [a-mí-ka-bol], *a.* Amigable, amistoso.

amicably ['æmɪkəblɪ] [a-mí-ka-bli], *adv.* Amigablemente, amistosamente.

amice [əˈmaɪs] [a-mais], *s.* Amito, el primero de los ornamentos sagrados que se pone el sacerdote cuando se reviste.

amid [əˈmɪd] [a-mid], **amidst** [əˈmɪdst] [a-mist], *prep.* 1. Entre, en medio de. **Amidships,** *(Mar.)* En medio del navío. 2. Mezclado con, rodeado por.

amide [əˈmaɪd] [a-maid] *s. (Quím.)* Amida.

amidol [əˈmɪdɒl] [a-mi-dol] *s. (Quím.)* Amidol.

amine [əˈmaɪn] [a-main] *s. (Quím.)* Amina.

amino [əˈmiːnəʊ] [a-mi-nou] *a.* Aminado.

amino acid [əˈmiːnəʊˈæsɪd] [a-mi-nou-á-sid] *s. (Quim)* Aminoácido.

amir [əˈmiː^r] [a-mi^r] *s.* Emir.

amiss [əˈmɪs] [a-mis], *adv.* Culpablemente, erradamente, mal impropiamente, fuera del caso. **It would not be amiss if you went there,** no sería malo que usted fuese allá. **It would not be amiss to do it,** no estaría de más el hacerlo. **Do not take it amiss,** no lo lleve usted a mal. **Nothing comes amiss to a hungry stomach,** a buen hambre no hay pan duro.

amiss, *a.* Vicioso, impuro, criminal; impropio; decaído de salud.

amity [əˈmɪtɪ] [a-mi-ti], *s.* Amistad, afecto recíproco entre dos o más personas.

ammeter [əˈmmiːtə^r] [am-mí-tar], *s. (Elec.)* Amperímetro.

ammonia [əˈməʊnɪə] [a-mou-nia], *s. (Quím.)* Alcali volátil, amoníaco.

ammoniac [əˈməʊnɪæk] [a-mou-niak], *s.* Amoníaco o sal amoniaca. **Gum ammoniac,** goma amoniaca.

ammoniacal [əˈməʊnɪækl] [a-mou-nia-kal], *a.* Amoniacal, lo que pertenece al amoníaco.

ammonite [əˈməʊnaɪt] [á-mou-nait], *s. (Geol.)* Amonita, caracol fósil perteneciente a un molusco extinguido.

ammonium [əˈməʊnɪəm] [a-mou-niam], *s.* Amonio.

ammunition [æmjʊˈnɪʃən] [a-miu-ní-shon], *s.* Munición, los pertrechos y bastimentos necesarios para la manutención de un ejército, una plaza, etc. *(Fig.)* Argumentos.

amnesia [æmˈniːzɪə] [am-ní-sia], *s.* Amnesia, pérdida de la memoria.

amnesic [æmˈniːzɪk] [am-né-sik] *a./s. (Med.)* Amnésico.

amnesty ['æmnɪstɪ] [am-né-si-ti], *s.* Amnistía, olvido general. *va.* Amnistiar.

amnion ['æmnɪən] [am-nion], **amnios** ['æmnɪəs] [am-nis], *s.* Amnios, la segunda membrana que envuelve al feto en el útero.

amniotic ['æmnɪɒtɪk] [am-nió-tik], *a. (Anat.)* Amniótico.

amoeba [əˈmiːbə] [a-mí-ba] *s. (Zool.)* ameba.

amoeboid [əˈmiːbɔɪd] [á-mi-boid], *a.* Semejante a la amibea; se dice especialmente del movimiento.

amok [ə'mɒk] [a-mok] *adv. (Fig.)* **They ran amok through the town,** atravesaron la ciudad destruyéndolo todo. **To run amok,** volverse loco.

amomun [ə'mɒmən] [a-mó-mam], *s.* Amomo, fruta de cierta planta en las Indias orientales.

among [ə'mʌŋ] [a-móng], **amongst** [ə'mʌŋst] [a-óngst], *prep.* y *adv.* Entre, mezclado con, o en medio de. **A house among the trees,** una casa entre los árboles. **A king among kings,** un rey entre reyes.

amontillado [ə'mɒn'tɪlɑdo] [a-mon-ti-la-do] *s.* Amontillado (sherry).

amoral [eɪ'mɒrəl] [a-mó-ral], *a.* Amoral, sin responsabilidad moral.

amoralism [eɪ'mɒrəlɪzm] [a-mo-ra-lí-sem] *s.* Amoralismo.

amorality [ˌeɪmɒ'rælɪtɪ] [a-mo-rá-li-ti] *s.* Amoralidad.

amoret [ə'mɒrɪt] [a-mó-rit], *s.* Amante.

amorette [ə'mɒri:t] [a-mó-rit], **amourette** [ə'mjʊərɪt] [a-miua-rit], *s.* 1. Amorío, intriga amorosa. 2. Cupido, amorcillo.

amorist [ə'mɒrɪst] [a-mó-rist], **amoroso,** *s.* Galanteador, amante, galán.

amornings [ə'mɔːnɪŋz] [a-mó-nins], *adv.* De mañana.

amorous [æ'mərəs] [á-mo-ros], *a.* 1. Enamorado, amoroso, tierno, apasionado, cariñoso. 2. Amatorio, lo que pertenece al amor. **Amorous looks,** miradas amorosas.

amorously [æ'mərəslɪ] [a-mó-ros-li], *adv.* Amorosamente, cariñosamente.

amorousness [æ'mərəsnɪs] [a-mó-ros-nis], *s.* Amor, cariño; la calidad de ser amoroso; galantería, terneza.

amorphism [æ'mərfɪzəm] [a-mor-fí-sem], *s.* Amorfia, carencia de forma, deformidad orgánica.

amorphous [ə'mɔːfəs] [a-mór-fos], *a.* Amorfo, informe, imperfecto, lo que no tiene la forma que le corresponde.

amort [ə'mɔːt] [a-mórt], *a.* Deprimido, abatido, amortiguado, mohíno, triste, taciturno.

amortization [əˌmɔːtɪ'zeɪʃən] [a-mor-ti-zéi-shon], **amortizement** [əˌmɔːtɪz'mənt] [a-mór-tis-ment], *s. (For.)* Amortización.

amortize [ə'mɔːtaɪz] [a-mór-tais], *va.* Amortizar, pasar los bienes a manos muertas.

amotion [ə'məʊʃən] [a-mó-shon], *s.* Remoción.

amount [ə'maʊnt] [a-máunt], *s.* Importe, la suma total del valor de una o muchas cosas. **Gross amount,** importe total. **Net amount,** importe neto. **To the amount of,** hasta la cantidad de, por la suma de. **Whole amount,** importe total. **The amount of what he said was this,** he aquí en sustancia lo que dijo. -*vn.* Alcanzar, ascender a, llegar a, sumar, equivaler, venir a ser, significar. **That amounts to fifty dollars,** eso suma cincuenta dólares. **His action amounts to treason,** su acción viene a ser una traición.

amour [ə'mʊəʳ] [a-múaʳ], *s.* Amores, amoríos, intriga de amor.

amove [ə'muːv] [a-múf], *va.* 1. Deponer, retirar o quitar a alguno del empleo que tiene. 2. Remover, mover, alterar, mudar.

amp [æmp] [ámp] *s. (Elec.)* Amperio.

amperage ['æmpərɪdʒ] [am-pé-rich], *s. (Elec.)* Amperaje, la fuerza de una corriente eléctrica en amperios.

ampere [æm'pɛːʳ] [am-péaʳ], *s. (Elec.)* Amperio, unidad de medida de corriente eléctrica.

ampere-hour [æmpə'aʊəʳ] [am-pe-auaʳ] *s. (Elec.)* Amperio hora.

amperemeter [æmpə'rɪmiːtəʳ] [am-pe-rí-mi-taʳ] *s.* Amperímetro.

ampere-second [æmpə'sekɒnd] [am-pa-sé-kond] *s. (Elec.)* Amperio segundo.

ampere-turn [æmpə'tɜːn] [am-per-térn] *s. (Elec.)* Amperio vuelta.

ampersand ['æmpəsænd] [am-pa-sánd], *s.* El signo & que significa *y.*

amphetamina [æm'fetəmiːnə] [am-fé-ta-mi-na] *s.* Anfetamina.

amphibia [æm'fɪbɪə] [am-fí-bia], *s. pl.* Anfibios, los animales que habitan así en el agua como en la tierra.

amphibious [æm'fɪbɪəs] [am-fí-bios] *a.* Anfibio.

amphibiousness [æm'fɪbɪəsnɪs] [am-fí-bios-nis], *s.* La calidad de ser anfibio.

amphibole [æm'fɪbəʊl] [am-fí-boul], *s. (Min.)* Anfíbol, género de sustancias minerales llamadas metasilicos, el cual comprende la hornblenda, el amianto o asbesto, etc.

amphibolite [æm'fɪbəlaɪt] [am-fí-bo-lait] *s. (Min.)* Anfibolita.

amphibological [æm'fɪbələdʒɪkl] [am-fi-bo-ló-chi-kal], *a.* Anfibológico, dudoso.

amphibologically [æm'fɪbələdʒɪklɪ] [am-fi-bo-ló-chi-kali], *adv.* Anfibológicamente.

amphibology [æm'fɪbələdʒɪ] [am-fi-bó-lo-chi], *s.* Anfibología, palabra o sentencia que se puede entender de dos modos.

amphibolous [æm'fɪbələs] [am-fí-bo-s], *a.* Impelido de una a otra parte.

amphibrach [æm'fɪbrætʃ] [am-fí-brak], *s.* Anfíbraco, pie de verso latino, de tres sílabas, la primera y la tercera breves y la segunda larga (+ * +).

amphictyons [æm'fɪktɪənz] [am-fík-tions], *s.* Anficciones, diputados de las ciudades de Grecia, que se reunían dos veces al año para resolver sobre los asuntos de la república.

amphictyony [æm'fɪktɪənɪ] [am-fík-tio-ni] *s.* Anficcionía.

amphioxus [æm'fɪksəs] [am-fió-ksus] *s. (Zool.)* Anfioxo.

amphipod [æm'fɪpɒd] [am-fí-pod], *s.* Orden de crustáceos, con cartorce pies.

amphisbaena [æm'fɪsbænə] [am-fis-ba-na], *s.* Anfisbena, especie de serpiente fabulosa, con una cabeza a cada extremo del cuerpo y capaz de moverse en una u otra dirección.

amphiscii [æm'fɪsɪ] [am-fi-si], *s. pl.* Anfíscios, los habitantes de la zona tórrida, porque su sombra se dirige ya al norte ya al mediodía, según las estaciones.

amphitheater, amphitheatre ['æmfɪθɪətəʳ] [am-fí-zi-á-tar], *s.* Anfiteatro, edificio de figura redonda u oval con gradas alrededor.

amphitheatrical ['æmfɪθɪətrɪkl] [am-fi-zi-á-tri-kal], *a.* Anfiteatral.

amphitrite [æm] [ám-fi-trait] N. Anfitrita.

amphitryon [æmf'trɪɒn] [ám-fi-trion] N. Anfitrión.

amphora ['æmfərə] [ám-fo-ra], *s.* ánfora, vaso antiguo de dos asas.

amphoric ['æmfərɪk] [am-fó-rik], *a.* Anfóreo: se dice de una cavidad en los pulmones que da sonido semejante al que se produce soplando en una garrafa vacía; como *amphoric resonance.*

ample ['æmpl] [ámpl], *a.* 1. Amplio, extendido, dilatado, extenso, ancho. 2. Liberal, largo, dadivoso; magnífico, ilimitado. **Ample room,** lugar amplio, espacio dilatado. **Ample resources,** abundantes recursos.

ampleness ['æmplnɪs] [ám-pel-nis], *s.* 1. Amplitud, anchura. 2. Abundancia, profusión, magnificencia.

ampliate ['æmplɪeɪt] [ám-pli-éit], *va.* Ampliar, extender, dilatar, aumentar, exagerar.

ampliation ['æmplɪeɪʃn] [am-pli-éi-shon], *s.* 1. Ampliación. 2. *(For.)* Plazo, término, prorrogación; respiro, plazo.

amplification [æmplɪfɪ'keɪʃən] [am-pli-fi-kéi-shon], *s.* 1. Amplificación, razonamiento en que se explican ampliamente las causas que influyen en lo que se quiere demostrar. 2. Extensión, ampliación; ampliación del microscopio. 3. Descripción prolija.

amplificative [æmplɪfɪ'kətɪv] [am-pli-fí-ka-tif], **amplificatory** [æmplɪfɪ'kətərɪ] [am-pli-fi-ka-tó-ri], *a.* Ampliativo, amplificador.

amplifier ['æmplɪfaɪəʳ] [am-pli-fáiaʳ] *s.* Amplificador.

amplify ['æmplɪfɑɪ] [ám-pli-fai], *va.* 1. *(Ret.)* Amplificar algún asunto o discurso con expresiones o imágenes. 2. Ampliar, extender, dilatar.

amplitude ['æmplɪtjuːd] [ám-pli-tiud], *s.* 1. Amplitud, extensión, dilatación. 2. Abundancia. 3. *(Astr.)* Amplitud. **Amplitude modulation,** (Radio) modulación de amplitud.

amply ['æmplɪ] [ám-pli], *adv.* Ampliamente, liberalmente, copiosamente. **Amply rewarded,** bien recompensado.

ampoule ['æmpuːl] [am-púl] *s.* Ampolla.

ampulla ['æmpʊlə] [am-pú-la], *s.* Ampolla: vaso de cuello angosto, y de cuerpo ancho y redondo.

ampullaceous ['æmpʊləsəs] [am-pu-lá-sos], *a.* Ampolláceo; semejante a una botella.

amputate ['æmpjʊteɪt] [ám-piu-teit], *va.* Amputar o cortar algún miembro del cuerpo humano.

amputation [æmpjʊ'teɪʃən] [am-piu-téi-shon], *s.* Amputación.

Amsterdam [æmpstə'dæm] [áms-ta-dam] N. *(Geogr.)* Amsterdam.

amuck [ə'mʌk] [a-mák], *adv.* Furiosamente, de una manera frenética. **To run amuck,** correr de acá para allá con propósito de matar a quien se encuentre al paso; atacar a ciegas, a troche y moche; también se escribe *amok*.

amulet ['æmjʊlɪt] [á-miu-leit], *s.* Amuleto, objeto portátil al que supersticiosamente se atribuye virtud para preservar de enfermedad o peligro.

amuse [ə'mkuːz] [a-miús], *va.* 1. Entretener, divertir. **The joke amused everyone,** el chiste divirtió a todo el mundo. **I am not amused,** no le veo la gracia. **To amuse one's guests,** entretener a sus invitados. 2. Embobar, entretener, engañar, adormecer, engaitar. -vn. Meditar.

amusement [ə'mkuːzmənt] [a-miús-ment], *s.* Diversión, entretenimiento, recreo, pasatiempo. **Amusement park,** parque de atracciones. **Look of amusement,** mirada divertida. **Place of amusement,** lugar de recreo.

amuser [ə'mkuːzəʳ] [a-miú-saʳ], *s.* Entretenedor, engañador, embaucador, engaitador.

amusing [ə'mkuːzɪŋ] [a-miú-sin] *a.* Divertido, gracioso, entretenido. **To be amusing,** tener gracia, ser divertido.

amusingly [ə'mkuːzɪŋlɪ] [a-miú-sin-li], *adv.* Divertidamente.

amusive [ə'mkuːzɪv] [a-miú-sif], *adv.* Divertido, lo que divierte, entretenido.

amusively [ə'mkuːzɪvlɪ] [a-miú-sif-li], *adv.* Entretenidamente.

amygdala [ə'mɪgdælə] [a-míg-da-la] *s. (Anat.)* Amígdala.

amygdalaceous [ə'mɪgdæləsəs] [a-mig-da-lá-sos] *a.* Amigdaláceo.

amygdalate [ə'mɪgdæl] [a-mig-da-leit], *a.* Hecho de almendras.

amygdaline [ə'mɪgdæliːn] [a-míg-da-lin], *a.* Almendrado, lo que se parece a la almendra en la figura. Amigdalino.

amygdaloids [ə'mɪgdælɔɪdʒ] [a-mig-da-loids], *s. pl.* *(Min.)* Piedras compuestas de varios pedazos como almendras.

amyl [ə'mɪl] [a-mil], *s. (Quím.)* Amilo: radical hidrocarbono, C_5H_{11}, de la serie parafina, y que se encuentra en el alcohol amílico.

amylaceous [ə'mɪləsəs] [a-mi-lá-sos] *a.* Amiláceo.

amylase [ə'ɪs] [a-mi-leis] *s.* Amilasa.

amylene [ə'mɪliːn] [a-mi-lin] *s. (Quím.)* Amileno.

amylic [ə'mɪlɪk] [a-mí-lik] *a.* Amílico.

amyloid [ə'mɪlɔɪd] [a-mi-loid] *a.* Amiloide.

amyloidosis [ə'mɪlɔɪdəsɪs] [a-mi-loi-do-sis] *s. (Med.)* Amilosis.

an [æn,ən] [an], *art.* Un, uno, una; es el mismo artículo indefinido, *A,* al cual se le añade la *n* cuando la voz que le sigue empieza por una vocal o *h* muda. **An eel,** una anguila. **An hour,** una hora. **A horse,** un caballo.

anabaptism [ænəbəp'tɪzəm] [a-na-bap-tísem], *s.* Herejía de los anabaptistas.

anabaptist [ænə'bəptɪst] [a-na-bap-tist], *s.* Anabaptista o anabatista, nombre de los sectarios.

anabaptistic [ænə'bəptɪstɪk] [a-na-bap-tís-tik], **anabaptistical** [ænə'bəptɪstɪkl] [a-na-bap-tís-ti-kal], *a.* Anabaptístico, lo que pertenece a los anabaptistas.

anabas ['ænəbəs] [a-na-bas], *s.* Género de peces que pueden andar por tierra y trepar árboles. V. CLIMBING-FISH. *(Gr.)*

anabasis ['ænəbəsɪs] [a-na-ba-sis] *s.* Anábasis.

anabolism [ænə'bɒlɪzm] [a-na-bo-lísem], *s.* El procedimiento de la asimilación de los alimentos.

anacamptic [ænə'kʌmtɪk] [a-na-kám-tik], *a.* Reverberado, reflejado. **An anacamptic hill,** monte o roca que produce un eco reflejando los sonidos.

anacardium [ænə'kɑːdɪəm] [a-na-kár-diom], *s.* Anacatártico, medicamento que opera por arriba.

anachoret [ænə'kərət] [a-ná-ko-ret], **anachorite** [æmɔkpɑ̈- ná-ko-rait], *s.* Anacoreta, el que vive en un lugar solitario, retirado del mundo.

anachorism [ænə'kərɪzm] [a-na-ko-rísem], *s.* Lo que no se aviene con las condiciones locales de un país.

anachronic [ə'nækrənik] [a-na-kró-nik] *a.* Anacrónico.

anachronism [ə,nækrənɪzəm] [a-na-kro-nísem], *s.* Anacronismo, error de cronología.

anachronistic [ə,nækrə'nɪstɪk] [a-na-kro-nís-tik], *a.* Anacronístico.

anaclastics [ə,næklɒstɪk] [a-na-klás-tiks], *s.* V. DIPTRICS.

anacoluthon [ænəkə'luːθɒn] [a-na-ko-lú-zon] *s. (Gram.)* Anacoluto.

anaconda [ænə'kɒndə] [a-na-kon-da], *s.* Anaconda, serpiente sudamericana.

anacreon [ə'nəkrɪən] [a-ná-krion] N. Anacreonte.

anacreontic [ə'nəkrɪəntɪk] [a-na-krion-tik], *a.* Anacreóntico.

anadromous [ə'nədrəməs] [a-na-dro-mos], *a.* Anadromo; se dice de los peces que, saliendo del mar, suben por los ríos en ciertas estaciones para procrear.

anaemia [ə'niːmɪə] [a-ní-mia], *s.* Anemia, disminución de los glóbulos de la sangre.

anaemic [ə'niːmɪk] [a-ní-mic], *a.* Anémico, en estado de anemia.

anaerobe [ə'nɛərəʊb] [a-neo-roub] *s.* Anaerobio.

anaerobic [ænɪs'rəʊbɪk] [a-neo-róu-bik] *a.* Anaerobio.

anaesthesia [ænɪs'θiːsɪə] [a-nis-zí-sha], *s.* Anestesia; pérdida del sentido; estado producido por enfermedad o por inspiración o aplicación de un anestésico.

anaesthetic [ænɪs'θetɪk] [a-nis-zé-tik], *a.* Anestésico, anestético; capaz de producir insensibilidad o pérdida completa del sentido. -s. Anestésico, lo que produce insensibilidad al dolor, como el cloroformo, la cocaína, etc.

an(a)esthetist [ænɪs'θetɪst] [a-nis-zé-tist], *a.* Anestesista, médico anestesista.

anaesthetization ['ænɪsθetɪ'zeɪʃən] [a-nes-zi-séi-shon] *s.* Anestesia.

an(a)esthetize [æ'nɪsθɪtɑɪz] [a-nis-zi-tais], *va.* Anestesiar.

anaglyph ['ænəglɪf] [á-na-glif], *s.* Anaglifo, sentido místico.

anagoge ['ænəgɒg] [á-na-gog] o **anagogy** [æ'nəgɒdʒɪ] [a-ná-go-chi] *s.* Anagoge, anagogía.

anagogics ['ænəgɒdʒɪks] [a-na-gó-chiks], *s.* Anagogía, sentido místico.

anagram ['ænəgræm] [á-na-gram], *s.* Anagrama, transposición de las letras de una palabra o sentencia, de la cual resulta otra palabra o sentencia distinta; v.g. *amor, ramo, mora.*

anagrammatical [ænəgrə'mætɪkl] [a-na-gra-má-ti-kal], *a.* Anagramático.

anagrammatist [ænə'græmətɪst] [a-na-gra-má-tist], *a.* Anagramatizador.

anagrammatize [ænə'græmətɑɪz] [a-na-gra-ma-tais], *vn.* Anagramatizar.

anal ['eɪnəl] [éi-nal], *a.* Anal; que tiene relación con el ano.

analect [ænə'ɛkt] [á-na-lekt], *s.* Fragmento escogido de un autor, se usa más en plural.

analepsis [æɪʃlɪs] [a-na-lép-sis], *s.* Analepsia, restauración de las fuerzas extenuadas.

analeptic [æ**n**əp**l**ɪk] [a-na-lép-tik], *a. (Med.)* Analéptico, restaurativo.

analgesia [ænæ'dʒiːsɪə] [a-nal-yí-sia] *s. (Med.)* Analgesia.

analgesic [ænæ'dʒiːsɪk] [a-nal-yí-sik], *s. y a. (Med.)* Analgésico.

analog computer ['ænəlɒɡ,kəm'pjuːtəʳ] [a-na-log-kom-piú-taʳ], *s.* Computadora analógica.

analogical [ænə'lɒdʒɪkl] [a-na-ló-chi-kal], *a.* Analógico.

analogically [ˌænə'lɒdʒɪklɪ] [a-na-ló-chi-ka-li], *adv.* La calidad de ser anfibio.

analogism [ænə'lɒdʒɪzm] [a-na-lo-yísem] *s.* Analogismo, argumento de la causa al efecto.

analogize [ænə'lɒdʒɑɪz] [a-ná-lo-chais], *va.* Analogizar, explicar por analogia. **To analogize with,** presentar analogías con.

analogous [ˌə'næləɡəs] [a-ná-lo-gos], *a.* Análogo; proporcional.

analogously [ˌə'næləɡəslɪ] [a-ná-lo-gos-li], *adv.* Analógicamente.

analogue [æ'nəlɒɡ] [á-na-log], *s.* Lo análogo, lo que guarda relación de semejanza con otra cosa o idea. **Analogue computer,** máquina calculadora de términos semejantes.

analogy [ə'nælədʒɪ] [a-ná-lo-chi], *s.* Analogía, proporción o semejanza de una cosa con otra, relación, conformidad.

analysable o **analyzable** [ænəlɪ'seɪbl] [a-na-li-sei-bol] *a.* Analizable.

analysand [ə'nælɪˌsænd] [a-na-li-sand] *s.* Persona que sigue un tratamiento de psicoanálisis.

analyse o **analyze** ['ænəlɑɪz] [á-na-lais], *va.* Analizar, hacer análisis.

analyser o **analyzer** ['ænəlɑɪzəʳ] [a-na-lái-saʳ] *s.* Analizador.

analysis ['ænəlɑɪzɪs] [a-ná-lai-sis], *s.* Análisis, *s. com.* separación de algún compuesto en las varias partes de que se compone.

analyst ['ænəlɪst] [á-na-list], *s.* Analizador.

analytic ['ænəlɪtɪk] [a-na-lí-tik], *a.* Método analítico.

analytical [ænə'lɪtɪkəl] [a-na-lí-ti-kal], *adv.* Analítico.

analytically ['ænəlɪtɪkəlɪ] [a-na-lí-ti-ka-li], *adv.* Analíticamente.

anamorphosis [ænəmɔː'fəʊsɪs] [a-mor-fóu-sis], *s.* Anamorfosis; la pintura que representa separadas, y al parecer informes, las varias partes de un objeto; pero que se hallan perfectas y en su propio lugar, cuando se mira desde cierto punto de vista.

ananas ['ænənəs] [a-na-nas], *s.* Anana, nombre dado en Europa a la piña de América.

anapestic ['ænəpɪstɪk] [a-na-pís-tik], *a.* Anapéstico.

anaphase ['ænəfeɪs] [á-na-feis] *s.* Anafase.

anaphora [ænə'fɒrə] [a-na-fo-ra], *s.* Anáfora, figura que consiste en la repetición de una misma palabra al principio de dos o más frases.

anaphrodisia [ænəfrə'dɪsɪə] [a-na-fro-dí-sia], *s.* Ausencia del apetito venéreo.

anaphrodisiac [ænəfrə'dɪsɪək] [a-na-fro-di-siak], *a.* Anafrodisíaco, calmante del deseo venéreo.

anaphylactic [ænəfɪ'læktɪk] [a-na-fi-lák-tik] *a.* Anafiláctico.

anaplasty [ænə'plæstɪ] [a-na-plas-ti], *s. (Med.)* Anaplastia, autoplastia, cirugía plástica.

anarchic ['ænəkɪk] [a-nár-kik], **anarchical** ['ænəkɪkl] [a-nár-ki-kal], *s.* Anárquico, confuso, desordenado.

anarchism ['ænəkɪzm] [a-nar-kí-sem] *s.* Anarquismo.

anarchist ['ænəkɪst] [á-nar-kist], **anarch** ['ænək] [a-nark], *s.* Anarquista.

anarchy ['ænəkɪ] [á-nar-ki] *s.* Anarquía.

anasarca ['ænə'səkə] [a-na-sá-ka], *s. (Med.)* Anasarca, especie de hidropesía.

anasarcous ['ænə'səkəs] [a-na-sá-kos], *a.* Hidrópico.

anastasis ['ænəstəsɪs] [a-nás-ta-sis], *s.* Resurrección.

anastatic [ænəstəsɪk] [a-nas-tá-tik], *a.* Anastático, en relieve. **Anastatic printing,** Impresión anastática; manera de obtener una copia en relieve de una página impresa, etc., sobre una plancha de zinc que sirve para la reimpresión.

anastomose [ænəstə'məʊz] [a-nás-to-mos], *vn.* Unirse por sus extremos las ramificaciones salientes de las arterias y venas; anastomarse.

anastomosis [ænəstə'məʊsɪs] [a-nas-to-móu-sis], *s. (Med.)* Anastomosis, unión de dos vasos sanguíneos o linfáticos.

anastomotic [ænəstə'məʊtɪk] [a-nas-to-móu-tik], *a.* Anastomótico; que forma anastomosis o se refiere a ella.

anastrophe [ænəstrəf] [a-nas-trouf], *s.* Anástrofe; inversión del orden usual de las palabras.

anathema [ə'næθɪmə] [a-na-zí-ma], *a.* Anatema, excomunión, execración. **It is anathema to him,** le es odioso.

anathematical [ə'næθɪmətɪkl] [a-na-zi-má-ti-kal], *a.* Lo perteneciente al anatema.

anathematically [ə'næθɪmkəlɪ] [a-na-zi-má-ti-ka-li], *adv.* A modo de anatema.

anathematization [ə'næθɪmətɪˈzeɪʃən] [a-na-zi-ma-ti-séi-shon], *s.* La acción de excomulgar.

anathematize [ə'næθɪmətaɪz] [a-na-zi-ma-tais], *va.* Anatematizar, excomulgar.

anathematizer [ə'næθɪmətaɪzəʳ] [a-na-zi-ma-tái-saʳ], *s.* Excomulgador, anatematizador.

anatocism [ə'nætɒsɪzm] [a-na-to-sízem], *s.* Contrato usuario, usura de la misma usura o interés del interés.

anatolia [ænə'təlɪə] [a-na-tó-lia] N. *(Geogr.)* Anatolia.

anatomical [ænə'tɒmɪkl] [a-na-tó-mi-kal], *a.* Anatómico.

anatomically [ænə'tɒmɪkəlɪ] [a-na-tó-mi-ka-li], *adv.* Anatómicamente.

anatomist [ænə'tɒmɪst] [a-na-to-mist], *s.* Anatomista o anatómico, el profesor de anatomía.

anatomize [ænə'tɒmaɪz] [a-na-to-mais], *va.* Anatomizar, hacer disección o anatomía de un cuerpo; disecar.

anatomy ['ænətɒmɪ] [a-na-to-mi], *s.* 1. Anatomía, parte de la medicina que trata de la descripción del cuerpo humano: se llama también así la disección de un cuerpo humano. 2. División de alguna cosa. 3. Esqueleto.

anatoxin [ænətəksɪn] [a-na-tok-sin] *s. (Med.)* Anatoxina.

anatropal [ænə'trəʊpəl] [a-na-tróu-pal] o **anatropous** ['ænə'trəʊpos] [a-na-tróu-pos] *a. (Bot.)* Anátropo.

anaxagoras ['ænəksæɡərəs] [a-nak-sá-go-ras] N. Anaxágoras.

anbury [æn'bʊrɪ] [an-bu-ri], *s.* Tumor blando y grumoso que se presenta en el cuerpo de las caballerías y los ganados.

ancestor ['ænsɪstəʳ] [an-sís-taʳ], *s.* Uno de los mayores, abuelos o antepasados de alguno, predecesor. **Ancestor worship,** el culto de los antepasados.

ancestral [æn'sestəl] [an-sís-tral] o **ancestrel** [æn'sestəl] [an-sís-trel], *a.* Hereditario. **Ancestral home,** casa solariega.

ancestry ['ænsɪstrɪ] [an-ses-tri], *s.* Linaje o serie de antepasados, extracción, raza, alcurnia.

ancientry [æn'sɪəntrɪ] [én-sian-tri], *s.* Antigüedad de una familia: dignidad antigua.

anchor ['æŋkəʳ] [an-kaʳ], *s.* 1. Ancla o áncora de una embarcación. **Best bower anchor,** ancla de ayuste. **Small bower anchor,** ancla sencilla. **Sheet anchor,** anclote o ancla de esperanza. **Anchor arms,** uñas del ancla. **Anchor back,** galga del ancla. **Anchor bill,** pico del ancla. **anchor cross,** cruz del ancla. **Anchor flukes,** orejas del ancla. **Anchor shank,** caña del ancla. **Anchor stock,** cepo del ancla. **to stock the anchor,** encepar el ancla. **At anchor,** al ancla. **Foul anchor,** ancla enredada con su cable. **Anchor beam,** serviola. **Anchor chocks,** calzos de ancla. **Anchor escapement,** escapa de áncora. **Anchor ground,** fondeadero. **Anchor stopper,** capón. **Drag anchor,** ancla flotante o de arrastre. **Foul anchor,** ancla encepada. **Kedge anchor,** anclote. **To ride at anchor,** estar al ancla. 2. *(Ant.)* V. ANACHORITE.

anchor, *vn.* Anclar, ancorar, echar las anclas. **to drop or let go anchor,** dar fondo. **To weigh anchor,** levar el ancla. **To**

drag the anchor, garrar o arrastrar el ancla. **Anchored,** anclado; formado como ancla. *-va.* Ancorar; fijar. **Anchoring,** anclaje. **Anchoring of a bridge,** amarras de un puente. **Anchoring ground,** agarradero; fondeadero.

anchorage ['æŋkɔreɪdʒ] [an-ka-reich], *s.* 1. Anclaje, el sitio o lugar para anclar: se llama también ancoraje o surgidero. 2. Anclaje, las áncoras de una embarcación. 3. Anclaje, el tributo o derecho que se paga en los puertos de mar por dar fondo en ellos.

anchoress ['æŋkɔres] [an-ka-res], *s.* Ermitaña, la mujer que vive en una ermita.

anchoret ['æŋkɔret] [an-ka-ret], **anchorite** ['æŋkɔraɪt] [an-ka-rait], *s.* Ermitaño, anacoreta. *V.* ANACHORITE.

anchor-hold ['æŋkɔhɔold] [an-ka-jóuld], *s.* 1. Agarro de ancla. 2. (*Fig.*) Seguridad.

anchorsmith ['æŋkɔzmɪθ] [an-kas-miz], *s.* Forjador de anclas.

anchovy ['æntʃɔvɪ] [an-chó-vi], *s.* Anchova o anchoa, pez pequeño, menor que la sardina.

anchylose, anchylosis ['æŋtʃɪləʊs/ɪs] [an-ki-lous/is] *V.* ANKYLOSE y ANKYLOSIS.

ancient ['eɪnʃənt] [éin-shant], *a.* Antiguo. *-s.* 1. (*Ant.*) Bandera; insignia. el porta-estandarte, porta-guión, o abanderado. 2. En plural, antepasados, mayores. **Ancient Greece,** Grecia Antigua. **Ancient customs,** costumbres antiguas. **The ancients,** los antiguos.

anciently ['eɪnʃəntlɪ] [éin-shant-li], *adv.* Antiguamente.

ancientness ['eɪnʃəntnɪs] [éin-shant-nis], *s.* Antigüedad de linaje.

ancillary [æn'sɪlɔrɪ] [an-sí-la-ri], *a.* El que sirve bajo otro sirviente. Ancilario; subordinado. **Surgery and ancillary services,** cirugía y servicios auxiliares. **Ancillary plants,** fábricas anexas.

ancipital, ancipitous [æn'sɪpɪtəl] [æn'sɪpɪtəs] [an-sí-pi-tal] [an-sí-pi-tos], *a.* 1. Con dos caras o formas. 2. De dos cortes.

ancon [æŋkɒn] [án-kon] *s.* Ancón.

ancoral [æŋkɒrəl] [án-ko-ral], *a.* 1. Perteneceinte o semejante a un áncora. 2. (*Zool.*) En forma de gancho, encorvado.

ancylostomiasis [æn sɪləstəmɪ'eɪsɪs] [an-si-los-to-mi-éi-sis] (*Med.*) Anquilostomiasis.

and [ænd] [and] (and), *conj.* Y, e, conjunción copulativa: aun, si, que, *a.* y *s.* Nombre del signo &. *V.* AMPERSAND. **Now and them,** de cuando en cuando, o de vez en cuando. **And therefore,** por esta razón, por tanto. **By and by,** luego, al instante. **Better and better,** cada vez mejor. **Here and there,** por aquí y por allí. **To go and see,** ir a ver. **And yet,** sin embargo, **With ifs and ands,** con dimes y diretes: con si y no. **And so forth,** y así sucesivamente.

Andalusia [ændə'luːzɪə] [an-da-lú-sia] *N.* (*Geogr.*) Andalucía.

Andalusian [ændə'luːzɪən] [an-da-lú-sian], *a.* Andaluz, andaluza; de Andalucía.

andante [ænˈdæntə] [an-dan-te], *a.* Andante, que significa distinto, primoroso, más vivo que larghetto y menos que allegretto.

andantino [ændənˈtiːnəʊ] [an-dan-tí-nou], *a.* Algo más lento que andante. Se usa algunas veces para denotar movimiento entre andante y allegretto.

Andean ['ændɪən] [án-dian], *a.* Andino, de los Andes.

Andes ['ændiz] [án-dis] *N. pl.* (*Geogr.*) Andes.

andesite ['ændɪzaɪt] [án-di-sait] *s.* Andesita.

andirons ['ændɪrənz] [án-di-rans], *s. pl.* Morillos, caballetes de hierro.

Andorra [ænˈdɔːrə] [an-do-ra] *N.* (*Geogr.*) Andorra.

Andorran [ænˈdɔːrən] [an-do-ran] *a./s.* Andorrano.

Andrew ['ændruː] [án-dru] *N.* Andrés. **St. Andrew's cross.** cruz de S. Andrés, aspa.

androecium [ændrəˈeʃəm] [an-dro-é-shom] *s.* (*Bot.*) Androceo.

androgen ['ændrədʒən] [an-dró-chen], *s.* (*Biol.*) Andrógeno.

androginal [ænˈdrɒdʒɪnəl] [an-dró-chi-nal], *a.* Andrógino. lo que pertenece a los hermafroditas.

androgynus [ænˈdrɒdʒɪnəs] [an-dró-chi-nos], **androgyne** ['ændrɒdʒiːn] [án-dro-chain], *s.* Hermafrodita, andrógino.

android ['ændrɔɪd] [an-dróid], *a.* Que tiene forma humana. *-s.* Hermafrodita, andrógino.

androtomy ['ændrɒtəmɪ] [an-dró-to-mi], *s.* Androtomía, la disección del cadáver de una persona.

anecdotal [ænɪkˈdəʊtəl] [a-nik-dou-tal] *a.* Anecdótico.

anecdote ['ænɪkdəʊt] [a-nik-dout], *s.* Anécdota, relación breve de un suceso curioso más o menos importante.

anecdotic [ænɪkˈdəʊtɪk] [a-nik-dou-tik] o **anecdotical** [ænɪkˈdəʊtɪkl] [a-nik-dou-ni-kal] *a.* Anecdótico.

anecdotist [ænɪkˈdəʊtɪst] [a-nik-dou-tist] *s.* Anecdotista.

anemia [əˈniːmɪə] [a-ní-mia] *s.* (*Med.*) Anemia.

anemic [əˈniːmɪk] [a-ní-mik] *a.* (*Med.*) Anémico.

anemograph [əˈnɪməgræf] [a-ni-mó-graf] *s.* (*Fís.*) Anemógrafo.

anemography [əˈnɪməgræfɪ] [a-ni-mó-gra-fi], *s.* Anemografía, descripción de los vientos.

anemometer [əˈnɪməmiːtər] [an-ni-mó-mi-tar], *s.* Anemómetro, instrumento para medir el viento y sus grados.

anemometry [əˈnɪməmetrɪ] [a-ni-mo-mi-tri], *s.* Anemometría, el arte de medir la fuerza del viento.

anemone [əˈnemənɪ] [a-né-mo-ni], *s.* (*Bot.*) Anémone, anémona, especie de flor; planta ranunculácea que contiene numerosas especies. **Sea-anemone,** actinia, anémona marina.

anemophilous [əˈneməfɪləs] [a-ne-mó-fi-los] *a.* (*Bot.*) Anemófilo.

anemoscope [əˈneməskəʊp] [a-né-mos-koup], *s.* anemoscopio, instrumento para indicar los cambios de dirección del aire.

anent [əˈnent] [a-nent], *prep.* 1. tocante, por lo concerniente. 2. Contra, opuesto.

aneroid [əˈnerɔɪd] [a-ne-roid], *a.* Aneroide: sin líquido. **Aneroid barometer,** barómetro aneroide.

anesthesia [ænɪsˈθiːzɪə] [a-nis-zí-sia] *s.* (*Med.*) Anestesia.

anesthetic [ænɪsˈθetɪk] [a-nis-zé-tik] *a.* (*Med.*) Anestésico.

anesthetist [ænɪsˈθetɪst] [a-nis-té-tist] *s.* Anestesista.

anesthetize [ænɪsˈθetaɪz] [a-nís-ze-tais] *va.* Anestesiar.

aneurism ['ænjəˌrɪzəm] [a-niu-rísem], *s.* Aneurisma, dilatación de las arterias.

aneurismal ['ænjəˌrɪzməl] [a-niu-rís-mal], *a.* Aneurismal.

anew [əˈnjuː] [a-niu], *adv.* 1. De nuevo, otra vez. 2. Nuevamente, de un modo nuevo, de refresco. *-N.B. Anew* se traduce elegantemente por el verbo *Volver. (irreg.)* v.g. **He writes anew,** el vuelve a escribir.

anfractuous [ænˈfræktʃʊəs] [an-frák-tuos], **anfractuose** [ænˈfræktʃʊəʊz] [an-frák-tuos], *a.* Tortuoso, sinuoso, anfractuoso, desigual.

anfractuosity [ænˈfræktʃʊɒsɪtɪ] [an-frak-tuó-si-ti], *s.* Desigualdad, sinuosidad, anfractuosidad.

angaria [ənˈgærɪə] [an-gá-ria] *s.* Angaria.

angel ['eɪndʒəl] [éin-chel], *s.* 1. Ángel. **Guardian angel,** ángel de la guarda. 2. Ángel, expresión de cariño para ponderar la hermosura de alguna persona. 3. Mensajero. *a.* Angélico, angelical. **What an angel you are!,** ¿qué cielo eres! **Fallen angel,** ángel caído. **To sing like an angel,** cantar como los ángeles.

angel-age ['eɪndʒəlˌeɪdʒ] [éin-chel-eich], *s.* Estado o existencia de los ángeles.

angelfish ['eɪndʒəlfɪʃ] [éin-chal-fish] *s.* (*Zool.*) Angelote.

angelic [eɪnˈdʒəlɪk] [ein-ché-lik] **angelical** [ein-ché-li-kal], *a.* Angelical, angélico.

angelica [eɪnˈdʒəlɪkə] [an-ché-li-ka], *s.* 1. (*Bot.*) Angélica, planta. 2. Cierto vino dulce de California.

angelicalness ['eɪndʒəlɪkəlnɪs] [an-ché-li-kal-nes], *s.* Excelencia sobrehumana, hermosura angelical.

angel-like ['eɪndʒəlaɪk] [éin-chal-laik], *a.* Angelical.

angelot ['eɪndʒəlɒt] [éin-cha-lot], *s.* 1. Instrumento músico, semejante al laúd. 2. Moneda acuñada por los ingleses, cuando los reyes de Inglaterra lo eran también de Francia. 3. Especie de queso my estimado que se hace en Normandía.

angel-shot ['eɪndʒəlʃɒt] [éin-chal-shot], *s.* Balas enramadas o encadenadas, palanquetas.

Angelus ['eɪndʒɪləs] [éin-yi-las], *s.* El Ave María, la oración de este nombre y el toque de campanas que indica esta oración.

angel-winged ['eɪndʒəl,wɪŋt] [ein-chal-uíngt], *a.* Alado como los ángeles.

angel-worship ['eɪndʒəl,wɔːʃɪp] [ein-chal-uor-ship], *s.* Culto de los ángeles.

anger ['æŋgəʳ] [án-gar], *s.* 1. Ira, cólera. 2. Inflamación de un órgano o tejido del cuerpo. 3. Enojo, enfado, disgusto. **A fit of anger,** un acceso **de** cólera. **To provoke to anger,** encolerizar, causar ira. **To speak in anger,** hablar furioso.

anger *va.* Provocar, enfurecer; enojar, irritar, encolerizar. *vn.* Encolerizarse, enfadarse, enojarse.

angina [æn'dʒaɪnə] [an-chái-na], *s.* Angina, afección inflamatoria de la faringe, la laringe, etc. **Angina pectoris,** angina de pecho, o esternalgia.

anginous [æn'dʒɪnəs] [án-chi-nos] *a.* (*Med.*) Anginoso.

angiocarpous [æn'dʒəkɑːpəs] [an-chio-kár-pus], *a.* Angiocarpio o angiocarpo; se dice de la planta cuyo fruto está contenido en una cubierta distinta y separada del fruto mismo.

angiography [æn'dʒəgræfɪ] [an-chió-gra-fi], *s.* Angiografía, descripción de los vasos del cuerpo humano.

angiology [æn'dʒəlɒdʒɪ] [an-chió-lo-yi], *s.* (*Anat.*) Angiología, parte de la anatomía que trata de los vasos.

angioma [æn'dʒəmə] [an-yió-ma] *s.* (*Med.*) Angioma.

angiomonospermous [æn'dʒəmənəs'pɜːməs] [an-chio-manas-pér-mos], *a.* Se dice de las plantas que tienen una semilla en su pericarpio.

angiosperm [ændʒɪə'spɜːm] [an-chios-perm], *s.* (*Bot.*) Angiosperma, orden de plantas cuya semilla está envuelta en vaina diferente del cáliz.

angiospermous ['ændʒɪəspɜːm] [an-chios-pér-mos], *a.* Angiosperma: fruto cuyos granos están encerrados en un pericarpio distinto o de diversa naturaleza.

angiosporous [ændʒɪəs'pɒrəs] [an-chios-po-ros], *a.* Angiospóreo; se dice de la planta cuyos esporos están contenidos en un receptáculo hueco, como ciertos hongos.

angle ['æŋgl] [ángel], *s.* 1. Ángulo, la inclinación de dos líneas que se cortan en un punto. 2. (*Geom.*) Ángulo, espacio comprendido entre dos líneas curvas o rectas que se reunen en un punto. 3. Esquina. 4. Caña de pescar. 5. Anzuelo. **Visual angle,** ángulo óptico. **Angle-bevel,** falsa escuadra. **Angle-brace,** cuadral. **Angle-brackets,** modillones angulares. **Angle-rafter,** lima. **Angle** (roofing) caballete.

angle, *va.* 1. Pescar con caña. 2. (*Met.*) Insinuarse, introducirse con maña para lograr de otro lo que se pretende. -*va.* Atraer, halagar. **To angle for,** ir a la caza de.

angled ['æŋglɪd] [án-glid], *a.* Anguloso.

angle iron ['æŋglaɪən] [angel-áion] *s.* Angular, ángulo.

angler ['æŋgləʳ] [án-glar], *s.* Pescador de caña.

angle-rod ['æŋglərɒd] [angla-rod], *s.* Trozo de la caña de pescar, al cual se afianzan el sedal y anzuelo del pescador.

angles ['æŋglz] [ángls] *N.* Anglos.

anglesite ['æŋgləzaɪt] [án-gla-sait] *s.* (*Min.*) Angiesita.

angle-worm ['æŋgl'wɔːm] [ángel-uém], *s.* Lombriz de tierra.

anglian ['æŋglɪən] [án-glian] *a./s.* Anglo.

Anglican ['æŋglɪkən] [án-gli-can], *a.* Anglicano. -*s.* Individuo de la iglesia anglicana.

Anglicanism ['æŋglɪkənɪzəm] [an-gli-ka-ní-sem] *s.* (*Rel.*) Anglicanismo.

Anglicism ['æŋglɪsɪzəm] [an-gli-sí-sem], *s.* Anglicismo, modo de hablar particular y privativo de la lengua inglesa.

Anglicist ['æŋglɪsɪst] [án-gli-sist] *s.* Anglicista.

anglicize ['æŋglɪsaɪz] [án-gli-sais], *va.* Traducir o convertir en inglés; dar a otra lengua los giros y el carácter del idioma inglés.

angling ['æŋglɪŋ] [án-gling], *s.* El arte o práctica de pescar con caña.

Anglo-American ['æŋgləə'merɪkæn] [an-glou-a-mé-ri-kan], *a.* y *s.* Angloamericano.

Anglo-Arab ['æŋgləʊ,ærəb] [an-glou-á-rab] *s.* Angloárabe.

Anglo-Arabian ['æŋgləʊ,ærəbɪən] [an-glou-a-rá-bian] *a.* Angloárabe.

Anglo-Indian ['æŋgləʊ'ɪndɪən] [an-glou-ín-dian], *a.* y *s.* Angloindio, relacionado con los ingleses y las Indias orientales.

anglomania ['æŋgləʊ,meɪnɪə] [an-glou-méi-nia], *s.* Anglomanía, admiración exagerada de los ingleses y de lo perteneciente a ellos.

anglomaniac ['æŋgləʊ,meɪnɪək] [an-glou-méi-niak], *a.* y *s.* Anglómano, el que imita servilmente a los ingleses o lo hace con extravagancia.

Anglo-Norman ['æŋgləʊ,nɔːmən] [an-glou-nór-man], *s.* y *a.* Anglonormando.

anglophil o **anglophile** ['æŋgləʊfaɪl] [an-glo-fail] *a./s.* Anglófilo.

anglophilia ['æŋgləʊfɪlɪə] [an-glo-fí-lia] *s.* Anglofilia.

anglophobe ['æŋgləʊfəʊb] [án-glo-foub] *a./s.* Anglófobo.

anglophobia ['æŋgləʊfəʊbɪə] [an-glou-fóu-bia] *s.* Anglofobia.

anglo-Saxon ['æŋgləʊsæksən] [an-glou-sák-son], *s.* y *a.* Anglosajón.

angolese ['æŋgəʊliːz] [an-go-lís] *a./s.* Angolés.

angora [æŋgərə] [an-go-ra], *s.* Angora, ciudad de Anatolia. **Angora cat, goat,** gato, cabra de Angora o Angola.

angostura [æŋgə'stjuərə] [an-gos-tiúa-ra] *s.* (*Bot.*) Angostura.

angrily [æŋgrɪlɪ] [an-gri-li], *adv.* Coléricamente, airadamente.

angry ['æŋgrɪ] [an-gri], *a.* 1. Colérico, irritado, enfadado, enojado, encolerizado, airado. 2. (*Med.*) Irritado, inflamado, que presenta inflamación. **They never spoke an angry word to each other,** jamás se han hablado con cólera. **To angry waves,** a las olas irritadas. **To get angry,** enfadarse, enojarse, enfurecerse. **I will be angry,** me enfadaré.

angstrom ['æŋgstrʌm] [ángs-trom] *s.* (*Fís.*) Angström.

anguilliform [æŋgwɪlɪ'fɔːm] [an-gui-li-form], *a.* En forma de anguila.

anguish ['æŋgwɪʃ] [an-güish], *s.* Ansia, pena, angustia, congoja, aflicción, dolor. **To be in anguish,** estar angustiado. *va.* Angustiar, acongojar.

anguished ['æŋgwɪʃt] [án-güisht], *a.* Atormentado, angustiado.

angular ['æŋgjʊləʳ] [an-giu-lar]. *a.* Angular, anguloso, lo que pertenece al ángulo o los tiene.

angularity [æŋgjʊ'lærɪtɪ] [an-guiu-lá-ri-ti], **angularness** ['æŋgjʊlənɪs] [an-guiu-lar-nis], **angulosity** ['æŋgjʊləsɪtɪ] [an-guiu-ló-si-ti], *s.* La propiedad de tener ángulos o esquinas.

angulate, angulated ['æŋgjʊlt] [án-guiu-lei-tid], *a.* (*Bot.*) Anguloso, angular.

anhelation [æn'leɪʃən] [a-ne-lei-shon], *s.* Jadeo, anhélito vehemente, anhelación.

anhydride [æn'haɪdraɪd] [an-ni-draid], *s.* Óxido que se convierte en ácido cuando se le añade agua; o ácido del cual se ha extraído el agua, y que forma sales.

anhydrite [æn'haɪdraɪt] [ani-drait] *s.* (*Min.*) Anidrita.

anhydrous ['ænɪdrəs] [a-ní-dros], *a.* Anhidro, que no contiene agua.

anil ['ænɪl] [a-nil], *s.* (*Bot.*) Añil, la planta de cuyas hojas y tallos se hace el índigo o añil.

anile ['ænɪl] [a-nil], *a.* Semejante a una vieja; falto de juicio, que chochea; chocha.

anilin o **aniline** ['ænɪlaɪn] [a-ni-lain], *s.* Anilina, base de la cual se obtienen muchos tintes brillantes. Líquido incoloro oleoso, obtenido hoy del alquitrán de carbón, pero originalmente del añil.

animadversion ['ænɪmədˈvɜːʃən] [a-ni-mad-vér-shon], s. 1. Animadversión, nota crítica o reparo. 2. Animadvertencia, advertencia u observación. 3. Reflexión, reprensión, castigo, apercibimiento.

animadversive ['ænɪmədˈvɜːsɪv] [a-ni-mad-vér-sif], a. Judicativo, lo que juzga o puede hacer juicio de algo.

animadversiveness ['ænɪmədˈvɜːsɪvnɪs] [a-ni-mad-vér-sif-nis], s. Poder o facultad de considerar o formar juicio. Censura, reproche.

animadvert ['ænɪmədˈvɜːt] [a-ni-mad-vért], vn. 1. Advertir, considerar, observar. 2. Censurar, formar juicio, dar dictamen, juzgar. 3. Reprochar, castigar.

animadverter ['ænɪmədˈvɜːtəʳ] [a-ni-mad-vér-tar], s. Censurador, crítico.

animal ['ænɪməl] [a-ni-mal], s. 1. Animal, cuerpo animado. 2. Animal, por injuria o desprecio se llama así al hombre incapaz o ignorante. -a. **Wild animal,** animal salvaje. **A stupid animal,** hombre estúpido; se dice por desprecio. **Animal kingdom,** el reino animal.

animalcular [ˌænɪməlˈkuːləʳ] [a-ni-mál-ku-lar], a. Animalcular, referente a los animálculos.

animalcule [ˌænɪməlˈkjuːl] [a-ni-mál-kiul], s. Animalillo microscópico: animálculo, como un infusorio or rotador.

animal husbandry [ˌænɪməlˈhəsbəndrɪ] [a-ni-mal-jás-ban-dri] s. Ganadería, cría de animales.

animalism ['ænɪməlɪzm] [a-ni-ma-lísem], s. 1. Animalismo, estado animal. 2. Sensualidad.

animalist ['ænɪməlɪst] [a-ní-ma-list] a./s. Animalista.

animality ['ænɪməlɪtɪ] [a-ni-má-li-ti]. s. El estado de la existencia animal, vida animal.

animalization [ˌænɪməlɪˈzeɪʃən] [a-ni-ma-li-séi-shon], s. Animalización.

animalize ['ænɪməlaɪz] [a-ní-ma-lais], va. 1. Animalizar, dotar de propiedades animales. 2. Asimilar los alimentos, convertirlos en materia animal.

animal power [ˈænɪməlˈpɑʊəʳ] [á-ni-mal-páuar] s. Fuerza de tracción animal.

animal spirits [ˌænɪməlsˈpɪrɪts] [a-ni-mals-pí-rits] s. Vitalidad, animación, vigor.

animate ['ænɪmɪt] [á-ni-meit], a. Viviente, animado. **Animate beings,** seres animados. va. Animar, alentar. **The soul animates the body,** el alma anima el cuerpo. **To animate the conversation,** animar la conversación.

animated ['ænɪmɪtɪd] [a-ni-méi-tid], a. 1. Animante, vivificante, excitante. 2. Alegre, divertido. **An animated street, person,** una calle, persona animada. **Animated cartoons,** dibujos animados.

animation [ˌænɪˈmeɪʃən] [a-ni-mei-shon], s. Animación. (Fig.) Viveza, espíritu.

animative ['ænɪmətɪv] [a-ní-ma-tif], s. Animador.

animator ['ænɪmeɪtəʳ] [á-ni-meit-ar] s. Animador.

anime ['ænɪmɪ] [a-ni-mi], **Gum anime,** a. 1. Anime, goma o resina del curbaril, árbol de Cayena y de las Indias. 2. Goma copal.

animism ['ænɪmɪzəm] [a-ni-mí-sem], s. 1. Animismo, creencia en el ser del espíritu, o alma, con independencia de la materia orgánica. 2. Sistema medicofisiológico que considera el alma como principio de acción y causa primera.

animist ['ænɪmɪst] [á-ni-mist] s. Animista.

animistic ['nɪmɪstɪk] [a-ni-mís-tik] a. Animista.

animosity ['ænɪˈmɒsɪtɪ] [a-ni-mó-si-ti], s. Animosidad, mala voluntad, ojeriza, rencor, odio, encono, aversión, aborrecimiento, rencilla.

animus ['ænɪməs] [á-ni-mos], s. ánimo, intención, designio.

anise ['ænɪs] [a-nis], s. (Bot.) Anís o matalahuva, planta anual umbelífera y su semilla. **Anise-seed,** anís o simiente de anís. **Indian aniseed,** badiana o anís de la China. **Star anise,** anís estrellado.

anisette [ænɪˈzet] [á-ni-set], s. (Fr.) Anisete, licor compuesto de aguardiente, azúcar y anís.

anisopetalous [ænɪsəˈpetələs] [a-ni-so-pé-ta-las] a. (Bot.) Anisopétalo.

anisophyllous [ænɪsəˈfɪləs] [a-ni-só-if-los] a. (Bot.) Anisófilo.

anisotropic [ænɪsəˈtrɒpɪk] [a-ni-so-tró-pik] a. Anisótropo.

anisotropy [ænɪsəˈtrɒpɪ] [a-ni-só-tro-pi] s. Anisotropía.

ankara ['æŋkərə] [an-ká-ra] N. (Geogr.) Ankara.

ankle ['æŋkl] [án-kel], s. Maléolo o tobillo del pie. **Ankle-bone,** hueso del tobillo. **Ankle support,** tobillera.

ankled ['æŋklɪd] [án-klid], a. Lo que pertenece al tobillo.

anklet ['æŋklɪt] [án-klit], s. 1. Aro de adorno para el tobillo. 2. Vendaje para mantener el tobillo en debida posición. 3. Medida tobillera.

ankylose [æŋkɪˈləʊs] [an-ki-lous], va. y vn. Anquilosar, fijar una articulación.

ankylosis [æŋkɪˈləʊsɪs] [an-ki-lóu-sis], s. Anquilosis, inflexibilidad de una articulación.

Ann o **Anne** [æn] [an] N. Ana.

annalist ['ænəlɪst] [á-na-list], s. Analista, el que escribe anales, cronista.

annalize ['ænəlaɪz] [á-na-lais], va. Escribir anales.

annals ['ænəlz] [á-nals], s. pl. 1. Anales, historia o relación de sucesos por años, de año en año. 2. Misas celebradas de tiempo en tiempo durante el año; y también las misas de aniversario.

annamite [ænəˈmaɪt] [á-na-mait] a./s. Anamita.

annats ['ænətʒ] [á-nats], s. Anata, la renta, frutos o emolumentos que produce en un año cualquier beneficio o empleo.

annatto ['ænətə] [a-na-to], s. Orellana, achiote; se dice del árbol y de la tintura.

anneal [əˈniːl] [a-níl], va. Templar el cristal o vidrio para que se penetren los colores; atemperar, frotar con aceite.

annealing [əˈniːlɪŋ] [a-ní-lin], s. 1. El acto o arte de templar el vidrio. 2. Recocción, destemple. **Annealing furnace** u **oven,** horno de recocido. **Annealing-pot,** crisol de templar.

annelid [əˈniːlɪd] [a-ní-lid] s. (Zool.) Anélido.

annex [əˈneks] [á-neks], va. Anexar, unir o agregar una cosa a otra con dependencia de ella; juntar, reunir.

annex o **annexe** [əˈneks] [á-neks] s. Anexo, dependencia, apéndice. (For.) Anexidades.

annexation [ænekˈseɪʃən] [a-nek-séi-shon], **annexment** [əˈneksmənt] [a-néks-ment], s. Anexión, la acción y efecto de anexar, o la misma cosa anexa; conjunción, adición, unión

annexationism [ænekˈseɪʃənɪzəm] [a-nek-sei-sho-nísem] s. Anexionismo.

annexationist [ænekˈseɪʃənɪst] [a-nek-séi-sho-nist] a./s. Anexionista.

annexed [əˈnekst] [a-nékst], pp. y a. Adjunto.

annexionism [əneksəˈnɪzəm] [a-nek-so-nízem] s. Anexionismo.

annexionist [əneksəˈnɪst] [a-nék-so-nist] a./s. Anexionista.

annexive ['əneksiːv] [a-nék-sif], a. Anexorio, que une o anexa, o que tiende a anexar.

annihilable [əˈnaɪələbl] [a-náia-bol], a. Destructible, lo que se puede destruir o aniquilar.

annihilate [əˈnaɪeɪt] [a-náia-leit], va. Aniquilar, reducir a la nada.

annihilation [əˈnaɪeɪʃən] [a-naia-léi-shon], s. Aniquilación, la acción y efecto de aniquilar.

anniversary [ænɪˈvɜːsərɪ] [a-ni-vér-sa-ri], s. 1. Aniversario, día en que se cumplen años de algún suceso. 2. Aniversario, la fiesta o ceremonia que se celebra en cierto día señalado de cada año. **Wedding anniversary,** aniversario de boda. **The anniversary of an event,** el aniversario de un suceso.

anniversary, a. Anual.

anno domini ['ænəʊˈdɒmɪnaɪ] [a-no-do-mi-ni], s. (Lat.) En el año de Nuestro Señor.

annomination ['ænəʊmɪˈneɪʃən] [a-no-mi-néi-shon], s. Agnominación o paronomasia.

anno mundi ['ænəʊ'muːndɪ] [a-no-mun-di], *s. (Lat.)* En el año del mundo.

annona ['ænənə] [a-no-na] *s. (Bot.)* Anona.

annotate ['ænəʊteɪt] [an',no,têt]. *va.* Anotar, comentar.

annotation [ænəʊ'teɪʃən] [a-no-téi-shon], *s.* Anotación o nota que se pone a algún escrito.

annotator ['ænəʊteɪtəᵣ] [a-no-téi-tar], **annotationist** [ˌænəʊ'teɪʃənɪʃt] [a-no-téi-sho-nist], *s.* Anotador, comentador, ilustrador.

annotto ['ænɒtə] [a-no-to], *s. (Bot.)* Orellana, achiote. Lo mismo que **annatto.**

announce [ə'naʊns] [a-náuns]. *va.* Anunciar, publicar, proclamar; declarar, jurídicamente. **To announce a piece of news,** anunciar una noticia. **To announce a guest,** anunciar a un invitado.

announcement [ə'naʊnsmənt] [a-náuns-ment], *s.* Aviso, advertencia, declaración. **To make an announcement to the public,** dar un aviso al público.

announcer [ə'naʊnsəᵣ] [a-náunsar], *s.* Anunciador. **Radio announcer,** locutor o anunciador de radio.

annoy [ə'nɔɪ] [a-noi], *va.* Molestar, incomodar, hacer mal, vejar, fastidiar. **The least sound annoys him,** el menor ruido le incomoda.

annoyance [ə'nɔɪəns] [a-nóians], *s.* Molestia, injuria, pena, incomodidad; disgusto, fastidio. **What an annoyance!,** ¡qué fastidio!, ¡qué molesto!

annoyer [ə'nɔɪəᵣ] [a-nóiar], *s.* Molestador, persona enojosa.

annoying [ə'nɔɪɪŋ] [a-nói-in], *pa.* Fastidioso, molesto, incómodo, importuno. **How annoying you are!,** ¡qué molesto eres!

annual ['ænjʊəl] [á-nual], **annuary** ['ænjʊərɪ] [a-nuá-ri], *a.* Anual, lo que se hace o sucede cada año; lo que dura sólo un año. **Annual income,** renta anual. **Annual ceremony,** ceremonia anual. *(Bot.)* **Annual ring,** capa cortical (of a tree).

annually ['ænjʊəlɪ] [á-nua-li], *adv.* Anualmente, de año en año, cada año.

annuitant [ə'njʊɪtənt] [a-niuí-tant], *s.* El que tiene una renta vitalicia.

annuity [ə'njuːɪtɪ] [á-niui-ti], *s.* Anualidad, renta vitalicia.

annul [ə'nʌl] [a-nál], *va.* 1. Anular, invalidar, revocar, dar por nulo. 2. Aniquilar, reducir a la nada alguna cosa.

annular [ə'nʌləᵣ] [á-niu-lar], *a.* Anular; que se parece al anillo en la figura.

annulary [ə'nʌlərɪ] [a-niú-la-ri], *a.* Adornado con anillo; se dice del dedo anular.

annulate, annulated [ə'ænt] [á-niu-leit], *a.* Anuloso, anillado; que se compone de anillos o lo parece.

annulet [ə'nʌlɪt] [á-niu-lit], *s.* Anillejo, sortijilla.

annulment [ə'nʌlmənt] [a-niúl-ment], *s.* Anulación, la acción de anular.

annulose [ə'nʌləʊz] [á-niu-los], *a.* 1. Anuloso, rodeado de anillos o rayas circulares. 2. Guarnecido de sortijas o anillos.

annum ['ænəm] [a-nam], *s.* Año; se emplea sólo en la locución, **Per annum.** al año, o por año.

annumerate [ænəme'reɪt] [a-ná-me-reit], *va.* Anumerar, añadir al número anterior, poner en el número, contar entre, comprender.

annunciate [ə'nʌnsɪeɪt] [á-nun-sieit], *va.* Anunciar, llevar o traer noticia o aviso.

annunciation [əˌnʌnsɪ'eɪʃən] [a-nun-siéi-shon], *s.* 1. Anunciación, día celebrado por la Iglesia en memoria de la embajada que el ángel trajo a la Virgen santísima; es el veinticinco de marzo. 2. Proclamación, promulgación.

annunciator [əˌnʌnsɪ'eɪtəᵣ] [a-nun-siéi-tar], *s.* 1. Proclamador. 2. Indicador (como en los hoteles); aparato para señalar un número, nombre, etc., cuando llaman.

anodal ['ænəʊdəl] [a-nou-dal], *a.* Que se refiere al ánodo.

anode ['ænəʊd] [a-noud], *s.* ánodo, polo positivo de una batería eléctrica. *(Gr.)*

anodic ['ænəʊdɪk] [a-nou-dik], *a.* Perteneciente al ánodo; que procede hacia arriba.

anodize ['ænəʊdaɪz] [á-nou-dais], *va.* Anodizar.

anodontia ['ænədɒʃə] [a-no-don-sha] *s.* Anodontia.

anodyne ['ænəʊdaɪn] [a-nou-dain], *a.* Anodino, lo que tiene virtud de suavizar y mitigar los dolores.

anodynia ['ænəʊdɪnɪə] [a-nou-dí-nia] *s. (Med.)* Anodinia.

anoint [ə'nɔɪnt] [a-noint], *va.* 1. Untar, pringar, aplicar a alguna cosa aceite u otra materia pingüe. 2. Ungir, signar con óleo sagrado. **To anoint a dying person,** administrar la extremaunción, u olear a un moribundo.

anointer [ə'nɔɪntəᵣ] [a-noin-tar], *s.* Untador, el que unta; también se puede entender del que unge.

anointing [ə'nɔɪntɪŋ] [a-noin-tin], **anointment** [ə'nɔɪntmənt] [a-noint-ment], *s.* Unción, el acto y el efecto de untar, o de ungir.

anomalism [ə'nɒməlɪzəm] [a-no-ma-lísem], *s.* Irregularidad, anomalía.

anomalistic, anomalistical [ə'nɒməlɪstɪk] [ə'nɒməlɪstɪk] [a-no-ma-lís-tik] [a-no-ma-lís-ti-kal], *a.* Anomalístico, perteneciente a la anomalía. **Anomalistic year,** año anomalístico, el tiempo que emplea la tierra en volver a un punto dado de su órbita.

anomalous [ə'nɒmələs] [a-nó-ma-los], *a.* Anómalo, irregular, que se separa de la regla común.

anomalously [ə'nɒmələslɪ] [a-nó-ma-los-li], *adv.* Irregularmente.

anomalousness [ə'nɒmələsnɪs] [a-nó-ma-los-nis], **anomaly** [ə'nɒmælɪ] [a-nó-ma-li], *s.* Anomalía, irregularidad.

anon [ə'nɒn] [a-non], *adv.* 1. Pronto, a poco. 2. De cuando en cuando. 3. A cada instante. 4. En seguida, immediatamente. **Ever and anon,** una y otra vez, a menudo.

anona [ə'nəʊnə] [a-nou-na] *s. (Bot.)* Anona.

anonym ['ænənɪm] [a-no-nim], *s.* 1. Persona o escritor anónimo. 2. Seudónimo.

anonymity [ˌænə'nɪmɪtɪ] [a-no-ni-mi-ti] *s.* Anónimo, anonimato.

anonymous [ə'nɒnɪməs] [a-nó-ni-mos], *a.* Anónimo, que no tiene nombre.

anonymously [ə'nɒnɪməslɪ] [a-nó-ni-mos-i], *adv.* Anónimamente.

anorak ['ænəræk] [a-no-rak] *s.* Anorak.

anorexia [ˌænə'reksɪə] [a-no-rék-sia], *s.* Anorexia, inapetencia.

anosmia ['ænɒzmɪə] [a-nós-mia], *s.* Anosmia, anosfresia, pérdida total o parcial del olfato.

another [ə'nʌðəᵣ] [a-nó-dar], *a.* 1. Otro, diferente, distino, **It is one thing to promise and another to perform,** una cosa es prometer y otra cumplir; del dicho al hecho hay gran trecho. 2. Uno más; otro. **He owns already four houses and how has bought another,** ya posee cuatro casas y ahora ha comprado una más. **Another time,** otro día, otra vez. **In another way,** de otra manera. **Give me another one,** déme otro. *-pron.* Otro, otra. **One another,** uno a otro. **Let's pass the ball one another,** pasémonos el balón el uno al otro. **May I have another?,** ¿puedo tomar otro?

anoxemia [ə'nɒksɪmɪə] [a-nok-sí-mia] *s. (Med.)* Anoxemia.

anoxia [ə'nɒksɪə] [a-nók-sia], *s. (Med.)* Anoxia, falta de oxígeno en los tejidos.

ansated [ən'seɪtɪd] [an-séi-tid], *a.* Con asas, ansato, que tiene asas.

anserine ['ænsəreɪn] [án-se-rain], *a.* 1. Anserino, que se refiere al ánsar o la oca. 2. Semejante al ánsar, como el cutis cuando está frío. 3. Tonto, necio, mentecato.

answer ['ɑːnsəᵣ] [án-sar], *vn.* 1. Responder, dar satisfacción a la pregunta, duda o dificultad que se propone. 2. Replicar. **Don't answer back!,** ¡no repliques!, ¡no seas respondón! 3. Responder, ser responsable. 4. Corresponder o venir bien una cosa con otra. **This year's crop does not answer our expectations,** la cosecha de este año no corresponde a nuestras esperanzas. 5. *(For.)* Comparecer. 6. Equivaler. 7. Salir bien, tener o dar buen resultado. **No, that will never answer,** no, eso no saldrá bien, no dará buen resultado. *-va.* 1. Responder, dar respuesta, contestar. 2. Satisfacer a, cumplir, obedecer. 3. Disputar, refutar. 4. Resolver (un problema. etc.) 5. Ser suficiente para; convenir a. **This answers my purpose,** esto conviene a mi designio. 6. Expiar. 7. Ser correlativo a, responder recíprocamente. 8. Otorgar, conceder una petición. 9. Talionar, pagar en la misma moneda. **To answer for,** (1) Fiar a, responder de. (2) Expiar (una falta). *(For.)* **To answer a charge,** defenderse contra una acusación. **To answer one's dreams,** realizar los sueños de uno.

answer, *s.* 1. Respuesta, contestación. 2. Refutación, réplica. 3. Solución correcta. **The answer is to study harder,** la solución es estudiar más. **In answer to,** en respuesta a, contestando a.

answerable ['ɑ:nsərəbl] [án-sa-ra-bol], *a.* 1. Aquello a que se puede responder. 2. Responsable, obligado a satisfacer por algún cargo. 3. Correspondiente; equivalente; conforme. 4. Refutable. **He is answerable to no one for what he does,** el no debe a nadie cuenta de su conducta.

answerably ['ɑ:nsərəbli], *adv.* Correspondientemente, proporcionadamente.

answerableness ['ɑ:nsərəblnɪs] [an-se-ra-bol-nis], *s.* Responsabilidad; también significa correspondencia o relación de una cosa con otra.

answerer ['ɑ:nsərər] [-an-se-rar], *s.* Fiador, el que da caución.

answering machine ['ɑ:nsərɪŋ,mətʃi:n] [án-se-rin-machin] o **answer phone** ['ɑ:nsəfəʊn] [-an-sa-foun] *s.* Contestador automático.

ant [ænt] [ant], *s.* Hormiga, insecto himenóptero, notable por su inteligencia; en este respecto tal vez el mejor dotado de todos los insectos. **White ant,** hormiga blanca, termita; insecto neuóptero.

a'n't o **ain't** [eɪnt] [éint], *v.* Contracción defectuosa de *am not, is not, are not. (Vulg.)*

anta ['æntə] [an-ta], *s. (Arq.)* Anta, pilastra saliente en los ángulos de un edificio (Plural ANTE o ANTES).

anta ['æntə] [an-ta], *s. (Zool.)* Danta, tapir.

antacid ['æntəsɪd] [an-ta-sid], *a.* y *s.* Antiácido, álcali. Remedio para la acidez del estómago.

antagonism [æn'tægənɪzəm] [an-ta-go-nísem], *s.* Contienda, oposición.

antagonist [æn'tægənɪst] [an-ta-go-nist], *s.* Antagonista, el que es opuesto o contrario a otro.

antagonistic [æn,tægə'nɪstɪk] [an-ta-go-nís-tik], *a.* Antagónico, perteneciente a los antagonistas; que implica o denota antagonismo.

antagonize [æn'tægənɑɪz] [an-ta-go-nais], *vn.* Competir con otro.

antalgic [æn'tældʒɪk] [an-tál-chik], *a.* Anodino, opuesto al dolor; antálgico. Equivalente, ANTALGESIC.

antaphrodisiac [æn,təfrɒdɪ'sɪək] [an-ta-fro-di-siak], *s.* y *a.* Antiafrodisíaco, que calma el apetito venéreo.

antaphroditic [æn,təfrɒ'dɪtɪk] [an-ta-fro-dái-tik], *a.* Antiafrodisíaco; se dice de los remedios para calmar el apetito venéreo.

antarctic [ænt'ɑ:ktɪk] [an-tár-tik], *a.* Antártico, lo que pertenece al polo meridional.

antarctica [ænt'ɑ:ktɪkə] [an-tár-ti-ka] *N. (Geogr.)* Antártida.

antarthritic [ænt'ɪkθr]an-tar-trí-tik]. *a. (Med.)* Antiartrítico: se dice de los remedios para la gota.

antasthmatic [ænt'əsmætɪk] [an-tas-má-tik], *a.* Antiasmático.

ant bear [ænt'bi:ər] [ant-bíar], *s.* Tamándoa o tamanuar, mamífero desdentado de la América tropical que se mantiene de hormigas. Oso hormiguero.

ante [æntɪ] [an-ti]. Preposición latina que se halla antes de varios nombres compuestos y que significa: ante, antes, que precede en tiempo o posición. *(Poker)* Apuesta inicial. *(Fam.)* Cuota. *vn.* Apostar. **To ante up,** contribuir.

ant-eater [ænt,i:tər] [ant-ítar], *s. (Zool.)* Oso hormiguero.

ante bellum [æntɪ'beləm] [an-ti-bé-lam], *a.* Antes de la guerra. En los Estados Unidos de Norte América, antes de la guerra civil.

antecede [æntɪsi:d] [an-te-síd], *vn.* Anteceder, preceder.

antecedence ['æntɪsɪdəns] [an-tí-si-dans], **antecedency** ['æntɪsɪdənsɪ] [an-ti-sí-dan-si], *s.* Precedencia, la acción y efecto de preceder o anteceder.

antecedent ['æntɪsɪdənt] [an-tí-si-dant], *a.* y *s.* Antecedente, precedente.

antecedently ['æntɪsɪdəntlɪ] [an-tí-si-dan-tli], *adv.* Anteriormente.

antecessor ['æntɪsɪsər] [an-ti-sí-sar], *s.* Antecesor, el que precede a otro.

antechamber ['æntɪ,tʃeɪmbər] [an-ti-cheim-bar], *s.* Antecámara, la pieza que está inmediata a la sala principal de alguna casa.

antechapel [æntɪ'tʃəpəl] [an-ti-chá-pal] *s.* Antecapilla.

antechoir [æntɪ'tʃʊər] [an-ti-chuar] *s.* Antecoro.

antedate ['æntɪdeɪt] [an-ti-déit], *va.* Antedatar, poner la fecha anticipada en alguna escritura o carta.

antedate, *s.* Anticipación; antedata.

antediluvian ['æntɪdɪ'lu:vɪən] [an-ti-di-lú-vian], *a.* y *s.* Antediluviano, lo que pertenece al tiempo anterior al diluvio.

antefix ['æntɪfɪks] [an-ti-fiks] *s. (Arq.)* Antefijo.

antelope ['æntɪləʊp] [an-tí-loup], *s.* Antílope, cuadrúpedo rumiante parecido al ciervo; hay varias especies.

antelucem ['æntɪlʌsəm] [an-ti-lú-sem], *a.* Temprano; antes del amanecer.

antemeridian [æntɪmɪ'ri:dɪən] [an-ti-mi-rí-dian], *a.* Antes de mediodía, por la mañana.

ante meridiem [æntɪmɪ'ri:dɪəm] [an-ti-mi-rí-diam], *loc. lat.* Antes del mediodía. Se usa comúnmente en la abreviatura A.M.; 9 A.M., las nueve de la mañana.

antemetic [æntɪ'mɪtɪk] [an-ti-mí-tik], *a.* Antiemético, remedio que hace cesar el vómito.

antemundane [æntɪmən'deɪn] [an-ti-mán-dein], *a.* Que antecedió a la creación del mundo.

antenatal [æntɪ'neɪtl] [an-ti-néital] *a.* Antenatal, prenatal.

antenna [æn'tenə] [an-te-na], *pl.* ANTENNAE, *s.* Antena, apéndice articulado de la cabeza, uno de los cuernecillos de algunos insectos y otros animales artrópodos.

antenumber [æn'tenəmbər] [an-te-nám-bar], *s.* Número anterior.

antenuptial [æn'tenəpʃəl] [an-te-náp-shal], *a.* Antenupcial, antes de la boda.

antepast [æn'tɪpæst] [an-te-past], *s. (Ant* o *poét.)* Anticipación; gusto anticipado.

antepenult [æntɪpɪ'nʌlt] [an-ti-pí-nalt] o **antepenultimate** [æntɪpɪ'nʌltɪmɪt] [an-ti-pi-nál-ti-meit], *a.* y *s.* Antepenúltima, la sílaba que está antes de la última.

antepileptic [æntɪɪp'tɪk] [an-ti-pi-lép-tik], *a. (Med.)* Antiepiléptico; remedios contra la epilepsia.

anteport [æntɪ'pɔ:t] [an-ti-pórt] o **antiport,** *a.* Antepuerta, puerta exterior.

anterior [æn'tɪərɪər] [an-tí-riar], *a.* Anterior, precedente.

anteriority [æn'tɪərɪtɪ] [an-ti-rió-ri-ti], *s.* Anterioridad; precedencia.

anteroom ['æntɪrʊm] [an-ti-rum], *s.* Antecámara, antesala, sala de espera.

antes [æn'tɪz] [án-tis], *s. pl. (Arq.)* Antas, pilastras.

anteversion [æntɪ'vɜ:ʃən] [an-ti-vér-shon], *s.* Anteroversión, posición anormal del útero, que consiste en dirigirse el fondo hacia el pubis y el cuello hacia el sacro.

antevert [æntɪ'vɜ:t] [an-ti-vert], *va.* Volver hacia adelante.

anteverted [æntɪ'vɜ:tɪd] [an-ti-ver-tid], *pp.* vuelto hacia adelante; en posición de anteroversión.

antehelmintic [æntɪ'elmɪntɪc] [an-ti-jel-min-tik], *a.* Antielmíntico, lo que mata las lombrices. Vermífugo.

anthem ['ænθəm] [án-zem], *s.* Antífona, motete. Himno. **National anthem,** himno nacional.

anthemis ['ænθəmɪs] [an-ze-mis], *s. (Bot.)* Género de plantas que comprende, entre otras numerosas especies, la manzanilla o camomila.

anthem-wise [ænθəm'waɪz] [an-zem-uais], *adv.* A modo de antífona.

anther ['ænθəʳ] [an-zar], *s. (Bot.)* Antera, el ápice del estambre que contiene el polen; es el órgano masculino de las plantas.

antheridium [ˌænθə'rɪdɪəm] [an-ze-rí-dium] *s. (Bot.)* Anteridia.

ant-hill ['ænthɪl] [ánt-jil], *s.* Hormiguero. *V.* FORMICARIUM.

anthological [ˌænθə'lɒdʒɪkl] [an-zo-ló-chi-cal], *a.* Antológico, lo perteneciente a la antología.

anthology [ˌænθə'lɒdʒɪ] [an-zó-lo-chi], *s.* 1. antología, florilegio; colección de trozos literarios selectos. 2. (Poco us.) Colección de flores.

Anthony ['æntənɪ] [án-zo-ni] *N.* Antonio.

Anthony's fire, *s.* Fuego de San Antón; erisipela.

anthozoa [æntə'zəʊ] [an-to-sou], *s.* Antozoarios, los pólipos, una clase de los zoófitos o coelenterados.

anthracene [ænθrə'siːn] [an-tra-sín] *s.* Antraceno.

anthracic [ænθrə'sɪk] [an-trá-sik], *a.* Que pertenece al ántrax, o que lo padece.

anthracite [ænθrə'saɪt] [an-tra-sait], *s.* Antracita, hulla lustrosa, carbón de piedra no bituminoso que arde sin humo y casi sin llama.

anthrax ['ænθræks] [an-zraks], *s.* 1. Antrax, carbunclo, avispero. 2. Fiebre contagiosa y maligna; se llama también fiebre esplénica.

anthrenus ['ænθrənəs] [an-zre-nas] *s. (Zool.)* Antreno.

anthropocentric [ˌænθrəʊpəʊ'sentrɪk] [an-zrou-pou-séntrik] *a.* Antropocéntrico.

anthropocentrism [ˌænθrəʊpəʊsen'trɪzəm] [an-zrou-pousen-trísem] *s.* Antropocentrismo.

anthropography [ˌænθrəʊpəʊ'græfɪ] [an-zrou-póu-gra-fi], *s.* Antropografía, la descripción del hombre.

anthropoid ['ænθrəʊpɔɪd] [an-zróu-poid], *s.* Antropoide, mono antropoídeo. *-a.* Antropoide, antropoideo.

anthropologic [ˌænθrəpə'lɒdʒɪk] [an-zro-po-ló-chik] *a.*

anthropological [ˌænθrəpə'lɒdʒɪkəl] [an-zro-po-ló-chi-kal] *a.* Antropológico.

anthropologist [ˌænθrəpə'lɒdʒɪst] [an-zro-pó-lo-chist] *s.* Antropólogo.

anthropology [ˌænθrəpə'lɒdʒɪ] [an-zro-pó-lo-chi], *s.* Antropología, la ciencia que trata del hombre física y moralmente considerado.

anthropometric [ˌænθrəpə'mɪtrɪk] [an-zro-po-mé-trik] o **anthropometrical** [ˌænθrəpə'mɪtrɪkl] [an-zro-po-mé-tri-kal] *a.* Antropométrico.

anthropometry [ˌænθrəpə'mɪtrɪ] [an-zro-pó-me-tri] *s.* Antropometría.

anthropomorph [ˌænθrəpə'mɔːf] [an-zro-po-mórf] *s.* Antropomorfo.

anthropomorphic [ˌænθrəpə'mɔːfɪk] [an-zro-po-mór-fik] *a.* Antropomórfico.

anthropomorphism [ˌænθrəpə'mɔːfɪzəm] [an-zro-po-morfísem], *s.* Antropomorfismo, doctrina u opinión de los que atribuyen a Dios cuerpo humano, o cualidades y sentimientos humanos.

anthropomorphite [ˌænθrəpə'mɔːfaɪt] [an-zro-po-mor-fáit] o **anthropomorphist** [ˌænθrəpə'mɔːfɪst] [an-zro-po-morfist] *s.* Antropomorfita.

anthropomorphous [ˌænθrəpə'mɔːfəs] [an-zro-po-mór-fos] *a.* Antropomorfo.

anthroponymy [ˌænθrəpənɪmɪ] [an-zro-pó-ni-mi], *s.* Antroponimia.

anthropophagi [ˌænθrəpəfəgaɪ] [an-zro-pó-fa-gai], *s.* Antropófagos, los que comen carne humana.

anthropophagous [ˌænθrəpəfəgəs] [an-zro-pó-fa-gos] *a.* Antropófago.

anthropophagy [ˌænθrəʊ'pəfədʒɪ] [an-zro-pó-fa-chi] *s.* Antropofagia.

anthropitecus [ˌænθrəpɪ'tekəs] [an-zro-pi-té-kos] *s.* Antropopiteco.

anthroposophy [ˌænθrə'pəsəfɪ] [an-zro-pó-so-fi], *s.* Antroposofía, ciencia de la naturaleza del hombre.

anti ['æntɪ] [an-ti], Partícula muy usada, compuesta con voces de derivación griega y significa *contra* o *contrario a.*

antiacid [æntɪ'eɪsɪd] [an-ti-éi-sid], *V.* ALKALI.

antiaircraft [æntɪ'ɛəkrɑːft] [an-ti-éa-kraft], *s.* Fuego o artillería antiaérea. *-a.* Antiaéreo. **Antiaircraft gun,** cañón antiaéreo.

antialcoholism [æntɪəl'kəʊhəlɪzm] [an-ti-al-kou-jo-lísem] *s.* Antialcoholismo.

anti-American [æntɪə'merɪkən] [an-ti-a-mé-ri-kan] *a.* Antiamericano.

antiapostle [æntɪə'pɒzl] [an-ti-a-pósel], *s.* Antiapóstol.

antiarthritic [æntɪɑː'θrɪtɪk] [an-ti-ar-zrí-tik], *a.* Antiartrítico, remedio contra la gota.

antibilious [æntɪ'bɪlɪəs] [an-ti-bí-lios], *a.* Antibilioso.

antibiotic [æntbaɪ'ɒtɪk] [an-ti-bió-tik], *s.* y *a.* Antibiótico.

antibody ['æntbɒdɪ] [an-ti-bo-di], *s. (Med.)* Anticuerpo.

antic ['æntɪk] [an-tic], *a.* Extraño, raro, ridículo, grotesco. - *s.* 1. Acción, fantástica o extravagante, cabriola, travesura. 2. Antigualla, figura o grupo grotesco. 3. Bufón, truhán, saltimbanco.

anticancerous [æntɪ'kænsɪrəs] [an-ti-kán-si-ros] *a.* Anticanceroso.

anticathode ['æntɪkɑθɒd] [an-ti-ká-zod] *s.* Anticátodo.

antichamber ['æntɪtʃʌmbəʳ] [an-ti-cheim-baʳ], *s. V.* ANTECHAMBER.

Antichrist ['æntɪkraɪst] [an-ti-kraist], *s.* Antecristo.

Antichristian ['æntɪkrɪstɪən] [an-ti-krís-chian], *s.* y *a.* Anticristiano.

anticipate [æn'tɪsɪpeɪt] [an-tí-si-peit], *va.* 1. Mirar a lo venidero, esperar, prever. 2. Anticipar, tomar alguna cosa antes que otro; adelantarse, prevenir. 3. Estar al frente de, en adelante. **He anticipated my wish,** se anticipó a mi deseo. **To anticipate criticism,** salir al paso de las críticas.

anticipation [ænˌtɪsɪ'peɪʃən] [an-ti-si-péi-shon], *s.* Anticipación, la acción y efecto de anticipar o anticiparse. **In anticipation of the future,** pensando en el futuro.

anticipator [æn'tɪsɪpeɪtəʳ] [an-ti-si-péi-tar], *s.* Anticipador.

anticipatory [æn'tɪsɪpeɪtərɪ] [an-ti-si-pa-tó-ri], *a.* Lo que anticipa.

anticlerical ['æntɪklækl] [an-ti-klé-ri-kal], *a.* Anticlerical.

anticlericalism ['æntɪklækklɪzəm] [an-ti-kle-ri-ka-lísem] *s.* Anticlericalismo.

anti-climax ['æntɪ'klɪmæks] [an-ti-klí-maks], *s. (Ret.)* Anticlímax, gradación descendente.

anticlinal ['æntɪ'klɪnəl] [an-ti-kli-nal], *a.* Anticlinal, que señala en la estratificación de los terrenos una inclinación en direcciones opuestas.

anticline [æntɪ'klaɪn] [an-ti-klain] *s. (Geol.)* Anticlinal.

anticly ['æntɪklaɪ] [an-ti-kli], *adv.* Ridículamente, por vía de travesura, grotescamente.

anticlockwise ['æntɪ'klɒkwaɪz] [an-ti-klok-uais] *a./adv.* En sentido contrario a las agujas del reloj.

anticoagulant ['æntɪ'kəʊɡjʊlənt] [an-ti-kou-giu-lant], *s.* y *a.* Anticoagulante.

anticolonialism ['æntɪkə'ləʊnɪəlɪzəm] [an-ti-ko-lou-nia-lísem], *s.* Anticolonialismo.

anticolonialist ['æntɪkə'ləʊnɪəlɪst] [an-ti-ko-lóu-nia-list] *a./s.* Anticolonialista.

anticommunism ['æntɪkɒ'mjɒnɪzəm] [an-ti-ko-miu-nísem], *s.* Anticomunismo.

anticommunist ['æntɪkɒ'mjɒnɪst] [an-ti-ko-miu-nist] *a. s.* Anticomunista.

anticonstitutional ['æntɪkɒnstɪ'tjuːʃənl] [an-ti-kons-ti-tiúsho-nal], *a.* Anticonstitucional, lo que es contra la constitución o sistema de gobierno establecido.

anticorrosive ['æntɪkə'rəʊzɪv] [an-ti-kó-rou-sif], *a.* Anticorrosivo, que obra contra la corrosión o la impide.

anticosmetic ['æntɪkəz'metɪk] [an-ti-kos-mé-tik], *a.* Anticosmético.

anticourt ['æntɪkɔːt] [an-ti-kórt], *a.* Lo que es opuesto a la corte.

antics ['æntɪks] [án-tiks] *s. pl.* Payasadas, bufonadas, travesuras, cabriolas. **To be up to one's antics,** estar haciendo de las suyas.

anticyclone ['æntɪ'saɪkləʊn] [an-ti-sái-kloun], *s.* Movimiento de la atmósfera, que por la dirección del viento y la distribución de la presión barométrica, se opone al de un ciclón.

anticyclonic ['æntɪ'saɪklɒnɪk] [an-ti-sai-klóu-nik] *a.* Anticiclonal.

antidazzle ['æntɪ'dæzl] [an-ti-dásel] *a.* Antideslumbrante.

antidemocrat ['æntɪ'dəmǝkræt] [an-ti-de-mó-krat] *s.* Antidemócrata.

antidemocratic ['æntɪ'dəmǝkrætɪk] [an-ti-de-mo-krá-tik] *a.* Antidemocrático.

antidotal ['æntɪ'dɒtǝl] [an-ti-do-tal], *a.* Perteneciente al antídoto.

antidotary ['æntɪ'dɒtǝrɪ] [an-ti-do-ta-ri] *a. (Ant.)* Antidotario; antídoto.

antidote ['æntɪ'dǝʊt] [an-ti-dout], *s.* Antídoto, contraveneno, preservativo.

antidysenteric ['æntɪ'dɪsǝntǝrɪk] [an-ti-di-sen-te-rik], *a.* Antidisentérico, que tiene virtud contra la disenteria.

antiemetic ['æntɪ'ɪmetɪk] [an-ti-i-mé-tik] *a. (Med.)* Antiemético.

antiepiscopal ['æntɪ'pɪskǝpǝl] [an-ti-i-pís-ko-pal], *a.* El que se opone al episcopado.

antiface ['æntɪ'feɪs] [an-ti-féis], *s.* Antifaz.

antifanatic ['æntɪ'fǝnætɪk] [an-ti-fa-ná-tik], *s.* Antifanático.

antifascism ['æntɪ'fæʃɪzǝm] [an-ti-fa-sí-sem] *s.* Antifascismo.

antifascist ['æntɪ'fæʃɪst] [an-ti-fa-shist] *a./s.* Antifascista.

antifebrile ['æntɪ'fiːbraɪl] [an-ti-fi-brail] *a. (Med.)* Antifebril, lo que sirve para corregir y curar las calenturas.

antifederalist ['æntɪ'fɪdǝrǝlɪst] [an-ti-fi-dé-ra-list] *s.* Antifederalista.

antifeminism ['æntɪ'femɪnɪzǝm] [an-ti-fe-mi-nísem] *s.* Antifeminismo.

antifeminist ['æntɪ'femɪnɪst] [an-ti-fe-mi-nist] *a./s.* Antifeminista.

antiferment ['æntɪ'fɜːmǝnt] [an-ti-fér-ment] *s.* Antifermento.

antifreeze ['æntɪ'friːz] [an-ti-frís], *s. y a.* Anticongelante.

antifriction ['æntɪ'frɪkʃǝn] [an-ti-frík-shon], *a.* Que disminuye el rozamiento. **Antifriction alloy, antifriction metal,** metal antifricción.

antigen ['æntɪdʒǝn] [an-ti-chan], *s.* Antígeno.

antiglare ['æntɪ'gleǝr] [an-ti-gléar] *a.* Antideslumbrante.

antigona [æn'tɪgǝnǝ] [an-ti-go-na] *N.* Antígona.

antigovernment [æntɪ'gʌvǝnmǝnt] [an-ti-go-vérn-ment] *a.* Antigubernamental.

antihistamine ['æntɪ'hɪstǝmiːn] [an-ti-jís-ta-min], *s. (Med.)* Antihistamina.

antihypnotic ['æntɪhɪp'nɒtɪk] [an-ti-jip-nó-tik], *a.* Antipnótico, lo que impide el sueño, sopor o letargo.

antihysteric ['æntɪhɪs'terɪk] [an-ti-jis-té-rik], *s.* Antihistérico, medicamento para las afecciones histéricas y espasmódicas.

antiinflationary ['æntɪen'flǝʃǝrɪ] [an-ti-in-fléi-sho-na-ri] *a.* Antiinflacionista.

antiknock ['æntɪnɒk] [an-ti-nok], *s. & a.* Antidetonante.

Antillean ['æntɪliːn] [an-ti-lín] *a./s.* Antillano.

Antilles ['æntɪliːz] [an-tils] *N. (Geogr.)* Antillas.

antilogarithm ['æntɪ'lɒgǝrɪθǝm] [an-ti-lo-ga-rizem] *s. (Mat.)* Antilogaritmo.

antilogy ['æntɪ'lɒdʒɪ] [an-tí-lo-chi], *s.* Antilogía, contradicción de palabras o de algunas sentencias o pasajes de un autor.

antimagnetic ['æntɪmæg'netɪk] [an-ti-mag-né-tik], *a.* Antimagnético.

antimalarial ['æntɪmǝ'leǝrɪǝl] [an-ti-ma-lá-rial], *a.* Antipalúdico, eficaz contra la malaria.

anti-masonic [æntɪmǝ'sɒnɪk] [an-ti-ma-só-nik] *a.* Antimasónico.

antimatter ['æntɪ‚mætǝr] [an-ti-má-tar], *s.* Antimateria.

antimilitarism [æntɪmɪ'lɪtǝrɪzm] [an-ti-mi-li-ta-rísem], *s.* Antimilitarismo.

antimilitarist [æntɪmɪ'lɪtǝrɪst] [an-ti-mi-lí-ta-rist], *s.* Antimilitarista.

antimissile [æntɪmɪsɪl] [an-ti-mi-sil], *a.* Antimisil. **Antimissile missile,** proyectil antimisil.

antimonarchic [æntɪmɒnǝkɪk] [an-ti-mo-na-kik], antimonarchical [an-ti-mo-ná-ki-kal], *a.* Antimonárquico, opuesto al gobierno monárquico.

antimonarchist [æntɪmɒnǝkɪst] [an-ti-mó-na-kist], *s.* Antimonárquico, el que es contrario al gobierno monárquico.

antimonial [æntɪmɒnɪǝl] [an-ti-mó-nial], *a.* Antimonial, hecho de antimonio o perteneciente a él.

antimoniate [æntɪmɒnɪeɪt] [an-ti-mo-nieit] *s, (Quím.)* Antimoniato.

antimoniated [æntɪmɒnɪeɪtɪd] [an-ti-mo-ni-éi-tid] *a. (Quím.)* Antimoniatado.

antimonic [æntɪmɒnɪk] [an-ti-mó-nik], *a.* Antimónico; que se refiere al antimonio.

antimony [æntɪmɒnɪ] [an-tí-mo-ni], *s.* Antimonio, metal duro, blanco argentino, cristalizable, brillante, que se usa mucho en la química, en la medicina y en las artes en forma de aleaciones. **Tartarized antimony o tartar emetic,** tártaro emético.

antimoralist [æntɪmɒrǝlɪst] [an-ti-mó-ra-list], *s.* Enemigo de la moralidad.

antinational [‚æntɪ'næʃnl] [an-ti-ná-sho-nal] *a.* Antinacional.

antineuralgic [æntɪnjʊ'rældʒɪk] [an-ti-niu-rál-chik] *a. (Med.)* Antineurálgico.

antineutron [‚æntɪ'njʊtrɒn] [an-ti-niú-tron], *s.* Antineutrón.

antinode [æntɪnǝʊd] [an-ti-noud] *s.* Antinodo.

antinomian [æntɪ'nǝmɪǝn] [an-ti-nó-mian], **antinomist** [æntɪnǝmɪst] [an-tí-no-mist], *s.* Herejes que negaban la obligación de la ley moral.

antinomianism [æntɪnǝmɪǝnɪzǝm] [an-ti-no-mia-nísem], *s.* Herejía por la cual se niega la virtud u obligación de la ley moral y la necesidad de las buenas obras.

antinomic [æntɪnǝmɪk] [an-ti-nó-mik] o **antinomical** [æntɪnǝmɪkl] [an-ti-nó-mi-kal] *a.* Antinómico.

antinomy [æntɪnǝmɪ] [an-tí-no-mi], *s.* 1. Antinomia, oposición o contrariedad de las leyes entre sí. 2. Incompatibilidad entre dos o más conclusiones que, sin embargo, parecen ser igualmente inevitables; paradoja.

antinucleon [æntɪ'njuːklɪǝn] [an,-ti-niú-klion], *s.* Antinucleón.

antioch ['æntɪɒk] [an-tiok] *N.* Antioquía.

antiparliamentarianism [æntɪ‚pɑːlɪǝ'mǝntǝrǝnɪzǝm] [an-ti-pa-lia-men-ta-ria-nísem] *s.* Antiparlamentarismo.

antiparliamentary [æntɪ‚pɑːlɪǝ'mǝntǝrɪ] [an-ti-pa-lia-men-ta-ri] *a.* Antiparlamentario.

antiparticle [æntɪ‚pɑːtɪkl] [an-ti-pa-tí-kel], *s.* Antipartícula.

antipasto [æntɪ‚pɑːstʊ] [an-ti-pas-to], *s.* Aperitivo.

antipathetic [æntɪpǝ'θetɪk] [an-ti-pa-zé-tik], **antipathetical** [an-ti-pa-zé-ti-kal], *a.* Antipático, que causa antipatía.

antipathetically [æntɪpǝθetɪklɪ] [an-ti-pa-zé-ti-ka-li], *adv.* De un modo contrario.

antipathic [æntɪ'pǝθɪk] [an-ti-pá-zik], *a.* Antipático, contrario, opuesto; adverso, naturalmente contrario.

antipathy [æn'tɪpǝθɪ] [an-tí-pa-zi], *s.* Antipatía, oposición natural, repugnancia instintiva entre personas, o de una persona hacia una cosa.

antipatriotic [æntɪpæ'rɪɒtɪk] [an-ti-pa-trió-tik] *a.* Antipatriota, antipatriótico.

antipatriotism [æntɪpætrɪɒ'tɪzǝm] [an-ti-pa-trio-tísem] *s.* Antipatriotismo.

antipendium [æntɪˈpendɪəm] [an-ti-pén-dium], *s.* Frontal de altar.

antiperiodic [ˌæntɪpɪərɪˈɒdɪk] [an-ti-pi-rió-dik], *a.* Antiperiódico; se dice de los medicamentos que sirven para evitar el acceso de una enfermedad intermitente.

Antipersonnel [ˌæntɪpɜːˈsɒnel] [an-ti-pé-so-nal], *a.* contrapersonal.

antiperspirant [ˌæntɪpɜːsˈpaɪrənt] [an-ti-pérs-pi-rant], *s.* Desodorante.

antipestilential [ˌæntɪpesˈtɪlʃəl] [an-ti-pes-ti-lén-shal], *a.* Antipestilencial.

antiphilosophic [ˌæntɪfɪləˈsɒfɪk] [an-ti-fi-lo-só-fik] o **antiphilosophical** [ˌæntɪfɪləˈsɒfɪkəl] [an-ti-fi-lo-só-fi-kal] *a.* Antifilosófico.

antiphlogistic [ˌæntɪfləˈdʒɪstɪk] [an-ti-flo-chis-tik], *s.* y *a.* Antiflogístico, el medicamento propio para calmar la inflamación.

antiphon [ˈæntɪfɒn] [an-ti-fon], **antiphony** [ænˈtɪfɒnɪ] [an-tí-fo-ni], *s.* Antífona; eco.

antiphonal [ænˈtɪfɒnl] [an-tí-fo-nal], **antiphonical** [ˌæntɪˈfɒnɪkl] [an-ti-fó-ni-kal], *a.* Antifonal, perteneciente a las antífonas.

antiphonal [ænˈtɪfɒnl] [an-tí-fo-nal], **antiphonar** [ˈæntɪfɑːr] [an-tí-fo-nar], *s.* Antifonal o antifonario.

antiphonary [ænˈtɪfɒnərɪ] [an-ti-fo-na-ri] *s.* Antifonario.

antiphrasis [ænˈtɪfreɪzɪz] [an-ti-fra-sis], *s.* Antífrasis o antífrase, figura irónica por la que diciendo una cosa se entiende la contraria.

antipodal [ænˈtɪpɒdl] [an-ti-po-dal], *a.* 1. Lo que es antípoda, que se halla al lado opuesto del globo. 2. Contrario; diametralmente opuesto.

antipode [ˈæntɪpɒd] [an-ti-pod], *s.* 1. Lo directamente contrario u opuesto; la cosa opuesta a otra. 2. Una de los antípodas.

antipodean [ænˈtɪpɒdɪən] [an-ti-pódian], *a.* Antipodal, lo que se refiere o pertenece a los antípodas.

antipodes [ænˈtɪpɒdz] [an-tí-po-dis], *s. pl.* 1. Antípodas, los que habitan en el otro lado del globo y tienen sus pies opuestos a los nuestros. 2. (*Fig.*) Antípoda, contrario, opuesto.

antipoison [ˈæntɪpɔɪzn] [an-ti-pói-son], *s.* Antídoto, contraveneno.

antipope [ˈæntɪpəʊp] [an-ti-poup], *s.* Antipapa, el que usurpa el papado.

antiprelatic [ˌæntɪpreˈlɪtɪk] [an-ti-pri-lá-tik], **antiprelatical** [ˌæntɪpreˈlɪtɪkl] [an-ti-pri-lá-ti-kal], *a.* Hostil o contrario a la prelacía.

antipriest [ˌæntɪˈpriːst] [an-ti-príst], *s.* Hostilidad a los sacerdotes.

antiprinciple [ˌæntɪˈprɪnsəpl] [an-ti-prín-si-pol]. *s.* Principio opuesto.

antiprogressive [ˌæntɪprəˈgresɪv] [an-ti-pro-gré-sif] *a./s.* Antiprogresista.

antiprohibitionist [ˌæntɪprəʊˈbɪʃənɪst] [an-ti-pro-ji-bí-shonist] *a./s.* Antiprohibicionista.

antiprotectionist [ˌæntɪprəˈtekʃənɪst] [an-ti-pro-ték-shonist] *a. s.* Antiproteccionista.

antiproton [ˈæntɪprəʊtɒn] [an-ti-pró-ton], *s.* Antiprotón.

antiputrefactive [ˌæntɪpjuːtrɪˈfæktɪv] [an-ti-piu-trí-fak-tif] *a.* (*Biol.*) Antipútrido.

antipyretic [ˌæntɪpaɪˈretɪk] [an-ti-pai-ré-tik], *a.* y *s.* Antipirético, febrífugo.

antipyrine [ˌæntɪˈpaɪriːn] [an-ti-pái-rin], *s.* Antipirina, medicamento compuesto blanco cristalizable ($C_{11}H_{12}N_2O$), usado para calmar la fiebre.

antiquarian [ˌæntɪˈkwɛərɪən] [an-ti-kué-rian], *a.* Anticuario, el que es aficionado al estudio de las antigüedades: relativo a lo antiguo.

antiquerianism [ˌæntɪkwɛərɪəˈnɪzəm] [an-ti-kue-ria-nísem], *s.* La afición a las antigüedades.

antiquary [ˈæntɪkwɛərɪ] [an-ti-kué-ri], *s.* Anticuario, el que se dedica al estudio especial de las cosas antiguas.

antiquate [ˈæntɪkweɪt] [an-ti-kuéit], *va.* Anticuar, abolir el uso de alguna cosa; anular.

antiquated [ˈæntɪkweɪtɪd] [an-ti-kuéi-tid], *a.* 1. Anticuado, fuera de uso, propio de tiempos pasados. 2. Añejo, viejo, fuera de servicio; imposibilitado.

antique [ænˈtɪk] [án-tik], *a.* Antiguo, lo que tiene antigüedad. *-s.* Antigüedad, monumento de tiempos antiguos o remotos; antigualla. **Antique dealer,** anticuario. **Antique shop,** tienda de antigüedades.

antiqueness [ænˈtɪknɪs] [an-tik-nis], *s.* Antigüedad, la calidad de ser antiguo.

antiquity [ænˈtɪkwɪtɪ] [an-ti-kui-ti], *s.* 1. Antigüedad, los tiempos antiguos. 2. Vestigios, de los tiempos antiguos. 3. Ancianidad, vejez, vetustez.

antirabic [ˌæntɪˈræbɪk] [an-ti-ra-bik] *a.* Antirrábico.

antirachitic [ˌæntɪrəˈkɑɪtɪk] [an-ti-ra-kái-tik] *a.* (*Med.*) Antirraquítico.

antiradar [ˌæntɪˈreɪdɑːr] [an-ti-réi-dar] *a.* Antirradar.

antireligious [ˌæntɪrɪˈlɪgɪəs] [an-ti-re-lí-chios] *a.* Antirreligioso.

antirepublican [ˌæntɪrɪˈpʌblɪkən] [an-ti-ri-pá-bli-kan] *a./s.* Antirrepublicano.

antirevolutionary [ˌæntɪrevəˈluːʃənərɪ] [an-ti-re-vo-lú-shona-ri], *a.* Antirrevolucionario.

antirevolutionist [ˌæntɪrevəˈluːʃənɪst] [an-ti-re-vo-lú-shonist], *s.* Antirrevolucionario.

antirheumatic [ˌæntɪruːˈmætɪk] [an-ti-ru-má-tik], *a.* Antirreumático, eficaz contra el reumatismo.

antirust [ˌæntɪrʌst] [an-ti-rast] *a.* Antioxidante.

antisacerdotal [ˌæntɪsæsəˈdəʊtl] [an-ti-sa-sá-dou-tal], *a.* Hostil a los sacerdotes.

antiscians [ænˈtɪsɪəns] [an-ti-sians] o **antiscii** [ˌæntɪsiː] [an-ti-si], *s. pl.* Antiscios, los pueblos que habitan en el hemisferio opuesto de la tierra.

antiscorbutic [ˌæntɪskɔːˈbjuːtɪk] [an-tis-kor-biú-tik], **antiscorbutical** [ˌæntɪskɔːˈbjuːtɪkl] [an-tis-kor-biú-ti-kal], *a.* Antiescorbútico, eficaz para curar el escorbuto.

antiscripturist [ˌæntɪskrɪpˈʃərɪst] [an-tis-krip-tu-rist], *s.* Antiescripturista, el que niega la revelación o impugna la sagrada escritura.

antisemite [ˌæntɪˈsiːmaɪt] [an-ti-si-mait] *s.* Antisemita.

antisemitic [ˌæntɪsɪˈmɪtɪk] [an-ti-si-mi-tik], *s.* y *a.* Antisemítico, antisemita.

antisemitism [ˌæntɪsəmɪˈtɪzəm] [an-ti-si-me-tísem], *s.* Antisemitismo.

antisepsis [ˌæntɪˈsepsɪs] [an-ti-sep-sis] *s.* (*Med.*) Antisepsia.

antiseptic [ˌæntɪˈseptɪk] [an-ti-sep-tik], *a.* Antiséptico, antipútrido, lo que impide la putrefacción o fermentación. También se usa como nombre.

antiseptical [ˌæntɪˈseptɪkl] [an-ti-sép-ti-kal], *a. V.* ANTISEPTIC.

antiseptically [ˌæntɪˈseptɪklɪ] [an-ti-sép-ti-ka-li], *adv.* De un modo antiséptico.

antiskid [ˈæntɪskɪd] [an-tis-kid] *a.* Antideslizante.

antislavery [ˌæntɪˈsleɪvərɪ] [an-tis-léi-va-ri], *a.* Partidario de la manumisión, opuesto a la esclavitud.

antisocial [ˌæntɪˈsəʊʃəl] [an-ti-sóu-shal], *a.* 1. Antisocial. 2. Antisociable.

antispasmodic [ˌæntɪspæzˈmɒdɪk] [an-tis-pas-mó-dik], *a.* Antiespasmódico, eficaz contra los espasmos.

antispastic [ˌæntɪsˈpæstɪk] [an-tis-pás-tik], *a.* Antispástico; se dice de los medicamentos que causan una revulsión de los humores.

antisplenetic [ˌæntɪsplɪˈnetɪk] [an-tis-ple-né-tik], *a.* Antiesplénico, lo que es eficaz contra las enfermedades del bazo.

antistrophe [ænˈtɪstrəʊfɪ] [an-tis-tróu-fi], *s.* 1. Antistrofa, la segunda parte del canto lírico en la poesía griega. 2. (*Ret.*) Inversión de voces en cláusulas sucesivas; de aquí, toda la inversión de relación.

antistrumatic [ˌæntɪstruˈmætɪk] [an-tis-tru-má-tik], *a.* Antiescrofuloso; se aplica a los medicamentos usados para curar lamparones.

antisubmarine [ˌæntɪsʌbˈməriːn] [an-ti-sáb-ma-rin] *a.* Antisubmarino.

antisyphilitic [ˌæntɪsɪfɪˈlɪtɪk] [an-ti-si-fi-lí-tik], *a.* y *n.* Antisifilítico, remedio contra la sífilis.

antitank [ˌæntɪˈtæŋk] [an-ti-tank], *a.* *(Mil.)* Antitanque.

antitetanic [ˌæntɪteˈtænɪk] [an-ti-te-tá-nik] *a.* *(Med.)* Antitetánico.

anti-theft device [ˌæntɪθeftdɪˈvaɪz] [an-ti-zéft-di-váis] *s.* Antirrobo.

antithesis [ænˈtɪθɪsɪs] [an-ti-zí-sis], *s.* 1. *(Ret.)* Antítesis, figura que consiste en contraponer una frase o una palabra a otra de contraria significación. 2. Antítesis, oposición, contrariedad, contraste.

antithetical [ˌæntɪˈθetɪkəl] [an-ti-zé-ti-kal], *a.* Antitético, lo que contiene antítesis.

antitoxin [ˈæntɪˈtɒksɪn] [an-ti-tok-sin], *s.* *(Med.)* Antitoxina.

antitrades [ˈæntɪˈreɪdz] [an-ti-tréids] *s. pl.* Contraalisios.

antitrinitarian [ˈæntɪtrɪnɪˈtəriən] [an-ti-tri-ni-tárian], *s.* Antitrinitario; se dice de los herejes que niegan la santísima Trinidad.

antitrust [ˈæntɪˈrʌst] [an-ti-trast], *a.* Contra los monopolios o los *trusts*.

antitubercular [ˈæntɪtʊˈbɜːkjʊlər] [an-ti-tu-bér-kiu-la] *a.* *(Med.)* Antituberculoso.

antitype [ˈæntɪtaɪp] [an-ti-taip], *s.* Antitipo, figura, imagen.

antitypical [ˈæntɪˈtɪpɪkl] [an-ti-tí-pi-kal], *a.* Antitípico.

antivenin [ˈæntɪˈvɪnɪn] [an-ti-vi-nin] *s.* *U.S.* Antitoxina.

antivenereal [ˈæntɪvɪˈnɪəriəl] [an-ti-vi-nía-rial] *a.* Antivenéreo.

antivirus [ˈæntɪˈvaɪərʌs] [an-ti-vái-ros], *s.* Antivirus.

antler [ˈæntlər] [an-tlar], *s.* 1. Cuerna, asta. 2. Mogote. 3. Candil. *-pl.* Cornamenta.

antlered [ˈæntləd] [ántlerd], *a.* Lo que tiene cercetas o astas ramosas.

ant-lion [ˈæntˈlaɪən] [ant-láion], *s.* Hormiga-león, insecto neuróptero, el mirmeleón; y particularmente, su larva que se alimenta de hormigas.

Antoinette [ˈæntwɑːnet] [an-tua-net] *N.* Antonia.

Antoninus [ˈæntɒnɪnəs] [an-to-ni-nas] *N.* Antonino.

antoeci [ænˈtaɪsaɪ] [an-ta-si], *s.* *(Geog.)* Antecos, los pueblos que habitan en lugares de una misma latitud y longitud, pero en lados opuestos del ecuador.

antonomasia [ˈæntɒnɒˈmɪziə] [an-to-no-má-sia], *s.* *(Ret.)* Antonomasia, figura retórica que consiste en usar el nombre apelativo por el propio o éste en lugar del apelativo.

Antony [ˈæntɒni] [án-to-ni] *N.* Antonio.

antonym [ˈæntɒnɪm] [an-tó-nim] *s.* Antónimo.

antrum [ˈæntrəm] [an-tram], *s.* Antro, cueva, caverna; con particularidad la cavidad o "antro de Highmore" en la cara.

Antwerp [ˈæntɜːp] [an-tuárp] *N.* *(Geogr.)* Amberes.

anuran [ˈænjuːrən] [a-niú-ran] *s.* *(Zool.)* Anuro.

anurous [ˈænjuːrəs] [á-niu-ras] *a.* Anuro.

anury [ˈænjuːri] [á-niu-ri] *s.* *(Med.)* Anuria.

anus [ˈeɪnəs] [-ei-nas], *s.* Ano, orificio por el cual se expele el excremento del cuerpo.

anvil [ˈænvɪl] [an-vil], *s.* Yunque, ayunque, bigornia. **The stock of an anvil,** cepo de yunque. *(Fig.)* **On the anvil,** sobre el tapete (under discussion), en el telar (in preparation).

anvilled [ˈænvɪld] [an-vild], *a.* Formado a modo de yunque.

anxiety [ænˈzaɪəti] [ánk-saia-ti], *s.* 1. Ansia, solicitud acerca de alguna cosa venidera. 2. Aflicción o abatimiento de ánimo. 3. Perplejidad, desasosiego, afán, anhelo, cavilación, inquietud, dificultad, ansiedad. **His anxiety to make good impression,** su ansia de dar buena impresión.

anxious [ˈæŋkʃəs] [ank-shos], *a.* Inquieto, perturbado, ansioso, anheloso, impaciente, penoso, roedor. **To be (o feel) anxious about,** estar inquieto a causa de, respecto a. **Anxious forebodings,** presentimientos alarmantes. **He is anxious to see you,** está deseoso de verte. **Anxious about the future,** preocupado por el futuro.

anxiously [ˈæŋkʃəsli] [ank-shos-li], *adv.* Ansiosamente, impacientemente. **Waiting anxiously for the results,** esperando con ansia los resultados.

anxiousness [ˈæŋkʃəsnɪs] [ank-shos-nis], *s.* Ansia, ansiedad, solicitud, anhelo.

any [ˈeni] [é-ni], *a.* Cualquier o cualquiera, algún, alguno, alguna, todo. **Any further,** más lejos. **Any more,** más aún. **Any longer,** más allá, todavía, mucho más tiempo. **Any thing,** algo. **Anywise,** *adv.* en o de algún modo. **Any,** después de negación o preposición privativa, Ninguno, na. **I have not seen any of your friends,** no he visto a ninguno de tus amigos. **Without any difficulty,** sin ninguna dificultad, sin la menor dificultad. **Any,** en sentido partitivo, no suele traducirse en castellano. **Have you any money?,** ¿tiene usted dinero? o ¿tiene usted algún dinero encima? **At any time,** en cualquier momento. **At any rate,** de todas formas.

anybody [ˈenɪbɒdɪ] [éni-badi], *pro.* 1. Alguno, alguien, cualquiera; con negación, nadie. 2. Todo el mundo, toda persona. **Is anybody at home?** ¿Hay alguien en casa? **Not anybody,** nadie. **Anybody can do that,** cualquiera puede hacer eso. **Hardly anybody thinks so,** casi nadie lo cree.

anyhow [ˈenɪhaʊ] [éni-jau], *adv.* 1. De todas formas, de cualquier modo que sea; bien que, sin embargo; en cualquier caso. 2. Con indiferencia, no importa como.

anymore [ˈenɪmɔːr] [éni-moar] *adv.* Nunca más, ya.

anyone [ˈenɪwʌn] [éni-uan] *pron.* See ANYBODY.

anything [ˈenɪθɪŋ] [éni-zin], *pro.* 1. Algo, alguna cosa, cualquier cosa; con negación, nada. 2. Todo, todo lo que. **Have you anything to do just now?** ¿Tiene Vd. algo que hacer ahora mismo? **I haven't got anything,** no tengo nada. **Anything you want,** todo lo que usted quiera. *(Fam.)* **To be as easy as anything,** ser coser y cantar, estar tirado. **To be anything but stupid,** no ser nada tonto. *adv.* Algo. **Is anything like his brother?** ¿Se parece algo a su hermano? **He is anything but clever,** es todo menos inteligente.

anyway [ˈenɪweɪ] [-eni-uei], *adv.* 1. Salga lo que saliere; sin embargo, con todo eso, sea lo que fuere. 2. De cualquier modo que sea; de todas formas.

anywhere [ˈenɪweər] [éni-uear], *adv.* Dondequiera, en cualquier parte, en todas partes. **Not anywhere,** en ninguna parte. **Put it anywhere,** ponlo en cualquier sitio. **Anywhere in the world,** en todas partes del mundo. **Anywhere from five to ten dollars,** entre cinco y diez dólares. **Miles from anywhere,** muy lejos, en el quinto pino.

anywise [ˈenɪwaɪz] [éni-uais] *a.* De cualquier manera, de cualquier modo, de cualquier forma. **Not anywise,** de ninguna manera, de ningún modo.

aorist [ˈeɪərɪst] [éa-rist], *s.* *Gram.* Aoristo.

aorist, aoristic, *a.* Parecido al aoristo; sin limitación de tiempo.

aorta [eɪˈɔːtə] [ei-orta], *s.* Aorta, la arteria mayor del cuerpo.

aortic [eɪˈɔːtɪk] [ei-or-tik], *a.* Aórtico, que pertenece a la aorta, o tiene relación con ella.

aortitis [eɪˈɔːtaɪtɪs] [ei-or-tái-tis] *s.* *(Med.)* Aortitis.

apace [əˈpeɪs] [a-péis], *adv.* Aprisa, con presteza o prontitud.

Apache [əˈpætʃi] [a-pá-chi] *s.* Apache.

apagoge [əpəˈɡɒɡ] [a-pa-gog], *s.* 1. *(Mat.)* El empleo de una proposición ya demostrada para probar otra. 2. Apagogía, razonamiento que sirve para probar la verdad de una proposición, demostrando lo absurdo de la contraria.

apagogical [əpəˈɡɒdʒɪkl] [a-pa-gó-chi-kal], *a.* Apagógico, lo que pertenece a la demostración de una proposición por lo absurdo de la contraria.

apanage [əpəˈneɪdʒ] [á-pa-neich] *s.* *(Hist.)* Infantado. Herencia, dependencia. **To be the apanage of,** ser privativo de, ser el patrimonio de.

apart [əˈpɑːt] [a-párt], *adv.* Aparte, a un lado, separadamente, por separado, aparte de. **He stood apart,** se mantuvo aparte. **Ten centimetres apart,** separados por diez centímetros.

Apart from the style, I quite like it, aparte del estilo, me gusta bastante. **To be miles apart,** estar a kilómetros de distancia. **To come apart,** desprenderse, ser desmontable, estropearse. **To live apart,** vivir apartado. **To stand with one's legs apart,** estar con las piernas separadas. **To tell two things apart,** distinguir dos cosas una de otra. **To set apart,** apartar, reservar. **Joking apart,** bromas aparte.

apartheid [əˈpɑːtjeɪd] [á-part-zeid] s. Apartheid, segregación racial.

apartment [əˈpɑːtmənt] [a-párt-ment], s. Departamento, apartamiento, vivienda, cuarto, habitación. **Apartment house,** casa de pisos.

apathetic [ˌæpəˈθetɪk] [a-pa-zé-tik], **apathistical** [æpəˈθɪstɪkl] [a-pa-zís-ti-kal], a. Apático, indolente, sin pasión por nada, indiferente, insensible.

apathist [ˌæpəˈθɪst] [á-pa-zist], s. Hombre apático o insensible.

apathy [ˈæpəθɪ] [á-pa-zi], s. Apatía, insensibilidad a toda pasión.

apatite [ˈæpəˈtaɪt] [á-pa-tait], s. Apatito, fosfato de cal nativo, cristalizado.

ape [eɪp] [éip], s. 1. Mono. 2. (Met.) Mono, el que imita o remeda.

ape, va. Hacer muecas o monadas, imitar, remedar.

apeak [əˈpiːk] [a-pík], adv. 1. En postura o ademán de penetrar la tierra. 2. (Mar.) A pique.

apelike [eɪpˈlaɪk] [éip-laik] a. Simiesco.

apennines [ˈæpɪnaɪnz] [á-pi-nains] N. (Geogr.) Apeninos.

apepsia, apepsy [ˈæpɪpˈsɪə] [a-píp-sia], s. (Med.) Apepsia mala digestión.

aper [eɪˈpɜːr] [a-pér], s. Imitador o mimo ridículo, bufón.

aperient [əˈpɪərɪənt] [a-pía-riant], **aperitive** [əˈperɪtɪv] [a-pé-ri-tif], a. Laxante.

aperiodic [əˈpɪrɪədɪk] [a-pi-rió-dik] a. Aperiódico.

apéritif [əˈperɪtɪv] [a-pé-ri-tif] s. Aperitivo (drink).

aperture [ˈæpətʃʊər] [a-pér-chuar], s. Abertura, paso, rendija, resquicio.

apery [əˈperɪ] [a-pe-ri] s. Mímica.

apetalous [əˈpetələs] [a-pé-ta-los], a. (Bot.) Apétalo, sin pétalos.

apex [ˈeɪpeks] [éi-peks], s. APEXES o APICES, pl. ápice, el extremo superior o la punta de alguna cosa, cima. **Apices of a flower,** (Bot.) ápices de los estambres de la flor.

aphaeresis [əˈfærezɪs] [a-fé-re-sis], s. Aféresis, supresión de lo superfluo.

aphaniptera [əfəˈnɪptərə] [a-fa-níp-ta-ra], s. Afanípteros, orden de insectos sin alas, como la pulga.

aphasia [æˈfeɪzɪə] [a-féi-sia], s. Afasia, pérdida de la facultad de hablar, quedando intactos los órganos vocales y sin alteración de la inteligencia. Resulta de enfermedad del cerebro.

aphasic [æˈfæzɪk] [a-fá-sik], a. Afásico.

aphelion [əˈfiːlɪən] [a-fí-lán-tro-pi], s. (Astr.) Afelio, el punto de la órbita de un planeta en que éste se halla más distante del sol.

aphesis [əˈfezɪs] [a-fé-sis] s. Gram.) Aféresis.

aphid [ˈeɪfɪd] [éi-fid], s. (Ento.) áfido.

aphilanthropy [əfɪˈlæntrəpɪ] [a-fi-lán-tro-pi], s. Falta de filantropía.

aphis [ˈeɪfɪs] [éi-fis], s. APHIDES, pl. Áfido, el pulgón; el género de los Áfidos; insecto del género Aphis.

aphonia [eɪˈfɒnɪə] [ei-fo-nia], **aphony** [eɪˈfɒnɪ] [éi-fo-ni], s. Afonía, pérdida de la voz a consecuencia de una afección de la laringe; ronquera crónica.

aphonic [eɪˈfɒnɪk] [ei-fó-nik], a. 1. Sin sonido; afónico, áfono. 2. Mudo, que no representa un sonido. **Aphonic letter,** letra muda.

aphorism [ˈæfərɪzəm] [a-fo-rísem], s. Aforismo, sentencia breve, máxima o regla general.

aphorismer [æfəˈrɪzmər] [a-fo-rís-mar], **aphorist** [ˈæfərɪst] [á-fo-rist], s. Escritor de aforismos.

aphorismic [ˌæfəˈrɪsmɪk] [a-fo-rís-mik] o **aphoristic** [ˌæfəˈrɪstɪk] [a-fo-rís-tik] a. Aforístico.

aphoristical [ˌæfəˈrɪstɪkl] [a-fo-rís-ti-kal], adv. Sentenciosamente.

aphrodisiac [æfrəʊˈdɪzɪæk] [a-frou-di-síak], **aphrodisiacal** [æfrəʊˈdɪzɪækl] [a-frou-dí-sia-kal], a. 1. Afrodisíaco, lo que conduce al apetito venéreo o lo excita. 2. Lascivo, lujurioso.

Aphrodite [æfrəʊˈdaɪtɪ] [á-frou-dait), s. 1. Afrodita, la diosa griega del amor; corresponde a la Venus latina. 2. Mariposa de hermosos colores de los Estados Unidos de América.

aphtha [ˈæftə] [áf-ta], pl. APHTHAE, s. Aftas, úlceras pequeñas y superficiales en la boca.

aphthong [ˈæftɒŋ] [áf-ton], s. Letra muda, o combinación de las mismas; como p en pseudo.

aphthous [ˈæftəs] [áf-tos], a. Aftoso, perteneciente a las aftas o afectado con ellas. **Aphthous fever,** fiebre aftosa.

aphyllous [əˈfɪləs] [a-fi-los], a. (Bot.) Afilo, que no tiene hojas.

apiarian [ˈeɪpɪərɪən] [ei-pi-á-rian] a. Apícola.

apiarist [ˈeɪpɪərɪst] [ei-pia-rist] s. Apicultor.

apiary [ˈeɪpɪərɪ] [ei-pia-ri], s. Colmenar, abejar, lugar en que se crían las abejas; colección de abejas, colmenas, utensilios, etc.

apical [ˈeɪpɪkl] [éi-pi-kal] s. Ápical, que está en la cumbre.

apices [ˈeɪpɪsiːz] [ei-pí-sis] s. pl. See APEX.

apicultural [ˈeɪpɪkʌltʃərəl] [ei-pi-kál-cha-ral] a. Apícola.

apiculture [ˈeɪpɪkʌltʃər] [ei-pi-kál-chaʳ], s. Apicultura, cuidado de las abejas.

apiculturist [ˈeɪpɪkʌltʃərɪst] [ei-pi-kál-cha-rist], s. Apicultor, el que cuida de las abejas.

apiece [əˈpiːs] [a-pís], adv. Por barba, por cabeza, por persona o cada uno. **We had two blankets apiece,** teníamos dos mantas cada uno. **He gave them one apiece,** les dio una a cada uno.

apis [əˈpɪs] [a-pis], s. 1. Apis, nombre del buey que adoraban como dios los antiguos egipcios. 2. Nombre científico de la abeja; género de insectos himenópteros interesantes por el gran desarrollo de su inteligencia.

apish [əˈpɪʃ] [a-pish], a. Gestero, bufón, monero; acostumbrado a hacer gestos y remedar como el mono; afectado, frívolo.

apishly [əˈpɪʃlɪ] [a-pish-li], adv. Afectadamente, frívolamente.

apishness [əˈpɪʃnɪs] [a-pish-nis], s. Monada, gesto o figura afectada y enfadosa.

apitpat [əˈpɪtpæt] [a-pit-pat], adv. Con palpitación acelerada: es voz vulgar. V. PIT-A-PAT.

apivorous [əˈpɪvərəs] [a-pí-vo-ros], a. Apívoro, que come abejas.

aplanatic [əpləˈnætɪk] [a-pla-ná-tik], a. Aplanático, exento de aberración esférica y cromática.

aplenty [əˈplentɪ] [a-plén-ti] adv. En abundancia.

aplomb [əˈplɒm] [a-plóm], s. 1. Confianza en sí mismo; aplomo. 2. Posición recta; postura vertical. (Gal.)

apnoea o **apnea** [əpˈniːə] [ap-nia] s. (Med.) Apnea.

apocalypse [əˈpɒkəlɪps] [a-po-ka-lips], s. Apocalipsis, revelación, el último libro del Nuevo Testamento.

apocalyptic [əˈpɒkəlɪptɪk] [a-po-ka-líp-tik], **apocalyptical** [əˈpɒkəlɪptɪkl] [a-po-ka-líp-ti-kal], a. Apocalíptico, lo que contiene revelaciones.

apochromatic [ˌæpɒkrəˈmætɪk] [a-po-kro-má-tik], a. Apocromático, corrector del espectro secundario.

apocopate [əˈpɒkəpeɪt] [a-pó-ko-peit], va. Gram.) Apocopar, cometer apócope.

apocopation [əˈpɒkəpeɪʃən] [a-po-ko-péi-shon] s. Gram.) Apócope.

apocope [əˈpɒkəʊpɪ] [a-pó-kou-pi], s. (Ret.) Apócope, figura por la cual se quita la última letra o sílaba de una dicción.

apocrypha [əˈpɒkrɪfə] [a-pó-kri-fa], s. pl. Libros apócrifos o no canónicos.

apocryphal [ə'pɒkrɪfəl] [a-pó-kri-fal], *a.* Apócrifo, no canónico, dudoso o falso.

apod, apodal ['əpɒd] ['əpɒdl] [a-pod] [a-po-dal], *a.* Ápodo, sin pies; sin aletas ventrales.

apodictic ['əpɒdɪktɪk] [a-po-dík-tik], **apodictical** ['əpɒdɪktɪkl] [a-po-dík-ti-kal], *a.* Apodíctico, demostrativo o convincente.

apodosis [ə'pɒdəʊsɪs] [a-po-dou-sis], *s.* Apódosis, segunda parte del período, en la que se completa el sentido que queda pendiente en la primera, llamada prótasis.

apodous ['əpɒdəs] [a-po-dos], *a.* ápodo, sin pies. V. APODAL.

apogee ['æpədʒɪ] [a-po-chi], *s.* Apogeo, el punto en que el sol o cualquier otro planeta se halla a la mayor distancia de la tierra en toda su revolución.

apoggiatura ['æpədʒətjʊrə] [a-po-chia-tu-ra], *s. (Mús.)* Apoyatura.

apograph [ə'pɒgræf] [a-po-graf], *s.* Apógrafo, copia de algún libro o escrito.

apolitical [ˌeɪpə'lɪtɪkəl] [ei-po-lí-ti-kal] *a.* Apolítico.

apoliticism [ˌeɪpə'lɪtɪsɪzm] [ei-pa-li-tísem] *s.* Apolitismo.

apollinarian [ˌeɪpə'lɪnærɪən] [ei-po-li-ná-rian], **apolinarist** [ˌeɪpə'lɪnærɪst] [ei-pó-li-na-rist], *s.* Apolinarista, hereje que negaba que Jesucristo hubiese formado carne en un cuerpo como el nuestro.

Apollo [ə'pɒləʊ] [a-po-lou] N. Apolo.

apollonian [ə'pɒləʊnɪən] [a-po-lou-nian] *a.* Apolíneo.

apologetic, apologetical [əˌpɒlə'dʒetɪk] [əˌpɒlə'dʒetɪkl] [a-po-lou-yé-tik] [a-po-lou-yé-ti-kal], *a.* Apologético. **An apologetic treatise,** un tratado apologético. **He was very apologetic about the incident,** me ofreció toda clase de disculpas por el incidente.

apologetically [əˌpɒlə'dʒetɪklɪ] [a-po-lou-yé-ti-ka-li], *adv.* Apologéticamente.

apologetics [əˌpɒlə'dʒetɪks] [a-po-lo-yé-tiks], *s.* 1. Apologética, ramo de la teología consagrado a la defensa de la religión cristiana. 2. Apologética, nombre dado a la defensa de los cristianos por Tertuliano.

apologia [ə'pɒlədʒɪə] [a-po-lo-chia] *s.* Apología.

apologist [ə'pɒlədʒɪst] [a-pó-lo-chist], *s.* Apologista.

apologize [ə'pɒlədʒaɪz] [a-pó-lo-chais], *va.* Apologizar, defender; excusar, disculpar o sacar la cara por, o en defensa de. -*vn.* Disculparse, excusarse.

apologizer [ə'pɒlədʒaɪzər] [a-po-lo-chái-sar], *s.* Defensor, defendedor, apologista.

apologue ['æpəlɒg] [a-po-log], *s.* Apólogo, fábula moral e instructiva.

apology [ə'pɒlədʒɪ] [a-pó-lo-chi], *s.* Apología, defensa; excusa, justificación. **My apologies,** mis disculpas. *(Fam.)* Birria. **What an apology for a house!,** ¡vaya birria de casa!

apomorphia [æpə'mɔːfɪə] [a-po-mor-fia], *s.* Apomorfina, alcaloide que se extrae del opio; emético enérgico.

aponeurosis [əpə'njuːrəsɪs] [a-po-niu-ró-sis], *s.* Aponeurosis, membrana fibrosa y resistente, destinada a mantener en su lugar los músculos que envuelve o a servirles de punto de inserción.

aponeurotic [əpə'njuːrətɪk] [a-po-niu-ró-tik], *a.* Aponeurótico.

apophasis [əpə'fæsɪs] [a-pó-fa-sis], *s.* Apófasis, refutación. Figura retórica en la cual el orador, negando un punto favorable, produce, no obstante, el efecto deseado.

apophlegmatic [æpə'flegmætɪk] [a-po-fleg-má-tik], *a.* Apoflemático, expectorante.

apophthegm ['æpəθegm] [a-po-zégm], *s.* V. APOTHEGM.

apophysis [ə'pɒfɪsɪs] [a-pó-fi-sis], *s. (Anat.)* Apófisis, eminencia o parte saliente de un órgano y particularmente de un hueso.

apoplectic [ˌæpə'plektɪk] [a-po-plék-tik], **apoplectical** [ˌæpə'plektɪkl] [a-po-plék-ti-kal], *a.* Apopléctico. *(Fig.)* **To get apoplectic,** ponerse furioso.

apoplexy ['æpəpleksɪ] [a-pó-plek-si], *s.* Apoplejía, privación súbita del sentido.

aporia [æ'pɒrɪə] [a-pó-ria] *s. (Fil.)* Aporía.

aport [æ'pɔːt] [a-pórt], *adv. (Mar.)* Ababor (el timón).

aposiopesis [əpəsɪə'pesɪs] [a-po-sio-pé-sis], *s.* Aposiópesis, reticencia; figura retórica que se comete cuando empezando a decir una cosa se interrumpe la frase y se deja el razonamiento por concluir.

apostasy [ə'pɒstəsɪ] [a-pós-ta-si], *s.* Apostasía, deserción o abandono de la religión que uno profesaba.

apostate [ə'pɒstɪt] [a-pos-teit], *s.* Apóstata, el que comete apostasía. -*a.* Falso, pérfido, rebelde.

apostatical [ə'pɒstətɪkl] [a-pos-tá-ti-kal], *a.* Apostático.

apostatize [ə'pɒstətaɪz] [a-pos-ta-tais], *vn.* Apostatar, abandonar la religión que uno profesaba.

apostem [ə'pɒstem] [a-pos-tem], **aposteme** [ə'pɒstem] [A,p<s',tîm], *s.* Apostema, absceso.

apostemate [əpɒs'temeɪt] [a-pos-te-meit], *vn. (Des.)* Apostemarse.

apostemation [əpɒste'meɪʃən] [a-pos-te-méi-shon], *s. (Med.)* Apostemación, apostema, absceso.

a posteriori ['ɑːpɒsterɪ'ɔːraɪ] [a-pos-te-ri-o-rai] *a./adv.* A posteriori.

apostil [ə'pɒstɪl] [a-pos-til] *s.* Apostilla, nota marginal.

apostle [ə'pɒsl] [a-pósel], *s.* Apóstol, enviado.

apostleship [ə'pɒslʃɪp] [a-pósel-ship], **apostolate** [ə'pɒstɒlət] [a-pós-to-leit], *s.* Apostolado.

apostolic [æpɒs'tɒlik] [a-pos-tó-lik], **apostolical** [æpɒs'tɒlikl] [a-pos-tó-li-kal], *a.* Apostólico. **Apostolic See,** sede apostólica.

apostolically [æpɒs'tɒliklɪ] [a-pos-tó-li-ka-li], *adv.* Apostólicamente.

apostolicalness [æpɒs'tɒliklnɪs] [a-pos-tó-li-kal-nis], *s.* La calidad de ser apostólico; autoridad apostólica.

apostrophe [ə'pɒstrəfɪ] [a-pos-tro-fi], *s.* 1. Apóstrofe, figura por la cual el orador suspende el discurso y dirige la palabra a una persona. 2. Apóstrofo, virgulilla que se pone para señalar alguna contracción, como *lov'd* por *loved, tho'* por *though;* también es la señal del caso genitivo, como *man's duty,* la obligación del hombre.

apostrophic [ə'pɒstrəfɪk] [a-pos-tró-fik], **apostrophical** [ə'pɒstrəfɪkl] [a-pos-tró-fi-kal], *a.* Lo perteneciente al apóstrofo.

apostrophize [ə'pɒstrəfaɪz] [a-pós-tro-fais], *va.* Apostrofar, dirigir o convertir el discurso con vehemencia a alguna persona o cosa. -*vn.* 1. Abreviar una palabra, suprimiendo una letra o letras. 2. Designar esta elisión por medio del apóstrofo.

apostume, *s.* V. APOSTEME.

apothecary [ə'pɒθɪkərɪ] [a-po-zi-ka-ri], *s.* Boticario. **An apothecary's shop,** botica.

apothegm [ə'pɒθegm] [a-po-zem], *s.* Apotegma, sentencia breve, dicha con agudeza.

apothegmatical [əpɒθeg'mætɪkl] [a-po-zeg-má-ti-kal], *a.* Apotegmático.

apothegmatist [əpɒθeg'mətɪst] [a-po-zeg-ma-tist], *s.* Apotegmatista, colector de apotegmas.

apothegmatize [ˌəpɒθeg'mətaɪz] [a-po-zeg-ma-tais], *vn.* Emplear o decir apotegmas.

apothem ['əpɒθem] [á-po-zem] *s. (Mat.)* Apotema.

apotheosis [əpɒθɪ'əʊsɪs] [a-po-zi-óu-sis], *va.* Deificar, poner entre los dioses.

apotheosize [əpɒθɪ'əʊsaɪz] [a-po-ziou-sais] *va.* Deificar, glorificar, idealizar.

apozem ['əpɒzem] [a-po-zem], *s.* Pócima, bebida medicinal.

appal, appall [ə'pɔːl] [a-pól], *va.* Espantar, aterrar; desmayar, desanimar. -*vn. (Des.)* Desmayar, debilitarse.

Appalachians [æpə'leɪʃənz] [a-pa-léi-shans] *N.* Apalaches.

appalling [ə'pɔːlɪŋ] [a-pó-lin], *a.* Espantoso, aterrador.

appanage [ə'pɔːneɪdʒ] [á-pa-neich], *s.* 1. Propiedad o territorio dependiente de otro, o de alguien. 2. Alimentos, la porción de rentas que corresponde a un hermano menor; heredamiento; infantazgo.

apparatus [æpə'reɪtəs] [a-pa-réi-tas], *s.* 1. Aparato, aparejo, apresto, prevención. 2. Tren, pompa, ostentación. 3.

Aparato, conjunto de piezas de una máquina; útiles empleados para la obtención de una cosa. **Digestive apparatus,** aparato digestivo. **Climbing apparatus,** equipo de montañismo. *(Fig.)* **The apparatus of government,** el aparato del gobierno.

apparel [ə'pærəl] [a-pa-rel], *s.* Atavío, indumentaria, ropa. *(Mar.)* Aparejo. **Wearing apparel,** vestidos, ropaje. *va.* Ataviar, vestir. *(Mar.)* Aparejar.

apparency [ə'pærənsɪ] [a-pa-ren-si], *s.* Calidad de evidente o claro.

apparent [ə'pærənt] [a-pa-rent], *a.* 1. Claro, patente, indubitable, evidente, manifiesto. **His sadness was very apparent,** su tristeza era muy evidente. 2. Aparente, lo que aparece y no es. **His apparent coldness is only shyness,** su aparente frialdad es sólo timidez. 3. Cierto. **The heir-apparent to the crown,** el heredero presunto de la corona.

apparently [ə'pærəntlɪ] [a-pa-ren-tli], *adv.* Evidentemente, claramente, al parecer.

apparentness [ə'pærəntnɪs] [a-pa-rent-nis], *s.* 1. Aparición o aparecimiento. 2. Aparición, visión, fantasma, espectro.

apparition [ˌæpə'rɪʃən] [a-pa-rí-shon] *s.* Aparición.

apparitor [ˌæpə'rɪtəʳ] [a-pa-rí-tar], *s.* 1. Alguacil de corona o de la curia, eclesiástica. 2. Macero o bedel de universidad.

appeach [ə'piːtʃ] [a-pích], *va. (Des.) V.* IMPEACH.

appeal [ə'piːl] [a-píl], *vn.* 1. Apelar, recurrir de un tribunal o juez inferior a otro superior; hacer a uno árbitro. **To appeal against a decision,** apelar una decisión. **To appeal to arms,** recurrir a las armas. 2. Llamar por testigo. **I appeal to God,** pongo a Dios por testigo. **The idea doesn't appeal to me,** la idea no me gusta.

appeal, *s.* 1. Apelación; recurso a un tribunal superior. 2. Rogación, súplica, petición, instancia. **An appeal for rebellion,** un llamamiento a la sublevación. **An appeal for help,** una llamada de socorro. *(For.)* **Appeal for annulment,** recurso de nulidad. **Court of appeal,** tribunal de apelación. **Right of appeal,** derecho de apelación.

appealable [ə'piːləbl] [a-pí-la-bol], *a.* Apelable.

appealer [ə'piːləʳ] [a-pí-lar], *s.* 1. Apelante. 2. Acusador.

appealing [ə'piːlɪŋ] [a-pí-lin] *a.* Suplicante, atrayente, atractivo. Conmovedor.

appear [ə'pɪəʳ] [a-píar], *vn.* 1. Aparecer o aparecerse, manifestarse, estar a la vista. **He was the last to appear,** fue el último en aparecer. 2. Comparecer, presentarse ante el juez; responder en persona o por procurador o abogado. **To appear in court,** comparecer ante un tribunal. 3. Parecer, dar alguna cosa muestras o señales de lo que es. **He appears to be very nice,** parece ser muy simpático. **I will make it appear,** yo lo haré constar. *(Fam.)* **As it appears,** a la cuenta, por lo que parece. 4. Evidenciarse, ser evidente, manifiesto, obvio. **To appear on the stage,** aparecer en escena.

appearance [ə'pɪərəns] [a-pía-rans], *s.* 1. Vista, la acción de dejarse ver alguna cosa; aparición, llegada, presentación al público. **To make an appearance,** aparecer, dejarse ver. 2. Apariencia, semejanza. 3. Apariencia, exterioridad. **His dishevelled appearance,** su aspecto desaliñado. 4. Comparecencia, el acto de comparecer ante el juez o tribunal. 5. Porte, la disposición, decencia o lucimiento de alguna persona. 6. Probabilidad, verisimilitud. 7. Aparición, fenómeno. **At first appearance,** a primera vista. **Appearances are deceptive,** las apariencias engañan.

appearer [ə'pɪərəʳ] [a-pía-rar], *s.* El que parece 2. *(For.)* Compareciente, la persona que comparece ante un juez.

appearing [ə'pɪərɪŋ] [a-pía-rin], *s.* 1. Aparición, la acción de aparecer. 2. *(For.)* Comparecencia, el acto de presentarse en juicio.

appeasable [ə'piːsəbl] [a-pí-sa-bol], *a.* Aplacable, reconciliable.

appeasableness [ə'piːsəblnɪs] [a-pi-sa-bol-nes], *s.* Aplacabilidad.

appease [ə'piːs] [a-pís], *va.* 1. Aliviar, aquietar el hambre o la sed, o el dolor. 2. Aplacar, apaciguar, pacificar, calmar, endulzar, aquietar.

apeasement [ə'piːsmənt] [a-pís-ment], *s.* Apaciguamiento, el acto y efecto de apaciguar o de aliviar; alivio, pacificación.

appeaser [ə'piːsəʳ] [a-pí-sar], *s.* Aplacador, apaciguador, reconciliador, pacificador.

appeasive [ə'piːsɪv] [a-pís-sif], *a.* El que o lo que aplaca, calma o pacifica; apaciguador, sosegador, pacificador.

appellancy [ə'pelənsɪ] [a-pé-lan-si], *s.* Apelación.

appellant [ə'pelənt] [a-pé-lant], *s.* Apelante; demandador, demandante. *-a.* Lo perteneciente al apelante o a la apelación.

appellate [ə'pelɪt] [a-pé-lit], *a.* De apelación; que tiene jurisdicción en las apelaciones; a que se puede recurrir.

appellation [ˌæpe'leɪʃən] [a-pe-léi-shon], *s.* Apelación, denominación, nombre. Apodo (nickname).

appellative [ə'pelətɪv] [a-pé-la-tif], *s.* Apelativo, nombre común que conviene a todos los individuos de una especie. *(Fam.)* Apellido. *-a.* Apelativo, común, usual, opuesto a propio o peculiar.

appellatively [ə'pelətɪvlɪ] [a-pe-la-tíf-li], *adv.* Apelativamente.

appellee [ə'peliː] [a-pe-li], *s.* Persona contra la cual se procede en apelación; demandado, acusado, apelado.

append [ə'pend] [a-pen], *va.* 1. Colgar, poner alguna cosa pendiente de otra. 2. Añadir o anexar; fijar, atar o ligar, p. ej. ponerle un sello a un documento.

appendage [ə'pendɪdʒ] [a-pen-dich], *s.* 1. Pertenencia, dependencia, cosa accesoria o dependiente de la principal y de ningún modo necesaria en su esencia. 2. *(Bot. y Zool.)* Apéndice.

appendant [ə'pendənt] [a-pen-dant], *a.* Pendiente, colgante, que cuelga de otra cosa; dependiente, anexo, accesorio, unido, pegado. *-s.* Pertenencia, dependencia.

appendectomy [ˌæpen'dektəmɪ] [a-pen-dék-to-mi], *s. (Med.)* Apendicectomía, extirpación del apéndice.

appendices [ə'pendɪzɪs] [a-pen-di-sis], *s.* Un plural de APPENDIX.

appendicitis [ˌəpendɪ'saɪtɪs] [a-pen-di-sái-tis], *a.* Apendicitis, inflamación del apéndice vermiforme.

appendix [ə'pendɪks] [a-pen-diks], *s. (pl.* APPENDIXES o APPENDICES). 1. Apéndice, adición o suplemento que se hace a alguna obra. 2. Accesoria, dependencia, parte suplementaria. *V.* APPENDAGE.

apperception [ˌæpə'sepʃən] [a-per-séip-shon], *s. (Fil.)* Percepción del conocimiento interior.

apperceive [əpə'siːv] [a-pér-sif] *va.* Percibir, apercibir.

appertain [ˌæpə'teɪn] [a-pér-tein], *vn.* Pertenecer, tocar a alguno por derecho o por naturaleza.

appertaining [ˌæpə'teɪnɪŋ] [a-per-téi-nin], **appertinent** [ˌæpə'tɪnənt] *(Des.)* [a-pér-ti-nent], *a.* Perteneciente.

appertenance [ˌæpə'tɪnəns] [a-pér-ti-nans], *s. (Ant.)* Pertenencia. *V.* APPURTENANCE.

appetence ['æpetens] [a-pá-tens], **appetency** ['æpətensɪ] [a-pé-tan-si], *s.* 1. Deseo ardiente; viva apetencia o apetito; inclinación. 2. Apetencia, instinto, tendencia natural. **The appetence of ducks for water,** la afición instintiva de los patos al agua.

appetent ['æpətent] [a-pé-tent], *a.* Apetecedor, my deseoso, ávido.

appetible ['æpətɪbl] [a-pe-ti-bol], *a.* Apetecible, deseable.

appetite ['æpɪtaɪt] [a-pi-tait], *s.* 1. Apetito, deseo natural de algún bien. **Appetite for power,** apetito de poder. 2. Sensualidad, concupiscencia. **Sexual appetite,** apetito carnal. 3. Antojo. 4. Apentito, hambre o gana de comer. **To whet the appetite,** estimular, abrir el apetito. **A good appetite is the best sauce,** a buen hambre no hay pan duro. **To eat with an appetite,** comer con mucho apetito.

appetitive [æpɪ'tɪtɪv] [a-pi-ti-tif], *a.* 1. Perteneciente o semejante al apetito; que tiene apetito. 2. Que estimula el apetito; atrayente, atractivo.

appetizer ['æpɪtaɪzə'] [a-pi-tái-sar], *s.* Lo que excita el apetito, aperitivo.

appetizing ['æpɪtaɪzɪŋ] [a-pi-tai-sin], *p. a.* 1. Grato, gustoso; tentador. 2. Que estimula un deseo cualquiera.

Appian Way [æpɪən'weɪ] [a-pian-uei] *N.* Via Apia.

applaud [ə'plɔːd] [a-plód], *va.* 1. Palmear, palmotear, aplaudir con palmoteos. 2. Aplaudir, alabar. *-vn.* Expresar aplauso o alabanza; dar palmadas.

applauder [ə'plɔːdə'] [a-pló-dar], *s.* El que aplaude o alaba.

applause [ə'plɔːdz] [a-plós], *s.* Aplauso, aprobación o alabanza pública con demostraciones de alegría. **Loud applause,** aplausos estrepitosos. **Applause** no se usa en plural. **To the applause of,** con el aplauso de. **A thunder of applause,** una salva de aplausos.

applausive [ə'plɔːzɪv] [a-pló-sif], *a.* Laudatorio.

apple ['æpl] [ápel], *s.* Manzana, fruta; manzano, le árbol que da esta fruta. **Apple of discord,** manzana de la discordia. **Apple-harvest,** cosecha de manzanas. **Apple-tart,** pastelillo de manzanas. **Apple-yard,** huerto. **Apple-tree,** *(Bot.)* manzano. **Apple-woman,** la mujer que vende manzanas. **The apple of the eye,** la pupila o niña del ojo y también el globo del ojo: y de aquí, cualquier cosa muy apreciada. **Apple-core,** corazón de manzana. **Apple-corer,** despepitador de manzanas. **Apple-fritter,** frituras de manzanas; fruta de sartén. **Apple-jack,** aguardiente de manzanas. **Apple-orchard,** manzanal. **Apple-pie,** pastel de manzanas. **In apple-pie order,** *(Coloq.)* en orden perfecto. **Apple-pealer,** mondador de manzanas. **Apple-sauce,** compota de manzanas. **Crab-apple,** manzana silvestre. **Oak-apple,** agalla de roble. **Thorn-apple,** estramonio. **Adam's apple,** nuez de la garganta.

appliance [ə'plɪəns] [a-plians], *s.* 1. Herramienta, instrumento, utensilio, medios; una cosa cualquiera por medio de la cual se efectúa algo instrumentalmente. 2. Aplicación: recurso. **Electrical appliance o home appliance,** electrodoméstico.

applicability [æplɪkə'bɪlɪtɪ] [a-pli-ka-bí-li-ti], *s.* Aplicabilidad.

applicable [ə'plɪkəbl] [a-plí-ka-bol], *a.* A propósito de, aplicable, pertinente; propio para.

applicableness [ə'plɪkəblnɪs] [a-pli-ká-bol-nis], *s.* La propiedad de ser aplicable.

applicably [ə'plɪkəblɪ] [a-plí-ka-bli], *adv.* De un modo aplicable.

applicant ['æplɪkənt] [á-pli-kant], *s.* El suplicante; pretendiente, candidato, aspirante. **Applicant for a job,** aspirante a un puesto.

applicate [æ'plɪkeɪt] [á-pli-keit], *s.* Línea coordenada de una sección cónica.

application [æplɪ'keɪʃən] [a-pli-kéi-shon], *s.* 1. Aplicación, la acción de aplicar una cosa a otra, y la cosa aplicada. 2. Súplica o petición. 3. Aplicación, la dedicación a un uso, demanda, o propósito particular; la aplicación de un principio o ley general al caso particular o a los negocios prácticos; empleo, uso, y la capacidad de ser empleado de esta manera. **The application of a theory,** la aplicación de una teoría. 4. Aplicación, estudio intenso o atención a alguna cosa particular. **To make application to,** recurrir a; dirigirse a. **A written application,** un memorial, una solicitud por escrito. **Application form,** formulario. *(Med.)* **For external application only,** para uso externo.

applicative [ə'plɪkətɪv] [a-plí-ka-tif], **applicatory** [ə'plɪkərɪ] [a-pli-ka-tó-ri], *a.* Aplicable.

applied [ə'plaɪd] [a-plaid], *pp.* y *a.* Aplicado; adaptado, utilizado. **Applied for,** pedido, encargado. **Applied science,** ciencia aplicada.

applier [ə'plaɪə'] [a-pláier], *s.* El que se aplica o adapta.

appliqué [æ'pliːkeɪ] [a-pli-kéi], *a.* Aplicado, pegado encima; se dice de los bordados.

apply [ə'plaɪ] [a-plái], *va.* 1. Aplicar, poner o juntar una cosa con otra. 2. Aplicar, apropiar, acomodar. 3. Aplicar, destinar a algún fin o para un uso particular; traer en relación con una persona o cosa; introducir en la práctica los principios de una ciencia, o valerse de una verdad general en el caso particular; utilizar. 4. Aplicarse, estudiar o dedicarse a algún estudio. 5. Recurrir, acudir a alguno como suplicante. **To apply colors,** dar color, aplicar colores sobre. **To apply a sum of money to,** destinar una suma de dinero a o para. **To apply one's attention to,** fijar su atención en. **Apply to me in case of need,** recurra usted a mí en caso de necesidad. **Apply to Mr. D.,** diríjase usted al Sr. D. *-vn.* 1. Pedir, dirigir una petición, hacer solicitud formal. 2. Dirigirse a, recurrir. 3. Convenir, acudir. **To apply oneself to,** aplicarse a, dirigirse a, recurrir a; aplicarse. **This rule applies to everyone,** esta regla se aplica a todos. **To apply for a job,** solicitar un trabajo.

appoint [ə'pɔɪnt] [a-point], *va.* 1. Señalar, determinar. 2. Decretar, establecer por decreto. 3. Surtir, equipar. 4. Nombrar, designar, elegir. **To appoint someone as Mayor,** nombrar a uno alcalde. **At the appointed time,** al tiempo prescrito o señalado, a la hora acordada. **Well appointed,** bien equipado, en buen estado. *-vn.* Ordenar.

appointee [əpɔɪn'tiː] [a-poin-ti], *s.* Funcionario, nombrado, designado.

appointer [ə'pɔɪntə'] [a-poin-tar], *s.* Ordenador, director, el que fija o determina alguna cosa o lugar.

appointment [ə'pɔɪntmənt] [a-point-ment], *s.* 1. Estipulación, acuerdo o convenio. 2. Decreto, establecimiento. 3. Dirección, orden o mandato. 4. Equipaje, aparato; equipo (de tropas). 5. Ración, sueldo, gajes, honorario, la cantidad de dinero que se paga a alguna persona por su servicio. 6. Cita. 7. Nombramiento. **Appointment book,** agenda de entrevistas. **To make an appointment,** pedir hora, citarse, quedar.

apportion [ə'pɔːʃən] [a-pór-shon], *va.* Proporcionar o dividir igualmente, prorratear.

apportioner [ə'pɔːʃənə'] [a-pór-sho-nar], *s.* Limitador.

apportionment [ə'pɔːʃənmənt] [a-pór-shon-ment], *s.* División en dos partes o porciones, prorrateo.

appose [ə'pəʊz] [a-póus], *va.* 1. Poner, fijar junto a, cerca de, aplicar. 2. Yuxtaponer. 3. *(Des.)* Cuestionar, examinar, considerar.

apposite ['æpəzɪt] [á-po-sit], *a.* 1. Adaptado, propio, proporcionado. 2. Justo, conforme: oportuno, a propósito.

appositely ['æpəzɪtlɪ] [a-po-sit-li], *adv.* Convenientemente, a propósito.

appositeness ['æpəzɪtnɪs] [a-po-sit-nis], *s.* Adaptación; propiedad.

apposition ['æpəzɪʃən] [a-po-sí-shon], *s.* 1. Añadidura, lo que se añade de nuevo a alguna cosa. 2. *Gram.)* Aposición, figura por la cual se ponen dos substantivos en el mismo caso sin conjunción. 3. Crecimiento o aumento por yuxtaposición. **Minerals grow by opposition,** los minerales crecen por aposición.

appositive ['æpəzɪtɪv] [a-pó-si-tif], *a.* 1. *Gram.)* Que se forma o construye por aposición. 2. Aplicable, propio.

appraisable [ə'preɪzəbl] [a-préi-sa-bol], *a.* Apreciable, estimable, ponderable, tasable.

appraisal [ə'preɪzəl] [a-préi-sal], o **appraisement** [ə'preɪzmənt] [a-préis-ment], *s.* Aprecio, avalúo, estimación, valuación, tasación.

appraise [ə'preɪz] [a-préis], *va.* Apreciar, valuar, poner precio o tasar alguna cosa; estimar, ponderar, dar valor.

appraiser [ə'preɪzə'] [a-préi-sar], *s.* Apreciador, tasador, avaluador. **Official appraiser,** perito tasador.

appreciable [ə'priːʃəbl] [a-prí-sha-bol], *a.* Apreciable, estimable, que admite estimación; perceptible, sensible.

appreciate [ə'priːʃɪeɪt] [a-prí-shieit], *va.* Apreciar, estimar, valuar, tasar alguna cosa. **To appreciate a good film,** apreciar una buena película. Agradecer. **I really appreciate**

your help, le agradezco mucho su ayuda. -vn. Subir en valor.

appreciation [əˌpriːˈʃɪˈeɪʃən] [a-pri-shi-éi-shon], s. 1. Valuación, estimación, tasa, aprecio, avalúo. 2. Alza, aumento de precio. 3. Susceptibilidad o sensibilidad que permite apreciar ligeros cambios o diferencias; percepción perspicaz de un punto o cosa no manifiestos.

appreciative, appreciatory [əˈpriːʃɪətɪv] [əˈpriːʃɪətərɪ] [a-pri-sha-tif] [a-pri-sha-to-ri], a. Que manifiesta aprecio, estimación.

apprehend [æˌprɪˈhend] [a-pri-jend], va. 1. Aprehender, asir. 2. Aprehender, prender, asegurar alguna persona delincuente. 3. Aprender, comprender, concebir alguna cosa. 4. Recelar, temer, desconfiar, sospechar. **I had reason to apprehend,** tenía motivos para recelar. 5. Notar. **As I apprehend,** según creo. **To apprehend ones meaning,** comprender lo que otro se propone o quiere decir.

apprehender [æˌprɪˈhendər] [a-pri-jén-dar], s. el que aprehende.

apprehensible [ˌæprɪˈhensɪbl] [a-pri-jén-si-bol], a. Comprensible, que puede comprenderse.

apprehension [ˌæprɪˈhenʃən] [a-pri-jén-shon], s. 1. Aprehensión, comprensión, el acto de entender o concebir las cosas. 2. Aprehensión, primera operación del entendimiento que no llega a formar juicio ni discurso. 3. Aprehensión, recelo, sospecha o temor. 4. Aprehensión, presa o captura; embargo. **To be dull of apprehension,** tener la cabeza dura, ser rudo de inteligencia. **Be under no apprehension on that account,** no tenga usted aprehensión a ese respecto.

apprehensive [ˌæprɪˈhensɪv] [a-pri-jén-sif], a. 1. Aprehensivo, agudo, penetrante, capaz o perspicaz. 2. Aprehensivo, receloso, tímido. 3. Sensible, que responde a las impresiones sobre los sentidos. **Apprehensive capacity,** capacidad de comprensión.

apprehensively [ˌæprɪˈhensɪvlɪ] [a-pri-jén-sif-li], adv. Aprehensivamente.

apprehensiveness [ˌæprɪˈhensɪvnɪs] [a-pri-jén-sif-nis], s. Estado de ansiedad o temor.

apprentice [əˈprentɪs] [a-pren-tis], s. 1. Aprendiz, el que aprende un arte u oficio. **Shoemaker's apprentice,** aprendiz de zapatero. 2. Tirón, novicio, principiante.

apprentice, va. Poner a alguno de aprendiz. **To be apprenticed to,** estar de aprendiz con.

apprenticeage [əˌprentɪˈseɪdʒ] [a-pren-ti-seich], s. Aprendizaje.

apprenticeship [əˈprentɪʃɪp] [a-pren-tis-ship], s. Aprendizaje, el tiempo fijado para estar de aprendiz. **To serve one's apprenticeship,** Hacer o pasar su aprendizaje.

apprise o **apprize** [əˈpraɪz] [a-prais], va. Informar, avisar, instruir, dar parte. 2. Valuar, apreciar, tasar. V. APPRAISE.

apprizement [əˈpraɪzmənt] [a-prais-ment], s. Avalúo, tasa, valuación, aprecio.

apprizer [əˈpraɪzər] [a-prai-sar], s. Valuador, tasador.

approach [əˈprəʊtʃ] [a-prouch], vn. Acercarse, aproximarse física o moralmente; parecerse a, ser parecido a. **The appointed hour was approaching,** se acercaba la hora señalada. -va. Acercar, poner una cosa o persona cerca de otra. Enfocar, considerar. **To approach a problem,** enfocar un problema. **A passion which approaches madness,** una pasión que se acerca o raya en la locura. **A man who is easy to approach,** un hombre de fácil acceso o abordable.

approach, s. 1. Acceso, la acción de llegar o acercarse. **The approach of the troops,** el acercamiento de las tropas. 2. Proximidad, condición de propincuidad. 3. Acceso, entradas, facilidad al trato y communicación con alguno. **Difficult of approach,** de difícil acceso. 4. Entrada, paso a una habitación; medios, camino o modo de acercarse. 5. **Approaches,** pl. (Fort.) Aproches, ataques, los trabajos que hacen los que sitian una plaza. **To make approaches to a country,** intentar entrar en contacto con un país.

approachability [əˌprəʊtʃəˈbɪlɪtɪ] [a-prou-cha-bí-li-ti] s. Accesibilidad.

approachable [əˈprəʊtʃəbl] [a-próu-cha-bol], a. Accesible, de fácil acceso.

approacher [əˈprəʊtʃər] [a-próu-char], s. El que se acerca o aproxima.

approaching [əˈprəʊtʃɪŋ] [a-próu-chin], a. Próximo, cercano. **The approaching convention,** la próxima convención.

approachless [əˈprəʊtʃlɪs] [a-próuch-lis] a. Inaccesible, inabordable.

approbate [əˈprəbeɪt] [a-pro-beit], va. 1. Aprobar (en este sentido se usa en los Estados Unidos y no en Inglaterra. 2. Licenciar, autorizar.

approbation [ˌæprəˈbeɪʃən] [a-pro-béi-shon], s. Aprobación.

approbative [əˈprəbətɪv] [a-pro-ba-tif], **approbatory** [əˈprəbətərɪ] [a-pro-ba-to-ri], a. Aprobatorio, que denota aprobación.

appropinquate [ˌæprəpɪnˈkweɪt] [a-pro-pin-kueit], vn. (Des.) Apropincuarse, aproximarse, acercarse.

appropriable [əˈprəʊprɪbl] [a-pro-pri-bol], a. Apropiable.

appropriate [əˈprəʊprɪeɪt] [a-pro-prieit], va. 1. Apropiar, destinar para algún objeto o uso particular. 2. Apropiar o apropiarse, alegar o ejercer dominio haciéndose dueño de alguna cosa. 3. Enajenar un beneficio. 4. Aplicar, acomodar, adaptar. **Appropriate funds,** asignar fondos.

appropriate, a. Apropiado, apto, destinado para algún uso, particular, peculiar.

appropriately [əˈprəʊprɪɪtlɪ] [a-pro-prit-li], adv. Propiamente, aptamente.

appropriateness [əˈprəʊprɪɪnɪs] [a-pro-prit-nis], s. Aptitud; propiedad de aplicación.

appropriation [əˌprəʊprɪˈeɪʃən] [a-pro-pri-éishon], s. 1. Apropiación; alguna cosa puesta aparte formal u oficialmente para uso particular; la acción y efecto de apropiar. 2. Enajenación de un beneficio.

appropriator [əˌprəʊprɪˈeɪtər] [a-pro-pri-éitar], s. Apropiador.

approprietary [əˌprəʊprɪəˈterɪ] [a-pro-pria-ta-ri], s. Apropiador secular.

approvable [əˈpruːvəbl] [a-pru-va-bol], a. Digno de aprobación, que merece aprobación.

approval [əˈpruːvəl] [a-pru-val], **approvance** (Ant.) [əˈpruːvəns] [a-pru-vans], **approvement** [əˈpruːvmənt] [a-pruf-ment], s. Aprobación. 1. El testimonio de un reo que confiesa su delito y acusa a sus cómplices. 2. Mejoramiento o cercamiento y cultivo de tierras incultas. **On approval, a** prueba (on trial), previa aceptación (previous acceptance).

approve [əˈpruːv] [a-prúf], va. 1. Gustar, aprobar, calificar o dar por bueno; consentir, dar el beneplácito. 2. Probar, hacer patente o manifiesta alguna cosa. **To approve oneself to one,** hacerse agradable a alguno. 3. Probar, ensayar. 4. Mejorar (las tierras). V. IMPROVE. -vn. Dar por bueno; estimar con favor, gracia; se emplea a menudo con of. **I approve of it,** lo doy por bueno.

approved school [əˈpruːvdˌskuːl] [a-prúf-skul] s. Reformatorio, correccional.

approver [əˈpruːvər] [a-prú-var], s. 1. Aprobador, aprobante. 2. (For. Ant.) El reo que acusa a sus cómplices.

approving [əˈpruːvɪŋ] [a-prú-vin] a. Aprobatorio, de aprobación.

approximant [əˈprɒksɪmənt] [a-prok-si-ment], **approximate** [ap,pr<c',si,m+ê t], a. 1. Casi perfecto o completo. 2. Próximo, inmediato, aproximativo.

approximate [əˈprɒksɪmɪt] [a-prok-si-meit], va. Aproximar. -vn. Acercarse.

approximation [əˌprɒksɪˈmeɪʃən] [a-prok-si-méi-shon], s. 1. Aproximación, el acto y efecto de aproximarse. 2. Aproximación, estimación aproximada de una cosa. 3.

(Mat.) Aproximación, cálculo que se acerca en lo posible al valor real de una cantidad.

approximative [əˈprɒksɪmətɪv] [a-prok-sí-ma-tif], *a.* Aproximativo, que aproxima, perteneciente a la aproximación; poco más o menos.

approximatively [əˈprɒksɪmətɪvlɪ] [a-prok-si-ma-tif-li], *adv.* Aproximativamente, por aproximación.

appulse [əˈpuːlz] [a-púls], *s.* Choque, el encuentro de una cosa con otra.

appurtenance [əˈpɜːtɪnəns] [a-pér-te-nans], *s. (For.)* Adjunto; pertenencia, cualquier cosa menor anexa a otra mayor; dependencia.

appurtenant [əˈpɜːtɪnənt] [a-pér-ti-nant], *a. (For.)* Perteneciente, lo que pertenece por derecho.

apricot [ˈeɪprɪkɒt] [éi-pri-kot], *s.* Albaricoque, fruta de hueso: damasco. **Apricot-tree**, albaricoque. *(Mex.)* Chabacano.

April [ˈeɪprəl] [éi-pril], *s.* Abril, el cuarto mes del año. **April-fool-day**, el mes de abril. **April-fool**, el que sufre inocentadas. V. ALL-FOOLS'-DAY. **April showers bring May flowers**, en abril, aguas mil.

apron [ˈeɪprən] [éi-pron], *s.* 1. Delantal, pieza que se usa en la cocina para cubrir la parte delantera de la ropa, y que se ata por la cintura. 2. Mandil, delantal tosco que usan ciertos artesanos. 3. Batiente de un dique; plataforma a la entrada de un dique; cuero para proteger las piernas. 4. *(Art.)* Planchada o plomada de cañón, pieza delgada de plomo que se pone sobre el fogón para que no entre la humedad. **Apron of the stem,** *(Mar.)* albitana o contrarroda, **Apronman,** el tendero o artesano que lleva delantal. **Apron-strings,** cintas del delantal. **To be tied to the apronstrings,** estar dominado por una mujer.

aproned [ˈeɪprənd] [éi-pron], *a.* Vestido con delantal.

apropos [ˌæprəˈpəʊ] [a-pró-pou], *adv.* A propósito, oportunamente.

apse, apsis [æps] [æpsɪs] [aps] [ap-sis], *s.* 1. *(Arq.)* Ábside, bóveda, nicho. 2. *(Astr.)* V. APSIS. **Apse aisle,** deambulatorio.

apsidal [ˈæpsɪdl] [ap-si-dal], *a.* Del ábside.

apsidiole [æpsɪdɪəl] [ap-si-dial] *s. (Arq.)* Absidiolo.

apsis [æpsɪs] [ap-sis], *s.* APSIDES, *pl.* 1. *(Astr.)* Ápside, cada uno de los dos puntos de la órbita de un planeta, que se llaman apogeo y perigeo. 2. V. APSE.

apt [æpt] [apt], *a.* 1. Apto, idóneo, propio. 2. Inclinado, dado a alguna cosa u ocasionado a ella. 3. Pronto, vivo. **Too apt to forgive,** muy indulgente. **Apt to break,** frágil. **An apt scholar,** un estudiante capaz.

apterous [ˈæptɪrəs] [ap-te-ros], *a.* 1. *(Ent.)* Áptero, sin alas; se dice de los insectos. 2. *(Bot.)* Desprovisto de alas o prolongaciones parecidas a alas.

apteryx [ˈæptɪrɪks] [ap-te-riks], *s.* Apterix, kivi, género de aves de la Nueva Zelanda, que sólo tienen rudimentos de alas y carecen de cola.

aptitude [ˈæptɪtjuːd] [ap-ti-tiud], *s.* 1. Aptitud, idoneidad. 2. Tendencia o disposición natural para alguna cosa; facilidad. **Aptitude test,** prueba de aptitud.

aptly [ˈæptlɪ] [ap-tli], *adv.* 1. Aptamente. 2. Prontamente, perspicazmente.

aptness [ˈæptnɪs] [ap-nis], *s.* V. APTITUDE.

aptote [ˈæptəʊt] [ap-tot], *s.* Nombre que no se declina.

apuleius [æpjəˈlɪəs] [a-pia-lias] N. Apuleyo.

apyretic [æpɪˈretɪk] [a-pi-ré-tik] *a. (Med.)* Apirético.

apyrexia [æpɪˈreksɪə] [a-pi-rék-sia], *s.* Apirexia, ausencia de fiebre.

apyrous [ˈæpɪrəs] [a-pi-ros], *a.* No alterado por el calor extremo, como la mica; se diferencia de refractario.

aqua [ˈækwə] [a-kua], *s.* Agua: voz muy empleada en la farmacia y la química antigua. *(Lat.)* **Aqua ammonix,** agua de amoníaco.

aquacade [ækwəˈkeɪd] [a-kua-keid], *s.* Ballet acuático.

aqua-fortis [ækwəˈfɔːtɪs] [a-kua-fór-tis], *s.* Agua fuerte, el licor que se saca por destilación al fuego del nitro purificado

y el ácido vitriólico. **Aqua vitae,** aguardiente. **Aqua regia,** agua regia, el ácido nitro-muriático.

aquafortist [ækwəˈfɔːtɪst] [a-kua-fór-tis] *s.* Acuafortista.

aqualung [ˈækwəlʌŋ] [a-kua-lun], *s.* Escafandra autónoma.

aquamarine [ˌækwəməˈriːn] [a-kua-ma-rin], *s.* Aguamarina. *-a.* De color de aguamarina.

aquanaut [ˈækwənɔːt] [a-kua-naut], *s.* Acuanauta.

aquaplane [ˈækwəpl] [a-kua-plein], *s.* Acuaplano, hidropatín.

aquarelle [ˈækwərəl] [a-kua-rel] *s. (Arte)* Acuarela.

aquarium [əˈkwɛərɪəm] [a-kua-rium], *s.* Acuario, receptáculo o depósito para conservar peces y plantas acuáticas.

aquarius [əˈkwɛərɪəs] [a-kua-rios], *s. (Astr.)* Acuario, el undécimo signo del zodíaco.

aquatic [əˈkwætɪk] [a-kua-tik], **aquatile** [əˈkwətaɪl] [a-kua-tail], *a.* Acuático o acuátil, lo que vive o se cría en el agua.

aquatint [ˈækwətɪnt] [a-kua-tint], *s.* Acuatinta, especie de grabado o estampado, semejante al dibujo de tinta de china.

aqueduct [ˈækwɪdʌkt] [a-kui-dakt], *s.* Acueducto, conducto de agua. *(Mex.)* Cañería.

aqueous [ˈeɪkwəs] [éi-kuos], **aquose** [ˈækwəʊz] [éi-kuous], *a.* Acueo, acuoso. **Aqueous humor,** humor acuoso.

aqueousness [ˈeɪkwəsnɪs] [éi-kuos-nis], **aquiferous** [ˈeɪkwəfərəs] [ei-kui-fe-ros], *a.* Que conduce o surte agua o fluido acuoso.

aquiform [ˈækwɪfɔːm] [éi-kui-form], *a.* Semejante al agua; líquido.

aquila [ˈækwɪlə] [a-kui-la] N. *(Astr.)* Águila.

aquiline [ˈækwɪlaɪn] [a-kui-lain], *a.* Aguileño, parecido al águila.

Aquitaine [ˈækwɪteɪn] [a-kui-tein] N. *(Geogr.)* Aquitania.

aquosity [ˈækwəsɪtɪ] [a-kuó-si-ti], *s.* Acuosidad..

-ar, *sufijo.* Perteneciente a: semejante; también la persona a quien pertenece algo.

ara [ˈærə] [a-ra] *s. (Zool.)* Guacamayo. *(Astr.)* Ara (constellation).

Arab [ˈærəb] [a-rab], **Arabian** [A,rê',bi,An], *s.* 1. Árabe, el natural de Arabia.

Arabesque [ærəˈbesk] [a-ra-besk], *a.* Arabesco, al estilo de los árabes. *-s.* 1. Arabescos, adornos primorosos usados en la pintura y escultura, hechos con figuras geométricas, caracteres cúficos u hojas y flores entrelazadas. 2. Adornos fantásticos en formas de animales y plantas, como se emplean en los estilos romano y del renacimiento.

Arabia [əˈreɪbɪə] [a-rei-bia] N. *(Geogr.)* Arabia.

Arabian [əˈreɪbɪən] [a-rei-bian], **Arabic** [ˈærəbɪk] [a-ra-bik], **Arabical** [ˈærəbɪkəl] [a-ra-bi-kal], *a.* Arábigo, arábico. **Arabian Gulf,** golfo arábico. **Arabian nights,** las mil y una noches.

Arabic [ˈærəbɪk] [a-ra-bik], *s.* Lengua arábiga. El árabe. **Arabic numerals,** numeración arábiga.

Arabically [ˈærəbɪklɪ] [a-ra-bi-ka-li], *adv.* A manera de los árabes.

Arabicism [ˈærəbɪsɪzm] [a-ra-bi-sísem] *s.* Arabismo.

Arabism [ˈærəbɪzm] [a-ra-bísem], *s.* Arabismo, giro propio de la lengua árabe, adoptado en otra.

Arabist [ˈærəbɪst] [a-ra-bist], *s.* Persona versada en la lengua arábiga.

Arabization [ˌærəbɪˈzeɪʃən] [a-ra-bi-séi-shon] *s.* Arabización.

Arabize [ˈærəbaɪz] [á-ra-bais] *va.* Arabizar.

arable [ˈærəbl] [a-rabol], *a.* Labrantío, dispuesto o apto para la labranza. **Arable ground,** tierra labrantía.

arachnida [əˈræknɪdə] [a-rak-ni-da], *s. pl. (Ento.)* Arácnidos o aracnéidos, una de las clases de los artrópodos. Comprende las arañas y otros artrópodos de ocho patas.

arachnoid [əˈræknɔɪd] [a-rak-noid], *a. y s. (Anat.)* Aracnoides, una de las tres membranas que envuelven el encéfalo.

arack [ə'ræk] [a-rak], s. (Des.) Aguardiente de azúcar. V. ARRACK.

aragonite [ˈærəgənaɪt] [a-ra-go-nait], s. Aragonito, cal carbonatada cristalina. Se llama vulgarmente, piedra de Santa Casilda.

Aramaic [ˌærəˈmeɪk] [a-ra-meik], a. Arameo, aramea, que se refiere al país de Aram. -s. Lengua aramea, nombre dado al asirio y al caldeo; la clase septentrional de las lenguas semíticas.

Aramean [ærəˈmiːn] [a-ra-min], a. V. ARAMAIC. -s. 1. Habitante de la Aramea (Siria y Mesopotamia). 2. Lengua aramea.

araneous [ærəˈnəʊs] [a-ra-nous], a. Semejante a la telaraña.

arapaima [ærəˈpaɪmə] [a-ra-pái-ma] s. (Zool.) Arapaima.

aration [æˈrəʃən] [a-rá-shon], s. (Ant.) Aradura, la acción o ejercicio de arar.

Araucanian [ærəʊˈkeɪnɪən] [a-rou-kéi-nian], a. y s. Araucano, relativo a los indígenas de la Araucania, en Chile, y a su lengua.

araucaria [ærəʊˈkeɪrɪə] [a-rou-kéi-ria] s. (Bot.) Araucaria.

arbalest, arbalist [ˈɑːbəlɪ] [ar-ba-list], s. Ballesta, arma para disparar flechas o saetas.

arbiter [ˈɑːbɪtəʳ] [ár-bi-tar], s. 1. Arbitrador, compromisario, el juez árbitro con quien las partes se avienen para que ajuste sus controversias. 2. árbitro, el que puede hacer una cosa por sí solo, sin dependencia de otro.

arbitrable [ˈɑːbɪtəbl] [ar-bái-tra-bol], a. Arbitrable, que pende del arbitraje; que se puede arbitrar.

arbitrably [ˈɑːbɪtəblɪ] [ar-bí-tra-bli], adv. A discreción.

arbitrage [ˈɑːbɪtrɪdʒ] [ár-bi-treich] s. Arbitraje.

arbitral [ˈɑːbɪtrəl] [ár-bi-tral] a. Arbitral.

arbitrament [ˈɑːbɪtrəmənt] [ar-bí-tre-ment], s. Arbitraje. V. ARBITRATION.

arbitrarily [ˈɑːbɪtərɪlɪ] [ar-bi-trá-ri-li], adv. Arbitrariamente.

arbitrariness [ˈɑːbɪtrərɪnɪs] [ar-bi-tra-ri-nis], s. Arbitrariedad, despotismo, poder absoluto.

arbitrarious [ˈɑːbɪtrərɪəs] [ar-bi-tra-rious], a. (Des.) V. ARBITRARY.

arbitrary [ˈɑːbɪtərɪ] [ar-bí-tra-ri], a. Arbitrario, despótico, absoluto.

arbitrate [ˈɑːbɪtreɪt] [ár-bi-treit], va. Arbitrar, juzgar o determinar como árbitro. -vn. Dar juicio, decidir como árbitro.

arbitration [ˌɑːbɪˈreɪʃən] [ar-bi-tréi-shon], s. Arbitramento, arbitraje, arbitración, la sentencia dada por un juez árbitro; la audiencia y determinación de una controversia ante una persona o personas mutuamente aceptadas por los interesados. **By arbitration**, por arbitraje, arbitralment. **Arbitration bond**, compromiso. **Arbitration of exchange**, arbitraje de cambio; operación de cambio de valores mercantiles, buscando la utilidad en los precios comparados de diferentes plazas.

arbitrator [ˈɑːbɪteɪtəʳ] [ar-bi-tréi-tar], sm. Arbitrador, árbitro.

arbitratix [ˈɑːbɪtrətɪks] [ar-bi-tra-tiks], **arbitress** [ˈɑːbɪtres] [ar-bi-tres], sf. Arbitradora.

arbitrement [ˈɑːbɪtrəbl] [ar-bi-tre-ment], s. Arbitrio, elección, determinación, compromiso.

arbor [ˈɑːbəʳ] [ár-bor], s. 1. árbol, eje de una rueda, de una máquina. 2. Árbol, en ciertos nombres botánicos, v.g. **Arborvitae**, q.v. **Arbor Dianae**, árbol de Diana; árbol de plata.

arbor, arbour, s. Emparrado, enramada; glorieta.

arbor-vitae [ˈɑːbəvɪte] [ar-bor-ví-te], s. 1. Tuya, árbol conífero. 2. (Anat.) Aspecto ramoso en una sección radial del cerebro.

arboreal, arboreous [ˈɑːbɔːrɪəl] [ar-bó-rial], **arborous** [ˈɑːbɔːrəs] [ar-bó-ros], a. Arbóreo.

arborescence [ˈɑːbərəsəns] [ar-bó-re-sans], s. 1. Arborescencia. 2. (Miner.) Arborización, ramaje dibujado naturalmente en algunos minerales y cristalizaciones.

arborescent [ˈɑːbərəsənt] [ar-bó-re-sant], a. Arborescente, que crece como un árbol; que va pareciendo árbol.

arboret [ˈɑːbərɪt] [ár-bo-rit], s. 1. Arbolillo, arbusto. 2. Soto, arboleda.

arboretum [ˈɑːbərɪtəs] [ar-bo-rí-tum], s. Plantel, almáciga, criadero de árboles.

arboriculture [ˈɑːbərɪkʌltʃəʳ] [ar-bo-ri-kál-char], s. Arboricultura, arte de cultivar los árboles y arbustos.

arboriculturist [ˈɑːbərɪkʌltʃərɪst] [ar-bo-ri-kál-cha-rist] s. Arboricultor.

arborist [ˈɑːbərɪst] [ár-bo-rist], s. Arbolista, el que se dedica por oficio al cultivo de los árboles.

arborization [ˈɑːbərɪzeishon] [ar-bo-ri-séi-shon] s. Arborización.

arbuscle [ˈɑːbʌskl] [ar-báskel], s. Arbustillo o arbusto pequeño.

arbute [ˈɑːbjuːt] [ar-biút], s. (Bot.) Fresal. V. ARBUTUS.

arbutean [ˈɑːbjuːtɪən] [ar-biú-tian], a. Lo perteneciente al fresal.

arbutus [ˈɑːbjuːtəs] [ar-bu-tus], s. 1. Madroño, reducido género de árboles y arbustos de la familia de las ericáceas. 2. **Trailing arbutus**, gayuba, planta rastrera de la p r i m a v e r a . V. MAYPLOWER.

arc [ɑːk] [árk], s. Arco de círculo. **Electric arc**, arco voltaico.

arc-light [ˈɑːkˌlaɪt] [ˈɑːkˌlaɪt] [ark-lait], s. Alumbrado eléctrico en que se usa el arco galvánico.

arcade [ˈɑːkeɪd] [ar-keid], s. 1. Arcada, bóveda continuada o una continuación de arcos. 2. Pasaje, galería cubierta llena de tiendas. **Shopping arcade**, galería comercial.

arcadia [ˈɑːkeɪdɪə] [ar-kéi-dia] N. Arcadia.

arcadian [ˈɑːkeɪdɪən] [ar-kéi-dian], a. Arcadio, árcade; idealmente rural o sencillo; pastoral. -s. Arcadio, habitante de Arcadia.

arcana [ˈɑːkənə] [ar-ka-na] s. pl. Arcanos.

arcane [ɑːˈkeɪn] [ar-kéin], a. Arcano, misterioso.

arcanum [ˈɑːkənʌm] [ar-ka-nom], s. Arcano. **Arcana**, misterios, arcanos.

arch [ɑːtʃ] [arch], s. Arco. 1. Arco de círculo. 2. Arco de puente. 3. Bóveda, obra de mampostería, etc., en forma de arco. 4. Arco del cielo. **The arch of heaven**, la bóveda celeste. **Arch of the aorta**, (Anat.) la curvatura de la aorta. **Segmental arch**, arco abocinado. **Gothic arch, pointed arch**, arco ojival, arco gótico. **Horse-shoe arch**, arco de herradura. **Semicircular arch**, arco de medio punto. **Triumphal arch**, arco de triunfo.

arch, va. 1. Arquear, formar en figura de arco; encorvar. 2. Abovedar, cubrir con bóvedas o arcos. -vn. Formar bóveda o bóvedas. **The trees arch overhead**, los árboles forman bóveda en lo alto.

arch, a. 1. Travieso, inquieto; picaresco, socarrón, astuto. 2. Principal, insigne, de primer orden, grande. **An arch wag**, un gran pillarín, un martagón. Se usa en composición como aumentativo. **An arch look**, una mirada picaresca.

archaelogical [ˌɑːkɪəˈlədʒɪkəl] [ar-kio-ló-chi-kal] a. Arqueológico.

archaeologist [ˌɑːkɪəˈlədʒɪst] [ar-kió-lo-chist] s. Arqueólogo.

archaeology [ˌɑːkɪəˈlədʒɪ] [ar-kió-lo-chi], s. Arqueología, discurso o tratado de cosas antiguas.

archaeopterix [ˌɑːkɪəpˈterɪks] [ar-keop-te-riks] s. (Zool.) Arqueoptérix.

archaic [ɑːˈkeɪk] [ar-keik], a. 1. Arcaico, anticuado, que va cayendo en desuso. 2. De un período anterior al desarrollo cumplido de un arte.

archaism [ˈɑːkeɪɪzəm] [ar-keisem], s. Arcaísmo, uso afectado de voces o frases anticuadas.

archaist [ˈɑːkeɪɪst] [ar-keist] s. Arcaísta.

archaistic [ˈɑːkeɪstɪk] [ar-keis-tik] a. Arcaizante.

archaize [ˈɑːkeɪz] [ar-keis] va./vn. Arcaizar.

archangel [ˈɑːkˌeɪndʒəl] [ar-kéin-chal], s. 1. Arcángel. 2. (Bot.) Ortiga muerta.

archangelical [ˈɑːkˌeɪndʒəlɪkl] [ar-kan-ché-li-kal], *a.* Arcangelical, arcangélico.

archapostle [ˈɑːkəposl] [ar-ka-pósel], *s.* Apóstol principal.

archarchitect [ˈɑːkərkɪtekt] [ar-kar-ki-tekt], *s.* Arquitecto supremo.

archbishop [ˈɑːtʃbɪʃəp] [arch-bí-shop], *s.* Arzobispo.

archbishopric [ˈɑːtʃbɪʃəprɪk] [arch-bí-shoprik], *s.* Arzobispado.

archbuilder [ˈɑːtʃbɪldəʳ] [arch-bíl-dar], *s.* Arquitecto o fabricador principal.

archchanter [ˈɑːtʃtʃɑːntəʳ] [arch-chan-tar], *s.* Cantor principal.

archconfraternity [ˈɑːtʃkʌnfrɑˌtɜːnɪtɪ] [arch-kon-fra-tér-ni-ti] *s.* Archicofradía.

archconspirator [ˈɑːtʃkɒnspɪˈrətəʳ] [arch-kons-pi-ré-tar], *s.* Conspirador principal.

archcritic [ˈɑːtʃkrɪtɪk] [arch-kri-tik], *s.* Criticón.

archdeacon [ˈɑːtʃdiːkən] [arch-dí-kon], *s.* Arcediano, antes el primero de los diáconos. Hoy es alta dignidad eclesiástica y tiene el primer rango después del obispo; auxiliar de un obispo.

archdeaconate [ˈɑːtʃdiːkənət] [arch-dí-ko-neit] *s.* (*Rel.*) Arcedianato.

archdeaconry [ˈɑːtʃdiːkənrɪ] [arch-dí-kon-ri], **archdeaconship** [ˈɑːtʃdiːkənʃɪp] [arch-dí-kon-ship], *s.* Arcedianato, la dignidad o jurisdicción del arcediano.

archdiocesan [ˈɑːtʃdaɪɒsɪsən] [arch-daia-sisen] *a.* (*Rel.*) Archidiocesano.

archdiocese [ˈɑːtʃdaɪəsɪs] [arch-daia-sis] *s.* Archidiócesis.

archdivine [ˈɑːtʃdɪvaɪn] [arch-di-vain], *s.* Teólogo principal.

archducal [ˈɑːtʃdjuːkəl] [arch-diú-kal], *a.* Archiducal.

archduchess [ˈɑːtʃdjuːtʃɪs] [arch-diú-chis], *sf.* Archiduquesa, princesa de Austria; la hija del emperador y la hija o mujer de un archiduque.

archduchy [ˈɑːtʃdjuːkɪ] [arch-diú-ki], *s.* Archiducado: distrito o dignidad de archiduque.

archduke [ˈɑːtʃdjuːk] [arch-diúk], *s.* Archiduque, título que se da a los príncipes de la casa de Austria.

archdukedom [ˈɑːtʃdjuːkdəm] [arch-diúk-dom], *s.* Archiducado.

archean, archaian [ˈɑːkaɪən] [ar-kaian], *a.* Arqueano, perteneciente a los estratos o al período más viejo de la historia geológica.

arched [ˈɑːtʃt] [archt], *a.* Arqueado, hecho en forma de arco.

archegonium [ˈɑːkɪɡəʊnɪəm] [ar-ki-go-niom] *s.* (*Bot.*) Arquegonio.

archenemy [ˈɑːkenɪmɪ] [ar-ke-ni-mi], *s.* El mayor enemigo; el demonio.

archeologian [ˈɑːkɪəlɒdʒɪən] [ar-kio-ló-chian], *s.* V. ARCHEOLOGIST.

archologic, archeological [ˈɑːkɪəlɒdʒɪk] [ˈɑːkɪəlɒdʒɪkl] [ar-kio-ló-chik] [ar-kio-ló-chi-kal], *a.* Arqueológico, relativo o la arqueología, o versado en ella.

archeologist [ˈɑːkɪəlɒdʒɪst] [ar-kió-lo-chist] *s.* Arqueólogo, el versado en la arqueología.

archeology [ˈɑːkɪəlɒdʒɪ] [ar-kió-lo-chi], *s.* Arqueología, estudio de monumentos, medallas, inscripciones, etc., de la antigüedad.

archer [ˈɑːtʃəʳ] [ár-char], *s.* Arquero, el que tira con arco o ballesta. (*Astr.*) **The archer,** el Sagitario.

archeress [ˈɑːtʃərɪs] [ár-che-res], *sf.* Arquera, ballestera.

archery [ˈɑːtʃərɪ] [ár-che-ri], *s.* El arte de tirar con arco y flecha.

arches-court [ˈɑːtʃɪzˌkɔːt] [ár-chis-kért], *s.* Un tribunal eclesiástico de Londres.

archetypal [ˈɑːkɪˈtaɪpl] [ar-ke-taipl], *a.* Lo perteneciente al arquetipo.

archetype [ˈɑːkɪtaɪp] [ár-ki-taip], *s.* Arquetipo, patróno o modelo.

archfelon [ˈɑːkfɪlon] [ark-fe-lon], *s.* Reo principal.

archfiend [ˈɑːkfiːnd] [ark-find], *s.* El demonio, el diablo, el enemigo mortal.

archflatterer [ˈɑːkflatərəʳ] [ark-fla-te-rar], *s.* Gran adulador.

archfounder [ˈɑːkfəʊndəʳ] [ark-faun-dar], *s.* Fundador principal.

archgovernor [ˈɑːkɡovənəʳ] [ark-go-ver-nor], *s.* Gobernador en jefe.

archheresy [ˈɑːkərəsɪ] [ar-ke-re-si], *s.* Herejía enorme.

archheretic [ˈɑːkərətɪk] [ar-ke-re-tik], *s.* Gran heresiarca.

archhypocrite [ˈɑːkɪpəkrɪt] [ark-i-po-krit], *s.* Hipocritón, santurrón.

archiater [ˈɑːkɪətəʳ] [ar-kia-tar], *s.* Protomédico.

arcical [ˈɑːkɪkəl] [ár-ki-kal], *a.* principal, primario.

archidiaconal [ˈɑːtʃɪdɪəkənəl] [ar-chi-dia-ko-nal], *a.* Perteneciente al arcediano.

archiepiscopacy [ˈɑːkɪepɪskɒpəsɪ] [ar-ki-e-pis-ko-pa-si], *s.* Rango, dignidad de arzobispo.

archiepiscopal [ˈɑːkɪepɪskɒpəl] [ar-ki-e-pis-ko-pal], *a.* Arquiepiscopal o arzobispal.

archiepiscopate [ˈɑːkɪepɪskɒpeɪt] [ar-ki-e-pis-ko-peit], *s.* Arzobispado, dignidad, jurisdicción de un arzobispo.

archil [ˈɑːkɪl] [ar-kil], *s.* 1. (*Bot.*) Archilla, especie de liquen del género Roccella. R. tinctoria. 2. Materia de tinte que se obtiene de esta planta. V. ORCHIL.

archimandrite [ˈɑːkɪməndraɪt] [ar-ki-man-drait], *s.* Archimandrita, superior de un monasterio en la iglesia griega.

Archimedes [ˌɑːkɪˈmiːdiːz] [ar-ki-mi-dis] *N.* Arquímedes. **Archimedes' screw,** tornillo de Arquímedes.

arching [ˈɑːkɪn] [ar-kin], *a.* Arqueado.

archipelago [ˌɑːkɪˈpelɪɡəʊ] [ar-ki-ple-li-gou], *s.* Archipiélago, parte del mar poblada de islas; por antonomasia (con mayúscula), las islas de Grecia en el Mar Egeo.

archips [ˈɑːkɪps] [ar-kips] *s.* (*Zool.*) Arquípteros.

architect [ˈɑːkɪtekt] [ar-ki-tect], *s.* 1. Arquitecto, alarife. 2. (*Fig.*) Artífice. **Landscape architect,** arquitecto paisajista.

architectonic [ˌɑːkɪtekˈtɒnɪk] [ar-ki-tek-to-nik], **architectonical** [ˌɑːkɪtekˈtɒnɪkl] [ar-ki-tek-to-ni-kal], *a.* Arquitectónico, versado en la arquitectura, o perteneciente a ella.

architectonics [ˌɑːkɪtekˈtɒnɪks] [ar-ki-tek-to-niks], *s.* Arquitectura, arte arquitectónico.

architectural [ˈɑːkɪtektʃərəl] [ar-ki-ték-cha-ral], *a.* Arquitectural, perteneciente a la arquitectura; constructor, que construye.

archecture [ˈɑːkɪtektʃəʳ] [ar-ki-ték-char], *s.* 1. Arquitectura, el arte de construir y hacer edificios. 2. Arquitectura, la obra ejecutada según las reglas del arte.

architrave [ˈɑːkɪteɪv] [ar-ki-treif], *s.* Arquitrabe, la parte inferior del cornisamento que descansa inmediatamente sobre el capitel de la columna.

archive [ˈɑːkaɪv] [ar-kaif], *s.* 1. Archivo, el paraje en que se guardan papeles, escrituras, instrumentos o documentos importantes. Más usado en plural. 2. Archivo, documento o escritura que se guarda en el lugar de ese nombre. **National Archives,** archivo nacional.

archivist [ˈɑːkɪvɪst] [ar-ki-vist], *s.* Archivero.

archivolt [ˈɑːkɪvəʊlt] [ar-ki-volt] *s.* (*Arq.*) Archivolta, arquivolta.

archlike [ˈɑːklaɪk] [ark-laik], *a.* Fabricado como arco.

archlute [ˈɑːklɒt] [ark-lut] *s.* (*Mús.*) Archilaúd.

archly [ˈɑːklɪ] [ar-kli], *adv.* Jocosamente, sutilmente.

archmagician [ˈɑːkmadʒɪʃən] [ark-ma-chi-shan], *s.* Mágico principal.

archness [ˈɑːknɪs] [ark-nis], *s.* Travesura, astucia, sutileza de ingenio.

archon [ˈɑːkɒn] [ar-kon], *s.* Arconte, magistrado supremo de la antigua Atenas.

archonship [ˈɑːkɒnʃɪp] [ar-kon-ship] o **archontate** [ˈɑːkɒnteɪt] [ar-kon-teit] *s.* Arcontado.

archpastor ['ɑːkpɑstəʳ] [ark-pas-tor], *s.* El Pastor de almas, Jesucristo.

archphilosopher ['ɑːkfɪləsəfəʳ] [ark-fi-ló-so-far], *s.* Arquifilósofo, filósofo principal.

archpillar ['ɑːkpɪləʳ] [ark-pi-lar], *s.* Columna principal.

archpoet, *s. V.* POET LAURFATE.

archpolitician ['ɑːkpɒlɪtɪʃən] [ark-po-li-ti-shan], *s.* Político profundo.

archprelate ['ɑːkprɪt] [ark-pri-leit], *s.* Arcipreste, el primero o principal de los presbíteros.

archpriest ['ɑːkpriːst] [ark-prist], *s.* Gran sacerdote. Arcipreste.

archpriesthood ['ɑːkpriːsthʊd] [ark-prist-jud] o **archpriestship** ['ɑːkpriːstʃɪp] [ark-prist-ship] *s.* Arciprestazgo.

archprimate ['ɑːkprɪt] [ark-pri-meit], *s.* Primado principal.

archprophet ['ɑːkprɒfɪt] [ark-pro-fit], *s.* profeta principal.

archrebel ['ɑːkrebl] [ark-re-bol], *s.* Rebelde principal; Satanás.

archtraitor ['ɑːkreɪtəʳ] [ark-trei-tar], *s.* Gran traidor; el demonio.

archtreasurer ['ɑːkreʒərəʳ] [ark-tre-sha-rar], *s.* Tesorero mayor.

archtyrant ['ɑːkˌtaɪrənt] [ark-tai-ran], *s.* El tirano o déspota por excelencia.

archvillain ['ɑːkvɪlən] [ark-vi-lan], *s.* Bellaconazo, picarón.

archvillainy ['ɑːkvɪlənɪ] [ark-vi-la-ni], *s.* Bellaquería grande.

archway ['ɑːtʃweɪ] [arch-uei] *s.* Arco, arcada.

archwise ['ɑːtʃwaɪz] [arch-uais], *a.* En figura de arco.

arc lamp ['ɑːklæmp] [ark-lamp] *s. (Elec.)* Lámpara de arco.

arcograph ['ɑːkɒgræf] [ar-ko-graf], *s.* Arcógrafo, instrumento con que se traza un arco circular sin punto céntrico.

arctation ['ɑːkteɪʃən] [ark-tei-shon], *s.* Angostura, estrechez.

Arctic ['ɑːktik] [ark-tik], *a.* Ártico, septentrional; que designa el polo septentrional o las regiones cercanas a él; frígido. **Arctic Circle,** Círculo Polar Ártico. **Arctic Ocean,** Océano ártico.

arctics ['ɑːktikz] [ark-tiks] *s. pl. U.S.* Botas impermeables.

Arcturus ['ɑːktʊrəs] [ark-turas], *s.* Arturo, estrella fija de primera magnitud, situada en la constelación Bootes.

arcuate ['ɑːkweit] [ar-kueit], *a.* Arqueado, formado en figura de arco.

arcuation ['ɑːkweɪʃən] [ar-kuei-shon], *s.* 1. encorvamiento, curvatura, calidad de corvo. 2. Obras encorvadas. 3. *(Hort.)* Acodadura. *V.* LAYERINO.

arc weld ['ɑːkˌweild] [ark-ueld], *s.* Soldadura de arco.

ardash ['ɑːdaʃ] [ar-dash], *s.* Ardaza, seda basta de Persia.

ardassine ['ɑːdasɪn] [ar-da-sin], *s.* Ardasina, seda finísima de Persia.

ardency ['ɑːdansɪ] [ar-dansi], **ardentness** ['ɑːdantnɪs] [ar-dant-sis], *s.* Ardor, vehemencia, ansia, anhelo, calor.

ardent ['ɑːdant] [ar-dant], *a.* 1. Ardiente, lo que arde. 2. Ardiente, vehemente. 3. Apasionado, vivo, ansioso.

ardently ['ɑːdanlɪ] [ar-dan-li], *adv.* Apasionadamente, ardientemente.

ardor, ardour ['ɑːdəʳ] [ar-daʳ], *s.* 1. Ardor, calor. 2. *(Fig.)* Ardor, pasión.

arduous ['ɑːdəs] [ar-dos], *a.* 1. Arduo, alto, inaccesible o difícil de subir. 2. Arduo, difícil.

arduously ['ɑːdəslɪ] [ar-dos-li], *adv.* Arduamente, difícilmente.

arduousness ['ɑːdəsnɪs] [ar-dos-nis] *s.* Dificultad.

are ['ɑːʳ] [aʳ], Plural del presente de indicativo del verbo To Be, **We are, you are, they are,** Somos, sois, son, o estamos, estáis, están.

Âre, *s.* Medida de superficie, cuadrado que tiene diez metros de lado.

area ['ɛərɪə] [ea-ria], *s.* 1. Área, la superficie comprendida entre ciertas líneas o límites. 2. Espacio o extensión superficial. **Area of a building,** área de un edificio, todo el espacio que ocupa. 3. Patio, corral; cualquier espacio cercado y no cubierto. 4. Un pequeño patio a nivel más bajo que el de la calle, delante de las puertas o ventanas del sótano. **Goal area,** área de gol. **Metropolitan area,** zona metropolitana.

area code ['ɛərɪəˌkəʊd] [ea-ria-koud] *s.* Prefijo (telephone).

areaway ['ɛərɪəweɪ] [ea-ria-uei] *s. U.S.* Patio.

areca ['ɑːrɪkə] [a-ri-ka], *s.* 1. Árbol de Malabar, especie de palma altísima. 2. Su fruta, que se masca como el betel.

arefaction [ɑːfækʃən] [ar-fak-shon], *s. (Des.)* La acción y efecto de secar o secarse.

arefy ['ɛərɪfaɪ] [ea-ri-fai], *va. (Des.)* Secar, extraer la humedad de algún cuerpo.

arena [əˈriːnə] [a-ri-na], *s.* Arena, sítio destinado a las luchas entre los antiguos. Campo de combate, círculo de acción.

arenaceous ['ɑːrɪnəʃəs] [a-ri-na-shos], **arenose** ['ɑːrɪnəʊs] [a-ri-nous], *a.* Arenisco, arenoso, lleno de arena o de arenillas.

arenicolous ['ærɪnɪkʌləs] [a-ri-ni-ko-los] *a. (Zool.)* Arenícola.

aren't [ɑːnt] [árnt] Contracción de *are not.*

areola [əˈriːələ] [a-ria-la], *s.* 1. *(Anat.)* Aréola, círculo mamario. 2. Círculo que rodea una pústula, un punto inflamado.

areolar [əˈriːələʳ] [a-ria-laʳ], *a.* Areolar. *V.* CONNECTIVE.

areole [əˈriːəl] [a-rial] *s.* Areola, aréola.

areometer [əˈriːəmɪtəʳ] [a-rio-mi-taʳ], *s.* Areómetro, instrumento para pesar los licores espirituosos.

arête [əˈriːt] [a-rit] *s.* Arista.

argal ['ɑːɡəl] [ar-gal], **argol** ['ɑːɡɒl] [ar-gol], *s.* Tártaro.

argand ['ɑːɡænd] [ar-gand], *a.* Perteneciente al alumbrado inventado por Aimé Argand, de Ginebra; se llama en España quinqué, del nombre del fabricante francés de dichas lámparas, Mr. Quinquet.

argent ['ɑːdʒənt] [ar-chant], *a. (Her.)* Blanco; plata, en los escudos de armas.

argentation [ɑːdʒənˈteɪʃən] [ar-chan-tei-shon], *s.* La acción de platear.

argentiferous ['ɑːdʒəntɪˌfərəs] [ar-chan-ti-fo-ros], *a.* Argentífero, que contiene plata.

Argentina [ɑːdʒənˈtiːnə] [ar-chan-ti-na], *N. (Geogr.)* Argentina.

Argentine [ɑːdʒənˈtiːn] [ar-chan-tin], *a.* 1. Argentino, sonoro como la plata, de color de plata. 2. Argentino, perteneciente a la República Argentina, o Río de la Plata. - *s.* 1. Metal blanco plateado. 2. Un precipitado de estaño y cinc. 3. La materia plateada del color de las escamas de los peces. 4. Argentino, natural de la República Argentina, o residente en ella.

Argentinean [ɑːdʒənˈtiːnən] [ar-chan-ti-nian], *a. /s.* Argentino.

argil ['ɑːdʒɪl] [ar-chil], *s.* Arcilla, tierra o barro que usan los alfareros. *V.* ALUMINA.

argillaceous ['ɑːdʒɪləʃəs] [ar-chi-la-shos], **argillous** ['ɑːdʒɪləs] [ar-chi-los], *a.* Arcilloso, lo que tiene arcilla o alúmina.

argive ['ɑːɡɪv] [ar-guif] *a./s. (Hist.)* Argivo.

Argon ['ɑːɡɒn] [ar-gon] *s. (Quím.)* Argón.

argonaut ['ɑːɡənɔːt] [ar-go-not], *s.* 1. Argonauta, uno de los compañeros de Jasón. 2. *(Zool.)* Argonauta, nautilo papiráceo: especie de molusco cefalópodo. Es una jibia octópoda con concha papirácea.

argosy ['ɑːɡɒsɪ] [ar-go-si], *s.* Bajel o buque grande mercante.

argot ['ɑːɡəʊ] [ar-gou], *s.* Jerga, jerigonza.

arguable ['ɑːɡkʊəbl] [ar-guiu-eibol] *a.* Defendible, discutible.

argue ['ɑːɡjuː] [ar-guiu], *vn.* Razonar, disputar, discurrir. **To argue with,** argüir, discutir con. -*va.* 1. probar, hacer ver, persuadir con razones. 2. Argüir, disputar; probar con argumentos.

arguer ['ɑːɡəʳ] [ar-gaʳ], *s.* Argumentador, el que arguye.

arguing [ˈɑːgʊɪŋ] [ar-güin], *s.* razonamiento, argumento.

argument [ˈɑːgjʊmənt] [ar-guiu-ment], *s.* 1. Argumento, tema o materia de algún discurso o escrito, asunto. 2. Argumento, la razón que se alega a favor o en contra de alguna cosa. (*For.*) Alegato. 3. Razonamiento, silogismo, prueba. 4. Argumento, el contenido de una obra en compendio o extracto. 5. (*Des.*) Argumento, controversia. **Let's no have any argument,** no discutamos. **It is beyond argument,** es indiscutible.

argumental [ˌɑːgjʊˈmentəl] [ar-guiu-men-tal], *a.* Argumentista, que pertenece a los argumentos.

argumentation [ˈɑːgjʊmənˌteɪʃən] [ar-guiu-men-teishon], *s.* Argumentación, raciocinio.

argumentative [ˈɑːgjʊˌmentətɪv] [ar-guiu-men-ta-tif], *a.* Argumentativo, demostrativo, aficionado a la argumentación; fundado en el raciocinio, que tiende a probar.

argumentatively [ˌɑːgjʊmentəˈtɪvlɪ] [ar-guiu-men-ta-tifli], *adv.* Argumentativamente.

argus [ˈɑːgəs] [ar-gos], *s.* 1. Argos, personaje fabuloso que tenía cien ojos. 2. Argos, faisán de China.

argute [ˈɑːgjuːt] [ar-guiut], *a.* 1. Agudo, sutil; astuto, perspicaz. 2. Agudo, penetrante (hablando de sonidos). 3. (*Bot.*) Provisto de dientes agudos como una hoja aserrada.

arguteness [ˈɑːgjuːtnɪs] [ar-guiut-nis], *s.* Argucia, agudeza, sutileza, perspicacia.

arhizal, arhizous [ˈɑːhɪzəl] [ar-ji-sal], *a.* (*Bot.*) V. ARRHIZOUS.

aria [ˈɑːrɪə] [a-ria], *s.* (*Mús.*) Aria, composición lírica para una sola voz.

Arian [ˈɑːrɪən] [a-rian], *s.* Arriano, el que sigue la herejía de Arrio.

Arianism [ˈɛərɪənɪzəm] [ea-ria-ni-sem], *s.* Arrianismo, la herejía de Arrio.

arid [ˈærɪd] [a-rid], *a.* árido, seco, sequizo, enjugado, enjuto.

aridity [ˈærɪdɪtɪ] [a-ri-di-ti] o **aridness** [ˈærɪdnɪs] [a-ridnis], *s.* 1. Aridez, gran sequedad de la tierra. 2. Sequedad; falta de devoción y fervor.

Aries [ˈɛəriːz] [a-ris], *s.* (*Astr.*) Aries, el primer signo del zodíaco; también, constelación del zodíaco.

arietta [ˈærɪɪtə] [a-ri-ita], *s.* (*Mús.*) Arieta, aria corta.

aright [əˈraɪt] [a-rait], *adv.* 1. Acertadamente. 2. Rectamente, puramente, bien. **To set aright,** rectificar, enderezar o poner una cosa o negocio en el estado que debe tener.

aril [ˈærɪl] [a-ril], **arillus** [ˈærɪlˌʌs] [A,ril',us], *s.* 1. Arilla, cubierta o zurrón del grano. 2. Arila, parte carnosa de un fruto.

arillated [ˈærɪlɪd] [a-ri-lei-tid], *a.* Arilado, que tiene arila.

ariolation [ˌærɪəˈleɪʃn] [a-rio-lei-shon], *s.* Adivinación.

arise [əˈraɪz] [a-rais], *vn.* (*Pret.* AROSE, *pp.* ARISEN) 1. Subir, elevarse. 2. Surgir, aparecer. 3. Levantarse, ponerse en pie. 4. Proceder (de); provenir (de). 5. Presentarse, ofrecerse, suscitarse, originarse. 6. Sublevarse, levantarse. **When the sun arose,** cuando salió el sol. **Another difficulty then arose,** entonces surgió otra dificultad. **The people arose against the tyrant,** el pueblo se sublevó contra el tirano.

arisen [əˈrɪzn] [a-ri-sen], *pp.* de ARISE.

arista [ˈærɪstə] [a-ris-ta], *s.* (*Bot.*) Arista. V. AWN.

aristarch [ˈærɪstɑːk] [a-ris-tark] *s.* Aristarco.

aristarchus [ˌærɪstɑːkəs] [a-ris-tar-kos], *s.* Aristarco, nombre que se da a los críticos severos.

aristocracy [ˌærɪsˈtɒkrəsɪ] [a-ris-to-kra-si], *s.* 1. Aristocracia, la clase noble, la nobleza hereditaria. 2. Aristocracia, gobierno en que sólo intervienen los nobles.

aristocrat [ˈærɪstəkræt] [a-ris-to-krat], *s.* Aristócrata, de familia noble, aficionado a la aristocracia y sostenedor de ella.

aristocratic [ˈærɪstəkrætɪk] [a-ris-to-kra-tik], **aristocratical** [ˈærɪstəˌkrætɪkl] [a-ris-to-kra-ti-kal], *a.* Aristocrático, lo perteneciente a la aristocracia.

aristocratically [ˈærɪstəˌkrætɪlɪ] [a-ris-to-kra-ti-li], *adv.* Aristocráticamente.

aristolochia [ˌærɪstələkɪə] [a-ris-to-lo-kia] *s.* (*Bot.*) Aristoloquia.

Aristophanes [ˌærɪsˈtɒfəniːs] [a-ris-to-fa-nis] *N.* Aristófanes.

Aristotelian [ˌærɪstəˈtiːlɪən] [a-ris-to-te-lian] *a./s.* Aristotélico.

Aristotelic [ˈærɪstətiːlɪk] [a-ris-to-te-lik], *a.* y *s.* Aristotélico, lo que pertenece al sistema filosófico de Aristóteles, y el que lo sigue.

Aristotle [ˈærɪstɒtl] [a-ris-totl] *N.* Aristóteles.

arithmancy [ˈærɪstəmænsɪ] [a-ris-to-man-si], *s.* Aritmancia, el arte de adivinar por los números.

arithmetic [əˈrɪθmetɪk] [a-riz-me-tik] *s./a.* (*Mat.*) Aritmética. **Mental arithmetic,** cálculo mental. **Arithmetic progression,** progresión aritmética.

arithmetical [ˌærɪθˈmetɪkəl] [a-riz-me-ti-kal], *a.* Aritmético, perteneciente a la aritmética, o según las reglas de la misma.

arithmetician [əˌrɪθməˈtɪʃən] [a-riz-me-ti-shan], *s.* Aritmético, el que sabe o enseña la aritmética.

ark [ɑːk] [ark], *s.* 1. Arca, la embarcación en que se salvaron Noé y su familia del diluvio. 2. Arca del Testamento. **Ark of the covenant,** el arca de la alianza. 3. Barco de transporte con fondo chato; lanchón.

arles [ˈɑːls] [arls], *s.* (Inglaterra del norte y Escocia) 1. Arras, parte del precio que se anticipa como prenda y señal de un contrato. 2. Prenda segura. V. EARNEST.

arlet [ˈɑːlɪt] [ar-lit], *s.* (*Bot.*) Especie de comino.

arm [ɑːm] [arm], *s.* 1. Brazo. 2. Miembro delantero de un vertebrado. 3. Vara o rama del árbol 4. Brazo de mar. 5. Brazo, poder, fuerza. **Arm's reach,** alcance. **An arm o elbow chair,** una silla de brazos. **Arm in arm,** (*Fam.*) del brazo. 6. Brazo (de un sillón). 7. Radio de una rueda. 8. Brazo, ramo, parte distinta. 9. (*Mar.*) Cabo de una verga. **At arm's length,** a una brazada. (*Fig.*) A distancia. **Forearm,** antebrazo.

arm, *s.* (*Mil.*) 1. Arma, instrumento de ataque o defensa. **The infantry arm,** el arma de infantería. V. ARMS. 2. Cada uno de los diferentes institutos o ramos del servico militar. **Arms race,** carrera de armamentos. **Coat of arms,** escudo de armas.

arm, *va.* 1. Armar. 2. Armar o reforzar. 3. Armar, aprestar. **Armed to the teeth,** armado hasta los dientes. **Armed with a hammer,** armado de un martillo. **Armed robbery,** atraco a mano armada. **Armed forces,** fuerzas armadas. *-vn.* Tomar las armas, levantarse las tropas; armarse.

armada [ɑːˈmɑːdə] [ar-ma-da], *s.* Armada, conjunto de las fuerzas marítimas; flota. **The Spanish armada,** la Armada Invencible.

armadillo [ˌɑːməˈdɪləʊ] [ar-ma-di-lou], *s.* Armadillo o tatuay, mamífero del orden de los desdentados, típico de América; tato. Para defenderse se enrolla como el erizo.

armament [ˈɑːməmənt] [ar-ma-ment], *s.* 1. Fuerza militar o naval. 2. Armamento de navío; equipo y pertrechos de guerra de una fortificación o de un navío.

armamentary [ˈɑːməmentərɪ] [ar-ma-men-ta-ri], *s.* Armería. V. ARMORY.

armature [ˈɑːmətjʊəʳ] [ar-ma-chuaʳ], *s.* 1. (*Elec.*) (1) Armadura, trozo de hierro que une los polos de un imán. (2) Centro de metal rodeado por un rollo de alambre, que gira cerca de los polos de un imán en una máquina dinamo eléctrica. 2. Armadura, arma defensiva, instrumento o medio de defensa u ofensa.

armband [ˈɑːmbænd] [arm-band] *s.* Brazalete.

armchair [ˈɑːmtʃeəʳ] [arm-cheaʳ] *a.* De sillón. *s.* Sillón, butaca. (*Fig.*) **Armchair strategist,** estratega de café.

armed [ˈɑːmd] [armd], *a.* 1. Armado, provisto de armas; en botánica, espinoso. 2. Eficaz. 3. (*Fís.*) Provisto de una armadura. **Long-armed, short-armed,** de brazos largos, de brazos cortos.

Armenia [ˈɑːmiːnɪə] [ar-mi-nia] *N.* Armenia.

Armenian [ˈɑːmiːnɪən] [ar-mi-nian], *a.* y *s.* Armenio.

Armenian bole [ˈɑːmiːnɪənˌbəʊl] [ar-mi-nian-boul], *s.* Bol arménico. V. BOLE.

armental ['ɑːməntəl] [ar-men-tal], **armentine** ['ɑːməntiːn] [ar-man-tin], **armentose** ['ɑːməntəs] [ar-men-tos], *a. (Des.)* Pecuario, lo perteneciente al ganado.

armful ['ɑːmfʊl] [arm-ful], *s.* Brazado, medida de lo que se puede abarcar con los brazos, o lo que se tiene en los brazos.

armhole ['ɑːmhəʊl] [arn-joul], *s.* Sobaco, abertura en los vestidos para el brazo. Escote (de camisa).

armiger ['ɑːmɪgəʳ] [ar-mi-gaʳ], *s.* 1. Armígero, caballero. 2. Escudero.

armigerous ['ɑːmɪgərəs] [ar-mi-go-ros], *a.* Armígero, el que lleva armas.

armillary ['ɑːmɪləri] [ar-mi-la-ri], *a.* Armilar, lo que se parece a brazalete; que consta de un anillo o de anillos. **Armillary sphere,** esfera armilar, la que representa los círculos de los movimientos de los astros.

armings ['ɑːmɪŋz] [ar-mins], *s. pl. (Mar.)* Empavesadas.

Arminian [ɑːmɪnɪən] [ar-mi-nian], *s. y a.* Arminiano, el que pertenece a la secta de Arminio.

Arminianism [ɑːmɪnɪə'nɪzm] [ar-mi-nia-nísem], *s.* Arminianismo, doctrina calvinista de Arminio.

armipotence ['ɑːmɪpəʊtəns] [ar-mi-pou-tens], *s.* Armipotencia.

armipotent ['ɑːmɪpəʊtənt] [ar-mi-pou-tent], *a.* Armipotente.

armisonous ['ɑːmɪsənəs] [ar-mi-so-nos], *a.* Sonoro como las armas o la armadura.

armistice ['ɑːmɪstɪs] [ar-mis-tis], *s.* Armisticio, suspensión de las hostilidades.

armless ['ɑːmlɪs] [arm-lis], *a.* Desarmado, desbrazado; sin armas; sin brazos.

armlet ['ɑːmlɪt] [arm-lit], *s.* 1. Brazuelo o brazo pequeño. 2. Brazal o brazalete, armadura de hierro que cubre y defiende el brazo.

armor, armour ['ɑːməʳ] [ar-moʳ], *s.* Armadura. **Armor plate,** plancha de coraza o blindaje.

armor, *va.* Acorazar, blindar con planchas de hierro o acero.

armor-bearer ['ɑːməbɪərəʳ] [ar-mor-bía-raʳ], *s.* Escudero, el que lleva la armadura.

armorer ['ɑːmərəʳ] [ar-mo-reʳ], *s.* 1. Armero, el artífice que fabrica armas. 2. Armador, el que arma, viste y pone a otro las armas.

armorial ['ɑːmərɪəl] [ar-mo-rial], *a.* Heráldico, que pertenece al escudo de armas de alguna familia. **Armorial bearings,** blasón, escudo de armas.

armoric ['ɑːmərɪk] [ar-mo-rik], **armorican** ['ɑːmərɪkən] [ar-mo-ri-kan], *a.* Armórico, lo que pertenece a la Armórica antigua, o la Baja Bretaña en Francia.

armorist ['ɑːmərɪst] [ar-mo-rist] *s. (Her.)* Heraldista.

armory ['ɑːməri] [ar-mo-ri], *s.* 1. Armería, el sitio en que se guardan las armas. 2. *(E.U.)* Arsenal en que se fabrican armas. 3. Armadura, armazón colectivamente. 4. Heráldica. 5. Escudo de armas.

armpit ['ɑːmpɪt] [arm-pit], *s.* Sobaco, la parte hueca que está debajo del hombro.

armrest ['ɑːmrest] [arm-rest] *s.* Brazo (of an armchair).

arms ['ɑːmz] [arms], *s. pl.* 1. Armas, instrumentos ofensivos o defensivos. **To arms!** ¡A las armas! 2. Hostilidad, guerra, como profesión, ciencia o arte. 3. Armas, partes u órganos defensivos, como púas, espinas, etc. 4. Armas, las insignias que usan las familias nobles en sus escudos, para distinguirse unas de otras. **Fire-arms,** armas de fuego. **Side-arms,** armas blancas, o armas que se llevan al costado, como espada y bayoneta. **Under arms,** con las armas listas para usarlas. **Man at arms,** hombre armado. **Present arms!** ¡presenten armas! **To lay down arms,** rendir las armas.

arm-soye ['ɑːmsɔɪ] [arm-soi], *s.* Escote. V. ARM-HOLE.

army [A$ rˈ,mi], *s.* 1. Ejército. 2. Multitud, muchedumbre. **Army chaplain,** capellán castrense.

army corps ['ɑːmɪˌkɔːpz] [ar-mi-korps], *s.* Cuerpo de ejército.

army register ['ɑːmɪˌredʒɪstəʳ] [ar-mi-re-chis-taʳ], *s.* Escalafón del ejército.

army-worm ['ɑːmwɔːm], *s.* 1. Oruga de una falena (mariposa nocturna) que a menudo pasa de un lugar a otro en grandísimo número, devorando la hierba, el grano y otras cosechas. La del norte de los Estados Unidos es la Leucania unipuncta. 2. La oruga llamada de las tiendas (tent-caterpillar) que se cría en los bosques.

arnatto ['ɑːnətə] [ar-na-to], **arnotto** ['ɑːnətə] [ar-no-to], V. ANNATTO.

arnica ['ɑːnɪkə], [ar-ni-ka] *s.* 1. Árnica, planta medicinal de flores amarillas, que así como la raíz, tienen sabor acre y aromático y olor fuerte. Pertenece a la familia de las sinantéreas. 2. Tintura que se obtiene de la raíz, hojas o flores de dicha planta.

aroint ['ɑːrɔɪnt] [a-roint], *vr.* Irse, apartarse: más usado en el imperativo y entonces equivale a fuera, afuera.

aroma [ə'rəʊmə] [a-rou-ma], *s. (Quím.)* Aroma, principio de odorífero agradable; fragancia de las plantas.

aromatic [ˌærəʊ'mætɪk] [a-rou-ma-tik], **aromatical** [ˌærəʊ'mætɪkl] [a-rou-ma-ti-kal], *a.* Aromático, lo que tiene fragancia o aroma; odorífero.

aromatize [ærəʊ'mətaɪz] [a-rou-ma-tais], *va.* Aromatizar, comunicar olor aromático a alguna cosa.

aromatizer [ˌærəʊmə'taɪzəʳ] [a-rou-ma-tai-saʳ], *s.* Aromatizador.

arose [ə'rəʊz] [a-rous], *pret.* del verbo TO ARISE.

around [ə'raʊnd] [a-raund], *prep.* En, cerca, a eso de, por. **Around five o' clock,** a eso de las cinco. **To go around town,** ir por la ciudad. -*adv.* Alrededor; por aquí, por allá, por todos lados, cerca, aproximadamente. **I don't get around much these days,** no salgo mucho actualmente. **The year around,** durante todo el año. **To get around,** viajar, salir, divulgarse.

arousal [ə'raʊsəl] [a-rau-sal] *s.* Despertamiento, acción de despertar.

arouse [ə'raʊz] [a-raus], *va.* 1. Despertar, quitar el sueño al que está durmiendo. 2. Despertar, excitar.

arow [ə'rəʊ] [a-rou], *adv. (Poét.)* En fila, en línea.

arpeggio [aː'pedʒɪəʊ] [ar-pe-chiou], *s.* Arpegio, la rápida sucesión de los sonidos de un acorde. -*vn.* Arpegiar.

arquebuse ['ɑːkɪbiuːs] [ar-ki-bius], *s.* Arcabuz, arma de fuego.

arquebusier [ˌɑːkɪ'biuːsjəʳ] [ar-ki-biu-siaʳ] *s.* Arcabucero.

arrack ['ærək] [a-rak], *s.* Arak, especie de licor fuerte y espirituoso. **Arrack-punch,** bebida o ponche hecho de arak.

arraign [ə'reɪn] [a-rein], *va.* 1. *(For.)* Citar, emplazar, delatar en justicia. 2. Acusar, hacer cargo de alguna cosa.

arraignment [ə'reɪnmənt] [a-rein-ment], *s.* 1. *(For.)* Emplazo, emplazamiento. 2. Acusación. 3. Proceso, autos. 4. Presentación al tribunal.

arrange [ə'reɪndʒ] [a-reinch], *va.* 1. Colocar, arreglar, poner en orden. 2. Preparar, disponer, aprestar; ajustar, convenir por lo que toca a los detalles de una cosa. 3. *(Mús.)* Cambiar, adaptar. -*vn.* 1. Prevenir, hacer preparaciones. 2. Concordar. **To arrange to meet someone,** quedar o citarse con alguien.

arrangement [ə'reɪndʒmənt] [a-reinch-ment], *s.* 1. Colocación, orden, arreglo. 2. *(Fig.)* Medida, providencia, disposición, cálculo, adaptación.

arranger [ə'reɪndʒəʳ] [a-reinch-chaʳ], *s.* Trazador, arreglador, ordenador.

arrant ['ærənt] [a-rant], *a.* Notorio, famoso; consumado, insigne. **An arrant thief,** ladrón famoso. **An arrant whore,** ramera infame. **An arrant fool,** *(Fam.)* tonto de remate.

arrantly ['ærəntlɪ] [a-ran-tli], *adv.* Corruptamente, vergonzosamente.

arras ['ærəs] [a-ras], *s.* Tapicería de Arras en Flandes. Tela rica figurada para cubrir las paredes.

array [ə'reɪ] [a-rei], *s.* 1. Orden regular o propio; arreglo en líneas o filas; **In battle array,** en orden de batalla. Pompa, aparato. 2. Formación, el cuerpo colectivo de personas, o cosas así colocadas; de aquí, una fuerza militar, una colocación de los jurados. 3. Adorno, vestido, atavío, particularmente si es rico. **In rich array,** con sus más ricos atavíos.

array, *va.* 1. Colocar, poner en orden de batalla; **To array the troops,** formar las tropas. 2. Vestir, adornar. 3. *(For.)* **To array the jury,** colocar los jurados.

arrear [əˈrɪəʳ] [a-riaʳ], *s.* 1. Caídos, lo que se debe por no haberlo pagado a su tiempo; se emplea generalmente en plural. 2. Atraso, calidad de atrasado o tardío. **To be in arrears,** estar atrasado.

arrearage [ˈærəreɪdʒ] [a-ria-reich], *s.* Atrasos, caídos: se entiende de rentas o sueldos devengados y no pagados, o pagados en parte.

arrect [ˈærəkt] [a-rekt], **arrected** [ar,rec',ted], *a. (Ant.)* Elevado, erguido.

arrentation [ˌærənˈteɪʃən] [a-ran-téi-shon], *s.* Licencia que concede el dueño de un bosque o monte para cercar las tierras que están sembradas en él.

arrest [əˈrest] [a-rest], *s.* Embargo de bienes; prisión o arresto de una persona; parada, interrupción; aprehensión, embargo. **Close arrest,** arresto mayor. **To be under arrest,** estar detenido, estar bajo arresto. **Under house arrest,** bajo arresto domiciliario.

arrest, *va.* 1. Impedir, detener, hacer cesar, atajar, reprimir. 2. Arrestar o prender a las personas; embargar las cosas. 3. Atraer y fijar la atención. **Her beauty arrested the attention of all present,** su belleza atrajo la atención de todos los presentes. 4. Suspender la ejecución de una sentencia, auto, etc.

arrester [əˈrestəʳ] [a-res-taʳ], *s.* 1. Lo que, o la persona que, arresta o detiene. 2. **Spark arrester,** chispero, sombrerete.

arresting [əˈrestɪŋ] [a-res-tin] *a.* Que llama la atención, llamativo.

arrhizous, arrhizal [əˈrɪʃəs] [a-ri-sos], *a.* Sin raíces; como ciertas plantas parásitas.

arrhythmia [əˈrɪθmɪə] [a-riz-mia] *s.* Arritmia.

arrhythmic [əˈrɪθmɪk] [a-riz-mik] *a.* Arrítmico.

arris [ˈærɪz] [a-ris], *s. (Arq.)* Esquina, ángulo externo; canto o lomo, especialmente el canto agudo entre dos estrías de una columna dórica.

arrival [əˈraɪvəl] [a-rai-val], *s.* 1. Arribo o llegada. 2. Logro, consecución de lo que se intenta; el fin de un viaje acabado o el principio de uno nuevo. 3. El que o lo que llega o arriba. **A new arrival,** un recién venido. **The first arrivals,** los primeros en llegar.

arrive [əˈraɪv] [a-raiv], *vn.* 1. Arribar, llegar a algún paraje por mar o por tierra. 2. Llevar a cabo, lograr, conseguir. 3. Suceder, acontecer. **To arrive at,** llegar a, lograr, alcanzar, conseguir. *-va. (Ant.)* Alcanzar, obtener: llegar a.

arrivism [əˈrɪvɪzm] [a-ri-vísem] *s.* Arribismo.

arriviste o **arrivist** [æriˈviːst] [a-ri-vist] *s.* Arribista.

arrogance [ˈærəgəns] [a-ro-gans], **arrogancy** [ˈærəgənsɪ] [a-ro-gan-si], **arrogantness** [ˈærəgəntnɪs] [a-ro-gant-nis], *s.* Arrogancia, orgullo, altivez, presunción, fiereza, insolencia.

arrogant [ˈærəgənt] [a-ro-gant], *a.* Arrogante, orgulloso, altivo, fiero, presuntuoso, insolente, soberbio, altanero.

arrogantly [ˈærəgəntlɪ] [a-ro-gan-tli], *adv.* Arrogantemente.

arrogate [ˈærəʊgeɪt] [a-rou-gueit], *va.* Arrogarse, usurpar o alegar algún derecho infundado; atribuirse, hacerse mérito de, presumir de sí, tener pretensiones.

arrogation [ˌærəgeɪʃən] [a-ro-guei-shon], *s.* Arrogación.

arrogative [ˈærəgətɪv] [a-ro-ga-tif], *a.* Arrogativo, lo que arroga o usurpa.

arrow [ˈærəʊ] [a-rou], *s.* Flecha, saeta. **Arrow-root** o **Indian arrow-root,** polvo nutritivo de la raíz de varias especies de la Maranta de los botánicos; también la planta que produce este almidón. **Arrow-grass,** triglóquin, planta acuática. Recibe su nombre de la forma de su cápsula después de hendida. **Arrow-head,** 1. Punta de flecha. 2. Flecha de agua, planta. **Arrow-headed, arrow-shaped,** aflechado, sagital. **Arrow-headed characters,** caracteres cuneiformes.

arrowy [ˈærəʊɪ] [a-roui], *a.* 1. Lo que consta de flechas o saetas. 2. Semejante a una flecha o saeta. 3. Rápido como la flecha.

arroyo [ˈærəʊdʒəʊ] [a-rou-you], *s.* Arroyo, el caudal corto de agua y el lecho seco por donde corre. *(Esp.)*

arse [ɑːs] [ars], *s.* Culo, trasero, nalgas, la parte posterior del cuerpo. *(Vulg.)*

arsenal [ˈɑːsɪnl] [ar-si-nal], *s.* Arsenal, depósito en que se guardan armas, pertrechos y municiones de guerra.

arsenate, arseniate [ˈɑːsɪneɪt] [ar-si-neit], *s.* Arseniato, sal formada de ácido arsénico con alguna base de tierra, álcali o metal.

arsenic [ˈɑːsɪnɪk] [ar-si-nik], *s.* Arsénico, mineral corrosivo y veneno violento.

arsenic, arsenical [ˈɑːsnɪk] [ˈɑːsnɪkl] [ar-si-nik] [ar-si-ni-kal], *a.* Arsenical, perteneciente al arsénico o que le contiene. **Arsenic oxide,** óxido de arsénico (AS_2O_5).

arsenid, arsenide [ˈɑːsɪnaɪd] [ar-si-naid], *s.* Compuesto de arsénico, en que el arsénico es el elemento negativo.

arsenious [ˈɑːsɪnɪəs] [ar-si-nios], *a.* Arsenioso, perteneciente al arsénico, o que le contiene en su equivalencia de tres. **Arsenious oxide,** óxido arsenioso (AS_2O_3).

arsenite [ˈɑːsɪnaɪt] [ar-si-nait], *s.* Arsenito, sal compuesta de ácido arsenioso y de una base.

arsine [ˈɑːsiːn] [ar-sin] *s.* Arsina.

arsis [ˈɑːsɪs] [ar-sis], *s.* 1. Arsis, la sílaba sobre la cual recae la fuerza del acento, en oposición al resto del verso, que se llama *thesis.* 2. *(Mús.)* La parte no acentuada de un compás.

arson [ˈɑːsn] [ar-son], *s.* Incendio premeditado; el delito de incendiar.

arsonist [ˈɑːsənɪst] [ar-so-nist] *s.* Incendiario.

art Antiguamente, segunda persona del presente de indicativo del verbo TO BE **Thou art,** tú eres, o tú estás.

art [ɑːt] [art], *s.* 1. Arte, la facultad de ejecutar alguna cosa por industria. 2. Arte, la aplicación práctica del c o n o c i m i e n t o o del talento natural; habilidad, maña, destreza; poder. **The art of cooking,** el arte culinario. 3. Arte, conjunto de reglas para hacer bien alguna cosa. 4. Los principios de la construcción artística y de la crítica estética. 5. Arte, la incorporación del pensamiento bello en formas que afectan los sentidos, como en mármol o en lenguaje; también, obras de las bellas artes. 6. Arte, oficio. 7. Arte, cautela, maña, astucia, artificio. **The fine arts,** las bellas artes. **The liberal arts,** las artes liberales. **The black art,** la magia negra. **Bachelor of Arts,** Licenciado en Letras.

artaxerxes [ɑːtəʃəˈɪs] [ar-ta-sher-shes]*n.* Artajerjes.

artefact [ˈɑːtɪfækt] [ar-ti-fakt] *s.* Artefacto.

arterial [ɑːtɪərɪəl] [ar-te-rial], *a.* Arterial, lo perteneciente a las arterias o lo contenido en ellas.

arterialize [ɑːˈtɪərɪəlaɪz] [ar-te-ria-lais], *va.* Arterializar, convertir la sangre venosa en arterial.

arterialization [ɑːtɪərɪələˈseɪʃən] [ar-te-ria-lai-séi-shon], *s.* Arterialización: acto y efecto de arterializar.

arteriosclerosis [ɑːˈtɪərɪəʊsklɪˈrəʊsɪs] [ar-te-rios-kli-rou-sis], *s. (Med.)* Arteriosclerosis, endurecimiento de las arterias.

arteriotomy [ɑːˈtɪərɪətɒmɪ] [ar-te-rio-to-mi], *s.* Arteriotomía, la acción de abrir una arteria para sacar sangre.

arteritis [ɑːˈtərɪtɪs] [ar-te-ri-tis], *a.* Inflamación de una arteria.

artery [ˈɑːtərɪ] [ar-te-ri], *s.* Arteria, canal destinado a recibir la sangre del corazón y distribuirla por todo el cuerpo.

artful [ˈɑːtful] [art-ful], *a.* 1. Artificioso, hecho con arte o según arte. 2. Artificial, no natural. 3. Artificioso, astuto, cauteloso. 4. Diestro, ingenioso, industrioso.

artfully [ˈɑːtfəlɪ] [art-fu-li], *adv.* Artificiosamente, diestramente; con arte; insidiosamente, con astucia y artificio.

artfulness [ˈɑːtfʊlnɪs] [art-ful-nis], *s.* Arte, astucia, habilidad, industria.

arthritic [ɑːˈθrɪtɪk] [ar-zri-tik], **arthritical** [ɑːˈθrɪtɪkl] [ar-zri-ti-kal], *a.* Artrítico, lo que pertenece a la gota, artritis o articulaciones; artético.

arthritis [ɑːˈθraɪtɪs] [ar-zrai-tis], *s.* Artritis. **Rheumatoid arthritis,** artritis reumática.

arthritism [ɑːˈθrɪtɪzm] [ar-zri-tísem] *s.* (*Med.*) Artritismo.

arthropod [ˈɑːθrəpɒd] [ar-zro-pod], *s.* Uno de los artrópodos. *V.* ARTHROPODA.

arthropoda [ˈɑːθrəpɒdə] [ar-zro-po-da], *s.* (*Zool.*) Artrópodos, un subreino de los animales; los articulados propiamente dichos (en oposición a los gusanos); presentan órganos de locomoción articulados, esto es, formados de varias piezas o artejos, y se dividen en cuatro clases: insectos, miriápodos, arácnidos y crustáceos.

arthropodal [ˈɑːθrəpɒdl] [ar-zro-po-dal], **arthropodous** [ˈɑːθrəpɒdəs] [ar-zro-po-dos], *a.* Relativo a los artrópodos o articulados propiamente dichos.

arthrosis [ˈɑːθrəʊsɪs] [ar-zrou-sis], *s.* Artrosis, articulación.

Arthur [ˈɑːθəʳ] [ar-zaʳ] N. Arturo.

artichoke [ˈɑːtɪtʃəʊk] [ar-ti-chouk], *s.* (*Bot.*) Alcachofa, planta muy parecida al cardo que arroja una cabeza a manera de piña, la que también se llama alcachofa. **Jerusalem artichoke,** (*Bot.*) especie de girasol; cotufa, chufa.

article [ˈɑːtɪkl] [ar-ti-kel], *s.* 1. Artículo, parte de la oración, como *el, la,* etc. 2. Artículo, una composición corta. 3. Artículo, parte o división de cualquier conjunto. 4. Artículo, término, o estipulación. 5. Articulación, coyuntura; parte entre dos nudos de una planta; segmento de un apéndice articulado. 6. (*Ant.*) Artículo, punto exacto de tiempo. **To surrender upon articles,** capitular. **Articles of merchandise,** mercaderías, mercancías, efectos, renglones. **Small articles,** Menudencias. **Trifling articles,** bagatelas. **To be under articles,** estar escriturado. **To sign articles,** escriturarse. **Articles of war,** el código penal militar. **The most necessary articles,** los objetos de primera necesidad.

article, *vn.* Capitular, pactar o contratar mutuamente, convenir. *-va.* Colocar en artículos distintos. **To article one for treason,** acusar y procesar a alguno por delito de lesa majestad o por alta traición. Contratar, poner a uno a trabajar en un oficio por contrata. **To article an apprentice to,** poner en aprendizaje.

articular [ˈɑːtɪkjələʳ] [ar-ti-kiu-laʳ], *a.* Articular, lo que pertenece a las junturas o articulaciones del cuerpo.

articularly [ˈɑːtɪkjəlalɪ] [ar-ti-kiu-lar-li], *adv.* Articuladamente.

articulate [ˈɑːtɪkjəlɪt] [ar-ti-kiu-lit], *a.* 1. Articulado, dividido en sílabas consecutivas; unido para formar el lenguaje. 2. Claro, distinto (palabras, sonidos). 3. Articulado que tiene articulaciones. 4. (*Zool.*) Articulado, perteneciente a los animales articulados. *-s.* Uno de los animales articulados. *-pl. s.* Articulados o entomozoos, una de las cuatro grandes divisiones del reino animal, que comprende los animales cuyo cuerpo está compuesto de segmentos unidos o articulados.

articulate, *va.* 1. Articular, pronunciar las palabras clara y distintamente. 2. Articular, formar algún convenio por artículos. 3. Formar nudos. *-vn.* Hablar distintamente.

articulately [ˈɑːtɪkjəlɪtlɪ] [ar-ti-kiu-lit-li], *adv.* Articuladamente.

articulateness [ˈɑːtɪkjəlɪtnɪs] [ar-ti-kiu-lit-nis], *s.* La calidad de ser articulado.

articulation [ˈɑːtɪkjəˈleɪʃən] [ar-ti-kiu-léishon], *s.* 1. Articulación, juego de las coyunturas de los huesos; nudo en las plantas. 2. Articulación, la acción de articular las palabras.

artifact [ˈɑːtɪfækt] [ar-ti-fakt], *s.* Artefacto.

artifice [ˈɑːtɪfɪs] [ar-ti-fis], *s.* 1. Artificio, engaño, fraude, estratagema, treta, destreza, habilidad, maña, artería. 2. (*Des.*) Arte, empleo u oficio mecánico, industria.

artificer [ˈɑːtɪfɪsəʳ] [ar-ti-fi-saʳ], *s.* Artífice, el que hace algún artefacto; el que construye o diseña; artesano hábil; también, inventor, autor.

artificial [ˈɑːtɪfɪʃəl] [ar-ti-fi-shal], **artificious** [ˈɑːtɪfɪʃəs] [ar-ti-fi-shos], *a.* 1. Artificial, hecho por arte. 2. Artificial, fingido. 3. Artificioso.

artificiality [ˈɑːtɪfɪʃəlɪtɪ] [ar-ti-fi-sha-li-ti], *s.* Carácter artificial, apariencia, arte, conducta artificiosa.

artificially [ˈɑːtɪfɪʃəlɪ] [ar-ti-fi-sha-li], *adv.* Artificialmente, artificiosamente.

artificialness [ˈɑːtɪfɪʃəlnɪs] [ar-ti-fi-shal-nis], *s.* Arte, astucia.

artillerist [ɑːˈtɪlərɪʃt] [ar-ti-le-rist], *s.* Artillero.

artillery [ɑːˈtɪlərɪ] [ar-ti-le-ri], *s.* 1. Arte de construir y usar las armas, máquinas y municiones de guerra. 2. Artillería, el tren de cañones, morteros y otras máquinas militares. **Artillery park,** parque de artillería. **Train of artillery,** tren de artillería. **Artillery-wagon,** carro de artillería, furgón. **Field, siege artillery,** artillería de campaña, de sitio. **Artilleryman,** artillero. **Artillery practice,** ejercicio de cañón.

artisan [ˈɑːtɪzæn] [ar-ti-san], *s.* Artesano, el que ejerce algún arte de mecánica.

artist [ˈɑːtɪst] [ar-tist], *s.* 1. Artista, el que profesa algún arte liberal. (Writer, painter, sculptor, musician, …).

artiste [ˈɑːtɪst] [ar-tist] *s.* Artista

artistic [ˈɑːtɪstɪk] [ar-tis-tik], *a.* Artístico, de las artes.

artistry [ˈɑːtɪstrɪ] [ar-tis-tri], *s.* Arte, habilidad artística.

artless [ˈɑːtlɪs] [art-lis], *a.* 1. Natural, sin arte, sencillo, simple; sin dolo. 2. (*Fam.*) Chabacano, hecho sin arte.

artlessy [ˈɑːtlɪsɪ] [art-li-si], *adv.* 1. Sencillamente, simplemente, naturalmente, sin arte; chabacanamente. 2. (*Fam.*) A la buena de Dios.

artlessness [ˈɑːtlɪsnɪs] [art-lis-nis], *s.* Sencillez, candidez, naturalidad.

arty [ˈɑːtɪ] [ar-ti] o **arty-crafty** [ˈɑːtɪˌkræftɪ] [ar-ti-kraf-ti] *a.* Que se las da de artista.

arum [ˈærəm] [a-ram], *a.* Arum, yaro, planta común parecida a la serpentaria.

arundinaceous [ˌærəndɪˈneɪʃəs] [a-ran-di-néi-shos], **arundineous** [ˈærəndɪnəs] [a-ran-di-nos], *a.* Arundináceo, hecho de cañas, lo que abunda de cañas.

aruspice [ˈærəspaɪz] [a-ras-pais], **aruspex** [ˈærəspeks] [a-ras-peks], *s.* Arúspice: entre los romanos, el sumo sacerdote que examinaba las entrañas de las víctimas para adivinar por ellas algún suceso.

aruspicy [ˈærəspɪsɪ] [a-ras-pi-si], *s.* Aruspicina, arte supersticiosa de adivinar los sucesos por la inspección de las entrañas de las víctimas.

aryan [ˈɛəɪən] [e-rian] *a./s.* Ario.

arytenoid [ˈɛəɪˈtɪnɔɪd] [e-ri-ti-noid], *a.* Aritenal, aritenóideo. **Arytenoid cartilages,** dos cartílagos situados en la parte posterior y superior de la laringe.

as [æz] [as], *conj.* 1. Como, del mismo modo que otra cosa. **As you please,** como usted quiera. **As good as,** tan bueno como. **As sure as can be,** sin duda alguna. **As I am informed,** por lo que he oído decir. 2. Mientras, cuando. **He arrived as you were leaving,** llegó cuando te estabas marchando. 3. Como, igualmente. **As I said yesterday,** como le dije ayer. 4. Se usa en sentido recíproco y corresponde con *so.* **As so,** así como, así también. 5. **As for, as to,** en cuanto a, por lo que toca a. 6. Según, como, a medida que. **I find it easier as I advance,** me encuentro más fácil a medida que adelanto. **As** indica el tiempo, y también el lugar, y entonces se traduce *como,* o *al,* y las más veces no se expresa; v.g. **As he was at the door,** estando él a la puerta. **As they were walking,** al ir ellos andando. **As I was there,** estando yo allá. **As far as,** hasta. **As soon as,** luego que. **As yet,** aún todavía. **As if** o **as though,** como si. **As well as,** tan bien. **As it is,** así como así. **As is the beginning, so is the end,** según es el principio, así es el fin. **As for me,** por lo que a mí toca; en cuanto a mí. **As big again,** dos veces tan grande. **As** después de *such* hace veces de los pronombres relativos *who* y *which.* **All such as went there,** todos los que fueron allí. *Prep.* En calidad de, como, por. **He came as an observer,** vino en calidad de observador. **As a rule,** por regla general.

asafoetida ['æsəfetidə] [a-sa-fe-ti-da], *s.* Asafétida, goma-resinosa, empleada en medicina, que se trae de las Indias orientales.

asbestine [æz'besti:n] [as-bes-tin], *a.* Asbestino, incombustible.

asbestos [æz'bestəs] [as-bes-tos], *s.* Asbesto o amianto, mineral fibroso y flexible, que tiene la propiedad singular de ser incombustible.

ascarides [æz'kɔridz] [as-ka-rids], *s.* Ascárides, lombricillas que se hallan en los intestinos, pero sobre todo en el recto. Se llaman también *thread-worms* o *pin-worms.* En el singular se escribe *ascaris* y *ascarid.*

ascend [ə'send] [a-send], *vn.* 1. Ascender, subir. 2. Adelantar, o subir de un grado de conocimiento a otro mayor. 3. Estar en grado ascendente de parentesco. *-va.* Ascender o subir. **To ascend a hill,** subir una colina o cuesta.

ascendable [ə'sendəbl] [a-sen-da-bol] *a.* Accessible, que se puede subir.

ascendance o **ascendence** [ə'sendəns] [a-sen-dans] *s.* Ascendiente, ascendencia.

ascendancy o **ascendency** [ə'sendənsi] [a-sen-dan-si] *s.* Ascendiente, ascendencia. Influjo, poder.

ascendant [ə'sendənt] [a-sen-dant], **ascendent,** *s.* 1. Altura, elevación. 2. Ascendiente, influjo, poder; el que tiene influencia. 3. Ascendiente, la persona de quien se desciende, antepasado.

ascendant, ascendent, *a.* 1. Ascendiente. 2. Superior, predominante.

ascension [ə'senʃən] [a-sen-shon], *s.* 1. Ascensión, la acción de ascender. 2. Ascensión, la subida de nuestro Redentor a los cielos. 3. Ascensión, la cosa que asciende o sube.

ascensional [ə'senʃənl] [a-sen-sho-nal], *a.* *(Astr.)* Ascensional

ascent [ə'sent] [a-sent], *s.* 1. Subida, la acción de subir. 2. Eminencia, paraje elevado, altura. 3. Cuesta, subida. **Line of ascent,** ascendencia.

ascertain [æsə'tein] [a-ser-tein], *va.* 1. Indagar, averiguar, hallar, descubrir por experimento o investigación. **I am going to ascertain what happened,** voy a averiguar lo que ha sucedido. 2. *(Ant.)* Asegurar, fijar, establecer, confirmar, afirmar. **To ascertain the price,** *(Ant.)* reglar o determinar el precio.

ascertainable [æsə'teinəbl] [a-ser-tei-na-bol], *a.* Averiguable, descubrible, comprobable.

ascertainer [æsə'teinəʳ] [a-ser-tei-naʳ], *s.* Averiguador, indagador.

ascertainment [æsə'teinmənt] [a-ser-tein-ment], *s.* 1. Averiguación, indagación. 2. *(Ant.)* Regla fija y determinada.

ascesis ['æsesis] [a-se-sis] *s.* Ascesis.

ascetic ['æsetik] [a-se-tik], *a.* Ascético, dedicado a la práctica de la devoción y mortificación. *-s.* Asceta.

ascetical ['æsetikl] [a-se-ti-kal] a. Ascético. *s.* Asceta.

asceticism [ə'setisizəm] [a-se-ti-sízem], *s.* Asceticismo, profesión de la vida ascética.

Ascians ['æsiəns] [a-sians], **ascii** ['æsi] [a-si], *s.* *(Geo.)* áscios, ascianos, habitantes de la zona tórrida que dos veces al año no hacen sombra al mediodía.

ascites ['æsits] [a-sits], *s.* Ascitis o hidropesía del abdomen.

ascitic ['æsitik] [a-si-tik], **ascitical** ['æsitikl] [a-si-ti-kal], *a.* Ascítico, hidrópico, el que padece ascitis.

ascititious ['æsitiʃəs] [a-si-ti-shos], *a.* Adicional, lo que se añade o suple. *V.* ADSCITITIOUS.

ascot ['æskɒt] [as-kot] *s.* Fular, pañuelo.

ascribable [ə'skraibəbl] [as-krai-ba-bol], *a.* Aplicable, imputable, que se puede atribuir, imputar o aplicar.

ascribe [ə'skraib] [as-kraib], *va.* 1. Adscribir. 2. Atribuir, achacar. 3. Aplicar, adjudicar.

ascription [ə'skripʃən] [as-krip-shon], *s.* Atribución; imputación.

ascus ['æskʌs] [as-kas], *s.* *(Bot.)* Asca.

asea [ə'si:] [a-sí], *adv.* Sobre el mar; hacia el mar.

asepsis [eɪ'sepsis] [a-sep-sis], *s.* Asepsia, no emponzoñamiento de la sangre; exención de la putrefacción y sus consecuencias.

aseptic [eɪ'septik] [a-sep-tik], *a.* Aséptico; preventivo de la putrefacción, y en particular del emponzoñamiento de la sangre.

asepticism [ˌeiseptɪ'sizm] [a-sep-ti-sí-zem] o **asepsis,** Estado o calidad de aséptico.

asepticize [eɪ'septisaiz] [a-sep-ti-sais] *va.* Esterilizar, volver aséptico, aseptizar.

asexual [eɪ'sekjuəl] [a-sek-siual], *a.* Asexual, sin reproducción sexual.

ash [æʃ] [ash], *s.* Singular de *ashes:* se usa principalmente en la formación de palabras compuestas. **Ash-pit, ash-pan,** cenicero, cenizal. **Ash-pail,** cubo para la ceniza. **Ash-tub,** coladero, cubeta de lejía. **That coal burns to a white ash,** ese carbón da ceniza blanca.

ash, *s.* *(Bot.)* Fresno, cualquier árbol del género Fraxinus. **Ash-grove,** fresneda. **Mountain-ash** o **rowan-tree,** serbal.

ashame [ə'ʃeim] [a-sheim], *va.* *V.* SHAME.

ashamed [ə'ʃeimd] [a-sheimd], *a.* Avergonzado, vergonzoso. **To be ashamed,** tener vergüenza, avergonzarse de, correrse de, sonrojarse.

ashamedly [ə'ʃeimdli] [a-sheimdli], *adv.* Vergonzosamente.

ash bin ['æʃbin] [ash-bin] *s.* Cubo de la basura.

ash can ['æʃkæn] [ash-can] *s.* Cubo de la basura.

ash colored ['æʃkʌləd] [ash-ca-lad], *a.* Ceniciento.

ashelf [ə'ʃelf] [a-shelf], *adv.* *(Mar.)* Arrimado sobre un peñasco o bajío.

ashen ['æʃn] [ashn], *a.* 1. Hecho de fresno. 2. Semejante a la ceniza; ceniciento, pálido.

ashes ['æʃs] [a-shes], *s. pl.* 1. Ceniza. 2. Ceniza o cenizas, los restos de un cadáver.

ashore [ə'ʃɔ:ʳ] [a-shoʳ], *adv.* En tierra, a tierra. **To get ashore,** desembarcar. **To run ashore,** encallar, echarse a la costa, hablando de un buque.

ashtray ['æʃtrei] [ash-trei] *s.* Cenicero.

ash-tub ['æʃtʌb] [ash-tab], *s.* Cenicero.

ash Wednesday [æʃ'wendzdei] [ash-uénds-dei], *a.* Miércoles de ceniza.

ash-weed [æʃ'wi:d] [ash-uíd], *s.* *(Bot.)* Angélica, planta.

ashy ['æʃi] [ashi], *a.* Cenizoso, ceniciento.

ashy-pale [æʃi'peil] [ashi-peil], *a.* Pálido como ceniza.

Asia ['eiʃə] [ei-sha] *n.* Asia. **Asia Minor,** Asia Menor.

Asian ['eiʃən] [ei-shan], *a.* **Asiatic** ['eiʃətik] [ei-sha-tik], *a.* Asiático. **Asiatic flu,** gripe asiática.

asiaticism [ˌeiʃəti'sizəm] [ei-sha-ti-sízem], *s.* Imitación de las costumbres asiáticas.

aside [ə'said] [a-said], *adv.* 1. Al lado, a un lado. 2. A parte. **To lay aside,** despreciar, no hacer caso, desechar, no admitir. *(Fam.)* Arrinconar. **To lay a project aside,** abandonar un proyecto. *(For.)* **To set aside a judgment,** anular una sentencia. **Joking aside,** bromas aparte. **Aside from,** además de, aparte de.

asinine ['æsinain] [a-si-nain], *a.* Asinino, asnal, lo perteneciente al asno. *(Fam.)* estúpido.

ask [ɑ:sk] [ask], *va.* 1. Pedir, rogar. 2. Preguntar, interrogar. **I must ask you one question,** tengo que hacer a usted una pregunta, o tengo que preguntar a usted 3. Pedir, invitar. **He asked me to come,** me pidió que viniese. **I asked them for dinner,** les invité a cenar. *-vn.* Buscar, inquirir, rogar. **To ask for** o **after one,** preguntar por alguno. **To ask in, up, down,** rogar (a una persona) que entre, suba o baje. **To ask for something back,** pedir que se devuelva algo. **To ask for trouble,** buscarse problemas.

askance [ə'skɑːns] [as-kans], *adv.* 1. Al sesgo, de soslayo, oblicuamente. 2. Con desdén. **To look askance at,** mirar con desconfianza, con recelo o con mala cara.

asker [ɑːskəʳ] [as-kaʳ], *s.* Inquiridor; suplicante. **Asker o ask,** especie de lagartija.

askew [ə'skjuː] [as-kiu], *adv.* Al lado; con desdén o desprecio; oblicuamente. De reojo, de soslayo.

asking ['ɑːskɪŋ] [as-kin], *s.* 1. Súplica, acción de pedir, demanda. 2. Publicación (de amonestaciones). **This is the third time of asking,** esta es la tercera amonestación.

aslant [ə'slɑːnt] [as-lant], *adv.* Oblicuamente. -*prep.* A través de.

asleep [ə'sliːp] [as-líp], *adv.* Dormido. **To fall asleep,** dormirse, quedarse dormido. **My foot is asleep,** se me ha entumecido o dormido un pie.

aslope [ə'sləʊp] [as-loup], *adv.* En declive, en pendiente.

asp [æsp] [asp], **aspic** [æspɪk] [as-pik], *s.* áspid, serpiente venenosa, cuya mordedura es mortal.

aspalathus [əspə'ləʊtəs] [as-pa-la-tus], *s.* (*Bot.*) Aspalato, palo de rosa o del águila.

asparagus [əs'pærəgəs] [as-pa-ra-gos], *s.* Espárrago, planta; y sus tallos tiernos que se comen antes de endurecerse.

aspect ['æspekt] [as-pekt], *s.* 1. Aspecto, semblante, cara. 2. Mirada, vista, ojeada. 3. Aspecto, postura o situación, disposición, dirección, traza, aire, ademán. 4. (*Astr.*) Aspecto, posición relativa de los planetas. **The house has a northern aspect,** la casa da o mira al norte. **From a personal aspect,** desde un punto de vista personal.

aspen ['æspən] [as-pen], *s.* Álamo temblón, árbol cuyas hojas siempre se están moviendo.

aspen, *a.* Perteneciente al álamo temblón o hecho de él.

asper, *s.* Aspro o áspero, moneda de Turquía.

asperate ['æspɪreɪt] [as-pi-reit], *va.* Hacer áspera alguna cosa.

asperation [ˌæspɪ'reɪʃən] [as-pi-rei-shon], *s.* El acto de hacer áspera alguna cosa.

asperges ['æspədʒ] [as-per-ches] *s.* (*Rel.*) Asperges.

aspergillum ['æspəgɪləm] [as-per-gui-lom] *s.* (*Rel.*) Hisopo, aspersorio.

aspergillus ['æspəgɪləs] [as-per-gui-los] *s.* (*Bot.*) Aspergilo.

asperifolious ['æspərɪfəljəs] [as-pe-ri-fo-lios], *a.* (*Bot.*) Se dice de las plantas que tienen ásperas las hojas.

asperity [æs'perɪtɪ] [as-pe-riti], *s.* Aspereza, desigualdad, rigidez, rudeza.

aspermous [æs'pɜːməs] [as-per-mos], **aspermatous,** *a.* (*Bot.*) Aspermo, sin semilla.

asperous [æs'perəs] [as-pe-ros] *a.* Áspero.

asperse [æs'pɜːs] [as-pers], *va.* Difamar, calumniar, denigrar, infamar. Hisopear, asperjar (to sprinkle).

asperser [æs'pɜːsəʳ] [as-persaʳ], *s.* Infamador.

aspersion [æs'pɜːʃən] [as-per-shon], *s.* Difamación, la acción de difamar o calumniar; mancha, mácula, tacha, deshonra, calumnia; aspersión, rociadura. (*Fam.*) Rociada, represión. **To cast aspersions on one,** difamar a alguno, calumniarle.

aspersive [əs'pɜːsɪv] [as-per-sif], *a.* Calumnioso, difamatorio.

aspersorium [əs'pɜːsərɪəm] [as-per-so-rium] *s.* (*Rel.*) Hisopo.

asphalt ['æsfælt] [as-falt] o **asphaltum** ['æsfæltəm] [as-fal-tam], *s.* Asfalto, especie de betún sólido. *va.* Asfaltar.

asphaltic ['æsfæltɪk] [as-fal-tik], *a.* Asfáltico, bituminoso.

asphalting ['æsfæltɪŋ] [as-fal-tin] *s.* Asfaltado.

asphodel ['æsfɒdəl] [as-fo-del], *s.* (*Bot.*) Asfódelo o gamón.

asphyxia [æs'fɪksɪə] [as-fik-sia], *s.* (*Med.*) Asfixia, privación de los sentidos por falta de respiración.

asphyxiate [æs'fɪksɪeɪt] [as-fik-sieit], *va.* Asfixiar, sofocar. -*vn.* Asfixiarse.

asphyxiated [æs'fɪksɪeɪtɪd] [as-fik-siei-tid], *pp.* Sofocado.

asphyxiation [æs'fɪksɪeɪʃən] [as-fik-siei-shon], *s.* Asfixia, sofocación.

aspic [æspɪk] [as-pik], (OIL OF), *s.* Aceite de espliego. V. LAVENDER.

aspic, *s.* Jalea gustosa que contiene picadillo de carne, pescado, huevos, etc.

aspidistra [æspɪ'dɪstə] [as-pi-dis-tra] *s.* (*Bot.*) Aspidistra.

aspirant ['æspɪrənt] [as-pi-rant], *s.* Aspirante, el que aspira, pretendiente, candidato.

aspirate ['æspərɪt] [as-pi-reit], *va.* 1. Aspirar, pronunciar con aspiración, como en las voces, *horse, hog* y otras. 2. (*Med.*) Extraer fluido, por ejemplo de la cavidad torácica, sin permitir la entrada al aire.

aspirate, *a.* Aspirado. -*s.* Acento señal, virgulilla. el signo (') en la lengua griega para indicar el sonido gutural de una letra.

aspiration [æspə'reɪʃən] [as-pi-rei-shon], *s.* 1. Anhelo, deseo vehemente. 2. Ambición, la pasión de aspirar a cosas elevadas, como dignidades, etc. 3. Aspiración, la acción de aspirar una vocal o darle más fuerza con el aliento. 4. Aspiración, acto de extraer fluido sin permitir la entrada al aire.

aspirator [æspə'reɪtəʳ] [as-pi-ra-taʳ], *s.* Aspirador, instrumento para la aspiración quirúrgica.

aspiratory [æspə'rətərɪ] [as-pi-ra-to-ri], *a.* Propio de la aspiración, lo que la produce; aspirante.

aspire [əs'paɪəʳ] [as-paiaʳ], *vn.* Aspirar, pretender, desear con ansia algún empleo o dignidad. **To aspire to high positions,** aspirar a o ambicionar altos cargos. -*va.* 1. Aspirar. 2. Soplar.

aspirer [əs'paɪrəʳ] [as-pai-raʳ], *s.* Aspirante, el que aspira.

aspirin [æsprɪn] [as-pi-rin], *s.* Aspirina.

aspiring [əs'paɪrɪŋ] [as-pai-rin], *s.* Pretensión, deseo de algún empleo o dignidad.

asplanchnic [əs'plæŋknɪk] [as-plank-nik], *a.* Sin canal alimenticio.

asplenium [əs'plɪnɪəm] [as-pli-ni-am], *s.* (*Bot.*) Asplenia, género de helechos que comprende muy numerosas especies; entre ellas, la doradilla, el culantrillo, etc.

asportation [əspə'teɪʃən] [as-por-tei-shon], *s.* Extracción.

asquint [əs'kwɪnt] [as-kuint], *adv.* De o al soslayo, de través.

ass [æs] [as], *s.* 1. Burro, borrico, asno, jumento. **A she-ass,** burra, borrica. **A young ass,** pollino. 2. (*Fig.*) Tonto, ignorante, bestia, asno, jumento, hablando de personas. **To make an ass of oneself,** ponerse en ridículo. (*Pop.*) Culo.

assail [ə'seɪl] [a-seil], *va.* Acometer, invadir, asaltar, atacar, embestir. **The beggars assailed him,** los mendigos le asaltaron.

assailable [ə'seɪləbl] [a-sei-la-bol], *a.* Lo que puede ser asaltado.

assailant [ə'seɪlənt] [a-sei-lant], *a.* El que acomete, acometedor, acometiente, *s.* Acometedor, asaltador, agresor, embestidor, chocador en una lid o contienda.

assailment [ə'seɪlmənt] [a-seil-ment], *s.* Asalto, acometimiento, acometida.

assart [ə'sɑːt] [a-sart], *va.* (GB) Rozar, desmontar y desbrotar la tierra.

assart, *s.* Rozo de la tierra, roza, tierra nuevamente rozada, para sembrar; árbol o planta arrancados.

assassin [ə'sæsɪn] [a-sa-sin], **assassinator** [ə'sæsɪneɪtəʳ] [a-sa-si-nei-taʳ], *s.* Asesino, el que mata alevosamente. **Hired assassin,** asesino pagado.

assassinate [ə'sæsɪneɪt] [a-sa-si-neit], *va.* Asesinar, matar alevosamente. -*vn.* Ser asesino, cometer asesinato.

assassination [əsæsɪ'neɪʃən] [a-sa-si-nei-shon], *s.* Asesinato, la acción y el delito de asesinar.

assault [ə'sɔːlt] [a-solt], *s.* 1. Asalto o acometimiento de alguna plaza. **Bayonet assault,** ataque a la bayoneta. 2. Asalto, invasión u hostilidad. 3. Acometimiento, la acción de acometer a otro con violencia, ataque, asalto, insulto. **Criminal assault,** intento de violación. (*For.*) **Assault and battery,** lesiones, vías de hecho. **To make an assault on,** asaltar a, dar el asalto a.

assault, *va.* Acometer, invadir, asaltar. **The thief assaulted him,** el ladrón le asaltó. (*For.*) Agredir, violar.

assaulter [ə'sɔːltəʳ] [a-sol-taʳ], *s.* Agresor o injusto invasor.

assay [əˈseɪ] [a-sei], *s.* 1. Ensayo, reconocimiento o examen. 2. Prueba o reconocimiento de pesos y medidas por el fiel. 3. Ensayo, estreno, experimento, tentativa, el primer acto de ejercer y poner por obra alguna cosa. 4. Valor. 5. Ensaye (of a metal), aquilatación. **Assay-furnace,** horno de copelación. **Assay-office,** oficina de ensayador.

assay, *va.* 1. Ensayar, hacer prueba de alguna cosa, experimentar. 2. Tentar o hacer tentativa, intentar. 3. Gustar, probar.

assayer [əˈseɪəʳ] [a-se-yaʳ], *s.* Ensayador, el que ensaya; en especial oficial de la casa de la moneda, cuyo deber es reconocer la ley de la plata u oro.

assaying [əˈseɪŋ] [a-seiyin], *s.* Ensaye, ensay (of metals). **Art of assaying,** docimástica, el arte de ensayar los metales y minerales.

assemblage [əˈsemblɪdʒ] [a-sem-blich], *s.* 1. Colección, agregado, compuesto o conjunto de muchas cosas. 2. Asamblea, multitud.

assemble [əˈsembl] [a-sem-bol], *va.* Reunir, congregar, convocar. -*vn.* Juntarse o unirse en junta o congreso.

assembler [əˈsembləʳ] [a-sem-blaʳ], *s.* El que se junta con otros.

assembly [əˈsemblɪ] [a-sem-bli], *s.* 1. Asamblea, junta, congreso. 2. (*Mil.*) Asamblea, toque de la caja, para que la tropa se recoja a sus cuerpos respectivos o al lugar designado. **General Assembly** (a) El más alto tribunal de justicia entre los presbiterianos o los de alguna otra denominación. (b) Legislatura, cuerpo legislativo. **Place of assembly,** lugar de reunión. **Assembly hall,** salón de actos. **Assembly line production,** producción en cadena. **Assembly shop,** taller de montaje.

assembly line [əˈsemblɪˌlaɪn] [a-sem-bli-lain], *s.* Línea de montaje.

assemblyman [əˈsemblɪˌmæn] [a-sem-bli-man], *s.* Individuo de un congreso o asamblea, y en especial de la cámara baja de la legislatura de un Estado.

asembly-room [əˈsemblɪˌruːm] [a-sem-bli-rum], *s.* Sala de juntas.

assent [əˈsent] [a-sent], *s.* Asenso, la acción y efecto de asentir, consentimiento; confesión, reconocimiento, declaración, aprobación, beneplácito.

assent, *vn.* Asentir, convenir en el juicio con otro, ser de un mismo dictamen; aprobar.

assentation [əˈsenteɪʃənt] [a-sen-tei-shon], *s.* Condescendencia a la opinión de otro por adulación o disimulo; lisonja, complacencia servil.

assenter [əˈsentəʳ] [a-sen-taʳ], *s.* Consentidor, favorecedor.

assentient [əˈsenʃənt] [a-sen-shant], *a.* 1. Que conviene o asiente. 2. *s.* Consentidor, el que aprueba.

assentingly [əˈsentɪŋlɪ] [əˈsent] [a-sen-tin-li], *adv.* 1. Con asenso, aprobación o consentimiento. 2. En signo de asentimiento.

assert [əˈsɜːt] [a-sert], *va.* 1. Sostener, mantener, defender, hacer bueno. 2. Afirmar, asegurar. 3. Alegar derecho o título a alguna cosa. **To assert oneself,** imponerse.

assertion [əˈsɜːʃən] [a-sershon], *s.* Aserción, afirmación. Reivindicación (of a right).

assertive [əˈsɜːtɪv] [a-ser-tif], *a.* Afirmativo, que afirma o envuelve aserción.

asserter, assertor [əˈsɜːtəʳ] [a-ser-taʳ], *s.* Afirmador, defensor, protector, libertador.

assertory [əˈsɜːtərɪ] [a-ser-to-ri], *a.* Afirmativo: declaratorio.

assess [əˈses] [a-ses], **assessment** [əˈsesmənt] [a-ses-ment], *s.* Amillaramiento, o tasa de los impuestos, cargas o gabelas, que se deben pagar por el importe de los bienes que se poseen, o por otros títulos. **The assessment came to twenty dollars,** la valoración fue de veinte dólares.

assess, *va.* Amillarar, declarar, señalar la cantidad que cada individuo debe pagar por el importe de los bienes que posee, o por otros títulos. **To assess damages,** fijar los daños y perjuicios.

assessable [əˈsesəbl] [a-se-sa-bol], *a.* Imponible, que puede ser amillarado.

assessionary [əˈseʃənərɪ] [a-se-so-na-ri], *a.* Lo perteneciente al asesor.

assessor [əˈsesəʳ] [a-se-saʳ], *s.* 1. Asesor, el letrado que acompaña al juez lego. 2. Tasador de impuestos o gabelas.

asset [ˈæsət] [a-set], *s.* 1. Cada una de las partidas que componen el caudal de una persona o corporación. 2. Ventaja. **Having a car is an asset in my profession,** tener coche es una ventaja en mi profesión.

assets [ˈæsets] [a-sets], *s. pl.* 1. Capital, o caudal en caja, o existente, fondos, créditos activos, cantidad o cantidades para pagar. 2. (*com.*) Activo, fondos de una quiebra, o de una sucesión. **Real assets,** bienes raíces. **Personal assets,** bienes muebles. **Assets in hand,** activo disponible.

asseverate [əˈsevəreɪt] [a-se-ve-reit], *va.* Aseverar, afirmar, asegurar solemnemente.

asseveration [əsevəˈreɪʃən] [a-se-ve-rei-shon], *s.* Aseveración, afirmación; protesta.

ass-head [əsˈhiːd] [as-jíd], *s.* (*Ant.*) Tonto, estúpido.

assibilate [əˈsɪbɪt] [a-si-bi-leit], *va.* Pronunciar con sonido sibilante; convertir en sibilante.

assiduity [əˈsɪdɔɪtɪ] [a-si-dui-ti], *s.* Asiduidad, aplicación y constancia, laboriosidad.

assiduous [əˈsɪdɪəs] [a-si-duos], *a.* Asiduo, constante, aplicado, continuo, laborioso.

assiduously [əˈsɪdɔəslɪ] [a-si-duos-li], *adv.* Constantemente, de continuo, sin cesar, perennemente, diligentemente.

assiduousness [əˈsɪdɪəsnɪs] [a-si-duos-nis], *s.* Diligencia, asiduidad.

assign [əˈsaɪn] [a-sain], *va.* 1. Asignar, señalar, destinar. 2. Dar la razón o motivo de alguna cosa; indicar, señalar, atribuir. 3. Probar, hacer ver. 4. (*For.*) Asignar, diputar; transferir, ceder, traspasar algún derecho a otro.

assign, *s.* (*For.*) Cesionario, la persona a cuyo favor se traspasa algún bien o derecho.

assignable [əˈsaɪnəbl] [a-sai-na-bol], *a.* Asignable, lo que se puede asignar.

assignation [æsɪgˈneɪʃən] [a-sig-nei-shon], *s.* 1. Asignación, cita o señalamiento de día, hora o lugar para verse o hablarse dos o más personas. 2. Renuncia, cesión o traslación de dominio. **House of assignation,** casa de asignación, casa de citas, prostíbulo.

assignee [æsaɪˈniː] [a-sai-ní], *s.* 1. Poderhabiente, apoderado. 2. (Der. *com.*) Síndico. Cesionario. *V.* ASSIGN.

assigner [æˈsaɪnəʳ] [a-sai-naʳ], *s.* Asignante, transferidor, el que asigna o transfiere.

assignment [æˈsaɪnmənt] [a-sain-ment], *s.* 1. Asignación, señalamiento, cesión. 2. (*For.*) Escritura de cesión de bienes, traspaso, renuncia, o traslación de dominio.

assignor [æsaɪˈnɔːʳ] [a-sai-noʳ], *s.* Cedente, el que asigna o transfiere.

assimilable [əˈsɪmɪləbl] [a-si-mi-la-bol], *a.* Semejable; asimilable, lo que puede asimilarse.

assimilate [əˈsɪmɪt] [a-si-mi-leit], *va.* 1. Asemejar, asimilar, hacer alguna cosa semejante a otra. 2. Convertir una cosa en la sustancia de otra. -*vn.* Convertir el alimento en quilo.

assimilation [əsɪmɪˈleɪʃən] [a-si-mi-lei-shon], *s.* 1. Asimilación, la conversión de una cosa en la sustancia de otra. 2. Asimilación, semejanza.

assimilative [əˈsɪmɪlətɪv] [a-si-mi-la-tif], *a.* Asimilativo.

assimulation [əsɪmjuˈleɪʃən] [a-si-miu-lei-shon], *V.* DISSIMULATION.

assist [əˈsɪst] [a-sist], *va.* Asistir, ayudar, socorrer, auxiliar. -*vn.* Asistir, hallarse presente, presenciar.

assistance [əˈsɪstəns] [a-sis-tans], *s.* Asistencia, auxilio, socorro, apoyo.

assistant [əˈsɪstənt] [a-sis-tant], *s.* Asistente o ayudante, el que está empleado en alguna cosa no como principal, sino como dependiente de otro. -*a.* Ayudador, que ayuda; auxiliar. **Assistant bishop,** obispo auxiliar. **Assistant teacher,** profesor auxiliar o adjunto. **Assistant engineer,** segundo maquinista, segundo ingeniero. **Assistant professor,** profesor agregado. **Assistant cameraman,**

ayudante de operador. **Assistant secretary,** subsecretario, secretario adjunto.

assistanship [əˈsɪstənʃɪp] [a-sis-tan-ship] s. Ayudantía.

assister [əˈsɪstəʳ] [a-sis-taʳ], s. Asistente, ayudador.

assistless [əˈsɪstlɪs] [a-sist-lis]

assizer [əˈsaɪzəʳ] [a-sai-saʳ], s. Fiel almotacén, la persona diputada para el reconocimiento de pesos y medidas.

ass-like [æsˈlaɪk] [as-laik], a. Semejante al asno, asinino, asnal; borricote.

associable [əˈsəʊʃəbl] [a-so-sha-bol], a. Sociable.

associate [əˈsəʊʃɪɪt] [a-sou-shiet], va. 1. Asociar, tomar por compañero o confederado a otro. 2. Asociar, acompañar. -vn. Asociarse. Unirse, tratarse, tratar. **I refuse to associate with them,** me niego a tratar con ellos.

associate, a. Asociado, confederado. -s. Socio o compañero. **Associate publishers,** editores asociados. **Associate member,** miembro asociado.

association [əˌsəʊsɪˈeɪʃən] [a-sou-si-ei-shon], s. Asociación, unión, sociedad, confederación, alianza, compañía, asamblea; cábala. **Religious association,** asociación religiosa. Recuerdo, relación. **Paris has happy associations for her,** París tiene recuerdos felices para ella. **Association of ideas,** asociación de ideas.

associator [əˌsəʊsɪˈeɪtəʳ] [a-sou-si-eitaʳ], s. Confederado.

associationism [əˌsəʊsɪəˈʃənɪzm] [a-sou-si-a-sho-nísem] s. Asociacionismo.

associative [əˈsəʊʃətɪv] [a-sou-sha-tif] a. De asociación.

assoil [æsɔɪl] [a-soil], va. 1. Resolver, responder. 2. Absolver, perdonar.

assonance [ˈæsənəns] [a-so-nans], s. Asonancia, similitud de sonidos. Asonancia, semejanza de sonido entre las últimas vocales de dos palabras, siendo las consonantes de sonido diferente. Esta clase de rima es exclusiva de la poesía española.

assonant [ˈæsənənt] [a-so-nant], a. Asonante, lo que hace asonancia.

assonate [ˈæsəneɪt] [a-so-neit] vn. Asonantar, asonar.

assonated [ˈæsəneɪtɪd] [a-so-nei-tid] a. Asonantado.

assort [əˈsɔːt] [a-sort], va. Colocar, ordenar, poner en orden; adecuar, proporcionar; clasificar.

assorted [əˈsɔːtɪd] [a-sor-tid] a. Clasificado, variado, surtido. **Ill-assorted couple,** matrimonio mal avenido. **Well-assorted couple,** matrimonio bien avenido.

assortment [əˈsɔːtmənt] [a-sort-ment], s. 1. Colección ordenada, surtido, variedad, clasificación. 2. El acto de arreglar o coordinar.

assuage [əˈsweɪdʒ] [a-sueich], va. Mitigar, apaciguar, calmar, suavizar, ablandar. -vn. Minorar, disminuir, deshincharse.

assuagement [əˈsweɪdʒmənt] [a-sueich-ment], s. Mitigación, calma.

assuager [əˈsweɪdʒəʳ] [a-sueichaʳ], s. Apaciguador.

assuasive [əˈswəsɪv] [a-sua-sif], a. Mitigativo, calmante.

assume [əˈsjuːm] [a-siúm], va. 1. Tomar, adoptar. **He assumed a foreign accent,** adoptó un acento extranjero. 2. Arrogar, apropiar, usurpar. 3. Presumir, suponer alguna cosa sin prueba o fundamento. **We assume him dead,** le damos por muerto. Manifestarse. **The disease assumes many forms,** la enfermedad se manifiesta de muchas maneras. Suponer. **I assume you will be there,** supongo que estarás allí. -vn. Arrogarse, atribuirse, apropiarse.

assumed [əˈsjuːmd] [a-siúmd], a. Afectado, fingido. **Assumed modesty,** modestia fingida.

assumer [əˈsjuːməʳ] [a-siú-maʳ], s. Persona arrogante.

assuming [əˈsjuːmɪŋ] [a-siú-min], a. Arrogante, altivo, presumido. **Assuming that,** suponiendo que, en el supuesto de que.

assumpsit [əˈsjuːmpsɪt] [a-siúm-sit], s. (For.) Promesa voluntaria y verbal, pacto, contrato.

assumption [əˈsjuːmpʃən] [a-siúm-shon], s. 1. Apropiación, la acción de apropiarse alguna cosa. 2. Asunción de la bienaventurada Virgen María, su tránsito y subida al cielo.

3. Asunción, proposición tomada sin prueba. **On the assumption that,** suponiendo que.

assumptive [əˈsjuːmptɪv] [a-siúm-tif], a. Apropiado; lo que puede ser supuesto.

assurance [əˈʃʊərəns] [a-shua-rans], s. 1. Seguridad, certeza. 2. Seguridad, firmeza. 3. Descaro, llaneza, demasiada confianza o falta de modestia. 4. Seguridad, fianza, garantía; convicción. 5. Intrepidez, arrojo, valor, ánimo, resolución. 6. Seguro de vida, contra incendios, etc. V. INSURANCE. **I gave my assurance that I would go,** le di palabra de que iría, le prometí que iría.

assure [əˈʃʊəʳ] [a-shuaʳ], va. 1. Asegurar, afirmar o dar seguridades de la certeza de lo que se refiere o promete. **Assure yourself that,** esté usted seguro. 2. Contratar un seguro contra pérdidas, perjuicios, etc.

assured [əˈʃʊəd] [a-shuad], a. 1. Seguro, cierto, indubitable. 2. Seguro, cierto, persuadido, libre de duda. 3. Descarado, atrevido, la persona que se toma demasiada confianza o llaneza. 4. Protegido por un contrato de seguro. **Rest assured that,** tenga la seguridad de que.

assuredly [əˈʃʊədlɪ] [a-shuad-li], adv. Ciertamente, indubitablemente, sin duda.

assuredness [əˈʃʊədnɪs] [a-shuad-nis] s. Certeza, seguridad.

assurer [əˈʃʊərəʳ] [a-shua-raʳ], s. Asegurador, el que asegura.

Assyria [əˈsɪrɪə] [a-si-ria] N. (Geogr.) Asiria.

Assyrian [əˈsɪrɪən] [a-si-rian], a. Asirio, de Asiria.

Assyriology [əˌsɪrɪəˈlɒdʒɪ] [a-si-ria-lo-chi] s. Asiriología.

astatic [æsˈtætɪk] [as-ta-tik], a. Astático, que no es estable, que no tiende a tomar dirección definida o fija. **Astatic needle,** aguja astática imantada.

aster [ˈæstəʳ] [as-taʳ], s. Aster, género de plantas radiadas (compuestas) con flores azuladas o blancas.

asterias [əstɪˈrɪəs] [as-ti-rias], s. (Zool.) Asteria, género de zoófitos, estrella de mar.

asterisk [ˈæstərɪsk] [as-te-risk], s. Asterisco, una estrellita que usan los impresores en los libros (*). va. Poner un asterisco a.

asterism [ˈæstərɪzm] [as-te-rísem], s. 1. (Astr.) Constelación, pequeño grupo de estrellas. 2. Grupo de astericos (******).

astern [əˈstɜːn] [as-térn], adv. (Mar.) Por la popa, a popa. Hacia atrás. **Astern of,** detrás de.

asteroid [ˈæstərɔɪd] [as-te-roid], s. Asteroide, planeta telescópico perteneciente a un grupo de 340 entre las órbitas de Marte y Júpiter.

asthenia [æsˈθiːnɪə] [as-zi-nia] s. (Med.) Astenia.

asthenic [æsˈθiːnɪk] [as-zi-nik], a. Asténico, flaco, débil.

asthma [ˈæsmə] [as-ma], s. Asma, enfermedad espasmódica del pecho, a menudo catarral.

asthmatic, asthmatical [æsˈmætɪk] [as-ma-tik], a. Asmático.

astigmat [æsˈtɪgmæt] [as-tig-mat] s. Astigmático.

astigmatic [æstɪgˈmætɪk] [as-tig-ma-tik], a. Astigmático, que tiene astigmatismo.

astigmatism [æsˈtɪgmætɪzm] [as-tig-ma-tí-sem], s. Astigmatismo, defecto de visión causado por falta de simetría en la córnea.

astir [əˈstɜːʳ] [as-téʳ], adv. En estado de movimiento o actividad; fuera de la cama.

astomatous [æsˈtəmætəʊs] [as-to-ma-tous], a. (Biol.) Sin boca, ni poros para respirar; ástomo, que carece de boca.

astonish [əˈstɒnɪʃ] [as-to-nish], va. Asombrar, pasmar, sorprender, enajenar. **To be astonished at** o **by,** quedarse asombrado o asombrarse de o por.

astonishingly [əˈstɒnɪʃɪŋlɪ] [as-to-ni-shin-li], adv. Pasmosamente, asombrosamente.

astonishingness [əˈstɒnɪʃɪŋnɪs] [as-to-ni-shin-nes], s. La calidad o propiedad pasmosa de alguna cosa.

astonishment [əˈstɒnɪʃmənt] [as-to-nish-ment], s. Pasmo, asombro, espanto, enajenamiento, sorpresa.

astound [əˈstaʊnd] [as-taund], va. 1. consternar, aturdir. 2. Asombrar, aterrar, sorprender. -vn. Temblar, enajenarse.

astounding [əˈstaʊndɪŋ] [as-taun-din], a. Asombroso, consternado.

astrachan [ˈæstrəˈkæn] [as-tra-kan] *s.* Astracán.

astraddle [æsˈrædl] [as-tra-del], *adv.* A horcajadas o a horcajadilas. **To ride astraddle,** montar a horcajadas.

astragal [æsˈrægæl] [as-tra-gal], *s.* 1. *(Arq.)* Astrágalo, cordón en forma de anillo, con que se adorna la parte superior e inferior de las columnas. 2. Astrágalo, empeine del pie. 3. *pl.* Dados: porque originalmente fueron tabas.

astragalus [æsˈrægæləs] [as-tra-ga-los], *s.* 1. *(Anat.)* Astrágalo, talón, empeine del pie, chita. 2. *(Bot.)* Astrágalo, alquitira, género de plantas papilionáceas.

astrakhan [æstrəˈkæn] [as-tra-kan], *a.* De Astracán en Rusia. -*s.* Piel de astracán. Escríbese también **Astrachan.**

astral [ˈæstrəl] [as-tral], *a.* Astral, que pertenece a los astros, o que viene de ellos. **Astral bodies,** cuerpos astrales.

astrand [ˈæstrənd] [as-trand], *adv. (Mar.)* Encallado, varado; echado sobre la costa.

astray [əˈstreɪ] [as-trei], *adv.* Desviado, errado, fuera del camino recto. **To go astray,** errar el camino; perderse, extraviarse. **To lead astray,** *(Fig.)* desviar, apartar, descaminar, descarriar, extraviar.

astrict [æsˈtrɪkt] [as-trikt], *va.* Astringir, apretar, estreñir.

astricted [æsˈrɪktɪd] [as-trik-tid] *a.* Astricto.

astriction [æsˈrɪkʃən] [as-trik-shon], *s.* Astricción, calidad o propiedad de una cosa astringente.

astride [æsˈraɪd] [as-traid], *adv.* A horcajadas, montado con una pierna a cada lado del caballo.

astringe [əsˈrɪndʒ] [as-trínch], *va.* Astringir, apretar, estreñir.

astringency [əsˈrɪndʒənsɪ] [as-trin-chan-si], *s.* 1. Astricción, el poder de astringir. 2. Aspereza de carácter.

astringent [əsˈrɪndʒənt] [as-trin-chent], *a.* 1. Astringente, que aprieta o astringe los tejidos blandos; estíptico; que detiene el vientre. 2. Áspero, agrio de genio, duro. **Astringent principle,** *(Quím.)* principio astringente, uno de los principios vegetales.

astrobiology [æstrəˌʊbaɪˈɒlədʒɪ] [as-trou-bai-o-lo-chi], *s.* Astrobiología.

astrography [æsˈrɒɡrəfɪ] [as-trou-gra-fi], *s.* Astrografía, descripción de los astros.

astrolabe [ˈæstrəleɪb] [as-trou-leib], *s.* Astrolabio, instrumento matemático que servía principalmente para observar, en el mar, la altura, lugar y movimientos de los astros.

astrologe [əsˈrɒlɒɡ] [as-trou-log], *s.* Astrólogo, el que profesa la astrología.

astrologic [əsˈrɒlədʒəʳ] [as-tro-lo-chaʳ], **astrological** [æstrɒˈlɒdʒɪkəl] [as-tro-lo-chi-kal], *a.* Astrológico.

astrologically [æstrɒˈlɒdʒɪkəlɪ] [as-tro-lo-chi-ka-li], *adv.* Astrológicamente.

astrology [əsˈrɒlədʒɪ] [as-tro-lo-chi], *s.* Astrología, el arte de pronosticar los sucesos por la situación de los planetas.

astronaut [ˈæstrənɔːt] [as-tro-not], *s.* Astronauta.

astronautics [æstrəˈʊnɔːtɪks] [as-tro-no-tiks], *s.* Astronáutica, viajes astronáuticos, viajes interestelares.

astronavigation [æstrənəvɪˈɡeɪʃən] [as-tro-na-vi-guéi-shon], *s.* Astronavegación. Navegación interplanetaria o espacial.

astronomer [əsˈrɒnəməʳ] [as-tro-no-maʳ], *s.* Astrónomo, el que profesa la astronomía. **Astronomer Royal,** director del observatorio astronómico de Greenwich.

astronomic [æstrəˈnɒmɪk] [as-tro-no-mik], **astronomical** [æstrəˈnɒmɪkəl] [as-tro-no-mi-kal], *a.* Astronómico. **Astronomic unit,** unidad astronómica. **Astronomical clock, telescope,** reloj, telescopio astronómico.

astronomically [æstrəˈnɒmɪklɪ] [as-tro-no-mi-kli], *adv.* Astronómicamente.

astronomize [æstrəˈnɒmaɪz] [as-tro-no-mais], *vn.* Estudiar la astronomía.

astronomy [əsˈrɒnəmɪ] [as-tro-no-mi], *s.* Astronomía, la ciencia que trata de la naturaleza, magnitud y movimiento de los cuerpos celestes.

astrophysicist [æstrəˈʊfɪzɪsɪst] [as-tro-fi-si-sist] *s.* Astrofísico.

astrophysics [æstrəˈʊfɪzɪks] [as-tro-fi-siks] *s.* Astrofísica.

astro-theology [æstrəʊˈθɪəlɒdʒɪ] [as-tro-zi-o-lo-chi]. Astroteología. Ciencia que demuestra por los astros el infinito poder, sabiduría y bondad de Dios.

astrut [ˈæstrət] [as-trot], *adv.* Hinchadamente, pomposamente.

astucious [æsˈtʊʃəs] [as-tú-shos] *a.* V. ASTUTE.

astute [əsˈtjuːt] [as-tiút], *a.* Astuto, agudo; aleve.

astuteness [əsˈtjuːtnɪs] [as-tiút-nis], *s.* Astucia, penetración, sutileza.

asunder [əˈsʌndəʳ] [a-sán-daʳ], *adv.* Separadamente, desunidamente, aparte. **To cut a thing asunder,** cortar alguna cosa en dos partes. **To come asunder,** separarse. **To tear asunder,** hacer pedazos.

aswim [əˈswɪm] [a-suín], *adv.* Flotante, nadando.

asylum [əˈsaɪləm] [a-sái-lam], *s.* Asilo, refugio. **To seek political asylum,** pedir asilo político. **To afford asylum to,** dar asilo a.

asymmetral [eɪˈsɪmɪtrəl] [ei-si-me-tral], **asymmetrical** [ˌeɪsɪˈmetrɪkəl] [ei-si-me-tral], *a.* Irregular, desproporcionado.

asymmetry [eɪˈsɪmɪtrɪ] [ei-si-me-tri], *s.* Asimetría, desproporción.

asymptote [əˈsɪmtɒt] [a-sim-tot], *s. (Mat.)* Asíntota, línea recta que se acerca a una curva sin jamás encontrarse con ella.

asymptotic [əˈsɪmtɒtɪk] [a-sim-to-tik] o **asymptotical** [əˈsɪmtɒtɪkl] [a-sim-to-ti-kal] *a.* Asintótico.

asynchronism [æˈsɪŋkrəˌnɪzm] [a-sin-kro-nísem], *s.* Asincronismo, divergencia o no coincidencia en tiempo o fechas.

asynchronous [æˈsɪŋkrənəs] [a-sin-kro-nos], *a.* Asincrónico, que no ocurre en la misma fecha.

asyndetic [ˈæsɪndetɪk] [a-sin-de-tik] *a.* Asindético.

asyndeton [ˈæsɪndetɒn] [a-sin-de-ton], *s. (Ret.)* Asíndeton, figura de locución que omite la conjunción copulativa.

at [æt] [at], *prep.* 1. A, en; preposición que antepuesta a lugar, denota el mismo lugar, denota el mismo lugar o su proximidad. **At the station,** en la estación. **I arrived at the office,** llegué a la oficina. **A man is at the house,** hay un hombre en la casa. 2. Antepuesta a una voz que signifique tiempo, denota la coexistencia de éste con lo que ha sucedido. **At nine o'clock there was an accident in this street,** a las nueve de esta mañana hubo un accidente en esta calle. **At first,** al principio, desde luego. **At last,** por último. **At that,** *(Fam.)* también; en adición. **At once,** de un golpe, a la vez, de una vez, al instante. **At no time,** nunca, jamás. **At last o at length,** por fin, al fin. 3. Delante de un superlativo significa el estado de la cosa. **At most,** a lo más, cuando más, a lo sumo. **At least,** a lo menos. **At best,** cuando mejor, a lo mejor. **At the worst,** a lo peor andar. 4. Significa la condición o estado particular del sujeto. **They are at peace,** están en paz. **He is at work,** está al trabajo o está trabajando. **He is at home,** está en casa. **He is at my command,** está a mi disposición. **At all,** en modo alguno; hasta cualquier grado; en todo caso; por cierto. **Is it at all likely?** ¿es probable en modo alguno? **At all events,** a todo trance, sea lo que fuere, en todo caso. **At large,** en general; sin limitación. **At sea,** (1) en el mar. (2) perplejo, turbado. **At hand,** a la mano. **At leisure,** despacio. **At ease,** descansadamente. **At play,** jugando. **At a push,** en una urgencia. **At a pinch,** en un apuro. **At a venture,** a lo que salga, a la buena ventura. **At a loss,** indeciso, perplejo, dudoso. **All at once,** de repente. **At a distance,** a lo lejos. **At the hazard of,** con peligro de. **At a mouthful,** de un bocado. **To be at.** Es un modo de hablar muy común que se usa para toda suerte de ocupación.

atabal [ˈætəbəl] [a-ta-bal], *s.* Atabal, especie de timbal usado por los moros.

ataghan [ˈætəɡæn] [a-ta-gan], *s.* Lo mismo que YATAGHAN.

atamasco [ˈætəməskəʊ] [a-ta-mas-kou], *s. (Bot.)* Lirio atamasco, planta norteamericana, de la familia de las amarilídeas, que produce una gran flor blanca y rojiza. (Nombre indio.)

ataraxia [ˈætəræksɪ] [a-ta-rak-si] o **ataraxy** [ˈætəræksɪə] [a-ta-rak-sia] s. Ataraxia.

atavic [ˈætəvɪk] [a-ta-vik] a. Atávico.

atavism [ˈætəvɪzəm] [a-ta-vísem], s. Atavismo, semejar de un animal o una planta con sus progenitores.

atavistic [ˌætəvɪstɪk] [a-ta-vis-tik] a. Atávico.

ataxia [əˈtæksɪə] [a-tak-sia] o **ataxy** [əˈtæksɪs] [a-tak-sis] s. Ataxia, irregularidad en las funciones del sistema muscular o en la marcha de una enfermedad.

ate [eɪt] [eit]. Pretérito del verbo TO EAT.

-ate. Sufijo que corresponde por lo general al español -ado.

atelier [ˈætəlɪəʳ] [a-te-liaʳ], s. Taller, estudio de un artista. *(Fr.)*

atellan [ˈætələn] [a-te-lan], s. y a. *(Ant.)* Representación dramática o satírica.

atheism [ˈeɪθɪɪzəm] [ei-ti-ísem], s. Ateísmo, opinión impía que niega la existencia de Dios.

atheist [ˈeɪθɪɪst] [ei-ti-ist], s. Ateo, el que niega la existencia de Dios.

atheistic [ˌeɪθɪˈɪstɪk] [ei-ti-is-tik], **atheistical** [ˌeɪθɪˈɪstɪkl] [ei-ti-is-ti-kal], a. Impío, ateo.

atheistically [ˌeɪθɪˈɪstɪklɪ] [ei-ti-is-ti-ka-li], adv. Impíamente.

Atheneum [əˈθɪnɪəm] [a-ti-niom], s. 1. Ateneo, lugar público de Atenas donde los escritores daban lectura a sus obras. 2. Ateneo, nombre que se da hoy a diversos establecimientos científicos y literarios, y a varias bibliotecas.

Athenian [əˈθɪnɪən] [a-ti-nion], a. Ateniense.

Athens [ˈæθəns] [á-zens] N. *(Geogr.)* Atenas.

Athermanous [əˈθɜːmənəs] [a-zer-ma-nos] a. Atérmano.

atheroma [əθɪˈrəʊmə] [a-zi-rou-ma], s. Ateroma, enfermedad de la túnica interior de una arteria que se caracteriza por espesamiento y degeneración crasa.

athirst [əˈθɜːst] [a-zérst], adv. Sediento.

athlete [ˈæθliːt] [a-zlít], s. Atleta, deportista. **All-round athlete,** atleta completo, deportista en todos los campos.

athletic [əˈθliːtɪk] [a-zlí-tik], a. 1. Atlético, que pertenece a la atlética o arte de luchar. 2. Fuerte, robusto, vigoroso.

athletics [əˈθliːtɪks] [a-zlí-tiks] s. Atletismo.

athwart [əˈθwɔːt] [az-uórt], **prep.** Al o a través, de través, por el través, de un modo atravesado. **Athwart the forefoot,** *(Mar.)* por el través de la gorja. **Atwart hawse,** *(Mar.)* por través de las barbas. **Atwart ship,** *(Mar,)* de babor a estribor. -adv. Contrariamente, a ciegas.

-atic. Sufijo: de, de la suerte de: usado en adjetivos de origen griego o latino, como *erratic,* errático; *grammatic,* gramático.

atilt [əˈtɪlt] [a-tilt], adv. 1. En postura de dar una lanzada; en ristre. 2. En la posición de un barril inclinado.

-ation [ˈeɪʃən] [ei-shon], Sufijo que forma nombres de acción: muchas veces equivale al nombre verbal o gerundio en *ing.*

Atlantean [əˈtlæntɪən] [at-lán-tian], a. Lo perteneciente al Atlante.

Atlantes [əˈtlæntɪs] [at-lán-tis] s. pl. *(Arq.)* Atlantes.

Atlantic [əˈtlæntɪk] [at-lán-tik], a. Atlántico. -s. El mar Atlántico.

Atlantis [əˈtlæntɪs] [at-lán-tis] N. Atlántida.

Atlas [ˈætləs] [at-las], s. 1. Atlas, el libro u obras geográficas que contiene todos los mapas del mundo. 2. *(Arq.)* Atlante o telamón. 3. Atlas, tela de seda. 4. Primera vértebra del cuello. 5. Atlas, cadena de montañas en África.

atmology [ˈætmɒlɒdʒɪ] [at-mo-lo-chi], s. Atmología, ciencia que trata de las leyes de los vapores acuosos.

atmosphere [ˈætməsfɪəʳ] [at-mos-fíaʳ], s. 1. Atmósfera, el aire que rodea la tierra por todos lados. 2. Alcance, o espacio a que se extienden las influencias ejercidas por una persona, cosa o idea. **An intellectual atmosphere,** un ambiente intelectual. 3. Unidad de fuerza o tensión fundada en la presión atmosférica.

atmospheric, atmospherical [ætməsˈferɪk] [at-mos-ferik], a. Atmosférico.

atmospherics [ætməsˈferɪks] [at-mos-fe-riks] s. pl. Perturbaciones atmosféricas, parásitos, interferencias.

atoll [ˈætɒl] [a-tol], **atollon,** s. Atol, atolón, isla madrepórica sumergida en su centro, de modo que aparece como un banco circular de coral que rodea una laguna central. Curiosa formación abundante en el Océano Pacífico.

atom [ˈætəm] [a-tom], s. 1. Átomo, un cuerpo tan pequeño que es físicamente indivisible. 2. Átomo, cualquier cosa sumamente pequeña. **Atom bomb,** bomba atómica. **Atom smasher,** acelerador de partículas atómicas.

atomic [ˈætɒmɪk] [a-to-mik], **atomica** [ˈætɒmɪkə] [a-to-mi-ka], a. Atómico. **Atomic age,** era atómica. **Atomic bomb,** bomba atómica. **Atomic energy,** energía atómica. **atomic dust,** polvo radiactivo. **Atomic number,** número atómico. **Atomic weight,** peso atómico.

atomicity [ˈætɒmɪsɪtɪ] [a-to-mi-si-ti] s. *(Quím.)* Atomicidad.

atomics [ˈætɒmɪks] [a-to-miks] s. Atomística.

atomism [ˈætɒmɪzm] [a-to-mi-sem], s. La doctrina de los átomos.

atomist [ˈætɒmɪst] [a-to-mist], s. Atomista, el que sigue o defiende el sistema de los átomos.

atomistic [ˈætɒmɪstɪk] [a-to-mis-tik] a. Atomístico.

atomization [ˌætɒmɪˈseɪʃən] [a-to-mi-séi-shon], s. Pulverización. Reducción a átomos o rocío (hablando de líquidos).

atomize [ˈætəmaɪz] [a-to-mais], va. Pulverizar, reducir a átomos o niebla (vapor visible), rociar.

atomizer [ˈætəmaɪzəʳ] [a-to-mai-saʳ], s. Pulverizador, aparato para reducir un líquido o partículas muy tenues, a manera de polvo, formando un rocío o vapor visible, con objeto de desinfectar, inhalar, perfumar, etc.

atom-like [ˈætəmˌlaɪk] [a-tom-laik], a. Semejante al átomo.

atom smasher [ˈætəmˌsmæʃəʳ] [a-tom-smá-saʳ], s. Pulverizador de átomos.

atomy [ˈætəmɪ] [a-to-mi], s. Átomo; motita. *(Fam.)* Enano.

atonal [æˈtəʊnl] [a-to-nal] a. *(Mús.)* Atonal.

atonality [əˈtəʊnælɪtɪ] [a-to-na-li-ti] s. Atonalidad.

atone [æˈtəʊn] [a-ton], va. Expiar, pagar las penas debidas por las culpas; apaciguar, aplacar. -vn. 1. Equivaler, corresponder una cosa con otra en la estimación, precio o valor. 2. *(Ant.)* Acordar, convenir una cosa con otra. **To atone with,** reconciliarse con.

atonement [æˈtəʊnmənt] [a-ton-ment] s. Expiación, reparación. **Day of atonement,** día de la expiación.

atoner [æˈtəʊnəʳ] [a-to-naʳ], s. Reconciliador, apaciguador.

atonic [æˈtɒnɪk] [a-to-nik], a. Atónico, que padece atonía, que está falto de vigor o elasticidad.

atony [ˈætɒnɪ] [a-to-ni], s. Atonía, debilidad de las fibras.

atop [əˈtɒp] [a-top], adv. Encima, en la punta o parte superior de alguna cosa.

-ator. Sufijo que denota agente, actor, como *arbitrator.*

-atory. Sufijo que denota perteneciente a; producente o producido por.

atrabilarian [ætrəbɪˈlærɪən] [a-tra-bi-la-rian], **atrabilarious** [ˌætrəbɪˈlærɪəs] [a-tra-bi-la-rias], a. Atrabiliario, atrabilioso, melancólico, hipocondríaco.

atrabiliar [ætrəˈbɪlɪəʳ] [a-tra-bi-liaʳ] a. Atrabiliario.

atrabilious [ætrəbɪˈlɪəs] [a-tra-bi-lios] a. Atrabiliario.

atramental [ætrəˈməntəl] [a-tra-men-tal], **atramentous** [ætrəˈməntəs] [a-tra-men-tos], a. Negro; perteneciente a la tinta.

atrip [ˈætrɪp] [a-trip] a. *(Mar.)* **With anchor atrip,** con el ancla levada.

atrium [ˈeɪtrɪəm] [ei-triom] s. *(Arq.)* Atrio. *(Med.)* Aurícula (of the heart).

atrocious [əˈtrəʊʃəs] [a-tro-shos], a. Atroz, enorme, extremadamente malo o cruel.

atrociously [əˈtrəʊʃəslɪ] [a-tro-shos-li], adv. Atrozmente.

atrociousness [ə'trəʊʃəsnɪs] [a-tro-shos-nis], **atrocity** [ə'trɒsɪtɪ] [a-tro-si-ti], s. Atrocidad, enormidad de algún delito; maldad horrible.

atrophic ['ætəfɪk] [a-tro-fik], a. Atrófico, concerniente a la atrofia, o afectado por ella; descaecido.

atrophous ['ætəfəs] [a-tro-fos], a. V. ATROPHIC.

atrophy ['ætəfɪ] [a-tro-fi], s. (Med.) Atrofia, enflaquecimiento. -vn. Atrofiarse, ir a menos, descaecer, decaer.

atropia ['ætəpɪə] [a-tro-pia], **atropine** ['ætəpɪn] [a-tro-pin], atropina, alcaloide venenoso que se extrae de la belladona.

attach [ə'tætʃ] [a-tach], va. 1. Pegar, juntar, atar, ligar; enganchar; conectar. **We are very attached to one another,** estamos muy unidos el uno al otro. 2. Prender, agarrar, pillar, asir, coger. 3. (For.) Embargar, secuestrar. 4. Ganar, lograr, adquirir, atraer a sí. 5. vr. Apegarse, adherirse. **To be attached to customs,** estar apegado a las costumbres. **To attach importance,** dar importancia a. **An expert attached to a delegation,** un experto agregado a una delegación.

attaché [ə'tæʃeɪ] [a-ta-shei] s. Agregado.

attaché case [ə'tæʃkeɪs] [a-ta-shei-keis] s. Maletín.

attachment [ə'tætʃmənt] [a-tach-ment], s. 1. Amistad, enlace, adherencia, afecto, apego, adhesión, afición; fidelidad; presa, aprehensión. **There is a strong attachment between them,** se tienen mucho apego. 2. (For.) Embargo, secuestro.

attack [ə'tæk] [a-tak], va. Atacar, acometer, embestir; impugnar, combatir. (Fig.) Asaltar. **Attacked by doubts,** asaltado por las dudas.

attack, s. Ataque, la acción de atacar, acometimiento, embestida. **To launch an attack,** iniciar un ataque. **Surprise attack,** ataque por sorpresa.

attackable [ə'tækəbl] [a-ta-ka-bol] a. Atacable.

attacker [ə'tækəʳ] [a-ta-krʳ], s. Atacador, acometedor.

attacking [ə'tækɪŋ] [a-ta-kin] a. Agresor. **Attacking army,** ejército agresor.

attain [ə'teɪn] [a-tein], va. Ganar, procurar, conseguir, lograr, alcanzar. -vn. Llegar a, obtener, alcanzar. **To attain to perfection,** alcanzar la perfección.

attainability [əteɪnə'bɪlɪtɪ] [a-tei-na-bi-li-ti] s. Accesibilidad.

attainable [ə'teɪnəbl] [a-tei-na-bol], a. Asequible, lo que se puede conseguir o alcanzar.

attainableness [ə'teɪnəblnɪs] [a-tei-na-bol-nis], s. Probabilidad o posibilidad de alcanzar alguna cosa.

attainder [ə'teɪndəʳ] [a-tein-daʳ], s. 1. (For.) Imputación de algún delito, deshonra; proscripción, muerte civil. **Bill of attainder,** decreto de proscripción. 2. (Ant.) Mancha, mácula, tacha.

attainment [ə'teɪnmənt] [a-tein-ment], s. 1. Logro, consecución de lo que se pretende. Adquisición. **Difficult of attainment],** de difícil consecución. 2. pl. Dotes, talento, conocimientos.

attaint [ə'teɪnt] [a-teint], va. 1. Convencer de algún delito, especialmente del de traición. 2. Corromper, viciar, manchar.

attaint, a. Convencido. -s. 1. Mancha, mácula. 2. (For.) Auto jurídico.

attaintment [ə'teɪntmənt] [a-teint-ment], s. El estado de haber sido convicto de algún delito.

attainture [ə'teɪntʃəʳ] [a-tein-chaʳ], s. (Des.) Deshonra. V. ATTAINDER.

attar [ə'tɑʳ] [a-taʳ], s. Aceite esencial fragante, en especial el de rosas. **Attar of roses,** esencia de rosas. V. OTTAR.

attemper [ə'tempəʳ] [a-tam-paʳ], va. Atemperar, diluir, molificar, mezclar; acomodar.

attempt [ə'tempt] [a-tempt], va. 1. Intentar, atentar; aventurar, arriesgar; atacar, embestir; tentar, tratar de (to try to). **He attempted to jump the wall,** intentó saltar el muro. 2. Probar, experimentar, ensayar, tratar de (hacer) (to try something.) **He attempted a smile,** intentó sonreír. **They attempted a rescue,** intentaron rescatarle. **Attempted**

murder, tentativa de asesinato. **To attempt the life of,** atentar contra la vida de. -vn. Procurar; hacer esfuerzos para conseguir algo, tirar a, pretender.

attempt, s. 1. Ataque, acometimiento, intento, tentativa (endeavor, try). **At the first attempt,** en el primer intento. 2. Empresa, atentado (attack) **attempt upon the security of the State,** atentado contra la seguridad del estado. Prueba, experimento peligroso, esfuerzo. **To make an attempt on the summit,** tratar de llegar a la cumbre. **It was a good attempt,** fue un esfuerzo digno de alabanza.

attemptable [ə'temptəbl] [a-temp-ta-bol], a. Sujeto o expuesto a ser atacado.

attempter [ə'temptəʳ] [a-temp-taʳ], s. Emprendedor, el que se esfuerza por hacer o conseguir alguna cosa.

attend [ə'tend] [a-tend], va. 1. Atender, estar con cuidado y aplicación a lo que se mira, oye, hace o dice; escuchar atentamente, poner atención. **Attend to what I say,** atienda usted a lo que digo. 2. Servir, asistir, cuidar, tratar, atender (to visit and treat). **To attend the sick,** cuidar al enfermo. 3. Acompañar. **His physician attended him through the whole journey,** su médico le acompañó durante todo el viaje. 4. Presentarse, acudir, comparecer, asistir. **He attended the meeting,** asistió a la reunión. **He attends evening classes,** asiste a clases nocturnas. 5. Acompañar o seguir como efecto necesario. 6. Esperar. 7. Traer tras de sí (to accompany as a result). **Success attended his every effort,** el éxito acompañaba todos sus esfuerzos. -vn. 1. Atender, prestar atención. **Are you being attended, sir?,** ¿le atienden, señor? 2. Esperar; tardar. 3. Considerar. **To attend to a business,** tener a su cargo un negocio. **To be attended with,** causar, ocasionar, acarrear.

attendance [ə'tendəns] [a-ten-dans], s. 1. Presencia, asistencia, concurrencia. **What was the attendance at the meeting?,** ¿cuántos asistieron a la reunión? (For.) comparecencia. **Your attendance is necessary,** la presencia de usted es necesaria. 2. Corte, obsequio. 3. Tren, séquito, comitiva, boato, acompañamiento. **To be on attendance on the minister,** acompañar al ministro, formar parte del séquito del ministro. 4. Servidumbre, asistencia, servicio. (Fam.) **To dance attendance,** estar de plantón o de postre, hacer antesala. **Lady in attendance,** Camarera mayor. 5. (Med.) Asistencia. **Cabs in attendance,** taxis en la parada. **To be on attendance,** estar de servicio.

attendant [ə'tendənt] [a-ten-dant], s. 1. Sirviente, servidor. 2. Cortesano. 3. Acompañante (companion). 4. Concomitante, lo que pertenece a otra cosa u obra con ella. 5. Criado, sirviente, asistente (person present). 6. Cortejo, galán, galanteador, obsequiante. 7. Acomodador (in cinema, theater). **Attendants,** subalternos (que acompañan a un ministro, u oficial superior). Tren, séquito. Servidumbre, criados, gentes de servicio. **Ignorance and its attendants, fear and prejudice,** la ignorancia y sus secuelas, el miedo y los prejuicios. -a. Concomitante (circumstances, etc.), acompañante. Asistente, presente. **Attendant on someone,** que sirve o acompaña a uno. **War and its attendant horrors,** la guerra y su secuela de horrores.

attender [ə'tendəʳ] [a-ten-daʳ], s. Compañero, socio, el que atiende.

attent [ə'tent] [a-tent], a. Atento, cuidadoso.

attentates [ə'tenteɪts] [a-ten-teits], a. Atento, cuidadoso.

attention [ə'tenʃən] [a-ten-shon], s. 1. Atención, miramiento, cuidado, aplicación, reflexión. **To pay attention to,** prestar atención a. **To attract, draw, call someone's attention,** llamar la atención de uno. **He received medical attention,** recibió cuidados médicos. **Attention!,** ¡cuidado! **For the attention of,** a la atención de. 2. Cortejo, galanteo, obsequio a una mujer. Más usado en el plural. **His constant attentions annoy me,** sus constantes atenciones me molestan. 3. (Mil.) Voz de mando con que se advierte que va a empezar cierta maniobra; la postura o actitud misma que toman los soldados al oír dicha voz. **Attention!,** ¡firmes! **To come to attention,** ponerse firme, cuadrarse. **To bring to attention,** dar la orden de cuadrarse. 4. Servicio (service in a shop, restaurant, etc.). **To be all attention,** estar muy atento. **Your attention, please!,** ¡atención!.

attentive [ə'tentɪv] [a-ten-tif], *a.* Atento, el que tiene o fija la atención en alguna cosa. **Attentive to the slightest sound,** atento al menor ruido. Aplicado, atento (industrious). **An attentive pupil,** un alumno aplicado. Atento (considerate, thoughtful).

attentively [ə'tentɪvlɪ] [a-ten-tif-li], *adv.* Atentamente, con atención y cuidado.

attentiveness [ə'tentɪvnɪs] [a-ten-tif-nes], *s.* 1. Calidad de atento; miramiento, circunspección, cuidado. 2. Cortesía, finura, afabilidad en los modales.

attenuant [ə'tenjʊənt] [a-te-niu-ant], *a.* Atenuante, lo que atenúa o adelgaza.

attenuate [ə'tenjʊeɪt] [a-te-niu-eit], *va.* Atenuar, adelgazar, disminuir; hacer más tenue, como se hace, por ejemplo, con un alambre.

attenuate, *a.* Atenuado, delgado, diminuto.

attenuation [ə,tenjʊ'eɪʃən] [a-te-niu-ei-shon], *s.* Atenuación, la acción de atenuar o adelgazar.

attest [ə'test] [a-test], *va.* 1. Atestiguar (to affirm, to bear witness to), deponer, declarar, afirmar como testigo alguna cosa. 2. Citar o llamar por testigo. 3. Confirmar, dar fe (to confirm as authentic), legalizar (document or signature), juramentar (to place on oath). *(For.)* **I attest,** doy fe. *vn.* Dar testimonio (*to,* de)

attest, attestation [ætes'teɪʃən] [a-tes-tei-shon], *s.* Atestación, evidencia o deposición de testigo; prueba, testimonio (act of bearing witness, testimony), confirmación. Atestado (document). Garantía. **That signature is sufficient attestation for us,** esa firma es garantía suficiente para nosotros. Prestación de juramento (oath).

attestor [ə'testər] [a-tes-tar], *s.* 1. Testigo, el que da testimonio. 2. Certificador, el que certifica.

attic ['ætɪk] [a-tik], *s.* 1. Desván (loft), guardilla; también piso de poca elevación construido sobre una cornisa o un entablamento. **Attic story,** el último piso o alto de la casa: ático (top floor). 2. Ático, el natural de Ática.

attic, attical ['ætɪkl] [a-tikl], *a.* Ático, agudo, juicioso, picante; se aplica al estilo.

Attica ['ætɪkə] *n. Geogr.* Ática.

Atticism ['ætɪsɪzm] [a-ti-síf-sem], *s.* Aticismo, la palidez, brevedad y elegancia de lenguaje que usaban los atenienses, así como a los romanos se llamó urbanidad.

Attila ['ætɪlə] [a-ti-la] *N.* Atila.

attire [ə'taɪər] [a-taia], *va.* Ataviar, componer, asear, adornar, vestir.

attire, *s.* 1. Atavío, el adorno y compostura de la persona; cofia, escofieta; traje, vestido en general. 2. *(Her.)* Astas de ciervo. 3. *(Ant.)* El pistilo y los estambres de las flores; sus partes interiores.

attiring [ə'taɪərɪŋ] [a-taia-rin], *s.* Cofia, escofieta; vestido en general.

attitude ['ætɪtjuːd] [a-ti-tiud], *s.* Postura (position), actitud (mental state). **Attitude of mind,** actitud mental. *(Aer.)* Posición. **To strike an attitude,** adoptar una postura teatral, tener una actitud estudiada.

attitudinal [ætɪ'tjuːdɪnəl] [a-ti-tiu-di-nal], *a.* De la actitud o referente a ella.

attitudinarian [ætɪ'tjuːdɪnɛrɪən] [a-ti-tiu-di-na-rian], *s.* Pintor o escultor que sobresale en el estudio y reproducción de las actitudes.

attitudinize [ætɪ'tjuːdɪnaɪz] [a-ti-tiu-di-nais], *vn.* Pavonearse, tomar posturas afectadas o académicas.

attollent ['ætɒlənt] [a-to-lent], *a.* Elevador, que levanta o eleva, por ejemplo un músculo.

attorn [ə'tɜːn] [a-térn], *vn..* (For. Ant.) Transferir los bienes o derechos a otro. *-va.* Reconocer a un nuevo poseedor de los bienes y aceptar sus poderes.

attorney [ə'tɜːnɪ] [a-ter-ni], *s.* 1. *(For.)* Abogado, procurador, apoderado; poderhabiente, el que en virtud de poder o facultad de otro ejecuta en su nombre alguna cosa. **Attorney general,** ministro de Justicia, (in Great Britain) fiscal del Tribunal Supremo. **District attorney,** fiscal. **Letter of attorney,** poder, procuración. 2. Procurador de la curia eclesiástica. *V.* PROCTOR Y SOLICITOR.

attorney-general [ə'tɜːnɪdʒənərəl] [a-ter-ni-yé-ne-ral], *s.* Fiscal, en los tribunales superiores; en los ayuntamientos, procurador, o síndico general.

attorneyship [ə'tɜːnɪʃɪp] [a-ter-ni-ship], *s.* Procuraduría, el oficio de procurador, agencia.

attract [ə'rækt] [a-trakt], *va.* 1. Atraer, traer hacia sí alguna cosa. 2. Atraer, inclinar o reducir a otro a su voluntad; granjear.

attractable [ə'ræktəbl] [a-trak-ta-bol], *a.* Atraíble, capaz de ser atraído, susceptible de atracción.

attracter, attractor [ə'ræktər] [a-trak-to], *s.* El agente que atrae.

attractile [ə'ræktɪl] [a-trak-til], *a.* Atractivo, con fuerza material de tracción o atracción; atráctil.

attractingly [ə'ræktɪŋlɪ] [a-trak-tin-li], **attractively** [a-trak-tif-li], *adv.* Atractivamente.

attraction [ə'rækʃən] [a-trak-shon], *s.* 1. Atracción, la acción o virtud de atraer a sí alguna cosa. 2. Atractivo, la fuerza con que se atrae la voluntad. **The main attraction of the fair,** la atracción principal de la feria. 3. Perturbación, desviación de las agujas imantadas. **Attraction of cohesion, molecular attraction,** atracción molecular. **Capilary attraction,** atracción capilar.

attractive [ə'ræktɪv] [a-trak-tif], *a.* 1. Atractivo, atrayente (interesting), lo que tiene la fuerza y virtud de traer. **Attractive offer,** oferta atractiva. 2. Atractivo (person), halagüeño (prospect), lo que se atrae o inclina a sí la voluntad.

attractive, *s.* Atractivo, incentivo, aliciente; encanto, embeleso.

attractiveness [ə'ræktɪvnɪs] [a-trak-tif-nis], *s.* Fuerza atractiva; gracia.

attrahent [ə'ræhənt] [a-tra-jent], *s.* Atrayente, lo que atrae o lleva hacia sí.

attributable [ə'trɪbjʊtəbl] [a-tri-biu-ta-bol], *a.* Imputable, lo que se puede imputar; lo que se puede aplicar o atribuir.

attribute ['ætrɪbjuːt] [a-tri-biut], *va.* 1. Atribuir, dar o aplicar. 2. Atribuir, achacar, imputar.

attribute, *s.* 1. Atributo, la cosa atribuida a otro. 2. Calidad o propiedad inherente. 3. Honra, reputación. **Reason is the attribute of man,** la razón es el atributo del hombre. *(Gram.)* Atributo.

attribution [ætrɪ'bjuːʃən] [a-tri-biu-shon], *s.* Calidades atribuidas, atributo; recomendación.

attributive [ætrɪ'bjuːtɪv] [a-tri-biu-tif], *a.* Atributivo, que atribuye. *-s.* La cosa atribuida.

attrite [ə'raɪt] [a-trit], *a.* 1. Estregado, frotado. Desgastado por el uso. 2. *(Teol.)* Pesaroso, atrito.

attrition [ə'trɪʃən] [a-tri-shon], *s.* 1. Rozadura, roce (rubbing), desgaste (wearing away, exhausting), colisión, trituración, o molimiento de una cosa contra otra. 2. Atrición, arrepentimiento por temor al castigo.

attune [ə'tjuːn] [a-triún], *va. (Mús.)* Afinar. Armonizar (to bring into harmony), acordar. *(Fig.)* Adaptar (to adapt). *V.* TUNE.

atwain [ə'tweɪn] [a-tuain], *adv.* Separadamente, en dos.

atwirl [ə'twɜːl] [a-tuérl], *a. y adv.* En rotación, girando, dando vueltas.

atwist [ə'twɪst] [a-tuist], *adv. y a.* Torcidamente, al través, sesgado.

atypic, atypical [eɪ'tɪpɪkəl] [ei-ti-pi-kal], *a.* Atipo, atípico, irregular, anormal.

aubade [əʊ'beɪd] [ou-beid] *s. (Mús. Poét.)* Alborada.

aubergine [əʊbədʒiːn] [au-bér-chin] *s. (Bot.)* Berenjena.

auburn ['ɔːbən] [o-bern], *a.* 1. Castaño; moreno rojizo; castaño es algo más obscuro que *auburn.* 2. Rojizo (del pelo).

auction [ˈɔːkʃən] [auk-shon], *s.* 1. Almoneda, venta pública en que uno puja el precio después de otro hasta rematarse en el que más ofrece. 2. Pública subasta. 3. Vendeja. *(Amer.)* Venduta. 4. La alhaja o cosa vendida en almoneda. **To put up for auction, to sell at auction,** subastar, poner o vender en pública subasta. **To be on auction,** salir a subasta.

auction, *va.* Subastar, vender a pública subasta. Almonedear, vender en almoneda.

auctionary [ˈɔːkʃənərɪ] [auk-sho-na-ri], *a.* Lo que pertenece a una almoneda.

auctioneer [ˌɔːkʃəˈnɪər] [auk-sho-niaʳ], *s.* Subastador, vendutero. *-va.* Vender a pública subasta.

auction room [ˈɔːkʃənrʊm] [auk-shon-rum] *s.* Sala de subastas.

audacious [ɔːˈdeɪʃəs] [au-dei-shos], *a.* 1. Audaz (daring), osado, atrevido (too daring), temerario. 2. Descarado, imprudente.

audaciously [ɔːˈdeɪʃəslɪ] [au-dei-shos-li], *adv.* Atrevidamente.

audaciousness [ɔːˈdeɪʃəsnɪs] [au-dei-shos-nis], *s.* Impudencia, descaro, temeridad, atrevimiento (impudence), audacia (boldness), desvergüenza, avilantez.

audacity [ɔːˈdæsɪtɪ] [au-da-si-ti], *s.* Audacia, osadía, atrevimiento. **To show, display audacity,** demostrar audacia.

audibility [ɔːdɪˈbɪlɪtɪ] [o-di-bi-li-ti] *s.* Audibilidad.

audible [ˈɔːdɪbl] [o-di-bol] *a.* Audible.

audibly [ˈɔːdɪblɪ] [o-di-bli], *adv.* De modo que se puede oír; alto.

audience [ˈɔːdɪəns] [o-dians], *s.* 1. Audiencia, la acción de oír a otro que habla, o la libertad que se concede a alguno para que diga lo que tiene que decir. 2. Auditorio, concurso de oyentes. 3. Audiencia, (official reception) el recibimiento que tiene el que lleva una embajada. Público, a u d i t o r i o (at show, etc.). Radioyentes (at radio), telespectadores (of television), lectores (of writer). **Audience-chamber,** sala o cámara de recepción. *(For.)* Audiencia.

audio frequency [ˌɔːdɪəʊˈfriːkwənsɪ] [o-diou-frí-kuan-si], *s.* (Radio) Audiofrecuencia.

audiogram [ˈɔːdɪəgræm] [o-dio-gram] *s.* Audiograma.

audiology [ˈɔːdɪɒlɒdʒɪ] [o-dio-lo-chi], *s.* Audiología.

audiometer [ˌɔːdɪˈɒmɪtəʳ] [o-dio-mi-taʳ], *s.* Audiómetro, instrumento para medir la agudeza del oído.

audion [ˈɔːdɪɒn] [o-dion], *s.* Audión (usado en transmisiones telefónicas y de radio a larga distancia).

audiophile [ˈɔːdɪəfaɪl] [o-dio-fail], *s.* El entusiasta de la música fonográfica, particularmente de la alta fidelidad. Audiófilo.

audio-visual [ˌɔːdɪəʊˈvɪzjʊəl] [ou-dio-vi-shual], *a.* Audiovisual. **Audio-visual aids,** medios audiovisuales.

audiphone [ˈɔːdɪfəʊn] [o-di-foun], *s.* Instrumento que, colocado contra los dientes, transmite el sonido a los oídos. Lo usan las personas algo sordas.

audit [ˈɔːdɪt] [o-dit], *s.* Remate de una cuenta. Revisión o intervención de cuentas. **Audit office,** tribunal de cuentas.

audit *va./vn.* Rematar; examinar; pelotear. Verificar o revisar la contabilidad. Ser oyente (to a class).

auditing [ˈɔːdɪtɪŋ] [o-di-tin] *s.* Intervención o revisión de cuentas.

audition [ɔːˈdɪʃən] [o-dí-shon], *s.* La acción de oír. La facultad de oír, el sentido del oído. *va./vn.* Dar una audición.

auditive [ˈɔːdɪtɪv] [o-di-tif], *a.* Auditivo. V. AUDITORY.

auditor [ˈɔːdɪtəʳ] [o-di-toʳ], *s.* 1. Radioyente, estudiante libre, oyente. 2. Contador, revisor de cuentas (accounts).

auditorium [ˌɔːdɪˈtɔːrɪəm] [o-di-to-rium], *s.* Auditorio, la parte de una iglesia, de un teatro, etc., destinada al auditorio. Sala (theater), paraninfo, auditorium (lecture hall, assembly hall). Nave (of a church). Locutorio, sala de visitas (of a convent).

auditorship [ˈɔːdɪtɔːʃɪp] [o-di-tor-ship], *s.* Auditorio, concurso de oyentes. *-a.* Auditivo, auditorio, que oye y lo

que sirve para oír. **Auditory canal, nerve,** Conducto, nervio auditivo.

auditory [ˈɔːdɪtərɪ] [o-di-to-ri] *a.* Auditivo.

auditress [ˈɔːdɪtres] [o-di-tres], *sf.* Oidora, la que oye.

Augean [ɔːˈdʒiːən] [o-chian], *a.* 1. Referente a Augeas, rey de Elida, cuyo establo contenía 3.000 bueyes, y no había sido limpiado en 30 años. Hércules lo limpió en un solo día. 2. Sucísimo, asqueroso, inmundo.

auger [ˈɔːdʒəʳ] [o-charʳ], *s.* Barrena, taladro, instrumento de carpintero para taladrar. **Bolting auger,** *(Mar.)* barrena de empernar. **Auger o auger-hole,** agujero; barreno. **Auger-bit,** gusanillo de rosca o de taladro. **Auger-handle,** mango, ástil de barrena. **Auger-shank,** vástago de barrena. **Expanding auger,** barrena de extensión. **Ground-auger,** barrena terrena. **Well-auger,** barrena de pocero.

aught [ɔːt] [ot], *pron.* Algo, alguna cosa: (con negación) nada. **For aught that I know it was not so,** en cuanto yo sé, no fue así. **For aught I care,** por mí.

augite [ˈɔːgaɪt] [o-gait] *s.* *(Min.)* Augita.

augment [ɔːɡˈment] [og-ment], *s.* Añadidura, aumento, acrecentamiento. *va./vn.* Aumentar.

augmentation [ˌɔːɡmənˈteɪʃən] [og-men-téi-shon], *s.* 1. Aumentación, la acción de aumentar. 2. Aumento, el efecto de ser aumentado. 3. Aumento, añadidura por la cual se hace una cosa mayor de lo que era.

augmentative [ɔːɡˈmentətɪv] [og-men-ta-tif], *a.* Aumentativo, que aumenta.

augur [ˈɔːgəʳ] [o-gaʳ], *s.*, **augurer** [ˈɔːgərəʳ] [o-ga-raʳ], *s.* Augur, agorero, adivino.

augur, augurate [ˈɔːgəreɪt] [o-ga-reit], *va.* Augurar, pronosticar, predecir. *-vn.* Augurar, agorar, pronosticar, adivinar por conjeturas. **To augur ill, well,** ser de mal, de buen agüero.

augural [ˈɔːgərəl] [o-ga-ral], *a.*, **augurial** [ˈɔːgərɪəl] [o-ga-rial], *a.* Augural, perteneciente a los agüeros o a los augures.

augury [ˈɔːgərɪ] [o-ga-ri], *s.* Agüero, adivinación o pronóstico ya sea favorable o contrario; presagio, auspicio, adivinación.

August [ˈɔːgəst] [o-gast], *a.* Augusto, grande, real, majestuoso.

August, Agosto, el octavo mes del año.

Augustan [ˈɔːgəstən] [o-gs-tan], *a.* Augusto, perteneciente al emperador Augusto o a su tiempo.

Auguste [ˈɔːgəst] [o-gast] *s.* Augusto (clown).

Augustine [ˈɔːgəstiːn] [o-gues-tin] *N.* Agustín.

Augustinian [ˌɔːgəsˈtiːnɪən] [o-gues-tí-nian], *a.* Agustiniano, Agustino: que se refiere o pertenece a San Agustín, a su doctrina o a la orden religiosa de su nombre.

Augustinianism [ˌɔːgəsˈtiːnɪənɪzm] [o-gues-ti-nia-nísem] o **augustinism** [ˌɔːgəsˈtiːnɪzən] [o-gues-ti-ní-sem] *s.* *(Rel.)* Agustinianismo.

augustness [ˈɔːgəstnɪs] [o-guest-nis], *s.* Majestuosidad, elevación de aire o porte, grandeza, majestad.

Augustus [ɔːˈgʌstəs] [o-gas-tas], *N.* Augusto.

auk [ɔːk] [ok], *s.* *(Orn.)* Alca, una ave marítima. V. Puffin.

auld lang syne [ˌɔːldlaŋˈʃaɪn] [ould-lain-shain], (Expresión escocesa) Frase que se usa para expresar los días pasados, antaño, tiempos que fueron.

aulic [ˈɔːlɪl] [o-lik], *a.* Aulico, lo que pertenece a la corte o palacio.

aunt [ɑːnt] [ant], *sf.* Tía, la hermana del padre o la madre. **Aunt-in-law,** tía política.

aunty [ˈɑːntɪ] [an-ti], *sf.* 1. Tía, comadre; mujer vieja. 2. (E. U. del Sur) Negra vieja. También se escribe AUNTIE.

au pair [əʊˈpeə] [o-péaʳ] *a./adv.* Au pair. *s.* Chica au pair, ayuda familiar.

aura [ˈɔːrə] [ó-ra], *s.* 1. Aura, ambiente (atmosphere), fluido, sutil exhalación o emanación de fuerza; influencia psíquica. 2. Sensación especial como de un vaho que procedente del tronco o de los miembros sube a la cabeza, síntoma monitorio de la epilepsia y de la histeria. 3. Céfiro, viento apacible y suave. 4. *(Rel.)* Aureola. *(Med.)* Aura.

aural [ˈɔːrəl] [ó-ral], *a.* Auditivo, auricular, que se refiere al oído.

aurated [ˈɔːrwɪtɪd] [ó-ri-tid], *a.* 1. Auriculado, que tiene apéndices como orejas. 2. Dorado, áureo.

aureate [ˈɔːrɪt] [ó-rit] *a.* Dorado.

aureola [ˈɔːrɪəul] [ó-rial], **aureole** [ˈɔːrɪəul] [ó-rial], *s.* Aureola, círculo de luz con que se representan las cabezas de los santos.

aureomycin [ˌɔːrɪəuˈmɪsiːn] [o-rio-mi-sin], *s.* (Trademark) Aureomicina.

auric [ˈɔːrɪk] [ó-rik] *a.* Aurico.

auricle [ˈɔːrɪkl] [ó-rikl], *s.* Oreja, el órgano exterior del oído. **Auricles,** *pl.* 1. Aurículas, las alas del corazón. 2. Las orejas o crestas que tienen algunas aves encima de los ojos, como el búho.

auricula [ˈɔːrɪkjələ] [o-rí-kiu-la], *s.* 1. (*Bot.*) Oreja de oso, una planta. 2. (*Biol.*) Pequeño apéndice en forma de oreja.

auricular [ˈɔːrɪkjələr] [o-rí-kiu-lar], *a.* 1. Auricular, lo que pertenece al oído; se aplica a la confesión de los católicos. 2. Secreto, dicho al oído. 3. Tradicional, lo que se sabe por tradición.

auricularly [ˈɔːrɪkjələlɪ] [o-rí-kiu-la-li], *adv.* Al oído, secretamente.

auriculate, auriculated [ˈɔːrɪkjɪt] [o-rí-kiu-leit], *a.* 1. Auriculífero, que tiene aurícula. 2. Auriculado, en forma de oreja; se dice de ciertos bivalvos y hojas.

auriferous [ˈɔːrɪfərəs] [o-rí-fe-ros], *a.* (*Poét.*) Aurífero, lo que produce oro, o contiene oro.

auriform [ˈɔːrɪfɔːm] [o-ri-fórm], *a.* Auriforme, en forma de oreja.

auriga [ˈɔːrɪgə] [o-ri-ga], *s.* Auriga, cochero; constelación boreal entre Perseo y Géminis.

aurigation [ˈɔːrɪgeɪʃən] [o-ri-géi-shon], *s.* El acto o la práctica de conducir carruajes.

aurist [ˈɔːrɪst] [o-rist], *s.* Aurista, el que tiene por profesión curar las enfermedades de los oídos.

aurochs [ˈɔːrɒks] [o-roks], *s.* (*Zool.*) Uro, auroch, toro bravío de la antigua Galia y Alemania. Hoy sólo quedan ejemplares en los bosques de Lituania y el Cáucaso. Bisonte europeo.

aurora [ˈɔːrɔːrə] [o-ro-ra], *s.* 1. Aurora, la primera luz que se descubre antes de salir el sol. 2. Crepúsculo de la mañana. 3. **Aurora australis,** aurora austral.

aurora borealis [ɔːˈrɔːrəbɔːrɪˈeɪlɪs] [o-ro-ra-bo-ri-éi-lis], *s.* Aurora boreal, *V.* NORTHERN LIGHTS.

auroral [ˈɔːrɔːrəl] [o-ro-ral], *a.* Producido por el alba o crepúsculo matutino, o semejante a la aurora; rosáceo.

aurous [ˈɔːrəs] [o-ros] *a.* Aurico.

auscultate [ˈɔːskjɔlteɪt] [os-kiul-teit], *va.* Auscultar, examinar por medio de la auscultación. *-vn.* Practicar la auscultación.

auscultation [ˈɔːskjɔlteɪʃən] [os-kiul-tei-shon], *s.* 1. Auscultación, acción y efecto de auscultar; aplicación del oído o el estetoscopio a ciertos puntos del cuerpo para explorar los sonidos y ruidos de los órganos del pecho, vientre, etc. 2. Atención, la acción de atender o escuchar lo que se dice.

auspice [ˈɔːspaɪs] [os-pais], *s.* 1. Auspicio, presagio de algún suceso por el vuelo de las aves. 2. Auspicio, protección, amparo, apoyo, autoridad. **Under the auspices of,** bajo los auspicios de.

auspicial [ˈɔːspɪʃəl] [os-pi-shal], *a.* Lo perteneciente a los pronósticos.

auspicious [ˈɔːspɪʃəs] [os-pi-shos], *a.* Próspero, feliz, favorable; benigno, propicio.

auspiciously [ˈɔːspɪʃəslɪ] [os-pi-shos-li], *adv.* Prósperamente, felizmente. Favorablemente, con buenos auspicios.

auspiciousness [ˈɔːspɪʃəsnɪs] [os-pi-shos-nis], *s.* Prosperidad, esperanza de felicidad. Buenos auspicios, carácter propicio.

austere [ɒˈtiːər] [os-tía], *a.* 1. Austero, severo, rígido; rudo. 2. Agrio, ácido, acerbo al gusto.

austerely [ɒsˈtiːlɪ] [os-tía-li], *adv.* Austeramente.

austereness [ɒsˈtiːnɪs] [os-tía-nis], *s.* Austeridad, crueldad, severidad.

austerity [ɒsˈterɪtɪ] [os-teriti], *s.* Austeridad. **Austerity program,** programa de austeridad.

austral [ˈɔːstrəl] [os-tral], *a.* Austral, lo que pertenece al austro o mediodía.

Australasia [ˌɔːstrəˈleɪʒə] [os-tra-lei-sia] *N.* (*Geogr.*) Australasia.

Australia [ɒsˈtreɪlɪə] [os-trei-lia] *N.* (*Geogr.*) Australia.

Australian [ɒsˈtreɪlɪən] [os-trei-lian], *a.* Australiano, perteneciente a Australia.

Austrasia [ɒsˈtreɪsɪə] [os-trei-sia] *N.* (*Geogr.*) Austrasia.

Austria [ˈɒstrɪə] [os-tria] *N.* (*Geogr.*) Austria.

Austrian [ˈɒstrɪən] [os-trian], *a.* Austriaco, de Austria.

autarchic [ˈɔːtɑːkɪk] [o-tar-kik] o **autarchical** [ˈɔːtɑːkɪkl] [o-tar-ki-kal] *a.* Autárquico.

autarchy [ˈɔːtɑːkɪ] [o-tar-ki], *s.* Autarquía, suficiencia económica nacional.

autarkic [ˈɔːtɑːkɪk] [o-tar-kik] o **autarkical** [ˈɔːtɑːkɪkl] [o-tar-ki-kal] *a.* Autárquico.

authentic [ɔːˈθentɪk] [o-zen-tik], **authentical** [ɔːˈθentɪkl] [o-zen-tikl], *a.* Auténtico, lo autorizado o legalizado públicamente; solemne, cierto, original.

authentically [ɔːˈθentɪkəlɪ] [o-zen-ti-ka-li], **authenticly** [ɔːˈθentɪklɪ] [o-zen-ti-kli], *adv.* Auténticamente.

authenticalness [ɔːˈθentɪkəlnɪs] [o-zen-ti-kal-nis], **authenticity** [ɔːˈθentɪsɪtɪ] [o-zen-ti-si-ti], **authenticness** [ɔːˈθentɪknɪs] [o-zen-tik-nis], *s.* Autenticidad.

authenticate [ɔːˈθentɪkeɪt] [o-zen-ti-keit], *va.* Autenticar, autentificar, hacer auténtico.

authentication [ɔːˌθentɪˈkeɪʃən] [o-zen-ti-kei-shon] *s.* Autenticación, autentificación.

author [ˈɔːθər] [o-zar], *s.* 1. Autor, el que es causa primera de alguna cosa. 2. Autor, el que es causa eficiente de alguna cosa. 3. Autor, el que ha compuesto alguna obra literaria, artística o científica, con respecto a la misma obra compuesta; escritor. 4. Conjunto de las obras o los escritos de un autor. **Author's royalties,** derechos de autor.

author, *va.* Ser autor de, hacer, escribir, inventar, crear.

authoress [ˈɔːθəres] [o-za-res], *sf.* Autora, escritora.

authoritarian [ˌɔːθɒrɪˈtɛərɪən] [o-zo-ri-ta-rian], *s.* y *a.* Autoritario.

authoritarianism [ˌɔːθɒrɪˈtɛərɪənɪəm] [o-zo-ri-ta-rianísem] *s.* Autoritarismo.

authoritative [ɔːˈθɒrɪtətɪv] [o-zo-ri-ta-tif], *a.* 1. Autorizado, que tiene la autoridad necesaria, que es una autoridad (book, document). 2. Que ejerce autoridad; positivo, perentorio, terminante. 3. Autoritario (with an air of command). Autorizado (source).

authoritatively [ɔːˈθɒrɪtətɪvlɪ] [o-zo-ri-ta-tif-li], *adv.* 1. Autorizadamente. 2. Autorizadamente.

authoritativeness [ɔːˈθɒrɪtətɪvnɪs] [o-zo-ri-ta-tif-nis], *s.* Autoridad debidamente sancionada; calidad de lo autorizado; apariencia autoritativa.

authority [ɔːˈθɒrɪtɪ] [o-zo-ri-ti], *s.* 1. Autoridad, potestad, facultad, poder legal. **To have authority over one's employees,** tener autoridad sobre sus empleados. **Authority of father,** patria potestad. **With complete authority,** con plena autoridad. 2. Crédito y fe que se da a alguna cosa. 3. Autoridad, el texto o palabras con que se apoya lo que se dice. **I have it from the best authority,** lo sé de muy buen original o de buena tinta; lo tengo de buena mano. **Printed by authority,** impreso con licencia. **On his own authority,** por su propia autoridad. **To apply to the proper authority,** dirigirse a la autoridad competente. **To be an authority,** ser una autoridad.

authorization [ˌɔːθɒrɪzeɪʃən] [o-zo-ri-séi-shon], *s.* Autorización, la acción y efecto de autorizar.

authorize [ˈɔːθəraɪz] [o-zo-rais], *va.* 1. Autorizar, dar autoridad o facultad para hacer alguna cosa. 2. Autorizar, legalizar algún instrumento de forma que haga fe pública. 3. Autorizar, sancionar, comprobar alguna cosa con autoridad. **Authorized Version,** traducción inglesa de la Biblia hecha en 1611, sancionada por el rey Jaime I, y que se dispuso fuera leída en las iglesias. *Cf.* REVISED VERSION.

authorized [ˈɔːzəraɪzd] [o-zo-aisd], *a.* Autorizado, facultado.

authorless [ˈɔːzərlɪs] [o-zo-lis], *a.* Desautorizado; sin autor. Anónimo.

authorship [ˈɔːzərʃɪp] [o-zo-ship], *s.* 1. El estado, la calidad o profesión de autor. Paternidad literaria. **I claim authorship of this book,** sostengo que soy el autor de este libro. **Of unknown authorship,** de autor desconocido. 2. Manantial, origen.

auto [ˈɔːtəʊ] [o-tou] *s.* (*Fam.*) Coche, auto, carro.

autobiographer [ˈɔːtəˌbaɪəʊˈgræfəʳ] [o-to-bai-ou-gra-faʳ] *s.* Autobiógrafo.

autobiographic [ˈɔːtəˌbaɪəʊˈgræfɪk] [o-to-bai-ou-gra-fik] o **autobiographical** [ˈɔːtəˌbaɪəʊˈgræfɪkl] [o-to-bai-ou-gra-fi-kal] *a.* Autobiográfico.

autobiography [ˈɔːtəˌbaɪəʊˈgræfɪ] [o-to-bai-ou-gra-fi], *s.* Autobiografía.

autobus [ˈɔːtəʊbʌs] [o-to-bas], *s.* Autobús, ómnibus, camioneta.

autocade [ˈɔːtəʊkeɪd] [o-to-keid], *s.* Caravana de automóviles.

autochthon [ɔːˈtɒkθən] [o-tok-zon] *s.* Autóctono.

autochthonous [ɔːˈtɒkθənəs] [o-tok-zo-nos] *a.* Autóctono.

autoclave [ˈɔːtəkleɪv] [o-to-kleif], *s.* Autoclave, aparato de esterilización por vapor y presión.

autocracy [ɔːˈtɒkrəsɪ] [o-to-kra-si], *s.* Autocracia, poder absoluto o independiente.

autocrat [ˈɔːtəʊkræt] [o-to-krat], *s.* Autócrata.

autocratical [ˈɔːtəʊkrætɪkl] [o-to-kra-ti-kal], *a.* Autocrático.

auto-da-fé o **auto-de-fé** [ˈɔːtəʊdɑːˈfeɪ] [o-to-da-fei] *s.* (*Rel.*) Auto de fe.

autodidact [ɔːtəʊdɪdækt] [o-to-di-dakt] *s.* Autodidacto.

autodidactic [ɔːtəʊdɪdæktɪk] [o-to-di-dak-tik] *a.* Autodidáctico, autodidacto.

autogamy [ɔːˈtɒgæmɪ] [o-to-ga-mi] *s.* (*Bot.*) Autogamia.

autogenous [ɔːˈtɒdʒɪnəs] [o-to-chi-nas] *a.* Autógeno. **Autogenous vaccine,** autovacuna.

autogiro, autogyro [ˈɔːtəˈdʒaɪrəʊ] [o-to-chaia-rou], *s.* (*Aer.*) Autogiro.

autograph [ˈɔːtəˈgrɑːf] [o-to-graf] *s.* Autógrafo, firma (signature).

autograph *va.* Poner un autógrafo a. Firmar (to sign).

autographical [ɔːtɪkl] [o-to-gra-fi-kal], *a.* Autográfico, escrito de propio puño. Autógrafo (letter, etc.).

autography [ɔːtəgrəfɪ] [o-to-grafi] *s.* Autografía.

autoinduction [ˌɔːtɔɪnˈdʌkʃən] [o-to-in-dák-shon] *s.* Autoinducción.

autoinfection [ˌɔːtɔɪnˈfekʃən] [o-to-in-fék-shon] *s.* Autoinfección.

autointoxication [ˌɔːtɔɪnˈtɒksɪˌkeɪʃən] [o-to-in-tok-si-kéi-shon] *s.* Autointoxicación.

autolysis [ˈɔːtəlaɪsɪs] [o-to-lai-sis] *s.* Autólisis.

automat [ˈɔːtəmæt] [o-to-mat], *s.* Restaurante en que la comida es distribuida por máquinas automáticas (restaurant). Aparato mecánico (machine).

automate [ˈɔːtəmeɪt] [o-to-meit] *va.* Automatizar.

automatic [ˌɔːtəˈmætɪk] [o-to-ma-tik], o **automatical** [ˌɔːtəˈmætɪkl] [o-to-ma-ti-kal], *a.* Automático, lo que se mueve por sí mismo. **Automatic brake,** freno automático. **Automatic tracking,** sistema de localización automática. *s.* Arma automática.

automaticity [ˌɔːtəˈmætɪsɪtɪ] [o-to-ma-ti-si-ti] *s.* Automaticidad.

automation [ˌɔːtəˈmeɪʃən] [o-to-méi-shon], *s.* Automatización.

automatism [ɔːˈtɒmətɪzəm] [o-to-ma-tísem] *s.* Automatismo.

automatize [ɔːˈtɒmətaɪs] [o-to-ma-tais] *va.* Automatizar.

automaton [ɔːˈtɒmətən] [o-to-ma-ton], *s.* Autómata, la máquina que se mueve por sí misma.

automobile [ˈɔːtəməbiːl] [o-to-mo-bil], *a.* Automóvil, que se mueve por sí mismo. *-s.* Carruaje de paseo, carretón o

vehículo para el transporte de mercancías, que tiene un mecanismo que lo pone en movimiento.

automotive [ˈɔːtəˈməʊtɪv] [o-to-mou-tif], *a.* Automotor, automotriz.

autonomic [ɔːˈtɒnəmɪk] [o-to-no-mik] *a.* Autonómico.

autonomist [ɔːˈtɒnəmɪst] [o-to-no-mist] *s.* Autonomista.

autonomous [ɔːˈtɒnəməs] [o-to-no-mos], *a.* Autónomo.

autonomy [ɔːˈtɒnəmɪ] [o-to-no-mi], *s.* Autonomía, derecho de gobernarse por sí mismo.

autopilot [ˈɔːtəʊpaɪlət] [o-to-pái-lot], *s.* (*Aer.*) Piloto automático.

autoplasty [ˈɔːtəplæstɪ] [o-to-plas-ti] *s.* Autoplastia.

autopsy [ˈɔːtəpsɪ] [o-top-si], *s.* Autopsia, examen anatómico un cadáver para descubrir la causa de la muerte. *va.* (*Med.*) Autopsiar.

autosuggestion [ˈɔːtəˌsəˈdʒestʃən] [o-to-sa-chés-shon], *s.* Autosugestión.

autotomy [ɔːˈtɒtəmɪ] [o-to-to-mi] *s.* Autotomía.

autotruck [ˈɔːtəʊrʌkt] [o-to-trakt], *s.* Autocamión.

autotype [ˈɔːtəʊtaɪp] [o-to-taip], *s.* 1. Autotipo, facsímil, copia exacta.

autovaccine [ˈɔːtəʊvæksiːn] [o-to-vak-sin] *s.* Autovacuna.

autumn [ˈɔːtəm] [o-tom], *s.* Otoño, la estación del año que media entre el verano y el invierno.

autumnal [ˈɔːtəmnəl] [o-tom-nal], *a.* Otoñal, lo perteneciente al otoño.

autumn crocus [ˈɔːtəmkrɒkəs] [o-tom-kro-kos] *s.* (*Bot.*) Cólquico.

auxiliar [ɔːgˈzɪlɪər] [ok-si-liar], *a.* Auxiliar, auxiliatorio.

auxiliary [ɔːgˈzɪlɪərɪ] [ok-si-lia-ri], *s.* Auxiliador. *a.* Auxiliar. **Auxiliary verb,** verbo auxiliar. (*Mil.*) Tropas auxiliares.

avail [əˈveɪl] [a-véil], *va.* 1. Aprovechar, emplear útilmente alguna cosa. 2. Promover, adelantar. **To avail oneself of an opportunity,** valerse de la ocasión. Aprovecharse de, sacar partido. *-vn.* Servir, importar, ser útil, ser ventajoso; ayudar. **It avails nothing to,** nada importa; de nada sirve.

avail, *s.* Provecho, ventaja, utilidad. *-pl.* Beneficios, producto (de una venta). **Of no avail,** sin efecto, inútil. **Of what avail** is it?, ¿de qué sirve? **To be of little avail,** no servir para mucho. **To no avail, without avail,** en vano.

availability [əˌveɪləˈbɪlɪtɪ] [a-vei-la-bi-li-ti], *s.* Eficacia, utilidad, actividad. Disponibilidad.

available [əˈveɪləbl] [a-véi-la-bol], *a.* 1. Útil, ventajoso, provechoso: (*com.*) disponible, que sirve (ready for use). Que se puede conseguir, obtenible (obtainable). Válido (ticket) 2. Eficaz, activo y poderoso en el obrar. **Available assets,** activo disponible. **By all available means,** por todos los medios posibles. **To make available to,** poner a la disposición de. **When will he be available?,** ¿cuándo estará libre?

availableness [əˈveɪləblnɪs] [a-vei-la-bol-nis], *s.* Eficacia, virtud, actividad, fuerza y poder para obrar; utilidad, ventaja.

availably [əˈveɪləblɪ] [a-véi-labli], *adv.* Eficazmente, provechosamente, útilmente.

avalanche [ˈævəlɑːʃ] [a-va-lanch], *s.* Avalancha o alud, masas grandes de nieve que se desprenden de las cumbres de las montañas, y cayendo en los valles o en el mar causan muchos daños.

avant-guard o **avant-garde** [ˈævɑːŋɡɑːd] [a-vant-gard], *s.* Vanguardia. *V.* VAN-GUARD.

avarice [ˈævərɪs] [a-va-ris], *f.* Avaricia, codicia.

avaricious [ævəˈrɪʃəs] [a-va-ri-shos], *s.* Avaro, avariento, miserable.

avariciously [ævəˈrɪʃəslɪ] [a-va-ri-shos-li], *adv.* Avaramente, avarientamente.

avariciousness [ævəˈrɪʃəsnɪs] [a-va-ri-shos-nis], *s.* Codicia, avaricia, la calidad de ser avaro.

avast [əˈvɑːst] [a-vast], *adv.* (*Mar.*) Forte. **Avast heaving,** (*Mar.*) forte al virar. También suele usarse en el sentido de ¡basta! ¡bueno está! ¡no más!

avatar [ˈævətəʳ] [a-va-taʳ] *s.* Avatar (in Hindu religion). (*Fam.*) Manifestación, materialización.

avaunt [ˈævɔːnt] [a-vont], inter. ¡Fuera! ¡Fuera de aquí! ¡Quita! ¡Quita allá! ¡Lejos de aquí! ¡Quítate de delante!

ave [æv] [av] s. Avemaría. **Ave Mary o Ave María,** s. Ave María; la salutación angélica.

avenaceous [ævɪˈnaʃəs] [a-vi-na-shos], a. Avenáceo, perteneciente a la avena; avenáceo, de la naturaleza de la avena.

avenge [əˈvendʒ] [a-vench], va. Vengarse, tomar satisfacción de un agravio o injuria; castigar algún delito. **To avenge oneself,** vengarse.

avengement [əˈvendʒmənt] [a-vench-ment], s. Venganza, satisfacción que se toma del agravio recibido.

avenger [əˈvendʒəʳ] [a-ven-chaʳ], s. 1. Castigador, el que castiga. 2. Vengador, el que venga o se venga.

avens [əˈvenz] [a-vens], s. (Bot.) Gariofilea, una planta cualquiera del género Geum, familia de las rosáceas.

aventurine, aventurin [əˈventoriːn] [a-ven-tu-rin], s. 1. Venturina, cuarzo con laminitas de mica amarilla. 2. Venturina artificial, cristal fundido con limaduras de cobre. 3. Un lacre moreno claro lleno de brillantes.

avenue [ˈævenjuː] [a-ven-niu], s. 1. Avenida, calle ancha o calle principal; calzada. 2. Calle de árboles, alameda, carrera. 3. Entrada, pasadizo. 4. (Fig.) Vía, senda, camino.

aver [əˈvəʳ] [a-vaʳ], va. Asegurar, afirmar, declarar, verificar, certificarse. (For.) Establecer la prueba de.

average [ˈævərɪdʒ] [a-ve-rich], s. 1. Promedio, tanteo, precio medio de una cosa o lo que ella vale o renta por un cómputo o cálculo prudencial o aproximado, ya relativamente a los diversos puntos donde se vende a un mismo tiempo, ya respecto de un quinquenio, lo que en castellano suele expresarse por una cosa con otra, un precio con otro, un año con otro. **On average,** por término medio, como promedio, como media. 2. Avería, daño que sufren las embarcaciones y sus cargamentos. 3. Capa o sombrero del capitán, el plus que se asigna al capitán de un buque en las pólizas de embarque por su cuidado de los efectos que se le entregan. 4. Parte igual o proporcional. 5. Servicio o servidumbre, obligación que contrae el vasallo de servir al rey personalmente, franqueándole el uso de sus bestias y carruajes. -a. 1. Medio, uno con otro, entre uno y otro. 2. Típico, ordinario, mediano. **A man of average build,** un hombre de estatura mediana. 3. Hecho o computado por un método de averías. **Average amount,** valor medio. **Average duties,** derechos de avería. **Average price,** precio medio. **Average weight,** peso aproximado.

average, va. 1. Comparar o cotejar y fijar un precio o término medio; proporcionar. 2. Costar, dar, tomar, tener, ocurrir, etc., como término medio. **He averages ten hours of work a day,** trabaja una media de diez horas diarias. **Sales average 1,000 copies a week,** las ventas arrojan un promedio de 1.000 ejemplares por semana. 3. Repartir proporcionalmente, prorratear. vn. **To average out at, to average up to,** ser por término medio, alcanzar un promedio de.

averment [ˈəvəmənt] [a-ver-ment], s. Afirmación o seguridad de alguna cosa de suerte que sea evidente; testimonio.

averrhoes o averroes [əˈverəoz] [a-ve-rous], N. Averroes.

averruncate [əˈverʌnkeɪt] [a-ve-ran-keit], va. Desarraigar, arrancar de raíz.

averse [əˈvəːs] [a-vérs], a. 1. Adverso, contrario. 2. Repugnante, opuesto; enemigo. **I am averse to drinking,** soy enemigo de la bebida.

aversely [əˈvəːslɪ] [a-vérs-li], adv. Repugnantemente.

averseness [əˈvəːsnɪs] [a-vérs-nes], s. Repugnancia, mala gana, aversión.

aversion [əˈvəːʃən] [a-vér-shon], s. Aversión, repugnancia, aborrecimiento, disgusto, odio. **Aversion for work,** aversión al trabajo. **Pet aversion,** pesadilla. **To take an aversion to someone,** tomar antipatía a alguien.

avert [əˈvəːt] [a-vért], va. Desviar, apartar, separar, alejar; prevenir. **To avert the danger,** prevenir, desviar el peligro. **To avert the eyes,** apartar los ojos o la mirada.

averter [əˈvəːtəʳ] [a-vér-taʳ], s. Apartador, el que desvía.

avian [ˈeɪvɪən] [éi-vian], a. Perteneciente a las aves. Aviar.

aviary [ˈeɪvɪərɪ] [éi-via-ri], s. Pajarera, jaula grande o aposento para criar o tener pájaros.

aviation [ˌeɪvɪˈeɪʃən] [ei-vi-éi-shon], s. Aviación.

aviator [ˈeɪvɪeɪtəʳ] [ei-vi-éi-taʳ] s. Aviador.

aviculture [ˌeɪvɪˈkʌltʃəʳ] [ei-vi-kál-chaʳ], s. Avicultura, cría de las aves.

avid [ˈævɪd] [á-vid], a. ávido, ansioso, codicioso.

avidity [ˈævɪdɪtɪ] [á-vi-di-ti], s. Voracidad, ansia, codicia, avidez.

Avignon [ˈævɪnjɒ] [a-vi-ñon] n. (Geogr.) Aviñón.

aviso [ˈævɪsəo] [a-vi-sou] s. (Mar.) Aviso (boat).

avitaminosis [ˌævɪtəmɪˈnəosɪs] [a-vi-ta-mi-nóu-sis] s. Avitaminosis.

avocado [ˌævəˈkɑːdəo] [a-vo-ka-dou], s. Aguacate, palta. (Mex.) Pagua. **Avocado pear,** aguacate. **Avocado plantation,** aguacatal.

avocation [ˌævəˈkeɪʃən] [a-vo-kéi-shon], s. 1. Evocación. 2. La acción de llamar o separar a uno de lo que está haciendo. 3. Estorbo, el asunto que llama o quita a uno de lo que está haciendo. 4. Obstáculo, impedimento, distracción. 5. Empleo, ocupación; uso familiar y común, pero impropio en lugar de vocation.

avocet, avoset [ˈævəsɪt] [a-vo-sit], s. (Orn.) Avoceta, ave del orden de las zancudas; tiene pies palmeados y pico encorvado hacia arriba.

avoid [əˈvɔɪd] [a-void], va. 1. Evitar, escapar, huir (to shun), esquivar, eludir (duty), dejar. **I can't avoid asking him to stay to dinner,** no puedo evitar pedirle que se quede a cenar. 2. Evacuar, desalojar; (For.) anular. -vn. 2. Retirarse. 2. Zafarse, escaparse.

avoidable [əˈvɔɪdəbl] [a-voi-da-bol], a. Evitable, que se puede evitar o huir. (For.) Revocable, anulable.

avoidance [əˈvɔɪdəns] [a-voi-dans], s. 1. El acto y efecto de evitar alguna cosa. (For.) Vacación. Evasión, refugio. 2. Anulación (de un acto), invalidación.

avoidless [əˈvɔɪdlɪs] [a-void-lis], a. Inevitable.

avoset [ˈævəset] [a-vo-set] s. (Zool.) Avoceta.

avouch [əˈvaotʃ] [a-vouch], va. Afirmar, justificar, sostener (to state); alegar en favor de otro; protestar. Garantizar (to guarantee), reconocer, confesar (to avow).

avouchable [əˈvaotʃəbl] [a-vou-cha-bol], a. Justificable, afirmable.

avoucher [əˈvaotʃəʳ] [a-vou-chaʳ], s. El que afirma, justifica, sostiene o alega a favor de otro.

avow [əˈvao] [a-vou], va. Declarar, manifestar abiertamente, protestar, confesar. Reconocer, admitir.

avowable [əˈvaoəbl] [a-voua-bol], a. Lo que se puede declarar abiertamente. Confesión.

avowal [əˈvaoəl] [a-voual], s. Declaración justificativa, aprobación, confesión, reconocimiento.

avowed [əˈvaod] [a-voud] a. Declarado, reconocido.

avowedly [əˈvaodlɪ] [a-voud-li], adv. Declaradamente, manifiestamente, abiertamente.

avowee [əˈvaoiː] [a-vouí], s. Patrono, el que tiene el patronato de alguna iglesia o beneficio.

avower [əˈvaoəʳ] [a-vouaʳ], s. Declarante, el que declara o justifica.

avowry [əˈvaorɪ] [a-vou-ri], s. (For.) Justificación de algún secuestro ya ejecutado, o el motivo que se alega para haberlo hecho.

avulsion [əˈvʌlʃən] [a-vál-shon], s. Avulsión. La acción de separar una cosa de otra.

awa [ɔːə] [oua], adv. (Esco.) Fuera, afuera, ausente.

awaft [ˈəoæft] [auáft], adv. (Mar.) Bandera amorronada, pabellón izado en lo alto del asta pero anudado de trecho en trecho.

await [əˈweɪt] [a-uéit], va. 1. Aguardar, esperar. 2. Esperar, estar aguardando alguna cosa.

awake [əˈweɪk] [a-uéik], va. Despertar, quitar el sueño al que está dormido. -vn. Despertarse (to stop sleeping). Darse cuenta (to realize).

awake, *a.* Despierto (not asleep). Alerta (alert). **To keep awake,** impedir el sueño, desvelar. **Wide-awake,** bien despierto, alerta.

awaken [ə'weɪkən] [a-uéiken], *vn. V.* AWAKE.

awakener [ə'weɪkənəʳ], *s.* Despertador.

awakening [ə'weɪkənɪŋ] [a-uéike-nin], *s.* Despertamiento, el acto de despertar.

awanting [ə'wɔːntɪŋ] [a-uón-tin], *pa.* (Esco. y poét.) Falto, necesitado, escaso.

award [ə'wɔːd] [a-uárd], *va.* Juzgar, sentenciar. Conceder, otorgar. (For.) Adjudicar, declarar a favor de alguno. *-vn.* Determinar.

award, *s.* (For.) Adjudicación, concesión. Sentencia, fallo (judgment). Premio, recompensa. (Mil.) Condecoración.

awardable [ə'wɔːdəbl] [a-uár-da-bol], *a.* Adjudicable.

awardee [ə'wɔːdiː] [a-uár-di] *s.* Adjudicatario.

awarder [ə'wɔːdəʳ] [a-uárdaʳ], *s.* Juez árbitro. adjudicador.

awarding [ə'wɔːdɪŋ] [a-uár-din] *s.* Atribución, concesión, otorgamiento.

aware [ə'wɛəʳ] [a-uéaʳ], *a.* Cauto, vigilante, que prevé; sabedor. Consciente (conscious). Al corriente (up to date). **He is not aware of such a thing,** no sabe tal cosa. **You are not aware who you are speaking to,** usted no sabe con quién habla. **No that I am aware of,** no que yo sepa. **To become aware of,** enterarse de (to find out), darse cuenta de, llegar a tener conciencia de (to realize).

awareness [ə'wɛənɪs] [a-uéa-nes] *s.* Conciencia, conocimiento.

awash [ə'wɒʃ] [a-uósh], *a.* y *adv.* (Mar.) A flor de agua. Inundado (flooded). Flotando (floating).

away [ə'weɪ] [a-uéi], *adv.* Ausente, afuera, fuera (in a different place). **He went away,** se marchó. **The house is ten miles away,** la casa está a diez millas. Lejos. **Away from the din,** lejos del bullicio. Incesantemente, sin parar. **He worked away for two days,** trabajó sin parar durante dos días. En sentido opuesto (in the opposite direction) **The arrow pointed away from the door,** la flecha apuntaba en sentido opuesto a la puerta. **Away** se emplea con gran número de verbos y denota en general la idea de alejamiento, aunque también expresa a veces continuación, persistencia. Por ejemplo: **To get away,** huir, evadirse. **To go away,** irse, marcharse. **To send away,** despedir. **To run away,** tomar las de Villadiego, escaparse. **To make away with oneself,** darse muerte, suicidarse. **Work away,** persista usted en el trabajo. **Write away,** escriba usted. sin cesar. **I'll do it right away,** lo haré inmediatamente. **To play away,** jugar fuera, en campo contrario. **Away match,** partido de ida. **Away team,** equipo de fuera.

away, *inter.* fuera, fuera de aquí, quita o quítate de aquí o de ahí. **Away with you!,** ¡márchate!, ¡quítate de delante!, ¡que no te vean mis ojos! **Away with it,** ¡quitádmelo de delante!, ¡basta, no más!.

awe [ɔː] [óu], *s.* 1. Miedo o temor reverencial (fear and respect). 2. Pavor. **He stands in awe of his father,** tiene un miedo pavoroso a su padre. 3. Asombro, admiración (wonder). **He looked in awe at the mountain,** contempló la montaña con admiración. **To keep one in awe,** tener sujeto a alguno, tener sometido por el terror.

awe, *va.* Amedrentar, asombrar, despavorir, atemorizar; infundir miedo, temor reverencial o pavor. **He was awed by his solemn words,** sus solemnes palabras le atemorizaron.

aweary [ə'wɛəri] [a-uéa-ri], *a.* (Poét.) Cansado, fatigado.

aweather [ə'wɛəðəʳ] [a-uéa-zaʳ], *adv.* (Mar.) A barlovento, por el lado del viento (en oposición a *alee,* sotavento).

awe-commanding [ɔː'kmændɪŋ] [ou-ko-mán-din], *a.* Lo que infunde respeto.

awe-inspiring ['ɔːɪnˌspaɪərɪŋ] [ou-ins-páia-rin], *a.* Impresionante, imponente.

awesome [ɔːsʌm] [ou-sam], *a.* 1. Terrible, temible, que infunde miedo; aterrador, pavoroso. 2. Reverencial, respetuoso.

awestricken [ɔːstrɪkɪŋ] [ou-strái-ken] *a.* Atemorizado.

awestruck [ɔːstrʌk] [ou-strák], *a.* Espantado, despavorido, dominado por el terror, o el respeto.

aweigh [ə'weɪ] [ou-uéi], *adv.* (Mar.) Pendiente, a plomo.

awful ['ɔːfəl] [ou-fol], *a.* 1. Tremendo; digno de respeto y reverencia. 2. Amedrentado, atemorizado. 3. Temible, funesto, horroroso, espantoso, terrible (appalling), atroz, horrible (ugly). 4. (Fam.) Muy malo, muy grande, enorme, tremendo (tremendous), horrendo. **An awful lot,** un montón, muchísimo. **How awful!,** ¡qué horror!

awfully ['ɔːfəlɪ] [ou-foli], *adv.* 1. Respetuosamente, con respeto y veneración; solemnemente, terriblemente, atrozmente. **He is awfully stupid,** es terriblemente estúpido. 2. (Fam.) Muy; excesivamente, muchísimo. **I am awfully sorry,** lo siento muchísimo. **Awfully good,** muy bueno. **That's awfully good of you,** es usted muy amable.

awful-eyed ['ɔːfəlˌaɪd] [ou-fol-aid], *s.* Veneración, respeto o temor reverencial que infunde alguna cosa por ser grande y majestuosa.

awfulness ['ɔːfʊlnɪs] [ou-ful-nes] *s.* Horror, atrocidad.

awhile [ə'waɪl] [a-uáil], *adv.* Un rato, algún tiempo. **Wait awhile,** espérese un rato. **Not for awhile,** todavía no, por ahora no. **Not yet awhile,** no tan pronto.

awhirl [ə'wɜːl] [a-uérl], *adv.* En rotación; en giro, en torbellino.

awkward [ɔːkwəd] [óuk-uard], *a.* 1. Zafio, tosco, inculto, rudo, zopenco, agreste. 2. Desmañado, desgarbado (graceless), falto de maña, torpe (clumsy), poco diestro. 3. Indócil, indómito. 4. Embarazoso, molesto (embarrassing), difícil, delicado; también, desgraciado, peligroso. 5. Inoportuno, inadecuado (inconvenient). **An awkward time to meet,** una hora inadecuada para encontrarse. **An awkward situation,** una situación embarazosa. **An awkward question,** una cuestión delicada. **An awkward customer,** un sujeto peligroso. **An awkward problem,** un problema difícil.

awkwardly [ɔːkwədlɪ] [óuk-uard-li], *adv.* 1. Groseramente, toscamente. 2. Torpemente, desmañadamente. 3. Embarazosamente, en una posición difícil, delicada. **Awkwardly placed,** en una posición embarazosa.

awkwardness [ɔːkwədnɪs] [óuk-uard-nes], *s.* Tosquedad, grosería, torpeza (clumsiness), poca habilidad o maña. Dificultad, molestia, carácter molesto, incomodidad (of a situation).

awl [ɔːl] [óul], *s.* Lesna, instrumento de hierro puntiagudo de que usan los zapateros y los carpinteros. **Brad-awl, lesna** para puntillas. **Scratch-awl,** punzón de marcar. **Pegging-awl,** estaquillador. **Sailmaker's-awl,** aguja de veleros. **Sewing-awl,** lesna de coser.

awless [ɔːlɪs] [óu-les], *a.* 1. Irreverente, el que falta a la reverencia y respeto que debe. 2. Lo que no causa ni infunde respeto o reverencia.

awl-shaped [ɔːl'ʃeɪpt] [óul-sheipt], *a.* Alesnado. (Bot.) Subulado.

awn [ɔːn] [óun], *s.* Arista, la barba de la espiga.

awning ['ɔːnɪŋ] [óunin], *s.* 1. (Mar.) Toldo, cubierta de lienzo u otra tela que se pone en la embarcación para guardarse del sol. 2. Toldo (de almacén o puesto de mercado; o de carro). 3. (Hort.) Abrigaña; estera para abrigar las plantas. **Awning stanchions,** (Mar,) candeleros de los toldos.

awoke [ə'wəʊk] [a-uóuk], Pretérito del verbo **to awake.**

awoken [ə'wəʊkən] [a-uóu-enk] *pp.* del verbo **to awake.**

awol ['eɪwɒl] [éi-uol] *adv./a.* Ausente sin permiso.

aworking [ə'wɜːkɪŋ] [a-uekin], *adv.* Trabajando, al trabajo.

awry [ə'raɪ] [a-rai], *adv./a.* 1. Oblicuamente, torcidamente, al través. Torcido. 2. Con la vista atravesada, de lado, de soslayo. **To go awry,** salir mal. **To look awry,** mirar de soslayo.

ax o axe [æks] [aks], *s.* Segur o hacha (tool). *(Fig.)* Reducción (of prices). *(Fam.)* **To get the ax,** ser despedido. **To have an ax to grind,** tener intereses personales. **A battle-axe,** hacha de guerra. **A pole-axe,** hacha de mano. **A pick-axe,** zapapico, azadón, piqueta. **Axe-head,** la cabeza o la parte cortante del hacha, destral. **Broad-axe, Cooper's axe,** doladera. *va.* Cortar (to cut). *(Fig.)* Reducir (to reduce). Suprimir (to do away with). Despedir (personnel).

axial ['æksɪəl] [ak-sial], *a.* Axial, perteneciente al eje o semejante a un eje: dispuesto alrededor de un eje común.

axil ['æksɪl] [ak-sil], *s. (Bot.)* Axila, ángulo formado por el lado superior de una hoja o de un ramo y el tallo o la rama de que nace.

axil, *a.* V. AXIAL.

axilla ['æksɪlə] [ak-si-la], *s.* 1. *(Anat.)* Sobaco (armpit). 2. Axila de las aves.

axillar ['æksɪləʳ] [ak-si-laʳ], **axillary** ['æksɪlərɪ] [ak-si-la-ri], *a.* 1. Axilar, lo que pertenece al sobaco. 2. *(Bot.)* Axilar, que crece en los ángulos de los ramos de las plantas.

axiom ['æksɪəm] [ak-siom], *s.* Axioma, proposición, sentencia o principio sentado. Verdad evidente.

axiomatic, axiomatical [æksɪəʊˈmætɪk] [ak-sio-ma-tik], *a.* Axiomático; evidente, irrefutable, patente.

axis ['æksɪs] [ak-sis], *s.* 1. Eje. 2. Pivote, centro de oscilación, 3. Axis, la segunda vértebra del cuello 4. Alianza. **The Axis Nations,** las Naciones del Eje. (Alemania, Italia y el Japón).

axle ['æksl] [aksl], **axle-tree** ['æksl,triː] [aksl-tri], *s.* Eje de una rueda. Árbol de una máquina. **Rear axle,** eje trasero.

axle box ['æksl,bɒks] [aksl-boks] *s. (Mec.)* Caja del eje. **Axle-clip,** *s.* Abrazadera que sujeta el cibicón al eje.

axolotl ['æksləʊtl] [aks-lotl], *s.* Axolote, reptil anfibio del lago de Méjico.

ay o aye [aɪ] [ai], *adv.* Sí, adverbio por el cual se responde afirmativamente. V. YES. **Ayes and noes,** votos a favor y en contra. **The ayes have it,** hay una mayoría de votos a favor.

aye [aɪ] [ai], *adv.* Siempre. **For aye,** para siempre.

aymara [aɪməˈraː] [ai-ma-ra] *s.* Aimara, aimará (people). *N.* Aimara, aimará (language).

aymaran ['aɪmərən] [ai-ma-ran] *a.* Aimara, aimará. *N.* Aimara, aimará (language).

ayry ['eɪrɪ] [eI-ri], *s.* El nido del halcón. V. EYRY.

azalea [əˈzeɪlɪə] [a-sei-lia], *s.* Azalea, arbusto de la familia de las ericáceas, género Azalea, notable por la belleza de sus flores.

azerole [əˈzerəʊl] [a-se-roul], *s. (Bot.)* Acerola.

azimuth [əˈzɪmɒθ] [a-si-muz], *s.* Azimut del sol o de una estrella; al arco del horizonte que hay entre el círculo vertical en que está el astro, y el meridiano del observador. **Azimuth-compass,** brújula de azimut.

azoic [əˈzɔɪk] [a-soik], *a.* Azóico.

azon bomb [əˈzɒnˈbɒmb] [a-son-bomb], *s.* Bomba aérea que puede ser guiada hacia la derecha o izquierda por radiocontrol.

azonic [əˈzɒnɪk] [a-so-nik], *a.* Azónico, no propio y peculiar de una zona o región; no local.

Azores [əˈzɔːz] [a-sors] *N. (Geogr.)* Azores.

azote [əˈzəʊt] [a-sout] *s. (Quím.)* Azoe, nitrógeno.

Aztec ['æztek] [as-tek], *a. y s.* Azteca, nombre que se da a los antiguos indígenas de Méjico, notables por su civilización; y también, a su lengua, etc.

azure ['eɪʒəʳ] [éi-saʳ], **azured** ['eɪʒəd] [éi-sard], *a.* Azulado claro; azul celeste. *(Her.)* Azur.

azure, *va.* Azular.

azurine [əˈzʊriːn] [a-surin], *a.* Azulado.

azygous [əˈzɪɡəs] [a-si-gos] *a. (Anat.) (Biol.)* Ácigos.

azyme [əˈzɪm] [a-sim] *s.* Pan ázimo.

B

b [biː] [bi], **B** (letter). Segunda, (in a series). (Mús.) Si. La B se usa como abreviatura; así B.A. quiere decir, Bachiller en Artes.

baa [baː] [bá], *s.* Balido (sheep).

baa, *vn.* Balar, dar balidos (sheep).

babbit ['bæbɪt] [ba-bit], *s.* Burgués, tradicionalista.

babbitt, babbitt metal ['bæbɪtˌmiːtəl] [ba-bit-me-tal], *s.* Metal de Babbitt, metal antifricción para cojinetes. *-va.* Revestir de metal antifricción.

babble ['bæbl] [babel], *vn.* 1. Balbucear, hablar como un niño. 2. Charlar, hablar mucho y sin sustancia. 3. Parlar, parlotear (people), revelar lo que se debe callar, cotillear (gossip). 4. Murmurar un arroyo. *-va.* Charlar. Farfullar (to utter incoherently). **To babble nonsense,** soltar necedades, Revelar (a secret).

babble, *s.* 1. Charla, conversación sin sustancia, cháchara (idle talk), farfulla (confused speech), balbuceo (of a baby) parla, charlatanería, parloteo (of people). 2. El susurro o murmullo de una corriente.

babbler ['bæbləʳ] [ba-blar], *s.* 1. Charlador, charlante, chacharero, charlatán, parlador, hablador, el que charla o habla mucho y sin sustancia. Parlanchín (chatterer). 2. Parlero, el que habla de lo que se debe callar. Cotilla (gossiper).

babbling ['bæblɪŋ] [ba-blin], *s.* Habla vana y sin provecho, cháchara, flujo de hablar.

babe [beɪb] [béib], *s.* Criatura, criaturita, infante, el niño pequeño que aún no está en edad de hablar. *(Fam.)* Nene. Bebé (baby), niño, niña (naïve person). Monada (attractive girl). **Babe in arms,** niño de pecho.

babel ['bæbəl] [béi-bel], *s.* Muchedumbre y confusión de pareceres; desorden, alboroto. Jaleo. **Tower of Babel,** torre de Babel.

babirusa o babiroussa [bæbɪˈrʊsə] [ba-bi-ru-sa] *s. (Zool.)* Babirusa.

babism ['bəbɪzm] [ba-bizem] *s.* Babismo (Persian religion).

baboon [bəˈbuːn] [ba-bún], *s.* Cinocéfalo, mono grande. Zambo, babuino (monkey).

babouche [bəˈbuːʃ] [ba-búsh], *s.* Babucha (slipper).

baby ['beɪbɪ] [bei-bi], *s.* 1. Criatura, infante, niño pequeño (young child), nene, cría (of an animal). 2. Muñeca, monada (attractive girl). Benjamín (youngest member of a family). *(Fam.)* **To be left holding the baby,** cargar con el muerto o con el mochuelo. *-a.* De niño (of a baby). Infantil (like a baby). **Baby face,** cara infantil. **A baby car,** un coche pequeño.

baby, *va.* Hacer o tratar como niño.

baby buggy ['beɪbɪˌbʌɡɪ] [bei-bi-bu-gi], *s.* Cochecito para niños.

baby carriage ['beɪbɪˌkærɪdʒ] [bei-bi- ca-rich], *s.* Cochecito para niños.

baby farm ['beɪbɪˌfaːm] [bei-bi-farm] *s.* Guardería infantil.

baby grand ['beɪbɪˈɡrænd] [bei-bi-grand] *s. (Mús.)* Piano de media cola.

babyhood ['beɪbɪhʊd] [bei-bi-jud], *s.* Niñez, el primer período de la infancia. También los niños colectivamente.

babyish ['beɪbɪʃ] [bei-bi-ish], *a.* De niño; pueril (childish). Infantil (infantile).

babyishness ['beɪbɪʃnɪs] [bei-bi-ish-nes], *s.* Puerilidad, niñada.

Babylon ['bæbɪlən] [ba-bi-lon] *N.* Babilonia (town). (kingdom).

babysit ['beɪbɪsɪt] [bei-bi-sit], *va.* Servir de niñera por horas.

baby-sitter ['beɪbɪˌsɪtəʳ] [bei-bi-si-taʳ], *s.* Canguro, niñera por horas.

baby sitting [ˈbeɪbɪˌsɪtɪŋ] [bei-bi-si-tin] *s.* Vigilancia de los niños.

baby tooth [ˈbeɪbɪˌtuːθ] [bei-bi-tuz] *s.* Diente de leche.

baby walker [ˈbeɪbɪˌwɔːkəʳ] [bei-bi-uó-kaʳ] *s.* Tacataca, tacatá, pollera.

baby-weighting scales [ˈbeɪbɪˌweɪtɪŋˈskeɪls] [bei-bi-ueitin-skéils] *s.* Pesabebés.

bacca [ˈbækə] [ba-ka] *s.* Baya.

baccalaureate [ˌbækəˈlɔːrɪɪt] [ba-ka-lo-ri-it], *a.* Bachillerato, el grado de bachiller. **Baccalaureate sermon,** sermón de despedida a los graduados de una clase. *(Amer.)*

baccarat [ˈbækərɑː] [ba-ka-rat] *s.* Cristal de Baccarat.

baccarat o **baccarra** [ˈbækərɑː] [ba-ka-rá] *s.* Bacarrá, bacará (gambling game).

baccate [ˈbækeɪt] [ba-keit], *a. (Bot.)* 1. Parecido a una baya (berry-shaped). 2. Que produce bayas.

bacchanal [ˈbækənəl] [ba-ka-nal], **bacchanalian** [ˌbækəˈneɪlɪən] [ba-ka-nei-lian], *s.* Un borracho, un alborotador. Bacante (follower of Bacchus) Bacanal (orgy). Juerguista (carouser). *-a.* Borracho, alborotado, relajado, licencioso, disoluto. Báquico.

bacchanalia [ˌbækəˈneɪlɪə] [ba-ka-nei-lia] *N. pl.* Bacanales.

bacchanalian [ˌbækəˈneɪlɪən] [ba-ka-nei-lian] *a.* Báquico.

bacchanals [ˈbækənəlz] [ba-ka-nals], *s. pl.* Bacanales, fiestas en honor de Baco.

bacchante [ˈbækæntɪ] [ba-kan-ti] *s.* Bacante, ménade.

Bacchic, bacchical [ˈbækɪk] [ba-ki-kal], *a.* Báquico.

Bacchus [ˈbækəs] [ba-cus], *s. (Mit.)* Baco, hijo de Júpiter y de Semele.

baccivorous [ˈbæksɪvərəs] [bak-si-vo-ros], *a.* Bacívoro, que come con mucha ansia las bayas de las plantas.

bach [bæk] [bak] *vn. (Fam.)* Llevar una vida de soltero.

bachelor [ˈbætʃələʳ] [ba-che-lor], *s.* 1. Soltero (unmarried man), célibe. **In my bachelor days,** en mi época de soltero. **Old bachelor,** solterón. 2. Bachiller (student), el que ha recibido el primer grado en alguna facultad. **Bachelor of Arts,** licenciado en letras. **Bachelor of Science,** licenciado en ciencias. **Bachelor girl,** soltera. **Bachelor's button,** *s. (Bot.)* Botón de oro, ranúnculo (yellow flower), aciano (blue flower). Azulejo, planta.

bachelorhood [ˈbætʃələhʊd] [ba-che-lor-jud] *s.* Soltería, celibato.

bachelorship [ˈbætʃələʃɪp] [ba-che-lor-ship], *s.* 1. Celibato, soltería. 2. Bachillerato, el grado de bachiller.

bacillar [bəˈsɪləʳ] [ba-si-laʳ] o **bacillary** [bəˈsɪlərɪ] [ba-si-la-ri] *a. (Med.)* Bacilar.

bacilliform [bəˈsɪlɪfɜːm] [ba-si-li-form] *a. (Med.)* Baciliforme.

bacillus [bəˈsɪləs] [ba-si-los], *s.* BACILLI, *pl.* Bacilos, variedad de las bacterias, organismo microscópico vegetal, en forma cilíndrica, virguliforme o filiforme.

bacitracin [bəˈsɪləs] [ba-si-trei-sin], *s.* Bacitracina.

back [bæk] [bak], *s.* 1. Espalda, espaldar, espinazo (of person). Lomo (of animal, book, sword), cerro, espinazo. 2. Metacarpo, dorso, reverso, respaldo (o sheet of paper). **Back of the hand,** el envés o el revés de la mano. 3. Recazo, lomo, canto, revés (of fabric), reverso (of medal). 4. Trasera, dorso. Parte posterior o de atrás (of head, house, car, mountain). **Back of a house,** trasera de una casa. **Back of beyond,** *(Fam.)* Quinto pino (remote place). **He lives in the back of beyond,** vive en el quinto pino. **Back of a chair,** respaldo de una silla. **Back of a coach,** trasera de un coche. **Back of a book,** lomo de un libro. **A back blow or a back stroke,** un revés. **Back yard,** patio interior. 5. Tina o enfriadera de cerveza. 6. *(Mar,)* Galga de ancla. 7. *(Mar.)* Espalda de un bote. 8. Fondo (of room), defensa, zaga (defensive position), zaguero (player). Dorso, respaldo (of cheque), foro (of stage). **On one's back,** a cuestas. **Back to back,** espalda con espalda. **To have a pain in the back,** tener dolor de espaldas, de cintura, de riñones. **To cast behind the back,** (1) perdonar y olvidar. (2) Desechar con desdén. **To see the back of,** desembarazarse o librarse de. **To turn the back,** huir. **To turn the back on,** abandonar,

desertar. *(Fam.)* **At the back of beyond,** en el quinto pino. **In back of,** detrás de. **Excuse my back,** perdone que le vuelva la espalda. **In the back of one's mind,** en lo más recóndito del pensamiento. **To be on one's back,** estar acostado boca arriba (to be lying), estar encamado (to be ill). **To break one's back,** deslomarse (to fall down, to overwork). *(Fig.)* **To break the back of a task,** hacer la parte más difícil de un trabajo. **To fall on one's back,** caerse de espaldas. *(Fig.)* **To get one's back up,** picarse (to become annoyed). **To put someone's back up,** picar a uno (to annoy). **To have a broad back,** tener anchas las espaldas. *(Fig.)* **To have one's back to the wall,** estar entre la espada y la pared. **To have someone on one's back,** tener a uno encima, tener que cargar con uno. **To know like the back of one's hand,** conocer como la palma de la mano. **To lend a back to,** aupar. *(Fig.)* **To put one's back into it,** echar el resto. **To stand with one's back to,** dar la espalda a. *(Fig.)* **To turn one's back to, on,** volver la espalda a. *-a.* 1. Trasero, posterior. **The back seat of a car,** el asiento trasero de un coche. Interior, de atrás o detrás, del interior (remote). Atrasado (in arrears). **Back rent,** alquiler atrasado. 2. Separado, apartado, lejano, extraviado. 3. Publicado en tiempo anterior al presente. 4. Que ha pasado del tiempo debido. **Back room,** cuarto interior, pieza apartada. **Back pension,** pensión debida, y no pagada todavía. **Back number,** entrega o ejemplar no muy reciente. V. NUMBER. **Back pay wages,** atrasos. *(Gram.)* Velar (vowel).

back, *adv.* 1. Atrás o detrás (To the rear). 2. De vuelta, de retorno. **Give me my money back,** devuélvame mi dinero. **When will you come back?,** ¿cuándo volverás? 3. Otra vez o segunda vez (again). Este adverbio, colocado después de un verbo, tiene el sentido de retrocesión o del prefijo español **re. To beat back,** rechazar (al enemigo). **To hold o keep back,** retener. **To come back,** volver otra vez, volver atrás o de nuevo. **To step back a pace,** dar un paso atrás. **Journey back,** viaje de vuelta. **Back from,** de vuelta o de regreso de (on returning), no alineado con (house). **Back in the forties,** allá por los años cuarenta. **To answer someone back,** replicar a uno. **To bow back to,** devolver el saludo a. **To get back,** volver (to return), recobrar (to recover). **To pay someone back,** devolverle el dinero a uno (to return money), pagarle a uno con la misma moneda (to avenge on someone). **To put back,** poner en su sitio. **To walk back,** volver andando. **Two years back,** hace dos años. **Years back,** años atrás. **Back and forth,** de acá para allá (to walk). Para adelante y para atrás (to sway). **Back and forth motion,** movimiento de vaivén. **To go back and forth,** ir y venir, ir de un sitio para otro.

back, *va.* 1. Montar a caballo; montar un caballo por primera vez. 2. Sostener, apoyar, respaldar (to support). **To back a colleague,** apoyar a un colega. **To back a venture,** respaldar una empresa. justificar, favorecer. 3. Mantener, soportar. Hacer retroceder, dar marcha atrás a (to cause to move bacwards). Dominar (to lie at the back of) **The hills that back the town,** las colinas que dominan la ciudad. Enlomar (a book), endosar (a check), avalar (a bill), hacer marcha atrás con (a car). **Foam-backed raincoat,** impermeable con un forro de espuma. **Leather-backed chair,** silla con un respaldo de cuero. **To back up,** apoyar. *(Mar.)* **To back water,** ciar. *vn.* Retroceder (to move backwards). Dar marcha atrás (a car). **To back down,** echarse atrás, volverse atrás. **To back out,** salir dando marcha atrás (in a car), retractarse, volverse atrás (of a commitment). **To back up,** retroceder.

back, *inter.* (abrev. de *go back*). ¡Atrás! ¡vuélvanse Uds.!

backache [ˈbækeɪk] [bak-eik] *s.* Dolor de espalda.

backband [bækˈbænd] [bak-band] *s.* Sufra (of harness), lomera (of book).

backbite [ˈbækbaɪt] [bak-bait], *va.* Murmurar, hablar mal del que está ausente; difamar, desacreditar.

backbiter [bækˈbaɪtəʳ] [bak-bai-taʳ] *s.* Maldiciente, murmurador.

backbiting [bæk'baɪtɪŋ] [bak-bai-tin], *s.* Detracción, difamación, maledicencia.

back-board ['bækbɔːd] [bak-bord], *s.* 1. *(Mar.)* Respaldo o escudo de boe. 2. Respaldo, espaldar (of bench), tabla trasera (of bookshelves), forro, materia delgada empleada en los espaldares de los espejos, cuadros, etc.

backbone ['bækbəʊn] [bak-boun], *s.* 1. Hueso dorsal, espinazo, columna vertebral. 2. Firmeza, decisión, principio moral. *(Fam.)* 3. *(Fig.)* Carácter (strength of character). Elemento principal, pilar (mainstay). **Farmers are the backbone of the nation,** los campesinos son el elemento principal de la nación. Lomo (of book). *(Fig.)* **English to the backbone,** inglés hasta la médula o los tuétanos.

backbreaking ['bækbreɪkɪŋ] [bak-brei-kin] *a. (Fam.)* Matador, deslomador. **Backbreaking task,** trabajo matador.

backchat ['bæktʃæt] [bak-chat] *s.* Impertinencia. **I want none of your backchat!,** ¡déjate de impertinencias!, ¡no seas tan respondón!

back-cloth ['bækklɒθ] [bak-kloz] *s.* Telón de foro.

back comb ['bækkəʊm] [bak-koum] *s.* Peineta.

back current ['bækkʌrənt] [bak-ka-rent] *s. (Elec.)* Contracorriente.

backdate ['bækdeɪt] [bak-deit] *s.* Antedatar (a document). Dar efecto retroactivo a (to make retroactive).

back door [bæk'dɔː] [bak-doaʳ], *s.* Puerta trasera. *(Fig.)* Puerta trasera o falsa. *-a.* De la puerta trasera. *(Fig.)* Clandestino, secreto (surreptitious).

backdown [bæk'daʊn] [bak-daun], *s. (Fam.)* Retractación. Cesión; rendición.

backdrop ['bækdrɒp] [bak-drop] *s.* Telón de foro (of theater). *(Fig.)* Fondo (background).

backed ['bækt] [bakt], *a.* 1. Lo que tiene dorso o espalda. 2. Apoyado, sostenido, autorizado.

backer ['bækəʳ] [ba-kaʳ], *s.* 1. Comanditario (financial supporter), fiador (guarantor), sostenedor, el que secunda o apoya a otro en una contienda. 2. Apostador (en las carreras de caballos).

backfire ['bækfaɪəʳ] [bak-faiaʳ], *s.* 1. Incendio provocado para contener el avance de otro. 2. Petardeo, explosión prematura, o en el escape, de motores de explosión. 3. Explosión hacia atrás de un arma de fuego. Retorno de llama (of Bunsen burner). Contrafuego (to stop a fire). *-vn.* Explotar prematuramente, petardear (engine). *(Fig.)* Resultar contraproducente. Fallar, salir rana (to fail). **The scheme backfired on us,** nos salió el tiro por la culata.

back-formation ['bækfɔːmeɪʃən] [bak-for-mei-shon] *s.* Derivación regresiva.

backgammon ['bækgæmən] [bak-ga-mon], *s.* Juego de chaquete. **Backgammon-board,** Tablas reales. *(Mex.)* Pretera.

background ['bækgraʊnd] [bak-graund], *s.* 1. Fondo. **Red triangles on a green background,** triángulos rojos en un fondo verde. **Background music, noise,** música, ruido de fondo. 2. Historial, antecedentes (events leading up to), educación, pasado (past life). **The background to the revolution,** los antecedentes de la revolución. 3. Cualidades, requisitos, calificaciones, conocimientos, experiencia. Origen. **He has an English backgroung,** es de origen inglés. Ambiente, medio (atmosphere). Último plano (of picture, photograph). *(Fig.)* Segundo plano, segundo término (less prominent situation).

backhand [bæk'hænd] [bak-jand] *a.* Dado con el dorso de la mano. **Backhand stroke,** revés (in tennis, etc.) *s.* Revés (blow, stroke). Letra inclinada hacia la izquierda (handwriting).

backhanded [bæk'hændɪd] [bak-jan-ded], *a.* 1. Referente al revés de la mano. 2. Falto de sinceridad, irónico, ambiguo, equívoco (compliment). **A backhanded compliment,** un cumplimiento poco sincero. 3. Inclinado a la izquierda (handwriting); v. g. **Backhanded letters,** letras inclinadas. 4. De revés. **A backhanded blow,** golpe de revés. Que vacila (hesitant). **He is not backhanded in asking for more,** no vacila en pedir más.

backing ['bækɪŋ] [ba-kin], *s.* 1. Apoyo dado a una persona o causa. 2. Retroceso. 3. Refuerzo (encuadernación). 4. Respaldo, forro, materia que forma el espaldar de alguna cosa. Refuerzo. **A cloth belt with a leather backing,** un cinturón de tela con un refuerzo de cuero. Entretela (in sewing). Refuerzo (of picture). **Financial backing,** respaldo financiero.

backlash ['bæklæʃ] [bak-lash] *s.* Retroceso (backward movement). Holgura, juego (looseness). Sacudida (jarring reaction). *(Fig.)* Reacción (antagonistic reaction).

backlighting [bæk'laɪtɪŋ] [bak-lai-tin] *s.* Contraluz.

backlog ['bæklɒg] [bak-log], *s.* 1. Leño en el fondo del hogar (of a fire). 2. *(Com.)* Pedidos pendientes por llenar. Reserva (reserve). **This backlog of orders assures the continued growth of the company,** esta reserva de pedidos garantiza el constante desarrollo de la compañía.

back number [bæk'nʌmbəʳ] [bak-nam-baʳ] *s.* Número atrasado (of a publication). *(Fig.)* Cosa o persona anticuada (old-fashioned). Vieja gloria (has been).

backpedal [bæk'pedl] [bak-pe-dal] *vn.* Pedalear hacia atrás. *(Fig.)* Volverse atrás (to back down).

backpiece ['bækpiːs] [bak-pis], *s.* Espaldar, armadura para cubrir la espalda.

backplate ['bækpleɪt] [bak-pleit] *s.* Espaldar.

backrest ['bækrest] [bak-rest] *s.* Respaldo (of a chair).

back room ['bækrʊm] [bak-rum] *s.* Cuarto trasero. *(Fig.)* **Decisions taken in the back room,** decisiones tomadas entre bastidores.

back scratcher ['bækˌskrætʃəʳ] [bak-skra-chaʳ] *s.* Rascador.

back seat ['bæksiːt] [bak-sit] *s.* Asiento trasero. **Back seat driver,** persona que abruma de consejos al conductor (in a car), persona entrometida (meddler). *(Fig.)* **To take a back seat,** pasar al segundo plano, estar en el segundo plano.

backset ['bækset] [bak-set], *s.* Contratiempo, revés (setback), infortunio; recaída. Contracorriente (of water).

back shop ['bækʃɒp] [bak-shop], *s.* 1. Trastienda, el cuarto o pieza que está más adentro de la tienda. 2. Trasero (de animal).

backside ['bæksaɪd] [bak-said], *s.* 1. *(Fam.)* Trasero. Espalda, la parte de atrás de cualquier cosa. 2. Trascorral o trasero.

backslapper ['bækˌslæpəʳ] [bak-sla-paʳ] *s.* Persona campechana.

backslide ['bækslaɪd] [bak-slaid], *vn.* 1. Resbalar o caer hacia atrás; torcerse; apostatar. 2. Recaer, hablando moralmente. Desviarse, salir al mal camino (to become corrupted). Reincidir volver a caer (to relapse).

backslider ['bækslaɪdəʳ] [bak-slai-daʳ], *s.* 1. Apóstata, 2. Reincidente.

backsliding ['bækslaɪdɪŋ] [bak-slai-din] *s.* Apostasía, reincidencia.

backspacer [ˌbæk'speɪsəʳ] [bak-spei-saʳ] *s.* Tecla de retroceso (of typewriter).

backspin ['bækspɪn] [bak-spin] *s.* Efecto. **To put a backspin on a ball,** dar efecto a una pelota.

backstaff ['bækstɑːf] [bak-staf], *s.* Instrumento para medir la altura del sol en el mar.

backstage ['bæksteɪdʒ] [bak-steich], *s. (Teat.)* Parte del escenario oculta a la vista del público. *-adv.* Entre bastidores. *-a.* en los camerinos (to or in the dressing rooms). *a.* De bastidores. *(Fig.)* De la vida privada (of theater people). Oculto, secreto. **Backstage deals,** acuerdos ocultos. **Backstage noises,** ruidos que vienen de los bastidores. **Backstage workers,** hombres que trabajan entre bastidores.

back stairs ['bækˈstɛəz] [bak-stears], *s. pl.* Escalera de servicio.

backstairs ['bækˈstɛəz] [bak-stears] *a. (Fig.)* Secreto (secret). Barato. **Backstairs novels,** novelas baratas.

Sórdido (sordid). *(Fig.)* **To get a job through backstairs influence,** conseguir un puesto por enchufe.

backstays ['bæk'steɪs] [bak-steis], *s.pl. (Mar.)* Brandales, ramales que mantienen los masteleros fijos, para que no caigan hacia proa. **Shifting backstays,** *(Mar.)* Brandales volantes. **Backstay-stools,** *(Mar.)* mesetas de los brandales. Soporte (support). Contrafuerte (of shoe).

backstitch ['bækstɪtʃ] [bak-stich], *s.* Pespunte (in sewing), punto atrás, puntada hecha clavando la aguja la mitad del largo de la puntada precedente. **To backstitch,** *va.* y *vn.* Pespuntear, coser al pespunte.

backstop ['bækstɒp] [bak-stop], *s.* 1. (Béisbol) Mampara colocada detrás del *home* para detener la pelota. 2. Cualquier cosa a que se recurra con propósito similares.

back street ['bækstriːt] [bak-strit] *s.* Calle pequeña, callejuela.

backstroke ['bækstrəʊk] [bak-strouk], *s.* En natación, brazada de dorso. Revés (in tennis).

backsword ['bæksɔːd] [bak-suod], *s.* Sable (sword). Bastón (singlestick). Alfanje.

back talk ['bæktɔːk] [bak-tok] *s.* See BACKCHAT.

backtrack ['bæktræk] [bak-trak], *va.* y *vn.* Seguir un rastro o huella en sentido inverso. Volver hacia atrás. *(Fig.)* Volverse atrás.

back-up light ['bækʌp'laɪt] [bak-ap-lait], *s.* Luz blanca para marcha atrás.

backward ['bækwəd] [bak-uod] *a.* Hacia atrás. **A backward glance,** una mirada hacia atrás. Atrasado. **A backward country, child,** un país, niño atrasado. Tardío (fruit). **Backward in,** tímido para (shy), remiso en (reluctant), tardo en (slow). **Backward motion,** retroceso. See BACKWARDS.

backward, *a.* 1. Opuesto, enemigo; el que hace alguna cosa de mala gana. 2. Lerdo, pesado, tardo, lento, negligente, perezoso.

backwardly ['bækwədlɪ] [bak-uodli], *adv.* Con repugnancia, de mala gana.

backwardness ['bækwədnɪs] [bak-uodnes], *s.* Torpeza, pesadez, tardanza, negligencia. Atraso, retraso (mental, economic). Timidez (shyness). Falta de entusiasmo (reluctance). Tardanza (slowness).

backwards ['bækwədz] [bak-uods] *adv.* Hacia atrás. **To lean backwards,** inclinarse hacia atrás. De espaldas. **To fall backwards,** caerse de espaldas. Al revés. **To do things backwards,** hacer las cosas del revés. **To know something backwards o backwards and forwards,** saber algo al dedillo o como el Padrenuestro. *(Fig.)* **To look backwards in time,** mirar hacia atrás. **To move backwards,** retroceder. **To read backwards,** leer al revés. **To stroke the cat backwards,** acariciar el gato a contrapelo.

backwash ['bækwɒʃ] [bak-uosh], *s.* 1. Estela, agua removida por hélices o remos. Remolinos de agua. Resaca (of waves). 2. Agitación resultante de algún acontecimiento. *(Fig.)* Repercusión.

backwater ['bækwɔːtəʳ] [bak-uota], *s.* 1. Agua que repele una rueda hidráulica. 2. Remanso (still water), agua estancada (de un río). Brazo de mar (of sea). *(Fig.)* Lugar apartado (remote place). Lugar apartado (remote place).

backwoods ['bækwʊdz] [bak-wuds], *s.* Región apartada de los centros de población o situada en fronteras lejanas, por lo general cubierta total o parcialmente de bosques. Selvas del interior (de América del Norte). *(Fig.)* Región apartada (remote area). Lugar apartado o perdido (remote place).

backwoodsman ['bækwʊdzmən] [bak-wuds-man] *s.* Persona que vive en un lugar perdido. Patán (peasant).

backwound ['bækwaʊnd] [bak-vund], *va. V.* BACKBITE.

backyard ['bæk'jɑːd] [bak-yard] *s.* Traspatio, patio interior.

bacon ['beɪkən] [bei-kon], *s.* Tocino entreverado; la carne salada del puerco. **Flitch of bacon,** hoja de tocino. **Gammon of bacon,** jamón, pernil. **Rusty bacon,** tocino rancio. *(Fig.)* **To bring home the bacon,** ganarse el cocido o el pan (to earn a living), llevarse la palma (to succeed). **To save one's bacon,** salvar el pellejo.

Baconian ['bəkənɪən] [ba-ko-nian] *a./s.* Baconiano.

bacteria [bæk'tɪərɪə] [bak-ti-ria], *s. pl.* Bacterias.

bacterial [bæk'tɪərɪəl] [bak-ti-rial], *a.* Bacterial, bactérico, perteneciente a las bacterias.

bactericidal [bækˌtɪərɪ'saɪdəl] [bak-ti-ri-si-dal], *a.* Destructor de las bacterias.

bactericide [bæk'tɪərɪsaɪd] [bak-ti-ri-said], *s. V.* GERMICIDE.

bacteriological [bækˌtɪərɪə'lɒdʒɪkəl] [bak-ti-ria-lo-yi-kal], *a.* Perteneciente a la bacteriología. **Bacteriological warfare,** guerra bacteriológica.

bacteriologist [bækˌtɪərɪ'ɒlədʒɪst] [bak-ti-ri-o-lo-yist], *n.* Bacteriólogo, el que se dedica al estudio de la bacteriología.

bacteriology [bækˌtɪərɪ'ɒlədʒɪ] [bak-ti-ri-o-lo-yi], *s.* Bacteriología, la ciencia que trata de las bacterias.

bacterium [bæk'tɪərɪəm] [bak-ti-rium], *s.* Singular de BACTERIA.

bad [bæd] [bad], *a.* 1. Mal, malo. **Bad habits,** malas costumbres. Viciado (blood). **Bad blood,** mala sangre. **To keep bad company,** tener malas compañías. **A bad light for reading,** una luz mala para leer. **These apples are bad,** estas manzanas están malas. **Bad news,** malas noticias. **Smoking is bad for the health,** el fumar es malo para la salud. 2. Perverso. Incobrable (debt). Severo, intenso (cold). 3. Infeliz, desgraciado, cruel (defeat). 4. Nocivo, dañoso, grave (mistake, accident, disease). 5. Indispuesto, malo. **To be bad of a fever,** estar con calentura. **To feel bad,** encontrarse mal. **From bad to worse,** de mal en peor. *(Fam.)* **Bad egg** o **bad lot,** mala persona. **He is a bad one,** es un tipo de cuidado, es un mal sujeto. **I am in bad with my friend,** mi amigo está enfadado conmigo. **In a bad sense,** en mal sentido. **In a bad way,** en mal estado (in a bad state), en un mal paso (in a tight spot). **It's not bad,** no está mal. **To go bad,** echarse a perder, estropearse. **To look bad,** tener mala cara. **Too bad! ,** ¡qué pena! (what a shame!), ¿qué le vamos a hacer? (never mind). **To use bad language,** ser mal hablado. *s.* Lo malo, gente mala (bad people). **I am ten pounds to the bad,** tengo un déficit de diez libras. **To go to the bad,** echarse a perder.

bad, bade [bæd] [beid], Pretérito del verbo *To bid.*

badge [bædʒ] [bach], *s.* Divisa, señal, distintivo (distinctive device), símbolo, insignia (of office). **Badge of honor,** divisa de honor. **Badges of the stern and quarters,** *(Mar,)* escudos de popa. **Red Cross badge,** brazalete de la Cruz Roja.

badge, *va.* Divisar, señalar con divisa.

badgeless ['bædʒlɪs] [bach-les], *a.* Sin divisa o señal.

badger ['bædʒəʳ] [ba-char], *s.* 1. Tejón, animal cuadrúpedo.

badger, *va.* Molestar, cansar, fatigar, fastidiar. Importunar, acosar (con preguntas).

badger-legged ['bædʒəˌlegd] [bad-cha-legd], *a.* Patituerto o estevado.

badinage ['bædɪnɑːʒ] [ba-di-nach], *s.* Gracejo, jocosidad, burla, chanza, chacota; cháchara. Discreteo (playful teasing). Broma (joking).

badlands ['bædlændz] [bad-lands] *s.* Páramos, tierras yermas.

bad-looking ['bædˌluːkɪŋ] [bad-lu-king] *a.* Feo.

badly ['bædlɪ] [bad-li], *adv.* Mal o malamente. **To behave badly,** portarse mal. Gravemente. **Badly hurt,** gravemente herido. Mucho. **To miss someone badly,** echar mucho de menos a alguien. **He needs money badly,** tiene mucha necesidad de dinero. **To be badly off,** andar mal de dinero (hard up). **To be badly off for,** andar mal de.

badminton ['bædmɪntən] [bad-min-ton], *s.* Badminton, juego parecido al tenis.

badness ['bædnɪs] [bad-nes], *s.* Maldad (of a person), falta de bondad, sea en lo físico o en lo moral; mala calidad de una cosa. Rigor (of climate, weather). Mal estado (of a road).

bad-tempered ['bæd'tempəd] [bad-tem-ped] *a.* De mal genio (permanently). De mal humor, malhumorado (occasionally).

baffle ['bæfl] [ba-fol], *va.* Desconcertar (to puzzle). Frustrar (to frustrate), interponiendo obstáculos, hacer inútil; eludir, huir de la dificultad. **To baffle all description,** escapar a cualquier descripción. Impedir (to hamper). Desviar (to deflect). Detener (to stop). -*vn.* Engañar, burlarse.

baffler ['bæflər] [ba-flar], *s.* Engañador, el que elude.

baffling ['bæflɪŋ] [baflin] *a.* Desconcertante.

bag ['bæg] [bag], *s.* 1. Saco (sack), talega, bolsa. **Shopping bag,** bolsa para la compra. **Paper bag,** bolsa de papel. Bolso (handbag), cartera (satchel) 2. Bolsita o vejiguilla en la que algunos animales tiene jugos particulares, como la víbora el veneno y la algalia el licor así llamado **Poison, ink bag,** bolsa de veneno, de tinta; ubre, teta (de vaca, de cabra, de oveja). **Game-bag,** morral, zurrón. **Cinnamon-bag,** churla de canela. **Cigar-bag,** petaquilla, cigarrera. **To pack up bag and baggage,** liar el hato, liar el petate, tomar el tole. *(Fig. Fam.)* **Bag of bones,** costal de huesos. **Bags of,** montones de, mucho. **Bags of money,** montones de dinero. **There's bags of room,** hay mucho sitio. **Diplomatic bag,** valija diplomática. *(Fam.)* **It's in the bag,** está en el bote. **To be left holding the bag,** cargar con el muerto. **Traveling bag,** bolsa de viaje. **Laundry bag,** bolsa para la ropa sucia. *(Fig.)* **The whole bag of tricks,** todo.

bag, *va.* 1. Ensacar (to put in bags), meter alguna cosa en sacos, empaquetar. 2. Entalegar, meter alguna cosa en talego o talega. *(Fig.)* Pescar, coger. **The police bagged the whole gang,** la policía pescó toda la banda. **He bagged the best seat,** cogió el mejor sitio. **Who has bagged my matches?,** ¿quién ha cogido mis cerillas? -*vn.* 1. Abotagarse, hincharse (to swell). 2. Hacer bolsa o pliegue (una prenda de vestir).

bagasse ['bægəs] [ba-gas] *s.* Bagazo (of grapes).

bagatelle [,bægə'tel] [ba-ga-tel], *s.* Bagatela, cosa de poca sustancia y valor, futesa, fruslería (trifle). Billar inglés (game).

bagful ['bægfʊl] [bag-ful] *s.* Bolsa, saco. **They picked three bagfuls of apples,** recogieron tres sacos de manzanas. Montón. **Bagfuls of money,** montones de dinero.

baggage ['bægɪdʒ] [ba-geich], *s.* 1. *(E.U.)* Equipaje (de un viajero); se llama *luggage,* en la Gran Bretaña. 2. Bagaje, equipaje de tropa. **Baggage check,** contraseña o talón de equipaje. **Baggage car,** carro furgón, de equipaje. **Baggage wagon,** furgón. **Baggage rack,** redecilla.

baggage, *s.* Zorra, pelleja *(Fam.)* coqueta; maula, buena alhaja. Picaruela (saucy girl). Ramera (prostitute).

bagging ['bægɪŋ] [ba-ging], *s.* Tela basta; arpillera.

baggy ['bægɪ] [ba-gi] *a.* Que hace bolsas. **A baggy suit,** un traje que hace bolsas. Holgado (loose). **Trousers baggy at the knees,** pantalón con rodilleras.

Baghdad [,bæg'dæd] [bag-dad] *N. (Geogr.)* Bagdad.

bagnio ['bægnɪə] [bag-nio], *s.* 1. Lupanar, burdel. 2. Casa de baños; baño. 3. Mazmorra de los esclavos en Turquía.

bagpipes ['bægpaɪpz] [bag-paips], *s.* Gaita, cornamusa.

bagpiper ['bægpaɪpər] [bag-pai-par], *s.* Gaitero.

baguette [bæ'get] [ba-guet] *s. (Arq.)* Junquillo.

bah [baː] [ba], inter. ¡Bah! exclamación de desprecio o enfado.

bail [beɪl] [beil], *s.* 1. Caución, fianza. **A bail of two hundred dollars,** una fianza de doscientos dólares.; caución juratoria; fianza carcelera. 2. El fiador o abonador de otro. **On bail,** bajo fianza. **To give bail,** sanear. **To forfeit bail,** perder la fianza. **To go bail o to put up bail for someone,** salir fiador por uno, dar fianza por uno. **To be on bail,** estar en libertad bajo fianza.

bail, *s.* 1. Asa (de un cubo, de una calera.). 2. División entre los compartimientos de un establo. Muro exterior (of castle). 3. *(G.B.)* Mojón, mojonera. 4. Achicador (for scooping water); cubo o vertedor para achicar.

bail, *va.* 1. Dar fianza o salir fiador por otro (to put up bail for). 2. *(For.)* Poner en libertad bajo fianza. 3. Desaguar, vaciar un estanque, achicar un bote (water out of a boat). **To**

bail out, vaciar; *(Aer.)* Lanzarse en paracaídas. *(Fig.)* **To bail out,** sacar de apuro.

bailable ['beɪləbl] [bei-la-bol], *a.* El que puede ser puesto en libertad bajo fianza; caucionable.

bail-bond [,beɪl'bɒnd] [beil-bond], *s.* Fianza de excarcelación; escritura de fianza.

bailee ['beiliː] [bei-lí], *s. (For.)* Depositario, el que recibe cierta propiedad mueble en depósito.

bailer ['beɪlər] [bei-lar], *s. (For.)* El que es fiador de otro. *(Mar.)* Achicador.

bailey ['beɪlɪ] [bei-li], *s.* Patio exterior de un castillo o cualquier patio de una fortaleza. **Old Bailey,** el tribunal central de lo criminal en Londres.

bailiff ['beɪlɪf] [bei-lif], *s.* 1. Alguacil (debt collector), corchete, ministro, inferior de justicia cuya obligación es prender o ejecutar prisiones. 2. Mayordomo (of state), administrador.

bailiwick ['beɪlɪwɪk] [bei-li-uik], *s.* Alguacilazgo; mayordomía.

bailment ['beɪlmənt] [beil-ment], *s. (For.)* 1. Depósito, entrega de alguna cosa a tercera persona. 2. Acción de procurar la libertad de un preso bajo fianza.

bailor ['beɪlər] [bei-lor], *s. (For.)* Fiador; el que da fianza por otro.

bain-marie [bemə'ri] [be-ma-ri] *s.* Baño maría, baño de maría.

bait [beɪt] [beit], *va.* 1. Cebar, dar cebo a los animales para engordarlos, o atraerlos. Poner el cebo en, encebar. **To bait the hook,** poner el cebo en el anzuelo. 2. Azuzar, incitar a los perros para que ataquen; molestar, hostigar (to torment), acosar, fatigar. -*vn.* 1. Hacer parada o alto para tomar un refrigerio. Dar un pienso a los animales en el camino. 2. Aletear, mover las alas con violencia. 3. Atraer, incitar.

bait, *s.* 1. Cebo, carnada (in fishing and hunting), la comida que se echa a los animales para atraerlos; anzuelo, añagaza, señuelo. 2. *(Fig.)* Cebo, señuelo (enticement), el formento de algún efecto o pasión; añagaza. 3. Refrigerio o refresco que se toma en los descansos que se hacen en una jornada. 4. Pienso, el alimento que se da a los animales. **To take the bait,** picar, tragar el anzuelo, caer en un lazo. **To lay the bait,** poner el cebo.

baize [beis] [beis], *s.* Bayeta, tela basta de lana. **Scarlet baize,** bayeta de grana. **Long-napped baize,** bayeta de pellón. **Green baize,** tapete verde (in games).

bake [beik] [beik], *s.* Cocción. *va.* 1. Cocer en horno (in an oven). **To bake a cake,** cocer un pastel en el horno. 2. Secar (to dry), desecar, endurecer (to harden), calcinar. **The earth is baked by the heat,** la tierra está desecada por el calor. **Baked bricks,** ladrillos cocidos. -*vn.* Hornear, ejercer el oficio de hornero. **Baked meat,** guisado, carne guisada o cocida al horno. Cocer, cocerse. *(Fig. Fam.)* **It's baking hot,** hace un calor achicharrante.

bakehouse ['beɪkhaʊs] [beik-jaus], *s.* Horno, panadería.

bakelite ['beɪkəlaɪt] [beika-lait], *s.* Bakelita, resina sintética.

baker ['beɪkər] [bei-kar], *s.* Hornero, panadero (who makes and sells bread). Pastelero (who makes and sells cakes). **Baker's,** panadería. **A baker's dozen,** trece por docena, docena de fraile.

bakery ['beɪkərɪ] [bei-ka-ri] *s.* Panadería, tahona.

baking ['beɪkɪŋ] [bei-kin], *s.* Hornada (Batch); cocimiento.

baking-pan ['beɪkɪŋpæn] [bei-kin-pan], *s.* Tortera o tartera.

baking powder ['beɪkɪŋˌpaʊdər] [bei-kin-pau-dar], *s.* Polvo de hornear, levadura en polvo.

baking soda ['beɪkɪŋˌsəʊdə] [bei-kin-sou-da], *s.* Bicarbonato de sosa o de soda.

balaclava [,bælə'klɑːvə] [ba-la-kla-va] *s.* **Balaclava helmet,** pasamontañas.

balalaika [,bælə'laɪkə] [ba-la-lai-ka] *s. (Mús.)* Balalaika.

balance ['bæləns] [ba-lans], *s.* 1. Balanza (apparatus), el peso compuesto de fiel, brazos y platillos. 2. Cotejo de una cosa con otra. 3. (physical) Equilibrio. **To keep, loose one's balance,** mantener, perder el equilibrio. **The blow caught**

him off **balance,** el golpe lo agarró o lo cogió desprevenido. **To throw somebody off balance** (disconcert), desconcertar a alguien, (topple) hacer que alguien pierda el equilibrio. Balance. **Bank balance,** saldo (difference, remainder, resto (of sum of money), saldo. 4. Volante de reloj. 5. *(Astr.)* Libra, el séptimo signo del zodíaco. **The balance of an account,** saldo de una cuenta, balance o ajuste final de ella (in accounting). **Balance sheet,** balance. **Balance weight,** contrapeso. **Balance wheel,** rueda catalina, volante, péndulo de reloj. **To strike a balance,** hacer o pasar balance.

balance, *va.* 1. Equilibrar, mantener o sostener en equilibrio. **He put out his arms to balance himself,** extendió los brazos para no perder el equilibrio. Igualar en peso, en poder, sopesar (weigh up). **You have to balance the risks against the likely profit,** tienes que sopesar los riesgos y los posibles beneficios. 2. Balancear, contrapesar. 3. Dar finiquito, saldar, satisfacer el alcance que resulta de una cuenta. **To balance the books,** hacer cuadrar las cuentas. 4. Pesar en balanza; pesar, considerar, examinar. *-vn.* 1. Estar en equilibrio; ser iguales en peso. 2. Balancear, dudar, estar perplejo en la resolución de alguna cosa. 3. Balancearse, agitarse, menearse de acá para allá. **Balance out,** compensarse. **It all balances out in the end,** al final una cosa compensa la otra. **The losses and the gains balance each other out,** las pérdidas y las ganancias se compensan.

balanced [ˈbælənst] [ba-lanst] *a.* Equilibrado.

balancing [ˈbælənsɪŋ] [ba-lan-sin], *s.* Equilibrio; la acción de pesar. **Balancing-pole,** balancín, contrapeso de los volantes y funámbulos. **To perform a balancing act,** hacer malabarismos.

balas ruby [ˈbæləsˌrʊbɪ] [ba-las-ru-bi], *s.* Balaje, rubí espinela de color vinoso.

balausta [ˈbæləstə] [ba-los-ta], *s.* Balaustra, fruto con el cáliz adnato, y que contiene numerosas semillas; o el del granado silvestre.

balcony [ˈbælkənɪ] [bal-ko-ni], *s.* 1. *(Arq.)* Balcón, plataforma rodeada de un antepecho de madera, piedra o hierro, que proyecta de una pared y suele ponerse delante de una puerta o ventana grande. (large) Terraza. 2. *(Teat.)* Platea alta, galería de los teatros, gallinero.

bald [bɔːld] [bold], *a.* 1. Calvo, falto de pelo. 2. Escueto, pelado; desnudo, pelón, raído, gastado, liso. **He is bald,** es calvo. **To go bald,** quedarse calvo. **Bald patch,** calva 3. Soso, desabrido, grosero, sin elegancia ni dignidad. **A bald translation,** una traducción grosera, sin elegancia. (Plain) **The bald truth,** la verdad pura y simple.

baldachin [ˈbældəntʃɪn] [bal-dan-chin], *s. (Arq.)* Dosel, baldaquín.

balderdash [ˈbɔːldədæʃ] [bol-dar-dash], *s. (Fam.)* 1. Disparate, jerga, jerigonza. 2. Mejunje, mezcolanza, especialmente de licores.

baldhead [bɔːldˈhed] [bold-jed], *s.* Calvo, sin pelo en la cabeza.

balding [ˈbɔːldɪŋ] [bol-din] *a.* **He is balding,** se está quedando calvo.

baldly [ˈbɔːldlɪ] [bold-li], *adv.* Chabacanamente, groseramente.

baldness [ˈbɔːldnɪs] [bold-nes], *s.* Calvez, calvicie, falta de pelo en la cabeza.

bald-pate, bald-pated [bɔːldˈpeɪt] [bold-peit], *a.* Tonsurado; calvo. **Baldpate,** cabeza pelada; se dice de los frailes.

baldric [ˈbɔːldrɪk] [bold-rik], *s.* 1. Zona, banda o faja. 2. *(Astr.)* Zodíaco.

bale [beɪl] [beil], *s.* 1. Bala o fardo de mercaderías. 2. Bala de papel que contiene diez resmas. 3. *(Ant.)* Calamidad, miseria. **Bale of fire,** lumbrada, luminaria, fuego.

bale, *vn.* Embalar, empaquetar, enfardar. *-va. (Mar.)* Achicar, sacar el agua del bote.

Balearic Islands [ˌbælɪˈærɪkˌaɪlandz] [ba-lia-rik-ai-lands] *N. (Geogr.)* las Islas Baleares.

baleen [ˈbəliːn] [ba-lín], *s. (Ant.)* Ballena.

baleful [ˈbeɪlfʊl] [beil-ful] *a.* Torvo.

balefully [ˈbeɪlfəlɪ] [beil-fu-li], *adv.* Desgraciadamente, tristemente.

bale out [ˈbeɪlaʊt] [beil-aut] See BAIL OUT.

balize [ˈbəlaɪs] [ba-lais], *s.* Baliza, boya o señal que se pone en algunos puntos del mar o de los ríos para indicar a las embarcaciones que hay peligro.

balk [bɔːk] [bolk], *s.* 1. Viga, madera larga y gruesa. 2. Lomo entre surcos. 3. Chasco, contratiempo, suceso contrario a lo que se esperaba. 4. Deshonor; desgracia. 5. Agravio, perjuicio.

balk, baulk, *va.* 1. Frustrar o dar chasco, faltar a la palabra. Obstaculizar (attempt, plan), evitar, eludir (avoid) (question, issue) 2. Amontonar en un bulto o lomo. *-vn.* Pararse obstinadamente; quedarse detenido; se dice de las caballerías. Mostrarse reacio a. **He balked at the suggestion,** se mostró reacio a aceptar la sugerencia.

Balkan [ˈbɔːlkən] [bal-kan] *a.* Balcánico. *N. (Geogr.)* **The Balkans,** los países balcánicos.

balky [ˈbɔːlkɪ] [bal-ki], *a.* Obstinado, porfiado, dispuesto a plantarse; se aplica más a las caballerías que se detienen de pronto y se niegan a seguir andando.

ball [bɔːl] [bol], *s.* 1. Bola, cuerpo redondo de cualquier materia, globo. **Eye-ball,** globo del ojo. 2. Pelota, bola (in baseball, golf), pelota, balón (in basketball, football), bola (in billiards). **The ball is in your court,** te corresponde a ti dar el próximo paso. *(Coloq,)* **To be on the ball,** ser muy espabilado, tener los ojos bien abiertos. **To carry the ball,** llevar la batuta o la voz cantante. (football) **To drop** o **fumble the ball,** flumbear. **You know he won't drop** o **fumble the ball,** ya sabes que no nos va a fallar. **To set, start, keep the ball rolling,** poner, mantener las cosas en marcha o en movimiento. **To play ball with somebody,** jugar a la pelota con alguien. 3. Bola (round mass), ovillo (of string, wool). **She was curled up in a wool,** estaba hecha un ovillo. *(Fam.)* **The whole ball of wax,** toda la historia. *(Anat.)* **The ball of the foot,** la parte anterior de la planta del pie. **Snow-ball,** bola de nieve. **Wash-ball,** bola de jabón. **Printer's ball,** bola de impresor. **The ball of the thumb,** eminencia en la base del dedo pulgar. **Ball of the foot,** eminencia carnosa en la base del dedo grueso del pie. 4. Baile, festejo en que se juntan varias personas para bailar. **To have a ball,** divertirse de lo lindo o como loco. **Fancy ball,** baile de trajes, en el que los concurrentes se presentan disfrazados. **Dress ball,** sarao; baile serio, o de etiqueta. **Masquerade ball,** baile de máscaras. **Ball bearings,** cojinete de bolas (de acero). 5. Balls *(Vul.) (testicles)* Huevos, pelotas, cojones, tanates. (Nonsense) Pendejadas, huevadas, gilipolleces, boludeces. *(Vul.)* **Ball up, balls up,** joder, fastidiar (spoil plans, task). Cagada, despelote. **He made a complete balls up of the arrangements,** se cargó la organización.

ballad [ˈbæləd] [ba-lad], *s.* Balada o balata (sentimental song), canción; jácara, romance (narrative poem, song).

ballad-maker, ballad-writer [ˈbælədˌmeɪkəʳ] [ba-lad-mei-kar], *s.* Coplero, coplista, jacarista, escritor de canciones.

ballad-monger [ˈbælədˌmʌŋgəʳ] [ba-lad-mon-guar], *s.* Coplero, el que trafica en baladas, coplas o canciones.

ballad-singer [ˈbælədˌsɪŋgəʳ] [ba-lad-sin-guar], *s.* Jacarero, cantor de jácaras o baladas.

ballad-tune [ˈbælədˌtjuːn] [ba-lad-tiún], *s.* Entonación o aire de balada.

ballast [ˈbæləst] [ba-last], *s.* 1. Lastre, el peso que se echa en el fondo del navío para que navegue. 2. *(F. C.)* Cascajo, balaste, arena y pedrisco para terraplenar. **To go in ballast,** ir en lastre. **Washed ballast,** lastre lavado o guijarro. **Ballast lighter,** lanchón de deslastrar. **Ballast ports,** portas de lastrar.

ballast, *va.* 1. Lastrar, echar lastre al navío. 2. Hacer o tener alguna cosa firme. *(F.C.)* Balastar, afirmar.

ballasting [ˈbæləstɪŋ] [ba-las-tin], s. 1. El acto de lastrar o de balastrar. 2. Material para terraplenes; balaste; afirmación. *(Mar.)* Lastre.

ballboy [ˈbɔːlbɔɪ] [bol-boi] s. Recogepelotas, recogebolas, pelotero.

ballerina [ˌbæləˈriːnə] [ba-le-ri-na], s. Bailarina de ballet. **Ballerina-length dress,** vestido de noche que llega un poco más arriba del tobillo.

ballet [ˈbæleɪ] [ba-lei], s. Ballet, baile clásico. **Ballet dancer,** bailarín de ballet.

ball game [ˈbɔːlˈɡeɪm] [bol-gueim] s. Juego de pelota. **Baseball game,** partido de béisbol. **Football game,** partido de fútbol, o fútbol americano. **No ball games,** prohibido jugar a la pelota. **It's a whole new ball game,** ha cambiado totalmente el panorama. **Ball game girl,** recogepelotas, recogebolas, pelotera.

ballistic [bəˈlɪstɪk] [ba-lis-tik] a. Balístico. **Ballistic missile,** *(Mil.)* Proyectil balístico.

ballistics [bəˈlɪstɪks] [ba-lis-tiks], s. Balística.

balloon [bəˈluːn] [ba-lún], s. Globo. **Balloon tire,** llanta o neumático balón. (Toy) Globo, bomba, chimbomba. *(Aer.)* Globo, aeróstato. **Meteorological** o **weather balloon,** globo sonda. *(Fam.)* **To go over/down like a lead balloon,** caer muy mal. **When the balloon goes up,** cuando estalle o reviente el asunto. Globo, bocadillo (in comic strip). *(Aer.)* **To go ballooning,** a) pasear en globo, b) hincharse (swell).

balloonist [bəˈluːnɪst] [ba-lu-nist], s. Aeronauta.

ballot [ˈbælət] [ba-lot], s. 1. Balota, bolilla o haba para votar. **2. Ballot paper,** papeleta impresa o manuscrita que sirve para votar. Número de votos (number of votes cast). 3. La acción de votar, votación (system of voting). **Ballot-box,** urna electoral; urna de escrutinio. **To hold, take a ballot on something,** someter algo a votación.

ballot, vn. 1. Balotar, votar con balotas. 2. Votar, en general; ejercer el derecho de sufragio. Invitar a votar (members). **To ballot somebody on something,** someter algo a la votación de alguien.

ball park [ˈbɔːlpɑːk] [bol-park] s. Estadio, parque de béisbol. **To be in the ball park: total costs will be in the 5 million ball park,** el costo total será del orden de cinco millones. **Several of the bids are in our ball park,** varias de las ofertas están a nuestro alcance. **A ball park figure,** una cifra aproximada.

ballplayer [ˈbɔːlˌpleɪəʳ] [bol-ple-yar], s. Jugador de pelota. Jugador de béisbol, beisbolista (in baseball). Jugador de fútbol, o de fútbol americano (in football). Jugador de baloncesto, baloncestista, basquetbolista (in basketball).

ball-point pen [ˈbɔːlpɔɪntˌpen] [bol-point-pen], s. Pluma de bola, pluma esferográfica. Bolígrafo.

ballroom [ˈbɔːlrʊm] [bol-rum], s. Salón de baile. **Ballroom dancing,** baile de salón.

ballyhoo [ˌbælɪˈhuː] [ba-li-ju], s. Bombo, exagerada publicidad, -va. Dar bombo, anunciar algo exageradamente, a bombo y platillo.

balm [bɑːm] [balm], s. 1. Bálsamo, el jugo o licor que se saca de un arbusto que se llama también *bálsamo*. 2. Bálsamo, cualquier ungüento precioso y fragrante. 3. Bálsamo, lo que mitiga y suaviza. **Balm of Gilead,** bálsamo de Canarias. 4. *(Bot.)* Balsamita mayor, toronjil. **Balm-gentle,** melisa.

balm, va. 1. Embalsamar. 2. Mitigar, suavizar, calmar.

balmy [ˈbɑːmɪ] [bal-mi], a. 1. Balsámico, lo que tiene las cualidades del bálsamo y lo que produce bálsamo. 2. Balsámico; untuoso; lo que mitiga y suaviza. 3. Fragrante. 4. *(Fig.)* Calmante, dulce, suave, reparador. **Balmy sleep,** sueño reparador. Templado y agradable (evening, air). Chiflado, rayado (crazy).

balneal [ˈbɑːnɪəl] [bal-nial], **balneary** [ˈbɑːnɪərɪ] [bal-nia-ri], a. Balneario, perteneciente a los baños públicos, o al baño.

baloney [bəˈləʊnɪ] [ba-lou-ni] s. Tonterías (nonsense), chorradas, macanas.

balsam [ˈbɔːlsəm] [bal-sam], s. 1. Bálsamo, sustancia oleosa, resinosa y aromática que se extrae de ciertas plantas y

árboles. **Balsam of Copaiba,** bálsamo de Copaiba. **Balsam of Peru,** bálsamo del Perú, o del Salvador. **Balsam of Tolu,** bálsamo de Tolú o de María. **Copal balsam,** bálsamo de copal. **Anada balsam (balsam of fir),** bálsamo del Canadá. 2. Planta anual de jardín, con hermosas flores; balsamina.

balsam-apple [ˈbɔːlsəmˌeɪpl] [bal-sam-eipol], s. *(Bot.)* Balsamina.

balsamic, balsamical [ˈbɔːlsəmɪk] [ˈbɔːlsəmɪkl] [bal-sa-mik] [ba-sa-mi-kal], a. Balsámico; untuoso; lo que mitiga y suaviza.

balsamine [ˈbɔːlsəmiːn] [bal-sa-min], s. Balsamina.

Baltic [ˈbɔːltɪk] [bal-tik] a. Báltico. *(Geogr.)* **The Baltic Sea,** el mar Báltico.

baluster [ˈbæləstəʳ] [ba-lus-tar], s. Balaustre, columna pequeña. **Balusters of a ship,** *(Mar.)* balaustres, pilares de madera colocados en el balcón de popa.

balustrade [ˌbæləsˈtreɪd] [ba-las-treid], s. Balaustrada.

bamboo [bæmˈbuː] [bam-bu], s. *(Bot.)* Bamboa, especie de caña o junco. **Bamboo shoots,** brotes de bambú.

bamboozle [bæmˈbuːzl] [bam-bu-sel], va. *(Vulg.)* Engañar; burlar, cansar, enredar. **He was bamboozled into financing their plan,** lo engatusaron para que financiara su plan.

bamboozler [bæmˈbuːzləʳ] [bam-bus-lar], s. *(Vulg.)* Engañador, el que engaña.

ban [bæn] [ban], s. 1. Bando, el acto de publicar algún edicto, ley o mandato; noticia pública dada a voz de pregonero; anuncio. 2. Excomunión. 3. Entredicho. 4. **Ban of the empire,** bando del imperio, censura pública por la cual se suspenden los privilegios de algún príncipe del imperio. **Bans of marriage,** amonestaciones, monición, proclama de casamiento que se hace antes de contraer matrimonio. Prohibición (prohibition). **To put, impose a ban on something,** prohibir algo.

ban, va. y vn. Maldecir, execrar. Prohibir (book, smoking), proscribir (organization). **Ban the bomb!,** ¡no a la bomba atómica! **He was banned from the club,** le prohibieron la entrada al club. (Sport) **He was banned from playing for one year,** lo suspendieron por un año.

banal [bəˈnɑːl] [ba-nal], a. 1. Trivial, vulgar, banal, insignificante. 2. Que pertenece al servicio feudal.

banality [bəˈnælɪtɪ] [ba-na-li-ti], s. 1. Trivialidad, banalidad. 2. En tiempos pasados, derecho del señor feudal a obligar a sus vasallos a que usaran su molino, lagar, etc.

banana [bəˈnɑːnə] [ba-na-na], s. *(Bot.)* Plátano, planta arbórea de gran tamaño que se cría en los países cálidos, cuya fruta se come. Banana, fruta del banano. Cambur. **Banana-tree,** banano, plátano. *(Fam.)* **To be top, second banana,** ser el mandamás, el segundo de a bordo. **Banana peel,** banana skin. **Republic banana,** república banana o bananera.

bananas [bəˈnɑːnəz] [ba-na-nas] a. *(Fam.)* **She's completely bananas,** está chiflada. **To go bananas,** perder la chaveta.

banana skin [bəˈnɑːnəskɪn] [ba-na-na-skin] s. Cáscara de plátano o de banana o de banano, piel de plátano, concha de cambur.

banc [bæŋk] [bank], s. Banco de la justicia. **Court in banc,** reunión completa de un tribunal.

band [bænd] [band], s. 1. Venda, tira o faja, que sirve para atar o ligar alguna cosa cubriéndola. Cinta (ribbon), banda, tira (strip of cloth), cinta (hat), franja (stripe). 2. Cadena o ramal, con que se sujeta algún animal. 3. Enlace, unión o conexión de unas cosas con otras. 4. Cuadrilla, gavilla, junta de muchas personas. Grupo (group), pandilla, banda (of thieves, youths). **Band of music,** banda de música. **Band in a church,** capilla. 5. Alzacuello, especie de cuello o corbata que usan los clérigos, abogados, legistas y estudiantes. 6. Filete o listón. **Bands,** fajas del arzón de una silla. 7. Banda de soldados. **Band-saw,** sierra de hoja sin fin, sierra continua. *(Mús.)* **Jazz band,** grupo o conjunto de jazz. **Rock band,** grupo o banda de rock. **Wave band,** (banda de) frecuencia. Anillo (ring). **Wedding band,** alianza, argolla. **Band together,** unirse, hacer causa común.

band, va. 1. Congregar, unir o juntar. 2. Vender, atar o ligar con venda. -vn. Asociarse.

bandage [ˈbændɪdʒ] [ban-deich], *s.* 1. Venda, tira o faja, que sirve para atar o ligar alguna cosa cubriéndola. 2. Vendaje, venda o faja, que se pone a algún miembro herido, roto o dislocado. *va.* Vendar. **She bandaged (up) my ankle,** me vendó el tobillo.

band-aid [bænˈeɪd] [band-eid] *s.* Curita o tirita.

bandanna o **bandana** [bænˈdænə] [ban-da-na], *s. (com.)* Bandana, pañuelo grande de colores vivos con manchas o figuras.

B & B *s.* Bed and breakfast.

bandbox [ˈbændbɒks] [band-boks], *s.* Caja de cartón, para sombreros, encajes, cintas y cosas de poco peso.

bandelet [ˈbændɪlɪt] [ban-di-let], *s. (Arq.)* Fajita.

bander [ˈbændəʳ] [ban-dar], *s.* El que se une con otros.

banderole [ˈbændərəʊl] [ban-de-roul], *s.* Banderola, bandera pequeña.

bandit [ˈbændɪt] [ban-dit], *s.* Un bandido o salteador de caminos. **One-armed bandit,** máquina tragaperras.

bandmaster [ˈbændmɑːstəʳ] [band-mas-tar], *s.* Músico mayor (de banda militar).

bandog [ˈbændɒg] [ban-dog], *s.* Mastín, perro grande y fornido.

bandoleers [ˈbændəlɪəz] [ban-do-lirs], *s. pl.* V. CARTRIDGE.

bandoline [ˈbændəliːn] [ban-do-lin], *s.* Bandolina, líquido espeso, adherente y perfumado, para fijar y asentar el pelo.

bandore [ˈbændɔː] [ban-dor], *s.* Bandurria, instrumento de música semejante al laúd.

bandrol [ˈbændrəl] [ban-drol], *s.* V. BANDEROLE.

bandstand [ˈbændstænd] [band-stand], *s.* Plataforma para banda de música. Quiosco.

bandwagon [ˈbændˌwægən] [band-va-gon], *s.* Vehículo para banda de música. **To get on the bandwagon,** adherirse a una candidatura probablemente triunfante. **To jump on the bandwagon,** subirse al carro o al tren.

bandy [ˈbændɪ] [ban-di], *s.* Palocorvo, especie de palo para botar una pelota. *a.* Arqueado, torcido.

bandy, *va.* 1. Botar la pelota con palocorvo. 2. Pelotear, arrojar una cosa de una parte a otra. Intercambiar (remarks, jokes). **To bandy words with somebody,** discutir con alguien. *-vn.* Contender, discutir, examinar atentamente; ligarse; cambiar; **To bandy compliments,** cumplimentarse mutuamente. **Bandy about, bandy around: A phrase that's bandied about a lot nowadays,** una frase que se maneja mucho hoy en día.

bandyleg [ˈbændɪleg] [ban-di-leg], *s.* Pierna zamba.

bandy-legged [ˈbændɪlegd] [ban-di-le-ged], *a.* Patizambo, el que es zambo de piernas.

bane [beɪn] [bein], *s.* 1. Veneno, tósigo, **Rat's bane,** arsénico. **Wolf's bane,** acónito. 2. Ruina, pesadilla. **To be the bane of somebody's life** o **existence,** ser la cruz de alguien. Destrucción, peste, muerte. **Henbane,** beleño.

baneful [ˈbeɪnʊl] [bein-ful], *a.* Venenoso, destructivo, mortal, funesto, mortífero.

banefulness [ˈbeɪnfəlnɪs] [bein-ful-nes], *s.* Calidad venenosa o perniciosa.

banewort [ˈbeɪnˌwɔːt] [bein-uort], *s. (Bot.)* Cualquier planta venenosa, especialmente la belladona, la hierbamora, y la francesilla.

bang [bↃ] [bang], *va.* 1. Lanzar, arrojar, golpear (strike). **She banged her forehead on the shelf,** se golpeó la frente con el estante. **He was banging his fist on the table,** golpeaba la mesa con el puño. (slam). **He banged the door,** dio un portazo. 2. Cascar, dar a uno con la mano, dar de puñadas, sacudir, zurrar. *-vn.* 1. Hacer estrépito; dar una cosa contra otra. **To bang into something,** darse contra alog. (Strike) **To bang on something,** golpear algo. (Slam) Cerrarse de golpe, dar un portazo. **The gate was banging in the wind,** la puerta daba golpes, o se golpeaba con el viento. (move noisily). **He was banging about the kitchen,** andaba por la cocina haciendo ruido. 2. Saltar.

bang, *va.* Cortar el cabello de la frente al través casi en línea recta.

bang, *s.* 1. Puñada, golpe que se da con el puño. (Blow) Golpe, trancazo, golpetazo. 2. Ruido de un golpe, estrépito (loud noise), explosión, estallido (explosion). **To go over, off with a bang/To go with a bang,** ser todo un éxito. **She returned to politics with a bang,** volvió a la política a lo grande. (Pleasure) **To get a bang out of something,** disfrutar como loco con algo. 3. (Bangs) El cabello corto. *(fringe* en Inglaterra). Flequillo, chasquilla, capul, fleco, pollina.

bang, *adv.* Con un golpe violento; estrepitosamente, estruendosamente. (Gun) **To go bang,** dispararse, hacer ¡bang! o ¡pum! **Bang went our holiday,** nuestras vacaciones se fueron al garete o al diablo. (As intensifier) **Bang in the middle,** justo o exactamente en el medio. **To be bang up to date,** estar muy al día. **Bang on time,** a la hora justa o exacta. **To be bang on,** dar en el blanco, acertar de lleno.

bang *interj.* ¡pum!, ¡bang! (Used to or by children) **Bang!bang! you're dead!,** ¡pum! ¡pum!, ¡te maté!

banger [ˈbæŋgəʳ] [ban-gar] *s.* Salchicha (sausage). Petardo (firework). Cacharro (car) (old banger).

Bangkok [bæŋˈkɒk] [bang-kok] *N. (Geogr.)* Bangkok.

Bangladesh [ˌbæŋgləˈdeʃ] [ban-gla-desh] *N. (Geogr.)* Bangladesh.

Bangladeshi [ˌbæŋgləˈdeʃɪ] [ban-gla-de-shi] *a./s.* Bangladesí.

bangle [ˈbæŋgl] [ban-guel], *s.* Brazalete delgado de la India oriental, y de África. Pulsera, esclava (thin, of gold or silver), aro.

banian [ˈbænɪən] [ba-nian], *s.* Se escribe también *banyan.* 1. *(Bot.)* Baniano, árbol de la India y de Persia. 2. El natural de la India oriental de la clase comerciante. 3. (Anglo-Ind.) Bata, ropa y talar, prenda de vestir holgada y cómoda.

banish [ˈbænɪʃ] [ba-nish], *va.* Desterrar (exile), echar a alguno de su propio país o territorio; echar fuera, despedir; deportar. Hacer olvidar, desvanecer (fear, doubts). Prohibir (prohibit).

banisher [ˈbænɪʃəʳ] [ba-nishar], *s.* El que destierra.

banishment [ˈbænɪʃmənt] [ba-nish-ment], *s.* Destierro, la acción y efecto de desterrar.

banister [ˈbænɪstəʳ] [ba-nis-tar], *V.* BALUSTER. Pasamanos, barandal.

banjo [ˈbændʒəʊ] [ban-yo], *s.* Banjo, instrumento músico de cinco cuerdas, algo parecido a la bandurria y la guitarra. (Corrupción de *bandore*). Es instrumento predilecto de los negros norteamericanos.

bank [bæŋk] [bank], *s.* 1. Orilla, ribera, márgen o banda de río (edge of river). 2. **Bank of earth/snow,** banco o montón de tierra/nieve. **Bank of clouds,** masa de nubes. 3. Banco de remeros en una galera. 4. Banco, el sitio, paraje o casa donde se deposita el dinero con interés o sin él 5. Banco, la compañía de los individuos que gobiernan el banco; directores del banco. **Bank-note,** cédula o billete de banco, papel moneda del banco. **Bank account,** cuenta bancaria. **Bank book,** libreta de ahorros. **Bank card,** tarjeta de crédito (expedida por un banco), tarjeta bancaria. **Bank clerk,** empleado de banco o banca. **Bank balance,** saldo. **Bank statement,** estado o extracto de cuenta. **Bank rate,** tipo o tasa de interés. **Bank roll,** fondos (funds), fajo de billetes (roll of money) 6. Dique. 7. Eminencia. **Bank of the sea,** escollo, banco de arena. 8. *(Mús.)* Teclado; hilera de teclas (piano y órgano). **Savings-bank,** caja de ahorros. *(Fam.)* **To laugh all the way to the bank,** morirse de risa. (In gambling) **The bank,** la banca. **One evening at the theater isn't going to break the bank,** ir una noche al teatro no nos va a arruinar. (Store, supply) **Blood/sperm bank,** banco de sangre/semen.

bank, *va.* 1. Poner, depositar o ingresar dinero en un banco. 2. Aislar o detener el agua con diques, o construirlos. 3. **To bank up a fire,** cubrir el fuego (como con cenizas o tierra).

-*vn*. Tener por banquero. **We bank with D. & Co.,** D. y Cía. son nuestros banqueros. **I bank with the National,** tengo la cuenta en el Nacional. *(Aer.)* Ladearse. **Bank on,** contar con (victory, help). **I wouldn't bank on it,** yo no me confiaría demasiado. **We were banking on them accepting our offer,** contábamos con, confiábamos en que aceptarían nuestra oferta.

bankable [ˈbæŋkəbl] [ban-ka-bol], *a*. Recibidero por un banco.

bankbill [ˈbæŋkbɪl] [bank-bil], *s*. Billete, vale o cédula de banco.

banker [ˈbæŋkəʳ] [ban-kar]. *s*. Banquero, cambista. (In gambling) Banca. **Banker's draft,** cheque o efecto bancario.

bank holiday [bæŋkˈhɒlədɪ] [bank-jo-li-dei] *s*. Día festivo, feriado.

banking [ˈbæŋkɪŋ] [ban-king] *s*. Banca (business). Bancario (charges, system).

banking-house [bæŋkˌhaʊs] [bank-jaus], *s*. Casa de banquero, banco particular.

bankrupt [ˈbæŋkrʌpt] [bank-rapt], *a*. Insolvente, en quiebra, en bancarrota. **To be bankrupt,** estar en quiebra o en bancarrota. **To go bankrupt,** quebrar, ir a la bancarrota. **A morally bankrupt country,** un país en (la) bancarrota moral. -*s*. Quebrado, fallido, el que hizo bancarrota o quiebra.

bankrupt, *va*. Quebrar, declararse insolvente. Llevar a la quiebra o a la bancarrota.

bankruptcy [ˈbæŋkrəptsɪ] [bank-rapt-si], *s*. Bancarrota, quiebra de un comerciante u hombre de negocios. **To go into bankruptcy,** quebrar.

bank-stock [ˈbæŋstɒk] [bank-stok], *s*. Acción de banco.

banner [ˈbænəʳ] [ba-nar], *s*. Bandera, insignia, estandarte, pancarta (in demonstration). *a*. Excepcional.

banner, *va*. Asignar una bandera o estandarte a; proveer de una bandera. -*a*. Digno de llevar la bandera; primero en dignidad.

banneret [ˈbænəret] [ba-ne-ret], *s*. Bandera pequeña.

bannerol [ˈbænərəl] [ba-ne-ret], *s*. Bandera pequeña. *V*. BANDEROL.

banning [ˈbænɪŋ] [ba-nin] *s*. Prohibición.

bannister [ˈbænɪstəʳ] [ba-nis-tar] *s. V*. BANISTER.

banns [ˈbænz] [bans], *s*. Amonestaciones. **To read the banns,** leer las amonestaciones. *V*. BAN.

banquet [ˈbæŋkwɪt] [ban-kuit], *s*. Banquete, comida espléndida a que concurren muchos convidados; festín.

banquet, *va*. Banquetear, dar banquetes o concurrir a ellos.

banquet-house [ˈbæŋkwɪtˌhaʊs] [ban-kuit-jaus], **banqueting-house** [ˈbæŋkwɪtɪŋˌhaʊs] [ban-kui-tin-jaus], *s*. Casa de banquetes o convites.

banqueting [ˈbæŋkwɪtɪŋ] [ban-kui-tin], *s*. El acto de banquetear.

banquette [bæŋˈket] [ban-ket], *s*. 1. *(Fort.)* Banqueta, banco corrido de tierra o mampostería, desde el cual pueden los soldados disparar a cubierto, detrás de muralla o parapeto. 2. (E.U. del Sur) Acera. 3. Andén de un puente; tongada en una trinchera (trabajos de ingeniería).

bantam [ˈbæntəm] [ban-tam], *s*. Gallina pequeña de Bantam, distrito de Java.

bantamweight [ˈbæntəmweɪt] [ban-tam-ueit], *s*. (Boxeo) Peso gallo.

banter [ˈbæntəʳ] [ban-tar], *va*. Zumbar o zumbarse, dar chasco o vaya a alguno; divertirse a costa de alguno.

banter, *s*. Zumba, vaya, burla, chasco, petardo, bromas.

banterer [ˈbæntərəʳ] [ban-ta-rar], *s*. Zumbón, el que se zumba, da vaya o chasco; burlón.

bantling [ˈbæntlɪŋ] [ban-tlin], *s*. Chicuelo o chicuela, criatura de poca edad.

banyan [ˈbænɪən] [ba-nian], *s*. Baniano, *V*. BANIAN.

baobab [ˈbeɪəbæb] [beio-bab], *s*. Baobal, árbol corpulento del África central.

baptism [ˈbæptɪzəm] [bap-tisem], *s*. Bautismo; bautizo, acción de bautizar.

baptismal [ˈbæptɪzməl] [bap-tis-mal], **baptistical** [ˈbæptɪztɪkl] [bap-tis-ti-kal], *a*. Bautismal, lo perteneciente al sacramento del bautismo.

baptist [ˈbæptɪst] [bap-tist], *s*. 1. El que administra al bautismo. **Saint John the Baptist,** San Juan Bautista. 2. Anabaptista, el sectario que sostiene que no debe bautizarse a los niños hasta que lleguen a la edad de la razón.

baptistery [ˈbæptɪstərɪ] [bap-tis-te-ri], *s*. Bautisterio, baptisterio, sitio donde está la pila bautismal.

baptize [bæpˈtaɪz] [bap-tais], *va*. Bautizar.

bar [baːʳ] [bar], *s*. 1. Palenque, barra. 2. Barra de metal, lingote. 3. Reja de una ventana, de una cárcel. **To put somebody/To be behind bars,** meter a alguien/estar entre rejas. 4. Tranca de puerta o ventana; barrote. 5. Impedimento, obstáculo. 6. Barra o banco de arena en un río o a su embocadura, o en la entrada de algún puerto. 7. *(Mús.)* Compás. Barra, raya perpendicular a las del pentagrama. La música que queda entre dos barras también se llama *bar*. 8. Estrado, foro, tribunal, el lugar en que se sientan los jueces para examinar y decidir las causas. 9. Conjunto de abogados en el tribunal; por extensión, la profesión del foro. (Law) **The Bar,** (legal profession), la abogacía (barristers). El conjunto de BARRISTERS. (In court) Banquillo. **The prisoner at the bar,** el acusado. 10. *(For.)* Excepción perentoria a alguna alegación. 11. Mostrador o banco de las tabernas, botillerías o cafés en donde se recibe el dinero. **Bar-maid,** criada de taberna o café. 12. Venda, varilla ancha, o raya: como **bar of light,** raya de luz. 13. Barandilla que separa al público de los vocales de una asamblea. **Bar iron,** hierro en barras. **Bar of gold,** lingote de oro. **Bar of chocolate,** barra o tableta de chocolate. **Bar of soap,** pastilla o barra de jabón. **Bar loom,** telar de barras. **Heel bar,** puesto de reparación rápida de calzado. **In bar of,** como excepción perentoria. **To be admitted to the bar,** *(E.U.)*, **to be called to the bar** (GB), recibirse de abogado. (Impediment) **Bar to something,** obstáculo o impedimento para algo. **Bar graph,** gráfico de barras. **Bar hop,** ir de bar en bar, ir de tascas.

bar, *va*. 1. Atrancar, cerrar con barras. (secure) (door, windows). 2. Impedir, obstar, estorbar, prohibir; exceptuar, excluir. **To bar in a harbor,** *(Mar.)* Encadenar la boca de un puerto. **To bar out,** Excluir, cerrar la puerta a. 3. Bloquear (block) (path, entrance). **A tree was barring our way,** un árbol nos bloqueaba el paso. 4. Prohibir (prohibit) (smoking, jeans). **Reporters were barred from the meeting,** se excluyó a los periodistas de la reunión. **His criminal record bars him from the job,** sus antecedentes penales le impiden acceder al puesto.

bar *Prep*. Salvo, excepto, a/con excepción de. **Bar none,** sin excepción.

barb [bAːb] [barb], *s*. 1. Púa que en los anzuelos y dardos proyecta en dirección opuesta a la punta, para impedir que ésta salga fácilmente de la herida; lengüeta de saeta o flecha. (of fishhook, arrow) 2. *(Bot.)* Barba, arista de espiga. 4. *(Des.)* Barda, arnés o armadura de caballo.

barb, *va*. 1. Armar flechas con lengüetas; hacer incisivo, mordaz, picante. 2. *(Des.)* Guarnecer a un caballo con barda.

Barbados [bɑːˈbeɪdɒs] [bar-bei-dos] *N. (Geogr.)* Barbados.

barbadoes [bɑːˈbeɪdɒs] [bar-bei-dos], *s*. Barbada, una de las Antillas. **Barbadoes leg,** mal de la Barbada, elefantíasis.

Barbadoes cherry [bɑːˈbeɪdɒsˌʃerɪ] [bar-bei-dos-she-ri], *s. (Bot.)* Guinda de Indias.

barbadoes tar [bɑːˈbeɪdɒsˌtɑːʳ] [bar-bei-dos-tar], *s*. Especie de petróleo o betún.

barbarian [bɑːˈbeərɪən] [bar-ba-rian], *s*. 1. Hombre bárbaro o salvaje. 2. Extranjero. 3. Hombre cruel o inhumano. -*a*. Bárbaro; en griego, no helénico; inculto.

barbaric [bɑːˈbærɪk] [bar-ba-rik], *a*. Extranjero, exótico, lo que viene de lejos; bárbaro, inculto. Primitivo (primitive). Brutal (brutal).

barbarism [ˈbɑːbərɪzəm] [bar-ba-ri-sem], *s*. 1. Barbarismo, vicio contra las reglas y pureza del lenguaje. 2. Barbaridad o barbarie, falta de cultura o política. 3. Crueldad, inhumanidad. 4. Ignorancia.

barbarity [bɑːˈbərɪtɪ] [bar-ba-ri-ti], *s.* 1. Barbaridad, falta de cultura (lack of cultivation), barbarie. 2. Ferocidad, inhumanidad, crueldad, brutalidad (brutality). **The barbarities of the regime,** las atrocidades del régimen. 3. Barbarismo.

barbarize [ˈbɑːbəraɪz] [bar-ba-rais], *va.* Barbarizar. *-vn.* Cometer barbarismos, viciar el lenguaje.

barbarous [ˈbɑːbərəs] [bar-ba-ros], *a.* 1. Bárbaro (tribes, rites), salvaje, brutal (punishment, captors), inculto. 2. Bárbaro, que emplea barbarismo en el lenguaje: no purista; no idiomático. 3. Cruel, inhumano. 4. Extranjero. 5. De sonido áspero y bronco.

barbarously [ˈbɑːbərəslɪ] [bar-ba-ros-li], *adv.* 1. Bárbaramente, ignorantemente. 2. Bárbaramente, con barbarismo. 3. Inhumanamente, cruelmente.

barbarousness [ˈbɑːbərəsnɪs] [bar-ba-ros-nes], *s.* V. BARBARISM.

barbary [ˈbɑːbərɪ] [bar-ba-ri], *s.* 1. Caballo berberisco. 2. Berbería.

barbate [ˈbɑːbeɪt] [bar-beit], *a.* 1. Barbado, que tiene púas, lengüetas, pelos o plumas. 2. *(Bot.)* Barbado, aristado.

barbecue [ˈbɑːbɪkjuː] [bar-bi-kiu], *va.* Aderezar, guisar o cocer un animal entero, sin despedazarle. *(Mex.)* Hacer barbacoa. Asar a la parrilla o a la brasa.

barbecue, *s.* Animal guisado sin despedazarle; (grid and fireplace) barbacoa, parrilla, asador, *(Amer.)* carne asada en un hoyo que se abre en tierra y se calienta como los hornos. **A barbecue-pig,** un cochinillo en barbacoa. (Social occasion) barbacoa, parrillada, asado.

barbed [bɑːbd] [barbd], *a.* 1. Mordaz. Barbado, armado con lengüetas, como las saetas, flechas, etc. 2. Barbado, armado con barda. V. BARD, *va.* **Barbed wire,** alambre de púas (para cercas).

barbel [ˈbɑːbəl] [bar-bel], *s.* 1. Uno de los apéndices blandos y filiformes, o barbillas, que crecen en las mandíbulas de ciertos peces. 2. Barbo, pez de río.

barbell [ˈbɑːbəl] [bar-bel], *s.* Haltera.

barber [ˈbɑːbər] [bar-bar] *s.* Barbero, peluquero.

barber-surgeon [ˌbɑːbəˈsɜːdʒən] [bar-ber-sur-yion], *s. (Ant.)* Barbero cirujano, flebotomiano.

barberry [ˈbɑːbərɪ] [bar-be-ri], *s. (Bot.)* Bérbero, berberís, agracejo, cualquier planta del género Berberis; arbusto.

barbet [ˈbɑːbɪt] [bar-bet], 1. Ave tropical de brillantes colores; barbudo, ave trepadora. 2. Variedad del perro de lanas. 3. Larva de un insecto que se alimenta de pulgones.

barbital [ˈbɑːbɪtəl] [bar-bi-tal], *s. (Quím.)* Barbital.

barbiturate [ˈbɑːbɪtəreɪt] [bar-bi-tu-reit], *(Quím.)* Barbitúrico.

barbican [ˈbɑːbɪkən] [bar-bi-kan], *s.* 1. Barbacana, fortificación, que en lo antiguo se colocaba delante de las murallas y después se llamó falsabraga. 2. Tronera, abertura que se hace en un parapeto para apuntar y disparar la artillería.

barbwire [ˈbɑːbwaɪər] [barb-uaiar] *s.* V. BARBED WIRE.

barcarolle [ˌbɑːkəˈrəʊl] [bar-ka-roul], *s.* 1. Barcarola, canción popular de los gondoleros italianos. 2. Composición musical del mismo carácter y puramente instrumental.

bar chart [ˈbɑːtʃɑːt] [bar-chart] *s.* Gráfico de barras. **Bar code,** código de barras.

bard [bɑːd] [bard], *s.* 1. Poeta, bardo, vate. 2. Barda, antigua armadura con que cubrían a los caballos. 3. **Bards,** las lonjas de tocino con que cubren las aves para asarlas. 4. Pez, mustela de río.

bard, *va.* 1. Guarnecer a un caballo con barda. 2. Guarnecer con lonjas delgadas de tocino.

bardic, bardish [ˈbɑːdɪk] [bar-dik], *a.* Lo que pertenece a los bardos o poetas, o lo que ellos dicen o escriben.

bare [beər] [bear], *a.* 1. Desnudo (uncovered), falto de vestido o abrigo, descalzo (foot). 2. Descubierto (head),

raso, pelado (tree), sin alfombrar (floorboards). 3. Liso, llano; sencillo, simple. 4. Descubierto, público. 5. Desnudo, pobre. 6. Mero, puro. 7. Raído, gastado, usado. 8. Puro, solo, no mezclado ni unido con otra cosa; desnudo (walls), con pocos muebles (room). **Bare of money,** sin un cuarto, sin blanca, sin dinero. **To lay bare,** desnudar, poner al descubierto. **To be bare of,** estar desprovisto de. **A bare account,** un relato pobre, sin interés, sin adorno. (Without details). **He gave me the bare facts,** se ciñó a los hechos. **The bare essentials,** lo estrictamente esencial (mere). **They earn the bare minimum,** ganan lo justo para vivir.

2. Bare, *va.* Desnudar, descubrir, privar, despojar. **To bare one's head,** descubrirse (la cabeza). **To bare one's chest,** mostrar el pecho. **The dog bared its teeth,** el perro enseñó o mostró los dientes. **He bared his soul/heart to me,** me abrió su corazón.

bare o **bore,** pretérito del verbo TO BEAR.

barebacked [beəˈbeɪkɪd] [bear-bakt], *a.* Sin silla (horse). **Bareback,** *a.* montado a pelo, sobre un caballo desensillado, (ride) a pelo. *-adv.* Sin silla o albarda, quitado el aparejo.

barebone [beəˈbəʊn] [bear-boun], *s.* Esqueleto, la persona muy flaca.

bareboned [beəˈbəʊnd] [bear-bound], *a.* Muy flaco, descarnado, amojamado, acecinado.

bare-chested [beəˈtʃestɪd] [bear-ches-tid] *a.* Desnudo de la cintura para arriba, sin camisa.

barefaced [beəˈfeɪst] [bear-feist], *a.* Descarado, desvergonzado, impudente, insolente, atrevido, cara de vaqueta.

barefacedly [beəˈfeɪstlɪ] [bear-feist-li], *adv.* Descaradamente, con descaro; con la cara descubierta, sin empacho ni miedo, al descubierto.

barefacedness [beəˈfeɪstnɪs] [ber-feist-nes], *s.* Descaro, desvergüenza, atrevimiento, insolencia, impudencia.

barefoot, barefooted [ˈbeəfʊt] [bear-fut], *a.* Descalzo. *adv.* **She ran barefoot,** corrió descalza.

bareheaded [beəˈhedɪd] [bear-je-did], *a.* Descubierto, con la cabeza al aire, sin sombrero ni gorra.

bare-legged [beəˈlegɪd] [bear-le-gid], *a.* Con las piernas descubiertas, sin medias.

barely [ˈbeəlɪ] [bear-li], *adv.* Meramente, simplemente, puramente, solamente, únicamente; pobremente, (hardly) apenas, (scantily). **A barely furnished room,** una habitación con pocos muebles.

barenecked [ˈbeənekt] [bear-nekt], *a.* El que tiene el cuello desnudo.

bareness [ˈbeənɪs] [bear-nes], *s.* 1. Desnudez (of body, walls, tree), falta de vestido, desabrigo, lo vacío (of room). 2. Flaqueza, falta de gordura. 3. Lacería, desnudez andrajosa.

bareribbed [ˈbeərɪbd] [bear-ribd], *a.* Muy flaco.

bargain [ˈbɑːgɪn] [bar-guein], *s.* 1. Ajuste, contrato, convenio, pacto, trato, acuerdo o concierto de compra o venta (deal, agreement). **It's a bargain!,** ¡trato hecho! 2. Compra o venta. 3. Ganga de ofertas, de oportunidades (cheap purchase), chiripa. **At a bargain,** baratísimo, por una bicoca, por casi nada. **To give into the bargain,** dar de más, de contra, de ñapa. *(Mex.)* Dar de pilón o de ganancia. **To strike a bargain, make a bargain,** cerrar un trato, efectuar una compra. **Into, in the bargain,** encima, por si fuera poco. **He drives a hard bargain,** sabe cómo conseguir lo que quiere. **Bargain basement,** sección de ofertas u oportunidades. **Bargain hunter,** cazador de gangas. **To go bargain hunting,** ir en busca de gangas.

bargain, *vn.* Pactar, ajustar, hacer contrato o convenio sobre la venta de alguna cosa; negociar, contratar; regatear, concertar. **We hadn't bargained for such an eventuality,** no habíamos tenido en cuenta esa posibilidad. **I got more than I had bargained for,** no me esperaba algo así.

bargainee [bɑːgɪˈniː] [bar-gui-ní], *s.* El que admite o acepta algún ajuste, pacto o convenio.

bargainer [ˈbɑːɡɪnəʳ] [bár-gui-nar], s. La persona que propone algún ajuste, pacto o convenio.

bargaining [ˈbɑːɡɪnɪŋ] [bár-gui-nin] s. Regateo (haggling), negociaciones (negotiating), negociador, de negociación (strategy, position).

barge [bɑːdʒ] [barch], s. 1. Alijador, lanchón de descarga, bote de fondo chato para la navegación en los puertos. 2. Falúa o faluca, bote muy adornado. 3. Gabarra, barco de transporte.

barge vn. (+ adv. compl.) **She barged through the crowd,** se abrió paso a empujones entre la multitud. **He barged past (me),** me dio un empujón para pasar. **He always barges in when we are trying to talk,** siempre se entromete cuando queremos hablar. **To barge into somebody,** chocar con alguien.

bargeman [ˈbɑːdʒmæn] [barch-man], **barger** [ˈbɑːdʒəʳ] [barchar], s. Barquero, el que gobierna o dirige un barco.

bargepole [ˈbɑːdʒpəʊl] [barch-poul] s. Pértiga, bichero. **I wouldn't touch him/it with a bargepole,** yo con él no me metería/eso no lo compraría (o aceptaría) ni aunque me pagaran.

baric [bɑːrɪk] [barik], a. 1. De bario, o que lo contiene. 2. Perteneciente al peso, especialmente al aire; barométrico.

barilla [bərɪlə] [ba-ri-la], s. 1. Barrilla, cualquier planta cuyas cenizas dan la sosa.

barite [ˈbærɪt] [ba-rit], s. Baritina, sulfato de bario. V. BARYTES.

baritone [ˈbærɪtəʊn] [ba-ri-toun], a. V. BARYTONE. s. Barítono.

barium [ˈbɛərɪəm] [ba-riom], s. (Quím.) Bario, el metal de barita.

bark [bɑːk] [bark], s. 1. (on tree) Corteza, la parte exterior del árbol. **Peruvian bark,** quina. **Angustura bark,** corteza de Angustura. 2. Barco, barca, embarcación pequeña. **Barklouse,** insecto de escama que infesta los árboles. **Oystershell, bark-louse,** Mytilaspis; se llama así por la forma de su escama, semejante a la concha de la ostra. **Tanner's oakbark,** casca, corteza del roble para el curtido de las pieles.

bark, s. Ladrido del perro; latido de la zorra; aullido del lobo. **Her/his bark is worse than her/his bite,** perro ladrador, poco mordedor.

bark, va. 1. Descortezar, quitar la corteza al árbol. 2. Raer, raspar, quitar raspando la piel u otra cubierta exterior. 3. Cubrir, dar una capa de corteza. Curtir o teñir en una infusión de corteza. 4. Aturdir o matar la caza menuda tirando a la corteza a la cual se agarra. Espetar (shout instructions, questions). **To bark (out) an order,** gritar una orden, dar una orden a gritos. -vn. 1. Ladrar, el perro. 2. Ladrar; cocear; latir, gañir como perro o zorra. **To bark at somebody/ something,** ladrarle a alguien/algo.

barkeeper [ˈbɑːkiːpəʳ] [bar-kí-par], s. (E.U.) El que sirve bebidas a los parroquianos sobre el mostrador de un café, tienda de vinos o taberna; tabernero (bar owner). Barman, camarero (male bartender). (Esp.) Mesera, camarera, moza (female bartender).

barker [ˈbɑːkəʳ] [bar-kar], s. 1. Ladrador. 2. Descortezador.

barking [ˈbɑːkɪŋ] [bar-kin], s. Ladrido.

barky [ˈbɑːkɪ] [bar-ki], a. Cortezudo, lo que tiene mucha corteza.

barley [ˈbɑːlɪ] [bar-li], s. Cebada. **Barley bread,** pan de cebada. **Barley broth,** caldo hecho con cebada; calducho. **Barley water,** agua de cebada. **Barley mow,** montón de cebada. **Pearl barley,** cebada perlada.

barleycorn [ˈbɑːlɪˌkɜːn] [bar-li-kern], s. 1. Grano de cebada. 2. Una medida que es la tercera parte de la pulgada.

barley-sugar [ˈbɑːlɪˌʃʊɡəʳ] [bar-li-shu-gar], s. 1. Azúcar clarificado con cebada. 2. Alfeñique, azúcar preparado con cáscara de limón.

barm [bɑːm] [barm], s. Jiste, el fermento de la cerveza; levadura, el fermento del pan.

barmy [ˈbɑːmɪ] [bar-mi], a. Que tiene jiste o levadura. V. BALMY.

barn [bɑːn] [barn], s. Granero (for crops), henil, pajar, establo (for livestock). (Mex.) Troje.

barnacle [ˈbɑːnəkl] [bar-na-kol], s. 1. Broma, escaramujo, especie de caracolillo marino que se adhiere al casco de las embarcaciones; percebe, cualquier crústaceo cirrípedo, especialmente el Goose-barnacle, Anatifa o Lepas Balanus. 2. Bernicla, branta o ánsar de Escocia, ave semejante al ganso. 3. Acial, instrumento con el cual los herradores sujetan a los caballos para herrarlos. **Barnacles,** (Vulg) anteojos, antiparras.

barn-dance [ˈbɑːnˌdɑːns] [barn-dans] s. Fiesta donde se baila música folclórica (dance party).

barn-door [ˈbɑːnˈdɔːʳ] [barn-dor], s. La puerta del granero. Cochera (for vehicles).

barn-floor [ˈbɑːnˈflɔːʳ] [barn-flor], s. Era, pajar.

barn-owl [ˈbɑːnˌaʊl] [barn-aul], s. Lechuza, zumaya. **Barnswallow,** golondrina que hace su nido entre las vigas de los graneros.

barn-storm [ˈbɑːnstɔːm] [barn-storm] vn. Recorrer zonas rurales durante una campaña electoral.

barn-yard [ˈbɑːnjɑːd] [barn-yard], s. Patio de granja.

barograph, barometrograph [bəˈrɒɡræf] [ba-ro-graf], s. Barógrafo, barometrógrafo, instrumento que registra y deja anotadas las variaciones de la presión atmosférica, de modo que puedan conocerse sin que sea necesaria la presencia de un operador u observador.

barometer [bəˈrɒmɪtəʳ] [ba-ro-mi-tar], s. Barómetro, instrumento para pesar la presión de la atmósfera. **Aneroid barometer,** barómetro aneroide. **Barometer reading,** indicación del barómetro.

barometrical [bəˈrɒmetrɪkl] [ba-ro-mé-tri-kal], a. Barométrico.

baron [ˈbærən] [ba-ron], s. 1. (nobleman) Barón, nombre de dignidad inferior a la de vizconde. 2. (For. Ant.) Varón, el marido en contraposición a la mujer. **A baron of the Exchequer,** un juez de la tesorería. **The lord chief baron,** el primer juez de la tesorería. Magnate (magnate). **Press baron,** magnate de la prensa.

baronage [ˈbærəneɪdʒ] [ba-ro-neich], s. Baronía, la dignidad del barón.

baroness [ˈbærənɪs] [ba-ro-nes], sf. Baronesa, la mujer del barón.

baronet [ˈbærənɪt] [ba-ro-nit], s. Título de honor inferior al de barón y superior al de caballero; es el último grado de los hereditarios en Inglaterra.

baronetage [ˈbærənɪteɪdʒ] [ba-ro-ne-teich], s. La dignidad de Baronet.

baronetcy, baronetship [ˈbærənɪtsɪ] [ˈbærənɪtʃɪp] [baro-net-si] [ba-ro-net-ship], s. La dignidad de barón; dominio o territorio de un barón, baronía.

baronial [bəˈrəʊnɪəl] [ba-ro-nial], a. Baronial, perteneciente a barón o baronía.

barony [ˈbærəʊnɪ] [ba-ro-ni], s. Baronía, señorío de barón.

baroque [bəˈrɒk] [ba↓rok] a. (also **Baroque**) (Arq., Art., Mús.) Barroco. s. **The baroque, Baroque,** el barroco.

baroscope [bəˈrɒskəʊp] [ba-ros-kop], s. Especie de barómetro; higrómetro.

barouche [bəˈruːʃ] [ba-rush], s. Birlocho, carruaje de cuatro asientos.

barracan [ˈbərəkæn] [ba-ra-kan], s. Barragán, especie de camelote basto.

barrack [ˈbærək] [ba-rak], s. Cuartel, edificio en que se alojan los soldados. **Barrack-master,** superintendente o jefe de cuartel. va. Alojar en barracones (soldiers). Abuchear (jeer, speaker, performer).

barracking [ˈbærəkɪŋ] [ba-rakin] s. Abucheo, silbatina.

barrack room [ˈbærəkrʊm] [ba-rak-rum] s. Barracón, barraca.

barracks [ˈbærəks] [ba-raks] s. Cuartel.

barracoon [ˈbærəkuːn] [ba-ra-kun], s. Barracón.

barracuda [ˌbærəˈkjuːdə] [ba-ra-kiu-da], s. Barracuda o esfirena, pez de cuerpo prolongado, parecido al sollo; becuna.

barrage [ˈbærɑːʒ] [ba-rach], s. 1. Dique de contención. 2. (Mil.) (action) Descarga. (Fire) Cortina o barrera de fuego. 3. Andanada. **Barrage balloon,** globo cautivo para formar barreras. (Deluge) Aluvión. **A barrage of criticism,** un aluvión de críticas.

barrator [ˈbærətəʳ] [ba-ratoʳ], s. Pleitista, camorrista, el que con ligero motivo mueve y ocasiona contiendas y pleitos; trapacero, altercador. (For. mar.) Empleado de a bordo culpable de baratería.

barratry [ˈbærətrɪ] [ba-ra-tri], s. 1. (For.) Pleito, o demanda fraudulenta. 2. Engaño, trapacería. 3. (Com.) Baratería, la pérdida causada a los dueños de un barco, o sus aseguradores, por dolo o malicia del capitán o tripulación.

barred [bɑːʳd] [bard] a. Con barrotes (windows).

barrel [ˈbærəl] [ba-ral], s. 1. Barril o tonel, barrica, vasija de madera que sirve para conservar licores y otros géneros (container). 2. Cañón de escopeta. Tubo (of cannon). 3. Cañón de pluma. 4. Cañón de bomba. 5. Tímpano del oído. 6. (Mar.) Cuerpo o eje de cabestrante o molinete. 7. Huso. V. FUSEE. 8. Caja de tambor. **It wasn't exactly a barrel of laughs,** no fue de lo más divertido. (Fam.) **It's like shooting fish in a barrel,** es pan comido. **To have somebody over a barrel,** tener a alguien entre la espada y la pared. **To scrape (the bottom) of the barrel,** no quedarle a uno más recursos. **Have you seen her new boyfriend? she's really scraping the barrel!,** ¿has visto con quién sale ahora?, ¡tiene que estar muy desesperada! **Barrel-organ,** organillo de cilindro.

barrel, va. Embarrilar, poner alguna cosa dentro de un barril. **To barrel up,** envasar. (Fam.) **Barrel along,** ir disparado o como un bólido.

barrelled [ˈbærəld] [ba-reld], pp. Embarrilado, entonelado. **Double-barrelled gun,** escopeta de dos cañones.

barren [ˈbærən] [ba-ren], a. (infertile, land, soil) Estéril, yermo (liter), infructuoso, erial, infecundo, infructífero. (Tree, plant, animal) (no comp) estéril. (woman, dated or liter) infecunda, estéril.

barrenly [ˈbærənlɪ] [ba-ren-li] v. Infructuosamente, estérilmente.

barrenness [ˈbærənɪs] [ba-ren-nes], s. Esterilidad, infructuosidad, infecundidad; falta de ingenio o de invención; tibieza.

barrenwort [ˈbærənwɔːθ] [ba-ren-uorz], s. (Bot.) Epimedio planta cuyas hojas se parecen a las de las hiedras.

barrette [bəˈret] [ba-ret], s. Pasador o broche para el cabello. Hebilla.

barricade, barricado [ˌbærɪˈkeɪd] [ba-ri-keid], s. Barrera, empalizada, barricada, estacada, parapeto para defenderse de los enemigos.

barricade, va. Barrear, empalizar, atrancar, cerrar con barricadas. **They barricaded themselves in the building,** se atrincheraron en el edificio.

barrier [ˈbærɪəʳ] [ba-riaʳ], s. 1. Barrera, muro (wall). **Crash barrier,** valla protectora. 2. Fortaleza. 3. Impedimento, obstáculo, estacada, embarazo; término. (Gate) Barrera. **Ticket barrier,** punto de acceso al andén, donde hay que presentar el billete. (Obstacle) **Language barrier,** barrera idiomática. (Crucial point) **The sound barrier,** la barrera del sonido.

Barrier Reef s. **The Great Barrier Reef,** el Gran Arrecife Coralino, la Gran Barrera Coral.

barring [ˈbærɪŋ] [ba-rin], pa. de To Bar. (Expresión adverbial) Amén de, aparte de, excepto. (prep.) **Barring accidents,** a menos que suceda algo imprevisto. **He said that barring delays,** dijo que, a menos que o salvo que hubiera algún retraso.

barrio [ˈbɑːrɪəʊ] [ba-rio] s. Barrio de hispanohablantes en una ciudad norteamericana.

barrister [ˈbærɪstəʳ] [ba-ris-taʳ], s. 1. Abogado. (Amer.) Licenciado. 2. Curial. (Great Britain) Abogado, habilitado para alegar ante un tribunal superior.

bar-room [ˈbɑːrʊm] [bar-rum], s. Sala con mostrador donde se sirven licores y refrescos; taberna.

barrow [ˈbærəʊ] [ba-rou], s. 1. Angarillas. 2. Marrano o puerco. 3. (Arq.) Túmulo, montón de tierra levantado en memoria de los que perecieron en una batalla; cementerio (grave mound). **Barrow hog,** barraco. **Barrow grease,** pringue de cerdo. **Wheel-barrow,** carretón o carretilla de una rueda. **Hand-barrow,** angarillas de mano, litera.

barshot [ˈbɑːʃɒt] [bar-shot], s. (Mar.) Palanqueta, barreta de hierro con dos cabezas que suele servir como carga de cañón para destrozar los aparejos y palos del enemigo.

barstool [ˈbɑːrstuːl] [bar-stul] s. Taburete.

bartender [ˈbɑːtəndəʳ] [bar-ten-daʳ], s. Cantinero, barman, camarero (male). Mesera, camarera, moza (female).

barter [ˈbɑːtəʳ] [bar-taʳ], vn. Baratar, trafagar o traficar permutando géneros. Hacer trueques. -va. Trocar, cambiar.

barter, s. 1. Cambio, trueque, permuta. 2. Tráfico, el acto de traficar.

barterer [ˈbɑːtərəʳ] [bar-te-raʳ], s. Traficante.

baryta [bærɪtə] [ba-ri-ta], s. (Quím.) Barita u óxido de bario.

barytes o barite [ˈbærɪtəz] [ba-ri-tas], s. Espato pesado, sulfato de bario.

barytic [bærɪtɪk] [ba-ri-tik], a. Barítico, lo perteneciente a la barita.

barytone [ˈbærɪtəʊn] [ba-ri-toun], s. 1. Barítono, voz media entre las de tenor y bajo.

barzah [ˈbɑːrsɑː] [bar-sa], s. El portal de una casa árabeafricana que sirve como sala de recepción.

basal [ˈbeɪsl] [bei-sal], a. Fundamental: lo que pertenece a la base o está situada en ella; básico. **Basal metabolism,** metabolismo basal.

basalt [ˈbæsɔːlt] [ba-solt], **basaltes** [ˈbæsɔːltz] [ba-solts], s. Basalto.

basaltic [ˈbæsɔːltɪk] [ba-sol-tik], a. Basáltico, que pertenece al basalto.

base [beɪs] [beis], a. 1. Bajo, humilde, despreciable, abyecto, innoble, vil, villano, ruin (conduct, motive). 2. Bajo de ley, hablando del oro y plata (inferior). **Base metal,** metal de baja ley. 3. Bajo, grave; hablando de instrumentos y voces. 4. Ilegítimo. 5. Vergonzoso, infame, indigno. 6. Poltrón, mandria, cobarde.

base, s. 1. Fondo o suelo; base (of spine, skull), pie (of mountain, tree, lamp): Base (foundation, basis). 2. Basa, pedestal o basamento de columna o estatua (of column, wall). 3. Bajo, la cuerda que lleva este punto. 4. (Quím.) Base, substancia que puede unirse con un ácido, formando una sal; en la farmacia, ingrediente principal. 5. (Geom.) Base, parte inferior de una figura de un sólido. 6. (Mús.) Bajo, grave. V. BASE. Voz de bajo. 7. Barrera o base en el juego de baseball. (wrong) **To be off base,** estar equivocado. (in baseball) (lit.) estar fuera de la base. (by surprise) **To catch somebody off base,** pillar o agarrar a alguien desprevenido. (in baseball) (lit) pillar o agarrar a alguien fuera de la base. **I called them just to touch base,** los llamé, para mantener el contacto. **Base camp** (for expedition), campamento base. Sede (of organization). (Culin.) **Dishes with a rice base,** platos a base de arroz (main ingredient).

base, va. 1. Envilecer, deteriorar. 2. Apoyar, fijar sobre alguna cosa, fundamentar, establecer (found). **To base something on/upon something,** basar o fundamentar algo en algo (opinion, conclusion). **The movie is based on a real event,** la película se basa o está basada en una historia real. Basar (locate). **The company is based in Madrid,** la compañía tiene su base en Madrid. **Where are you based now?,** ¿dónde estás (vives, etc.) ahora?

baseball [ˈbeɪsbɔːl] [beis-bol], s. 1. (game) Béisbol. **Baseball bat,** bate de béisbol. 2. La pelota que se usa en este juego.

baseboard [ˈbeɪsbɔːd] [beis-bord] s. Zócalo, rodapié.

base-born [ˈbeɪsbɔːn] [beis-boun], a. 1. Bastardo, espurio, hijo natural. 2. Vil, bajo. **Base-burner, base-burning stove,** estufa de alimentación automática.

base-court [ˈbeɪskɔːt] [beis-kort], s. Patio, el espacio que en algunas casas se deja al descubierto, empedrado o enlosado, y cerrado por paredes, columnas, galerías o corredores, detrás del patio principal.

based [beɪst] [beist] *(Suf.)* Having its base in. **London-based,** con sede en Londres. Having as basis. **Acrylic-based,** con base de acrílico.

base hit [beɪsˈhɪt] [beis-jit], *s.* Sencillo. En el béisbol, golpe del bateador a la pelota que le permite llegar a primera base.

baseless [ˈbeɪslɪs] [beis-les], *a.* Desfondado: sin apoyo, sin fondo; sin fundamento. Infundado.

baseline [ˈbeɪslaɪn] [beis-lain] *s.* Línea de fondo o de saque.

basely [ˈbeɪslɪ] [beis-li], *adv.* Bajamente, con bajeza o vileza. **Basely born,** de vil cuna u origen.

baseman [ˈbeɪsmən] [beis-man], *s.* En el béisbol, cada uno de los jugadores que protegen las bases. **First, second, third baseman,** jugador de primera, segunda, tercera base.

basement [ˈbeɪsmənt] [beis-ment], *s. (Arq.)* Basamento. El cuarto bajo de una casa. En Madrid y algunas otras partes de España lo llaman *sótano vividero.*

base-minded [beɪsˈmaɪndɪd] [beis-main-ded], *a.* Ruin, vil, el que tiene bajos pensamientos.

base-mindedness [beɪsˈmaɪndidnɪs] [beis-main-ded-nes], *s.* Bajeza de ánimo, abyección.

baseness [ˈbeɪsnɪs] [beis-nes], *s.* 1. Bajeza, vileza, infamia, bastardía. 2. Ilegitimidad de nacimiento. 3. Avaricia, mezquinería, tacañería.

basepay [ˈbeɪspeɪ] [beis-pei] *s.* Sueldo base o básico.

baserate [ˈbeɪsreɪt] [beis-reit] *s.* Tipo o tasa base.

bases [ˈbeɪsɪs] [bei-sis] *Pl. of* BASIS.

bases *pl. of* BASE.

base string [beɪsˈstrɪŋ] [beis-strin], *s. (Mús.)* Bajo segundo.

base o **bass-viol** [beɪs] [bAːsˈvaɪ@l] [beis] [bas-vaiol], *s.* Violón o violoncelo.

bash [bæʃ] [bash] *s.* Golpe, madrazo (blow) *(Méx.) (Fam.)*. Abolladura, madrazo (dent). Juerga (party). (Attempt) (GB) **Come on, have a bash!,** ¡vamos, inténtalo o haz la prueba. **I'll give it a bash,** lo intentaré, haré la prueba.

bash *va.* Pegarle a (hit). *(Fam.)* **I bashed my knee on, against the door,** me golpeé o me reventé la rodilla contra la puerta. **Bash around,** *(GB)* **bash about,** tratar a golpes o a patadas. **Bash in,** echar abajo (door). Abollar (dent, box, car). *(Fam.)* **To bash somebody's head in,** romperle la cabeza o la crisma a alguien.

bashful [ˈbæʃfʊl] [bash-ful], *a.* Vergonzoso, modesto, tímido, penoso, corto, encogido; esquivo.

bashfully [ˈbæʃfʊlɪ] [bash-fu-li], *adv.* Vergonzosamente, modestamente. Con timidez.

bashfulness [ˈbæʃfʊlnɪs] [bash-ful-nes], *s.* Vergüenza, modestia, timidez, cortedad; esquivez.

basic [ˈbeɪsɪk] [bei-sik], *a.* Básico, relativo a una base química, u otra. Fundamental (fundamental). **To be basic to something,** ser fundamental para algo. Básico, fundamental (knowledge). Básico, esencial (hotel, food) Sencillo. (Econ.) Básico (pay).

basic, *s.* Lo básico, lo esencial. **We must get back to basics,** tenemos que replantearnos todo esto desde cero. **Basic English,** *s.* Inglés básico.

basically [ˈbeɪsɪklɪ] [bei-si-kli] *adv.* Fundamentalmente. **I was lucky, basically,** más que nada o fundamentalmente, tuve suerte. **What went wrong? Basically, we made a mistake,** ¿qué pasó? -en dos palabras: nos equivocamos.

basify [ˈbeɪsɪfaɪ] [bei-si-fai], *va.* Convertir en base por medios químicos.

basil [ˈbæzl] [basel], *s.* 1. *(Bot.)* Albahaca. 2. *(Carp.)* Filo achaflanado de escoplo o cepillo. 3. Badana, la piel curtida del carnero u oveja.

basilic [ˈbæzɪlɪk] [ba-si-lik], *s. (Anat.)* Basílica, la vena media o central del brazo.

basilic, basilical [ˈbæzɪlɪkl] [ba-si-li-kal], *a.* 1. *(Anat.)* Lo que pertenece a la vena basílica. 2. Real, regio.

basilica [bəˈzɪlɪkə] [ba-si-li-ka], *s.* Basílica, iglesia o templo magnífico; iglesia principal.

basilicon [ˈbæzɪlɪkən] [ba-si-li-kon], *s.* Basilicón, ungüento amarillo de resina.

basilisk [ˈbæzɪlɪsk] [ba-si-lisk], *s.* 1. Basilisco, animal fabuloso. 2. Basilisco, pieza antigua de artillería.

basin [beɪsn] [beisn], *s.* 1. Jofaina o aljofaina, bacía, palangana, lebrillo, vasija en que se echa agua para varios usos. Cuenco, bol, tazón (for liquid, food). 2. Reserva de un dique, reserva o concha de un puerto; arca de agua o depósito, estanque. 3. Cavidad de la pelvis. 4. Tazón de una fuente. 5. Platillo de balanza. 6. Vasija redonda que usan como molde los ópticos y sombrereros. 7. *(Geogr., Geol.)* Cuenca de un río. 8. Hoya, valle extenso, cuyo fondo comúnmente contiene agua. Formación geológica cuyas capas se inclinan interiormente hacia el centro. 9. Pilón de fuente o surtidor. 10. Represa de un molino. 11. Taza más grande que las usuales; tazón. (GB) **Hand basin,** lavamanos, lavabo, pileta.

basined [ˈbeɪznd] [beisnd], *a.* Situado o encerrado en una hoya u hondonada.

basinet [ˈbeɪznɪt] [beisi-net], *s.* Bacinete, capacete, pieza de la armadura antigua que cubría la cabeza.

basis [ˈbeɪsɪs] [bei-sis] 1. Basa, el fundamento de cualquier cosa. 2. Basa de columna, pedestal. 3. Base, fundamento (foundation, grounds). **On what basis do you make this assertions?,** ¿en qué se basa usted para afirmar eso? **On the basis that...,** partiendo de la base de que... 4. (System, level) **We meet on a regular/monthly basis,** nos reunimos regularmente/mensualmente. **On a regional/national basis,** a nivel regional, nacional.

bask [bɑːsk] [bask], *va.* Asolear, calentar alguna cosa al sol. *-vn.* Ponerse a tomar el sol. **To bask in the sun,** disfrutar (del color) del sol. **She basked in their adulation,** se deleitaba o se regodeaba con su adulación.

basket [ˈbɑːskɪt] [bas-kit], *s.* (for shopping) Cesta, canasta; cesto, cestón; espuerta, cuévano, capacha, capacho. (in basketball) (goal) canasta, cesto. (score) canasta, enceste. **Wicker basket,** cuévano, cesta o canasta de mimbres. **A basket coach,** carrito de junco. **Basket-work,** (1) trabajos o tejido hechos con mimbres, o una imitación de cestería en metal. (2) *(Mil.)* Cestón, cestonada, tejido de mimbres o ramas lleno de tierra que sirve como defensa. **Basket-hilt,** la guarnición de la espada o florete que cubre toda la mano. *(Prov.)* La taza de la espada. **Basket-maker,** cestero. **Basket-making,** cestería. **Basket-salt,** sal gema filtrada en cestas. - *sf.* **Basket-woman,** cestera, la mujer del cestero o la que vende cestas.

basketball [ˈbɑːskɪtbɔːl] [bas-kit-bol], *s.* (game) **Basketball,** baloncesto, básquetbol. (ball) Pelota de básquetbol o balón de baloncesto.

basketful [ˈbɑːskɪtfʊl] [bas-kit-ful], *s.* Cestada.

bason [beɪsn] [bei-son], *s. V.* BASIN.

Basque [bæsk] [bask], *a.* 1. Vascongado, da. **The Basque Country,** el País Vasco, Euskadi. 2. La lengua del país vascongado, vascuence, euskera. 3. *s.* Vasco. (person) (language) euskera, vasco, vascuence.

bas-relief [ˈbæsrɪˌliːf] · [bas-ri-lif], **basso-relievo** [bæsəˈriliːvəʊ] [ba-so-ri-lí-vo], *s.* Bajo relieve, especie de escultura: llámase también algunas veces *low relief.*

bass [bæs] [bas], o **striped bass** [strɪptˈbˈ{s] [stript-bas], *a.* Lubina, pez delicioso.

bass, *s. (Mús.)* (voice, singer) Bajo, grave. **Bass o bass-viol,** violoncelo. **Double-bass,** contrabajo; bordón. **Bass player,** (contra) bajo, (contra) bajista. (Audio) graves. *a.* (voice) De bajo. **Bass clef,** clave de fa. **Bass drum,** bombo. **Bass guitar,** contrabajo.

bass, bassock [ˈbæsɒk] [ba-sok], *s.* 1. Esparto. 2. Estera de iglesia.

bass, *s.* 1. *V.* BASSWOOD. 2. *V.* BAST.

basset [ˈbæsɪt] [ba-set], *s.* Baceta, en el juego de naipes. **Basset-horn,** clarinete de tenor.

basset, *vn. (Min.)* Apoyarse; se dice de los ramos de metales o lechos de piedras que estriban sobre otros.

bassinet [ˈbeɪsɪnɪt] [ba-si-net], *s.* 1. Moisés. cuna de mecer niños (cradle). 2. *(Mil.)* Bacinete, almete.

basso [bæˈsə] [ba-so], *s.* 1. Bajo, el que canta con voz de bajo. 2. La parte baja, bajo.

bassoon [bə'suːn] [ba-sun], *s. (Mús.)* Bajón. Instrumento de viento, fagot.

basswood ['bæswʊd] [bas-wud], *s.* Tilo americano, llamado también *whitewood-tree* (árbol de madera blanca).

bast [bæst] [bast], *s.* 1. Corteza interior textil del tilo y otros árboles. 2. Estera, cuerda, etc., hecha con esta corteza.

bastard ['bɑːstəd] [bas-tard], *s.* 1. Bastardo, espurio, la persona procreada fuera de legítimo matrimonio (illegitimate child). *(Coll. o vulg.)* Cabrón. *(Fam. o vulg.)* Hijo de puta. 2. *(Mar.)* Vela grande de galera para navegar con poco viento.

bastard, *a.* 1. Bastardo, ilegítimo (child, son). 2. Bastardo, degenerado, lo que degenera de su origen y naturaleza.

bastardize ['bɑːstədaɪz] [bas-tar-dais], *va.* 1. Probar que alguno es bastardo. 2. Procrear hijos bastardos. 3. Depravar, alterar, bastardear, envilecer, prostituir.

bastardly ['bɑːstədlɪ] [bas-tard-li], *adv.* Como bastardo.

baste [beɪst] [beist], *va.* 1. Apalear, cascar, dar golpes con palo o bastón en las plantas de los pies. 3. *(Culin.)* Pringar o untar la carne en el asador. Rociar con su jugo o con mantequilla durante la cocción 3. Hilvanar, asegurar con hilo lo que se ha de coser después. 4. Bastear.

bastile ['bɑːstɪl] [bas-til], *s.* Castillo, fortaleza, prisión.

bastinade, bastinado ['bæstɪneɪd] [bas-ti-neid], *s.* Paliza, zurra de palos en las plantas de los pies; bastonazo, bastonada.

bastinade, bastinado, *va. V.* BASTE.

basting ['beɪstɪŋ] [beis-tin], *s.* 1. Hilván. 2. *(Fam.)* Apaleamiento, paliza.

bastion ['bæstɪən] [bas-tion], *s. (Fort.)* Bastión o baluarte.

bat [bæt] [bat], *s.* 1. Garrote o maza. 2. *(Zool.)* Murciélago. **Like a bat out of hell,** como alma que lleva el diablo. **To be (as) blind as a bat,** ser más ciego que un topo. (Hag, colloq.) **Old bat,** vieja. 3. (Beisbol, cricket) Bate. (Table tennis) Paleta, raqueta. **To be at bat,** ser bateador (in baseball). **Off one's own bat,** de motu proprio, por su cuenta, por iniciativa propia. **To go bat for somebody,** echarle una mano a alguien.

bat. *va.* Golpear o impeler con una maza o porra. (Hit) Golpear, darle. (average in baseball) Tener un promedio de. *-vn.* Usar de una maza en cierto juego de pelota. *(Sport)* Batear.

bat, *va.* (E.U. y prov. en Inglaterra) Pestañear; moverse, agitarse. **To bat one's eyelashes** o (GB) **eyelids at somebody,** hacerle ojitos o caídas de ojos a alguien. **No to bat an eyelash** o (GB) **an eyelid, an eye,** no pestañear, no inmutarse.

batable ['bætəbl] [ba-ta-bol], *a.* Disputable, lo que se puede controvertir, disputar o defender por ambas p rtes. **Batavian** ['bætəvɪən] [ba-ta-vian], *a.* Báta o, va.

bat-fowling [bæt'faʊlɪŋ] [bat-fou-lin], *s.* Caza de pájaros por la noche.

batch [bætʃ] [bach], *s.* 1. (of cakes) Cochura, hornada, tanda, la cantidad de pan que de una vez se cuece en el horno. 2. Número o cantidad de cosas que se reciben, se despachan o se coleccionan de una vez. Lote (of goods). Grupo, tanda (trainees, candidates). Pila, montón. (mail, paperwork). Lote *(Comput.)* **Batch processing,** procesamiento por lotes.

bate [beɪt] [beit], *s.* Contienda, altercación, debate, disputa. **Make-bate,** cizañero, soplón, cuentero; bufón.

bate, *va.* 1. Minorar, disminuir. 2. Rebajar o bajar el precio de alguna cosa. *-vn.* Minorarse, mermar.

bate, *va.* Remojar, como un cuero o piel; separar y ablandar, como henequén, jute.

bated ['beɪtɪd] [bei-tid] *a.* **With bated breath,** con ansiedad, conteniendo la respiración.

bateful ['beɪtfʊl] [beit-ful], *a.* Contencioso, controvertible.

batement ['beɪtmənt] [beit-ment], *s.* Disminución, merma o menoscabo.

bath [bɑːθ] [baz], *s.* 1. (wash) Baño. **To have, to take a bath,** bañarse, darse un baño. **To give somebody a bath,** bañar a alguien. (Tub) Bañera, tina. **I was in the bath when**

you rang, me estaba bañando cuando llamaste. (bathwater) **To run a bath,** preparar un baño. 2. Cuarto de baño. **Hot baths,** baños calientes o termas. **Cold baths,** baños fríos. **Dry bath,** estufa. **Water bath,** *(Quím.)* baño de María, calentamiento del líquido contenido en una vasija poniendo ésta dentro de otra que contiene agua caliente. **Sand bath,** baño de arena, vasija con arena caliente en que se ponen retortas para la destilación de algún líquido. **Knight of the Bath,** o en abreviatura después de los nombres, K. B., caballero de la orden del Baño, orden de caballería de Inglaterra. **Baths** (swimming) (GB) Piscina, alberca, pileta. **Public baths,** baños públicos (for washing).

bath *va.* Bañar (GB). *vn.* Bañarse.

bath-brick [bɑːθ'brɪk] [baz-brik], *s.* Piedra para limpiar cuchillos. Toma su nombre de la ciudad de Bath en Inglaterra.

bathe [beɪð] [beiz], *va.* Bañar, lavar en baño (wound, eyes). Lavar, bañar (baby, dog). **To be bathed in something,** estar bañado en algo (tears, light). *-vn.* Bañarse, estar en el baño. (take bath, go swimming).

bather ['beɪðəʳ] [beiza'] *s.* (GB) Bañista.

bathing [bɑː'θɪŋ] [ba-zing], *s.* Baño, la acción de bañar o bañarse. *-a.* De baño. **Bathing beach,** balneario, playa para bañarse. **Bathing resort,** balneario. **Bathing suit,** (GB) **Bathing costume,** traje de baño, bañador, malla de baño, vestido de baño.

bathmat ['bɑːθmæt] [baz-mat] *s.* Alfombrilla, tapete o piso de baño.

bathrobe ['bɑːθrəʊb] [baz-roub], *s.* Bata de baño, albornoz.

bathroom ['bɑːθrʊm] [baz-rum], *s.* Cuarto de baño (room with bath). Baño, servicio (Toilet). **To go to the bathroom,** ir al baño o al servicio. **Bathroom tub, bañera,** tina, bañadera.

bath-tub ['bɑːθtʌb] [baz-tab], (más usado) o **bathing-tub** ['bɑːθɪŋtʌb] [ba-zin-tab], *s.* Baño, bañera, pieza grande de madera, metal o mármol para bañarse. *(Mex.)* Tina.

bathymetry ['bɑːθɪmɪtrɪ] [ba-ti-me-tri], *s.* Batimetría.

bathyscaphe ['bɑːθɪskeɪf] [ba-zis-keif], *s.* Batíscafo.

batik [bə'tɪk] [ba-tik], *s.* Batik, arte malayo para teñir telas con cera.

bating ['bətɪŋ] [ba-tin], *prep.* Excepto, exceptuando, menos, fuera de, amen de.

batiste [bæ'tiːst] [ba-tist], *s.* Batista, lino fino; olán.

batlet ['bætlɪt] [ba-tlet], *s.* Paleta de lavandera.

baton ['bætən] [ba-ton], *s.* 1. Bastón (truncheon), testigo (in relay race), bastón de mando (officer's) (GB), bastón (drum's major). 2. *(Mús.)* Batuta.

baton, *va.* Bastonear, golpear con un bastón.

batoon [bə'tuːn] [ba-tún], *s.* 1. Clava o palo grande. 2. Bastón o insignia de mando. 3. *(Her.)* Señal de nacimiento ilegítimo en el escudo de armas. *(Des.)*

batrachia [bə'treɪkɪə] [ba-trei-kia], *s. pl.* Los batracios o anfibios, una de las clases de los vertebrados.

batrachian [bə'treɪkɪən] [ba-trei-kian], *a.* Batracio, relativo o perteneciente a las ranas. *-s.* Uno de los batracios.

batsman ['bætsmən] [bats-man] *s.* Bateador.

battalia [bə'tælɪə] [ba-ta-lia], *s. (Ant.)* Orden de batalla, parte principal de un ejército.

battalion [bə'tælɪən] [ba-ta-lion], *s.* Batallón, un cuerpo de infantería.

batten ['bætn] [ba-ten], *s.* Lata, tabla de chilla, listón de madera; alfajía, tablilla.

batten, *va.* Construir con lata, tablillas, o tablas de chilla. **To batten down the hatches,** *(Mar.)* cerrar las escotillas y asegurarlas con listones de madera.

batten, *va.* 1. Cebar, dar cebo para engordar. 2. Reparar, rehacer, restablecer las fuerzas o el vigor perdido. *-vn.* Engordar, ponerse gordo; revolcarse.

batter ['bætəʳ] [ba-ta'], *va.* 1. Apalear, dar de palos, cascar, golpear, aporrear (beat) (victim, opponent); maltratar, pegarle a (child, wife). 2. Batir, cañonear; romper, desmenuzar; destruir, demoler, derribar. **Boats battered by the storm,** barcos azotados por la tormenta. *-vn. (Mec.)*

Hacer barriga o comba. **Batter around,** (GB) **Batter about,** maltratar, pegarle a. **Batter down,** derribar a golpes.

batter, *s.* Batido, mezcla de varios ingredientes batidos y trabados; pasta culinaria. *(Culin.)* Rebozado, pasta para rebozar (for fried fish). **Cover with batter,** rebozar. Masa (for cakes, pancakes)

batter, *s.* El que da con la maza, o *bat,* en el juego de pelota llamado *base-ball* y otros. Bateador.

batter, *s.* 1. Golpazo; golpes repetidos. 2. Batidor de yeso. 3. *(Tip.)* Rotura o mutilación de los tipos o de una plancha. 4. Declive de un parapeto.

battered [ˈbætəd] [ba-terd] *a.* Abollado (car), estropeado (hat, suitcase), maltrecho (reputation, image), maltratado, que recibe o ha recibido malos tratos (baby, wife). **Her battered pride,** su orgullo herido.

batterer [ˈbætərəʳ] [ba-te-red] *s.* Apaleador.

battering [ˈbætərɪŋ] [ba-te-rin] *s.* Paliza.

battering-piece [ˈbætərɪŋˌpiːs] [ba-te-rin-pis], *s. (Art.)* Pieza de batir. **Battering-ram,** ariete, máquina usada antiguamente para demoler las murallas.

battering-train [ˈbætərɪŋˌtreɪn] [ba-te-rin-trein], *s.* Tren de batir, cureña de sitio.

battery [ˈbætərɪ] [ba-te-ri], *s.* 1. *(Elec.)* Batería, acumulador (car, motorcycle), pila (radio, lamp). **To recharge one's batteries,** cargar las baterías, recuperar la energía. **Battery acid,** electrolito. **Battery charger,** cargador de pilas, cargador de baterías. 2. *(Mil.)* Batería. 3. Violencia, asalto. **Batery cell,** pila eléctrica. *(Agr.)* Batería, conjunto de jaulas instaladas para la explotación avícola intensiva. De criadero, de batería (eggs, hens). **Battery farming,** cría intensiva. **A battery of tests,** una serie de tests (array, set). **A battery of questions,** una sarta de preguntas. *(Law)* Lesiones.

batting [ˈbætɪŋ] [ba-tin], *s.* 1. Agramaje, espadillaje; *(Cer.)* moldeaje. 2. Algodón o lana en hojas o capas. 3. El acto de apalear, y la manera de usar un garrote o cachiporra. Bateo. **Cotton batting,** algodón en rama.

battle [ˈbætl] [ba-tel], *s.* 1. *(Mil.)* Batalla. 2. *(Des.)* El centro o la parte principal del ejército. **To do battle,** luchar. **Battle cry,** grito de guerra. Lucha (struggle). **A battle of wits,** una lucha de ingenio. **That's half the battle (won),** eso ya es un gran paso adelante. **To fight a losing battle,** luchar por una causa perdida.

battle, *vn.* Batallar, pelear en batalla, combatir. **Battle on,** seguir luchando. **To battle it out,** seguir luchando hasta el final.

battle-array [ˈbætlərei] [ba-tel-a-rei], *s.* Orden de batalla.

battle-axe [ˈbætlæks] [ba-tel-aks], *s.* Hacha de guerra (weapon). Sargenta (woman) *(Coloq.),* sisebuta *(Fam.).*

battledoor [ˈbætldɔːʳ] [ba-teldoʳ], *s.* Pala o raqueta, el instrumento que impele la pelota o volante. **Battledoor and shuttlecock,** la raqueta y el volante.

battlefield [ˈbætlfiːld] [ba-tel-fild], *s.* Campo de batalla.

battlefront [ˈbætlfrɒnt] [ba-tel-front] *s.* Frente de batalla.

battleground [ˈbætlɡraʊnd] [ba-tel-graund] *s.* Campo de batalla.

battlement [ˈbætlmənt] [ba-tel-ment], *s.* Muralla almenada o con almenas y boquillas.

battle-piece [ˈbætlpiːs] [ba-tel-pis], *s.* Cuadro que representa una batalla.

battleship [ˈbætlʃɪp] [ba-tel-ship], *s.* Acorazado.

battling [ˈbætlɪŋ] [ba-tlin], *s.* Conflicto, combate.

battologize [ˈbætəlɒdʒaɪz] [ba-to-lo-yais], *vn.* Repetir palabras inútil y enojosamente.

battology [ˈbætəlɒdʒɪ] [ba-to-lo-yi], *s.* Batología, repetición inútil de palabras.

battue [ˈbætjuː] [ba-tiu], *s.* 1. Batida, montería de caza mayor. 2. Matanza inexcusable.

batty [ˈbætɪ] [ba-ti] *a.* Chiflado *(Coloq.),* rayado *(Fam.).* **To go batty,** chiflarse, rayarse.

bauble, bawble [ˈbɔːbl] [bo-bel], *s.* Chuchería, miriñaque, cosa de poca importancia, pero pulida y delicada (for decoration). Adorno (on Christmas tree).

baud [bɔːd] [bod] *s. (Comput.)* Baudio. **Baud rate,** velocidad media de transferencia.

baulk [bɔːlk] [bolk], *va./vn.* V. BALK.

bauxite [ˈbɔːksaɪt] [bok-sait], *s.* Bauxita, compuesto de aluminio y óxido férrico.

bavarian [bəˈbeərɪən] [ba-va-rian], *a.* y *s.* Bávaro, perteneciente a Baviera; natural de este reino.

bavaroy [ˈbavərɔɪ] [ba-va-roi], *s.* Tudesco, especie de capote.

bavin [ˈbævɪn] [ba-vin], *s.* Fagina, hacecillo de leña menuda.

bawd [bɔːd] [bod], *s.* Alcahuete o alcahueta.

bawd, *vn.* Alcahuetear, servir de alcahuete o alcahueta. *-va.* Ensuciar.

bawdily [ˈbɔːdɪlɪ] [bo-di-li], *adv.* obscenamente.

bawdiness [ˈbɔːdɪnɪs] [bo-di-nes], *s.* obscenidad; alcahuetería; suciedad.

bawdrick [ˈbɔːdrɪk] [bo-drik], *s.* Cinturón; cuerda; tahalí. V. BALDRIC.

bawdry [ˈbɔːdrɪ] [bo-dri], *s.* Alcahuetería, el acto de alcahuetear.

bawdy [ˈbɔːdɪ] [bo-di], *a.* Obsceno, impuro, torpe; sucio, impúdico, deshonesto, infame. Subido de tono.

bawdy-house [ˈbɔːdɪhaʊs] [bo-di-jaus], *s.* Lupanar, burdel.

bawl [bɔːl] [bol], *vn.* Gritar, vocear, vociferar, desgañitarse (shout). **To bawl at somebody,** gritarle a uno. Ladrar, chillar, berrear (cry noisily). *-va.* Pregonar; publicar a voces. Gritar (insults). Dar a gritos (order). **Bawl out,** (insults) gritar, regañar, retar (scold).

bawler [ˈbɔːləʳ] [bolaʳ], *s.* Voceador, vocinglero, alborotador.

bawsin, bauson [ˈbɔːsɪn] [bo-sin], *s.* Tejón, animal cuadrúpedo.

bay [beɪ] [bei], *a.* Bayo, de color rojizo parecido al castaño (horses).

bay, *s.* 1. Bahía, rada, puerto abierto, donde se abrigan las embarcaciones. Muelle o plataforma de carga (loading). 2. Bahía, brazo de mar. 3. *(Bot.)* Laurel, planta. 4. La situación del que se halla rodeado de enemigos. **To be at bay,** estar rodeado de enemigos; hallarse en el último aprieto; estar en el mayor peligro. **To keep at bay,** tener a raya; contener; tener a distancia. 5. División de un edificio. Parte saliente de una ventana o un balcón en forma de mirador *(Bay window).* 6. Laurel, lauro, el premio de la victoria. 7. Compuerta. 7. Espacio (area, recess). **Parking bay,** plaza de estacionamiento o de aparcamiento.

bay, *vn.* 1. Aullar, dar ladridos ahogado. 2. Balar. *-va.* 1. Encerrar.

bayard [beɪəd] [beiard], *s.* 1. Caballo bayo. 2. Bausán, boquiabierto.

bayardly [ˈbeɪədlɪ] [beiard-li], *a.* Estúpido, ciego.

bayberry [ˈbeɪbərɪ] [bei-beri], *s. (Bot.)* 1. árbol de la cera, arbusto de las miriáceas. 2. Laurel.

bayberry tallow [ˈbeɪbərɪˌtæləʊ] [bei-beri-ta-lou], *s.* Sustancia que se obtiene del árbol de la cera.

baying [ˈbeɪɪŋ] [bei-ing], *s.* Ladrido; balido.

bayleaf [ˈbeɪliːf] [bei-lif] *s.* Hoja de laurel.

bayonet [ˈbeɪənɪt] [ba-yo-net], *s.* Bayoneta.

bayou [ˈbaɪjuː] [ba-yu], *s.* Canalizo: brazo de río de escasa corriente. Pantano. (E.U. del Sur.)

bay run [ˈbeɪrʌn] [bei-ran], *s.* Ron con aceite escencial de laurel o de malgueta.

bay-salt [ˈbeɪsɔːlt] [bei-solt], *s.* Sal morena o sal marina.

bay-window [ˈbeɪˈwɪndəʊ] [bei-uin-dou], *s.* ventana salidiza, mirador.

bazaar, bazar [bəˈzaːʳ] [ba-saʳ], *s.* 1. Bazar (oriental market). Venta benéfica (charity sale). 2. Baño, lugar donde se encerraba a los esclavos.

bazooka [bəˈzuːkə] [ba-sú-ka], *s.* Lanzador portátil de proyectiles-cohete.

BBC *s.* British Broadcasting Corporation. **The BBC,** la BBC. **bC** (Before Christ) Antes de Cristo. (written form) aC, a. de C., a. de J. C.

bedellium [ˈbdəlɪəm] [be-de-liom], *s.* 1. Bedelio, el árbol y la resina que éste produce. 2. Joya, tal vez perla, pero con más probabilidad el ámbar.

be [biː] [bi], *vn.* 1. Ser o estar, tener algún estado, condición o calidad. (followed by an adjective) **She's French/ intelligent,** es francesa, inteligente. **He's worried/furious,** está preocupado/furioso. **He's blind,** es o está ciego. **He's short and fat,** es bajo y gordo. **He's so fat he can't get into his clothes any more,** está tan gordo que ya no le cabe la ropa. **These shoes are new,** estos zapatos son nuevos. **Have you never had gazpacho? it's delicious!,** ¿nunca has comido gazpacho? ¡es delicioso! **The cake is delicious, did you make it yourself?,** el pastel está delicioso, ¿lo hiciste tú? **She was very rude to me,** estuvo o fue muy grosera conmigo. **She's very rude,** es muy grosera. **Be good,** sé bueno. **Don't be silly!,** ¡no seas tonto! (Talking about marital status) **Tony is married/divorced/single,** Tony está o es casado/divorciado/soltero. **We've been married for eight years,** llevamos ocho años casados. (Followed by a noun) **She's a lawyer,** es abogada. **He's a Catholic,** es católico. **He was Prime Minister for eleven years,** fue Primer Ministr durante once años. **Who was Prime Minister at the time?,** ¿quién era Primer Ministro en ese momento? **It's me/Daniel,** soy yo/ es Daniel. **If I were you I'd stay,** yo que tú o yo en tu lugar me quedaría. (Play the role of) hacer de. **I was Juliet in the school play,** hice de Julieta en la obra del colegio. (Talking about mental and physical states) **How are you?,** ¿cómo estás? **I'm much better,** estoy o me encuentro mucho mejor. **She's pregnant/tired,** está embarazada/cansada. 2. Tener, en algunas significaciones, v.g. **To be hungry,** tener hambre. **To be cold/thirsty/sleepy,** tener frío, sed, sueño. (Talking about age) Tener. **How old are you?,** ¿cuántos años tienes? **I'm 31,** tengo 31 años. **Paul was four last Monday,** Paul cumplió cuatro años el lunes pasado. (Giving cost, measurement, weight) **How much is that?-That will be $15 please,** ¿cuánto es?- Son 15 dólares por favor. **Two plus two is four,** dos más dos son cuatro. **How tall/heavy is he?,** ¿cuánto mide/pesa? (Exist, live) **I think, therefore I am,** pienso, luego existo. **To be or not to be,** ser o no ser. **Her husband-to-be,** su futuro marido. (in expressions of time). **Don't be too long,** no tardes mucho, no te demores mucho. **How long will dinner be?,** ¿cuánto falta para la cena? (Take place) **The party is tomorrow,** la fiesta es mañana. (Be situated, present) Estar. **Where is the library?,** ¿dónde está o queda la biblioteca? **Where are you?,** ¿dónde estás? **Who's in the movie?,** ¿quién actúa o trabaja en la película? **How long are you in Chicago (for)?** ¿cuánto (tiempo) te vas a quedar en Chicago? (only in perfect tenses) (visit) Estar. **I've never been to India,** nunca he estado en la India. **Have you been to the exhibition yet?,** ¿ya has estado en o has ido a la exposición? *V. impers.* (talking about physical conditions, circumstances). **It's sunny/cold/hot,** hace sol/frío/ calor. **It's cloudy,** está nublado. **It was two degrees below zero,** hacía dos grados bajo cero. **It's so noisy/quiet in here!,** ¡qué ruido/silencio hay aquí! (in expressions of time) Ser. **It's three o'clock,** son las tres. **It's one o'clock,** es la una. **It was still very early,** todavía era muy temprano. **It's Monday today,** hoy es lunes. (Talking about distance) Estar. **It's 50 miles from here to New York,** Nueva York queda o está a 50 millas de aquí. (introducing person, object) **It was me who told them,** fui yo quien se lo dije o dijo, fui yo el que se lo dije o dijo. (in conditional use) Ser. **If it hadn't been o had it not been for Peter, we would have been killed,** si no hubiera sido por Pedro o de no ser por Pedro, nos habríamos matado. *To be* es el verbo auxiliar que sirve para formar la voz pasiva, y las acciones en progreso. **What was I saying?** ¿qué estaba diciendo? **She was leaving when...** se iba cuando... **How long have you been waiting?** ¿cuánto (tiempo) hace que esperas? ¿cuánto (tiempo) llevas esperando? *(with future reference)* **He is o will be arriving tomorrow,** llega mañana. **She will be staying at the Hilton,** se va a alojar en el Hilton. **It was built in 1903,** fue construido en 1913, se construyó en 1913, lo construyeron en 1903. **She was told that...,** le dijeron o se le dijo que... **It's known that...,** se sabe que...

(with future reference) **I'm to be met at the airport by Mary,** María me irá a buscar al aeropuerto. **The dessert is (still) to come,** todavía falta el postre. (expressing possibility) **What are we to do?,** ¿qué podemos hacer? **He wasn't to know,** no tenía cómo saberlo. (expressing obligation) Deber. **Tell her she's to stay here,** dile que debe quedarse aquí o tiene que quedarse aquí, dile que se quede aquí. **You are not to tell Susan!,** ¡no debes decírselo a Susana! **I'm not to be disturbed!,** ¡que nadie me moleste! (in hypotheses) **What would happen if she o was to die?,** ¿qué pasaría si ella muriera? (in tag questions) **She's right, isn't she?,** tiene razón, ¿no? o ¿verdad? o ¿no es cierto? **So that's what you think, is it?,** de manera que es eso lo que piensas. (in elliptical uses) **Are you disappointed? Yes, I am/No, I'm not,** ¿estás desilusionado? Sí, (lo estoy)/No, (no lo estoy). **She was told the news, and so was he/but I wasn't,** a ella le dieron la noticia, y también a él/pero a mí no. **I'm surprised, are you?/aren't you?,** estoy sorprendido, ¿y tú?/¿tú no? **To be for,** inclinarse a. **To be out,** cortarse o perderse en alguna recitación, confundirse. **To be a great way off,** estar muy distante. **To be off,** *(Fam.)* irse a la francesa; echarse fuera; tomar las de Villadiego. **He is on and off,** tan pronto quiere como no quiere. **To be up to everything,** ser para todo, no asustarse por nada. **To be gone,** irse, haberse ido. **To be being,** estarse haciendo. **Secret meetings were being held,** se estaban celebrando juntas secretas. **To let, a house that is being finished in Fifth Street,** se alquila una casa que se está acabando, o está para acabarse, en la Calle Quinta.

be, prefijo. Por; cerca de; sobre. Sirve para hacer verbos activos de los neutros; para hacer más intenso el sentido del verbo: para formar verbos de adjetivos o sustantivos, etc.

beach [biːtʃ] [bich],s. Costa, ribera, playa, orilla; cabo. **A day at the beach,** un día en la playa. **Beach ball,** pelota de playa.

beach, *va.* Impeler a la playa, o arrastrar sobre ella. (boat). Hacer embarrancar (whale). *-vn.* Desembarcar en una playa o costa.

beachhead ['biːtʃhed] [bich-jed], s. Cabeza de playa.

beachy ['biːtʃɪ] [bi-chi], a. Que tiene riberas o playas.

beacon ['biːkən] [bi-kon], s. *(Mar.)* Faro (light), final, baliza, almenara (fire), señal que se pone o que se hace para dirigir a los navegantes u otros.

beaconage ['biːkɔeɪdʒ] [bi-ko-neich], s. Balizaje, derecho que se paga para mantener los fanales, balizas o almenaras.

beaconed ['biːkɔnd] [bi-kond], a. Lo que tiene balizas o almenaras.

bead [biːd] [bid], s. 1. Cuenta, cada una de las bolitas ensartadas, que componen el rosario. 2. Cuenta o cuentas, bolitas ensartadas formando collares (necklace, bracelet). 3. Cualquier cuerpo globoso. 4. Ornamento formado de una hilera de cuentas. **Glass bead,** mostacilla, chaquira, abalorio. **Steel beads,** abalorios de acero. 5. *(Carp.)* Filete, nervio, astrágalo. 6. *(Arq.)* Perla. 7. *(Joy.)* Grano, perla, cuenta. 8. Burbuja, espuma sobre un líquido. Gota (drop). **Beads of sweat,** gotas de sudor. **To draw a bead on,** apuntar cuidadosamente con un arma de fuego. **To tell o say, one's beads,** rezar el rosario.

bead, va. 1. Adornar con abalorios. 2. Ensartar cuentas. 3. En tornería, hacer rizos o filetes en la madera.

beading ['biːdɪŋ] [bi-din], s. 1. Guarnición o adorno de abalorios. *(Arq.)* Listón, pestaña, borde. 2. Preparación para formar espuma sobre licores. 3. Conjunto de cuentas o abalorios.

bead-tree [biːd'triː] [bid-tri], s. *(Bot.)* Coco de Indias, el árbol con cuyas semillas se hacen los rosarios.

beadle ['biːdl] [bidel], s. Pertiguero o macero en las catedrales; muñidor en las parroquias o cofradías; bedel en las universidades; y alguacil, ministro o ministril en los tribunales.

beadleship ['biːdlʃɪp] [bidel-ship], s. Bedelía.

beadroll ['biːdrɒl] [bid-rol], s. Catálogo o lista de los cofrades del rosario.

beadsman ['bi:dsmən] [bids-man], *s.* Hombre empleado en rezar por otros.

beadwork [bi:dʷwɜːk] [bid-uek], *s.* 1. Abalorio. 2. *(Arq.)* Listón, reborde.

beady ['bi:dɪ] [bi-di], *a.* 1. Parecido a cuentas. 2. Cubierto de cuentas. 3. Lo que tiene espuma o está cubierto de burbujas. **Beady eyes,** ojos redondos y brillantes.

beagle ['bi:gl] [bigel], *s.* 1. Sabueso, perro con el cual se cazan las liebres. 2. Alguacil. 3. Tiburón pequeño de ciertas especies.

beak [bi:k] [bik], *s.* 1. Pico, el extremo de la cabeza del ave que le sirve como de boca (of bird). 2. Pico o cañón de alambique. 3. *(Mar.)* Saltillo de proa; espolón de navío. 4. Pico, hocico, cualquier cosa que remata en punta. 5. Cabo, promontorio. *(Fam.)* (nose) Napia.

beaked [bi:kt] [bikt], *a.* Picudo, lo que tiene pico; encorvado.

beaker ['bi:kəʳ] [bikaʳ], *s.* 1. Taza con pico. 2. *(Quím.)* Bocal con pico; vaso cilíndrico con fondo llano, de vidrio delgado; se usa en los análisis. (GB) Taza (alta y sin asa) (cup).

be-all ['bi:ɔːl] [bi-ol] *s.* **It's the be-all and end-all of his life,** es su razón de ser. **Work isn't the be-all and end-all,** el trabajo no lo es todo.

beam [bi:m] [bim], *s.* 1. *(Arq.)* Viga maestra de un edificio (in building). 2. Astil, brazo del peso de cruz, de cuyos extremos penden las balanzas. 3. Madero cilíndrico, en el cual los tejedores arrollan la tela al paso que la van tejiendo; enjullo o vara de empaño. 4. Rayo de luz (ray); haz de luz (broad). **A ray of light,** un rayo de luz. **Keep the headlights on high** o (GB) **full/main beam,** deja las (luces) largas (auto). 5. Lanza de coche. 6. Rama de venado. 7. Brazos de balanza. 8. Barra sueca o de equilibrio (in gymnastics). **Beams,** *(Mar.)* baos, vigas gruesas que mantienen firmes los costados del navío y sobre las cuales se asientan las cubiertas (in ship). Manga (widest part of ship. **Beams of the upper decks,** baos de las cubiertas altas. **Aftermost beam,** bao popero. **Foremost beam,** bao proel. **Midship beam,** bao maestro. **On the beam,** por el través. **Before the beam,** por la proa del través. **Abaft the beam,** por la popa del través. *(Fam.)* **To be broad in the beam,** ser culón, tener un buen trasero.

beam, *vn.* Emitir o arrojar rayos. Brillar (shine). Sonreír abiertamente (smile). **A beaming smile,** una sonrisa radiante. *va.* Transmitir (broadcast).

beaming [bi:mɪŋ] [bi-min], *a.* Radiante, que despide rayos de luz; luciente, luminoso; alegre, vivo.

beamless ['bi:mles] [bim-les], *a.* Sin rayos.

beamy [bi:mɪ] [bi-mi], *a.* 1. Radiante, lo que despide y arroja de sí rayos de luz. 2. Alegre, vivo. 3. Parecido a una viga; pesado como una lanza. 4. *(Mar.)* Que tiene baos anchos.

bean [bi:n] [bin], *s.* 1. Haba, 2. Judía, habichuela, fréjol, alubia. (Mex., Cuba) Frijol (dried). **String beans,** *(Mex.)* ejotes; habichuelas o judías tiernas o verdes (fresh, in pod) **Green bean. To be full of beans,** estar lleno de vida. **To spill the beans,** descubrir el pastel, levantar la liebre/la perdiz. **Coffee bean,** grano de café. (GB) *(Coloq.)* **It isn't worth a bean,** no vale nada (scrap, trace). *(Fam.)* **Not to have a bean,** estar pelado. **Not to know beans about something,** no saber ni papa de algo. Coco, mate (head). **Beanbag** (chair), sillón formado por una gran bolsa de cuentas de poliestireno, etc. Pequeño saco relleno que se arroja para que otro lo ataje (toy). **Bean curd,** tofu, queso de soja. **Beanpole,** rodrigón (person). **She's a beanpole,** es un espárrago, es muy larguirucha. **Beanshoot, bean sprout,** frijol germinado o judía germinada o poroto germinado. Brote germinado de soya o soja (of soy bean).

bean *va.* **To bean somebody,** darle un mamporro en la cabeza a alguien.

bean-fed [bi:nfed] [bin-fed], *a.* Alimentado con habas.

bear [bɜəʳ] [beaʳ], *va. (pret.* BORE, *pp.* BORNE, o BORN). 1. Llevar alguna cosa como carga. 2. Llevar o mudar alguna cosa de una parte a otra (carry). **Our raft was borne along** by the current, la corriente arrastraba nuestra balsa. **She's not one to bear a grudge,** no es rencorosa o resentida (harbor). 3. Usar alguna insignia de autoridad o distinción. **To bear a crown,** ceñirse una corona. 4. Cargar, llevar alguna cosa como carga; cargar con, imponerse una carga u obligación (responsibility). **You shall bear the guilt, UD.** cargará con la responsabilidad. 5. Sostener, apoyar, mantener alguna cosa para que no caiga (support). 6. Tener amor u odio a uno. **I can't bear her,** no la soporto, no la aguanto, no la puedo ver. 7. Padecer, sufrir, aguantar, soportar, tolerar (endure) **The pain was too much to bear,** el dolor se hizo insoportable. **I can't bear to watch,** no puedo mirar. 8. Llevar, producir. 9. Parir, dar a luz. **She bore him six children,** le dio seis hijos. En este sentido, el participio de *bear* es *born.* 10. Entretener, engañar. 11. Poseer poder u honra. 12. Animar, impeler. 13. *(Com.)* Hacer bajar el valor, jugar a la baja. **Bear a hand!** *(Mar.),* socorrer pronto; coger, agarrar.

bear away, vencer, sobrepujar.

bear back, retirarse, hacerse atrás. **To bear company,** acompañar. **To bear date,** llevar fecha, estar fechado. **To bear in mind,** acordarse. -*vn.* 1. Padecer o sufrir algún dolor. 2. Aguantar, tolerar. 3. Tener virtud generativa, criar; llevar fruto. 4. Dirigirse o encaminarse a algún paraje, determinado. **To bear and forbear,** llevar y conllevar.

bear down, arrastrar; ahondar; tropezar, derribar, derrocar, echar por tierra, hacer bajar por fuerza: se dice de la mujer que está de parto.

bear off, (a) desviar el golpe o evitarle. (b) *(Mar.)* hacerse mar adentro.

bear in, ir a, dirigirse a.

bear out, mantener, sostener, apoyar; sacar de paso; justificar, afirmar; avanzar.

bear up, llevar, transportar, conducir, sostener; resistir; subir, crecer, elevarse, alzarse, sostenerse.

bear up against, resistir, oponerse fuertemente, hacer esfuerzos contra alguna cosa, arrostrar, mantenerse tieso o firme. **To bear up to a ship,** transportar a un navío.

bear upon, estribar.

To bring to bear upon, apuntar los cañones contra. **To bear a good price,** tener buen precio. **To bear a part,** paticipar, tener parte. **To bear faith,** ser fiel. **To bear likeness,** parecerse. **To bear resemblance to,** tener semejanza con, parecerse a. **To bear one a grudge, spite** o **ill-will,** querer mal a alguno, tenerle ojeriza. **To bear one good-will,** tener buena voluntad a alguno. **To bear sway** o **rule,** gobernar, dominar, mandar, tener el poder en su mano. **To bear the charges,** pagar los gastos, llevar las cargas. **To bear too hard upon one,** tratar a alguno con sobrada dureza. **To bear with one,** sufrir a alguno, perdonarle, ser indulgente para con él. **To bear witness,** atestiguar, testificar, dar testimonio, ser testigo. **To bear away,** *(Mar.)* arribar. **To bear away before the wind,** *(Mar.)* arribar todo o amollar viento en popa. **To bear away large,** *(Mar.)* arribar a escota larga. **To bear down on a ship,** *(Mar.)* arribar sobre un bajel. **Past bearing,** improductivo (hablando de árboles frutales y de animales); infecunda, la mujer que ha pasado la edad crítica.

bear, *s.* 1. Oso, animal fiero. **He's a regular bear in the morning,** por la mañana está de un humor de perros. **To be like a bear with a sore head,** estar de un humor de perros. **To be loaded for bear,** estar listo para el ataque. **Bear cub,** osezno. 2. Bajista, el jugador de bolsa que juega a la baja de los fondos públicos u otros valores. **Great and Little Bear,** *(Astr.)* Osa Mayor y Menor. 3. *(Ento.)* Oruga lanuda del *tiger-moth.* **Brown bear,** oso pardo. **White** o **polar bear,** oso blanco, oso gris de América. **The Bear,** Rusia.

bearable ['bɛərəbl] [bea-rabol], *a.* Sufrible, soportable.

bear-berry ['bɛərberɪ] [bear-beri], *s.* 1. *(Bot.)* Gayuba, hierba medicinal. Uva, ursi. 2. La cáscara sagrada de California y el arbusto que la produce. Se llama también *bearwood.*

bear-binder [ˈbɛəbɪndəʳ] [bear-bin-daʳ], *s.* *(Bot.)* Correhuela.

beard [bɪəd] [bíard], *s.* 1. Barba (of person), el pelo que nace en la parte inferior de la cara. **A man with a beard,** un hombre con barba o de barba. **To have/wear a beard,** tener barba. 2. Cara, rostro. 3. *(Bot.)* Arista de espiga. 4. Barba de flecha.

beard, *va.* 1. Desbarbar, agarrar a uno por la barba, arrancarle las barbas. 2. Hacer frente, subirse a las barbas; oponerse fuertemente.

bearded [ˈbɪədɪd] [bíarded], *a.* 1. Barbado, el que tiene barbas (man). 2. Barbado, lo que tiene barbas, o aristas como el maíz y otras espigas de grano. 3. Armado con lengüetas, como la saeta, etc.

beardless [ˈbɪədlɪs] [bíard-les], *a.* 1. Imberbe, joven; barbilampiño. 2. Derraspado: se dice del trigo.

bearer [ˈbɛərəʳ] [bearaʳ], *s.* 1. Portador, el que lleva o trae alguna cosa (carrier, porter). 2. Faquín, el que sirve para llevar cargas. 3. Sepulturero. 4. Árbol frutífero. 5. Apoyo, lo que sostiene alguna cosa, sostén, gancho, soporte. **A cross-bearer,** crucífero o crucero. **An ensign-bearer,** portaestandarte. Portador (of news), (holder of check). Titular (of passport).

bear-herd [ˈbɛəhəd] [bear-jed], *s.* Guarda de osos, el que los cuida.

bear hug [ˈbɛəhʌg] [bear-jeg], *s.* **He gave me a bear hug,** me estrechó fuertemente entre sus brazos.

bearing [ˈbɛərɪŋ] [bea-rin], *s.* 1. Situación, colocación de una cosa respecto de otra. 2. Saledizo. 3. Porte exterior (way of standing), maneras, presencia. 4. Donaire, aire; gracia. 5. Relación, conexión, fuerza, valor de una expresión. **I do not see the bearing of that remark,** no veo la fuerza de esa observación. 6. *(Mec.)* Manga de eje, cojinete, soporte. 7. *(Arq.)* Apoyo, apuntalamiento. 8. *(Top.)* ángulo formado en el punto de observación entre el meridiano magnético y el objeto; orientación. 9. *(Agr.)* Fruto. **Armorial bearing,** *(Her.)* escudo de armas. **Past bearing,** insufrible, inaguantable, insoportable, demasiado. Demora *(Aer.)* **To find/get one's bearings,** orientarse. **To lose one's bearings,** desorientarse, perderse. **That has no bearing on the subject,** eso no tiene ninguna relación con el tema (relevance).

bearish [ˈbɛərɪʃ] [bea-rish], *a.* Rudo, áspero, feroz como un oso.

bearlike [ˈbɛəlaɪk] [beaʳ-laik], *a.* Semejante o parecido al oso.

bear's ear [ˈbɛəzɪəʳ] [bears-iaʳ] *s.* *(Bot.)* Oreja de oso.

bear's-foot [ˈbɛəzfuːt] [bears-fut], *s.* *(Bot.)* Eléboro negro.

bearsking [ˈbɛəskɪŋ] [bear-skin], *s.* Piel de oso, especie de peletería.

bearwood [ˈbɛəwʊd] [bear-vud], *s.* Nombre común del arbusto, cuya corteza es la cáscara sagrada de California.

bearwort [ˈbɛəwɔːt] [bear-uort], *s.* *(Bot.)* V. BALDMONEY.

beast [ˈbiːst] [bist], *s.* 1. Bestia, animal cuadrúpedo. 2. Animal irracional, a distinción del hombre. **Beast of burden,** bestia de carga, acémila. 3. Bestia, hombre brutal (unkind person). *(Fam.)* **Don't be such a beast!,** ¡no seas malo o asqueroso! **Wild beast,** bestia feroz, fiera.

beastlike [ˈbiːstlaɪk] [bist-laik], *a.* Bestial, abrutado.

beastliness [ˈbiːstlɪnɪs] [bist-li-nes], *s.* Bestialidad, brutalidad, suciedad.

beastly [ˈbiːstlɪ] [bistli], *a.* Bestial, brutal, irracional; sucio. *(Fam.)* **That beastly brother of hers,** el asqueroso de su hermano. **What a beastly thing to say!,** ¡qué cosa más horrorosa de decir! *-adv.* Brutalmente, bestialmente.

beat [biːt] [bit], *va.* 1. Apalear, golpear (hit repeatedly), sacudir (carpet), dar de palos. **He beats his children,** pega a sus hijos, maltrata a sus hijos (inflict blows on). 2. *(Mús.)* Llevar el compás. 3. Batir el soto o el monte. 4. Batir, mezclar unas cosas con otras, agitándolas y golpeándolas con frecuencia. 5. *(Mil.)* Batir una muralla o plaza. 6. Ganar, vencer o exceder a otro en alguna cosa. 7. Batir las alas. 8.

Tocar un tambor. 9. Rebajar el precio que se pide por alguna cosa. Batir, superar (be better than), record. **Our prices can't be beaten,** nuestros precios son imbatibles. 10. Pisar la senda. 11. Deprimir, abatir. 12. Empujar con violencia. Derrotar, vencer. **He always beats me at chess,** siempre me gana al ajedrez (defeat, opponent). *-vn.* 1. Moverse con pulsación o con movimiento pulsativo, como un reloj, las arterias, etc.; latir, palpitar (pulsate). 2. Rozar una cosa con otra. 3. Batir, golpear; batir, hablando del sol, del aire, del mar, etc.: dar o herir en alguna parte sin impedimento alguno. 4. Fluctuar, estar en movimiento. 5. Tentar el vado, buscar todos los medios para la consecución de alguna cosa. 6. Dar con violencia con alguna cosa. **To beat up for o to raise soldiers,** *(Mil.)* reclutar tropas.

beat against, estrellarse, echarse contra o sobre.

beat away, ahuyentar a alguno a fuerza de golpes.

beat back, reverberar, rechazar.

beat down, abatir, derribar, demoler, destruir. Rebajar (seam). Rebajar, disminuir (price). (Art. y Of.) Apilar, amontonar.

beat in, cascar, machacar, moler: echar dentro. Hundir, echar hacia abajo o hacia dentro; desfondar, quitar el fondo.

beat into, inculcar, hacer entrar.

beat off, echar, arrojar, despedir, rechazar.

beat out, arrancar, lanzar. **To beat to powder,** reducir a polvo. **To beat black and blue,** acardenalar. **To beat one's brains,** romper a alguno los cascos, hacerle saltar la tapa de los sesos.

beat up, batir (eggs), sorprender (enemy). *-vn.* Dar una batida, levantar tropas.

beat upon, echarse contra, estrellarse; batir (sun). *(Fam.)* **He beats all,** el los gana a todos. **That beats all,** eso es más que todo.

beat, *a.* Fatigado, agotado, reventado, molido (exhausted). **To be dead beat,** estar reventado o molido.

beat, *s.* 1. Golpe o modo de golpear. 2. Pulsación, latido. *(Mús.)* Tiempo, ritmo (rhythmic accent) 3. Oscilación del péndulo de un reloj. 4. Toque de tambor, sonido. 5. Quiebro de la voz. 6. Ronda (of policeman), el distrito o cuartel al cuidado de un alguacil, o sereno.

beatchick [ˈbiːtʃɪk] [bit-chik], *s.* Tipo fémino que corresponde al de *Beatnik,* bohemio estrafalario de los E.U.A.

beaten [ˈbiːtn] [bi-ten], *part. adj.* Trillado, pisado. *-pp.* Batido, golpeado, apaleado: derrotado, vencido, etc.

beater [ˈbiːtəʳ] [bitaʳ], *s.* 1. Martillo, maza, pisón, golpeador, batidor, el instrumento con que se bate, pisa o golpea. 2. Apaleador, el que apalea. **Egg-beater,** batidor de huevos.

beatific, beatifical [ˌbiːəˈtɪfɪk] [bia-ti-fik], *a.* Beatífico, lo que constituye la última felicidad.

beatifically [ˌbiːəˈtɪfɪklɪ] [bia-ti-fi-ka-li], *adv.* Beatíficamente.

beatification [biːætɪfɪˈkeɪʃən] [bia-ti-fi-kei-shon], *s.* Beatificación, declaración del Papa de que alguna persona goza de la eterna bienaventuranza después de su muerte.

beatify [biːˈætɪfaɪ] [bia-ti-fai], *va.* Beatificar, declarar bienaventurado.

beating [ˈbiːtɪŋ] [bi-tin], *s.* Paliza (thrashing) (defeat), zurra, de palos o golpes. Corrección; pulsación. Golpeo, batidura. **They gave us/we took a beating,** nos dieron una paliza. **Her time will take some/a lot of beating,** va a ser difícil/muy difícil superar su marca.

beatitude [biːˈætɪtjuːd] [bi-ati-tiud], *s.* Beatitud, felicidad. **The Beatitudes,** las Bienaventuranzas.

beatnik [ˈbiːtnɪk] [bit-nik], *s.* Bohemio estrafalario de los E.U.A.

beat-up [ˈbiːtʌp] [bit-ap] *a.* Destartalado (furniture), andrajoso (clothes).

beau [bəʊ] [bou], *s.* (en pl. BEAUX y BEAUS). 1. Petimetre, pisaverde, currutaco. *(Fr.)* **Beau-monde,** gente de moda. 2. Galán, chichisveador, cortejo, pretendiente.

beau-ideal [bəʊˈaɪdɪəl] [bou-ai-dial], *s.* Bello ideal, concepción de la belleza perfecta tal como sólo existe en la imaginación.

beauish [ˈbəʊɪʃ] [bouish], *a.* Guapo, galán, lucido; lo que es propio de un petimetre o pisaverde.

beauteous [ˈbjuːtɪəs] [biu-tios], *a.* Bello, hermoso, lo perfecto en su línea.

beauteously [ˈbjuːtɪəslɪ] [biu-tios-li], *adv.* V. BEAUTIFULLY.

beauteousness [ˈbjuːtɪəsnɪs] [biu-tios-nes], *s.* Belleza, encantos; gracia, elegancia.

beautician [bjuːˈtɪʃən] [biu-ti-shan] *s.* Esteticista.

beautification [ˈbjuːtɪfɪˈkeɪʃən] [biu-ti-fi-kei-shon], *s.* Acción y efecto de hermosear o adornar.

beautifier [ˈbjuːtɪfaɪəʳ] [biu-ti-faiaʳ], *s.* Hermoseador.

beautiful [ˈbjuːtɪfʊl] [biu-ti-ful], *a.* Hermoso, precioso, bello (scenery, poem, colors). Precioso, guapísimo, hermoso, bello (woman, child, hair, voice). Estupendo, buenísimo (meal, weather). Encantador (person). **Small is beautiful,** lo bueno viene en frascos pequeños. -*s.* Lo bello.

beautifully [ˈbjuːtɪfʊlɪ] [biu-ti-fu-li], *adv.* Hermosamente, con belleza, con perfección. Maravillosamente (bien) (excellently, very well). **She was beautifully dressed,** iba elegantísima. **The children behaved beautifully,** los niños se portaron estupendamente o a las mil maravillas. **The water was beautifully cool,** el agua estaba deliciosamente fresca (as intensifier).

beautifulness [ˈbjuːtɪfʊlnɪs] [biu-ti-ful-nes], *s.* Hermosura, belleza.

beautify [ˈbjuːtɪfaɪ] [biu-ti-fai], *va.* Hermosear, acicalar, componer, adornar, embellecer.

beautifying [ˈbjuːtɪfaɪɪŋ] [biu-ti-fain], *s.* La acción de adornar o hermosear una cosa: afeite, compostura, adorno, aderezo.

beautiless [ˈbjuːtɪlɪs] [biu-ti-les], *a.* Feo, falto de belleza.

beauty [ˈbjuːtɪ] [biu-ti], *s.* 1. Belleza, hermosura. 2. Hermosura, persona hermosa o bella. 3. Encanto, gracia. 4. (*Fam.*) Lo mejor, lo gracioso, lo singular. **The beauty of the story was,** lo mejor de cuento fue. **Beauty contest, beauty pageant,** concurso de belleza. **Beauty salon, Beauty parlor,** salón de belleza.

beautydom [ˈbjuːtɪdʌm] [biu-ti-dam], *s.* Conjunto de hermosuras (mujeres bellas).

beauty-spot [ˈbjuːtɪspɒt] [biu-ti-spot], *s.* Parche o lunar postizo (on face). Lugar pintoresco (place).

beaver [ˈbiːvəʳ] [bi-vaʳ], *s.* 1. (*Zool.*) Castor, animal cuadrúpedo anfibio. 2. Sombrero de castor, sombrero hecho de pelo de castor. 3. Visera, la parte de a armadura que cubre la cara. **To be an eager beaver,** ser muy entusiasta y trabajador. **Beaver away,** trabajar como una hormiguita.

beaverteen [ˈbiːvətiːn] [bi-var-tín], *s.* Piel de tusa, especie de fustán.

bebop [ˈbiːbɒp] [bi-bop], *s.* Variedad de jazz.

becalin [ˈbɪkəlɪn] [bi-ka-lin], *va.* 1. Serenar o calmar alguna tempestad o borrasca. 2. Serenar el ánimo, sosegar. (*Mar.*) Calmar, quedarse en calma.

becalming [ˈbɪkɑːmɪŋ] [bi-kal-min], *s.* Calma.

became [bɪˈkeɪm] [bi-keim], Pretérito del verbo TO BECOME.

because [bɪˈkɒz] [bi-kos], *conj.* Porque, por esta razón, a causa de. **Because he loves her, he doesn't see it,** como la quiere, no se da cuenta. **because of** (*prep.*) Por, a causa de. **I was late because of him,** llegué tarde por su culpa.

bechance [bɪˈtʃæns] [bi-chans], *va.* y *vn.* Acaecer, suceder, acontecer.

becharm [bɪˈtɑːm] [bi-charm], *va.* Encantar, captar, cautivar.

beck [bek] [bek], *va.* y *vn.* Hacer señas con la cabeza.

beck, *s.* 1. V. NOD. 2. Riachuelo. 3. Tanque para lejía, tinte o jabón. **To be at somebody's beck and call,** estar siempre a entera disposición de alguien.

becket [ˈbekɪt] [be-ket], *n.* (*Mar.*) Vinatera, arraigado o manzanillo de aparejo.

beckon [ˈbekən] [be-kon], *vn.* Hacer seña con la cabeza. **She beckoned to him to follow,** le hizo señas para que le siguiera. -*va.* Hacer seña a. **To beckon with the hand,** hacer una seña con la mano. **To beckon somebody in/over,** hacerle señas a alguien para que entre o se acerque.

beckon, *s.* Seña con la cabeza.

becloud [ˈbɪklaʊd] [bi-klaud], *va.* Obscurecer, cubrir como con una nube, anublar. También se usa en sentido figurado. **Beclouded intellect,** una inteligencia obscurecida.

become [bɪˈkʌm] [bi-kam], *va.* Convenir, parecer, sentar, caer bien, ser propio, estar bien. -*vn.* 1. Hacerse, volverse, pasar de un estado o condición a otro, convertirse, venir a parar; ser lo que no era; ponerse a, meterse a. 2. **To become of,** parar en algo. **What will become of me?,** ¿qué será de mí? **What has become of my hat?,** ¿qué ha sido de mi sombrero? **To become warm in,** acalorarse en. **To become forfeited,** incurrir en alguna pena, confiscación o multa. **To become crazy,** perder el juicio, volverse loco; perder la chaveta. **Become** *o* **come to be,** llegar a ser. El verbo inglés *become* con un adjetivo se expresa a veces en español por medio de los prefijos *a o en;* p. ej. **To become warm,** enardecerse, acalorarse.

becoming [bɪˈkʌmɪŋ] [bi-ka-min], *pa.* 1. Gracioso, primoroso, decoroso, propio; decente, conveniente, acomodado, justo. 2. Lo que adorna, que sienta bien, que va bien. **A becoming dress,** un vestido que sienta bien. Apropiado, favorecedor.

becomingly [bɪˈkʌmɪŋlɪ] [bi-ka-min-li], *adv.* Decorosamente, decentemente, con garbo y elegancia, a propósito.

becomingness [bɪˈkʌmɪŋnɪs] [bi-ka-min-nes], *s.* Decencia, elegancia, en los modales; propiedad, garbo, compostura.

becurl [ˈbekɜːl] [be-kerl], *va.* Formar rizos.

bed [bed] [bed], *s.* 1. Cama, lecho; el armazón de madera o hierro, ya por sí solo ya con ropa y colchones. **Bed of state,** cama de respeto. **Feather-bed,** colchón de plumas, plumón. **Flock-bed,** colchón de borra. **Straw-bed,** jergón de paja. **Folding-bed,** cama plegadiza. **Death-bed,** lecho mortuorio. 2. Cuadro de jardín; era, tablar, de una huerta. 3. Lecho, tongada, la capa o cama con que por su orden se ponen unas cosas sobre otras. 4. Madre de río, cauce, lecho. 5. Afuste de mortero. 6. Almohadilla de cureña. 7. Capa minera horizontal. 8. (*Carp.*) Asiento, armadura. 9. Mesa (de billar). **To lay to bed,** partear, ayudar la partera o comadrón al parto. **To be brought to bed,** (*Fam.*) Parir. **To make the bed,** hacer la cama. **A crazy bed,** una cama desvencijada, una mala cama. **To go to bed,** ir a acostarse. **To jump out of bed,** saltar de la cama. **To lie late in bed,** levantarse tarde. **To make one's (own) bed,** quien mala cama hace, en ella se yace.

bed, *va.* 1. Meter en la cama, acostar. 2. Acostarse, o irse a la cama con otra persona. 3. sembrar o plantar. 4. Poner una cosa en togadas o capas sobrepuestas. -*vn.* Cohabitar, hacer vida en común.

bedabble [ˈbedəbl] [be-da-bol], *va.* Rociar, mojar.

bed and breakfast [ˈbedænˈbrekfəst] [bed-and-brek-fast] *s.* **They do bed and breakfast,** dan alojamiento y desayuno. Pensión (establishment).

bedawi [ˈbedəwɪ] [be-da-ui], *s.* (*pl.* BEDAWIN). V. BEDOUIN.

bedazzle [bɪˈdæzəl] [bi-dasel], *va.* Deslumbrar, desvistar, quitar la vista o confundirla con el resplandor.

bedbug [ˈbedbʌg] [bed-bag], *s.* Chinche.

bedchamber [ˈbedˌtʃeɪmbəʳ] [bed-cheim-baʳ], *s.* Dormitorio, la alcoba o el aposento donde se duerme. (*Mex.*) Recámara. **A gentleman of the king's bedchamber,** gentilhombre de cámara.

bedclothes [ˈbedkləʊðz] [bed-klouds], *s. pl.* coberturas de cama, ropa de cama, mantas y sábanas.

bedded [ˈbedɪd] [be-ded], *pp.* 1. Con una o varias camas. **A single-bedded, a double-bedded room,** alcoba de una cama, de dos camas. 2. (*Geol.*) Estratificado, dividido en capas. 3. Que crece en tongadas, lechos o tablares; reunión o recogido en un tablar, lecho o tongada (oysters, plants, etc.)

bedder [ˈbedəʳ] [be-daʳ], **bedetter** [ˈbedətəʳ] [be-de-taʳ], *s.* Piedra de los molinos sobre la cual se mueve la muela.

bedding [ˈbedɪŋ] [be-din], *s*. Ajuar o ropa de cama. Cama (for animals).

bedeck [brˈdek] [bi-dek], *va*. Adornar, asear. **To be bedecked with something,** estar adornado o engalanado con algo.

bedehouse [ˈbedhaʊs] [bed-jaus], *s*. Casa de misericordia.

bedel [ˈbedəl] [be-del], *s*. *(Ant.)* V. BEADLE.

bedelry [ˈbedəlrɪ] [be-del-ri], *s*. Jurisdicción del bedel.

bedevil [brˈdevəl] [bi-de-val], *va*. 1. Endemoniar, endiablar, maleficiar; hechizar; enloquecer, volver loco o demente. 2. Endiablar, dañar, hacer sufrir abuso o tratamiento diabólico. **The project was bedeviled with problems,** el proyecto estaba plagado de problemas.

bedew [brˈdjuː] [bi-diu], *va*. Rociar, esparcir alguna cosa sobre la tierra con la misma suavidad con que cae el rocío; regar.

bedfellow [ˈbedfeləʊ] [bed-fe-lou], *s*. Compañero o compañera de cama. **To make strange bedfellows,** hacer una extraña pareja.

bedhangings [bedˈhæŋgɪŋs] [bed-jan-gings], *s*. Cortinas de cama.

bedhead [ˈbedhed] [bed-jed], *s*. Cabecera de cama.

bedight [brˈdaɪt], *va*. (*pret*. y *pp*. BEDIGHT o BEDIGHTED). Adornar, hermosear.

bedim [brˈdɪm] [be-dim], *va*. Oscurecer, ofuscar; desvistar, deslumbrar.

bedizen [brˈdɪzən] [be-di-sen], *va*. *(Vulg.* Adornar, aderezar, acicalar.

bedlam [ˈbedləm] [bed-lam], *s*. 1. Casa de orates, aquella en que hay mucho bullicio y poco gobierno; un gran tropel o bullicio, desbarajuste. 2. Casa de locos. **There was bedlam when he announced the news,** se armó la de S. Quintín cuando anunció la noticia. **It was bedlam in there!,** aquello era una locura.

bedlamite [ˈbedləmaɪt] [bed-la-mit], *s*. Loco.

bedmaker [ˈbedmeɪkəʳ] [bed-mei-kaʳ], *s*. Criada o persona que hace las camas.

bedmate [ˈbedmeɪt] [bed-meit], *s*. Compañero o compañera de cama.

bedmoulding [ˈbedməʊldɪŋ] [bed-moul-din], *s*. Moldura de cornisa.

bedouin [ˈbedɔɪn] [be-duin], *s*. 1. Beduino, árabe del desierto. 2. Vagabundo callejero.

bed-pan [ˈbedpæn] [bed-pan], *s*. 1. Vasija de loza para uso de los enfermos en el lecho. 2. Calentador de cama. *(Med.)* Cuña, chata.

bedplate [ˈbedpleɪt] [bed-pleit], *s*. Bancaza o cama de una máquina.

bedpost [ˈbedpəʊst] [bed-poust], *s*. Pilar o columna que sostiene el cielo de la cama.

bedpresser [ˈbedpresəʳ] [bed-pre-saʳ], *s*. Dormilón, el que duerme mucho.

bed-quilt [ˈbedkilt] [bed-kilt], *s*. Cobertor de cama.

bedraggle [brˈdrægl] [bi-draguel], *va*. Ensuciar o manchar la ropa.

bedraggled [brˈdrægld] [bi-dragueld] *a*. Desaliñado, despeinado, enmarañado.

bedrench [brˈdrentʃ] [bi-drench], *va*. empapar, embeber.

bedrid o bedridden [ˈbedrɪdl] [be-drid], *a*. Postrado en cama, por vejez o enfermedad.

bed-right o bed-rite [ˈbedraɪt] [bed-rait], *s*. Derecho conyugal.

bed-rock [ˈbedrɒk] [bed-rok], *s*. La roca sólida que está debajo de minerales, etc. **The bed-rock of his theory,** los cimientos o la base de su teoría.

bedroom [ˈbedrɒm] [bed-rum], *s*. Recámara, dormitorio, alcoba. **Bedroom slippers,** pantuflas, zapatillas.

bedrop [ˈbedrɒp] [bed-rop], *va*. Rociar, salpicar.

bedside [ˈbedsaɪd] [bed-said], *s*. Lado de cama. **Bedside table,** mesita de noche, mesilla.

bedsit [ˈbedsɪt] [bed-sit] **bedsitter** [ˈbedˈsɪtəʳ] [bed-si-taʳ] *s*. Habitación amueblada cuyo alquiler suele incluir el uso de baño y cocina comunes.

bedsore [ˈbedsɔːʳ] [bed-soʳ], *s*. Escara, úlcera de decúbito. Llaga causada por la prolongada permanencia en el lecho.

bedspread [ˈbedspred] [bed-spred], *s*. Colcha de cama; cubrecama.

bedspring [ˈbedsprɪŋ] [bed-sprin], *s*. Colchón de muelles o de resortes.

bedstead [ˈbedsted] [bed-sted], *s*. Armazón de cama, el catre o tablas con sus pies.

bed-straw [ˈbedstrɔː] [bed-stro], *s*. 1. Paja de o para jergón. 2. *(Bot.)* cuajaleche, galio, hierba del género Galium.

bedswerver [ˈbedswɜːvəʳ] [bed-suer-vaʳ], *s*. *(Des.)* Adúltero o adúltera.

bedtick, bedticking [ˈbedtɪk] [bed-tik], *s*. Cutí, tela para colchones.

bedtime [ˈbedtaɪm] [bed-taim], *s*. La hora de irse a la cama o de recogerse, de acostarse.

beduck [ˈbedʌk] [be-dak], *va*. Sumergir debajo del agua.

bedung [ˈbedʌŋ] [be-dan], *va*. Estercolar, cubrir con estiércol, engrasar y beneficiar la tierra con estiércol.

bedust [ˈbedʌst] [be-dast], *va*. Empolvar, polvorear, esparcir polvo o llenar de polvo.

bedward [ˈbedwɔːd] [bed-uord], *adv*. Hacia la cama.

bedwarf [ˈbedwɔːf] [bed-uorf], *va*. Achicar, reducir a menos el tamaño de alguna cosa.

bedwork [ˈbedwɜːk] [bed-uek], *s*. Obra hecha en la cama; obra hecha sin trabajo, o la que no cuesta pena ni fatiga.

bee [biː] [bí], *s*. 1. Abeja, insecto social himenóptero que fabrica la cera y la miel; en especial, la Apis mellifica. 2. *(Fam.)* reunión de vecinos o amigos para hacer algún trabajo o para divertirse. **Queen-bee,** abeja madre o reina. **Worker-bee,** abeja obrera. **Bee-bread,** polen almacenado. **Bee-fly,** mosca, abeja, díptero del género Bombylius. También, pero incorrectamente, la Eristalis, o *drone-fly.* **Swarm of bees,** enjambre de abejas. **Bee-culture,** cultivo o cuidado de las abejas, apicultura. **To have a bee in one's bonnet about something,** tener manía a algo, tener algo metido entre ceja y ceja.

beech [biːtʃ] [bích], *s*. *(Bot.)* Haya, árbol alto, grueso y copudo, de corteza blanca y madera tenaz y flexible.

beechen [ˈbiːtʃən] [bí-chen], *a*. De haya, compuesto o hecho de haya.

beech-mast o beech-nut [biːtʃmɑːst] [biːtʃmɑːstnʌt] [bích-mast] [bích-nat], *s*. Fabuco, el fruto que produce la haya.

beech-oil [biːtʃɔɪl] [bích-oil], *s*. Aceite de fabuco, que se saca del fruto de la haya.

bee-eater [biːtʃɪtəʳ] [bích-ítaʳ], *s*. *(Orn.)* Abejaruco, pájaro que se come las abejas y destruye los colmenares.

beef [biːf] [bíf], *s*. Carne de res. **Beef broth,** consomé, caldo de carne. **Beef steak,** bistec, lomo de carne. **Roast beef,** carne de res para asar. **Beefburger,** hamburguesa.

beefeater [ˈbiːˌiːtəʳ] [bíf-ítaʳ], *s*. 1. Alabardero, especie de guardia del rey de Inglaterra. Corrupción de "buffeteer", el que sirve en el "buffet" o aparador; criado rollizo.

beef-witted [ˈbiːfwɪtd] [bíf-uíted], *a*. Lerdo, estúpido.

beefy [ˈbiːfɪ] [bí-fi] *a*. Fornido.

bee-garden [biːˈɡɑːdn] [bí-gar-den], *s*. Abejar, colmenar.

bee-glue [biːˈɡluː] [bí-glu], *s*. Cera aleda. V. PROPOLIS.

bee-hive [ˈbiːhaɪv] [bí-jaiv], *s*. Colmena, especie de caja en que se crían las abejas y donde labran la miel y la cera.

bee-line [biːˈlaɪn] [bí-lain], *s*. Línea recta. **To make a bee-line for somebody/something,** irse derechito a alguien/algo.

bee-master [biːˈmɑːstəʳ] [bí-mas-taʳ], *s*. Colmenero o abejero, el que tiene abejas y colmenas, o el que las cuida.

bee-moth [ˈbiːmoθ] [bí-moz], *s*. Mariposa cuyas larvas se crían en los colmenares y destruyen los panales.

been [biːn] [bín], *pp*. del verbo TO BE.

beep [biːp] [bíp] *s*. Pitido. *va/vn*. Pitar. **To beep one's horn,** pitar.

beeper [ˈbiːpəʳ] [bípaʳ] *s*. Buscapersonas, busca, bip, bíper.

beer [bɪəʳ] [bíaʳ], *s*. Cerveza, bebida fermentada que se hace de cebada y hombrecillo o lúpulo. **Small beer,** cerveza floja. **Strong beer,** cerveza fuerte. **Stale beer,** cerveza agriada. **Lager beer,** cerveza que contiene poco lúpulo. *V.* LAGER. **Pale beer,** cerveza blanca. *(Fam.)* **Beer belly, beer gut,** panza (de bebedor de cerveza). **Beer garden,** jardín o patio abierto de un bar. **Beer mat,** posavasos (de cartón).

beer-house, *s. V.* ALE-HOUSE.

beestings, biestings ['biːstɪŋz] [bís-tings], *s.* Calostro, la primera leche que se ordeña de la vaca después de parir.

beeswax ['biːzwæks] [bís-uaks], *s.* Cera de abejas.

beet [biːt] *s. (Bot.)* Acelga, remolacha. *(Mex.)* Betabel. **Sugar-beet,** remolacha. **Beet-sugar,** azúcar de remolacha. **As red as a beet,** rojo o colorado como la grana o como un tomate.

beetle ['biːtl] [bí-tel], *s.* 1. *(Zool.)* Escarabajo, o cualquier insecto coleóptero. 2. Pisón, maza, instrumento que sirve para apretar la tierra, piedras, etc. **Colorado beetle,** dorífera, insecto del Colorado, coleóptero que causa grandes destrozos en la patata. Llamado también potato-bug.

beetle, *vn.* 1. Hacer barriga; colgar sobre. 2. Sobresalir.

beetle-browed ['biːtl'braʊd] [bí-tel-braud], *a.* Cejudo, el que tiene las cejas muy salidas.

beetle-headed ['biːtl'hedɪd] [bí-tel-je-did], *a.* Lerdo, pesado.

beetle-stock ['biːtl'stɒk] [bí-tel-stok], *s.* Mango de pisón.

beetling ['biːtlɪŋ] [bí-tlin], *a.* Saliente, pendiente, colgante.

beetling-machine ['biːtlɪŋ'matʃɪn] [bí-tlin-machín], *s.* Sacabocados mecánico, estampador mecánico.

beet-radish ['biːt'radɪʃ] [bít-radish], **beet-rave** ['biːt'reɪv] [bít-reiv], *s.* Betarraga o remolacha.

beetroot ['biːtruːt] [bi-trut] *s.* (GB) *V.* BEET.

beet-sugar ['biːtʃʊgə'] [bit-shu-ga'], *s.* Azúcar de remolacha.

beeves ['biːvz] [bívs], *s. pl.* Ganado mayor.

befall [bɪ'fɔːl] [bi-fol], *vn. (pret.* BEFELL, *pp.* BEFALLEN). Suceder, acontecer, sobrevenir. Se usa generalmente para significar un acontecimiento desgraciado. **Whatever befalls,** suceda lo que quiera. **The worst that can befall,** lo peor que puede acontecer.

befit [bɪ'fɪt] [bi-fit], *va.* Venir bien, convenir, acomodarse a. **As befits a princess,** como corresponde a una princesa.

befitting [bɪ'fɪtɪŋ] [bi-fi-tin], *pa.* y *a.* Conveniente, propio, digno, que se aviene con. **With a magnificence befitting the occasion,** con un esplendor acorde con/a la ocasión.

befoamed [bɪ'fəʊmd] [bi-foumd], *a.* Cubierto de espuma.

befog [bɪ'fɒg] [bi-fog], *va.* Envolver en niebla; confundir, oscurecer.

befool [bɪ'fuːl] [bi-ful], *va.* Infatuar, entontecer.

before [bɪ'fɔː'] [bi-fo'], *prep.* 1. Más adelante, hablando de lugar. 2. Delante, enfrente. 3. Delante, ante, en presencia de una persona (in front of). 4. Antes de (preceding in time). **Before nightfall,** antes de anochecer. 5. Antes o delante. **Look before you leap,** antes que te cases, mira lo que haces. 6. Anterior a; superior a. *-adv.* 1. Antes, primero, hablando de tiempo (preceding). **I was there before him,** yo estuve allí ántes que él. 2. Antes, en tiempo pasado. **I have never seen him before,** nunca le he visto antes de ahora. 3. Antes, en algún tiempo recién pasado. **A little before,** poco antes. 4. Antes, hasta ahora. **Before it was not so,** antes no era así. 5. Ya. **To get before one,** adelantarse a alguno. **I told you so before,** ya se lo he dicho a usted **Before cited,** ya citado. **Before mentioned,** mencionado más arriba, de que queda hecha mención. **She puts her work before her family,** antepone el trabajo a su familia (in rank, priority).

beforehand [bɪ'fɔːhænd] [bi-for-jand], *adv.* 1. De antemano (in advance), a prevención, anticipadamente. **To be beforehand with one,** llevar la delantera a uno. 2. Primeramente, antes (earlier), ya. 3. Con muchos ahorros. **I know beforehand that,** ya sé que.

beforetime [bɪ'fɔːtaɪm] [bi-for-taim], *adv.* En tiempo pasado, en otro tiempo, tiempo atrás.

befoul [bɪ'faʊl] [bi-faul], *va.* Ensuciar, emporcar, embadurnar.

befriend [bɪ'frend] [bi-frend], *va.* Favorecer, patrocinar, amparar, ayudar, proteger. **To befriend oneself,** mirar por sí; hacerse amigo de.

befringe [bɪ'frɪndʒ] [bi-frinch], *va.* Guarnecer con franjas.

befuddle [bɪ'fʌdl] [bi-fadel] *va.* Aturdir, ofuscar. **He was befuddled by drink,** estaba ofuscado por la bebida.

beg [beg] [beg], *vn.* Mendigar, pordiosear vivir de la limosna; hacer la cuestación o colecta (money, food). *-va.* 1. Rogar, pedir con sumisión suplicar. **I beg it as a favor,** se lo suplico a usted por favor. Suplicarle a, rogarle a (person). **I beg you!,** ¡te lo suplico!, ¡te lo ruego! **They live by begging,** viven de la mendicidad. **She taught the dog to beg,** enseñó al perro a levantar las patitas. **To beg for mercy,** pedir o suplicar clemencia. 2. Suponer, dar por supuesto. (Lógica) **To beg the question,** dar por admitido el punto que se discute, dar por supuesto.

began [bɪ'gæn] [bi↓gan] *pret.* del verbo TO BEGIN.

beget [bɪ'get] [bi-guet], *va. (pret.* BEGA *-ant.*BEGAT *-pp.* BEGOTTEN). 1 Engendrar (father). 2 Producir, causar, provocar (give raise to). **To beget strifes,** suscitar contiendas.

begetter [bɪ'getə'] [bi-gue-ta'], *s.* Engendrador, el que engendra.

begetting ['bɪ'getɪŋ] [bi-gue-tin], *s.* Generación; producción.

beggar ['begə'] [be-ga'], *s.* 1. Mendigo, el pobre que pide limosna y vive de ella. 2. Suplicante. 3. Miserable; gorrón. *(Prov.)* **It is better to be a king among beggars than a beggar among kings,** más vale ser cabeza de ratón que cola de león. **Beggars can't be choosers,** a veces no se está en situación de elegir nada. *(Coloq.)* **You lucky beggar!,** ¡qué suertudo eres!, ¡qué potra tienes!

beggar, *va.* 1. Empobrecer, arruinar, reducir a pobreza o mendicidad. 2. Apurar, agotar. **To beggar description,** ser indescriptible, no haber palabras para describir.

beggarliness ['begəlɪnɪs] [be-gar-li-nes], *s.* Mezquindad, pobreza, miseria, mendicidad.

beggarly ['begəlɪ] [be-gar-li] *a.* Pobre, miserable. **Beggarly action,** bajeza. *-adv.* Mezquinamente, pobremente.

beggary ['begərɪ] [be-gar-ri], *s.* Mendicidad o mendiguez.

begging ['begɪŋ] [be-guin], *a.* Mendicante. **To go begging,** pedir limosna. *(Met.)* Carecer de valor; no hallar comprador.

begilt ['begɪlt] [be-guilt], *pa.* Dorado.

begin [bɪ'gɪn] [bi-guin], *va.* Empezar, comenzar, principiar, dar principio a alguna cosa. **To begin the world,** empezar a vivir. **To begin one's march,** ponerse en camino. **To begin afresh** o **again,** volver a empezar o empezar de nuevo; proseguir lo que se había empezado y dejado. *-vn.* Nacer, principiar a existir.

beginner [bɪ'gɪnə'] [bi-gui-na'], *s.* 1. Autor, inventor, el que da principio a alguna cosa. 2. Principiante, el sujeto que empieza a aprender o ejercer algún arte o facultad. **Beginner's lack,** la suerte del principiante.

beginning [bɪ'gɪnɪŋ] [bi-gui-nin], *s.* 1. Principio, origen o causa (in time, place) **The beginning of the end,** el principio del fin. **From beginning to end,** de principio a fin. 2. Principios o rudimentos de alguna facultad.

begird [bɪ'gɜːd] [bi-guerd], **begirt** [bɪ'gɜːt] [bi-guert], *va. (pret.* y *pp.* BEGIRT). 1. Ceñir, atar. 2. Ceñir, rodear, abrazar al rededor. 3. Sitiar o poner sitio a alguna plaza.

begnaw [beg'nɔ] [beg-no], *a.* Roer.

begone! [bɪ'gɒn] [bi-gon], *inter.* ¡Fuera, apártate de ahí, quita allá!

begonia [bɪ'gəʊnɪə] [bi-go-nia], *s.* Begonia.

begored [bɪ'gɔːd] [bi-gord], *a.* Manchado con sangre.

begot [bɪ'gɒt] [bi-got], *pret.* **Begotten,** *pp.* del verbo TO BEGET.

begrime [bɪ'graɪm] [bi-graim], *va.* Encenagar, ensuciar con cieno; ennegrecer.

begrudge [bɪ'grʌdʒ] [bi-grach], *va.* Envidiar la posesión de (envy); repugnar. **I don't begrudge your success,** no te envidio del éxito que tienes (resent). **I begrudge paying so much,** me da rabia o me duele pagar tanto.

beguile

beguile [bɪˈgaɪl] [bi-gail], *va.* Engañar (deceive), seducir, cautivar (charm); entretener con falsas esperanzas. **To beguile the time,** hacer pasar el tiempo. **He was beguiled into signing the contract,** le engatusaron para que firmara el contrato.

beguiler [bɪˈgaɪləʳ] [bi-gai-laʳ], *s.* Engañador, seductor, impostor.

begum [bɪˈgʌm] [bi-gam], *va.* Engomar, empapar o cubrir de goma.

begun [bɪˈgʌn] [bi-gan], *pp.* del verbo TO BEGIN.

behalf [bɪˈhɑːf] [bi-jalf], *s.* 1. Favor, patrocinio, consideración, beneficio. **In behalf of,** a favor o en nombre de. 2. Defensa, amparo. **In his behalf,** en su defensa.

behave [bɪˈheɪv] [bi-jeiv], *va.* y *s.* Proceder, obrar, conducirse, comportarse o portarse bien o mal (act, esp. of children). **He behaves very ill,** él se porta muy mal. *(Fam.)* **Behave!** ¡estése usted quieto!, ¡no moleste usted! *(Fam.)* ¡no sea Vd. majadero! **Well-behaved,** de buena conducta, de buenas maneras. **Ill-behaved,** de mala conducta. **To behave oneself,** portarse bien, comportarse. **Behave yourself!,** ¡pórtate bien!

behavior, behaviour [bɪˈheɪvjəʳ] [bi-jei-vioʳ], *s.* 1. Proceder, conducta, el modo de portarse o de gobernarse uno en sus acciones. 2. Continente, gesto. 3. Modal, acción particular y propia de algún sujeto con que se hace reparar. 4. Crianza; porte, maneras, aire. **What extraordinary behavior!** ¡qué proceder tan extraordinario! **He was on his best behavior,** se portó mejor que nunca.

behavioral, behavioural [bɪˈheɪvjərəl] [bi-jei-vio-ral] *a.* De conducta, conductual.

behead [bɪˈhed] [bi-jed], *va.* Degollar, decapitar.

beheading [bɪˈhedɪŋ] [bi-je-din], *s.* Decapitación, degollación, acto y efecto de decapitar.

beheld [bɪˈheld] [bi-jeld], *pret.* y *pp.* del verbo TO BEHOLD.

behest [bɪˈhest] [bi-jest], *s.* Mandato, precepto, requirimiento. **At the behest of somebody/At somebody's behest,** a instancias de alguien.

behind [bɪˈhaɪnd] [bi-jaind], *prep.* 1. Detrás, tras (to the rear of). **Behind the curtain,** detrás del telón, en la escena o entre bastidores. **Behind one's back,** en ausencia o a espaldas de una persona. **She's well behind the rest of the class,** está muy atrasada con respecto al resto de la clase. 2. Atrás (to the other side of) 3. Inferior. **To ride behind one,** montar a las ancas o en ancas. **I know who's behind this,** yo sé quién está detrás de esto (responsible for). **The theory behind it is that…,** la teoría sobre la que se basa es que… (underlying). **We're all behind the police,** todos respaldamos a la policía (in support of). **I'm behind schedule,** voy atrasado o retrasado. *-adv.* 1. Atrás, detrás (to the rear, behind). **To follow behind,** ir o seguir atrás de otro. **I was attacked from behind,** me atacaron por la espalda. **Keep an eye on the car behind,** no pierdas de vista al coche de atrás. 2. Atrasadamente. 3. No a la vista; sin tocar, de reserva. **England was two goals behind,** Inglaterra iba perdiendo por dos goles (in race, competition). **I'm behind my work,** estoy atrasado con el trabajo (in arrears). **Buenos Aires is five hours behind,** Buenos Aires tiene cinco horas de retraso (in time). *(Fam.)* Trasero.

behindhand [bɪˈhaɪndhænd] [bi-jaind-jand], *adv.* Atrasadamente, con atraso.

behold [bɪˈhəʊld] [bi-jold] *va.* Ver, mirar, contemplar, considerar, notar. *vn.* (only in imperative) Mirar. See LO. **behold!** ¡He! ¡he aquí! ¡aquí está! ¡vele ahí!

beholden [bɪˈhəʊldən] [bi-jol-den], *a.* Deudor, obligado por gratitud. **To be beholden to somebody,** estar en deuda con alguien.

beholder [bɪˈhəʊldəʳ] [bi-jol-daʳ], *s.* Espectador, mirón.

beholding [bɪˈhəʊldɪŋ] [bi-jol-din], *a.* Obligado, deudor.

behoney [bɪˈhʌni] [bi-ja-ni], *va.* Dulcificar, endulzar (con miel).

behoof [bɪˈhuːf] [bi-júf], *s.* Provecho, utilidad, ventaja.

behoove, behove [bɪˈhuːv] [bi-júv], *vn.* Este verbo sólo se usa impersonalmente, y significa convenir, importar, ser útil, ser necesario. **It behoves us to be prepared for death,** nos importa estar preparados para la muerte. **It behoves us to support him,** nos corresponde apoyarlo.

behooveful, behoveful [bɪˈhuːvfʊl] [bi-júv-ful], *a.* Provechoso, útil; idóneo, necesario, expediente.

behovable [bɪˈhəʊvəbl] [bi-jo-va-bol], *a.* Ganancioso, útil.

beige [beɪʒ] [beish], *s.* Beige, color natural de la lana. Color arena, entre gris y pardo.

Beijing [ˈbeɪˈdʒɪŋ] [bei-yin] *N. (Geogr.)* Beijing.

beild [biːld] [biild], *v.* y *s.* V. BIELD.

being [ˈbiːɪŋ] [bí-ing], *s.* 1. Existencia, el ser o esencia actual de alguna cosa (existence, life). 2. Estado o condición particular. 3. Ente, ser (person, creature). 4. Vivienda, morada, habitación. **A man's first being,** el primer momento de la vida. **The well-being,** la felicidad, el bienestar. *-conj.* Ya que, puesto que, supuesto. *-part.* del verbo TO BE. **I do no good by being here,** mi presencia no sirve de nada aquí, yo no hago aquí nada. **To keep a thing from being done,** impedir que una cosa se haga; no dejar hacer una cosa. **Such being the case,** ya que tal es el caso. **For the time being,** por el momento.

bejade [bɪˈdʒeɪd] [bi-yeid], *va.* Cansar.

bejeweled, (GB) bejewelled [bɪˈdʒuːəld] [bi-yueld] *a.* Enjoyado.

bel [bel] [bel], *s.* El dios supremo, o uno de los dioses principales de los Babilonios: forma caldaica de *Baal,* y aun el mismo Baal según algunos escritores.

belabor, belabour [bɪˈleɪbəʳ] [bi-la-boʳ], *va.* Apalear, dar de puñadas cascar, fustigar.

belaced [bɪˈleɪst] [bi-leist], *a.* Adornado con encaje, galoneado.

belarus [beləˈrʊs] [be-la-ros] *N. (Geogr.)* Bielorrusia.

belate [bɪˈleɪt] [bi-leit], *va.* 1. Tardar, retardar hasta pasada la hora debida, o de costumbre. 2. Cogerle uno la noche.

belated [bɪˈleɪtɪd] [bi-lei-tid], *a.* El que anda de noche, el que llega tarde; retardado, tardío.

belatedly [bɪˈleɪtɪdlɪ] [bi-lei-tid-li] *adv.* Con retraso (arrive). Tardíamente (respond).

belatedness [bɪˈleɪtɪdnɪs] [bi-lei-tid-nes], *s.* Tardanza; frialdad.

belay [bɪˈleɪ] [bi-lei], *va.* 1. Bloquear. 2. Asechar, poner asechanzas, armar emboscadas. 3. *(Mar.)* Amarrar o dar vuelta. **To belay a running rope,** amarrar un cabo de labor. **Belaying-pins,** cavillas.

belch [beltʃ] [belch], *vn.* 1. Regoldar, eructar (person); vomitar. 2. Salir o aparecer violentamente de dentro a fuera, como salen, por ejemplo, las llamas de un horno. *-va.* Arrojar, echar de sí (flames, shots). **Belch out,** escupir.

belch, belching [ˈbeltʃɪŋ] [bel-chin], *s.* Regüeldo, eructo, eructación, la acción de regoldar.

beldam, beldamo [beldəm] [bel-dam], *f.* 1. Vejezuela, la mujer vieja, fea o maliciosa. 2. Bruja.

beleaguer [bɪˈliːgəʳ] [bi-li-gaʳ], *va.* Asediar (besiege), sitiar, bloquear, oprimir. **Beleaguered,** atribulado (harassed).

belee [bɪˈliː] [bi-lí], *va. (Mar.)* Sotaventar.

belemnite [beleˈnaɪt] [be-lem-nait], *s. (Min.)* Belerunita, molusco fósil, puntiagudo, en forma de dedo; cefalópodo.

belfry [ˈbelfrɪ] [bel-fri], *s.* Campanario, la torre o paraje en que están las campanas.

Belgian [ˈbeldʒən] [bel-chan], *a.* De Bélgica. *-s.* Belga.

Belgium [ˈbeldʒəm] [bel-yam] *N. (Geogr.)* Bélgica.

belgrade [belˈgreɪd] [bel-greid] *N. (Geogr.)* Belgrado.

Belial [bɪˈlɪəl] [bi-lial], *s.* Belial, Satanás, el espíritu del mal.

belibel [bɪˈlɪbəl] [bi-li-bal], *va.* Calumniar.

belie [bɪˈlaɪ] [bi-lai], *va.* 1. Contrahacer, fingir, remedar. No dejar traslucir, ocultar (disguise). 2. Desmentir, decirle a uno que miente. 3. Calumniar, acusar falsamente. 4. Representar alguna cosa falsamente. **To belie oneself,** contradecirse; cortarse. **His looks belie his words,** sus miradas desmienten sus palabras.

belief [bɪˈliːf] [bi-líf], *s.* 1. Fe, creencia que se da respecto de las cosas que no vemos (conviction, opinion). **Contrary to popular belief,** contrariamente a lo que comúnmente se cree. **It's my belief that he lied,** creo que mintió. **He acted in the belief that…,** actuó convencido de que… **Their attitude irritated me beyond belief,** su actitud me irritó increíblemente o sobremanera. 2. Creencia, lo que cada uno cree en su religión. 3. Credo. 4. Opinión, parecer, sentimiento. **Past all belief,** increíble. **Light of belief,** crédulo. **Hard of belief,** incrédulo. **In the firm belief that,** en la firme creencia (o convicción) de que.

believable [bɪˈliːvəbl] [bi-lí-va-bol], *a.* Creíble, que se puede creer (story, account).

believe [bɪˈliːv] [bi-lív], *va.* Creer, dar asenso o crédito a alguna cosa (statement, story). **I don't believe a word he says,** no le creo ni una palabra. **I don't believe he's capable of that,** no le creo capaz de eso. **Believe it or not,** aunque no lo creas, aunque parezca mentira. **Don't you believe it!,** ¡créetelo! *(Coloq,)* **Would you believe it!,** ¡habráse visto!,¡será posible! **I don't believe it!,** ¡no puedo creerlo! **Believe you me!,** ¡te lo juro! -*vn.* 1. Creer, estar firmemente persuadido de la verdad de alguna cosa. **I believe in discipline,** soy partidario de la disciplina. 2. Creer, ejercer la virtud teologal de la fe. **To believe in God,** creer en Dios. 3. Pensar, imaginar, creer (think). **I believe so/not,** creo que sí/no, tengo entendido que sí/no. **The police believe him to be dangerous,** la policía cree que es peligroso. **It was believed to be harmless,** se creía que era inofensivo. 4. Fiarse.

believer [bɪˈliːvəʳ] [bi-lí-va-ʳ], *s.* 1. Creyente, el que cree o da crédito a lo que se le dice. 2. *(Rel.)* Creyente, fiel, cristiano, el que profesa la ley de Cristo.

believing [bɪˈliːvɪŋ] [bi-lí-vin], *s.* Fe, creencia.

believingly [bɪˈliːvɪŋlɪ] [bi-lí-vin-li], *adv.* Con fe o creencia.

belike [bɪˈlaɪk] [bi-laik], *adv.* Probablemente, quizá, acaso; aparentemente.

belime [bɪˈlaɪm] [bi-laim], *va.* Enligar, enviscar, untar con liga.

belittle [bɪˈlɪt] [bi-li-tel], *va.* Deprimir, hacer poco caso, dar escasa importancia. Menospreciar (achievements). Denigrar, rebajar (person). **To belittle oneself,** menospreciarse, tenerse en menos.

Belize [beˈliːz] [be-lis] *N. (Geogr.)* Belice.

bell [bel] [bel], *s.* 1. Campana (of church, clock). **Clapper of a bell,** badajo de campana. **Wing of bells,** son o toque de campanas. **Passing-bell,** campana que toca a muerto. 2. Campana, cualquier cosa que tiene semejanza de campana. **Diving** *o* **diver's bell,** campana de buzo, aparato para bucear. 3. Cascabel (on cat, toy). **To bear away the bell,** llevar el cencerro; ser el primero, ganar el premio. **To lose the bell,** ser vencido; rendirse. 4. Pabellón de un instrumento de viento. 5. Timbre (door, bicycle, telephone, timer). **Chime of bells,** repique de campanas, juego de campanas. **To set the bells going,** echar las campanas al vuelo. **To ring the bell,** (a) tocar la campana, tocar a rebato. (b) Tirar de la campanilla. **His voice was as clear as a bell,** lo oía como si estuviera a mi lado. **The name rings a bell,** me suena el nombre. **Bell tower,** campanario. **He was saved by the bell,** lo salvó la campana. **Bell-bottoms,** pantalones de pata de elefante.

bell, *vn. (Bot.)* Crecer una planta o una parte de la planta en figura de campana.

belladonna [ˌbeləˈdɒnə] [be-la-do-na], *s. (Bot.)* Belladama o belladona; hierba mora.

bellboy [ˈbelbɔɪ] [bel-boi], *s.* Botones, mozo de hotel.

bell-buoy [ˈbelbɔɪ] [bel-boi], *s.* Boya de campana.

belle [bel] [bel], *sf.* Señorita : una mujer joven y hermosa. Belleza, beldad. **The belle of the ball,** la reina de la fiesta.

bellhop [ˈbelhɒp] [bel-jop] *s.* Botones.

belles-lettres [ˈbelˈletr] [bel-letr], *s.* Bellas letras, literatura.

bell-fashioned [ˈbelˈfaʃənd] [bel-fa-shond], *a.* Campaniforme, lo que tiene la forma o figura de campana.

bell-flower [ˈbelflaʊəʳ] [bel-flauaʳ], *s. (Bot.)* 1. Ruiponce o repónchigo; campanilla. 2. Variedad de manzana.

bell-founder [ˈbelfaʊndəʳ] [bel-faun-daʳ], *s.* Campanero, el artífice que vacía y funde las campanas.

bell-glass [ˈbelglɑːs] [bel-glas], *s.* Campana de cristal.

bell-hanger [ˈbelhæŋəʳ] [bel-jan-gaʳ], *s.* Campanillero, instalador de campanillas.

bell-horse [ˈbelhɔːs] [bel-jors], *s. Cf.* BELLWETHER.

bellicose [ˈbelɪkəʊs] [be-li-kous], *a.* Belicoso, bélico, guerrero.

bellied [ˈbeliːd] [be-lid], *a.* 1. Ventrudo. 2. *(Arq.)* Combado, acombado, con barriga, convexo.

belligerent [bɪˈlɪdʒərənt] [bi-li-che-rent], *a.* Beligerante, belicoso, marcial, guerrero, agresivo.

belligerently [bɪˈlɪdʒərəntlɪ] [bi-li-che-rent-li] *adv.* Agresivamente.

bellipotent [bɪˈlɪpɒtənt] [bi-li-po-tent], *a.* Poderoso en la guerra.

bell-man [ˈbelmən] [bel-man], *s.* Pregonero de campana, el que pregona alguna cosa al son de una campana, avisador, despertador al toque de campana.

bell-metal [ˈbelmetl] [bel-me-tal], *s.* Metal campanil, el metal de que se hacen las campanas.

bell-mouthed [ˈbelmaʊθ] [bel-mauz], *a.* 1. Abocinado, de boca de campana. 2. De voz sonora y profunda.

bellow [ˈbeləʊ] [be-lou], *vn.* 1. Bramar. 2. Vociferar, gritar. 3. Bramar, embravecerse o estar agitado el mar o el viento. **To bellow at somebody,** gritarle a alguien.

bellower [ˈbeləʊəʳ] [be-lou-aʳ], *s.* Bramador, gritador.

bellow, bellowing [ˈbeləʊɪŋ] [be-louin], *s.* Bramido, rugido; grito.

bellows [ˈbeləʊz] [be-lous], *s.* Fuelle, instrumento para soplar y encender el fuego; fuelle del órgano.

bell pepper [ˈbelˈpepəʳ] [bel-pe-paʳ], *s.* CAPSICUM.

bell-pull [ˈbelpʊl] [bel-pul], *s.* Botón, tirador de campanilla. *V.* BELL-ROPE.

bell-punch [ˈbelpʌntʃ] [bel-panch], *s.* Sacabocados.

bell-ringer [ˈbelrɪŋəʳ] [bel-rin-gaʳ], *s.* Campanero, tocador de campana.

bell-rope [ˈbelrəʊp] [bel-roup], *s.* Cuerda o soga de campana.

bell-shaped [ˈbelʃeɪpt] [bel-sheipt], *a.* Campaniforme.

belluine [ˈbelʊɪn] [be-luin], *a. (Ant.)* Bestial, brutal.

bell-wether [ˈbelweðəʳ] [bel-ue-daʳ], *s.* Manso, el carnero que lleva el cencerro, y va delante, guiando a los demás.

belly [ˈbelɪ] [be-li], *s.* 1. Vientre, barriga (of person), panza (of animal), la parte del cuerpo humano desde el pecho al empeine. 2. Seno, entrañas. 3. Barriga, la parte de alguna cosa que sobresale a lo demás de ella. **Belly-band,** cincha, ventrera, cinto. **Bellyful,** panzada, hartazgo de comida, hartura. **Belly-god,** glotón, el que come mucho y desordenadamente. **Belly-slave,** esclavo de su apetito. **Belly-worm,** lombriz del vientre. -*a.* **Belly-bound,** estreñido de vientre. **Belly-pinched,** hambriento. **Belly button,** ombligo. **belly dance,** danza del vientre. **A belly laugh,** una sonora carcajada.

belly, *vn.* Hacer barriga; hartarse. -*a.* Llenar, inflar, hinchar.

bellyache [ˈbelɪeɪk] [be-li-eik] *s.* Cólico o dolor de vientre. *vn.* Rezongar, refunfuñar. **To bellyache about somebody/ something,** quejarse constantemente de alguien/algo.

bellyful [ˈbelɪfʊl] [be-li-ful] *s.* **To have had a bellyful (of somebody/something),** estar hasta la coronilla (de alguien/algo).

belong [bɪˈlɒŋ] [bi-lon], *vn.* 1. Pertenecer, tocar a alguno o ser propia de él alguna cosa (be property). **It belongs to her,** es de ella, le pertenece (a ella). **Does this belong to you?,** ¿esto es tuyo? 2. Tocar a alguno por oficio u obligación. 3. Concernir, mirar a, tocar a. 4. Residir, estar domiciliado en, ser natural de; tener lugar o esfera apropiada. **He belongs in Quito,** reside en Quito. **That jug belongs in the cupboard,** esa jarra va en el armario (have as usual place). **It belongs to the reptile family,** pertenece a la familia de los reptiles (in category). **I don't feel I belong here,** no me siento a gusto aquí (socially).

belongings [bɪˈlɒŋɪŋz] [bi-lon-guings], *s.* pl. Efectos, enseres, posesiones. **You and all your belongings,** usted y todo lo que le pertenece. **Personal belongings,** efectos u objetos personales.

belove [ˈbɪlʌv] [bi-lav], *va.* Amar; usado solamente en la voz pasiva.

beloved [bɪˈlʌvɪd] [bi-la-vid], *a/s.* Querido, amado. *pp.* de BELOVE.

below [bɪˈləʊ] [bi-lou], *prep.* 1. Debajo, en par (under). 2. Debajo, inferior en dignidad o excelencia (inferior, junior to). **The room directly below this one,** la habitación justo debajo o abajo de ésta. -*adv.* Abajo (underneath), por bajo, por debajo de (less than). **Below average,** inferior a o por debajo de la media. **Below zero,** bajo cero. **Put it on the shelf below,** ponlo en el estante de abajo. **See diagram below,** véase el diagrama más abajo (in text). **He is there below,** él está allá abajo. **The regions below,** las regiones infernales. **Below par,** desigual; a descuento; pierde o está más bajo que el valor figurado, hablando de letras de cambio o del papel moneda.

belt [belt] [belt], *s.* 1. Cinto o cinturón, faja (clothing). **To have something under one's belt,** tener algo a las espaldas, tener algo en el haber. **To hit below the belt,** dar un golpe bajo. **To tighten one's belt,** apretarse el cinturón. 2. Correa de transmisión. 3. Zona, región ancha sobre un globo o esfera; extensión considerable de terreno que tiene forma de banda (area). **A belt of low pressure,** un frente de bajas presiones. **The industrial belt,** el cinturón industrial. **The cotton belt,** la zona o región algodonera. 4. Toda fuerza o influencia que restriñe. **Sword-belt,** biricú, o cinturón. **Shoulder-belt,** tahalí.

belt, *va.* 1. Cercar, rodear con una correa. 2. Azotar con una correa, dar latigazos. Darle una paliza a. **He belted me on the ear** o **(GB) round the ear,** me dio un tortazo o un trancazo. *Vn. (Fam.)* **To belt along/in,** ir/entrar zumbando. **To belt down,** tomarse una. **He's belting them down,** está empinando el codo. **Belt out,** cantar a grito pelado (sing); tocar muy fuerte (play). *(Fam.)* **Belt up,** callarse la boca, cerrar el pico (be quiet). Ponerse el cinturón (auto).

belt-saw [beltˈsɔː] [belt-so], *s.* Sierra sin fin, sierra de cinta. *V.* BAND-BAW.

belting [ˈbeltɪŋ] [bel-tin], *s.* 1. Correaje, correas motoras o de transmisión. 2. Material de que se hacen las correas. *(Coloq,)* Paliza.

beltway [ˈbeltweɪ] [belt-uei] *s.* Carretera o ronda de circunvalación, periférico.

beluga [beˈlɔɡə] [be-lu-ga], *s.* 1. La ballena blanca de los mares árticos. 2. El gran esturión blanco.

belvedere [ˈbelvədərə] [bel-ve-de-re], *s.* Belvedere, glorieta.

bemangle [ˈbemæŋl] [be-man-gel], *va.* Lacerar. *V.* MANGLE.

bemask [ˈbɪmɑːsk] [bi-maks], *va.* Esconder, tapar, ocultar.

bemaze [ˈbɪmeɪz] [bi-meis], *va.* Confundir, enredar; descaminar.

bemire [ˈbɪmaɪəʳ] [bi-maiaʳ], *va.* Enlodar, encenegar, emporcar.

bemoan [bɪˈməʊn] [bi-moun], *va.* Lamentar, deplorar, plañir.

bemoanable [bɪˈməʊnəbl] [bi-mouna-bol], *a.* Lamentable.

bemoaner [bɪˈməʊnəʳ] [bi-mounaʳ], *s.* Lamentador, plañidor.

bemoaning [bɪˈməʊnɪŋ] [bi-mounin], *s.* Lamentación.

bemock [ˈbɪmɒk] [bi-mok], *va.* Mofarse, reírse de.

bemuse [bɪˈmjuːz] [bi-mius], *va.* Embriagar ligeramente, dejar algo atontado, como con los efectos del licor. Desconcertar (puzzle). **Bemused,** de desconcierto (expression).

bench [bentʃ] [bench], *s.* 1. Banco (seat), asiento largo con respaldo o sin él. **Work bench,** mesa de trabajo. 2. *(Law)* Tribunal de justicia en Inglaterra. **The bench** o **the Bench,** la judicatura (judges collectively); el tribunal (tribunal). *s.* Las personas sentadas en un banco. **King's** o **Queen's**

Bench, un tribunal principal de justicia, y una prisión de Londres. **Bench show,** exposición de perros, bajo cubierto, en casetas colocadas sobre bancos. **Bench warrant,** auto de prisión expedido por uno de los tribunales superiores. **To play to empty benches,** representar para las butacas, es decir, ante muy reducido público. **The bench,** el banquillo o la banca (sport).

bench *va.* 1. Hacer bancos o asientos. 2. Asentar sobre un banco. 3. Mandar al banquillo o a la banca.

bencher [bentʃəʳ] [ben-chaʳ], *s.* 1. Nombre de los decanos de los colegios de abogados. 2. Individuo de algún ayuntamiento. 3. Asesor.

bend [bend] [bend], *va.* (*pret.* y *pp.* BENT). 1. Encorvar, doblar, plegar o torcer alguna cosa poniéndola corva. **Do not bend,** no doblar. **He was bent double with pain,** se retorcía de dolor. 2. Dirigir, inclinar o encaminar a cierto o determinado paraje. 3. Sujetar, vencer. 4. Tender, estirar. 5. *(Fig.)* Dirigir, aplicar; concentrar (energies, attention). 6. *(Mar.)* Entalingar, amarrar (cable), envergar (sail). -*vn.* 1. Encorvarse, doblarse. 2. Inclinarse, bajar o encorvar el cuerpo para significar rendimiento, sumisión o cortesía. 3. Ceder, doblarse. **The beam bent under the weight,** la viga cedió bajo el peso. **Bent on mischief,** determinado a hacer mal. **To bend back,** encorvar o doblar hacia atrás. **To bend one's brows,** fruncir o arrugar las cejas. **To bend the head,** inclinar o bajar la cabeza. **To bend the knee,** doblar la rodilla. **To bend one's efforts** o **endeavors,** dirigir o encaminar sus esfuerzos. **To bend down,** inclinarse, torcerse, pandearse, ladearse. **To bend to something,** ceder a algo (submit). **Bend down,** agacharse. **Bend over,** inclinarse.

bend *s.* 1. Comba, encorvadura. 2. Venda. Bends, *(Mar.)* Las ligazones de cada una de las cuadernas de una embarcación, desde la quilla hasta el remate del costado. *(Her.)* Bandas. **Bend sinister,** *(Her.)* Barm, figura ordinaria del escudo que coge desde el ángulo izquierdo superior al derecho inferior.

bendable [ˈbendəbl] [ben-da-bol], *a.* Flexible, se puede doblar; plegable.

bender [ˈbendəʳ] [ben-daʳ], *s.* El que encorva o tuerce alguna cosa. *(Coloq,)* Juerga. **To go on a bender,** irse de juerga.

bending [ˈbendɪŋ] [ben-din], *s.* Pliegue, doblez, encorvadura, comba; pendiente, declive; rodeo vuelta.

bendlet [ˈbendlɪt] [bend-let], *s. (Her.)* Banda pequeña, de media anchura.

bendwith [ˈbendwɪt] [bend-uit], *s. (Bot.)* Viburno, especie de arbusto.

beneaped [ˈbeniːpt] [be-nípt], *a. (Mar.)* Varado, encallado.

beneath [bɪˈniːθ] [bi-níz], *adv.* y *prep.* Bajo o en paraje más bajo, debajo, abajo; del centro, de lo más hondo (under). **The city lay spread out beneath us,** la ciudad se extendía a nuestros pies. **Those beneath him,** los que están por debajo de él (inferior to). **She married beneath her,** no se casó bien. **It's beneath her,** es indigno de ella (unworthy of). **You're beneath contempt,** no mereces ni desprecio. **I wondered what lay beneath,** me preguntaba qué habría debajo o abajo.

benedictine [ˌbenɪˈdɪktɪn] [be-ni-dik-tin], *s.* y *a.* Benedictino, benito.

benediction [ˌbenɪˈdɪkʃən] [be-ni-dik-shon], *s.* Bendición.

benefactor [ˈbenɪfæktəʳ] [be-ni-fak-toʳ], *s.* Bienhechor, benefactor; fundador; patrón.

benefaction [ˈbenɪfækʃən] [be-ni-fak-shon], *s.* Beneficio, favor, gracia.

benefactress [ˈbenɪfækreɪs] [be-ni-fak-tres], *sf.* Bienhechora, benefactora; fundadora, patrona.

benefice [ˈbenɪfɪs] [be-ne-fis], *s.* 1. Beneficio, el bien que se hace a otro. 2. Beneficio eclesiástico.

beneficed [ˈbenɪfɪst] [be-ne-fist], *a.* Beneficiado, el que goza algún beneficio eclesiástico.

beneficence [bɪˈnrfɪsəns] [bi-ni-fi-sens], *s.* Beneficencia; liberalidad, largueza.

beneficent [bɪˈnɪrfɪsənt] [bi-ni-fi-sent], *a.* Benéfico, el que o lo que hace bien.

beneficently [bɪˈnɪrfɪsəntlɪ] [bi-ni-fi-sent-li], *adv.* Benéficamente.

beneficial [ˌbenɪˈfɪʃəl] [be-ni-fi-shal], *a.* Beneficioso, provechoso, útil, ventajoso. **To be beneficial to somebody/something,** ser beneficioso para alguien/algo.

beneficially [ˌbenɪˈfɪʃəlɪ] [be-ni-fi-sha-li], *adv.* Beneficamente, provechosamente.

beneficialness [ˌbenɪˈfɪʃəlnɪs] [be-ni-fi-shal-nes], *s.* Utilidad, provecho.

beneficiary [ˌbenɪˈfɪʃərɪ] [be-ni-fi-sha-ri], *s.* 1. Beneficiario, persona que recibe un beneficio, a manera de privilegio o concesión caritativa. 2. Beneficiado, el que está en posesión de algún beneficio eclesiástico.

benefit [ˈbenɪfɪt] [be-ni-fit], *s.* 1. Beneficio (good), el bien que se hace o recibe; bondad, favor, gracia, servicio. 2. Utilidad, provecho, ventaja (advantage). **It will be of great benefit to them,** será muy beneficioso para ellos, les beneficiará mucho. **To give somebody the benefit of the doubt,** darle a alguien el beneficio de la duda. 3. Prestación. **He's on unemployment benefits,** recibe subsidio de desempleo o de cesantía, está cobrando el paro. Beneficio o ventaja (extrasalarial).

benefit, *va.* Beneficiar, hacer bien. *-vn.* Aprovecharse a utilizarse, prevalerse, beneficiarse. **He didn't benefit much from the experience,** no sacó mucho (provecho) de la experiencia. **You will all benefit from the change,** todos se van a beneficiar con el cambio.

Benelux [ˈbenɪlʌks] [be-ni-luks] *N.* (*Geogr.*) Benelux.

benet [ˈbenet] [be-net], *va.* Asechar, hacer caer en el lazo: poner asechanzas, lazos.

benevolence [bɪˈnevələns] [bi-ne-vo-lans], *s.* 1. Benevolencia, bondad, amor, buena voluntad, afecto, amistad. 2. Benevolencia, el bien hecho o recibido; donativo gratuito, servicio.

benevolent [bɪˈnevələnt] [bi-ne-vo-lent], *a.* Benévolo (person, smile), el que tiene buena voluntad o afecto a otro; dulce, clemente. De benevolencia (gesture). Benéfico, de beneficencia (society, organization).

benevolently [bɪˈnevələntlɪ] [bi-ne-vo-lent-li], *adv.* Benignamente, con benevolencia.

bengal [benˈgɔːl] [ben-gal], *s.* Bengala, especie de tela delgada de Bengala. **Bengal light,** luz de Bengala.

Bengali [benˈgɔːlɪ] [ben-ga-lí], *s.* Bengalí, lengua que se habla en Bengala. *-a.* Bengalí, de Bengala.

benight [bɪˈnaɪt] [bi-nait], *va.* Cogerle a uno la noche, anochecerse a uno; oscurecer.

benighted [bɪˈnaɪtɪd] [bi-nai-tid], *pp.* Anochecido. **We were benighted about four miles from town,** nos anocheció a unas cuatro millas de la ciudad. (*Fig.*) **To be benighted,** (a) estar ciego o sin luz, descarriado, extraviado, errante. (b) Estar sin saber, ignorante.

benign [bɪˈnaɪn] [bi-nain], *a.* 1. Benigno, afable, generoso, liberal, dulce, humano, obsequioso, servicial, benévolo (person, attitude). 2. Benigno, saludable.

benignant [bɪˈnɪgnənt] [bi-nig-nant], *a.* Benéfico, propicio.

benignity [bɪˈnɪgnɪtɪ] [bi-nig-ni-ti], *s.* 1. Benignidad, bondad, dulzura. 2. Benignidad, salubridad.

benignly [bɪˈnaɪnlɪ] [bi-nain-li], *adv.* Benignamente, con benevolencia, benévolamente.

benison [bɪˈnɪsən] [bi-ni-son], *s. V.* BENEDICTION.

benjamin [ˈbendʒəmɪn] [ben-ya-min], *s.* Corrupción de BENZOIN.

bennet, herb bennet [ˈbenet] [be-net], *s.* (*Bot.*) Gariofilata o gariofilea.

ben-nut [ˈbenʌt] [be-nat], *s.* Nuez de ben o behén de que se saca un aceite fragante.

benorth [ˈbɪnɔːθ] [bi-norz], *prep.* (*Esco.*) Al norte de.

bent [bent] [bent], *s.* 1. Encorvadura, la acción de poner o estar una cosa en figura corva y torcida. 2. Último esfuerzo. 3. Disposición, inclinación propensión, determinación, dirección, tendencia (determined). **To be bent on doing**

something, estar empeñado en hacer algo. 4. Pendiente, declive, cuesta. 5. (*Carp.*) Una sección del maderamen de un edificio que se arma y concierta en tierra, y luego se alza y coloca en posición de una vez. También, una viga grande. **To follow one's bent,** seguir su inclinación, sus gustos. **People with an artistic bent,** personas con inclinaciones artísticas. **To be bent,** ser del otro bando (homosexual).

bent, *pp.* 1. Dirigido o inclinado a determinado paraje. 3. Determinado, resuelto. *V.* BEND. 3. Inclinado, encorvado, tendido. **To be bent upon,** tener mucho empeño en; estar determinado o decidido a; no penar más que en.

benumb [bɪˈnʌmb] [bi-namb], *va.* Entorpecer, dejar torpe o casi sin movimiento. **Benumbed with cold,** yerto, traspasado de frío.

benumbedness [bɪˈnʌmbɪdnɪs] [bi-nam-bid-nes], *s.* Entorpecimiento.

benzene [ˈbenziːn] [ben-sín], *s. V.* BENZOLE.

benzin, benzine [ˈbænziːn] [ben-sín], *s.* Bencina, sustancia, líquida, incolora, de olor penetrante, inflamable y algo volátil, compuesta de carbono y de hidrógeno; la cual se obtiene de varias materias y principalmente de la brea o del aceite de hulla.

benzoic [ˈbenzɔɪk] [ben-soik], *a.* Benzoico, perteneciente o relativo al benjuí.

benzoin [ˈbenzɔɪn] [ben-soin], *s.* 1. Benjuí o menjuí, especie de resina aromática y medicinal que viene de las Indias orientales. *V.* STYRAX. 2. *V.* SPICEBUSH. 3. (*Quím.*) Compuesto cristalizable ($C_{14}H_{12}O_2$) que se obtiene por diversos procedimientos.

benzole [ˈbensɔəl] [ben-soul], o **benzol,** *s.* Benzole, líquido volátil, muy inflamable, obtenido por destilación de ácido benzoico.

bepaint [bɪˈpeɪnt] [bi-peint], *va.* Colorar, dar color, teñir alguna cosa.

bepinch [beˈpɪntʃ] [be-pinch], *va.* Pellicar, señalar con pellizcos.

bepowder [bɪˈpaʊdəʳ] [bi-pau-daʳ], *va.* Empolvar (los cabellos).

bepraise [bɪˈpreɪs] [bi-preis], *va.* Lisonjear hiperbólicamente.

bepurple [bɪˈpɜːpl] [bi-par-pel], *va.* Purpurar, teñir de púrpura.

bequeath [bɪˈkwiːð] [bi-kuiz], *va.* 1. Mandar, legar o donar alguna cosa a otro en testamento. 2. Transmitir a la posteridad.

bequeath [bɪˈkwiːðəʳ] [bi-kuizaʳ], *s. V.* TESTATOR.

bequest [bɪˈkwest] [bi-kuest], *s.* Manda, donación legado que alguno deja a otro en su testamento.

berate [bɪˈreɪt] [bi-reit], *va.* Zaherir, reñir, poner a uno como nuevo. **To berate somebody,** reprender o amonestar a alguien.

berber [ˈbɜːbəʳ] [ber-baʳ], *s.* Berberí o Bereber.

berberry [ˈbɜːberɪ] [ber-beri], *s.* Berberís, agracejo. *V.* BARBERRY.

bere [ˈbɜːʳ] [baʳ], *s.* (*Esco.*) Especie de cebada, farro.

bereave [bɪˈriːv] [bi-rív], *va.* 1. Despojar, quitar o privar a alguno de lo que goza y tiene, o desposeerle con violencia de ello; arrebatar. 2. Desolar, acongojar.

bereaved [bɪˈriːvd] [bi-rívd] *a.* Desconsolado, afligido (due to a death). *s.* **The bereaved,** los deudos, la familia del difunto.

bereavement [bɪˈriːvmənt] [bi-rív-ment], *s.* Privación, despojo, desamparo: aflicción, dolor, pesar (for a death). **They have suffered o had a bereavement in the family,** han sufrido la pérdida de un familiar.

bereft [bɪˈreft] [bi-reft] *a.* **To be bereft of something,** verse privado de algo. **Totally bereft of inspiration,** desprovisto de toda inspiración.

beret [ˈbereɪ] [be-rei], *s.* Boina.

berg [bɜːg] [berg], *s.* Gran masa o témpano de hielo.

bergamot [ˈbɜːgəmɒt] [ber-ga-mot], *s.* (*Bot.*) 1. Bergamota, variedad de pera. 2. Bergamota, especie de lima muy aromática, de cuya corteza se extrae el aceite esencial de su nombre. 3. Especie de rapé o tabaco en polvo rociado con la esencia de bergamota.

bergmaster [ˈbɜːɡmɑːstəʳ] [berg-mas-taʳ], s. Burgomaestre, bailío.

berhyme [ˈbɜːhaɪm] [ber-jaim], va. Elogiar a uno en verso rimado.

berk [bɜːk] [berk] s. (GB) Imbécil.

Berlin [bɜːˈlɪn] [ber-lin], s. Berlina, coche de dos asientos. **Berlin blue,** azul de Prusia. **Berlin wool,** estambre. N. (Geogr.) Berlín.

bermuda shorts [bɜːˈmjuːdə] [ber-miu-da], s. pl. Cierto estilo de calzones que llegan a la rodilla. N. las (islas) Bermudas. **The Bermuda Triangle,** el triángulo de las Bermudas.

Bermudas [bɜːˈmjuːdəz] [ber-miu-das] s. pl. Bermudas.

Bern, Berne [bɜːn] [bern] N. (Geogr.) Berna.

bernicle [ˈbɜːnɪkl] [ber-ni-kel], s. Bernacho, especie de ánsar.

berry [ˈberɪ] [be-ri], s. (Bot.) Baya, fruta pequeña, que crían varios árboles y arbustos: grano. (Culin.) Fresas, frambuesas, moras, etc. **As brown as a berry,** negro como el carbón. **Avignon, French** o **yellow berries,** granas de Aviñón, pizacantas.

berry, vn. Producir bayas.

berry-bearing [ˈberɪˈbeərɪŋ] [be-ri-bea-rin], a. Bacífero, que lleva bayas; se dice de los árboles.

berserk [ˈbɜːsɜːk] [ber-sek] a. **To go bersek,** ponerse como una fiera o como un loco.

berth [bɜːθ] [berz], s. 1. Camarote de marinero (cabin). 2. Anclaje, estación de un buque. 3. (Fam.) Empleo, destino. 4. Cada una de las literas, camas o catres fijos construídos en los camarotes de los buques; cama en coche dormitorio de ferrocarril (couchette, bunk). 5. Atracadero (mooring). **To give somebody a wide berth,** eludir o rehuir a alguien. **A starting berth,** un puesto de (jugador) titular (sport).

berth, va. Proporcionar o dar un berth, ya en sentido literal ya en el de colocación, destino o empleo.

bertha [bɜːθə] [ber-ta], s. 1. Berta, pañoleta de mujer. 2. Bert, nombre propio.

berthage [ˈbɜːθeɪɡ] [ber-zeich], s. 1. Derechos de anclaje o de estación de un buque. 2. El lugar destinado a cada buque en un puerto.

bertram [ˈbɜːtrəm] [ber-tram], s. (Bot.) Agerato o alterreina.

beryl [ˈberɪl] [be-ril], s. Berilo, piedra preciosa; agua marina.

berylline [ˈberɪliːn] [be-ri-lin], a. Lo perteneciente al berilo.

bescrawl [ˈbeskrɔːl] [bes-krol], va. Escarabajear, garabatear, garrapatear.

bescribble [ˈbeskrɪbl] [bes-kri-bol], va. Borrajear.

beseech [bɪˈsiːtʃ] [bi-sich], va. Suplicar, rogar, pedir, implorar, hacer instancias, conjurar.

beseecher [bɪˈsiːtʃəʳ] [bi-si-chaʳ], s. Rogador, suplicante, implorante.

beseeching [bɪˈsiːtʃɪŋ] [bi-si-chin], s. Ruego, instancia, súplica.

beseem [bɪˈsiːm] [bi-sim], va. Convenir, parecer bien. -vn. Aparecerse, parecer.

beseeming [bɪˈsiːmɪŋ] [bi-si-min], s. Gracia, donaire, decencia, decoro, bienparecer, propiedad. -part. adj. Conveniente, decoroso.

beseemly [bɪˈsiːmlɪ] [bi-sim-li], a. Decoroso, gracioso, decente.

beset [bɪˈset] [bi-set], va. (pret. y pp. BESET). 1. Sitiar, rodear. 2. Acosar, perseguir, acechar, espiar. **Beset with troubles,** lleno de disgustos. **A besetting sin,** vicio habitual y dominante, flaco de una persona. **He was besetted by doubts,** lo acosaban las dudas. **The way ahead is besetted with difficulties,** tenemos (o tienen) muchos obstáculos por delante.

beside [bɪˈsaɪd] [bi-said], prep. 1. Cerca, al lado de otro (at the side of). **She's the one beside me in the photograph,** es la que está a mi lado o junto a mí en la foto. 2. Excepto. 3. Sobre; fuera de. -adv. Además, a más de esto, por otra

parte, aun, fuera de esto o ello, fuera de que. **To be beside oneself,** estar loco o fuera de sí, haber perdido la cabeza o el juicio; estar desatinado. **That's beside the point,** eso no tiene nada que ver, eso no viene al caso.

besides [bɪˈsaɪdz] [bi-saids] prep. Además de (in addition to) **There are five others coming besides you,** además de o aparte de ti, vienen otros cinco. Excepto, aparte de, fuera de (apart from). **No one knows besides you,** nadie lo sabe aparte de ti, excepto tú o fuera de ti. adv. Además. **And plenty more besides,** y mucho más todavía.

besiege [bɪˈsiːdʒ] [bi-sidch], va. 1. Sitiar, poner sitio a alguna plaza. 2. (Met.) Sitiar, asediar, acosar a alguno. **Besieged by applicants for office,** asediado de pretendientes. **An angry crowd besieged the embassy,** una muchedumbre enfurecida rodeó o cercó la embajada. **The village was besieged by reporters,** el pueblo se vio asediado por periodistas.

besieger [bɪˈsiːdʒəʳ] [bi-sichaʳ], s. Sitiador, el que pone sitio a alguna plaza.

besieging [bɪˈsiːdʒɪŋ] [bi-si-chin], s. Sitio, cerco.

beslave [bɪˈsleɪv] [bis-leiv], va. Esclavizar.

beslobber [bɪˈslɒbəʳ] [bis-lo-baʳ], va. Salpicar o ensuciar.

besmear [bɪˈsmiːəʳ] [bis-miaʳ], va. 1. Salpicar, ensuciar. 2. Embadurnar.

besmearer [bɪˈsmiːərəʳ] [bis-mia-raʳ], s. Ensuciador.

besmirch [bɪˈsmɜːtʃ] [bis-merch], va. 1. Manchar, ensuciar. 2. Deshonrar, despreciar, mancillar.

besmoke [bɪˈsmək] [bis-mouk], va. 1. Ahumar, llenar de humo alguna cosa. 2. Ahumar, poner al humo alguna cosa para que la cure.

besmut [bɪˈsmʌt] [bis-mat], va. Tiznar con humo u hollín.

besnuffed [bɪˈsnʌft] [bis-naf], a. Manchado con tabaco en polvo o rapé.

besom [ˈbiːzəm] [bi-sem], s. Escoba, manojo de ramillas que se usa para barrer.

besot [bɪˈsɒt] [bi-sot], va. Infatuar, entontecer; embrutecer.

besotted [bɪˈsɒtɪd] [bi-so-tid] a. **He's totally besotted with her,** está perdidamente enamorado de ella, está loco por ella.

besottedly [bɪˈsɒtɪdlɪ] [bi-so-tid-li], adv. Tontamente.

besottedness [bɪˈsɒtɪdnɪs] [bi-so-tid-nes], s. Entontecimiento, fatuidad; embrutecimiento.

besought [bɪˈsɔːt] [bi-sot], pret. y pp. del verbo TO BESEECH.

bespangle [bɪˈspæŋɡl] [bis-pangel], va. Matizar, adornar con matices o con lentejuelas.

bespatter [bɪˈspætəʳ] [bi-spa-taʳ], va. 1. Salpicar, manchar con agua, lodo o suciedad. 2. Disfamar, desacreditar.

bespeak [bɪˈspiːk] [bis-pik], va. 1. Encomendar, mandar, ordenar, encargar a otro alguna cosa para que la haga; apalabrar alguna cosa. Mandar hacer; apalabrar. **To bespeak a pair of shoes,** encargar un par de zapatos. 2. Predecir, adivinar. 3. Hablar a alguno. 4. Demostrar, da a conocer. **His behaviour bespeaks a composed mind,** su porte demuestra un ánimo tranquilo 5. Alquilar. 6. Prevenir, advertir.

bespeaker [bɪˈspiːkəʳ] [bis-pikaʳ], s. El que encarga alguna cosa.

bespeckle [bɪˈspekl] [bis-pi-kel], va. Abigarrar, gayar, pintorrear o pintarrajear alguna cosa.

bespectacled [bɪˈspektɪkld] [bis-pek-ta-kled] a. De anteojos o lentes, con gafas.

bespew [bɪˈspjuː] [bis-piu], va. Ensuciar alguna cosa con vómito.

bespice [bɪˈspiːs] [bis-pis], va. Condimentar, sazonar con especias o condimentos.

bespit [bɪˈspɪt] [bis-pit], va. Escupir; ensuciar con saliva, escupidura o gargajos. -s. Salivazo.

bespoke [bɪˈspək] [bis-pouk], bespoken, pret. y pp. del verbo TO BESPEAK. Mandado, ordenado, alquilado, prevenido; mandado a hacer. (GB) **Bespoke tailor,** trajes a medida.

bespot [bɪ'spɒt] [bis-pot], *va.* Abigarrar, salpicar de manchitas.

bespread [bɪ'spred] [bis-pred], *va.* Cubrir, tender una cosa sobre otra.

besprent [bɪ'sprent] [bis-prent], *a. (Poét.)* Rociado, esparcido.

besprinkle [bɪ'sprɪŋkl] [bis-prinkl], *va.* Rociar, esparcir alguna cosa sobre otra.

besprinkler [bɪ'sprɪŋklər] [bis-prinklaʳ], *s.* Rociador, el que rocía o esparce.

besputter [bɪ'spʌtər] [bis-pa-taʳ], *va.* Salpicar o ensuciar con escupiduras o saliva.

best [best] [best], *a.* Superlativo de *Good* (bueno). óptimo, superior, lo mejor, lo más bueno. **He was the best,** él era el mejor. **For the best part of an hour,** durante casi una hora. **Best of all was the windsurfing,** lo mejor de todo fue el windsurf. **The best things in life are free,** los mejores placeres no cuestan dinero (set phrase). **May the best man/team win,** que gane el mejor (set phrase). **She knows what's the best for you,** ella sabe qué es lo que más te conviene. **Best before July 29,** consumir preferentemente antes del 29 de julio. *-adv.* (sup. of WELL) Más bien, mejor y rectamente, más oportunamente. **Which color suits me the best?,** ¿qué color me queda mejor? **I love that best of all,** prefiero aquello a todo lo demás. **To do one's best,** hacer todo lo que se puede, o cuanto se puede. **The second best,** el segundo en los premios, es decir, el mejor después del primero. **To make the best of a bad game,** salir de un mal paso o negocio lo mejor posible. **He had the best of it,** se llevó la mayor parte, sacó para sí toda la ventaja. **At best, at the best,** a lo más, lo más; cuando mejor. **It's best forgotten,** más vale olvidarlo. *-s.* Lo mejor. **Choose ABC hotels when only the best will do,** si usted exige lo mejor, escoja hoteles ABC. **He is in the best of health,** está en excelente estado de salud. **It's the best I can do,** no lo puedo hacer mejor. **To the best of my knowledge,** que yo sepa. **It all turned out for the best in the end,** al final todo fue para bien. **Even the best of us are wrong sometimes,** todos nos equivocamos. **They're the best of friends,** son de lo más amigos. **She's not at her best in the morning,** la mañana no es su mejor momento del día. **It's British theater at its best,** es un magnífico exponente del teatro británico. **The roses were past their best,** las rosas ya no estaban en su mejor momento. **All the best!,** ¡buena suerte!, ¡que te vaya bien! (in greetings). Récord. **A personal best for Flynn,** un récord para Flynn (sport).

bestain ['besteɪn] [bes-tein], *va.* Manchar, llenar de manchas.

bestial ['bestɪəl] [bes-tial], *a.* Bestial, brutal; carnal. Salvaje (cruelty, crime).

bestiality [ˌbestɪ'ælɪtɪ] [bes-tia-li-ti], *s.* Bestialidad, brutalidad, irracionalidad (cruelty). Bestialidad (sex with animals).

bestialize ['bestɪəlaɪz] [bes-tia-lais], *va.* Obrar como bestia.

bestir [bɪ'stɜːʳ] [bis-taʳ], *va.* Mover, menear, incitar. *-vn.* Removerse, intrigar.

best man [ˌbes'mæn] [best-man], *s.* Padrino de boda. Amigo que acompaña al novio el día de la boda. Padrino, testigo.

bestow [bɪ'stəʊ] [bis-tou], *va.* 1. Dar, conferir, otorgar (title, award). 2. Dar de limosna. 3. Dar en matrimonio. 4. Regalar, dar como presente o dádiva. 5. Emplear, gastar. **He bestowed his affections on her,** la hizo depositaria de su amor.

bestowal [bɪ'stəʊəl] [bis-toual], *s.* Acción de dar, o presentar; dádiva presentación.

bestower [bɪ'stəʊəʳ] [bis-touaʳ], *s.* Regalador.

bestraddle [bɪ'strædl] [bis-tra-del], **bestride** [bɪ'straɪd] [bis-traid], *va.* 1. Montar a horcajadas. 2. Zanquear, atrancar. 3. Atravesar. *V.* STRIDE. *-pret.* BESTODE, *pp.* BESTRIDDEN.

bestrew, bestrow [bɪ'struː] [bis-tru], *va.* Rociar, esparcir, derramar sobre.

best-seller ['best'selər] [best-se-laʳ] *s.* Bestseller, superventas (book). Superventas (product). Autor de bestsellers (author).

best-selling ['best'selɪŋ] [best-se-lin] *a.* **A best-selling book,** un libro de gran éxito de ventas, un superventas. **A best-selling writer,** un escritor que tiene gran éxito de ventas.

bet [bet] [bet], *s.* Apuesta, acción de apostar (wager); cantidad o premio de la apuesta. **I had/made a bet with Charlie that Brazil would win,** le aposté a Charlie que ganaría Brasil. **Your best bet is to stay here,** lo mejor que puedes hacer es quedarte aquí (option). **It's a pretty/good fair bet that someone here speaks English,** es casi seguro que aquí alguien habla inglés. **To hedge one's bets,** cubrirse. 1**bet,** *va.* Apostar (gamble). **How much will you bet?** ¿cuánto quiere usted apostar? **David bet him $5 the Liberals would win,** David le apostó cinco dólares a que ganaban los liberales. Jugarse, apostar (be sure). **I bet he doesn't even remember my name,** apuesto a que ni se acuerda de mi nombre. **I had a hard time persuading him-I'll bet you did!,** me costó mucho convencerlo- ¡me lo puedo imaginar! **I can do it!- I bet you can't!,** ¡a que puedo hacerlo!, ¡a que no! *(Fam.)* **You can bet your life** o **your bottom dollar,** apuesto o me juego la cabeza o camisa. *-vn.* Jugar (gamble). **I'm not a betting man, but…,** no soy jugador, pero… **I wouldn't bet on it,** yo no estaría tan seguro, no me fiaría (be sure). **Do you want to bet?,** ¿qué o cuánto te apuestas?, ¿quieres apostar? *(Coloq.)* **I bet!,** sí, seguro. 1**betake** [bɪ'teɪk] [bi-teik], *va.* (*pret.* BETOOK, *pp.* BETAKEN. 1. Recurrir, acudir. 2. Irse a un lugar o punto determinado. **To betake oneself to study,** aplicarse o darse al estudio. **To betake oneself to one's heels,** huir, escapar, tomar las de Villadiego.

beta particle ['biːtəˌpɑːtɪkl] [bi-ta-par-ti-kel], *s.* Partícula beta.

beta ray [biːtə'reɪ] [bi-ta-rei], *s.* Rayo beta.

betaron ['betərən] [be-ta-ron], *s.* Betatrón.

betel o betle ['biːtəl] [bi-tel], *s. (Bot.)* Betel.

bête noire ['beɪt'nwɑːʳ] [beit-nuaʳ], *s.* Coco, espantajo; objeto espantoso que causa terror. *(Gal.)* Bestia negra (period).

bethel ['beθəl] [be-zel], *s.* 1. Iglesia o capilla para marineros. 2. En Inglaterra, capilla de los disidentes. 3. Lugar santificado por la presencia de Dios.

bethink [bɪ'θɪŋk] [bi-zink], *va.* Recapacitar, recordar algo, volver a reflexionar sobre alguna cosa. *-vn.* Considerar, pensar, examinar.

Bethlehem ['beθlɪhem] [bez-li-jem], *s.* Belén. *V.* BEDLAM.

Bethlehemite ['beθlɪhemaɪt] [bez-li-je-mait], *s. V.* BEDLAMITE.

bethought [bɪ'θɔːt] [bi-zot], *pret.* y *pp.* del verbo TO BETHINK.

bethump [bɪ'θʌmp] [bi-zamp], *va.* Dar de puñadas.

betide [bɪ'taɪd] [bi-taid], *vn.* Suceder, acontecer, acaecer, llegar al lance, verificarse alguna cosa. *-va.* Presagiar, indicar. (liter. & arch.) WOE.

betime [bɪ'taɪm] [bi-taim], **betimes** [bɪ'taɪmz] [bi-taims], *adv.* 1. Con tiempo, en sazón. 2. Pronto, antes de mucho. 3. Temprano.

betoken [bɪ'təʊkən] [bi-tou-ken], *va.* 1. Significar, representar. 2. Anunciar, pronosticar, presagiar. 3. Marcar, designar.

betokening [bɪ'təʊkənɪŋ] [bi-tou-ke-nin], *s.* Presagio, pronóstico.

betony [bɪ'təʊnɪ] [bi-to-ni], *s. (Bot.)* Betónica., planta labiada. Stachys Betonica.

betook [bɪ'tʊk] [bi-tuk], *pret.* del verbo *To* BETAKE.

betoss [bɪ'tɒs] [bi-tos], *va.* Agitar, mover alguna cosa con violencia.

betray [bɪ'treɪ] [bi-trei], *va.* 1. Traicionar, hacer traición, vender a uno o entregarle alevosamente en manos del enemigo. **He betrayed us to the enemy,** nos vendió al enemigo. **To betray somebody's trust,** defraudar la confianza que alguien ha puesto en uno. 2. Revelar, delatar (reveal), descubrir o divulgar algún secreto. **His voice betrayed him,** su propia voz le descubrió o le vendió. 3. Exponer, arriesgar. 4. Mostrar, hacer ver.

betrayal [bɪˈtreɪəl] [bi-treial], *s.* Traición (of secrets), delación. La acción y efecto de traicionar, de revelar, de mostrar, etc. **A betrayal of confidence/trust,** abuso de confianza.

betrayed [bɪˈtreɪd] [bi-treid], *pp.* Vendido, descubierto engañado alevosamente. V. BETRAY.

betrayer [bɪˈtreɪər] [bi-treiar], *s.* Traidor.

betrim [bɪˈtrɪm] [bi-trim], *va.* Acicalar, pulir, adornar.

betroth [bɪˈtraʊð] [bi-trouz], *va.* 1. Desposar, contraer esponsales. 2. Dar palabra de casamiento, prometer en matrimonio.

betrothal [bɪˈtraʊðəl] [bi-trou-zal], *s.* Esponsales, promesa de matrimonio; el acto de contraer esponsales.

better [ˈbetər] [be-tar], *a.* (comp. of GOOD) Mejor, lo que es superior a otra cosa con que se compara. **He's better at playing the guitar than at singing,** toca la guitarra mejor de lo que canta. **Fruit's much better for you than candy,** la fruta es mucho más sana que los caramelos. **Things couldn't be better,** todo va de maravilla. **To get better,** mejorar. **The bigger the better,** cuanto más grande, mejor. **The best said about it the better,** cuanto menos se hable del tema mejor. **If they can both come, so much the better,** si pueden venir los dos, mucho/tanto mejor -*adv.* (comp. of WELL) Mejor, más bien. **She swims better than I do/me,** nada mejor que yo. **We get on better than before,** nos llevamos mejor que antes. **To be better,** estar mejor de salud; ser de mejor conducta; valer más. **To make better,** mejorar una cosa o hacerla de más valor de lo que era; enmendar, corregir, reformar. **To grow better,** irse mejorando alguna cosa, enmendarse. **To grow better and better,** ir de mejor a mejor. **The better way is to,** el mejor modo o medio es. **To be better off,** estar en mejor posición, más acomodado. **Had better**(ought). **Hadn't you better phone them?,** ¿no deberías llamarlos? **Well, I'd better be off,** bueno, me tengo que ir. **You'd better not complain!,** ¡más te vale no quejarte! *(Coloq,)* **You'd better believe it!,** más vale que lo creas. **It cost me better than $100,** me costó más de 100 dólares.

better, *va.* 1. Mejorar (improve), adelantar, reformar, aumentar. 2. Sobrepujar, exceder. 3. Mejorar, superar (surpass) (record, score). **To better oneself,** superarse.

better, *s.* 1. El mejor o lo mejor, de más suposición; ventaja, mejoría (superior of two). **The better of the two,** el mejor de los dos. **For the better,** para bien, para mejor. **Things took a turn for the better,** las cosas dieron un giro positivo. **My curiosity got the better of me,** la curiosidad fue más fuerte que yo/pudo más que yo. 2. Superior, persona de rango más elevado o de mayor mérito. Superiores (superiors). **Our betters,** nuestros superiores. **His elders and betters,** sus mayores.

better, *s.* Apostador.

bettering [ˈbetərɪŋ] [be-te-rin], *s.* Mejoría.

betterment [ˈbetərmənt] [be-ter-ment], *s.* Mejora, mejoramiento, en especial de bienes raíces.

better-off [ˈbetərˌɒf] [be-ter-of] *a.* De mejor posición económica (financially). **He's better-off than her,** tiene mejor posición económica que ella, es de posición más acomodada que ella. Mejor (emotionally, physically). **I'm better-off divorced,** estoy mejor divorciado.

betting [ˈbetɪŋ] [be-tin], *s.* Apuesta. **What's the betting he won't turn up?,** ¿qué (te) apuestas (a) que no viene? **Betting shop,** agencia de apuestas.

bettor [ˈbetər] [be-tar], *s.* Apostador.

betty [ˈbetɪ] [be-ti], *s.* 1. Maricón, cominero, el hombre que se entremete en los quehaceres de mujeres. 2. *(E.U.)* Matraz, botella que tiene el cuello muy largo. 3. *(Ger.)* Pie de cabra, instrumento de hierro para romper y derribar puertas; ganzúa romana, corchete, garabato. -*n. pr.* Belica, Belita, dim. de *Elizabeth.*

between [bɪˈtwiːn] [bi-tuin], *prep.* 1. Entre, en medio de una y otra cosa (between two points, times, numbers). **Between now and Thursday,** de aquí al jueves. **It's closed between 1 and 3,** está cerrado de 1 a 3. **Nothing can come between us,** nada podrá separarnos. **Between decks,** *(Mar.)* entre puentes. 2. Entre, perteneciente a dos que están en compañía. **Between whiles,** *(Vulg.)* a ratos. **The space between,** intermedio, espacio, hueco. **Between now and then,** de aquí a allá. **They divided the money between the two,** se repartieron el dinero entre los dos. **This is strictly between you and me,** esto debe quedar entre nosotros. **We spent $250 between us,** gastamos 250 dólares entre los dos (jointly, in combination). **Between them they managed to lift it,** entre los dos consiguieron levantarlo. **Between working and training I've no time for reading,** entre el trabajo y el entrenamiento no tengo tiempo para leer (what with). *adv.* **The one between,** el/la de en medio. **There are very large houses and very small apartments and nothing (in) between,** hay casas muy grandes o apartamentos muy pequeños, pero no hay nada entre ambos.

betwixt [bɪˈtwɪkst] [bi-tuikst], *prep.* (liter. & arch.) Entre V. BETWEEN. *adv.* **They're betwixt and between, neither children nor adults,** no son ni una cosa ni otra, ni niños ni adultos.

bevatron [ˈbevətrɒn] [be-va-tron], *s. (Fís.)* Bevatrón.

bevel [ˈbevəl] [be-vel], *s.* Cartabón, instrumento que sirve para medir y formar ángulos de toda especie. **Bevel edge,** borde biselado, bisel, chaflán. **Bevel gear,** engranaje cónico: ruedas o piñones cónicos o en ángulo. **Bevel rule,** falsa regla, falsa escuadra.

bevel, *va.* Cortar un ángulo al sesgo o en chaflán, chaflanar, achaflanar, biselar.

bevelling [ˈbevəlɪŋ] [be-ve-lin], *s.* Sesgadura, chaflán, bisel, bies, corte al sesgo.

beverage [ˈbevərɪdʒ] [be-va-rich], *s.* 1. Brebaje, bebida. 2. Estrena. 3. (Dial. brit.) Propina.

bevy [ˈbevɪ] [be-vi], *s.* 1. Bandada, número crecido de aves o pájaros que vuelan juntos. 2. Compañía o junta de mujeres; corro, corrillo.

bewail [bɪˈweɪl] [bi-ueil] *va.* Llorar (loss), lamentar, lamentarse de (lack, decline), sentir, deplorar. *vn.* Plañir.

bewailing [bɪˈweɪlɪŋ] [bi-uei-lin] *s.* Lamentación, lloro, sentimiento, pesar, pena.

beware [bɪˈweər] [bi-uear], *va.* Cuidar de, mirar por. -*vn.* Guardarse, recelarse y precaverse de algún riesgo o peligro; recatarse. **Beware!,** ¡(ten) cuidado!, ¡atención! **Beware of the dog,** cuidado con el perro. **He was told to beware of pickpokets,** le dijeron que se cuidara de los carteristas o bolsistas. **Beware of imitations,** desconfíe de las imitaciones.

beweep [bɪˈwiːp] [bi-uip], *va.* Llorar, lamentar con lágrimas. -*vn.* Plañir.

bewet [bɪˈwet] [bi-uet], *va.* Mojar, humedecer alguna cosa.

bewilder [bɪˈwɪldər] [bi-uil-dar], *va.* Descaminar, descarriar, separar del camino recto o hacer perder a uno en parajes escabrosos y sin salida. Desconcertar (confuse), dejar perplejo, apabullar (overwhelm).

bewildered [bɪˈwɪldəd] [bi-uil-ded] *a.* Desconcertado, perplejo, apabullado (overwhelmed).

bewildering [bɪˈwɪldərɪŋ] [bi-uil-de-rin] *a.* Desconcertante, apabullante (overwhelming).

bewilderment [bɪˈwɪldəmənt] [bi-uil-der-ment] *s.* Perplejidad, desconcierto. **The children looked around in bewilderment,** los niños miraban perplejos a su alrededor.

bewitch [bɪˈwɪtʃ] [bi-uich], *va.* 1. Encantar, maleficiar, embrujar, hechizar (cast spell on). 2. Encantar, embelesar, cegar, hechizar, arrobar, cautivar (entrance, delight).

bewitcher [bɪˈwɪtʃər] [bi-ui-cha], *s.* 1. Encantador, brujo, hechicero. 2. Halagador, encantador, hechicero.

bewitchery [bɪˈwɪtʃərɪ] [bi-uiche-ri], **bewitchment** [bɪˈwɪtʃmənt] [bi-uich-ment], *s.* Encantamiento, hechizo; embeleso, encanto, gracia.

bewitching [bɪˈwɪtʃɪŋ] [bi-ui-chin], s. Encanto, hechizo; halago, embeleso. -a. Atractivo; encantador, hechicero (smile), cautivador (beauty).

bewitchingly [bɪˈwɪtʃɪŋlɪ] [bi-ui-chin-gli], adv. Halagüeñamente.

bewray [bɪˈwrɪ] [bi-vrei], va. (Des.) 1. Traicionar, hacer traición. 2. Hacer ver, descubrir.

bewrayer [bɪˈwreɪəʳ] [bi-reiaʳ], s. Traidor.

bey [beɪ] [bei], s. Bey, el gobernador entre los turcos.

beyond [bɪˈjɒnd] [bi-yond,], prep. 1. (on the other side of) Más allá, a la parte de allá, allende, más adelante. **I live just beyond the station,** vivo justo pasando la estación. **Beyond this point,** de aquí en adelante, más allá. 2. (further than) Fuera. **Beyond my reach,** fuera de mis alcances. **Beyond the hour,** pasada la hora. **Beyond measure,** desmesuradamente. **Beyond dispute,** incontestable. **Beyond doubt,** fuera de duda. **Beyond comprehension,** incomprensible. **I can't tell you anything beyond that,** no te puedo decir nada más que eso (more than, apart from). **It's beyond repair,** ya no tiene arreglo (past, no longer permitting). **Beyond the reach of the law,** fuera del alcance de la ley (outside reach, scope of). **Circumstances beyond our control,** circunstancias ajenas a nuestra voluntad. **His integrity is beyond question,** su integridad está fuera de toda duda. **To live beyond one's means,** vivir por encima de sus (o mis, etc.) posibilidades (surpassing). **It's beyond belief,** es increíble, es de no creer. -adv. Lejos. Más allá (in space, time) **We're planning for the year 2010 and beyond,** estamos haciendo planes para el 2010 y más allá del 2010.

bezel, bezil [ˈbɪzɪl] [bi-sil], s. Chatón, la parte de un anillo en que se engasta la piedra.

bezel [ˈbɪzɪl] [bi-sil], va. 1. Cortar un ángulo al sesgo. 2. Poner chatón, engarzar.

bezique [bɪˈziːk] [bi-saik], s. Juego de naipes.

bezoar [ˈbɪzɔːʳ] [bi-soʳ], s. Bezar, bezaar o bezoar, piedra medicinal.

bezoardic [ˈbɪzɔːdɪk] [bi-sor-dik], a. Bezoárdico.

bhp = brake horsepower.

bi- [baɪ] [bai], prefijo que significa dos, dos veces o doble. Algunas veces *bin*, por eufonía.

biangular [baɪˈæŋgjuːləʳ] [bai-an-giu-laʳ], (preferido) o **biangulated** [baɪˈæŋgjuːleɪtɪd] [bai-an-giu-lei-tid], a. Biangular, lo que tiene dos ángulos.

biannual [baɪˈænjʊəl] [bai-a-niual], a. Semestral (report), semianual. Que se celebra dos veces al año (event, festival).

biannually [baɪˈænjʊəlɪ] [bai-a-niua-li] adv. Dos veces al año.

bias [ˈbaɪəs] [baias], s. 1. Sesgo, sentido oblicuo, oblicuidad. 2. Carga o peso que se echa en un lado de un bolo para que al tirarlo se desvíe de la línea recta. 3. Propensión, inclinación, disposición; sesgo. **His scientific bias,** su inclinación por las ciencias (leanings, tendency). 4. (Fig.) Preocupación, prejuicio, parcialidad (prejudice, unfairness). **To be without bias,** ser imparcial, no ser tendencioso o parcial. **The firm's bias in favor of younger applicants,** la preferencia de la compañía por los candidatos más jóvenes. -adv. Al sesgo. **To cut on the bias,** cortar al sesgo (in sewing).

bias va. 1. Inclinar, ladear hacia una parte determinada. **Passions bias the judgment,** las pasiones arrastran o tuercen el juicio. 2. Prevenir, preocupar. 3. Ganar, atraer la voluntad de alguno. (Fig.) Preocupar, inducir a una opinión o juicio sin el debido examen. Influir en, afectar (judgment).

biased, biassed [ˈbaɪəst] [baiast], a. Tendencioso, parcial (report, criticism, judge). **To be biased against something/somebody,** estar predispuesto en contra de algo/alguien, tener prejuicio en contra de algo/alguien. **To be biased towards something/somebody,** estar predispuesto a favor de algo/alguien.

bib [bɪb] [bib], s. Babador, babero (for baby), un pedazo de lienzo que para más limpieza se pone a los niños en el

pecho. **To put on one's best bib and tucker,** ponerse sus mejores galas.

bib, va. Beber frecuentemente, beborrotear.

bibacious [bɪˈbeɪʃəs] [bi-bei-shos], a. Dado al vicio de beber, bebedor, borracho. (Fam.) Cuero.

bibasic [bɪˈbeɪsɪk] [bi-bei-sik], a. (Quím.) Bibásico, de dos bases o de doble base.

bibb [bɪb] [bib], o **bibecock,** s. Grifo, llave curva de agua.

Bible [ˈbaɪbl] [bai-bol], s. 1. Biblia, la Sagrada Escritura; ejemplar de la Biblia; también, una edición particular de las Escrituras. 2. Los libros sagrados de cualquier pueblo. **The Holy Bible,** la Sagrada o Santa Biblia. **The feminist's bible,** la biblia o el libro de cabecera de las feministas.

Bible Belt [ˈbaɪblˌbelt] [bai-bol-belt], s. Zona de los EEUU donde impera un fundamentalismo protestante.

biblical [ˈbɪblɪkəl] [bi-bli-kal], a. 1. Bíblico, que pertenece a la Biblia. 2. En consonancia con la Biblia.

bibliographer [ˌbɪblɪˈɒgrəfəʳ] [bi-blio-gra-faʳ], o s. Bibliógrafo.

bibliographical [ˌbɪblɪəʊˈgræfɪkəl] [bi-bliou-gra-fi-kal], **bibliographic** [ˌbɪblɪəʊˈgræfɪk] [bi-bliou-gra-fik] a. Bibliográfico.

bibliography [ˌbɪblɪˈɒgrəfɪ] [bi-blio-gra-fi], s. Bibliografía.

bibliomania [ˌbɪblɪəʊˈmeɪnɪə] [bi-bliou-mei-nia], s. Bibliomanía.

bibliomaniac [ˌbɪblɪəʊˈmeɪnɪæk] [bi-bliou-mei-niak], s. Bibliómano.

bibliophile [ˈbɪblɪəʊfaɪl] [bi-bliou-afil], s. Bibliófilo, aficionado a los libros.

bibliopolist [ˌbɪblɪəʊˈpɒlɪst] [bi-bliou-po-list], s. Librero.

bibulous [ˈbɪbjʊləs] [bi-biu-los], a. 1. Poroso, esponjoso. **Bibulous paper,** papel secante, papel de filtro. 2. Bebedor, borrachín.

bicapsular [baɪˈkæpsələʳ] [bi-kap-su-laʳ], a. (Bot.) Bicápsula, la planta cuya cápsula está dividida en dos partes.

bicarbonate [baɪˈkɑːbənɪt] [bai-kar-bo-neit], s. Bicarbonato, sal que contiene doble cantidad de ácido carbónico que el carbonato neutro. **Bicarbonate of soda,** bicarbonato de sodio, o de soda, o de sosa.

bice [baɪs] [bais], s. Azul de Armenia.

bicentenary [ˌbaɪsenˈtiːnərɪ] [bai-sen-ti-na-ri], **bicentennial** [ˌbaɪsenˈtenɪəl] [bai-sen-te-nial] s. Bicentenario.

bicephalous [ˈbaɪsefələs] [bai-se-fa-los], a. Bicéfalo de dos cabezas.

biceps [ˈbaɪseps] [bai-seps], s. Biceps.

bichloride [baɪˈklɔːraɪd] [bi-klo-raid], s. (Quím.) Bicloruro. Se llama también DI-CHLORID.

bichromate [ˈbaɪkrɒmeɪt] [bi-kro-meit], s. (Quím.) Bicromato.

bicipital, bicipitous [ˈbaɪsɪpɪtəl] [bai-si-pi-tal], s. Bicípite, lo que tiene dos cabezas.

bicker [ˈbɪkəʳ] [bi-kaʳ], vn. 1. Escaramucear, pelear a veces acometiendo y a veces retirándose; reñir, disputar. 2. Correr rápidamente con algún ruido, como un arroyo; chisporrotear; charlar, gorjear como los pájaros. -va. Dar o golpear muchas veces.

bicker. s. (GB) Vasija de madera para alimento y bebidas.

bickerer [ˈbɪkərəʳ] [bi-ke-raʳ], s. Escaramuzador, el que pelea haciendo escaramuzas; pendenciero.

bickering [ˈbɪkərɪŋ] [bi-ke-rin], s. Escaramuza; pendencia, riña, disputa, contestación, Peleas, discusiones.

bickern [ˈbɪkɜːn] [bi-kern], s. Pico de bigornia.

bicolor [ˈbɪkələʳ] [bi-ko-loʳ], a. Bicolor, de dos colores.

biconcave [ˈbɪkɒnkeɪv] [bi-kon-keiv], a. Bicóncavo, de dos caras cóncavas.

biconvex [ˈbɪkɒnveks] [bi-kon-veks], a. Biconvexo, de dos caras convexas.

bicornous [ˈbɪkɔːnəs] [bi-kor-nos], a. Bicorne, que tiene dos cuernos.

bicorporal [ˈbɪkɔːpərəl] [bi-kor-po-ral], a. Bicorpóreo, de dos cuerpos.

bicuspid [baɪˈkʌspɪd] [bai-kas-pid], *a*. Bicúspide, que tiene dos cúspides. *-s*. La muela inmediata al colmillo.

bicycle [ˈbaɪsɪkl] [bai-si-kol], *s*. Bicicleta, biciclo. **To ride a bicycle,** andar o montar en bicicleta. **Bicycle race,** carrera ciclista o de bicicletas. *vn*. Ir en bicicleta.

bicycling [ˈbaɪsɪklɪŋ] [bai-si-klin], *s*. Ciclismo, arte y práctica de andar en bicicleta.

bicyclist, bicycler [ˈbaɪsɪklɪst] [bsi-si-klist], *s*. Ciclista.

bid [bɪd] [bid], *s*. 1. Postura, el precio o valor que se ofrece en una venta, o almoneda pública. Oferta, puja (at auction). 2. La puja o valor que se ofrece sobre otra puja. 3. Declaración (in bridge). **No bid,** paso. 4. Intento, tentativa (attempt); intentona, conato, intento, tentativa (successful). **An escape bid,** un conato o intentona de fuga. **Their bid for power,** su intento de hacerse con el poder. **He made one last bid for freedom,** hizo un último intento de escapar.

bid, *va*. (pret. BADE, BAD o BID; *pp*. BIDDEN o BID). 1. Pedir, rogar, convidar. 2. Mandar, ordenar. 3. Ofrecer, proponer, dar, pujar (at auction). **To bid for something,** pujar por algo. 4. Sobrepujar, exceder. 5. Pronunciar, publicar, declarar (in bridge). **To bid adieu/ farewell,** despedirse. **To bid defiance to,** atreverse con. **To bid somebody welcome,** darle la bienvenida a alguien (wish, say). **To bid somebody to,** pedirle a alguien algo (request).

bidden [ˈbɪdn] [biden], *pp*. del verbo TO BID. Invitado; comandado.

bidder [ˈbɪdəʳ] [bidaʳ], *s*. El postor, el que ofrece, propone o puja el precio de alguna cosa. **The highest bidder,** el mejor postor.

bidding [ˈbɪdɪŋ] [bi-din], *s*. 1. Orden, mandato. 2. Ofrecimiento de precio por alguna cosa, postura. **Who will open the bidding at $1,000?,** ¿quién ofrece 1.000 dólares para empezar? **Bidding was brisk,** la puja estaba muy animada. **They had servants to do their bidding,** tenían criados para lo que se les antojara (wishes). **At his father's bidding,** a petición de su padre.

bide [baɪd] [baid], *va*. Sufrir, aguantar. *-vn*. Residir, vivir de asiento en alguna parte. **To bide one's time,** esperar o aguardar el momento oportuno.

bidental [baɪˈdentl] [bai-den-tal], *a*. Bidentado, que tiene dos dientes.

bidentate [baɪˈdenteɪt] [bai-den-teit], *a*. De dos dientes, bidentado.

bidet [ˈbiːdeɪ] [bi-dei], *s*. 1. Bidé, bañadera de asiento para uso de las señoras. 2. Jaca, caballo pequeño.

biding [ˈbaɪdɪŋ] [bai-din], *s*. Residencia, mansión.

biennial [baɪˈenɪəl] [bai-enial], *a*. Bienal, que dura dos años o que sucede cada dos años. *-s*. 1. Planta bienal que produce hojas y raíces el primer año, y flores con fruto el segundo, y enseguida muere. 2. Examen que se verifica una vez cada dos años en los colegios.

bier [bɪəʳ] [biaʳ], *s*. Andas, féretro, el ataúd en que llevan a enterrar los muertos. **On a bier,** en andas.

biff [bɪf] [bif] *s*. (Coloq.) Puñetazo. *va*. (Coloq.) Pegarle un puñetazo a.

bifarious [ˈbɪfərɪəs] [bi-fa-rios], *a*. Duplicado; de dos maneras.

bifer [bɪfəʳ] [bi-faʳ], *s*. Planta que produce flores o frutos dos veces al año.

biferous [ˈbɪfərəs] [bi-fe-ros], *s*. Que da dos cosechas al año.

bifocal [ˈbaɪfəʊkəl] [bai-fou-kal], *a*. Bifocal. **Bifocal glasses,** lentes o anteojos bifocales.

bifocals [ˈbaɪfəʊkəlz] [bai-fou-kals] *s. pl.* Anteojos o gafas bifocales.

bifold [ˈbaɪfəʊld] [bai-fould], *a*. Doble.

biform [ˈbaɪfɔːm] [bai-form], **biformed** [ˈbaɪfɔːmd] [bai-formd], *a*. Biforme, que tiene dos formas.

bifurcate [ˈbaɪfəkeɪt] [bai-for-keit], o **bifurcated** [ˈbaɪfəkeɪtɪd] [bai-for-kei-tid], *a*. Bifurcado, que tiene dos cabezas; que está dividido a modo de horca.

bifurcation [ˈbaɪfəkeɪʃən] [bai-for-kei-shon], *s*. División en dos partes, bifurcación.

big [bɪg] [big], *a*. 1. Grande (in size), abultado, espeso, lleno, grueso. **A big garden,** un jardín grande, un gran jardín. **Her big blue eyes,** sus grandes ojos azules. 2. Embarazada. **A woman big with child,** una mujer embarazada. 3. Hinchado, inflado. **To talk big,** echar bravatas, fanfarronadas. **To look big,** entonarse. 4. Grande, noble, generoso, valeroso, magnánimo. **Big bug,** persona de importancia o que cree serlo. **The big bang,** el big bang, la gran explosión. **Big-bellied,** ventrudo, ventroso; preñado. **Big-bodied,** grueso, gordo, repleto. **Big-boned,** huesudo, robusto. **Big business,** el gran capital. **Big cheese,** pez gordo. **Big Dipper,** la Osa Mayor. **Big-corned,** lleno de granos muy gruesos. **Big gun,** pez gordo. **Big-head,** (Vulg.) estado de presumido y arrogante. **Big-hearted,** de gran corazón, generoso. **Big-sounding,** altisonante. **Big league,** liga mayor. **Big mouth,** fanfarrón, chismoso, cotilla, hocicón. **Big-name,** de renombre, importante. **Big-swollen,** túmido, hinchado. **Big shot,** pez gordo. **Bigwig,** *s*. (Vulg.) Persona de importancia. **She's really big in Europe,** es muy conocida en Europa. **He's getting too big for his boots/breeches,** se le han subido los humos a la cabeza. **My big brother,** mi hermano mayor (older, grown up). **A big decision,** una gran decisión, una decisión importante (significant, serious). **I'm a big fan of his,** soy un gran admirador suyo (great). **A big explosion,** una gran explosión (in scale, intensity). *adv*. **To think big,** ser ambicioso, planear las cosas a lo grande (ambitiously). **To make it big,** tener un gran éxito. **Big-screen,** para la pantalla grande (version), de la pantalla grande (actor). **Big-ticket,** caro, costoso. **The big time,** el estrellato. **Big top,** carpa de circo. **Big wheel,** rueda gigante, o de la fortuna, o de Chicago, noria.

bigg, *s*. (Bot.) Especie de cebada.

bigamist [ˈbɪgəmɪst] [bi-ga-mist], *s*. Bígamo, el que tiene dos mujeres a un tiempo.

bigamous [ˈbɪgəməs] [bi-ga-mos] *a*. Bígamo.

bigamy [ˈbɪgəmɪ] [bi-ga-mi], *s*. 1. Bigamia, el delito de tener dos mujeres a un tiempo. 2. Bigamia, el estado de ser casado dos veces.

biggin [ˈbɪgɪn] [bi-guin], *s*. 1. Cafetera. 2. Capillo de niño.

biggish [ˈbɪgɪʃ] [bi-guish], *a*. Algo grande o grueso.

bighearted [ˈbɪgˈhɑːtɪd] [big-jar-tid], *a*. Generoso, magnánimo, de gran corazón.

bighorn [ˈbɪghɔːn] [big-jorn], *s*. (Zool.) Carnero de grandes cuernos de las Montañas Roqueñas, América del Norte.

bight [baɪt] [bait], *s*. (Mar.) 1. Seno de un cabo. 2. Caleta, pequeña ensenada.

bigly [ˈbɪglɪ] [bi-gli], *adv*. Orgullosamente, con orgullo y altivez, extremadamente.

bigness [ˈbɪgnɪs] [big-nes], *s*. 1. Grandeza, el exceso que tiene alguna cosa sobre lo regular y común. 2. Grandor, espesor, grosor, el tamaño de alguna cosa, sea pequeña o grande.

bigot [ˈbɪgət] [bi-got], *s*. 1. Intolerante. Fanático, el hombre que sigue un partido u opinión religiosa con preocupación y entusiasmo. 2. Beatón, santurrón, hipócrita, mojigato.

bigoted [ˈbɪgətɪd] [bi-go-tid], *a*. Ciegamente preocupado a favor de alguna cosa. Intolerante, prejuicioso.

bigotry [ˈbɪgətrɪ] [bi-go-tri], *s*. 1. Fanatismo, celo indiscreto y excesivo o preocupación en materias religiosas. 2. Hipocresía. Intolerancia.

bijou [ˈbiːdʒuː] [bi-yu] *a*. (GB) Monísimo.

bike [baɪk] [baik] (Coloq.) Bici (bicycle). Moto (motorcycle).

biker [ˈbaɪkəʳ] [bai-kaʳ] *s*. Motociclista, motorista.

bikini [brˈkiːnɪ] [bi-ki-ni], *s*. Bikini, brevísimo traje de baño femenino. **Bikini bottom/top,** parte de abajo/arriba del bikini. **Bikini line,** entrepierna, ingle.

bilander [brˈlændəʳ] [bi-lan-daʳ], *s*. Embarcación pequeña de dos palos que se usa para portear géneros.

bilateral [baɪˈlætərəl] [bai-la-te-ral], *a*. Bilateral, de dos lados.

bilberry [ˈbɪlbərɪ] [bil-be-ri], *s.* Arándano, fruta silvestre; mirtil.

bilbo [ˈbɪlbə] [bil-bo], *s.* Estoque.

bile [baɪl] [bail], *s.* 1. Bilis. 2. *(Met.)* Cólera, ira, enojo; mal genio (bad temper).

bile-duct [baɪlˈdʌkt] [bail-dakt], *s.* Conducto biliar, por donde pasa la bilis.

bilge [bɪldʒ] [bilch], *vn. (Mar.)* Hacer agua.

bilge, *s. (Mar.)* 1. Pantoque (part of hull). **Bilge-water,** agua de pantoque. **Bilge-pumps,** bombas de carena. 2. Barriga de barril. 3. *(Coloq,)* (GB) Paparruchas.

biliary [ˈbɪlɪərɪ] [bi-lia-ri], *a.* Biliario, que pertenece a los órganos que secretan la bilis.

bilingual [baɪˈlɪŋgwəl] [bai-lin-gual], *a.* 1. Bilingüe, en dos lenguas. 2. Que habla dos idiomas.

bilious [ˈbɪlɪəs] [bi-lios], *a.* Bilioso, lo que abunda en bilis. **To feel bilious,** sentirse descompuesto. **Bilious attack,** ataque al/de hígado.

biliousness [ˈbɪlɪəsnɪs] [bi-lios-nes], *s.* Biliosidad, estado bilioso.

bilk [bɪlk] [bilk], *va.* Engañar, defraudar, pegarla, chasquear, no pagar lo que se debe.

bilk, *s.* 1. Traición, engaño, 2. *(Vulg.)* Engañador, trampista, el que defrauda a sus acreedores.

bill [bɪl] [bil], *s.* 1. Pico de ave. 2. Honcejo o podadera corva. **Bill-hook** *o* **hedging bill,** podadera corva con dos filos. 3. Papel, escrito, billete, cédula. 4. *(Com.)* Cuenta, factura (invoice). **The telephone bill,** la cuenta o el recibo del teléfono. Cuenta, nota, adición (in a restaurant). 5. Billete (banknote), pagaré, letra. **A dollar bill,** un billete de un dólar. **Bill of exchange,** letra de cambio. 6. **Private bill,** proyecto de ley o estatuto, que se presenta al Parlamento de Inglaterra o al Congreso de los Estados Unidos para su aprobación. 7. Cartel, anuncio, (poster), programa (program). **To head/top the bill,** encabezar el reparto. 8. Hacha de armas. **Bill-broker,** corredor de cambios. **Bill of rights,** una de las leyes fundamentales de Inglaterra. **Play-bill,** cartel de teatro. **Bill of lading,** conocimiento de embarque; resguardo de un capitán de buque. **Bill of fare,** lista de los manjares dispuestos para comer. **Bill of health,** patente de sanidad. **Bill of mortality,** lista o relación de los muertos que ha habido en algún distrito en un tiempo determinado. **Bills payable,** letras pagaderas. **Bills receivable,** letras a cobrar. **Bill head,** encabezamiento de factura. **To sell somebody a bill of goods,** darle, pasarle, meterle gato por liebre a alguien.

bill, *vn.* Arrullar, como las palomas cuando se enamoran; acariciar. **To bill and coo,** estar como dos tortolitos. *-va.* 1. Avisar al público o publicar alguna cosa por medio de periódicos, carteles, etc. (advertise) (play, performer). 2. Pasarle la cuenta o la factura a (invoice, charge).

bill of sale [bɪlˌɒfˈseɪl] [bil-of-seil], *s.* Escritura de venta. (certificate).

billboard [ˈbɪlbɔːd] [bil-bord], *s.* Cartelera, cartel para anuncios. Valla publicitaria.

billet [ˈbɪlɪt] [bi-lit], *s.* 1. Billete, esquela. 2. Zoquete de leña para chimenea u horno. 3. Boleta.

billet, *va.* Alojar o aposentar soldados.

billet-doux [ˈbɪleɪˈduː] [bi-lit-du], *s.* Carta o esquela amorosa.

billfold [ˈbɪlfəʊld] [bil-fould], *s.* Billetera, cartera.

billiard [ˈbɪlɪəd] [bi-liard] *a.* De billar. **A billiard ball/table,** una bola/mesa de billar.

billiards [ˈbɪlɪədz] [bi-liards], *s.* Billar, juego a modo del de los trucos. **Billiard ball,** billa, bola de billar. **Billiard cue,** taco. **Billiard-cloth,** paño de billar. **Billiard-pocket,** tronera de billar. **Billiard-table,** mesa de billar.

billing [ˈbɪlɪŋ] [bi-lin] *s.* Orden de importancia en un reparto.

billion [ˈbɪlɪən] [bi-lion], *s. (Arit.)* 1. Billón, millón de millones. 2. Mil millones, en el sistema de enumeración actual, que es el francés y americano; un millón de millones en el inglés y español.

billionaire [ˌbɪlɪəˈnɛər] [bi-lio-niar], *s.* Billonario, multimillonario.

billionth [ˈbɪlɪənθ] [bi-lionz], *a.* Billonésimo.

billow [ˈbɪləʊ] [bi-lou], *s.* Oleada, ola grande.

billow, *vn.* Crecer o hincharse como una ola. **Billow out,** hincharse, inflarse (sail, parachute). **Smoke billowed from the window,** nubes de humo salían de/por la ventana. **Billowing,** hinchado, inflado. **Billowing smoke,** nubes de humo.

billowy [ˈbɪləʊɪ] [bi-loui], *a.* Hinchado como las olas.

billposter [ˈbɪlˌpəʊstər] [bil-pous-ta] (GB) **billsticker** [ˈbɪlstɪkər] [bil-sti-ka] *s.* Persona que pega carteles.

billy [ˈbɪlɪ] [bi-li], *s.* Macho cabrío (goat). **Billy can,** cacerola, cazo. **Billy club,** palo corto con extremidad gruesa; cachiporra de agente de policía.

bilobate [ˈbɪləbeɪt] [bi-lo-beit], *a.* De dos lóbulos; bilobulado.

bilocular [bɪˈlɒkjuːlər] [bi-lo-kiu-la], *a.* Bilocular, de dos celdillas.

bimana [ˈbɪmənə] [bi-ma-na], *s. (Zool.)* Bimano, el orden más elevado de los mamíferos: es decir, el hombre.

bimbo [ˈbɪmbəʊ] [bim-bou] *s. (Coloq,)* Joven bonita y tonta.

bimetallic [ˌbɪmɪˈtælɪk] [bi-me-ta-lik], *a.* Bimetálico, que consiste de dos metales o se refiere a ellos.

bimetallism [ˈbɪmɪtælɪzm] [bi-me-ta-lisem], *s.* Uso del oro y la plata como dinero, en una razón fija.

bimonthly [baɪˈmʌnθlɪ] [bai-monzli], *a.* Bimestral (every two months), bimensual, quincenal (twice a month). *adv.* Bimestralmente (every two months), bimensualmente, quincenalmente (twice a month).

bin [bɪn] [bin], *s.* 1. El lugar o sitio donde se guarda pan, vino, carbón o granos. 2. Hucha, arcón, arca. 3. Cubo, tacho, bote, caneca o tobo de la basura (for kitchen refuse, etc.); papelera, papelero, caneca, basurero (litter bin).

binary [ˈbaɪnærɪ] [bai-na-ri], *a.* Binario, doble, el número que consta de dos unidades. **Binary code,** código binario.

binaural [ˈbɪnərəl] [bi-no-ral], *a.* 1. Para los dos oídos. 2. De dos orejas.

bind [baɪnd] [baind], *va.* 1. Atar, apretar, amarrar con cadenas u otra cosa (tie, fasten). **The ties that bind us,** los lazos que nos unen. 2. Ceñir, envolver, ribetear, galonear. 3. *(Culin.)* Unir, ligar juntar una cosa con otra. 4. Encuadernar, empastar (book). 5. Vendar una herida. 6. Obligar (law), precisar, constreñir, empeñar. 7. Estreñir, desecar. 8. Impedir, embarazar. 9. Poner a uno a servir. **To bind one apprentice,** escriturar a alguno como aprendiz de un oficio. 10. **To bind over,** obligar a comparecer ante el juez. **They were bound over to keep the peace,** quedaron bajo apercibimiento. *-(For.)* Condenar a. *-vn.* 1. Encogerse una cosa poniéndose dura. 2. Astringir, estreñir. 3. Ser obligatorio.

bind *s.* 1. Tallo o vástago de lúpulo. 2. Aprieto, apuro (difficult situation). **To be in a bind,** estar en un aprieto o apuro, estar metido en un lío. 3. *(Fam.)* Lata, plomo, rollo (nuisance).

binder [ˈbaɪndər] [bain-da], *s.* 1. Encuadernador, el que encuaderna libros. 2. Atadero, lo que sirve para atar alguna cosa. 3. Atador, entre los segadores el que ata los haces en gavillas; en particular, agavilladora, apéndice de una máquina segadora para agavillar las mieses. 4. *(Carp.)* Traviesa, ligazón, amarra. 5. Carpeta (file, folder).

bindery [ˈbaɪndərɪ] [bain-de-ri], *s.* Taller de encuadernación.

binding [ˈbaɪndɪŋ] [bain-din], *s.* 1. Venda, tira, faja, cinta ancha y larga que sirve para atar o ligar cubriendo alguna cosa. **Bindings,** *(Mar.)* herrajes de las vigas. 2. Ribete de costura (tape). 3. Encuadernación. 4. Tapa, cubierta (book cover).

binding, *a.* 1. Obligatorio, lo que obliga, vinculante (law). Que hay que cumplir (promise, commitment) 2. Astringente, lo que estriñe. **Binding screw,** *(Elec.)* Tornillo de conexión.

bindweed [ˈbaɪndwiːd] [baind-uíd] *s.* Convólvulo, correhuela.

binge [bɪndʒ] [bindch] *s. (Coloq,)* **To go on a binge,** irse de juerga o parranda o farra. **She dieted for two weeks and**

then had a huge binge, estuvo dos semanas a régimen y después se dio una tremenda comilona. -*vn.* Darse una comilona. **To binge on something,** atiborrarse o hartarse de algo.

bingo ['bɪŋgəʊ] [bin-gou] *s.* Bingo, lotería (de cartones). *interj.* ¡Zas!, ¡sorpresa! (describing sudden effect).

binliner ['bɪnlaɪnəʳ] [bin-lai-naʳ] *s.* Bolsa de la basura.

binnacle ['bɪnəkl] [bi-na-kol], *s. (Mar.)* Bitácora, la caja en que se pone la aguja de marear.

binocle ['bɪnəkl] [bi-na-kol], *s. (Opt.)* Binóculo, anteojo doble de larga vista, gemelo.

binocular [bɪ'nɒkjuləʳ] [bi-no-kiu-laʳ], *a.* Binocular. **Binoculars,** *s. pl.* Gemelos, binóculares, prismáticos, largavistas, anteojos de larga vista.

binomial [baɪ'nəʊmɪəl] [bai-nou-mial], *s. (Alg.)* Raíz binomia, la que consta de dos partes o números.

bio- ['baɪəʊ] [baiou] *pref.* Bio-

biochemical [ˌbaɪəʊ'kemɪkəl] [baiou-ke-mi-kal], *a.* Bioquímico.

biochemist ['baɪəʊ'kemɪst] [baiou-ke-mist] *s.* Bioquímico.

biochemistry ['baɪəʊ'kemɪstrɪ] [baiou-ke-mis-tri]. Bioquímica.

biodegradable [ˌbaɪədɪ'greɪdəbl] [baio-di-grei-da-bol] *a.* Biodegradable, hecho de compuestos que se descomponen por la acción de bacterias.

biodynamics ['baɪəʊdɪnæmɪks] [baio-di-na-miks], *s.* Biodinámica.

bioecology ['baɪəʊɪkələdʒɪ] [baio-e-ko-lo-chi], *s.* Bioecología.

biogenesis ['baɪəʊdʒenɪsɪs] [baio-ye-ni-sis], *s.* Biogénesis, doctrina de que la vida se produce únicamente por medio de seres vivientes.

biogeny ['baɪəʊdʒenɪ] [baio-ye-ni], *s.* Biogenia, la evolución de los organismos o cosas vivientes.

biographer [baɪ'ɒgrəfəʳ] [baiou-gra-faʳ], *s.* Biógrafo, escritor de vidas.

biographical [baɪ'ɒgrəfɪkl] [baiou-gra-fi-kal] **biographic** [baɪ'ɒgrəfɪk] [baiou-gra-fik] *a.* Biográfico.

biography [baɪ'ɒgrəfɪ] [baiou-gra-fi], *s.* Biografía.

biologic, biological [ˌbaɪə'lɒdʒɪk] [baio-lo-chik], *a.* Biológico, perteneciente a la biología. **biologist** [baɪ'ɒlədʒɪst] [baio-lo-chist], *s.* Biólogo.

biology [baɪ'ɒlədʒɪ] [baio-lo-chi], *s.* Biología, ciencia de la vida, o de los organismos vivientes; comprende la zoología y la botánica.

bionic [baɪ'ɒnɪk] [baio-nik] *a.* Biónico.

bionics [baɪ'ɒnɪkz] [baio-niks], *s. (Biol.)* Biónica.

bionomy [baɪ'ɒnəmɪ] [baio-no-mi], *s.* Bionomía, ciencia de las leyes a que obedecen las funciones de los seres vivientes.

biophysical [ˌbaɪəʊ'fɪzɪkl] [baio-fi-si-kal], *a.* Biofísico.

biophysics [ˌbaɪəʊ'fɪzɪks] [baio-fi-siks], *s.* Biofísica.

biopsy ['baɪɒpsɪ] [baiop-si], *s.* Biopsia.

biorhythm ['baɪəʊrɪðəm] [baiou-ri-zem] *s.* Biorritmo.

biosphere ['baɪəsfɪəʳ] [baios-fiaʳ], *s.* Biosfera.

biotin ['baɪətɪn] [baio-tin], *s.* Biotina.

biotechnology [ˌbaɪəʊ'teknɒlədʒɪ] [baiou-tek-no-lo-yi] *s.* Biotecnología (in industry). Ergonomía (ergonomics).

biparous ['bɪpərəs] [bi-pa-ros], *a.* La hembra que pare dos hijos a un tiempo.

bipartisan [ˌbaɪ'pɑːtɪzən] [bai-par-ti-san], *a.* Representante de dos partidos políticos.

bipartition [ˌbaɪ'pɑːtɪʃən] [bai-par-ti-shon], *s.* División en dos pedazos o partes.

bipartite [baɪ'pɑːtaɪt] [bai-par-tait], *a.* Que consta de dos partes correspondientes. Bipartito (bilateral) (contract, treaty).

biped ['baɪped] [bai-ped], *s.* Bípedo, animal de dos pies.

bipedal ['baɪpedl] [bai-pe-dal], *a.* Bípede, que tiene dos pies.

bipennated ['baɪpeneɪtɪd] [bai-pe-nei-tid], *a.* Que tiene dos alas.

bipetalous ['baɪpetələs] [bai-pe-ta-los], *a.* Bipétalo, que tiene dos pétalos.

biplane ['baɪpleɪn] [bai-plein], *s.* Biplano.

bipolar [baɪ'pəʊləʳ] [bai-pou-laʳ], *a.* Bipolar, que tiene dos polos.

bipyramidal [ˌbaɪpɪ'ræmɪdl] [bai-pi-ra-mi-dal], *a.* Bipiramidal, formado por dos pirámides, unidas por sus bases.

biquadrate ['baɪkwadreɪt] [bai-kua-dreit], **biquadratic** ['baɪkwadreɪtɪk] [bai-kua-drei-tik], *s. (Alg.)* Bicuadrática, la cuarta potencia que proviene de la multiplicación del cuadrado por sí mismo.

birch [bɜːtʃ] [berch], *s.* 1. Abedul, cualquier árbol o arbusto del género Betula, de las cupulíferas. 2. Varilla de abedul para azotar a los niños.

birchen ['bɜːtʃən] [ber-chen], *a.* Abedulino, perteneciente al abedul; hecho de abedul.

bird [bɜːd] [berd], *s.* Ave (large), término general para todo animal de pluma que vuela; pájaro (small). **Bird of passage,** ave de paso. **Bird of prey,** ave de rapiña. **Song bird,** pájaro cantor. **Birds of a feather,** pájaros de una misma pluma, gente de una calaña. **A bird in the hand is worth two in the bush,** más vale pájaro en mano que ciento volando. **A little bird told me,** me lo dijo un pajarito. **The bird has flown,** el pájaro ha volado (set phrase). **He told us about the birds and the bees,** nos contó de dónde venían los niños. **To kill two birds with one stone,** matar dos pájaros de un tiro. **It's the early bird that catches the worm,** a quien madruga Dios le ayuda. **He's an odd bird,** es un bicho raro. **Bird of paradise,** ave del Paraíso. **Bird seed,** alpiste.

bird, *vn.* Andar a caza de pájaros.

bird-bolt ['bɜːdbɒlt] [berd-bolt], *s.* 1. Saetilla o dardo pequeñito. 2. *V.* BURBOT.

bird-brained ['bɜːdbreɪnd] [berd-brein] *a. (Fam.)* Lelo.

bird-cage ['bɜːdkeɪdʒ] [berd-keich], *s.* Jaula de pájaros.

bird-call ['bɜːdkɔːl] [berd-kol], *s.* Reclamo.

bird-catcher ['bɜːdkatʃəʳ] [berd-ka-chaʳ], **birder** ['bɜːdəʳ] [berdaʳ], *s.* Pajarero, el que caza pájaros.

bird-dog ['bɜːddɒg] [berd-dog] *va.* Controlar, vigilar. *s.* Perro de caza (in hunting). Guardián, guardiana (person).

bird-eyed ['bɜːdaɪd] [berd-aid], *a.* Dotado de ojo vivo como el de los pájaros.

bird-fancier ['bɜːdfænsɪəʳ] [berd-fan-siar], *s.* 1. El aficionado a los pájaros. 2. Pajarero, el que se dedica a la cría y venta de pájaros.

birdie ['bɜːdɪ] [ber-di], *s.* 1. En el juego de golf, golpe menos de par en un agujero. 2. Pajarito (used esp. to or by children).

bird-like ['bɜːdlaɪk] [berd-laik], *a.* Semejante a pájaro.

bird-lime ['bɜːdlaɪm] [berd-laim], *s.* Liga, materia viscosa con la cual, untando unas varillas o espartos, se cazan pájaros; ajonje.

bird-limed ['bɜːdlaɪmd] [berd-laimd], *a. (Fig.)* Cogido como con liga.

bird-man ['bɜːdmən] [berd-man], *a.* Pajarero; dedicado al estudio de las aves.

bird's-eye ['bɜːdzaɪ] [berds-ai], *s. (Bot.)* Ojo de pájaro. **Bird's-eye view,** vista de pájaro. **Bird's-eye diaper,** género moteado. (lienzo adamascado). **Bird's-eye maple,** arce moteado. -*a.* 1. Moteado, salpicado de motas que semejan ojos de pájaro. 2. Visto de una ojeada, y desde lo alto, como ven los pájaros.

bird's-foot ['bɜːdzfiːt] [berds-fút], *s. (Bot.)* Pie de pájaro, planta del género Ornithopus.

bird's-nest ['bɜːdznest] [berds-nest], *s.* 1. Nido de ave. 2. *(Bot.)* Planta.

bird watcher ['bɜːdwɒtʃəʳ] [berd-uo-chaʳ] *s.* Observador de aves. **Bird watching,** observación de las aves (como hobby).

birgander ['bɜːgændəʳ] [ber-gan-daʳ], *s. (Orn.)* Ganso silvestre.

Biro ['baɪrəʊ] [bai-rou] s. (GB) Bolígrafo, lápiz de pasta, boli.

birr [bɪr] [bir], s. Zumbido, ruido continuado, como el que hace el torno al hilar.

birr, vn. Zumbar, moverse con ruido continuado y bronco.

birt [bɪrt] [birt], s. V. TURBOT.

birth [bɜːθ] [berz], s. 1. Nacimiento, el acto de nacer. 2. Nacimiento, alcurnia, el origen y descendencia de alguna persona en orden a su calidad. **He is a gentleman by birth**, es caballero de nacimiento. Parto, el feto que ha nacido. 4. Parto, la acción o acto de parir (childbirth). **To give birth**, dar a luz, parir. **At birth**, al nacer. 5. Camada. 6. Causa, principio. **To give birth to something**, dar origen a algo. **A new birth**, renacimiento, regeneración. **Birth certificate**, partida, acta, certificado de nacimiento. **Date of birth**, fecha de nacimiento. **Birth right**, derecho de nacimiento; primogenitura (of the eldest child).

birth control ['bɜːθkənˈtrəʊl] [berz-kon-troul], s. Control de natalidad.

birthday ['bɜːθdeɪ] [berzdei], s. Cumpleaños, el aniversario del día en que alguno ha nacido. Cumpleaños (of person), aniversario (of institution). **Birthday present**, cuelga, regalo. **Happy birthday!**, ¡feliz cumpleaños! De cumpleaños (cake, card, party). **The boy/girl birthday**, el (niño), la (niña) del cumpleaños, el cumpleañero, la cumpleañera. **In one's birthday suit**, tal como Dios lo trajo al mundo, tal como vino al mundo, en traje de Adán/Eva.

birthdom ['bɜːθdɒm] [berz-dom], s. Derechos de nacimiento, los privilegios que corresponden a uno por su nacimiento.

birth-mark ['bɜːθmɑːk] [berz-mark], s. Marca o señal corporal de nacimiento, antojo.

birthnight ['bɜːθnaɪt] [berz-nait], s. La noche en que alguno nace.

birthplace ['bɜːθpleɪs] [berz-pleis], s. Suelo nativo, el paraje donde uno nace. Lugar de nacimiento (of person); cuna (of movement, fashion, idea).

birth rate ['bɜːθreɪt] [berz-reit], s. Natalidad (índice o tasa).

birthright ['bɜːθraɪt] [berz-rait], s. 1. Derechos de nacimiento, los privilegios que corresponden a uno por su nacimiento. 2. Primogenitura, la prerrogativa del primogénito. 3. Mayorazgo.

birthwort ['bɜːθwɔːt] [berz-uort], s. (Bot.) Aristoloquia.

bis-. Prefijo latino que equivale a dos veces.

Biscay ['bɪskeɪ] [bis-kei] N. (Geogr.) **The Bay of Biscay**, el Golfo de Vizcaya.

Biscayan ['bɪskeɪən] [bis-keian], a. Vizcaíno, de Vizcaya.

biscuit ['bɪskɪt] [bis-kit], s. 1. Galleta o bizcocho, pan que se cuece una segunda vez para que dure por mucho tiempo. Galleta, galletita (cracker). 2. Bizcocho, masa compuesta de la flor de harina, almendras y azúcar. 3. Porcelana cocida antes de ser vidriada. **To take the biscuit**, ser el colmo o el acabóse, llevarse la palma (person).

bise. V. BICE.

bisect [baɪˈsekt] [bai-sekt], va. Dividir en dos partes iguales. Bisecar.

bisection [baɪˈsekʃən] [bai-sek-shon], s. Bisección, la división de alguna cantidad en dos partes iguales.

bisector [baɪˈsektər] [bai-sek-tor], s. Bisector, bisectriz.

bisexual ['baɪˈseksjʊəl] [bai-seksiual], a./s. (Bot.) De dos órganos; flor que tiene estambres y pistilos.

bishop ['bɪʃəp] [bi-shop], s. 1. (Rel.) Obispo, prelado. 2. Alfil, pieza de juego de ajedrez (in chess). 3. Bebida compuesta de vino, azúcar y zumo de naranjas. **Bishop's lawn**, linón, batista; especie de tela muy fina.

bishop, va. Confirmar o administrar la confirmación.

bishop-like ['bɪʃəplaɪk] [bi-shop-laik], **bishoply** ['bɪʃəplɪ] [bi-sho-pli], a. Episcopal, lo que es propio de un obispo o pertenece a él.

bishopric ['bɪʃəprɪk] [bi-sho-prik], s. Obispado, el territorio o distrito asignado a cada obispo; diócesis.

bishopsweed ['bɪʃəpswiːd] [bi-shop-suíd], **bishopswort** ['bɪʃəpswɔːt] [bi-shop-suort], s. (Bot.) Amijistro.

bisk [bɪsk] [bisk], s. Sopa o caldo; guisado a modo de pepitoria.

bismuth ['bɪzməθ] [bis-maz], s. Bismuto, metal de color blanco rojizo. **Magistery of bismuth o pearl white**, el nitrato de bismuto.

bison ['baɪsən] [bai-son], s. Bisonte, o búfalo de la América del Norte, muy parecido al toro : raza casi extinguida.

bisque [bɪsk] [bisk], s. Porcelana blanca no vidriada. (De BISCUIT, 3ª acep.)

bissextile [baɪˈsekstaɪl] [bai-seks-tail], s. y a. Bisiesto.

bister o bialre ['bɪstər] [bis-tar], s. Tinta de China: hollín desleído.

bistort ['bɪstɔːt] [bis-tort], s. (Bot.) Bistorta, dragoncia o dragúnculo.

bistoury ['bɪstərɪ] [bis-to-ri], s. Bisturí.

bisulcous ['bɪsʌlkəs] [bi-sal-kous], a. Partihendido, bisulco.

bisulphate ['bɪsʌlfeɪt] [bi-sal-feit], s. Bisulfato.

bit [bɪt] [bit], s. 1. Bocado. **Tit-bit**, trozo delicado. 2. Pedacito, pedazo pequeño de alguna cosa, trozo (fragment, scrap). **In tiny bits**, en trocitos o pedacitos. **Bits and pieces**, cosas (assorted items), bártulos (belongings), pedazos (broken fragments). **A bit of**, un poco de (some, little). **A bit of peace**, un poco de paz. **We had a bit of difficulty finding a hotel**, nos resultó algo difícil encontrar un hotel. **We had a bit of an argument**, tuvimos una pequeña discusión. **She's a bit of an expert**, es casi una experta. **A bit** (as an adverb). Un poco (somewhat). **a bit faster**, un poco más rápido. **The town has changed a bit**, la ciudad ha cambiado algo/un poco. **Were you worried?-Not a bit**, ¿estabas preocupado?- en absoluto. **Two bits**, veinticinco centavos de dólar. **I don't care/give two bits what she thinks**, me importa un bledo/un comino lo que piense. **A 50p bit**, una moneda de 50 peniques. 3. Barrena de berbiquí. 4. Freno, brida. **Bit of a bridle**, bocado del freno. **Bit of a key**, paletón de llave. **Bit of an auger**, gusanillo de taladro. **Bit of a cable**, (Mar.) bitadura del cable. **Bits**, (Mar.) V. BITTS. **Not a bit**, nada, ni miaja. **Extension o expansion bit**, (Mec.) barrena de extensión. **Taper-bit**, alisador cónico. **Bit by bit**, poco a poco. **I'm every bit as disappointed as you**, estoy tan decepcionado como tú. **He was champing at the bit**, lo consumía la impaciencia, estaba que no se podía aguantar. **She has the bit between her teeth**, está que no la para nadie. (Comp.) Bit. 1**bit**, va. 1. Enfrenar, echar el freno al caballo. 2. (Mar.) Tomar la bitadura con el cable, bitar.

bit, pret. y pp. del verbo TO BITE.

bitch [bɪtʃ] [bich], sf. 1. Perra, la hembra del perro. 2. (Vulg.) Zorra, nombre contumelioso que se da a las mujeres perdidas (spiteful woman). (Ame) (vulg.), (GB) (sl.) Puta, (vulg.) bruja, (Fam.) arpía. Lata, coñazo, chingadera (difficult, unpleasant thing). (Fam.) **To have a malicious bitch**, chismear de lo lindo (malicious talk). (Coloq,) Queja (complaint).

bitch, vn. (Coloq,) Quejarse, refunfuñar (complain). **To bitch about something/somebody**, quejarse de algo/alguien. (Fam.) (GB) Chismear (talk maliciously). **To bitch about something/somebody**, hablar pestes de algo/alguien.

bitchy ['bɪtʃɪ] [bi-chi] a. (Coloq,) Malicioso, rencoroso, de mala leche (remark).

bite [baɪt] [bait], va/vn. (pret. BIT, pp. BITTEN o BIT). 1. Morder, asir con los dientes haciendo presa con ellos, o cortando y despedazando alguna cosa; roer (person, dog). **To bite one's nails**, morderse/comerse las uñas. **The dog bit his finger off**, el perro le arrancó el dedo de un mordisco. **To bite off more than one can chew**, tratar de abarcar más de lo que se puede. **Once bitten, twice shy**, el gato escaldado del agua fría huye. **To bite the dust**, morder el polvo, morir, caer vencido. **To bite the bait**, picar el anzuelo. 2. Punzar, picar (bug). **This mustard bites my tongue**, esta mostaza me quema la boca. 3. Murmurar o satirizar, hiriendo la fama de alguno. 4. Engañar, clavar, defraudar. **To bite into something**, darle un mordisco a algo, hincarle el diente a algo. **To bite on something**, morder algo. **He bit back his words,** se mordió la lengua, fue a decir algo pero se contuvo.

bite, s. 1. Mordedura (act), tarascada (fierce), la acción de morder. **Take a bite of this,** prueba esto. **To have/get two bites at the cherry,** tener una segunda oportunidad. 2. Mordedura, la acción de picar el pez el cebo del anzuelo. 3. Bocado. 4. Engaño. 5. (*Ger.*) Engañador, impostor, ladrón, ratero. 6. Picadura (wound from insect). Mordedura (dog, snake). 7. Bocado (snack). **To have a snack (to eat),** comer un bocado, comer algo. 8. Lo fuerte (of flavor). Mordacidad (sharpness).

biter ['baɪtəʳ] [baita'], s. 1. Mordedor, el que muerde. 2. Pez que muerde o pica el cebo. 3. Engañador, impostor.

biting ['baɪtɪŋ] [bai-tin], s. 1. Mordimiento, mordedura, tarascada. 2. El acto de dañar a uno censurándoles. Mordaz (sarcasm, criticism); picante. Cortante, penetrante (wind).

bitingly ['baɪtɪŋlɪ] [bai-tin-li], adv. Mordazmente, con mofa; satíricamente.

bit part s. Papel pequeño.

bitt [bɪt] [bit], s. V. BITTS.

bitten [bɪtn] [bi-ten], pp. del verbo TO BITE.

bitter ['bɪtəʳ] [bi-ta'], a. 1. Amargo (in taste), áspero, lo que tiene un gusto desapacible. 2. Amargo, cruel, severo. Glacial, muy frío (weather). Cortante, penetrante (wind, frost). **It's bitter,** hace un frío glacial. 3. Calamitoso, miserable. Resentido, amargo (person). 4. Mordaz, satírico, rudo. 5. Penoso, desagradable. **Bitter words,** palabras mayores, frases picantes, insultos. -s. Alguna cosa amarga. **To taste bitter,** ser de gusto amargo. **A bitter criticism,** o **critique,** una crítica amarga, severa, mordaz. **Bitter enmity,** odio encarnizado. **Bitter cold,** frío picante. **Bitters,** licor en cuya composición entran diversa plantas y raíces amargas. Tipo de cerveza ligeramente amarga. **They fought on to the bitter end,** lucharon valientemente hasta el final.

bitterish ['bɪtərɪʃ] [bi-te-rish], a. Amargoso. ligeramente amargo.

bitterly ['bɪtəlɪ] [bi-ter-li], adv. 1. Amargamente, con amargura o sabor amargo. 2. Con angustia o pena. 3. Agriamente, severamente. **It was bitterly cold,** hacía un frío glacial.

bittern ['bɪtɜːn] [bi-tern], s. 1. (*Orn.*) Alcaraván o bitor, especie de garza. 2. Agua madre de sal que contiene sulfato de magnesia.

bitterness ['bɪtɜːnɪs] [bi-ter-nes], s. 1. Amargor o amargura, sabor o gusto amargo (of taste). 2. Odio, rencor, tirria, ojeriza, mala voluntad. 3. Severidad, dureza de genio. 4. Mordacidad lenguaje que zahiere. 5. Pena, dolor, angustia, amargura (of disappointment), resentimiento (of person).

bitters ['bɪtəz] [bi-ters], V. BITTER, ad finem.

bittersweet ['bɪtəswiːt] [bi-ter-suít], s. Dulcamara, planta de las solanáceas. Agridulce; amargo (chocolate).

bitterwort ['bɪtəwɔːt] [bi-ter-uort], s. (*Bot.*) Genciana, una planta.

bitts [bɪts] [bits], s. pl. (*Mar.*) Bitas, barraganetes, dos pedazos de vigas alrededor de los cuales se asegura el cable cuando se ha aferrado el áncora. **Lining of the bitts,** forro de las bitas. **Pawl bitts,** bitas del linguete. **Top-sail bitts,** abitones.

bitumen ['bɪtjʊmɪn] [bi-tiu-min], s. Betún, materia combustible, algo semejante a las resinas.

bituminize ['bɪtjʊmɪnaɪz] [bi-tiu-mi-nais], va. Embetunar, cubrir o impregnar de betún.

bituminous ['bɪtjʊmɪnəs] [bi-tiu-mi-nos], a. Bituminoso, que contiene betún o participa de él.

bivalence, bivalency ['baɪ'veɪləns] [bai-vei-lans], s. Equivalencia de dos en los compuestos químicos.

bivalent ['baɪ'veɪlənt] [bai-vei-lant], a. (*QUIM.*) Que tiene el valer o poder de dos, en sus combinaciones.

bivalve ['baɪvælv] [bai-valv], **bivalvular** ['baɪvælvjʊləʳ] [bai-val-viu-la'], a. 1. Bivalvo, de dos conchas, que tiene dos conchas, como las ostras, etc. 2. (*Bot.*) Vaina de dos ventanas.

bivouac ['bɪvɔæk] [bi-vuak], s. (*Mil.*) Vivac o vivaque, guardia extraordinaria que se hace de noche para la seguridad de un campo, de una plaza o de un puesto militar. Campamento.

bivouac, vn. (*Mil.*) Vivaquear, pasar la noche al sereno o a campo raso.

biweekly ['baɪ'wiːklɪ] [bai-uí-kli], a. Quincenal, cada dos semanas. Bisemanal (twice a week) -adv. Quincenalmente, cada dos semanas (every two weeks). Bisemanalmente, dos veces por semana (twice a week). -s. Publicación quincenal.

bizarre [bɪ'zɑːʳ] [bi-za'], a. Raro, caprichoso. Extraño (story, coincidence). Estrambótico, estrafalario (appearance, behavior).

blab [blæb] [blab], va. Parlar, revelar, decir o divulgar lo que se debía callar. Descubrir el pastel (reveal secrets). Parlotear (prattle). -vn. Chismear.

blab, blabber ['blæbəʳ] [bla-ba'], s. Chismoso, el que se emplea en traer y llevar chismes. Hablador. **Blabbermouth,** bocazas.

blabbing ['blæbɪŋ] [bla-bin], s. Habladuría.

black [blæk] [blak], va. Dar de negro. (*Fig.*) Denigrar, deshonrar. **To black somebody's eye,** ponerle el ojo morado a alguien (bruise). Boicotear (boycott). **Black out,** perder el conocimiento (lose consciousness). V. BLACKEN.

black, s. 1. Negro, el efecto producido en la vista por la falta de luz. 2. Luto. 3. Negro, el etíope. **Bone-black,** negro animal. **Ivory black,** negro de marfil (marfil carbonizado). **Lampblack** negro de humo. **Black and blue,** cardenal, contusión. **To be in the black,** no estar en números rojos (freedom from debt). **It's here in black and white,** aquí está escrito bien claro. **She sees things in black and white,** para ella no hay términos medios. **Black-and-white,** en blanco y negro.

black, a. 1. Negro, obscuro (dress, hair, drink, sky)) **Black cloud,** nubarrón, nube negra.. 2. Ceñudo, tétrico, grave y melancólico. 3. Horrible, malvado, atroz. 4. Triste, funesto. 5. Negro, sucísimo (dirty). 6. Negro, solo, tinto, puro, sin leche (coffee). **Black and blue,** lívido, amoratado. **To look black at,** mirar de través, con ceño. **The black economy,** la economía informal/paralela, la economía sumergida. **Things were looking pretty black,** las cosas tomaban mal cariz o se estaban poniendo feas (sad, hopeless).

blackamoor ['blækəmʊəʳ] [blak-a-mua'], s. Negro, el etíope.

black art ['blækɑːt] [blak-art], s. Nigromancia, magia negra.

blackball ['blækbɔːl] [blak-bol], s. Bola negra para votar.

blackball, va. Echar o dar bola negra; votar en contra.

black bear ['blækbɛəʳ] [blak-ba'] s. Oso negro americano.

black belt ['blækbelt] [blak-belt] s. Cinturón negro, cinta negra.

blackberry ['blækberɪ] [blak-be-ri], s. 1. (*Bot.*) Zarza, mata espinosa. 2. Zarzamora, el fruto de la zarza. **To go blackberrying,** ir a recoger moras.

blackbird ['blækbɜːd] [blak-berd], s. (*Orn.*) Mirlo o merla. Totí.

blackboard ['blækbɔːd] [blak-bord], s. Pizarra, encerado de las escuelas, pizarrón, tablero.

black box ['blækbɒks] [blak-boks] s. (*Aer.*) Caja negra.

black-browed ['blækbraʊd] [blak-braud], s. Cejinegro; triste, tenebroso.

black-cap ['blækkæp] [blak-cap], s. 1. El que lleva una gorra negra. 2. Alondra, silvia, de cabeza negra. 3. Frambueso negro y su fruta. 4. Enea, espadaña común.

black cattle ['blækkætl] [blak-ka-tel], s. Ganado vacuno.

black-cock ['blækkɒk] [blak-kok], s. Gallo silvestre.

black currant ['blækkʌrənt] [blak-ka-rent], s. Grosella negra.

black death ['blækdeθ] [blak-dez] s. La peste negra.

black draught ['blækdrɑːt] [blak-drot], s. Infusión de sen.

blacken ['blækən] [blaken], va. 1. Dar de negro o teñir de negro. 2. Tildar, obscurecer o difamar. **To blacken one's**

character, denigrar, quitar a uno la estimación. 3. Negrecer o ennegrecer.

blackener [ˈblækənəʳ] [bla-ke-naʳ], *s.* Ennegrecedor, el que ennegrece alguna cosa; denigrador.

black eye [ˈblækaɪ] [blak-ai] *s.* Ojo morado, ojo a la funerala, ojo en compota, ojo en tinta (bruise). **To give somebody a black eye,** ponerle un ojo morado (o a la funerala, etc.) a alguien. Mala fama (bad reputation).

black-eyed [ˈblækaɪd] [blak-aid], *a.* Ojinegro.

black-faced [ˈblækfeɪst] [blak-feist], **black-visaged** [ˈblækvɪseɪdʒ] [blak-vi-seich], *a.* Carinegro, moreno.

black flag [ˈblækflæg] [blak-flag], *s.* Bandera negra, pabellón pirata.

Black Forest *s.* **The Black Forest,** la Selva Negra.

black friars [ˈblækfrɪəz] [blak-friars], *s.* 1. Frailes negros, apodo dado a los domicanos.

blackguard [ˈblækgɑːd] [blak-gard], *s. (Faro.)* Pillastrón, pelagatos, galopo, tunante, pillo. Villano (dated). Canalla.

black-haired [ˈblækhɛəd] [blak-jead], *a.* Pelinegro.

blackhead [ˈblækhed] [blak-jed], *s.* Espinilla, punto negro, comedón.

black hole [ˈblækhəʊl] [blak-joul], *s.* Agujero negro.

black ice [ˈblækaɪs] [blak-ais], *s.* Capa fina de hielo en las carreteras.

blacking [ˈblækɪŋ] [bla-kin], *s.* Betún, unto o lustre de zapatos; bola.

blackish [ˈblækɪʃ] [bla-kish], *a.* Negruzco, lo que tira a negro.

black-jack [ˈblækdʒæk] [blak-yak], *s.* 1. Pequeño roble. 2. *V.* BLENDE. 3. Pabellón pirata. 4. Cachiporra pequeña. 5. Jarro o escudilla charolada que era antiguamente de piel

black-lead [ˈblækliːd] [blak-lid], *s.* Lápiz-plomo, mineral que se usa para lapiceros; es el grafito de los mineralogistas.

blackleg [ˈblækleg] [blak-leg], *s.* 1. Petardista, fullero, tramposo. 2. Enfermedad pestilente del ganado vacuno; morriña negra. 3. Esquirol (strikebreaker).

black-letter [ˈblækletəʳ] [blak-le-taʳ], *s.* Letra gótica antigua de imprenta: impresión en caracteres góticos: p.ej., Esta línea está en black-letter.

black list [ˈblæklɪst] [blak-list], *s.* Lista negra. *va.* Poner en la lista negra.

blackly [ˈblæklɪ] [blak-li], *adv.* Atrozmente.

blackmail [ˈblækmeɪl] [blak-meil], *s.* Chantaje, extorsión de dinero amenazando con escándalo, denuncia o censura. *-va.* Chantajear, amenazar con chantaje.

blackmailer [ˈblækmeɪləʳ] [blak-mei-laʳ], *s.* Chantajista, persona que practica el chantaje.

Black Maria [ˈblækmərɪə] [blak-ma-ria] *s.* Coche o furgón celular, cuca, jaula, julia.

black mark [ˈblækmɑːk] [blak-mark], *s.* Punto en contra.

black market [ˈblækmɑːkɪt] [blak-mar-ket], *s.* Mercado negro.

black-mouthed [ˈblækmaʊθɪd] [blak-mau-zid], *a.* Grosero, vil, bajo, el que usa de un lenguaje indecente.

blackness [ˈblæknɪʃ] [blak-nes], *s.* 1. Negrura color negro. 2. Oscuridad.

blackout [ˈblækaʊt] [blak-aut], *s.* Oscurecimiento. *(Mex.)* Apagón (power failure). **A news blackout,** un bloqueo informativo (embargo). Desvanecimiento, desmayo (loss of consciousness). **To have a blackout,** tener o sufrir un desvanecimiento. Oscurecimiento de la ciudad para que ésta no sea visible desde los aviones (in wartime).

black-pudding [ˈblækpʊdɪŋ] [blak-pu-din], *s.* Morcilla.

Black Sea *s.* El Mar Negro.

black-sheep [ˈblækʃiːp] [blak-ship], *s.* Oveja sarnosa. *(Met.)* El peor entre todos, el malo entre los buenos.

blacksmith [ˈblæksmɪθ] [blak-smiz], *s.* Herrero.

blacksonake [ˈblæksɒneɪk] [blak-so-neik], *s.* 1. Cierta clase de serpiente negra o negruzca. 2. Azote pesado, flexible, hecho de cuero acordonado.

blackthorn [ˈblækθɔːn] [blak-zorn], *s.* Endrino, el árbol que lleva las endrinas.

black tie [ˈblæktaɪ] [blak-tai], *s.* Traje de etiqueta, smoking, esmoquin (on invitation).

blacktop [ˈblæktɒp] [blak-top] *s.* Asfalto (material); pista (surface). *va.* Asfaltar, pavimentar.

black vomit [ˈblækvəmɪt] [blak-vo-mit], *s.* Vómito negro, de la fiebre amarilla.

blackwell hall [ˈblækwelhɔːl] [blak-uel-jol], *s.* Sala donde se vende paño o telas de lana. **Blackwell-hall factor,** factor o agente de los fabricantes de lana.

black widow [ˈblækwɪdəʊ] [blak-ui-dou], *s.* Viuda negra.

blad [blæd] [blad], *va. (Esco.)* Herir, dar: dar una bofetada, golpear; de aquí, maltratar.

blad, *s.* 1. Pedazo o porción grande. 2. Teleta, papel secante. 3. Manotada, golpe dado con la mano.

bladder [ˈblædəʳ] [bla-daʳ], *s.* 1. Vejiga, bolsa muscular y membranosa que sirve de receptáculo a la orina. 2. Vejiga, ampolla. **Bladder-senna,** *(Bot.)* Espantalobos.

bladdered [ˈblædəd] [bla-de-red], *a.* Hinchado como vejiga.

bladderwort [ˈblædəwɔːt] [bla-der-uort], *s.* Utricularia, planta acuática.

blade [bleɪd] [bleid], *s.* 1. La punta tierna del grano antes de granar. 2. Hoja, la parte cortante de algún arma o instrumento (of knife, razor). 3. Pala de remo. 4. Jaquetón, el valentón y guapo. **Cunning blade,** zorrastrón. **Old blade,** viejo muy experto y marrullero. **Stout blade,** bravo, valiente. **Blade of a propeller,** ala o paleta de la hélice. **Blade of grass,** tallo de hierba.

blade-bone [ˈbleɪdbəʊn] [bleid-boun], *s.* Escápula, espaldilla u omoplato.

bladed [ˈbleɪdɪd] [blei-did], *a.* Entallecido, lo que tiene tallos.

bladesmith [ˈbleɪdsmɪθ] [bleids-miz], *s.* Espadero, fabricante de espadas.

blah [blɑː] [bla] *s. (Coloq,)* Pamplinas (nonsense). *interj.* **blah, blah, blah,** bla, bla, bla, etcétera, etcétera. **To have the blahs,** estar con la depre. *a. (Fam.)* Pesado, plomizo.

blamable [ˈbleɪməbl] [blei-ma-bol], *a.* Culpable, digno de culpa, vituperable.

blamableness [ˈbleɪməblnɪs] [blei-ma-bol-nes], *s.* Culpabilidad.

blame [bleɪm] [bleim], *va.* Culpar, echar la culpa; condenar, vituperar, reprender; censurar; tachar. **Don't blame me,** no me eches la culpa a mí, no me culpes a mí. **To blame somebody for something,** culpar a alguien de algo, echarle la culpa de algo a alguien. **She blames herself for the accident,** se siente culpable del accidente. **To be to blame for something,** tener la culpa de algo. **No one's to blame,** no es culpa de nadie. **I'm not having any more to do with him- I don't blame you,** no quiero saber nada más de él y con toda la razón (disagree, criticize). **You can't blame me for getting upset,** es normal que me molestara ¿no?

blame, *s.* 1. Culpa, vituperación, imputación de algún delito o defecto, reprobación, censura. 2. Culpa, delito (responsibility). **It's always me that gets the blame,** siempre me echan la culpa a mí. **To take the blame for something,** asumir la responsabilidad de algo.

blameful [ˈbleɪmfʊl] [bleim-ful], *a.* Reo, culpable.

blameless [ˈbleɪmlɪs] [bleim-les], *a.* Inocente, el que está libre de culpa, irreprensible, puro (guiltless). Intachable, sin tacha (irreproachable).

blamelessly [ˈbleɪmlɪslɪ] [bleim-les-li], *adv.* Inocentemente, sin culpa.

blamelesness [ˈbleɪmlɪsnɪs] [bleim-les-nes], *s.* Inocencia, carencia de culpa.

blamer [ˈbleɪməʳ] [blei-maʳ], *s.* Represor, censurador.

blameworthy [ˈbleɪmwɜːθɪ] [bleim-uer-zi], *a.* Culpable (person). Censurable (act).

blameworthiness [ˈbleɪmwɜːθɪnɪs] [bleim-uer-zi-nes], *s.* Culpabilidad.

blanch [blɑːntʃ] [blanch], *va.* 1. Blanquear, poner blanca alguna cosa. *(Culin.)* Escaldar, blanquear. 2. Pelar, mondar, quitar la cascarilla. 3. Dejar o pasar en blanco. 4. Eludir, paliar, colorear, cohonestar. *-vn.* Blanquear, ponerse blanco, perder el color; palidecer (person). **He blanched at the sight of the body,** palideció al ver el cadáver.

blanch, s. Mineral de plomo incrustado en la roca.

blancher ['blɑːntʃəʳ] [blan-cha'], s. Blanqueador, el que blanquea

blanching ['blɑːntʃɪŋ] [blan-chin], s. Blanquición, la operación de blanquear la moneda, blanqueo. **Blanching liquor,** agua de blanquear, solución de cloruro de cal.

blanc-mange [blə'mɒnʒ] [bla-manch], s. Manjar blanco, compuesto de gelatina, musgo marino u otra sustancia viscosa, fécula de maíz, leche, azúcar, etc.

bland [blænd] [bland], a. Blando, suave, dulce (mild; diet, food). Soso, insípido, desabrido (food, taste). Soso, insulso, desabrido (colors, music). Anodino, que no dice nada (statement, reply). Insulso (smile, manner).

blandation ['blændeɪʃən] [blan-dei-shon], s. Blandura, lisonja, caricia.

blandiloquence ['blændɪləkwens] [blan-di-lo-kuens], s. Agasajo; blandura; lenguaje lisonjero, cumplimiento, lisonja.

blandish ['blændɪʃ] [blan-dish], va. 1. Ablandar, suavizar. 2. Engatusar, acariciar, halagar, lisonjear.

blandisher ['blændɪʃəʳ] [blan-di-sha'], s. Halagador, lisonjero.

blandishing ['blændɪʃɪŋ] [blan-di-shin], s. Blandura, caricia. V. BLANDISHMENT.

blandishment ['blændɪʃmənt] [blan-dish-ment], s. Halago, requiebro, caricia, agasajo, demostración afectuosa. sea de palabra o de obra, lisonjas (flatteries). Incentivos (inducements).

blandly ['blændlɪ] [blan-dli] adv. De manera insulsa (smile).

blank [blæŋk] [blank], a. 1. Blanco. 2. En blanco, no escrito (page, space) (empty); virgen (tape). **The screen went blank,** se fue la imagen de la pantalla. **My mind went blank,** se me quedó en blanco. **A blank expression,** un rostro carente de expresión (lifeless). **He stared at me in blank amazement,** me miró perplejo. 3. (Poet.) Suelto o sin rima, hablando de verdad. 4. Confuso, turbado, desconcertado, pálido. Rotundo, tajante (uncompromising) (refusal, rejection). (Mil.) De fogueo (ammunition). **Blank out,** borrar. -s. 1. Blanco, espacio, hueco. 2. Suerte o cédula de la lotería que no gana nada. 3. Papel en blanco. 4. Blanco, la señal fija y determinada a que se tira. 5. Pedazo de plata u oro destinado a la acuñación. 6. Carta blanca, el naipe sin figura. **Blank cards,** tarjetas. **Blank-book,** libro en blanco. **Blank cartridge,** cartucho sin bala. **To draw a blank,** no obtener ningún resultado. (Mil.) Cartucho de fogueo.

blank, va. 1. Perturbar, confundir. 2. Anular, cancelar, borrar.

blank check ['blæŋktʃek] [blank-chek], (GB) **cheque** s. Cheque en blanco. **To give somebody a blank check,** dar a alguien carta blanca.

blanket ['blæŋkɪt] [blan-ket], s. 1. Manta, cubierta de lana para la cama y otros usos; cobertor, colcha o cobertura. (Mex.) cobija. **A blanket of snow,** un manto de nieve. 2. Mantilla, envoltura de las criaturas. 3. Mantilla, el cordelate que se pone en las imprentas entre el tímpano y timpanillo. a. Global (measure).

blanket, va. 1. Cubrir con manta. 2. Mantear, levantar en el aire a alguna persona poniéndola en una manta.

blanketing ['blæŋkɪtɪŋ] [blan-ke-tin], s. Manteamiento, el acto de mantear.

blankly ['blæŋklɪ] [blan-kli], adv. En blanco. **To look at somebody blankly,** mirar a alguien sin comprender.

blankness ['blæŋknɪs] [blank-nes]. 1. Blanco, hueco. 2. Turbación, confusión. **Blank verse** s. Verso blanco.

blare [bleəʳ] [bla'], s. Ruido, fragor; sonido como de trompeta. Estridencia, estruendo. vn. Atronar. **Blaring horns,** bocinas atronadoras. **The radio was blaring out music,** la radio emitía música retumbante. **To blare out an order,** dar una orden a gritos. Resonar, bramar (voice).

blarney ['blɑːnɪ] [blar-ni], s. Lenguaje adulador, zalamería, caricia mentida, labia, coba.

blasé ['blɑːzeɪ] [bla-sei], a. Hastiado de placeres o disipación. (Gal.). Disciplente (manner, remark). **You sound very blasé about your exams,** no parecen preocuparte mucho tus exámenes.

blaspheme [blæs'fiːm] [blas-fim], va. 1. Blasfemar, hablar con impiedad de Dios y de todo lo sagrado. 2. Hablar mal de alguna persona. -vn. Decir blasfemias, jurar.

blasphemer [blæs'fiːməʳ] [blas-fi-ma'], s. Blasfemo, blasfemador.

blaspheming [blæs'fiːmɪŋ] [blas-fi-min], s. Blasfemia, la acción de blasfemar.

blasphemous [blæs'fiːməs] [blas-fi-mos], a. Blasfemo, impío.

blasphemously [blæs'fiːməslɪ] [blas-fi-mos-li], adv. Blasfemamente, impíamente, con blasfemia o impiedad.

blasphemy [blæs'fiːmɪ] [blas-fi-mi], s. Blasfemia, palabra injuriosa contra Dios o cualquier cosa sagrada.

blast [blɑːst] [blast], s. 1. Ráfaga, ventarrón, golpe de aire, (air, wind). Chorro (water). 2. Ventolera. 3. Soplo, aire impelido por un fuelle, soplete, etc. 4. Carga de pólvora o dinamita; explosión (de una mina), vuelo. Explosión (explosion), onda expansiva (shock wave). 5. Son de cualquier instrumento músico de viento. 6. Golpe o influjo de astro maligno. 7. Tizón, añublo. **He had the TV on full blast,** tenía la tele a todo lo que daba (sound). **It will be a blast.** será el desmadre (enjoyable event).

blast, va. 1. Castigar con alguna calamidad repentina. 2. Infamar. 3. Marchitar, secar. 4. Espantar, atacar, arremeter contra. 5. Volar, dar barreno, abrir las rocas con pólvora. **They used dynamite to blast the safe open,** usaron dinamita para volar o hacer saltar la caja fuerte. 6. Arruinar. 7. Anieblar, anublar, atizonar los granos. **Blast it!,** ¡maldición! (expressing annoyance). **Blast the exam!,** ¡al diablo el examen! **Blast off,** despegar. **Blast out,** emitir a todo volumen (message); tocar a todo lo que da (music).

blasted ['blɑːstɪd] [blas-tid] a. Maldito, condenado.

blaster ['blɑːstəʳ] [blasta'], s. El que arruina, infama o marchita repentinamente.

blast furnace ['blɑːst'fɜːnɪs] [blast-fer-nis], s. Alto horno.

blasting ['blɑːstɪŋ] [blas-tin], s. 1. El acto de abrir o hender las rocas. 2. Voladura.

blastoderm ['blɑːstədɜːm] [blas-to-derm], s. Blastoderma, membrana germinal del embrión.

blast-off ['blɑːstɒf] [blast-of], s. (Aer.) Despegue.

blatant ['bleɪtənt] [blei-tant], a. Mugiente o bramante a manera de becerro. Vocinglero. Descarado, ostensible, flagrante (prejudice, disrespect) (unconcealed). **They're so blatant about it,** lo hacen o dicen con tanto descaro o tanta desfachatez. Patente (obvious) (incompetence).

blatantly ['bleɪtəntlɪ] [blei-tant-li] adv. Descaradamente, abiertamente, ostensiblemente (openly). **It's blatantly untrue,** está claro que no es cierto (clearly). **It's blatantly obvious that…,** está clarísimo que...

blate ['bleɪt] [bleit], a. (GB) 1. Sin agudeza de ingenio o ánimo; tonto. 2. Atrasado o vergonzoso.

blather ['blæðəʳ] [bla-da'], va. y vn. Charlar, hablar mucho sin sustancia; balbucear, parlotear. **What are you blathering (on) about?,** ¿qué tonterías dices? -s. Charla, desatino, disparate.

blatherskite ['blæðəskaɪt] [bla-da-skait], s. (E.U. y Esco.) 1. Matamoros, fanfarrón. 2. Fanfarronada, baladronada.

blaw [blɔː] [blo], va. (Esco.) 1. Jactarse, fanfarronear. 2. Adular, lisonjear.

blaze [bleɪz] [bleis], s. 1. Llama o llamarada (flames). Fuego (in grate), fogata, hoguera (bonfire). Incendio (dangerous fire). 2. Publicación o divulgación de alguna cosa. 3. Ruido, rumor. 4. Estrella, la mancha blanca en la frente del caballo o la vaca. 5. Mancha, estrella o señal hecha en los troncos do los árboles, comúnmente por los agrimensores y cazadores, para servirles de marca o guía. **A blaze of glory,** una gloria brillante. **A blaze of color,** un derroche de color (dazzling display). (Fam.) **How/what the blazes…?,**

¿cómo/qué demonios o diablos…? *(Fam.)* **Like blazes,** como un bólido (very fast).

blaze, *vn.* 1. Encenderse en llama. 2. Brillar, resplandecer, lucir (lights), arder (fire). **The sun blazed down,** el sol abrasaba. Centellear (eyes). **She blazed with anger,** ardía de indignación. -*va.* 1. Inflamar o hacer llama. 2. Publicar, divulgar. 3. Marcar los árboles 4. Fuego o concortes y seriales, para que sirvan de guía.

blazer [ˈbleɪsəʳ] [blei-saʳ], *s.* 1. Prenda de vestir, chaqueta ligera de franela o seda, que se usa comúnmente en los juegos al aire libre. 2. Brasero, braserillo. 3. Charlador, cuentero.

blazing [ˈbleɪzɪŋ] [bleisin], *a.* Flameante, en llamas; resplandeciente (lights), deslumbrador. Abrasador (sun), centelleante (eyes), *(Coloq.)* violento (row). **Blazing-star,** (a) Cometa. (b) *(E. U.)* Hierba de las liliáceas.

blazon [ˈbleɪzn] [bleisn], *va.* 1. Blasonar, disponer los escudos de armas según las reglas del arte. 2. Explicar la significación de los escudos de armas. 3. Adornar, decorar. 4. Celebrar, alabar. 5. Publicar o hacer notorio, explicar.

blazon, *s.* 1. *V.* BLAZONRY. 2. Divulgación, publicación, celebración.

blazoner [ˈbleɪzənəʳ] [blei-so-naʳ], *s.* 1. Autor de heráldica. 2. Genealogista, heraldo. 3. Difamador, Infamador.

blazonry [ˈbleɪzənrɪ] [blei-son-ri], *s.* Blasón, el arte de explicar y describir los escudos de armas.

bleach [bliːtʃ] [blích], *va.* Blanquear al sol, poner blanca alguna cosa. -*m.* Blanquear (with bleach).

bleacher [ˈbliːtʃəʳ] [blí-chaʳ], *s.* 1. Blanqueador, lejía, lavandina. *V.* BLEACHERY. 2. pl. *(E.U.)* Gradas o asientos descubiertos para espectadores.

bleachery [ˈbliːtʃərɪ] [blí-cha-ri], *s.* Blanquería, el sitio donde se ponen las cosas a blanquear.

bleaching [ˈbliːtʃɪŋ] [blí-chin], *s.* Blanqueo, blanqueamiento, blanqueadua.

bleak [bliːk] [blík], *a.* 1. Abierto, desabrigado, expuesto a la intemperie. 2. Frío, helado.

bleak, *s.* Albur, pez pequeño de río. *a.* Inhóspito (landscape), lóbrego (room), crudo (winter), gris y deprimente (day). Sombrío, funesto (miserable, cheerless) (prospects, news).

bleakly [ˈbliːklɪ] [blíkli] *adv.* Sombríamente.

bleakness [ˈbliːknɪs] [blík-nes], *s.* Intemperie, destemplanza; frío, frialdad.

blear [blɪəʳ] [blíaʳ], **bleared** [blɪːəd] [blíad], *a.* Lagañoso o legañoso.

blear, *va.* Hacer legañoso; ofuscar la vista.

blear-eyed [bliːəaɪd] [blíad-aid], *a.* 1. Legañoso. 2. Confuso de entendimiento.

bleardness [ˈbliːədnɪs] [blíad-nes], *s.* Legaña; ofuscación o turbación que padece la vista.

bleary [ˈblɪərɪ] [blía-ri] *a.* **Bleary with tears,** tenía los ojos empañados o nublados de lágrimas.

bleary-eyed [ˈblɪərəaɪd] [blía-aid] *a.* Con cara de sueño. **To be bleary-eyed from sleep,** tener cara de sueño.

bleat [bliːt] [blít], *s.* Balido, la voz que forman la oveja, el carnero y el cordero.

bleat, *vn.* Balar, dar balidos la oveja o el cordero.

bleating [ˈbliːtɪŋ] [blí-tin], *s.* Balido, el acto de balar.

bleb [bleb] [bleb], *s.* Ampolla, vejiga.

bled, *pret.* y *pp.* del verbo TO BLEED.

bleed [bliːd] [blíd], *vn.* 1. Sangrar, echar sangre. **My nose is bleeding,** me sale sangre de la nariz. 2. Morir, fallecer. -*va.* Sangrar, sacar sangre, chorrear sangre. *(Fig.)* Renovarse, abrirse otra vez, presentarse, hacerse sentir de nuevo. 3. Perder el jugo o la savia (hablando de la vid, o de los árboles). -*va.* Arrancar dinero de una persona. **To bleed to death,** morir de una hemorragia. **My heart bleeds for you,** ¡qué lástima me das! **To bleed somebody dry,** chuparle la sangre a alguien.

bleeder [ˈbliːdəʳ] [blí-daʳ], *s.* Sangrador, el que sangra.

bleeding [ˈbliːdɪŋ] [blí-din], *s.* Sangría; fin. Hemorragia. **A bleeding heart,** un corazón traspasado de dolor. -*a.* Tierno, afectuoso, simpático. *a./adv.* BLOODY.

bleep [bliːp] [blíp] *s.* Pitido. *vn.* Emitir un pitido.

bleeper [ˈbliːpəʳ] [blí-paʳ] *s.* Buscapersonas, busca, bip, bíper.

blemish [ˈblemɪʃ] [ble-mish], *va.* 1. Afear, poner fea alguna cosa, manchar, ensuciar, ajar. 2. Denigrar, deshonrar, infamar, quitar el crédito (honor, reputation).

blemish, *s.* 1. Tacha o defecto físico. Imperfección (on skin). 2. Deshonra, infamia, mancha en la reputación, tacha en las cualidades morales. **Without blemish** *or* **defect,** sano y sin tacha. **A blemish on his reputation,** una mancha en su reputación.

blemishless [ˈblemɪʃlɪs] [ble-mish-les], *a.* Irreprensible, sin defecto.

blench [blentʃ] [blench], *vn.* 1. Cejar, recular, retroceder; estremecerse (recoil), palidecer (turn pale). 2. *(Obs.)* Obstruir, impedir.

blencher [ˈblentʃəʳ] [blenchaʳ], *s.* El que espanta o sobresalta.

blend [blend] [blend], *va.* (*pret.* BLENDED, *pp.* BLENDED o BLENT). 1. Mezclar, trabar unas cosas con otras o confundirlas. Licuar (colors). 2. Manchar, echar a perder. 3. *(Pint.)* Mezclar, combinar, casar colores. -*vn.* Unirse, casarse; se dice de los colores. **Blend together,** armonizar (flavors, colors). **The house blends (in) well with its surroundings,** la casa forma un conjunto armonioso con su entorno. **He learned to blend into the background,** aprendió a pasar desapercibido. **Blend in,** añadir, agregar, mezclar (ingredients). Difuminar, extender (make-up). Armonizar, no desentonar.

blend, *s.* Acción y efecto de mezclar; mezcla, mixtura (colors, hues).

blended [ˈblendɪd] [blen-ded] *a.* De mezcla (whisky).

blender [ˈblendəʳ] [blen-daʳ], *s.* 1. Mezclador, licuadora. 2. Brocha para casar.

blennorrhoea [ˈblenərɪə] [ble-no-ria], *s.* *(Med.)* Blenorrea, flujo abundante mucoso; leucorrea.

blent [blent] [blent], *pret.* y *pp.* de BLEND.

bless [bles] [bles], *va.* 1. Bendecir (give benediction), prosperar, hacer feliz. 2. Bendecir, desear o pedir la felicidad y prosperidad de otra persona. 3. Alabar, dar alabanzas por los beneficios recibidos. **He's blessed with good health,** goza de buena salud. **Bless you!,** ¡salud!, ¡Jesús! (to somebody who sneezes), muchísimas gracias (expressing gratitude). **Bless me/my soul!,** ¡válgame Dios! **Bless the Lord!,** ¡bendito, alabado sea el Señor!

bless me, [ˈblesmɪ] [bles-mi], *inter.* ¡Buen Dios! ¡Gran Dios! ¡Válgame Dios!

blessed [ˈblesɪd] [ble-sid], *a.* 1. Bendito, santo; dichoso. 2. Bienaventurado el que goza de la eterna felicidad. **Blessed thistle,** *(Bot.)* cardo bendito. **The blessed Virgin,** la Santísima Virgen. **Blessed are the poor,** bienaventurados los pobres (fortunate, happy). **It's a blessed nuisance,** es un latazo.

blessedly [ˈblesɪdlɪ] [ble-sid-li], *adv.* Bienaventuradamente, dichosamente, felizmente.

blessedness [ˈblesɪdnɪs] [ble-sid-nes], *s.* Felicidad, santidad, beatitud.

blesser [ˈblesəʳ] [ble-saʳ], *s.* El que bendice.

blessing [ˈblesɪŋ] [ble-sin], *s.* Bendición (benediction), la acción de bendecir; bien, prosperidad; gracias, favores del cielo. Aprobación, consentimiento (approval). Consagración (bread, wine). Bendición del cielo (fortunate thing). **This may turn out to be a blessing in disguise,** puede que todo sea para bien o para mejor. **To be a mixed blessing,** tener sus pros y sus contras. **You should count your blessings,** deberías dar gracias por lo que tienes.

blest [blest] [blest], *part. adj.* *V.* BLESSED.

blet [blet] [blet], *vn.* Pasarse, echarse a perder (fruit).

blet, *s.* Picadura, mancha de una fruta demasiado madura; podredumbre incipiente.

blether [ˈbleðəʳ] [blezaʳ] *vn.* BLATHER.

blethering [ˈblezerɪŋ] [ble-ze-rin], *a.* Chirlador, chirladora.

blew [blu:] [blu], *pret.* del verbo TO BLOW.

blight [blaɪt] [blait], *s.* 1. Tizón; pulgón. 2. *(Agr.)* Añublo; alheña, roña. 3. Todo lo que marchita las esperanzas o expectativas. 4. Peste (loosely), plaga, cáncer (curse).

blight, *va.* 1. Atizonar, abrasar, esterilizar, anieblar las mieses. Arruinar, infestar (plant, crop), asolar (region). Arruinar (career, health), malograr (hopes). 2. Ajar, marchitar. *-vn* Atizonarse.

blighter [ˈblaɪtəʳ] [blai-taʳ], *s. (Fam.)* Tipo. **You lucky blighter!,** ¡qué suertudo eres!, ¡qué potra tienes!

blimey [ˈblaɪmɪ] [blai-mi] *interj.* ¡Caray!

blimp [blɪmp] [blimp], *s.* **Blimp,** pequeño dirigible.

blind [blaɪnd] [blaind], *a.* 1. Ciego, privado de la vista. **Blind of one eye,** tuerto. **He's been blind since birth,** es ciego de nacimiento. **To go blind,** quedarse ciego. **How could I have been so blind?,** ¿cómo pude haber sido tan ciego? **Nobody took a blind bit of notice,** nadie le hizo ni p zca de caso. 2. Ignorante, insensato.

blind, *va.* Cegar, quitar la vista; turbar o extinguir la luz de la razón, deslumbrar. **He was blinded in an accident,** perdió la vista en un accidente. Cegar, enceguecer (passion, ambition). Deslumbrar, encandilar (light, wealth). **He was blinded by her beauty,** su belleza lo deslumbró o encandiló. **Love blinded her to his faults,** el amor le impedía ver sus defectos.

blind, *s.* 1. Velo, cualquier cosa que estorba la vista u ofusca el entendimiento. 2. Escondite. 3. Pretexto. 4. Máscara. 5. Tabla, biombo, etc. **Window-blind,** transparente, persianas. **Purblind,** muy corto de vista. **Blinds,** *pl. (For.)* Rindajes. **Venetian blinds,** celosías. **The blind,** los ciegos, los invidentes. **It's a case of the blind leading the blind,** tan poco sabe el uno como el otro.

blind *adv.* **To swear blind that...,** jurar y perjurar que... (as intensifier). **To be blind drunk,** estar más borracho que una cuba.

blind alley [blaɪndˈælɪ] [blaind-a-li], *s.* 1. Callejón sin salida. 2. Atolladero, atascadero, obstáculo insuperable.

blind date [ˈblaɪndeɪt] [blaind-eit] *s.* Cita con un desconocido.

blinders [ˈblaɪndəz] [blain-ders], *s. pl.* Anteojeras, viseras de caballo.

blind flying [ˈblaɪndflaɪŋ] [blaind-flai-in], *s.* 1. Vuelo a ciegas, vuelo ciego. 2. Vuelo dirigido por radar.

blindfold [ˈblaɪndfəʊld] [blaind-foul], *va.* Vendar los ojos.

blindfold, *a.* Que tiene los ojos vendados. *-adv.* Con los ojos vendados. **I could do it blindfold,** podría hacerlo con los ojos vendados.

blindfolded [ˈblaɪndfəʊldɪd] [blaind-foul-ded] *a.* Con los ojos vendados.

blinding [ˈblaɪndɪŋ] [blain-din] *a.* Cegador, deslumbrador, enceguecedor (light). Atroz (headache, pain).

blindly [ˈblaɪndlɪ] [blaind-li], *adv.* Ciegamente, a ciegas, precipitadamente, sin conocimiento ni reflexión.

blindman's-buff [ˈblaɪndmænzˈbʌf] [blainds-baf], *s.* Juego de la gallina ciega.

blindness [ˈblaɪndnɪs] [blain-nes], *s.* 1. Ceguedad o ceguera, privación o falta de la vista. 2. Ceguedad, alucinación, afecto que ofusca y obscurece la razón.

blind side [ˈblaɪnsaɪd] [blain-said], *s.* Debilidad, fragilidad, flaqueza, el flaco o la parte débil de una persona.

blind spot [ˈblaɪnspɒt] [blain-spot] *s.* Punto flaco o débil (weak point). Punto ciego (auto).

blind-worm [ˈblaɪndwɜːm] [blain-uerm], *s.* Cecilia, serpiente pequeña que parece ciega.

blink [blɪŋk] [blink], *vn.* 1. Pestañear, parpadear. 2. Cerrar los ojos, disimular; eludir, evadir. *-va.* 1. Eludir. 2. Paliar, colorear, cohonestar. 3. Guiñar. **If you blink, you'll miss it,** si te descuidas, te lo pierdes. **To blink back tears,** contener las lágrimas.

blink, *s.* Ojeada, mirada pronta y ligera; vislumbre. Parpadeo, pestañeo. En plural significa las ramas que se rompen cazando. **To be on the blink,** no marchar, no andar. **To go on the blink,** estropearse, descomponerse.

blinker [ˈblɪŋkəʳ] [blin-kaʳ], *s.* Luz intermitente. *-pl.* Anteojeras.

blinkered [ˈblɪŋkəd] [blin-ked] *a.* De miras estrechas (attitude). Estrecho (view, outlook).

blinking [ˈblɪŋkɪŋ] [blin-kin] *a.* Intermitente (light). **What a blinking nerve!,** ¡qué cara! **What a blinking idiot!,** ¡qué tipo más imbécil!

blip [blɪp] [blip] *s.* Pitido, bip (sound). Accidente (irregularity). Problema pasajero (problem).

bliss [blɪs] [blis], *s.* 1. Gloria, bienaventuranza, felicidad eterna. 2. Gusto y placer vehemente.

blissful [ˈblɪsfʊl] [blis-ful], *a.* Bienaventurado, feliz en sumo grado, dichoso.

blissfully [ˈblɪsfəlɪ] [blis-fu-li], *adv.* Felizmente. Con gran felicidad. **They were blissfully happy,** eran completamente felices.

blissfulness [ˈblɪsfəlnɪs] [blis-ful-nes], *s.* Suprema felicidad. *V.* BLISS.

blissless [ˈblɪsnɪs] [blis-nes], *a.* Infeliz, desgraciado.

blister [ˈblɪstəʳ] [blis-taʳ], *s.* 1. Vejiga, ampolla, flictena. 2. Vejigatorio, cantárida. 3. Ampolla o burbuja de aire. **These shoes give me blisters,** estos zapatos me hacen ampollas.

blister, *vn.* Ampollarse, levantarse ampollas en alguna parte del cuerpo. *-va.* Ampollar, hacer ampollas, aplicar un vejigatorio o cantárida.

blistering [ˈblɪstərɪŋ] [blis-te-rin] *a.* Abrasador (heat, sun). **A blistering hot day,** un día de calor achicharrante. Virulento (harsh, angry) (attack). **Blistering plaster,** *s.* Vejigatorio o parche de cantáridas.

blithe [blaɪð] [blaiz], **blitheful** [ˈblaɪðfʊl] [blaiz-ful], *a.* Alegre, contento, gozoso, lleno de alegría natural. Despreocupado (unconcerned), risueño (happy, carefree).

blithely [ˈblaɪðlɪ] [blaiz-li], *adv.* Alegremente, con alegría. **They seemed blithely unconcerned,** tenían un aire risueño y despreocupado.

blitheness [ˈblaɪðnɪs] [blaiz-nes], **blithesomeness** [ˈblaɪðsʌmnɪs] [blaiz-som-nes], *s.* Alegría, júbilo, contento del ánimo.

blithering [ˈblaɪðərɪŋ] [blai-ze-rin] *a.* **You blithering idiot!,** ¡imbécil!

blithesome [ˈblaɪðsʌm] [blaiz-som], *a. V.* BLITHE.

blitz [blɪts] [blits] *s. (Aer. Mil.)* Bombardeo aéreo. **The Blitz,** el bombardeo alemán de Londres en 1940-41. **This weekend we're going to hav a blitz on the garden,** este fin de semana vamos a atacar el jardín. Carga (defensiva) (in American football).

blitz, *va.* Bombardear desde el aire (area). *(Sport)* Hacerle una carga defensiva a (quarterback).

blitzkrieg [ˈblɪtskriːg] [blits-krig], *s.* **Blitz-krieg,** guerra relámpago. *(Al.)*

blizzard [ˈblɪzəd] [bli-sard], *s. (E.U.)* 1. Viento huracanado y agudamente frío, con abundante nevada. 2. Descarga ruidosa de armas de fuego; golpe que echa a tierra; desastre repentino.

bloat [bləʊt] [blout], *va.* Hinchar. *-vn.* Entumecerse, hincharse.

bloat, *va.* Ahumar, curar por medio del humo, como se hace con el arenque.

bloat, *a.* Ahumado.

bloatedness [ˈbləʊtɪdnɪs] [blou-tid-nes], *s.* Turgencia, hinchazón con encendimiento del cutis.

bloated [ˈbləʊtɪd] [blou-tid] *a.* Hinchado, abotagado. **I feel bloated after all that food,** me siento hinchado de tanto comer.

bloater [ˈbləʊtəʳ] [blou-taʳ], *s.* Arenque ahumado.

blob [blɒb] [blob], *s.* 1. Gota, masa esférica blanda. 2. Burbuja, ampolla de aire. 3. Masa redonda de hierro que sirve de base a un poste de hierro en los buques. Gota, goterón (drip), mancha, borrón (indistinct shape).

blobber [ˈblɒbəʳ] [blo-baʳ], *s.* Burbuja, la ampolla que se levanta en el agua.

blobber-lip [ˈblɒbəlɪp] [blo-ber-lip], *s.* Bezo, labio grueso.

bloc [blɒk] [blok], *s.* Bloque, agrupación de fuerzas políticas.

block [blɒk] [blok], *s.* 1. Zoquete, pedazo de madera grueso y corto. **Hatter's block,** horma de sombrero. 2. Tajo, pedazo de madera sobre el cual eran degollados los reos. **The executioner's block,** el tajo del verdugo. **To knock somebody's block off,** romperle la crisma a alguien. **Chopping-block,** tajo de cocina. 3. Boliche. 4. *(Mar.)* Motón, garrucha de madera de diversas formas y tamaños por donde laborean los cabos. **Block and block,** *(Mar.)* abesar. 5. Modrego, el sujeto desmañado y que no tiene habilidad. 6. Obstáculo, impedimento. 7. Canto, piedra, trozo de granito, trozo de mármol sin pulir. 8. Polea, garrucha. 9. Molde. 10. *(Mar.)* Motón, cuaderna. **Block of houses,** manzana de casas. **An office block,** un edificio de oficinas. **Block and tackle,** polea con aparejo. **Double block,** motón de dos ojos. **Single block,** motón sencillo. **Snatch block,** pasteca. **Swivel block,** motón giratorio. **Block letter,** tipo de madera. **Block pulley,** carillo, motón, polea. **To be first off the blocks,** ser el primero en la salida.

block, *va.* Bloquear, poner bloqueo a alguna plaza o costa. **To block up,** bloquear, obstruir, cerrar, tapiar, condenar una puerta o ventana. *(Tip.)* Montar una plancha. *(Art y Of.)* Conformar un sombrero. **You're blocking my way,** me estás impidiendo o bloqueando el paso. **This fat man is blocking my view,** ese gordo no me deja ver. **My nose is blocked,** tengo la nariz tapada. **Block in,** cerrarle el paso a (hem in). **Block off,** cortar (street). **Block out,** ahuyentar, borrar de la mente (shut out) (thought). Tapar (obstruct) (light). **Block up,** cerrar, tapiar (seal) (entrance, window). Atascar, tapar (cause obstruction in) (drain, sink). Atascarse, taparse (become obstructed).

blockade [blɒˈkeɪd] [blo-keid], *s.* Cerco que se pone a alguna plaza, bloqueo de un puerto o litoral.

blockade, *va.* Bloquear, poner bloqueo o cerco a alguna plaza.

blockage [ˈblɒkɪdʒ] [blo-keich] *s.* Obstrucción (in pipe, road). *(Med.)* Oclusión.

blockbuster [ˈblɒkˌbʌstəʳ] [blok-bas-taʳ] *s.* Éxito de taquilla (movie). Bestseller, superventas (book).

block capitals [ˈblɒkˌkæpɪtəls] [blok-ka-pi-tals] *s. pl.* Letras mayúsculas de imprenta.

blocked [ˈblɒkt] [blokt] *a.* Obstruido (pipe, artery). Bloqueado, cerrado (road). Bloqueado o congelado (account, currency).

blockhead [ˈblɒkhed] [blok-jed], *s.* Bruto, necio, tonto, bolonio.

blockheaded [ˈblɒkhedɪd] [blok-je-ded], *a.* Lerdo; tardo, estúpido, tonto.

blockheadly [ˈblɒkhedlɪ] [blok-jed-li], *adv.* Lerdamente, tontamente.

block-house [ˈblɒkhaʊs] [blok-jaus], *s.* Fortaleza colocada en medio de un paso para cerrarlo; blocao.

blockish [ˈblɒkɪʃ] [blo-kish], *a.* Estúpido, tonto, bobo, estólido.

blockishness [ˈblɒkɪʃnɪs] [blo-kish-nes], *s.* Estolidez, incapacidad, estupidez, grosería, tontería, necedad; indecencia.

block-like [ˈblɒklaɪk] [blok-laik], *a.* Como un tonto; parecido a un zoquete.

block system [ˈblɒksɪstəm] [blok-sis-tem], *s.* División de una vía férrea en trozos o tramos, para organizar y dirigir el movimiento de los trenes por medio de determinadas señales.

block tin [ˈblɒktɪn] [blok-tin], *s.* Estaño puro, tejo.

bloke [bləʊk] [blouk] *s. (Fam.)* Tipo, tío.

blond, blonde [blɒnd] [blond], *a. y o.* Rubio, rubia. *(Mex.)* Güero, güera, mono, catire.

blond-lace [ˈblɒndleɪs] [blond-leis], *s.* Encaje o blonda hecha de seda.

blood [blʌd] [blad], *s.* 1. Sangre. 2. Sangre, alcurnia, linaje o parentesco. 3. Ira, cólera, indignación. 4. Jugo o zumo de alguna cosa. 5. Vida. 6. Asesinato, muerte violenta. 7. Hombre animoso. **To let blood,** sangrar. **Blue blood,** casta pura; linaje aristocrático. **Music is in his blood,** lleva la música en la sangre. **Bad blood,** resentimiento, animosidad. **Blood and guts,** violencia. **In cold blood,** a sangre fría. **You can't get blood out of a stone,** no se le puede pedir peras al olmo. **I makes my blood boil to think that…,** me hierve la sangre cuando pienso que… **His laugh made my blood run cold,** su risa hizo que se me helara la sangre. **To sweat blood,** sudar sangre o tinta, sudar la gota gorda (hard work). **Blood donor,** donante de sangre. **We're not blood relations,** no tenemos lazos de sangre. **Blood bath,** masacre. **Bloodcurdling,** espeluznante, aterrador. **Bloodhound,** sabueso.

blood, *va.* 1. Ensangrentar, teñir o manchar con sangre. 2. Ensangrentar, exasperar. 3. Sangrar, sacar sangre.

bloodbank [ˈblʌdbæŋk] [blad-bank], *s.* Banco de sangre.

blood-consuming [ˈblʌdkənsjuːmɪŋ] [blad-kon-siu-min], *a.* Lo que gasta sangre.

blooded [ˈblʌdɪd] [bla-did], *a.* 1. Que tiene sangre de tal o cual carácter determinado. **Fishes are cold-blooded,** los peces tienen la sangre fría. 2. De pura casta, de buena raza.

blood-flower [ˈblʌdflaʊəʳ] [blad-flauaʳ], *s. (Bot.)* Flor de la sangre.

blood-frozen [ˈblʌdfrəʊzn] [blad-frousn], *s.* El que tiene la sangre helada.

blood-guiltiness [ˈblʌdˈɡɪltɪnɪs] [blad-guil-ti-nes], *s.* Homicidio, asesinato.

blood-heat [ˈblʌdhiːt] [blad-jít], *s.* El calor natural de la sangre: es decir, 37.6° C/100° Fahr.

blood-horse [ˈblʌdhɔːz] [blad-jors], *s.* Caballo de buena casta, especialmente de la raza anglo-árabe.

bloodhound [ˈblʌdhaʊnd] [blad-jaund], *s.* Sabueso, especie de podenco.

bloodily [ˈblʌdɪlɪ] [bla-di-li], *adv.* Cruelmente, inhumanamente. **The rebellion was bloodily suppressed,** la rebelión fue sofocada de forma sangrienta.

bloodiness [ˈblʌdɪnɪs] [bla-di-nes], *s.* 1. El estado de lo que echa sangre o está sanguinolento. 2. Crueldad.

bloodless [ˈblʌdlɪs] [blad-les], *a.* 1. Exangüe, desangrado, muerto. 2. Sin efusión de sangre. Sin derramamiento de sangre (without blooshed). Sin sangre en las venas (person) (lacking vitality).

bloodletter [ˈblʌdletəʳ] [blad-le-taʳ], *s.* Sangrador, flebotomista.

bloodletting [ˈblʌdˌletɪŋ] [blad-le-tin], *s.* Sangría, flebotomía, abertura de una vena para sacar sangre.

blood mobile [ˈblʌdˈməʊbaɪl] [blad-mou-bail] *s.* Unidad móvil de extracción de sangre.

blood-money [ˈblʌdmʌnɪ] [blad-ma-ni], *s.* Precio de un homicidio.

blood orange [ˈblʌdˌɒrɪndʒ] [blad-o-rindch] *s.* Naranja sanguina o de sangre.

blood platelet [ˈblʌdplətlɪt] [blad-plat-lit], *s.* Plaqueta, plaqueta sanguínea.

blood poisoning [ˈblʌdˌpɔɪznɪŋ] [blad-poi-so-nin], *s.* Envenenamiento de la sangre, septicemia.

blood pressure [ˈblʌdˌpreʃəʳ] [blad-pre-shaʳ], *s.* Presión arterial. **High blood pressure,** hipertensión, presión alta.

blood-red [ˈblʌdˈred] [blad-red], *a.* Encarnado o rojo como la sangre.

blood-relation [ˈblʌdrɪˈleɪʃən] [blad-ri-lei-shon], *s.* Pariente consanguíneo.

blood-relationship [ˌblʌdrɪˈleɪʃənʃɪp] [blad-ri-lei-shon-ship], *s.* Parentesco de consanguinidad.

blood-root [ˈblʌdˈruːt] [blad-rut], *s.* Sanguinaria, planta medicinal perenne de América. Sanguinaria Canadensis.

bloodshed [ˈblʌdʃed] [blad-shed], *s.* Efusión de sangre; matanza.

bloodshedder [ˈblʌdʃedəʳ] [blad-she-daʳ], *s.* Homicida, asesino.

bloodshedding [ˈblʌdʃedɪŋ] [blad-she-din], *s.* Derramamiento de sangre.

bloodshot [ˈblʌdʃɒt] [blad-shot], *a.* Ensangrentado. Inyectado de sangre: se dice, por lo común, de los ojos.

bloodsport [ˈblʌdspɔːt] [blad-sport] *s.* Deporte sangriento.

blood-stained [ˈblʌdsteɪnd] [blad-steind], *a.* Manchado con sangre; cruel.

bloodstone [ˈblʌdstəʊn] [blad-stoun], *s.* Hematites, piedra de color verde con venas o manchas sanguinolentas.

bloodstream [ˈblʌdstriːm] [blad-strím] *s.* El torrente sanguíneo.

bloodsucker [ˈblʌdsʌkəʳ] [blad-sa-kaʳ], *s.* 1. Sanguijuela. 2. Homicida, asesino. 3. Avaro.

bloodsucking [ˈblʌdsʌkɪŋ] [blad-sa-kin], *a.* Que chupa sangre.

bloodthirstiness [ˈblʌdˌθɜːstɪnɪs] [blad-zers-ti-nes], *s.* Inclinación, tendencia y prontitud a derramar sangre.

bloodthirsty [ˈblʌdθɜːstɪ] [blad-zers-ti], *a.* Sanguinario, cruel, inclinado a derramar sangre.

blood transfusion [ˈblʌdtrænsˈfjuːʒən] [blad-trans-fiu-shon], *s.* Transfusión de sangre.

blood-type [ˈblʌdtaɪp] [blad-taip], *va.* Determinar el tipo de sangre.

blood vessels [ˈblʌdˈveslz] [blad-veséls], *s. pl.* Vasos sanguíneos. **She nearly burst a blood vessel when he told her,** casi le dio un ataque cuando se enteró.

blood-warm [ˈblʌdwɔːm] [blad-uorm], *a.* A la temperatura de la sangre.

bloody [ˈblʌdɪ] [bladi], *a.* Sangriento, manchado con sangre, ensangrentado (hands, clothes); cruel. Que sangra, sangrante (wound). Sangriento (battle). *(Vulg. o Coloq.)* (GB) **Where's that bloody dog?,** ¿dónde está ese maldito o puñetero perro? (expressing annoyance, surprise). *(Fam.)* **I didn't understand a bloody word,** no entendí ni jota. *(Vulg.)* **Bloody hell!,** ¡coño!, ¡chingado! **Bloody-faced,** el que tiene cara de asesino. **Bloody flux,** disentería. **Bloody-minded,** cruel, sanguinario. **Bloody-red,** sanguíneo rojo obscuro. **Bloody-sceptred,** el de centro o corona ensangrentada.

bloody, *adv. (Vulg. o Colloq,)* (GB) **The weather was bloody awful!,** ¡hizo un tiempo horrible! **Not bloody likely!,** ¡ni loco!

bloody, *va.* Ensangrentar, manchar con sangre.

bloody-minded [ˈblʌdɪˈmaɪndɪd] [bladi-main-ded] *a.* Difícil, empecinado, atravesado.

bloody-mindedness [ˈblʌdˈmaɪndɪdnɪs] [bladi-main-ded-nes] *s.* Empecinamiento. **He did it out of sheer bloody-mindedness,** lo hizo sólo para fastidiar.

bloom [bluːm] [blúm], *s.* 1. Flor de los árboles y plantas. 2. Flor, hablando de la edad; belleza, lindeza, frescura. 3. Changote, trozo de hierro en bruto o después de la primera operación del mazo. 4. Pelusilla muy suave que cubre algunas frutas y hojas. **To be in bloom,** estar en flor. **To be in full bloom,** estar en plena floración. **To lose one's bloom,** ajarse.

bloom, *va.* Echar o producir flor. *-vn.* 1. Florecer. 2. Ser joven.

bloomery [ˈbluːmərɪ] [blú-me-ri], *s.* La primera forjadura del hierro en goas o changotes.

bloomer [ˈbluːməʳ] [blú-maʳ] *s. (Coloq,)* (GB) Metedura o metida de pata (mistake).

bloomers [ˈbluːməz] [blú-maʳ], *s. pl.* Pantalones bombachos de mujer.

blooming [ˈbluːmɪŋ] [blú-min] *a.* **I missed the blooming bus!,** ¡perdí el condenado o maldito autobús! Radiante (happy and healthy).

bloomingly [ˈbluːmɪŋlɪ] [blú-min-li], *adv.* Floridamente.

blooper [ˈbluːpəʳ] [blú-paʳ] *s.* Metedura o metida de pata.

blossom [ˈblɒsəm] [blo-som], *s.* La flor de los árboles y plantas (mass of flowers). Flor (by single bloom).

blossom, *vn.* Florecer, echar flor. Alcanzar su plenitud (person, relationship). **Our friendship blossomed into love,** nuestra amistad se transformó en amor.

blot [blɒt] [blot], *va.* 1. Borrar, testar o tachar lo escrito. 2. Cancelar. 3. Manchar, ensuciar, empañar. 4. Denigrar. **To blot out,** rayar lo escrito, testar o borrar. Emborronar,

borronear (stain, smear) (page, word). Secar con papel secante (ink).

blot, *s.* 1. Canceladura de alguna cosa escrita, testadura. 2. Borrón, mancha (of ink). **The factory is a blot on the landscape,** la fábrica afea o estropea el paisaje.

blotch [blɒtʃ] [bloch], *s.* 1. Mancha (on skin), borrón, manchón (of paint), lunar, pintarrojo. 2. Roncha, mancha, el bultillo que se eleva en el cutis.

blotch, *va.* Marcar o cubrir con manchas o ronchas. Emborronar, borronear (page).

blotchy [ˈblɒtʃɪ] [blo-chi] *a.* Lleno de manchas (skin).

blotter [ˈblɒtəʳ] [blo-taʳ], *s.* 1. Borrador, libro en que los mercaderes y hombres de negocios hacen sus anotaciones (record book). 2. Papel secante. 3. Carpeta, cartapacio (on desktop). **Police blotter,** fichero de la policía.

blotting [ˈblɒtɪŋ] [blo-tin], *s.* El acto de manchar o borronear papel.

blotting paper [ˈblɒtɪŋˌpeɪpəʳ] [blo-tin-pei-paʳ], *s.* Papel secante, teleta.

blotto [ˈblɒtəʊ] [blo-tou] *a. (Coloq,)* Como una cuba, tomado.

blouse [blaʊz] [blaus], *s.* Blusa.

blow [bləʊ] [blou], *s.* 1. Golpe (shock, setback). **His death came as a blow to us,** su muerte fue un duro golpe para nosotros. **Blows of fortune,** reveses de fortuna. 2. Acaecimiento repentino, desastre, desdicha. 3. Florescencia, estado de florecer las plantas; las flores en general. 4. Ventarrón. 5. Huevo de mosca depositado en carne. Esta voz se expresa a menudo en español por el sufijo -azo, así: **Blow with the fist,** puñetazo. **Blow with a stick,** bastonazo. **To come to blows,** venir a las manos. **At a blow, at a single blow,** de un golpe, de un solo golpe, de una vez. **To give one's nose a blow,** sonarse la nariz.

blow, *vn. (pret.* BLEW. *pp.* BLOWN). 1. Soplar el viento haciéndose sentir. **A gust blew the door shut,** una ráfaga de viento cerró la puerta. **Her umbrella was blown away by the wind,** el viento tiró lejos su paraguas. 2. Jadear, arrojar con vehemencia y congoja el aliento o respiración. 3. Sonar, hacer ruido armonioso algún instrumento músico de viento. 4. Florecer, abrirse las flores. 5. Pasar. *-va.* 1. Soplar, impeler alguna cosa a fuerza de aire. **She blew the ash into the floor,** sopló y echó la ceniza al suelo. **To blow bubbles,** hacer pompas de jabón. 2. Inflar, henchir algo de aire. 3. Dar figura a alguna cosa llenándola de aire. 4. Hacer sonar a un instrumento de viento. 5. Calentar algo con el aliento. 6. Divulgar algo. 7. Hacer florecer.

blow away, apartar o llevar soplando.

blow down, hacer caer alguna cosa soplándola; derribar, echar por tierra.

blow in, (1) introducir alguna cosa soplando. (2) (Jerga E.U.) Gastar inconsideradamente, malgastar, despilfarrar.

blow off, disipar con soplos.

blow out, expeler o separar a soplos. **To blow out a candle,** apagar una vela a soplos o soplarla.

blow over, derribar (tree), tumbar (crops), calmarse (storm), olvidarse (scandal).

blow up, volar (destroy), ampliar (photo), reventar (to burst), aventar (fire).

blow it upon, dañar, desacreditar, disfamar. **To blow a trompet,** tocar una trompeta. **To blow one's nose,** sonarse las narices. *-v. imp.* **It blows,** hace viento. **To blow fresh,** refrescar el viento.

blow-by-blow [bləʊbaʳˈbləʊ] [blou-bai-blou] *a.* Con pelos y señales (account).

blow-dry [ˈbləʊˌdraɪ] [blou-drai] *va.* **To blow-dry one's hair,** hacerse un brushing (secarse el pelo con secador de mano y cepillo). *s.* Brushing.

blower [ˈbləʊəʳ] [blouaʳ], *s.* Soplador, el que sopla; aventador, fuelle. Calefactor (fan). Teléfono (telephone).

blow-fly [ˈbləʊflaɪ] [blou-flai], *s.* Coríndia, mosca grande que deposita sus huevos sobre carne.

blow-gun [ˈbləʊɡʌn] [blou-gan], s. Bodoquera; cañuto con el cual se puede arrojar una flecha soplando con fuerza; cerbatana.

blowhard [ˈbləʊhɑːd] [blou-jard] s. Fanfarrón.

blowing [ˈbləʊɪŋ] [blouin], s. Soplo, soplido; sonido de la respiración bronca. Sopleo de vidrio. -a. Que sopla. **Blowing weather,** tiempo tempestuoso. **Blowing-fan,** aventador.

blown [bləʊn] [bloun], pp. del verbo TO BLOW.

blowout [bləʊˈəʊt] [blou-aut], s. Reventón de neumático o de llanta. Comilona.

blow-pipe [ˈbləʊpaɪp] [blou-paip], s. Soplete. **Glass-blower's pipe,** cafia, cartón desoplar. Cerbatana.

blowsy [ˈbləʊzɪ] [blou-si] a. BLOWZY.

blowtorch [ˈbləʊtɔːtʃ] [blou-torch], s. Soplete para soldar.

blow up [ˈbləʊʌp] [blou-ap] s. (Coloq.) (phot.) Ampliación.

blowy [ˈbləʊɪ] [bloui] a. Ventoso, de mucho viento (day).

blowzy [ˈbləʊzɪ] [blaousi], a. 1. Quemado o tostado por el sol 2. Desaliñado, puerco. **A blowzy woman,** una mujer con pinta de ordinaria.

blubber [ˈblʌbəʳ] [bla-baʳ], s. 1. Grasa o untura de ballena (whale fat). (Coloq,) Grasa (on person). 2. Ortiga marina. 3. Gimoteo, acción de gimotear.

blubber, vn. y a. Llorar hasta hincharse los carrillos; gimotear, lloriquear.

bludgeon [ˈblʌdʒən] [blad-yion], s. Cachiporra o porra, palo corto que tiene un extremo grueso. va. Aporrear (strike). Coaccionar (bully).

blue [bluː] [blú], s. 1. Azul, uno de los siete colores originales. 2. Materia colorante que se emplea para dar un color azul. **The blues,** esplín, melancolía, abatimiento de espíritu. -a. 1. Azul, de color azul, (dress, sea, sky).; cerúleo. 2. Abatido, desalentado. falto de buen humor; triste, melancólico, desconfiado. 3. Severo, estricto, puritánico. 4. Fiel, leal, genuino. 5. Lívido, amoratado, como por una contusión. 6. Pedante; se dice de las mujeres. 7. Que designa el polo sur de un imán: opuesto a rojo. 8. Verde, porno, colorado (pornography). **Blue with cold,** amoratado de frío. **She went blue in the face,** se le amorató la cara. **Sky blue,** azul celeste. **To look blue,** quedarse confuso, chafado, aturullado o consternado. **Blue devils, blues,** dolencia del bazo; hipocondría. **Blue-gum,** eucalipto. **True blue,** leal, constante, adicto; fiel; sin mezcla, sincero, recto. **Blue grass,** hierba del género Poa, particularmente la de Kentucky. **Blue light,** (a) Luz de señales. (b) Preparación pirotécnica que arde con llama azul resplandeciente. **Blue-stone,** sulfato de cobre.

blue, va. 1. Azular, teñir de azul. 2. Pavonar, dar color azulado oscuro al hierro o acero.

blue baby [ˈbluːbeɪbɪ] [blú-bei-bi], s. Niño atacado de cianosis congénita.

blue-bell [ˈbluːbel] [blú-bel], **bluebottle** [ˈbluːbɒtl] [blú-bo-tel], s. (Bot.) Campanilla o coronilla, flor. Jacinto silvestre.

blueberry [ˈbluːberɪ] [blu-be-ri], s. (Bot.) Arándano azul.

blue-bird [ˈbluːbɜːd] [blú-berd], s. Pájaro cantor, muy común en los Estados Unidos; azulejillo, azulejo.

blue-blooded [ˈbluːblʌdɪd] [blu-bla-ded] a. De sangre azul.

bluebottle [ˈbluːbɒtl] [blú-bo-tel], s. (Ent.) Corónida, mosca de vientre azul.

blue-collar [ˈbluːkɒləʳ] [blu-ko-laʳ] a. Obrero (union). Manual (job). **Blue-collar workers,** los obreros.

blue-eyed [ˈbluːaɪd] [blú-aid], a. Ojizarco, ojiazul. De ojos azules. **Blue-eyed boy,** niño mimado.

blue grass [ˈbluːgrɑːs] [blu-gras] s. Hierba que se usa como forraje.

bluejeans [ˈbluːdʒiːnz] [blu-yins] s. vaqueros (pantalones); jeans (jeans).

blueness [ˈbluːnɪs] [blu-nes], s. Propiedad del color azul.

bluenose [ˈbluːnəʊz] [blú-nous] s. (Coloq.) Puritano.

blueprint [ˈbluːprɪnt] [blu-print], s. 1. Cianotipia, cianotipo; heliografía. 2. Plan detallado. 3. Plano, proyecto (of technical drawing); programa (plan of action).

blueprint, va. Copiar a la cianotipia.

blue-ribbon [ˈbluːrɪbɒn] [blu-ri-bon] a. De élite, selecto (goup, panel).

blues [bluːz] [blús], s. pl. 1. (Fam.) Melancolía, tristeza (depression). **To have the blues,** estar deprimido. 2. Canciones con letra triste y ritmo sincopado.

blue tit [ˈbluːtɪt] [blu-tit] s. Alionín, herrerillo.

bluff [blʌf] [blaf], a. 1. Agreste, áspero, rústico. 2. (Mar.) Obtuso. 3. Rudo, firme. 4. Escarpado, amogotado. 5. (Fam.) Francote, campechano (person).

bluff, s. 1. Colina o risco escarpado, por lo general inmediato a las orillas de un río o del mar (cliff). 2. Fanfarronada. **Bluff, blof** (pretence). **To call somebody's bluff,** poner a alguien en evidencia.

bluff, va. Engañar simulando recursos de que se carece. Alardear, fanfarronear. Hacer un bluff o blof. **He managed to bluff his way out of it,** logró salir del apuro embaucándolos.

bluffness [ˈblʌfnɪʃ] [blaf-nes], s. Asperidad.

bluing [ˈbluːɪŋ] [bluin], s. 1. Sustancia colorante azul como el añil, que se emplea en el lavado de ropa; azul en pasta para lavandera. 2. Acto o procedimiento de dar un matiz azul al hierro o acero; el mismo matiz azul.

bluish [ˈbluːɪʃ] [bluish], a. Azulado, lo que tira a azul.

blunder [ˈblʌndəʳ] [blan-daʳ], vn. 1. Desatinar, disparatar, hacer o decir desatinos o despropósitos. 3. Desatinar, perder el tino (move clumsily, stumble) **He blundered into the table,** se tropezó con la mesa. **He blundered around in the dark,** andaba dando tumbos en la oscuridad. 4. Cometer un error garrafal (make a mistake). (Fam.) **That blundering idiot!,** ¡ese idiota perdido! -va. Confundir una cosa con otra sin consideración. **To blunder about,** hacer las cosas a tientas. **To blunder a thing out,** divulgar alguna cosa inconsideradamente; dejar escapar algún secreto sin pensar. **To blunder upon a thing,** desatinar sobre algo, razonar sin conocimiento acerca de una cosa.

blunder, s. Desatino, disparate, despropósito, error craso (mistake); atolondramiento, ligereza, indiscreción, falta. Metedura o metida de pata.

blunderbuss [ˈblʌndəbʌs] [blan-der-bas], s. Trabuco, escopeta corta y de boca ancha que calza muchas balas a un tiempo.

blunderer [ˈblʌndərəʳ] [blan-de-raʳ], **blunderhead** [ˈblʌndəhed] [blan-der-jed], s. Desatinado, imprudente.

blunderingly [ˈblʌndərɪŋlɪ] [blan-de-rin-li], adv. Desatinadamente.

blunge [blʌndʒ] [blandch], va. (Art. y Of.) Mezclar (arcilla) con agua por medio de un Blunger o en una artesa. Cf. PLUNGE.

blunger [ˈblʌndʒəʳ] [bland-chaʳ], s. Paleta para mezclar la pasta.

blunt [blʌnt] [blant], a. 1. Embotado, falto de filo, obtuso; desafilado, que no tiene punta, mocho (knife). Romo (tip, edge). **A blunt instrument,** un objeto contundente. 2. Lerdo, tardo. 3. Bronco, áspero, descortés, tosco, grosero, rudo. Directo, franco (straightforward) (person). Rotundo, categórico (refusal). **To grow blunt,** entorpecerse, embrutecerse, hablando de personas; embotarse, hablando de instrumento.

blunt, va. 1. Embotar, engrosar los filos o puntas de las armas y otros instrumentos cortantes o agudos. 2. Enervar, debilitar. 3. Adormecer, calmar o mitigar un dolor. Despuntar (pencil), desafilar (knife, scissors). Embotar (make dull) (senses, intellect).

bluntly [ˈblʌntlɪ] [blant-li], adv. 1. Sin filo. 2. Lisa y llanamente, sin artificio; sin rodeos, claramente (say); bruscamente, sin delicadeza. 3. Obtusamente, rotundamente (refuse). **To put it bluntly, you bore me,** hablando en plata, me aburres.

bluntness [ˈblʌntnɪs] [blant-nes], s. 1. Embotadura o embotamiento, falta de filo (of blade) o punta en algún arma o instrumento; lo poco afilado, lo mocho (of point). Franqueza (straightfowardness). 2. Grosería, falta de urbanidad; prontitud o viveza de genio con sequedad, aspereza.

blunt-witted [ˈblʌntwɪtd] [blant-uited], *a.* Estúpido, lerdo.

blur [blɜːʳ] [blaʳ], *s.* 1. Apariencia, forma indistinta o confusa. 2. Borrón o mancha. **Everything became a blur,** todo se volvió borroso. **A blur of colors,** una masa de colores indistintos.

blur, *va.* 1. Hacer obscuro o indistinto; desdibujar, hacer borroso (outline). Hacer menos claro (distinction). Hacer borroso (memory). 2. Embotar, entorpecer. 3. Manchar. *vn.* Desdibujarse, hacerse borroso (outline).

blurb [blɜːb] [blerb] *s.* Propaganda, nota publicitaria (en folleto, tapa de libro, etc.)

blurred [blɜːd] [blerd] *a.* Borroso (outline, vision). **The photos were blurred,** las fotos habían salido mal enfocadas. **I felt dizzy and then everything went blurred,** me mareé y empecé a verlo todo borroso.

blurry [blɜrɪ] [bla-ri] *a.* Borroso.

blurt [blɜːt] [blert] *va.* Decir o soltar alguna cosa de una manera abrupta e inesperada. **To blurt out,** hablar sin consideración.

blush [blʌʃ] [blash], *vn.* Abochornarse, sonrojarse, ponerse colorado, mostrar en la cara rubor, vergüenza o confusión tener empacho o vergüenza. *-va.* Sonrojar, abochornar a alguno.

blush, *s.* 1. Rubor, bochorno, sonrojo, los colores que la vergüenza pinta en la cara. **Spare my blushes!,** no me hagas pasar vergüenza, no hagas que me ruborice. 2. Color rojo o purpúreo.

blusher [blʌʃəʳ] [bla-shaʳ] *s.* Colorete, rubor.

blushing [ˈblʌʃɪŋ] [bla-shin], *s.* Sonrojo, sonroseo, bochorno.

blushless [blʌʃlɪs] [blash-les], *a.* Desvergonzado, descarado.

bluster, blustering [ˈblʌstəʳ] [blas-taʳ] [ˈblʌstərɪŋ] [blas-te-rin], *s.* Ruido, tumulto; jactancia. **Blustering weather,** tempestad, tiempo tempestuoso. **A blustering wind,** viento fuerte, vehemente o furioso. **A blustering fellow,** espíritu violento, inquieto o turbulento. **A blustering style,** estilo hinchado.

bluster, *vn.* 1. Bramar, rugir (wind) hacer ruido tempestuoso. 2. Bravear, echar fieros o bravatas, bravuconear (talk threateningly). *-va.* Proferir, articular ruidosa y coléricamente.

bluster, *s.* Bravatas, bravuconería.

blusterer [ˈblʌstərəʳ] [blas-te-raʳ], *s.* Matasiete, el fanfarrón que se precia de valiente y animoso.

blustery [ˈblʌstərɪ] [blas-te-ri], *a.* Borrascoso (wind); tempestuoso (night).

blvd. = Boulevard, Blvar., Br.

b-movie [ˈbɪˌmuːviː] [bi-mu-vi], *s.* Película de serie B o de bajo presupuesto.

bn = billion.

boa [bɔː] [bo], *s.* 1. (*Zool.*) Boa. 2. Boa, cuello de pieles que usan las mujeres. **A boa constrictor,** una boa constrictor.

boar [bɔːʳ] [boʳ], *s.* Verraco, el cerdo padre (pig). **A wild boar,** jabalí.

board [bɔːd] [bord], *s.* 1. Tabla, tablón (plank), pedazo de madera más ancho y largo que grueso; tabla del suelo (floor). **As stiff as a board,** más tieso que un palo, o que una tabla. **To tread the boards,** pisar las tablas. Tabla de madera (for chopping). Tabla, base (circuit). Trampolín (diving). Tabla de surf (for surfing, windsurfing). Tablero (games). **To sweep the boards,** arrasar con o llevarse todos los premios. Tablero de anuncios (notice); letrero, cartel, (sign). Marcador (score). Pizarra, pizarrón, tablero (blackboard). 2. Mesa. 3. La mesa a que se sientan para despachar los ministros de algún tribunal. 4. Tribunal, consejo, junta (committee). **Board of admiralty,** el consejo del almirantazgo. **Board of trade,** junta de comercio. **Board of trustees,** junta directiva. **Board of Education,** junta de Educación. **Board of Health,** junta de Sanidad; la que, con carácter oficial, cuida de mantener y mejorar las

condiciones sanitarias de una población. 5. *(Mar.)* Bordo, el lado o costado de un navío. Bordada, el camino o derrota que recorre una embarcación entre dos viradas, para ganar el barlovento. **To make a good board,** barloventear bien. **On board,** a bordo. **To board to a ship,** embarcarse. 6. Alimento; pensión (provision of meals). **Board and lodging,** comida y alojamiento. **Full/half board,** pensión completa/media pensión. 7. Cartón. *(Enc.)* **Bound in boards,** encartonado. **Bristol-board,** cartulina de Bristol. **Cardboard,** cartón. **Free on board** (f. o. b.) libre de gastos a bordo. *-pl.* **Boards,** las tablas, la escena de un teatro. **Head-board,** cabecera de cama. **Paddle-boards,** paletas (de las ruedas). **Straw board,** cartón de paja. **Chess-board,** tablero para jugar al ajedrez. **Falling board,** trampa. **Side-board,** alacena, bufete. **Sounding-board,** tornavoz. **To go by the board,** *(Mar.)* (1) caer un mástil roto por el costado del buque. (2) Arruinarse por completo. **They have promised to reduce taxation across the board,** han prometido una reducción general de impuestos. **All these precautions tend to go by the board,** todas estas precauciones suelen dejarse a un lado. **To take something on board,** asumir algo.

board, *va.* 1. *(Mar.)* Abordar. 2. Acometer, acercarse a. 3. Entablar, entarimar, cubrir el suelo con tarimas o tablas. *-vn.* 1. Estar de pupilo. 2. Tomar pupilos. **Board up,** cerrar con tablas.

boardable [ˈbɔːdəbl] [bor-da-bol], *a.* Accesible.

board game [ˈbɔːdgeɪm] [bord-gueim] *s.* Juego de mesa.

boarder [ˈbɔːdəʳ] [bor-daʳ], *s.* Pensionista, huésped, pupilo.

boarding [ˈbɔːdɪŋ] [bor-din], *s.* *(Mar.)* Abordaje. **Boarding-pikes,** chuzos.

boarding card [ˈbɔːdɪŋkɑːd] [bor-din-kard] *s.* BOARDING PASS.

boarding-house [ˈbɔːdɪŋhaʊs] [bor-din-jaus], *s.* Casa de pupilos o de huéspedes, posada.

boarding pass [ˈbɔːdɪŋpɑːs] [bor-din-pas] *s.* Tarjeta de embarque, pase de abordar.

boarding pupil [ˈbɔːdɪŋpʊpɪl] [bor-din-pu-pil], *s.* Interno, discípulo, pensionista.

boarding-school [ˈbɔːdɪŋskuːl] [bor-din-skúl], *s.* Internado.

boardroom [ˈbɔːdrʊm] [bord-rum] *s.* Sala o salón de juntas.

boardwalk [ˈbɔːdwɔːk] [bord-uok] *s.* Paseo marítimo entarimado.

boarish [ˈbɔːrɪʃ] [bo-rish], *a.* Brutal, cruel, áspero, bronco.

boast [bəʊst] [boust], *vn.* Jactarse, vanagloriarse, alabarse, prorrumpir en alabanzas propias. **To boast about/of something,** alardear, jactarse o vanagloriarse de algo. *-va.* 1. Ponderar. 2. Exaltar, magnificar. 3. Alabar excesivamente, decantar.

boast, *s.* Alarde, fanfarronada (claim); *(Fam.)* **It's her proud boast that…,** se jacta de que… (cause of pride).

boaster [ˈbəʊstəʳ] [bous-taʳ], *s.* Fanfarrón, jactancioso, presumido.

boastful [ˈbəʊstfʊl] [boust-ful], *a.* Jactancioso, baladrón.

boasting [ˈbəʊstɪŋ] [bous-tin], *s.* Jactancia, expresión de ostentación, vanagloria, bravata.

boastingly [ˈbəʊstɪŋlɪ] [bous-tin-li], *adv.* Jactanciosamente, ostentosamente.

boastless [ˈbəʊstlɪs] [boustles], *a.* Simple, sencillo.

boat [bəʊt] [bout], *s.* Bote, barca o lancha, batel, chalupa (small). Vapor de río. **Ballast-boat,** *(Mar.)* bote de lastrar. **Ferry-boat,** bote de pasaje. **Fishing boat,** bote de pescar. **Shipwright's boat,** bote de maestranza. **Boat in frame,** bote en piezas de armazón. **To bale the boat,** *(Mar.)* achicar el bote. **To trim the boat.** *(Mar.)* adrizar el bote. **To moor the boat,** *(Mar.)* Amarrar el bote. **Boat-rope,** cordel de bote. **Packet-boat,** paquebote o paquebot. **Boat-hook,** bichero, botador. **Boat-house,** casilla de botes. **Boat-load,** barcada. **Gun-boat,** lancha cañonera. **Jolly-boat,** canoa pequeña y ligera. **Life-boat,** bote salvavidas. **Steamboat,** bote de vapor. **Tow-boat** o **tug** (boat), remolcador.

boating ['bəʊtɪŋ] [bou-tin], s. 1. El acto de guiar o manejar un bote, ir en bote. 2. Transporte de carga o pasajeros en bote.

boatload ['bəʊtləʊd] [bout-loud] s. cargamento. **A boatload of tourists,** un barco cargado de turistas.

boatman ['bəʊtmən] [bout-man], **boatsman** ['bəʊtzmən] [bouts-man], s. Barquero.

boat race ['bəʊtreɪs] [bout-reis] s. Regata.

boatswain ['bəʊtsn] [bout-suein], s. Contramaestre. **Boatswain's mate,** segundo contramaestre.

bob [bɒb] [bob], va. 1. Apalear, golpear con algún objeto redondeado o nudoso. 2. Sacudir con el codo o la mano. 3. va. y vn. Mover, agitar, mover(se) de un lado a otro, o de arriba abajo, de una manera súbita y rápida. **The cork bobbed up and down on the water,** el corcho cabeceaba en el agua. 4. Cortar la cola de un caballo. (Coloq,) **Bob up,** aparecer. -vn. 1. Bambolear, moverse alguna cosa de un lado a otro sin salir de su sitio; estar pendiente, colgar. 2. Pescar con boya o flotador ligero de corcho o madera.

bob, s. 1. Pingajo o colgajo; pendiente de oreja. 2. Estrambote, copla añadida a alguna composición poética. 3. Golpe. 4. Un toque de campanas. 5. Corcho de caña para pescar. Cebo para pescar. 6. Lenteja, disco o parte más pesada del péndulo. 7. (Fam.) Chelín (en Inglaterra hasta 1.971). **She's not short of a few bob/bob or two,** está forrada. 8. Balancín de bomba o de máquina de vapor. 9. La cola cortada de un caballo. 10. Inclinación (movement of head), reverencia (curtsy). 11. Melena (haircut).

bob, (Coloq,) (GB) **Bob's your uncle!,** ¡listo!, ¡ya está!

bobbin ['bɒbɪn] [bo-bin], s. 1. Bolillo, pedacito de palo delgado con una cabecilla. 2. Canilla, en que los tejedores devanan el hilo o la seda; broca entre bordadores; carrete diminuto de algunas máquinas de coser. **Lace bobbins,** palillos o majaderitos. **Bobbin-work,** obra o fábrica hecha con palillos, canillas o brocas. 3. Carrete, bobina. (Elec.) Rollo de alambre aislado que contiene generalmente un centro de hierro dulce, el cual se magnetiza cuando atraviesa el alambre una corriente eléctrica.

bobbinet (o **bobbin net**) ['bɒbɪnet] [bo-bi-net], s. Punto de bobiné, labor de adorno.

bobble ['bɒbl] [bo-bel] s. Borla, pompón (on hat). (Sport) Fomble.

bobby ['bɒbɪ] [bo-bi] s. Bobby, policía británico.

bobby pin ['bɒbɪˌpɪn] [bo-bi-pin], s. Variedad de horquilla para el pelo.

bobby socks, bobby sox ['bɒbɪsɒks] [bo-bi-soks], s. pl. Tobilleras, medias tobilleras, calcetines cortos.

bobbysoxer ['bɒbɪsɒksəʳ] [bo-bi-sok-saʳ] s. (Coloq,) (Fam.) Quinceañera, calcetinera.

bobcat ['bɒbkæt] [bob-kat], s. (Zool.) Variedad de lince. Lince rojo.

bobolink ['bɒbəlɪŋk] [bo-bo-link], s. Pájaro migratorio famoso por su canto alegre y retozón.

bobsled ['bɒbsled] [bob-sled], (GB) **bobsleigh** ['bɒbsleɪh] [bob-slei] s. Trineo.

bob-stay ['bɒbsteɪ] [bob-stei], s. (Mar.) Barbiquejo. **Bob-stay-holes,** grueras de tajamar.

bobtail ['bɒbteɪl] [bob-teil], s. Rabón, descolado; cola cortada. **Bobtail car,** (Fam.) Carro urbano pequeño, sin conductor o cobrador y por lo general con un solo caballo.

bobtailed ['bɒbteɪld] [bob-tei-lid], a. Rabón, descolado; con cola cortada.

bob-white ['bɒbwaɪt] [bob-uait], s. Codorniz, perdiz.

bobwig ['bɒbwɪg] [bob-uig], s. Peluca redonda; peluquín.

bocasine ['bɒkəsiːn] [bo-ka-sin], s. 1. Especie de bocací delgado. 2. V. CALLIMANCO.

bod [bɒd] [bod] s. Cuerpo, figura (body). (GB) Tipo (person). (Fam.) **An odd bod,** un bicho raro.

bodacious ['bɒdəʃəs] [bo-da-shos] a. Voraz (appetite); espantoso (hurry).

bode [bəʊd] [boud], va. Presagiar, pronosticar. **To bode well/ill,** ser buena/mala señal. -vn. Predecir.

bodega [bɒʊˈdeɪgə] [bou-dei-ga] s. Tienda de comestibles o de abarrotes; almacén (grocery store).

bodement ['bɒʊdmənt] [boud-ment], s. Presagio, pronóstico.

bodice ['bɒdɪs] [bo-dis], s. Corpiño (undergarment), jubón ajustado al cuerpo, parte del vestido de mujer; almilla atada con cordones. Canesú (of dress).

bodied ['bɒdɪd] [bo-did], a. Corpóreo, lo que tiene cuerpo. **Big-bodied,** corpulento. **Green-bodied,** de cuerpo verde. See also ABLE-BODIED.

bodiless ['bɒdɪlɪs] [bo-di-les], a. Incorpóreo, lo que no tiene cuerpo.

bodily ['bɒdɪlɪ] [bo-di-li], adv. Corpóreo, corporal, real, verdadero. **Bodily functions,** funciones fisiológicas.

bodily, adv. Corporalmente, con el cuerpo. **They dragged him bodily into the car,** lo agarraron y lo metieron en el coche a la fuerza.

boding ['bɒdɪŋ] [bo-din], s. Presagio, pronóstico.

bodkin ['bɒdkɪn] [bod-kin], s. 1. Punzón de sastre. 2. Agujeta o aguja de jareta. 3. (Ant.) Daga, puñal. 4. Horquilla para los cabellos. 5. (Tipo.) Punzón para sacar tipos de una forma.

body ['bɒdɪ] [bo-di], s. 1. Cuerpo, la sustancia material del hombre y de los demás animales. **Body and soul,** en cuerpo y alma. **Body language,** lenguaje corporal. 2. Tronco, el cuerpo humano con excepción de la cabeza, brazos y piernas (trunk); cadáver (corpse). **A dead body,** un cadáver. **Over my dead body!,** ¡tendrán que pasar por encima de mi cadáver. 3. Materia, en oposición al espíritu. 4. Una persona, un individuo. 5. Realidad, como opuesta a una mera representación. 6. Cuerpo, la masa colectiva o el agregado de las partes que componen un todo, el grueso de algo (majority, bulk). 7. Cuerpo o gremio, el agregado de personas que forman un pueblo, república o comunidad. 8. Cuerpo, la parte principal de alguna cosa (main part); carrocería (auto), fuselaje (plane), casco (ship). **Body shop,** taller de carrocería. 9. Colección general. 10. Cuerpo, espesor, fortaleza. **They walked out in a body,** salieron en masa o en bloque (unit). **A body of evidence,** un conjunto de pruebas (colection). **Foreign body,** cuerpo extraño (object). **Heavenly body,** cuerpo celeste. **A busybody,** entremetido. **Anybody,** Cualquiera. **Somebody,** alguien, alguno, **Everybody,** cada uno, todos. **Nobody,** Ninguno, nadie. **Body of a church,** nave de una iglsia. **Body of a tree,** tronco. **The main body of an army,** el grueso de un ejército. **Body-clothes,** manta que se pone a los caballos. **Body-color,** primera mano de color. **Body-guard,** (1) Guardia de corps. (2) (Fig.) Seguridad. Salvaguardia. **Body builder,** fisiculturista. **Body building,** fisiculturismo. **Body search,** cacheo. **Body shirt,** blusa (blouse); body, maillot (leotard). **Body stocking,** body. **Body work,** carrocería; trabajo de carrocería (repairing).

body, va, Dar cuerpo, forma u orden a alguna cosa. Able-bodied, Sano, robusto, sin tacha.

boetian ['bɒʊʃən] [bou-shan], a. De Beocia, provincia de Grecia; beocio.

boer ['bɒʊəʳ] [bauaʳ], s. Agricultor holandés; persona blanca de raza holandesa en la República del Transvaal.

bog [bɒg] [bog], s. Pantano, ciénaga (swamp). **To be bogged down with work,** estar inundado de trabajo. **Bog-bean,** (Bot.) trifolio fibrino. **Bog-moss,** esfagno, musgo de pantano. **Bog-ore, bog-iron** ore, limonita, peróxido de hierro hidratado. **Bog-land,** el que vive en país pantanoso. Tierra pantanosa. **Bog-oak,** lignito de encina. **Bog-trotter,** el que vive entre pantanos. (GB) (Sl.) Retrete (lavatory).

bogey o bogy ['bəʊgɪ] [bou-gui], s. Duende, espantajo (evil spirit) BOGEYMAN. (GB) Moco.

bogeyman ['bəʊgɪˌmæn] [bo-gui-man] s. (Fam.) Coco, cuco.

boggle ['bɒgl] [bogl], vn. 1. Recular, cejar, retroceder. 2. Cejar, fluctuar, titubear, vacilar, balancear. **The mind boggles,** uno se queda helado o pasmado, uno alucina.

boggle, s. Fantasma, espectro, objeto espantoso.

bogglish ['bɒglɪʃ] [bo-glish], a. Irresoluto, indeciso.

boggy ['bɒgɪ] [bo-gui], *a.* Pantanoso, lleno de pantanos, cenagoso.

bogie ['bəʊgɪ] [bou-gui], *s.* Carretilla. **Bogie-engine,** Locomotora de balaste.

bogus ['bəʊgəs] [bo-gus], *a.* Falso (claim, name), espúreo; postizo. Falaz (argumento). **A bogus company,** una empresa fantasma.

bohemian [bəʊˈhiːmɪən] [bou-í-mian], *s.* Bohemio (unconventional), bohemiano, de Bohemia.

boil [bɔɪl] [boil], *vn.* Hervir, cocer; se dice de todo lo que hierve o cuece (be at boiling point) (water, vegetables). **The rice has boiled dry,** el arroz se ha quedado sin agua. 2. Bullir; se dice de los líquidos. **Boiling water,** agua hirviendo. 3. Estar extraordinariamente agitado o hervirle a uno la sangre (be excited). **He was boiling with rage,** le hervía la sangre de rabia. 4. Estar lleno de fervor. **To boil away,** consumir un líquido a fuerza de cocerlo, reducir (stock, sauce). **To boil down to,** reducirse a. **What it boils down to is,** en resumidas cuentas, lo que pasa es esto. **To boil down,** reducir por medio de la cocción (milk, pan). Perder el control (person). **To boil over,** bullir o salirse fuera de la vasija con el calor. **To boil up,** estarse preparando. *-va.* Cocer (cook in boiling water) (vegetables). **Boil the eggs for three minutes,** cocer o hervir los huevos tres minutos. Hervir (bring to boiling point); dejar hervir (keep to boiling point). **Boiled,** hervido (potatoes, rice), cocido (ham), pasado por agua (egg) (soft), duro (hard). **Boiled sweet,** caramelo de fruta.

boil, *s.* (*Med.*) Divieso, furúnculo, tumor doloroso. (Cuba) Nacido. (*Mex.*) Clacote. **The vegetables are on the boil,** las verduras se están haciendo (boiling point). **He has another project on the boil,** tiene un nuevo proyecto entre manos. **Bring the water to the boil,** dejar que el agua rompa el hervor. **Interest in the affair has gone off the boil,** ha decaído el interés en el asunto.

boiler ['bɔɪləʳ] [boi-laʳ], *s.* 1. Cocedor, el que cuece alguna cosa. 2. Marmita, olla o caldero. 3. Caldera, calentador (water, heater), caldera (in steam engine). **Large boiler,** cazo, caldera, paila. **Steam-boiler,** hervidero para vaho; caldera de vapor. **Sugar boilers,** (Cuba) tachos. **Boiler compound,** pasta o polvos desincrustadores para las calderas. **Boiler-shell o jacket,** camisa o cubierta de una caldera. **Boiler-iron,** hierro en planchas para calderas.

boiler maker ['bɔɪləˈmeɪkəʳ] [boilar-mei-kaʳ], *s.* Calderero. (*Fam.*) Whisky con cerveza. **Boilermaker room,** sala de calderas. **Boilermaker suit,** mono, overol.

boilery ['bɔɪlərɪ] [boi-le-ri], *s.* En las salinas, el lugar donde está el caldero para secar la sal.

boiling ['bɔɪlɪŋ] [boi-lin], *s.* Hervor; ebullición; cocción, acción de hervir. *a.* (*Coloq*) **This coffee is boiling,** este café está hirviendo. (*Fam.*) **I'm boiling,** estoy asado. **It's boiling hot today,** hace un calor espantoso hoy.

boiling, *va.* Hirviendo. **Boiling hot,** hirviendo a borbollones o borbotones. **Boiling-kettle,** caldera. **Boiling-point,** punto de ebullición (del agua), centígrado, 100°; Fahrenheit 212°; Réaumur, 80°, al nivel del mar. **To be at/reach boiling point,** estar, ponerse al rojo vivo (situation).

boisterous ['bɔɪstərəs] [bois-te-ros], *a.* 1. Vociglero rudo, clamoroso, ruidoso, tumultuoso, bullicioso (child/game). 2. Borrascoso, tempestuoso. **A boisterous youth,** un aturdido.

boisterously ['bɔɪstərəslɪ] [bois-te-ros-li], *adv.* Ruidosamente, tumultuosamente, curiosamente.

boisterousnes ['bɔɪstərəsnɪs] [bois-te-ros-nes], *s.* Turbulencia, tumulto, vociglería; vehemencia, impetuosidad.

bold [bəʊld] [bould], *a.* 1. Intrépido, arrojado, ardiente, falto de temor, bravo, valiente. 2. Audaz, atrevido, osado, temerario (daring). 3. Impudente, descarado, desvergonzado (smile, advances). **If I may be so bold as to...,** si me permite el atrevimiento... 4. (*Mar.*) Saltado, alto, escarpado, acantilado; se dice de la ribera del mar. 5. Llamativo (pattern); fuerte, vivo (color).

bold-face ['bəʊldfeɪs] [bould-feis], *s.* 1. Descaro, desvergüenza, impudencia. 2. Negrita.

bold-faced ['bəʊldfeɪst] [bould-fei-sid], *a.* Descarado, desvergonzado. **Bold-faced type,** letra negra, negrita, como ésta: **Bold-face.** Lo mismo que FULL-fACE.

boldly ['bəʊldlɪ] [bould-li], *adv.* 1. Intrépidamente, audazmente (daringly). 2. Descaradamente, con descaro (impudently).

boldnes ['bəʊldnɪs] [bould-nes], *s.* 1. Arresto, arrojo o determinación para comprender alguna cosa árdua; intrepidez, aliento, ánimo, resolución, valentía. 2. Descaro, desvergüenza (impudence). 3. Libertad, atrevimiento, avilantez, osadía (daring). 4. Confianza en Dios.

bole [bəʊl] [boul], *s.* 1. Tronco, la parte inferior de un árbol. 2. Bol o bolo, especie de tierra que se usa para los tintes, las pinturas y el bruñido de oro. 3. Antigua medida inglesa para grano, de seis fanegas; dos hectolitros.

bolero [bəˈleərəʊ] [bo-le-rou], *s.* 1. Bolero, aire musical popular español y el baile correspondiente. 2. Bolero, chaquetilla corta de señora, abierta al frente.

bolide ['bɒlɪd] [bo-lid], *s.* Bólido, meteoro ígneo que cruza el espacio con gran velocidad. (*Gal.*)

Bolivian [bəˈlɪvɪən] [bo-li-vian] *a./s.* Boliviano.

boll [bəʊl] [bol], *s.* Tallo. **Boll of flax** o **hemp,** tallo o cápsula de lino o cáñamo. **Boll** o **bole of salt,** medida de sal que consta de dos fanegas.

bollard ['bəʊləd] [bou-lard] *s.* Noray, bolardo. (GB) Baliza (by road).

bollix ['bəʊlɪks] [bou-liks] *va.* (AmE) (*Sl.*) **Try not to bollix up this time!,** ¡esta vez intenta no cagarla! **The numbers are all bollixed up,** los números están todos liados.

bolloking ['bɒləkɪŋ] [bo-la-kin] *s.* (GB) (*Sl.*) **To give somebody a bollocking,** echarle una bronca a alguien.

bollocks ['bɒləks] [bo-loks] *s. pl.* (GB) (*Vulg.*) Huevos, pelotas, cojones, (testicles). Pendejadas o gilipolleces, pelotudeces, boludeces, huevadas (nonsense).

boll weevil ['bəʊlwiːvɪl] [boul-ui-vil], *s.* Picudo, gorgojo del algodón.

Bologna [bəˈləʊnɪə] [bo-lou-nia] *s.* Tipo de salchicha ahumada. **Bologna sausage,** salchichón de Bolonia.

bolognese [bɒləˈnjeɪz] [bo-lo-ñeis], *a.* Bolonés, de Bolonia. **Bolognese sauce,** salsa boloñesa, tuco.

Bolshevik ['bɒlʃəvɪk] [bol-she-vik], *s.* y *a.* Bolchevique.

Bolshevism ['bɒlʃəvɪzəm] [bol-she-visem], *s.* Bolchevismo.

bolshie, bloshy ['bɒlʃɪ] [bol-shi] *a.* (GB) (*Coloq,*) Rebelde, díscolo.

bolster ['bəʊlstəʳ] [bouls-taʳ], *s.* 1. Travesero, almohadón para recostar la cabeza en la cama; almohada de forma cilíndrica. 2. Colcha. 3. Cabezal, lienzo de varios dobleces que se pone encima de la herida. 4. (*Mar.*) Almohada de los palos. 5. Borrenes, las almohadillas de la silla de montar. 6. Solera de carro. (*F.C.*) 7. Nabo; cancelillo; caballete.

bolster, *va.* 1. Recostar la cabeza en el travesero. 2. Aplicar el cabezal a una herida. 3. Sostener, mantener, apoyar; reforzar (popularity, economy), reafirmar (argument), levantar (morale).

bolsterer ['bəʊlstərəʳ] [bouls-te-raʳ], *s.* Mantenedor, sostenedor.

bolstering ['bəʊlstərɪŋ] [bouls-te-rin], *s.* Apoyadero, apoyo.

bolt [bəʊlt] [boult], *s.* 1. Dardo, flecha. 2. Rayo; proyectil largo y cilíndrico para un cañón; lo que aparece o sobreviene de repente. 3. Cerrojo, pasador de una puerta. 4. Pestillo de cerradura. 5. (*E.U.*) Disidencia, acto de separarse de un partido político, o de negarse a apoyar a un candidato, medida o política de un partido. 6. Partida o salto repentino. **A bolt for home,** partida súbita de una persona con rumbo a su casa. 7. Rollo (de tela). 8. (*Mar.*) Perno, cavillas de hierro. **Bolts,** grillos, prisiones para los pies. 9. Clavija, perno, tolete. 10. Tamiz muy fino para separar la harina del salvado. 11. Relámpago, rayo (of lightning). **Bolt of cloth,** rollo. **Bolt and nut,** perno y tuerca. **Countersunk bolt,** perno de cabeza perdida. **Round-headed bolt,** perno de cabeza de hongo. **Square-headed bolt,** perno de cabeza, de diamante. **Bolt up right,** derecho, recto como un dardo.

bolt, va. 1. Cerrar con cerrojo. 2. Cerner, separar con el cedazo las partes más finas de cualquier materia reducida a polvo. 3 Examinar, escudriñar. 4 (E.U) Rehusar uno su apoyo al partido político a que pertenece; rechazar candidato o una medida de partido. 5. Charlar, hablar sin discreción ni tacto, descubrir por imprudencia lo que se debe callar. 6. Engullir, tragar sin mascar. 7. Lanzar, arrojar, echar, expeler de repente. **To bolt together,** asegurar con pernos (fasten with bolts). **To bolt down,** engullir (food, meal). -vn. 1. Saltar de repente. 2. Lanzarse, arrojarse. 3. Caer como un rayo. **To bolt in,** entrar de repente. **To bolt oral,** salir de golpe.

bolt, adv. **Bolt upright,** muy erguido. **He suddenly sat bolt upright in bed,** se irguió de repente en la cama.

bolter [ˈbɔʊltəʳ] [boul-taʳ], s. 1. Cedazo. 2. Especie de red. 3. El que niega su apoyo a una candidatura debidamente acordada o designada.

bolthead [ˈbɔʊlthed] [boult-jed], s. (Quím.) Recipiente.

bolting [ˈbɔʊltɪŋ] [boul-tin], s. 1. Cernido o cernidura, la acción de pasar por cedazo. 2. Cerramiento. 3. Acción de negar su apoyo a un candidato o a una medida de partido. **Bolting-cloth,** cedazo, tamiz, criba. **Bolting-house.** cernedero. **Bolting-hutch, bolting-tub,** tina para cerner harina.

bolus [ˈbɔləs] [bo-lus], s. 1. Bolo, píldora gruesa; de aquí, dosis o medicamento difícil de tomar. 2. Cuerpo esférico de cualquier materia.

bomb [bɔm] [bom], s. Bomba (explosive device). **Bomb scare.** amenaza de bomba. **Bomb squad,** brigada antiexplosivos o de explosivos. **The room looked as if a bomb had hit it,** la habitación estaba toda patas arriba. (GB) (Coloq,) **To cost a bomb,** costar un dineral (large sum).

bomb, vn. Zumbar, sonar como una bomba. (Fam.) Ser un fracaso, tronar (flop, play). (GB) (Fam.) **To bomb along,** ir a todo lo que da (go fast). -va. Bombardear (from air). Colocar una bomba en (plant bomb in). (Fam.) Poner por los suelos (condemn).

bomb-chest [ˈbɔmtʃest] [bom-ches], s. Caja de bombas que se pone en algún paraje subterráneo para volarlo.

bombard [bɔmˈbɑːd] [bom-bard], s. 1. Bombarda, una máquina militar antigua. 2. (Ant.) Vasija para conservar vino.

bombard, va. (Mil.) Bombardear, tirar bombas (assail). **She was bombarded with questions,** la acribillaron o bombardearon a preguntas.

bombardier [ˌbɔmbəˈdɪəʳ] [bom-bar-diaʳ], s. Bombardero. **Bombardier beetle,** escarabajo bombardero o escopetero.

bombardment [bɔmˈbɑːdmənt] [bom-bard-ment], s. Bombardeo, el acto de bombardear.

bombast [ˈbɔmbɑːst] [bom-bast], s. 1. Hinchazón, estilo hinchado. 2. Especie de estofa blanda y ligera.

bombast, bombastic, a. Altisonante, pomposo, retumbante, hinchado. Grandilocuente, bombástico.

bombax [ˈbɔmbɑːks] [bom-baks], s. Árbol americano de los trópicos, familia de las malváceas; la ceiba de Cuba. Bombax.

bombazette [ˈbɔmbəziːt] [bom-ba-síf], s. Alepín.

bombazine [ˈbɔmbəziːn] [bom-ba-sín], s. Alepín, tela fina de lana y seda.

bomb disposal [ˈbɔmdɪsˈpəʊzəl] [bomb-dis-pou-sal] s. Desactivación de explosivos. **Bomb disposal expert,** artificiero.

bombed [ˈbɔmd] [bombd] a. (Fam.) **To be bombed,** estar como una cuba, estar tomado.

bomber [ˈbɔməʳ] [bom-baʳ], s. 1. Bombardero, avión de bombardeo (aircraft). 2. Terrorista que perpetra atentados colocando bombas (terrorist). **Bomber jacket,** chaqueta, cazadora, chamarra o campera de aviador.

bombic [ˈbɔmbɪk] [bom-bik], a. Perteneciente al gusano de seda (bombice) o que se deriva de él.

bombing [ˈbɔmbɪŋ] [bom-bin] s. Bombardeo (from aircraft). Atentado terrorista (from terrorists).

bomb-proof [ˈbɔmpruːf] [bomb-prúf], a. (Mil.) A prueba de bomba. **Bomb release,** s. (Acr.) Lanzabombas.

bombshell [ˈbɔmʃel] [bomb-shel], s. 1. Bomba, granada. 2. (fig.) Sorpresa devastadora. **The news about their divorce came as a bombshell,** la noticia de su divorcio cayó como una bomba. (Coloq,) **A blonde bombshell,** una rubia explosiva.

bomb shelter [ˈbɔmˌʃeltəʳ] [bomb-shel-taʳ], s. Refugio antiaéreo.

bombsight [ˈbɔmsaɪt] [bom-sait], s. Mira de bombadero, visor.

bombyx [ˈbɔmbɪks] [bom-biks], s. (Ent.) Gusano de seda en el estado de mariposa, bómbice.

bona-fide [ˈbɔʊnəˈfaɪdɪ] [bouna-faidi], (Lat.) De buena fe, sin engaño. (Coro.) Verdad sabida, y buena fe guardada. Genuino, auténtico.

bonanza [bəˈnænzə] [bo-nan-sa] s. Filón, mina de oro (piece of luck). Superabundancia, gran oferta (plentiful supply).

bonbon [ˈbɔnbən] [bon-bon], s. Confite, dulce, caramelo.

bond [bɔnd] [bond] s. 1. La cadena o soga con que está atado alguno. 2. Ligadura, vínculo, unión (link). **The bond between mother and child,** el vínculo afectivo entre madre e hijo. s. Prisión, cautiverio. 4. Obligación, la escritura, promesa o cédula que uno hace a favor de otro, de que cumplirá aquello que ofrece o a que se obliga. **My word is my bond,** puedes fiar o de confiar en mi palabra. 5. Bono, obligación (debt certificate); título de la deuda de una corporación o una nación. **To bond,** poner en depósito. **In bond,** en depósito. 6. Depósito. -a. Cautivo, siervo. **Bonds,** cadenas (fetters).

bond, vn. Adherirse (stick); establecer vínculos o lazos afectivos (form relationship). va. **To bond something to something,** adherir o pegar algo a algo.

bondage [ˈbɔndɪdʒ] [bon-dich], s. Cautiverio, esclavitud, servidumbre, estado a que pasa la persona que, perdida su libertad, vive en poder de otro (enslavement); obligación.

bonded [ˈbɔndɪd] [bon-did], pp. 1. Garantizado por obligación escrita; asegurado; protegido por seguro de infidelidad (guard/salesperson). 2. En depósito aduanero (goods). **Bonded goods,** mercancías en depósito **Bonded-warehouse,** almacén en depósito. **Bond-holder,** almacén de depósito. **Bond-holder,** tenedor de bonos u obligaciones.

bondmaid [ˈbɔndmeɪd] [bond-meid], s. Esclava, sierva, mujer puesta en esclavitud.

bondman [ˈbɔndmən] [bond-man], s. Esclavo, siervo.

bondservant [bɔndˈsɜːvənt] [bond-ser-vant], s. El esclavo o esclava que sirve como tal.

bondservice [bɔndˈsɜːvɪs] [bond-ser-vis], s. Esclavitud.

bondslave [ˈbɔndsleɪv] [bond-sleiv], s. V. BOND-MAN.

bondsman [ˈbɔndsmən] [bonds-man], s. 1. Fiador, seguridad, el que da fianza por otro. 2. Esclavo.

bone [bəʊn] [boun], s. 1. Hueso, la parte sólida y dura del animal. 2. Raspa o espina del pez. 3. Hueso, fragmento de carne. **I can feel it in my bones,** tengo ese presentimiento. **To pick a bone,** roer un hueso. **To have a bone to pick with anyone,** tener que hacer con alguno; tener alguna queja de él, alguna diferencia, o satisfacción que pedirle. **A Spaniard to the backbone,** español de pies a cabeza. **He makes no bones about being an atheist,** no esconde o no oculta que es ateo. **To be close to the bone,** pasarse de castaño oscuro. 4. Dado. **The back-bone,** la espina dorsal. **The cheek-bone,** el hueso malar, apófisis del pómulo. **The jaw-bone,** la quijada. **To be skin and bones,** no tener más que la piel y los huesos. **Whale-bone,** barba de ballenas. **Boneblack,** negro animal. **Bones,** restos, huesos (of dead person).

bone, va. 1. Desosar, quitar o apartar los huesos de la carne; quitar las espinas a (fish). 2. Emballenar, poner ballenas a un corpiño, corsé, etc. 3. Abonar con huesos pulverizados. (Coloq,) **Bone up on,** estudiar. **Bone china,** porcelana fina. **Bone dry,** completamente seco. **Bonehead, boneheaded,** estúpido. (GB) (Coloq,) **Bone idle,** haragán, flojo.

bone, -*va.* Nivelar con un instrumento.

bone-ache [bəʊnˈeɪk] [boun-eik], *s.* Dolor de huesos.

boned [bəʊnd] [bound], *a.* Osudo, huesudo, ososo; robusto.

bonelace [ˈbəʊnleɪs] [boun-leis], *s.* Encaje de hilo.

boneless [ˈbəʊnlɪs] [boun-les], *s.* Pulposo, sin huesos.

boner [ˈbəʊnəʳ] [bounaʳ] *s. (Coloq.)* Metedura o metida de pata.

boneset [ˈbəʊnset] [boun-set], *s.* Eupatorio, hierba medicinal amarga y tónica. Eupatorium perfoliatum.

bone-setter [ˈbəʊnsetəʳ] [boun-se-taʳ], *s.* Cirujano, curandero, el que concierta los huesos dislocados.

bonfire [ˈbɒnfaɪəʳ] [bon-faiaʳ], *s.* Hoguera o fogata encendida al aire libre, ya para quemar basura, ya por diversión o en señal de regocijo. **Bonfire night,** (in UK) GUY FAWKES NIGHT.

bonhomie [ˈbɒnɒmiː] [bon-o-mi] *s.* Cordialidad.

bonito [bɒnˈiːtə] [bo-ni-to], *s.* Pez semejante al atún.

bonk [bɒŋk] [bonk] *vn. (Coloq,)* **To bonk somebody on the nose,** pegarle o darle a alguien en la nariz.

bonkers [ˈbɒŋkəz] [bon-kers] *a.* **To be bonkers,** estar chiflado. **To go bonkers,** perder la chaveta.

bonnet [ˈbɒnɪt] [bo-nit], *s.* 1. Gorra, gorro; sombrero de mujer (clothing). 2. Solideo, bonete. 3. *(Fort.)* Bonete de clérigo, pequeño baluarte avanzado. 4. *(Mar,)* Borietas, los pedazos de velas que se añaden por la parte inferior a la vela mayor, mesina y trinquete.

bonnily [ˈbɒnɪlɪ] [bouni-li], *adv.* Bonitamente, alegremente, hermosamente.

bonny [ˈbɒnɪ] [bo-ni], *a.* 1. Bonito, lindo, galán, gentil. 2. Alegre, festivo. Es voz usada hoy casi exclusivamente en Escocia.

bon-ton [bɒnˈtɒn] [bon-ton], *s.* 1. El gran mundo, la alta sociedad. 2. Buen tono, buenas maneras. (Gal,)

bonus [ˈbəʊnəs] [bo-nos], *s.* 1. Adehala, lo que se da de gracia sobre el precio principal. 2. Regalo en dinero para obtener un favor, un privilegio o suministro. 3. Prima; bonificación (payment to employee). **For a bonus of two points,** para ganar dos puntos extra (in competition).

bony [ˈbəʊnɪ] [bou-ni], *a.* Huesudo (knee); óseo (made of bone).

boo [buː] [bú] *interj.* (GB) ¡Bu! **He wouldn't say boo to a goose,** es incapaz de matar una mosca. *s.* Silba, rechifla.

boo, boos, booing, booed, *va.* **She was booed off the stage,** le abuchearon y tuvo que abandonar el escenario. -*vn.* Abuchear.

boob [buːb] [búb] *s. (Coloq,)* Metedura o metida de pata (blunder). *(Fam.)* **To make a boob,** meter la pata. *(Fam. o vulg.)* Teta, pechuga (breast). Bobo (foolish person).

boo-boo [buːˈbuː] [bú-bu] *s.* BOOB.

booby [ˈbuːbɪ] [bú-bi], *s.* Zote, hombre bobo, necio e ignorante. **Booby hatch,** loquero. **Booby prize,** premio al peor.

booby trap [ˈbuːbɪtræp] [bu-bi-trap], *s. (Mil.)* Granada o mina disimulada que estalla al moverse el objeto que la oculta. Bomba trampa. **His car was booby trapped,** le pusieron una bomba en el coche.

boodle [ˈbuːdl] [bú-del], *s.* (Ger. E. U.) 1. Dinero, especialmente dinero pagado como soborno; producto de un hurto o malversación. 2. Agregado, totalidad, colección; cuadrilla. Se escribe también *caboodle.* Se dice más comúnmente de personas. 3. *(Ger.)* Moneda falsa.

booger [ˈbuːgəʳ] [bú-gaʳ] *s.* Moco (seco).

boogey-man [ˈbuːgɪmən] [bu-gui-man] *s.* BOGEYMAN.

boogie [ˈbuːgɪ] [bú-gui] *vn. (Coloq,)* Bailar.

boogie-woogie [ˈbuːgɪˌwuːgɪ] [bu-gui-vu-gui], *s.* Forma de tocar *blues* en el piano caracterizada por un ritmo grave y persistente.

boo-hoo [buːˈhuː] [bu-ju] *interj.* ¡buuah!

booing [ˈbuːɪŋ] [buin] *s.* Abucheo.

book [bʊk] [buk], *s.* 1. Libro (printed book), volumen de papel cosido y cubierto para leer o escribir en él; cuaderno (exercise book), libreta o cuaderno de apuntes (notebook); Guía, directorio (telephone book). Muestrario (set of samples); librito (of matches, stamps) 2. Libro, las partes principales en que se divide algún volumen o tratado. 3. Libro de asiento, el libro en que un negociante asienta sus cuentas. **To keep the books,** llevar los libros, la contabilidad. Registro (of club, agency) **Are you on our books?,** ¿está usted inscrito aquí? **Day-book,** diario. **Invoice-book,** libro de facturas. **Pocket-book,** cartera. **Memorandum-book,** librito de memoria. **Cash-book,** libro de caja. **Old book,** maulán, maula. **A paperbook,** libro en blanco. **Second-hand books,** libros de ocasión. **Schoolbooks,** libros de enseñanza. **It sounds like something out of a book,** parece de cuento. **The good Book,** la Biblia. **By/according to the book,** ciñéndose a las reglas o normas. **In my book,** a mi modo de ver. **To be a closed book to somebody,** ser un misterio para alguien. **To be an open book,** ser (como) un libro abierto. **I'm in her bad books now,** en este momento no soy santo de su devoción. **To bring somebody to book,** pedirle cuentas a alguien. **To be brought to book,** tener que rendir cuentas. **Don't tell me stories, I can read you like a book,** a mí no me vengas con historias, que yo ya te conozco. **To throw the book at somebody,** castigar a alguien duramente. **Book club,** club del libro, círculo de lectores. **Book review,** reseña de un libro. **I'd make books they'll lose the game!,** me apuesto/juego la cabeza a que pierden el partido.

book, *va.* Asentar en un libro, notar en un registro. **To book one's place,** retener un asiento (en un carruaje público, etc.). Reservar (room, seat, flight). **The hotel/flight is fully booked,** el hotel/vuelo está completo. **We're fully booked until June,** hasta junio no nos queda nada. Concertar (appointment). Multar, ponerle una multa a (record charge against). Amonestar (in soccer). **Book in,** inscribirse, registrarse (register arrival). **She'd booked us in at the Hilton,** nos había reservado habitación en el Hilton (reserve room for).

book up: The hotels are all booked up, los hoteles están todos completos. **Tonight's performance is booked up,** no quedan localidades para la función de esta noche.

bookable [ˈbʊkəbl] [bu-ka-bol] *a.* Que se puede reservar (seat). Que se sanciona con tarjeta amarilla (sport, offence).

bookbinder [ˈbʊkˌbaɪndəʳ] [buk-bain-daʳ], *s.* Encuadernador de libros.

bookbinding [ˈbʊkˌbaɪndɪŋ] [buk-bain-din], *s.* Encuadernación de libros. **Bookbinding case,** biblioteca, estantería, librería, librero. **Bookbinding end,** sujetalibros.

bookcase [ˈbʊkkeɪs] [buk-keis], *s.* Armario o estante para libros; biblioteca.

bookie [ˈbʊkɪ] [bu-ki], *s. (Fam.)* Corredor de apuestas (en las carreras de caballos). BOOKMAKER.

booking [ˈbʊkɪŋ] [bu-kin], *s.* Registro, asiento. **Booking clerk,** *(Ingl.)* vendedor de billetes de pasaje o teatro. **Booking office,** *(Ingl.)* registro y despacho de pasajes, expendeduría de billetes. Reserva, reservación (reservation). **Booking fee,** suplemento, recargo. Compromiso (engagement). **Booking office,** (GB) *(Teat.)* Taquilla, boletería.

bookish [ˈbʊkɪʃ] [bu-kish], *a.* 1. Estudioso, aficionado a los libros; entendido o versado en libros. 2. Teórico, poco práctico, especulativo. Libresco (style). **One of those bookish types,** un ratón de biblioteca.

bookishness [ˈbʊkɪʃnɪs] [bu-kish-nes], *s.* Aplicación intensa a los libros; estudiosidad; falta de sentido práctico.

bookkeeper [ˈbʊkˌkiːpəʳ] [buk-kí-paʳ], *s.* Tenedor de libros, el dependiente que en una casa de comercio está encargado de los libros; contable.

bookkeeping [ˈbʊkˌkiːpɪŋ] [buk-kí-pin], *s.* La teneduría de libros, el arte de hacerlos asientos en los libros de comercio; contabilidad.

book-learned [ˈbʊkˌlɜːnɪd] [buk-ler-nid], *a.* Leído, versado en libros, erudito.

book-learning [ˈbʊkˌlɜːnɪŋ] [buk-ler-nin], *s.* Literatura, conocimiento de las letras o ciencias.

bookless [ˈbʊklɪs] [buk-lis], *a.* Sin libros; desaplicado.

booklist [ˈbʊklɪst] [buk-list] *s.* Catálogo de libros (of bookseller, publisher); bibliografía (reading list).

bookmaker [ˈbʊkmeɪkəʳ] [buk-mei-kaʳ], *s.* 1. El que compila o escribe libros sólo por la ganancia o lucro; el que los imprime y encuaderna. 2. Apostador de profesión; se dice en especial del que solicita y anota apuestas en las carreras de caballos.

bookmaking [ˈbʊkmeɪkɪŋ] [buk-mei-kin], *s.* La ocupación de compilar o escribir libros a destajo.

bookman [ˈbʊkmən] [buk-man], *s.* Hombre estudioso o dedicado al estudio.

bookmark [ˈbʊkmɑːk] [buk-mark], *s.* Marcador de libros, señalador.

bookmate [ˈbʊkmeɪt] [buk-meit], *s.* Condiscípulo.

bookmobile [ˈbʊkməʊˌbiːl] [buk-mou-bil] *s.* Biblioteca ambulante.

book-muslin [ˈbʊkməslɪn] [buk-mus-lin], *s.* Percalina plegada en la pieza a manera de libro.

bookplate [ˈbʊkpleɪt] [buk-pleit] *s.* ex libris.

bookseller [ˈbʊkˌseləʳ] [buk-se-laʳ], *s.* Librero, el que vende libros. **Book trade,** el comercio de libros. **Book-store,** librería, almacén de libros.

bookshelf [ˈbʊkʃelf] [buk-shelf] *s.* Estante, balda para libros (shelf).

bookshop [ˈbʊkʃɒp] [buk-shop] *s.* Librería.

bookstall [ˈbʊkstɔːl] [buk-stol] *s.* Quiosco de prensa y libros (in station).

bookstand [ˈbʊkstænd] [buk-stand], *s.* Puesto de libros.

bookstore [ˈbʊkstɔːʳ] [buk-stoʳ], *s.* Librería.

book token [ˈbʊkˌtəʊkən] [buk-tou-ken] *s.* (GB) Cheque regalo, vale canjeable por libros.

bookworm [ˈbʊkwɜːm] [buk-uerm], *s.* 1. Polilla o gusano que roe los libros. 2. *(Met.)* Estudiante demasiado aplicado a los libros; buquinista, ratón de biblioteca.

boom [buːm] [bum], *s.* 1. *(Mar.)* Botalón, palo largo con un motón hecho firme en una cabeza para pasar las escotas de las alas. 2. Cadena para cerrar un puerto. 3. Estampido, estrépito, estruendo (of guns, explosion), bramido (sound of waves, wind). 4. Jirafa (de micrófono). 5. Bonanza, auge, prosperidad repentina. **Boom town,** ciudad que está en auge. **Boom times,** época de gran prosperidad comercial. **Boom industry,** industria en auge.

boom, *vn.* 1. Hacer ruido profundo y resonante, como el de las olas del mar, o el estampido de un cañón; tronar, retumbar. 2. Moverse con violencia; ir a velas desplegadas. 3. (Fam. E.U.) Aumentar rápidamente de valor en el mercado o ganar en favor. Vivir un boom (market, industry). *-va.* Favorecer, anunciar o fomentar algo muy enérgicamente. **Boom out,** retumbar, resonar.

boomerang [ˈbuːməræŋ] [bu-me-ran], *s.* 1. Bumerang, arma arrojadiza muy singular de los indígenas de Australia y de algunas partes de la India. 2. Todo acto o proceder cuyas malas consecuencias recaen sobre el autor del mismo. *-vn.* Tener el efecto contrario al buscado.

booming [ˈbuːmɪŋ] [bu-min] *a.* Retumbante (sound). En auge (industry).

boon [buːn] [bun], *s.* Dádiva, presente, regalo; gracia, merced, favor; dicha, bendición (blessing).

boon, *a.* 1. Alegre, festivo. 2. Liberal, generoso. 3. Dichoso, afortunado, próspero.

boondocks [ˈbuːndɒks] [bun-doks], **boonies** [ˈbuːnɪs] [bu-nis] *s. pl.* **The boondocks/boonies,** los quintos infiernos.

boondoggle [ˈbuːndɒgl] [bun-do-gol] *s.* *(Coloq.)* Despilfarro.

boor [bʊəʳ] [buaʳ], *s.* 1. Patán, aldeano, villano, grosero.

boorish [ˈbʊərɪʃ] [bua-rish], *a.* Rústico, agreste ; grosero, zafio.

boorishly [ˈbʊərɪʃnɪs] [bua-rish-li], *adv.* Rústicamente, toscamente.

boorishness [ˈbʊərɪʃnɪs] [bua-rish-nes], *s.* Rusticidad, tosquedad, falta de cultura.

boose [buːz] [bus], *s.* (Prov. Ingl.) 1. Boyeriza, establo para los bueyes. 2. Cierta mezcla de tierra y minerales.

boost [buːst] [bust], *va.* (Fam. E. U.) Empujar, levantar, alzar desde abajo. Estimular (economy, production); aumentar, incrementar (sales); levantar (morale). **To boost somebody's confidence,** darle más confianza en sí mismo a alguien. *s.* Alza; ayuda, asistencia. **To give a boost to something,** dar empuje a algo, estimular algo (uplift). **It was a tremendous boost to her confidence,** le dio mucha más confianza en sí misma.

booster [ˈbuːstəʳ] [bus-taʳ], *s.* Fomentador, secuaz. **Booster rocket,** cohete impulsor. **Booster shot,** *(Med.)* inyección estimulante, vacuna de refuerzo. Repetidor (Rad., Telec., TV). Booster (auto). **Booster cable,** cable de arranque.

boot [buːt] [but], *va.* y *vn.* 1. Aprovechar, ser de algún uso o utilidad, valer, servir, ser útil, importar. 2. Calzarse las botas, ganar. 3. Darle un puntapié a. **He booted the ball into the net,** metió el balón en la red de una patada. *(Comput.)* **Boot up,** cargar, hacer el cebado de. *(Coloq,)* **Boot out,** echar, poner de patitas en la calle.

boot, *s.* 1. Ganancia, provecho, utilidad, ventaja. 2. Bota (clothing), botín (short), todo calzado que cubre parte de la pierna. **A pair of boots,** unas botas, un par de botas. **The boot's on the other foot now,** se ha vuelto la tortilla. **To die with/in one's boots,** morir con las botas puestas. *(Coloq,)* **To lick somebody's boots,** adular a alguien, hacerle la pelota, la barba o la pata a alguien; chuparle las medias a alguien, lambonear a alguien. (GB) *(Coloq,)* **To put/stick the boot in,** dar patadas. *(Coloq,)* **To give somebody the boot,** echar a alguien, darle la patada a alguien. **Boot-jack,** sacabotas. **Boot-legs,** Cortes de botas. **Boot-hose,** calcetones. **Boot-tree,** horma de botas. *(Fam.)* **To boot** (Cuba), De ñapa, de contra; de más a más; encima. *(Mex.)* De ganancia, de pilón. 3. Pesebrón de un coche. Maletero, portamaletas, cajuela, baúl, maleta, maletera (Auto). **To boot,** para rematarla, por si fuera poco (hum) (as linker).

bootblack [ˈbuːtblæk] [but-blak], *s.* Limpiabotas. *(Mex.)* Bolero.

boot camp [ˈbuːtkæmp] [but-kamp] *s.* Campamento de entrenamiento de reclutas de Marina.

booted [ˈbuːtɪd] [bu-ted], *a.* Puesto de botas, calzado con botas.

bootee [buːˈtiː] [bu-ti], o **bootie** *s.* Botita de lana para infantes (for baby). Botín (for woman).

booth [buːθ] [buz], *s.* 1. Barraca (stall at fair) o casa hecha de tablas, choza, cabaña. 2. Puesto, stand (at exhibition), tabladillo, mesilla de feria o mercado. Cabina (cabin). **Ticket booth,** taquilla, boletería. **Photo booth,** fotomatón. **Polling booth,** cabina de votación. **Telephone booth,** cabina de teléfono.

bootleg [ˈbuːtleg] [but-leg], *va.* y *vn.* Contrabandear, dedicarse al contrabando (esp. en licores). **To bootleg tapes,** grabar y vender cintas piratas.

bootleg, *a.* De contrabando (liquor); pirata (tape).

bootlegger [ˈbuːtlegəʳ] [but-legaʳ], *s.* Contrabandista (esp. de licores).

bootlegging [ˈbuːtlegɪŋ] [but-le-guin], *s.* Contrabando (esp. de licores).

bootless [ˈbuːtlɪs] [but-les], *a.* 1. Inútil, sin provecho. 2. Sin botas.

boots [buːts] [buts], *s.* Limpiabotas (de una fonda).

booty [ˈbuːtɪ] [bu-ti], *s.* Botín, presa, saqueo. **To play booty,** jugar fraudulentamente, o estar de inteligencia con uno para engañar a otro.

booze [buːz] [bus], *vn.* Embriagarse, emborracharse. *-s.* Borrachera; bebida espirituosa.

boozer [ˈbuːzəʳ] [bu-saʳ] *s.* *(Coloq,)* Borrachín. (GB) bar (pub).

booze-up [ˈbuːzˌʌp] [bus-ap] *s.* *(Coloq,)* (GB) Juerga.

boozy[ˈbuːzɪ] [busi], *a.* Embriagado, beodo. **A boozy meal,** una comida regada con abundante alcohol.

bop [bɒp] [bop] *s. (Coloq,)* (GB) **To go for a bop,** ir a bailar. **A bop on the head,** un coscorrón (blow). *vn.* Bailar.

bopeep [ˈbɒpiːp] [bo-pip], *s.* 1. El acto de mirar al soslayo, de harto o de reo. 2. Escondite.

boracic acid [bəˈræsɪk] [bo-ra-sik], *s.* Acido borácico, o bórico.

boracite [bəˈrəsaɪt] [bo-ra-sait], *s. (Min.)* Borácita o borato de magnesia.

borate [ˈbəreɪt] [bo-reit], *s.* Borato, sal compuesta de ácido borácico unido a alguna base.

boratto [bəˈreɪtə] [bo-rei-to], *s.* Tela de seda y lana semejante a bombasí o alepín.

borax [ˈbɔːræks] [bo-raks], Bórax, atíncar mineral compuesto de borato de sosa y agua.

borborygm [bɔːbəˈrɪdʒm] [bor-bo-ri-chem], *s.* Borborigmo, ruido de tripas.

bordello [ˈbədelə] [bor-de-lo] *s.* Burdel.

border [ˈbɔːdəʳ] [bor-daʳ], *s.* 1. Orilla, borde (edge), margen o extremidad de alguna cosa. 2. *(Pol.)* Frontera, límite o confín de algún país. **Paraguay has borders with three countries,** Paraguay limita con tres países. Fronterizo (dispute, town). 3. Guarnición de vestido, florón, ribete, cenefa (edging-on fabric, plate), franja, farfalá. 4. Borde o lomo de un jardín plantado de flores; arriate, cantero (in garden).

border, *vn.* 1. Confinar, lindar. 2. Aproximarse, acercarse. - *va.* 1. Guarnecer, ribetear (edge with ribbon, binding). **The plates were bordered with a blue band,** los platos tenían una cenefa azul. 2. Alcanzar, tocar o lindar con (fields, lands); limitar con (country, state). **To border on/upon,** confinar, tocar, limitar. **France borders upon Spain,** Francia confina con España. De aquí, acercarse en carácter, asemejarse.

bordering [ˈbɔːdərɪŋ] [bor-de-rin], *s.* Guarnicionado. -*a.* Fronterizo, contiguo, cercano, vencino. **A bordering town,** ciudad fronteriza.

borderland [ˈbɔːdələænd] [bor-der-land] *s.* Zona fronteriza.

borderline [ˈbɔːdəlaɪn] [bor-der-lain], *s.* Límite, orilla, frontera. -*a.* Incierto, dudoso (case, score); en el límite entre el aprobado y el reprobado o el suspenso (candidate). **A borderline pass,** un aprobado muy justo. **A borderline case,** caso entre lo normal y lo subnormal.

bore [ˈbɔːʳ] [boʳ], *va.* Taladrar; barrenar, excavar, abrir (shaft, tunnel). **They bore a hole into the rock,** hicieron una perforación en la roca. -*vn.* 1. Hacer agujeros, perforar, taladrar. **They are boring for oil,** están haciendo perforaciones en busca de petróleo. 2. Adelantarse avanzar gradualmente. 3. Llevar la cabeza baja los caballos. *(Fam.)* **To bore,** molestar, incomodar, jorobar, aburrir (weary).

bore, *pret.* del verbo TO BEAR.

bore, *s.* 1. Taladro, barreno, el agujero que se hace taladrando o barrenando. 2. Taladro, barreno o barrena, el instrumento con que se taladra o barrena. 3. Calibre, el hueco de un cañón (of cylinder, gun barrel). (GB) **12-bore shotgun,** escopeta de calibre 12. 4. *(Fam.)* **A bore,** o **A perfect bore,** majadero, jorobón, pelma, pesado, molienda, insufrible, pelmazo, plomo (person). Aburrimiento, pesadez, lata (thing). 5. Ola que forma la subida de la marea por el cauce de un río.

boreal [ˈbɔːrɪəl] [bor-rial], *a.* Septentrional, boreal.

boreas [ˈbɔːrɪəz] [bor-dias], *s.* Norte, uno de los vientos.

borecole [ˈbɔːkəʊl] [bor-koul], *s. (Bot.)* Especie de berza.

bored [ˈbɔːd] [bord] *a.* Aburrido. **To be bored with something,** estar aburrido de algo. **To get bored,** aburrirse.

boredom [ˈbɔːdəm] [bor-dom], *s.* 1. Los pesados, y majaderos, como clase. 2. La condición de verse y estar fastidiado y molestado. Aburrimiento.

borer [ˈbɔːrəʳ] [boraʳ]], *s.* 1. Barreno o taladro. 2. Lo que excava, como escarabajo, cansado.

boresome [ˈbɔːsʌm] [bor-som], *a.* Fastidioso, aburrido. 2. *(Fam.)* Latoso.

boring [ˈbɔːrɪŋ] [bo-rin] *a.* Aburrido, aburridor.

born [ˈbɔːn] [born], *pp.* of BEAR. Nacido; destinado. **To be born,** nacer. **Since I was born,** desde que nací. **To be born again,** renacer. **The first-born,** el primogénito. **High-born, low-born,** de elevado, de humilde nacimiento. **To be born lucky,** nacer con suerte. **Poets are born not made,** los poetas nacen, no se hacen. **He was born (to a life) of luxury,** nació para ser rico. **I wasn't born yesterday, you know!,** ¡oye, que no nací ayer! **There's one born every minute!,** hay tontos para repartir.

born, *a.* Nato (teacher/leader). *(Coloq,)* **In all my born days,** en toda mi vida. **He's a born looser,** siempre ha sido y será un perdedor.

-born *suff.* **Austrianborn/Dallasborn,** nacido en/oriundo de Austria/Dallas.

born-again [ˈbɔːnəˌgen] [born-e-guein] *a.* **Born-again Christian,** cristiano convertido especialmente a una secta evangélica.

borne [ˈbɔːn] [born], *pp.* de TO BEAR. Llevado, sostenido.

boron [ˈbɔːrɒn] [bo-ron], *s.* Boro, elemento químico no metálico; origen del ácido bórico.

borough [ˈbʌrə] [ba-ro], *s.* 1. Ciudad o villa. 2. *(Ingl.)* Corporación municipal, no una ciudad, dotada por real cédula de ciertos privilegios (municipal borough). Municipio (in New York, London). **The five Boroughs,** la ciudad de Nueva York. 3. *(Ingl.)* Pueblo constituido o no en corporación legal, pero con derecho de representación en el Parlamento (parliamentary borough). 4. Distrito municipal (in US), municipio (in UK), condado (in Alaska).

borrow [ˈbɒrəʊ] [bo-rou], *va.* 1. Tomar fiado o prestado. 2. Pedir prestado (have on loan); lo contrario de *to lend,* prestar. **May I borrow your pencil?,** ¿me prestas o me dejas el lápiz? **The ladder is borrowed,** la escalera es prestada. **I borrowed $5,000 from the bank,** pedí un préstamo de 5.000 dólares al banco. **He was living on borrowed time,** tenía los días contados. 3. Usar prendas ajenas, servirse de lo que pertenece a otro. Sacar (from library) (idea). Tomar (word). **A term borrowed from German,** un préstamo del alemán, una palabra tomada del alemán.

borrower [ˈbɒrəʊəʳ] [bo-rouaʳ], *s.* El que pide prestado. *(Fin.)* Prestatario, Usuario (from library).

borrowing [ˈbɒrəʊɪŋ] [bo-rouin], *s.* Empréstito, préstamo, el acto de pedir prestado o la cosa que se pide prestada.

borstal [ˈbɔːstl] [borstal] *s.* Reformatorio (formerly in UK).

boscage [ˈbɒskeɪdʒ] [bos-keich], *s.* 1. Boscaje, soto, floresta, arboleda, el conjunto de árboles y plantas. 2. *(Pint.)* Paisaje poblado de árboles.

bosh [bɒʃ] [bosh], *s.* 1. Galimatías, necedad. 2. Atalaje de alto horno; embudo del cabilote. (Turco).

bosk [ˈbɒsk] [bosk], *s.* Bosque pequeño; matorral.

bosket [ˈbɒskɪt] [bos-kit], *s.* Bosquecillo, bosquete, grupo de árboles en un jardín extenso.

Bosnia Herzegovina [ˈbɒznɪəhɜːtsəgəˈviːnə] [bos-nia-jer-se-gou-vi-na] *N. (Geogr.)* Bosnia Herzegovina.

Bosnian [ˈbɒznɪən] [bos-nian], *a./s.* Bosnio, de Bosnia.

bosom [ˈbʊzəm] [bo-som], *s.* 1. Seno, (heart, center), el pecho, (breast, chest, bust), el corazón. 2. Amor, inclinación, afecto, cariño. **Bosom friend,** amigo íntimo o de la mayor confianza. 3. Pecho, la parte del vestido de mujer que está sobre el pecho. **Bosom of the church,** El gremio de la Iglesia. 4. Pechera, en costura. **Bosom of a shirt,** Pechera de la camisa.

bosom, *va.* 1. Guardar en el pecho. 2. Ocultar o tener secreta alguna cosa.

boson [ˈbɒsən] [bo-son], *s. V.* BOATSWAIN.

Bosphorus [ˈbɒsfərəs] [bos-fo-ros], *s.* Bósforo, el estrecho, canal o garganta de mar entre dos tierras firmes, por donde un mar se comunica con otro.

boss [bɒs] [bos], *s.* 1. Clavo o tachón; giba, joroba, corcova, abolladura. **Boss of a bridle,** copa de freno. **Boss of a book,** lomo de un libro. 2. Patrón (employer, factory owner), maestro: capataz de obreros. Jefe (superior). **You decide, you're the boss,** decídelo tú que eres el que manda. **I want to be my own boss,** quiero ser mi propio patrón. 3. Dictador o cacique político. Dirigente (leader). **Union bosses,** dirigentes sindicales. **A Mafia boss,** un capo de la Mafia. **Boss around,** (GB) **boss about,** *(Coloq.)* Mandonear.

boss, *va.* 1. Trabajar en relieve. V. EMBOSS. 2. *(Fam.) (E.U.)* (a) Dirigir obras. (b) Tener y ejercer poder o influencia.

bossage ['bɒsɪdʒ] [bo-sich], *s.* Relieve o proyectura de alguna piedra.

bossed ['bɒst] [bost], **bossy** ['bɒsɪ] [bo-si], *a.* Saltado, tachonado; turgente, abultado, saliente.

bossily ['bɒsɪlɪ] [bo-si-li] *adv.* En tono autoritario (say); de manera autoritaria (behave).

bossy ['bɒsɪnɪs] [bo-si-nis] *a. (Coloq.)* Mandón.

bosun ['bəʊsən] [bou-son] *s.* V. BOATSWAIN.

bot [bɒt] [bot], *s.* 1. Larva de estro. 2. Estro. V. BOT-FLY.

botanic, botanical [bəˈtænɪk] [bo-ta-nik] [bəˈtænɪkl] [bo-ta-nikl], *a.* Botánico, que pertenece a la botánica. **Botanic gardens,** jardín botánico.

botanically [bəˈtænɪklɪ] [bo-ta-nikli], *adv.* Botánicamente.

botanist ['bɒtənɪst] [bo-ta-nist], *s.* Botánico, el que profesa la botánica o tiene conocimiento de las plantas.

botanize ['bɒtənaɪz] [bo-ta-nais], *va.* Explorar en busca de ejemplares botánicos o para estudiar la vida de plantas. *-vn.* Herborizar, buscar plantas y estudiarlas; ocuparse en botánica.

botany ['bɒtənɪ] [bo-ta-ni], *s.* Botánica, la parte de la biología que trata de las plantas, sus clases, géneros y especies (subject). Flora (of particular place).

botch [bɒtʃ] [boch], *s.* 1. Roncha, el bultillo que se eleva en el cuerpo del animal. 2. Remiendo, cualquiera cosa mal acabada añadida a otra. 3. Landre, úlcera. 4. *(Poét.)* ripio. **To make a botch-up of something,** hacer una chapuza de algo.

botch, *va.* 1. Remendar ropa chapuceramente (repair). 2. Juntar o unir alguna cosa chabacanamente. 3. Chapuzar, chafallar, hacer un trabajo apresuradamente. Estropear (plan). 4. *(Poét.)* Llenar de ripios el verso.

botcher ['bɒtʃəʳ] [bo-chaʳ], *s.* Sastre remendón.

botchy ['bɒtʃɪ] [bo-chi] *a.* Señalado con ronchas.

bot-fly ['bɒtˈflaɪ] [bot-flai], *s.* Estro, insecto díptero de la familia Oestridae, de muchas especies diferentes; algunas de ellas son nocivas al caballo, al buey y a la oveja, en cuyos cuerpos depositan sus huevos.

both [bəʊθ] [bouz], *a.* Ambos, los dos, entrambos, ambos a dos. **On both sides,** por ambos lados, por ambas partes, de uno y otro lado. **Both of them,** ellos dos. **Both of us,** nosotros dos. **Both his sons,** sus dos hijos.

both, *conj.* Tanto como, así como. **Both in time of peace and war,** tanto en tiempo de paz como de guerra. **Both Paul and John are in Italy,** tanto Paul como John están en Italia, Paul y John están los dos en Italia.

both, *pron.* Ambos, ambas, los dos, las dos. **Both of them wanted to go,** los dos o ambos querían ir. **Both of my brothers can swim,** mis dos hermanos saben nadar. **We both like chess,** a los dos nos gusta el ajedrez. **The coats are both too big,** los dos abrigos son demasiado grandes. **She sends her love to you both,** les manda recuerdos a los dos.

bother ['bɒðəʳ] [bo-zaʳ], *va. (Fam.)* Aturrullar, confundir, perturbar, enojar, aturdir con ruido; molestar (irritate), incomodar, jorobar, fastidiar (pester). **Does my smoking bother you?,** ¿te molesta que fume? **Sorry to bother you,** perdone (que le moleste). Preocupar (trouble). **What's bothering you?,** ¿qué es lo que te preocupa? **She's very quiet, but don't let it bother you,** es muy callada, no te inquietes por ello. **Don't bother writing a long letter,** no hace falta que escribas una carta larga (making effort). **I**

don't bother cooking any more, ya no me molesto en cocinar más. *-vn.* Molestarse (make effort). **You shouldn't have bothered,** no debiste haberte molestado. **Why bother?,** ¿para qué molestarse? **I don't usually bother with lunch,** normalmente no como nada al mediodía. **To bother about something/somebody,** preocuparse por algo/alguien (worry).

bother, *s.* Molestia (trouble), trabajo (work), problemas (problems). **It isn't worth the bother,** no vale la pena. (GB) *(Coloq.)* **A spot of bother,** un problemita. **If it isn't too much of a bother for you,** si no es mucho problema o demasiada molestia para usted (nuisance).

bother, *interj. (Coloq.)* (GB) Bother (it)!, ¡maldito sea!

bothered ['bɒðəd] [bo-derd] *a.* **I can't be bothered to go,** me da pereza ir. **She yelled at him, but he wasn't a bit bothered,** le pegó un berrido, pero él ni se inmutó. (GB) **I'm not bothered,** me da igual o lo mismo (I don't mind).

bothersome ['bɒðəsʌm] [bo-der-sam] *a.* Molesto (demands); pesado, fastidioso (person).

Bothnian ['bɒθnɪən] [boz-nian], *a.* Botniano.

botryoidal ['bɒtrɪɔɪdəl] [bo-troi-dal], *a.* Botrioideo, que tiene la forma de un racimo; se aplica comúnmente a los minerales. (Gr. botrys, racimo).

bots [bɒts] [bots], *s. pl.* Lombrices en las entrañas de los caballos. Larvas de varias especies de moscas *(botfly),* que molestan a las caballerías.

bottle ['bɒtl] [botel], *s.* 1. Botella (container, contents), frasco (of perfume), redoma de vidrio. **Return empty bottles,** devuelva los envases o los cascos. **A milk bottle,** una botella de leche (el envase). 2. Botella, la cantidad de vino que se echa en dicha vasija, que viene a ser algo menos de dos cuartillos. 3. Haz o gavilla de heno o verde. **Bottle friend o companion,** compañero en el beber, bebedor. **Nursing-bottle o baby's/feeding bottle,** mamadera, biberón, tetero, mamila. **Stone bottle,** botella de greda. **Bottle brush,** cepillo o escobilla para limpiar botellas. **Bottle opener,** abrebotellas, destapador. *(Coloq,)* **To hit the bottle,** darle a la bebida, al trago (alcohol). (GB) *(Coloq,)* Agallas (courage, nerve). *(Fam.)* **To lose one's bottle,** achicarse.

bottle, *va.* 1. Embotellar (wine, milk), enfrascar, poner alguna cosa en botellas o frascos. **Bottled milk,** leche en o de botella. **Bottled water,** agua embotellada. 2. Agavillar. 3. (GB) Poner en conserva (fruit, vegetables). **Bottle out,** rajarse, acobardarse. **Bottle up,** reprimir (emotion), **Don't bottle it all up inside you,** no te lo guardes dentro. **Bottle bank,** contenedor de recogida de vidrio. **Bottlefeed,** alimentar o criar con biberón, mamila, mamadera o tetero.

bottled ['bɒtld] [boteld], *a.* Embotellado, enfrascado.

bottleflower ['bɒtlˈflaʊəʳ] [botel-flauaʳ], *s. (Bot.)* Centaurea.

bottlegreen ['bɒtlˈgriːn] [botel-grín], *s.* Verde botella, un color.

bottleneck ['bɒtlnek] [botel-nek], *s.* 1. Cuello de botella (narrow stretch of road). 2. Cuello de estrangulación (en el tránsito); embotellamiento (hold-up). 3. *(Fig.)* Angostura, obstrucción. *va.* Obstaculizar.

bottlescrew ['bɒtlskruː] [botel-skrú], *s.* Tirabuzón o sacatrapos para extraer los tapones de los frascos y botellas.

bottling ['bɒtlɪŋ] [bo-tlin], *s.* Embotellamiento.

bottom ['bɒtəm] [bo-tom], *s.* 1. Fondo (box, bottle, drawer), suelo, la parte inferior o más baja de alguna cosa (underneath). Final, pie (of page). Parte de abajo (of pile). **At the bottom of the list,** al final de la lista. *(Coloq,)* **Bottoms up!,** ¡al centro y pa'dentro! **From the bottom of one's heart,** de todo corazón. **To get to the bottom of something,** llegar al fondo de algo. **To knock the bottom out of something,** echar por tierra algo. 2. Zanja, el cimiento o fundamento de alguna cosa. Fondo (of garden, sea, river, lake). **To hit/touch bottom,** tocar fondo. 3. Cañada o valle. 4. Hondonada, ovillo, globo o pelota compuesta de hilo, seda, etc. 5. Embarcación o buque. 6. Fin, designio, motivo. 7. Culo, trasero (of person), traste.

The bottom of the belly, el empeine. 8. Asentaderas, nalgas. 9. Asiento de una silla. 10. Pie (hill, stairs); base, fundamento. 11. Pantalón, pantalones (of pyjamas, tracksuit); parte de abajo (of bikini). 12. Parte baja, segunda (in baseball). **Bottoms,** valle, vega (river valley). **Bottom out,** tocar fondo. **He's at the bottom of the class,** es el último de la clase (of hierarchy). **The team is at the bottom of the league,** el equipo está a la cola de la liga. **She started out at the bottom,** empezó desde abajo.

bottom, a. De más abajo (shelf, layer); más bajo (grade); inferior, de abajo (part/edge/lip). **The bottom left-hand corner,** el ángulo inferior izquierdo.

bottomed [ˈbɒtəmd] [bo-tomd], a. Lo que tiene fondo o suelo. Forrado.

bottomless [ˈbɒtəmlɪs] [bo-tom-les], a. 1. Insondable, lo que no se puede sondear. Sin fondo (well, shaft). **Bottomless pit,** abismo. **He's a bottomless pit,** tiene la solitaria, es un barril sin fondo. 2. Excesivo, desmesurado, impenetrable.

bottom line [ˈbɒtəmlaɪn] [bo-tom-lain] s. **The bottom line is that…,** en pocas palabras o en resumidas cuentas, esto implica que… (result).

bottomry [ˈbɒtəmrɪ] [bo-tom-ri], s. (Mar.) Casco y quilla, el acto de tomar dinero prestado hipotecando todo el barco.

botulism [ˈbɒtjʊlɪzəm] [bo-tiu-lisem], s. Botulismo.

boudoir [ˈbuːdwɑːʳ] [bu-duaʳ], s. Tocador o recámara de señora.

bouffe [ˈbuːf] [buf], a. Cómico. V. **OPERA.**

bough [bɔː] [bo], s. Brazo del árbol, las ramas mayores que parten del tronco.

bought pret. y pp. del verbo TO BUY.

bought [bɔːt] [bot], s. 1. Torcedura, nudo, corvadura o curvatura. 2. La parte de la honda que contiene la piedra.

bougie [ˈbɑdʒiː] [bo-chi], s. 1. Candelilla, cilindro flexible para superar obstrucciones de la uretra, esófago u otros conductos del cuerpo, o para dilatarlos en casos de estrechez. 2. Candelilla de gelatina, u otra substancia, impregnada de un medicamento para su introducción en la uretra, u otro conducto. (Gal.)

bouillon [ˈbuːjɒn] [bui-yon], s. Caldo claro de carne. (Gal.)

boulder o bowlder [ˈbəʊldəʳ] [boul-daʳ], s. Peña, piedra desprendida de una masa de roca. Guijarro grande. Roca grande alisada por la erosión.

boulder-wall [ˈbəʊldəˈwɔːl] [boul-deʳ-uol], s. (Arq.) Muralla o pared compuesta de grandes cantos rodados.

boulevard [ˈbuːləvɑːʳ] [bu-le-var], s. Bulevar, avenida ancha o paseo público.

bounce [baʊns] [bauns], vn. 1. Arremeter, acometer con ímpetu. 2. Brincar, saltar, dar un salto repentino; rebotar, picar, botar (ball, object). **The box was bouncing around on the back seat,** la caja iba dando tumbos en el asiento de atrás. **The child was bouncing up and down on the sofa,** el niño saltaba o daba brincos en el sofá. **She bounced into the room,** entró a la habitación saltando, brincando, dando brincos. 3. Bravear, echar fieros o bravatas; jactarse. 4. Ser devuelto o rechazado, rebotar (check). **Bouncing,** sano, rozagante (baby). -va. 1. Hacer saltar o botar, darle botes a, hacer picar. **She bounced the child on her knee,** le hacía el caballito al niño. 2. (Fam. E. U.) Despedir, privar de algún empleo u oficio; echar, botar (drunk, employee). 3. Devolver, rechazar (check). (Coloq,) **Bounce back,** levantarse, recuperarse (recover).

bounce, s. 1. Golpazo, golpe fuerte. 2. Estallido, ruido o estruendo. 3. Bravata, fanfarronada, amenaza con arrogancia para intimidar a otro. 4. Brinco. 5. Bote, salto de una pelota u otro cuerpo elástico; rebote, bote, pique (action). **He hit the ball on the bounce,** le dio a la pelota de rebote. **This shampoo puts the bounce back into your hair,** este champú les da nueva vida a sus cabellos (springiness, vitality). **She's full of bounce,** es una persona llena de vida. (Coloq,) **To give somebody the bounce,** poner a alguien de patitas en la calle, botar a alguien (dismissal). 6. Bola, mentira grosera.

bouncer [ˈbaʊnsəʳ] [baun-saʳ], s. El guapo que echa bravatas y fieros; fanfarrón. (Coloq,) Gorila, sacabullas.

bouncing [ˈbaʊnsɪŋ] [baun-sin], a. 1. Fuerte, vigoroso, bien formado. **A bouncing baby,** un niño robusto. 2. Exagerado, desmesurado. 3. Fanfarrón, valentón; mentiroso.

bouncy [ˈbaʊnsɪ] [baun-si] a. Que rebota o bota bien (ball); firme y elástico (mattress); movido (ride). Animado, lleno de vida (person) (cheerful, lively); alegre (tune).

bound [baʊnd] [baund], s. 1. Límite, término, confín o lindero. 2. Bote, brinco, corcovo, salto (jump). 3. Resalto, repercusión. **Bounds,** límites. **Her generosity knows no bounds,** su generosidad no tiene límite(s). **Within the bounds of possibility,** dentro de lo posible.

bound, vn. 1. Deslindar o poner límites, delimitar (area, country). 2. Confinar. 3. Limitar, ceñir. 4. Hacer saltar. -va. 1. Saltar, dar saltos (leap). **The dog bounded along behind the bicycle,** el perro iba dando saltos detrás de la bicicleta. 2. Resaltar. 3. Botar. **To bound in/out/away,** entrar/salir/ irse dando saltos.

bound, a; pret. y pp. del verbo TO BIND. 1. Atado, amarrado (tied up), ligado; confinado. **My hands were bound,** tenía las manos atadas o amarradas. 2. Moralmente o legalmente obligado o forzado (obliged). **You're still bound by your promise,** sigues estando obligado a cumplir lo que prometiste. **He felt bound to tell his mother what happened,** se sintió obligado a decirle a su madre lo que había sucedido. 3. Encuadernado, o que tiene cobertura. 4. (Fam.) Destinado; sentenciado (certain). **It was bound to happen sooner or later,** tarde o temprano tenía que suceder. **She's bound to be elected,** seguro que sale elegida. **It was bound to go wrong,** no cabía duda de que iba a salir mal. 5. (Fam. E.U.) Decidido, resuelto. 6. Puesto en aprendizaje. 7. Estreñido, cerrado de vientre. -a. Destinado (headed). **Our ship is bound for Venice,** nuestra embarcación está destinada a Venecia o va a Venecia. **The truck was bound for Italy,** el camión iba rumbo a Italia.

-bound [] suff. **Passengers for the Birmingham-bound train,** los pasajeros con destino a Birmingham (headed for). **It crashed into the Moscow-bound train,** chocó con el tren que se dirigía a Moscú. (Publ.) **Leather-bound,** encuadernado en cuero. **Snow-bound,** paralizado por la nieve (immobilized by). **Wheelchair-bound,** confinado a una silla de ruedas (confined to).

boundary [ˈbaʊndərɪ] [baun-de-ri], s. Límite o linde, frontera. **Boundary line,** línea divisoria, linde.

bounden [ˈbaʊndn] [baun-den], a. Obligado, precisado; indispensable.

bounder [ˈbaʊndəʳ] [baun-daʳ], s. El que pone límites, medidor.

bounding-stone [ˈbaʊndɪŋˈstəʊn] [baun-din-stoun], **boundstone** [ˈbaʊndstəʊn] [baund-stoun], s. 1. Mojón, piedra que sirve como señal para dividir los términos, lindes o caminos. 2. Piedra de jugar, piedra de saque.

boundless [ˈbaʊndlɪs] [baund-les], a. Ilimitado, inagotable (resources), lo que no tiene límites ni término; infinito (universe). Sin límites (love, patience).

boundlessness [ˈbaʊndlɪsnɪ] [baund-les-nes], s. Inmensidad, infinidad de espacio.

bounteous [ˈbaʊntɪəs] [baun-tios], a. Liberal, generoso.

bounteously [ˈbaʊntɪəslɪ] [baun-tios-li], adv. Liberalmente, generosamente.

bounteousness [ˈbaʊntɪəsnɪs] [baun-tios-nes], s. Munificencia, liberalidad, generosidad.

bounteth [ˈbaʊntɪθ] [baun-tez], s. (Esco.) Propina, recompensa sobre el salario regular.

bountiful [ˈbaʊntɪfəl] [baun-ti-ful], a. Liberal, generoso, bienhechor. Munificente, pródigo (king, nature); copioso, abundante (harvest, gifts). (GB) **To play Lady Bountiful,** hacerse la dadivosa.

bountifully [ˈbaʊntɪfəlɪ] [baun-ti-fuli], *adv.* Liberalmente, generosamente, copiosamente.

bountifulness [ˈbaʊntɪfəlnɪs] [baun-ti-ful-nes], *s.* Generosidad, lberalidad, largueza.

bounty [ˈbaʊntɪ] [baun-ti], *s.* 1. Generosidad, liberalidad, munificencia (generosity); bondad. 2. Premio, recompensa (reward). 3. Ayuda de costa. **Bounty money,** enganche. **Bounty hunter,** cazador de recompensas.

bouquet [ˈbʊkeɪ] [bu-kei], *s.* 1. Ramo de flores; ramillete (small). 2. Perfume, bouquet (of wine), aroma del vino.

bouquet garni [ˈbʊkeɪˌgɑːnɪ] [bu-kei-gar-ni] *s.* Ramito compuesto.

Bourbon [ˈbʊəbən] [bur-bon], *s.* 1. Borbón, miembro de la antigua casa de Borbón en Francia; o de sus ramas en España y Nápoles. 2. (Ger. E.U.) Porfiado en sus ideas políticas conservadoras; opuesto al progreso. 3. Bourbon.

bourdon [ˈbʊədən] [bur-don], *s.* (*Fr.*) Bordón, registro de órgano.

bourgeois [ˈbʊəʒwɑː] [bur-yua], *a.* Burgués, el que pertenece a la clase media o comercial; de aquí, común, ordinario, poco cultivado. -*s.* Burgués, ciudadano de la clase media; vecino de una ciudad; comerciante, tendero. (*Gal.*)

bourgeois, *s.* Tipo medio entre breviario y entredós; carácter de nueve puntos.

bourgeoisie [ˈbʊəʒwɑːˈziː] [bur-yua-si], *s.* Burguesía. (*Fr.*)

bourgeon [ˈbʊːʒən] [bur-yon], *vn.* Brotar o echar ramas. -*s.* Yema. (*Fr.*)

bourn [bɔːn] [born], *s.* 1. Límite o linde. 2. Arroyo.

bourse [bɔːs] [bors], *s.* 1. Bolsa, lonja; especialmente la de París. 2. (*Anat.*) Cualquier receptáculo en forma de bolsa, como el pericardio.

bouse [ˈbuːz] [bus], *vn.* Beber con intemperancia. V. **BOOZE.**

bousy [ˈbuːsɪ] [bu-si], *a.* Borracho, embriagado. V. **BOOZY.**

bout [baʊt] [baut], *s.* 1. Vez, la relación de una cosa con otra sucesiva o anterior; un rato. 2. Ataque de borrachera, o de enfermedad (period, spell). **I had a bout of flu,** tuve una gripe muy mala. **Bouts of depression,** frecuentes depresiones. **A bout of activity,** una racha de actividad. **A drinking bout,** una borrachera o juerga. 3. Curva o vuelta de una cuerda. 4. Combate, encuentro (in boxing, wrestling). **A bout at fencing,** un asalto de esgrima.

boutique [buːˈtiːk] [bu-tik] *s.* Boutique.

bovate [ˈbəʊveɪt] [bo-veit], *s.* El espacio de tierra que puede arar un par de bueyes en un año; medida antigua.

bovine [ˈbəʊvaɪn] [bou-vain], *a.* Bovino, relativo al buey, o al ganado vacuno.

bow [bəʊ] [bau], *va.* 1. Hacer reverencia o cortesía: expresar por medio de la inclinación del cuerpo. **To bow to somebody,** hacerle una reverencia a alguien, inclinarse ante a l g u i e n . **We must bow to her experience,** debemos tratarla con la deferencia que su experiencia merece. 2. Escoltar o acompañar haciendo reverencias. 3. Agobiar, oprimir, agravar. -*vn.* 1. Doblarse, torcerse o encorvarse. 2. Agobiarse. 3. Ceder, someterse. **He bowed his head,** inclinó la cabeza. **Bow down,** doblegarse. **To bow down to somebody/something,** someterse a algo/alguien. **Bow out,** retirarse.

bow, *s.* 1. Reverencia, cortesía, inclinación del cuerpo o parte de él que se hace en señal de respeto (movement). **The actress took a bow,** la actriz salió a saludar al público/hizo una reverencia. 2. (*Mar.*) Proa, toda la figura exterior de la embarcación de la nave a la roda. **On the bow,** (*Mar.*) por la serviola. **Bow-oar, -***s.* el remo más cercano a la proa de una lancha, o la persona que lo maneja. **To make a bow,** saludar, hacer un saludo.

bow, *s.* 1. Arco, arma para disparar flechas (weapon). **Bow and arrow,** arco y flecha. 2. El arco iris. 3. (*Mús.*) Arco, el instrumento con que se tocan los violines y violones. 4. Lazo, de corbata, de cinta, etc. (knot). **To tie a bow,** hacer un lazo. 5. Arzón de silla.

bow, *va.* Encorvar en forma de arco; doblar y torcer alguna cosa. Arquear (branch, beam). -*vn.* Arquearse, doblarse, pandearse (branch, plank).

bow-bent [bəʊˈbent] [bau-bent], *a.* Arqueado.

bowdlerize [ˈbaʊdləraɪz] [baudla-rais] *va.* (*Pej.*) Expurgar.

bowel [ˈbaʊəl] [bauel], *va.* (*Des.*) Traspasar las entrañas, destripar, despanzurrar.

bowel, *s.* 1. (*Anat.*) Intestino, entraña, tripa. **Large bowel,** intestino grueso. 2. *pl.* Entrañas, lo más escondido o más interior de una cosa. **In the bowels of the earth,** en las entrañas de la tierra. 3. (*Ant.*) Entrañas, ternura, compasión. **To open the bowels,** hacer moverse el vientre. **A bowel complaint,** enfermedad de los intestinos.

bowelless [ˈbaʊəlɪs] [baue-les], *a.* Inhumano, sin ternura o compasión.

bower [ˈbaʊəʳ] [bauaʳ], *s.* 1. Glorieta, emparrado o enramada de jardín; bóveda. 2. Morada, domicilio; retrete, aposento retirado. **Bower-bird,** ave de enramada; tilonorinco, pájaro australiano de la familia de los córvidos, notable por la pequeña enramada o choza que construye en el suelo aparte de su nido, y que adorna con conchas, plumas, huesos y objetos de colores brillantes.

bower, *s.* 1. Tocador con arco. 2. Arquero. V. **BOWYER.**

bower, *s.* **Right bower, left bower,** los dos naipes más altos en el juego llamado euchre.

bower, *va.* EMBOWER.

bower-anchor [ˈbaʊəˌæŋkəʳ] [bauer-an-koʳ], *s.* (*Mar.*) Ancla de servidumbre.

bowery [ˈbaʊərɪ] [baue-ri], *a.* Lleno de emparrados o enramadas; sombrío.

bow-hand [ˈbaʊhænd] [bau-jand], *s.* La mano del arco, la que tiene el arco para herir las cuerdas de los instrumentos músicos.

bowie-knife [ˈbaʊɪnaɪf], [baui-naif], *s.* Cuchillo de monte; puñal largo y ancho.

bowing [ˈbaʊɪŋ] [bauin], *a.* Inclinado.

bow-knot [ˈbaʊnɒt] [bau-not], *s.* Lazo corredizo, o escurridizo.

bowl [bəʊl] [boul], *s.* 1. (*Culin.*) Taza, cuenca, bol, tazón (container); palangana, barreño (for washing). **Fruit bowl,** frutero. **Soup bowl,** sopero. 2. Hueco o cóncavo de alguna cosa. 3. Tazón de fuente. 4. Bolo, esfera de madera o hierro que se hace rodar por el suelo para jugar a los bolos o a las bochas. **Bowl of a pipe,** hornillo de la pipa. **Bowl of a spoon,** paleta de la cuchara. 5. *pl.* Juego de bolos. 6. Taza, inodoro (of toilet).

bowl, *va.* 1. Voltear como una bola. 2. Bolear, tirar los bolos. Lanzar (ball). Eliminar (in cricket, batsman). -*vn.* Jugar a las bochas. Lanzar (throw); **To go bowling,** ir a jugar a los bolos, la petanca, las bochas, etc. **Bowl over,** derribar, tirar al suelo (knock down). **We were bowled over by the beauty of the island,** la belleza de la isla nos dejó pasmados o boquiabiertos (impress).

bowlder. V. BOULDER.

bow-legged [ˈbəʊˌlegɪd] [bou-legd], *a.* Patiestevado, el que tiene las piernas estevadas; patizambo. **Bowleg,** pierna corva.

bowler [ˈbəʊləʳ] [bou-laʳ], *s.* Jugador de bochas o de bolos. Lanzador (in cricket); jugador (in bowlin, bowls).

bowline [ˈbəʊlɪn] [bou-lin], **bowling** [ˈbəʊlɪn] [bou-lin], *s.* (*Mar.*) Bolina, cabo que se fija en las púas que nacen de las relingas de las velas mayores. **To haul the bowlines,** (*Mar.*) polinear.

bowling [ˈbəʊlɪŋ] [bou-lin], *s.* Bolos (in bowling alley); V. BOWLS (in grass). El arte o acto de jugar a las bochas; el juego de bolos. **Bowling-alley,** bolera, sitio cubierto para jugar a los bolos. **Bowling-green, bowling-ground,** plano para jugar a las bochas, juego de bolos; calle en los jardines cubierta de césped.

bowls [ˈbəʊlz] [bouls] *s.* Juego semejante a la petanca que se juega sobre césped.

bowman [ˈbəʊmən] [bou-man], *s.* Arquero, el soldado que peleaba con arco y flechas.

bownet [bəʊˈnet] [bou-net], *s.* Nasa o cesta para pescar.

bowse [bəʊs] [bous], *vn.* (*Mar.*) Halar a un tiempo.

bow-shot [ˈbəʊʃɒt] [bou-shot], *s.* La distancia a que una flecha puede ser arrojada del arco.

bowsprit [ˈbəʊsprɪt] [bou-sprit], *s.* (*Mar*) Bauprés, palo que sale inclinado de la proa de un bajel.

bowstring [ˈbəʊstrɪŋ] [bous-trin], *s.* Cuerda de arco.

bow tie [ˈbəʊˈtaɪ] [bou-tai] *s.* Corbata de moño, pajarita.

bow-window [ˈbəʊˈwɪndəʊ] [bou-uin-dou], *s.* Ventana arqueada o saliente en forma de arco.

box [bɒks] [boks], *s.* 1. (*Bot.*) Box o boj, árbol cuya madera se llama también así. 2. Caja, cajita o cajón; excusabaraja; pieza hueca de madera, metal, piedra u otra materia para meter dentro alguna cosa (container, contents); cajón (large); estuche (for pen, watch); urna (ballot box); alcancía, hucha (collection box); joyero, alhajero (jewelry box); caja de herramientas (tool box). 3. (*Mar.*) Bitácora. 4. Palco de teatro. Cabina (booth). **Witness box,** estrado. 5. Puñete, manotada o puñada dada en la cabeza. 6. Cuarto muy reducido en una taberna o botillería. 7. Cajetín en las imprentas. 8. Banquillo de castigo (in ice hockey penalty box); área de penalty o de castigo (in soccer); área (in baseball). (*Fam.*) **The box,** la tele. **What's on the box?,** ¿qué dan en la tele? **A box around the ears,** un sopapo (thump). **Band-box,** caja de cartón. **Hat-box,** sombrerera. **Jewel-box,** caja para joyas. **Letter-box,** buzón del correo. **Strong box,** cofre fuerte. **Box car,** carro de cajón, furgón. **Christmas-box,** aguinaldo. **Alms-box,** cepillo de limosna. **Coach-box,** pescante de coche. **Dice-box,** cubilete. **Dust-box,** salvadera. **Snuff-box,** tabaquera. **Box of a pump,** émbolo de una bomba. **Box plaiting,** (*Cost.*) plegado que consiste en dobleces o pliegues hechos a derecha e izquierda alternadamente. **Box-elder,** árbol norteamericano semejante al arce, pero con hojas de tres o cinco hojuelas.

box, *va.* 1. Encajonar, poner en una caja, embalar (put in boxes). 2. Apuñear, dar manotazos. -*vn.* (*Sport*) Boxear (fight); combatir o pelear a puñadas, andar a trompis. **To box somebody around the ears,** darle un sopapo a alguien (hit). **To box the compass,** (*Mar.*) cuartear. **Box in,** cerrarle el paso a (restrict, surround); esconder tapando con una tabla, etc. (enclose pipes).

boxen [ˈbɒksən] [box-sen], *a.* Hecho de boj o semejante a él.

boxer [ˈbɒksəʳ] [bok-saʳ], *s.* 1. Púgil, boxeador, el que combate a puñadas. 3. El que pone géneros en cajas. 4. Bóxer (dog).

boxer shorts [bɒksəˈʃɒts] [bok-ser-shorts] *s.* Calzoncillos, calzones interiores.

boxhaul [ˈbɒkshɔːl] [boks-joul], *va.* (*Mar.*) dar vuelta la nave cuando no se puede virar.

boxing [ˈbɒksɪŋ] [bok-sin], *s.* Boxeo, pugilato. **Boxing ring,** cuadrilátero.

Boxing Day [ˈbɒksɪŋdeɪ] [bok-sin-dei] *s.* El 26 de diciembre, día festivo en Gran Bretaña.

box number [ˈbɒksˌnʌmbəʳ] [boks-nam-baʳ] *s.* Apartado de correos, apartado postal, casilla postal o de correo (at post office).

box office [ˈbɒksɒfɪs] [boks-o-fis], *s.* Taquilla, boletería.

box seat [ˈbɒksiːt] [bok-sít], *s.* Palco (en un teatro).

boxwood [ˈbɒkswʊd] [boks-wud], *s.* Madera, amarillenta del box; también, el mismo árbol.

boy [bɔɪ] [boi], *s.* 1. Muchacho o niño, chico (baby, child). **Is it a boy or a girl?,** ¿es niño o niña?, ¿es varón o nena? **Boys will be boys,** así son los chicos o los niños. **His wife was delivered of a boy,** su mujer parió un varón. 2. Muchacho, el que no ha llegado a la edad adulta y ha pasado de la de niño (young man). (*Coloq.*) **A good old boy,** un sureño típico. **A night out with the boys,** una noche de juerga con los muchachos. (GB) (*Coloq.*) **Jobs for the boys,** amiguismo. **The boys in blue,** la policía. 3. Muchacho, voz de desprecio con que se moteja a los

jóvenes. 4. Criado, lacayo, mozo (servant). **Cabin-boy,** paje de escoba. **School-boy,** muchacho de escuela. **Choir-boy,** niño de coro. **Soldier's boy,** galopín, galopo. **A little boy,** muchachito, chico. **My dear boy,** mi querido niño. **Bad, naughty boy,** chico travieso. **Boy's play,** pasatiempo o juego de muchachos.

boy, *interj.* ¡vaya!

boycott [ˈbɔɪkɒt] [boi-kot], *va.* Boicotear. Desacreditar, excluir, coligarse contra una persona, por ejemplo, un propietario o tendero. (Del capitán Boycott, así tratado en Irlanda en 1880).

boycott *s.* Boicoteo. Coalición organizada contra un propietario, comerciante u otra persona, negándose a sostener con ella relaciones sociales o de negocios.

boyfriend [ˈbɔɪfrend] [boi-frend] *s.* Novio, amigo.

boyhood [ˈbɔɪhʊd] [boi-jud], *s.* Muchachez, el estado de muchacho; niñez.

boyish [ˈbɔɪʃ] [boi-ish], *a.* Pueril, propio de niño (enthusiasm, smile). **His boyish looks,** su aspecto juvenil o de chico. De muchacho, de chico (used of woman).

boyishly [ˈbɔɪʃlɪ] [boi-ishli], *adv.* Puerilmente, como niño.

boyishness [ˈbɔɪʃnɪʃ] [boi-ish-nes], *s.* Puerilidad, muchachada, niñada o cosa propia de niños.

boy scout [ˌbɔɪˈskaʊt] [boi-skaut], *s.* Explorador, muchacho o niño explorador.

bozo [ˈbɒzə] [bo-so] *s.* (*pej.*) Sujeto.

bra [brɑː] [bra] *s.* Sostén, sujetador, brasier, corpiño, soutien.

brabble [ˈbræbl] [bra-bel], *vn.* Armar camorra. -*s.* Camorra, riña o pendencia; debate.

braccate [ˈbrɑːkeɪt] [bra-keit], *a.* (*Orn.*) Paticalzado, el ave que tiene las patas cubiertas de plumas.

brace [breɪs] [breis], *va.* 1. Atar, ligar, amarrar. 2. (*Mar.*) Bracear, halar las brazas o poner las vergas según es menester. 3. Cercar, rodear. 4. Fortificar, vigorizar (los nervios). Apuntalar (support). **Brace up,** animarse. **Brace up!,** ¡arriba ese ánimo! *vn.* **To brace for something,** prepararse para algo.

brace, *s.* 1. Abrazadera, laña, grapón, broche, lo que mantiene alguna cosa firme (support). **Carpenter's brace,** barbiquejo; berbiquí (drill), barbiquí; tornapunta. **Brace and bits,** berbiquí con sus barrenas. 2. Tirante, la vigueta que va de solera a solera en una fábrica. 3. Sopanda de coche, cada una de las correas que sostienen la caja. 4. Par. **Brace of partridges,** un par de perdices. 5. (*Imp.*) Corchete, llave, rasgo que abraza dos o más renglones en lo escrito o impreso. 6. (*Arq.*) Anclaje, silla, mordaza; can, canecillo. -**Braces of a rudder,** (*Mar.*) hembras del timón. (2) Tirantes del pantalón; cargadores, tiraderas, suspensores. (*Dent.*) Aparatos, fierros, frenos, frenillos. (GB) Par (pair).

bracelet [ˈbreɪslɪt] [breis-let], *s.* 1. Brazalete, adorno para el brazo. (*Méx.*) Pulsera, manilla. 2. Brazalete, brazal, armadura del brazo.

bracer [ˈbreɪsəʳ] [brei-saʳ], *s.* 1. Brazal, armadura del brazo. 2. (*Med.*) Un medicamento tónico, fortificante y astringente. 3. Abrazadera, laña; cinto, venda. 4. Braguero.

braces [ˈbreɪsɪs] [brei-sis], *s. pl.* Abrazadera, freno para dientes.

brachial [ˈbræɪkəl] [bra-kial], *a.* Braquial, que pertenece o toca el brazo.

brachiopod [ˈbrækɪəpəd] [bra-kio-pod], *s.* Braquiópodo, ejemplar de la familia de moluscos bivalvos que tienen dos brazos carnosos dotados de extensión y contractilidd, que les sirven para moverse.

brachium [ˈbreɪkɪəm] [bra-kiom], *s. pl.* BRACHIA. El brazo superior o lo que lo representa en cualquier animal.

brachygrapher [ˈbrækɪɡræfəʳ] [bra-ki-gra-faʳ], *s.* Braquiógrafo, el que escribe en abreviatura.

brachygraphy [ˈbrækɪɡræfɪ] [bra-ki-gra-fi], *s.* Braquiografía, el arte de escribir en abreviatura.

bracing [ˈbreɪsɪŋ] [brei-sin], *a.* Fortificante, tónico, confortante. -*s.* (*Tec.*) Amarra, ligazón, refuerzo trabazón.

brack [ˈbræk] [brak], s. Rotura; pelo o mancha en los metales.

bracken [ˈbrækən] [braken], s. (Bot.) 1. Helecho grande de las regiones templadas; en particular la Pteris aquilina. 2. Helechal, sitio poblado de helechos.

bracket [ˈbrækɪt] [bra-ket], s. 1. Puntal, el madero en cuya corona o cabeza estriba otra cosa; listón, listoncillo; can, repisa. **Can-head brackets,** (Mar.) Aletas de las serviolas. 2. Paréntesis, angulares; así [], corchete (square bracket). (GB) Paréntesis (parenthesis). **In brackets,** entre paréntesis. 3. (Mec.) Bloque, garfio. 4. Repisa, rinconera, codillo. 5. Brazo de lámpara. **Tax bracket,** banda impositiva (category). **Income bracket,** nivel de ingresos. **The best car in this price bracket,** el mejor coche dentro de esta gama de precios.

bracket va. Poner entre corchetes (word, phrase); poner entre paréntesis (in parentheses). Catalogar (categorize). **You can't bracket these two cases together,** no se puede equiparar estos dos casos.

brackish [ˈbrækɪʃ] [bra-kish], a. Salobre, que por naturaleza tiene sabor de sal; áspero.

brackishness [ˈbrækɪʃnɪs] [bra-kish-nes], s. Sabor salobre; saladura; aspereza.

bract [ˈbrækt] [brakt], s. (Bot.) Bráctea, hoja de cuya axila se levanta un tallo de flor, o pedúnculo.

bractlet [ˈbræktlɪt] [brakt-let], s. (Bot.) Bracteola, bractea pequeña o secundaria.

brad [bræd] [brad], s. Clavo de ala de mosca; puntilla.

brad-awl [ˈbrædɔːl] [brad-oul], s. Punzón afilado, lesna.

brag [bræg] [brag], s. 1. Jactancia. 2. La cosa de que se jacta uno. 3. Un juego de naipes.

brag, vn. Jactarse, fanfarronear. (Fam.) **To brag about/of something,** alardear o jactarse de algo. **That's nothing to brag about,** eso no es como para enorgullecerse. va. Fanfarronear. (Fam.) **To brag that,** hacer alarde o jactarse de que.

braggadocio [bræɡəˈdɔːsɪə] [bra-ga-do-sio], s. Fanfarrón, el que echa fanfarronadas.

braggardism [ˈbræɡɑːdɪzm] [bra-gar-disem], s. Jactancia, vana ostentación.

braggart [ˈbræɡət] [bra-gart], a. Jactancioso, el que se jacta, fanfarrón.

braggart, bragger [ˈbræɡər] [bra-gar], s. Fanfarrón, el que echa fanfarronadas.

bragget [ˈbræɡet] [bra-guet], s. Aguamiel, una bebida dulce.

braggingly [ˈbræɡɪŋlɪ] [bra-guin-li], adv. Jactanciosamente.

Brahman [ˈbrɑːmən] [bra-man], s. Bracmán, nombre que se da a los filósfos y sacerdotes de la India.

Brahmanical, Braminical [brɑːˈmənɪkəl] [bra-ma-ni-kal], a. Bracmánico, perteneciente a los bracmanes. V. BRAHMAN.

braid [breɪd] [breid], va. 1. Trenzar, hacer trenzas. 2. Acordonar, bordar con cordoncillo o de realce; galonear.

braid, s. 1. Galón, fleco, alamar. 2. Trenza (of hair); cordoncillo. **She wears her hair in braids,** lleva el pelo trenzado. -a. Astuto, fraudulento, falso. (Esco.) Ancho. **Braidclaith,** paño ancho.

brail [breɪl] [breil], va. (Mar.) Cargar las velas; halar por medio de candelizas.

Braille [breɪl] [breil] s. Braille.

brails [breɪlz] [breils], va. (Mar.) Candelizas o cargaderas, los cabos pequeños que pasan por los motones.

brain [breɪn] [brein], s. 1. Cerebro (organ), sesos, la colección de vasos y órganos contenidos en la cavidad del cráneo. **Brain damage,** lesión cerebral. **Brain surgeon,** neurocirujano. **Brain tumor,** tumor cerebral. 2. Entendimiento, seso, juicio, cordura, talento; cerebro (clever person). **The brain drain,** la fuga de cerebros. **She's got a good brain,** es muy inteligente (intellect). (Coloq.) **To have something on the brain,** tener algo metido en la cabeza. **To blow out one's brains,** levantarse la tapa de los sesos. V. BRAINS.

brain, va. Descerebrar, matar a uno haciéndole saltar la tapa de los sesos. (Coloq.) Romperle la crisma a. **Hare-brained,**

aturdido, sin seso. (Ant.) **Scatter-brained,** o **shittle-brained,** veleidoso, voltario, ligero, inconstante. (GB) (Coloq.) **Brain box,** cerebrito. **Brainchild,** creación. **Brain-dead,** clínicamente muerto.

brainish [ˈbreɪnɪʃ] [brei-nish], a. Loco, furioso.

brainless [ˈbreɪnlɪs] [brein-les], a. Tonto, insensato; estúpido.

brainpan [breɪnˈpæn] [brein-pan], s. Cráneo o casco.

brains [breɪnz] [breins] s. Sesos (substance). (Culin.) Sesos. Inteligencia (intelligence). **I'd like to pick your brains about something,** quisiera hacerte unas preguntas o consultas acerca de algo. **To rack one's brains (over something),** devanarse los sesos (con algo). Cerebro, autor, intelectual (mastermind). **She's the brains behind the operation,** es el cerebro o la autora intelectual de la operación. **He's the brains of the family,** es la lumbrera de la familia.

brainsick [ˈbreɪnsɪk] [brein-sik], a. Alegre de cascos, inconstante, mala cabeza; frenético.

brainsickly [ˈbreɪnsɪklɪ] [brein-sik-li], adv. Con debilidad de cabeza.

brainsickness [ˈbreɪnsɪknɪs] [brein-sik-nes], s. Inconstancia, instabilidad; vértigo, veleidad, ligereza.

brainstorm [ˈbreɪnstɔːm] [breins-torm], s. 1. Agitación transitoria. 2. Confusión mental. (GB) (Coloq.) **He had a brainstorm,** se le cruzaron los cables. 3. Repentina idea genial.

brainteaser [ˈbreɪnˌtiːzər] [brein-tí-sar] s. Rompecabezas.

brain trust [ˈbreɪnˌtrʌst] [brein-trast] s. Grupo de expertos.

brainwash [ˈbreɪnwɒʃ] [brein-uosh] va. Hacerle un lavado de cerebro a, lavarle el cerebro a.

brainwashing [ˈbreɪnˌwɒʃɪŋ] [brein-uoshin], s. Lavado cerebral imposición por persuasión o tortura de ciertas ideas políticas.

brainwave [ˈbreɪnweɪv] [brein-ueiv] s. (Coloq.) Idea genial o brillante, lamparazo.

brainy [ˈbreɪnɪ] [breini] a. Coloq.) Inteligente, listo.

braise [breɪz] [breis] va. Estofar.

brake [breɪk] [breik], s. 1. Helecho del género Pteris, particularmente Pteris aquilina. V. BRACKEN. 2. Agramadera, instrumento para agramar lino o cáñamo. 3. Maleza, zarzal, matorral. 4. (F.C.) Freno; retranca (on vehicle). Freno de mano (handbrake). (Coloq.) **To put the brakes/a brake on something,** poner freno a algo. **Brake lights,** luces de freno o de frenado. 5. (Mar.) Guimbalete de bomba. 6. Amasadera, la artesa de amasar. 7. Bocado de canutillo para caballo. 8. Palanca, espeque. **Brake beam,** barra del freno. **Brake-man,** guardafreno, retranquero. **Air-brake,** freno atmosférico o de aire. **Automatic brake,** freno automático.

brake, va./vn. Frenar. pret. del verbo TO BREAK.

braking [ˈbreɪkɪŋ] [brei-kin] s. Frenado. **Braking distance,** distancia de frenado.

braky [ˈbreɪkɪ] [breiki], a. Espinoso, áspero, lleno de malezas.

bramble [ˈbræmbl] [bram-bol], s. Zarza o cualquier otro arbusto espinoso. Zarzamora (blackberry bush)

brambled [ˈbræmbld] [bram-bold], a. Breñoso, zarzoso, cubierto de zarzas o arbustos espinosos.

brambling [ˈbræmblɪŋ] [bram-blin], s. Pinzón, especie de pájaro.

brambly [ˈbræmblɪ] [bram-bli], a. Zarzoso, lleno de zarzas.

bran [bræn] [bran], s. Salvado, la cáscara del trigo después de molido; afrecho.

bran-new [brænˈnjuː] [bran-niu], a. Enteramente nuevo, flamante.

branch [brɑːntʃ] [branch], s. 1. Rama o ramo del árbol. 2. Ramo, la parte separada de algún otro con dependencia y relación a él. 3. Brazo, parte de un río que desemboca en otro mayor. 4. Rama, cualquier persona con relación al tronco de que trae su descendencia u origen. Rama (of family, field of study). 5. Pitón, asta. 6. Cama del freno. 7. Brazo del candelero. 8. Brazo de trompeta. **Vine Branch**

sarmiento. **Branch pease,** arvejones enramados. 9. Sucursal (of company, bank). **The American branch of the company,** la división americana de la compañía. 10. *(F. C.)* Ramal, bifurcación (of river, road, railway). **Branches,** (colectivamente) Ramas, ramaje. **The three branches of the armed forces,** los tres cuerpos del ejército. *-a.* Divergente de un tronco o parte principal o tributario de ella.

branch, *vn.* 1. Ramificarse, esparcirse y dividirse en ramas alguna cosa (river, family); bifurcarse (road). **A path branches (off) to the right,** un sendero sale a la derecha. **Branch out,** diversificar sus actividades (take on new activity). **The company has branched out into publishing,** la compañía ha diversificado sus actividades lanzándose al campo editorial. 2. Hablar difusamente. **He has branched out on his own,** se ha establecido por su cuenta (business partner - become independent). 3. Echar pitones, astas o ramas. *-va.* 1. Ramificar, dividir en ramas. 2. Bordar alguna cosa con figuras de ramos.

brancher ['brænt∫əʳ] [bran-chaʳ], *s.* 1. El que divide en ramos. 2. *(Cetr.)* Halcón ramero.

branchery ['brænt∫ərɪ] [bran-che-ri], *s.* Las partes vasculosas de algunos frutos.

branchiae ['bræŋkɪə] [bran-kia], *s. pl.* Branquias, órganos respiratorios de los peces, crustáceos y muchos moluscos.

branchial ['bræŋkɪəl] [bran-kial], *a.* Branquial.

branchiness ['brænt∫ɪnɪs] [bran-chi-nes], *s.* Frondosidad.

branchless ['brænt∫lɪs] [branch-les], *a.* Sin ramas; desnudo.

branchlet ['brænt∫lɪt] [branch-let], *s. dim.* Rama pequeña, ramilla.

branchy ['brænt∫ɪ] [bran-chi], *a.* Ramoso, lo que tiene muchos ramos o ramas.

brand [brænd] [brand], *s.* 1. Tizón o tea, palo encendido o propio para encenderse (torch). 2. Espada. 3. Rayo. 4. Marca o sello que se pone a las reses y que se ponía a los reos con un hierro ardiendo (identification mark). Marca; tipo (type); estilo (style). **Her brand of socialism,** su tipo de socialismo. 5. Tizón, nota de infamia. **To cast a brand upon one,** difamar a alguno, quitarle la reputación.

brand, *va.* 1. Herrar, marcar o sellar con un hierro ardiendo (cattle). 2. Tiznar, infamar, desdorar, manchar, empañar la reputación. **To brand something/somebody as something,** tachar o tildar algo/a alguien de algo (label). **Branded gray horse,** caballo con manchas irregulares.

brand goose [brænd'guːz] [brand-gús], *s.* Oca silvestre. V. BRANT.

brandiron ['brændɪrən] [bran-di-ron], **branding iron,** *s.* Marca, el hierro para marcar a los animales o a los malhechores.

brandish ['brændɪ∫] [bran-dish], *va.* Blandir, jugar con; sacudir la mano.

brandish, *s.* Floreo; movimiento rápido y de corta duración.

brandling ['brændlɪŋ] [brand-lin], *s.* Especie de gusano que sirve para cebo.

brand name [brænd'neɪm] [brand-neim] *s.* Marca.

brand new ['brænd'njuː] [brand-niu] *a.* Nuevo, flamante (toy, car).

brandrith ['brændrɪθ] [brand-riz], *s.* Antepecho o brocal de pozo.

brandy, brandy-wine ['brændɪ] [bran-di], *s.* Aguardiente, coñac, brandy.

brandyshop ['brændɪ∫ɒp] [bran-di-shop], *s.* Aguardentería, la tienda en que se vende aguardiente.

brangle ['bræŋgl] [bran-guel], *vn.* Vocinglear, disputarse. V. WRANGLE.

brank [bræŋk] [brank], *s.* (Dial. ingl.) V. BUCKKWHEAT.

brankursine ['bræŋkɜːsaɪn] [bran-kur-sain], *s.* *(Bot.)* Branca ursina, acanto.

branlin ['brænlɪn] [bran-lin], *s.* Salmón pequeño antes de ir al mar.

branny ['brænɪ] [bra-ni], *a.* Casposo, parecido al salvado.

brant [brænt] [brant], *s.* Especie de ganso, u oca silvestre. Se llama también *brent.*

brasen, brazen [breɪsn] [brei-sen], *a.* Hecho de bronce.

brash [bræ∫] [brash], *a.* Impetuoso, temerario. Excesivamente desenvuelto, de gran desparpajo. *-s.* 1. Ramas sueltas de árboles. 2. Enfermedad repentina.

brasier, brazier ['breɪzɪəʳ] [brei-siaʳ], *s.* 1. Latonero, el que trabaja en latón, azófar, alambre o cobre. 2. Brasero o coda.

Brasil, Brazil ['brɒsɪl] [bra-sil], *s.* Palo del Brasil.

brass [bræs] [bras], *s.* 1. Latón, cobre (metal). Dorado (button). 2. Descaro, desvergüenza. **To be as bold as brass,** ser muy descarado. 3. *(Fam.)* Altos jefes militares. 4. *(Mús.)* Bronces, metales. **Brass instrument,** instrumento de metal. **The brass section,** los bronces, los metales. **Brass band,** banda de instrumentos de viento, charanga.

brassfounder [bræs'faʊndəʳ] [bras-faun-daʳ], *s.* Fundidor de bronce.

brassie [bræsɪ] [bra-si], *s.* Maza que se emplea en el juego de golf.

brassiere ['bræsɪəʳ] [brasiaʳ], *s.* Brassière, soporte para senos.

brassiness ['bræsɪnɪs] [bra-si-nes], *s.* Bronceada, apariencia de bronce.

brass knuckles [brɑːs'nʌklz] [bras-nakols] *s. pl.* Nudilleras de metal, manoplas.

brass rubbing [brɑːs'rʌbɪŋ] [bras-ra-bin] *s.* Técnica de calcar por frotación un BRASS 2 (activity); calco por frotación de un BRASS 2 (product).

brass-visaged [brɑːs'vɪseɪdʒ] [bras-vi-seich], *a.* Descarado, descocado, desvergonzado.

brassy ['brɑːsɪ] [bra-si], *a.* 1. Que participa de la naturaleza del latón. 2. Descarado, desvergonzado, ordinario, chabacano. 3. V. BRAZEN.

brat [bræt] [brat], *s.* 1. Rapaz, el muchacho pequeño de edad; chulo, chiquillo; angelito; mocoso (child), niño mimado (spoilt person). 2. (Despect.) Prole.

brattle ['brætl] [bratel], *vn.* Hacer ruido rápidamente repetido y poco sonoro ; correr con estruendo; poner en polvorosa.

brattle, *s.* Ruido resonante, como el de un tambor, el correr de personas o el de un ataque. (Onomatopéyico.)

bravado [brə'vɑːdəʊ] [bra-va-dou], *s.* Bravata, baladronada, bravuconada.

brave [breɪv] [breiv], *a.* 1. Bravo, valiente, esforzado, animoso, atrevido, intrépido. **That was brave of you!,** ¡qué valiente! 2. Garboso, airoso. 3. Bravo, elegante, hábil, honrado.

brave, *va.* 1. Desafiar, provocar a duelo. 2. Bravear, echar bravatas. 3. Ofender, insultar. 4. Arrostrar. Afrontar, hacer frente a. **To brave the weather,** hacer frente al mal tiempo.

brave, *s.* 1. Bravonel, el guapo que echa bravatas y fieros, fanfarrón. 2. Bravata, amenaza con arrogancia. 3. Guerrero piel roja (North American Indian). **The brave,** los valientes.

bravely ['breɪvlɪ] [breiv-li], *adv.* Bravamente, valientemente, con valor; perfectamente.

bravery ['breɪvərɪ] [brei-ve-ri], *s.* 1. Esfuerzo, valentía, valor, coraje, ánimo. 2. Lustre, galantería, esplendor, magnificencia. 3. Pompa, ostentación. 4. Bravata.

bravingly ['breɪvɪŋlɪ] [brei-vin-li], *adv.* En desafío.

bravo ['brɑːvəʊ] [bra-vou], *s.* Asesino asalariado. *-inter.* Voz de aplauso. ¡Bueno; bueno; bravo va!

bravura [brə'vʊərə] [bra-vua-ra], *s.* *(Mús.)* Aire o canción difícil de cantar.

braw [brɔː] [bro], *a.* *(Esco.)* Bravo, garboso, elegantemente vestido; espléndido, hermoso.

brawl [brɔːl] [brol], *s.* 1. Quimera, alboroto, disputa, camorra, pelea, reyerta. 2. Baile, y la música que lo acompaña.

brawl, *vn.* 1. Alborotar, armar quimera con voces desentonadas; vocinglear; pelearse, armar camorra. 2. Hacer ruido. *-va.* Expeler por medio de ruido; aterrar.

brawler ['brɔːləʳ] [brou-laʳ], *s.* Quimerista o camorrista.

brawling ['brɔːlɪŋ] [brou-lin], *s.* Alboroto, el acto de alborotar, vocinglería.

brawn [brɔːn] [bron], *s.* 1. Pulpa, carne mollar, la parte carnosa y muscular del cuerpo. Músculos (strength). 2. El brazo, llamado así por ser musculoso. 3. Carnosidad, carne maciza y musculosa. 4. Carne de verraco o cerdo padre.

brawner [ˈbrɔːnəʳ] [bro-naʳ], *s.* El verraco que se mata para comer.

brawniness [ˈbrɔːnɪnɪs] [bro-ni-nes], *s.* Fortaleza o dureza de músculos; partes carnosas.

brawny [ˈbrɔːnɪ] [bro-ni], *a.* Carnoso, musculoso, membrudo.

braxy [ˈbræksɪ] [braksi], *s.* Fiebre carbuncular de los carneros y las ovejas; también una res lanar atacada de este mal. *-a.* Atacado de dicha fiebre.

bray [breɪ] [brei], *va.* 1. Majar, triturar, moler, machacar o pulverizar. 2. Emitir. *-vn.* 1. Rebuznar (donkey); cacarear (person). 2. Hacer ruido desapacible.

bray, *s.* 1. Rebuzno, la voz desapacible del asno. 2. Ruido bronco. 3. Monte de tierra, trinchera. **False bray,** *(Mil.)* Falsabraga.

brayer [ˈbreɪəʳ] [breiaʳ], *s.* Rebuznador. 2. *(Imp.)* Moledor de tinta.

braying [ˈbreɪɪŋ] [brei-in], *s.* Grito, clamor; rebuzno.

braze [breɪz] [breis], *va.* 1. Soldar con latón o azófar. 2. Broncear. 3. Hacer desvergonzado o descarado a alguno.

brazen [ˈbreɪzn] [breisn], *a.* 1. Bronceado; hecho de bronce. 2. Descarado, desvergonzado. **The brazen hussy!,** ¡esa fresca o descarada!

brazen, *va.* Hacerse descarado. **To brazen out a thing,** sostener alguna cosa con impudencia. **To brazen one down,** desconcertar, aturdir, confundir a uno.

brazen-browed [ˈbreɪznˌbraʊd] [breisn-broud], **brazen-faced** [ˈbreɪznˌfeɪst] [breisn-feist], *a.* Descarado, desvergonzado, impudente.

brazen-face [ˈbreɪznˌfeɪs] [breisn-feis], *s.* Cara de vaqueta, la persona que no tiene vergüenza.

brazeness [ˈbreɪznɪs] [breis-nes], *s.* Descaro, desvergüenza.

brazier [ˈbreɪzɪəʳ] [brei-siaʳ], *s.* Brasero. V. BRASIER.

Brazil [brəˈzɪl] [bra-sil] *N. (Geogr.)* Brasil.

Brazilian [brəˈzɪlɪən] [bra-si-lian] *a./s.* Brasileño.

Brazil (nut) [brəzɪlˈnʌt] [bra-sil-nat] *s.* Coquito del Brasil, castaña del Pará.

Brazil-wood [brəzɪlˈwuːd] [bra-sil-wud], *s.* Madera palo del Brasil.

braziletto [ˈbrəzɪletə] [bra-si-le-to], *s.* Brasilete madera inferior al brasil.

breach [briːtʃ] [brích], *s.* 1. Rotura o rompimiento, el acto de romper alguna cosa; ruptura (break). 2. Brecha, la rotura o abertura que se hace en la muralla (gap, opening). **To step into/fill the breach,** llenar el hueco. 3. Contravención de alguna ley o contrato, infracción, violación (of law); ofensa, perjuicio, detrimento de la honra, reputación, derechos o privilegios. **Breach of contract,** incumplimiento de contrato. **A breach of confidence,** un abuso de confianza. **Breach of promise,** falta de palabra. **Breach of duty,** violación del deber.

breach, *va.* Infringir, violar (rule); poner en peligro (security). Abrir una brecha en (defenses).

bread [bred] [bred], *s.* 1. Pan, alimento que se hace de la harina de diversas semillas. 2. Pan, todo lo que en general sirve para el sustento diario del hombre. 3. *(Sl. & dated)* Guita, lana, pasta (money). **Bread and butter,** pan con mantequilla. **Teaching is his bread and butter,** se gana la vida enseñando. **To take the bread out of somebody's mouth,** quitarle el pan de la boca a alguien. **To want one's bread buttered on both sides,** querer el oro y el moro. **To earn one's bread,** ganarse la vida. **Household bread,** pan casero, pan bazo. **Light bread,** pan esponjoso. **Shipbread,** galleta, bizcocho de mar. **Batch of bread,** hornada de pan. **Soft bread,** mollete. **Sow bread,** criadilla de tierra. **Unleavened bread,** ázimo. **Bread-stuffs,** la harina, trigo, maíz, y en general todos los granos que sirven para hacer pan. **New bread,** pan tierno. **Stale bread,** pan duro o

sentado. **Slice of bread,** rebanada de pan. **Corn bread,** pan de maíz. **Brown bread,** pan moreno.

breadbasket [ˈbredˌbɑːskɪt] [bred-baskit] *s.* Panera (container).

breadbin [ˈbredbɪn] [bred-bin], **breadbox** [ˈbredbɒks] [bred-boks] *s.* Panera para guardar el pan.

breadboard [ˈbredbɔːd] [bred-bord], *s.* Tabla para cortar el pan o para amasarlo.

bread-corn [ˈbredkɔːn] [bred-korn], *s.* Pan, la semilla de que se hace pan.

breadcrumb [ˈbredkrʌm] [bred-kram] *s.* Miga de pan. *(Culin.)* **Breadcrumbs,** pan rallado o molido.

breaden [ˈbredn] [breden], *a.* (Poco us.) Hecho de pan.

bread-fruit [ˈbredfruːt] [bred-frut], *s.* Árbol del pan y su fruto.

bread line [ˈbredlaɪn] [bred-lain], *s.* Cola que se forma para recibir alimentos gratuitamente. *(Coloq.)* **They're on the bread line,** apenas tienen/les alcanza para vivir.

bread room [ˈbredrʊm] [bred-rum], *s. (Mar.)* Pañol del pan.

breadstuff [ˈbredstʌf] [bred-staf], *s.* Material para hacer pan; grano, harina, etc.

breadth [bredθ] [bredz], *s.* 1. Anchura, la dimensión contrapuesta a lo largo (width); amplitud (extent). **The breadth and length of anything,** lo ancho y largo de alguna cosa. 2. Catolicidad, liberalidad. 3. Paño, lo ancho de una tela. **There are five breadths in that skirt,** hay cinco paños en esa saya o falda.

breadthwise [ˈbredθwaɪz] [bredz-uais], *adv.* A lo ancho.

bread-winner [ˈbredˌwɪnəʳ] [bred-wi-naʳ], *s.* El que se mantiene a sí mismo y a otros con su sueldo, jornal o ganancias; productor. **She's the breadwinner of the family,** es la que mantiene/sostiene a la familia.

break [breɪk] [breik], *va. (pret.* BROKE o BRAKE *(Poét.); pp.* BROKEN o BROKE. 1. Romper (window, plate), partir, quebrar (stick), abrir o hender alguna cosa a la fuerza. Forzar (get into/safe). **We broke the toolbox open,** abrimos la caja de herramientas forzándola. **I've broken my pencil,** se me ha roto la punta del lápiz. **He broke his wrist,** se rompió la muñeca. 2. Vencer, sobrepujar. 3. Abrir brechas batiendo; horadar. Roturar (breach/pierce). 4. Quebrantar o destruir alguna cosa. Romper, descomponer (render useless - machine). 5. Abatir el espíritu. 6. Imposibilitar, inutilizar. 7. Domar (tame/horse). 8. Causar quiebra o bancarrota. 9. Quebrantar, violar algún contrato o promesa; infringir, quebrantar una ley (rule); no cumplir, faltar a (promise). Incumplir, romper (promise). 10. Arruinar o destruir a uno (ruin) (person, company); destroza, deshacer (crush-person), marchitar. 11. Interceptar, interrumpir, cortar (interrupt/circuit); romper (fast/silence), impedir. Poner fin a (end) (strike); desarticular (drug ring); salir de (impasse); dejar (habit). Escaparse o fugarse (escape from). *-vn.* 1. Romperse (window, plate), partirse, quebrarse (stick), dividirse una cosa. **My watch broke,** se me rompió el reloj. 2. Abrirse, reventarse algún tumor, descargando materia. 3. Prorrumpir, exclamar. 4. Quebrar, hacer bancarrota. 5. Decaer, tener la salud o las fuerzas quebrantadas. Desmoronarse, venirse abajo (give in/resistance). **She broke under constant interrogation,** no resistió el constante interrogatorio. 6. Romper, enemistarse. 7. Separarse, apartarse con violencia. 8. Entrar de repente, apuntar, abrir (p. ej. el día). 9. Estallar (v. gr. una tempestad), romper, apuntar, despuntar (day). Cambiar (change) (weather). 10. Mudar, perder calidad música, hablando de la voz. 11. Parar, hacer una pausa. **To break for lunch,** parar para almorzar. 12. Abrir el juego (in snooker, pool). **Things are breaking well for me,** me están saliendo bien las cosas. **To break asunder,** partir, dividir, separar en dos partes. **To break cover,** salir de un bosque, de la espesura (hablando de la caza), de un escondite. **To break forth,** brotar, saltar, salir de la tierra. **To break open,** romper, fracturar. **To break the law,** infringir la ley. **To break open a door,** desherrajar una puerta. *(Mar.)*

Desbaratar. **To break a business,** abrir una disensión, proponer un asunto. **To break a custom,** desacostumbrar, hacer perder algún hábito o costumbre. **To break a horse,** domar un caballo. **To break a jest,** decir un chiste de repente. **To break prison,** forzar o escalar la cárcel. **To break bulk,** sacar parte de la carga. **To break ground,** abrir la trinchera; arar. *(Fig.)* Comenzar una empresa, un trabajo. **To break a lance with,** oponerse a, entrar en la lucha contra. **To break loose,** desatar o desatarse, escapar, huir. **To break one's back,** derrengar. **To break one's fast,** desayunarse. **To break one's heart,** matar a pesadumbres. **To die broken hearted,** morir de pesadumbre, o de pena. **To break the spirit,** deprimir, abatir el espíritu o el corazón. **To break one's oath,** ser traidor o perjuro, faltar al juramento. **To break the bank,** hacer saltar la banca (en el juego). **To break open a house,** forzar una casa. **To break with sorrow,** consumirse de tristeza. **To break wind,** peer, ventosear, soltar el preso.

break away, desprenderse (piece); escindirse o separarse (faction/region). **The boat broke away from its moorings,** el barco se soltó de las amarras.

break down, abatir, derribar, demoler, arruinar; (y como neutro) caer, desplomarse, arruinarse; volcar (un carruaje); cortarse (en un discurso). Estropearse, averiarse, descomponerse, quedarse varado/en pana (vehicle/machine); fallar, venirse abajo (system); fracasar (talks). Perder el control (lose composure). **It breaks down as follows,** el total puede desglosarse de la siguiente manera. Echar abajo, derribar (door/barrier). Desglosar (divide up / expenditure); descomponer (sentence). **The process can be broken down into three steps,** el proceso puede dividirse en tres pasos.

break in o **into,** arrojarse, asaltar, acometer; horadar; forzar; penetrar adentro, entrar por fuerza, meterse para robar (intruder). **our house was broken into,** nos entraron a robar. Cargar al enemigo o cerrar con él; mezclarse en negocios de otros; interrumpir al que está ocupado (interrupt). **I didn't mean to break in on your conversation,** no quería interrumpirles la conversación. **To break in,** enseñar, acostumbrar, formar; domar un caballo. Cambiar (banknote). **They had to break into their savings,** tuvieron que echar mano de sus ahorros. **To break into a run,** echarse a correr. **To break into applause,** romper o prorrumpir en aplausos.

break off, romper (engagement/ diplomatic relations); dejar por acabar, sin concluir; desgajar, desprenderse (snap off, come free). **The handle broke off,** se le rompió el asa. Partir (detach); parar de hablar, detenerse (stop talking) **To break of,** (una cosa) corregir, reforzar.

break out, desenfrenarse, darse o entregarse a los vicios; salir o dejarse ver; llenarse de úlceras. **A rash broke out on his face,** le salió un sarpullido en la cara. **He broke out in spots,** le salieron granos. **To break out in a sweat,** empezar a sudar. Estallar (war, epidemic, rioting); reventar, rebosar, salir de madre; exclamar, prorrumpir; declararse; encolerizarse; abrir camino; salir con violencia; escalar la cárcel, escaparse, fugarse (prisoner).

break through, pasar por medio de, romper, superar, abrirse camino, vencer dificultades o peligros. *(Mil.)* Penetrar en las defensas enemigas. Salir (sun). **The sun broke through the clouds,** el sol se abrió paso entre las nubes.

break up, 1. *va.* Demoler, derribar, abatir; romper, desgarrar, partir. 2. *vn.* Decampar, levantar el campo, tomar las de Villadiego, poner pies en polvorosa; principiar las vacaciones en las escuelas. **We break up on the 21st.,** las clases terminan el 21. 3. Levantar una sesión; interrumpir; disolver (demonstration), despedir una asamblea, terminar (meeting), dispersarse (crowd). **He broke up the fight,** separó a los niños (o los hombres, etc.), que se estaban peleando. Separarse (lovers, band). **Their marriage broke up,** su matrimonio fracasó. **To break up with somebody,** romper o terminar con alguien. **To break up an officer,** *(Mil.)* desaforar a un oficial, echarle del regimiento. **To**

break up an army, licenciar las tropas. Romperse, deshacerse (boat, ship).

break with, romper con (tradition).

break, *s.* 1. Rotura, abertura, fractura (fracture). 2. Pausa (Rad., TV) (comercial), parada, intervalo, interrupción (gap), vacío. *(Teat.)* Entreacto, intermedio. Descanso (rest period); recreo (at school). **We have a coffee break at 11,** a las once paramos para tomar un café. Vacaciones (short vacation); cambio (change, respite). **I need a break from all this,** necesito descansar de todo esto; necesito un cambio de aires (a holiday). Ruptura, corte (in circuit). Oportunidad (chance, opportunity). **He got a break,** se le presentó una oportunidad. Ruptura (separation, rift). **To make a clean break,** cortar por lo sano. **He made a break for the door,** corrió hacia la puerta (sudden move). Tacada, serie (in snooker, pool); ruptura, quiebre (in tennis). 3. Una línea que ponen los ingleses al fin de algunas oraciones para denotar que no está completo su sentido. 4. Blanco en los escritos. **The break of the day,** la aurora.

breakable ['breɪkəbl] [breik-abol] *a.* Quebradizo, frágil.

breakables ['breɪkəblz] [breikabols] *s. pl.* Objetos frágiles.

breakage ['breɪkeɪdʒ] [breik-eich], *s.* 1. Fractura, rotura o quebrantamiento (action). 2. Objetos quebrados, roturas (objects broken). 3. Indemnización por cosas quebradas.

breakaway ['breɪkəweɪ] [breik-auei] *s.* Ruptura, escisión (separation). Disidente, escindido (faction). *(Sport)* Escapada.

breakdown ['breɪkdaʊn] [breik-daun], *s.* 1. Parada imprevista, avería repentina, pana (failure of car, machine). **They had a breakdown on the highway,** se les estropeó el coche en la autopista. **Breakdown service,** servicio de asistencia en carretera. Interrupción (of service, communications); fracaso, ruptura. (of negotiations). *(Comput.)* **The system suffered a complete breakdown,** el sistema colapsó. 2. *(Med.)* Colapso, crisis. **Nervous breakdown,** crisis nerviosa. 3. Derrumbamiento, falta de éxito o mal éxito, fracaso. 4. *(Quím.)* Descomposición (into constituent elements), análisis. **A breakdown of expenditure,** un desglose de los gastos.

breaker ['breɪkər] [brei-car], *s.* 1. El que rompe o labra tierra de labor. 2. Infractor, quebrador, rompedor. **-Breakers,** *pl.* Embate de las olas, cuando se retiran de los escollos. Reventazones, rompientes. (GB) *(Auto)* **Breaker's yard,** cementerio de automóviles.

break-even point [ˌbreɪkˈiːvənˌpɔɪnt] [breik-iven-point], *s.* Punto en que un negocio empieza a cubrir los gastos que ocasiona.

breakfast ['brekfəst] [brek-fast], *vn.* Desayunar, almorzar.

breakfast, *s.* Desayuno, almuerzo, el alimento que se toma por la mañana; alimento. **To have breakfast,** desayunar, tomar el desayuno. **Breakfast television,** televisión matinal.

breakfront ['breɪkfrɒnt] [breik-front] *s.* Mueble con estantes en la parte superior y armarios cerrados debajo.

break-in ['breɪkˌɪn] [breik-in] *s.* Robo (con escalamiento). **They had a break-in next door,** entraron a robar en la casa de al lado.

breaking ['breɪkɪŋ] [breikin], *s.* 1. Bancarrota. 2. Irrupción; disolución. 3. Rompimiento de tierra. 4. Principio de las vacaciones en las escuelas. 5. Fractura, rompimiento. **Breaking up of the Parliament,** suspensión de las sesiones del Parlamento. **Breaking and entering,** allanamiento de morada. **Breaking point,** límite. **The soldiers were at breaking point,** los soldados habían llegado al límite de sus fuerzas.

breakneck ['breɪknek] [breik-nek], *s.* Despeñadero, paraje en que está alguno expuesto a despegarse; precipicio, ruina. *-a.* Precipitado, rápido. **At breakneck speed,** a una velocidad vertiginosa.

breakout ['breɪkaʊt] [breik-aut], *s.* fuga, evasión (from prison).

breakthrough ['breɪkθruː] [breik-zru], *s.* 1. Descubrimiento o hipótesis que permite un adelanto científico o tecnológico. **A major breakthrough,** un avance o adelanto importantísimo. 2. *(Mil.)* Ruptura, brecha. 3. Oportunidad.

breakup ['breɪkʌp] [breik-ap] *s.* Desintegración (of structure, family); desmembramiento (of empire, company); disolución (of political parties); fracaso (talks). **The breakup of their marriage,** su separación o ruptura.

breakvow ['breɪkvəʊ] [breik-vau], *s.* El que falta a sus votos; embustero.

breakwater ['breɪkˌwɔːtəʳ] [breik-uotaʳ], *s.* Rompeolas, tajamar, muralla o construcción de piedra a la entrada de un puerto para impedir las oleadas.

bream [briːm] [brím], *s.* Sargo, pez de agua dulce. **Sea bream,** besugo.

bream, *va.* Limpiar algo, p. ej. los fondos de un buque, de conchas, algas, fango, etc., por medio de fuego y raedura. Cf. BROOM.

breast [brest] [brest], *s.* 1. Pecho, seno, la parte del cuerpo humano desde la garganta hasta el estómago. 2. Testera, los extremos delanteros de las gualderas de una cureña de campaña. 3. Pecho o teta en la mujer. **Breast cancer,** cáncer de mama o de pecho. 4. Pecho, el corazón, el interior del hombre. **To beat one's breast,** darse golpes de pecho. **To make a clean breast of something,** confesar algo. 5. Toro, moldura del pie de la columna. 6. Frente o cara de veta o filón. 7. Comba del cubo de una rueda. **A child at the breast,** un niño de pecho. 8. Pechuga (of chicken, turkey); **breast of lamb,** pecho de cordero.

breast, *va.* Acometer de frente o presentarse de frente.

breastbone ['brestbəʊn] [brest-boun], *s.* Esternón, el hueso que constituye la parte anterior del pecho.

breast-deep ['brestˈdiːp] [brest-díp], **breast-high** ['brestˈhaɪ] [brest-jai], *a.* Alto hasta el pecho; antepecho.

breasted ['brestɪd] [bres-tid], *a.* Lo que tiene pecho. **Narrow-breasted,** hundido de pecho. **Pigeon-breasted,** de pecho abultado.

breastfeed ['brestfiːd] [brest-fid] *va.* Darle el pecho a, darle de mamar a, amamantar. **A breastfed baby,** un niño amamantado. *vn.* Dar el pecho a, dar de mamar a.

breasthooks ['bresthuːks] [brest-juks], *s. (Mar.)* Buzardas, piezas de madera que se colocan en la proa para sujetar la unión de los costados.

breastknot ['brestnɒt] [brest-not], *s.* Lazo o lazada, adorno de cintas en forma de lazo que llevan las mujeres al pecho.

breastpin ['brestpɪn] [brest-pin], *s.* Broche, alfiler de pecho, sostén y adorno de diferentes formas que llevan las mujeres al pecho.

breastplate ['brestpleɪt] [brest-pleit], *s.* 1. Peto, armadura del pecho. 2. Pretal de una cabalgadura. 3. Pectoral.

breast-plow o **breast-plough** ['brestplɔː] [brest-plou], *s.* Arado de pecho, especie de arado pequeño que se empuja a fuerza de pecho.

breast-pump ['brestpʌmp] [brest-pamp], *s.* Extractor de leche.

breastrail ['brestreɪl] [brest-tril], *s. (Mar.)* Antepecho.

breastrope ['brestrəʊp] [brest-roup], *s.* 1. *(Mar.)* Guardamancebo de sondar. 2. *(Mar.)* Nervio de las redes de combate.

breaststroke ['brestrəʊk] [bres-trouk] *s.* Pecho, braza (estilo).

breast-wheel ['brestwiːl] [brest-uíl], *s.* Rueda hidráulica de costado.

breastwork ['brestwɜːk] [brest-uek], *s.* 1. *(Fort.)* Parapeto, terraplén que defiende el pecho contra los golpes del enemigo. 2. *(Mar.)* Propao.

breath [breθ] [brez], *s.* 1. Aliento (air exhaled or inhaled), respiración, resuello, huelgo. 2. Soplo de aire. 3. Vida. 4. Pausa; sobreseimiento. 5. Instante; un momento. **To have bad breath,** tener mal aliento. **Take a deep breath,** respire hondo. **To be short of breath,** ser corto de resuello, respirar con dificultad **Under one's breath,** en voz baja. **In a breath,** de un tirón, de una vez. **At every breath,** a cada instante. **To gasp for breath,** jadear. **To be out of breath,** estar sin aliento, sofocado. **To run oneself out of breath,** correr hasta perder el aliento. **Foul breath,** mal aliento. **To waste one's breath,** gastar saliva. **With bated breath,** con el corazón en un puño.

breathable ['briːðəbl] [bri-za-bol], *a.* Respirable, que se puede respirar.

breathalyze ['breθəlaɪz] [bre-za-lais] *va.* (GB) Hacerle la prueba del alcohol o de la alcoholemia a.

breathalyzer, breathalyser ['breθəlaɪzəʳ] [bre-za-laisaʳ] *s.* Alcohómetro, alcoholímetro. **Breathalyzer test,** prueba del alcohol o de la alcoholemia.

breathe [briːð] [bríz], *vn.* 1. Alentar, respirar o arrojar el aliento (person, animal). **To breath deeply,** respirar hondo. Dejar pasar el aire (fabric, leather). 2. Vivir. 3. Respirar, descansar. 4. Soplar, arrojar el aliento dentro de alguna cosa. 5. Exhalar, echar el aliento hacia fuera. 6. Secar al aire. *-va.* 1. Inspirar, respirar (air, fumes); exhalar (exhale) **She breathed garlic all over me,** me echó todo su aliento a ajo; dar aire o desahogo. 2. Decir o revelar secretamente alguna cosa. **To breathe after,** anhelar, desear, ansiar. **To breathe a vein,** abrir las venas, sangrar. **To breathe one's last,** dar el último suspiro, morir. **Don't breathe a word of this to anyone,** no le digas ni una palabra de esto a nadie. **Breathe in,** aspirar, respirar (air, fumes). **Breathe out,** espirar. Expeler (smoke); exhalar, expulsar (air).

breather ['briːðəʳ] [brí-zaʳ], *s.* 1. El que respira o vive. 2. Revelador. 3. El que inspira. **To have/take a breather,** tomar un respiro o descanso.

breathful ['briːðfʊl] [bríz-ful], *a.* Lleno de aire, lleno de olor.

breathing ['briːðɪŋ], [brí-zin], *s.* 1. Aspiración. 2. Respiradero, abertura por donde entra o sale el aire. 3. Respiración.

breathing-place ['briːðɪŋpleɪs] [brí-zin-pleis], *s.* Pausa, respiradero, descanso, parada.

breathing space ['briːðɪŋspeɪs] [brí-zin-speis], *s.* Respiro.

breathing spell ['briːðɪŋspel] [brí-zin-spel], *s.* Reposo, lapso para descansar.

breathing-time ['briːðɪŋtaɪm] [brí-zin-taim], *s.* Relajación, reposo; el tiempo de alentar o descansar; descanso, parada; interrupción o cesación del trabajo; intervalo, intermisión, alivio en el dolor.

breathless ['breθlɪs] [brezles], *a.* 1. Falto de aliento, sin aliento; desalentado. **The blow left me breathless,** el golpe me dejó sin aliento. **He arrived breathless,** llegó jadeando. 2. Muerto.

breathlessly ['breθlɪslɪ] [brezles-li] *adv.* Entrecortadamente, jadeando.

breathlessness ['breθlɪsnɪs] [brezles-les-nes], *s.* Desaliento, muerte. Dificultad al respirar.

breathtaking ['breθteɪkɪŋ] [brez-tei-kin], *a.* Fascinador, emocionante, conmovedor. Impresionante, imponente.

breccia ['bretʃia] [bre-chia], *s. (Min.)* Piedras conglutinadas o compuestas, como el mármol colorado.

brechan ['bretʃən] [bre-chan], *s. (Esco.)* V. BRACKEN.

bred [bred] [bred], *pret. y pp.* del verbo TO BREED.

breech [briːtʃ] [brích], *s.* 1. Trasero, nalgas, posaderas. 2. Culata de cañón o fusil ; recámara. *a.* De nalgas (birth).

breech, *va.* 1. Poner los calzones a uno. 2. Azotar. 3. Poner culata a un cañón o fusil.

breeches ['briːtʃɪz] [brí-ches], *s. pl.* Calzones, parte del vestido del hombre, que cubre desde la cintura hasta la rodilla, bombachos (knee breeches). Pantalones de montar (riding breeches). **To wear the breeches,** ponerse los calzones; se dice de la mujer que gobierna a su marido.

breeches-buoy ['briːtʃɪzbʊɔɪ] [bríchis-buoi], *s.* Aparato salvavidas que consiste en unas bragas de lona aseguradas por la cintura a una boya de salvamento, la cual pende de un cable tendido desde la orilla a un buque náufrago.

breeching ['briːtʃɪŋ] [bríchin], *s.* 1. Grupera del arnés. 2. *(Mar.)* Bragueros de cañón.

breech-loader ['briːtʃˌləʊdəʳ] [brich-lou-daʳ], *s.* Arma de retrocarga, que se carga por la recámara.

breech-loading [ˈbriːtʃˌləʊdɪŋ] [brich-lou-din], *a.* Que se carga por la recámara (hablando de armas).

breed [briːd] [brid], *va.* 1. Criar, procrear, engendrar, multiplicar (animals). 2. Ocasionar, causar, producir, engendrar, generar (violence). **Success breeds success,** el éxito llama al éxito. 3. Criar, educar, enseñar (raise, educate). **I'm a Londoner born and bred,** nací y me crié en Londres. -*vn.* Criar. hacer cría o multiplicarla. Reproducirse.

breed, *s.* 1. Casta, raza, progenie (of animals); variedad (of plants). 2. Progenie, generación. **A new breed of athletes,** una nueva generación de atletas. **A dying breed,** una especie en vías de extinción.

breeder [ˈbriːdəʳ] [brí-daʳ], *s.* 1. Lo que cría o produce alguna cosa. 2. La persona que cría y educa a otro. 3. Paridera, la hembra fecunda de cualquier especie. 4. Criador, el que cría caballos, mulas u otros animales. Cultivador (of plants). **Breeder reactor,** reactor reproductor.

breeding [ˈbriːdɪŋ] [brídin], *s.* 1. Crianza, urbanidad. atención, cortesía. 2. Educación, enseñanza, forma dada a la inteligencia y a los modales (upbringing). 3. Reproducción (reproduction); cría (raising of animals); cultivo (of plants). **A woman of breeding,** una mujer de buena cuna. **Politness is a sign of good breeding,** la cortesía es señal de buena educación. **Breeding-cage,** jaula de criar, criadera. **Cross breeding,** cruzamiento de razas. **Good breeding,** buena educación. **Bad breeding,** modales groseros, de mal tono.

breeding ground [ˈbriːdɪŋɡraʊnd] [brídin-graund] *s.* (*Zool.*) Lugar de cría. **A breeding ground for revolutionaries,** un semillero de revolucionarios. **A breeding ground for violence,** un caldo de cultivo para la violencia.

breeze [briːz] [brís] **breeze-fly** *s.* Tábano, especie de moscón. Se escribe también *breese y brize.*

breeze, *s.* 1. Brisa, viento suave (light wind). 2. (*Fam.*) Ligera agitación o alarma; confusión, quimera. (*Coloq.*) **To be a breeze,** ser pan comido, ser un bollo (something easy).

breeze, *s.* Cenizas calientes, rescoldo. Carboncillo, cisco de *coke.* (*Ingl.*)

breeze, *vn.* (*Coloq.*) **To breeze in/out,** entrar/salir tan campante, tan pancho. (*Fam.*) **He breezed into the office,** entró en la oficina como Pedro o Perico por su casa.

breeze through [ˈbriːzθruː] [brís-tru], (*Coloq.*) **They breezed through the exam,** el examen les resultó un paseo.

breezeless [ˈbriːzlɪs] [bríz-les], *a.* Inmoble, sin movimiento o brisa.

breezily [ˈbriːzɪlɪ] [brí-si-li], *adv.* Alegremente, jovialmente (cheerfully).

breezy [ˈbriːzɪ] [brí-si], *a.* Refrescado con brisas. Ventoso (spot - windy). **It was pleasantly breezy,** soplaba una agradable brisa. **It's a bit breezy today,** hace un poco de vientecito hoy. (*Coloq.*) Dinámico (lively - person); alegre y simpático (smile/greeting).

brent [brent] [brent], *a.* Liso, no arrugado; también, alto, prominente.

brethren [ˈbreθrɪn] [brez-ren], *s. pl.* de BROTHER. Hermanos, en estilo grave o hablando de todos los hombres.

Breton [ˈbretən] [bre-ton], *a.* Natural de la Bretaña francesa, o perteneciente a ella; bretón. -*s.* 1. Un bretón. 2. Idioma de los bretones.

breve [briːv] [briv], *s.* (*Mús*) 1. Breve, nota de música: hoy poco usada. 2. V. BRIEF.

brevet [briˈvɪt] [brívit], *va.* En el ejército, la milicia y la marina, conceder un grado superior al empleo efectivo; dar un ascenso honorífico.

brevet, *s.* (*Mil.*) Nombramiento o comisión honoraria, grado honorífico. **Brevet rank,** graduación militar sin el sueldo correspondiente ni empleo efectivo. **Brevet colonel,** coronel graduado.

breviary [ˈbriːvɪərɪ] [brívia-ri], *s.* 1. Compendio, extracto, epítome, resumen. 2. Breviario, el libro que contiene el rezo u oficio divino diario de todo el año.

breviate [ˈbriːvɪeɪt] [brívi-eit], *s.* 1. Compendio corto. 2. *V.* BRIEF.

brevier [briˈvɪəʳ] [brivia ʳ], *s.* Breviario, grado de letra muy menuda, tipo o carácter de letra de ocho puntos. El de nueve puntos se llama en inglés *bourgeois.*

brevirostrate, brevirostral [ˈbrevɪrəstreɪt] [bre-vi-ros-treit], *a.* Que tiene pico corto.

brevity [ˈbrevɪtɪ] [bre-vi-ti], *s.* Brevedad (shortness), concisión (conciseness). **Brevity is the soul of wit,** lo bueno, si breve, dos veces bueno.

brew [bruː] [brú], *va.* 1. Hacer licores mezclando varios ingredientes; fabricar, hacer (beer); preparar, hacer (tea). 2. Urdir o tramar algún designio, maquinar, fraguar (mischief). 3. Menear a fuerza de brazo; batir, preparar; mezclar. **A storm is brewing,** se prepara una tempestad; habrá borrasca. -*vn.* Hacer o fabricar cerveza (make beer); fermentar los licores. **The tea is brewing,** el té se está haciendo. Avecinarse (storm); gestarse (trouble).

brew, *s.* Mezcla; modo de mezclar o de hacer fermentar los licores; brebaje.

brewage [ˈbruːeɪdʒ] [brúeich], Brebaje, bebida en que entran muchos ingredientes.

brewer [ˈbruːəʳ] [brúar], *s.* Cervecero.

brewery [ˈbruːərɪ] [brúeri], **brew-house** [ˈbruːhaʊs] [brújaus], *s.* Cervecería, la casa o fábrica en que se hace la cerveza.

brewing [ˈbruːɪŋ] [brúin], *s.* 1. La cantidad de cerveza que se hace de una vez. 2. (*Mar.*) Apariencia de borrasca; reunión de nubes negruzcas.

brewis [ˈbruːɪs] [brúis], *s.* Rebanada de pan mojada en caldo de vaca salada mientras está hirviendo.

briar [ˈbraɪəʳ] [braiaʳ] *s. V.* BRIER.

bribe [braɪb] [braib], *s.* Cohecho, soborno. **To take/accept a bribe,** dejarse sobornar, aceptar un soborno.

bribe *va.* Cohechar, sobornar, ganar para un fin malo, corromper. **To bribe somebody to,** sobornar a alguien para que.

briber [ˈbraɪbəʳ] [brai-baʳ], *s.* Cohechador, sobornador, corruptor.

bribery [ˈbraɪbərɪ] [brai-be-ri], *s.* Cohecho, soborno.

bric-a-brac [ˈbrɪkəbræk] [brik-a-brak], *s.* Bric-a-brac: objetos de arte, artículos curiosos y de gusto. Baratijas, chucherías.

brick [brɪk] [brik], *s.* 1. (*Const.*) Ladrillo, pedazo de tierra amasado y cocido. 2. Ladrillo de pan; una clase de pan que tiene la figura de un ladrillo. **Sundried brick,** (*Mex.*) adobe. 3. (*Ger.*) Un buen sujeto, un real mozo. **Bath** o **Bristol brick,** piedra hecha de arena muy fina, en forma de ladrillo, para limpiar cuchillos. (GB) **To drop a brick,** meter la pata.

brick, *va.* Enladrillar, solar o cubrir alguna cosa con ladrillos. **To brick a floor,** enladrillar el suelo. **Brick in, brick up,** tabicar, tapiar.

brickbat [ˈbrɪkbæt] [brik-bat], Pedazo de ladrillo.

brick-clay [ˈbrɪkkleɪ] [brik-klei], **brick-earth** [ˈbrɪkɜːθ] [brik-erz], *s.* Tierra para hacer ladrillos.

brickdust [ˈbrɪkdʌst] [brik-dast], *s.* Ladrillo molido.

brick-kiln [ˈbrɪkkɪln] [brik-kiln], *s.* Horno de ladrillo, que se llama también ladrillar o ladrillal.

bricklayer [ˈbrɪkleɪəʳ] [brik-leiaʳ], *s.* Albañil, el que hace paredes u otras fábricas de ladrillo. **Bricklayer's boy,** peón de albañil.

brickmaker [ˈbrɪkmeɪkəʳ] [brik-mei-kaʳ], *s.* Ladrillero, el que hace ladrillos.

brickred [ˈbrɪkred] [brik-red] *a.* Rojo teja, rojo ladrillo.

brickwork [ˈbrɪkwɜːk] [brik-uek], *s.* Enladrillado, obra de ladrillos (bricks). Aparejo (way bricks are laid).

bricky [ˈbrɪkɪ] [briki], *a.* Ladrilloso, lleno de ladrillos.

brickyard [ˈbrɪkjɑːd] [brik-yard], *s.* Ladrillar.

bridal [ˈbraɪdl] [braidal], *a.* Nupcial, perteneciente a las bodas; nupcial (procession); para novias (shop). **Bridal gown,** traje de novia. -*s.* Boda, fiesta nupcial. **Bridal song,** epitalamio.

bride ['braɪd] [braid], *s.* Novia, desposada, la mujer recién casada, o la que va a casarse. **The bride and groom,** los novios; los recién casados, los novios (after ceremony). **Bride-bed,** tálamo, la cama de los desposados. **Bride-cake,** torta o pan de la boda. **Bride-chamber,** cámara nupcial.

bridegroom ['braɪdgrʊm] [braid-grum], *s.* Novio, el recién casado, o el que va a casarse.

bridesmaid ['braɪdzmeɪd] [braids-meid], *sf.* Madrina de boda; dama de honor. Niña que acompaña a la novia (child).

bridesman ['braɪdzmən] [braids-man], *s.* Padrino de boda, el que acompaña al novio en la ceremonia del matrimonio. Son nombres más usuales los de *best man y groomsman*.

bridge [brɪdʒ] [brich], *s.* 1. Puente, fábrica construida sobre los ríos, fosos, etc., para pasarlos. **Drawbridge,** puente levadizo. **Bridge of boats,** puente de barcas. **To build bridges,** tender un puente de unión. **We'll cross that bridge when we come to it,** ese problema lo resolveremos cuando llegue el momento. 2. El caballete de la nariz (of nose); puente (of glasses). 3. Puente de violín, violón, guitarra u otro instrumento de cuerda. 4. Balanza de Wheatstone, artificio para medir la resistencia eléctrica. **Cantilever bridge,** puente de contra peso. **Suspension bridge,** puente colgante. *(Dent.)* Puente. Bridge (card game).

bridge, *va.* Construir o levantar un puente en algún paraje. Tender o construir un puente (river); salvar (differences).

bridgehead ['brɪdʒhed] [brich-jed], *s.* Cabecera de puente, entrada de puente.

bridgeward ['brɪdʒwɑːd] [brich-uard], *s.* 1. Custodio de puente. 2. Guarda principal de una llave.

bridgework ['brɪdʒwɜːk] [brich-uek], *s.* 1. Construcción de puentes. 2. Puente dental.

bridle ['braɪdl] [brai-dol], *s.* 1. Brida o freno. 2. Freno, sujeción. **Bridle-cutter,** el que corta cuero para los silleros y freneros. **Bridle hand,** mano izquierda, la mano del jinete que tiene las riendas. **Bridle-path,** senda angosta, que sólo permite pasar a las caballerías o acémilas una tras otra. Camino de herradura.

bridle, *va.* 1. Guiar un caballo con el freno. 2. Embridar, poner la brida a un caballo. 3. Reprimir, refrenar. *-vn.* Levantar la cabeza. **To bridle it,** remilgarse, erguirse. **To bridle at something,** molestarse por algo.

bridler ['braɪdlər] [braidlar], *s.* El que gobierna, dirige o refrena.

bridles ['braɪdlz] [braidels], *s. pl. (Mar.)* Poas.

brief [briːf] [bríf], *a.* Breve (interlude, reign), conciso (statement, summary), corto, sucinto, sumario; estrecho. **His report was brief and to the point,** su informe era breve e iba al grano. **In brief,** en resumen. Diminuto (scanty).

brief, *s.* 1. Epítome, resumen o compendio. 2. *(Law)* Alegato, memorial ajustado, informe, el apuntamiento en que se contiene todo el hecho de algún pleito o causa; auto jurídico. Expediente entregado por el abogado al BARRISTER. 3. *(Mús.)* Breve, nota que vale dos compases del tiempo que se llama compasillo. 4. Breve, buleto apostólico. 5. Despacho, sumario, informe. Licencia para pedir socorros públicamente por alguna pérdida o desgracia. 6. Instrucciones (instructions); competencia (area of responsibility).

brief, *va.* Instruir (lawyer); darle instrucciones u órdenes a (pilot/spy); informar (committee). **The president had been badly briefed for the meeting,** el presidente no había sido bien preparado para la reunión.

brief case ['briːfkeɪs] [bríf-keis], *s.* Cartera grande, portafolio, maletín.

briefing ['briːfɪŋ] [brífin], *s.* Instrucciones breves. Sesión para dar instrucciones (briefing session). Reunión informativa para la prensa (press briefing).

briefless ['briːflɪs] [bríf-les], *a.* Sin causas o pleitos: sin clientes.

briefly ['briːflɪ] [brífli], *adv.* Brevemente, sucintamente (reply/speak), compendiosamente, en pocas palabras, en resumen (indep). Por poco tiempo (visit/rule). **She biefly**

wondered what he was doing there, se preguntó por un momento qué hacía él allí.

briefness ['briːfnɪs] [bríf-nes], *s.* Brevedad, concisión.

briefs ['briːfz] [brífs] *s. pl.* Calzoncillos, slip (man's); calzones, bragas, bombachas, pantaletas (woman's).

brier ['braɪər] [braiar], *s.* 1. Escaramujo, agavanzo, rosal silvestre (wild rose). 2. Zarza, mata espinosa (thornbush).

briery ['braɪərɪ] [braie-ri], *a.* Zarzoso, lleno de zarzas.

brig, brigantine [brɪg] [brig] ['brɪgətiːn] [bri-gan-tin], *s. (Mar.)* Bergantín. **Brig,** calabozo (prison).

brigade [brɪ'geɪd] [bri-gueid], *s.* Brigada, cierto número de batallones o escuadrones. *(Coloq,)* **The brown rice brigade,** los fanáticos de la cocina macrobiótica.

brigadier [ˌbrɪgə'dɪər] [briga-diar] *s.* General de brigada (in UK). **Brigadier general,** *s.* Brigadier, el oficial que tiene el grado inmediatamente inferior al de mariscal de campo. General de brigada (in US).

brigand ['brɪgənd] [bri-gand], *s.* Ladrón público, salteador de caminos, bandido, bandolero.

brigandine ['brɪgəndaɪn] [bri-gan-dain], *s.* Cota de malla de que usaban antes los ladrones y rufianes y algunas tropas ligeras.

brigantine ['brɪgəntiːn] [bri-gan-tin], *s.* V. BRIG.

bright [braɪt] [brait], *a.* 1. Claro, reluciente, luciente, resplandeciente, lustroso, brillante (star); brillante, fuerte (light); con mucha luz (room). **Draw the curtains, it's too bright,** corre las cortinas, hay demasiada luz. **It was a bright, sunny day,** era un día de sol radiante. Fuerte, vivo, brillante (color). **A bright red shirt,** una camisa de un rojo fuerte, vivo o brillante. 2. Claro, evidente. 3. Esclarecido, ilustre. 4. Ingenioso, agudo, perspicaz, vivo; lleno de vida, vivaracho (cheerful/eyes). **To make bright,** pulimentar, poner brillante, reluciente. *(Coloq,)* **To get up bright and early,** levantarse tempranito. Prometedor (hopeful/future). **The prospects are not very bright,** las perspectivas no son muy prometedoras. **To look on the brighter side of something,** mirar o ver el lado bueno de algo. Inteligente (intelligent/person). **Whose bright idea was it to…?,** ¿quién tuvo la brillante idea de…?

brighten ['braɪtn] [brai-ten], *va.* 1. Pulir, bruñir, dar lustre. 2. Avivar, dar viveza. 3. Ilustrar, ennoblecer. 4. Aguzar el ingenio. 5. Iluminar (make brighter). **Brighten up,** alegrar (room); animar (occasion/party). *-vn.* Aclarar, ponerse claro lo que estaba obscuro, realzar. Hacerse más brillante o más fuerte (become brighter). **Her eyes brightened,** se le iluminaron los ojos. Animarse, alegrarse (person/become cheerful); mejorar (situation/prospects). **It brightened up in the afternoon,** por la tarde salió el sol.

bright-eyed ['braɪtaɪd] [brait-aid], *a.* Ojialegre. De ojos vivos o vivarachos. **Bright-eyed and bushy tailed,** lleno de vida y energía.

bright-haired ['braɪtheəd] [brait-jead], *a.* Que tiene los cabellos relucientes.

bright-harnessed [braɪt'hɑːnest] [brait-jar-nest], *a.* El de armadura brillante.

brightly ['braɪtlɪ] [braitli], *adv.* Espléndidamente, con esplendor y lustre. Intensamente, vivamente (shine). **A brightly polished table,** una mesa resplandeciente. Alegremente (say/smile).

brightness ['braɪtnɪs] [braitnis], *s.* 1. Lustre, esplendor, brillo, brillantes. 2. Agudeza o viveza de ingenio. 3. Resplandor, brillo (of light, star), claridad, luminosidad (of morning). Alegría (cheerfulness); inteligencia (intelligence).

brights ['braɪts] [braits], *s. pl. (Auto)* Luces de carretera.

bright's disease ['braɪtzdɪsiːs] [braits-di-sis], *s.* Mal de Bright, nefritis crónica.

bright spark ['braɪtspɑːk] [brait-spark] *s.* (GB) Lumbrera, genio (iro.).

brill [brɪl] [bril], *s.* Mero, pez semejante al rodaballo, muy estimado como alimento. V. BRET.

brilliance ['brɪljəns] [bri-lians], **brilliancy** ['brɪljənsɪ] [briliansi], *s.* Brillantez, brillo, el resplandor o luz que da de sí alguna cosa (brightness); esplendor, lustre. Brillantez (skill, intelligence).

brilliant ['brɪljənt] [bri-liant], *a.* Brillante, lo que brilla (light); radiante (sunshine); brillante, luminoso (red/green). (GB) *(Coloq.)* Genial, fenomenal (person/party). **¡Brilliant!,** ¡genial! *-s.* 1. Brillante, el diamante abrillantado. 2. El tipo de menor tamaño que se funde y se emplea en la impresión: 31/2 puntos. 3. Tela de algodón, con dibujo alzado y tejido.

brilliantine ['brɪljənti:n] [bri-lian-tin], *s.* Brillantina, para tela vestidos parecida a la alpaca, pero de calidad superior.

brilliantly ['brɪljəntlɪ] [bri-liantli], *adv.* Espléndidamente. Intensamente (shine); con brillantez (write); extraordinariamente (funny). *(Coloq,)* **He played brilliantly,** jugó genial o fenomenal.

brilliantness ['brɪljəntnɪs] [bri-liant-nes], *s.* Brillantez.

brills ['brɪls] [brils], *s. pl. (Des.)* Las pestañas del caballo.

brim [brɪm] [brim], *s.* Borde, extremo u orilla de alguna cosa (of vessel); labio de un vaso; ala de sombrero.

brim, *va.* Llenar hasta el borde. *-vn.* Estar de bote en bote; estar llena alguna vasija hasta no caber más. **Her eyes were brimming with tears,** tenía los ojos llenos de lágrimas. **To be brimming with happiness,** estar rebosante o desbordante de felicidad. **Brim over,** desbordarse, rebosar (cup). **He was brimming over with enthusiasm,** estaba rebosante o desbordante de entusiasmo.

brimmer ['brɪmər] [bri-mar], *s.* Copa o vaso lleno.

brimful ['brɪm'fʊl] [brim-ful], *a.* Lleno hasta el borde, lleno de bote en bote. **To be brimful of something,** estar repleto de algo (of ideas); estar rebosante o desbordante de algo (of energy).

brimfulness ['brɪm'fʊlnɪs] [brim-ful-nes], *s.* El estado de estar lleno hasta el borde.

brimming ['brɪmɪŋ] [bri-min], *a.* Sin labio o borde.

brimming, *a.* Lleno hasta el borde.

brimstone ['brɪmstəʊn] [brim-stoun], *s.* Azufre se dice del azufre vivo o amoldado en canelones. *V.* FIRE.

brindle ['brɪndl] [brin-dol], *s.* Variedad de colores como la que tiene el tigre.

brindled ['brɪndld] [brin-dold], *a.* Abigarrado. *V.* BRINDED.

brine [braɪn] [brain], *s.* 1. Salmuera (saltwater); agua salada o de mar (seawater). 2. *(Poét)* El mar (the sea). **The brine,** el piélago. 3. Lágrimas.

brine, *va. (Agr.)* Embeber en salmuera el trigo antes de sembrarlo, para impedir el tizón.

brinepit ['braɪnpɪt] [brain-pit], *s.* Pozo de salina o de agua salada.

bring [brɪŋ] [brin], *va. (pret. y pp.* BROUGHT). 1. Llevar o traer. **Bring this to the kitchen,** lleva esto a la cocina. 2. Traer (convey, carry), hacer venir. **She's bringing Lucy with her,** va a venir con Lucy, o va a traer a Lucy. **Bring your passport with you,** traiga el pasaporte. **Bring her,** hazla pasar o entrar. 3. Atraer, traer hacia sí alguna cosa; acarrear; recoger. Atraer (attract, cause to come). **What brings you here?,** ¿qué te trae por aquí? Traer (result in, produce). **It will bring enormous benefits,** va a traer o reportar enormes beneficios. **You've brought so much happiness to those children,** les has dado tanta alegría a esos niños. **To bring a smile to somebody's face,** hacer sonreír a alguien. **It brought tears to my eyes,** hizo que se me llenaran los ojos de lágrimas. 4. Poner en un estado determinado. 5. Inducir, persuadir (persuade). **I couldn't bring myself to do it,** no pude hacerlo. **To bring pressure to bear on somebody,** ejercer presión sobre alguien. **He brought his experience to bear on the problem,** hizo uso de toda su experiencia para resolver el problema.

bring about, efectuar, poner por obra, salir con el intento. Dar lugar, ocasionar (cause/downfall, crisis). **To try to bring about change in society,** tratar de lograr que se produzcan cambios en la sociedad.

bring again, volver, conducir o traer de nuevo.

bring along, traer.

bring around, traer (take along). Convencer (persuade). **We finally brought her around to our point of view,** finalmente conseguimos convencerla. **I brought the conversation around to James,** llevé la conversación al tema de James (steer). Hacer volver en sí (restore consciousness).

bring away, llevarse, quitar, sacar una cosa de donde estaba; hacer salir; alzar.

bring back, (return). **I'll bring your book back tomorrow,** te devolveré o te regresaré el libro mañana. **Crying won't bring him back,** con llorar no vas a conseguir que vuelva. **To bring back to life again,** volver a la vida, hacer revivir. **To bring back,** traer de vuelta, devolver. Traer (gift/souvenir); volver a introducir (reintroduce/custom); recordar (recall). **It brought back memories,** me trajo recuerdos.

bring by the lee, *(Mar.)* tomar por la luna sobre la arribada.

bring down, abatir, deprimir, humillar; disminuir; reducir, hacer bajar (lower/price); hacer bajar (temperature); llevar una cosa baja; bajar; tirar o echar abajo; (cause to fall/tree, wall); derribar (player, opponent, plane); derrocar, hacer caer (government). **To bring down the house,** derribar la casa.

bring forth, producir (fruit), dar de sí, parir; dar a luz (child); poner de manifiesto.

bring forward, empujar, dar empuje. *(Com.)* Llevar una suma a otra cuenta. **Brought forward,** suma y sigue, referencia, partida referente. Hacer comparecer (witness); presentar (evidence, idea); adelantar (to earlier time/appointment).

bring home, her letter brought home to me the seriousness of the situation, su carta me hizo dar cuenta cabal de la gravedad de la situación.

bring in, reclamar; dejar utilidad o ganancia (earn). **His job doesn't bring in much money,** no saca mucho dinero con su trabajo; reducir; introducir, implantar (introduce) (regulation/system); presentar (bill); meter. *(Law)* **To bring in a verdict of guilty,** declarar culpable a alguien. Atraer (attract/customers). **They had to bring the police in,** tuvieron que hacer intervenir a la policía (involve). **We have to bring in extra staff in the summer,** tenemos que contratar personal extra en verano. Servir (una comida). **To bring dinner in,** servir la cena. Introducir (una moda).

bring into, comprometer.

bring low, abatir, humillar; debilitar. **To bring word,** informar, dar noticia.

bring off, desempeñar o desempeñarse; rescatar; desembarazar ; disuadir, desviar, apartar. Conseguir, lograr (feat, victory); llevar a cabo (plan); conseguir (deal).

bring on, transportar; agigantar empeñar, inducir; empeñarse, obligarse. Provocar (cause/attack/breakdown). **What brought this on?,** ¿esto a qué se debe? Hacer salir (introduce/player). **He brought it all on himself,** él (mismo) se lo buscó (cause to befall).

bring out, salir; recitar; mostrar, echar fuera, descubrir; hacer salir, sacar, extraer. Sacar al mercado (product, model); publicar, sacar (edition, book). **Children bring out the best in her,** el trato con los niños hace resaltar o pone de manifiesto sus mejores cualidades (accentuate). Hacer florecer (make bloom). (GB) **It brought me out in spots,** hizo que me salieran granos. **I tried to bring her out a bit,** traté de ayudarla a vencer su timidez (make less shy).

bring over, ganar, atraer a alguno a su partido; transportar, hacer atravesar.

bring round, *V.* BRING AROUND.

bring to, someter; resolver; llevar a. Ponerse a la capa. **To bring to bed,** parir.

bring together, *(Fig.)* reunir, reconciliar. **The conference will bring together scientists from all over the world,** el congreso reunirá o congregará a científicos de todo el mundo. **A tragedy like this can bring a family together,** una tragedia así puede unir a una familia. **They were brought together by chance,** el destino quiso que se conocieran (o se encontraran, etc.).

bring under, sojuzgar, sujetar, avasallar, someter a su mando. **To bring an action,** poner una demanda.

bring up, hacer subir, hacer avanzar o adelantarse; poner a la moda; llevar en alto; educar, enseñar, criar (rear a child). **I was brought up in India,** me crié en la India. **You were badly brought up,** te criaron muy mal. **They brought us up to respect authority,** desde niños nos enseñaron a respetar la autoridad. Sacar (mention/subject). **Did you have to bring that up?,** ¿por qué tuviste que sacar ese tema? **I wanted to bring out the matter of...,** quería mencionar el asunto de... Vomitar, devolver (vomit).

bring upon, atraer; exponer. **To bring upon oneself,** buscarse (cause to befall), causarse, atraerse, procurarse.

bringer ['brɪŋəʳ] [brin-gaʳ], s. Portador, la persona que lleva o trae alguna cosa. **Bringer in,** el que introduce alguna cosa. **Bringer up,** instructor. (Mil.) El soldado postrero de cada fila. **Bringing forth,** producción.

brinish ['braɪnɪʃ] [brai-nish], a. Salado, lo que tiene sabor de sal.

brink [brɪŋk] [brink], s. Orilla, margen, borde. **The country stood on the brink of war,** el país estaba al borde de la guerra. **To be on the brink of,** estar a punto de. Extremidad, extremo. **Brink of a well,** pozal o brocal de pozo.

brinkmanship ['brɪŋkmənʃɪp] [brink-man-ship] s. Política arriesgada o suicida.

briny ['braɪnɪ] [brai-ni], a. Salado, del sabor del agua del mar. Salobre. **The briny deep,** mar, el océano.

briquette [brɪ'ket] [bri-ket], s. Briqueta, conglomerado de carbón en forma de ladrillo.

brisk [brɪsk] [brisk], s. 1. Vivo, alegre, despejado, jovial, festivo, juguetón. 2. Vigoroso, fuerte. 3. Enamorado, alegre de cucos, alegrillo, alumbrado por haber bebido un poco más de lo regular. 4. Rápido y enérgico, brioso (pace/lively, quick); a paso ligero (walk). **Ice-cream sellers did a brisk trade,** los vendedores de helado vendieron muchísimo. 5. Enérgico, dinámico y eficiente (efficient, person/manner). Fresco (wind, morning). **A brisk gale of wind,** viento fresco.

brisk up, vn. Avanzar con viveza presentarse con garbo y aire; regocijarse, alegrarse. -va. Vivificar, avivar.

brisket ['brɪskɪt] [bris-ket], s. El pecho de un animal o un pedazo cortado de él (corte de carne del cuarto delantero).

briskly ['brɪsklɪ] [briskli], adv. Vigorosamente; alegremente. Con brío (walk); con tono de eficiencia (say). **It's selling briskly,** se está vendiendo muy bien.

briskness ['brɪsknɪs] [brisk-nes], s. 1. Viveza, actividad, vigor, vivacidad. 2. Viveza, garbo, gallardía. 3. Alegría, humorada. 4. Desenvoltura, desahogo.

bristle [brɪsl] [brisel], s. 1. Cerda, seta, el pelo duro y recio que crían los cerdos. 2. Pelusa, especie de vello de ciertas plantas. **His face was covered in bristle(s),** tenía la barba crecida.

bristle, va. Erizar, levantar o poner derechas las cerdas o púas el animal que las tiene. -vn. Erizarse, ponerse derechas las cerdas o púas de un animal, como las del cerdo y del erizo. Erizarse, ponerse de punta (stand up/hair). **She bristled at his rudeness,** su grosería la irritó. **The place was bristling with tourists,** el lugar estaba repleto o plagado de turistas (have many). **To bristle with difficulties,** estar erizado de dificultades. **To bristle a thread,** poner seta al hilo del zapatero.

bristly ['brɪslɪ] [brisli], a. Cerdoso, lleno de cerdas. Hirsuto (beard). **Don't kiss me, you're too bristly,** no me beses, que tu barba está muy rasposa.

Bristol-board ['brɪstəl'bɔːd] [bristol-bord], s. Cartulina; calidad fina de cartón satinado. (De Bristol, ciudad inglesa)

Bristol-stone ['brɪstəl'stəʊn] [bristol-stoun], s. Diamante de Bristol.

brit [brɪt] [brit], s. 1. El alimento de las ballenas; consta de entomostráceos y otros animalillos que nadan en la superficie. 2. Arenque pequeño. (Coloq,) Británico.

Britain ['brɪtən] [briten] N. Gran Bretaña.

Britannia [brɪ'tænɪə] [bri-ta-nia], (Metal.) s. Metal inglés, liga de estaño, antimonio, bismuto y cobre.

Britannic [brɪ'tænɪk] [bri-ta-nik], a. Británico, de la Gran Bretaña.

britches ['brɪtʃəz] [bri-ches] s. pl. V. BREECHES.

brite [braɪt] [brait], va. (Prov. Ingl.) Modorrarse, madurarse demasiado; desgranarse las mieses.

British ['brɪtɪʃ] [british], a. Británico, lo que pertenece a Gran Bretaña. **The British language,** la lengua de los antiguos celtas de la Gran Bretaña. **British Lion,** el león británico, emblema de la Gran Bretaña. **British Thermal Unit,** unidad termal británica.

Britisher ['brɪtɪʃəʳ] [britishaʳ], s. (Fest.) Inglés; particularmente un soldado o marinero inglés. Británico.

British Isles ['brɪtɪʃ'aɪlz] [british-ails], s. pl. Las Islas Británicas. **British Isles Summer Time,** hora de verano en Gran Bretaña, adelantada una hora con respecto a la hora de Greenwich.

Briton ['brɪtən] [bri-ton], a. y s. El natural de la Gran Bretaña, o lo que pertenece a este país. Ciudadano británico. **The ancient Britons,** los antiguos britanos.

Brittany ['brɪtənɪ] [bri-ta-ni], N. Bretaña.

brittle ['brɪtl] [bri-tol], a. Quebradizo, que con facilidad se quiebra (twigs, bones); frágil, precario (peace); crispado (laugh, voice).

brittleness ['brɪtlnɪs] [britel-nes], s. Fragilidad.

broach [brəʊtʃ] [brouch], s. 1. Asador. 2. Lezna, punzón. 3. Terraja, herramienta de gancho; broche. 5. (Carp.) Brocha, mecha. 6. (Arq.) Aguja, chapitel.

broach, va. 1. Mencionar por primera vez; introducir; hacer público. 2. Espetar, atravesar alguna cosa con otra que sea puntiaguda, como se atraviesa la carne con el asador. 3. Barrenar el tonel u otra vasija que tenga vino o cualquier licor, para sacarlo; barrenar, decentar. 4. Empezar a gastar alguna cosa que se tenía guardada o intacta. 5. Proferir; decir alguna cosa de la que es uno autor; inventar o propagar mentiras; sembrar una especie. 6. **To broach to,** (Mar.) tomar por la luna, por avante.

broacher ['brəʊtʃəʳ] [brou-chaʳ], s. 1. Asador. 2. Autor o inventor de alguna cosa.

broad [brɔːd] [broud], a. 1. Ancho (avenue); lo contrapuesto a lo angosto; extenso, amplio; grande (valley); despejado, amplio (forehead). De oreja a oreja (grin). **She has broad hips,** es ancha de caderas. Amplio (extensive/syllabus); numeroso, variado (interests). **In its broadest sense,** en su sentido más amplio. General (general/guidelines, conclusions). **A broad hint,** una indirecta muy clara, o muy directa. Cerrado (accent). 2. Claro, abierto. 3. Comprensivo; liberal, tolerante, de amplias miras e ideas. 4. Grosero, poco delicado, inmodesto, impuro. 5. Descomedido, atrevido; rudo de hablar, que habla un dialecto. (Fam.) Tipa, vieja (woman). **Broad as long,** igual en todo. **To grow broad,** ensancharse. **To speak broad,** hablar groseramente. **In broad day,** en pleno día: a la luz del día. **Broad Scotch,** el dialecto escocés fuertemente marcado. **Broad-blown,** enteramente formado. **Broad-breasted,** ancho de pechos. **Broad-brimmed,** que tiene el borde ancho; de alas anchas, hablando de sombreros. **Broad-eyed,** el que tiene vista muy larga. **Broad-faced, broad-fronted,** cariancho. **Broad-horned,** que tiene cuernos grandes o anchos. **Broad-leaved,** (Bot.) que tiene las hojas anchas. **Broad-shouldered,** espalducho, la persona que tiene grandes espaldas, rechoncho. **Broad-tailed,** cosa o animal de cola ancha.

broad-axe [brɔːd'æks] [broud-aks], s. Hacha ancha de carpintero; doladera (de tonelería).

broad bean [brɔːd'biːn] [broud-bin] s. Haba.

broad-brim ['brɔːdbrɪm] [broud-brim], s. 1. Sombrero de ala ancha. 2. (Fam.) Cuákero.

broadcast ['brɔːdkɑːst] [broud-kast], s. 1. Radiodifusión. Programa, emisión. 2. (Agr.) Siembra al vuelo. -va. 1. Radiodifundir. Transmitir, emitir (program). **The fight was broadcast live,** la pelea se transmitió o se retransmitió en directo. Difundir, divulgar (make known). 2. (Agr.) Sembrar al vuelo. 3. Esparcir a lo lejos, diseminar a gran distancia. vn. Transmitir, emitir.

broadcaster [ˈbrɔːdkɑːstəʳ] [broud-kas-taʳ], s. Radiodifusor. Presentador, locutor de radio o televisión.

broadcasting [ˈbrɔːdkɑːstɪŋ] [broud-kastin], s. Radiodifusión; televisión (TV).

broadcloth [ˈbrɔːdklɒθ] [broud-kloz], s. Paño fino de más de 29 pulgadas de ancho.

broaden [ˈbrɔːdn] [brouden], vn. Ensancharse, ponerse más ancha alguna cosa. Ampliarse (scope, interests); ensancharse (river). va. Ampliar (scope, horizons, interests). **Travel broadens the mind,** los viajes amplían los horizontes.

broad gauge [ˈbrɔːdˈɡeɪdʒ] [broud-gueich], a. 1. (F.C.) Vía ancha, de más de 564 pulgadas inglesas. 2. V. BROADMINDED.

broadish [ˈbrɔːdɪʃ] [broudish], a. Algo ancho.

broad jump [ˈbrɔːdˈdʒʌmp] [broud-jamp], s. Salto de longitud.

broadloom [ˈbrɔːdluːm] [broud-lúm], a. Tejido en telar ancho. **Broadloom rug,** alfombra de un solo color.

broadly [ˈbrɔːdlɪ] [broud-li], adv. Anchamente. **The two systems are broadly similar,** en líneas generales, los dos sistemas son similares (generally, approximately). **Generally speaking,** en líneas generales, hablando en términos generales. De oreja a oreja (grin).

broad-minded [ˈbrɔːdˈmaɪndɪd] [broud-maindid], a. Tolerante, de ideas liberales. De criterio amplio.

broadmindedness [ˈbrɔːdˈmaɪndɪdnɪs] [broud-maindidnes], s. Tolerancia, amplitud de miras.

broadness [ˈbrɔːdnɪs] [broud-nes], s. 1. Ancho o anchura. 2. Grosería, falta de urbanidad.

broadsheet [ˈbrɔːdʃiːt] [broud-shit] s. Periódico de formato grande.

broadshouldered [ˈbrɔːdˈʃəʊldəd] [broud-shoulded] a. Ancho de espaldas.

broadside [ˈbrɔːdsaɪd] [broud-said], s. (Mar.) 1. Costado de un buque. 2. Andanada (volley), la descarga de todos los cañones del costado de un navío hecha de una vez. 3. (Imp.) Cada lado de un pliego de papel. 4. Ataque, invectiva (verbal or written attack).

broadside, broadside on, adv. De lado, de costado.

broadsword [ˈbrɔːdsbɔːd] [broud-suord], s. Espada ancha, espadón.

broadwise [ˈbrɔːdwaɪz] [broud-uais], adv. A lo ancho, o por lo ancho.

brocade [brəʊˈkeɪd] [brokeid], s. Brocado, tela de seda tejida con oro o plata.

brocade, va. Tejer o hacer labor con dibujo de relieve; decorar; adornar como un brocado.

brocaded [brəʊˈkeɪdɪd] [bro-kei-ded], a. Vestido de brocado; tejido como brocado.

brocage o **brokage** [brəʊˈkeɪdʒ] [brokeidch], s. V. BROKERAGE.

brocatel [brəʊˈkətəl] [bro-ka-tel], s. Brocatel, tejido basto adamascado de seda y lana, cáñamo o algodón, que se emplea en muebles y colgaduras.

broccoli [ˈbrɒkəlɪ] [bro-ko-li], s. Bróculi, brécol, especie de bretón.

brochure [ˈbrəʊsjʊəʳ] [brou-shiuaʳ], s. Librito de pocas hojas; folleto.

brock [brɒk] [brok], s. 1. Tejón, animal, cuadrúpedo. 2. Hombre sucio.

brocket [ˈbrɒkɪt] [broket], s. Gamo de dos años.

brodekin [ˈbrɒdəkɪn] [bro-de-kin], s. Borceguí.

brogan [ˈbrɒɡæn] [bro-gan], s. Zapato pesado y basto.

broggle [ˈbrɒɡl] [bro-guel], vn. Enturbiar el agua para pescar anguilas.

brogue [brəʊɡ] [broug], s. 1. Especie de calzado. V. BROGAN. 2. Idioma corrompido, jerigonza, jerga, particularmente de los irlandeses.

brogue-maker [brəʊɡˈmeɪkəʳ] [broug-mei-kaʳ], a. Zapatero.

broidery [ˈbrɔɪdərɪ] [broi-de-ri], s. Bordadura, bordado. V. EMBROIDERY.

broil [brɔɪl] [broil], s. 1. Tumulto, quimera, camorra, riña, disensión. 2. Alboroto, debate; sedición; división.

broil, va. Asar carne sobre las ascuas o en parrilla; soasar. vn. Asarse, padecer calor.

broiler [ˈbrɔɪləʳ] [broilaʳ], s. 1. Quimerista. 2. Parrilla, grill. 3. Pollo a propósito para asar.

broiling [ˈbrɔɪlɪŋ] [broi-lin], a. Extremadamente cálido; tórrido.

broke [brəʊk] [brouk], pret. de TO BREAK. -a. (vul.) En quiebra, sin dinero. **To be broke** (Mex.) estar bruja. **To be flat/stony/stone broke,** estar pelado, planchado o sin un duro.

broken [ˈbrəʊkən] [brouken], pp. Quebrado, roto (bone); interrumpido. Roto (window, vase, chair). **Broken glass,** vidrios o cristales rotos. Roto (not working). **Broken English,** inglés mal pronunciado, chapurrado. **Broken meat,** fragmentos de viandas, carne cortada. **A broken week,** una semana que tiene días de fiesta. **A broken voice,** una voz interrumpida. **Broken-bellied,** a. Quebrado, entrecortado (emotionally/voice). **He's a broken man,** está destrozado. Quebrado, el que padece hernias (poco usado). **Broken-backed,** (Mar.) quebrantado. Deshecho (home, marriage). Roto (not fulfilled/promise, contract); defraudado (trust). Accidentado (ground/irregular, rough).

broken-down, a. arruinado, quebrantado, descompuesto, deshecho. Averiado, en pana, varado (car, machine). Destartalado (shed, gate).

broken-handed, a. manco.

broken-hearted, a. aburrido de pesadumbre; contrito de corazón, traspasado de dolor. Destrozado, deshecho. **She died of a broken heart,** murió de pena.

broken language, lenguaje chapurrado o tosco. **broken line,** una línea discontinua.

broken sleep, sueño interrumpido. **She'd only had a few hours' broken sleep,** había dormido poco y mal, despertándose cada dos por tres (interrupted).

broken spirit, espíritu decaído, amilanado. **Broken winded,** corto de aliento.

brokenly [ˈbrəʊkənlɪ] [brou-ken-li], adv. Interrumpidamente, a ratos y no de seguido.

brokenness [ˈbrəʊkənnɪs] [brouken-nes], s. Desigualdad.

broker [ˈbrəʊkəʳ] [broukaʳ], s. 1. Corredor, el que por oficio interviene en ajustes, compras y ventas de todo género de cosas. Agente (agent). **Insurance broker,** agente de seguros. Corredor de bolsa (stock broker). 2. Chamarilero, almonedero, ropavejero, el que vive de comprar y vender cuadros y trastos viejos, o ropa usada. 3. Alcahuete. 4. Trujamán.

broker, va. Hacer corretaje de (bonds, commodities).

brokerage [ˈbrəʊkərɪdʒ] [brou-ke-reich], s. 1. Corretaje, el pago que se da al corredor por su diligencia y trabajo en los ajustes y ventas. 2. Corretaje, el estipendio que se da a los alcahuetes, espías y a otras personas empleadas para algún fin depravado o ilícito. 3. Ropavejería. 4. Comercio de mercancías viejas.

brokery [ˈbrəʊkərɪ] [brou-ke-ri], s. Corredoría, trujamanía.

brolly [ˈbrɒlɪ] [bro-li] s. (Coloq.) (GB) Paraguas.

bromate [ˈbrɒmeɪt] [bro-meit], va. Combinar con el bromo. -s. Sal formada con el ácido brómico.

bromide [ˈbrɒmaɪd] [bro-maid], s. Bromuro.

bromine [ˈbrɒmiːn] [bro-min], s. Bromo, elemento químico, que se relaciona con el cloro y el iodo. Es un líquido de olor sofocante.

bromoform [ˈbrɒməfɔːm] [bro-mo-form], s. Bromoformo: análogo al cloroformo.

bronchi [ˈbrɒŋkɪ] [bron-ki], pl. de BRONCHUS.

bronchial [ˈbrɒŋkɪəl] [bron-kial], **bronchic** [ˈbrɒŋkɪk] [bron-kik], a. Bronquial, que pertenece a los bronquios. **Bronchial tubes,** bronquios.

bronchitis [ˈbrɒŋkaɪtɪs] [bron-kai-tis], s. Bronquitis, inflamación de la membrana mucosa que reviste los bronquios.

bronchopneumonia [ˌbrɒŋkənjuːˈməʊnɪə] [bron-ko-niu-mo-nia], *s. (Med.)* Bronconeumonía.

bronchotomy [ˈbrɒŋkətəmɪ] [bron-ko-to-mi], *s. (Cir.)* Broncotomía. El acto de cortar la tráquea, o traquearteria.

bronchus [ˈbrɒŋkəs] [bron-kos], *pl.* BRONCHI, *s.* Bronquio, ramal de la tráquea y sus subdivisiones. Las más pequeñas se llaman *bronchioles*.

bronco [ˈbrɒŋkəʊ] [bron-kou] *s.* Potro salvaje.

bronze [brɒnzd] [bronz], *s.* 1. *(Metal.)* Bronce, liga de cobre y estaño, de color moreno rojizo; a veces contiene otros metales en pequeña proporción. 2. Figura o estatua en bronce. 3. Color preparado para imitar al bronce. **The Bronze Age,** la Edad de Bronce. **Bronze medal,** medalla de bronce.

bronze, *va.* 1. Broncear, poner moreno, tostar por el sol. 2. Broncear, pavonar.

bronzed [brɒnzd] [bronzd] *a.* Bronceado.

broo [bruː] [brú], *s.* 1. *(Esco.)* La frente; opinión favorable. 2. Zumo; líquido, caldo.

brooch [brəʊtʃ] [brouch], 1. Broche o piocha de diamantes. 2. Aguada, diseño o dibujo hecho de un color.

brooch, *va.* Adornar con joyas o diamantes.

brood, *s.* 1. *(bruːd)* [brúd], *vn.* 1. Empollar, ponerse las aves sobre los huevos. 2. Cobijar, tapar los pollos con las alas, como las gallinas. 3. Considerar, pensar o rumiar alguna cosa con cuidado. **She sat brooding on the unfairness of life,** rumiaba lo injusta que era la vida. **Stop brooding on/ over it,** deja de darle vueltas al asunto. 4. Madurar alguna cosa con cuidado. *-va.* Criar con cuidado.

brood, *s.* 1. Progenie, generación, raza, casta, ralea; hablando de personas se toma en mala parte. Prole (of children). 2. Nidada (of birds), el conjunto de huevos puestos en el nido. Camada (of mammals). 3. Cría, los pajarillos o pollos criados a un tiempo o de una vez. 4. Producción, cualquier cosa producida.

brooder [ˈbruːdəʳ], [brú-daʳ], *s.* 1. Incubadora. 2. Gallina clueca.

broody [ˈbruːdɪ] [brúdi], *a.* Clueca o llueca. **Broody hen,** gallina clueca. *(Coloq.)* (GB) **It makes me feel broody,** me despierta el instinto maternal. Meditabundo (moody).

brook [brʊk] [bruk], *s.* Arroyo.

brook, *va.* Sufrir, aguantar, tolerar, admitir, llevar con paciencia.

brooklet [ˈbrʊklɪt] [bruk-let], *s.* Arroyuelo.

brooklime [ˈbrʊklaɪm] [bruk-laim], *s. (Bot.)* Becabunga o becabunca, especie de planta medicinal.

brookmint [ˈbrʊkmɪnt] [bruk-mint], *s. (Bot.)* Menta de agua.

brooky [ˈbrʊkɪ] [bru-ki], *a.* Lo que tiene muchos arroyos.

broom [brʊm] [brum], *s.* 1. *(Bot.)* Hiniesta, retama. 2. Escoba de hiniesta o retama (brush). **A new broom sweeps clean,** escoba nueva barre bien. **Broom cupboard/closet,** armario de los artículos de limpieza.

broom, *va. (Mar.)* V. CAREEN.

broom corn [ˈbrʊmˌkɔːn] [brum-korn], *s.* Millo de escoba. Variedad de sorgo semejante al maíz, de que se usa para hacer escobas.

broom-land [ˈbrʊmlænd] [brum-land], *s.* Retamal, el lugar o sitio en que se cría la retama.

broomstaff [ˈbrʊmstɑːf] [brum-staf], **broomstick** [ˈbrʊmstɪk] [brum-stik], *s.* Palo de escoba.

broomy [ˈbrʊmɪ] [bru-mi]*a.* Retamoso, lleno de retamas.

broth [ˈbrɒθ] [broz], *s.* Caldo, el agua en que se ha cocido carne.

brothel, brothel-house [ˈbrɒðl] [brozl], *s.* Burdel, la casa pública de mujeres mundanas; mancebía.

brother [ˈbrʌðəʳ] [bro-daʳ], *sm.* 1. Hermano, el que ha sido engendrado del mismo padre y madre que otro (relative). **Do you have any brothers and sisters?,** ¿tienes hermanos? **Brother-in-law,** cuñado. **Foster brother,** hermano de leche. 2. Hermano, el que está íntimamente unido con otro. 3. El que tiene la misma profesión que otro. Compañero (comrade). **Brother lawyer,** *(Fam.)* compañero, colega.

Half-brother, hermanastro, medio hermano o hermano solamente por parte de padre o de madre. *(Coloq,)* Hermano, tío, mano (as form of address).

brother *interj.* **(oh) brother!,** ¡Dios mío!

brotherhood [ˈbrʌðəhʊd] [brader-jud], 1. Hermandad. 2. Fraternidad, el parentesco que hay entre los hermanos. 3. Hermandad, cofradía, reunión de hombres con un mismo objeto y bajo las mismas reglas (association). 4. Confraternidad (fellowship). *(Rel.)* Cofradía.

brother-in-law [ˈbrʌðərɪnlɔː] [bro-daʳ-in-loa] *s.* Cuñado.

brotherless [ˈbrʌðəlɪs] [bro-der-les], *a.* Se dice de la persona que no tiene ningún hermano.

brotherlike [ˈbrʌðəlaɪk] [bro-dar-laik], *a.* Fraternal.

brotherly [ˈbrʌðəlɪ] [bro-der-li], *a.* Fraternal, lo que es propio de hermanos. *-adv.* Fraternalmente.

brougham [ˈbrɔːɡəm] [bro-gam], *s.* Coche cerrado de cuatro ruedas, para dos o cuatro personas.

brought [brɔːt] [brot], *pret.* y *pp.* del verbo TO BRING. **Brought forward,** pasa al frente, o suma del frente; suma y sigue. **Brought over,** suma de la vuelta.

brow [braʊ] [brau], *s.* 1. Ceja, una porción de pelo corto en figura de arco que guarnece la extremidad superior del cóncavo del ojo. 2. Frente o rostro. 3. Cara o semblante. Frente (forehead). 4. Ceja, cima (of hill), la parte superior o la cumbre del monte o sierra. 5. Atrevimiento. 6. *(Met.)* Brow, sien, usado siempre en plural. **His brow was encircled with laurel,** sus sienes estaban coronadas de laurel. **To knit the brows,** fruncir las cejas, arrugar el entrecejo.

brow, *va.* Estar al borde o al canto de.

browbeat [ˈbraʊbiːt] [brau-bit], *va.* 1. Imponer, intimidar. **They tried to browbeat me into joining them,** intentaron intimidarme para que me uniera a ellos. 2. Mirar con ceño; mirar con fiereza.

browbeating [ˈbraʊbiːtɪŋ] [brau-bi-tin], *s.* Acto de mirar con ceño o desdén.

browbound [ˈbraʊbaʊnd] [brau-baund], *a.* Coronado, el que tiene las sienes ceñidas con corona.

browless [ˈbraʊlɪs] [brau-les], *a.* Descarado.

brown [braʊn] [braun], *a.* Moreno, castaño, bazo, que tira a encarnado o medio entre encarnado y negro, como el color de la pasa; pardo. Marrón, café, carmelito (shoe, dress, eyes); castaño (hair); moreno (naturally/skin, person); bronceado, moreno (suntanned). **To get brown,** broncearse, ponerse moreno. *-s.* Color moreno o pardo; el obtenido mezclando rojo, amarillo y negro en diferentes proporciones; matiz de las hojas marchitas. Marrón, café, carmelito. *va. (Culin.)* Dorar. Broncear (tan). *vn. (Culin.)* Dorarse. Broncearse, ponerse moreno (tan).

brown bear, oso pardo.

brown bread, pan bazo o moreno. Pan de harina de centeno con maíz; o de trigo con centeno y maíz.

brown coal, lignito, combustible fósil V. LIGNITE.

browned-off [braʊndɒf] [braund-of] *a.* (GB) *(Coloq,)* **To be browned-off,** estar harto.

brownian [ˈbraʊnɪən] [brau-nian], *a.* V. BRUNONIAN.

brownie [ˈbraʊnɪ] [brau-ni], *s.* 1. Especie de duende moreno, bondadoso, del que se supone que frecuenta las granjas y hace labores útiles por la noche. (Fam. de Escocia). 2. Bizcocho de chocolate y nueces. 3. **Brownie,** alita (in UK). **To earn Brownie points,** marcarse o anotarse puntos.

brownish [ˈbraʊnɪʃ] [brau-nesh], *a.* Lo que tira a moreno o castaño.

brown-linnet [braʊnˈlɪnɪt] [brau-ni-li-net], *s. (Orn.)* Pardillo.

brownness [ˈbraʊnnɪs] [braun-nes], *s.* Color moreno.

brownout [braʊnˈaʊt] [braun-aut], *s.* Apagón (parcial).

brown paper [braʊnˈpeɪpəʳ] [braun-pei-paʳ], papel de estraza.

brown-red o **red ochre,** V. OCHRE.

brown rice [ˈbraʊnraɪz] [braun-rais], arroz integral.

brown sauce [ˈbraʊnsɔːs] [braun-sos], salsa hecha con jugo de carne (thickened stock). (GB) Salsa agridulce con especias (spicy relish).

brown stone ['braʊnstəʊn] [braun-stoun], s. Variedad de piedra arenisca, muy usada en la construcción de edificios. Piedra rojiza (stone); casa de piedra rojiza (building).

brown sugar ['braʊnʃʊgəʳ] [braun-shu-gaʳ], azúcar terciado; azúcar moreno.

brownwort ['braʊnwɔːt] [braun-uort], s. (Bot.) Escrofularia.

browse [braʊz] [braus], va. Ramonear, pacer, cortar o comer las ramas, pimpollos o renuevos, como hacen los venados, cabras, etc. -vn. Alimentarse. Mirar en una tienda, catálogo, etc. (look). **She was browsing through the records/a magazine,** estaba echando un vistazo a los discos/hojeando una revista.

browsing ['braʊzɪŋ] [brau-sin], s. El alimento o comida de los venados.

browst ['braʊst] [braust], s. (Esco.) Braceaje, trabajo de preparación de la cerveza.

brucia, brucine ['bruːʃə] [bru-sha] ['brɒsiːn] [bru-sin], s. Brucina, alcaloide vegetal que se halla en la nuez vómica.

bruin ['bruɪn] [bruin], s. Oso; nombre usado en los cuentos populares.

bruise [bruːz] [brus], va. Magullar, mallugar (fruit), machacar, abollar, majar; pulverizar. Contusionar (body, arm); herir (feelings, ego). vn. Magullarse, mallugarse (fruit). **He bruises very easily,** le salen moratones o cardenales con mucha facilidad.

bruise, s. Magulladura, contusión, golpe, y también el cardenal que queda señalado, moretón, morado; confusión.

bruiser ['bruːzəʳ] [bru-saʳ], s. 1. Un instrumento de los ópticos. 2. (Fest.) Púgil. 3. (Coloq,) Muchachote; matón (aggressive).

bruisewort ['bruːzwɔːt] [brus-uort], s. Consuelda o suelda consuelda.

bruit [bruːt] [brut], s. 1. Ruido, rumor, noticia, fama. 2. (Med.) Sonido generalmente irregular y anómalo que se oye por la auscultación.

bruit, va. Esparcir, divulgar, pregonar, publicar; echar voz, dar fama.

brumal ['bruːməl] [bru-mal], a. Brumal, perteneciente al invierno.

brumous ['bruːməs] [bru-mos], a. Brumal, nebuloso, brumoso, invernal.

brunch [brʌntʃ] [branch], s. (Coloq,) Combinación de desayuno y almuerzo o comida.

brunette [bruːˈnet] [bru-net], sf. Morena, trigueña, mujer agraciada de tez morena.

brunonian ['bruːnəʊnɪən] [bru-nou-nian], a. Lo que pertence al Doctor John Brown, de Edimburgo: hallado o inventado por él.

brunswick black [brʌnsˈwɪkˈblæak] [brun-suik-blak], s. Charol negro. Se llama también *Japan black.*

brunt [brʌnt] [brant], s. 1. Choque o encuentro violento, combate, esfuerzo. 2. Golpe. 3. Desastre, accidente, desgracia. **To bear/take the brunt of something,** sufrir algo. **I had to bear the brunt of his anger,** tuve que sufrir su cólera. **The city has taken the full brunt of the recession,** la ciudad es la que más ha sufrido la crisis.

brush [brʌʃ] [brash], s. 1. Cepillo (for cleaning/hair), escobilla, limpiadera, bruza, pincel (paint), brocha (large). **To be tarred with the same brush,** estar cortados por la misma tijera o por el mismo patrón. Cola (of fox). 2. Asalto, choque, combate, zacapela, sarracina, riña de voces y golpes. 3. Haz de leña menuda. 4. Matorral, monte, breñal. Maleza (scrub); broza (cut branches). **I gave my hair a brush,** me cepillé el pelo. Roce (faint touch). **Brush with something/somebody,** roce con algo/alguien (encounter/with the law, the police). **She had had several brushes with death,** ha visto la muerte de cerca en varias ocasiones.

brush, va. 1. Acepillar, limpiar con el cepillo o escobilla (clean/groom; jacket, hair); restregar; rasar. 2. Pintar con brocha. **To brush one's teeth,** lavarse o cepillarse los dientes. **He brushed the crumbs off the table,** quitó las migas de la mesa (sweep). Rozar (touch lightly). -vn. 1. (Joc.) Mover apresuradamente. 2. Pasar ligeramente por encima. **To brush away,** quitar, como con cepillo. **To brush by one,** pasar bruscamente cerca de alguno sin hacer caso de él.

brush aside, apartar (person, obstacle); desdeñar (objection, suggestion).

brush down, (GB) Cepillar.

brusher ['brʌʃəʳ] [bra-shaʳ], s. Acepillador, limpiador.

brushfire war [brʌʃfaɪəʳ] [brash-faiaʳ], s. Guerra de escaramuzas, guerra limitada o acción militar menor.

brush off, quitar cepillando (mud, hair). No hacer caso de, hacer caso omiso de (advances, suggestions).

brush-off, s. (Coloq,) **To give somebody the brush-off,** darle calabazas a alguien.

brush stroke, s. Pincelada.

brush up, (Coloq,) darle un repaso a. **To brush up on something,** darle un repaso a algo.

brush-up, s. (GB) **To have a wash and brush-up,** lavarse y arreglarse un poco.

brushwood ['brʌʃwʊd] [brash-vud], s. Matorral, breñal, zarzal. Broza (cut branches); maleza (scrub).

brushy ['brʌʃɪ] [bra-shi], a. Cerdoso, cerdudo; áspero como el cepillo de cerdas; velludo, hablando de personas.

brusk [brʌsk] [brask], o **brusque,** a. Áspero, rudo.

brusquely ['brʌsklɪ] [brask-li] adv. Con brusquedad.

Brussels ['brʌslz] [bra-sels], n. pr. Bruselas, la capital de Bélgica. Da su nombre a varios artículos de comercio: **Brussels carpet,** alfombra de Bruselas. **Brussels lace,** encaje de Bruselas. **Brussels sprouts,** s. pl. Coles de Bruselas.

brutal ['bruːtl] [bru-tal], a. 1. Brutal (killer, attack), lo que pertenece a los brutos. 2. Salvaje, cruel, inhumnano. Crudo (truth, frankness); atroz (conditions). **A brutal sport,** un deporte salvaje.

brutality [bruːˈtælɪtɪ] [bru-ta-li-ti], s. Brutalidad, la propiedad del bruto. **Police brutality,** malos tratos por parte de la policía.

brutalize ['bruːtəlaɪz] [bru-ta-lais], vn. Embrutecerse, entorpecerse. Insensibilizar, endurecer.

brutally ['bruːtəlɪ] [bru-ta-li], adv. Brutalmente (attack, treat). Crudamente, despiadadamente (mercilessly/frank, honest).

brute [bruːt] [brut], s. Bruto, animal, bestia (person). **He's a big brute of a man,** es un animal, un bestia. Bestia (animal).

brute, a. Salvaje, silvestre, montaraz, irracional, áspero, feroz, bestial. **Brute force,** fuerza bruta.

brute, va. V. BRUIT.

brutify ['bruːtɪfaɪ] [bru-ti-fai], va. Embrutecer, entorpecer.

brutish ['bruːtɪʃ] [bru-tish], a. 1. Brutal, bestial. 2. Brutal, fiero, feroz, salvaje (cruel), bruto (coarse). 3. Brutal, grosero, ignorante. 4. Insensible; frívolo. 5. Sensual.

brutishly ['bruːtɪʃlɪ] [bru-tish-li], adv. Brutalmente.

brutishness ['bruːtɪʃnɪs] [bru-tish-nes], s. Brutalidad.

BS s. = **Bachelor of Science.**

BSc s. (GB) = **Bachelor of Science.**

BSE = **(bovine spongiform encephalopathy)** Encefalopatía espongiforme bovina.

BSI s. = **British Standards Institution.**

BST = **British Summer Time.**

bryology ['braɪɒlɒdʒɪ] [brai-o-lod-chi], s. La parte de la bótanica que trata de los musgos.

bryozca ['braɪɒskə] [brai-os-ka], s. pl. V. POLYZOA.

bub [bʌb] [bab], s. 1. Muchachito. 2. (Ger.) Cerveza doble o fuerte.

bubble [bʌbl] [babel], s. 1. Burbuja, la ampolla que se levanta en el agua (of air, gas); pompa (of soap); ampolla (in paintwork). **To blow bubbles,** hacer pompas. **Speech/thought bubble,** bocadillo, globito (en una historieta). 2. Bagatela, cosa de poca o ninguna firmeza. 3. Engañifa, apariencia falsa.

bubble, *vn.* 1. Burbujear, hacer burbujas o ampollas el agua; bullir (form bubbles); burbujear (champagne). **She bubbles with enthusiasm,** rebosa (de) o desborda entusiasmo, el entusiasmo le sale por los poros (person). 2. Correr con ruido manso. *-va.* Engañar.

bubble over, *(Coloq,)* **She was bubbling over with enthusiasm,** no cabía en sí de entusiasmo.

bubble bath [ˈbʌblˌbɑːθ] [babel-baz] *s.* Baño de burbujas o espuma.

bubble gum [ˈbʌblɡʌm] [ba.bel-gam] *s.* Chicle (de globos), chicle de bomba, chicle globero.

bubbler [ˈbʌbləʳ] [ba-blaʳ], *s.* Engañador, fullero.

bubbly [ˈbʌblɪ] [ba-bli], *a.* Espumoso. Lleno de vida (person); efervescente (personality). Burbujeante (full of bubbles).

bubbly, *s. (Coloq,)* Champán, champaña.

bubby [ˈbʌbɪ] [ba-bi], *s.* 1. Voz cariñosa que se aplica a un muchachito. Es corrupción de *brother.* 2. *(Vul.)* Teta o pecho de mujer.

bubo [ˈbjuːbʊ] [biu-bo], *s.* Incordio, bubón, tumor que se forma en la ingle, producido generalmente por el virus venéreo.

bubonic [bjuːˈbɒnɪk] [biu-bo-nik], *a.* Bubónico. **Bubonic plague,** peste bubóncia.

buccal [ˈbjuːkl] [biu-kal], *a.* Bocal, de la boca.

buccaneers [ˌbʌkəˈnɪəz] [ba-ka-niars], *s. pl.* Filibusteros, nombre que tuvieron en otro tiempo los piratas de las Antillas. Bucaneros.

bucentaur [ˈbjuːsɒntəʳ] [biu-sen-toʳ], *s.* 1. Bucentauro, animal mitológico, mitad toro, mitad hombre. 2. Bucentauro, galera del dux de Venecia.

buchu [ˈbʊkuː] [bu-kú], *s.* Buchú, arbusto del África del Sur, con hojas pequeñas usadas en medicina. (Barosma).

buck [bʌk] [bak], *s.* 1. Gamo, animal parecido al ciervo. 2. El macho de algunos animales, como el ciervo, el antílope, la liebre, el conejo, etc. Indio o negro varón y adulto. *(Fam. E.U.A.)* 3. Petimetre atrevido y descarado. 4. Banquillo de aserrador de leña. *(Coloq,)* Dólar, verde (dollar). **To make a fast/quick buck,** hacer dinero o plata fácil. *(Coloq,)* **To pass the buck,** pasar la pelota (responsibility). **The buck stops here,** la responsabilidad es mía.

buck, *s.* 1. Lejía o colada en que se limpia y blanquea la ropa. 2. Colada, la porción de ropa que hay en la lejía.

buck, *va.* 1. Colar, lavar ropa en la colada. 2. *(Mil.)* Castigar atando entre sí los codos, las muñecas y las rodillas del delincuente, obligándolo a permanecer encorvado y en cuclillas. 3. Resistirse, oponerse a (trend). **To buck to the system,** ir contra la corriente, *-vn.* 1. Juntarse gamo y gama en tiempo de brama. 2. Saltar violentamente, cayendo con las patas delanteras rígidas, y la cabeza lo más baja posible: se dice del caballo o el mulo vicioso. Corcovear (horse). Dar sacudidas (move jerkly - car, deck). **To buck against something/somebody,** rebelarse contra algo/alguien (resist, oppose), *-va.* y *vn.* Romper el mineral con martillo. **Buck up,** levantar el ánimo (become cheerful). **Buck up!,** ¡levanta el ánimo!, ¡arriba ese ánimo! Esforzarse (make effort); (GB) Moverse, acelerar (hurry). Levantarle el ánimo a (person - cheer up). (GB) **To buck one's ideas up,** mejorar el comportamiento, ponerse a trabajar en serio.

buckbean [ˈbʌkbiːn] [bak-bin], *s.* Trifolio palustre o trébol de pantano.

buckboard [ˈbʌkbɔːd] [bak-bord], *s. (E.U.)* Carretón de cuatro ruedas, sin muelles.

bucket [ˈbʌkɪt] [ba-ket], *s.* 1. Cubo, pozal, balde, herrada, vasija para sacar agua de los pozos; cubeta, tobo, balde. **A bucket of water,** un balde (cubo, etc.) de agua. **To rain buckets,** llover a cántaros. **To cry buckets,** llorar a lágrima viva o a moco tendido. *(Coloq,)* **To kick the bucket,** estirar la pata. 2. Cangilón de noria, arcaduz. 3. Paleta de rueda; válvula de bomba.

bucket, *vn.* (GB) *(Coloq,)* **It's bucking (down),** está lloviendo a cántaros.

bucketful [ˈbʌkɪtfʊl] [baket-ful] *s.* Cantidad que puede contener un cubo.

bucket shop [ˈbʌkɪtʃɒp] [baket-shop], *s.* Agencia informativa de bolsa. (GB) *(Coloq,)* Agencia de viajes que vende boletos de avión a precios reducidos.

buckeye [ˈbʌkaɪ] [bak-ai] *s.* Nombre de ciertos árboles y arbustos americanos del género Aesculus y parecidos al Castaño de Indias.

buckle [ˈbʌkl] [bakel], *s.* 1. Hebilla, pieza de metal que sirve para prender las correas y para otros usos. 2. Bucle, el rizo de pelo en forma de anillo o sortija.

buckle, *va.* 1. Hebillar, afianzar alguna cosa con hebilla. Abrochar (fasten). Torcer, combar (bend). 2. Afianzar, agarrar, no soltar. 3. Juntar en batalla. 4. Hacer rizos en el pelo. *-vn.* Doblarse, encorvarse. Torcerse, combarse (bend, crumple/wheel, metal). **His knees buckled beneath him,** se le doblaron las rodillas. **To buckle to,** someterse, aplicarse a. **To buckle with,** empeñarse, encontrarse con. **To buckle for,** prepararse. **Buckle down,** ponerse a trabajar en serio. **Buckle up,** ponerse o abrocharse el cinturón de seguridad.

buckler [ˈbʌkləʳ] [baklaʳ], *s.* Escudo, broquel, adarga, arma defensiva.

buckmast [ˈbʌkmɑːst] [bak-mast], *s.* Fabuco.

buck private [bʌkˈpraɪvɪt] [bak-pri-veit], *s. (Fam.)* Soldado raso.

buckram [ˈbʌkrəm] [bak-ram], *s.* Bocací, tela de lino engomada.

bucksaw [ˈbʌksɔː] [bak-so], *s.* Sierra de bastidor.

buckshorn [ˈbʌkzhɔːn] [baks-jorn], *s. (Bot.)* Estrellamar, planta parecida en algo al llantén.

buckshot [ˈbʌkʃɒt] [bak-shot], *s.* Posta, perdigón.

buckskin [ˈbʌkskɪn] [bak-skin], *s.* Ante, el cuero de gamo curtido; también un cuero flexible, fuerte, pardo, amarillento, que hoy se hace principalmente de pieles de carnero. Gamuza. *-a.* Hecho de este cuero.

buckstall [ˈbʌkstɔːl] [bak-stol], *s.* Red tumbadera.

buckteeth [ˈbʌktiːθ] [bak-tiz], *s. pl.* **To have buckteeth,** tener los dientes salidos.

buckthorn [ˈbʌkθɔːn] [bak-zorn], *s. (Bot.)* Cambrón, espino cerval.

buckwheat [ˈbʌkwiːt] [bak-uit], *s.* Trigo negro o sarraceno, alforfón.

bucolic, bucolical [bjuːˈkɒlɪk] [biu-ko-lik], *a.* Bucólico, pastoril.

bud [bʌd] [bad], *s.* 1. Pimpollo, vástago, botón o yema de las plantas; capullo de una flor. **To be in bud,** tener brotes. *(Coloq,)* **To nip something in the bud,** cortar algo de raíz. 2. El acto o estado de brotar. 3. *(Zool.)* Parte parecida a un pimpollo o botón; prominencia semejante a un botón en varios animales, como los pólipos, etc., que se desarrolla y transforma en un nuevo individuo. 4. Lo que se asemeja a un pimpollo. 5. Algo no desarrollado. *(Fam.)* Una joven al ser presentada por primera vez en sociedad. *(Coloq,)* BUDDY (as form of address).

bud, *vn.* 1. Brotar, abotonar, arrojar el árbol o las plantas sus hojas, flores, botones o renuevos. 2. Estar en flor. *-va.* Inocular, ingertar o ingerir, de escudete.

Buddha [ˈbʊdə] [bu-da], *s.* Buda, dios de la India. Gautama Siddartha, apellidado Buda.

Buddhism [ˈbʊdɪzəm] [bu-disem], *s.* Budismo, culto de Buda, doctrina religiosa en Asia.

Buddhist [ˈbʊdɪst] [bu-dist], *s.* Budista, persona que profesa las doctrinas del Budismo.

budding [ˈbʌdɪŋ] [badin], *s.* Injerto de escudete, la operación de injertar un botón o yema. *a.* En ciernes (artist, genius).

buddle [ˈbʌdl] [badel], *s.* Lavadero, artesa grande para lavar el mineral.

buddy [ˈbʌdɪ] [badi] *s.* Amigo compinche, cuate; hermano, macho, güey, gallo (as form of address).

buddy-buddy [bʌdɪˈbʌdɪ] [badi-badi] *a.* Muy compinche, cuate. **To be buddy-buddy with somebody,** estar a partir un piñón o a partir un confite con alguien.

budge [ˈbʌdʒ] [badch], *va.* Mover un poco. Correr (move). Convencer, hacer cambiar de opinión (persuade). *-vn.*

Moverse, menearse, mudar de posición; hacer lugar. **He stood there and refused to budge,** se plantificó ahí y no hubo quien lo moviera. Cambiar de opinión (change opinion).

budge *a.* 1. Guarnecido con piel curtida de cordero o que la lleva. 2. Pomposo, imponente, formal. *-s.* 1. Piel curtida de cordero o cabrito. 2. *(Des.)* Ratero, ladronzuelo.

budgerigar [ˈbʌdʒərɪɡɑːʳ] [badche-ri-gaʳ] *s.* Periquito.

budget [ˈbʌdʒɪt] [bachet] *s.* 1. Talego portátil, mochila. 2. Provisión de alguna cosa. 3. Presupuesto, cómputo de los ingresos y gastos de un estado. **The Budget,** los presupuestos generales del Estado (in UK). **The project ran over budget,** el proyecto costó más de lo presupuestado o excedió el presupuesto. **A big/low-budget production,** una producción con un gran presupuesto/con un presupuesto reducido.

budget, *vn.* Administrarse. **To learn to budget,** aprender a administrar el dinero. **I hadn't budgeted for staying in a hotel,** no había contado con, o no había previsto gastos de hotel.

budgie [ˈbʌdʒɪ] [bad-chi] *s.* (GB) *(Coloq.)* Periquito.

buff [bʌf] [baf], *s.* 1. Ante, la piel adobada y curtida del búfalo y algunos otros animales, de la cual se hacen ciertas prendas de vestir, cinturones, etc. **Buff leather,** gamuza. **In the buff,** en cueros (bare skin). 2. Búfalo. 3. Coleto de soldado hecho de cuero grueso. 4. Color amarillo ligero, beige. 5. Linfa cuajada. 6. *(Coloq.)* Aficionado (enthusiast). **Film buff,** cinéfilo. **Jazz buff,** aficionado al jazz. *-a.* 1. De color de ante, beige (buff colored). De gamuza (made of buff). 2. Sólido, firme, que no cede.

buff, *va.* Pulimentar con ante. Pulir (metal); sacar brillo a (shoes). 2. Adelgazar el cuero. 3. Disminuir la velocidd del movimiento, amortiguar los efectos de un choque. **Buffing-block,** cojinete o tope para amortiguar el choque entre los vagones de un tren.

buffalo [ˈbʌfələʊ] [ba-fa-lou], *s.* Búfalo, especie de toro salvaje (wild ox). Búfalo de agua, carabao (water buffalo). También se da este nombre al bisonte norteamericano, ya casi extinto. Bisonte (bison).

buffalo-moth [ˈbʌfələʊˌmɒθ] [ba-fa-lou-moz], *s.* Antreno, insecto coleóptero cuya larva ataca y destruye las alfombras. **Buffalo-robe,** piel del bisonte norteamericano adobada y con pelo, que se usa como manta de coche y de viaje.

buffer [ˈbʌfəʳ] [ba-faʳ], 1. Resorte, muelle en espiral. 2. *(F.C.)* Resortes para choques tope. Parachoques, paragolpes (auto). (GB) Tope (on train- rail); parachoques, amortiguador de choques (in station). **Buffer state,** estado tapón. **Buffer zone,** zona parachoques. *(Comput.)* Memoria intermedia o interfaz, tampón.

buffet [ˈbʌfɪt] [ba-fet], *s.* Puñada, el golpe que se da con el puño cerrado. Buffet (meal). (GB) Bar (in train). **Buffet car,** coche restaurante, coche comedor, vagón restaurante. Bar (cafetería, en una estación).

buffet, *va.* Combatir a puñadas. Zarandear, sacudir.

buffeting [ˈbʌfɪtɪŋ] [ba-fe-tin], *s.* Golpe: puñada. **The buffeting of the waves,** el embate de las olas. **The area took a buffeting during the storm,** la zona fue azotada o castigada por la tormenta.

buffoon [bəˈfuːn] [ba-fun], *s.* Bufón, payaso, truhán, chocarrero, juglar, que sirve de hazmerreír; gracioso en los teatros.

buffoon, *va.* Burlar, chocarrear, chulear.

buffoonery [bəˈfuːnərɪ] [ba-fu-ne-ri], **buffooning** [bəˈfuːnɪŋ] [ba-fu-nin], *s.* Bufonada, bufonería, dicho o acción de bufón; chanzas bajas; chocarrería; majadería.

buffoonlike [bəˈfuːnlaɪk] [ba-fun-laik], *a.* Truhanesco, chocarrero, burlesco, licencioso.

buffy [ˈbʌfɪ] [ba-fi], *a.* De color amarillo ligero; parecido al ante.

bug [bʌɡ] [bag], *s.* Chinche, insecto asqueroso y hediondo (biting insect); bicho (any insect). **To be as snug as a bug in a rug,** estar en la gloria. Nombre dado en general en inglés a los insectos hemípteros. **Potato-bug,** doryphora.

Esta voz se usa también a menudo inexactamente para designar ciertos escarabajos, como *lady-bu* (mariquita o vaquilla de San Martín); o algunos crustáceos, como *sowbug,* corredera; y aun como sinónimo de insecto en general. *(Coloq.)* **He caught/picked up a stomach bug,** se agarró algo al estómago (germ, disease). **She got the travel bug,** le entró la fiebre de los viajes (obsession). **A movie bug,** un cinéfilo, un amante del cine (enthusiast). *(Coloq.)* Micrófono oculto (listening device). Problema (fault).

bug, *va.* Colocar micrófonos ocultos en (room/telephone). Fastidiar (irritate, bother). **It really bugs me when you do that,** me saca de quicio que hagas eso. **What's bugging you?,** ¿qué mosca te ha picado? *-vn.* Salirse de las órbitas (eyes).

bugaboo o **bugbear** [ˈbʌɡəbuː] [ba-ga-bú] [ˈbʌɡbɪəʳ] [bag-biaʳ], *s.* Fantasma, objeto espantoso que causa terror; espantajo, coco. Pesadilla.

bugger [ˈbʌɡəʳ] [ba-gaʳ] *s.* (GB) *(Vulg.)* Hijo de puta (unpleasant person). *(Sl.)* **Poor bugger!,** ¡pobre tipo! (GB) *(Sl.)* **The exam was a real bugger,** el examen fue jodidísimo. *(Vulg.)* **She did bugger all,** no hizo un carajo.

bugger, *va.* *(Vulg.)* **(I'm) buggered if I know!,** ¡no tengo ni puta idea! (in interj. phrases). *(Vulg.)* Joder, chingar (spoil, ruin). Sodomizar (commit buggery with).

bugger about, (GB) *(Vulg.)* Joder (act foolishly) (inconvenience).

bugger off, (GB) *(Vulg.)* **Bugger off!,** ¡vete a la mierda! **He buggered off,** se largó.

bugger up, (GB) *(Vulg.)* Joder. **I buggered up my exam,** la cagué en el examen.

bugger, *interj,* ¡carajo!

buggery [ˈbʌɡərɪ] [ba-gue-ri] *s.* Sodomía.

bugging device [ˈbʌɡɪŋˈdevaɪz] [ba-guin-de-vais] *s.* Micrófono oculto.

buggy [ˈbʌɡɪ] [ba-gui], *a.* Chinchero, chinchoso, lleno de chinches.

buggy, *s.* Calesín, carruaje ligero de cuatro ruedas. Calesa (horse-drawn vehicle). Cochecito (baby carriage). (GB) Sillita de paseo (plegable) (pushchair).

bugle, buglehorn [ˈbʌɡəlhɔːn] [baguel-jorn], *s.* Corneta de monte o trompa de caza; instrumento músico militar, corneta de órdenes. Clarín.

bugle, *s.* 1. Bolita de vidrio negro. **Bugles,** abalorios, 2. Búgula o consuelda media; planta.

bugler [ˈbjuːɡləʳ] [biu-glaʳ], *s.* Corneta, trompetero.

bugloss [ˈbʌɡlɒs] [ba-glos], *s.* *(Bot.)* Buglosa, lengua de buey.

buhl [bʌl] [bal], **buhlwork** [ˈbʌlvɜːk] [bal-uek], *s.* Taracea, marquetería decorativa.

build [bɪld] [bild], *s.* Estructura, la forma o figura de algún edificio o fábrica. Complexión. **With a slim build,** de complexión delgada. **The build of a swimmer,** el físico de un nadador.

build, *va.* Construir, edificar, hacer (house). Construir (bridge, road, ship). Construir, levantar, hacer (wall). Hacer (fire, nest). Forjarse (career). Levantar, construir (empire). *-vn.* Edificar (erect buildings). Aumentar (increase/tension, pressure). **Build on,** agregar (extension, kitchen). **Build up,** fortalecer (make bigger, stronger/muscles). **To build up one's strength,** fortalecerse. Acumular (accumulate/supplies, experience); acrecentar (reserves). **They're building up their forces in the area,** están intensificando su presencia militar en la zona. Forjarse (develop/reputation); desarrollar (confidence); agarrar o coger (speed). **To build up one's hopes,** hacerse ilusiones. **He built the firm up from nothing,** levantó la empresa de la nada. Poner por las nubes (praise). Acumularse, juntarse (dirt/accumulate). **Their debts had built up,** sus deudas se habían ido acumulando. Ir en aumento (increase/pressure, noise). **The tension builds up to a climax,** la tensión va en aumento hasta llegar a un punto culminante.

builder [ˈbɪldəʳ] [bil-daʳ], s. Arquitecto, alarife, maestro de obras. Contratista.

building [ˈbɪldɪŋ] [bild-in], s. Fábrica, edificio, inmueble (edifice). Construcción (construction). **Building contractor**, contratista de obras. **Building site**, obra. **The building trade**, la industria de la construcción. **Ship-building**, construcción de buques o arquitectura naval. **The art of building**, arquitectura. **Building society**, sociedad de crédito hipotecario.

buildup [ˈbɪldʌp] [bild-ap], s. Incremento; publicidad destinada a realzar una persona, producto u organización, popularización, propaganda, bombo (publicity). Aumento, intensificación, concentración (of tension, pressure). Acumulación (accumulation). Concentración (of troops).

built [bɪlt] [bilt], prep. y pp. del verbo TO BUILD.

built, a. **The school is built around a courtyard**, la escuela está construida alrededor de un patio (constructed). **To be built of/out of something**, estar hecho de algo. **He's built like an ox**, es muy corpulento (physically). **She's heavily built**, es de complexión robusta. **Athletically built**, con físico de atleta.

-built, suff. **Brickbuilt/stonebuilt**, hecho de ladrillo/piedra. **Sturdily built**, de complexión sólida.

built-in, a. Empotrado, encastrado (bookcase, desk). Fijo (equipment). Incorporado (mechanism, feature). Intrínseco (inherent/weakness, tendency). **Built-in furniture**, muebles empotrados.

built-up [ˈbɪltʌp] [bilt-ap] a. Urbanizado (area).

bulb [bʌlb] [balb], s. (Bot.) 1. Bulbo o cebolla, la raíz redonda formada de cascos o cubierta de telas. Bulbo, papa (of flower); cabeza (of garlic). 2. Cubeta del barómetro. 3.Ampolleta del termómetro. 4. Bombilla, foco, bombillo, bombita o lamparita, ampolleta, bujía (light bulb).

bulbar [ˈbʌlbəʳ] [balbaʳ], a. Perteneciente a un bulbo, y especialmente a la médula espinal.

bulbous [ˈbʌlbəs] [bal-bos], a. Bulboso, lo que tiene bulbos (growth); protuberante (nose).

Bulgarian [bʌlˈgeərɪən] [bal-guea-rian], a./s. Búlgaro, de Bulgaria (person, language).

bulge [bʌldʒ] [balch], s. Parte prominente o la más convexa; comba. Bulto. (Mar.) Abertura de agua.

bulge, vn. 1. (Mar.) Hacer agua la embarcación. 2. (Arq.) Hacer barriga o comba el muro o la pared. Sobresalir (protrude). **Her eyes bulged at the thought**, los ojos se le salían de las órbitas de sólo pensarlo. **The bag was bulging with books**, la bolsa estaba repleta de libros. **Bulging**, repleto (pocket, bag); saltón (eyes).

bulimia (nervosa) [bjuːˈlɪmɪə] [biu-li-mia] s. Bulimia (nerviosa).

bulimic [bjuːˈlɪmɪk] [biu-li-mik] a. Bulímico.

bulk [bʌlk] [balk], s. 1. Tamaño, bulto, masa, volumen, magnitud, grosor, el grandor de alguna cosa. Mole (large mass). 2. Corpulencia, talle. 3. La mayor parte. 4. Cabida de una fábrica. 5. Capacidad o carga de un buque. **By the bulk**, en grueso, por mayor. **In bulk**, en grandes cantidades (large quantity). **The bulk of something**, la mayor parte de algo, gran parte de algo (largest part).

bulk, s. (Ingl.) Barriga o comba en algún edificio; banco delante de las tiendas donde se ponen mercancías a vender.

bulkhead [ˈbʌlkhed] [balk-jed], s. (Mar.) Mampara, división de tablas que se forman en diferentes partes de la embarcación.

bulkiness [ˈbʌlkɪnɪs] [balki-nes], s. Volumen o bulto, masa, magnitud. V. BULK.

bulky [ˈbʌlkɪ] [balki], a. Voluminoso, grande (package); corpulento (person); macizo, repleto, pesado, abultado, grueso, gordo (sweater).

bull [bʊl] [bul], s. 1. Toro, el padre del ganado vacuno (male bovine). **To be like a bull in a china shop**, ser como un elefante en una cristalería. **To take the bull by the horns**, agarrar o coger al toro por los cuernos. Macho (male of other species). 2. (Astr.) Tauro, el segundo signo de los doce del zodíaco. 3. Bula pontificia. 4. Disparate, bola, dicho fuera de propósito, dicho absurdo; contradicción

manifiesta, incongruidad, inconsecuencia. (Sl.) Estupideces, chorradas, macanas, jaladas. 5. Alcista, jugador a la alza. John bull, (Fest.) Apodo dado a la nación inglesa.

bulla [bʊlə] [bu-la], s. Flictena, ampolla, vejigüela cutánea transparente, que contiene un humor seroso.

bullace [ˈbʊleɪs] [bu-leis], s. Ciruela silvestre o bruna.

bullary [ˈbʊlərɪ] [bu-la-ri], s. Bulario, recopilación de las bulas de los Papas.

bull-baiting [ˈbʊlbeɪtɪŋ] [bul-bai-tin], s. Combate de toros y perros.

bull-beef [ˈbʊlbiːf] [bul-bif], s. Carne de toro.

bull-calf [ˈbʊlkɑːf] [bul-kaf], s. 1. Ternero. 2. El hombre tosco y pusilánime.

bull-dog [ˈbʊldɒg] [bul-dog], s. 1. Alano, perro dogo o de presa. 2. Revólver de calibre grande.

bulldoze [ˈbʊldəʊz] [bul-dous], va. (Ger. E.U.) Intimidar con amenazas o violencia física: echar fieros. Demoler, derribar. **To bulldoze somebody into something**, forzar a alguien a algo.

bulldozer [ˈbʊldəʊzəʳ] [bul-dou-saʳ], s. 1. Niveladora, maquinaria empleada para movimiento y desplazamiento de tierra. Bulldozer, topadora. 2. (Fam.) Valentón, matón.

bullen [ˈbʊlən] [bu-len], s. Cañamiza; cañamazo.

bullet [ˈbʊlɪt] [bulit], s. Bala de metal.

bulletin [ˈbʊlɪtɪn] [bu-li-tin], s. 1. Boletín (newsletter); anuncio, comunicado (notice); noticias del día. Boletín informativo (report). 2. Publicación periódica sobre asunto o ramo especial. (Fr.)

bulletin board [ˈbʊlɪtɪnbɔːd] [bu-li-tin-bord], s. Tablero para noticias. Tablón de anuncios, diario mural.

bullet-proof [ˈbʊlɪtpruːf] [bu-let-pruf], a. A prueba de bala. Antibalas (vest). Blindado (car).

bull-faced [ˈbʊlfeɪst] [bul-feist], a. Cariancho.

bull-feast [ˈbʊlfiːst] [bul-físt], **bull-fight** [ˈbʊlfaɪt] [bulfait], s. Corrida de toros o fiesta de toros.

bullfight, s. Corrida de toros.

bullfighter [ˈbʊlfaɪtəʳ] [bul-fai-taʳ] s. Torero.

bullgighting [ˈbʊlfaɪtɪŋ] [bul-fai-tin] s. (Deporte de) los toros. Toreo, tauromaquia. **Bullfighting is very popular here**, los toros o las corridas de toros son muy populares aquí.

bullfinch [ˈbʊlfɪntʃ] [bul-finch], s. Pinzón real; pájaro cantor del género Pyrrhula.

bullfrog [ˈbʊlfrɒg] [bul-frog], s. Rana norteamericana de unas ocho pulgadas de largo, y de estruendoso graznido. Rana catesbiana.

bull-head [ˈbʊlhed] [bul-jed], s. 1. Cabeza redonda, el de rudo entendimiento. 2. Gobio, pez. V. CATFISH. 3. Chorlito, ave zancuda.

bullhorn [ˈbʊlhɔːn] [bul-jorn] s. Megáfono.

bullion [ˈbʊljən] [bulion], s. 1. Oro en tejos, o plata en barras y sin labrar. **Gold/silver bullion**, oro/plata en lingotes. 2. Canutillo briscado. **Bullion fringe**, franja de oro.

bullish [ˈbʊlɪʃ] [bu-lish], a. Disparatado.

bullock [ˈbʊlək] [bu-lok], s. Buey, en especial el de más de cuatro años (castrated bull). Novillo (younger bull).

bullpen [ˈbʊlpen] [bul-pen] s. Bull pen, zona de calentamiento en un diamante de béisbol (place) (in baseball). Píchers o lanzadores de reserva. (Coloq.) Calabozo (prison cell).

bullring [ˈbʊlrɪŋ] [bul-rin] s. Plaza de toros.

bull session [ˈbʊlseʃən] [bul-se-shon] s. Charla.

bullseye [ˈbʊlzaɪ] [buls-ai] s. Diana. **To score a bullseye**, dar en el blanco, hacer diana.

bull's eye [ˈbʊlzaɪ] [buls-ai], s. 1. Claraboya, tragaluz, ventana redonda ú ovalada. 2. Linterna sorda. 3. Centro de blanco y tiro que da en el blanco. 4. (Astr.) Aldebarán estrella principal de la constelación de Tauro. 5. (Mar.) Ojo de buey u ojo de ciego.

bullshit [ˈbʊlʃɪt] [bul-shit] s. (Vulg.) Sandeces, pendejadas, gilipolleces, huevadas, boludeces, mamadas (nonsense).

bullshit, vn. Decir sandeces (o gilipolleces) (talk nonsense). Tirarse un farol (boast, brag).

bullshitter [ˈbʊlʃɪtəʳ] [bul-shi-taʳ] s. (Sl.) Farolero, fantasma, mandaparte, hocicón.

bull terrier [ˌbʊlˈterɪəʳ] [bul-teriaʳ] s. Bulterrier.

bull-weed [ˈbʊlwiːd] [bul-uíd], s. (Bot.) Escoba, una mata.

bully [ˈbʊlɪ] [buli], s. Espadachín, el preciado de guapo y valentón, alborotador y amigo de pendencias, quimerista; matón, bravucón (thug, tyrant); rufián, tahur. Bully, salida (in field hockey).

bully, a. (Ger.) 1. Jovial; vistoso. 2. Magnífico, excelente.

bully, va. Echar plantas, fieros o bravatas; insultar. Intimidar, matonear. **She bullied him into doing it,** lo acosó hasta que lo hizo. -vn. Reñir, fanfarronear. **Bully off,** sacar (in field hockey).

bully, interj. **Bully for you/him!,** ¡bravo!

bullying [ˈbʊlɪɪŋ] [buliin] s. Intimidación, acoso.

bulrush [ˈbʊlrʌʃ] [bul-rash], s. Junco, enea, anea, totora, planta que se cría en los parajes acuosos. Junco marinero (rush).

bulwark [ˈbʊlwək] [bul-uork], s. 1. Baluarte, cuerpo de fábrica que en las plazas fortificadas se coloca en los ángulos para defender las murallas (defense). 2. (Met.) Baluarte, lo que sirve de amparo o defensa. **Bulwarks,** (Naut.) macarrones.

bulwark, va. Hacer girar y zumbar (una peonza). -vn. (Fam. E.U.) 1. Holgazanear, estar ocioso o hacer vida disipada (con la preposición around). 2. Beber a pote.

bum [bʌm] [bum], s. 1. Holgazán, vago (worthless person); vagabundo (vagrant). **Ski/tennis bum,** loco del esquí/tenis (enthusiast). **He's a beach bum,** se pasa el día en la playa. 2. (vul.) Nalgas, trasero, trasero, culo, traste, poto (buttocks).

bum, va. (Sl.) **To bum something form/off somebody,** gorronearle o gorrearle algo a alguien, pecharle a alguien. -vn. **To bum around,** vagabundear. **To bum off somebody,** gorronearle, gorrearle, garronearle o pecharle a alguien (cadge).

bum, a. (Sl.) De porquería (job, place). **A bum rap,** una acusación falsa. **It turned out to be a bum deal,** resultó ser un chanchullo.

bumbailiff [bʌmˈbaɪlɪf] [bum-bai-lif], s. Corchete, el ministro de justicia que lleva los presos a la cárcel.

bumble-bee o **bumble-bee** [bʌmblˈbiː] [bam-bol-bi], s. Abejorro, abejón; abeja grande social del género Bombus; se llama así a causa de su zumbido.

bumbling [ˈbʌmblɪŋ] [bamblin] a. Torpe, incompetente.

bumboat [ˈbʌmbəʊt] [bam-boat], s. (Mar.) Bote vivandero.

bumf [bʌmf] [bamf] s. (Coloq.) (GB) Papelerío, papeles.

bumkin [ˈbʌmkɪn] [bam-kin], **boomkin** [ˈbʊmkɪn] [bum-kin], s. (Mar.) Pescante de la amura del trinquete.

bummer [ˈbʌməʳ] [bu-maʳ], s. Holgazán, ocioso, pillo. (Sl.) Latazo, plomo, plomazo, coñazo.

bump [bʌmp] [bamp], s. Hinchazón o bulto, protuberancia (lump in surface); giba joroba, corcova hablando de animales; bollo, chichón (on head); bodoque de golpes dados en la cabeza; abolladura, en el metal; barriga, en una pared. Bache (on road). Golpe (blow); sacudida (jolt); topetazo (collision). **That brought me back to reality with a bump,** eso me devolvió de golpe a la realidad. Golpe (sound). **Things that go bump in the night,** cosas que dan miedo.

bump, va. Dar estallido como una bomba. Golpear, dar golpes. **I bumped my elbow on/against the door,** me dí en el codo con/contra la puerta. **I bumped the post as I was reversing,** choqué con/contra el poste al dar marcha atrás (hit, knock lightly). Echar (remove, throw out). **We got bumped from the flight,** nos quedamos sin plaza en el vuelo. -vn. **To bump against something/somebody,** darse o chocar contra algo/alguien (hit, knock).

bump into, darse o chocar contra (collide with). (Coloq.) toparse o tropezarse con, encontrarse con (meet by chance).

bump off, (Sl.) Liquidar.

bump up, (Coloq,) Aumentar.

bumper [ˈbʌmpəʳ] [bam-paʳ], s. 1. Lo que da golpes. 2. Tope para amortiguar los choques. 3. (Auto) Defensa o parachoques de un automóvil. **The cars were bumper to bumper,** los coches iban pegados unos a otros. **Bumper crop,** (Fam.) cosecha abundante.

bumper, a. Récord, extraordinario (crop, year); extra (edition); gigante (pack).

bumper car s. Coche de choque, carrito chocón, autito chocador, carro loco.

bumph [bʌmf] [bamf] s. V. BUMF.

bumpkin [ˈbʌmpkɪn] [bam-kin], s. Patán, el hombre zafio, tosco y campesino; villano, rústico. **(Country) bumpkin,** pueblerino, paleto, pajuerano.

bumpkinly [ˈbʌmpkɪnlɪ] [bam-kin-li], a. Zafio, rústico.

bumptious [ˈbʌmpʃəs] [bamp-shos], a. (Fam.) Engreído, envanecido, presuntuoso.

bumpy [ˈbʌmpɪ] [bam-pi], a. Desigual, con desniveles (uneven/surface); lleno de baches (road). **We had a bumpy flight,** el avión se movió mucho (rough). **It was a bumpy ride and she felt sick,** se mareó con el traqueteo del autobús/coche.

bun [bʌn] [ban], s. 1. Bollo en forma de panecillo (sweetened). **Currant bun,** bollo con pasas. Panecillo, pancito, bolillo (bread roll). 2. Moño, rodete, chongo (hairstyle). **Buns,** (Coloq,) trasero, culo, traste, poto.

bunch [bʌntʃ] [banch], s. 1. Nudo, bulto o tumor, giba, corcova. 2. Racimo, (of bananas/grapes), penca, ristra, cacho. 3. Manojo (of keys), grupo (group), atado, hacecillo, gavilla; ramo (of flowers), ramillete (small), boncho. **They're a bunch of idiots,** son una panda de idiotas. **They're an odd bunch,** son gente de lo más rara. 4. Puñado, montón de hierba. 5. Penacho. 6. Montón, porrón, chorro (a lot). **Thanks a bunch!,** ¡gracias mil! **Bunch-grass,** ejemplar de varias plantas gramíneas del Oeste de la América del Norte, que crecen comúnmente en grupos. **Bunches,** (GB) coletas (hairstyle).

bunch, vn. Formar giba o corcova. **Bunch (together),** amontonarse (runners, cars); fruncirse (cloth).

bunchbacked [ˈbʌntʃbakt] [banch-bakt], a. Gibado, corcovado.

bunchiness [ˈbʌntʃɪnɪs] [ban-chi-nes], s. La calidad de ser racimoso o nudoso.

bunchy [ˈbʌntʃɪ] [ban-chi], a. Racimoso, lo que se va formando en racimos; corcovado, gibado, giboso.

bunco, bunko [ˈbʌŋkəʊ] [ban-kou], s. Lenguaje o discurso altisonante y ampuloso, sin más objeto que ganar el aplauso del público.

bundle [ˈbʌndl] [bandel], s. Atado, lío, fardo (of clothes); mazo, envoltorio; paquete (of newspapers, letters); fajo (of money); haz, atado (of sticks). **Software bundle,** paquete de software. **That child is a bundle of mischief,** ese niño es un diablillo. **She's a bundle of nerves,** es un manojo de nervios. **The play isn't exactly a bundle of laughs,** la obra no es precisamente muy cómica. (Coloq,) **A bundle,** un dineral, un platal, un pastón, un lanón (large sum of money).

bundle, va. Liar, atar, hacer un lío o atado (make into a bundle); empaquetar, envolver. **She bundled them off to school,** los despachó al colegio. **They bundled him into the car,** lo metieron a empujones en el coche.

bundle up, liar (clothes, paper); abrigarse.

bung [bʌŋ] [bang], s. Tapón o tarugo que se pone en la parte superior de las cubas o barriles.

bung, va. Taponar (put bung). (GB) (Coloq,) Poner, meter (put). **Just bung it out,** tíralo (a la basura). **Bung up,** (GB) (Coloq,) atascar, tapar (sink, pipe). **I'm really bunged up,** tengo la nariz tapada.

bungalow [ˈbʌŋgələʊ] [ban-ga-lou], s. Casa, habitación de un solo piso rodeada de galerías o portales cubiertos.

bungee jumping [ˈbʌndʒiː] [ban-yi] s. Banyi.

bunghole [ˈbʌŋhəʊl] [bang-joul], s. Boca, el agujero por el cual se envasan los licores en las pipas, toneles y barriles, y se tapa con el tapón.

bungle [ˈbʌŋgl] [bangl], *va.* Chapucear, chafallar, hacer alguna cosa chapuceramente; echar a perder una cosa, estropear. **A bungled attempt,** un intento fallido. *-vn.* Hacer algo chabacanamente.

bungler [ˈbʌŋglər] [ban-glaʳ], *s.* Chapucero, chambón, el que hace mal y toscamente las cosas de su oficio.

bungling [ˈbʌŋglɪŋ] [ban-glin] *a.* Torpe.

bunglingly [ˈbʌŋglɪŋlɪ] [ban-glin-li], *adv.* Chapuceramente, chabacanamente, groseramente, toscamente.

bungy jumping, *s.* V. BUNGEE JUMPING.

bunion o bunyon [ˈbʌnjən] [ba-nion], *s.* Juanete del pie.

bunk [bʌŋk] [bank], *s.* 1. Tarima para dormir; litera (bed). 2. *(Fam.)* Palabrería, faramalla, (GB) *(Sl.)* Largarse. **Bunk off,** V. SKIVE OFF.

bunk bed *s.* Litera.

bunker [ˈbʌŋkər] [ban-kaʳ], *s.* 1. *(Mil.)* Fortín. 2. *(Mar.)* Carbonera.

bunkum [ˈbʌŋkəm] [ban-kom] *s.* *(Coloq,)* Bobadas.

bunny [ˈbʌnɪ] [bani], **bunny rabbit** *s.* *(Fam.)* Un conejo, o una ardilla. Conejito (used to or by children).

bunt [bʌnt] [bant], *vn.* *(Mar.)* Hincharse.

bunt, *s.* Hongo parásito, especie de tizón que convierte el interior de los granos de trigo en fétido polvo negro. (burnt).

bunt, *va.* 1. Dar o empujar con la cabeza; topetar. 2. (Baseball) Golpear la pelota con la maza de una manera especial.

bunter [ˈbʌntər] [ban-taʳ], *s.* Mujercilla, mujer vil y despreciable.

bunting [ˈbʌntɪŋ] [ban-tin], *s.* *(Mar.)* Lanilla, tejido del cual se hacen por lo común las banderas.

bunting, *s.* Pájaro del género Emberiza, del que hay varias especies. Verderón pintado.

bunting-iron [ˈbʌntɪŋaɪrən] [ban-tin-airon], *s.* Soplete de vidrio.

buntlines [ˈbʌntlaɪnz] [bant-lains], *s.* *(Mar.)* Brioles, cuerdas que sirven para cargar o recoger las velas de un buque.

buoy [buːɔɪ] [buoi], *s.* 1. *(Mar.)* Boya, el palo, corcho u otro objeto flotante que nada sobre el agua, sujeto a algún peso. 2. Boya, señal flotante para señalar la posición de algún objeto situado bajo el agua; o para indicar a los buques la dirección de un paso o canal. **Can-buoy,** boya cónica de baliza. **Wooden buoy,** boya de madera. **Buoy-rope,** orinque. **Buoy-slings,** eslingas o guarnimiento de la boya. **Bell-buoy,** boya de campana. **Whistling-buoy,** boya de pito de alarma. **Life-buoy,** boya salvavidas; guíndola.

buoy, *va.* Boyar, mantener sobre al agua. **To buoy the cable,** *(Mar.)* boyar el cable. **Buoy up,** mantener a flote (boat, person); animar (keep cheerful). **To buoy one up,** apoyar o sostener a alguno.

buoyage [ˈbɔɪədʒ] [boiach], *s.* Conjunto de boyas; sistema de boyas; acción de proveer de boyas.

buoyancy [ˈbɔɪənsɪ] [boian-si], *s.* Fluctuación, la propiedad de sobrenadar o flotar en el agua o de mantenerse sobre un gas. Flotabilidad (ability to float); sustentación hidráulica (of liquid); optimismo (resilience); *(Fin.)* solidez (of currency); tendencia alcista (of market).

buoyant [ˈbɔɪənt] [boiant], *a.* Boyante, lo que nada sobre el agua y no se va a fondo; flotante (able to float). Optimista (mood, spirits). *(Fin.)* Fuerte (currency); tendencia alcista (of market).

buprestis [ˈbʌprestɪs] [ba-pres-tis], *s.* Bupresto, insecto coleóptero, notable por la riqueza de sus colores. En estado de larva es muy perjudicial a los árboles.

bur [bɜːʳ] [baʳ], *s.* 1. Cadillo o cabeza áspera de alguna planta, como la de la cardencha. 2. Envoltura de algunos frutos. V. BURR.

bur, *va.* 1. Desmontar, quitar los cadillos a la lana. 2. Disponer una cavidad con el buril del dentista.

burble [ˈbɜːbl] [ber-bol] *vn.* Borbotar, borbotear (stream, spring); parlotear, cotorrear (talk meaningless); hablar atropelladamente (talk excitedly).

burbot [ˈbɜːbət] [ber-bot], *s.* *(Ict.)* Mustela de río o agua dulce.

burdelais [ˈbɜːdəlɪs] [ber-de-les], *s.* Uva de parra gruesa, morada o blanca, que vulgarmente llaman de San Diego.

burden [ˈbɜːdn] [ber-den], *s.* 1. Carga, el peso que lleva sobre sí el hombre o la bestia (load). 2. Carga, cuidados y aflicciones del ánimo (encumbrance). **Life is a burden to him,** está cansado de vivir. 3. Carga o cargazón de buque. 4. Estrambote, estribillo, verso o copla que se repite al fin de alguna canción o estancia. **Beast of burden,** acémila, bestia de carga. **To be a burden on,** ser una carga para. **The burden of responsibility,** el peso de la responsabilidad.

burden, *va.* Cargar, agobiar, embarazar, oprimir. **To burden somebody with something,** cargarle a alguien con algo (with work). **I don't want to burden you with my problems,** no te quiero preocupar con mis problemas.

burdener [ˈbɜːdənəʳ] [ber-de-naʳ], *s.* Cargador, el que carga; opresor, el que oprime.

burdensome [ˈbɜːdnsʌm] [ber-den-som], *a.* Gravoso, pesado, molesto, incómodo. Oneroso.

burdensomeness [ˈbɜːdnsʌmnɪs] [ber-den-som-nes], *s.* Molestia, pesadez.

burdock [ˈbɜːdɒk] [ber-dok], *s.* *(Bot.)* Badana.

bureau [bjʊəˈrəʊ] [biua-rou], *s.* 1. Armario con cajones, cómoda (chest of drawers); escritorio, buró (desk), bufete, papelera, escaparate. 2. Escritorio, oficina, despacho. **The Weather Bureau,** el departamento de Señales Meteorológicas en el Ministerio de Agricultura, (Estados Unidos de N.A.) 3. Agencia (agency); departamento (government department). **Bureau de change,** (casa de) cambio.

bureaucracy [bjʊəˈrɒkrəsɪ] [biua-rou-kra-si], *s.* Sistema de gobierno por medio de oficinas departamentales, cada una de ellas bajo el jefe respectivo. Burocracia.

bureaucratic [ˌbjʊərəʊˈkrætɪk] [biua-rou-kra-tik], *a.* Perteneciente o relativo a las oficinas públicas, a los empleados en general, y al sistema en que predomina esa clase de gobierno. Burocrático.

burette [bjʊˈrɪt] [biu-rit], *s.* *(Fr.)* Bureta, probeta para dividir los líquidos en partes decimales.

burg [bɜːg] [berg], *s.* Villa, aldea. V. BOROUGH.

burgage [ˈbɜːgeɪdʒ] [ber-gueich], *s.* Una clase de arriendo de tierras.

burgamot [ˈbɜːgəmɒt] [ber-ga-mot], *s.* V. BERGAMOT.

burganet [ˈbɜːgənɪt] [ber-ga-net], o **burgonet,** *s.* Borgoñota, armadura antigua de la cabeza.

burgeon [ˈbɜːdʒən] [ber-yon] *vn.* Florecer (grow, flourish).

burgeoning [ˈbɜːdʒənɪŋ] [ber-yo-nin], creciente (demand); pujante, floreciente (market).

burger [ˈbɜːgəʳ] [ber-gaʳ] *s.* *(Coloq,)* Hamburguesa.

burgess [ˈbɜːdʒɪs] [ber-guis], *s.* 1. Ciudadano, el que goza ciertos privilegios en alguna ciudad. 2. El diputado de la cámara de los comunes que representa uno de los pueblos que gozan del derecho de enviar diputados al Parlamento.

burgess-ship [ˈbɜːdʒɪsʃɪp] [ber-guis-ship], *s.* Oficio y calidad de diputado de villa o ciudad con derecho de representación.

burgh [ˈbʌrə] [bara], *s.* V. BOROUGH.

burgher [ˈbɜːgəʳ] [ber- gaʳ], *s.* Ciudadano, vecino.

burghership [ˈbɜːgəʃɪp] [ber-guar-ship], *s.* Ciudadanía, privilegio de ciudadanía.

burglar [ˈbɜːgləʳ] [ber-glaʳ], *s.* Ladrón, ratero, salteador. **Burglar alarm,** alarma contra ladrones.

burglarious [ˈbɜːglərɪəs] [ber-gla-rious], *s.* Lo que pertenece al robo de casas por la noche: del robo en poblado.

burglarize [ˈbɜːgləraɪz] [ber-gla-rais] *va.* Robar.

burglary [ˈbɜːglərɪ] [ber-gla-ri], *s.* Robo, acción de robar. **Burglary insurance,** seguro contra robos.

burgle [ˈbɜːgl] [ber-guel] *va.* Robar. **Our house was/we were burgled,** nos entraron ladrones en casa, nos entraron a robar.

burgomaster [ˈbɜːɡɒmɑːstər] [ber-go-mas-taʳ], *s.* Burgomaestre, el primer magistrado alguna ciudad, particularmente en los Países Bajos.

Burgundy [ˈbɜːɡəndɪ] [ber-gan-di], *s.* Borgoña, antiguo ducado francés. **Burgundy wine,** vino de Borgoña. **Burgundy helmet,** celada borgoñona. **Burgundy pitch,** pez de Borgoña.

burial [ˈberɪəl] [berial], *s.* 1. Entierro, el acto de enterrar y dar sepultura a los cuerpos difuntos. 2. Enterramiento, la acción de poner alguna cosa debajo de la tierra. 3. Oficio de difuntos, exequias, las honras funerales que se hacen a los difuntos. **Burial rites,** ritos funerarios.

burial-ground [ˈberɪəlɡraʊnd] [berial-graund], o **burial-place** [ˈberɪəlpleɪs] [berial-pleis], *s.* Cementerio.

burier [ˈberɪəʳ] [beriaʳ], *s.* Enterrador, sepulturero.

burin [ˈbɜːrɪn] [berin], *s.* Buril, instrumento para grabar.

burl [ˈbɜːl] [berl], *va.* Batanar, golpear paños o telas en el batán; desnudar o quitar los nudos en el paño.

burlap [ˈbɜːlæp] [ber-lap], o **burlaps,** *s.* Especie de aspillera; tela basta de cáñamo, jute o lino.

burler [ˈbɜːləʳ] [ber-laʳ], *s.* El que quita los nudos en el paño.

burlesque [bɜːˈlesk] [ber-lesk], *s. y a.* Lengua burlesca; burlesco, lo que mueve a risa. Obra burlesca.

burlesquer [bɜːˈleskəʳ] [ber-les-kaʳ], *s.* Burlador.

burletta [bɜːˈliːtə] [ber-li-ta], *s.* Entremés con música. (*Ital.*)

burliness [ˈbɜːlɪnɪs] [ber-li-nes], *s.* 1. Tosquedad. 2. Volumen.

burly [ˈbɜːlɪ] [ber-li], *a.* Voluminoso, túmido: jactancioso; turbulento; nudoso, repleto; gordo. Fornido, corpulento.

Burmese [bɜːˈmiːz] [ber-mís] *a.* Birmano. *s.* Birmano (person/language).

burn [bɜːn] [bern], *va. (pret. y pp.* BURNED o BURNT). 1. Quemar, abrasar o consumir con fuego (letter, rubbish). 2. Quemar, herir con fuego; incendiar (building, town). **I burned a hole in my sleeve,** me quemé la manga (con un cigarrillo). **To burn one's boats/bridges,** quemar las naves. **I've burned the cake,** se me ha quemado el pastel (overcook). -*vn.* 1. Quemarse, arder (fire, flame, building) (wood, coal). Quemarse (food/skin in sun). **Something is burning!,** ¡se está quemando algo! **I can smell burning,** huele o hay olor a quemado. 2. Estar enardecido por una pasión; secarse, consumirse. **She was burning with curiosity,** ardía de curiosidad. **She burned for revenge,** deseaba ardientemente vengarse. 3. Reducirse a cenizas. **To burn to ashes,** reducir a cenizas.

burn away, consumir una cosa quemándola.

burn down, incendiar, incendiarse.

burn off, quitar con llama (paint/varnish); quemar (gas, calories).

burn out, apagarse (fire, candle); quemarse (motor). **He's burnt himself out,** está acabado o quemado.

burn up, consumir (consume/fuel); quemar (calories). (*Coloq.,*) Enfermar, poner enfermo (annoy, anger). Desintegrarse (meteorite/rocket).

burn with, abrasarse de o en. **He burnt his fingers there,** no le tuvo cuenta allí; se llevó chasco. **To burn to do a thing,** arder en deseo de hacer una cosa. **To burn oneself,** quemarse (injure). **I've burned my tongue,** me he quemado la lengua. **To be burned to death,** morir abrasado. Estafar, timar (swindle).

burn, *s.* 1. Quemadura, la llaga o herida que hace el fuego o una cosa muy caliente (on skin, surface). 2. (Esco. é Ingl. del Norte) Arroyo, riachuelo. 3. Un incendio y sus consecuencias.

burnable [ˈbɜːnəbl] [ber-na-bol], *a.* Combustible.

burner [ˈbɜːnəʳ] [ber-naʳ], *s.* 1. Quemador, el que quema alguna cosa. 2. Quemador de lámpara piquera, mechero. **Bat's wing o butterfly burner,** quemador de abanico.

burnet [ˈbɜːnɪt] [ber-net], *s. (Bot.)* Sanguisorba; pimpinela.

burning [ˈbɜːnɪŋ] [ber-nin], *s.* 1. Ardor, inflamación. 2. Quemadura, abrasamiento, quema, incendio. **Burning-glass,** espejo o vidrio ustorio. -*a.* Abrasador (sun), ardiente (sand), vehemente; ardiente (intense/desire); violento (hatred); candente (urgent/issue, question). **It is a burning shame,** es una gran vergüenza. **It's burning hot,** está muy caliente, está ardiendo. **The burning hot sand,** la arena caliente.

burnish [ˈbɜːnɪʃ] [ber-nish], *va.* Bruñir, pulir o dar lustre a alguna cosa; gratar; satinar. -*vn.* 1. Tomar lustre. 2. Crecer, aumentarse.

burnisher [ˈbɜːnɪʃəʳ] [ber-ni-shaʳ], *s.* 1. Bruñidor, pulidor, el que bruñe. 2. Bruñidor, instrumento para bruñir; acicalador; satinador.

burnoose, burnous [ˈbɜːnuːz] [ber-nús], *s.* Albornoz, o capote de los árabes.

burnout [ˈbɜːnaʊt] [bern-aut] *s. (Coloq.)* Agotamiento, surmenage.

burnt [bɜːnt] [bernt], *pp.* del verbo TO BURN. *a.* 1. Quemado (food, toast), abrasado; a quemado (smell, taste). 2. Consumido, reducido a cenizas. 3. Cocido. **A burnt child dreads the fire,** gato escaldado del agua fría huye.

burn-out [ˈbɜːnaʊt] [bern-aut] *a.* Calcinado.

burp [bɜːp] [berp] *s.* Eructo.

burp, *vn.* Eructar, soltar un eructo.

burr [bɜːʳ] [baʳ], *s.* 1. El filo delgado, o lomo, dejado por una herramienta al cortar o modelar el metal. 2. El capullo o cáscara de algunos frutos, como de la castaña; cadillo de la cardencha. 3. *(Dent.)* Buril. 4. *(Carp.)* Rondana de perno, virola. 5. Lóbulo o pulpejo de la oreja. 6. Raíz de las astas de un ciervo.

burr, *va. y vn.* Pronunciar o hablar con deje gutural, dejando oír el sonido de la erre. -*s.* 1. Articulación bronca gutural, como en un dialecto; en particular, el sonido gutural de la erre común en el Norte de Inglaterra. 2. Zumbido, zumbo.

burrel [ˈbɜːrəl] [berel], *s.* 1. Manteca de oro, especie de pera. (<su corol, buriel.) 2. **Burrel fly,** mosca de burro, especie de mosca muy molesta a los animales; el tábano del ganado: Hypoderma bovis. 3. **Burrel shot,** especie de metralla.

burrow [ˈbʌrəʊ] [ba-rou], *s.* 1. Madriguera, conejera (of rabbits). 2. Montón de tierra. 3. *(Des.)* V. BOROUGH.

burrow, *vn.* Minar como los conejos; esconderse en la madriguera. Cavar (in sand, soil); hurgar, escarbar (in handbag, drawer).

burrowing-owl [ˈbʌrəwɪŋɔːl] [ba-rowuin-oul], *s.* Búho peculiar de América.

burr-stone [ˈbʌrstəʊn] [bar-stoun], *s.* Roca silícea de la cual se obtienen las mejores piedras de molino.

bursa [ˈbʌrsə] [bar-sa], *s.* Bolsillo, bolsa o saco; particularmente un hueco sinovial situado entre los tendones y eminencias huesosas.

bursar [ˈbʌrsəʳ] [bar-saʳ], *s.* 1. Tesorero de un colegio; administrador. 2. Colegial de beca en los colegios de Escocia.

bursarship [ˈbʌrsəʃɪp] [bar-sar-ship], *s.* 1. Tesorería de una institución pública o una orden religosa. 2. Fondo para mantener a los estudiantes necesitados.

burse [ˈbʌrs] [bers], *s.* 1. Bolsa, divisa oficial del Lord Canciller de Inglaterra. 2. Cubierta, para cáliz, etc. 3. Fondo para mantener a los estudiantes necesitados.

burst [bɜːst] [berst], *vn. (Pret. y pp.* BURST). Reventar, estallar, abrirse alguna cosa por el impulso de otra interior (pipe); rebosar; echarse con violencia; principiar repentinamente; prorrumpir. Reventarse (balloon, tire); romperse (dam). **To burst open,** abrirse de golpe. **They burst into the room,** entraron de sopetón en la habitación. -*va.* Romper, quebrar alguna cosa, haciéndola reventar o saltar de repente. Reventar (balloon, bubble).

burst in, entrar de sopetón. **Don't come bursting in like that!,** ¡no se entra así de sopetón, sin llamar! **They burst in on the meeting,** irrumpieron en la reunión.

burst into. To burst into tears, deshacerse en lágrimas, prorrumpir en llanto. **To burst into flames,** estallar en llamas.

burst out, reventar, prorrumpir; brotar. **You're lying!, she burst out suddenly,** ¡estás mintiendo!, saltó de repente (cry). **He burst out laughing,** se echó a reír (start). Salir (exit).

burst, s. 1. Reventón, estallido, el acto de reventar o abrirse alguna cosa; rebosadura. 2. Esfuerzo repentino, carrera precipitada. Salva (of applause) (short surge). Arrebato, arranque (of activity). **A burst of energy,** un arranque de energía. **There was a burst of laughter from the table in the corner,** se oyeron carcajadas en la mesa del rincón. Ráfaga (of gunfire). Rotura (of pipe).

bursting [ˈbɜːstɪŋ] [bers-tin] a. **To be bursting with something,** estar repleto de algo (overflowing). **He was bursting with energy,** rebosaba energía. *(Coloq,)* **I'm bursting,** estoy que reviento (have eaten too much). **To be bursting to,** morirse por (anxious, impatient).

bursting (point), s. **To be filled/full to bursting (point) with something,** estar (lleno) hasta los topes o hasta el tope de algo.

burstwort [ˈbɜːstwɔːt] [berst-uort], s. Herniaria, planta que se usaba para curar las hernias.

burthen [ˈbɜːðən] [berzen], s. V. BURDEN.

burton [ˈbɜːtn] [berton], s. *(Mar.)* Aparejo o palanquín de polea y gancho. (GB) *(Coloq,)* **To go for a burton,** irse al traste o al diablo o al cuerno (plan).

bury [ˈberɪ] [be-ri], va. 1. Enterrar, sepultar, dar sepultura a los cuerpos de los difuntos. **To bury somebody at sea,** dar sepultura a alguien en el mar. 2. Sepultar, esconder, ocultar. **The village was buried by the avalanche,** el pueblo fue sepultado por la avalancha. **To bury the hatchet,** poner a un lado las armas de la guerra, y hacer la paz. Débese esta frase a una costumbre de los indios norteamericanos. **She buried the knife in his chest.** le enterró, hundió o clavó el cuchillo en el pecho (plunge, thrust). **He buried his head in his hands,** ocultó la cabeza entre las manos. **To bury oneself in something,** enfrascarse en algo (immerse oneself in one's work/books, etc.).

burying [ˈberɪŋ] [be-rin], s. Entierro; exequias.

burying-ground o **burying-place** [ˈberɪŋˌgraʊnd] [be-rin-graund], s. Cementerio, campo santo.

bus [bʌs] [bas]. s. Autobús, ómnibus, bus, camión, colectivo, micro, guagua. **To look like/have a face like the back (end) of a bus,** ser feo con ganas. **Bus conductor,** cobrador, guarda de autobuses. **Bus driver,** conductor, chófer de autobús, camionero, colectivero, microbusero. **Bus stop,** parada, paradero de autobús (bus, etc.). Autobús, autocar, pullman (long distance).

bus, va. Transportar en autobús (o bus, etc.). Transportar a colegios fuera de su zona para favorecer la integración racial (schoolchildren).

busboy [ˈbʌsbɔɪ] [bas-boi] s. Ayudante de camarero.

bush [bʊʃ] [bash], s. 1. Arbusto, mata; espinal, breña; matorral, zarza. **To beat about the bush,** andarse con rodeos. **Stop beating about the bush!,** ¡déjate de rodeos! 2. Ramo, señal que se pone a las puertas de las tabernas. 3. Cola de zorra. 4. Guedeja. **Bushes,** matorrales, maleza. **To beat the bushes for something,** buscar algo por todas partes.

bush, a. Poco profesional.

bush, vn. Crecer espeso o contiguo. -va. 1. Aforrar con otro material, como se hace con la cámara del cañón, el cojinete del eje, etc. 2. Apoyar, sostener con matas. 3. Gradar o igualar el terreno arrastrando matas sobre él. 4. Labrar (piedra) a escuadra con un martillo de canto de acero.

bushbaby [ˈbʊʃˌbeɪbɪ] [bush-beibi] s. Gálago.

bushed [bʊʃt] [busht] a. *(Coloq,)* Hecho polvo, agotado.

bushel [ˈbʊʃl] [bushl], s. Fanega, medida de granos y otras semillas. *El bushel* imperial inglés equivale a 36,35 litros; el americano a 35 litros.

bushelage [ˈbʊʃledʒ] [bush-lech], s. Derecho que se paga por fanega.

bushiness [ˈbʊʃɪnɪs] [bu-shi-nes], s. 1. Espesor formado por los arbustos. 2. Estado de lo lanudo o peludo.

bushing [ˈbʊʃɪŋ] [bu-shin], s. Encaje de una pieza de metal dentro de otra; boquilla, anillo de guía.

bush league [ˈbʊʃliːg] [bush-líg] s. **Liga menor.**

bushy [ˈbʊʃɪ] [bushi], a. 1. Espeso, cerrado como el monte o arboleda cuyos arbustos o ramos están muy juntos y unidos; lleno de arbustos. 2. Lanudo; peludo. Poblado, espeso (beard); tupido, poblado (eyebrows); espeso (undergrowth).

busily [ˈbɪzɪlɪ] [bi-si-li], adv. Solícitamente, diligentemente; apresuradamente. **They were all working busily,** todos trabajaban afanosamente. **She was busily writing her journal,** estaba muy ocupada escribiendo en su diario.

business [ˈbɪznɪs] [bis-nes], s. Empleo, oficio; asunto (affair, situation, activity); **What's all this business about you leaving?,** ¿qué es eso de que te vas? **To give somebody the business,** echarle la bronca a alguien (reprimand); tomarle el pelo a alguien (tease). Negocio, empresa (firm); ocupación. **I'm in the insurance/antique business,** trabajo en el ramo de los seguros/en la compra y venta de antigüedades (branch of commerce). **She's the best designer in the business,** es la mejor diseñadora del ramo. **It's been a pleasure to do business with you,** ha sido un placer trabajar con usted (transactions). **She's away on business,** está fuera por negocios. **To mix business with pleasure,** mezclar el trabajo con la diversión. **Business before pleasure,** antes es la obligación que la devoción, primero el deber (y después el placer). **To get down to business,** ir al grano, entrar en materia. **To mean business,** decir algo muy en serio. **To talk business,** hablar de negocios. Negocios (world of commerce, finance). **Business studies,** (ciencias) empresariales. **Business school,** escuela de administración o gestión de empresas. **A course in business German,** un curso de alemán comercial. Comercio (commercial activity, trading). **The firm has been in business for 50 years,** la empresa tiene 50 años de actividad comercial. **To set up in business,** montar o poner un negocio. **They went into business together,** montaron o pusieron un negocio juntos. **To go out of business,** cerrar. **Business is good,** el negocio anda o marcha bien. **We open for business at nine o'clock,** abrimos al público a las nueve. **To lose business,** perder clientes o clientela (clients, custom). **What is your business here?,** ¿qué le trae a Ud. acá? **To do the business for,** liquidar (una cuenta) completamente; acabar; de aquí, matar o arruinar a alguno. Asunto, incumbencia (rightful occupation, concern). **It is not my business,** eso no me atañe; nada tengo que ver con eso. **Mind your own business!,** ¡no te metas en lo que no te importa! **I shall make it my business to find out,** yo me ocuparé o me encargaré de averiguarlo. *(Coloq,)* **She was getting through those chocolates like nobody's business,** les estaba dando duro a los bombones. **He was dashing around like nobody's business,** estaba corriendo como un loco de aquí para allá. **To attend to business,** aplicarse a los negocios. **To carry on business,** comerciar. **To do business,** hacer negocios. **To give up business,** retirarse del comercio. **Beginning business,** establecerse. **In business,** estar establecido. **Line of business,** ramo de negocios. De trabajo, de negocios (appointment, lunch). **Business letter,** carta comercial. **Business trip,** viaje de negocios. Asuntos, temas (items of agenda). **Any other business,** otros asuntos, ruegos y preguntas.

business-class, adv. En clase preferente o business-class.

businesslike, a. Formal, serio (serious/ person, manner); eficiente (efficient); serio (discussion).

businessman [ˈbɪznɪsmæn] [bis-nes-man], s. Hombre de negocios, negociante, comerciante, empresario.

businesswoman [ˈbɪznɪsˌwʊmən] [bis-nes-uo-man], s. Mujer de negocios, empresaria.

busk [bʌsk] [bask], s. 1. Palo de cotilla. 2. Ballena de corsé.

busk, vn. (GB) *(Coloq,)* Cantar o tocar un instrumento en la calle o en estaciones del transporte público.

busker [ˈbʌskəʳ] [bas-kaʳ], s. (GB) Músico callejero.

buskin ['bʌskɪn] [bas-kin], *s.* Borceguí, especie de calzado; botín que llega a la mitad de la pierna; coturno.

buskined ['bʌskɪnd] [bas-kind], *a.* Calzado con borceguíes.

busload ['bʌsləʊd] [bas-loud] *s.* **A busload of schoolchildren,** un autobús (lleno) de escolares. **Tourists were arriving by the busload/in busloads,** iban llegando autocares (o autobuses, etc.) llenos de turistas.

buss [bʌs] [bas], *s.* 1. Beso, el acto o efecto de besarse. 2. (*Mar.*) Bucha pescadora.

buss, *va.* (Ant. o Prov.) Besar.

bust [bʌst] [bast], *s.* 1. Busto, estatua que representa medio cuerpo humano hasta el pecho (sculpture). 2. El pecho, particularmente el de mujer (bosom). 3. Caída, descalabro (collapse).

bust, *a.* (*Coloq,*) **To go bust,** quebrar, irse a la bancarrota, fundirse (bankrupt). **It's a gold medal or bust,** o la medalla de oro o nada (games). (GB) Roto, estropeado.

bust, *va.* (*Coloq,*) Romper (break). (*Sl.*) Agarrar, trincar (raid/ person); hacer una redada en (premises). (*Coloq,*) Dejar sin un centavo, o sin blanca, o sin un quinto (bankrupt). Darle un puñetazo a (punch). (*Sl.*) **Bust down,** degradar (demote). *vn.* Romperse, estropearse, sonar (object, machine).

bustard ['bʌstəd] [bas-tad], *s.* Avutarda, especie de pavo silvestre.

busted ['bʌstɪd] [bas-tid] *a.* Roto, estropeado.

buster ['bʌstəʳ] [bas-taʳ] *s.* (*Coloq,*) Fulano, macho, güey, che (as form of address).

bustle ['bʌsl] [ba-sel], *vn.* Bullir, menearse con extrema viveza; no parar; hacer ruido o estruendo; entremeterse. **I could hear the bustling along the corridor,** le oía ir y venir afanosamente por el corredor. **To bustle around,** ir de aquí para allá, trajinar. **To bustle with something,** bullir de algo (be crowded, lively/ street, store).

bustle, *s.* 1. Bullicio, ruido, alboroto, ajetreo (activity). 2. Polisón, miriñaque (clothing, Hist.).

bustler ['bʌsləʳ] [bas-laʳ], *s.* Bullebulle, hombre inquieto y excesivamente vivo.

bustling ['bʌslɪŋ] [bast-lin] *a.* Animado, de mucho movimiento (street, shop).

busto, *s. V.* BUST.

bust-up ['bʌsʌp] [bast-ap] *s.* Ruptura (breakup). (GB) (*Coloq.*) Pelea, bronca (quarrel).

busty ['bʌstɪ] [bas-ti] *a.* (*Coloq.*) Pechugona.

busy ['bɪzɪ] [bi-si], *a.* 1. Ocupado, aplicado o empleado en alguna cosa (person/ occupied). **The children keep me very busy,** los niños me tienen muy atareada, o me dan mucho que hacer. **To get busy,** ponerse a trabajar. **I was busy writing a letter,** estaba ocupada escribiendo una carta. 2. Bullicioso, entremetido. Concurrido, de mucho movimiento (street, market). **I've had a busy day,** he tenido un día de mucho trabajo. **I've a busy schedule,** tengo un programa muy apretado. **A busy road,** una carretera con mucho tráfico o muy transitada. 3. (*Telec.*) Ocupado, comunicando.

busy, *v. refl.* **To busy oneself,** ponerse a. **To busy oneself with something,** entretenerse con algo.

busybody ['bɪzɪbɒdɪ] [bi-si-bo-di], *s.* Entremetido, el que se mete en todo sin ser llamado; metomentodo, metiche. **Busybody signal,** tono o señal de ocupado, señal de comunicando.

busybrain ['bɪzɪbreɪn] [bi-si-brein], *s.* Ingenio inventivo; proyectista.

but [bʌt] [bat], *conj.* 1. Excepto, menos. 2. Pero (however), mas, sin embargo, no obstante. **She was fired, but they were not,** la despidieron a ella, pero no a ellos. (*Coloq,*) **You're really bugging me but good!,** ¡qué manera de darme la lata! **But what made you say it?,** ¿pero por qué lo dijiste? (used for introductory emphasis) **Surely he doesn't believe that?-oh, but he does!,** no puede ser que se crea eso- pues sí que se lo cree. Pero (however, still). **But then** (as linker); pero entonces (in that case). **But then you never were very ambitious, were you?,** pero la verdad es que tú nunca fuiste muy ambicioso ¿no? **I don't want to,**

but then again I do, no quiero, pero a la vez o al mismo tiempo sí quiero. 3. Solamente, no más que, que no. **I cannot but go,** no puedo dejar de ir. **He is but just gone,** no ha hecho más que salir. **But for,** si no fuera por, a no ser por. **It is but a poor shift,** es un pobre efugio. **But little,** muy poco. **But few,** muy pocos. **But yet,** sin embargo. **The last but one,** el penúltimo. **But a while since,** hace poco. **But just now,** inmediatamente. 4. (*Lóg.*) Es así que. **Not... but...,** no... sino...; **It appears that she's not Greek but Albanian,** parece que no es griega, sino albanesa. **Not only did she hit him, but she also...,** no sólo le pegó, sino que también... -*prep.* Sin, excepto (except). **Everyone but me,** todos menos yo o excepto yo o salvo yo. **The last street but one,** la penúltima calle. **The next street but one,** la próxima calle no, la siguiente. **I had no alternative but to go,** no me quedó otra alternativa que irme. **There's nothing we can do but wait,** no podemos hacer otra cosa sino esperar, lo único que podemos hacer es esperar. **But for them, we'd have lost everything,** de no haber sido o si no hubiera sido por ellos, habríamos perdido todo. -*adv.* Solamente. **We can but try,** con intentarlo no se pierde nada. **He's but a child,** no es más que un niño. **One can't help but admire her audacity,** uno no puede (por) menos que admirar su audacia. -*inter.* Exclamación de sorpresa o admiración. *s.* **No buts: come here at once!,** no hay pero que valga, ¡ven aquí inmediatamente!

butane ['bjuːteɪn] [biu-tein] *s.* Butano.

butch [bʊtʃ] [buch] *a.* (*Coloq.*) Machote (man); hombruna, machota (woman).

butcher ['bʊtʃəʳ] [bu-chaʳ], *s.* 1. Carnicero, el que mata animales y vende su carne (meat dealer). 2. Carnicero, el hombre cruel, sanguinario o inhumano. Asesino (murderer). **Butcher's (shop),** carnicería.

butcher, *va.* Matar atrozmente, hacer una carnicería, hacer pedazos, dar muerte cruel. Matar, carnear (cattle, pig). Masacrar (people).

butcher-bird ['bʊtʃəbɜːd] [bu-char-berd], *s.* Pegareborda, alcaudón, especie de marica. Se llama así por su costumbre de impalar su presa, avecillas, insectos, etc., en espinas, para devorarla más fácilmente.

buchtering ['bʊtʃərɪŋ] [bu-che-rin], *s.* El acto de matar de un modo cruel; carnicería, matanza. -*a.* Cruel, inhumano.

butcherly ['bʊtʃəlɪ] [bu-cher-li], *a.* Sanguinario, bárbaro, cruel.

butchery ['bʊtʃərɪ] [bu-che-ri], *s.* 1. El trato y oficio de carnicero. 2. Carnicería o destrozo, mortandad de gente; degüello. 3. Matadero, el paraje en donde se matan las reses.

butler ['bʌtləʳ] [batlaʳ], *s.* 1. Mayordomo que sirve a la mesa. 2. Despensero, el que provee la mesa de vinos y los tiene a su cargo. **Butler's pantry,** despensa situada entre el comedor y la cocina.

butlerage ['bʌtləreɪdʒ] [batler-eich], *s.* 1. Departamento del despensero. 2. (*Ingl.*) Antiguamente, derecho sobre vinos.

butlership ['bʌtləʃɪp] [batlar-ship], *s.* Oficio de despensero; sumillería.

butlery ['bʌtlərɪ] [ba-tle-ri], *s.* Despensa.

butment ['bʌtmənt] [bat-ment], *s.* Estribo de un arco.

butt [bʌt] [bat], *s.* 1. Terreno, el objeto o blanco que se pone para tirar a él. 2. Blanco, hito, el fin u objeto a que se dirigen las acciones de alguno. 3. Hazmerreír, el que es objeto de la irrisión de otros (target of jokes or criticism). 4. Bota, pipa. 5. Culata (rifle). 6. Topetazo (from goat). (*Coloq,*) Trasero, culo, traste, poto. **To get off one's butt,** ponerse a trabajar. **Butt-leather,** cuero de buey. **Butt-end,** cabo o mango de alguna cosa; término más pesado de alguna cosa. Regatón, contera. **Cigar-butt,** punta de cigarro.

butt, *va.* Topar o topetar, dar con la cabeza en alguna cosa; darle un topetazo a (goat). **Butt in,** interrumpir, meter la cuchara.

butt-ends ['bʌtendz] [bat-ends], **butts** [bötz] [bats], *s. pl.* Pie de árbol, la unión de dos extremos de los tablones.

butte [ˈbʌtɪ] [bati], s. Colina o altura, aislada por lo general, que se destaca conspicuamente a manera de torre natural.

butter [ˈbʌtəʳ] [ba-taʳ], s. 1. Manteca; (Amer.) mantequilla. 2. (Quím.) Manteca, nombre que se daba antiguamente a varias preparaciones por su consistencia semejante a la de la manteca, como manteca de antimonio, arsénico, estaño, etc. **Fresh o salt butter,** manteca fresca o salada. **Draw butter,** manteca derretida. **Butter-boat,** bote o vasija para mantequilla derretida en la mesa. **Apple butter,** mermelada o dulce de manzana. **Butter wouldn't melt in his/her mouth,** es una mosquita muerta.

butter, va. 1. Untar con manteca o mantequilla, ponerle mantequilla a (bread). **Buttered toast,** tostadas con mantequilla. 2. Doblar las puestas, en el juego. **His bread is buttered on both sides,** él come a dos carrillos, o tiene un empleo que le da dobles emolumentos. **He knows on which side his bread is buttered,** él sabe por dónde va el agua al molino. **His bread is well buttered,** tiene el riñón bien cubierto, está rico. (Coloq.) **Butter up,** darle jabón a, hacerle la barba a, hacerle la pata a.

butter bean [ˈbʌtəˌbiːn] [bater-bín] s. Tipo de frijol blanco, poroto de manteca. Tipo de frijol fresco con vaina amarilla (wax bean).

butterbur [ˈbʌtəbɜːʳ] [bater-baʳ], s. (Bot.) Fárfara o uña de caballo.

buttercup [ˈbʌtəkʌp] [bater-kap], s. Ranúnculo, botón de oro.

butter dish [ˈbʌtədɪʃ] [bater-dish], s. Mantequillera.

butterfat [ˈbʌtəfɑːt] [bater-fat], s. 1. Nata de la leche. 2. Grasa de la mantequilla.

butterfingers [ˈbʌtəˌfɪŋgədz] [bater-fin-guers] s. (Coloq.) Torpe, patoso.

butterfly [ˈbʌtəflaɪ] [ba-taʳ-flai], s. (Zool.) Mariposa, nombre general de los lepidópteros diurnos. Estilo de mariposa (swimming stroke). **Butterflies,** nervios (nervous feeling). **To get/have butterflies in one's stomach,** ponerse/estar nervioso.

butterin(e) [ˈbʌtəriːn] [ba-te-rin], s. Manteca artificial. V. OLEOMARGARINE.

buttermilk [ˈbʌtəmɪlk] [ba-taʳ-milk], s. Suero de manteca. Suero de la leche.

buttermold [ˈbʌtəməʊld] [ba-taʳ-mould], **butter-print** [ˈbʌtəprɪnt] [bater-prInt], s. Molde para manteca, pieza de madera en que se vacía la figura de lo que se quiere estampar en las mantequillas.

butternut [ˈbʌtənʌt] [ba-taʳ-nat], s. Nuez oleaginosa, comestible, del nogal blanco americano; el árbol que la produce.

butterscotch [ˈbʌtəskɒtʃ] [ba-taʳ-skcoch], s. Mezcla de mantequilla y azúcar morena. Caramelo duro hecho con azúcar y mantequilla.

buttertooth [ˈbʌtətuːθ] [ba-taʳ-túz], s. Diente incisivo.

butterwife [ˈbʌtəwaɪf] [ba-taʳ-uaif], **butter-woman,** [ˈbʌtəwʊmən] [ba-taʳ-uo-man], sf. Mantequera, vendedora de manteca.

butterwort [ˈbʌtəwɔːt] [ba-taʳ-uort], s. (Bot.) Sanícula, hierba sin tallo del género Pinguicula. Sus hojas son anchas y gruesas y segregan una substancia oleosa.

buttery [ˈbʌtərɪ] [ba-te-ri], s. Despensa, el lugar o sitio donde se guardan los comestibles.

buttock [ˈbʌtək] [ba-tok], s. 1. Nalga, trasero. 2. (Mar.) Cucharros o llenos de popa, la parte de la embarcación comprendida entre el yugo principal y la línea superior del agua.

button [ˈbʌtn] [baton], s. 1. Botón (clothing), el que se pone al canto de los vestidos para que los afiance y abroche. 2. (Art.) Cascabel, el remate en forma casi esférica que tiene por la parte posterior el cañón de artillería. 3. (Prov. Ingl.) Botón o capullo que echan las plantas o flores. 4. Apéndice parecido a un nudo, como el término de la cola de la serpiente de cascabel, o la extremidad posterior de las orugas de ciertas mariposas. 5. Toda protuberancia parecida a un botón, como el llamador de un timbre eléctrico o el botón de un florete. 6. Botón, pequeño glóbulo o disco de metal que se halla en el crisol después de la fusión. **Button-hook,** abotonador, abrochador. **Button-maker,** botonero. **His answer was right on the button,** dio en el clavo con su respuesta. **She arrived on the button,** llegó en el punto o muy puntual. **To be as bright as a button,** ser muy despierto, ser más listo que el hambre. **Button mushroom,** champiñón pequeño. **Button nose,** nariz chata y pequeña.

button va. Abotonar, abrochar. -vn. Abotonarse, abrocharse. **Button up,** abotonar, abrochar.

button-down [ˈbʌtndaʊn] [baton-daun] a. **Button-down collar,** cuello cuyas puntas se abotonan a la camisa.

buttoned-down [ˈbʌtndˌdaʊn] [batond-daun] a. (Coloq.) Acartonado (staid, conventional).

button-hole [ˈbʌtnhəʊl] [baton-joul], s. Ojal. (GB) Flor que se lleva en el ojal (flower). -va. 1. Hacer o abrir ojales. 2. Asir a uno por la solapa a tiempo que se habla con él; fastidiar. **Button-hole scissors,** tijeras para hacer ojales.

button-wood [ˈbʌtndwuːd] [ba-ton-wud], s. 1. El plátano de América, o de Occidente. 2. Pequeño árbol siempre verde de las Antillas.

buttress [ˈbʌtrɪs] [ba-tres], s. 1. (Arq.) Contrafuerte, estribo, machón, arbotante, pedazo de pared fuerte a manera de pilar, que se pone arrimado a la misma pared o muralla para sostenerla. 2. Apoyo, sostén. **Flying buttress,** arbotante.

buttress, va. Estribar, afianzar con estribo. Reforzar con un contrafuerte (wall). Respaldar, apoyar (support/argument, case).

butty [ˈbʌtɪ] [ba-ti] s. (Coloq.) (GB) Sandwich, bocata.

butyric [ˈbʌtɪrɪk] [ba-ti-rik], a. Perteneciente a la manteca, o derivado de ella.

buxom [ˈbʌksəm] [bak-som], a. 1. Vivo, alegre, jovial, juguetón. **A buxom lass,** moza retozona o juguetona. 2. Rollizo, regordete. 3. (Des.) Obediente, obsequioso, dócil; amoroso. 4. Con mucho pecho o busto.

buxomly [ˈbʌksəmlɪ] [bak-som-li], adv. Vivamente, jovialmente; amorosamente.

buy [baɪ] [bai], va. (pret. y pp. BOUGHT). Comprar, adquirir por dinero el dominio de alguna cosa (purchase). **Money can't buy happiness,** el dinero no hace la felicidad. **To buy somebody something,** comprarle algo a alguien. **Let me buy you a drink,** déjame invitarte a una copa. **I bought myself a hat,** me compré un sombrero. **To buy something from somebody,** comprarle algo a alguien. **I bought the radio from/off a friend,** le compré la radio a un amigo. **To buy something for somebody,** comprar algo para alguien. **To buy upon trust, upon credit,** comprar al fiado. (Coloq.) Tragarse (accept, believe). -vn. Tratar de compra. **Buy in,** comprar para abastecerse (food, supplies). **Buy into,** adquirir participación en, comprar acciones en (company). **Buy off,** sobornar, comprar. **To buy one off,** ganar a alguno con presentes; corromperle, comprarle. **Buy out,** comprarle su parte a (partner, share-holder). **Buy up,** comprarse todas las existencias de.

buy, s. Compra.

buyer [ˈbaɪəʳ] [baiaʳ], s. Comprador, el que compra (customer). Encargado de compras (buying agent).

buz [bʌz] [bas], inter. Exclamación de disgusto al oír alguna cosa ya sabida.

buzz [bʌz] [bas], s. Susurro, soplo; zumbido (of insect); rumor, murmullo (of voices). **There was a buzz of excitement in the hall,** hubo un murmullo de agitación en la sala. Zumbido (as signal). (Coloq.) **To give somebody a buzz,** darle o pegarle o echarle un telefonazo a alguien, darle un toque a alguien (phone call). **I get a buzz out of surfing,** el surf me vuelve loco (thrill).

buzz, vn. 1. Zumbar, hacer un ruido sordo, como las abejas y moscardones. **My ears were buzzing,** me zumbaban los oídos. Sonar (telephone, alarm clock). **The town was buzzing with rumors,** la ciudad era un hervidero de rumores (be animated). **The Boston arts scene is really**

buzzing, hay una actividad febril en el mundo artístico de Boston. 2. Cuchuchear, llevar chismes, o cuchichear, hablar al oído de alguno. *-va. (Aer.)* Bordonear. Llamar por el interfono (call on intercom). *(Coloq,)* Darle o pegarle o echarle un telefonazo a, darle un toque a (call on the phone). *(Coloq,)* **Buzz off,** largarse, picar (usu. in imperative).

buzzard ['bʌzəd] [baserd], *s.* 1. Buaro, especie de milano. 2. Modrego, majadero. **To be betwixt hawk and buzzard,** no ser ni carne ni pescado, nadar entre dos aguas. águila ratonera (hawk); aura, gallinazo, zopilote (vulture).

buzzer ['bʌzəʳ] [ba-saʳ], **s.** *(Elec.)* Zumbador, vibrador. Timbre, chicharra.

buzz saw [bʌzˌsɔ:] [bas-so], *s.* Sierra circular.

buzzword ['bʌzˌwɜːd] [bas-ued] *s.* Palabra de moda.

b/w = black and white.

by [baɪ] [bai], *prep.* 1. Por, preposición que significa el agente, el instrumento, la causa, el modo y el medio por el cual se ejecuta alguna cosa (via, through). **I came in by the back door,** entré por la puerta de atrás. **By land/sea/air,** por tierra/mar/avión. Por (indicating agent, cause) (with passive verbs). **She was brought up by her grandmother,** la crió su abuela, fue criada por su abuela. **She was accompanied by her father,** iba acompañada de su padre. **A play by Shakespeare,** una obra de Shakespeare. **It was written by Pinter,** fue escrita por Pinter. **Made by hand,** hecho a mano (indicating means, method). **To travel by car/train,** viajar en coche/tren. **To pay by credit card,** pagar con tarjeta de crédito. **By moonlight,** a la luz de la luna. **I'll begin by introducing myself,** empezaré por presentarme. **By chance,** por casualidad (owing to, from). **She's Spanish by birth,** es española de nacimiento. **He had two children by his second wife,** tuvo dos hijos con o de su segunda mujer. **By specializing, he has limited his options,** al especializarse, ha restringido sus posibilidades. **By that clock it's almost half past,** según ese reloj son casi y media (according to). **By the look of things,** por lo visto o al parecer. **That's fine by me,** por mí no hay problema. **I swear by Almighty God…,** juro por Dios Todopoderoso (in oaths). **By God you'll be sorry you said that!,** te juro que te vas a arrepentir de haber dicho eso. Por (indicating rate). **We're paid by the hour,** nos pagan por hora(s). **They make them by the thousand,** hacen miles y miles de ellos. **She broke the record by several seconds,** batió el récord en o por varios segundos (indicating extent of difference). **One by one,** uno por uno (indicating gradual progression). **They went in two by two,** entraron de dos en dos. **Little by little,** poco a poco, de poco a poco. *(Mat.)* **Multiply two by three,** multiplica dos por tres. **Divide six by three,** divide seis por o entre tres. **North by northeast,** nornor(d)este (in compass directions). **By oneself,** solo (alone, without assistance). **I need to be by myself,** necesito estar solo o a solas. **They do their homework by themselves,** hacen los deberes solos. 2. A, en algún paraje. **By the river's side,** a la orilla del río. 3. Con, partícula que denota la diferencia de dos cosas cotejadas entre sí. 4. A: de, con, en. **By the laws of Castile,** a ley de Castilla. **By stealth,** a hurtadillas. **By dint of,** a fuerza de. **By all means,** absolutamente, cueste lo que cueste. **By no means,** de ningún modo. **By much,** con mucho. **I always keep some money by me,** siempre llevo algo de dinero encima (to hand). **By this time,** en este tiempo. **He told her to be home by eleven,** le dijo que volviera antes de las once (not later than). **They should be there by now,** ya deberían estar allí. **Will it be ready by 5?,** ¿estará listo para las 5? **By the time he arrived, Ann had left,** cuando llegó, Ann se había ido. 5. Cerca, junto; al lado de, junto a (at the side of, near to). **Come and sit by me,** ven a sentarte a mi lado o junto a mí. **It's right by the door,** está justo al lado de la puerta. **By day/night,** de día/noche (during, at). **Rome by night,** Roma de noche. *a.* **To sit by the fire,** sentarse cerca del fuego. 6. A solas. 7. Por, partícula con que se expresa el juramento. **To swear by God,** jurar por Dios. 8. A la mano. 9. Por, partícula que se usa en los ruegos o súplicas. 10. De. **He is abhorred by**

everybody, es aborrecido de todos. **By this time twelve months,** de aquí a un año. **By day, by night,** de día, de noche. **By proxy,** por poder, por procuración. *-adv.* 1. Cerca. **My house is hard by,** mi casa está aquí cerca. 2. Presente, delante. **By and by,** pronto, luego, de aquí a poco, ahora. **By and by they came to the clearing,** al poco rato llegaron al claro. **It's going to rain by and by,** va a llover dentro de poco. 3. Al lado de. **By reason** o **by reason that,** porque. **By reason of,** a causa de, a fuerza de. **By then,** para entonces, en ese tiempo, o antes de él. **By the way,** (1) en el camino, junto al camino, o cerca de él; (2) de paso; entre paréntesis. **By and large,** por lo general, en general. **By oneself,** solo, aparte. **Set it by itself,** póngalo Vd. a un lado, aparte. **By and large,** por todos conceptos, de todos modos. **Let me by!,** ¡déjenme pasar! **She rushed by without seeing me,** pasó corriendo y no me vió. **They watched the parade march by,** vieron pasar el desfile. **To stand by,** (1) sostener, defender, apoyar; (2) *(Mar.)* mantenerse cerca, estar o quedarse allí; estar listo, pronto o preparado. **I put a little money by each week,** ahorro un poco de dinero cada semana (aside, in reserve). **Call/stop by on your way to work,** pasa por casa de camino al trabajo (to somebody's residence).

by, *s.* Asunto accidental o el que no es el objeto principal de la atención. **By the by,** de paso; entre paréntesis; escríbese también, *by the bye.*

by-blow [baɪˈblɔ:] [bai-blo], *s.* 1. Accidente imprevisto; chiripa. 2. Hijo natural, ilegítimo.

by-book [baɪˈbʊk] [bai-buk], *s.* Libro de memoria.

by-corner [baɪˈkɔ:n@ʳ] [bai-kor-naʳ], *s.* Esquina retirada.

by-design [baɪˈdesɪn] [bai-de-sin], *s.* Designio casual o secreto.

bye [baɪ] [bai] *s.* **He mentioned it by the bye,** lo mencionó de pasada.

bye, *interj. (Coloq,)* ¡adiós!, ¡chao o chau!

bye-bye ['baɪˈbaɪ] [bai-bai] *interj. (Coloq,)* ¡adiós!, ¡chucito!, ¡cháito!

bygone ['baɪgəʊn] [bai-goun], *a.* Pasado, de antaño (age, days). **Let bygones be bygones,** olvidemos lo pasado. (GB) **Bygone law,** ordenanza municipal.

by-lane [baɪˈleɪn] [bai-lein], *s.* Camino retirado y fuera del principal.

by-law ['baɪlɔ:] [bai-lo], *s.* Ley privada o particular; estatutos o reglamentos interiores de un cuerpo o una sociedad.

by-matter [baɪˈmɑːtəʳ] [bai-ma-taʳ], *s.* Alguna cosa accidental.

by-name [baɪˈneɪm] [bai-neim], *s.* Apodo.

by-pass ['baɪpɑːs] [bai-pas], *s.* Desvío, desviación. (GB) Carretera de circunvalación, bypass, libramiento, carretera circunvalar. *(Med.)* Bypass. *-va.* 1. Desviar. 2. Pasar por alto. *-vn* Eludir (circumvent/person, difficulty). *(Transp.)* Circunvalar (road); evitar entrar en (driver).

by-past ['baɪpɑːst] [bai-past], *a.* Pasado.

by-path ['baɪpɑːθ] [bai-paz], *s.* Senda descarriada.

by-play ['baɪpleɪ] [bai-plei], *s.* Aparte escénico, acción o palabras de un actor, suponiendo que no le ven ni le oyen los demás.

by-product ['baɪˌprɒdəkt] [bai-pro-dukt], *s.* Subproducto, derivado, producto accesorio (in manufacture). Consecuencia (consequence). **Coal tar is a by-product in the manufacture of gas,** el alquitrán de hulla es un subproducto de la fabricación de gas.

by-road ['baɪrəʊd] [bai-roud], *s.* Camino apartado o no frecuentado. Carretera secundaria o vecinal.

by-speech [baɪˈspiːtʃ] [bai-spích], *s.* Digresión o arenga pronunciada por incidencia o casualidad.

byssus ['baɪsəs] [bai-sas], *s.* 1. Lienzo fino de Egipto. 2. Cirro de filamentos sedosos secretados por el pie de algunos moluscos, como los mejillones y que les sirve para adherirse a las peñas.

bystander ['baɪstændəʳ] [bai-stan-daʳ], *s.* Mirón, mirador; uno que está presente. **They opened fire, killing innocent**

bystanders, abrieron fuego y mataron a varias personas inocentes o a varios transeúntes.

by-street [baɪˈstriːt] [bai-strít], *s.* Calle desviada.

byte [baɪt] [bait] *s. (Comp.)* Byte, octeto.

by-town [baɪˈtaʊn] [bai-taun], *s.* Pueblo que no está en el camino principal o de posta.

by-turning [baɪˈtɜːnɪŋ] [bai-ter-nin], *s.* Senda obscura; rodeo.

by-view [baɪˈvjuː] [bai-viu], *s.* Fin particular o propio interés.

by-walk [baɪˈwɔːk] [bai-uok], *s.* Paseo oculto, privado o reservado.

byway [ˈbaɪweɪ] [bai-uei], *s.* Camino desviado.

by-wipe [ˈbaɪwaɪp] [bai-uaip], *s.* Sarcasmo de dos sentidos, uno de los cuales es satírico y el otro puede tomarse a buena parte.

byword [ˈbaɪwɜːd] [bai-ued], *s.* 1. Locución, persona, etc., que ha llegado a ser objeto de irrisión o escarnio. 2. Apodo, mote. 3. Dicho trillado. **To be a byword for something,** ser sinónimo de algo. **By-your-leave, -s. Without so much as a by-your-leave,** sin (ni) siquiera pedir permiso.

Byzant, Bizantine [baɪˈzæntaɪn] [bai-sen-tain], *s.* Besante, antigua moneda de oro acuñada en Bizancio (ahora Constantinopla), de un valor aproximado de 360 pesetas.

Byzantian, Byzantine [baɪˈzæntaɪn] [bai-sen-tain], *a.* Bizantino, de Bizancio.

Byzantium [baɪˈzænʒəm] [bai-sen-shom] *N.* Bizancio.

C

c [siː] [si], Tiene tres sonidos; el primero como la *c* castellana cuando precede a las letras *a, o, u, l, r;* v.g. en *cap, come, coo, clap, crop;* El segundo a modo de una *s* pronunciada con dulzura, como en *chap, chess, chin, chop, choose, much.* Las letras *ch* en las voces que se derivan del griego ó del latín, se pronuncian generalmente como *c* ó *k,* ó *que, qui,* como en castellano, v.g. *character, christian, monarchy, archaeology* (cáracter, crístian, mónarqui, arqueóloyi); y en las tomadas del francés se les da el sonido que tienen en esta lengua, como en *chaise, machine* (chéis, mashín).

c, vale ciento en los números romanos. *(Mús.)* Do, nota tónica de la gama natural, sin sostenido ni bemol. *Middle C,* el *do* que se halla en el centro del piano ú órgano entre el soprano y el bajo.

c *(Corresp.)* (= **copy to**): **c H. Palmer,** copia a H. Palmer. **cent(s),** centavo(s) (in US). **circa: c. 800 B.C.,** hacia el 800 aC.

c (= **Celsius** o **centigrade**) C; 20°C, 20°C.

ca = **circa.**

CA, ca = **California**

CAA *s.* (in UK) = **Civil Aviation Authority.**

cab [kæb] [kab], *s.* 1. Cab, medida hebraica. 2. Cabriolé, coche de alquiler de uno ó dos asientos, con pescante y por lo general de un solo caballo. 3. Garita, casilla del maquinista; la parte cubierta de una locomotora. Cabina (driver's compartment). 4. Taxímetro. Taxi. **To call a cab,** llamar a un taxi. **Cab driver,** taxista.

CAB *s.* = **Civil Aeronautics Board** (in US). **Citizens' Advice Bureau** (in UK).

cabal [kəˈbæl] [ka-bal], *s.* 1. Cábala, la ciencia secreta de los rabinos. 2. Cábala, junta o sociedad de personas unidas para alguna conjuración o intriga. Conciliábulo (group); conspiración (plot). 3. Maquinación, trama, partido, manejo.

cabal, *vn.* Maquinar, tramar, enredar a uno ó muchos, formar alguna conjuración o partido.

cabala [ˈkæbələ] [ka-ba-la], *s.* Cábala de los judíos.

cabalism [ˈkæbəlɪzm] [ka-ba-lisem], *s.* Cabalismo, ciencia de la cábala.

cabalist [ˈkæbəlist] [ka-ba-list], *s.* Cabalista, el que está versado en las tradiciones judaicas.

cabalistic, cabalistical [ˈkæbəlistik] [ka-ba-lis-tik], *a.* Cabalístico, oculto, secreto. **cabalistically** [kəbæˈlistikəli] [ka-ba-lis-ti-ka-li], *adv.* Cabalísticamente.

caballer [ˈkəbælər] [ka-ba-laʳ], *s.* Pandillero, maquinador, sedicioso, pandillista, fomentador de tramas y partidos.

cabana [ˈkəbænə] [ka-ba-na], *s.* Cabaña.

cabaret [ˈkæbərei] [ka-ba-rei], *s.* Cabaret, club nocturno.

cabas [ˈkæbəs] [ka-bas], *s.* 1. Bolsa de labor de mujer; saco de mano pequeño. 2. En Francia, esportilla o capacho para llevar higos, uvas, etc.

cabbage [ˈkæbɪdʒ] [ka-beich], *s.* 1. Berza, repollo, col (vegetable). **A head of cabbage,** repollo. **I found him in the cabbage patch,** lo trajo la cigüeña. 2. Los retales que los sastres se apropian de las telas que se les entregan. **Cabbage butterfly,** mariposa de berza del género Pieris, cuyas orugas devoran las hojas de la berza, y otras plantas parecidas. **Cabbage fly,** mosca que en estado de larva ataca las raíces de la berza. **(GB)** *(Coloq.)* Vegetal (person).

cabbage, *va.* Cercenar o hurtar retazos, como hacen los sastres; ratear, hurtar. *(Ger.) -vn.* Formar una cabeza redonda como la de las berzas, acogollase, apiñarse, apretarse las berzas y lechugas.

cabbage-tree [ˈkæbɪdʒtriː] [ka-beich-trí], *s. (Bot.)* Especie de palma, un árbol grande de las Antillas.

cabbage-worm [ˈkæbɪdʒwɜːm] [ka-beich-uerm], *s.* Gusano de berza, oruga de algunas especies de falensa y mariposas que devoran las hojas de la col.

cabby, cabbie [ˈkæbɪ] [ka-bi] *s. (Coloq.)* Taxista, ruletero, tachero.

cabdriver [ˈkæbˌdraɪvər] [kab-drai-veʳ], *s.* 1. *(Auto)* Taxista. 2. (Carruaje) Cochero.

cabin [ˈkæbɪn] [ka-bin], *s.* 1. Cabaña, choza (hut); bungalow (in motel). 2. *(Mar.)* Camarote. 3. *(Aerosp, Auto, Aviat.)* Cabina. **Cabin steward,** camarero.

cabin, *vn.* Vivir en cabaña o choza.

cabin-boy [ˈkæbɪnbɔɪ] [ka-bin-boi], *s.* 1. *(Mar.)* Paje de escoba de la cámara del capitán. 2. Muchacho de cámara; grumete. **Cabin cruiser,** yate de motor.

cabinet [ˈkæbɪnɪt] [ka-bi-net], *s.* 1. Gabinete, escritorio, conjunto de cajones y anaqueles en que se guardan cosas. Armario (cupboard). **Glass cabinet,** vitrina. **Medicine cabinet,** botiquín. 2. Gabinete, paraje retirado en una casa para tratar negocios, o para consultas. 3. Gabinete ministerial, ministerio, el cuerpo de ministros del Estado. **Cabinet minister,** ministro, secretario de Estado. 4. Caja, estuche. **Cabinet organ,** órgano de salón. **Cabinet piano,** gran piano vertical. **Cabinet-council,** consejo privado. **Cabinet-maker,** ebanista, el que trabaja en ébano y en otras maderas finas. **Cabinet-work,** ebanistería.

cabinet, *va. V. ENCLOSE.*

cable [ˈkeɪbl] [kei-bol], *s.* 1. *(Mar.)* Cable, maroma muy gruesa que se asegura al ancla para dar fondo. 2. Cable, medida longitudinal. *V. CABLE'S-LENGTH.* 3. Cualquier maroma pesada de alambre. 4. Cable, conductor eléctrico, subacuático, aéreo o subterráneo, envuelto en una cubierta aisladora. *(Telec.)* Cable, telegrama. **Best bower cable,** cable del ayuste. **Small bower cable,** cable sencillo o de leva. **Sheet cable,** cable de esperanza. **Stream cable,** calabrote. **Cable-bit,** bitadura o media bitadura. **Weather-bit of a cable,** bitadura entera de cable. **To bit the cable,** tomar la bitadura con el cable. **To clap a messenger on the cable,** tomar margarita sobre el cable. **To heave in the cable,** virar el cable para abordo. **To pay away the cable,** arriar cable para afuera. **To part the cables,** partir los cables. **To serve the cable,** aforrar el cable. **To slip the cable,** alargar el cable por ojo o por el chicote. **Cable-car,** carro o vagón que corre sobre carriles movido por tracción de cable. **Cable grip,** grapa, fiador de cable. **Cable-laid,** guindaleza acalabrotada. **Cable's-length,** cable, medida longitudinal equivalente al décimo de una milla marina o 120 brazas. **Cable rail-road,** ferrocarril en el cual la fuerza motriz, producida por una máquina fija, se communica a un cable continuo que está situado debajo del pavimento o en una depresión del mismo. Los carros toman o sueltan el cable por medio de una grapa especial que pasa por una muesca en la calzada. Fué inventado en San Francisco de California. **Submarine cable,** cable telegráfico submarino.

cable, va. *(Telec.)* Cablegrafiar, telegrafiar (message, news). **She cabled me $2,000,** me envió un giro telegráfico de 2.000 dólares.

cable address ['keɪblˌədres] [kei-bol-a-drés], *s.* Dirección cablegráfica.

cable car ['keɪblkɑːr] [kei-bol-kaʳ], *s.* Teleférico (suspended); funicular (funicular); tranvía (streetcar).

cabled ['keɪbld] [kei-bold], *a.* Atado o afirmado con cable.

cablegram ['keɪblgræm] [kei-bol-gram], *s. (Fam.)* Mensaje telegráfico enviado por cable; cablegrama.

cable railway ['keɪbl'reɪweɪ] [kei-bol-reil-uei] *s.* Funicular.

cable television ['keɪbl'televɪʃən] [kei-bol-te-le-vi-shon] *s.* Televisión por cable, cablevisión.

cabman ['kæbmən] [kab-man], *s.* Cochero de cabriolé; calesero, simón.

cabob ['kɔbɒb] [ka-bob], *va.* Asar un lomo de carnero.

cabob, *s.* Pierna de carnero con salsa de arenques. Carne asada, en general. **caboodle** [kə'buːdl] [ka-budl] *s. (Coloq.)* **The whole caboodle,** absolutamente todo.

caboose [kə'buːz] [ka-bus], *s.* 1. *(Mar.)* El fogón o cocina a bordo de un barco. 2. *(F.C.)* Carro de conductor enganchado a un tren de mercancías. Furgón de cola, cabús.

cabotage ['kæbəteɪdʒ] [ka-bo-teich], *s. (Mar.)* Cabotaje, la navegación o el tráfico que se hace sin desviarse mucho de la costa del mar.

cabriolet ['kæbrɪəlɪt] [ka-brio-let], *s.* Cabriolé, especie de coche ligero de dos ruedas; corresponde también a birlocho, silla volante o carrocín. V. *CAB* y *GIG.*

caburn ['kæbɜːn] [ka-bern], *s. (Mar.)* Cajeta, trenza de filástica o meollar, de la cual se hacen tomadores y rizos.

cacao [kə'kɑːəʊ] [ka-kau], *s. (Bot.)* Cacao, árbol de la América tropical y su simiente, una almendra carnosa que se emplea como principal ingrediente del chocolate.

cachalot ['kætʃəlɒt] [ka-cha-lot], *s.* Cachalote, especie de ballena.

cache [kæʃ] [kash], *va.* Depositar en un escondrijo; ocultar en la tierra, o debajo de un montón de piedras.

cache, *s.* 1. Escondite, escondrijo, lugar recóndito y a propósito para ocultar alguna cosa. 2. Alijo (of provisions). 3. *(Inform.)* Cache.

cachectic, cachectical ['kæʃetkɪk] [ka-shek-tik], *a.* Caquéctico, el que padece caquexia.

cachexia ['kæʃəksɪə] [ka-shek-sia], o **cachexy** ['kæʃəksɪ] [ka-shek-si], *s.* Caquexia, estado del cuerpo en el que está impedida la nutrición y por consiguiente debilitadas las funciones vitales y animales.

cachinnation ['kækɪnəʃən] [ka-ki-nei-shon], *s.* Carcajada, risotada.

cackhanded ['kæk'hændɪd] [kak-jen-ded] *a. (Coloq.)* (GB) Torpe, patoso.

cackle ['kækl] [kakol], *vn.* 1. Cacarear, cloquear la gallina, o graznar. 2. Reírse socarronamente (person). 3. Chacharear, picotear, hablar mucho y sin sustancia.

cackle, *s.* 1. El cacareo, la voz de la gallina u otra ave que cacarea. 2. Charla, cháchara. 3. Risa socarrona (laugh). *(Coloq.)* **Cut the cackle!,** ¡menos charla!

cackler ['kæklər] [kaklaʳ], *s.* 1. Cacareador, pájaro o ave que cacarea. 2. Cacareador, hablador, chismoso, parlanchín.

cackling ['kæklɪŋ] [ka-klin], *s.* 1. Cloqueo de la gallina. 2. Cháchara, parla.

cacochymic, cacochymical [kə'kɒkɪmɪk] [ka-ko-ki-mik], *a.* Cacoquímico, lleno de malos humores.

cacodemon [kæ'kɒdɪmɒn] [ka-ko-di-mon], *s.* Diablo, espíritu maligno.

cacoethes ['kækəθz] [ka-kezs], *s.* Mala costumbre; comezón.

cacography [kə'kɒgræfɪ] [ka-ko-gra-fi], *s.* Cacografía, mala ortografía.

cacophony [kə'kɒfənɪ] [ka-ko-fo-ni], *s. (Ling.)* Cacofonía, sonido desagradable al oído. Disonancia, algarabía (dissonance).

cactus ['kæktəs] [kak-tus], *s. (pl.* CACTI o CACTUSES*).* Cacto, género de plantas vasculares, crasas y perennes, de hojas carnosas y espinosas, familia de las cácteas; tales son la higuera de Indias y el nopal.

cacumen [kə'kjuːmən] [ka-kiu-men], *s.* Ápice, cumbre.

cacuminate [kə'kjuːmɪnɪt] [ka-kiu-mi-neit], *va.* Aguzar, acabar o terminar alguna cosa en punta o figura piramidal.

cad [kæd] [kad], *s.* 1. Hombre vulgar y malcriado, cualquiera que sea su posición social. Femenino, CADDESS. 2. Demandadero, mozo de esquina o de cordel. 3. *(Ingl.)* Conductor de ómnibus. 4. *(Coloq.)* Canalla, sinvergüenza.

CAD *s.* (= **Computer-aided design**) CAD.

cadaver [kə'deɪvər] [ka-dei-vaʳ], *s.* Cadáver, el cuerpo muerto.

cadaverous [kə'dævərəs] [ka-da-ve-rous], *a.* Cadavérico, pálido.

caddie ['kædɪ] [ka-di], *s. (Esco.)* Mensajero, recadero; dícese, especialmente del muchacho que en el juego llamado *golf* lleva los bastones o mazas de que se sirven los jugadores.

caddie *vn.* Hacer de caddie. **To caddie for somebody,** ser el caddie de alguien.

caddis ['kædɪs] [ka-dis], *s.* 1. Jerguilla de lana. 2. Especie de cinta hecha de seda y estambre. 3. Gusano de la paja, larva de la frigana estriada, insecto neuróptero. Se escribe también, en este sentido, *caddis-worm.*

caddow ['kædəʊ] [ka-dou], *s.* 1. *(Orn.)* V. *JACKDAW.* 2. Vestidura basta de lana.

caddy ['kædɪ] [ka-di], *s.* Botecito, cajita para té (tea caddy). Carrito de la compra (for shopping). V. *CADDIE.*

caddy *vn.* V. *CADDIE.*

cade ['keɪd] [keid], *a.* Manso, domesticado, delicado, criado a la mano.

cade, *s.* 1. Barril; banasta. 2. Enebro. **Cade-oil,** aceite de enebro.

cade, *va.* Criar con blandura, mimar.

cadence ['keɪdəns] [keidans], *va.* Regular por medida música.

cadence, *s.* 1. Caída, declinación. 2. Cadencia, en la música, en la poesía o en las frases.

cadent ['keɪdənt] [keidant], *a.* Cayente.

cadet [kə'det] [ka-det], *s.* 1. Cadete, de un cuerpo militar. 2. El hermano menor con relación a otro mayor.

cadge [kædʒ] [kadch] *va. (Coloq.)* **To cadge something from/off somebody,** gorronearle, gorrearle, garronearle o bolsearle algo a alguien. Llevar un fardo. *-vn.* **To cadge from/off somebody,** gorronearle, gorrearle, garronearle o bolsearle a alguien.

cadger ['kædʒər] [kadchaʳ], *s.* Placero, regatón. V. *HUCKSTER.*

cadi ['kædɪ] [kadi], *s.* Cadí, un magistrado entre los mahometanos.

Cadiz [kə'dɪz] [ka-dis] *N.* Cádiz.

cadmium ['kædmɪəm] [kad-mium], *s.* Cadmio, cuerpo simple metálico, parecido al estaño.

cadre ['kɑːdə] [ka-daʳ] *s.* Cuadro.

caduceus [kə'djuːʃəs] [ka-diu-shos], *s.* Caduceo, la vara de Mercurio.

caducity [kə'djuːsɪtɪ] [ka-diu-si-ti], *s.* Caducidad; lo que amenaza ruina; fragilidad.

caducous [kə'djuːkəs] [ka-diu-kos], *a.* 1. Caduco, perecedero, poco durable 2. En el derecho romano significaba lo que estaba sujeto a las leyes sobre herencias.

caecal ['siːkl] [sí-kal], *a.* Cecal, del intestino ciego.

caecum ['siːkəm] [sí-kum], *s.* Intestino ciego, el mayor de los intestinos gruesos.

Caesar ['siːzər] [sí-saʳ] *N.* César.

caesarean ['siːzərɪən] [si-sa-rian], **caesarean operation,** *s. (Med.)* Operación cesárea.

caesura [sɪ'sjʊərə] [si-sua-ra], *s. (Poét.)* Cesura, o pausa en un verso.

caesural [sɪ'sjʊərəl] [si-su-ral], *a.* Lo que pertenece a la cesura.

café [ˈkæfeɪ] [ka-fei], s. 1. Café, cafetería (coffee bar); restaurante económico (restaurant). 2. Cantina.

cafeteria [ˌkæfɪˈtɪərɪə] [ka-fi-tia-ria], s. Cafetería, cantina (in hospital, college); restaurante en que se sirve uno mismo, autoservicio (self-service).

caffeine [ˈkæfiːn] [ka-fin], s. Cafeína, alcaloide cristalizable que se extrae del café.

caftan [ˈkæftæn] [kaf-tan], s. Vestimenta que se estila entre los persas.

cage [keɪdʒ] [keidch], s. 1. Jaula. 2. Jaula para fieras. 3. Jaula o cárcel, trena, prisión. 4. *(Anat.)* **Rib cage,** caja torácica. 5. Canasta, cesta (in basketball). 6. Portería, meta, arco (in ice hockey).

cage, va. Enjaular, encerrar en jaula.

cagey [ˈkeɪdʒɪ] [kei-dchi] a. *(Coloq.)* Reservado, cauteloso (reply).

cagily [ˈkeɪdʒɪlɪ] [kei-chi-li] adv. Cautelosamente (reply).

cagy [ˈkeɪdʒɪ] [kei-chi] a. V. CAGEY.

cahoots [kəˈhuːts] [ka-huts]», s. pl. *(Coloq.)* **In cahoots,** cómplices, aliados. **To be in cahoots with,** conspirar con, complotar con.

caic o caique [ˈkeɪk] [keik], s. Caique, esquife destinado al servicio de las galeras; lancha de los cosacos en el Mar Negro.

caiman [ˈkeɪmən] [kei-man], s. Caimán, nombre que dan los americanos a una especie de cocodrilo.

cain [ˈkeɪn] [kein] N. Caín. *(Coloq.)* **To raise Cain,** armar la de Dios es Cristo.

cairn [kɜən] [kearn], s. Montón de piedras sobre el sepulcro de alguna persona distinguida.

Cairo [ˈkaɪərəʊ] [kai-rou] N. El Cairo.

caisson [ˈkeɪzən] [kei-son], s. 1. Arcón o cajón grande, que sirve en los ejércitos para las municiones, víveres, etc. 2. Cajón dentro del cual se hacen los estribos de los puentes. 3. *(Mar.)* Camello, aparato para poner un barco a flote, o para levantarlo y carenarlo.

cajeput, cajuput [ˈkeɪdʒpɒt] [keich-put], s. Cayeput, árbol pequeño de las Molucas, familia de las mirtáceas, del cual se obtiene un aceite que destruye los insectos y se usa contra el dolor de muelas.

cajole [kəˈdʒəʊl] [ka-youl], va. Lisonjear, adular; requebrar, engatusar, acariciar. Convencer con zalamerías o halagos.

cajolery [kəˈdʒəʊlərɪ] [ka-you-le-ri], s. Adulación, lisonja; requiebro, zalamería.

Cajun [ˈkeɪdʒən] [kei-yon] a. Cajún.

Cajun s. Cajún (person); descendiente de inmigrantes franceses en el estado norteamericano de Luisiana. *(Ling.)* Dialecto del francés hablado por los CAJUN.

cake [keɪk] [keik], vn. 1. Cocer o endurecer, pegarse. 2. Formar costra. **Our shoes were caked with mud,** teníamos los zapatos cubiertos de barro endurecido.

cake, s. *(Culin.)* Bollo, especie de pan delicado, tortita, hojaldre, pastellillo, masa (small, individual). Pastel, tarta, torta (large). **Cake of wax,** pan de cera. **Bride-cake, wedding cake,** tarta o pastel de boda. **Plum-cake, fruit-cake,** torta con pasas de Corinto. **Sponge cake,** bizcocho, queque, bizcochuelo, ponqué, panque. **The icing/frosting on the cake,** un extra. *(Coloq.)* **To be a piece of cake,** ser pan comido. **To take the cake,** ser el colmo; llevarse la palma (person). **To go/sell like hot cakes,** venderse como pan caliente o como rosquillas. **You can't have your cake and eat it too,** no puedes tenerlo todo, tienes que elegir. **Cake walk,** diversión originaria de los negros del Sur de los Estados Unidos; marcha o paseo en el que se da un pastel como premio a la pareja que mejor y más graciosamente se contonea. **Cake of soap,** pastilla de jabón.

cake tin [ˈkeɪktɪn] [keik-tin] s. (GB) Molde para pastel (for baking). Lata para guardar pasteles (for storage).

cal (= **calorie(s)**) cal.

cal (= **Calorie(s)**) kcal.; = **California.**

CAL s. = **computer-aided learning.**

calabash [ˈkæləbæʃ] [ka-la-bash], s. 1. Calabaza, güira, tapara, totumo. 2. Calabacera, taparo.

caladium [kəˈlædɪəm] [ka-la-dium], s. Caladio, planta que se da en los terrenos húmedos de la América del Sur. Se cultiva por sus hojas grandes, multicolores y sagitadas.

calamanco [kæləˈmæŋkəʊ] [ka-la-man-kou], s. Calamaco, especie de tela de lana.

calamar, calamary [ˈkælmər] [kal-ma'], s. 1. Calamar, molusco que posee una secreción negra llamada tinta. 2. Su concha interior o casco córneo. *V. SQUID.*

calamine [ˈkæləmaɪn] [ka-la-main], s. Calamina o piedra calaminar. **Calamine lotion,** loción de calamina.

calamint [ˈkæləmɪnt] [ka-la-mint], s. *(Bot.)* Calamento.

calamitous [ˈkæləmɪtəs] [ka-la-mi-tos], a. Calamitoso, miserable, desgraciado, infeliz.

calamitousness [ˈkæləmɪtəsnɪs] [ka-la-mi-tos-nes] **calamity** [ˈkælmɪtɪ] [ka-la-mi-ti], s. Calamidad, infortunio, trabajo, miseria, desastre, desgracia.

calamus [ˈkæləməs] [ka-la-mos], s. *(Bot.)* Cálamo aromático.

calash [ˈkæləʃ] [ka-lash], s. 1. Calesa, carruaje pequeño. 2. Gorra que llevan las señoras en la cabeza para guardar el peinado.

calcarious [kælˈkɛərɪəs] [kal-kea-rios], a. Calcáreo, que tiene propiedad de cal.

calceated [ˈkælsiːtɪd] [kal-si-tid], a. Calzado, el que tiene puestos los zapatos.

calcedony [ˈkælsɪdənɪ] [kal-si-do-ni], s. Calcedonia, piedra preciosa.

calciferous [ˈkælsɪfərəs] [kal-si-fe-ros], a. Que produce o contiene cal.

calcification [ˌkælsɪfɪˈkeɪʃən] [kal-si-fi-kei-shon], s. Conversión en sustancia pétrea por la deposición de sales de cal; v. gr. una petrificación.

calcify [ˈkælsɪfaɪ] [kal-si-fai], va. y vn. Calcificar, calcificarse.

calcimine [ˈkælsɪmiːn] [kal-si-min], s. Pintura de cola, lechada, mezcla de yeso o cal con cola y agua; a menudo se le mezcla también algún color. -va. Dar lechada, aplicar esta mezcla a las paredes o techos. Se escribe también KALSOMINE.

calcinable [ˈkælsɪnəbl] [kal-si-na-bol], a. Calcinable, capaz de ser calcinado.

calcination [ˌkælsɪnəˈʃən] [kal-si-nei-shon], s. Calcinación, la acción de calcinar.

calcinatory [ˈkælsɪnətərɪ] [kal-si-na-to-ri], s. Calcinatorio, vasija que se usa para calcinar.

calcine [ˈkælsiːn] [kal-sín], va. Calcinar, reducir a cal o ceniza los metales, piedras, etc.; quemar. -vn. Calcinarse.

calcite [ˈkælsaɪt] [kal-sait], s. Espato calcáreo, carbonato de cal.

calcitrate [ˈkælsɪtreɪt] [kal-si-treit], vn. Acocear, hollar, patear.

calcium [ˈkælsɪəm] [kal-siom], s. Calcio, metal ligero amarillo que combinado con el oxígeno, forma la cal.

calc-spar [ˈkælkspɑːr] [kalk-spa'], s. Espato calcáreo.

calculable [ˈkælkjələbl] [kal-kiu-la-bol], a. Calculable.

calculate [ˈkælkjəleɪt] [kal-kiu-leit], va. Calcular (compute, estimate); contar, suputar; adaptar. -vn. Hacer cálculos. *(Fam.)* **Well calculated,** muy a propósito. **It is well calculated,** es lo que se necesita. **His remarks were calculated to offend,** lo dijo con la intención o el propósito de ofender.

calculated [ˈkælkjəleɪtɪd] [kal-kiu-lei-ted] a. Calculado (risk); deliberado (act); dicho con toda intención (insult).

calculating [ˈkælkjəleɪtɪŋ] [kal-kiu-lei-tin] a. Calculador.

calculation [ˌkælkjəˈleɪʃən] [kal-kiu-lei-shon], s. Calculación, cálculo. **According to my calculation(s),** según mis cálculos.

calculative [ˈkælkjələtɪv] [kal-kiu-la-tiv], a. Lo que pertenece al cálculo.

calculator ['kælkjʊleɪtər] [kal-kiu-lei-toᵣ], s. 1. Calculador, persona que calcula. 2. Máquina calculadora. **Pocket calculator,** calculadora de bolsillo.

calculatory ['kælkjʊlətərɪ] [kal-kiu-la-to-ri], a. Lo que pertenece al cálculo.

calculous ['kælkjʊləs] [kal-kiu-los], **calculose** ['kælkjʊləs] [kal-kiu-los], a. Pedregoso, arenoso; calculoso.

calculus ['kælkjʊləs] [kal-kiu-los], s. Cálculo, piedra en la vejiga o en los riñones. *Calculi,* cálculos.

caldron, (GB) **cauldron** ['kɔːldrən] [kal-dron], s. Caldera o caldero.

caledonian [ˌkælɪ'dəʊnɪən] [ka-li-dou-nian], a. Escocés, natural de, o perteneciente a Escocia.

calefacient ['kælɪfeɪʃənt] [ka-li-fei-shent], a. Lo que produce calefacción, que da calor.

calefaction ['kælɪfækʃən] [ka-li-fak-shon], s. Calefacción, la acción y efecto de calentar o calentarse.

calefactive ['kælɪfæktɪv] [ka-li-fak-tiv], **calefactory** ['kælɪfæktərɪ] [ka-li-fak-to-ri], a. Calefaciente, que calienta.

calefy ['kælɪfaɪ] [ka-li-fai], vn. (Des.) Calentarse, caldearse. -va. Calentar.

calendar ['kæləndər] [ka-len-daᵣ], s. 1. Calendario o almanaque. 2. Lista o tabla de los pleitos o causas que están para verse en los tribunales. **Calendar of events,** programa de actos. **Calendar month,** mes (del calendario).

calendar, va. Entrar o insertar en el calendario.

calender, s. Calandria o prensa recargada, máquina para dar lustre a las telas de seda o para satinar papel.

calender, va. Prensar con calandria, lustrar el papel o las telas pasándolas entre dos cilindros.

calenderer ['kæləndərər] [ka-len-de-raᵣ], s. Aprensador, el que aprensa con calandria.

calends ['kæləndz] [ka-lends], s. pl. Calenda o calendas, el primer día de cada mes en el antiguo cómputo romano.

calendula ['kæləndjuːlə] [ka-len-diu-la], s. Caléndula, maravilla, planta crisantema del orden de las compuestas.

calendulin ['kæləndjʊliːn] [ka-len-diu-lin], s. Calendulin, goma o sustancia mucilaginosa, que se extrae de la caléndula.

calenture ['kæləntʃər] [ka-len-chaᵣ], s. Calentura, fiebre tropical violenta.

calf [kɑːf] [kalf], s. (pl. CALVES [kɑːvz] [kalvs]). 1. (*Zool.*) Ternero o ternera; cervatillo (animal). **To kill the fatted calf,** celebrar una gran fiesta de bienvenida. 2. (*Anat.*) Pantorrilla, la parte posterior de la pierna, la más carnosa y abultada. 3. Tonto; cobarde. **Calf's foot jelly,** gelatina de manos de ternero.

calfskin ['kɑːfskɪn] [kalfskin], s. Becerrillo, becerros o piel de ternero.

caliber, calibre ['kælɪbər] [ka-li-beᵣ], s. 1. Calibre, la abertura, hueco y diámetro del cañón de un arma de fuego. 2. Grado de capacidad, mérito o facultades intelectuales (quality). **A writer of his caliber,** un escritor de su calibre. 3. Peso total del armamento de un buque.

calibrate ['kælɪbreɪt] [ka-li-breit], va. Calibrar.

calibration ['kælɪbreɪʃən] [ka-li-brei-shon], s. Calibración, calibrado.

calico ['kælɪkəʊ] [ka-li-kou], s. 1. Calicó, indiana, una especie de tela de algodón estampada, percal; (GB) Lienzo, percal (white cotton). 2. Zaraza. (*Mex.*) Angaripola.

calico-printer ['kælɪkəʊˌprɪntər] [ka-li-kou-prin-taᵣ], s. Estampador de tela de algodón.

calid ['kælɪd] [ka-lid], a. (Des.) Caliente; cálido, ardiente.

calidity ['kælɪdɪtɪ] [ka-li-di-ti], **calidness** ['kælɪdnɪs] [ka-lid-nes], s. (Des.) Calor, encendimiento.

calif, caliph ['kælɪf] [ka-lif], s. Califa, título que tomaron los sucesores de Mahoma.

Calif = California

California [ˌkælɪ'fɔːnɪə] [ka-li-for-nia]. N. California.

Californian [ˌkælɪ'fɔːnɪən] [ka-li-for-nian], a. Califórnico, perteneciente a California. -s. Californio, californiа, natural de California, californiano.

caligraphy ['kælɪɡræfɪ] [ka-li-gra-fi], s. V. CALLIGRAPHY.

calipash ['kælɪpɑːʃ] [ka-li-pash], s. Cierta parte de la tortuga próxima a la concha superior; una sustancia gelatinosa verdusca.

calipee ['kælɪpɪ] [ka-li-pi], s. Parte de la tortuga próxima a la concha inferior; sustancia gelatinosa amarillenta.

calipers, (GB) **callipers** ['kælɪpəz] [ka-li-pars], s. Compás, calibrador (for measuring). **Inside calipers,** compás de calibres. **Outside calipers,** compás de espesores. (*Med.*) Aparato ortopédico para la pierna.

caliphate ['kælɪfeɪt] [ka-li-feit], s. Califato, dignidad o jurisdicción del califa.

calisaya ['kælɪsəɪə] [ka-li-sa-ya], s. Variedad de quina de las más estimadas.

calisthenic [ˌkælɪs'θenɪks] [ka-lis-ze-niks], a. V. CALLISTHENIC.

caliver ['kælɪvər] [ka-li-vaᵣ], s. (*Ant.*) Una especie de escopeta; pedrero, cantero.

calix ['kælɪks] [ka-liks], s. 1. Órgano o cavidad en forma de copa. 2. V. CALYX.

calk, caulk ['kɔːk] [kolk], va. 1. (*Mar.*) Calafatear un buque. **Calking mallet,** maceta de calafate. **Calking iron,** escoplo de calafate. 2. (*Vet.*) Hacer talones o proyecciones en la herradura del caballo.

calk, va. y vn. Marcar con tiza; de aquí, calcar, pasar un dibujo.

calker ['kɔːkər] [kolkeᵣ], s. Calafate. **Calker's boy,** calafatín. **Calker's tool-box,** banqueta de calafate.

calkin ['kɔːkɪn] [kol-kin], s. (*Vet.*) La parte saliente en la herradura de los caballos para impedir que tropiecen.

calking ['kɔːkɪŋ] [kol-kin], s. Calafateo, acción y efecto de calafatear.

call [kɔːl] [kol], va. 1. Llamar, nombrar (shout). **To call somebody's name,** llamar a alguien. Llamar (name, describe as). **We call her Betty,** la llamamos o le decimos Betty. **What are you going to call the baby?,** ¿qué nombre le van a poner al bebé? **What is this called in Italian?,** ¿cómo se llama esto en italiano? **Are you calling me a liar?,** ¿me estás llamando mentiroso? 2. Llamar, decir a uno que venga (police, taxi, doctor). Llamar (contact by telephone, radio). **For more information call us on/at 341-6920,** para más información llame o llámenos al (teléfono) 341-6920. **Don't call us, we'll call you,** ya lo llamaremos. 3. Convocar (strike), citar, juntar, congregar. 4. Llamar, inspirar. 5. Invocar o apelar. 6. Proclamar, publicar, pregonar. 7. Poner apodos. 8. Visitar a uno; llamar a uno o darle voces. 9. Excitar, traer a la vista. 10. Ver (in poker); declarar (in bridge). -vn. 1. Pararse un rato: hacer visita. 2. Llamar (person). **She called to me for help,** me llamó para que la ayudara. Gritar. **To call after one,** llamar a alguno a voces. 3. Llamar (by telephone, radio). **Who's calling, please?,** ¿de parte de quién, por favor? **Madrid calling,** aquí Madrid. **To call again,** volver a llamar; hacer volver. **To call aloud,** dar voces, gritar. **To call aside,** llamar aparte, sacar aparte. **To call down,** hacer bajar. **To call over,** repasar, leer algo, leer alguna lista o catálogo. **To call to account,** pedir cuentas. **To call witness,** tomar por testigo.

call around, (*Telec.*) llamar (a varias personas). Pasar por casa (visit).

call at, parar, pasar por. **This train calls at all stations,** este tren para en todas las estaciones. **I called at your place yesterday,** ayer pasé por tu casa.

call away, hacer salir, echar fuera; llevar consigo. **She was called away from the meeting,** la llamaron y tuvo que salir de la reunión. **He was called away on business,** tuvo que ausentarse por motivos de trabajo.

call back, mandar volver, hacer volver, llamar a uno para que vuelva al punto de donde ha salido, o decirle que vuelva. **Can I call you back?,** ¿puedo llamarte más tarde? (*Telec.*) volver a llamar.

call for, llamar, preguntar por alguno, ir a buscarle. Requerir, exigir (require/skill, courage). **You won! This calls for**

champagne!, ¿ganaste? ¡esto hay que celebrarlo con champán! Pedir (demand); pedir a gritos (shout for). Pasar a buscar o a recoger (collect/goods, person).

call forth, hacer salir o venir. Provocar, dar lugar a (protest, criticism); inspirar (emotion).

call in, reasumir, volver atrás, llamar (summon/doctor, expert); introducir; retirar de circulación (withdraw); revocar. **He has called in his money,** ha retirado sus fondos. **To call in question,** poner en duda. **I'll call in later,** me paso luego (visit). **Shall we call in on the Rowsons?,** ¿por qué no pasamos a ver o a visitar a los Rowson?

call off, disuadir; divertir (la atención). Suspender (cancel). Retirar (men/order to stop); llamar (dog). **If that's what you feel, let's call the whole thing off,** mira, si eso es lo que piensas mejor olvidémoslo.

call on, solicitar; pronunciar con solemnidad el nombre de algún muerto o ausente llamándole; visitar a alguno, ir a ver a alguno (visit). V. CALL UPON.

call out, desafiar; llamar a uno para que salga; llamar fuerte, gritar. Llamar (summon/fire brigade); hacer intervenir a (army); llamar, hacer venir (doctor).(GB) Llamar a la huelga (on strike). **He called out her name,** la llamó, pronunció su nombre (utter).

call round, (GB) pasar (visit). *(Telec.)* Llamar a varias personas.

call up, traer a la memoria, evocar (cause to return/memory, image). Invocar, llamar (spirits). Llamar (telephone). *(Mil.)* Llamar a filas.

call upon, implorar, rogar, pedir; visitar; exhortar, animar; invocar. Apelar a (appeal to). **To call upon somebody to speak,** dar la palabra a alguien (invite).

call, *s.* 1. Llamada, la acción de llamar (by telephone). **To make a call,** hacer una llamada telefónica. **To give somebody a call,** llamar a alguien por teléfono. **Will you take the call?,** ¿le paso la llamada? (talk to somebody); ¿acepta la llamada? (accept charges). **Local/long distance call,** llamada urbana/interurbana. *(Fam.)* Visita (visit). **To pay a visit on somebody,** hacerle una visita a alguien. **I have some calls to make,** tengo que hacer algunas visitas. Llamada, llamado (of person- cry); grito (shout). 2. Instancia, llamamiento, llamado (demand). **There were calls for his resignation,** pidieron su dimisión; vocación. 3. Pretensión o alegación de derecho a alguna cosa. 4. Reclamo, instrumento para llamar los pájaros. **Call-bird,** pájaro de reclamo. 5. Inspiración divina. 6. *(Mar.)* Pito de contramaestre. 7. Demanda (de fondos). 8. *(Sport)* Decisión, cobro. **Be within call,** esté Vd. al alcance de la voz. **He had no call to do it,** él no tenía derecho a hacerlo. Motivo (reason). **He had no call to be rude,** no tenía por qué ser grosero. **There's not much call for this product,** no hay mucha demanda para este producto (demand). **There are too many calls on my time,** muchas cosas reclaman mi atención (claim). **To be on call,** estar de guardia (summons). **Beyond the call of duty,** más de lo que el deber exigía (o exige). **To answer/obey the call of nature,** hacer sus (o mis, etc.) necesidades. Llamada, atracción (lure).

call box [ˈkɔːlbɒks] [kol-boks] *s.* (GB) Cabina telefónica.

caller [ˈkɔːlər] [kole] *s.* Llamador, el que llama. **We didn't have many callers,** no vino mucha gente; *(Telec.)* no tuvimos o no hubo muchas llamadas. **The caller didn't leave his name,** la persona que llamó no dejó su nombre.

callgirl [ˈkɔːlgɜːl] [kol-guerl] *s.* *(Coloq.)* Call-girl, prostituta que da citas por teléfono.

callid [ˈkɔːlɪd] [ka-led], *a.* Astuto, sagaz.

calligraph [ˈkəlɪgræf] [ka-li-graf], *s.* Ejemplar o muestra de buena escritura.

calligraphic [ˌkəlɪˈgræfɪk] [ka-li-gra-fik], *a.* Caligráfico, relativo a la caligrafía.

calligraphy [kəˈlɪgræfɪ] [ka-li-gra-fi], *s.* Bella escritura, letra hermosa y elegante; caligrafía en general.

callimanco, *s.* V. CALAMANCO.

call-in [ˈkɔːlɪn] [ko-lin] *s.* Programa de radio o TV en el que el público participa por teléfono.

calling [ˈkɔːlɪŋ] [ko-lin], *s.* Profesión, vocación, el modo de vida que cada uno tiene, usa y ejerce públicamente; clase; oficio, ejercicio. **Calling card,** tarjeta de visita.

calliope [ˈkəlɪɒp] [ka-liop], *s.* Instrumento musical compuesto de una serie de silbatos que tocan mediante un teclado.

callipers [ˈkalɪpəz] [ka-lipers], *s.* Compás calibrador. V. CALIPER.

callisthenic [ˌkælɪsˈtenik] [ka-lis-te-nik], *a.* Calisténico; perteneciente a la calistenia; lo que favorece la gracia y soltura del cuerpo.

callisthenics [ˌkælɪsˈtenikz] [ka-lis-te-niks], *s.* Calistenia, ligeros ejercicios gimnásticos a propósito para las niñas y jóvenes, con objeto de aumentar la agilidad y el donaire del cuerpo.

callosity [kæˈlɒsɪtɪ] [ka-lo-si-ti], **callousness** [ˈkæləsnɪs] [ka-los-nes], *s.* Callosidad, dureza; insensibilidad.

callous [ˈkæləs] [ka-los], *a.* 1. Calloso, endurecido. 2. Insensible, cruel.

callously [ˈkæləslɪ] [ka-los-li], *adv.* Insensiblemente, duramente, cruelmente.

call-out [ˈkɔːlˈaʊt] [kol-aut] *a.* (GB) Por desplazamiento (charge, fee); a domicilio (service).

callow [ˈkæləʊ] [ka-lou], *a.* 1. Pelado, desplumado. 2. Sin experiencia del mundo, joven. Inmaduro, inexperto.

callus [ˈkæləs] [ka-los], *s.* *(Med.)* Callo, callosidad, dureza en alguna parte del cuerpo; el punto por donde se unen otra vez los huesos después de rotos.

calm [kɑːm] [kalm], *s.* Calma (stillness); serenidad, tranquilidad (peace, tranquillity); quietud, bonanza, reposo, sosiego. **The calm before the storm,** la calma que precede a la tormenta. **Dead calm,** *(Mar.)* calma chicha. -*a.* Quieto, tranquilo, sosegado, sereno (person, voice). En calma, tranquilo, calmo (sea). **Keep calm!,** ¡tranquilo!, ¡calma! **To become calm,** *(Mar.)* calmar o comenzar a hacer calma.

calm, *va.* Tranquilizar, aquietar; apaciguar, calmar; aplacar, sosegar. **I had a drink to calm my nerves,** me tomé una copa para tranquilizarme o calmarme.

calm down, tranquilizar, calmar. Tranquilizarse. **Calm down!,** ¡tranquilízate!, ¡tranquilo!

calmer [ˈkɑːmər] [kal-ma], *s.* tranquilizador, apaciguador, sosegador, aquietador, pacificador.

calming [ˈkɑːmɪŋ] [kal-min] *a.* Tranquilizante.

calmly [ˈkɑːmlɪ] [kalm-li], *adv.* Serenamente, con serenidad, con calma.

calmness [ˈkɑːmnɪs] [kalm-nes], *s.* Tranquilidad, serenidad, calma (of person). Calma (of sea, wind).

calmy [ˈkɑːmɪ] [kal-mi], *a.* Tranquilo, pacífico.

calomel [ˈkɑːləməl] [ka-lo-mel], *s.* Calomelanos, calomel, cloruro mercurioso (Hg2, Cl2).

calor gas [ˈkɑːləgæz] [ka-lor-gas] *s.* (GB) Butano, supergás (gas).

caloric [kɑːˈlɒrɪk] [ka-lo-rik], *s.* *(Quim.)* Calórico.

calorie [ˈkɑːlərɪ] [ka-lo-ri], *s.* *(Fís.)* Caloría. *(Culin.)* **Calorie,** (kilo)caloría. **A calorie-controlled diet,** una dieta o un régimen bajo en calorías.

calorific [ˌkæləˈrɪfɪk] [ka-lo-ri-fik], *a.* Calorífico. **Calorific value,** contenido calorífico (of food).

calorimeter [ˌkæləˈrɪmɪtər] [ka-lo-ri-mi-ta], *s.* Calorímetro, instrumento para medir el calor.

caltha [ˈkəlθə] [kal-za], *s.* *(Bot.)* Hierba centella, calta.

caltrop [ˈkɔltrɒp] [kal-trop], *s.* 1. *(Mil.)* Abrojo, pieza de hierro con tres o cuatro puntas, una de las cuales queda siempre hacia arriba; se usa para impedir el paso de infantes y caballos, mutilándoles los pies. 2. *(Bot.)* Tríbulo, abrojo.

calumet [ˈkæljʊmɪt] [ka-liu-met], *s.* Pipa de los aborígenes de la América del Norte. Tiene la taza o cabeza de piedra y el tubo de caña.

calumniate [kəˈlʌmnɪeɪt] [ka-lum-nieit], *va./vn.* Calumniar.

calumniation [ˈkəlʌmnɪeɪʃən] [ka-lum-niei-shon], *s.* Calumnia.

calumniator [ˈkəlʌmnɪeɪtər] [ka-lum-nieitoʳ], *s.* Calumniador, el que calumnia o acusa falsamente.

calumniatory [ˈkəlʌmnɪətərɪ] [ka-lum-nia-to-ri], **calumnious** [ˈkəlʌmnəʊs] [ka-lum-nous], *a.* Calumnioso, injurioso.

calumniously [ˈkəlʌmnəʊslɪ] [ka-lum-nous-li], *adv.* Injuriosamente, calumniosamente.

calumny [ˈkəlʌmnɪ] [ka-lum-ni], *s.* Calumnia.

calvary [ˈkəlvərɪ] [kal-va-ri], *s.* 1. Calvario, el lugar del suplicio de Jesucristo. 2. Calvario, Via crucis.

calve [kɑːv] [kalv], *vn.* Parir la vaca.

calves [kɑːvz] [kalvs] *pl.* of CALF.

calvinism [ˈkælvɪnɪzəm] [kal-vi-nisem], *s.* Calvinismo, la doctrina de Calvino.

calvinist [ˈkælvɪnɪst] [kal-vi-nist], *s.* Calvinista.

calvinize [ˈkælvɪnaɪz] [kal-vi-nais], *va.* Enseñar la doctrina de Calvino.

calvish [ˈkælvɪʃ] [kal-vish], *a.* Aternerado.

calvity [ˈkælvɪtɪ] [kal-viti], *s.* V. BALDNESS.

calx [kælks] [kalks], *s. (pl.* CALXES o CALCES). 1. Cenizas o residuos procedentes de la calcinación de minerales. 2. *(Anat.)* El hueso calcáreo, que forma el talón o calcañar.

calycle [ˈkælaɪkl] [ka-lai-kol], *s.* Calículo, cáliz accesorio de algunas flores.

calypso [kəˈlɪpsəʊ] [ka-lip-sou], *s.* 1. *(Bot.)* Calipso. 2. *(Mús.)* Calipso, ritmo afro-antillano originario de la isla de Trinidad.

calyx [ˈkeɪlɪks] [ka-liks], *s.* 1. *(Bot.)* Cáliz, envoltura exterior de las flores. 2. *(Anat.)* Pelvis del riñón.

cam [kæm] [kam], *s. (Mec.)* Álabe, excéntrica, leva.

camaraderie [ˌkæməˈrɑːdərɪ] [ka-ma-ra-de-ri] *s.* Camaradería, compañerismo.

camber [ˈkæmbər] [kam-baʳ], *s. (Mar.)* Comba, combadura, alabeo de la cubierta. *-vn.* y *va.* Combar, hacer comba o tener arqueo hacia arriba.

cambist [ˈkæmbɪst] [kam-bist], *s. (Com.)* 1. Cambista, el que tiene por oficio dar o aceptar letras de cambio. 2. Cambiador, el que cambia las monedas.

cambium [ˈkæmbɪəm] [kam-bium], *s. (Bot.)* Sustancia viscosa, que se encuentra entre la albura y la corteza de los árboles.

cambric [ˈkeɪmbrɪk] [kam-brik], *s.* Batosta, olán batista.

camcorder [ˈkæmkɔːdər] [kam-kor-daʳ] *s.* Videocámara, camcórder.

came [keɪm] [keim], *pret.* del verbo TO COME.

camel [ˈkæməl] [ka-mel], *s.* 1. *(Zool.)* Camello, bestia de carga en áfrica y Oriente. **Camel's hair,** pelo o lana de camello. **Camel's hair pencil,** pincel de pelo de camello. **Camel's hay,** esquinante o esquinanto, junco oloroso medicinal. 2. *(Mar.)* Camello, aparato a manera de bote o barco, herméticamente cerrado, que sirve para levantar buques en los diques y para poner a floté las embarcaciones sumergidas. 3. Beige (color).

camellia [kəˈmiːlɪə] [ka-mi-lia], *s.* Camelia, planta y flor.

camelopard [ˈkəmɪləpɑːd] [ka-mi-lo-pard], *s.* Camello pardal, jirafa, animal algo parecido al camello.

cameo [ˈkæmɪəʊ] [ka-miou], *s.* 1. Camafeo, piedra preciosa con figuras labradas en relieve (jewelry). 2. Actuación especial (cine, TV). **A cameo performance,** una actuación especial.

camera [ˈkæmərə] [ka-me-ra], *s.* 1. Cámara, caja en la cual se refleja la imagen de los objetos exteriores sobre una superficie plana, por medio de una lente, o lentes. 2. *(Anat.)* Cavidad, como las del corazón. 3. (Ley inglesa) Cámara particular para los jueces. **Folding camera,** cámara plegadiza. **Hand camera,** cámara (fotográfica) de mano. **Camera stand,** pie, sostén de la cámara fotográfica. **Stereoscopic camera,** cámara estereoscópica. **Camera lucida,** cámara lúcida. **Camera obscura,** cámara obscura, aparato para mirar, trazar o fotografiar.

cameral [ˈkæmərəl] [ka-me-ral], *a.* Relativo a una cámara, un cuarto, oficina pública, o tesorería.

cameralistic [ˈkæmərəlɪstɪk] [ka-me-ra-lis-tik], *a.* Perteneciente a la hacienda y rentas del Estado.

cameraman [ˈkæmərəmæn] [ka-me-ra-man], *s.* Camarógrafo, cameraman, cámara.

camera-shy [ˈkæmərəˌʃaɪ] [ka-me-ra-shai] *a.* He's camera-shy, se cohíbe frente a una cámara.

camerated [ˈkæmərətɪd] [ka-me-ra-tid], *a.* Arqueado, abovedado.

cameration [ˈkæmərəʃən] [ka-me-ra-shon], *s.* Arqueo, abovedación.

camerawork [ˈkæmərəˌwɜːk] [ka-me-ra-uek] *s.* Fotografía.

Cameroon [ˌkæməˈruːn] [ka-me-rún] *N.* Camerún.

camisado [ˈkæmɪsədəʊ] [ka-mi-sei-dou], *s. (Ant.)* Encamisado, una estratagema militar.

camisated [ˈkæmɪseɪtɪd] [ka-mi-sei-tid], *a.* Encamisado, el que tiene la camisa puesta sobre el vestido.

camise [ˈkæmiːz] [ka-mís], *s.* Camisa holgada que usan los orientales; también una bata ligera y holgada. *Cf.* CHEMISE.

camisole [ˈkæmɪsəʊl] [ka-mi-soul] *s.* Camisola.

camlet [ˈkæmlɪt] [kam-lit], *s.* 1. Camelote o chamelote. 2. Barragán.

cammock [ˈkæmɒk] [ka-mok], *s. (Bot.)* Detienebuey, gatuña. (Ononis.)

camomile [ˈkæməʊmaɪl] [ka-mo-mail], *s. (Bot.)* Manzanilla, camomila, hierba amarga de flores medicinales.

camouflage [ˈkæməflɑːz] [ka-mu-flash], *s.* Camuflaje, simulación, engaño. *-va.* Recurrir al camuflaje, fingir, simular (algo).

camp [kæmp] [kamp], *s. (Mil.)* Campo, campamento (tropa y terreno). **Summer camp,** campamento de verano, colonia de vacaciones o verano. **Army camp,** campamento militar. Bando (group, position). Amaneramiento, afectación (affected behavior, style).

camp, *vn. (Mil.)* Acampar, colocarse el ejército en tiendas. *-va.* Alojar un ejército; acampar. **To go camping,** ir de camping, de campamento o de acampada. **To camp out,** acampar. **To camp up,** actuar amaneradamente o con afectación.

camp, *a.* Amanerado, afeminado (effeminate). Afectado, exagerado (performance).

campaign [kæmˈpeɪn] [kam-pein], *s.* 1. Campaña, campiña, campo raso, llanura rasa. 2. *(Mil.)* Campaña, el tiempo que el ejército se mantiene en el campo. **To open the campaign,** empezar la campaña.

campaign, *vn.* Servir en campaña. **To campaign for/against something,** hacer una campaña a favor/en contra de algo.

campaigner [kæmˈpeɪnər] [kam-pei-neʳ], *s.* Campeador; veterano. *(Pol., Sociol.)* Defensor. **An old campaigner,** un veterano.

campaniform [ˌkæmpənɪˈfɔːm] [kam-pa-ni-form], **campanulate** [kæmˈpənjʊleɪt] [kam-pa-niu-leit], *a. (Bot.)* Campaniforme o campanuda, flor que tiene la figura de campana.

campanile [ˌkæmpəˈniːlɪ] [kam-pa-ni-li], *s.* Campanario de iglesia, especialmente cuando la torre se destaca aislada.

campanology [ˌkæmpəˈnɒlədʒɪ] [kam-pa-no-lo-yi], *s.* Campanología, el arte de tocar o repicar las campanas.

campanula [kæmˈpænjʊlə] [kam-pa-niu-la], *s. (Bot.)* Campánula.

campanulate [kæmˈpænjʊleɪt] [kam-pa-niu-leit], *a.* V. CAMPANIFORM.

campeachy-wood [ˌkæmpiːˈtʃɪˈwuːd] [kam-pi-chi-wud, *s.* Palo de Campeche o Palo campeche.

camper [ˈkæmpər] [kam-paʳ] *s.* Campista, acampante (in tent). *(Transp.)* Cámper.

campfire [ˈkæmpˌfaɪə] [kamp-faia], *s.* Hoguera en un campamento. Fogata, fogón.

campfollower [ˈkæmpəˌfɒləʊər] [kamp-fo-loueʳ] *s.* Simpatizante (sympathizer). *(Mil.)* Prostituta (prostitute).

campground [ˈkæmpgraʊnd] [kamp-graund] *s.* Camping.

camphine [ˈkæmpfiːn] [kamp-fin], *s.* Aceite de trementina rectificado, que se usó antiguamente para el alumbrado.

camphor [ˈkæmfər] [kam-foʳ], *s.* Alcanfor, sustancia blanca, volátil, parecida a la goma, de un olor característico, que se extrae del alcanforado, o laurel-alcanfor. **Camphor-tree,** alcanforero, alcanforado, o laurel alcanfor.

camphor, camphorate, *va.* Alcanforar, impregnar o lavar con alcanfor.

camphorate, *a.* Alcanforado.

camping [ˈkæmpɪŋ] [kam-pin], *s.* 1. Campamento. 2. *(Des.)* Antiguo juego de pelota con los pies. **I like camping,** me gusta ir de camping, de campamento o de acampada. **No camping,** prohibido acampar.

campion [ˈkæmpɪən] [kam-pion], *a. (Bot.)* Colleja, hierba de las cariofileas.

campsite [ˈkæmpsaɪt] [kamp-sait] *s.* Camping.

campus [ˈkæmpəs] [kam-pus], *s.* *(E.U.)* Terreno perteneciente a un colegio e inmediato a él, o el patio rodeado por los edificios dle colegio o universidad.

camshaft [ˈkæmʃɑːft] [kamp-shaft], *s. (Mec.)* Árbol de levas, eje de levas.

camwood [ˈkæmpwuːd] [kamp-wud], *s.* Madera roja de África y del Brasil.

can [kæn] [kan], *s.* Lata, bote, tarro (container). **Can opener,** abridor de latas, abrelatas. **A can of worms,** un problema complicado. Bidón (for petrol, water); cubo, tacho, caneca, bote, tobo de la basura (for garbage). (GB) *(Coloq.)* **To carry the can,** pagar el pato. Cárcel, cana, bote, trullo (prison). **To be in the can,** estar a la sombra. Trono (toilet). *(Fam./vulg.)* Culo, trasero (buttocks).

can, *v mod.* (pret.COULD). 1. Poder (indicating ability). **She couldn't answer the question,** no pudo contestar la pregunta. **We can but try,** con intentarlo no se pierde nada. **If I can but see him,** con tal que yo le pueda ver. **As sure as can be,** sin duda, indudablemente, segurísimo. **As soon as can be,** al instante que se pueda; lo más pronto posible. **It can not be,** es imposible, no puede ser. **He can't (can not) pay,** él no puede pagar. **He is as like his father as can be,** el es tan parecido a su padre que más no puede ser. 2. Saber (referring to particular skills). **Can you swim/speak German?,** ¿sabes nadar/(hablar) alemán? **She can read and write,** ella sabe leer y escribir. **Nobody can tell,** nadie sabe nada. **I can't see very well,** no veo muy bien (with verbs of perception). **Can you hear me?,** ¿me oyes? **I can't understand it,** no lo entiendo, no logro o no puedo entenderlo (with verbs of mental activity). **Can't you tell he's lying?,** ¿no te das cuenta de que está mintiendo? Poder (indicating, asking etc. permission). **Can I come with you?,** ¿puedo ir contigo? **You can stay as long as you like,** te puedes quedar todo el tiempo o todo lo que quieras. Poder (in requests). **Can you turn that music down, please?,** ¿puedes bajar esa música, por favor? **Can I have two salads, please?,** ¿me trae dos ensaladas, por favor? **Can I help you?,** ¿me permite? (in offers); ¿le atienden?, ¿qué desea? (in shop). **Can I carry that for you?,** ¿quieres que te lleve eso? Poder (allow oneself to). **You can't blame her,** no puedes echarle la culpa. **I couldn't very well tell him just then,** no se lo podía decir justo en ese momento. **How could you?,** pero, ¿cómo se te ocurrió hacer una cosa así?, pero, ¿cómo pudiste hacer (o decir) una cosa así? **Can't you give it another try?,** ¿por qué no lo vuelves a intentar? (in suggestions, advice). **For a start, you can clean all this up,** puedes empezar por limpiar todo esto (in orders). Poder (indicating possibility). **Anything can happen now,** ahora puede pasar cualquier cosa. **What can she be doing in there?,** ¿qué estará haciendo ahí?; ¿qué puede estar haciendo ahí? **It can't be true!,** ¡no puede ser!, ¡no es posible! **You can't be serious!,** ¡no lo dirás en serio! **She can be charming when she wants to,** es encantadora cuando quiere, o cuando se lo propone (indicating characteristic). **She's as happy as can be,** está contentísima, está de lo más contenta.

can, *va.* Guardar algo en cajas de hoja de lata para conservarlo en buen estado. Enlatar (put in cans); preparar conservas de (fruit). **Canned goods,** carne preparada, hortalizas, pescado o frutas encerrados herméticamente en receptáculos de hoja de lata o de vidrio. Llámense generalmente en la Gran Bretaña, *tinned goods.* *(Coloq.)* Echar, correr (dismiss). **Can it!,** ¡basta ya! (stop).

Canada [ˈkænədə] [ka-na-da] *N.* Canadá.

canada balsam, *s. V. BALSAM.*

canadian [kəˈneɪdɪən] [ka-nei-dian], *a./s.* Canadiense, del Canadá.

canal [kəˈnæl] [ka-nal], *s.* 1. Canal; conducto artifical por donde corre el agua (irrigation). 2. Canal, de navegación (for transport). 3. *(Anat.)* Canal, conducto por donde circulan la sangre y otros humores del cuerpo. 4. *(Arq.)* Estría, media caña.

canalage [kəˈnæleɪdʒ] [ka-na-leich], *s.* 1. Construcción de canales. 2. Coste, gastos del transporte por un canal.

canaliculate [kəˈnælɪkjʊleɪt] [ka-na-li-kiu-leit], *a.* Acanalado, estriado, abierto en forma de media caña.

canaliculus [kəˈnælɪkjʊləs] [ka-na-li-kiu-lus], *s.* Canal, o tubo, diminuto como los que hay en un hueso.

canard [kæˈnɑːd] [ka-nard], *s.* Embuste; noticia falsa, principalmente en un periódico.

Canaries [kəˈnɛərɪz] [ka-na-ris] *N.* **The Canaries,** (las) Canarias.

canary [kəˈnɛərɪ] [ka-na-ri], *s.* 1. Vino de Canarias. 2. Canario, un baile antiguo. 3. *(Fam.)* Soplón, chivato.

canary-bird [ˈkənɛərɪˌbɜːd] [ka-na-ri-berd], *s.* Canario, pájaro pequeño que canta primorosamente.

Canary Islands [kəˈnɛərɪˌaɪləndz] [ka-na-ri-ailands], *s.* las Islas Canarias.

canary-seed [kəˈnɛərɪˌsiːd] [ka-na-ri-síd], *s.* Alpiste.

canary-yellow [kəˌnɛərɪˈjeləʊ] [ka-na-ri-ye-lou], *a.* amarillo canario o patito.

canasta [kəˈnæstə] [ka-nas-ta], *s.* Canasta (juego de naipes).

can-buoy [kænˈbɔɪ] [kan-boi], *s. (Mar.)* Boya cónica de barril.

can-hooks [kænˈhuːkz] [kan-juks], *s. pl. (Mar.)* Gafas.

cancel [ˈkænsəl] [kan-sel], *va.* 1. Cancelar (meeting, subscription, flight); borrar. 2. Cancelar un escrito. 3. Invalidar, anular (command, decree, check). 4. Limitar, encerrar, estrechar, poner límites. 5. *(Mat.)* Eliminar. *-vn.* **He cancelled at the last minute,** a último momento canceló la cita (o el viaje) (call off).

cancel out, *(Mat.)* Anular. Compensar (offset/deficit, loss); cancelar (debt). **Those advantages are called out by the practical difficulties,** las dificultades de orden práctico anulan estas ventajas.

cancel, *s. (Imp.)* Cartón, cuartilla, la hoja o las páginas que se rehacen, sea por corrección o por errata.

cancellate [ˈkænsəlɪt] [kan-se-leit], *a.* Reticular, celular, poroso como algunos huesos.

cancellation [ˈkænsəleɪʃən] [kan-se-lei-shon], *s.* Canceladura, cancelación. *(Teat.)* **There may be some cancellations on the night,** quizás haya alguna devolución esa misma noche.

cancer [ˈkænsər] [kan-saʳ], *s.* 1. *(Med.)* Cáncer, tumor maligno (disease). 2. *(Astr.)* Cáncer, el signo de solsticio de estío. Cáncer o canceriano (person). 3. Cangrejo.

cancerate [ˈkænsəreɪt] [kan-se-reit], *vn.* Cancerarse o encancerarse.

canceration [ˈkænsəreɪʃən] [kan-se-rei-shon], **cancerousness** [ˈkænsərəsnɪs] [kan-se-rous-nes], *s.* Principio de cáncer, el estado o calidad cancerosa.

cancer-fighting [ˌkænsəˈfaɪtɪŋ] [kan-ser-fai-tin], *a.* Anticanceroso.

cancerous [ˈkænsərəs] [kan-se-rous], *a.* Canceroso, lo que tiene la malignidad de cáncer; virulento.

candelabrum [ˌkændɪˈlæbrəm] [kan-di-la-brum], *s.* CANDELABRA, *pl.* 1. Hachero, blandón, el pie o soporte en que los antiguos ponían la lámpara. 2. Candelero con varios mecheros, mechero. Candelabro.

candent [ˈkændənt] [kan-dent], *a. (Ant.)* Candente, que está hecho un ascua.

candid ['kændɪd] [kan-ded], *a*. 1. Cándido, sencillo, ingenuo, sincero, franco, íntegro, abierto, sin doblez. 2. (*Des.*) Blanco.

candidacy ['kændɪdəsɪ] [kan-di-da-si] *s*. Candidatura.

candidate ['kændɪdeɪt] [kan-di-deit], *s*. Candidato, el que aspira a algún empleo; pretendiente, opositor, aspirante.

candidateship ['kændɪdeɪtʃɪp] [kan-di-deit-ship], *s*. Candidatura, estado de candidato.

candid camera ['kændɪdˌkæmərə] [kan-did-ka-me-ra], *s*. Pequeña máquina fotográfica utilizada para tomar instantáneas inadvertidamente.

candidly ['kændɪdlɪ] [kan-did-li], *adv*. Cándidamente, ingenuamente, francamente.

candidness ['kændɪdnɪs] [kan-did-nes], *s*. Candidez, candor, sinceridad, pureza de ánimo.

candied ['kændɪd] [kan-did], *pp*. y *a*. Confitado, bañado en azúcar o conservado en almíbar. *V. CANDY.*

candle ['kændl] [kan-dol], *s*. 1. Candela, vela (for domestic use); cirio (for altar). 2. Luz. 3. Bujía. **To burn the candles at both ends,** tratar de abarcar demasiado, hacer de la noche día. **She can't/doesn't hold a candle to her sister,** no le llega ni a la suela del zapato a la hermana. **Candle power,** fuerza de iluminación de una standard candle. **Standard candle, (a)** vela de esperma que quema dos granos por minuto: se usa como tipo y medida de la luz; (b) la cantidad de luz que da esa vela o bujía. (c) La cantidad de luz emitida por 1/20 milímetro cuadrado de platino derretido. **Roman candle,** vela romana, juego artificial. **The game is not worth the candle,** no vale la pena. **To hold a candle to,** comparar una persona o cosa con otra. **Candle-holder,** palmatoria, portavela (for birthday cakes, etc.). **Candle-snuffers,** despabiladeras, instrumento para despabilar; cuando se aplica a personas, denota inutilidad o estupidez.

candlelight ['kændllaɪt] [kan-del-lait], la luz de una vela, bujía o candela; luz artificial, en general. **By candlelight,** a la luz de una vela/de las velas. **At early candlelight,** al punto de las oraciones; al tiempo preciso de encender las luces.

candlelit ['kændllɪt] [kan-del-lit], *a*. alumbrado con velas (room, restaurant). **A candlelit dinner,** una cena íntima a la luz de las velas.

candleberry-tree ['kændlberɪˌtriː] [kan-del-be-ri-trí], *s*. (*Bot.*) Árbol de la cera.

Candlemas ['kændlmæs] [kan-del-mas], *s*. Candelaria, fiesta que celebra la iglesia en honra de la Purificación de la Virgen.

candlepower ['kændlˌpaʊər] [kan-del-paua'], *s*. (*Elec.*) Bujías.

candlestick ['kændlstɪk] [kan-del-stik], *s*. Candelero. **Chamber candlestick,** palmatoria. **Branched candlestick,** araña. (*Mex.*) Candil.

candlewick ['kændlwɪk] [kan-del-uik], *s*. Chenilla, mecha.

candor, candour ['kændər] [kan-do'], *s*. Candor, sinceridad, integridad, sencillez, ingenuidad, franqueza.

C & W *s*. = **country and western.**

candy ['kændɪ] [kan-di], *va*. 1. Confitar, cubrir las frutas o pastas con un baño de azúcar o cocerlas en almíbar. **Lemon candy,** caramelos. **Peanut candy,** pepitoria. **Candied almonds,** almendras garapiñadas. 2. Garapiñar. *-vn*. Cristalizar (el azúcar); secarse o endurecerse los dulces.

candy, *s*. Confite, confitura, dulce, golosina (confectionery). Caramelo, dulce (individual piece). **Candy bar,** golosina en barra. **Candy box,** caja de dulces o confites. **Candy dish,** confitera.

candy apple ['kændɪˌeɪpəl] [kan-di-eipol] *s*. Manzana acaramelada.

candyfloss ['kændɪflɒs] [kan-di-flos] *s*. Algodón (de azúcar).

candystriped ['kændɪstraɪpt] [kan-di-straipt] *a*. A rayas.

candytuft ['kændɪtʌft] [kan-di-taft], *s*. (*Bot.*) Carraspique ibéride, planta crucífera que se cultiva en los jardines como de adorno.

cane [keɪn] [kein], *s*. 1. Caña o junco de Indias, caña de Bengala (of bamboo). 2. Caña de azúcar (sugar cane). 3. Lanza, caña. 4. Junco o bastón (walking stick); palmeta (for punishment). **He got the cane,** le dieron con la palmeta. 5. Caña, planta hueca y nudosa que se cría en los lugares húmedos. Mimbre (for wickerwork). 6. Caña o bastón de caña de Bengala. 7. Rodrigón, tutor (for supporting plants). **Head of a cane,** puño de bastón. **Cane-brake,** cañaveral espeso. **Cane-field,** cañaveral. **Cane-juice,** zumo de la caña de azúcar, llamado en Cuba guarapo. **Canemill,** ingenio de azúcar.

cane, *va*. Apalear, dar de palos con un bastón o caña. Castigar con la palmeta.

canella ['kæniːlə] [ka-ni-la], *s*. 1. Canelero, canelo. 2. Canela, corteza aromática.

canescent ['kænəsənt] [ka-nesent], *a*. Que se pone blanco o cano.

canicular ['kænɪkjolər] [ka-ni-kiu-la'], *a*. Canicular, perteneciente a la canícula.

canine ['kænaɪn] [ka-nain], *s*. (*Zool.*) Canino, cánido, perruno. **Canine tooth,** diente canino, colmillo. *-a*. Canino.

caning ['keɪnɪŋ] [kei-nin] *s*. **To give somebody a caning,** castigar a alguien con la palmeta.

canister ['kænɪstər] [ka-nis-ta'], *s*. 1. Canastillo, cesta pequeña. 2. Bote, frasco, o caja, de plata u hoja de lata para guardar té, tabaco, etc. 3. (*Mil.*) Bote (de humo, metralla, etc.)

canker ['kæŋkər] [kan-ka'], *s*. 1. Una llaga ulcerosa con tendencia a la gangrena; especialmente una pequeña úlcera en la boca. 2. Gangrena, enfermedad que padecen los árboles. **Canker sore,** afta.

canker, *vn*. Gangrenarse, corromperse, roerse. *-va*. Gangrenar, roer, corromper; contaminar.

cankerous ['kæŋkərəs] [kan-ke-rus], *a*. Gangrenoso, corrosivo, canceroso.

cankerworm ['kæŋkəwɔːm] [kan-ker-uerm], *s*. Oruga que destruye los árboles y frutas, especialmente las larvas del género Anisopterix.

cannabis ['kænəbɪs] [ka-na-bis], *s*. 1. Cáñamo, planta de las cannabineas, antiguo orden incluido hoy en la familia de las urticáceas. **Cannabis plant,** cáñamo índico. 2. Hachís, cannabis (drug).

canned ['kænd] [kand] *a*. 1. Enlatado, en o de lata, en conserva (food). 2. (*Coloq.*) Enlatado (pre-recorded/music); grabado (laughter).

canned goods ['kændˌguːdz] [kand-guds], *s*. *pl*. Conservas enlatadas, artículos enlatados.

cannel ['kænl] [kanel], *s*. Carbón duro. *V. COAL.*

cannelloni [ˌkænɪˈləʊnɪ] [ka-ni-lou-ni] *s*. Canelones.

canner ['kænər] [ka-na'], *s*. Enlatador.

cannery ['kænərɪ] [ka-ne-ri] *s*. Fábrica de conservas o enlatados.

cannibal ['kænɪbəl] [ka-ni-bal], *s*. Caníbal, caribe, antropófago, el que come carne humana.

cannibalism ['kænɪbəlɪzəm] [ka-ni-ba-lísem], *s*. Canibalismo, antropofagia, carácter y costumbres de los caníbales.

cannibalize ['kænɪbəlaɪz] [ka-ni-ba-lais] *va*. Canibalizar (machine, car); fusilarse, plagiar (material).

cannon ['kænən] [ka-non], *s*. 1. Cañón de artillería. 2. (*Ingl.*) Carambola en el juego de billar. **Cannon fodder,** carne de cañón. **Within cannon-shot,** a tiro de cañón. **Cannon-ball** o **Cannon-shot,** bala de cañón. **Cannon metal,** metal para cañones, que es generalmente bronce, pero algunas veces de hierro y acero.

cannon-hole ['kænənhəʊl] [ka-non-joul], *s*. (*Mar.*) Tronera.

cannon-proof ['kænənpruːf] [ka-non-pruf] *a*. A prueba de cañón.

cannonade [ˌkænəˈneɪd] [ka-no-neid], *va*. Cañonear o acañonar, batir a cañonazos. *-s*. Cañoneo, acto de cañonear; la repetición de cañonazos.

cannoneer ['kænənɪər] [ka-no-nia'], *va*. Cañonear.

cannoneer, *s.* Cañonero o artillero, el que carga, apunta y dispara el cañón.

cannot [ˈkænɒt] [ka-not], *vn.* De can y*not.* No poder. *V. CAN.*

canny, cannie [ˈkænɪ] [ka-ni], *a. (Esco.)* 1. Sagaz, prudente, cuerdo. Astuto (shrewd). 2. Agradable, placentero; garboso; digno.

canoe [kəˈnuː] [ka-nu], *s.* Canoa, piragua.

canoe, *vn.* Ir en canoa o piragua.

canoeing [kəˈnuːɪŋ] [ka-nuin] *s.* Piragüismo, canotaje.

canoeist [kəˈnuːɪst] [ka-nuist] *s.* Piragüista, remero de canoas, canoero.

canon [ˈkænən] [ka-non], *s.* 1. Canon, regla, ley, estatuto (standard, criterion). 2. Canon o cánones, leyes establecidas por los concilios, que tratan de la disciplina eclesiástica (church decree). **Canon law,** derecho canónico. 3. Canónigo, el que posee una prebenda o canongía en las catedrales o colegiatas. 4. Canon, catálogo de los libros sagrados y auténticos aceptados por la Iglesia. 5. Canon, un grado de la letra de imprenta, letra gruesa. 6. Canónigo (clergyman).

canoness [ˈkænənnɪs] [ka-no-nes], *sf.* Canonesa, la doncella que posee una de las prebendas que hay en algunas partes, destinadas a mujeres.

canonic, canonical [kəˈnɒnɪkəl] [ka-no-ni-kal], *a.* Canónico, según los cánones o según las leyes eclesiásticas; espiritual.

canonically [kəˈnɒnɪkəlɪ] [ka-no-ni-ka-li], *adv.* Canónicamente.

canonicals [kəˈnɒnɪkəlz] [ka-no-ni-kals], *s. pl.* Hábitos eclesiásticos, vestidos clericales.

canonicate [kəˈnɒnɪkeɪt] [ka-no-ni-keit], *s.* Canonicato.

canonist [kəˈnɒnɪst] [ka-no-nist], *s.* Canonista, profesor de derecho canónico.

canonization [ˌkænənaɪˈzeɪʃən] [ka-no-nai-sei-shon], *s.* Canonización, declaración del Sumo Pontífice, por la cual se pone en el número de los santos a alguno que ha vivido ejemplarmente.

canonize [ˈkænənaɪz] [ka-no-nais], *va.* Canonizar, poner en el número de los santos.

canonry [ˈkænənrɪ] [ka-non-ri], **canonship** [ˈkænənʃɪp] [ka-non-ship], *s.* Canongía o canonicato; prebenda.

canoodle [kəˈnuːdl] [ka-nudel] *vn. (Coloq.)* Besuquearse.

canopied [ˈkænəpaɪd] [ka-no-paid], *a.* Endoselado.

canopy [ˈkænəpɪ] [ka-no-pi], *s.* Dosel, baldaquín, baldaquino (over bed, throne); pabellón. Palio, dosel (over person). *(Aer.)* Cabina cerrada, transparente. **Cannopy of a bed,** cielo de cama colgada.

canopy, *va.* Endoselar, cubrir con dosel.

canorous [ˈkænərəs] [ka-no-ros], *a.* Canoro, lo que produce un sonido agradable al oído; melodioso, musical.

canst [ˈkænst] [kanst] *s. (Arq.)* 2nd pers. sing. pres. of CAN.

cant [ˈkænt] [kant], *s.* 1. Jerigonza, germanía, modo de hablar usado entre gitanos y gente baja. Jerga (jargon). 2. Hipocresía (insincere talk); fingimiento de piedad, virtud o devoción. 3. Almoneda pública. 4. Sesgo, posición oblicua, desviación de la línea vertical u horizontal. 5. *(Ant.)* Esquina, ángulo; escuadra.

can't [ˈkænt] [kant]. *(Fam.)* Abreviación de *cannot. V. CAN.*

cantaloup o cantaloupe [ˈkæntəluːp] [kan-ta-lup], *s. Cantaloup,* variedad de melón de cáscara rugosa y pulpa anaranjada.

cantankerous [kænˈtæŋkərəs] [kan-tan-ke-rus], *a. (Fam.)* Quimerista, pendenciero, propenso a poner faltas. Cascarrabias.

cantata [kænˈtɑːtə] [kan-ta-ta], *s.* Cantata, canción. *(Ital.)*

canted [ˈkæntɪd] [kan-ted], *a.* Oblicuo, inclinado.

canteen [kænˈtiːn] [kan-tin], *s.* 1. *(Mil.)* Cantina, bote de hoja de lata en que los soldados llevan agua o licor; cantimplora (water bottle). 2. Cantina, puesto en el campo donde se vende vino, cerveza y licores. 3. (GB) Cantina, comedor, casino (en un lugar de trabajo, colegio, etc.) (dining hall). 4. Estuche para guardar un juego de cubiertos. **Canteen of cutlery,** juego de cubiertos, cubertería.

cantel [ˈkæntl] [kan-tel], *s. V. CANTLE,* 1ª acep.

canter [ˈkæntər] [kan-teʳ], *s.* Medio galope.

canter, *vn.* Andar el caballo a paso largo y sentado.

cant-frames [ˈkæntfreɪmz] [kant-freims], *s. pl. (Mar.)* Cuadernas reviradas. **Cant-timbers,** o **cant-crotches,** piques capuchinos o reviradas.

cantharides [kænˈθærɪdiːs] [kan-za-ri-dis], *s.* Cantáridas.

canthus [ˈkænθəs] [kan-zus], *s.* Canto o ángulo del ojo.

canticle [ˈkæntɪkl] [kan-ti-kol], *s.* 1. Cántico, canto o canción. 2. El Cantar de los Cantares de Salomón.

cantilever [ˈkæntɪliːvər] [kan-ti-le-vaʳ], *s. (Arq.)* Ménsula, viga voladiza. **Cantilever bridge,** puente voladizo.

cantingly [ˈkæntɪŋlɪ] [kan-tin.li], *adv.* Hipócritamente.

cantle, cantlet [ˈkæntl] [kan-tel] [ˈkæntlɪt] [kan-tlit], *s.* 1. Pedazo, fragmento o residuo. 2. Borrén, trasero del arzón de una silla de montar.

canto [ˈkæntəʊ] [kan-tou], *s.* Canto, parte de algún poema u obra de poesía.

canton [ˈkæntɒn] [kan-ton], *s.* Cantón, porción de territorio con el correspondiente número de habitantes; una de las 22 divisiones de la Confederación Suiza.

canton, cantonize [ˈkæntənaɪz] [kan-to-nais], *va.* Acantonar, acuartelar, distribuir en cuarteles separados.

cantonment [ˈkæntɒnmənt] [kan-ton-ment], *s.* Acuartelamiento, acantonamiento.

cantor [ˈkæntər] [kan-toʳ], *s.* Chantre, cantor principal.

canty [ˈkæntɪ] [kan-ti], *a. (Esco.)* Alegre, jovial, festivo.

canuck [kæˈnɒk] [ka-nuk] *s. (Slang)* Canadiense.

canvas [ˈkænvəs] [kan-vas], *s.* 1. Lona, tela tosca y fuerte hecha de cáñamo o algodón (cloth). **Under canvas,** en una tienda de campaña o en una carpa (in a tent). 2. Cañamazo, tela gruesa y clara sobre la que se borda con seda o lana. 3. Lienzo, tela tendida sobre y preparada para recibir colores (for painting). 4. *(Mar.)* Lona, vela, velamen.

canvas-back [ˈkænvəsˌbæk] [kan-vas-bak], *s.* Pato marino de la América del Norte, muy estimado por su carne.

canvass [ˈkænvəs] [kan-vas], *s.* 1. El acto de solicitar votos para lograr algún destino; pretensión. 2. Examen, inspección oficial de alguna cosa. 3. Investigación circunstanciada.

canvass, *va.* 1. Escudriñar, examinar. 2. Disputar, conrovertir. **To canvass voters in an area,** hacer campaña entre los votantes de una zona. Sondear, hacer un sondeo de (opinion). **To canvass the votes,** hacer el escrutinio de los votos (scrutinize). *-vn.* Solicitar votos para lograr algún destino, pretender, ser candidato en alguna elección; ambicionar, escudriñar. Hacer campaña, hacer propaganda electoral. **To canvass for somebody,** hacer campaña a o en favor de alguien.

canvasser [ˈkænvəsər] [kan-va-seʳ], *s.* 1. Solicitador; particularmente el que solicita comercio o negocios yendo de casa en casa. 2. *(E.U.)* Agente electoral. Persona que solicita votos durante una campaña electoral.

canvassing [ˈkænvəsɪŋ] [kan-va-sin] *s.* Solicitación de votos.

canyon [ˈkænjən] [ka-nion], *s.* Cañón, desfiladero.

canzonet [ˈkænzənɪt] [kan-so-net], *s.* Cancioneta o cancioncilla, canción pequeña.

caoutchouc [ˈkaʊtɒk] [kau-chuk], *s.* Goma elástica, hule; jugo resinoso y lechoso de varios árboles tropicales.

cap [kæp] [kap], *s.* 1. Gorro o gorra, que se pone en la cabeza (hat). **Swimming cap,** gorro o gorra de baño. **Baseball/golf cap,** gorra de béisbol/golf. **Cap and gown,** toga y birrete. **If the cap fits wear it,** al que le caiga o le venga el sayo o saco, que se lo ponga; el que se pica ajos come. *(Coloq.)* **To put one's thinking cap on,** usar la materia gris. 2. Birreta o capelo, la insignia de cardenal. 3. Tapa (de lente). Tapa, tapón (of bottle); chapa, tapa (metal); capuchón, tapa (of pen). **Gas/petrol cap,** tapa del depósito o tanque de gasolina. (BrE) Diafragma (diaphragm). Tope (upper limit). **To put a cap on something,** poner un límite a algo. 4. *(Mar.)* Tamboretes, tablones gruesos, que se ponen al remate del palo. 5. Sombrero de mortero. 6. Reverencia hecha con la gorra. 7. Cima, cumbre, el punto más elevado. **Fool's cap,** (a) Nombre de una especie de papel para escribir, cuya dimensión corresponde al marquilla español. (b) (En las escuelas) Orejas de burro. **Percussion cap,** cápsula, pistón fulminante (for toy gun). **The cap fits,** viene de perilla. **To set one's cap for,** proponerse o procurar conquistarse el amor de un hombre; dícese de la mujer que anda en busca de marido. **Cap paper,** papel a propósito para escribir. *V. PAPER.*

cap. *va.* 1. Poner cima o remate a; cubrir la punta de. Tapar (bottle, tube). 2. Cubrir la cabeza. 3. Saludar a uno. 4. Dar la última mano, acabar; también, sobrepujar. 5. Rematar, coronar (crown, complete). **To cap it all off,** o (GB) **To cap it all...** para colmo de desgracias o de males..., para rematarla... 6. Poner un tope a, limitar (set upper limit) (expenditure). *(Dent.)* **To have a tooth capped,** ponerse una funda o una corona. **They were always trying to cap each other's jokes,** estaban siempre tratando de contar un chiste mejor que el del otro (outdo). *-vn.* Quitarse el gorro en señal de reverencia o cortesía. **To cap verses,** recitar versos.

cap (= **capital city**) Cap.

CAP *s.* (= **Common Agricultural Policy**) PAC.

capability [ˌkeɪpəˈbɪlɪtɪ] [ka-pa-bi-li-ti], *s.* Capacidad, idoneidad, aptitud, inteligencia. **Capability to,** capacidad para. **Capabilities,** aptitudes (potential).

capable [ˈkeɪpəbl] [kei-pa-bol], *a.* 1. Capaz, idóneo, competente (competent). **I'll leave you in the capable hands of Mr. Smith,** lo dejo con el Sr. Smith que lo ayudará en todo lo que necesite. 2. Capaz, inteligente. 3. Capaz, lo que puede contener alguna cosa. 4. Suficiente, bastante, apto, bueno, propio. **To be capable of,** ser capaz de (able).

capableness [ˈkeɪpəblnɪs] [kei-pa-bol-nes], *s.* Capacidad, la propiedad de ser capaz.

capably [ˈkeɪpəblɪ] [kei-pa-bli] *adv.* Competentemente.

capacious [kəˈpeɪʃəs] [ka-pei-shos], *a.* 1. Capaz, ancho. 2. Capaz, extensivo, espacioso, extenso, grande, vasto.

capaciously [kəˈpeɪʃəslɪ] [ka-pei-shos-li], *adv.* Extensivamente.

capaciousness [kəˈpeɪʃəsnɪs] [ka-pei-shos-nes], *s.* Capacidad, cabida.

capacitate [kəˈpæsɪteɪt] [ka-pa-si-teit], *va.* Habilidad, hacer capaz, investir de autoridad conforme a la ley.

capacity [kəˈpæsɪtɪ] [ka-pa-si-ti], *s.* 1. Capacidad, cabida (maximum content). **A capacity crowd,** un lleno completo o total. Capacidad (output). **To operate at full capacity,** funcionar al límite de capacidad o a pleno rendimiento. 2. Inteligencia, poder, habilidad, capacidad, comprehensión, saber. **The job was beyond her capacity,** el trabajo estaba por encima de su capacidad. 3. Calidad (role), estado, condición, carácter. **In his capacity as union delegate,** en su calidad de delegado del sindicato. 4. Calidad, empleo, destino. **Cap and gown,** toga y birrete.

cap-a-pie [kæpəˈpaɪ] [kap-a-pai], *adv.* De pies a cabeza, de punta en blanco.

caparison [kəˈpærɪsn] [ka-pa-ri-son], *s.* Caparazón, cubierta que se pone a los caballos para tapar la silla y el aderezo.

caparison, *va.* 1. Enjaezar un caballo. 2. *(Fam.)* Vestir soberbiamente.

cape [keɪp] [keip], *s.* 1. Cabo, promontorio o punta de tierra. **To double o sail round a cape,** *(Mar.)* doblar o montar un cabo. **Cape Horn,** el Cabo de Hornos. **The Cape of Good Hope,** el Cabo de Buena Esperanza. 2. Capa corta, esclavina, manteleta (clothing).

caper [ˈkeɪpər] [kei-pe'], *s.* 1. Cabriola, salto o brinco (jump). 2. *(Bot., Culin.)* Alcaparra, fruta del alcaparro. 3. Corsario holandés del siglo XVII. 4. Travesura, broma (prank). **Cross capers,** desgracias, trabajos. **To cut a caper,** cabriolar, dar un brinco súbito.

caper, *vn.* 1. Cabriolar, cabriolear, hacer cabriolas. 2. *(Fam.)* Bailotear, brincar.

caperbush [ˈkeɪpəbʌʃ] [kei-per-bash], *s.* Danzador, saltador.

caper-spurge [keɪpˈspɜːdʒ] [kei-per-sperch], *s. (Bot.)* Tártago o catapacia menor.

Cape Town [keɪptaʊn] [keip-taun] *N.* Ciudad del Cabo.

capful [ˈkæpfʊl] [kap-ful] *s.* Contenido de una tapa (o un tapón, etc.).

capias [ˈkæpɪəs] [ka-pias], *s.* Auto ejecutivo o de ejecución. *(Lat.)*

capillaceous [kæpɪˈleɪʃəs] [ka-pi-la-shos], *a.* Capilar, delgado, semejante a un cabello.

capillaire [ˈkæpɪlər] [ka-pi-la'], *s.* Jarabe de culantrillo.

capillament [ˌkæpɪˈlæmənt>] [ka-pi-la-ment], *s.* Estambre o hebra de flor.

capillarity [ˌkæpɪˈlærɪtɪ] [ka-pi-la-ri-ti], *s.* Capilaridad, atracción capilar.

capillary [kəˈpɪlərɪ] [ka-pi-la-ri], *a.* 1. Semejante a un cabello, capilar, delgado. 2. Que pertenece a los vasos capilares. 3. Que pertenece a los fenómenos que se observan en los líquidos contenidos en tubos muy delgados, y a otros de atracción molecular. *-s. (Anat.)* Vaso capilar.

capillose [ˈkæpɪləʊz] [ka-pi-lous], *a.* Cabelludo.

capillation [ˈkæpɪleɪʃən] [ka-pi-lei-shon], *s.* Ramificación pequeña de vasos.

capital [ˈkæpɪtl] [ka-pi-tal], *a.* 1. Capital, que pertenece a la cabeza. 2. *(Law)* Que está sancionado con la pena de muerte; criminal, capital. **Capital punishment,** pena capital o de muerte. 3. *(Print.)* Mayúscula, hablando de letras. **He's into art with a capital A,** le interesa el Arte con mayúscula. 4. Excelente, brillante, magnífico. 5. Principal, primordial (major). *(Geog., Pol.)* **Capital city,** capital. *-s.* 1. Capitel o chapitel de una columna. 2. Capital, la ciudad principal o cabeza de algún gobierno (city). 3. *(Fin.)* Capital, fondo, principal, caudal productivo. **To make capital (out) of something,** sacar provecho o partido de algo. **Capital expenditure/investment,** gasto/inversión de capital. **Capital gains tax,** impuesto sobre la plusvalía. **Capital punishment,** Pena capital, pena de muerte.

capitalism [ˈkæpɪtəlɪzəm] [ka-pi-ta-lísem], *s.* Capitalismo.

capitalist [ˈkæpɪtəlɪst] [ka-pi-ta-list], *s.* Capitalista, el dueño de un capital, fondo o caudal productivo.

capitalize [kəˈpɪtəlaɪz] [ka-pi-ta-lais], *va.* 1. *(Fin.)* Capitalizar, agregar al capital el importe de los intereses; reducir la renta al capital. 2. *(Print.)* Principiar una palabra con mayúscula.

capitalize on, sacar provecho o partido de, capitalizar.

capitally [ˈkæpɪtəlɪ] [ka-pi-ta-li], *adv.* 1. Excelentemente, admirablemente. 2. Capitalmente con pena de muerte.

capitate [ˈkæpɪteɪt] [ka-pi-teit], *a. (Bot.)* Capitado, dispuesto en forma de cabezuela.

capitation [ˈkæpɪteɪʃən] [ka-pi-tei-shon], *s.* Encabezamiento o empadronamiento.

capitol [ˈkæpɪtɒl] [ka-pi-tol], *s.* 1. Capitolio, ciudadela antigua de Roma. 2. **Capitol Hill,** Capitolio, palacio del congreso en Washington, Estados Unidos de América; y edificio del poder legislativo en los diferentes Estados de la Unión.

capitoline [ˈkæpɪtɒliːn] [ka-pi-to-lin], *a.* Perteneciente al capitolio romano, capitolino.

capitular [ˈkæpɪtjɒlər] [ka-pi-tiu-la'], *s.* Estatutos capitulares, o el libro capitular en que se ponen.

capitularly [ˈkəpɪtjɒləlɪ] [ka-pi-tiu-lar-li], *adv.* Capitularmente.

capitulary [ˈkəpɪtjɒlərɪ] [ka-pi-tiu-la-ri], *a.* Capitular.

capitulate [kəˈpɪtjɒleɪt] [ka-pi-tiu-leit], *vn.* 1. *(Mil.)* Capitular, rendirse o entregarse bajo ciertas condiciones. 2. *(Des.)* Escribir alguna cosa dividiéndola en capítulos.

capitulation [kəˌpɪtjʊˈleɪsən] [ka-pi-tiu-lei-shon], *s.* 1. Capitulación, tratado, condición o términos con que se entrega alguna ciudad o plaza. 2. El acto de escribir por capítulos.

capitulator [kəˈpɪtjʊleɪtər] [ka-pi-tiu-lei-to*r*], *s.* Capitulante, el que capitula.

caplet [ˈkæplɪt] [kap-let] *s.* Comprimido de forma ovalada.

capnomancy [ˈkæpnɒmənsɪ] [kap-no-man-si], *s.* Capnomancia, pretendida adivinación por medio de las formas y la dirección del humo.

capo [ˈkeɪpə] [kei-po] *s.* Capotasto, ceja (for guitar).

capon [ˈkeɪpən] [kei-pon], *s.* Capón o pollo castrado.

capot [ˈkeɪpət] [kei-pot], *s.* Capote, en varios juegos es cuando un jugador no deja baza al contrario, así como en otros se llama bola.

capote [ˈkəpəʊt] [ka-pout], *s.* Capote, capota.

cappadine [ˈkəpədiːn] [ka-pa-din], *s.* Cadarzo, seda basta de capullo.

capparidaceous [ˌkəpærɪˈdeɪʃəs] [ka-pa-di-ri-dei-shos], *a.* Caparídeo, que se parece o refiere al género alcaparra.

capper [ˈkəpər] [ka-pe*r*], *s.* 1. Gorrero, el que hace o vende gorras. 2. El que en las fábricas para conservar frutas, etc., solda las tapas sobre los botes de hoja de lata. 3. Herramienta para fijar las cápsulas en la cabeza de una granada.

capreolate [ˈkəprəleɪt] [ka-pro-leit], *a. (Bot.)* Que tiene zarcillos o se asemeja a ellos. Se dice de las vides y otras plantas.

caprice [kəˈpriːs] [ka-pris], *s.* Capricho, extravagancia; antojo, humor.

capricious [kəˈprɪʃəs] [ka-pri-shos], *a.* Caprichoso, caprichudo; antojadizo, extravagante (person); variable (weather).

capriciously [kəˈprɪʃəslɪ] [ka-pri-shos-li], *adv.* Caprichosamente o caprichudamente.

capriciousness [kəˈprɪʃəsnɪs] [ka-pri-shos-nis], *s.* Capricho. *V. CAPRICE.*

Capricorn [ˈkæprɪkɔːn] [ka-pri-korn], *s. (Astr.)* Capricornio (sign); capricornio, capricorniano (person). **Capricorn-beetle,** *(Ent.)* Capricornio, especie de escarabajo.

caprification [ˌkæprɪfɪˈkeɪʃən] [ka-pri-fi-kei-shon], *s.* Caprificación, la acción de impregnar a la higuera hembra con el polen de la higuera macho, para que se madure el fruto.

capriole [ˈkəprɪəʊl] [ka-prioul], *s.* Corveta, cabriola, salto que da un caballo.

caps = capital letters

capsicum [ˈkæpsɪkəm] [kap-si-kum], *s. (Bot.)* Pimiento, pimentero; pimiento de Guinea. Pimentón, ají.

capsize [kæpˈsaɪz] [kap-sais], *va.* y *vn.* Trabucar, trastornar, volcar, poner patas arriba, volver de arriba abajo, acostar, tumbar, quedar dormido, zozobrar. Hacer volcar; hacer dar una vuelta de campana (right over). Volcarse, dar una vuelta de campana (right over).

capstan [ˈkæpstən] [kap-stan] o **capstern** [ˈkæpstɜːn] [kap-stern], *s.* 1. Cabrestante, para levantar cosas de peso. 2. *(Mar.)* Cabrestante, máquina a bordo de un buque, por medio de la cual se levan las áncoras y se descargan los fardos más pesados. **Capstan-barrel,** cuerpo o eje de cabrestante. **Capstan-whelps,** guarda-infantes. **Capstan-chocks,** cuñas de cabrestante. **Capstan-drumhead,** cabeza de cabrestante. **Capstan-spindle,** pínola del cabrestante. **Step of the capstan,** concha o carlinga del cabrestante. **Capstan-bars,** barras del cabrestante. **Capstan-pins,** pernillos del cabrestante. **To rig the capstan,** guarnir el cabrestante. **To heave the capstan,** virar el cabrestante. **To pawl the capstan,** pasar linguete. En las minas de Méjico, *Malacate.*

capstone [ˈkæpstəʊn] [kap-stoun], *s.* Piedra que corona y remata un edificio o monumento.

capsular [ˈkæpsjʊlər] [kap-siu-la*r*], **capsulary** [ˈkæpsjʊlərɪ] [kap-siu-la-ri], *a.* Capsular, en forma de bolsa o caja.

capsulate, capsulated [ˈkæpsjʊleɪt] [kap-siu-leit], *a.* Cerrado en forma de cápsula.

capsule [ˈkæpsjʊl] [kap-siul], *s.* 1. *(Bot.)* Cápsula, hollejo que cubre el fruto de alguna planta. 2. *(Quím.)* Crisol para ensayar los minerales. 3. Cajita, bolsita. **Space capsule,** cápsula espacial.

capt = Captain (title).

captain [ˈkæptɪn] [kap-tein], *s. (Mil.)* 1. Capitán, el oficial que manda una compañía de soldados (rank). 2. Jefe, comandante (person in command); comandante (of airline plane). 3. Maître, jefe de comedor, capitán de meseros (headwater). **Captain of a ship of the line,** *(Mar.)* capitán de navío. **Captain of the top,** gaviero mayor.

captain, *va. (Naut., Sport)* Capitanear.

captaincy [ˈkæptənsɪ] [kap-tein-si], **captainship** [ˈkæptənʃɪp] [kap-tein-ship], *s.* Capitanía, el grado y empleo de capitán.

caption [ˈkæpʃən] [kap-shon], *s.* 1. Título, rótulo, introducción de un documento legal (headline); leyenda (pie de foto o ilustración). 2. Membrete, encabezamiento. 3. Captura, prisión, la acción de prender a alguno.

captious [ˈkæpʃəs] [kap-shos], *a.* 1. Susceptible, quisquilloso, caviloso. 2. Capcioso, sofístico, falaz.

captiousness [ˈkæpʃəsnɪs] [kap-shos-nes], *s.* Espíritu de contradicción; humor pendenciero o querellista.

captivate [ˈkæptɪveɪt] [kap-ti-veit], *va.* 1. Cautivar, hacer a alguno cautivo; esclavizar. 2. Cautivar, atraer la voluntad.

captivating [ˈkæptɪveɪtɪŋ] [kap-ti-vei-tin], *a.* Encantador, seductor, seductivo, atractivo.

captvation [ˈkæptɪveɪʃən] [kap-ti-vei-shon], *s.* Captura, la ación de hacer a uno prisionero o cautivo.

captive [ˈkæptɪv] [kap-tiv], *s.* 1. Cautivo o esclavo. 2. Prisionero. *-a.* Cautivo. **To hold somebody captive,** mantener cautivo o prisionero a alguien. **To have a captive audience,** tener un público que no tiene más remedio que escuchar.

captivity [kæpˈtɪvɪtɪ] [kap-ti-vi-ti], *s.* 1. Cautiverio o cautividad, prisión. 2. Sujeción mental; influencia ejercida por una persona sobre la mente o la voluntad de otra.

captor [ˈkæptər] [kap-to*r*], *s.* Apresador, el que coge un prisionero o una presa.

capture [ˈkæptʃər] [kap-cha*r*], *s.* 1. Captura, la acción de prender (of person, animal); conquista, toma (of city); apresamiento (of ship). 2. Presa, botín, apresamiento.

capture, *va.* 1. Apresar, capturar (seize by force/person, animal); apresar (ship); tomar (city). 2. Captar, atraer (attract, hold/attention, interest). Captar, reproducir (preserve, record/ mood, atmosphere).

capuchin [ˈkæpjʊʃɪn] [ka-piu-shin], *s.* 1. Capuchino, religioso reformado de la orden de San Francisco. 2. Capucha y capotillo, especie de vestido exterior de señoras, algo parecido al de los capuchinos. 3. *(Orn.)* Especie de copete de plumas sobre la cabeza de los pájaros, en forma de capucha. 4. Capuchino, mono de la América del Sur, sapajú con el pelo de la cabeza en forma de capucha de fraile.

capucin [ˈkæpjʊʃɪn] [ka-piu-shin], 1. Color rojizo anaranjado. 2. Capuchina, planta trepadora, y su flor.

car [kɑːr] [ka*r*], *s.* 1. *(Rail, Transp.)* Vagón, coche, carro de ferrocarril; coche, automóvil, carro (Auto). **To go by car,** ir en coche, carro, etc. **Car bomb,** coche bomba. **Car seat,** asiento del coche (part of a car); asiento de bebé para el coche (for infant). 2. Carreta o carro de dos ruedas. 3. Carro militar, con que combatían antiguamente los héroes. 4. Caja de un ascensor, cabina (of elevator). 5. **Car of a balloon,** barquilla de globo aerostático. **Baggage-car,** coche de equipaje. **Dining-car,** coche comedor. **Flat car,** carro de plataforma. **Express car,** coche del expreso, para bultos y paquetes. **Sleeping-car,** coche dormitorio. **Cable-car,** *V. CABLE.* **Postal car,** coche estafeta. **Street car,** coche de tranvía, carro urbano.

carabine ['kærəbi:n] [ka-ra-bin], **carbine** ['kærbi:n] [kar-bin], s. Carabina, arma de fuego pequeña.

carabineer, carabinier ['kærəbɪnɪər] [ka-ra-bi-nia'], s. V. *CARBINEER.*

carac ['kærək] [ka-rak], s. Carraca, navío grande y tardo en navegar.

caracole ['kærəkəol] [ka-ra-koul], s. 1. Caracol, la vuelta que hace el jinete con el caballo, como en medio torno. 2. Escalera de caracol.

caracole, vn. Caracolear.

carafe [kə'ræf] [ka-raf], s. Garrafa, botella de cristal (for wine); botella de boca ancha (for water).

caramel ['kærəməl] [ka-ra-mel], s. 1. Caramelo, pasta de azúcar hecho almíbar al fuego y endurecido (burnt sugar). **Caramel sauce,** caramelo hecho a base de leche y azúcar (confectionery). 2. Caramelo, azúcar quemado para colorar licores.

carapace ['kærəpeɪs] [ka-ra-peis], s. Carapacho, la concha (superior) de las tortugas y algunos otros animales.

carat ['kærət] [ka-rat], s. Quilate, ley, grado de bondad y perfección del oro; peso de cuatro granos con que se pesan los diamantes y perlas. **18-carat gold,** oro de 18 quilates.

caravan ['kærəvæn] [ka-ra-van], s. 1. Caravana, multitud de viajeros, peregrinos, traficantes, etc., que se juntaban para cruzar los desiertos (group). 2. Caravana, cada una de las cuatro campañas de mar que hacían los caballeros de Malta. 3. (GB) Caravana, rulot, casa rodante, tráiler (vehicle). **Gypsy caravan,** carromato de gitanos. **Caravan park/site,** camping para caravanas.

caravel [kærə'vel] [ka-ra-vel], **carvel** ['kærvel] [kar-vel], s. Carabela, antigua embarcación larga y angosta, de una cubierta, tres mástiles y espolón a proa.

caraway o **caraway-seed** ['kærəweɪ] [ka-ra-uei], s. (Bot.) Alcaravea. Carvi.

carbid(e) ['ka:baɪd] [kar-baid], s. Carburo, combinación de carbón y un elemento positivo.

carbine ['ka:baɪn] [kar-bain], s. Carabina, fusil pequeño.

carbineer ['ka:bɪnɪər] [kar-bi-nia'], s. Carabinero, soldado de caballería ligera armado con carabina.

carbohydrate ['ka:bəo'haɪdreɪt] [kar-bou-hai-dreit], s. Carbohidrato, hidrato de carbono.

carbolic [ka:'bɒlɪk] [kar-bo-lik], a. Perteneciente al aceite de alquitrán. **Carbolic acid,** ácido carbólico o fénico. Llámase también *phenol.*

carbolize ['ka:bɒlaɪz] [kar-bo-lais], va. Impregnar con ácido carbólico.

carbon ['ka:bən] [kar-bon], s. (Quím.) Carbón o carbono. V. CARBON PAPER (paper); V. CARBON COPY (copy).

carbonate ['ka:bənɪt] [kar-bo-neit], s. Carbonato, sal formada por el ácido carbónico unido a alguna base.

carbonated ['ka:bənɪtɪd] [kar-bo-nei-ted], a. Carbonatado (water); gaseoso (drink).

carbon copy ['ka:bənkəpɪ] [kar-bon-ko-pi], s. Copia hecha con papel carbón. **To be a carbon copy of somebody/ something,** ser un calco de alguien/algo.

carbon dating ['ka:bəndeɪtɪŋ] [kar-bon-dei-tin] s. Datación mediante el método del carbono 14.

carbon dioxide [ˌka:bəndaɪ'ɒksaɪd] [kar-bon-dai-ok-said], s. (Quím.) Anhídrido carbónico, bióxido (o dióxido) de carbono.

carbon 14 ['ka:bənfɔ:ti:n] [kar-bon-for-tin], s. Carbono 14.

carbonic ['ka:bɒnɪk] [kar-bo-nik], a. Carbónico.

carboniferous ['ka:bɒnɪfərəs] [kar-bo-ni-fe-ros], a. Carbonífero, que contiene o da carbón o hulla.

carbonization [ˌka:bɒnaɪ'zeɪʃən] [kar-bo-nai-sei-shon], s. Carbonización, acción y efecto de carbonizar.

carbonize ['ka:bɒnaɪz] [kar-bo-nais], va. 1. Carbonizar, reducir a carbón. 2. Cubrir papel con carbón, negro de humo, etc.

carbon monoxide ['ka:bənmənɒksaɪd] [kar-bon-mo-nok-said] s. Monóxido de carbono.

carbon paper ['ka:bənˌpeipər] [kar-bon-pei-pa'], s. Papel carbón; papel de calco.

carborundum [ˌka:bə'rʌndəm] [kar-bo-ran-dom], s. (Quím.) Carborundo.

carbuncle ['ka:bʌŋkl] [kar-ban-kel], s. 1. Carbúnculo o carbunclo, piedra preciosa que brilla en la obscuridad. 2. (Med.) Carbunco, tumor puntiagudo y maligno con inflamación y dolor; forúnculo.

carbuncled ['ka:bʌŋklɪd] [kar-ban-klid], a. 1. Engastado con carbunclos. 2. Lleno de granos.

carbuncular ['ka:bʌŋkjɒlər] [kar-ban-kiu-la'], a. Encarnado como un carbunclo.

carburet ['ka:bjɒret] [kar-biu-ret], s. Carbureto, combinación del carbono con una base. V. CARBIDE.

carburetor, (BrE) **carburettor** [ˌka:bjɒ'retər] [kar-biu-re-ta'], s. Carburador.

carburize ['ka:bjɒraɪz] [kar-biu-rais], va. Combinar o impregnar con carbón.

carcanet ['ka:kənɪt] [kar-ka-nit], s. Collar o gargantilla de perlas o de otras piedras.

carcass, carcase ['ka:ləs] [kar-kas], s. 1. Res muerta o el cuerpo de un animal muerto (dead animal); caparazón, hablando de aves ; res muerta (for meat); huesos (of poultry). 2. Armazón de una casa. 3. (Mar.) Casco o armazón de un embarcación. 4. (Art.) Carcasa, especie de bomba oblonga.

carcer ['ka:sər] [kar-se'], s. Cárcel, lugar de encierro. (Lat.)

carceral ['ka:sərəl] [kar-se-ral], a. Lo que pertenece a la cárcel.

carcinogen [ka:'sɪnədʒen] [kar-si-no-yen], s. (Med.) Carcinógeno.

carcinogenic [ˌka:sɪnə'dʒenɪk] [kar-si-no-ye-nik] a. Cancerígeno, carcinógeno.

carcinoma ['ka:sɪ'nəomə] [kar-si-nou-ma], s. Carcinoma, cáncer.

carcinomatous ['ka:sɪ'nəomətəs] [kar-si-nou-ma-tos], a. Carcinomatoso, canceroso.

card [ka:d] [kard], s. 1. Naipe, carta, cartón pintado con diversos colores y figuras para jugar a varios juegos. **Pack of cards,** una baraja de naipes. **To shuffle the cards,** barajar las cartas. **To deal the cards,** dar cartas. **To cut the cards,** alzar o cortar las cartas para darlas. **Court card,** figura. **Small card,** carta sencilla. **Trump card,** triunfo. **Card-table,** mesa de juego. **To play cards,** jugar a las cartas. **To lay/put one's cards on the table,** poner las cartas boca arriba o sobre la mesa. **To play one's cards right,** jugar bien sus cartas. **It was in/on the cards that something like this would happen,** se veía venir o era seguro que iba a pasar algo así. **Postal card,** tarjeta postal. 2. Rosa naútica, la división que se hace en un círculo de cartón para señalar los vientos; llámase también rosa de los vientos. 3. Tarjeta (for identification, access). **Business card,** tarjeta de visita. **Credit card,** tarjeta de crédito. (GB) (Coloq.) **To give somebody their cards,** echar a alguien, darle la patada a alguien. **Greeting card,** tarjeta de felicitación. **Birthday card,** tarjeta de cumpleaños. **Christmas card,** tarjeta de Navidad, tarjeta de Pascua. **Card catalog/index,** fichero. Cromo, estampa (for collecting); lámina, figurita. Cartulina (thin cardboard). 4. Cardencha, carda, instrumento para cardar lana.

card, va. 1. Cardar lana; mezclar; desenredar. 2. Peinar y limpiar el pelo de los caballos con una carda.

cardamine ['ka:dəmaɪn] [kar-da-main], s. (Bot.) Mastuerzo de prado, hierba de las crucíferas.

cardamom ['ka:dəmən] [kar-da-mon], s. Cardamomo o grana del paraíso.

cardass ['ka:dəs] [kar-das], s. 1. Alanquia, carda grande de peinar seda. 2. Cardencha, carda para la lana.

cardboard ['ka:dbɔ:d] [kard-bord], s. Cartón (stiff); cartulina (thin). **Cardboard box,** caja de cartón. **Cardobard**

binding, encuadernación en cartoné, encuadernación con pastas de cartón.

cardcarrying [ˈkɑːdˌkærɪŋ] [kard-ka-rin] *a.* **He's a cardcarrying member of the party,** está afiliado al partido, es un miembro activo del partido.

card catalogue, *s.* Catálogo de tarjetas o fichas.

carder [ˈkɑːdər] [kardeʳ], *s.* 1. Cardador. 2. **Carder,** o **carder-bee,** abejorro que carda y fieltra el musgo para su nido.

cardholder [ˈkɑːdˌhəʊldər] [kard-joul-daʳ] *s.* Titular de una tarjeta de crédito.

cardiac [ˈkɑːdɪæk] [kar-diak], *a.* Cardíaco (condition). **Cardiac arrest,** paro cardíaco.

cardialgia, cardialgy [ˈkɑːdɪældʒɪə] [kar-dial-yia], *s. (Med.)* Cardialgia.

cardigan [ˈkɑːdɪɡən] [kar-di-gan] *s.* Cárdigan, chaqueta de punto, rebeca, saco, chaleca. **Cardigan sweater,** suéter o chaqueta tejida con botonadura al frente.

cardinal [ˈkɑːdɪnl] [kar-di-nal], *a.* 1. Cardinal, principal, primero. Fundamental, esencial (rule, idea). **Cardinal sin,** pecado capital. **Cardinal virtue,** virtud cardinal. **Cardinal point,** punto cardinal. 2. De color rojo vivo como el ropaje de los cardenales; bermellón. -*s.* 1. *(Rel.)* Cardenal, prelado de la Iglesia romana que tiene voz activa y pasiva en el cónclave para la elección del Pontífice. 2. Capa de mujer, del siglo XVIII. **Cardinal number,** número cardinal. **Cardinal-bird,** cardenal, pájaro rojo de la familia de los fringílidos. Cardinalis cardinales. **Cardinal-flower,** escurripa, hierba perenne norteamericana con flores de color rojo vivo.

cardinalate [ˈkɑːdɪnəleɪt] [kar-di-na-leit], **cardinalship** [ˈkɑːdɪnəlʃɪp] [kar-di-nal-ship], *s.* Cardenalato, empleo o dignidad de cardenal.

card index, *s.* Fichero, tarjetero.

carding [ˈkɑːdɪŋ] [kar-din], *s.* 1. El juego de naipes. 2. Cardadura, el acto de cardar lana o algodón.

cardiograph [ˈkɑːdɪəɡræf] [kar-dio-graf], *s.* Cardiógrafo.

cardiogram [ˈkɑːdɪəʊˌɡræm] [kar-dio-gram], *s.* Cardiograma.

cardiologist [ˌkɑːdɪˈɒlədʒɪst] [kar-dio-lo-yist] *s.* Cardiólogo.

cardiology [ˌkɑːdɪˈɒlədʒɪ] [kar-dio-lo-yi], *s.* Cardiología.

cardmaker [ˈkɑːdmeɪkər] [kard-mei-kaʳ], *s.* Fabricante de naipes o de cardenchas.

cardoon [ˈkɑːduːn] [kar-dún], *s. (Bot.)* Cardo silvestre.

card-party [kɑːdˈpɑːtɪ] [kard-par-ti], *s.* Partido o partida, el conjunto de los que participan en un juego de naipes.

cardphone [ˈkɑːdˌfəʊn] [kard-foun] *s.* (GB) Teléfono público que funciona mediante tarjetas prepagadas y/o de crédito.

cardsharp, cardshark [ˈkɑːdˌʃɑːp] [kard-sharp], Tahúr, tramposo, fulero.

care [kɛər] [keaʳ], *s.* 1. Cuidado, solicitud, inquietud, zozobra, desasosiego. 2. Cuidado, cautela, atención (attention, carefulness). 3. Cuidado, cargo, objeto de cuidado. **Handle with care,** frágil. **To take care,** tener cuidado. **Take care!** ¡ten cuidado! **He took care that all the figures were correct,** se aseguró de que todas las cifras eran las correctas. **To cast away care,** olvidar penas, alegrarse, regocijarse. **Care-crazed,** consumido de cuidados. **Care-worn,** devorado de inquietud, lleno de zozobra. **Medical care,** asistencia médica (of people); cuidado (of animals, things). *(Soc. Admin.)* (GB) **Her children were taken into care,** le quitaron la patria potestad. **In care of,** (GB) care of, en casa de (on letters). **To take care of somebody/something,** atender a alguien, cuidar de alguien (look after/of patient); cuidar de alguien, ocuparse o encargarse de alguien (of children). Cuidar algo (pet, plant, machine). **Take care!,** ¡cuídate!, ¡que estés bien! (saying goodbye). **I can take care of myself,** yo sé cuidarme. Ocuparse o encargarse de alguien o de algo (deal with). **That takes care of that!,** ¡listo!, ¡esto ya está! Preocupación (worry).

care, *vn.* 1. Cuidar, tener cuidado o pena, inquietarse o fatigarse de o por alguna cosa. Preocuparse por algo. **All he cares about is sport,** lo único que le interesa es el deporte.

2. Estimar, apreciar, hacer caso. **Who cares!,** ¡y a mí qué!; **see if I care!,** ¡me da igual! **What care I?,** ¿a mí qué me importa? **Will you come to walk? I don't care if I do,** ¿quiere Vd. venir a pasear? como Vd. quiera; me importa poco el hacerlo o no; me es indiferente. **I do not care,** no se me da nada; no me importa, no me da cuidado. **He does not care to be seen there,** él se ríe de que le vean allí. **Not to take care of one,** no hacer caso de alguno, despreciarle, desairarle. -*va.* **I couldn't care less what he does,** me tiene o me trae sin cuidado lo que haga, no me importa en absoluto lo que haga. **Who cares what she thinks?,** ¿y a quién le importa lo que ella piense? **Would you care to join us for dinner?,** ¿le gustaría cenar con nosotros? (wish). **He needs her more than he cares to admit,** la necesita más de lo que está dispuesto a reconocer. **Care for,** cuidar de, atender (look after/patient); cuidar, encargarse, ocuparse de (house, garden). **Well cared for,** bien cuidado. Querer, sentir afecto o cariño por (be fond of). **The house was lovely, but I didn't care for the furniture,** la casa era preciosa, pero los muebles no me gustaron o no eran de mi gusto (like). **Would you care for a cigar?,** ¿puedo ofrecerle un puro? (in offers).

careen [kəˈriːn] [ka-rín], *va. (Mar.)* Carenar o dar carena al navío, dar de lado a un barco para carenarle, o componerle. **Careening gear,** aparejo de carenar. **Careening wharf,** muelle de carenaje. -*vn.* Echarse de costado, dar a la banda. Ir a toda velocidad.

careening [kəˈriːnɪŋ] [ka-rí-nin], *s. (Mar.)* Carenamiento, el acto y efecto de carenar.

career [kəˈrɪər] [ka-riaʳ], *s.* 1. Carrera o curso de alguna cosa. 2. Carrera, el acto de correr rápidamente. 3. Carrera, profesión (armas, letras o ciencias). **He made a career for himself as a journalist,** se forjó una carrera como periodista. **Career girl/woman,** mujer de carrera. 4. *(Des.)* Carrera o estadio, el terreno en que se corre una carrera.

career, *vn.* Correr a carrera tendida o a todo galope.

carefree [ˈkɛəfriː] [kea-fri], *a.* Despreocupado, sin cuidados.

careful [ˈkɛəfʊl] [kea-ful], *a.* 1. Cuidadoso, ansioso, lleno de cuidados, inquieto, prudente (cautious). **You should be more careful in future,** tendrías que tener más cuidado en el futuro. **You can't be too careful,** toda prudencia es poca. **Be careful,** ten cuidado. **Be careful what you say,** cuidado con lo que dices. 2. Diligente, cauteloso, vigilante, avisado, prudente, solícito. Cuidadoso (painstaking/planning); cuidado, esmerado, bien hecho (work); meticuloso (worker). **After careful consideration of all the options,** después de considerar detenidamente todas las opciones.

carefully [ˈkɛəfəlɪ] [kea-fu-li], *adv.* Cuidadosamente, con cuidado (handle, drive); detenidamente, cuidadosamente (plan, examine); con esmero (designed, chosen). **Think it over carefully,** piénsatelo bien. **Listen carefully,** presta atención.

carefulness [ˈkɛəfəlnɪs] [kea-ful-nes], *s.* Cuidado, vigilancia; cautela, atención, diligencia; ansiedad.

careless [ˈkɛəlɪs] [kea-les], *a.* 1. Descuidado, poco cuidadoso (inattentive, negligent/person); negligente (driving); omiso, indiferente, abandonado; poco cuidado (work). **You made some careless mistakes,** cometiste errores por descuido. **She seems careless of the danger,** no parece importarle o preocuparle el peligro (indifferent). 2. Alegre, tranquilo. 3. Desenfadado; sencillo. 4. Dejado, flojo, indolente, perezoso. 5. Inconsiderado, hecho o dicho sin reflexión.

carelessly [ˈkɛəlɪslɪ] [kea-les-li], *adv.* Descuidadamente, negligentemente; con indiferencia. Sin la debida atención (inattentively); de manera despreocupada (casually).

carelessness [ˈkɛəlɪsnɪs] [kea-lis-nes], *s.* Descuido, negligencia, abandono, indiferencia, dejadez, flojedad, incuria. Falta de atención o cuidado.

carer [ˈkɛərər] [kea-reʳ] *s.* Persona que tiene a su cuidado a un anciano o a un incapacitado sin recibir por ello remuneración.

caress [kəˈres] [ka-res], *va.* Acariciar, halagar.

caress, *s.* Caricia, halago.

caret [ˈkærət] [ka-ret], *s.* Nota de corrección interlineal.

caretaker [ˈkeəˌteɪkər] [kea-tei-kaʳ] *s.* Conserje. Provisional (government).

careworn [ˈkeəwɔːn] [kea-uorn] *a.* Agobiado por las preocupaciones.

carfare [ˈkɑːfeəʳ] [kar-feaʳ] *s.* Precio del boleto o del billete.

carful [ˈkɑːfʊl] [kar-ful] *s.* V. CARLOAD.

cargo [ˈkɑːgəʊ] [kar-gou], *s.* Carga, cargazón cargamento de un buque (load). Carga (goods). **Cargo ship,** carguero, barco de carga.

carhop [ˈkɑːhɒp] [kar-jop] *s.* (in US) Persona que atiende a los clientes en sus coches (in drive-in restaurants).

Caribbean [ˌkærɪˈbiːən] [ka-ri-bian] *a.* Caribeño, del caribe. **caribbean,** *s.* **The Caribbean Sea,** el (mar) Caribe. **The Caribbean,** el Caribe, las Antillas (region).

caribou [ˈkærɪbuː] [ka-ri-bu], *s.* El reno norteamericano.

caricature [ˈkærɪkətʃʊər] [ka-ri-ka-chuaʳ], *s.* Caricatura.

caricature, *va.* Caricaturizar.

caricaturist [ˌkærɪkəˈtjʊərɪst] [ka-ri-ka-chua-rist], *s.* El que hace caricaturas.

caries [ˈkeəriːz] [kea-ris], **cariosity** [ˈkeərɪəsɪtɪ] [kea-rio-si-ti], *s.* Caries, ulceración o corrosión de los huesos o dientes.

carina [ˈkərɪnɑː] [ka-ri-na], *s.* Carena, pétalo inferior de ciertas flores; prolongación del tallo en las hojas.

carinate [ˈkərɪneɪt] [ka-ri-neit], *a.* Carenado; dícese de la flor que presenta la forma de una carena o quilla de buque.

caring [ˈkeərɪŋ] [kea-rin] *a.* Humanitario (society, approach); bondadoso, generoso (person/kindly); comprensivo (sympathetic). **In the caring professions,** en las profesiones de vocación social.

carious [ˈkeərɪəs] [kea-rious], *a.* Carioso, lo que tiene caries.

cark [kɑːk] [kark], *vn. (Ant.)* Ser muy cuidadoso; estar consumido a fuerza de cuidados.

carking [ˈkɑːkɪŋ] [kar-kin], *a.* Devorador, acerbo que causa cuidado o inquietud; penoso.

carl [kɑːl] [karl], *s.* Patán, rústico; hombre ruin, grosero, villano.

carline, carling [ˈkɑːlɪŋ] [kar-lin], *s.* Carlinga, madero fijo sobre la quilla, en el que entra la mecha del palo. *(Mar.)* Atravesaños de las latas. **Carlings of the hatchways,** *(Mar.)* galeotas de las escotillas.

carload [ˈkɑːkləʊd] [kar-loud], *s. (F.C.)* Furgón entero. **We were driving with a carload of children,** íbamos con el coche lleno de niños (auto). **A carload of oranges,** un vagón lleno o cargado de naranjas.

carlock [ˈkɑːlɒk] [kar-lok], *s.* Variedad de colapez rusa.

carman [ˈkɑːmæn] [kar-man], *s.* Carretero, carromatero.

carmelite [ˈkɑːməlaɪt] [kar-me-lait], *s.* 1. Carmelita, religioso o religiosa del Carmen. 2. Tela fina de lana, ordinariamente de color gris. 3. Especie de pera.

carminative [ˈkɑːmɪnəti:v] [kar-mi-na-tiv], *a.* Carminante o carminativo, lo que pertenece a los remedios contra los flatos.

carmine [ˈkɑːmaɪn] [kar-main], *s.* Carmín, color rojo muy encendido; la materia colorante de la cochinilla.

carnage [ˈkɑːnɪdʒ] [kar-neich], *s.* Carnicería, mortandad.

carnal [ˈkɑːnl] [kar-nal], *a.* 1. Carnal, lo que pertenece a la carne por contraposición a lo que es espiritual. 2. Carnal, lujurioso, sensual, brutal. **Carnal-minded,** sensual, mundano.

carnalist [ˈkɑːnəlɪst] [kar-na-list], *s.* El que es lujurioso o lascivo.

carnality [ˈkɑːnəlɪtɪ] [kar-na-li-ti], *s.* 1. Carnalidad, sensualidad, lujuria, concupiscencia, lascivia. 2. Propensión o acto carnal.

carnalize [ˈkɑːnəlaɪz] [kar-na-lais], *va.* Hacer carnal, excitar la sensualidad; atribuir carnalidad.

carnally [ˈkɑːnəlɪ] [kar-na-li], *adv.* Carnalmente.

carnation [kɑːˈneɪʃən] [kar-nei-shon], *s.* 1. *(Pint.)* Encarnación, color natural de la carne. 2. Clavel doble, flor muy fragante y hermosa.

carnationed [kɑːˈneɪʃənd] [kar-nei-shond], *a.* Encarnado como un clavel.

carnelian [kɑːˈniːlɪən] [kar-ni-lian], *s.* Cornerina, piedra preciosa, variedad de calcedonia.

carneous [ˈkɑːnəʊs] [kar-nous], *a.* Carnoso, carnudo, lleno de carne.

carnification [ˌkɑːnɪfɪˈkeɪʃən] [kar-ni-fi-kei-shon], *s.* Carnificación, una alteración patológica de los órganos.

carnify [ˈkɑːnɪfaɪ] [kar-ni-fai], *vn.* Carnificarse, criar carne.

carnival [ˈkɑːnɪvəl] [kar-ni-val], *s.* 1. Carnaval (festival); feria ambulante (traveling fair). 2. Parque de atracciones.

carnivora [ˈkɑːnɪvərə] [kar-ni-vo-ra], *s. pl.* Carnívoros, orden de animales que se alimenta de carne. -CARNIVOR, uno de los carnívoros.

carnivore [ˈkɑːnɪvəːr] [kar-ni-voʳ] *s.* Carnívoro.

carnosity [ˈkɑːnəsɪtɪ] [kar-no-si-ti], *s.* Carnosidad.

carnous [ˈkɑːnəs] [kar-nous], *a.* Carnoso, carnudo. V. CARNEOUS.

carob [ˈkærəb] [ka-rob], *s. (Bot.)* 1. Algarroba, árbol, y su fruto. 2. Algarroba, planta anal y su semilla.

carob-bean [ˈkærəbiən] [ka-ro-bin], *s.* Algarroba, el fruto del algarrobo.

carol [ˈkærəl] [ka-rol], *s.* Villancico, canción alegre y piadosa.

carol, *va.* Cantar, celebrar la Navidad con canciones o villancicos.

carom [ˈkærəm] [ka-rom], *s.* Carambola (en el juego de billar). -*vn.* Hacer carambola (in billiards). **The car caromed off the fence into a tree,** el coche rebotó contra la valla y dio contra un árbol.

carotid, carotidal [kəˈrɒtɪd] [ka-ro-tid], *a.* Carótidas, dos arterias que nacen del tronco ascendente de la aorta.

carousal [kəˈraʊzəl] [ka-rou-sal], *s.* 1. Festín, o función de alboroto y gresca. 2. Francachela, comida alegre entre amigos. 3. Jarana, gresca.

carouse [kəˈraʊz] [ka-rous] *va. y s.* Jaranear, alborotar. *(Fam.)* Correrla. Beber excesivamente, embriagarse.

carouse, *s.* Borrachera, jarana. *vn.* Estar de juerga o jarana.

carousel [ˌkæruːˈsel] [ka-ru-sel], *s.* 1. V. MERRY-GO-ROUND. 2. Liza, justa o torneo. 3. Cinta o correa transportadora, carrusel (for baggage). Expositor giratorio (in shops).

carouser [ˌkæruːˈser] [ka-ru-saʳ], *s.* Bebedor, jaranero.

carp [kɑːp] [karp], *s.* Carpa, pez de agua dulce.

carp, *vn.* Censurar, criticar (find fault); vituperar, afear; sutilizar; regañar. Quejarse (complain).

carpal [ˈkɑːpəl] [kar-pal], *a.* De, o cerca de la muñeca. -*s.* Hueso de la muñeca.

car park [ˈkɑːpɑːk] [kar-park] *s.* (GB) V. PARKING LOT (open space). V. PARKING GARAGE (Building).

Carpathians [kɑːˈpeɪθɪənz] [kar-pei-shians] *N.* **The Carpathians,** los (montes) Cárpatos.

carpel [ˈkɑːpl] [kar-pel], *s. (Bot.)* Carpelo, cada uno de los frutos o pistilos parciales de una misma flor.

carpenter [ˈkɑːpɪntər] [kar-pen-taʳ], *s.* Carpintero. **Ship-carpenter,** carpintero de ribera o de buque.

carpentry [ˈkɑːpɪntrɪ] [kar-pen-tri], *s.* 1. Carpintería. 2. Maderaje, maderamen. **Carpenter and joiner,** carpintero ensamblador, ebanista.

carper [ˈkɑːpər] [kar-paʳ], *s.* Regañón, criticón, censurador; maldiciente, murmurador.

carpet [ˈkɑːpɪt] [kar-pet], *s.* 1. Tapete de mesa. 2. Alfombra o tapiz; moqueta, moquette (wall-to-wall). Alfombra (of flowers, leaves, moss). **Carpet beater,** sacudidor de alfombras. **To be on the carpet,** estar examinándose algún negocio o cuestión; hablarse mucho de alguna cosa; traer a alguna persona o suceso de boca en boca. **Carpet-beetle,** antreno, escarabajo cuya larva destruye alfombras y telas de lana.

carpet, *va.* Alfombrar, entapizar, enmoquetar (floor, room).

carpetbagger [ˈkɑːpɪtˌbægər] [kar-pet-ba-guaʳ] *s.* Político oportunista que logra o pretende representar a una localidad que no es la suya.

carpet bombing [ˈkɑːpɪtˌbɒmɪŋ] [kar-pet-bom-bin] *s.* Bombardeo por saturación.

carpeting [ˈkɑːpɪtɪŋ] [kar-pe-tin], *s.* 1. Materia o tela para alfombras; alfombra o tapete, en general. 2. El acto o la acción de alfombrar.

carpet slipper [ˈkɑːpɪtˌslɪpər] [kar-pet-sli-paʳ] *s.* Zapatilla o pantufla de felpa.

carpet sweeper [ˈkɑːpɪtˌswiːpər] [kar-pet-sui-paʳ], *s.* Barredor de alfombras.

carpet-walk [ˈkɑːpetˌwɔːk] [kar-pet-uok], **carpet-way** [ˈkɑːpɪtweɪ] [kar-pet-uei], *s.* Camino alfombrado o cubierto de césped.

carphology [kɑːˈfɒlɒdʒɪ] [kar-fo-lo-yi], *s. (Med.)* Carfología, acción inconsciente de arañar y plegar el enfermo las ropas de la cama; obsérvase en casos de delirio y fiebre lenta y se considera como síntoma mortal.

carphone [ˈkɑːfəʊn] [kar-foun] *s.* Teléfono de automóvil.

carping [ˈkɑːpɪŋ] [kar-pin], *a.* Capcioso, porfiado, caviloso, criticón. *-s.* Efugio, censura.

carpingly [ˈkɑːpɪŋlɪ] [kar-pin-li], *adv.* Mordazmente.

car pool [ˈkɑːpuːl] [kar-pul], *s.* Transporte colectivo en automóvil a prorrata. Acuerdo entre varias personas que se trasladan juntas al lugar de trabajo, etc. utilizando por turnos el coche de cada uno.

car-pool *vn.* Organizar o formar un CAR POOL.

carport [ˈkɑːpɔːt] [kar-port], *s.* Cobertizo para automóvil.

carpus [ˈkɑːpəs] [kar-pus], *s.* Carpo, muñeca, la parte que está entre el antebrazo y la palma de la mano.

carriage [ˈkærɪdʒ] [ka-rich], *s.* 1. Porte, conducción, acarreo o transporte de alguna cosa de una parte a otra. 2. Porte, presencia, continente, aire de una persona. 3. Porte, conducta o modo de proceder. 4. Coche, carroza; vehículo, carruaje (horse-drawn). Cochecito, carriola (baby carriage). 5. Carga. 6. Cureña de cañón. 7. En la Gran Bretaña, vagón de ferrocarril. 8. Pieza de una máquina sobre la cual descansa y funciona otra, como en los tornos, taladros, etc. **Carriage paid,** porte pagado. **Carriage free,** franco de porte. **Carriage and four,** carroza de cuatro caballos.

carrier [ˈkærɪər] [ka-riaʳ], *s.* 1. Portador, el que lleva alguna cosa. Portador (of disease, gene). 2. Arriero, ordinario, carretero o conductor de mercaderías. 3. Mensajero, el que lleva algún recado, despacho o noticia de otro. Compañía o empresa de transportes (company). *(Aviat.)* Línea aérea. (GB) **Carrier bag,** bolsa de plástico o papel. **Carrier-pigeon,** paloma mensajera.

carrion [ˈkærɪən] [ka-rion], *s.* 1. Carroña, la carne corrompida. 2. Carne muerta que no sirve para alimento. 3. Pulpón, pelleja, desollada; dícese de una mujer abandonada. *-a.* Mortecino, podrido.

carron-oil [ˌkærənˈɔɪl] [ka-ron-oil], *s.* Mezcla de una parte de agua de cal y dos de aceite de linaza: se usa en casos de quemaduras recientes.

carrot [ˈkærət] [ka-rot], *s. (Bot.)* Zanahoria.

carroty [ˈkærətɪ] [ka-ro-ti], *a.* Pelirrojo, el que tiene el pelo de color de zanahoria.

carry [ˈkærɪ] [ka-ri], *va.* 1. Llevar, conducir de una parte a otra. Llevar (bear, take). **I can't carry this, it's too heavy,** no puedo llevar esto, pesa demasiado. **She was carrying her baby in her arms,** llevaba a su hijo en brazos. Llevar, transportar, acarrear (convey/goods, passengers). **The car can carry four people,** el coche tiene cabida para cuatro personas, en el coche caben cuatro personas. **She was carried along by the crowd,** fue arrastrada por la multitud. **As fast as his legs would carry him,** tan rápido como pudo. Llevar (channel, transmit/oil, water, sewage). **The wind carried her voice to him,** el viento le hizo llegar su voz. Ser portador de (disease). Soportar, resistir (support, weight). Cargar con (take responsibility for/cost, blame). 2. Llevar

encima (have with one), tener consigo (be provided with) (guarantee). **Every pack carries the logo of the company,** todos los paquetes vienen con o traen el logotipo de la compañía. 3. Llevar, arrebatar o quitar. 4. Llevar a efecto alguna cosa. Aprobar (gain support for/bill, motion). *(Pol.)* Hacerse con (win/constituency, city). **Carry all before one,** hacerse dueño de todo; vencer o sobrepujar todos los obstáculos, apoderarse de todo, alcanzar cuanto se desea, arrasar con todo. 5. Llevar adelante. **The leading actress carried the play,** la protagonista sacó la obra adelante (sustain). 6. Buscar y traer, como hacen los perros de agua. 7. Conseguir, lograr. 8. Contener, importar, mostrar. Tener, vender (stock, model); *(Journ.)* Traer, publicar (include). Conllevar (involve, entail/responsibility); Acarrear, traer aparejado (consequences, penalty). 9. Estar embarazada o encinta de (be pregnant with). **The fighting was carried over the border,** la lucha se extendió más allá de la frontera (extend, continue). **Never carry a diet too far,** no hay que exagerar con los regímenes. *-v. refl.* **Carry oneself: She carries herself well,** tiene buen porte (in bearing). Comportarse, actuar (behave). *-vn.* Alcanzar, llegar (hablando de armas de fuego). **Sound carries further in the mountains,** en la montaña los sonidos llegan más lejos. **Her voice carries well,** su voz tiene mucha proyección.

carry about, llevar de un lado a otro, o llevar de una parte a otra.

carry along, alzar, llevarse una cosa. **To carry arms,** (a) pertenecer al ejército; (b) llevar o portar armas. (c) *(Mil.)* Cuadrarse, sosteniendo el fusil, espada u otra arma en posición vertical, a lo largo del cuerpo y apoyada contra el hombro.

carry away, llevarse, quitar, mudar una cosa de un lugar a otro, alzar. **To carry away by force,** arrebatar, quitar de delante, tomar por fuerza, llevar tras sí con violencia alguna cosa, robar. **They were carried away by the excitement of the occasion,** se dejaron llevar por lo emocionante de la ocasión. **I got carried away and painted the window as well,** me entusiasmé y pinté la ventana también. **There is no need to get carried away,** no te pases.

carry back, restituir, traer a la mano, volver a llevar, traer o sacar, devolver, acompañar a alguno al paraje de donde se le había sacado. **To carry coals to Newcastle,** llevar leña al monte; llevar géneros a donde los hay de sobra.

carry down, hacer bajar, descender, conducir, acarrear, portear.

carry forth, sacar, mostrar, hacer parecer, hacer salir de alguna parte, hacer progresar una cosa; sostener una opinión.

carry forward, llevar a la columna o página siguiente (total). **Carried forward,** (en las cuentas), pasa al frente, o pasa a la vuelta; suma y sigue.

carry in, introducir meter o llevar adentro, hacer entrar.

carry into, llevar a efecto, poner en ejecución o en planta.

carry off, alzar, llevarse una cosa; arrastrar, disipar. Llevarse (abduct/victim, hostage). Kill (disease). Hacerse con (win/trophy, cup). **She carried off all the prizes,** barrió o arrasó con todos los premios. **She carried the interview off very well,** salió muy airosa o muy bien parada de la entrevista (succeed with). **She tried to appear disinterested but failed to carry it off,** intentó aparentar desinterés pero no lo logró o consiguió.

carry on, mantener (conversation, correspondence); sostener, fomentar; promover, continuar, seguir (continue); mantener, sostener, conducir, llevar adelante, empujar; proseguir. **To carry on with something,** seguir con algo. *(Coloq.)* **What a way to carry on!,** ¡qué manera de hacer escándalo, por favor! (make a fuss). **There's no need to carry on about it!,** ¡no hay necesidad de seguir dale que te dale con el asunto! *(Coloq.)* **They've been carrying on for years,** hacía años que tenían un enredo (have affair).

carry out, llevar a cabo, desarrollar, realizar, hacer (work, repairs); sacar, mostrar, hacer parecer, hacer salir de alguna parte; hacer progresar alguna cosa; sostener una opinión. Cumplir (order); cumplir con (duty).

carry over, transportar; hacer atravesar. Postergar, posponer (business); transferir (surplus, debt).

carry through, sostener; vencer dificultades, llevar a cabo o a buen término, ejecutar (bring to completion); realizar (reform); poner en práctica (idea). **Enough supplies to carry them through the winter,** suficientes provisiones que les permitan sobrevivir el invierno (enable to survive). **His determination carried him through,** su resolución lo alentó a seguir.

carry to and fro, llevar de un lado a otro o llevar de aquí para allí.

carry up, hacer subir, elevar. *(Fam.)* Dejar atrás, echar el pie atrás a. **Carry it high,** afectar señorío o grandeza, hacer de persona. **To carry the cause,** ganar la sentencia. **To carry the day,** quedar victorioso, alcanzar victoria. **To carry oneself well,** saber vivir, conducirse debidamente, portarse bien. **A pillar that carries false,** una columna que falsea o se está cayendo.

Carry, *s. (Prov.)* Movimiento de las nubes.

carry-all [ˌkærɪˈɔl] [ka-ri-ol], *s.* 1. *(E.U.)* Carruaje de familia, ligero, cubierto, de cuatro ruedas y generalmente tirado por un solo caballo. 2. Bolso de viaje, bolsón.

carrycot [ˈkærɪkɒt] [ka-ri-kot] *s.* (GB) Cuna portátil, capazo.

carryings-on [ˈkærɪɪŋˈɒn] [ka-ri-ins-on] *s. pl. (Coloq.)* Enredos, líos.

carry-on, [ˌkærɪˈɒn] [ka-ri-on] *s.* (GB) *(Coloq.)* Lío, jaleo, follón. *a.* De mano (bag, baggage).

carryout [ˈkærɪˌaʊt] [ka-ri-aut] *s.* Comida preparada o bebida que se vende para consumir fuera del lugar de venta.

carsick [ˈkɑːsɪk] [kar-sik] *a.* Mareado. **I get carsick,** me mareo (cuando viajo) en coche.

cart [kɑːt] [kart], *s.* Carro, carreta (waggon); carromato, carruaje. Carrito (in supermarket, airport). **Cart-horse,** caballo de tiro. **Cart-wheel,** rueda de carro. **Garbage** o **Offal cart,** carro de basura. **Cart-load,** carretada, carga de carro o carreta. **Cart-rope,** cuerda gorda. **Cart-way,** carril, camino carretero. **To put the cart before the horse,** empezar la casa por el tejado. **Handcart,** carretilla.

cart, *va.* Carretear, acarrear con carros o carretas. *(Coloq.)* **I had to cart the books around all day,** tuve que cargar con los libros todo el día. **They were carted off to prison,** se los llevaron a la cárcel. *-vn.* Usar carretas o carros.

cartage [ˈkɑːtɪdʒ] [kart-eich], *s.* Carretaje, paga por el uso de un carro.

carte-blanche [ˈkɑːtˌblɑːnʃ] [kart-blansh], *s.* 1. Carta blanca, papel o firma en blanco, para que ponga en él lo que quiera la persona a quien se da. 2. Autorización verbal o escrita ilimitada; amplias facultades.

cartel [kɑːˈtel] [kar-tel], *s.* 1. Cartel, reglas acordadas entre dos enemigos para el rescate, canje o cambio de prisioneros; se llama también así el buque que lleva prisioneros canjeados. 2. Cartel de desafío. 3. Cartel, papel escrito o cartelón impreso; anuncio, tablilla.

carter [ˈkɑːtər] [kar-teʳ], *s.* Carretero.

cartesian [kɑːˈtiːzɪən] [kar-ti-sian], *s. y a.* Cartesiano, el que sigue el sistema filosófico de Cartesio o Descartes y de sus discípulos.

carthorse [ˈkɑːthɔːs] [kart-jors] *s.* Caballo de tiro.

carthusian [kɑːˈθjuːzɪən] [kar-ziu-sian], *s.* Cartujo, el monje de la orden de San Bruno.

cartilage [ˈkɑːtɪlɪdʒ] [kar-ti-leich], *s. (Anat.)* Cartílago, ternilla.

cartilaginous [ˌkɑːtɪˈlædʒɪns] [kar-ti-la-yi-nous], *a.* Cartilaginoso, ternilloso.

cartographer [kɑːˈtɒɡræfər] [kar-to-gra-faʳ], *s.* Cartógrafo. Véase su equivalente CHARTOGRAPHER.

cartography [kɑːˈtɒɡrəfɪ] [kar-to-gra-fi], *s.* Cartografía, dibujo de mapas.

carton [ˈkɑːtən] [kar-ton], *s.* Caja de cartón fino, o el cartón para hacer esas cajas. Envase de cartón (of milk, fruit juice, eggs); cartón (of cigarettes).

cartoon [kɑːˈtuːn] [kar-tún], *s.* 1. Cartón, dibujo hecho en papel grueso, que representa el asunto o adorno que después ha de ejecutarse en pintura al fresco, mosaicos, tapices, vidrios, etc. 2. Dibujo o caricatura, por lo general de carácter político o satírico. Chiste (humourous drawing); viñeta, mono (gráfico); *(Cin.)* dibujos animados. (GB) Historieta, tira cómica, monitos (strip cartoon).

cartouch [ˈkɑːtuːtʃ] [kar-túch], *s.* 1. Cartucho de balas o metralla. 2. Cartuchera. 3. Cartón, adorno de diferentes formas con una inscripción en el centro.

cartridge [ˈkɑːtrɪdʒ] [kar-tridch], *s.* Cartucho de pólvora para cargar cañones o fusiles. **Cartridge-box,** cartuchera, caja para llevar cartuchos. **Blank cartridge,** cartucho sin bala. Cartucho (for gun, pen). **Cartridge belt,** cartuchera.

cart-rut [ˈkɑːtˌrɒt] [kart-rut], *s.* Carril, rodada, el vestigio o señal que deja la rueda de un carro.

cartulary [ˈkɑːtɒlərɪ] [kar-tu-la-ri], *s.* 1. Cartulario, el libro donde se asientan y copian los privilegios y donaciones otorgados a favor de una iglesia o convento. 2. Guarda de cartulario. 3. Papelera.

cartwheel [ˈkɑːtwiːl] [kart-uil] *s.* Voltereta lateral (in gymnastics); rueda, vuelta de carro, rueda de carro, medialuna.

cartwright [ˈkɑːtraɪt] [kart-rait], *s.* Carretero, el carpintero que hace carros, carretas y carretones.

caruncle [ˈkɑːrʌŋkl] [ka-run-kel], *s.* Carúncula, excrecencia pequeña de carne.

carve [kɑːv] [karv], *va.* 1. *(Art.)* Esculpir en madera o piedra; cincelar, tallar, entallar; abrir de talla; embutir. Esculpir, tallar (figure, bust). **Carved work,** entallado, obra de talla. 2. Trinchar, cortar o dividir las viandas en la mesa. 3. Grabar (initials). 4. Distribuir. 5. Apropiar. *-vn.* 1. Cortar cualquier material. 2. Trinchar, cortar (meat).

carve out, forjarse (reputation); hacerse (name).

carve up, dividir, repartir (divide/country, company).

carvel [ˈkɑːvl] [kar-vel], *s. (Mar.)* Carabela. V. CARAVEL.

carven [ˈkɑːvn] [kar-ven], *a. (Poét.)* Esculpido, entallado, grabado.

carver [ˈkɑːvər] [kar-vaʳ], *s.* 1. Escultor, el artífice que esculpe en madera o piedra; grabador, entallador, tallista. 2. Trinchante, el que trincha las viandas en la mesa.

carving [ˈkɑːvɪŋ] [kar-vin], *s.* 1. Escultura o figuras esculpidas; talla. 2. El arte de trinchar. 3. La acción de trinchar. **Carving knife,** trinchante, cuchillo de trinchar.

caryatid [ˌkærɪˈætɪd] [ka-ri-a-tid], **caryatides** [ˌkærɪˈætɪdz] [ka-ri-a-tids], *s. pl.* Cariátide, especie de columna o pilastra en figura de mujer, que sirve para sostener el arquitrabe.

casal [ˈkeɪsəl] [kei-sal], *a. (Gram.)* Perteneciente a un caso o casos.

Casanova [ˌkæsəˈnəʊvə] [ka-sa-nou-va] *N.* Casanova. *(Coloq.)* **He's a real Casanova,** es un casanova o un Don Juan.

cascabel [ˈkæskəbəl] [kas-ka-bel], *s.* 1. Cascabel, remate esférico de la parte posterior del cañón de artillería. 2. Serpiente de cascabel, o el cascabel mismo.

cascade [kæsˈkeɪd] [kas-keid], *s.* Cascada, salto o despeñadero de agua desde un lugar elevado.

cascade, *vn.* Caer en cascada.

cascara sagrada [kæsˈkɑːrə] [kas-ka-ra], *s. (Bot.)* Cáscara sagrada.

cascarilla [kæsˈkɑːrɪjə] [kas-ka-ri-ya], *s.* Cascarilla, corteza aromática de un arbusto de las Antillas.

case [keɪs] [keis], *s.* 1. Caso (matter); suceso, acontecimiento. **The Greene case,** el caso Greene. **to lose/win a case,** perder/ganar un pleito o juicio. **An open-and-shut case,** un caso claro. **To be on somebody's case,** estar encima de alguien. **Get off my case!,** ¡déjame tranquilo o en paz! **To make a federal case out of something,** hacer un drama de algo. 2.

Casualidad, caso, lance, coyuntura. 3. Estado o condición de alguna cosa; situación. **It was a case of doing what we were told,** era cuestión de hacer lo que se nos mandara. **As the case may be,** según (sea) el caso. **That is the case,** así es, esa es la cuestión. **In that case, I'm not interested,** en ese caso, no me interesa. 4. Enfermedad, mal. *(Coloq.)* **A hopeless case,** un caso perdido. 5. Contingencia. 6. Caso, cuestión relativa a personas o cosas particulares. 7. *(Gram.)* Caso, las diversas inflexiones de los nombres. **The case in point,** el caso en cuestión, el asunto de que se trata. **In any case,** a todo evento, en todo caso; de todas maneras, de cualquier modo, en cualquier caso. **In the case of,** en cuanto a, respecto a. **In a sad case,** en una triste posición. **To make out one's case,** demostrar lo que uno se proponía. **A case in law,** un proceso, una causa, un pleito. **In case,** si acaso. **Make a note in case you forget,** apúntalo por si te olvidas. **In case of,** en caso de. *(Fam.)* Gordo o lucio. **The case for the prosecution/defense,** la acusación/la defensa (argument). **She has a good/strong case,** sus argumentos son buenos/poderosos. **There's a case for doing nothing,** hay razones para no hacer nada. **To make (out) a case for something,** exponer los argumentos a favor de algo. **To put/state one's case,** dar/exponer sus razones. **I rest my case,** a las pruebas me remito.

case, *s.* 1. Caja (hard container for large objects), estuche (for small objects); vaina, funda (soft container); cubierta. Caja, cajón, jaba (crate). Maleta, petaca, valija (suitcase); maletín (attaché case). 2. Caja, y el contenido de ella. Caja de 12 botellas (of wine, liquor). 3. Caja de imprenta. **Upper case,** caja alta, de mayúsculas o versales, versalita y signos. **Lower case,** caja baja, de minúsculas, números, puntuación y espacios. **Book-case,** estante de libros. **Dressing-case,** tocador. **Jewel-case,** cofrecito de joyas. **Needle-case,** alfiletero. **Glass-case,** vidriera, mostruario. **Cigar-case,** tabaquera. **Pillow-case,** funda de almohada. **Pistol-case,** pistolera, funda de pistolas. **Case-knife,** cuchillo de mesa.

case *va.* 1. Encajar, poner en caja o estuche alguna cosa. 2. Cubrir, resguardar. *(Sl.)* **To case the joint,** reconocer el terreno (antes de cometer un delito).

casebook [ˈkeɪsbʊk] [keis-buk] *s.* Registro.

caseharden [keɪsˈhɑːdn] [keis-jar-den], *va.* Endurecer por fuera, templar la superficie del hierro, convirtiéndola en acero.

case history [ˈkeɪsˈhɪstərɪ] [keis-jis-to-ri] *(Med.)* Historial médico o clínico, historia clínica.

casein [ˈkeɪsiːn] [kei-sin], *s.* 1. Caseína, principio albuminoso de la leche de que se forma el queso. 2. Legúmina, albúmina vegetal.

caseload [ˈkeɪsləʊd] [keis-loud] *s.* Número de casos (atendidos por un médico, abogado, etc.).

casemate [ˈkeɪsmeɪt] [keis-meit], *s. (Fort.)* Casamata, caserna, construcción abovedada para protección de las tropas, depósito de víveres, etc.; también, mampara acorazada de a bordo horadada para los cañones de banda.

casement [ˈkeɪsmənt] [keis-ment], *s.* 1. Puerta ventana. Marco (de ventana con bisagras). **Casement window,** ventana cuya hoja u hojas se abren por medio de bisagras. 2. *(Fort.)* Barbacana. 3. Cubierta, caja.

casern [ˈkəsɜːn] [ka-sern], *s.* 1. Caserna, alojamiento inmediato al terraplén. 2. Cuartel, edificio donde se alojan los soldados de una guarnición.

case-shot [keɪsˈʃɒt] [keis-shot], *s.* Balas encajonadas.

case study [ˈkeɪsˌstʌdɪ] [keis-sta-di] *s.* Estudio, monografía, trabajo.

casework [ˈkeɪswɜːk] [keis-uek] *s.* Trabajo de asistencia social individual.

case-worker [ˈkeɪsˌwɜːkər] [keis-uor-ka^r], *s.* 1. Investigador, estudioso de los antecedentes de un caso sociológico. 2. Asistente social.

cash [kæʃ] [kash], *s.* 1. Dinero contante, dinero contante y sonante; dinero (en) efectivo (notes and coins). **We pay cash for gold,** compramos oro al contado. **(In) cash,** en efectivo,

en metálico. **Cash on delivery,** entrega contra reembolso. **Cash in hand,** (saldo de) caja. *(Coloq.)* **Cash on the barrelhead,** dinero contante y sonante, dinero en mano. En efectivo (payment); al contado (refund). **A cash sale,** una venta pagada en efectivo. 2. Fondos disponibles. **Cash discount,** descuento en efectivo. 3. *(Coloq.)* Dinero, lana, plata, tela (funds).

cash, *va.* Cambiar, convertir en moneda o dinero contante (un billete, un cupón, etc.); hacer efectiva (una letra). Cobrar (check). **Cash in,** canjear, cobrar (exchange for money). **To cash in (on something),** aprovecharse o sacar provecho (de algo), sacar tajada (de algo).

cash and carry [ˈkæʃænˈkærɪ] [kash-and-ka-ri] *s.* Tienda de venta al por mayor.

cash-book [ˈkæʃbʊk] [kash-buk] *s.* Libro de caja.

cashbox [ˈkæʃbɒks] [kash-boks] *s.* Caja (del dinero).

cashcard [ˈkæʃkɑːd] [kash-kard] *s.* (GB) Tarjeta del cajero automático.

cash crop [ˈkæʃkrɒp] [kash-krop] *s.* Cultivo industrial o comercial.

cash desk [ˈkæʃdesk] [kash-desk] *s.* (GB) Caja.

cash dispenser [ˈkæʃdɪsˌpensər] [kash-dis-pen-sa^r] *s.* Cajero automático.

cashew [kæˈʃuː] [ka-shu], *s.* Anacardo, árbol de las Antillas. **Cashew-nut,** anacardo, fruto medicinal del árbol del mismo nombre; castaña de cajú, nuez de la India.

cash flow [ˈkæʃˌfləʊ] [kash-flou] *s.* Flujo de caja, cash-flow. **Cash flow problem,** problema de liquidez.

cashier [kæˈʃɪər] [ka-shia^r], *s.* Cajero, el que guarda o tiene a su cargo el dinero.

cashier, *va.* Destituir, quitarle a uno su empleo. *(Mil.)* Desaforar, esto es, arrojar ignominiosamente de un regimiento o cuerpo a uno de sus oficiales.

cashier's check [kæˈʃɪərˈʃek] [kashiar-chek] *s.* Cheque de caja, o gerencia, o bancario.

cashmere [kæʃˈmɪər] [kash-mia^r], *s.* 1. Casimir, tela fina y suave de lana para vestidos. 2. Tela fina suave y costosa hecha con lana de cabras de Cachemira, en la India. 3. Mantón o chal de cachemira.

cash on delivery [ˈkæʃˌɒfˈdelɪvərɪ] [kash-of-de-li-ve-ri], *s.* Entrega contra reembolso, cóbrese al entregar.

cashoo [ˈkæʃuː] [ka-shu], *s. V.* CATECHU.

cashpoint [ˈkæʃpɔɪnt] [kash-point] *s.* (GB) Cajero automático.

cash register [ˈkæʃˌredʒɪstər] [kash-re-chis-ta^r], *s.* Caja registradora.

casing [ˈkeɪsɪŋ] [kei-sin], *s.* 1. Cubierta, lo que recubre o afora (cover); caja (case); estuche, envoltura. 2. Guarnición de una ventana o puerta.

casings [ˈkeɪsɪŋz] [kei-sins], *s. pl.* Boñiga seca para combustible.

casino [kəˈsiːnəʊ] [ka-si-nou], *s.* 1. Casino, salón de baile y de juego. 2. Casino, club social. 3. Variedad de juego de naipes.

cask [kɑːsk] [kask], *s.* 1. Barril o tonel; cuba; casco. 2. Casco o casquete.

cask, *va.* Entonelar.

casket [ˈkɑːskɪt] [kas-ket], *s.* 1. Cajita para joyas, casquete, estuche. **Wedding-casket,** las donas. 2. *(E.U.)* Ataúd de metal o madera, pero de igual anchura en toda su extensión (coffin).

casket, *va.* Poner en cajita.

caskets [ˈkɑːskɪts] [kas-kets], *s. (Mar.) V.* GASKET.

Caspian Sea [ˈkæspɪənˌsiː] [kaspian-si] *N.* **The Caspian Sea,** el mar Caspio.

casque [kɑːsk] [kask], *s.* Casquete o casco, armadura que cubre y protege la cabeza. Antiguamente almete, capacete, morrión, casquete.

cassation [kəˈseɪʃən] [ka-sei-shon], *s.* 1. La acción de anular alguna cosa. 2. *(For.)* Casación, anulación de una sentencia o de un fallo judicial.

cassava [kəˈsɑːvə] [ka-sa-va], *s. (Bot.)* Cazabe, harina gruesa de América, hecha con la raíz de la yuca. Mandioca.

casserole, [ˈkæsərəʊl] [ka-se-roul], *s.* Cacerola, cazuela, fuente de horno (con tapa). (*Food*) Guiso, guisado. **Casserole, casserole dish,** guiso a la cacerola.

cassette [kæˈset] [ka-set] *s.* (*Audio*) Cassette. **Cassette deck,** platina, pletina. **Cassette player,** pasacintas, cassette, pasacassettes, tocacassettes. **Cassette recorder,** grabadora o grabador (de cassettes), cassette. (*Video*) Videocassette, cinta de video, videocinta.

cassia [ˈkæsɪə] [ka-sia], *s.* Casia, especie de canela, **Cassia buds,** flores de casia.

cassimere [ˈkæsɪmɪər] [ka-si-miaʳ], *s.* Casimir, casimira o casimiro, tela de lana muy fina.

cassino [kəˈsiːnəʊ] [ka-si-nou], *s.* Un juego de naipes. *V.* CASINO.

cassiterite [kæsɪtəriːt] [ka-si-te-rit], *s.* Casiterita, óxido de estaño; el más importante mineral de estaño.

cassock [ˈkæsək] [ka-sok], *s.* Sotana o balandrán, vestidura talar que usan los eclesiásticos debajo del manteo.

cassoon [ˈkæsuːn] [ka-sún], *s.* (*Arq.*) Artesón, que se pone ordinariamente en las bóvedas o vueltas de los arcos.

cassowary [ˈkæsəveərɪ] [ka-so-ua-ri], *s.* (*Zool.*) Casoar, ave zancuda parecida al avestruz.

cassweed [ˈkæsuiːd] [ka-suid], *s.* (*Bot.*) Bolsa de pastor.

cast [kɑːst] [kast], *va.* (*pret.* y *pp.* CAST). 1. Tirar, arrojar, lanzar alguna cosa con la mano (stone). Lanzar (line); echar (net). Proyectar (shadow, light). Emitir (vote). **To cast doubt on something,** poner algo en duda. **To cast your eye over this,** échale una mirada o una ojeada o un vistazo a esto. 2. Tirar alguna cosa como inútil o dañosa. 3. Echar, verter. 4. Tirar dados o echar suertes. 5. Tumbar o derribar a uno luchando con él. 6. Mudar o estar de muda (shed/skin, snake). **The horse cast a shoe,** al caballo se le salió una herradura. 7. Desechar ropa. 8. Sobrepujar o exceder en el peso. 9. Ganar el pleito a su adversario. 10. (*Metal*) Fundir, derretir; (*Art.*) vaciar (mold). 11. Abortar, hablando de animales. 12. Modelar. 13. Comunicar por reflexión. 14. Ceder enteramente. 15. Imponer una pena. 16. Adicionar (an account), computar, calcular. 17. (*Cine, Teat.*) Asignar, distribuir (in a comedy, etc.) **She was cast as the princess,** le dieron el papel de la princesa. **He's well cast as Iago,** está bien elegido para el papel de Yago. -*vn.* 1. Idear o maquinar alguna cosa, discurriendo los medios para ejecutarla. 2. Amoldarse, recibir otra forma o figura. 3. Alabearse o torcerse la madera. 4. Vomitar.

cast about, esparcir, derramar, arrojar por todos los lados; considerar, meditar, revolver proyectos en la imaginación. **Cast about for,** tratar de encontrar, buscar (for idea, excuse).

cast against, reprochar, dar en rostro, echar en cara, vituperar, afear.

cast aside, desechar, dejar o poner a un lado. **To cast away,** desechar, apartar de sí (doubts, worries); dejar, abandonar; desterrar; echar a un lado, dejar de lado (person); arrojar.

cast away, naufragar. **They were cast away on a desert island,** llegaron a una isla desierta tras naufragar.

cast back, Cast your mind back, trata de recordar, rememora.

cast down, abatir, derribar, echar por tierra: (*fig.*) Afligir, desanimar; abatir, humillar.

cast forth, exhalar; centellear, relumbrar, echar rayos de luz.

cast off, abandonar, dejar (abandon/friend, lover); desamparar; despojar; mudar la pluma; descartar; echar de sí. Cerrar (in knitting/stitch). (*Naut.*) Soltar amarras.

cast on, poner o montar los puntos (in knitting). Montar, poner (stitch).

cast out, echar fuera, arrojar; espantar. Expulsar (expel).

cast up, calcular, sumar o ajustar alguna cuenta; vomitar; improperar; exhalar. **To cast up a bank,** construir un dique. **To cast up one's eyes,** levantar los ojos.

cast upon, empañar, deslucir; recurrir, acudir. **To cast a fault upon,** culpar, echar la culpa. **To cast an account,** ajustar una cuenta. **To cast headlong,** precipitar. **To cast her young,**

malparir (se dice de los animales). **To cast his coat,** mudar pellejo. **To cast into a form,** dar la forma de. **To cast into sleep,** adormecer. **To cast one behind,** adelantarse a alguno, dejarle atrás. **To cast scorn upon,** despreciar. **To cast the eyes on,** mirar, poner la vista a los ojos; echar la vista o los ojos. **Cast it in his teeth,** arrójele Vd. eso al rostro, o a la faz. **To cast lots,** echar suertes. **To cast a glance at** o **on,** echar una ojeada hacia o sobre. **To cast a statue in bronze,** vaciar una estatua en bronce. **Casting vote,** voto decisivo o de calidad. **Casting-house,** fundería, fundición. **Castingnet,** esparavel, red redonda para pescar.

cast, *s.* 1. Tiro, golpe. 2. Ojeada o mirada. 3. Molde, forma (mold). (*Art*) Vaciado (molded object). **A plaster cast of the footprint,** un molde de yeso de la huella. Yeso, escayola (for broken limb). 4. Aire o modo de presentarse; también, tinte, tono, matiz. 5. Modo de echar o tirar. 6. Echamiento. 7. Tendencia a; apariencia exterior, aspecto, semblante, mirada. 8. Temple. 9. Fundición. (*Metal*) Pieza fundida. 10. La distribución de los papeles para la representación de alguna pieza en el teatro. Reparto, elenco. **She met the cast,** le presentaron a los actores. **That has a greenish cast,** eso tiene un tinte verdusco. **To have a cast in one's eye,** bizcar, torcer la vista, mirar bizco o atravesado.

castanets [ˌkæstəˈnets] [kas-ta-nets], *s. pl.* Castañetas o castañuelas.

castaway [ˈkɑːstəweɪ] [kas-ta-uei], *s.* 1. Náufrago. 2. Desecho, zupia, desperdicio. 3. Réprobo.

caste [kɑːst] [kast], *s.* 1. Casta, raza; clase hereditaria del Indostán. 2. Clase social, división de la sociedad en virtud de principios convencionales, como el derecho hereditario, la riqueza, etc...

castellan [ˈkæstəleɪn] [kas-te-lein], *s.* Castellano, el alcaide de un castillo.

castellany [ˈkæstələnɪ] [kas-te-la-ni], *s.* Castellanía.

castellated [ˈkəstəleɪtɪd] [kas-te-lei-tid], *a.* Hecho en forma de castillo; encerrado dentro de murallas, encastillado.

castelry [ˈkæstəlrɪ] [kas-tel-ri], *s.* El gobierno, derecho de posesión o jurisdicción de un castillo; territorio sometido al señor del castillo.

caster, castor [ˈkɑːstər] [kas-taʳ], *s.* 1. Tirador, el que tira. 2. Adivino; calculador. 3. Fundidor. 4. Ruedecilla con eje de eslabón giratorio para rodar por todos lados (wheel). 5. Ampolleta destinada a contener aceite, vinagre pimienta o sal para el servicio de la mesa. **Casters,** vinagreras.

caster sugar [ˌkæstəˈʃugər] [kas-ter-shu-gaʳ] *s.* (GB) Azúcar blanca de granulado muy fino.

castigate [ˈkæstɪgeɪt] [kas-ti-gueit], *va.* Castigar; corregir. Reprender (pupil); fustigar, criticar severamente (government).

castigation [ˌkæstɪˈgeɪʃən] [kas-ti-guei-shon], *s.* 1. Castigo o pena. 2. Corrección, enmienda.

castigator [ˌkæstɪˈgeɪtər] [kas-ti-guei-toʳ], *s.* Enmendador, castigador.

castigatory [ˌkæstɪˈgətərɪ] [kas-ti-ga-to-ri], *a.* Penal, lo que sirve para castigar.

Castile [ˈkæstiːl] [kas-til], *s.* Castilla, una provincia de España.

Castilian [ˈkæstiːlɪən] [kas-ti-lian], *s.* y *a.* Castellano, habitante o natural de Castilla, y su idioma. Castellano (person, language).

casting [ˈkɑːstɪŋ] [kas-tin], *s.* 1. Tiro, el acto de tirar o arrojar. 2. Invención, distribución, arreglo; plan, modelo. 3. Fundición. 4. Moldaje, forma que se da a un metal vaciado; y la operación de dejar correr el metal y vaciarlo. 5. Curalle, medicamento usado en cetrería.

casting vote [ˈkæstɪŋvəʊt] [kas-tin-vout] *s.* Voto de castidad.

cast-iron [ˈkæstaɪrɒn] [kast-aironl], *s.* Hierro fundido o colado. *a.* 1. Hecho de hierro colado. 2. Parecido al hierro colado; rígido, que no cede, inflexible. Sólido (guarantee);

férreo (will); irrefutable (evidence); a toda prueba (alibi). **A cast-iron constitution,** una salud de hierro.

castle [ˈkɑːsl] [ka-sel], s. 1. Castillo, fortaleza. 2. Palacio, morada de un hombre opulento. 3. Roque o torre, cierta pieza del juego de ajedrez. -va. Enrocar (en el juego de ajedrez). **(To build) castles in the air/in Spain,** (construir) castillos en el aire.

castle-builder [ˈkɑːslbɪldər] [ka-sel-bil-da'], s. Proyectista imaginario, el que hace castillos en el aire.

castled [ˈkɑːsld] [ka-seld], a. Lleno de castillos; fortificado con castillo.

castleguard [ˈkɑːslˌwɑːd] [ka-sel-guard], s. Especie de feudo.

castlet [ˈkɑːslɪt] [kas-lit], s. Castilluelo, castillejo.

castling [ˈkɑːslɪŋ] [kas-lin], s. Aborto, lo que nace antes de tiempo.

castoff [ˈkɑːstɒf] [kast-of] s. **She gave me her castoffs,** me dio la ropa que ya no quería.

castor [ˈkɑːstər] [kas-tor], s. 1. Castor, animal anfibio. 2. Sombrero fino hecho del pelo de castor. 3. Castóreo. V. CASTOREUM. 4. V. CASTER. **Castor and pollux,** (Meteor.) 1. Cástor y Pólux, especie de meteoro que los marineros llaman fuego de Santelmo. 2. Constelación de los Gemelos (Gemini).

castoreum [ˈkɑːstərɪəm] [kas-to-rium], s. Castóreo, sustancia aceitosa y de olor fuerte que tiene el castor en bolsas en el vientre.

castor-oil [ˈkɑːstəɔɪl] [kas-tor-oil], s. Aceite de palmacristi o ricino; aceite de castor, usado en la medicina como purgante.

castrametation [ˈkæstrəmɪtreɪʃən] [kas-tra-mi-trei-shon], s. (Mil.) Castrametación, arte de acampar un ejército con ventaja.

castrate [kæsˈtreɪt] [kas-treit], va. 1. Castrar, capar. 2. Expurgar un escrito.

castration [kæsˈtreɪʃən] [kas-treishon], s. Capadura, la acción de capar.

castrel [ˈkætrəl] [kas-trel], s. (Orn.) Especie de halcón. V. KESTREL.

castrensian [ˈkæstrənsɪən] [kas-tren-sian], a. Castrense.

casual [ˈkæʒjʊəl] [ka-shiual], a. Casual, fortuito, accidental. Superficial (inspection). **A casual acquaintance,** un conocido, una conocida. **Casual sex,** relaciones sexuales promiscuas. Ocasional (chance/visit, caller, reader); Informal (informal); de sport, informal (clothes). Despreocupado (unconcerned/attitude, tone); hecho al pasar (remark). **She seemed very casual about the whole thing,** parecía como si no tuviera nada que ver con ella. Eventual, ocasional (not regular/employment, labor). **Casual worker,** jornalero (on farm); obrero, eventual (in factory).

casually [ˈkæʒjʊəlɪ] [ka-shiua-li], adv. Casualmente, fortuitamente. De manera informal, informalmente (informally/dressed); informalmente (chat). Con indiferencia (with indifference).

casualness [ˈkæʒjʊəlnɪs] [ka-shiual-nes], s. Contingencia.

casuals [ˈkæʒjʊəlz] [ka-shiuals] s. pl. Ropa de sport (clothing).

casualty [ˈkæʒjʊəltɪ] [ka-shiual-ti], s. Casualidad, aventura, contingencia, acaso, accidente. Herido (injured person); víctima (dead person); (Mil.) Baja. (GB) Urgencias (hospital department).

casuist [ˈkæzjʊɪst] [ka-shuist], s. Casuista, el que escribe, trata o estudia casos de conciencia, y los resuelve y determina.

casuistical [ˈkæzjʊɪstɪkl] [ka-shuis-ti-kal], a. Casuístico, lo que pertenece a casos de conciencia.

casuistry [ˈkæzjʊɪstrɪ] [ka-shuis-tri], s. Teología moral, la ciencia de los casuistas. Casuística.

casus [ˈkæsəs] [ka-sus], s. (Lat.) Contingencia, acaecimiento, suceso. **Casus belli,** caso o motivo de guerra.

cat [kæt] [kat], s. 1. Gato (domestic animal); felino (lion, tiger). **The big cats,** los felinos mayores. **A wild cat,** un gato montés. **To bell the cat,** poner el cascabel al gato. (Coloq.) **Has the cat got your tongue?,** ¿te ha comido la lengua el gato? **He thinks he's the cat's whiskers/ pajamas,** se cree el no va más. **You look like something the cat dragged in,** ¡parece que vinieras de la guerra! (GB) (Coloq.) **Not to have a cat in hell's chance,** no tener la más mínima posibilidad. **There's not enough/no room to swing a cat,** no cabe ni un alfiler. **To fight like cat and dog,** andar como el perro y el gato. **To grin like a Cheshire cat,** sonreír de oreja a oreja. **To let the cat out of the bag,** descubrir el pastel, levantar la liebre o la perdiz. **To play cat and mouse (with somebody),** jugar al gato y al ratón (con alguien). **To rain cats and dogs,** llover a cántaros o a mares. **To set/put the cat among the pigeons,** levantar un revuelo. **Civetcat,** algalia. **Polecat,** veso, animal cuadrúpedo parecido a la garduña, pero de pelo negro. 2. (Mar.) Gata. **Cat-tackle,** (Mar.) aparejo de gata. **Cat-harpings,** (Mar.) jaretas. **Cat-heads,** (Mar.) serviolas. **Cat's-paw,** (Mar.) soplo. (Fam.) Mano de gato: se aplica al que se deja engañar y sirve, sin conocerlo, de medio o anzuelo para que otro consiga lo que desea. (Fam.) **To make one a cat's-paw,** sacar las castañas del fuego con mano de gato. **Cat-o'-nine-tails,** disciplina o azote con nueve ramales. **Cat's-eye,** (Min.) ojo de gato; especie de ágata. **Cat's-foot,** (Bot.) hiedra terrestre.

catabolism [kæˈtæbɒlɪzm] [ka-ta-bo-lisem], s. Catabolismo.

catachresis [ˈkætəkrɪsɪs] [ka-ta-kri-sis], s. Catacresis, empleo defectuoso de metáforas o epítetos.

cataclysm [ˈkætəklɪzəm] [ka-ta-kli-sem], s. Cataclismo, diluvio, inundación.

cataclysmal, cataclysmic [ˈkætəklɪsməl] [ka-ta-klis-mal], a. Lo que se refiere al cataclismo.

catacombs [ˈkætəkuːmz] [ka-ta-kums], s. pl. Catacumbas, lugares subterráneos y especie de grutas para enterrar a los muertos.

catacoustics [ˈkætəkʊstɪks] [ka-ta-kus-tiks], s. Catacústica, ciencia de los sonidos reflejos.

catadioptric, catadioptrical [ˈkætədaɪˌɒptrɪk] [ka-ta-dai-op-trik], a. Catadióptrico.

catafalque [ˈkætəfælk] [ka-ta-falk], s. Catafalco, túmulo muy elevado y magnífico para las exequias de altos personajes.

Catalan [ˈkætələn] [ka-ta-lan] a./s. Catalán (person, language).

catalectic [ˈkætəlektɪk] [ka-ta-lek-tik], a. (Ret.) Cataléctico, verso falto de una sílaba.

catalepsy [ˈkætəlepsɪ] [ka-ta-lep-si], s. Catalepsia, suspensión de las sensaciones e inmovilidad del cuerpo, debidas a un accidente nervioso repentino.

cataleptic [ˌkætəˈleptɪk] [ka-ta-lep-tik], a. Cataléptico, referente a la catalepsia; que la padece.

catalog, catalogue [ˈkætəlɒg] [ka-ta-log], s. Catálogo, lista o memoria que contiene muchos nombres propios de hombres, títulos de libros u otros objetos (list, book). **A catalog of disasters,** un desastre detrás de otro.

catalog, catalogue, va. Catalogar, poner en catálogo.

Catalonia [ˌkætəˈləʊnɪə] [ka-ta-lou-nia] N. Cataluña.

Catalonian [ˌkætəˈləʊnɪən] [ka-ta-lou-nian] a. Catalán.

catalpa [ˈkætəlpə] [ka-tal-pa], s. Árbol de adorno, originario de la América del Norte. Tiene hojas ovaladas y acorazonadas de gran tamaño y flores grandes y campaniformes.

catalysis [kəˈtælɪsɪs] [ka-ta-li-sis], s. 1. (Quím.) Catálisis, descomposición y nueva combinación de los cuerpos químicos compuestos, efectuadas por un agente que permanece inalterable. 2. V. DISSOLUTION.

catalyst [ˈkætəlɪst] [ka-ta-list], s. Catalizador, agente catalítico.

catalytic [ˌkætəˈlɪktɪk] [ka-ta-lik-tik], a. Catalítico, perteneciente a la catálisis. **Catalytic converter,** s. Catalizador.

catalyzer [ˈkætəlaɪzər] [ka-ta-li-sa'], s. (Quím.) Catalizador.

catamaran [ˌkætəməˈræn] [ka-ta-ma-ran], s. 1. Almadía larga y estrecha de la India. 2. Embarcación de vela o vapor formada por dos cascos paralelos unidos entre sí; catamarán.

catamenia

catamenia [ˌkætəˈmiːniə] [ka-ta-mi-nia], *s.* Menstruación, reglas.

catamite [ˈkætəmaɪt] [ka-ta-mait], *s.* Catamita, sodomita.

catamount [ˈkætəmaʊnt] [ka-ta-maunt], *s.* Gato montés.

cataphract [ˈkætəfrakt] [ka-ta-frakt], *s.* Armadura antigua hecha con chapas de metal a manera de escamas, fijadas sobre cuero, etc.

cataplasm [ˈkætəplɑːzm] [ka-ta-plasm], *s.* Cataplasma.

catapult [ˈkætəpʌlt] [ka-ta-palt], *s.* Catapulta, máquina antigua de guerra para arrojar piedras, lanzas, etc… *(Aviat., Mil.)* Catapulta; (GB) tirachinas, honda, resortera, cauchera, tiragomas.

catapult, *va.* Catapultar. **The crash catapulted her through the windshield,** el choque la hizo saltar disparada por el parabrisas.

cataract [ˈkætərækt] [ka-ta-rakt], *s.* 1. Cascada, catarata (over a precipice); rápido (in a river). 2. *(Med.)* Catarata, opacidad de la lente cristalina del ojo o de su cápsula, que produce la ceguera, parcial o total. *(Fam.)* **A cataract of tears,** un diluvio de lágrimas.

catarrh [kəˈtɑːr] [ka-taʳ], *s.* Catarro, romadizo, resfriado, constipado, fluxión, reuma.

catarrhal [kəˈtɑːrəl] [ka-ta-ral], **catarrhous** [kæˈtɑːrəs] [ka-ta-rous], *a.* Catarral.

catastrophe [kəˈtæstrɒfɪ] [ka-tas-tro-fi], *s.* 1. Catástrofe, la mutación o revolución imprevista que se hace en un poema dramático y que por lo común le da fin. 2. Catástrofe, por lo común cosa infeliz, desgraciada y funesta.

catastrophic [kəˈtæstrɒfɪk] [ka-tas-tro-fik] *a.* Catastrófico.

catatonic [ˌkætəˈtɒnɪk] [ka-ta-to-nik] *a.* Catatónico.

catbird [ˈkætbɜːd] [kat-berd], *s.* Tordo mimo, de color de pizarra; se halla desde el Canadá hasta Méjico y Cuba.

cat burglar [ˈkætbɜːɡlər] [kat-ber-glaʳ] *s.* Ladrón que escala paredes para entrar a un edificio.

catcall [ˈkætkɔːl] [kat-kol], *s.* 1. Silbo, silbido, con que se hace burla de lo que se desaprueba en las representaciones públicas. *(Max.)* Chiflido, chiflo y el silbido que sirve para avisar cuando deben correrse o descorrerse los telones. 2. Reclamo. **Catcalls,** abucheo, silbatina.

catch [kætʃ] [kach], *va. (pp. y pret.* CAUGHT). 1. Coger, agarrar (ball, object); asir, arrebatar. **He caught her by the arm,** la agarró o cogió del brazo. 2. Coger al vuelo. 3. Coger, alcanzar (intercept/person). **Catch you later,** nos vemos. Tomar, coger (take/train, plane); alcanzar (be in time for). **I only just caught it,** lo alcancé con el tiempo justo, por poco lo pierdo. **We'll just catch the end of the game,** todavía podemos pescar el final del partido. **We could catch a movie before dinner,** podríamos ir al cine antes de cenar. 4. Coger o detener alguna cosa para que no caiga. 5. Coger, atrapar (capture/mouse, lion); pescar, coger (fish); atrapar (thief). **I caught my skirt on a nail,** se me enganchó o atoró, o se me atoró la falda en un clavo (entangle, trap). **I caught my finger in the drawer,** me pillé o me agarré el dedo en el cajón. **I got caught in a traffic jam,** me agarró o me cogió un atasco. 6. Comprender, discernir. 7. Agradar, dar gusto. 8. Coger algún mal por infección o por contagio; contagiarse de (become infected with/disease). **To catch a cold,** resfriarse, agarrar o coger, pescar o pillar un resfriado. **I caught the measles from him,** me contagió o me pegó el sarampión. 9. Asir repentinamente o ansiosamente. 10. Pillar, agarrar, pescar (take by surprise); clavar; albardar. **To catch somebody in the act,** agarrar o pillar a alguien infraganti o con las manos en la masa. **She caught him reading her mail,** lo pilló leyendo sus cartas. *(Coloq.)* **You won't catch me going there again!,** ¡a mí no me vuelven a ver el pelo por ahí! **We got caught in the rain,** nos sorprendió o nos pilló o nos pescó la lluvia. 11. Sorprender. 12. Ganar. **To catch a tartar,** caer en la trampa que se ha puesto para otro. **Try to catch his attention,** trata de atraer su atención (attract). **The dress caught her fancy,** se encaprichó con el vestido. **Did you catch what she said?,** ¿oíste o entendiste lo que dijo? (hear or understand clearly).

Captar, reflejar (mood, likeness). **He caught his head on the beam,** se dio en la cabeza con la viga (hit). **You really catch it if he sees you!,** ¡si te ve, te mata! **He caught his breath in surprise,** se le cortó la respiración de sorpresa (hold back). **To catch oneself,** contenerse (restrain). *-vn.* 1. Agarrarse a; con *at.* Agarrar, coger (grasp). 2. Cerrarse, enredarse o engancharse algo (become hooked); engranar (bite, take hold). Prender, agarrar (fire/ignite). 3. Pegarse, ser pegajoso o contagioso. **To catch a cold,** resfriarse. **To catch a distemper,** Infeccionarse, contagiarse; enfermar. **To catch one's death,** causarse la muerte.

catch at, buscar, inquirir, procurar, coger u obtener una cosa, en sentido figurado; y llevar las manos hacia alguna cosa con intención de agarrarla, en sentido propio. **To catch hold of,** agarrarse a, apoderarse de. **To catch it,** *(Fam.)* ganarse una zurra, una reprimenda, etc.

catch on, *(Fam.)* entender, comprender, caer (understand). **To catch on to something,** darse cuenta de algo, entender algo. Imponerse (become popular/fashion, idea). Ponerse de moda (game, style).

catch out, pillar, agarrar (trick). **To catch somebody out,** pillar o agarrar a alguien desprevenido.

catch up, coger, asir, empuñar; alcanzar (physically). **To catch up with somebody/something,** alcanzar a alguien/algo. Ponerse al corriente de algo (on gossip/news). **She had to catch up with/on the rest of the class,** tuvo que ponerse al nivel del resto de la clase. **I missed three weeks' classes, and it was a struggle to catch up,** perdí tres semanas de clase y me costó ponerme al día (draw level). **All those late nights eventually caught up on/with me,** todas esas trasnochadas finalmente pudieron más que yo. Alcanzar (draw level with); recoger (pick up). **To be/get caught up in something,** estar/quedar enganchado/atrapado en algo (trap, involve/in barbed wire, thorns); verse envuelto en algo (scandal, dispute); estar absorto o ensimismado en algo (in thoughts); contagiarse de algo (in excitement, enthusiasm).

catch, *s.* 1. Presa, captura, prisión o prendimiento; es también aprensión, hablando de contrabandos; la acción de prender o coger. Pesca (of fish). *(Sport)* Atrapada, parada, atajada. Trampa (hidden drawback). **I knew there'd be a catch in/to it somewhere,** ya sabía yo que tenía que haber gato encerrado. 2. Taravilla de picaporte. Pestillo, pasador (fastening device/on door). Cierre (on window, box, necklace). **Safety catch,** seguro. 3. Provecho, ventaja; atracción. **It is no great catch,** no es gran cosa, no vale la pena. *(Coloq.)* **He/she's a good catch,** es un buen partido (potential partner). 4. Alzaprima, palanca de rueda. 5. Gancho. 6. Canción con estribillo. 7. Cuaiche, especie de embarcación de dos palos o masteleros. *V.* KETCH. Temblor (in voice). **With a catch in her voice,** con la voz entrecortada o temblorosa. **To be** o **lie upon the catch,** espiar o acechar la presa.

catchable [ˈkætʃəbl] [ka-cha-bol], *a.* Expuesto a ser pillado o cogido.

catch-all [ˈkætʃɔːl] [kach-ol], *s. (Fam.)* Armario, cesto, cajón o saco destinado a recibir indistintamente toda clase de objetos, retazos, etc. Cajón de sastre. Comodín (clause, phrase, term).

catcher [ˈkætʃər] [ka-chaʳ], *s.* 1. Cogedor, el que coge o con lo que se coge alguna cosa. 2. Agarrador. 3. Jugador de pelota. Receptor, catcher (in baseball).

catchfly [ˈkætʃflaɪ] [kach-flai], *s. (Bot.)* Especie de colleja.

catching [ˈkætʃɪŋ] [ka-chin], *s.* 1. El endentado de una rueda en que deben entrar o engranar los dientes de otra. 2. Presa, captura. *-a.* Contagioso.

catchment [ˈkætʃmənt] [kach-ment], *s.* Desagüe. **Catchment basin,** cuenca o territorio desaguado por un río.

catchment area [ˌkætʃmənˈtæɪ̩ə] [kach-ment-e-ria] s. Zona de captación (of hospital, school). Distrito que corresponde a un hospital, colegio, etc.).

catchpenny [ˈkætʃˌpenɪ] [kach-pe-ni], s. Engañifa, baratija, alguna cosa de poco valor hecha para venderse muy barata.

catchphrase [ˈkætʃfreɪz] [kach-freis] s. Latiguillo (of person); eslogan (political party).

catchpoll [ˈkætʃˌpɔːl] [kach-pol], s. Corchete, alguacíl.

catchup [ˈkætʃʌp] [ka-chap], s. Salsa picante hecha de setas o tomates. *V.* CATSUP.

catchword [ˈkætʃwɜːd] [kach-ued], s. Reclamo, la palabra o sílaba que se pone al fin de cada plana, que es la misma con que ha de empezar la plana siguiente. 2. Palabra o frase de efecto destinada a llamar la atención pública. Eslogan (slogan).

catchy [ˈkætʃɪ] [ka-chi] a. Pegadizo, pegajoso.

catechetic, catechetical [ˈkætɪketɪk] [ka-ti-ke-tik], a. 1. Catequístico, lo que tiene preguntas y respuestas.

catechetically [ˈkætɪketɪklɪ] [ka-ti-ke-ti-ka-li], adv. Por preguntas y respuestas.

catechism [ˈkætɪkɪzəm] [ka-ti-kisem], s. 1. Catecismo, compendio de un credo religioso puesto en forma de preguntas y respuestas. 2. Manual de instrucción en forma de diálogo. Catequesis (instruction); catecismo (book).

catechist [ˈkætɪkɪst] [ka-ti-kist], s. Catequista o catequizante.

catechistical [ˈkætɪkɪstɪkl] [ka-ti-kis-ti-kal], s. Catequístico.

catechize [ˈkætɪkaɪz] [ka-ti-kais], va. 1. Catequizar, preguntar, examinar. 2. Catequizar, instruir en los artículos fundamentales de la religión cristiana.

catechizer [ˈkætɪkaɪzər] [ka-ti-kai-sa'], s. Catequizante.

catechizing [ˈkætɪkaɪzɪŋ] [ka-ti-kai-sin], s. Examen, interrogación.

catechu [ˈkætɪkjʊ] [ka-ti-kiu], s. Cato, tierra japónica o catecú, un medicamento astringente.

catechumen [ˈkætɪkjʊmən] [ka-ti-kiu-men], s. Catecúmeno, el que aprende los principios de la religión.

catechumenical [ˈkætɪkjʊmɪnɪkl] [ka-ti-kiu-mi-ni-kal], a. Catecuménico, lo que pertenece a los catecúmenos.

categoric, categorical [ˌkætɪˈgɒrɪk] [ka-ti-go-rik] [ˌkætɪˈgɒrɪkl] [ka-ti-go-ri-kal], a. Categórico, absoluto, positivo, explícito. Terminante, rotundo (refusal).

categorically [əkætɪˈgɒrɪkəlɪ] [ka-ti-go-ri-ka-li], adv. Categóricamente (state, say); rotundamente (refuse, deny).

categorize [ˈkætɪgəraɪz] [ka-ti-go-rais] va. Clasificar (things); catalogar, calificar (people).

category [ˈkætɪgɒrɪ] [ka-ti-go-ri], s. Categoría, clase; orden de ideas; predicamento.

catenary [ˈkætɪnærɪ] [ka-ti-na-ri], s. (Geom.) La línea curva formada por una cuerda o cadena perfectamente flexible, suspendida por ambos extremos.

catenate [ˈkætɪneɪt] [ka-ti-neit], va. Encadenar.

catenation [ˈkætɪneɪʃən] [ka-ti-nei-shon], s. Encadenamiento, encadenadura.

cater [ˈkeɪtər] [kei-ta'], vn. Abastecer, proveer de víveres o procurar diversión y entretenimiento. (Culin.) Encargarse del servicio de comida y bebida para fiestas, cafeterías, etc. -va. Encargarse del buffet de. **Cater to,** (GB) **cater for people of all ages,** ofrecer servicios para gente de todas las edades. **We try to cater to/for all needs,** tratamos de satisfacer todas las necesidades.

cater-corner [ˈkeɪtəˌkɔːnər] [keita-kor-na'], **cater-cornered** [ˈkeɪtəˈkɔːnəd] [keita-kor-nad] a. Diagonal.

cater-cousin [ˈkeɪtəˈkuːzɪn] [keita-ku-sin], s. 1. Un favorito. 2. Primo cuarto, dícese familiarmente de dos que son parientes en grado muy remoto.

caterer [ˈkeɪtərər] [kei-ta-ra'], s. Proveedor, abastecedor. En el estilo familiar significa propiamente la persona que va a la plaza a comprar los mejores comestibles; y en el figurado, el sujeto que procura las mejores divesiones, etc. Persona o

firma que se encarga del servicio de comida y bebida para fiestas, cafeterías, etc.

cateress [ˈkeɪtərəs] [kei-ta-res], sf. Proveedora, abastecedora.

catering [ˈkeɪtərɪŋ] [kei-ta-rin] s. **To do the catering,** encargarse del servicio de comida y bebida (provision of food). Restauración (trade, department).

caterpillar [ˈkeɪtəˌpɪlər] [keita-pi-la'], s. 1. Oruga, gusanillo muy nocivo que se engendra en las hojas y frutas; larva de un insecto himenóptero. 2. (Bot.) Oruga. **Caterpillar tractor,** tractor de oruga.

caterwaul [ˈkætəˈwɔːl] [keita-uol], vn. 1. Maullar, como los gatos en celo. 2. Dar chillidos o hacer algún ruido desapacible, como el maullido de los gatos.

cates [ˈkeɪtz] [keits], s. pl. Provisiones en general, y especialmente platos o manjares delicados.

cat-eyed [ˈkætˌaɪd] [kat-aid], a. El que tiene ojos de gato o como gato.

catfish [ˈkætfɪʃ] [kat-fish], s. Siluro, pez de cabeza ancha; barbo.

catflap [ˈkætˌflæp] [kat-flap] s, Gatera.

catgut [ˈkætˌgʌt] [kat-gat], s. 1. Hilo que se forma de tripa de carnero retorcida y sirve en los instrumentos músicos de cuerda. 2. Merli, especie de tela (del siglo XVIII) más basta que la gasa.

catharist [ˈkæθərɪst] [ka-za-rist], s. Puritano, persona que hace gran ostentación de pureza de vida o de principios.

catharsis [kəˈθɑːsɪs] [ka-zar-sis], s. (Med.) Catarsis, operación de purgar.

cathartic, cathartical [kəˈθɑːtɪk] [ka-zar-tik], a. Catártico, purgante.

cathartic s. Catártico o medicina purgante.

catharticalness [ˈkəˈθɑːtɪkəlnɪs] [ka-zar-ti-kal-nes], s. Calidad purgante de alguna cosa.

cathedra [kəˈθiːdrə] [ka-zi-dra], s. 1. Sillón de un obispo en la iglesia catedral de su diócesis. 2. Silla de profesor o catedrático.

cathedral [kəˈθiːdrəl] [ka-zi-dral], s. Catedral, iglesia principal o matriz de un obispado.

catherine-wheel [kəˈθəriːnˌwiːl] [ka-zi-rin-uil], s. (Arq.) 1. Rosa, gran ventana circular, cerrada por lo común con vidrieras de colores. 2. Rueda de fuegos artificiales; girándula.

catheter [ˈkæθɪtər] [ka-zi-ta'], s. Catéter, algalia, instrumento hueco de que se usa para dar curso a la orina, cuando hay una retención de ella, o para introducir en otros conductos del cuerpo.

catheterize [ˈkæθɪtəˌraɪz] [ka-zi-ta-ra-is], va. Introducir el catéter.

cathetus [ˈkæθɪtəs] [ka-zi-tos], s. (Geom.) Línea perpendicular imaginaria que pasa por el centro de un cuerpo cilíndrico.

cathode [ˈkæθəʊd] [ka-zoud], s. Polo negativo de una batería galvánica; opuesto a *anode.* **Cathode rays,** cf. ROENTGEN RAYS. **Cathode-ray tube,** tubo o válvula de rayos catódicos.

catholic [ˈkæθəlɪk] [ka-zo-lik], a. 1. Católico, universal o general; ortodoxo. 2. Perteneciente a la iglesia romana, a la anglicana, o a la griega. 3. Liberal, de amplias miras e ideas. **The Roman Catholic Church,** la iglesia católica (apostólica romana). Variado (interests, tastes). -s. Católico romano, el que profesa la religión católica.

catholicism [kəˈθɒlɪsɪzəm] [ka-zo-li-si-zem], s. Catolicismo, la profesión de la religión católica.

catholicize [kəˈθɒlɪzaɪz] [ka-zo-li-sais], vn. Hacerse católico.

catholicly [kəˈθɒlɪklɪ] [ka-zo-li-kli], adv. Católicamente, generalmente.

catholicness [kəˈθɒlɪknɪs] [ka-zo-lik-nes], s. (Des.) Universalidad. *V.* CATHOLICITY.

catkin [ˈkætkɪn] [kat-kin], s. Trama, amento, flores imperfectas que cuelgan de los árboles a manera de látigo, como se ve en los sauces; candelilla. *V.* AMENT.

catlike [ˈkætlaɪk] [kat-laik], *a.* Gateado, gatuno.

catling [ˈkætlɪŋ] [kat-lin], *s.* 1. Legra, especie de cuchillo de que se sirven los cirujanos. 2. Cuerdas de violón o guitarra.

catmint [ˈkætmɪnt] [kat-mint], **catnip** [ˈkætnɪp] [kat-nip], *s. (Bot.)* Gatera, calamento, calaminta, especie de planta del género Nepeta.

catnap [ˈkætnæp] [kat-nap], *s.* Siesta, siesta corta, cabezada, sueño ligero o corto, somnolencia, modorra. **To have/take a catnap,** echarse una siestecita o cabezada.

catnap, *vn.* Adormecerse, dormitar, estar amodorrado.

catnip [ˈkætnɪp] [kat-nip], *s.* Calamento. Nébeda.

catonian [kætəniən] [ka-to-nian], *a.* Grave, serio; riguroso.

cat-o'-nine-tails, *s.* Látigo de tiras con nueve nudos.

catoptrical [ˈkætəptrɪkəl] [ka-top-tri-kal], *a.* Catóptrico.

catoptrics [ˈkætəptrɪks] [ka-top-triks], *s.* Catóptrica, ciencia que enseña el modo de ver los objetos por medio de la reflexión de los rayos de la luz en los espejos y otras superficies tersas.

cat's cradle [ˈkætksˌkreɪdl] [kats-kradel] *s.* **To play cat's cradle,** jugar a hacer cunitas.

cat's eyes [ˈkætsˌaɪz] [kats-ais] *s. (Transp.)* Catafaros, ojo de gato, estoperol.

catsilver [ˈkætsɪlvər] [kat-sil-vaʳ], *s. (Min. Ant.) V.* MICA.

cat's-tail [ˈkætsˌteɪl] [kats-teil] o **cattail** [ˈkæteɪl] [ka-teil], *s. (Bot.)* Espadaña, hierba acuática.

cat suit [ˈkætsuːt] [kat-sut] *s. (GB)* Malla (entera).

catsup [ˈkætsəp] [kat-sap], *s.* Salsa de setas o de tomate. *V.* CATCHUP. *V.* KETCHUP.

cattail [ˈkæteɪl] [ka-teil] *s.* Enea, totora.

cattish [ˈkætɪʃ] [ka-tish], *a.* Gatuno, gatesco.

cattle [ˈkætl] [katel], *s.* 1. Ganado, reses, toda especie de bestias que pacen juntas. **Neat cattle,** black cattle, o **honed cattle,** ganado vacuno. 2. Se dice por desprecio de las personas. **Small cattle,** ganado lanar y cabrío. **Cattle plague,** fiebre tifoidea contagiosa que ataca al ganado vacuno. **Cattle range,** terreno dilatado y no cercado para apacentar el ganado mayor. **Cattle breeder,** ganadero. **Cattle breeding,** ganadería. **Cattle guard,** (GB) **grid,** rejilla en la carretera que permite pasar a los vehículos pero no al ganado.

cattle car [ˈkætlˌkɑːr] [katel-kar] *s.* Vagón de ganado.

cattle market [ˈkætlˌmɑːkɪt] [katel-mar-ket] *s.* Feria de ganado.

cattle truck [ˈkætlˌtrʌk] [katel-trak] *s. (Transp.)* Camión de ganado. (GB) *(Rail.)* Vagón de ganado.

catty [ˈkætɪ] [ka-ti], *s.* Cati, medida de peso de la China que equivale a 6 hectogramos. *a. (Coloq.)* Malicioso, venenoso.

catwalk [ˈkætˌwɔːk] [kat-uok] *s.* Pasarela (for models, on scaffolding).

caucasian [kɔːˈkeɪzɪən] [kou-kei-shian], *a.* Caucásico, del Cáucaso. Caucasiano. *s.* Caucásico. **The suspect is a male Caucasian,** el sospechoso es un hombre de raza blanca.

caucasus [ˈkɔːkəsəs] [kou-ka-sus] *N.* **The Caucasus (Mountains),** el Cáucaso.

caucus [ˈkɔːkəs] [kou-kos], *s.* 1. Conventículo o junta secreta de los directores o accionistas de una compañía, banco, ferrocarril o sociedad, para resolver en todo lo que se relaciona con la empresa. 2. Junta privada para designar candidatos o discutir medidas o asuntos políticos. 3. Entruchada.

caudad [ˈkɔːdəd] [kou-dad], *adv.* Hacia la cola.

caudal [ˈkɔːdl] [kou-dal], *a.* Lo que pertenece a la cola.

caudex [ˈkɔːdeks] [kou-deks], *s. (pl.* CAUDICES). Tallo en forma de cola; tallo de una palma.

caudle [ˈkɔːdl] [koudel], *s.* Bebida confortante, compuesta de vino y otros ingredientes, que se da a las recién paridas y a otros enfermos.

caudle, *va.* Componer una bebida confortante; confortar.

cauf [ˈkɔːf] [kof], *s.* Vivero de pescado, canasta o cajón lleno de agujeros en que se tienen peces vivos dentro del agua.

caught, *pret.* y *pp.* del verbo TO CATCH.

caul [ˈkɔːl] [koul], *s.* 1. Redecilla, cofia o toca, red en que las mujeres recogen el pelo. 2. Redecilla, cualquier red pequeña. 3. Membrana o tela que cubre la cabeza de algunas criaturas cuando nacen. 4. Omento.

cauldron [ˈkɔːldrən] [kol-dron] *s. (GB) V.* CALDRON.

caulescent [kɔːˈlesənt] [kou-lesent], *a. (Bot.)* Cuadelescente, que tiene un tallo bien definido.

cauliferous [kɔːˈlifərəs] [kou-li-fe-ros], *a.* Colífero; se dice de las plantas que tienen tallos como la coliflor.

cauliflower [ˈkɒlɪflaʊər] [kou-li-flauaʳ], *s.* Coliflor, especie de col o berza. (GB) **Cauliflower cheese,** colifor gratinada con queso. **To have a cauliflower ear,** tener la oreja deformada (por golpes).

caulk, *va. V.* CALK.

cauma [ˈkɔːmə] [kou-ma], *s. (Ant.)* Calor de fiebre; fiebre.

caup [ˈkəʊp] [koup], *va.* Cambiar, trocar.

caup, *s. (Esco.)* Copa; taza.

causable [ˈkɔːzəbl] [kou-sa-bol], *a.* Causable.

causal [ˈkɔːzəl] [kou-sal], *a.* Causal, perteneciente a una causa.

causality [ˈkɔːzəlɪtɪ] [kou-sa-li-ti], **causation** [kɔːˈzeɪʃən] [kou-sei-shon], *s.* Causalidad; causa, origen, principio, modo o acción con que se causa u obra un efecto.

causally [ˈkɔːzəlɪ] [kou-sa-li], *adv.* De un modo causal.

causative [ˈkɔːzətɪv] [kou-sa-tiv], *a.* Causal, causativo, causante.

causatively [ˈkɔːzətɪvlɪ] [kou-sa-tiv-li], *adv.* Efectivamente.

cause [ˈkɔːz] [kous], *s.* 1. Causa, origen, principio (of accident, event, death). **Cause and effect,** causa y efecto. 2. Autor, causa; motivo, razón (reason, grounds); pretexto. **There's some cause for concern,** existen motivos o razones para preocuparse. **There's no cause for concern,** no hay por qué preocuparse. **Without (good) cause,** sin causa (justificada) o motivo (justificado). 3. Acción o pleito incoado ante un tribunal, y también todo un procedimiento judicial. 4. Partido. **The cause is over,** se ha visto la causa. **To espouse one's cause,** abrazar la causa de alguno, tomar su partido. Causa (ideal, movement). **To fight/die for the cause,** luchar/morir por la causa. **It's a good cause,** es una buena causa. **They fought in the cause of freedom,** lucharon en pro de la libertad.

cause, *va.* Causar, hacer, excitar, producir algún efecto. **To cause love,** inspirar amor. **To cause sorrow,** dar pesadumbre. **To cause to,** hacer, expedir. **To cause somebody problems,** causarle u ocasionarle problemas a alguien.

cause célèbre [ˌkɔːzseɪˈlebr] [kos-sei-lebr] *s.* Caso famoso o célebre. **The strike became a cause célèbre,** la huelga dio mucho que hablar.

causeless [ˈkɔːslɪs] [kos-les], *a.* 1. Que tiene su origen en sí mismo y no reconoce causa. 2. Infundado, injusto, sin razón.

causelessly [ˈkɔːslɪslɪ] [kos-lis-li], *adv.* Infundadamente, sin causa, motivo ni fundamento.

causelessness [ˈkɔːslɪsnɪs] [kos-les-nes], *s.* Motivo o causa injusta.

causer [ˈkɔːzər] [kou-saʳ], *s.* 1. Causador. 2. Autor.

causeway [ˈkɔːzweɪ] [kos-uei], **causey** [ˈkɔːzeɪ] [kous-ei], *s.* Arrecife, camino real, o calzada empedrada. Paso elevado (path); carretera elevada (road).

causidical [ˈkɔːsɪdɪkl] [kou-si-di-kal], *a.* Causídico, perteneciente a la prosecución de causas y pleitos.

caustic, caustical [ˈkɔːstɪk] [kous-tik], *a. (Quím.)* Cáustico, que quema y destruye todo aquello a que se aplica. Cáustico, mordaz (wit, remark).

caustic, *s.* Cáustico, medicamento corrosivo.

causticity [ˈkɔːstɪsɪtɪ] [kos-ti-si-ti], *s.* Mordacidad; calidad de cáustico.

causticness [ˈkɔːstɪknɪs] [kos-tik-nes], *s. V.* CAUSTICITY.

cautelous [ˈkɔːtɪləs] [ko-ti-lous], *a.* Cauteloso, cauto, astuto, prudente, socarrón.

cauterant [ˈkɔːtɪrənt] [ko-te-rant], *s.* y *a.* Cauterio, medicamento cáustico.

cauterism [ˈkɔːtərɪzəm] [kau-te-risem], **cauterization** [ˈkɔːtərɪseɪʃən] [kau-te-ri-sei-shon], s. Cauterización, cauterio.

cauterize [ˈkɔːtəraɪz] [kau-te-rais], va. Cauterizar, dar cauterio.

cauterizing [ˈkɔːtəraɪzɪŋ] [kau-te-raisin], s. Cauterización.

cautery [ˈkɔːtərɪ] [kau-te-ri], s. Cauterio.

caution [ˈkɔːʃən] [kau-shon], s. 1. Caución, cautela, prudencia (care, prudence), precaución, circunspección, atención. **To use/exercise caution,** tener mucho cuidado. **To throw caution to the wind(s),** echar la precaución por la borda. 2. Amonestación (Law, Sport); prevención; advertencia, aviso (warning). 3. Aviso, miramiento, recato.

caution, va. 1. Caucionar, precaver, prevenir; advertir (warn); avisar, amonestar. 2. Caucionar, afianzar, dar fianza. 3. Informar de sus derechos (inform of rights). **To caution somebody about something,** llamarle la atención a alguien por algo (reprimand). *(Law, Sport)* **To caution somebody for,** amonestar a alguien por.

cautionary [ˈkɔːʃənərɪ] [ko-sho-na-ri], a. 1. Amonestador, admonitorio, avisador; que amonesta. 2. Caucionado, dado en fianza o en rehenes; aviso. **Cautionary words/remarks,** advertencias. **Cautionary tale,** cuento con moraleja.

cautious [ˈkɔːʃəs] [ko-shos], a. Cauto, vigilante, circunspecto, cauteloso. **The senator was cautious about committing himself,** el senador se cuidó de comprometerse.

cautiously [ˈkɔːʃəslɪ] [ko-shos-li], adv. Cautamente, prudentemente, cautelosamente. **I'm cautiously optimistic,** soy prudentemente optimista.

cautiousness [ˈkɔːʃəsnɪs] [ko-shos-nes], s. Cautela, vigilancia, circunspección, previsión, prudencia, precaución.

cavalcade [ˌkævəlˈkeɪd] [ka-val-keid], s. Cabalgata o procesión a caballo.

cavalier [ˌkævəˈlɪər] [ka-va-lieʳ], s. 1. Caballero. Cuando las guerras civiles de Inglaterra en el reinado de Carlos I, se llamaron *Cavaliers* los realistas, y los del partido contrario *Round-heads;* así como en España en el tiempo de las Comunidades llamaron *caballeros* a los que seguían el partido del rey, y *comuneros* a los que seguían al pueblo. 2. Hombre galante, que sirve de escolta a una dama o de pareja en el baile. 3. Jinete, caballero, y especialmente un jinete armado. 4. *(Fort.)* Caballero, el terraplén que se levanta para colocar los cañones. -a. 1. Caballeresco, bravo, belicoso. Disciplente. 2. Altivo, desdeñoso, alegre, libre.

cavaliery [ˌkævəˈlɪərɪ] [ka-va-lie-ri], adv. Altívamente, a lo caballero, caballerosamente.

cavalry [ˈkævəlrɪ] [ka-val-ri], s. Caballería, cuerpo de milicia que va a caballo.

cavalryman [ˈkævəlrɪmən] [ka-val-ri-man], s. *(Mil.)* Soldado de caballería.

cavatina [ˈkævətiːnə] [ka-va-ti-na], s. Aria corta y sencilla; pieza musical cantada por una sola persona.

cave [keɪv] [keiv], s. Cueva, caverna, antro; bodega; cualquier lugar hueco y subterráneo. **Cave dweller,** cavernícola, troglodita (prehistoric); habitante de las cuevas (modern). **Cave painting,** pintura rupestre.

cave, vn. 1. Hundirse, abismarse. 2. *(Fam.)* Ceder, rendirse. -va. Excavar. **To cave in,** caer en un hoyo. Derrumbarse, hundirse (collapse/roof, tunnel). *(Coloq.)* Ceder (person/yield).

caveat [ˈkeɪvɪæt] [kei-viet], s. 1. *(For.)* Intimación o notificación formal hecha a un juez o funcionario público, para que suspenda todo procedimiento ulterior hasta haber oído al peticionario. 2. *(E.U.)* Descripción de un invento no perfeccionado todavía, archivada en la Oficina de Patentes en Washington. 3. Advertencia (warning). **With the caveat that...,** con la salvedad de que...

caveman [ˈkeɪvmæn] [keiv-man] s. Hombre de las cavernas (prehistoric).

cavendishe [ˈkeɪvəndɪʃ] [keivan-dish], s. Un tabaco norteamericano.

cavern [ˈkævən] [ka-vern], s. Caverna, concavidad hecha en la tierra.

cavernede [ˈkævəniːd] [ka-ver-nid], **cavernouse** [ˈkævənəʊz] [ka-ver-nous], a. 1. Cavernoso, lleno de cavernas o concavidades. **Caverned,** el que vive en caverna o cueva. 2. Grande y tenebroso (building, hall); profundo y oscuro como la boca de un lobo (pit).

cavessone [ˈkeɪvsən] [keiv-son], s. Cabezón, cabezada con muserola y provista de argolla para rienda o cuerda, por medio de la cual se obliga al caballo a trotar o andar en círculo, entorno del domador.

caviar, caviaree [ˈkævɪɑːr] [ka-viar] [ˈkævɪəriː] [ka-via-ri], s. Cavial, caviar, especie de embuchado que se hace con las huevas de esturión saladas.

cavil [ˈkævɪl] [ka-vil], s. Efugio, evasión, cavilación, sofistería, vanas sutilezas, quisquillas: triquiñuelas en el juego; trampa legal.

cavil, vn. Cavilar, querer hallar dificultades donde no las hay: armar pleitos o enredos; sutilizar o buscar escapatorias para salir de alguna dificultad. Buscar quisquillas. (GB) **To cavil at/about something,** ponerle reparos a algo. -va. Poner faltas quisquillosamente.

caviller [ˈkævɪlər] [ka-vi-laʳ], s. Sofista; trapacero, enredador.

cavilling [ˈkævɪlɪŋ] [ka-vi-lin], s. Cavilación, sofistería. V. CAVIL.

cavillingly [ˈkævɪlɪŋlɪ] [ka-vi-lin-li], adv. Cavilosamente.

cavilous [ˈkævɪləs] [ka-vi-los], a. Caviloso, quisquilloso.

caving [ˈkeɪvɪŋ] [kei-vin] s. Espeleología.

cavitary [ˈkævɪtərɪ] [ka-vi-ta-ri], a. Que tiene una cavidad, hueco; que tiene un conducto intestinal, como ciertos gusanos.

cavity [ˈkævɪtɪ] [ka-vi-ti], s. Cavidad, espacio cóncavo o vacío. *(Dent.)* Caries.

cavort [kəˈvɔːt] [ka-vort], vn. *(E.U.)* Cabriolar como el caballo. Retozar. **He's cavorting with his secretary,** está tonteando con su secretaria.

caw [kɔː] [ko], vn. Graznar, crascitar, como el grajo o el cuervo; jadear. s. Graznido.

cay [keɪ] [kei], s. Cayo, peñasco o isleta en las Antillas. Cf. KEY.

cayenne pepper [ˈkeɪenˌpepər] [keie-pe-paʳ], s. *(Bot.)* Pimentón; pimiento, guindilla. Pimienta de cayena.

cayman [ˈkeɪmən] [kei-man], s. Caimán, cocodrilo de América.

CBS s. (in US) = **Columbia Broadcasting System,** la CBS.

cc (= **cubic centimeter** o (GB) **centimeter**), c.c.; **copies to** (corresp.).

CD s. (= **compact disc/disk**) CD.

cease [siːs] [sis], vn. 1. Cesar (noise); desistir, parar. 2. Fenecer, acabarse; interrumpirse (production); detenerse (work). 3. Descansar. -va. Parar, suspender, interrumpir (production, publication). **His naiveté never ceases to amaze me,** no me explico cómo puede ser tan ingenuo.

cease-fire [ˌsiːsˈfaɪər] [sis-faiaʳ], s. Alto el fuego, cese del fuego.

ceaseless [ˈsiːslɪs] [sis-les], a. Incesante, perpetuo, continuo, perenne.

ceaselessly [ˈsiːslɪslɪ] [sis-lis-li], adv. Perpetuamente, incesantemente.

ceasing [ˈsiːsɪŋ] [sisin], s. Cesación.

cecils [ˈsesɪls] [se-sils], s. pl. Pisto, picadillo de carne.

cecity [ˈsesɪtɪ] [se-si-ti], s. Ceguedad, ceguera, privación de la vista.

cedar [ˈsiːdər] [si-daʳ], s. Cedro, árbol fragante de las coníferas; también, tuya.

cedar-bird [ˈsiːdəbɜːn] [si-dar-berd], s. *(Orn.)* Pájaro del cedro (de América).

cedarlike [ˈsiːdəˈlaɪk] [si-dar-laik], *a.* Semejante al cedro.

cedarn [ˈsiːdən] [si-darn], *a.* 1. *V.* CEDRINE. 2. Hecho o revestido con cedros.

cede [siːd] [sid], *va.* Ceder, traspasar a otro una cosa o un derecho; transferir territorio. **To cede something to somebody,** cederle algo a alguien.

cedilla [sɪˈdɪlə] [si-di-la], *s.* Zedilla, virgulilla debajo de una *c*, que servía para expresar un sonido parecido al de la zeda.

cedrine [sɪˈdraɪn] [si-drain], *a.* Cedrino, que se refiere o pertenece al cedro.

ceil [siːl] [sil], *va.* Cubrir o techar con cielo raso.

ceiling [ˈsiːlɪŋ] [si-lin], *s.* 1. Techo o cielo raso de una habitación. 2. *(Mar.)* Revestimiento interior de la bodega. 3. *(Aer.)* Cielo, cielo máximo, techo. Límite, tope (upper limit).

ceiling price [siːlɪŋˌpraɪz] [si-lin-prais], *s.* Precio tope.

celature [ˈselətʃʊər] [se-la-chua], *s.* Grabado, el arte de grabar sobre los metales.

celebrant [ˈselɪbrənt] [se-li-brant], *s.* Celebrante, el sacerdote que dice la misa.

celebrate [ˈselɪbreɪt] [se-li-breit], *va.* 1. Celebrar, festejar (birthday, success); alabar, aplaudir, loar (praise/virtues, deeds). 2. Celebrar, solemnizar. 3. Hacer elogio o elogiar. *vn.* **We won: let's celebrate!,** ¡ganamos, vamos a celebrarlo!

celebrated [ˈselɪbreɪtɪd] [se-li-brei-ted], *a.* Célebre, famoso.

celebration [ˌselɪˈbreɪʃən] [se-li-brei-shon], *s.* 1. Celebración, acción hecha con solemnidad; tiempo de celebrar. Fiesta (event). **He attended the celebrations,** asistió a los festejos o festividades. **We ought to have a little celebration,** deberíamos celebrarlo o festejarlo. 2. Celebración (praise); celebridad, aplauso. **The play is a celebration of life,** la obra es un canto o una loa a la vida. 3. Elogio, panegírico, alabanza.

celebrator [ˈselɪbreɪtər] [se-li-brei-to], *s.* Celebrador, celebrante.

celebratory [ˌselɪˈbreɪtəri] [se-li-brei-to-ri] *a.* **We had a celebratory drink,** nos tomamos una copa para celebrarlo o festejarlo.

celebrious [ˈselɪbrɪəs] [se-li-brios], *a.* Célebre, famoso, renombrado

celebrity [sɪˈlebrɪti] [se-li-bri-ti], *s.* Celebridad, fama, renombre. 2. Personaje, persona renombrada.

celeriac [səˈlerɪæk] [se-li-riak], *s. (Bot.)* Apio napiforme.

celerity [sɪˈlerɪti] [se-li-ri-ti], *s.* Celeridad, ligereza, prontitud, velocidad, rapidez.

celery [ˈseləri] [se-le-ri], *s. (Bot.)* Apio. **A stick/head of celery,** una rama/mata de apio.

celestial [sɪˈlestɪəl] [si-les-tial], *a.* 1. Celestial, célico, celeste. 2. Divino, excelente. -*s.* 1. Habitador del cielo. 2. Chino.

celestial mechanics [sɪˈlestɪəlˌmætʃiːnz] [si-les-tial-me-ka-niks], *s.* Mecánica celeste.

celestialize [sɪˈlestɪəlaɪz] [si-les-tia-lais], *va.* Hacer celestial o celeste.

celestially [sɪˈlestɪəli] [si-les-tia-li], *adv.* Celestialmente.

celestins [ˈsɪlestɪnz] [si-les-tins], *s.* Celestinos, una orden religiosa.

celiac [ˈsɪlɪæk] [si-liak], *a. (Med.)* Celíaco, perteneciente al vientre. **Celiac axis,** arteria corta que surte al hígado, al estómago y al bazo.

celibacy [ˈselɪbəsi] [se-li-ba-si], *s.* Celibato, soltería, el estado de los que no están casados.

celibate [ˈselɪbɪt] [se-li-beit], *a.* Célibe, soltero. -*s.* 1. Celibato, estado de la persona que no ha tomado estado de matrimonio. 2. Célibe.

cell [sel] [sel], *s.* 1. *(Biol.)* Célula, el elemento mínimo de planta o animal que manifiesta libre acción vital; unidad de estructura. Celular (division, wall). 2. Nicho, cavidad pequeña; alveolo. 3. Celdilla de abejas en los panales. 4. Celda, habitación de un religioso o religiosa. Celda (in prison, monastery, honeycomb). 5. Celdilla, cavidad donde se hallan encerradas ciertas semillas. 6. *(Ant.)* Cavidad de los tejidos esponjosos. 7. Celda, par de una batería galvánica. *(Elec.)* Célula; elemento, pila (in battery).

cellar [ˈselər] [se-la], *s.* Sótano, bodega de una casa (for wine); carbonera (for coal). *(Coloq.)* **To be/ finish in the cellar,** estar/llegar en el último lugar.

cellarage [ˈselərɪdʒ] [se-la-reich], *s.* 1. Cueva, sótano, la parte subterránea de un edificio destinada a poner el carbón, el vino y otras cosas. 2. Alquiler que se paga por poner el vino en la bodega de otro.

cellarer [ˈselərər] [se-la-ra], **cellarist** [ˈselərɪst] [se-la-rist], *s.* Cillerero, el despensero de un monasterio.

cellaret [ˈselərɪt] [se-la-rit], *s.* Frasquera, caja de licores.

cellist [ˈselɪst] [se-list] *s.* Violoncelista, violonchelista, chelista.

cello [ˈtʃeləʊ] [che-lou], *s.* Violoncelo, bajo; abreviatura de violoncello. Violonchelo, chelo.

cellophane [ˈseləfeɪn] [se-lo-fein], *s.* Celofán.

cellphone [ˈselfəʊn] [sel-foun] *s.* Teléfono celular.

cellular [ˈseljʊlər] [se-liu-la], *a.* Celular, lo que se compone de varias celdillas o cavidades.

cellule [ˈseljʊl] [se-liul], *s.* Celdita.

cellulite [ˈseljʊlaɪt] [se-la-lait] *s.* Celulitis.

celluloid [ˈseljʊlɔɪd] [se-liu-loid], *s.* Celuloide, compuesto duro elástico, que se forma sometiendo algodón pólvora, alcanfor y otras sustancias a presión hidráulica.

cellulose [ˈseljʊləʊs] [se-liu-lous], *s.* Celulosa, sustancia insoluble en agua que cubre las células; materia fundamental de las plantas.

celsitude [ˈselsɪtjuːd] [sel-si-tiud], *s.* Celsitud, elevación, altura, alteza.

celsius [ˈselsɪəs] [sel-sius] *a.* **20 degrees Celsius,** 20 grados centígrados o Celsio(s).

celt, kelt [kelt] [kelt], *s.* Celta, nombre de los antiguos habitantes de la parte occidental de Europa.

celtic [ˈkeltɪk] [kel-tik], **keltic** [ˈkeltɪk] [kel-tik], *a.* Céltico, lo que pertenece a los celtas.

celticism [ˈkeltɪsɪzm] [kel-ti-sizem], *s.* Celticismo, costumbre de los celtas.

cement [səˈmənt] [se-ment], *s.* 1. Cemento, argamasa o mezlca muy fuerte para pegar, tapar, etc. 2. Cal arcillosa que se endurece en el agua. 3. Lo que sirve para unir dos cuerpos entre sí. 4. Enlace o vínculo de amistad.

cement, *va. (Const.)* Pegar, unir una cosa con otra por medio de una mezcla; argamasar; asegurar, estrechar, solidar. **To cement something (over),** revestir algo de cemento, cementar algo. Consolidar, fortalecer (make firm/ friendship, alliance). -*vn.* Unirse, hacer liga.

cementation [ˌsiːmənˈteɪʃən] [si-men-tei-shon], *s.* 1. Ligazón, la acción de unirse una cosa con otra. 2. *(Quím.)* Cimentación, afinación de un metal por medio de un cemento; se dice particularmente de la transformación del hierro en acero.

cementer [sɪˈməntər] [si-men-ta], *s.* Ligador, pegador.

cement mixer [ˈsəmənt,mɪksər] [se-ment-mik-sa] *s.* Hormigonera.

cemetery [ˈsemɪtri] [se-mi-tri], *s.* Cementerio.

cenobite [ˈsenəbaɪt] [se-no-bait], *s.* Cenobita, religioso o monje.

cenobitic o cenobitical [senəbaɪtɪk] [se-no-bi-tic], *a.* Cenobítico, el que vive en comunidad.

cenobium [ˈsenəbɪəm] [se-no-bium], *s.* 1. Morada de cenobitas. 2. *(Zool.)* Grupo o colonia de protozoarios. 3. *(Bot.)* Entre las algas unicelulares, colonia de individuos independientes unidos por una matriz común.

cenotaph [ˈsenətɑːf] [se-no-taf], *s.* Cenotafio, monumento sepulcral erigido para honrar la memoria de algún difunto.

cense [sens] [sens], *va.* Incensar, perfumar con incienso.

censer [sensər] [sen-sa], *s.* Incensario, braserillo con que se inciensa.

censor [sensər] [sen-sa], *s.* 1. Censor, magistrado de Roma que formaba el censo y tenía cuidado de la corrección de las costumbres. 2. Censor, el que todo lo censura y critica. -va. Censurar.

censorial ['sənsərɪəl] [sen-so-rial], **censorian** ['sənsərɪən] [sen-so-rian], a. Censorio, lo perteneciente al censor o a su oficio.

censorious ['sənsɔ:rɪəs] [sen-so-rios], a. Severo, rígido; crítico, maldiciente, sofístico.

censoriously ['sənsɔ:rɪəslɪ] [sen-so-rios-li], adv. Severamente, críticamente.

censorship ['sənsəʃɪp] [sen-sor-ship], s. Censura, el oficio o dignidad de censar.

censual ['sənsʊəl] [sen-sual], a. Censual, lo perteneciente al censo.

censurable ['sənʃərəbl] [sen-shu-ra-bol], a. Censurable, digno de censura.

censurableness ['sənʃərəblnɪs] [sen-shu-ra-bol-nes], s. La calidad de ser censurable.

censurably ['sənʃərəblɪ] [sen-shu-ra-bli], adv. Censurablemente.

censure ['senʃər] [sen-shaʳ], s. 1. Censura, reprensión, crítica. 2. Censura, parecer, opinión. 3. Censura, pena espiritual o eclesiástica como la excomunión, suspensión, etc.

censure, va. 1. Censurar, culpar, reprender. 2. Criticar, condenar. 3. Juzgar.

censurer ['senʃərər] [sen-sha-raʳ] s. Censurador, censurante.

censuring ['sensərɪŋ] [sen-sha-rin], s. Improperio, censura.

census ['sensəs] [sen-sas], s. Censo.

cent [sent] [sent], s. 1. Centavo, moneda de cobre de los Estados Unidos, cuyo valor es un centavo o la centésima parte de un peso o dólar. 2. Ciento, en la frase *per cent,* que quiere decir por ciento. **Six per cent** (interés de), seis por ciento. 3. Centésima parte de la unidad en otros sistemas monetarios, como céntimo de franco. **I don't have/it isn't worth a red cent,** no tengo/no vale ni un céntimo o centavo. **To put in one's two cent's worth,** meter baza o cuchara, dar su opinión.

cental ['sentl] [sen-tal], s. Quintal, peso de cien libras. -a. Perteneciente a un ciento.

centare ['sentɑ:r] [sen-taʳ], s. Centiárea, la centésima parte de un área, o sea el metro cuadrado. 1 1/3 yardas cuadradas.

centaur ['sentɔ:r] [sen-toʳ], s. 1. (Poét.) Centauro, monstruo mitad hombre y mitad caballo. 2. Centauro, un signo del zodíaco.

centaurea ['sentɔrɪə] [se-tau-ria], s. (Bot.) Centaurea, género de plantas compuestas.

centaury ['sentɔ:rɪ] [sen-to-ri], s. (Bot.) Centaura, o centaurea, planta medicinal.

centenarian [sentɪ'nɛərɪən] [sen-ti-nea-rian], s. Centenario, la persona que llega a la edad de cien años.

centenary [sen'ti:nərɪ] [sen-ti-na-ri], s. Centena, centenar, centenario, tiempo o plazo de cien años.

centennial [sen'tenɪəl] [sen-te-nial], a. Del centenario. s. Centenario.

center, (GB) centre ['sentər] [sen-taʳ], s. 1. Centro, punto que está en medio de una esfera o de una figura circular; el punto medio de otras figuras (middle point, area). **To be the center of attention,** ser el centro de atención. 2. Punto de atracción o convergencia; punto focal. 3. Punto de emanación; núcleo, origen. 4. Cimbra. 5. (Pol.) **He's left of center,** es de centro izquierda. 6. Relleno (filling). **Community center,** centro cívico (site of activity). (Sport) Centro (in US football, rugby); pivot, pivote (basketball).

center, (GB) centre, va. Centrar, colocar o fijar en un centro (position); (Sport) lanzar un centro con (ball). **To center something on something/somebody,** centrar algo en algo/alguien (concentrate, focus). **The major industries are centered on Chicago,** las principales industrias están concentradas en Chicago y sus alrededores. -vn. 1. Descansar o reposar sobre alguna cosa. 2. Terminar, rematar, confinar; reunirse. **To center on/upon something/somebody,** centrarse en algo/alguien. **His hopes centered**

on being promoted, cifraba todas sus esperanzas en que lo ascendieran. **To center on/around something/somebody,** girar alrededor de o en torno a algo/alguien. -vr. Colocarse en el centro o en medio.

center-board ['sentə'bɔ:d] [sen-tar-bord], s. (Mar.) Orza de deriva, usada especialmente en los yates.

centered ['sentəd] [sen-te-red], pp. Concentrado, reunido en centro.

center field [sentə'fi:ld] [sen-tar-fild] s. Jardín central, centro campo (area/in baseball).

center fielder ['sentəˌfi:ldər] [sen-ter-fil-daʳ] s. Jardinero centro, centro campo (in baseball).

centerfold [sentə'fəʊld] [sen-ter-fould] s. Póster o encarte central.

center forward [sentə'fɔ:wɑ:d] [sen-ter-for-uard] s. Delantero centro.

center half [sentə'hɑ:f] [sen-ter-jalf] s. Medio centro.

centering ['sentərɪŋ] [sen-te-rin], s. 1. Acto u operación de colocar un objeto en el foco del microscopio o anteojo. 2. Acto de practicar un hueco poco profundo en el centro de un objeto. 3. (Arq.) Cimbra de arco o bóveda.

center of gravity [sentə'ɒfgrævɪtɪ] [sen-tar-of-gra-vi-ti] s. Centro de gravedad.

centerpiece ['sentəpi:s] [sen-ta-pis] s. Centro de mesa (decoration); eje (main feature).

centesimal [sen'təsɪməl] [sen-te-si-mal], a. Centésimo que llega al número de ciento.

centi- [sentɪ] [sen-ti] pref. Centi-

centifolious [sentɪ'fəlɪəs] [sen-ti-fo-lios], a. Centifolio, que tiene cien hojas.

centigrade ['sentɪgreɪd] [sen-ti-greid], a. Centígrado, de cien grados. En el termómetro centígrado el punto de congelación se marca cero y el de ebullición del agua 100°. **20 degrees centigrades,** 20 grados centígrades.

centigram (o Centigramme) ['sentɪgræm] [sen-ti-gram], s. Centígramo, el peso de la centésima parte de un gramo.

centiliter o centilitre ['sentɪˌli:tər] [sen-ti-li-taʳ], s. Centilitro, la centésima parte de un litro.

centimeter o centimetre ['sentɪˌmi:tər] [sen-ti-mi-taʳ], s. Centímetro, la centésima parte de un metro.

centipede ['sentɪpi:d] [sen-ti-pid], s. Cientopiés o ciempiés, insecto venenoso.

centner [sentnər] [sent-neʳ], s. 1. Peso de cien libras = 45.36 kilos. 2. En docimástica, una dracma.

cento ['sentə] [sen-to], s. Centón, obra literaria compuesta por la mayor parte de pensamientos entresacados de diferentes autores.

centrad ['sentrəd] [sen-trad], adv. (Zool.) Hacia el centro.

central ['sentrəl] [sen-tral], a. 1. Central, lo que se refiere o pertenece al centro. Central (main); fundamental, principal (problem). **This is central to the success of the project,** esto es fundamental para que el proyecto sea un éxito. 2. Céntrico (in the center/area, street). **Our office is very central,** nuestra oficina está en una zona céntrica o en un lugar muy céntrico. **In central Chicago,** en el centro de Chicago.

Central African Republic [ˌsentrəlˌæfrɪkənrɪ'pʌblɪk] [sen-tral-a-fri-kan-ri-pa-blik] N. La República Centroafricana.

Central America ['sentrələ'merɪkə] [sen-tral-a-me-ri-ka] N. Centroamérica, América Central.

Central American ['sentrələ'merɪkən] [sen-tral-a-me-ri-kan] a./s. Centroamericano, de América Central.

Central Europe ['sentrəl'jʊərəp] [sen-tral-iu-rop] N. Europa Central.

Central European ['sentrəl'jʊərəpɪən] [sen-tral-iu-ro-pian] a./s. Centroeuropeo, de Europa Central.

central heating ['sentrəl'hi:tɪŋ] [sen-tral-ji-tin] s. Calefacción central.

centralism ['sentrəlɪzm] [sen-tra-lisem], s. Centralización.

centrality [sen'trælɪtɪ] [sen-tra-li-ti], s. Centralidad, posición central.

centralization [ˌsentrəlaɪˈzeɪʃən] [sen-tra-lai-sei-shon], *s.* Centralización.

centralize [ˈsentrəlaɪz] [sen-tra-lais], *va.* Centralizar.

centrally [ˈsentrəlɪ] [sen-tra-li], *adv.* Centralmente. **Centrally heated,** con calefacción central. **It's centrally located,** está en una zona céntrica o en un lugar céntrico.

central reservation [ˈsentrəlˌrezəˈveɪʃən] [sen-tral-re-ser-vei-shon] *s.* (GB) Mediana, bandejón (central).

Central Standard Time [ˈsentrəlˌstændədˈtaɪm] [sen-tral-stan-dard-taim] *s.* Horario de la zona central.

centre [ˈsentər] [sen-taʳ] (GB) *V.* CENTER.

centric, centrical [ˈsentrɪk] [sen-trik], *a.* Central.

centrically [ˈsentrɪkəlɪ] [sen-tri-ka-li], *adv.* Centralmente.

centricalness [ˈsentrɪkəlnɪs] [sen-tri-kal-nes], *s.* Situación central.

centrifugal [senˈtrɪfjʊɡəl] [sen-tri-fiu-gal], *a.* Centrífugo, lo que se aparta o se aleja del centro.

centrifuge [ˈsentrɪfjuːʒ] [sen-tri-fiush] *s.* Centrifugador.

centripetal [senˈtrɪpɪtl] [sen-tri-pi-tal], *a.* Centrípeta, lo que se acerca o tiene tendencia al centro.

centuple [ˈsentʌpl] [sen-ta-pel], *a.* Céntuplo, centuplicado, cien veces tanto.

centuplicate [ˈsentʌplɪkeɪt] [sen-ta-pli-keit], *va.* Centuplicar, aumentar cien veces más alguna cosa.

centurial [senˈtjʊrɪəl] [sen-iu-rial], *a.* 1. Perteneciente a una centuria del pueblo romano. 2. Secular, referente a un espacio de cien años.

centuriator [ˈsentjʊrɪətər] [sen-tiu-ria-toʳ], **centurist** [sen-tiu-rist], *s.* El que distingue los tiempos por siglos.

centurion [ˈsentjʊrɪən] [sen-tiu-rion], *s.* Centurión, capitán, oficial militar romano que mandaba cien hombres.

century [ˈsentjʊrɪ] [sen-tiu-ri], *s.* 1. Centuria, siglo; el número de cien años. **In the 19th,** en el siglo XIX. **A centuries-old tradition,** una tradición secular o de siglos. Centena (in cricket). 2. Centuria, cuerpo o fuerza militar romano que un tiempo constó de cien hombres.

CEO *s.* = chief executive officer

cephalalgia [ˈsefəlældʒɪə] [sen-tral], *s.* Cefalagia, dolor de cabeza.

cephalic [ˈsefəlɪk] [se-fa-lik], *a.* Cefálico, útil o perteneciente a la cabeza.

cephalopod [ˈsefəlɒpɒd] [se-fa-lo-pod], *a.* Perteneciente a los cefalópodos.

cephalopoda [ˈsefəlɒpɒdə] [se-fa-lo-po-da]», *s. pl.* Cefalópodos, clase de moluscos caracterizados por largos brazos o tentáculos.

cepheus [ˈsefɪəs] [se-fios], *s.* Cefeo, constelación boreal, cerca del Dragón y Casiopea.

ceraceous [ˈserəʃəs] [se-ra-shos], *a.* Ceráceo, de la naturaleza de la cera o semejante a ella.

ceramic [ˈseræmɪk] [se-ra-mik], *a.* Cerámico, relativo al arte de la fabricación de objetos de tierra, loza y porcelana. De cerámica (pot). **Ceramic tile,** azulejo (for walls); baldosa (for floors). **Ceramic art,** arte cerámica.

ceramics [ˈseræmɪks] [se-ra-miks], *s.* 1. Arte cerámica, alfarería; el arte de modelar barro, etc. (art, process). 2. Alfarería, los objetos hechos de barro o porcelana (objects).

cerasin [ˈserəsiːn] [se-ra-sin], *s.* Cersina, goma del cerezo, ciruelo, etc.

cerastes [ˈserəstəs] [se-ras-tes], *s.* Cerasta o cerastes, una especie de culebra venenosa de África.

cerate [ˈsereɪt] [se-reit], *s.* Cerato, composición de cera, aceite o resina, con medicamentos; permanece siempre sólida.

cerated [ˈsereɪtɪd] [se-rai-tid], *a.* Encerado.

cerberean [ˈsərbɪrɪən] [ser-bi-rian]», *a.* Parecido al cancerbero o relativo a él.

cere [ˈsiːr] [siʳ], *va.* Encerar, dar con cera.

cereal [ˈsɪərɪəl] [si-rial], *a.* Cereal, lo que pertenece a los granos farináceos. -*s.* Planta farinácea, como el trigo, centeno, cebada, etc., y el grano que produce. Cereal (plant, grain); cereales (breakfast).

cerebellar [ˈserɪbelər] [se-ri-be-laʳ], *a.* Relativo o perteneciente al cerebelo.

cerebellum [ˈserɪbeləm] [se-ri-be-lum], *s.* Cerebelo, la parte posterior del cerebro.

cerebral [ˈsentrəl] [sen-tral], *a.* Cerebral. **Cerebral palsy,** parálisis cerebral, diplejía espástica.

cerebrate [ˈserɪbreɪt] [se-ri-breit], *vn.* Exhibir actividad mental, pensar.

cerebration [ˌserɪˈbreɪʃən] [se-ri-brei-shon], *s.* Función cerebral, sea o no consciente y voluntaria.

cerebrum [ˈserəbrəm] [se-ri-brum], *s.* Cerebro; encéfalo.

cerecloth [ˈserɪklɒθ] [se-ri-kloz], *s.* Encerado, hule, lienzo aderezado con cera, goma o cualquier otra materia glutinosa.

ceremonial [ˌserɪˈməʊnɪəl] [se-ri-mou-nial], *a.* y *s.* Ceremonial; rito externo; conjunto de formalidades o ceremonias de un acto público y solemne (occasion). Ceremonial (robes).

ceremonialness [ˌserɪˈməʊnɪəlnɪs] [se-ri-mou-nial-nes], **ceremoniousness,** [ˌserɪˈməʊnɪəsnɪs] [se-ri-mou-nios-nes], *s.* Ceremoniosidad.

ceremonious [ˌserɪˈməʊnɪəs] [se-ri-mou-nios], *a.* 1. Ceremonial, lo que toca o pertenece al uso de ceremonias. 2. Ceremonioso, cumplimentero, etiquetero. 3. Ceremoniático, importuno a fuerza de ceremonias.

ceremoniously [ˌserɪˈməʊnɪəslɪ] [se-ri-mou-nios-li], *adv.* Ceremoniosamente.

ceremony [ˈserɪmənɪ] [se-ri-mo-ni], *s.* 1. Ceremonia, los ritos y fórmulas que se usan en el culto divino. 2. Ceremonia, cumplido, especie de cortesía que usan los hombres unos con otros. 3. Ceremonias, fórmulas exteriores que se observan por razón de estado. **The book of ceremonies,** ceremonia. **Without ceremony,** con franqueza, con toda libertad. **Master of ceremonies,** maestro de ceremonias. **To stand on ceremony,** ser muy ceremonioso. **Don't stand on ceremony,** déjate de ceremonias.

cereous [ˈserɪəs] [se-rious], *a.* Hecho de cera o parecido a ella.

cereus [ˈsiːrɪəs] [si-rios], *s.* Género de los cactos con flores grandes, laterales, tubulares y a menudo nocturnas. El *Cereus giganteus,* de Arizona, es a veces de sesenta pies de alto y dos de diámetro.

cerinthian [ˈserɪntɪən] [se-rin-zian], *s.* Cerintio, el que sigue la herejía de Cerinto, mezcla de cristianismo, judaísmo y paganismo.

cerise [səˈriːz] [se-ris] *a./s.* Color guinda.

cerite [səˈraɪt] [se-rait], *s.* Cerita, silicato de cerio, mineral muy escaso, resinoso.

cerium [səˈrɪəm] [se-rium], *s.* Cerio.

cernuous [səˈnʊəs] [ser-nuos], *a.* Que tiene la extremidad superior inclinada; que se dobla e inclina, como una flor.

cerograph [ˈserəɡræf] [se-ro-graf], *s.* Grabado o escritura sobre cera.

ceroplastic [serəˈplæstɪk] [se-ro-plas-tik], *s.* Ceroplástica, arte de modelar en cera.

cerris [səˈriːz] [se-ris], *s.* (*Bot.*) Especie de encina.

cert [sɜːt] [sert] *s.* (GB) (*Sl.*) **He's a dead cert to win an award,** seguro que se lleva un premio.

certain [ˈsɜːtən] [ser-tein], *a.* 1. Cierto, claro, evidente, manifiesto, indudable, incontestable, lo que no admite duda. Seguro (definite). **They were heading for certain death,** iban a una muerte segura. **She made certain of a good seat by arriving early,** llegó temprano para asegurarse una buena localidad. **It's not certain (that) they'll approve of the idea,** no es seguro que aprueben la idea. **It's certain to rain,** seguro que llueve. **For certain,** con certeza. **I can't say for certain,** no lo puedo decir a ciencia cierta. 2. Cierto, alguno, un tal. **A certain Jill Brown,** una tal Jill Brown. 3. Cierto, determinado, fijo. **It's only open certain days,** está abierto solamente ciertos días. **He has a certain something,** tiene un no sé qué o un algo especial. **A certain person refused to go,** cierta persona se negó a ir, alguien que yo conozco se negó a ir. 4. Cierto, seguro. **To be certain for something,** estar seguro de algo (convinced). **I feel certain that it was a mistake,** tengo la seguridad o la certeza de que fue un error. **I checked the list to make certain (that)...,** revisé la lista para asegurarme de que...

certain, *pron.* **Certain of his colleagues/her works,** ciertos colegas suyos/ciertas obras suyas.

certainly ['sɜːtənlɪ] [ser-tein-li], *adv.* 1. Ciertamente, indudablemente, sin duda, a la verdad. 2. Seguramente, sin falta. **We're almost certainly going to win,** es casi seguro que vamos a ganar (definitely). **Do you see what I mean?-Certainly,** ¿te das cuenta de lo que quiero decir?-desde luego. **He's certainly intelligent but...,** no hay duda de que es inteligente, pero...; es cierto que es inteligente, pero... **I certainly won't be buying anything there again!,** por cierto que, o por supuesto que no voy a volver a comprar nada allí (emphatic). **He may be rich, but he certainly isn't generous,** será rico, pero de generoso no tiene nada. **Certainly, sir,** por supuesto o cómo no, señor. **Certainly not!,** ¡de ninguna manera!, ¡por supuesto que no!

certainness ['sɜːtənnɪs] [ser-tein-nes], **certainty** ['sɜːtəntɪ] [ser-tein-ti], *s.* 1. Certeza, seguridad (conviction); certidumbre, conocimiento cierto de alguna cosa y que excluye toda duda. 2. Seguridad, verdad. **There is no certainty in him,** no se puede tener confianza en él; no hay que confiar en él. **Defeat is now a certainty,** la derrota es algo seguro o es cosa segura (certain event).

certes ['sɜːtəs] [ser-tes], *adv. (Ant.)* Ciertamente, en verdad.

certifiable [,sɜːtɪ'faɪəbl] [ser-ti-fai-eibol] *a.* Demente.

certificate [sə'tɪfɪkɪt] [ser-ti-fi-ket], **certification** [,sɜːtɪfɪ'keɪʃən] [ser-ti-fi-kei-shon], *s.* Certificación, testimonio, certificado. **Certificate of baptism,** Fe de bautismo.

certificate, *va.* Certificar.

certify ['sɜːtɪfaɪ] [ser-ti-fai], *va.* Certificar (facts, claim, death); atestiguar, afirmar. **This is to certify that...,** por la presente certifico o doy fe de que... Declarar demente (declare insane). **He isn't certified to teach in this state,** no está habilitado para ejercer la docencia en este estado (license). **Certified milk,** leche con garantía sanitaria. **Certified public accountant,** contador público, censor jurado, de cuentas.

certiorari [,sɜːtɪɔ'rɑːrɪ] [ser-tio-ra-ri], *s. (For.)* Auto de uno de los tribunales superiores de justicia avocando a sí la causa que pende en un tribunal inferior.

certitude ['sɜːtɪtjuːd] [ser-ti-tiud], *s.* Certidumbre, certeza.

cerulean [sɪ'ruːlɪən] [si-ru-lian], *a.* Cerúleo, azul obscuro.

cerulific ['sɪrəlɪfɪk] [si-ru-li-fik], *a.* Lo que puede dar color cerúleo.

cerumen [sɪ'ruːmen] [se-ru-men], *s.* Cera de los oídos, cerilla.

ceruse ['sɜːruːs] [se-rus], *a.* 1. Cosa que tiene albayalde. 2. Mujer que usa el albayalde u otro afeite.

cervical ['sɜːvɪkəl] [ser-vi-kal], *a.* Cervical, lo que pertenece al cuello. Del cuello del útero. **Cervical smear,** citología.

cervix ['sɜːvɪks] [ser-viks], *s.* Cerviz, el cuello, o lo que a él se parece, y en especial la parte posterior del cuello. Cuello del útero.

cesarean (section) [sɪ'zɛərɪən] [si-sea-rian] *s.* Cesárea.

cespititious ['sespɪtɪʃəs] [ses-pi-ti-shos], *a.* Hecho de césped.

cespitose ['sespɪtəs] [ses-pi-tous], *a.* De césped, lo que crece en grupos o espesuras como el césped.

cess [ses] [ses], *va.* Amillarar.

cessation ['sezeɪʃən] [se-sei-shon], *s.* Cesación, interrupción, suspensión, intermisión, parada.

cession ['seʃən] [se-shon], *s.* Cesión, la acción de ceder o la acción con que un hombre cede a otro el derecho que tiene alguna cosa.

cessionary ['seʃənərɪ] [se-sho-na-ri], *a.* y *s.* Cesionario, que hace cesión.

cessor ['seʃər] [se-shoᵣ], *s. (For.)* 1. El que descuida cumplir con lo que debe dentro del término legal. 2. Asesor. 3. Tasador. 4. Repartidor, amillarador.

cesspool o cesspit ['sespuːl] [ses-pul] ['sespɪt] [ses-pit], *s.* Sumidero, pozo de letrina, hoyo cubierto para recibir las inmundicias de un edificio. Pozo negro, séptico, o ciego.

cest [sest] [sest], *s.* Ceñidor.

cestus ['sestəs] [ses-tus], *s.* 1. Ceñidor de Venus. 2. Manopla guarnecida de hierro.

cesura, *s.* V. CAESURA.

cetacean ['setəʃən] [se-ta-shan], *s.* Uno de los cetáceos, como la ballena.

cetaceous ['setəʃəs] [se-ta-shos], *a.* Cetáceo, de la especie de la ballena.

Ceylon [sɪ'lɒn] [si-lon] *s. (Hist.)* Ceilán.

cf (compare) cf.

CFC *s.* = **chlorofluorocarbon**

ch *s. (pl.* **chs**) (= **chapter**) c.

cha ['tʃɑː] [cha], *s.* El té; especie de té arrollado que se usa en el Asia central.

chablis ['tʃɑːblɪs] [cha-blis], *s.* Nombre de un vino blanco hecho cerca de Chablis, en Francia.

chafe [tʃeɪf] [cheif], *va.* 1. Rozar, frotar, estregar, ludir, escaldar, calentar alguna cosa frotándola. 2. Enojar, enfadar, irritar. -*vn.* 1. Enojarse, enfadarse, acalorarse; fricarse; desollarse. 2. Rozar (rub). 3. Irritarse. **He chafed at the restrictions,** le irritaban las trabas.

chafe *s.* Acaloramiento, rabia, furor, cólera, ardor.

chafer ['tʃɑːfər] [cha-feᵣ], *s.* 1. Especie de escarabajo. 2. Escalfador, jarro de metal para calentar agua.

chafery ['tʃɑːfərɪ] [cha-fe-ri] *s.* Fragua o forja en la herrería.

chaff [tʃɑːf] [chaf], *s.* 1. Zurrón u hollejo, la cáscara del grano que se separa después de trillado y aventado. 2. Arista, cascabillo, gluma o funda exterior de las gramíneas; también paja menuda. 3. *(Met.)* Paja, broza, tamo, lo que es de ningún valor o entidad (worthless material). Barcia, ahechaduras (husks). 4. Befa, burla, zumba.

chaffer ['tʃɑːfər] [cha-faᵣ], *vn.* Regatear, baratear.

chaffinch ['tʃæfɪntʃ] [cha-finch], *s. (Orn.)* Pinzón, pájaro. Fringilla coelebs.

chaffless ['tʃɑːflɪs] [chaf-les], *a.* 1. Sin zurrón u hollejo; mondado. 2. Sólido, profundo, lo que no tiene paja.

chaffy ['tʃɑːfɪ] [cha-fi], *a.* Pajizo, lleno de zurrón u hollejo.

chafing ['tʃɑːfɪŋ] [cha-fin], *s.* Desolladura, escaldadura, fricción.

chafing dish ['tʃɑːfɪŋdɪʃ] [cha-fin-dish], *s.* Infiernillo, anafe.

chagas' disease [,tʃɑːgæs'dɪsiːs] [cha-gas-di-sís], Enfermedad de Chagas.

chagrin ['ʃægrɪn] [sha-grin], *s.* 1. Mal humor o mala condición, enfado, pesadumbre, disgusto, desazón, pena. 2. Disgusto, desilusión. **To my/his chagrin,** para mi/su disgusto.

chagrin *va.* Enfadar o provocar la ira, vejar, entristecer, desazonar, enfadar, amohinar.

chain [tʃeɪn] [chein], *s.* 1. Cadena, serie de muchos anillos o eslabones unidos unos a otros; serie o sucesión (series). **A chain of events,** una cadena o concatenación de acontecimientos. **Mountain chain,** cadena montañosa o de montañas. **To be in chains,** estar encadenado. **Chain of office,** collar que es atributo de un cargo oficial. 2. Encadenamiento, enlace de causas, ideas, etc. 3. Cadena, grillete. 4. Cadena de agrimensor; también medida de 66 pies ingleses o 20.1164 metros. 5. Cadena entre los tejedores; los hilos por donde pasa la trama. **Chain of rocks,** arrecife de piedras. En plural es servidumbre, cautiverio, esclavitud. **Chain-gang,** cadena de presidiarios. **Chain-plates,** *(Mar.)*

cadenas de las vigotas. **Chain-pump,** *(Mar.)* bomba de cadena. **Chain-shot,** *(Art.)* balas encadenadas o balas entramadas.

chain, *va.* 1. Encadenar. 2. Esclavizar. 3. Poner cadena a alguna cosa. 4. Enlazar, unir, juntar. **To chain something/ somebody to something,** encadenar algo/alguien a algo. **Chain up,** encadenar.

chain letter [ˈtʃeɪnˌletər] [chein-le-tar] *s.* Carta (de una cadena).

chain mail [ˈtʃeɪnˈmeɪl] [chein-meil] *s.* Cota de malla.

chain reaction [ˈtʃeɪnriːˈækʃən] [chein-riak-shon], *s.* Reacción en cadena.

chain saw [ˈtʃeɪnˌsɔː] [chein-so] *s.* Motosierra, sierra de cadena.

chainsmoke [ˈtʃeɪnʃsməʊk] [chein-smouk] *vn.* Fumar un cigarrillo tras otro.

chainsmoker [ˈtʃeɪnsməʊkər] [cheins-mou-ka^r] *s.* Persona que fuma un cigarrillo tras otro.

chainstore [ˈtʃeɪnstɔːr] [cheinsto^r] *s.* Tienda de una cadena.

chainwork [ˈtʃeɪnˌwɔːk] [chein-uork], *s.* Cadeneta, labor o trabajo hecho en figura de cadena.

chair [tʃeər] [chea^r], *s.* 1. Silla o taburete, asiento portátil (seat). 2. Silla, asiento de juez u otra persona constituida en autoridad. 3. Silla de manos. 4. Sillón, asiento de la presidencia en una asamblea o cuerpo legislativo: por extensión, presidente (de una asamblea o congreso). **Arm chair,** silla de brazos o poltrona; sillón, butaca. **Privy-chair,** sillico o servicio. 5. Silla volante. **Hair-bottomed chairs,** sillas con asientos de crin. **Cane-bottomed chairs,** sillas de junquillo. **Rocking-chair,** mecedora. (Cuba) Columpio. **Pivot-chair,** silla giratoria. 6. Calesín, volanta o volante, quitrín. 7. Cojinete (de ferrocarril). **The chair is taken,** se ha abierto la sesión. **Professor's chair,** cátedra (at university). **To be in/take the chair,** presidir.

chair lift [ˈtʃeəlɪft] [chea-lift], *s.* 1. Telesilla, telesquí. 2. Montaescaleras.

chairman [ˈtʃeəmən] [chear-man], *s.* 1. Presidente de una junta o reunión. 2. Silletero, el que está asalariado para llevar silla de manos; o sillero, el que hace o vende sillas.

chairmanship [ˈtʃeəmənʃɪp] [chear-man-ship], *s.* Presidencia (de un comité, una asamblea, etc.)

chairperson [ˈtʃeəˌpɜːsn] [chea-per-son] *s.* Presidente, presidenta.

chairwoman [ˈtʃeəˌwʊmən] [chea-uo-man] *s.* Presidenta.

chaise [ˈʃeɪz] [sheis], *s.* 1. Silla volante. 2. Coche de cuatro ruedas. **Post-chaise,** silla de posta.

chaise longue [ˈʃeɪz] [sheis], *s.* Canapé, tipo de sofá muy cómodo.

chalaza [ˈʃələsə] [sha-la-sa], *s.* 1. *(Zool.)* Chalaza, cada uno de los ligamentos que unen la yema del huevo a los polos del mismo. 2. *(Bot.)* Chalaza, cordón de algunas semillas.

chalcedony [ˈtʃælsɪdɒnɪ] [chal-si-do-ni], *s.* Calcedonia, cuarzo no cristalizado y muy translúcido.

chaldaic [ˈtʃəldaɪk] [chal-daik], **chaldean** [chal-dian], *a.* Caldaico, caldeo, lo que pertenece a Caldea. -*s.* **Chaldaic, chaldee,** idioma caldeo.

chaldron [ˈtʃældrɒn] [chal-dron], *s.* Chaldrón, peso o medida de carbón y cok.

chalet [ˈʃæleɪ] [sha-lei], *s.* 1. Casita de labrador suizo. 2. Quinta de forma y construcción parecidas a las de las casas suizas. 3. Chalet de montaña (cabin). 4. (GB) Bungalow (in motel).

chalice [ˈtʃælɪs] [cha-lis], *s.* Cáliz.

chalk [tʃɔːk] [chok], *s.* *(Geol.)* Creta, caliza. **To be as different as chalk and cheese,** ser (como) la noche y el día o (como) el día y la noche. Greda, marga; clarión, tiza (for writing). **A piece of chalk,** una tiza. (GB) *(Coloq.)* **Not by a long chalk,** ni mucho menos. *(Amer.)* Tizate. **French chalk,** espuma de mar. Jaboncillo de sastre, esteatita usada para marcar sobre telas. **Chalk-cutter,** cavador de greda. **Chalk-**

pit, pozo del que se saca la greda. **Chalk-stone,** pedazo de greda, o tiza.

chalk, *va.* 1. Engredar. 2. Señalar, marcar o dibujar con lápiz o yeso; escribir con tiza (write with chalk). 3. Margar, abonar con greda o con marga.

chalk up, Escribir, anotar (write on blackboard). Apuntarse, anotarse (win, success). *(Coloq.)* **To chalk something up to somebody,** anotar algo en la cuenta de alguien.

chalkboard [ˈtʃɔːkbɔːd] [cholk-bord] *s. V.* BLACKBOARD.

chalky [ˈtʃɔːkɪ] [chol-ki], *a.* Gredoso, yesoso, lo que tiene greda o yeso; calcáreo (containing chalk); terroso (like chalk); lleno de tiza (covered in chalk).

challenge [ˈtʃælɪndʒ] [cha-lendch], *va.* 1. Desafiar, retar, provocar a combate o desafío: poner a prueba (summon). **To challenge somebody to,** desafiar a alguien a. **No one can challenge the leaders,** nadie puede hacer peligrar la posición de los líderes. 2. Acusar, imputar. Cuestionar (question/authority, findings); poner en entredicho o en duda o en tela de juicio (assumption/theory). 3. Recusar, tachar o poner excepción a un juez, ministro o testigo. 4. Alegar derecho a alguna cosa; pedir pretender. 5. Citar a uno para el cumplimiento de alguna condición. 6. *(Mil.)* Dar el quién vive; darle el alto a (stop). 7. Suponer o constituir un reto o desafío para (stimulate/job).

challenge, *s.* 1. Desafío, reto (to duel, race); el papel, billete o cartel de desafío. **To issue a challenge to somebody,** desafiar o retar a alguien. 2. Demanda, pretensión, la acción de pedir lo que se debe. 3. Recusación 4. Concurso, de los que se disputan algún premio o destino; reto, desafío (stimulation). 5. Alto (by policeman, sentry).

challengeable [ˈtʃælɪndʒəbl] [cha-len-cha-bol], *a.* Sujeto o expuesto a desafío o acusación, recusable.

challenger [ˈtʃælɪndʒər] [cha-len-ye^r], *s.* Desafiador, duelista, agresor; demandante. Contendiente, rival. **The challenger for the title,** el/la aspirante al título.

challenging [ˈtʃælɪndʒɪŋ] [cha-lind-yin] *a.* 1. Que da que pensar, que cuestiona ideas establecidas (movie, book). 2. Que supone o constituye un reto o un desafío (task). 3. Desafiante, retador (look, tone).

challis [ˈtʃælɪs] [cha-lis], *s.* Chalí, tela ligera de lana.

chalumeau [ˈtʃæləmɔː] [cha-lu-mo], *s.* El registro más bajo del clarinete.

chalybean [ˈtʃælɪbiːn] [cha-li-bin], *a.* Calibeado, lo perteneciente a los antiguos calibes en Asia menor, famosos artífices en hierro y acero.

chalybeate [ˈtʃælɪbiːt] [cha-li-bit], *a.* Impregnado con hierro o acero. -*s.* Agua ferruginosa.

chama [ˈtʃæmə] [cha-ma], *s.* El molusco de mayor tamaño conocido hasta el día, que llega a pesar 500 libras.

chamade [ˈtʃæmɑːd] [cha-mad], *s. (Mil.)* Llamada, señal que se hace con la caja o clarín para parlamentar y a veces para rendirse.

chamber [ˈtʃeɪmbər] [cheim-ba^r], *s.* 1. Cámara, cuarto, habitación, aposento, pieza habitable de una casa. **Bed-chamber,** alcoba, dormitorio. *(Mex.)* Recámara. **Chamber-pot,** orinal. 2. Cámara, tribunal o sala de justicia. 3. **Chamber of commerce,** Cámara de Comercio. **4. Chamber of a pump,** *(Mar.)* almacén de una bomba. 5. *(Art.)* Cámara, la parte hueca del cañón que ocupa la carga, recámara (of gun). 6. *(Art.)* Cámara de mina, la cavidad en donde se pone pólvora en una mina. **Chamber of London,** cámara o ayuntamiento de Londres, o su tesoro público. **Chamber of presence,** sala de estrado. **Judge's chamber,** gabinete del juez. **Condensing chamber,** condensador. **Chamber-council** (a) comunicación confidencial; (b) junta o consejo secreto. **Chamber-counsel,** jurisconsulto, abogado que da su parecer sin presentarse ante el tribunal. **Chamber-organ,** órgano portátil. **Chamber-practice,** la práctica del jurisconsulto o consejero que da su parecer sin presentarse en los tribunales.

chamber, va. 1. Hacer la cámara de un cañón. 2. Ajustar a la cámara. -vn. 1. Ajustarse de una manera compacta los perdigones de un cartucho. 2. (Ant.) Entregarse a la lascivia.

chamberer ['tʃeɪmbərər] [cheim-ba-ra^r], s. (Ant.) Galancete, hombre faldero, mujeriego y galanteador; libertino, disoluto.

chamber-fellow ['tʃeɪmbə'feləʊ] [cheim-ba-fe-lou], s. Compañero de cuarto, el que duerme en la misma pieza que otro.

chambering ['tʃeɪmbərɪŋ] [cheim-ba-rin], s. 1. División en compartimientos. 2. (Des.) Lascivia, liviandad.

chamberlain ['tʃeɪmbəlɪn] [cheim-ba-lin], s. 1. Jefe de cámara. **Lord chamberlain,** gran chambelán; camarlengo o camarero mayor. 2. Recibidor de rentas.

chamberlainship ['tʃeɪmbəlɪnʃɪp] [cheim-ba-lin-ship], s. Oficio de camarero.

chamber-lye, s. V. URINE.

chamber-maid ['tʃeɪmbə'meɪd] [cheim-ba-meid], sf. 1. Doncella de una señora; camarera. 2. Criada de sala.

chamber music ['tʃeɪmbəmju:sɪk] [cheim-ba-miu-sik] s. Música de cámara.

chambray ['tʃæmbreɪ] [cham-brei], s. Cambray, o batista, lienzo blanco muy delgado.

chameleon [kə'mi:lɪən] [ca-mi-lion], s. Camaleón, especie de lagarto.

chamfer ['tʃæmfər] [cham-fa^r], va. Acanalar, arrugar, estriar.

chamfer, chamfret ['tʃæmfret] [cham-fret], s. Canal, arruga, estría, bisel.

chamfrain ['tʃæmfreɪn] [cham-frein], s. Testera, armadura para la frente de un caballo de guerra o de batalla. Cf. CHANFRIN.

chamois ['ʃæmwɑ:] [sha-mua], s. (Zool.) Gamuza, especie de cabra montés. **Chamois leather,** gamuza.

chamomile ['kæməʊmaɪl] [ka-mou-mail], s. Manzanilla, camomila, hierba de flores medicinales. **Chamomile tea,** manzanilla.

champ [tʃæmp] [champ], va. Morder, mascar, mordiscar (chew).

champ, s. (Coloq.) Campeón.

champagne [ʃæm'peɪn] [sham-pein], s. 1. Vino de Champaña; champán. Color champán (color). 2. s. Campiña, campo descubierto, llanura.

champak ['tʃəmpæk] [cham-pak], s. Árbol sagrado del Indostán con flores color de oro y muy fragantes. Pertenece a las magnoliáceas.

champertor ['ʃæmpektər] [sham-pek-to^r], s. Pleitista o litigante que quiere tener parte de la cosa litigada.

champerty ['ʃæmpətɪ] [sham-per-ti], s. Mantenimiento de un pleito para recibir parte de la cosa litigada.

champion ['tʃæmpɪən] [cham-pion], s. 1. Defensor de una causa, doctrina o persona. **She's a champion of lost causes** es una defensora de pleitos perdidos o de causas perdidas. 2. (Hist.) Paladín, campeón, el que mantenía contienda o batalla por medio de las armas. 3. Héroe, guerrero. 4. (Sport) Campeón.

champion, va. Abogar por, defender.

championess ['tʃæmpɪənnɪs] [cham-pion-nes], s. Campeona, defensora; abogada.

championship ['tʃæmpɪənʃɪp] [cham-pion-ship] s. (Sport) Campeonato.

chance [tʃɑ:ns] [chans], s. 1. Fortuna, ventura, suerte. 2. Acaso, suceso, lance, accidente, casualidad, azar (fate), contingencia. **It was pure chance that we met,** nos encontramos por pura casualidad. **To leave nothing to chance,** no dejar nada al azar. 3. Riesgo, peligro (risk). **Don't take any chances,** no te arriesgues, no corras riesgos. 4. (Mat.) Probabilidades. 5. Oportunidad, ocasión (opportunity). **To jump/leap at the chance,** aprovechar o no dejar escapar la oportunidad u ocasión. **The chance of a lifetime,** la oportunidad de su vida. **Give them half a chance and they'll fleece you,** en cuanto te descuidas te desplumán. 6. Posibilidad, chance (likelihood). **They don't**

stand much of a chance, lo tienen difícil. (Coloq.) **Not a chance/no chance!,** ¡ni en broma! **It's a million-to-one chance** o **a chance in a million,** las posibilidades son muy remotas. (Coloq.) **(The) chances are (that)…,** lo más probable es que… (GB) **To be in with a chance,** tener posibilidades o chances. **By chance,** por ventura, casualmente, por acaso, por casualidad. **Have you seen my hat by any chance?,** ¿has visto mi sombrero por casualidad? **There is no chance,** no hay esperanza, remedio, escape. **He met me by chance,** me encontró por casualidad. **The main chance,** lo sólido, lo esencial. **To stand a chance,** tener suerte. **To take one's chance,** correr el riesgo, aventurarse. **The doctrine of chances,** el cálculo de las probabilidades.

chance, a. Fortuito, casual (meeting, occurrence); accidental. -adv. Casualmente, por acaso.

chance, vn. Acaecer, suceder, acontecer. **If my letter should chance to be lost,** si acaso se perdiese mi carta. va. **To chance it,** arriesgarse, correr el riesgo (risk). **I just chanced to be passing your office,** pasaba por tu oficina por casualidad (happen). **Chance on, chance upon,** encontrar por casualidad (object); encontrarse por casualidad con (person).

chancel ['tʃɑ:nsəl] [chan-sel], s. Presbiterio en la iglesia.

chancellor ['tʃɑ:nsələr] [chan-se-lo^r], s. 1. Canciller (premier); cancelario. **Chancellor of the Exchequer,** (Ingl.) ministro de hacienda. **Lord High Chancellor,** ministro de Justicia o gran canciller. 2. Rector (at university).

chancellorship ['tʃɑ:nsələʃɪp] [chan-se-lor-ship], s. Cancillería, el empleo y la dignidad de canciller.

chance-medley [tʃɑ:ns'medlɪ] [chans-med-li], s. (For.) Homicidio, casual; propiamete, es el homicidio cometido en defensa propia en una riña repentina.

chancery ['tʃɑ:nsərɪ] [chan-se-ri], s. 1. Cancillería. 2. Tribunal de justicia que conoce de casos no contemplados por el derecho consuetudinario o el escrito.

chancre ['ʃæŋkər] [shan-ke^r], s. Úlcera venérea. (Vul.) Chancro.

chancrous ['tʃæŋkrəs] [chan-kros], a. Ulceroso.

chancy ['tʃɑ:nsɪ] [chan-si], a. (Fam.) Expuesto a riesgo; incierto; aventurado, peligroso.

chandelier [ʃændəlɪər] [shan-de-lia^r], s. Araña de luces, candelero cornupia. (Méx.) Candil.

chandler ['tʃɑ:ndlər] [chand-la^r], s. Cerero o velero, el que hace o vende velas de cera o sebo. **Chandler's shop,** lonja, abacería, tienda de víveres. (Am.) Pulpería. (Mex.) Tienda. **Ship-chandlery,** abastecedor de buques. **Wax-chandler,** cerero. **Tallow-chandler,** velero. **Corn-chandler,** triguero, el que vende trigo y granos.

chandlery ['tʃɑ:ndlərɪ] [chand-le-ri], s. Todas las cosas que se venden en las tiendas de granos, velas, etc.; mercería. **Ship-chandlery,** almacén donde se vende toda especie de artículos necesarios para los barcos.

chanfrin ['tʃɑ:nfrɪn] [chan-frin], s. Frente o faz del caballo.

change [tʃeɪndʒ] [cheinch], va. 1. Poner una cosa en lugar de otra. 2. Cambiar, trocar una cosa por otra. 3. Cambiar, reducir una moneda mayor a varias menores (into smaller denominations). **Can anyone change $20?,** ¿alguin me puede cambiar 20 dólares? **To change something into something,** cambiar algo en algo o a algo (into foreign currency). 4. Convertir, transmutar, cambiar (appearance, rules; situation/tire, oil, sheets). **The sorcerer changed him into a stone,** el mago le convirtió en piedra. **To change one's address/doctor,** cambiar de dirección/médico. **To change one's clothes,** cambiarse de ropa. **To change color,** cambiar de color. **Let's change the subject,** cambiemos de tema. **I wouldn't want to change places with her,** no quisiera verme en su lugar (exchange). **He changed it for a red one,** lo cambió por uno rojo. 5. Mudar de genio o de vida. 6. (Transp.) **You have to change trains at Nice,** tienes que hacer transbordo o cambiar de trenes en Niza. -vn. 1. Mudar, variar, alterarse, corregirse. Cambiar (become different). **I can't believe how much she has changed,** me parece increíble lo mucho que ha cambiado. **To change into something,** convertirse o transformarse en algo. **The scene changes to wartime Rome,** la escena pasa o se traslada a Roma durante la guerra (from one thing to another). **Changing,** cambiante (needs, role, moods). 2. Cambiarse (put on different clothes). **She changed into a black dress,** se cambió y se puso un vestido negro. **I'm going to change into something more comfortable,** me voy a poner algo más cómodo. **To get changed,** cambiarse. *(Transp.)* Cambiar, hacer transbordo.

change around [ˌtʃeɪndʒəˈraʊnd] [cheinch-araund] Cambiar de sitio o de lugar (rearrange). Cambiar.

change over [ˌtʃeɪndʒəˈəʊvər] [cheinch-ou-var] Cambiar (change function, system). **To change over to something,** cambiar a algo, adoptar algo.

change round, *V.* CHANGE AROUND.

change, *s.* 1. Mudanza, variedad, conversión, variación de estado que tienen las cosas; cambio (alteration). Muda (of clothes). **A change in temperature,** un cambio de temperatura. **There's been a change in the weather,** ha cambiado el tiempo. **To make changes to something,** hacerle cambios a algo. **A change for the better/worse,** un cambio para mejor/peor. **A change of address,** un cambio de dirección (replacement). **To have a change of heart,** cambiar de idea. **For a change,** para variar. **To ring the changes,** introducir variaciones. **A change is as good as a rest,** con un cambio de actividad se renuevan las energías. 2. Vicisitud. 3. Cambio, dinero menudo, sencillo, feria, menudo (coins). **One dollar in change,** un dólar en monedas. Cambio, vuelto, vuelta, vueltas (money returned). **Keep the change,** quédese con el cambio. **You won't get much change from/out of $1,000,** no te costará mucho menos de 1.000 dólares. 4. Lonja o bolsa, lugar donde se reunen los comerciantes a tratar sus negocios. En este sentido es abreviatura de EXCHANGE. **I have no change,** no tengo suelto o no tengo cambio. **Change of the moon,** interlunio, cuarto de luna. **Change of clothes,** muda de ropa. **Change of life,** la edad crítica, cesación final del menstruo.

changeability [ˌtʃeɪndʒəˈbɪlɪtɪ] [cheinch-a-bi-li-ti], *s.* Mutabilidad.

changeable [ˈtʃeɪndʒəbl] [chein-cha-bol], *a.* 1. Voluble, variable, inconstante, veleidoso. 2. Mudable, lo que se puede mudar. 3. Cambiante, tornasolado, hablando de géneros.

chageableness [ˈtʃeɪndʒəblnɪs] [chein-cha-bol-nes], *s.* Mutabilidad, volubilidad, inconstancia.

changeably [ˈtʃeɪndʒəblɪ] [chein-cha-bli], *adv.* Inconstantemente.

changeful [ˈtʃeɪndʒfʊl] [cheinch-ful], *a.* Inconstante, variable, voltario, veleidoso.

changeless [ˈtʃeɪndʒlɪs] [cheinch-les], *a.* Constante, inmutable.

changeling [ˈtʃeɪndʒəlɪŋ] [chein-cha-lin], *s.* 1. Un niño cambiado por otro, sea por equivocación o de intento. 2. Loco, tonto. 3. Inconstante, el que es mudable, persona irresoluta, sin carácter.

changeover [ˈtʃeɪndʒəʊvər] [cheinch-ou-var] *s.* **Changeover from something to something,** cambio de algo a algo (transition). **Changeover purse,** monedero, portamonedas.

changing room [ˈtʃeɪndʒɪŋˌrʊm] [chein-yin-rum] *s.* (GB) *(Sport)* Vestuario, vestidor. Probador (in shop).

channel [ˈtʃænl] [cha-nel], *s.* 1. Canal (strait); álveo, la madre de un río. Cauce (course of river). Canal (navigable course). 2. Canal, cualquier cavidad hecha longitudinalmente. *(Arq.)* Estría, mediacaña. Acequia (for irrigation). 3. Canal, trozo de mar estrecho. **British Channel,** el canal de la Mancha. 4. Vía (system, method). **Through diplomatic channels,** por la vía diplomática. **You must go through the official channels,** tiene que hacer el trámite por los conductos o las vías oficiales. **Distribution channels,** canales de distribución. 5. *(Comput, TV)* Canal. **Channels,** *(Mar.)* mesas de guarnición. **Fire-**

channels, *(Mar.)* canales de fuego. **Channel out of soundings,** *(Mar.)* Foso. **Channel of a block,** *(Mar.)* cajera.

channel, *va.* 1. Acanalar, estriar; surcar. 2. Conducir o llevar por, o como por un canal; canalizar, encauzar, dirigir.

Channel Islands [ˈtʃænlˌaɪlændz] [cha-nel-ailands] *s. pl.* Las Islas Anglonormandas, las islas del Canal de la Mancha.

channel-surf. *vn.* (TV) Hacer zapping.

Channel Tunnel [ˈtʃænlˌtʌnl] [cha-nel-ta-nel] *s.* El eurotúnel, el túnel del Canal de la Mancha.

channer [ˈtʃænər] [cha-ner], *vn.* *(Esco.)* Refunfuñar, quejarse.

chant [tʃɑːnt] [chant], *va. y vn.* 1. Cantar. 2. *(Mús., Relig.)* Salmodiar, cantar el servicio en una iglesia catedral. 3. Gritar (crowd).

chant *s.* Canto; canto llano, melodía. Consigna (of demonstrators); alirón, canción (of sports fans).

chanter [ˈtʃɑːntər] [chan-ta^r], *s.* 1. Cantor, el que canta. 2. Chantre.

chantey [ˈʃæntɪ] [shan-ti], *s.* Canto monótono de los marineros cuando halan y en otras maniobras.

chanticleer [ˈʃæntɪkliːər] [shan-ti-klie^r], *s.* Quiquiriquí, el gallo, así llamado por su modo de cantar.

chantress [ˈʃɑːntrɪs] [shan-tres], *s.* Cantora, cantante, cantatriz.

chantry [ˈʃæntrɪ] [shan-tri], *s.* 1. Capilla, especialmente una dotada para decirse en ella misas diarias. 2. Vallado, enrejado o estructura que contiene una tumba.

chanukah [ˈʃæjuːkɑː] [sha-nu-ka] *s. V.* HANUKKAH.

chaos [ˈkeɪɒs] [keios], *s.* 1. Caos, la mezcla confusa en que se hallaban todos los elementos antes de la creación. 2. Caos, confusión, mezcla irregular, desorden.

chaotic [ˈkeɪɒtɪk] [keio-tik], *a.* Caótico, confuso, desordenado, irregular.

chap [tʃæp] [chap], *va.* Hender, rajar, resquebrajar; abrir grietas o rajas en el cutis, en la madera, etc. -*vn.* 1. Rajarse o hendirse la tierra por el excesivo calor. 2. Hacerse grietas en la cara o en las manos por la frialdad. 3. *(Esco.) V.* CHEAPEN.

chap *s.* 1. Grieta, abertura, rendija, hendidura. 2. *(Esco.)* Golpe seco sobre la puerta; choque. 3. Mozo, joven, muchacho. **Chap-book,** folleto vendido por un pacotillero. 4. *(Fam.)* Mozo, chico. En este sentido es abreviatura de «chapman». **A queer chap,** un original, un hombre extravagante. *(Coloq.)* Tipo (man). **The poor little chap!,** ¡pobrecito!

chap *s.* 1. Mandíbula, quijada inferior o superior de un animal. *V.* CHOP. 2. Quijada de un tornillo de banco.

chap. *s.* (*pl.* **chaps**) = (**chapter**) c.; cap.

chaparral [ˈtʃæpərəl] [cha-pa-ral], *s.* (E.U. del Oeste) Chaparral, el sitio poblado de chaparros.

chape [tʃeɪp] [cheip], *s.* Chapa de cinturón; contera de espada; charnela de hebilla.

chapel [ˈtʃæpəl] [cha-pel], *s.* 1. Capilla, iglesia pequeña (building). 2. Capilla, dependencia de una iglesia con su altar (area in church). 3. Edificio consagrado al culto de los disidentes. Templo (nonconformist church). 4. El cuerpo organizado de los cajistas e impresores de una imprenta dada. **Chapel-master,** maestro de capilla. *V.* KAPELLMEISTER.

chapeless [ˈtʃeɪplɪs] [cheip-les], *a.* Sin contera.

chapelet [ˈtʃeɪplɪt] [cheip-let], *s.* 1. *(Equit.)* Doble estribo. 2. Máquina para elevar agua, o para dragar el fondo de un puerto, por medio de cubos sujetos a una cadena sin fin.

chapelry [ˈtʃeɪplrɪ] [chei-pel-ri], *s.* La jurisdicción o límites de una capilla.

chaperon, chaperone [ˈʃæpərəʊn] [sha-pe-roun], *s.* 1. Señora que acompaña a una o más jóvenes en público, o en reuniones, viajes, etc.; acompañante (for children). Rodrigón, hombre de edad que acompaña a una señora, por el buen parecer. Acompañante (of young lady). 2. Caperuza, capirote.

chaperon, chaperone, *va.* Acompañar a una o más señoras a las tertulias o reuniones o tener cuidado de ellas.

chapfallen, chopfallen ['tʃæpfɔːlən] [chap-fo-len], *a.* Boquihundido, el que tiene hundidos los labios. *(Fig.)* **To be chapfallen,** estar triste, abatido, desanimado. *(Fam.)* estar con las orejas gachas.

chapiter ['tʃæpɪtər] [cha-pi-taʳ], *s. (Arq.)* Capitel. V. CAPITAL.

chaplain ['tʃæplɪn] [chaplin], *s.* 1. Capellán, el sacerdote que se dedica al servicio de una capilla; limosnero. 2. Capellán castrense.

chaplaincy ['tʃæplənsɪ] [cha-plan-si], **chaplainship** ['tʃəplənʃɪp] [cha-plan-ship], *s.* Capellanía.

chapless ['tʃeɪplɪs] [cheip-les], *a.* Boquiseco.

chaplet ['tʃæplɪt] [chap-let], *s.* 1. Guirnalda, corona de flores. 2. Rosario. 3. *(Arq.)* Moldura de cuentas. 4. Penacho. 5. Capilleja.

chapman ['tʃæpmən] [chap-man], *s.* Buhonero, vendero, traficante en géneros baratos; pacotillero.

chapped [tʃæpt] [chapt] *a.* Agrietado, partido (lips).

chaps [tʃæps] [chaps] *s. pl.* Zahones, chaparreras, p(i)erneras, zamarros.

chapter ['tʃæptər] [chap-taʳ], *s.* 1. Capítulo, una de las partes de que se compone un libro. 2. Capítulo, categoría, lista, serie; asunto de que se trata. 3. Capítulo, cabildo, junta del clero de una catedral. 4. Ramificación o sucursal de una sociedad o confraternidad. **And so on to the end of the chapter,** y así lo demás. **Chapter-house,** sala capitular. **To read one a chapter** *(fig.)* poner a alguno como nuevo, zaherirle. **To the end of the chapter,** hasta el fin. **To quote chapter and verse,** citar textualmente o palabra por palabra.

char ['tʃɑːr] [chaʳ], *va.* 1. Hacer carbón de leña; carbonizar. 2. Trabajar a jornal.

char, *s.* 1. *(Des.)* Jornal, trabajo a jornal. (GB) Mujer de la limpieza, asistenta (cleaner). 2. Umbra, especie de pescado de agua dulce.

character ['kærɪktər] [ca-rak-taʳ], *s.* 1. Carácter, la índole, genio y condición de cada uno (temperament, nature/of person). **To be in/out of character,** ser/no ser típico. **She's a good judge of character,** es buena psicóloga. 2. Carácter, nombre, fama, calidad, reputación. **Character reference,** referencias. 3. Informe, testimonio de conducta. 4. Retrato, descripción, representación de una pesona o cosa. Carácter (of place, thing). **Her face is full of character,** tiene una cara con mucha personalidad. 5. Personaje, persona, individualidad. Carácter (strength of personality). 6. Papel, la parte de un actor en el teatro; personaje, carácter (in novel, play, movie). **He doesn't react in character,** su reacción no es la que cabría esperar de su personaje. 7. Carácter, marca, distintivo o señal (symbol). 8. Carácter o forma de la letra. **Persons of bad character,** personas de mala vida o reputación. 8. Tipo (person). Caso (eccentric person). **He's a nasty character,** es un mal tipo. **Character,** *va.* Grabar, esculpir, señalar, imprimir.

character-assassination ['kærɪktəəsæsɪˈneɪʃən] [ka-rak-ta-a-sa-si-nei-shon], *s.* Difamación, calumnia, descrédito público (public slander).

characteristic, characteristical [ˌkærɪktəˈrɪstɪk] [ka-rak-te-ris-tik] [ˌkærɪktəˈrɪstɪkl] [ka-rak-te-ris-ti-kal], *a.* Característico.

characteristic *s.* Característico.

characteristically [ˌkærɪktəˈrɪstɪklɪ] [ka-rak-te-ris-ti-ka-li], *adv.* Característicamente.

characteristicalness [ˌkærɪktəˈrɪstɪkəlnɪs] [ka-rak-te-ris-ti-kal-nes], *s.* Propiedad característica.

characterization [ˌkærɪktərɪˈzeɪʃən] [ka-rak-te-ri-sei-shon], *s.* El acto, procedimiento o efecto de caracterizar.

characterize ['kærɪktəraɪz] [ka-rak-te-rais], *va.* 1. Caracterizar (be typical of); calificar (describe). **To**

characterize something/somebody as something, calificar algo/a alguien de algo. 2. Grabar, esculpir, señalar.

characterless ['kærɪktəlɪs] [ka-rak-ter-les], *a.* Sin carácter (restaurant, town).

charactery ['kærɪktərɪ] [ka-rak-te-ri], *s.* 1. Carácter, impresión o señal. 2. Sistema de caracteres; representación.

charade [ʃəˈrɑːd] [sha-rad], *s.* Charada (game), especie de enigma, acertijo. Farsa (farse), payasada.

charbon ['kɑːbən] [kar-bon], *s.* 1. Fiebre esplénica, ántrax. 2. Mancha negra en los dientes de los caballos después que cierran.

charcoal ['tʃɑːkəʊl] [kar-koul], *s.* Carbón (vegetal). Carbón de leña. **Animal charcoal,** carbón animal, negro de marfil. *(Art)* Carboncillo, carbonilla.

chard [tʃɑːd] [chard], *s. (Bot.)* 1. Hoja de alcachofa, o acelga, aporcada. 2. Acelga suiza.

chardoon ['tʃɑːdɒn] [char-dun], *s. V.* CARDOON.

charge [tʃɑːdʒ] [charch], *va.* 1. Cargar, poner una carga o peso sobre alguna cosa. 2. Cargar, introducir la carga en un arma de fuego. 3. Encargar, comisionar, confiar al cuidado de alguno. 4. Cargar, poner en cuenta; poner precio, pedir por; cobrar (ask payment). **They charged him $15 for a haircut,** le cobraron 15 dólares por el corte de pelo. **She never carries cash, she just charges everything,** nunca lleva dinero, lo compra todo con tarjeta (de crédito)/lo carga todo a su cuenta (obtain on credit). **To charge something to somebody,** cargar algo a la cuenta de alguien. 5. Cargar, atarear. 6. Cargar, acometer. *(Mil.)* Cargar contra. Embestir o arremeter contra (animal). 7. Censurar, acusar, imputar, denunciar. **To charge somebody with something,** acusar a alguien de algo (accuse). 8. Mandar, exhortar, instruir. Encomendar (entrust). **To charge somebody with something,** encomendarle a alguien algo. **To charge somebody to,** ordenarle a alguien que (command). Aducir (allege). 9. Hacer gastar. 10 *(Elec.)* Cargar (battery). *-vn.* 1. Demandar o fijar precio. 2. Atacar. *(Mil.)* Cargar; arremeter o embestir (animal). **Charge!,** ¡al ataque!, ¡a la carga! *(Coloq.)* **He charged straight into me,** se abalanzó hacia mí (rush). **Don't all charge off at the end of the lesson,** no salgan en estampida al acabar la clase. 3. Agacharse, acuclillarse; dícese de los perros de caza.

charge, *s.* 1. Carga, tiro, la cantidad de pólvora y balas con que se carga un arma de fuego (of explosive). 2. Cargo, partida, cláusula. 4. Precepto, mandato, orden, instrucción (command, commission); cargo, comisión. **Who's in charge?,** ¿quién es el/la responsable? **I left Paul in charge,** dejé a Paul a cargo. **To be in charge of something/ somebody,** tener algo/a alguien a cargo. **In the charge of somebody, in somebody's charge,** a cargo de alguien. **She took charge of the situation,** se hizo cargo de la situación. 5. *(Law)* Cargo, acusación. **He's being tried on a charge of murder,** se le juzga por homicidio. **To bring/press charges against somebody,** formular o presentar cargos contra alguien. **To drop charges,** retirar la acusación o los cargos. 6. Ataque, embestida, carga (attack). Ofensiva en la que se gana mucho terreno (in US football). 7. Carga, medicina que se aplica a los caballos. 8. Encargo, depósito. 9. Acto y posición de agacharse los perros de caza o la orden de agacharse. 10. Precio (price); honorario (fee). **There is no charge for the service,** no se cobra por el servicio, el servicio es gratis. **Free of/without charge,** gratuitamente, gratis, sin cargo. **At no extra charge,** sin cargo adicional. **Electricity charges are going up again,** las tarifas eléctricas vuelven a subir. 11. *(Elec., Phys.)* Carga.

chargeable ['tʃɑːdʒəbl] [char-ye-bol], *a.* 1. Imputable, lo que se puede imputar, como una deuda o un delito. 2. Acusable, sujeto a cargos y acusaciones. 3. *(Ant.)* Costoso, caro, dispendioso, lo que cuesta mucho.

chargeableness ['tʃɑːdʒəblnɪs] [char-yei-bol-nes], *s.* Gasto, coste.

charge account [ˌtʃɑːdʒˈakaʊnt] [charch-a-kaunt], s. Cuenta corriente, cuenta de crédito.

charge card [tʃɑːdʒˈkaːd] s. Tarjeta de pago.

charged [tʃɑːdʒd] [chardchd] a. Cargado. **A voice charged with emotion,** una voz cargada de emoción.

chargé d'affaires [ˌtʃɑːdʒeɪdæˈfɛɑr] [char-yei-da-fears] s. Encargado de negocios.

charger [ˈtʃɑːdʒər] [char-ya], s. 1. Fuente o plato grande. 2. Corcel, caballo criado para la guerra. 3. Cargador (battery).

charily [ˈtʃɛərɪlɪ] [chea-ri-li] adv. Cautelosamente, cuidadosamente.

chariness [ˈtʃærɪnɪs] [cha-ri-nes], s. Cautela, cuidado, precaución.

chariot [ˈtʃærɪət] [cha-riot], s. 1. Carroza de paseo o de ceremonia. (Prov.) Faetón o carrocín; 2. Carro militar, en que combatían antiguamente. 3. Coche ligero o cochecillo. **Chariot-race,** carrera de carros.

charioteer [ˌtʃærɪəˈtɪər] [cha-rio-tia'], s. Cochero; carretero; auriga.

charisma [kæˈrɪzmə] [ka-ris-ma] s. Carisma.

charismatic [kæˈrɪzmətɪk] [ka-ris-ma-tik] a. Carismático.

charitable [ˈtʃærɪtəbl] [cha-ri-ta-bol], a. 1. Caritativo, limosnero (generous, giving). 2. Benigno, bueno (kind/ person); benévolo, generoso (interpretation). **A charitable organization,** una organización de beneficencia, una obra benéfica (for charity).

charitableness [ˈtʃærɪtəblnɪs] [cha-ri-ta-bol-nes], s. Caridad.

charitably [ˈtʃærɪtəblɪ] [cha-ri-ta-bli], adv. Caritativamente; benignamente, con caridad o generosidad.

charity [ˈtʃærɪtɪ] [cha-ri-ti], s. 1. Caridad, ternura, benevolencia, amor. 2. Caridad, virtud teologal que consiste en amar a Dios y al prójimo. 3. Caridad, limosna, el socorro que se da a los pobres (generosity, kindness). 4. Organización benéfica o de beneficencia, obra benéfica (organization); obras de beneficencia (relief). **To raise money for charity,** recaudar dinero para un fin benéfico. **A charity performance,** una función benéfica o de beneficencia, un beneficio. **To be in charity with all men,** querer a todo el mundo, no desear el mal de nadie. **Charity begins at home,** la caridad bien ordenada empieza por uno mismo.

charivari [ˈʃærɪvɑrɪ] [sha-ri-va-ri], s. Cencerrada, ruido discorde para dar broma a los recién casados.

chark [tʃɑːk] [chark], va. Carbonizar, reducir a carbón. Cf. CHAR.

charlady [ˈtʃɑːleɪdɪ] [char-lei-di] s. (GB) Mujer de la limpieza.

charlatan [ˈʃɑːlətən] [shar-la-tan], s. Charlatán, saltimbanco, curandero, empírico.

charlatanic [ˈʃɑːlətənɪk] [shar-la-ta-nik], a. Empírico, propio de un charlatán.

charlatanry [ˈʃɑːlətənrɪ] [shar-la-tan-ri], s. Charlatanería, engaño; picotería.

Charles' wain [tʃɑːlz] [chals], s. (Astr.) Osa mayor, constelación boreal.

charley horse [ˈtʃɑːlɪhɔːs] [char-li-jors] s. Calambre.

charlock [ˈtʃɑːlɒk] [char-lok], s. (Ingl.) Mostaza silvestre, planta común en los sembrados.

charlotte [ˈʃɑːlət] [shar-lot], s. Compota de fruta, nata, etc., contenida en un molde de bizcocho. **Charlotte russe,** nata batida o flan en un molde de bizcocho.

charm [tʃɑːm] [charm], s. 1. Encanto, atractivo (attractiveness); hechizo o maleficio. **To turn on the charm,** ponerse encantador. 2. Embeleso, atractivo, gracia, hechizo (spell); encanto (attractive quality, feature). **To work/ go like a charm,** funcionar, ir o andar a las mil maravillas. 3. Amuleto, fetiche (amulet); dije (on bracelet).

charm, va. 1. Ensalmar, hechizar, encantar (bewitch/ snake). 2. Encantar, embelesar, cautivar, atraer, hechizar, arrobar (delight); captar o arrebatar la vista, los oídos o el

ánimo. **He can charm the birds off/out of the trees,** es capaz de convencer a cualquiera con sus encantos. **To lead a charmed life,** tener mucha suerte en la vida. -vn. Sonar armoniosamente.

charmed [tʃɑːmd] [sharmd], a. Encantado; complacido, embelesado.

charmer [ˈtʃɑːmər] [char-ma'], s. 1. Encantador, hechicero. 2. Hechicero, la persona que atrae las voluntades. 3. Persona encantadora, encanto.

charmful [ˈtʃɑːmfʊl] [charm-ful], a. Lleno de encantos, gracioso.

charming [ˈtʃɑːmɪŋ] [char-min], a. Agradable, hechicero, encantador, maravilloso, pasmoso (person); precioso, encantador (room, house).

charmingly [ˈtʃɑːmɪŋlɪ] [char-min-li], adv. Agradablemente, deleitosamente.

charmingness [ˈtʃɑːmɪŋnɪs] [char-min-nes], s. Encanto, embeleso, atractivo.

charm school [ˈtʃɑːmˌskuːl] [charm-skul] s. Escuela para señoritas donde se enseña a comportarse en sociedad.

charnel [ˈtʃɑːnl] [char-nel], a. Del osario, lo que contiene huesos de difuntos.

charnel-house [ˈtʃɑːnlhaʊs] [char-nel-jaus], s. Carnero, u osario, el paraje en que se ponen los huesos de los difuntos.

charpie [ˈtʃɑːpɪ] [char-pi], s. Hilas, las hebras que se van sacando de los trapos de lienzo.

charr [tʃɑːr] [cha'], s. Umbra, trucha asalmonada, pez de agua dulce.

charry [ˈtʃɑːrɪ] [cha-ri], a. Carbonoso, de la naturaleza del carbón.

chart [tʃɑːt] [chart], va. Poner en una carta hidrográfica. Trazar el mapa de (make map of); trazar (plan, plot); seguir atentamente (follow closely/progress, changes); registrar gráficamente (record). -s. (Mar.) Carta de navegar o de mareas; carta hidrográfica. (Meteo) Mapa, carta; gráfico (diagram, graph); tabla (table). **The charts,** la lista de éxitos, el hit parade (best-selling records).

chartaceous [tʃɑːˈteɪʃəs] [char-ta-shos], a. Que tiene la textura de papel de escribir.

charter [ˈtʃɑːtər] [char-ta'], s. 1. Escritura auténtica. Estatutos (of university); fuero (of city); escritura de constitución (of company). 2. Cédula, título, privilegio, exclusivo (guarantee of rights). 3. Carta constitucional. 4. (Transp.) Contrato de fletamento; chárter (flight, plane).

charter, va. 1. Establecer por ley, incorporar o reconocer como un cuerpo legítimo. Aprobar los estatutos de (grant charter to). 2. (Mar.) Fletar un barco por un tanto. Fletar, alquilar (plane, ship, bus). (GB) **Chartered,** colegiado (engineer, surveyor). **Chartered accountant,** contador público, censor jurado, de cuentas.

chartered [ˈtʃɑːtəd] [char-ted], a. Privilegiado. (Mar.) Fletado.

charter-party [ˌtʃɑːtəˈpɑːtɪ] [char-ta'-par-ti], s. Contrata, instrumento o papel con que las partes aseguran algún convenio, quedándose cada una con una copia.

chartography, cartography [ˈkɑːtəgræfɪ] [kar-to-gra-fi], s. Cartografía, arte de construir las cartas marinas o mapas.

chartreuse [ˈkɑːtrəs] [kar-tros], s. 1. Cartuja, monasterio de cartujos. V. CARTHUSIAN. 2. Un licor estomacal.

chartulary, s. V. CARTULARY.

char-woman [ˈtʃɑːˌwʊmən] [char-uo-man], s. Mujer asalariada para las faenas domésticas por uno o pocos días.

chary [ˈtʃɛərɪ] [chea-ri], a. Cuidadoso, cauteloso, circunspecto; económico, frugal. **She's chary of making commitments,** es reacia a contraer compromisos.

chasable [ˈtʃeɪsəbl] [chei-sa-bol], a. Cazadero, cazable.

chase [tʃeɪs] [cheis], va. 1. Cazar. 2. Dar caza, perseguir o seguir al enemigo por mar o tierra (follow, pursue/thief). (Coloq.) **They're both chasing the same woman,** ambos andan detrás de la misma mujer. 3. Engastar, montar una piedra preciosa. 4. Cincelar (el oro y la plata). V. ENCHASE. 5. Seguir. **To chase away,** hacer huir, espantar. **To chase after,** correr tras de, o en seguimiento de. *-vn.* **We chased after the thief,** fuimos o salimos tras el ladrón. **To chase after girls,** ir o andar detrás de las chicas.

chase up [tʃeɪsˈʌp] [cheis-ap] *(Coloq.)* **Chase up this order for me, please,** averíguame qué pasó con este pedido, por favor. **I'll have to chase him up about the report,** voy a tener que recordarle lo del informe.

chase, *s.* 1. Caza. 2. Caza, seguimiento o la acción de seguir al enemigo; persecución (pursuit). **Car chase,** persecución en coche. **to give chase,** salir en persecución de alguien/ algo, ir tras alguien/algo, darle caza a alguien/algo. 3. Caza, los animales o aves que se cazan. 4. Cazadero, el sitio en que se hace la caza. 5. Partida de cazadores que van a cazar. 6. *(Mar.)* Caza. **Bow-chase,** cañón de mira. **Stern-chase,** guardatimón, cañón de a popa. **Wild-goose chase,** a caza de ilusiones, en seguimiento de lo inasequible. **The chase,** la caza (hunting).

chase, *s.* 1. Rama, cerco de hierro, con que se sujeta el molde en la prensa. 2. Cualquier muesca o encaje. 3. *(Art.)* Calibre de un cañón.

chaser [ˈtʃeɪsər] [chei-sa^r], *s.* 1. Cazador. 2. Engastador.

chasing [ˈtʃeɪsɪŋ] [chei-sin], *s.* 1. Cinceladura, arte de cincelar; trabajo en relieve. 2. Seguimiento, caza.

chasm [ˈkæzəm] [kasem], *s.* 1. Hendidura, grieta, rajadura, abertura. 2. Vacío, hueco, cóncavo u hondo. Abismo. 3. En los libros de cuentas, laguna, falta, blanco.

chasmed [ˈkæzəmd] [kasemd], *a.* Hendido, rajado, lleno de grietas.

chassis [ˈʃæsɪ] [sha-sis], *s. (Auto)* Chasis, armazón, bastidor.

chaste [tʃeɪst] [cheist], *a.* 1. Casto, puro, honesto, continente, púdico, opuesto a la sensualidad. 2. Castizo, neto, limpio y puro; dícese del estilo.

chaste-eyed [ˌtʃeɪstˈaɪd] [cheist-aid], *a.* El que tiene el mirar modesto.

chastely [ˈtʃeɪstlɪ] [cheist-li], *adv.* 1. Castamente; decorosamente. 2. Correctamente, de una manera castiza (hablando del estilo).

chasten [ˈtʃeɪsn] [chei-sen], *va.* 1. Corregir, castigar. 2. Depurar, limpiar, las faltas o errores; purificar por medio de aflicción. 3. Limpiar, elevar.

chastener [ˈtʃeɪsənər] [chei-se-na^r] Castigador, corrector, depurador, limpiador.

chasteness [ˈtʃeɪstnɪs] [cheist-nes], *s.* Pureza, castidad, continencia.

chastening [ˈtʃeɪstnɪŋ] [cheist-nin], *s.* Castigo, corrección, reprimenda; disciplina.

chaste-tree [ˈtʃeɪstˌtriː] [cheist-tri], *s. (Bot.)* Agnocasto, sauzgatillo o pimiento loco.

chastisable [ˈtʃæstɪsəbl] [chas-ti-sa-bol], *a.* Punible, castigable.

chastise [tʃæsˈtiːs] [chas-tis], *va.* Castigar, reformar, corregir. Reprender, reprobar (verbally); castigar (physically).

chastisement [ˈtʃæstɪzmənt] [chas-tis-ment], *s.* Castigo, pena, corrección.

chastiser [ˈtʃæstɪsər] [chas-ti-sa^r], *s.* Castigador, castigadora.

chastity [ˈtʃæstɪtɪ] [chas-ti-ti], *s.* Castidad, pureza, continencia. **Chastity belt,** cinturón de castidad.

chasuble [ˈtʃæzjʊbl] [cha-su-bol], *s.* Casulla, vestidura sagrada que se pone el sacerdote sobre el alba; manta sin mangas.

chat [tʃæt] [chat], *vn.* Charlar, parlotear. **To chat to/with somebody,** charla, hablar, conversar o platicar con alguien.

chat up [tʃætˈʌp] [chat-ap] (GB) *(Coloq.)* Tratar de ligar con, llevarle la carga a.

chat *s.* 1. Charla, locuacidad, cháchara, parla, lujo de hablar, garrulidad. **To have a chat with somebody,** charlar o hablar o conversar o platicar con alguien. 2. Pájaro cantor americano.

chateau [ˈtʃætɔː] [cha-to], *s. V.* CASTLE.

chatelaine [ˈtʃætlaɪn] [chat-lain], *s.* 1. Cadena o cadenas que cuelgan del cinturón de la mujer. *(Fr.)* 2. Castellana, la señora de un castillo.

chatellany [ˈtʃætlænɪ] [chat-la-ni], *s.* Castellanía.

chat show [tʃætˈʃɔː] [chat-sho] *s.* (GB) Programa de entrevistas.

chattel [ˈtʃætl] [chatel], *s.* Bienes muebles.

chatter [ˈtʃætər] [cha-ta^r], *vn.* 1. Cotorrear, parlar como una cotorra (birds); parlotear (monkeys). 2. Rechinar los dientes. 3. Charlar, parlotear, parlar, chacharear, cotorrear (person). **His teeth are chattering,** le castañean los dientes.

chatter, *s.* 1. Chirrido. 2. Charla, cháchara, parloteo, parla; conversación ociosa (idle talk).

chatterbox [ˈtʃætəbɒks] [cha-ter-boks], *s.* Parlero, parlador, charlatán, charlador, guapetón, hablador; especialmente un niño.

chatterer [ˈtʃætərər] [cha-te-ra^r], *s.* Charlador o charlante, garrulo.

chattering [ˈtʃætərɪŋ] [cha-te-rin], *s.* 1. Chirrido de los pájaros. 2. Rechinamiento de dientes. 3. Garrulidad.

chattering, *a.* Locuaz, hablanchín.

chatty [ˈtʃætɪ] [cha-ti], *a.* Dispuesto a hablar; conversador, hablador (person); informal, llano (style); simpático y lleno de noticias (letter). *-s.* (Anglo-indio) Jarra, olla porosa de la India.

chauffeur [ˈʃəʊfər] [sho-fa^r], *s.* Chofer o chófer. **A chauffeur-driven limousine,** una limusina con chofer o con chófer.

chauffeur, *va.* Hacer de chófer para. **A chauffeured car,** un coche con chófer.

chauvinism [ˈʃəʊvɪnɪzəm] [sho-vi-nisem] *s.* Chauvinismo (chovinismo), patriotería (jingoism). **Male chauvinism,** machismo (sexism).

chauvinist [ˈʃəʊvɪnɪst] [sho-vi-nist], *s.* El que demuestra celo exagerado por la honra y el buen nombre de su patria. Chovinista, patriotero (jingoist). **Male chauvinist,** machista (sexist).

cheap [tʃiːp] [chip]. *a.* 1. Barato, lo que se vende o compra a poco precio (inexpensive); económico (restaurant, hotel). (GB) Económico, de precio reducido (fare/ticket). **It's cheap at the price,** a ese precio resulta barato, a ese precio resulta económico. **Cheap and cheerful,** bonito y barato. **On the cheap,** gastando lo menos posible. 2. Barato, lo que no tiene estimación. Ordinario, de baratillo (shoddy/merchandise, jewelry); chapucero (mechanic, electrician). 3. Común, de poco valor, de poco aprecio. De mal gusto (vulgar, contemptible/joke, gimmick). Bajo, rastrero (trick, tactics); vil (liar, crook). 4. Fácil. (worthless/flattery, promises). **Words are cheap,** es fácil hablar. *(Coloq.)* Agarrado, apretado (stingy). *-s. (Des.)* Mercado; compra, una cosa barata. *adv.* **The house was going cheap,** la casa se vendía barata.

cheapen [ˈtʃiːpən] [chi-pen], *va.* 1. Regatear alguna cosa antes de comprarla. 2. Abaratar, minorar o rebajar el precio de alguna cosa. 3. Quitarle valor a, degradar. **To cheap oneself,** rebajarse, degradarse.

cheapener [ˈtʃiːpnər] [ʻchi-pe-na^r], *s.* Regatón, traficante.

cheaply [ˈtʃiːplɪ] [chipli], *adv.* Barato, a bajo precio. (buy, sell, get); con poco dinero, económicamente (dress, eat, live).

cheapness [ˈtʃiːpnɪs] [chip-nes], *s.* Baratura.

cheap shot [ˈtʃiːpʃɒt] [chip-shot] *s.* Glope bajo.

cheapskate [ˈtʃiːpskeɪt] [chip-skeit] *a. (Coloq.)* Agarrado, apretado.

cheat [tʃiːt] [chit], *va.* 1. Engañar, defraudar, estafar, entrampar, cometer fraude o engaño, timar (deceive). **They were cheated (out) of their land,** los estafaron, engañaron o timaron quitándoles las tierras. 2. Trampear, trapacear, no jugar limpio o hacer fullerías en el juego. 3. Chasquear. 4. Burlar (avoid). **He cheated death,** burló a la muerte. *-vn.* Hacer trampas (act deceitfully). **To cheat on somebody,** engañar a alguien (be unfaithful).

cheat, *s.* 1. Trampa, fraude, estafa (trick, fraude); impostura, engaño, ratería, droga. 2. Trampista, petardista, droguero. Estafador (swindler); tramposo, fulero (at cards); tramposo (in exam). **Cheat-bread,** pan blanco.

cheatableness ['tʃiːtəblnɪs] [chi-ta-bol-nes], *s.* Engaño, trapacería, fullería, impostura, fraude.

cheater ['tʃiːtər] [chi-taʳ], *s.* Tramposo, bribón, estafador, ratero, petardista, fullero, trapacero.

cheatery ['tʃiːtəri] [chi-te-ri], *s.* Fraude sistemático; trampa, fullería (en el juego).

cheating ['tʃiːtɪŋ] [chi-tin], *pa. y s.* Engaño, fraude, trampa, añagaza.

check [tʃek] [chek], *va.* 1. Reprimir, refrenar (restrain/ enemy advance); moderar, detener; contener, controlar (anger, impulse); atajar, sofocar, ahogar, 2. Confrontar o examinar un talón de banco, las partidas de una cuenta, los nombres de una lista, etc. Revisar, controlar (inspect/ passport, ticket); inspeccionar (machine, product); controlar (quality); comprobar, chequear, checar (temperature, pressure, volume); revisar, comprobar (accounts, bill); comprobar, verificar (verify/facts; information). **To check something against something,** cotejar o chequear algo con algo. **Check that it's closed,** asegúrate de que o comprueba que esté cerrado. 3. Dar jaque en el juego de ajedrez. 4. Poner talón o contraseña a un bulto u objeto, para su expedición. Marcar, hacer un tic, poner un visto en (tick). 5. (*Ant.*) Regañar, reñir, desaprobar algún dicho o hecho. 6. Dejar en el guardarropa (deposit/in cloakroom); dejar o depositar en consigna (in baggage office); (*Aviat.*) facturar, chequear (register/ baggage). *-vn.* 1. Pararse o detenerse. 2. Meterse o mezclarse en alguna cosa. 3. Comprobar, verificar, chequear, checar. **Just checking!,** sólo me quería asegurar. **To check with something,** coincidir o concordar con algo (tally).

check in, 1. Facturar o chequear el equipaje (register/at airport); registrarse (at hotel). **He usually checks in after lunch,** generalmente llama/pasa después de comer (make routine contact). 2. Facturar, chequear (register/luggage). **The girl who checked us in,** la chica que nos atendió (o nos facturó el equipaje). Devolver (return/book, equipment).

check off, Ir marcando (items, details).

check out, 1. **He checked out (of the hotel) this morning,** dejó el hotel esta mañana (habiendo pasado la factura, etc.). 2. Cuadrar (story/tally). 3. Verificar, comprobar, chequear, checar (facts, story). (*Coloq.*) **We must check out the new film,** tenemos que ir a ver qué tal es la nueva película. 4. Pagar (shopping/customer); cobrar (cashier).

check up, Have you been checking up on me?, ¿me has estado vigilando o espiando? **We checked up and found out he was lying,** hicimos averiguaciones y comprobamos que mentía. **Can you check up on that?,** ¿puedes comprobarlo o confirmarlo?

check, *s.* 1. Rechazo, resistencia. 2. Restricción, control, freno (stop, restrain). **To keep/hold something/somebody in check,** controlar a alguien o contener algo. **To put a check to something,** impedir algo. 3. Obstáculo, impedimento; contratiempo, descalabro, derrota. 4. La persona, cosa o causa que impide; alguna interrupción. 5. (*Fin.*) (GB) **cheque** Cheque, documento en forma de mandato de pago, para recibir dinero de un banco. **To pay by check,** pagar con cheque o con talón. **A check for $50,** un cheque de 50 dólares o por valor de 50 dólares. 6. Talón, conocimiento o contraseña de que se usa en los ferrocarriles. 7. Contraseña, billete de salida en los entreactos de los teatros. 8. Jaque, en el ajedrez. 9. Listado, lienzo tejido en cuadros o listas de azul y blanco; paño de varios colores (cloth); a cuadros (jacket, shirt). 10. Control, revisión (inspection/of passport,

documents); examen, revisión (of work); inspección (of machine, product). **To keep a check on something,** controlar o vigilar algo. Verificación (of facts). 11. Cuenta, adición (restaurant, bill). 12. Marca, tic, visto, palomita. **Check-book,** libro de cheques o talones. **Check-list,** check-roll, lista para la confrontación de nombres, lista de electores, rol de obreros, etc.

check, *interj.* ¡Jaque! (in chess). (*Coloq.*) ¡sí, señor! (expressing confirmation).

checkbook, (GB) **chequebook** ['tʃekbʊk] [chek-buk], *s.* Talonario, libro talonario, libro talonado, talonario de cheques.

checked [tʃekt] [chekt] *a.* A cuadros (material, shirt).

checker o **chequer** ['tʃekər] [che-keʳ], *va.* 1. Taracear, formar cuadros de varios colores. 2. Diversificar.

checker o **chequer,** *s.* 1. Una de las piezas usadas en el juego de damas, por lo común un pequeño disco. 2. Uno de los cuadros en una superficie taraceada. 3. Represor, amonestador. 4. *pl.* Damas, juego de damas; nombre más común en los Estados Unidos que *draughts.* V. DRAUGHTS. 5. Cajero (cashier). **Checker-board,** tablero.

checkered ['tʃekəd] [che-kerd], (GB) **chequered,** *pp. y a.* 1. Dividido en cuadros de diferentes colores; ataraceado. A cuadros (pattern, design). 2. Diversificado, variado entre lo bueno y lo malo. 3. Accidentado, con altibajos (career, history).

checkers ['tʃekəz] [che-kaʳz] *s.* Damas.

check-in ['tʃekɪn] [chek-in] *s.* Facturación de equipajes (at airport). **Check-in desk/counter,** mostrador de facturación (at airport); recepción (in hotel). **Check-in time,** hora de facturación.

checking account ['tʃekɪŋəkaʊnt] [che-kin-a-kaunt], *s.* Cuenta corriente.

checkless ['tʃekləs] [chek-les], *a.* Violento, desgobernado.

checklist ['tʃeklɪst] [chek-list] *s.* Lista de control.

checkmate ['tʃekmeɪt] [chek-meit], *va.* 1. Dar jaque mate. 2. Deshacer, derrotar completamente al enemigo. *-s.* Mate, jaque mate, el último lance del ajedrez.

checkout ['tʃekaʊt] [chek-aut] *s.* Caja (in supermarket). **Checkout counter,** caja. **Checkout girl,** cajera. **Checkout time,** hora en que se debe dejar libre la habitación (in hotel).

checkpoint ['tʃekpɔɪnt] [chek-point], *s.* Sitio o lugar de revisión o inspección. Control.

check room ['tʃekrʊm] [chek-rum], *s.* Guardarropa. **Check-room attendant,** guardarropa.

check stub ['tʃekstʌb] [chek-stab], *s.* Talón. *-pl.* Libro talonario, talonario.

checkup ['tʃekʌp] [chek-ap] *s.* (*Med.*) Chequeo, revisión, reconocimiento médico. **To have a checkup,** hacerse un chequeo. (*Dent.*) Chequeo, revisión. (*Auto*) Revisión, servicio.

cheddar ['tʃedər] [che-dar] *s.* Queso (de) Cheddar.

cheek [tʃiːk] [chík], *s.* 1. Carrillo, mejilla, cachete (of the face). (*Coloq.*) Nalga, cachete (buttock). **Cheeks of a window** o **door,** jambas de ventana o puerta; derrame. 2. (*Art.*) Gualdera de cureña. 3. **Checks of a mast,** (*Mar.*) cacholas, guarnición de madera que se pone sobre el cuello de los palos mayores. **Cheek of the pump,** (*Mar.*) picota. **Cheeks of the head,** (*Mar.*) tajamar. **Cheek by jowl,** (*Vul.*) cara a cara. **To turn the other cheek,** dar la otra mejilla. 4. (*Ger.*) Descaro, frescura, cara, desvergüenza, impudencia. **To have plenty of cheek,** tener cara de baqueta, ser desvergonzado. **What a cheek!,** ¡qué cara (más dura)!, ¡qué caradura es!

cheek-bone ['tʃiːkbəʊn] [chík-boun], *s.* Pómulo, juanete de la mejilla.

cheekily ['tʃiːkɪli] [chi-ki-li] *adv.* Descaradamente.

cheeky ['tʃiːkɪ] [chí-ki] *a.* Fresco, atrevido, descarado (boy, girl); pícaro (grin); impertinente (remark).

cheep [tʃiːp] [chíp], *vn.* Piar, chirriar, las aves pequeñas. *-s.* Gorjeo débil. Piada, piído.

cheer [tʃɪər] [chiaʳ], *s.* 1. Banquete, festín. 2. Convite a un festín o banquete. 3. Alegría, buen humor; ánimo, vigor. 4. Gesto, aire, ademán. 5. Vivas, vítores, aplausos. Ovación, aclamación (of encouragement, approval). **To give three cheers for somebody,** vitorear a alguien. **Three cheers for Fred!,** ¡viva Fred! 6. Hurra (cheerleaders' routine). 7. **Cheers,** ¡salud! (drinking toast). (GB) *(Coloq.)* Gracias (thanks). Alegría, animación (cheerfulness). **Be of good cheers,** ¡ánimo!, ¡levanta el ánimo!

cheer, *va.* 1. Excitar, animar, alentar, dar ánimos (shout encouragement at). 2. Consolar, alegrar, dar consuelo o alegría; reconfortar (gladden, comfort). 3. Vitorear, aclamar (shout in approval); aplaudir. *-vn.* Alegrarse, ponerse alegre. **To cheer up,** tomar o cobrar ánimo. **Cheer up!** ¡vamos, valor! Aplaudir, gritar entusiasmadamente.

cheer up, Animarse; animar, levantarle el ánimo a (person). **Some bright curtains would cheer the room up,** unas cortinas en colores vivos alegrarían el cuarto.

cheerer [tʃɪərər] [chia-raʳ], *s.* Alegrador, regocijador, vitoreador, aplaudidor.

cheerful [tʃɪəfʊl] [chiaʳ-ful], **cheerly** [tʃɪəlɪ] [chiaʳ-li], *a.* Alegre, vivo, lleno de ánimo. 2. Placentero, jovial. 3. Alentador (news, prospect).

cheerfully [tʃɪəfʊlɪ] [chiaʳ-fu-li], **cheerly** [tʃɪəlɪ] [chiaʳ-li] *adv.* Alegremente, con alegría. **I could have cheerfully murdered him,** lo hubiera matado.

cheerfulness [tʃɪəfʊlnɪs] [chiaʳ-ful-nes] *s.* Alegría, buen humor, jovialidad.

cheerily [tʃɪərɪlɪ] [chia-ri-li] *adv* Con alegría.

cheering [tʃɪərɪŋ] [chia-rin] *a.* Alentador. *s.* Ovaciones, aplausos, vítores.

cheerio [tʃɪrɪˈəʊ] [chi-ri-ou] *interj* (GB) *(Coloq.)* Hasta luego, chao (goodbye).

cheerleader [tʃɪəˌliːdər] [chia-lí-daʳ] *s.* Animador, animadora (en encuentros deportivos, mítines políticos); porrista.

Cheerless [tʃɪəlɪs] [chiaʳ-les], *a.* Triste, melancólico, falto de alegría. Triste, sin alegría (room, house). Triste (day, landscape).

cheery [tʃɪərɪ] [chia-ri] *a.* De felicidad, alegre (smile); lleno de alegría (greeting); risueño y optimista (manner).

cheese [tʃiːz] [chís], *s.* Queso. **Cream cheese,** queso fresco. **Cheese curds,** cuajadas. **Cheese-mite,** ácaro de queso. **Cheese rennet,** cuajaleche, gallote, género de plantas rubiáceas. **Cheese-cake,** quesadilla. **Cheese-monger,** quesero, el que hace o vende queso. **Cheese-paring,** raedura de queso. **Cheese-parings and candle-ends,** gajes del oficio. **Cheese-press,** prensa de queso. **Cheese-vat,** quesera, la tabla formada a propósito para hacer queso. *(Fotog.)* **Say cheese!,** ¡sonría!, (o ¡sonrían!, etc.). **Hard cheese,** mala pata.

cheese off, *(Coloq.)* **To be cheesed off,** estar mosqueado.

cheeseboard [tʃiːzbɔːd] [chís-bord] *s.* Tabla de quesos (course).

cheeseburger [tʃiːzbɜːgər] [chís-ber-gaʳ], *s.* Emparedado de queso y carne molida. Hamburguesa con queso.

cheesecake [tʃiːzkeɪk] [chis-keik], *s.* 1. Pastel de queso. 2. *(Fam.)* Fotografías que exhiben desnudeces femeninas.

cheese cloth [tʃiːzklɒθ] [chis-kloz], *s.* Estopilla (tela). Bambula.

cheeseparing [tʃiːzˌpɛərɪŋ] [chis-pea-rin] *a.* Tacaño.

cheesy [tʃiːzɪ] [chí-si], *a.* Caseoso, de la calidad del queso. (Como) a queso (smell, taste). De mala calidad, rasca (shoddy).

cheetah [tʃiːtə] [chí-ta], *s.* Leopardo de Asia y norte de áfrica; suele adiestrarse para la caza. Guepardo, chita.

chef [ʃef] [shef] *s.* Chef, jefe de cocina.

chemical [kemɪkəl] [ke-mi-kal], *a.* Químico. *-s.* Producto químico.

chemise [ʃəˈmiːz] [she-mis], *s.* 1. Camisa de mujer. 2. *(Fort.)* Camisa o revestimiento exterior de la muralla. 3. (Art. y of.) La manga de hierro laminado de que se usa para hacer los cañones de escopeta.

chemisette [ʃəmiˈsiːt] [she-mi-sít], *s.* Prenda de ropa interior de mujer, que sólo cubre el cuello y los hombros.

chemism [kemɪzm] [ke-misem], *s.* Afinidad química.

chemist [kemɪst] [kemist], *s.* Químico, el que profesa la química (scientist). (GB) Farmacéutico (pharmacist). **Dispensing chemist,** farmacéutico. **At the chemist's,** en la farmacia.

chemistry [kemɪstrɪ] [ke-mis-tri], *s.* Química (science). Sintonía, vibraciones (interaction). **Good/bad chemistry,** buena/mala sintonía.

chemotherapy [keməʊˈθerəpɪ] [ke-mou-ze-ra-pi] *s.* Quimioterapia.

chenille [ʃəˈniːl] [she-nil], *s.* Felpilla, cordón tejido con pelo, como la felpa, y lecho de algodón, seda, estambre o lana.

chenopodium [kenəˈpɒdɪəm] [ke-no-po-diom]. *s.* Ceñiglo, hierba común.

cheque [tʃek] [chek], *s.* Cheque o talón (GB). V. CHECK, quinta acepción. **Write a cheque,** extender un cheque.

chequebook [tʃekbʊk] [chek-buk] *s.* (GB) V. CHECKBOOK.

chequered [tʃekəd] [che-ked] *a.* V. CHECKERED.

cherish [tʃerɪʃ] [che-rish], *va.* 1. Criar, mantener, fomentar, proteger. 2. Mantener, preservar vivo, mantener (cling to/ memory, hope); apreciar, estimar, valorar (care for, value); acordarse con placer. Abrigar, acariciar (illusion, dream). **Cherised,** preciado. **A long cherished ambition,** una ambición albergada durante largo tiempo.

cherisher [tʃerɪʃər] [che-ri-shaʳ], *s.* Entrañable.

cherishing [tʃerɪʃɪŋ] [che-ri-shin], *s.* Apoyo, fomento, protección, estima.

cheroot [ʃəˈruːt] [she-rut], *s.* Filipino, especie de cigarro puro de perilla cortada. Puro cortado en ambos extremos.

cherry [tʃerɪ] [cherri], *s.* 1. Cereza, la fruta del cerezo. 2. Cerezo, árbol de varias especies del género Prunus. 3. La madera del cerezo. **Cherry-stone,** cuesco o hueso de cereza. **Cherry-tree,** cerezo. **Black cherry,** guinda. **Cherry brandy,** aguardiente de cerezas. **Cherry blossom,** flor de cerezo. **Cherry orchard,** cerezal.

cherry, *a.* Lo que tiene color de cereza. **Cherry-cheeks,** mejillas encarnadas. **Cherry-brandy,** aguardiente de cerezas.

cherry-pit [tʃerɪpɪt] [cherri-pit], *s.* 1. Hueso de cereza. 2. Hoyuelo, juego de niños.

cherry-red [tʃerɪred] [cherri-red] *a.* Rojo cereza, color guinda.

chert [tʃert] [chert], *s. (Min.)* Horsteno, variedad de cuarzo.

cherty [tʃertɪ] [cher-ti], *a.* Lo que tiene cuarzo o pedernal.

cherub [tʃerəb] [che-rab], *s.* Querubín, espíritu angélico. *-pl.* CHERUBIM, Querubines.

cherubic, cherubical [tʃeˈruːbɪk] [che-ru-bik], *a.* Angelical.

chervil [tʃɜːvɪl] [cher-vil], *s. (Bot.)* Perifolio o cerafolio, hierba semejante al perejil.

chess [tʃes] [ches], *s.* El juego del ajedrez. **Chess-board,** ajedrez, el tablero en que se juega a dicho juego. **Chessman,** pieza de ajedrez. **Chess-player,** jugador de ajedrez.

chess-trees [tʃestriːs] [ches-tris], *s. pl. (Mar.)* Castañuelas de las amuras.

chest [tʃest] [chest], *s.* 1. Arca, arcón, caja de madera u otro material (box). 2. (Art. y Of.) Receptáculo para gases o líquidos: como **steam-chest,** caja de vapor. 3. *(Com.)* Caja, cantidad determinada. 4. *(Anat.)* Pecho, tórax. 5. Tesorería (treasury); fondos (funds). **To get something off one's chest,** desahogarse contando/confesando algo. **To play/keep one's cards close to one's chest,** no soltar prenda. **Chest of drawers,** cómoda, buró, guardarropa con cajones; armario con gavetas. En los Estados Unidos se llama generalmente *bureau.*

chest, *va.* Depositar o meter alguna cosa en una cómoda.

chested ['tʃestɪd] [ches-ted], *a.* De pecho; usado en composición: como, **Narrow-chested,** estrecho de pecho. **Hollow-chested,** de pecho hundido.

chestnut ['tʃesnʌt] [ches-nat], *s.* 1. Castaña (nut). 2. Color de castaña. 3. Pequeña callosidad en la superficie interior de la pierna del caballo. 4. (E.U., fest.) Broma vetusta, chanza o dicho muy repetido y sabido de todos. *(Coloq.)* **An old chestnut,** una historia muy vieja o pasada (old story).

chestnut, *a.* Castaño, zaino (horse); castaño (hair).

chestnut-tree ['tʃesnʌttri:] [ches-nat-tri], *s. (Bot.)* Castaño.

chesty ['tʃestɪ] [ches-ti] *a.* (GB) *(Med.)* De pecho (cough, cold).

cheval ['ʃəvæl] [she-val], *s.* Caballo, caballete; apoyo, sostén. **Cheval-glass,** psiquis, espejo que gira sobre un eje horizontal. **Cheval-de-frise,** *V.* CHEVAUX-DE-FRISE.

chevalier ['ʃəvælɪər] [she-va-liar], *s.* Caballero.

chevaux-de-frise ['ʃəvɔːˌdefiːs] [she-vo-de-fris, *s. (Mil.)* Caballo de frisa, madero con púas que se usa como defensa contra la caballería.

cheveril ['ʃevərɪl] [she-ve-ril], *s. (Des.)* 1. Cabritillo o cabrito, choto. 2. Cabritilla, la piel del cabrito.

chevron ['ʃevrən] [she-vron], *s.* 1. Galón, figura de dos o tres barras en forma de V, que llevan en las mangas las clases del ejército. 2. Cheurrón, cabrio, la figura o pieza en forma de ángulo que se pone en los escudos.

chew [tʃuː] [chu], *va.* 1. Mascar, masticar o desmenuzar con los dientes (food); morder (nails, pencils); mascar (tobacco, gum). 2. Rumiar, meditar, considerar despacio; reflexionar. *(Coloq.)* **To chew the fat/rag,** charlar, conversar, platicar. *-vn.* Rumiar. **To chew at/on something,** mordiscar o mordisquear algo.

chew out Regañar, reñir (scold, reprimand).

chew over *(Coloq.)* Considerar (suggestion, offer); darle vueltas a (problem).

chew up Masticar o mascar bien (when eating). **The dog had chewed up the carpet,** el perro había destrozado la alfombra a mordiscos.

chew, *s.* Mascadura, y la cosa masticada.

chewing ['tʃuːɪŋ] [chuin], *s.* Masticación.

chewing gum ['tʃuːɪŋgʌm] [chuin-gam], *s.* Chicle, goma de mascar.

chewink ['tʃuːɪŋk] [chuink], *s. (Orn.)* Emberiza.

chewy ['tʃuːɪ] [chui] *a.* Duro, correoso, latiguido; masticable (candy).

chiaroscuro [kɪˌɑːrəsˈkuərəʊ] [kia-ros-kua-rou], *s.* Claroscuro, acertada distribución de la luz y sombras de un cuadro.

chic [tʃɪk] [chik], *a.* 1. Gentil, bonito, bien hecho, bien parecido, elegante. 2. Vivo, listo, impertinente; mono, fino. *-s.* 1. Elegancia, buen tono, originalidad y buen gusto, como en decorar y vestirse. 2. Facilidad y habilidad de ejecución. 3. Viveza, vivacidad y petulancia de maneras.

chicane [tʃɪˈkeɪn] [chi-kein], *s.* Tramoya, enredo, embrollo, cavilación, trampa, artificio. *(For.)* Trampa legal.

chicane *vn.* 1. Entretener, tener a uno en suspenso dilatando la decisión de algún pleito o demanda. 2. Armar enredos, sutilizar, buscar escapatorias.

chicaner ['tʃɪkənər] [chi-ka-ne'], *s.* Sofista, trampista, enredador, trapacero.

chicanery ['tʃɪkənərɪ] [chi-ka-ne-ri], *s.* Sofistería, trapacería, enredo, trapaza, embrollo, trampa legal, efugio, quisquilla, vanas sutilezas; argucia.

chick [tʃɪk] [chik] *s.* Polluelo, pichón (young bird); pollito (young chicken). Muchacha, chavala, pebeta, cabra (young woman).

chickadee ['tʃɪkədiː] [chi-ka-di], *s.* Pavo americano sin cresta, y con el cuello y parte superior de la cabeza negros.

chicken ['tʃɪkɪn] [chi-ken], *s.* 1. Polluelo o pollo; gallina (hen); pollo (as generic term). **To play chicken,** jugar a ver quién es más gallito. **Don't count your chickens (before they're hatched),** no cantes victoria antes de tiempo. 2.

(Fig.) Jovencito; niño. **She's no (spring) chicken,** no es ninguna niña/nena.

chicken out *(Coloq.)* Acobardarse, achicarse, rajarse. **She chickened out of telling him,** no se atrevió a decírselo.

chicken *a. (Coloq.)* Gallina.

chickenfeed ['tʃɪkɪnfiːd] [chi-kin-fíd] *s. (Coloq.)* Una miseria, calderilla.

chicken-hearted ['tʃɪkɪnˌhɑːtɪd] [chi-kin-jar-tid], *a.* Cobarde, miedoso, gallina, medroso, mandria.

chicken-pox ['tʃɪkɪnpɒks] [chi-kin-poks], *s.* Viruelas locas. Varicela.

chicken wire ['tʃɪkɪnˌwaɪər] [chi-kin-uaia'] *s.* Alambrera.

chickling ['tʃɪklɪŋ] [chi-klin], *s.* Pollito, polluelo.

chickpea ['tʃɪkpiː] [chik-pí], *s. (Bot.)* Garbanzo.

chickweed ['tʃɪkwiːd] [chik-uíd], *s. (Bot.)* Alsine, planta anual.

chicle ['tʃɪkl] [chikol], *s. (Bot.)* Chicle, goma de mascar.

chicory ['tʃɪkərɪ] [chi-ko-ri], *s. (Bot.)* Endivia. Achicoria (in coffee); planta, cuya raíz se usa para la adulteración del café.

chide [tʃaɪd] [chaid], *va. (pret.* CHID o CHODE, *pp.* CHID o CHIDDEN). Reprobar, culpar, echar en cara, regañar, refunfuñar. **To chide somebody for something,** reprender o censurar a alguien por algo. *-vn.* Regañar, reñir, alborotar.

chide, *s.* Murmullo, reprensión, reprimenda.

chider ['tʃaɪdər] [chai-da'], *s.* Regañón, regañador.

chiding ['tʃaɪdɪŋ] [chai-din], *s.* Reprensión, regaño, reprimenda.

chidingly ['tʃaɪdɪŋlɪ] [chai-din-li], *adv.* Con reprensión o reprimenda.

chief [tʃiːf] [chíf], *a.* 1. Principal (main), capital, eminente, jefe. 2. Superior, supremo (highest in rank). **Chief constable,** jefe de policía. **The chief man in the town,** el primer personaje de la población. **Our chief happiness,** nuestra mayor felicidad. **Chief-clerk,** oficial mayor; primer dependiente. **Chief-justice,** presidente de sala o del tribunal.

chief, *s.* 1. Jefe, líder (head), principal; cabeza de tribu, familia, ejército, escuadra, departamento del Estado, etc.; el que tiene autoridad. **Chief of police,** jefe de policía. 2. Actor, agente principal. 3. Parte principal, la mayor parte de una cosa.

chiefest ['tʃiːfəst] [chí-fest], *a. sup. (Ant.)* Principalísimo.

chiefless ['tʃiːflɪs] [chíf-les], *a.* Sin jefe o superior.

chiefly, chief, *(Poét.),* ['tʃiːflɪ] [chíf-li], *adv.* Principalmente, particularmente, sobre todo.

chieftain ['tʃiːftən] [chíf-ten], *s.* 1. Jefe, comandante. 2. Caudillo, capitán; cabeza de bando. 3. Cacique (of tribe).

chieftainship ['tʃiːftənʃɪp] [chíf-ten-ship], *s.* Jefatura, la dignidad u oficio de jefe.

chiffer, chiffre [tʃiːf] [chíf], *s.* Cifra, como en música escrita con números.

chiffon ['ʃɪfɒn] [shi-fon], *s.* Gasa, tela de seda muy transparente.

chiffonier ['ʃɪfɒnɪər] [shi-fo-nia'], *s.* Cómoda, cajonería, guardarropa con cajones.

chignon ['ʃiːnjɔːŋ] [shi-ñon], *s.* Penca o moño de pelo que llevaban las mujeres.

chigoe ['ʃɪguː] [shi-gu], *s.* Nigua, pulga pequeñísima de las Antillas y Sudamérica.

chilblains ['tʃɪlbleɪnz] [chil-bleins], *s. pl.* Sabañones.

child [tʃaɪld] [chaild], *s. (pl.* CHILDREN). 1. Infante, el niño pequeño y de muy poca edad. Infantil (psychology). 2. Hijo (son) o hija (daughter). Niño (boy); niña (girl). 3. Parto, el efecto o producto de otra cosa. **From a child,** desde niño. **With child,** preñada, embarazada. **To be child's play,** ser un juego de niños. **Child benefit,** (in UK) Prestación que se recibe del Estado por cada hijo independientemente del ingreso de los padres; asignación familiar. **Child labor,** trabajo de menores; *V.* ABUSE. **Have you any children?,** ¿tiene hijos?

childbearing ['tʃaɪldˌbɛərɪŋ] [chaild-bea-rin], *s.* Parto. Maternidad. **To be of childbearing age,** estar en edad fértil

childbed ['tʃaɪldbed] [chaild-bed], *s.* Sobreparto.

childbirth ['tʃaɪldbɜ:θ] [chaild-berz], s. Parto o dolores de parto. Alumbramiento. **To die in childbirth,** morir de parto.

childcare ['tʃaɪldkeər] [chaild-kea'] s. Cuidado de los niños, puericultura.

childermas-day [,tʃaɪldəmæs'deɪ] [chail-der-mas-dei], s. Día de inocentes, el 28 de Diciembre.

childhood ['tʃaɪldhʊd] [chaild-jud], s. Infancia, niñez; puerilidad, niñería.

childish ['tʃaɪdɪʃ] [chaild-dish], a. Frívolo, trivial; infantil, pueril, propio de niño (immature). Infantil (typical of a child). **Childish trick,** muchachada.

childishly ['tʃaɪldɪʃlɪ] [chaild-dish-li], adv. Puerilmente. De una manera infantil o pueril, como un niño.

childishness ['tʃaɪldɪʃnɪs] [chaild-dish-nes], s. Puerilidad, cosa propia de niños.

childless ['tʃaɪldlɪs] [chaild-les]», a. Sin hijos, infecundo.

childlike ['tʃaɪldlaɪk] [chaild-laik], a. Pueril, propio de niño o muchacho. Ingenuo, de niño.

childminder ['tʃaɪld,maɪndər] [chaildmain-de'] s. (GB) Niñero, niñera que cuida a un niño mientras sus padres trabajan; madre del día.

child molester ['tʃaɪld,mɒləstər] [chaild-mo-les-ta'] s. Persona que somete a un niño a abusos deshonestos.

childproof ['tʃaɪldpru:f] [chaild-pruf] a. A prueba de niños.

children ['tʃɪldrən] [chil-dren], s. pl. de CHILD. Niños. (Prov.) **Children and fools speak the truth,** los niños y los locos dicen las verdades.

Chile ['tʃɪlɪ] [chi-li] N. (Geogr.) Chile.

chilean ['tʃɪlɪən] [chi-lian], a. y s. Chileno, chileño.

chiliast ['tʃɪlɪəst] [chi-liast], s. Milenario, sectario que espera la venida de un período de mil años, en que todo el mundo será justo y vivirá feliz.

chili, chilli ['tʃɪlɪ] [chi-li] s. Ají, chile. **Chili powder,** ají o chile en polvo.

chili sauce ['tʃɪlɪ,sɔːs] [chi-li-sos], s. Salsa de tomate con chile.

chill [tʃɪl] [chil], a. 1. Frío, friolento. 2. Desanimado, desalentado, abatido; rudo. -s. Frío, fresco (coldness, weather); escalofrío, sensación de frío que a veces precede a la fiebre. (Med.) Enfriamiento, resfriado. **To catch a chill,** resfriarse. **To take the chill off/out of something,** quitar el frío, templar o calentar algo. (Fig.) Estremecimiento. **A chill came over the assembly,** un estremecimiento recorrió la asamblea.

chill, va. 1. Enfriar, poner fría alguna cosa. Poner a efriar (wine, food). **Serve chilled,** sírvase frío. **We were chilled to the bone,** estábamos congelados (de frío). 2. helar. 3. Desanimar, desalentar, -vn. Escalofriarse.

chilli s. V. CHILI.

chilliness ['tʃɪlɪnɪs] [chi-li-nes] s. Principio o entrada del escalofrío; tiritón.

chilling ['tʃɪlɪŋ] [chi-lin] a. Escalofriante, espeluznante.

chillness ['tʃɪlnɪs] [chil-nes], s. Frío, falta de calor.

chilly ['tʃɪlɪ] [chi-li], a. Friolento. Frío (room, weather). **Chilly today, isn't it?,** hace fresquito hoy ¿no? Frío (greeting). -adv. Fríamente.

chimaera s. V. CHIMERA.

chimaphila ['kaɪməfɪlə] [kai-ma-fi-la], s. Quimafila.

chime [tʃaɪm] [chaim], s. 1. Armonía de sonidos, como los de las campanas o de un instrumento; melodía; ritmo (de un discurso o poema). Repique (sound/of bells); campanada (of clock); campanilla (of doorbell). Carillón (device). 2. Juego de campanas dispuestas de modo que producen sonidos armónicos. 3. Conformidad, analogía.

chime, s. 1. Jable o gárgol de tonel, barril o cuba, salida dormada por las extremidades de las duelas. 2. Muesca, ranura de la duela.

chime, vn. 1. Sonar con armonía; repicar (bell); dar la hora, sonar (clock). 2. Convenir, concordar. 3. Tañer, repicar las campanas. -va. Tocar o mover alguna cosa con compás y armonía (tune).

chime in (Coloq.) Meter (la) cuchara.

chimer ['tʃaɪmər] [chai-ma'], s. Campanero; repicador o tañedor de campanas.

chimera [kaɪ'mɪərə] [kai-mia-ra], s. 1. Quimera, monstruo fabuloso. 2. Quimera, ilusión, imaginación vana.

chimere [kaɪ'mɪər] [kai-mia'], s. Sobrepelliz, vestidura exterior y sin mangas de un obispo.

chimerical [kaɪ'merɪkəl] [kai-me-ri-kal], Quimérico, imaginario.

chimerically [kaɪ'merɪkəlɪ] [kai-me-ri-ka-li], adv. Quiméricamente.

chimney ['tʃɪmnɪ] [chim-ni], s. 1. Cañón de chimenea. 2. Chimenea u hogar, lugar en que se enciende el fuego en las casas. 3. Tubo o cañón de vidrio, para las lámparas. **Flue of a chimney,** cañón, humero de una chimenea. **Mantlepiece of a chimney,** campana de la chimenea; repisa. (Coloq.) **To smoke like a chimney,** fumar como una chimenea.

chimney-corner ['tʃɪmnɪ,kɔːnər] [chim-ni-kor-na'], s. Rincón de chimenea.

chimney-piece ['tʃɪmnɪpiːs] [chim-ni-pis], s. Las jambas y el dintel que sirven para adorno de las chimeneas.

chimney-sweeper ['tʃɪmnɪswiːpər] [chim-ni-sui-pa'], s. Deshollinador o limpiachimeneas.

chimney-top ['tʃɪmnɪtɒp] [chim-ni-top], s. La parte superior del cañón de la chimenea.

chimp [tʃɪmp] [chimp] s. (Coloq.) Chimpancé.

chimpanzee [,tʃɪmpæn'ziː] [chim-pan-si], s. Chimpancé, mono antropomorfo.

chin [tʃɪn] [chin], s. Barba. Barbilla, mentón, pera. **To keep one's chin up,** no perder el ánimo. (Coloq.) **Chin up!,** ¡ánimo! **To take it on the chin,** sufrir las consecuencias, pagar el pato. (GB) **To take something on the chin,** aguantar algo con resignación (suffer stoically). **Chin-cloth** o **bib,** babero.

China ['tʃaɪnə] [chaina] N. (Geogr.) China.

china, chinaware ['tʃaɪnəweər] [chai-na-uea'], s. China, porcelana loza de China. **China o India ink,** s. Tinta de China.

china-root ['tʃaɪnəruːt] [chai-na-rut], s. (Bot.) China, planta y raíz que se trae de la China.

chinchilla [tʃɪn'tʃɪlə] [chin-chi-la], s. Chinchilla y su piel.

chincough ['tʃɪnkɔː] [chin-ko], s. (Des.) Tos convulsiva, tos ferina.

chine ['tʃaɪn] [chain], s. 1. Espinazo. 2. Lomo en los animales. 3. Solomo.

chine, va. Deslomar, romper por el espinazo.

chinese [tʃaɪ'niːz] [chai-nís], a. Chino, chinesco, de la China, o parecido a las cosas de aquel país. **Chinese white,** blanco de China, óxido de cinc. -s. 1. Chino, natural de la China. 2. La lengua china.

chink [tʃɪŋk] [chink], s. 1. Grieta, abertura (crack/in fence, wall); rendija, resquicio (of door); hendedura, rajadura, abertura. **A chink of light entered through the shutters,** la luz entraba por las rendijas de la persiana. 2. **They found a chink in his armor,** le encontraron un punto flaco o débil. 3. Tintineo (of glasses).

chink vn. Henderse, abrirse; sonar, resonar. Hacer tintinear (glasses); hacer sonar o tintinear (coins).

chinkapin ['tʃɪŋkəpɪn] [chin-ka-pin], s. Castaño enano, y su fruto; arbusto del Este de los Estados Unidos.

chinky ['tʃɪŋkɪ] [chin-ki], a. Hendido, rajado, lleno de hendeduras.

chinned ['tʃɪnɪd] [chi-nid], a. Barbado.

chinse [tʃɪnz] [chins], va. (Mar.) Calafatear.

chints, chintz [tʃɪnts] [chints], s. Zaraza, tela de algodón con dibujos en colores.

chintzy ['tʃɪntsɪ] [chin-tsi] a. Barato, ordinario (shoddy, cheap); coquetón (flowery, pretty/decor, furnishings).

chinwag ['tʃɪnwæg] [chin-uag] s. (Coloq.) Cháchara. **To have a chinwag,** chacharear.

chip [tʃɪp] [chip], va. 1. Desmenuzar, hacer pedazos menudos una cosa; es hacer astillas, si se habla de leña o madera, y picar, si de carne. Desportillar, cascar, saltar (damage/crockery); romper un trocito de (tooth); hacer, abrir (hole/cut, break). **I chipped off the old plaster,** quité el yeso viejo quebrándolo. 2. *(Culin.)* Cortar (slice). **Chipped beef,** carne de vaca ahumada y cortada en rodajas finas. 3. Levantar la pelota mediante un golpe corto y preciso (in golf, tennis, soccer). *-vn.* 1. Romperse, abrirse; dícese de los huevos empollados. 2. Quebrarse; dícese de la loza o del vidrio. Desportillarse, cascarse, saltarse (china/cup); saltarse, desconcharse (paint, varnish).

chip in *(Coloq.)* Meter la cuchara (speak); contribuir (contribute).

chip, *s.* 1. Brizna, astilla (of wood); esquirla (of stone); raspaduras de la corteza del pan; barbas de los libros cuando se igualan sus cortes; viruta de la madera cuando se cepilla, llamada también doladura o cepilladura. Desportilladura, muesca (crack, break). **To have a chip on one's shoulder,** ser un resentido. 2. *(Culin.)* Papas o patatas fritas, patatas a la inglesa, papas chip (thin, crisp, slice); (French fry). **Chip shop,** pescadería donde se vende pescado frito y papas fritas. 3. Ficha (games). **To be in the chips,** ser rico o boyante. (GB) *(Coloq.)* **I thought I'd had my chips,** creí que me había llegado la hora. **When the chips are down,** a la hora de la verdad. 4. *(Comput., Electron.)* chip. **Silicon chip,** pastilla de silicio. **Chip-axe,** azuela. **Chip-hat,** sombrero de virutas, o de hoja de palma; sombrero jíbaro. **Chip of the same block,** de tal palo tal astilla.

chipboard [ˈtʃɪpbɔːd] [chip-bord] *s.* Madera prensada o aglomerada, aglomerado (of wood); cartón prensado (of paper).

chipmunk [ˈtʃɪpmʌŋk] [chip-mank], *s.* Ardilla terrícola listada.

chipper [ˈtʃɪpər] [chi-pa'], *a.* (E.U.Fam.) Vivo, alegre, jovial; sano, robusto.

chipping [ˈtʃɪpɪŋ] [chi-pin], *s.* 1. Brizna, la parte pequeña que se separa de alguna cosa. 2. Acto de desmenuzar. 3. (GB) Gravilla, cascajo.

chirk [tʃɜːk] [cherk], *a.* (Fam.) Alegre, jovial.

chirk, *s.* Petrosílex, horsteno. V. CHERT.

chirograph [ˈkaɪrəʊgræf] [kai-rou-graf], *s.* 1. Contrato que se hacía formando dos copias idénticas sobre un mismo pergamino y cortándolas o separándolas después. 2. Quirógrafo, documento autorizado con una firma autógrafa.

chirographer [kaɪˈrəʊgræfər] [kai-rou-gra-fa'], *s.* Escribano, escribiente; el vale o escritura hecho de propia mano.

chirography [kaɪˈrəʊgræfɪ] [kai-rou-gra-fi], *s.* Quirografía; el arte de escribir y la atestación de escribir de propia mano; modo de escribir.

chiromancer [ˈkaɪərəmænsər] [kai-ro-man-sa'], *s.* Quiromántico, el que profesa la quiromancia.

chiromancy [ˈkaɪərəmænsɪ] [kaia-ro-man-si], *s.* Quiromancia, supuesta adivinación por las rayas de la mano.

chironomy [kɪˈrɒnəmɪ] [ki-ro-no-mi], *s.* Quironomía, arte o teoría de los movimientos y de la gesticulación dramática y oratoria.

chiropodist [kɪˈrɒpədɪst] [ki-ro-po-dist], *s.* Pedicuro, el que tiene por oficio la extirpación y curación de los callos y uñeros y otras dolencias de los pies. Podólogo, callista.

chiropody [kɪˈrɒpədɪ] [ki-ro-po-di] *s.* Podología.

chiropractor [ˈkaɪrəʊˌpræktər] [kai-rou-prak-to'], *s.* Quiropráctico.

chirp [tʃɜːp] [cherp], *vn.* Gorjear o piar como los pájaros; chirriar, como los insectos. *va.* Decir alegremente.

chirp, *s.* 1. Chirrido, gorjeo. 2. Canto, piada, pído (of birds).

chirper [ˈtʃɜːpər] [cher-pa'], *s.* Chirriador, el que chirría o gorjea.

chirping [ˈtʃɜːpɪŋ] [cher-pin], *s.* Chirrido, el canto sin melodía de los pájaros e insectos.

chirpy [ˈtʃɜːpɪ] [cher-pi] *a.* *(Coloq.)* (GB) Alegre, animado.

chirrup [ˈtʃɪrəp] [chi-rop], *va.* y *vn.* Gorjear, con nota sostenida; trinar.

chirurgeon [kɪˈrɜːdʒɪən] [ki-rur-yion], *s.* Cirujano. V. SURGEON.

chirurgery [kɪˈrɜːdʒərɪ] [ki-rur-ye-ri], *s.* Cirugía. V. SURGERY.

chirurgical [kɪˈrɜːdʒɪkl] [ki-rur-yi-kal], *a.* Quirúrgico. V. SURGICAL.

chisel [ˈtʃɪzl] [chisol], *s.* Escoplo o formón (for wood); cincel (for stone).

chisel, *va.* Escoplear o cincelar, esculpir. Cincelar (stone); labrar, tallar (wood). **His finely chiseled features,** sus finamente cincelados o dibujados rasgos.

chiseler [ˈtʃɪzlər] [chi-se-la'], *s.* Estafador.

chit [tʃɪt] [chit], *s.* 1. Chiquilla, muchacha. 2. Tallo, germen, botones, yema, el pitoncillo que arroja el grano. 3. Peca en la cara. 4. Recibo, resguardo (receipt); nota (note); vale (to exchange for something).

chit *va.* Quitar los brotes o tallos tiernos de los bulbos, tubérculos y plantas. *-vn.* Brotar, echar botones o yemas las plantas.

chitchat [ˈtʃɪtʃæt] [chit-chat], *s.* Charla. *(Fam.)* Cuchicheo, palique, cháchara.

chitin [ˈtʃɪtɪn] [chi-tin], *s.* Quitina, la parte esencial del carapacho de los insectos y crustáceos.

chitinous [ˈtʃɪtɪnəs] [chi-ti-nos], *a.* Quitinoso.

chitterlings [ˈtʃɪtəlɪŋz] [chi-ter-lins], *s. pl.* 1. Despojos; el vientre, asadura, cabeza y manos de las reses que se matan en las carnicerías. 2. Pechera, guirindola o chorrera de camisola.

chitty [ˈtʃɪtɪ] [chi-ti], *a.* 1. Lo que tiene gérmenes o botones. 2. *(Des.)* Pecoso.

chivalric [ˈʃɪvəlrɪk] [shi-val-rik], *a.* Caballeresco, perteneciente a la caballería.

chivalrous [ˈʃɪvəlrəs] [shi-val-rous], *a.* Caballeroso, cortés, propio de caballero.

chivalry [ˈʃɪvəlrɪ] [shi-val-ri], *s.* 1. *(Hist.)* Caballería, grado y dignidad de caballero militar. 2. Caballería andante; caballerosidad, cortesía, hidalguía (in conduct). 3. Proeza, hazaña.

chive [tʃaɪv] [chaiv], *s.* 1. Cebolleta, cebollino, especie de cebolla pequeña. 2. *(Des.)* Estambre, filamento.

chivvy [ˈtʃɪvɪ] [chi-vi] *va.* V. CHIVY.

chivy [ˈtʃɪvɪ] [chi-vi] *va. (Coloq.)* Meterle prisa a, apurar (person). **She had to chivy me into applying,** me tuvo que empujar para que hiciera la solicitud.

chlamys [ˈklæmɪz] [kla-mis], *s.* 1. Clámide, capa corta y ligera de los griegos y romanos. 2. Capa pluvial de color de púrpura.

chloracetic [ˈklɔːrəsɪtɪk] [klo-ra-se-tik], *a. (Quím.)* Cloracético. **Chloracetic acid,** ácido cloracético, obtenido por la acción del cloro sobre el ácido acético.

chloral [ˈklɔːrəl] [klo-ral], *s.* Cloral, líquido incoloro, aceitoso, con olor penetrante; obtenido por la acción del cloro sobre el alcohol. **Chloral hydrate** (o simplemente *chloral*), hidrato de cloral, compuesto blanco, cristalizado, picante, que se usa en medicina como narcótico.

chloramphenicol [ˈklɔːrəˌfenɪkl] [klo-ra-fe-ni-kol], *s. (Med.)* Cloramfenicol.

chlorate [ˈklɔːreɪt] [klo-reit], *s.* Clorato, sal de ácido clórico.

chloremia [klɔːˈriːmɪə] [klo-ri-mia], *s. (Med.)* Cloremia.

chloric [ˈklɔːrɪk] [klo-rik], *a.* Clórico, combinado con el cloro. **Chloric acid,** ácido clórico.

chlord, chloride [ˈklɔːraɪd] [klo-raid], *s.* Cloruro, combinación del cloro con metal o metaloide.

chlorinate [ˈklɒrɪneɪt] [klo-ri-neit] *va.* Clorar, tratar con cloro.

chlorination [ˌklɔːrɪˈneɪʃən] [klo-ri-nei-shon], *s.* Tratamiento al cloro.

chlorine [ˈklɔːriːn] [klo-rin], *s. (Quím.)* Cloro, gas amarillo verdoso, venenoso y de olor desagradable.

chlorite [ˈklɔːraɪt] [klo-rait], *s. (Min.)* Clorita, ejemplar de varios silicatos hidratados, de color verdoso.

chlorofluorocarbon [ˈklɔːrəʊˈflʊərəʊˈkɑːbən] [klo-ro-fluo-ro-kar-bon] *s.* Clorofluorocarbono.

chloroform [ˈklɔːrəfɔːm] [klo-ro-form], *s.* Cloroformo, líquido incoloro, volátil, algo dulce, que se emplea como poderoso anestésico y anodino. *-va.* Administrar cloroformo: cloroformizar.

chloromycetin [ˈklɔːrəˌmɪsətɪn] [klo-ro-mi-se-tin], *s. (Med.)* Cloromicetina.

chlorophyl, chlorophyll [ˈklɔːrəfɪl] [klo-ro-fil], *s.* Clorofila, la materia colorante verde de las hojas de los vegetales.

chlorosis [ˈklɔːrəʊsɪs] [klo-rou-sis], *s. (Med.)* Clorosis, enfermedad de las adolescentes caracterizada por palidez del rostro y empobrecimiento de la sangre, y comúnmente por amenorrea.

chlorotic [ˈklɔːrətɪk] [klo-ro-tik], *a.* Clorótico, clorótica, perteneciente o relativo a la clorosis. Se dice de la mujer que la padece.

clorous [ˈklɔːrəs] [klo-rus], *a.* Combinado con el cloro y en especial en su valor de tres.

choc-ice [ˈtʃɒkaɪs] [chok-ais] *s.* (GB) Bombón helado.

chock [tʃɒk] [chok] 1. Calzo, cuña, pedazo de madera u otro objeto a propósito para calzar un barril tonel, etc. 2. *(Mar.)* Choque, calzo fijo sobre la cubierta de un buque o sobre un muelle, con quijadas por las cuales se puede pasar un cable o cadena. 3. *V.* CHUCK.

chock, *va.* 1. Afianzar, soportar, proveer con calzos. *-vn.* Cerrar, tapar, llenar un hueco o juntura.

chock-a-block [tʃɒk] [chok] *a. (Coloq.)* **To be chock-a-block with something/somebody,** estar hasta los topes de algo/alguien.

chock-full, chuck-full [tʃɒk] [chok], *a.* Colmado, lleno hasta el tope; de bote en bote. **To be chock-full of/with something,** estar hasta los topes de algo.

chocolate [ˈtʃɒklɪt] [choklit], *s.* 1. Chocolate, pasta hecha de cacao, azúcar, etc.; bombón (candy, sweet). **Milk/dark** o (GB) **plain chocolate,** chocolate con/sin leche. De chocolate (egg, cake). **Chocolate bar,** chocolatina, chocolatín. **Chocolate-chip cookie,** galleta con pedacitos de chocolate. **Chocolate liqueur,** bombón de licor. 2. Chocolate, el compuesto líquido de la pasta desleída por medio de agua caliente o leche. **A cup of hot chocolate,** una taza de chocolate caliente. 3. Color chocolate, marrón, café o carmelito oscuro (color).

chocolate *a.* Color chocolate, marrón, café o carmelito oscuro (in color).

choice [tʃɔɪs] [chois], *s.* 1. Escogimiento, elección (act, option); preferencia; el acto, facultad o cuidado de elegir, escoger o preferir una cosa a otra. **I had no choice but to obey,** no tuve más remedio o alternativa que obedecer. **To make one's choice,** elegir, escoger. **I'm single by choice,** no me he casado porque no me querido o por decisión propia. **You can take any two books of your choice,** puede llevarse dos libros a elección. 2. La cosa elegida, lo selecto, lo más escogido (de personas). **She's a possible choice for the job,** es una de las candidatas posibles para el puesto (person, thing chosen). **It was an unfortunate choice of words,** no fue la mejor manera de decirlo. Surtido, selección (variety). **To be spoiled for choice,** tener mucho donde elegir. **Hobson's choice,** o tal cosa, o nada; o tomarlo o dejarlo.

choice, *a.* 1. Escogido, selecto (fruit, vegetables, wine); de primera (beef, veal); exquisito (language, phrase); excelente. **He used some choice language when he found out,** soltó unas perlitas cuando se enteró *(iró.)* 2. Cuidadoso, frugal, parco, económico.

choiceless [ˈtʃɔɪslɪs] [chois-les], *a.* Limitado, el que no tiene facultad de elegir.

choir [ˈkwaɪər] [kuaiar], *s.* 1. Coro, unión o conjunto de voces. 2. Coro, los que cantan salmos, himnos y otras composiciones sagradas. 3. Coro, la parte de la iglesia en que se juntan los que cantan. **Choir-service,** oficio de coro.

choirboy [ˈkwaɪəbɔɪ] [kuaia-boi] *s.* Niño que canta en un coro de iglesia.

choke [tʃəʊk] [chouk], *va.* 1. Ahogar, sofocar, quitar la respiración. Estrangular, ahogar, asfixiar (stifle). **A voice choked by sobs,** una voz ahogada en llanto. 2. Cerrar alguna comunicación o paso. 3. Suprimir, oprimir. **To choke up,** obstruir, tapar. **The garden is choked with weeds,** el jardín está invadido de malezas (overwhelm). *-vn.* Ahogarse, asfixiarse. **To choke on something,** atragantarse o atorarse con algo.

choke back Contener, tragarse (tears). **I choked back my anger,** me contuve.

choke up Obstruir, atascar, tapar (block/drain, pipe). *(Coloq.)* Fallar (fail).

choke, *s.* 1. Hebra de alcachofa. 2. *(Auto)* Choke, estárter, cebador, chupete.

choked [tʃəʊkt] [choukt] *a.* **Goodbye, he said in a choked voice,** adiós - dijo, con la voz entrecortada por la emoción.

choke-full [ˈtʃəʊkfʊl] [chouk-ful], *a.* Lleno enteramente hasta los bordes. *V.* CHOCK-FULL.

choke-pear [ˈtʃəʊkpɪər] [chouk-pia^r], *s.* 1. Ahogadera, especie de pera áspera al paladar. 2. # *(Met.)* Tapaboca, cualquier dicho picante que obliga a alguno a callarse.

choker [ˈtʃəʊkər] [chou-ka^r], *s.* 1. Ahogador, el que ahoga; el que hace callar a otro; tapaboca, argumento sin réplica. 2. Corbata grande. 3. Gargantilla (necklace).

choky [ˈtʃəʊkɪ] [chou-ki], *a.* Lo que puede ahogar; sofocante.

choler [ˈkɒlər] [ko-la^r], *s.* Ira, enojo.

cholera [ˈkɒlərə] [ko-le-ra], *s.* 1. *(Med.)* Cólera-morbo, enfermedad aguda, epidémica, causada por un bacilo; cólera asiático. 2. Cólera-morbo, enfermedad no epidémica, esporádica. *Cholera morbus, V.* 2ª acep.

choleric [ˈkɒlərɪk] [ko-le-rik], *a.* Colérico, enojado.

cholericness [ˈkɒlərɪknɪs] [ko-le-rik-nes], *s.* Cólera, ira, enojo.

cholerine [ˈkɒləriːn] [ko-le-rin], *s.* 1. Colerina, primer período del cólera epidémico. 2. Tipo ligero de esta enfermedad; diarrea coleriforme.

cholesterol [kəˈlestərɒl] [ko-les-te-rol], *s.* (Bioquímica) Colesterol.

chomp [tʃɒmp] [chomp] *va.* Mascar, masticar.

chondroid [ˈkɒndrɔɪd] [kon-droid], *a.* Parecido al cartílago.

choose [tʃuːz] [chus], *va.* Escoger, optar; tomar o elegir con preferencia (select); predestinar. Elegir (candidate). **To choose to,** decidir, optar por (decide). *-vn.* Tener facultad para elegir, hacer o dejar de hacer alguna cosa; preferir, querer. Elegir, escoger. **You can choose from this range,** puede elegir o escoger dentro de esta gama. **There's little o not much to choose between them,** no hay gran diferencia entre ellos. **Why don't you tell me your age?-because I don't choose,** ¿por qué no me dice Ud. su edad? -porque no quiero, porque no me place. **To choose rather,** preferir. **The chosen ones,** los mejores, los más granados, los escogidos.

chooser [ˈtʃuːzər] [chu-sa^r], *s.* Escogedor; elector.

choosing [ˈtʃuːzɪŋ] [chu-sin], *s.* Escogimiento, elección.

choosy [ˈtʃuːzɪ] [chu-si] *a. (Coloq.)* Exigente, difícil de contentar.

chop [tʃɒp] [chop], *va.* 1. Tajar, cortar o separar; picar; desbastar un madero. Cortar (cut/wood); cortar en trozos pequeños (meat, apple); picar (parsley, onion). **Chopped,** picado (onions, herbs); molido o picado (meat). 2. Rajar, hender. 3. Mudar, cambiar, trocar; comprar. 4. Articular de un modo rápido y entrecortado. *-vn.* Hacer alguna cosa con movimiento veloz; tropezar. Golpear, cortar (strike). Cambiar, variar, mudarse; dícese del viento. **Chop-logic,** argumentación llena de argucias y sutilezas. *(Coloq.)* **To chop and change,** cambiar continuamente. **To chop off,** tronchar. **To chop at,** pillar, zampar, atrapar con la boca. **To**

chop in, entrar de repente con la intención de sorprender. **To chop about,** girar, rodear, mudar. **To chop meat,** picar la carne. **Chopped hands,** manos agrietadas.

chop down Cortar, talar (tree); cortar (branch, pole).

chop off Cortar (branch); cortar, cercenar (finger).

chop up Picar (onion, parsley); cortar en trozos pequeños (meat, apple).

chop, s. 1. Porción, parte; tajada de carne; chuleta o costilla de ternera, carnero, etc.; raja. 2. Hachazo (with ax, cleaver); manotazo (with hand); (*Sport*) golpe cortado; (in karate). (GB) (*Coloq.*) **To give somebody the chop,** echar a alguien (dismissal, cancellation). **They all got the chop,** los echaron a todos. 3. (*Coloq.*) **Chops,** boca, jeta, morro (of person). **To lick/smack one's chops,** relamerse. **To bust somebody's chops,** arremeter contra alguien.

chop-fallen V. CHAP-FALLEN.

chop-house [ˌtʃɒpˈhaʊs] [chop-jaus], s. Bodegón, figón.

chopper [ˈtʃɒpər] [cho-pərˈ], s. 1. Cuchilla de carnicero; hacha pequeña (hatchet). 2. (*Coloq.*) Helicóptero (helicopter). 3. (*Coloq.*) **Choppers,** dientes postizos, comedor.

chopping [ˈtʃɒpɪŋ] [cho-pin], a. 1. Que se cambia de repente a otra dirección (viento). 2. Lleno de olas pequeñas. 3. (*Ant.*) Rollizo, robusto. -s. Tajadura, cortadura. **Chopping-block,** tajo de cocina, tajadera. **Chopping-board,** tajador; tabla de picar. **Chopping-knife,** cuchilla, tajadera.

choppy [ˈtʃɒpɪ] [cho-pi], a. 1. Rajado, hendido, lleno de grietas, agujereado. 2. Lleno de olas pequeñas y agitadas; picado (sea).

chops [tʃɒpz] [chops], s. (*Vul.*) Boca; quijadas. **Chops of the channel,** (*Mar.*) boca de un canal.

chop-sticks [ˈtʃɒpstɪks] [chop-stiks], s. pl. Varillas delgadas, de que se sirven los chinos y japoneses para llevar los alimentos a la boca; palillos.

chop suey [ˌtʃɒpˈsʊɪ] [chop-sui], s. Guiso popular en E.U. que se supone de origen chino.

choral [ˈkɔːrəl] [ko-ral], a. Coral, perteneciente al coro; cantado en coro.

chord [kɔːd] [kord], s. 1. (*Mús.*) Cuerda. Cuando esta voz quiere decir cordel o soga se escribe *cord.* 2. (*Mús.*) Acorde, combinación de sonidos escogidos según las leyes de la armonía. 3. (*Geom.*) Cuerda, línea recta que une los dos extremos de un arco de círculo. **That struck a chord with her,** eso le tocó la fibra sensible. **His speech struck the right chord with the audience,** su discurso estuvo en perfecta sintonía con el sentir del público.

chord, va. (*Mús.*) Encordar, poner cuerdas en alguna cosa.

chore [tʃɔːr] [choʳ], s. Tarea o trabajo de poco momento; especialmente del servicio doméstico (routine task). Lata (tedious task).

choreographer [ˌkɒrɪˈɒɡrəfər] [ko-ri-o-gra-feʳ], s. Coreógrafo, maestro de baile.

choreography [ˌkɒrɪˈɒɡrəfɪ] [ko-ri-o-gra-fi], s. Coreografía.

choriambic [ˌkɒrɪˈæmbrɪk] [ko-ri-am-brik], s. Coriambo. -a. Coriámbico.

chorion [ˈkɒrɪən] [ko-rion], s. (*Anat.*) Corion, membrana exterior que envuelve el feto en el útero.

chorographer [kɒˈrɒɡrəfər] [ko-ro-gra-feʳ], s. Corógrafo.

chorography [kɒˈrɒɡrəfɪ] [ko-ro-gra-fi], s. Corografía, ciencia que enseña a formar el mapa particular de una región o provincia.

choroid [ˈkɒrɔɪd] [ko-roid], a. Coroideo, parecido al corion. -s. Túnica media del ojo.

chortle [ˈtʃɔːtl] [chor-tel] vn. **To chortle over something,** reírse de algo.

chortle s. Risa de satisfacción.

chorus [ˈkɔːrəs] [ko-rus], s. 1. Coro (in musical, opera, tragedy). **Chorus girl,** corista. **Chorus line,** coro. 2. Coro, estrambote o estribillo (refrain); coral (choral piece). 3. Coro (outburst). **A chorus of protest,** un coro de protestas.

chose, chosen, *pret.* y *pp.* del verbo TO CHOOSE.

chose [tʃəʊz] [chous], s. (*For.*) Cada uno de los objetos que constituyen propiedad mueble. **Chose in action,** derecho de una persona sobre propiedad mueble o dinero no en su posesión pero reivindicable por medio de procedimiento legal.

chosen [ˈtʃəʊzən] [chousen] a. **Only a chosen few were invited to attend,** sólo invitaron a una selecta minoría. **God's chosen people,** el pueblo elegido.

chough [tʃʌf] [chaf], s. (*Orn.*) Chova, especie de grajo de color negro y patas rojas.

chouse [tʃuːz] [chus], va. Engañar, embaucar, engatusar.

chouse, s. 1. Primo, tonto, bobalicón, el bobo o simple que se deja engañar. 2. Engaño, fraude, chasco, pieza, burla.

chousing [ˈtʃaʊzɪŋ] [chou-sin], s. Bellaquería, engaño, fraude.

chow [tʃaʊ] [chau] s. (*Sl.*) Comida (food).

chow-chow [ˌtʃaʊˈtʃaʊ] [chau-chau], s. Mezcla, olla podrida; alimentos divididos a la manera china; en especial, encurtidos de diferentes legumbres con mostaza. (Chino)

chowder [ˈtʃaʊdər] [chau-daʳ], s. Sopa de pescado o de mariscos.

chow mein [ˌtʃaʊˈmeɪn] [chau-mein], s. Guiso de tallarines chinos, carne y verduras. Se supone de origen chino.

chrestomthy [ˈtʃrestɒmθɪ] [chres-tom-zi], s. Crestomatía, colección de escritos selectos, especialmente la destinada a la enseñanza en un idioma determinado.

chrism [krɪzm] [krisem], s. Crisma, aceite consagrado.

chrismatory [ˈkrɪzmətərɪ] [kris-ma-to-ri], s. Crismera.

Chrissake [ˈkrɪseɪk] [kri-seik] interj. (*Sl.*) **For Chrissake!,** ¡por Dios!, ¡por favor!

Christ [kraɪst] [kraist], s. (*Rel.*) Cristo o Jesucristo, nuestro Salvador. (*Coloq.*) ¡Jesús! (as interj.); **for Christ sake!,** ¡por amor de Dios!

christ-cross-row [ˈkraɪstˈkrɒsrɔː] [kraist-kros-ro], s. (*Ant.*) El Crístus o la cartilla.

christen [ˈkrɪzn] [kr-isen], va. 1. Dar nombre al tiempo de bautizar. 2. Bautizar, practicar las ceremonias por medio de las cuales uno se hace cristiano (baptize). 3. Cristianar, hacer cristiano por medio del bautismo. 4. (*Fam.*) Estrenar, empezar a usar una cosa (use for first time).

christendom [ˈkrɪsndəm] [kri-sen-dom], s. Cristianismo, cristiandad.

christening [ˈkrɪsnɪŋ] [kris-nin] s. Bautismo, bautizo. -a. Bautismal.

christian [ˈkrɪstɪən] [kris-tian], s. Cristiano, el que profesa la fe de Jesucristo, -a. Cristiano, lo que pertenece a la religión cristiana. **Christian name,** nombre de bautismo o de pila. **Christian Scientist,** científico cristiano.

christianism [ˈkrɪstɪənɪzm] [kris-tia-nisem], **christianity** [ˈkrɪstɪənɪtɪ] [kri-tia-ni-ti], s. Cristianismo (faith); los cristianos, el cristianismo (believers).

christianization [ˌkrɪstɪənaɪˈzeɪʃən] [kris-tia-nai-zi-shon], s. Cristianización.

christianize [ˈkrɪstɪənaɪz] [kris-tia-nais], va. Cristianizar, cristianar.

christianlike [ˈkrɪstɪənlaɪk] [kris-tian-laik], a. Propio de cristiano.

christianly [ˈkrɪstɪənlɪ] [kris-tian-li], adv. Cristianamente.

christless [ˈkrɪstlɪs] [krist-les], a. Anticristiano, impío, herético.

Christmas [ˈkrɪsməs] [kris-mas], s. 1. La Navidad o Natividad, conmemoración anual del nacimiento de nuestro Señor Jesucristo. Pascua; las Navidades, la Navidad, la Pascua (Christmas time). **Merry** (GB) **happy Christmas!,** ¡Feliz Navidad!, ¡Felices Pascuas! 2. El día de Navidad. 3. Aguinaldo o regalo de Navidad. **Christmas pudding,** pudin de Navidad. **Christmas carol,** villancico, cántico de Navidad. **Christmas card,** tarjeta de Navidad, tarjeta de Pascua, crismas. **Christmas cracker,** sorpresa que se abre durante la comida de Navidad. **Christmas Day,** día de Navidad o de Pascua. **Christmas Eve,** la víspera de Navidad; Nochebuena (evening). **Christmas holidays,**

vacaciones de Pascuas. **Christmas tree,** árbol de Navidad o de Pascua.

christmas-box [ˈkrɪsməsbɒks] [kris-mas-boks], *s.* Cajita para recoger el aguinaldo; el aguinaldo mismo.

christ's-thorn [ˈkraɪsˈθɜːn] [kraist-zern], *s. (Bot.)* Espino amarillo.

chroma [ˈkrəmə] [kro-ma], *s.* Intensidad de color; el mayor o menor grado de color respecto del blanco.

chromate [krəˈmeɪt] [kro-meit], *s.* Cromato, sal del ácido crómico.

chromatic [krəˈmætɪk] [kro-ma-tik], *a.* 1. Cromático, relativo a los colores. 2. *(Mús.)* Cromático, que procede por semitonos. -*s. (Mús.)* Nota modificada por un bemol o sostenido.

chromatics [krəˈmætɪkz] [kro-ma-tiks], *s.* Cromática, ciencia del colorido.

chromatography [ˌkrəʊməˈtɒɡrəfɪ] [kro-ma-to-gra-fi], *s.* Cromatografía, descripción de los colores.

chrome [krəʊm] [kroum], *s.* 1. Cromo. 2. *V.* CHROMIUM.

chromic [ˈkrəʊmɪk] [kro-mik], *a.* Crómico, que pertenece al cromio en su mayor grado de combinación con otros cuerpos. **Chromic acid,** *(Quím.)* Acido crómico.

chromium [ˈkrəʊmɪəm] [kro-mium], *s. (Quím.)* Cromio, metal que se halla mineralizado con plomo, hierro y piedras preciosas. **Chromium plating,** cromado.

chromo [ˈkrəʊmə] [krou-mo], *s. V.* CHROMO-LITHOGRAPH.

chromo lithograph [ˈkrəʊməlɪˈtɒɡræf] [krou-mo-li-to-graf], *s.* Estampa o lámina en colores, obtenida por la cromolitografía.

chromosome [ˈkrəʊməsəʊm] [krou-mo-soum], *s. (Biol.)* Cromosoma.

chronic, chronical [ˈkrɒnɪk] [kro-nik] [ˈkrɒnɪkl] [kro-ni-kal], *a.* 1. Crónico, lo que pertenece al tiempo. Crónico (employment, shortages); empedernido (smoker, liar). 2. *(Med.)* Crónico, de larga duración. 3. *(GB) (Coloq.)* Pésimo, terrible (terrible).

chronicity [ˈkrɒnɪsɪtɪ] [kro-ni-si-ti], *s.* Estado o calidad de crónico.

chronicle [ˈkrɒnɪkl] [kro-nikl], *s.* Crónica, historia compuesta por orden de fechas.

chronicler [ˈkrɒnɪklər] [kro-niklaᵣ], *s.* Cronista, historiador.

chronogram [ˈkrɒnəɡræm] [kro-no-gram], *s.* Cronograma, inscripción en la que las letras numerales forman la fecha de algún suceso.

chronograph [ˈkrɒnəɡræf] [kro-no-graf], *s.* Cronógrafo, aparato eléctrico indicador del tiempo o duración de un acontecimiento.

chronographer [ˈkrɒnəɡræfər] [kro-no-gra-feᵣ], *s.* Cronologista.

chronography [ˈkrɒnəɡræfɪ] [kro-no-gra-fi], *s.* Cronografía, descripción del tiempo pasado.

chronologer [ˈkrɒnələɡər] [kro-no-lo-gaᵣ], **chronologist** [ˈkrɒnələdʒɪst] [kro-no-lo-yist], *s.* Cronologista, cronólogo, el que es versado en la cronología.

chronologic, chronological [krəˈnɒlədʒɪ] [kro-no-lo-yi], *a.* Cronológico. **In chronological order,** en orden cronológico.

chronologically [ˌkrɒnəˈlɒdʒɪkəlɪ] [kro-no-lo-yi-ka-li], *adv.* Cronológicamente.

chronology [krəˈnɒlədʒɪ] [kro-no-lo-yi], *s.* 1. Cronología, ciencia que determina el orden y fecha de los sucesos históricos. 2. Manera de computar los tiempos.

chronometer [krɒˈnəmɪtər] [kro-no-mi-taᵣ], *s.* Cronómetro, instrumento para medir el tiempo; reloj de longitudes que mide exactamente el tiempo.

chronometric, chronometrical [krəˈnɒmɪtrɪk] [kro-no-mi-trik], *a.* Cronométrico, referente al cronómetro o determinado por medio de él.

chronometry [krəˈnɒmɪtrɪ] [kro-no-mi-tri], *s.* Cronometría, la acción de medir el tiempo; ciencia de la medición del tiempo.

chronoscope [ˈkrɒnəskəʊp] [kro-nos-koup], *s.* Cronógrafo, u otro instrumento para medir un intervalo muy corto de tiempo.

chrysalis [ˈkrɪsəlɪs] [kri-sa-lis], *s.* Crisálida, ninfa o dormida, la oruga y otros insectos en su capullo antes de transformarse en mariposas.

chrysanthemun [krɪˈsænθəməm] [kri-san-ze-mum], *s. (Bot.)* Crisantemo, género de plantas compuestas que se cultivan como de adorno.

chrysoberyl [ˈkrɪsɒbərɪl] [kri-so-be-ril], *s. (Min.)* Crisoberilo, piedra preciosa.

chrysolite [ˈkrɪsəlaɪt] [kri-so-lait], *s.* Crisólito, piedra preciosa.

chrysoprace [ˈkrɪsɒpreɪs] [kri-so-preis], *s. (Min.)* Crisoprasa o crisopracio, especie de calcedonia de color verde manzana.

chub [tʃʌb] [chab], *s.* Coto, pez de agua dulce. **Chub-faced,** cariancho.

chubbed [tʃʌbd] [cha-bed], *a.* Cabezudo, el que tiene cabeza grande. *V.* CHUBBY.

chubby [ˈtʃʌbɪ] [cha-bi], *a.* Gordo, gordiflón, regordete. rechoncho (person); regordete (legs, cheeks, face). **Chubby-cheeked,** mofletudo.

chuck [tʃʌk] [chak], *vn.* Cloquear, cacarear la gallina cuando está clueca. -*va.* 1. Dar una sobarbada o golpe debajo de la barba a alguno. **To chuck somebody under the chin,** darle una palmadita en la barbilla a alguien. 2. Arrojar diestramente. 3. Cloquear, llamar la gallina a sus pollos. 4. *(Coloq.)* Tirar, aventar (throw); tirar, botar (throw away); dejar, plantar (give up/job); plantar, botar, largar (boyfriend/girlfriend).

chuck away *(Coloq.)* Derrochar, despilfarrar, tirar (squander, waste/money); desperdiciar (opportunity). *V.* CHUCK OUT.

chuck in *(GB) (Coloq.)* Dejar, mandar al diablo (job, studies).

chuck out 1. *(Coloq.)* Tirar, botar (rubbish); rechazar (reject/plan, suggestion). 2. Echar (expel).

chuck up *(Sl.)* Abandonar, renunciar, vomitar.

chuck, *s.* 1. Cloqueo. 2. Cariño. 3. Sobarbada. 4. Rumor repentino. 5. Corte de carne vacuna del cuarto delantero.

chuck, *s. (Art. y Of.)* 1. Mandril, mangote, plato de un torno; invento para asir un objeto de tal manera que pueda girar. 2. Cuña, calzo.

chuck-farthing [tʃʌkˈfɑːθɪŋ] [chak-far-zin], *s.* Hoyuelo, especie de juego de los muchachos en que meten el dinero en un hoyo.

chuckle [ˈtʃʌkl] [cha-kel], *vn.* Reír entre dientes; sonreír de satisfacción; fisgar sonriéndose. -*va.* 1. Cloquear, llamar la gallina a sus pollos. 2. Acariciar, hacer fiestas a alguno; requebrar.

chuckle, *s.* Risa ahogada, risita. **They had a chuckle over/about that,** se estuvieron riendo de eso. -*a.* Grueso o tosco (hablando de la cabeza). **Chuckle-head,** tonto, estúpido, cabeza de chorlito.

chuck wagon [tʃʌkˈweɪɡɒn] [chak-ua-gon] *s.* Furgón en el que se transportan víveres y utensilios de cocina.

chuff [tʃʌf] [chaf], *s. (Ant.)* Patán, rústico.

chuffed [tʃʌft] [chaft] *a.* (GB) *(Coloq.)* Contento.

chuffily [ˈtʃʌfɪlɪ] [cha-fi-li], *adv.* Groseramente.

chuffiness [ˈtʃʌfɪnɪs] [cha-fi-nis], *s.* Rusticidad, falta de urbanidad.

chuffy [ˈtʃʌfɪ] [cha-fi], *a.* Grosero, desatento.

chug [tʃʌɡ] [chag] *vn.* **The engine chugged up the hill,** la locomotora subió la cuesta dando resoplidos. **The project is chugging along,** el proyecto sigue marchando.

chugalug [ˈtʃʌɡəlʌɡ] [cha-ga-lag] *va. (Coloq.)* Beberse o tomarse de un trago.

chum [tʃʌm] [cham], *vn.* Compartir una habitación con otro; ser íntimo. -*s.* 1. Camarada, compañero; condiscípulo. *(Coloq.)* Amigo, compinche. 2. Carnada, cebo (bait).

chump [tʃʌmp] [champ], *s.* 1. Tajo, tronco, leño grueso. 2. La extremidad gruesa de alguna cosa, por ejemplo, el lomo del carnero. 3. *(Ger.)* Leño, tonto, naranjo, mastuerzo.

chunk [tʃʌŋk] [chank], *s.* 1. Pedazo grueso y corto; persona o bestia rechoncha. 2. Pedazo, trozo, cacho (of bread, meat). **A chunk of bread,** un zoquete de pan.

chunky [tʃʌŋkɪ] [chan-ki], *a.* 1. Corto, rechoncho, abundante en carnes. *(E.U.)* Fornido, macizo (person); grueso, gordo (sweater). 2. Con trozos grandes de cáscara (marmalade).

chunnel [tʃʌnl] [cha-nel] *s. (Coloq.)* **The Chunnel,** el Eurotúnel, el túnel del canal de la Mancha.

church [tʃɜːtʃ] [cherch], *s.* 1. Iglesia, templo, edificio consagrado al culto (building). 2. Iglesia, la congregación de los fieles; cuerpo determinado de cristianos. 3. Culto público, oficio divino regular. 4. El clero; la Iglesia (as organization). **The church of England/Scotland,** la iglesia Anglicana/Presbiteriana Escocesa. **To go to church,** ir a misa, asistir al oficio divino. **A church service,** un oficio religioso. **He wants a church wedding,** quiere casarse por la Iglesia. **Eastern Church,** la Iglesia griega. *V.* GREEK CHURCH. **Western Church,** la iglesia del imperio romano de occidente en la edad media, hoy la Iglesia católica romana. **Church of Jesus Christ of Latter-day Saints,** Título oficial de la iglesia de Mormón, que quiere decir: Iglesia de Jesucristo de los Modernos Santos. **Church militant,** la iglesia militante, congregación de los fieles que viven en este mundo. **Church-ale,** aniversario o fiesta solemne en memoria de la consagración de una iglesia **Church-book, church register,** registro de parroquia, libro de bautizos. **Church-burial.** entierro, según los ritos de la iglesia. **Church-land,** tierras beneficiales, bienes eclesiásticos. **Church-music,** Música sagrada. **Church-preferment,** beneficio o renta eclesiástica. **Church-robbing,** sacrilegio. **Church-way,** camino a la iglesia. **Church-work,** la obra del Escorial; dícese de algún trabajo que procede lentamente.

church, *va.* Purificar, ejecutar las ceremonias de la purificación de una mujer recién parida.

churchdom [tʃɜːtʃdʌm] [cherch-dam], *s.* Dominio o autoridad de la iglesia.

churchgoer [tʃɜːtʃgəʊər] [cherch-goua'] *s.* Practicante, feligrés.

churchlike [tʃɜːtʃlaɪk] [cherch-laik], *a.* Eclesiástico, propio de un sacerdote.

churchman [tʃɜːtʃmən] [cherch-man], *s.* Sacerdote, eclesiástico; miembro de la Iglesia anglicana o católica.

churchwardens [tʃɜːwɔːdnz] [cherch-uardens], *s. pl.* Mayordomos, los que se eligen anualmente para que cuiden de las cosas de la iglesia, capilleros.

chuchyard [tʃɜːtʃjɑːd] [cherch-yard], *s.* Cementerio de parroquia.

churl [tʃɜːl] [cherl], *s.* Patán, rústico, payo. Charro; hombre ruin, miserable tacaño.

churlish [tʃɜːlɪʃ] [cher-lish], *a.* Rudo, agreste; ruin, escaso, rústico, grosero, maleducado, brutal, avaro.

churlishly [tʃɜːlɪʃlɪ] [cher-lish-li], *adv.* Rudamente, brutalmente.

churlishness [tʃɜːlɪʃnɪs] [cher-lish-nes], *s.* Rusticidad; rudeza, grosería, descortesía.

churn [tʃɜːn] [chern], *s.* Mantequera, vasija en que se hace la manteca.

churn, *va.* 1. Agitar o menear alguna cosa con violencia. 2. Batir o menear la nata de la leche para hacer manteca. Batir (milk); hacer (butter); agitar, revolver (water, mud). *-vn.* Arremolinarse (water). **My stomach was churning,** tenía un nudo en el estómago (with nerves); tenía el estómago revuelto (with nausea).

churn out *(Coloq.)* Producir como salchichas.

churn up Revolver.

churning [tʃɜːnɪŋ] [cher-nin], *s.* Batido.

churn-staff [tʃɜːnstɑːf] [chern-staf], *s.* Batidera, instrumento con el cual se bate la nata en la mantequera.

chuse, *v. V.* CHOOSE.

chute [ʃuːt] [shut], *s.* 1. Caída, plano inclinado o cualquier conducto de arriba hacia abajo. *(Fr.)* 2. Tolva, vertedor;

tobogán, rodadero (in swimming pool, amusement park). **Chutes and ladders** *s.* Juego de la oca, serpientes y escaleras.

chutney [ˈʃʌtnɪ] [shat-ni] *s.* Chutney, conserva agridulce que se come con carnes, queso, etc.

chylaceous [ˈkɪləʃəs] [ki-la-shos], *a.* Quiloso.

chyle [kiːl] [kil], *s.* Quilo, fluido lechoso que se extrae del quimo y que se mezcla con la sangre.

chylifaction, chylification [ˈkɪlɪfækʃən] [ki-li-fak-shon], *s.* Quilificación.

chylifactive [ˈkɪlɪfækti:v] [ki-li-fak-tiv], *a.* Quilificativo.

chylopoietic [ˈkɪləɔɪətɪk] [ki-lo-poi-e-tik], *a.* Quilopoyético, que tiene poder de hacer quilo.

chylous [ˈkɪləs] [ki-lous], *a.* Quiloso.

chyme [kiːm] [kim], *s.* Quimo, la masa de alimentos disgregados y reblandecidos por la digestión, de que se forma el quilo.

chymic [ˈkɪmɪk] [ki-mik], **Chymistry,** etc., *a. V.* CHEMIC, etc.

CIA *s.* (= **Central Intelligence Agency**) CIA

cibol [ˈsɪbəl] [si-bol], *s.* 1. Cebolleta, cebolla gala o puerro de piedra. 2. Chalota, especie de ajo.

ciborium [ˈsɪbərɪəm] [si-bo-rium], *s.* 1. Dosel de altar. 2. Copón, vaso que encierra el Santísimo Sacramento en el sagrario.

cicada [sɪˈkɑːdə] [si-ka-da], *s.* Cigarra, insecto hemíptero; llámase también *harvest-fly.*

cicatrice [ˈsɪkətri:z] [si-ka-tris], **cicatrix** [ˈsɪkətri:z] [si-ka-tris], *s.* Cicatriz.

cicatrisant [ˈsɪkətri:zənt] [si-ka-tri-sant], *s.* Cicatrizante.

cicatrisive [ˈsɪkətrɪzɪv] [si-ka-tri-siv], *a.* Cicatrizativo.

cicatrization [ˈsɪkətri:zeɪʃən] [si-ka-tri-sei-shon], *s.* Cicatrización.

cicatrize [ˈsɪkətraɪz] [si-ka-trais], *va.* Cicatrizar.

cicely [ˈsɪsəlɪ] [si-se-li], *s.* Perifollo, cerafollo, planta de las umbelíferas. **Sweet cicely,** perifollo, planta aromática.

cicerone [ˈsɪsərəʊn] [si-se-roun], *s.* Guía que enseña los monumentos, las instituciones y cosas dignas de verse en algún lugar. Se dice en plural *ciceroni,* y es voz moderna italiana.

cicuta [ˈsɪkuːtə] [si-ku-ta], *s.* Cicuta, hierba umbelífera cuya raíz es venenosa.

CID *s.* (in UK) = **Criminal Investigation Department**

cider [ˈsaɪdər] [sai-da'], *s.* Sidra (alcoholic); Sidra, bebida hecha del zumo de manzanas (non-alcoholic). **Sweet cider,** jugo o zumo de manzana. **Hard cider,** sidra fermentada.

ciderist [ˈsaɪdərɪst] [sai-de-rist], *s.* Fabricante o conocedor de sidra.

ciderkin [ˈsaɪdəkɪn] [sai-der-kin], *s.* Aguapié, la sidra que se saca de la manzana ya exprimida.

ci-devant [sɪˈdiːvənt] [si-di-vant], *a.* Del tiempo pasado; anterior, antecedente.

cigar [sɪˈgɑːr] [si-ga'], *s.* Cigarro, puro, tabaco. **Cigar store,** cigarrería, tabaquería, estanco de cigarros.

cigarette [ˌsɪgəˈret] [si-ga-ret], *s.* Cigarrillo, cigarro. **Cigarette case,** cigarrera. **Cigarette lighter,** encendedor automático. **Cigarette paper,** librillo. **Cigarette butt/end,** colilla. **Cigarette holder,** boquilla.

cilia [ˈsɪlɪə] [si-lia], *s.* Plural de CILIUM.

ciliary [ˈsɪlɪərɪ] [si-lia-ri], *a.* Ciliar, lo que pertenece o se refiere a las pestañas.

ciliate [ˈsɪlɪeɪt] [si-lieit], *a.* Ciliado, pestañoso, provisto de pelitos.

cilicious [ˈsɪlɪəs] [si-li-sios], *a.* Cerdoso.

cilium [ˈsɪlɪəm] [si-liom], *s.* (Más usado en plural) 1. Pelito, por lo común microscópico, semejante a una pestaña. 2. Pestaña; barbilla de las plantas.

cima [ˈsɪmə] [si-ma], *s. V.* CYMA.

cimbric [ˈsɪmbrɪk] [sim-brik], *s.* Címbrico, el lenguaje de los antiguos habitantes de Jutlandia.

cimeter [ˈsɪmɪtər] [si-mi-ta'], *s.* Cimitarra, arma de acero a manera de sable, de hoja ancha y corva.

cimmerian ['sɪmərɪən] [si-me-rian], *a.* Lo perteneciente a los cimerios, pueblos de Italia de los que relata Homero que vivían en obscuridad perpetua. **Cimmerian darkness,** obscuridad espantosa.

cinch [sɪntʃ] [sinch], *va.* (Fam. E.U.) Cinchar; apretar, forzar; asegurar (make sure of). -*s.* 1. Cincha (de cabalgadura). 2. (*Fam.*) Cosa segura, cosa hecha; ganga. (*Coloq.*) **It's a cinch,** es pan comido, es tirado, es una papa o un bollo, es botado. **It's a cinch that she will get the part,** (de) fijo que le dan el papel (certainty).

cinchona [sɪŋˈkɔʊnə] [sin-kou-na], *s.* Cinchona, nombre científico de la quina.

cincture ['sɪŋktʃər] [sink-chaᵣ], *va.* Ceñir, como con un cinto o ceñidor; cercar, rodear. -*s.* Cinto, ceñidor, cíngulo, cincho; cercado, cerca.

cinder ['sɪndər] [sin-daᵣ], *s.* 1. Carbón, cualquier cosa quemada al fuego, pero no reducida a cenizas. Carbonilla, carboncillo (ember). 2. Cernada o ceniza gruesa y caliente. **The dinner was burnt to a cinder,** la cena estaba carbonizada. **Cinders,** ceniza, rescoldo (ashes).

Cinderella [sɪndəˈrelə] [sin-de-re-la] *s.* (la) Cenicienta.

cinder track ['sɪndətræk] [sin-der-trak] *s.* Pista de ceniza.

cinecamera ['sɪnɪˈkæmərə] [si-ni-ka-me-ra] *s.* (GB) Filmadora, tomavistas; cámara cinematográfica (large, professional).

cinema ['sɪnəmə] [si-ne-ma], *s.* Cinema, cinematógrafo; cine (building). **What's on at the cinema?,** ¿qué echan en el cine? Cine (films). **French cinema,** el cine francés.

cinemagoer ['sɪnəməˌɡəʊər] [si-ne-ma-go-aᵣ] *s.* **He's a keen cinemagoer,** es muy aficionado al cine.

cineraceous ['sɪnərəsəs] [si-ne-ra-sous], *a.* Cinéreo, de ceniza o parecido a ella.

cineraria ['sɪnərərɪə] [si-ne-ra-ria], *s.* Cineraria.

cinerary ['sɪnərərɪ] [si-ne-ra-ri], *a.* Cinerario, relativo a las cenizas o que contiene cenizas.

cinereous ['sɪnərəs] [si-ne-rous], *a.* Ceniciento, cinéreo.

cineritious ['sɪnərɪʃəs] [si-ne-ri-shos], *a.* Cenizoso, cineríceo, de la naturaleza de las cenizas; de su color.

cinnabar ['sɪnəbər] [si-ne-baᵣ], *s.* Cinabrio o bermellón, sulfuro rojo de mercurio.

cinnamic ['sɪnəmɪk] [si-na-mik], *a.* De la canela, o derivado de canela.

cinnamon ['sɪnəmən] [si-na-mon], *s.* Canela, la corteza fragante de un árbol que se cría en la isla de Ceilán. **Cinnamon bag,** churla de canela. **Cinnamon stick,** trozo de canela en rama. Canela (color).

cinnamon-tree ['sɪnəmənˌtriː] [si-na-mon-trí], *s.* Árbol de la canela.

cinquefoil ['sɪŋkwəˈfɔɪl] [sin-cue-foil], *s.* 1. (*Arq.*) Pentalóbulo, adorno o ventana de cinco puntas. 2. (*Bot.*) Cincoenrama, planta del género Potentilla.

cion ['sɪən] [sion], *s.* V. SCION.

cipher ['saɪfər] [sai-far], *s.* 1. Cifra, carácter aritmético. 2. Cero, cifra aritmética que ni por sí, ni puesta antes de otro número, tiene valor alguno. 3. Cifra, código, carácter arbitrario y convenido con que se escriben dos personas en secreto. Clave (code). 4. Cifra, enlace de letras para expresar un nombre en abreviatura. 5. (*Mús.*) Prolongación indebida del sonido de un cañón de órgano, causada por el imperfecto funcionamiento de una válvula. **He is a mere cipher,** es un cero a la izquierda.

cipher, *va.* 1. Numerar, usar de cifras o números para contar o formar algún cómputo. 2. Sonar un cañón de órgano, sin que el organista toque la tecla correspondiente. -*va.* Cifrar, escribir en cifra.

circa ['sɜːkə] [ser-ka], *prep.* Alrededor de, hacia.

circensial ['sɜːˈsənsɪəl] [ser-sen-sial], **circensian** ['sɜːˈsənsɪən] [ser-sen-sian], *a.* Cirense, relativo a los juegos o espectáculos de los romanos en el circo.

circinate ['sɜːsɪneɪt] [ser-si-neit], *a.* (*Bot.*) Arrollado hacia dentro; se aplica a la vernación.

circle ['sɜːkl] [ser-kel], *s.* 1. Círculo (shape), circunferencia, curva planta, cerrada, cuyos puntos equidistan de otro interior llamado centro. **To come/go full circle,** volver al punto de partida. **The negotiations seem to be going around in circles,** las negociaciones están estancadas o en un impasse. **I was running around in circles trying to get everything ready,** estaba (dando vueltas) como loco tratando de tenerlo todo listo. 2. Círculo, área o superficie contenida dentro de la circunferencia. 3. Corro, corrillo, el cerco formado por un número de personas reunidas formando círculo (group). **Their circle of friends,** su círculo de amigos. **In business circles,** en el mundo de los negocios. 4. Reunión, asamblea, junta, congreso de muchos en un mismo lugar. 5. Circunlocución, circunloquio, rodeo, ambages. 6. Círculo, cinturón, circunloquio, rodeo, (around eye). 7. (GB) (*Teat.*) **Dress circle,** primer piso, platea alta. **Upper circle,** segundo piso.

circle, *va.* 1. Mover alguna cosa circularmente. 2. Circundar, rodear, cercar (be around); dar vueltas alrededor de (move around). **We circled the landing site,** sobrevolamos en círculo el lugar de aterrizaje. 3. Cercar, ceñir, abrazar todo alrededor. 4. Trazar un círculo alrededor de (draw circle around). -*vn.* Circular, dar vueltas como en círculo. Volar en círculos, circunvolar (aircraft, bird). **To circle around something,** dar vueltas alrededor de algo.

circled ['sɜːkld] [ser-klid], *a.* Redondo, en forma de círculo.

circlet ['sɜːklɪt] [ser-klit], *s.* 1. Círculo pequeño, anillo. 2. Disco; corona.

circling ['sɜːklɪŋ] [ser-klin], *a.* Circular, redondo.

circuit ['sɜːkɪt] [ser-kit], *s.* 1. Circuito, revolución, la vuelta que se da alrededor de alguna cosa. Recorrido, vuelta (passage around). **The athlete ran six circuits of the track,** el atleta dio seis vueltas a la pista. 2. Circuito, recinto, el espacio contenido dentro de un círculo. Autódromo, pista (motor racing track). 3. (*Elec. y Radio*) Circuito. **Circuit breaker,** (*Elec.*) cortacircuitos.

circuit, *vn.* Moverse circularmente. -*va.* Andar alrededor.

circuit board ['sɜːkɪtˌbɔːd] [ser-kit-bord] *s.* Placa base.

circuiteer ['sɜːkɪtɪər] [ser-ki-tiaᵣ], *s.* El juez que recorre un distrito para administrar justicia.

circuitous ['sɜːkjɔɪtəs] [ser-kui-tos], *a.* Tortuoso, rodeado, indirecto. Poco directo (route); que no conduce a nada (argument).

circuitously ['sɜːkjɔɪtəslə] [ser-kui-tos-li], *adv.* Tortuosamente.

circuit training ['sɜːkɪt'treɪnɪŋ] [ser-kit-trei-nin] *s.* Tabla de gimnasia.

circuitry ['sɜːkɔɪtrɪ] [ser-kui-tri] *s.* Sistema de circuitos.

circulable ['sɜːkjʊləbl] [ser-kiu-la-bol], *a.* Capaz de ser puesto en circulación.

circular ['sɜːkjʊlər] [ser-kiu-laᵣ], *a.* 1. Circular. redondo (round); de circunvalación (making a circuit/route). **A circular tour,** un circuito. 2. Circular, lo que siempre vuelve al punto donde empieza. 3. Viciado (argument). **Circular letter,** circular, carta, aviso, orden, etc., que se envía a muchas personas a un tiempo, dándoles conocimiento de alguna cosa. -*s.* Circular, carta o aviso circular.

circularity [sɜːkjʊˈlærɪtɪ] [ser-kiu-la-ri-ti], *s.* Forma o figura circular.

circularize ['sɜːkjʊləraɪz] [ser-kiu-la-rais], *va.* Hacer circular (algo).

circular saw ['sɜːkjʊlərˈsɔː] [ser-kiu-lar-so] *s.* Sierra circular.

circulate ['sɜːkjʊleɪt] [ser-kiu-leit], *va.* 1. Hacer circular, esparcir; diseminar; poner en circulación. 2. Cercar, circundar. -*vn.* 1. Circular, dar vueltas como en círculo, moverse alrededor. 2. Circular, pasar de mano en mano, propagarse, esparcirse. Hacer circular, divulgar (disseminate/report, news). 3. Pasar de un sitio a otro por curso indirecto, como el vapor por un sistema de tubos. **Circulating decimal,** fracción continua o periódica.

Circulating medium, moneda corriente. **Circulating library,** librería circulante, esto es, librería en donde depositando el precio del libro, y por un pequeño interés, se prestan los libros por tiempo determinado.

circulation ['sɜːkjʊleɪʃən] [ser-kiu-lei-shon], s. 1. Circulación. 2. Mudanza recíproca de sentido. 3. Circulación de moneda. **To be in/out of circulation,** estar en/fuera de circulación.

circulatory ['sɜːkjʊlətərɪ] [ser-kiu-la-to-ri], a. Circular, circulante.

circum, Prefijo latino que significa alrededor.

circumambiency ['sɜːkəmæmˌbɪənsɪ] [ser-kum-am-bien-si], s. Circumambiencia.

circumambient ['sɜːkəmæmbɪənt] [ser-kum-am-bient], vn. Circumambular, pasear o andar alrededor.

circumcise ['sɜːkəmsaɪz] [ser-kum-sais], va. Circuncidar.

circumciser ['sɜːkəmsɪsər] [ser-kum-si-sar], s. Circuncidador.

circumcision [ˌsɜːkəm'sazən] [ser-kum-si-son], s. 1. Circuncisión. 2. Purificación espiritual. 3. Los judíos, como pueblo circuncidado.

circumduct ['sɜːkəmdʌkt] [ser-kum-dakt], va. 1. Circunducir. 2. Contravenir; anular, revocar, abrogar.

circumduction ['sɜːkəmdʌkʃən] [ser-kum-dak-shon], s. 1. Anulación, abolición. 2. Circunducción.

circumference [səˈkəmfərəns] [ser-kum-fe-rens], s. Circunferencia, periferia; perímetro, cerco, circuito.

circumferential [səkəmfəˈrənʃəl] [ser-kum-fe-ren-shal], a. Circunferencial

circumferentor ['sɜːkəmfərəntər] [ser-kum-fe-ren-tor], s. 1. Grafómetro, instrumento para medir tierras. 2. Plancheta, instrumento para levantar planos.

circumflex ['sɜːkəmfleks] [ser-kum-fleks], s. Acento circunflejo. -a. 1. (Gram.) Pronunciado o marcado con el acento llamado circunflejo. 2. (Anat.) Circunflejo, encorvado en forma curvilínea, arqueado; como algunos vasos y nervios.

circumflexion ['sɜːkəmflekʃən] [ser-kum-flek-shon], s. Encorvamiento, encorvadura, acción de encorvar, de dar a un objeto forma o dirección curvilínea.

circumfluence ['sɜːkəmflʊəns] [ser-kum-fluens], s. Acción de correr las aguas en torno de algo, rodeándolo.

circumfluent ['sɜːkəmflʊənt] [ser-kum-fluent], a. Circunfluente.

circumfluous ['sɜːkəmfləs] [ser-kum-flos], a. Lo que rodea o circunda con agua.

circumfuse ['sɜːkəmfjuːz] [ser-kum-fius], va. Verter o derramar alrededor.

circumfusile ['sɜːkəmfjʊsɪl] [ser-kum-fiu-sil], a. Lo que puede vaciarse o verterse alrededor.

circumfusion ['sɜːkəmfjʊʃən] [ser-kum-fiu-shon], s. El acto de esparcir alguna cosa en torno de otra.

circumgyrate ['sɜːkəmgɪreɪt] [ser-kum-gui-reit], va. Girar, dar vueltas alrededor.

circumgyration ['sɜːkəmgɪreɪʃən] [ser-kum-gui-rei-shon], s. Giro o vuelta alrededor.

circumjacent ['sɜːkəmjʊsənt] [ser-kum-ya-sent], a. Lo que está en torno de alguna cosa.

circumlittoral ['sɜːkəmlɪtərəl] [ser-kum-li-to-ral], a. Circunlitoral, adyacente a la costa.

circumlocution [ˌsɜːkəmləˈkjuːʃən] [ser-kum-lo-kiu-shon], s. Circunlocución, circunloquio, rodeo de palabras, perífrasis.

circumlocutory [ˌsɜːkəmləˈkjuːtərɪ] [ser-kum-lo-kiu-to-ri], a. Circunlocutorio.

circummure ['sɜːkəmmɪʊər] [ser-kum-miua'], va. Rodear de murallas.

circumnavigable [ˌsɜːkəmˈnævɪgəbl] [ser-kum-na-vi-ga-bol], a. Navegable alrededor.

circumnavigate [ˌsɜːkəmˈnævɪgeɪt] [ser-kum-na-vi-gueit] va. Circunnavegar.

circumnavigation [ˌsɜːkəmˈnævɪgeɪʃən] [ser-kum-na-vi-guei-shon], s. Navegación alrededor.

circumnavigator [ˌsɜːkəmˈnævɪgeɪtər] [ser-kum-na-vi-guei-to'], s. El que navega alrededor.

circumoral ['sɜːkəmərəl] [ser-kum-mo-ral], a. Que rodea o circunda la boca.

circumpolar ['sɜːkəmpʊlər] [ser-kum-po-la'], a. Circumpolar, alrededor del polo.

circumposition ['sɜːkəmpɒsɪʃən] [ser-kum-po-si-shon], s. Colocación circular de alguna cosa.

circumrenal ['sɜːkəmriːnl] [ser-kum-ri-nal], a. Que rodea o circunda los riñones.

circumrotation ['sɜːkəmrɒˈteɪʃən] [ser-kum-ro-tei-shon], s. Rotación; circunvolución.

circumrotatory ['sɜːkəmˈrɒtətərɪ] [ser-kum-ro-ta-to-ri], a. Giratorio, lo que se mueve en rotación.

circumscissile ['sɜːkəmsɪsɪl] [ser-kum-si-sil], a. (Bot.) Dehiscente, separable a manera de cápsula.

circumscribe ['sɜːkəmskraɪb] [ser-kum-skraib], va. Circunscribir. Limitar, restringir.

cirumscription ['sɜːkəmskrɪpʃən] [ser-kum-skrip-shon], s. 1. Circunscripción. 2. Limitación. 3. Inscripción circular.

circumscriptive ['sɜːkəmskrɪptɪv] [ser-kums-krip-tiv], a. Circunscriptivo.

circumspect ['sɜːkəmspekt] [ser-kums-pekt], a. Circunspecto, prudente, cauto, mirado, reservado, discreto, recatado, contenido.

circumspection ['sɜːkəmspekʃən] [ser-kum-spek-shon], s. Circunspección, miramiento, prudencia, reserva, comedimiento, recato, moderación.

circumspective ['sɜːkəmspektɪv] [ser-kum-spek-tiv], a. Circunspecto, mirado.

circumspectively ['sɜːkəmspektɪvlɪ] [ser-kum-spek-tiv-li], **circumnspectly** ['sɜːkəmspektlɪ] [ser-kum-spek-tli], adv. Circunspectamente, con cautela y vigilancia.

circumspectness ['sɜːkəmspektnɪs] [ser-kum-spekt-nes], s. Cautela, vigilancia, recato.

circumstance ['sɜːkəmstəns] [ser-kum-stans], s. 1. Accidente, cosa adventicia, incidente, acontecimiento; lo que sucede o existe incidentalmente. 2. Circunstancia, incidente, estado o condición en que se halla alguna cosa (condition, fact). **Circumstances beyond our control,** circunstancias ajenas a nuestra voluntad. **In/under no circumstances,** dadas las circunstancias. **In/under no circumstances,** bajo ningún concepto, bajo ninguna circunstancia. 3. Circunstancia; tomado absolutamente en plural es el estado o condición de los negocios públicos (financial position). **A person in my circumstances,** una persona en mi situación o posición económica. **To be in easy circumstances,** estar acomodado, en buena posición.

circumstance, va. Colocar en buen o mal estado, en una posición cualquiera; se usa comúnmente en el participio pasado. **Circumstanced as we were, we could not escape,** en las circunstancias en que nos encontrábamos, era imposible escapar.

circumstantial ['sɜːkəmstənʃəl] [ser-kum-stan-shal], a. 1. Accidental, casual; accesorio. Circunstancial (evidence). 2. Circunstanciado, puesto con todas las circunstancias y menudencias precisas; particular.

circumstantiality ['sɜːkəmstənʃəlɪtɪ] [ser-kum-stan-sha-li-ti], s. 1. Circunstancialidad. 2. Detalles minuciosos.

circumstantially ['sɜːkəmstənʃəlɪ] [ser-kum-stan-sha-li] adv. Circunstanciadamente, con toda menudencia. 2. Eventualmente, según las circunstancias.

circumstantiate ['sɜːkəmstənʃeɪt] [ser-kum-stan-sieit], va. 1. Contar, referir o explicar una cosa con todas su circunstancias. 2. Notar o señalar las circunstancias de cualquier cosa, circunstanciar, detallar.

circumterraneous ['sɜːkəmtɪrənɪəs] [ser-kum-ti-ra-nious], a. Lo que está alrededor de la tierra.

circumvallate ['sɜːkəmvaleɪt] [ser-kum-va-leit], *va.* Circunvalar, rodear algún paraje con trincheras o fortificaciones.

circumvallation ['sɜːkəmvə'leɪʃən] [ser-kum-va-lei-shon], *s.* Circunvalación, cerco o línea de defensa o ataque de una plaza fuerte, campamento.

circumvent [ˌsɜːkəm'vent] [ser-kum-vent], *va.* Entrampar, enredar, engañar a alguno con artificio; burlar (law, rule); sortear, salvar (difficulty, obstacle).

circumvention [ˌsɜːkəm'venʃən] [ser-kum-ven-shon], *s.* Engaño, fraude, impostura, trampa, enredo, embrollo.

circumventive [ˌsɜːkəm'ventɪv] [ser-kum-ven-tiv], *a.* Engañoso, delusorio.

circumvolation [ˌsɜːkəmvə'leɪʃən] [ser-kum-vo-lei-shon], *s.* Vuelo alrededor.

circumvolution [ˈsɜːkəmvəljʊʃən] [ser-kum-vo-liu-shon], *s.* Circunvolución, la vuelta que en redondo hace una cosa.

circumvolve ['sɜːkəmvɔːv] [ser-kum-volv], *va.* Enrollar una cosa en torno de otra.

circus ['sɜːkəs] [ser-kus], *s.* 1. Circo, recinto circular destinado a los ejercicios de equitación y de gimnástica. 2. Circo, edificio que servía entre los romanos para carreras, juegos y otros espectáculos. 3. *(Teat.)* Circo.

cirrhosis [sɪ'rəʊsɪs] [si-rou-sis], *s. (Med.)* Cirrosis, lesión en las vísceras, especialmente en el hígado. **Cirrhosis of the liver,** cirrosis del hígado o hepática.

cirripeds, cirripedia [sɪ'rɪpeds] [si-ri-peds], *s. pl.* Cirrópodos, orden de crustáceos encerrados en envolturas calcáreas.

cirro-, forma de combinación. *V.* CIRRUS.

cirrus ['sɪrəs] [si-rus], *s.* 1. Cirrus: nombre dado a las nubes que presentan el aspecto de fibras extendidas como los hilos de una madeja. 2. *(Bot.)* Cirro, zarcillo, el apéndice en forma de espiral que tienen muchas plantas. 3. *(Anat.)* Apéndice parecido a un zarcillo o hilo que sirve como órgano del tacto. **Cirro-cumulus, cirro-stratus,** nubes que parecen ser mezclas de cirrus con cúmulos o estratus. El primero se llama vulgarmente cielo aborregado.

CIS *s.* (= **Commonwealth of Independent States**) CEI.

Cisalpine ['sɪsˌɑlpiːn] [sis-al-pin], *a.* Cisalpino.

cissy ['sɪsɪ] [si-si], *s.* (GB) *V.* SISSY.

cist [sɪst] [sist], *s. (Ant.)* 1. Cista, o canastillo de ofrendas. 2. Caja de metal para contener artículos de tocador.

cistercian [sɪs'tɜːʃən] [sis-ter-shan], *s.* Cisterciense, religioso de la orden de San Bernardo.

cistern ['sɪstɜːn] [sis-tern], *s.* 1. Cisterna, aljibe, receptáculo de agua (water tank); (GB) cisterna (of lavatory). 2. Arca de agua.

cistoscope ['sɪstəskɔːp] [sis-tos-koup], *s.* Cistoscopio.

cistus ['sɪstəs] [sis-tus], *s. (Bot.)* Cisto, jara, juagarzo, estepa, planta ramosa.

cit [sɪt] [sit], *s. (Fam.)* Ciudadano. *V.* CITIZEN.

citable ['sɪtəbl] [si-ta-bol], *a.* Citable, que se puede citar, o digno de ser citado.

citadel ['sɪtədl] [si-ta-del], *s.* Ciudadela.

citation [saɪ'teɪʃən] [sai-tei-shon], *s.* 1. Citación, comparendo, emplazamiento judicial, con señalamiento de tiempo y circunstancia. 2. Cita, la acción de alegar o citar alguna ley o autor. 3. Mención de alguna cosa (commendation); cita (quotation).

citatory ['saɪtətɔrɪ] [sai-ta-to-ri], *a.* Citatorio, que cita.

cite [saɪt] [sait], *va.* 1. Citar a juicio, llamar a alguno ante el juez. 2. Alegar alguna ley, autoridad, texto e ejemplo. 3. Citar, referirse, mencionar (quote).

citer ['saɪtər] [sai-ta'], *s.* Citador.

cithara ['sɪθərə] [si-za-ra], *s.* Cítara, especie de laúd.

citified ['sɪtɪfaɪd] [si-ti-faid], *a.* Con las maneras propias de la ciudad.

citizen ['sɪtɪzn] [si-tisen], *s.* 1. Ciudadano, el que goza de los derechos civiles. 2. Habitante o vecino de una ciudad. **Fellow-citizen,** conciudadano. **The citizens of Cuenca,** los habitantes o vecinos de Cuenca, los conquenses.

citizen's arrest ['sɪtɪzn.ərest] [si-tisen-a-rest] *s.* Detención llevada a cabo por un ciudadano común.

citizen's band ['sɪtɪznzbænd] [si-tisens-band] *s. (Rad.)* Banda ciudadana.

citizenship ['sɪtɪznʃɪp] [si-tisen-ship], *s.* Ciudadanía, naturalización. **Citizenship papers,** documentos de naturalización.

citrate ['sɪtreɪt] [si-treit], *s. (Quím.)* Citrato, sal formada del ácido cítrico unido a una base.

citric ['sɪtrɪk] [si-trik], *a. (Quím.)* Cítrico, derivado del limón o frutas semejantes. **Citric acid,** ácido cítrico.

citrine ['sɪtriːn] [si-trin], *a.* 1. Cetrino, color de limón. 2. Perteneciente al limón.

citron ['sɪtrən] [si-tron], *s.* Cidra, toronja, fruta semejante al limón.

citron-tree ['sɪtrən.triː] [si-tron-tri], *s.* Cidro, acitrón, toronjal, árbol que produce las cidras.

citron-water ['sɪtrən.wɔːtər] [si-tron-uo-ta'], *s.* Aguardiente destilado de cidras.

citrus ['sɪtrəs] [si-trus], *a. (Bot.)* Auranciáceo, cítrico. **Citrus fruits,** agrios, frutas agrias (como el limón, la toronja, la naranja, etc.)

city ['sɪtɪ] [si-ti], *s.* Ciudad. En Gran Bretaña tienen el nombre de *city* todas las poblaciones donde hay silla episcopal; en los Estados Unidos toda población que tiene ayuntamiento establecido por las leyes del respectivo estado. **City center,** centro de la ciudad. **City council,** ayuntamiento, municipio. **City planner,** urbanista. **City planning,** urbanismo. (in UK) **The City,** la City (de Londres), el centro financiero londinense. *-a.* Ciudadano.

city fathers ['sɪtɪ.fɑːðəz] [si-ti-fa-dars] *s.* Concejales y mandatarios municipales.

city hall ['sɪtɪ.hɔːl] [si-ti-jol], *s.* Palacio municipal, ayuntamiento, casa consistorial, municipio.

city planning ['sɪtɪ.plɑːnɪŋ] [si-ti-pla-nin], *s.* Urbanización, planificación.

citywide ['sɪtɪ.waɪd] [si-ti-uaid] *a.* Que abarca toda la ciudad (network).

civet ['sɪvɪt] [si-vit], *s.* 1. Civeta, gato de algalia. 2. Algalia, el perfume que despide de sí la civeta.

civic ['sɪvɪk] [si-vik], *a.* Cívico, lo que pertenece o se refiere a una ciudad, a un ciudadano o a la ciudadanía. Civil (authorities); de la ciudad (leader); cívico (duty, virtues). **Civic center,** edificios municipales.

civics ['sɪvɪks] [si-viks], *s.* Instrucción cívica.

civies ['sɪvɪz] [si-vis] *s. pl. V.* CIVVIES

civil ['sɪvɪl] [si-vil], *a.* 1. Civil, lo que pertenece al gobierno, vida o intereses de los ciudadanos de un estado (of society, citizens). **Civil unrest,** malestar social. 2. Civil, lo contrario a criminal en términos forenses, y lo que no es eclesiástico ni militar. **Civil death,** la privación de los derechos civiles a consecuencia de una sentencia o pena. 3. Civil, intestino, doméstico. 4. Civil, atento, urbano, cortés (polite), afable. **That's very civil of you,** es muy gentil de su parte. **Civil service,** los departamentos del servicio público que no son militares ni navales. **Civil law,** *V.* LAW. **Civil defense,** (GB) **defence,** defensa civil. **Civil disobedience,** desobediencia civil.

civil engineer ['sɪvlendʒɪ'nɪər] [si-vil-en-yi-nia'], *s.* Ingeniero civil o de caminos.

civilian [sɪ'vɪlɪən] [si-vi-lian], *s.* 1. El que no pertenece al ejército, la marina ni el clero. 2. Jurisperito, jurisconsulto, el que está versado en el derecho civil. *a.* Entre la población civil (casualties). *(Mil.)* **In civilian dress,** vestido de civil o de paisano.

civility [sɪ'vɪlɪtɪ] [si-vi-li-ti], *s.* Civilidad, urbanidad, cortesía, buena crianza, educación (courtesy); política, sociabilidad; decoro, afabilidad, atención. Cortesía, cumplido (act, utterance).

civilization [ˌsɪvɪlaɪ'zeɪʃən] [si-vi-lai-sei-shon], *s.* Civilización.

civilize ['sɪvɪlaɪz] [si-vi-lais], *va.* Civilizar, instruir; suavizar el lenguaje, la condición y las costumbres de alguno; hacer razonables, cultas y sociables a las personas o naciones; humanizar.

civilized ['sɪvɪlaɪzd] [si-vi-laisd], *pp.* y *a.* Civilizado, el que ya se ha acostumbrado al lenguaje, usos y modales de la gente culta; en estado de civilización (society). Educado (person). **Please call back at a more civilized hour,** por favor llame a una hora más decente.

civilizer ['sɪvɪlaɪzər] [si-vi-lai-ser], *s.* Civilizador, el o lo que civiliza.

civil liberties ['sɪvɪlˌlɪbətiːz] [si-vi-li-ber-tis] *s. pl.* Derechos civiles.

civil list ['sɪvɪlˌlɪst] [si-vil-list] *s.* **The civil list** (in UK), presupuesto anual asignado por el Parlamento a la familia real.

civilly ['sɪvɪlɪ] [si-vi-li], *adv.* Civilmente, cortésmente.

civil rights ['sɪvɪlˌraɪts] [si-vil-raits] *s. pl.* Derechos civiles.

civil servant ['sɪvɪlˌsɜːvənt] [si-vil-ser-vant] *s.* Funcionario (del Estado).

civil service ['sɪvɪlˌsɜːvɪs] [si-vil-ser-vis] *s.* **The civil service,** la administración pública; el funcionariado del Estado (employees).

civil war ['sɪvɪlwɑːr] [si-vil-uaʳ] *s.* Guerra civil. **The Civil War,** la guerra civil; (in US) la guerra de Secesión.

civism ['sɪvɪzm] [si-vism], *s.* 1. Civismo, patriotismo, devoción al interés público. 2. Ciudadanía.

civvies ['sɪvɪs] [si-vis] *s. pl. (Coloq.)* **In civvies,** de civil, de paisano.

cl (= centiliter(s), (GB) centilitre(s)) **cl.**

clabber, bonny-clabber ['klæbər] [kla-baʳ], *s.* Cuajo, leche cuajada. *-vn.* Cuajarse, como la leche.

clack [klæk] [klak], *s.* Cualquier cosa que hace un ruido o estrépito continuo e importuno.

clack, *vn.* 1. Cencerrear, hacer un ruido importuno; crujir, restallar; castañetear. Tabletear, taconear (high heels). 2. Charlar, picotear, hablar demasiado.

clad [klæd] [klad], *a.* Vestido, cubierto, aderezado. **Scantily clad,** ligero de ropa. **Clad in something,** vestido de algo. *(Arq.)* Past and past p. of CLOTHE.

-clad *suff.* Con ropa de cuero.

claim [kleɪm] [kleim], *va.* 1. Demandar, pedir en juicio, reclamar, reivindicar, pretender como cosa debida. Reclamar (assert title to/throne, inheritance, land); reivindicar (right). **To claim diplomatic immunity,** alegar inmunidad diplomática. Reclamar (lost property/ demand as being one's own). **The earthquake claimed many lives,** el terremoto se cobró muchas vidas. Solicitar (apply for/social security, benefits); cobrar (receive). **He's going to claim compensation,** va a exigir que se lo indemnice, va a reclamar una indemnización. **You can claim your expenses back,** pudes pedir que te reembolsen los gastos. 2. **No one has claimed responsibility for the attack,** nadie ha reivindicado el atentado (allege, profess). **No one can yet claim victory,** nadie puede cantar victoria todavía. **He claimed (that) he knew nothing about it,** aseguraba o afirmaba no saber nada de ello. **They claim to have found the cure,** dicen o aseguran haber encontrado la cura. **I can't claim to be an intellectual,** no pretendo ser un intelectual. 3. Reclamar (attention, interest). *-vn.* Presentar una reclamación. **To claim for something,** reclamar algo. **You can claim on the insurance,** puedes reclamar al seguro.

claim, *s.* 1. Pretensión, título, derecho, reclamación, reivindicación (to right, title). **Claim to something,** derecho a algo. **That's her only claim to fame,** eso es lo único por lo que se destaca. **To lay claim to something,** reivindicar algo. **Wage/pay claim,** reivindicación salarial, demanda de aumento salarial (demand). **Insurance claim,** reclamación al seguro. **To put in a claim for expenses,** presentar una solicitud de reembolso de gastos. **She makes enormous claims on my time,** me quita muchísimo tiempo. 2. Demanda, la acción o propuesta que se hace a un juez para que ponga al demandante en posesión de lo que otro tiene.

claimable ['kleɪməbl] [klei-ma-bol.], *a.* Lo que se puede demandar o pedir en justicia como debido.

claimant ['kleɪmənt] [klei-mant], **claimer** [kleimaʳ], *s.* Demandante, el que demanda o pide. Solicitante (Soc. Adm.); pretendiente (to throne).

clairvoyance [klɛə'vɔɪəns] [klea-voians], *s.* Lucidez, facultad atribuida a las personas magnetizadas de ver los objetos distantes u ocultos.

clairvoyant [klɛə'vɔɪənt] [klea-voiant], *a.* Lúcido, en estado de lucidez magnética, vidente; clarividente.

clam [klæm] [kl{m], *s.* Marisco, almeja, molusco de dos conchas, muy estimado como alimento. *(Coloq.)* **To shut up like a clam,** quedarse como una tumba.

clam, *va. (Prov.)* Empastar, pegar con alguna cosa viscosa o glutinosa. *-vn.* 1. Mojarse; hambrear. 2. Excavar para sacar de la playa los moluscos llamados *clams* 3. Repicar, echar las campanas a vuelo.

clam up *(Coloq.)* Ponerse muy poco comunicativo.

clamant ['klæmənt] [kla-mant], *a.* 1. Clamante, que da voces lastimosas pidiendo auxilio. 2. *(Poét.)* Clamoroso; resonante.

clambake ['klæmbeɪk] [klam-beik] *s.* (in US) Picnic en la playa en el que se cuecen almejas.

clamber ['klæmbər] [klam-baʳ], *vn.* Gatear, trepar, encaramarse. **They clambed over the wall,** treparon o se encaramaron al muro y saltaron.

clamminess ['klæmɪnɪs] [kla-mi-nes], *s.* Viscosidad, materia viscosa.

clammy ['klæmɪ] [kla-mi], *a.* Viscoso, pegajoso. Húmedo (handshake); bochornoso, pegajoso (weather). *-s.* 1. Clamor, grito, vociferación. 2. Clamoreo. 3. Algarabía, alboroto.

clamor, (GB) **clamour** *vn.* Gritar. **To claim for justice,** clamar por justicia.

clamorous ['klæmərəs] [kla-mo-ros], *a.* Clamoroso, ruidoso, tumultuoso, estrepitoso.

clamorously ['klæmərəslɪ] [kla-mo-rous-li], *adv.* Clamorosamente; ruidosamente.

clamp [klæmp] [klamp], *s.* 1. Torno de mano, tornillo. Tornillo de banco (in carpentry). 2. Abrazadera (const); cuchillero. 3. *(Med.)* Pinza hemostática, clamp. (GB) **Wheel clamp,** cepo.

clamp, *va.* 1. Sujetar con abrazadera (join, fasten). 2. Asegurar con el torno de mano. 3. Imponer. **To clamp down on,** apretar los tornillos a; cohibir, refrenar, reprimir. (GB) *(Coloq. Auto)* **To clamp a car,** ponerle el cepo a un coche.

clampdown ['klæmpdaʊn] [klamp-daun], *s.* Cohibición, refrenamiento, represión. *(Coloq.)* **A clampdown on illegal immigrants,** medidas drásticas contra los inmigrantes ilegales. **There's been a clampdown on loans,** se ha restringido severamente la concesión de créditos.

clan [klæn] [klan], *s.* 1. Clan. Familia, tribu, casta o raza de muchas personas enlazadas por sangre o parentesco. 2. Secta, grupo.

clandestine [klæn'destɪn] [klan-des-tin], *a.* Clandestino, secreto, oculto.

clandestinely [klæn'destɪnlɪ] [klan-des-tin-li], *adv.* Clandestinamente.

clandestineness [klæn'destɪnnɪs] [klan-des-tin-nes], *s.* Secreto, estado oculto.

clang [klæŋ] [klang], *s.* 1. Rechino, sonido desapacible resultante del choque de una cosa con otra. Sonido metálico fuerte. 2. Ruido de armas, de cadenas, etc. 3. V. CLANGTINT.

clang, *vn.* Rechinar, hacer o causar un sonido agudo y retumbante; sonar, repicar (bells). **The gate clanged shut,** la verja se cerró con gran estruendo. *-va.* Hacer resonar, tocar.

clanger ['klæŋər] [klan-guaʳ] *s.* (GB) *(Coloq.)* Metedura de pata. **To drop a clanger,** meter la pata.

clangor, clangour [ˈklæŋər] [klan-gaʳ], *s.* Ruido estridente, agudo, penetrante; ruido de armas, cadenas o campanas; clamor.

clang-tint [klæŋtɪnt] [klang-tint], *s.* Calidad de sonido; timbre: color acústico.

clank [klæŋk] [klank] *s.* Rechinamiento, ruido estridente, poco musical, pero no retumbante como el *clang;* producido por el choque de metales entre sí.

clank, *vn.* Rechinar, producir un ruido agudo y penetrante. - *va.* Hacer rechinar, hacer sonar.

clannish [ˈklænɪʃ] [kla-nish], *a.* Del *clan* o tribu o semejante a él; estrechamente unido.

clansman [ˈklænzmən] [klans-man], *s.* Miembro de un *clan.*

clap [klæp] [klap], *va.* 1. Batir, golpear una cosa contra otra. 2 Pegar, encajar, encasquetar una cosa a otra; juntar, aplicar. 3. Palmear, palmotear, vitorear. **She clapped her hands together,** batió palmas o dio una palmada de alegría o de satisfacción. **To clap up,** concluir una cosa instantáneamente. **To clap up a peace,** hacer una paz simulada. **To clap up together,** empaquetar. **To clap in prison,** encarcelar. **To clap up a bargain,** rematar un trato o ajuste. **To clap in,** empujar, hacer entrar por fuerza. -*vn.* 1. Cerrarse ruidosamente. 2. Arrojarse con violencia o impetuosidad en. 3. Aplaudir, dar palmadas. **He clapped me on the back,** me dio una palmada en la espalda (slap). **To clap on all the sails,** cargar todas las velas. **To clap the door to,** cerrar la puerta con violencia. **To clap spurs to one's horse,** poner espuelas al caballo. **He clapped his hand over my eyes,** me tapó los ojos con la mano (put, place).

clap, *s.* 1. Estrépito, ruido o golpe causado por el encuentro repentino de dos cuerpos. 2. Trueno, el estruendo o ruido que causa la exhalación eléctrica al dividir el aire. 3. Palmoteo, palmada, el acto de palmotear, aplauso. **To give somebody a clap,** aplaudir a alguien (applaud). 4. *(Vul.)* gonorrea o purgaciones. **Clap of thunder,** trueno, rayo.

clapboard [ˈklæpbɔːd] [klap-bord], *s.* Tabla de chilla, comúnmente más gruesa en su borde inferior que en el superior.

clapped-out [ˌklæptˈaut] [klapt-aut] *a.* (GB) *(Coloq.)* Destartalado (machine). **A clapped-out car,** un cacharro, una carcacha, una tartana. **To be/feel clapped-out,** estar reventado o hecho polvo.

clapper [ˈklæpər] [kla-paʳ], *s.* 1. Palmoteador, el que palmea o palmotea. 2. Badajo de campana. 3. Taravilla o cítola de molino. 4. Aldaba de una puerta. 5. *(Mar.)* Chapaleta de la bomba. 6. *(Mar.)* Chapaletas de los imbornales. (GB) *(Coloq.)* **It was going like the clappers,** iba como una bala o como un bólido.

clapperboard [ˈklæpəbɔːd] [kla-per-bord] *s.* Claqueta.

clapper-claw [klæpəˈklɔː] [kla-per-klo], *va. (Vul.)* 1. Golpear (con la mano), rascar y desgarrar; atacar con el pico y las uñas. 2. Regañar; maltratar de palabra.

clapping [ˈklæpɪŋ] [kla-pin], *s.* Aleteo; palmoteo, palmada, aplauso.

clap-trap [klæpˈtræp] [klap-trap], *a.* Engañador, que causa sensación, pero sin mérito verdadero. -*s.* Recurso, lenguaje, conducta encaminados a evocar aplauso; artificio indigno. *(Coloq.)* Paparruchas.

claque [klæk] [klak], *s. (Teat.)* Claque, aplaudidores pagados.

clarabella [ˈklærəbelə] [kla-ra-be-la], *s.* Clarabela, registro melodioso del órgano; se hace de madera.

clarence [ˈklærəns] [kla-rens], *s.* Cupé, clarence, carruaje de cuatro ruedas, provisto comúnmente de un frente de vidrio.

clarendon [ˈklærəndən] [kla-ren-don], *s.* Carácter de tipo algo grueso y compacto. La voz CLARENDON a la cabeza de este título está impresa en dicha letra, negrita.

clare-obscure [klærəbsˈkjuər] [kla-robs-kiuaʳ], *s.* Claroscuro.

claret [ˈklærət] [kla-ret], *s.* Clarete, vino tinto o rojo; vino tinto de Burdeos. Granate (color).

clarification [ˌklærɪfɪˈkeɪʃən] [kla-ri-fi-kei-shon], *s.* Clarificación. Aclaración (explanation).

clarify [ˈklærɪfaɪ] [kla-ri-fai], *va.* 1. Clarificar, aclarar, poner claro lo que está turbio (purify/fat, wine). Aclarar (explain, make clear). 2. Ilustrar, dar lustre o esplendor a alguna cosa.

clarinet [ˌklærɪˈnet] [kla-ri-net], *s.* Clarinete, instrumento músico de viento.

clarinettist [ˌklærɪˈnetɪst] [kla-ri-ne-tist], *s.* Clarinetista, el que toca el clarinete.

clarion [ˈklærɪən] [kla-rion], *s.* Clarín, instrumento de música, especie de trompeta de agudo sonido.

clarionet [ˈklærɪənɪt] [kla-rio-net], *s.* V. CLARINET.

clarity [ˈklærɪtɪ] [kla-ri-ti], *s.* Claridad, resplandor, luz. Claridad (of thought, expression).

clary [ˈklærɪ] [kla-ri], *s. (Bot.)* Salvia silvestre.

clash [klæʃ] [klash], *vn.* 1. Chocar, entrechocarse, tropezar o encontrarse con violencia. 2. Encontrarse; contradecir, oponerse. Estar en conflicto o en pugna (aims, interests); chocar (personalities); desentonar (colors, patterns). 3. Chocar (armies, factions, leaders). **To clash with somebody over something,** chocar con alguien acerca de algo. **Police clashed with demonstrators,** hubo choques entre la policía y los manifestantes. 4. Coincidir (dates). **The concert clashes with the film tonight,** el concierto y la película de esta noche son a la misma hora. 5. Sonar al entrechocar (make noise/cymbals, swords); chocar (collide). -*va.* Batir, golpear una cosa contra otra, entrechocar (weapons); tocar (cymbals).

clash, *s.* 1. Choque, fragor, crujido colisión de una cosa contra otra con ruido o estrépito. 2. Oposición, contradicción; disputa, debate, choque (of cultures, personality); conflicto (of interests); disparidad (of opinions, views). **I missed the lecture because of a timetable clash,** me perdí la conferencia porque tenía otra cosa a la misma hora o por un problema de coincidencia de horarios. 2. Enfrentamiento, choque (between armies, factions). 3. **The clash of swords,** el sonido de choque de espadas. **The clash of the cymbals,** el sonido de los platillos (noise).

clashing [ˈklæʃɪŋ] [kla-shin], *s.* Oposición, contradicción, enemistad, contienda; choque, ruido.

clashingly [ˈklæʃɪŋlɪ] [kla-shin-li], *adv.* En oposición en contradicción.

clasp [klɑːsp] [klasp], *s.* 1. Broche, cierre (fastening); chapeta, botoncito, especie de corchete que sirve para abrochar y asegurar alguna cosa; hebilla. 2. Abrazo.

clasp, *va.* 1. Abrochar, cerrar o unir con broche o corchete. 2. Abrazar, coger alguna cosa entre los brazos (grip, embrace). **She clasped her bag firmly,** sujetó o agarró firmemente el bolso. **They clasped hands,** se dieron un fuerte apretón de manos. **He clasped her in his arms,** la estrechó entre sus brazos. 3. Cercar, incluir.

clasp-knife [klɑːspnaɪf] [klasp-naif], *s.* Navaja, especie de cuchillo que se dobla entrando el corte en el mango.

class [klɑːs] [klas], *s.* 1. Clase, orden o número de personas del mismo grado, calidad y oficio (social stratum). **The class struggle,** la lucha de clases. 2. Rango, categoría; *(Coloq.)* Clase, estilo (style). 2. Clase en las escuelas (lesson); conjunto de personas que se han graduado juntas en un colegio o universidad, o que esperan graduarse a la vez; cada clase toma el nombre del año de su graduación, y así se dice, por ejemplo, la clase de 1998 (group of students). **The class of '98,** la promoción del 98. 4. Orden de cosas pertenecientes a una misma especie (group, type). **To be in a class of one's/its own,** ser único o inigualable. **They're not in the same class as their opponents,** no están a la altura de sus contrincantes. 5. *(Biol.)* Clase, subdivisión intermedia entre reino y género. 6. *(Transp.)* Clase; (in UK) *(Post.)* **Send the letter first/second class,** mandar la carta por correo preferente/normal; *(Educ.)* Tipo de título que se concede según las calificaciones obtenidas durante la carrera y/o exámenes finales. **He got a first class degree,** se recibió con la nota más alta, sacó matrícula de honor en la carrera. **The**

working class, la clase trabajadora, los artesanos, operarios, etc. **The upper class,** la clase alta, la clase elevada. **Class-room,** sala de enseñanza, local de una clase.

class, va. Clasificar, coordinar, ordenar, distribuir, catalogar.

class-conscious [ˈklaːsˈkɒnʃəs] [klas-kon-shous] *a. (Pol., Soc.)* Con conciencia de clase; clasista, consciente de las condiciones sociales (classist).

classic [ˈklæsɪk] [kla-sik] *a.* Clásico; memorable (scene, line). *s.* Autor clásico. Clásico (play, film, book). *V.* CLASSICS. Prenda clásica (clothing).

classical [ˈklæsɪkəl] [kla-si-kal], *a.* 1. Clásico (of Greece, Rome), relativo a los antiguos autores griegos y latinos de primer orden, y a los de primer rango entre los modernos. **A classical scholar,** un humanista especializado en lenguas clásicas. 2. Clásico, de primera clase, en la literatura o arte. 3. Compuesto por los grandes maestros de música. Clásico (traditional). **Classical music,** música clásica.

classically [ˈklæsɪkəlɪ] [kla-si-ka-li], *adv.* Clásicamente.

classicism [ˈklæsɪsɪzəm] [kla-si-sisem], *s.* 1. Clasicismo, estilo o idiotismo clásico. 2. Erudición clásica.

classicist [ˈklæsɪsɪst] [kla-si-sist], *s.* Clásico, el partidario de las obras de la antigüedad; el que sigue las doctrinas del clasicismo.

classics [ˈklæsɪks] [kla-siks] *s.* Clásicas.

classification [ˌklæsɪfɪˈkeɪʃən] [kla-si-fi-kei-shon], *s.* Clasificación; coordinación o distribución de algunas cosas en clases.

classified [ˈklæsɪfaɪd] [kla-si-faid] *a.* 1. Clasificado (categorized). **Classified advertising,** anuncios por palabras, avisos clasificados. 2. Secreto, confidencial (secret/information).

classify [ˈklæsɪfaɪ] [kla-si-fai], *va.* Clasificar, coordinar o distribuir algunas cosas en clases (categorize/books, data).

classis [ˈklaːsɪs] [kla-sis], *s.* 1. Consejo o tribunal en algunas iglesias reformadas. 2. Clase biológica.

classist [ˈklaːsɪst] [kla-sist] *a.* Clasista.

classless [ˈklaːslɪs] [klas-les] *a.* Sin clases (society).

classmate [ˈklaːsmeɪt] [klas-meit], *s.* Condiscípulo, compañero de clase.

classroom [ˈklaːsrʊm] [klas-rum], *s.* Sala de clase, aula.

classy [ˈklaːsɪ] [kla-si] *a. (Coloq.)* Con estilo o clase.

clastic [ˈklaːstɪk] [klas-tik], *a.* 1. Que se rompe en partes. 2. Compuesto de fragmentos.

clatter [ˈklætər] [kla-taʳ], *vn.* 1. Resonar, hacer sonido o ruido (pans); chacolotear, hacer sonido (hooves); repiquetear (typewriter). 2. Charlar, picotear; disputar. *-va.* 1. Golpear alguna cosa haciéndola retumbar; hacer ruido con (pans, cutlery). 2. Gritar, vocear, reñir.

clatter, *s.* 1. Ruido, estruendo, fracaso. 2. Gresca, trapisonda, alboroto, bulla y confusión. 3. Traqueteo (of trains); repiqueteo (of typewriters); chacoloteo (of hooves).

clatterer [ˈklætərər] [kla-te-raʳ], *s.* El que hace ruido; soplón.

claudicate [ˈklɔːdɪkeɪt] [klo-di-keit], *vn.* Claudicar, cojear, ser o estar defectuoso.

clause [klɔːz] [klos], *s.* 1. Cláusula, punto, miembro de un período. 2. Artículo, estipulación particular de un contrato. 3. Condición. 4. *(Ling.)* Oración, cláusula.

claustral [ˈklɔːstrəl] [klos-tral], *a.* Claustral.

claustrophobia [ˌklɔːstrəˈfəʊbɪə] [klos-tro-fou-bia] *s.* Claustrofobia.

claustrophobic [ˌklɔːstrəˈfəʊbɪk] [klos-tro-fo-bik] *a.* Claustrofóbico.

clausure [ˈklɔːʒər] [klo-shaʳ], *s.* 1. Clausura, encierro. 2. Broche para libro.

clavate [ˈkæveɪt] [kla-veit], **clavated** [kla-vei-tid], *a.* 1. Clavado, en forma de maza o clava. 2. Claveteado.

clavichord [ˈklævɪkɔːd] [kla-vi-kord], *s.* Clavicordio, instrumento músico de cuerda que precedió al piano.

clavicle [ˈklævɪkl] [kla-vi-kol], *s.* Clavícula, hueso que está sobre el pecho más abajo del cuello.

clavicular [ˈklævɪkjələr] [ka-vi-kiu-laʳ], *a.* Clavicular, de las clavículas.

clavier [ˈklæviər] [kla-viaʳ], *s.* 1. *(Mús.)* Teclado (del órgano). 2. Instrumento con teclado, particularmente el clavicordio o el piano de mesa u horizontal.

claw [klɔː] [klo], *s.* 1. Garra; garfa. Zarpa, garra (of tiger, lion); garra (of eagle); pinza (of crab, lobster). *(Coloq.)* **He won't stand a chance if she gets her claws into him,** es hombre muerto si cae en sus garras. 2. Garra, la mano del hombre; en este sentido es voz despectiva. 3. *(Mar.)* Uñas de espeque o pie de cabra. 4. *(Bot.)* Uña de un pétalo. **Claw-bar,** palanca de uña. **Claw-hammer,** martillo de orejas. **Claw-hammer coat,** frac, casaca de cola de bacalao; llámase así por su forma. **Claw for tacks,** arrancador de puntillas.

claw, *va.* 1. Desgarrar. 2. Arañar, rasgar, despedazar. **The cat had clawed the rug to shreds,** el gato había destrozado la alfombra con las uñas. 3. Reñir, regañar. 4. *(Des.)* Lisonjear. 5. **To claw off,** *(Mar.)* desempeñarse de una costa; por extensión, escapar. **To claw it off,** hacer una cosa con diligencia. **They clawed their way through the rubble,** se abrieron camino como pudieron entre los escombros. **He clawed his way to the top,** no reparó en medios para llegar a la cima. *-vn.* Arañar. **To claw at something,** arañar algo.

claw back (esp. GB) Recuperar (money, revenue).

clawed [klɔːd] [klod], *a.* Armado de garras o zarpas.

clay [kleɪ] [klei], *s.* Arcilla, tierra crasa y pegajosa. Plastilina, plasticina (for children). **Potter's clay,** marga, barro de olleros o alfareros. **Clay-stone,** concreción de diversas formas que se halla en la arcilla aluvial. **Clay-ground,** tierra arcillosa. **Clay-marl,** marga, tierra gredosa. **Clay-pit,** barrizal, el paraje de donde se saca barro, tierra o arcilla. *(Sport)* **Clay court,** cancha de arcilla, pista de tierra batida. **Clay pipe,** pipa de cerámica o barro. *-a.* **Clay-cold,** frío, sin vida.

clay, *va.* Cubrir alguna cosa con arcilla; abonar las tierras con arcilla.

clayey [ˈkleɪɪ] [kleiyi], **clayish** [ˈkleɪɪʃ] [klei-yish], *a.* Arcilloso, lleno de arcilla o barro.

claymore [ˈkleɪmɔːr] [klei-moʳ], *s.* Espada de dos filos, larga y ancha, de los antiguos escoceses.

clay pigeon [ˈkleɪˈpɪdʒən] [klei-pichon] *s.* Plato (de tiro). **Clay pigeon shooting,** tiro al plato.

cleading [ˈkliːdɪŋ] [kli-din], *s. (Art. y Of.)* Cubierta o envoltura exterior de tablas, forro de fieltro, u otro material para dar mayor resistencia e impermeabilidad. Se aplica a la presa de un molino, a una caldera de vapor, al pozo o galería de un ascensor, etc.

clean [kliːn] [klin], *a.* 1. Limpio, claro, exento de suciedad (not soiled). **Are your hands clean?,** ¿tienes las manos limpias? **She wiped the table clean,** limpió la mesa. 2. Limpio, casto, inocente (morally/joke). **Keep it clean,** no te pases. Limpio (fair/game, player). 3. Curioso, aseado; desembarazado, despejado, claro, distinto. 4. Entero. Limpio (not used/clothes, towel). **Use a clean sheet of paper,** usa una hoja de papel nueva. Limpio, puro (pure, non-polluting/ air, water). A limpio (smell); refrescante (taste). 5. Diestro; donde no constan infracciones (unblemished/driver's license). *(Coloq.)* **To come clean about something,** confesar algo. 6. Bien proporcionado, que tiene simetría. Bien definido, nítido (well defined/stroke, features). **A clean break,** una fractura limpia. **She made a clean break with the past,** cortó radicalmente con el pasado. *-adv.* Enteramente, perfectamente, completamente. **I clean forgot about it,** se me olvidó por completo. **They got clean away,** se escaparon sin dejar ni rastro. Limpio, limpiamente (fairly/fight, play). **To make clean,** limpiar. **To make a clean breast,** hacer una confesión plena y sin reservas; aliviar el ánimo. **Clean up,** (a) aseo general; (b) la acción de recoger el oro después de lavado y triturado; y el oro así recogido. **To show a clean pair of heels,** escapar huyendo, dejar atrás en fuga.

clean, *va.* Limpiar (remove dirt from); asear, desembarazar de toda suciedad o materia extraña; **To clean one's teeth,** lavarse los dientes. **She cleaned the splashes off the windows,** limpió las salpicaduras que había en las ventanas. Desenlodar; lavar (la vajilla, etc.); borrar, limpiar (blackboard); desengrasar las telas; depurar (el oro). Limpiar en seco, llevar a la tintorería (dry-clean). Limpiar (fish, chicken). -*vn.* Limpiar (remove dirt/substance, device).

clean out 1. Vaciar y limpiar a fondo (clean thoroughly). 2. *(Coloq.)* Dejar pelado (leave with no money); desplumar (steal everything from).

clean up 1. Limpiar (make clean/room, garden). **I'll just clean myself up a bit,** voy a arreglarme o lavarme un poco. Limpiar (morally). 2. Limpiar (make clean). **I'm tired of cleaning up after you,** estoy harto de limpiar lo que tú ensucias.

clean, *s. (Coloq.)* Limpieza. **Just give it a quick clean,** dale una repasadita.

clean-cut [kli:n'kʌt] [klin-kat], *a.* 1. Cortado con claridad. 2. Bien definido, nítido. **Clean-cut person,** persona de aspecto nítido y agradable (appearance).

cleaner [kli:n] [klin]kli:nər] [kli-naʳ], *s.* Limpiador, el que limpia (person); producto de limpieza (substance); tintorero (dry cleaner). **Take it to the cleaner's/cleaners,** llévalo a la tintorería. *(Coloq.)* **To take somebody to the cleaner's/ cleaners,** dejar limpio o pelado a alguien.

cleaning [ˈkli:nɪŋ] [kli-nin], *s.* Limpieza, aseo. **Dry-cleaning,** tintorería, lavado en seco. **Cleaning rod,** baqueta para limpiar (armas de fuego). **Cleaning fluid,** líquido limpiador. **The cleaning lady/woman,** la señora o mujer de la limpieza.

cleanliness [ˈkli:nlɪnɪs] [klin-li-nes], *s.* 1. Limpieza, aseo (bodily hygiene); limpieza (of surroundings). **Personal cleanliness,** el aseo personal. 2. Curiosidad en el vestir.

clean-living [kli:n'li:vɪŋ] [klin-li-vin] *a.* Sin vicios, de vida sana.

cleanly [ˈkli:nlɪ] [klin-li], *a.* Limpio, aseado; puro, delicado. -*adv.* Primorosamente, aseadamente. Limpiamente (evenly/cut, snap). Limpio, limpiamente, con limpieza (fairly/fight, play).

cleanness [ˈkli:nnɪs] [klin-nes], *s.* Limpieza, aseo (absence of dirt); pureza (of air, water); inocencia.

cleanse [klenz] [klens], *va.* 1. Limpiar, purificar. 2. Purgar de algún reato o delito. 3. Librar de malos humores. 4. Fregar, limpiar.

cleanser [ˈklenzər] [klen-sar], *s.* Evacuante, purgante. Producto de limpieza (for household use); leche o crema limpiadora o de limpieza (for skin).

clean-shaven [kli:ˈʃeɪvən] [klin-shei-ven] *a.* Bien afeitado o rasurado (face). **A clean-shaven man,** un hombre sin barba ni bigote.

cleansing [ˈklenzɪŋ] [klen-sin], *s.* Purificación; limpieza. *a.* Limpiador. **Cleansing lotion,** loción limpiadora o de limpieza.

cleanup [ˈklenʌp] [klenap] *s.* Limpieza (clean). *(Coloq.)* Tajada (large profit).

clear [klɪər] [kliaʳ], *a.* 1. Claro, transparente, diáfano. Despejado, claro (sky); despejado (day); transparente (liquid, glass). **Clear soup,** consomé. **To have a clear conscience,** tener la conciencia tranquila o limpia. **She has very clean skin,** tiene muy buen cutis. **To keep a clean head,** mantener la mente despejada. 2. Alegre, sereno. 3. Evidente, indisputable, palpable (plain, evident). **It's a clear case of suicide,** es un caso evidente o claro de suicidio. **The Bears are clear favorites,** los Osos son, sin lugar a dudas, el equipo favorito. **It became clear that...,** se hizo evidente que... 4. Patente, manifiesto, claro, fácil de comprender (explanations, instructions). **Is that clear?,** ¿está claro? **Let's get this clear,** entendámonos bien. **Do I make myself clear?,** ¿me explico?, ¿está claro? 5. Libre de culpa, puro, inocente, fuera de riesgo. 6. Neto, líquido. **We've got two clear days,** tenemos dos días enteros. **He makes a clear $650 a week,** saca 650 dólares netos o limpios a la semana.

7. Desempeñado, sin deudas. 8. Desenredado. Despejado (free, unobstructed/space, road). **Keep clear,** no obstruya el paso. **All clear!,** ¡el campo está libre! 9. Claro, sonoro; nítido, claro (distinct/outline, picture); claro (voice). **Clear reputation,** reputación sin mancha, buen nombre. **To be in the clear,** estar fuera de peligro (free from danger); estar libre de deudas (free from debt); estar libre de toda sospecha (free from suspicion). Sin faltas (in showjumping/round). **A clear sky,** un cielo despejado. **A clear style,** un estilo claro, inteligible. **Clear weather,** tiempo sereno, apacible.

clear *adv.* 1. Claramente, enteramente, absolutamente. **Once you're clear of the town,** una vez que hayas salido de la ciudad (beyond, outside). **Stand clear of the doors,** manténganse alejados de las puertas. **He leapt clear of the oncoming car,** se apartó de un salto del coche que venía. **The curtains should hang clear of the radiators,** las cortinas no deben tocar los radiadores. 2. (As intensifier) **The cargo sank clear to the bottom,** la carga se fue a pique hasta el fondo. **He fell clear through the ceiling,** se cayó y atravesó el techo. 3. **To keep/stay/steer clear of something,** mantenerse alejado de algo. **Keep clear!,** ¡no se acerquen! **I advised her to steer clear of him,** le aconsejé que no tuviera nada que ver con él. 4. (Distinctly) *V.* LOUD.

clear, *s.* Claro, el espacio no interrumpido entre dos cosas.

clear, *va.* 1. Clarificar, dar lustre y esplendor a alguna cosa. 2. Aclarar, disipar alguna obscuridad. Vaciar (make free, unobstructed/room); despejar (surface); desatascar, destapar (drain, pipe); desalojar (building). **To clear the table,** levantar o quitar la mesa. **To clear one's throat,** carraspear, aclararse la voz. **To clear a space for something,** hacer sitio o lugar para algo. **An agreement that clears away for increasing trade,** un acuerdo que abre camino para un mayor intercambio comercial. **Let's clear all this paper off the desk,** quitemos todos estos papeles del escritorio. *(Inform.)* Despejar (screen); borrar (data). 3. Justificar, purificar, absolver de una acusación (free from suspicion). **He was cleared of all charges,** lo absolvieron de todos los cargos. **She's determined to clear her name,** está decidida a limpiar su nombre. 4. Desembarazar o librar de lo que ofende. 5. Clarificar, poner claro algún licor. 6. Limpiar, blanquear. 7. Sacar los géneros de la aduana. 8. Desembrollar (un negocio); satisfacer (una hipoteca). Liquidar, saldar (settle/debt, account); sacar (earn); liquidar (sell off/stock). (GB) **Reduced to clear,** rebajas por liquidación. 9. Saltar por encima; pasar por encima de algo, sin tocarlo (fence, ditch). **The plane just cleared the trees,** el avión pasó casi rozando los árboles. **To clear customs,** pasar por la aduana. 10. Cortar o arrancar los árboles y malezas de un terreno; preparar para la labranza; despoblar de árboles, desmontar (land). 11. *(Sport)* Despejar (ball, puck). -*vn.* 1. Aclararse, volver a ponerse claro lo que estaba obscuro. Despejarse (sky, weather); aclararse (water). **Her head began to clear,** se le empezó a despejar la cabeza. Levantarse, disiparse (disperse/fog, smoke); despejarse (traffic, congestion). 2. Desembarazarse, desenredarse. 3. *(Fin.)* Ser compensado (check). **It clears up,** va aclarando. **To clear the room,** desocupar un cuarto, hacer salir de él a los que están dentro. **To clear the way,** abrir camino. **To clear accounts,** liquidar cuentas. **To clear off,** desbastar, pulir. **To clear a vessel or merchandise in the custom-house,** despachar un barco o géneros en la aduana. **To clear a wood,** desmontar un bosque.

clear off 1. *(Coloq.)* Largarse (go away). 2. Liquidar (pay/debt); echar de (remove).

clear out 1. Vaciar y ordenar (cupboard). 2. *(Coloq.)* Largarse (leave).

clear up 1. Esclarecer, resolver (resolve, crime); aclarar (misunderstandings, doubts); recoger (tidy/rubbish). **Can you clear up this mess?,** ¿puedes ordenar todo esto? 2. Ordenar (tidy); despejar (weather); mejorarse, irse (get better/cough, cold). **The rash has cleared up,** se le ha ido el sarpullido.

clearage [ˈklɪəreɪdʒ] [klia-reich], *s.* El acto de remover alguna cosa; despejo.

clearance ['klɪərəns] [klia-rans], *s.* 1. Despejo; desmonte, despeje (of building, land). 2. (*Com.*) Despacho de aduana (from customs); autorización (authorization). 3. (*Com.*) Utilidad líquida. 4. (*Aer.*) Espacio (free space). 5. Liquidación (of stock). **Clearance sale,** liquidación, barata. 6. Compensación (of check).

clear-cut ['klɪəkʌt] [kliar-kat], *a.* Claro, bien definido.

clearer ['klɪərər] [klia-raʳ], *s.* Lo que aclara, purifica o ilumina.

clear-headed ['klɪəhedɪd] [klia-je-ded] *a.* Lúcido.

clearing ['klɪərɪŋ] [klia-rin], *s.* 1. Justificación, vindicación. 2. Claro, raso, sitio sin árboles en un bosque. 3. Arreglo, liquidación de los balances en el banco de liquidación.

clearing bank ['klɪərɪŋbæŋk] [kliarin-bank] *s.* (in UK) Banco de compensación.

clearing house ['klɪərɪŋhaʊz] [kliarin-jaus], *s.* (*Com.*) Bolsa o banco de compensación; cámara de compensación.

clearly ['klɪəli] [klia-li], *adv.* Claramente (distinctly/visible, marked); con claridad, claramente (write, speak, think)/ (without ambiguity/speak, show); evidentemente (obviously) **It's clearly impossible,** es a todas luces imposible, está claro que es imposible. **Clearly, this must stop,** evidentemente, o desde luego, esto se tiene que terminar. Libremente; llanamente; abiertamente, sin reserva.

clearness ['klɪənɪs] [klia-nes], *s.* 1. Claridad, transparencia; lustre, esplendor; luz. 2. Perspicuidad, perspicacia. 3. Sinceridad. **Clearness of the air,** serenidad del aire.

clear-out ['klɪəraʊt] [klia-aut] *s.* (GB) (*Coloq.*) Limpieza (deshaciéndose de trastos, etc.).

clear-sighted ['klɪə'saɪtɪd] [klia-sai-tid], *a.* Previsor, perspicaz, juicioso, despierto, avispado, de gran lucidez.

clear-sightedness ['klɪə'saɪtɪdnɪs] [klia-sai-tid-nes], *s.* Perspicacia, discernimiento, penetración.

clearstarch ['klɪəsta:tʃ] [klia-starch], *va.* Almidonar.

clearstarcher ['klɪəsta:tʃər] [klia-star-cheʳ], *s.* Almidonador, la persona que almidona ropa fina.

clearstory ['klɪəstɔrɪ] [klia-sto-ri], *s.* 1. Piso más alto de la nave y del coro de una iglesia, con una serie de pequeñas ventanas. 2. Piso semejante en edificios de otro carácter, o sobretecho de un coche de ferrocarril con claraboyas a los costados para darle luz y ventilación.

clear-voiced ['klɪəvɔɪsd] [klia-voisd], *a.* El que tiene la voz clara.

clearway ['klɪəweɪ] [klia-uei] *s.* (in UK) Tramo de carretera en el que está prohibido detenerse.

clearwing ['klɪəwɪŋ] [klia-uin], *s.* Falena diurna con alas casi transparentes.

cleat [kli:t] [klit], *s.* 1. Listón de madera o hierro que se asegura sobre otro material para sujetarlo, cubrirlo, impedir que se deslice. 2. (*Mar.*) Tojino. 3. (*Mar.*) Galápago de las palomas.

cleavage ['kli:vɪdʒ] [klia-vich], *s.* 1. La acción de hendirse o el estado de hendido o hendidura, división. 2. Tendencia de una roca o cristal a partirse en determinadas direcciones. 3. Escote (bosom).

cleave [kli:v] [kliv], *vn.* 1. Pegarse o unirse una cosa a otra. 2. Ajustarse una cosa con otra. 3. Adherir, arrimarse, atenerse al dictamen o parecer de otro. 4. Abrirse en rajas, dividirse. **To cleave through something,** abrirse camino a través de algo (crowd, enemy); surcar (waves). **To cleave to something/somebody,** serle fiel a algo/alguien (be faithful). -*va.* Rajar, hender, partir naturalmente.

cleaver ['kli:vər] [kli-vaʳ], *s.* 1. Cuchilla de carnicero. Hacha para rajar madera.

cleavers ['kli:vəz] [kli-vers], *s. pl.* (*Bot.*) Galio. V. BEDSTRAW.

cleek [kli:k] [klik], *s.* 1. Gancho. 2. Maza empleada para el juego de golf.

clef [klef] [klef], *s.* (*Mús.*) Clave, signo que indica el tono al principio de la pauta.

cleft [kleft] [kleft], *past and past p. of* CLEAVE. *s.* Rajadura, hendedura, abertura, grieta. **Clefts,** grietas, aberturas que se forman en los pies de las caballerías. *a.* Partido (chin). **Cleft palate,** fisura del paladar.

cleftgraft [kleft'graft] [kleft-graft], *va.* Injertar en tronco.

clematis ['klemətɪs] [kle-ma-tis], *s.* (*Bot.*) Clemátide, género de plantas de las ranunculáceas.

clemency ['klemənsɪ] [kle-man-si], *s.* Clemencia (mercy); misericordia, indulgencia, bondad; benignidad (of weather).

clement ['klemənt] [kle-ment], *a.* Clemente, piadoso, benigno, indulgente, misericordioso.

clementine ['kleməntaɪn] [kle-men-tain] *s.* (GB) Clementina.

clench [klentʃ] [klench], *va.* 1. Asir fuertemente o resueltamente; apretar, agarrar (grip). 2. Cerrar con estrechez o convulsivamente, como el puño o los dientes; apretar (close/fist, jaw). **He spoke through clenched teeth,** masculló algo, dijo algo entre dientes. 3. Hacer firme, asegurar. 4. V. CLINCH. -*s.* La acción de asir fuertemente.

clencher ['klentʃər] [klen-chaʳ], *s.* 1. El que o lo que ase; herramienta para asir. 2. (*Fig.*) Argumento sin réplica.

clepsydra ['klepsɪdrə] [klep-si-dra], *s.* Clepsidra, reloj de agua.

clerestory ['klɪərəstɔrɪ] [kle-res-to-ri], *s.* V. CLEAR-STORY.

clergy ['klɜ:dʒɪ] [kler-yi], *s.* Clero.

clergyman ['klɜ:dʒɪmən] [kler-yi-man], *s.* Clérigo, eclesiástico.

cleric ['klerɪk] [kle-rik], *s.* Clérigo, eclesiástico. -*a.* Clerical.

clerical ['klerɪkəl] [kle-ri-kal], *a.* 1. (*Rel.*) Clerical, eclesiástico. 2. De oficina (of a clerk/job, work). **Clerical assistant,** oficinista, empleado, **Clerical staff,** personal administrativo.

clerk [klɜ:rk] [klerk], *s.* 1. Oficial de secretaría; amanuense, escribiente. 2. Dependiente, mancebo de tienda (sales clerk); empleado de oficina; empleado administrativo, oficinista (in office); empleado bancario (in bank); recepcionista (desk clerk). 3. Eclesiástico, clérigo. 4. Escolar, estudiante. **Clerk of a ship,** contador de navío. **Clerk of a parish,** sacristán. **The clerk of the king's great wardrobe,** el primer ayuda de cámara del rey. **Clerk of a countinghouse or shop,** dependiente, cajero, mancebo, mozo de tienda o almacén. **Clerk of a court of justice,** escribano de cámara o secretario de tribunal.

clerk *vn.* Trabajar de dependiente (o de oficinista, etc.).

clerkly ['klɜ:klɪ] [kler-kli], *a.* Diestro, literato. -*adv.* Ingeniosamente.

clerkship ['klɜ:kʃɪp] [klerk-ship], *s.* 1. Literatura, educación literaria. 2. El oficio, empleo u ocupación de dependiente, clérigo, estudiante o escribiente. 3. Escribanía de cámara, secretaría.

clever ['klevər] [kle-veʳ], *a.* 1. Diestro, experto, hábil, ingenioso (skilful, adept/player, politician); ingenioso (invention, solution); avispado, mañoso; listo, inteligente (intelligent); capaz, listo (artful). **Don't try to be clever with me,** no te hagas el listo conmigo. 2. (Fam. E.U.) bien dispuesto, complaciente. 3. (*Ant.*) Justo, apropiado, cómodo, apto, propio. **To be clever at something,** ser bueno para algo. **She's clever with her hands,** es hábil con las manos.

clever dick, clever Dick *s.* (GB) (*Coloq.*) Sabelotodo, sabihondo.

cleverly ['klevəli] [kle-ver-li], *adv.* Diestramente, hábilmente, ingeniosamente.

cleverness ['klevənɪs] [kle-vr-nes], *s.* Destreza, habilidad (skill); conocimiento, maña; garbo, gracia. Lo ingenioso (of design, plan); inteligencia (of person/intelligence).

clevis ['klevɪs] [kle-vis], *s.* Abrazadera, pieza de hierro sujeta al timón del arado o a las boleas de un coche, y a la cual se asegura la cadena de tiro. (*Mec.*) Correón.

clew [klu:] [klú], *s.* 1. Hilo ovillado, ovillo de hilo, seda o lana. 2. Guía, norte. En sentido de guía, escríbese a menudo «clue» **To give a clew to,** guiar, enseñar el camino. 3. **Clew of a sail** *(Mar.)* puño, extremo o ángulo donde forman gazas las relingas de las velas.

clew-lines [ˈkluːlaɪnz] [klu-lains], *s. pl. (Mar.)* Chafaldetes de los puños.

cliché [ˈkliːʃeɪ] [kli-shé], *s.* 1. Clisé, pieza de metal de imprenta con letra o dibujo, clisada para imprimir. 2. Negativo fotográfico. 3. Lugar común, cliché, tópico.

clichéd [ˈkliːʃeɪd] [kli-sheid] *a.* Estereotipado.

click [klɪk] [klik], *va.* Retiñir, hacer un ruido acompasado y sucesivo como el del reloj. Chasquear, tronar (fingers); chasquear (tongue). **To click one's heels,** dar un taconazo. - *vn.* 1. Hacer un ruidito seco, hacer «clic» (make clicking sound). **It clicks into place,** encaja en su lugar haciendo «clic». 2. *(Coloq.)* **It suddenly clicked,** de repente caí en la cuenta o lo vi todo claro (strike home). Congeniar (relate well). **We just clicked,** congeniamos o nos entendimos desde un principio. Tener éxito (succeed).

click, *s.* 1. Sonido breve, agudo y seco que es comúnmente resultado de un choque o golpe; chasquido (sound/of fingers, tongue); taconazo (of heels); clic (of camera, switch). 2. Linguete, retén o fiador de rueda. 3. Articulación especial a manera de chasquido.

clicker [ˈklɪkər] [kli-kaʳ], *s.* 1. El que hace o lo que produce el sonido seco llamado *click*. 2. *(Impr.)* Compaginador.

clicket [ˈklɪkɪt] [kli-ket], *s.* Llamador o aldaba de puerta.

client [ˈklaɪənt] [klaient], *s.* 1. Cliente, el litigante que se aconseja con un letrado para que le defienda. 2. Ahijado, hechura, protegido, el que debe su fortuna o empleo a la protección de algún poderoso.

cliental [klaɪˈəntəl] [klai-en-tal], *a.* Dependiente.

cliented [klaɪˈəntɪd] [klai-en-tid], *a.* Provisto de clientes.

clientele [ˌkliːɑːnˈtel] [klian-tél], *s.* 1. Clientela, conjunto de personas acogidas a la protección de un poderoso o de una institución. 2. Conjunto de personas que se valen de los servicios de un médico o letrado, o que concurren de ordinario a un mismo establecimiento o tienda, hotel, teatro, etc.

clientship [ˈklaɪəntʃɪp] [klaiant-ship], *s.* Clientela, patrocinio.

cliff [klɪf] [klif], *s.* Peñasco, roca escarpada; costa acantilada; acantilado, precipicio.

cliffhanger [ˈklɪfˌhæŋər] [klif-jan-gaʳ] *s.* Situación de suspenso o suspense (at end of episode).

cliffy [ˈklɪfɪ] [kli-fi], **clifty** [klif-ti], *a.* Acantilado, escarpado; escabroso.

clift [klɪft] [klift], *s.* 1. *(Ant.) V.* CLIFF. 2. *(Des.) V.* CLEFT.

climacteric [klaɪˈmæktərɪk] [klai-mak-te-rik], *s.* Época peligrosa y crítica. **Grand climacteric,** la edad de sesenta y tres años.

climacteric [klaɪˈmæktərɪk] [klai-mak-te-rik], **climaterical** [klaɪˈmæktərɪkl] [klai-mak-te-ri-kal], *a.* Climatérico, perteneciente a un clima.

climate [ˈklaɪmɪt] [klai-met], **climature** [ˈklaɪmətʃ] [klai-ma-chuaʳ], *s.* 1. Clima, las condiciones atmosféricas de una región. 2. Clima, país diferente de otro por razón de su temperatura, humedad, etc.

climatic [klaɪˈmætɪk] [klai-ma-tik], **climatical** [klai-ma-ti-kal], *a.* Del clima, relativo al clima. Climático, climatológico.

climatology [klaɪməˈtɒlədʒɪ] [klai-ma-to-lo-yi], *s.* Climatología, el estudio o tratado de los climas.

climax [ˈklaɪmæks] [klai-maks], *s.* 1. Clímax, figura retórica por la cual una sentencia va ascendiendo por grados. 2. Colmo, culminación, cenit, punto más alto o de mayor intensidad en una progresión ascendente; punto culminante, orgasmo (orgasm).

climb [klaɪm] [klaim], *va.* Trepar, subir ayudándose de pies y manos, o (una planta) por medio de zarcillos; escalar, subir a (mountain); trepar a, subirse a, treparse a (tree); subir (stairs). *-vn.* 1. Trepar, treparse (clamber); ascender,

subir (rise); elevarse. 2. Elevarse, ascender regularmente (en posición o dignidad) por medio de continuo esfuerzo. *(Sport)* **To go climbing,** hacer alpinismo o andinismo, ir a escalar o de escalada. **She climbed onto the table,** se subió a la mesa, trepó o se trepó a la mesa. **To climb into/out of bed,** meterse en/levantarse de la cama. **He climbed into his pajamas,** se puso el pijama.

climb down 1. Bajarse por (descend/rope); bajarse de (tree). 2. Bajar(se), descender (descend). *(Coloq.)* Ceder (withdraw, concede).

climb up 1. Trepar a treparse a (tree); subir (hill); escalar (rockface); subir o trepar por (rope). 2. Subir.

climb [klaɪm] [klaim] *s.* Subida (ascent); *(Sport)* escalada. Ascenso, subida (gradient). *(Aviat.)* Ascenso.

climbable [klaɪm] [klaim], *a.* Lo que se puede ascender.

climb-down [klaɪm] [klaim] *s.* (GB) Marcha o vuelta atrás.

climber [ˈklaɪmər] [klaimaʳ], *s.* 1. Trepador, escalador (rock climber); alpinista, andinista (mountaineer). 2. Enredadera, planta trepadora. 3. *(Zool.)* Trepador, nombre genérico de un orden de pájaros. 4. *(Pej.)* Arribista, trepador (social climber).

climbing [ˈklaɪmɪŋ] [klaimin], *s.* Subida, el acto de subir. *(Sport)* Alpinismo, montañismo, andinismo. *a.* Trepador.

clime [klaɪm] [klaim], *s. (Poét.)* 1. Porción o región de la tierra. 2. *(Des.)* Clima.

clinch [klɪnt] [klinch], *va.* 1. Remachar un clavo. 2. Agarrarse, pelear forcejeando. 3. Afirmar, fijar, afianzar, establecer, confirmar. *(Mar.)* Entalingar. 4. *V.* CLENCH. 5. Cerrar (deal); ganar, hacerse con (title). **This clinched the argument,** esto resolvió la discusión de forma contundente. *-vn.* 1. Agarrarse. 2. Remacharse, ser remachado. 3. Ganar (assure victory).

clinch, *s.* 1. Remache, o lo que remacha; *(fig.)* argumento sin réplica. 2. *(Mar.)* Entalingadura, la parte del cable que se ata al ancla. 3. *(E.U.)* Forcejeo, lucha, cuerpo a cuerpo. 4. *(Des.) V.* PUN. 5. Clinch (in boxing); *(Coloq.)* abrazo, achuchón, apercolle, apapacho (embrace).

clincher [ˈklɪntʃər] [klin-chaʳ], *s.* Laña. *V.* CRAMP.

clinching [ˈklɪtʃɪŋ] [klin-chin], *s. (Mar.)* Solapadura, especie de calafateo ligero.

cling [klɪŋ] [kling], *vn.* (pret. y pp. CLUNG). 1. Adherirse, pegarse, unirse, fuertemente una cosa a otra. 2. Adherirse, unirse o amistarse por interés o afecto. 3. *(Prov.)* Secarse, consumirse. **To cling to something/somebody,** estar aferrado a algo/alguien. **She still clings to that hope/belief,** sigue aferrada a esa esperanza/creencia. **The boy clung on to her hand,** el niño no le soltaba la mano. **To cling to somebody,** pegársele a alguien (be dependent). **To cling to something,** pegarse o adherirse a algo (stick) *-va. (Ant.)* Encoger, estrechar.

clingfilm [ˈklɪŋfɪlm] [kling-film] *s.* (GB) Plástico para envolver alimentos.

clinging [ˈklɪŋɪŋ] [klin.guin] *a.* Poco independiente (child); pegajoso, pesado (person); que se pega o se ciñe al cuerpo (dress).

clingstone [ˈklɪŋstəʊn] [kling-stoun], *a.* Que se pega al hueso; se dice de un melocotón. *-s.* Pavía, variedad del pérsico, cuya pulpa se pega al hueso.

clingy [ˈklɪŋɪ] [klin-gui], *a.* Colgante, pendiente, adhesivo.

clinic [ˈklɪnɪk] [kli-nik], *s. (Med.)* Clínica (private hospital); consultorio (in state hospital). **Dental clinic,** clínica dental.

clinical [ˈklɪnɪkəl] [kli-ni-kal], *a.* Un enfermo habitual que guarda cama, y el que le asiste. **Clinical lecture,** lectura médica hecha a la cabecera de los enfermos. *(Med.)* Clínico. Frío (unemotional/manner, detachment).

clink [klɪŋk] [klink], *vn.* Retiñir, resonar, retumbar, tañer, tocar. *-va.* Hacer tintinear. **We clinked glasses,** entrechocamos los vasos.

clink, *s.* 1. Tañido, retintín, sonido o golpe que deja la campana u otro cuerpo metálico sonoro; tintineo (sound). 2. Cárcel, trullo, bote, cana.

clinker [ˈklɪnkər] [klin-kaʳ], *s.* 1. Lo que retiñe; específicamente, escoria de fundición. 2. Lava irregular porosa, semejante a la escoria de los hornos. 3. Ladrillo refractario. 4. Baldosa de Holanda. 5. *(Sl.)* Metedura o metida de pata, pifia, pifiada. Porquería, basura (bad product).

clinometer [klɪnɒˈmiːtər] [kli-no-mi-taʳ], *s.* Clinómetro, instrumento para medir la inclinación de toda línea o plano con respecto a un plano horizontal.

clinometric [klɪnɒˈmɪtrɪk] [kli-no-me-trik], *a.* Clinométrico, del clinómetro y de su medida.

clinometry [klɪnɒˈmɪtrɪ] [kli-no-me-tri], *s.* Clinometría, arte de medir la inclinación de las capas o estratos.

clinquant [ˈklɪŋkwənt] [klin-kuant], *a.* Brillante, reluciente. - *s.* Oropel.

clip [klɪp] [klip], *va.* 1. Trasquilar o cortar con tijeras, esquilar (sheep, dog); cortar (cut/hair, nails, grass, hedge); recortarle el pelo a (dog); picar, perforar (punch, ticket). Recortar (cut out). 2. Cortar a raíz; escatimar, acortar; omitir sílabas de las palabras; chapurrear, estropear un idioma. 3. Cercenar o minorar alguna cosa. **To clip a coin,** tallar o cercenar una moneda. 4. Abrazar, dar un abrazo. 5. Confinar, tener agarrado. 6. Golpear (hit). **To clip somebody round the ear,** darle una torta o un tortazo a alguien. 7. Sujetar con un clip (attach). *-vn.* **The lid clips on,** la tapa se ajusta con unos ganchos.

clip, *s.* 1. Tijereteada, tijeretazo, talla. 2. Esquileo, y el producto de esta operación; la acción de esquilar. 3. Cercenadura. 4. Abrazo.

clip, *s.* 1. Pieza o herramienta que sirve para asir o tener firme; grapa, pinza (fotográfica), grapas de resorte, sujetapapeles. 2. Clip, gancho (device). *V.* HAIRCLIP, PAPERCLIP. 3. Fragmento, clip (from film). 4. Bloqueo por la espalda (fuera de la zona legal) (foul). 5. **To give somebody a clip on/round the ear,** darle una torta o un tortazo a alguien (blow). 6. *(Coloq.)* **A clip,** cada uno (item).

clipboard [ˈklɪpbɔːd] [klip-bord] *s.* Tablilla con sujetapapeles.

clip-clop [ˈklɪpˈklɒp] [klip-klop] *s.* Ruido de cascos.

clip-on [klɪpˈɒn] [klip-on] *a.* Que se engancha (brooch, sunglasses); de clip (earrings).

clipped [klɪpt] [klipt] *a.* Cortado (accent, speech).

clipper [ˈklɪpər] [kli-paʳ], *s.* 1. Tallador, cercenador de monedas, el que las cercena en circuito para dejarlas en su peso. 2. Maquinilla o aparato que se usa para cortar el pelo, particularmente de los caballos. 3. Esquilador. 4. Barco de vela de mucho andar; clíper.

clippers [ˈklɪpəz] [kli-pers], *s. pl.* Maquinilla para cortar el pelo (for hair); cortauñas (for nails); podadera, tijeras de podar (for hedge, lawn).

clipping [ˈklɪpɪŋ] [kli-pin], *s.* Cercenadura, cortadura, retal; tijereteo. Recorte de prensa (press clipping). **Clipping-machine,** maquinilla de atusar. *V.* CLIPPER. 2ª acep. **Clippings,** recortes, pedazos (clipped pieces). **Grass clippings,** hierba cortada. **Nail clippings,** pedazos de uñas.

clique [kliːk] [klik], *s.* Corrillo, pandilla, pequeña reunión de personas, por lo común de gente aviesa, camarilla.

clitoris [ˈklɪtərɪs] [kli-to-ris] *s.* Clítoris.

cloaca [ˈkləʊəkə] [klou-a-ka], *s.* 1. *(Zool.)* Cloaca, cavidad en la que convergen el canal alimenticio y los conductos urinarios y genitales de las aves y de algunos peces, insectos, etc. 2. Cloaca, conducto por donde van las aguas sucias.

cloak [kləʊk] [klouk], *s.* 1. Capa (clothing); tapadera (disguise). 2. Capa, cualquier cosa que tapa o encubre. 3. Pretexto, excusa. **Cloak-bag,** portamanteo, especie de maleta para llevar ropa. **Cloak-loop,** cordoncillo para atar la capa.

cloak, *vn.* 1. Encapotar. 2. Ocultar, encubrir (purpose, activities); paliar. **To be cloaked in something,** estar envuelto en algo (in darkness, mist). **The whole affair was cloaked in secrecy,** todo el asunto estuvo rodeado de un velo o un manto secreto.

cloakroom [ˈkləʊkrʊm] [klouk-rum] *s.* Guardarropa (for coats). (GB) Lavabo, baño de las visitas (lavatory).

clobber [ˈklɒbər] [klouk] *va.* *(Coloq.)* Darle una paliza a, cascar. Darle una paliza a (defeat heavily).

clobber *s.* (GB) *(Coloq.)* Bártulos.

clock [klɒk] [klok], *s.* 1. Reloj, máquina para medir el tiempo (timepiece). **To work around/round the clock,** trabajar las veinticuatro horas del día, trabajar día y noche. **Around-the-clock/round-the-clock surveillance,** vigilancia las veinticuatro horas del día. **To put the clocks back/forward,** atrasar/adelantar los relojes. **To turn/put the clock back,** volver atrás. **Tower clock,** reloj de torre. **Alarm-clock,** *V.* ALARM. **What time is it?** ¿qué hora es? **Nine o'clock in the morning,** las nueve de la mañana. **To wind up a clock,** dar cuerda a un reloj. 2. Cuadrado, adorno que se pone en las medias. 3. Reloj registrador o checador (time clock); *(Auto.)* *(Coloq.)* Cuentakilómetros (mileometer); velocímetro (speedometer); taxímetro (in taxi). **Clock-maker,** relojero. **Clock-setter,** el que da cuerda y arregla el reloj.

clock, *va.* *(Coloq.)* Registrar, hacer (achieve, reach/speed, time); cronometrar (time/athlete, race). (Gran Bretaña) *V.* CLUCK.

clock in, (GB) **clock on** Fichar, marcar o checar tarjeta al entrar al trabajo (register time of arrival). Entrar al trabajo (arrive at work).

clock out, (GB) **clock off** Fichar, marcar o checar tarjeta al salir del trabajo (register time of departure). Salir del trabajo (leave work).

clock up *(Coloq.)* Hacer (accumulate/miles, hours); apuntarse, anotarse (successes).

clock radio [klɒkˈreɪdɪəʊ] [klok-rei-diou] *s.* Radio despertador.

clocktower [ˈklɒkˌtaʊər] [klok-tauaʳ] *s.* Torre de reloj.

clockwise [ˈklɒkwaɪz] [klok-uais], *a. y adv.* Con movimiento circular a la derecha. Dirección/en el sentido de las agujas del reloj.

clockwork [ˈklɒkwɜːk] [klok-uek], *s.* Movimiento causado por medio de pesos y resortes, como el del reloj. Mecanismo de relojería. **The organization runs like clockwork,** la organización funciona como un reloj. *(Coloq.)* **As regular as clockwork,** como un reloj. **Clockwork toy,** juguete de cuerda. *-a.* Que tiene regularidad de movimiento; que se mueve con precisión automática.

clod [klɒd] [klod], *s.* 1. Terrón (of earth), césped; y de aquí tierra, suelo. 2. Masa, trozo de alguna cosa. 3. El cuerpo del hombre. 4. Cualquier cosa baja, vil y despreciable. 5. Idiota, zoquete, zopenco (oaf). **Clod-crusher,** desterronador.

clod, *vn.* Convertirse en terrones. *-va.* Tirar terrones.

cloddy [ˈklɒdɪ] [klo-di], *a.* 1. Lleno de terrones. 2. *(Fig.)* Terrenal, bajo, grosero.

clodhopper [ˈklɒdˌhɒpər] [klod-jo-paʳ], **clodpoll** [ˈklɒdpɒl] [klod-pol], *s.* Zoquete, rústico. Patán (yokel). Zapatón (heavy shoe).

clodpate [ˈklɒdpeɪt] [klod-peit], *s.* Idiota, zoquete.

clodpated [klɒdˈpeɪtɪd] [klod-pei-ted], *a.* Negado, necio, ignorante.

clog [klɒg] [klog], *va.* Cargar, embarazar, empachar, impedir, cargar con alguna cosa que impide el movimiento. Obstruir, atascar (pipe, filter); atascar (wheels). *-vn.* 1. Apiñarse, atestarse, agolparse, estrecharse y unirse una cosa con otra. Obstruirse, atascarse (pipe); atascarse (wheel). 2. Embarazarse, hallarse embarazada o impedido.

clog, *s.* 1. Traba, embarazo, impedimento, obstáculo. 2. Carga, hipoteca. 3. Galocha, especie de calzado como zueco o chapín que se usa para andar por el lodo, la nieve o el agua; zuecos, chanclos.

clogginess [ˈklɒdʒɪnɪs] [klo-yi-nes], *s.* Embarazo, impedimento, obstáculo.

cloggy [ˈklɒdʒɪ] [klo-yi], *a.* Embarazoso.

cloister [ˈklɔɪstər] [klois-taʳ], *s.* 1. Claustro, galería que cerca el patio. 2. Monasterio, convento.

cloisteral [ˈklɔɪstərəl] [klois-te-ral], **cloistral** *a.* Claustral, del claustro; solitario, retirado.

cloistered [ˈklɔɪstəd] [klois-terd], *a.* 1. Solitario, enclaustrado. **He had led a cloistered existence,** había vivido muy enclaustrado. 2. Cercado de tránsitos, columnas o galerías.

cloisterer [ˈklɔɪstərər] [klois-te-raʳ], *s.* Monje, religioso.

cloisteress [ˈklɔɪstərəs] [klois-te-res], *sf.* Monja, una religiosa.

cloke [ˈkləʊk] [klouk] *s. (Des.) V.* CLOAK.

clomb, *pp.* de TO CLIMB.

clone [kləʊn] [klaun] *s.* Clon.

clone *va.* Clonar.

clonic [ˈklɒnɪk] [klo-nik], *a.* Clónico, convulsivo, relajante. **Clonic spasm,** espasmo clónico.

close [kləʊs] [klous], *va.* 1. Cerrar (window, book, value); **He closed his mouth/eyes,** cerró la boca/los ojos. Juntar, unir, consolidar. 2. Cerrar, ajustar (terminate, wind up/branch, file, account), encajar, poner en contacto, hacer continuo. 3. Concluir, terminar, acabar, poner fin a (conclude/deal, debate, meeting). 4. Incluir, contener. 5. Unir o juntar los pedazos rotos de alguna cosa. 6. *(Ant.)* Encerrar. *V.* INCLOSE. 7. Cerrar (block/road). -*vn.* 1. Cerrarse, unirse las partes que estaban separadas (door, window). Cerrarse (gap, wound). **Her eyes closed and she fell asleep,** se le cerraron los ojos y se quedó dormida. 2. Convenirse, estar de acuerdo. 3. Darse a partido. 4. Cerrar (shop, library, museum). 5. Terminar, concluir (finish, end/lecture, book). 6. Acercarse (get closer). **To close on somebody/something,** acercarse a algo/alguien. **To close in,** cercar (un jardín), poner una cerca. **To close with one,** acordarse o estar de acuerdo con uno. **To close in with the people,** ser el partido del pueblo. **To close in,** encerrar. **To close up,** cerrar completamente. **To close up a wound,** cicatrizar una herida.

close down 1. Cerrar (factory, shop). 2. Cerrar (cease operations/shop, factory).

close in Acercarse, aproximarse (pursuers, enemy). **To close in on something/somebody,** cercar algo/a alguien. Acercarse (winter). **Night was closing in,** estaba oscureciendo o anocheciendo, caía la noche. Acortarse (get shorter/days).

close off Clausurar, cerrar.

close on Acercarse a (reduce gap).

close out Liquidar.

close up Cerrar (shop, museum). Cerrarse, cicatrizar (wound/gash). **Come on, everybody close up a bit!** ¡vamos, pongánse un poco más juntos!

close with Enfrentarse a (engage/enemy).

close, *s.* 1. Fin, conclusión, término (conclusion, end). **To come/draw to a close,** llegar/acercarse a su fin. **To bring something to a close,** poner o dar fin a algo. **At the close of day,** al caer el día. 2. Pausa, cesación. 3. Riña, lucha cuerpo a cuerpo. 4. Cierre, la manera de cerrarse. 5. (GB) Calle sin salida (in residential area).

close, *s.* 1. Cercado, huerta, prado u otro sitio rodeado de vallado o tapias. 2. Atrio, el espacio cercado que hay en algunas iglesias y abadías.

close, *a.* 1. Cerrado, apretado, perfectamente ajustado, sin abertura. 2. Sofocante, sin respiradero. 3. Compacto, denso. Detenido, detallado (careful/examination). **To pay close attention to something,** prestar mucha atención a algo. **To keep a close watch on something/somebody,** vigilar algo/a alguien de cerca. 4. Incomunicado (hablando de un preso). 5. Inmediato, contiguo; unido. Próximo, cercano (near). **At close range/quarters,** de cerca. **Close to something/somebody,** Próximo o cercano a algo/alguien, cerca de algo/alguien. Estrecho (link, connection); directo (contact); cercano (relative). **They're close friends,** son muy amigos, son amigos íntimos. **They've always been very close,** siempre han sido o estado muy unidos. **Sources close to the government,** fuentes allegadas o cercanas al gobierno. 6. Estrecho, angosto; ajustado. Al ras, apurado (shave). *(Coloq.)* **That was a close shave/call,** se salvó por un pelo

o por los pelos. 7. Breve, compendioso. 8. Oculto, secreto. **It was kept a close secret,** se mantuvo en el más absoluto o riguroso secreto (strictly guarded). 9. Apretado, avaro, interesado, tacaño. 10. Retirado, solitario; aplicado. 11. Nublado, obscuro, cubierto. 12. Reservado, callado. 13. Casi a la par o igual. **A close election,** una elección muy reñida. **It's not the same color but it's a close match,** no es el mismo color, pero es casi igual (in similarity). **He bears a close resemblance to his brother,** tiene un gran parecido con su hermano. **That's the closest thing to a hammer I've got,** esto es lo más parecido a un martillo que tengo 14. *(Com.* y *fam.)* Difícil de obtener: se dice del dinero. 15. Limitado a determinadas personas, restringido, o cerrado por la ley; no abierto o libre. 16. Que se ajusta estrechamente. Ajustado, ceñido (fit). 17. Observador atento, riguroso. 18. Reñido (contest/finish). **He finished a close second,** llegó en segundo lugar, muy cerca del ganador. **Close study,** aplicación. **Close connection,** intimidad. **Close substance,** sustancia compacta. **Close piece of cloth,** paño tupido. **Close weather,** tiempo pesado, sofocante, bochornoso (weather, atmosphere). **Close discourse,** discurso conciso. **Close-fisted,** escaso, tacaño, poco dispuesto a dar. **Close-grained,** denso, compacto, sólido. **Close-hauled,** *(Mar.)* de bolina, ciñendo el viento. **Close-season,** la época del año en que la ley prohibe la caza o pesca de ciertos animales, para favorecer su propagación.

close, *adv.* De cerca, estrechamente, apretadamente. Cerca (in position). **To draw/get/come close,** acercarse. **To hold somebody close,** abrazar a alguien. **They're following close behind,** nos siguen de cerca. **Phew, that was close!,** ¡uf, nos salvamos por poco o por los pelos! (In intimacy) **The tragedy brought them closer together/to each other,** la tragedia los acercó o unió más. (In approximation) **It's not my favorite but it comes pretty close,** no es mi favorito pero casi. **The temperature is close to …,** la temperatura es de casi … **He must be close to 50,** debe tener cerca de 50 años. **He was close to tears,** estaba a punto de llorar. **To live close,** vivir económicamente. **To study close,** estudiar con mucha aplicación. **Close to the ground,** pegado a la tierra, a raíz de la tierra. **Close by,** muy arrimado, pegado, junto, cerca. **To sail close to the wind,** ceñir el viento, navegar de bolina. **Close together,** juntos (physically). **Our birthdays are close together,** nuestros cumpleaños caen por las mismas fechas o muy cerca. **Close up,** de cerca.

close-bodied [kləʊsˈbʌdɪd] [klous-bo-did], *a.* Ajustado al cuerpo.

closecropped [ˈkləʊskrɒpt] [klous-kropt] *a.* Muy corto (grass). **To have a closecropped hair, to be closecropped,** llevar el pelo (cortado) al rape.

close-curtained [kləʊsˈkɜːteɪnd] [klous-ker-teind], *a.* Rodeado de cortinas.

closed [kləʊst] [kloust] *a.* 1. Cerrado (door, book, flower). **His eyes were closed,** tenía los ojos cerrados. 1. Cerrado (not operating, trading). 3. Cerrado (road); a puerta(s) cerrada(s) (meeting). 4. Cerrado (case, matter).

closed-circuit [kləʊzdˈsɜːkwɪt] [klous-ser-kuit], *a. (Elec.)* En circuito cerrado. **Closed-circuit television,** televisión en circuito cerrado. **Closed-circuit door.** A puerta(s) cerrada(s) (meeting, briefing).

close-down [ˈkləʊzdaʊn] [klous-daun] *s.* Cierre (of factory).

closed shop [kləʊzdˈʃɒp] [klous-shop], *s.* Contrato de trabajo según el cual pueden ocuparse sólo obreros sindicalizados.

close-fisted [ˈkləʊsˈfɪstɪd] [klous-fis-tid], **close-handed** [klous-jan-ded], *a.* Apretado, avariento, mezquino, tacaño, agarrado.

close-fitting [kləʊsˈfɪtɪŋ] [klous-fi-tin], *a.* Entallado, ajustado al cuerpo, ceñido.

close-knit [ˈkləʊsnɪt] [klous-nit] *a.* Unido.

closely ['kləʊslɪ] [klous-li], *adv.* 1. Estrechamente (connected, associated); contiguamente. **We're closely related,** somos parientes cercanos. **They worked closely with the French,** trabajaron en estrecha colaboración con los franceses. 2. Estrechamente, fuertemente, sólidamente. 3. Estrictamente, exactamente. 4. Secretamente, atentamente. 5. De cerca (at a short distance/follow, mark). Detenidamente (carefully/ study, examine). De cerca, atentamente (watch); a fondo (question). **A closely guarded secret,** un secreto muy bien guardado. 6. **Somebody who resembled her closely,** alguien que se le parecía mucho (in approximation). **A closely fought/contested game,** un partido muy reñido (nearly equally). **To pursue any one closely,** irle a uno a los alcances, seguirle de cerca. **Closely packed,** sólidamente empaquetado. **A page closely printed,** una página de impresión compacta. **To examine closely,** examinar atentamente, de cerca.

closemouthed [kləʊs'maʊθd] [klous-mau-zd], *a.* Reservado, discreto, incomunicativo.

closeness ['kləʊsnɪs] [klous-nis], *s.* 1. Encierro. 2. Estrechez, falta de lugar. 3. Espesura, condensación, apretamiento. 4. Falta de aire o ventilación. 5. Solidez, firmeza. 6. Reclusión, soledad; secreto. 7. Tacañería, avaricia, ruindad. 8. Conexión, dependencia, unión. 9. Amistad, intimidad. 10. Exactitud, fidelidad (copy, translation).

closeout [kləʊsaʊt] [klous-aut]*s.* Liquidación.

close-pent [kləʊspent] [klous-pent], *a.* Cerrado estrechamente.

close quarters [kləʊs'kwɔːtəz] [klous-kuar-tars], *s. pl.* Espacio limitado, lugar estrecho.

close-run [ˌkləʊs'rʌn] [klous-ran] *a.* Muy reñido (race).

closer ['kləʊsər] [klou-saʳ], *s.* El que acaba o concluye.

close-set ['kləʊs‚set] [klous-set] *a.* Junto (eyes).

closet ['klɒzɪt] [klo-sit], *s.* 1. Retrete, cuarto pequeño; habitación retirada de una casa. 2. Gabinete. 3. Secreta, común, excusado, letrina (a la inglesa; abreviación de *water-closed*). 4. Armario, placard (cupboard); armario, closet, placard (for clothes). *(Coloq.)* **To come out of the closet,** destaparse, declararse abiertamente homosexual. **Understairs closet,** covacha.

closet *a.* Encubierto, de closet, de tapadillo (gay, racist).

closet, *va.* Encerrar o esconder en un retrete o gabinete; deliberar o conferenciar en gabinete. **To closet oneself** o **to be closeted,** Encerrarse. **To be closeted with somebody,** estar encerrado con alguien.

close-tongued [kləʊs'tɒŋd] [klous-tongd], *a.* Cauteloso en el hablar.

close-up ['kləʊsʌp] [klous-ap], *s.* 1. Fotografía de cerca; primer plano. 2. Algo visto muy de cerca.

closing ['kləʊzɪŋ] [klousin], *s.* 1. Cierre. 2. Clausura.

closing date [kləʊzɪŋ'deɪt] [klousin-deit] *s.* Fecha límite, fecha tope.

closing time [kləʊzɪŋ'taɪm] [klousin-taim] *s.* Hora de cierre.

closure ['kləʊʒəʳ] [klou-saʳ], *s.* 1. *(Neol.)* Procedimiento por el cual se pone fin al debate en un cuerpo deliberante. 2. Cierre; cerca. V. INCLOSURE. 3. Fin, conclusión. 4. Completamiento de un circuito eléctrico. 5. Cierre (of hospital, factory, road).

clot [klɒt] [klot], *s.* 1. Grumo, parte de lo líquido que se coagula. 2. Cuajarón de sangre; coágulo (of blood). 3. (GB) *(Coloq.)* Bobalicón (idiot).

clot, *vn.* 1. Coagularse, cuajarse (blood). 2. Engrumecerse, hacerse grumos el líquido.

cloth [klɒθ] [kloz], *s.* 1. Tela, género (fabric); paño, tela de lana (thick, woolen); seda, lino, algodón, etc., tejida en telar. **To be made (up) out of whole cloth,** ser pura invención o puro invento. Trapo (for cleaning). 2. Porción o parte de una de esas telas, como un mantel o manteles (tablecloth). 3. Vestido o ropa clerical; y de aquí, el clero, el conjunto de eclesiásticos en general. **The cloth,** el clero. **A man of the cloth,** un clérigo. **Cloth-prover,** contador, cuentahilos, microscopio de tejedores para contar el

número de hilos en una pulgada cuadrada. **Cloth-yard,** antigua medida para el paño, de 27 pulgadas. **Cloth-shearer,** tundidor de paños.

cloth binding [klɒθ'bɪndɪŋ] [kloz-bin-din], *s.* Encuadernación en tela.

clothe [kləʊð] [klouz], *va.* 1. Vestir, cubrir el cuerpo con vestido, adornar con vestidos (provide clothes for); vestir, ataviar (dress). V. CLAD. 2. Cubrir; investir. **To clothe with authority,** investir de autoridad. -*vn.* Llevar ropa.

cloth-eared ['klɒθɪəd] [kloz-iad] *a. (Coloq.)* Sordo como una tapia.

clothes ['kləʊðz] [klouzs], *s. pl.* 1. Vestido, vestidura, ropaje, vestuario, ropa de toda especie. **To put on/take off one's clothes,** ponerse/quitarse la ropa. **She jumped in with her clothes on,** se metió vestida. **He had no clothes on,** estaba desnudo. **Clothes brush,** cepillo para o de la ropa, escobilla de ropa. 2. Ropa de cama. **Cast-off clothes,** ropa usada. **A suit of clothes,** un vestido completo. **Clothes-horse,** percha de colgar ropa. **Clothes-line,** tendedera. **Clothes-pins,** ganchos de tendedera. **Clothes-press,** guardarropa, gabinete para vestidos. **Clothes-wringer,** exprimidor de ropa. **Clothes shop,** tienda o casa de modas. **Clothes tree,** perchero.

clothesbrush ['kləʊðzbrʌʃ] [klozs-brash], *s.* Cepillo de ropa.

clothes hanger ['kləʊðz‚hæŋər] [klozs-jan-gaʳ], *s.* Colgador o gancho de ropa.

clothesman ['kləʊðzmæn] [klozs-man], *s.* 1. Ropero. 2. Ropavejero.

clothier ['kləʊðɪər] [klou-ziaʳ], *s.* Fabricante de paños; pañero.

clothing ['kləʊðɪŋ] [klou-zin], *s.* 1. Vestidos, ropa de toda especie. **The clothing industry,** la industria de la confección. 2. Revestimiento o cubierta no conductora que envuelve el cilindro de una máquina de vapor, una cañería o una caldera.

clotted, clotty [klɒtd] [klotid] [klɒtɪ] [kloti], *a.* Grumoso, coagulado. **Clotted cream.** Crema muy espesa.

cloud [klaʊd] [klaud], *s.* 1. *(Meteo.)* Nube (single); nubes, nubosidad (mass). **There's not a cloud in the sky,** está totalmente despejado. **The only cloud on the horizon is my exam,** la única nube en el horizonte o el único nubarrón es mi examen. *(Coloq.)* **To be on cloud nine,** estar en el séptimo cielo o en la gloria. **Under a cloud,** en circunstancias sospechosas o poco claras. **Every cloud has a silver lining,** no hay mal que por bien no venga. 2. Nublado, nublo, nubarrón; se dice de la nube obscura o de tempestad. 3. Nube, manchita, sombra que se nota en algunas piedras preciosas y en otros cuerpos. Nube (of gas, smoke, dust); halo, nube (of suspicion, ambiguity). 4. Cualquier cosa que obscurece o encubre a otra. 5. Acumulación o hacinamiento parecido al de las nubes: muchedumbre, multitud, montón. **A cloud of witnesses,** una multitud de testigos.

cloud, *va.* 1. Anublar, encubrir la luz del sol. 2. Anublar, obscurecer, cegar. Nublar (dim, blur/view, vision). **Emotion clouded his judgement,** la emoción lo ofuscaba, estaba obnubilado por la emoción. **To cloud the issue,** embrollar el asunto, crear confusión. Empañar (spoil, mar/enjoyment, relationship). 3. Abigarrar con venas obscuras. 4. Manchar, difamar. -*vn.* Anublarse; obscurecerse, tomar aire sombrío y triste.

cloud over Nublarse.

cloudberry ['klaʊdbərɪ] [klaud-be-ri], *s. (Bot.)* Camemoro.

cloudburst ['klaʊdbɜːst] [klaud-berst], *s.* Turbión, chaparrón, tormenta de lluvia, aguacero.

cloud-capt [klaʊd'kæpt] [klaud-kapt], **cloud-covered** [klaʊd'kʌvəd] [klaud-ka-verd], **cloud-topt** [klaʊd'tɒpt] [klaud-topt], *a.* Nublado, cubierto de nubes.

cloud-cuckoo-land [klaʊd'kukuˌlænd] [klaud-ku-ku-land] *s.* **She lives in cloud-cuckoo-land,** vive en las nubes o en otro mundo.

cloud-dispelling [klaʊd'dɪspəlɪŋ] [klaud-dis-pe-lin], *a.* Lo que disipa y separa las nubes.

cloud-kissing [klaʊdˈkɪsɪŋ] [klaud-ki-sin], *a.* Lo que es tan alto que llega a las nubes; dícese de las cumbres más elevadas de los montes.

cloudily [ˈklaʊdɪlɪ] [klau-di-li], *adv.* Obscuramente; con mucha niebla.

cloudiness [ˈklaʊdɪnɪs] [klau-di-nes], *s.* 1. Nebulosidad, calidad de nebuloso, obscurecido por las nubes. 2. Obscuridad, falta de claridad o brillantez.

cloudless [ˈklaʊdlɪs] [klau-les], *a.* Sin nubes, claro, sereno, despejado.

cloudy [ˈklaʊdɪ] [klau-di], *a.* 1. Nublado, nubloso, obscurecido por las nubes (day); nublado, nuboso (sky). Turbio (liquid); poco claro (memory). 2. Obscuro, difícil de entenderse. 3. Tétrico, sombrío, triste, melancólico. 4. Nubarrado, colorido en figura de nubes.

clout [klaʊt] [klaut] *s.* 1. *(Coloq.)* Tortazo (blow). 2. Peso, influencia (power, influence).

clout, *va.* 1. Remendar toscamente alguna cosa. 2. Tapar o cubrir con algún paño o trapo. 3. Chapucear. 4. Abofetear. *(Coloq.)* **To clout somebody,** darle un tortazo a alguien.

clove [kləʊv] [klouv], *s.* 1. Clavo, especia aromática (spice). 2. Diente de ajo, las partes en que se divide la cabeza del ajo (of garlic). 3. *(Prov.)* Peso de siete libras, usado para pesar lana o queso.

clove *(Arq.)* Past of CLEAVE.

cloven [ˈkləʊvn] [klauvn] *(Arq.)* Past p. of CLEAVE.

cloven-foot, cloven-footed [ˌkləʊvnˈfʊt] [klau-ven-fut], **cloven-hoofed** [ˌkləʊvnˈhuːfd] [klau-ven-jufd], *a.* Patihendido, el animal que tiene el pie dividido en dos partes. **To betray o show the cloven foot,** *(Fam.)* eneseñar la oreja, sacar la pata.

cloven hoof [kləʊvnˈhuːf] [klauvn-juf] *s.* Pezuña partida o hendida.

clove-gilly-flower [kləʊvˈgɪlɪˌflaʊər] [klauv-gui-li-flauaʳ], *s.* *(Bot.)* Especie de clavel de flores dobles. Se llama también *Clove-pink.*

clove-hitch [ˈkləʊvhɪtʃ] [klauv-jich], *s.* *(Mar.)* Trincafía, ballestrinque.

clover [ˈkləʊvər] [klo-veʳ], *s.* *(Bot.)* Una de varias especies de trébol. **To be o live in clover,** vivir lujosamente, en la abundancia. **Four-leaf o four-leaved clover,** trébol de cuatro hojas.

clovered [ˈkləʊvəd] [klau-ved], *a.* Cubierto con trébol.

cloverleaf [ˈkləʊvəliːf] [klauver-lif], *s.* Hoja de trébol. **Cloverleaf (highway intersection),** hoja de trébol (en la carretera).

clove-tree [ˈkləʊvtriː] [klov-tri], *s.* Árbol del clavo, clavero.

clown [klaʊn] [klaun], *s.* Patán, hombre zafio, rústico y agreste; el gracioso de teatro; el payaso de los circos ecuestres.

clown *vn.* **Clown around/about,** hacer payasadas, payasear, hacer el payaso.

clownery [ˈklaʊnərɪ] [klau-ne-ri], *s.* 1. Rusticidad, mala crianza. 2. Bufonada, payasada.

clownish [ˈklaʊnɪʃ] [klau-nish], *a.* 1. Villano, rústico, agreste. 2. Rudo, malcriado, grosero. 3. Tosco, basto, desmañado, inculto.

clownishly [ˈklaʊnɪʃlɪ] [klau-nish-li], *adv.* Toscamente, groseramente.

clownishness [ˈklaʊnɪʃnɪs] [klau-nish-nes], *s.* Rusticidad, falta de crianza, grosería, brutalidad, impolítica, rustiquez.

cloy [klɔɪ] [kloi], *va.* 1. Saciar, hartar, ahitar, empalagar. 2. Clavar cañones. 3. *(Des.)* Tapar, obstruir. 4. Clavar, punzar a un caballo herrándole.

cloying [ˈklɔɪɪŋ] [kloiin] *a.* Empalagoso.

cloyless [ˈklɔɪlɪs] [kloi-les], *a.* Ligero, lo que no puede ahitar.

cloyment [ˈklɔɪmənt] [kloi-ment], *s.* Saciedad, hartura.

club [klʌb] [klab], *s.* 1. Clava, cachiporra, garrote (cudgel); tranca, maza. **Golf club,** palo de golf. 2. *(Games.)* Basto o bastos, uno de los cuatro palos de que se compone la baraja de naipes; tréboles. 3. Escote, la parte o cantidad que a prorrata cabe a cada uno de los que se han divertido o comido juntos. 4. Club, junta de personas para elegir los oficiales o funcionarios públicos, o para otras medidas en los asuntos de una sociedad o de una población (society, association). **Sports club,** club deportivo. **To join a club,** hacerse socio de un club. **I'm fed up-join the club!,** estoy harto-¡no eres el único!, ¡ya somos dos! 5. Tertulia, junta de cierto número de personas. **Club of hair,** castaña. **Club-house,** el edificio de un casino o tertulia. **Club-moss,** *(Bot.)* pinillo. **Indian clubs,** mazas de hacer gimnasia.

club, *vn.* 1. Contribuir, o concurrir a gastos comunes, unirse o juntarse para un mismo fin. **To go clubbing,** ir de nightclubs (visit nightclubs). *-va.* 1. Escotar, pagar a prorrata la parte que a cada uno le toca. 2. Aporrear, darle garrotazos a.

club together (GB) **They clubbed together to buy her a present,** le compraron un regalo entre todos (contribute money).

clubbed [ˈklʌbɪd] [kla-bed], *a.* En forma de clava o maza, más grueso hacia un extremo: v.g. *Clubbed antennae,* Antenas en forma de maza. *-pp.* de TO CLUB.

clubbist [ˈklʌbɪst] [kla-bist], *s.* Individuo de algún club o junta, reunión o tertulia particular; socio de un casino.

club-foot [ˈklʌbˈfʊt] [klab-fut], *s.* Pateta, patitueto, el que tiene un torcimiento congénito de los pies. Pie deforme.

club-footed [ˈklʌbˌfʊtɪd] [klab-fu-ted], *a.* Patituerto.

club-headed [ˈklʌbˈhedɪd] [klab-je-did], *a.* Cabezudo, cabezorro.

clubhouse [ˈklʌbhaʊs] [klab-jaus] *s.* Casa club (building for club); club de tribuna (of grandstand, stadium).

club-law [ˈklʌbˈlɔː] [klab-loa], *s.* La ley del más fuerte.

club-room [ˈklʌbrʊm] [klab-rum], *s.* La pieza o sala en donde se reune la junta o tertulia llamada club.

club sandwich [ˈklʌbˈsændwɪtʃ] [klab-san-uich] *s.* Sandwich club o de dos pisos.

cluck [klʌk] [klak], *vn.* Cloquear la gallina, dar su voz cuando llama a los pollos (hen); chascar o chasquear la lengua (person). *-va.* Cloquear.

cluck *s.* 1. Cloqueo (of hen); chasquido de la lengua (of person). 2. *(Coloq.)* Idiota (fool).

clue [kluː] [klu], *s.* 1. Guía, norte; todo lo que sirve de guía en medio de la duda o perplejidad. 2. Cualquier indicio provechoso; indicación, aviso; pista (indication); clave (in crosswords); rastro. **Not to have a clue,** no tener ni la más mínima o menor idea (not know, be incompetent). En sentido náutico y como verbo. *V.* CLEW.

clued-up [kluːdˈʌp] [klud-ap] *a.* *(Coloq.)* **To be clued-up about something,** estar muy al tanto de algo.

clueless [ˈkluːlɪs] [klu-les] *a.* Sin pistas (not having found clue). (GB) *(Coloq.)* Negado (incompetent).

clump [ˈklʌmp] [klamp], *s.* 1. Grupo (de árboles o arbustos); macizo (of flowers); terrón (of earth). 2. Trozo de madera, etc., sin forma de figura particular.

clump *vn.* *(Coloq.)* Caminar pisando fuerte (walk heavily).

clumsily [ˈklʌmsɪlɪ] [klam-si-li], *adv.* Zafiamente, groseramente. Torpemente, con torpeza (handle, apologize); toscamente (made); con poca fluidez (written).

clumsiness [ˈklʌmsɪnɪs] [klam-si-nes], *s.* Zafiedad, falta de destreza; tosquedad, rusticidad, rustiquez, grosería. Torpeza (of movement, words); tosquedad (of construction, design).

clumsy [ˈklʌmsɪ] [klam-si], *a.* Basto, ordinario, tosco, pesado; inculto, sin arte. Torpe, patoso (person, movement); tosco (tool, shape); burdo (translation, forgery); falto de fluidez (writing).

clung, *pret. y pp.* del verbo TO CLING.

cluniac [ˈkluːnɪæk] [klu-ni-ak], *s.* Cluniacense, monje benedictino de Cluni en Borgoña.

clunk [klʌŋk] [klank] *vn.* Golpetear.

clunk *s.* Golpetazo (metal).

cluster [ˈklʌstər] [klas-ta^r], *s.* 1. Racimo. 2. Manada, hato, caterva o multitud de animales que se juntan en un paraje; enjambre de abejas. 3. Agregado, colección por regla general de limitado número. 4. Grupo (of people, buildings); racimo (of berries, bananas); grupo (of stars). 5. *(Fam.)* Piña. **Cluster-cups,** pequeñas cápsulas amarillentas y por lo general agrupadas, que contienen esporos.

cluster, *vn.* Arracimarse, agruparse, apiñarse. *-va.* Apiñar, juntar y estrechar unas cosas con otras. **All the hotels are clustered around the station,** todos los hoteles están agrupados o concentrados alrededor de la estación.

clustery [ˈklʌstərɪ] [klas-te-ri], *a.* Arracimado; apiñado; agrupado.

clutch [klʌtʃ] [klach], *va.* 1. Agarrar o asir con la mano. 2. Empuñar, agarrar con el puño cerrado; apretar.

clutch *s.* 1. Toma, presa, apresamiento. 2. Garra, mano. **To be in/fall into somebody's clutches,** estar/caer en las garras de alguien. 3. Embrague, clutch (de un automóvil) (device). **Clutch pedal,** pedal del embrague. **To let out the clutch,** desembragar, soltar el embrague. 4. Nidada (of eggs); puñado (group, bunch). *(Coloq.)* **In the clutch,** en las emergencias (difficult, crucial situation). **Clutch situation,** situación de emergencia.

clutch *va.* Tener firmemente agarrado. **She clutched the child to her breast,** estrechó o apretó al niño contra su pecho. *-vn.* **To clutch at something,** tratar de agarrarse a algo.

clutch bag [klʌtʃˈbæg] [klach-bag] *s.* Bolso sin asas, sobre.

clutter [ˈklʌtər] [kla-ta^r], *s.* *(Fam.)* 1. Baraúnda, ruido y confusión grande, batahola. 2. Desorden, enredo, confusión. **The room was full of clutter,** la habitación estaba abarrotada o atestada de cosas. **A clutter of books and papers,** un revoltijo de libros y papeles.

clutter, *vn.* Alborotar, hacer ruido o estrépito; atroparse, reunirse en desorden. **Clutter up,** abarrotar. **To clutter something with something,** abarrotar algo de algo. **Don't clutter your essay with unnecessary detail,** no recargues el trabajo con detalles superfluos.

cluttered [ˈklʌtəd] [kla-ted] *a.* Abarrotado o atestado de cosas.

clyster [ˈklɪstər] [klis-te^r], *s.* Clístel o clíster, jeringazo; lavativa.

cm (= **centimeter(s)** o (GB) **centimetre(s)** cm.

cmdr = **Commander** (title).

CND *s.* (in UK) (= **Campaign for Nuclear Disarmament**) Campaña pro Desarme Nuclear.

c/o (= **in care of,** (GB) **care of**). **John Smith, c/o Ana Mas,** John Smith, en casa de Ana Mas, para entregar a John Smith.

Co (Company) Cía. *(Geog.)* **County**

CO 1. *(Geog.)* = Colorado 2. *(Mil.)* = **Commanding Officer.**

coach [kəʊtʃ] [kouch], *s.* 1. Coche, carroza, carruaje, coche de caballos (horse-drawn carriage); diligencia (stage coach). Autobús, autocar, pullman (long distance bus). 2. Preceptor que prepara a un pupilo para un examen, profesor particular (tutor); entrenador, director técnico, el que dirige los ejercicios preparatorios de los que han de participar en regatas, carreras, etc. (team manager). 3. *(Rail)* Coche o carro de viajeros en los ferrocarriles. Vagón de tercera clase; de tercera (fare, passanger). **Hackney-coach,** coche de alquiler o coche simón. **Coach and four,** coche tirado por cuatro caballos. **Coach-box,** pescante de coche. **Coach-dog,** perro dalmático, que corre debajo o a lo largo de un coche. **Coach-hire,** alquiler de coche. **Coach-horse,** caballo de tiro. **Coach-house,** cochera. **Coach-maker,** carrocero. **Coach-office,** administración de diligencias. **Coach-stand,** estación de carruajes.

coach, *va.* 1. Instruir, enseñar; adiestrar. Preparar, darle clases a (a pupil, student, singer). Entrenar (team, player). 2. Llevar en coche. *-vn.* 1. Pasearse en coche. 2. Estudiar con un preceptor.

coaching [ˈkəʊtʃɪŋ] [kou-chin] *s.* Entrenamiento (training); preparación, clases (tutoring); ayuda (prompting).

coachload [ˈkəʊtʃləʊd] [kouch-laud] *s.* (GB) V. BUSLOAD.

coachman [ˈkəʊtʃmæn] [kouch-man], *s.* Cochero.

coachmanship [ˈkəʊtʃmænʃɪp] [kouch-man-ship], *s.* El arte de cochear.

coact [kəʊkt] [koukt], *va.* Forzar juntamente, compeler o refrenar. *-vn.* Cooperar, obrar de acuerdo o de concierto.

coaction [ˈkəʊækʃən] [kouak-shon], *s.* 1. Coacción, necesidad, fuerza. 2. Acción concertada.

coactive [ˈkəʊæktiːv] [kou-ak-tiv], *a.* Coactivo; cooperante.

coadjument [kəʊædˈjʌdʒmən] [kouad-ya-ment], *s.* Mutua y recíproca asistencia.

coadjutant [ˈkəʊædjʊtənt] [kouad-yu-tant], *a.* Coadyuvante, auxiliar, lo que coadyuva o auxilia.

coadjutor [ˈkəʊædjuːtər] [kouad-yu-to^r], *s.* 1. Coadjutor, compañero. 2. Coadjunctor, el que ayuda a una persona en dignidad, regularmente eclesiástica, a ejercer sus funciones.

coadjutrix [kəʊædˈju:trɪks] [kouad-yu-triks], *sf.* Coadjutora; abadesa.

coadjuvancy [kəʊtdjuːvænsɪ] [kod-yu-van-si], *s.* Coadjutoría; ayuda, socorro.

coadunation [ˈkəʊʊdənəɪʃən] [kou-du-nei-shon], **coadunition** [ˈkəʊʊdənɪʃən] [kou-du-ni-shon], *s.* Coadunación, unión.

coagent [kəʊˈɑːdʒent] [kou-ad-yent], *s.* Coagente, cooperador.

coagulability [ˌkəʊægjʊləˈbɪlɪtɪ] [kou-a-guiu-la-bi-li-ti], *s.* La propiedad de coagularse.

coagulable [kəʊˈægjʊləb] [kou-a-guiu-la-bol], *a.* Coagulable.

coagulant [kaʊˈægjʊlænt] [kou-a-guiu-lant], *a. y s.* Coagulante, lo que produce la coagulación.

coagulate [kəʊˈægjʊleɪt] [kou-a-guiu-leit], *va.* Coagular, cuajar, condensar. *-vn.* Coagularse, cuajarse, espesarse (blood).

coagulation [kəʊ͵ægjʊleɪʃən] [kou-a-guiu-lei-shon], *s.* Coagulación; coágulo; espesamiento.

coagulative [kəʊˈægjʊlətɪv] [kou-a-guiu-la-tiv], *a.* Coagulativo.

coagulator [kəʊˈægjʊleɪtər] [kou-a-guiu-lei-to^r], *s.* Coágulo, lo que causa la coagulación.

coagulum [kəʊˈægjʊləm] [kou-a-guiu-lum], *s.* Coágulo, masa coagulada; dícese comúnmente de un cuajarón de sangre.

coak [kəʊk] [kouk], *s.* 1. Dado o macho de madera dura para unir piezas de la arboladura. 2. *(Mar.)* Dado de roldana. 3. V. COKE.

coak, *va.* Unir por medio de dados.

coal [kəʊl] [koul], *s.* 1. Carbón de piedra. **Anthracite coal,** carbón de antracita, mineral muy duro, sin humo, y de un ardor intenso. **Tibuminous coal,** carbón bituminoso, hulla. **Cannel coal,** hulla grasa. 2. Brasa, fuego, alguna cosa inflamada o encendida. *(Prov.)* **To carry coals to Newcastle,** llevar hierro a Vizcaya, llevar algo allí donde lo hay de sobra. **Coal-black,** negro como el carbón. **Coal-box,** caja del carbón, carbonera. **Coal-hole,** carbonera. **Coal-man,** carbonero. **Coal-mine,** mina de carbón. **Coal-miner,** carbonero. V. COLLIER. **Coal-pit,** carbonera, hoya de donde se saca el carbón de piedra. **Coal-ship,** barco carbonero. V. COLLIER. **Coal-tar,** alquitrán de hulla. Produce los tintes de anilina, y compuestos semejantes. **Coal-work,** carbonera, obras en las minas de carbón. **To haul somebody over the coals,** reprender severamente a alguien. **Coal bin/bunker,** carbonera. **Coal cellar,** carbonera. **Coal dust,** carbonilla. **Coal fire,** fuego de o a carbón. **Coal shed,** carbonera.

coal, *va.* 1. Proveer de carbón. 2. Reducir a carbón, carbonizar. 3. Dibujar o señalar con carbón. *-vn.* Hacer provisión de carbón.

coal-black [ˈkəʊlˈblæk] [koul-blak], *a.* Negro como el carbón.

coalesce [ˌkəʊəˈles] [kou-les], *vn.* Unirse, juntarse, incorporarse.

coalescence [ˌkəʊəˈlesəns] [kouk], *s.* Unión, enlace, coyuntura, coalescencia.

coalface [ˈkəʊlˈfeɪs] [koul-feis], *s.* Tajo, frente de explotación del carbón.

coalfield [ˈkəʊlfiːld] [koul-fild], *s.* Yacimiento de carbón; área o zona de minas (area of working mines).

coalheaver [kəʊlˈhiːvər] [koul-ji-va^r], s. Trabajador que descarga los barcos de carbón.

coalition [ˌkəʊəˈlɪʃən] [koua-li-shon], s. 1. Unión, enlace, o trabazón de unas cosas con otras. 2. Coalición, confederación.

coalman [ˈkəʊlmən] [koul-man] s. Carbonero.

coal mining [kəʊlˈmaɪnɪŋ] [koul-mai-nin] s. Explotación hullera o de las minas de carbón. **Coal-mining area,** zona minera.

coal scuttle [ˈkəʊlskʌtl] [koul-ska-tel] s. Cubo del carbón.

coal tar [ˈkəʊlˈtɑːr] [koul-ta^r] s. Alquitrán de hulla. **Coal tar soap,** jabón de brea.

coaming [ˈkəʊmɪŋ] [kou-min], s. Brazola de escotilla; brocal de un pozo.

coaptation [ˌkəʊæpˈteɪʃən] [kou-ap-tei-shon], s. Arreglo, ajuste, el acto de ajustar o proporcionar las partes de un todo para que venga bien.

coarctate [ˈkɔːkteɪt] [kork-teit], a. Comprimido, estrechado; contraído, especialmente en la base.

coarctation [ˈkɔːkteɪʃən] [kork-tei-shon], s. (Med.) Contracción, estrechamiento de un canal.

coarse [kɔːs] [kors], a. 1. Grueso (sand, filter); basto (bread); ordinario. Tosco (features). 2. Tosco, rústico, grosero; bajo, vil, descortés (person); ordinario, basto, tosco (manners); ordinario, basto, grosero (language, joke). 3. Grueso, gordo, basto, hablando de tejidos.

coarsely [ˈkɔːsəlɪ] [kor-se-li], adv. Toscamente (weave); groseramente. En trozos grandes (chop); de manera ordinaria, con ordinariez (speak, behave).

coarsen [ˈkɔːsən] [kor-sen] va. Poner áspero (skin); volver ordinario, tosco o basto (person, manners). vn. Volverse áspero (skin); volverse más ordinario o basto (person, language).

coarseness [ˈkɔːsnɪs] [kor-se-nes], s. 1. Tosquedad, falta de finura. 2. Grosería, falta de crianza; bajeza.

coassume [ˌkəʊæˈzjuːm] [kou-a-sium], va. Asumir en unión de otro juntamente.

coast [kəʊst] [koust], s. 1. Costa, ribera u orilla del mar (shoreline). Costa, litoral (region). **From coast to coast,** de costa a costa. 2. (Ant.) Término, límite; lado. **The coast is clear,** ha pasado el peligro, no hay moros en la costa.

coast, vn. 1. (Mar.) Costear, ir navegando por la costa. 2. (E.U.) Bajar una cuesta o declive, v.gr. en un trineo. -va. Costear algún país o litoral. Deslizarse sin llevar el motor en marcha (freewheel/car). **She coasted through her exams,** superó fácilmente los exámenes (proceed effortlessly).

coastal [ˈkəʊstəl] [kous-tal] a. Costero.

coaster [ˈkəʊstər] [kous-ta^r], s. 1. Piloto práctico en las costas. 2. Bajel o buque costanero. Barco de cabotaje (ship). 3. Posavasos (drink mat).

coaster brake [kəʊstəˈbreɪk] [kous-ter-breik], s. Freno de bicicleta.

coastguard [ˈkəʊstɡɑːd] [koust-gard] s. **The Coastguard,** los guardacostas (organization). Guardacostas (person).

coasguardsman [ˈkəʊstɡɑːdmən] [koust-gard-man] s. V. COASTGUARD.

coasting [ˈkəʊstɪŋ] [kous-tin], s. Cabotaje, navegación costera.

coast line [kəʊstˈlaɪn] [koust-lain], s. Costa, litoral. **Coastline to coastline,** a lo largo y ancho del país.

coastwise [kəʊstˈwaɪz] [koust-uais], a. y adv. A lo largo de la costa.

coat [kəʊt] [kout], s. 1. Levita, casaca, frac; chaqueta (jacket), chaquetón (heavier); prenda de vestir que cubre la parte superior del cuerpo: llevado comúnmente por los hombres. 2. Cubierta o envoltura, como el pelo, lana y plumas que cubren a los animales y aves; túnica del ojo; capa o mano de pintura, yeso, alquitrán, etc. **Coat of mail,** cota de malla. **Great-coat, overcoat, top-coat,** sobretodo, abrigo. **Dress-coat,** frac, casaca. **Coat of arms,** escudo de armas. **Frock-coat,** levita. **To turn one's coat,** (Met.) volver casaca, mudar de partido, cambiar de opinión. **White coat,** bata blanca (doctors). **To cut one's coat according to one's cloth,** vivir según sus posibilidades, adaptarse a las circunstancias. **Coat hanger,** percha. **Coat stand,** perchero.

coat, va. Cubrir, vestir. **Sugar-coated,** garapiñado, cubierto con azúcar.

-coated suff. (Culin.) Sugarcoated, cubierto de azúcar. **Chocolatecoated,** cubierto de chocolate, bañado en chocolate.

coatee [ˈkəʊtiː] [koutí], s. Casaquilla, levitín, casaca muy corta.

coating [ˈkəʊtɪŋ] [kou-tin], s. Revestimiento, capa, mano de pintura, barniz, cal, etc., sobre una pared u otra superficie cualquiera. Capa (of dust, grease). (Culin.) Capa, baño. **Protective coating,** revestimiento de protección.

coat of arms [kəʊtɒfˈɑːmz] [kout-of-arms] s. Escudo de armas.

coax [kəʊks] [kouks], va. Engaitar, engatusar, mimar, acariciar, halagar. **I coaxed the child into going to bed,** convencí al niño para que se acostara. **I coaxed the animal into the cage,** con paciencia logré que el animal se metiera en la jaula. **She coaxed them to eat,** con paciencia intentó que comieran. **To coax something from/out of somebody,** sonsacarle algo a alguien. **A coaxing voice,** una voz persuasiva.

coaxer [ˈkəʊksər] [kouk-sa^r], s. Engatusador, mimador, gaitero.

coaxial [ˌkəʊˈæksɪəl] [kou-aksial], a. Coaxial. **Coaxial cable,** cable coaxial.

coaxing [ˈkəʊksɪŋ] [kouksin], s. Engatusamiento, adulación, caricia. Persuasión, mano izquierda.

cob [kɒb] [kob], s. 1. Masa casi redonda, montón; cabeza. 2. Mazorca de maíz, choclo, elote (corncob). 3. Jaco, caballo fuerte, rechoncho y de piernas cortas. 4. El cisne. 5. Araña. 6. Peso duro de España. 7. Gaviota de Inglaterra. 8. Mezcla de arcilla y paja para hacer paredes y la pared hecha con ella.

cob, va. (Mar.) Azotar con una paleta. **Cobbing-board,** paleta de azotar.

cobalt [ˈkəʊbɒlt] [kou-bolt], s. Cobalto, un metal duro, de color gris, estimado por los colores azules que produce.

cobalt bomb [kəʊbɒltˈbɒm] [kobu-bolt-bomb], s. Bomba de cobalto.

cobble [ˈkɒbl] [kobel], va. 1. Chapucear, remendar o hacer alguna cosa sin pulidez. 2. Remendar zapatos. **Cobbled,** adoquinado (street).

cobble together (Coloq.) Improvisar (meal); redactar a las carreras (essay, speech).

cobbler [ˈkɒblər] [kobla^r], s. 1. Zapatero de viejo, remendón (shoe repairer). 2. Chapucero, chambón, mal oficial. 3. Galopín, persona vil y baja. **Cobblers,** (GB) (Sl.) Estupideces (nonsense).

cobblestone [kɒblˈstəʊn] [ko-ble-stoun], s. Guijarro, piedra, redondeada por la acción del agua. Adoquín.

cobelligerent [kɒˈbəlɪdʒərənt] [ko-be-li-ye-rent], a. y s. Cobeligerante, que hace la guerra en unión y de acuerdo con otra potencia.

cobirons [ˈkɒbɪrənz] [ko-bi-rons], s. pl. (Prov.) Morillos, caballetes de hierro que se ponen en el hogar para sustentar la leña o el asador.

cobishop [ˈkɒbɪʃɒp] [ko-bi-shop], s. Obispo coadjutor o auxiliar.

cobra [ˈkɒbrə] [kou-bra], s. (Zool.) Cobra.

cobwed [ˈkɒbweb] [kob-ueb], s. 1. Telaraña. 2. Trama, tramoya.

cobwebbed [ˈkɒbwebd] [ko-uebd], a. Entelarañado, cubierto con telarañas.

coca [ˈkəʊkə] [kou-ka], s. Coca, las hojas del arbusto Erythroxylon Coca, estimulante enérgico procedente de América del Sur.

cocain, cocaine [kəˈkeɪn] [ko-kein], s. Cocaína, acaloide blanco, amargo, cristalino, que se halla en la coca: muy empleada en medicina como anestésico local.

cocainize [kəˈkeɪniːz] [ko-kei-nis], va. Poner bajo la infuencia anestésica de la cocaína.

cocciferous [ˈkɒksɪfərəs] [kok-si-fe-ros], *a.* Lo que produce o cría bayas.

cocculus indicus [kɒkələsˈɪndɪkəs] [ko-ku-lus-in-di-kus], *s. (Bot.)* Baya narcótica que se usa para emborrachar los peces.

coccus [ˈkɒkəs] [ko-kus], *s.* 1. Bacteria, esférica, o casi esférica. 2. Cóccido, insecto escamoso del orden de los hemípteros.

coccygeal [ˈkɒksɪdʒɪəl] [kok-si-yial], *a.* Relativo, o cerca del coxis o la cola.

coccyx [ˈkɒksɪks] [kok-sis], *s.* Coxis, hueso en que termina la columna vertebral.

cochineal [ˈkɒtʃɪniːl] [ko-chi-nil], *s.* 1. Cochinilla, insecto del cual se obtine el color de grana. 2. Cochinilla, el color que se obtiene de este insecto.

cochlea [ˈkɒklɪə] [ko-klia], *s.* Cóclea, conducto interior del oído, generalmente de forma espiral.

cochleary [ˈkɒklɪərɪ] [ko-klia-ri], **cochleated** [kɒklɪˈeɪtɪd] [ko-kli-ei-ted], *a.* Caracoleado.

cock [kɒk] [kok], *s.* 1. Gallo, el macho de la gallina (male fowl). 2. Macho, ave del sexo masculino entre los pájaros (male bird); en este sentido se usa ordinariamente en composición. 3. Veleta, giraldilla, pedazo de hierro que señala la dirección del viento. 4. Llave, instrumento de metal que sirve para sacar los licores de las vasijas o el agua de las fuentes; grifo, grifón, espita. 5. *(Ingl.)* Caudillo, campeón. 6. Montoncillo de heno 7. Pie de gato de escopeta; y la posición en que se halla el gatillo cuando está levantado. 8. Estilo de reloj de sol. 9. Armazón de sombrero. 10. Aguja de romana. 11. *(Vulg.)* Verga, pija, polla, pico (penis). **A cock and bull story,** cuento pesado; embuste. **Cockspurs,** navajas de gallo. **Cock-sparrow,** gorrión. **Turkey-cock,** pavo, guanajo.

cock, *va.* 1. Enderezar o poner derecho hacia arriba. Ladear (head); levantar, parar (ears). **The dog cocked its leg at each tree,** el perro levantaba la pata en cada árbol. 2. Encandilar el sombrero, armar el sombrero. 3. Amartillar, preparar un arma de fuego para dispararla (gun). 4. Hacinar o amontonar heno. -*vn.* 1. Entonarse, engreírse. 2. Criar o enseñar gallos para pelear. **Cocked hat,** (a) sombrero de tres picos; (b) juego de bochas con tres piezas que se ponen en los ángulos de un triángulo. **To knock into a cocked hat,** *(Vul.)* aporrear, dar de palos de suerte que algo pierda su forma; vencer; demoler.

cock up (GB) *(Sl.)* Fastidiar, joder.

cockade [kɒˈkeɪd] [ko-keid], *s.* Escarapela o cucarda.

cock-a-doodle-doo [ˈkɒkəduːdlˈduː] [ko-ka-du-del-du] *interj.* ¡quiquiriquí!

cock-a-hoop [ˈkɒkəˈhuːp] [kok-a-jup] *a.* **To be cock-a-hoop about something,** estar contentísimo o como unas castañuelas con algo (exultant).

cockamamy [ˈkɒkəməmɪ] [ko-ka-ma-mi] *a. (Coloq.)* Absurdo, disparatado.

cock-and-bull [ˈkɒkənˈbɒl] [kok-an-bul] *a. (Coloq.)* **Cock-and-bull story/tale,** cuento chino, camelo.

cockatoo [ˌkɒkəˈtuː] [kok-a-tu], *s. (Orn.)* Cacatoes, especie de papagayo de la India y Australia, que tiene un copete eréctil. Cacatúa.

cockatrice [ˈkɒkətriːz] [ko-ka-tris], *s.* Basilisco; animal fabuloso.

cockboat [ˈkɒkbəʊt] [kok-bout], *s. (Mar.)* Bote pequeño de remo.

cock-brained [kɒkˈbreɪnd] [kok-breind], *s.* Ligero, temerario, travieso.

cock-broth [kɒkˈbrɒθ] [kok-broz], *s.* Caldo de gallo.

cockchafer [ˈkɒktʃeɪfər] [kok-chei-far], *s. (Ento.)* Abejorro, escarabajo.

cock-crowing [kɒkˈkrəʊɪŋ] [kok-krouin], *s.* El canto del gallo; la aurora.

cocked hat [kɒktˈhɑːtk] [kokt-jat] *s.* **To knock somebody/something into a cocked hat,** darle cien o cien mil vueltas a alguien/algo, ser muchísimo mejor que alguien/algo.

cocker [ˈkɒkər] [kokar], *va.* Acariciar, mimar.

cocker, *s.* 1. Sabueso pequeño que se emplea para cazar la chochaperdiz y otras aves. 2. El que es aficionado a las peleas de gallos.

cockerel [ˈkɒkrəl] [ko-krel], *s.* Gallipollo; gallito.

cockering [ˈkɒkərɪŋ] [ko-ke-rin], *s.* Indulgencia excesiva, mimo.

cocker spaniel [kɒkəˈspaːnɪəl] [ko-ker-spa-niel] *s.* Cocker (spaniel).

cocket [ˈkɒkɪt] [ko-ket], *s.* 1. Sello de la aduana. 2. Certificación de pago de la aduana. -*a. (Des.)* Vivo; atrevido.

cock-eyed [kɒkˈaɪd] [kok-aid], *a.* 1. Bizco. 2. Disparatado (ridiculous). 3. Torcido, chueco (askew).

cock-fight, cock-fighting [ˈkɒkfaɪt] [kok-fait], *s.* 1. Riña o pelea de gallos. 2. Juego de gallos.

cock-fighter [ˈkɒkfaɪtər] [kok-fai-tar], **cock-master**, *s.* Gallero, el que tiene y cría gallos para pelear.

cockfighting [ˈkɒkfaɪtɪŋ] [kok-fai-tin] *s.* Peleas de gallos, riñas de gallos.

cock-horse [kɒkˈhɔːz] [kok-jors], *s.* Caballito mecedor de juguete; palo o caña con que juegan los niños montándolo a horcajadas.

cocking [ˈkɒkɪŋ] [ko-kin], *s.* La riña de gallos.

cockle [ˈkɒkl] [kokel], *s.* 1. *(Zool.)* Berberecho, una especie de caracol de mar comestible. 2. *(Bot.)* Vallico, zizaña, joyo, hierba que nace entre los trigos y cebadas. **To warm the cockles of somebody's heart,** enternecer a alguien.

cockle, *va.* Arrugar, hacer arrugas; doblar una cosa en figura espiral. -Plegarse, doblarse.

cockled [ˈkɒkld] [kokeld], *a.* Espiral, hecho en figura de caracol.

cockler [ˈkɒklər] [koklaʳ], *s.* El que vende los caracoles de mar llamados *cockle.*

cock-loft [kɒkˈlɒft] [kok-loft], *s.* Desván, zaquizamí.

cock-match [kɒkˈmaːtʃ] [kok-mach], *s.* Riña o pelea de gallos.

cockney [ˈkɒknɪ] [kok-ni], *s.* 1. Londinense, tradicionalmente de clase obrera. 2. Hombre afeminado.

cockpit [ˈkɒkpɪt] [kok-pit], *s.* 1. Reñidero de gallos. Gallera, reñidero, palenque (for cockfights). 2. *(Mar.)* Entarimado del sollado. 3. *(Aviat.)* Cabina de mando. *(Naut.)* Puente de mando. Cabina (in racing car).

cockroach [ˈkɒkrəʊtʃ] [kokrouch], *s.* Cucaracha, corredera, insecto ortóptero que infesta las cocinas y despensas.

cockscomb [ˈkɒkskəʊm] [kok-skoum], *s. (Bot.)* 1. Amaranto, moco de pavo, flor. 2. V. COXCOMB.

cockspur [ˈkɒkspɜːr] [kokspar], *s.* 1. Espolón natural o navaja de gallo. 2. *(Bot.)* Especie de níspero.

cock-sure [ˈkɒkˈʃʊər] [kok-shuar], *a. (Vul.)* Confiado, cierto, seguro. *(Coloq.)* Creído, petulante, engreído.

cockswain [ˈkɒkzweɪn] [koks-uein], *s. (Mar.)* Patrón de bote. V. COXSWAIN.

cocktail [ˈkɒkteɪl] [kok-teil], *s.* Cóctel, bebida alcohólica compuesta (drink). **Cocktail bar,** coctelería. **Cocktail cabinet,** mueble-bar. **Cocktail party,** cóctel. **Cocktail stick,** palillo, mondadientes, escarbadientes. **Shrimp** o (GB) **prawn cocktail,** cóctel de camarones o de gambas o de langostinos, langostinos con salsa golf (food).

cock-up [ˈkɒkʌp] [kok-ap] *s.* (GB) *(Coloq.)* Lío, follón. **I made a cock-up of it,** la fastidié, la embarré.

cocky [ˈkɒkɪ] [ko-ki] *a. (Coloq.)* Gallito, chulo.

cocoa [ˈkəʊkəʊ] [kou-kou], *s.* 1. Coco, palma de América. 2. Cacao, árbol de América y la bebida preparada con sus simientes. Cacao, cocoa (powder); chocolate, cocoa (drink).

cocoa-nut, coconut [ˈkəʊkənʌt] [ko-ko-nat], *s.* 1. Coco, fruto del árbol llamado coco. 2. Cacao, el fruto del cacao. **Coconut milk,** agua de coco. **Coconut palm,** cocotero, palma de coco. **Coconut shy,** tiro al coco. **Coconut tree.** V. COCONUT PALM.

cocoon [kəˈkuːn] [ko-kun], *s. (Zool.)* Capullo del gusano de seda, y de otros insectos en estado de oruga.

cocoon, *va.* **To cocoon somebody in something,** arrebujar o arropar a alguien con algo.

coction ['kɒkʃən] [kok-shon], *s.* Cocción, la acción de cocer, el acto de hervir.

cod, codfish [kɒd] [kod], *s.* Abadejo, bacalao. **Cod-liver oil,** aceite de hígado de bacalao.

cod, *s.* 1. *(Bot.)* Vaina, vainilla, la corteza tierna y larga en que están encerradas algunas legumbres o semillas. *V.* POD. 2. *(Anat.)* Bolsa; panza; el escroto.

cod, *va.* Envainar, encerrar en vaina u hollejo.

C.O.D., Abreviatura de **cash/collect on delivery,** entrega contra reembolso, cóbrese al entregar.

coddle ['kɒdl] [ko-del], *va.* 1. Cuidar con mucho cuidado o ternura; mimar. 2. Cocer a medias.

code [kəʊd] [koud], *s.* 1. Código, compilación de leyes (Law). 2. Clave, sistema de señales o de caracteres para representar palabras o frases. Código (for identification). *(Telec.)* Código, prefijo. *(Inform.)* Código. Clave, código (cipher). **In code,** en clave, cifrado. 3. Colección de preceptos o reglas de conducta: como **Code of honor,** código de honor. Código (social, moral). **Code of practice,** código de práctica.

code *va.* Cifrar, poner en clave (encipher). Codificar (give identifying number, mark). *(Inform.)* Codificar.

codein ['kəʊdɪn] [kou-dein], *s.* Codeína, alcaloide obtenido del opio.

codger ['kɒdʒər] [kod-yaʳ], *s.* Hombre tacaño y avariento; se usa despreciativamente. *(Coloq.)* **Old codger,** vejete.

codicil ['kɒdɪsɪl] [ko-di-sil], *s.* Codicilo, escrito auténtico por el cual se quita o añade algo a un testamento.

codification [ˌkəʊdɪfɪ'keɪʃən] [kou-di-fi-kei-shon], *s.* Codificación (de las leyes).

codify ['kəʊdɪfaɪ] [kou-di-fai], *va.* Codificar, compilar leyes, formar códigos de leyes, señales o reglas.

coding ['kəʊdɪŋ] [kou-din] *s.* Cifrado, notación en clave. *(Inform.)* Codificación.

codling ['kɒdlɪŋ] [kodlin], *s.* Manzana medio cocida. **Codling- (o codlin) moth,** mariposa tortrícida cuya oruga es el gusano de la manzana.

co-driver ['kəʊdraɪvər] [kou-drai-var] *s.* Copiloto.

codswallop ['kɒdzwɒləp] [kad-sua-lop] *s.* (GB) *(Coloq.)* Paparruchas.

coeducation ['kəʊˌedjʊ'keɪʃən] [kou-e-diu-kei-shon], *s.* Coeducación.

coeducational ['kəʊˌedjʊ'keɪʃnl] [kou-e-diu-kei-sho-nal], **coed** [kəʊed] [koued] *a.* Coeducativo. Mixto.

coefficiency [ˌkəʊɪ'fɪʃənsɪ] [kou-i-fi-shen-si], *s.* Cooperación, concurso.

coefficient [ˌkəʊɪ'fɪʃənt] [kou-i-fi-shient], *a.* Coeficiente.

coefficiently [ˌkəʊɪ'fɪʃəntlɪ] [kou-i-fi-shient-li], *adv.* Cooperativamente.

coemption ['kəʊempʃən] [kou-emp-shon], *s.* Compra mutua, cierta forma de matrimonio en el derecho romano.

coequal [kəʊ'ɪkwəl] [kou-i-kual], *a.* Igual. Coigual, hablando de las personas de la Santísima Trinidad.

coerce [kəʊ'ɜːs] [kou-ers], *va.* 1. Forzar, obligar. 2. Contener, refrenar. **To coerce somebody into,** coaccionar a alguien para que, compeler a alguien.

coercible [kəʊ'ɜːsɪbl] [kou-er-si-bol], *a.* Lo que puede o debe ser refrenado.

coercion [kəʊ'ɜːʃən] [kou-ershon], *s.* Coerción, violencia, fuerza, sujeción, opresión. Coacción.

coercive [kəʊ'ɜːsɪv] [kou-er-siv], *a.* Coercitivo; coactivo.

coessential [kəʊɪ'senʃəl] [kou-i-sen-shal], *a.* Coesencial.

coessentially [kəʊɪ'senʃəlɪ] [kou-i-sen-sha-li], *adv.* Coesencialmente.

coetaneous [kəʊɪ'teɪnɪəs] [kou-i-ta-nious], *a.* Coetáneo, contemporáneo.

coeternal [kəʊɪ'tɜːnl] [kou-i-ter-nal], *s.* Coeternidad.

coeval [kəʊ'iːvəl] [kou-i-val], *a.* Coevo, contemporáneo. -*s. V.* CONTEMPORARY.

coexist ['kəʊɪg'zɪst] [kou-ik-sist], *vn.* Coexistir. **To coexist with somebody/something,** coexistir o convivir con alguien/algo.

coexistence ['kəʊɪg'zɪstəns] [kou-ik-sis-tans], *s.* Coexistencia, convivencia.

coexistent ['kəʊɪg'zɪstənt] [kou-ik-sis-tant], *a.* Coexistente.

coextend ['kəʊɪkstend] [kou-iks-tend], *va.* Coextenderse.

coextension ['kəʊɪk'stenʃən] [kou-iks-ten-shon], *s.* Coextensión.

coextensive [ˌkəʊɪks'tensɪv] [kou-iks-ten-siv], *a.* Coextensivo.

coextensively ['kəʊɪks'tensɪvlɪ] [kou-iks-ten-siv-li], *adv.* Coextensivamente.

coffee ['kɒfɪ] [ko-fi], *s.* 1. Café, haba o haya del árbol así llamado. 2. Café, bebida hecha con las bayas de café tostadas, molidas e infundidas en agua hirviendo. Café (beans, granules, drink). 3. Café con leche (color). **Coffee-bean** o **berry,** grano de café. **Coffee break,** pausa para tomar café. **Coffee mill/grinder,** molinillo de café. **Coffee plantation,** cafetal, plantillo de café. **Coffee planter** o **seller,** cafetero. **Coffee store,** cafetería. **Coffee table,** mesita para el servicio de café en las salas. **Black coffee,** café negro, solo, puro o tinto. **White coffee,** café con leche. **Coffee percolator,** cafetera de filtro.

coffee bar ['kɒfɪ'bɑːr] [ko-fi-baʳ] *s.* (GB) Cafetería.

coffee cake ['kɒfɪ'keɪk] [ko-fi-keik] *s.* Bizcocho con fruta seca (in US); pastel de café (in UK).

coffee-house ['kɒfɪˌhaʊs] [ko-fi-jaus], *s.* Café, casa o sitio donde se vende café.

coffee klatsch ['kɒfɪˌklɑːtʃ] [ko-fi-klash] *s.* Tertulia.

coffee maker ['kɒfɪˌmeɪkər] [ko-fi-mei-keʳ] *s.* Cafetera, máquina para preparar café.

coffee-pot ['kɒfɪpɒt] [ko-fi-pot], *s.* Cafetera, vasija en que se hace el café.

coffee table ['kɒfɪˌteɪbl] [ko-fi-tei-bol] *s.* Mesa de centro, mesa ratona. **Coffee-table book,** libro ilustrado de gran formato.

coffee-tree ['kɒfɪtriː] [ko-fi-tri], *s. (Bot.)* Cafeto, el árbol que produce el café.

coffer ['kɒfər] [ko-feʳ], *s.* 1. Arca, cofre o caja (chest). 2. *(Fort.)* Cofre, cierta excavación que se hace en medio del foso seco, para contener al enemigo al llegar a la contraescarpa. 3. Tesoro; en este sentido se usa más comúnmente en plural. **Coffers,** fondos (funds). 4. *(Arq.)* Artesón hondo. *V.* CAISSON.

coffer *va.* 1. Atesorar o meter dinero en arcas. 2. Adornar con artesones. 3. Proveer de un cofre o cofres.

coffer-dam ['kɒfədæm] [ko-fer-dam], *s.* Represa encofrada, malecón, construcción que se introduce en el agua para que los trabajadores puedan hacer los estribos de los puentes y otras obras parecidas.

coffin ['kɒfɪn] [ko-fin], *s.* 1. Ataúd, féretro, cajón. 2. La parte de casco del caballo que cubre un hueso. **Coffin-bone,** el hueso que se halla dentro del casco del caballo.

coffin-maker ['kɒfɪnˌmeɪkər] [ko-fin-mei-kaʳ], *s.* El que hace ataúdes.

cofounder ['kəʊ'faʊndər] [ko-faun-daʳ], *s.* El que funda alguna cosa con otro u otros.

cog [kɒg] [kog], *va.* 1. Puntear una rueda, ponerle puntos o dientes. 2. Engañar, engaitar, trampear. **To cog a dice,** cargar un dado, poner plomo en él para que se incline a un lado. - *vn.* Mentir engañar con lisonjas.

cog, *s.* 1. Punto, diente de rueda con el cual se mueven otras. Piñón, rueda dentada (wheel). Diente (tooth). **To be a cog in the machine,** ser una pieza más en el engranaje del organismo (o del partido.). 2. Fraude, engaño. 3. Ramplón de herradura. 4. Botequín, o barca de pescador.

cogency ['kəʊdʒənsɪ] [ko-yen-si], *s.* Fuerza lógica o moral, urgencia, evidencia.

cogenial, *a. V.* CONGENIAL.

cogent ['kəʊdʒənt] [kou-yent], *a.* 1. Convincente, poderoso, urgente. Contundente. 2. Fuerte, potente (en sentido físico).

cogently [ˈkəʊdʒəntlɪ] [kou-yent-li], *adv.* Convincentemente.

cogger [ˈkɒɡər] [ko-gua'], *s.* Adulador, engañador, lisonjero; fullero, tahur.

cogging [ˈkɒɡɪŋ] [ko-guin], *s.* Lisonja, adulación, fullería.

cogitable [ˈkɒdʒɪtəbl] [ko-yi-ta-bol], *a.* Cogitable, lo que puede ser objeto del pensamiento.

cogitate [ˈkɒdʒɪteɪt] [ko-yi-teit], *vn.* Pensar, meditar, reflexionar. **To cogitate on/upon something,** cavilar o meditar sobre algo.

cogitation [ˈkɒdʒɪteɪʃən] [ko-yi-tei-shon], *s.* Pensamiento, reflexión, meditación.

cogitative [ˈkɒdʒɪtətɪv] [ko-yi-ta-tiv], *a.* Discursivo, pensativo, reflexivo.

cogglestone [ˈkɒɡlɪstəʊn] [kog-lis-toun], *s.* Guijarro.

cognac [ˈkɒnjæk] [kog-nak], *s.* Coñac, aguardiente francés.

cognate [ˈkɒɡneɪt] [kog-neit], *a.* 1. Cognado, consanguíneo. 2. Semejante, análogo. 3. Pariente colateral por la línea femenina.

cognation [ˈkɒɡneɪʃən] [kog-nei-shon], *s.* Cognación, parentesco de consanguinidad.

cognition [kɒɡˈnɪʃən] [kog-ni-shon], *s.* Conocimiento, experiencia, convicción.

cognitive [ˈkɒɡnɪtɪv] [kog-ni-tiv], *a.* Cognoscitivo, capaz de conocer.

cognizable [ˈkɒɡnɪzəbl] [kog-ni-za-bol], *a.* 1. Lo que se puede comprender, percibir o conocer. **Cognizable by the senses,** perceptible por medio de los sentidos. 2. Lo que se puede examinar jurídicamente; de la competencia.

cognizance [ˈkɒɡnɪzəns] [kog-ni-sans], *s.* 1. Conocimiento, acto de conocer o juzgar una cosa. 2. Divisa, señal o distintivo con que uno es conocido. 3. *(For.)* Conocimiento, competencia, derecho a conocer de una causa o negocio.

cognizant [ˈkɒɡnɪzənt] [kog-ni-sant], *a.* Que nota o advierte; sabedor, que tiene conocimiento.

cognizee [ˈkɒɡɪziː] [kog-ni-si], *s. (For. Ant.)* El censualista que tiene derecho de cobrar una multa por la venta o trueque de las tierras o posesiones sujetas al pago del censo.

cognizor [ˈkɒɡnɪzər] [kog-ni-so'], *s. (For. Ant.)* El censualista que pasa su derecho de cobrar multas por ventas o trueques o otra persona.

cognominal [ˈkɒɡnəʊmɪnl] [kog-nou-mi-nal], *a.* Tocayo.

cognominate, *va. V.* DENOMINATE.

cognomination [ˈkɒɡnəʊmɪneɪʃən] [kog-nou-mi-nei-shon], *s.* Sobrenombre que se da a alguno a casua de sus virtudes o vicios, v.g. *Alfonso el Sabio.*

cognosce [ˈkɒɡnəs] [kog-nos], *va. y vn.* Conocer o entender jurídicamente, adjudicar.

cognoscible [ˈkɒɡnəsɪbl] [kog-nos-si-bol], *a.* Conocible, cognoscible.

cognoscitive [ˈkɒɡnəsɪtɪv] [kog-nos-si-tiv], *a.* Cognoscitivo, lo que es capaz de conocer.

cognovit [ˈkɒɡnəvɪt] [kog-no-vit], *s. (For.)* Convenio o acuerdo escrito por el cual el demandado reconoce justa la reclamación del demandante, o parte de ella, y acepta la decisión del tribunal.

cog-wheel [ˈkɒɡwiːl] [kog-uil], *s.* Rueda dentada.

cohabit [kəʊˈhæbɪt] [kou-ja-bit], *vn.* 1. *(Ant.)* Vivir en compañía de otro. 2. Cohabitar, vivir como marido y mujer. **To cohabit with somebody,** cohabitar con alguien.

cohabitant [kəʊˈhæbɪtənt] [kou-ja-bi-tant], *s.* El que es convecino de otro.

cohabitation [kəʊˈhæbɪteɪʃən] [kou-ja-bi-tei-shon], *s.* 1. El estado de vivir en compañía. 2. Cohabitación, vida maridable.

coheir [kəʊˈheər] [ko-jea'], *s.* Coheredero.

coheiress [ˈkəʊheəres] [kou-jea-res], *sf.* Coheredera.

cohere [kəʊˈhɪər] [kou-jia'], *vn.* Adherirse, pegarse, unirse, adaptarse. *(Des.)* Convenir, conformarse. Formar una unidad (form unit). **To cohere with something,** se coherente o congruente con algo.

coherence, coherency [ˈkəʊhɪərəns] [kou-jia-rans], *s.* Cohesión, coherencia, conexión, unión (logical conexion); consecuencia; consistencia, relación. Cohesión (of group).

coherent [kəʊˈhɪərent] [kou-jia-rent], *a.* Coherente, congruente; consecuente, consiguiente; ligado, unido.

cohesion [ˈkəʊhiːʒən] [kou-ji-shon], *s.* 1. Cohesión, coherencia, adherencia. 2. Cohesión, fuerza de adherencia entre las moléculas de un cuerpo 3. Hilación, enlace, conexión.

cohesive [ˈkəʊhiːsɪv] [kou-ji-siv], *a.* Coherente, adherente. *a.* Unido (group).

cohesively [ˈkəʊhiːsɪvlɪ] [kou-ji-siv-li], *adv.* Coherentemente.

cohesiveness [ˈkəʊhiːsɪvnɪs] [kou-ji-siv-nes], *s.* Calidad o propiedad coherente.

cohibit [ˈkəʊhiːbɪt] [kou-ji-bit], *va.* (Raro) Cohibir, refrenar, impedir.

cohobate [ˈkəʊhəʊbeɪt] [kou-jo-beit], *va. (Quím.)* Destilar repetidas veces una misma cosa.

cohort [ˈkəʊhɔːt] [kou-jort], *s. (Hist., Mil.)* Cohorte. Seguidor (follower).

coif [kɔɪf] [koif], *va.* Adornar la cabeza con una cofia.

coifed [ˈkɔɪfd] [koi-fid], *a.* Lo que tiene o está adornado con cofia o escofieta.

coiffure, *s.* Tocado, peinado. *V.* HEADDRESS.

coil [kɔɪl] [koil], *va.* Recoger, doblar en redondo; arrollar en espiral. Enrollar (rope, wire). **To coil something/oneself around something,** enrollar algo/enrollarse o enroscarse alrededor de algo. **To coil a cable,** *(Mar.)* adujar un cable. - *vn.* Formar círculos. **Smoke coiled into the air,** el humo se alzaba en volutas o en espiral.

coil, *s.* 1. Rollo, serie de círculos o espiral, que se forma doblando algo en redondo (series of loops - of rope, wire). Espiral, volutas (of smoke). Moño, chongo, rodete (of hair). 2. *(Mar.)* Adujada, cable o cabo adujado. 3. Pliegue (de serpiente o culebra); lío (de cuerdas). 4. *(Elec.)* Alambre conductor enrollado en un carrete. 5. Lazada, vuelta (single loop). 6. (GB) Espiral (contraceptive).

coiling [ˈkɔɪlɪŋ] [koi-lin], *s. (Mec.)* Arrollamiento.

coin [kɔɪn] [koin], *va.* 1. Acuñar moneda. 2. Falsificar, contrahacer. Acuñar (invent/word, expression). **To coin words,** inventar palabras. **To coin a lie,** forjar una mentira. **To coin a phrase,** como se suele decir (set phrase).

coin, *s.* 1. Moneda acuñada con cuño real o autoridad pública. **The other side of the coin,** la otra cara de la moneda. 2. Pago de dinero contante. 3. *(Arq.)* Rincón, cuando significa el ángulo entrante; esquina, cuando indica el ángulo saliente. *V.* QUOIN.

coinage [ˈkɔɪnɪdʒ] [koi-nich], *s.* 1. Acuñación. 2. Moneda, dinero. Sistema monetario (system). 3. Braceaje, los gastos de acuñación. 4. Falsificación, la acción de falsear o contrahacer alguna cosa. 5. Invención, cuento forjado. 6. Palabra o frase de nuevo cuño (invented word, phrase).

coin box [ˈkɔɪnbɒks] [koin-boks] *s.* Depósito de monedas.

coincide [ˌkəʊɪnˈsaɪd] [kouin-said], *vn.* 1. Coincidir, concurrir, convenir. 2. Con *with:* convenirse, estar o ponerse de acuerdo.

coincidence [kəʊˈɪnsɪdəns] [kouin-si-dans], *s.* 1. Coincidencia, concurrencia, casualidad. **By coincidence he was there,** dio la casualidad de que estaba allí. 2. Contemporaneidad.

coincidency [kəʊˈɪnsɪdənsɪ] [kouin-si-dan-si], *s.* 1. Concurrencia, acaecimiento o concurso de varios sucesos al mismo tiempo. 2. Tendencia de muchas cosas al mismo fin.

coincident [kəʊˈɪnsɪdənt] [kouin-si-dans], *a.* Coincidente, concurrente.

coincidental [kəʊˈɪnsɪdəntəl] [kouin-si-den-tal] *a.* Casual, fortuito.

coincidentally [ˌkəʊɪnsɪˈdentəlɪ] [kouin-si-den-ta-li] *adv.* Por casualidad, casualmente.

coincider [kəʊˈɪnsɪdər] [kouin-si-da'], *s.* Lo que coincide con otro.

coindicant [kəʊˈɪnsɪkænt] [kouin-di-kant], *a.* Concurrente, confirmante de otra indicación previa.

coindication [ˌkəʊɪndɪˈkeɪʃən] [kouin-di-kei-shon], *s.* Coindicante.

coined [ˈkɔɪnd] [koind], *pp.* 1. Acuñado. 2. Inventado, forjado. **Newly coined words,** palabras nuevamente introducidas, neologismos.

coiner [ˈkɔɪnər] [koi-naʳ], *s.* 1. Acuñador de moneda. 2. Monedero falso. 3. Inventor, fabricador.

coin-operated [ˈkɔɪnˈɒpɪreɪtɪd] [koin-o-pe-rei-ted] *a.* Que funciona con monedas.

coir [kɔːr] [koʳ], *s.* Estopa de coco, la cáscara fibrosa de su nuez y la cuerda hecha con esa fibra.

coition [ˈkɔɪʃən] [koi-shon], *s.* La acción de juntarse; especialmente el coito, la cópula.

coitus [ˈkɔɪtəs] [koi-tos] *s.* Coito.

cojuror [ˈkjʊərər] [ko-yuo-roʳ], *s.* Compurgador, el que confirma bajo juramento la declaración de otro.

coke [kəʊk] [kouk], *s.* 1. Cok, coque, hulla calcinada en hornos o retortas. Carbón de coque (fuel). 2. *(Coloq.)* Coca (cocaine). 3. *(Coloq.)* Coke, Coca-cola.

coke, *va. y vn.* Cambiar o cambiarse en coque.

col (= **Colonel**) Coronel. (title).

colaborer [ˈkɒləbərər] [ko-la-bo-raʳ], *s.* Colaborador, el que trabaja con otro.

colander [ˈkʌˈlændər] [ka-lan-daʳ], *s.* Coladera, coladero, coldador, cedazo. Escurridor (de pasta, verduras).

colation [ˈkʌleɪʃən] [ka-lei-shon], **colature** [ˈkʌlətʃər] [ko-la-chuaʳ], *s.* Coladura, la acción y efecto de colar.

colchicum [ˈkɔːlkɪkəm] [kol-ki-kum], *s.* *(Bot.)* Cólquico, azafrán rumí o bastardo; planta medicinal; *(ant.)* villorita.

colcothar [ˈkɔːlkəθər] [kol-ko-zaʳ], *s.* *(Quím.)* Colcótar, peróxido de hierro rojo que se prepara calcinando la caparrosa. Cf. CROCUS y ROUGE.

cold [kəʊld] [kould], *a.* 1. Frío (water, weather, drink). **I'm cold,** tengo frío. **My feet are cold,** tengo los pies fríos, tengo frío en los pies. **It's cold today/in here,** hoy/aquí hace frío. **The soup is cold,** la sopa está fría. **I'm getting cold,** me está entrando frío. **It's getting cold,** está empezando a hacer frío. **The engine starts straight from cold,** el motor arranca en frío. **The trail had gone cold,** se habían borrado las huellas. 2. Frío, indiferente, insensible; sereno; casto, sin pasiones (unfriendly, unenthusiastic). **I got a very cold reception,** me recibieron con mucha frialdad o muy fríamente. **To be cold to/with somebody,** tratar a alguien con frialdad, estar/ser frío con alguien. *(Coloq.)* **That leaves me cold,** (eso) me deja frío o tal cual, (eso) no me da ni frío ni calor. 3. Frío, insulso, soso, desagradable, sin energía ni gracia. 4. Frío, tibio, flojo. 5. Reservado, esquivo, serio, poco tratable, seco en el trato. Frío (impersonal, logic). **To be cold,** tener frío (hablando de personas); hacer frío (hablando del tiempo). **In cold blood,** a sangre fría. **To turn the cold shoulder,** proceder con tibieza; ser indiferente. **To throw cold water on,** desanimar con tibieza o frialdad. **Cold-chisel,** cortafrío. **Cold-cream,** pomada o ungüento para el cutis. (El ungüento de agua rosada.) **I came to the job cold,** empecé el trabajo sin ninguna preparación (without preparation).

cold, *s.* 1. Frío (low temperature). **To shiver with cold,** temblar de frío. **To feel the cold,** ser friolero, sentir el frío. 2. Frío, frialdad, sensación de frío. 3. *(Med.)* Resfriado, constipado, catarro, resfrío. **To have a cold,** estar resfriado. **To catch a cold,** resfriarse, coger un resfriado; constiparse, tener una fluxión. **A cold in the head,** un romadizo. **To leave out in the cold,** dejar a uno a la luna de Valencia; menospreciar con premeditación.

cold, *adv.* (as intensifier). **I've got the part down cold now,** ahora me sé el papel perfectamente o de pe a pa.

cold-blooded [ˈkəʊldˈblʌdɪd] [kould-bla-ded], *a.* 1. De sangre fría; deficiente en calor vital. 2. *(Zool.)* Que tiene una temperatura baja casi igual a aquella en la que viven; dícese

de los peces y reptiles. 3. Inhumano, atroz, cruel, despiadado, desalmado (killer). A sangre fría (murder).

cold calling [ˈkəʊldˈkɔːlɪŋ] s. Venta en frío.

cold cream [ˈkəʊldˈkriːm] [kould-krím] s. Crema limpiadora o de limpieza, cold cream.

cold cuts [ˈkəʊldˈkʌts] [kould-kats] s. Fiambres.

cold-hearted [ˈkəʊldˈhɑːtɪd] [kould-jar-ted], *a.* Insensible, frío, desamorado, hurón.

coldly [ˈkəʊldlɪ] [kould-li], *adv.* Fríamente; indiferentemente, con frialdad.

coldness [ˈkəʊldnɪs] [kould-nes], *s.* 1. Frialdad (of person, attitude). Frío (temperature). 2. Tibieza, indiferencia, lentitud, descuido. 3. Frialdad, esquivez. 4. Castidad.

cold shoulder [ˈkəʊldˈʃəʊldər] [kould-shoul-dar] *vn.* *(Coloq.)* Hacerle el vacío a.

cold sore [ˈkəʊldˈsɔːr] [kould-shoa] s. Herpes (labial), boquera, fuego, pupa.

cold storage [ˈkəʊldˈstɔːreɪdʒ] [kould-sto-reich], *s.* Cámara frigorífica. Almacenamiento en cámaras frigoríficas.

cold turkey [ˈkəʊldˈtɜːkɪ] [kould-ter-ki] *adv.* *(Sl.)* **To go cold turkey,** estar con el mono.

cold war [ˈkəʊldˈwɑːr] [kould-uaʳ], *s.* Guerra fría.

cole [kəʊl] [koul], *s.* *(Bot.)* Col, berza.

coleoptera [kəʊlɪˈɒptɪrə] [kou-li-op-ti-ra], *s. pl.* Coleópteros, orden de insectos cuyas alas anteriores son córneas y forman como un estuche; los escarabajos.

coleopterous [kəʊlɪˈɒptɪrəs] [kou-li-op-ti-rus], *a.* Coleoptéreo, con las alas encerradas en un estuche.

coleslaw [kəʊlsˈlɔː] [kou-lis-loa], *s.* Ensalada de col cortada menudamente. Ensalada de repollo, zanahoria y cebolla con mayonesa.

colessee [kəʊlɪsiː] [kou-li-si], *s.* Mediero, el que toma a medias una finca en arriendo.

colessor [ˈkəʊlɪsər] [kou-li-saʳ], *s.* Una de dos o más personas que otorgan un contrato de arrendamiento.

colewort [ˈkəʊlwɔːt] [kou-li-uort], *s.* *(Bot.)* Especie de berza.

colic [ˈkɒlɪk] [ko-lik], *s.* Cólico o dolor cólico. -*a.* Cólico, que afecta al intestino grueso.

colitis [kɒˈlaɪtɪs] [ko-lai-tis], *s.* *(Med.)* Colitis.

collaborate [kəˈlæbəreɪt] [ko-la-bo-reit], *vn.* Colaborar.

collaboration [kəˈlæbəreɪʃən] [ko-la-bo-rei-shon], *s.* Colaboración (cooperation); colaboracionismo (with enemy). **In collaboration with,** en colaboración con.

collaborator [kəˈlæbəreɪtər] [ko-la-bo-rei-taʳ], *s.* Colaborador (partner); colaboracionista (with enemy).

collage [kɒˈlɑːdʒ] [ko-lech], *s.* *(Gal.)* Arte de colaje.

collapse [kəˈlæps] [ko-laps], *va.* Hacer derrumbarse, contraerse o decaer. -*vn.* 1. Desplomarse, desmoronarse, derrumbarse, hundirse por completo (fall down/building). 2. Salir con mal éxito; acabarse desastrosamente. Fracasar, venirse abajo (fail). 3. Postrarse, debilitarse. 4. Desalentarse, desanimarse; quedar rendido. Desplomarse (fall/person). **We collapsed with laughter,** nos desternillamos de risa. *(Med.)* Sufrir un colapso (person). 5. Plegarse (fold/table, chair). **Collapsing,** plegable (table, chair).

collapse, *s.* 1. Derrumbamiento, desplome, hundimiento, caída completa y simultánea (de un edificio.) (of building). 2. *(Med.)* Colapso, ostración repentina de la energía cerebral y de las fuerzas vitales. 3. Fracaso, mal resultado (of plan); ruina, quiebra (company).

collapsible [kəˈlæpsɪbl] [ko-lap-si-bol] *a.* Plegable (table, bed).

collar [ˈkɒlər] [ko-laʳ], *s.* 1. Cuello, parte de ciertas prendas de vestir que rodea el pescuezo; cuello de camisa, frac, levita, etc. (clothing). *(Med.)* Collarín, cuello ortopédico. 2. Collar, cadena que rodea el pescuezo del cuello de ciertos animales. 3. Collera, el collar para las caballerías de tiro. 4. Collar, insignia que usan los caballeros de varias órdenes militares. 5. *(Mar.)* Collar, encapilladura. 6. *(Arq.)* Anillo, moldura convexa. **To slip the collar,** escaparse, desenlazarse, desenredarse, librarse de alguna dificultad. **To get hot under the collar, sulfurarse,** ponerse hecho una furia.

collar, *va.* 1. Agarrar a uno por los cabezones. 2. Proveer de un cuello o collar. **To collar beef,** arrollar y ceñir un pedazo de carne. *(Coloq.)* **He collared me as I was leaving,** me agarró o pescó cuando salía.

collar-bone [ˈkɒləˌbəʊn] [ko-lar-boun], *s.* Clavícula, hueso transversal de la parte superior y anterior del pecho.

collate [kɒˈleɪt] [ko-leit], *va.* 1. Comparar, confrontar, cotejar una cosa con otra de la misma especie. 2. Colar un beneficio, conferirle canónicamente. 3. Reunir, recopilar (assemble); poner en orden, compaginar (order).

collateral [kɒˈlætərəl] [ko-la-te-ral], *a.* 1. Colateral. 2. Colateral, el pariente que lo es por línea transversal. 3. Indirecto, accesorio. 4. Subsidiario. **Collateral security,** garantía subsidiaria. 5. *(Fin.)* Garantía, fianza.

collaterally [kɒˈlætərəlɪ] [ko-la-te-ra-li], *adv.* Colateralmente, indirectamente, transversalmente, subsidiariamente.

collateralness [kɒˈlætərəlnɪs] [ko-la-te-ral-nes], *s.* Colateralidad.

collation [kɒˈleɪʃən] [ko-lei-shon], *s.* 1. Cotejo, comparación, paralelo de una copia con el original o con otra copia para asegurarse de que se hallan conformes. 2. Colación, título o provisión de un beneficio. 3. Colación, merienda; originalmente, refacción que se solía tomar por la noche cuando se ayunaba.

collative [kɒˈlætətɪv] [ko-la-tiv], *a.* Colativo, dícese del patronato de un beneficio cuando el patrón y el obispo son la misma persona.

collator [kɒˈlætər] [ko-lei-tor], *s.* 1. El que coteja copias o manuscritos. 2. Colador de beneficio.

colleague [kɒˈliːg] [ko-lig], *va.* Unir, juntar, reunir. -*vn.* Coligarse.

colleague, *s.* Colega, compañero.

collect [kəˈlekt] [ko-lekt], *va.* 1. Recoger, juntar; coleccionar (plantas, libros, insectos, monedas.) (as hobby). Reunir, recopilar (gather together/information, evidence, data). **We're collecting old clothes for charity,** estamos juntando ropa usada para una obra benéfica. **We collected (up) our belongings,** recogimos nuestras cosas. Acumular, juntar (attract, accumulate, dust). *(Coloq.)* Sacarse, ganarse (earn). 2. Sumar, juntar muchos números para saber cuánto componen. 3. Cobrar (obtain payment/rent, fine, subscription); recaudar (taxes). 4. *(Des.)* Colegir, inferir, deducir. **To collect himself,** volver en sí; sosegarse, reponerse, reposarse. 5. Recoger (fetch, pick up) **They collect the garbage every Monday,** todos los lunes pasan a recoger la basura. **She collects her from school every day,** la recoge del colegio, o la va a buscar al colegio todos los días. **Give me some time to collect my thoughts,** déjame pensar un momento (put in order). -*vn.* 1. Congregarse, reunirse (gather, assemble/people); acumularse, juntarse (accumulate/dust, water). 2. Recaudar dinero, hacer una colecta (solicit contributions).

collect, *s.* Colecta, oración breve.

collect *a./adv.* A cobro revertido, por cobrar (call, cable).

collectable, *v.* COLLECTABLE.

collectaneous [kəˈlektənɪəs] [ko-lek-ta-nious], *a.* Congregado, juntado, unido.

collected [kəˈlektɪd] [ko-lek-ted], *a.* 1. Reunido, junto. 2. Sosegado, vuelto en sí. Sereno, compuesto (composed). **The collected works of Jane Austen,** las obras completas de Jane Austen. -*pp.* de COLLECT.

collectedly [kəˈlektɪdlɪ] [ko-lek-tid-li], *adv.* Juntamente, todo unido a la vista.

collectedness [kəˈlektɪdnɪs] [ko-lek-ted-nes], *s.* El acto de rehacerse de una sorpresa.

collectible [kəˈlektɪbl] [ko-lek-ti-bol], *a.* Cobrable, que puede cobrarse, recaudarse o recogerse.

collection [kəˈlekʃən] [ko-lek-shon], *s.* 1. Colección, el conjunto de las cosas recogidas. 2. Colección; recopilación (of evidence), cobro (of debts, rent), recaudación (of taxes). **A debt collection agency,** una agencia de cobro a morosos. 3. Cuestación o colecta, petición con objeto piadoso y la suma recogida (of money). **To make/hold a collection for something,** hacer una colecta para algo. **Collection box,** alcancía, hucha. *(Rel.)* **Collection plate,** bandeja, cepillo. 4. Compilación. **The goods are ready for collection,** puede recoger o pasar a buscar las mercancías (act of fetching). 5. Recogida (of mail, refuse). 6. Colección (group of objects); grupo (of people).

collective [kəˈlektɪv] [ko-lek-tiv], *a.* 1. Colectivo, congregado, agregado; opuesto a individual. 2. Lo que siendo en sí singular denota pluralidad. **People, army are collective nouns,** pueblo, ejército son nombres colectivos. 3. Que puede juntar o unir.

collective *s.* Colectivo, cooperativa.

collectively [kəˈlektɪvlɪ] [ko-lek-tiv-li], *adv.* Colectivamente, en masa.

collectivism [kəˈlektɪvɪzm] [ko-lek-ti-visem], *s.* Colectivismo.

collectivization [kəˌlektɪvaɪˈzeɪʃən] [ko-lek-ti-vai-zei-shon], *s.* Colectivización.

collectivize [kəˈlektɪvaɪz] [ko-lek-ti-vais], *va.* Colectivizar.

collector [kəˈlektər] [ko-lek-to'], *s.* 1. Colector, el que recoge. 2. Colector, recaudador de contribuciones, cobrador (official). **Tax collector,** recaudador de impuestos. 3. Compilador. 4. Coleccionista. **A collector's item/piece,** una pieza de colección.

collectorate [kəˈlektəreɪt] [ko-lek-to-reit], **collectorship** [kəˈlektəʃɪp] [ko-lek-tor-ship], *s.* Colecturía, oficio o jurisdicción de colector o recaudador.

college [ˈkɒlɪdʒ] [ko-lech], *s.* 1. Colegio, casa de educación. Universidad (university); universitario (education, life, lecturer). Escuela, instituto (for vocational training). *V.* TEACHERS COLLEGE. Facultad, departamento (department of university); colegio universitario (in Britain). 2. Edifico o serie de edificios poseídos y usados por un colegio. 3. Colegio, cuerpo de asociados, colegas o compañeros; como el colegio de cardenales.

college-like [ˈkɒlɪdʒˌlaɪk] [ko-lich-laik], *a.* Colegial.

collegial [ˈkɒlɪdʒɪəl] [ko-li-yial], *a.* Colegial, lo que pertenece a colegio.

collegian [ˈkɒlɪdʒɪən] [ko-li-yian], **collegiate** [kəˈliːdʒɪɪt] [ko-li-yeit], *a.* Colegiado, lo que pertence a un colegio. Universitario.

collet [ˈkɒlɪt] [ko-lit], *s.* 1. Cuello o collar. 2. Engaste, la parte de la sortija en que está engastada la piedra.

collide [kəˈlaɪd] [ko-laid], *vn.* 1. Chocar; colisionar (crash/vehicle). **To collide with something/somebody,** chocar con algo/alguien. 2. Contradecir, estar en oposición. **To collide with somebody over something,** tener un enfrentamiento con alguien acerca/sobre algo (disagree).

collie [ˈkɒlɪ] [ko-li], *s.* Perro pastor, procedente de Escocia.

collier [ˈkɒlɪər] [ko-lia'], *s.* 1. Minero, carbonero o cavador de carbón de piedra. 2. Barco carbonero. 3. Mercader de carbón. 4. Carbonero, el que hace o vende carbón.

colliery [ˈkɒlɪərɪ] [ko-lie-ri], *s.* Carbonera, mina de carbón. 2. Comercio de carbón.

colliflower [ˈkɒlɪflaʊər] [ko-li-flaua'], *s.* *(Des.)* Coliflor. *V.* CAULIFLOWER.

colligate [ˈkɒlɪgeɪt] [ko-li-gueit], *va.* Atar, juntar, amarrar, una cosa con otra.

colligation [ˈkɒlɪgeɪʃən] [ko-li-guei-shon], *s.* Coligación, la acción y efecto de coligarse.

collimate [ˈkɒlɪmeɪt] [ko-li-meit], *va.* Poner en línea, como los ejes de dos lentes; hacer paralelos (rayos de luz); ajustar la visual de un telescopio.

collimation [ˈkɒlɪmeɪʃən] [ko-li-mei-shon], *s.* Acción de poner en línea recta.

collimator [ˈkɒlɪmeɪtər] [ko-li-mei-to'], *s.* 1. Telescopio fijo que se emplea para ajustar otro. 2. Tubo del espectroscopio que hace paralelos los rayos de luz.

collineate [ˈkɒlɪnɪɪt] [ko-li-nieit], *va.* *V.* COLLIMATE. -*vn.* Hallarse en línea recta.

collineation [ˈkɒlɪnɪɪʃən] [ko-lini-i-shon], *s.* Acción o procedimiento de alinear; posición en línea recta.

collinsia [ˈkɒlɪnsɪə] [ko-lin-sia], s. (Bot.) Género de plantas de las escrofulariáceas, que se cultivan para adorno.

colliquate [ˈkɒlɪkweɪt] [ko-li-kueit], va. Colicuar, derretir. - vn. Colicuarse.

colliquative [ˈkɒlɪkwətɪv] [ko-li-kua-tiv], a. Colicuante, colicuativo.

colliquefaction [ˌkɒlɪkwəˈfækʃən] [ko-li-kue-fak-shon], s. Colicuefacción, el acto de colicuar o colicuarse muchas cosas juntas.

collish [ˈkɒlɪʃ] [ko-lish], s. (Art. y Of.) Herramienta para pulir las suelas de calzado.

collision [kəˈluːʃən] [ko-lu-shon], s. Colisión, ludimiento; choque, encuentro (crash/of cars, trains); abordaje, colisión (of boats). **To be in collision with something,** chocar o colisionar con algo. **The two ships were on a collision course,** los dos barcos llevaban rumbo de colisión. 2. Oposición, contradicción; enfrentamiento, confrontación (disagreement).

collocate [ˈkɒləkeɪt] [ko-lo-keit], va. Colocar.

collocate, a. Colocado; puesto.

collocation [ˌkɒləˈkeɪʃən] [ko-lo-kei-shon], s. Colocación, situación.

collocution [ˌkɒləˌkjuːˈʃən] [ko-lo-kiu-shon], s. Conferencia, conversación.

collocutor [ˈkɒləkjuːtər] [ko-lo-kiu-toʳ], s. Interlocutor, dialoguista.

collodion [ˈkɒlədɪən] [ko-lo-dion], s. Colodio, solución de algodón pólvora en éter y alcohol, que se emplea en cirugía y fotografía.

colloid [ˈkɒlɔɪd] [ko-loid], s. y a. (Quím.) Coloide.

collop [ˈkɒləp] [ko-lop], s. 1. Bocado delicado, tajada pequeña de carne. **A collop of bacon,** torrezno. 2. Pedacito, pequeña porción de cualquier cosa.

colloquial [kəˈləʊkwɪəl] [ko-lou-kial], a. Familiar, de uso común, en contraposición al literario.

colloquialism [kəˈləʊkwɪəlɪzəm] [ko-lou-kia-lisem], s. Vulgarismo, expresión familiar.

colloquially [kəˈləʊkwɪəlɪ] [ko-lou-kia-li] adv. Coloquialmente.

colloquist [ˈkɒlɪkwɪst] [ko-lo-kist], s. Interlocutor.

colloquy [ˈkɒləkwɪ] [ko-lo-ki], s. Coloquio, conversación, plática.

collotype [ˈkɒlətaɪp] [ko-lo-taip], s. Colotipia.

collude [kəˈluːd] [ko-lud], vn. Obrar de concierto, convenirse o entenderse secretamente con una de las partes litigantes en perjuicio de la otra.

colluder [kəˈluːdər] [ko-lu-deʳ], s. Colusor, cómplice en un engaño.

collusion [kəˈluːʒən] [ko-lu-shon], s. Colusión, inteligencia fraudulenta entre dos o más personas; connivencia. **To be in collusion with somebody,** estar coludido con alguien, estar en colusión o connivencia con alguien.

collusive [kəˈluːsɪv] [ko-lu-siv], a. Colusorio, concertado con fraude y en daño de tercero.

collusively [kəˈluːsɪvlɪ] [ko-lu-siv-li], adv. Colusoriamente.

collusiveness [kəˈluːsɪvnɪs] [ko-lu-siv-nes], s. Convenio fraudulento, colusión.

collusory [kəˈluːʃərɪ] [ko-lu-so-ri], a. Colusorio.

colly [ˈkɒlɪ] [ko-li], va. (Des.) Manchar, ennegrecer o ensuciar con hollín.

collyrium [ˈkɒlɪrɪəm] [ko-li-rium], s. Colirio, remedio para los males de los ojos.

collywobbles [ˈkɒlɪˌwɒblz] [ko-li-uolbols] s. pl. **To have the collywobbles,** estar nerviosísimo, tener canguelo, tener culillo, tener ñáñaras (nerves).

colo = Colorado

colocynth [ˈkɒləsɪnθ] [ko-losinz], s. (Bot.) Coloquíntida, especie de cohombro, y su fruto; purgante violento.

cologne [kəˈləʊn] [ko-loun] s. Colonia (eau de cologne).

Colombia [kəˈlɒmbɪə] [ko-lom-bia] N. (Geogr.) Colombia.

colombian [kəˈlɒmbɪən] [ko-lom-bian] a./s. Colombiano.

colon [ˈkəʊlən] [kou-lon], s. 1. (Gram.) Dos puntos (:). 2. (Anat.) Colon, parte del intestino grueso.

colonel [ˈkɜːln] [ko-lo-nel], s. Coronel, el jefe de un regimiento.

colonelcy [kɜːnəlsɪ] [ko-lo-nel-si], **colonelship** [kɜːnəlʃɪp] [ko-lo-nel-ship], s. Coronelía.

colonial [kəˈləʊnɪəl] [ko-lou-nial], a. Colonial.

colonialism [kəˈləʊnɪəlɪzəm] [ko-lou-nia-lisem], s. Colonialismo.

colonialist [kəˈləʊnɪəlɪst] [ko-lou-nia-list], s. & a. Colonialista.

colonist [ˈkɒlənɪst] [ko-lo-nist], s. Colono, habitante de una colonia.

colonization [ˌkɒlənaɪˈzeɪʃən] [ko-lo-nai-sei-shon], **colonizing** [ˈkɒlənaɪzɪŋ] [ko-lo-nai-sin], s. Colonización.

colonize [ˈkɒlənaɪz] [ko-lo-nais], va. Colonizar, formar o establecer colonias. -vn. Establecerse en un país lejano.

colonizer [ˈkɒlənaɪzər] [ko-lo-nai-saʳ], s. Colonizador, uno de los fundadores de una colonia.

colonnade [ˈkɒləneɪd] [ko-lo-neid], s. Columnario o persitilo, columnata.

colony [ˈkɒlənɪ] [ko-lo-ni], s. 1. Colonia, conjunto de colonos. 2. Colonia, el país habitado por colonos.

colophon [ˈkɒləfən] [ko-lo-fon], s. La fecha de una impresión y el nombre de lugar e impresor puestos al fin del libro; colofón.

colophony [ˈkɒləfənɪ] [ko-lo-fo-ni], s. Colofonía, especie de resina negra.

color, colour [ˈkʌlər] [ko-loʳ], s. 1. Color (shade). **What color is the ball?,** ¿de qué color es la pelota? **Her hair is reddish-brown in color,** tiene el pelo (de color) castañorojizo. Color (not monochrome) **In full color,** a todo color. En colores o a color (photograph/television). **Color supplement,** suplemento a todo color o en color. Color, colorido (vividness). **Local color,** el color local. 2. Color, colores, la coloración de la tez, la tez misma (racial feature). **Color prejudice,** prejuicio racial. 3. Color o colores, materiales de varios colores que preparan los pintores para pintar. 4. Color, pretexto, motivo, colorido, excusa. 5. Palo, en los naipes. -**Colors,** pl. bandera, la insignia bajo la cual militan los soldados. **To hoist the colors,** (Mar.) enarbolar la bandera. **The colors of the regiment,** el estandarte del regimiento. **She showed her true colors,** se mostró tal cual era en realidad. (Sports) (GB) **The team colors,** los colores del equipo. **Oil-color,** color al óleo. **Water-color,** acuarela. **Under color of,** so color de, bajo capa o con pretexto de. **There was no color of excuse,** no tenía ni sombra de excusa. **With flying colors,** a banderas desplegadas. **To bring the color back to somebody's cheeks,** devolverle el color o los colores a alguien. V. OFF-COLOR.

color, colour va. 1. Colorar, colorir, teñir o dar color (dye); dar los colores a lo que se pinta; iluminar un dibujo. (Art) Pintar, colorear. **To color something blue,** pintar algo de azul. 2. Paliar, extenuar. Empañar (atmosphere/influence). **You shouldn't let that color your judgment,** no deberías dejar que eso influyera en tu opinión. -vn. 1. Colorearse, tomar color. 2. Ponerse colorado, ruborizarse, encenderse, sonrojarse (blush).

color in Colorear.

colorableness [ˈkʌləreɪblnɪs] [ko-lo-rei-bol-nes], s. Lo que es plausible.

colorably [ˈkʌlərəblɪ] [ka-lo-ra-bli], adv. Plausiblemente, especiosamente.

colorado beetle [ˈkɒləˈraːdəʊˌbiːtl] [ko-lo-ra-dobi-tel] s. Escarabajo de la papa o patata.

coloration [ˌkʌləˈreɪʃən] [ko-lo-rei-shon], s. Coloración.

colorature [ˈkʌlərətʊər] [ko-lo-ra-tuar], s. Floreos, variaciones y cadencias caprichosas en el canto.

color-blind [ˈkʌləblaɪnd] [ko-lor-blaind], a. Daltoniano, daltónico.

color blindness [ˈkʌlə,blaɪndnɪs] [ko-lor-blaind-nes], s. Daltonismo.

colorcast [ˈkʌləkɑːst] [ko-lor-kast], *s.* Un programa de televisión en color.

colorcast, *va.* Transmitir en color un programa de televisión.

color-coded [ˈkʌləkəʊdɪd] [ko-lor-kou-did] *a.* Codificado con colores.

color-coordinated [ˈkʌləkɔːdɪˌneɪtɪd] [ko-lor-kor-di-nei-tid] *a.* Haciendo juego, con colores coordinados.

colored, coloured [ˌkʌləd] [ko-lord], *a.* 1. Colorado, que tiene color; pintado o teñido. De color (walls, blouse). 2. Persona de color, (non-white); mestizo (in S Africa). 3. Especioso, embellecido, exagerado. 4. Parcial (biased).

colored, coloured *s.* Persona de color (non-white/often offensive). Hijo de padres de distinta raza (Cape Colored/in S Africa). **Coloreds** *pl.* Ropa de color.

-colored, -coloured, *suff.* **Slate/colar colored,** de color pizarra/coral. **A dark colored hat,** un sombrero de (un) color oscuro.

colorfast, colourfast [ˈkʌləfɑːst] [ko-lor-fast] *a.* Que no destiñe, de colores sólidos o inalterables.

colorful, colourful [ˈkʌləfəl] [ko-lor-ful] *a.* De colores muy vivos o vistosos (clothes, plumage); lleno de color o de colorido, vistoso (parade/description). **He's a very colorful character,** es un hombre de lo más pintoresco u original.

colorfully, colourfully [ˈkʌləfʊlɪ] [ko-lor-fu-li] *adv.* Vistosamente, con colores vivos o brillantes (with bright colors); con gran colorido (in vivid terms).

colorific [ˌkʌlərɪfɪk] [ko-lo-ri-fik], *a.* Colorativo, lo que tiene virtud para producir colores.

colorimeter [ˌkʌlərɪˈmiːtər] [ko-lo-ri-mi-ta^r], *s.* Colorímetro, aparato para medir la intensidad de los colores.

coloring, colouring [ˈkʌlərɪŋ] [ko-lo-rin], *s.* 1. Colorante, lo que da color o tinte (food coloring); coloración, acción de colorar. 2. Estilo o aire particular. 3. *(Pint.)* Colorido (of picture). **Coloring book,** libro o para colorear. 4. Color, tono (of skin); colorido (of fur, plumage).

colorist [ˈkʌlərɪst] [ko-lo-rist], *s.* Colorista, el que es hábil en dar colorido.

colorless, colourless [ˈkʌləlɪs] [ko-lor-les], *a.* Descolorido, sin color, incoloro. Anodino, gris (dull/person, life).

colorman [ˈkʌləmæn] [ko-lor-man], *s.* El que hace y vende toda especie de colores, barniz, afeite, aceites, etc.

color scheme, colour scheme [ˈkʌləskiːm] [ko-lor-skím] *s.* Combinación de colores.

colossal [kəˈlɒsl] [ko-lo-sal], **colossean** [kəˈlɒsɪən] [ko-lo-sian], *a. (Coloq.)* Colosal, descomunal.

colosseum [kəˈlɒsɪəm] [ko-lo-sium], *s.* Coliseo, el anfiteatro de Vespasiano en Roma.

colossus [kəˈlɒsəs] [ko-lo-sus], *s.* Coloso, estatua de magnitud desmesurada.

colostrum [kəˈlɒstrəm] [ko-los-trum], *s.* Calostro, la primera leche de las recién paridas.

colour, *s.* y v.*V.* COLOR. Así se escribe generalmente en Inglaterra.

colt [kəʊlt] [koult], *s. (Equ.)* 1. Potro, caballo que no pasa de cuatro años. 2. Mozuelo sin juicio. 3. Soga, con un nudo al extremo, para castigar. 4. Revólver.

colter [ˈkəʊltər] [koul-ta^r], *s.* Cuchilla, reja de arado.

coltish [ˈkɒltɪʃ] [koul-tish], *a.* Juguetón, retozón.

colt's-foot [ˈkəʊltsfʊt] [koults-fut], *s. (Bot.)* Tusílago, fárfara.

colt's-tooth [ˈkəʊltstuːθ] [koults-tuz], *s.* 1. Diente imperfecto del potro. 2. Niñada o niñadas, placeres pueriles, boberías.

colubrine [ˈkɒlʊbriːn] [ko-lu-brin], *a.* Culebrino; astuto.

columbian [ˈkɒlʌmbɪən] [ko-lom-bian], *a.* 1. Colombiano, de la República de Colombia. 2. Relativo a Cristóbal Colón; colombino.

columbine [ˈkɒləmbaɪn] [ko-lom-bain], *s.* 1. *(Bot.)* Aguileña o pajarilla, planta de las ranunculáceas. 2. La actriz que hace el papel de graciosa en las pantomimas.

columbium [ˈkɒlʌmbɪəm] [ko-lom-bium], *s. (Min.)* Columbio, elemento metálico, de color gris; se llama también niobio.

columbo [ˈkɒləmbə] [ko-lom-bo], *s.* Medicamento tónico hecho de columbo o colombo.

Columbus [kəˈlʌmbəs] [ko-lom-bos] *s.* **Christopher Columbus,** Cristóbal Colón.

Columbus Day [kəˈlʌmbəsˌdeɪ] [ko-lom-bos-dei] *s.* (in US) El día de la Raza o de la Hispanidad.

columella [ˈkɒləmbəs] [ko-lom-bos], *s.* 1. *(Anat. y Zool.)* Varita, pequeña columna o eje central; como la varilla central de la cóclea. 2. *(Bot.)* Eje central, como el de un musgo.

column [ˈkɒləm] [ko-lum], *s.* 1. *(Arq.)* Columna, especie de pilar cilíndrico, que sirve para sostener o adornar algún edificio, altar, etc. 2. *(Fig.)* Columna, cantidad de fluido de figura cilíndrica. 3. Algo parecido a una columna; sostén. En anatomía, la espina dorsal. 4. *(Imp.)* Columna, división perpendicular de una página (on grid, chart, screen). **He writes a column for «The Globe»,** es columnista de «The Globe». 5. *(Mil.)* Columna, cuerpo de tropas formadas en secciones de poco frente y mucho fondo.

columnar [ˈkɒləmnɑːr] [ko-lum-na^r], *a.* Columnario, en forma de columna; parecido al fuste de columna; con columnas.

columned [ˈkɒləmnd] [ko-lum-nd], *a.* Con columnas, o arreglado en columnas.

columnist [ˈkɒləmnɪst] [ko-lum-nist] *s.* Articulista, columnista, encargado de una sección especial de un periódico.

colure [ˈkɒlʊər] [ko-lua^r], *s. (Astr.)* Coluro, uno de los dos círculos máximos que en la esfera se cortan en ángulos rectos por los polos del globo, pasando por los signos Aries y Libra.

colza [ˈkɒlzə] [kol-sa], *s.* Colza, especie de berza de que se extrae un aceite estimado.

com-, Prefijo, que en composición significa con o en compañía de otro.

coma [ˈkəʊmə] [kou-ma], *s.* 1. *(Med.)* Coma, letargo, sopor profundo con estertor. **To be in/to go into coma,** estar/entrar o caer en coma. 2. *(Astr.)* Cabellera, atmósfera luminosa que rodea o sigue al núcleo de un cometa. 3. *(Bot.)* Manojito de hebras sedosas que hay al extremo de algunas semillas.

comate [ˈkəʊmeɪt] [kou-meit], *s.* Camarada, compañero.

comate, *a.* Cabelludo. *V.* HAIRY.

comatose [ˈkəʊmətəʊs] [kou-ma-tous], *a. (Med.)* Comatoso, letárgico.

comb [kəʊm] [koum], *s.* 1. Peine, instrumento con que se limpia y compone el pelo. Peineta (worn in hair). **Carved or cut shell comb,** peineta de carey calada. **Braid shell comb,** peineta de carey para rizo. **Carved horn comb,** peineta de cuerno calada. **Cockscomb,** cresta de gallo. **Honey-comb,** panal de miel. **Flax-comb,** rastrillo. 2. Carda, rastrillo, para preparar el lino, el cáñamo, o la lana. 3. Cresta carnosa o carúncula del gallo o de la gallina. 4. Alvéolo, celdilla donde la abeja deposita su miel. *V.* HONEY-COMB. 5. CURRY-COMB. **Fine-toothed comb,** peine fino, lendrera. **To go over something with a fine-toothed comb,** examinar o revisar algo minuciosamente o con lupa. **Comb-foundation,** hoja delgada de cera, copia exacta de la pared media del panal, sobre la cual acaban las abejas el panal. **Your hair needs a comb,** tienes que peinarte.

comb, *va.* 1. Peinar, limpiar y componer el pelo; cardar la lana; rastrillar el lino. **To comb somebody's hair,** peinar a alguien. **To comb one's hair,** peinarse (pass a comb through). 2. Peinar, rastrear (search/area, field); rebuscar en (files, archives). **They combed the area for survivors,** peinaron o rastrearon la zona en busca de supervivientes.

combat [ˈkɒmbæt] [kom-bat], *s.* Combate, batalla, pelea, desafío. **Single combat,** duelo, desafío, combate singular. **Combat jacket,** guerrera.

combat, *vn.* Combatir, luchar. *-va.* Resistir, impugnar.

combatant [ˈkɒmbətənt] [kom-ba-tant], *s.* Combatiente; campéon. -*a.* Dispuesto a pelear.

combater [ˈkɒmbətər] [kom-ba-tar], *s.* Combatidor, campeador.

combative [ˈkɒmbətɪv] [kom-ba-tiv], *a.* Dispuesto a combatir.

combativeness [ˈkɒmbətɪvnɪs] [kom-ba-tiv-nes], *s.* Combatividad, predisposición a la lucha.

comb-bursh [ˈkɒmbɜːʃ] [kom-bersh], *s.* Limpiadera, bruza para limpiar los peines, cepillo de peines.

comber [ˈkɒmbər] [kom-baʳ], *s.* 1. Cardador o peinador de lana. 2. Ola de cresta (o cumbre) larga; marejada. V. BREAKER.

combinable [ˈkɒmbɪnəbl] [kom-bi-na-bol], *a.* Combinable, que se puede combinar.

combination [ˌkɒmbɪˈneɪʃən] [kom-bi-nei-shon], *s.* Combinación, unión, liga; mezcla (mixture). Combinación (of lock). **Combination lock,** cerradura de combinación.

combinative [ˈkɒmbɪnətɪv] [kom-bi-na-tiv], *a.* Combinatorio.

combine [ˈkɒmbaɪn] [kom-bain], *va.* Combinar (elements), juntar, unir; ajustar. (*Culin.*) Mezclar (ingredients). Aunar (efforts). **She combines charm and intelligence,** reúne encanto e inteligencia. **This, combined with the fact that…,** esto, unido o sumado al hecho de que… -*vn.* Unirse, juntarse; maquinar, conspirar. Combinarse (elements); mezclarse (ingredients); unirse (teams, forces).

combine *s.* 1. (*Agr.*) Cosechadora (combine harvester). 2. Alianza, coalición (coalition).

combined [kəmˈbaɪnd] [kom-baind] *a.* Conjunto. **Our combined efforts led to success,** la suma de nuestros esfuerzos nos condujo al éxito. **It's a pen, watch and calculator combined,** es bolígrafo, reloj y calculadora a la vez.

combing [ˈkɒmbɪŋ] [kom-bin], *s.* 1. La acción de peinar, de cardar, de rastrillar, etc. 2. Postizo, cabello sobrepuesto para cubir la calva.

combless [ˈkɒmblɪs] [kom-les], *a.* Descrestado.

comb-maker [ˈkɒmbmeɪkər] [kom-mei-kaʳ], *s.* Peinero, el que hace peines.

combo [ˈkɒmbəʊ] [kom-bou], *s.* Pequeña orquesta de jazz, con combinación especial de instrumentos.

combustibility [ˌkɒmbʌstɪˈbɪlɪti] [kom-bas-ti-bi-li-bi], *s.* Combustibilidad.

combustible [ˈkɒmbʌstɪbl] [kom-bas-ti-bol], *a.* Combustible, inflamable. -*s.* Combustible, todo lo que puede servir para mantener el fuego.

combustibleness [ˌkɒmbʌstɪblnɪs] [kom-bas-ti-bol-nes], *s.* Combustibilidad.

combustion [kəmˈbʌstʃən] [kom-bas-chun], *s.* 1. Combustión, quema, incendio, acción del fuego sobre las sustancias inflamables. 2. Combustión, combinación química acompañada de calor y luz. **Combustion engine,** motor de combustión.

combustion chamber [ˈkəmˈbʌstʃənˌtʃæmbər] [kom-bas-chun-cham-baʳ], *s.* (*Mec.*) Cámara de combustión.

come [kʌm] [kam], *vn.* (*pret.* CAME, *pp.* COME). 1. Venir, llegar, aproximarse (advance, approach, travel). **Come here,** ven aquí. **Have you come far?,** ¿vienes de lejos? **As I was coming up/down the stairs,** cuando subía/bajaba por las escaleras. **We've come a long way since…,** hemos avanzado mucho desde que… (made much progress), ha llovido mucho desde que… (many things have happened). **He came running into the room,** entró corriendo en la habitación. **Come and look at this,** ven a ver esto. Venir (be present, visit, accompany). **Can I come with you?,** ¿puedo ir contigo?, ¿te puedo acompañar? **Sue's coming as a clown,** Sue va a venir (vestida) de payaso. 2. Moverse a la vista; hacerse perceptible. 3. Llegar, estar presente, existir; llegar a ser o conseguir alguna cosa (become). **It's come loose,** se ha aflojado. **My dream has come true,** mi sueño se ha hecho realidad. **It'll come, just keep practicing,** ya te va a salir o lo vas a lograr, sigue practicando (be gained). **Sugar comes in half-pound bags,** el azúcar viene en paquetes de media libra (be available, obtainable). **The car comes with the job,** el coche te lo dan con el trabajo. **It comes with instructions,** viene con o trae instrucciones. **He's as silly as they come,** es de lo más tonto que hay. 4. Proceder, venir (arrive). **What time are you coming?,** ¿a qué hora vas a venir? **After a while, you'll come to a crossroads,** al cabo de un rato llegarás a un cruce. **I'm coming, I won't be a moment,** enseguida voy. **To come about something,** venir por algo. **To come for something/somebody,** venir a buscar algo/a alguien; venir a por algo/alguien. **To come and go,** ir y venir. **You can come and go as you please,** puedes salir y entrar a tu antojo. (*Fam.*) **She doesn't know whether she's coming or going,** está hecha un lío. **Three o'clock came and went and he still hadn't arrived,** pasaron las tres y no llegaba. 5. Acontecer, suceder (occur in time, context). **Christmas comes but once a year,** sólo es Navidad una vez al año. **Christmas is coming,** ya llega Navidad. **This coming Friday,** este viernes que viene. **It came as a complete surprise,** fue una sorpresa total. **To take life as it comes,** aceptar la vida tal (y) como se presenta. **Come what may,** pase lo que pase. **He had it coming (to him),** se lo tenía merecido. Para (as prep.). **I'll be tired out come Friday,** estaré agotado para el viernes. **To come** (in the future/as adverb). **In years to come,** en años venideros, en el futuro. **A taste of things to come,** una muestra de lo que nos espera. **The best is yet to come,** todavía nos queda lo mejor. 6. Llegar (extend, reach). **The water only came up to our knees,** el agua sólo nos llegaba a las rodillas. 7. (in sequence, list, structure). **Cancer comes between Gemini and Leo,** Cáncer está entre Géminis y Leo. Llegar (in race, competition). **To come first,** llegar el primero (in a race); quedar o salir el primero (in an exam). Estar (be ranked). **My children come first,** primero están mis hijos. 8. (*Coloq.*) Venirse, correrse o acabar (have orgasm). *va.* **Don't come the victim with me!,** no te hagas la víctima conmigo. *Come,* en imperativo, sirve para llamar la atención o animar. **Come on!,** ¡vamos! ¡adelante! ¡valor! ¡ánimo!, expresión que se usa para alentar a alguno. **To come on,** adelantarse, avanzar; aprovechar en el estudio; cerrar con el enemigo; engordar.

come about, girar, rodear; acontecer, acaecer, suceder; efectuar, conseguir; venir por rodeo; ocurrir, suceder (happen). **How does it come about that…?,** ¿cómo es que…?

come across, encontrar, hallar por casualidad. **He eats nothing but what comes up,** vomita cuanto come. **How comes that?,** ¿cómo es eso? **To come,** por venir. **In time to come,** en tiempo venidero. **In the world to come,** en el otro mundo. **come across** 1. Encontrar(se) (find); encontrarse con (meet/person). **I'd never come across the word before,** era la primera vez que oía o leía la palabra. 2. Ser comprendido (comunicate, be comunicated/meaning); transmitirse (feelings). **He came across very well in the interview,** hizo muy buena impresión en la entrevista.

come after, seguir, venir detrás, venir después. **To come after one,** suceder a, o ser sucesor de alguno.

come again, volver, venir otra vez.

come asunder, deshacerse, hacerse pedazos, desunirse; dislocarse, desnucarse.

come along 1. (Hurry up/in imperative) **Come along, children!,** ¡vamos, niños!, ¡de prisa, niños!, ¡apúrense, niños! **Come along!,** ¡vamos! (as encouragement, rebuke). 2. Andar, caminar con otro (accompany). **Come along with me,** venga Vd. conmigo. Llegar (arrive). **You came along just at the right time,** llegaste justo en el momento adecuado. **Grab the first taxi that comes along,** toma el primer taxi que pase o venga. 3. Ir, marchar (progress).

come apart Deshacerse (fall apart); desmontarse, desarmarse (have detachable parts).

come around, (GB) come round 1. Tomar (bend); doblar (corner). 2. Venir (visit). Volver en sí (recover consciousness). **He'll come around eventually,** ya se va a convencer (change mind). **To come around to somebody's point,** aceptar el punto de vista de alguien. **Winter is coming around again,** ya vuelve el invierno (occur). **To come round,** venir por rodeos; llegar a ser, conseguir una cosa, obtener el puesto que se esperaba ocupar; convenir, asentir, después de haber hecho oposición; restablecerse, cobrar nuevo vigor. *(Fam.)* Obrar con doblez.

come at, alcanzar, conseguir, adquirir, obtener, tener, ganar, llegar a.

come away 1. Salir (leave, depart). **To come away from something,** salir de algo (from meeting, stadium). **I came away with the impression that...,** me quedé con la impresión de que... **Come away from there!,** ¡apártate de ahí!, ¡no te acerques ahí! 2. Salirse (become detached/handle); despegarse (wallpaper). **To come away,** retirarse, irse.

come back, volver, retroceder. **come back** 1. Volver (return). **To come back,** volver, venir otra vez. **To come back again,** volver a venir. **Would you like to come back to my place for a drink?,** ¿quieres venir a casa a tomar algo? **It's all coming back to me,** estoy volviendo a recordarlo todo (remember). 2. **I'll come back to you with the results,** ya le comunicaré los resultados (with reply, comment).

come before, llegar antes, anteponerse, ponerse delante.

come between, interponerse entre, separar; intervenir, sobrevenir.

come by, conseguir, hacerse con (get, acquire). **How did you come by it?,** ¿cómo lo ha obtenido? **To be easy/hard to come by,** ser fácil/difícil de conseguir. **To come by,** pasar junto, cerca o arrimado a; obtener.

come down 1. Bajar (descend). Llegar (reach). **Her hair came down to her waist,** el pelo le llegaba hasta la cintura. Caerse, venirse abajo (collapse/ceiling, wall). Aterrizar (plane); caer (in accident). Bajar, descender; desplomarse, desmoronarse. **To come down again,** volver a bajar. **To come down on** o **upon,** caerse pesadamente. 2. Bajar (decrease/price). **She's come down in my estimation,** ha bajado en mi estima. **They've come down in the world,** (se) han venido a menos. 3. Venir (from the north). 4. **To come down against/in favor of something/somebody,** fallar en contra/a favor de algo/alguien (decide/judge, court). 5. **The ring came down to her from her mother,** heredó el anillo de su madre (be passed down, inherited). 6. **The firm comes down severely on absenteeism,** la empresa trata el ausentismo con mano dura (deal with).

come down to, ser cuestión de (be a question of).

come down with, caer enfermo de (become ill with).

come for, venir a buscar, venir por.

come forth, salir, aparecer; adelantarse.

come forward, presentarse, salir al frente. **Come forward,** presentarse (witness); ofrecerse, presentarse (volunteer). **To come forward with a solution,** ofrecer o sugerir una solución. **To come forward,** adelantar, aprovechar, hacer progresos; adelantarse, llegar primero.

come from 1. Venir de (originate from); ser de (person). **Where do you come from?,** ¿de dónde eres? **I want to know where you're coming from on this,** quiero saber qué te propones con esto. 2. Resultar de, surgir de.

come home to (strike, convince). **It suddenly came home to him that...,** de pronto se dio cuenta de que...

come high o **low,** venderse caro o barato. **To come home,** volver a casa. *(Fig.)* Dar en la tecla, tocar la cuerda sensible.

come in, entrar, llegar; desembocar; ceder, rendirse, someterse, acceder; venir a parar, hacerse de moda una cosa; llegar a hacerse parte de una cosa; adelantar o medrar en

intereses; parir la vaca; empezar a dar leche. **To come in as an heir,** presentarse como heredero, reclamar una herencia. **To come in the way,** presentarse al paso, ofrecerse; sobrevenir. **To come in for,** pretender. **To come in for a share,** tocar a uno cierta porción de cualquier cosa repartida. 1. Entrar (enter). **Come in!,** ¡adelante!, ¡pase! 2. Llegar (arrive/boat). Subir (tide). Venir (to work). Llegar (in race). **She came in last,** llegó la última. 3. Recibirse (be received/signal). Llegar (applications/reports/donations). Entrar, recibirse (as income/revenue). **They have $600 coming in each month,** les entran 600 dólares al mes. 4. Entrar en vigor (be implemented/law); entrar en vigencia (regulations). Ponerse de moda (become fashionable). 5. Intervenir (join in). **They came in on the deal,** participaron en el negocio. **Where do I come in?,** ¿cuál es mi papel? (play useful role). **To come in handy,** venir bien, resultar útil. 6. Subir al poder (come to power). **Come in for,** ser objeto de (be subject to/criticism).

come into, entrar en, entrar a (enter into). Heredar (inherit). **Principles don't come into it,** no es cuestión de principios (be become relevant). **I want to know where I come into this,** quiero saber cuál es mi papel en todo esto. **Come into,** juntarse a socorrer, venir al socorro; consentir, condescender; acordarse o ponerse de acuerdo en una cosa. **To come into business,** comenzar a negociar; comenzar a tener salida o despacho en la venta de los géneros, o principiar a tener parroquianos, corresponsales, clientes, etc. **To come into trouble,** meterse en líos, tomar algún empeño trabajoso. **To come into danger,** exponerse al peligro. **To come into the world,** venir al mundo, nacer. **To come in unto,** tener coito el hombre con la mujer. **To come it,** *(Fam.)* manejar o efectuar algo. **To come near,** acercarse, allegarse. **To come next,** venir inmediatamente después, seguir inmediatamente.

come of, proceder, venir de. **It was a good idea, but nothing came of it,** era una buena idea, pero todo quedó en la nada (result). **No good can come of it,** nada bueno puede salir de ello.

come off 1. Soltarse (detach itself/handle); desprenderse, caerse (button); despegarse (wallpaper); quitarse, salir (dirt, grease). Caerse de (fall off/horse, motorcycle). 2. Suceder (take place). Tener éxito (succeed). **To come off badly,** salir mal parado (fare, acquit oneself). **He always comes off worst,** siempre sale perdiendo. **She doesn't come off as very bright,** no da la impresión de ser muy inteligente (appear, seem). 3. Dejar de tomar (stop taking/drug). *(Coloq.)* **Come off it!,** ¡anda!, ¡no digas tonterías! (be serious). **To come off,** librarse, desembarazarse, separarse, salir de un cuidado, negocio, etc.; caer; acontecer, suceder. (Fam. E. U.) Dejarse de necedades; ser razonable. (Úsase en imperativo). **Come off from,** dejar, omitir.

come on 1. (urging/only in imperative). **Come on!,** ¡vamos!, ¡date prisa!, ¡apúrate!, ¡órale! **Come on! you can do it!,** ¡vamos, que lo puedes hacer! **Hi! come on in/up,** hola, pasa/sube (inviting somebody). Avanzar (advance). 2. Entrar, empezar (begin/night, winter). **I can feel a headache coming on,** me está empezando un dolor de cabeza. Encenderse, ponerse en funcionamiento (begin to operate/heating, appliance); encenderse (light). 3. Avanzar (progress). 4. Aparecer, salir a escena (actor/performer). Empezar, salir al aire (Radio, TV). *(Sport)* Entrar (player).

come out, salir, trascender, parecer; apuntar el día, brotar las plantas; salir algo a luz: descubrirse o hacerse una cosa pública. **To come short of,** faltar, salir mal de, ser desafortunado. **Come out with,** dar salida, dejar escapar, soltar aflojar. **come on to,** pasar a. **Come out** 1. Salir (from inside, indoors). **To come out of something,** salir de algo. **If you take this route, you come out at Park Lane,** por este camino se sale a Park Lane. Salir (from prison, hospital). 2. Caerse (tooth, hair); salir (stain). 3. Salir (appear/sun, stars). Florecer, salir (flowers). 4. Salir (be said, spoken). **I tried to say it in French but it came out all wrong,** quise decirlo en francés, pero me salió mal. **I didn't mean to say it, it just**

came out, no lo dije a propósito, se me escapó. Revelarse, salir a la luz (be revealed, emphasized/secret, truth). 5. Declararse (declare oneself). **To come out on strike,** declararse en huelga, ir a la huelga. Destaparse, declararse abiertamente homosexual (as being gay). 6. Salir (be published, become available/newspaper, record, product). 7. Salir (have as outcome, total). **Everything came out right in the end,** al final todo salió bien. **To come out well/badly,** salir bien/mal parado (fare, acquit oneself). 8. *(Fot.)* Salir. **come out in, I/she came out in spots,** me/le salieron granos. **He came out in a cold sweat,** le entró un sudor frío.
come out with 1. Salir con (say/excuse, allegation).
come over (to somebody's home). **Telephone me, or better still, come over,** llámame o, mejor aún, pásate o ven por casa. Venir (from overseas). **She came over to our side,** se pasó a nuestro bando (change sides, opinions). **He came over all shivery,** de repente le dieron escalofríos (have sudden feeling). **2. A feeling of nausea came over her,** le dieron náuseas (affect, afflict). **I don't know what came over me,** no sé qué me pasó.
come over, volver, disiparse, irse; alborotarse; atravesar, pasar; volver disiparse, irse. *(Fam.)* Sorprender, engañar.
come round (GB) *V.* COME AROUND.
come through Pasar (into room, office, etc.). Llegar (be received/message, news, supplies). **You're coming through loud and clear,** te recibimos u oímos muy bien. **In the end they came through with the money,** al final pusieron el dinero (not fail). **When the chips where down, you came through for me,** a la hora de la verdad, tú no me fallaste. 2. Penetrar, entrar (penetrate/water, light); oírse (sound, noise). 3. Salir de (survive/ordeal, illness); sobrevivir (war). **He came through the ordeal greatly scarred,** salió de la experiencia muy marcado.
come to, acercarse; llegar a obtener, alcanzar (reach certain state); consentir; llegar a, lograr, conseguir; estar reducido a; pasar a alguna parte; ascender, montar o importar cuando se trata de cantidades; parar en. **How do you come to here?,** ¿cómo es que estás aquí? **To come to an estate,** heredar, suceder a uno en la posesión de una hacienda. **To come to and fro,** pasar y repasar. **To come to grief,** salir mal parado. **To come to hand,** ser recibido, llegar a manos de; ofrecerse. **To come to himself,** volver en sí. **To come to nothing,** reducirse a nada una conversación, discurso, etc.; no quedar en nada, no valer nada, echarse a perder, ir en decadencia. **To come to an end,** estar a punto de acabarse, morir. **To come to life,** nacer. **To come to life again,** resucitar. **To come to mind,** ocurrir, presentarse a la memoria. **To come to pass,** acontecer, acaecer, suceder. **To come to terms,** someterse a algunas condiciones. **To come to one,** acercarse o llegar a uno, dirigirse a él. **To come short,** estar bajo la dependencia de otro; ser desafortunado; faltar.
come to 1. Llegar a (reach). **What's the world coming to!,** ¡hasta dónde vamos a llegar!, ¡adónde vamos a ir a parar! Ocurrirse (occur/idea, answer, name). **It come to me in a flash,** se me ocurrió de repente. **When it comes to…,** cuando se trata de… (be a question of). 2. Ascender a (amount to/total). **It comes to $15 exactly,** son 15 dólares justos. **The pian never came to anything,** el plan nunca llegó a nada. **I comes to the same thing,** viene a ser lo mismo. 3. Volver en sí, recobrar el conocimiento (recover consciousness).
come together, 1. venir junto, juntarse; casarse; 2. reunirse (group, people). Cuajar (idea, plan).
come under Caer bajo (domination/spell). Ir bajo (be classified under).
come up 1. Subir (ascend, rise/person); salir (sun/moon). Acercarse (approach). **To come up to somebody,** acercársele a alguien. 2. Crecer (grow/seed, plant). Quedar (after cleaning). **The sheets have come up beautifully,** las sábanas han quedado muy bien. (GB) Hincharse (swell). 3. Surgir, presentarse (occur, arise/problem). **Something important has just come up,** acaba de surgir algo importante. **Two**

hamburgers, coming up, dos hamburguesas, marchando. Surgir (be raised, mentioned/subject, point); ser mencionado (name). *(Law)* **My case comes up next Wednesday,** mi caso se ve el próximo miércoles. **come up,** subir; aparecer; establecerse una cosa; brotar o nacer las plantas. **To come up to,** acercarse a, llegar a, subir a; juntarse con; abordar un buque. **To come up with,** alcanzar a uno.
come up against Enfrentarse a, toparse o tropezarse con (opposition, prejudice).
come up for. The car is coming up for its annual service, dentro de poco hay que hacerle la revisión anual al coche. **I should come up for promotion next year,** me deberían considerar para un ascenso el año que viene. **To come up for re-election,** presentarse a la re-elección.
come upon Encontrarse con (encounter, reach). **Come upon,** embestir, atacar, sorprender, coger de repente; agarrar, asir, coger.
come up to Llegar a o hasta. **The water came up to my chest,** el agua me llegaba al pecho. Alcanzar, llegar a (attain/standard). **Her performance didn't come up to expectations,** su actuación no estuvo a la altura de lo que se esperaba. **It's coming up to four o'clock,** son cerca de las cuatro (be nearly). **We're coming up to the end of this stage,** nos estamos acercando al final de esta etapa.
come up with Idear (find/plan, scheme); presentar, plantear (proposal); conseguir (money). **If you can come up with a better idea,** si a ti se te ocurre algo mejor.
comeback ['kʌmbæk] [kam-bak] *s.* 1. Vuelta, retorno (return, revival). **He made/staged a comeback at 60,** volvió a la escena (o a la política.) a los 60 (años). 2. **The trouble is that you have no comeback at all,** el problema es que no puedes hacer ninguna reclamación o no puedes exigir reparación (redress). 3. Respuesta, réplica (retort).
comedian [kə'miːdɪən] [ko-mi-dian] *s.* 1. Comediante, representante, cómico, actor o actriz; humorista. 2. Escrito de comedias. *V.* DRAMATIST.
comedienne [kə,miːdɪ'en] [kam] *s.* Cómica, actriz, humorista.
comedown ['kʌmdaʊn] [kam-daun] *s. (Fam.)* Cambio desfavorable de circunstancias, descenso en la escala social. Degradación, humillación.
comedy ['kɒmɪdɪ] [ko-mi-di] *s.* Comedia (play, film); humorismo (comic entertainment); humorístico, de humor (show, program); comicidad, lo cómico (of situation.
comelily ['kʌmɪlɪlɪ] [ko-mi-li-li], *adv.* Donosamente, cortésmente.
comeliness ['kʌmɪlɪnɪs] [ko-mi-li-nes], *s.* 1. Gracia, donaire, hermosura, garbo, modestia. 2. Honestidad, decencia.
comely ['kʌmlɪ] [kam-li], *a.* Garboso, bien parecido, hermoso, decente, honesto, modesto. Bonito, lindo. *-adv.* 1. *V.* COMELILY. 2. Decentemente.
come-off [kʌm'ɒf] [kam-of], *s.* Salida, pretexto, excusa, escapatoria.
come-on [kʌm,ɒm] [kam-on] *s. (Coloq.)* **To give somebody the come-on,** insinuársele a alguien, tirarle los tejos a alguien.
comer ['kʌmər] [ka-ma'], *s.* Viniente, el que viene. **The contest is open to all comers,** el certamen está abierto al público en general o a todos los que quieran participar. *(Coloq.)* **She/he/it looks like a comer,** parece que tiene posibilidades o futuro, parece prometedor (promising person, thing).
comestible [kə'mestɪbl] [ko-mes-ti-bol], *a.* Comestible. *-zs.* Comestible, mantenimiento.
comet ['kɒmɪt] [ko-mit], *s.* 1. Cometa, cuerpo celeste. 2. Cometa, juego de naipes.
cometarium ['kɒmɪtərɪəm] [ko-mi-ta-rium], *s.* Instrumento para mostrar la revolución de un cometa.
cometary ['kɒmɪtərɪ] [ko-mi-ta-ri], *a.* Perteneciente a un cometa.

comet-like [ˈkɒmɪtˌlaɪk] [ko-mit-laik], *a.* Semejante a un cometa; cosa que causa espanto o admiración.

cometography [ˌkɒmɪˈtɒɡræfɪ] [ko-mi-tou-gra-fi], *s.* Cometografía.

come-uppance [ˌkʌmˈʌpəns] [kam-a-pans] *s.* (*Coloq.*) **To get one's come-uppance,** llevarse su merecido.

comfit [ˈkɒmfɪt] [kom-fit], *s.* Confite, pasta echa de azúcar.

comfit, *va.* Confitar.

comfiture [ˈkɒmfɪtʃʊər] [kom-fi-chuaʳ], *s.* Confitura.

comfort [ˈkʌmfət] [kom-fort], *va.* 1. Confortar, fortificar, dar fuerza, espíritu y vigor. 2. Animar, alentar, consolar al afligido (bereaved person); consolar (child). **I was comforted by the knowledge that you'd be there,** me reconfortaba saber que estarías allí. 3. Alegrar, divertir, dar gozo y placer al que está triste. 4. (*For.*) Ayudar, apoyar. Cf. ABET.

comfort, *s.* 1. Confortación, auxilio, asistencia, favor, ayuda. 2. Consuelo, alivio, en alguna pena o aflicción (mental); placer, satisfacción. **He was a great comfort to me,** me sirvió de mucho consuelo. **To give aid and comfort to terrorists,** cooperar con terroristas. **To make comfort from something.** consolarse con algo. **Too close for comfort,** peligrosamente cerca. **To be cold comfort,** no servir de consuelo. 3. Comodidad, confort (physical, material); conveniencia, regalo. **To live in comfort,** vivir desahogadamente o con holgura. Comodidad (something pleasant, luxury). 4. (*For.*) Ayuda, apoyo en la perpetración de un crimen.

comfortable [ˈkʌmfətəbl] [kom-for-ta-bol], *a.* 1. Agradable, cómodo, consolador, consolatorio, consolante, dulce. 2. Cómodo (chair/clothes); confortable, cómodo (house, room). **I'm not very comfortable in this dress,** no estoy muy cómoda con este vestido. **Make yourself comfortable!,** ¡ponte cómodo! (*Med.*) Estable. Cómodo (at ease). **To feel comfortable with somebody,** sentirse cómodo o a gusto con alguien. 3. Bueno (income). **A comfortable lifestyle,** una vida desahogada. 4. Amplio, holgado (margin, majority). -*s.* (*E.U.*) Bufanda.

comfortableness [ˈkʌmfətəblnɪs] [kom-for-tei-bol-nes], *s.* 1. Comodidad, bienestar. 2. Consuelo, dulzura, agrado.

comfortably [ˈkʌmfətəblɪ] [kom-for-ta-bli], *adv.* Agradablemente; cómodamente, confortablemente (lie, sit). Holgadamente, con holgura (live). **To be comfortably off,** vivir holgadamente, tener una posición desahogada. Holgadamente, sin problemas (win).

comforter [ˈkʌmfətər] [kom-for-taʳ], *s.* 1. Consolador. 2. El Espíritu Santo. 3. (*E.U.*) Sobrecama o manta acolchada; edredón (bedcover). 4. Bufanda larga de lana. 5. (BrE) *V.* PACIFIER (for baby).

comforting [ˈkʌmfətɪŋ] [kom-for-tin], *a.* Consolador, confortante. De consuelo, reconfortante (words). **It's a comforting thought,** es reconfortante pensarlo o es un consuelo pensarlo.

comfortless [ˈkʌmfətlɪs] [kom-fort-les], *a.* Desconsolado, sin consuelo, inconsolable, desesperado, desagradable.

comfortress [ˈkʌmfətres] [kom-for-tres], *sf.* Consoladora.

comfort station [ˈkʌmfətˌsteɪʃən] [kom-fort-stei-shon] *s.* Baño público, servicios públicos.

comfy [ˈkʌmfɪ] [kom-fi] *a.* (*Coloq.*) Cómodo.

comic [ˈkɒmɪk] [ko-mik] *a.* Cómico (actor, scene); humorístico (writer). **Comic opera,** ópera bufa o cómica. **Comic relief,** toque de humor.

comic *s.* 1. Cómico, humorista (comedian). 2. (GB) Comic, libro de historietas (book); *V.* COMIC BOOK (magazine). **Comics,** *pl.* tiras cómicas, historietas, monitos.

comical [ˈkɒmɪkəl] [ko-mi-kal], *a.* Cómico, burlesco, alegre.

comically [ˈkɒmɪkəlɪ] [ko-mi-ka-li], *adv.* Burlescamente, cómicamente.

comic book [ˈkɒmɪkbʊk] [ko-mik-buk] *s.* Revista de historietas, tebeo, revista de chistes; comic (for adults).

comic strip [ˈkɒmɪkstrɪp] [ko-mik-strip], *s.* Historieta, tira cómica.

coming [ˈkʌmɪŋ] [ka-min], *s.* 1. Venida, llegada. 2. (*Rel.*) Advenimiento. **There was a lot of coming and going,** había mucho ir y venir de gente, había mucho movimiento.

coming, *a.* 1. El o lo que viene, venidero, viniente. 2. En camino de la celebridad o del poder. 3. Próximo, entrante (approaching/week, year). **This coming Monday,** este lunes, el lunes que viene. **The coming election,** las próximas elecciones.

coming-in [ˈkʌmɪŋˌɪn] [ko-min-in], 1. Introducción, principio, entrada. 2. Renta. 3. sumisión.

coming-of-age [ˈkʌmɪŋəvˈeɪdʒ] [ko-min-eich] *s.* Mayoría de edad.

coming-out [ˈkʌmɪŋˈaʊt] [ko-min-aut] *s.* Presentación en sociedad, puesta de largo (of debutante).

comitative [ˈkɒmɪtətɪv] [ko-mi-ta-tiv], *a.* Que indica asociación o acompañamiento.

comitial [ˈkɒmɪʃəl] [ko-mi-shial], *a.* Perteneciente a comicios o asambleas.

comity [ˈkɒmɪtɪ] [ko-mi-ti], *s.* Cortesía, urbanidad.

comma [ˈkɒmə] [ko-ma], *s.* 1. Coma, el signo (,) que sirve para dividir los miembros más cortos del período. 2. (*Mús.*) Coma, ligera diferencia en el tono. **Turned comma.** (') virgulilla. *V.* QUOTATION-MARK.

command [kəˈmɑːnd] [ko-mand], *va.* 1. Mandar, comandar, ordenar, regir, gobernar (order). **To command somebody to,** ordenarle a alguien que. Estar al o tener el mando de (army, ship). 2. Dominar, hablando de un paraje elevado con relación a las llanuras que lo rodean. 3. Contar con, disponer de (wealth, resources). 4. Imponer, infundir, inspirar (respect); exigir (fee); alcanzar (price). -*vn.* Tener poder o autoridad suprema, gobernar.

command, *s.* 1. Mando (authority); poder, dominio (mastery); comando. 2. Mandamiento; orden (order). **To be at somebody's command,** estar a las órdenes de alguien. **Who's in command of this ship?,** ¿quién manda en este barco? **She's in command of the situation,** es dueña de la situación. **Under somebody's command,** bajo las órdenes de alguien. 3. Autoridad, imperio. 4. Cuerpo de tropas bajo un comandante. 5. Dominació y de aquí, alcance de vista. 6. Facilidad, recursos. 7. Mando (leadership). **Command post,** puesto de mando. 8. (*Inform.*) Orden, comando. **To have command of** o **over oneself,** saber dominarse. **Yours to command,** su seguro servidor.

commandant [ˌkəmɑːnˈdænt] [ko-man-deʳ], *s.* Comandante.

commandeer [kəˈmɑːndɪər] [ko-man-diaʳ], *va.* (*Mil.*) Confiscar, expropiar. Reclutar forzosamente (personnel). Requisar (vehicle, building, supplies). Apropiarse de (take arbitrarily).

commander [kəˈmɑːndər] [ko-man-daʳ], *s.* 1. Comandante (officer in command). Capitán de fragata (navy rank). 2. Maza o mazo para empedrar.

commander-in-chief [kəˈmɑːndərɪnˈtʃiːf] [ko-man-der-in-chif], *s.* Comandante en jefe.

commandery [kəˈmɑːndərɪ] [ko-man-de-ri] *s.* 1. Comandancia, el cuerpo de los caballeros de Malta de una misma nación. 2. Residencia de algún cuerpo de caballeros. 3. Encomienda, en las órdenes militares.

commanding [ˈkɒmə] [ko-ma], *pa.* 1. Dominante, imperativo. 2. Imponente. 3. (*Mil.*) Comandante. **A commanding presence,** una presencia imponente. **The commanding officer,** comandante en jefe. *a.* De superioridad, dominante (dominant, position) considerable (lead). Que impone (authoritative/presence); autoritario, imperioso (tone). Prominente (overlooking/ position).

commandingly [kəˈmɑːndɪŋlɪ] [ko-man-din-li], *adv.* Imperativamente, en tono de mando.

commanding officer [kə'mɑ:ndɪŋ'ɒfɪsər] [ko-man-din-o-fi-sar] *s.* Oficial al mando.

commandment ['kɒmndmənt] [ko-mand-mant], *s.* Mandato, precepto. **The ten Commandments,** los diez Mandamientos.

commando [kə'mɑ:ndəʊ] [ko-man-dou], *s.* Comando, comandos, soldado o tropa entrenados especialmente para misiones difíciles (unit, soldier).

commandress [kə'mɑ:ndres] [ko-man-dres], *sf.* Comendadora, mandante.

commatism ['kɒmætɪzm] [ko-ma-tisem], *s.* Concisión, brevedad.

commeasurable [kə'mɪɜʒərəbl] [ko-mia-su-rei-bol], *a.* Conmensurable.

commemorable [kə'memərəbl] [ko-me-mo-ra-bol], *a.* Memorable, digno de ser recordado.

commemorate [kə'meməreɪt] [ko-me-mo-reit], *va.* Conmemorar, recordar.

commemoration [kə,memə'reɪʃən] [ko-me-mo-reishon], *s.* Conmemoración, recuerdo.

commemorative [kə'memərətɪv] [ko-me-mo-ra-tiv], *a.* Conmemorativo.

commemoratory [kə'memərətərɪ] [ko-mè-mo-ra-to-ri], *a.* Conmemoratorio.

commence [kə'mens] [ko-mens], *vn.* Comenzar, empezar. Dar comienzo, iniciarse (session, celebration); comenzar (person). -*va.* Comenzar, principiar, entablar. Dar comienzo a, iniciar, comenzar (work, discussion).

commencement [kə'mensmənt] [ko-mens-ment], *s.* 1. Principio, inicio, comienzo (beginning). 2. El día de recibir grados en las universidades y la celebración que hacen los graduados en ese día. Ceremonia de graduación.

commend [kə'mend] [ko-mend], *va.* 1. Encomendar, recomendar; encargar algún negocio o persona al cuidado de otro (entrust). **To commend somebody/something to somebody,** encomendarle alguien/algo a alguien. 2. Alabar, hablar en favor de alguna persona; elogiar (praise). **To commend somebody for something,** elogiar a alguien por algo. **Highly commended,** mención de honor, accésit. 3. Ensalzar, 4. Enviar. 5. Recomendar (recommend). **It has little/much to commend it,** tiene pocos/muchos méritos. **To commend something to somebody,** recomendar(le) algo a alguien.

commendable [kə'mendəbl] [ko-men-da-bol], *a.* Recomendable, loable, encomiable, digno de alabanza.

commendably [kə'mendəblɪ] [ko-men-da-bli], *adv.* Loablemente.

commendatary [kə'mendətərɪ] [ko-men-da-ta-ri], *s.* Comendatario, beneficiado.

commendation [,kɒmen'deɪʃən] [ko-men-dei-shon], *s.* Recomendación, encomio, alabanza, elogios (praise). Mención de honor, accésit (award).

commendator [kə'mendeɪtər] [ko-men-dei-to'], *s.* Comendatario, el eclesiástico que tenía en encomienda algún beneficio.

commendatory [kə'mendətərɪ] [ko-men-da-to-ri], *a.* 1. Recomendatorio. 2. Encomendero. -*s.* Encomio, recomendación.

commender [kə'mendər] [ko-men-da'], *s.* La persona que recomienda; alabador.

commensal [kə'mensl] [ko-men-sal], *a.* 1. Comensal, el que come a la mesa y a expensas de otro. 2. *(Biol.)* Asociado a otro o que vive con él, pero no como parásito; por ejemplo, una anémona marina y un cangrejo ermitaño.

commensalism [kə'mensəlɪɜm] [ko-men-sa-lisem], o **commensality** [kə'mensəlɪtɪ] [ko-men-sa-li-ti], *s.* Comensalía, la compañía de casa y mesa.

commensurability [kə'menʃərəbɪlɪtɪ] [ko-men-shu-ra-bi-li-ti], **commensurableness** [kə'menʃərəblnɪs] [ko-men-shu-ra-bol-nes], *s.* Comensurabilidad.

commensurable [kə'menʃərəbl] [ko-men-shu-ra-bol], *a.* 1. Conmensurable, o que tiene una medida común. 2. Proporcionado, a propósito.

commensurate [kə'menʃərɪt] [ko-men-shu-reit], *va.* Conmensurar, medir o tomar la proporción de alguna cosa reduciéndola a medida común.

commensurate, *a.* Conmensurativo, proporcionado. Acorde. **Commensurate with something,** acorde o en proporción con algo.

commensurately [kə'menʃərɪtlɪ] [ko-men-shu-reit-li], *adv.* Proporcionadamente.

comment ['kɒment] [ko-ment], *va.* 1. *(Ant.)* Comentar, hacer un comentario, glosar, observar. 2. -*vn.* Anotar, hacer notas críticas, explicar. **To comment on something,** hacer comentarios sobre algo.

comment *s.* 1. Comento, explicación, glosa, exposición. 2. Comentario, observación (remark). **The film is a comment on modern society,** la película es una reflexión sobre la sociedad actual. Comentarios (reaction). **To pass comment on something,** hacer comentarios sobre algo. **The minister is unavailable for comment,** el ministro no desea hacer ningún comentario. **No comment,** sin comentarios.

commentary ['kɒmentərɪ] [ko-men-ta-ri], *s.* 1. Comentario, glosa; interpretación. *(Rad, TV, Sport)* Comentarios, crónica. Comentario (anlysis). 2. Comentario, relación histórica de alguna expedición. 3. Notas explicatorias del texto, escolio.

commentate ['kɒmenteɪt] [ko-men-teit], *vn.* Glosar, anotar. **To commentate on something,** hacer los comentarios o la crónica de algo.

commentator ['kɒmenteɪtər] [ko-men-tei-to'], **commenter** ['kɒmentər] [ko-men-ta'], *s.* Comentador, expositor. Comentarista.

commentitious ['kɒmentɪʃəs] [ko-men-ti-shos], *a.* Imaginario, fingido, falso.

commerce ['kɒmɜːs] [ko-mers], *s.* 1. Comercio (trade), negociación, tráfico. 2. Trato familiar, correspondencia, amistad, unión amistosa. 3. Comercio, un juego de naipes. **Foreign commerce,** comercio exterior. **Domestic commerce,** comercio interior. **To enter into commerce with,** entrar en relaciones con. **To carry on a commerce,** hacer tráfico de, comerciar en.

commerce, *vn.* 1. Mantener trato o correspondencia. 2. *(Des.)* Comerciar, traficar, negociar, tratar con.

commercial [kə'mɜːʃəl] [ko-mer-shal], *a.* Comercial, comerciante, mercantil. **Commercial flying,** aviación comercial. **Commercial law,** derecho mercantil o comercial -*s.* Anuncio comercial (en la radio, en la televisión, etc.). Spot publicitario.

commercialism [kə'mɜːʃəlɪzəm] [ko-mer-sha-lisem] *s.* Comercialismo.

commercialize [kə'mɜːʃəlaɪz] [ko-mer-sha-lais], *va.* 1. Mercantilizar. Comercializar. 2. Explotar un negocio. 3. Comerciar un producto.

commercially [kə'mɜːʃəlɪ] [ko-mer-sha-li], *adv.* Comercialmente (manufacture, sell). **Commercially viable,** rentable.

commercial paper ['kɒmɜːʃəl'peɪpər] [ko-mer-shal-pei-pa'] *s.* Efectos negociables, papel comercial.

commercial traveler ['kɒmɜːʃəl'trævlər] [ko-mer-shal-trav-le'] *s.* (GB) Viajante de comercio, corredor.

commerge ['kɒmɜːdʒ] [ko-merch], *va. y vn.* Mezclar, unir o unirse.

commie, commie ['kɒmɪ'kɒmɪ] [ko-mi-ko-mi] *s. (Sl.)* Rojo, comunista.

commigrate ['kɒmɪgreɪt] [ko-mi-greit], *vn.* Emigrar juntos, en compañía de otros.

commination ['kɒmɪneɪʃən] [ko-mi-nei-shon], *s.* Conminación, amenaza.

comminatory [ˈkɒmɪnətərɪ] [ko-mi-na-to-ri], *a.* Conminatorio.

commingle [ˈkɒmɪŋl] [ko-mingl], *va.* Mezclar, hacer mezcla de cosas diversas. *-vn.* Mezclarse, unirse una cosa con otra.

comminute [ˈkɒmɪnuːt] [ko-mi-nut], *va.* Moler, pulverizar, desmenuzar, romper, quebrar, dividir. **Comminuted fracture,** fractura conminuta, rotura del hueso en varios fragmentos.

comminution [ˈkɒmɪnuːʃən] [ko-mi-nu-shon], *s.* 1. Pulverización; división. 2. *(Cir.)* Fractura conminuta. 3. Atenuación, pérdida gradual.

commiserable [ˈkəmɪzərəbl] [ko-mi-se-ra-bol], *a.* Lastimoso, digno de compasión.

commiserate [kəˈmɪzəreɪt] [ko-mi-se-reit], *va.* Apiadarse, tener lástima o compasión, compadecerse. *vn.* **I commiserated with him about losing his job,** le dije cuánto sentía que se hubiera quedado sin trabajo.

commiseration [kəˌmɪzəˈreɪʃən] [ko-mi-se-rei-shon], *s.* Conmiseración, compasión, piedad.

commiserative [kəˈmɪzərətɪv] [ko-mi-se-ra-tiv], *a.* Compasivo.

commiserator [kəˈmɪzəreɪtər] [ko-mi-sa-rei-to'], *s.* Apiadador.

commissariat [ˌkɒmɪseərɪət] [ko-mi-sea-riat], *s.* 1. Comisaría, el empleo o la oficina del comisario. 2. El cuerpo de Administración Militar, que se encarga de proveer a la subsistencia del ejército. 3. Los víveres y demás artículos necesarios abastecidos por la Administración Militar.

commissary [ˈkɒmɪsərɪ] [ko-mi-sa-ri], *s.* Comisario, delegado. 2. *(Mil.)* Comisario de guerra, oficial que tiene a su cargo el aprovisionamiento de las tropas. **Commissary-general,** jefe superior de Administración Militar.

commissaryship [ˈkɒmɪsərɪʃɪp] [ko-mi-sa-ri-ship], *s.* Comisaría, comisariato.

commission [kəˈmɪʃən] [ko-mi-shon], *s.* 1. Comisión, la acción de cometer a otro alguna cosa. 2. Comisión, encargo. (for music, painting, building). Cargo (office). 3. Patente, despacho, nombramiento en virtud del cual se designa o constituye a un oficial en algún empleo militar. 4. Comisionados, cierto número de personas a quienes se les confía alguna comisión. Comisión (grupo). **The European Commission,** la Comisión Europea o de las Comunidades Europeas. 5. *(Com.)* Mando o autoridad de algún comisionista o agente. 6. Paga o sueldo de comisionista. Comisión (for sales). **To sell something on commission,** vender algo a comisión. 7. Comisión, perpetración. **To put in o into commission,** poner un buque de guerra bajo el mando directo de un oficial determinado para el servicio activo. 8. Servicio (use). **To be out of commission,** estar fuera de servicio (ship); no funcionar (machine).

commission, *va.* 1. Comisionar, dar comisión o poder a alguno para que en su virtud obre; autorizar, encargar, apoderar. Encargar, comisionar (painting, novel, study). **To commission somebody to,** encargarle a alguien que (artist, writer, researcher). 2. *(Mil.)* Nombrar oficial. **Commissioned officer,** oficial del ejército con grado de teniente o superior a teniente. *(Naut.)* Poner en servicio (ship).

commission agent [kəˈmɪʃənˈeɪdʒənt] [ko-mi-shon-ei-yent], *s.* Agente comisionista.

commissionaire [kəˌmɪʃəˈnɛər] [ko-mi-sho-nea'] *s.* (GB) Conserje, portero.

commissional [kəˈmɪʃənəl] [ko-mi-sho-nal], **commissionary** [kəˈmɪʃənərɪ] [ko-mi-sho-na-ri], *a.* Comisionado.

commissioner [kəˈmɪʃənər] [ko-mi-sho-na'], *s.* Comisionado, apoderado. Comisionado, miembro de la comisión (committee member). **EC Commissioner,** comisario de la CE. (GB) Inspector, jefe (of police). *(Sport)* Presidente de una federación deportiva.

commissure [ˈkɒmɪʃər] [ko-mi-shua'], *s. (Anat.)* Comisura, punto de unión de ciertas partes similares del cuerpo, como

los labios y los párpados. El adjetivo de este vocablo es *Commissural.*

commit [kəˈmɪt] [ko-mit], *va.* 1. Cometer, perpetrar algún delito o yerro (perpetrate/crime, error, sin). **To commit suicide,** suicidarse. 2. Cometer, confiar. 3. Depositar, entregar (send). **To commit somebody to an asylum,** internar a alguien en un manicomio. **She was committed to trial,** se dictó auto de procesamiento o auto de sujeción a proceso contra ella. 4. Encarcelar, poner preso. 5. Encargar, encomendar. Asignar, consignar (funds, time, resources). **To commit something to paper/writing,** poner/consignar algo por escrito. **To commit something to somebody's care,** confiar algo al cuidado de alguien. 6. Aprender de memoria. **To commit something to memory,** memorizar algo. 7. Comprometer, obligar (bind). *v. refl.* **To commit oneself,** comprometerse (bind). Comprometerse (state views). **He wouldn't commit himself,** no quiso comprometerse.

commitment [kəˈmɪtmənt] [ko-mit-ment], *s.* 1. Auto de prisión. 2. Fianza, seguridad, prenda. 3. Perpetración (de un delito). 4. Remisión de un proyecto de ley a una comisión. 5. Responsabilidad (responsibility); obligación (obligation). **Family commitments,** obligaciones o cargas familiares. **There's no commitment to join,** no hay (ninguna) obligación de afiliarse. Compromiso (engagement). 6. **Commitment to something,** dedicación o entrega a algo (dedication).

committal [kəˈmɪtl] [ko-mi-tal], *s.* 1. *V.* COMMITMENT, 1ª y 3ª aceps. 2. Consignación. 3. Encarcelamiento.

committed [kəˈmɪtɪd] [ko-mi-tid] *a.* Comprometido (dedicated/Christian, Communist, feminist); entregado a su trabajo, dedicado (teacher, worker). Comprometido (under obligation, pledged). **I am committed to helping her,** me he comprometido a ayudarla.

committee [kəˈmɪtɪ] [ko-mi-ti], *s.* Junta de comisión o meramente comisión encargada de un negocio particular. Comité (of club, society); comisión (of parliament). **To be on a committee,** ser miembro de un comité o una comisión. **Committee of arrangements,** comisión de arreglos, junta o diputación de personas para disponer una función. **Committee,** *(For.)* guardián o cuidador judicial de la persona o bienes de un lunático o un menor. Del comité o de la comisión (meeting, member).

committeeman [kəˈmɪtɪmən] [ko-mi-ti-man] *s.* Miembro de una comisión o de un comité.

committee woman [kəˈmɪtɪwʊmən] [ko-mi-ti-uo-man] *sf.* Miembro de una comisión o de un comité.

commiteeship [kəˈmɪtɪʃɪp] [ko-mi-ti-ship], *s.* El empleo de comisión.

committer [kəˈmɪtər] [ko-mi-ta'], *s.* Perpetrador, agresor, el que hace o comete algún delito; autor.

committible [kəˈmɪtɪbl] [ko-mi-ti-bol] *a.* Lo que se puede cometer.

commix [kəˈmɪks] [ko-miks], *va.* Mezclar. *-vn.* Unir.

commixture [kəˈmɪkstʃər] [ko-miks-chuar], *s.* Mezcla, mixtura, compuesto.

commode [kəˈməʊd] [ko-moud], *s.* 1. Cómoda, mueble con cajones para guardar ropa y otras cosas (chest of drawers). 2. Lavabo cubierto con aljofaina, etc. 3. Sillico o servicio. Silla con orinal (for invalid). Inodoro, taza (toilet). 4. Tocado que usaron las mujeres por los años de 1700.

commodious [kəˈməʊdɪəs] [ko-mou-dios], *a.* Cómodo, conveniente, útil, apropiado para su objeto, especialmente en el sentido de espacioso, dilatado. Espacioso, amplio.

commodiously [kəˈməʊdɪəslɪ] [ko-mou-dios-li], *adv.* Cómodamente, aptamente.

commodiousness [kəˈməʊdɪəsnɪs] [ko-mou-dios-nes], *s.* Conveniencia, comodidad; extensión.

commodity [kəˈmɒdɪtɪ] [ko-mo-di-ti], *s.* 1. Interés, ventaja, utilidad, provecho. 2. Comodidad, conveniencia de tiempo o lugar. 3. *pl.* Géneros, mercaderías, productos, frutos, producciones (product). *(Fin.)* Materia prima.

commodore [ˈkɒmədɔːr] [ko-mo-dor], *s. (Mar.)* Comodoro, grado inmediatamente inferior al de contraalmirante; jefe de escuadra.

common [ˈkɒmən] [ko-mon], *a.* 1. Común, corriente, usual (widespread, prevalent). **The commom cold,** el resfriado común. **To be in common use,** ser de uso corriente. **The common man,** el hombre medio o de la calle (average, normal). **The common people,** la gente común y corriente. **I was treated like a common criminal,** me trataron como a un vulgar delincuente. **It's common decency,** es una cuestión de elemental (buena) educación. 2. Común, ordinario, vulgar (low class, vulgar). 3. Público, general. 4. Bajo, inferior, de poco valor. 5. Común (shared, mutual). **Common ground,** puntos en común o de coincidencia. **To be common to something,** ser común a. **It's common knowledge,** todo el mundo lo sabe (public). **By common consent he's the best,** todos coinciden en que es el mejor. **The common good,** el bien común o de todos. *-adv. V.* COMMONLY. **Common council,** ayuntamiento, consejo. **Common councilman,** regidor. **Common hall,** casa consistorial. **Common Pleas Court,** uno de los tribunales de justicia para las causas civiles. **Common law,** la ley no escrita (de Inglaterra), costumbre que tiene fuerza de ley. **Common Prayer,** liturgia de la Iglesia anglicana. **Common sense,** sentido común, sensatez, inteligencia práctica. **Common crier,** pregonero. **Common carrier,** conductor público de mercancías de un lugar a otro; en particular un ferrocarril, vapor, o compañía de expreso. **Common sewer,** albañal. **Common soldier,** soldado raso. **Common-place topics,** lugares u observaciones comunes.

common, *s.* 1. Común, comunal, pastos comunes; terreno perteneciente al municipio. 2. **In common,** en común. **To have something in common with somebody,** tener algo en común con alguien. **In common with** (as prep.) al igual que. *V.* COMMONS.

commonable [ˈkɒmənəbl] [ko-mo-na-bol], *a.* Común, comunal.

commonage [ˈkɒmənɪdʒ] [ko-mo-neich], *s.* Derecho de pastar ganados en terreno común.

commonality [ˈkɒmənælɪtɪ] [ko-mo-na-li-ti], *(Des.),* **commonalty** [ˈkɒmənæltɪ] [ko-mo-nal-ti], *s.* El común, el vulgo o pueblo; la mayor parte del género humano; sociedad, comunidad.

commoner [ˈkɒmənər] [ko-mo-naʳ], *s.* 1. Plebeyo, el que es del estado llano. 2. Individuo o miembro de la cámara baja o de los comunes en Inglaterra. 3. Estudiante de segunda clase en la universidad inglesa de Oxford. 4. Comunero, el que tiene parte en alguna heredad o pasto común.

common law [ˈkɒmənˌlɔː] [ko-mon-lo] *s.* Derecho consuetudinario. **Common-law wife,** concubina, conviviente.

commonly [ˈkɒmənlɪ] [ko-mon-li], *adv.* Comúnmente, frecuentemente. **A commonly held belief,** una creencia muy generalizada o extendida.

Common Market [ˈkɒmənˌmɑːkɪt] [ko-mon-mar-ket] *s.* El Mercado Común.

commonness [ˈkɒmənnɪs] [ko-mon-nes], *s.* 1. Comunidad; igual participación de una cosa entre muchos. 2. Frecuencia (frequency). Ordinariez (vulgarity).

common-or-garden [ˈkɒmənɔːˌɡɑːdn] [ko-mon-or-garden] *a.* (GB) *(Coloq.)* Vulgar o común y corriente.

commonplace [ˈkɒmənpleɪs] [ko-mon-pleis], *a.* Común, vulgar, trivial, corriente (ordinary); banal, trillado (trite). *-s.* 1. Memento, nota. 2. Lugares comunes, en los escritos. Tópico (platitude). Cosa frecuente, común o corriente (common occurrence).

commonplace, *va.* Escribir en libros de memoria.

commons [ˈkɒmənz] [ko-mons], *s. pl.* 1. El vulgo o pueblo bajo. 2. La cámara baja en Inglaterra; **The Commons,** la Cámara de los Comunes. 3. Ordinario, la comida usual de todos los días.

commonsense [ˈkɒmənˌsens] [ko-mon-sens] *a.* Lleno de sentido común. **He has a commonsense attitude to things,** ve las cosas con mucho sentido común. **Common sense,** *s.* sentido común.

common stock [ˈkɒmənstɒk] [ko-mon-stok], *s. (Com.)* Acciones ordinarias.

commonwealth [ˈkɒmənwelθ] [ko-mon-uelz], *s.* 1. Todo el pueblo del Estado, el cuerpo político. 2. República, gobierno en el cual el poder supremo reside en el pueblo. **The British Commonwealth,** la Commonwealth.

commorance [ˈkɒmərəns] [ko-mo-rans], **commorancy** [ˈkɒmərənsɪ] [ko-mo-ran-si], *s. (For.)* Morada, estancia, residencia.

commorant [ˈkɒmərənt] [ko-mo-rant], *a. (For.)* Residente, habitante, vecino.

commotion [kəˈməʊʃən] [ko-mou-shon], *s.* 1. Agitación, movimiento del mar y de aquí perturbación del ánimo. 2. Conmoción, levantamiento, tumulto, sublevación, sedición. Alboroto, jaleo (noise). Conmoción (outrage). **To cause a commotion,** producir o causar una conmoción.

commotioner [kəˈməʊʃənər] [ko-mou-sho-naʳ], *s.* Commovedor, perturbador, revolucionario, agitador.

commove [kəˈmuːv] [ko-muv], *va.* Conmover, perturbar, turbar, agitar, revolver.

communal [ˈkɒmjuːnl] [ko-miu-nal], *a.* 1. Referente a un distrito municipal (de Francia) llamado *commune.* 2. Que pertenece a la comunidad; comunal, público (shared/land, ownership); común (kitchen, bathroom); comunitario (in community/life). Interno, intestino (between groups/ violence).

communally [ˈkɒmjuːnəlɪ] [ko-miu-na-li] *adv.* En comunidad.

commune [ˈkɒmjuːn] [ko-miun], *s.* 1. La menor división política de Francia, distrito municipal. 2. Comunidad organizada para gobernarse por sí misma. Comuna. 3. Plática íntima.

commune, *vn.* 1. Conversar, platicar, conferir, hablar familiarmente. 2. Comulgar, recibir la comunión. **To commune with God/nature,** estar en íntima comunión con Dios/la naturaleza.

communicability [kəˈmjuːnɪkəˈbɪlɪtɪ] [ko-miu-ni-ka-bi-li-ti], **communicableness** [kəˈmjuːnɪˈkeɪblnɪs] [ko-miu-ni-kei-bol-nes], *s.* Comunicabilidad.

communicable [kəˈmjuːnɪkəbl] [ko-miu-ni-ka-bol], *a.* 1. Comunicable, lo que se puede comunicar, susceptible de comunicarse o pasar de uno a otro; transmisible. 2. Distribuído, poseído con otros. 3. *V.* COMMUNICATIVE.

communicant [kəˈmjuːnɪkənt] [ko-miu-ni-kant], *s.* Comunicante, comulgante, el que recibe la comunión.

communicate [kəˈmjuːnɪkeɪt] [ko-miu-ni-keit], *va.* 1. Comunicar, decir a otro lo que uno sabe. **To communicate something to somebody,** comunicarle algo a alguien (make known/knowledge, idea); transmitirle o comunicarle algo a alguien (transmit/feeling). 2. Descubrir, revelar o enseñar a uno; paticipar, transmitir. *-vn.* 1. Comulgar. 2. Comunicarse, tener comunicación (person, aircraft). **To communicate with something,** comunicarse con algo (conect, room). **Communicating,** que se comunican (rooms); de comunicación (doors).

communication [kəˌmjuːnɪˈkeɪʃən] [ko-miu-ni-kei-shon], *s.* 1. Comunicación (act). **To be in/get into communication with somebody,** estar/ponerse en comunicación o en contacto con alguien. *(Educ.)* **Communication skills,** aptitud para comunicarse. 2. Comunicación, entrada, paso de un lugar a otro. 3. Participación recíproca de lo que se sabe. 4. Trato o correspondencia entre dos o más personas; plática, conversación. **Communications,** *pl.* comunicaciones (means of communication). **Communications satellite,** satélite de comunicaciones.

communicative [kəˈmjuːnɪkətɪv] [ko-miu-ni-ka-tiv], *a.* 1. Comunicativo, el que tiene aptitud, inclinación y propensión natural a comunicar a otros lo que sabe, o a dividir lo que posee. 2. Franco, sociable, accesible al trato de los demás.

communicativeness [kəˈmjuːnɪkətɪvnɪs] [ko-miu-ni-ka-tiv-nes], Comunicabilidad.

communicatory [kəˈmjuːnɪkətərɪ] [ko-miu-ni-ka-to-ri], *a.* Comunicatorio, que da a conocer.

communion [kəˈmjuːnɪən] [ko-miu-nion], *s.* 1. Comunión, trato familiar; relaciones amistosas (exchange of ideas, fellowship); confraternidad. 2. *(Rel.)* Comunión, el acto de recibir la sagrada eucaristía. **Holy Communion,** la Santa o Sagrada Comunión. **To take Communion,** recibir la comunión o la eucaristía, comulgar. 3. Comunión, congregación de muchas personas unidas por una creencia uniforme.

communiqué [kəˈmjuːnɪkeɪ] [ko-miu-ni-kei], *s.* Comunicación oficial; comunicado.

communism [ˈkɒmjʊnɪzəm] [ko-miu-ni-sem], *s.* 1. El sistema social de la comunidad de bienes. 2. Comunismo, doctrina que proclama la abolición del derecho de propiedad particular y la absoluta autoridad del cuerpo político para dirigir todo lo relativo al trabajo, la religión, las relaciones sociales, etc.

communist [ˈkɒmjʊnɪst] [ko-miu-nist], *s.* Comunista, el partidario del comunismo.

communistic [kəˈmjuːnɪstɪk] [ko-miu-nis-tik], *a.* 1. Perteneciente al comunismo. 2. Dividido en común.

community [kəˈmjuːnɪtɪ] [ko-miu-ni-ti], *s.* 1. Comunidad, el cuerpo político, el público; la sociedad en general. **The community,** la comunidad (society at large). **Community service,** trabajo comunitario prestado en lugar de cumplir una pena de prisión. **Community spirit,** espíritu de comunidad. 2. Conjunto de personas que tienen intereses comunes, por ejemplo una comunidad de frailes; comunidad (people in a locality). Colectividad (large grouping). **The city's black community,** la población o comunidad negra de la ciudad. 3. Comunidad, propiedad o goce común de una cosa; igualdad, conformidad. Comuna (people living together).

community center, (GB) **centre** *s.* Centro social.

community chest [kəˈmjuːnɪtɪˌtʃest] [ko-miu-ni-ti-chest], *s.* Fondo de caridad para beneficio de la comunidad.

community college [kəˈmjuːnɪtɪˌkʌlɪdʒ] [ko-miu-ni-ti-ko-lech] *s.* (in US) Establecimiento donde se imparten cursos de nivel terciario de dos años de duración.

community property [kəˈmjuːnɪtɪˌprɒpəːtɪ] [ko-miu-ni-ti-pro-per-ti] *s.* (in US) Bien ganancial.

commutable [kəˈmjuːtəbl] [ko-miu-ta-bol], *a.* Conmutable.

commutation [ˈkɒmjʊˈteɪʃən] [ko-miu-tei-shon], *s.* 1. Mudanza, alteración. 2. Cambio, trueque, el acto de dar una cosa por otra. 3. Conmutación, el trueque de una pena corporal en otra pecuniaria. 4. Iguala, ajuste, el precio que se da por la franquicia de pasar un río, camino, etc., por cierto tiempo. **Commutation ticket,** billete de abono, válido para viajar por tiempo determinado, a precio reducido.

commutative [kəˈmjuːtətɪv] [ko-miu-ta-tiv], *a.* Conmutativo.

commutatively [kəˈmjuːtətɪvlɪ] [ko-miu-ta-tiv-li], *adv.* Conmutativamente.

commutator [kəˈmjuːteɪtər] [ko-miu-tei-toʳ], *s.* Conmutador, aparato para cambiar la corriente en una máquina dinamoeléctrica.

commute [kəˈmjuːt] [ko-miuti], *va.* 1. Conmutar, permutar, trocar, cambiar; rescatar. Conmutar (sentence, punishment). **To commute something to something,** conmutar algo por algo. 2. Igualarse, ajustarse, pagar un tanto por ciento tiempo por el peaje, pasaje de un río, etc. con el objeto de no tener que hacerlo cada vez. -*vn.* 1. Conmutar, resarcir por medio de conmutación. 2. Viajar todos los días entre el lugar de residencia y el de trabajo.

commuter [kəˈmjuːtər] [ko-miu-taʳ], *s.* La persona que viaja con billete de abono, a precio reducido. Persona que viaja diariamente una distancia considerable entre su lugar de

residencia y el de trabajo. **The commuter belt,** los barrios periféricos.

commutual [kəˈmjuːtʊəl] [ko-miu-tual], *a.* Mutuo, recíproco.

comose [kəˈməʊz] [ko-mous], *a.* Peludo.

compact [ˈkɒmpækt] [kom-pakt], *s.* 1. Pacto, convenio, concierto, ajuste, acuerdo (agreement). 2. **Powder compact,** polvera. 3. **Compact car,** coche compacto.

compact, *va.* 1. Consolidar, juntar y unir unas cosas con otras con solidez y firmeza. 2. Pactar, hacer algún pacto o convenio. 3. Compaginar, ordenar y componer unas cosas con otras hasta reducirlas a sistema. 4. Compactar, comprimir (soil, snow).

compact, *vn.* Coligarse, unirse a o con.

compact, *a.* 1. Compacto (small and neat); firme, sólido, denso; cerrado, apretado (tightly packed). 2. Breve, compendioso. Conciso (concise/style of writing). 3. Pulido, hermoso. 4. Compuesto o hecho de, consistente en.

compact disc, compact disk [ˈkɒmpæktˌdɪsk] [kom-pakt-disk] *s.* Disco compacto, compact-disc. **Compact disc player,** reproductor de compact-disc.

compacted [ˈkɒmpæktɪd] [kom-pak-ted], *a.* Consolidado, apretado, firme.

compactedly [kəmˈpæktɪdlɪ] [kom-pak-ted-li], *adv.* V. COMPACTLY.

compactedness [kəmˈpæktɪdnɪs] [kom-pak-ted-nes], *s.* Firmeza, estrechez, solidez, densidad.

compactible [ˈkɒmpæktɪbl] [kom-pak-ti-bol], *a.* Lo que se puede unir, estrechar, hacer compacto.

compactly [kəmˈpæktlɪ] [kom-pakt-li], *adv.* Estrechamente, unidamente, pulidamente, en pocas palabras.

compactness [kəmˈpæktnɪs] [kom-pakt-nes], *s.* Firmeza, densidad, unión, estrechez, pulidez.

compages [ˈkɒmpeɪdʒəs] [kom-pei-yes], *s.* Trabazón, juntura, enlazamiento, enlace.

compaginate [kɒmˈpædʒɪneɪt] [kom-pa-yi-neit], *va.* Compaginar, juntar, adaptar.

compagination [ˌkɒmpædʒɪˈneɪʃən] [kom-pa-yi-nei-shon], *s.* Compaginación.

companion [kəmˈpænɪən] [kom-pa-nion], *s.* 1. Compañero, socio (associate, comrade). **A traveling companion,** un compañero de viaje. **A boon companion,** un compañero alegre y jovial. 2. Compañero, camarada, la persona con quien uno se acompaña; compañero, pareja (accompanying item). 3. Caballero de una orden. 4. Dama de compañía, señorita/señora de compañía. 5. Guía, manual (guide).

companion, *s. (Mar.)* 1. Lumbrera, chupeta de escala en los buques mercantes. 2. Carroza, cubierta de popa. **Companion-ladder,** escala de toldilla. **Companion-way,** escalera de la cámara.

companionable [kəmˈpænɪəbl] [kom-pa-nia-bol], *a.* Sociable, amigable.

companionably [kəmˈpænɪəblɪ] [kom-pa-nia-bli], *adv.* Sociablemente.

companionship [kəmˈpænɪənʃɪp] [kom-pa-nion-ship], *s.* Sociedad, compañía, reunión de amigos; camaradería, compañerismo (fellowship); compañía (company of others).

company [ˈkʌmpənɪ] [kom-pa-ni], *s.* 1. *(Busn.)* Compañía o sociedad; empresa. 2. Compañía, junta o tertulia de personas que se reunen para divertirse o hablar de algún asunto (companionship). **In somebody's company,** en compañía de alguien. **The dog will be company for her,** el perro le hará compañía (companion, companions). **She's excelent company,** es muy agradable o divertido estar con ella. **Present company excepted,** exceptuando a los presentes, mejorando lo presente. **We've got company,** tenemos visita (guests). 3. Compañía, número de personas que se unen para un fin determinado. 4. Compañía de comercio. 5. Gremio, cuerpo. 6. *(Mil.)* Compañía, cierto número de soldados que militan al mando de un capitán. 7. *(Mar.)* **Ship's company,** tripulación, dotación. **To join company,** *(Mar.)* incorporarse. 8. *(Theat).* Compañía. **To keep company,** frecuentar. **To**

keep company with, (a) asociarse, acompañar; (b) *(Prov.)* cortejar, galantear o recibir galanteos. **To bear company,** acompañar, o asistir. *a.* **A joint stock company,** una sociedad por acciones. **Limited company,** V. LIABILITY *(limited).* **To part company (with),** separarse. **By companies,** en cuadrilla, en tropel.

company, *va.* V. ACCOMPANY. *-vn.* Asociarse. V. ACCOMPANY.

comparable ['kɒmpərəbl] [kom-pa-ra-bol], *a.* Comparable, equiparable. **Comparable with/to something,** comparable o equiparable a algo.

comparably ['kɒmpərəblɪ] [kom-pa-ra-bli], *adv.* Comparablemente. De modo análogo o similar.

comparate ['kɒmpəreɪt] [kom-pa-reit], *s.* Una cosa que está comparada con otra.

comparative [kəm'pærətɪv] [kom-pa-ra-tiv], *a.* 1. Comparativo, respectivo, relativo, no absoluto (relative). 2. Comparativo, lo que tiene capacidad para comparar. 3. Comparado (literature, linguistics); comparativo, comparado (analysis, study). **Comparative degree,** *(Gram.)* Comparativo, grado que expresa la mayor o menor intensidad de calidad en una cosa que en otra; v.g. Juan es menos hábil que Pedro; la mano derecha es más fuerte que la izquierda.

comparative, *s. (Ling.)* Comparativo.

comparatively [kəm'pærətɪvlɪ] [kom-pa-ra-tiv-li], *adv.* Comparativamente, relativamente.

compare [kəm'pɛər] [kom-peaʳ], *va.* Comparar, cotejar, confrontar, colacionar, comprobar. Comparar (make comparison between). **To compare something/somebody to** o **with something/somebody,** comparar algo/a alguien con algo/alguien. **It's tiny compared to your house,** es pequeñísima comparada o en comparación con tu casa. *-vn.* **How do the two models compare for speed?,** en cuanto a velocidad, ¿qué diferencia hay entre los dos modelos? **Nothing compares with good home cooking,** la comida casera no se puede comparar con nada. **It compares favorably with your previous efforts,** este trabajo está mejor que los anteriores.

compare, *s.* (Poét. o Ant.) Comparación, cotejo, comprobación; símil. **Beyond compare,** sin comparación, incomparable.

comparer [kəm'pɛərər] [kom-pea-raʳ], *s.* Comparador.

comparing [kəm'pɛərɪŋ] [kom-pea-rin], *s.* Comparación.

comparison [kəm'pærɪsn] [kom-pa-rison], *s.* 1. Comparación, la acción y efecto de comparar, cotejo, confrontación, comprobación. 2. Símil; parábola. **Beyond comparison,** sin comparación; sin igual. **There's no comparison between them,** no tienen comparación, no hay ni punto de comparación entre ellos. **By/in comparison with something/somebody,** en comparación con algo/alguien.

compart [kəm'pɑːt] [kom-part], *va.* Compartir, dividir, distribuir.

compartment [kəm'pɑːtmənt] [kom-part-ment], *s.* 1. Compartimiento o compartimento (of bag, desk, refrigerator); cada una de las partes en que se subdivide un espacio cerrado, por ejemplo el interior de un buque. (GB) *(Rail)* Compartimiento (in train). 2. Compartimiento, división o distribución de una pintura o diseño. 3. Cajoncito, gaveta de un escaparate o cómoda. 4. *(Her.)* División de un escudo de armas, cuartel.

compartmentalize [ˌkɒmpɑːˈmentəlaɪz] [kom-par-men-ta-lais] *va.* Compartimentar.

compartition [kəm'pɑːtɪʃən] [kom-par-ti-shon], *s.* Compartimiento; división.

compass ['kʌmpəs] [kom-pas], *va.* 1. Conseguir, lograr, alcanzar, obtener. 2. Trazar, idear, maquinar, conspirar contra. 3. Comprender, entender, concebir. 4. *(Ant.)* Circuir, cercar, rodear, circundar; sitiar.

compass, *s.* 1. Círculo, circuito, ámbito; alcance; extensión, espacio encerrado entre límites. 2. Circunferencia. 3. Moderación, límites, la justa medida y término razonable que deben tener las cosas. Alcance (limits, scope). **It falls within the compass of the board,** cae dentro de la competencia de la junta. 4. Compás de la voz o de un instrumento. 5. Intención, designio, propósito. 6. Compás, instrumento que sirve para formar círculos, tirar líneas y otros usos. En este sentido se usa generalmente en plural. **A pair of compasses,** un compás. **Caliber compasses,** compás de calibres. **Proportional compasses,** compás de reducción. 7 Compás de mar, brújula, aguja de marcar (magnetic compass). **The points of the compass,** los puntos cardinales. **Azimuth compass,** brújula de azimut. **Hanging compass,** brújula revirada de cámara. **Compass-box,** caja de brújula. **Compass-card,** rosa de los vientos. **Compass-timber,** *(Mar.)* madera de vuelta. **Compass-saw,** *(Carp.)* serrucho angosto para cortar circularmente.

compassable ['kʌmpəsəbl] [kom-pa-sa-bol], *a.* Asequible, que se puede alcanzar u obtener.

compassion [kəm'pæʃən] [kom-pa-shon], *s.* Compasión, conmiseración, piedad. **Compassion toward somebody,** compasión con alguien.

compasssionable [kəm'pæʃənəbl] [kom-pa-sho-na-bol], *a.* Lastimoso, digno de compasión.

compassionate [kəm'pæʃənɪt] [kom-pa-sho-neit], *a.* Compasivo, el que con facilidad se mueve a compasión. (GB) **Compassionate leave,** permiso por motivos familiares.

compassionately [kəm'pæʃənɪtlɪ] [kom-pa-sho-neit-li], *adv.* Tiernamente.

compaternity [kɒmpə'tɜːnɪtɪ] [kom-pa-ter-ni-ti], *s.* Compaternidad, compadrazgo.

compatibility [kəm,pætə'bɪlɪtɪ] [kom-pa-te-bi-li-ti], **compatibleness** [kəm'pætɪblnɪs] [kom-pa-ti-bol-nes], *s.* Compatibilidad, cualidad de las cosas que no se oponen entre sí.

compatible [kəm'pætɪbl] [kom-pa-ti-bol], *a.* Compatible, que puede coexitir (people, ideas, principles); congruo, apto. **To be compatible with somebody/something,** ser compatible con alguien/algo. *(Inform.)* Compatible. **An IBM compatible computer,** una computadora o un ordenador compatible con IBM.

compatibly [kəm'pætɪblɪ] [kom-pa-ti-bli], *adv.* Compatiblemente.

compatriot [kəm'pætrɪət] [kom-pa-triot], *s.* Compatriota. *-a.* Lo que es de la misma patria.

compeer [kəm'pɪər] [kom-piaʳ], *s.* Compañero, colega; compadre.

compel [kəm'pel] [kom-pel], *va.* 1. Compeler, obligar, constreñir, precisar, forzar. 2. Predominar. 3. Arrancar, tomar por fuerza o con violencia. 4. Imponer (command/obedience, respect). **To compel somebody to,** obligar o forzar a alguien a (force). **I feel compelled to warn you that…,** me veo en la obligación de advertirle que…

compellable [kəm'peləbl] [kom-pe-la-bol], *a.* Lo que puede ser compelido, obligado o violentado.

compellably [kəm'peləblɪ] [kom-pe-la-bli], *adv.* A viva fuerza.

compellation [kəm'peleɪʃən] [kom-pe-lei-shon], *s.* 1. Tratamiento, el título de cortesía que se da a alguno; apóstrofe. 2. Acción de dirigir la palabra.

compeller [kəm'pelər] [kom-pe-laʳ], *s.* Compulsor, el que compele.

compelling [kəm'pelɪŋ] [kom-pe-lin] *a.* Convincente, persuasivo (argument, evidence); absorbente (book); imperioso (need).

compend [kəm'pend] [kom-pend], *s.* Compendio, resumen, epítome, sumario que se hace de un libro, causa o proceso.

compendiarious [kəm'pendɪærɪəs] [kom-pen-dia-rious], *a.* V. COMPENDIOUS.

compendious [kəm'pendɪəs] [kom-pen-dious], *a.* 1. Compendioso, breve, sucinto, reducido. 2. *(Des.)* Directo, sin rodeos.

compendiously [kəmˈpendɪəslɪ] [kom-pen-dious-li], *adv.* Compendiosamente.

compendiousness [kəmˈpendɪəsnɪs] [kom-pen-dious-nes], *s.* Brevedad.

compendium [kəmˈpendɪəm] [kom-pen-dium], *s.* 1. Compendio (book); resumen, epítome, extracto. 2. Juegos reunidos (of games).

compensable [ˈkɒmpensəbl] [kom-pen-sa-bol], *a.* Compensable.

compensate [ˈkɒmpenseɪt] [kom-pen-seit], *va.* Compensar, dar o tomar el equivalente de una cosa; indemnizar, resarcir, reparar (indemnify). **To compensate somebody for something,** indemnizar o compensar a alguien por algo, resarcir a alguien de algo. -*vn.* (Con la preposición for.) Compensarse las pérdidas con las ganacias, o los males con los bienes. **To compensate for something,** compensar algo.

compensation [ˌkɒmpenˈseɪʃən] [kom-pen-sei-shon], *s.* Compensación, acción con que una cosa se sustituye y compensa con otra equivalente; indemnización, resarcimiento, reparación. **Compensation for something,** indemnización o compensación por algo (recompense). **I received $20,000 as/in compensation for the damage,** me dieron 20.000 dólares de indemnización o en compensación por los daños. Remuneración, retribución (remuneration). **Compensation package,** paquete salarial. **Compensation balance, bar o pendulum,** volante o balanza, barra o péndulo de compensación de un reloj.

compensative [ˈkɒmpensətɪv] [kom-pen-sa-tiv], **compensatory** [ˈkɒmpensətərɪ] [kom-pen-sa-to-ri], *a.* Equivalente, lo que compensa.

compensator [ˈkɒmpenseɪtər] [kom-pen-sei-toʳ], *s.* El que o lo que compensa, compensador, v.g. de una brújula.

compense [ˈkɒmpəns] [kom-pens], *va.* V. COMPENSATE.

compere, compère [ˈkɒmpɛər] [kom-peaʳ] *s.* (GB) Presentador, animador. *va.* Presentar, animar.

compete [kəmˈpiːt] [kom-pít], *vn.* Competir, participar, contender dos o más sujetos entre sí, aspirar unos y otros con empeño a una misma cosa. **To compete with,** competir, rivalizar con. **To compete for something,** competir por algo, disputarse algo. **To compete against somebody/something,** competir contra alguien/algo. **We can't compete with the big firms,** no podemos competir con las grandes firmas, no podemos hacerle la competencia a las grandes firmas.

competence, competency [ˈkɒmpɪtəns] [kom-pi-tens], *s.* 1. Lo bastante, lo suficiente; tanto cuanto basta. 2. Lo necesario, bienes suficientes para un mediano pasar. 3. *(Law)* Competencia, la jurisdicción que pertenece a un juez o tribunal (jurisdiction). 4. Competencia, capacidad (ability). **Level of competence in French,** nivel (de conocimientos) de francés.

competent [ˈkɒmpɪtənt] [kom-pi-tent], *a.* Competente, adecuado, bastante, suficiente, capaz, propio, apto, calificado (person). **To be competent to,** estar capacitado para. Aceptable (adequate). *(Law)* Competente (court); hábil (witness).

competently [ˈkɒmpɪtəntlɪ] [kom-pi-tent-li] *adv.* Competentemente.

competition [ˌkɒmpɪˈtɪʃən] [kom-pi-ti-shon], *s.* 1. Competencia, competición, disputa o contienda entre dos o más personas acerca de alguna cosa que se pretende; rivalidad, concurrencia en un mismo empeño (competing). **To be in competition with somebody/something,** competir con alguien/algo. Competencia (opposition). 2. Concurso (contest); certamen, concurso (literary); *(Sport)* Competencia, competición.

competitive [kəmˈpetɪtɪv] [kom-pe-ti-tiv], *a.* De la competencia, referente a la competencia. Competitivo. **Competitive examination,** examen de concurso u oposición.

competitively [kəmˈpetɪtɪvlɪ] [kom-pe-ti-tiv-li] *adv.* Con espíritu competitivo (play). *(Busn.)* **Competitively priced,** a precios competitivos.

competitor [kəmˈpetɪtər] [kom-pe-ti-toʳ], *s.* 1. Competidor, rival, antagonista (rival). 2. Participante, concursante (contestant). *(Sport)* Contrincante, rival.

competitress [kəmˈpetɪtres] [kom-pe-ti-tres], **competitrix** [kəmˈpetɪtrɪks] [kom-pe-ti-triks], *sf.* Competidora.

compilation [ˌkɒmpɪˈleɪʃən] [kom-pi-lei-shon], *s.* Compilación, colección de varios autores; conjunto de algunas cosas (of list); recopilación (of information); recopilación (collection).

compilator [ˌkɒmpɪˈleɪtər] [kom-pi-lei-toʳ], **compiler** [ˌkɒmpɪlər] [kom-pi-lar], *s.* Compilador; redactor.

compilatory [ˈkɒmpɪlətərɪ] [kom-pi-la-to-ri], *a.* Perteneciente a un compilador o a una compilación.

compile [kəmˈpaɪl] [kom-pail], *va.* Compilar, juntar en un cuerpo varias noticias o materias (dictionary, index); recopilar, reunir, recabar (information). *(Inform.)* Compilar (program).

compilement [kəmˈpaɪlmənt] [kom-pail-ment], *s.* Compilación.

complacence, complacency [kəmˈpleɪsəns] [kom-plei-sens], *s.* Complacencia, placer, gusto, satisfacción; deferencia al gusto o parecer de otro; condescendencia. **Self-complacency,** satisfacción de sí mismo.

complacent [kəmˈpleɪsənt] [kom-plei-sent], *a.* Afable, cortés, urbano, condescendiente. Satisfecho de sí mismo (person); disiplente (attitude).

complacently [kəmˈpleɪsəntlɪ] [kom-plei-sent-li], *adv.* Afablemente, urbanamente. Con suficiencia (smile).

complain [kəmˈpleɪn] [kom-plein], *vn.* 1. Quejarse, lamentarse, querellarse. **To complain to somebody about something,** quejarse a alguien por algo. **I can't complain,** no me puedo quejar. **To complain of something,** quejarse de algo. 2. *(For.)* Querellarse, poner acusación contra alguno en justicia, por agravio, injuria o delito; demandar, por daños y perjuicios. 3. Quejarse, afirmar que se siente dolor; estar enfermo. *va.* **You're hurting me, she complained,** me haces daño-protestó o se quejó. **He complained that…,** se quejó de que…

complainable [kəmˈpleɪnəbl] [kom-plei-na-bol], *a.* Lastimero.

complainant [kəmˈpleɪnənt] [kom-plei-nant], *s.* Querellante, demandante.

complainer [kəmˈpleɪnər] [kom-plei-naʳ], *s.* Lamentador.

complaining [kəmˈpleɪnɪŋ] [kom-pleinin], *s.* Lamento.

complaint [kəmˈpleɪnt] [kom-pleint], *s.* 1. Queja, expresión de dolor, pena o sentimiento; lamento, llanto, quejido (grievance). **To make a complaint,** quejarse, reclamar. 2. Causa u objeto de algún agravio. 3. Mal, enfermedad. Dolencia (ailment). 4. Queja, querella. **Ground of complaint,** motivo de queja. 5. *(For.)* Demanda. **To lodge a complaint,** presentar una demanda en justicia.

complaisance [kəmˈpleɪzəns] [kom-plei-sans], **complaisantness** [kəmˈpleɪzəntnɪs] [kom-plei-sant-nes], *s.* Civilidad, cortesía, urbanidad, cumplimiento y muchas veces adulación.

complaisant [kəmˈpleɪzənt] [kom-plei-sant], *a.* 1. Cortés, atento, complaciente. 2. Cumplimentero.

complaisantly [kəmˈpleɪzəntlɪ] [kom-plei-sant-li], *adv.* Cortésmente.

complanate [kəmˈpləneɪt] [kom-pla-neit], *va.* Aplanar, allanar. -*a.* Aplanado, llano; que está situado en el mismo plano.

complected [kəmˈplektɪd] [kom-plek-ted], *a.* Entretejido, enlazado, complicado.

complement [ˈkɒmplɪmənt] [kom-pli-ment], *s.* 1. Complemento, perfección o colmo de alguna cosa. 2. Complemento, lo que acaba de completar alguna cosa. *(Mil.)* Contingente, fuerza numérica. 3. Apéndice, o cosa accesoria que sirve de adorno. 4. Colmo, total. **The orchestra had the full complement of strings,** la orquesta contaba con una sección de cuerdas completa (full number). **Complement of the course,**

(Mar.) complemento de la derrota, los puntos que faltan a la derrota para ser igual a noventa grados o a ocho rumbos, que son los que componen el cuarto del compás de la brújula. **The ship's complement,** la tripulación o dotación completa.

complement, *va.* Suplir una falta, acabar, hacer perfecto o cabal. Complementar. **Those colors complement each other,** esos colores se complementan entre sí.

complemental [ˈkɒmplɪmentl] [kom-pli-men-tal], *a.* Completivo, lo que completa o llena.

complementary [ˌkɒmplɪˈmentərɪ] [kom-pli-men-ta-ri], *a.* Complementario, que completa, que suple lo que falta. -*s.* Algo que suple lo que falta; color complementario.

complete [kəmˈpliːt] [kom-plít], *a.* 1. Completo (set, edition/entire); acabado, perfecto, cabal, consumado. **It comes complete with batteries,** viene con las pilas incluidas. Terminado, concluido (finished). 2. Total, completo (thorough, absolute). **It came as a complete surprise,** fue una auténtica sorpresa. **A complete waste of time,** una pérdida de tiempo total y absoluta.

complete, *va.* Completar, acabar, concluir, consumar. Acabar, terminar (finish/building, education); cumplir (sentence); completar, concluir (investigations). Completar (make whole/set, collection). Llenar, rellenar (fill in/form).

completely [kəmˈpliːtlɪ] [kom-plít-li], *adv.* Completamente, perfectamente, totalmente. **I completely forgot,** me olvidé completamente.

completement [kəmˈpliːtmənt] [kom-plít-ment], *s.* Complemento, acabamiento.

completeness [kəmˈpliːtnɪs] [kom-plít-nes], *s.* Perfección, complemento.

completion [kəmˈpliːʃən] [kom-plí-shon], *s.* Complemento, acabamiento, colmo. Finalización, terminación. **To bring something to completion,** terminar algo, llevar algo a término. **The building is nearing completion,** falta poco para terminar el edificio.

completive [kəmˈpliːtɪv] [kom-plí-tiv], **completory** [kəmˈpliːtərɪ] [kom-li-to-ri], *a.* Completivo.

completory [kəmˈpliːtərɪ] [kom-li-to-ri], *s.* Completas. *(Ant.)* V. COMPLIN.

complex [ˈkɒmpleks] [kom-pleks], *a.* Complejo, compuesto; complicado, enredado (complicated/person, issue, situation). Complejo (intricate/system, pattern, design).

complex, *s.* 1. Complicación, suma, total; reunión, colección. 2. Complejo (buildings); *(Psych.)* Complejo.

complexion [kəmˈplekʃən] [kom-plek-shon], *s.* 1. Tez, color de las partes exteriores del cuerpo, y particularmente del rostro. 2. Aspecto general, estado; carácter o calidad. **Political complexion of a legislature,** carácter político de un cuerpo legislativo. **To put a different/new complexion on something,** darle otro/un nuevo cariz a algo. 3. *(Ant.)* Complexión, temperamento y constitución de los humores del cuerpo humano. 4. *(Ant.)* Complejo, el conjunto de varias cosas. **A fine complexion,** un hermoso cutis, un bello color. **A fresh complexion,** una tez fresca, rosada.

complexional [ˈkɒmpleʃənl] [kom-plek-sho-nal], *a.* Complexional.

complexionally [kəmˈplekʃənlɪ] [kom-plek-sho-na-li], *adv.* Por complexión.

complexioned [kəmˈplekʃənd] [kom-plek-shond], *a.* De tal o cual tez; dotado de cierto color. **Dark-complexioned,** de tez morena.

complexity [kəmˈpleksɪtɪ] [kom-plek-si-ti], **complexness** [kəmˈpleksnɪs] [kom-pleks-nes], *s.* Complejidad, estado complejo.

complexly [ˈkɒmplekslɪ] [kom-pleks-li], *adv.* Complexamente.

complexus [ˈkɒmpleksəs] [kom-plek-sus], *s.* 1. Complicación, sistema complicado. 2. Complexo, gran músculo del cuello y de la espalda.

compliable [kəmˈplaɪəbl] [kom-plaia-bol], *a.* Complaciente, rendido, sumiso; acorde, conforme.

compliance [kəmˈplaɪəns] [kom-plaians], *s.* 1. Sumisión, obediencia. Conformidad (acquiescence). **In compliance with your wishes,** conforme a o en conformidad con sus deseos. Docilidad (submissiveness). 2. Cumplimiento, rendimiento, condescendencia, consentimiento, complacencia.

compliant [kəmˈplaɪənt] [kom-plaiant], *a.* Rendido, sumiso; atento, cortés, condescendiente, fácil, complaciente, oficioso, obsequioso, servicial, galante. Dispuesto a acatar los deseos de otros.

compliantly [kəmˈplaɪəntlɪ] [kom-plaiant-li], *adv.* Rendidamente.

complicacy [ˈkɒmplɪkəsɪ] [kom-pli-ka-si], *s.* Complicación, lo que es complicado y el estado o la calidad de serlo.

complicate [ˈkɒmplɪkeɪt] [kom-pli-keit], *va.* 1. Complicar, enredar una cosa con otra. 2. Mezclar, confundir, embrollar, crear dificultades.

complicated [ˈkɒmplɪkeɪtɪd] [kom-pli-kei-ted] *a.* Complicado, enredado; difícil de entender o explicar.

complicately [ˈkɒmplɪkeɪtlɪ] [kom-pli-keitli], *adv.* Complicadamente.

complicateness [ˈkɒmplɪkeɪtnɪs] [kom-pli-keit-nes], *s.* Complicación, perplejidad, enredo.

complication [ˌkɒmplɪˈkeɪʃən] [kom-pli-kei-shon], *s.* Complicación. **Complications set in,** surgieron complicaciones.

complicative [ˈkɒmplɪkətɪv] [kom-pli-ka-tiv], *a.* Que produce, o puede producir, complicaciones.

complice [ˈkɒmplɪs] [kom-plis], *s.* Cómplice, compañero en el delito.

complicity [kəmˈplɪsɪtɪ] [kom-pli-si-ti], *s.* 1. Complicidad, la calidad de cómplice. 2. Estado complexo.

complier [ˈkɒmplɪər] [kom-plia'], *s.* Hombre dócil, condescendiente y complaciente; consentidor, contemporizador.

compliment [ˈkɒmplɪmənt] [kom-pli-ment], *s.* 1. Cumplimiento, obsequio, regalo, fineza que se hace por urbanidad o cortesía. Cumplido, halago (expression of praise). **To pay somebody a compliment,** hacerle un cumplido a alguien, halagar a alguien. **She returned the compliment,** me devolvió el cumplido. **My compliments to the chef,** felicitaciones al cocinero. 2. Cumplimiento, cumplido, muestra de urbanidad; más usado en plural. **Compliments,** saludos (best wishes). **With the compliments of the management,** gentileza o cortesía de la casa, con los mejores deseos de la dirección. **Compliments slip,** tarjeta.

compliment, *va.* 1. Cumplimentar, dirigir frases de cortesía o afecto; felicitar; hacer un regalo por cumplido o muestra de afeto. 2. Cumplimentar, obsequiar, lisonjear. **To compliment somebody on something,** felicitar a alguien por algo. **She complimented him on his new suit,** le alabó el traje nuevo. -*vn.* Hacer cumplimientos, usar de ceremonias.

complimental [ˈkɒmplɪmentl] [kom-pli-men-tal], *a. (Ant.)* V. COMPLIMENTARY.

complimentary [ˌkɒmplɪˈmentərɪ] [kom-pli-men-ta-ri], *a.* 1. Cumplido, cortés, obsequioso. 2. Cumplimentero, ceremonioso. Elogioso, halagüeño (flattering/remark, review). **She wasn't very complimentary about her teacher,** no habló muy bien de su profesora. 3. De obsequio o regalo (free/copy).

complin, compline [ˈkɒmplɪn] [kom-plin], *s.* Completas, la parte del oficio divino con que determinan las horas canónicas del día.

complore [ˈkɒmplɔːr] [kom-plo'], *vn.* Condolerse.

complot [ˈkɒmplɒt] [kom-plot], *s.* Trama, confederación o conspiración secreta; maquinación, cábala.

complot, *va.* Tramar, conspirar, conjurar.

complotment [ˈkɒmplɒtmənt] [kom-plot-ment], *s.* Conjuración, conspiración.

complotter [ˈkɒmplɒtər] [kom-plo-ta'], *s.* Conspirador, conjurado.

comply [kəm'plaɪ] [kom-plai], *vn.* Cumplir, obedecer, satisfacer, llenar; ceder, condescender, consentir, someterse, conformarse, acomodarse. A menudo va seguido de la preposición *with*. **To comply with the necessary formalities,** llenar las formalidades necesarias. **To comply with the times,** contemporizar. **To comply with a request,** acceder a una solicitud. **To comply with an order,** cumplir una orden. **To comply with the law,** acatar la ley. **All machinery must comply with safety regulations,** toda la maquinaria debe cumplir con o llenar los requisitos de seguridad.

component [kəm'pəʊnənt] [kom-pou-nent], *a.* Componente, lo que compone o entra en la composición de un todo. Constituyente (element). **Component part,** componente, parte integrante. *-s.* Parte constitutiva (constituent part); *(Auto)* pieza. *(Electron.)* Componente.

comport [kəm'pɔːt] [kom-port], *vn.* y *va.* 1. Convenir, concordar. 2. *(Des.)* Sufrir, tolerar, aguantar. 3. Comportarse, portarse.

comportable [kəm'pɔːtəbl] [kom-por-ta-bol], *a.* Conforme.

comportment [kəm'pɔːtmənt] [kom-port-ment], *s.* Porte, conducta, comportamiento.

compose [kəm'pəʊz] [kom-pous], *va.* 1. Componer, formar de varias cosas una juntándolas con método. 2. Colocar alguna cosa en su debida forma y según método. **To be composed of something,** estar compuesto de algo, componerse de algo (constitute). 3. Componer, hacer alguna obra de ingenio; escribir, inventar. Componer (music); redactar (letter). 4. Apaciguar, sosegar, serenar, calmar. **To compose one's thoughts,** poner en orden sus ideas (calm, control). **To compose oneself,** serenarse, recobrar la compostura. 5. Ajustar, concertar, reglar, ordenar. 6. *(Imp.)* Componer, formar dicciones colocando las letras o caracteres. 7. Componer, poner alguna cosa en música. *-vn.* Ocuparse en la composición de obras literarias o musicales, o en componer o parar tipo de imprenta. **Composing frame o stand,** chivalete de imprenta. **Composing rule,** regleta o filete de cajista. **Composing-stick,** componedor de cajista.

composed [kəm'pəʊzd] [kom-pousd], *a.* Compuesto, sosegado, tranquilo, cachazudo, sereno. *-pp.* de COMPOSE.

composedly [kəm'pəʊzɪdlɪ] [kom-pou-sid-li], *adv.* Tranquilamente, serenamente, sosegadamente.

composedness [kəm'pəʊzɪdnɪs] [kom-pou-sid-nes], *s.* Compostura, modestia, tranquilidad, serenidad, calma.

composer [kəm'pəʊzər] [kom-pou-saʳ], *s.* 1. Autor, escritor, compositor (de música); cajista. 2. Conciliador, el que arregla una diferencia, la persona que calma, apacigua y serena.

composite ['kɒmpəzɪt] [kom-pou-sit], *a.* 1. Compuesto, formado de partes distintas, mezclado, no sencillo. 2. *(Arq.)* Compuesto, uno de los cinco órdenes de arquitectura. *-s.* 1. Compuesto, mezcla o unión de varios miembros. 2. *(Bot.)* Una de las flores o plantas compuestas.

composition [ˌkɒmpə'zɪʃən] [kom-pou-si-shon], *s.* 1. Composición. 2. Compuesto, la masa que resulta de la mezcla de varios ingredientes. 3. Composición, obra compuesta, escrita o impresa. 4. Composición, el acto de quedar el deudor solvente con el acreedor pagándole solamente parte de la deuda. 5. Convención, acomodamiento, ajuste.

compositive ['kɒmpəzɪtɪv] [kom-pou-si-tiv], *a.* Componente, que puede combinar o componer, sintético.

compositor [kəm'pɒzɪtər] [kom-pou-si-toʳ], *a.* 1. *(Imp.)* Compositor, cajista. 2. El que arregla o pone en orden.

compossible ['kɒmpəzɪbl] [kom-pou-si-bol], *a.* Que puede existir con otra cosa.

compost ['kɒmpɒst] [kom-post], *s.* Abono, estiércol; mezcla para abonar la tierra; abono orgánico o vegetal. **Compost heap,** lugar donde se amontonan desechos para preparar abono.

composure [kəm'pəʊʒər] [kom-pou-shaʳ], *s.* 1. Compostura, serenidad, tranquilidad, calma, sangre fría, presencia de espíritu. **To lose/regain one's composure,** perder/recobrar la compostura. 2. *(Des.)* Colocación, combinación; hechura. 3. *(Des.)* Composición o compostura, trato amigable con que se avienen las partes en un pleito o desavenencia.

compound ['kɒmpaʊnd] [kom-paund], *va.* 1. Componer, formar de varias cosas una mezclándolas; arreglar, acomodar. **To be compounded with something,** ir acompañado de algo (combine). 2. Componer un pleito o desavenencia. 3. Componerse un deudor con sus acreedores pagándoles solamente parte de la deuda. 4. Agravar, exacerbar (make worse/problem); acrecentar, aumentar (risk, difficulties). *-vn.* 1. Componerse, concertarse, rebajando una de las partes o ambas alguna cosa. 2. Ajustar, comprar o vender por entero. 3. Capitular.

compound, *a.* Compuesto (number, interest, leaf). Compuesto, formado de dos o más ingredientes, de varias partes. *(Gram.)* Formado de dos o más palabras. *-s.* 1. Mezcla, compuesto, agregado de varias cosas que componen un todo. *(Quím.)* Compuesto. 2. Palabra compuesta (word). 3. Complejo habitacional (residence); barracones (for prisoners).

compoundable ['kɒmpaʊndəbl] [kom-paun-da-bol], *a.* Componible, que se puede componer, arreglar o conciliar.

compounder ['kɒmpaʊndər] [kom-paun-daʳ], *s.* 1. Compositor, mezclador. 2. Arbitrador, mediador.

comprehend [ˌkɒmprɪ'hend] [kom-pri-jend], *va.* 1. Comprender, contener, encerrar, incluir en sí alguna cosa, abarcar (include). 2. Comprender, conocer, entender, penetrar, concebir (understand).

comprehensible [ˌkɒmprɪ'hensəbl] [kom-pri-jen-si-bol], *a.* 1. Comprensible, inteligible, fácil de comprender. 2. *(Des.)* Comprensible, que puede ser comprendido, contenido o incluído en otra cosa.

comprehensibleness [ˌkɒmprɪ'hensəblnɪs] [kom-pri-jen-si-bol-nes], *s.* Comprensibilidad.

comprehensibly [ˌkɒmprɪ'hensɪblɪ] [kom-pri-jen-si-bli], *adv.* Comprensiblemente.

comprehension [ˌkɒmprɪ'henʃən] [kom-pri-jen-shon], *s.* 1. Comprensión, el acto o propiedad de comprender, contener o incluir. 2. Comprensión, inteligencia, concepción, conocimiento (understanding). **It's beyond my comprehension,** me resulta incomprensible. (GB) Ejercicio de comprensión (school exercise). 3. *V.* COMPREHENSIVENESS.

comprehensive [ˌkɒmprɪ'hensɪv] [kom-pri-jen-siv], *a.* 1. Comprensivo, inclusivo, de mucha cabida, de gran alcance de inteligencia, de gran amplitud de simpatías, de miras, etc. 2. Compendioso, corto. Exhaustivo, global (survey, report); integral, de conjunto (view); completo (list, range); contra todo riesgo (insurance, cover). 3. *(Biol.)* Sintético. 4. *(Educ.)* (in UK) Relativo al sistema educativo en el cual no se separa a los alumnos según su nivel de aptitud.

comprehensively [ˌkɒmprɪ'hensɪvlɪ] [kom-pri-jen-siv-li], *adv.* Comprensivamente.

comprehensiveness [ˌkɒmprɪ'hensɪvnɪs] [kom-pri-jen-siv-nes], *s.* 1. Extensión, alcance, cabida. 2. Comprensión, perspicacia y capacidad para comprender o penetrar. 3. Energía, precisión, brevedad, cualidad de contener mucho en pocas palabras.

comprehensive (school) *s.* (in UK) Instituto de segunda enseñanza para alumnos de cualquier nivel de aptitud.

compress ['kɒmpres] [kom-pres], *va.* 1. Comprimir, apretar, estrechar, condensar. 2. Abreviar, reducir, hacer breve o acortar una cosa. **Compressed air,** aire comprimido.

compress ['kɒmpres] [kom-pres], *s.* Cabezal, compresa, lienzo de varios dobleces que se pone encima de una herida.

compressibility [ˌkɒmpresɪˈbɪlɪtɪ] [kom-pre-si-bi-li-ti], **compressibleness** [ˈkɒmpres] [kom-pres], *s.* Compresibilidad.

compressible [ˈkɒmpresɪbl] [kom-pre-si-bol], *a.* Compresible, comprimible.

compression [kəmˈpreʃən] [kom-pre-shon], *s.* Compresión, la acción de estrechar, apretar y unir la partes de un cuerpo con violencia; condensación, construcción.

compressive [kəmˈpresɪv] [kom-pre-siv], *a.* Compresivo, que puede comprimir.

compressor [kəmˈpresər] [kom-pre-so'], *s.* El o lo que comprime; en particular: 1. Máquina o aparato para comprimir el aire, gases u otras sustancias, como el heno o algodón. 2. Compresor, instrumento para comprimir los vasos o un miembro en las operaciones quirúrgicas. 3. Aparato para el microscopio que produce una presión graduada sobre el objeto que se examina. En este sentido se llama a menudo **Compressorium.**

compressure [ˈkɒmpreʃər] [kom-pre-sha'], *s.* Compresión.

comprisal [kəmˈpraɪsl] [kom-prai-sal], *s.* Inclusión, comprensión.

comprise [kəmˈpraɪz] [kom-prais], *va.* Comprender, contener, incluir, encerrar, constar de (consist of); componer (constitute, make up).

compromise [ˈkɒmprəmaɪz] [kom-pro-mais], *s.* Compromiso, el acto y efecto de comprometerse; convenio entre litigantes por el cual ajustan o zanjan su litigio mediante concesiones recíprocas; arreglo, acuerdo mutuo (agreement). **To come to/to reach a compromise,** llegar a un acuerdo mutuo.

compromise, *va.* 1. Comprometer, comprometerse, allanarse o convenir en la decisión de un tercero; terminar un desacuerdo por medio de concesiones mutuas. Comprometer (discredit/person, organization, reputation). 2. Comprometer, exponer, arriesgar un negocio por algún acto o declaración, poner en peligro (endanger). *-vn.* Transigir, transar, someterse a un compromiso (make concessions). **We cannot compromise on this point,** en este punto no podemos ceder o transigir (give way).

compromiser [ˈkɒmprəmaɪzər] [kom-pro-mai-sa'], *s.* Compromisario.

compromising [ˈkɒmprəmaɪzɪŋ] [kom-pro-mai-sin] *a.* Comprometedor (evidence); comprometido (situation).

compromissorial [ˈkɒmprəmɪsərɪəl] [kom-pro-mi-so-rial], *a.* Compromisario.

compromit, *va. (Ant.)* Comprometer.

comprovincial [ˈkɒmprəvɪnʃəl] [kom-pro-vin-shal], *a. (Ant.)* Comprovincial.

compt [kɒmpt] [kompt], *s. (Des.)* Cuenta, cálculo.

comptometer [kənˈtɒmiːtər] [kon-to-mi-ta'], *s.* Contómetro, máquina calculadora.

comptrol, v. y *s. V.* CONTROL.

comptroller [kənˈtrəʊlər] [kon-trou-la'], *s.* Controlador, interventor, inspector.

comptrollership [kənˈtrəʊləʃɪp] [kon-trou-ler-ship], *s.* Contraloría.

compulsative [kəmˈpʌlsɪv] [kom-pal-siv], **compulsatory** [kəmˈpʌlsətərɪ] [kom-pal-sa-to-ri]*a.* Compulsorio, coactivo, que tiene fuerza o autoridad para compeler.

compulsatively [kəmˈpʌlsətɪvlɪ] [kom-pal-sa-tiv-li], **compulsively** [kəmˈpʌlsɪvlɪ] [kom-pal-siv-li], *adv.* Por fuerza.

compulsion [kəmˈpʌlʃən] [kom-pal-shon], **compulsiveness** [kəmˈpʌlsɪvnɪs] [kom-pal-siv-nes], *s.* Compulsión (obsession); apremio, coacción (force, duress).

compulsive [kəmˈpʌlsɪv] [kom-pal-siv] *a.* **The book is compulsive reading,** es uno de esos libros que se empiezan y no se pueden dejar. **The film is compulsive viewing,** es una película que no hay que perderse (compelling). Compulsivo (obsessive/behavior). **He's a compulsive eater/liar,** come/miente por compulsión. **A compulsive gambler,** un jugador empedernido.

compulsory [kəmˈpʌlsərɪ] [kom-pal-so-ri], *a.* Compulsorio. Obligatorio (attendance); forzoso (retirement). **Compulsory purchase,** (GB) expropiación.

compulsively [kəmˈpʌlsɪvlɪ] [kom-pal-siv-li], **compulsorily** [kəmˈpʌlsərɪlɪ] [kom-pal-so-ri-li], *adv.* Por fuerza.

compunction [kəmˈpʌŋkʃən] [kom-pank-shon], *s.* Compunción, contrición, arrepentimiento, remordimiento. Reparo. **To have no compunction about,** no tener ningún reparo en.

compunctious [kəmˈpʌŋkʃəs] [kom-pank-shos], *a.* Compungido, arrepentido, contrito.

compurgation [kəmˈpɜːgeɪʃən] [kom-per-guei-shon], *s.* Compurgación, justificación de la veracidad de alguno por medio del testimonio del otro.

compurgator [kəmˈpɜːgeɪtər] [kom-per-guei-tar], *s.* Compurgador, el que en la prueba llamada compurgación canónica, afirmaba bajo juramento la inocencia de un acusado.

computable [kəmˈpjʊtəbl] [kom-piu-ta-bol], *a.* Computable, estimable, que se puede computar o calcular.

computation [ˌkɒmpjʊˈteɪʃən] [kom-piu-tei-shon], *s.* Computación, cómputo, cuenta, cálculo.

compute [ˈkɒmpjʊt] [kom-piut], *va.* Computar, contar, calcular, estimar.

computer [kəmˈpjuːtər] [kom-piu-ta'], *s.* Calculador, computador, computista; máquina calculadora; computador, ordenador. **All the data is on computer,** todos los datos están computarizados o computerizados. De la informática (society, age, revolution); de computadora o de ordenador (program, game); por computadora o por ordenador (graphics, animation). **Computer programmer,** programador. **Computer programming,** programación. **Computer science,** informática. **Computer studies,** informática, computación.

computer-aided [ˌkəmpjʊtəˈaɪdɪd] [kom-piu-ter-aidid], **computer-assisted** [ˌkəmpjʊtəˈæsɪstɪd] [kom-piu-ter-a-sis-ted] *a.* Asistido por computadora o por ordenador (learning/design).

computerization [kəmˈpjʊtəbl] [kom-piu-ta-bol] *s.* Computarización, computerización (of data); informatización (of business).

computerize [kəmˌpjuːtəraɪˈzeɪʃən] [kom-piu-te-rai-sei-shon], *va.* Habilitar con computadoras. Computarizar, computerizar; informatizar (company/department).

computer-operated [ˌkəmpjuːtəˈɒpereɪtɪd] [kom-piu-ter-o-pe-rei-ted] *a.* Operado por computadora o por ordenador, computarizado, computerizado.

computing [kəmˈpjuːtɪŋ] [kom-piu-tin] *s.* Informática, computación. **Computing skills,** competencia en el uso de computadoras u ordenadores.

comrade [ˈkɒmrɪd] [kom-rid], *s.* Camarada, compañero, asociado o amigo.

comradeship [ˈkɒmrɪdʃɪp] [kom-rid-ship], *s.* Camaradería.

con [kɒn] [kon], *prep.* Con, partícula inseparable, como en *concourse,* concurso. Toma la forma de COMP- antes de c, de, f, g, i, j, n, q, s, t, w. Este prefijo indica en general ya la unión, como en *conjoin,* juntar, ya la compañía de otro como en *contend,* discutir; *consort,* asociarse. *V.* COM-.

con, *adv.* Contra. **Neither pro nor con,** ni a favor ni en contra.

con, *va.* 1. Estudiar, reflexionar, meditar, fijar en la memoria. 2. *(Mar.)* Dirigir la acción de gobernar el buque. 3. *(Des.)* Conocer, saber. 4. *(Coloq.)* Timar, estafar (deceive); engatusar, embaucar, camelar (sweet-talk). **I was conned into it,** me embaucaron o me camelaron para que lo hiciera (o para que fuera, etc.). **I was conned into thinking that…,** me engatusaron haciéndome creer que… **He conned the old ladies out of their savings,** embaucó a las ancianas y les quitó los ahorros.

concamerate [kɒnˈkæməreɪt] [kon-ka-me-reit], *va.* 1. Dividir en cámaras. 2. *(Des.)* Abovedar, cubrir con bóveda.

concamerated [ˌkɒnkæməˈreɪtɪd] [kon-ka-me-rei-tid], *a.* (*Zool.*) Dividido en cámaras, como una concha o un hueso.

concameration [kɒnˈkæməreɪʃən] [kon-ka-me-rei-shon], *s.* (*Zool.*) 1. División en cámaras, y la cámara misma. 2. Arco, bóveda; firmamento.

concatenate [kɒnˈkætɪˌneɪt] [kon-ka-te-neit], *va.* Concatenar, encadenar.

concatenation [kɒnˌkætɪˈneɪʃən] [kon-ka-ti-nei-shon], *s.* Concatenación.

concave [ˈkɒnˈkeɪv] [kon-keiv], *a.* Cóncavo, hueco, vacío, lo contrario de convexo.

concave, *va.* Hacer cóncava alguna cosa.

concave, *s.* Hueco, hondón.

concaveness [ˈkɒnˈkeɪvnɪs] [kon-keiv-nes], *s.* Concavidad.

concavity [ˈkɒnˈkævɪtɪ] [kon-ka-vi-ti], *s.* Concavidad, profundidad.

concavo-concave [ˈkɒnˈkævəkɒnkeɪv] [kon-ka-vo-kon-keiv], *s.* Cóncavo-cóncavo, esto es, por ambos lados.

concavo-convex [ˈkɒnˈkævəˈkɒnveks] [kon-ka-vo-kon-veks], *s.* Cóncavo-convexo, cóncavo por un lado y convexo por el otro.

concavous [ˈkɒnˈkævəs] [kon-ka-vos], *a.* (*Des.*) V. CONCAVE.

concavously [ˈkɒnˈkævəslɪ] [kon-ka-vos-li], *adv.* (*Des.*) Con hueco.

conceal [kənˈsiːl] [kon-sil], *va.* Callar, tapar; ocultar (object, fact, truth); esconder, tener secreto; disimular, ocultar (emotions). **With barely concealed hatred,** con mal disimulado odio. **Concealed weapons,** armas prohibidas que se llevan ocultamente, en violación de la ley. **Concealed,** *past p.* Oculto (door, camera); indirecto (lighting).

conceable [kənˈsiːləbl] [kon-si-la-bol], *a.* Ocultable, escondible.

concealedness [kənˈsiːldnɪs] [kon-sild-nes], *s.* Obscuridad, secreto, retiro.

concealer [kənˈsiːlər] [kon-si-laʳ], *s.* Ocultador, encubridor.

concealing [kənˈsiːlɪŋ] [kon-si-lin], *s.* 1. Escondimiento, ocultación. 2. Disimulo, acción de ocultar; encubrimiento (de una cosa robada).

concealment [kənˈsiːlmənt] [kon-sil-ment], *s.* 1. Ocultación, secreto, encubrimiento. 2. Escondrijo, escondite. 3. Reticencia. 4. Retiro, misterio.

concede [kənˈsiːd] [kon-sid], *va.* Conceder (allow/right, privilege); asentir, convenir en lo que otro dice o afirma; reconocer (admit). Conceder (give away/game, penalty). **To concede defeat,** admitir la derrota, darse por vencido. *-vn.* Admitir la derrota, darse por vencido (admit defeat).

conceit [kənˈsiːt] [kon-sit], *s.* 1. Amor propio, presunción, arrogancia, alto concepto de sí mismo, engreimiento, encaprichamiento. 2. Concepto, capricho, fantasía, imaginación, pensamiento. 3. Concepción, facilidad o aptitud del entendimiento para comprender. 4. Concepción pensamiento, idea. (*Ant.* o *Amer.*) **To be out of conceit with anything,** perder el gusto por alguna cosa. **Idle conceits,** boberías, necedades.

conceited [kənˈsiːtɪd] [kon-si-ted], *a.* Engreído, presuntuoso, creído. Afectado, vano, porfiado, vanaglorioso, fantástico, presumido, caprichoso. (*Prov.*) Conceptuoso, ingenioso.

conceitedly [kənˈsiːtɪdlɪ] [kon-si-tid-li], *adv.* Vanamente, fantásticamente, afectadamente.

conceitedless [kənˈsiːtɪdlɪs] [kon-si-tid-lnes] *a.* Atolondrado, estúpido, sin ideas.

conceitedness [kənˈsiːtɪdnɪs] [kon-si-tid-nes] *s.* Presunción, amor propio, pertinacia, porfía, obstinación, vanidad.

conceivable [kənˈsiːvəbl] [kon-si-va-bol] *a.* Concebible, lo que se puede concebir o imaginar; inteligible, creíble. Imaginable. **Every conceivable means,** todos los medios imaginables. **It's just conceivable that he forgot,** cabe la posibilidad de que se haya olvidado.

conceivably [kənˈsiːvəblɪ] [kon-si-va-bli] *adv.* De un modo conceptible. **They may conceivably have decided to sell it,** cabe la posibilidad de que hayan decidido venderlo.

conceive [kənˈsiːv] [kon-siv] *va.* 1. Concebir (devise, plan); formar idea, entender alguna cosa, comprender. 2. Recibir, abrigar en el espíritu ciertas impresiones y afectos. 3. Crear, imaginar, pensar (imagine); darse cuenta de. Considerar (consider). 4. Engendrar, originar. Concebir (child). 5. Expresar, formular (hablando de palabras). **I can't conceive why you did it,** no concibo o no me cabe en la cabeza por qué lo hiciste. *vn.* 1. Concebir, imaginar, pensar. 2. Concebir, hacerse preñada la hembra (become pregnant).

conceive of, imaginar, concebir.

conceiver [kənˈsiːvər] [kon-si-vaʳ] *s.* El que concibe o comprende.

conceiving [kənˈsiːvɪŋ] [kon-si-vin] *s.* Entendimiento, comprensión, concepción.

concent [kənˈsent] [kon-sent] *s.* Armonía, concepto, consonancia.

concentrate [ˈkɒnsəntreɪt] [kon-sen-treit] *va.* Concentrar, impeler alguna cosa hacia el centro. **To concentrate something (on something),** concentrar algo (en algo) (energies, attention). **To concentrate something in/into something,** concentrar algo en algo (gather, bring together). *-vn.* 1. Concentrarse (focus attention/person). **Concentrate on getting this finished,** concéntrate en terminar esto. 1. Concentrarse (converge/people).

concentrate *s.* Concentrado.

concentrated [ˈkɒnsəntreɪtɪd] [kon-sen-trei-ted] *a.* Intenso y continuado (effort); concentrado (solution, juice).

concentration [ˈkɒnsəntreɪʃən] [kon-sen-trei-shon] *s.* Concentración. **Concentration camp,** campo de concentración. **Power of concentration,** poder de concentración.

concentrator [ˈkɒnsəntreɪtər] [kon-sen-trei-toʳ] *s.* Concentrador, máquina o aparato para concentrar o separar los minerales.

concentre [ˈkɒnsəntər] [kon-sen-taʳ] *vn.* Reconcentrarse. *va.* Concentrar. **Concentred all in self,** reconcentrado en sí mismo.

concentric, concentrical [ˈkɒnsəntrɪk] [kon-sen-trik] *a.* Concéntrico.

concentrically [ˈkɒsəntrɪkəlɪ] [kon-sen-tri-ka-li] *adv.* Concéntricamente.

concentricity [ˈkɒnsəntrɪsɪtɪ] [kon-sen-tri-si-ti] *s.* Concentricidad, estado concéntrico.

concentual [ˈkɒnsəntəəl] [kon-sen-tual] *a.* (*Des.*) Armonioso.

concept [ˈkɒnsept] [kon-sept] *s.* 1. Concepto, idea general que comprende todos los atributos comunes a los individuos que componen una clase. 2. En acepción menos propia, concepto, idea que concibe o forma la inteligencia.

conceptacle [ˈkɒnseptəkl] [kon-sep-ta-kol] *s.* 1. Receptáculo. 2. Cavidad que contiene esporos reproductores en muchas algas, hongos, helechos, etc.

conception [kənˈsepʃən] [kon-sep-shon] *s.* 1. Concepción, la acción de concebir la hembra (of baby). Concepción (of plan). 2. Concepción, idea que se forma, imagen, noción (idea). **They have no conception of…,** no tienen noción o idea de… 3. Concepto, sentimiento. 4. Conocimiento, comprensión.

conceptive [ˈkɒnseptɪv] [kon-sep-tiv] *a.* Conceptible.

conceptual [kənˈseptəəl] [kon-sep-tual] *a.* Referente a una concepción o idea general.

conceptualize [kənˈseptəəlaɪz] [kon-sep-tua-lais] *va.* Conceptuar.

concern [kənˈsɜːn] [kon-sern] *va.* 1. Concernir, tocar, importar o pertenecer, interesar, incumbir (affect, involve). **The people concerned,** la gente en cuestión. **Those concerned know who they are,** los interesados ya saben quiénes son. **To be concerned with something,** ocuparse de algo. **Where money is concerned…,** en lo que respecta al dinero… **As far as I'm concerned,** en lo que a mí respecta, por mi parte. 2. Mover, excitar alguna de las pasiones humanas, interesar. 3. Inquietar, preocupar (worry, bother).

4. Interesar (interest). **I'm more concerned with quality than quantity,** me interesa más la calidad que la cantidad. **To be concerned for,** tomar mucho interés por. **To be much concerned,** sentir vivamente, en el alma; estar muy interesado. **What does it concern you?,** ¿qué le va o le viene a Vd. en eso?, ¿qué le importa a Vd. eso? 5. **My fears concerning her health were unfounded,** mis temores en cuanto a o respecto a su salud eran infundados. **Item one concerns the new office,** el primer punto trata de la nueva oficina. *v. refl.* **To concern oneself about somebody/something,** preocuparse por alguien/algo. **To concern oneself with something,** ocuparse de algo (be busy with something). **I don't concern myself with their affairs,** yo no me inmiscuyo en sus asuntos.

concern *s.* 1. Negocio, ocupación. Asunto (business, affair). **That's no concern of yours,** eso no es asunto tuyo. 2. Interés o parte que se tiene en alguna cosa, incumbencia. **Concern for somebody/something,** interés por alguien/algo (interest). **To be of concern to somebody,** importarle o preocuparle a alguien. 3. Empresa, casa de comercio, negocio (firm). 4. Importancia, consecuencia. 5. Afecto, amor, cariño. 6. Inquietud, sentimiento, pesar, preocupación (anxiety). **Cause for concern,** motivos de preocupación o para preocuparse. **That is no concern of mine,** eso no es cuenta mía, no es de mi incumbencia, o no me concierne.

concerned [kən'sɜːnd] [kon-sernd] *a.* 1. Interesado, comprometido. 2. Inquieto, apesarado. Preocupado (person). De preocupación (look). **To be concerned about/for somebody/something,** estar preocupado por alguien/algo.

concernedly [kən'sɜːndlɪ] [kon-sernd-li] *adv.* Tiernamente, con cariño.

concerning [kən'sɜːnɪŋ] [kon-ser-nin] *prep.* Por lo concerniente, tocante a, respecto a. Sobre, acerca de, con respecto a. *s. (Des.)* Negocio, interés.

concernment [kən'sɜːnmənt] [kon-sern-ment] *s.* Interés, negocio; importancia, momento, entidad; pena, cuidado; pasión; interposición; trato; influencia, relación.

concert [kən'sɜːt] [kon-sert] *va.* 1. Concertar, acordar, ajustar. 2. Concertar, tomar medida en unión con otros; deliberar de común acuerdo. **We made a concerted effort,** coordinamos o concertamos nuestros esfuerzos para…

concert *s.* 1. Concierto, convenio; comunicación de designios. 2. Concierto de música (performance). **Concert hall,** sala de conciertos, auditorio. **Concert pianist,** concertista de piano. **In concert,** en vivo, en concierto (performing live). **To act in concert with,** obrar de concierto o de inteligencia con. **Concert pitch,** *V.* PITCH

concertina [ˌkɒnsə'tiːnə] [kon-ser-ti-na] *s.* Concertina, instrumento músico parecido a un acordeón, pero de forma poligonal.

concertina *vn.* Aplastarse como un acordeón.

concertmaster ['kɒnsətˌmɑːstər] [kon-sert-mas-taʳ] *s.* Primer violín, concertino.

concerto [kən'tʃɛətəʊ] [kon-cher-tou] *s.* Concierto, composición de música de varios instrumentos, en que uno desempeña la parte principal. *(Ital.)* **Violin concerto,** concierto para violín.

concession [kən'seʃən] [kon-se-shon] *s.* Concesión, gracia, licencia, cesión, privilegio.

concessionary [kən'seʃənərɪ] [kon-se-sho-na-ri] *s.* Concesionario, la persona a quien se hace una concesión. *a.* Otorgado por concesión; de una concesión. A precio reducido, con descuento (fare).

concessive [kən'sesɪv] [kon-se-siv] *a.* Que contiene o denota concesión: concedido, implicando concesión o gracia. *s.* Palabra o cláusula que concede.

concessively [kən'sesɪvlɪ] [kon-se-siv-li] *adv.* Por vía de concesión.

concessory [kən'seʃərɪ] [kon-se-sho-ri] *a.* Concedente, otorgante.

conch [kɒntʃ] [konch] *s.* 1. Concha. 2. Caracol marino de gran tamaño que se usa como bocina. 3. *(Arq.)* Concha, bóveda de concha. 4. *V.* CONCHA

concha [kən'tʃə] [kon-cha] *s.* 1. Concha, la cavidad que se halla en el fondo del pabellón de la oreja. 2. Uno de los cornetes o láminas huesosas de la nariz. 3. *(Arq.) V.* CONCH

conchite [kən'tʃiːt] [kon-chit] *s.* Conchita, concha petrificada.

conchoid [kən'kɔɪd] [kon-koid] *s.* Concoide, especie de curva de cuarto grado.

conchoidal [kən'kɔɪdl] [kon-koi-dal] *a.* Lo que pertenece a la concoide.

conchologist [kən'kɒlədʒɪst] [kon-ko-lo-yist] *s.* Conquiliólogo, la persona versada en la conquiliología, o estudio y clasificación de las conchas.

conchology [kən'kɒlədʒɪ] [kon-ko-lo-yi] *s. (Zool.)* Conquiliología, ramo de la zoología que trata de las conchas de los moluscos.

concierge [ˌkɒnsɪ'eəʒ] [kon-sierch] *s. V.* JANITOR. *(Fr.)*

conciliate [kən'sɪlɪeɪt] [kon-si-lieit] *va.* Conciliar, granjear, ganar, atraer.

conciliation [kən'sɪlɪeɪʃən] [kon-si-liei-shon] *s.* Conciliación.

conciliator [kən'sɪlɪeɪtər] [kon-si-liei-toʳ] *s.* Conciliador.

conciliatory [kən'sɪlɪətərɪ] [kon-si-lia-to-ri] *a.* Reconciliatorio, conciliador, conciliatorio.

concinnity [kən'sɪnɪtɪ] [kon-si-ni-ti] *s.* 1. Aptitud, decencia, propiedad. 2. Armonía.

concinnous [kən'sɪnəs] [kon-si-nous] *a.* Decente, apto, propio, armonioso.

concise [kən'saɪs] [kon-sais] *a.* Conciso (instructions, writing); breve, compendioso, lacónico, sucinto, corto. **Concise dictionary,** diccionario abreviado.

concisely [kən'saɪslɪ] [kon-sais-li] *adv.* Concisamente, lacónicamente, en pocas palabras.

conciseness [kən'saɪsnɪs] [kon-sais-nes] *s.* Concisión, brevedad, laconismo.

concision [kən'sɪʒən] [kon-si-shon] *s.* 1. Corte, cortadura. 2. Concisión. *V.* CONCISENESS. 3. *(Ant. Biblia)* Circuncisión.

concitation [kənsɪ'teɪʃən] [kon-si-tei-shon] *s. (Des.)* Revuelta, alteración, conmoción.

conclamation [ˌkɒnklə'meɪʃən] [kon-kla-mei-shon] *s.* Clamor, vocería, griterío.

conclave ['kɒnkleɪv] [kon-kleiv] *s.* 1. Conclave, el lugar en que se hace la elección del Papa, y la asamblea de todos los cardenales para dicha elección. 2. Conclave, junta o congreso de gentes que se reunen para tratar de algún asunto.

conclude [kən'kluːd] [kon-klud] *va.* 1. Concluir, inferir por raciocinio (infer). 2. Decidir, determinar. Cerrar (settle/deal); llegar a (agreement); firmar (treaty); pactar (alliance). 3. Concluir, terminar, acabar, finalizar (end). 4. Restringir, coartar; en derecho, y por lo regular en forma pasiva. 5. *(Ant.)* Incluir. *vn.* 1. Finalizar. Concluir, terminar (come to an end). **To conclude, I would like to…,** para concluir, querría. 2. Argumentar, juzgar, decidir. **Concluding** *pres p.* Final (remarks, chapter).

concluder [kən'kluːdər] [kon-klu-daʳ] *s.* El que determina o decide.

concludible [kən'kluːdɪbl] [kon-klu-di-bol] *a.* Determinable.

concludingly [kən'kluːdɪŋlɪ] [kon-klu-din-li] *adv.* Con evidencia incontrovertible, concluyentemente.

conclusion [kən'kluːʒən] [kon-klu-shon], *s.* 1. Conclusión (end), determinación. **In conclusion,** para concluir, como conclusión. 2. Terminación, término, fin o remate de alguna cosa, desenlace, catástrofe. 3. Consecuencia sacada de las premisas. Conclusión (decision, judgment). **To come to/reach a conclusion,** llegar a una conclusión. **I've come to the conclusion that…,** he llegado a la conclusión de que… **To draw a conclusion,** sacar una conclusión. **To jump to conclusions,** precipitarse (a sacar conclusiones).

conclusive [kən'kluːsɪv] [kon-klu-siv], *a*. Concluyente (evidence, argument); decisivo, contundente (victory); final, conclusivo.

conclusively [kən'kluːsɪvlɪ] [kon-klu-siv-li], *a*. Concluyentemente; de manera concluyente.

conclusiveness [kən'kluːsɪvnɪs] [kon-klu-siv-nes], *s*. Resolución o determinación.

conclusory [kən'kluːʒərɪ] [kon-klu-so-ri], *a*. V. CONCLUSIVE.

concoct [kən'kɒkt] [kon-kokt], *va*. 1. Preparar algo mezclando sus ingredientes, como una bebida, una sopa, etc. 2. *(Fig)* Trazar, proyectar, urdir, tramar (plan); inventarse (story). 3. *(Des)* Cocer, digerir, purificar con fuego o calor; madurar.

concoction [kən'kɒkʃən] [kon-kok-shon], *s*. 1. La acción y efecto de mezclar ingredientes, mezcla. 2. Maquinación, trama; trazo. **I'm not eating/drinking that concoction,** yo no me como ese mejunje/bebo ese brebaje. **One of Pierre's delicious concoctions,** una de las exquisitas creaciones de Pierre.

concoctive [kən'kɒktɪv] [kon-kok-tiv], *a*. Perteneciente a una mezcla, o un trazo.

concomitance, concomitancy [kən'kɒmɪtəns] [kon-ko-mi-tans], *s*. Concomitancia, concurrencia de una cosa con otra.

concomitant [kən'kɒmɪtənt] [kon-ko-mi-tant], *a*. Concomitante. -*s*. Compañero; persona o cosa concomitante.

concomitantly [kən'kɒmɪtəntlɪ] [kon-ko-mi-tant-li], *adv*. Concomitantemente, en compañía de otros.

concord [kɒŋkɔːd] [kon-kord], *s*. 1. Concordia, unión. 2. Concordia, paz, unión, armonía, buena inteligencia (harmony). 3. Concordancia, armonía en la música. 4. *(For)* Pacto, convención, convenio. 5. *(Gram.)* Concordancia, correspondencia de las palabras según las reglas gramaticales.

concordal [kɒŋ'kɔːdəl] [kon-kor-dal], *a*. *(Gram.)* Relativo a la concordancia.

concordance [kən'kɔːdəns] [kon-kor-dans], *s*. 1. Concordancia, índice alfabético de todas las palabras de la Biblia, con citas de los lugares en que se hallan, para buscar y cotejar lo que convenga. 2. Concordancia, conformidad, unión.

concordant [kɒn'kɔːdənt] [kon-kor-dant], *a*. Concordante, consonante, conforme. -*s*. Correspondiente.

concordantly [kɒŋ'kɔːdəntlɪ] [kon-kor-dant-li], *adv*. Concordemente, de común acuerdo.

concordat [kɒn'kɔːdæt] [kon-kor-dat], *s*. Concordato, el tratado o convenio que hace el gobierno de un Estado con la Santa Sede, acerca de asuntos eclesiásticos.

concourse ['kɒŋkɔːs] [kon-kors], *s*. 1. Concurso, confluencia, concurrencia (gathering). 2. Junta, el conjunto de personas unidas multitud de personas unidas, multitud, gentío, muchedumbre. 3. Explanada (large hall).

concrement [kɒn'krɪmənt] [kon-kri-ment], *s*. Concremento; masa formada por concreción.

concresce ['kɒnkriːs] [kon-kris], *vn*. Unirse, aficionarse; estar estrechamente unidos, juntarse en una masa.

concrescence ['kɒnkriːsəns] [kon-kri-sens], *s*. Concescencia, crecimiento.

concrescible ['kɒnkriːsɪbl] [kon-kri-si-bol], *a*. Concrescible, susceptible de hacerse concreto; condensable.

concrescive ['kɒnkriːsɪv] [kon-kri-siv], *a*. Uniéndose, que forma estrecha unión.

concrete ['kɒnkriːt] [kon-krit], *vn*. Cuajar, unirse o juntarse en una masa. -*va*. 1. Concretar, unir y juntar unas cosas con otras formando de ellas una masa. 2. Poner en forma concreta. 3. Cubrir con cemento o argamasa. Pavimentar con hormigón o concreto (path).

concrete, *a*. 1. Concreto; cuajado, formado en una masa por crecimiento o unión. 2. Concreto que existe actualmente en el sujeto, opuesto a abstracto. 3. Hecho de hormigón, hecho de cemento (Sp. Am). -*s*. 1. Concreción. 2. Hormigón, concreto (Sp. Am). Cemento (in loose usage). De hormigón

o concreto (building). 3. Lo concreto. **Concrete mixer,** hormigonera. **Concrete number,** número concreto. **Concrete paint,** pintura para hormigón. **Reinforced concrete,** hormigón armado.

concretely ['kɒnkriːtlɪ] [kon-krit-li], *adv*. Concretamente.

concreteness ['kɒnkriːtnɪs] [kon-krit-nes], *s*. Calidad de lo concreto

concretion ['kɒnkriːʃən] [kon-kri-shon], *s*. 1. Concreción, agregado de diversas partículas en una masa. 2. *(Geol.)* Agregado de materia inorgánica de nudillo o disco, alrededor de un centro llamado núcleo. 3. *(Med.)* Concreción, cálculo.

concretionary ['kɒnkriːʃənərɪ] [kon-kri-sho-na-ri], *a*. Perteneciente a una concreción.

concretive ['kɒnkrɪtɪv] [kon-kri-tiv], *a*. Formando concreciones.

concubinage [kɒŋ'kjʊbaɪneɪdʒ] [kon-kiu-bai-neich], *s*. Concubinato, amancebamiento.

concubine ['kɒŋkjʊbaɪn] [kon-kiu-bain], *sf*. Concubina.

concupiscence [kən'kjuːpɪsəns] [kon-kiu-pi-sens], *s*. Concupiscencia, apetito desordenado de placeres deshonestos.

concupiscent [kən'kjuːpɪsənt] [kon-kiu-pi-sent], *a*. Libidinoso, lascivo.

concur [kən'kɜːr] [kon-ker], *vn*. 1. Concurrir, encontrarse en un mismo punto. 2. Juntarse, obrar juntamente con otros. 3. Convenir, conformarse, estar de acuerdo. **To concur with somebody/something,** coincidir o estar de acuerdo con alguien/algo.

concurrence o concurrency [kən'kʌrəns] [kon-ka-rens], *s*. 1. Concurrencia, combinación, acuerdo. 2. Concurrencia, auxilio, asistencia, ayuda. 3. Concurrencia, pretensión recíproca de dos o más personas a un mismo empleo y otra cosa a que tienen igual derecho. 4. Consentimiento, relación aprobación.

concurrent [kən'kʌrənt] [kon-ka-rent], *a*. Concurrente, simultáneo (event); concomitante, coexistente.

concurrently [kən'kʌrəntlɪ] [kon-ka-rent-li], *adv*. Concurrentemente, simultáneamente.

concuss [kən'kʌs] [kon-kas], *va*. 1. Afectar o dañar (el cerebro) por concusión. **To be concussed,** sufrir una conmoción (cerebral) o una concusión. 2. Sacudir, agitar.

concussion [kən'kʌʃən] [kon-ka-shon], *s*. 1. Concusión, conmoción cerebral, impulso. 2. Peculado, cohecho.

concussive [kən'kʌsɪv] [kon-ka-siv], *a*. Lo que conmueve o sacude violentamente.

cond [kɒnd] [kond], *va*. *(Des. Mar.)* Guiar o gobernar un bajel. V. CON. *(Mar.)*

condemn [kən'dem] [kon-dem], *va*. 1. Desaprobar, censurar (censure); culpar, vituperar, reprobar, afear. 2. Condenar, sentenciar a una pena (sentence). **He was condemned to death,** lo condenaron o fue condenado a muerte. **The condemned man,** el condenado a muerte. 3. Prohibir oficialmente el uso de algo o el consumo de determinados comestibles o bebidas. 4. Ordenar jurídicamente la toma de posesión de algo para el uso público; declarar confiscado, expropiar por motivos de utilidad pública (building) (in US: convert to public use). Declarar ruinoso (declare unusable).

condemnable [kən'demneɪbl] [kon-dem-nei-bol], *a*. Culpable, censurable, vituperable, condenable.

condemnation [ˌkɒndem'neɪʃən] [kon-dem-nei-shon], *s*. Condenación, acción y efecto de condenar o condenarse. Condena, repulsa.

condemnatory [ˌkɒndem'neɪtərɪ] [kon-dem-nei-to-ri], *a*. Condenatorio, que contiene censura o represión; que expresa sentencia o condenación.

condemner [kən'demnər] [kon-dem-nar], *s*. Condenador.

condensable [ˌkɒnden'seɪbl] [kon-den-sei-bol], *a*. Condensable.

condensate ['kɒndenseɪt] [kon-den-seit], *va*. y *vn*. Condensar, condensarse. V. CONDENSE.

condensate, *a*. Condensado, comprimido, espesado.

condensation [ˌkɒndenˈseɪʃən] [kon-den-sei-shon], *s.* 1. Condensación (process); vapor, vaho (on windows, etc.). 2. Condensación (abridgment).

condesative [ˈkɒndensətɪv] [kon-den-sa-tiv], *a.* Lo que tiene poder de condensar.

condense [kənˈdens] [kon-dens], *va.* 1. Condensar, comprimir, compendiar, resumir (abridge/ book, article). *(Quím.)* Condensar. 2. Hacer más denso, espeso o compacto, consolidar. 3. Abreviar, epitomar. -*vn.* Condensarse, comprimirse, espesarse. *(Quím.)* Condensarse.

condensed [kənˈdensd] [kon-densd], *a.* Condensado, resumido. **Condensed milk,** leche condensada. **Condensed soup,** sopa concentrada.

condenser [kənˈdensər] [kon-den-saᵣ], *s.* Condensador; cualquier invento, máquina o aparato para condensar. 1. Recipiente de una máquina de vapor de condensación. 2. Recipiente de aire de una bomba. 3. Lente o lentes para concentrar lo rayos de luz, en un microscopio, linterna óptica, faro, etc. 4. Aparato para acumular electricidad. 5. Aparato para eliminar las adulteraciones de gas del aiumbrado por medio de la condensación. **Bull's-eye condenser,** lente gruesa plano-convexa para el microscopio.

condenser pipe [kənˈdensəˌpaɪp] [kon-den-ser-paip], *s.* Tubo de condensador.

condensing [kənˈdensɪŋ] [kon-den-sin], *pa.* Condensante. **Condensing engine,** máquina de condensación.

condensity [kənˈdensɪtɪ] [kon-den-si-ti], *s. (Ant.)* Densidad.

conder [ˈkɒndər] [kon-daᵣ], *s.* El que avisa desde la costa a los pescadores de arenques el camino que lleva el cardume.

condescend [kənˈdesənd] [kon-de-send], *vn.* 1. Condescender, hacer más de lo que quiere la justicia, consentir. **To condescend to,** dignarse o condescender a (deign). **To condescend to somebody,** tratar a alguien con condescendencia (patronize). 2. Acomodarse a la voluntad de otro, someterse.

condescendence [kənˈdesəndəns] [kon-de-sen-dens], **condescension** [kənˈdesənd] [kon-de-send], *s.* Condescendencia.

condescending [kənˈdesəndɪŋ] [kon-de-sen-din], *s.* Condescendencia. *a.* Condescendiente (tone, smile). **To be condescending to/towards somebody,** tratar a alguien con condescendencia.

condescendingly [kənˈdesəndɪŋlɪ] [kon-de-sen-din-li], *adv.* Cortésmente, condescendientemente.

condescension [kənˈdesənʃən] [kon-de-sen-shon] *s.* Condescendencia.

condign [kənˈdaɪn] [kon-dain], *a.* Condigno, merecido: se dice del castigo.

condignity [ˈkɒndaɪnɪtɪ] [kon-dai-ni-ti], *(Teol.)* **condignness** [ˈkɒndaɪnnɪs] [kon-dig-nis], *s.* Condignidad, merecimiento.

condignly [ˈkɒndaɪnlɪ] [kon-dain-li], *adv.* Merecidamente.

condiment [ˈkɒndɪmənt] [kon-di-ment], *s.* Condimento, aliño, aderezo, guiso, salsa (relish).

condisciple [kənˈdɪsɪpl] [kon-dis-si-pol], *s.* Condiscípulo, compañero, discípulo de un mismo maestro.

condite [ˈkɒndaɪt] [kon-dait], *va. (Des.)* Escabechar, adobar, condimentar, sazonar.

condition [kənˈdɪʃən] [kon-di-shon], *s.* 1. Condición, cualidad. 2. Condición natural o genio de los hombres. 3. Condición, situación, estado, circunstancias; la naturaleza o constitución de las cosas. **Conditions** *pl.* Condiciones (circumstances). **Working/housing conditions,** condiciones de trabajo/vivienda. *(Meteo.)* **Weather conditions are good,** el estado del tiempo es bueno. 4. Condición, rango, esfera, calidad del nacimiento o estado de alguno (state). **To be in no condition to,** no estar en condiciones de. **To be in/out of condition,** estar/no estar en forma (state of fitness). *(Med.)* Afección, enfermedad. **A heart/liver condition,** una afección cardíaca/hepática. 5. Condición, artículo o cláusula de alguna escritura (stipulation, requirement). **On one condition,** con una

condición. On condition that, con la condición de que, a condición de que. 6. Requisito necesario, dato necesario, condición *sine qua non.*

condition *va.* 1. Condicionar (influence, determine). **To condition somebody to,** condicionar a alguien a. Acondicionar (make healthy/hair). 2. Requerir antes, constituir la condición de algo. 3. Estipular, pactar.

conditional [kənˈdɪʃənl] [kon-di-sho-nal], *a.* Condicional, lo que incluye y lleva consigo alguna condición o requisito; no absoluto (provisional/agreement, acceptance). **To be conditional on/upon something,** estar condicionado o supeditado a algo. *(Ling.)* Condicional. -*s.* Palabra, cláusula, etc. significativa de condición.

conditionally [kənˈdɪʃənəlɪ] [kon-di-sho-na-li], *adv.* Condicionalmente.

conditionary [kənˈdɪʃənərɪ] [kon-di-sho-na-ri], *a.* Estipulado, convenido, pactado.

conditionate [kənˈdɪʃəneɪt] [kon-di-sho-neit], *va.* Calificar, regular.

conditionate *a.* Condicionado, establecido con alguna condición.

conditioned [kənˈdɪʃənd] [kon-di-shond], *a.* Acondicionado, en buen o mal estado, de buena o mala condición.

conditioner [kənˈdɪʃənər] [kon-di-sho-naᵣ] *s.* Acondicionador, enjuague, suavizante, bálsamo (hair conditioner); suavizante (fabric conditioner).

conditioning [kənˈdɪʃənɪŋ] [kon-di-shon-in] *s. (Psych.)* Condicionamiento.

condo [ˈkɒndəʊ] [kon-dou] *s. (Coloq.)* V. CONDOMINIUM.

condolatory [kənˈdəʊlətərɪ] [kon-do-la-to-ri], *a.* Que expresa pésame o duelo.

condole [kənˈdəʊl] [kon-doul], *vn.* Condolerse, dolerse con otro, simpatizar con, dar el pésame.

condolence [kənˈdəʊləns] [kon-dou-lens], *s.* 1. Compasión, lástima, dolor o pena por la aflicción ajena. 2. El pésame que se da a otro por haber perdido algún pariente o persona querida. **Letter of condolence,** carta de condolencia (sympathy). **Condolences** *pl.* Condolencias, pésame. **He offered/sent his condolences to the widow,** le dio/envió el pésame o sus condolencias a la viuda.

condoler [kənˈdəʊlər] [kon-dou-ler], *s.* El que da el pésame a otro.

condom [ˈkɒndəm] [kon-dom] *s.* Preservativo, condón.

condominium [ˈkɒndəˈmɪnɪəm] [kon-do-mi-nium], *s.* Condominio, cooperativa, propiedad en condominio, propiedad horizontal (ownership). Condominio, bloque de pisos (building); apartamento, piso (en régimen de propiedad horizontal) (apartment).

condonation. condonement [ˈkɒndəneɪʃən] [kon-do-nei-shon], *s.* Condonación, perdón, indulto.

condone [kənˈdəʊn] [kon-doun], *va.* Condonar, perdonar o remitir alguna pena. Aprobar (violence, conduct).

condor [ˈkɒndɔːr] [kon-doᵣ], *s.* Cóndor, especie de buitre grande que habita en los Andes.

conduce [kənˈdjuːs] [kon-dius], *vn.* Conducir, convenir, ser a propósito para el logro de alguna cosa (seguido de la preposicion to). -*va. (Des.)* Conducir, efectuar.

conducible [kənˈdjuːsɪbl] [kon-diu-si-bol], *a.* Conducente, útil, ventajoso.

conducibleness [kənˈdjuːsɪblnɪs] [kon-diu-si-bol-nes], **conduciveness** [kənˈdjuːsɪvnɪs] [kon-diu-siv-nes], *s.* La calidad de conducir o ser a propósito para el logro de alguna cosa; utilidad, conducencia.

conducibly [kənˈdjuːsɪblɪ] [kon-diu-si-bli], *adv.* Conducentemente.

conducive [kənˈdjuːsɪv] [kon-diu-siv], *a.* Conducente, oportuno, útil, conveniente. **To be conducive to something,** ser propósito para algo.

conduct [ˈkɒndʌkt] [kon-dakt], *s.* 1. Conducta, manejo, gobierno, economía. 2. Conducción de tropas. 3. Conducta o convoy. 4. Conducta, proceder, porte, manera como uno dirige su vida y acciones, comportamiento (behavior). **Her**

conduct of the investigation, la manera o el modo en que condujo la investigación (management).

conduct, *va.* 1. Conducir (heat, electricity); guiar (visitor, tour, party); dirigir, acompañar. 2. *(Mús.)* Dirigir, manejar. 3. Mandar un ejército. 4. Llevar a cabo, realizar (inquiry, experiment); mantener (conversation). **To conduct business,** llevar a cabo actividades comerciales. *vn. (Mús.)* Dirigir. *v. refl.* **To conduct oneself,** conducirse, comportarse.

conductible ['kɒndʌktɪbl] [kon-dak-ti-bol], *a.* Conductible, que se puede conducir.

conduction ['kɒndʌkʃən] [kon-dak-shon], *s.* Transmisión del sonido, el calórico o la electricidad por medio de un cuerpo conductor, sin movimiento de dicho cuerpo; conducción en general.

conductive ['kɒndʌktɪv] [kon-dak-tiv], *a.* 1. Conductivo, que tiene la facultad de conducir. 2. *(Elec.)* Que procede por conducción.

conductivity [ˌkɒndʌk'tɪvɪtɪ] [kon-dak-ti-vi-ti], *s.* Conductividad, virtud de conducir; conductibilidad.

conductor ['kɒnkʌktər] [kon-dak-to'], *s.* 1. Conductor. 2. Jefe o general de un ejército. 3. Conductor, guía, director. *(Mús.)* Director de orquesta. 4. *(E.U.)* Conductor de un tren o de un carro de ferrocarril urbana o tranvía. Cobrador, guarda (on bus, train). *Cf. GUARD.* 5. Ductor; instrumento de cirugía. 6. Conductor eléctrico.

conductress [kən'dʌktrɪs] [kon-dak-tres], *sf.* Conductora. Cobradora, guarda (on bus, train).

conduit ['kɒndɪt] [kon-dit], *s.* 1. Conducto, encañado. 2. Caño, el tubo o cañón por el cual se saca el agua de una fuente.

conduplicate ['kɒndjʊplɪkeɪt] [kon-diu-pli-keit], *va.* Duplicar, replegar. *-a.* Duplicado, replegado.

conduplication [kɒnˌdiuplɪ'keɪʃən] [kon-diu-pli-kei-shon], *s.* Duplicación, duplicado.

condyle ['kɒndaɪl] [kon-dail], *s. (Anat.)* Cóndilo, nudillo de las articulaciones.

condyloma ['kɒndaɪləmə] [kon-dai-lo-ma], *s. (Med.)* Condiloma, excrecencia como una verruga que suele formarse cerca del ano o de los órganos genitales de uno y otro sexo.

cone [kəʊn] [koun], *s.* 1. *(Auto, Math)* Cono, cuerpo sólido que tiene un círculo por base y termina por la parte superior en vértice o punta. 2. Piña, el fruto y simiente de algunas especies de pinos. 3. Cima simétrica de una montaña. 4. Cucurucho, barquillo, barquilla o cono (ice-cream cone). **Cone wheel,** rueda cónica. **Friction cone,** cono de fricción. **Cone-shaped,** cónico, en forma de cono.

coney *s. V.* CONY.

confabcone [kɒnfæb'kəʊn] [koun-fab-koun], *s. (Fam.)* Abreviatura de *Confabulation. (Coloq.)* Charla.

confabulatecone [kən'fæbjʊleɪtˌkəʊn] [kon-fa-biu-leit-koun], *vn.* Confabular, hablar dos o más personas juntas; platicar, hablar familiarmente.

confabulation [kənˌfæbjʊ'leɪʃən] [kon-fa-biu-lei-shon], *s.* Confabulación, plática.

confabulatory [kən'fæbjʊlətərɪ] [kon-fa-biu-la-to-ri], *a.* Lo que pertenece a la confabulación.

confarreation [kɒnfærɪ'ækʃən] [koun-fa-ri-ak-shon], *s.* Confarreación, una de las formas de matrimonio entre los antiguos romanos.

confect ['kɒnfekt] [koun-fekt], *va.* 1 Confitar. 2. Preparar, confite.

confection [kən'fekʃən] [kon-fek-shon], *s.* Confitura, confección, dulce; la fruta que está confitada.

confectionary [kən'fekʃənərɪ] [kon-fek-sho-na-ri], *a.* Perteneciente a los confites, o parecido a ellos.

confectioner [kən'fekʃənər] [kon-fek-sho-na'], *s.* 1. Confitero, el que tiene por oficio vender y hacer dulces y confituras. 2. Confeccionador.

confectionery [kən'fekʃənərɪ] [kon-fek-sho-ne-ri], *s.* 1. Confitura, confite, dulce. Productos de confitería. 2. Confitería, tienda de confitero.

confederacy [kən'fedərəsɪ] [kon-fe-de-ra-si], **confederation** [kən'fekʃən] [kon-fek-shon], *s.* Confederación, alianza, liga, unión: cábala.

confederate [kən'fedərɪt] [kon-fe-de-rit], *va.* Confederar, unir, formar una liga o confederación. *-vn.* Confederarse, unirse, aliarse.

confederate, *a. y s.* Confederado, aliado, ligado.

confer [kən'fɜːr] [kon-fa'], *vn.* Conferenciar, conferir, hablar o tratar con otro sobre algún asunto. Consultar (discuss). **To confer with somebody about something,** consultar algo con alguien. *-va.* 1. Conferir, comparar, confrontar, cotejar. 2. Conferir; dar. Conceder, conferir (bestow). **To confer something on/upon somebody/something,** concederle o conferirle algo a alguien/algo. 3. Conducir, convenir, ser conducente o conveniente.

conference ['kɒnfərəns] [kon-fe-rens], *s.* 1. Conferencia, conversación formal en que se trata algún asunto o negocio. Congreso, conferencia (large assembly, convention). **Conference center** o (GB) **centre,** centro de conferencias. **To be in conference with somebody,** estar reunido o en reunión, o en conferencia con alguien. **Conference room,** sala de juntas o reuniones. **At the conference table,** en la mesa de negociaciones. 2. Cuerpo organizado de predicadores y legos; y en la Iglesia católica, asamblea de clérigos para discutir cuestiones teológicas. 3. *(Sport)* Liga.

conferrable [kən'ferəbl] [kon-fe-ra-bol], *a.* Que puede ser conferido.

conferrer [kən'ferər], [Kon-fer-ra'], *s.* 1. Conferidor, colador. 2. Regalador, el que regala.

conferring [kən'ferɪŋ] [kon-fe-rin], *s.* Colocación, acción de conferir.

conferva [kən'fɜːvə] [kon-fer-va], *s. (Bot.)* Conferva, el tejido de filamentos verdes que sobrenadan sobre el agua estancada; género de algas, terrestres o de agua dulce.

confervoid [kən'fɜːvɔɪd] [kon-fer-void], *a.* Parecido a una conferva.

confess [kən'fes] [kon-fes], *va.* 1. Confesar, manifestar algún delito; reconocer y declarar una falta. 2. Confesar, oír en confesión, oír las culpas del penitente. 3. Declarar abiertamente, Reconocer; probar. **I must confess,** debo decir. *-vn.* 1. *(Rel.)* Confesarse. 2. Confesar (admit). **He confessed to five murders,** confesó haber cometido cinco asesinatos.

confessant, confessary [kən'fesənt] [kon-fe-sant], *s.* 1. El que confiesa o hace una confesión. 2. Penitente, el que confiesa.

confessed [kən'fest] [kon-fest], *a.* 1. Incontestable, indudable, evidente. 2. Confesado, declarado, manifiesto (thief, liar).

confessedly [kən'fesdlɪ] [kon-fes-li], *adv.* 1. Conocidamente, cierta e infaliblemente, sin contradicción. 2. Manifiestamente, por confesión propia.

confession [kən'feʃən] [kon-fe-shon], *s.* 1. Confesión, declaración de algún delito (statement). **A signed confession,** una confesión por escrito. 2. Confesión, profesión de fe. 3. Confesión sacramental (of sins). **To go to confession,** ir a confesarse. 4. Reconocimiento de una falta.

confessionary [kən'feʃənərɪ] [kon-fe-sho-na-ri], *s.* Confesionario, el lugar destinado para oír la confesión sacramental.

confessionary *a.* Lo que pertenece a la confesión.

confessor [kən'fesər] [kon-fe-so'], *s.* 1. Confesor, el que declara su fe. 2. Confesor, el sacerdote que oye en confesión. 3. Penitente; confeso, el que confiesa sus delitos.

confest [kən'fest] [kon-fest], *a. (Ant.* o *poét.)* Confesado, manifiesto, reconocido por todos. *V.* CONFESSED.

confetti [kən'fetiː] [kon-fe-ti], *s.* Confeti, chaya o papel picado, papelillos.

confidant [ˌkɒnfɪˈdænt] [kon-fi-dent], *s.* Confidente, amigo íntimo a quien se confían los secretos.

confidante [ˌkɒnfɪˈdænt] [kon-fi-dent] *s.f.* Confidente.

confide [kənˈfaɪd] [kon-faid], *vn.* Confiar, fiarse, entregarse o referirse a la fidelidad de otro. **To confide in somebody,** confiarse a alguien (tell secrets). **To confide in somebody/something,** confiar en alguien/algo (trust). *-va.* Confiar, depositar, decir o dar a guardar a otro alguna cosa sin otra seguridad que la buena fe. **To confide something to somebody,** confiarle algo a alguien.

confidence [ˈkɒnfɪdəns] [kon-fi-dens], *s.* 1. Confianza, seguridad fundada en la discreción o probidad de otro (trust, faith). **Confidence in somebody/something,** confianza en alguien/algo. 2. Confianza, ánimo, aliento y valor. Confianza en sí mismo, seguridad en sí mismo (self-confidence). 3. Atrevimiento; presunción. 4. Conversación particular; secreto, confidencia (secret). **They exchanged confidences,** se hicieron confidencias. **He took her into his confidence,** se confió a ella (confidenciality). **In confidence,** en confianza. **In strict confidence,** con absoluta reserva.

confidence game, confidence trick *s.* Estafa, timo.

confident [ˈkɒnfɪdənt] [kon-fi-dent], *a.* 1. Cierto, seguro. Hecho con confianza y seguridad (sure/statement). **I am confident she won't disappoint us,** tengo (la) plena confianza de que no nos defraudará. **To be confident of something,** confiar en algo. 2. Confiado, terco, dogmático. Seguro de sí mismo (self-confident/person). 3. *(Ant.)* Descarado, atrevido, resuelto. *-s.* Confidente, a quien se confía un secreto.

confidential [ˈkɒnfɪdənʃəl] [kon-fi-den-shal], *a.* 1. Reservado, secreto, confidencial (secret/information). 2. Seguro; de confianza (private/secretary); íntimo, confidencial (intimate/tone).

confidentiality [ˌkɒnfɪdenʃɪˈælɪtɪ] [kon-fi-den-sha-li-ti] *s.* Confidencialidad.

confidentially [ˌkɒnfɪˈdənʃəlɪ] [kon-fi-den-sha-li] *adv.* Confidencialmente.

confidently [ˈkɒnfɪdəntlɪ] [kon-fi-dent-li], *adv.* Confidentemente, confidencialmente, secretamente. Con seguridad o confianza.

confider [ˈkɒnfɪdər] [kon-fi-dar], *s.* El que confía.

confiding [ˈkɒnfɪdɪŋ] [kon-fi-din], *a.* Fiel, seguro.

configurate [ˈkɒnfɪgjʊreɪt] [kon-fi-guiu-reit], *va.* Configurar, dar forma o figura. *-vn.* Ser congruo o apto.

configuration [kənˌfɪgjʊˈreɪʃən] [kon-fi-guiu-rei-shon], *s.* 1. Configuración, figura, forma exterior. 2. *(Astr.)* Aspecto, posición relativa de los planetas.

configure [ˈkɒngjʊr] [kon-fi-gar], *va.* Configurar, dar forma o figura.

confinable [ˈkɒnfɪnəbl] [kon-fi-na-bol], *a.* Limitable, lo que se puede limitar.

confine [kənˈfaɪn] [kon-fain], *s.* Confín, límite, término, frontera o línea que divide un teritorio de otro.

confine, *vn.* Confinar, lindar, estar contiguo o inmediato a otro territorio. *-va.* 1. Limitar, poner límite a alguna cosa (limit, restrict). **To confine something to something,** limitar o restringir algo a algo. **Drug addiction is not confined to large cities,** la drogadicción no afecta únicamente a las grandes ciudades. **The fire was confined to the basement,** el incendio sólo afectó al sótano. 2. Encerrar, aprisionar, poner preso. Confinar, recluir (shut in, imprison/person); encerrar (animal). 3. Restringir, estrechar, reducir. **He is confined to his bed,** no puede dejar la cama, o está enfermo en cama. **To be confined,** estar de parto.

confined [kənˈfaɪnd] [kon-faind] *a.* Limitado, reducido (space).

confineless [kənˈfaɪnlɪs] [kon-fain-les], *a.* Ilimitado.

confinement [kənˈfaɪnmənt] [kon-fain-ment], *s.* 1. Prisión, encierro, destierro, cautividad. Reclusión, confinamiento (act, state). 2. Estreñimiento, restricción dentro de determinados límites; abstención de salir por causa de enfermedad. 3. Parto; sobreparto, tiempo que la parida guarda cama (in childbirth).

confiner [ˈkɒnfaɪnər] [kon-fai-na^r], *s.* 1. La persona o cosa que limita, encierra, o restringe. 2. *(Des.)* Vecino; la cosa que está confinante o rayando con otra.

confines [ˈkɒnfaɪnz] [kon-fains] *s. pl.* Confines, límites.

confinity [kənˈfaɪnɪtɪ] [kon-fai-ni-ti], *s.* Cercanía, comarca, proximidad, inmediación.

confirm [kənˈfɜːm] [kon-ferm], *va.* 1. Confirmar, comprobar, corroborar (substantiate/report, reservation). 2. *(Rel.)* Confirmar, administrar la confirmación. 3. Establecer; revalidar, ratificar (ratify/treaty, agreement). 4. Confirmar, fortificar, dar mayor firmeza y seguridad.

confirmable [kənˈfɜːməbl] [kon-fer-ma-bol], *a.* Capaz de ser confirmado o ratificado.

confirmation [ˌkɒnfəˈmeɪʃən] [kon-fer-mei-shon], *s.* 1. Confirmación, la acción de confirmar o corroborar la verdad de una cosa; prueba, testimonio convincente (substantiation); ratificación (ratification). 2. *(Rel.)* Confirmación, la acción de confirmar por la imposición de manos del obispo. 3. Revalidación.

confirmative [kənˈfɜːmətɪv] [kon-fer-ma-tiv], *a.* Confirmativo.

confirmatory [kənˈfɜːmətərɪ] [kon-fer-ma-to-ri], *a.* Confirmativo o confirmatorio.

confirmed [kənˈfɜːmd] [kon-fermd], *a. y pp.* 1. Comprobado, corroborado; ratificado. 2. Establecido, demostrado. 3. Inveterado, consumado, empedernido (bachelor, liar).

confirmedness [kənˈfɜːmdnɪs] [kon-fermd-nes], *s.* Certeza, firmeza.

confirmer [kənˈfɜːmər] [kon-fer-ma^r], *s.* Confirmador, establecedor.

confirmingly [kənˈfɜːmɪŋlɪ] [kon-fer-min-li], *adv.* Confirmativamente.

confiscable [kənˈfɪskəbl] [kon-fis-ka-bol], *a.* Confiscable, lo que puede ser confiscado.

confiscate [ˈkɒnfɪskeɪt] [kon-fis-keit], *va.* Confiscar, privar de sus bienes a algún reo y aplicarlos al fisco; decomisar. **To confiscate something from somebody,** confiscarle o decomisarle algo a alguien.

confiscate, confiscated [ˈkɒnfɪskeɪtɪd] [kon-fis-kei-tid], *a.* Confiscado, entregado al fisco.

confiscation [ˌkɒnfɪsˈkeɪʃən] [kon-fis-kei-shon], *s.* Confiscación, decomiso, la adjudicación de los bienes de un reo al fisco.

confiscator [ˈkɒnfɪskeɪtər] [kon-fis-kei-to^r], *s.* Confiscador.

confiscatory [ˈkɒnfɪskətərɪ] [kon-fis-ka-to-ri], *a.* Lo que se confisca.

confiture [ˈkɒnfɪtʃʊər] [kon-fi-chua^r], *s.* Confitura, dulce.

confix [ˈkɒnfɪks] [kon-fiks], *va.* Atar, ligar, enclavar una cosa con otra.

confixure [ˈkɒnfɪksər] [kon-fiksua^r], *s.* Atadura, aseguramiento.

conflagrant [ˈkɒnfləgrænt] [kon-fla-grant], *a.* Incendiado.

conflagration [ˌkɒnfləˈgreɪʃən] [kon-fla-grei-shon], *s.* Conflagración, fuego o incendio general.

conflate [kənˈfleɪt] [kon-fleit], *va.* Combinar varias lecciones, lecturas o párrafos para componer con ellos una sola lección; se usa en forma pasiva. Refundir, combinar.

conflation [kənˈfleɪʃn] [kon-flei-shon], *s.* 1. Combinación de dos lecciones variantes para formar una nueva lección. 2. Toque de muchos instrumentos de viento a tiempo.

conflict [ˈkɒnflɪkt] [kon-flikt], *vn.* Luchar, contender, combatir; estar en oposición; chocar, entrechocar. Discrepar, estar reñido.

conflict, *s.* 1. Conflicto, encuentro violento de una cosa con otra; combate, pelea, contienda. 2. Conflicto, combate o angustia de ánimo, pena, dolor, pesar. **To come into conflict with something/somebody,** estar en conflicto con algo/alguien. **A conflict of interests,** un conflicto de intereses.

conflicting [ˈkɒnflɪktɪŋ] [kon-flik-tin] *a.* Opuesto, encontrado (interests); contradictorio (views, accounts, emotions).

confluence [ˈkɒnfluəns] [kon-fluens], *s.* 1. Confluencia, el lugar o sitio en que un río se une con otro. 2. Concurso, concurrencia de muchas personas o cosas.

confluent [ˈkɒnfluənt] [kon-fluent], *a.* 1. Confluente, que confluye o se junta. 2. Confluente; dícese de la erupción simultánea de granos, pústulas, etc. **Confluent smallpox,** viruela confluente. -s. Corriente que se une con otra; confluencia de un río.

conflux [ˈkɒnflʌks] [kon-fluks], *s.* Confluencia de varios ríos; concurso o concurrencia de muchas personas o cosas.

confocal [ˈkɒnfəʊkəl] [kon-fou-kal], *a.* Que tiene foco o focos comunes.

conform [kənˈfɔːm] [kon-form], *va.* Conformar hacer una cosa conforme o semejante; ajustar, concordar. -vn. 1. Conformarse, allanarse, cumplir con algún rito, ceremonia, uso o costumbre. **To conform to/with something,** ajustarse a o cumplir con algo (be in accordance). 2. Conformarse, ceder, someterse. Ser conformista (act in a conformist way). **He usually conforms to their wishes,** por lo general se aviene a sus deseos.

conformability, conformableness [kənˌfɔːməˈbɪlɪtɪ] [kon-for-ma-bi-li-ti], *s.* Conformidad, cualidad o estado de lo que es conforme, correspondiente, consistente, armonioso o semejante.

conform, conformable [kənˈfɔːməbl] [kon-for-ma-bol], *a.* Conforme semejante; conveniente, proporcionado; dócil, obsequioso.

conformably [kənˈfɔːməblɪ] [kon-for-ma-bli], *adv.* Conformemente.

conformation [kənˈfɔːmeɪʃən] [kon-for-mei-shon], *s.* Conformación, figura, arreglo.

conformer [kənˈfɔːmər] [kon-for-maʳ], *s.* El que conforma.

conformist [kənˈfɔːmɪst] [kon-for-mist], *s.* 1. Conformista, el que se conforma con el culto autorizado por las leyes de Inglaterra o con los ritos de la Iglesia anglicana. 2. El que se somete. *a.* Conformista.

conformity [kənˈfɔːmɪtɪ] [kon-for-mi-ti], *s.* Conformidad, consistencia, conveniencia, igualdad. **In conformity with,** conforme a, en conformidad con.

confound [kənˈfaʊnd] [kon-faund], *va.* 1. Confundir, desconcertar (perplex/person); frustrar (thwart/attempt); echar por tierra (plan). 2. Enredar, embrollar; turbar, consternar. 3. *(Ant.)* Atolondrar, atontar; desconcertar, avergonzar. 4. *(Des.)* Destruir, arruinar. *(Coloq.)* **Confound it!,** ¡maldita sea! (damn).

confounded [kənˈfaʊndɪd] [kon-faun-ded], *a.* Maldito, abominable, detestable, aborrecible, odioso, enorme. *(Coloq.)* Maldito, condenado.

confoundedly [kənˈfaʊndɪdlɪ] [kon-faun-did-li], *adv.* Destestablemente, horriblemente.

confoundedness [kənˈfaʊndɪdnɪs] [kon-faun-did-nis], *s.* Abatimiento, confusión.

confounder [kənˈfaʊndər] [kon-faun-daʳ], *s.* 1. Enredador. 2. Exterminador, desolador.

confraternity [ˌkɒnfrəˈtɜːnɪtɪ] [kon-fra-ter-ni-ti], *s.* 1. Cofradía, confraternidad, hermandad, sociedad. 2. Confraternidad, relaciones amistosas entre los individuos de una sociedad.

confrère [kənˈfrɛər] [kon-freaʳ], *s.* Compañero, colega.

confrication [ˌkɒnfrɪˈkeɪʃən] [kon-fri-kei-shon], *s. (Des.)* Confricación, acción y efecto de estregar.

confront [kənˈfrʌnt] [kon-front], *va.* 1. Confrontar, afrontar, hacer frente a (come face to face with/danger, problem). **Police were confronted by a group of demonstrators,** la policía se vio enfrentada a un grupo de manifestantes. Hacer frente a, enfrentarse a (face up to/enemy, fear, crisis). **I decided to confront him on the matter,** decidí plantearle la cuestión cara a cara. **I intend to confront him with it tomorrow,** pienso encararme con

él mañana y decírselo. 2. Carear. 3. Cotejar o comparar una cosa con otra.

confrontation [ˌkɒnfrənˈteɪʃən] [kon-fron-tei-shon], *s.* Confrontación, careo (encounter); enfrentamiento, confrontación (conflict).

confucian [kənˈfjuːʃən] [kon-fiu-shan]; *a.* Relativo a Confucio, el sabio chino.

confuse [kənˈfjuːz] [kon-fius], *va.* 1. Confundir, desconcertar (bewilder); complicar, enredar (blur/situation) obscurecer. 2. Inquietar, atropellar. 3. Confundir (mix up, be unable to distinguish/ideas, sounds). **To confuse something/somebody with something/somebody,** confundir algo/a alguien con algo/alguien.

confused [kənˈfjuːzd] [kon-fiusd], *a.* 1. Confuso, confundido, desorientado, perplejo (perplexed). **To get confused,** confundirse. **What are you confused about?,** ¿qué es lo que te tiene confundido? 2. Confuso (unclear/argument).

confusedness [kənˈfjuːznɪs] [kon-fius-nis], *s.* Atropellamiento, confusión, desorden.

confusing [kənˈfjuːzɪŋ] [kon-fiu-sin] *a.* Confuso, poco claro.

confusion [kənˈfjuːʒən] [kon-fiu-shon], *s.* 1. Confusión (turmoil); desorden (disorder); tumulto, caos, embarazo. **The meeting ended in confusion,** la reunión terminó en medio de la confusión general. 2. Perturbación, vergüenza. Confusión, desconcierto (perplexity); turbación (embarrassment). **Her presence threw him into confusion,** su presencia lo turbó. 3. *(Des.)* Ruina, destrucción.

confutable [kənˈfjuːtəbl] [kon-fiu-ta-bol], *a.* Refutable.

confutant [kənˈfjuːtənt] [kon-fiu-tant], *s.* Refutador

confutation [ˌkɒnfjuːˈteɪʃən] [kon-fiu-tei-shon], *s.* Confutación, refutación.

confute [kənˈfjuːt] [kon-fiut], *va.* Confutar, impugnar, refutar.

conga [ˈkɒŋɡə] [kon-ga], *s.* Conga, ritmo y baile afro-cubanos.

con game [kənˈɡeɪm] [kon-gueim] *s.* Timo, estafa.

congé [kənˈdʒeɪ] [kon-yei], *s.* Salutación, reverencia; el acto de despedir o despedirse, despedida.

congeal [kənˈdʒiːl] [kon-yil], *va.* 1. Congelar, helar o cuajar alguna cosa líquida. 2. Helar, dejar a uno suspenso, pasmarle, sobrecogerle. -vn. Congelarse, helarse, cuajarse alguna cosa líquida. Solidificarse, cuajar (fat). **Congealed blood,** sangre coagulada.

congealable [kənˈdʒiːləbl] [kon-yi-la-bol], *a.* Congelable, que es capaz de congelarse.

congealment [kənˈdʒiːlmənt] [kon-yil-ment], *s.* Congelación.

congee [kənˈdʒeɪ] [kon-yei], *vn.* Despedirse cortésmente; saludar.

congee [kənˈdʒiː] [kon-yíi] **conjee,** *s. (Ind.)* Atole o gachas de arroz, maíz, etc.

congelation [kənˈdʒəleɪʃən] [kon-ye-lei-shon], *s.* Congelación.

congener [kənˈdʒənər] [kon-ye-naʳ], **congeneric** [kənˈdʒənərɪk] [kon-ye-ne-rik], **congenerous** [kənˈdʒɪnərɪəs] [kon-yi-ne-rous], *a.* Congénere, idéntico, de la misma especie o género; congénérico.

congeneracy [kənˈdʒənərəsɪ] [kon-ye-ne-ra-si], **congenerousness** [kənˈdʒənərəsnɪs] [kon-ye-ne-ros-nis], *s.* Descendencia de un mismo origen, congeneración.

congenetic [kənˈdʒənətɪk] [kon-ye-ne-tik], *a.* Semejante en origen.

congenial [kənˈdʒiːnɪəl] [kon-yi-nial], *a.* 1. Congenial, análogo, de especie o naturaleza semejante, cognado. 2. Congenial, de igual genio o inclinaciones. 3. Simpático, agradable (person). **A congenial atmosphere,** un ambiente amigable.

congeniality [kənˈdʒenɪəlɪtɪ] [kon-ye-nia-li-ti], **congenialness** [kənˈdʒenɪəlnɪs] [kon-ye-nial-nes], *s.* Semejanza de genio.

congenital [kənˈdʒenɪtl] [kon-ye-ni-tal], *a.* Congénito, que nace con el individuo o existe desde el nacimiento.

conger, conger-eel [ˈkɒŋgər] [kon-yaʳ], *s.* Congrio, pescado de mar.

congeries [kənˈdʒɪrɪəs] [kon-yi-ries], *s.* Congerie, cúmulo o montón de cosas.

congest [kənˈdʒest] [kon-yest], *vn.* Hacerse obstruido, acumular, amontonar.

congested [kənˈdʒestɪd] [kon-yes-tid] *pa. (Med.)* 1. Congestionado, obstruido por sangre o humores. 2. *(Fig.)* Apretado, apiñado, obstruido por la muchedumbre como sucede en las calles. Congestionado (with traffic); abarrotado o repleto de gente (with people).

congestible [kənˈdʒestɪbl] [kon-yes-ti-bol], *a.* Acumulable, amontonable.

congestion [kənˈdʒestʃən] [kon-yes-chon], *s.* Congestión (with traffic); abarrotamiento (with people). *(Med.)* Congestión.

congestive [kənˈdʒestɪv] [kon-yes-tiv], *a. (Med.)* Perteneciente a la congestión. **Congestive chill,** escalofrío congestivo.

congiary [kənˈdʒɪərɪ] [kon-yia-ri], *s.* Congiario, don que solían distribuir al pueblo los emperadores romanos.

conglobate [kənˈgləbeɪt] [kon-glo-beit], *a.* Conglobado, amontonado en forma esférica más o menos perfecta.

conglobate, *va.* Conglobar, formar en figura de globo.

conglobately [kənˈgləbeɪtlɪ] [kon-glo-beit-li], *adv.* Conglobosamente.

conglobation [kənˈgləbeɪʃən] [kon-glo-bei-shon] *s.* Conglobación, globo.

conglobulate [kənˈgləbjʊleɪt] [kon-glo-biu-leit], *vn.* Conglobarse.

conglomerate [kənˈglɒmərɪt] [kon-glo-me-reit], *va.* Conglomerar, aglomerar, redondear.

conglomerate, *a.* Conglomerado; congregado, redondeado. - *s.* 1. Masa o colección de sustancias heterogéneas; colección de cosas o de ideas, confusamente acumuladas. 2. Roca compuesta de guijarros redondeados y desgastados por las aguas; se llama también *pudding-stone.* 3. *(Neg.)* Conglomerado de empresas.

conglomeration [kənˌglɒməˈreɪʃən] [kon-glo-me-rei-shon], *s.* 1. Conglomeración. Acumulación, conglomerado. 2. Entretejedura, mezcla.

conglomeritic, conglomeratic [kənˈglɒmərɪtɪk] [kon-glo-me-ri-tik], *a.* De una roca conglomerada o parecido a ella; formado por conglomeración.

conglutinate [kənˈglətɪneɪt] [kon-glu-ti-neit], *a.* Conglutinado, unido por medio de una sustancia viscosa.

conglutination [kənˌglətɪˈneɪʃən] [kon-glu-ti-nei-shon], *s.* Conglutinación.

conglutinative [kənˈglətɪnətɪv] [kon-glu-ti-na-tiv], *a.* Conglutinativo, que tiene virtud de conglutinar.

conglutinator [kənˌglətɪˈneɪtər] [kon-glu-ti-nei-toʳ], *s.* Conglutinador, agente medicinal que sirve para unir o cerrar los bordes de las heridas.

Congo [ˈkɒŋgəʊ] [kon-gou] *N. (Geogr.)* El Congo.

congratulant [kənˈgrætjʊlənt] [kon-gra-tiu-lant], *a.* Congratulorio, que expresa congratulación.

congratulate [kənˈgrætjʊleɪt] [kon-gra-tiu-leit], *va.* Congratular, felicitar. **To congratulate somebody on something,** felicitar o darle la enhorabuen a alguien por algo. *-vn. (Des.)* Congratularse, alegrarse *vr. refl.* **To congratulate oneself on something,** felicitarse o congratularse por algo o de algo.

congratulation [kənˌgrætjʊˈleɪʃən] [kon-gra-tiu-lei-shon], *s.* Congratulación; felicitación (praise). **Congratulations,** *pl.* enhorabuena, felicitaciones. **(My) congratulations!,** ¡enhorabuena!, ¡felicitaciones!

congratulator [kənˈgrætjʊleɪtər] [kon-gra-tiu-lei-toʳ], *s.* Congratulador; congraciador.

congratulatory [kənˈgrætjʊlətərɪ] [kon-gra-tiu-la-to-ri], *a.* Congratulatorio, que expresa congratulación. De enhorabuena o felicitación.

congregate [ˈkɒŋgrɪgeɪt] [kon-gri-gueit], *va.* Congregar, convocar, reunir. *-vn.* Juntarse.

congregate, a Agregado, reunido.

congregation [ˈkɒŋgrɪgeɪʃən] [kon-gri-guei-shon], *s.* 1. Congregación, concurso, auditorio, asamblea, reunión. 2. Agregado, colección, masa. 3. *(Rel.)* Fieles (attending service); feligreses (parishioners).

congregational [ˌkɒŋgrɪˈgeɪʃənl] [kon-gri-guei-sho-nal], *a.* 1. Lo que pertenece a alguna congregación o asamblea de cristianos. 2. Congregacional, perteneciente a la denominación protestante del congregacionalismo o a los congregacionalistas.

congregationalism [ˌkɒŋgrɪˈgeɪʃnlɪzm] [kon-gri-guei-sho-na-lisem], *s.* 1. Congregacionalismo, la forma de gobierno eclesiástico que reconoce como suprema la autoridad de la congregación local dentro de su jurisdicción. 2. Sistema de creencia y práctica de la secta congregacionalista.

congregationalist [ˌkɒŋgrɪˈgeɪʃnlɪst] [kon-gri-guei-shona-list], *s.* Partidario del congregacionalismo; miembro de la Iglesia congregacionalista.

congress [ˈkɒŋgres] [kon-gres], *s.* 1. Congreso, junta de soberanos o ministros para tratar asuntos comunes (conference). 2. Congreso, cámara de los diputados. En los Estados Unidos del Norte, Cámara de Representantes y Senado, el cuerpo legislativo nacional. 3. Conferencia, entrevista, congreso de varias personas; como acepción especial, ayuntamiento de hombre y mujer.

congression [ˈkɒŋgreʃən] [kon-gre-shon], *s.* Compañía, asamblea.

congressional [ˈkɒŋgreʃnl] [kon-gre-sho-nal], *a.* Del congreso, relativo a un congreso, congresional (committee). **Congressional district,** distrito electoral. **Congressional elections,** elecciones parlamentarias. **Congressional debates,** debates del congreso. **The Congressional Record,** las Actas del Congreso (de los EEUU).

congressive [ˈkɒŋgresɪv] [kon-gre-siv], *a.* Juntado, unido, pegado.

congressman [ˈkɒŋgresmən] [kon-gres-man], *s.* Miembro del congreso de los Estados Unidos; especialmemte uno de los diputados.

congresswoman [ˈkɒŋgresˌwʊmən] [kon-gres-uo-man] *s.f.* (in US) Miembro del Congreso.

congruence, congruency [ˈkɒŋgrʊəns] [kon-gruens], **congruity** [ˈkɒŋgrʊɪtɪ] [kon-grui-ti], Congruencia, congruidad, conformidad.

congruent [ˈkɒŋgrʊənt] [kon-gruent], *a.* Congruente, conveniente, conforme.

congruous [ˈkɒŋgrʊəs] [kon-gruos], *a.* Congruo, apto, proporcionado.

congruously [ˈkɒŋgrʊəslɪ] [kon-gruos-li], *adv.* Congruentemente.

conic, conical [ˈkɒnɪk] [ko-nik], *a.* Cónico.

conically [ˈkɒnɪklɪ] [ko-ni-ka-li], *adv.* En forma cónica.

conicalness [ˈkɒnɪkəlnɪs] [ko-ni-kal-nes], *s.* Conicidad, calidad de cónico.

Conic section [ˈkɒnɪkˌsekʃən] [ko-nik-sek-shon], *s. (Geom.)* Sección cónica. **Conics,** la ciencia de medir conos y sus curvas.

conifer [ˈkɒnɪfər] [ko-ni-faʳ], *s.* Conífero, el árbol que produce fruto en forma de cono.

coniferae [ˈkɒnɪfərə] [ko-ni-fe-ra], *s. pl.* Coníferas, orden de plantas resinosas, siempre verdes por lo común, que dan el fruto en forma de cono; v.g. el pino, el cedro, el abeto, etc.

coniferous [ˈkɒnɪfərəs] [ko-ni-fe-ros], *a.* Conífero, que produce pericarpos de forma cónica. De coníferas (forest). **A coniferous tree,** una conífera.

coniform [ˈkɒnɪfɔːm] [ko-ni-form], *a.* Coniforme, cónico.

conirostral ['kɒnɪrəstrəl] [ko-ni-ros-tral], *a.* Conirrostra, ave de pico cónico.

conium ['kɒnɪəm] [ko-nium], *s.* Cicuta, planta venenosa de las umbelíferas.

conjecturable ['kən'dʒektʃərəbl] [kon-yek-cha-re-bol], *a.* Conjeturable.

conjectural ['kən'dʒektʃərəl] [ko-yek-cha-ral], *a.* Conjetural.

conjecturally ['kən'dʒektʃərəlɪ] [kon-yek-chua-ra-li], *adv.* Conjecturalmente, por conjetura, sin prueba.

conjecture ['kən'dʒektʃʊər] [ko-yek-chua'], *s.* Conjetura (guess); apariencia, suposición, sospecha. **Conjecture was at fault,** salieron fallidas las conjeturas. **It's pure conjecture,** no son más que conjeturas o suposiciones (guesswork).

conjecture *va.* Conjeturar; sospechar, pronosticar.

conjecturer ['kən'dʒektʃʊərər] [ko-yek-chua-re'], *s.* Conjeturador.

conjoin [kən'dʒɔɪn] [ko-yoin], *va.* 1. Juntar, unir; asociar. 2. Asociar, conectar. -*vn.* Confederarse, unirse, ligarse.

conjoint [kən'dʒɔɪnt] [ko-yoint], *a.* Asociado, confederado.

conjointly [kən'dʒɔɪntlɪ] [ko-yoint-li], *adv.* Unidamente, de mancomún.

conjugable [kən'dʒʊgəbl] [ko-yu-ga-bol], *a.* (Gram.) Que puede ser conjugado.

conjugal ['kɒndʒugəl] [ko-yu-gal], *a.* Conyugal, matrimonial.

conjugally ['kɒndʒugəlɪ] [ko-yu-ga-li], *adv.* Conyugalmente.

conjugate ['kɒndʒugeɪt] [ko-yu-geuit], *va.* 1. (Gram.) Conjugar, variar las terminaciones de los verbos. 2. Juntar, unir (en matrimonio). -*vn.* 1. Conjugarse (verb). 2. (Biol.) Unirse en conjugación.

conjugate, *s.* La palabra que tiene la misma derivación que otras. -*a.* 1. Juntado en pares, apareado. 2. (Mat.) Conjugado, recíprocamente coordinado, recíproco.

conjugation [ˌkɒndʒuˈgeɪʃən] [ko-yu-guei-shon], *s.* 1. Conjución, unión. 2. (Gram.) Conjugación. 3. (Biol.) Unión o fusión de dos o más celdillas o individuos para la reproducción, como sucede con los animales y las plantas más sencillos, *p. ej.* las algas.

conjunct [kɒn'dʒʌŋkt] [ko-yankt] *a.* Conjunto, allegado, unido.

conjunction [ˈkɒndʒʌŋkʃən] [ko-yank-shon] *s.* 1. Conjunción, unión, asociación, liga Combination. 2. (Gram.) Conjunción. 3. (Astr.) Conjunción de dos planetas.

conjunctiva [kən'dʒʌktɪvə] [ko-yak-ti-va], *s.* Conjuntiva, membrana mucosa que cubre la superficie posterior de los párpados y la parte anterior del globo del ojo.

conjunctival ['kɒndʒəktɪvl] [ko-yak-ti-val], *a.* Relativo a la conjuntiva.

conjunctive ['kɒndʒʌŋktɪv] [ko-yank-tiv], *a.* 1. Conjunto; conjuntivo. 2. (Gram.) Subjuntivo. **Conjunctive mode,** modo subjuntivo.

conjunctively ['kɒndʒʌŋktɪvlɪ] [ko-yank-tiv-li], *adv.* Conjuntamete, de mancomún.

conjunctivitis ['kɒndʒʌŋktɪˈvaɪtɪs] [ko-yank-ti-vai-tis], *s.* Inflamación de la conjuntiva, conjuntivitis.

conjunctly ['kɒndʒʌŋktlɪ] [ko-yankt-li], *adv.* Juntamente.

conjuncture [kən'dʒʌŋktʃər] [ko-yank-cha'], *s.* 1. Conyuntura. 2. Ocasión, sazón, crisis. 3. Modo de unión, Conexión.

conjuration [ˌkɒndʒʊəˈreɪʃən] [ko-yua-rei-shon], *s.* 1. Depreciación, petición, súplica ardiente. 2. Conjuro, imprecación, conspiración. 3. Conjuración, conspiración. 4. La forma o acto de citar a alguno en nombre de Dios.

conjure ['kɒndʒʊər] [ko-yua'], *va.* 1. Hechizar, encantar, efectuar algo por arte mágica. 2. Citar, ahuyentar, por arte supranatural o mágica. **To conjure something out of thin air,** hacer aparecer algo como por arte de magia. -*vn.* Practicar la mágica, hacer juegos de manos. Hacer magia (perform tricks). **To conjure away,** exorcizar. **To conjure**

up, evocar, llamar con invocaciones supersticiosas. **To conjure up difficulties,** suscitar dificultades u obstáculos.

conjure, *va.* 1. Conjurar o citar en nombre de Dios; pedir con instancia y ruegos. 2. (Des.) Conjurarse, conspirar. 3. (Ant.) Encantar, hechizar.

conjure up Evocar, traer a la memoria (evoke). **It conjures up images of...,** hace pensar en...

conjurer ['kən'dʒʊərər] [ko-yua-ra'], *s.* 1. Conjurador, encantador. Prestidigitador, mago. 2. (Irón.) Hombre sagaz. **He is not a conjurer,** no es adivino.

conjuring ['kən'dʒʊərɪŋ] [ko-yua-rin] *s.* Prestidigitación, magia. **Conjuring trick,** truco de magia.

conjuror *s.* V. CONJURER

conker ['kɒŋkər] [kon-ka'] *s.* (GB) (Coloq.) Castaña de Indias.

conk out ['kɒŋk'aʊt] [konk-aut] *vn.* (Coloq.) Averiarse, descomponerse (engine, car).

con man ['kɒnmæn] [kon-man] *s.* Estafador, timador.

conn = Connecticut

connate ['kɒneɪt] [ko-neit], *a.* 1. Del mismo parto, nacido con otro. 2. (Bot.) Connato, unido desde su origen, formando un mismo cuerpo. 3. Innato, que se tiene al nacer.

connation ['kɒneɪʃən] [ko-nei-shon], *s.* Calidad de connato; unión congénita.

connatural ['kɒnætjʊrəl] [ko-na-tu-ral], *a.* Connatural.

connaturality ['kɒnætəˈrælɪtɪ] [ko-na-tu-ra-li-ti], **connaturalness** ['kɒnætərəlnɪs] [ko-na-tu-ral-nes], *s.* Participación de la misma naturaleza.

connaturalize ['kɒnætʃərəlaɪz] [ko-na-chua-lais], *va.* Unir con iazos naturales, con los que impone la naturaleza.

connaturally ['kɒnætʃəlɪ] [ko-na-chua-li], *adv.* Connaturalmente.

connect [kə'nekt] [ko-nekt], *va.* 1 Juntar, unir, enlazar, atar, trabar. **To connect something to something,** conectar algo a algo (attach). Comunicar (link together/ rooms, buildings); conectar (towns). 2. Coordinar, combinar, poner en orden y método alguna cosa. 3. Aparear, juntar, reunir; relacionar, asociar (associate/people, ideas, events). (Mec.) Engargantar, poner en comunicación dos ruedas, dos piezas de una máquina. (Telec.) **I'm trying to connect you,** un momento que lo comunico o le pongo el número. Conectar (phone, gas). -*vn.* 1. Comunicarse (be joined together/rooms); empalmar (pipes). **To connect to something,** estar conectado a algo (be fitted). 2. (Transp.) **To connect with something,** enlazar con algo, conectar con algo (train, flight). 3. Unirse, juntarse; asociarse. **Connecting-rod,** biela, barra de conexión, biela motriz, vástago oscilante de un émbolo.

connect up 1. Conectar (wires, apparatus). 2. Conectarse (wires). **It all connects up,** todo está relacionado.

connected [kə'nektɪd] [ko-nek-ted] *a.* Relacionado (ideas, events). **The two firms are in no way connected,** las dos empresas no tienen conexión o relación alguna. **She's very well connected,** está muy bien relacionada o conectada, tiene muy buenas conexiones. **To be connected with something,** estar relacionado o conectado con algo.

connecting [kə'nektɪŋ] [ko-nek-tin] *a.* **Connecting rooms,** habitaciones que se comunican entre sí. **The connecting door was locked,** la puerta que comunicaba las dos habitaciones estaba cerrada con llave. **Connecting flight,** vuelo de enlace.

connection [kə'nekʃən] [ko-nek-shon], *s.* 1. Conexión, enlace (link). (Elec.) Conexión. 2. Atadura, trabazón. 3. Afinidad, parentesco; familia. Conexión (relationship). 4. Conjunto de personas reunidas; compañía; secta o comunión religiosa. 5. Relación, analogía, conexión (relation). **She's wanted in connection with the killing,** se la busca en conexión o en relación con el asesinato. 6. (Transp.) Conexión o enlace; empalme, traspaso de un ferrocarril a otro sin demora. **I missed my conexion,** perdí la combinación o conexión. **Connections,** *pl.* Lazos (links, ties); contactos, conexiones (influential people); familiares, parientes (relations).

connective [kəˈnɛktɪv] [ko-nek-tiv], *a.* Conexivo. **Connective tissue,** *(Anat.)* El tejido fibroso que atraviesa el cuerpo entero y sirve para unir y sostener las diversas partes. -*s.* 1. *(Gram.)* Conjunción. 2. *(Bot.)* La parte del estambre que une los lóbulos de la antena. 3. *(Zool.)* Pieza de conexión.

connectively [kəˈnɛktɪvlɪ] [ko-nek-tiv-li], *adv.* Conjuntamente, unidamente.

conner [ˈkɒnər] [ko-naʳ], *s.* 1. El que examina atentamente; inspector. 2. El que dirige el gobierno y rumbo de un buque desde un punto elevado o conveniente. 3. (a) Esparo, crenilabro, pez europeo; (b) *V.* CUNNER.

connexion [kəˈnɛkʃən] [ko-nek-shon], *s.* 1. Conexión, unión, coherencia, ligazón, corespondencia, enlace. 2. *(Mar.)* Ligazón. *V.* CONNECTION.

connexive [kəˈnɛksɪv] [ko-nek-siv], *a.* Conexivo, conjuntivo.

conning tower [ˌkɒnɪŋˈtaʊər] [ko-nin-taueʳ], *s.* Caseta blindada del piloto en barco de guerra.

conniption, conniption fit [kəˈnɪpʃən] [ko-nip-shon], *s.* *(Fam.)* Pataleta, rabieta, ataque de histerismo.

connivance [kəˈnaɪvæns] [ko-nai-vans], *s.* Connivencia, complicidad, disimulo, permisión tácita de un delito.

connive [kəˈnaɪv] [ko-naiv], *vn.* 1. Tolerar, disimular una falta; permitir, hacer la vista gorda. 2. Disimular, fingir ceguedad o ignorancia. **To connive with somebody,** actuar en complicidad o en connivencia con alguien (plot). **To connive at something,** ser cómplice en algo.

connivence, connivency, *s. V.* CONNIVANCE.

connivent [kəˈnaɪvənt] [ko-nai-vent], *a.* Descuidado, disimulado.

conniver [kəˈnaɪvər] [ko-nai-vaʳ], *s.* Cómplice, el que está en connivencia con otro.

conniving [kəˈnaɪvɪŋ] [ko-nai-vin] *a.* Maniobrero, maquinador.

connnoisseur [ˌkɒnəˈsɜːr] [ko-no-siʳ], *s.* Perito, entendido, conocedor, inteligente.

connoisseurship [ˌkɒnəsɜːˈʃɪp] [ko-no-ser-ship], *s.* Inteligencia, pericia, conocimiento, habilidad por juzgar de una cosa.

connotate [ˈkɒnəʊteɪt] [ko-nou-teit], *va.* 1. Designar indirectamente. 2. *(Lóg.)* Connotar, significar algo más de lo que las palabras expresan por sí mismas.

connotation [ˌkɒnəʊˈteɪʃən] [ko-nou-tei-shon], *s.* *(Lóg.)* Connotación, designación indirecta.

connote [kɒˈnəʊt] [ko-nout], *va.* *(Lóg.)* Connotar, significar indirectamente.

connubial [kəˈnjuːbɪəl] [ko-niu-bial], *a.* Conyugal, matrimonial.

connumeration [ˌkɒnjʊməˈreɪʃən] [ko-niu-me-rei-shon], *s.* Connumeración.

conoid [ˈkɒnɔɪd] [ko-noid], *s.* 1. Conoide, cuerpo que se semeja al cono y cuya base es una elipse. 2. Conoide, sólido formado por la revolución de una sección cónica sobre su eje.

conoidal [ˈkɒnɔɪdəl] [ko-noi-dal], **conoidical** [ˈkɒnɔɪdɪkl] [ko-noi-di-kal], *a.* Conoidal, lo que pertenece al conoide.

conquer [ˈkɒŋkər] [kon-keʳ], *va.* 1. Conquistar (country, mountain). 2. Vencer (enemy); rendir, sujetar, sojuzgar, domar; superar, véncer (fear). **The conquering army,** el ejército victorioso. -*vn.* Vencer, ganar la victoria.

conquerable [ˈkɒŋkərəbl] [kon-ke-ra-bol], *a.* Vencible, conquistable, domable.

conqueress [ˈkɒŋkərəs] [kon-ke-res], *sf.* Conquistadora.

conquering [ˈkɒŋkərɪŋ] [kon-ke-rin], *a.* Victorioso, triunfador, triunfante.

conqueror [ˈkɒŋkərər] [kon-ke-roʳ], *s.* Vencedor, conquistador.

conquest [ˈkɒŋkwɛst] [kon-kuest], *s.* 1. Conquista. 2. Conquista, la cosa conquistada.

conquistador [kɒnˈkwɪstədɔː] [kon-kuis-ta-doʳ] *s.* Conquistador.

consanguineous [ˌkɒnsæŋˈgwɪnɪəs] [kon-san-gui-nios], *a.* 1. Consanguíneo, que tiene parentesco de consanguinidad. 2. Se dice en inglés de los que tienen el mismo padre, pero diferentes madres.

consanguinity [ˌkɒnsæŋˈgwɪnɪti] [kon-san-gui-ni-ti], *s.* Consanguinidad, parentesco natural o de sangre.

conscience [ˈkɒnʃəns] [kon-sens], *s.* 1. Conciencia, ciencia o conocimiento íntimo e interior del bien que debemos hacer y del mal que debemos evitar. **To have a clean conscience,** tener la conciencia tranquila o limpia. **She has a guilty conscience,** no tiene la conciencia tranquila, le remuerde la conciencia. **Her conscience was troubling her,** le remordía la conciencia. **I don't want that on my conscience,** no quiero tener ese cargo de conciencia. 2. Escrúpulo, dificultad; justicia; veracidad. 3. *(Fam.)* Razón. **For conscience' sake, to satisfy one's conscience,** para descargo de la conciencia.

conscienced [ˈkɒnʃənst] [kon-senst], *a.* Concienzudo.

conscientious [ˌkɒnʃənˈʃəs] [kon-sen-shos], *a.* 1. Concienzudo, serio (work); aplicado, serio (student). 2. Escrupuloso. **Conscientious objector,** objetor de conciencia.

conscientiously [ˌkɒnʃɪˈɛnʃəslɪ] [kon-si-en-shos-li], *adv.* Escrupulosamente. A conciencia, concienzudamente.

conscientiousness [ˌkɒnʃɪˈɛnʃəsnɪs] [kon-si-en-shos-nes], *s.* 1. Rectitud de conciencia, equidad, justicia. 2. Escrúpulo.

conscionable [ˈkɒnʃənəbl] [kon-sho-na-bol], *a.* Justo, razonable.

conscionably [ˈkɒnʃənəblɪ] [kon-sho-na-bli], *adv.* En conciencia razonablemente.

conscious [ˈkɒnʃəs] [kon-shos], *a.* 1. Consciente, sabedor de sus propios pensamientos y acciones; que tiene conciencia de sus actos (awake, alert). **To be conscious of something,** ser o estar consciente de algo, tener conciencia de algo (aware). **To become conscious of something,** tomar conciencia de algo. 2. Que tiene excesiva conciencia de sí mismo; turbado o cohibido por el sentimiento exagerado de la propia individualidad. 3. *V.* COGNIZANT. **I am concious of it,** lo sé muy bien o estoy convencido de ello; estoy cierto de ello, lo conozco. 4. Deliberado (deliberate/decision). **She made a conscious effort to be nice,** se esforzó por ser amable.

-conscious *suff.* **Safety-conscious,** preocupado por la seguridad. **A fashion-conscious girl,** una chica que sigue o siempre va a la última moda. *V.* CLASS-CONSCIOUS.

consciously [ˈkɒnʃəslɪ] [kon-shos-li], *adv.* Con cierta ciencia o conocimiento de sus propias acciones; a sabiendas sinceramente. Deliberadamente (choose, avoid).

consciousness [ˈkɒnʃəsnɪs] [kon-shos-nes], *s.* 1. Ciencia o conocimiento interior, sentimiento interior. 2. Conocimiento (state of being awake, alert) **To recover** o **return to consciousness,** recobrar el sentido, volver en sí. 3. Conciencia (awareness). **To raise somebody's consciousness,** concientizar o concienciar a alguien.

consciousness-raising *s.* Concientización, concienciación.

conscript [ˈkɒnskrɪpt] [kons-kript], *a.* Conscripto; registrado, notado en algún registro. **Conscript fathers,** padres conscriptos, los senadores de la antigua Roma. -*s.* Conscripto, recluta francés.

conscript, *va.* Reclutar, obligar al servicio militar (soldiers, army). **He was conscripted into the army,** lo llamaron a filas; lo llamaron a cumplir el servicio militar (for national service).

conscription [ˈkɒnskrɪpʃən] [kons-krip-shon], *s.* Reclutamiento, quinta, alistamiento forzoso del ejército.

consecrate [ˈkɒnsɪkreɪt] [kon-si-kreit], *va.* 1. Consagrar, destinar una cosa profana a usos piadosos; dedicar, poner aparte solemnemente. 2. Dedicar o destinar alguna cosa a un fin particular. 3. Canonizar. 4. Hacer reverendo o venerable.

consecrate, *a.* (*Poét.*) Consagrado.

consecration [ˌkɒnsɪˈkreɪʃən] [kon-si-krei-shon], *s.* 1. Consagración, el rito de consagrar o destinar alguna cosa al servicio de Dios. 2. Canonización.

consecrator [ˌkɒnsɪˈkreɪtər] [kon-si-krei-toʳ], *s.* Consagrante, consagrador.

consecratory [ˈkɒnsɪkrətərɪ] [kon-si-kra-to-ri], *a.* Sacramental, lo que pertenece a la consagración.

consecutive [kənˈsekjʊtɪv] [kon-se-kiu-tiv], *s.* 1. Consecutivo, consiguiente; sucesivo (successive/numbers). **He was absent on three consecutive days,** faltó tres días seguidos. 2. Consecuente; con la preposición *to.*

consecutively [kənˈsekjʊtɪvlɪ] [kon-se-kiu-tiv-li], *adv.* Consecutivametne.

consension [kənˈsenʃən] [kon-sen-shon], *s.* (*Ant.*) Convenio, ajuste, reconocimiento.

consensual [kənˈsensjʊəl] [kon-sen-siual], *a.* 1. (*For.*) Que existe solamente a causa de aquiescencia o consentimiento. 2. (*Fisiol.*) Excitado por medio de acción simpática o refleja.

consensus [kənˈsensəs] [kon-sen-sus], *s.* 1. Consenso, opinión colectiva, consentimiento general. 2. (*Fisiol.*) La relación simpática de los órganos del cuerpo en la ejecución de una función cualquiera.

consent [ˈkənsent] [kon-sent], *s.* 1. Consentimiento, asenso, convenio, correspondencia, conexión; aprobación, permiso, beneplácito, acuerdo, **Silence gives consent,** quien calla otorga. **By mutual consent,** de común acuerdo. **He gave his consent to their marriage,** dio su consentimiento para que se casaran. (*Law*) **Age of consent,** edad a partir de la cual es válido el consentimiento que se da para tener relaciones sexuales. 2. (*Ant.*) V. CONSENSUS.

consent, *vn.* Consentir, cooperar; obrar de concierto con otro; conceder, permitir; avenirse. Acceder. **To consent to something,** acceder a o consentir en algo. (*Law*) **Consenting adult,** adulto que realiza un acto por su propia y libre voluntad.

consentaneous [ˈkənsentənɪəs] [kon-sen-ta-nious], *a.* Conforme, conveniente, acorde, consentáneo, de acuerdo con; simultáneo.

consentaneously [ˌkənsenˈtənɪəslɪ] [kon-sen-ta-nious-li], *adv.* Conformemente, convenientemente.

consentaneousness [ˌkənsenˈtənɪəsnɪs] [kon-sen-ta-nious-nes], *s.* Conformidad, proporción, correspondencia.

consenter [ˈkənsentər] [kon-sen-taʳ], *s.* Consentidor.

consentient [ˈkənsenʃənt] [kon-sen-shent], *a.* Acorde, unido y convenido en el modo de pensar; uniforme, de opinión unánime.

consenting [ˈkənsentɪŋ] [kon-sen-tin], *s.* Consentimiento.

consequence [ˈkənsɪkwəns] [kon-si-kuens], *s.* 1. Consecuencia, resulta, efecto (result). **To be a consequence of something,** ser consecuencia o resultado de algo. **To have consequences,** tener o traer consecuencias. **To take consequences,** atenerse a o aceptar las consecuencias. **He neglected the business, with the consequences that...,** descuidó el negocio y a consecuencia de ello... 2. Consecuencia, proposición sacada de las premisas de un silogismo. 3. Consecuencia, encadenamiento de causas y efectos. 4. Importancia, momento; influencia, tendencia; trascendencia (importance). **To be of consequence to somebody,** tener trascendencia o ser de importancia para alguien. **That's of no consequence,** eso no tiene importancia. **By o in consequence,** de consiguiente. **In consequence,** en, a, o por consecuencia.

consequent [ˈkənsɪkwənt] [kon-si-kuet], *a.* 1. Consiguiente, lo que sigue, depende o se deduce de otra cosa. 2. Lógico, lo que está caracterizado por la exactitud del raciocinio. *-s.* 1. Consecuencia, efecto. 2. Consiguiente, la segunda proposición de un entimema.

consequential [ˈkənsɪkwənʃəl] [kon-si-kuen-shal], *a.* 1. Consecutivo, consiguiente, concluyente, resultante (resultant). 2. Necesario, lógico, producido por el encadenamiento de los efectos con las causas. 3. Pomposo, altivo, importante, trascendental (important).

consequentially [ˈkənsɪkwənʃəlɪ] [kon-si-kuen-sha-li], *adv.* Consiguientemente, consecuentemente; pomposamente.

consequentialness [ˈkənsɪkwənʃəlnɪs] [kon-si-kuen-shal-nes], *s.* Coherencia, conexión.

consequently [ˈkənsɪkwəntlɪ] [kon-si-kuent-li], *adv.* Consiguientemente, por consiguiente.

conservable [kənˈsɜːvəbl] [kon-ser-va-bol], *a.* Lo que se puede conservar.

conservancy [kənˈsɜːvənsɪ] [kon-ser-van-si], *s.* 1. Conservación. 2. Junta para la conservación y fomento de las pesquerías.

conservant [ˈkənsɜːvənt] [kon-ser-vant], *a.* Lo que conserva.

conservation [ˈkənsɜːveɪʃən] [kon-ser-vei-shon], *s.* Conservación, el acto de conservar, continuar o guardar; preservación, defensa, protección. (*Ecol.*) Protección o conservación del medio ambiente; conservacionista (group, scheme). **Conservation area,** (GB) zona protegida por su interés ecológico o arquitectónico.

conservationist [ˌkɒnsəˈveɪʃənɪst] [kon-ser-vei-sho-nist] *s.* Conservacionista.

conservatism [ˈkənsɜːvətɪzm] [kon-ser-va-tisem], *s.* Disposición a ser conservador, opuesto a la mudanza. Conservadurismo.

conservative [kənˈsɜːvətɪv] [kon-ser-va-tiv] *a.* 1. Conservador, que se adhiere al orden actual de cosas; opuesto a la mudanza y en cierto modo al progreso (traditional). **The Conservative (and Unionist) Party,** el Partido Conservador. 2. Conservativo, preservativo, que tiene el poder de preservar. 3. Cauteloso, prudente (cautious). **At a conservative estimate,** calculando por lo bajo.

conservative *s.* Conservador (traditionalist). **The Conservatives,** los conservadores, el Partido Conservador.

conservator [kənˈsɜːvəteɪtər] [kon-ser-vei-toʳ], *s.* Conservador, defensor, protector.

conservatory [kənˈsɜːvətərɪ] [kon-ser-va-to-ri], *a.* Conservatorio, a propósito para conservar. *-s.* 1. Invernáculo, pieza o casa cubierta y abrigada artificialmente para conservar las plantas delicadas; jardín de invierno (greenhouse). 2. Conservatorio, establecimiento público para enseñar y fomentar la música u otras artes (school of music).

conservatrix [kənˈsɜːvətrɪks] [kon-ser-va-triks], *sf.* Conservadora.

conserve [kənˈsɜːv] [kon-serv], *va.* 1. Conservar, cuidar, guardar, mantener alguna cosa paa que no se pierda o consuma. Proteger, conservar (preserve/wildlife, rivers). Conservar (save/energy, resources). **To conserve one's strength,** ahorrar energías. 2. Disponer las frutas para hacer conserva.

conserve, *s.* 1. Conserva dulce que se hace con frutas y azúcar. 2. (*Farm.*) Confección.

conserver [kənˈsɜːvər] [kon-ser-vaʳ], *s.* Conservador; confitero.

consider [kənˈsɪdər] [kon-si-daʳ], *va.* 1. Considerar, pensar, meditar, examinar, reflexionar (examine/advantages, offer). **It's my considered opinion that...,** lo he pensado mucho y considero u opino que... Considerar, plantearse, contemplar (contemplate, possibility). **I wouldn't even consider it!,** ¡yo ni me lo plantearía! **We're considering Ann for the job,** estamos pensando en Ann para el puesto. Tener en cuenta, considerar (take into account). **All things considered, I think that...,** bien considerado o bien mirado, creo que... 2. Recompensar, atender o premiar el trabajo o mérito de alguno. 3. Estimar, querer (regard as). **It's considered to be the best of its class,** está considerado como el mejor de su clase. **Consider yourself lucky!,** puedes darte por afortunado. **Consider it done!,** ¡dalo por hecho! 4. Ser de opinión, creer; seguido de una cláusula complemental. *-vn.* 1. Considerar, pensar con madurez. 2.

Considerar, deliberar, dudar, resolver consigo mismo. **To consider of,** examinar, deliberar, discutir o pensar detenidamente. **To consider again,** pensar o deliberar de nuevo. **To consider one,** considerar o estimar a alguno, mostrarle consideración. **Consider what you do,** mire Vd. lo que hace.

considerable [kən'sɪdərəbl] [kon-si-de-ra-bol], a. 1. Considerable, digno de consideración; respetable. 2. Importante, notable, considerable (achievement, risk). 3. Considerable, cuantioso, importante (sum). **With considerable difficulty,** con bastante dificultad. **To a considerable extent,** en gran parte.

considerableness [kən'sɪdərəblnɪs] [kon-si-de-ra-bol-nes], s. Importancia, entidad, valor.

considerably [kən'sɪdərəblɪ] [kon-si-de-ra-bli], adv. Considerablemente, importantemente.

considerate [kən'sɪdərɪt] [kon-si-de-reit] a. Atento, considerado.

considerateness [kən'sɪdəreɪtnɪs] [kon-si-de-reit-nes], s. Prudencia, circunspección, moderación.

consideration [kən,sɪde'reɪʃən] [kon-si-de-reishon], s. 1. Consideración (thoughtfulness). 2. Consideración, reflexión, miramiento; examen, deliberación (attention, thought). **Their case has been given careful consideration,** su caso ha sido estudiado o considerado detenidamente. **The report is under consideration,** el informe está siendo estudiado. **In consideration of,** en consideración a. 3. Importancia, valor, mérito, consecuencia (importance). **Of little/no importance,** de poca/ninguna importancia o trascendencia. 4. Recompensa, remuneración (payment). **For a small consideration,** por una módica suma o cantidad. 5. (For.) Motivo, respeto, razón, causa; la condición de un contrato sin la cual es nulo. **To take into consideration,** cuidar de; tomar en consideración. **A major consideration is the cost,** un factor muy a tener en cuenta es el costo (factor).

considerative [kən'sɪdərətɪv] [kon-si-de-ra-tiv], a. (Ant.) Considerado.

considerer [kən'sɪdərər] [kon-si-de-raʳ], s. Hombre de reflexión; considerador.

considering [kən'sɪdərɪŋ] [kon-si-de-rin] prep. y conj. En atención a, en consideración a, a causa de, visto que, en razón a; teniendo en cuenta. Por origen es participio. **Considering she is a woman,** visto que es mujer. **Considering she is only two years,** teniendo en cuenta que sólo tiene dos años. -a. Pensativo, considerado, juicioso. adv. (Coloq.) **It's not too bad considering,** no está tan mal, si te pones a pensar o después de todo.

consideringly [kən'sɪdərɪŋlɪ] [kon-si-de-rin-li], adv. Seriamente, atinadamente.

consign [kən'saɪn] [kon-sain], va. 1. Consignar o entregar a otro alguna cosa. 2. (For. y Com.) Cosignar, enviar, confiar, o fiar a otro mercaderías u objetos para vender, transferir o guardar (send/goods). 3. Ceder, transferir a otro el dominio de alguna cosa; entregar, relegar. **The boy was consigned to the care of his aunt,** el niño fue encomendado a su tía, el niño fue confiado al cuidado de su tía. **To consign one to punishment,** castigar a uno; entregarle a la ley.

consignation ['kənsaɪ'neɪʃən] [kon-sai-nei-shon], s. 1. Consignación, el acto de consignar o entregar. 2. (Des.) El acto de firmar. 3. En las Iglesias griega, asiria, cóptica y nestoriana, la acción de consagrar o bendecir con la señal de la cruz.

consignatory [kən'saɪnətərɪ] [kon-sai-na-to-ri], s. El que firma en unión con otros.

consignee [kən'saɪni:] [kon-sai-ni], s. Consignatorio, corresponsal, depositario.

consigner [kən'saɪnər] [kon-sai-naʳ], s. (Com.) Consignador. V. CONSIGNOR.

consignification [,kənsaɪnɪfɪ'keɪʃən] [kon-sai-ni-fi-kei-shon], s. Significación semejante a otra.

consignify [kən'saɪnɪfaɪ] [kon-sai-ni-fai], va. y vn. 1. Significar, con otro vocablo (el mismo sentido); como

«negociar» y «pactar». 2. Significar un sentido, en unión con otra palabra o señal.

consignment [kən'saɪnmənt] [kon-sain-ment], s. 1. Consignación, la acción de consignar, dar, entregar o ceder. 2. La propiedad o los ojetos consignados y la escritura de consignación, cesión o traspaso. 3. Envío, remesa (goods sent); envío (sending).

consignor [kən'saɪnər] [kon-sai-noʳ], s. Consignador, el que consigna sus mercancías o buques a un corresponsal suyo.

consiliary [kən'sɪlɪərɪ] [kon-si-lia-ri], a. Relativo o perteneciente a consejo, aviso o dictamen.

consimilar [kən'sɪmɪlər] [kon-si-mi-laʳ], a. Semejante, igual, parecido.

consist [kə'sɪst] [kon-sist], vn. 1. Consistir, subsistir, permanecer, continuar. 2. Componerse, constar, estar contenido en otra cosa. 3. Coexistir. 4. Convenir, corresponder, acordarse. **Consisting,** compuesto. **To consist of,** consistir en, estar compuesto de, componerse de. **To consist with,** ser compatible, acordarse o estar de acuerdo y conformidad.

consistence, consistency [kə'sɪstəns] [kon-sis-tens], s. 1. Consistencia, conformidad; estado o existencia de alguna cosa. 2. Grado de densidad o raridad; consistencia (of mixture). 3. Forma sustancial. 4. Permanencia, estabilidad, regularidad (regularity). 5. Relación, compatibilidad, conveniencia.

consistent [kən'sɪstənt] [kon-sis-tent], a. 1. Consistente, conveniente, conforme. 2. Firme, sólido, estable, constante (constant/excellence, failure); sistemático, constante (denial). **We have to be consistent in our approach,** tenemos que ser coherentes o consecuentes en el enfoque. 3. Compatible; plausible. **To be consistent with something,** concordar con algo (compatible/statements, beliefs).

consistently [kən'sɪstəntlɪ] [kon-sis-tent-li], adv. Conformemente; consecuentemente (behave); coherentemente (without change); sistemáticamente, constantemente (constantly/claim, refuse).

consistorial [kən'sɪstərɪəl] [kon-sis-to-rial], a. Consistorial.

consistory [kən'sɪstərɪ] [kon-sis-to-ri], s. 1. Tribunal, sala de justicia de una curia eclesiástica. 2. Consistorio, la junta o consejo que celebra el Papa con asistencia de los cardenales. 3. Junta, asamblea, congreso.

consociate [kən'səʃɪeɪt] [kon-so-shieit], vn. Juntar, unir, pegar. -vn. Asociarse, unirse, juntarse con otros.

consociate, a. Asociado, confederado, unido.

consociation [kən'səʃɪeɪʃən] [kon-so-shiei-shon], s. Alianza, liga; unión, intimidad; asociación, sociedad.

consol [kən'səl] [kon-sol], s. V. CONSOLS.

consolable [kən'sələbl] [kon-so-la-bol], a. Consolable.

consolate [kən'səleɪt] [kon-so-leit], va. Consolar. V. CONSOLE.

consolation [kən'sələɪʃən] [kon-so-lei-shon], s. Consolación, consuelo, alivio. **If it's any consolation to you,** si te sirve de consuelo. **Consolation prize,** premio de consolación, premio de consuelo.

consolatory [kən'sələtərɪ] [kon-so-la-to-ri], s. Consolador, consolatorio, que da consuelo o tiende a consolar. -s. Discurso o escrito consolatorio.

console [kən'səʊl] [kon-soul] s. Consola (control panel).

console, va. Consolar; confortar, aliviar la tristeza o la pena. **I consoled myself with the thought that…,** me consolé pensando que…

consoler [kən'səʊlər] [kon-sou-laʳ], s. Consolador, el o la que consuela.

consolidant [kən'səʊlɪdənt] [kon-so-li-dant], a. Consolidativo, lo que tiene virtud de consolidar.

consolidate [kən'sɒlɪdeɪt] [kon-so-li-deit], va. 1. Consolidar, dar firmeza y solidez a alguna cosa (reinforce/ support, position). 2. Reunir dos beneficios. Fusionar (combine companies); consolidar (debts). -vn. Consolidarse, ponerse firme, dura o sólida alguna cosa. **Consolidated annuities,** V. CONSOLS.

consolidation [kənˌsɒlɪˈdeɪʃən] [kon-so-li-dei-shon], s. Consolidación, reunión, conjunción (reinforcement). Fusión (merging of companies).

consolidative [kənˈsɒlɪdətɪv] [kon-so-li-da-tiv], a. Consolidativo.

consoling [kənˈsəʊlɪŋ] [kon-so-lin] a. De consuelo (words).

consommé [kənˈsɒmeɪ] [kon-so-mei], s. Consomé, caldo de carne. **Chicken consommé,** consommé de pollo, caldo de pollo.

consonance [ˈkɒnsənəns] [kon-so-nans], **consonancy** [ˈkɒnsənənsɪ] [kon-so-nan-si], s. Consonancia, congruencia, conformidad; rima, armonía; relación.

consonant [ˈkɒnsənənt] [kon-so-nant], a. 1. Consonante, conforme, cónsono. 2. V. CONSONANTAL.

consonant, s. (Gram.) Consonante, letra que no puede pronunciarse sin el auxilio de alguna vocal.

consonantal [ˌkɒnsəˈnæntl] [kon-so-nan-tal], a. Perteneciente a una consonante.

consonantly [ˈkɒnsənəntlɪ] [kon-so-nan-tli], adv. Conformemente.

consonantness [ˈkɒnsənəntnɪs] [kon-so-nant-nes], s. Consonancia, conformidad.

consonous [ˈkɒnsənəs] [kon-so-nos], a. (Mús.) Cónsono, acorde, armonioso.

consopite [ˈkɒnsəpaɪt] [kon-so-pait], va. Adormecer, arrullar para hacer dormir.

consort [ˈkɒnsɔːt] [kon-sort] s. Consorte (spouse). **Prince consort,** príncipe consorte.

consort with Tener trato con (associate with). **To consort with the enemy,** confraternizar con el enemigo.

consort, vn. Asociarse, acompañarse. -va. 1. Casar, unir el hombre a la mujer por medio del matrimonio. 2. Acompañar, hacer compañía a otro, vivir juntos.

consortable [ˈkɒnsɔːtəbl] [kon-sor-ta-bol], s. Compañía, estado de consorte.

consortium [kənˈsɔːʃəm] [kon-sor-shium] s. Consorcio.

conspectus [kənˈspektəs] [kons-pek-tus], s. 1. Ojeada abarcadora y completa; vista general. 2. Resumen, compendio, digesto.

conspicuity [kənˈspɪkwɪtɪ] [kons-pi-kui-ti], s. Claridad, visibilidad; evidencia; eminencia.

conspicuous [kənˈspɪkjʊəs] [kons-pi-kuos], a. 1. Conspicuo, claro, visible, aparente. 2. Eminente, ilustre, esclarecido, notable, famoso, distinguido. 3. Llamativo (hat, badge); manifiesto, evidente (differences, omissions). **To make oneself conspicuous,** llamar la atención. **To be conspicuous by one's absence,** brillar por su ausencia. **To be conspicuous for something,** destacar por algo (for bravery, loyalty).

conspicuously [kənˈspɪkjʊəslɪ] [kons-pi-kuos-li], adv. 1. Visiblemente, manifiestamente. 2. Claramente, eminentemente. **She was conspicuously dressed,** iba vestida de forma muy llamativa.

conspicuousness [kənˈspɪkjʊəsnɪs] [kons-pi-kuos-nes], s. Claridad, celebridad, fama, nombre, reputación.

conspiracy [kənˈspɪrəsɪ] [kons-pi-ra-si], s. 1. Conspiración, cooperación, conjuración. 2. Concurrencia.

conspirant [kənˈspɪrənt] [kons-pi-rant], a. Conjurado, conspirador.

conspiration [kənˈspɪreʃənɪs] [kons-pi-rei-shon], s. Conspiración; unión.

conspirator [kənˈspɪrətər] [kons-pi-ra-to^r], s. Conspirado, conspirador.

conspiratorial [kənˌspɪrəˈtɔːrɪəl] [kons-pi-ra-to-rial] a. De complicidad.

conspire [kənˈspaɪər] [kons-paia^r], vn. Conspirar, maquinar (plot); concurrir, convenir; ligarse, conjurarse. **Conspiring,** conspirante. **Conspiring powers,** (Mec.) fuerzas conspirantes, todas las que obran simultáneamente para producir un movimiento o un resultado cualquiera. **To conspire against somebody,** conspirar contra alguien.

conspirer [kənˈspaɪərər] [kons-paia-ra^r], s. Conspirador.

conspiringly [kənˈspɪrɪŋlɪ] [kons-pi-rin-li], adv. Conspirando criminalmente.

constable [ˈkʌnstəbl] [kons-ta-bol], s. 1. Condestable. 2. Comisario de barrio. (GB) Agente de policía. **Constable of the Tower,** gobernador de la Torre de Londres. En los Estados Unidos constable es simplemente un alguacil. **First constable,** alguacil mayor.

constableship [ˈkʌnstəblʃɪp] [kons-ta-bol-ship], s. Condestablía.

constablewick [ˈkʌnstəblwɪk] [kons-ta-bol-uik], s. La jurisdicción del condestable o la de un comisario de barrio.

constabulary [kənsˈtæbjʊlərɪ] [kons-ta-bu-la-ri], a. Perteneciente a un alguacil o esbirro; que se compone de ellos. -s. El conjunto de alguaciles; fuerza militar de policía. (GB) Policía.

constancy [ˈkɒnstənsɪ] [kons-tan-si], s. 1. Constancia (steadfastness); perseverancia, firmeza, fuerza; fidelidad, lealtad (fidelity); permanencia, estabilidad. 2. Fortaleza de alma, intrepidez. 3. Realidad, veracidad.

constant [ˈkɒnstənt] [kons-tant], a. 1. Constante, firme, sólido; permanente. Constante, continuo (continual/pain, complaints). **It's in constant use,** se usa continuamente. 2. Firme, resuelto, inmutable, perseverante, invariable; cierto, indudable. Constante (unchanging/temperature, speed). Fiel, leal (loyal).

constant s. Constante.

constantly [ˈkɒnstəntlɪ] [kons-tant-li], adv. 1. Constantemente, igualmente, invariablemente; asiduamente. **A constantly changing world,** un mundo en constante cambio. 2. Ciertamente, indudablemente.

constellate [ˈkɒnstəleɪt] [kons-te-leit], vn. (Ant.) Resplandecer o lucir en gurpos, brillar como una constelación. -va. Unir o juntar varios cuerpos resplandecientes en uno.

constellation [ˈkɒnstəleɪʃən] [kons-te-lei-shon], s. 1. (Astr.) Constelación, grupo de estrellas fijas. 2. Conjunto de resplandores o excelencias.

consternation [ˌkɒnstəˈneɪʃən] [kons-ter-nei-shon], s. Consternación, atolondramiento, aturdimiento, terror, sorpresa.

constipate [ˈkɒnstɪpeɪt] [kons-ti-peit], va. 1. Cerrar alguna cosa en paraje estrecho. 2. (Des.) Espesar, condensar; obstruir. -vn. 1. Constiparse. 2. Estreñirse el vientre.

constipated [ˈkɒnstɪpeɪtɪd] [kons-ti-pei-tid] a. Estreñido.

constipation [ˈkɒnstɪpeɪʃən] [kons-ti-pei-shon], s. 1. Apretura de alguna cosa en paraje estrecho. 2. Estreñimiento de vientre que los médicos suelen llamar constipación. 3. (Des.) Condensación, obstrucción.

constituency [kənˈstɪtjʊənsɪ] [kons-ti-tuen-si] s. Circunscripción o distrito electoral (area). Electores potenciales (supporters).

constituent [kənˈstɪtjʊənt] [kons-ti-tuent], s. 1. Elector, votante. 2. Constituyente (el que diputa o sustituye a otro para que en su nombre haga alguna cosa), comitente, delegante, poderdante. 3. Constitutivo, parte o elemento necesario, componente (component). -a. Constituyente, elemental, esencial, constitutivo (part, element).

constitute [ˈkɒnstɪtjʊt] [kons-ti-tiut], va. 1. Constituir, formar un todo, o ser de la sustancia de; componer (compose, make up). 2. Constituir, señalar (represent). 3. Erigir, establecer (establish). 4. Constituir, diputar, dar poder en forma.

constituter [ˈkɒnstɪtjʊtər] [kons-ti-tiu-ta^r], s. Constituidor.

constitution [ˈkɒnstɪtjʊʃən] [kons-ti-tiu-shon], s. 1. Constitución (of country). 2. Estado, situación o conjunto de circunstancias. 3. Constitución, ley fundamental, estatutos (of association, party). 4. Constitución, ley, ordenanza. 5. Complexión, temperamento, constitución, hablando de personas.

constitutional [ˌkɒnstɪˈtjʊʃənl] [kons-ti-tiu-sho-nal], a. 1. Constitucional, relativo a la constitución o composición de una persona o cosa en general; inherente a la constitución o complexión corporal o al carácter del individuo. 2. Constitucional, legal, conforme a la Constitución de un Estado. -*s.* (*Fam.*) Paseo a pie por motivos de salud, como recurso higiénico.

constitutionalist [ˌkɒnstɪˈtjuːʃənəlɪst] [kons-ti-tiu-sho-na-list], *s.* Constitucional, el partidario de la constitución de un Estado.

constitutionally [ˌkɒnstɪˈtjuːʃənəlɪ] [kons-ti-tiu-sho-na-li], *adv.* Constitucionalmente, legalmente.

constitutionist [ˌkɒnstɪˈtjəʃənɪst] [kons-ti-tiu-sho-nist], *s.* Constitucional, el defensor celoso de la constitución de su país.

constitutive [ˌkɒnstɪˈtjʊtɪv] [kons-ti-tiu-tiv], *a.* Constitutivo, legislativo; esencial.

constrain [kənˈstreɪn] [kons-trein], *va.* 1. Constreñir, obligar, forzar (compel). **She felt constrained to be polite,** se sintió obligada a ser cortés. 2. Restringir, impedir, detener. 3. Comprimir, apretar.

constrainable [kənˈstreɪnəbl] [kons-trei-na-bol], *a.* Constreñible.

constrainedly [kənˈstreɪndlɪ] [kons-trei-ned-li], *adv.* Constreñidamente; por compulsión, por fuerza.

constrainer [kənˈstreɪnər] [kons-trei-nar], *s.* El que obliga o precisa.

constraint [kənˈstreɪnt] [kons-treint], *s.* 1. Constreñimiento, coartación, apremio; compulsión, fuerza, violencia, tormento. Coacción (compulsion). 2. Incomodidad; necesidad. 3. Restricción, limitación (restriction). **Without constraint,** sin restricciones o limitaciones.

constrict [kənˈstrɪkt] [kons-trikt], *va.* 1. Constreñir, apretar, ligar, atar. 2. Constreñir, estrechar (opening/channel); arrugar, encoger. Dificultar (flow, breathing). Coartar, restringir (freedom). 3. Sofocar o sufocar.

constricted [kənˈstrɪktɪd] [kons-trik-tid] *a.* Estrecho, angosto (opening/channel); coartado (inhibited).

constriction [kənˈstrɪkʃən] [kons-trik-shon], *s.* Contracción, encogimiento, constricción, sofocación. Estrechamiento (narrow part); opresión (tightness). (*Med.*) Constricción. Restricción, limitación (limitation, hampering).

constrictive [kənˈstrɪktɪv] [kons-trik-tiv], *a.* Constrictivo, que tiende a constreñir o sofocar.

constrictor [kənˈstrɪktər] [kons-trik-toʳ], *s.* 1. Constrictor, constringente, sofocante. 2. (*Anat.*) Constrictor, músculo que estrecha o cierra ciertos conductos o cavidades del cuerpo. 3. (*Zool.*) Boa constrictor.

constringe [kənˈstrɪndʒ] [kons-trinch], *va.* Constreñir, comprimir, estrechar, ligar.

constringent [kənˈstrɪndʒənt] [kons-trin-yent], *a.* Constrictivo, constringente.

construct [kənˈstrʌkt] [kons-trakt], *va.* 1. Construir, edificar (build); hacer o formar alguna cosa, montar, armar (put together/model). 2. Idear, imaginar, componer: v.g. **To construct a theory,** idear una teoría.

construct, *a.* Relativo a, o que expresa construcción. **Construct state,** anexión, estado constructo, en la gramática semítica, expresión de la relación del genitivo.

constructer, constructor [kənˈstrʌktəʳ] [kons-trak-toʳ], *s.* Constructor, el que construye.

construction [kənˈstrʌkʃən] [kons-trak-shon], *s.* 1. Construcción, la acción de construir (of building); de la construcción (industry, worker). 2. (*Gram.*) Construcción, colocación y régimen de las palabras según las reglas de la sintaxis. 3. Interpretación, explicación.

consubstantiate [ˌkɒnsəbˈstænsɪˈeɪt] [kon-subs-tan-sieit], *va.* Unir en una misma sustancia o naturaleza.

consubstantiation [kənˌsəbstænsɪˈeɪʃən] [kon-subs-tan-siei-shon], *s.* Consubstanciación.

consuetude [kənˈsuːətuːd] [kon-sue-tud], *s.* Costumbre; (*ant.*) consuetud; asociación.

consuetudinary [kənˈsuːətuːdrˈnæri] [kon-sue-tu-di-na-ri], *a.* Consuetudinario, lo que es de costumbre; lo que viene de uso

inmemorial. -*s.* Ritual de las devociones ordinarias o de costumbre.

consul [ˈkɒnsəl] [kon-sul], *s.* 1. Cónsul, nombre de dos magistrados que tenían la primera autoridad con la república romana. 2. Cónsul, oficial o empleado público nombrado por el gobierno para proteger el comercio, la navegación y los súbditos o ciudadanos de un país en los puertos y plazas principales de otras naciones.

consular [ˈkɒnsjʊlər] [kon-su-laʳ], *a.* Consular, perteneciente a un cónsul.

consulate [ˈkɒnsəleɪt] [kon-su-leit] *s.* Consulado.

consult [kənˈsʌlt] [kon-sult], *vn.* 1. Consultarse, pedir parecer uno a otro recíprocamente. **They consulted and decided to leave,** se consultaron entre sí y decidieron irse. 2. Aconsejarse con o de. **I ought to consult with my wife first,** primero debería consultárselo a o consultarlo con mi mujer. -*va.* 1. Consultar, pedir parecer, dictamen o consejo a otro. **We were not consulted about the office move,** no se nos consultó sobre el traslado de la oficina. 2. Mirar, escudriñar, examinar. 3. Idear, deliberar, discurrir.

consult, *s.* 1. Consulta, parecer o dictamen que se pide o se da sobre una cosa. 2. Consulta, junta de personas para deliberar y determinar algún asunto.

consultancy [kənˈsʌltənsɪ] [kon-sul-tan-si] *s.* (*Busn.*) Asesoría, consultoría. **Consultancy fees,** honorarios por asesoría.

consultant [kənˈsʌltənt] [kon-sul-tant], *a.* Consultante. -*s.* 1. Consultante, el que consulta con otro. 2. Asesor, consultor (adviser). 3. (*Med.*) (GB) Especialista.

consultation [ˌkɒnsʌlˈteɪʃən] [kon-sul-tei-shon], *s.* 1. Consulta, junta, número de personas unidas a quienes se pide parecer. **Consultation of physicians,** junta de médicos. 2. Deliberación, opinión o parecer dado en consulta. Consulta (with doctor, lawyer); consulta (of dictionary, notes). **There was no consultation with the tenants,** no se consultó a los inquilinos. **In consultation with somebody,** en conferencia con alguien.

consultative, consultatory [kənˈsʌltərɪ] [kon-sul-to-ri], *a.* Consultivo.

consulter [kənˈsʌlt] [kon-sult], *s.* Consultante.

consulting [kənˈsʌltɪŋ] [kon-sul-tin], *a.* Consultor, consultora, el que da su parecer, consultado sobre algún asunto. (*Med.*) **Consulting hours,** horario u horas de consulta. **Consulting room,** consultorio, consulta.

consumable [kənˈsjuːməbl] [kon-siu-ma-bol], *a.* Consumible.

consume [kənˈsjuːm] [kon-sium], *va.* Consumir, acabar, destruir, disipar, gastar (eat, drink); consumir (use up/electricity, resources, energy). (*Econ.*) Consumir (commodity, product). Reducir a cenizas (destroy/fire). **He was consumed by/with jealousy,** lo consumían los celos. -*vn.* Consumirse, deshacerse, acabarse, aniquilarse, perecer.

consumer [kənˈsjuːmər] [kon-siu-maʳ], *s.* 1. Consumidor; disipador. 2. (Econ. Polit.) Consumidor, comprador; el que consume un artículo de valor variable. **Consumer demand,** demanda de consumo. **Consumer goods,** artículos o bienes de consumo. **Consumer research,** estudio de mercado. **Consumer rights,** derechos del consumidor. **The consumer society,** la sociedad de consumo. **Consumer Price Index,** índice de precios al consumo o al consumidor.

consuming [kənˈsjuːmɪŋ] [kon-siu-min] *a.* Devorador (passion); arrollador, absorbente (interest).

consummate [kənˈsjuːmɪt] [kon-siu-mit], *va.* Consumar, acabar, terminar, completar.

consummate, *a.* Consumado (actor, liar); completo, perfecto, cabal.

consummately [kənˈsjuːmɪtlɪ] [kon-siu-mit-li], *adv.* Consumadamente.

consummation [ˌkɒnsʌˈmeɪʃən] [kon-siu-]ei-shon], *s.* Consumación, perfección completa; desarrollo perfecto, fin.

consumption [kənˈsʌmpʃəm] [kon-samp-shon], *s.* 1. Consunción, disipación, destrucción, ruina; consumo, gasto. 2. Consunción, tisis (tuberculosis); marasmo. **To be in a consumption,** estar tísico. 3. (Econ. Polít.) Consumo, destrucción o gasto que se hace de comestibles, telas y otros géneros que ofrece el mercado, para el uso individual (eating, drinking). **It's fit/unfit for human consumption,** es/no es apto para el consumo. Consumo (use). **Water consumption,** consumo de agua.

consumptive [kənˈsʌmptɪv] [kon-sam-tiv], *a.* Consuntivo, destructivo; hético. Tísico.

consumptively [kənˈsʌmptɪvlɪ] [kon-sam-tiv-li], *adv.* A manera de consunción.

consumptiveness [kənˈsʌmptɪvnɪs] [kon-sam-tiv-nis], *s.* Principio de consunción.

cont (= continued) sigue.

contabescence [ˈkɒntæbənsns] [kon-ta-be-sens], *s.* 1. (*Med.*) Tabes, marasmo, atrofia. 2. (*Bot.*) Esterilidad de los estambres y el polen; ocurre a menudo en las plantas híbridas.

contact [ˈkɒntækt] [kon-takt], *s.* 1. Contacto, tocamiento (physical). **To come in/into contact with something,** hacer contacto con algo. **The plane's wheels made contact with the ground,** las ruedas del avión tocaron tierra. **Point of contact,** punto de contacto. **Contact sport,** deporte de choque. 2. Contacto (communication). **To come in/into contact with somebody,** tratar a alguien. **To be/get in contact with somebody,** estar/ponerse en contacto con alguien. **To lose contact with somebody,** perder el contacto con alguien. 3. (*Elec.*) Contacto. 4. Contacto (influential person).

contact *va.* Ponerse en contacto con, contactar con.

contact lens [ˈkɒntæktˌlenz] [kon-takt-lens], *s.* Lente de contacto.

contact print [ˈkɒntæktˌprɪnt] [kon-takt-print] *s.* Contacto.

contagion [kənˈteɪdʒən] [kon-tei-chon], *s.* 1. Contagio, peste, pestilencia, infección. 2. Contagio, infición, el daño y corrupción que propagan las malas doctrinas o el mal ejemplo. 3. Contagión, el medio de transmisión de una enfermedad específica.

contagious [kənˈteɪdʒəs] [kon-tei-chos], *a.* Contagioso, que se pega y comunica por contagio.

contagiousness [kənˈteɪdʒəsnɪs] [kon-tei-chos-nes], *s.* Carácter contagioso.

contain [kənˈteɪn] [kon-tein], *va.* 1. Contener, comprender, caber; incluir, abrazar, encerrar (hold). **That bottle contains six pints,** en aquella botella caben seis cuartillos. 2. Reprimir, contener, refrenar (enemy, fire, epidemic); contener (anger, laughter). **To contain oneself,** contenerse, aguantarse. 3. (*Mat.*) Ser exactamente divisible. *-vn.* Contenerse, abstenerse, vivir en continencia.

containable [kənˈteɪnəbl] [kon-tei-na-bol], *a.* Contenible.

container [kənˈteɪnər] [kon-tei-naʳ], *s.* 1. Envase (as. packaging). 2. Recipiente (receptacle). 3. (*Transp.*) Contenedor, contáiner. **Container ship,** buque portacontenedores.

containment [kənˈteɪnmənt] [kon-tein-ment] *s.* Contención.

contaminate [kənˈtæmɪneɪt] [kon-ta-mi-neit], *vn.* 1. Contaminar, manchar, corromper; contagiar, inficionar. **To become contaminated,** contaminarse. 2. Corromper, viciar, pervertir.

contaminate, *a.* Contaminado, manchado, corrompido.

contamination [kənˌtæmɪˈneɪʃən] [kon-ta-mi-nei-shon], *s.* Contaminación.

contd (= continued) sigue.

contemn [kənˈtem] [kon-tem], *va.* Despreciar, menospreciar, desestimar, tener en poco alguna cosa.

contemper [kənˈtempər] [kon-tem-paʳ], *va.* Contemperar, templar, moderar.

contemplate [ˈkɒntempleɪt] [kon-tem-pleit], *va.* 1. Contemplar, estudiar, meditar (ponder/position, alternatives).

2. Proyectar, formar intención. **She's contemplating a trip to China,** está pensando o proyectando hacer un viaje a la China (consider possibility). **I contemplated phoning her,** pensé (en) llamarla. 3. Contemplar (look at). *-vn.* Contemplar, detener el entendimiento en la consideración de alguna cosa; meditar, divagar.

contemplation [ˌkɒntemˈpleɪʃən] [kon-tem-plei-shon], *s.* 1. Contemplación (observation); meditación estudiosa; estudio, consideración, reflexión (reflection). 2. Proyecto; expectación. 3. Meditación sagrada.

contemplative [kənˈtemplətɪv] [kon-tem-pla-tiv], *a.* 1. Contemplativo, estudioso, discursivo. 2. Pensativo, meditabundo.

contemplatively [kənˈtemplətɪvlɪ] [kon-tem-pla-tiv-li], *adv.* Con atención y cuidado.

contemplator [ˌkɒntemˈpleɪtər] [kon-tem-plei-toʳ], *s.* Contemplador.

contemporaneity, contemporariness [kənˌtempəræˈnɪtɪ] [kon-tem-po-ra-ni-ti], [kənˌtempəræˈrɪnɪs] [kon-tem-po-ra-ri-nes], *s.* Contemporaneidad, sincronismo, existencia al mismo tiempo.

contemporaneous [kənˌtempəˈreɪnɪəs] [kon-tem-po-rei-nios], *a.* Contemporáneo, que existe al mismo tiempo que una persona o cosa. V. CONTEMPORARAY,

contemporaneously [kənˌtempəˈreɪnɪəslɪ] [kon-tem-po-rei-nios-li], *adv.* Contemporáneamente, al mismo tiempo, en una misma época.

contemporary [kənˌtempərərɪ] [kon-tem-po-ra-ri], *a.* Contemporáneo, coetáneo (person/of the same period); de la época (object). **To be contemporary with somebody/something,** ser contemporáneo o coetáneo de alguien/algo. Contemporáneo, actual (present day).

contemporary *s.* Contemporáneo, coetáneo (somebody living at same time). *Contemporaneous,* se dice principalmente de hechos y sucesos; *contemporary,* de personas. **He looks older than his contemporaries,** parece mayor que la gente de su edad o generación.

contemporize [kənˌtempərəraɪz] [kon-tem-po-ra-rais], *va.* Hacer dos o más cosas de un mismo siglo o era; considerar como contemporáneo.

contempt [kənˈtempt] [kon-tempt], *s.* Desprecio, desdén (scorn); menosprecio, vilipendio. **To hold something/somebody in contempt,** despreciar, desdeñar algo/a alguien. **To be beneath contempt,** ser despreciable o deleznable. (*Law*) **Contempt of court,** contumacia; rebeldía. Desacato al tribunal.

contemptibility [kənˌtemptɪˈblɪ] [kon-temp-ti-bli], *s.* V. CONTEMPTIBLENESS.

contemptible [kənˈtemptəbl] [kon-temp-ta-bol], *a.* Despreciable, deleznable, despreciado, desestimado, vil.

contemptibleness [kənˈtemptəblnɪs] [kon-temp-ta-bol-nes], *s.* Vileza, bajeza, abyección; torpeza.

contemptibly [kənˈtemptəblɪ] [kon-temp-ti-bli], *adv.* Vilmente.

contemptuous [kənˈtemptʊəs] [kon-temp-tuos], *a.* Desdeñoso, despectivo, altivo, insolente, despreciador. **Contemptuous words,** palabras ofensivas. **To be contemptuous of something/somebody,** despreciar o desdeñar algo/a alguien.

contemptuously [kənˈtemptʊəslɪ] [kon-temp-tuos-li], *adv.* Desdeñosamente, con menosprecio, con desdén.

contemptuousness [kənˈtemptʊəsnɪs] [kon-temp-tuos-nes], *s.* Desdén, desprecio, altanería.

contend [kənˈtend] [kon-tend], *va.* Sostener, argüir, afirmar; va seguido de *that* con una cláusula complemental. *-vn.* Contender, pleitear, disputar, pretender; competir, lidiar, altercar. **Contending parties,** partes contenciosas, o litigantes. **To contend with somebody for something,** competir con alguien por algo (compete). **To contend with something,** lidiar con o enfrentarse a algo (face). **Contending,** contrario, rival (teams); en pugna, antagónico, opuesto (interests).

content [kən'tent] [kon-tent], *a.* Cotento, satisfecho. **To be content with something,** estar contento con algo. **Not content with raising taxes…,** no contentos con subir los impuestos… En la Cámara de los Pares de Inglaterra, voto afirmativo. **The contents have it,** la proposición queda aprobada.

content, *va.* Contentar, satisfacer, complacer, agradar. *v. refl.* **To content oneself with something,** contentarse o conformarse con algo.

content, *s.* 1. Contento, contentamiento, satisfacción, agrado (contentment). **Content is the philosopher's stone, that turns all it touches into gold,** el contento es un tesoro, es la verdadera piedra filosofal. 2. Contenido, lo que se encierra en una cosa; cabida, capacidad; generalmente en plural (amount contained). Contenido (substance). **Sugar content,** contenido de azúcar. 3. *(Geom.)* Area contenida, extensión; cabida. **Table of contents,** tabla de materias de un libro en el orden en que se suceden, lo cual la diferencia de un índice alfabético. **Contents,** el o lo contenido, tabla de materias. Contenido (of box, bottle, book). **She read the contents of the letter,** leyó la carta. **Table of contents,** índice de materias, sumario (of book); sumario (in magazine).

contented [kən'tentɪd] [kon-ten-tid], *a.* 1. Contento, satisfecho, agradado, tranquilo. 2. Resignado, paciente. 3. De satisfacción (sigh/purr); satisfecho (person, workforce). **To be contented with something,** contentarse o conformarse con algo.

contentedly [kən'tentɪdlɪ] [kon-ten-tid-li], *adv.* Tranquilamente, contentamente; con satisfacción.

contentedness [kən'tentɪdnɪs] [kon-ten-tid-nes], *s.* Contento, satisfacción.

contentful [kən'təntful] [kon-tent-ful], *a.* Perfectamente contento, dichoso, feliz.

[kən'tenʃən] [kon-ten-shon] *s.* 1. Contención, contienda, debate, competencia, contestación, altercado; esfuerzo. **There's considerable contention over…,** existe un gran desacuerdo sobre… (dispute). 2. Opinión (assertion). **It's her contention that…,** ella sostiene que… 3. **All three cyclists are in contention for the title,** los tres ciclistas compiten por el título.

contentious [kən'tenʃəs] [kon-ten-shos], *a.* Contencioso, litigioso; polémico, muy discutido (issue). Discutidor (person).

contentiously [kən'tenʃəslɪ] [kon-ten-shos-li], *adv.* Contenciosamente.

contentless [kən'tentlɪs] [kon-tent-les], *a.* 1. Sin contenido o significación. 2., Descontento, desagradado.

contentment [kən'tentmənt] [kon-tent-ment], *s.* Contentamiento, contento, gusto, satisfacción.

conterminable [kən'tɜːmɪnəbl] [kon-ter-mi-na-bol], *a.* Lo que es capaz de ser contenido en los mismos límites que otra cosa.

conterminal [kən'tɜːmɪnl] [kon-ter-mi-nal], *a.* V. CONTERMINOUS.

conterminate [kən'tɜːmɪneɪt] [kon-ter-mi-neit], *a.* Lo que tiene el mismo límite que otra cosa.

conterminous [kən'tɜːmɪnəs] [kon-ter-mi-nos], *a.* 1. Contérmino, vecino, limítrofe. 2. Contendio dentro de los mismos límites, coextensivo. Lo mismo significa *Coterminous.*

contest [ˈkɒntest] [kon-test], *s.* Concurso (games/competition). *(Sport)* Competencia o competición; combate (in boxing). Lucha, contienda (struggle).

contest, *va.* 1. Contestar, disputar, litigar. Refutar (allegation); impugnar (will); protestar contra (decision). 2. Presentarse como candidato a (election). *-vn.* Contender, competir; emular.

contestable [ˈkɒntestəbl] [kon-tes-ta-bol], *a.* Contestable, disputable; dudoso, contencioso.

contestant [kən'testənt] [kon-tes-tant], *s.* 1. Contestante, disputador, litigante; especialmente el que disputa una elección o un testamento. 2. Concursante.

contestation [ˈkɒntesˌteɪʃˌn] [kon-tes-tei-shon], *s.* 1. Contestación. 2. Testimonio, prueba.

contestingly [ˈkɒntestɪŋlɪ] [kon-tes-tin-li], *adv.* Contenciosamente.

contestless [ˈkɒntestlɪs] [kon-test-les], *a.* Indisputable, incontestable.

context [ˈkɒntekst] [kon-tekst], *s.* Contexto, contenido; contextura. **Out of context,** fuera de contexto.

contextual [kɒn'tekstjʊəl] [kon-teks-tual], *a.* Del contexto, relativo al contexto.

contextural [ˈkɒntekstərəl] [kon-teks-tu-ral], *a.* Perteneciente a la contextura o entretejido.

contexture [ˈkɒntekstʃʊəʳ] [kon-teks-chuaʳ], *s.* Contextura, orden o disposición de las partes entre sí, tejido, entretejido, enlazamiento.

contignation [ˈkɒntɪgneɪʃən] [kon-tig-nei-shon], *s.* *(Arq.)* Contignación, trabazón de vigas que forma los pisos y techos. *V.* FRAMEWORK.

contiguity [ˈkɒntɪgjuːɪtɪ] [kon-ti-güi-ti], *s.* Contigüidad, inmediación de una cosa a otra.

contiguous [kən'tɪgjʊəs] [kon-ti-guos-li], *adv.* Contiguo, junto.

contiguously [kən'tɪgjʊəslɪ] [kon-ti-guos-li], *adv.* Contiguamente.

contiguousness [kən'tɪgjʊəsnɪs] [kon-ti-guos-nes], *s.* Contigüidad, vecindad.

continence o continency [ˈkɒntɪnəns] [kon-ti-nens], *s.* Continencia, temperancia, templanza, castidad; dominio sobre sí mismo, especialmente respecto a la pasión sexual.

continent [ˈkɒntɪnənt] [kon-ti-nent], *a.* 1. Continente, casto, puro. 2. *(Ant.)* Lo que contiene alguna cosa.

continent, *s.* Continente, gran exptensión de tierra, mayor de lo que suelen ser las islas y penínsulas (land mass). **The Continent,** Europa (continental).

continental [ˌkɒntɪ'nentl] [kon-ti-nen-tal], *a.* 1. *(Geogr.)* Continental. 2. **Continental** (European) de Europa (continental). **Continental breakfast,** desayuno continental (café o té y bollos con mantequilla y mermelada).

continently [ˈkɒntɪnentlɪ] [kon-ti-nent-li], *adv.* Castamente.

contingence o contingency [kən'tɪndʒəns] [kon-tin-yens], *s.* 1. Contingencia, acontecimiento o cosa que puede suceder o no. 2. Eventualidad, accidente o caso imprevisto (eventuality). De emergencia, para imprevistos (fund). **We've made contingency plans,** hemos tomado medidas previendo cualquier contingencia o eventualidad.

contingent [kən'tɪndʒəns] [kon-tin-yens], *s.* 1. Contingencia, casualidad. 2. Contingente, cuota.

contingent, *a.* Contingente, casual, accidental. **To be contingent on something,** estar supeditado a algo, depender de algo (dependent).

contingently [kən'tɪndʒəntlɪ] [kon-tin-yent-li], *adv.* Contingentemente, casualmente, accidentalmente.

contingentness [kən'tɪndʒəntnɪs] [kon-tin-yent-nes], *s.* Contingencia, casualidad.

continual [kən'tɪnjʊəl] [kon-ti-niual], *a.* 1. Continuo, frecuente, repetido a menudo. 2. Continuo, que dura o se hace sin interrupción; sin intermisión, incesante.

continually [kən'tɪnjʊəlɪ] [kon-ti-niua-li], *adv.* Continuamente, constantemente.

continualness [kən'tɪnjʊəlnɪs] [kon-ti-niual-nes], *s.* Permanencia.

continuance [kən'tɪnjʊəns] [kon-ti-niuans], *s.* 1. Continuación, permanencia. 2. Demora, duración, dilación, perseverancia. 2. Continuidad o coherencia; plazo. 4. Morada.

continuate [kən'tɪnjʊeɪt] [kon-ti-niu-eit], *a.* Continuado, unido inmediatamente, no interrumpido.

continuation [kən'tɪnjʊ'eɪʃən] [kon-ti-niu-ei-shon] *s.* 1. Continuación, duración, seguida, serie. 2. Mantenimiento (maintenance). Reanudación, continuación (resumption). 3. Prolongación, continuación (extension/of street, canal). Continuación (of story, film).

continuative [kənˈtɪnjʊətɪv] [kon-ti-niua-tiv], s. Expresión que denota continuación o permanencia.

continuator [kənˈtɪnjʊeɪtər] [kon-ti-niu-ei-tóʳ], s. Continuador, el que o lo que continúa o prosigue una obra o sucesión.

continue [kənˈtɪnjuː] [kon-ti-niu], vn. 1. Continuar, seguir (carry on) durar, ser durable. **We continued on our way,** reanudamos el camino 2. Permanecer en un estado o lugar. 3. Perseverar; detenerse; persistir, morar. 4. Continuar, seguir, proseguir (resume). 5. Continuar, seguir (go, extend/road, canal). -va. 1. Continuar; prolongar, perpetuar. 2. Continuar, seguir con (keep on). **Her health continues to improve,** su salud continúa o sigue mejorando. 3. Continuar, seguir con, proseguir (resume). **To be continued,** continuará. **Continued on page 96,** continúa en la pág. 96. 4. Prolongar (extend, prolong).

continued [kənˈtɪnjuːd] [kon-ti-niud], a. Continuo, no interrumpido (success); constante (support). **A continued fever,** fiebre continua. -pp. de CONTINUE.

continuedly [kənˈtɪnjuːdlɪ] [kon-ti-niud-li], adv. Continuadamente.

continuer [kənˈtɪnjuːər] [kon-ti-niuaʳ], s. Continuador, perseverador.

continuing [kənˈtɪnjʊɪŋ] [kon-ti-niuin] a. Continuado.

continuity [ˌkɒntɪˈnjuːɪtɪ] [kon-ti-nui-ti], s. 1. Continuidad, continuación, coherencia. 2. Unión, enlace, dependencia. **Solution of continuity,** (Med.) solución de continuidad, la división o destrucción de alguna parte del cuerpo humano.

continuous [kənˈtɪnjʊəs] [kon-ti-niuos], a. 1. Continuo, unido o sin espacio intermedio o interrupción aparente (line). (Cin.) **Continuous performance,** función continua, sesión continua, función continuada. 2. (Ling.) Continuo.

continuous s. (Ling.) **The continuous,** el continuo.

continuously [kənˈtɪnjʊəslɪ] [kon-ti-niuos-li] adv. Continuamente, sin interrupción.

continuum [kənˈtɪnjʊəm] [kon-ti-niuom] s. Continuo.

contort [kənˈtɔːt] [kon-tort], va. Torcer, contorcer. Contraer, crispar (face). **To contort one's body,** contorsionarse. V. CONTORTED. vn. Crisparse, contraerse. **His face contorted with pain,** se le crispó o se le contrajo el rostro de dolor.

contorted [kənˈtɔːtɪd] [kon-tor-ted], a. y pp. 1. Torcido, retorcido. **His face was contorted with pain,** tenía el rostro contraído o crispado de dolor (twisted). 2. (Bot.) Arrollado, envuelto. V. CONVOLUTE.

contortion [kənˈtɔːʃən] [kon-tor-shon], s. 1. Contorsión, retorcimiento. 2. Dislocación parcial. 3. (Bot.) Retorcimiento irregular del tallo o ramas de las plantas, a causa de interrupción en su crecimiento.

contortionist [kənˈtɔːʃənɪst] [kon-tor-sho-nist], s. Acróbata ejercitado en retorcer cuerpo o miembros. Contorsionista.

contour [ˈkɒntʊər] [kon-tuaʳ], s. Contorno o perfil (outline). **Contours,** pl. Curvas (curves). **Contour line,** curva de nivel, cota. **Contour map,** mapa acotado o topográfico.

contra [ˈkɒntrə] [kon-tra] prep. insep. Contra.

contraband [ˈkɒntrəbænd] [kon-tra-band], s. Contrabando, matute. **Contraband goods,** géneros de contrabando o prohibidos. -a. Prohibido, ilegal.

contrabandism [ˈkɒntrəbændɪzm] [kon-tra-ban-disem], s. Contrabando, importación de géneros prohibidos.

contrabandist [ˈkɒntrəbændɪst] [kon-tra-ban-dist], s. Contrabandista, matutero.

contrabass [ˈkɒntrəbɑːs] [kon-tra-bas], s. Contrabajo, instrumento de cuerda, una octava más bajo que el violón.

contraception [ˌkɒntrəˈsepʃən] [kon-tra-sep-shon], s. Medidas anticoncepcionales. Anticoncepción.

contraceptive [ˌkɒntrəˈseptɪv] [kon-tra-sep-tiv], s. y a. Contraceptivo, anticoncepcional; anticonceptivo, contraconceptivo.

contract [ˈkɒntrækt] [kon-trakt], va. 1. Contraer, apretar, estrechar, encoger, plegar; abreviar, compendiar. 2. Contraer algún vicio, hábito o costumbre. Contraer (debt, disease, muscle). 3. Contratar (person/place under contract). 4. Contraer esponsales. -vn. 1. Contraerse, encogerse (become smaller). 2. Contratar, pactar. **To contract with somebody for something,** celebrar un contrato con alguien para algo (enter into an agreement).

contract out Subcontratar (job, work).

contract, s. 1. Contrato, pacto, convención o convenio entre partes (agreement, document). Contrata (for public works, services). **To be under contract to somebody/something,** estar bajo contrato con alguien/algo. **To put something out to contract,** otorgar la contrata de o para algo. **To exchange contracts,** suscribir el contrato de compraventa (in UK: on property deal). **Contract law,** derecho contractual. **To sign a contract,** firmar o suscribir un contrato. 2. Esponsales. 3. Contra, escritura. 4. **To put out a contract on somebody,** ponerle precio a la cabeza de alguien (for murder). **Contract killer,** asesino a sueldo, sicario. -a. Prometido, afianzado.

contracted [ˈkɒntræktɪd] [kon-trak-ted], a. 1. No ancho o amplio; encogido. 2. Contraído, apretado, estrecho.

contractedly [ˈkɒntræktɪdlɪ] [kon-trak-tid-li], adv. De una manera apretada, contraída.

contractedness [ˈkɒntræktɪdnɪs] [kon-trak-tid-nes], s. 1. Contracción: apretamiento, opresión. 2. Estrechez de miras, ruindad, mezquindad.

contractibility [ˌkɒntræktɪˈbɪlɪtɪ] [kon-trak-ti-bi-li-ti], **contractibleness** [ˌkɒntrækˈtəblnɪs] [kon-trak-ta-bol-nes], s. Contractilidad.

contractible [ˈkɒntræktɪbl] [kon-trak-ti-bol], a. Que se puede contraer, susceptible de contracción.

contractile [ˈkɒntræktɪl] [kon-trak-til], a. (Med.) Contráctil, lo que puede contraerse; lo que puede producir contracción.

contracting [ˈkɒntræktɪŋ] [kon-trak-tin], a. Contratante. **The contracting parties,** las partes contratantes, los contrayentes.

contraction [ˈkɒntrækʃən] [kon-trak-shon], s. 1. Contracción. 2. (Gram.) La reducción de dos vocales o sílabas en una; abreviatura o abreviación.

contractor [ˈkɒntræktər] [kon-trak-toʳ], s. 1. Contratante. 2. Contratista, persona que por contrata ejecuta una obra material. **A firm of building contractors,** una empresa de construcciones.

contract-dance [ˈkɒntræktˌdɑːns] [kon-trakt-dans], s. Contradanza y la música de ese baile.

contradict [ˌkɒntrəˈdɪkt] [kon-tra-dikt], va. 1. Contradecir, negar lo que otro da por cierto; oponerse, contrariar (assert the opposite of/statement, person). **To contradict oneself,** contradecirse. 2. Contradecirse con (be inconsistent with/principles, spirit).

contradicter [ˌkɒntrəˈdɪktər] [kon-tra-dik-taʳ], s. Contradictor, el que contradice o se opone.

contradiction [ˌkɒntrəˈdɪkʃən] [kon-tra-dik-shon], s. Contradicción, oposición, implicación, contrariedad, incongruencia, repugnancia. **A contradiction in terms,** un contrasentido.

contradictorily [ˌkɒntrədɪkˈtərɪlɪ] [kon-tra-dik-to-ri-li], adv. Contradictoriamente.

contradictory [ˌkɒntrəˈdɪktərɪ] [kon-tra-dik-to-ri], a. Contradictorio, contrario, opuesto, que implica contradicción. -s. Contrariedad, inconsistencia. (Lóg.) Contradictoria, una de dos proposiciones, de las cuales la una afirma lo que la otra niega y no pueden ser a un mismo tiempo verdaderas, ni a un mismo tiempo falsas. **Contradictory temper,** espíritu de contradicción.

contradistinct [ˌkɒntrədɪˈstɪŋkt] [kon-tra-dis-tinkt], a. Distinguido por calidades opuestas, contradistinto.

contradistinction [ˌkɒntrədɪsˈtɪŋkʃən] [kon-tra-dis-tink-shon], s. Distinción por calidades opuestas. **In contradistinction,** por oposición, por contradistinción.

contradistinctive [ˌkɒntrəˈdɪstɪŋktɪv] [kon-tra-dis-tink-tiv], *a.* Contradistintivo.

contradistinguish [ˌkɒntrəˈdɪstɪŋgwɪʃ] [kon-tra-dis-tin-güish], *va.* Contradistinguir. *-vn.* Poner en oposición, distinguir por calidades opuestas.

contrafissure [ˌkɒntrəˈfɪʃʊər] [kon-tra-fi-shuaʳ], *s.* Contrafractura, abertura del cráneo por la parte opuesta a aquella donde se ha recibido un golpe.

contrail [ˈkɒntreɪl] [kon-treil], *s.* Estela de vapor.

contraindicant [ˌkɒntrəˈɪndɪkənt] [kon-tra-in-di-kant], **contraindication** [ˌkɒntrə,ɪndɪˈkeɪʃən] [kon-tra-in-di-kei-shon], *s.* Contraindicante, contraindicación, síntoma que indica la impropiedad de un remedio dado o tratamiento seguido.

contraindicate, *va.* Contraindicar.

contralto [kənˈtræltəʊ] [kon-tral-tou], *s. y a.* Contralto, la voz media entre el tiple y el tenor.

contranatural [ˌkɒntrəˈnætʃrəl] [kon-tra-na-tu-ral], *a.* Contranatural.

contraposition [ˌkɒntrəˈpɒsɪʃən] [kon-tra-po-si-shon], *s.* Contraposición.

contraption [kənˈtræpʃən] [kon-trap-shon] *s. (Coloq.)* Artilugio, artefacto.

contraregularity [kɒn,trəregjʊˈlærɪtɪ] [kon-tra-re-guiu-la-ri-ti], *s.* Contrariedad.

contrariant [kənˈtrɛərɪən] [kon-trea-rian], *a.* Repugnante, contradictorio.

contraries [kənˈtrɛərɪəs] [kon-tra-ries], *s. pl.* Contrarios, calidades o proposiciones opuestas o contrarias.

contrariety [kənˈtrətɪətɪ] [kon-tra-rie-ti], *s.* Contrariedad, repugnancia, oposición, inconsistencia, incompatibilidad.

contrarily [kənˈtrɛərɪlɪ] [kon-trea-ri-li], *adv.* Contrariamente, en contrario. **She behaves so contrarily,** hace todo lo contrario de lo que se le dice.

contrariness [kənˈtrɛərɪnəs] [kon-tra-ri-nes], *s.* Contrariedad.

contrariwise [kənˈtrɛərɪwaɪz] [kon-tra-uais], *adv.* Al contrario, al revés.

contrary [kənˈtrɛərɪ] [kon-tra-ri], *a.* Contrario, opuesto (opposed, opposite); contradictorio, discorde. **To be contrary to something,** ir en contra de algo. **Contrary to** (as prep.), contrariamente a, al contrario de. **He's so contrary,** siempre tiene que llevar la contraria (child, person). *-s.* Contrario (opposite). **The contrary,** lo contrario. **On the contrary,** al contrario o por el contrario. **I can say nothing to the contrary,** nada tengo que oponer a eso. **Unless you hear to the contrary,** a menos que se te informe de lo contrario. **Despite his assertions to the contrary...,** a pesar de sus declaraciones en sentido contrario...

contrary, *va. (Prov.)* Oponer, contradecir, impedir.

contrary-minded [kənˈtrɛərɪˌmaɪndɪd] [kon-tra-ri-main-did], *a.* De diverso parecer.

contrast [ˈkɒntrɑːst] [kon-trast], *s.* 1. Contraste, oposición. 2. Oposición, diferencia (difference). 3. *(Ret.)* Cf. ANTITHESIS. 4. *(Art, Cin., Fot.)* Contraste. **To be a contrast to somebody/something,** contrastar con alguien/algo. **By contrast,** por contraste, en comparación. **In contrast to/with,** en contraste con, a diferencia de.

contrast, *va.* Contrastar, comparar, oponer, demostrar desemejanza. **To contrast something/somebody with something/somebody,** comparar algo/a alguien con algo/alguien. *-vn.* Variar, quedar claramente diferenciado de otra cosa por medio de comparación (con la prep. *with*). Contrastar (differ). **Contrasting,** contrastante, opuesto (opinions, approaches).

contravallation [ˌkɒntrəvəˈleɪʃən] [kon-tra-va-lei-shon], *s.* Contravalación, construcción de una línea fortificada por el frente de los sitiadores de una plaza.

contravene [ˌkɒntrəˈviːn] [kon-tra-vin], *va.* Contravenir, ir en contra de lo que está mandado y dispuesto, infringir o violar un mandato o una ley.

contravener [ˌkɒntrəˈviːnər] [kon-tra-vi-naʳ], *s.* Contraventor, infractor; el que contraviene.

contravention [ˌkɒntrəˈvenʃən] [kon-tra-ven-shon], *s.* Contravención, infracción, quebrantamiento de lo mandado.

contraversion [ˌkɒntrəˈvɜːʃən] [kon-tra-ver-shon], *s.* Vuelta al lado opuesto.

contrayerva [ˌkɒntrəˈjɜːvə] [kon-tra-yer-va], *s. (Bot.)* Contrahierba, dorstenia, planta medicinal de la América tropical.

contretemps [ˌkɒntrəˈtɒmpz] [kon-tre-temps] *s.* Contratiempo.

contributary [kənˈtrɪbjʊtərɪ] [kon-tri-biu-ta-ri], *a. (Poco us.)* Contribuyente, contributario.

contribute [kənˈtrɪbjuːt] [kon-tri-biut], *va.* Contribuir, dar o pagar cada uno la cuota que le corresponde. Contribuir con, aportar, hacer una aportación o un aporte de (money, time). Aportar (suggestions, ideas). Escribir (article, poem, paper). *-vn.* Contribuir, ayudar, cooperar o concurrir con otros al logro de algún fin. **To contribute to something,** contribuir a algo (play significant part). Contribuir (give money). **They all contributed to his present,** todos contribuyeron con dinero para su regalo. **To contribute to something,** participar en algo. *(Journ.)* **To contribute to something,** escribir para algo.

contributer, *s. V.* CONTRIBUTOR.

contribution [ˌkɒntrɪˈbjuːʃən] [kon-tri-biu-shon], *s.* 1. Cooperación, contribución, la acción de contribuir o suministrar con otros para algún fin; también lo que se contribuye; la cuota o cantidad que se da entre muchos para algún fin público. Contribución (participation, part played). **To make a contribution to something,** hacer una contribución a algo. **His contribution to the debate,** su intervención en el debate. **Contribution-box,** caja para recibir dádivas o cuotas, p. ej. en una reunión pública. 2. Contribución (payment, donation); aportación, aporte (to a fund).

contributive [kənˈtrɪbjuːtɪv] [kon-tri-biu-tiv], *a.* Cooperante, lo que coopera; contribuyente, contribuidor.

contributor [kənˈtrɪbjʊtər] [kon-tri-biu-toʳ], *s.* Contribuidor, contribuyente. Colaborador (writer). **He's a regular contributor to the local paper,** escribe regularmente para el periódico local. Donante (donor).

contributory [kənˈtrɪbjʊtərɪ] [kon-tri-biu-to-ri], *a.* 1. Cooperante o contribuyente. 2. Que contribuye (factor, circumstance). De aportación obligatoria por parte del empleado (pension plan).

con trick [kənˈtrɪkt] [kon-trikt] *s. (Coloq.)* Timo, estafa.

contrite [ˈkɒntraɪt] [kon-trait], *a.* 1. Contrito, pesaroso, arrepentido, penitente. *Contrite,* entre los teólogos, es el penitente que tiene dolor de contricción, y *attrite,* el que tiene dolor de atrición. 2. *(Des.)* Quebrantado, machacado, magullado.

contriteness [ˈkɒntraɪtnɪs] [kon-trait-nes], *s.* Contrición, arrepentimiento.

contrition [kənˈtrɪʃən] [kon-tri-shon], *s.* 1. Contrición, arrepentimiento, pesar de haber ofendido a Dios por ser quien es. 2. *(Des.)* Pulverización.

contriturate [kənˈtrɪtjʊrəns] [kon-tri-tiu-rans], *va.* Triturar, pulverizar juntamente (con otra cosa).

contrivable [kənˈtraɪvəbl] [kon-trai-va-bol], *a.* Imaginable, que puede inventarse o proyectarse.

contrivance [kənˈtraɪvəns] [kon-trai-vans], *s.* 1. Idea, plan, designio, discurso, invención. Artilugio, aparato (device). 2. Traza, maña, treta, artificio (stratagem); concepto, maquinación.

contrive [kənˈtraɪv] [kon-traiv], *va.* 1. Idear, inventar, imaginar, discurrir medios para el logro de algún intento, darse maña. 2. Maquinar, tramar. *-vn.* Trazar, delinear, concertar, buscar un medio, maquinar.

contrivement [kənˈtraɪvmənt] [kon-traiv-ment], *s.* Traza, invención.

contriver [kənˈtraɪvər] [kon-trai-vaʳ], *s.* Trazador, autor, inventor.

control

control [kən'trəʊl] [kon-troul], *s*. 1. Control, contrarregistro que se tiene en algunas oficinas para servir de comprobante. 2. Sujeción, freno, dominio; control (ability to control, restrain); autoridad (authority). **To be beyond somebody's control,** estar fuera del control de alguien. **Circumstances beyond our control,** circunstancias ajenas a nuestra voluntad. **To be out of control,** estar fuera de control. **To get out of control,** descontrolarse. **He lost control of the car,** perdió el control del coche. 3. Censura, inspección (regulation, restriction). **Price control(s),** control de precios. 4. Poder, autoridad, control (command). **Who's in control here?,** ¿quién manda aquí? **To be in control of something,** dominar o controlar algo. **To gain/take control of something,** hacerse con el control de algo. **To have/lose control of something,** tener/perder el control de algo. **Without control,** sin control, sin límites. **Remote control,** control remoto. **He has no self-control,** carece de dominio sobre sí mismo, no puede contenerse. **To control oneself,** dominarse, contenerse, controlarse. **He is under control,** lograron dominarlo. 5. Botón de control (knob, switch). **Controls,** *pl.* mandos (of vehicle). 6. Control (headquarters, checkpoint). 7. Patrón de comparación (in experiment). **Control group,** grupo de control. 8. Dominio (skill, mastery).

control, *va*. 1. Reprimir, restringir, predominar; gobernar; refutar. 2. Registrar; examinar, criticar. 3. Controlar, ejercer control sobre (command/country, people); controlar, regular (regulate/temperature, flow); dirigir (traffic); controlar (inflation, growth). 3. Controlar (curb, hold in check/animal, fire); controlar, dominar (emotion). **To control oneself,** controlarse, dominarse. Controlar (manage, steer/vehicle, boat); controlar, dominar (horse). **Controlling interest,** *(Com.)* mayoría, interés predominante.

control column [kən'trəʊl,kʌləm] *s*. Palanca de mando.

control key [kən'trəʊl'ki:] [kon-troul-ki] *s*. Tecla de control.

controllable [kən'trəʊləbl] [kon-trou-la-bol], *a*. Sujeto a vista, registro, inspección o examen. **Controllable by,** sometido al imperio de.

controller [kən'trəʊlər] [kon-trou-laʳ], *s*. 1. Contralor, director, superintendente, mayordomo, veedor, registrador, censurador. **Controller of the Currency,** *(E. U.)* funcionario del gobierno que ejerce superintendencia sobre los bancos nacionales. 2. Controlador (device).

controllership [kən'trəʊləʃɪp] [kon-troulaʳ-ship], *s*. Contraloría, oficio y oficina de contralor; mayordomía, veeduría.

controlling [kən'trəʊlɪŋ] [kon-trou-lin] *a*. **Controlling interest,** participación mayoritaria o de control.

controlment [kən'trəʊlmənt] [kon-troul-ment], *s*. Restricción, sujeción.

control room [kən'trəʊl,rʊm] [kon-troul-rum] *s. (Mil., Naut.)* Centro de operaciones. *(Audio, Rad., TV)* Sala de control.

control tower [kən'trəʊl,taʊər] [kon-troul-tauaʳ], *s. (Aer.)* Torre de control.

controversial [ˌkɒntrə'vɜːʃəl] [kon-tro-ver-shal], *a*. Perteneciente a las controversias o disputas; polémico, contencioso, controvertido.

controversialist [ˌkɒntrə'vɜːʃəlɪst] [kon-tro-ver-sha-list], *s*. Controversista, contendor literario.

controversy [kɒn'trɒvəsi] [kon-tro-ver-si] *s*. Controversia, disputa, debate, pleito, contradicción.

controvert ['kɒntrəvɜːt] [kon-tro-vert], *va*. Controvertir, disputar o altercar sobre alguna cosa.

controverter ['kɒntrəvɜːtər] [kon-tro-ver-taʳ], **controvertist** ['kɒntrəvɜːtɪst] [kon-tro-ver-tist], *s*. Controversista, argumentador.

controvertible ['kɒntrəvɜːtɪbl] [kon-tro-ver-ti-bol], *a*. Controvertible, disputable.

contumacious [ˌkɒntjʊ'meɪʃəs] [kon-tu-mei-shos], *a*. Contumaz, rebelde, porfiado, obstinado, terco, tenaz, inflexible.

contumaciously [ˌkɒntjʊ'meɪʃəslɪ] [kon-tiu-mei-shos-li], *adv*. Contumazmente, pertinazmente.

contumaciousness [ˌkɒntjʊ'meɪʃəsnɪs] [kon-tiu-mei-shos-nis], *s*. Contumacia, obstinación, terquedad.

contumacy ['kɒntjʊməsɪ] [kon-tiu-ma-si], *s*. 1. Contumacia, rebeldía, resistencia a comparecer en juicio o a obedecer la ley. 2. Contumacia, tenacidad, dureza, terquedad; obstinación, porfía.

contumelious [ˌkɒntjʊ'məlɪəs] [kon-tiu-me-lios] *a*. Contumelioso, sarcástico, afrentoso.

contumeliousness [ˌkɒntjʊ'məlɪəsnɪs] [kon-tiu-me-lios-nes], **contumely** ['kɒntjʊməlɪ] [kon-tiu-me-li], *s*. Contumelia, baldón, ultraje, desprecio, injuria, menosprecio, insulto.

contuse [kɒn'tju:z] [kon-tius], *va*. Contundir, magullar, machacar, causar o hacer contusión.

contusion [kən'tju:ʒən] [kon-tiu-shon], *s*. 1. Contusión, magullamiento. 2. Golpe y el cardenal que de él resulta.

conundrum [kə'nʌndrəm] [ko-nan-drom], *s*. 1. Acertijo, adivinanza. 2. Cuestión o cosa intrincada.

conurbation [ˌkɒnɜː'beɪʃən] [ko-nur-bei-shon] *s*. Conurbación.

conure [kɒ'nʊər] [ko-nueʳ], *s*. Papagayo americano del género Conurus; a él pertenece la cotorra de Carolina.

convalesce [ˌkɒnvə'les] [kon-va-les] *vn*. Recuperarse, convalecer. **To convalesce after/from something,** convalecer o recuperarse de algo.

convalescence o convalescency [ˌkɒnvə'lesəns] [kon-va-le-sens], *s*. Convalecencia, restablecimiento de la salud, mejoría de una enfermedad.

convalescent [ˌkɒnvə'lesənt] [kon-va-le-sent], *a*. Convaleciente.

convalescent *s*. Convaleciente. **Convalescent home,** clínica de reposo.

convallaria [ˌkɒnvə'læriə] [kon-va-la-ria], *s. (Bot.)* Convalaria, el lirio de los valles.

convection [kən'vekʃən] [kon-vek-shon], *s*. El acto de llevar o transportar; convección, difusión del calor por un líquido o gas por medio del movimiento de sus partes componentes, lo cual la diferencia de la conducción. **Convection heater,** estufa o calentador de convección.

convective [kən'vektɪv] [kon-vek-tiv], *a*. Perteneciente o relativo a la difusión por convección.

convector [kən'vektər] [kon-vek-taʳ]*s*. Estufa o calentador de convección.

convenable [kən'vi:nəbl] [kon-vi-na-bol], *a*. Lo que puede juntarse.

convene [kən'vi:n] [kon-vin], *va*. 1. Convocar, congregar, juntar, unir. 2. Citar, emplazar o convocar jurídicamente. - *vn*. Convenir, juntarse, reunirse.

convener [kən'vi:nər] [kon-vi-naʳ], *s*. Convocador, el que convoca a una reunión.

convenience o conveniency [kən'vi:nɪəns] [kon-vi-niens], *s*. Conveniencia, comodidad (comfort, practicality); oportunidad, conformidad. **Does it suit your convenience?,** ¿le conviene a Vd.? **It is a great convenience,** es de gran comodidad. **At your convenience,** cuando le resulte conveniente. *(Corresp.)* **At your earliest convenience,** a la mayor brevedad posible, a la brevedad. **With every modern convenience,** con todas las comodidades modernas (amenity, appliance).

convenience food [kən'vi:nɪəns'fʊd] [kon-vi-niens-fud] *s*. Comida de preparación rápida.

convenient [kən'vi:nɪənt] [kon-vi-nient], *a*. Conveniente, apto, cómodo, oportuno, conforme, propio (opportune, suitable). **Would it be convenient for me to call tomorrow?,** ¿estaría bien que pasara mañana? **His resignation was most convenient for the firm,** su dimisión fue muy oportuna para la firma. Práctico, cómodo (neat, practical). **It's very convenient having the school so near,** resulta muy práctico tener la escuela tan cerca (handy).

conveniently, *adv.* Cómodamente; convenientemente (handily); útil y oportunamente. **It's conveniently situated,** está convenientemente situada. **The government conveniently forgets its election promises,** le resulta muy cómodo al gobierno olvidarse de sus promesas electorales. **Conveniently for him, the banks were closed,** le vino muy bien o le convino que los bancos estuvieran cerrados.

convening [kən'viːnɪŋ] [kon-vi-nin], *s.* Convención; reunión.

convent ['kɒnvənt] [kon-vent], *s.* 1. Convento; comunidad de personas religiosas que viven en una misma casa. 2. Casa que habita una comunidad. **Convent school,** colegio de monjas.

convent, *va.* *(Des.)* Citar o emplazar delante del juez. *-vn.* Concurrir, juntar.

conventicle ['kɒnvəntɪkl] [kon-ven-ti-kol], *s.* Conventículo, conciliábulo, junta clandestina e ilícita.

conventicler ['kɒnvəntɪklər] [kon-ven-ti-klaʳ], *s.* El que sostiene o frecuenta conventículos o conciliábulos.

convention [kən'venʃən] [kon-ven-shon], *s.* 1. Convención, asamblea, congreso, junta. 2. El acto de juntarse; cita, conferencia (conference). 3. Asenso o convenio general o tácito. 4. Contrato, capitulación, tratado, convención (agreement). 5. Convenciones, convencionalismos (social code). **Convention dictates that one should wear black on such occasions,** es costumbre vestir de negro en tales ocasiones. 6. Convención (established practice). **Literaty convention,** convención literaria.

conventional [kən'venʃənl] [kon-ven-sho-nal], *a.* 1. Convencional, estipulado (behavior, method, arms). 2. Convenido, establecido por costumbre, formal. 3. Elegido o considerado arbitrariamente como emblemático de alguna cosa. 4. (Bellas artes) Aceptado como habitual y acostumbrado, pero no necesariamente verdadero y natural; basado sobre la tradición. Tradicional, clásico (design, style).

conventionalism [kən'venʃənəlɪzm] [kon-ven-sho-na-lisem], *s.* Consideración y respeto para con lo que es de uso y costumbre; artificio, forma o ficción aceptada generalmente.

conventionality [kən'venʃənælɪtɪ] [kon-ven-sho-na-li-ti], *s.* Carácter artificial; algo establecido y aceptado por costumbre.

conventionally [kən'venʃənəlɪ] [kon-ven-sho-na-li] *adv.* De manera convencional (dress, behave); de manera tradicional o clásica (built, designed).

conventionist [kən'venʃənɪst] [kon-ven-sho-nist], *s.* Contratista.

conventual [kən'ventʃʊəl] [kon-ven-shual], *s.* Conventual, el que reside en un convento o es individuo de una comunidad. *-a.* Conventual, lo que pertenece al convento.

converge [kən'vɜːdʒ] [kon-verch], *vn.* Converger, dirigirse a un mismo punto, convergir (lines, roads); reunirse (crowd, armies). **They all converged on the square,** todos se reunieron en la plaza.

convergence, convergency [kən'vɜːdʒəns] [kon-ver-chens] *s.* Convergencia, tendencia hacia un mismo punto.

convergent [kən'vɜːdʒənt] [kon-ver-chent], **converging** [kən'vɜːdʒɪŋ] [kon-ver-chin], *a.* Convergente, que tiende hacia un mismo punto.

conversable [kən'vɜːsəbl] [kon-ver-sa-bol], *a.* Conversable, sociable.

conversableness [kən'vɜːsəblnɪs] [kon-ver-sa-bol-nes], *s.* Sociabilidad.

conversably [kən'vɜːsəblɪ] [kon-ver-sa-bli], *adv.* Sociablemente, afablemente.

conversant [kən'vɜːsənt] [kon-ver-sant], *a.* 1. Versado en, experimentado, familiar, conocedor de. 2. Empleado activamente, ocupado en, interesado. **To be conversant with something,** ser versado en algo.

conversation [ˌkɒnvə'seɪʃən] [kon-ver-sei-shon], *s.* 1. Conversación, conferencia, trato, familiaridad. **They were deep in conversation,** estaban en plena conversación. **To make polite conversation,** conversar como un gesto de amabilidad. **Conversation piece,** tema de conversación. 2. Conducta, porte. 3. Trato carnal.

conversational [ˌkɒnvə'seɪʃənl] [kon-ver-sei-sho-nal] *a.* Familiar, coloquial (manner, tone).

conversationalist [ˌkɒnvə'seɪʃnəlɪst] [kon-ver-sei-shona-list] *s.* Conversador. **He's not much of a conversationalist,** no es muy buen conversador.

conversative [kɒn'vɜːsətɪv] [kon-ver-sa-tiv], *a.* Conversable, sociable.

converse [kən'vɜːs] [kon-vers], *vn.* 1. Conversar, vivir con otro y tratar con él. 2. Conversar, tener conocimiento con alguno. 3. Platicar, hablar familiarmente sobre algún asunto. **To converse on/about something,** conversar sobre/acerca de algo. 4. Tratar con, tener trato ilícito con persona de otro sexo.

converse, *s.* 1. Conversación, plática, comunicación, familiaridad, trato, comercio. 2. Conversa, proposición opuesta a la directa; lo que existe en relación recíproca a otra cosa. 3. **The converse,** lo contrario o lo opuesto.

converse *a.* Contrario, inverso.

conversely [kɒn'vɜːsəlɪ] [kon-ver-se-li], *adv.* 1. Mutuamente, recíprocamente. 2. A la inversa (as linker).

conversion [kɒn'vɜːʃən] [kon-ver-shon], *s.* 1. Conversión, transmutación de una cosa a otra (transformation). **Conversion table,** table de conversión o de equivalencias. **Conversion from something to something,** conversión de algo a algo (change, switch). 2. Conversión, arrepentimiento. 3. *(Rel.)* Mudanza de una religión a otra; cambio de opinión, de partido. 4. *(For)* Apropiación ilícita de los bienes de otro para uso propio.

conversive [kɒn'vɜːsɪv] [kon-ver-siv], *a.* Conversivo, que causa conversión o que resulta de ella.

convert ['kɒnvɜːt] [kon-vert], *va.* 1. Convertir, transmutar. Remodelar, reformar (building); transformar (vehicle). **A converted barn,** un granero convertido en vivienda. **To convert pounds into/to kilos,** convertir libras a/en kilos. 2. Convertir, reducir al vicioso a la prática de las buenas costumbres (cause to change view). **To convert somebody to something,** convertir a alguien a algo. **A converted Jew,** un judío converso. 3. Convertir, volver, dirigir una cosa hacia una parte diversa de donde estaba antes. 4. Dar una cosa destino diverso del que antes tenía. 5. *(Com.)* Convertir o cambiar en valor de otra forma. 6. *(Sport)* Transformar, convertir. *-vn.* Convertirse, transformarse en algo (change into); mudarse.

convert, *s.* Converso o convertido, la persona que se ha convertido de una religión o parecer a otro diferente. **New convert,** neófito, recién convertido, converso, convertido; religioso lego.

converter, convertor [kən'vɜːtər] [kon-ver-tor], *s.* 1. Convertidor, el que convierte. 2. *(Metal.)* Convertido, retorta de cementación, aparato de Bessemer par convertir el hierro en acero. 3. Convertidor, transformador eléctrico. *V.* TRANSFORMER.

convertibility [kənˌvɜːtə'bɪlɪtɪ] [kon-ver-ti-bi-li-ti], *s.* Capacidad de conversión.

convertible [kən'vɜːtəbl] [kon-ver-ti-bol], *a.* Convertible, transmutable. *-s.* Convertible, automóvil convertible, descapotable. Sofá-cama (sofa bed).

convertibly [kən'vɜːtɪblɪ] [kon-ver-ti-bli], *adv.* Recíprocamente, mutuamente.

convertite [kən'vɜːtaɪt] [kon-ver-tait], *s.* Neófito, recién convertido.

convex [kɒn'veks] [kon-veks], *a.* Convexo, que tiene superficie curva más elevada en el centro que en los bordes u orillas; es lo contrario de cóncavo. *-s.* Cuerpo o superficie convexa.

convexed [kɒnˈvekst] [kon-vekst], *a.* Convexo, elevado en figura circular.

convexedly [kɒnˈveksdlɪ] [kon-vek-sed-li], *adv.* En forma o figura convexa.

convexity [kɒnˈveksɪtɪ] [kon-vek-si-ti], *s.* 1. Convexidad, superficie exterior de un cuerpo convexo; forma esférica o convexa. 2. Combadura, comba.

convexly [kɒnˈvekslɪ] [kon-veks-li], *adv.* Convexamente.

convexness [kɒnˈveksnɪs] [kon-veks-nes], *s.* Convexidad.

convexo-concave [ˈkɒnˈveksəˈkɒnˌkeɪv] [kon-veksou-kon-keiv], *a.* Convexo-cóncavo.

convey [kənˈveɪ] [kon-vei], *va.* 1. Transportar, conducir o llevar una parte a otra (goods, people, electricity). 2. Transmitir, llevar (sound); enviar; expresar, transmitir (opinion, feeling); hacer llegar (thanks). 3. Transferir, traspasar a otro. 4. Participar, dar parte o noticia de alguna cosa. 5. Comunicar, expresar (el sentido de las palabras). **To convey away,** quitar del miedo, hacer desaparecer, llevarse una cosa, ocultar. **To convey out,** poner fuera de alcance, salvar. **To convey out of danger,** sacar del peligro. **To convey his sense,** expresar su pensamiento.

conveyable [kənˈveɪəbl] [kon-ve-ya-bol], *a.* Capaz de ser transportado o conducido.

conveyance [kənˈveɪəns] [kon-ve-yans], *s.* 1. Conducción, transporte (transport); vehículo, medio de transporte (vehicle). 2. Conducción, modo o manera de conducir o transportar. 3. Entrega. 4. Traspaso o traslación de dominio. 5. Escritura de traspaso.

conveyancer [kənˈveɪənsər] [kon-ve-yan-saʳ], *s.* El escribano que hace la escritura de traspaso, enajenación o traslación de dominio.

conveyancing [kənˈveɪənsɪŋ] [kon-ve-yan-sin], *s.* El oficio de preparar las escrituras de traspaso, incluyendo la pesquisa de títulos.

conveyor [kənˈveɪər] [kon-ve-yaʳ], *s.* 1. Conductor, mensajero. 2. Portador, invento mecánico para transportar material, como en molinos, elevadores, etc. 3. *(Des.)* Truhán, impostor; ladrón. **Conveyor belt,** correa o cinta transportadora, banda transportadora.

convict [ˈkɒnvɪkt] [kon-vikt], *va.* 1. Convencer, probar la culpabilidad; declarar culpable después de un proceso judicial, condenar. **A convicted murderer,** un asesino convicto. **To be convicted of something,** ser condenado por algo. 2. Confutar, refutar, destruir los argumentos del contrario.

convict, *s.* Convicto, el reo a quien legalmente se le ha probado su delito; recluso, presidiario.

convictible [ˈkɒnvɪktɪbl] [kon-vik-ti-bol], *a.* Convencible.

conviction [kənˈvɪkʃən] [kon-vik-shon], *s.* 1. Convicción, demostración de culpabilidad; juicio basado en pruebas suficientes: proposición firmemente creída. 2. Convicción, la prueba de un delito. 3. Confutación, refutación. 4. *(Law)* Condena. 5. Convicción (certainty, strong belief). **To speak without conviction,** hablar sin convicción. **Their claims carry little conviction,** lo que sostienen es poco convincente.

convictive [kɒnˈvɪktɪv] [kon-vik-tiv], *a.* (Poco us.) Convincente.

convictively [kɒnˈvɪktɪvlɪ] [kon-vik-tiv-li], *adv.* Convincentemente.

convince [kənˈvɪns] [kon-vins], *va.* 1. Convencer, precisar a otro con razones a que mude de dictamen; hacer creer. **To convince somebody of something,** convencer a alguien de algo. **To convince somebody that,** convencer a alguien de que. **To convince somebody to,** convencer a alguien para que. 2. Poner en evidencia, juzgar. 3. *(Des.)* Declarar culpable. V. CONVICT.

convinced [kənˈvɪnst] [kon-vinst] *a.* **To be convinced of something,** estar convencido de algo. **To be convinced that,** estar convencido de que.

convincement [kənˈvɪnsmənt] [kon-vins-ment], *s.* Convicción.

convincer [kənˈvɪnsər] [kon-vin-saʳ], *s.* El lo que convence.

convincible [kənˈvɪnsəbl] [kon-vin-se-bol], *a.* Convencible; convincente, incontestable.

convincing [kənˈvɪnsɪŋ] [kon-vin-sin] *a.* Convincente.

convincingly [kənˈvɪnsɪŋlɪ] [kon-vin-sin-li], *adv.* Convincentemente.

convincingness [kənˈvɪnsɪŋnɪs] [kon-vin-sin-nes], *s.* Convicción, evidencia y fuerza de la razón que convence.

convivial [kənˈvɪvɪəl] [kon-vi-vial], *a.* 1. Festivo relativo a festín o convite. 2. Convivial, festivo, jovial. 3. Cordial, de camaradería (atmosphere); simpático, sociable (person).

conviviality [kənˈvɪvɪəlɪtɪ] [kon-vi-via-li-ti], *s.* Jovialidad, buen humor.

convocate [ˈkɒnvəkeɪt] [kon-vo-keit], *va.* Convocar, citar, llamar a muchos que deben juntarse en un lugar determinado para algún fin.

convocation [ˌkɒnvəˈkeɪʃən] [kon-vo-kei-shon], *a.* 1. Convocación, acción de convocar o de reunir. 2. Asamblea así convocada, especialmente junta de clero o sínodo.

convoke [ˈkɒnvəʊk] [kon-vouk], *va.* Convocar, citar, juntar, reunir.

convolute, convoluted [ˈkɒnvəˌluːt] [kon-vo-lut], *a.* 1. Arrollado, envuelto, replegado. 2. Intrincado, enrevesado (story, argument). *-s.* Lo que está arrollado.

convolution [ˌkɒnvəˈluːʃən] [kon-vo-lu-shon], *s.* 1. La acción de arrollar o envolver. 2. Repliegue, enroscadura. *(Anat.)* Una de las sinuosidades o senos de un órgano, especialmente del cerebro o del intestino.

convolve [ˈkɒnvɔːlv] [kon-volv], *va.* Arrollar, revolver, retorcer una cosa en sí misma. *-vn.* Revolver o enlazarse sobre sí mismo.

convolvulaceous [kənˈvɒlvjʊələʃəs] [kon-vol-viu-la-shos], *a.* *(Bot.)* Convolvuláceo, semejante o relativo al convólvulo.

convolvulus [kənˈvɒlvjʊləs] [kon-vol-viu-lus], *s.* Convólvulo, género de plantas cuyo tipo es la correhuela o albohol y que comprende también el dondiego, la batata, la jalapa, etc.

convoy [ˈkɒnvɔɪ] [kon-voi], *va.* Convoyar, escoltar lo que se conduce por mar o por tierra para que vaya resguardado.

convoy, *s.* 1. Convoy o conserva, escolta o guardia que se destina para la segura conducción por mar o por tierra. 2. Convoy, los efectos, valores o pertrechos que van escoltados (of ship, vehicles). 3. La acción de convoyar; el estado de ser convoyado.

convulse [kənˈvʌls] [kon-vals], *va.* 1. Convulsar, causar la contradicción de los músculos; afectar espasmódicamente; agitar violentamente. **He was convulsed with pain,** se retorcía de dolor (contort). **Their antics convulsed the audience,** el público se desternillaba de risa con sus payasadas. 2. Convulsionar, sacudir (shake, rock). *-vn.* Convelerse, convulsarse, irritarse, alterarse o ponerse en convulsión las fibras del cuerpo **To be convulsed with laughter,** morirse de risa.

convulsion [kənˈvʌlʃən] [kon-val-shon], *s.* 1. Convulsión, espasmo (spasm). **Their antics had us in convulsions,** nos desternillamos de risa con sus payasadas. 2. Agitación violenta, inquietud. 3. Conmoción, alboroto, revolución, tumulto. 4. *(Geol.)* V. CATACLYSM.

convulsionary [kənˈvʌlʃənərɪ] [kon-val-sho-na-ri], *a.* De la convulsión; que causa convulsiones o es resultado de ellas.

convulsive [kənˈvʌlsɪv] [kon-val-siv], *a.* Convulsivo. **He collapsed into convulsive laughter,** le dio un ataque de risa.

convulsively [kənˈvʌlsɪvlɪ] [kon-val-siv-li], *adv.* Tumultuariamente; convulsivamente.

cony [ˈkəʊnɪ] [kou-ni], *s.* Conejo. **Cony-skins** o **Wool,** V. RABBIT-SKINS O WOOL.

cony-burrow [ˈkəʊnɪˈbʌrəʊ], *s.* Conejera, vivar o madriguera donde se crían los conejos.

coo [kuː] [ku], *vn.* 1. Arrullar, cantar, como paloma o tórtola o zurear (dove, pigeon). **Everyone was cooing over the baby,**

todos estaban bobos con el bebé. 2. Decir ternezas. (Fam.) Enamorar. va. Susurrar.

cooing ['kuːɪŋ] [kuin], s. 1. Arrullo de palomas o tórtolas. 2. (Fig.) Arrullo, halago, caricia.

cook [kʊk] [kuk], va. 1. Cocinar, guisar, aderezar las viandas. Hacer, preparar (food, meal). 2. Falsificar, alterar para engañar, amañar (falsify/books, accounts). -vn. Guisar, cocinar (prepare food); hacerse (become ready/food).

cook up, Tramar, maquinar en secreto (scheme); inventarse (alibi).

cook s. Cocinero. **He's a good cook,** cocina muy bien, es muy buen cocinero. **Too many cooks spoil the broth,** muchas manos en un plato hacen mucho garabato. **Cook's shop,** bodegón. **Cook-maid,** cocinera. **Cook-room,** cocina; (Mar.) fogón de un buque.

cookbook ['kʊkbʊk] [kuk-buk] s. Libro de cocina o de recetas, recetario.

cooked [kʊkt] [kukt] a. Cocido (ham); caliente (meal, breakfast). **It's not quite cooked yet,** le falta un poco todavía. **Cooked meats,** fiambres.

cooker ['kʊkər] [ku-kaʳ] s. (GB) Cocina o estufa (stove).

cookery ['kʊkərɪ] [ku-ke-ri], s. Arte de cocina, el arte de componer las viandas; también, lugar para cocinar. **Cookery book,** V. COOKBOOK.

cookie ['kʊkɪ] [ku-ki] s. Galleta, galletita (biscuit). **That's the way the cookie crumbles,** ¡qué se le va a hacer!, ¡así es la vida! **He was caught with his hand in the cookie jar,** lo agarraron o lo pillaron con las manos en la masa. (Coloq.) **She's a smart cookie,** es más lista que el hambre (person). **He's a tough cookie,** es un tipo durísimo.

cooking ['kʊkɪŋ] [ku-kin], s. 1. Cocina, arte de cocinar. **To do the cooking,** cocinar. **It's used in cooking,** se usa para cocinar o en cocina. **Home cooking,** la cocina casera. **His cooking is awful,** cocina muy mal. **Spanish cooking,** la cocina o la gastronomía española. 2. Comestible (oil); para cocinar (sherry, apple); de cocina (utensils). -a. De cocina. **Cooking range, cooking stove,** estufa, cocina económica. **Cooking utensils,** batería o enseres de cocina.

cookout ['kʊkaʊt] [kuk-aut] s. Comida al aire libre.

cooky ['kʊkɪ] [ku-ki], s. Pequeño bollo dulce. V. COOKIE.

cool [kuːl] [kul], a. 1. Frío, fresco (drink); fresco (cold/climate, air, clothes). **It's cool outside,** hace o está fresco fuera. 2. Tibio, flojo, indiferente, poco fervoroso (reserved, hostile/reception, behavior). **To be cool to/toward somebody,** estar frío con alguien. 3. Sereno, tranquilo (calm). **Keep cool!,** ¡tranquilo!, no te pongas nervioso. **Cool, calm and collected,** tranquilo y sereno. **To play it cool,** tomarse las cosas con calma. 4. Impasible (unperturbed). **He's a very cool customer,** tiene una sangre fría impresionante. (Sl.) **She's really cool,** está muy en la onda (trendy, laid-back). (Coloq.) **A cool one million dollars,** la friolera de un millón de dólares.

cool s. 1. Frescura o fresco. **Let's stay here in the cool,** quedémonos aquí al fresco (low temperature). **In the cool of the evening,** por la tarde cuando está o hace fresco. 2. Calma (composure). **To keep/lose one's cool,** mantener/perder la calma.

cool, va. Enfriar, refrescar, entibiar, atemperar, dulcificar, sosegar o templar la ira (enthusiasm); enfriar (engine, food); refrigerar (air, room). **To cool somebody's temper,** apaciguar a alguien. **Cool it, you two! we don't want any fights in here,** ya está bien, que aquí no queremos peleas. **Cool it! he's watching us,** disimula, que nos está mirando. -vn. 1. Refrescar, enfriarse, templarse, moderar el enojo o cualquier pasión. **To cool the heels,** estar aguardando mucho tiempo, hacer antesala cansada y larga. 2. Refrigerarse (air, room); enfriarse (engine, food, enthusiasm). **To cool toward somebody/something,** perder el entusiasmo por alguien/algo.

cool down 1. Enfriarse (become cooler/food, iron); refrescarse (person); calmarse (become calmer/temper,

person). 2. Enfriar (make cooler/food); refrescar (person); calmar (make calmer/person).

cool off Refrescarse (become cooler/person); calmarse (become calmer); enfriarse (lose enthusiasm, passion).

coolant ['kuːlənt] [ku-lant] s. Líquido refrigerante.

cool-cup [kuːl'kʌp] [kul-kap] s. Bebida hecha de vino, agua, azúcar y borraja.

-cooled [kuːld] [kuld] suff. **Air/water-cooled,** enfriado por aire/agua. **Gas-cooled reactor,** reactor enfriado por gas.

cooler ['kuːlər] [ku-laʳ], s. 1. Enfriadera garapiñera, garrafa. La vasija en que se enfría alguna cosa. Refrigerador (container, device). 2. (Med.) Regrigerante. (Sl.) **In the cooler,** a la sombra (in jail); en el calabozo (in a cell).

cool-headed ['kuːlˌhedɪd] [kul-je-did], a. Tibio, no fácilmente perturbado o excitado; que obra con calma y deliberación. Sereno.

coolie ['kuːlɪ] [ku-li], s. Peón chino o de la India que trabaja con contrata.

cooling ['kuːlɪŋ] [ku-lin], a. 1. Refrescante, fresco, refrigerativo (drink, swim). 2. Tibio, flojo.

cooling-off [ˌkuːlɪŋ'ɒf] [ku-lin-of] s. Enfriamiento. **Cooling-off period,** período de reflexión. **Cooling-off tower,** torre de refrigeración.

coolish ['kuːlɪʃ] [ku-lish], a. Fresco, un poco frío.

coolly ['kuːlɪ] [ku-li], adv. Frescamente, serenamente, fríamente, con frialdad (with reserve, hostility). Con serenidad o calma (calmly); descaradamente, con la mayor frescura (boldly).

coolness ['kuːlnɪs] [kul-nes], s. 1. Fresco, frío; frescor, frescura (in temperature). 2. Frialdad, tibieza. 3. Frescura, serenidad de ánimo; sangre fría (calmness); descaro, frescura (boldness). 4. Frialdad (reserve, hostility).

coom [kuːm] [kum], s. 1. Hollín de horno. 2. El unto negro que despiden los ejes de las ruedas de carros y coches.

coomb [kuːm] [kum], s. Antigua medida inglesa de cuatro fanegas.

coon [kuːn] [kun], s. V. RACCOON. **A coon's age,** mucho tiempo. **An old coon,** persona astuta y mañosa. **A gone coon,** (E.U.) persona o cosa en situación o condición desesperada.

coop [kuːp] [kup], s. 1. Caponera, gallinero, jaula para capones y otras aves. **Chicken/hen coop,** gallinero. 2. Redil para ganado lanar. 2. Tonel, barril grande de madera para líquidos. 4. (Esco.) Chirrión. V. TUMBREL.

coop, va. Enjaular, encarcelar.

coop up Encerrar.

co-op ['kəʊ'ɒp] [kou-op] s. Cooperativa.

cooper ['kuːpər] [ku-peʳ], s. Tonelero, el que hace o fabrica toneles, pipas o cubas.

cooperage ['kuːpərɪdʒ] [ku-pe-rich], s. 1. Jornal de tonelero, el dinero que se le da por su trabajo. 2. Todo lo perteneciente a la tonelería.

cooperant [kəʊ'ɒpərənt] [kou-o-pe-rant], a. Cooperante, el que o lo que coopera.

cooperate [kəʊ'ɒpəreɪt] [kou-o-pe-reit], vn. 1. Cooperar, colaborar, obrar de consumo para un mismo fin. 2. Contribuir con algo o de alguna manera para la perfección o consecución de una cosa y objeto.

cooperation [kəʊˌɒpə'reɪʃən] [kou-o-pe-rei-shon], s. Cooperación, colaboración.

cooperative [kəʊ'ɒpərətɪv] [kou-o-pe-ra-tiv], a. 1. Cooperativo; cooperante. De colaboración, cooperativo (obliging/attitude). **He was very cooperative,** se mostró muy dispuesto a cooperar o colaborar. 2. Conjunto (effort, venture); en régimen de cooperativa (collective/farm). **Cooperative society/store,** cooperativa.

cooperative, s. Cooperativa.

cooperator ['kəʊ'ɒpəreɪtər] [kou-o-pe-rei-toʳ], s. Cooperador.

coopering [kəˈʊpərɪŋ] [kou-o-pe-rin], *s.* Tonelería el arte de tonelero.

co-opt [ˈkəʊˈɒpt] [kou-opt] *va.* **To co-opt somebody onto a committee,** invitar a alguien a formar parte de una comisión.

co-optate [ˈkəʊˈɒpteɪt] [kou-op-teit], *va.* Adoptar por acción mutua, admitir, agregar.

coordinate [ˈkəʊˈɔːdɪnɪt] [kou-or-di-neit] *a.* Coordinado. *s.* (*Mat.*) Coordenada. **Coordinates,** *pl.* prendas para combinar, coordinados.

coordinate *va.* 1. Coordinar (make function together). 2. Combinar, coordinar (clothes).

coordinately [ˈkəʊˈɔːdɪnɪtlɪ] [kou-or-di-neit-li], *adv.* Coordinadamente.

coordinateness [ˈkəʊˈɔːdɪnɪtnɪd] [kou-or-di-neit-nes], **coordination** [kəʊˌɔːdɪˈneɪʃən] [kou-or-di-nei-shon], *s.* Coordinación, método, colocación o distribución de alguna cosa.

coordinator [ˈkəʊˈɔːdɪneɪtər] [kou-or-di-nei-toˈ] *s.* Coordinador.

coot [kuːt] [kut], *s.* (*Orn.*) Negreta, especie de ánade de color muy obscuro.

cootie [ˈkuːtɪ] [ku-ti] *s.* (*Sl.*) Piojo (louse).

cop [kɒp] [kop], *s.* 1. Cima, cumbre, punta. 2. Moño, copa, copete. 3. (*Art. y Of.*) Penacho, manojito de hilos que se forma sobre el huso de una máquina de hilar.

cop, *s.* (*Ger.*) 1. Agente de policía. (*Coloq.*) Poli, tira, cana, cachaco, paco, bofia, madero (police officer). **To play cops and robbers,** jugar a policías y ladrones. 2. **To be not much cop,** no ser nada del otro mundo o del otro jueves (good, use).

cop *va.* 1. Llevarse (win/medal, prize). (*Coloq.*) (GB) **Cop (a load of) this/him/her!** ¡no te lo pierdas! (get). **You'll cop it if they find out,** como se enteren estás arreglado, o te vas a llevar una buena. 2. Agarrar, pillar, pescar (catch, seize).

cop out (*Sl.*) Rajarse, evadirse. **To cop out of something,** escabullirse de algo, sacarle el cuerpo a algo (of responsibility, task).

copal [ˈkɒpəl] [ko-pal], *s.* Goma copal o ánime; resina dura y transparente empleada para barnices.

coparcenary [ˈkɒpɑːsənərɪ] [ko-par-se-na-ri], **coparceny** [ˈkɒpɑːsənɪ] [ko-par-se-ni], *s.* (*For.*) Derecho igual por sucesión a alguna herencia.

copartner [ˈkɒpɑːtnər] [ko-part-naˈ], *s.* Compañero, socio, asociado, el que tiene parte en una empresa o comercio.

copartnership [ˈkɒpɑːtnəˈʃɪp] [ko-part-ner-ship], *s.* Compañía, sociedad, asociación; parte o interés en una empresa, negocio, etc.

cope [kəʊp] [koup], *s.* 1. Lo que cubre formando arco o curva, como la bóveda del cielo, la cima de cúpulas, paredes, etc.; albardilla. 2. Capa pluvial.

cope, *va.* (*Des.*) Contener, disputar, pleitear. *-vn.* Competir o lidiar con otro en condiciones iguales; hacer cara; sobresalir. **To cope with stress,** saber sobrellevar el estrés. **I can't cope with all this work,** no doy abasto o no puedo con tanto trabajo. **How do you cope without a washing machine?,** ¿cómo te las arreglas sin lavadora? **I just can't cope any more,** ya no puedo más.

cope, *va.* 1. Cubrir o vestir con capa pluvial. 2. Poner albardilla o caballete sobre un muro. 3. (*Ant.*) Recompensar, dar en cambio, cambiar, trocar.

copeck [ˈkəʊpek] [ko-pek], *s.* Moneda rusa de un rublo. *V.* KOPEK.

Copenhagen [ˌkəʊpnˈheɪɡən] [kou-pen-ja-guen] *N.* (*Geogr.*) Copenhague.

copernican [kəˈpɜːnɪkn] [ko-per-ni-kan], *a.* Copernicano, lo que pertenece al sistema de Copérnico.

copestone [ˈkəʊpstəʊn] [koup-stoun], *s.* Piedra de una pared que sirve de cima o tope.

copier [ˈkɒpɪər] [ko-piaˈ], *s.* 1. Copiante, copista. 2. Copiador, plagiario. 3. Fotocopiadora.

copilot [ˈkəʊˈpaɪlət] [kou-pai-lot] *s.* Copiloto.

coping [ˈkəʊpɪŋ] [kou-pin], *s.* Albardilla, el caballete que se forma sobre una pared para que no la penetren y calen las lluvias; cumbre de edificio.

copious [ˈkəʊpɪəs] [kou-pios], *a.* Copioso, abundante, difuso, rico.

copiously [ˈkəʊpɪəslɪ] [kou-pios-li], *adv.* Copiosamente, ampliamente.

copiousness [ˈkəʊpɪəsnɪs] [kou-pios-nes], *s.* Abundancia, redundancia; difusión; profusión, copia.

copivi [ˈkəʊpɪvɪ] [ko-pi-vi], *s. V.* COPAIBA.

cop-out [ˈkɒpaʊt] [kop-aut] *s.* (*Coloq.*) **That's just a cop-out,** eso es evadirse.

copped [ˈkɒpt] [kopt], *a.* Copado, copetudo.

coppel [ˈkɒpəl] [kou-pel], *s. V.* CUPEL.

copper [ˈkɒpər] [ko-paˈ], *s.* 1. Cobre, un metal, rojizo y dúctil. 2. Calderón, caldera grande. 3. Vellón, moneda de cobre; centavo, penique. **Coppers,** *pl.* peniques, perras, quintos, chauchas, vintenes. **Copper-colored,** color cobrizo; se aplica especialmente a los indios americanos. **Copper-nickel,** *V.* NICOOLITE. 4. *V.* COP (police officer).

copper, *va.* 1. Encobrar, cubrir o revestir con hojas de cobre; forrar de cobre un buque. 2. En el juego de faraón, poner un centavo sobre las monedas o las fichas apuntadas a una carta; lo cual significa apostar en contra.

copperas [ˈkɒpərəs] [ko-pe-ras], *s.* Caparrosa, vitriolo verde, sulfato de hierro.

copperhead [ˈkɒpəhed] [ko-per-jed], *s.* Culebra norteamericana muy venenosa, parecida a la cascabel.

copperish [ˈkɒpərɪʃ] [ko-pe-rish], **coppery** [ˈkɒpərɪ] [ko-pe-ri], *a.* Cobrizo, cobreño, lo que contiene cobre, se le asemeja o es de su color.

copperplate [ˈkɒpəpleɪt] [ko-paˈ-pleit], *s.* Lámina de cobre, la plancha de cobre de que se sirven los grabadores para grabar. **Copperplate prints,** estampas, láminas o grabados. **Copperplate handwriting,** letra de caligrafía.

coppersmith [ˈkɒpəsmɪθ] [ko-pes-miz], *s.* Calderero.

copper sulphate [ˈkɒpəsʌlfeɪt] [ko-per-sal-feit], *s.* Sulfato de cobre, vitriolo azul.

copper-work [ˈkɒpəwɔːk] [ko-per-uek] *s.* Fábrica de cobre.

copperworm [ˈkɒpəwɔːm] [ko-per-uem], *s.* 1 Broma, gusano que agujerea la madera de los buques. 2. Polilla, insecto que roe la ropa. 3. Arador, insecto que produce comezón en la piel.

coppice [ˈkɒpɪs] [ko-pis], **copse** [ˈkɒpz] [ko-z] *s.* Bosquecillo. Soto, tallar, monte bajo, bosque que se corta a menudo.

copple-dust [kɒplˈdʌst] [ko-pel-dast], *s. V.* CUPELDUST.

coppied [ˈkɒpɪd] [ko-pid], *a.* Lo que se eleva en forma cónica. *V.* COPPED.

copra [ˈkɒprə] [ko-pra], *s.* Copra, médula del coco de la palma.

coproprietor [ˌkɒprəprɪˈeɪtər] [ko-pro-pi-ei-toˈ], *s.* Copropietario, el que posee juntamente con otro alguna cosa.

copse [kɒps] [kops], *va.* Conservar los bosques recién cortados.

copsy [ˈkɒpsɪ] [kop-si], *a.* Lo que pertenece a los montes bajos.

copt [kɒpt] [kopt], *s.* Copto, descendiente de los antiguos egipcios.

coptic [ˈkɒptɪk] [kop-tik], *a.* Cóptico, relativo a los coptos. - *s.* Copto, la lengua antigua de los egipcios cristianos.

copula [ˈkɒpjʊlə] [ko-piu-la], *s.* (*Gram. y Lóg.*) 1. Cópula, el verbo que une el predicado con el sujeto. 2. En un órgano, *V.* COUPLER. 3. (*Anat.*) Parte que une o junta.

copulate [ˈkɒpjʊleɪt] [ko-piu-leit], *va.* Unir, juntar o estrechar una cosa con otra de modo que no pueda haber mediación o cosa intermedia. *-vn.* Ayuntarse o unirse; tener coito el macho con la hembra o una mujer.

copulation [kɒpjʊˈleɪʃən] [ko-piu-lei-shon], *s.* Cópula, coito, unión del macho con la hembra y en particular del hombre con la mujer; conjunción.

copulative [ˈkɒpjʊlətɪv] [ko-piu-la-tiv], *a. (Gram.)* Copulativo, conjuntivo. -*s. (Gram.)* Conjunción.

copulatory [ˈkɒpjʊlətərɪ] [ko-piu-la-to-ri], *a.* 1. De la cópula o perteneciente a ella. 2. *V.* COPULATIVE.

copy [ˈkɒpɪ] [ko-pi], *s.* 1. Copia, traslado sacado a la letra de cualquier escrito original. 2. Original, el manuscrito que se da a imprimir (unprinted matter). 3. Instrumento legal de entrega. 4. Copia de una pintura o modelo de una estatua. 5. Ejemplar de algún libro (of newspaper, book). **Back copy,** número atrasado. 6. Muestra. **A fair copy,** copia en limpio. **Rough copy,** borrador, minuta. **Good news doesn't make good copy,** las buenas noticias no se venden bien.

copy, *va.* Copiar, trasladar algún escrito (reproduce, transcribe); imitar, copiarle a (imitate/painter, singer); copiar (style, behavior). **To copy something from/off somebody,** copiarle algo a alguien. **To copy something from/out of something,** copiar algo de algo. Fotocopiar (photocopy). -*vn.* Imitar, contrahacer.

copybook [ˈkɒpɪbʊk] [ko-pi-buk], *s.* 1. Cuaderno para planas u otros usos. 2. Cuaderno de escritura; copiador de cartas, libro en que se copian las cartas. **To blot one's copybook,** manchar su reputación.

copycat [ˈkɒpɪkæt] [ko-pi-kat] *s.* Copión, imitamonos; inspirado en otros (journ./murder).

copyer [ˈkɒpɪər] [ko-pie^r], **copyist** [ˈkɒpɪɪst] [ko-pi-ist], *V.* COPIER.

copyhold [ˈkɒpɪhəʊld] [ko-pi-jold], *s. (For.)* Especie de enfiteusis, arrendamiento temporal, tenencia de tierras por censo o por feudo.

copyholder [ˌkɒpɪˈhəʊldər] [ko-pi-jol-da^r], *s.* 1. Aparato para colocar el original (en las imprentas). 2. El que lee en voz alta al corrector de pruebas. 3. *(For.)* Arrendador.

copying [ˈkɒpɪɪŋ] [ko-pi-in], *s.* y *pa.* de TO COPY. **Copying-ink,** tinta de copiar, que contiene azúcar, glicerina o sustancia parecida, y se usa en la prensa de copiar. **Copying-paper,** papel muy delgado que se usa en el copiador de cartas. **Copying-press,** prensa de copiar o copiador de cartas; también, aparato que sirve para sacar numerosas reproducciones de cartas, circulares, etc.

copyright [ˈkɒpɪraɪt] [ko-pi-rait], *s.* La propiedad de una obra literaria. Copyright, derechos de reproducción. **Copyright law,** ley de propiedad intelectual.

copywriter [ˈkɒpɪraɪtər] [ko-pi-rai-ta^r] *s.* Redactor publicitario.

coquet [ˈkɒket] [ko-ket], *va.* y *vn.* 1. Coquetear, hacer coqueterías, tener ademanes o conducta de coqueta. 2. Cocar, hacer cocos, requebrar, cortejar, galantear.

coquetry [ˈkɒketrɪ] [ko-ke-tri], *s.* Coquetería, afectación en el vestir y hablar para agradar y perecer bien; insconstancia o veleidad en las mujeres.

coquette [kəˈket] [ko-ket], *sf.* 1. Coqueta, dama presumida de hermosa, petimetra. 2. Carantoñera, mujer que gusta verse cortejada, y hace lo posible para serlo de muchos a un tiempo.

coquettish [kəˈketɪʃ] [ko-ke-tish], *a.* De coqueta; dispuesta a hacer coqueterías.

coracoid [ˈkɒrəkɔɪd] [ko-ra-koid], *s. (Anat.)* Coracoides, apófisis del omoplato.

coral [ˈkɒrəl] [ko-ral], *s.* 1. Coral, despojo sólido de una agregación de pólipos. 2. Coral, género de pólipo zoofitario cuyo polípero es arborizado. **Coral reef,** arrecife de coral, barrera coralina. 3. Coral (color). -*a.* Coralino, de coral; parecido al coral.

coralline [ˈkɒrəliːn] [ko-ra-lin], *a.* Coralino, lo que tiene coral. -*s.* Coralina, musgo marino, planta de mar; es una concha de zoófitos, así como el coral.

coralloid, coralloidal [ˈkɒrəlɔɪd] [ko-ra-loid] *a.* Coralino.

corban [ˈkɔːbən] [kor-ban], *s.* 1. Entre los antiguos judíos, ofrenda a Dios, especialmente en cumplimiento de un voto. 2. Cepillo o cestillo para pedir limosna.

corbeil [ˈkɔːbeɪl] [kor-beil], *s. (Mil.)* Cestón, tejido de mimbres lleno de tierra para parapetarse contra el fuego del enemigo.

corbel [ˈkɔːbəl] [kor-bel], **corbil** [ˈkɔːbɪl] [kor-bil], *s. (Arq.)* Cesta sobre la cabeza de la cariátide. 2. *(Arq.)* Saledizo fuera de las paredes.

corbie [ˈkɔːbɪ] [kor-bi], *s. (Esco.)* Cuervo.

cord [kɔːd] [kord], *s.* 1. Cuerda, cuerdecita, bramante, cabo; cordel, lazo (string, rope). 2. Cordoncillo, en los tejidos (of pajamas, curtains). *(Elec.)* Cordón, cable. 3. Cuerda, haz o montón de leña para quemar, que tiene ocho pies de largo, cuatro de alto y cuatro de ancho. **Spermatic cord, spinal cord, umbilical cord,** véanse los adjetivos. 4. Pana, corderoy, cotelé. **Cords,** pantalones de pana (clothing).

cord, *va.* Encordelar, atar o amarrar con cordeles o cuerdas.

cordage [ˈkɔːdeɪdʒ] [kor-deich], *s.* Cordaje. **Twicelaid cordage,** cabos contrahechos. **Plaited cordage,** cajetas.

cordate [ˈkɔːdeɪt] [kor-deit], *a.* Cordiforme, en forma de corazón.

corded [ˈkɔːdɪd] [kor-ded], *a.* Hecho de cuerdas.

cordelier [ˈkɔːdəlɪər] [kor-de-lia^r], *s.* Fraile franciscano.

cordial [ˈkɔːdɪəl] [kor-dial], *s.* Cordial, remedio confortativo; refresco concentrado (soft drink).

cordial, *a.* 1. Sincero, de corazón, amistoso, afectuoso. 2. Cordial, confortativo.

cordiality [ˌkɔːdɪˈælɪtɪ] [kor-dia-li-ti], *s.* Cordialidad, sinceridad.

cordially [ˈkɔːdɪəlɪ] [kor-dia-li], *adv.* Cordialmente, sinceramente.

cordialness [ˈkɔːdɪəlnɪs] [kor-dial-nes], *s.* Sinceridad, afecto cordial.

cordiform [ˈkɔːdɪfɔːm] [kor-di-form], *a. V.* CORDATE.

cordite [ˈkɔːdaɪt] [kor-dait], *s. (Quím.)* Cordita.

cordless [ˈkɔːdlɪs] [kord-les] *a.* Inalámbrico.

cord-maker [ˈkɔːˌmeɪkər] [kord-mei-ka^r], *s.* Cordelero, soguero.

cordon [ˈkɔːdn] [kordn], *s.* 1. Cordón, serie o línea extensa de hombres o buques, colocados de tal manera que bloqueen una entrada o dominen una frontera. 2. Cordón, cíngulo. 3. *(Arq.)* Cordón, moldura saliente y horizontal.

cordon off Acordonar.

cordovan [ˈkɔːdəvən] [kor-do-van], **cordwain** [ˈkɔːweɪn] [kord-uein], *s.* Cordobán, para hacer zapatos; cuero curtido de caballo.

corduroy [ˈkɔːdərɔɪ] [kor-du-roi], *s.* Pana, tela gruesa y durable de algodón, acordonada o rayada. **Corduroy road,** camino con piso de troncos. **Corduroys,** *pl.* pantalones de pana (clothing).

cordwainer [ˈkɔːweɪnər] [kord-uei-na^r], *s.* Zapatero.

cord-wood [ˈkɔːdˈwʊd] [kord-wud], *s.* Cuerda de leña, la porción que está ya medida y hacinada para vender.

core [kɔːr] [ko^r], *s.* 1. Corazón; fondo, interior o centro de una cosa (of apple, pear); centro, núcleo (of Earth); núcleo (of nuclear reactor. **The organization is rotten to the core,** la organización está totalmente corrompida. 2. Cuesco o hueso, lo que está debajo de la carne de la fruta y encierra la almendra o semilla. 3. Anima, macho de un molde. 4. Cascote o roca cilíndrica que se saca con un taladro anular. 5. Corazón, los alambres asilados de conducción de un cable eléctrico. Alma (of electric cable). 6. Enfermedad del ganado lanar. 7. Núcleo (central, essential part); meollo (of problem). **A hard core of resistance,** un foco de resistencia férrea. *(Educ.)* Básico (subject, vocabulary). **Core curriculum,** plan de estudios común. *(Inform.)* Núcleo magnético. **Core memory,** memoria central.

core *va.* Quitarle el corazón o el centro a (apple).

coregency [ˌkɔːrəˈdʒənsɪ] [ko-re-yen-si], *s.* Corregencia, calidad del que es regente con otro.

corelative *a. V.* CORRELATIVE.

coreopsis [ˌkɔːrɪˈɒpsɪs] [ko-ri-op-sis], *s. (Bot.)* Género de plantas americanas de la familia de las compuestas, con hermosas flores amarillas y color de rosa; corcópsida, planta de este género.

corer [ˈkɔːrər] [ko-ra^r], *s.* Despepitador; instrumento para quitar las pepitas o los huesos de las frutas.

correspondent [ˌkɔːrɪsˈpɒndənt] [kou-ris-pon-dent], *s.* 1. *(For.)* Correspondiente, el que responde con otros. 2. *(For.)* La persona a quien se acusa como cómplice del demandado en una demanda de divorcio.

coriaceous [ˌkɔrɪˈeɪʃəs] [ko-ri-ei-shos], *a.* Coriáceo, de cuero o parecido al cuero; correoso.

coriander [ˌkɔrɪˈændər] [ko-ri-an-daʳ], *s. (Bot.)* Cilandro, culantro.

corinthian [ˈkɔrɪnθɪən] [ko-rin-zian], *a.* 1. *(Arq.)* Corintio, el cuarto orden de arquitectura. 2. Libidinoso.

corival [ˈkɔrɪvəl] [ko-ri-val], *s.* Rival, competidor juntamente con dos o más personas. -*va.* Rivalizar.

cork [kɔːk] [kork], *s.* 1. Alcornoque, árbol parecido a la encina. 2. Corcho, la corteza del alcornoque. 3. Corcho, tapón de botella.

cork, *va.* Tapar botellas con corchos.

corkage [ˈkɔːkɪdʒ] [kor-kich] *s.* Precio que cobra un restaurante por abrir botellas que el cliente trae consigo.

corkcutter [kɔːkˈkʌtər] [kor-ka-taʳ], *s.* Taponero, el que hace tapones de corcho; también la heramienta especial que usa.

corkscrew [ˈkɔːkskruː] [kork-skru], *s.* Tirabuzón, sacacorchos, instrumento para sacar los corchos de las botellas. -*a.* En forma de tirabuzón, en espiral.

cork-tree [ˈkɔːktriː] [kork-tri], *s.* Alcornoque.

corm [kɔːm] [korm] *s.* Bulbo.

cormorant [ˈkɔːmərənt] [kor-mo-rant], *s.* 1. Corvejón, cuervo marino; cormorán. 2. *(Fig.)* Glotón o avaro.

corn [kɔːn] [korn], *s.* 1. Grano, fruto y semilla de las mieses (cereal crop in general); en Inglaterra, trigo, cebada, avena (oats) y centeno, especialmente el trigo (wheat). En Escocia, la avena por lo general. En América, el maíz (maize), cereal propio del hemisferio occidental. **Green corn,** mazorca de maíz tierno. *(Mex.)* Helote. 2. Mies que aún está por segar o trillar. 3. Cualquier partícula menuda. **Corn-cob,** mazorca de maíz, la espiga alrededor de la cual crecen los granos del maíz. **Corn-crib,** granero de rejilla para el maíz. **Corn-meal,** harina de maíz. **Corn-shuck** o **husk,** cáscara o vaina del maíz. **Corn-starch,** almidón de maíz, especialmente purificado para la mesa. **Corn-sheller,** desgranadora de maíz. **Broom corn,** millo de scoba. **Indian corn,** maíz.

corn *s.* Callo, dureza que se forma en los pies.

corn *va.* 1. Salar. 2. Desmenuzar alguna cosa hasta reducirla a granos pequeños.

cornage [ˈkɔːnɪdʒ] [kor-neich], *s.* La obligación que en lo antiguo tenían ciertas personas de tocar la corneta cuando invadían los enemigos.

corn-bind [kɔːnˈbaɪnd] [korn-baind], *s. (Bot.)* Especie de correhuela.

cornchandler [kɔːnˈtʃændlər] [korn-chand-laʳ] Revendedor de granos.

corn-crake [ˈkɔːnkreɪk] [korn-kreik] *s. (Orn.)* V. LAND-RAIL.

corn-cutter [ˈkɔːnkʌtər] [korn-ka-taʳ], *s.* 1. Máquina para cortar el maíz. 2. Pedicuro, callista.

cornea [ˈkɔːnɪə] [kor-nia], *s.* Córnea, la parte anterior transparente del ojo.

corned [kɔːnd] [kornd] *a.* 1. Salado, conservado en salmuera. **Corned beef,** carne de vaca en media salmuera. 2. Borracho, chispo.

cornel [kɔːnl] [kornl], **o cornelian-tree** [kɔːnəlɪənˈtriː] [kor-ne-lian-tri], *s. (Bot.)* Cornejo, corno.

cornelian [kɔːˈnəlɪən] [kor-ne-lian], *s.* Cornerina, piedra preciosa. V. CARNELIAN.

cornemuse [ˈkɔːnəmuːz] [kor-ne-mus], *s.* 1. Cornamusa. 2. Gaita. 3. Oboe.

corneous [ˈkɔːnɪəs] [kor-nios], *a.* 1. Córneo, hecho de cuerno. 2. Calloso.

corner [ˈkɔːnər] [kor-naʳ], *s.* 1. Ángulo, esquina (outside angle/of street, page); esquina, punta (of table); curva (bend in road). **He took the corner too fast,** tomó la curva demasiado rápido. **The inner corner,** rincón. **The outer**

corner, esquina. 2. Rincón (inside angle/of room, cupboard); esquina (of field); comisura (of mouth). Rincón, escondrijo o lugar retirado. **A quiet corner of Hampshire,** un tranquilo rincón de Hampshire. 3. Extremidad, la parte más remota de alguna cosa. 4. Aprieto, apuro situación difícil. 5. *(E.U.)* Estado del mercado respecto a un valor o artículo que ha sido monopolizado en gran parte para especular con él. **In all corners of the earth,** por toda la tierra. **Corner house,** casa en la esquina de la calle. **Corners of a river,** vueltas, rodeos o sinuosidades de un río. **In a corner,** secretamente; en situación difícil. **Out of the corner of one's eyes,** con el rabillo del ojo. **Around the corner,** a la vuelta de la esquina. **Corner shop,** tienda de la esquina, tienda de barrio. 6. Córner, tiro o saque de esquina (in soccer). 6. Esquina (in boxing).

corner, *va.* 1. Arrinconar, forzar o empujar hacia un rincón. Acorralar (trap). **I cornered her in the corridor,** la abordé en el pasillo. 2. Poner en situación difícil o embarazosa. 3. *(E.U.)* Monopolizar, comprar o contratar la compra de ciertos valores o de un artículo de necesario consumo, para dominar el mercado y dictar el precio de dichos valores o mercaderías; acaparar (monopolize). -*vn.* Lindar con una esquina. Tomar una curva. **This car corners well,** este coche tiene buen agarre en las curvas.

cornered [ˈkɔːnəd] [kor-nerd], *a.* Angulado, esquinado. **Three-cornered hat,** sombrero de tres candiles.

cornerstone [ˈkɔːnəstəʊn] [kor-ner-stoun], *s.* 1. *(Arq.)* Piedra angular; mocheta. 2. Algo fundamental y de primera importancia.

cornerwise [ˈkɔːnəwaɪz] [kor-ner-uais], *adv.* Diagonalmente.

cornet [ˈkɔːnɪt] [kor-net], *s.* 1. Corneta, instrumento de música y boca. 2. Portaestandarte, oficial de caballería que lleva el estandarte. 3. Toca de mujer. 4. Cucurucho, papel arrollado en forma de cono para envolver géneros menudos. 5. V CORONET, 3ª acep.

cornetcy [ˈkɔːnetsɪ] [kor-net-si], *s.* Empleo y grado de portaestandarte.

corneter [ˈkɔːnətər] [kor-ne-taʳ], *s.* El que toca la corneta.

cornfield [ˈkɔːnfiːld] [korn-fild], *s.* Sembrado, el pedazo de terreno sembrado de granos. Maizal (in US); Trigal (in UK/of wheat); avenal (in UK/of oats).

cornflag [ˈkɔːnflæg] [korn-flag], *s. (Bot.)* Gladiolo, gladio o espadaña.

cornflakes [ˈkɔːnfleɪkz] [korn-fleiks] *s.* Copos u hojuelas de maíz.

corn-floor [ˈkɔːnflɔːr] [korn-floʳ], *s.* Suelo de granero.

cornflour [ˈkɔːnflaʊər] [korn-flaueʳ] *s.* Maizena.

cornflower [ˈkɔːnflaʊər] [korn-flaueʳ], Azulejo, aciano, coronilla, flores que nacen en los sembrados.

corn-heap [ˈkɔːnhiːp] [korn-jip], *s.* Hacina, pila de grano.

cornice [ˈkɔːnɪs] [kor-nis], *s.* 1. *(Arq.)* Cornisa. 2. Sobrepuerta.

cornicle [ˈkɔːnɪkl] [kor-ni-kel], *s.* Cuernecito.

corniculate [ˈkɔːnɪkjʊleɪt] [kor-ni-kiu-leit], *a. (Bot.)* Flor corniculada.

corniflic [ˈkɔːnɪflɪk] [kor-ni-flik], *a.* Cornífico, que produce cuernos o sustancia córnea.

cornigerous [ˈkɔːnɪdʒərəs] [kor-ni-ye-ros], *a.* Cornígero, que tiene cuernos.

corning-house [ˈkɔːnɪŋhaʊs] [kor-nin-jaus], *s.* La casa donde se reduce a grano la pólvora.

cornish [ˈkɔːnɪʃ] [kor-nish], *a.* Perteneciente al condado de Cornuelles o Cornwall, Inglaterra. -*s.* Antiguo dialecto céltico de Cornualles.

cornish *s.* Córnico.

corn-land [ˈkɔːnlænd] [korn-land], *s.* Tierra sembrada o destinada y a propósito para sembrar; tierra de pan llevar.

corn-loft [ˈkɔːnlɒft] [korn-loft], *s.* Granero, cámara donde se encierran los granos.

corn-marigold [kɔːnˈmærɪgəʊld] [korn-ma-ri-gould], *s. (Bot.)* Especie de caléndula.

corn-meter [kɔːnˈmiːtər] [korn-mi- taʳ], *s.* Antiguamente, medidor de granos.

corn-mill [ˈkɔːnmɪl] [korn-mil], *s.* Molino, máquina para moler el trigo y otros granos, o el edificio donde se muelen.

corn-pipe [ˈkɔːnpaɪp] [korn-paip], *s.* Especie de silbato hecho con el tallo del trigo o de la avena.

corn-plaster [kɔːn] [korn], *s.* Emplasto para los callos.

corn-popper [kɔːn] [korn], *s.* Tostador de maíz.

corn-poppy [kɔːn] [korn], *s.* (*Bot.*) Ababa, abadol, amapola, planta que nace en los sembrados.

corn-rose [kɔːnrəʊz] [korn-rous], *s.* (*Bot.*) Ababa, abadol, amapola.

corn-salad [ˈkɔːnsæləd] [korn-sa-lad], *s.* (*Bot.*) Macha, valerianilla.

cornstarch [ˈkɔːnstɑːtʃ] [korn-starch] *s.* Maizena.

cornucopia [ˌkɔːnjʊˈkəʊpɪə] [kor-niu-ko-pia], *s.* 1. Cornucopia, cuerno de la abundancia. 2. Alcartaz, cucurucho.

cornuted [ˈkɔːnjʊtɪd] [kor-niu-tid], *a.* Cornudo, lo que tiene cuernos; en figura de cuerno.

cornuto [ˈkɔːnjʊtə] [kor-niu-to], *s.* Cornudo, el marido cuya mujer ha faltado a la fidelidad conyugal.

corn-violet *s.* (*Bot.*) Especie de campánula.

cornwall [ˈkɔːnwəl] [korn-uol] *N.* (*Geogr.*) Cornualles.

corny [ˈkɔːnɪ] [kor-ni], *a.* 1. Hecho de cuerno, córneo, calloso. 2. Que produce o contiene grano. 3. (*Coloq.*) Cursi, sensiblero (song, movie); (GB) malo (joke).

corolla [kəˈrɒlə] [ko-ro-la], *s.* Corola.

corollary [kəˈrɒlərɪ] [ko-ro-la-ri], *s.* 1. Corolario, consectario. 2. Sobrante.

corona [kəˈrəʊnə] [ko-rou-na], *s.* 1. (*Arq.*) Corona de entablamento, una de las partes de que se compone la cornisa. 2. Corona, halo, especie de meteoro circular que aparece alrededor del sol o de la luna. 3. (*Bot.*) Eminencia parecida a una corona en el ápice de algunos pétalos. (*Biol.*) Parte o estructura parecida a una corona.

coronal [kəˈrəʊnəl] [ko-rou-nal], *s.* Coronal, el hueso de la frente; corona, guirnalda. -*a.* Coronal, lo perteneciente al hueso coronal.

coronary [ˈkɒrənərɪ] [ko-rou-na-ri], *a.* Coronario, lo que pertenece a la corona.

coronary *s.* Infarto de miocardio.

coronation [ˌkɒrəˈneɪʃən] [ko-ro-nei-shon], *s.* Coronación.

coroner [ˈkɒrənər] [ko-rou-naʳ], *s.* Córoner; se llama así un empleado cuyo deber es indagar las causas de las muertes repentinas y violentas, con presencia indispensablemente del cadáver. Juez de instrucción.

coronet [ˈkɒrənɪt] [ko-ro-net], *s.* 1. La corona particular que corresponde a los títulos nobiliarios según su clase. Corona de príncipe, duque, etc. (small crown); diadema (tiara). 2. Guirnalda para la cabeza. 3. Margen superior del casco del cabello.

corp = corporation

corporal [ˈkɔːpərəl] [kor-po-ral], *s.* Cabo o caporal, el que manda una de las escuadras en que se divide la compañía. -*a.* 1. Corporal, corpóreo, lo que pertenece al cuerpo. 2. Material, no espiritual.

corporality [ˈkɔːpərəlɪtɪ] [kor-po-ra-li-ti], *s.* Corporalidad, corporeidad.

corporally [ˈkɔːpərəlɪ] [kor-po-ra-li], *adv.* Corporalmente.

corporal punishment [ˈkɔːpərəlˌpʌnɪʃmənt] [kor-po-ral-pu-nish-ment] *s.* Castigos corporales.

corporate [ˈkɔːpərɪt] [kor-po-reit] 1. Formado en cuerpo o en comunidad. 2. General; unido. 3. Perteneciente a una corporación; colectivo (join, collective/action, decision). 4. De la empresa o compañía (of a company/headquarters, lawyer). **The corporate image,** la imagen de la empresa o compañía. Empresarial (mentality, jargon).

corporately [ˈkɔːpərɪtlɪ] [kor-po-reit-li], *adv.* 1. Corporalmente; unidamente. 2. En cuerpo.

corporateness [ˈkɔːpərɪtnɪs] [kor-po-reit-nes], *s.* Comunidad, incorporación.

corporation [ˌkɔːpəˈreɪʃən] [kor-po-rei-shon], *s.* 1. Corporación, cuerpo político o civil, con capacidad legal para obrar como una sola persona. Sociedad anónima (in US/company); compañía, empresa, corporación (in GB). 2. Cabildo, ayuntamiento, corporación municipal, municipio (municipal council); comunidad de personas eclesiásticas o seculares; cuerpo, sociedad, gremio, v. gr. gremio de sastres, zapateros, etc. 3. (*Fest.*) El cuerpo humano cuando es grande y pesado.

corporeal [kɔːˈpɔːrɪəl] [kor-po-rial], *a.* 1. Corpóreo; material, lo opuesto a inmaterial o espiritual. 2. (*For.*) Perceptible por los sentidos corporales, sustancial y permanente; material, tangible.

corporealist [ˈkɔːpərɪəlɪst] [kor-po-ria-list], *s.* Materialista, el que niega la inmaterialidad del alma.

corporeality [ˈkɔːpərɪˈælɪtɪ] [kor-po-ri-a-li-ti] *s.* Corporeidad.

corporeally [ˈkɔːpərɪəlɪ] [kor-po-ria-li], *adv.* Materialmente, corporalmente.

corporeity [ˈkɔːpərɪtɪ] [kor-po-rei-ti], *s.* Corporeidad, materialidad.

corporeus [ˈkɔːpərɪəs] [kor-po-rios], *a.* Corpóreo.

corporosity [ˈkɔːpərəsɪtɪ] [kor-po-ro-si-ti], *s.* (*Ger.E.U.*) El cuerpo de una persona; Corpulenta, gran barriga.

corposant [ˈkɔːpəsənt] [kor-po-sant], *s.* (*Mar.*) Fuego de Santelmo, meteoro de naturaleza eléctrica que aparece en noches tempestuosas sobre los palos o las vergas de los buques.

corps [kɔːps] [korps], *s.* 1. Número de personas que obran juntas de algún modo. 2. Cuerpo del ejército; cuerpo de guardia.

corpse [kɔːps] [korps], *s.* Cadáver, el cuerpo muerto de una persona.

corpulence, corpulency [ˈkɔːpjuːləns] [kor-piu-lens], *s.* Corpulencia, la magnitud del cuerpo; gordura, espesor.

corpulent [ˈkɔːpjʊlənt][kor-piu-lent], *a.* Corpulento, gordo, repleto.

corpus [ˈkɔːpəs][kor-pus], *s.* 1. Cuerpo. 2. (For.) Objeto material, especialmente bienes tangibles, corporales. Los hechos o elementos de un caso legal estimados colectivamente. **Corpus delicti,** El cuerpo del delito, el hecho fundamental y esencial de la perpetración de un crimen.

corpuscle [ˈkɔːpəsl][kor-pu-sel], *s.* 1. Corpúsculo, átomo. 2. Cuerpo diminuto, celdilla, como las de la sangre.

corpuscular [kɔːˈpəskjʊləʳ][kor-pus-kiu-laʳ], **Corpuscularian** [, *a.* Corpuscular.

corrade [kəˈreɪd][ko-reid], *va.* Desagregar, rocas por solución y ludimiento: dícese de los ríos.

corradiate [kəˈreɪdieɪt][ko-rei-dieit], *va..* Concentrar los rayos de luz en un mismo punto.

corradiation [kəreɪdiˈeɪən][ko-rei-diei-shon], *s.* Unión de los rayos en un mismo punto.

corral [kəˈræl][ko-ral] , *s.* Corral.—*va.* Acorralar.

correct [kɔːˈrekt][ko-rekt], *va.* 1. Corregir, rectificar, enmendar lo que está errado. 2. Corregir, reprender, castigar; enmendar, amonestar. 3. remediar, neutralizar la acción de lo que es perjudicial o dañoso.

correct, *a.* Correcto, revisto o acabado con exactitud; exacto, justo.

correction [kɔːˈrekʃən][ko-rek-shon], *s.* Corrección, castigo, enmienda, lima, reforma; censura, pena. House of correction, Casa de corrección, en que se castiga a los adolescentes de uno y otro sexo.

correctional [kɔːˈrekʃənəl][ko-rek-sho-nal], *a.* Correccional, lo que conduce a la corrección.

corrective [kɔːˈrektɪv][ko-rek-tiv], *a.* Corrective, lo que corrige.—*a.* Correctivo, limitación, restricción, excepción.

correctly [kɔːˈrektlɪ][ko-rekt-li], *adv.* Correctamente.

correctness [kɔːˈrektnɪs][ko-rekt-li], *s.* Exactitud, corrección.

corrector [kɔːˈrektəʳ][ko-rek-taʳ], *s.* Corrector, reformador, revisor.

correlate [ˈkɔːreleɪt][ko-re-leit], *va.* Poner en correlación o relación recíproca. —*vn.* Tener correlación o relación recíproca.

correlate, *s.* La persona que tiene correlación con otra.

correlation [kɔːreˈleɪʃən][ko-ri-lei-shon], *s.* 1. Correlación, relación recíproca que tienen entre sí dos o más cosas. 2. La acción de poner en unión, correspondencia, o acción intermedia.

correlative [kɔːˈrelətɪv][ko-ri-la-tiv], *a.* y *s.* Correlativo.

correlativeness [kɔːˈrelətɪvnɪs][ko-ri-la-tiv-nes], *s.* Correlación, correspondencia, analogía o relación recíproca.

correspond [kɔːrəsˈpɒnd][ko-ris-pond], *vn.* 1. Corresponder, tener proporción una cosa con otra. 2. Estar de acuerdo, o de inteligencia. 3. Corresponderse, tener correspondencia con una persona ausente.

correspondence, correspondency [kɔːrəsˈpɒndəns][ko-ris-pon-dans], *s.* 1. Correspondencia, relación recíproca. 2. Inteligencia. 3. Correspondencia, amistad o comercio mútuo.

correspondent [kɔːrəsˈpɒndənt][ko-ris-pon-dant], *a.* Correspondiente, conforme, conveniente.—*s.* Correspondiente, corresponsal.

correspondently [kɔːrəsˈpɒndəntlɪ][ko-ris-pon-dant-li], *adv.* Correspondientemente.

corridor [ˈkɔːrɪdɔːʳ][ko-ri-doʳ], *s.* 1. Corredor, especie de galería alrededor de una casa. 2. (Mil.) Corredor, camino cubierto alrededor de una fortificación. 3. Pasillo.

corrigent [ˈkɔːrɪdʒənt][ko-ri-yent] *a.* (Med.) Correctivo; dulcificante.—*s.* Correctivo, medicamento modificado ; adición a una receta para modificar la acción de otros ingredientes.

corrigible [ˈkɔːrɪdʒɪbl][ko-ri-yi-bol], *a.* Corrigible, lo que es capaz de corrección.

corrival [kɔːˈrɑɪvəl][ko-rai-val], *a.* Émulo; contrario.—*s.* Competidor, rival.

corrivalry [kɔːˈrɑɪvəlrɪ][ko-rai-val-ri], *s.* (Poco us.) Competencia, disputa, contienda, rivalidad.

corroborant [kɔːˈrɒbɒrənt][ko-ro-bo-rant], *a.* Corroborante.—*s.* Corroborante, el medicamento que tiene virtud de corroborar o fortificar.

corroborate [kɔːˈrɒbəreɪt][ko-ro-bo-reit], *va.* Corroborar, confortar, fortalecer; confirmar, fortificar, apoyar.

corroboration [kɔːrɒbəˈreɪʃən][ko-ro-bo-rei-shon], *s.* Corroboración, confirmación; apoyo.

corroborative [kɔːˈrɒbərətɪv][ko-ro-bo-ri-tiv], *a.* Corroborative, corroborante.—*s.* Confortativo.

corrode [kɔːˈrəʊd][ko-roud], *va.* Corroer, roer poco a poco alguna cosa.

corrodent [kɔːˈrəʊdənt][ko-roud], *a.* y *s.* (Poco us.) Corrosivo.

corrodibility [kɔːrəʊdɪˈbɪlɪtɪ][ko-rou-di-bi-li-ti] **Corrosibility** [kɔːrəʊsɪˈbɪlɪtɪ], *s.* La calidad de ser corrosible.

corrodible, corrosible [kɔːˈrəʊdɪbl][ko-rou-di-bol], *a.* Corrosible, capaz de corrosión.

corrosibleness, *s.* V. CORRODiBILITY.

corrosion [kɔːˈrəʊʃən][ko-rou-shon], *s.* Corrosión.

corrosive [kɔːˈrəʊzɪv][ko-rou-siv], *a.* y *s.* 1. Corrosivo, lo que corroe o destruye. 2. Corrosivo, mordaz, picante. Corrosive sublimate, Sublimado corrosivo, solimán, bicloruro de mercurio (HgCl2).

corrosiveness [kɔːˈrəʊsɪvnɪs][ko-rou-sif-nis], *s.* Calidad de corosivo o mordicante; también se usa figuradamente con relación al tiempo, al pesar, etc.

corrugant [ˈkɔːrəgənt][ko-ru-gant], *a.* Lo que arruga o hace arrugas.

corrugate [ˈkɔːrəgeɪt][ko-ru-gueit], *va.* Arrugar, plegar, hacer pliegues o arrugas; acanalar; encarrujar.

corrugate, *a.* Encogido, arrugado; acanalado.

corrugated [ˈkɔːrəgeɪtɪd][ko-ru-guei-tid], *a.* Corrugado, acanalado. Corrugated carton, cartón corrugado.

corrugation [kɔːrəˈgeɪʃən][ko-ru-guei-shon], *a.* Corrugación, contracción, encogimiento.

corrugator [kɔːrəˈgeɪtəʳ][ko-ru-guei-taʳ], *s.* El o lo que arruga. 1. (Anat.) Contractor, músculo que arruga la piel. 2. Máquina de encarrujar.

corrupt [kɔːˈrʌpt][ko-rapt], *a.* 1. Corrompido, corrupto, podrido en estado de descomposición. 2. (Fig.) Corrompido, depravado, viciado. 3. Seducido, sobornado. 4. Lleno de errores, falsificado, erróneo; v. g. un texto falsificado.

corrupt, *va.* 1. Corromper, malear, adulterar, viciar una cosa. 2. Corromper, sobornar, seducir, pervertir a una persona. 3. Estragar las costumbres. 4. Infectar, echar a perder, podrir.—*vn.* Corromperse, podrirse.

corrupter [kɔːˈrʌptəʳ][ko-rap-taʳ], *s.* Corruptor, seductor. corrompedor, sobornador.

corruptibility [kɔːrʌptɪˈbɪlɪtɪ][ko-rap-ti-bi-li-ti], *a.* Corruptibilidad.

corruptible [kɔːˈrʌptɪbl][ko-rap-ti-bol], *adv.* Corruptible, lo que se puede corromper, depravar o viciar.

corruptibleness [kɔːˈrʌptɪblnɪs][ko-rap-ti-bol-nis], *s.* Corruptibilidad.

corruptibly [kɔːˈrʌptɪblɪ][ko-rap-ti-bli], *adv.* De un modo corruptible.

corrupting [kɔːˈrʌptɪŋ][ko-rap-tin], *s.* Corrupción, adulteración.

corruption [kɔːˈrʌpʃən][ko-rap-shon], *a.* 1. Corrupción, la acción de corromper o el estado de corrompido; destrucción por causa de descomposición, disolución o muerte. 2. Corrupción, vicio, hediondez; podredumbre; depravación, iniquidad, ruindad, maldad. 3. Pus, materia. 4. Seducción, soborno. 5. Corrupción, alteración de un texto o lenguaje, o del buen gusto.

corruptive [kɔːˈrʌptɪv][ko-rap-tiv], *a.* Corruptivo.

corruptless [kɔːˈrʌptles][ko-rapt-les], *a.* Incorruptible, íntegro, recto.

corruptly [kɔːˈrʌptlɪ][ko-rapt-li], *adj.* Corrompidamente, viciosamente.

Corruptness [kɔːˈrʌptnɪs][ko-rapt-nes], *s.* Corruptela, corrupción, putrefacción, infección, vicio.

corruptress [kɔːˈrʌptrɪs][ko-rap-tres], *sf.* Corrompedora.

corsage [kɔːˈsɑːdʒ][kor-sach] *s.* Corpiño, jubón, justillo del vestido de mujer. (Fr.)

corsair [ˈkɔːrsəʳ][kor-saʳ], *s.* Corsario, pirata.

corse [ˈkɔːrs][kors], *s.* 1. Cinta usada para hábitos y vestiduras. 2. (Ant.) Cadáver, cuerpo muerto.

corselet [ˈkɔːrslet][kors-let], *s.* 1. Coselete, peto, armadura que cubre la parte anterior del cuerpo, 2. (Ent.) Corselete, el pecho de todo insecto y artrópodo.

corset [kɔːˈset][kor-set], *s.* Corsé, especie de cotilla interior con que se ajustan el talle las mujeres. **Corset-maker,** Corsetera, corsetero.

corsican [ˈkɔːrsɪkən][kor-si-kan], *a.* Corso.

cortège [ˈkɔːrtedʒ][kor-tesh], *s.* Comitiva, séquito, acompañamiento.

cortes [ˈkɔːrtes][kor-tes], *s.* Cortes, la reunión de los representantes del pueblo español o portugués.

cortex [ˈkɔːrteks][kor-teks], *s.* Corteza.

cortical [ˈkɔːrtɪkəl][kor-ti-kal], *a.* 1. Cortical, lo que pertenece a la corteza. 2. (Anat.) Cortical, exterior, de la envoltura exterior.

corticate [ˈkɔːrtɪkeɪt][kor-ti-keit], **Corticated** [cer'-ti-kê-ted], *a.* Cortezudo; que tiene corteza, corticoso.

corticose [ˈkɔːrtɪkəʊs][kor-ti-kous], *a.* Corticoso, corticiforme, semejante a o de la naturaleza de la corteza.

cortisone [ˈkɔːrtɪsəʊn][kor-ti-soun], *s.* (Med.) Cortisona.

corundum [kɔːˈrʌndʌm][ko-run-dum], *s.* Corindón, mineral de extrema dureza que se compone casi de alúmina pura, y se usa para pulir. Las variedades coloradas son piedras preciosas; v. g. el zafiro, el rubí oriental, el topacio, la esmeralda y la amatista. El esmeril es la variedad granular.

coruscant [ˈkɔːrʌskənt][ko-rus-kant], *a.* Coruscante, resplandeciente.

coruscate [ˈkɔːrʌskeɪt][ko-rus-keit], *vn* Relucir, resplandecer.

coruscation [kɔːrʌsˈkeɪʃən][ko-rus-kei-shon], *s.* 1. Relámpago, especie de meteoro ígneo de una llama muy pronta. 2. Resplandor, brillo.

corvette [kɔːrˈvet][kor-vet], *s.* Corbeta, buque de guerra que en orden de tamaño venía después de la fragata.

corvetto [kɔːrˈvetəʊ][kor-ve-to], *s.* Corveta. V. CURVET.

corvine [kɔːrˈvɑɪn][kor-vain], *a.* Corvino, perteneciente al cuervo; semejante al cuervo.

corybantes [kɔːriːˈbɒntɪs][ko-ri-ban-tis], *s.* Coribantes, sacerdotes de la diosa Cibeles.

corybantic [kɔːriːˈbɒntɪk][ko-ri-ban-tik], *a.* Lo que pertenece a los coribantes; maniático.

corymb [ˈkɔːrɪmb][ko-rimb] *s.* (Bot.) Corimbo, maceta, una de las especies de inflorescencia o posición de las flores en las plantas.

corymbiate, carymbiated [kɔːˈrɪmbɪeɪt][ko-rimb], *a.* (Bot.) Corímbeo, en forma de ramillete o corimbo, arbusto cuyas flores forman corimbo.

corymbiferous [kɔːrɪmˈbɪfərəs][ko-rim-bi-fe-ros], *a.* (Bot.) Corimbífero, lo que lleva Corimbo.

corypheus [kɔːrɪˈfiːəs][ko-ri-fios], *a.* Corifeo; director, guía, jefe, principal.

coryza [kɔːˈrɑɪzə][ko-rai-sa], *s.* (Med.) Coriza, inflamación de las membranas mucosas de la nariz y las cavidades contiguas.

coscinomancy [kəʊsɪnəʊˈmænsɪ][ko-si-no-man-si], *s.* Adivinación por medio de una criba o cedazo.

cosecant [kəʊˈsiːkənt][ko-si-kant], *s.* (Geom.) Cosecante.

cosen, *va.* V. COZEN.

cosentient [kəʊˈsenʃənt][ko-sen-shant], *a.* Que percibe o siente con otro.

cosey [ˈkəʊsɪ][ko-si], *a.* V. Cozy.

cosher [ˈkəʊʃər][ko-shaʳ] (Fam.), *va.* Dar de comer dulces y bocados regalados; de aquí, acariciar, mimar.—*vn.* Ser compadre o comadre de; chismear.

cosine [ˈkəʊsɑɪn][ko-sain], *s.* (Geom.) Coseno, el seno de un arco que es el complemento de otro.

cosmetic [kɒsˈmetɪk][kos-me-tik], *a.* y *s.* Cosmético, afeite que usan las mujeres para hermosear la cara.

cosmic, cosmical [ˈkɒsmɪk][kos-mik], *a.* 1. Cósmico, lo que pertenece al mundo; metódico; opuesto a caótico. 2. Lo que sale con el sol o inmediatamente antes. 3. Perteneciente al universo material; vasto en extensión o duración.

cosmically [ˈkɒsmɪkəlɪ][kos-mi-ka-li], *adv.* Con el sol.

cosmic ray [ˈkɒsmɪkreɪ][kos-mik rei], *s.* Rayo cósmico.

cosmogony [kɒsˈmɒdʒɪnɪ][kos-mo-yi-ni], *s.* Cosmogonía, la ciencia o sistema de la formación del universo.

cosmogonist [kɒsˈmɒdʒɪnɪst][kos-mo-yo-nist], *s.* Cosmogonista, el que sabe o profesa la cosmogonía.

cosmographer [kɒsˈmɒɡrəfər][kos-mo-gra-faʳ], *s.* Cosmógrafo, el que ha escrito, sabe o enseña la estructura y delineación del mundo.

cosmographical [kɒsˈmɒɡræfɪkəl][kos-mo-gra-fi-kal], *a.* Cosmográfico.

cosmography [kɒsˈmɒɡrəfɪ][kos-mo-gra-fi], *s.* Cosmografía, la descripción del mundo, o la ciencia que enseña la figura, construcción y disposición de todas sus partes.

cosmological [kɒsmɒˈlɒdʒɪkəl][kos-mo-lo-yi-kal], *a.* Cosmológico, referente a la cosmología.

cosmologist [kɒsˈmɒlədʒɪst][kos-mo-lo-yist], *s.* Cosmólogo, el que es versado en la cosmología.

cosmology [kɒsˈmɒlədʒɪ][kos-mo-lo-yi], *s.* Cosmología, ciencia de las leyes que gobiernan el mundo físico.

cosmopolitan [kɒsmɒˈpɒlɪtən][kos-mo-po-li-tan], **cosmopolite** [kɒsˈmɒpəlɪt][kos-mo-po-lit], *a.* 1. Cosmopolita, que considera a todo el mundo como patria suya; común a todo el mundo. 2. (Biol.) De extensa distribución; p. ej. un género.—*s.* Cosmopolita, ciudadano del mundo.

cosmos [ˈkɒsməs][kos-mos], *s.* 1. El mundo o el universo, estimado como sistema perfecto en orden y arreglo; opuesto a caos. 2. Cualquier sistema harmonioso y completo. 3. (Bot.) Planta de las compuestas, y su flor, cultivada como de adorno; de la familia de las dalias. (Gr.)

cosmotron [ˈkɒsmətrɒn][kos-mo-tron] *s.* Cosmotrón.

cossacks [ˈkɒsæks][ko-saks], *s.* Cosacos, caballería ligera e irregular de Rusia; también es el nombre de los habitantes de algunas provincias del imperio ruso.

cosset [ˈkɒset][ko-set], *s.* Cordero, criado sin la madre; se dice también de los terneros y novillos.—*va.* Acariciar, mimar.

cost [ˈkɒst][kost], *s.* 1. Coste, precio ; expensas, gastos. 2. Costa, daño, pérdida. **To my cost,** A mis expensas. **At cost,** Al costo, o a coste y costas.

cost, *vn.* Costar, tener alguna cosa un coste o precio. **Cost what it may,** Cueste lo que cueste, o costare. **To cost dear,** Causar grandes gastos, incomodidad o pérdidas y perjuicios de consideración.

costal [ˈkəʊstəl][kos-tal], *a.* Costal, lo perteneciente a las costillas.

costermonger, Costard-monger, *s.* Buhonero, vendedor ambulante de frutas y legumbres.

costive [ˈkɒstɪv][kos-tiv], *a.* 1. Estreñido de cuerpo o vientre. 2. (Des.) Impervio; dícese de la tierra arcillosa.

costiveness [ˈkɒstɪvnɪs][kos-tiv-nes], *s.* Constipación o estreñimiento de vientre.

costless [ˈkɒstles][kost-les], *a.* Sin coste o precio, de balde.

costliness [ˈkɒstlɪnes][kost-li-nes], *s.* Suntuosidad.

costly [ˈkɒstlɪ][kost-li], *a.* 1. Costoso, caro, dispendioso. 2. Magnífico, espléndido, suntuoso.

costmary [ˈkɒstmærɪ][kost-ma-ri], *s.* (Bot.) Especie de tanaceto.

costrel [ˈkɒstrəl][kos-trel], *s.* Botella o frasco (de peregrino) con asas.

costume [ˈkɒstjuːm][kos-tum], *s.* 1. Traje, vestido; el traje de cierto país, época, clase, etc.; modo de vestir en general. 2. La usanza o estilo de diferentes países a que debe atenerse un pintor o un poeta para guardar propiedad; color local.

costumer [ˈkɒstjuːmər][kos-tum-aʳ], *s.* El que hace, vende o alquila trajes para el teatro.

cosy, *a.* V. Cozy.

cot [ˈkɒt][kot], *s.* 1. Cabaña, choza, casa pequeña o albergue de gente pobre. 2. Hamaca, coy, cama suspendida a bordo de los barcos. 3. Camita, cuna; catre. 4. Dedal. 5. (Irlanda) Barquillo. 6. Desecho o desperdicio de lana.

cotabulate, *va.* V. CONTABULATE.

cotangent [ˈkəʊtændʒent][ko-tan-yent], *s.* (Geom.) Cotangente.

cote [ˈkəʊt][kout], *s.* 1. Corral, redil. 2. Casita para refugio; voz usada sólo en composición, como **dove-cote,** palomar; **sheep-cote,** redil.

cotemporaneous [kəʊtempəˈreɪnɪəs][ko-tem-po-ra-nios], *a.* V. CONTEMPORANEOUS.

cotemporary [kəʊˈtempəˈrərɪ][ko-tem-po-ra-ri], *a.* Contemporáneo, coetáneo. Es preferible **Contemporary.**

coterie [kəʊˈtərɪ][ko-te-ri], *s.* Corrillo, corro, corro de ociosos, tertulia, junta casera de diversión o de amigos.

coterminous [kəʊˈtɜːmɪnəs][ko-ter-mi-nos], *a.* V. CONTERMINOUS.

cothurnus [kəʊˈθɜːnəs][ko-zer-nos], *s.* Coturno. V. BUSKIN.

cotillon [kəʊˈtɪljən][ko-til-yon], *s.* Cotillón, especie de contradanza entre ocho doce o diez y seis personas.

cotland [ˈkɒtlænd][kot-land], *s.* Pedazo de terreno contiguo a una choza.

cotquean [ˈkɒtkiːn][kot-kuin], *s.* Maricón cazolero, maricasera, el hombre que se entremete en los quehaceres de las mujeres.

cotrustee [kəʊtrʌsˈtiː][ko-tras-tii], *s.* El que ejerce el cargo de síndico, fideicomisario o curador en unión de otra persona.

cotswold [ˈkɒtswəʊld][kots-uould], *s.* Redil de campo llano y abierto.

cotta [ˈkɒtə][ko-ta], *s.* Cota, sobrepelliz corta, vestidura eclesiástica.

cottage [ˈkɒtɪdʒ][ko-tich], *s.* 1. Casa humilde, de un solo piso; también, casa situada en las afueras de una población; casucha. 2. Casa de campo, a veces grande y suntuosa.

cottage cheese [ˈkɒtɪdʒtʃiːz][ko-tich chis], *s.* Requesón.

cottaged [ˈkɒtɪdʒd][ko-tichd]. *a.* Poblado de casas humildes o suburbanas.

cottager [ˈkɒtɪdʒəʳ][ko-ti-gaʳ], **Cotter** [ˈkɒtəʳ], *s.* Rústico, aldeano payo. (Cuba) Montero.

cotter pin [ˈkɒtəʳpɪn][ko-taʳ pin], *s.* (Mec.) Chaveta.

cotton [ˈkɒtn][ko-ton], *s.* 1. Algodón 2. Cotonía, una tela de algodón. **Absorbent cotton**, Algodón absorbente, purificado, que se usa en cirugía. **Upland cotton**,Algodón de pellón largo. **Raw cotton**, Algodón en rama. **Cotton bagging**, Lienzo de algodón para sacos. **Cotton balls**, Hilo de algodón en bolas. **Cotton-gin**, Almarraes, desmotadora de algodón. **Cotton jeans**, Coquillos, cotíes de algodón. **Cotton-seed oil**, Aceite de semilla de algodón. **Cotton-waste**, Desperdicios de algodón. **Cotton-plant**, Algodonero, algodonal, la planta que produce el algodón. Gossypium. **Spool-cotton**, Hilo de algodón en carreteles o canillas. **Cotton yarn** (para tejedores), Hilaza de algodón; (para costureras) Hilo de torzal o de pelo. **Cotton cambric**, Muselina finísima. (Amer.) Coco muy fino, estopilla de algodón. **Cotton-wool**, Algodón en rama. (cotón.)

cotton, *vn.* 1. Levantar pelusa; cubrirse de pelusa o borra. 2. Acordarse, salir bien.—*va.* Acolchar, rellenar con algodón.

cottonlike [ˈkɒtnlaɪk][ko-ton-laik], **Cottony** [cetʼ-¬n-i], *a.* Lleno de algodón, semejante al algodón; blando, velloso; acolchado.

cottonwood [ˈkɒtnwʊd][ko-ton-wud], *s.* Cada una de las varias especies americanas del álamo.

cotyla [ˈkɒtələ][ko-ti-la], **cotyle** [ˈkɒtəl][ko-til], *s.* (Anat.) Cotila, la cavidad de un hueso que recibe la cabeza de otro hueso.

cotyledon [kɒˈtəliːdən][ko-ti-li-don], *s.* (Bot.) 1. Cotiledón o paleta de la semilla. 2. Cotiledón, cada uno de los lóbulos que, unidos, forman la placenta.

cotyloid [ˈkɒtələɔːd][ko-ti-loid], *a.* Cotiloidea, en forma de copa; dícese de la cavidad articular de la cadera.

couch [kaʊtʃ][kauch], *vn.* 1. Acostarse, recostarse, echarse; arrodillarse como las bestias para descansar. 2. Agacharse o inclinarse con intención de ocultarse. 3. Agobiarse, encorvarse de miedo o dolor.—*va.* 1. Colocar sobre una cama u otro sitio de descanso. 2. Colocar una cosa sobre otra en capas o tongadas. 3. Solapar, encubrir o disimular; incluir. 4. (Cir.) Batir las cataratas o nubes de los ojos. To couch in writing, Poner por escrito. **To couch the lance**, Enristrar, poner la lanza en ristre.

couch, *s.* 1. Silla poltrona, silla de descanso; lecho, canapé. 2. Lecho o lechos, tongada, capas o camas de las cosas que se ponen unas sobre otras.

couchant [ˈkaʊtʃənt][kau-chant], *a.* Acostado, agachado.

coucher [ˈkaʊtʃəʳ][kau-chaʳ], *s.* 1. El que bate las cataratas de los ojos. 2. Cartulario.

couch-fellow [ˈkaʊtʃfeləʊ][kauch-fe-lou], *s.* Compañero de cama.

couching [ˈkaʊtʃɪŋ][kau-chin], *s.* 1. La operación de batir las cataratas con aguja. 2. Encorvamiento.

cougar [ˈkuːgəʳ][ku-gaʳ], *s.* Cuguar, puma, la pantera de América. Felis concolor.

cough [kɒf][kof] *s.* Tos. **To have a cough**, tener tos. **He gave a loud cough**, tosió ruidosamente. **Cough drop**, pastilla para la tos. **Cough mixture/syrup**, jarabe para la tos. **Cough sweet**, caramelo para la tos. **Whooping-cough**, tos ferina, sofocante, o convulsiva.

cough *vn.* Toser. -*va.* Arrancar o arrojar del pecho lo que a uno le molesta, a fuerza de toser. **Cough (up)**, expectorar, esputar.

cough up *(Coloq.)* Soltar, aflojar (pay, money). Soltar la plata, la pasta o la lana.

coughing [ˈkɒfɪŋ] [ko-fin] *s.* Tosidura, acción y efecto de toser. **Fit of coughing**, acceso de tos.

could [kʊd] [kud], *pret.* imp. del verbo CAN. 1. Poder (indicating possibility). **If I took a taxi, I could get there on time**, si tomara un taxi, podría llegar a tiempo. **I would help you if I could**, te ayudaría si pudiera. **You could be right**, puede que tengas razón. **They couldn't be happier**, están contentos a más no poder. **I could not do it**, no pude o no podría hacerlo. **Could you do it?**, ¿podría Vd. hacerlo? *Could*, y su presente *Can*, corresponden frecuentemente a *saber*; v.g. **He did not sign, because he could not write**, no firmó por no saber escribir. 2. **Could I use your phone?**, ¿podría o me permitiría usar el teléfono? (asking permission). **Could you sign here, please?**, ¿quiere firmar aquí por favor? (in requests). 3. Poder (in suggestions). **You could try doing it this way**, podrías tratar de hacerlo de esta manera. **You could at least apologize!**, ¡al menos podrías pedir perdón! Poder (indicating strong desire). **I could have killed her**, la hubiera matado; la podría o podía haber matado.

couldn't = could not

coulomb [ˈkuːlɒm] [ku-lom] *s.* Culombio.

coulter [ˈkuːltər] [kul-teʳ] *s.* Cuchilla, reja de arado. V. COLTER.

council [ˈkaʊnsl] [kaun-sil] *s.* 1. Concilio o consejo (advisory group), junta de personas que se unen para consultar y deliberar; ayuntamiento, municipio. **Council housing**, viviendas de alquiler subvencionadas por el ayuntamiento. 2. Sínodo, junta del clero. **Common council**, ayuntamiento, cuerpo legislativo municipal. **Councilman**, concejal, individuo de un consejo municipal. **The Council of Europe**, el Consejo de Europa.

council-board [ˈkaʊnslbɔːd] [kaun-sil-bord] *s.* Reunión o sesión del consejo.

councilor, councillor [ˈkaʊnslər] [kaun-si-loʳ] *s.* Consejero, concejal.

council tax [ˈkaʊnsltæks] [kaun-sil-taks] *s.* Contribución municipal o inmobiliaria.

councilwoman [ˈkaʊnslwʊmən] [kaun-sil-vu-man] *s.* Concejala.

counsel [ˈkaʊnsəl] [kaun-sel] *s.* 1. Consejo (advice); aviso, parecer, dictamen, deliberación, determinación. **To hold/take counsel with somebody**, asesorarse o aconsejarse con alguien. **To keep one's own counsel**, reservarse la opinión. 2. Prudencia, secreto, sigilo. 3. Trama, designio. 4. *(Law)* Abogado. **Counsel for the defense**, abogado defensor. **Counsel for the prosecution**, fiscal. 5. Consultor.

counsel *va.* Aconsejar, recomendar, dirigir, avisar. **To counsel somebody to**, aconsejar a alguien que.

counseling, (GB) **counselling** [ˈkaʊnsəlɪŋ] [kaun-se-lin] *s.* *(Educ., Psych)* Orientación psicopedagógica.

counsel-keeper [ˈkaʊnslkiːpər] [kaun-sel-ki-paʳ] *s.* El que guarda un secreto.

counselor, (GB) **counsellor** [ˈkaʊnsələr] [kaun-se-loʳ] *s.* 1. *(Educ., Psych)* Consejero, aconsejador, orientador. 2. Confidente. 3. *(Law)* Consejero; abogado.

counselor-at-law [ˈkaʊnsələˈætlɔː] [kaun-se-lor-at-loa] *s.* Abogado.

counsellable [ˈkaʊnsələbl] [kaun-se-la-bol] *a.* Dócil, dispuesto a recibir y seguir los consejos de otro.

counsellorship [ˈkaʊnsələʃɪp] [kaun-se-lor-ship] *s.* El empleo, oficio, plaza o dignidad de consejero.

count [ˈkaʊnt] [kaunt] *va.* 1. Contar, numerar (enumerate, add up). **I'm counting the hours till he arrives**, 2. Considerar, calcular, reputar, contar (include). **Not counting the driver**, sin contar el conductor. **There will be fourteen of us, counting you and me**, seremos catorce, tú y yo incluidos. **He counts himself a learned man**, él se tiene por hombre docto. **To count oneself lucky,** darse por afortunado. 3. Imputar, atribuir. -*vn.* 1. Idear, trazar, tramar. 2. Contar, confiar o poner la esperanza en alguna cosa. 3. Contar (enumerate); contar (be valid matter. **That doesn't count,** eso no cuenta o no vale. **Every minute counts,** cada minuto cuenta.

count against Perjudicar. **His age counted against him,** su edad fue un factor negativo o lo perjudicó.

count for Contar. **Your opinion counts for a great deal/won't count for much,** tu opinión importa mucho/no va a contar mucho.

count in Incluir. **You can count me in,** yo me apunto, yo me anoto, cuenten conmigo.

count on 1. Contar con (rely on (friend, help). **I wouldn't count on it,** yo que tú no me confiaría. **We were counting on her for support,** contábamos con que nos apoyaría. 2. Esperar (expect). **We hadn't counted on that happening.** no esperábamos que fuera a pasar eso.

count out 1. **You can count me out,** a mí no me incluyan, no cuenten conmigo. 2. Contar uno por uno (money, objects).

count toward, (GB) **count towards** Contar para.

count *s.* 1. Cuenta o cálculo, partida, cláusula. 2. El acto de dar atención a los detalles; cuidado. 3. *(For.)* Demanda, cargo, capítulo. **To be found guilty on all counts,** ser declarado culpable de todos los cargos (point). **It's been criticized on several counts,** ha sido criticado por varios motivos. 4. Recuento, cómputo (act of counting); escrutinio, recuento, cómputo, conteo (of votes); cuenta, conteo (in boxing). **At the last count,** en el último recuento. **We'll begin at the count of four,** a los cuatro empezamos. **To be out for the count,** estar fuera de combate. 5. Total (total). **The final count,** el recuento o cómputo final (of votes).

count, *s.* Conde, título de nobleza que desde el principio correspondió al de *earl* en Inglaterra (rank).

countable [ˈkaʊntəbl] [kaun-te-bol] *a.* Contadero, contable. *(Ling.)* Numerable.

countdown [ˈkaʊntdaʊn] [kaunt-daun] *s. (Aer.)* Cuenta inversa. Se usa especialmente para explosiones nucleares y lanzamientos de cohetes. Cuenta atrás o regresiva, conteo regresivo. **In the countdown to the Olympic Games,** en los días que precedieron o preceden a los Juegos Olímpicos.

countenance [ˈkaʊntɪnəns] [kaun-ti-nans] *s.* 1. Semblante, cara, rostro, continente, aspecto (face, expression). 2. Buena o mala cara, en cuanto indica el estado de ánimo de una persona. 3. Patrocinio, amparo, protección, apoyo, favor. 4. Aire de presunción y arrogancia. **Out of countenance,** abochornado, desconcertado, turbado, consternado, confuso, corrido, chafado. **To be out of countenance,** -*vr.* abochornarse, correrse, desconcertarse, turbarse, confundirse; sonrojarse. **To give countenance,** apoyar, favorecer, proteger, auxiliar.

countenance *va.* Sostener, patrocinar, apoyar, proteger, fomentar, favorecer, mantener. Tolerar, aceptar.

counter [ˈkaʊntər] [kaun-taʳ] *s.* 1. Contador, contante. 2. Mostrador (in shop); barra (in café); ventanilla (in bank, post office); encimera (in kitchen); tablero, contador. **That drug is not available over the counter,** esa medicina no se puede comprar sin receta. 3. Ficha (games); tanto, monedilla que sirve para contar. **Counter,** tantos, fichas, piedras. 4. *(Mar.)* Bovedilla. **Upper counter,** *(Mar.)* bovedilla superior. 5. Lo opuesto, lo contrario. 6. La porción del zapato que ciñe el talón. 7. Pecho del caballo. 8. *(Mús.)* La parte de canto puesta en contraste inmediato con el tono.

counter *adv.* Contra, al contrario, al revés. También es partícula que se usa en composición, y por lo común significa oposición o contrariedad. **To run counter,** Oponerse; violar, faltar a.

counter *va.* Contrarrestar (oppose, trend). Rebatir, refutar (in debate/idea, statement). **To counter that,** responder o replicar que.

counter- *pref.* Contra.

counteract [ˌkaʊntəˈækt] [kaun-tar-akt] *va.* Contrariar, impedir, estorbar el efecto de alguna cosa, frustrar. Contrarrestar.

counteraction [ˌkaʊntəˈækʃən] [kaun-tar-ak-shon] *s.* Oposición; impedimiento.

counteractive [ˌkaʊntəˈæktɪv] [kaun-tar-ak-tiv] *a.* Que tiende a contrariar o frustrar; contrario, opuesto. -*s.* Opositor.

counter-approach [ˌkaʊntəˈprəʊtʃ] [kaun-tar-a-prouch] *s. (Fort.)* Contraaproches o contraataques, trabajos con que los sitiados impiden que los sitiadores se acerquen.

counterattack [ˈkaʊntərəˌtæk] [kaun-tar-a-tak] *s.* Contraataque.

counterattack *vn.* Contraatacar.

counter-attraction [ˌkaʊntərəˈtrækʃən] [kaun-tar-a-trak-shon] *s.* Atracción opuesta.

counterbalance [ˈkaʊntəˌbæləns] [kaun-tar-ba-lans] *s.* Contrapeso, equilibrio, compensación.

counterbalance *va.* Contrapesar, servir de contrapeso.

counter-bond [ˈkaʊntəbɒnd] [kaun-tar-bond] *s.* Contrafianza, obligación dada a un fiador por la persona a quien fio.

counterbuff [ˈkaʊntəbʌf] [kaun-tar-buf] *va.* Rechazar, repeler.

counterbuff, *s.* Rechazo.

counterchange [ˈkaʊntətʃændʒ] [kaun-tar-cheinch] *s.* Contracambio, recompensa recíproca.

counterchange, *va.* Trocar, cambiar, dar y tomar recíprocamente.

countercharge [ˈkaʊntətʃɑːdʒ] [kaun-tar-charch] *s.* Recriminación, acusación del acusado contra el que acusa.

countercharge, *va.* 1. *(Mil.)* Cargar, atacar a los que dan una carga. 2. Hacer cargos, el acusado contra el acusador.

countercharm [ˈkaʊntətʃɑːm] [kaun-tar-charm] *s.* Desencanto.

countercharm, *va.* Desencantar.

countercheck [ˈkaʊntətʃek] [kaun-tar-chek] *va.* Contrastar, contrarrestar.

countercheck, *s.* Oposición, repulsa.

counterclaim [ˈkaʊntəkleɪm] [kaun-ter-kleim] *s.* Contrarreclamación.

counter clerk [ˈkaʊntəklɜːk] [kaun-tar-klerk] *s.* Empleado (in post office); (GB) cajero (in bank).

counterclockwise [ˈkaʊntəˈklɒwaɪz] [kaun-tar-klok-uais] *a.* y *adv.* Con movimiento circular a la izquierda. En sentido contrario a las agujas del reloj.

countercunning [ˈkaʊntəkʌnɪŋ] [kaun-tar-ka-nin] *s.* Contraastucia, astucia opuesta a otra.

countercurrent [ˈkaʊntəkʌrənt] [kaun-tar-ka-rent] *s.* Contracorriente, corriente contraria a otra.

counterdeed [ˈkaʊntədiːd] [kaun-tar-did] *s.* Contraescritura, escrito o acto particular que deshace en todo o en parte algún otro acto público.

counterdistinction *s.* V. CONTRADISTINCTION.

counterdraw [ˈkaʊntədrɔː] [kaun-tar-dro] *va.* Calcar, pasar un dibujo por medio de un material transparente.

counterespionage [ˈkaʊntərˈespɪɑːdʒ] [kaun-tar-es-pio-nech] *s.* Contraespionaje.

counterevidence [ˈkaʊntərˈevɪdəns] [kaun-ter-e-vi-dens] *s.* Contraevidencia, el testimonio de un segundo testigo, opuesto al que otro dio antes.

counterfeit [ˈkaʊntəfiːt] [kaun-ter-fit] *va.* 1. Falsear, contrahacer, copiar alguna cosa con intención de pasarla por original. 2. Imitar, falsificar, forjar; hacer una cosa tan parecida a otra que con dificultad se distingan. -*vn.* Fingir, disimular.

counterfeit, *s.* 1. Impostura, engaño, falsificación, contrahacimiento. 2. Mentira, disimulo, artimaña, bellaquería, trapacería. 3. Falseador, impostor, falsificador. -*a.* Contrahecho, falsificado, falseado, engañoso, fingido. **Counterfeit coin,** moneda falsa.

counterfeiter [ˈkaʊntəfiːtər] [kaun-tar-fi-taʳ] s. Falsario, falsificador, contrahacedor, forjador, flaseador, imitador. **Counterfeiter of coin,** monedero falso.

counterfeitly [ˈkaʊntəfiːtlɪ] [kaun-ter-fit-li] adv. Falsamente, fingidamente.

counterfoil [ˈkaʊntəfɔɪl] [kaun-ter-foil] s. Talón, matriz.

counterguard [ˈkaʊntəgɑːd] [kaun-ter-gard] s. (Fort.) Contraguardia, obra exterior compuesta de dos caras que forman ángulo, edificiada delante de los baluartes.

counterinfluence [ˈkaʊntərɪnˈfluːəns] [kaun-ter-in-fluens] va. Influir en contrario.

counterinfluence s. Influencia opuesta.

counterintelligence [ˈkaʊntərɪnˌtelɪdʒəns] [kaun-ter-in-te-li-yens] s. Contraespionaje.

counter-irritant [ˈkaʊntərˌɪrɪtənt] [kaun-ter-i-ri-tant] s. Agente medicinal que se emplea para excitar irritación en una parte del cuerpo a fin de aliviar el dolor en otra parte.

counterlight [ˈkaʊntəlaɪt] [kaun-ter-lait] s. Contraluz, la luz contraria a la propia para ver el objeto que se presenta.

countermand [ˈkaʊntəmænd] [kaun-tar-mand] va. Contramandar; revocar, invalidar; retirar las invitaciones para un convite, una junta, etc.

countermand, s. Contramandato, contraorden; nulidad.

countermarch [ˈkaʊntəmɑːtʃ] [kaun-tar-march] s. 1. Contramarcha, retroceso del camino andado. 2. Contramarcha, cambio de frente. 3. Mudanza de ideas o conducta.

countermarch, vn. Contramarcha, desandar lo andado.

countermark [ˈkaʊntəmɑːk] [kaun-tar-mark] s. 1. Contramarca, segunda o tercera señal que se hace sobre una bala o un fardo de mercaderías. 2. Contramarca del gremio de plateros en Inglaterra.

countermine [ˈkaʊntəmaɪn] [kaun-tar-main] s. 1. Contramina, la mina que se hace en oposición a las del enemigo, a fin de inutilizarlas. 2. Contramina, medida adoptada para frustrar el intento de otro.

countermine,» va. 1. Contraminar, hacer minas para encontrar las del enemigo. 2. Deshacer o impedir la ejecución de lo que otro intenta, estorbar.

countermotion [ˈkaʊntəmoʊʃən] [kaun-tar-moushon] s. 1. Movimiento contrario. 2. Proposición contraria.

countermove [ˈkaʊntəmuːv] [kaun-tar-muv] va. y vn. Mover o moverse en dirección contraria u opuesta a otra.

countermovement [ˈkaʊntəmuːvmənt] [kaun-tar-muv-ment] s. Movimiento opuesto a otro.

countermure [ˈkaʊntəmʊər] [kaun-tar-muar] s. Contramuro, falsabraga.

counternatural [ˈkaʊntəˌnætjʊərəl] [kaun-ter-na-tiu-ral] a. Contranatural.

counternoise [ˈkaʊntənɔɪs] [kaun-tar-nois] s. Un sonido que impide que se oiga otro.

counteroffensive [ˈkaʊntərəˈfensɪv] [kaun-taro-fen-siv] s. Contraofensiva.

counteropening [ˈkaʊntərˈɒpənɪŋ] [kaun-tar-o-pe-nin] s. (Cir.) Contraabertura.

counterpace [ˈkaʊntəpeɪs] [kaun-tar-peis] s. Contrapaso.

counterpane [ˈkaʊntəpeɪn] [kaun-tar-pein] s. Colcha de cama, sobrecama; cobertor.

counterpart [ˈkaʊntəpɑːt] [kaun-tar-part] s. 1. Contraparte; duplicado, traslado, copia, imagen. 2. Homólogo (person); equivalente (thing).

counterpetition [ˈkaʊntəpeˈtɪʃən] [kaun-tar-pe-ti-shon] s. Petición opuesta, contrainstancia.

counterpetition vn. Hacer una petición o súplica contraria a otra.

counterplea [ˈkaʊntəpliː] [kaun-tar-pli] s. Segunda instancia.

counterplot [ˈkaʊntəplɒt] [kaun-tar-plot] va. Contraminar; oponer una astucia a otra.

counterplotting [ˈkaʊntəplɒtɪŋ] [kaun-tar-plo-tin] s. Trama inventada para contrarrestar otra.

counterpoint [ˈkaʊntəpɔɪnt] [kaun-tar-point] s. 1. (Mús.) Contrapunto, concordancia armoniosa de voces contrapuestas. 2. Punto o método opuesto.

counterpoise [ˈkaʊntəpɔɪz] [kaun-tar-pois] va. Contrapesar, contrarrestar, contrabalancear.

counterpoise, s. 1. Contrapeso. 2. Equilibrio. 3. Pilón, pesa movible que corre por el ástil de una romana y determina el peso de una cosa igualando el fiel.

counterpoison [ˈkaʊntəpɔɪzn] [kaun-tar-poi-son] s. Contraveneno; antídoto.

counterpractice [ˈkaʊntəpræktɪs] [kaun-tar-prak-tis] s. Práctica en oposición a otra.

counterpressure [ˈkaʊntəpreʒər] [kaun-tar-pre-shaʳ] s. Fuerza opuesta o contraria.

counterproductive [ˈkaʊntəfiːt] [kaun-tar-fit] a. Contraproducente.

counteproject [ˈkaʊntəprəjekt] [kaun-tar-pro-yekt] s. Proyecto opuesto a otro.

counterproof [ˈkaʊntəpruːf] [kaun-tar-pruf] s. Contraprueba, la segunda prueba que sacan los impresores, grabadores y estampadores.

counterprove [ˈkaʊntəpruːv] [kaun-tar-pruv] va. Sacar los perfiles de una estampa o dibujo calcándolo.

counterrevolution [ˈkaʊntərəveˈluːʃən] [kaun-tar-re-vo-lu-shon] s. Contrarrevolución.

counterrevolutionary [ˈkaʊntərəveˈluːʃənərɪ] [kaun-tar-re-vo-lu-sho-na-ri] a. Contrarrevolucionario.

counterrevolutionist [ˈkaʊntərəveˈluːʃənɪst] [kaun-tar-re-vo-lu-sho-nist] s. Contrarrevolucionario.

countersalute [ˈkaʊntəˌsəljuːt] [kaun-tar-sa-liut] s. Contrasalva, salva en respuesta a otra hecha anteriormente.

counterscarf [ˈkaʊntəskɑːf] [kaun-tar-skarf] s., **counterscarp** [ˈkaʊntəskɑːp] [kaun-tar-skarp], s. (Fort.) Contraescarpa, el declive hecho junto al foso, al lado de la esplanada y opuesto a la escarpa.

counterseal [ˈkaʊntəsiːl] [kaun-tar-sil] va. Contrasellar.

countersecure [ˈkaʊntəˌsekjuːr] [kaun-tar-se-kiuʳ] va. Asegurar más.

countersense [ˈkaʊntəsəns] [kaun-tar-sens] s. Contrasentido, sentido opuesto.

countersign [ˈkaʊntəsaɪn] [kaun-tar-sain] va. Refrendar, firmar algún decreto o despacho de alguna autoridad superior para darle mayor autenticidad (document).

countersign, s. 1. (Mil.) Santo y seña, contraseña. 2. Refrendata, la firma del que subscribe por autoridad pública después del superior.

countersignal [ˈkaʊntəsaɪnəl] [kaun-tar-sig-nal] s. (Mar.) Señal que corresponde a otra.

countersignature [ˈkaʊntəsaɪnəˌtʃʊər] [kaun-tar-sig-na-chuaʳ] s. V. COUNTERSIGN, 2a acep.

countersink [ˈkaʊntəsɪŋk] [kaun-tar-sink] va. Avellanar. - s. 1. Avellanador. 2. Dilatación de un hueco para recibir la cabeza de un tornillo, de un perno, etc.

counterstatute [ˈkaʊntəstətjuːt] [kaun-tar-sta-tiut] s. Ordenanza o estatuto contrario a otro.

counterstroke [ˈkaʊntəstroʊk] [kaun-tar-strouk] s. Golpe retornado.

countersway [ˈkaʊntəzweɪ] [kaun-tars-uei] s. Influencia que obra en oposición de otra.

counter-surety s. V. COUNTER-BOND

counter-tally [ˈkaʊntətælɪ] [kaun-tar-ta-li] s. Contratarja.

counter-taste [ˈkaʊntəteɪst] [kaun-tar-teist] s. Gusto falso o ficticio.

counter-tenor [ˈkaʊntəˌtenər] [kaun-tar-te-nor] s. (Mús.) Contralto.

counter-tide [ˈkaʊntətaɪd] [kaun-tar-taid] s. (Mar.) Contramarea, una marea contraria a otra.

countertime [ˈkaʊntətaɪm] [kaun-tar-taim] s. Defensa, oposición; contratiempo.

countertop [ˈkaʊntəstɒp] [kaun-tar-top] s. Encimera.

counter-trench [ˈkaʊntətrentʃ] [kaun-tar-trench] s. (Mil.) Contratrinchera.

counter-turn ['kaʊntətɜːn] [kaun-tar-tern] *s.* Desenlace, desenredo de un lance de comedia.

countervail ['kaʊntəveɪl] [kaun-tar-veil] *va.* Contrapesar, contrarrestar, compensar.

counter-view ['kaʊntəvɪuː] [kaun-tar-viu] *s.* Postura en que dos personas se miran cara a cara, o se hallan frente a frente.

counter-vote ['kaʊntəvəʊt] [kaun-tar-vout] *va.* Oponer, ganar por pluralidad de votos.

counter-weigh [ˌkaʊntə'weɪ] [kaun-tar-uei] *vn.* Contrapesar.

counter-weight [ˌkaʊntə'weɪt] [kaun-tar-ueit] *s.* Contrapeso.

counter-wheel ['kaʊntəwiːl] [kaun-tar-uil] *va. (Mil.)* Evolucionar en diversas direcciones.

counter-work ['kaʊntəwɜːk] [kaun-tter-uek] *va.* Contrarrestar, contrariar, resistir o impedir, contraminar.

countess ['kaʊntes] [kaun-tes] *sf.* Condesa, la esposa del conde, o la que por sí tiene este título.

counting-house ['kaʊntɪŋˌhaʊs] [kaun-tin-jaus] *s.* Despacho, escritorio, en que los comerciantes tienen sus libros y cuentas.

countless ['kaʊntles] [kaunt-les] *a.* Innumerables, sin número, incontables (stars, hours).

countrified ['kaʊntrɪfaɪd] [kaun-tri-faid] *a. y pp.* Rústico, campesino, rural.

countrify ['kaʊntrɪfaɪ] [ken-tri-fai] *va.* hacer rústico o campesino, especialmente en el aspecto.

country ['kaʊntrɪ] [ken-tri] *s.* 1. País, región; pueblo (people). 2. Campo, campiña (en oposición a ciudad); provincia, región (en oposición a capital o metrópoli). **The country, el campo (rural area). To go into the country,** ir al campo. 3. País (nation), patria (native land), tierra; el país natal o el suelo nativo de alguno. 4. Los habitantes de algún país. 5. *(For.)* La comunidad donde se convocan o de donde proceden los miembros de un jurado; y de aquí el jurado mismo. 6. Terreno, territorio (region). **Cattle-farming country,** región ganadera. *-a.* Rústico, rural, campesino, rudo, agreste, campestre. **Country merchant,** comerciante del interior, o de tierra adentro.

country-and-western ['kaʊntrɪænd'westɜːn] [ken-tri-anues-tern] *s.* Música country.

country bumpkin ['kaʊntrɪˌbʌmpkɪn] [ken-tri-bamp-kin] *s.* Pueblerino, paleto, pajuerano.

country cousin ['kaʊntrɪkʌzn] [ken-tri-kasn] *s.* Pueblerino.

country-dance ['kaʊntrɪdæns] [ken-tri-dans] *s.* Contradanza. *V.* CONTRA-DANCE.

country dancing ['kaʊntrɪˌdænsɪŋ] [ken-tri-dan-sin] *s. (BrE)* Danzas folklóricas.

country-house ['kaʊntrɪhaʊs] [ken-tri-jaus] *s.* Casa de campo, granja, quinta. **The king's country palace,** real sitio.

countryman ['kaʊntrɪmæn] [ken-tri-man] *(pl.* COUNTTRYMEN) *s.* 1. Paisano, compatriota, conciudadano. 2. Paisano, aldeano, patán; labrador. 3. Ganso, paleto. (Cuba) Montero, guajiro. *(Mex.)* Payo.

country mile ['kaʊntrɪmaɪl] [ken-tri-mail] *s. (Coloq.)* **To miss something by a country mile,** errar por mucho o por una legua, errarle feo.

countryside ['kaʊntrɪsaɪd] [ken-tri-said] *s.* Campiña, campo.

country squire ['kaʊntrɪskwaɪər] [ken-tri-skuai-aʳ] *s.* Caballero de provincia.

country store ['kaʊntrɪstɔːr] [ken-tri] *s.* Tienda de pueblo en la que se vende de todo.

countrywide ['kaʊntrɪ] [ken-tri-uaid] *a./adv.* A escala nacional.

country-woman ['kaʊntrɪˌwʊmən] [kaun-tri-uo-man] *sf.* Compatriota, paisana; aldeana. *V.* COUNTRYMAN.

county ['kaʊntɪ] [kaun-ti] *s.* Condado, distrito territorial. En los Estados Unidos, subdivisión civil de un estado; también, sus habitantes. En Inglaterra se llama también *county* al *shire. V.* SHIRE. **County line,** límite del condado. **County-seat,** capital de condado o distrito, cabeza de partido. **County town,** capital del condado.

county council ['kaʊntɪˌkaʊnsl] [kaun-ti-kaun-sil] *s.* Corporación de gobierno a nivel de condado. **County court,** (in US) juzgado comarcal; (in UK) juzgado comarcal que conoce de causas de derecho civil.

coup [kuː] [ku] *s.* Golpe maestro (successful action). *(Pol.)* **Coup d' état,** golpe de estado. **Coup de grâce,** golpe de gracia.

couple ['kʌpl] [kapol] *s.* 1. Par, dos seres o cosas de cualquier especie, siendo de igual calidad. Un par de algo (two or small number). **I think he'd had a couple,** creo que ha tomado unas copas de más. **A couple hundred books,** unos doscientos libros. 2. Par, macho y hembra. **Married couple,** matrimonio, marido y mujer. 3. Pareja, compañero y compañera, dos personas unidas temporalmente, p. ej. en un baile; dos animales apareados. **The happy couple,** la feliz pareja, los recién casados.

couple *va.* 1. Parear, unir, juntar, encadenar; *(Rail)* enganchar (connect); asociar (theories, events). **To couple something/somebody with something/somebody,** asociar algo/a alguien con algo/alguien. **The fall in demand, coupled with competition from abroad,** el descenso de la demanda, unido a la competencia extranjera. 2. Casar, solemnizar el matrimonio, el sacerdote o funcionario autorizado para ello. *- vn.* Tener cópula o coito, unirse o juntarse carnalmente.

couple up Enganchar.

couple-beggar ['kʌplˌbegər] [kapl-be-gaʳ] *s.* El clérigo o funcionario que casa clandestinamente.

coupler ['kʌplər] [ka-pleʳ] *s.* Aparato de conexión; enganche, acopladura.

couplet ['kʌpl] [kapl] *s.* 1. Par, pareja. 2. Copla; pareado, el verso que rima con el que le sigue.

coupling ['kʌplɪŋ] [ka-plin] *s.* 1. Ayuntamiento, cópula. 2. Lazo, unión, enganche; ensambladura, conexión. **Coupling-pin,** *(F. C.)* pasador del enganche. **Friction-coupling,** manguito de fricción, unión friccional. **Shaft-coupling,** embrague, conexión de los ejes de transmisión.

coupon ['kuːpɒn] [ku-pon] *s.* Cupón, parte de un vale o crédito con interés; parte separable de un billete, etc. (voucher for discount); cupón de racionamiento (in rationing). Cupón (form/in advertisement); boleto (for competition).

courage ['kʌrɪdʒ] [ka-rich] *s.* Coraje, valor, intrepidez, brío, bravura. **To have/lack the courage of one's convictions,** ser/no ser fiel a sus convicciones. **To lose one's courage,** acobardarse. **He took courage from her smile,** su sonrisa le dio ánimo. **To take one's courage in both hands,** hacer de tripas corazón.

courageous [kəˈreɪdʒəs] [ko-rei-chos] *a.* Animoso, valiente, valeroso, brioso, intrépido (person); valiente (words); valeroso, de valor o de valentía (act).

courageously [kəˈreɪdʒəsli] [ko-rei-chos-li] *adv.* Valerosamente, con valor o valentía.

courageousness [kəˈreɪdʒəsnɪs] [ko-rei-chos-nes] *s.* Ánimo, aliento, valor, intrepidez.

courgette [kɔːˈdʒeɪ] [kor-yei] *s.* (GB) *V.* ZUCCHINI. Calabacín.

courier ['kʊrɪər] [ku-rieʳ] *s.* Correo, expreso, ordinario. Guía (guide); mensajero, correo, rutero (messenger). **Courier service,** servicio de mensajero.

course [kɔːs] [kors] *s.* 1. Corrida, curso, carrera. Curso (of river); recorrido (of road). **The only course open to us,** el único camino que tenemos, nuestra única opción (ways of proceeding). **In the normal course of events,** normalmente, en circunstancias normales (progress). **In the course of time,** con el tiempo. **I changed the course of history,** cambió el curso de la historia. **To run/take its course,** seguir su curso. 2. Tránsito, paso de un paraje a otro, camino, ruta, tirada, paseo; viaje, correría, excursión. 3. Estadio. *(Sport)* Hipódromo, pista (de carreras); campo o cancha de golf (golf course). **To last/stay the course,** aguantar hasta el final (persist to the end). 4. *(Mar.)* Rumbo, derrotero o derrota de una embarcación. **To set course for,** poner rumbo a. **To go off course,** desviarse de rumbo. **To change course,** cambiar de rumbo. 5. Curso, los principios y elemento de alguna ciencia o arte explicados metódicamente. *(Educ.)* Curso. **A short course,** un cursillo. **To take/do a course,** hacer un curso. **To go on a course,** ir a hacer un curso. *(Med.)* **A course of treatment,** un tratamiento. 6. Método o género de vida o modo de obrar; conducta, porte, costumbre. 7. Entrada, servicio, cubierto, el número de platos que se ponen de una vez en la mesa. Plato (part of a meal). **Main course,** plato principal o fuerte o central. **As a/for the first course,** de primer plato, de entrada. **Dinner of ten courses,** comida o mesa de diez entradas. 8. Indole. 9. Estructura regular; serie o hilera de piedras o ladrillos en una pared. 10. Regularidad, orden; marcha, progresión; medios ordenados para alcanzar alguna cosa. 11. Ceremonia, cumplimientos. *-pl.* 1. *(Mar.)* Papahigos o velas mayores. **To be under the courses,** andar con los papahigos. 2. *(Fam.)* Reglas, menstruación. **Of course,** por supuesto, sin duda, indudablemente, por sabido por descontado, por consiguiente, de juro. **Matter of course,** cosa de cajón. **Course of physic,** método curativo. **Main course,** *(Mar.)* la vela mayor de un buque. **Words of course,** ceremonias, cumplimientos. **The last course,** los postres. **Everyone in his course,** cada uno a su vez. **It is our common course,** es nuestro modo de obrar, es nuestra costumbre.

course *va.* 1. Correr por, o sobre. 2. Hacer correr, excitar a correr. 3. Cazar, dar caza, perseguir. *-vn.* Corretear, andar de casa en casa o de calle en calle, disputar, argumentar. **To course over,** ir encima de. **He felt the blood coursing through his veins,** sentía correr la sangre por sus venas.

courser [ˈkɔːsər] [kor-saʳ] *s.* 1. Corcel ligero o veloz. 2. Corredor o cazador de liebres, el que las corre con perros.

courses *s. pl. V.* COURSE.

coursing [ˈkɔːsɪŋ] [kor-sin] *s.* La caza.

court [kɔːt] [kort] *s.* 1. Corte, comitiva. 2. Corte, el lugar donde reside el monarca; palacio. 3. Corte, se toma por el soberano y sus ministros, y en esta significación se llama también gabinete. 4. Corte, consejo, tribunal de justicia, el conjunto de jueces que forman un tribunal y la sala, donde se juntan a administrar justicia, que también se llama estrados. *(For.)* **Supreme Court,** consejo o tribunal supremo; en los Estados Unidos y en cada uno de los estados es el tribunal de último recurso. **Superior court,** en los Estados Unidos, tribunal de segunda instancia, correspondiente a la Audiencia. **Court of Common Pleas,** juzgado o tribunal de primera instancia. **Court-martial,** consejo de guerra, tribunal militar. **To appear in court,** comparecer ante el tribunal o los tribunales. **To take somebody to court,** demandar a alguien, llevar a alguien a juicio. **The court is adjourned,** se levanta la sesión. **Court case,** causa, juicio. **Court order,** orden judicial. **Court guide,** guía de forasteros. 5. Corte, el acompañamiento obsequioso que se hace a alguna persona constituida en dignidad. 6. Corte, cortejo, el obsequio o galanteo que se hace a una mujer. 7. Patio, atrio de una casa (courtyard). 8. *(Sport)* Cancha, pista.

court *va.* 1. Cortejar, enamorar, requebrar, acariciar; hacer la corte; engatusar. 2. Solicitar, adular, rogar. 3. Buscar (seek/danger, favor); exponerse a (disaster). *-vn.* Estar de novios, noviar, pololear (dated).

court-breeding [ˈkɔːtˌbriːdɪŋ] [kort-bri-din] *s.* Educación de corte, cortesanía.

court-card [ˈkɔːtkɑːd] [kort-kard] *s.* Una figura en los naipes. Es corrupción de *coat-card.*

court-chaplain [ˈkɔːtˌtʃɑːpleɪn] [kort-cha-plein] *s.* Capellán de palacio.

court-cupboard [ˈkɔːtkʌpˌbɔːd] [kort-kap-bord] *s.* Especie de alacena.

court-day [ˈkɔːtdeɪ] [kort-dei] *s.* 1. Día de junta general de los tribunales de justicia. 2. Día de besamanos.

court-dress [ˈkɔːtdres] [kort-dres] *s.* 1. Ayuda de cámara o camarista de las personas de la corte. 2. Lisonjeador.

courteous [ˈkɜːtɪəs] [kor-tios] *a.* Cortés, atento, político, civil, sociable, afable, urbano, bien criado; benigno, humano, benévolo; cortesano.

courteously [ˈkɜːtəslɪ] [kor-tios-li] *adv.* Cortésmente, con cortesía, civilmente.

courteousness [ˈkɜːtəsnɪs] [kor-tios-nes] *s.* Cortesía, cortesanía, atención, agrado, urbanidad, buena crianza, benevolencia.

courter [ˈkɔːtər] [kortaʳ] *s.* 1. Cortejador, cortesano. 2. Pretendiente, aspirante.

courtesan [ˌkɔːtɪˈzæn] [ker-ti-san] *sf.* Cortesana, mujer pública.

courtesy [ˈkɜːtɪsɪ] [ker-ti-si] *s.* 1. Cortesía (politeness). **It's common courtesy,** es de (simple) cortesía o de buena educación. **You could have had the courtesy to inform us,** podría haber tenido la gentileza de avisarnos. 2. Gracia, favor, merced; atención, gentileza (favor). **By courtesy of,** por atención o gentileza de. 3. Bondad, benignidad. 4. Cortesía, reverencia que hacen las mujeres. **They exchanged courtesies,** se saludaron con las cortesías de rigor (greeting). *V.* CURTSY.

courtesy *vn.* Hacer una cortesía o reverencia. *-va.* Hablar o tratar con cortesía.

court-fashion [ˈkɔːtfæʃən] [kort-fa-shion] *s.* Moda o traje de corte.

court-favor [ˈkɔːtfeɪvər] [kort-fei-vor] *s.* Gracia, merced o distinción que dispensa el poder supremo.

court-hand [ˈkɔːthænd] [kort-jand] *s.* Letra de curia.

court-house [ˈkɔːthaʊs] [kort-jaus] *s.* Edificio público destinado a las funciones judiciales. En los estados del sur se llama también así a la capital de condado.

courtier [ˈkɔːtɪər] [kort-tier] *s.* Cortesano, palaciego; cortejo, cortejante.

court-lady [ˈkɔːtleɪd] [kort-leidi] *s.* Dama de corte o de palacio.

courtlike [ˈkɔːtlaɪk] [kort-laik] *a.* Cortesano, propio de corte, elegante, urbano.

courtliness [ˈkɔːtlaɪnəs] [kert-lai-nes] *s.* Cortesanía, cortesía, urbanidad; elegancia, gracia.

courtly [ˈkɔːtlɪ] [kort-li] *a.* Cortesano, elegante, insinuante, cortés; distinguido, fino. **Courtly love,** el amor cortés.

court-martial [ˈkɔːtˈmɑːʃəl] [kort-mar-shal] *s.* Consejo de guerra.

court-martial *va.* Formarle consejo de guerra a (a soldier).

court-minion [ˈkɔːtmiːnɪən] [kort-mi-nion] *s.* Valido, privado, favorito.

court-plaster [ˈkɔːtplɑːstər] [kort-plas-taʳ] *s.* Tafetán inglés.

courtroom [ˈkɔːtrɔm] [kort-rum] *s.* Sala de un tribunal.

courtship [ˈkɔːtʃɪp] [kort-ship] *s.* 1. Corte, cortejo; galantería, obsequio y galanteo; el acto de pretender a una mujer en matrimonio. 2. *(Zool.)* Cortejo.

court shoe [ˈkɔːtʃuː] [kort-shu] *s.* Zapato de salón.

courtyard [ˈkɔːtjɑːd] [kort-yard] *s.* Patio.

cousin [ˈkʌzn] [ka-sin] *s.* Primo o prima. **Cousin german** o **first cousin,** primo hermano. **Second cousin,** primo segundo.

cove [kʌv] [kav] *s.* 1. *(Mar.)* Caleta, ensenada. 2. *(Arq.)* Bovedilla, toda especie de moldura cóncava. 3. *(Ger.)* Hombre, mozo, chaval.

cove *va.* Abovedar, arquear.

coven [ˈkʌvən] [ka-ven] *s.* Aquelarre.

covenant [ˈkʌvɪnənt] [ka-ve-nant] *s.* Contrato, convención, estipulación, pacto, tratado, ajuste; alianza, liga; escritura de contrato. **The new covenant,** el nuevo testamento, o la nueva alianza.

covenant *va.* Estipular, contratar. *-vn.* Convenir, pactar, estipular.

covenantee [ˌkʌvɪnənˈtiː] [ka-vi-nan-ti] *s.* Contratante.

covenanter, covenantor [ˈkʌvɪnəntər] [ka-vi-nan-tor] *s.* Confederado, coligado, conjurado.

Coventry [ˈkɒvəntrɪ] [ko-ven-tri] *s.* Nombre de una ciudad en Warwickshire, Inglaterra. **Coventry blue,** hilo de marcar. **To send to Coventry,** desterrar, echar de la sociedad.

cover [ˈkʌvər] [ka-vaʳ] *va.* 1. Cubrir, tender una cosa sobre otra (overlay); tapar, ocultar; abrigar, proteger. **To be covered in something,** estar cubierto de algo. Tapar (hole, saucepan). Poner una funda a (cushion); forrar (book); tapizar, recubrir (sofa). Techar, cubrir (passage, terrace). 2. Empollar, ponerse las aves sobre los huevos para sacar cría. 3. Resarcir, compensar, indemnizar. *(Fin.)* Cubrir (cost, expenses); hacer frente a (liabilities). **Will $100 cover it?,** ¿alcanzará con 100 dólares? Cubrir, asegurar (insurance). 4. Apuntar y retener a uno al alcance de un arma de fuego; dominar tropas o cañones; apuntarle a (point gun at). **We've got you covered!,** ¡te estamos apuntando! Cubrir (guard, protect). **I'll keep you covered,** yo te cubro. *(Sport)* Marcar (opponent); cubrir (shot, base). 5. Pasar, atravesar; dícese de un espacio o distancia. Recorrer, cubrir (travel, distance); llenar (page); cubrir (extend over/area, floor). 6. Cubrir, juntarse el macho de algunos animales con la hembra. 7. Cubrirse, ponerse el sombrero; tapar (hide). **She covered her eyes,** se tapó los ojos. **To cover one's head,** cubrirse (la cabeza). 8. Paliar, disfrazar, disimular (mask/surprise, ignorance); ocultar, tapar (mistake). 9. Cubrir (deal with/syllabus); tratar (topic); contemplar (eventuality). *(Journ.)* Cubrir (report on). **Covered way,** camino cubierto. *-vn.* **To cover for somebody,** sustituir a alguien (deputize); encubrir a alguien (conceal truth). *vr.* **To cover oneself,** cubrirse las espaldas.

cover over 1. Techar, cubrir (roof). 2. Tapar, cubrir (conceal).

cover up 1. Cubrir, tapar (cover completely); ocultar, tapar (conceal/facts, truth); disimular (mistake). 2. Disimular (conceal error). **To cover up for somebody,** encubrir a alguien (conceal truth).

cover *s.* 1. Cubierta, tapadera (lid, casing); tapa, cubierta (of book); portada, carátula (of magazine). **Back cover,** contraportada. **Cover of a letter,** cubierta de una carta, sobre, sobrescrito. **To read something from cover to cover,** leer algo de cabo a rabo. **Under separate cover,** por separado (envelope). 2. Capa o pretexto, velo. 3. Cubierta, lo que cubre o defiende, abrigo, techado, albergue, cobertizo. **Under cover,** (a) bajo cubierto; al abrigo; (b) bajo sobre, cerrado (pliego, carta). 4. Cubierto (tenedor, cuchillo y cuchara) (in restaurant); consumición mínima (in nightclub). 5. Funda (cushion, sofa, typewriter); forro (book); cubrecama, colcha (bed cover). **Covers,** (bedclothes). **The covers,** las mantas, las cobijas, las frazadas. 6. Maleza, matorral. **Cover-glass,** cubierta de vidrio muy delgado para muestras microscópicas. 7. Cobertura (insurance). **To take cover,** guarecerse o ponerse a cubierto (shelter, protection). **To run for cover,** correr a guarecerse o a ponerse a cubierto. **Under cover of darkness/night,** al abrigo o amparo de la oscuridad o de la noche.

coverage [ˈkʌvərɪdʒ] [ka-ve-rich] *s.* *(Journ.)* Cobertura. **Press/television/news coverage,** cobertura periodística, televisiva, informativa. **There will be live coverage of the game,** el partido será transmitido o retransmitido en directo.

coveralls [ˈkʌvərɔːlz] [ka-va-rols] *s. pl.* Mono de trabajo.

coverer [ˈkʌvərər] [ka-ve-raʳ] *s.* Lo que cubre o protege.

cover girl [ˈkʌvəgɜːl] [ka-ver-guel] *s.* Modelo de portada.

covering [ˈkʌvərɪŋ] [ka-ve-rin] *s.* Ropa o vestido, lo que cubre el cuerpo para abrigarle. **Use it as a covering for the floor,** úsalo para cubrir o tapar el suelo. **A covering of dust,** una capa de polvo.

covering letter [kʌvərɪŋˌletər] [ka-ve-rin-le-taʳ] *s.* Carta adjunta.

coverlet, covelid [ˈkʌvəlɪt] [ka-ve-lit] *s.* Colcha, sobrecama o cobertura de cama.

coversed sine [kʌvɜːstˈsaɪn] [ka-verst-sain] *s.* *(Mat.)* Coseno verso, seno verso del complemento de un ángulo o de un arco.

cover story [ˈkʌvəstɔːrɪ] [ka-va-sto-ri] *s.* Tema de portada (in magazine); noticia de primera plana (in newspaper).

covert [ˈkʌvət] [ka-vert] *s.* 1. Cubierto o cubierta. 2. Refugio, asilo, guarida. 3. Matorral o espesura de matas en que se oculta o se esconde alguno. 4. Bandada, en la caza de aves. *-a.* 1. Cubierto, oculto, tapado, secreto, escondido.

covertly [ˈkʌvətlɪ] [ka-vert-li] *adv.* Secretamente, en secreto.

covertness [ˈkʌvətnɪs] [ko-vert-nes] *s.* Secreto, sigilo; escondrijo.

coverture [ˈkʌvətʃʊər] [ka-ver-chuaʳ] *s.* Escondrijo, escondite; antiguamente, cubierta.

covert-way [kʌvətˈweɪ] [ka-vert-uei] *s.* *(Fort.)* Camino cubierto, el espacio que media entre la contraescarpa y la esplanada. Lo mismo que *covered way.*

cover-up [ˈkʌvərʌp] [ka-ver-ap] *s.* Encubrimiento (of crime). **There has been a cover-up,** ha habido una maniobra para encubrir el asunto.

covet [ˈkʌvɪt] [ka-vit] *va.* Codiciar, desear con ansia, apetecer, ambicionar. *-vn.* Desear, anhelar, aspirar.

covetable [ˈkʌvɪtəbl] [ka-vi-ta-bol] *a.* Codiciable.

coveted [ˈkʌvɪtɪd] [ka-vit-nes] *a.* Codiciado.

coveting [ˈkʌvɪtɪŋ] [ka-vi-tin] *s.* Codicia desordenada.

covetingly [ˈkʌvɪtɪŋlɪ] [ka-vi-tin-li] *adv.* Codiciosamente.

covetous [ˈkʌvɪtəs] [ka-vi-tos] *a.* Codicioso, avariento, ambicioso, sórdido, interesado, avaro, roñoso, mezquino, mísero, ávido, ansioso. **To be covetous of something,** codiciar algo.

covetously [ˈkʌvɪtəslɪ] [ka-vi-tos-li] *adv.* Codiciosamente.

covetousness [ˈkʌvɪəsnɪs] [ka-vi-tos-nes] *s.* Codicia, avaricia; ambición, avidez, mezquindad, miseria, sordidez.

covey [ˈkʌvɪ] [kavi] *s.* Nidada, pollada; banda o bandada, número crecido de aves o pájaros que vuelan juntos.

cow [kaʊ] [kau] *va.* Acobardar, amedrentar, intimidar, causar o poner miedo. **He wasn't cowed by their treats,** no se dejó acobardar o intimidar por sus amenazas. **A cowed look,** una mirada acobardada.

cow 1. Vaca. **Milch-cow,** vaca de leche. *(Coloq.)* **Till/until the cows come home,** hasta el día del juicio final. 2. Hembra (female whale, elephant, seal). (GB) *(Coloq.)* **Stupid cow!,** ¡imbécil! (woman).

coward [ˈkaʊəd] [kaued] *s.* Cobarde, collón. *(Vul.)* Pendejo. *-a.* Cobarde, medroso, pusilánime.

cowardice [ˈkaʊədɪs] [kaued-is], **cowardliness** [ˈkaʊədlɪnɪs] [kaued-li-nes] *s.* Cobardía, timidez, poquedad de alma, pusilanimidad, pendejada.

cowardlike [ˈkaʊədlaɪk] [kaued-laik] *a.* Acobardado, amilanado.

cowardly [ˈkaʊədlɪ] [kauedli] *a.* Cobarde, medroso, miedoso, pusilánime, tímido. **Cowardly action,** acción vil. *-adv.* Cobardemente.

cowboy [ˈkaʊbɔɪ] [kau-boi] *s.* 1. Muchacho empleado como pastor de vacas. Vaquero, gaucho. 2. *(E.U.)* Vaquero montado. **To play cowboys and Indians,** jugar a indios y vaqueros. 3. De vaquero, de cowboy (hat). **Cowboy boots,** botas camperas o tejanas. (GB) *(Coloq.)* Pillo, pirata (unscrupulous trader).

cow-catcher [ˈkaʊəˌkɑːtʃər] [kau-ka-cher] *s.* Botaganado o trompa de locomotora; armazón en forma de cuña que iba al frente de la locomotora. V. PILOT.

cower [ˈkaʊər] [kauaʳ] *vn.* Agacharse, bajarse doblando las rodillas. Encogerse de miedo.

cowgirl [ˈkaʊəgɜːl] [kaua-guel] *s.* Vaquera.

cowhand [ˈkaʊəhænd] [kau-jand] *s.* Peón de campo.

cow-herd [ˈkaʊhɜːd] [kau-jerd] *s.* Vaquero, pastor del ganado vacuno.

cowhide [ˈkaʊhaɪd] [kau-jaid] *s.* Cuero, piel de vaca curtida. *-va.* Azotar, dar azotes con un látigo de cueros.

cow-house [ˈkaʊhaʊs] [kau-jaus] *s.* Boyera, boyeriza, el establo en que se guardan vacas o bueyes.

cow-keeper [ˈkaʊˌkiːpər] [kau-ki-paʳ] *s.* Vaquero, el que tiene vacas de leche.

cowl [kaʊl] [kaul] s. 1. Cogulla de monje, capuz, capilla, capucha de fraile. Hábito con capucha (monk's cloak). **To throw off the cowl,** colgar los hábitos. 2. Caperuza de chimenea. 3. Tina, vasija para agua; cuba, cubeta.

cowled [ˈkaʊld] [kauld] a. Lo que tiene cogulla o capucha.

cowlick [ˈkaʊlɪk] [kau-lik] s. Tupé, mechón de cabellos levantado sobre la parte superior de la frente; remolino.

cowlike [ˈkaʊlaɪk] [kau-laik] a. Semejante a una vaca.

cowl-staff [ˈkaʊlstɑːf] [kaul-staf] s. Palo para llevar alguna cosa entre dos hombres.

cowman [ˈkaʊmən] [kau-man] s. (in US) Ganadero (ranch owner); vaquero, peón (ranch worker).

coworker [kaʊˈwɔːkər] [kau-uor-ke^r] s. V. FELLOW-LABORER. Colega, compañero de trabajo (workmate); colaborador (collaborator).

cowpat [ˈkaʊpæt] [kau-pat] s. Boñiga, bosta de vaca.

cowpoke [ˈkaʊpəʊk] [kau-pouk] s. (Coloq.) Vaquero.

cowpox [ˈkaʊpɒks] [kau-poks] s. Vacuna, viruela que sale a las vacas en las tetas. V. VACCINE.

cowry, cowrie [ˈkaʊrɪ] [kau-ri] s. Cuaris, concha usada como dinero en Africa y en la India.

cowshed [ˈkaʊʃed] [kau-shed] s. Establo de las vacas.

cowslip [ˈkaʊslɪp] [kau-slip] s. Prímula o primavera, vellorita.

cow-wheat [ˈkaʊwiːt] [kau-wit] s. Trigo vacuno.

coxcomb [ˈkɒkskəʊm] [koks-kom] s. 1. Mequetrefe, mozuelo prsumido, pisaverde; currutaco; lechuguino. 2. (Des.) Coronilla, la parte más alta de la cabeza; cresta de gallo.

coxcombly [ˈkɒkskəʊmblɪ] [koks-kom-bli], **coxcomical** [ˈkɒkskəʊmɪkl] [koks-ko-mi-kal] a. Presumido, fantástico, fatuo, impertinente, currutaco.

coxcombry [ˈkɒkskəʊmbrɪ] [koks-kom-bri] s. Presunción, petimetrería, currutaquería.

coxswain [ˈkɒkswɛɪn] [koks-wein] s. (Naut.) Timonel.

coy, coyish [kɔɪ] [koi] a. Recatado, modesto; reservado, esquivo; retrechero. Tímido (shy); evasivo (evasive). **A coy little smile,** una sonrisita tímida y coqueta.

coy va. Halagar, lisonjear, acariciar. -vn. Esquivarse, desdeñarse.

coyly [ˈkɔɪlɪ] [koi-li] adv. Con esquivez. Con (coqueta) timidez.

coyness [ˈkɔɪnɪs] [koi-nes] s. Esquivez, despego, extrañeza; recato, modestia.

coyote [kɔɪˈəʊtɪ] [koi-ou-ti] s. Coyote.

coypu [ˈkɔɪpuː] [koi-pu] s. Coipo.

coz [kʌz] [koz] s. Voz familiar que significa lo mismo que *cousin*. V. COUSIN.

cozen [ˈkʌzn] [kozn] va. Engañar, defraudar.

cozenage [ˈkʌzɪnɪdʒ] [kou-zi-nis] s. Fraude, engaño, trampa, superchería.

cozener [ˈkʌzənər] [kou-ze-na^r] s. Engañador, defraudador.

cozily [ˈkəʊzɪlɪ] [kou-zi-li] adv. Reducida pero cómodamente. Agradablemente.

cozy [ˈkəʊzɪ] [kou-zi] a. 1. Cómodo, manejable, agradable; sociable, tranquilamente instalado. 1. Acogedor (room). **In her cozy bed,** en su cama cómoda y calentita. 3. Intimo y agradable (chat). 4. (Pej.) De lo más conveniente (convenient).

cozy, (BrE) **cosy** s. **Tea cozy,** cubreteteras.

cozy up to Adular, tratar de quedar bien con.

CPA s. (in US) = **Certified Public Accountant**

cpl (title) = **Corporal**

CPU s. = **(central processing unit)** CPU

crab [kræb] [krab] a. Agrio, áspero. -s. 1. Cangrejo, jaiba (animal, meat). 2. Manzana silvestre. 3. Hombre de mal genio. 4. (Mar.) Cabrestante sencillo o volante. 5. (Astr.) Cáncer. **Crab-apple,** manzana pequeña y agria que sirve principalmente para hacer conservas. V. 2ª acep. **Crabs,** pl. ladillas (public lice). **Crab-louse,** ladilla. **To catch a crab,** hundir demasiado el remo o no tocar con él en el agua, y caerse hacia atrás al dar la remada.

crabbed [ˈkræbɪd] [kra-bid] a. Impertinente, áspero, ceñudo, duro, severo, austero, bronco, tosco; escabroso, desigual.

crabbedly [ˈkræbɪdlɪ] [kra-bid-li] adv. Impertinentemente; ásperamente, secamente.

crabbedness [ˈkræbɪdnɪs] [kra-bid-nes] s. 1. Aspereza. 2. Rigidez o austeridad.

crabby [ˈkræbɪ] [kra-bi] a. (Coloq.) Rezongón, refunfuñón.

crabs'-eyes [ˈkræbzˈaɪs] [krabs-ais] s. pl. (Fam.) Ojos de cangrejo. V. CRABSTONE.

crabsidle [ˈkræbsɪdl] [krab-sidol] vn. (Fest.) Moverse de lado, como un cangrejo.

crabstone [ˈkræbstəʊn] [krab-stoun] s. Ojo de cangrejo, concreción calcárea que se forma en el estómago de los cangrejos cuando están para mudar la piel.

crack [kræk] [krak] s. 1. Hendedura, rendija (chink, slit); grieta (in ice, wall, pavement); raja, rajadura (in glass, china); quebraja, rotura. **To paper/paste over the cracks,** ponerle parches al problema o a la situación. 2. Crujido (of bones); chasquido (sound/of whip, twig); castañetazo, estallido (of rifle shot); estruendo (of thunder); estampido. **(GB) To give somebody a fair crack of the whip,** darle todas las oportunidades a alguien. 3. Golpe retumbante (blow). 4. Locura, mentecatez. 5. La mudanza de la voz al llegar a la pubertad. 6. Persona de viso en cierto concepto o esfera. 7. (Ant. Ger.) Impureza, cochinada, indecencia. 8. Intento. (Coloq.) **To have a crack at something,** intentar algo (attempt). 9. Comentario socarrón (wisecrack). 10. Crack (drug). **At the crack of dawn,** al amanecer, al despuntar el día (instant). -a. (Fam.) De calidad superior; de primer orden. De primera (shot, troops).

crack va. 1. Hender, rajar (cup, glass); agrietar, resquebrajar (ground, earth); agrietar (skin). **He cracked a rib,** se fracturó una costilla. 2. Decir alguna cosa con jovialidad; contar (joke). 3. Romper, destruir. Cascar, romper (break open/egg); cascar, partir (nut); forzar (safe); desmantelar, desarticular (drugs ring, spy ring). **To crack a bottle,** despachar una botella. (Coloq.) **To crack a book,** abrir un libro. **To crack a smile,** sonreír. 4. Volverle a uno el juicio, volverle loco. (Amer.) Chiflarse. 5. Descifrar, dar con (decipher, solve/code); resolver (problem). (Coloq.) **I've cracked it!,** ¡ya lo tengo! 6. Hacer chasquear o restallar (make cracking sound with/whip); hacer crujir (finger, knuckle). -vn. 1. Reventar, saltar, abrirse alguna cosa. Rajarse (cup, glass); agrietarse (rock, paint, skin). 2. (Fam.) Arruinarse. 3. Crujir, dar crujidos algún cuerpo cuando se rompe; estallar. Chasquear, restallar (make cracking sound); crujir (bones, twigs). Quebrarse (voice). 4. (Ant.) Jactarse, echar bravatas o balandronadas. **She cracked under the strain,** sufrió una crisis nerviosa a causa de la tensión (break down). (Coloq.) **To get cracking,** ponerse manos a la obra. **Come on, get cracking!,** ¡vamos, muévete!

crack down, To crack down on somebody/something, tomar medidas enérgicas contra alguien/algo.

crack up 1. Sufrir un ataque de nervios, sucumbir a la presión (person/break down). (Coloq.) Soltar una carcajada (burst out laughing). 2. (Coloq.) Matar de la risa (make laugh). 3. **It isn't all it's cracked up to be,** no es tan bueno como lo pintan.

crack-brained [krækˈbreɪnd] [krak-breind] a. Alocado, alelado, mentecato, estúpido, chiflado.

crackdown [ˈkrækdaʊn] [krak-daun] s. **Crackdown on something/somebody,** ofensiva o campaña contra algo/alguien. Medidas enérgicas contra algo/alguien.

cracked [krækt] [krakt] pp. de CRACK. **Cracked wheat,** trigo resquebrajado.

cracked a. Rajado (cup, glass); fracturado (rib); con grietas, resquebrajado (wall, ceiling); partido, agrietado (lips); agrietado (skin). (Coloq.) Loco, chiflado (crazy/person). Cascado (voice).

cracker [ˈkrækər] [kra-ka^r] s. 1. Lo que da crujidos. 2. Cohete de China; triquitraque; petardo (firecracker). (GB) Sorpresa que estalla al abrirla. 3. (Amer.) Galletica, bizcocho delgado y quebradizo; cracker, galleta salada (biscuit). 4. Anade marino o faisán acuátil. 5. El pedacito de papel que se pone en cada rizo para hacerlo.

cracker-barrel [ˈkrækəˈbærəl] [kra-kar-ba-rel] *a.* Sin sofisticaciones (humor, philosopher).

crackerjack [ˈkrækədʒæk] [kra-ker-jak] *s. (Coloq.)* As; fuera de serie (person, idea, car).

crackers [ˈkrækəz] [kra-kars] *a.* (GB) *Coloq.* Chiflado (crazy).

crack-hemp [krækˈhemp] [krak-jemp], **crack-rop** [ˈkrækrɒp] [krak-rop] *s.* Hombre digno de ser ahorcado.

cracking [ˈkrækɪŋ] [kra-kin] *a. (Coloq.)* **At a cracking pace,** a toda pastilla, a un ritmo endemoniado.

crackle [ˈkrækl] [krakol] *vn.* Crujir (twigs, paper); chasquear, das chasquidos. Crepitar, chisporrotear (fire). **The line is cracling a lot,** hay mucho ruido en la línea.

cracle *s.* Crujido (of twigs, paper); chisporroteo (of fire).

crackling [ˈkræklɪŋ] [kra-klin] *s.* 1. Estallido; crujido (noise of paper); chisporroteo (of fire). 2. *(Culin.)* Piel crujiente y tostada del cerdo asado. **Cracklings,** chicharrones. *-pa.* de CRACKLE.

cracknel [ˈkræknɪl] [krak-nel] *s.* Especie de rosca o bollo duro y quebradizo.

crackpot [ˈkrækpɒt] [krak-pot] *a. (Coloq.)* Chiflado, chalado. **A crackpot idea,** una idea descabellada.

crackup [ˈkrækʌp] [krak-ap] *s.* Crisis nerviosa (mental breakdown); choque (collision).

cradle [ˈkrædl] [kra-del] *s.* 1. Cuna (for baby). **To rock the cradle,** mecer o mover la cuna. 2. Niñez, infancia; *(fig.)* cuna, origen o principio de alguna cosa. 3. *(Cir.)* Caja o tablilla para un hueso roto. 4. *(Agr.)* Segadora de mano; arco unido al mango de la guadaña. 5. *(Min.)* Andamio colgante; artesa móvil para lavar el oro. 6. Carro salvavidas. 7. *(Mar.)* Cuna, parte del aparato empleado para lanzar un buque al agua. 8. Horquilla (for telephone receiver). **Cradle scythe,** hoz de rastra.

cradle *va.* 1 Meter en cuna; acostar a un niño en la cuna; acunar, mecer (baby); sostener contra el pecho (guitar). 2. Segar las mieses con segadora de mano. *-vn.* Reposar como en cuna.

cradle-clothes [ˈkrædlˈklɒðs] [kra-del-klozs] *s. pl.* Ropa de cuna.

craft [krɑːft] [kraft] *s.* 1. Arte (skill), oficio (trade), el trabajo y ejercicio en que se emplean los artesanos. **Craft fair,** feria artesanal o de artesanía. **Crafts,** *pl.* artesanía. 2. Arte, maña, artificio, astucia, treta, fraude, engaño; artimañas (guile, deceit). 3. Embarcación, barco; cualquier género de nave. También es el conjunto de naves. **Small craft,** *(Mar.)* navichuelos, sean barcos, barcas, bateles, esquifes o lanchas.

craft *va.* Trabajar.

craftily [ˈkrɑːftɪlɪ] [kraf-ti-li] *adv.* Astutamente, con astucia (act); artificiosamente, mañosamente.

craftiness [ˈkrɑːftɪnɪs] [kraf-ti-nes] *s.* Astucia, treta, estratagema, maña.

craftsman [ˈkrɑːftsmæn] [krafts-man] *s.* Artífice, artesano.

craftsmanship [ˈkrɑːftsmænʃɪp] [krafts-man-ship] *s.* Destreza, conocimiento del oficio (skill). Trabajo (workmanship).

craftsmaster [ˈkrɑːftsˌmɑːstər] [krafts-mas-teʳ] *s.* Maestro, el artífice o artesano.

crafty [ˈkrɑːftɪ] [kraf-it] *a.* Astuto, artificioso, taimado (person); hábil, artero (methods, tactics).

crag [kræg] [krag] *s.* 1. Despeñadero, risco, roca o peñasco lleno de precipicios. 2. Cima de un despeñadero.

cragged [ˈkrægɪd] [kra-guid] *a.* Escabroso, áspero, peñascoso.

craggedness [ˈkrægɪdnɪs] [kra-guid-nes], **cragginess** [ˈkrægɪnɪs] [kra-gui-nes] *s.* Escabrosidad, desigualdad, aspereza, fragosidad.

craggy [ˈkrægɪ] [kra-gui], *a.* Escabroso, áspero, desigual, fragoso, escarpado (rocks, mountains). **He had a craggy,**

weather-beaten face, tenía un rostro curtido y de facciones bien marcadas.

cram [kræm] [kram], *va.* 1. Rellenar, henchir. 2. Atestar, llenar demasiado (stuff). **I crammed all my things into a case,** metí o embutí todas mis cosas en una maleta. **The room was crammed with people/books,** la habitación estaba abarrotada o atiborrada de gente/libros. 3. Atracar, embutir, llenar una cosa hasta no poder más; hartar, atracar de comida. **To cram oneself with food,** atiborrarse de comida. 4. Empujar, meter una cosa en otra con fuerza y violencia. *-vn.* 1. Atracarse de comida. **To cram poultry,** engordar o cebar capones o pavos. 2. Sobrecargar la inteligencia y la memoria con un cúmulo de conocimientos adquiridos apresuradamente. Empollar, zambutir, tragar, matearse, empacarse (for exam). 3. Meterse (get in). **We all crammed into the room,** nos metimos todos en la habitación.

crambo [ˈkræmbəʊ] [kram-bou], *s.* Un juego en el cual dada una palabra hay que hallar una consonante para ella.

cramming [ˈkræmɪŋ] [kra-min], *s.* Repaso; término usado en los colegios para designar la acción de preparar a un estudiante para los exámenes.

cramp [kræmp] [kramp], *s.* 1. Calambre, rampa, pasmo o encogimiento de nervios que impide el movimiento. **I've got a cramp in my leg,** me ha dado un calambre o una rampa en la pierna. **Stomach cramps,** retorcijones o retortijones en el estómago. 2. Sujeción, estrechez, aprieto. 3. Laña, especie de grapa de hierro que sirve para unir y trabajar dos cosas. *-a.* Dificultoso, nudoso.

cramp, *va.* 1. Dar o causar calambre. 2. Sujetar, tener en sujeción. 3. Lañar, trabar, asegurar, unir o afianzar con lañas. 4. Constreñir, apretar, enganchar, aferrar. Entorpecer (limit/work, progress). **To cramp somebody's style,** cortarle los vuelos a alguien. **To cramp out,** arrancar.

cramped [kræmpt] [krampt] *a.* Apretado (handwriting). **I'm cramped for space,** tengo poco sitio o lugar. **They work in cramped conditions,** están muy estrechos en el trabajo. **We were a bit cramped in the car,** íbamos algo apretujados o apretados en el coche.

cramp-fish [ˈkræmpfɪʃ] [kramp-fish], *s.* Torpedo, tremielga.

cramp-iron [kræmpˈaɪrən] [kramp-airon], *s.* Gatillo de hierro, laña. *V.* CRAMP.

crampon, crampoon [ˈkræmpən] [kram-pon], *s.* 1. Un hierro con garfio en la punta que sirve para levantar con la grúa los maderos, piedras y otras cosas de peso. 2. Raíz aérea para trepar, como en la hiedra. 3. Púa asegurada al calzado para andar sobre el hielo o para escalar postes o muros.

cranage [ˈkrænɪdʒ] [kra-nich], *s.* 1. Permiso para tener pescante o grúa en algún muelle. 2. Derechos de grúa o pescante, el dinero que se paga por sacar géneros de alguna embarcación con la grúa.

cranberry [ˈkrænbərɪ] [kran-be-ri], *s. (Bot.)* Arándano.

crane [kreɪn] [krein], *s.* 1. *(Zool.)* Grulla, ave de paso, de alto vuelo, con pico largo, recto y agudo. 2. Grúa, máquina para elevar toda clase de pesos (for lifting). 3. Pescante, instrumento compuesto de poleas, cuerdas y ganchos, para subir y levantar cosas de peso. **Wheel-crane,** pescante o grúa con rueda. 4. Sifón, cañón o tubo corvo que sirve para sacar licores de una vasija. 5. Cigüeña o aguilón de chimenea.

crane *va.* **To crane one's neck,** estirar el cuello. **To crane up,** subir una cosa con la grúa o el pescante. *-vn.* Estirarse.

crane-fly [ˈkreɪnflaɪ] [krein-flai], *s. (Ent.)* Especie de típula; zancudo.

crane's-bill [kreɪnzˈbɪl] [kreins-bil], *s.* 1. *(Bot.)* Geranio, pico de cigüeña. 2. Tenazas puntiagudas de los cirujanos.

cranial [ˈkræniəl] [kra-nial], *a.* Del cráneo o perteneciente a él.

craniology [krænɪˈɒlɒdʒɪ] [kra-nio-lo-yi], *s.* Craneología.

cranium [ˈkræniəm] [kra-nium], *s.* Cráneo, casco de la cabeza.

crank [kræŋk] [krank], *s.* 1. *(Mech Eng.)* Biela, manubrio, cigüeñal; invento para comunicar movimiento de rotación a un eje, o para convertir el movimiento rotatorio en recíproco, y vice versa. 2. Cigüeñal, el hierro a que se asegura el cordel de la campana para tocarla. 3. Capricho, concepto. 4. (E.U. Fam.) Mentecato, maniático, raro; cascarrabias (bad-tempered person). **He is a crank,** está algo tocado, le falta un tornillo. **Crank-pin,** botón de manubrio. -*a.* 1. Sano, alegre; vigoroso, dispuesto. 2. *(Mar.)* V. CRANK-SIDED.

crank, *va.* 1. *(Auto)* Poner en marcha (un motor) con biela o manubrio (car). 2. Encorvar para dar forma de manubrio.

crankcase [ˈkræŋkkeɪs] [krank-keis] *s. (Mec.)* Cárter (de un automóvil).

crankness [ˈkræŋknɪs] [krank-nes] *s.* Salud, robustez, vigor; alegría, vivacidad.

crankshaft [ˈkræŋkʃɑːft] [krank-shaft] *s. (Mec.)* Cigüeñal.

crank-sided [kræŋkˈsaɪdɪd] *a. (Mar.)* Celoso, el bajel que con facilidad se tumba a la banda y no aguanta la vela, si el viento es algo recio y viene por el costado.

cranky [ˈkræŋkɪ] [kran-ik] *a.* 1. Caprichoso, lleno de extravagancias, lunático; maniático, raro (eccentric); estrafalario, raro (idea); malhumorado (bad-tempered). 2. Torcido, corvo. 3. Destartalado, titubeante, expuesto a venirse a abajo.

crannied [ˈkrænɪəd] [kra-nied] *a.* Hendido, abierto, lleno de grietas o aberturas.

cranny [ˈkrænɪ] [kra-ni] *s.* Grieta, hendedura, raja, abertura, agujero.

crap [kræp] [krap] *s. (Vulg.)* Mierda (excrement); estupideces, gilipolleces, pendejadas, huevadas, boludeces (nonsense).

crape [kreɪp] [kreip] *s.* 1. Crespón, tela de seda a modo de gasa. 2. Cendal. *(Amer.)* Espumilla. **Canton crape,** burato.

crape, *va.* 1. Encrespar, rizar el cabello encrespándolo. 2. Revestir con crespón, poner crespón como señal de luto.

crappy [kræpɪ] [kra-pi] *a. (Vulg.)* Malo, de porquería, de mierda.

craps [kræpz] [krasp] *s.* Un juego de dados. **To shoot craps,** jugar al crap.

crapshooting [kæpˈʃuːtɪŋ] [krap-shu-tin] *s.* Un juego de dados.

crapula [ˈkræpjʊlə] [kra-piu-la] *s.* Crápula, glotonería, embriaguez o borrachera.

crapulent [ˈkræpjʊlənt] [kra-piu-lent] **crapulous** [ˈkræpjʊləs] [kra-piu-los] *a.* Crapuloso, dado a la crápula; borracho, el que anda en borracheras o comilonas.

crash [kræʃ] [krash] *va.* 1. Estrellar, hacer añicos (smash). **He crashed the car,** tuvo un accidente con el coche, chocó. 2. *(Fam.)* Colarse en. **To crash a party,** colarse en una fiesta. -*vn.* 1. *(Aer.)* Estrellarse (collide). **To crash into something,** estrellarse o chocar contra algo. 2. Desplomarse con gran estrépito. 3. Chocar. 4. Dar estallido, retumbar (make loud noise/thunder). **The dishes crashed to the floor,** los platos se cayeron al suelo estrepitosamente. 5. *(Fin.)* Caer a pique, colapsar (shares). 6. *(Coloq.)* Quedarse a dormir (spend the night). 7. *(Inform.)* Fallar.

crash out, quedarse a dormir.

crash, *s.* 1. Estrépito, estruendo, estampido (loud noise). **The crash of the waves,** el estruendo de las olas al romper. 2. Fracaso repentino. 3. Choque, accidente (collision, accident). **Plane/car crash,** accidente aéreo/de automóvil. 4. Derrumbe, desplome. 5. Crac, crack (financial failure). 6. *(Aer.)* Aterrizaje violento.

crash barrier *s.* Barrera de protección.

crash helmet *s.* Casco protector.

crash-landing *s.* Aterrizaje forzoso o de emergencia.

crass [kræs] [kras] *a.* 1. Grueso, gordo; basto, tosco, grosero (remark); espeso; burdo (joke). 2. Rudo, torpe, tardo en comprender.

crassamentum [kræsəˈmentəm] [kra-sa-men-tum] *s.* Parte espesa y coagulable de la sangre.

crassitude [ˈkræsɪtjuːd] [kra-si-tiud] *s.* Crasitud, tosquedad; espesor, espesura.

crate [kreɪt] [kreit] *s.* Cuévano, cesto grande; también la carga o suma de objetos que contiene. **Crate of earthenware,** canasto de loza. *(Mex.)* Guacal de loza. *(Amer.)* Jaba, cajón de embalaje, jaula (container). *(Sl.)* Cascajo, cacharro (old plane, car).

crater [ˈkreɪtər] [krei-ta^r] *s.* 1. Cráter, boca de volcán. 2. Copa en antigüedades clásicas. 3. La Copa, constelación del hemisferio astral.

cravat [krəˈvæt] [kra-vat] *s.* Corbata.

crave [kreɪv] [kreiv] *va.* Rogar, suplicar, implorar, pedir, encarecidamente, desear con antojo; importunar; ansiar (admiration, flattery); tener ansias de (affection); morirse por (food, drink). **To crave indulgence,** implorar indulgencia.

craven [ˈkreɪvn] [krei-ven] *s.* Un bajo cobarde. -*a.* Acobardado, pusilánime.

craven, *va.* Amilanar, acobardar, intimidar.

craver [ˈkreɪvər] [krei-va^r] *s.* Pedidor, pedigón, el que es pedigüeño o pide con importunidad.

craving [ˈkreɪvɪŋ] [krei-vin] *s.* Deseo vehemente, ardiente; ansias, sed (strong desire); antojo (in pregnancy). -*a.* Insaciable; pedigüeño.

craw [krɔː] [kro] *s.* Buche, bolsa o seno en que reciben las aves la comida.

crawfish [ˈkrɔːfɪʃ] [kro-fish] *s.* Cangrejo de agua dulce; crustáceo parecido a la langosta. -*vn.* (Fam. E. U.) Andar hacia atrás, como el cangrejo; de aquí, recular, retroceder, abandonar la posición o actitud que antes se tenía.

crawl [krɔːl] [krol] 1. Arrastrar, moverse con lentitud (creep). 2. Gatear (baby); andar (insect); avanzar muy lentamente (go slowly/traffic, train). 3. *(Coloq.)* Arrastrarse, rebajarse (demean oneself). **To crawl to somebody,** arrastrarse o rebajarse ante alguien. **To crawl up,** trepar. **To crawl forth,** avanzar rastreando. **The beach was crawling with tourists,** la playa estaba plagada de turistas, la playa hervía de turistas (teem).

crawl, *s.* 1. Arrastre, movimiento lento. **To go at a crawl,** avanzar muy lentamente, ir a paso de tortuga. 2. Acto de gatear. 3. Brazada de pecho (en natación); crol (swimming stroke).

crawler [ˈkrɔːlər] [kro-le^r] *s.* 1. Reptil, el que va arrastrándose como los reptiles. 2. *(Coloq.)* Pelota, chupamedias, lambiscón, lambón.

crayfish [ˈkreɪfɪʃ] [krei-fish] *s.* Cangrejo de río, ástaco (freshwater); langosta pequeña (marine); cigala. V. CRAWFISH.

crayon [ˈkreɪən] [kre-yon] *s.* 1. Lápiz, piedra o pasta de varios colores para dibujar al pastel. 2. Dibujo de lápiz. 3. Clarión, tiza.

craze [kreɪz] [kreis] *va.* 1. Alelar, embobar, entontecer. 2. Hacer pequeñas grietas o hendeduras en; literal y figuradamente. 3. *(Des.)* Quebrantar, debilitar. -*vn.* Henderse, llenarse de grietas la alfarería.

craze, *s.* 1. Locura, demencia, manía. 2. Extravagancia loca de la moda; capricho. 3. Antojo, capricho, fantasía o manía que no raciocina. 4. Grieta, falta, defecto en el lustre de la alfarería o vajilla de barro.

crazed [kreɪzd] [kreist] *a.* De loco (expression); enloquecido (person).

crazedness [kreɪz] [kreines] *s.* 1. Calidad de loco. 2. Calidad de grietoso.

craziness [ˈkreɪzɪnɪs] [krei-si-nes] *s.* Debilidad, sea de cuerpo o entendimiento; locura; enajenación mental; condición de lo desvencijado.

crazy [ˈkreɪzɪ] [krei-si] *a.* 1. Lelo, fatuo, simple, loco; acometido de enajenación mental (mad, foolish). **That's crazy,** es una locura. **To go crazy,** volverse loco. **To drive somebody crazy,** volver loco a alguien. **Like crazy,** como un loco. 2. Quebrantado, decrépito, cascado, caduco. 3. **A crazy thing** or **article,** alguna cosa desvencijada, coja o imperfecta; miserable, pobre. 4. *(Fam.)* Exageradamente deseoso o ansioso; deseoso de un modo insensato (very enthusiastic). **To be crazy about/for/over somebody,** estar loco por alguien. **I'm not crazy about the idea,** la idea no me enloquece o no me vuelve loco.

crazy paving *s.* Enlosado de diseño irregular.

crazy quilt *s.* Colcha de patchwork o de retazos, centón.

creak [kriːk] [krik], *vn.* Crujir, hacer un ruido áspero (bedsprings/floorboards/joints); estallar. Chirriar (door).

creak *s.* Chirrido, crujido.

creaking [ˈkriːkɪŋ] [kri-kin], *s.* Crujido, estallido.

creaky [ˈkriːkɪ] [kri-ki] *a.* Que chirría, chirriante (door); que cruje (stairs).

cream [kriːm] [krim], *s.* 1. Crema, la nata y flor de la leche. **Light/single cream,** crema líquida. **Heavy/double cream,** crema doble, nata para montar. **Cream tea,** té servido con scones, mermelada y crema batida (in UK). 2. Lo mejor, lo más estimado y escogido de alguna cosa (elite). **The cream of society,** la flor y nata o la crema de la sociedad. 3. Crema (lotion). **Face cream,** crema para la cara. 4. Color cema (color). **Cream of tartar,** crémor tártaro, bitartrato de potasa. **Whipped cream,** nata batida. **Cold-cream,** V. COLD.

cream *a.* Color crema.

cream, *vn.* Hacer nata. levantar espuma. *-va.* 1. Quitar la crema de la leche o la flor de cualquier cosa. 2. Batir hasta obtener una consistencia cremosa (sugar, butter). **Creamed potatoes,** puré de papas o de patatas.

cream off, *(Coloq.)* (GB) Llevarse, quedarse con (profits).

cream cake *s.* Tarta o torta con crema o con nata (gateau); pastel o bollo de crema o de nata, masa de crema (individual).

cream cheese [kriːmˈtʃiːs] [krim-chis] *s.* Queso crema, queso para untar.

cream cracker [kriːmˈkrækər] [krim-kra-keʳ] *s.* (GB) Galleta salada, cracker.

creamer [ˈkriːmər] [kri-maʳ] *s.* 1. Jarrita para crema (jug). 2. Leche en polvo (powder).

cream soda [kriːmˈsəʊdə] [krim-so-da] *s.* Gaseosa con sabor a vainilla.

creamery [ˈkriːmərɪ] [kri-me-ri], *s.* 1. El edificio y la habitación donde se conserva la leche a la debida temperatura para obtener la nata. 2. Establecimiento donde se hace la manteca o mantequilla. 3. Lechería, lugar donde se vende la nata.

creamy [ˈkriːmɪ] [kri-mi], *a.* Parecido a la crema o nata o que la contiene; cremoso.

crease [kriːs] [kris], *s.* Pliegue, la doblez o arruga que se hace en alguna cosa; plegadura.

crease, *va.* Plegar, señalar con pliegues (paper); arrugar (clothes). *vn.* Arrugarse.

crease up *(Coloq.)* (GB) Desternillarse o partirse de risa (laugh).

creassote, *s.* V. OBEOSOTE.

create [kriːˈeɪt] [kri-eit], *va.* 1. Criar o crear, producir algo de la nada; dar ser a lo que antes no lo tenía (bring into existence). **To create jobs,** crear o generar empleo. 2. Criar, producir, ocasionar, causar. 3. Engendrar, procrear. 4. Crear, elevar a alguna nueva dignidad, constituir, elegir. *vn.* Armar jaleo (make a fuss).

creation [kriːˈeɪʃən] [kri-ei-shon], *s.* 1. Cración, el acto de crear o sacar alguna cosa de la nada. 2. Elevación a nueva dignidad, nombramiento, elección. 3. Cración; el universo. 4. Cualquier cosa producida o causada; los seres creados; especie.

creative [kriːˈeɪtɪv] [kri-ei-tiv], *a.* Creativo, creador, lo que puede crear. **Creative writing,** creación literaria.

creativeness [kriːˈeɪtɪvnɪs] [kri-ei-tiv-nes], *s.* Facultad creadora, genio inventivo.

creativity [kriː ˈeɪtɪvɪtɪ] [kri-ei-ti-vi-ti] *s.* Creatividad.

creator [kriːˈeɪtər] [kri-ei-tor], *s.* 1. Creador, Criador, el Ser supremo que creó todas las cosas. 2. Lo que crea o causa.

creatress [kriːˈətres] [kri-a-tres], *s.* Creadora.

creature [ˈkriːtʃər] [kri-chaʳ], *s.* 1. Criatura, ente criado o creado. 2. Criatura, voz de desprecio que a veces se aplica a una persona. 3. Criatura, voz que expresa ternura o compasión. **Poor creature!** ¡pobrecito! 4. Criatura, hechura, el que debe a otro su elevación, empleo o fortuna; dependiente. 5. Bestia, animal. **Our fellow-creatures,** nuestros semejantes. **Creature comforts,** las cosas que confortan o refrescan el cuerpo.

creatureship [kriːtʃəˈʃɪp] [kri-char-ship], *s.* Estado de criatura.

creche, créche [kreɪʃ] [kreish] *s.* 1. Orfanato, orfelinato, orfanatorio (hospital for foundings). Guardería infantil (day nursery). 2. Nacimiento, pesebre, belén (Nativity scene).

credence [ˈkriːdəns] [kri-dans], *s.* Creencia, asenso, fe; crédito. **To give/lend credence to something,** dar crédito a algo.

credendum, plur. CREDENDA [kriːˈdendəm] [kri-den-dom], *s.* Creencia; artículos de fe.

credent [ˈkriːdəns] [kri-dans], *a.* (Ant.) Creyente, crédulo, acreditado.

credentials [krɪˈdenʃəlz] [kri-den-shals], **credential letters,** *s. pl.* Cartas credenciales (of ambassador); referencias (references); documentos de identidad (identifying papers).

credibility [ˌkredəˈbɪlətɪ] [kre-di-bi-li-ti], *s.* Credibilidad, probabilidad, verosimilitud.

credible [ˈkredɪbl] [kre-di-bol], *a.* Creíble, probable, verosímil; digno de confianza.

credibleness [ˈkredɪbnɪsl] [kre-di-bol-nes], *s.* Credibilidad; veracidad.

credibly [ˈkredɪblɪ] [kre-di-bli], *adv.* Creíblemente, probablemente.

credit [ˈkredɪt] [kre-dit], *s.* 1. Crédito, asenso, fe, creencia. 2. Crédito, reputación, buena opinión; influencia. Mérito (honor, recognition). **She deserves some credit for trying,** merece que se le reconozca el mérito de haberlo intentado. **Your children are a credit for you,** puedes estar orgulloso de tus hijos. **The results do credit to the school,** los resultados hablan muy bien del colegio o le hacen honor al colegio. 3. Confianza, seguridad que uno tiene en otro. 4. Influjo, autoridad, poder, aunque no coactivo. 5. *(Fin.)* Crédito (in store). **Credit account,** credicuenta, cuenta de o a crédito. **Credit balance,** saldo positivo. **If your account is in credit…,** si está en números negros…, si tiene fondos en su cuenta… **Letter of credit,** carta de crédito. **Open credit,** letra abierta. **To buy goods on credit,** comprar géneros al fiado. **To sell on credit,** vender al fiado. 6. *(Educ.)* Crédito, unidad de valor de una asignatura dentro de un programa de estudios. 7. *(Cine, TV, Video)* **Credits,** créditos, rótulos de crédito.

credit, *va.* 1. Creer, honrar, fiar, confiar, acreditar, dar fama, dar fe, dar crédito a (believe). **Can you credit it?,** ¿te lo puedes creer?, ¿no te parece increíble? **I credited you with more common sense,** te creía con más sentido común (ascribe to). **They are credited with having invented the game,** se les atribuye la invención del juego. 2. Prestar o vender a crédito, dar al fiado. 3. *(Com.)* Acreditar, abonar una partida en el libro de cuentas (sum, funds). **To credit something to something,** abonar o ingresar algo en algo.

creditable [ˈkredɪtəbl] [kre-di-ta-bol], *a.* Apreciable, estimable, honorífico; encomiable, meritorio.

creditableness [ˈkredɪtəblnɪs] [ˈkredɪtəblnɪs] [kre-di-ta-bol-nes], *s.* Reputación, estimación.

creditably [ˈkredɪtəblɪ] [kre-di-ta-bli], *adv.* Honorablemente, honrosamente.

credit balance [ˈkredɪtˈbæləns] [kre-dit-ba-lans], *s.* Saldo acreedor.

credit card [ˈkredɪtˌkɑːd] [kre-dit-kard], *s.* Tarjeta de crédito.

credited [ˈkredɪtɪd] [kre-di-tid], *pp.* y *a.* 1. Acreditado, estimado, tenido en buena opinión. 2. Creído. 3. *(Com.)* Acreditado, abonado en cuenta; abonado al haber.

creditor [ˈkredɪtər] [kre-di-toʳ], *s.* 1. Acreedor. 2. *Com.* Haber, una de las dos partes en que se dividen las cuentas corrientes.

creditress o **creditrix** [ˈkredtrɪs] [kre-di-tris], *sf.* Acreedora.

creditworthy [ˈkredɪtˈwɔːθɪ] [kre-dit-uor-zi] *a.* Con capacidad de pago, solvente.

credo [ˈkredəʊ] [kre-dou], *s.* 1. Credo, profesión, especialmente la de los Apóstoles. 2. Música para cantar el credo.

credulity [ˈkrediʊlɪtɪ] [kre-diu-li-ti], *s.* Credulidad, demasiada facilidad en creer.

credulous [ˈkredjʊləs], *a.* Crédulo, que cree fácilmente; sin desconfianza.

credulousness [ˈkredjʊləsnɪs] [kre-diu-los-nes], *s.* Credulidad.

creed [kriːd] [krid], *s.* Credo, creencia, símbolo. **There is my creed,** esa es mi profesión de fe.

creek [kriːk] [krik], *s.* 1. Cala, caleta, ensenada. 2. *(E.U.)* Corriente formada por la marea creciente o que cursa por un valle y cuya dimensión varia entre arroyo y río. **To be up the creek,** estar mal, estar equivocado. *(Coloq., vulg.)* **To be up shit creek (without a paddle),** estar en aprietos o en apuros, estar jodido (in difficulty)

Creek, *n. pr.* Tribu de indios norteamericanos que en otro tiempo habitaron gran parte de los Estados de Georgia y Alabama.

creeky [ˈkriːkɪ] [kri-ki], *a.* Tortuoso, lleno de caletas o entradas.

creel [kriːl] [kril], *s.* 1. Cesta de pescador. 2. Jaula de mimbres, para coger langostas. 3. Estizola de urdidor.

creep [kriːp] [krip], *vn. (pret. y pp.* CREPT). 1. Arrastrar, serpear, ratear. Arrastrarse (crawl). 2. Andar lenta o imperceptiblemente; andar secretamente; insinuarse, entrar a escondidas (move stealthily). **To creep into a room,** entrar en un cuarto sigilosamente. **Several mistakes have crept in,** se han deslizado varios errores. 3. Tener sensación nerviosa como de hormigueo sobre la piel. 4. Incensar, lisonjear, adular con bajeza, complacer bajamente (ingratiate oneself). **To creep to somebody,** adular a alguien, hacerle la pelota a alguien, hacerle la pata a alguien, chuparle las medias a alguien. **To creep in** o **into,** insinuarse; deslizarse en; *(fam.)* escaparse de; meterse en, escurrirse. **To creep out,** salir sin hacer ruido. **To creep on,** acercarse insensiblemente. **To creep and crouch,** hacer la gata ensogada. **To creep up,** trepar a; encaramarse. *-s.* 1. Acción de serpear. 2. *pl.* Sensación nerviosa como de hormigueo sobre la piel.

creep up on, They crept up on him, se le acercaron sigilosamente. **Old age creeps up on you,** vas envejeciendo sin darte cuenta.

creep *s.* 1. *(Coloq.)* Asqueroso (unpleasant person); adulador, pelota, chupamedias, lambiscón, lambón (favor-seeking person). 2. **Creeps,** *pl. (Coloq.)* **To give somebody the creeps,** ponerle los pelos de punta a alguien, darle escalofríos a alguien.

creeper [ˈkriːpər] [kri-par], *s.* 1. El que o lo que anda arrastrándose. 2. *(Bot.)* Planta enredadera; solano trepador. 3. Un ave pequeña; las hay de varias especies. 4. Garfio, garabato para sacar objetos de un pozo o estanque. 5. Ramplón de zapato. Cf. CRAMPON, acep. 3.

creep-hole [ˈkriːpˈhəʊl] [krip-joul], *s.* 1. Huronera, hueco o agujero que sirve de refugio a un animal cualquiera. 2. Pretexto excusa, escapatoria.

creepingly [ˈkriːpɪŋlɪ] [kri-pin-li], *adv.* A paso de tortuga, muy lentamente.

creepy [ˈkriːpɪ] [kri-pi] *a. (Coloq.)* Escalofriante, espeluznante (story, film); repulsivo, asqueroso (person).

creepy-crawly [kriːpɪˈkrɔːlɪ] [kri-pi-kro-li] *s. (Coloq.)* Bicho.

cremate [krɪˈmeɪt] [kri-meit], *va.* Quemar (los cadáveres, los desechos, etc.), reducir a cenizas; incinerar.

cremation [krɪˈmeɪʃən] [kri-mei-shon], *s.* Cremación, quema, el acto de quemar, especialmente de quemar los cadáveres.

crematorium [ˌkreməˈtɔːrɪəm] [kre-ma-to-rium] *s.* Crematorio.

crematory [ˈkremətərɪ] [kre-ma-to-ri], *s.* Crematorio, quemadero, lugar para quemar los cadáveres; el edifico y el horno.

crème caramel [ˈkremˈkærəməl] [krem-ka-ra-mel] *s.* Flan.

crème de la crème [ˈkremˈdəlɑːˈkrem] [krem-da-la-krem] *s.* La flor y nata, la crema.

crème de menthe [ˈkremdəmɒːnθ] [kem-de-monz] *s.* Crema de menta.

cremor [ˈkremər] [kre-moʳ], *s.* Crémor.

crenate, crenated [krɪˈneɪt] [kri-neit], *a. (Bot.)* Crenífero, dentado con dientes redondeados.

crenelate [ˈkrenɪleɪt] [kre-ni-leit], *va.* 1. Almenar, coronar de almenas un edificio, muralla, etc. 2. Dentar, festonear, recortar en festón.

creole [ˈkriːəʊl] [kri-oul], *s.* y *a.* Criollo.

creosote [ˈkrɪəsəʊt] [krio-sout], *s.* Creosota.

crepe, crêpe [kreɪp] [kreip], *s.* 1. Crep, crepé (fabric). Crespón. **Crêpe de chine,** crespón de seda. 2. *(Culin.)* Crep, crêpe, panqueque, crepa (pancake).

crêpe paper [kreɪpˈpeɪpər] [krep-pei-paʳ], *s.* Papel crepé.

crepitate [ˈkrepɪteɪt] [kre-pi-teit], *vn.* Crepitar, chisporrotear, arder chispeando, como la sal en el fuego; chirriar.

crept, *pret.* y *pp.* de TO CREEP.

crepuscule [krɪˈpʌskjʊl] [kri-pius-kiul], *s.* Crepúsculo.

crepuscular, crepusculine [krɪˈpʌskjʊlər] [kri-pius-kiu-laʳ], **crepusculous** [krɪˈpʌskjʊləs] [kri-pius-kiu-los], *a.* Crepuscular.

crescendo [krɪˈʃendəʊ] [kri-shen-dou], *a. (Mús.)* Que va aumentándose gradualmente en fuerza. *-s.* Aumento gradual del volumen del sonido. Punto culminante (climax).

crescent [ˈkresnt] [kresnt], *a.* Creciente. *-s.* 1. Creciente, el primer cuarto de la luna. 2. Cualquier cosa que tiene figura semicircular. Media luna (shape).

crescive [ˈkresɪv] [kre-siv], *a. (Ant.)* Creciente.

cress [kres] [kres], *s. (Bot.)* Lepidio, mastuerzo. **Water-cress,** berro.

cresset [ˈkresɪt] [kre-sit], *s.* 1. Fanal o farol. 2. Antorcha, lámpara. 3. Trébedes.

crest [krest] [krest], *s.* 1. Crestón de celada o cimera de morrión, cresta o copete. 2. Orgullo, altanería. **Crest of a horse,** el cuello del caballo. 3. *(Her.)* Emblema, divisa. **Crest of a coat of arms,** cimera sobre el escudo de armas. 4. Cresta (of wave); cima of mountain. **To be on/ride (on) the crest of a wave,** estar en la cresta de la ola.

crest, *va.* Señalar alguna cosa con rayas; coronar; encopetar, erguir.

crested [ˈkrestɪd] [kres-tid], *a.* Crestado, encopetado, coronado.

crestfallen [ˈkrestfɔːlən] [krest-fo-len], *a.* Acobardado, amedrentado, amilanado, abatido de espíritu, caído; con el rabo entre las piernas; con las orejas gachas.

crestless [ˈkrestlɪs] [krest-les], *a.* Sin cimera, sin divisa; sin escudo de armas, de humilde estirpe.

cretaceous [krɪˈteɪʃəs] [kri-tei-shos], *a.* Gredoso, cretáceo, de la naturaleza de la greda.

cretan [ˈkriːtən] [kri-tan], *a.* Cretense, perteneciente a la isla de Creta.

cretated [kriˈteɪtɪd [kri-tei-tid], *a.* Dado de greda.

cretin [ˈkretɪn] [kre-tin], *s.* 1. *(Med.)* Cretino, la persona afectada de cretinismo. 2. Estúpido, imbécil (stupid person).

cretinism [ˈkretɪnɪzm] [kre-ti-nisem], *s.* Cretinismo, enfermedad incurable, caracterizada por deformidad del cuerpo y alteración de la mente. Ataca a los habitantes de regiones montañosas.

cretonne [kreˈtɒn] [kre-ton], *s.* Cretona, tela de algodón, de superficie mate y estampada en colores.

cretose [kreˈtəʊs] [kre-tous], *a.* Cretáceo, gredoso.

crevasse [krɪˈvæs] [kri-vas], *s.* 1. Grieta, hendedura profunda en un ventisquero. 2. *(E.U.)* Brecha en el dique de un río.

crevice [krɪˈvaɪs] [kri-vais], *s.* Raja, hendedura, grieta, abertura.

crevice, *va. V.* CRACK.

crew [kruː] [kru], *s.* 1. Cuadrilla, banda, tropa, reunión de personas congregadas para algún intento, (gag, band). 2. *(Mar. Aer.)* Tripulación. **Cabin/flight/ground crew,** personal de cabina/vuelo/tierra. **Crew member,** miembro de la tripulación, tripulante. 3. Equipo (team). *(Cin.)* **Crew film,** equipo de rodaje o filmación.

crew, *pret. ant. del verbo* TO CROW.

crewcut [ˈkruːkʌt] [kru-kat], *s.* Corte de pelo al cepillo.

crewneck [ˈkruːnek] [kru-nek] *s.* Cuello redondo.

crewel [ˈkruːəl] [kruel], *s.* Ovillo de estambre.

crib [krɪb] [krib], *s.* 1. Pesebre, belén, nacimiento (Nativity's scene). Camita de niño con barandilla por los lados. Cuna (child's bed). **Rattan crib,** camita de junquillo o bambú. 3. Arcón, arca para las mieses; granero de rejilla (for storing grain). 4. *(Min.)* Brocal de entibación. 5. *(Hid.)* Cofre, cajón; balsa pequeña. 6. Fuerte base o estribo flotante. 7. Robo de menor cuantía, y el objeto robado; plagio. 8. *(Des.)* Choza, casucha, chiribitil. 9. *(Coloq.)* Chuleta o acordeón o torpedo (for cheating in exam). Refrito, plagio (plagiarism). Traducción (translation).

crib, *va.* 1. Enjaular, encerrar como en un pesebre. 2. Quitar, hurtar. 3. Copiar (answer). *vn.* Copiar.

cribbage [ˈkrɪbɪdʒ] [kri-bich], *s.* Un juego de naipes.

crib death [ˈkrɪbdeθ] [krib-dez] *s.* Muerte de cuna, muerte súbita (infantil).

cribble [ˈkrɪbl] [kribol], *s.* Criba, harnero; aventador.

crible, *va.* Cerner, pasar por el cedazo o criba.

cribriform [ˈkrɪbrɪfɔːm] [kri-bri-form], *a.* Cribiforme, que tiene forma de criba.

crick [krɪk] [krik], *s.* 1. Chirrido o chirrio. 2. Calambre, afección espasmódica local del cuello o espalda. **Crick in the neck,** tortícoli.

crick *va.* **To crick one's neck,** hacer un mal movimiento con el cuello.

cricket [ˈkrɪkɪt] [kri-ket], *s.* 1. *(Ent.)* Grillo. 2. Vilorta, un juego. *(Sport)* Críquet (game). **That's not cricket,** eso no es jugar limpio. 3. Cáncana, banquillo, escabelito.

cricketer [ˈkrɪkɪtər] [kri-ki-taʳ], *s.* Vilortero.

crier [ˈkraɪər] [kraiaʳ], *s.* Pregonero.

crime [kraɪm] [kraim], *s.* 1. Crimen (murder); delito (wrongful act); culpa. **It's a crime to waste such talent,** es un crimen o un pecado desperdiciar un talento así. 2. Delincuencia (criminal activity). **Crime doesn't pay,** no hay crimen sin castigo. De criminalidad (rate, figures). **Crime wave,** ola delictiva.

criminal [ˈkrɪmɪnl] [kri-mi-nal], *a.* 1. *(Law)* Delictivo (act/ of crime); criminal (organization, mind). **Criminal court,** juzgado en lo penal. **Criminal law,** derecho penal. **Criminal lawyer,** abogado criminalista o penalista. **To start criminal proceedings against somebody,** iniciar proceso criminal o enjuiciamiento contra alguien. 2. *(Coloq.)* Vergonzoso (shameful).

criminal *s.* Delincuente; criminal (serious offender).

criminality [ˌkrɪmɪˈnælɪtɪ] [kri-mi-na-li-ti], *s.* Criminalidad.

criminally [ˈkrɪmɪnəlɪ] [kri-mi-na-li], *adv.* Criminalmente. **An institution for the criminally insane,** una institución penitenciaria para delincuentes psicóticos.

criminalness [ˈkrɪmɪnəlnɪs] [kri-mi-nal-nes], *s.* Criminalidad.

criminal record *s.* Antecedentes penales, prontuario.

criminate [ˈkrɪmɪneɪt] [kri-mi-neit], *va.* Acriminar, acusar.

crimination [ˈkrɪmɪneɪʃən] [kri-mi-nei-shon], *s.* Criminación o acriminación.

criminatory [ˈkrɪmɪnətərɪ] [kri-mi-na-to-ri], *a.* Acriminatorio, acusatorio.

criminology [ˌkrɪmɪˈnɒlədʒɪ] [kri-mi-no-lo-yi], *s.* Criminología, estudio e investigación científicos de materias referentes a los crímenes y a los delincuentes.

criminous [ˈkrɪmɪnəs] [kri-mi-nos], *a.* Criminal, malvado, inicuo, criminoso.

criminously [ˈkrɪmɪnəslɪ] [kri-mi-nos-li], *adv.* Criminalmente.

crimosin *(Des.) V.* CRIMSON.

crimp [krɪmp] [krimp], *a.* 1. Quebradizo, desmenuzable, fácil de desmenuzarse. 2. Contradictorio, fácil de contradecir. 3. Tieso, rígido, como almidonado y planchado.

crimp, *s.* 1. Lo que está encrespado; rizo; se usa en plural. 2. Aparato o instrumento para rizar o encrespar. 3. Sargento que engancha reclutas; también el que con engaño conduce a otros a un sitio determinado para robarlos o maltratarlos. *(Coloq.)* **To put a crimp in something,** obstaculizar o dificultar algo.

crimp, *va.* Torcer, rizar o encrespar; alechugar, dar una forma ondeada. Rizar, ondular con tenacillas (hair).

crimping [ˈkrɪmpɪŋ] [krim-pin], *pa. de* TO CRIMP. **Crimping-iron,** tenacillas, hierros para rizar. **Crimping-machine,** máquina de estampar en relieve.

crimple [krɪmpl] [krimpl], *va.* Encrespar, encoger, arrugar, rizar.

crimpy [ˈkrɪmpɪ] [krim-pi] *a.* Que presenta la aparición de rizado; encrespado.

crimson [ˈkrɪmzn] [krim-son], *a.* Carmesí. **To turn/flush crimson,** ponerse colorado o rojo. *-s.* Carmesí.

crimson, *va.* Teñir de carmesí.

cringe [krɪndʒ] [krinch], *s.* Bajeza.

cringe, *vn.* 1. Incensar, lisonjear, adular con bajeza. 2. Encogerse (shrink, cower). **I cringed at his jokes,** sus chistes me hacían sentir vergüenza ajena. 3. Arrastrarse (grovel). *-va.* Estrechar.

cringer [ˈkrɪndʒər] [krin-chaʳ], *s.* Adulador servil.

cringing [ˈkrɪndʒɪŋ] [krin-chin], *a.* Bajo, vil.

crinigerous [krɪˈnɪdʒərəs] [kri-ni-che-ros], *a.* Peludo, lleno de pelo, cabelludo.

crinkle [ˈkrɪŋkl] [krin-kol], *vn.* Serpentear; arrugar. *-va.* Hacer desigualdades, arrugarse.

crinkle, *s.* 1. Vuelta y revuelta, recodo; sinuosidad. 2. Arruga.

crinkly [ˈkrɪŋklɪ] [krin-kli] *a.* Arrugado (material, face); rizado (hair).

crinoid [ˈkrɪnɔɪd] [kri-noid], *s.* Crinóideo, género de equinodermos.

crinoline [ˈkrɪnəlaɪn] [kri-no-lain], *s.* 1. Tela de crin. 2. Crinolina, ahuecador o miriñaque de mujer, de tela de crin.

crinose [ˈkrɪnəʊs] [kri-nous], *a.* Peloso, peludo, cabelludo.

cripple [krɪpl] [kri-pel], *s. y a.* Cojo, manco, tullido, estropeado. *(Mar.)* Desarbolado, desmantelado.

cripple, *va.* 1. Derengar, estropear, encojar, tullir, baldar, estropear. **He was crippled for life,** quedó lisiado de por vida (lame, disable). **He's crippled with arthritis,** la artritis lo tiene casi inmovilizado. **A crippled arm,** un brazo tullido. 2. Inutilizar (make inactive, ineffective/ship, plane); paralizar (industry).

crippling [ˈkrɪplɪŋ] [kri-plin] *a.* Agobiante (costs, debts); de consecuencias catastroóficas (losses, strike); atroz (pain).

crisis [ˈkraɪsɪs] [krai-sis], *s.* Crisis; momento crítico; cambio decisivo en una enfermedad, negocio, etc. **An identity crisis,** una crisis de identidad. **She's good in a crisis,** reacciona bien en los momentos difíciles. **To reach crisis point,** hacer crisis.

crisp [krɪsp] [krisp], *a.* 1. Crespo, rizado. 2. Vivo; quebradizo, frágil. 3. Achicharrado, tostado. **Crisp almonds,** almendras tostadas. 3. Crujiente, crocante (brittle/toast, bacon); fresco (fresh/lettuce); limpio y almidonado (sheets). 4. Frío y vigorizante (cold/air). 5. Seco (brisk, concise/manner); escueto (style).

crisp *s.* Papa o patata frita de bolsa, chip. **To burn something to a crisp,** achicharrar algo.

crisp, *va.* 1. Crespar, encrespar, torcer, rizar; ondular. 2. Hacer quebradizo o frágil. 3. Trenzar, entrelazar.

crispate [ˈkrɪspeɪt] [kris-peit], *a.* Desigual, sinuoso, arrugado.

crispation [ˈkrɪspeɪʃən] [kris-pei-shon], *s.* 1. Contracción ligera o constricción espasmódica; acción de arrugar. 2. *(Des.)* Encrespadura, crispatura.

crispbread [ˈkrɪspbred] [krisp-bred] *s.* Galleta delgada y crujiente, generalmente de centeno.

crisping-iron [ˈkrɪspɪŋˌaɪrən] [kris-pin-ai-on], **crisping-pin** [ˈkrɪspɪŋˌpɪn] [kris-pin-pin], *s.* Encrespador.

crispness [ˈkrɪspnɪs] [krisp-nes], *s.* Rizado, encrespadura, fragilidad.

crispy [ˈkrɪspɪ] [kris-pi], *a.* Crespo, rizado, desmenuzable, frágil.

crisscross [ˈkrɪskrɒs] [kris-kros], *a.* Cruzado o entrelazado en diferentes direcciones; dícese de líneas, etc. -*s.* 1. Cruz o firma del que no sabe escribir. 2. Líneas cruzadas entre sí. 3. Juego de niños. -*va.* Cruzar líneas. Entrecruzar.

criss-cross-row [ˈkrɪskrɒsˌrəʊd] [kris-kros-roud], *s.* Cristus. V. CHRIST-CROSS-ROW.

criterion [krɪˈtɪərɪən] [kri-te-rion], *s.* Crisis, crítica o criterio.

critic, critical [ˈkrɪtɪk] [kri-tik], *a.* 1. Crítico, exacto, escrupuloso (censorious/remark, report). **Critical affair**, negocio delicado. **To be critical of something/somebody**, criticar a algo/alguien. 2. *(Med.)* Crítico, que indica una crisis; difícil, peligroso, decisivo. 3. Crítico, relativo al examen y censura de las obras literarias o de arte. 4. Quisquilloso, caviloso. 5. Crítico (very serious/condition, shortage); crítico (decisive, crucial/period); de importancia fundamental (decision).

critic, *s.* 1. *(Art, Theat., Lit.)* Crítico, censor. 2. Crítica, observación crítica, examen crítico.

critically [ˈkrɪtɪkəlɪ] [kri-ti-ka-li], *adv.* 1. Exactamente, rigurosamente. **She looked critically at her reflection,** miró con ojo crítico la imagen que le devolvía el espejo. **She spoke rather critically of him,** habló de él en tono de crítica (censoriously). 2. Gravemente (ill).

criticalness [ˈkrɪtɪkəlnɪs] [kri-ti-kal-nes], *s.* Crítica.

criticism [ˈkrɪtɪsɪzəm] [kri-ti-si-zem], *s.* 1. Crítica, juicio fundado en las reglas del buen gusto. 2. Crítica, censura de las acciones ajenas.

criticize, criticise [ˈkrɪtɪsaɪz] [kri-ti-sais], *vn.* Criticar. -*va.* Censurar.

criticizer [ˈkrɪtɪsaɪzər] [kri-ti-sai-sar], *s.* Crítico.

critique [krɪˈtiːk] [kri-tik], *s.* 1. Crítica, examen crítico de alguna cosa; revista. 2. Crítica, el arte de juzgar el mérito de las obras.

critter [ˈkrɪtər] [kri-tar] *s.* *(Sl.)* Bicho.

croak [krəʊk] [krouk], *vn.* 1. Graznar, crascitar o crocitar (raven); cantar, croar (frog); hablar con voz ronca (person). 2. Gruñir, murmurar entre dientes, presagiar mal. 3. *(Sl.)* Estirar la pata (die). *va.* Decir con voz ronca (utter).

croak, *s.* Graznido (of raven); croar, canto (of frog); voz ronca, graznido (of person).

croaker [ˈkrəʊkər] [krou-kar], *s.* Gruñidor, refunfuñador; nombre de desprecio con que se moteja al que da demasiada importancia a los acontecimientos políticos.

croaking [ˈkrəʊkɪŋ] [krou-kin], *pa.* de TO CROCROAK. -*s.* 1. Graznido del cuervo; canto de la rana. 2. *(Fam.)* Gruñido, refunfuño.

croat [ˈkrəʊt] [krout], *s.* Croata, habitante o natural de Croacia.

croatian [ˈkrəʊˈeɪʃɪən] [krou-ei-shian], *a.* Croata, de Croacia. *s.* Croata.

croceous [ˈkrəʊsɪəs] [krou-sios], *a.* (Poco us.) Azafranado.

crochet [ˈkrəʊʃeɪ] [krou-shei], *va. y vn.* Tejer con gancho, hacer cierta labor de aguja con hilo de lana, seda o algodón. -*s.* Tejido de gancho; crochet, ganchillo. **Crochet needle**, gancho para tejer.

crock [krɒk] [krok], *s.* 1. Escudilla, cazuela, orza; olla de barro (earthen vessel). 2. *(Sl.)* **Ain't that a crock!,** ¡qué estupidez! (nonsense). Antigualla, cacharro (decrepit thing); *(GB Coloq.)* Vejestorio (decrepit person).

crockery [ˈkrɒkərɪ] [kro-ke-ri], *s.* Vidriado, loza, todo género de vasijas de barro; vajilla.

crocodile [ˈkrɒkədaɪl] [kro-ko-dail], *s.* Cocodrilo, crocodilo o caimán. **To shed/weep crocodile tears,** derramar o llorar lágrimas de cocodrilo.

crocus [ˈkrəʊkəs] [krou-kos], *s.* 1. *(Bot.)* Azafrán. 2. Azafrán croco o de Marte; rojo de pulir.

croft [krɒft] [kroft], *s.* Campo pequeño cercano a una casa; huerta o tierra pequeña cercada.

croissant [ˈkrwʌsɑːŋ] [krua-san] *s.* Croissant, medialuna, cachito, cuernito.

cromlech [ˈkrɒmleʧ] [krom-lech], *s.* Círculo de piedras verticales que a menudo rodean un dolmen; monumento megalítico. V. DOLMEN.

crone [krəʊn] [kroun], *s.* 1. Mujer vieja. *(Fam.)* Una tía, una comadre. 2. Oveja vieja.

crony [ˈkrəʊnɪ] [krou-ni], *s.* Compinche, camarada, amigo y conocido antiguo. **An old crony,** un amigo de muchos años; un conocido viejo.

crook [krʊk] [kruk], *s.* 1. Curvatura, curva; cosa encorvada. Parte interior del codo (of the arm). 2. Gancho, garfio. 3. Gancho o cayado de pastor. 4. Artificio, trampa. 5. *(Fam.)* Un criminal de profesión; fullero, petardista; sinvergüenza, pillo (criminal).

crook, *va.* 1. Encorvar, torcer. Doblar (finger, arm). 2. *(Ant.)* Pervertir, separar del camino recto. -*vn.* Estar encorvado.

crook-backed [ˈkrʊkˌbeɪkɪd] [kruk-bei-kid], *a.* Jorobado, corcovado, gibado, giboso.

crooked [ˈkrʊkɪd] [kru-kid], *a.* 1. Corvo, encorvado (back); torcido, chueco (line, legs); oblicuo. Sinuoso, lleno de curvas (path). Torcido (smile). **She gave me a crooked grin,** me hizo una mueca. 2. *(Fig.)* Perverso, pervertido, malvado. *(Coloq.)* Deshonesto, chueco (dishonest/person, deal). **Crooked legs,** patituerto o piernas tuertas. **Crooked line,** línea curva. **To go crooked,** encorvarse, torcerse.

crookedly [ˈkrʊkɪdlɪ] [kru-kid-li], *adv.* Torcidamente, de través; de mala gana.

crookedness [ˈkrʊkɪdnɪs] [kru-kid-nes], *s.* 1. Corvadura, corcova. 2. Perversidad, maldad, iniquidad. 3. Vueltas, sinuosidades, anfractuosidades.

crook-neck [ˈkrʊknek] [kruk-nek], *a.* Que tiene el cuello torcido. -*s.* Variedad de calabaza que toma el nombre de cuello largo y retorcido.

croon [kruːn] [krun], *va.* Cantar o canturrear suavemente, con delicadeza. -*vn.* 1. Cantar en tono bajo y monótono. 2. Gruñir sordamente.

crooner [ˈkruːnər] [kru-ner] *s.* Cantante melódico.

crop [krɒp] [krop], *s.* 1. Cosecha (quantity of produce); cultivo (type of produce); las mieses. **Crop rotation,** rotación de cultivos. *(Coloq.)* Tanda (batch). 2. Crecimiento de cabellos o barba. 3. Cortadura. Corte de pelo muy corto (haircut). 4. Empuñadura de látigo; fusta, fuete (riding crop). 5. Caballo desorejado. 6. Buche de ave.

crop, *va.* 1. Segar o cortar las mieses o hierba. 2. Pacer o roer la hierba. 3. Desorejar, cortar las orejas o los cabellos; esquilar (los perros o las caballerías). Cortar muy corto (cut/hair).

crop up *(Coloq.)* Surgir (occur, present itself). **Something must have cropped up at work,** debe haber surgido algún problema en el trabajo. **One phrase that crops up again and again,** una frase que se repite constantemente.

crop-eared [ˈkrɒpˈɛərd] [krop-eard], *a.* Desorejado.

cropful [ˈkrɒpfʊl] [krop-ful], *a.* Harto, hartado, ahíto.

cropper [ˈkrɒpər] [kro-par], *s.* 1. Especie de paloma que tiene el buche grande. V. POUTER. 2. *(Coloq.)* **To come a cropper,** darse o pegarse un porrazo (fall). Fracasar por completo (suffer defeat, disaster).

cropping [ˈkrɒpɪŋ] [krop-pin], *s.* 1. Corta, acción de cortar. 2. Pasto, acción de pastar. 3. Esquileo de los animales. 4. Siega, cultivación de una cosecha. 5. Porción aparente de un estrato en un terreno.

cropsick [ˈkrɒpsɪk] [krop-sik], *a.* Ahíto, ahitado, relleno.

croquet [ˈkrəʊkeɪ] [krou-kei], *s.* Raqueta, croquet, juego al aire libre con bolas, mazos y arcos de alambre. Pueden jugarlo de dos a ocho personas. *-va.* Hacer cierta jugada especial en el juego de este nombre.

croquette [krəʊˈket] [krou-ket], *s.* Croqueta. **Chicken croquettes,** croquetas de pollo.

crosier [ˈkrəʊʒər] [krou-siaʳ], *s. V.* CROZIER.

cross [krɒs] [kros], *s.* 1. Cruz, instrumento de suplicio entre los antiguos. 2. *(Rel.)* Cruz, emblema del cristianismo. **To make the sign of the cross,** hacer la señal de la cruz. 3. Peso, carga, trabajo; oposición; pena, aflicción, desgracia, tormento, revés. **We all have our cross to bear,** todos cargamos con o llevamos nuestra cruz. 4. Cruz, insignia honorífica de algunas órdenes militares y civiles (mark, sign). 5. *(Biol.)* Cruce, mezcla de las diferentes especies de plantas o de las castas de animales (hybrid). 6. *(Sport)* Pase cruzado (in soccer). Cruzado, cross (in boxing). **Crosses are ladders leading to heaven,** *(Prov.)* las cruces llevan al cielo. **The cross on the breast and the devil in action,** la cruz en la frente y el diablo en la obra. **The Southern Cross,** la Cruz del Sur, constelación del hemisferio austral.

cross, *a.* 1. Contrario, opuesto, atravesado. 2. Malhumorado, enojado, enfadado, picado; caprichoso, cabezudo, impertinente, revoltoso, regañón. **To get cross,** enojarse, enfadarse. **It makes me cross,** me da rabia. **To be cross about something,** estar enojado o enfadado por algo. 3. Desgraciado, infausto. 4. Alternado, cruzado; dícese de una raza o linaje. 5. Displicente, desabrido, de mal genio o natural. *(For.)* **Cross-question, cross-interrogatory,** repregunta, examen de la parte contraria.

cross, *prep.* Al través; de una parte a otra.

cross, *va.* 1. Trazar una línea al través de. **To cross the t,** ponerle el palito a la t (put line through). 2. Borrar, cancelar, rayar: con las preposiciones *off* o *out.* 3. Cruzar, poner o trazar en forma de cruz. Cruzar (arms, legs). *(Telec.)* **We have a crossed line,** se han cruzado las líneas. *(Coloq.)* **I think maybe we've got our wires crossed,** me parece que no hablamos de lo mismo. **The two streets cross each other,** las dos calles se cruzan. 4. Atravesar, cruzar, pasar de una parte a otra (go across/road). Cruzar, atravesar (river, desert). **It crossed my mind that...,** se me ocurrió que..., me pasó por la cabeza que... 5. Señalar con la señal de la cruz. 6. Vejar; frustrar (plans); desbaratar. Contrariar (go against/person). 7. Contradecirse uno a sí mismo. 8. Cruzar, mezclar las castas (plants, breeds). *(Sport)* Cruzar, tirar cruzado (ball). *-vn.* Estar al través, cruzarse (paths, roads, letters). **To cross over,** atravesar de un lado a otro pasando por encima de una cosa; pasar del lado de allá al de acá. *-vr.* **To cross oneself,** persignarse, santiguarse, hacerse la señal de la cruz.

cross off Tachar (name, item). **She crossed it off the list,** lo tachó de la lista.

cross out Tachar (name, item).

cross-armed [krɒsˈɑːmd] [kros-armd], *a.* 1. Cruzado de brazos. 2. *(Bot.)* Los árboles y arbustos, cuyas ramas se cruzan.

crossbar [ˈkrɒsbɑːr] [kros-baʳ], *s.* Barra (on bicycle); larguero, travesaño horizontal (of goal); listón (in pole vaulting, high jump).

cross-barred [ˈkrɒsbɑːrəd] [kros-ba-red], *a.* Atravesado, atorado.

cross-bar-shot [ˌkrɒsbɑːˈʃɒt] [kros-bar-shot], *s. (Mar.)* Palanqueta.

cross-bearer [krɒsˈbɪərər] [kros-bea-raʳ], *s.* Crucífero.

cross-bill [ˈkrɒsbɪl] [kros-bil], *s.* 1. Escrito o cargo producido por el demandado contra el demandante. 2. **Cross-bill** o **cross-beak** *(Orn.)* picogordo.

cross-bow [ˈkrɒsbəʊ] [kros-bou], *s.* Ballesta.

cross-bower [ˈkrɒsbəʊər] [kros-bouaʳ], **cross-bowman** [ˈkrɒsbəʊmən] [kros-bou-man], *s.* Ballestero.

crossbred [ˈkrɒsbred] [kros-bred] *a.* Cruzado.

crossbreed [ˈkrɒsbriːd] [kros-brid] *s.* Cruce, cruza.

cross-bun [ˈkrɒsbʌn] [kros-ban], *s.* Bollo señalado con una cruz.

cross-chanel [ˈkrɒsˌtʃænl] [kros-cha-nel] *a.* Que cruza el Canal de la Mancha (ferry/traffic).

cross-check [ˈkrɒstʃek] [kros-chek] *va.* Verificar consultando otras fuentes (facts, references). **To cross-check something against something,** cotejar algo con algo. *-vn.* Hacer una comprobación o verificación.

cross-check *s.* Comprobación, verificación.

cross-country [ˈkrɒsˈkʌntrɪ] [kros-ken-tri] *a.* Campo a través, a campo traviesa, a campo través (across countryside/route, drive); de fondo (skiing). **Country-cross race,** cross.

cross-country *adv.* Campo través, a campo traviesa, a campo través (across countryside/travel, drive).

cross-cut [ˈkrɒskʌt] [kros-kat], *va.* Intersectar, cortar al través. *-s.* Senda traviesa, camino más corto.

cross-examination [ˈkrɒsɪgˌzæmɪˈneɪʃən] [kros-ek-sa-mi-nei-shon], *s. (For.)* Repreguntas que se hacen a un testigo sobre la declaración que ha dado.

cross-examine [ˈkrɒsɪgˈzæmɪn] [kros-ek-sa-min], *va.* Examinar o repreguntar a un testigo sobre su declaración.

cross-eye [ˈkrɒsaɪ] [kros-ai], *s.* Estrabismo.

cross-eyed [ˈkrɒsaɪd] [kros-aid], *a.* Bizco, bisojo.

cross-fertilize [ˈkrɒsˈfɜːtɪlaɪz] [kros-fer-ti-lais], *va.* Fertilizar una flor por medio del polen de otra.

crossfire [ˈkrɒsfaɪər] [kros-faiaʳ] *s.* Fuego cruzado.

cross-flow [ˈkrɒsfləʊ] [kros-flau], *vn.* Fluir o correr en dirección contraria, al través de.

cross-grained [ˈkrɒsgreɪnd] [kros-greind], *a.* 1. Vetado o veteado; (madero) de fibras atravesadas y difícil de cortar y trabajar. 2. *(Fig.)* Perverso, intratable, desabrido, de mal natural.

crossing [ˈkrɒsɪŋ] [kro-sin] *s.* 1. El acto de señalar con la cruz, oposición. 2. Travesía, paso; lugar donde se puede cruzar, pasar o vadear algo. 3. Cruzado de una tela; encrucijada, cuatro calles; en los ferrocarriles, cruce de vía, vía diagonal.

cross-jack [ˈkrɒsjæk] [kros-yak], *s. (Mar.)* Vela seca.

cross-legged [ˈkrɒslegd] [kros-legd], *a.* Patizambo. *-adv.* Con las piernas cruzadas.

crossly [ˈkrɒslɪ] [kros-li], *adv.* Contrariamente; enojadamente. **No, she said crossly,** no, dijo enojada.

crossness [ˈkrɒsnɪs] [kros-nes], *s.* 1. Mal humor; enfado, enojo. 2. Malicia, perversidad. 3. Travesía.

cross-piece [ˈkrɒspiːs] [kros-pis], *s. (Mar.)* Cruz de las bitas; *(Carp.)* Travesaño, cruceta. **Cross-piece of the forecastle,** *(Mar.)* atravesaño del propao del castillo.

cross-purpose [ˈkrɒspɜːpəs] [kros-per-pos], *s.* 1. Disposición contraria. **We're talking at cross-purposes,** estamos hablando de cosas distintas. 2. Enigma, juego, diversión casera.

cross-question [ˈkrɒsˈkwestʃən] [kros-kues-tion], *va. (For.)* Repreguntar. *V.* CROSS-EXAMINE.

cross reference [ˈkrɒsˈrefərəns] [kros-re-fe-rens], *s.* Referencia cruzada, remisión del lector de una parte de un texto a otra.

cross-road [ˈkrɒsrəʊd] [kros-roud], *s.* Atajo, trocha, camino que acorta una distancia. **Cross-roads,** encrucijada, cuatro caminos; ocurre a menudo en las aldeas pequeñas.

cross-row [ˈkrɒsrəʊ] [kros-rou], *s.* Alfabeto, cartilla.

cross-section [ˈkrɒsˈsekʃən] [kros-sek-shon], *s.* Corte transversal. Sección. **A cross-section of society,** una muestra representativa de los distintos estratos sociales.

cross-staff [ˈkrɒsstæf] [kros-staf], *(Mar.)* Ballestilla.

crosstown [ˈkrɒsstaʊn] [kros-staun] *a.* Que cruza o atraviesa la ciudad.

cross-trees [ˈkrɒstriːs] [kros-tris], *s. pl. (Mar.)* Crucetas, baos de gavia.

crosswalk [ˈkrɒswɔːk] [kros-uok], *s.* Cruce o paso de peatones.

cross-way [ˈkrɒsweɪ] [kros-uei], *s.* Senda; camino de travesía. *V.* CROSS-ROAD.

cross-wind [ˈkrɒswɪnd] [kros-uind], *s.* Viento atravesado.

crosswise [ˈkrɒswaɪz] [kros-uais], *adv.* 1. De través, al través; de una parte a otra. 2. En forma de cruz.

crossword puzzle [ˈkrɒswɔːdˈpʌzl] [kros-ued-pasol], *s.* Crucigrama.

crosswort [ˈkrɒswɔːt] [kros-uort], *s. (Bot.)* Cruzciata.

crotch [krɒtʃ] [kroch], *s.* 1. Gancho, corchete; horquilla, cruz. 2. Entrepierna.

crotchet [ˈkrɒtʃɪt] [kros-chit], *s.* 1. Capricho, entusiasmo; idea o pensamiento extravagante. **It/he has its/his little crotchets!,** ¡tiene sus mañas! 2. Corchea, nota musical cuyo valor es una cuarta parte de la semibreve. 3. Garfio pequeño. 4. Corchete, carácter o signo de imprenta así []. *V.* BRACKET. 5. Instrumento de obstetricia.

crotchety [ˈkrɒtʃɪtɪ] [kro-chi-ti], *a.* Caprichoso, extravagante, raro. Cascarrabias, malhumorado.

crouch [krautʃ] [krouch], *va.* Agacharse, ponerse en cuclillas (person) **To crouch down,** agacharse; abatirse, bajarse; adular con bajeza.

croup [kruːp] [krup], *s.* 1. Obispillo o rabadilla de ave; anca, grupa (de caballo). 2. Crup, garrotillo, enfermedad de los conductos respiratorios que ataca a los niños.

croupier [ˈkruːpɪəɪ] [kru-piei] *s.* Crupier, croupier.

crouton [ˈkruːtən] [kru-ton], *s.* Crutón, picatoste.

crow [krəʊ] [krou], *s.* 1. *(Zool.)* Cuervo, ave de rapiña. 2. **Crow, crowbar,** barra, palanca de hierro; pie de cabra. 3. Cacareo (cry/of rooster). **As the crow flies,** en línea recta. **To eat crow,** *(E.U.)* desdecir uno sus palabras, contradecirse.

crow, *vn.* 1. Cantar el gallo. 2. Gallear, jactarse, cantar victoria, hacer alarde de, pavonearse (exult). **To crow over one,** afectar superioridad sobre alguno; bravear, echar bravatas. *-va.* Alardear.

crowd [kraud] [kraud], *s.* 1. Tropel, gentío, turba, concurso; apretura; muchedumbre, tumulto, (gathering of people); populacho, vulgo. **There was quite a crowd,** había mucha gente. **Crowd of shoppers,** multitud de clientes. 2. Antiguo instrumento músico de Irlanda y Gales, parecido al violín. Fue el primero de su clase que se tocó con arco. **To get through the crowd,** atravesar o abrirse camino por medio del gentío. **To go with/follow the crowd,** seguir a la manada, dejarse arrastrar o llevar por la corriente (masses, average folk). *(Coloq.)* **They're a nice crowd,** son gente simpática (group, set).

crowd *vn.* Aglomerarse. **They crowded around him,** se aglomeraron a su alrededor. **They crowded into the hall,** entraron en tropel a la sala. *-va.* Llenar, abarrotar (people/hall, entrance). **Don't try to crowd everything onto one page,** no trates de meter todo en una página.

crowded [ˈkraudɪd] [krau-ded] *a.* Abarrotado, atestado, lleno de gente (street, room, bus). **The beach gets very crowded,** la playa se llena de gente.

crowd-puller [ˈkraudˌpʊləɪ] [kraud-pu-laʳ] *s. (Coloq.)* Gran atracción, espectáculo o persona que atrae mucho público.

crowfoot [ˈkrəʊfʊt] [krou-fut], *s.* 1. *(Bot.)* Ranúnculo. 2. *(Mar.)* Araña. 3. *(Mil.)* Abrojo. V. CALTROP. 4. *(Elec.)* Cierta clase de cinc de batería que se usa en una celda de gravedad.

crown [kraun] [kraun], *s.* 1. Corona, ornamento honorífico de los reyes y príncipes soberanos; y por extensión, la monarquía, el poder real y la dignidad de monarca. *(Law, Govt.)* **The Crown,** la corona. 2. Premio. 3. Guirnalda de flores. 4. Coronilla (of head); copa (of hat). 5. Copa (of tree); cima (top/of hill). Centro (of road). 6. Complemento, colmo. 7. *(Fin.)* Moneda de plata en Inglaterra del valor de cinco chelines. 8. Corona, parte del diente que se halla fuera de la encía. 9. *(Arq.)* Corona, coronamiento de bóveda o arco; parte de la cornisa que está debajo del cimacio y la gola. **Crown lands,** *(Ingl.)* bienes raíces que pertenecen al soberano.

crown, *va.* 1. Coronar (make monarch); recompensar, premiar; completar, dar la última mano. 2. Coronar, rematar (surmount). Coronar (be culmination of). **To crown it all, I lost my wallet,** y para rematarla, perdí la billetera. 3.

(Dent.) Poner una corona en (tooth). 4. *(Coloq.)* Darle un coscorrón a (hit).

crown court [krauŋˈkɔːt] [kraun-kort] *s.* (in UK) Juzgado que conoce de causas de derecho penal.

crownet, *s. V.* CORONET.

crown-glass [ˈkraunglɑːs] [kraun-glas], *s.* Vidrio fino para vidrieras. V. GLASS.

crowning [ˈkraunɪŋ] [krau-nin], *s. (Arq.)* Remate. *a.* Supremo, mayor (success, achievement).

crown jewels [kraunˈjuːəlz] [kraun-yuels] *s. pl.* Joyas de la corona.

crown prince [ˈkraunprɪns] [kraun-prins] *s.* Príncipe heredero.

crown princess [kraunˈprɪnsəs] [kraun-prin-ses] *s.* Princesa heredera.

crown-wheel [ˈkraunwiːl] [kraun-uil], *s.* Rueda superior próxima al volante del reloj.

crown-works [ˈkraunwɜːks] [kraun-uerks], *s.* Obra coronada, la que está separada del cuerpo de la plaza para defender algún puesto.

crow's-foot [ˈkrəʊzfʊt] [krous-fut], *s.* 1. Pata de gallo, arruga que se forma en el ángulo externo del ojo. 2. Abrojo. V. CALTROP. 3. Punto de hacer bordado.

crozier [ˈkruːzɪəɪ] [kru-siaʳ], *a.* Cayado o báculo pastoral del obispo.

crucial [ˈkruːʃəl] [kru-shal], *a.* 1. Decisivo, conclusivo, final; que determina absolutamente la verdad o la falsedad de algo. 2. Cruzado, atravesado.

cruciate [ˈkruːʃɪeɪt] [kru-shieit], *a.* 1. Cruciforme, en forma de cruz. 2. Atormentado.

crucible [ˈkruːsɪbl] [kru-sibol], *s.* Crisol, vasija que resiste la acción del fuego y sirve para fundir metales y otras cosas.

cruciferous [ˈkruːsɪfərəs] [kru-si-fe-ros], **crucigercus** [ˈkruːsɪɡɜːkəs] [kru-si-guer-kus], *a.* 1. Crucífero, lo que lleva cruz. 2. *(Bot.)* Crucíferas, familia de plantas con flores de cuatro pétalos que forman cruz.

crucifier [ˈkruːsɪfəɪ] [kru-si-fiaʳ], *s.* Crucificador.

crucifix [ˈkruːsɪfɪks] [kru-si-fiks], *s.* Crucifijo, la efigie o imagen de nuestro Señor crucificado.

crucifixion [ˌkruːsɪˈfɪkʃən] [kru-si-fik-shon], *s.* Crucifixión.

cruciform [ˈkruːsɪfɔːm] [kru-si-form], *a.* Cruciforme, en forma de cruz.

crucify [ˈkruːsɪfaɪ] [kru-si-fai], *va.* 1. Crucificar (execute). 2. Atormentar, enojar. 3. *(Coloq.)* **They were crucified in the press,** la prensa los destrozó (treat severely).

crud [krʌd] [krad], *s.* 1. Porquería (impurities). 2. V. CURD.

crude [kruːd] [krud], *a.* 1. Crudo, indigesto, imperfecto. 2. Crudo, no refinado (oil/containing impurities); en estado que necesita preparación antes de ser usado. Rudimentario, burdo (unsophisticated). 3. *(Fig.)* Imperfecto, mal elaborado, mal concebido, superficial. 4. Ordinario, grosero (vulgar). *s.* Crudo.

crudely [ˈkruːdəlɪ] [kru-de-li] *adv.* 1. Groseramente (vulgarly). **To put it crudely,** hablando en plata. 2. De un modo rudimentario (roughly).

crudeness [kruːdnɪs] [krud-nes], **crudity** [ˈkruːdɪtɪ] [kru-di-ti], *s.* Crudeza, falta de madurez, imperfección. **Crudity,** lo crudo, lo indigesto o informe.

cruel [krɔəl] [kruel], *a.* Cruel, inhumano, bárbaro, terrible, feroz, sanguinario, despiadado, inclemente, atroz. Crudo (winter); duro (blow). **To be cruel to somebody,** ser cruel con alguien.

cruelly [ˈkrɔəlɪ] [krue-li], *adv.* Cruelmente, dolorosamente, inhumanamente.

cruelness [ˈkrɔəlnɪs] [kruel-nes], **cruelty** [ˈkrɔəltɪ] [kruel-ti], *s.* Crueldad, inhumanidad, barbarie; tiranía, dureza.

cruet [ˈkruːɪt] [kruit], *s.* Ampolleta para aceite o vinagre; vinagrera, aceitera, alcuza.

cruet-stand [ˈkruːɪtstænd] [kruit-stand], *s.* Angarillas, vinagreras, salvilla en que se colocan las ampolletas de aceite, vinagre, mostaza, etc.

cruise [kru:z] [krus], *s.* 1. Travesía marítima. **To go on a cruise,** hacer un crucero. 2. Paseo por tierra. 3. Viaje en avión.

cruise, *vn.* 1. *(Mar.)* Navegar por el mar o a lo largo de la costa, hacer un crucero. 2. Patrullar (police car). 3. Volar, desplazarse (travel at a steady speed/plane); ir a una velocidad constante (car).

cruiser ['kru:zər] [kru-se^r], *s.* La persona o nave que hace viaje por mar; especialmente crucero, buque de guerra próximo en fuerza al *battle-ship* o acorazado y más ligero que éste.

cruising speed ['kru:zɪŋspi:d] [kru-sin-spid], *s.* Velocidad de crucero.

crum o crumb [krʌm] [kram], *s.* Miga, migajón (of bread, cake).

crum, crumb, *va.* 1. Migar, desmigajar, reducir a migajas. 2. Desmenuzar.

crumble ['krʌmbl] [kram-bel], *va.* Migar, desmigajar (bread); desmenuzar (earth, cake). -*vn.* Desmigajarse; desmoronarse (wall). Desmenuzarse (cake, soil); desmoronarse, derrumbarse (democracy, resolve). **To crumble pieces,** irse desmoronando.

crummy ['krʌmɪ] [kra-mi], *a.* 1. Blando, tierno; que tiene mucha miga; que se desmigaja. 2. *(Coloq.)* Malo, horrible.

crump ['krʌmp] [kramp], *a.* 1. *V.* CRISP. 2. *(des.)* Corcovado, gibado, giboso, el que tiene giba o corcova.

crumpet ['krʌmpɪt] [kram-pit], *s.* Buñuelo o bollo blando. Panecillo de levadura que se come tostado.

crumple ['krʌmpl] [kram-pol] *va.* Arrugar (paper, clothes); abollar (metal). **She crumpled the sheet of paper into a ball,** hizo una bola estrujando la hoja de papel. -*vn.* Arrugarse (become creased/fabric, shirt).

crumpled ['krʌmpld] [kram-peld], *pp.* y *a.* Arrugado, ajado; contraído.

crumpling ['krʌmplɪŋ] [kram-plin], *s.* Manzana pequeña arrugada.

crunch [krʌntʃ] [kranch], *va.* Mascar, ronchar, ronzar (eat noisily); crujir, cascar con los dientes. Aplastar haciendo crujir (crash). **To crunch something up,** triturar algo. *vn.* Mascar, ronchar, ronzar (eat noisily). **Our footsteps crunched on the gravel,** nuestros pasos hacían crujir la grava.

crunch *s.* 1. Crujido (noise). 2. **When it comes/came to the crunch,** a la hora de la verdad (crisis).

crunchy ['krʌntʃɪ] [kran-chi] *a.* Crujiente.

cruor ['kruər] [kruo^r], *s.* Cruor, sangre coagulada.

crupper ['krʌpər] [kra-pa^r], *s.* 1. Crupera, ataharre. 2. Grupa.

crural ['krʊrəl] [kru-ral], *a.* Crural, perteneciente a la pierna o al muslo. **Crural artery,** arteria crural.

crus [kru:s] [krus], *s.* 1. Pierna, la parte del animal que está entre el pie y la rodilla. 2. Parte parecida a la pierna; pedúnculo; comúnmente en plural, CRURA.

crusade [kru:'seɪd] [kru-seid], **crusado** ['kru:seɪdəʊ] [kru-sei-dou], *s.* *(Hist.)* Cruzada; cruzada, campaña (campaign). -**Crusado,** cruzado, moneda de Portugal.

crusader [kru:'seɪdər] [kru-sei-da^r], *s.* *(Hist.)* Cruzado; defensor (campaigner).

cruse ['kru:'] [kru:s], *s.* Ampolleta, cantarillo, frasco, redomita, botellita.

cruset ['kru:sɪt] [kru-sit], *s.* Crisol de orífice o platero.

crush [krʌʃ] [krash], *va.* 1. Aplastar (squash/box, car, person, fingers); machacar (garlic); moler; prensar, pisar (grapes); arrugar (dress, suit). Triturar (pound, pulverize). **Crushed ice,** hielo picado o frappé. *(Fam.)* Despachurrar. 2. Apretar, comprimir, oprimir. Aplastar (subdue/resistance, enemy). 3. Amilanar, arruinar, trastornar, destruir; sojuzgar completamente. -*vn.* Estar comprimido: condensarse. Arrugarse (fabric).

crush, *s.* 1. Colisión, choque. 2. Aglomeración (crowd). **Three people were injured in the crush,** tres personas resultaron heridas en el tumulto. 3. *(Coloq.)* Enamoramiento (infatuation). **To have a crush on somebody,** estar chiflado por alguien. 4. **Orange crush,** naranjada. **Lemon crush,** limonada (drink).

crush barrier ['krʌʃˌbærɪər] [krash-ba-ria^r] *s.* Valla de protección o de contención.

crusher ['krʌʃər] [kra-sha^r], *s.* 1. Apretador; opresor. 2. Bocarte, triturador, instrumento para machacar el mineral antes de fundirlo.

crushing ['krʌʃɪŋ] [kra-shin] *a.* Aplastante (defeat); apabullante (reply, contempt).

crust [krʌst] [krast], *s.* 1. Costra. 2. Corteza. **The earth's crust,** la corteza terrestre. 3. Pedazo o fragmento de pan ya duro. **A crust of bread,** un mendrugo. *(Coloq.)* **To earn a/one's crust,** ganarse el pan o los garbanzos. 4. Pasta de una torta, de un pastel. 5. Capa (del globo). 6. Carapacho, concha: el tegumento duro de los cangrejos e insectos.

crust, *va.* Encostrar, cubrir con costra, revestir, incrustar. -*vn.* Encostrarse.

crustacea [krʌs'teɪʃɪə] [kras-tei-shia], *s. pl.* *(Zool.)* Crustáceos, clase de animales articulados que comprende langostas, cangrejos, langostinos, camarones, percebes y otros.

crustacean [krʌs'teɪʃən] [kras-tei-shan], *a.* y *s.* Crustáceo. *V.* CRUSTACEA.

crustaceous [krʌs'teɪʃəs] [kras-tei-shos], *a.* Crustáceo; conchado, cubierto de conchas.

crustate ['krʌsteɪt] [kras-teit], *a.* Cubierto con corteza o costra.

crustation [krʌs'teɪʃən] [kras-tei-shon], *s.* Incrustación, cobertura.

crustily ['krʌstɪlɪ] [kras-ti-li], *adv.* Enojadamente, broncamente.

crustiness ['krʌstɪnɪs] [kras-ti-nes], *s.* 1. Dureza de la costra. 2. Mal genio, aspereza de carácter.

crusty ['krʌstɪ] [kras-ti], *s.* 1. Costroso. 2. Bronco, rudo, impertinente, inquieto; brusco, áspero. Malhumorado (irascible). 3. Crujiente (crispy/bread).

crutch [krʌtʃ] [krach], *s.* 1. Muleta (walking aid). **To be/ walk on crutches,** andar con muletas. 2. *(Mar.)* Horquilla del cangrejo. -**Cruches,** *(Mar.)* Horquetas. 3. Muleta, apoyo (support). **Crutched man,** un cojitranco.

crutch, *va.* Andar con muletas.

crux [krʌks] [kraks] *s.* Quid. **The crux of the matter,** el quid de la cuestión.

cry [kraɪ] [krai], *vn.* 1. Gritar, vocear, llamar a voces (person); chillar (bird). *(Coloq.)* **For crying out loud!,** ¡por el amor de Dios! 2. Pregonar, publicar. 3. Exclamar: lamentarse. 4. Llorar (weep), gimotear. 5. Aullar, bramar. -*va.* 1. Llorar (weep). **He cried himself to sleep,** lloró hasta quedarse dormido. 2. Gritar (call). 3. Pregonar, publicar la pérdida o hallazgo de alguna cosa. **To cry aloud,** levantar la voz; llorar a gritos. **To cry down,** culpar; hacer callar a uno a fuerza de voces; menospreciar; reprimir; rebatir o responder con demasiada violencia; prohibir. **To cry for,** (a) gritar, pedir llorando; (b) llorar a causa de. **To cry for joy,** llorar de alegría. **To cry off,** renunciar, no querer más. **To cry out,** gritar fuertemente, vocear, exclamar; llorar dando quejidos; estar de parto; publicar las faltas de alguno. **To cry out upon one,** avergonzar a alguno. **To cry one's eyes out,** llorar amargamente. **To cry unto,** invocar, reclamar. **To cry up,** aplaudir, alabar; pondear, exagerar, exaltar. **To cry one up for a saint,** hacer pasar a alguno por santo.

cry off Echarse atrás. **Several of the guests cried off at the last minute,** a último momento varios de los invitados dijeron que no podían venir.

cry out Gritar (call out). **To cry out for something,** pedir algo a gritos (need).

cry, *s. (pl.* CRIES) 1. Alarido, grito (exclamation). **To give/ let out a cry,** dar/soltar un grito. **She heard cries for help,** oyó gritos de socorro. 2. Lamento, lloro o llanto (weep). **To have a cry,** llorar. 3. Gritería, clamor, grito; aplauso. Chillido (call of seagull). 4. Pregón (of street vendor; promulgación, publicación. Lema, slogan (slogan). 5.

Aclamación. 6. Llamada importuna. 7. Muta, cuadrilla de perros de caza. **A far cry,** camino largo. **Great cry and little wool,** mucho ruido y pocas nueces.

cry-baby [ˈkraɪˌbeɪbɪ] [krai-bei-bi], *s.* Niño llorón.

cryer [ˈkraɪər] [kraia'], *s.* 1. *V.* CRIER. 2. Halcón gentil, neblí.

crying [ˈkraɪɪŋ] [krai-in], *s.* Grito, lloro, dolores de parto. **Crying down,** desestimación, desprecio, hablando de personas; desaprecio, ningún aprecio, hablando de cosas. *-a.* 1. Enorme, atroz, lo que pide venganza al cielo por injusto o tiránico. 2. Apremiante (need, urgency). **It's a crying shame!,** es una verdadera pena o lástima.

cryogenics [kraɪəˈdʒenɪks] [kraio-ye-niks], *s.* Criogenía, física de muy bajas temperaturas.

crypt [krɪpt] [kript], *s.* 1. Bóveda subterránea en que antiguamente acostumbraban enterrar los muertos y a la que llamaban cript. 2. *(Anat.)* Cripta, pequeño folículo, saquillo secretorio de la piel o de las membranas mucosas.

cryptic, cryptical [ˈkrɪptɪkəlɪ] [krip-ti-kal], *a.* Escondido, secreto. Enigmático, críptico (remark, reference); críptico (crossword).

cryptically [ˈkrɪptɪkəlɪ] [krip-ti-ka-li], *adv.* Ocultamente.

crypto-. del griego cryptos, oculto: forma de combinación.

cryptogam [ˈkrɪptəʊgæm] [krip-to-gam], *s.* Criptógama, planta de la clase de ese nombre.

criptogamia [ˈkrɪptəʊgæmɪə] [krip-to-ga-mia], *s. pl.* Criptogamia, la clase de plantas cuyos órganos sexuales están ocultos o son poco aparentes.

cryptogram [ˈkrɪptəʊgræm] [krip-to-gram], *s.* Escritura secreta por medio de signos convenidos, cifra.

criptography [ˈkrɪptɒgræfɪ] [krip-to-gra-fi], *s.* Criptografía; caracteres secretos, el arte de escribir en cifra.

criptology [ˈkrɪptɒlədʒɪ] [krip-to-lo-yi], *s.* Criptología, lenguaje enigmático.

crystal [ˈkrɪstl] [kris-tal], *s.* 1. Cristal, forma regular poliedra en que se presentan las sales, piedras, metales y otros cuerpos. 2. Cristal, vidrio incoloro y muy transparente. 3. *V.* GLASS (Flint). 4. Cristal de reloj.

crystal, crystalline [ˈkrɪstəlaɪn] [kris-ta-lain], *a.* 1. Cristalino, hecho o compuesto de cristal. 2. Claro, transparente.

crystal ball [ˈkrɪstlbəl] [kris-tal-bol] *s.* Bola de cristal.

crystal-clear [ˈkrɪstlˈklɪər] [kris-tal-klia'] *a.* Cristalino (water); nítido, claro (sound, image). **It's crystal-clear that…,** está clarísimo que…, está más claro que el agua que…

crystallizable [ˈkrɪstəlaɪzəbl] [kris-ta-lai-sa-bol], *a.* Cristalizable.

crystallization [ˈkrɪstəlaɪzeɪʃən] [kris-ta-lai-se-shon], *s.* Cristalización.

crystallize [ˈkrɪstəlaɪz] [kris-ta-lais], *va. (Quím., Geol.)* Cristalizar; materializar (idea, plan). *(Culin.)* Confitar, escarchar, abrillantar, cristalizar (fruit). *-vn.* Cristalizarse, formar un sólido cristalino.

crystallizer [ˈkrɪstəlaɪzər] [kris-ta-lai-sa'], *s.* Lo que ayuda a cristalizarse; receptáculo para cristalizarse.

crystalloid [ˈkrɪstəlɔɪd] [kris-ta-loid], *a.* Cristaloide, parecido a un cristal. *-s.* Ejemplar de una sustancia cristalizable, cuyas soluciones son de fácil difusión: lo opuesto a *colloid*.

CS gas *s.* Gas lacrimógeno.

CST (in US) **= Central Standard Time**

CT = Connecticut

cu = cubic

cub [kʌb] [kab], *s.* 1. Cachorro (young animal). 2. Ballenato, el hijuelo de la ballena. 3. Cachorro, voz con que se motejaba a un zopenco o a un hombre de modales rudos. 4. (Prov. Ingl.) Establo de ganado.

cub, *vn.* Parir la osa o zorra.

Cuba [ˈkjuːbəb] [kiu-ba] *N. (Geogr.)* Cuba.

Cuban [ˈkjuːbən] [kiu-ban], *s. y a.* Cubano, de Cuba; natural de Cuba.

cubation [kjuːˈbeɪʃən] [kiu-bei-shon], *s.* 1. *V.* CUBATURE. 2. *(Des.)* Acostamiento, el acto de acostarse.

cubature [ˈkjuːbətʃər] [kiu-ba-cha'], *s. (Geom.)* Cubicación.

cubbyhole [ˈkʌbɪhəʊl] [ka-bi-joul], *s.* Casilla, compartimiento pequeño. Cuchitril (for storage).

cube [kjuːb] [kiub], *s.* 1. Cubo, el sólido cuyas caras son seis cuadrados perfectos (solid shape); dado, cubito (of meat, cheese); terrón (of sugar). 2. Cubo, la tercera potencia de una cantidad, el producto de tres factores iguales. *-va.* 1. *(Mat.)* Cubicar, elevar a la tercera potencia. **Cube root,** raíz cúbica. 2. Cortar en dados o cubitos (cut into cubes).

cubeb [ˈkjuːbɪb] [kiu-bib], *s.* Cubeba o carpo, semilla aromática.

cubic, cubical [ˈkjuːbɪk] [kiu-bik], *a.* Cúbico (of mesure, shape). **Cubic capacity,** volumen; cilindrada, cubicaje (of engine).

cubically [ˈkjuːbɪkəlɪ] [kiu-bi-ka-li], *adv.* Cúbicamente.

cubicle [ˈkjuːbɪkəl] [kiu-bi-kol] *s.* Cubículo (in dormitory, toilets); cabina (booth); probador (in store).

cubicular [kjuːbɪˈkjɒlər] [kiu-bi-kiu-la'], *a.* Lo perteneciente a la alcoba.

cubiform [ˈkjuːbɪfɔːm] [kiu-bi-form], *a.* Cúbico.

cubism [ˈkjuːbɪzm] [kiu-bism], *s.* Cubismo.

cubist [ˈkjuːbɪst] [kiu-bist] *a.* Cubista.

cubit [ˈkjuːbət] [kiu-bit], *s.* Codo, antigua medida lineal que se tomó de la distancia que media desde el codo a la extremidad de la mano.

cubital [ˈkjuːbɪtəl] [kiu-bi-tal], *a.* Cubital, lo que tiene la medida de un codo; relativo o perteneciente al codo.

cubited [ˈkjuːbɪtɪd] [kiu-bi-tid], *a.* Lo que tiene un codo de largo.

cub scout [ˈkjuːbˌskaʊt] [kiub-skaut], *s.* Cachorro, lobato, (de los exploradores).

cuckold [ˈkʌkəld] [ka-kold], *s.* Cornudo, el marido de una adúltera. Se llama así del cuco o cuclillo, a causa de la costumbre de esa ave de poner sus huevos en el nido de otra.

cuckold, *va.* Hacer cornudo. Ponerle los cuernos a.

cuckoldmaker [ˈkʌkəldˌmeɪkər] [ka-kold-mei-ka'], *s.* Encornudador.

cuckoldom [ˈkʌkəldɒm] [ka-kol-dom], *s.* 1. Adulterio, el acto de cometer adulterio. 2. El estado y la calidad de cornudo.

cuckoldly [ˈkʌkəldlɪ] [ka-kold-li], *a.* Vil, despreciable, cobarde.

cuckoo [ˈkuːkuː] [ku-ku], *s. (Orn.)* Cuclillo o cuco (bird). **A cuckoo in the nest,** un usurpador. *a. (Coloq.)* Chiflado, chalado.

cuckoo clock [ˈkuːkuːklɒk] [ku-ku-klok] *s.* Reloj de cuco o cucú.

cuckoo-flower [ˈkuːkuːflaʊər] [ku-ku-flaua'], *s. (Bot.)* Cardámina.

cuckoo-spittle [ˈkuːkuːspɪtl] [ku-ku-spitl], *s.* Baba de cuclillo, exudación que se halla sobre algunas plantas y que proviene de las larvas de ciertos insectos.

cucullate, cucullated [ˈkʊkəleɪt] [ku-ku-leit], *a.* Cubierto con capilla; en forma de capucho o capucha.

cucumber [ˈkʊkʌmbər] [ku-kam-ba'], *s.* Cohombro o pepino. **As cool as a cucumber,** fresco como una lechuga.

cucurbit [ˈkʊkɜːbɪt] [ku-ker-bit], *s.* 1. Cucúrbita, retorta de alambique en forma de calabaza. 2. Una planta cualquiera de la familia cuyo tipo es la calabaza.

cucurbitaceous [ˈkʊkəbrɪˈteɪʃəs] [ku-kur-bi-tei-shos], *s. (Bot.)* Cucurbitáceo.

cud [kʌd] [kad], *s.* 1. El alimento contenido en el estómago de los animales rumiantes, antes de masticarlo por segunda vez. **To chew the cud,** rumiar, meditar, reflexionar. 2. *(Vul.)* Chicote, pedazo de tabaco para mascar. *V.* QUID. 3. Rumen, el primer estómago de un rumiante.

cudbear [ˈkʌdbɪər] [kad-bea'], *s.* 1. Tinte purpúreo parecido a la orchilla, que se hace de algunas especies de líquenes. 2. El liquen mismo.

cuddle [kʌdl] [kadol], *va.* Proteger, acariciar, abrazar. *-vn.* Agacharse, agazaparse, esconder el cuerpo para no ser visto. **To cuddle up to somebody,** acurrucarse contra alguien.

cuddle, *s.* Abrazo.

cuddly [ˈkʌdlɪ] [kadli] *a.* Adorable (person/baby). **Cuddly toy,** muñeco de peluche.

cuddy [ˈkʌdɪ] [ka-di], *s. (Mar.)* 1. Camarote de proa: carroza de barco abierto. 2. Pañol del cocinero. 3. Rústico, patán.

cudgel [ˈkʌdʒəl] [kad-yel], *s.* Garrote o palo, porra.

cudgel, *va.* Apalear, dar golpes con garrote, palo o bastón. **To cudgel one's brains,** devanarse los sesos.

crudgel-play [ˈkʌdʒəlpleɪ] [kad-yel-plei], *s.* Juego con garrotes.

cudgel-proof [ˈkʌdʒəlprʊf] [kad-yel-pruf], *a.* A prueba de garrotazos.

cudgeller [ˈkʌdʒələr] [kad-ye-laʳ], *s.* Apaleador.

cudweed [ˈkʌdwiːd] [kad-uid], **cudwort** [ˈkʌdwɔːd] [kaduort], *s. (Bot.)* Gnafalio, algodonera.

cue [kjuː] [kiu], *s.* 1. Cola, rabo, la punta o extremidad de alguna cosa: particularmente una larga trenza de cabello. En este sentido se escribe a menudo *queue.* 2. *(Mús.)* Entrada. *(Teat.)* Pie, apunte, el acto de leer o indicar el apuntador al actor lo que ha de decir. **To miss one's cue,** no salir a escena en el momento debido. **To take one's cue from somebody,** seguir el ejemplo de alguien. 3. Indirecta, sugestión. 4. Genio, humor. 5. Taco de billar. **Cue ball,** bola blanca.

cue *va.* Darle el pie a (actor); darle entrada a (musician).

cuff [kʌf] [kaf], *s.* 1. Puñada, manotada o bofetón: golpe (blow on face); coscorrón (on head). 2. Puño de camisa: vuelta o bocamanga de una prenda de vestir; bastilla, dobladillo. **A cuff on the ear,** un sopapo. **To go to cuffs,** principiar a darse golpes. **Handcuffs,** manillas, esposas con que se maniata a los reos. **He spoke off the cuff,** habló improvisando. **An off-the-cuff speech,** un discurso improvisado. **He let me have the beer on the cuff,** me fió la cerveza.

cuff, *va.* Golpear con la mano abierta: dar golpes, abofetear (strike). *-vn.* Dar de puñadas, luchar, boxear: herir con las garras como suelen hacer las aves de rapiña.

cuff-links [ˈkʌflɪŋkz] [kaf-links], *s. pl.* Gemelos (para los puños de camisa).

cuirass [ˈkwɪræs] [kui-ras], *s.* Coraza, armadura que cubre el pecho y la espalda.

cuirassier [ˈkwɪræsɪər] [kui-ra-siaʳ], *s.* Coracero, soldado armado de coraza.

cuish [kwɪʃ] [kuish], *s.* Escarcela, quijote, armadura de los muslos.

cuisine [kwɪziːn] [kui-sin], *s.* La cocina, pieza o piezas de una casa destinadas a guisar: el departamento culinario. 2. Cocina, estilo o clase de cocina, manera de guisar. *(Fr.)*

cul-de-sac [ˈkʌldəsæk] [kal-de-sak] *s.* Calle sin salida o ciega o cortada.

culinary [ˈkʌlɪnərɪ] [ka-li-na-ri], *a.* Culinario, perteneciente a la cocina.

cull [kʌl] [kal], *va.* 1. Escoger, elegir, echar mano de lo mejor, entresacar, extraer; seleccionar (facts, information). 2. Sacrificar de forma selectiva (seals, deer).

cullender [ˈkʌləndər] [ka-len-daʳ], *s. V.* COLANDER.

culler [ˈkʌlər] [ka-laʳ], *s.* El que escoge o elige.

cullion [ˈkʌlɪən] [ka-lion], *s.* 1. Raíz semejante a un bulbo: órquide. 2. *(Vul.)* Belitre, pícaro, tunante.

cullis [ˈkʌlɪs] [ka-lis], *s.* 1. Gotera, canalón en un tejado. 2. Muesca, como para un bastidor de teatro.

cully [kʌlɪ] [ka-li], *va.* Engaitar, engañar. engatusar.

cully, *s.* Bobo, el que se deja engañar.

culm [kʌlm] [kalm], *s.* 1. *(Bot.)* Caña, especie particular de tallo propio de las gramas. 2. Carbón de piedra en polvo; cisco.

culmen, *s. V.* SUMMIT.

culmiferous [ˈkʌlmɪfərəs] [kal-mi-fe-ros], *a.* Culmífero: dícese de las plantas cuyo tallo está articulado y envainado por la base de las hojas.

culminate [ˈkʌlmɪneɪt] [kal-mi-neit], *vn.* 1. Culminar, pasar por el meridiano. 2. Lograr, alcanzar el punto o grado más

alto (reach peak). **To culminate in something,** culminar en algo. *va.* Ser la culminación de.

culmination [ˌkʌlmɪˈneɪʃən] [kal-mi-nei-shon], *s.* 1. Culminación, el punto del paso de un astro por el meridiano. 2. Apogeo, la situación o el punto más alto a que puede llegar una persona o cosa. Punto culminante (of events, efforts).

culpability [ˌkʌlpəˈbɪlɪtɪ] [kal-pa-bi-li-ti], *s.* Culpabilidad.

culpable [ˈkʌlpəbl] [kal-pa-bol], *a.* Culpable, el que es delincuente, criminal.

culpableness [ˈkʌlpəbl] [kal-pa-bol], *s.* Culpa, delito.

culpably [ˈkʌlpəblɪ] [kal-pa-bli], *adv.* Culpablemente, criminalmente.

culpatory [ˈkʌlpətərɪ] [kal-pa-to-ri], *a.* Lo que culpa o reprende.

culprit [ˈkʌlprɪt] [kal-prit], *s.* Reo, culpado, criminal.

cult [kʌlt] [kalt], *s.* 1. Culto, sistema de prácticas religiosas (belief, worship); secta (sect); culto (craze). 2. Adoración de una persona o una cosa: homenaje extravagante. 3. El objeto de gran admiración o devoción. **Personality cult,** el culto a la personalidad. **Cult figure,** ídolo. **Cult movie,** película de culto.

cultivable [ˈkʌltɪvəbl] [kal-ti-va-bol], *a.* Cultivable.

cultivate [ˈkʌltɪveɪt] [kal-ti-veit], *va.* 1. Cultivar, labrar: mejorar la tierra con el cultivo. 2. Adelantar, perfeccionar por el estudio o instrucción y ejercicio. **She cultivated an air of indiference,** adoptaba un estudiado aire de indiferencia. 3. Prestar atención asidua: consagrarse.

cultivated [ˈkʌltɪveɪtɪd] [kal-ti-vei-tid] *a.* Cultivado.

cultivation [ˌkʌltɪˈveɪʃən] [kal-ti-vei-shon], *s.* 1. *(Agr., Hort.)* Cultivación, cultivo: las labores y beneficios que se dan a la tierra y a las plantas. **Under cultivation,** en cultivo. 2. Mejora, adelantamiento. 3. Cultura, el estudio y enseñanza con que se perfecciona y mejora. Cultivo (of friendship); refinamiento (refinement).

cultivator [ˈkʌltɪveɪtər] [kal-ti-vei-toʳ], *s.* 1. Cultivador, labrador, agricultor. 2. Cultivadora, arado de cultivar; especie de mielga.

cultural [ˈkʌltʃərəl] [kal-chu-ral], *a.* Perteneciente a la cultura o al cultivo.

culture [ˈkʌltʃər] [kal-chaʳ], *s.* 1. Cultura (civilization). **Culture shock,** choque cultural o de culturas. Cultura (intellectual activity). 2. Arte de mejorar las tierras, artes, ciencias o costumbres. 3. *(Agr., Biol.)* Cultivo.

culture, *va.* Educar, enseñar, criar; refinar. Cultivar.

cultured [ˈkʌltʃəd] [kal-cherd] *a.* Culto (person, mind); refinado, propio de una persona culta (tastes). **Cultured pearls,** perlas cultivadas o de cultivo.

culture vulture [ˈkʌltʃəvʌltʃər] [kal-cha-val-chaʳ] *s. (Coloq.)* Devorador de cultura.

culverin [ˈkʌlvərɪn] [kal-ve-rin], *s.* Culebrina, pieza de artillería usada en el siglo XVI.

culvert [ˈkʌlvət] [kal-vert], *s.* Alcantarilla, conducto artificial para el paso de las aguas construido debajo de un camino o ferrocarril.

culvertail, *s. V.* DOVETAIL.

cum [kʌm] [kam] *prep.* **A study-cum-library,** un estudio-biblioteca. **My secretary-cum-assistant,** mi secretaria y ayudante a la vez.

cumbent [ˈkʌmbənt] [kam-bent], *a.* Acostado, recostado.

cumber [ˈkʌmbər] [kam-baʳ], *va.* Embarazar, obstruir, embrollar, estorbar: impedir; incomodar; sujetar.

cumbersome [ˈkʌmbəsəm] [kam-be-som], *a.* Engorroso, embarazoso, enfadoso, pesado, incómodo, fastidioso, molesto. Pesado y torpe (movements, gait).

cumbersomely [ˈkʌmbəsəmlɪ] [kam-be-som-li], *adv.* Embarazosamente.

cumbersomeness [ˈkʌmbəsəmnɪs] [kam-be-som-nes], *s.* Embarazo, impedimento.

cumbrance [ˈkʌmbrəns] [kam-brans], *s.* Carga, peso, impedimento, obstáculo, molestia.

cumbrous [ˈkʌmbrəs] [kam-bros], *a.* Engorroso, pesado, confuso.

cumbrously ['kʌmbrəslɪ] [kam-bros-li], *adv.* Pesadamente, fastidiosamente.

cumfrey ['kʌmfrɪ] [kam-bri], *s. (Bot.)* Consuelda.

cumin ['kʌmɪn] [ka-min], *s. (Bot.)* Comino, planta anual que produce semillas de olor aromático y sabor acre. La simiente es medicinal y se usa también como condimento.

cum laude [kʊmˈlaʊdeɪ] [kum-lau-dei] *adv.* Cum laude.

cummerbund ['kʌməbʌnd] [ka-mer-bund] *s.* Faja de smoking.

cumulate ['kuːmjʊleɪt] [kiu-miu-leit], *va.* Acumular, cumular, amontonar, hacinar.

cumulation ['kjuːmjʊleɪʃən] [kiu-miu-lei-shon], *s.* Acumulación, amontonamiento, hacinamiento.

cumulative ['kjuːmjʊlətɪv] [kiu-miu-la-tiv], *a.* Acumulativo.

cumulus ['kjuːmjʊləs] [kiu-miu-los] *s.* Cúmulo.

cunctation [kʌŋkˈteɪʃən] [kank-tei-shon], *s.* Demora, tardanza, retardo.

cuneal ['kjuːnɪəl] [kiu-nial], *a.* Lo que pertenece a cuña: en forma de cuña.

cuneiform ['kjuːnɪfɔːm] [kiu-ni-form], *a.* Cuneiforme, en forma de cuña: (a) Nombre de tres huesos del tobillo. (b) Antiguos caracteres asirios inscritos sobre bronce, hierro, ladrillos, piedra y otros materiales.

cunner ['kʌnər] [ka-naʳ], *s.* Pez lábrido muy abundante en la costa atlántica de Norte América.

cunning ['kʌnɪŋ] [ka-nin], *a.* 1. Sabio, experto. 2. Artificioso, mañoso, ingenioso (ingenious/device); astuto (clever, sly); malicioso (smile); maulero, artero, marrullero, trapacero, sutil, diestro, hábil: disimulado, capcioso, intrigante, sagaz. 3. *(E. U.)* Fino, gracioso, divertido, mono. **A cunning child,** un niño gracioso. **A cunning guy,** un tipo guapo o buen mozo (cute, attractive). -*s.* 1. Astucia, ardid, maña, treta, disimulo, artificio, manejo, artimaña, maulería, bellaquería, marrullería, artería, trapaza. 2. *(Ant.)* Arte, habilidad, destreza, sutileza.

cunningly ['kʌnɪŋlɪ] [ka-nin-li], *adv.* Astutamente: expertamente.

cunningness ['kʌnɪŋnɪs] [ka-nin-nes], *s.* Astucia, fraude, engaño, maña, treta. *V.* CUNNING.

cunt [kʌnt] [kant] *s. (Vulg.)* Coño, concha, pucha.

cup [kʌp] [kap], *s.* 1. Copa (goblet); taza, jícara (container, contents, cupful). **He isn't my cup of tea,** no es santo de mi devoción. **A cup of tea** o **coffee,** una taza de té o café. **A cup of chocolate,** una jícara de chocolate. **Cup made of a gourd,** (Cuba) güiro. *(Mex.)* Tecomate. **Cup and can,** la maza y la mona. **Cups,** convite de bebedores. 2. Cáliz, que sirve en la misa para echar el vino que ha de consagrarse: y el vino mismo. 3. *(Fig.)* Suerte, fortuna: toda aflicción o alegría extraordinaria. 4. Bebida embriagante. 5. Premio, comúnmente una copa de oro o plata que se da al vencedor en las carreras o juegos atléticos, tiro al blanco y regatas (trophy). **The cup final,** la final de copa. 6. Cualquier objeto o cavidad en forma de copa. 7. *(Med.)* Ventosa. *V.* CUPPING-GLASS. **There's many a slip 'twixt the cup and the lip,** de la mano a la boca se pierde la sopa.

cup, *va.* 1. Pegar, echar o aplicar ventosas sajadas o secas. 2. *(Art. y Of.)* Ahuecar en forma de taza. **To cup one's hands,** ahuecar las manos (to drink); hacer bocina con las manos (to shout).

cupbearer ['kʌpbɪərər] [kap-bia-raʳ], *s.* Copero o escanciador.

cupboard ['kʌpbɔːd] [kap-bord], *s.* Armario o alacena con anaqueles para guardar loza o comestibles. Aparador (in dining-room); armario, closet o placard (cabinet). Armario, closet o placard (full-length, built-in).

cupboard love ['kʌpbɔːlʌv] [kap-lov] *s. (GB)* Cariño interesado.

cupel [kʌpl] [ka-pel], *s.* Copela, vaso pequeño preparado para ensayar y afinar el oro y la plata.

cupel-dust [kʌpl'dʌst] [ka-pel-dast], *s.* Polvo de copela.

cupellation [kʌpə'leɪʃən] [ka-pe-lei-shon], *s. (Quím.)* Copeiación, afinación del oro y de la plata en una copela.

cupful ['kʌpfʊl] [kap-ful], *s.* El contenido de una taza o copa.

cupid ['kjuːpɪd] [kiu-pid], *s.* Cupido, el dios del amor de los antiguos romanos.

cupidity ['kjuːpɪdɪtɪ] [kiu-pi-di-ti], *s.* 1. Apetito, deseo inmoderado de poseer: codicia, avaricia. 2. (Poco us.) Concupiscencia.

cupola ['kjuːpələ] [kiu-po-la], *s.* 1. Cúpula, bóveda o media esfera que remata algunos grandes edificios. 2. Horno de fundición para el hierro. 3. Torre blindada giratoria, provista de cañones de grueso calibre, v. gr. la de un monitor (buque de guerra).

cuppa ['kʌpə] [ka-pa] *s. (GB) (Coloq.)* Taza de té.

cupper ['kʌpər] [ka-pAʳ], *s.* Aplicador de ventosas sajadas o secas.

cupping-glass ['kʌpɪŋglɑːs] [ka-pin-glas], *s. (Cir.)* Ventosa, escarificador.

cupreous ['kʌprɪəs] [ka-prios], *a.* Cobrizo, cosa de cobre o que tiene su color.

cupric ['kʌprɪk] [ka-prik], *a. (Quím.)* Cúprico, relativo al cobre.

cuprous ['kʌprəs] [ka-pros], *a. (Quím.)* Del cobre en su menor facultad de combinación.

cup-shaped [kʌp'ʃeɪpt] [kap-sheipt], *a.* Acopado, en forma de copa.

cupule ['kjuːpʊl] [kiu-pul], *s.* 1. Hueco acopado o cóncavo. 2. *(Bot.)* Parte acopada: cúpula o copa, la cascarilla que rodea la base de la bellota, avellana, etc.

cur [kɜːr] [keʳ], *s.* 1. Perro inútil o de mala ralea; perro callejero. 2. Perro, hombre vil y despreciable; bellaco (despicable man).

curable ['kjʊərəbl] [kiu-ra-bol], *a.* Curable.

curableness ['kjʊərəblnɪs] [kiu-ra-bol-nes], *s.* Capacidad de curarse.

curacy ['kjʊərəsɪ] [kiu-ra-si], *s.* Tenencia, vicariato, vicaría.

curare [kjʊə'rɑːrɪ] [kiu-a-ra-ri], *s.* Curare, veneno vegetal muy violento que preparan y usan los indios de América del Sur.

curate ['kjʊəreɪt] [kiu-reit], *s.* Teniente de cura: beneficiado. Coadjutor.

curateship, *s. V.* CURACY.

curative ['kjʊərətɪv] [kiu-ra-tiv], *a.* Curativo.

curator [kjʊə'reɪtər] [kiu-ra-toʳ], *s.* Curador; guardián, conservador (of museum, art gallery); comisario (of exhibition).

curb [kɜːb] [kerb], *s.* 1. Barbada, cadena de hierro que abraza al barboquejo del caballo para sujetarle. 2. Freno, sujeción, restricción (restraint). **To put a curb on something,** poner freno o coto a algo. 3. Brocal de pozo: orilla (de una acera); borde de la banqueta, cuneta, sardinel, cordón de la vereda. *V.* CURB-STONE.

curb, *va.* Refrenar, dominar (control/anger); contener, reprimir; poner freno a, moderar (spending/prices).

curbable ['kɜːbəbl] [ker-ba-bol], *a.* (Poco us.) Restringible.

curbing ['kɜːbɪŋ] [ker-bin], *s.* Obstáculo, restricción, freno, oposición.

curb-stone ['kɜːbstəʊn] [kerb-stoun], *s.* Cada una de las piedras gruesas, o el conjunto de ellas, que se ponen verticalmente donde termina el empedrado de las calles y que forman el reborde, canto u orilla de la acera; guardacantón.

curd [kɜːd] [kerd], *s.* 1. Cuajada (from milk). 2. Requesón. (GB) **Bean curd,** tofu, queso de soja (paste). **Lemon curd,** crema de limón.

curd, *va.* Cuajar, coagular, condensar.

curdle ['kɜːdl] [kerdl], *vn.* Cuajarse (milk/from curds); coagularse, espesarse, condensarse. Cortarse (go bad, separate/milk, sauce). -*va.* Coagular, cuajar (cause to form curds); espesar. Cortar (cause to go bad).

curdy ['kɜːdɪ] [ker-di], *a.* Cuajado, coagulado, espeso.

cure [kjʊər] [kiuaʳ], *s.* 1. Cura (remedy for disease); remedio (for problem); restablecimiento, curación (return to health); medicina, medicamento. 2. Cura de almas. 3. Salazón de pescados o carnes.

cure, *va.* 1. (*Med.*) Curar, sanar. **To cure somebody of something,** curar a alguien de algo; quitarle algo a alguien (of habit, idea). Remediar, poner remedio a (problem). 2. Preservar; salar, ahumar: preparar, componer, curar (meat). Vulcanizar (rubber).

cure-all ['kjʊərɔːl] [kiua-rol], *s.* Panacea, curalotodo. **Cured** "[kiürd]", *a.* Salado. **Cured fish,** pescado salado.

cureless ['kjʊəlɪs] [kiua-les], *a.* Incurable.

curer ['kjʊərər] [kiua-ra'], *s.* 1. El que prepara alguna cosa para que se conserve. 2. Médico.

curfew ['kɜːfjuː] [ker-fiu], *s.* Toque de queda. La retreta, la queda.

curia ['kjʊrɪə] [kiu-ria], *s.* Curia, tribunal de justicia.

curio ['kjʊərɪəʊ] [kiu-riou], *s.* Curiosidad, objeto curioso y raro: cosa de bric-a-brac (Abreviación de *curiosity*).

curiosity [ˌkjʊrɪˈɒsɪtɪ] [kiu-ri-o-si-ti], *s.* 1. Curiosidad, deseo de saber o averiguar alguna cosa (inquisitive interest). **Curiosity killed the cat,** por querer saber, la zorra perdió la cola. 2. Curiosidad, objeto curioso y raro, rareza. Curiosidad (novelty). **Curiosity value,** valor de pieza rara.

curioso, *s.* V. VIRTUOSO.

curious ['kjʊrɪəs] [kiu-rios], *a.* 1. Curioso, deseoso de saber y averiguar las cosas (inquisitive). **Why do you ask? -oh, I'm just curious,** ¿por qué lo preguntas?-sólo por curiosidad. 2. Cuidadoso, exacto. 3. Delicado, primoroso, exquisito, admirable, raro, singular, extraño (strange); elegante. 4. (*Des.*) Difícil de agradar; riguroso.

curiously ['kjʊrɪəslɪ] [kiu-rios-li], *adv.* Con curiosidad (with curiosity); curiosamente (strangely). **Curiously enough,** curiosamente…, aunque parezca mentira…

curiousness ['kjʊrɪəsnɪs] [kiu-rios-nes], *s.* Curiosidad, exactitud, delicadeza, primor.

curl [kɜːl] [kerl], *s.* 1. Bucle o rizo, rulo, chino (of hair); bucle, tirabuzón (ringlet). Voluta (of smoke). 2. Tortuosidad, sinuosidad, ondulación. (Cuba) Crespo. 3. Enfermedad de los melocotones. 4. Alabeo (of wood).

curl, *va.* 1. Rizar o encrespar, formar rizos o bucles, enchinar, enrular (hair). 2. Ensortijar, torcer. 3. Ondear, formar ondas u ondulaciones en alguna cosa. **To curl the lip,** fruncir el labio, hacer una mueca, torcer el gesto (twist, bend). **The snake curled itself around the branch,** la serpiente se enroscó en la rama. -*vn.* Rizarse, ensortijarse, encresparse, enchinarse, enrularse (hair); ondearse, enroscarse, ondularse, rizarse (paper, leaf, edge). Formar o hacer volutas, subir en espirales (smoke).

curl up Ondularse, rizarse (twist/leaf, pages). **The cat curled up in front of the fire,** el gato se hizo un ovillo frente a la chimenea. **To curl up in a chair,** acurrucarse en un sillón. (*Coloq.*) **I wanted to curl up and die,** quería que la tierra me tragara.

curled pate [kɜːldˈpeɪt] [kerld-peit], **curly-headed,** *a.* El que tiene rizado el pelo.

curler ['kɜːlər] [ker-la'] *s.* Rulo, rulero, marrón, tubo (for hair).

curlew ['kɜːljuː] [ker-liu], *s.* Chorlito, ave acuátil.

curlicue ['kɜːlɪkjuː] [ker-li-kiu], *s.* 1. Algo ondeado o torcido de un modo raro, como los rasgos o adornos hechos con una pluma. 2. Cabriola, brinco.

curliness ['kɜːlɪnɪs] [ker-li-nes], *s.* El estado de las cosas rizadas o formadas en bucles.

curling-irons [kɜːlɪŋˈaɪrɒnz] [ker-lin-ai-rons], **curling-tongs** [kɜːlɪŋˈtɒŋz] [ker-lin-tongs], *s.* Encrespador, tenacillas de hierro para rizar el pelo. **Curl-paper,** papel a propósito para hacer rizos.

curlingly ['kɜːlɪŋlɪ] [ker-lin-li], *adv.* A manera de rizos.

curly ['kɜːlɪ] [ker-li], *a.* Lo que cae en forma de rizos o sortijas, y lo que es fácil de rizarse. Rizado, ensortijado, crespo, chino (hair); enroscado (tail).

curmudgeon ['kɜːlmʌdʒən] [ker-mad-yion], *s.* Hombre tacaño, mezquino y miserable.

curmudgeonly ['kɜːmʌdʒənlɪ] [ker-mad-yon-li], *a.* Codicioso, mezquino, avariento.

currant ['kʌrənt] [ka-rent], *a.* 1. Grosellero, el arbusto que produce la grosella. 2. Grosella, fruta del grosellero. 3. Uva o pasa de Corinto.

currency ['kʌrənsɪ] [ka-ren-si], *s.* El medio circulante, la moneda que está en circulación, ya sea acuñada o en papel. Moneda (type of money). **Foreign currency,** moneda extranjera, divisas. 2. Circulación. 3. Aceptación general o uso corriente de alguna cosa. Difusión (prevalence). **To gain currency,** extenderse, ganar adeptos (view, fashion). 4. Valor corriente de alguna cosa. **Fractional currency,** menudo, moneda de valor menor que la moneda tipo, ya sea ésta el peso o dolar, el franco, la peseta, etc. **Paper currency,** papel moneda.

current ['kʌrənt] [ka-rent], *a.* 1. Corriente, común; admitido, en boga; en general popular. 2. Presente, del día, de actualidad. Actual (existing/situation, prices); en curso (year); último (most recent/issue). **The current year,** el año corriente. 3. Vigente (valid/license, membership); corriente, común, habitual (prevailing/opinion, practice). -*s.* 1. Corriente (flow of water, air). **Against the current,** contra la corriente. **With the current,** en el sentido de la corriente. Corriente (general trend). **To go with the current,** dejarse llevar por la corriente. 2. Curso, progresión, marcha. 3. (*Elec.*) Corriente. **To run off household current,** funcionar con electricidad.

current account ['kʌrəntəˌkaʊnt] [ka-rent-a-kaunt] *s.* (GB) Cuenta corriente.

current affairs ['kʌrəntəˈfɛəʒ] [ka-rent-a-fears] *s. pl.* Sucesos de actualidad.

currently ['kʌrəntlɪ] [ka-rent-li], *adv.* Corrientemente; generalmente, a la moda. Actualmente (at present); comúnmente (commonly).

currentness ['kʌrəntnɪs] [ka-rent-nes], *s.* Circulación; facilidad en pronunciar; aceptación general.

curricle ['kʌrɪkl] [ka-ri-kel], *s.* Carro abierto de dos ruedas, con lanza o pértiga.

curriculum [kəˈrɪkjʊləm] [ka-ri-kiu-lom], *s.* Curso de estudios en un colegio; plan de estudios (range of courses); programa de estudio, currículo, currículum (for single course).

curriculum vitae [kəˈrɪkjʊləmˌviːte] [ka-ri-kiu-lo-vi-tem *s.* (GB) Currículum, historial personal, hoja de vida.

currier ['kʌrɪər] [ka-ria'], *s.* Curtidor, zurrador.

currish ['kʌrɪʃ] [ka-rish], *a.* 1. Perruno, parecido a un perro; arisco; dispuesto a morder. 2. (*Fig.*) Brutal, regañón, áspero.

currishly ['kʌrɪʃlɪ] [ka-rish-li], *adv.* Brutalmente, ásperamente.

currishness ['kʌrɪʃnɪs] [ka-rish-nes], *s.* Morosidad, malignidad, mezquindad: carácter arisco.

curry ['kʌrɪ] [ka-ri], *va.* 1. Zurrar, adobar el cuero después de curtido; prepararlo para usarlo. 2. Zurrar, dar una zurra. 3. Almohazar, estregar las caballerías con las almohazas para limpiarlas. 4. Hacer cosquillas; agradar, lisonjear. **To curry favor,** insinuarse, ganar el ánimo o la voluntad de alguno. **To curry with one,** cortejar a alguno. 5. (*Culin.*) Preparar al curry. **Curried chicken,** pollo al curry.

curry, *s.* Curri, sa sa picante muy usada en la India; guisado preparado con esta salsa. **Curry-powder,** polvo de ciertas especias para preparar el curri.

curry-comb ['kʌrɪkɒm] [ka-ri-kom], *s.* Almohaza, instrumento para limpiar las caballerías.

currying ['kʌrɪɪŋ] [ka-ri-in], *s.* 1. El acto de almohazar. 2. Zurrar, el acto de zurrar las pieles después de curtirlas: remojarlas y desengrasarlas.

curse [kɜːs] [kers], *va.* 1. Maldecir (put spell on/express annoyance at); echar maldiciones a alguno. **Curse her!,** ¡maldita sea! 2. Afligir, atormentar. 3. Insultar (swear at). **To be cursed with something,** estar aquejado de algo, padecer de algo (afflict). -*vn.* Imprecar, negar o afirmar con imprecaciones, blasfemar; maldecir, soltar palabrotas.

curse, *s.* 1. Maldición (evil spell); juramento, palabrota (oath); imprecación, anatema. **To put a curse on somebody,**

echar una maldición a alguien. 2. Castigo, pena, grave aflicción; maldición (burden) **The curse of unemployment,** la lacra del desempleo. **The curse,** la regla (menstruation).

cursed [ˈkɜːst] [kerst], a. Maldito, aborrecible, perverso, malvado, detestable, abominable, execrable: molesto, enfadoso.

cursedly [ˈkɜːsɪdlɪ] [ker-sid-li], adv. Miserablemente, abominablemente.

cursedness [ˈkɜːsɪdnɪs] [ker-sid-nes], s. Estado de maldición; malicia, perversidad; abominación.

curser [ˈkɜːsər] [ker-saʳ], s. Maldiciente.

curship [ˈkɜːʃɪp] [ker-ship], s. Vileza, bajeza, ruindad, brutalidad.

cursing [ˈkɜːsɪŋ] [ker-sin], s. Execración, maldición.

cursitor [ˈkɜːsɪtər] [ker-si-toʳ], s. Antiguamente un empleado en el tribunal de la Chancillería que extendía los originales.

cursive [ˈkɜːsɪv] [ker-siv], a. y s. Cursivo, corriente.

cursor [ˈkɜːsər] [ker-soʳ] s. Cursor.

cursorily [ˈkɜːsərɪlɪ] [ker-so-ri-li], adv. Precipitadamente, de paso.

cursory [ˈkɜːsərɪ] [ker-so-ri], a. Precipitado, inconsiderado. Rápido (glance); somero (description); superficial (interest). **Cursory view,** vista por encima, o de paso.

curt [kɜːt] [kert], a. Corto, conciso, lacónico; brusco en su expresión. Cortante, seco.

curtail [kɜːteɪl] [ker-teil], va. Cortar, abreviar (cut short); restringir (restrict); reducir (reduce); cercenar, mutilar; estrecharse, economizar; desmembrar. **To curtail a privilege,** restringir un privilegio.

curtailing [ˈkɜːtɪlɪŋ] [ker-tei-lin], s. Abreviatura.

curtailment [ˈkɜːteɪlmənt] [ker-teil-ment], s. Reducción (of spending); restricción (of freedom); abreviación, acortamiento (cutting short).

curtain [ˈkɜːtn] [ker-ten], s. 1. Cortina (at window); cualquier cosa que tapa u oculta como una cortina. **Curtain-lecture,** reconvención de la mujer a su marido en particular; originalmente, regaño dado en la cama. **To draw the curtain,** correr la cortina; correr un velo, ocultar. 2. (Fort.) Cortina, el lienzo de muralla que está entre dos bastiones. 3. (Teat.) Telón de boca en los teatros. **Curtain in a play-house,** telón de teatro. **To raise the curtain,** levantar el telón. **To drop the curtain,** correr o bajar el telón. 4. Cortina (of rain); manto (of fog); halo, velo (of mystery, secrecy). (Coloq.) **It's curtains for you,** estás acabado.

curtain off Separar con una cortina.

curtain, va. Rodear o proveer de cortinas.

curtain call [ˈkɜːtnkɔːl] [ker-ten-kol] s. Salida a escena o al escenario para saludar.

curtly [ˈkɜːtlɪ] [kert-li], adv. Brevemente, lacónicamente. De manera cortante.

curtness [ˈkɜːtnɪs] [kert-nes], s. Concisión, brevedad; brusquedad.

curtsy [ˈkɜːtsɪ] [kert-si], s. Reverencia o saludo especial que solían hacer las mujeres doblando las rodillas.

curtsy, vn. Hacer una reverencia.

curule [ˈkɜːrjuːl] [ke-riul], a. Curul, de la magistratura romana. **Curule chair,** silla curul, asiento oficial de los magistrados romanos de más alto rango.

curvate, curvated [ˈkɜːveɪt] [ker-veit], a. Corvo, encorvado.

curvature [ˈkɜːvətʃʊər] [ker-va-chuaʳ], s. Curvatura, comba combadura, cimbra. **Curvature of the spine,** desviación de columna.

curve [ˈkɜːv] [kerv], va. Encorvar, formar curva o curvatura. - vn. Estar curvado o combado (surface); describir una curva (river, ball). **The path curves down to the sea,** el sendero tuerce y baja hacia el mar.

curve, a. Corvo, torcido, encorvado. -s. Corva, curva, comba o combadura. **To throw somebody a curve,** agarrar o coger a alguien desprevenido.

curved [ˈkɜːvd] [kervd] a. Curvo.

curvet [ˈkɜːvɪt] [ker-vit], s. 1. Corveta, corcovo, salto que da el caballo. 2. Ventolera, capricho.

curvet, vn. 1. Corcovear, dar corcovos. 2. Cabriolar, hacer cabriolas. 3. Saltar de alegría: ser revoltoso.

curvilinear [ˈkɜːvɪliːnɪər] [ker-vi-li-niaʳ], a. Curvilíneo.

curvity [ˈkɜːvɪtɪ] [ker-vi-ti], s. Curvatura, combadura.

curvy [ˈkɜːvɪ] [ker-vi] a. Curvo (line); curvilíneo (figure).

cushat [ˈkʌʃæt] [ker-shat], s. Paloma torcaz.

cushion [ˈkʊʃən] [ku-shion], s. 1. Cojín, almohadón (of chair). **Cushion cover,** funda de almoadón o cojín. 2. (Mec.) Cojinete, soporte, chumacera.

cushion, va. 1. Amortiguar, amortecer, suavizar (blow). **To cushion something/somebody against something,** proteger algo/a alguien contra algo (protect). 2. Mitigar, disminuir. 3. Colocar sobre cojines.

cushioned [ˈkʊʃənd] [ku-shiond], a. Encojinado.

cushionet [ˈkʊʃənɪt] [ku-shio-nit], s. Cojinete, cojinillo.

cushy [ˈkʊʃɪ] [ku-shi] a. (Coloq.) Cómodo, fácil.

cusp [kʌsp] [kasp], s. 1. Punta o cuerno de la luna u otro astro. 2. Punta o cúspide de un diente, o una planta.

cuspated [ˈkʌspeɪtɪd] [kas-pei-tid], V. CUSPIDATE.

cuspidal [ˈkʌspɪdl] [kas-pi-dal], a. Puntiagudo, lo que remata en punta.

cuspidate, va. V. SHARPEN.

cuspidate, cuspidated [ˈkʌspɪdeɪt] [kas-pi-deit], a. Cuspidada o apuntillada, dícese de las plantas.

cuspidor [ˈkʌspɪdər] [kas-pi-doʳ], s. Escupidera.

cuspis [ˈkʌspɪs] [kas-pis], s. Cúspide, remate puntiagudo.

cuss [kʌs] [kas] s. (Fam. E. U.) Corrupción de CURSE. Palabrota, mala palabra, taco (curse). **I don't give/care a cuss,** me importa un comino.

cuss va. **She cussed us for being late,** nos puso de vuelta y media por llegar tarde. -vn. Despotricar (complain). Maldecir, soltar palabrotas (swear).

cuss word [ˈkʌswɔːd] [kas-uord] s. Palabrota, mala palabra, taco.

custard [ˈkʌstəd] [kas-tard], s. Flan, leche crema o quemada; crema confeccionada con huevos y azúcar, especie de flan (egg sauce). Natillas (cold, set). Crema (sauce).

custodial [ˈkʌstədɪəl] [kas-to-dial], a. Lo que pertenece a la custodia o guarda.

custodian [ˈkʌstədɪən] [kas-to-dian] s. Conservador (of museum, library).

custody [ˈkʌstədɪ] [kas-to-di], s. 1. Custodia, encierro, prisión, cárcel: cuidado; seguridad. **To be in custody,** estar detenido (detention). **To take somebody into custody,** detener a alguien. 2. Custodia (of child); custodia, cuidado (safekeeping).

custom [ˈkʌstəm] [kas-tom], s. 1. Costumbre, uso (conventio, tradition, habit). **He broke with custom,** rompió con la tradición. 2. Costumbre de comprar lo que uno necesita de ciertas personas o en determinadas tiendas: parroquia de una tienda. **If they value our custom,** si no nos quieren perder como clientes. **I'll take my custom elsewhere,** dejaré de ser su cliente. 3. Venta, salida, despacho. 4. (For.) Consuetud, ley o derecho no escrito, pero establecido por el uso de cien años. 5. plur. Derechos de aduana o arancelarios (tax). **Custom-free,** libre de derechos. Aduana (organization, place). **To go through customs,** pasar por la aduana. **Customs officer/official,** agente u oficial de aduanas.

custom a. Que trabaja por encargo (tailor); A la medida (suit); hecho de encargo (car).

custombale [ˈkʌstəmbeɪl] [kas-tom-beil], a. Común, habitual.

customableness [ˈkʌstəmeɪblnɪs] [kas-to-mei-bol-nes], s. Frecuencia, costumbre, hábito.

customably [ˈkʌstəməblɪ] [kas-to-ma-bli], adv. Según costumbre.

customarily [ˈkʌstəmərɪlɪ] [kas-to-ma-ri-li], adv. Comúnmente, ordinariamente; habitualmente.

customariness [ˈkʌstəmərɪnɪs] [kas-to-ma-ri-nes], s. Frecuencia, hábito, costumbre.

customary [ˈkʌstəmərɪ] [kas-to-ma-ri], *a.* 1. Usual, acostumbrado, habitual, ordinario, usado. 2. *(For. Ingl.)* Consuetudinario, de costumbre, a fuero.

custom built [ˈkʌstəmˌbɪlt] [kastom-bilt], *a.* Hecho a la orden o a la medida.

customed [ˈkʌstəmd] [kas-tomd], *a. (Poét.)* Acostumbrado, ordinario, común, acreditado.

customer [ˈkʌstəmər] [kas-to-maʳ], *s.* 1. Parroquiano, marchante. 2. *(Fam.)* Persona con quien uno se habla, trata o se encuentra; se usa comúnmente con adjetivo. **An ugly customer,** (a) un bribón, un mal pájaro. (b) Adversario temible, duro de pelar. 3. Cliente (client).

custom-house [ˈkʌstəmhaʊs] [kas-tom-jaus], *s.* Aduana. **Custom-house officer,** aduanero, vista de la aduana.

custom made [ˈkʌstəmˈmeɪd] [kas-tom-meid], *a.* Hecho a la orden o a la medida (suit, shoes). Hecho de encargo (furnishings, furniture).

custrel [ˈkʌstrɪl] [kas-tril], *s.* 1. Escudero. 2. Vasija de vino.

cut [kʌt] [kat], *va.* 1. Cortar (wood, paper, wire, rope); hender; esculpir, tallar (shape/stone, glass), hacer (key). **They cut a path through the undergrowth,** abrieron un camino a través de la maleza. **To cut something in half,** cortar algo por la mitad. **I cut my finger,** me corté el dedo. 2. Separar, destruir, estropear, herir, mutilar. 3. Partir, dividir; reducir (reduce/level, number); rebajar, reducir (price, rate); recortar (budget); hacer recortes en (service, workforce). 4. Picar, preparar por medio de un instrumento cortante. 5. Quitar, separar. *V. To cut away o to cut off.* 6. Encontrar o pasar a alguno intencionadamente aparentando no conocerlo (ignore). *(Coloq.)* **To cut somebody dead,** dejar a uno con el saludo en la boca. 7. Desunir, interrumpir una relación o conexión. 8. Castrar. 9. Alzar o cortar los naipes. 10. Cortar (trim/hair, nails); cortar, segar (grass, corn). **To get one's hair cut,** cortarse el pelo. 11. Acortar (shorten/text); cortar (remove/scene); editar (film/edit); hacer cortes en (censors). **A tunnel cut into the mountain,** un túnel excavado en la montaña (excavate). *-vn.* 1. Hacer cortadura, operar por incisión. Cortar (knife, scissors). **The rope cut into her wrists,** la cuerda le estaba cortando o lastimando las muñecas. **To cut loose,** romper las ataduras (break free). **Her remarks cut deep,** sus palabras lo (o la etc.) hirieron en lo más vivo. **It cuts easily,** se corta fácilmente (be cuttable). 2. Ser a propósito para dividir o dividirse. 3. Cortar, perforar las encías (dícese de los dientes). 4. *(Ger.)* Tomar soleta, tomar el tole. 5. *(Cin., Rad.)* **Cut!,** ¡corte! 6. Cortar (in cards). **To cut asunder,** rasgar, hacer pedazos, destrozar, despedazar, quebrar. **To cut away,** quitar, cercenar, separar. **To cut short,** acortar, cercenar, disminuir; interrumpir, cortar la palabra; abreviar, resumir, compendiar. **To cut to,** cortar de raíz. picar; afligir, lastimar, herir profundamente. **To cut capers,** cabriolar. **To cut small,** desmenuzar. **To cut to the heart,** afligir, enojar, enfadar, molestar. **To cut a figure,** hacer papel o también hacer figura. **To cut the lots,** echar pajas. **To cut over the face,** acuchillar la cara. **To cut one's hair too short,** pelar al rape. **To cut the ground,** abrir la tierra, labrarla por la primera vez.

cut across Cortar al través, tomar por el atajo (take shortcut across); trascender (cross boundaries off).

cut back 1. Podar, recortar (prune/hedge); recortar, reducir (reduce/spending). 2. Hacer economías constreñirse (make reductions). **To cut back on something,** reducir algo.

cut down 1. Abatir; aserrar; cortar una cosa hasta que caiga al suelo, derribar, echar abajo, cortar, talar (fell/tree); destrozar un ejército; exceder, sobrepujar. 2. Matar (kill). **He was cut down in his prime,** su vida fue segada en flor. 3. Reducir, recortar (reduce/expenditure); reducir, disminuir (consumption). **Cigarette?-no, thanks, I'm trying to cut down,** ¿un cigarrillo?-no, gracias, estoy tratando de fumar menos. **You should cut down on carbohydrates,** deberías reducir el consumo de hidratos de carbono.

cut in Interrumpir (interrupt); atravesarse (auto).

cut off Cortar completamente, hacer pedazos, destruir, extirpar, cortar (sever/branch, limb); separar, tajar, trinchar; matar a alguno; interceptar; poner fin a una cosa; interrumpir, cortar (interrupt, block/supply, route); abreviar; imponer silencio a uno que está hablando. Aislar (separate, isolate). **To feel cut off,** sentirse aislado. **The town was cut off,** la ciudad quedó sin comunicaciones. **We were cut off,** se cortó la comunicación (telephone). **To cut off a leg,** amputar una pierna. **To cut off an heir,** desheredar a alguno. **To cut off all contentions,** prevenir o impedir toda disputa. **To cut off delays,** despacharse, apresurarse.

cut out Tajar o cortar; formar, hacer, proporcionar o disponer alguna cosa en debida proporción; proyectar, trazar; adoptar; excluir, privar; exceder, aventajar. Recortar (article, photograph). Cortar (dress, cookies). Eliminar, suprimir (exclude/noise, carbohydrates). **He cut me out of his will,** me excluyó de su testamento. **Cut it out!,** ¡basta ya! **I'm not cut out to be a teacher,** no estoy hecho para la enseñanza. Pararse, calarse (stop working/engine). Apagarse (switch off).

cut through Abrirse camino por entre (overcome). Cortar camino por, atajar por (take shortcut).

cut up Cortar, partir, trinchar, hacer tajadas, cortar en pedazos (vegetables, wood); disecar; arrancar de raíz, desarraigar. *(Fam.)* Hacer de las suyas, travesear. *(Coloq.)* **To be cut up about something,** estar disgustado por algo.

cut, *a.* 1. Cortado (flowers); tajado. 2. Interceptado, interrumpido. 3. Trinchado; tallado (glass). 4. Preparado.

cut, *s.* 1. Corte, cortadura, tajo (wound); corte (incision). Corte (of meat/type); trozo (piece). **A wage cut,** un recorte salarial (reduction). **To make cuts in essential services,** hacer recortes en los servicios esenciales. 2. Atajo de camino. 3. Estampa o grabado. 4. Hechura, forma, figura. 5. Tajada, parte (share); lonja. 6. Cuchillada (blow/with knife), herida; hendedura. 7. Corto, pasaje o paso. 8. Desgracia, afrenta. *(Coloq.)* **He thinks himself a cut above the rest,** se cree superior a los demás.

cut-and-dried [ ] *a.* Preparado de antemano (arrangements). Preconcebido (opinions). **Her election isn't cut and dried,** no se puede dar por sentado que vaya a salir elegida.

cutaneous [kjuːˈteɪnɪəs] [kiu-tei-nios], *a.* Cutáneo.

cutback [ˈkʌtbæk] [kat-bak] *s.* Corte, reducción (reduction).

cute [kjuːt] [kiut], *a.* (Contracción de ACUTE). *(Fam.)* Atractivo, gracioso, mono, cuco, rico (sweet/baby, face). Guapo (attractive). Listo, vivo (clever, person). Afectado, efectista (contrived).

cutesy [ˈkjuːtsɪ] [kiu-te-si] *a.* Cursi.

cut glass [ˈkʌtɡlaːs] [kat-glas], *s.* Cristal cortado. *a.* De cristal tallado.

cuticle [ˈkʌtɪkl] [ka-ti-kel], *s.,* 1. Cutícula, epidermis, lapa. 2. Película, viscosidad que cubre algunas plantas; capa que se forma en la superficie de un líquido.

cuticular [kjuːtɪkjələʳ] [kiu-ti-kiu-laʳ], *a.* Cuticular, de la epidermis.

cutie [kjuːtɪ] [kiu-ti] *s. (Coloq.)* Bombón, churro (woman). **He/She's a little cutie,** es una monada (child).

cutlass [ˈkʌtləs] [kat-las], *s.* Alfanje, machete.

cutler [ˈkʌtlər] [ka-tlaʳ], *s.* Cuchillero.

cutlery [ˈkʌtlərɪ] [kat-le-ri], *s.* Cuchillería, mercadería o géneros de cuchilleros, cubertería, cubiertos.

cutlet [ˈkʌtlɪt] [kat-lit], *s.* Chuleta, costilla o costillita asada de carnero, ternera, etc.

cutoff [ˈkʌtɒf] [kat-of], *s. (E. U.)* 1. Atajo de un camino (shorcut). 2. Cortavapor, invento para interceptar el vapor en el cilindro en un punto fijo. 3. Límite. **Cutoff date,** fecha límite o tope. **Cutoffs,** shorts, vaqueros.

cutout [ˈkʌtaʊt] [kat-aut] *s.* Recortable, figura para recortar (image, silhouette).

cut-price [ˈkʌtpraɪs] [kat-prais], **cut-rate** [ˌkʌtˈreɪt] [kat-reit] *a.* (GB) A precio rebajado (goods, travel); de ocasión (shop).

cutpurse [ˈkʌtpɜːs] [kat-pers], *s.* Cortabolsa, ladrón, un ratero.

cutter ['kʌtər] [ka-ta^r], *s.* 1. Cortador (worker). 2. Lo que corta; herramienta o máquina para cortar, tenazas (tool for wire). 3. Cúter, embarcación ligera o velera semejante a una falúa. 4. Buque guardacostas. 5. *(E. U.)* Pequeño trineo.

cutthroat ['kʌtθrəʊt] [kat-zrout], *s.* Asesino, el que mata o quita la vida a otro alevosamente (murderer). **Cutthroat razor,** (GB) navaja. *-a.* 1. Cruel, bárbaro. 2. Feroz, salvaje (competition).

cutting ['kʌtɪŋ] [ka-tin], *'s.* 1. Cortadura; incisión. 2. *(Cir.)* Talla, operación de la piedra. 3. Alce de naipes. 4. Algo obtenido o hecho por cortadura; recorte (from newspaper); esqueje (from plant); cercenadura, viruta, retazo. 5. Zanja (GB) (for road, railway). 6. *(Cin., Rad., TV)* Montaje, edición. **Cutting down,** *(Mar.)* astilla muerta. **Cutting-down line,** *(Mar.)* arrufo de astilla muerta. **Cutting of the teeth,** dentición, salida de los dientes.

cutting, *a.* 1. Cortante, que corta (tool, blade). 2. Helado, picante, áspero, cortante (cold, wind). 3. Incisivo, mordaz, picante, satírico, hiriente (hurtful, remark). **At the cutting edge of technology,** a la vanguardia de la tecnología.

cuttle ['kʌtl] [katel], o **cuttle-fish,** *s.* Jibia, sepia, molusco marino, voraz, carnívoro, del género de los cefalópodos, del cual se extrae el color llamado sepia. V. CUTTLE-BONE.

cuttle-bone [kʌtl'bəʊn] [ka-tel-boun], *s.* Jibión.

CV *s.* = **curriculum vitae**

cut-water [kʌt'wɔːtər] [kat-uo-ta^r], *s. (Mar.)* Tajamar, un tablón algo corvo que sale de la quilla y va endentado en la parte exterior de la roda, cuyo uso es cortar el agua. **Beak of the cut-water,** *(Mar.)* espolón del tajamar. **Forepiece of the cut-water,** *(Mar.)* azafrán del tajamar. **Doublings of the cut-water,** *(Mar.)* batideros de proa.

cut-work ['kʌtwɔːk] [kat-uek], *s.* 1. Obra de bordadura. 2. Impresión de grabados y láminas.

cut-worm ['kʌtwɔːm] [kat-uem], *s.* Larva de una mariposa (Agrotis) que por las noches destroza las plantas tiernas, por lo general cerca de la superficie y roe las yemas de los árboles.

cyanic ['saɪənɪk] [sai-a-nin], *a.* Ciánico, perteneciente al cianógeno. **Cyanic acid,** ácido ciánico.

cyanid, cyanide ['saɪənɪd] [sai-a-nid], *s.* Cianuro, compuesto de cianógeno y un metal.

cyanogen ['saɪənɒdʒən] [sai-a-no-yen], *s.* Cianógeno, gas incoloro, venenoso y licuable (C_2N_2) de olor semejante al de la almendra y que arde con llama purpúrea. Entra en la composición del azul de Prusia.

cyanuret ['saɪənʊret] [sai-a-nu-ret], *s.* Antiguo nombre del *cyanide* o cianuro.

cybernetics [ˌsaɪbə'netɪkz] [sai-ba-ne-tiks], *s. (Med., Elec.)* Cibernética.

cyberspace ['saɪbəspeɪs] [sai-ba-speis] *s.* Ciberespacio.

cyclamen ['sɪkləmən] [si-kla-men], *s. (Bot.)* Pamporcino, ciclamino, artanita, planta de adorno.

cycle ['saɪkl] [sai-kel], *s.* 1. V. CIRCLE. 2. *(Astr.)* Ciclo (process), período de tiempo o número de años que, acabados, se vuelven a contar de nuevo, y durante los cuales se reproducen fenómenos idénticos a los del período anterior. **The life cycle,** el ciclo de la vida. 3. Curso. 4. Bicicleta o triciclo; bicicleta (bicycle). 5. Programa (of washing machine). 6. *(Elec., Comput.)* Ciclo.

cycle *vn.* Ir en bicicleta (person).

cyclic, cyclical ['saɪklɪk] [sai-klik], *a.* Cíclico, perteneciente a un ciclo o período.

cycling ['saɪklɪŋ] [sai-klin] *s.* Ciclismo. **To go cycling,** salir en bicicleta, ir a andar en bicicleta.

cyclist ['saɪklɪst] [sai-klist], *s.* El que va montado en un biciclo o triciclo.

cycloid ['saɪklɔɪd] [sai-kloid], *s. (Geom.)* Cicloide, curva geométrica.

cyclometer ['saɪklɒmiːtər] [sai-klo-mi-ta^r], *s.* 1. Ciclómetro. 2. Odómetro.

cyclometry ['saɪkləmɪtrɪ] [sai-klo-mi-tri], *s.* El arte de medir ciclos o círculos.

cyclone ['saɪkləʊn] [sai-kloun], *s.* 1. Ciclón, torbellino espiral (storm). 2. *(Fam.)* Huracán, tifón. 3. Zona de bajas presiones (low-pressure area).

cyclopaedia ['saɪklə'piːdɪə] [sai-klo-pi-dia], *s.* Enciclopedia, colección de todas las ciencias.

cyclopean ['saɪkləpɪən] [sai-klo-pian], **cyclopic** [saɪkləprk] [sai-klo-pik], *a.* 1. Gigantesco, enorme; de gran dificultad. 2. Perteneciente a los cíclopes.

cyclops ['saɪklɒps] [sai-klops], *s.* Cíclope, gigante fabuloso que tenía un ojo en la frente.

cyclotron ['saɪklətrən] [sai-klo-tron], *s. (Elec.)* Ciclotrón.

cygnet ['sɪɡnɪt] [saig-net], *s.* Pollo del cisne.

cylinder ['sɪlɪndər] [si-lin-da^r], *s.* 1. *(Mat.)* Cilindro. 2. Rollo, rollete, tambor (component/of gun). 3. Tanque, bombona, garrafa, balón (container/for liquid gas). 4. Cilindro (of engine).

cylindric, cylindrical ['sɪlɪndrɪk] [si-lin-drik], *a.* Cilíndrico.

cylindroid ['sɪlɪndrɔɪd] [si-lin-droid], *s. (Geom.)* Cilindroide, cilindro con bases elípticas.

cyma ['saɪmə] [sai-ma], **cymatium** ['sɪmeɪʃən] [si-mei-shon], *s. (Arq.)* Cimacio, moldura.

cymbal ['sɪmbəl] [sim-bal], *s.* Címbalo, platillo, instrumento de percusión.

cyme ['saɪm] [saim], *s.* 1. *(Bot.)* Cima, grupo o ramo de flores que en su parte superior forman una superfice plana: corimbo. 2. *(Arq.)* Cimacio.

cynegetic ['saɪnə'dʒetɪk] [sai-ner-ye-tik], *a.* Perteneciente o relativo a la caza con perros.

cynic, cynical ['sɪnɪk] [si-nik], *a.* Cínico.

cynic, *s.* Cínico, filósofo secuaz de Diógenes: misántropo.

cynically ['sɪnɪkəlɪ] [si-ni-ka-li] *adv.* Cínicamente.

cynicism ['sɪnɪsɪzm] [si-ni-si-zem], *s.* Cinismo.

cinosure ['sɪnəʃʊər] [si-no-shua^r], *s.* 1. Objeto o centro de la atención o las miradas de todos. 2. *(Astr.)* Osa Menor.

cypher, *s.* V. CIPHER.

cypress ['saɪprɪs] [sai-pris], *s. (Bot.)* Ciprés. **Cypress,** *(Fig.)* luto.

Cyprian ['sɪprɪən] [si-prian], *a.* 1. Ciprio, chipriota, de la isla de Chipre. 2. Lascivo. *-s.* 1. Chipriota, natural o el idioma de Chipre. 2. Cortesana.

Cypriot ['sɪprɪət] [si-priot], *s.* 1. Ciprio, chipriota, natural o habitante de Chipre. 2. La antigua lengua de Chipre, dialecto del griego.

Cyprus ['saɪprəs] [sai-prus] *N. (Geogr.)* Chipre.

cyrillic [sɪ'rɪlɪk] [si-ri-lik] *a.* Cirílico.

cyst, cystis ['ɪst] [sist], *s.* Quiste o quisto, saco o vejiga membranosa.

cystic ['sɪstɪk] [sis-tik], *a.* 1. Cístico, contenido en el quiste. 2. Que tiene quistes. **Cystic fibrosis,** fibrosis cística o pancreática.

cystitis ['sɪstaɪtɪs] [sistai-tis], *s. (Med.)* Cistitis.

cytase ['sɪstəs] [sis-tas], *s.* Citasa.

cytisus ['sɪtɪsəs] [si-ti-sos], *s. (Bot.)* Citiso, cantueso.

cytological ['saɪtə'lɒdʒɪkl] [si-to-lo-yi-kal], *a.* Citológico.

cytology ['saɪtələdʒɪ] [si-to-lo-yi], *s.* Citología.

czar [zɑːr] [za^r], *s.* Zar, emperador de Rusia.

czardas ['zɑːdəs] [zar-das], *s.* Danza nacional de los magiares, en dos tiempos, uno lento y otro rápido.

Czarevitch, Czarowitz ['zarevɪtʃ] [za-re-vich], *s.* Zarevitz, título que se da al hijo primogénito del zar de Rusia: antiguamente cualquier hijo del zar.

czarina ['zɑːriːnə] [za-ri-na], *sf.* Zarina o zaritza, la esposa del zar de Rusia.

czarish ['zɑːrɪʃ] [za-rish], *a.* Zariano.

czech [ ] *a./s.* Checo (person/language).

Czechoslovakia ['tʃekəʊsləʊvækɪə] [che-kous-lou-va-kia] *N. (Geogr.)* Checoslovaquia.

czechoslovakian ['tʃekəʊsləʊvækɪən] [che-kous-lou-va-kian] *a.* Checoslovaco.

Czech Republic *s.* La République Checa.

D

d [dɪ] [di], Se pronuncia en inglés como la *d* española en Castilla. La D usada como abreviatura, quiere decir, *doctor;* **D.D.,** doctor en Teología; **I.L.D.,** doctor en Leyes, o en ambos derechos; **D.M.,** doctor en Medicina; como numeral romano vale 500. *(Mus.)* Re.

da *s.* (in US) District attorney.

dab [dæb] [dab], *va.* Dar o estregar suavemente con alguna cosa húmeda o blanda. **Dab antiseptic on the cut,** dése unos toques de antiséptico en la herida.

dab, *s.* 1. Pedazo pequeño de alguna cosa. 2. Salpicadura; cualquier golpe dado con alguna cosa blanda. 3. Barbada, pez marino en figura de rombo. 4. *(Vul.)* Artista. 5. Toque (small amount/cream, paint). **He gave his tie a dab with a damp cloth,** se frotó un poco la corbata con un trapo húmedo (pat).

dabber [ˈdæbəʳ] [da-baʳ], *s.* El que o lo que da suavemente; clisador del impresor.

dabbing [ˈdæblɪŋ] [da-blin], *s.* La acción de indentar la superficie de una piedra.

dabble [dæbl] [da-bol], *va.* Rociar, salpicar; mojar, humedecer. **We dabbled our hands/feet in the river,** chapoteamos en el río. *vn.* Chapotear, golpear en el agua o lodo de modo que salpique; entrometerse, meterse alguno donde no le llaman. **To dabble in politics/journalism,** tener escarceos con la política/el periodismo.

dabbler [ˈdæbləʳ] [da-blaʳ], *s.* 1. Chapuzador; chapucero. 2. Chisgarabís, el que se mete en lo que no sabe ni debe.

dab hand [dæbˈhænd] [dab-jand] *s.* (GB) *(Coloq.)* **To be a dab hand at something,** tener buena mano para algo.

dabster [ˈdæbstəʳ] [dabs-taʳ], *s.* La persona diestra, hábil, experta.

dace [ˈdeɪs] [deis], *s.* Albur, pez de río.

dachshund [ˈdækshʊnd] [dak-shund], *s.* Dachshund, perro tejonero alemán.

dacker [ˈdækəʳ] [da-kaʳ], *vn.* 1. Hacer trabajo de pieza, 2. Trocar, traficar permutando géneros. 3. Asir. 4. *V.* LOITER. 5. *V.* Ransack.

dactyl [ˈdæktɪl] [dak-til], *s. (Poét.)* Dáctilo, pie de verso que consta de tres sílabas, la primera larga y las otras dos breves.

dactylic [ˈdæktɪlɪk] [dak-ti-lik], *a.* Dactílico.

dactylist [ˈdæktɪlɪst] [dak-ti-list], *s.* El que escribe versos con pies dáctilos.

dactylology [ˈdæktɪl] [dak-tilo-lo-chi], *s.* Dactilogía, el arte de hablar con los dedos.

dactylonomy [ˈdæktɪˌlənɒmɪ] [dak-ti-lo-no-mi], *s.* Dactilonomía, la ciencia de contar por los dedos.

dactyloscopic [ˈdæktɪˌləskɒpɪk] [dak-ti-los-ko-pik], *a.* Dactiloscópico, relativo a las huellas digitales.

dad, daddy [dæd] [dad] [ˈdædɪ] [da-di], *s.* Papá. *(Fam.)* Tata, taitica, padrecito. Palabra usada solamente entre niños y rústicos.

dadaism [ˈdɑːdɑːɪzəm] [da-da-ism], *s.* Dadaísmo, movimiento literario.

daddy longlegs [ˈdædɪ] [da-di], *s.* 1. Arácnido de cuerpo corto y largas patas. 2. Típula. *V.* CRANEFLY. 3. Segador, falangio (harvestman).

dado [ˈdædəʊ] [da-dou], *s. (Arch.)* Dado, cubo.

daemon [ˈdæmən] [da-mon], *s.* Demonio. *V.* DEMON.

daffodil, daffodilly [ˈdæfədɪl] [da-fo-dil], *s. (Bot.),* Narciso.

daft [dæft] [daft] *a.* (GB) *(Coloq.)* Tonto, bobo. **That was a daft thing to do/say,** hiciste una tontería, decir eso fue una tontería.

dagger [ˈdægəʳ] [da-gaʳ], *s.* 1. Daga, puñal. **To look o to speak daggers to one,** comerse a uno con los ojos. 2. *(Imp.)* Cruz [#].

dago [ˈdeɪgəʊ] [dei-gou], *s.* (Ger. E.U.) Extranjero de piel morena; especialmente un italiano, español o portugués.

daguerreotype [dəˈgɛrəʊˌtaɪp] [da-gue-rou-taip], *s.* Daguerrotipo, procedimiento primitivo para nombrar las imágenes obtenidas en la cámara oscura y fijarlas sobre una plancha metálica plateada. También, la imagen misma así obtenida.

dahlia [ˈdælɪə] [da-lia], *s.* 1. Dalia, planta y flor. 2. Color violado obtenido del alquitrán de carbón.

daily [ˈdeɪlɪ] [dei-li], *a.* Diario (newspaper, prayers); diario, cotidiano (walk, visit). **Employed/paid on a daily basis,** contratado/pagado por días. *-adv.* Diariamente, cada día; con frecuencia. *s.* Diario, periódico.

dainties [ˈdeɪntɪs] [dein-tis], *s.* Chochos, confites, golosinas.

daintily [ˈdeɪntɪlɪ] [dein-ti-li], *adv.* Regaladamente, delicadamente.

daintiness [ˈdeɪntɪnɪs] [dein-ti-nis], *s.* Elegancia, pulidez, delicadeza, golosina, afectación.

dainty [ˈdeɪntɪ] [dein-ti], *a.* 1. Delicado (delicate/flowers, vase); delicado, refinado (appearance); delicado (physique); espléndido, elegante. 2. Regalado, sabroso, exquisito (delicious). 3. Melindroso; afectado. *s.* Regalo, manjar delicado, bocado exquisito, golosina; se usaba antiguamente como expresión de cariño.

daiquiri [ˈdaɪkɪrɪ] [dai-ki-ri], *s.* Daiquirí, bebida alohólica compuesta.

dairy [ˈdɛərɪ] [dea-ri], *s.* 1. Lechería (on farm); lugar donde se prepara la leche para hacer queso y manteca; quesera o quesería, el lugar donde se prepara la leche para hacer quesos. 2. Lácteo (produce); de granja (butter, cream); lechero (cow/industry). 3. Lechería (shop); central lechera (company). **Dairy farm,** granja lechera. **Dairyman,** lechero.

dairymaid [ˈdɛərɪˌmeɪd] [dea-ri-meid], *sf.* Lechera, mantequera, la mujer que trabaja en una lechería o vende la leche.

dais [ˈdeɪs] [deiis], *s.* 1. Tablado o gradas a la cabecera de un salón; tarima, estrado (rostrum). **2. Silla elevada, bajo dosel.**

daisy [ˈdeɪzɪ] [dei-si], *s.* 1. *(Bot.)* Margarita (cultivated); margarita de los prados, maya (wild). **As fresh as a daisy,** tan fresco como una lechuga. **To be pushing up (the) daisies,** estar criando malvas. 2. *(Ger.)* Persona o cosa muy admirada.

daisy wheel *s.* Margarita, impresora de margarita.

dale [ˈdeɪl] [deil], *s.* Cañada, valle pequeño, llanura de tierra entre montes.

dalliance [ˈdeɪlɪəns] [dei-lians], *s.* 1. Regodeo, diversión, fiesta; trato familiar enre los casados; juguete, retozo; devaneo, escarceos. 2. Tardanza, dilación.

dallier [ˈdeɪlɪəʳ] [dei-liaʳ], *s.* Retozón o juguetón.

dally [ˈdælɪ] [da-li], *vn.* 1. Bobear, acariciarse, juguetear, requebrar, divertirse; retozar. 2. Burlarse, hacer mofa de; retardarse, retrasarse, tardar. *-va.* Dilatar, suspender; hacer pasar el tiempo con gusto.

dalmatian [dælˈmeɪʃən] [dal-mei-shan], *a. y s.* Dálmata, de la Dalmacia, dalmático.

dalmatic [ˈdælmætɪk] [dál-ma-tik], *s.* Dalmática, vestidura sagrada de los diáconos.

dam [dæm] [dam], *s.* 1. La madre en los animales; yegua. (Despectivo) Madre, mujer. 2. Presa o represa de agua, dique. 3. Límite, linde.

dam, *va.* Represar, detener o estancar el agua corriente; cerrar, tapar. **To dam up,** contener el agua con diques. **To dam a neighbor's lights,** impedir la libre entrada de la luz en casa de un vecino.

damage [ˈdæmɪdʒ] [da-mich], *s.* 1. Daño, perjuicio, detrimento (to reputation, cause). Daño (to object). **Storm/fire damage,** daños ocasionados por una tormenta/un incendio. **The damage is done,** el daño ya está hecho. 2. Resarcimiento de daño. 3. Pérdida; retribución. 4. Desventaja. 5. *(Com.)* Avería. *-pl. (Law)* Daños y perjuicios.

damage, *va.* Dañar (building, vehicle); perjudicar, ser perjudicial para la salud (health); perjudicar, dañar (reputation, cause). **Damaged,** dañado, averiado (stock). - *vn.* Dañarse, averiarse.

damageable ['dæmɪdʒəbl] [da-mi-cha-bol], *a.* Susceptible de daño; perjudicial, pernicioso, dañoso, dañino.

damaging ['dæmɪdʒɪŋ] [da-ma-chin] *a.* Perjudicial. **To be damaging to somebody/something,** ser perjudicial para alguien/algo.

damascene ['dæməsiːn] [da-ma-sin], *va. V.* DAMASKEEN. *a.* Damasceno de la ciudad de Damasco.

Damascus ['dæmɪskəs] [da-mas-kus] *N. (Geogr.)* Damasco.

damask ['dæməsk] [da-mask], *s.* 1. Damasco, tela de seda o lino bastante doble, con dibujo del mismo color. 2. Damasco, tela de lino que se llama así por la semejanza de sus flores a las del damasco de seda. **Damask tablecloth,** mantel adamascado o alemanisco. **Damask steel,** acero damasquino.

damask, *va.* 1. Adamascar. *V.* DAMESKEEN. 2 Tejer con patrones abundantes en flores. 3. Diversificar, matizar.

damask-plum ['dæməsk‚pləm] [da-mask-plum], *s.* Ciruela damascena.

damask-rose ['dæməsk‚rəʊz] [da-mask-rous], *s.* Rosa de damasco o encarnada.

damaskeen ['dæməsiːn] [da-mas-kin], *va.* Adornar con incrustaciones metálicas una superficie de hierro o acero; ataujiar; adornar un metal con líneas ondeantes.

damaskeening ['dæməskiːnɪŋ] [da-mas-ki-nin], *s.* Ataujía, el arte o acto de embutir unos metales en otros.

damassin ['dæməsiːn] [da-ma-sin], *s.* Damasina, tejido de seda parecido al damasco en el dibujo y la labor.

dame [deɪm] [deim], *sf.* 1. Dama, señora, ama. *(Fam.)* Tía. 2. Maestra de niñas.

dame's-violet [deɪmz'vaɪələt] [deims-vaio-let], *s. (Bot.)* Violeta matronal, hespéride, planta aromática de las crucíferas.

dammar ['dæmər] [da-mar], *s.* Damar, resina usada en las artes.

dammit ['dæmɪt] [da-mit] *interj. (Coloq.)* ¡Caray! **As near as dammit,** poco más o menos.

damn [dæm] [dam], *va.* 1. *(Rel.)* Condenar, castigar con las penas eternas del infierno. Condenar (condemn). 2. Maldecir, echar maldiciones. 3. Vituperar; silbar o reprobar; mofar, despreciar. *(Coloq.)* **(God) damn it!,** ¡caray!, ¡maldita sea! **Well, I'll be damned!,** ¡vaya! -*s.* Maldición. **I don't give a damn what they think,** me importa un bledo o un pito o un comino lo que piensen. -*a.* Condenado, maldito, pinche.

damnable ['dæmnəbl] [dam-na-bol], *a.* 1. Damnable, condenable. 2. Detestable, pernicioso; infame.

damnably ['dæmnəblɪ] [dam-na-bli], *adv.* Horriblemente, de un modo indigno, infame o abominable.

damnation [dæm'neɪʃən] [dam-nei-shon], *s.* Damnación, condenación.

damnatory ['dæmnətərɪ] [dam-na-to-ri], *a.* Condenatorio.

damned [dæmd] [damnd], *a.* Condenado (souls); maldito; detestable, aborrecible; reprobado; dañado; silbado. **The damned,** los condenados.

damnedest ['dæmnɪdest] [dam-ni-dest] *s. (Coloq.)* **She did her damnedest to stop it,** hizo todo lo que pudo para impedirlo.

damnify ['dæmnɪfaɪ] [dam-ni-fai], *va.* Dañar, injuriar; debilitar, malear. (Más usado como voz forense.)

damning ['dæmnɪŋ] [dam-nin] *a.* Condenatorio (condemnatory/evidence). Crítico (critical/appraisal).

damp [dæmp] [damp], *a.* 1. Húmedo. **There are damp patches on the ceiling,** hay manchas de humedad en el techo. **To smell damp,** oler a humedad. 2. Triste, abatido, melancólico, amilanado. *s.* 1. Niebla, humedad; exhalación nociva. Como exhalación nociva se llama también *Chokeamp.* 2. Desaliento, cobardía, pusilanimidad, abatimiento, aflicción, consternación.

damp, *va.* 1. Mojar, humedecer. 2. Desanimar, abatir, acobardar; entorpecer; entibiar, aflojar, amainar, amortiguar,

apagar. 3. Sofocar (fire); apagar, enfriar (enthusiasm, excitement).

dampen ['dæmpən] [dam-pen], *va.* 1. Humedecer, poner húmedo, mojar (moisten). 2. Enfriar, desanimar, desalentar (discourage/hopes, enthusiasm); poner el apagador sobre algo, apagar. **To dampen somebody's spirits,** desanimar o desalentar a alguien.

dampened ['dæmpənd] [dam-pend], *a.* Humedecido. 2. Desanimado, desalentado.

damper ['dæmpər] [dam-par], *s.* 1. Lo que se apaga o reprime; registro, llave del humero de una chimenea para regular el tiro; regulador de tiro. 2. Apagador del piano; sordina. 3. Desalentador, el que desalienta. **The bad news put a damper on the celebrations,** la mala noticia estropeó las fiestas.

dampish ['dæmpɪʃ] [dam-pish], *a.* Algo humedecido.

dampishness ['dæmpɪʃnɪs] [dam-pish-nes], **dampness** ['dæmpnɪs], *s.* Humedad.

damp-proof ['dæmppruːf] [damp-pruf] *va.* Proteger contra la humedad.

damsel ['dæmzəl] [dam-sel], *sf.* 1. Damisela, señorita; en lo antiguo, doncel y doncella. 2. Reborde de la muela.

damson ['dæmsən] [dam-son], *s.* Ciruela damascena.

dan [dæn] [dan], *s.* 1. Palabra antigua que equivale a Master. Cf. DON. 2. Carretón, en las minas de carbón de piedra.

dance [dɑːns] [dans] *vn.* 1. Bailar, danzar. 2. Saltar, brincar (skip). -*va.* Hacer bailar; hacer saltar. **To dance attendance,** *(Vul.)* servir con prontitud y atención, hacer plantón. **They danced the night away,** bailaron durante toda la noche.

dance, *s.* Danza, baile. **To lead somebody a merry dance,** darle a alguien quebraderos de cabeza.

dance hall ['dɑːnshɔːl] [dans-jol], *s.* Salón de baile.

dancer ['dɑːnsər] [dan-sar], *s.* 1. Danzador, bailador. 2 Danzarín, bailarín.

dancing ['dɑːnsɪŋ] [dan-sin], *s.* La acción de danzar o bailar. **Dancing-master,** maestro de baile o danza. **Dancing-school,** escuela de baile. **Dancing-room,** sala de baile.

dandelion ['dɑːndɪlaɪən] [dan-di-laion], *s. (Bot.)* Diente de león, o amargón.

dander ['dɑːndər] [dan-dar], *s.* 1, *V.* DANDRUFF. 2. *(Vul.)* Ira, cólera.

dandify ['dɑːndɪfaɪ] [dan-di-fai], *va.* Hacer a otro petimetre o currutaco; vestirlo con elegancia exagerada, a lo lechuguino.

dandiprat ['dɑːndɪpræt] [dan-di-prat], *s. (Ant.)* Hombrecito; hombrezuelo cachigordete.

dandle ['dændl] [dan-del], *va.* 1. Mecer, menear a un niño en los brazos o sobre las rodillas; hacer saltar sobre las rodillas. 2. Mimar, acariciar; tratar a uno como a un niño. 3. Entretener, dar largas.

dandler ['dændlər] [dan-dlar], *s.* Niñero.

dandruff ['dændrəf] [dan-druf], *s.* Caspa, escamilla que se forma en la cabeza.

dandy ['dændɪ] [dan-di], *s.* 1. Petimetre, currutaco, elegante exagerado en el vestir y afectado en sus maneras, 2. *(Ger.)* Cualquier cosa especialmente fina o agradable en su clase. *V.* DAISY. 3. **Dandy** o **dandy-fever,** *V.* DENGUE.

Dane [deɪn] [dein], *s.* Danés, dinamarqués, natural o ciudadano de Dinamarca. **Great Dane,** perro danés, de raza grande y fuerte.

dang [dæŋ] [dan], *va.* Maldecir; eufemismo rústico en lugar de *damn.*

danger ['deɪndʒər] [dein-char], *s.* Peligro, riesgo, contingencia. *(Fam.)* **There is no danger,** no hay miedo, no hay cuidado. **Out of danger,** fuera de peligro. **To be on/off the danger list,** encontrarse en estado grave/estar fuera de peligro. **Danger signal/zone,** señal/zona de peligro.

danger money *s.* (GB) Plus o prima de peligrosidad.

dangerless ['deɪndʒəlɪs] [dein-char-les], *a.* Seguro, sin peligro.

dangerous ['deɪndʒrəs] [dein-che-ros], *a.* Peligroso, arriesgado. **Dangerous driving,** conducción con imprudencia temeraria.

dangerously ['deɪndʒrəsli] [dein-che-ros-li], *adv.* Peligrosamente. **To live dangerously,** llevar una vida arriesgada. **She came dangerously close to losing her life,** estuvo a un paso de la muerte.

dangerousness ['deɪndʒrəsnɪs] [dein-che-ros-nes], *s.* Peligro, calidad de peligroso.

dangle ['dæŋgl] [dan-gol], *va.* 1. Colgar algo libremente en el aire. 2. Hacer oscilar. **He dangled the possibility of promotion in front of her,** quiso tentarla con la posibilidad de un ascenso. -*vn.* 1. Pender, fluctuar, bambolearse; estar colgado en el aire. 2. Hacer a alguno la corte con adulación.

dangler ['dæŋglər] [dan-glar], *s.* Juan de las damas, el que continuamente está haciendo la corte a las damas; Perico entre ellas, Don Precioso.

Danish ['dænɪʃ] [da-nish], *a.* Danés, dinamarqués, perteneciente a Dinamarca. *s.* Idioma de Dinamarca.

danish blue *s.* Tipo de queso azul. **Danish pastry,** bollo cubierto de azúcar glaseado.

dank [dæŋk] [dank], *a.* Frío y húmedo. V. DAMP.

dankish ['dæŋkɪʃ] [dan-kish], *a.* Algo húmedo.

dankness, *s.* V. DAMPNESS.

dantesque ['dæntesk] [dan-tesk], *a.* Dantesco, propio y característico de Dante, poeta insigne italiano.

Danube ['dænjuːb] [da-niub] *s.* **The Danube,** el Danubio.

dap [dæp] [dap], **dape** [deɪp] [deip], *vn.* Dejar caer alguna cosa muy despacio en el agua; pescar con caña en la superficie del agua.

daphne ['dæfnɪ] [daf-ni], *s.* 1. Dafne, ninfa de Diana, transformada en laurel. 2. Dafne, género de arbustos de la familia de las timéleas.

dapper ['dæpər] [da-par], *a.* Gentil, bonito, limpio, aseado; gallardo; pequeño y vivaz.

dapperling ['dæpəlɪŋ] [da-per-lin], *s.* Enano, chicuelo, monigote.

dapple, *va.* Varetear, señalar con varios colores, abigarrar.

dapple, *a.* Vareteado, rucio. **Dapple-gray horse,** rucio rodado, o moro azul.

dappled ['dæplt] [da-pelt] *a.* Rodado, pinto (horse); veteado (pattern).

dare, dart, *s.* (Local, Ingl.) V. DACE.

dare [deər] [dear], *vn.* (*pret.* DURST o DARED; *pp.* DARED). Osar, atreverse, arriesgarse, emprender alguna cosa con atrevimiento. **Just you dare!,** ¡atrévete y verás! **How dare you!,** ¡cómo te atreves! **I dare say you've had enough,** estarás harto (me imagino). -*va.* 1. Arrostrar, hacer frente. 2. Desafiar, provocar contender o competir con otro. **To dare larks,** (*Des.*) coger calandrias con espejo.

dare, *s.* Desafío, reto. **She did it on/for a dare,** lo hizo porque la retaron o la desafiaron. V. CHALLENGE.

dare-devil ['deədevl] [dea-de-vil], *a.* y *s.* Atrevido, temerario (feat, exploit); descuidado, atolondrado.

dareful ['deərfʊl] [dea-ful], *a.* Atrevido, osado.

darer ['deərər] [dea-rar], *s.* Desafiador.

darg [dɑːg] [darg], *s.* (*Esco.*) El trabajo de un día; trabajo cansado.

daring ['deərɪŋ] [dea-rin], *a.* Osado, atrevido, intrépido, arriesgado, temerario, emprendedor (explorer, pilot); audaz (plan); atrevido (dress, film).

daringly ['deərɪŋlɪ] [dea-rin-li], *adv.* Atrevidamente, osadamente.

dark [dɑːk] [dark], *a.* 1. Desprovisto de luz en parte o totalmente; opaco; oscuro (unlit/room, night). **It's getting dark,** está oscureciendo, se está haciendo de noche. **The dark side of the moon,** el lado oculto de la luna. **Dark blue,** azul oscuro. 2. Moreno, bruno, lo que tira a negro; oscuro (in color). **Dark chocolate,** chocolate sin leche. 3. Oscuro (evil, sinister/deeds, threats); difícil de entenderse, enigmático; secreto. **There's a dark side to his nature/his activities,** hay algo de siniestro en él/sus actividades. Sombrío (somber/thoughts). **To keep something dark,** mantener algo en secreto. 4. Ignorante, falto de conocimiento.

5. Triste, melancólico, tétrico. 6. Moreno de tez morena. 7. (*Poét.*) Ciego, ignorante. **Dark room,** pieza o cuarto oscuro, falto de luz actínica; a propósito para trabajos fotográficos. **The dark ages,** la época de la superstición y la ignorancia. **A dark saying,** enigma. **Dark lantern,** linterna sorda.

dark, *s.* 1. Oscuridad, tinieblas (absence of light). **The dark,** la oscuridad. **To wait until dark,** esperar hasta que anochezca. **After dark,** de noche. 2. Ignorancia, falta de ciencia o conocimiento; mancha. **To leave one in the dark,** dejar a uno a oscuras.

Dark Ages *s. pl.* La Alta Edad Media, la Edad de las tinieblas. **They're living in the Dark Ages,** viven en la prehistoria.

darken ['dɑːkən] [dar-ken], *va.* 1. Oscurecer (make dark); poner oscuro, sombrío, ensombrecer (make somber). 2. Anublar, cubrir de nubes. 3. Confundir, embrollar. 4. Denigrar, manchar. 5. (*Fig.*) Contristar, entristecer. -*vn.* Oscurecerse (grow dark/room, colour); oscurecerse, nublarse (sky). Ensombrecerse (grow somber).

darkener ['dɑːkənər] [dar-ke-nar], *s.* El que oscurece o confunde.

dark-field microscope ['dɑːkfiːlˌmaɪkrəskəʊp] [dark-fil-mai-kros-koup], *s.* Ultramicroscopio.

dark horse ['dɑːkhɔːs] [dark-jors], *s.* 1. En la política, candidato de transacción que surge inesperadamente; ganador sorpresa (surprise victor). 2. Enigma (unknown quantity).

darkish ['dɑːkɪʃ] [dar-kish], *a.* Algo oscuro, ofusco.

darkling ['dɑːklɪŋ] [dar-klin], *a.* 1. Oscurecido, visto ofuscadamente; lo que está en tinieblas. 2. Incapaz de ver.

darkly ['dɑːklɪ] [dar-kli], *adv.* Oscuramente, secretamente, misteriosamente (hint).

darkness ['dɑːknɪs] [dark-nes], *s.* 1. Oscuridad (of night, room); tinieblas; densidad, opacidad. **The building was in complete/total darkness,** el edificio estaba totalmente a oscuras. **When darkness fall,** al caer la noche. 2. Ignorancia; secreto; dominio de Satanás. 3. Tinieblas (evil). **The powers of dark,** los poderes del mal.

dark room ['dɑːkrʊm] [dark-rum], *s.* Cuarto oscuro, cámara oscura (para fotografías).

dark-skinned [ˌdɑːkˈskɪnd] [dark-skind] *a.* De piel oscura.

darksome ['dɑːksəm] [dark-som], *a.* (*Poét.*) Oscuro, opaco, sombrío.

darling ['dɑːlɪŋ] [dar-lin], *s.* El predilecto, el querido, el favorito; cariño (as form of address). **She was the darling of the public,** era la niña mimada del público. *a.* Querido, amado (beloved); mono (delightful).

darn [dɑːn] [dan], *va.* Zurcir (mend). *interj.* (*Coloq.*) **Darn it!,** ¡caray!

darn, *va.* Maldecir: (forma atenuada de *damn*).

darn, darned ['dɑːnd] [darnd] *a.* (*Coloq.*) Maldito. **I can't see a darn/darned thing,** no veo ni medio. -*adv.* (as intensifier). **He's too darn/darned clever,** se pasa de listo.

darnel ['dɑːnl] [dar-nel], *s.* (*Bot.*) Zizaña, cizaña, una planta cualquiera del género Lolium.

darner ['dɑːnər] [dar-nar], *s.* Zurcidor o zurcidora.

darning ['dɑːnɪŋ] [dar-nin], *s.* Zurcidura. Zurcido (action). Ropa para zurcir (things to be darned).

dart [dɑːt] [dart], *s.* Dardo (weapon, Games); venablo. Pinza (clothing).

dart, *va.* Lanzar (look); arrojar, tirar, echar de sí alguna cosa con violencia. -*vn.* Lanzarse, arrojarse, precipitarse; volar como dardo o saeta. **To dart into/out of a room,** entrar como una flecha en/salir como una flecha de una habitación.

dartars ['dɑːtəz] [dar-tars], *s.* Roña o llaga que padecen los corderos.

dartboard ['dɑːtbɔːd] [dart-bord] *s.* Diana.

darter ['dɑːtər] [dar-tar], *s.* 1. El que arroja dardos. 2. Pez pequeño americano, de vivos colores. 3. El pájaro-culebra americano.

darts ['dɑːts] [darts] *s. pl.* Dardos.

Darwinism ['dɑːvɪnɪzəm] [dar-vi-nisem], *s.* Darwinismo, transformismo, sistema de Darwin que explica el origen de las especies animales mediante la transformación y la selección natural.

dash [dæʃ] [dash], *va.* 1. Arrojar, tirar con ímpetu alguna cosa contra otra. 2. Estrellar, chocar, romper; magullar. **She dashed the plate to pieces,** hizo añicos o trizas el plato. **The ship was dashed against the rocks,** el barco se estrelló contra las rocas. 3. Rociar, salpicar con agua u otro líquido. 4. Mezclar, mudar alguna cosa por medio de alguna mezcla. 5. Bosquejar, escribir apresuradamente (con *off*). 6. Confundir, avergonzar; frustrar; defraudar (disappoint/hopes). -*vn.* 1. Chocar, estrellarse, romperse (crash/waves). **I dashed to the rescue,** me lancé al rescate. **I must dash,** tengo que irme corriendo. 2. Saltar, dar un salto. 3. Estallar, saltar en pedazos dando un estallido. 4. Zambullirse en el agua de golpe haciéndola saltar.

dash away, desechar, arrojar de sí.

dash down, rechazar; precipitar; volcar, echar por tierra.

dash out, levantar la tapa de los sesos; hacer saltar; borrar o testar lo escrito; salir precipitadamente. **To dash one's confidence,** turbar a alguno, cortarle, desconcertarle. **To dash to pieces,** hacerse añicos, hacerse una tortilla.

dash off 1. Escribir corriendo (write hurriedly). 2. Irse corriendo (leave hastily).

dash, *s.* 1. Movimiento repentino hacia adelante (sudden movement); arranque, ataque; incursión. **To make a dash for safety/shelter,** correr a ponerse a salvo/a cobijarse. **To make a dash for it,** salir a toda velocidad. 2. Colisión, choque, encuentro violento de dos cuerpos. 3. Guión (-), raya o línea, señal que se usa en lo escrito y en lo impreso (punctuation mark); Raya (in Morse code). 4. Ostentación vanagloriosa, gran papel. 5. Infusión, mezcla, tintura. 6. Golpe; rasgo. **Dash of a pen,** rasgo de pluma. 7. Poquito (small amount). **A dash of milk/salt,** un chorrito de leche/una pizca de sal. 8. Brío (nerve, spirit). *(Dep.)* **The 100 m dash,** los 100 metros lisos.

dashboard [ˈdæʃbɔːd] [dash-bord], *s.* 1. Guardafango. 2. Tablero de instrumentos (en un automóvil o avión).

dashing [ˈdæʃɪŋ] [da-shin], *a.* Precipitado, arrojado; gallardo (lively); elegante (smart).

dastard [ˈdæstɑːd] [das-tard], *s.* Collón, hombre bajo y cobarde.

dastardize [ˈdæstədaɪz] [das-tar-dais], *va.* Acobardar, amedrentar.

dastardly [ˈdæstədlɪ] [das-tard-li], *a.* Cobarde, pusilánime, tímido; ruin (deed).

dastardliness [ˈdæstədlɪnɪs] [das-tard-li-nis], **dastardy** [ˈdæstədɪ] [das-tar-di], *s.* Cobardía, pusilanimidad.

data [ˈdeɪtə] [dei-ta], *s. pl.* (de DATUM, V. infra). 1. Cosas o principios dados, fijos o determinados; datos, información (facts, information). 2. *(Inform.)* Datos. **A piece of data,** un dato. **Data bank,** banco de datos. **Data capture,** toma de datos. **Data protection,** protección de datos o de la información.

database [ˈdeɪtəbeɪs] [dei-ta-beis] *s.* Base de datos.

data processing [deɪtəˈprəsesɪŋ] [dei-ta-pro-se-sin], *s.* Procesamiento de información; proceso de acumulación, ordenación y presentación de datos.

datary [ˈdætərɪ] [da-ta-ri], *s.* Datario; dataría.

date [deɪt] [deit], *s.* 1. Data, fecha (of appointment, battle). **What's the date today?,** ¿a qué fecha estamos?. 2. Duración, continuación; fin, conclusión. **A thing out of date,** cosa que no se estila, fuera de uso. 3. *(Coloq.)* Cita (appointment). **Greg has a date with Ana on Sunday,** Greg sale con Ana el domingo. **He's my regular date,** estoy saliendo con él (person). **He's playing three dates in London,** tiene que actuar tres veces en Londres (booking).

date, *s.* 1. Dátil, el fruto de la palmera. 2. Palmera. V. DATE-PALM.

date, *va.* 1. Datar, fechar (mark with date); notar la data de alguna escritura o acaecimiento (give date to/remains, pottery, fossil). *(Coloq.)* **That song really dates you,** eso demuestra tu

edad, eso demuestra lo viejo que eres. 2. Salir con (go out with). -*vn.* 1. Contar, computar. 2. Datar (originate in). **It dates from the 14th century,** data del siglo XIV. 3. Pasar de moda (become old-fashioned). 4. Salir con chicas, chicos (go on dates).

dated [ˈdeɪtɪd] [dei-ted] *a.* Anticuado (fashion, word). **His plays are dated,** sus obras han perdido actualidad.

dateless [ˈdeɪtlɪs] [deit-les], *a.* Sin data, fecha o tiempo señalado.

date line [ˈdeɪtlaɪn] [deit-lain], *s.* 1. Línea internacional de cambio de fecha. 2. Fecha de publicación de un periódico, una revista, etc.

date-palm o date-tree [ˈdeɪtpɑːm] [deit-palm] [deɪtˈtriː] [deit-tri], *s. (Bot.)* Palmera, el árbol que produce los dátiles.

dater [ˈdeɪtər] [dei-taʳ], **date stamp** [ˈdeɪtstæmp] [deit-stamp] *s.* Sello fechador.

date rape [ˈdeɪtreɪp] [deit-reip] *s.* Violación cometida durante una cita.

dative [ˈdeɪtɪv] [dei-tiv], *a. y s.* Dativo el tercer caso del nombre. -*a. (For.)* Lo que es dado, en posesión a lo que es hereditario.

datum [ˈdeɪtəm] [dei-tum], *s.* Dato, algo asumido o conocido; fundamento para formar juicio o deducir consecuencias. -*pl.* DATA.

daub [dɔːb] [dob], *va.* 1. Embadurnar (smear); untar con alguna substancia pegajosa; bañar, cubrir con yeso; de aquí manchar, ensuciar, embarrar; 2. Pintorrear, pintar toscamente. 3. Cubrir, disfrazar. 4. *(Des.)* Adular con vileza.

daub *s.* 1. Aplicación viscosa; mancha grasienta (smear). V. WATTLE. 2. Argamasa barata. 3. Pintarrajo, mamarracho.

daubing [ˈdɔːbɪŋ] [do-bin], *s.* Mortero, estuco; afeite.

dauby [ˈdɔːbɪ] [do-bi], *a.* Viscoso, glutinoso, pegajoso.

daugther [ˈdɔːtər] [do-taʳ], *sf.* Hija. **Daughter-in-law,** nuera. **Grand-daugther,** nieta. **God-daugther,** ahijada.

daugterly [ˈdɔːtəlɪ] [do-tar-li], *a.* Semejante a hija; obediente.

daunt [dɔːnt] [dont], *va.* Acobardar, desanimar, amilanar; espantar, intimidar, atemorizar. **Nothing daunted, we carried on,** impertérritos, seguimos adelante.

daunting [ˈdɔːntɪŋ] [duon-tin] *a.* Desalentador, sobrecogedor (prospect); de enormes proporciones (task).

dauntless [ˈdɔːntlɪs] [daunt-les], *a.* Intrépido.

dauntlessness [ˈdɔːntlɪsnɪs] [dont-lis-nes], *s.* Intrepidez, valor.

dauphin [ˈdɔːfɪn] [do-fin], *s.* Delfín, título que se daba en otro tiempo al primogénito y heredero del rey de Francia.

dauphiness [ˈdɔːfɪnɪs] [do-fi-nes], *sf.* Delfina, la mujer del delfín.

davenport [ˈdævnpɔːt] [daven-port] *s.* Sofá grande.

davit [ˈdævɪt] [da-vit], *s. (Mar.)* Pescante de bote, cada una de las pequeñas grúas en forma de efe que van en pares a los costados del buque.

daw [dɔː] [do], *s.* Corneja.

dawdle [ˈdɔːdl] [do-del], *vn.* Gastar tiempo; holgazanear, haraganear; entretenerse. **She dawdled over her meal,** comió con gran parsimonia.

dawdler [ˈdɔːdlər] [do-dlaʳ] *s.* Persona lenta o cachazuda, lerdo.

dawn [dɔːn] [don], *vn.* 1 Amanecer, apuntar el día. 2. Empezar lentamente a manifestar lustre o brillo. 3. Apuntar, comenzar a crecer, a espaciarse, a dar muestras de inteligencia. **To dawn on, It gradually dawned on me that…,** fui cayendo en la cuenta de que…

dawn *s.* 1. Alba, albor, amanecer (daybreak). **At dawn,** al amanecer, al alba. **From dawn till dask,** de sol a sol. **Since the dawn of civilization,** desde los albores de la civilización. De madrugada (patrol, start). 2. Principio u origen de alguna cosa. **The dawn of reason,** la luz de la razón.

dawning [ˈdɔːnɪŋ] [do-nin], *s.* Alba, el amanecer.

day [deɪ] [dei] *s.* 1. Día (unit of time); luz. **Twice a day,** dos veces al día. **A tree-day-old chick,** un pollito de tres días. 2. Día, el espacio de tiempo que emplea la tierra (o un astro) en dar una vuelta completa sobre su eje (daylight hours). **All day,** todo el día. **We went to the beach for the day,** fuimos a pasar el día a la playa. **Day and night,** día y noche. 2. La parte del día destinada al trabajo. 4. Tiempo o período (period of time); siglo. **Up to the present day,** hasta el día de hoy. **The burning issues of the day,** los temas candentes del día. **In days to come,** en días venideros. **In the old days,** antiguamente. 5. Jornada, batalla. 6. Día señalado o en el que ha sucedido alguna cosa extraordinaria (point in time). **What day is it today?,** ¿qué día es hoy? **Every day,** todos los días. 7. Vida. **Days,** lifetime. **His days are numbered,** tiene los días contados. **In our days,** en nuestros tiempos. **To gain the day,** ganar la batalla. **Daytime,** día, el tiempo que hay luz natural. **By day,** de día. **From day to day,** de día en día; de un día para otro; sin certeza o continuación. **St. John's Day,** día de San Juan. **Every other day,** cada tercer día, un día sí y otro no. **Today,** hoy. **To this day,** hasta el día de hoy. **The day before yesterday,** antes de ayer, anteayer. **This day week,** hoy hace ocho días; de hoy en ocho días. **Dog-days,** la canícula. **At daybreak,** al romper el día, al ser de día. **Days of grace,** días de gracia o de cortesía, cierto número de días que se concede para el pago de una letra de cambio después de haber vencido. **The day before,** la víspera. **All day long,** todo el día. **Good-day!,** ¡buenos días! **To gain the day,** ganar la batalla. **The Lord's Day,** el domingo, el día del Señor. **Work day,** día de trabajo. **A meagre day,** día de vigilia. **A fast-day,** día de ayuno. **Lay days,** (*Mar.*) días de demora o de estadía. **An off day,** un día de más, no del número. **To carry/win the day,** prevalecer (contest). **Her quick thinking saved the day,** su rapidez mental nos sacó del apuro. **That will be the day,** cuando las ranas críen pelo.

day-book ['deɪbʊk] [dei-buk], *s.* Diario, libro de mercaderes o mercantes.

daybreak ['deɪbreɪk] [dei-breik], *s.* Alba, amanecer. **At daybreak,** al alba, al amanecer. V. DAWN.

day care ['deɪkɛəʳ] [dei-keaʳ] *s.* 1. Servicio de guardería infantil (for children). 2. (GB) Atención prestada durante el día a ancianos, minusválidos, etc. (for old/disabled people). **Day-care center,** guardería infantil. (GB) **Day-care centre,** centro diurno para ancianos, minusválidos, etc.

daydream ['deɪdriːm] [dei-drim], *vn.* Soñar despierto, hacerse ilusiones. -*s.* Sueño, ilusión, quimera.

day-labor (GB) **day-labour** [deɪləbəʳ] [dei-la-baʳ], *s.* 1. El trabajo de un día; jornada. 2. Jornal.

day-laborer, (GB) **day-labourer** [deɪləbərəʳ] [dei-la-bo-raʳ] *s.* Jornalero, gañán.

dayletter ['deɪletəʳ] [dei-le-taʳ], *s.* Carta telegráfica diurna.

daylight ['deɪlaɪt] [dei-lait], *s.* 1. Luz del día, luz. 2. Amanecer, alba. **To scare the daylighs out of,** (*Fam.*) meter los monos a. **That dog scares the daylights out of me,** ese perro me da pánico o terror. **In broad daylight,** a plena luz del día. **Before daylight,** antes de que amanezca.

daylight-saving time [deɪlaɪtˈseɪvɪŋˌtaɪm] [dei-lat-sei-vin-taim], *s.* Hora oficial (para aprovechar mejor la luz del día).

day nursery [deɪˌnɜːsərɪ] [dei-ner-se-ri], *s.* Guardería, casa cuna para niños cuyas madres trabajan.

day release [ˌdeɪrɪˈliːs] [dei-re-lis] *s.* Sistema que permite a un empleado ausentarse regularmente de su trabajo para seguir estudios relacionados con el mismo.

dayroom ['deɪrʊm] [dei-rum] *s.* Sala de estar comunal en hospitales, prisiones, etc.

day's run [deɪsˈrʌn] [deis-ran], *s.* (*Mar.*) Singladura, el camino que hace un buque en 24 horas.

day-scholar [deɪˈskɒləʳ] [dei-sko-laʳ], *s.* Externo, alumno de una escuela que no vive en ella.

day school [deɪskuːl] [dei-skul], *s.* Escuela diurna.

day service ['deɪsɜːvɪs] [dei-ser-vis], *s.* Servicio diurno.

dayspring ['deɪsprɪŋ] [dei-sprin], *s.* Alba, primera luz del día.

day-star ['deɪstaːʳ] [dei-staʳ], *s.* Lucero.

daytime ['deɪtaɪm] [dei-taim] *s.* **In/during daytime,** de día o durante el día. **Daytime trip,** excursión de un día. **Daytime-tripper,** excursionista.

day work ['deɪwɜːk] [dei-uek], *s.* Trabajo diurno.

daze [deɪz] [deis], *va.* Deslumbrar, ofuscar con una luz demasiado viva. -*s.* Deslumbramiento, ofuscamiento. **To go about in a daze,** estar en las nubes.

dazed [deɪzt] [deist] *a.* Aturdido.

dazzle ['dæzl] [da-sel], *va.* 1. Deslumbrar, ofuscar con luz intensa. 2. Ofuscar, turbar, encantar, v.g. con brillantes promesas o expectativas. (*Vul.*) Encandilar.

dazzle, *s.* Resplandor, brillo (of lights); hechizo (of publicity).

dazzlement ['dæzlmənt] [da-sel-ment], *s.* Deslumbramiento; desvanecimiento, ofuscamiento.

dazzling ['dæzlɪŋ] [das-lin], *a.* Deslumbrador, resplandeciente, que encandila (bright/light, glare); deslumbrante, deslumbrador (impressive/wit, looks).

db, dB (= decibel) dB.

d-day ['diːdeɪ] [di-dei] *s.* Día D, día del desembarco aliado en Normandía (in World War ll); el día señalado (important day).

D.D.T. ['dɪdɪtɪ] [di-di-ti], D.D.T.

DEA *s.* (= **Drug Enforcement Administration**) DEA.

deacon ['diːkən] [di-kon], *s.* 1. Diácono. 2. Sobrestante de pobres en Escocia.

deaconry ['diːkənrɪ] [di-kon-ri], **deaconship** ['diːkənʃɪp] [di-kon-ship], *s.* Diaconato.

deactivate [diːˈæktɪveɪt] [di-ak-ti-veit], *va.* Desactivar.

dead [ded] [ded], *a.* 1. Muerto, sin vida (no longer alive). **He's dead,** está muerto. **Dead body,** cadáver, cuerpo sin vida. **He was dead on arrival at the hospital,** cuando llegó al hospital ya había muerto, ingresó cadáver. **To drop dead,** caerse muerto. **When I'm dead and gone,** cuando yo me muera. 2. (*Coloq.*) Muerto (very tired, ill); flojo, entorpecido, pesado. Dormido (numb). **To go dead,** dormirse (limb). **To be dead to something,** ser sordo a algo (unresponsive). 3. Vacío, lo que está desocupado; inútil estéril. 4. Apagado, sin fuego; (*Fig.*) sin espíritu. Desolado, despoblado; marchito, que no está animado. 5. Apagado, sin brillo; mate. 6. Sin variación, plano, monótono. 7. Completo, acabado, absoluto. Muerto (obsolete/language); en desuso (custom); pasado (past, finished with/issue); 8. Cierto, seguro, indudable. 9. No para ser contado. 10. Que no da luz; que no permite abrirse. Desconectado (not functioning/wire, circuit); desconectado, cortado (telephone); descargado (battery). **The line went dead,** se cortó la comunicación. Apagado (not alight/fire, match). Muerto (not busy/town, hotel, party). 11. Que no da movimiento; gastado, frío. 12. Sumido en el pecado. 13. (*For.*) Desprovisto de la vida civil. 14. (*Elec.*) Que no transmite corriente. 15. Que ya no fermenta. 16. Sin elasticidad: sin eco, no retumbante (un suelo, techo, etc.). 17. (*Tip.*) Material muerto o para distribuir. -*s.* 1. Personas muertas. **The dead,** los muertos. **In the** o (GB) **at the dead of night,** a altas horas de la noche o de la madrugada. 2. Silencio profundo; el centro o medio de alguna cosa. **A dead calm,** una calma profunda. (*Mar.*) Calma chicha. **A dead town,** una ciudad muerta, sin movimiento, sin animación. **A dead coal,** carbón apagado. **Dead-drunk,** borracho, hecho un cuero.

dead *adv.* 1. Justo (exactly). (GB) **She was dead on time,** llegó puntualísima. Justo, directamente (directly). **Dead ahead,** justo delante. **To stop dead,** parar en seco (suddenly). 2. (*Coloq.*) Completamente (absolutely/straight, level). **Dead slow,** lentísimo. **Dead tired,** muerto de cansancio, cansadísimo. **You're dead right,** tienes toda la razón. **To be dead certain/sure,** estar totalmente seguro. (*Sl.*) **It was dead easy,** estuvo regalado o tirado. **Dead boring/expensive,** aburridísimo/carísimo.

deadbeat ['dedˈbiːt] [ded-bit] *s.* (*Coloq.*) Vago, bueno para nada, flojo (lazy person); aprovechado, gorrón (scrounger).

deaden ['dedn] [de-den], *va.* 1. Amortiguar, amortecer, quitar las fuerzas o espíritu de alguna cosa (impact). 2. Retardar, disminuir la velocidad del movimiento. Reducir (noise, vibration); atenuar, aliviar (pain); insensibilizar (nerve); entorpecer (faculties). 3. Hacer incapaz de transmitir el sonido; como una pared o un piso. 4. Apagar o quitar el brillo, la viveza del colorido o del pulimento. 5. Hacer insípido (el vino, la cerveza).

dead end ['ded'end] [ded-end] s. Callejón sin salida. *(Coloq.)* **A dead-end job,** un trabajo sin porvenir o futuro.

dead head ['dedhed] [ded-jed] s. *(Coloq.)* Pánfilo.

dead-killing [ded'ki:lɪŋ] [ded-ki-lin], a. Que mata instantáneamente.

dead-letter office [dedletə'əfɪs] [ded-le-ta-o-fis], s. El departamento de la administración general de correos donde se examinan las cartas no reclamadas, para remitirlas a los que las franquearon o para destruirlas, según el caso.

dead lift ['dedlɪft] [ded-lift], s. El acto de alzar algo en peso, sin ayuda alguna; de aquí, esfuerzo inútil o hecho en condiciones adversas.

dead-lights ['dedlaɪts] [ded-laits], s. *(Mar.)* Postigos o portas de correr que se colocan exteriormente en las ventanas de popa.

deadline ['dedlaɪn] [ded-lain], s. 1. Fecha y hora de cierre de una publicación. 2. Límite de fecha para terminar alguna operación, transacción; plazo, término. **To meet a deadline,** entregar un trabajo dentro del plazo previsto.

deadliness ['dedlaɪnɪs] [ded-lai-nes], s. Peligro mortal; calidad de venenoso, destructivo o mortífero.

dead load ['dedloʊd] [ded-loud], s. Carga fija o permanente.

deadlock ['dedlɒk] [ded-lok], s. Paro, interrupción o estancamiento por desacuerdo. Punto muerto, impasse.

deadly ['dedlɪ] [ded-li], a. 1. Destructivo, mortal (fatal/disease, poison); mortífero (weapon); terrible, implacable. Enorme (seriousness); a muerte (enemy, rival). **A deadly silence,** un silencio sepulcral. 2. *(Coloq.)* Aburridísimo, terriblemente aburrido (dull). -adv. Mortalmente, implacablemente. Terriblemente (dull). **I'm deadly serious,** lo digo muy en serio. Se usa a veces como argumentativo.

deadness ['dednɪs] [ded-nes], s. Frío, frialdad, debilidad, flojedad, inercia; pérdida de vida; amortiguamiento.

dead-nettle ['dednetl] [ded-ne-tel], s. *(Bot.)* Ortiga muerta.

deadpan ['dedpæn] [ded-pan] a. De póquer o de palo (expression); deliberadamente inexpresivo (voice, delivery).

dead-reckoning ['dedrekənɪŋ] [ded-re-ko-nin], s. *(Mar.)* Estima, juicio que forma el piloto del camino que ha andado la embarcación y del paraje en que se halla, sin observación de los cuerpos celestes, y sólo por medio de la barquilla y corredera.

dead-rising ['dedraɪsɪŋ] [ded-rai-sin], s. *(Mar.)* Línea del arrufo del cuerpo principal.

Dead Sea ['dedsi:] [ded-si] s. El Mar Muerto.

dead-struck ['dedstrʌk] [ded-strak], a. Espantado, confundido, aterrado, anonadado.

dead water ['dedwɔ:tər] [ded-uo-tar], s. *(Mar.)* Reveses de las aguas de un bajel.

dead weight ['dedweɪt] [ded-ueit], s. 1. Peso muerto. 2. Carga onerosa.

deadwood ['ded'wʊd] [ded-wud], s. 1. Leña seca; ramas secas (dead branches). 2. Material inutilizable. 3. Miembros ineficientes de una organización. **To get rid of the deadwood among the staff,** sacarse de encima al personal inútil.

dead-work ['dedwɜ:k] [ded-uek], s. *(Mar.)* Obras muertas.

deaf [def] [def], a. Sordo, el que está privado del sentido del oído. **To make deaf,** aturdir, ensordecer, dejar sordo. **To turn a deaf ear,** hacerse el sordo. **Born deaf,** sordo de nacimiento. **Deaf and dumb,** sordomudo. **The deaf,** los sordos.

deaf, deafen [defn] [de-fen], va. Ensordar, ensordecer.

deaf-aid ['defeɪd] [def-eid] s. (GB) Audífono.

deafening [defnɪŋ] [def-nin] a. Ensordecedor.

deafly [deflɪ] [de-fli], adv. Sordamente; oscuramente.

deaf-mute [def'mju:t] [def-miut], s. Sordomudo; especialmente el que es mudo a causa de sordera.

deafness [defnɪs] [def-nes] s. Sordera.

deal [di:l] [dil], s. 1. Parte; cantidad indefinida, grado de más o menos, poco o mucho. **It makes a great/good deal of**

difference, cambia mucho/bastante las cosas. **I've given it a great deal of thought,** he reflexionado mucho sobre el asunto. **A great deal of money,** mucho dinero. 2. *(Games)* Mano, distribución de las cartas en juego. **It's my deal,** me toca a mí dar o repartir, doy o reparto yo. 3. Madera de pino, tabla, tabla de chilla. 4. *(E.U.)* Pacto o convenio secreto en la política o en el comercio, en provecho exclusivo de los interesados. Trato, acuerdo (agreement). **It's a deal!,** ¡trato hecho! *(Coloq.)* **What's the deal?,** ¿qué pasa?. Acuerdo (financial arrangement). **She got a very good deal when she left the company,** llegó a un buen arreglo económico al dejar la compañía. **You'll get a better deal if you shop around,** lo conseguirás más barato si vas a otras tiendas (bargain). **A great deal,** mucho. **A good deal,** bastante. **A great deal better,** mucho mejor.

deal, va. (pret. y pp. DEALT). 1. Distribuir, repartir, desparramar, esparcir, 2. Dar, hablando de repartir naipes en el juego (cards). -vn. 1. Traficar, comerciar, tratar, negociar. 2. Intervenir, mediar. 3. Portarse bien o mal en cualquier asunto. 4. *(Games)* Dar, repartir. **To deal in contraband goods,** hacer contrabando. **To deal in all sorts of commodities,** comerciar en todo género de mercancías. **To deal with,** tratar con; contender con. **To deal by,** portarse, conducirse de cierto modo; usar de. **To deal in,** mezclarse en, ocuparse en; usar de; comerciar en.

deal in *(Neg.)* Dedicarse a la compra y venta de, comerciar en.

deal out Repartir, distribuir (gifts, money). **The punishment that was dealt out to them,** el castigo que se les aplicó o impuso.

deal with 1. Tener relaciones comerciales con (do business with/company). **I prefer to deal with her,** yo prefiero tratar con ella. **To deal fairly with somebody,** tratar a alguien con justicia (behave toward). 2. Ocuparse de, atender (tackle, handle/complaint); manejar (situation). **The problem must be dealt with now,** hay que ocuparse del o hay que resolver el problema ahora mismo. **I know how to deal with him,** yo sé cómo tratarlo. **Let me deal with her,** yo me encargo de ella. Ocuparse o encargarse de (be responsible for). **Your mother will deal with you,** ya te las verás con tu madre (punish). 3. Tratar (issue/discuss, treat); tratar de (have as subject).

dealbate ['di:lbeɪt] [dil-beit], a. *(Bot.)* Blanqueado; cubierto con polvo blanco.

dealer ['di:lər] [di-lar], s. 1. Interventor. 2. Comerciante, mercader, negociante, traficante (trader). **A dealer in livestock,** un consignatario o tratante de ganado. **She's a car dealer,** se dedica a la compra-venta de coches. **Drug dealer,** traficante de drogas. 3. *(Games)* **The dealer,** el que da las cartas en el juego; repartidor. *(Fin.)* Corredor de bolsa o de valores. **Plain-dealer,** hombre sincero. **False dealer,** hombre doble. **Double-dealer,** hombre de dos caras, engañador; que come a dos carrillos.

dealership ['di:ləʃɪp] [di-ler-ship] s. Concesión, representación.

dealing ['di:lɪŋ] [di-lin], s. 1. Modo de obrar o proceder, conducta (business methods). **Honest dealing,** hombre de bien. 2. Trato, comunicación. 3. Tráfico, comercio, negocio (trafficking). (GB) Transacciones (on stock exchange). 4. pl. Negocios relaciones de adquisición y de venta; relaciones, trato. **The company has dealings with the Far East,** la compañía tiene negocios en el Lejano Oriente. **Fair dealing,** buena fe. **Foul dealing,** doblez.

dealt [delt] [delt], pret. y pp. de TO DEAL. **Easy to be dealt with,** tratable, fácil de contentar. **Hard to be dealt,** descontentadizo.

dean [di:n] [din], s. 1. Deán, dignidad eclesiástica. En la iglesia católica el cabeza del cabildo después del obispo. 2. Decano de un colegio o universidad, o de una facultad.

deanery ['di:nərɪ] [di-ne-ri], **deanship,** s. Decanato.

dear [dɪəʳ] [diaʳ], *a.* 1. Querido (loved); predilecto, caro, amado. **Dear (old) Jane,** la buena de Jane. **Memories that are very dear to him,** recuerdos que le son muy queridos o que significan mucho para él. 2. Caro, costoso (expensive). **Was it very dear?,** ¿te costó muy caro? 3. Escaso; difícil de hallar. 4. *(Des.)* Peligroso, fatal. **A dear creature,** buena alhaja. 5. Adorable (lovable). **He's such a dear little thing!,** ¡es una ricura o monada de niño! **Dear Mr. Jones,** estimado Sr. Jones. **Dear Jimmy,** querido Jimmy (in letter writing). *s.* 1. Querido, voz expresiva de cariño (as form of address). **My dear,** querido mío, querida mía. **Dear me!,** ¡de veras! ¡cierto! ¡Dios mío! ¡Válgame Dios! 2. *(Coloq.)* **He's such a dear,** es un ángel o un cielo. *interj.* **Oh, dear!,** ¡ay!, ¡qué cosa!

dear-bought [ˌdɪəˈbɔʊt] [dia-bot], *a.* Caro, lo que ha costado mucho.

dear-loved [ˌdɪəˈlʌvd] [dia-lavd], *a.* Muy amado.

dearly [ˈdɪəlɪ] [dia-li], *adv.* 1. Caramente, tiernamente, cariñosamente, amorosamente. **I love him dearly,** lo quiero mucho o de verdad. *(Rel.)* **Dear beloved,** amados hermanos (as form of address). 2. Caro (at great cost). **He paid dearly for his generosity,** pagó cara su generosidad.

dearness [ˈdɪənɪs] [diar-nes], *s.* 1. Cariño, amor, afecto, benevolencia. 2. Carestía, el precio muy subido de las cosas.

dearth [dɜːθ] [derz], *s.* 1. Carestía. 2. Hambre, carestía y falta de bastimentos; esterilidad.

dearticulate [ˌdɪəˈtɪˈkjʊleɪt] [diar-ti-kiu-leit], *va.* Desmembrar, desunir, separar.

deary [ˈdɪərɪ] [dia-ri], *s.* Expresión de cariño; queridito.

death [deθ] [dez], *s.* 1. Muerte, fallecimiento, mortalidad. **He died a horrible death,** tuvo una muerte horrible. **To put somebody to death,** ejecutar a alguien. **At death's door,** a las puertas de la muerte. **To be the death of somebody,** acabar con alguien. 2. Mortandad, estrago causado por la muerte. 3. Asesinato. 4. Condenación, muerte eterna. **At the point of death,** a las puertas de la muerte. **On pain of death,** bajo pena de muerte. **To grieve oneself to death,** morirse de pesadumbre.

deathbed [ˈdeθbed] [dez-bed], *s.* Lecho de muerte; agonía. In extremis, in artículo mortis (confession).

death blow [ˈdeθblə] [dez-blo] *s.* Golpe mortal.

death-boding [ˈdeθbədɪŋ] [dez-bo-din], *a.* Lo que pronostica la muerte.

death certificate [deθˈsɜːtɪfɪkeɪt] [dez-ser-ti-fi-keit] *s.* Certificado de defunción.

death dealing [ˈdeθdiːlɪŋ] [dez-di-lin] *a.* Mortífero.

death duties [ˈdeθdɪʊtɪs] [dez-diu-tis] *s. pl.* (GB) Impuesto sobre sucesiones o a la herencia.

deathful [ˈdeθfʊl] [dez-ful], *a.* Mortal, mortífero.

deathfulness [ˈdeθfʊlnɪs] [dez-ful-nes], *s.* Apariencia de muerte.

deathless [ˈdeθlɪs] [dez-les], *a.* Inmortal.

deathlike [ˈdeθlaɪk] [dez-laik], *a.* Quedo, inmóvil, silencioso como la muerte; letárgico; cadavérico.

deathly [ˈdeθlɪ] [dez-li] *a.* De muerte, sepulcral (silence); cadavérico (pallor). *adv.* **She looked deathly white/pale,** estaba blanca como el/un papel, estaba lívida.

death penalty [deθˈpenəltɪ] [dez-pe-nal-ti] *s.* **The death penalty,** la pena de muerte.

death row [ˈdeθrɔː] [dez-rou] *s.* Pabellón de los condenados a muerte, corredor de la muerte.

death's door [ˈdeθsdɔːʳ] [dezs-doʳ] *s. (Fam.)* Las puertas de la muerte, cercanía a la muerte; agonía. **He has been at death's door,** ha estado en las garras de la muerte, al borde de la tumba.

death-shadowed [deθˈʃədəʊd] [dez-sha-doud], *a.* Rodeado de las sombras de la muerte.

death's-head [ˈdeθshed] [dezs-jed], *s.* Calavera, armazón de los huesos de la cabeza. **Death's-head moth,** atropos mariposa «cabeza de muerto».

death's-man [ˈdeθsmæn] [dezs-man] *s.* Verdugo. **Man of death,** asesino.

death squad [ˈdeθskɔd] [dez-skuod] *s.* Escuadrón de la muerte.

death throes [deθˈθruːs] [dez-zrus] *s. pl.* Agonía. **To be in one's death throes,** agonizar.

death-token [deθˈtəʊkən] [dez-tou-ken], *s.* Presagio de muerte.

death toll [ˈdeθtɔːl] [dez-tol] *s.* Número de víctimas mortales o de muertos.

death trap [ˈdeθtræp] [dez-trap] *s.* Edificio, vehículo, etc. muy poco seguro.

deathward [ˈdeθwɔːd] [dez-uord], *adv.* A la muerte.

death-warrant [ˈdeθwərənt] [dez-ua-rant], *s.* 1. Orden oficial para la ejecución de un reo; sentencia de muerte. 2. El fin de toda esperanza.

deathwatch [ˈdeθwɔtʃ] [dez-uach], *s.* 1. Últimas horas pasadas acompañando a un moribundo; velación de un cadáver. 2. Guardia que se pone a vigilar al reo antes de su ejecución.

deathwatch *s. (Ento.)* Carcoma; anobio, insecto coleóptero que produce un sonido acompasado parecido al tic-tac de un reloj y al que los supersticiosos consideran como precursor de próxima muerte.

death-wound [ˈdeθwʊnd] [dez-vund], *s.* Herida mortal.

deaurate [ˈdeəreɪt] [deo-reit], *va.* Dorar.

deaurate, *a. (Ento.)* Dorado.

debacle [deɪˈbaːkl] [dei-bakol], *s.* Desbordamiento de las aguas fuera de sus límites naturales. 2. Terror pánico; caída, ruina. Debacle, descalabro.

debar [dɪˈbaːʳ] [di-baʳ], *va.* Excluir, no admitir, privar, prohibir. **The fact that she didn't have a degree debarred her from promotion,** el hecho de no tener un título universitario le impedía ascender. **He was debarred from taking his final exam,** se le prohibió rendir el examen final.

debark [dɪˈbaːk] [di-bark], *va.* Desembarcar. V. DISEMBARK.

debarkation [dɪˈbaːkeɪʃən] [di-bar-kei-shon], *s.* Desembarco.

debase [dɪˈbeɪs] [di-beis], *va.* 1 Abatir, deprimir, humillar, envilecer, degradar, deshonrar (devalue/ideal, principle); corromper, viciar (language); degradar, rebajar (demean/person). 2. Adulterar, viciar, falsificar, alterar.

debasement [dɪˈbeɪsmənt] [di-beis-ment], *s.* Abatimiento, envilecimiento; adulteración, falsificación.

debaser [dɪˈbeɪsəʳ] [di-bei-saʳ], *s.* El que abate o envilece; falsificador.

debatable [dɪˈbeɪtəbl] [di-bei-ta-bol], *a.* Disputable; discutido, sujeto a controversia.

debate [dɪˈbeɪt] [di-beit], *s.* 1. Discusión, debate, contienda, disputa, contestación, controversia (discussion); debate (public, parliamentary). 2. *(Des.)* Querella, conflicto. *va.* Debatir, discutir (question, topic, motion); darle vueltas a, considerar (weigh up/idea, possibility).

debateful [dɪˈbeɪtfʊl] [di-beit-ful], *a.* Litigioso; reñido.

debatefully [dɪˈbeɪtfʊlɪ] [di-beit-fu-li], *adv.* Litigiosamente.

debater [dɪˈbeɪtəʳ] [di-bei-taʳ], *s.* Controversista, el que debate.

debating [dɪˈbeɪtɪŋ] [di-bei-tin] *s.* Discusión. **Debating society,** círculo de debate y discusión.

debauch [dɪˈbɔːtʃ] [di-boch], *va.* 1. Corromper, viciar, relajar, pervertir, estragar. 2. Corromper o seducir a una doncella; sobornar o sonsacar criados, dependientes, etc.

debauch, *s.* 1. Exceso, desorden, desarreglo, especialmente en comer y beber. 2. Vida disoluta, el vicio de la lujuria.

debauched [dɪˈbɔːtʃt] [di-bocht] *a.* Vicioso, libertino.

debauchedly [dɪˈbɔːtʃflɪ] [di-boch-li], *adv.* Licenciosamente, de una manera disoluta.

debauchedness [dɪˈbɔːtʃnɪs] [di-boch-nes], *s.* Intemperancia, lascivia.

debauchee [dɪˈbɔːtʃiː] [di-bo-chi], *s.* Hombre libertino, disoluto, licencioso, desarreglado, relajado.

debaucher [dɪˈbɔːtʃər] [di-bo-chaʳ], *s.* Seductor, corrompedor.

debauchery [dɪˈbɔːtʃrɪ] [di-bo-che-ri], *s.* Disolución, libertinaje, desorden, licencia, relajación. **To lead a life of debauchery,** llevar una vida disipada o disoluta.

debauchment [dɪˈbɔːtʃmənt] [di-boch-ment], *s.* Corrupción, corrompimiento.

debenture [dɪˈbentʃər] [di-ben-chaʳ], *s.* *(Com.)* 1. Vale, acción, obligación, papel que hace constar el crédito que uno tiene contra otro y en cuya virtud lo reclama. 2. Remisión o restitución de los derechos al tiempo de exportar los géneros que se han importado anteriormente. 3. Orden de pago del gobierno.

debile [ˈdɪbɪl] [di-bil], *a.* Débil.

debilitate [dɪˈbɪlɪteɪt] [di-bi-li-teit], *va.* Debilitar, extenuar, enervar.

debilitating [dɪˈbɪlɪteɪtɪŋ] [di-bi-li-tei-tin] *a.* Debilitante (disease); extenuante (climate). **Her debilitating shyness,** su timidez enfermiza.

debilitation [dɪˈbɪlɪteɪʃən] [di-bi-li-tei-shon] *s.* Debilitación, extenuación.

debility [dɪˈbɪlɪtɪ] [di-bi-li-ti], *s.* Debilidad, extenuación, imbecilidad, languidez.

debit [ˈdebɪt] [de-bit], *s.* Balance o alcance; débito, cargo. **Debit balance,** saldo deudor. **Debit card,** tarjeta de cobro automático. **Debit note,** nota de cargo.

debit *va. (Fin.)* Adeudar, cargar.

debit balance [ˈdebɪtˌbələns] [de-bit-ba-lans], *s.* Saldo deudor.

debonair [ˌdebəˈnɛər] [de-bo-neaʳ], *a.* Garboso, cortés, afable (courteous); urbano, bien criado; elegante, desenvuelto (suave); político, honrado, dulce, complaciente.

debonairness [ˈdebənɛnɪs] [de-bo-near-nes], *s.* Civilidad, cortesía.

debouch [dɪˈbaʊtʃ] [di-bauch], *va.* Desembocar, descargar; salir.

debouchure [dɪˈbaʊtʃər] [di-bau-chaʳ], *s.* Salida, boca de un desfiladero. etc. *(Fr.)*

debrief [ˌdiːˈbriːf] [di-brif] *va.* **He was debriefed by his captain,** rindió informe o dio parte de su misión al capitán.

debriefing [ˌdiːˈbriːfɪŋ] [di-bri-fin] *s.* **They were sent for debriefing,** los llamaron para que rindiesen informe o diesen parte de su misión.

debris [ˈdebriː] [de-bri], *s.* 1. Restos, ruinas. Escombros (rubble); restos (of plane, ship); desechos (rubbish). 2. *(Geol.)* Despojos, detritos, restos de las rocas.

debt [debt] [debt], *s.* 1. Deuda o débito; endeudamiento (indebtedness). **I'm $200 in debt,** debo 200 dólares, tengo deudas por 200 dólares. **To be in somebody's debt/in debt to somebody,** estarle en deuda a alguien, estar en deuda con alguien. **To get/be out of debt,** salir de/no tener deudas. Deuda (money owning). **Foreign debt,** deuda externa. **A debt of honor,** una deuda de honor. 2. Obligación, lo que uno debe hacer por buena correspondencia. **A small debt,** deudilla. **Debt collector,** cobrador de deudas o de morosos.

debted, *a. V.* INDEBTED.

debtless [ˈdebtlɪs] [debt-les], *a.* Sin deuda o débito.

debtor [ˈdebtər] [deb-taʳ], *s.* 1. Deudor. 2. Cargo, el lado de las cuentas en que se sientan las partidas que debe una persona.

debug [diːˈbʌg] [di-bag] *va.* 1. *(Inform.)* Depurar. 2. Localizar y retirar los micrófonos de (room, building).

debunk [diːˈbʌŋk] [di-bank] *va. (Coloq.)* Desacreditar.

début [ˈdeɪbuː] [dei-bu], *s.* Estreno de actor, cantatriz, etc.; primer paso, entrada en la sociedad. **To make one's début,** debutar, hacer su debut (on stage, etc.).

débutant, *m.* **débutante** [ˈdeɪbuːtənt] [dei-bu-tant] *f.* Principiante, el que se presenta al público por primera vez.

decade [ˈdekeɪd] [di-keid] *s.* 1. Decenio, curso de diez años. 2. Década, decena.

decadence, decadency [ˈdekədəns] [de-ka-dens], *s.* Decadencia, descaecimiento.

decadent [ˈdekədənt] [de-ka-dent] *a.* Decadente.

decaffeinated [ˌdiːˈkæfɪneɪtɪd] [di-ka-fi-nei-tid] *a.* Descafeinado.

decagon [ˈdiːkægən] [di-ka-gon], *s. (Geom.)* Decágono.

decagram, decagrame [ˈdekəgræm] [de-ka-gram], *s.* Decagramo, peso de diez gramos.

decahedron [ˌdɪkəˈiːdrən] [di-ka-i-dron], *s.* Decaedro, figura que tiene diez caras planas.

decal [dɪkl] [d-kal] *s.* Calcomanía.

decaliter, decalitre [ˈdekəˌliːtər] [di-ka-li-taʳ], *s.* Decalitro, medida de diez litros.

decalogist [deˈkɔlədʒɪst] [de-ka-lo-yist], *s.* Decalogista, expositor del decálogo.

decalogue [ˈdekəlɒg] [de-ka-log], *s.* Decálogo, los diez mandamientos de la ley de Dios dados a Moisés.

decameter, decametre [ˈdekəmiːtər] [di-ka-mi-taʳ], *s.* Decámetro, medida de diez metros.

decamp [dɪˈkæmp] [di-kamp], *vn.* 1. *(Mil.)* Decampar, levantar el campo; mudar un ejército de campamento. 2. Escapar, tomar las de Villadiego, poner pies en polvorosa. Esfumarse, hacerse humo (abscond, hum).

decampment [dɪˈkæmpmənt] [di-kamp-ment], *s.* El acto de levantar un campo o campamento; la acción de decampar.

decanal [dɪˈkænəl] [di-ka-nal], *a.* Lo que pertenece al decanato.

decant [dɪˈkænt] [di-kant], *va.* Decantar, mudar los licores u otros líquidos de una vasija a otra, quedando las heces en la primera; trasegar.

decantation [dɪˈkænteɪʃən] [di-kan-tei-shon], *s.* Decantación; trasiego.

decanter [dɪˈkæntər] [di-kan-taʳ], *s.* 1. Botella par el vino, etc. de cristal, garrafa adornada. 2. Vaso para líquidos trasegados.

decapitate [dɪˈkæpɪteɪt] [di-ka-pi-teit], *va.* Degollar, decapitar.

decapitation [dɪˌkæpɪˈteɪʃən] [di-ka-pi-tei-shon], *s.* Decagüello, decapitación.

decapod [dɪˈkæpɒd] [di-ka-pod], *s.* Decápodo, crustáceo que tiene diez patas.

decarbonize, decarburize [diːˈkɑːbənaɪz] [di-kar-bo-nais], *va.* Descarbonizar, descarburar.

decasyllable [ˈdekəsɪləbl] [de-ka-si-la-bol], *s.* Decasílabo, línea o verso de diez sílabas.

decathlon [dɪˈkæθlən] [di-ka-zlon] *s.* Decatlón.

decay [dɪˈkeɪ] [di-kei], *vn.* 1. Decaer, descaecer, declinar (empire, culture, civilization); empeorar, ir a menos; deteriorarse (deteriorate/building, machine); pudrir, degenerar, pasarse, marchitarse. 2. Descomponerse, pudrirse (rot/foodstuffs, corpse); pudrirse (wood); cariarse, picarse (tooth). *-va.* Arruinar, destruir, echar a perder. Descomponer (rot/food, corpse). Pudrir (wood); picar, cariar (tooth).

decay, *s.* 1. Descaecimiento, menoscabo, decadencia, declinación, caimiento, disminución; pobreza. 2. Deterioro (of building); decadencia (of culture). 3. Descomposición (of organic matter); caries (tooth decay).

decayer [dɪˈkeɪər] [di-keiaʳ], *s.* Lo que produce decadencia.

decaying [dɪˈkeɪɪŋ] [di-keiin], *s.* Decadencia.

decease [dɪˈsiːs] [di-sis], *s.* Muerte, fallecimiento.

decease *vn.* Morir, fallecer.

deceased [dɪˈsiːst] [di-síst], *a.* Difunto, muerto, fallecido. - *s.* Finado, difunto, fallecido. **Her deceased husband,** su difunto marido. **William Jones, deceased,** el difunto Willian Jones.

decedent [ˈdɪsɪdənt] [di-si-dent], *s. (For.)* Una persona fallecida, y en especial una persona cuyos bienes están en manos de un administrador.

deceit [dɪˈsiːt] [di-sit], *s.* 1. Engaño, dolo, fraude, falacia; impostura, superchería. 2. Artificio, treta, estratagema.

deceitful [dɪˈsiːtfʊl] [di-sit-ful], *a.* Fraudulento, engañoso (action); falso, embustero (person); ilusorio, falaz.

deceitfully [dɪˈsiːtfʊlɪ] [di-sit-fu-li], *adv.* Fraudulentamente, falsamente.

deceitfulness [dɪˈsiːtfʊlnɪs] [di-sit-ful-nes], *s.* Falsedad; atractivos falaces.

deceivable [dɪˈsiːvəbl] [di-si-va-bol], *a.* 1. Engañadizo, bobalicón. 2. Engañoso.

deceive [dɪˈsiːv] [di-siv], *va.* Engañar, alucinar, burlar; defraudar; privar de toda esperanza. **He was deceived by her story,** se dejó engañar por lo que le contó. **To deceive oneself,** engañarse.

deceiver [dɪˈsiːvəʳ] [di-si-vaʳ], *s.* Engañador, impostor.

deceiving [dɪˈsiːvɪŋ] [di-si-vin], *a.* Engañador.

decelerate [dɪˈseləreɪt] [di-se-le-reit] *vn.* Reducir o aminorar la velocidad (vehicle, driver).

deceleration [ˈdiːˌseləˈreɪʃən] [di-se-la-rei-shon], *s.* Deceleración, desceleración.

December [dɪˈsembəʳ] [di-sem-baʳ], *s.* 1. Diciembre, el último mes del año. 2. *(Fig.)* Época de decadencia; vejez.

decempedal [dɪˈsempedəl] [di-sem-pe-dal], *a.* 1. Que tiene diez patas. 2. *(Des.)* Lo que tiene diez pies de largo.

decemvir [dɪˈsemvɪʳ] [di-sem-viʳ], *s. (pl.* VIRS [verz] o VIRI [Vi-rai]). 1. Decenviro, uno de los diez magistrados superiores de la antigua Roma. 2. Miembro de un cuerpo cualquiera compuesto de diez personas.

decemvirate [dɪˈsemvɪːreɪt] [di-sem-vi-reit], *s.* Decemvirato.

decency [ˈdiːsənsɪ] [di-sen-si] *s.* 1. Decencia, decoro, adorno (of dress, conduct); buena educación, consideración (propriety). **She didn't even have the decency to ask me,** ni siquiera tuvo la consideración de preguntarme. 2. Recato, modestia, decoro; propiedad. 3. **Decencies,** *pl.* **To observe the decencies,** guardar las formas (proper conduct).

decennary [dɪˈsenərɪ] [di-se-na-ri], *a.* Que contiene diez, o pertenece al diezmo.

decennial [dɪˈsenɪəl] [di-si-nial], *a.* Decenal, lo que comprende o dura diez años; que sucede cada diez años.

decent [ˈdiːsənt] [di-sent], *a.* 1. Decente, decoroso, razonable (appropriate/language, conduct, dress); acomodado, propio, conveniente. **Are you decent?,** ¿estás presentable? **To do the decent thing,** hacer lo que corresponde o es correcto. Decente (respectable). 2. Pasable, aceptable (acceptable/person); decente, como es debido (meal, housing). 3. Amable (kind). **He's being very decent about it all,** se está portando muy bien.

decently [ˈdiːsəntlɪ] [di-sent-li], *adv.* 1. Decentemente, con decencia (respectably/dress, behave). **We couldn't recently refuse,** hubiera sido descortés o una descortesía el no aceptar (reasonably). 2. Bastante bien (acceptably/perform, cook). 3. Amablemente (kindly).

decentness [ˈdiːsəntnɪs] [di-sent-nes], *s.* Decencia, modestia, decoro; propiedad.

decentralization [diːˌsentr@laɪˈzeIS@n] [di-sen-tra-lai-sei-shon], *s.* Descentralización.

decentralize [ˈdiːsentrəlaɪz] [di-sen-tra-lais], *va.* Descentralizar.

deception [dɪˈsepʃən] [di-sepshon] *s.* Decepción, engaño, impostura, superchería, dolo, fraude; charlatanería. **To obtain something by deception,** obtener algo mediante o valiéndose de engaños.

deceptive [dɪˈseptɪv] [di-sep-tiv], *a.* Falaz, engañoso. **Appearances can be deceptive,** las apariencias engañan.

deceptively [dɪˈseptɪvlɪ] [di-sep-tiv-li], *adv.* Falsamente, de una manera engañosa. **It's deceptively simple,** es aparentemente simple.

decern [dɪˈsɜːn] [di-sern], *va.* 1. *(For., Esco)* Juzgar, decretar. 2. *(Des.)* V. DISCERN.

decharm [dɪˈtʃɑːm] [di-charm], *va.* Desencantar.

decibel [ˈdesɪbel] [de-si-bel] *s. (Fis.)* Decibel, decibelio.

decidable [dɪˈsaɪdəbl] [di-sai-da-bol], *a.* Decidible.

decide [dɪˈsaɪd] [di-said], *va. y vn.* 1. Decidir (make up one's mind); determinar, resolver, juzgar. **I can't decide which I prefer,** no puedo decidir cuál prefiero, no sé por cual

decidirme. **What finally decided me was the price,** lo que me decidió o me hizo decidir fue el precio. 2. Acabar o poner término a alguna cosa. Decidir (settle/ question, issue); determinar (outcome). 3. Sentenciar algún caso, duda, cuestión o pleito. 4. Decidirse. **We decided in favor of the cheaper one,** nos decidimos por el más barato. **She decided against buying,** decidió no comprarlo.

decide on, decide upon Decidir (date/venue); decidirse por (candidate).

decided [dɪˈsaɪdɪd] [di-sai-did], *a.* 1. Decidido (determined/ character, tone); terminado, resuelto, incontestable, indudable. 2. Claro, marcado (definite/improvement, advantage).

decidedly [dɪˈsaɪdɪdlɪ] [di-sai-did-li], *adv.* 1. Decididamente (definitely); con decisión (determinedly/speak, act). 2. Determinadamente. 3. Indudablemente.

decider [dɪˈsaɪdəʳ] [di-sai-daʳ], *s.* 1. árbitro, determinante. *(Dep.)* El partido de desempate (match); el tanto decisivo (point, goal).

deciding [dɪˈsaɪdɪŋ] [di-sai-din] *a.* Decisivo (factor).

deciduous [dɪˈsɪdjʊəs] [di-si-duos], *a.* Deciduo, decedente, que se desprende y cae algún tiempo después de su desarrollo; sujeto a desprenderse en épocas periódicas, v.g. las hojas, los cuernos, los dientes, etc.; de hoja caduca.

deciduousness [dɪˈsɪdjʊəsnɪs] [di-si-duos-nes], *s.* La facilidad en ser caedizo o en caer; la caída de las hojas en el otoño.

decigram, decigramme [ˈdesɪɡræm] [de-si-gram], *s.* Decigramo, peso de un décimo de gramo: cerca de 1.54 gramos.

deciliter, decilitre [ˈdesɪˌlɪtəʳ] [de-si-li-taʳ], *s* Decilitro, medida de un décimo de litro.

decimal [ˈdesɪməl] [de-si-mal], *a.* Decimal, cuya base es diez; lo que se aumenta o disminuye por decenas. **Accurate to three decimal places,** exacto hasta la tercera cifra decimal. -*s.* Decimal, fracción decimal.

decimalization [ˌdesɪmələɪˈzeɪʃən] [de-si-ma-lai-sei-shon] *s,* Decimalización, conversión al sistema decimal.

decimalize [ˈdesɪmələɪz] [de-si-ma-lais] *va.* Decimalizar, convertir al sistema decimal.

decimally [ˈdesɪməlɪ] [de-si-ma-li], *adv.* Por decenas; por medio de los decimales.

decimal point [ˈdesɪməlˌpɔɪnt] [de-si-mal-point] *s.* Coma decimal o de los decimales; punto decimal.

decimate [ˈdesɪmeɪt] [de-si-meit], *va.* 1 Matar uno de cada diez; *(Fam.)* destruir gran parte de una población. 2. *(Des.)* Diezmar.

decimation [ˌdesɪˈmeɪʃən] [de-si-mei-shon], La acción y efecto de matar uno de cada diez; gran destrucción.

decimator [ˈdesɪmeɪtəʳ] [de-si-mei-taʳ], *s.* Gran destructor.

decimeter, decimetre [ˈdesɪˌmiːtəʳ] [de-si-mi-taʳ] *s.* Decímetro, la décima parte de un metro.

decipher [dɪˈsaɪfəʳ] [di-sai-faʳ], *va.* 1. Descifrar. 2. Cifrar, poner en cifra. 3. Estampar o señalar con caracteres. 4. Desenrollar, desembrollar, desenmarañar. 5. Aclarar o interpretar lo que está oscuro, describir lo oculto, explicar lo dudoso.

decipherable [dɪˈsaɪfərəbl] [di-sai-fe-ra-bol], *a.* Descifrable, que se puede descifrar o aclarar.

decipherer [dɪˈsaɪfərəʳ] [di-sai-fe-raʳ], *s.* Descifrador.

decision [dɪˈsɪʒən] [di-si-shon], *s.* 1. Decisión, determinación, resolución. **To make/take a decision,** tomar una decisión. **On/by a decision**

decision-making [dɪˈsɪʒənˌmeɪkɪŋ] [di-si-shon-mei-kin] *s.* Toma de decisiones; decisorio (body/process).

decisive [dɪˈsaɪsɪv] [di-sai-siv] *a.* 1. Decisivo (conclusive/battel, factor); conclusivo, terminante, contundente (victory). 2. Decidido, resuelto (purposeful, person); firme (lidership, answer).

decisively [dɪˈsaɪsɪvlɪ] [di-sai-siv-li], *adv.* Decisivamente; contundentemente (convincingly/beat, win); con decisión (purposefully/speak, act).

decisiveness [dɪˈsaɪsɪvnɪs] [di-sai-siv-nes], *s.* Autoridad decisiva.

decisory [dɪˈsaɪsərɪ] [di-sai-so-ri], *a.* Decisorio, decisivo.

deck [dek] [dek], *va.* 1. Cubrir. 2. Ataviar, componer, asear, adornar, embellecer. **To deck something (out) with something,** engalanar o adornar algo con algo (adorn). **He was all decked out in his Sunday best,** iba muy endomingado, iba de punta en blanco. 3. *(Coloq.)* Tumbar (knock dowm).

deck *s.* 1. *(Mar.)* Cubierta, cada uno de los suelos que dividen las estancias de un buque. **Between decks,** entre puentes. 2. Tejado de un coche o carro. 3. *(Min.)* Plataforma de jaula. 4. *(Games)* Baraja, el conjunto de cartas de que consta el juego de naipes. *(Inform.)* Lote, paquete. 5. (GB) Piso (of bus) **Gun-deck,** cubierta principal, batería. **On deck,** sobre cubierta. **Quarter-deck,** alcázar, castillo de proa. **Spardeck,** cubierta alta o de guindaste. **Deck-hand,** estibador en buque de vapor, marinero. **To be on deck,** estar esperando turno, estar en el círculo de espera (in baseball); estar a mano (ready, to hand). **Let's clear the decks before we start the new project,** despejemos el camino antes de embarcarnos en el nuevo proyecto. *(Sl.)* **To hit the deck,** caerse al suelo (fall flat).

deck chair [ˈdek,tʃɛər] [dek-chear], *s.* Silla de cubierta (en un barco); silla de playa, perezosa, reposera.

decker [ˈdekər] [de-kar], *s.* 1. Cubridor, adornador, aseador. 2. Navío, carro, etc., con cubierta; se usa solamente en composición. **A two-decker,** navío de dos puentes.

decking [ˈdekɪŋ] [de-kin], *s.* Adorno.

deckle [dekl] [de-kel], *s.* 1. En la fabricación de papel, cubierta, bastidor rectangular. 2. Banda de caucho flexible y continua. 3. Barba, borde sin cortar del papel hecho a mano.

declaim [dɪˈkleɪm] [di-kleim], *va.* Recitar en público. *-vn.* 1. Declamar, recitar de una manera oratoria, arengar. 2. Recitar (de memoria).

declaimer [dɪˈkleɪmər] [di-klei-mar] *s.* Declamador.

declaiming [dɪˈkleɪmɪŋ] [di-klei-min] *s.* Arenga, oración.

declamation [ˌdekləˈmeɪʃən] [de-kla-mei-shon] *s.* Declamación, arenga.

declamatory [dɪˈklæmətərɪ] [di-kla-ma-to-ri] *a.* Declamatorio.

declarable [ˈdekləreɪbl] [de-kla-rei-bol] *a.* Lo que se puede declarar.

declaration [ˌdekləˈreɪʃən] [de-kla-rei-shon] *s.* 1. Declaración (statement); manifestación, publicación; explicación, exposición. **A customs declaration,** una declaración de aduanas. 2. *(Law)* Pronunciamiento oficial (finding); declaración (statement).

declarative [deˈklərətɪv] [di-kla-ra-tiv] *a.* Declaratorio, expositivo.

declaratorily [deˈklərətərɪlɪ] [de-kla-ra-to-ri-li] *adv.* En forma de declaración.

declaratory [deˈklərətərɪ] [de-kla-ra-to-ri] *a.* Declaratorio; afirmativo, demostrativo.

declare [dɪˈkleər] [di-klear] *va.* 1. Declarar, (state, announce/intention); manifestar (opinion). **To declare war,** declarar la guerra. **The museum was oficially declared open,** el museo fue inaugurado oficialmente. Declarar (tax, goods, income). **Nothing to declare,** nada que declarar. 2. Publicar, proclamar. 3. Afirmar, asegurar, confesar. *-vn.* 1. Declarar, deponer, testificar; decidirse en favor de. **To declare for/against somebody/something,** declararse o pronunciarse a favor/en contra de alguien/algo. 2. Anunciar su (o mi, etc.) candidatura.

declared [dɪˈkleəd] [di-kleard] *a.* Declarado (aim, motive).

declaredly [dɪˈkleədlɪ] [di-klead-li] *adv.* Declaradamente, deponente.

declarer [dɪˈkleərər] [di-klea-rar], *s.* Declarador, declarante, deponente.

declaring [dɪˈkleərɪŋ] [di-klea-rin], *s.* Declaración.

declension [dɪˈklenʃən] [di-klen-shon] *s.* 1. Declinación, decadencia, caimiento, disminución, decremento, menoscabo. 2. *(Gram.)* Declinación, la serie de los casos del nombre. 3. Inclinación, oblicuidad, declivio.

declinable [dɪˈklaɪnəbl] [di-klai-na-bol] *a.* Declinable.

declination [ˌdɪklaɪˈneɪʃən] [di-klai-nei-shon] *s.* 1. Declinación; descenso, declive; inclinación. 2. Decadencia, decremento; desvío. 3. *(Mar.)* declinación de la aguja de marear, lo que la aguja se aparta de la dirección al polo hacia oriente o poniente. 4. *(Gram.)* Declinación. 5. Negativa: falta de aceptación excusa.

declinator [dɪˈklaɪneɪtər] [di-klai-nei-tar], **Declinatory** *s.* Declinatorio, instrumento para medir el ángulo de declinación.

declinatory [dɪˈklaɪnətərɪ] [di-klai-na-to-ri] *a.* Que envuelve o lleva excusa. **Declinatory plea,** *(For.)* Declinatoria.

decline [dɪˈklaɪn] [di-klain] *va.* 1. Rehusar, rechazar, repulsar (refuse/offer, invitation). **He declined to comment,** declinó hacer declaraciones. 2. Inclinar una cosa hacia abajo, bajarla. 3. *(Gram.)* Declinar. 4. *(Ant.)* Huir, evitar. *-vn.* 1. Rehusar, rechazar (refuse). **I invited him, but he declined,** lo invité pero rehusó o declinó mi invitación. 2. Declinar, inclinarse hacia abajo. 3. Decaer, desmejorar. 4. Huir, eludir, desviar. 5. Disminuir, decrecer (decrease/ production, strength); disminuir, decaer (interest). **To decline in importance,** perder importancia. **Declining,** en declive, en decadencia (industry, region, standards). **In his declining years,** en sus últimos años.

decline *s.* 1. Declinación, decadencia, caimiento; descenso, disminución (decrease). 2. *(Med.)* Enfermedad que va cediendo de su violencia. 3. Menoscabo, decadencia de las fuerzas físicas o mentales por causa de enfermedad; *(Fam.)* consunción. 4. Declive, decadencia, deterioro (downward trend). **To be in decline,** estar en declive o en decadencia. **To go into a decline,** entrar en decadencia.

declivity [dɪˈklɪvɪtɪ] [di-kli-vi-ti] *s.* Declive, declivio, pendiente de algún terreno.

declivitous, declivous [dɪˈklɪvɪtəs] [di-kli-vi-tos], *a.* Inclinado, que está en declive o en pendiente.

declutch [dɪˈklʌtʃ] [di-klatch] *vn.* Desembragar, sacar el clutch.

decoct [dɪˈkɒkt] [di-kokt], *va.* 1. Cocer, hervir. 2. *(Ant.)* Asimilar, digerir.

decoction [dɪˈkɒkʃən] [di-kok-shon], *s.* 1 Cocción o hervor. 2. Decocción de plantas o drogas para sacar la substancia.

decocture [dɪˈkɒktʃər] [di-kok-char], *s.* 1. Cocción o hervor. 2. Decocción V. DECOCTION.

decode [ˈdiːkəʊd] [di-koud] *va.* Descifrar (message); descodificar (signal).

decoder [ˈdiːkəʊdər] [di-kou-dar] *s.* Descodificador.

decollate [ˌdiːkəˈleɪt] [di-ko-leit] *va.* Degollar.

decollation [ˌdiːkəˈleɪʃən] [di-ko-lei-shon] *s.* Degollación.

decolor, decolour, decolorate [ˌdiːkələr] [di-ko-lor] *va.* Quitar el color, blanquear; clarificar (azúcar).

decoloration [ˌdiːkələˈreɪʃən] [di-ko-lo-rei-shon], *s.* Descoloramiento.

decompose [ˌdiːkəmˈpəʊz] [di-kom-pous] *va.* Descomponer, reducir un cuerpo a sus principios, separar las partes de algún cuerpo o mezcla, destruir la unión química de las partículas de los cuerpos; pudrir. *-vn.* Pudrirse, corromperse, descomponerse.

decomposite [ˌdiːkɒmˈpəsaɪt] [di-kom-po-sait] *a.* Compuesto de nuevo.

decomposition [ˌdiːkɒmpəˈzɪʃən] [di-kom-po-si-shon] *s.* 1. Descomposición, separación. 2. Segunda composición, combinación de cosas ya compuestas.

decompound [ˌdiːkəmˈpaʊnd] [di-kom-pound] *va.* 1. Componer de cosas ya compuestas. 2. Descomponer, separar cosas compuestas.

decompound, *a.* *(Bot.)* Dos veces compuesto.

decompression [ˌdiːkəmˈpreʃən] [di-kom-pre-shon] *s.* *(Mar.)* Descompresión. **Decompression chamber,** cámara de descompresión.

decongestant [ˌdiːkənˈdʒestənt] [di-kon-yes-tant] *s.* Descongestionante, anticongestivo.

decontaminate [ˌdiːkən↓təmɪneɪt] [di-kon-ta-mi-neit] *va.* Descontaminar.

decontamination [ˌdiːkənˈtəmɪneɪʃən] [di-kon-ta-mi-nei-shon] *s.* Descontaminación.

decor, décor [ˈdeɪkɔːʳ] [dei-koʳ] *s.* Decoración (furnishings). *(Teat.)* Decorado, escenografía.

decorate [ˈdekəreɪt] [de-ko-reit] *va.* Decorar (cake); hermosear, adornar (Christmas tree); pulir; pintar (room/house/with paint); empapelar (with wallpaper). **To decorate somebody for something,** condecorar a alguien por algo (award medal). *vn.* Pintar (paint); empapelar (hang wallpaper).

decorating [ˈdekəreɪtɪŋ] [de-ko-rei-tin] *s.* **He helped me with the decorating,** me ayudó a decorar la casa.

decoration [ˈdekəreɪʃən] [de-ko-rei-shon], *s.* 1. Decoración, adorno o lustre; ornamento (ornamentation); decoración (act). **For decoration,** de adorno. 2. Divisa (de honor). **Decoration Day,** *(E.U.)* el 30 de Mayo, día señalado para decorar las sepulturas de los soldados y marinos que murieron en la guerra civil (1861-65). 3. *(Mil.)* Condecoración.

decorative [ˈdekərətɪv] [de-ko-ra-tiv] *a.* Ornamental, de adorno (object). **The decorative arts,** las artes decorativas.

decorator [ˈdekəreɪtəʳ] [de-ko-rei-toʳ], *s.* Decorador, adornista, interiorista (designer); pintor (painter); empapelador (paperhanger).

decorous [ˈdekərəs] [de-ko-ros], *a.* Decente. decoroso, honesto; convincente.

decorously [ˈdekərəslɪ] [de-ko-ros-li], *adv.* Decorosamente.

decorousness [ˈdekərəsnɪs] [de-ko-ros-nes], *s.* Decoro, circunspección, conveniencia de conducta.

decorticate [ˈdekɔːtɪkeɪt] [de-kor-ti-keit], *va.* 1. Descortezar. 2. Pelar, mondar.

decortication [ˈdekɔːtɪkeɪʃən] [de-kor-ti-kei-shon], *s.* Descortezamiento.

decorum [ˈdekərəm] [de-ko-rum] *s.* Decoro, honor, decencia, compostura; propiedad, conveniencia.

decoy [ˈdiːkɔɪ] [di-koi], *va.* 1. Atraer algún pájaro a la jaula con señuelo o añagaza (lure). 2. Atraer con falsos halagos, embaucar, engañar, pillar, clavar.

decoy *s.* 1. Seducción, incitación a hacer alguna cosa mala. 2. Cazadero con señuelo (lure/in hunting).

decoy-duck [ˈdiːkɔɪˌdʌk] [di-koi-dak] *s.* Pato de reclamo.

decrease [diːˈkriːs] [di-kris] *vn.* 1. Decrecer, menguar, ir a menos, minorarse, disminuir (in quantity/amount, numbers); bajar (prices); disminuir (speed). 2. Disminuir, bajar (in intensity, quality); disminuir, decrecer (power, effectiveness); disminuir, decaer (interest). *-va.* Disminuir, minorar, reducir.

decrease *s.* 1. Decremento, disminución; descaecimiento, decadencia, descrecimiento, mengua, merma, bajada. **Crime is on the decrease,** la delincuencia está disminuyendo. 2. Menguante de la luna.

decreasing [diːˈkriːsɪŋ] [di-kri-sin] *a.* Decreciente.

decree [diːˈkriː] [di-kri] *vn.* Decretar, mandar por decreto o edicto; determinarse, resolverse. *-va.* Decretar, determinar, mandar, ordenar.

decree *s.* 1. *(Law)* Decreto (command), ley, edicto, mandato; regla establecida. 2. Decreto, resolución, determinación, decisión de algún pleito. 3. Decreto del Papa y sus cardenales.

decrement [diːˈkriːmənt] [di-kri-ment] *s.* Decremento, disminución.

decrepit [diˈkrepɪt] [di-kre-pit] *a.* 1. Decrépito, cargado de años, consumido por la vejez (infirm/person, animal). 2. Destartalado (dilapidated/bus, furniture); deteriorado, viejo y en mal estado.

decrepitate [diˈkrepɪteɪt] [di-kre-pi-teit] *va.* y *vn.* Decrepitar, henderse o saltar con ruido alguna cosa echada al fuego, como la sal, etc.

decrepitation [diˈkrepɪteɪʃən] [di-kre-pi-tei-shon] *s.* *(Quím.)* Decrepitación.

decrepitness [diˈkrepɪtnɪs] [di-kre-pit-nes], **decrepitude** [diˈkrepɪtjuːd] [di-kre-pi-tiud], *s.* Decrepitud (infirmity); senectud, caducidad. Deterioro (dilapidation).

decrescendo [diˈkresəndəʊ] [di-kres-sen-dou], *a., s.* y *adv.* *(Ital.)* V. DIMINUENDO.

decrescent [diˈkresənt] [di-kre-sent], *a.* Lo que decrece o mengua.

decretal [diˈkretəl] [di-kre-tal], *s.* 1. Decretal, epístola pontificia en la que el Papa declara alguna duda. 2. Decretero, libro de decretos; rescripto. *a.* Decretal, lo que pertenece a un decreto.

decretion [diˈkreʃən] [di-kre-shon], *s.* Minoración, merma.

decretist [diˈkretɪst] [di-kre-tist], *s.* Decretista, decretalista, expositor o intérprete de las decretales.

decretive [diˈkretɪv] [di-kre-tiv], *a.* Decretal, decretivo, de la naturaleza de un decreto.

decretorily [diˈkretərɪlɪ] [di-kre-to-ri-li], *adv.* Definitivamente.

decretory [diˈkretərɪ] [di-kre-to-ri], *a.* Decretorio, definitivo, decisivo, perentorio; crítico.

decrial [diˈkrɪəl] [di-krial], *s.* Gritería y confusión contra alguna persona; insulto.

decrier [diˈkrɪəʳ] [di-kriaʳ], *s.* El que censura precipitadamente o ruidosamente.

decriminalize [diˈkrɪmɪnəlaɪz] [di-kri-mi-na-lais] *va.* Despenalizar.

decrown [diˈkraʊn] [di-kraun], *va.* V. DISCROWN.

decrustation [diˈkrʌsteɪʃən] [di-kras-tei-shon], *s.* La acción de quitar la costra.

decry [diˈkraɪ] [di-krai], *va.* Desacreditar, culpar o censurar públicamente; gritar contra alguna persona o cosa. Condenar, censurar (condemn); menospreciar (disparage).

decubation [diˈkjuːbeɪʃən] [di-kiu-bei-shon], *s.* El acto de acostarse.

decubitus [diˈkjuːbɪtəs] [di-kiu-bi-tos], *s.* Decúbito, posición del cuerpo de una persona echada o recostada; posición del enfermo en la cama.

decumbence, decumbency [diˈkʌmbəns] [di-kam-bens], *s.* La acción de estar acostado y la postura que se tiene en la cama.

decumbent [diˈkʌmbənt] [di-kam-bent] *a.* 1. V. RECUMBENT. 2. Echado en la cama; enfermo.

decumbiture [diˈkʌmbɪtʃəʳ] [di-kam-ba-chuaʳ], *s.* 1. Tiempo que el enfermo guarda cama. 2. *(Astrol.)* Pronóstico que se toma del aspecto del cielo para predecir la mejoría o la muerte del enfermo.

decuple [ˈdɪkʌpl] [di-ka-pel] *a.* Décuplo, diez veces tanto como otra cantidad.

decurion [diˈkjuːrɪən] [di-kiu-rion] *s.* Decurión, el jefe de diez soldados entre los romanos.

decurrent [diˈkʌrənt] [di-ka-rent], *a.* *(Bot.)* Decurrente; se dice de la hoja cuyo limbo se prolonga a lo largo del tallo, adhiriéndose a él.

decursive [diˈkɜːsɪv] [di-ker-siv], *a.* V DECURRENT.

decussate [diˈkjuːseɪt] [di-kiu-seit], *vn.* Cortarse dos líneas en ángulos agudos o en forma de X; cruzarse como las mallas de una red. *a.* Entrecuzado; en botánica, decusativo; se dice de las hojas opuestas cuyos pares se cruzan formando ángulo recto.

decussation [ˌdɪkjʊˈseɪʃən] [di-kiu-sei-shon], *s.* Decusación, el punto donde se cruzan varias líneas o radios; se dice particularmente de los nervios del ojo.

dedal, daedal [ˈdɪdəl] [di-dal], *a.* 1. Primorosamente hecho, intricado, artístico, ingenioso. 2. Artificioso, taimado, engañoso.

dedicate [ˈdedɪkeɪt] [de-di-keit], *va.* 1. Dedicar, aplicar, consagrar alguna cosa a Dios (devote). 2. Dedicar, destinar una persona a algún empleo u ocupación, o una cosa a alguna persona o uso determinado (consecrate/church, shrine, memorial); inaugurar (declare open/building, fair). 3. Dedicar (poem, book), ofrecer alguna obra o trabajo de la inteligencia a un personaje para que lo patrocine.

dedicated

dedicated [ˈdedɪkeɪtɪd] [de-di-kei-tid] *a.* 1. Consagrado, dedicado, de gran dedicación, entregado a su trabajo (musician, nurse, teacher). 2. *(Inform.)* Dedicado.

dedication [ˌdedɪˈkeɪʃən] [de-di-kei-shon] *s.* 1. Dedicación, consagración, entrega (devotion). 2. Dedicatoria que precede a una obra (written message). 3. Dedicación (consecration); inauguración (opening).

dedicator [ˈdedɪkeɪtəʳ] [de-di-kei-taʳ] *s.* Dedicante, el que dedica.

dedicatory [ˈdedɪkətərɪ] [de-di-ka-to-ri] *a.* Que contiene o presenta la forma de dedicatoria; que se refiere o pertenece a la dedicatoria.

deduce [dɪˈdjuːs] [di-dius] *va.* Deducir, sacar por orden o serie regular y conexa; concluir o inferir por consecuencias legítimas, derivar; substraer.

deducement [dɪˈdjuːsmənt] [di-dius-ment] *s.* Deducción, conclusión, consecuencia.

deducible [dɪˈdjuːsɪbl] [di-diu-si-bol] *a.* Deducible, que puede ser deducido, inferido.

deducive [dɪˈdjuːsɪv] [di-diu-siv] *a.* Deductivo; concluyente, ilativo.

deduct [dɪˈdʌkt] [di-dakt] *va.* Deducir, substraer, descontar, rebajar, bajar, desfalcar, rebatir.

deductible [dɪˈdʌktɪbl] [di-dak-ti-bol] *a.* Deducible, desgravable. *s.* Franquicia.

deduction [dɪˈdʌkʃən] [di-dak-shon] *s.* 1. Deducción, ilación, consecuencia (reasoning, conclusion). 2. Deducción, descuento (substraction), rebaja, desfalco. **He gets $260 a week after deductions,** gana 260 dólares semanales netos.

deductive [dɪˈdʌktɪv] [di-dak-tiv] *a.* Deductivo que obra o procede por deducción, ilativo.

deductively [dɪˈdʌktɪvlɪ] [di-dak-tiv-li] *adv.* Por ilación o consecuencia.

deed [diːd] [did] *s.* 1 Acción, operación, acto, hecho (action); realidad. **Deeds, not words,** hechos y no palabras. **Good deeds,** buenas acciones, buenas obras. 2. Hazaña, acción heroica. 3. Instrumento auténtico que hace fe. **In deed, in very deed,** de veras, en verdad; de hecho. 4. *(Law)* Escritura. **The deed/deeds to the house,** la escritura de la casa. *-va.* Ceder, transferir.

deedless [ˈdiːdlɪs] [did-les] *a.* Omiso, descuidado, inerte, oscuro, sin nombre, que no se ha dado a conocer por ningún hecho.

deedy [ˈdiːdɪ] [didi] *a.* Activo, industrioso.

deejay [ˈdiːdʒeɪ] [di-yei] *s.* *(Coloq.)* Disc-jockey, pinchadiscos.

deem [diːm] [dim] *va. y vn.* Juzgar, hacer o formar dictamen o juicio de alguna cosa, imaginar, suponer, pensar, creer, estimar; determinar.

deemster [ˈdiːmstəʳ] [dims-taʳ] *s.* Juez, magistrado en la isla inglesa de Man.

deep [diːp] [dip] *a.* 1. Hondo, profundo, lo que se considera medido desde lo más alto a lo más bajo (water, hole, pit). Profundo (gash); hondo (dish); alto (pan). **The ditch is 6 ft deep,** la zanja tiene 6 pies de profundidad. Profundo (horizontally/shelf). **The soldiers were standing 12 deep,** los soldados formaban columnas de 12 en fondo. Ancho (broad/edge). 2. Profundo, lo que profundiza o penetra mucho (thoughts, mystery, secret). *(Coloq.)* **She's a deep one,** es un enigma. 3. Sagaz, hábil, penetrador. 4. Artificioso, insidioso. 5. Grave, oscuro. 6. Profundo, silencioso, taciturno. Profundo, hondo (sigh/groan). **Take a deep breath,** respire hondo. **Deep in debt,** cargado de deudas. 7. Oscuro (se dice del color). 8. Grave, en sonido, profundo (voice); grave (note). Intenso, subido (color). Profundo (intense/sleep, love, impression). **It's with deep regret that…,** es con gran o profundo pesar que… **To be in deep trouble,** estar en un serio apuro o en un buen lío. 9. Cenagoso, lodoso; se dice, p.ej., de un camino. *-s.* 1. Piélago, abismo, lo más profundo del mar o de alguna cosa. 2. Misterio. **Deep of night,** el horror de las tinieblas, la oscuridad más profunda.

deep *adv.* 1. **To dig deep,** cavar hondo. **He thrust his hands deep into his pockets,** hundió las manos en los bolsillos (of penetration). **To go deeper into something,** ahondar o profundizar más en algo (thoroughly). 2. **Deep in the forest,** en lo profundo del bosque (situated far from edge). **Deep down you know I'm right,** en el fondo sabes que tengo razón. **I found her deep in her book,** la encontré absorta o ensimismada en su libro (greatly involved). *(Coloq.)* **You're in this too deep,** estás metido en esto hasta el cuello. 3. **To drink deep of something,** embeberse de o en algo (extensively).

deep-drawing [diːpˈdrɔːɪŋ] [dip-drouin], *a.* Que está muy profundo en el agua; de mucho calado.

deepen [ˈdiːpən] [di-pen], *va.* 1. Profundizar o ahondar en (knowledge); aumentar (concern); estrechar (friendship); hacer más profundo u hondo (canal, well). 2. Oscurecer. 3. Entristecer. *-vn.* 1. Descender gradualmente; profundizarse, hacerse o volverse más hondo o profundo (gorge, river). 2. Hacerse más profundo, aumentar (concern, love); estrecharse (friendship); crecer, aumentar (mystery); acentuarse (crisis); hacerse más profundo (darkness).

deep end [diːpˈend] [dip-end] *s.* **The deep end,** la parte honda, lo hondo (of swimming pool). *(Coloq.)* **To go/jump off the deep end,** ponerse hecho una furia. **To throw somebody in (at) the deep end,** meter a alguien de lleno en lo más difícil.

deepening [ˈdiːpənɪŋ] [di-pe-nin] *a.* Cada vez más profundo (waters, darkness, mystery); creciente, cada vez mayor (crisis, dismay).

deep freeze [diːpˈfriːz] [dip-fris] *s.* 1. Congelación rápida. 2. Congelador (in shop, home). **The proposal is in deep freeze,** la propuesta ha sido congelada (state).

deep-freeze, *va.* Congelar, almacenar en congeladora; ultracongelar (commercially). **Deep-frozen cod,** bacalao ultracongelado.

deeply [ˈdiːplɪ] [di-pli] *adv.* 1. Profundamente, muy hondo, a una gran profundidad. 2. Profundamente (sigh); sumamente, en sumo grado. **To breathe deeply,** respirar hondo. **He cut deeply into the wood,** hizo un corte profundo en la madera. 3. Gravemente, tristemente, oscuramente. 4. Sagazmente, con profunda atención; a fondo (think); profundamente (concerned); sumamente (interested). **I was deeply offended by his remarks,** me sentí muy ofendida por sus comentarios.

deep-mouthed [diːpˈmaʊθɪd] [dip-mau-zid], *a.* Ronco, el que tiene la voz profunda y bronca.

deep-musing [diːpˈmʌsɪŋ] [dip-ma-sin], *a.* Pensativo, contemplativo.

deepness [ˈdiːpnɪs] [dip-nes], *s.* Profundidad, la extensión de cualquier cosa de su superficie hasta su fondo.

deep-read [ˈdiːpred] [dip-red], *a.* Muy leído, profundamente versado en los libros.

deep-rooted [ˈdiːpˈruːtɪd] [dip-ru-tid] *a.* Profundamente arraigado (belief).

deep-sea diving [ˌdiːpsiːˈdaɪvɪŋ] [dip-si-dai-vin] Buceo de altura o en alta mar.

deep-sea fishing [ˌdiːpsiːˈfɪʃɪŋ] [dip-si-fi-shin], *s.* Pesca de alta mar.

deep-sea-line [ˌdiːpsiːˈlaɪn] [dip-si-lain] *s.* *(Mar.)* Escandallo, sonda o plomada para medir la cantidad de brazas de agua que hay hasta el fondo.

deep-seated [ˈdiːpˈsiːtɪd] [dip-si-tid] *a.* Profundamente arraigado (prejudice, conviction); profundo, de raíces profundas (problem).

deer [dɪəʳ] [diaʳ] *s.* Ciervo o venado, un animal cualquiera del género cerval. **Fallow deer,** gamo, gama. **Red deer** ciervo común. **Deer-fold,** parque de ciervos. **Deerhound,** galgo, perro corredor. **Deer-skin,** gamuza, piel de gamo. **Deer-stalking,** caza al acecho.

deerstalker [ˈdɪəstɔːkəʳ] [dias-to-kaʳ] *s.* Gorra de cazador.

de-escalate [ˌdiːˈeskəleɪt] [di-es-ka-leit] *va.* Desescalar, reducir (bombing); desacelerar (crisis). *-vn.* Disminuir, reducirse (violence); mejorar (situation).

deface [dɪˈfeɪs] [di-feis] *va.* 1. Desfigurar, mutilar la faz o la superficie de una cosa. Pintarrajear (wall, notice). 2. Borrar, destruir, afear.

defacement [dɪˈfeɪsmənt] [di-feis-ment] *s.* Violación, injuria; rasadura, destrucción, ruina.

defacer [dɪˈfeɪsəʳ] [di-fei-saʳ] *s.* Destructor o destruidor.

de facto [deɪˈfæktəʊ] [de-fak-tou] *a./adv.* De hecho, actual, en oposición a *de jure.*

defalcate [ˈdiːfælˈkeɪt] [di-fal-keit] *va.* Desfalcar, descabalar, deducir, quitar parte o porción de alguna cosa. *-vn.* Tomar para sí, apropiarse uno el dinero.

defalcation [ˌdiːfælˈkeɪʃən] [di-fal-kei-shon] *s.* 1. Desfalco, malversación, hurto. 2. Deducción, disminución. 3. Déficit.

defamation [ˌdefəˈmeɪʃən] [de-fa-mei-shon] *s.* Difamación, disfamación, calumnia.

defamatory [dɪˈfæmətərɪ] [di-fa-ma-to-ri] *a.* Infamatorio, calumnioso, difamatorio.

defame [dɪˈfeɪm] [di-feim], *va.* Difamar, desacreditar, deshonrar, denigrar; calumniar.

defamer [dɪˈfeɪməʳ] [di-fei-maʳ] *s.* Infamador, calumniador.

defaming *s.* V. DEFAMATION.

default [dɪˈfɔːlt] [di-folt], *s.* 1. Omisión (omission), descuido, negligencia, mora (on payments); incomparecencia (failure to appear). *(Dep.)* **She won by default,** ganó por incomparecencia de su rival. 2. Culpa, delito. 3. Defecto, falta. **In default whereof,** en cuyo defecto. 4. *(For.)* Rebeldía, la acción de no comparecer en juicio dentro del plazo de la citación. 5. Falta (lack). **He was elected by default,** fue elegido por ausencia de otros candidatos. *(Inform.)* **Default option,** opción por defecto.

default *va.* Faltar, no cumplir algún contrato o estipulación. *-vn.* 1. *(Law)* Caer en rebeldía o contumacia. 2. *(Des.)* Ofender, ser descuidado. 3. *(Fin.)* **To default on something,** no pagar algo. 4. *(Dep.)* No presentarse.

defaulter [dɪˈfɔːltəʳ] [di-fol-taʳ] *s.* El que falta o no cumple su deber. 1. *(For.)* Rebelde, contumaz, el que no comparece en juicio dentro del término de la citación. 2. *(Fin.)* Malversador, moroso.

defeasible [dɪˈfiːsɪbl] [di-fi-si-bol] *a.* Anulable, revocable.

defeat [dɪˈfiːt] [di-fit] *s.* Derrota (by opponent); rota, vencimiento, destrucción o ruina; p. ej. de un ejército o un partido. Rechazo (of motion, bill). **To accept/admit defeat,** darse por vencido.

defeat *va.* 1. Derrotar, vencer (opponent); deshacer, destruir. 2. Frustrar (hopes, plans); privar a alguno de lo que se le debía o esperaba. **That would defeat the object of the exercise,** eso iría en contra de lo que se pretende lograr. 3. *(For.)* Anular, abrogar. 4. *(Des.)* Abolir, exterminar. 5. Derrotar (opposition); rechazar (bill, motion). *(Coloq.)* **It defeats me,** no alcanzo a comprenderlo.

defeatism [dɪˈfiːtɪzm] [di-fi-ti-sem] *s.* Derrotismo.

defeatist [dɪˈfiːtɪst] [di-fi-tist] *s./a.* Derrotista.

defecate [ˈdefəkeɪt] [de-fe-keit] *va.* Purgar, purificar, limpiar; depurar. *-vn.* 1. Limpiarse de impurezas. 2. Exonerar el vientre, defecar.

defecate *a.* Depurado, aclarado.

defecation [ˌdefəˈkeɪʃən] [de-fe-kei-shon] *s.* 1. Defecación, se dice de los líquidos cuando se van aclarando por irse posando las heces en el fondo; purificación, clarificación. 2. Exoneración del vientre, defecación.

defect [ˈdiːfekt] [di-fekt] *s.* Defecto, falta, tacha, imperfección; omisión. **A speech/birth defect,** un defecto en el habla/de nacimiento.

defect *vn.* Desertar. defeccionar (period). **Their key man has defected to a rival team,** su mejor hombre se ha pasado a un equipo rival.

defectible [ˈdiːfektɪbl] [di-fek-ti-bol] *a.* Defectible; imperfecto.

defection [dɪˈfekʃən] [di-fek-shon] *s.* 1. Defección, apostasía; conjuración, rebeldía, desobediencia,

levantamiento, sublevación. 2. Separación, deserción, abandono.

defective [dɪˈfektɪv] [di-fek-tiv] *a.* Defectivo, defectuoso, imperfecto, culpable.

defectively [dɪˈfektɪvlɪ] [di-fek-tiv-li] *adv.* Defectuosamente.

defectiveness [dɪˈfektɪvnɪs] [di-fek-tiv-nes] *s.* Defecto, culpa, falta, delito.

defence [dɪˈfens] [di-fens], *f.* defensa.

defend [dɪˈfend] [di-fend] *va.* 1. Defender, preservar, proteger, conservar. **To defend oneself,** defenderse. 2. Sostener alguna opinión. 3. Fortalecer, asegurar. 4. Repeler. *vn.* 1. *(Law)* Actuar por la defensa. 2. *(Dep.)* **He's better at defending,** juega mejor como defensa.

defendable [dɪˈfendəbl] [di-fen-da-bol] *a.* Defendible.

defendant [dɪˈfendənt] [di-fen-dant] *a.* Defensivo. *s.* 1. *(For.)* El demandado (in civil case); acusado (in criminal case). 2. El que defiende.

defender [dɪˈfendəʳ] [di-fen-daʳ] *s.* 1. Defensor (of cause, course of action, opinion); abogado; campeón; afirmador, protector, patrón. 2. *(Dep.)* Defensa.

defending [dɪˈfendɪŋ] [di-fen-din] *a.* **The defending champion,** el actual campeón. *(Law)* **Defending counsel,** abogado defensor.

defensative [dɪˈfensətɪv] [di-fen-sa-tiv] *s.* *(Ant.)* Defensiva, defensa, guardia, reparo.

defense, defence [dɪˈfens] [di-fens], *s.* 1. Defensa, la acción y afecto de defender, protección (protection); sostén, apoyo. (in US) **Secretary of Defense,** Ministro, Secretario de Defensa. (in UK) **Defence Minister,** Ministro o Secretario de Defensa. 2. Defensa, vindicación, justificación, apología. 3. Resistencia, resguardo con que se evita o repele algún riesgo; cualquier cosa que defiende *(Dep.)* Defensa. Defensa (in chess). 4. *(For.)* Defensa, la respuesta del demandado. **Defense councel,** abogado defensor. 5. *(Mil., Med., Psych.)* **Defenses,** *pl.* defensas. **To low/drop one's defenses,** bajar la guardia.

defenseless [dɪˈfenslɪs] [di-fens-les] *a.* Indefenso, sin armas, sin defensa, impotente: incapaz de resistir.

defenselessness [dɪˈfenslɪsnɪs] [di-fens-les-nes] *s.* Desvalimiento, desamparo, abandono.

defensible [dɪˈfensɪbl] [di-fen-si-bol] *a.* Defendible, que se puede defender o sostener (theory, conduct).

defensive [dɪˈfensɪv] [di-fen-siv] *a.* Defensivo. *s.* Defensiva, la situación o estado del que sólo trata de defenderse. **To be/to stand upon the defensive,** estar o ponerse a la defensiva.

defensively [dɪˈfensɪvlɪ] [di-fen-siv-li] *adv.* Defensivamente.

defensory [dɪˈfensərɪ] [di-fen-so-ri], *a.* Defensivo, justificativo.

defer [dɪˈfɜːʳ] [di-faʳ] *vn.* 1. Diferir, dilater, suspender, posponer. 2. Deferir, ceder, condescender por atención o respeto. *-va.* 1. Diferir, retardar, atrasar. 2. Remitirse al parecer de otro; ofrecer. *(Fin.)* **Deferred,** diferido (charges, taxation); de dividendo diferido (shares). *(Law)* Aplazado (sentence). **He was deferred on medical grounds,** le concedieron una prórroga por razones médicas.

defer to Deferir a.

deference [dɪˈferəns] [di-fe-rens] *s.* Deferencia, sumisión, respeto, consideración, condescendencia. **Out of deference,** por deferencia, en consideración a.

deferent [dɪˈferənt] [di-fe-rent], *a.* 1. Deferente, que lleva o se lleva. 2. V. DEFERENTIAL. *-s.* Vehículo, lo que lleva o conduce. *(Anat.)* Canal deferente, conducto excretor.

deferential [ˌdefəˈrenʃəl] [de-fe-ren-shal] *a.* Deferente, respetuoso.

deferment [dɪˈfɜːmənt] [di-fer-ment] *s.* Dilatación, tardanza. Aplazamiento (of decision, payment). *(Mil.)* Prórroga.

deferrer [dɪˈfɜːrəʳ] [di-fe-raʳ] *s.* Tardador, holgazán; el que difiere o dilata.

deferring [dɪˈfɜːrɪŋ] [di-fe-rin] *s.* Dilatación, la acción de diferir.

defiance [dɪˈfaɪəns] [di-faians] *s.* 1. Desafío, cartel o reto, provocación a duelo o combate. **An act of defiance,** un desafío, un acto de rebeldía. **In defiance of her orders,** haciendo caso omiso de sus órdenes. 2. El acto de retar a otro a que pruebe una acusación. 3. Expresión de menosprecio o vilipendio. **To bid defiance,** retar, provocar a desafío; bravear, echar plantas, fieros o bravatas; contradecir, oponerse abiertamente o cara a cara. **To set at defiance,** befar, hacer befa o mofa.

defiant [dɪˈfaɪənt] [di-faiant] *a.* Desafiante (attitude, tone); rebelde (person).

defiantly [dɪˈfaɪəntlɪ] [di-faiant-li] *adv.* Con actitud desafiante.

defibrinate [dɪˈfɪbrɪneɪt] [di-fi-bri-neit] *va.* Desfibrinar, quitar la fibrina de la sangre.

deficiency, deficience [dɪˈfɪʃənsɪ] [di-fi-shen-si] *s.* 1. Defecto, imperfección. 2. Falta; defecto, deficiencia (shortcoming). 3. Escasez, déficit (shortage). *(Med.)* Deficiencia.

deficient [dɪˈfɪʃənt] [di-fi-shent] *a.* Deficiente, insuficiente, defectuoso, falto, incompleto. **Foods deficient in vitamins,** alimento de bajo contenido vitamínico. **A plan deficient in imagination,** un plan carente de imaginación.

deficiently [dɪˈfɪʃəntlɪ] [di-fi-shent-li] *adv.* Defectuosamente.

deficit [ˈdefɪsɪt] [de-fi-sit] *s.* Déficit, la falta, alcance o descubierto que resulta comparando el haber con el fondo puesto en la empresa; o la cantidad que falta para pagar las cargas del Estado; descubierto con el fisco.

defile [dɪˈfaɪl] [di-fail] *va.* 1. Manchar, ensuciar. 2. Violar; *(Rel.)* profanar; viciar. 3. Corromper, envilecer (mind, spirit); violar, deshonrar (woman). Profanar (memory). *-vn.* Desfilar, marchar o ir en filas.

defile, *s.* Desfiladero, sitio o pasaje estrecho. **A defile between two hills,** garganta de montaña.

defilement [dɪˈfaɪlmənt] [di-fail-ment] *s.* Contaminación, violación, suciedad, corrupción, profanación.

defiler [dɪˈfaɪləʳ] [di-fai-laʳ] *s.* Corruptor, violador, contaminador, profanador.

defiling [dɪˈfaɪlɪŋ] [di-fai-lin] *s.* Contaminación, corrupción, profanamiento.

definable [dɪˈfaɪnəbl] [di-fai-na-bol] *a.* Definible, lo que se puede definir.

define [dɪˈfaɪn] [di-fain] *va.* 1. Definir, describir (state meaning of, describe/word, position). 2. Circunscribir, señalar términos o límites; determinar, delimitar (powers, duties). Distinguir (characterize). Definir (outline). *-vn.* Decidir, juzgar.

definer [dɪˈfaɪnəʳ] [di-fai-naʳ] *s.* Definidor, el que explica o define una cosa.

definite [ˈdefɪnɪt] [de-fi-nit] *a.* 1. Definido, exacto, preciso, determinado, limitado, cierto; seguro, confirmado (certain). 2. Definitivo, en firme (final/date, price, offer). 3. Firme, terminante (firm, categorical/tone). **She was very definite about wanting to come,** dijo categóricamente que quería venir. **It's a definite advantage/possibility,** es, sin duda, una ventaja/posibilidad. *(Gram.)* **Definite article,** artículo determinado o definido. *-s.* Definido, la cosa definida.

definitely [ˈdefɪnɪtlɪ] [de-fi-nit-li] *adv.* Definitivamente (definitively/arrange, agree); determinantemente, categóricamente (firmly/speak, say); con firmeza (act); ciertamente (without doubt). **It's definitely true/an improvement,** es indudablemente cierto/una mejoría. **He definitely said we should meet here.** seguro que dijo que nos encontráramos aquí.

definiteness [ˈdefɪnɪtnɪs] [de-fi-nit-nes] *s.* Limitación fija de alguna cosa.

definition [ˈdefɪnɪsən] [de-fi-ni-shon] *s.* 1. Definición, descripción breve y clara (statement of meaning). **What's your definition of good music?,** ¿tú qué entiendes por buena música?. **By definition,** por definición. 2. Decisión, determinación. 3. *(Opt.)* Propiedad de una lente de dar una

imagen clara y distinta. *(Cin., Phot., TV)* Nitidez, definición. **The plot lacked definition,** la trama argumental no estaba bien definida (focus). 4. Definición, delimitación (categorization).

definitive [dɪˈfɪnɪtɪv] [di-fi-ni-tiv] *a.* Definitivo (final/victory, verdict); decisivo, perentorio. De mayor autoridad (authoritative/biography, study). *-s.* Lo que define.

definitively [dɪˈfɪnɪtɪvlɪ] [di-fi-ni-tiv-li] *adv.* Definitivamente, decisivamente, resolutivamente.

definitiveness [dɪˈfɪnɪtɪvnɪs] [di-fi-ni-tiv-nes] *s.* Autoridad decisiva.

deflagrable [ˈdefləgrəbl] [de-fla-gra-bol] *a.* Combustible.

deflagrate [ˈdefləgreɪt] [de-fla-greit] *va.* Incendiar, abrasar, efectuar una combustión, especialmente si es repentina y rápida. *-vn.* Arder con combustión repentina y rápida; crepitar.

deflagration [ˈdefləgreɪʃən] [de-fla-grei-shon] *s.* Deflagración, combustión total por medio del fuego.

deflagrator [ˈdefləgreɪtəʳ] [de-fla-grei-toʳ] *s. (Elec.)* Deflagrador, instrumento para efectuar muy rápida combustión.

deflate [diːˈfleɪt] [di-fleit] *va.* 1. Desinflar (balloon, tire). **To deflate somebody/somebody's ego,** bajarle los humos a alguien (humble). Deprimir (depress). **I felt deflated,** me sentí por los suelos. 2. *(Econ.)* Deflactar. *vn.* Desinflarse (balloon, tire).

deflation [dɪˈfleɪʃən] [di-flei-shon] *s.* Desinflación, deflación.

deflect [dɪˈflekt] [di-flekt] *va.* Desviar, apartar, separar del camino o curso. *-vn.* Desviarse, apartarse, ladearse, separarse del camino o carrera que se llevaba.

deflection, deflexion [dɪˈflekʃən] [di-flek-shon], *s.* 1. Desvío, rodeo, desviación (of ball, bullet); refracción (of light); deflexión (of particle). 2. Declinación de la aguja de marear.

deflex [dɪˈfleks] [di-fleks] *va.* Desviar, ladear, doblar repentinamente hacia abajo.

deflexure [dɪˈflekʃəʳ] [di-flek-shaʳ] *s.* Combadura, torcimiento.

deflorate [dɪˈflɔreɪt] [di-flo-reit] *a. (Bot.)* 1. Se dice de la planta que ha cesado de florecer. 2. Que ha emitido o depositado su polen.

defloration [dɪˈflɔreɪʃən] [di-flo-rei-shon] *s.* 1. Defloración. 2. Escogimiento, elección de lo más florido o precioso.

deflower [diːˈflaʊəʳ] [di-flauaʳ] *va.* 1. Quitar la flor de las plantas. 2. Ajar, deslustrar, quitar la flor o lustre a alguna cosa. 3. Desflorar, estuprar, corromper o forzar a una doncella.

deflowerer [diːˈflaʊərəʳ] [di-flou-e-raʳ] *s.* Estuprador.

defluxion [diːˈflʌkʃən] [di-flak-shon] *s.* Fluxión copiosa o abundante, destilación; derramamiento por demasiada abundacia.

defog [diːˈfɒg] [di-fog] *va.* Desempañar.

defogger [diːˈfɒgəʳ] [di-fo-guaʳ] *s.* Desempañador.

defoliate [diːˈfəʊlɪeɪt] [di-fou-lieit] *a.* Deshojado, privado do hojas. *-va.* Quitar o privar de las hojas; deshojar.

defoliation [ˌdiːfəʊlɪˈeɪʃən] [di-fou-liei-shon] *s. (Bot.)* época de la caída de las hojas.

deforce [dɪˈfɔːs] [di-fors] *va.* Usurpar la posesión de bienes raíces.

deforcement [dɪˈfɔːsmənt] [di-fors-ment] *s.* Usurpación, posesión ilegítima de los bienes de otro.

deforest [diːˈfɒrɪst] [di-fo-rest] *va.* Desboscar, arrancar árboles, talar bosques.

deforestation [diːˌfɒrəˈsteɪʃən] [di-fo-res-tei-shon] *s.* Deforestación, despoblación forestal.

deform [dɪˈfɔːm] [di-form] *va.* 1. Deformar, desfigurar, afear. 2. Deshonrar, quitar el honro, estimación o fama.

deformation [dɪˈfɔːmeɪʃən] [di-for-mei-shon] *s.* Deformación, alteración.

deformed [dɪˈfɔːmd] [di-formd] *a.* 1. Deformado, desfigurado; contrahecho. 2. *(Des.)* Feo; bajo, vergonzoso.

deformedness [dɪˈfɔːmɪdnɪs] [di-for-mid-nes], **deformity** [dɪˈfɔːmɪtɪ] [di-for-mi-ti] *s.* 1. Deformidad (disfigurement, malformation), fealdad; ridiculez. Deformación (of mind, character). 2. Deshonor; acción o idea disparatada y opuesta al buen sentido.

defraud [dɪˈfrɔːd] [di-frod] *va.* Defraudar, usurpar fraudulentamente a alguna persona lo que le toca y pertenece de derecho; frustrar. Estafar (person). **To defraud the state,** defraudar al estado. **To defraud somebody of something,** estafarle algo a alguien.

defraudation [dɪˈfrɔːdeɪʃən] [di-fro-dei-shon] *s.* Defraudación.

defrauder [dɪˈfrɔːdəʳ] [di-fro-daʳ] *s.* Defraudador, engañador.

defrauding [dɪˈfrɔːdɪŋ] [di-fro-din], **defraudment** [dɪˈfrɔːdmənt] [di-frod-ment] *s.* Defraudación, fraude.

defray [dɪˈfreɪ] [di-frei] *va.* Costear, hacer el gasto o la costa de alguna cosa; satisfacer, sufragar (cost).

defrayer [dɪˈfreɪəʳ] [di-freiaʳ] *s.* El que hace la costa o el gasto de alguna cosa.

defrayment [dɪˈfreɪmənt] [di-frei-ment] *s.* Gasto, el pago de lo que se ha gastado.

defrock [diːˈfrɒk] [di-frok] *va. (Rel.)* **He was defrocked,** lo apartaron del sacerdocio.

defrost [diːˈfrɒst] [di-frost] *va.* Descongelar (food); deshelar, descongelar (refrigerator); desempañar (wind-shield). *-vn.* Descongelarse (meat); deshelarse, descongelarse (refrigertator).

defroster [diːˈfrɒstəʳ] [di-fros-taʳ], *s.* Descongelador.

deft [deft] [deft] *s.* Diestro, gallardo, hábil (movement); mañoso, apto.

deftly [ˈdeftlɪ] [deft-li] *adv.* Hábilmente, con destreza.

deftness [ˈdeftnɪs] [deft-nes] *s.* Garbo, gracia, maña en hacer una cosa.

defunct [dɪˈfʌŋkt] [di-fankt] *a.* 1. Difunto, muerto (dead). 2. Caduco (extinct/idea, theory); desaparecido, extinto, fenecido (institution). *-s.* Difunto.

defunctionalize [deˌfʌŋkʃənəˈlaɪz] [de-fan-sho-na-lais] *va.* Privar de una función o funciones.

defuse [diːˈfjuːz] [di-fius] *va.* Desactivar (bomb); distender (situation); calmar (crisis).

defy [dɪˈfaɪ] [di-fai], *va.* 1. Desafiar, ignorar (danger, death); provocar a singular combate, retar; arrostrar. 2. Despreciar, tratar con desprecio. 3. *(Des.)* Desdeñar, negar, renunciar. 4. Desacatar, desobedecer (order, authority). **To defy understanding/description,** ser incomprensible/indescriptible (resist). **To defy all logic/reason,** no tener ninguna lógica, ir en contra de toda lógica.

degeneracy [dɪˈdʒenərəsɪ] [di-ye-ne-ra-si] *s.* 1. Degeneración, bastardía, abandono, bajeza. 2. Despravación, corrupción, envilecimiento.

degenerate [dɪˈdʒenərɪt] [di-ye-ne-reit] *vn.* 1. Degenerar, no corresponder a las virtudes de los antepasados. 2. Degenerar, descaecer, desdecir. Deteriorarse (health). 3. Degenerar, ir perdiendo una cosa su primera calidad o naturaleza por deteriorarse, como sucede con algunos animales, semillas y plantas.

degenerate *a.* Degenerado, el que degenera de sus antepasados; vil, bajo, indigno, infame. *-s.* Degenerado.

degenerately [dɪˈdʒenərɪtlɪ] [di-ye-ne-reit-li] *adv.* Bajamente, indignamente.

degenerateness [dɪˈdʒenərɪtnɪs] [di-ye-ne-reit-nes] *s.* Degeneración, abandono

degenerating [dɪˈdʒenərɪtɪŋ] [di-ye-ne-rei-tin] *s.* La acción de degenerar.

degeneration [dɪˌdʒenəˈreɪʃən] [di-ye-ne-rei-shon] *s.* Degeneración, empeoramiento, deterioración (deterioration); envilecimiento. *(Med.)* Degeneración (of tissue, organs).

degenerative [dɪˈdʒenərətɪv] [di-ye-ne-ra-tiv] *a.* Degenerativo.

deglutinate [dɪˈglʊtɪneɪt] [di-glu-ti-neit] *va.* 1. Despegar, separar las substancias adheridas entre sí. 2. Extraer o separar el gluten, ej. del trigo.

deglutition [dɪˈglʊtɪʃən] [di-glu-ti-shon] *s.* Deglución, la acción de tragar los alimentos.

degradation [ˌdegrəˈdeɪʃən] [de-gra-dei-shon] *s.* 1. Degradación, privación de grado y honores, deposición. 2. Degeneración. 3. Disminución de fuerza o valor. 4. Envilecimiento, corrupción. 5. *(Pint.)* Degradación de tintas, colores y sombras.

degrade [dɪˈgreɪd] [di-greid] *va.* 1. Degradar, privar, deponer a alguna persona de las dignidades, honores y privilegios que tenía. **To degrade oneself,** degradarse, rebajarse. 2. Minorar, rebajar, reducir. 3. Envilecer, deshonrar, hacer despreciable una cosa. 4. *(Pint.)* Degradar, atenuar colores o tintas. 5. *(Biol.)* Reducir de rango superior a uno inferior. *-vn.* 1. Degenerar. 2. *(Biol.)* Degenerar. pasar de rango superior a uno inferior.

degrading [dɪˈgreɪdɪŋ] [di-grei-din] *a.* Degradante.

degradingly [dɪˈgreɪdɪŋlɪ] [di-grei-din-li] *adv.* Degradantemente.

degree [dɪˈgriː] [di-gri] *s.* 1. Grado, calidad. estimación de una cosa; grado, nivel (level, amount). **It's a matter/ question of degree,** es cuestión de grados. **There's a degree of truth in what she says,** hay cierta verdad en lo que dice. **To a certain/limited degree,** hasta cierto punto. **To a degree,** en grado sumo (extremely); hasta cierto punto (to some extent). 2. Estado, rango, condición; grado (grade, step). **First/third degree burns,** quemaduras de primer/tercer grado. **First/second degree murder,** homicidio en primer/ segundo grado. 3. Grado, escalón. 4. Grado de parentesco. 5. Grado, proporción. 6. Grado, la graduación y título que se da a quien ha cursado en alguna universidad. **First degree,** licenciatura. **To take a philosophy degree,** hacer la carrera de filosofía, licenciarse en filosofía. 7. *(Gram.)* Grado (de comparación). 8. *(Math., Geog., Meteo., Phys.)* Grado; cada una de los 360 partes en que se divide el círculo, en álgebra, la potencia de un término; es también la medida de calor, frío, humedad, etc. **It was 40 degrees in the shade,** hacía 40 grados a la sombra. **12 degrees below zero,** 12 grados bajo cero. 9. *(Mús.)* Grado, línea o espacio del pentagrama. **To take one's degrees,** graduarse. **By degrees,** *adv.* gradualmente.

dehisce [dɪˈhɪs] [di-his] *vn.* Hendirse, abrirse en grietas.

dehiscence [dɪˈhɪsəns] [di-hi-sens] *s.* 1. Hendidura, grieta. 2. *(Bot.)* Dehiscencia, la manera y acto de abrirse los frutos para dar salida a las semillas.

dehiscent [dɪˈhɪsənt] [di-hi-sent] *a.* Dehiscente, (ovario) que se abre espontáneamente.

dehorn [dɪˈhɔːn] [di-jorn] *va.* Descornar, quitar los cuernos a un animal.

dehort [dɪˈhɔːt] [di-jort] *va.* Disuadir, desaconsejar.

dehortation [dɪˈhɔːteɪʃən] [di-hor-tei-shon] *s.* Disuasión; distracción.

dehorter [dɪˈhɔːtəʳ] [di-jor-taʳ] *s.* El que disuade.

dehumanize [dɪːˈhjuːmənaɪz] [di-jiu-ma-nais] *va.* Privar de las cualidades a los atributos humanos, embrutecer.

dehumidify [ˌdiːhjuːˈmɪdɪfaɪ] [di-jiu-mi-di-fais] *va.* Deshumedecer.

dehydrate [diːˈhaɪdreɪt] [di-jai-dreit] *va.* Deshidratar.

dehydrated [diːˈhaɪdreɪtɪd] [di-jai-drei-tid] *a.* Deshidratado. **To become dehydrated,** deshidratarse.

dehydration [diːˈhaɪdreɪʃən] [di-jai-drei-shon] *s.* Deshidratación.

dehydrogenate [diːˈhaɪdredʒeneɪt] [di-jai-dro-ye-neit] *va.* Deshidrogenar.

deice [diːˈaɪs] [di-ais] *va.* Descongelar, deshelar.

deicer [diːˈaɪsəʳ] [di-ai-saʳ] *s.* Descongelante.

deictic [ˈdaɪktɪk] [daik-tik] *a.* Lo que prueba por razonamiento directo; lo que es directo.

deific, deifical [diːˈɪfɪk] [di-i-fik] *a.* 1. Que deifica. 2. Deífico, de los dioses; divino.

deification [ˌdiːɪfɪˈkeɪʃən] [di-i-fi-kei-shon] *s.* Deificación, la acción de deificar; apoteosis.

deifier [ˈdiːɪfaɪəʳ] [di-i-faiaʳ] *s.* El que deifica; idólatra.

deiform [ˈdiːɪfɔːm] [di-i-form] *a.* Deiforme, divino.

deify ['diːɪfaɪ] [di-i-fai] *va*. 1. Deificar, colocar a alguno en el número de los dioses, adorarle como Dios. 2. Endiosar, divinizar, alabar a alguno hasta ponerle en las nubes. 3. Adorar como a un Dios.

deign [deɪn] [dein] *va*. Conceder, admitir, permitir; considerar digno. -*vn*. Dignarse, condescender. **He did not deign to speak to me,** tuvo a menos hablarme.

deigning ['deɪnɪŋ] [dei-nin] *s*. El acto de condescender o considerar digno.

deipara ['diːpərə] [di-ipa-ra] *a*. Deípara, epíteto de la madre de Dios. Equivale al griego Theotokos.

deism ['diːɪzəm] [di-i-sem] *s*. Deísmo, la opinión de los que creen en un Dios sin admitir la religión revelada ni el cistianismo.

deist ['diːɪst] [di-ist] *s*. Deísta, partidario del deísmo.

deistical ['diːɪstɪkəl] [di-is-ti-kal] *a*. Deístico.

deity ['diːɪtɪ] [di-i-ti] *s*. 1. Deidad, dibinidad, naturaleza divina, calidades divinas. 2. Dios fabuloso; falsa deidad de los idólatras. **The Deity,** Dios.

déjà vu [deɪdʒɑːˈvuː] [dei-ya-vu] *s*. Ya visto.

deject [dɪˈdʒekt] [di-yekt] *va*. Abatir, afligir, contristar, entristecer: desanimar, desalentar, acobardar, descorazonar.

deject, dejected [dɪˈdʒektɪd] [di-yek-tid], *a*. Abatido, acobardado, amilanado, desanimado, desalentado, afligido. **To look dejected,** mostrar en el semblante aflicción o consternación.

dejecta [dɪˈdʒektə] [di-yek-ta], *s.pl*. Excrementos; materias evacuadas.

dejectedly [dɪˈdʒektɪdlɪ] [di-yek-tid-li] *adv*. Abatidamente, tristemente; con desaliento o desánimo.

dejectedness [dɪˈdʒektɪdnɪs] [di-yek-tid-nes] *s*. Abatimiento, desaliento, amilanamiento.

dejecter [dɪˈdʒektəʳ] [di-yek-taʳ] *s*. El que abate, aflige o envilece.

dejection [dɪˈdʒekʃən] [di-yek-shon] *s*. 1. Melancolía, tristeza, aflicción, abatimiento de espíritu, desánimo. 2. Debilidad, extenuación. 3.(*Med.*) Deyección, cámara, la deposición de un enfermo.

dejectory [dɪˈdʒektərɪ] [di-yek-to-ri] *a*. 1. Que tiende a abatir o descorazonar. 2. (*Med.*) Lo que produce cámaras o las promueve.

dejecture [dɪˈdʒektʃəʳ] [di-yek-chaʳ] *s*. (*Med.*) Excremento, deyección.

de jure [deɪˈdʒʊərɪ] [dei-yua-ri] (*For.*) Legalmente, legítimamente; en contraposiciíon a de facto.

dekagram, dekaliter, etc. V. DECAGRAM, etc.

delaine [dɪˈleɪn] [di-lein] *s*. Muselina de lana; chalí.

delapsed [dɪˈlæpsd] [di-laps] *a*. (*Med.*) Caído, inclinado hacia abajo.

delate [dɪˈleɪt] [di-leit] *va*. 1. (Ley escocesa ecles.) Delatar, denunciar, acusar. 2. (*Des.*) Llevar, conducir.

delation [dɪˈleɪʃən] [di-lei-shon] *s*. 1. (*For.*) Delación, acusación, denunciación. 2. (*Ant.*) Porte, conducción.

delator [dɪˈleɪtəʳ] [di-lei-toʳ] *s*. Delator, delatante, denunciador.

delay [dɪˈleɪ] [di-lei] *va*. 1. Dilatar, diferir, suspender. Retrasar, demorar (defer/decision, payment). **We delaying signing the contract,** retrasamos o demoramos la firma del contrato. 2. Retardar, retrasar, demorar (make late, hold up); estorbar. **I don't want to delay you,** no quiero entretenerte. **Delaying,** *pres. p*. dilatorio (action, tactics). **Delayed,** *past p*. retardado (action, effect, reaction). -*vn*. Detenerse, pararse, cesar de obrar; tardar, demorar. **There's no point in delaying any longer,** no tiene sentido esperar más tiempo.

delay *s*. 1 Dilación, tardanza, demora (waiting); plaza, aplazamiento, prórroga (extra time); lapso, intervalo (interval). **And now, without further delay...,** y ahora, sin más preámbulos... 2. Detención, demora, retraso (holdup); retardo, retardación; atraso. **Delays can be expected on major roads,** se puede esperar embotellamientos en las principales carreteras.

delayed action [dɪˈleɪdˈækʃən] [di-leid-ak-shon] *s*. Acción retardada. **Delayed-action mechanism,** mecanismo de acción retardada.

delayer [dɪˈleɪəʳ] [di-leiaʳ] *s*. Temporizador, entretenedor, que gana tiempo dilatando.

dele [dɪˈliː] [di-li] Borrar, tachar.

deleble ['dɪləbl] [di-le-bol] *a*. Lo que se puede borrar.

delectable [dɪˈlektəbl] [di-lek-ta-bol] *a*. Deleitable, delicioso, exquisito (delicious); delicioso, encantador (delightful).

delectableness [dɪˈlektəblnɪs] [di-lek-ta-bol-nes] *s*. Delicia, gusto o placer especial que se percibe en alguna cosa.

delectably [dɪˈlektəblɪ] [di-lek-ta-bli] *adv*. Deleitosamente.

delectation [diːlekˈteɪʃən] [di-lek-tei-shon] *s*. Delectación o deleitación, deleite, placer vivo.

delegate ['delɪgɪt] [de-le-gueit] *va*. 1. Delegar, diputar, dar sus veces a otro (duties, powers, responsibility). 2. Enviar a una embajada. 3. Comisionar, señalar o nombrar un representante. -*vn*. Delegar.

delegate *s*. Delegado, diputado, comisionado, comisario. **Court of delegates,** un tribunal de apelación en Inglaterra. -*a*. Delegado, diputado.

delegation [delɪˈgeɪʃən] [de-le-guei-shon] *s*. 1. Delegación (deputation), diputación, comisión. (in US) Grupo de representantes de un estado en el Congreso. 2. Delegación (act of delegating).

delete [dɪˈliːt] [di-lit] *va*. Borrar, testar, tachar (by crossing out); suprimir, eliminar.

deleterious [delɪˈtɪərɪəs] [de-li-ti-rious] *a*. Deletéreo, mortal, mortífero, destructivo, emponzoñado, venenoso; pernicioso, nocivo, perjudicial.

deletion [dɪˈliːʃən] [di-li-shon] *s*. Canceladura, la acción de cancelar o borrar; destrucción, ruina.

deletory [dɪˈliːtərɪ] [di-li-to-ri], *s*. Lo que borra.

delf [delf] [delf] *s*. 1. Desaguadero; zanja de derivación. 2. Césped, hierba menuda y espesa. 3. (*Ant.*) Mina, cantera.

delf, delft [delft] [delft] *s*. Loza fina que se parece a la china. Delftware, loza vidriada.

Delfic, Delphian ['delfɪk] [del-fik] ['delfɪən] [del-fian] *a*. Délfico, referente a Delfos y al célebre oráculo de su templo.

deliberate [dɪˈlɪbəreɪt] [di-li-be-reit] *va*. Deliberar, discurrir, considerar, premeditar, determinar alguna cosa con premeditación. -*vn*. Pausar, pensar, dudar, deliberar sobre.

deliberate *a*. 1. Pensado, reflexionado, hecho con reflexión y madurez; circunspecto, cauto. Deliberado, intencionado (act, attempt). **It was a deliberate insult,** lo dijo (o lo hizo) con (la) intención de insultar. 2. Tardo, lento, pausado. 3. Prudente, avisado.

deliberately [dɪˈlɪbərɪtlɪ] [di-li-be-reit-li] *adv*. 1. Deliberadamente, prudentemente, gradualmente. Adrede, a propósito (intentionally). 2. Pausadamente, con parsimonia (unhurriedly).

deliberateness [dɪˈlɪbərɪtnɪs] [di-li-be-reit-nes] *s*. Deliberación, circunspección, cautela, precaución, reflexión, premeditación, sangre fría.

deliberation [dɪˌlɪbəˈreɪʃən] [di-li-be-rei-shon] *s*. 1. Deliberación (consideration), el acto de consultar con otro acerca del mejor modo de hacer una cosa. **After long deliberation,** tras largas deliberaciones o una larga deliberación. **Deliberations,** *pl*. deliberaciones (decision-making). 2. Parsimonia, calma (unhurried manner).

deliberative [dɪˈlɪbərətɪv] [di-li-be-ra-tiv] *a*. 1. Deliberativo, de la naturaleza de deliberación. 2. Deliberante, el que delibera. -*s*. Discurso deliberativo.

delicacy ['delɪkəsɪ] [di-li-ka-si] *s*. 1. Delicadeza, lo que es delicado fino, frágil o tenue (fineness, intricacy); finura, delicadeza, flaqueza, falta de vigor o robustez; fragilidad (fragility). 2. Delicadeza, nimiedad, escrupulosidad en el comer. 3. Delicadeza, la cosa que agrada a los sentidos. 4. Hermosura mujeril, blandura. 5. Aseo y gusto en el vestir, elegancia. 6. Urbanidad, cortesía; suavidad, dulzura, consideración para con otros. Delicadeza (tact); lo delicado (subtleness). 7. Ternura; escrupulosidad. 8. Manjar, exquisitez (choice food).

delicate [ˈdelɪkɪt] [de-li-keit] *a.* 1. Delicado (fine, intricate/lace, features); fino y ligero en textura, esmerado (workmanship); armonioso en color y figura; hermoso; regalado. 2. Delicado (subtle/shade, taste); exquisito, escogido, excelente. 3. Cortés, urbano, suave, que manifiesta consideración para con otros; delicado, discreto (tactful). 4. Afeminado, incapaz de aguantar fatiga o trabajo. 5. Puro, claro; fino, casto. 6. Tierno, sensible; frágil, flaco; delicado (fragile, needing care). **A delicate child,** un niño delicado de salud. 7. Delicado, difícil, expuesto a contingencias (needing skill).

delicately [ˈdelɪkɪtlɪ] [di-li-keit-li], *adv.* 1. Delicadamente, con delicadeza (carve, paint). 2. Exquisitamente, cortésmente, afeminadamente, con delicadeza (behave, treat). 3. Delicadamente (patterned, perfumed).

delicateness [ˈdelɪkɪtnɪs] [di-li-keit-nes] *s.* Delicadeza, molicie.

delicatessen [ˌdelɪkəˈtesn] [de-li-ka-tesn] *s. pl.* Delicadezas, golosinas, manjares delicados. (*Al.*) Charcutería, rotisería, salsamentaría, salchichonería.

delicious [dɪˈlɪʃəs] [di-li-shos] *a.* Delicioso, ameno, agradable, exquisito, riquísimo (food, smell). **It tastes/it's delicious,** está delicioso, o exquisito, o riquísimo. Delicioso (delightful/breeze, feeling).

deliciously [dɪˈlɪʃəslɪ] [di-li-shos-li] *adv.* Deliciosamente, gustosamente.

deliciousness [dɪˈlɪʃəsnɪs] [di-li-shos-nes] *s.* Delicia, suavidad, gusto, placer.

deligation [dɪˈlaɪɡeɪʃən] [di-li-guei-shon] *s.* Ligadura, la acción de ligar.

delight [dɪˈlaɪt] [di-lait] *s.* Delicia, deleite, placer, gozo, alegría (joy); satisfacción, encanto. **To take delight in reading,** tener gusto en leer. **Her happiness was a delight to see,** era un placer o daba gusto verla tan feliz.

delight *va.* Deleitar (give pleasure to); agradar, contentar, causar placer, divertir; llenar de alegría (make very happy). **His success delighted them,** su éxito los llenó de alegría. **The clown delighted the children,** el payaso hizo las delicias de o deleitó a los niños. *-vn.* Deleitarse, tener deleite en alguna cosa; divertirse, complacerse.

delighted [dɪˈlaɪtɪd] [di-lai-ted] *a.* De alegría (grin, look). **I told him the news and he was delighted,** le di la noticia y se alegró muchísimo. **I'm delighted that you can come,** me alegra mucho que puedas venir. **To be delighted with something/somebody,** estar encantado con algo/alguien.

delighter [dɪˈlaɪtəʳ] [di-lai-taʳ] *s.* El que se complace o deleita en alguna cosa.

delightful [dɪˈlaɪtfʊl] [di-lait-ful] *a.* Delicioso, deleitoso, ameno, agradable, deleitable, grato, divertido, encantador (person); embelesador, exquisito, precioso (dress). Muy agradable, delicioso (weather, evening).

delightfully [dɪˈlaɪtfʊlɪ] [di-lait-fu-li] *adv.* Deliciosamente, deleitosamente; divinamente, de maravilla.

delightfulness [dɪˈlaɪtfʊlnɪs] [di-lait-ful-nes] *s.* Delicia, suavidad, placer, encanto.

delightless [dɪˈlaɪtlɪs] [di-lait-les] *a.* Sin placer o deleite.

delightsome [dɪˈlaɪtsɒm] [di-lait-som] *a.* Delicioso, deleitoso, placentero.

delightsomely [dɪˈlaɪtsɒmlɪ] [di-lait-som-li] *adv.* Deliciosamente, deleitablemente.

delightsomeness [dɪˈlaɪtsɒmnɪs] [di-lait-som-nes] *s.* Delicia, gusto delicioso, deleite, amenidad.

delimit [ˈdelɪmɪt] [de-li-mit] *va.* Delimitar.

delineament [dɪˈlɪnɪmənt] [de-li-ni-ment] *s.* Delineamiento, representación por líneas; bosquejo; descripción verbal.

delineate [dɪˈlɪnɪeɪt] [de-li-nieit] *va.* 1. Delinear, trazar, diseñar, dibujar (draw). 2. Pintar con diversos colores. 3. Representar alguna cosa como es. 4. Delinear, describir. 5. Definir, describir (problem).

delineation [dɪˈlɪnɪeɪʃən] [de-li-nei-shon] *s.* 1. Delineación, delineamiento. 2. Bosquejo, esquicio; descripción, pintura, representación por medio de la palabra.

delineator [dɪˈlɪnɪeɪtəʳ] [de-li-nei-taʳ] *s.* Delineador, dibujante, descriptor.

delinquency [dɪˈlɪŋkwənsɪ] [di-lin-kuen-si] *s.* Descuido u omisión en el cumplimiento del deber; delito, culpa, falta. (*Law, Sociol.*) Delincuencia.

delinquent [dɪˈlɪŋkwənt] [di-lin-kuent] *a.* 1. Descuidado, negligente en sus deberes, culpable, defectuoso. 2. Debido y no pagado; se dice de las contribuciones de un gobierno, del pago de intereses, censos, etc. 3. Delincuente (youth); delictivo (activities). *-s.* Delincuente, el que descuida su obligación; criminal.

deliquate [ˈdɪlɪkweɪt] [di-li-kueit] *vn.* Derretirse, liquidarse. *-va.* Disolver. V. DELIQUESCE.

deliquation [ˈdɪlɪkweɪʃən] [di-li-kuei-shon] *s.* Derretimiento, liquidación, el acto de derretir o liquidarse alguna cosa.

deliquesce [ˈdɪlɪkwəs] [di-li-kues] *vn.* Liquidarse, hacerse líquido; deshacerse poco a poco por la acción de la humedad.

deliquescence [ˈdɪlɪkwəsəns] [di-li-kue-sens] *s.* (*Quím.*) Derretimiento, delicuescencia, la tendencia de algunas sales a derretirse, y el estado líquido a que se reducen a consecuencia de esta tendencia.

deliquescent [ˈdɪlɪkwəsənt] [di-li-kue-sent] *a.* Delicuescente, se dice de las sales que se liquidan expuestas al aire.

deliquiate [ˈdɪlɪkieɪt] [di-li-kieit] *vn.* V. DELIQUATE.

deliquium [ˈdɪlɪkiom] [di-li-kium] *s.* 1. Liquidación; estado líquido de alguna sal. 2. Defecto, estado debilitado de la mente. 3. (*Des.*) Deliquio.

deliriant [dɪˈlɪrɪənt] [di-li-riant] *s.* (*Med.*) 1. Veneno que produce un delirio persistente. 2. Delirante, el que delira.

delirious [dɪˈlɪrɪəs] [di-li-rios] *a.* Delirante, el que delira o desvaría. **To be delirious,** delirar, desvariar. (*Coloq.*) Loco de alegría (wildly excited, happy).

deliriously [dɪˈlɪrɪəslɪ] [di-li-rios-li] *adv.* Delirantemente (mutter). (*Coloq.*) **She was deliriously happy,** estaba loca de alegría.

delirium [dɪˈlɪrɪəm] [di-li-riom] *s.* (*Med.*) Delirio, perturbación del cerebro; locura, demencia, destemple de la imaginación o fantasía. **Delirium tremens,** delírium tremens, enfermedad del cerebro producida por el abuso de bebidas alcohólicas o de narcóticos.

delitescence [dɪˈlɪtəsəns] [di-li-te-sens] *s.* (*Ant.*) 1. Disminución repentina de una inflamación. 2. Retiro, oscuridad.

deliver [dɪˈlɪvəʳ] [di-li-vaʳ] *va.* 1. Librar (save); libertar, salvar, soltar a un preso, poner a alguno en libertad, sustraerlo a la sujeción o el predominio de otro. **To deliver somebody from something,** librar a alguien de algo. 2. Dar, entregar (hand over); repartir a domicilio (distribute); ceder, rendir. **We have our paper delivered every day,** nos traen el periódico a casa todos los días. 3. (*Med.*) Partear, ayudar o asistir facultativamente a un parto (se usa a menudo con la prep. of). **Her husband delivered the baby,** su marido la asistió en el parto. 4. Recitar, hablar, decir, relatar. 5. Tirar, arrojar. (*Dep.*) Lanzar (ball). 6.- Propinar, asestar (administer/ blow, punch); dar (issue/ultimatum, lecture, sermon); hacer (warning); pronunciar (speech); dictar, pronunciar, emitir (judgment). **He promised much, but he delivered little,** cumplió muy poco de lo mucho que había prometido (produce, provide). **To deliver over,** transmitir; poner entre las manos de otro; pasar. **To deliver up,** entregar, resignar, abandonar. *vn.* 1. (*Neg.*) **We deliver free of charge,** hacemos reparto(s) a domicilio gratuitamente. 2. (*Coloq.*) Cumplir (produce the necessary).

deliverance [dɪˈlɪvərəns] [di-li-ve-rans] *s.* 1. Rescate; salida de prisión o cautiverio; preservación de un mal, de un peligro. 2. Prolación, la acción de proferir o pronunciar; expresión de parecer u opinión. V. DELIVERY. 3. Parto, el acto de parir.

deliverer [dɪˈlɪvərəʳ] [di-li-ve-raʳ] *s.* 1. El que entrega. 2. Libertador, salvador. 3. Narrador, relator, el que narra o relata.

delivery [dɪˈlɪvərɪ] [di-li-ve-ri] *s.* 1. Libramiento, rescate, la acción de librar o libertar. Liberación (freeing). 2. Entrega (act). **Cash on delivery,** entrega contra reembolso. **To take delivery of something,** recibir algo. **Delivery man,** repartidor. **Delivery note,** nota de entrega, albarán de entrega. **Delivery period,** plazo de entrega. **Delivery service,** servicio de reparto a domicilio. Reparto (occasion). **Is there a delivery on Saturdays?,** ¿hay reparto los sábados?. 3. Rendición, el acto de rendir alguna cosa. 4. Alumbramiento, parto, el acto de parir. **Delivery room,** sala de partos. 5. Prolación, la acción de proferir palabras; el modo de producirse. Expresión oral (manner of speaking). 6. Expedición, desembarazo, la facilidad en producirse. 7. *(For.)* Entrega, el acto de poner en posesión. *(Com.)* Remesa, partida (consignment). 8. Proyección, descarga; fuerza propulsora; descarga de un cañón. 9. *(Dep.)* Lanzamiento (throw); estilo de lanzamiento (manner of trowing).

dell [del] [del] *s.* Barranco, paraje profundo; valle hondo, hondonada, foso.

delouse *va.* Despiojar

delphian *a.* V. DELFIC.

delta [ˈdeltə] [del-ta] *s.* 1. Delta, cuarta letra del alfabeto griego que corresponde a la D. 2. Delta, isla de figura triangular formada en la desembocadura de algunos ríos; depósito aluvial.

deltoid [ˈdeltɔɪd] [del-toid] *a.* Deltoide, triangular, en forma de delta. -*s.* *(Anat.)* Deltoides; se dice de uno de los músculos que levantan el brazo.

deludable [dɪˈljuːdəbl] [di-liu-da-bol] *a.* Engañadizo.

delude [dɪˈluːd] [di-lud] *va.* Engañar, entrampar, chasquear, embaucar; frustrar. **They deluded him into believing that he had talent,** le hicieron creer que tenía talento. **To delude oneself,** hacerse ilusión.

deluded [dɪˈluːdɪd] [di-lu-did] *a.* Engañado.

deluder [dɪˈluːdər] [di-ludaʳ] *s.* Delusor, engañador, impostor.

deluding [dɪˈluːdɪŋ] [di-lu-din] *s.* Colusión, falsedad, engaño, impostor.

deluge [ˈdeljuːdʒ] [de-ludch] *s.* 1. Diluvio (downpour); inundación (flood), copiosa abundancia de agua e inundación de la tierra. **The Deluge,** el diluvio universal. 2. Creciente avenida, el aumento de agua que toman los ríos. 3. Golpe, infortunio, calamidad, desgracia o infelicidad repentina. 4. Aluvión, avalancha (of protests, questions, letters).

deluge *va.* 1. Diluviar, llover a cántaros. Inundar (flood). 2. Abrumar, oprimir (overwhelm). **They were deluged with protests/letters,** recibieron un aluvión de protestas/cartas. **He was deluged with offers,** le llovieron las ofertas.

delusion [dɪˈluːʒn] [di-liu-shon] *s.* 1. Error (mistaken idea), el estado del que está engañado. 2. Ilusión, prestigio, falsa imaginación, falsa ilusión (vain hope). 3. Dolo, decepción, engaño, acción de engañar. 4. *(Psych)* Idea delirante. **He has delusions of grandeur,** tiene delirios de grandeza.

delusive [dɪˈluːsɪv] [di-liu-siv] **delusory** [dɪˈluːsərɪ] [di-liu-so-ri], *a.* Engañoso, falaz, fraudulento, ilusorio.

de luxe [dɪˈlʌks] [di-laks] *a.* De lujo.

delve [delv] [delv] *va.* 1. Cavar, levantar y mover la tierra con la azada o azadón. 2. Sondear, inquirir, rastrear con cautela (research). **To delve into the past,** ahondar en el pasado. 3. Hurgar, escarbar (rummage).

delve, *s.* Foso, hoyo, barranco, hondón; zanja; madriguera.

delver [ˈdelvər] [del-vaʳ] *s.* Cavador, el que tiene por oficio cavar la tierra.

demagnetize [diːˈmæɡnɪtaɪz] [di-mag-ni-tais] *va.* Desmagnetizar, privar del magnetismo.

demagog, (GB) **demagogue** [ˈdeməɡɒɡ] [de-ma-gog] *s.* Demagogo.

demagogic [deməˈɡɒɡɪk] [de-ma-go-guik] *a.* Demagógico, perteneciente a la demagogia o al demagogo.

demagogism [ˈdeməɡɒɡɪsm] [de-ma-go-guism] *s.* Demagogia, dominación tiránica de la plebe o de una facción popular.

demain [ˈdɪmeɪn] [di-mein], **demesne** [dɪˈmesn] [di-mesn] *s.* Tierras patrimoniales, las que uno posee heredadas; tierra solariega.

demand [dɪˈmɑːnd] [di-mand] *s.* 1. Demanda, súplica, petición, pedido (request); exigencia (claim). *(Lab Rel., Pol.)* Reivindicación, reclamo. **By popular demand,** a petición o pedido del público. **The demands of the job,** las exigencias del trabajo. **Abortion on demand,** libre aborto. **Payable on demand,** pagadero a la vista. 2. Alegación de derecho a alguna cosa. 3. *(Ant.)* Demanda, pregunta, interrogación. 4. Petición jurídica de una deuda. 5. Venta continuada, buen despacho. Demanda (requirement). **These shoes are much in demand,** estos zapatos tienen gran demanda o se venden mucho. **He's in great demand,** está muy solicitado, es muy popular. **In full of all demands,** ajustadas todas las cuentas.

demand, *va.* 1. Demandar, reclamar, pedir con autoridad o exigir como de derecho (person/call on, insist on); procesar. **The unions are demanding better conditions,** los sindicatos reclaman mejores condiciones. **She demanded to know the reason,** quiso saber el porqué, exigió que se le dijera el porqué. 2. Demandar, exigir con urgencia, necesitar. 3. *(Ant.)* Preguntar, interrogar. 4. Exigir, requerir (require/determination, perseverance).

demandable [dɪˈmɑːndəbl] [di-man-da-bol] *a.* Exigible, demandable.

demandant [dɪˈmɑːndənt] [di-man-dant] *s.* *(For.)* Demandante, demandador.

demander [dɪˈmɑːndər] [di-man-daʳ] *s.* 1. Exactor, demandador, el que pide, demanda o requiere alguna cosa con autoridad. 2. Pedigüeño, pedigón, el que pide con importunidad.

demanding [dɪˈmɑːndɪŋ] [di-man-din] *a.* Que exige mucho (job); difícil (book, music); exigente (teacher). **She's a very demanding child,** es una niña que exige mucha atención. **It's physically demanding,** es agotador.

demandress [dɪˈmɑːndrɪs] [di-man-res] *sf.* Demandadora.

demarcate [diːˈmɑːkeɪt] [di-mar-keit] *va.* Demarcar (frontier, area, limit); delimitar (concept).

demarcation [diːmɑːˈkeɪʃən] [di-mar-kei-shon] *s.* 1. Demarcación (delimitation), señalamiento de confines o límites; separación, distinción. **Demarcation line,** línea de demarcación. 2. Límite, confín. 3. (GB) (Lab Rel) Delimitación de atribuciones.

demarch [dɪˈmɑːch] [di-march] *s.* *(Des.)* El paso, el andar o modo de andar.

demean [dɪˈmiːn] [di-min] *va.* y *vr.* 1 Portarse, gobernarse bien o mal, conducirse. 2. *(Ant.)* Dirigir, conducir; registrar. -*va.* Envilecer, desestimar, degradar. **To demean oneself,** rebajarse, degradarse.

demean, *vr.* Rebajarse, degradarse; acepción errónea de *Demean.*

demeanor, demeanour [dɪˈmiːnər] [di-mi-noʳ] *s.* Porte (bearing); conducta, comportamiento, el modo de gobernarse, portarse o conducirse (behavior).

demency [dɪˈmənsɪ] [di-men-si] *s.* V. DEMENTIA.

dement [dɪˈmənt] [di-ment] *va.* Enloquecer, volver loco o demente, trastornar a uno el juicio.

dementate [dɪˈmənteɪt] [di-men-teit] *vn.* Dementarse, volverse loco.

demented [dɪˈməntɪd] [di-men-tid] *pp.* y *a.* Demente (insane/person), falto de razón, loco. Enloquecido, de demente (screams, mutterings). *(Coloq.)* Histérico (very worried, irritated).

dementia [dɪˈmenʃə] [di-men-sha] *s.* Demencia, locura, pérdida o trastorno de la facultad de pensar con coherencia.

demephitize [dɪˈmɪfɪtaɪz] [di-mi-fi-tais] *va.* Desinfectar, purificar el aire mefítico o malsano.

demerit [diːˈmerɪt] [di-me-rit] *s.* Demérito (fault), desmerecimiento; lo que es opuesto al mérito. Sanción (black mark).

demerit *va.* Desmerecer, hacerse indigno de algún bien.

demersed [dɪˈmɜːst] [di-merst] *a.* (*Bot.*) Sumergido, situado en el agua o que crece en ella.

demersion [dɪˈmɜːʃən] [di-mer-shon] *s.* 1. (*Ant.*) Inmersión, sumersión o sufocación en el agua. 2. El acto de poner una medicina en algún menstruo o disolvente.

demi [ˈdemɪ] [de-mi] Partícula inseparable que significa la mitad de alguna cosa, y a veces también lo mismo que casi.

demi-devil [ˈdemɪdevɪl] [de-mi-de-vil] *s.* Medio demonio.

demi-god [ˈdemɪɡɒd] [de-mi-god] *s.* Semidiós.

demijohn [ˈdemɪjɒn] [de-mi-yon] *s.* Garrafón, damajuana.

demi-lance [ˈdemɪlæns] [de-mi-lans] *s.* Lanza ligera.

demilitarize [ˈdiːˈmɪlɪtəraɪz] [di-mi-li-ta-rais] *va.* Desmilitarizar. **Demilitarized zone,** zona desmilitarizada.

demi-monde [ˈdemɪmɒːnd] [de-mi-mond] *s.* Cierta clase de persona de reputación equívoca: se aplica en especial a las queridas o concubinas que no son mujeres públicas.

demi-rep [ˈdemɪrep] [de-mi-rep] *sf.* Mujer sospechada, pero no convicta de incontinencia.

demise [dɪˈmaɪz] [di-mais] *s.* 1. Muerte, fallecimiento, deceso (death). Desaparición (end). 2. Transmisión de la corona o de la autoridad real. 3. (*For.*) Traslación de dominio por arriendo o legado.

demise, *va.* 1. Legar, dejar en testamento. 2. Transferir, ceder el derecho o dominio que se tiene sobre una cosa; arrendar, dar en arriendo.

demission [ˈdemɪʃən] [de-mi-shon], *s.* Degradación, destitución de una dignidad, dimisión; decadencia.

demissory *a.* V. DIMISSORY.

demist [ˈdemɪst] [de-mist] *va.* (GB) Desempañar.

demister [ˈdemɪstəʳ] [de-mis-taʳ] *s.* (GB) Desempañador.

demit [ˈdemɪt] [de-mit], *va.* 1. Ceder, renunciar, resignar. 2. (*Des.*) Soltar; despedir. 3. (*Des.*) Deprimir, abatir, envilecer, humillar.

demi-wolf [ˈdemɪwʊlf] [de-mi-vulf] *s.* Mediolobo; cruzado de perro y loba.

demo [ˈdeməʊ] [de-mou] *s.* 1. (*Mus.*) Demostración. **Demo tape,** cinta de demostración. 2. (GB) (*Coloq.*) Manifestación (protest).

demobilize [diːˈməʊbɪlaɪz] [di-mou-bi-lais] *va.* (*Mil.*) Desmovilizar.

democracy [dɪˈmɒkrəsɪ] [de-mo-kra-si] *s.* Democracia, gobierno en que el pueblo ejerce la soberanía.

democrat [ˈdeməkræt] [de-mo-krat] *s.* Demócrata, el partidario de la democracia (believer in democracy).

democratic, democratical [ˈdeməkrætɪk] [de-mo-kra-tik] *a.* Democrático (country, election).

democratically [ˈdeməkrætɪklɪ] [de-mo-kra-ti-ka-li] *adv.* Democráticamente.

democratization [dɪˌmɒkrətaɪˈzeɪʃən] [de-mo-kra-tai-sei-shon] *s.* Democratización.

democratize [dɪˈmɒkrətaɪz] [de-mo-kra-tais] *va.* Democratizar.

demographer [dɪˈmɒɡrəfəʳ] [de-mo-gra-faʳ] *s.* Demógrafo.

demographic [ˌdeməˈɡræfɪk] [de-mo-gra-fik] *a.* Demográfico.

demography [dɪˈmɒɡrəfɪ] [di-mo-gra-fi] *s.* Demografía.

demoiselle [ˈdeməʊəsel] [de-mua-sel] *s.* V. DAMSEL. Damisela, doncella.

demolish [dɪˈmɒlɪʃ] [di-mo-lish] *va.* 1. Demoler, derribar, echar abajo (structure, building); deshacer, arruínar, echar por tierra (argument, theory); arrasar. 2. (*Coloq.*) Hacer polvo (defeat); zamparse (eat up).

demolisher [dɪˈmɒlɪʃəʳ] [di-mo-li-shaʳ] *s.* Arruinador, destructor, el que demuele.

demolishment [dɪˈmɒlɪʃmənt] [di-mo-lish-ment] *s.* Destrucción, ruina.

demolition [ˌdeməˈlɪʃən] [di-mo-li-shon] *s.* Demolición, derribo (of building); demolición, destrucción (of theory). **Demolition squad,** cuadrilla de demolición.

demon [ˈdiːmən] [di-mon] *s.* Demonio, espíritu maligno, diablo. (*Coloq.*) **She worked like a demon all week,** trabajó como una bestia toda la semana.

demoness [ˈdiːmənɪs] [di-mo-nes] *sf.* Mujer diabólica.

demonetize [diːˈmʌnɪtaɪz] [di-ma-ni-tais] *va.* Desmonetizar, quitar su valor legal a la moneda o papel moneda.

demoniac, demoniacal [dɪˈməʊniæk] [di-mou-niak] [ˌdiːməˈnaɪəkəl] [di-mo-nai-a-kal] *a.* 1. Demoníaco, perteneciente al demonio. 2. Poseso, obseso, endemoniado, afligido o atormentado por el espíritu maligno.

demoniac *s.* Energúmeno, el que está poseído del demonio.

demonism [ˈdiːmənɪzm] [di-mo-nísem] *s.* 1. La creencia en demonios. 2. Naturaleza o carácter de demonio.

demonocracy [ˌdiːməˈnɒkrəsɪ] [di-mo-no-kra-si] *s.* Poder o gobierno del demonio.

demonolatry [ˌdiːməˈnɒlətrɪ] [di-mo-no-la-tri] *s.* Culto del demonio.

demonology [ˌdiːməˈnɒlədʒɪ] [di-mo-no-lo-yi] *s.* Demonología, demonomanía.

demonstrable [ˈdemənstrəbl] [de-mons-tra-bol] *a.* Demostrable.

demonstrableness [ˈdemənstrəblnɪs] [de-mons-tra-bol-nes] *s.* Capacidad de demostración

demonstrably [ˈdemənstrəblɪ] [de-mons-tra-bli] *adv.* Demostrablemente, demostrativamente; ciertamente. **A demonstrably true/false statement,** una afirmación cuya verdad/falsedad es demostrable.

demonstrate [ˈdemənstreɪt] [de-mons-treit] *va.* Demostrar (show/need, ability); probar y hacer ver alguna cosa con el mayor grado de certeza. Hacer una demostración de (Marketing)-vn. (*Pol.*) Manifestarse.

demonstration [ˌdemənˈstreɪʃən] [de-mons-trei-shon] *s.* 1. Demostración, muestra, evidencia, prueba de alguna cosa por principios ciertos (expression). 2. Manifestación, señalamiento. 3.(*Mil.*) Demostración o despliegue de fuerza: especialmente en un ataque simulado. 4. Manifestación pública, sea aprobatoria o condenatoria; asamblea en masa. 5. Demostración (display).

demonstrative [dɪˈmɒnstrətɪv] [di-mons-tra-tiv], *a.* 1. Demostrativo, que prueba de una manera evidente. 2. Demostrativo, el que declara con gran fuerza de expresión sus ideas o sentimientos; efusivo, expresivo (expressive). 3. (*Gram.*) Demostrativo.

demonstrator [ˈdemənstreɪtəʳ] [de-mons-trei-tʳ], *s.* 1. Demostrador, mostrador, enseñador (Marketing). 2. (*Pol.*) Manifestante.

demonstratory [ˌdemənsˈtrætərɪ] [de-mons-tra-to-ri] *a.* Lo que tiende a demostrar.

demoralization [dɪˌmɒrəlaɪˈzeɪʃən] [de-mo-ra-lai-sei-shon] *s.* Desmoralización; corrupción, estragamiento de costumbres.

demoralize [dɪˈmɒrəlaɪz] [di-mo-ra-lais] *va.* 1. Desmoralizar, hacer perder la buena moral, corromper las costumbres. 2. Desanimar, descorazonar, acobardar. p.ej. a un ejército, a una multitud.

demoralizing [dɪˈmɒrəlaɪzɪŋ] [di-mo-ra-lai-sin] *a.* Desalentador, desmoralizante.

demote [dɪˈməʊt] [di-mout] *va.* Bajar de categoría (in organization); (*Mil.*) Degradar.

demotic [dɪˈmɒʊtɪk] [di-mou-tik] *a.* Demótico, que concierne al pueblo; escrito con caracteres usuales, en contraposición a lo escrito en los jeroglíficos que usaban los sacerdotes egipcios.

demotion [dɪˈməʊʃən] [di-mou-shon] *s.* 1. (*Mil.*) Degradación. 2. Descenso de rango o categoría (in organization).

demountable [dɪˈməʊntəbl] [di-moun-ta-bol], *a.* Desarmable, desmontable.

demulcent [dɪˈmʌlsənt] [di-mal-sent] *a. (Med.)* Emoliente, demulcente, dulcificante, *-s.* Emoliente, medicamento dulcificante, como las substancias mucilaginosas y untuosas.

demur [dɪˈmɜːʳ] [di-maʳ] *vn.* 1. Objetar, poner tachas, objeciones o reparos; suspender el curso de alguna instancia en un tribunal con objeciones y dudas. 2. Vacilar, fluctuar; tener escrúpulo sobre alguna cosa *-va. (Ant.)* Dudar, tener duda de alguna cosa.

demur *s.* Duda, escrúpulo, hesitación, perplejidad, vacilación. **Without demur,** sin poner objeciones o reparos.

demure [dɪˈmjʊəʳ] [di-miuaʳ] *a.* 1. Sobrio, moderado; reservado; decente. 2. Grave, serio, formal. 3. Gazmoño, modesto con afectación; pacato, recatado.

demurely [dɪˈmjʊəlɪ] [di-miua-li] *adv.* Modestamente, con gazmoñería; recatadamente, con recato.

demureness [dɪˈmjʊənɪs] [di-miua-nes] *s.* Gazmoñería, modestia afectada o verdadera, seriedad, gravedad de aspecto.

demurrage [dɪˈmʌrɪdʒ] [di-ma-rich] *s.* Demora o gastos de demora, gastos extraordinarios que debe abonar el comerciante al patrón de un buque por el tiempo que se detiene en un puerto fuera de lo estipulado; estadía.

demurral [dɪˈmʌrəl] [di-ma-ral] *s.* Demora, detención; sobreseimiento, cesación; interrupción o tardanza en sentenciar un pleito a causa de alguna duda.

demurrer [dɪˈmʌrəʳ] [di-ma-raʳ] *s.* 1. El que pone tachas, objeciones o reparos. 2. *(For.)* Excepción perentoria, cuestación de derecho; alegación que admite los hechos alegados por la parte contraria, pero niega que constituyen causa suficiente de acción.

demy [dɪˈmɪ] [di-mi] *s.* Marquilla, nombre de una clase de papel.

demystify [diˈmɪstɪfaɪ] [di-mis-ti-fai] *va.* Desmistificar.

den [den] [den] *s.* Caverna, antro; cueva de fieras. Guarida, cubil (lair), guarida (of thieves). **A den of iniquity,** un antro de perdición. *(Coloq.)* Cuarto de estar; estudio, gabinete (for study, work).

denary [dɪˈnɑrɪ] [di-na-ri] *a.* Lo que contiene diez; decimal. *-s.* Decena.

denationalize [diːˈnæʃnəlaɪz] [di-na-sho-na-laiz] *va.* Desnacionalizar, quitar a uno los privilegios de la nación a que pertenece.

denatured [diːˈneɪtʃəd] [di-nei-ched] *a.* Desnaturalizado. **Denatured alcohol,** alcohol desnaturalizado.

dendriform [ˌdendrɪˈfɔːm] [den-dri-form] *a. V.* DENDRITIC.

dendrite [ˈdendraɪt] [den-drait] *s. (Min.)* Dendrita, piedra con figuras estampadas de árboles y plantas.

dendritic [denˈdraɪtɪk] [den-drai-tik] *a.* Dendrítico, con arborizaciones que imitan la forma de un arbusto.

dendrology [denˈdrɒlɒdʒɪ] [den-dro-lo-yi] *s.* Dendrología, historia natural de los árboles.

dengue [ˈdeŋgɪ] [den-gui] *s.* Dengue, enfermedad tropical aguda y epidémica. Se llama también *break-bone fever o dandy-fever.*

deniable [dɪˈnaɪəbl] [di-naia-bol] **a.** Negable, lo que se puede negar.

denial [dɪˈnaɪəl] [di-naial] *s.* 1. Denegación (of request, rights). 2. Negación, rechazo, repulsa (repudiation). 3. Renuncia, abnegación (abstinence). **Self-denial,** abnegación de sí mismo. **To issue a denial of something,** desmentir algo (of accusation, fact).

denier [dɪˈnaɪəʳ] [di-naiaʳ] *s.* Contradictor, negador.

denier, *s.* Dinero, antigua moneda de plata en Francia, que valía un penique.

denigrate [ˈdenɪgreɪt] [de-ni-greit] *va.* Denegrecer, denegrir, ennegrecer; denigrar (character, person); infamar. Menospreciar (effort).

denim [ˈdenɪm] [de-nim] *s.* Mezclilla, tela basta y resistente de algodón; tela vaquera o de jeans. Vaquero, tejano, de

mezclilla (jacket, shirt). **Denims,** *(Coloq.)* vaqueros, jeans, bluyines (jeans); pantalón de peto, mono, overol (overalls).

denization [denɪˈzeɪʃən] [de-ni-sei-shon] *s.* Naturalización, ciudadanía acción de naturalizar a uno en Inglaterra.

denizen [ˈdenɪzn] [de-nisen], *s.* 1. Ciudadano, habitante, residente. 2. (Der.ingl.) El extranjero naturalizado.

denizen, *va.* 1. Naturalizar. 2. Eximir, otorgar ciertos privilegios al extremo naturalizado.

Denmark [ˈdenmɑːk] [de-mark] *N. (Geogr.)* Dinamarca.

denominate [dɪˈnɒmɪneɪt] [di-no-mi-neit], *va.* Denominar, nombrar.

denomination [dɪˌnɒmɪˈneɪʃən] [di-no-mi-nei-shon], *s.* 1. Denominación, título, nombre, designación. 2. Secta, grupo de cristianos que no está de acuerdo con una Iglesia establecida. 3. *(Rel.)* Confesión. 4. Valor, denominación (of currency). **Bills in $10 and $20 denominations,** billetes de 10 y 20 dólares.

denominational [dɪˌnɒmɪˈneɪʃənl] [di-no-mi], *a.* Confesional.

denominative [dɪˌnɒmɪˈnætɪv] [di-no-mi-na-tiv], *a.* Denominativo.

denominator [dɪˈnɒmɪneɪtəʳ] [di-no-mi-nei-toʳ], *s. (Arit.)* Denominador.

denotable [dɪˈnəʊtəbl] [di-nou-ta-bol], *a.* Capaz de ser notado o distinguido.

denotation [ˌdiːnəʊˈteɪʃən] [di-nou-tei-shon], *s.* Designación, marca, señal, indicio, notabilidad.

denote [dɪˈnəʊt] [di-nout], *va.* Denotar, indicar, anunciar, significar, designar, marcar, señalar.

denotement [dɪˈnəʊtmənt] [di-nout-ment], *s.* Señal, indicación.

denouement [deɪˈnuːmɒn] [di-nu-men], *s.* éxito, salida, fin; desenredo, desenlace.

denounce [dɪˈnaʊns] [di-nauns], *va.* Denunciar, delatar. 2. Acusar; amenazar; proclamar con amenazas. 3. Promulgar, publicar, declarar alguna cosa solemnemente.

denouncement [dɪˈnaʊsmənt] [di-nauns-ment], *s.* Denunciación; acusación o delatación.

denouncer [dɪˈnaʊnsəʳ] [di-naun-saʳ], *s.* 1. Denunciador, acusador. 2. Amenazador.

dense [dens] [dens], *a.* 1. Denso, espeso (closely spaced/ forest, jungle); compacto, cerrado, apretado (crowd). Denso (population, traffic). Denso, espeso (thick/fog, mist, smoke). Denso (complicated/prose, article). 2. *(Coloq.)* Burro; duro de entenderas (stupid).

densely [ˈdenslɪ] [dens-li] *adv.* Densamente (populated, forested); apretadamente (packed).

densimeter [ˌdensɪˈmiːtəʳ] [den-si-mi-taʳ], *s.* Densímetro, aerómetro.

density [ˈdensɪtɪ] [den-si-ti], *s.* Densidad, solidez. Lo espeso, densidad (fog).

dent [dent] [dent], *s.* Abolladura, abollón (in metal); marca (in wood). *(Coloq.)* **It's made a big dent in our savings,** se ha llevado o se ha comido una buena parte de nuestros ahorros.

dent, *va.* Abollar (metal); hacer una marca en (wood). Afectar (popularity); hacer mella en (pride). *vn.* Abollarse (metal). *V.* INDENT.

dental [ˈdentl] [den-tal], *a.* 1. Dental, lo que pertenece a los dientes. **Dental floss,** hilo o seda dental. **Dental surgeon,** cirujano, dentista. 2. *(Gram.)* Dental, la letra cuya pronunciación requiere que la lengua toque en los dientes, como la d y th. *-s. (Ict.)* Dentón, pescado.

dentate, dentated [ˈdenteɪt] [den-teit] *a.* Dentado.

dentelli *s. V.* MODILLIONS.

denticle [ˈdentɪkl] [den-ti-kol], *s.* Dientecillo, punto saliente.

denticulate [denˈtɪkjʊleɪt] [den-ti-kiu-leit], **denticulated** [denˈtɪkjʊleɪtɪd] [den-ti-kiu-lei-tid], *a. (Bot.)* Dentado, provisto de pequeños dientes.

denticulation [denˈtɪkjʊleɪʃən] [den-ti-kiu-lei-shon], *s.* Dentadura, la fila de dientes pequeños que tienen algunas máquinas o instrumentos.

dentifrice ['dentɪfrɪs] [den-ti-fris], *s.* Dentífrico, lo que sirve para limpiar los dientes.

dentil ['dentɪl] [den-til], *s. (Arq.)* Dentículo, moldura o adorno en figura de diente.

dentirostral [ˌdentɪ'rɒstrəl] [den-ti-ros-tral], *a.* Dentirrostro, (pájaro) de pico dentado.

dentist ['dentɪst] [den-tist], *s.* Dentista, odontólogo. **To go to the dentist('s),** ir al dentista.

dentistry ['dentɪstrɪ] [den-tis-tri] *s.* Odontología.

dentition ['dentɪʃən] [den-ti-shon], *s.* 1. Dentición, el procedimiento o la época de endentecer. 2. Dentadura peculiar a un animal.

dentoid ['dentɔɪd] [den-toid], *a.* Parecido a un diente; en figura de diente.

denture ['dentʃəʳ] [den-chaʳ] *s.* Prótesis dental (dental plate). **Dentures,** *pl.* dentadura postiza. **A set of dentures,** una dentadura postiza.

denudate [dɪ'njuːdeɪt] [di-niu-deit], *a.* Desnudo; despojado, quitado; en especial, sin escamas, follaje u otra cubierta.

denudation [dɪˌnjuː'deɪʃən] [di-niu-dei-shon], *s.* 1. Despojo de ropa, la acción de desnudar o quitar la ropa. 2. *(Cir.)* Denudación. 3. *(Geol.)* Erosión, desprendimiento de la parte sólida de la tierra de suerte que los estratos en otro tiempo cubiertos quedan expulsados a la vista.

denude [dɪ'njuːd] [di-niud], *va.* Desnudar, despojar, privar.

denunciate [dɪ'nʌnsɪeɪt] [di-nan-sieit], *vn.* Denunciar, amenazar

denunciation [dɪˌnʌnsɪ'eɪʃən] [di-nan-si-ei-shon], *s.* 1. Denunciación, acusación; proceso, autos. 2. Publicación, declaración.

denunciator [dɪ'nʌnsɪeɪtəʳ] [di-nan-siei-toʳ], *s.* Denunciador, denunciante, delator.

deny [dɪ'naɪ] [di-nai], *va.* 1. Negar (accusation, fact); contradecir, desmentir (rumors). **There's no denying that...,** es innegable, o no se puede negar que... **She denied stealing/having stolen it,** negó haberlo robado. 2. Rehusar, no conceder. 3. Renunciar, renegar de (disavow/faith, country); no reconocer, desconocer. 4. Abjurar, renegar (refuse/request); desdecirse. 5. Negarse a, no dejarse ver de -*vn.* Decir que no; replicar negativamente; declarar algo no verdadero. **To deny oneself,** (a) Hacer abnegación de sí mismo, negarse lo agradable o lo necesario; (b) negarse, no dejarse ver de, no recibir a.

deobstruct [dɪ'ɒbstrʌkt] [di-obs-trakt], *va.* Desembarazar, desobstruir, abrir.

deodant [dɪ'əʊdənt] [di-ou-dant], *s.* (Ant. Ley inglesa) El animal o cosa causante de la muerte de una persona y que, por lo mismo, era confiscada a favor de la corona para usos piadosos.

deodorant [diː'əʊdərənt] [di-ou-do-rant], *s.* Desodorante, agente que destruye los malos olores.

deodorize [diː'əʊdəraɪz] [di-ou-do-rais], *va.* Modificar o disipar el olor de algo, p.ej. con el empleo de desinfectante; se dice especialmente de olores perjudiciales a la salud.

deontology [ˌdiːɒn'tɒlədʒɪ] [di-on-to-lo-yi], *s.* Deontología, ciencia que trata de los deberes y obligaciones morales.

deoxidize [diː'ɒksɪdaɪz] [di-ok-si-dais], **deoxidate** [diː'ɒksɪdeɪt] [di-ok-si-deit], *va. (Quím.)* Desoxigenar, desoxidar.

deoxyribonucleic acid [dɪ'ɒksɪˌraɪbəʊnjuˈkleɪɪkˌæsɪd] [di-ok-si-rai-bo-niu-kleik-a-sid], *s.* Ácido deoxiribonucleico.

depaint [dɪ'peɪnt] [di-peint] *(Ant.)* Pintar, describir, representar una cosa.

depart [dɪ'pɑːt] [di-part], *vn.* 1. Parti, marcharse, empezar a caminar. 2. Desistir, renunciar o dejar alguna cosa a que uno estaba antes acostumbrado; desviarse, 3. Perderse, desaparecer. 4. Desertar, apostatar. 5. Apartarse de algún intento u opinión. 6. Morir, fallecer. -*va.(Ant.)* Dejar. **To depart from,** desviarse, alejarse, apartarse, desistir.

departed [dɪ'pɑːtɪd] [di-par-ted] *a.* Difunto (dead); perdido (happiness, joys, youth). *s.* **The departed,** el difunto, los difuntos.

departer [dɪ'pɑːtəʳ] [di-par-taʳ], *s.* 1. El que se marcha. 2. Refinador de metales.

departing [dɪ'pɑːtɪŋ] [di-par-tin], *s.* Partida, ida.

department [dɪ'pɑːtmənt] [di-part-ment], *s.* 1. Departamento, parte de un todo muy extenso; sudivisión de una empresa, organización o gobierno; ramo de una ciencia. 2. Negociado, despacho. Ministerio, secretaría. **The Department of Education,** el Ministerio de Educación. **The police/fire department,** el cuerpo de policía/bomberos. 3. Departamento, provincia o distrito de algún país; distrito de marina. 4. Sección (of store); departamento, sección (of company). 5. *(Coloq.)* **Cooking is my husband's department,** la cocina es cosa de mi marido (area of competence, responsibility).

departmental [ˌdiːpɑː'mentl] [di-part-men-tal], *a.* Departamental.

department store *s.* Grandes almacenes, tienda de departamentos.

departure [dɪ'pɑːtʃəʳ] [di-par-chaʳ], *s.* 1. *(Transp.)* Partida, el acto de partir, de alejarse de un lugar. **Point of departure,** punto de partida. **Departure time,** hora de salida. **Departure gate/lounge,** puerta/sala de embarque. 2. Muerte. 3. Partida, ida (of person). 4. Desamparo, abandono; desistimiento. 5. *(Mar.)* Diferencia de meridiano. 6. **A departure from the norm,** una desviación de la norma (deviation). **It's a new departure for this government,** es una nueva orientación de este gobierno.

depauperate [dɪ'pɔːpəreɪt] [di-po-pe-reit], *va.* Empobrecer, hacer pobre a alguno.

depend [dɪ'pend] [di-pend], *vn.* 1. Pender, colgar, estar alguna cosa pendiente de otra. 2. Depender, estar sujeto o dependiente de algún superior (rely, be dependent). **To depend on something,** depender de algo (be determined by). 3. Necesitar del auxilio o apoyo de alguna persona. **To depend on/upon,** contar con (count on), confiar, esperar con confianza, descuidar en una persona, dejar a su cuidado una cosa, estar seguro de

dependable [dɪ'pendəbl] [di-pen-da-bol], *a.* Digno de confianza, seguro, formal (person). Digno de confianza, con el que se puede contar (ally, workman).

dependance, dependancy, *s. V.* DEPENDENCE, DEPENDENCY.

dependant [dɪ'pendənt] [di-pend] **dependent** [dɪ'pend] [di-pen-dant], *s.* Dependiente, subalterno. **Your children and other dependants,** sus hijos y otras personas a su cargo/cargas familiares -*a.* 1. Dependiente, subalterno. Dependiente (territory). **To be dependant on something/somebody,** depender de algo/alguien (reliant). 2. Contingente, causal, accidental. 3. Que necesita socorro o ayuda; necesitado. **Dependant relative,** carga familiar, familiar a su (o mi, etc.) cargo. 4. Pendiente, colgante, que cuelga.

dependence [dɪ'pendəns] [di-pen-dans] *s.* 1. Dependencia, estado de dependiente; de aquí, seguridad, esperanza firme (reliance). 2. Dependencia, sujeción, inferioridad. *(Med.)* Dependencia (addiction). **Drug dependence,** drogodependencia. 3. Aquello con que uno cuenta, o en que confía, o en lo que descansa; apoyo. **He was their main dependence,** el que fue su principal apoyo. 4. La acción y efecto de pender o estar una cosa pendiente de otra.

dependency [dɪ'pendənsɪ] [di-pen-dan-si], *s.* 1. La cosa dependiente de otra. 2. Lugar, territorio o estado sometido a otro. 3. Edificio auxiliar, cerca del principal. 4. Dependencia, sujeción.

depender [dɪ'pendəʳ] [di-pen-daʳ], *s.* Dependiente.

depending [dɪ'pendɪŋ] [di-pen-din], *pa.* Pendiente.

depersonalize [diː'pɜːsənəlaɪz] [di-per-so-na-lais], *va.* Hacer impersonal. Despersonalizar.

depehlegmate [dɪ'peləgmeɪt] [di-pe-leg-meit], *va. (Quím.)* Deflegmar, separar la parte acuosa contenida en los líquidos espirituosos.

depict [dɪ'pɪkt] [di-pikt], *va.* Pintar, representar, retratar, describir (portray); describir, pintar (describe).

depiction [dɪ'pɪkʃən] [di-pik-shon] *s.* Representación (representation); descripción (description).

depicture [dɪ'pɪktʃəʳ] [di-pik-chaʳ], *va.* Representar por medio de la pintura o de las palabras; pintar, retratar, describir.

depilate [dɪ'pɪleɪt] [di-pi-leit], *va.* Quitar el vello o pelo.

depilation [ˌdɪpɪ'leɪʃən] [di-pi-lei-shon], *s.* La acción y el efecto de arrancar o quitar el vello o pelo.

depilatory [dɪ'pɪlətərɪ] [di-pi-la-to-ri], *s.* Atanquía, ungüento para hacer caer el cabello. -*a.* Depilatorio.

deplane [diː'pleɪn] [di-plein] *vn.* Desembarcar, descender del avión.

deplete [dɪ'pliːt] [di-plit], *va.* 1. Reducir (reduce/supply, stock); disminuir, agotar (exhaust/energy, source); disipar; vaciar. 2. Disminuir la cantidad de sangre, p. ej. en los vasos del cuerpo.

depletion [dɪ'pliːʃən] [di-pli-shon], *s.* 1. Vaciamiento. Reducción, disminución (reduction); agotamiento (exhaustion). 2. *(Med.)* Depleción, la acción de disminuir la cantidad de sangre en los vasos del cuerpo.

depletive, depletory [dɪ'pliːtɪv] [di-pli-tiv], *a.* Depletivo, que causa la depleción o tiende a ella.

deplorable [dɪ'plɔːrəbl] [di-plo-ra-bol], *a.* 1. Deplorable, vergonzoso (disgraceful); lamentable (regrettable); miserable. 2. Despreciado; lastimoso.

deplorableness [dɪ'plɔːrəblnɪs] [di-plo-ra-bol-nes], *s.* Estado deplorable.

deplorably [dɪ'plɔːrəblɪ] [di-plo-ra-bli], *adv.* Deplorablemente, lastimosamente, infelizmente.

deplore [dɪ'plɔːʳ] [di-ploʳ], *va.* Deplorar, condenar (condemn); lamentar, llorar, deplorar (regret).

deploredly [dɪ'plɔːrɪdlɪ] [di-plo-rid-li], *adv.* Vilmente.

deplorer [dɪ'plɔːrəʳ] [di-plo-raʳ], *s.* Lamentador, llorón.

deploy [dɪ'plɔɪ] [di-ploi], *va. y vn.* 1. *(Mil.)* Desplegar (position), extender el frente de batalla; marchar a la derecha o a la izquierda o por ambos lados. 2. Utilizar, hacer uso de (distribute, use) -*s.* Acción de desplegar.

deployment [dɪ'plɔɪmənt] [di-ploi-ment] *s.* 1. *(Mil.)* Despliegue. 2. Utilización (distribution, use).

deplumation [dɪ'pluːmeɪʃən] [di-plu-mei-shon], *s.* 1. Muda, tiempo o acto de mudar las aves sus plumas. 2. Caída de las pestañas.

deplume [dɪ'pluːm] [di-plim], *va.* Desplumar, quitar las plumas; despojar de plumaje.

depolarization [diːˌpəʊlərɑɪ'zeɪʃən] [di-pou-la-rai-sei-shon], *s.* Despolarización.

depone [dɪ'pəʊn] [di-poun], *va.* Deponer, testificar, declarar en justicia.

deponent [dɪ'pəʊnənt] [di-pou-nent], *s.* 1. Deponente, declarante. 2. *(Gram.)* Verbo deponente.

depopulate [dɪ'pɒpjʊleɪt] [di-po-piu-leit], *va.* Despoblar, devastar, asolar, destruir, arruinar -*vn.* Despoblarse.

depopulation [ˈdiːˌpɒpjʊ'leɪʃən] [di-po-piu-lei-shon], *s.* Despoblación; devastación.

depopulator [diː'pɒpjʊleɪtəʳ] [di-po-piu-lei-toʳ], *s.* Despoblador, asolador.

deport [dɪ'pɔːt] [di-port], *va.* Deportar, desterrar por castigo a un punto lejano.- *vr. (Con oneself)* Portarse, conducirse, gobernarse.

deportation [ˌdiːpɔː'teɪʃən] [di-por-tei-shon], *s.* Deportación, destierro, estrañamiento de un país.

deportment [dɪ'pɔːtmənt] [di-port-ment], *s.* Porte (carriage), conducta (conduct); manejo.

deposable [dɪ'pəʊzəbl] [di-po-sa-bol], *a.* Capaz de ser depuesto.

deposal [dɪ'pəʊzəl] [di-pou-sal], *s. (Ant.)* Destronamiento, deposición; destitución, degradación de honores.

depose [dɪ'pəʊz] [di-poz], *va.* 1. Deponer. 2. Destronar, privar del trono; derrocar (overthrow, unseat/dictator, rules); destronar (champion, king). 3. Deponer, degradar o destituir

a alguna persona de los empleos, dignidades y honores que tenía. 4. Deponer, testificar. -*vn.* Ser testigo.

deposer [dɪ'pəʊzəʳ] [di-pou-saʳ], *s.* 1. Desposeedor, el que depone o degrada. 2. Testigo, deponente.

deposing [dɪ'pəʊzɪŋ] [di-pou-sin], *s.* Deposición.

deposit [dɪ'pɒzɪt] [di-po-sit], *va.* 1. Depositar, poner (set down); resguardar; consignar; apartar. 2. Confiar a la guarda de alguien; poner dinero en un banco, depositar (leave). **I deposited the will with my lawyer,** dejé el testamento en manos de mi abogado. Depositar, ingresar (money). 3. *(Geol.)* Depositar (silt).

deposit *s.* 1. Depósito (accumulation of silt, mud); capa (of dust); sedimiento, poso, heces, precipitado. 2. Depósito, cosa confiada como fianza; fianza, prenda (security). Depósito, entrega inicial (down payment/on large amounts); depósito, señal, seña (on small amounts). 3. Depósito, ingreso (payment into account). **Deposit slip,** comprobante o boleta de depósito, resguardo de ingreso. 4. *(Min.)* Depósito (of gas); yacimiento (of gold, copper).

deposit account *s.* Cuenta de ahorros.

depositary [dɪ'pɒzɪtərɪ] [di-po-si-ta-ri], *s.* 1. Depositario, guardián. 2. Almacén sitio o paraje donde se hacen los depósitos.

depositing [dɪ'pɒzɪtɪŋ] [di-po-si-tin], *s.* El acto de apartar o depositar.

deposition [ˌdiːpɒ'zɪʃən] [di-po-si-shon], *s.* 1. *(Law)* Deposición, testimonio, declaración ante juez o escribano. 2. Deposición, el acto de deponer o desposeer a un príncipe de su corona. 3. Destitución (of leader), privación del empleo u honores que gozaba alguna persona. Destronamiento (of king).

depositor [dɪ'pɒzɪtəʳ] [di-po-si-toʳ], *s.* Depositante (en un banco, etc.). Inversionista, ahorrista, ahorrante.

depository [dɪ'pɒzɪtərɪ] [di-po-si-to-ri], *s.* 1. Depositaría, sitio o paraje donde se hacen los depósitos. 2. (Poco us.) Depositario.

depositum *s. V.* DEPOSIT.

depot ['depəʊ] [de-pau], *s.* 1. Pósito, almacén público o principal (storehouse). 2. Despacho, oficina de la administración de diligencias, coches de camino, etc.; en los E.U del Norte, estación de un ferrocarril. En este sentido la palabra es menos usada que otro tiempo. Terminal o estación de autobuses (bus station); estación (train station). 3. Estación, almacén o depósito militar. 4. Garaje, cochera, depósito (storage area/for buses); depósito de locomotoras (for trains).

depravation [ˌdeprə'veɪʃən] [de-pra-vei-shon], *s.* 1. El acto de depravar. 2. Depravación, corrupción, estragamiento del gusto o costumbres.

deprave [dɪ'preɪv] [di-preiv], *va.* Depravar, pervertir. corromper, viciar, estrangar; alterar, falsificar; difamar.

depraved [dɪ'preɪvd] [di-preivd], *a.* Depravado, viciado, abandonado, corrompido.

depravedly [dɪ'preɪvdlɪ] [di-preivd-li], *adv.* Corrompidamente, depravadamente.

depravedness [dɪ'preɪvdnɪs] [di-preivd-nes], *s.* Depravación, corrupción, estragamiento, malignidad.

depraver [dɪ'preɪvəʳ] [di-prei-vaʳ], *s.* Depravador.

depraving [dɪ'preɪvɪŋ] [di-prei-vin], *s.* Depravación.

depravity [dɪ'prævɪtɪ] [di-pra-vi-ti], *s.* Depravación, desorden, estragamiento de costumbres, gusto. etc; corrupción, desorden; maldad, ruindad, malignidad.

deprecable ['deprɪkəbl] [de-pri-ka-bol], *a.* Capaz de ser suplicado.

deprecate ['deprɪkeɪt] [de-pri-keit], *va.* 1. Deprecar, rogar, suplicar con eficacia o instancia; pedir o desear que no suceda algún mal o verse libre de él. 2. Reprobar, criticar (express disapproval of); menospreciar, despreciar (belittle).

deprecating ['deprɪkeɪtɪŋ] [de-pri-kei-tin] *a.* De desaprobación, reprobatorio (disapproving/remark); de desprecio (belittling/smile, laugh).

deprecation ['deprɪkeɪʃən] [de-pri-kei-shon], *s.* Súplica para conjurar o evitar los males; deprecación, ruego, petición.

deprecative ['deprɪkətɪv] [de-pri-ka-tiv], **deprecatory** ['deprɪkətərɪ] [de-pri-ka-to-ri], *a.* Deprecativo, deprecatorio, suplicante.

deprecator ['deprɪkeɪtər] [de-pri-kei-to'], *s.* Deprecante.

depreciate [dɪ'priːʃɪeɪt] [di-pri-shieit], *va.* 1. Rebajar el valor o precio de alguna cosa. *(Fin.)* Depreciar. 2. Despreciar, menospreciar, deprimir. *-vn.* Desvalorizarse, amortizar. *(Fin.)* Depreciarse.

depreciation [dɪˌpriːʃɪ'eɪʃən] [di-pri-shiei-shon], *s.* Depreciación, descrédito, desestimación; baja, reducción de precio. *(Fin.)* Depreciación.

depreciative, depreciatory [dɪ'priːʃɪətɪv] [di-pri-shia-tiv] [dɪ'priːʃɪətərɪ] [di-pri-shia-to-ri], Despreciativo, que causa desprecio.

depreciator [dɪ'priːʃɪeɪtər] [di-pri-shiei-to'], *s.* Despreciador.

depredate ['deprɪdeɪt] [de-pri-deit], *va.* 1. Saquear, robar, pillar. 2. Desolar, destruir, arruinar, asolar.

depredation ['deprɪdeɪʃən] [de-pri-dei-shon], *s.* Depredación, pillaje, saqueo, saco, devastación.

depredator ['deprɪdeɪtər] [de-pri-dei-to'], *s.* Saqueador; rapiñador, ladrón.

depredatory ['deprɪdətərɪ] [de-pri-da-to-ri], *a.* Que pilla, roba o saquea.

depress [dɪ'pres] [di-pres], *va.* 1. Bajar (press down/lever), comprimir, apretar hacia abajo, pulsar (button); dejar caer. 2. Bajar, minorar, disminuir; reducir el precio. 3. Desalentar, desanimar; entristecer. Deprimir, abatir (sadden). 4. *(Econ.)* Deprimir (market); reducir, hacer bajar (prices, wages).

depressed [dɪ'prest] [di-prest], *a.* 1. Deprimido, comprimido. 2. Rebajado, disminuido. 3. Desanimado, entristecido, deprimido, abatido (dejected). **To get/become depressed,** deprimirse, dejarse abatir. 4. *(Biol.)* Deprimido, hundido, hondo. 5. *(Econ.)* Deprimido, en crisis (economy, market); deprimido, de gran desempleo (area). 6. De calidad inferior (substandard/stock). **His reading skills are depressed,** en lectura está por debajo de lo normal.

depressing [dɪ'presɪŋ] [di-pre-sin] *a.* Deprimente.

depressingly [dɪ'presɪŋlɪ] [di-pre-sin-li] *adv.* **The crime rate is depressingly high,** el índice de criminalidad ha alcanzado unos niveles deprimentes.

depression [dɪ'preʃən] [di-pre-shon], *s.* 1. Compresión, la acción de comprimir o apretar hacia abajo. 2. Depresión, abatimiento (despondency). **To suffer from depression,** sufrir depresiones. 3. Lo que está apretado hacia abajo; concavidad ligera, hueco poco profundo. Depresión (in flat surface). 4. *(Econ.)* Depresión, crisis. 5. *(Meteo.)* Depresión atmosférica, borrasca.

depressive [dɪ'presɪv] [di-pre-siv], *a.* Depresivo.

depressor [dɪ'presər] [di-pre-so'], *s.* 1. Depresor. 2. Opresor.

depressurize [dɪ'preʃəraɪz] [di-pre-sha-rais] *va.* Despresurizar.

deprivation [ˌdeprɪ'veɪʃən] [de-pri-vei-shon], *s.* 1. Privación (lack, loss); privaciones, penurias (hardship). **To suffer deprivation(s),** pasar o sufrir privaciones o penurias. 2. Pérdida. 3. Amovilidad.

deprive [dɪ'praɪv] [di-praiv], *va.* 1. Privar, despojar, quitar a uno algo. **To deprive oneself of something,** privarse de algo. 2. Excluir; impedir. 3. Librar, libertar.

deprived [dɪ'praɪvd] [di-praivd] *a.* Carenciado, desventajado (child); carenciado (region).

depriver [dɪ'praɪvər] [di-prai-va'], *s.* El que priva, despoja o quita.

depth [depθ] [depz], *s.* 1. Hondura, profundidad (of hole, water); abismo. **When it comes to computers I'm out of my depth,** estoy muy flojo en informática. **Don't go out of your depth,** no vayas donde no haces pie o no tocas fondo (in water). Profundidad. fondo (of shelf. cupboard); ancho (of hem). *(Dep.)* Alcance (of shot). 2. Espesor; extensión o distancia hacia dentro, hacia atrás o hacia arriba (del cielo). 3. Centro, punto medio, corazón, fondo de una cosa. **In the**

depth of winter, en el rigor del invierno. 4. Oscuridad o riqueza, viveza, del color: gravedad del sonido. 5. Sagacidad, penetración, conocimiento; profundidad (of emotion, knowledge). **To study something in depth,** estudiar algo a fondo o en profundidad. 6. Profundidad, extrema extensión; inmensidad. Profundidad (of voice); intensidad (of sound). **Beyond one's depth,** *(Fig.)* más allá o fuera, en exceso de las fuerzas o la capacidad de uno. **Depths,** *s. pl.* **In the depths of the ocean/forest,** en las profundidades del océano/ la espesura del bosque. **In the depths of despair,** en lo más hondo de la desesperación. **To plumb the depths of despair,** hundirse en la desesperación.

depth bomb [depθ'bɒm] [depz-bom], *s.* Bomba de profundidad.

depthless ['depθlɪs] [depz-les], *a.* Superficial, sin profundidad.

depurant ['depjuːrænt] [de-piu-rant], *a.* Depuratorio, depurativo.

depurate ['depjuːreɪt] [de-piu-reit], *va.* Depurar, limpiar, purgar, purificar.

depurate. *a.* Depurado, limpio, purificado, puro; libre.

depuration ['depjuːreɪʃən] [de-piu-rei-shon], *s.* Depuración.

depurative ['depjuːrətɪv] [de-piu-ra-tiv], *a.* V. DEPURANT.

deputation [ˌdepjoˈteɪʃən] [de-piu-tei-shon], *s.* Diputación, comisión, delegación.

depute [dɪ'pjuːt] [di-piut], *va.* Diputar, destinar, señalar, enviar, detener. **To depute somebody to something,** encomendarle algo a alguien, comisionar a alguien para algo.

deputize ['depjotaɪz] [de-piu-tais], *va. (E.U.)* Diputar. V. DEPUTE. Nombrar como segundo (appoint as deputy). *vn.* **To deputize for somebody,** desempeñar las funciones de alguien.

deputy ['depjotɪ] [de-piu-ti], *s.* 1. Diputado, comisario, delegado, enviado, agente. **Lord deputy,** virrey. **Deputy governor,** teniente gobernador. 2. Segundo (second-in-command); suplente, reemplazo (substitute). **Deputy director,** subdirector, director adjunto.

deracinate [dɪ'ræsɪneɪt] [di-ra-si-neit], *va.* Desarraigar, arrancar de raíz; abolir, extirpar.

derail [dɪ'reɪl] [di-reil], *va.* Hacer descarrilar, echar fuera de los carriles (train); desbaratar (upset/plan). *-vn.* Descarrilarse, o desviarse del carril en las vías férreas.

derailment [dɪ'reɪlmənt] [di-reil-ment], *s.* Descarrilamiento, desvío de los carriles.

derange [dɪ'reɪndʒ] [di-reinch], *va.* Desarreglar, desordenar, desconcertar.

deranged [dɪ'reɪndʒd] [di-rein-chd] *a.* Trastornado, desquiciado.

derangement [dɪ'reɪndʒmənt] [di-reinch-ment], *s.* Desarreglo, desorden; enajenamiento del ánimo: confusión, desbarato.

derby ['dɑːbɪ] [da-bi], *s.* 1. Derby, famosa carrera anual de caballos en Epsom, condado de Surrey. **A local derby,** enfrentamiento de dos equipos vecinos a nivel nacional (in soccer). 2. *(E.U.)* Sombrero hongo, bombín (hat).

deregulate [diː'regjoleɪt] [di-re-guiu-leit] *va.* Desregular, liberalizar.

deregulation [diːˌregjoˈleɪʃən] [di-re-guiu-lei-shon] *s.* Desregulación, liberalización.

derelict ['derɪlɪkt] [de-ri-likt], *a.* Abandonado y en ruinas. *-s.* 1. *(For.)* Toda propiedad abandonada voluntariamente al mar. 2. Marginado (vagrant).

dereliction [ˌderɪ'lɪkʃən] [de-ri-lik-shon], *s.* 1. Desamparo, abandono (of property, area). 2. **Dereliction of duty,** negligencia en el cumplimiento del deber.

deride [dɪ'raɪd] [di-raid], *va.* Burlar, mofar, escarnecer; zumbar o dar zumba, poner en ridículo.

derider [dɪ'raɪdər] [di-rai-da'], *s.* Burlón, zumbón, soflamero.

deridingly [dɪˈraɪdɪŋlɪ] [di-rai-din-li], *adv.* Irrisoriamente, con zumba.

de rigueur [dərɪˈgɜːʳ] [da-ri-gaʳ] *a.* **To be de rigueur,** ser de rigor.

derision [dɪˈrɪʒən] [de-ri-shon], *s.* Irrisión, mofa, escarnio, burla, chulada. **To make something/somebody the object of derision,** ridiculizar algo/a alguien.

derisive [dɪˈraɪsɪv] [di-rai-siv], **derisory** [dɪˈraɪsərɪ], [di-rai-so-ri], *a.* Irrisorio, hecho por mofa o escarnio. Burlón (smile, laughter); desdeñoso y burlón (attitude, remark).

derisively [dɪˈraɪsɪvlɪ] [di-rai-siv-li], *adv.* Irrisoriamente, burlonamente, con sorna.

derivable [ˈderɪvəbl] [de-ri-va-bol], *a.* 1. Lo que se puede adquirir por derecho de descendencia. 2. Derivable, deducible, lo que se puede derivar o deducir.

derivation [ˌderɪˈveɪʃən] [de-ri-vei-shon], *s.* 1. Derivación, (process); origen (origin). 2. Etimología de una voz. 3. (*Biol.*) Derivación, descendencia. 4. (*Med.*) Derivación, reducción de la inflamación por medio de un vejigatorio. 5. (*Des.*) La acción de sacar o desviar agua de un río para formar una acequia.

derivate [ˈderɪveɪt] [de-ri-veit], *a.* 1. Derivativo. 2. Carente de originalidad (unoriginal/novel); manido, trillado (plot/theme); adocenado (artist/writer). *s.* Derivado (in industry); derivado (word); lengua derivada (language).

derive [dɪˈraɪv] [di-raiv], *va.* 1. Derivar, repartir o distribuir el agua de algún canal en otros muchos. 2. Derivar, deducir o sacar una cosa de algún origen, causa o principio: recibir por transmisión. **Children can derive great enjoyment from the simplest things,** las cosas más simples pueden dar enorme placer a un niño. **Penicillin is derived from mold,** la penicilina se obtiene del moho. **The name is derived from the Greek,** el nombre viene o deriva del griego. 3. Comunicar. *-vn.* (Con *from.*) Derivar, derivarse, nacer; descender, proceder (stem from/attitude, problem); participar.

deriver [dɪˈraɪvəʳ] [di-rai-vaʳ], *s.* El que deriva o deduce.

derm [dɜːm] [derm], *s.* Dermis, cutis. Equivalentes: DERMA, DERMIS.

dermal, dermic [ˈdɜːməl] [der-mal], *a.* Dérmico, cutáneo, perteneciente al cutis.

derma-, dermato-, dermo. Prefijos o bien formas de combinación en voces científicas y que significan cutis.

dermatitis [ˌdɜːməˈtaɪtɪs] [der-ma-tai-tis] *s.* Dermatitis.

dermatologist [ˌdɜːməˈtɒlədʒɪst] [der-ma-to-lo-yist], *s.* Dermatólogo.

dermatology [ˌdɜːməˈtɒlədʒɪ] [der-ma-to-lo-yi], *s.* Dermatología o dermología, ciencia que trata de la piel y sus enfermedades.

derogate [ˈderɒgeɪt] [di-ro-gueit], *va.* 1. Menospreciar, anular, abrogar, invalidar-*vn.* (Con *from*) Detraer, detractar.

derogate, *a.* Derogado; desacreditado, envilecido.

derogately [dɪˈrɒgeɪtlɪ] [di-ro-gueit-li], **derogatorily** [dɪˈrɒgeɪt] [di-ro-gueit], *adv.* Derogativamente.

derogation [dɪˈrɒgeɪʃən] [di-ro-guei-shon], *s.* Derogación; desestimación.

derogative [dɪˈrɒgətɪv] [di-ro-ga-tiv], *a.* Derogatorio, derogativo.

derogatoriness [dɪˈrɒgətərɪnɪs] [di-ro-ga-to-ri-nes], *s.* Derogación; detracción.

derogatory [dɪˈrɒgətərɪ] [di-ro-ga-to-ri], *a.* Derogatorio, despectivo, peyorativo.

derrick [ˈderɪk] [de-rik], *s.* 1. Grúa (derrick crane). 2. Torre de perforación (over oil well).

dervish [ˈdɜːvɪʃ] [der-vish], *s.* 1. Derviche, fakir, santón mendicante mahometano. 2. (*Neol.*) Partidario del Madí en el Sudán. (Turco)

descale [ˈdeskeɪl] [des-keil] *va.* Quitarle el sarro a.

descant [ˈdeskænt] [des-kant], *s.* 1. (*Mús.*) Discante, melodía; variación, modulación. 2. Discurso, comentario, paráfrasis, disertación.

descant, *vn.* Discantar: Discurrir, comentar larga y pesadamente.

descanting [ˈdeskæntɪŋ] [des-kan-tin], *s.* Conjetura, presunción.

descend [dɪˈsend] [di-send], *vn.* 1. Descender, bajar (move downwards); descender (set in/mist); caer (rain); abatirse (silence/gloom). 2. Descender, derivarse, traer o tomar su origen. Rebajarse a algo (stoop). **Don't descend to his level,** no te pongas a su nivel. 3. Descender, tocar o venir a algún sucesor por orden de herencia (be descended). **To descend from somebody,** descender de alguien, ser descendiente de alguien. 4. Pasar de lo general a lo particular. **In descending order of importance,** en orden decreciente o descendiente de importancia. *-va.* Descender, andar hacia abajo. **To descend to/into,** descender o entrar en; bajarse a. **To descend into oneself,** entrar en sí mismo.

descend on, descend upon. Lanzarse o caer sobre (attack). **A plague descended on the town,** una plaga se abatió sobre la ciudad. Invadir (invade). **The whole family will be descending on us at Christmas,** nos va a invadir o nos va a caer toda la familia para Navidad.

descendable, *a. V.* DESCENDIBLE.

descendant [dɪˈsend] [di-send], *s.* 1. Descendiente. 2. Descendencia, posteridad.

descended [dɪˈsendɪd] [di-sen-did] *a.* **To be descended from somebody,** ser descendiente de alguien, descender de alguien.

descendent [dɪˈsendənt] [di-sen-dent], *a.* 1. Descendente, lo que se cae, hunde o viene abajo. 2. Descendiente que desciende de otro.

descendibility [dɪˌsendəˈbɪlɪtɪ] [di-sen-da-bi-li-ti], *s.* Cualidad de ser transmisible como una herencia; conformidad con las leyes de descendencia.

descendible [dɪˈsendɪbl] [di-sen-di-bol], *a.* Lo que puede descender, bajar o bajarse; transmisible.

descension [dɪˈsenʃən] [di-sen-shon], *s.* 1. Descendimiento, descensión, descenso, declinación caída. 2. Degradación.

descent [dɪˈsent] [di-sent], *s.* 1. Descenso, bajada (by climbers, plane); descendimiento; descensión; pendiente, declive, bajada (in terrain). 2. Alcurnia, descendencia, origen, nacimiento, linaje, ascendencia (lineage). 3. Descendencia, posteridad, herederos. **Of a noble descent,** de nacimiento ilustre. 4. Descendencia, sucesión. 5. Invasión, acción de invadir el enemigo. 6. Oblicuidad, inclinación, caída (decline); degradación.

descramble [ˈdiːˈskræmbl] [dis-kram-bol] *va.* Descodificar.

descrambler [ˈdiːˈskræmbləʳ] [dis-kram-blaʳ] *s.* Descodificador.

describe [dɪsˈkraɪb] [dis-kraib], *va.* 1. Describir (put into words); delinear, figurar; explicar, definir, representar. 2. (*Math*) Trazar (draw); describir (move in shape of/curve, arc). 3. **He describes himself as a socialist,** se define como socialista (characterize). **I would describe the book as dull and repetitive,** yo diría que es un libro soso y repetitivo.

decriber [dɪsˈkraɪbəʳ] [dis-krai-baʳ], *s.* descriptor.

descrier [dɪsˈkraɪəʳ] [dis-kraiaʳ], *s.* Descubridor; averiguador.

description [dɪsˈkrɪpʃən] [dis-krip-shon], *s.* 1. Descripción, representación. **Powers of description,** talento para describir. **Her beauty was beyond description,** su belleza era indescriptible. 2. Clase, género, naturaleza, calidad. **We don't have anything of that description,** no tenemos nada de ese tipo.

descriptive [dɪsˈkrɪptɪv] [dis-krip-tiv], *a.* Descriptivo (passage, powers); calificativo (adjective).

descry [dɪsˈkraɪ] [dis-krai], *va.* 1. Espiar, observar, reconocer de lejos. 2. Columbrar, avistar, divisar; describir; averiguar.

desecrate [ˈdesɪkreɪt] [de-si-kreit], *va.* Profanar.

desecration [ˌdesɪˈkreɪʃən] [de-si-krei-shon], *s.* Profanación. **Desecration of a grave,** profanación de sepultura.

desegregation [ˌdesɪˈgreɪʃən] [de-si-grei-shon], *s.* Supresión de la segregación racial.

desert [dɪˈzɜːt] [di-sert], *s.* Desierto, yermo; soledad. *-a.* Desierto, desamparado, despoblado, inhabilitado, solitario. Desértico (region, climate); del desierto (tribe, sand).

desert, *s.* (Muy usado en plural) 1. Merecimiento. 2. Mérito, virtud.

desert, *va.* 1. Desamparar, dejar, abandonar (family); huir de (place). 2. Desertar de (cause). *-vn. (Mil.)* Desertar; ausentarse; apartarse.

deserted [dɪˈzɜːtɪd] [di-ser-ted] *a.* Desierto (street, village); abandonado (husband, wife).

deserter [dɪˈzɜːtəʳ] [di-ser-taʳ], *s.* Desertor; tránsfuga.

desertion [dɪˈzɜːʃən] [di-ser-shon], *s. (Mil.)* Deserción; abandono (of family, place).

desertless [dɪˈzɜːtlɪs] [di-sert-les], *a.* Indigno, sin mérito.

desertlessly [dɪˈzɜːtlɪslɪ] [di-sert-les-li], *adv.* Desmerecidamente.

deserts [dɪˈzɜːts] [di-serts] *s. pl.* **To get one's just deserts,** recibir su (o tu, etc.) merecido.

deserve [dɪˈzɜːv] [di-serv], *va.* Merecer, tener derecho a (success, praise, criticism). **They deserve each other,** ser tal para cual. **They got what they deserved,** se llevaron su merecido. Merecer, ser digno de (attention, investigation) *vn.* **They deserved better of us all,** merecían que los tratáramos mejor.

deservedly [dɪˈzɜːvdlɪ] [di-ser-ved-li] *adv.* Merecidamente.

deserving [dɪˈzɜːvɪŋ] [di-ser-vin], *a.* Meritorio, digno de recompensa o de elogio (cause, case). **The deserving poor,** los pobres dignos de ayuda. **To be deserving of something,** ser merecedor de algo. *-s.* Mérito. *V.* DESERT.

deservingly [dɪˈzɜːvɪŋlɪ] [di-ser-vin-li], *adv.* Dignamente, merecidamente.

desiccant [desɪˈkænt] [de-si-kant], *a.* Desecante, que enjuga o deseca. *-s. (Med.)* Desecante.

desiccate [desɪˈkeɪt] [de-si-keit], *va.* Desecar, enjugar, quitar la humedad a alguna cosa, hacer evaporar; secar, hacer secar. *-vn.* Secarse.

desiccative [deˈsɪkətɪv] [de-si-ka-tiv], *a.* Desecativo, que tiene la propiedad de desecar.

desideratum [dɪˌzɪdəˈrɑːtuːm] [de-si-de-ra-tum], *s.* Desiderátum, lo que hace mucha falta o que mucho se desea.

design [dɪˈzaɪn] [di-sain], *va.* 1. Proponer, pensar, tener intención de; dedicar. 2. Diseñar, hacer el diseño de alguna cosa (dress, product); planear, estructurar (course, program). 3. Designar, idear, determinar, proyectar (devise/house, garden). 4. Tramar, maquinar. **Designed,** diseñado (created). **A well designed chair/machine,** una silla/máquina bien diseñada o de buen diseño. *-vn.* 1. Proponerse. 2. Tener por empleo hacer diseños, ya sean artísticos o para la industria.

design, *s.* 1. Dibujo, diseño (of product, car, machine); trazo. Diseño, boceto (drawing). **A design fault,** un defecto de diseño. Diseño, motivo, dibujo (pattern, decoration). Modelo (product, model). 2. Designio, mira, intento, intención 3. Empresa; fin, motivo, objeto. 4. Plan, proyecto; treta en perjuicio de otro. **Through design,** expresadamente, con toda intención, adrede. **Designs,** *pl.* propósitos, designios. **To have designs on something/somebody,** tener los ojos puestos en algo/alguien.

designable [dɪˈzaɪnəbl] [di-sai-na-bol], *a.* Lo que se puede designar o señalar; distinguible.

designate [dɪˈzaɪnɪt] [di-sai-nit], *va.* 1. Apuntar, señalar; distinguir. 2. Designar (call), nombrar, identificar por el nombre; indicar (indicate). 3. Designar, destinar alguna persona o cosa para determinado fin (name officially). **The area was designated a national park,** la zona fue declarada parque nacional.

designate *a.* **The governor designate,** quien ha sido nombrado gobernador.

designation [ˌdezɪgˈneɪʃən] [di-sai-nei-shon], *s.* 1. Designación, señalamiento, título. 2. Nombramiento, nominación, designación (naming); denominación, nombre (name). 3. Nombramiento, designación (appointment). 4. *(Ant.)* Descripción, carácter, suerte o clase.

designative [deˈzɪgnətɪv] [di-sai-na-tiv], *a.* Designativo, especificante.

designedly [dɪˈzaɪnɪdlɪ] [di-sai-nid-li], *adv.* Adrede, de propósito, de caso pensado, de intento.

designer [dɪˈzaɪnəʳ] [di-sai-naʳ], *s.* 1. Dibujante, diseñador; inventor; proyectista. **A fashion/furniture designer,** un diseñador de modas/muebles. De diseño exclusivo (clothes, jeans); de diseño (furniture, pen). 2. Maquinador.

designing [dɪˈzaɪnɪŋ] [di-sai-nin], *a.* Insidioso, mal intencionado; astuto, artero. *-s.* Dibujo, diseño, acto o arte de diseñar.

designingly [dɪˈzaɪnɪŋlɪ] [di-sai-nin-li], *adv.* Insidiosamente.

designless [dɪˈzaɪnlɪs] [di-sain-lis], *a.* Inadvertido; sin intención.

desinence [dɪˈzaɪnəns] [di-sai-nens], *s.* Terminación, sufijo, afijo, desinencia.

desirability [dɪˌzaɪrəˈbɪlɪtɪ] [di-sai-ra-bi-li-ti], *s.* Calidad de lo apetecible. Conveniencia (of action, idea); atractivo (of person). *V.* DESIRABLENESS.

desirable [dɪˈzaɪərəbl] [di-saia-ra-bol], *a.* 1. Agradable, gustoso, deseable, apetecible, atractivo (sexually/man, woman). 2. Deseable, conveniente (outcome); conveniente, aconsejable (option). 3. Atractivo (property, location).

desirableness [dɪˈzaɪrəblnɪs] [di-sai-ra-bol-nes], *s.* Ansia, afán; calidad de apetecible.

desirably [dɪˈzaɪrəblɪ] [di-saia-ra-bli] *a.* De manera deseable o ideal. **Desirably located,** en una situación ideal.

desire [dɪˈzaɪəʳ] [di-saiaʳ], *s.* Deseo, anhelo (wish); ansia, apetito. Deseo (lust). **He expressed a desire to see his family,** dijo que deseaba ver a su familia. **It leaves much to be desired,** deja muchoa que desear.

desire, *va.* Desear (want/happiness, success); apetecer, rogar, suplicar, pedir. Desear (lust after/person). **To leave nothing to be desired,** no dejar nada que desear. **I desire you to come immediately,** ruego a Ud. que venga en seguida. **To have the desired effect,** surtir el efecto deseado.

desireless [dɪˈzaɪəlɪs] [di-saia-les], *a.* Sin deseo, sin ansia, indiferente.

desirer [dɪˈzaɪərəʳ] [di-saia-raʳ], *s.* Deseador.

desiring [dɪˈzaɪərɪŋ] [di-saia-rin], *s.* Deseo.

desirous [dɪˈzaɪərəs] [di-saia-ros], *a.* Desesoso, ansioso. **To be desirous of honors or riches,** tener ambición de honores o riquezas. **To be desirous that,** querer que.

desirously [dɪˈzaɪərəslɪ] [di-saia-ros-li], *adv.* Ansiosamente.

desirousness [dɪˈzaɪərəsnɪs] [di-saia-ros-nes], *s.* Deseo vivo, anhelo.

desist [dɪˈzɪst] [di-sist], *vn.* Desistir, dejar o cesar de hacer alguna cosa; detenerse, abstenerse (abstain). **To desist from something,** desistir de algo.

desistance [dɪˈzɪstəns] [di-sis-tans], *s.* Desistencia, desistimiento, cesación.

desk [desk] [desk], *s.* 1. Bufete, mesa de escribir, escritorio (table). 2. Pupitre (in school); de escritorio, de sobremesa (lamp). **Roll-top desk,** escritorio de tapa corrediza. **Desk diary,** agenda de escritorio. **A desk job,** un trabajo de oficina. 3. Mostrador (service counter). **Information desk,** mostrador de información. **Reception desk,** recepción.

deskbound [ˈdeskbaʊnd] [desk-baund] *a.* Sedentario.

deskclerk [ˈdeskklɜːk] [des-klerk] *s.* Recepcionista.

desktop [ˈdesktɒp] [desk-top] *a.* De escritorio, de sobremesa (calculator, computer).

desmid [ˈdesmɪd] [des-mid], *s.* Desmidia, planta de hermoso color verde, tipo de un orden de algas microscópicas.

desmo-. Forma de combinación, derivada del griego desmos, lazo, ligamento.

desmography [ˈdesmɒgrəfɪ] [des-mo-gra-fi], *s.* Desmografía, descripción de los ligamentos del cuerpo.

desolate [ˈdesəlɪt] [de-so-lit], *a.* Desolado, desierto (deserted/place, landscape); despoblado, solitario, abandonado, arruinado, destruido. Desconsolado, desolado (person); sombrío, lúgubre (outlook, existence).

desolate, *va.* Desolar, despoblar, devastar, arruinar.

desolately ['desəlɪtlɪ] [de-so-lit-li], *adv.* De un modo desolador.

desolateness ['desəlɪtnɪs] [de-so-lit-nes], *s.* Desolación condición desolada.

desolater, desolator ['desəlɪtəʳ] [de-so-li-taʳ], *s.* Desolador, asolador.

desolating ['desəlɪtɪŋ] [de-so-li-tin], *s.* El acto de desolar.

desolation [,desə'lɪʃən] [de-so-li-shon], *s.* 1. Desolación (of land, area); desolamiento, estrago, ruina, destrucción. 2. Desolación, aflicción, desconsuelo (misery); melancolía; destitución. 3. Desierto.

despair [dɪs'pɛəʳ] [dis-peaʳ], *s.* Desconfianza, desesperación. **To be in despair,** estar desesperado.

despair, *vn.* Desesperar, perder la esperanza. **He despaired of ever seeing his family again,** perdió las esperanzas de volver a ver a su familia. **Don't despair!,** ¡ánimo!

despairer [dɪs'pɛərəʳ] [dis-pea-raʳ], *s.* Desesperado.

despairing [dɪs'pɛərɪŋ] [dis-pea-rin] *a.* Desesperado (look, cry). **His despairing mother,** su desconsolada madre.

despairingly [dɪs'pɛərɪŋlɪ] [dis-pea-rin-li], *adv.* Desesperadamente.

despatch [dɪs'pætʃ] [dis-pach], *va.* 1. Despachar, aviar, enviar con prisa y diligencia. 2. Despachar, matar, quitar la vida. 3. Despachar, abreviar, concluir una cosa con prontitud.

despatch, dispatch, *s.* 1. Despacho, embarque. 2. Expedición, prontitud. 3. Despacho, oficio o mensaje enviado rápidamente, generalmente por medio del telégrafo. **Despatch boat,** aviso, embarcación ligera para llevar despachos de gobierno o de un buque de guerra a otro. *-va.* Despachar, embarcar, remitir, enviar.

despatcher [dɪs'pætʃəʳ] [dis-pa-chaʳ], *s.* 1. Despachador, el que despacha. 2. Expedidor, el que envía géneros de un punto a otro. 3. El que ejecuta algún negocio.

despatchful [dɪs'pætʃfʊl] [dis-pach-ful], *a.* Diligente, expedito.

desperado [,despə'rɑːdəʊ] [des-pe-ra-dou], *s.* Hombre desesperado, atrevido, furioso; un rufián, un perdido.

desperate ['despərɪt] [des-pe-reit], *a.* 1. Desesperado, sin esperanza (frantic, reckless/person, attempt). **To be desperate,** estar desesperado. 2. Arrojado, arriesgado. 3. Desesperado, grave, lo que no tiene remedio (critical/state, situation); apremiante (need). 4. Furioso, inconsiderado, violento, terrible. 5. *(Fam.)* Consumado, rematado. *-s.* Perdido, el que es atrevido y no tiene esperanza ni miedo.

desperately ['despərɪtlɪ] [des-pe-reit-li], *adv.* Desesperadamente (struggle); furiosamente. Urgentemente, con urgencia (need). **She's desperately ill,** está gravemente enferma. **They desperately need it,** lo necesitan urgentemente.

desperateness ['despərɪtnɪs] [des-pe-reit-nes], *s.* Precipitación, temeridad, arrojo, furia, violencia.

desperation [,despə'reɪʃən] [des-pa-rei-shon], *s.* Desesperación, furor, encarnizamiento.

despicable ['despɪkəbl] [des-pi-ka-bol], *a.* Despreciable, vil, bajo.

despicableness ['despɪkəblnɪs] [des-pi-ka-bol-nes], *s.* Bajeza, vileza.

despicably ['despɪkəblɪ] [des-pi-ka-bli], *adv.* Vilmente, bajamente.

despisable [dɪs'paɪsəbl] [des-pi-sa-bol], *a.* Despreciable.

despisal [dɪs'paɪsəl] [des-pi-sal], *s.* Desdén, desprecio.

despise [dɪs'paɪs] [des-pais], *va.* Despreciar, desestimar, menospreciar; desdeñar.

despised [dɪs'paɪst] [des-paist], *a.* Desestimado, despreciado; detestado.

despisedness [dɪs'paɪsnɪs] [des-pai-nes], *s.* Envilecimiento, bajeza, abatimiento.

despiser [dɪs'paɪsəʳ] [des-pai-saʳ], *s.* Despreciador.

despising [dɪs'paɪsɪŋ] [des-pai-sin], *s.* Desdén, desprecio.

despite [dɪs'paɪt] [des-pait], *s.* Despecho, ira, enojo; desdén con reto; malicia, malignidad, malevolencia.

despite, *va. (Ant.)* Molestar, enfadar.

despite, *prep.* A despecho de, a pesar de.

despiteful [dɪs'paɪtfʊl] [des-pait-ful], *a.* Malicioso, rencoroso, vengativo, maligno.

despitefully [dɪs'paɪtfʊlɪ] [des-pait-fu-li], *adv.* Malignamente, maliciosamente.

despitefulness [dɪs'paɪtfʊlnɪs] [des-pait-ful-nes], *s.* Malignidad, rencor, odio, mala voluntad, malicia.

despoil [dɪs'pɔɪl] [des-poil], *va.* (Con *of*) 1. Despojar, saquear; privar. 2. *(Ant.)* Desnudar.

despoiler [dɪs'pɔɪləʳ] [des-poi-laʳ], *s.* Pillador, saqueador, robador.

despoliation [dɪs,pɒlɪ'eɪʃən] [des-po-li-ei-shon], *s.* Despojo, la acción de despojar.

despond [dɪs'pɒnd] [des-pond], *vn.* Desconfiar, desalentarse, abatirse; desesperanzar, decaer de ánimo.

despondency [dɪs'pɒndənsɪ] [des-pon-den-si], *s.* Desconfianza, temor; desaliento, abatimiento, desmayo; decaimiento de ánimo. Se escribe también **Despondence.**

despondent [dɪs'pɒndənt] [des-pon-dent], *a.* Abatido, melancólico, desanimado.

desponder [dɪs'pɒndəʳ] [des-pon-daʳ], *s.* El que no tiene esperanza.

despondingly [dɪs'pɒndɪŋlɪ] [des-pon-din-li], *adv.* Desconfiadamente.

despot [dɪs'pɒt] [des-pot], *s.* Déspota, señor, absoluto.

despotic, despotical [dɪs'pɒtɪk] [des-po-tik], *a.* Despótico, absoluto, independiente.

despotically [dɪs'pɒtɪklɪ] [des-po-tik-li], *adv.* Despóticamente, arbitrariamente.

despoticalness [dɪs'pɒtɪklnɪs] [des-po-ti-kal-nes], *s.* Despotismo, absolutismo.

despotism [dɪs'pɒtɪzm] [des-po-tísem], *s.* Despotismo, tiranía, gobierno arbitrario.

despumate [dɪs'pjʊmeɪt] [des-piu-meit], *vn.* Arrojar, desembarazarse de las impurezas en forma de espuma. *-va.* Espumar, despumar, quitar la espuma de algún líquido.

despumation [,dɪspjʊ'meɪʃən] [des-piu-mei-shon], *s.* Despumación.

desquamate [dɪs'kwəmeɪt] [des-kua-meit], *vn.* Despojarse de las escamas o de la epidermis; exfoliarse.

desquamation [,dɪskwə'meɪʃən] [des-kua-mei-shon], *s.* Descamación, exfoliación de la epidermis, como en el sarampión y la escarlatina.

dessert [dɪ'zɜːt] [di-sert], *s.* Postres, las frutas, dulces y otras cosas que se sirven al fin de las comidas; ramillete en las mesas de lujo.

destabilization [diːˌsteɪbɪlaɪ'zeɪʃən] [dis-tei-bi-lai-sei-shon] *s.* Desestabilización.

destabilize [dɪs'teɪbɪlaɪz] [dis-ta-bi-lais] *a.* Desestabilizar.

destinate ['destɪneɪt] [des-ti-neit], *va. (Des.)* V. DESTINE.

destination [,destɪ'neɪʃən] [des-ti-nei-shon], *s.* Destinación, destino (end of journey); paradero. Meta (purpose).

destine ['destɪn] [des-tin], *va.* 1. Destinar, señalar, determinar. 2. Dedicar, consagrar. 3. Preordinar, predestinar, prescribir, decrtar.

destined ['destɪnd] [des-tind] *a.* 1. **It was destined to fail,** estaba condenado al fracaso (fated). 2. **Destined for the West Indies,** con destino al Caribe (bound, on way).

destiny ['destɪnɪ] [des-ti-ni], *s.* Destino, hado, fatalidad, fortuna, suerte; signo, estrella, hablando vulgarmente.

destitute ['destɪtjuːt] [des-ti-tiut], *a.* Destituído, abandonado, desamparado; falto, desprovisto, privado; olvidado, indigente. **She was left destitute,** quedó en la indigencia o miseria.

destitution [destɪ'tjuːʃən] [des-ti-tiu-shon], *s.* 1. Destitución, privación, desamparo, abandono. 2. Pobreza extrema.

destroy [dɪs'trɔɪ] [dis-troi], *va.* 1. Destruir (ruin, wreck/building, forest); asolar, arrasar, demoler; arruinar, destrozar (life); matar, quitar la vida, sacrificar (animal); acabar con (reputation, confidence); aniquilar. 2. Demostrar ser falso; confutar. 3. *(Coloq.)* Aplastar, darle una paliza a (defeat/opposition); decepcionar (disappoint).

destroyable [dɪs'trɔɪəbl] [dis-troia-bol], *a*. Destruíble.

destroyer [dɪs'trɔɪəʳ] [dis-troia^r], *s*. 1. Torpedo de alta mar. 2. Destructor.

destruct [dɪ'strʌkt] [dis-trakt] *s*. *(Aerosp., Mil.)* (auto)destrucción; de (auto)destrucción (mechanism, system).

destructibility [dɪs'trʌtɪbɪlɪtɪ] [dis-trak-ti-bi-li-ti], *s*. Destructibilidad.

destructible [dɪs'trʌktɪbl] [dis-trak-ti-bol], *a*. Destruíble, destructible.

destruction [dɪs'trʌkʃən] [dis-trak-shon], *s*. 1. Destrucción (of city, books, forest); ruina (of reputation, civilization); asolamiento, exterminación (slaughter). 2. Mortandad, destrozos, estragos, destrucción (damage). 3. Causa de desolación. 4. Perdición, ruina (cause of downfall); muerte eterna.

destructive [dɪs'trʌktɪv] [dis-trak-tiv], *a*. Destructivo (tendency), destructor (storm, weapon), ruinoso, fatal. Destrozón (child); destructivo, negativo (criticism).

destructively [dɪs'trʌktɪvlɪ] [dis-trak-tiv-li], *adv*. Destructivamente.

destructiveness [dɪs'trʌktɪvnɪs] [dis-trak-tiv-nes], *s*. 1. Propiedad de destruír. 2. *(Frenol.)* Destructibilidad, inclinación a destruir o matar.

destructor [dɪs'trʌktəʳ] [dis-trak-to^r], *s*. 1. Horno para quemar los desperdicios. 2 *(Des.)* Destructor, consumidor.

desudation [dɪ'sjʊdeɪʃən] [di-siu-dei-shon], *s*. Sudor excesivo.

desuetude [dɪ'sjʊɪtjuːd] [di-siui-tiud], *s*. Desuso; desuetud. **To fall into desuetude,** caer en desuso.

desultoriness ['desəltərɪnɪs] [de-sal-ta-ri-nes], *s*. 1. Inconstancia, el estado de ser inconstante, irregular o variable. 2. Variación: falta de ilación, orden y método.

desultory ['desəltərɪ] [de-sal-ta-ri], *a*. 1. Pasajero, mudable, variable, irregular, inconstante. 2. Vago, suelto, inconexo, no seguido; desganado (effort, attempt). **In a desultory fashion,** sin estusiasmo, con desgana o desgano.

detach [dɪ'tætʃ] [di-tach], *va*. 1. Separar, apartar, quitar (separate); despegar (unstick). **The headrest can be detached,** el apoyacabezas se puede desmontar o quitar. 2. Destacar, separar un número de soldados del cuerpo principal.

detachable [dɪ'tætʃəbl] [di-ta-cha-bol] *a*. De quita y pon, de quitar y poner (cover); desmontable (lining).

detached [dɪ'tætʃəbl] [di-ta-cha-bol], *pp*. de DETACH. -*a*. 1. Suelto, distinto, aparte. 2. Distante, indiferente (person, manner/aloof); objetivo, imparcial (objective). 3. No adosado (house).

detaching [dɪ'tætʃɪŋ] [di-ta-cha-chin], *s*. El acto de separar o destacar.

detachment [dɪ'tætʃmənt] [di-tach-ment], *s*. 1. Separación, apartamiento, distancia, indiferencia (aloofness); objetividad, imparcialidad (objectivity). 2. Lo que está apartado o separado. 3. *(Mil.)* Destacamento, cuerpo de tropas separadas del ejército, o parte de una escuadra, para servicio especial. 4. Desprendimiento (act of detaching).

detail ['diːteɪl] [di-teil], *va*. 1. Detallar, especificar, particularizar, referir por menor, circunstanciar, contar con sus pelos y señales (describe). 2. *(Mil.)* Destacar.

detail, *s*. 1. Detalle, pormenor, cuenta circunstanciada de alguna cosa (particular). **He asked for further details,** pidió más información o información más detallada. Detalle (embellishment); minucia, detalle sin importancia (insignificant matter). 2. Detalles (minutiae). **To go into detail,** entrar en detalles o pormenores. **To describe/explain something in detail,** describir/explicar algo detalladamente o minuciosamente. 3. *(Mil.)* Destacamento poco numeroso (de tropas), cuadrilla. 3. *(Arte y Arq.)* Porción menor y accesoria de una obra: detalle.

detain [dɪ'teɪn] [di-tein], *va*. 1 Detener (arrest), retardar, suspender, impedir. **Don't let me detain you,** no quiero

entretenerlo o demorarlo. Detener (in custody). 2. Retener, guardar o conservar lo que pertenece a otro.

detainee ['diːteɪniː] [di-tei-ni] *s*. Detenido.

detainer ['diːteɪnəʳ] [di-tei-na^r], *s*. *(For.)* Detentador, retenedor; detención.

detect [dɪ'tekt] [di-tekt], *va*. Descubrir, averiguar algún delito, fraude o trama; revelar, declarar, manifestar; detectar (object, substance). **I detected a note of sarcasm in his voice,** noté cierto tonillo sarcástico en su voz.

detectable [dɪ'tektəbl] [di-tek-ta-bol] *a*. Perceptible, detectable.

detecter [dɪ'tektəʳ] [di-tek-ta^r], *s*. Descubridor, averiguador, revelador, delator.

detection [dɪ'tekʃən] [di-tek-shon], *s*. 1. Averiguación, descubrimiento (of act, crime, criminal); manifestación revelación, declaración. **To escape detection,** pasar desapercibido o inadvertido. 2. Detección (of substance).

detective [dɪ'tektɪv] [di-tek-tiv], *a*. 1. Con aptitud especial para descubrir lo que es secreto. 2. Denunciador, delator de una cosa secreta; referente a la policía secreta; espía asalariado. 3. Detective (private); agente oficial (in police force). **Detective story,** novela policíaca o policial. **Detective work,** pesquisas, investigaciones.

detent ['dɪtent] [de-tent], *s*. Fiador, retén seguro; escape de un reloj.

detention [dɪ'tenʃən] [de-ten-shon], *s*. 1: Detención (in custody), retención; limitación; encierro, cautividad; tardanza. **Detention order,** orden de arresto. 2. *(Educ.)* **To be in detention,** estar castigado. **Detention home, detention center,** reformatorio, correccional o de menores.

detentive [dɪ'tentɪv] [di-ten-tiv], *a*. Que puede detener, detenedor; o que sirve y se emplea para asir, retener o afianzar.

deter [dɪ'təʳ] [di-ta^r], *va*. 1. Desanimar, desalentar, acobardar; disuadir, hacer disuadir (person); impedir (crime, war). 2. Disminuir, desviar, impedir. **Don't let him deter you,** no dejes que te desanime.

detege [dɪ'tedʒ] [di-tech], *va*. Limpiar una llaga.

detergent [dɪ'tɜːdʒənt] [di-ter-yent], *a*. *(Quím.)* Detergente, lo que tiene poder de limpiar. -*s*. Detersorio, detergente (for clothes); lavavajillas (for dishes).

deteriorate [dɪ'tɪərɪəreɪt] [di-tia-rio-reit], *va*. desmejorar, deteriorar. *vn*. Deteriorarse (health, relationship, material); empeorar (weather, work). **To deteriorate into something,** degenerar en algo.

deterioration [dɪ'tɪərɪəreɪʃən] [di-tia-rio-rei-shon], *s*. Deterioración, deterioro, desmejoramiento.

determent [dɪ'tɜːmənt] [di-ter-ment], *s*. La acción y efecto de desanimar; lo que impide o desalienta; desaliento, descaecimiento de ánimo; impedimento.

determinable [dɪ'tɜːmɪnəbl] [di-ter-mi-na-bol], *a*. Determinable, lo que puede determinarse o decidirse.

determinably [dɪ'tɜːmɪnəblɪ] [di-ter-mi-na-bli], *adv*. Determinadamente, resueltamente.

determinant [dɪ'tɜːmɪnənt] [di-ter-mi-nant], *a*. Determinante, que hace tomar una determinación. -*s*. 1. Lo que causa una determinación. 2. *(Biol.)* Una de las unidades secundarias del plasma, del germen o substancia hereditaria.

determinate [dɪ'tɜːmɪnɪt] [di-ter-mi-neit], *a*.

determinately [dɪ'tɜːmɪnətlɪ] [di-ter-mi-na-tli], *adv*. Determinadamente, inmutablemente.

determination [dɪ'tɜːmɪneɪʃən] [di-ter-mi-nei-shon], *s*. 1. Determinación, resolución, decisión (resoluteness). **With an air of determination,** con aire resuelto o decidido. 2. Resolución, entereza. 3. *(For.)* Auto definitivo, decisión judicial. 4. *(Lóg.)* Especificación. 5. *(Med.)* Congestión, acumulación de sangre o humores en alguna parte del cuerpo. 6. *(Ant.)* Terminación, término.

determinative [dɪ'tɜːmɪnətɪv] [di-ter-mi-na-tiv], *a*. Determinativo.

determinator [dɪ'tɜːmɪneɪtəʳ] [di-ter-mi-nei-to^r], *s*. Determinante; juez árbitro.

determine [dɪ'tɜ:mɪn] [di-ter-min], *va.* 1. Determinar, fijar (date); limitar, reglar, establecer (ascertain); decidir (resolve), juzgar, resolver definitivamente. 2. Determinar, condicionar (influence). **Determining factor,** factor determinante. Definir, demarcar (mark/boundary, limit). -*vn.* Terminar, acabar, concluir; determinarse, resolverse, decidirse, tomar una resolución. **To be determined by,** depender de. **To determine what is to be done,** decidir lo que se debe hacer. **Determine on, determine upon** Decidirse por.

determined [dɪ'tɜ:mɪnd] [di-ter-mind], *a.* Decidido, resuelto (mood/person). **We must make a determined effort to prevent it,** debemos poner todo nuestro empeño en impedirlo.

determiner [dɪ'tɜ:mɪnə'] [di-ter-mi-na'], *s.* El que toma alguna determinación.

determining [dɪ'tɜ:mɪnɪŋ] [di-ter-mi-nin] *a.* Determinante, decisivo.

deterration [dɪ'tərɛɪʃən] [di-te-rei-shon], *s.* Desentierro, desenterramiento.

deterrence [dɪ'tərəns] [di-te-rens], *s.* Disuasión.

deterrent [dɪ'tərənt] [di-te-rent], *a.* Disuasivo; que refrena o impide. -*s.* Elemento disuasivo. **It may act as a deterrent to thieves,** puede servir para disuadir a los ladrones. **The nuclear deterrent,** las armas nucleares como fuerza disuasoria. **To act as a deterrent to,** ser una amenaza a, servir como freno para.

detersion [dɪ'tərʃən] [di-ter-shon], *s.* Detersión, el acto y efecto de limpiar y purificar, p.ej. una llaga.

detersive [dɪ'tərsɪv] [di-ter-sin], *a.* Detersivo, detersorio, detergente. -*s.* Remedio detersivo.

detest [dɪ'test] [di-test], *va.* Detestar, abominar, aborrecer, odiar, execrar.

detestable [dɪ'testəbl] [di-tes-ta-bol], *a.* Detestable, aborrecible, abominable, odioso, exerable.

detestably [dɪ'təstəblɪ] [di-tes-ta-bli], *adv.* Detestablemente.

detestation [,di:tes'teɪʃən] [di-tes-tei-shon] *sf.* Aborrecimiento, odio. **To hold in detestation,** odiar, aborrecer.

detester [dɪ'testə'] [di-tes-ta'], *s.* Aborrecedor, el que aborrece.

dethrone [di:'θrəʊn] [di-zroun], *va.* Destronar, privar a alguno del trono y la potestad real.

dethronement [di:'θrəʊnmənt] [di-zroun-ment], *s.* Destronamiento.

detinue [di:'tɪnu:] [di-ti-nu], *s.* *(For.)* Auto contra el detentador de alguna cosa.

detonate ['detəneɪt] [de-to-neit], *va.* Hacer detonar o estallar súbitamente. -*vn.* Detonar, inflamarse súbitamente y con estrépito.

detonation [,detə'neɪʃən] [de-to-nei-shon], *s.* Detonación, fulminación.

detonator ['detəneɪtə'] [de-to-nei-ta'], *s.* Detonador, fulminante.

detorsion ['dɪtɔ:ʃən] [di-tor-shon], *s.* Apartamiento, separación o desvío del primer designio.

detour ['di:tʊə'] [di-tua'], *s.* 1. Vuelta, rodeo (deviation), revuelta, recodo. *(Transp.)* Desvío, desviación. **To make a detour,** dar un rodeo, desviarse. 2. Rodeo, tergiversación, subterfugio.

detour *va.* Desviar (traffic).

detoxicate [di:'tɒksɪkeɪt] [di-tok-si-keit] *vt.* Desintoxicar.

detoxification [,di:tɒksɪfɪ'keɪʃən] [di-tok-si-fi-kei-shon] *s.* Desintoxicación (of addict); eliminación de la toxicidad (substance, material).

detoxify [di:'tɒksɪfaɪ] [di-tok-si-fai] *va.* Desintoxicar (addict, alcoholic); eliminar la toxicidad de (substance, material).

detract [dɪ'trækt] [di-trakt], *va.* Detraer, disminuir, quitar. -*vn.* Detraer, detractar, infamar, quitar el crédito, denigrar (con *from.* por lo común). **I didn't wish to detract from her achievement,** no quise quitarle méritos o restarle valor a su logro.

detracter [dɪ'træktə'] [di-trak-ta'], *s.* Detractor, infamador, murmurador.

detraction [dɪ'trækʃən] [di-trak-shon], *s.* 1. La acción de detraer, de quitar parte de alguna cosa. 2. Detracción, maledicencia, murmuración, calumnia, denigración.

detractive [dɪ'træktɪv] [di-trak-tiv], *a.* Difamatorio, derogarotio, denigrante, que lastima la reputación.

detractor [dɪ'træktə'] [di-trak-ta'], *s.* Difamador; detractor.

detractress [dɪ'træktrɪs] [di-trak-tres], *sf.* Detractora, murmuradora.

detrain [dɪ'treɪn] [di-trein], *va.* y *vn.* Salir o hacer salir un tren.

detriment ['detrɪmənt] [de-tri-ment], *s.* Detrimento, daño, perjuicio, pérdida. **To the detriment of somebody/something,** en detrimento o perjuicio de alguien/algo. **Without detriment to,** sin perjuicio de.

detrimental [,detrɪ'mentl] [de-tri-men-tal], *a.* Perjudicial; desventajoso, dañoso.

detrital ['detrɪtəl] [de-tri-tal], *a.* Detrítico, compuesto de detritus o perteneciente a ellos.

detrition ['detrɪʃən] [de-tri-shon], *s.* Rozadura, desgaste por frotamiento.

detritus [dɪ'traɪtəs] [di-trai-tus], *s.* 1. *(Geol.)* Detritus, los restos del desgaste de las rocas y del deterioro de los vegetales esparcidos por la superfie de la tierra. 2. Cualquier conjunto de substancias desagregadas; desperdicios; inmundicias.

de trop [də'trəʊ] [de-trou] *adv.* **To be de trop,** sobrar, estar de más.

detrude [de'trju:d] [de-triud], *va.* Hundir, empujar alguna cosa hacia abjo; precipitar.

detruncate ['detrʌnkeɪt] [de-tran-keit], *va.* Podar, cortar, quitar las ramas superfluas de ls árboles.

detruncation ['detrʌnkeɪʃən] [de-tran-kei-shon], *s.* Poda.

detrusion ['detrʌʃən] [de-tra-shon], *s.* La acción de precipitar alguna cosa.

deturbation [,detɜ:'beɪʃən] [de-tar-bei-shon], *s.* 1. El acto de arrojar al suelo alguna cosa. 2. Degradación.

deuce [dju:s] [dius], *s.* 1. Dos en los juegos, como para decir, dos ases, el dos de espadas; dos puntos en dados; deuce, cuarenta iguales (in tennis). 2. *(Vul.)* El demonio, el diantre, dianhe. **How the deuce!,** ¡cómo diablos! **The deuce take me if I have not forgotten it!,** ¡el diablo me lleve si no lo he olvidado!

deuterium [dju:'tɪərɪəm] [diu-tia-rium], *s.* *(Quím.)* Deuterio.

deutero-, deuto-, forma de combinación derivada del griego *deuteros,* segundo.

deuterogamy [dju:tərə'gæmɪ] [diu-te-ro-ga-mi],

devalue ['di:'vælju:] [di-va-liu] *vt.* Devaluar, desvalorizar.

devaluation [dɪ,vælju:'eɪʃən] [di-va-liu-ei-shon] *sf.* Desvalorización.

devastate ['devəsteɪt] [de-vas-teit] *vt.* 1. Asolar, devastar. 2. Deprimirse, hundir en depresión (person).

devastating ['devəsteɪtɪŋ] [de-vas-tei-tin] *a.* Devastador, arrollador (argument, news), contundente (defeat), irresistible (beautiful, charm).

devastation ['devəsteɪʃən] [de-vas-tei-shon] *sf.* Devastación, desolación, destrucción, ruina, saqueo.

develop [dɪ'veləp] [di-ve-lop], *va.* 1. Desenvolver, desarrollar, descoger, abrir, desplegar; descubrir. 2. En fotografía, revelar, desarrollar, hacer visible la imagen latente. -*vn.* 1. Progresar; avanzar, pasar de un estado inferior al superior. 2. Hacerse patente, descubrirse (el enredo de una novela); asomar (la imagen fotográfica).

developed [dɪ'veləpt] [di-ve-lopt] *a.* Desarrollado (country), profundo.

developer [dɪ'veləpə'] [di-ve-lo-pa'], *s.* Revelador, desarrollador; baño químico para revelar una fotografía.

developing [dɪ'veləpɪŋ] [di-ve-lo-pin] *a.* **Developing country,** país en vías de desarrollo.

development [dɪ'veləpmənt] [di-ve-lop-ment], *s.* 1. Desarrollo, revelación. Acción de descubrir lo oculto o secreto. 2. Desarrollo, revelación *(fot.)* 3. Adelanto, progreso, mejoría, evolución, desarrollo (progress).

devest [dɪ'vest] [di-vest], *va.* 1. *(Des.)* Desnudar. 2. *(For.)* Privar de los bienes o del título; enajenar.-*vn.* Perderse o enajenarse (el título o la herencia).

deviate ['diːvɪeɪt] [di-vi-eit], *vn.* 1. Desviarse, salir del camino derecho. 2. Descarriarse, ir errando; pecar.

deviation [ˌdiːvɪ'eɪʃən] [di-vi-ei-shon], *s.* 1. Desvío, la acción y efecto de desviarse; extravío, error; falta, pecado. 2. Mala conducta. 3. *(Astr.)* Deviación.

device [dɪ'vaɪs] [di-vais], *s.* 1. Plan, proyecto. 2. Dispositivo. 3. Estratagema, ardid. 4. Divisa, lema.

deviceful [dɪ'vaɪsfʊl] [di-vais-ful], *a.* Inventivo, ingenioso, especulativo.

devicefully [dɪ'vaɪsfʊlɪ] [di-vais-fu-li], *adv.* Curiosamente ideado.

devil ['devl] [de-vil], *s.* 1. Diablo, demonio, espíritu maligno. 2. Diablo, hombre o mujer del mal natural. 3. Se usa como interjección, para indicar sorpresa o enfado. 2. Aprendiz de impresor. **The devil!** ¡demonio! ¡diantre! **The devil take you!** ¡el diablo te lleve! ¡vete al diablo! **Devil-fish,** animal marino de gran tamaño y repulsivo aspecto, especialmente el octópodo o pulpo. **The devil to pay,** gran confusión o mala suerte, perplejidad. **To whip the devil round the stump,** la cupa del asno, echarla a la albarda. **To play the devil with,** causar gran perjuicio o daño. **To go to the devil,** llevárselo a uno la trampa, insecto neuróptero; (2) Peine de Venus, planta umbelífera.

devil, *va.* 1. Condimentar, preparar pescados y carnes para la mesa sazonándolos con pimienta y mostaza, etc. y sobreasándolos o friéndolos. 2. Hacer diabólico. **Deviled ham,** jamón en latas, con salsa muy picante.

deviled eggs [ˌdevɪld'egs] [de-vi-lid-egs], *s. pl.* Huevos cocidos y rellenos con salsa picante.

deviling ['devlɪŋ] [de-vi-lin], *s.* Diablillo.

devilish ['devlɪʃ] [de-vi-lish], *a.* 1. Diabólico. 2. Excesivo; se dice en burla. 3. Epíteto para expresar aborrecimiento o desprecio.

devilishly ['devlɪʃlɪ] [de-vi-lish-li], *adv.* Diabólicamente, endiabladamente.

devilishness ['devlɪʃnɪs] [de-vi-lish-nes], *s.* Diablura.

devilkin ['devlkɪn] [de-vil-kin], *s.* Diablillo.

devilship ['devlʃɪp] [de-vil-ship], *s.* Calidad o estado de demonio o diablo.

deviltry ['devltrɪ] [de-vil-tri], *s.* Diablura, diablería, y el espíritu que conduce al mal.

devious ['diːvɪəs] [di-vios], *a.* Desviado, descarriado, descaminado, extraviado, errado, tortuoso; errante.

deviously ['diːvɪəslɪ] [di-vios-li], *adv.* A través, de una manera torcida; tortuosamente.

deviousness ['diːvɪəsnɪs] [di-vios-nes], *s.* Extravío, descarrío; desviación del camino recto.

devisable [dɪ'vaɪzəbl] [di-vai-sa-bol], *a.* 1. Imaginable, lo que se puede trazar o idear. 2. Transmisible, lo que se puede legar por testamento.

devisal [dɪ'vaɪzl] [di-vai-sal], *s.* El acto de inventar; el de legar por testamento.

devise [dɪ'vaɪz] [di-vais], *va.* 1. Trazar, idear, inventar, proyectar, pensar (invent, think), tener ánimo o intención de alguna cosa. 2. Legar. -*vn.* Pensar, considerar, maquinar.

devise, *s. (For.)* 1. Legado, manda de bienes ríces. 2. Testamento o cláusula del mismo que lega bienes raíces.

devisee [dɪ'vaɪziː] [di-vai-si], *s.* Legatario.

deviser [dɪ'vaɪzər] [di-vai-sar], *s.* Inventor, autor.

devisor [dɪ'vaɪzər] [di-vai-sor], *s.* Testador, el que deja un legado de bienes raíces.

devitalize [diː'vaɪtəlaɪz] [di-vai-ta-lais], *va.* Privar del poder vital o de la fuerza para sostener la vida.

devoid [dɪ'vɔɪd] [di-void], *s.* 1. Obsequio. 2. Cumplimiento, cumplido.

devoir [dɪ'vɔər] [di-vuar], *s.* 1. Obsequio. 2. Cumplimiento, cumplido.

devolution [ˌdiːvə'luːʃən] [di-vo-lu-shon], *s.* 1. Mudanza de mano en mano; transmisión, traspaso a un sucesor. *(For.)*

Devolución o derecho devoluto. 2. *(Neol.)* Denegación, lo contrario de *evolution.*

devolve [dɪ'vɒlv] [di-volv], *va.* 1. Transmitir, traspasar, remitir, pasar de una mano a otra. 2. *(Ant.)* Rodar hacia abajo o hacia adelante. -*vn.* Recaer en alguno por devolución o derecho devoluto (seguido de *to, on* o *upon*).

devonian [de'vəʊnɪən] [de-vou-nian], *a.* Devoniano, perteneciente al condado de Devon en Inglaterra. **Devonian age,** *(Geol.)* edad devoniana o de los peces, subsiguiente a la silúrica.

devote [dɪ'vəʊt] [di-vout], *va.* 1. Dedicar, consagrar; aplicar, entregar completamente. 2. Maldecir, execrar.

devoted [dɪ'vəʊtɪd] [di-vou-tid], *a.* 1. Dedicado, consagrado, aplicado, destinado. 2. Apegado, aficionado, consagrado a. 3. Infeliz, malhadado, desdichado.

devotedly [dɪ'vəʊtɪdlɪ] [di-vou-tid-li] *adv.* Con devoción.

devotedness [dɪ'vəʊtɪdnɪs] [di-vou-tid-nes], *s.* 1. Devoción, dedicación, afecto a alguna persona. 2. Sacrificio voluntario.

devotee [ˌdevəʊ'tiː] [de-vou-ti], *s.* 1. Devoto, devota, partidario. 2. Santón, saturrón, majigato.

devoter [dɪ'vəʊtər] [di-vou-tar], *s.* 1. El que dedica o consagra. 2. *(Des.)* Adorador.

devotion [dɪ'vəʊʃən] [di-vou-shon], *s.* 1. Devoción, piedad. 2. Adoración, lealtad, veneración. 3. Oración (preach). 4. Elevación del alma a Dios reconociéndose su criatura. 5. Disposición. 6. Oblación de caridad. 7. Afecto o amor ardiente (love). 8. Ardor, anhelo, ansia.

devotional [dɪ'vəʊʃənl] [di-vou-sho-nal], *a.* Devoto, religioso, piadoso.

devotionalist [dɪ'vəʊʃənlɪst] [di-vou-sho-na-list], *s.* Santón, santurrón.

devotionist [dɪ'vəʊʃənɪst] [di-vou-sho-nist], *s.* Santón; persona piadosa.

devour [dɪ'vəʊər] [di-vuar], *va.* 1. Devorar, tragar, engullir; comer con avidez, con voracidad, como un animal carnívoro. 2. Devorar, destruir, consumir, consumir sin reparo, deshacerse temerariamente de algo. 3. Mirar con avidez o deleite, devorar con la vista. **To be devoured with jealous,** morirse de celos.

devourer [dɪ'vəʊərər] [di-voua-rar], *s.* Devorador, tragón; destructor.

devouring [dɪ'vəʊərɪŋ] [di-voua-rin] *a.* Absorbente.

devouringly [dɪ'vəʊərɪŋlɪ] [di-voua-rin-li], *adv.* De un modo devorador.

devout [dɪ'vəʊt] [di-vout], *a.* Devoto, piadoso, fervoroso.-*s.* V. DEVOTEE.

devoutlessness [dɪ'vəʊtlɪsnɪs] [di-vout-les-nes], *s.* Falta de devoción, tibieza en las cosas espirituales.

devoutly [dɪ'vəʊtlɪ] [di-vout-li], *adv.* Devotamente, piadosamente.

devoutness [dɪ'vəʊtnɪs] [di-vout-nes], *s.* Piedad, devoción.

dew [djuː] [diu], *s.* Rocío, relente, rocío.

dew *va.* Rociar, mojar como son rocío; de aquí, apaciguar, refrescar.

dew-bent [djuː'bent] [diu-bent], *a.* Inclinado con el rocío, cargado de rocío.

dewberry [djuː'berɪ] [diu-be-ri], *s. (Bot.)* Zarzamora, el fruto de la zarza rastrera, y la planta de la misma.

dew-besprent [djuː'besprent] [diu-bes-prent], *a.* Rociado.

dewdrop ['djuːdrɒp] [diu-drop], *s.* Gota de rocío.

dew-dropping [djuː'drɒpɪŋ] [diu-dro-pin], *a.* Lo que cae a gotas como el rocío; lo que deja caer el rocío.

dew-impearled [djuːɪm'pɜːld] [diu-im-perld], *a.* Aljofarado, cubierto con las gotas de rocío.

dewlap ['djuːlæp] [diu-lap], *s.* Papada.

dewlapt ['djuːlæpt] [diu-lapt], *a.* Papudo, el que tiene papada.

dew-plant ['djuːplænt] [diu-plant], *s.* Planta de adorno con gruesas hojas relucientes.

dew-point [djuː'pɔɪnt] [diu-point], *s.* La temperatura a que se forma el rocío, humedad relativa de cien grados.

dew-pond ['dju:pɒnd] [diu-pond] *sf.* Charca que forma el rocío.

dew-worn ['dju:wɔ:n] [diu-uorn], *s.* Lombriz de tierra.

dewy ['dju:ɪ] [diui], *a.* Rociado, humedecido con rocío; semejante al rocío, lleno de rocío.

dexter ['dekstə^r] [deks-ta^r], *a.* 1. Diestro o derecho. 2. Favorable, propicio.

dexterity ['deksterɪtɪ] [deks-te-ri-ti], *s.* Destreza, agilidad, habilidad, maña y arte; primor, gracia.

dexterous ['dekstərəs] [deks-te-ros], *a.* Diestro, sagaz, hábil, experto.

dexterously ['dekstərəslɪ] [deks-te-ros-li], *adv.* Diestramente, hábilmente.

dexterousness ['dekstərəsnɪs] [deks-te-ros-nes], *s.* Habilidad, conocimiento práctico.

dextrad ['dekstræd] [deks-trad], *adv.* A la derecha; al lado derecho.

dextral ['dekstrəl] [deks-tral], *a.* Derecho, diestro.

dextrality ['dekstrælɪtɪ] [deks-tra-li-ti], *s.* Situación a la mano derecha.

dextrin, dextrine ['dekstri:n] [deks-trin], *s. (Quím.)* Dextrina, substancia parecida a la goma, y que se usa en sustitución de la goma arábiga.

dextrose ['dekstrəs] [deks-tros], *s.* Dextrosa, glucosa, azúcar de uvas. Azúcar contenida en la miel de abejas y en muchas frutas. Se utiliza en dulces y en la fermentación del tabaco.

dey [deɪ] [dei], *s.* Bey o dey, el jefe supremo de Argel antes de la conquista francesa de 1830. Los gobernantes de Túnez y Trípoli.

dg Abreviatura de **decigram**, decigramo.

diabetes [ˌdaɪə'bi:ti:z] [daia-bi-tis], *s. (Med.)* Diabetes, enfermedad caracterizada por una secreción abundante de orina más o menos cargada de glucosa.

diabetic [ˌdaɪə'betɪk] [daia-be-tik], *a.* Diabético, de la diabetes o relativo a ella.

diabolic, diabolical [ˌdaɪə'bɒlɪk] [daia-bo-lik] [daia-bo-li-kal], *a.* Diabólico.

diabolically [ˌdaɪə'bɒlɪkəlɪ] [daia-bo-li-ka-li], *adv.* Diabólicamente.

diabolicalness [ˌdaɪə'bɒlɪkəlnɪs] [daia-bo-li-kal-nes], *s.* La calidad de diablo.

diabolism [ˌdaɪə'bɒlɪzm] [daia-bo-li-sem], *s.* 1. Diablura. 2. Posesión, el estar poseído por los demonios.

diachylon [ˌdaɪə'kɪlɒn] [daia-ki-lon], **diachylum** [ˌdaɪə'kɪləm] [daia-ki-lum], *s.* Diaquilón, ungüento con que se hacen emplastos, compuesto de óxido de plomo, aceite y agua.

diaconal [ˌdaɪə'kɒnl] [daia-ko-nal], *a.* Diaconal, relativo o perteneciente a un diácono o diaconato.

diacoustics [ˌdaɪə'kʌstɪks] [daia-kas-tiks], *s.* Diacústica, ciencia que trata de la refracción de los sonidos.

diacritic, diacritical [ˌdaɪə'krɪtɪk] [daia-kri-tik], *a.* Diacrítico, distinguido por un punto, signo o señal.

diadem ['daɪədem] [daia-dem], *s.* Diadema, corona.

diademed ['daɪədemd] [daia-de-md], *a.* 1. Coronado. 2. *(Her.)* Diademado.

diaeresis o dieresis [daɪ'erɪsɪs] [dai-e-ri-sis], *s. (Gram.)* Diéresis, figura por la cual se disuelve un diptongo, formando sus vocales dos sílabas en vez de una.

diagnose ['daɪəgnəʊz] [daiag-nous], *va. (Med.)* Diagnosticar, formar el diagnóstico de una enfermedad.

diagnosis ['daɪəgnəʊsɪs] [daiag-nou-sis], *s.* 1. *(Med.)* Diagnosis, conocimiento de los síntomas característicos de las enfermedades. 2. Discernimiento entre cosas o condiciones de análoga naturaleza.

diagnostic [ˌdaɪəg'nɒstɪk] [daiag-nos-tik], *s. (Med.)* Diagnóstico, signo característico por el cual se distingue una enfermedad de otra. -*a.* Diagnóstico, distintivo, característico.

diagnostics [ˌdaɪəg'nɒstɪks] [daiag-nos-tiks] *sf.* Diagnóstica.

diagnosticate [ˌdaɪəg'nɒstɪkeɪt] [daiag-nos-ti-keit], *va.* Diagnosticar, distinguir entre las enfermedades.

diagonal [daɪ'ægənl] [dai-a-go-nal], *a.* Diagonal. -*s.* Diagonal.

diagonally [daɪ'ægənəlɪ] [dai-a-go-na-li], *adv.* Diagonalmente.

diagram ['daɪəgræm] [dai-a-gram], *s.* Diagrama; perfil, bosquejo, recorte, traza; borrón o diseño de un mapa o de una proyección.

diagrammatic [ˌdaɪəgrə'mætɪk] [dai-a-gra-ma-tik] *a.* Esquemático.

diagraph ['daɪəgræf] [dai-a-graf], *s.* Diágrafo, instrumento de reducción de un imagen con el que puede trazar toda clase de líneas y figuras.

diagraphic o diagraphical ['daɪəgræfɪk] [dai-a-gra-fik] ['daɪəgræfɪkl] [dai-a-gra-fi-kal], *a.* Descriptivo.

dial ['daɪəl] [daial], *s.* 1. Reloj de sol. 2. Esfera (de un reloj). 3. Brújula. **Dial code,** prefijo. **Dial phone,** teléfono automático. **Dial tone,** tono (de marcación). **Luminous dial,** esfera luminosa (de un reloj).

dial, *va,* Marcar.

dialect ['daɪəlekt] [daia-lekt], *s.* Dialecto, lenguaje propio de una provincia o región; variedad de un idioma, a diferencia de la lengua general y literaria.

dialectic [ˌdaɪə'lektɪk] [daia-lek-tik], s, Dialéctica. -*a.* Arguyente.

dialectical [ˌdaɪə'lektɪkəl] [daia-lek-ti-kal], *a.* Dialéctico.

dialectician [ˌdaɪəlek'tɪʒən] [daia-lek-ti-shan], *s.* Dialéctico.

dialist ['daɪəlɪst] [daia-list], *s.* Constructor de relojes solares.

dialling ['daɪəlɪŋ] [daia-lin], *s.* 1. Marcación. 2. Gnomónica, la ciencia de hacer relojes de sol o cuadrantes.

dialog ['daɪəlɒg] [daia-log] *s.* y *vn.* Diálogo.

dialogism ['daɪəlɒgɪzm] [daia-lo-gui-sem], *s.* Dialogismo, el arte del diálogo.

dialogist ['daɪəlɒgɪst] [daia-lo-guist], *s.* Dialoguista, el que pone en diálogo una cosa.

dialogistically ['daɪəlɒgɪstɪkəlɪ] [daia-lo-guis-ti-ka-li], *adv.* A manera de diálogo.

dialogize ['daɪəlɒgaɪz] [daia-lo-gais], *vn.* Dialogar, dialogizar, hacer diálogos.

dialogue ['daɪəlɒg] [daia-log], *s.* Diálogo, interlocución; conversación, conferencia, coloquio.

dialogue *vn.* Dialogar.

dialogue-writer ['daɪəlɒgˌwraɪtə^r] [daia-log-vrai-ta^r], *s.* Dialoguista.

dial-plate ['daɪəlˌpleɪt] [daial-pleit], *s.* Muestra de un reloj.

dial telephone ['daɪəlˌtelɪfəʊn] [daial-te-li-foun], *s.* Teléfono automático.

dial tone ['daɪəlˌtəʊn] [daial-toun] *s.* Tono de marcar o de discado.

dialysis [daɪ'æləsɪs] [daia-li-sis], *s.* 1. Diálisis, separación de partes; solución de continuidad. 2. *(Quím.)* Diálisis, procedimiento de separación fundamento en la propiedad que ciertas substancias poseen de atravesar fácilmente las membranas porosas, en tanto que otras quedan retenidas por dichas membranas. 3. *(Gram.)* Diéresis, crema. 4. *(Ret.)* Asíndeton. 5. *(Méd.)* Disolución, languidez, dificultad de mover los miembros. 6. *(Cir.)* Herida abierta.

dialytic [daɪ'ælɪtɪl] [daia-li-tik], *a.* Dialítico, perteciente a la diálisis.

dialyze [daɪ'ælaɪs] [daia-lais], *va.* Dialisar, separar las substancias susceptibles de desprenderse de una mezcla.

dialyzer [daɪ'ælaɪzə^r] [daia-lai-sa^r], *s.* Dialisador, instrumento propio para practicar la diálisis.

diamentine [di:'əmentaɪn] [dia-men-tain], *a.* Adamantino, diamantino.

diameter [daɪ'æmɪtə^r] [daia-mi-ta^r], *s.* Diámetro.

diametral [daɪ'æmɪtrəl] [daia-mi-tral], *a.* Diametral; opuesto, contrario.

diametrically [ˌdaɪə'metrɪkəlɪ] [daia-mi-tri-ka-li], *adv.* Diametralmente.

diamond ['daɪəmənd] [daia-mond], *s. (Min.)* Diamante, piedra preciosa; brillante, diamante (cut). **Diamond ring,** anillo o sortija de brillantes o diamantes. 2. Punta de diamante, instrumento que sirve para cortar vidrio. 3. Oros, uno de los palos de que se compone la baraja de naipes. 4. Nombre de un grado muy pequeño de letra de imprenta, muy próximo a la letra "brillante" 4 0 4 1/2 puntos, corpus cuatro. 5. *(Geom.)* Rombo (shape). 6. Diamante, cuadro; rombo del juego de pelota llamado baseball (area inside bases). Campo de béisbol (entire field). **Diamond-cutter,** diamantista. **Diamond-drill,** taladro de punta de diamante.

diamond, *a.* Diamantado: adiamantado

diapason [ˌdaɪəˈpeɪzən] [daia-pei-son], *s.* 1. Diapasón, registro fundamentalmente del órgano. 2. Diapasón, armonía comprensiva o fundamental; tono justo, acuerdo.

diaper [ˈdaɪəpəʳ] [daia-paʳ], *s.* 1. Lienzo adamascado; servilleta. 2. Arabesco, adorno en pintura y escultura, hecho con dibujos de flores, figuras geométricas, etc. 3. Pañal, sabanilla de niño. **She has diaper rash,** está escaldada o rozada.

diaper, *va.* 1. Matizar una tela de diferentes colores. 2. Adamascar.

diaphaneity [ˌdaɪəfəˈnɪtɪ] [daia-fa-ni-ti], *s.* Diafanidad, transparencia.

diaphanous [daɪˈæfənəs] [dai-a-fa-nos], *a.* Diáfano, transparente, terso, claro.

diaphoresis [ˌdaɪəfəˈrɪsɪs] [daia-fo-ri-sis], *s. (Med.)* Diaforesi, transpiración copiosa, sudor (en especial la transpiración artificial).

diaphoretic, diaphoretical [ˌdaɪəfəˈretɪk] [daia-fo-re-tik], *a.* Diaforético, sudorífico.

diaphragm [ˈdaɪəfræm] [daia-fram], *s.* 1. *(Anat.)* Diafragma, músculo que sirve para la respiración y que separa el tórax del abdomen; es característico de los mamíferos. 2. Diafragma; división o separación, como el diafragma vibratorio del teléfono. 3. Diagragma (contraceptive).

diaphragmatic [ˌdaɪəfrəˈmætɪk] [daia-fra-ma-tik], *a.* Diafragmático, perteneciente al diafragma.

diarrhea, diarrhoea [ˌdaɪəˈriːə] [daia-ria], *s.* Diarrea, flujo de vientre, cámaras, despeño. *(Vul.)* Evacuaciones, cursos. **Verbal diarrhea,** verborrea, diarrea verbal.

diarist [ˈdaɪərɪst] [daia-rist], *s.* Diarista.

diary [ˈdaɪərɪ] [daia-ri], *s.* 1. Diario, relación de los acontecimientos de cada día (personal record). 2. Agenda (book for appointments).

diastase [ˈdaɪəstɑːs] [daias-tas], *s.* Diastasa, principio componente de la saliva, que se halla también en los cereales en estado de germinación; es un fermento que convierte el almidón en dextrina y azúcar.

diastyle [ˈdaɪəstaɪl] [daia-fram], *s. (Arq.)* Diástilo.

diatessaron [ˌdaɪəˈtesərən] [daia-te-sa-ron], *s.* Diatesarón, el intervalo compuesto de dos tonos, mayor y menor, y de un semitono mayor: también es cuarta en la música.

diathermy [ˈdaɪəθɜːmɪ] [daia-zer-mi], *s.* Diatermina.

diatom [ˈdaɪətɒm] [daia-tom], *s.* Diátomo, planta unicelular del orden de las Diatomáceas, algas microscópicas. Crecen en las aguas dulces y saladas y se distinguen de las desmidias por sus válvulas silicosas y su color aureo pardo u oscuro.

diatomaceous [ˌdaɪətəˈmeɪʃəs] [daia-to-mei-shos], *a.* Diatomáceo, perteneciente a los diátomos.

diatomic [ˌdaɪəˈtɒmɪk] [daia-to-mik], *a. (Quim.)* 1. Diatómico, que consiste sólo de dos átomos. 2. Bivalente, cuyo poder de combinación es de dos unidades.

diatribe [ˈdaɪətrɪb] [daia-trib], *s.* Diatriba, invectiva, sátira mordaz.

dibble [ˈdɪbl] [di-bel], *s.* Plantador, almocafre, instrumento que sirve a los jardineros y hortelanos par plantar.

dibs [dɪbz] [dibs], *s.* Jarabe que se hace hirviendo el zumo de uvas o dátiles. *V.* DIBSTONE.

dibstone [ˈdɪbztəʊn] [dib'stoun], *s.* Piedra que los niños usan en uno de sus juegos para mover a otras; taba.

dice [daɪs] [dais], *s. pl.* de DIE. Dados.

dice, *vn.* Jugar con o a los dados. **To dice with death,** jugar con la muerte. *va. (Culin.)* Cortar en dados o cubitos.

dice-box [ˈdaɪsbɒks] [dais-boks], *s.* Cubilete de dados.

dicer [ˈdaɪsəʳ] [dai-saʳ], *s.* Jugador de dados.

dicey [ˈdaɪsɪ] [dai-si] *a. (Coloq.)* Arriesgado, riesgoso (risky); dudoso, incierto (uncertain).

dichotomize [dɪˈkɒtəmaɪz] [di-ko-to-mais], *va.* Separar, dividir.

dichotomous [dɪˈkɒtəməs] [di-ko-to-mus], *a.* Dicotómico, lo que se divide y subdivide por parejas, de dos en dos.

dichotomy [dɪˈkɒtəmɪ] [di-ko-to-mi], *s.* Dicotomía, distribución de una cosa en dos partes.

dick [dɪk] [dik] *s. (Vulg.)* Verga, pija, polla, pico.

dickens [ˈdɪkɪnz] [di-kens], *s. (Vul.)* Diantre, dianche, demonio.

dicker [ˈdɪkəʳ] [di-kaʳ], *va. (E.U.)* Hacer un trueque sin importancia: regatear. -*s.* 1. Cambio, trueque de poca monta. 2. *(Des.)* Decenar o decenario.

dickey [ˈdɪkɪ] [di-ki], *s.* Peto, pechera.

dickhead [ˈdɪkhed] [dik-jed] *s. (Vul.)* Huevón, pelotudo, pendejo, gilipollas.

dicky [ˈdɪkɪ] [di-ki] *a.* (GB) *(Coloq.)* **He's got a dicky heart,** tiene problemas cardíacos.

dicotyledon [ˌdɪkɒˈtɪlɪdən] [di-ko-li-li-don], *s.* Dicotiledón, vegetal que tiene dos lóbulos o cotiledones.

dicotyledonous [ˌdɪkɒtɪˈliːdənəs] [di-ko-li-li-nos], *a.* Dicotiledóneo. *V.* DICOTYLEDON.

dictate [ˈdɪkteɪt] [dik-teit], *va.* 1. Dictar, declarar a otro alguna cosa con autoridad. Establecer, dictar (prescribe, lay down); dictar (common sense). **To dictate terms,** imponer condiciones. 2. Dictar, decir a otro lo que ha de escribir o hablar (read out). *vn.* Dictar.

dictate to Mandar, darle órdenes a.

dictate, *s.* Dictamen, máxima autorizada, precepto; sugestión; lección, doctrina, documento; dictado, nota, mandato.

dictation [dɪkˈteɪʃən] [dik-tei-shon], *s.* 1. *(Corresp.)* Dictado, acción de dictar. **She asked her secretary to take dictation,** llamó a la secretaria para dictarle una carta (o informe, etc.). *(Educ.)* Dictado. 2. Precepto, prescripción.

dictator [dɪkˈteɪtəʳ] [dik-tei-toʳ], *s.* 1. Dictador, el que ejerce una autoridad absoluta, especialmente en época turbulenta o peligrosa. 2. Dictador, el que dicta o prescribe.

dictatorial [ˌdɪktəˈtɔːrɪəl] [dik-ta-to-rial], *a.* Autoritativo, arrogante, altivo, imperioso, absoluto, magistral, dogmático, dictatorial.

dictatorship [dɪkˈteɪtəʃɪp] [dik-tei-tor-ship], *s.* Dictadura; arrogancia, presunción.

dictatory [dɪkˈteɪtərɪ] [dik-tei-to-ri], *a.* Dominante, arrogante, dogmático.

diction [ˈdɪkʃən] [dik-shon], *s.* Dicción, estilo, expresión; locución, lenguaje.

dictionary [ˈdɪkʃənərɪ] [dik-sho-na-ri], *s.* Diccionario, colección alfabética de las palabras de una lengua, arte o ciencia, con sus definiciones o explicaciones.

dictograph [ˈdɪktəɡræf] [dik-to-graf], *s.* Máquina para dictar.

dictum [ˈdɪktəm] [dik-tum], *s.* (*pl.* DICTA). Sentencia o dicho positivo o dogmático. 2. *(For.)* Fallo, la sentencia de un juez, sobre un punto no esencial a la decisión del juicio principal.

did, *pret.* del verbo TO DO, hacer. -Did se emplea como indicación del tiempo pasado de los verbos, particularmente en las frases interrogativas y negativas.

didactic, didactical [daɪˈdæktɪk] [dai-dak-tik] [daɪˈdæktɪkl] [dai-dak-ti-kal], *a.* Didáctico.

didapper [ˈdaɪdæpəʳ] [dai-da-paʳ], *s.* Somorgujo, somormujo o somormujón, ave acuática.

diddle [ˈdɪdl] [di-dol], *va. (Coloq.)* Engañar, entrampar, estafar, timar. **He diddled me out of $50,** me sacó o me estafó 50 dólares. -*vn. (Prov.)* Vacilar, anadear.

die [daɪ] [dai], *vn.* (pa.DYING, *pret.* & *pp.* DIED). 1. Morir, expirar (stop living); matarse, morir (violently). **He died of cancer,** (se) murió de cáncer. *(Coloq.)* Morirse (be overcome). **To die laughing,** morirse de risa. 2. Fenecer, acabar del todo. 3. Padecer violentamente algún afecto o pasión; padecer la muerte. 4. Marchitarse, perder el jugo y secarse los vegetales. 5. Evaporar o evaporarse, perder el espíritu y fuerza los licores. 6. *(Teol.)* Perecer eternamente. 7. Descaecer; desmadejarse, devanecerse. 8. Cesar, extinguirse (hablando de las pasiones y de afectos morales). Extinguirse, apagarse (be extinguished/fire, light). Apagarse, dejar de funcionar (stop functioning/engine, motor). 9. *(Coloq.)* Quedarse embasado, ser dejado de base (in baseball). *(Coloq.)* **To be dying for something,** morirse por algo (want very much). *va.* **To die a natural death,** morir de muerte natural. **To die a violent death,** tener o sufrir una muerte violenta. (GB) *(Coloq.)* **To die a death,** quedar en la nada.

die away, debilitarse gradualmente; extinguirse, caer, cesar; disiparse; borrarse, desaparecer. Amainar (storm, wind); pasar (anger). **Her voice died away,** su voz se fue apagando o extinguiendo.

die down, irse apagando (fire, noise); amainar (storm/wind); calmarse (anger, excitement).

die off, ir muriendo.

die out, extinguirse (race, species); morir, caer en desuso (custom).

die, *s.* 1. Dado, pieza de hueso u otra materia que se usa para jugar: en este sentido su plural es *dice.* **The die is cast,** la suerte está echada. 2. Dado, suerte. **To cog a die,** cargar un dado para que se ladee o se incline. 3. Cuño, el sello con que se acuña la moneda: su plural en este sentido es *dies.* 4. *(Arq.)* Cubo. **Die-sinker,** Grabador en hueco.

dieresis, *s. V.* DIAERESIS.

diesel [ˈdiːzəl] [di-sel] *s.* Coche (o camión, etc.) diesel. Diesel, gasóleo, gas-oil (fuel).

diesel engine [ˈdiːzəlˌendʒɪn] [di-sel-en-yin], *s.* Locomotora Diesel.

diet [ˈdaɪət] [daiet], *s.* 1. Alimento, comida, manjar, vianda; alimentación, dieta alimenticia (nourishment). **They live on a diet of rice and fish,** se alimentan de arroz y pescado. 2. Dieta, régimen (special food). **To be/go on a diet,** estar/ponerse a régimen o a dieta. 3. Ración de víveres. 4. Dieta, asamblea de los príncipes y estados del imperio de Alemania.

diet, *vn.* Estar a o de dieta, poner a dieta; comer, alimentarse. *va.* 1. Comer parcamente. 2. Dar de comer.

dietary [ˈdaɪətərɪ] [daie-ta-ri], *a.* Dietético (fiber); alimenticio (habits). -*s.* Dieta medicinal.

diet-drink [ˈdaɪətdrɪŋk] [daiet-drink], *s.* Bebida medicinal.

dieter [ˈdaɪətəʳ] [daie-taʳ], *s.* El que da reglas para guardar la dieta.

dietetic, dietetical [ˈdaɪətɪk] [daie-tik], *a.* Dietético.

dietetics [ˈdaɪətɪks] [daie-tiks], *s.* Dietética.

dietician, dietitian [ˌdaɪəˈtɪʃən] [daie-ti-shan] *s.* Dietista, experto en dietética.

dieting [ˈdaɪətɪŋ] [daie-tin], *s.* Adietación.

diffarreation [ˌdaɪfərɪˈækʃən] [dai-fa-ri-ak-shon], *s.* Difarreación, la ceremonia que hacían los romanos de partir un bollo cuando se divorciaban.

differ [ˈdɪfəʳ] [di-faʳ], *vn.* 1. Diferenciarse, distinguirse; diferir (be at variance). **How do they differ?,** ¿en qué difieren? Ser distinto o diferente (be unlike). 2. Contener, lidiar, altercar. 3. Contradecir; discrepar, diferir (disagree). **I beg to differ, but...,** lamento discrepar (de su opinión), pero... -*va.* Diferenciar, variar.

difference [ˈdɪfrəns] [di-frens], *s.* 1. Diferencia (dissimilarity); diversidad, distinción, desemejanza, disparidad. **To tell the difference,** notar o ver la diferencia. **It will no difference to you,** a ti no te va a afectar. *(Mat.)* **To split the difference,** dividirse la diferencia (a partes iguales). 2. Diferencia (disagreement); riña, pendencia. **To settle/resolve one's differences,** saldar o resolver sus diferencias. 3. Distinción.

difference, *va.* Diferencia, hacer diferencia, distinguir.

different [ˈdɪfrənt] [di-ferent], *a.* 1. Diferente, distinto, diverso; desemejante (not the same). 2. Diferente, original (unusual).

differential [ˌdɪfəˈrenʃəl] [di-fe-ren-shal], *a. (Mat., Fin.)* Diferencial. **Differential calculus,** cálculo diferencial. -*s. (Mec.)* Diferencial.

differentiate [ˌdɪfəˈrenʃɪeɪt] [di-fe-ren-shiet], *va.* 1. Diferenciar, hacer diferencia. 2. Constituir diferencia entre; ser señal distintiva. 3. *(Biol.)* Hacer diferencia, hacer especial en forma o función; desarrollar variación en (plantas que se cultivan. etc.).-*vn.* Adquirir carácter diverso y diferente. Distinguir.

differently [ˈdɪfrəntlɪ] [di-fren-tli], **differingly** [ˈdɪfərɪŋlɪ] [di-fe-rin-li], *adv.* Diferentemente. **They think differently,** no piensan igual o del mismo modo.

difficult [ˈdɪfɪkəlt] [di-fi-kult], *a.* 1. Difícil, dificultoso, oscuro; penoso. **We'll make things difficult for him,** le haremos la vida imposible. **He's difficult to live with,** es difícil convivir con él. 2. áspero, agrio de condición, difícil de contentar.

difficulty [ˈdɪfɪkəltɪ] [di-fi-kul-ti], *s.* 1. Dificultad (of situation, task). **He has difficulty in understanding English,** tiene dificultad para entender el inglés. 2. Oposición, obstáculo, repugnancia; calamidad. 3. Dificultad, enredo, problema (problem). **To be in difficulties,** estar en apuros. **To make difficulties,** crear problemas. 4. Duda, argumento, reparo, objeción.

diffide [ˈdɪfaɪd] [di-faid], *vn.* Desconfiar, recelarse de alguno.

diffidence [ˈdɪfɪdəns] [di-fi-dens], *s.* Difidencia, desconfianza; timidez, pusilanimidad; falta de seguridad en sí mismo, retraimiento.

diffident [ˈdɪfɪdənt] [di-fi-dent], *a.* 1. Corto, corto de genio, vergonzoso, tímido. 2. *(Ant.)* Desconfiado, dudoso, receloso. 3. Poco seguro de sí mismo (person); tímido (smile).

diffidently [ˈdɪfɪdəntlɪ] [di-fi-dent-li], *adv.* Modestamente, tímidamente.

diffluence, diffluency [ˈdɪfluəns] [di-flu-ens], *s.* Fluidez.

diffluent [ˈdɪfluənt] [di-flu-ent], *a.* Que fluye por todas partes; que difluye o se difunde; que se deslíe o disuelve.

difform [ˈdɪfɔːm] [di-form], *a.* Disforme, deforme.

difformity [ˈdɪfɔːmɪtɪ] [di-for-mi-ti], *s.* Deformidad, irregularidad; diversidad de forma.

diffraction [ˈdɪfrækʃən] [di-frak-shon], *s.* Difracción, fenómeno luminoso producido por el cambio de dirección que experimentan los rayos solares cuando rozan los borde de un cuerpo muy tenue o penetran por una hendidura muy estrecha.

diffranchisement [ˈdɪfrænʃɪsmənt] [di-fran-shis-ment], *s.* El acto de privar a alguna ciudad de sus franquicias o privilegios. *V.* DISFRANCHISEMENT.

diffuse [ˈdɪfjuːz] [di-fius], *va.* Difundir, esparcir (heat); esparramar; derramar, verter; repartir; propagar, publicar, difundir (knowledge). Tamizar, difuminar (light). *vn.* Difundirse. *a.* Difuso.

diffused [ˈdɪfjuːzd] [di-fiusd], *a.* Difundido, extendido, derramado. 2. *(Zool.)* Que se desvanece por los bordes, como sucede con las manchas o colores de algunos animales1; borroso.

diffusedly [ˈdɪfjuːzdlɪ] [di-fiusd-li], *adv.* Difusamente, latamente.

diffusedness [ˈdɪfjuːzdnɪs] [di-fiusd-nes], *s.* Dispersión, esparcimiento, separación.

diffusely [ˈdɪfjuːzlɪ] [di-fius-li], *adv.* Extensivamente. copiosamente, ampliamente, prolijamente.

diffuser [ˈdɪfjuːzəʳ] [di-fiu-saʳ], *s.* Difundidor, esparcidor.

diffusible [ˈdɪfjuːzɪbl] [di-fiu-si-bol], *a.* Difusivo, capaz de difusión o extensión.

diffusion [ˈdɪfjuːʒən] [di-fiu-shon], **s.** Difusión, prolijidad; esparcimiento, dispersión, diseminación.

diffusive [ˈdɪfjuːsɪv] [di-fiu-siv], *a.* Difusivo, difundido, difuso, extendido; esparcido.

diffusively [ˈdɪfjuːsɪvlɪ] [di-fiu-siv-li], *adv.* Difusamente.

diffusiveness [ˈdɪfjuːsɪvnɪs] [di-fiu-siv-nes], *s.* Dispersión; difusión, extensión.

dig [dɪg] [dig], *va. (pret.* y *pp.* DUG o DIGGED). 1. Cavar o ahondar (ground); cavar (by hand/hole, trench); excavar (by machine). **To dig the garden,** cavar en el jardín. 2. Cultivar la tierra; sacar (potatoes). 3. Extraer, sacar de la tierra; beneficiar una mina. *(Archeol.)* Excavar. 4. Penetrar con una punta. 5. *(Fig.)* Buscar y extraer por medio del trabajo. **To dig again,** binar. **To dig deeper,** profundizar. **To dig out/up,** desenterrar. **He dug his way out,** escapó cavándose una salida. **To dig somebody in the ribs,** darle o pegarle un codazo en las costillas a alguien (jab, thrust). *-vn.* 1. Trabajar con azadón o azada; cavar (by hand/excavate); escarbar (dog). **To dig for oil,** hacer prospecciones petrolíferas. *(Arheol.)* Hacer excavaciones, excavar. 2. Buscar (search). **She dug in her pockets for the key,** buscó la llave en los bolsillos.

dig around *(Coloq.)* Revolver, escarbar buscando algo.

dig in *(Mil.)* Atrincherarse. *(Coloq.)* **Dig in!,** ¡al ataque!, ¡ataquen! (start eating).

dig into *(Coloq.)* 1. Atacar (start eating). 2. Investigar (investigate). 3. Echar mano de (resources, reserves).

dig out 1. Sacar de entre los escombros, la nieve, etc. (remove); desenterrar (from soil). 2. *(Coloq.)* sacar, desempolvar (find).

dig up 1. Levantar (lawn); arrancar (weeds, tree). 2. Desenterrar (body, treasure). 3. *(Coloq.)* Sacar a la luz (facts).

dig *s.* 1. *(Archeol.)* Excavación. 2. Codazo (jab/with elbow); pinchazo (with pin). **To give somebody a dig in the ribs,** darle un codazo en las costillas a alguien. 3. *(Coloq.)* Pulla (critical remark); indirecta (hint). **To have a dig at somebody/something,** meterse con alguien/algo. (GB) **To live in digs,** vivir en una habitación alquilada, una pensión, etc. (lodgings).

digamma ['dɪgæmə] [di-ga-ma], *s.* Digama, la letra F, sexta del alfabeto griego originalmente, pero que muy pronto cayó en desuso.

digastric ['dɪgæstrɪk] [di-gas-trik], *a.* Digástrico, se dice de dos músculos de la quijada inferior.

digest ['daɪdʒest] [dai-yest], *s.* 1. Digesto, recopilación de las decisiones de la jurisprudencia romana; también, resumen o extracto de escritos literarios u otros. 2. Compendio (summary); boletín, revista (journal).

digest, *va.* 1. Digerir el alimento en el estómago para convertirlo en quimo y quilo (food). 2. Digerir, pensar, meditar, rumiar. 3. Digerir, sufrir con paciencia, tragar o tolerar una afrenta (assimilate mentally). 4. Digerir, ordenar, disponer, distribuir, colocar. 5. *(Quím.)* Digerir, cocer alguna cosa por medio de un calor templado. *-vn.* 1. *(Quím.)* Ser preparado por medio del calor y de la humedad para ulterior manipulación. 2. *(Cir.)* Supurar.

digester ['daɪdʒestə'] [dai-yes-tA'], *s.* 1. El que digiere lo que come. 2. Digeridor; aparato para reducir los huesos y toda la materia animal o vegetal a jalea o líquido. 3. Cualquier cosa que ayuda la digestión.

digestible [dɪ'dʒestɪbl] [di-yes-ti-bol], *a.* 1. *(Physiol.)* Digerible, que es fácil de digerir. 2. Fácil de asimilar o digerir (comprehensible). **Easily digestible,** fácil de digerir.

digestion [daɪ'dʒestʃən] [dai-yes-chon], *s.* 1. Digestión, la acción y efecto de digerir. 2. La acción de ordenar y colocar metódicamente o de reducir a método u orden: recepción y asimilación mentales. 3. *(Quím.)* Fermentación lenta que se produce por medio de un calor artificial. 4. Maduración de un tumor para que supure, por medio de medicinas.

digestive [dɪ'dʒestɪv] [di-yes-tiv], *a.* Digestivo; metódico. **The digestive system,** el aparato digestivo. *-s.* Medicamento digestivo.

diggable ['dɪgəbl] [di-ga-bol], *a.* Que puede ser cavado.

digger ['dɪgə'] [di-ga'], *s.* Cavador. **Gravedigger,** sepulturero. Excavadora (machine); excavador (person).

dight ['daɪt] [dait], *va.* 1. (Poét. o Prov.) Adornar, embellecer, vestir. 2. Preparar; alisar, limpiar.

digit ['dɪdʒɪt] [di-yit], *s.* 1. *(Anat.)* Dedo (de la mano o del pie). 2. Cualquier número denotado con una cifra solamente. 3. *(Astr.)* Dígito, la duodécima parte del diámetro del sol o de la luna. 4. *(Mat.)* Dígito, antigua medida longitudinal de tres cuartos de pulgada.

digital ['dɪdʒɪtəl] [di-yi-tal], *a.* Digital

digital computer [‚dɪdʒɪtəlkɒm'pju:tə'] [di-yit], *s.* Computadora digital, máquina calculadora digital.

digitalis [‚dɪdʒɪ'teɪlɪs] [di-yi-tei-lis], *s.* Dedalera, digital purpúrea, planta medicinal y sus hojas, usadas como tónico cardíaco.

digitate [‚dɪdʒɪ'teɪt] [di-yi-tet], **digitated** [‚dɪdʒɪ'teɪtɪd] [di-yi-te-tid], *a.* Dividido como los dedos.

digitrigade [‚dɪdʒɪ'trɪgeɪd] [di-yi-tri-gueid], *a.* Digitígrado, que anda sobre los dedos.

diglyph ['dɪglɪf] [di-glif], *s. (Arq.)* Diglifo, cartela ornada en su frete con dos muescas, semejantes a las tres del triglifo.

dignified ['dɪgnɪfaɪd] [dig-ni-faid], *a.* Dignificado. Digno, circunspecto (person, reply); digno (silence, attitude). **It's not very dignified,** no es muy decoroso o elegante. Majestuoso (stately).

dignify ['dɪgnɪfaɪ] [dig-ni-fai], *va.* 1. Dignificar (grace); exaltar, condecorar, elevar, promover. 2. Darle categoría a (make respectable). **I would not dignify that question with an answer,** esa pregunta no es digna de respuesta.

dignitary ['dɪgnɪtərɪ] [dig-ni-ta-ri], *s.* Dignidad, el que en alguna iglesia catedral obtiene alguna dignidad o beneficio preeminente. Dignatario.

dignity ['dɪgnɪtɪ] [dig-ni-ti], *s.* 1. Dignidad (dignified air/of person); cargo, empleo; rango, elevación; carácter, aire noble, aire de grandeza; solemnidad (of occasion). **To stand on one's dignity,** mantener las distancias. 2. Dignidad, categoría (status, worth). **She considers it to be beneath her dignity,** lo considera una degradación.

digress [daɪ'gres] [dai-gres], *vn.* Hacer digresión, separarse o apartarse del asunto, extraviarse. **If I may digress for a moment,** si me permiten hacer un breve inciso o paréntesis. **But I digress,** pero estoy divagando.

digression [daɪ'greʃən] [dai-gre-shon], *s.* 1. Digresión. 2. Desvío, separación. **By way of a digression,** a modo de inciso o paréntesis.

digressional [daɪ'greʃənl] [dai-gre-sho-nal], *a.* Lo que se separa del asunto principal; caracterizado por la digresión.

digressive [daɪ'gresɪv] [dai-gre-siv], *a.* Digresivo, discursivo.

digressively [daɪ'gresɪvlɪ] [dai-gre-siv-li], *adv.* Por vía de digresión.

dihedral [daɪ'hɪdrəl] [dai-hi-dral], *a.* Diedro (ángulo) formado por dos superficies planas.

dijudicate [dɪ'dʒɔdɪkeɪt] [di-yu-di-keit], *va.* 1. Fijar con autoridad, juzgar entre dos partes, decidir. 2. Discernir, distinguir, desarrollar.

dike [daɪk] [daik], *a.* 1. Dique (to keep out water); malecón, defensa contra el ímpetu de las aguas; terraplén (causeway); acequia (ditch). 2. *(Min.)* Vena o pared de otra materia que corta o impide la del mineral en alguna mina. 3. *(Ant.)* Canal de desagüe.

dike, *va.* Represar, contener por medio de un dique o represa; abrir un canal de desagüe.

dilacerate [dɪ'ləsəreɪt] [di-la-se-reit], *va.* Dilacerar, romper, rasgar, lacerar, despedazar.

dilaceration [dɪ'ləsəreɪʃən] [di-la-se-rei-shon], *s.* Despedazamiento, dilaceración.

dilapidate [dɪ'ləpɪdeɪt] [di-la-pi-deit], *va.* Dilapidar, arruinar, destruir, derribar. *-vn.* Arruinarse.

dilapidated [dɪ'ləpɪdeɪtɪd] [di-la-pi-dei-ted] *a.* Ruinoso (building); destartalado, desvencijado (car).

dilapidation [dɪ‚læpɪ'deɪʃən] [di-la-pi-dei-shon], *s.* Dilapidación, destrucción, daño; deterioro.

dilapidator [dɪ'ləpɪdeɪtə'] [di-la-pi-dei-to'], *s.* Dilapidador.

dilatability [dɪləta'bɪlɪtɪ] [di-la-ta-bi-li-ti], *s.* Dilatabilidad, la capacidad de dilatación.

dilatable [daɪ'lətəbl] [dai-la-te-bol], *a.* Dilatable.

dilatant [daɪ'lətənt] [dai-la-tant], *a.* Dilatador, que dilata o extiende. *-s.* Instrumento o substancia usada para dilatar.

dilatation [daɪ'lateɪʃən] [dai-la-tei-shon], *s.* Dilatación, extensión.

dilate [daɪˈleɪt] [dai-leit], *va.* y *vn.* 1. Dilatar, extender, alargar. 2. Hablar difusamente. 3. Dilatarse, explayarse o extenderse. 4. Dilatarse, ensancharse, extenderse.

dilated [daɪˈleɪtɪd] [dai-lei-tid], *pp.* y *a.* 1. Dilatado, extendido. 2. Explayado, prolijo, difuso. **His pupils were dilated,** tenía las pupilas dilatadas.

dilater [daɪˈleɪtəʳ] [dai-lei-taʳ], *s.* Dilatador, el que dilata o agranda.

dilation [daɪˈleɪʃən] [dai-lei-shon], **dilatation** [daɪˈləteɪʃən] [dai-la-tei-shon] *s.* 1. Dilatación. 2. (*Des.*) Dilatación, retardación. (*Med.*) **Dilation and curettage,** dilatación y legrado o raspaje.

dilative [daɪˈlətɪv] [dai-la-tiv], *a.* Dilativo, que tiene virtud de dilatar o de causar extensión.

dilatorily [daɪˈlərəlɪ] [dai-la-to-ri-li], *adv.* Lentamente, perezosamente.

dilatoriness [daɪˈlərənɪs] [dai-la-to-ri-nes], *a.* Lentitud, tardanza, pesadez.

dilatory [daɪˈlərɪ] [dai-la-to-ri] *a.* Dilatorio (causing delay); tardío (not prompt).

dilemma [daɪˈlemə] [dai-le-ma], *s.* 1. Dilema. 2. Suspensión, dificultad o duda en escoger o elegir; embarazo.

dilettante [ˌdɪlɪˈtænti] [di-li-tan-ti], *s.* Diletante, aficionado a las artes y ciencias. Voz italiana cuyo plural es *dilettanti.*

diligence [ˈdɪlɪdʒəns] [di-li-yens], *s.* 1. Asiduidad, aplicación al trabajo. 2. Diligencia, cuidado, esmero, exactitud. 3. (Der.) (a) Citación, orden, mandato; (b) embargo, secuestro por deudas.

diligence, *s.* Diligencia, coche grande dividido en dos o tres departamentos, que cubre la carrera ordinaria con relativa rapidez. Tiran de ella cuatro, seis o más caballos o mulas.

diligent [ˈdɪlɪdʒənt] [di-li-yent], *a.* Diligente, cumplidor (worker); aplicado, diligente (student); asiduo, activo, exacto, cuidadoso; esmerado, concienzudo (work, study).

diligently [ˈdɪlɪdʒəntlɪ] [di-li-yent-li], *adv.* Diligentemente, cuidadosamente.

dill [dɪl] [dil], *s.* (*Bot.*) Eneldo, hierba umbelífera anual, con semillas aromáticas.

dilly-dally [ˈdɪlɪdælɪ] [di-li-da-li], *vn.* (*Fam.*) Malgastar el tiempo; entretenerse en bagatelas.

dilucidate [daɪˈluːsɪdeɪt] [dai-lu-si-deit], *va.* Dilucidar, aclarar. *V.* ELUCIDATE.

diluent [dɪˈluːənt] [di-luent], *a.* y *s.* Diluyente, lo que diluye.

dilute [daɪˈluːt] [dai-lut], *va.* 1. Desleír, diluir, deshacer, disolver; atenuar. 2. Templar, debilitar. 3. Remojar, clarificar. *-vn.* Desleírse, deshacerse, hacerse menos concentrado.

dilute, *a.* Atenuado, diluído; desleído, disuelto, adelgazado, templado.

diluter [daɪˈluːtəʳ] [dai-lu-taʳ], *s.* Diluyente, lo que diluye.

dilution [daɪˈluːʃən] [dai-lu-shon], *s.* Desleidura, dilución.

diluvial, diluvian [dɪˈluːvɪən] [di-lu-vian], *a.* Diluviano, lo que pertenece al diluvio: producido por medio de un diluvio o inundación. **Diluvian,** en sentido geológico significa arcaico, antiguo.

dim [dɪm] [dim], *a.* 1. Oscuro, poco iluminado (dark/room); opaco, falto de brillo; débil, tenue (light). Borroso (indistinct/memory, shape). Vago (idea). **In the dim and distant past,** en el pasado remoto. 2. Confuso, indistinto; sombrío, nublado. 3. Turbio de vista; corto de vista; lerdo, falto de inteligencia, tardo en comprender (stupid). 4. Falto de brillantez, deslumbrado. Nada halagüeño, nada prometedor (gloomy).

dim, *va.* Ofuscar, quitar la luz, atenuar (lights); oscurecer, hacer alguna cosa menos resplandeciente; ofuscar, turbar la inteligencia o debilitando (eyesight); ir borrando (memory). **To dim one's headlights,** poner las luces cortas o de cruce o luces bajas. *vn.* Irse atenuando (light); irse borrando (memory); irse debilitando (sight).

dime [daɪm] [daim], *s.* 1. Moneda de plata de los Estados Unidos cuyo valor es diez centavos o dos reales de vellón. **It's not worth a dime,** no vale nada. **They are a dime a**

dozen, son baratísimos (very cheap); los hay a patadas o a montones (very common). 2. Décimo, el número diez.

dimension [dɪˈmenʃən] [di-men-shon], *s.* 1. Dimensión, medida, extensión. **A problem of enormous dimensions,** un problema de enormes dimensiones. 2. (*Alg.*) Dimensión, grado de una potencia o ecuación; cantidad que entra como factor de un término algebraico.

dimensionless [dɪˈmenʃənlɪs] [di-men-shon-les], *a.* Lo que no tiene dimensión determinada.

dimensity [dɪˈmensɪtɪ] [di-men-si-ti], *s.* (Poco us.) Extensión, capacidad.

dimensive [dɪˈmensɪv] [di-men-siv], *a.* Lo que señala las dimensiones.

dime store [daɪmˈstɔːʳ] [daim-stoʳ] *s.* Tienda que vende artículos de bajo precio.

dimeter [dɪˈmiːtəʳ] [di-mi-taʳ], *a.* y *s.* Verso que consta de dos medidas o cuatro pies.

dimidiate [ˈdɪmɪdɪeɪt] [di-mi-dieit], *va.* Dimidiar, promediar, partir en dos mitades.

diminish [dɪˈmɪnɪʃ] [di-mi-nish], *va.* 1. Disminuir, reducir (size, cost); minorar. Disminuir (enthusiasm). 2. Desmejorar, debilitar. *-vn.* Disminuirse, reducirse (cost, number); decrecer; debilitarse; degenerar. Disminuir, apagarse (enthusiasm). **To diminish in value,** disminuir de valor, depreciarse. **Diminishing,** cada vez menor (amount, importance). (*Econ.*) **The law of diminishing returns,** la ley de los rendimientos decrecientes.

diminished [dɪˈmɪnɪʃt] [di-mi-nisht] *a.* Más limitado (expectations). **To plead diminished responsibility,** alegar una atenuante de responsabilidad.

diminishingly [dɪˈmɪnɪʃɪŋlɪ] [di-mi-ni-shin-li], *adv.* Escasamente.

diminuendo [dɪˌmɪnjɪˈendəʊ] [di-mi-niu-en-dou], *a.* y *adv.* (*Mús.*) Que va disminuyendo gradualmente en volumen del sonido; lo opuesto a crescendo y denominado pro dim., dimin, o el signo.

diminution [ˌdɪmɪˈnjuːʃən] [di-mi-niu-shon], *s.* Disminución; degradación,; descrédito.

diminutive [dɪˈmɪnjʊtɪv] [di-mi-niu-tiv], *s.* y *a.* 1. Diminutivo; pequeño; mezquino; diminuto, minúsculo. 2. Diminutivo, lo que tiene cualidad de disminuir o reducir a menos alguna cosa.

diminutively [dɪˈmɪnjʊtɪvlɪ] [di-mi-niu-tiv-li], *adv.* Diminutivamente.

diminutiveness [dɪˈmɪnjʊtɪvnɪs] [di-mi-niu-tiv-nes], *s.* Pequeñez.

dimissory [dɪˈmɪsərɪ] [di-mi-so-ri], *a.* 1. Dimisorio. 2. Lo que da permiso para retirarse.

dimity [ˈdɪmɪtɪ] [di-mi-ti], *s.* Fustán, cotonía.

dimly [ˈdɪmlɪ] [dim-li], *adv.* Ofuscadamente, oscuramente. Débilmente (shine). **A dimly lit room,** una habitación poco iluminada o iluminada por una luz tenue.

dimmed headlight [dɪmˈhedlaɪt] [dim-jed-lait], *s.* Faro de automóvil con luz amortiguada.

dimmer [ˈdɪməʳ] [di-maʳ], *s.* Amortiguador (de la luz de un automóvil). Potenciómetro, dimmer. (*Elec.*) **Dimmer switch,** potenciómetro, conmutador de las luces.

dimming [ˈdɪmɪŋ] [di-min], *s.* Oscuridad.

dimmish [ˈdɪmɪʃ] [di-mish], *a.* Algo ofuscado, oscuro o bobio.

dimness [ˈdɪmnɪs] [dim-nes], *s.* 1. Ofuscamiento u oscurecimiento de la vista. 2. Torpeza, estupidez.

dimorph [ˈdɪmɔːf] [di-morf], *s.* Una de las formas de una substancia dimorfa.

dimorphism [ˈdɪmɔːfɪzm] [di-mor-fi-sem], *s.* Diformismo, propiedad de existir en dos formas como la tienen ciertas substancias cristalizables, ciertos insectos, una palabra de doble ortografía (v. g. *quay* y *key*), etc.

dimorphous [ˈdɪmɔːfəs] [di-mor-fos], *a.* Dimorfo, lo que existe o se presenta en dos formas; caracterizado por el dimorfismo.

dimple ['dɪmpl] [dim-pel], s. Hoyuelo, cavidad pequeñas en la mejilla, barba u otra parte (in cheeks, chin).

dimple, vn. Formarse hoyos en alguna parte del cuerpo.

dimpled ['dɪmpld] [dim-peld], **dimply** ['dɪmplɪ] [dim-pli], a. Lleno de hoyos.

dims [dɪmz] [dims], s. pl. Luces de cruce.

dim-sighted ['dɪmˌsaɪtəd] [dim-sai-tid], a. Cegato.

dimwit ['dɪmwɪt] [dim-uit] s. (Coloq.) Tarado mental.

dimwitted ['dɪmˈwɪtɪd] [dim-ui-ted] a. (Coloq.) Tonto, idiota.

din [dɪn] [din], s. Ruido violento y continuado; barullo, bulla (of conversation, voices); son, sonido; estruendo, ruido (of drill, traffic).

din, va. Atolondrar o aturdir con ruido.

dine [daɪn] [dain], vn. Hacer o tomar la comida principal del día. -va. Dar de comer, proveer con la comida principal, dar un convite.

dine out Cenar (a) fuera. **You'll be dining out on that for years,** te va a dar tema de conversación para quién sabe cuántas ocasiones.

diner ['daɪnəʳ] [di-naʳ], s. 1. Carro comedor (trains). 2. Comensal (person). 3. Cafetería (restaurant).

dinette set [dɪ'netˌset] [di-net-set] Juego de comedor diario.

ding [dɪŋ] [ding], va. 1. Instar, urgir repetidamente. 2. Arrojar violentamente, chocar con violencia. -vn. 1. Echar fieros o bravatas. 2. Resonar a intervalos regulares, como los toques de una campana; repicar.

ding-dong ['dɪŋˈdɒŋ] [din-don], s. Dindán, tintín, voz onomatopéyica para imitar el sonido de las campanas.

dinghy, dingy o dingey ['dɪndʒɪ] [din-yi], s. 1. Bote de remos de las Indias Orientales. 2. Esquife. 3. Bote salvavidas.

dingle ['dɪŋl] [din-gol], s. Cañada, espacio entre dos alturas.

dingle-dangle [dɪŋl'dæŋl] [dingl-danguel], adv. (Vul.) Se dice de lo que está mal colgado o que estando pendiente se menea por no estar bien firme.

dinginess ['dɪdʒɪnɪs] [din-yi-nes], s. La calidad de ser deslustrado o moreno.

dingy ['dɪdʒɪ] [din-yi], a. 1. Empañado, deslucido (furnishings); manchado, sucio (dirty). Lúgubre, deprimente (building, room). 2. Moreno, oscuro, negruzco.

dining car ['daɪnɪŋkɑːʳ] [dai-nin-kaʳ] s. Carro comedor trains.

dining hall ['daɪnɪŋhɔːl] [dai-nin-jol] s. Refectorio.

dinning room ['daɪnɪŋrʊm] [dai-nin-rum], s. Comedor, la pieza destinada para comer; refectorio, en los conventos, colegios, etc.

dining table ['daɪnɪŋˌteɪbl] [dai-nin-tei-bol] s. Mesa de comedor.

dinky ['dɪŋkɪ] [din-ki] a. 1. (Coloq.) De mala muerte (town). **A dinky appartment/room,** un cuchitril. 2. (Coloq.) (GB) Mono, lindo (cute).

dinna ['dɪnə] [di-na], v. (Esco.) No hacer.

dinner ['dɪnəʳ] [di-naʳ], s. 1. La comida principal del día; el acto de comer; cena, comida (in evening). **To eat/have dinner,** cenar, comer. **To go out to dinner,** salir a cenar fuera. 2. Banquete, cena de gala (formal). 3. Almuerzo, comida (at midday). (Coloq.) **He's had more girlfriends than you've had hot dinners,** ¡cambia de novia como de camisa!

dinner dance ['dɪnəˌdæns] [di-nar-dans] s. Cena con baile, comida bailable, cena-baile.

dinner jacket ['dɪnəˌdʒækɪt] [di-na-ya-kit] s. (GB) Esmoquin, smoking.

dinner party ['dɪnəˌpɑːtɪ] [di-na-par-ti] s. Cena, comida.

dinner plate ['dɪnəˌpleɪt] [di-na-pleit] s. Plato llano o plano, playo o bajo.

dinner service, dinner set s. Vajilla.

dinnertime ['dɪnətaɪm] [di-na-taim], s. La hora de comer o almorzar (at midday); la hora de cenar (in evening).

dinosaur ['daɪnəsɔːʳ] [dai-na-soʳ], s. Dinosaurio; pieza de museo (outdated thing).

dint [dɪnt] [dint], s. 1. Abolladura, marca, señal o impresión de un golpe. 2. Fuerza, violencia, poder. 3. (Des.) Golpe, choque. **By dint of argument,** a fuerza de argumentos.

dint, va. V.DENT.

diocesan [daɪ'sɪsən] [daio-si-san], s. Diocesano. -a. Diocesano.

diocese [daɪ'sɪs] [daio-sis], s. Diócesis, distrito o territorio de la jurisdicción espiritual de un obispo; distrito.

diode ['daɪəʊd] [daioud] s. Diodo.

dioecious [daɪ'sɪsəs] [daio-si-shos], a. (Biol.) Dioico, dioica; se dice de las plantas y de los moluscos cuyos sexos se hallan en distintos individuos.

dioicous [daɪ'ɔɪkəs] [daioi-kos], a. V. DIOECIOUS.

dioptic, dioptical [daɪ'ɒptrɪk] [dai-op-trik], **dioptric, dioptrical** [daɪ'ɒptrɪkl] [dai-op-tri-kal], a. Dióptrico.

dioptrics [daɪ'ɒptrɪkz] [dai-op-triks], s. Dióptrica, la ciencia que trata de la refracción de la luz.

diorama [daɪ'ræmə] [dai-o-ra-ma], s. Diorama, vistas de perspectiva, y el local donde se enseñan o exponen.

dioramic [daɪ'ræmɪk] [dai-o-ra-mik], a. Diorámico, relativo al diorama.

diorite [daɪ'ɒraɪt] [dai-o-rait], s. Diorita, roca plutónica compuesta de feldespato y anfíbol.

dioxide [daɪ'ɒksaɪd] [dai-ok-said], s. (Quím.) Bióxido, óxido de segundo grado. Se llama también binoxide.

dioxin [daɪ'ɒksɪn] [dai-ok-sin] s. Dioxina.

dip [dɪp] [dip] va. 1. Mojar, remojar, bañar, chapuzar, zampuzar, chapotear, sumergir; mojar en algo (into liquid). **Dip it in flour,** páselo por harina, enharínelo. 2. Ojear, repasar ligeramente algún libro, escrito, etc.; examinar de prisa alguna cosa. 3. Bajar o volver a alzar un objeto, p. ej. una bandera; agachar, bajar (lower/head). (GB) (Auto) To **dip one's headlights,** poner las luces cortas o de cruce o bajas. 4. Alzar, levantar para vaciar; sacar líquidos. 5. (Des.) Hipotecar, empeñar, dar alguna cosa en hipoteca o prenda. (Agr.) Desinfectar (haciendo pasar por un baño) (sheep). vn. 1. Sumergirse, meterse debajo del agua. 2. Empeñarse o meterse en algún negocio. 3. Declinar, inclinarse hacia abajo. Bajar (decrease/sales, prices). Bajar en picado (move downward/aircraft, bird). **The sun dipped below the horizon,** el sol desapareció o se escondió tras el horizonte. Descender, bajar (slope, land). 4. (Geol.) Yacer, quedarse o hallarse formando ángulo con el horizonte; se dice de las capas de terreno, estratos, etc.

dip into Echar mano de (reserves, savings); hojear, leer por encima (book).

dip, s. 1. Inmersión, la acción de sumergir; baño corto, chapuzón (swim). **To take a dip,** darse un chapuzón. 2. La acción del verbo dip en cualquiera de sus acepciones; depresión, hondonada (depression, hollow). Caída, descenso (in sales, production). 3. Baño, líquido en que algo está sumergido. 4. Inclinación de la aguja magnética (vertical), de una capa o estrato, de un eje de carruaje, etc. 5. Profundidad de inmersión de una rueda de paleta, de un hélice, etc. 6. (Culin.) Salsa en la que se mojan diferentes bocaditos (en una fiesta, etc.).

dipetalous [dɪ'petələs] [di-pe-ta-los], a. (Bot.) Dipétalo o dipétala.

diphtheria [dɪf'θɪərɪə] [dif-zia-ria], s. Difteria, difteritis, enfermedad caracterizada por la formación de falsas membranas.

diphthong ['dɪfθɒŋ] [dif-zong], s. (Gram.) Diptongo.

diploe ['dɪplɔː] [di-plo], s. 1. Diploe, tejido esponjoso de los huesos del cráneo. 2. (Bot.) Parenquima de una hoja entre dos capas epidérmicas.

diploma [dɪ'pləʊmə] [di-plou-ma], s. Diploma, despacho, privilegio, título, autorizado con sello.

diplomacy [dɪ'pləʊməsɪ] [di-plou-ma-si], s. 1. Diplomacia, conocimiento de los intereses o relaciones de unas potencias con otras. 2. El cuerpo de los embajadores o ministros extranjeros.

diplomat [dɪ'pləʊmæt] [di-plou-mat], s. Diplomático, representante de un Estado soberano en la capital o en la corte de otro; miembro de una legación.

diplomatic [ˌdɪpləʊ'mætɪk] [di-plou-ma-tik], a. 1. Diplomático, relativo o perteneciente a la diplomacia. **The diplomatic corps,** el cuerpo diplomático. **Diplomatic**

immunity, inmunidad diplomática. 2. Diplomático, lo que pertenece al estudio de los diplomas y documentos antiguos o importantes. 3. Diplomático (tactful).

diplomatics [ˌdɪpləʊˈmætɪkz] [di-plou-ma-tiks], s. (Arqueología) Diplomática, el arte de conocer y distinguir los diplomas y otros documentos de importancia.

diplomatist [ˌdɪpləʊˈmætɪst] [di-plou-ma-tist], s. 1. V. DIPLOMAT. 2. Diplomático, el que es versado y hábil en diplomacia. 3. Se dice de la persona disimulada, astuta y sagaz.

diplopia [dɪˈpləʊpɪə] [di-plou-pia], s. (Med.) Diplopia, visión doble; fenómeno morboso que hace ver dobles los objetos.

dipper [ˈdɪpəʳ] [di-paʳ], s. 1. El que moja, sumerge o baña. 2. Cucharón para sacar líquidos en cantidad (ladle). 3. Echa y saca líquidos. 4. (Fam.) Osa mayor. 5. (Zool.) Tordo de agua.

dipping-needle [ˌdɪpɪŋˈniːdl] [di-pin-ni-dol], s. Aguja magnética sobre un eje horizontal.

dipsas [ˈdɪpsəs] [dip-sas], s. Serpiente fabulosa, cuya mordedura producía una sed inextinguible.

dipsomania [ˌdɪpsəʊˈmeɪnɪə] [dip-sou-mei-nia], s. Dipsomanía, deseo irresistible de bebidas alcohólicas.

dipsomaniac [ˌdɪpsəʊˈmeɪnɪæk] [dip-sou-mei-niak]] a. Dipsómano.

dipterous [ˈdɪptərəs] [dip-te-ros], a. (Ent.) Díptero, se dice de los insectos que tienen dos alas.

dipstick [ˈdɪpstɪk] [dip-stik] s. Varilla medidora del aceite.

dip switch [ˈdɪpswɪtʃ] [dip-suich] s. (GB) Conmutador de las luces.

diptych [ˈdɪptɪk] [dip-tik], s. Díptica, registro de obispos y mártires.

dire [ˈdaɪəʳ] [daiaʳ], a. 1. Horrendo, horroroso, horrible, espantoso, atroz (very bad); cruel, inhumano; funesto, nefasto (news, consequences). **To be in dire straits,** estar en una situación desesperada. 2. Serio, grave (ominous, warning). 3. Extremo (desperate/need, misery).

direct [daɪˈrekt] [dai-rekt], a. 1. Directo (route, flight); derecho (contact); directo (cause, consequence). (Telec.) **Direct dialing,** (GB) dialling, servicio automático, discado directo o automático. (Elec.) **Direct current,** corriente continua. **He's a direct descendant of the duke,** desciende del duque por línea directa (in genealogy). 2. Abierto, claro, patente; franco, directo (frank, straightforward/person, manner); directo (question). 3. Exacto (exact/equivalent, quotation). **To score a direct hit,** dar en el blanco. 4. (Gram.) En estilo directo (question, command). **Direct discourse,** (GB) **speech,** estilo directo. - adv. 1. En línea recta; directamente (write, phone); directo, directamente (go, travel). (Telec.) **To dial direct,** marcar o discar directamente el número. 2. Directamente (straight). (Rad., TV) **Direct from Paris,** en directo desde París. 3. Directamente, sin rodeos (straightforwardly).

direct, va. 1. Dirigir (aim); apuntar, enseñar, enderezar, guiar. **It was directed at us,** iba dirigido a nosotros. 2. Dirigir, mostrar la dirección; indicarle el camino a (give direction); mandar, dirigir (address/letter, parcel). 3. Dirigir (play, orchestra, traffic); gobernar, regir, reglar, conducir, ordenar. -vn. (Cin., Teat.) Dirigir.

direct access [daɪˌrektˈæksəs] [dai-rekt-ak-ses] s. Acceso directo.

direct action [daɪˌrektˈækʃən] [dai-rekt-ak-shon] s. Acción directa.

direct billing [daɪˈrektbɪlɪŋ] [dai-rekt-bi-lin] s. Débito bancario o domiciliación de pagos.

direct current [daɪˌrektˈkʌrənt] [dai-rekt-ka-rent] s. Corriente continua.

direction [dɪˈrekʃən] [dai-rek-shon], s. 1. Dirección, la acción y efecto de dirigir, encaminar, etc. 2. Dirección (course, compass, point); movimiento causado por algún impulso. **Sense of direction,** sentido de la orientación. **It's**

a step in the right direction, es un paso positivo. 3. Dirección (supervision), consejo; orden, instrucción, mandato, 4. Curso de una línea, rumbo, dirección. 5. Designio, mira, fin; tendencia. **He lacks direction,** no tiene un norte (purpose). 6. El sobrescrito o sobre de una carta; señas, dirección, residencia. **Directions,** indicaciones (for route); instrucciones, indicaciones (for task, use, assembly).

directional signal [dɪˈrekʃənˌsaɪnl] [dai-rek-sho-nal-sai-nal], s. Luz intermitente, luz direccional.

direction indicator [dɪˈrekʃənˌɪndɪkeɪtəʳ] [dai-rek-shon-in-di-kei-toʳ], s. (Aer.) Indicador de dirección.

directive [dɪˈrektɪv] [dai-rek-tiv], s. Directiva, directorio. -a. Directivo, que dirige; indicativo.

directly [dɪˈrektlɪ] [dai-rekt-li], adv. 1. Directamente, en línea recta. Directamente (without stopping/go, drive, fly). 2. Sin medianero, sin intervención de tercero; directamente (without intermediaries/report, deal). **He's directly responsible,** es el responsable directo. 3. Inmediatamente, en seguida; al instante, ahora mismo (now, at once). 4. Por línea directa (in genealogy/related, descended). 5. Directamente, (frankly, straightforwardly/ask); con franqueza (speak).

direct mail [ˌdaɪrektˈmeɪl] [dai-rekt-meil] s. Publicidad por correo.

directness [daɪˈrektnɪs] [dai-rekt-nes], s. 1. Derechura, línea recta. 2. Franqueza (of character, remark); lo directo (of aim, attack).

director [daɪˈrektəʳ] [dai-rek-taʳ], s. Director (of department, project); directivo (of company). 2. Regla, ordenanza. 3. Director, el que dirige o instruye; director espiritual. 4. (Cin., Teat.) Director.

directorate [daɪˈrektərɪt] [dai-rek-to-reit], s. Dirección, el cuerpo de directores de un ramo, empresa o institución.

directorial [daɪrekˈtɔːrɪəl] [dai-rek-to-rial], a. 1. Directorio, directivo. 2. De dirección (techniques, tricks); en dirección, como director (experience); como director (debut).

directorship [dɪˈrektəʃɪp] [di-rek-tor-ship] s. Dirección, cargo de director.

directory [dɪˈrektərɪ] [dai-rek-to-ri], s. 1. Directorio, guía (index, yearbook); guía de forasteros. **A city,** (BG) **street directory,** una guía de calles, un callejero. 2. Añalejo, librito que señala el orden del rezo y oficio divino. 3. Directorio comercial, lista alfabética de los habitantes de una ciudad. Guía telefónica o de teléfonos, directorio telefónico. **Directory assistance,** (GB) **enquiries,** servicio de información telefónica. 4. Directorio, nombre del poder ejecutivo en Francia en 1795.

direful [ˈdaɪrəfʊl] [daia-ful], a.

direfulness [ˈdaɪrəfʊlnɪs] [daia-ful-nes], s. Horribilidad, espanto; fiereza, crueldad.

direness [ˈdaɪrənɪs] [daia-nes], s. Horror, espanto; fiereza.

dirge [ˈdɜːdʒ] [derch], s. Endecha; canto fúnebre; canción triste y lamentosa.

dirigible [ˈdaɪrɪdʒəbl] [dai-ri-yi-bol], s. Dirigible, globo dirigible.

dirk [dɜːk] [derk], s. Especie de daga.

dirt [dɜːt] [dert], s. 1. Cieno, lodo, barro, basura. Suciedad, mugre (unclean substance). 2. Excremento. 3. Tierra suelta (earth, soil). **To hit the dirt,** caerse al suelo. De tierra (road, track). 4. Vileza, bajeza. 5. **To dig up dirt on/about somebody,** sacarle los trapos sucios a relucir o al sol a alguien (scandal); (Coloq.) Inmundicia (obscenity). **Dirt cheap,** (fam.) excesivamente barato. **Dirt farmer,** agricultor que trabaja su propia tierra.

dirtily [ˈdɜːtɪlɪ] [der-ti-li], adv. 1. Puercamente, suciamente, vilmente, indignamente. 2. Lascivamente (laugh, leer); sin modales (eat).

dirtiness [ˈdɜːtɪnɪs] [der-ti-nes], s. Suciedad; sordidez, bajeza, villanía.

dirty [ˈdɜːtɪ] [der-ti], a. 1. Sucio (soiled). **The floor is dirty,** el suelo está sucio. **My hands are dirty,** tengo las manos sucias. **To get dirty,** ensuciarse. Puerco, asqueroso, cochino (obscene/story, book); lascivo (leer, grin); verde o colorado (joke); porno (magazine). **To have a dirty mind,** tener una mente de cloaca. Sucio (shameful/job, work). **Dirty money,** dinero sucio o negro. **To do somebody's dirty work,** hacerle el trabajo sucio a alguien. 2. Sórdido, vil, bajo, despreciable, villano, indigno. **He played a dirty trick on me,** me jugó una mala pasada (despicable). Sucio (unfair, tactis). **He's a dirty player,** juega sucio. 3. **A dirty look,** una mirada asesina (angry, accusing).

dirty *va.* Ensuciar; manchar (reputation).

dirty *adv.* 1. *(Coloq.)* Sucio (unfairly/fight, play). **To talk dirty,** decir cochinadas (indecently). 2. (as intensifier) **Dirty great,** tremendo.

dirty old man *s. (Coloq.)* Viejo verde.

dirty tricks *s. pl.* Chanchullos.

dirty word *s.* Palabrota, mala palabra.

dis [dɪs] [dis], **des** [dɪs] [dis], Partícula prepositiva que quiere decir aparte; denota separación, negación o fuerza intensiva.

disability [ˌdɪsə'bɪlɪtɪ] [di-sa-bi-li-ti], *s.* Impotencia; inhabilidad, incapacidad; discapacidad, invalidez (state). Por invalidez (pension, allowance); problema (particular handicap).

disable [dɪs'eɪbl] [di-sei-bol], *va.* 1. Disminuir las fuerzas naturales. Dejar inválido (illness, accident, injury). 2. Inhabilitar, inutilizar (machine, weapon); incapacitar; arruinar. **To disable a ship,** *(Mar.)* desaparejar un navío. **To disable the guns of battery,** desmontar una batería. 3. Incapacitar legalmente.

disabled [dɪs'eɪbld] [di-sei-bold] *a.* Discapacitado, minusválido.

disabled *s. pl.* **The disabled,** los discapacitados, los minusválidos.

disablement [dɪs'eɪblmənt] [di-sei-bol-ment], *s.* Impedimento legal; inhabilitación.

disabuse [ˌdɪsə'bjuːz] [di-sa-bius], *va.* Enmendar, desengañar, sacar de un error. **I tried to disabuse him of the notion that...,** intenté sacarlo del error de que...

dissaccommodate [ˌdɪsə'kɒmədeɪt] [di-sa-ko-mo-deit], *va.* *(Ant.)* Incomodar.

disaccommodation [dɪsəˌkəmə'deɪʃən] [di-sa-ko-mo-dei-shon], *s.* Ineptitud.

disaccord [ˌdɪsə'kɔːd] [di-sa-kord], *va.* Desacordar, discordar.

disaccustom [ˌdɪsə'kʌstəm] [di-sa-kas-tom] *va.* Desacostumbrar, deshabituar.

disadjust [dɪs'ədʒʌst] [dis-ad-yast], *va.* Transtornar el arreglo ordenado de algo; desarreglar, poner en desorden.

disadorn [dɪs'ədɔːn] [dis-a-dorn], *va.* Desadornar.

disadvantage [ˌdɪsəd'vɑːntɪdʒ] [dis-ad-van-tich], *s.* 1. Desventaja, inconveniente (hindrance, drawback); menoscabo o pérdida. **To be at a disadvantage,** estar en desventaja. 2. Disminución de alguna cosa apreciable. 3. Desprevención.

disadvantage, *va.* Menoscabar, dañar, perjudicar.

disadvantaged [ˌdɪsəd'vɑːntɪdʒd] [dis-ad-van-tichd] *a.* Desfavorecido, carenciado (children, area).

disadvantageous [ˌdɪsædvɑːn'teɪdʒəs] [dis-ad-van-tei-chos] *a.* Desventajoso, desfavorable.

disadvantageously [ˌdɪsædvɑːn'teɪdʒəslɪ] [dis-ad-van-tei-chos-li], *adv.* Desventajosamente.

disadvantageousness [ˌdɪsædvɑːn'teɪdʒəsnɪs] [dis-ad-van-tei-chos-nes], *s.* Menoscabo, desventaja.

dissaffect [ˌdɪsə'fekt] [dis-a-fekt], *va.* Descontentar; inquietar, tener hastío, enfermar; desaprobar; indisponer; malquistar.

disaffected [ˌdɪsə'fektɪd] [dis-a-fek-tid], *a.* Desaficionado, desinclinado, disgustado, descontento, desafecto; mal intencionado.

disaffectedness [ˌdɪsə'fektɪdnɪs] [dis-a-fek-tid-nes], *s.* Desafecto, desamor.

disaffection [ˌdɪsə'fekʃən] [dis-a-fek-shon], *s.* Desafecto, deslealtad, desamor, descontento, desafección.

disaffectionate [ˌdɪsə'fekʃənɪt] [dis-a-fek-sho-neit], *a.* Desaficionado.

disaffirm [ˌdɪsə'fɜːm] [dis-a-ferm], *va.* 1. Contradecir, negar, impugnar una afirmación. 2. *(For.)* Invalidar, anular, hacer nulo; desconocer, renunciar, rechazar.

disaffirmance [ˌdɪsə'fɜːməns] [dis-a-fer-mens], *s.* Confutación, impugnación.

disaffirmation [dɪsəfɜː'meɪʃən] [dis-a-fer-mei-shon], *s.* V. DISAFFIRMANCE.

disafforest [ˌdɪsə'fɒrɪst] [dis-a-fo-rest], *va.* (Der. inglés) Abrir un bosque o hacerlo de uso común.

disaggregate [ˌdɪsə'grəgeɪt] [dis-a-gri-gueit], *va.* Desagregar, separar en sus partes constitutivas.

disagree ['dɪsə'griː] [disa-gri], *vn.* 1. Desconvenir; discordiar, oponerse mutuamente, desavenirse; no estar de acuerdo con algo, discrepar de algo (differ in opinion). 3. Contender, lidiar, ser contrario; altercar, discutir con alguien (quarrel). 3. No ser conveniente, no sentar bien, ser dañoso o perjudicial (cause discomfort). **Onions disagree with her,** las cebollas le sientan o le caen mal. 4. No coincidir, discrepar (conflict/figures, accounts).

disagreeable [ˌdɪsə'griːəbl] [disa-gri-a-bol], *a.* 1. Contrario, opuesto. 2. Desagradable (smell, experience, person); ofensivo. Ingrato, desagradable (task, job).

disagreeableness [ˌdɪsə'griːəblnɪs] [disa-gri-a-bol-nes], *s.* Oposición, desagrado, disgusto, desplacer.

disagreeably [ˌdɪsə'griːəblɪ] [disa-gri-a-bli], *adv.* Desagradablemente; de mala manera, de manera desagradable (look, say). **It was disagreeable hot,** hacía un calor desagradable.

disagreement [ˌdɪsə'griːmənt] [disa-gri-ment], *s.* 1. Desacuerdo, disconformidad (difference of opinion); desavenencia, disensión, discusión (quarrel). 2. Desemejanza, diferencia; discrepancia (disparity). 3. Discordia, contrariedad.

disallow [ˌdɪsə'lao] [dis-a-lou], *va.* 1. Negar la autoridad de alguno. *(Law)* Rechazar, desestimar (claim, evidence); anular (goal). 2. Desaprobar, reprobar, censurar, culpar. *-vn.* Negar o no dar permiso, prohibir.

disallowable ['dɪsə'laoəbl] [di-sa-loua-bol], *a.* Negable; inadmisible; culpable, censurable.

disallowance ['dɪsə'laoəns] [di-sa-louans], *s.* Prohibición, vedamiento.

disanimate ['dɪsə'nɪmeɪt] [di-sa-ni-meit], *va.* 1. *(Ant.)* Desanimar, desalentar, acobardar. 2. *(Des.)* Matar.

disannul [ˌdɪsə'nʌl] [di-sa-nul], *va. (Ant.)* Anular, invalidar.

disannuller [ˌdɪsə'nʌlər] [di-sa-nu-lar], *s.* Anulador.

disannulling [ˌdɪsə'nʌlɪŋ] [di-sa-nu-lin], *s.* Anulación.

disannulment [ˌdɪsə'nʌlmənt] [di-sa-nul-ment], *s.* Anulación.

disanoint [ˌdɪsə'nɔɪnt] [di-sa-noint], *va.* Profanar; degradar al que está ordenado.

disapparel [ˌdɪsə'pɛərəl] [di-sa-pea-rel], *va.* Desnudar, quitar el vestido; desguarnecer.

disappear [ˌdɪsə'pɪər] [di-sa-piar], *vn.* Desaparecer, perderse de vista (become invisible); ausentarse. **The ship disappeared over the horizon,** el barco desapareció o se perdió en el horizonte. Desaparecer, irse (go away/pain, problems); desvanecerse (worries, fears).

disappearance [ˌdɪsə'pɪərəns] [di-sa-pia-rans],

disappearing [ˌdɪsə'pɪərɪŋ] [di-sa-pia-rin], *s.* Desaparecimiento, desaparición.

disappoint [ˌdɪsə'pɔɪnt] [di-sa-point], *va.* Frustrar, privar a alguno de lo que esperaba o dejar sin efecto su intento; faltar a la palabra; engañar; chasquear. Decepcionar (person); defraudar (hopes, desires). **To be disappointed,** llevarse chasco, salir mal en una empresa; ser contrariado. *(Fam.)* Quedar o dejar plantado, colgado o chasqueado; petardear.

disappointed [ˌdɪsə'pɔɪntɪd] [di-sa-poin-tid] *a.* De desilusión (look, sigh). **She was disappointed at losing the match,** se llevó una desilusión al perder el partido. **I'm disappointed with the results,** los resultados me han decepcionado. **She**

was disappointed in love, tuvo un desengaño amoroso. **I'm disappointed in you,** me has decepcionado o defraudado.

disappointing [ˌdɪsə'pɔɪntɪŋ] [di-sa-poin-tin] *a.* Decepcionante.

disappointment [ˌdɪsə'pɔɪntmənt] [di-sa-point-ment], *s.* Chasco, decepción (letdown); contratiempo, petardo, revés, disgusto. Desilusión decepción (emotion). **Much to my disappointment,** para mi gran desilusión.

disapprobation [ˌdɪsəprə'beɪʃən] [di-sa-pro-bei-shon], *s.* Desaprobación, reprobación.

disapprobatory [ˌdɪsə'prəbətəri] [di-sa-pro-ba-to-ri], *s.* Desaprobador, que desaprueba.

disapproval [ˌdɪsə'pruːvəl] [di-sa-pru-val], *s.* 1. Desaprobación (dislike). **To voice/express one's disapproval of somebody/something,** mostrar o expresar su desaprobación respecto de alguien/algo. 2. No aprobación (rejection/of bill); denegación (of grant).

disapprove [ˌdɪsə'pruːv] [di-sa-pruv], *vn.* 1. Desaprobar, reprobar, condenar, censurar (Usase a menudo con *of*). **She wants to be a singer but her parents disapprove,** quiere ser cantante pero a sus padres no les parece bien o sus padres desaprueban la idea. **He disapproves of smoking,** está en contra del tabaco o del cigarrillo. 2. Invalidar, revocar. *va.* Rechazar, no aprobar (plan, expenditure).

disapproving [ˌdɪsə'pruːvɪŋ] [di-sa-pru-vin] *a.* De reproche (tone, look).

disapprovingly [ˌdɪsə'pruːvɪŋlɪ] [di-sa-pru-vin-li] *adv.* Con desaprobación.

disarm [dɪs'aːm] [dis-arm], *va.* 1. Desarmar, despojar de armas (troops, opposition); desactivar (bomb, mine); desbaratar (criticism). 2. Privar del poder de hacer daño; calmar, apaciguar; desarmar (win confidence of). *-vn.* Desechar o poner a un lado las armas, desarmarse; licenciar tropas o fuerzas marítimas, ponerlas en pie de paz.

disarmament [dɪs'aːməmənt] [dis-ar-ma-ment], *s.* Desarme. **Nuclear disarmament,** desarme nuclear. **Total disarmament,** desarme total.

disarmer [dɪs'aːmər] [dis-ar-mar], *s.* El que desarma.

disarming [dɪs'aːmɪŋ] [dis-ar-min], *s.* Desarme, desarmadura; que desarma.

disarmingly [dɪs'aːmɪŋlɪ] [dis-ar-min-li] *adv.* **She's disarmingly frank,** es de una franqueza que desarma.

disarrange [ˌdɪsə'reɪndʒ] [di-sa-reindch], *va.* Desarreglar, desordenar.

disarrangement [ˌdɪsə'reɪndʒmənt] [di-sa-reindch-ment], *s.* Desarreglo, desorden, confusión.

disarray [ˌdɪsə'reɪ] [di-sa-rei], **s.** 1. Desarreglo, desorden, confusión; desorganización (of political party); desaliño (of appearance). **The troops were in disarray,** entre las tropas reinaba la confusión o el caos. **Her papers were in total disarray,** sus papeles estaban completamente desordenados. 2. Ropa de levantar, paños menores, trapillo, desabillé.

disarray, *va.* Desnudar; desarreglar; derrotar, desordenar.

disarticulate [ˌdɪsaː'tɪkjʊleɪt] [di-sar-ti-kiu-leit], *va.* Desarticulr, separar las articulaciones. *-vn.* Desarticularse, descoyuntarse.

disassociate [ˌdɪsə'səʊʃɪeɪt] [di-sa-sou-shieit], *va.* Desunir.

disaster [dɪ'zaːstər] [di-sas-tar], *s.* 1. Desastre, mala estrella. 2. Desgracia, aflicción, miseria, desdicha, infortunio, revés (misfortune). **Disaster struck,** ocurrió o se produjo una catástrofe. 3. Catástrofe, desastre (flood, earthquake); siniestro, desastre (crash, sinking). **Disaster fund,** fondo para los damnificados. 4. Desastre (fiasco); *(Coloq.)* Desastre (hopeless person).

disaster area [dɪ'zaːstə'æərɪə] [di-sas-ter-a-ria] *s.* Zona siniestrada, zona de desastre. **My room is a real disaster area,** mi habitación está hecha un desastre.

disastrous [dɪ'zaːstrəs] [di-sas-tros], *a.* Desastroso, infeliz, desgraciado, desastrado, ominoso, calamitoso, infausto, funesto, triste, fatal.

disastrously [dɪ'zaːstrəslɪ] [di-sas-tros-li], *adv.* Desastrosamente.

disastrousness [dɪ'zaːstrəsnɪs] [di-sas-tros-nes], *s.* Desgracia, desdicha.

disavouch [ˌdɪza'svoːtʃ] [di-sa-voch], *va. (Ant.)* Retractar, desdecirse.

disavow ['dɪsə'vaʊ] [di-sa-vau], *va.* Denegar, negar; desconocer; desaprobar.

disavowal [ˌdɪsə'vaʊəl] [di-sa-vauel], **disavowment** [ˌdɪsə'vaʊmənt] [di-sa-vau-ment], *s.* Denegación.

disauthorize ['dɪsə'θəraɪz] [di-so-zo-rais], *va.* Desautorizar.

disband [dɪs'bænd] [dis-band], *va.* Despedir de un servicio colectivo, especialmente licenciar del servicio militar. Disolver (organization); licenciar (army). *-vn.* Retirarse, separarse, desmandarse; desbandarse (group); disolverse (organization).

disbar [dɪs'baːr] [dis-baʳ], *va.* Excluir del colegio de abogados; privar del derecho de comparecer ante un juez o tribunal como abogado.

disbarment [dɪs'baːmənt] [dis-bar-ment], *s.* La acción y efecto de excluir a uno del colegio de abogados.

disbark [dɪs'baːk] [dis-bark], *va. (Mar.)* Desembarcar.

disbelief ['dɪsbə'liːf] [dis-bi-lif], *s.* Incredulidad, repugnancia en creer, falta de fe, terquedad en no creer; escepticismo. **She looked at me in disbelief,** me miró incrédula o sin dar crédito a lo que veía (u oía, etc.).

disbelieve ['dɪsbə'liːv] [dis-bi-liv], *va.* Descreer, no creer (statement); desconfiar, dudar; no creerle a (person).*-vn.* Rehusar, no consentir en creer (p. ej. una doctrina religiosa).

disbeliever ['dɪsbə'liːvər] [dis-bi-li-vaʳ], *s.* Descreído, incrédulo.

disbelieving ['dɪsbə'liːvɪŋ] [dis-bi-li-vin] *a.* Incrédulo.

disbench ['dɪsbentʃ] [dis-bench], *va.* (Der. inglés) Desbancar.

disbowel ['dɪsbəʊəl] [dis-bouel], *va. (Ant.)* V. DISEMBOWEL.

disbranch ['dɪsbræntʃ] [dis-branch], *va. (Ant.)* Desgajar, arrancar las ramas del tronco.

disbud ['dɪsbʌd] [dis-bad], *va.* Desyemar, desborrar, quitar los botones o tallos a las plantas.

disburden [dɪs'bəːdn] [dis-bar-den], *va.* Descargar, aligerar, desembarazar de un peso. *-vn.* Descargar o aquietar el ánimo.

disbursable [dɪs'bəːsəbl] [dis-bar-sa-bol], *a.* Desembolsable, pagable, que se puede desembolsar.

disburse [dɪs'bəːs] [dis-bers] *va.* Desembolsar.

disbursement [dɪs'bəːsmənt] [dis-bers-ment] *s.* Desembolso (payment). **Disbursements,** *pl.* gastos (expenses).

disburser [dɪs'bəːsər] [dis-ber-saʳ], *s.* El que desembolsa, pagador.

disc, *s.* V. DISK.

discal ['dɪskəl] [dis-kal], *a.* De disco; perteneciente o parecido a un disco.

discalced ['dɪskəlst] [dis-kalst], *a.* Descalzado, descalzo (se aplica a los carmelitas).

discant [dɪs'kænt] [dis-kant], *v.* y *s.* V. DESCANT.

discard ['dɪskaːd] [dis-kard], *va.* 1. Descartar, desechar como inútil, deshacerse de (dispose of); desechar (idea, belief); despedir o echar a un criado. Mudar (shed/skin, leaves); Desembarazarse de (take off/clothing). 2. Descartar, deponer, apear de algún empleo o destino. *-vn.* Descartarse (en el juego de naipes).

discase ['dɪskeɪs] [dis-keis], *va. (Ant.)* Desenvainar, quitar la cubierta; desnudar.

discern [dɪ'sɜːn] [di-sern], *va.* 1. Columbrar, alcanzar a ver de lejos. 2. Discernir, conocer, percibir, descubrir. *-vn.* Discernir, distinguir.

discerner [dɪ'sɜːnər] [di-ser-naʳ], *s.* Discernidor, el que discierne.

discernible [dɪ'sɜːnɪbl] [di-ser-ni-bol], *a.* Perceptible (fault, drawback); aparente, visible, sensible; apreciable, ostensible (likeness/change).

discernibleness [dɪ'sɜːnɪblnɪs] [di-ser-ni-bol-nes], *s.* Visibilidad, perceptibilidad.

discernibly [dɪˈsɜːnɪblɪ] [di-ser-ni-bli], *adv.* Perceptiblemente, visiblemente.

discerning [dɪˈsɜːnɪŋ] [di-ser-nin], *a.* Juicioso, sagaz, perspicaz, despierto, avisado, advertido; exigente, con criterio (reader, customer); exigente, fino (palate, taste); educado (ear, eye). *-s.* Discernimiento.

discerningly [dɪˈsɜːnɪŋlɪ] [di-ser-nin-li], *adv.* Juiciosamente.

discernment [dɪˈsɜːnmənt] [di-sern-ment], *s.* Discernimiento, conocimiento; gusto; agudeza, juicio recto.

discerp [dɪˈsɜːp] [di-serp], *va.* (*Ant.*) Despedazar; separar, escoger.

discerptible [dɪˈsɜːptɪbl] [di-serp-ti-bol], *a.* Separable.

discerption [dɪˈsɜːpʃən] [di-serp-shon], *s.* Despedazamiento; separación.

discharge [dɪˈtʃɑːdʒ] [di-charch], *va.* 1. Descargar o aliviar la carga. 2. Descargar o sacar a tierra la carga de una embarcación (unload/cargo). 3. Descargar, soltar; disparar (shoot/volley, broadside). 4. Pagar una deuda, saldar, liquidar (debt); cumplir con (duty). 5. Exonerar, eximir de alguna obligación, dispensar; absolver, dar libertad (release/prisoner); desembarazar de alguna dificultad. Dar de alta (patient); dispensar (juror); rehabilitar (bankrupt). **I discharged myself from hospital,** me di de alta yo mismo del hospital. 6. Ejecutar, cumplir. 7. Cancelar, borrar. 8. Descartar, despedir, privar de algún empleo u oficio (dismiss); desempeñar, cumplir, llenar bien. 9. Emitir, despedir (send out/fumes); descargar (electricity); verter (sewage, waste).. *-vn.* 1. Descargarse, soltarse. **To discharge the officers and crew,** despedir la tripulación de un buque. **To discharge one's duty,** cumplir con su obligación. 2. Desembocar, descargar (river). Descargarse (battery).

**discharge, ** *s.* 1. (*Elec.*) Descarga. 2. Descargo, finiquito, carta de pago; liquidación, pago (of debt, liabilities); cumplimiento (of duty). 3. Dimisión de algún empleo; exención. 4. Descargo, absolución; puesta en libertad (from prison); baja (release/from army); descargo (from army). 5. Perdón de algún delito. 6. Rescate. 7. Ejecución. 8. Derrame, desagüe, cantidad o volumen de agua que sale por un orificio en un tiempo dado; emisión (of toxic fumes, gases); vertido (of sewage, waste).

discharger [dɪˈtʃɑːdʒəʳ] [di-char-aʳ], *s.* Descargador, disparador.

disciple [dɪˈsɪpl] [di-si-pol], *s.* 1. Discípulo, alumno, estudiante. 2. Discípulo, partidario, el que sigue una doctrina.

**disciple, ** *va.* Disciplinar, criar, amaestrar.

disciple-like [dɪˈsɪplˌlaɪk] [di-si-pol-laik], *a.* Semejante a un discípulo, o propio de él.

discipleship [dɪˈsɪplʃɪp] [di-si-pol-ship], *a.* Disciplinable, lo que es capaz o digno de disciplina o corección.

disciplinableness [dɪˈsɪplɪnəblnɪs] [di-si-pli-na-bol-nes], *s.* Capacidad de instrucción o de ser instruído.

disciplinant [dɪˈsɪplɪnənt] [di-si-pli-nant], *s.* Disciplinante.

disciplinarian [dɪˈsɪplɪnærɪən] [di-si-pli-na-rian],

disciplinary [dɪˈsɪplɪnərɪ] [di-si-pli-na-ri], *a.* Lo que pertenece a la disciplina.

**disciplinarian, ** *s.* 1. El que gobierna y enseña con rigor y exactitud. 2. (*Des.*) Puritano, presbiteriano.

discipline [dɪˈsɪplɪn] [di-si-plin], *s.* 1. Disciplina, doctrina, instrucción, enseñanza; orden, regla, conducta, educación; arte, ciencia. 2. Rigor, castigo; mortificación, corrección.

**discipline, ** *va.* 1. Disciplinar, educar, instruir (control/child, pupils); controlar (emotions). 2. Reglar, gobernar, tener en orden. 3. Castigar, corregir, reformar; sancionar (punish/employee); disciplinar (train/body, mind).

disciplined [dɪˈsɪplɪnd] [di-si-plind] *a.* Disciplinado.

disc jockey [ˈdɪskˌdʒɒkɪ] [disk-jo-ki], *s.* Anunciador de programas de radio a base de discos fonográficos. Pinchadiscos.

disclaim [dɪsˈkleɪm] [dis-kleim], *va.* 1. Negar, desconocer, renunciar, rechazar. 2. (*For.*) Denegar, renunciar (pretensión, derecho); declinar; negar, desconocer (responsabilidad de un acto). **He disclaimed any connection with him,** negó tener ninguna relación con él.

disclaimer [dɪsˈkleɪməʳ] [dis-klei-maʳ], *s.* 1. Negador, desconocedor. 2. (*For.*) Renuncia, abandono; el acto, la declaración o escritura en que se hace renuncia o denegación.

disclose [dɪsˈkləʊz] [dis-klous], *vn.* 1. Descubrir, destapar; abrir. 2. Revelar, publicar.

discloser [dɪsˈkləʊzəʳ] [dis-klou-saʳ], *s.* Descubridor, revelador.

disclosure [dɪsˈkləʊʒəʳ] [dis-klou-shaʳ], *s.* Descubrimiento, revelación, declaración.

disco [ˈdɪskəʊ] [dis-kou] *s.* Discoteca, disco.

discoid [ˈdɪskɔɪd] [dis-koid], **discoidal** [ˈdɪskɔɪdl] [dis-koi-dal], *a.* Que tiene la figura de un disco; perteneciente a un disco.

discolor [dɪsˈkʌləʳ] [dis-ka-loʳ], *va.* 1. Descolorar, amortiguar, quitar o comer el color a una cosa (fade); descolorir, dejar amarillento, manchar (stain). 2. Descolorar, descolorir, apagar, robar el color, dar color no natural; se dice de las cosas y personas. Decolorarse (lose color); volverse amarillento (become stained).

discoloration [dɪsˌkʌləˈreɪʃən] [dis-ka-lo-rei-shon], *s.* Descoloramiento (fading); mancha, alteración de color (stain).

discolored [dɪsˈkʌləd] [dis-ka-led], *a.* Descolorido, descolorado, manchado, emborronado, empañado.

discomfit [dɪsˈkʌmfɪt] [dis-kam-fit], *va.* 1. Derrotar, vencer, deshacer, romper un ejército o tropas. 2. Turbar, desconcertar.

discomfiture [dɪsˈkʌmfɪtʃəʳ] [dis-kam-fi-chaʳ], *s.* 1. Derrota, vencimiento. 2. Turbación, desconcierto.

discomfort [dɪsˈkʌmfət] [dis-kom-fort], *s.* 1. Incomodidad, malestar (lack of comfort); inquietud, pesar, desasosiego (emotional, mental); molestia, malestar (pain). **To be in discomfort,** tener molestias. 2. Desconsuelo, aflicción.

**discomfort, ** *va.* Incomodar, molestar; desconsolar, apesadumbrar, afligir, entristecer.

discommend [dɪsˈkʌmənd] [dis-ko-mend], *va.* (*Ant.*) Vituperar, censurar, culpar.

discommendable [dɪsˈkʌməndəbl] [dis-ko-men-da-bol], *a.* Culpable, censurable.

discommendation [dɪsˌkʌmənˈdeɪʃən] [dis-ko-men-dei-shon], *s.* Culpa, censura; oprobio.

discommender [dɪsˈkʌməndəʳ] [dis-ko-men-daʳ], *s.* Censor, censurador.

discommode [dɪsˈkʌməd] [dis-ko-mod], *va.* Incomodar, molestar, hacer mala obra.

discommodious [dɪsˈkʌmədɪəs] [dis-ko-mo-dios], *a.* Incómodo, molesto, importuno.

discommodity [dɪsˈkʌmədɪtɪ] [dis-ko-mo-di-ti], *s.* Incomodidad, inconveniente.

discommon [dɪsˈkʌmən] [dis-ko-mon], *va.* Privar de algún prvilegio común.

discompose [dɪsˈkʌmpəs] [dis-kom-pous], *va.* 1. Descomponer, desconcertar, sacar de quicio. 2. Turbar, inmutar, inquietar, ofender. 3. Desordenar, desarreglar.

discomposure [ˌdɪskəmˈpəʊʒəʳ] [dis-kom-pou-shaʳ], *s.* Descomposición, confusión, desorden, desarreglo; emoción, inquietud.

disconcert [ˌdɪskənˈsɜːt] [dis-kon-sert], *va.* Desconcertar, descomponer, confundir, turbar, perturbar; hacer perder a uno el tino; avergonzar, correr, cortar.

disconcerting [ˌdɪskənˈsɜːtɪŋ] [dis-kon-ser-tin], *a.* Desconcertante, perturbador.

disconformity [ˌdɪskənˈfɔːmɪtɪ] [dis-kon-for-mi-ti], *s.* (*Ant.*) Desconformidad, desconveniencia. *V.* NONCONFORMITY.

discongruity [ˌdɪskənˈgrɔɪtɪ] [dis-kon-grui-ti], *s.* Incongruencia, incongruidad. *V.* INCONGRUITY.

disconnect [ˌdɪskəˈnekt] [dis-ko-nekt], *va.* Desunir, separar. Desconectar. **I didn't pay my bills, so I was disconnected,** me cortaron el teléfono (o el gas, etc.) por no pagar.

disconnected [ˌdɪskəˈnektɪd] [dis-ko-nek-tid] *a.* Inconexo, sin ilación (remarks, thoughts).

disconnection [ˌdɪskəˈnekʃən] [dis-ko-nek-shon], *s.* Desunión, separación.

disconsolate [dɪsˈkɒnsəlɪt] [dis-kon-so-lit], *a.* Desconsolado, apesadumbrado, inconsolable, triste, abatido, afligido.

disconsolately [dɪsˈkɒnsəlɪtlɪ] [dis-kon-so-lit-li], *adv.* Desconsoladamente.

disconsolateness [dɪsˈkɒnsəlɪtnɪs] [dis-kon-so-lit-nes], *s.* Desconsuelo, tristeza.

discontent [ˈdɪskənˈtent] [dis-kon-tent], *s.* Descontento (dissatisfaction); sinsabor, desagrado. **Discontents,** *pl.* quejas (grievances). *-a.* Descontento, malcontento, desazonado, disgustado.

discontent, *va.* Descontentar, desagradar, inquietar.

discontented [ˈdɪskənˈtentɪd] [dis-kon-ten-tid], *a.* Descontentadizo, disgustado; malcontento.

discontentedly [ˈdɪskənˈtentɪdlɪ] [dis-kon-ten-tid-li], *adv.* De mala gana, a regañadientes.

discontentedness [ˈdɪskənˈtentɪnɪs] [dis-kon-ten-tid-nes], *s.* Descontento, inquietud.

discontenting [ˈdɪskənˈtentɪŋ] [dis-kon-ten-tin], *a.* Disgustado, malcontento.

discontentment [ˈdɪskənˈtentmənt] [dis-kon-tent-ment], *s.* Descontentamiento.

discontinuance [ˈdɪskənˈtɪnjuəns] [dis-kon-ti-nuens], *s.* 1. Descontinuación, cesación, interrupción, intermisión. 2. Desunión, separación, división.

discontinuation [ˈdɪskənˌtɪnjuˈeɪʃən] [dis-kon-ti-nu-ei-shon], *s.* 1. Descontinuación, el acto y efecto de descontinuar. 2. Desunión, separación.

discontinue [ˈdɪskənˈtɪnjuː] [dis-kon-ti-niu], *va. y vn.* 1. Descontinuar o discontinuar; interrumpir, suspender (production); separarse, cesar. 2. Cesar de recibir un periódico. 3. *(Law)* Desistir de (action, suit).

discontinuity [ˈdɪskɒnˈtɪnjuːɪtɪ] [dis-kon-ti-nui-ti], *s.* Desunión, falta de coherencia o de continuidad.

discontinuous [ˈdɪskənˈtɪnjuəs] [dis-kon-ti-nuos], *a.* Descontinuo, interrumpido; separado, no continuo, abierto.

discord [ˈdɪskɔːd] [dis-kord], *s.* 1. Discordia (conflict); disensión. 2. Desacuerdo, discordancia, falta de acuerdo. 3. *(Mús.)* Discordancia, disonancia, sonido desagradable que ofende al oído (lack of harmony); acorde disonante (chord).

discordance, discordancy [ˈdɪskɔːdəns] [dis-kor-dans], *s.* Discordancia, contrariedad, disensión.

discordant [ˈdɪskɔːdənt] [dis-kor-dant], *a.* Discorde, incompatible, incongruo, inconsecuente; discordante (music, color); de discordia (atmosphere).

discordantly [ˈdɪskɔːdəntlɪ] [dis-kor-dant-li], *adv.* Incongruentemente.

discotheque [ˈdɪskəʊtek] [dis-kou-tek], *s.* Discoteca.

discount [ˈdɪskaʊnt] [dis-kaunt], *s.* Descuento, rebaja, desfalco. **I got a 10% discount/a discount of 10%,** me hicieron un 10% de descuento/un descuento del 10%. **Cash discount,** descuento por pago en efectivo o al contado. **At a discount,** con descuento, a precio reducido (sell); de saldos (store); de saldo (goods).

discount, *va.* 1. Descontar (amount), rebajar (goods), reducir (price). 2. Descontar una letra de cambio. 3. Descartar (disregard/possibility); pasar por alto, no tener en cuenta (claim, criticism). **Discount rate,** tasa de descuento.

discountable [ˈdɪskaʊntəbl] [dis-kaun-ta-bol], *a. (Com.)* Descontable, que se puede descontar.

discountenance [ˈdɪskaʊntənəns] [dis-kaun-te-nans], *va.* 1. Poner mala cara, reprobar, condenar, desalentar. 2. *(Ant.)* Avergonzar, sonrojar; mirar de reojo.

discountenancer [ˈdɪskaʊntəˌnænsəʳ] [dis-kaun-te-nan-saʳ], *s.* Desalentador, el que desalienta a otro con su mala acogida; un vinagre.

discounter [ˈdɪskaʊntəʳ] [dis-kaun-taʳ], *s.* Prestamista, el que presta dinero a interés.

discourage [dɪsˈkʌrɪdʒ] [dis-kau-rich], *va.* 1. Desalentar, desanimar (depress); acobardar, amedrentar, intimidar. **To become discouraged,** desanimarse. 2. Reprimir, impedir, frustrar; apartar de un propósito (con *from*); poner freno a (deter/crime, speculation); ahuyentar, disuadir (burglar). **He discouraged me from taking the exam,** trató de convencerme de que no me presentara al examen (dissuade).

discouragement [dɪsˈkʌrɪdʒmənt] [dis-kau-rich-ment], *s.* Desaliento, desánimo (dejection); descaecimiento de ánimo; cobardía; freno (deterrent); impedimento (obstacle).

discourager [dɪsˈkʌrɪdʒəʳ] [dis-kau-ri-chaʳ], *s.* Desalentador, desanimador.

discouraging [dɪsˈkʌrɪdʒɪŋ] [dis-kau-ri-chin] *a.* Desalentador, descorazonador (news, result).

discourse [ˈdɪskɔːs] [dis-kors], *s.* 1. Discurso, plática, conversación (talk); disertación (dissertation). 2. *(Log.)* Razonamiento.

discourse, *va.* 1. Conversar, hablar. 2. Discurrir. *-va.* Hablar de; pronunciar.

discoursing [ˈdɪskɔːsɪŋ] [dis-kor-sin], *s.* Discurso, plática, conversación.

discourteous [ˈdɪskɔːtəs] [dis-kor-tos], *a.* Descortés, grosero.

discourteously [ˈdɪskɔːtəslɪ] [dis-kor-tos-li], *adv.* Descortésmente.

discourtesy [ˈdɪskɜːtɪsɪ] [dis-kor-ti-si], *s.* Descortesía, grosería.

discous [ˈdɪskəs] [dis-kos], *a.* Discoidal, discoide, a manera o en forma de disco. *V.* DISCOID.

discover [dɪsˈkʌvəʳ] [dis-ko-vaʳ], *va.* 1. Descubrir (find/planet, cure); descubrir, darse cuenta de (error); descubrir, hallar (find out/reason, solution, culprit); descubrir (talent, star). 2. Revelar, manifestar; exhibir o exponer a la vista, descorrer el velo, hacer patente. 3. Descubrir, ver alguna cosa a lo lejos o de lejos. **To discover ahead,** *(Mar.)* descubrir por la proa.

discoverable [dɪsˈkʌvərəbl] [dis-ka-ve-ra-bol], *a.* 1. Lo que se puede descubrir. 2. Patente, manifiesto.

discoverer [dɪsˈkʌvərəʳ] [dis-ka-ve-raʳ], *s.* Descubridor, explorador.

discovery [dɪsˈkʌvərɪ] [dis-ka-ve-ri], *s.* 1. Descubrimiento, invento, hallazgo. **She's Hollywood's newest discovery,** es el último descubrimiento o la última revelación de Hollywood. 2. Revelación, manifestación.

discredit [dɪsˈkredɪt] [dis-kre-dit], *s.* 1. Descrédito, diminución o pérdida de la reputación; deshonor, oprobio, ignominia. 2. Desconfianza.

discredit, *va.* 1. Discreer, dudar. 2. Desacreditar, infamar, deshonrar, difamar.

discreditable [dɪsˈkredɪtəbl] [dis-kre-di-ta-bol], *a.* Vergonzoso, ignominioso.

discreet [dɪsˈkriːt] [dis-kriit], *a.* 1. Discreto (tactful/person, inquiries); cuerdo, circunspecto. **I followed at a discreet distance,** seguí a una distancia prudencial. 2. Discreto, sobrio (restrained/elegance, colors).

discreetly [dɪsˈkriːtlɪ] [dis-kriit-li], *adv.* Discretamente, cuerdamente.

discreetness [dɪsˈkriːtnɪs] [dis-kriit-nes], *s.* Discreción, prudencia, juicio, seso.

discrepance, discrepancy [dɪsˈkrepəns] [dis-kre-pans], *s.* Discrepancia, diferencia; divergencia, desacuerdo. (La forma *Discrepance* es menos usada).

discrepant [dɪsˈkrepənt] [dis-kre-pant], *a.* Discrepante.

discrete [dɪsˈkriːt] [dis-kriit], *a.* 1. Distinto, diferenciado (events, units); desunido, separado, hecho de distintas unidades: *(Med.)* discreto. 2. Descontinuo. 3. Contrario, que denota oposición.

discretion [dɪsˈkreʃən] [dis-kre-shon], *s.* 1. Discreción (tact), prudencia, miramiento, circunspección. 2. Arbitrio, criterio (judgment). **Use your discretion,** usa tu criterio, haz lo que mejor te parezca. **Discretion is the better part of the valor,** la prudencia es la madre de la ciencia. **Age of discretion,** *(For.)* la edad legal, cumplida la cual se responde criminalmente ante los tribunales de justicia. Varía en los diferentes países.

discretional [dɪsˈkreʃənl] [dis-kre-sho-nal], discretionary [dɪsˈkreʃənərɪ] [dis-kre-sho-na-ri], a. Discrecional, arbitrario, ilimitado, que se hace libre y prudencialmente.

discretionally [dɪsˈkreʃənlɪ] [dis-kre-sho-na-li], adv. Discrecionalmente, a discreción.

discretive [dɪsˈkretɪv] [dis-kre-tiv], a. 1. Disyuntivo, que denota oposición lógica. 2. Distinto; separado.

discretively [dɪsˈkretɪvlɪ] [dis-kre-tiv-li], adv. Disyuntivamente, separadamente, cada cosa de por sí.

discriminable [dɪsˈkrɪmɪnəbl] [dis-kri-mi-na-bol], a. Discernible, distinguible.

discriminate [dɪsˈkrɪmɪneɪt] [dis-kri-mi-neit], vn. 1. Discriminar, distinguir (distinguish); discernir, utilizar el sentido crítico (be discerning). 2. Discriminar, hacer discriminaciones (act with predudice).

discriminate, a. 1. Que nota o advierte diferencias; escogedor, que distingue. 2. Distinguido, diferenciado, escogido entre otros.

discriminately [dɪsˈkrɪmɪneɪtlɪ] [dis-kri-mi-neit-li], adv. Distintamente; particularmente.

discriminateness [dɪsˈkrɪmɪneɪtnɪs] [dis-kri-mi-neit-nes], s. Diversidad, diferencia.

discriminating [dɪsˈkrɪmɪneɪtɪŋ] [dis-kri-mi-nei-tin], pa. 1. Capaz de distinguir claramente; mirado, fino, exigente (discerning/critic, customer); sagaz (judgment); refinado, educado, que sabe distinguir (taste). 2. Distintivo, particular, que sirve para distinguir. 3. Lo que establece distinción; diferencial.

discrimination [dɪsˌkrɪmɪˈneɪʃən] [dis-kri-mi-nei-shon], s. 1. Discriminación, distinción; criterio, discernimiento (discernment). 2. Discriminación (unfair treatment). Racial/sexual discrimination, discriminación racial/sexual.

discriminative [dɪsˈkrɪmɪnətɪv] [dis-kri-mi-na-tiv], a. Distintivo, característico.

discriminatively [dɪsˈkrɪmɪnətɪvlɪ] [dis-kri-mi-na-tiv-li], adv. De un modo distintivo.

discriminatory [dɪsˈkrɪmɪnətərɪ] [dis-kri-mi-na-to-ri], a. Discriminador.

discrown [dɪsˈkraʊn] [dis-kraun], va. Destronar, privar de la corona.

discubitory [dɪsˈkjʊbɪtərɪ] [dis-kiu-bi-to-ri], a. Reclinatroio.

disculpate [dɪsˈkʌlpeɪt] [dis-kal-peit], va. Disculpar. V. EXCULPATE.

discumbency [dɪsˈkʌmbənsɪ] [dis-kam-ben-si], s. (Ant.) Reclinación, acción de recostarse para comer, como lo hacían los antiguos.

discurrent [dɪsˈkʌrənt] [dis-ka-rent], a. Estancado, no corriente.

discursion [dɪsˈkɜːʃən] [dis-ker-shon], s. 1. «Razonamiento, el acto de razonar. 2. (Des.) El acto de andar o correr de una parte a otra.

discursive [dɪsˈkɜːsɪv] [dis-ker-siv], a. 1. Errante, vagabundo; discursivo. 2. Que raciocina; que denota pensamiento conexo.

discursively [dɪsˈkɜːsɪvlɪ] [dis-ker-siv-li], adv. Por ilación, por deducción, por inferencia.

discursiveness [dɪsˈkɜːsɪvnɪs] [dis-ker-siv-nes], s. 1. Calidad de digresivo. 2. El hilo o curso de un argumento.

discursory [dɪsˈkɜːsərɪ] [dis-ker-so-ri], a. Argumentativo, racional, dircursivo.

discus [dɪsˈkʌs] [dis-kas], s. (pl. DISCI). 1. Disco, tejo de metal o piedra usado en los juegos gimnásticos. 2. (Biol.) Disco. V. DISK.

discuss [dɪsˈkʌs] [dis-kas], va. 1. Examinar alguna cosa; discutir, agitar o ventilar. Hablar de (talk about/person); hablar de, tratar (topic); debatir (debate); discutir (plan, problem). 2. (Fam.) Catar; probar o juzgar una cosa comiéndola o bebiéndola; p. ej. una comida.

discusser [dɪsˈkʌsər] [dis-ka-sar], s. El que discute o examina.

discussing [dɪsˈkʌsɪŋ] [dis-ka-sin], s. Examen; debate.

discussion [dɪsˈkʌʃən] [dis-ka-shon], s. Discusión, examen, debate. It's still under discussion, todavía se está discutiendo o estudiando. She suggested a topic for discussion, sugirió un tema para debatir.

discussive [dɪsˈkʌsɪv] [dis-ka-siv], a. (Med.) Discusivo.

discutient [dɪsˈkʌʃənt] [dis-ka-shent], s. Resolutivo o resolvente.

disdain [dɪsˈdeɪn] [dis-dein], va. Desdeñar, menospreciar, despreciar, tener a o en menos.

disdain, s. Desdén, desprecio, menosprecio.

disdainful [dɪsˈdeɪnfʊl] [dis-dein-ful], a. Desdeñoso, despectivo (manner, tone); altivo, altanero.

disdainfully [dɪsˈdeɪnfəlɪ] [dis-dein-fu-li], adv. Desdeñosamente, con desprecio, con desdén, de una manera altiva.

disdainfulness [dɪsˈdeɪnfʌnɪs] [dis-dein-ful-nes], s. Desprecio altanero.

disdaining [dɪsˈdeɪnɪŋ] [dis-dei-nin], s. Vilipendio, desprecio.

disease [dɪˈziːz] [di-sis], s. 1. Mal, enfermedad, achaque, indisposición. 2. Malestar, sufrimiento.

disease, va. 1. Enfermar, causar enfermedad, contagiar. 2. (Des.) Afligir, incomodar; hacer daño.

diseased [dɪˈziːzt] [di-sist] a. Afectado (organ, tissue); enfermo (plant, animal); enfermizo, morboso (abnormal, mind); enfermo (society).

diseasedness [dɪˈziːztnɪs] [di-sist-nes], s. Enfermedad, indisposición.

disedge [dɪˈzedʒ] [di-sedch], va. Desafilar, embotar.

disembark [ˌdɪsɪmˈbɑːk] [di-sim-bark], vn. Desembarcar. -va. Desembarcar, sacar a tierra lo que está embarcado.

disembarkation, disembarcation [ˌdɪsɪmbɑːˈkeɪʃən] [di-sim-bar-kei-shon], s. Desembarque (of cargo); desembarco (of people).

disembarrass [ˌdɪsɪmˈbærɑːs] [di-sim-ba-ras], va. Desembarazar.

disembarrassment [ˌdɪsɪmˈbærɑːsmənt] [di-sim-ba-ras-ment], s. Desembarazo.

disembay [ˈdɪsɪmbeɪ] [di-sim-bei], va. Salir de la bahía.

disembitter [ˌdɪsɪmˈbɪtər] [di-sim-bi-tar], va. Dulzurar, dulcificar.

disembodied [ˈdɪsɪmˈbɒdɪd] [di-sim-bo-did], a. Separado del cuerpo; incorpóreo.

disembody [ˈdɪsɪmˈbɒdɪ] [di-sim-bo-di], va. 1. Librar, separar del cuerpo o de la carnalidad. 2. Licenciar temporalmente algún cuerpo de ejército o de milicias.

disembogue [ˈdɪsɪmˈbɒg] [di-sim-bog], va. Desembocar, descargar o desaguar en algún río o en el mar. -vn. (Mar.) Desembocar, salir de una bahía o un estrecho.

disembosom [ˈdɪsɪmˈbɒsəm] [di-sim-bo-som], va. Sacar del seno o del fondo del corazón.

disembowel [ˌdɪsɪmˈbaʊəl] [di-sim-bauel], va. Desentrañar, destripar.

disembroil [ˈdɪsɪmˈbrɔɪl] [di-sim-broil], va. Desembrollar, desenredar, desenmarañar.

disenable [ˈdɪsɪnəbl] [di-si-na-bol], va. (Des.) Debilitar, incapacitar.

disenchant [ˈdɪsɪnˈtʃɑːnt] [di-sin-chan-t], va. Desencantar.

disenchantment [ˈdɪsɪnˈtʃɑːntmənt] [di-sin-chant-ment] s. Desencanto, desilusión.

disenclose [ˈdɪsɪnˈkləʊz] [di-sin-klous], va. Descercar.

disencumber [ˈdɪsɪnˈkʌmbər] [di-sin-kam-bar], va. Desembarazar, librar de obstáculos o estorbos.

disencumbrance [ˈdɪsɪnˈkʌmbrəns] [di-sin-kam-brans], s. Desembarazo.

disenfranchise [ˈdɪsɪnˈfræntʃaɪz] [di-sin-fran-chais] va. Privar del derecho al voto (person); privar del derecho de representación (place).

disengage [ˈdɪsɪnˈgeɪdʒ] [di-sin-gueich], va. Desunir; desocupar; libertar de poder u obligación; desenredar, librar a alguno de un embarazo o peligro. He disengaged his hand from hers, se soltó de su mano. 2. (Mil.) Retirar (troops, forces). 3. (Tech.) Desconectar (gears, mechanism).

To disengage the clutch, desembragar, soltar el embrague. *-vn.* 1. Libertarse de, separarse, desembarazarse. 2. *(Tech.)* Desconectarse (gears, mechanism).

disengaged [ˈdɪsɪnˈgeɪdʒt] [di-sin-gueicht], *a.* Desembarazado, libre; desunido; desocupado; sin empeño.

disengagedness [ˈdɪsɪnˈgeɪdʒnɪs] [di-sin-gueich-nes], *s.* Desembarazo; desocupación.

disengagement [ˈdɪsɪnˈgeɪdʒmənt] [di-sin-gueich-ment], *s.* Desempeño, desembarazo; vacío.

disennoble [ˈdɪsɪnɒbl] [di-si-no-bel], *va. (Ant.)* Desennoblecer, degradar, envilecer.

disenroll [ˈdɪsɪnrəʊl] [di-sin-roul], *va. (Ant.)* Borrar algún nombre de una lista.

disenslave [ˈdɪsɪnˈsleɪv] [di-sin-sleiv], *va.* Rescatar de esclavitud.

disentangle [ˈdɪsɪnˈtæŋgl] [di-sin-tan-guel], *va.* Desenredar, desenlazar, desasir, desenmarañar (rope, hair, wool); separar cosas revueltas o mezcladas sin orden, desembarazar; esclarecer, desentrañar (mistery).

disentanglement [ˈdɪsɪnˈtæŋglmənt] [di-sin-tan-guel-ment], *s.* Desenredo, desembarazo, desempeño.

disentail [ˈdɪsɪnˈteɪl] [di-sin-teil], *va.* Anular el vínculo u orden de sucesión, librar del vínculo.

disenthrall [ˈdɪsɪnˈθrɔl] [di-sin-zrol], *va.* Libertar, sacar de la esclavitud, librar de la opresión, emancipar. Se escribe también, **Disenthral.**

disenthrone [ˈdɪsɪnˈθrəʊn] [di-sin-zroun], *va.* Destronar.

disentitle [ˈdɪsɪnˈtaɪtl] [di-sin-tai-tol], *va.* Privar de un título o derecho.

disentrance [ˈdɪsɪnˈtræns] [di-sin-trans], *va.* Despertar de un sueño profundo; hacer volver a alguno en sí.

disepalous [ˈdɪsɪpələs] [di-si-pa-los], *a.* Disépalo, de dos sépalos.

disespouse [ˈdɪsɪspəʊs] [di-sis-pous], *va. (Poét.)* Invalidar, anular los esponsales de presente o de futuro.

disestablish [ˈdɪsɪsˈtæblɪʃ] [di-sis-ta-blish], *va.* Privar del estado o carácter establecido; quitar a una Iglesia el apoyo del Estado.

disestablishment [ˈdɪsɪsˈtæblɪʃmənt] [di-sis-ta-blish-ment], *s.* La acción y efecto de privar del apoyo de un Estado.

disesteem [ˈdɪsɪsˈtiːm] [di-sis-tim], *s.* Desestima, desestimación.

disesteem, *va.* Desestimar, tener en poco, desaprobar, no apreciar alguna cosa.

disestimation [ˈdɪsɪsˈtɪmeɪʃən] [di-sis-ti-mei-shon], *s.* Desestimación.

disfame [dɪsˈfeɪm] [dis-feim], *s.* Descrédito, infamia, mala reputación.

disfavor [dɪsˈfeɪvəʳ] [dis-fei-vaʳ], *va.* Desairar; desfavorecer, privar a alguno del favor que gozaba; desfigurar, afear o poner fea a alguna persona.

disfavor, *s.* Disfavor, disgusto; fealdad, deformidad. Desaprobación. **To view/look on something with disfavor,** desaprobar algo, no ver algo con buenos ojos. **To fall into disfavor,** caer en desgracia (person).

disfavorer [dɪsˈfeɪvərəʳ] [dis-fei-vo-raʳ], *s.* Desfavorecedor.

disfiguration [ˌdɪsfɪgəˈreɪʃən] [dis-fi-gu-rei-shon], *s.* Desfiguración, deformidad.

disfigure [dɪsˈfɪgəʳ] [dis-fi-gaʳ], *va.* Desfigurar (face, person); afear, estropear (landscape, building).

disfigurement [dɪsˈfɪgəmənt] [dis-fi-ga-ment], *s.* Desfiguración (of person); afeamiento (of scenery, building).

disforest [dɪsˈfɒrɪst] [dis-fo-rest], *va.* 1. Desmontar, privar de árboles. 2. *V.* DISAFFOREST.

disfranchise [ˈdɪsˈfræntʃaɪz] [dis-fran-chais], *va.* Privar de los derechos de ciudadano: quitar franquicias, privilegios o inmunidades.

disfranchisement [ˈdɪsˈfræntʃaɪzmənt] [dis-fran-chais-ment], *s.* Privación de los derechos de ciudadanía y de otros privilegios e inmunidades.

disfurnish [dɪsˈfɜːnɪʃ] [dis-fer-nish], *va. (Ant.)* Desproveer, despojar, desamueblar.

disgarnish [ˈdɪsˈgɑːnɪʃ] [dis-gar-nish], *va. (Ant.)* Desguarnecer.

disgarrison *va.* Desguarnicionar.

disgorge [ˈdɪsˈgɔːdʒ] [dis-gorch], *va.* 1. Vomitar. 2. Arrojar con violencia. 3. Entregar o devolver por fuerza, necesidad o temor.

disgorgement [ˈdɪsˈgɔːdʒənt] [dis-gorch-ment], *s.* Vómito; entrega, devolución.

disgrace [dɪsˈgreɪs] [dis-greis], *s.* Ignominia, infamia, oprobio, deshonra; vergüenza. **It's a disgrace,** es una vergüenza, es un escándalo. **He brought disgrace on his family,** trajo la deshonra a su familia. **To be a disgrace,** ser una vergüenza.

disgrace, *va.* 1. Deshonrar, disfamar, atraer vergüenza, causar oprobio (bring shame on/person, family, school). **I disgraced myself by getting drank,** hice un papelón emborrachándome. 2. Hacer caer en desgracia; despedir con ignominia. Desacreditar (destroy reputation of/enemy, politician).

disgraceful [dɪsˈgreɪsfʊl] [dis-greis-ful], *a.* Vergonzoso, deshonroso, oprobioso, ignominioso.

disgracefully [dɪsˈgreɪsfʊlɪ] [dis-greis-fu-li], *adv.* Vergonzosamente.

disgracefulness [dɪsˈgreɪsfʊlnɪs] [dis-greis-ful-nes], *s.* Ignominia, afrenta.

disgracer [dɪsˈgreɪsəʳ] [dis-grei-saʳ], *s.* Deshonrador.

disgruntle [dɪsˈgrʌntl] [dis-gran-tel], *va. (Fam.)* Descontentar; dejar plantado, enfadar.

disgruntled [dɪsˈgrʌntld] [dis-gran-teld] *a.* Contrariado (child, look); descontento (employee).

disguise [dɪsˈgaɪz] [dis-gais], *va.* 1. Disfrazar, enmascarar (person); cambiar (voice). **To disguise oneself as something,** disfrazarse de algo. 2. Encubrir, solapar, tapar, ocultar (conceal/mistake); disimular (disapproval, contempt); desfigurar, alterar la forma. 3. Embriagar (eufemismo).

disguise *s.* Disfraz. **In disguise,** disfrazado.

disguiser [dɪsˈgaɪzəʳ] [dis-gai-saʳ], *s.* El que disfraza, encubre, etc.

disguising [dɪsˈgaɪzɪŋ] [dis-gai-sin], *s.* 1. Máscara. 2. El acto de dar apariencia de verdad a lo que es falso.

disgust [dɪsˈgʌst] [dis-gast], *s.* Disgusto, desazón; repugnancia, asco (physical, stronger); displicencia, sinsabor, aversión, tedio; indignación (revulsion). **Much to my disgust, they ate it raw,** se lo comieron crudo, lo cual me dio un asco espantoso. **She stormed out of the meeting in disgust,** salió indignada o furiosa de la reunión.

disgust, *va.* Disgustar, repugnar, enfadar; darle asco a.

disgusted [dɪsˈgʌstɪd] [dis-gas-ted] *a.* Indignado; asqueado (stronger). **She's disgusted with him,** está indignada o furiosa con él.

disgustful [dɪsˈgʌstfʊl] [dis-gast-ful], *a.* Desabrido, fastidioso, enfadoso, asqueroso, desagradable.

disgusting [dɪsˈgʌstɪŋ] [dis-gas-tin] *a.* 1. Asqueroso, repugnante (smell, taste, food). **How disgusting!,** ¡qué asco! 2. Vergonzoso (conduct, attitude).

disgustingly [dɪsˈgʌstɪŋlɪ] [dis-gas-tin-li], *adv.* Desagradablemente, asquerosamente, desabridamente. **He's disgustingly rich,** está podrido de dinero, está podrido en plata.

dish [dɪʃ] [dish], *s.* 1. Fuente (serving dish); plato grande o platón (plate). 2. Plato, la vianda o manjar que se sirve en los platos (amount). 3. Concavidad de la forma; copera, reborde de llanta. **A chafing-dish,** chofeta, escalfador. **Side dish,** un plato de entrada, principio. **Soupdish,** sopera. *-pl.* **Dishes,** vajilla, servicio de mesa (crokery). **To wash/do the dishes,** lavar los platos. *(Telec.)* Antena parabólica.

dish, *va.* 1. Servir las viandas en fuente o plato grande. 2. Ponerle copera a una rueda. 3. *(Ger.)* Atrapar, engañar, dar gato por liebre.

dish out 1. *(Culin.)* Servir. 2. *(Coloq.)* Repartir (distribute); dar (advice).

dish up *(Culin.)* Servir.

dishabille [ˌdɪsæˈbiːl] [di-sa-bil], *s.* Paños menores, trapillo; ropa de mañana o de casa.

disharmonious [ˌdɪsˈhaːmənɪəs] [dis-ar-mo-nios], *a.* Desacordado, destemplado, desafinado.

disharmony [ˌdɪsˈhaːmənɪ] [dis-ar-mo-ni], *s.* Discordancia, disonancia.

dishcloth [ˈdɪʃklɒθ] [dish-kloz], *s.* Paño para lavar los platos.

dishclout [dɪʃˈklaʊt] [dish-klaut], *s.* Rodilla, el trapo con que se limpian los platos.

dishearten [dɪsˈhaːtn] [dis-jar-ten], *va.* Desanimar, desalentar, descorazonar.

disheartening [dɪsˈhaːtnɪŋ] [dis-jar-te-nin] *a.* Descorazonador, desalentador.

dished [ˈdɪʃt] [disht], *pp.* de DISH. 1. Servido en un plato; puesto en la mesa. 2. Se dice de la rueda con copera.

dishevel [dɪˈʃevəl] [dish-e-vel], *va.* Desgreñar, desmelenar.

disheveled [dɪˈʃevəld] [dish-e-veld] *a.* Despeinado.

dishful [ˈdɪʃfʊl] [dish-ful], *s.* Cantidad que puede contener un plato; el contenido de un plato lleno.

dishing [ˈdɪʃɪŋ] [di-shin], *a.* Cóncavo.

dishonest [dɪsˈɒnɪst] [dis-ho-nest], *a.* 1. Pícaro, malo; desleal, falto de integridad, indigno de confianza; deshonest (person, answer). 2. Fraudulento, falso, injusto, deshonesto (dealings, means). 3. *(Des.)* Lascivo, impuro, deshonesto.

dishonestly [dɪsˈɒnɪstlɪ] [dis-ho-nes-tli], *adv.* Fraudulentamente, de mala fe; injustamente.

dishonesty [dɪsˈɒnɪstɪ] [dis-ho-nes-ti], *s.* 1. Picardía, dolo, fraude. Deshonestidad, falta de honradez; falsedad (of statement); fraudulencia (of dealings). 2. Violación de la confianza o del fideicomiso.

dishonor [dɪsˈɒnəʳ] [dis-ho-naʳ], *s.* Deshonor, deshonra, ignominia (disgrace).

dishonor, *va.* 1. Deshonrar, infamar (bring disgrace on). 2. Desflorar. 3. Despreciar; desadornar. 4. No respetar (renege on/agreement, treaty); no cumplir, faltar a (promise).

dishonorable [dɪsˈɒnərəbl] [dis-ho-no-ra-bol], *a.* 1. Deshonroso, afrentoso, indecoroso. 2. Deshonrado, infamado, sin honra; de reputación perdida.

dishonorably [dɪsˈɒnərəblɪ] [dis-ho-no-ra-bli], *adv.* Ignominiosamente; de manera deshonrosa. **To be dishonorably discharged,** ser dado de baja con deshonor.

dishonorer [dɪsˈɒnərəʳ] [dis-ho-no-raʳ], *s.* 1. Seductor. 2. Deshonrador.

dishouse [dɪsˈhaʊz] [dis-haus], *va.* Privar de la casa; desalojar.

dishpan [dɪʃˈpæn] [dish-pan] *s.* Palangana para lavar los platos. **Dishpan hands,** manos de fregona.

dishrag [ˈdɪʃræg] [dish-rag], *s.* Paño o trapo para lavar los platos.

dish soap [ˈdɪʃsəʊp] [dish-soup] *s.* Lavavajillas, detergente.

dishwasher [ˈdɪʃˌwɒʃəʳ] [dis-uo-shaʳ], *s.* 1. Lavaplatos, lavador o lavadora de platos. 2. Lavadora de platos (machine).

dishwater [ˈdɪʃˌwɒtəʳ] [dis-uo-taʳ], *s.* Agua en que se lavan los platos.

disillusion, disillusionize [dɪsɪˈluːʃən] [di-si-lu-shon] [dɪsɪˈluːʃənaɪz] [di-sí-lu-sho-nais], *va.* Desencantar, quitar la ilusión; desilusionar. -*s.* Desilusión, pérdida de la ilusión.

disincarcerate [ˈdɪsɪnˈkaːsɪreɪt] [di-sin-kar-se-reit], *va.* Desencarcelar.

disincentive [ˌdɪsɪnˈsentɪv] [di-sin-sen-tiv] *s.* Falta de incentivos. **It's a disincentive to savers,** no fomenta el ahorro.

disinclination [ˌdɪsɪnlɪˈneɪʃən] [di-sin-kli-nei-shon], *s.* Desafecto, desamor; aversión.

disincline [ˈdɪsɪnˈklaɪn] [di-sin-klain], *va.* Desinclinar, desviar la inclinación o afecto de alguno.

disinclined [ˈdɪsɪnˈklaɪnd] [di-sin-klaind], *a.* Desinclinado, averso, indispuesto con. **She was disinclined to listen to him,** no se sentía inclinada a escucharlo.

disincorporate [ˌdɪsɪnˈkɔːpərɪt] [di-sin-kor-po-reit], *va.* 1. Desincorporar, quitar las franquicias de una corporación. 2. Disolver una corporación.

disinfect [ˌdɪsɪnˈfekt] [di-sin-fekt], *va.* Desinfectar, destruir la infección.

disinfectant [ˌdɪsɪnˈfektənt] [di-sin-fek-tant], *a.* Desinfectante. -*s.* Desinfectante, substancia usada para desinfectar; como el cloro, el ácido sulfuroso, o la formalina.

disinfection [ˌdɪsɪnˈfekʃən] [di-sin-fek-shon], *s.* Desinfección, el acto y efecto de desinfectar.

disinfector [ˌdɪsɪnˈfektəʳ] [di-sin-fek-toʳ], *s.* Agente o aparato desinfectante. 2. Desinfectador, el que desinfecta.

disinflation [ˌdɪsɪnˈfleɪʃən] [di-sin-flei-shon] *s.* Desinflación.

disinformation [ˌdɪsɪnfəˈmeɪʃən] [di-sin-for-mei-shon] *s.* Desinformación.

disingenuous [ˌdɪsɪnˈdʒenjʊəs] [di-sin-ye-ni-os], *a.* Doble, falso, disimulado, insincero.

disingenuously [ˌdɪsɪnˈdʒenjʊəslɪ] [di-sin-ye-nios-li], *adv.* Doblemente, falsamente, traidoramente.

disinhabited [ˌdɪsɪnˈhæbɪtɪd] [di-sin-ja-bi-ted], *a.* Despoblado, desierto, deshabitado.

disinherison [ˌdɪsɪnˈherɪʃən] [di-sin-je-ri-shon], *s.* Desheredamiento. *V.* DISINHERITANCE.

disinherit [ˈdɪsɪnˈherɪt] [di-sin-je-rit], *va.* Desheredar (heir). **To disinherit somebody of/from something,** despojar a alguien de algo (deprive).

disinheritance [ˌdɪsɪnˈherɪtəns] [di-sin-je-ri-tans], *s.* Desheredación, acción de desheredar.

disintegrate [dɪsˈɪntɪgreɪt] [dis-in-ti-greit], *va.* Desagregar, desintegrar, desmoronar. -*vn.* Desmoronarse, desintegrarse (fragment), desagregarse, hacerse o caerse a pedazos.

disintegration [dɪsˌɪntɪˈgreɪʃən] [dis-in-ti-grei-shon], *s.* Desagregación, desintegración, desmoronamiento.

disinter [dɪsˈɪntəʳ] , [dis-in-taʳ], *va.* Exhumar, desenterrar.

disinterested [dɪsˈɪntrɪstɪd] [dis-in-te-res-tid], *a.* Desinteresado (action); neutral, imparcial (decision, advice).

disinterestedly [dɪsˈɪntrɪstɪdlɪ] [dis-in-te-res-tid-li], *adv.* Desinteresadamente.

disinterestedness [dɪsˈɪntrɪstɪdnɪs] [dis-in-te-res-tid-nes], *s.* Desinterés, abnegación.

disinterment [ˌdɪsɪnˈtɜːmənt] [dis-in-ter-ment], *s.* Exhumación, desenterramiento.

disinthrall, *va. V.* DISENTHRALL.

disintricate [ˌdɪsɪnˈtrɪkeɪt] [dis-in-tri-keit], *va.* Desenredar.

disinvolve [ˌdɪsɪnˈvɒlv] [dis-in-volv], *va.* Desenredar, destapar.

disjoin [dɪsˈdʒɔɪn] [dis-yoin], *va.* Desunir, desasir, apartar, separar.

disjoint [dɪsˈdʒɔɪnt] [dis-yoint], *va.* 1. Dislocar, descoyuntar, desencajar, desmembrar. 2. Desunir, separar, desarreglar, desordenar. Trinchar un ave. -*vn.* Desmembrarse, caer a pedazos.

disjont, disjointed [dɪsˈdʒɔɪntɪd] [dis-yoin-ted], *a.* Dividido; inconexo, deshilvanado.

disjointly [dɪsˈdʒɔɪnlɪ] [dis-yoin-tli], *adv.* Desunidamente.

disjunct [dɪsˈdʒʌŋkt] [dis-yankt], *a.* Descoyuntado, dislocado.

disjunction [dɪsˈdʒʌŋkʃən] [dis-yank-shon], *s.* Disyunción, descoyuntamiento, dislocación.

disjunctive [dɪsˈdʒʌŋktɪv] [dis-yank-tiv], *a. y s.* disyuntivo.

disjunctively [dɪsˈdʒʌŋktɪvlɪ] [dis-yank-tiv-li], *adv.* Disyuntivamente.

disk [dɪsk] [disk], *s.* 1. Disco, figura circular y plana; superficie circular o casi circular y achatada. *(Comp.)* Disco. 2. *(Bot.)* Disco, cualquier órgano casi plano y circular, centro de una flor compuesta. 3. Patena, platillo sagrado de la eucaristía. 4. *(Anat./Zool.)* Parte o estructura circular y achatada. 5. *V.* DISCUS y QUOIT. 6. *(Art. y Ofic.)* Disco; rueda de vidrio de la máquina eléctrica.

disk drive [dɪskˈdraɪv] [disk-draiv] *s.* Unidad de disco.

diskette [dɪsˈket] [dis-ket] *s.* Disquete.

diskindness [dɪsˈkaɪndnɪs] [dis-kaind-nes], s. (Poco us.) Descariño; agravio ligero.

dislike [dɪsˈlaɪk] [dis-laik], s. Aversión, aborrecimiento, repugnancia, antipatía. **To take a dislike to anyone,** tener o tomar a uno entre ojos o entre ceja y ceja. **I have a strong dislike of dogs,** no me gustan nada los perros. **You'll have to tell us all your likes and dislikes,** tendrás que decirnos lo que te gusta y lo que no te gusta.

dislike, va. Tener aversión a alguna persona, desaprobar. **I dislike dogs,** no me gustan los perros. **He disliked her intensely,** no la podía ver, le tenía verdadera aversión. **He dislikes wearing a tie,** le desagrada o no le gusta llevar corbata.

disliker [dɪsˈlaɪkəʳ] [dis-lai-k], s. El que desaprueba algo.

dislimb [dɪsˈlɪmb] [dis-limb], va. Desmembrar.

dislimn [dɪsˈlɪm] [dis-lim], va. (Ant.) Borrar una pintura.

dislocate [ˈdɪsləʊkeɪt] [dis-lou-keit], va. (Med.) Dislocar, descoyuntar.

dislocation [ˈdɪsləʊkeɪʃən] [dis-lou-keit-shon], s. (Med.) Dislocación, descoyuntamiento.

dislodge [dɪsˈlɒdʒ] [dis-lodch], va. 1. Desalojar, sacar o hacer salir de un lugar a una persona o cosa (shift, remove). **The wind dislodged some tiles,** el viento causó que se soltaran varias tejas. 2. Desalojar, echar al enemigo de algún puesto. -vn. Desalojar, mudarse a otra parte.

disloyal [dɪsˈlɔɪəl] [dis-loial], a. 1. Desleal. 2. Infiel, falso.

disloyally [dɪsˈlɔɪəlɪ] [dis-loia-li], adv. Deslealmente.

disloyalty [dɪsˈlɔɪəltɪ] [dis-loial-ti], s. Deslealtad, infidelidad; perfidia, inconstancia.

dismal [ˈdɪzməl] [dis-mal], a. Triste, funesto (very bad/news, prophecy); sombrío, deprimente, lúgubre (gloomy/place, tone) deplorable, espantoso, malísimo (weather); pésimo (results, performance); horrendo, horroroso, terrible, infeliz, aciago.

dismally [ˈdɪzməlɪ] [dis-mal-li], adv. Funestamente, tristemente.

dismalness [ˈdɪzməlnɪs] [dis-mal-nes], s. Tristeza, melancolía; aspecto siniestro, infelicidad.

disman [ˈdɪzmən] [dis-man], va. 1. Privar de hombres, desguarnecer. 2. (Des.) V. UNMAN.

dismantle [dɪsˈmæntl] [dis-man-tel], va. Desguarnecer, desamueblar; desmantelar una plaza, desaparejar una embarcación; despojar de adornos, etc. Desmontar (machinery, furniture); desmantelar (organization).

dismantling [dɪsˈmæntlɪŋ] [dis-man-tlin], s. El acto de desmantelar.

dismast [dɪsˈmɑːst] [dis-mast], va. Desarbolar un bajel.

dismay [dɪsˈmeɪ] [dis-mei], s. Desmayo, deliquio, congoja, espanto, terror, consternación. **They looked at him in dismay,** lo miraron consternados. **Much to my dismay,** para mi desgracia.

dismay, va. Desmayar, espantar, desanimar, consternar. **I was dismayed at her reaction,** su reacción me dejó consternado.

dismayedness [dɪsˈmeɪdnɪs] [dis-meid-nes], s. Desmayo, desaliento, aterramiento, espanto, deliquio.

dismember [dɪsˈmembəʳ] [dis-mem-baʳ], va. 1. Desmembrar, separar un miembro del cuerpo, despedazar. 2. Separar del cuerpo de una sociedad, iglesia, etc.

dismemberment [dɪsˈmembəmənt] [dis-mem-ba-ment], s. Desmembramiento.

dismettled [dɪsˈmetld] [dis-me-teld], a. (Des.) Desanimado, sin espíritu o animación.

dismiss [dɪsˈmɪs] [dis-mis], va. 1. Despedir, echar (employee); destituir (executive, minister); licenciar a un soldado; dejar salir (send away/class). 2. Descartar, desechar (possibility, suggestion); despachar, enviar; desestimar, rechazar (request, petition, claim). (Law) Desestimar (charge, appeal). **To dismiss a case,** sobreseer una causa. 3. Disolver una reunión, asamblea, etc. 4. Repudiar, rechazar. **To dismiss**

abruptly, echar a uno con cajas destempladas. **To dismiss/send one about his business,** enviar a uno a paseo. vn. **Dismiss!,** ¡rompan filas!

dismissal [dɪsˈmɪsəl] [dis-mi-sal], s. 1. Dimisión; despido (of employee); destitución (of executive, minister). 2. Permiso para salir, marcharse o retirarse (sending away). 3. Rechazo (of theory, request). 4. (Law) Desestimación.

dismission [dɪsˈmɪʃən] [dis-mi-shon], s. 1. Despedimiento, despedida. 2. Dimisión; deposició, privación, de un empleo.

dismissory, dismissive [dɪsˈmɪsərɪ] [dis-mi-so-ri], a. 1. Que despide, destituye o licencia; dimisorio. 2. Desdeñoso (attitude, smile); disciplente (tone).

dismount [dɪsˈmaʊnt] [dis-maunt], va. 1. Desmontar, sacar el caballo de la silla a su jinete. 2. Hacer que los soldados de a caballo presten servicio a pie. 3. Desmontar, desarmar una máquina, un cañón, etc., quitándole su montaje. -vn. Desmontar, apearse del caballo, bajar, descender.

disnaturalize [dɪsˈnætrəlaɪz] [dis-na-tu-ra-lais], va. Desnaturalizar.

disobedience [ˌdɪsəˈbiːdɪəns] [dis-o-bi-dians], s. Desobediencia.

disobedient [ˌdɪsəˈbiːdɪənt] [dis-o-bi-dians], s. Desobediente.

disobey [ˈdɪsəˈbeɪ] [dis-o-bei], va. y vn. Desobedecer.

disoblige [ˈdɪsəˈblaɪdʒ] [dis-o-blaidch], va. Desobligar, disgustar; librar de la obligación.

disobliger [ˈdɪsəˈblaɪdʒəʳ] [dis-o-blai-yaʳ], s. Ofensor.

disobliging [ˈdɪsəˈblaɪdʒɪŋ] [dis-o-blai-yin], a. Desagradable, ofensivo.

disobligingly [ˈdɪsəˈblaɪdʒɪŋlɪ] [dis-o-blai-yin-li], adv. Desagradablemente.

disobligingness [ˈdɪsəˈblaɪdʒɪŋnɪs] [dis-o-blai-yin-nes], s. Desagrado, desatención.

disorder [dɪsˈɔːdəʳ] [dis-or-daʳ], s. 1. Desorden, desarreglo, confusión, desconcierto (confusion); desórdenes, disturbios (unrest). 2. Indisposición, desazón, disgusto. 3. Enfermedad, indisposición; enajenamiento del ánimo. 4. Motín o tumulto; alboroto.

disorder,, va. 1. Desordenar, confundir, descomponer, desconcertar. 2. Causar alguna enfermedad. 3. Inquietar, perturbar el ánimo, enojar, enfadar, alterar.

disordered [dɪsˈɔːdəd] [dis-or-de-red], a. Desordenado, disoluto, confuso.

disorderedness [dɪsˈɔːdənɪs] [dis-or-de-red-nes], s. Irregularidad, confusión.

disorderly [dɪsˈɔːdəlɪ] [dis-or-der-li], a. Desordenado, desarreglado (untidy); confuso, ilegal; alborotado (unruly/crowd); revoltoso (person). -adv. Desordenamente, ilegalmente.

disorganization [dɪsˈɔːɡənaɪˈzeɪən] [dis-or-ga-nai-sei-shon], s. Desorganización.

disorganize [dɪsˈɔːɡənaɪz] [dis-or-ga-nais], va. Desorganizar, destruir o romper la estructura orgánica de, derribar.

disorganized [dɪsˈɔːɡənaɪzt] [dis-or-ga-naist] a. Desorganizado.

disorganizer [dɪsˈɔːɡənaɪzəʳ] [dis-or-ga-nai-saʳ], s. Desorganizador.

disorient, disorientate [dɪsˈɔːrɪent] [dis-o-ri-ent] [dɪsˈɔːrɪenteɪt] [dis-o-rien-teit], va. 1. Desviar del este; en especial, construir una iglesia sin el altar al lado oriente. V. ORIENTATE. 2. Desorientar, hacer perder el conocimiento de la posición que se ocupa en el terreno; de aquí (Fig.) extraviar, confundir, hacer confuso en la mente. **To become disoriented,** desorientarse.

disorientated [dɪsˌɔːrɪenˈteɪtɪd] [dis-o-rien-tei-ted], a. Desorientado, desatentado.

disorientation [dɪsˌɔːrɪenˈteɪən] [dis-o-rien-tei-shon] s. Desorientación.

disown [dɪsˈəʊn] [dis-oun], *va.* Negar, desconocer, renunciar, no reconocer (deny responsibility for); renegar de, repudiar (repudiate).

disparage [dɪsˈpærɪdʒ] [dis-pa-rich], *va.* 1. Rebajar, difamar, injuriar a alguno por compararle o juntarle con otro inferior, rebajar, disminuir el valor de una cosa comparándola con otra de mala calidad. *V.* BELITTLE. 2. Desdorar, quitar el crédito de alguna persona.

disparagement [dɪsˈpærɪdʒmənt] [dis-pa-rich-ment], *s.* 1. Desdoro; unión o comparación injuriosa de una cosa inferior con otra superior. 2. Censura, infamia. 3. Desprecio, murmuración, conversación denigrativa.

disparager [dɪsˈpærɪdʒəʳ] [dis-pa-ri-chaʳ], *s.* El que desdora, mancilla o deslustra.

disparaging [dɪsˈpærɪdʒɪŋ] [dis-pa-ri-chin] *a.* Desdeñoso, despreciativo. **She was very disparaging about their efforts,** habló de sus intentos en tono desdeñoso o despreciativo.

disparagingly [dɪsˈpærɪdʒɪŋlɪ] [dis-pa-ri-chin-li], *adv.* Desdeñadamente, de un modo que rebaja y desdora; en tono desdeñoso o despreciativo.

disparate [dɪsˈpærɪt] [dis-pa-rit], *a.* Desigual, discorde, desemejante, dispar (varied); distinto (distinct, separate).

disparates [dɪsˈpærɪtz] [dis-pa-rits], *s. pl.* Cosas tan desemejantes que no admiten comparación entre sí.

disparity [dɪsˈpærɪtɪ] [dis-pa-ri-ti], *s.* Disparidad, desigualdad; desemejanza (inequality); discrepancia (difference).

dispark [dɪsˈpɑːk] [dis-park], *va. (Ant.)* Descercar, abrir una cerca.

dispart [dɪsˈpɑːt] [dis-part], *va.* 1. Despartir, apartar, dividir, separar. 2. Señalar el punto de mira en los cañones. *-vn.* Partirse, dividirse, rajarse.

dispart, *s.* 1. Mira, pieza del cañón que sirve para dirigir la vista y asegurar la puntería. Se llama también DISPART-SIGHT. 2. Vivo de un cañón.

dispassion [dɪsˈpæʃən] [dis-pa-shon], *s. (Ant.)* Calma, serenidad de ánimo.

dispassionate [dɪsˈpæʃənɪt] [dis-pa-sho-nit], *a.* Desapasionado, objetivo (account); sereno, fresco, templado, sosegado; imparcial (adjudication, onlooker); moderado.

dispassionately [dɪsˈpæʃənɪtlɪ] [dis-pa-sho-nit-li], *adv.* Serenamente, tranquilamente, sin apasionamiento.

dispassioned [dɪsˈpæʃənd] [dis-pa-shond], *a.* (Poco us.) Sereno. *V.* DISPASSIONATE.

dispatch [dɪsˈpætʃ] [dis-pach], *va.* 1. Despachar, enviar (send). 2. Despachar (carry out/task, duty); despachar (kill/person, animal); despacharse (consume/food, drink). *s.* 1. Despacho (message); *(Mil.)* Parte. 2. Despacho, envío, expedición (sending). **To be mentioned in dispatches,** recibir una mención de honor. *V.* DESPATCH.

dispatch case [dɪsˈpætʃkeɪs] [dis-pach-keis] *s.* Portafolios.

dispatch rider [dɪsˈpætʃˌraɪdəʳ] [dis-pach-rai-daʳ] *s.* Mensajero (on motorcycle).

dispel [dɪsˈpel] [dis-pel], *va.* Dispersar, esparcir; disipar, hacer desvanecer (doubts, fear); disipar (fog); expeler, desechar.

dispend [dɪsˈpend] [dis-pend], *va.* Gastar.

dispensable [dɪsˈpensəbl] [dis-pen-sa-bol], *a.* Dispensable, prescindible.

dispensableness [dɪsˈpensəblnɪs] [dis-pen-sa-bol-nes], *s.* La calidad de dispensable.

dispensary [dɪsˈpensərɪ] [dis-pen-sa-ri], *s.* 1. Dispensario, farmacia (in hospital); enfermería (in school). 2. Casa o botica de barrio o distrito donde los enfermos pobres reciben gratuitamente o a precio barato los auxilios facultativos y los medicamentos que necesitan.

dispensation [ˌdɪspenˈseɪʃən] [dis-pen-sei-shon], *s.* 1. Distribución o reparto de alguna cosa. Administración (of justice). 2. Dispensación, dispensa; exención (exemption). **He was granted a dispensation from military service,** lo declararon exento del servicio militar.

3. Dispensación o ley divina; sistema de principios o ritos prescritos en una religión.

dispensative [dɪsˈpensətɪv] [dis-pen-sa-tiv], *a. (Ant.)* Lo que dispensa.

dispensator [dɪsˈpenseɪtəʳ] [dis-pen-sei-toʳ], *s.* Dispensador.

dispensatory [dɪsˈpensətərɪ] [dis-pen-sa-to-ri], *s.* Farmacopea, el libro que prescribe la composición de las medicinas. *-a.* Lo que tiene poder de dispensar o dar dispensas.

dispense [dɪsˈpens] [dis-pens], *va.* 1. Dispensar, distribuir, repartir; ofrecer, dar (advice); dar (grants, alms); conceder (favors); expender (machine/coffee, soap). 2. Componer un medicamento de varios ingredientes; despachar, preparar (drugs, prescription). 3. Dispensar, exceptuar; excusar. 4. Administrar (justice). **To dispense with,** dispensar de, permitir que no se haga alguna cosa, renunciar la observancia de; privarse de alguna cosa, ceder, dejar, renunciar a algo.

dispenser [dɪsˈpensəʳ] [dis-pen-saʳ], *s.* 1. Dispensador, el que inventa disculpas para no hacer alguna cosa. 2. **A cash dispenser,** un cajero automático (device). 3. Farmacéutico (pharmacist).

dispeople [dɪsˈpiːpl] [dis-pi-pol], *va.* Despoblar.

dispeopler [dɪsˈpiːpləʳ] [dis-pi-plaʳ], *s.* Despoblador.

dispersal [dɪsˈpɜːsəl] [dis-per-sal], *s. V.* DISPERSION.

disperse [dɪsˈpɜːs] [dis-pers], *va.* 1. Dispersar, esparcir, desparramar. 2. Disipar. 3. Distribuir. 4. Separar la luz en sus colores componentes. *-vn.* 1. Dispersarse, separarse, retirarse. 2. Disiparse; desaparecer.

dispersedly [dɪsˈpɜːsɪdlɪ] [dis-per-sid-li], *adv.* Esparcidamente.

dispersedness [dɪsˈpɜːsɪdnɪs] [dis-per-sid-nes], *s.* Dispersión.

disperser [dɪsˈpɜːsəʳ] [dis-per-saʳ], *s.* Esparcidor, sembrador.

dispersion [dɪsˈpɜːʃən] [dis-per-shon], *s.* 1. Dispersión, esparcimiento, acción y efecto de dispersar. 2. Desviación de los rayos de luz.

dispersive [dɪsˈpɜːsɪv] [dis-per-siv], *a.* Esparcidor, lo que tiene el poder de esparcir.

dispirit [dɪsˈpɪrɪt] [dis-pi-rit], *va.* Desalentar, desanimar, amilanar.

dispirited [dɪsˈpɪrɪtɪd] [dis-pi-ri-tid] *a.* Desanimado, abatido (person). **To become dispirited,** desanimarse.

dispiritedness [dɪsˈpɪrɪtɪdnɪs] [dis-pi-ri-tid-nes], *s.* Desaliento, desánimo.

dispiriting [dɪsˈpɪrɪtɪŋ] [dis-pi-ri-tin] *a.* Desalentador, descorazonador.

displace [dɪsˈpleɪs] [dis-pleis], *va.* 1. Dislocar, desordenar; desplazar (liquid, volume). 2. Tomar el lugar de (destituyendo); reemplazar (replace). 3. Desplazar (force from home/refugees, workers).

displaced person [dɪsˈpleɪstˈpɜːsən] [dis-pleist-per-son], *s.* Persona desplazada.

displacement [dɪsˈpleɪsmənt] [dis-pleis-ment], *s.* 1. Desarreglo, trastorno, mudanza; desplazamiento (of refugees); sustitución, reemplazo (replacement). 2. Cambio aparente de posición, v. gr. de una estrella. 3. *(Mar.)* Desplazamiento, el peso del agua que desaloja el casco de un buque. 4. *(Quím. y Farm.)* Coladura. *V.* PERCOLATION. 5. *(Geol.)* Falla. *V.* FAULT.

displacer [dɪsˈpleɪsəʳ] [dis-plei-saʳ], *s.* 1. El que desordena. 2. *(Quím.)* Colador. *V.* PERCOLATOR.

displant [dɪsˈplænt] [dis-plant], *va.* Transplantar, trasponer; expeler; arrancar.

displantation [ˌdɪsplænˈteɪʃən] [dis-plan-tei-shon], *s.* 1. Trasplante, trasplantación. 2. *(Fig.)* Expulsión (de una raza, de un pueblo).

displanting [dɪsˈplæntɪŋ] [dis-plan-tin], *s.* Deposición, expulsión.

display [dɪsˈpleɪ] [dis-plei], *va.*

display, *s.* 1. Despliegue (of courage, strength, knowledge); acción de desplegar o extender; ostentación, manifestación, fausto; demostración (of ignorance). Exposición, muestra (exhibition); show (show). **Fireworks display,** fuegos artificiales. **To be on display,** estar expuesto (painting, wares). **A display of flowers,** un arreglo floral (arrangement); exteriorización, demostración (of feelings). 2. *(Inform., Electron.)* Display, visualizador. **Digital/analog display,** visualizador digital/analógico; de visualización de datos (screen, panel). 3. *(Journ., Print)* **Display advertising,** anuncios destacados.

displayer [dɪsˈpleɪəʳ] [dis-pleiaʳ], *s.* Ostentador.

display window [dɪsˈpleɪˌwɪndəʊ] [dis-plei-uni-dou], *s.* Vitrina, aparador.

displeasant [dɪsˈpliːsənt] [dis-pli-sant], *a.* Desagradable, ofensivo.

displease [dɪsˈpliːz] [dis-plis], *va. y vn.* Desplacer, enfadar, desazonar, incomodar, inquietar; ofender; desagradar, contrariar.

displeased [dɪsˈpliːzt] [dis-plist], *a.* Ofendido, disgustado, incomodado, enojado.

displeasing [dɪsˈpliːzɪŋ] [dis-pli-sin], *pa.* Displicente, ofensivo; desagradable.

displeasingness [dɪsˈpliːzɪŋnɪs] [dis-pli-sin-nes], *s.* Ofensa, displicencia.

displeasure [dɪsˈpleʒəʳ] [dis-pli-shaʳ], *s.* Desplacer, disgusto, inquietud, ofensa; indignación, desgracia, disfavor. **He incurred the king's displeasure,** contrarió al rey.

displeasure, *va. (Ant.)* Desagradar, disgustar.

displode [dɪsˈpləʊd] [dis-ploud], *va.* V. EXPLODE.

dispondee [dɪsˈpɒndiː] [dis-pon-di], *s.* Dispondeo, pie de verso que consta de dos espondeos o cuatro sílabas largas.

disport [dɪsˈpɔːt] [dis-port], *s.* Diversión, pasatiempo.

disport, *va.* Juguetear, travesear. *-vn.* Entretenerse, retozar, divertirse, recrearse.

disposable [dɪsˈpəʊzəbl] [dis-pou-sabl], *a.* 1. Disponible (income). 2. Desechable, de usar y tirar (cup, razor, pen).

disposal [dɪsˈpəʊzəl] [dis-pou-sal], *s.* 1. Disposición, colocación, arreglo. Desactivación (of bomb). *(Fin.)* Enajenación. 2. Venta; donación; desembolso; libramiento. **The problem of the disposal of waste,** el problema de cómo deshacerse de residuos (removal, riddance). 3. Poder de restringir, gobierno, dirección. 4. Despliegue (of troops). 5. Disposición (power to use). **To have something at one's disposal,** disponer de algo, tener algo a su disposición.

dispose [dɪsˈpəʊz] [dis-pous], *va.* 1. Disponer, dar, colocar, adaptar, arreglar. 2. Cultivar el entendimiento. **dispose of** 1. Aplicar; transferir; vender, enajenar (sell/house, car, land); entregar; desembarazarse de, deshacerse de (get rid of/refuse, evidence); deshacerse de, liquidar (rival, opponent); dar; dirigir; conducir; poner en alguna condición. Despachar (deal with). 2. Disponer de (have use of/funds, resources). **To dispose of a house,** ceder, transferir, vender una casa. **To dispose of another man's money,** servirse del dinero ajeno. **To dispose of one,** librarse o zafarse de uno. *(Fig.)* Matar a uno. **To dispose of one's time,** emplear su tiempo.

disposed [dɪsˈpəʊzt] [dis-poust], *pp.* Dispuesto, preparado, inclinado. **Disposed of,** dado, dispuesto a (inclined); vendido; alquilado. **I don't feel disposed to help him,** no me siento inclinada a ayudarlo. **To be disposed to something,** ser propenso a algo, tener propensión a algo.

disposer [dɪsˈpəʊzəʳ] [dis-pou-saʳ], *s.* Disponedor, regulador, director.

disposing [dɪsˈpəʊzɪŋ] [dis-pou-sin], *s.* Dirección. *-part. adj.* Disponente.

disposition [ˌdɪspəˈzɪʃən] [dis-po-si-shon], *s.* 1. Disposición, orden, método (arrangement). 2. Aptitud, proporción. 3. Genio, natural, índole; manera o modo de ser, temperamento (personality). 4. Buena o mala intención. 5. Inclinación dominante. **Disposition of body,** el estado de salud.

disposses [ˈdɪspəˈzes] [dis-po-ses], *va.* Desposeer, privar a uno de la posesión o goce de alguna cosa.

dispossession [ˈdɪspəˈzeʃən] [dis-po-se-shon], *s.* Desposeimiento, despojo.

disposure [dɪsˈpəʊʃəʳ] [dis-po-shaʳ], *s.* V. DISPOSAL Y DISPOSITION.

dispraise [ˈdɪspreɪs] [dis-preis], *va. (Des.)* Vituperar, condenar, afear.

dispraise, *s.* Desprecio, censura, vituperación, reprobación.

dispraiser [ˈdɪspreɪsəʳ] [dis-prei-saʳ], *s.* Censor.

dispraisingly [ˈdɪspreɪsɪŋlɪ] [dis-prei-sin-li], *adv.* Vituperiosamente.

dispread [ˈdɪspred] [dis-pred], *va.* Desplegar. *-vn.* Extenderse.

dispreader [ˈdɪspredəʳ] [dis-pre-daʳ] *s.* Pregonero, publicador.

disprize [ˈdɪspreɪs] [dis-prais], *va. (Ant.)* Despreciar.

disprofit [ˈdɪsprɒfɪt] [dis-pro-fit], *s. (Ant.)* Pérdida, daño.

disproof [ˈdɪspruːf] [dis-pruf], *s.* 1. Confutación. 2. Refutación, impugnación.

disproperty [ˈdɪsprɒpətɪ] [dis-pro-per-ti], *va.* Desposesionar, desposeer a uno de la posesión o dominio de alguna finca.

disproportion [ˌdɪsprəˈpɔːʃən] [dis-pro-por-shon], *s.* Desproporción, desigualdad.

disproportion, *va.* Desproporcionar.

disproportionable [ˌdɪsprəˈpɔːʃənbl] [dis-pro-por-sho-na-bol], **disproportional** [ˌdɪsprəˈpɔːʃənl] [dis-pro-por-sho-nal]. Out of proportion **disproportionate** [ˌdɪsprəˈpɔːnɪt] [dis-pro-por-sho-nit], *a.* 1. Desproporcionado (number, size); desigual, falta de proporción y simetría. 2. Insuficiente.

disproportionableness [ˌdɪsprəˈpɔːʃənblnɪʃ] [dis-pro-por-sho-na-bol-nes], **disproportionality** [ˌdɪsprəˈpɔːʃənlɪtɪ] [dis-pro-por-sho-na-li-ti], **disproportionateness** [ˌdɪsprəˈpɔːʃənɪtnɪs] [dis-pro-por-sho-nit-nes], *s.* Desproporción, desigualdad.

disproportionably [ˌdɪsprəˈpɔːʃənblɪ] [dis-pro-por-sho-na-bli], **disproportionally** [ˌdɪsprəˈpɔːʃənlɪ] [dis-pro-por-sho-na-li], **disproportionately** [ˌdɪsprəˈpɔːʃənɪtlɪ] [dis-pro-por-sho-neit-li], *adv.* Desproporcionadamente.

disprovable [dɪsˈprəvəbl] [dis-pro-va-bol], *a.* Refutable, que puede refutarse o impugnarse.

disprove [dɪsˈpruːv] [dis-pruv], *va.* Confutar; desaprobar, impugnar. Desmentir (claim, assertion, charge); rebatir, refutar (doctrine, theory).

disprover [dɪsˈpruːvəʳ] [dis-pru-vAʳ], *s.* Impugnador; censurador.

dispunishable [dɪsˈpʌnɪʃəbl] [dis-pu-ni-sha-bol], *a. (Ant.)* No punible.

disputability, disputableness [dɪsˈpjʊtəˌbɪlɪtɪ] [dis-piu-ta-bi-li-ti] [dɪsˈpjuːtəblnɪs] [dis-piu-ta-bol-nes], *s.* Disputabilidad, condición que permite controversia.

disputable [dɪsˈpjuːtəbl] [dis-piu-ta-bol], *a.* Disputable, controvertible, problemático.

disputant [dɪsˈpjuːtənt] [dis-piu-tant], *a.* Disputante. *-s.* Disputador.

disputation [dɪsˈpjuːteɪʃən] [dis-piu-tei-shon], *s.* Disputa, controversia.

disputatious [dɪsˈpjuːteɪʃəs] [dis-piu-tei-shos], **disputative** [dɪsˈpjuːtætɪv] [dis-piu-ta-tiv], *a.* Disputador; quisquilloso; caviloso.

dispute [dɪsˈpjuːt] [dis-piut], *vn.* Disputar, controvertir. *-va.* 1. Disputar, pleitear; argüir. Impugnar (will, decision). 2. Contestar, resistir. 3. Discutir, cuestionar (contest). **I don't dispute that it was a mistake,** no discuto que fue un error. 4. Debatir, discutir (argue/point, question). **Disputed,** discutido, polémico (decision); en litigio (territory).

dispute, *s.* 1. Disputa, controversia, polémica (controversy, clash). 2. Discusión, debate (debate); disputa (quarrel); contienda, altercación, 3. *(Lab Rel)* Conflicto laboral. **An industrial dispute,** un conflicto laboral. **The territory**

in/under dispute, el territorio en litigio. **Beyond/without dispute,** sin disputa, sin la menor duda.

disputeless [dɪsˈpjuːtlɪs] [dis-piut-les], *a.* Indisputable.

disputer [dɪsˈpjuːtəʳ] [dis-piu-taʳ], *s.* Disputador; controversista.

disputing [dɪsˈpjuːtɪŋ] [dis-piu-tin], *s.* Disputa, altercación.

disqualification [dɪsˌkwɒlɪfɪˈkeɪʃən] [dis-kua-li-fi-kei-shon], *s.* Inhabilitación (from office, service); inhabilidad, incapacidad. Descalificación (from exam, competition). **A tree-year disqualification from driving,** la inhabilitación para manejar o conducir por tres años.

disqualify [dɪsˈkwɒlɪfaɪ] [dis-kuo-li-fai], *va.* Inhabilitar, declarar a uno inhábil para una cosa (incapaz de ejercer los derechos de ciudadano, etc.); imposibilitar; privar. *(Dep.)* Descalificar (debar). **As a professional she was disqualified from entering the Olympics,** el hecho de ser profesional le impedía participar en las Olimpíadas.

disquiet [dɪsˈkwaɪət] [dis-kua-iet], *s.* Inquietud, intranquilidad, desasosiego, desazón. *-a.* Inquieto, desasosegado.

disquiet, *va.* Inquietar, desasosegar, molestar, atormentar, no dejar en paz.

disquieter [dɪsˈkwaɪətəʳ] [dis-kua-ietaʳ], *s.* Inquietador.

disquietful [dɪsˈkwaɪətfʊl] [dis-kua-iet-ful], *a.* Que produce inquietud o molestia.

disquieting [dɪsˈkwaɪətɪŋ] [dis-kua-ietin], *s.* Vejación, molestia. *-pa.* de DISQUIET. *a.* Inquietante, intranquilizante.

disquietly [dɪsˈkwaɪətlɪ] [dis-kua-iet-li], *adv.* Inquietamente.

disquietness [dɪsˈkwaɪətnɪs] [dis-kua-iet-nes], **disquietude** [dɪsˈkwaɪɪtjuːd] [dis-kua-ietiud], *s.* Inquietud, desasosiego.

disquisition [ˌdɪskwɪˈzɪʃən] [dis-kui-si-shon], *s.* Disertación, ensayo, tratado o discurso sistemático sobre cualquier materia.

disrate [dɪsˈreɪt] [dis-reit], *va.* *(Mar.)* Degradar, rebajar del grado.

disregard [ˈdɪsrɪˈgɑːd] [dis-ri-gard], *va.* Destender, no hacer caso, descuidar, pasar por alto, menospreciar. Ignorar, despreciar (danger, difficulty); hacer caso omiso de, no prestar atención a (advice); no tener en cuenta (feelings, wishes).

disregard *s.* Desatención, descuido, omisión, negligencia, desprecio, indiferencia. **With complete disregard for her own safety,** sin ni siquiera considerar su propia seguridad.

disregarder [ˈdɪsrɪˈgɑːdəʳ] [dis-ri-gar-daʳ] *s.* Despreciador, menospreciador.

disregardful [ˈdɪsrɪˈgɑːdfʊl] [dis-ri-gard-ful] *a.* Desatento, negligente.

disregardfully [ˈdɪsrɪˈgɑːdfʊlɪ] [dis-ri-gard-fu-li], *adv.* Desatentamente.

disrelish [ˈdɪsrelɪʃ] [dis-re-lish], *s.* 1. Disgusto, desazón, desabrimiento causado en el paladar. 2. Desgana, tedio, hastío, aversión, inapetencia.

disrelish, *va.* 1. Disgustar, causar disgusto y desabrimiento al paladar. 2. Dar un gusto desabrido o ingrato a alguna cosa; tener tedio o aversión.

disrepair [ˈdɪsrɪˈpeəʳ] [dis-ri-peaʳ] *s.* Mal estado. **To be in/fall into (a state of) disrepair,** estar en mal estado/deteriorarse.

disreputable [dɪsˈrepjʊtəbl] [dis-re-piu-tei-bol], *a.* Deshonroso, dañoso a la reputación; desacreditado, despreciado. De dudosa reputación, de mala fama (person, firm); de mala fama (nightclub, district); vergonzoso (conduct, action).

disrepute [ˈdɪsrɪˈpjuːt] [dis-ri-piut], *s.* Descrédito, ignominia, mala fama, mal nombre. **To fall into disrepute,** caer en descrédito.

disrepute, *va.* Deshonrar, quitar el crédito; desatender.

disrespect [ˈdɪsrɪsˈpekt] [dis-ris-pekt], *s.* Irreverencia, desacato, falta de respeto; desatención.

disrespect, *va. (Fam.)* Desacatar, desatender, despreciar.

disrespectful [ˈdɪsrɪsˈpektfʊl] [dis-ris-pekt-ful], *a.* Irreverente (attitude); descortés, irrespetuoso (person); desatento, falto de respeto.

disrespectfully [ˈdɪsrɪsˈpektfʊlɪ] [dis-ris-pekt-fu-li], *adv.* Desacatadamente, irreverentemente, desatentamente.

disrober [ˈdɪsrɒbəʳ] [dis-ro-baʳ], *s.* Desnudador.

disroot [ˈdɪsruːt] [dis-rut], *va.* Desarraigar, arrancar de raíz; arrancar de los cimientos.

disrupt [dɪsˈrʌpt] [dis-rapt], *va.* Romper, hacer pedazos, rajar. Perturbar el desarrollo de (meeting, class); crear problemas de, afectar a (traffic, communications); desbaratar, trastocar (plans).

disruption [dɪsˈrʌpʃən] [dis-rap-shon], *s.* Rompimiento; dilaceración; reventón; trastorno. **This caused serious disruption to our schedules,** esto desbarató nuestro calendario de trabajo, esto ocasionó graves trastornos en nuestro calendario de trabajo.

disruptive [dɪsˈrʌptɪv] [dis-rap-tiv], *a.* Rajante, que revienta o estalla. Perjudicial, negativo (influence). **A disruptive pupil,** un alumno problema.

dissatisfaction [ˈdɪsˌsætɪsˈfækʃən] [di-sa-tis-fak-shon] *s.* Descontento, insatisfacción, disgusto.

dissatisfactoriness [ˈdɪsˌsætɪsˈfæktərɪnɪs] [di-sa-tis-fak-to-ri-nes], *s.* Incapacidad de contentar.

dissatisfactory [ˈdɪsˌsætɪsˈfæktərɪ] [di-sa-tis-fak-to-ri], **a.** Desplaciente, enojoso, fastidioso.

dissatisfied [ˈdɪsˈsætɪsfaɪd] [di-sa-tis-faid] *a.* Descontento, insatisfecho (customer).

dissatisfy [ˈdɪsˈsætɪsfaɪ] [di-sa-tis-fai], *va.* Descontentar, desagradar.

disseat [dɪsˈsiːt] [di-sit], *va.* Echar del asiento.

dissect [dɪˈsekt] [di-sekt], *va.* 1. Cortar o dividir en pedazos; dividir y examinar por menor, anatomizar, disecar. Diseccionar, hacer la disección de (cut up/animal, body). 2. *(Fig.)* Criticar, analizar minuciosamente, diseccionar (analyze/theory, book).

dissection [dɪˈsekʃən] [di-sek-shon], *s.* 1. Disección, anatomía. 2. Examen minucioso de una cosa, análisis. 3. Objeto disecado, preparación anatómica.

dissector [dɪˈsektəʳ] [di-sek-toʳ], *s.* Anatómico, disector.

disseize [dɪˈsaɪz] [di-sais], *va. (For.)* Desposeer, usurpar el dominio.

disseisin [dɪˈsaɪsɪn] [di-sai-sin], *s. (For.)* Usurpación de las tierras o heredades ajenas.

disseizor [dɪˈsaɪzəʳ] [di-sai-saʳ], *s. (For.)* Usurpador, el que desposee a otro de su propiedad.

dissemblance [dɪˈsembləns] [di-sem-blans], *s. (Ant.)* Desemejanza, disimilitud.

dissemble [dɪˈsembl] [di-sem-bel], *va.* Disimular (emotions); ocultar (truth, motive); encubrir, dar a entender lo que no es. *-vn.* Disimular, ocultar, hacer el papel de hipócrita. Fingir.

dissembler [dɪˈsembləʳ] [di-sem-blaʳ], *s.* Hipócrita, disimulador.

dissembling [dɪˈsemblɪŋ] [di-sem-blin], *s.* Disimulación.

dissemblingly [dɪˈsemblɪŋlɪ] [di-sem-blin-li], *adv.* Disimuladamente.

disseminate [dɪˈsemɪneɪt] [di-se-mi-neit], *va.* Diseminar (virus, spores); sembrar, esparcir; *(fig.)* diseminar, divulgar, promulgar, difundir (idea, information).

dissemination [dɪˈsemɪneɪʃən] [di-se-mi-nei-shon], *s.* Diseminación, sembradura; divulgación.

disseminator [dɪˈsemɪneɪtəʳ] [di-se-mi-nei-toʳ], *s.* Diseminador; sembrador.

dissension [dɪˈsenʃən] [di-sen-shon], *s.* Disensión, contienda, desunión, pendencia, cizaña, querella, división, discordia; oposición.

dissensious [dɪˈsenʃəs] [di-sen-shos], *a.* V. DISSENTIOUS.

dissent [dɪˈsent] [di-sent], *vn.* 1. Disentir, discrepar, diferir de opinión, variar, diferenciarse, disidir. 2. Rehusar, adhesión a una iglesia establecida.

dissent, *s.* Disensión, oposición, o contrariedad en los pareceres. Desacuerdo, disconformidad.

dissentaneous [dɪˈsenteɪnəs] [di-sen-tei-nos], *a.* Discorde; contrario.

dissenter [dɪ'sentə^r] [di-sen-ta^r], *s.* 1. Disidente, el que se separa del modo de pensar del mayor número. 2. Disidente, hereje entre los católicos; no conformista.

dissentient [dɪ'senʃɪənt] [di-sen-shient], *a.* Desconforme, opuesto.

dissenting [dɪ'sentɪŋ] [di-sen-tin], *s.* Declaración de un parecer u opinión diferente; discrepante.

dissentous [dɪ'sentəs] [di-sen-tos], *a.* Contencioso, pendenciero.

dissertation [ˌdɪsə'teɪʃən] [di-ser-tei-shon] *s.* Disertación, discurso en que se presentan razones a favor de una opinión y se impugnan las contrarias. Tesis doctoral (in US; for PhD); tesis, tesina (in UK; for lower degree).

dissertator [ˌdɪsə'teɪtə^r] [di-ser-tei-ta^r] *s.* Disertador.

disserve [dɪ'sɜːv] [di-serv] *va.* Dañar, injuriar, perjudicar.

disservice [dɪs'sɜːvɪs] [di-ser-vis] *s.* Deservicio, perjuicio. **This report does him a disservice,** este informe no le hace justicia.

disserviceable [ˈdɪs'sɜːvɪsəbl] [di-ser-vi-sa-bol] *a.* Perjudicial, dañoso.

disserviceableness [ˈdɪs'sɜːvɪsəblnɪs] [di-ser-vi-sa-bol-nes] *s.* Injuria, daño.

dissettle [ˈdɪsetl] [di-se-tel], *va.* Descomponer. *V.* UNSETTLE.

dissever [dɪ'sevə^r] [di-se-va^r], *va.* Partir, dividir en dos partes, separar, desunir, desmembrar.

dissevering [ˈdɪsevərɪŋ] [di-se-ve-rin], *s.* Separación, desunión.

dissidence [ˈdɪsɪdəns] [di-si-dens], *s.* Discordia, disidencia, desunión.

dissident [ˈdɪsɪdənt] [di-si-dent], *a.* Opuesto, desconforme, disidente.

dissilience, dissiliency [ˈdɪsɪlɪəns] [di-si-liens], *s.* Reventón, el acto de reventar, o abrirse súbitamente.

dissilient [ˈdɪsɪlɪənt] [di-si-lient], *a.* Reventado, lo que se abre en dos partes o revienta.

dissimilar [dɪ'sɪmɪlə^r] [di-si-mi-la^r], *a.* Desemejante, diferente, heterogéneo.

dissimilarity [ˌdɪsɪmɪ'lærɪtɪ] [di-si-mi-la-ri-ti], **dissimilitude** [ˌdɪsɪmɪ'lɪtjuːd] [di-si-mi-li-tiud] *s.* 1. Desemejanza, disimilitud, diversidad, diferencia. 2. Comparación entre dos cosas contrarias.

dissimulation [dɪˌsɪmjʊ'leɪʃən] [di-si-miu-lei-shon], *s.* Disimulación, hipocresía.

dissimulate [dɪˌsɪmjʊ'leɪt] [di-si-miu-leit] *va.* Disimular, encubrir (feelings, intention).

dissipable [ˈdɪsɪpəbl] [di-si-pei-bol], *a.* Disipable, lo que es fácil de disiparse o esparcirse.

dissipate [ˈdɪsɪpeɪt] [di-si-peit], *va.* 1. Disipar, dilapidar (squander, inheritance); esparcir, dispersar; disipar, hacer desvanecer (dispel, anxiety). 2. Desparramar, desperdiciar (enery, talents); malgastar, derrochar. *-vn.* 1. Disiparse, desvanecerse (anger, doubts); esparcirse, evaporarse, desaparecer. 2. Ser pródigo o disoluto.

dissipated [ˈdɪsɪpeɪtɪd] [di-si-pei-ted], *a.* Disipado, disoluto, perdido, relajado. *-pp.* de DISSIPATE.

dissipation [ˌdɪsɪ'peɪʃən] [di-si-pei-shon], *s.* 1. Disipación, la acción y efecto de disipar; evaporación, pérdida. 2. Distracción, dispersión. 3. Relajación, devaneo, vida relajada, disoluta.

dissociable [dɪ'səʊʃɪeɪbl] [di-sou-shiei-bol], *a.* 1. Que no está bien ordenado o asociado, incongruo, insociable. 2. Que permite separarse o desunirse.

dissocial [dɪ'səʊʃɪəl] [di-sou-shial], *a.* Insociable, intratable, huraño.

dissociate [dɪ'səʊʃɪeɪt] [di-sou-shieit], *va.* Desunir, disociar, dividir, separar; separar las partes cuya aglomeración forma un cuerpo.

dissociation [dɪˌsəʊʃɪ'eɪʃən] [di-sou-shiei-shon], *s.* Disociación, separación, desunión. Desvinculación (from opinion, act).

dissoluble [dɪ'sɒljʊbl] [di-so-liu-bol], *(Quím.) a.* 1. Disoluble. 2. Separable en partes.

dissolubility [dɪˌsɒljʊ'bɪrɪtɪ] [di-so-liu-bi-li-ti], *s.* Disolubilidad.

dissolute [ˈdɪsəljuːt] [di-so-liut], *a.* Disoluto, libertino, licencioso.

dissolutely [ˈdɪsəljuːtlɪ] [di-so-liut-li], *adv.* Disolutamente.

dissoluteness [ˈdɪsəljuːtnɪs] [di-so-liut-nes], *s.* Disolución, relajación de la vida y costumbres, enviciamiento.

dissolution [ˌdɪsə'ljuːʃən] [di-so-liu-shon], *s.* 1. Disolución, acción de disolver, de desleír. 2. *(Quím.)* Descomposición, separación de las moléculas que componen un cuerpo; desagregación. 3. Disolución de una sociedad o de un parlamento; desintegración (of empire). 4. Muerte.

dissolvable, dissolvible [dɪ'zɒlvəbl] [di-sol-va-bol], *a.* Disoluble, que se puede disolver o desatar.

dissolve [dɪ'zɒlv] [di-solv], *va.* 1. Disolver (in liquid), deshacer, desleír. 2. Disolver, terminar una asamblea; levantar una sesión (dismiss/assembly, parliament). 3. Desencantar. 4. *(For.)* Anular, abrogar; disolver (break up/company, marriage). 5. Desatar, deshacer un lazo o nudo, separar, desunir, relajar. 6. Destruir. *-vn.* 1. Disolverse (in liquid), derretirse, evaporarse. 2. Descomponerse; desvanecerse (vanish). **To dissolve into tears,** deshacerse en lágrimas (emotionally). 3. Descaecer, ir a menos, perderse de vista. 4. Languidecer, enervarse, aniquilarse.

dissolvent [dɪ'zɒlvənt] [di-sol-vent], *a.* y *s.* Disolvente, resolutivo.

dissolver [dɪ'zɒlvə^r] [di-sol-va^r], *s.* 1. Disolvente. 2. El que resuelve una dificultad.

dissonance, dissonancy [ˈdɪsənəns] [di-so-nans], *s. (Mus.)* Disonancia; desconcierto, discordia; discordancia (lack of agreement).

dissonant [ˈdɪsənənt] [di-so-nant], *a.* Disonante, discordante (discordant/music); contrario, diferente, opuesto. Discrepante (dissenting/opinions, beliefs). Discordante (clashing/colors, characteristics).

dissuade [dɪ'sweɪd] [di-sueid], *va.* Disuadir, desviar, procurar apartar a uno de su intento o hacerle mudar de dictamen (con *from*).

dissuader [dɪ'sweɪdə^r] [di-suei-da^r], *s.* Disuadidor.

dissuasion [dɪ'sweɪʒən] [di-suei-shon], *s.* Disuasión, consejo o persuasión.

dissuasive [dɪ'sweɪsɪv] [di-sua-siv], *a.* Disuasivo. *-s.* Disuasión, consejo.

dissyllabic [dɪ'sɪlæbɪk] [di-si-la-bik], *a.* Disílabo, que consta de dos sílabas.

dissyllable [dɪ'sɪləbl] [di-si-la-bol], *s. (Gram.)* Disílabo.

distad [ˈdɪstəd] [dis-tad], *adv. (Anat.)* Hacia la periferia o la extremidad.

distaff [ˈdɪstɑːf] [dis-taf], *s.* 1. Rueca. 2. *(Fig.)* El sexo femenino. **On the distaff side,** por línea materna, por parte de madre.

distain [ˈdɪsteɪn] [dis-tein], *va.* Manchar, teñir; deslustrar.

distal [ˈdɪstəl] [dis-tal], *a.* Relativamente distante del cuerpo o del punto de adherencia.

distance [ˈdɪstəns] [dis-tans], *s.* 1. Distancia (space between two points). **Within easy distance walking,** a poca distancia a pie. **From a distance of 12 miles,** a una distancia de 12 millas. **I can't walk long distances,** no puedo caminar mucho. Distancia (in time). **From a distance of ten years,** a diez años de distancia, después de diez años. 2. Alejamiento; distanciamiento (emotional). **To keep one's distance,** guardar las distancias (remain aloof). 3. Lontananza. 4. Respeto, miramiento. 5. Esquivez, extrañeza; frialdad, altivez. 6. Contrariedad. 7. *(Dep.)* Distancia. **Distance runner,** corredor de fondo. **The fight went the distance,** la pelea duró hasta el último round. **At a distance,** de lejos o a lo lejos. **Not to come within any distance from anyone,** no llegarle a la suela del zapato. **To keep at a distance,** tener a distancia, no tratar con familiaridad.

distance, *va.* Alejar, apartar, desviar; sobrepasar; espaciar; tomar la delantera, dejar atrás, sobresalir. **To distance oneself from somebody/something,** distanciarse de alguien/algo (emotionally); desvincularse de alguien/algo (deny involvement). *-vn.* Adelantarse.

distant ['dɪstənt] [dis-tant], *a.* 1. Distante, apartado, lejano, remoto (in space/spot, country). **I could hear the distant sound of bells,** oía campanas a lo lejos. **In the distant past/future,** en el pasado remoto/en un futuro lejano (in time). 2. Esquivo, extraño; distante, frío (aloof); ausente, ido (absent-minded/expression, tone). 3. Lejano (relative); remoto (resemblance, connection). **To be distant with one,** tratar a uno con frialdad. **A distant relative,** un pariente lejano. **A distant hope,** una esperanza remota. **Distant manners,** maneras reservadas.

distantly ['dɪstəntlɪ] [dis-tan-tli], *adv.* 1. A distancia, de lejos; en lontananza, en la lejanía (in the distance/hear, see). **We're distantly related,** somos parientes lejanos (loosely). 2. Con frialdad (coldly/nod, greet). **Yes, she replied distantly,** -sí-respondió distante (absent-mindedly).

distaste ['dɪsteɪst] [dis-teist], *s.* Hastío, fastidio, aversión, disgusto, tedio, desagrado.

distasteful ['dɪsteɪstful] [dis-teist-ful], *a.* Desabrido, enfadoso, desagradable (unpleasant/task, chore); maligno. De mal gusto (offensive/remark, picture).

distastefulness ['dɪsteɪstfulnɪs] [dis-teist-ful-nes], *s.* Aversión, desagrado.

distemper [dɪs'tempəʳ] [dis-tem-paʳ], *s.* 1. Mal, indisposición, incomodidad, enfermedad; se aplica principalmente a los animales, moquillo. 2. Perversidad de ánimo. 3. Inquietud, desasosiego. 4. *(Pint.)* Distemple; pintura al temple. 5. Falta de la proporción debida.

distemper, *va.* Destemplar, desordenar, perturbar; causar una enfermedad.

distemperature ['dɪstempətʃəʳ] [dis-tem-pa-chaʳ], *s.* 1. Destemplanza, perturbación, confusión, agitación de espíritu, desarreglo. 2. Indisposición, dolencia o desarreglo del cuerpo. 3. Desorden, mezcla de elementos incongruos.

distend [dɪs'tend] [dis-tend], *va.* Extender, ensanchar; inflar, hinchar con aire; dilatar, hinchar. *vn.* Dilatarse, hincharse.

distensible [dɪs'tensɪbl] [dis-ten-si-bol], *a.* Dilatable, que se puede dilatar o extender.

distension, distention [dɪs'tenʃən] [dis-ten-shon], *s.* Ensanche, dilatación, anchura.

distich ['dɪstɪk] [dis-tik], *s.* Dístico; dos versos que forman sentido completo.

distil, distill [dɪs'tɪl] [dis-til], *va.* 1. Destilar (liquid, spirits); extraer o producir por medio de la vaporización y la condensación. **Distilled water,** agua destilada. 2. Purificar, rectificar. 3. Dar, emitir, exhalar en gotas. 4. Extraer (information, ideas). *-vn.* 1. Destilar, gotear, caer gota a gota, manar poco a poco. 2. Extraer substancias volátiles por medio de la vaporización y la condensación.

distillable [dɪs'tɪləbl] [dis-ti-la-bol], *a.* Destilable.

distillate [dɪs'tɪleɪt] [dis-ti-leit], *s.* Destilado, el producto separado o condensado por la destilación.

distillation [ˌdɪstɪ'leɪʃən] [dis-ti-lei-shon], *s.* 1. Destilación (process), el acto de destilar o de caer gota a gota. Destilado (product). 2. Síntesis (of facts, experiencies).

distillatory [dɪs'tɪlətərɪ] [dis-ti-la-to-ri], *a.* Destilatorio, lo que toca a la destilación. *-s.* Aparato para destilar; alambique.

distiller [dɪs'tɪləʳ] [dis-ti-laʳ], *s.* Destilador, refinador.

distillery [dɪs'tɪlərɪ] [dis-ti-le-ri], *s.* Destilatorio, establecimiento en que se hacen las destilaciones; destilería.

distinct [dɪs'tɪŋkt] [dis-tinkt], *a.* 1. Distinto, diferente, diverso (different, separate); inconfundible (unmistakable). **We're talking about English people as distinct from British people,** nos referimos a los ingleses en particular y no a los británicos. 2. Preciso, expreso; formal, exacto, ajustado; definido, claro, nítido (shape, outline); obvio,

marcado (likeness); decidido, marcado (improvement); nada desdeñable (possibility).

distinction [dɪs'tɪŋkʃən] [dis-tink-shon], *s.* 1. Distinción, diferencia (difference); distinción (act of differenciating). **Without distinction of race or creed,** sin distinción de raza o credo. 2. Prerrogativa. 3. Discernimiento, juicio, penetración. 4. Seña o designación de honor (merit, excellence). **A writer of distinction,** un distinguido o destacado escritor. **A car of distinction,** un coche de categoría. Distinción (distinguished appearance). **He has an air of distinction,** tiene un aire distinguido o de distinción. Honor, distinción (mark of recognition). 5. Superioridad de cualquier clase o forma; posición honorífica.

distinctive [dɪs'tɪŋktɪv] [dis-tink-tiv], *a.* Distintivo, característico (marking, plumage); personal, inconfundible (gesture, laugh); particular (decor, dress).

distinctively [dɪs'tɪŋktɪvlɪ] [dis-tink-tiv-li], **distinctly** [dɪs'tɪŋktlɪ] [dis-tink-tli], *adv.* Distintamente, claramente. De manera muy particular o personal (dress, behave); con personalidad (dressed, furnished).

distinctly [dɪs'tɪŋktlɪ] [dis-tink-tli] *adv.* Con claridad (speak, enunciate); perfectamente, claramente (hear). **I distinctly remember telling you,** me acuerdo perfectamente o muy bien de que te lo dije. **He sounded distinctly Scottish,** tenía un inconfundible acento escocés (decidedly).

distinctness [dɪs'tɪŋktnɪs] [dis-tinkt-nes], *s.* Distinción, claridad.

distinguish [dɪs'tɪŋgwɪʃ] [dis-tin-güish], *va.* 1. Distinguir, conocer la diferencia que hay entre las cosas (differentiate). 2. Distinguir, marcar, hacer que una cosa se diferencie de otra (make out). 3. Distinguir, manifestar con el aprecio o estima la preeminencia de alguna cosa. 4. Distinguir, hacer particular estimación de una persona o cosa. 5. Discernir. *vn.* Distinguir. **He can't distinguish between green and blue,** no distingue entre el verde y el azul.

distinguishable [dɪs'tɪŋgwɪʃəbl] [dis-tin-güi-sha-bol], *a.* Distinguible, que se puede distinguir, perceptible.

distinguished [dɪs'tɪŋgwɪʃt] [dis-tin-güisht], *a.* 1. Distinguido, eminente, notable, famoso, ilustre. 2. Especial, marcado, señalado.

distinguisher [dɪs'tɪŋgwɪʃəʳ] [dis-tin-güi-shaʳ], *s.* Hombre de discernimiento.

distinguishingly [dɪs'tɪŋgwɪʃɪŋlɪ] [dis-tin-gü-shin-li], *adv.* Distintamente.

distinguishment [dɪs'tɪŋgwɪʃmənt] [dis-tin-güish-ment], *s.* Distinción.

distort [dɪs'tɔːt] [dis-tort], *va.* Tergiversar, falsear, interpretar o describir falsamente (misrepresent/facts, statement). Deformar (deform/metal, object). **His face was distorted by/with pain,** tenía el rostro crispado de dolor. Deformar, distorsionar (image, reflection); *(Electron.)* distorsionar (signal, sound).

distort, *a. (Des.)* Torcido.

distortion [dɪs'tɔːʃən] [dis-tor-shon], *s.* 1. Esguince, contorsión, torcimiento; deformación (of metal, object); distorsión (of features). 2. Perversión, alteración de la significación; tergiversación, distorsión (of facts, news).

distract [dɪs'trækt] [dis-trakt], *va.* 1. Distraer, apartar la atención de (divert/person). 2. Separar, apartar. 3. Perturbar, enloquecer, poner fuera de sí. 4. Interrumpir. 5. Entretener, distraer (amuse).

distracted [dɪs'træktɪd] [dis-trak-tid] *a.* Trastornado (person); enajenado (look).

distractedly [dɪs'træktɪdlɪ] [dis-trak-tid-li], *adv.* Locamente, como un loco.

distractedness [dɪs'træktɪdnɪs] [dis-trak-tid-nes], *s.* 1. Turbación, embarazo. 2. Locura, demencia.

distracter [dɪs'træktəʳ] [dis-trak-taʳ], *s.* Perturbador, interruptor.

distraction [dɪs'trækʃən] [dis-trak-shon], *s.* 1. Distracción (interruption); confusión. 2. Perturbación de ánimo. 3.

Frenesí. 4. Discordia. 5. Entretenimiento, distracción (entertainment). 6. **To drive somebody to distraction,** sacar a alguien de quicio. **To love somebody to distraction,** estar perdidamente enamorado de alguien (madness).

distractive [dɪsˈtræktɪv] [dis-trak-tiv], *a*. Lo que perturba o confunde.

distrain [dɪsˈtreɪn] [dis-trein], *va. y vn. (For.)* Embargar, secuestrar.

distrainer [dɪsˈtreɪnəʳ] [dis-trei-naʳ], *s*. Embargador.

distraint [dɪsˈtreɪnt] [dis-treint], *s*. Embargo, secuestro.

distraught [dɪsˈtrɔːt] [dis-trot], *a*. Distraído, atolondrado; turbado, desconcertado; consternado, angustiado (voice, person). **To be distraught with grief/worry,** estar consternado por el dolor/por la preocupación.

distream [dɪsˈtriːm] [dis-trim], *vn. (Des. Poét.)* Fluir.

distress [dɪsˈtres] [dis-tres], *s*. 1. Pena, dolor, sufrimiento agudo; angustia, aflicción (mental). **He was in great distress,** sufría mucho. **In distress,** en peligro (danger). De socorro (call, signal). 2. Calamidad, miseria, apuro, conflicto, escasez. 3. *(For.)* Embargo, secuestro. **To put in in distress,** *(Mar.)* entrar de arribada.

distress, *va*. 1. Angustiar, afligir, congojar (upset); consternar (grieve). **Please, don't distress yourself,** por favor no se aflija. 2. Constreñir, obligar por medio de la miseria o la penuria. 3. *(For.)* Embargar, secuestrar.

distressed [dɪsˈtres] [dis-tres], *a*. Afligido (upset); envejecido (leather, wood). **To be in distressed circumstances,** pasar estrecheces (poor).

distressedness [dɪsˈtrestnɪs] [dis-trest-nes], *s*. Aflicción, congoja, angustia, apuro, conflicto.

distressful [dɪsˈtresfʊl] [dis-tres-ful], *a*. Miserable, desdichado, lleno de trabajos.

distressfully [dɪsˈtresfʊlɪ] [dis-tres-fu-li], *adv*. Miserablemente, infelizmente.

distressing [dɪsˈtresɪŋ] [dis-tre-sin], *a*. Penoso, congojoso, aflictivo, angustiante (news, circumstance). **It was distressing to see him like that,** daba angustia verlo así.

distribute [dɪsˈtrɪbjuːt] [dis-tri-biut], *va*. 1. Distribuir, repartir (hand out/leaflets, food); dividir, repartir (share out/profits); distribuir (tasks, responsibilities). *(Neg.)* Distribuir (supply). Distribuir (spread out). **The weight must be evenly distributed,** el peso debe estar bien distribuido. 2. Clasificar, arreglar en orden; separar de una colección y localizar. 3. *(Lóg.)* Aplicar a todos los miembros de una clase tomados separadamente; opuesto a "usar colectivamente". *-vn*. 1. Hacer distribución; hacer un acto de caridad, dar limosna. 2. *(Imp.)* Distribuir, deshacer los moldes, repartiendo las letras entre los cajetines.

distributer [dɪsˈtrɪbjuːtəʳ] [dis-tri-biu-taʳ], *s*. Distribuidor, repartidor.

distribution [dɪsˈtrɪbjuːʃən] [dis-tri-biu-shon], *s*. 1. Distribución, repartimiento, división; reparto (of dividends). **Distribution network,** red de distribuidores. 2. Arreglo, disposición, colocación oportuna; esparcimiento. 3. Distribución, lo que está distribuído. 4. *(Arq.)* Colocación y dependencia mutua de las subdivisiones interiores, etc.; en este sentido se distingue de *disposition*.

distributive [dɪsˈtrɪbjuːtɪv] [dis-tri-biu-tiv], *a*. Distributivo. **The distributive trades,** el sector de la distribución.

distributively [dɪsˈtrɪbjuːtɪvlɪ] [dis-tri-biu-tiv-li], *adv*. Distributivamente.

distributiveness [dɪsˈtrɪbjuːtɪvnɪs] [dis-tri-biu-tiv-nes], *s*. El deseo de distribuir.

distributor [dɪsˈtrɪbjuːtəʳ] [dis-tri-biu-taʳ], *s*. 1. *(Neg.)* Distribuidor. *(Cin.)* Distribuidora. 2. *(Auto, Elec.)* Distribuidor del encendido.

district [ˈdɪstrɪkt] [dis-trikt], *s*. Distrito, comarca o territorio; región, zona (region); jurisdicción; barrio (locality). **Financial district,** distrito financiero. **District attorney,** fiscal del distrito (in US). **District court,** tribunal de distrito (in US). **District nurse,** enfermero que tiene a su cuidado a los pacientes de un distrito (in UK).

distrust [dɪsˈtrʌst] [dis-trast], *va*. Desconfiar, sospechar, rehusar la confianza en (alguien o algo).

distrust, *s*. Desconfianza, recelo, sospecha.

distrustful [dɪsˈtrʌstfʊl] [dis-trast-ful], *a*. 1. Desconfiado, receloso; sospechoso. 2. Modesto, que desconfía de sí mismo.

distrustfully [dɪsˈtrʌstfʊlɪ] [dis-trast-fu-li], *adv*. Desconfiadamente.

distrustfulness [dɪsˈtrʌstfʊlnɪs] [dis-trast-ful-nes], *s*. Desconfianza, sospecha.

distrusting [dɪsˈtrʌstɪŋ] [dis-tras-tin], *s*. Estado de desconfianza.

distrustless [dɪsˈtrʌstlɪs] [dis-trast-les], *a*. Sin sospecha, confiado.

disturb [dɪsˈtɜːb] [dis-terb], *va*. 1. Perturbar, inquietar, llenar de inquietud (trouble); desordenar (disarrange); estorbar, interrumpir (interrupt). **The noise disturbed my concentration,** el ruido me hizo perder la concentración. **He found that his papers had been disturbed,** notó que alguien había tocado sus papeles. 2. Molestar (inconvenience); atormentar, inquietar; sorprender (burst in upon). **I'm sorry to disturb you, but...,** perdone que le moleste, pero...

disturbance [dɪsˈtɜːbəns] [dis-ter-bans], *s*. Disturbio, confusión, desorden, alboroto, tumulto (riot); perplejidad, irresolución; Alteración (of routine); interrupción (interruption). **To cause/create a disturbance,** provocar/armar un alboroto (noisy disruption). **The aircraft are a continual disturbance,** los aviones son una molestia constante.

disturbed [dɪsˈtɜːbd] [dis-terbd] *a*. 1. Trastornado (person, mind). **She's emotionally disturbed,** tiene problemas emocionales. **I was greatly disturbed to hear of his misfortunes,** la noticia de su desgracia me impresionó o afectó muchísimo (perturbed). 2. Agitado, inquieto (restless/sleep). **I had a disturbed night,** dormí muy mal.

disturber [dɪsˈtɜːbəʳ] [dis-ter-baʳ], *s*. Perturbador, inquietador.

disturbing [dɪsˈtɜːbɪŋ] [dis-ter-bin] *a*. Inquietante, perturbador (worrying, upsetting); alarmante (alarming).

disulfid, disulphid, disulphide [dɪˈsʌlfɪd] [di-sul-fid], *s*. Bisulfuro. Equivalente. **disulphure.**

disuniform [dɪsˈjuːnɪfɔːm] [di-siu-ni-form], *a*. Heterogéneo.

disunion [dɪsˈjuːnɪən] [dis-iu-nion], *s*. Desunión, discordia, desavenencia, división, separación.

disunite [dɪsˈjuːnaɪt] [dis-iu-nait], *va*. Desunir, dividir, separar, enajenar, desavenir. *-vn*. Desunirse, separarse, desavenirse.

disuniter [ˈdɪsjuːnaɪtəʳ] [dis-iu-nai-taʳ], *s*. El que desune.

disunity [ˌdɪsˈjuːnɪtɪ] [dis-iu-ni-ti], *s*. Desunión, separación.

disusage [dɪsˈjuːsədʒ] [dis-iu-sach], *s*. Desuso, falta de uso o ejercicio.

disuse [dɪsˈjuːs] [dis-ius], *s*. Desuso, cesación de algún uso o costumbre. **To fall into disuse,** caer en desuso (costums, words); dejar de utilizarse (building, port).

disuse, *va*. Desusar, desacostumbrar.

disused [ˈdɪsjuːst] [dis-iust] *a*. Abandonado (factory, quarry); en desuso (machinery).

disvaluation [ˌdɪsvæljʊˈeɪʃən] [dis-va-liu-ei-shon], **disvalue** [dɪsˈvæljuː] [dis-va-liu], *s*. Desestimación.

disvalue, *va*. Desapreciar.

disyoke [ˈdɪsdʒəʊk] [dis-youk], *va*. Quitar el yugo a; desuncir.

dit [dɪt] [dit], *va. (Esco.)* Cerrar.

ditch [dɪtʃ] [dich], *s*. 1. Zanja, canal que se hace en la tierra para proteger los sembrados, etc; cuneta (at roadside); acequia (for irrigation). 2. *(Fort.)* Foso, zanja que circunda alguna plaza o fortaleza.

ditch, *va*. 1. Abrir zanjas o fosos. 2. *(Coloq.)* Plantar, botar (girlfriend, boyfriend); deshacerse de, botar, tirar (object);

abandonar, desechar (plan). 3. *(Aviat.)* **To ditch a plane,** hacer un amarizaje o amerizaje forzoso. *-vn.* Hacer fosos, especialmente como ocupación habitual.

ditcher [ˈdɪtʃəʳ] [di-cha^r], *s.* Cavador de zanjas o fosos.

ditheism [ˈdɪθeɪzm] [di-ze-isem], *s.* Diteísmo, doctrina de los que admiten dos dioses iguales; maniqueísmo, sistema de Zoroastro.

dither [ˈdɪðəʳ] [di-za^r] *vn. (Coloq.)* Ponerse muy nervioso (become agitated); titubear, vacilar (be indecisive). **I was dithering over whether to go or not,** no sabía si ir o no ir.

dithyramb [ˌdɪðɪˈræm] [di-zi-ram], *s.* Ditirambo, himno en honor de Baco.

dithyrambic [ˌdɪðɪˈræmbɪk] [di-zi-ram-bik], *s.* Ditirambo. - *a.* Ditirámbico, en forma de ditirambo; apasionado.

dittany [ˈdɪtənɪ] [di-ta-ni], *s. (Bót.)* 1. Pequeño arbusto perenne americano. Cunila Mariana. 2. Cualquier planta del género Dictamnus. **Dittany of Crete,** díctamo. **White dittany,** fraxinela.

dittied [ˈdɪtɪɪd] [di-ti-id], *a.* Cantado, adaptado a la música.

ditto [ˈdɪtəʊ] [di-tou], *a.* Dicho o dicha, lo mismo, palabra que se usa más frecuentemente en los libros de comercio y cuentas, y equivale a *idem*. **I'm fed up - ditto!,** estoy harto - ¡y yo ídem de ídem!.

ditty [ˈdɪtɪ] [di-ti], *s.* Cancioneta, composición música corta y sencilla para cantar.

diuresis [ˌdaɪjʊəˈresɪs] [dai-ua-re-sis], *s. (Med.)* Diuresis, secreción excesiva de la orina.

diuretic [ˌdaɪjʊəˈretɪk] [dai-ua-re-tik], *a. y s.* Diurético, lo que tiene virtud para facilitar la secreción de la orina.

diurnal [daɪˈɜːnl] [dai-er-nal], *a.* 1. Diurno, diario, cotidiano. 2. Diurno, que pertenece al día. 3. *(Zool.)* Activo durante el día. 4. *(Bot.)* Que se abre de día y se cierra por la noche; que dura solamente veinticuatro horas, efímero. *-s.* 1. Diurno, libro del rezo eclesiástico que contiene las horas menores. 2. *(Des.)* Diario, jornal, libro en que se escribe lo que se hace cada día.

diurnalist, *s. V.* JOURNALIST.

diurnally [daɪˈɜːnlɪ] [dai-er-na-li], *adv.* Diariamente.

diuturnal [daɪˈtɜːnl] [dai-ter-nal], *a.* Diuturno, que ha durado mucho tiempo.

diuturnity [daɪˈtɜːnɪtɪ] [dai-ter-ni-ti], *s.* Diuturnidad, espacio dilatado de tiempo.

divan [dɪˈvæn] [di-van], *s.* 1. Diván, el supremo consejo entre los turcos. 2. Cámara del consejo. 3. Café, cuarto de fumar. 4. Diván, especie de sofá sin respaldo y con cojines. Cama turca.

divaricate [dɪˈværɪkeɪt] [di-va-ri-keit] *vn. y va.* 1. Dividirse en dos partes o ramos. 2. *(Biol.)* Divergir marcadamente. *V.* DIVERGE.

divarication [dɪˈværɪˌkeɪʃən] [di-va-ri-kei-shon], *s.* División en dos partes; extensión.

dive [daɪv] [daiv], *vn.* 1. Zambullirse, sumergirse o meterse voluntariamente debajo del agua, tirarse al agua (from height). Sumergirse, zambullirse (from surface/person, whale); sumergirse (submarine). **She dived into the water,** se zambulló, se tiró al agua. 2. Bucear, sacar alguna cosa de lo profundo del agua. Bajar en picado (swoop/plane, bird). **To dive for treasure,** bucear buscando tesoros. **To go diving,** ir a hacer submarinismo o a bucear. 3. Sumergirse, enfrascarse en los negocios, etc. 4. Profundizar o estudiar a fondo alguna cuestión o ciencia. 5. Caer en picada o en picado, pegar un bajón (drop sharply/currency, sales). 6. **He dived for cover under the table,** se tiró o se metió debajo de la mesa para protegerse (lunge, move suddenly).

dive in *(Coloq.)* Tirarse de cabeza al agua, tirarse o echarse un clavado (into water).

dive, *s.* 1. Zambullidura, clavado (into water). *(Dep.)* Salto de trampolín, clavado. Inmersión (of submarine, whale). Descenso en picado (swoop). 2. Buceo, acción de bucear o mantenerse debajo del agua. 3. Enfrascamiento, absorción en los negocios, etc. 4. *(Fam.)* Timba, leonera, antro (disreputable club, bar). 5. *(Coloq.)* **He made a dive**

for the gun, se abalanzó sobre la pistola (lunge, sudden movement).

dive bomber [ˈdaɪvˌbɒməʳ] [daiv-bom-ba^r], *s. (Aer.)* Bombardero en picado.

diver [ˈdaɪvəʳ] [dai-va^r], *s.* 1. Buzo, submarinista (deep-sea); saltador, clavadista (from diving board). 2. Ave que se zambulle; en especial, el colimbo, especie de mergio.

diverge [daɪˈvɜːdʒ] [dai-verch], *vn.* 1. Divergir, divergirse, apartarse (lines, paths); divergir (opinions, explanations). 2. Desviarse de un rumbo, dirección o modelo dado. 3. *V.* DIFFER.

divergence, divergency [daɪˈvɜːdʒəns] [dai-ver-yens], *s.* Divergencia.

divergent [daɪˈvɜːdʒənt] [dai-ver-yent], *a.* Divergente.

divers [ˈdaɪvɜːz] [dai-vers], *a.* Varios, diversos, diferentes, muchos, más de uno, pero no numerosos.

divers-colored [ˈdaɪvɜːzˌkʌləd] [dai-vers-ka-led], *a.* De muchos o varios colores.

diverse [ˈdaɪvɜːs] [dai-vers], *a.* 1. Diverso, diferente, distinto, multiforme, variado (interests, tastes). **Plant life in the area is extremely diverse,** la vegetación en la zona es muy variada. 2. Diferente, distinto (unlike).

diversely [ˈdaɪvɜːslɪ] [dai-vers-li], *adv.* Diversamente, distintamente, en diferentes direcciones.

diversification [daɪˌvɜːsɪfɪˈkeɪʃən] [dai-ver-si-fi-kei-shon], *s.* Diversificación, acción de diversificar; variación o variedad de formas o colores.

diversify [daɪˈvɜːsɪfaɪ] [dai-ver-si-fai], *va.* Diversificar, variar, cambiar, diferenciar; matizar, abigarrar. *vn.* Diversificarse. **They diversified into sportswear,** diversificaron su producción introduciéndose en el mercado de ropa de deporte.

diversion [daɪˈvɜːʃən] [dai-ver-shon], *s.* 1. Desviación (of river); malversación (of funds). 2. Diversión, entretenimiento, pasatiempo (amusement). 3. *(Mil.)* Diversión, divertimento estratégico (distraction). **You create a diversion and I'll make my escape,** tú los distraes mientras yo me escapo.

diversity [daɪˈvɜːsɪtɪ] [dai-ver-si-ti], *s.* Diversidad, variedad, diferencia, desemejanza.

divert [ˈdaɪvɜːt] [dai-vert], *va.* 1. Desviar, apartar, alejar, divertir (redirect/stream, flow, traffic); eludir, esquivar (ward off/blow, attack). **I tried to divert the conversation away from the topic,** intenté desviar la conversación hacia otro tema. 2. Desviar, distraer (distract/attention, thoughts). 3. Divertir, regocijar, recrear, entretener (amuse).

diverter [ˈdaɪvɜːtəʳ] [dai-ver-ta^r], *s.* Quitapesares, consuelo, alivio.

diverticle [daɪˈvɜːtɪkl] [dai-ver-ti-kol], *s.* Camino o senda desviada, vuelta.

diverticulum [ˌdaɪvɜːˈtɪkjʊləm] [dai-ver-ti-kiu-lum], *(pl.* LA) *s. (Biol.)* Divertículo, apéndice (vertical); bolsillo ciego.

divertisement [daɪˈvɜːtɪzmənt] [dai-ver-tis-ment], *s.* 1. Diversión, holgura. 2. Intermedio de baile (en los teatros).

divertive [ˈdaɪvɜːtɪv] [dai-ver-tiv], *a.* Divertido.

divest [daɪˈvest] [dai-vest], *va.* Desnudar, privar de autoridad; despojar, desposeer.

divestiture [daɪˈvestɪtʃəʳ] [dai-ves-ti-cha^r], *s.* 1. Despojo. 2. *(For.)* Desposeimiento, el acto y efecto de privar a alguno de sus bienes o hacienda.

dividable [dɪˈvaɪdəbl] [di-vai-da-bol], *a.* Divisible.

divide [dɪˈvaɪd] [di-vaid], *va.* 1. Dividir (split up); distribuir, repartir (share/cake, money, work). **I divide my time between England and Italy,** paso parte del tiempo en Inglaterra y parte en Italia. 2. Desunir, separar, dividir (cause to disagree). 3. *(Mat.)* Dividir. **To divide 10 by 5,** dividir 10 entre 5. **10 divided by 5 is 2,** 10 dividido entre 5 es (igual a) 2. *-vn.* 1. Romper, reñir con alguno; desunirse, dividirse. 2. Dividirse (fork/road, river); dividirse (split/group, particles, cells). 3. *(Mat.)* Dividir.

divide off, separar.

divide up 1. Dividir. 2. Dividirse.

divide, *s.* Vertiente de una montaña; línea divisoria de las aguas. **The Great Divide,** *(Fam. E. U.)* la vertiente de las Montañas Rocosas.

divided [dɪ'vaɪdɪd] [di-vai-did] *a.* Dividido (opinion). **They are divided on the issue,** sus opiniones al respecto están muy divididas.

divided highway [dɪ'vaɪdɪd͵haɪweɪ] [di-vai-did-jai-uei] *s.* Autovía.

divided skirt [dɪ'vaɪdɪd͵skɜːt] [di-vai-did-skert] *s.* Falda pantalón, pollera pantalón.

dividedly [dɪ'vaɪdɪdlɪ] [di-vai-did-li], *adv.* Separadamente, por separado.

dividend ['dɪvɪdend] [di-vi-dend], *s.* 1. Dividendo, la parte o porción que toca a cada uno en el repartimiento de alguna cosa. **To pay dividends,** pagar dividendos, reportar beneficios. 2. *(Arit.)* Dividendo.

divider [dɪ'vaɪdəʳ] [di-vai-daʳ], *s.* 1. Partidor, el instrumento que parte; mampara (screen); separador (in filing system). **Dividers,** compás de división. 2. Partidor el que parte o divide. 3. *(Arit.)* Divisor, partidor. 4. Distribuidor, repartidor.

dividing [dɪ'vaɪdɪdɪŋ] [di-vai-di-din], *s.* Separación. **Dividing line,** línea divisoria.

dividual [dɪ'vɪdjuːəl] [di-vi-dual], *a. (Ant.)* Dividido.

divination [͵dɪvɪ'neɪʃən] [di-vi-nei-shon], *s.* Divinación, adivinación.

divinator [dɪvɪ'neɪtəʳ] [di-vi-nei-taʳ], *s.* Adivinador, adivino.

divinatory [dɪ'vɪnətərɪ] [di-vi-na-to-ri], *a.* Divinatorio.

divine [dɪ'vaɪn] [di-van], *a.* 1. Divino, lo que pertenece a Dios o a los falsos dioses. **It was divine justice,** fue un castigo de Dios. 2. Divino, admirable, sublime, precioso (wonderful). -*s.* Predicador, teólogo.

divine, *va.* Adivinar (discover, guess); descubrir con una varita de zahorí (minerals, water). -*vn.* Conjeturar, presentir, pronosticar, profetizar; sospechar.

divinely [dɪ'vaɪnlɪ] [di-vain-li], *adv.* Divinamente; excelentemente.

divineness [dɪ'vaɪnnɪs] [di-vain-nes], *s.* 1. Divinidad, participación de la naturaleza divina. 2. Excelencia, perfección.

diviner [dɪ'vaɪnəʳ] [di-vai-naʳ], *s.* Adivino, adivinador, conjeturador.

diving ['daɪvɪŋ] [dai-vin], *s.* 1. Buceo, 2. Zambullimiento, zambullida, zambullidura. 3. Saltos de trampolín, clavados (from height); submarinismo, buceo (under water). **Diving bell,** campana de buzo, campana de salvamento. **Diving board,** trampolín. **Diving suit,** escafandra.

divining rod [dɪ'vaɪnɪŋrɒd] [di-vai-nin-rod] *s.* Varita de zahorí.

divinity [dɪ'vɪnɪtɪ] [di-vi-ni-ti], *s.* 1. Divinidad (divine nature, being). 2. Dios (verdadero o falso). 3. La teología (theology). 4. Atributo, virtud o cualidad que se supone ser de carácter divino.

divisibility [͵dɪvɪsɪ'bɪlɪtɪ] [di-vi-si-bi-li-ti], **divisibleness.** Divisibilidad.

divisible [dɪ'vɪzəbl] [di-vi-sa-bol], *a.* Divisible. **21 is divisible by 3,** 21 es divisible entre o por 3.

division [dɪ'vɪʒən] [di-vi-shon], *s.* 1. División, la acción o efecto de dividir, separar o repartir (distribution). **The division of labor,** la división del trabajo. División (boundary). **Linguistic/classes division,** divisiones lingüísticas/de clase. 2. División, separación, desunión, discordia, desacuerdo (disagreement). 3. *(Arit.)* División, partición. **Long division,** división larga o desarrollada. 4. *(Mil.)* División, parte de un ejército o de una armada que obran o marchan separadamente. 5. Lo que separa o divide; división, sección (department). 6. Votación de un cuerpo legislativo (como del Parlamento británico). 7. *(Dep.)* Categoría (in boxing); zona (in US: area); división (in UK: by standard).

divisional, divisionary [dɪ'vɪʒənl] [di-vi-sho-nal], *a.* Divisional, referente a la división.

divisive [dɪ'vaɪsɪv] [di-vi-siv], *a.* Divisivo, que sirve para dividir.

divisor [dɪ'vaɪʒəʳ] [di-vi-saʳ], *s. (Arit.)* Divisor.

divorce [dɪ'vɔːs] [di-vors], *s.* 1. Divorcio, disolución legal del matrimonio. 2. Divorcio, separación, desunión. **Divorce proceedings,** trámites de divorcio. **To get a divorce from somebody,** conseguir el divorcio de alguien

divorce, *va.* 1. Divorciar, autorizar la separación de dos esposos, pronunciar el divorcio. *(Law)* Divorciarse de. **To get divorced,** divorciarse. 2. Divorciar; separar alguna cosa de lo que estaba unido con ella; arrancar violentamente una cosa de otra (separate).

divorced [dɪ'vɔːst] [di-vorst] *a. (Law)* Divorciado. **To be divorced from something,** estar divorciado de algo (detached).

divorcee [dɪ'vɔːsiː] [di-vor-si] *s.* Divorciado.

divorcement [dɪ'vɔːsmənt] [di-vors-ment], *s.* Divorcio.

divorcer [dɪ'vɔːsəʳ] [di-vor-saʳ], *s.* Divorciador; el que o lo que divorcia.

divorcive [dɪ'vɔːsɪv] [di-vor-siv], *a.* Lo que tiene poder de divorciar.

divulgate [daɪ'vʌlgeɪt] [di-val-gueit], *va. (Des.)* Divulgar, publicar.

divulge [daɪ'vʌldʒ] [dai-valch], *va.* 1. Divulgar, publicar, descubrir, revelar. **To divulge something to somebody,** revelarle algo a alguien. 2. Proclamar, pregonar.

divulger [daɪ'vʌldʒəʳ] [dai-val-yaʳ], *s.* Divulgador; pregonero.

divulsion [daɪ'vʌlʒən] [dai-val-shon], *s.* Arranque, la acción y efecto de arrancar.

divulsive [daɪ'vʌlsɪv] [dai-val-siv], *a. (Des.)* Divulsivo, lo que tiene poder de arrancar o separar violentamente una cosa de otra.

diwan [daɪ'wɒn] [dai-uan], *s.* Colección de poemas cortos de un solo autor; ciclo, antología. (Persa)

dixie o dixieland ['dɪksɪ] [dik-si], *s.* 1. Región integrada por los estados del sur de E. U. 2. Canto de guerra de dicha región en la Guerra de Secesión.

DIY *s.* (GB) (= **do-it-yourself**) bricolaje.

dizen [daɪ'zən] [dai-sen], *va.* 1. Ataviar, adornar. 2. Poner el lino en la rueca (Uso propio).

dizziness ['dɪzɪnɪs] [di-si-nes], *s.* Vértigo, vahido, desvanecimiento, mareo.

dizzy ['dɪzɪ] [di-si], *a.* 1. Vertiginoso (causing dizziness/ speed). De vértigo (height) 2. Desvanecido, atacado de un vértigo; que causa vértigo; de mareo (sensation/giddy). **I had a dizzy spell,** me dio un mareo. **To feel dizzy,** estar mareado. 3. *(Ant.)* Ligero, voluble, aturdido. *(Coloq.)* Tarambana (scatterbrained).

dizzy, *va.* Causar vértigos o vahidos de cabeza, girar alrededor. -*vn.* Aturdirse, desvanecerse, írsele a uno la cabeza.

DJ *s.* = **disc jockey**

DNA *s.* (= **deoxyribonucleic acid**) ADN, DNA.

do [duː] [du], *va. (pret.* DID, *pp.* DONE). 1. Hacer, ejecutar, obrar. **Do something!,** ¡haz algo! **Are you doing anything this evening?,** ¿vas a hacer algo esta noche? **It was a silly thing to do,** fue una estupidez. **Can I do anything to help?,** ¿puedo ayudar en algo? 2. Finalizar, concluir (achieve, bring about); despachar, rematar, hacer (carry out/job, task). **To do the cooking,** cocinar. **Let me do the talking,** déjame hablar a mí. **She's done it: it's a new world record,** lo ha logrado: es una nueva marca mundial. **What do you do?,** ¿usted qué hace o a qué se dedica? (as job). 3. Producir algún efecto; preparar, hacer (meal); arreglar, modificar (fix, arrange, repair); verter, traducir, hacer (drawing, translation). **He doesn't do live concerts any more,** ya no da más conciertos en vivo. **I have to do my nails,** me tengo que arreglar las uñas. Lavar (clean, dishes); limpiar (brass, windows). 4. Servir, aprovechar; emplear el poder, alargar la mano. 5. *(Ger.)* Estafar, petardear; engañar (cheat); también, injuriar, agraviar, matar. **I've been done!,** ¡me han estafado o timado!

6. *(Teat.)* Hacer el papel de (play role of); actuar en (play, take part in); imitar (impersonate). 7. *(Fam.)* Bastar, ser suficiente para (suffice for, suit). **Fifty dollars will do me for the present,** me bastarán cincuenta pesos por ahora. 8. **The car has only done 4,000 miles,** el coche sólo tiene 4.000 millas (travel). 9. Estudiar (study); visitar (visit/sights, museum). **We're doing Balzac,** estamos estudiando Balzac. **We did Europe last year,** el año pasado recorrimos Europa. 10. Cumplir (serve in prison). **He's doing eight years for armed robbery,** está cumpliendo ocho años por atraco a mano armada. 11. Agarrar (catch, prosecute). **He was done for speeding,** le encajaron una multa por exceso de velocidad. 12. **To do drugs,** drogarse, consumir drogas (use). 13. *(Coloq.)* Terminar (finish), **have you done complaining?,** ¿has terminado de quejarte? -vn. 1. Conducirse, comportarse, portarse, proceder, hacer (act, behave). **Do as you are told!,** ¡haz lo que se te dice! 2. Pasarlo, estar, hallarse, cuando se trata de la salud o de un empeño (get along, manage). V. FARE. **How do you do?** ¿cómo le va a Ud.?, ¿cómo se halla Ud.?, ¿cómo está Ud.? (as greeting). **She did well/badly in her exams,** le fue bien/mal en los exámenes. **He's done well for himself,** ha sabido abrirse camino. 3. Salir bien o mal en una cosa: v. g. **In the drawing I did badly,** salí mal en el sorteo. **He does well in his new enterprise,** sale bien en su nuevo empleo. 4. Darse maña, discurrir trazas para adelantar, ingeniarse. 5. Servir al designio de uno; ser a propósito. 6. **Look, this won't do!,** ¡mira, esto no puede ser! **It's not ideal, but it will do,** no es lo ideal, pero sirve (be suitable, acceptable). 7. Ser suficiente, alcanzar, bastar (be enough). **One bottle will do,** con una botella basta o es suficiente. **One egg will do for me,** un huevo es suficiente para mí. 8. Terminar (finish). **I haven't done it yet!,** no he terminado todavía. 9. His concern to do well for his son, su preocupación por hacer todo lo posible por su hijo. **Do as you would be done by,** trata a los demás como tú quisieras ser tratado. -Este verbo es auxiliar, y se emplea como tal en los tiempos presente y pasado para señalar la negación o la interrogación. **I do not read,** no leo. **I did not read,** no leí. **Do I read?,** ¿leo yo? **Did my brother go?,** ¿fue mi hermano? -En las oraciones afirmativas se emplea *To do* para dar más energía a la oración, para expresar con más fuerza la oposición y como expletivo. **I do hate him,** le aborrezco de veras. **I did love her, but I scorn her now,** la amé ciertamente, mas ahora la aborrezco. -También se usa para evitar repeticiones. **I shall come, but if I do not, go away,** yo vendré, mas si no vengo, márchate. -Se emplea también para mandar con imperio o pedir una cosa con ansia. **Make haste, do,** vamos, dése Ud. prisa, despáchese. **Do, pray, go and tell him I am here,** tenga Ud. la bondad de ir a decirle que estoy aquí. **To do again,** rehacer, volver a hacer. **To do off,** deshacer; quitar; sacar. **To do on,** poner una cosa sobre otra; meter. **To do one's best,** esmerarse. **To do one's utmost,** hacer cuanto es posible. **That will do,** eso es bastante, suficiente o a propósito. **That won't do,** eso no vale, eso no sirve; ni por esas. **To have done with,** dejar o abandonar; cesar, descontinuar. **Parents wish their children to do well,** los padres desean que sus hijos prosperen o sean felices.

do away with, abolir, suprimir (abolish/privilege, tax); eliminar, acabar con (need); llevar, borrar. *(Coloq.)* Eliminar, liquidar (kill).

do down Menospreciar, hacer de menos.

do for, ser a propósito, servir para; tener cuidado de, cuidar del bienestar personal o intereses de; *(Ger.)* matar, herir o lastimar mortalmente. **He is done for,** han acabado con él. **They've spotted us, we're done for!,** ¡nos han visto, estamos perdidos! (cause collapse of). **To do for oneself,** sostenerse sin ayuda ajena, ganarse la vida.

do in 1. *(Coloq.)* Eliminar, liquidar (kill); agotar, reventar (tire out). **To be done in,** estar reventado o molido o hecho polvo. 2. Hacerse daño en, embromarse (injure, ruin/back, shoulder); estropear, arruinar, cargarse (engine).

do out Hacer una limpieza a fondo de (clean out/room). **The bedroom was done out in pink,** el dormitorio estaba pintado de/empapelado en rosa.

do out of *(Coloq.)* Quitar, birlar. **He was done out of his share,** le quitaron o le birlaron su parte.

do over 1. Hacer de nuevo, volver a hacer; cubrir completamente con algún material extendido o disuelto. 2. Darle una paliza a, sacarle la mugre a (beat up). **To do over with gold,** dorar. **To do over with silver,** platear.

do up Liar, empaquetar, envolver (wrap up/parcel); arreglar, enrollar, como los cabellos; almidonar y planchar, como una tela; fatigarse, cansarse. Abrochar (fasten/coat, necklace, button); subir (zipper). Arreglar (pintando, etc.)(hous). **To do up one's shoes,** atarse los cordones o las agujetas o los pasadores de los zapatos. **Do up your tie,** hazte el nudo de la corbata. **She was all done up,** estaba muy elegante.

do with Conducirse, arreglarse para; disponer de; usar en provecho de (benefit from). **That door could do with a coat of paint,** no le vendría mal una mano de pintura a esa puerta. **You could do with a change,** te hace falta o te vendría bien un cambio. **What's that got to do with it?,** ¿y eso qué tiene que ver? **It's to do with your son,** se trata de su hijo (expressing connection).

do without, Pasar sin; dispensar de. Arreglárselas. **Her coming to stay is something I can do without!,** ¡ni falta que me hace que ella se venga a quedar! **You really think you could do without me?,** ¿te las puedes arreglar sin mí?, ¿te las puedes arreglar sólo?.

do, *s.* 1. Do, primera voz de la escala musical que sustituye al *ut.* 2. *(Coloq.)* Fiesta, reunión (party, gathering). 3. *(Coloq.)* **Fair does all round,** a partes iguales para todos; ¡seamos justos! (state of affairs). 4. **do's and don'ts,** normas (rules). **The do's and don'ts of foreign travel,** qué hacer y qué evitar cuando se viaja al extranjero.

DOA *a.* = **dead on arrival**

DOB *s.* = **date of birth**

doc *s. (Coloq.)* Doctor.

docibility [dɒsɪ'bɪlɪtɪ] [do-si-bi-li-ti], *s.* Docilidad.

docible [dəʊ'sɪbl] [dou-si-bol], *a.* Dócil, flexible, obediente, deferente; el que aprende con facilidad lo que le enseñan.

docile ['dəʊsaɪl] [dou-sail], *a.* Dócil, sumiso; apacible.

docility [dəʊ'sɪlɪtɪ] [dou-si-li-ti], *s.* Docilidad.

docimastic [dəʊsɪ'mæstɪk] [dou-si-mas-tik], *a.* Docimástico, referente a la docimasia.

docimasy, docimacy [dəʊ'sɪməsɪ] [dou-si-ma-si], *s.* Docimasia, docimástica, el arte de ensayar los minerales para determinar los metales que contienen y en qué proporción.

dock [dɒk] [dok], *s.* 1. Muelle, desembarcadero (wharf, quay); dársena (for cargo ships); portuario (worker, strike). **To be in dock,** estar en puerto. **Dry dock,** astillero, dique seco. **Docks,** puerto. 2. *(Law)* **The dock,** el banquillo de los acusados. 3. *(Bot.)* Acedera.

dock, *va.* 1. Entrar en muelle; fondear, atracar (vessel, ship). 2. Rescindir (wages). **To dock one's wages,** descontar a alguien parte de su sueldo. 3. Descolar, quitar o cortar la cola al animal. 4. Cercenar, cortar, rebajar. 5. *(Mar.)* Meter o poner una embarcación en el dique. *vn. (Naut.)* Atracar, fondear (ship, vessel). *(Aerosp.)* Acoplarse.

dockage ['dɒkeɪdʒ] [do-keich] *s.* 1. La acción de poner un buque en el dique. 2. Cantidad que se paga por el uso de un dique.

docket ['dɒkɪt] [do-kit], *s.* 1. Rótulo, extracto, etiqueta (label); resguardo de entrega (delivery note). **To strike a docket,** *(Com.)* declarar a un comerciante en bancarrota. 2. *(For.)* Lista, tablilla, enumeración o registro de los pleitos y causas pendientes. 3. Marbete.

docket, *va.* 1. Extractar, hacer el sumario de una obra, papeles o documentos. 2. Rotular, poner rótulo o nombre a un cuaderno, paquete, etc., indicando su contenido. 3. Incluir en la lista o registro de las causas y pleitos pendientes.

docking ['dɒkɪŋ] [do-kin] *s. (Aerosp.)* Acoplamiento.

dockland ['dɒklænd] [dok-land] s. Zona portuaria.

dock-yard ['dɒkjɑːd] [dok-yard], s. (Mar.) Arsenal; astillero.

doctor ['dɒktəʳ] [dok-taʳ], s. 1. Doctor, médico, facultativo. 2. Doctor, el que ha recibido en una universidad el grado más alto en una facultad, como derecho, teología, etc. **Doctor's office,** consultorio del médico o del doctor. **Doctor of Law,** doctor en Leyes. **Medical doctor,** doctor en Medicina. **Doctor of Philosophy,** doctor en Filosofía.

doctor, va. 1. (Fam.) Medicinar, recetar. 2. Alterar, adulterar (food, drink). 3. Reparar, componer, arreglar (text); falsificar, amañar (results, evidence). 4. Operar (neuter/cat, dog). -vn. 1. Tomar medicinas o recibir tratamiento médico. 2. Practicar la medicina.

doctoral ['dɒktərəl] [dok-to-ral], a. Doctoral que pertenece al grado de doctor (thesis, dissertation).

doctorally ['dɒktərəlɪ] [dok-to-ra-li], adv. A modo de doctor.

doctorate ['dɒktərɪt] [dok-to-rit], s. Doctorado.

doctorate, va. Doctorar, conferir el grado de doctor.

doctoress ['dɒktərɪs] [dok-to-res], sf. Doctora.

doctorship ['dɒktəʃɪp] [dok-tor-ship], s. Doctorado.

doctrinaire [ˌdɒktrɪˈneəʳ] [dok-tri-neaʳ], a. y s. Doctrinario.

doctrinal [dɒkˈtraɪnl] [dok-trainl], a. 1. Doctrinal, lo que contiene o pertenece a la doctrina. 2. Didáctico, referente a la enseñanza; instructivo. -s. Parte de doctrina; doctrinal.

doctrinally ['dɒktraɪnəlɪ] [dok-trai-na-li], adv. Magistralmente.

doctrine ['dɒktrɪl] [dok-trin], s. 1. Doctrina, dogma, creencia, especialmente en religión. 2. (Ant.) Enseñanza, erudición, saber.

document ['dɒkjʊmənt] [do-kiu-ment], s. Documento, escritura, testimonio, documento auténtico.

document, va. Documentar, proveer de documentos; probar por medio de documentos o escrituras.

documental [ˌdɒkjʊˈmentl] [do-kiu-men-tal], a. Documental, procedente de los documentos.

documentary [ˌdɒkjʊˈmentərɪ] [do-kiu-men-ta-ri], a. Documental.

documentation [ˌdɒkjʊmenˈteɪʃən] [do-kiu-men-tei-shon], s. Documentación.

dodder ['dɒdəʳ] [do-daʳ], s. (Bot.) Cuscuta, planta parásita sin hojas, que se usa en medicina. vn. (Coloq.) Andar tambaleándose o con paso inseguro (totter). (Fam., pej.) **Doddering,** chocho.

doddered ['dɒdəd] [do-derd], a. Cubierto de cuscuta o plantas parásitas.

doddery ['dɒdərɪ] [do-de-ri] a. (Coloq.) Temblequeante.

doddle ['dɒdl] [do-del] s. (Fam.) **It's a doddle,** está tirado, está regalado.

dodecagon ['dɒdəkægɒn] [do-de-ka-gon], s. (Geom.) Dodecágono, figura que consta de doce lados iguales.

dodecahedron ['dɒdəkæˌhiːdrən] [do-de-ka-ji-dron], s. (Geom.) Dodecaedro.

dodecatemory ['dɒdəkəˌtemərɪ] [do-de-ka-te-mo-ri], s. (Astr.) Dodecatemoria, la duodécima parte de un círculo o signo del zodíaco.

dodge [dɒdʒ] [dodch], va. 1. Escabullirse, escapar mediante un cambio súbito de posición; evadir, diestramente; eludir (pursuer); esquivar (blow); esquivar, soslayar (question); soslayar (problem, issue); eludir (work, responsibility); evadir (tax). **We dodged our fare,** viajamos sin pagar. 2. Seguir o perseguir mañosa y evasivamente. -vn. Moverse rápidamente a un lado, apartarse. **She dodged behind the car,** se escondió rápidamente detrás del coche. 2. Trampear, entrampar.

dodge s. 1. (Coloq.) Treta, truco, artimaña (trick). 2. Esquive (sidestep).

dodger ['dɒdʒəʳ] [dod-chaʳ], s. 1. Trampista, el que saca de continuo dinero con engaños y estafas. **Tax dodger,** evasor de impuestos. **Fare dodger,** persona que intenta viajar sin pagar en un medio de transporte público. 2. (E. U.) Cartel o anuncio pequeño.

dodgy ['dɒdʒɪ] [dod-chi] a. Arriesgado, riesgoso (risky). **The brakes are a bit dodgy,** los frenos no andan muy bien (unreliable, dubious). **He's a dodgy character,** no es un tipo de fiar.

dodman ['dɒdmən] [dod-man], s. Especie de pescado; caracol.

dodo ['dəʊdəʊ] [dou-dou], s. (Orn.) Dido, ave algo parecida a un palomo de gran tamaño, con alas rudimentarias.

doe [dəʊ] [dou], sf. Gama, la hembra del gamo (of deer); de la liebre, del conejo (of rabbit); del canguro y del antílope.

doer ['duːəʳ] [douaʳ], s. 1. Hacedor, el que hace o ejecuta alguna cosa. **He is a great talker but little doer,** todo se le va por el pico. 2. Actor, agente. 3. La persona que es activa o valiente, emprendedora o dinámica (active person). **Evil-doer,** el que hace mal.

does [dʌz] [das], Tercera persona del verbo TO DO.

doeskin ['dəʊskɪn] [dous-kin], s. 1. Ante, la piel de una gama. 2. Tejido fino de lana.

doff [dɒf] [dof], va. Quitar la ropa, deshacer, sacar. **He doffed the cassock for the cuirass,** él cambió la sotana por la coraza. **To doff one's hat to somebody,** quitarse el sombrero ante alguien. (Contracción de do off).

dog [dɒg] [dog], s. 1. Perro, perra. **Bull-dog,** perro de presa. **Setting-dog,** podenco. **Lap-dog,** perro faldero o perrito de faldas. 2. Perro, nombre que se da por ignominia y afrenta o jocosamente a un hombre. 3. Se usa para designar el macho de algunos animales, v. g. **The dog fox,** el zorro. 4. Herramienta, pequeña pieza que sirve para asir y asegurar, fiador, retén. 5. Morillo, caballete de hierro que se pone en el hogar para sostener la leña. 6. Gatillo de un arma de fuego. **To give/send to the dogs,** echar a perros, dar a los diablos, tirar por la ventana, disipar la hacienda, malbaratar. **To go to the dogs,** estar arruinado. **To make dog's ears in books,** (Fam.) hacer orejones. **To play the dog in the manger,** ser como el perro del hortelano. **A dog's life,** una vida de perros. **It's a case of dog eat dog,** hay una competencia brutal. **To treat somebody like a dog,** tratar a alguien como a un perro. **You can't teach an old dog new tricks,** loro viejo no aprende a hablar. **Dog show,** exposición canina.

dog, va.

dog-bane [dɒgˈbeɪn] [dog-bein], s. (Bot.) Matacán.

dog-brier [dɒgˈbraɪəʳ] [dog-braiAʳ], s. (Bot.) Zarza perruna, escaramujo.

dog-cart ['dɒgkɑːt] [dog-kart], s. Coche de dos ruedas para un caballo, con dos asientos unidos por el respaldo, y espacio para perros debajo de los asientos.

dog-cheap [dɒgˈtʃiːp] [dog-chip], a. Muy barato, a bajo precio, por nada. (Cuba.) De guagua.

dog collar ['dɒgkɒləʳ] [dog-ko-laʳ] s. Alzacuello, clergyman (clerical collar).

dog-days ['dɒgdeɪz] [dog-deis], s. pl. La canícula, los días caniculares, del 15 de Julio al 25 de Agosto.

doge [dəʊdʒ] [douch], s. Dux, jefe de las antiguas repúblicas de Venecia y Génova.

dog-eared ['dɒgɪəd] [dog-iad] a. Sobado y con las esquinas dobladas.

dog-end ['dɒgend] [dog-end] s. Colilla, pucho.

dog-fight ['dɒgfaɪt] [dog-fait], s. Riña de perros (between dogs). (Aviat.) Combate aéreo.

dog-fish ['dɒgfɪʃ] [dog-fish], s. Tiburón.

dogged ['dɒgɪd] [do-guid], a. 1. Duro, inflexible, tenaz; obstinado, emperrado. 2. (Des.) Ceñudo, intratable, áspero.

doggedly ['dɒgɪdlɪ] [do-guid-li], adv. Tenazmente, con dureza; obstinadamente.

doggedness ['dɒgɪdnɪs] [do-guid-nes], s. Tenacidad, inflexibilidad.

dogger ['dɒgəʳ] [do-gaʳ], s. (Mar.) Barca de pescador.

doggerel ['dɒgərəl] [do-gue-rel], a. Prosaico, de bajo estilo, bajo, hablando de versos. -s. Coplas de ciego. Ripios.

doggish ['dɒgɪʃ] [do-guish], a. Perruno, brutal, regañón.

doggo ['dɒgəʊ] [do-gou] adv. **To lie doggo,** quedarse escondido sin hacer ruido.

doggone [ˌdɒgˈgɒn] [do-goun] a. Maldito.

doggy ['dɒgɪ] [do-gui] *s.* Guauguau, perrito (used to or by children). **Doggy bag,** bolsita que proporcionan en algunos restaurantes para llevarse las sobras a casa.

dog-hearted ['dɒgˌhɑːtɪd] [dog-jar-ted], *a.* Sanguinario, cruel, inhumano.

dog-hole ['dɒgˌhəʊl] [dog-joul], **dog-kennel** *s.* **Perrera,** casa de perros; la casa en que se encierran los perros de caza; tabuco, camaranchón.

doghouse ['dɒghaʊs] [dog-jaus] *s.* Casa o casilla, caseta o casucha del perro, perrera. **To be in the doghouse,** haber caído en desgracia. **Don't be a doghouse in the manger,** no seas como el perro del hortelano (que ni come ni deja comer).

dogie ['dɒgɪ] [do-gui], *s.* Ternero huérfano.

dog-keeper ['dɒgkɪːpəʳ] [dog-ki-paʳ], *s.* Perrero.

Dog-Latin ['dɒg'lætɪn] [dog-la-tin], *s.* Latín bárbaro o macarrónico.

dog-leech ['dɒgliːtʃ] [dog-lich], *s.* El albéitar que cura los males de los perros. Se dice también de los malos médicos o cirujanos, por desprecio.

dog-louse ['dɒgləʊz] [dog-lous], *s.* Piojo perruno.

dogma ['dɒgmə] [dog-ma], *s.* Dogma, máxima, axioma; punto de doctrina.

dogmatic, dogmatical [dɒg'mætɪk] [dog-ma-tik] [dɒg'mætɪkl] [dog-ma-ti-kal], *a.* Dogmático, magistral; autoritario, arrogante.

dogmatically [dɒg'mætɪklɪ] [dog-ma-ti-ka-li], *adv.* Dogmáticamente.

dogmaticalness [dɒg'mætɪkəlnɪs] [dog-ma-ti-kal-nes], *s.* Magisterio, calidad de dogmático.

dogmatism ['dɒgmætɪzəm] [dog-ma-ti-sem], *s.* 1. Presunción de los que quieren que sus teorías o aseveraciones, expresadas con imperio y arrogancia, sean aceptadas sin discusión. 2. Escuela filosófica opuesta al escepticismo. 3. Sistema médico de la antigua escuela dogmática.

dogmatist ['dɒgmætɪst] [dog-ma-tist], *s.* Dogmatista, dogmatizador, dogmatizante.

dogmatize ['dɒgmætaɪz] [dog-ma-tais], *vn.* Dogmatizar; afirmar.

dogmatizer ['dɒgmætaɪzəʳ] [dog-ma-tai-saʳ], *s.* Dogmatizador.

do-gooder ['duːˌgʊdəʳ] [du-gu-daʳ] *s.* Hacedor de buenas obras.

dog paddle ['dɒgˌpædl] [dog-pa-del] *s.* Estilo de perro o perrito.

dogsbody ['dɒgzbɒdɪ] [dogs-bo-di] *s.* (*Coloq.*) **I'm just the general dodsbody around here,** yo aquí no soy más que el botones. **I'm fed up with being his dogsbody,** estoy harta de ser su sirvienta.

dog-rose ['dɒgrəʊz] [dog-rous], *s.* (*Bot.*) Escaramujo, rosal silvestre.

dog's-ears ['dɒgzˌɪəz] [dog-iars], *s. pl.* Orejones en los ángulos de las hojas de un libro.

dog-sick ['dɒgsɪk] [dog-sik], *a.* Enfermo o malo como un perro.

dog-skin ['dɒgskɪn] [dog-skin], *a.* Hecho de pellejo de perro.

dog-sleep ['dɒgsliːp] [dog-slip], *s.* Sueño fingido.

dog's-meat ['dɒgzmiːt] [dogs-mit], *s.* Perruna, pan para perros.

dog-star ['dɒgstɑːʳ] [dog-staʳ], *s.* Sirio, canícula, la más brillante de las estrellas fijas; su salida coincide con la del sol en los días caniculares.

dog's-tongue ['dɒgztɒŋ] [dogs-tong], *s.* (*Bot.*) Cinoglosa, hierba medicinal.

dog's tooth ['dɒgztuːθ] [dogs-tuz], *s.* (*Bot.*) Diente de perro.

dog tag ['dɒgtæg] [dog-tag] *s.* (*Mil.*) Placa de identificación.

dog-teeth ['dɒgtiːθ] [dog-tiz], *s. pl.* Dientes caninos.

dog-tired ['dɒgtaɪəd] [dog-taiad], *a.* Rendido de cansancio.

dog-trick ['dɒgtrɪk] [dog-trik], *s.* Perrería, tratamiento brutal.

dog-trot ['dɒgtrɒt] [dog-trot], *s.* Trote lento, como el de un perro.

dog-watch ['dɒgwɒtʃ] [dog-uach], *s.* (*Mar.*) Una de las dos guardias de a bordo, de dos horas cada una, entre las cuatro de la tarde y las ocho de la noche.

dog-weary ['dɒgwɛərɪ] [dog-uea-ri], *a.* Cansado como un perro.

doily ['dɔɪlɪ] [doi-li], *a.* 1. Especie de servilleta pequeña para los postres, o para colocar sobre ellas floreros, jarrones, etc.; tapete, pañito, carpeta (under plate, ornament); blonda (on plate). 2. (*Des.*) Especie de tela de lana.

doing ['duːɪŋ] [duin] *s.* **It'll take a bit/lot of doing,** va a dar un poco de/mucho trabajo. **That takes some doing,** eso no es nada fácil. **It was none of our doing,** nosotros no tuvimos nada que ver (action).

doings ['duːɪŋz] [duins], *s. pl.* Hechos, acciones; eventos; acontecimientos; bullicio; función. Actividades (activities, events).

doit ['dɔɪt] [duit], *s.* Moneda pequeña de muy poco valor.

do-it-yourself ['duːɪtjəˈself] [duit-yur-self] *s.* Bricolaje. **Do-it-yourself enthusiast,** aficionado al bricolaje, bricolero.

doldrums ['dɒldrəmz] [dol-drams] *s.* **To be in the doldrums,** estar de capa caída.

dole [dəʊl] [doul], *s.* 1. Distribución, repartimiento. **The dole,** el subsidio de desempleo, el paro, la cesantía. **To be on the dole,** estar cobrando subsidio de desempleo o de cesantía, estar en el paro. 2. Parte, porción; dádiva, don. 3. Limosna u otra cosa repartida. 4. Dolor, angustia, congoja. 5. Golpes. 6. (*Ant.*) Miseria. 7. Límite, linde. 8. Vacío en la cría de ganado.

dole, *va.* Repartir, distribuir.

dole out Dar, repartir (food, money).

doleful ['dəʊlfʊl] [doul-ful], *a.* Doloroso, lastimoso, lúgubre (sound, voice); triste, compungido (face, look).

dolefulness ['dəʊlfəlnɪs] [doul-ful-nes], *s.* Tristeza, melancolía; miseria.

dolent ['dəʊlənt] [dou-lent], *a.* Doliente.

dolerite ['dəʊlərɪt] [dou-le-rit], *s.* (*Min.*) Dolerita, roca granítica de color negruzco.

dolesome ['dəʊlsʌm] [doul-sam], *a.* Lastimoso, triste.

dolesomely [dəʊl'sʌməlɪ] [doul-sa-me-li], *adv.* Desconsoladamente, tristemente.

do-little ['duːlɪtl] [du-litel], *s.* Capitán araña, manda mucho y no hace nada; nombre despectivo con que se moteja al que hablando mucho obra poco.

doll [dɒl] [dol], *s.* 1. Muñeca (toy). 2. Muñeca (pretty little girl); muñeca (attractive woman); encanto (pleasant person). 3. Abreviatura de Dorothy o Dorotea.

dollar ['dɒləʳ] [do-laʳ], *s.* Dólar, moneda de los Estados Unidos de América y el Canadá. **Hard dollar,** peso duro o fuerte. **Current dollar,** peso sencillo. **It's dollars to doughnuts they'll come,** te apuesto lo que quieras a que vienen. (*Coloq.*) **To be as sound as a dollar,** funcionar como un reloj (heart, engine); estar como un toro (person). **She looked like a million dollars,** estaba despampanante. **Top dollar,** el mejor precio, sueldo, etc.

dollhouse ['dɒlhaʊs] [dol-jaus] (GB) **doll's house** *s.* Casa de muñecas.

dollop ['dɒləp] [do-lop] *s.* (*Coloq.*) Cucharada (served with a spoon); porción (serving, mesure).

dolly ['dɒlɪ] [do-li], *s.* 1. Muñequita (used to or by children). 2. Relinchador. 3. Plataforma con rodillos para cargar cosas pesadas.

dolman ['dəʊlmæn] [doul-man], *s.* 1. Dolmán, prenda exterior de vestir de los turcos, larga, abierta por delante y de mangas ceñidas. 2. Dormán, especie de chaqueta corta, adornada con alamares; chaqueta de húsar. 3. Capa de mangas perdidas que usan las mujeres.

dolmen ['dəʊlmən] [dol-men], *s.* Dolmen, monumento druídico consistente en una gran piedra sobrepuesta a dos o más verticales.

dolomite ['dɒləmaɪt] [do-lo-mait], *s.* Dolomita, caliza magnesiana.

dolomitic ['dɒləmaɪtɪk] [do-lo-mai-tik], *a.* Dolomítico, que contiene dolomita o es parecido a ella.

dolor [ˈdɒlərˀ] [do-laˀ], *s.* Dolor, angustia; llanto.

doloriferous [ˈdɒlərɪfərəs] [do-lo-ri-fe-ros], **dolorific, dolorifical** [ˈdɒlərɪfɪk] [do-lo-ri-fik], *a.* Doloroso; triste, lúgubre.

dolorous [ˈdɒlərəs] [do-lo-ros], *s.* Doloroso, lastimoso, lamentable.

dolphin [ˈdɒlfɪn] [dol-fin], *s.* 1. Delfín, cetáceo. Cf PORPOISE. 2. Pez grande de alta mar, notable por sus cambios de color cuando se le saca del agua. 3. La constelación boreal Delfín.

dolt [ˈdəʊlt] [doult], *s.* El hombre bobo, tonto o imbécil.

doltishness [ˈdəʊltɪʃnɪs] [doul-tish-nes], *s.* Estupidez, tontería, imbecilidad.

domain [dəˈmeɪn] [dou-mein], *s.* 1. Dominio, imperio, soberanía. 2. Bienes, estados, posesión de tierras. 3. Campo, esfera (sphere of influence, activity). **In the public domain,** del dominio público.

domal [ˈdəʊməl] [dou-mal] *a.* Lo perteneciente a la casa; se usa en astrología.

dome [ˈdəʊm] [doum], *s.* 1. (*Arq.*) Cúpula, cimborrio, dombo, domo, media naranja. 2. Toda cubierta en forma de copa invertida o de cimborrio. 3. (*Poét.*) Casa, edificio majestuoso.

domed [ˈdəʊmd] [doumd] *a.* Con cúpula (building); abovedado (roof).

domestic, domestical [dəˈmestɪk] [do-mes-tik] *a.* 1. Doméstico, de la casa, de la familia; familiar (life, problems); casero, hogareño (home-loving). **They live in domestic bliss,** la felicidad de su hogar es perfecta. **Domestic violence,** violencia en el hogar. 2. Civil, intestino. 3. Domesticado y domado por el hombre (animal). 4. (*Econ., Pol.*) Interno (affairs, policy, market); nacional (produce). **Domestic flight,** vuelo nacional.

domestic, *s.* Doméstico, criado, sirviente.

domestically [dəˈmestɪkəlɪ] [do-mes-ti-ka-li], *adv.* Domésticamente.

domesticate [dəˈmestɪkeɪt] [do-mes-ti-keit], *va.* Domesticar, acostumbrar a un animal salvaje a la vista y compañía del hombre. -*vn.* Adquirir costumbres y gustos domésticos.

domesticated [dəˈmestɪkeɪtɪd] [do-mes-ti-kei-tid] *a.* 1. Domesticado (animal, species). 2. **He's not very domesticated,** no es un hombre muy de su casa (of person).

domesticity [ˌdəʊmesˈtɪsɪtɪ] [do-mes-ti-si-ti], *s.* Calidad de doméstico, domesticidad.

domestic science *s.* Economía doméstica.

domicile [ˈdɒmɪsaɪl] [do-mi-sail], *s.* Domicilio, casa, habitación permanente de un individuo o una familia. **To have domicile in England,** estar domiciliado en Inglaterra. -*va.* Domiciliarse, establecer una residencia fija.

dominance [ˈdɒmɪnəns] [do-mi-nans] *s.* 1. Dominio, dominación (supremacy). 2. Predominio, preponderancia (predominance).

dominant [ˈdɒmɪnənt] [do-mi-nant], *a.* 1. Dominante (more powerful/nation, influence). 2. Predominante, preponderante (predominant/crop, industry). 3. (*Biol., Ecol.*) Dominante.

dominate [ˈdɒmɪneɪt] [do-mi-neit], *vn.* Dominar, predominar. -*va.* Gobernar, dominar (have control). **To dominate over something,** predominar sobre algo (predominate).

domination [ˌdɒmɪˈneɪʃən] [do-mi-nei-shon], *s.* Dominación, imperio; tiranía; gobierno, autoridad.

dominative [ˈdɒmɪnətɪv] [do-mi-na-tiv], *a.* Dominativo, dominante; imperioso, altivo.

dominator [ˈdɒmɪneɪtərˀ] [do-mi-nei-taˀ], *s.* Dominador; gobernador.

domine [ˈdɒmɪn] [do-min], *s.* Clérigo, eclesiástico.

domineer [ˌdɒmɪˈnɪərˀ] [do-mi-niaˀ], *vn.* Dominar, señorear, mandar, avasallar. -*va.* Gobernar.

domineering [ˌdɒmɪˈnɪərɪŋ] [do-mi-nia-rin] *a.* Dominante.

dominical [dəˈmɪnɪkl] [do-mi-ni-kal], *a.* Dominical, perteneciente a los días consagrados al Señor. -*s.* Domínica.

Dominican [dəˈmɪnɪkən] [do-mi-ni-kan] *a.* 1. (*Rel.*) Dominico, domínico. 2. Dominicano (from the Dominican Republic).

Dominican Republic [dəˈmɪnɪkənrɪˈpʌblɪk] [do-mi-ni-kan-ri-pa-blik] *s.* La República Dominicana.

dominie [dəˈmɪniː] [do-mi-ni], *s.* 1. Dómine, maestro de escuela, pedagogo. 2.(*Fam.*) V. DOMINE.

dominion [dəˈmɪnɪən] [do-mi-nion], *s.* 1. Dominio (power); soberanía, imperio, gobierno; potencia. **To have/hold dominion over something/somebody,** tener/mantener algo/a alguien bajo dominio. 2. Territorio, distrito. 3. Predominio, ascendiente.

domino [ˈdɒmɪnəʊ] [do-mi-nou], *s.* 1. Dominó, traje talar para máscaras. 2. Pieza del juego de dominó (counter). 3. *pl.* DOMINOES. Dominó, juego en que se emplean veintiocho fichas rectangulares, numeradas de uno a seis. **Domino effect,** efecto dominó.

don [dɒn] [don], *va.* Vestir, revestir; ponerse una prenda sobre otra. Abrev. de *Do on.*

don, *s.* 1. Don, antes título honorífico y de dignidad en España y hoy tratamiento usual y corriente, como Señor, o Mister en inglés. 2. Profesor universitario (esp. in Oxford and Cambridge). *va.* Ponerse (put on).

donary [ˈdɒnərɪ] [do-na-ri], *s.* Donación piadosa.

donate [dəˈneɪt] [dou-neit], *va.* Donar, hacer una donación o dádiva, particularmente cuando es de considerable valor.

donation [dəˈneɪʃən] [dou-nei-shon], *s.* Donación (act); don, dádiva, presente, regalo (gift).

donatism [ˈdɒnətɪzm] [do-na-tisem], *s.* Donatismo, herejía de los donatistas.

donatist [ˈdɒnətɪst] [do-na-tist], *s.* Donatista.

donative [ˈdɒnətɪv] [do-na-tiv], *s.* Donativo, don, presente, dádiva.

donator [ˈdɒneɪtərˀ] [do-nei-taˀ], *s.* Donador.

done [dʌn] [dan], *pp.* del verbo TO DO. 1. Hecho, ejecutado, llevado a cabo (finished). **I must have this done by five o'clock,** tengo que tener esto hecho o terminado para las cinco. 2. Acabado, concluído. 3. Bien cocido o asado (cooked). 4. Fatigado, consumido; lastimado mortalmente o gravemente enfermo. **That may be done,** lo que es factible, lo que puede hacerse (accepted). **That turkey is not done enough,** ese pavo no está bastante cocido o asado. **To have done with,** finalizar, concluir, acabar; cesar de, cortar relaciones. -*adv.* (*Fam.*) De acuerdo; corriente, convenido, adelante.

done, *inter.* Cosa hecha, muy bien; ya está; expresión que denota conformidad con lo que alguno dice o propone, o bien la conclusión de alguna cosa. ¡Trato hecho!, ¡vale!

donee [dəˈniː] [do-ni], *s.* Donatario, el que recibe una donación.

donjon, *s. V.* DUNGEON.

donkey [ˈdɒŋkɪ] [don-ki], *s.* Asno, burro, borrico. (*Coloq.*) **Donkey's years,** siglos. **Donkey jacket,** chaquetón de trabajo con un refuerzo impermeable en los hombros. (*Coloq.*) **Donkey work,** trabajo pesado.

donnerd [ˈdɒnɜːd] [do-nerd], *s.* (*Esco.*) Persona perezosa e inútil; diablo.

donor [ˈdɒnərˀ] [do-noˀ], *s.* Donador, dador.

donship [ˈdɒnʃɪp] [don-ship], *s.* Nobleza, caballería, la calidad o rango de caballero.

don't *abrev.de DO NOT.*

donzel, *s.* (*Des.*) Paje, doncel.

doodle [ˈduːdl] [du-del], *va.* y *vn.* Borrajear, garrapatear, garabatear. *s.* Garabato.

doom [duːm] [dum], *va.* 1. Sentenciar, mandar, juzgar, ordenar judicialmente. 2. Destinar, determinar, resolver absolutamente; condenar (fate). **The project was doomed from the start,** el proyecto estaba condenado al fracaso desde el principio. **Doomed,** condenado, sentenciado (man). **Doomed to failure,** predestinado o condenado al fracaso.

doom, *s.* 1. Sentencia, juicio, condena. 2. Determinación. 3. Suerte, destino, hado; sino (fate); muerte (death); fatalidad (ruin). 4. Perdición, ruina. **The crack of doom,** la señal del juicio final. **The profets of doom,** los catastrofistas o agoreros.

doomsday ['duːmzdeɪ] [dums-dei], *s.* Día del juicio universal.

doomsday-book [,duːmzdeɪ'bʊk] [dums-dei-buk], *s.* Gran catastro de Inglaterra, libro hecho por orden del rey Guillermo I de Inglaterra, en el cual se registraban todas las tierras feudales del reino.

door [dɔːʳ] [doʳ], *s.* 1. Puerta. **To knock at the door,** tocar o llamar a la puerta. **To turn out of doors,** echar de casa. **She was at the door,** estaba en la puerta. **The meeting went on behind closed doors,** la reunión se celebró a puerta(s) cerrada(s). 2. Portal o zaguán; entrada, pasillo (doorway, entrance). **Tickets are available at the door,** se pueden comprar las localidades en la puerta o a la entrada. **Doors open at six,** entrada a partir de las seis. 3. Avenida. 4. *(Fam.)* Casa. **Back door,** puerta trasera. *(Fam.)* Puerta falsa. 5. Puerta (means of access). **When one door shuts, another opens,** donde una puerta se cierra, otra se abre. **To lock the door,** cerrar la puerta con llave; echar llave a la puerta. **Out of doors,** fuera de casa, en la calle, al aire libre. **Doorbell,** campanilla de puerta; timbre. **Door-jam,** jamba de puerta, quicial. **Door knob,** pomo de la puerta. **Doormat,** felpudo de puerta, estera para limpiarse los pies. **I'm fed up with being a doormat,** estoy harta de que me pisoteen. **Doorplate,** plancha con el nombre del que habita una casa. **Doorsill, doorstep,** umbral. **To lie at one's door,** ser carga para alguno, imponerle responsabilidad. **To go from door to door,** ir de puerta en puerta.

doorcase ['dɔːkeɪs] [dor-keis], *s.* Marco de la puerta.

doorframe ['dɔːfreɪm] [dor-freim], *s.* Dintel o marco de una puerta.

doorkeeper ['dɔːkiːpəʳ] [dor-ki-paʳ], *s.* Portero.

door-nail ['dɔːneɪl] [dor-neil], *s.* Clavo sobre el cual golpea el aldabón o llamador de una puerta.

door-post ['dɔːpəʊst] [dor-poust], *s.* Jamba, puerta.

doorway ['dɔːweɪ] [dor-uei] *s.* Entrada, puerta, portal. **The doorway to fulfillment,** la senda o el camino que lleva a la realización.

dope [dəʊp] [doup], *s.* 1. Narcótico, droga heroica (drugs); hachís, chocolate (cannabis). 2. *(Fam.)* Información, datos sobre alguna cosa (information). **So what's the dope on Brian?,** ¿qué hay de Brian? 3. *(Fam.)* Zonzo, tonto; imbécil, tarugo (stupid person). 4. *(Dep.)* Estimulante, droga, doping; antidoping (test).

dope *va. (Coloq.)* Dopar, drogar (person, racehorse); poner droga en (food, drink).

dopehead ['dəʊphed] [doup-jed] *s. (Sl.)* Drogata, pichicatero, grifo.

dopey, dopy ['dəʊpɪ] [dou-pi] *a. (Coloq.)* Lelo, bobo (stupid); atontado, grogui (befuddled).

dor, dor-bug [dɔːbʌg] [dor-bag], *s.* Escarabajo estercolero que produce fuerte zumbido al volar.

dorian ['dɔːrɪən] [do-rian], **doric** [do-rik] *a.* Dórico, lo que pertenece a los dóricos.

doricism ['dɔːrɪsɪzm] [do-ri-si-zem], **dorism** ['dɔːrɪzm] [do-ri-sem] *s.* Frase peculiar del dialecto dórico.

dormancy ['dɔːmənsɪ] [dor-man-si], *s.* Quietud, descanso.

dormant ['dɔːmənt] [dor-mant], *a.* 1. Durmiente. 2. Secreto, oculto; latente (idea, emotion). 3. Sin movimiento, parado, sin giro. Aletargado (animal, plant); inactivo (volcano). 4. Inusitado; ineficaz.

dormant, dormer ['dɔːməʳ] [dor-maʳ], *s.* 1. Viga maestra. 2. **Dormer-window,** buharda, ventana de guardilla o desván.

dormitory ['dɔːmɪtərɪ] [dor-mi-to-ri], *s.* 1. Dormitorio (in school, hostel); edificio perteneciente a un colegio o escuela y destinado a estudiar y dormir, también, cualquier pieza de gran tamaño donde duermen varias personas. **Dormitory town/suburb,** ciudad/barrio dormitorio. 2. Residencia de estudiantes (students' residence). *(Mex.)* Recámara.

dormouse ['dɔːmaʊs] [dor-maus], *s.* Lirón; en plural DORMICE

dorr [dɔːʳ] [doʳ], *s.* V. DOR.

dorsad ['dɔːsæd] [dor-sad], *adv. (Anat. y Zool.)* Hacia la espalda, atrás.

dorsal ['dɔːsl] [dor-sal], *a.* Dorsal, perteneciente al dorso, espalda o lomo; colocado en o cerca de la espalda.

dorsel, dorser *s.* Serón, especie de sera o espuerta.

dorsiferous, dorsiparous ['dɔːsɪfərəs] [dor-si-fe-ros], *a.* 1. Que lleva algo a la espalda o lomo. 2. *(Bot.)* Dorsífero, se dice de las plantas que tienen las semillas en el dorso de las hojas.

dorsum ['dɔːsəm] [dor-som], *s.* 1. Dorso, revés o espalda de alguna cosa. 2. Cuesta.

DOS *s.* (= disc-operating system) DOS.

dosage ['dəʊsɪdʒ] [dou-sidch], *s.* La administración de un medicamento en dosis regulares. **Dosage: one every three hours,** posología: uno cada tres horas.

dose [dəʊs] [dous], *s.* 1. Dosis (of medication). **He's fine in small doses,** se le puede aguantar en pequeñas dosis. *(Coloq.)* **Like a dose of salts,** en menos que canta un gallo. 2. Porción (portion, amount). *(Coloq.)* **A bad dose of flu,** una gripe muy mala.

dose, *va.* Disponer las dosis de un remedio cualquiera; proporcionar un medicamento al estado o fuerza del enfermo. **I'm all dosed up with painkillers,** me he tomado no sé cuántos analgésicos.

doss [dɒs] [dos] *vn. (Coloq.)* Dormir (sleep); haraganear, rascarse, flojear (be lazy).

dossal, dosel ['dɒsl] [dou-sal], *s.* Retablo, colgaduras o tapices ricos colocados detrás del altar.

dosser ['dɒsəʳ] [dou-saʳ] *s. (Coloq.)* Vagabundo (tramp); vago, flojo, manta (idler).

dosshouse ['dɒshaʊs] [dos-haus] *s.* (GB) *(Coloq.)* Albergue para vagabundos o pobres.

dossier ['dɒsɪeɪ] [do-siei] *s.* Dossier, expediente.

dost [dʌst] [dost], Segunda persona del singular del presente indicativo del verbo *To Do;* forma solemne o arcaica.

dot [dɒt] [dot] *s.* 1. Tilde, vírgula o nota que se pone sobre alguna letra; punto (spot). **On the dot,** en punto. **Dot dot dot,** puntos suspensivos. 2. *(Mús.)* Punto que puesto después de una nota aumenta o prolonga su valor en una mitad. 3. Punto (in Morse code).

dot, *va.* 1. Tildar, poner tildes a las letras que los deben tener; puntuar. 2. Salpicar (scatter). **Her family is dotted about all over Europe,** su familia está desperdigada por toda Europa. **Dotted,** de puntos (line). **To sign on the dotted line,** firmar la línea punteada o de puntos. 3. *(Mús.)* Con puntillo (note).

dotage ['dəʊtɪdʒ] [dou-tich], *s.* 1. Chochera, chochez, debilidad de juicio. **To be in one's dotage,** estar chocho, chochear. 2. Cariño excesivo. 3. Extravagancia, delirio, visiones, desvarío.

dotal [dɒtl] [do-tal], *a.* Dotal, lo que pertenece a la dote.

dotard ['dɒtɑːd] [do-tard], *s.* El viejo que chochea.

dotardly ['dɒtɑːdlɪ] [do-tard-li], *a.* Estúpido, chocho.

dotation [dɒ'teɪʃən] [do-tei-shon], *s.* 1. Dotación, la acción y efecto de dotar. 2. Dotación, la consignación de renta perpetua para algún establecimiento, fundación, etc.

dote [dəʊt] [dout], *vn.* Chochear, caducar. **To dote upon,** amar con exceso; poner el corazón en alguna persona.

doter ['dəʊtəʳ] [dou-taʳ] *s.* El que ama con exceso. V. DOTARD.

doth [dʌθ] [doz], Tercera persona del singular del presente indicativo del verbo *To Do;* forma solemne o arcaica.

doting ['dəʊtɪŋ] [dou-tin], *a.* Choco, excesivamente cariñoso. **His doting mother,** su madre, que lo adora.

dotingly ['dəʊtɪŋlɪ] [dou-tin-li], *adv.* Con cariño excesivo, ciegamente.

dot matrix [dɒt'meɪtrɪks] [dot-mei-triks] *s.* Matriz de puntos. **Dot-matrix printer,** impresora matricial.

dottard ['dɒtɑːd] [do-tard], *s. (Ant.)* Árbol bajo o decaído.

dotterel ['dɒtərəl] [do-te-rel], *s. (Orn.)* Calandria marina.

dotty ['dɒtɪ] [do-ti] *a. (Coloq.)* Chiflado (person); descabellada (idea).

double ['dʌbl] [da-bel], *a.* 1. Doble, doblado, duplicado. **A double brandy,** un coñac doble. **We get double pay on**

Sundays, los domingos nos pagan el doble. **To be double the age of,** tener doble edad que. 2. Doble (dual); falso (false); traidor, engañoso. **A double purpose,** un doble propósito. **To lead a double life,** llevar una doble vida. 3. Doble (for two/room); de matrimonio, de dos plazas (bed). 4. Doble (folded). **To fold something double,** doblar algo por la mitad. **He was bent double with the pain,** se retorcía de dolor. -*adv.* Dos veces; el doble (twice as much/pay, earn, cost). **She spends double what she earns,** gasta el doble de lo que gana. **To see double,** ver el doble (two together).

double, *va.* 1. Doblar, duplicar, multiplicar por dos (increase twofold/earnings, profits). Redoblar (efforts). **I'd double the amount of sugar,** yo le pondría el doble de azúcar. **I'll double that offer,** yo ofrezco el doble. 2. Doblar, plegar; por lo común con *up, over, etc.* 3. Redoblar, repetir. 4. Ser dos veces otra cosa. 5. *(Games)* Doblar (stake, call, bid). **To double a cape** *(Mar.)* doblar o montar un cabo. **To double a ship's bottom,** *(Mar.)* Embonar. -*vn.* 1. Doblarse, duplicarse (increase twofold/price, amount). 2. Jugar una mala partida o pegar petardo. 3. Disimular, usar de artificios, obrar con doblez. 4. Volver atrás. 5. **The table doubles as a desk,** la mesa también se usa como escritorio (have dual role).

double back Volver sobre sus pasos (person, animal). **The path doubled back on itself,** el camino doblaba sobre sí mismo.

double up 1. Doblar (redouble). 2. **To double up with laughter,** morirse o desternillarse de risa (bend). **She was doubled up with pain,** se retorcía de dolor.

double, *s.* 1. Doble (hotel room); duplo. Doble (of spirits). **I'll have a double,** déme uno doble. 2. Pliegue, doblez en la ropa. 3. Doblez; impostura, engaño, treta, artificio. 4. Duplicado, semejanza, homónimo, doble (lookalike); *(Fig.)* aparecido, fantasma. **His double,** su mismo retrato. 5. Doble (in bridge, dice, dominoes, darts); doble, doblete (in baseball). 6. *(Mil.)* **At/on the double,** a paso ligero. **Come here at the double!,** ¡ven aquí inmediatamente!

doubleact [ˈdʌblˈækt] [da-bel-akt] *s.* **They do/are a doubleact,** actuan en pareja.

double agent [ˈdʌblˈeɪdʒənt] [da-bel-ei-yent] *s.* Doble agente.

double-barreled [ˈdʌblˈbærəld] [da-bel-ba-reld], *a.* 1. De dos cañones (shotgun). 2. *(Fig.)* De dos propósitos. 3. Compuesto (surname).

double-bass [ˈdʌblˈbeɪs] [da-bel-beis], *s.* Contrabajo, instrumento grande de cuerda, de la figura de un violín.

double bill [ˈdʌblˈbɪl] [da-bel-bil] *s.* Programa doble.

double boiler [ˈdʌblˈbɔɪləʳ] [da-bel-boi-laʳ], *s.* Baño María.

double-book [ˈdʌblˈbʊk] [da-bel-buk] *va.* **The room had been double-booked,** la habitación ha sido reservada para dos personas distintas. **Double booking,** doble reserva. **We have a double booking for the 27th,** nos hemos comprometido con dos personas a la vez para el 27.

double-buttoned [ˈdʌblˈbʌtənd] [da-bel-ba-tond], *a.* Lo que tiene dos hileras de botones.

double-charge [ˈdʌblˈtʃɑːdʒ] [da-bel-charch], *va.* Echar doble carga.

double-check [ˈdʌblˈtʃek] [da-bel-chek] *vn.* Volver a mirar, verificar dos veces. *va.* Volver a revisar (facts, information).

double-chin [ˈdʌblˈtʃɪn] [da-bel-chin], *s.* Papada.

double cream [ˈdʌblˈkriːm] [da-bel-krim] *s.* Crema doble, nata para montar, doble crema.

double-dealer [ˌdʌblˈdiːləʳ] [da-bel-di-laʳ], *s.* Hombre doble, traidor y falso; engañador, embustero.

double-dealing [ˈdʌblˈdiːlɪŋ] [da-bel-di-lin], *s.* Doblez, trato doble, simulación, dolo, fraude.

double-decker (bus) [ˈdʌblˈdekəʳ] [da-bel-de-kaʳ], Autobús de dos pisos. **Double-decker (sandwich),** sandwich doble o de dos pisos.

double-dye [ˈdʌblˈdaɪ] [da-bel-dai], *va.* Reteñir.

double-eagle [ˌdʌblˈiːgl] [da-bel-i-guel], *s.* Moneda de oro de los Estados Unidos; su valor es de dos águilas o 20 pesos.

double-edged [ˈdʌblˈedʒd] [da-bel-echt], *a.* Instrumento de dos cortes o filos; de doble filo (knife, blade, scheme); de doble sentido (remark, comment).

double-ender [ˈdʌblˈendəʳ] [da-bel-en-daʳ], *s.* Lo que tiene las dos extremidades parecidas, como un vapor de río, una canoa.

double-entry [ˈdʌblˈentrɪ] [da-bel-en-tri], *s.* *(Com.)* Partida doble.

double-eyed [ˈdʌblˈaɪd] [da-bel-aid], *a.* El que mostrando bondad en su semblante es áspero y cruel.

double-faced [ˈdʌblˈfeɪst] [da-bel-feist], *a.* De dos caras: pérfido, doble.

double feature [ˈdʌblˈfiːtʃəʳ] [da-bel-fi-chaʳ], *s.* Dos películas cinematográficas en una sola función, programa doble.

double-formed [ˈdʌblˈfɔːmd] [da-bel-formd], *a.* Biforme.

double-glaze [ˌdʌblˈgleɪz] [da-bel-gleis] *va.* Instalar doble ventana en. **Double glazing,** doble ventana.

double-hearted [ˈdʌblˈhɑːtɪd] [da-bel-jar-tid], *a.* Pérfido, doble, disimulado.

double-lock [ˈdʌblˈlɒk] [da-bel-lok], *va.* Echar dos vueltas a la llave.

double-meaning [ˈdʌblˈmiːnɪŋ] [da-bel-mi-nin], *s.* Ambigüedad, equívoco, sentido doble. -*a.* Con dos sentidos, ambiguo, de doble sentido.

double-minded [ˈdʌblˈmaɪndɪd] [da-bel-main-did], *a.* Insidioso, doloso, indeciso, irresoluto. *(Fam.)* Dos caras.

doubleness [ˈdʌblnɪs] [da-bel-nes], *s.* Doblez, dobladura.

double-parked [ˌdʌblˈpɑːkt] [da-bel-parkt] *a.* Estacionado o aparcado en doble fila.

double play [ˌdʌblˈpleɪ] [da-bel-plei], *s.* Maniobra en el beisbol que pone fuera de juego a dos jugadores.

double-quick [ˌdʌblˈkwɪk] [da-bel-kuik], *a.* *(Mil.)* A paso redoblado. -*s.* Marcha o movimiento a razón de unos 165 a 180 pasos por minuto, cada paso de una vara (33 pulgadas). Hoy sustituído en los Estados Unidos por *double-time. adv.* *(Coloq.)* Volando.

doubler [ˈdʌbləʳ] [da-blaʳ], *s.* El que dobla alguna cosa.

doubles [ˈdʌblz] [da-bels], *s. pl.* Juego de dobles en el tenis.

double standard [ˌdʌblˈstædəd] [da-bel-stan-dard] *s.* **To apply/have double standards,** aplicar una ley para unos y otra para otros.

doublet [ˈdʌblɪt] [da-blit], *s.* 1. Par, pareja. 2. Justillo, almilla; casaca; prenda de vestir de los siglos XV a XVII.

double time [ˌdʌblˈtaɪm] [da-bel-taim], *s.* 1. *(Mil.)* Paso doble, muy rápido. 2. *(Neg.)* Paga doble. **On Sundays we're on double time,** los domingos nos dan paga doble o nos pagan el doble.

double-tongued [ˌdʌblˈtɒŋd] [da-bel-tongd], *a.* Doble, falso, engañoso. *(Fam.)* Doslenguas.

doubling [ˈdʌblɪŋ] [da-blin], *s.* Vuelta para huir, rodeo; artificio. **Doubling of the gits,** *(Mar.)* Almohadas de las bitas. **Doubling of a ship's bottom,** *(Mar.)* embón, refuerzo del fondo de un buque. **Doubling of the cutwater,** *(Mar.)* batideros de proa.

doubloon [ˈdʌbluːn] [da-blun], *s.* Doblón, moneda antigua de oro.

doubly [ˈdʌblɪ] [da-bli], *adv.* 1. Doblemente, en doble, por duplicado (difficult, dangerous, interesting). **Make doubly sure you lock the door,** asegúrate bien de cerrar la puerta. 2. Con doblez, disimuladamente, dolosamente.

doubt [daʊt] [daut], *vn.* Dudar, temer, recelar, sospechar, vacilar. -*va.* Dudar de (fact, truth); dudar (consider unlikely); temer, desconfiar. **I doubted my own eyes,** no daba crédito a mis propios ojos. **I very much doubt it,** lo dudo mucho. **I doubt he'll agree,** dudo que vaya a acceder.

doubt, *s.* Duda, incertidumbre (uncertainty); escrúpulo, sospecha, dificultad, reparo. **No doubt she'll phone,** con seguridad que llama, seguro que llama. **To entertain doubts of, as to,** recelarse de, concebir dudas sobre. *(Law)* **Beyond reasonable doubt,** más allá de toda duda fundada. **When in doubt,** en caso de duda. **I have my doubts,** tengo mis dudas.

doubtable [ˈdaʊtəbl] [dau-ta-bol], *a.* Dudable.

doubter [ˈdaʊtəʳ] [dau-taʳ], *s.* El que duda, escéptico.

doubtful [ˈdaʊtfʊl] [daut-ful], *a.* 1. Dudoso (in doubt); dudable, ambiguo, incierto, receloso. **The outcome remains doubtful,** el resultado sigue siendo dudoso o incierto. 2. De indecisión o duda, dubitativo. **I'm doubtful as to its value,** tengo mis dudas acerca de su valor. 3. Dudoso (questionable). **A man of doubtful character,** un hombre de moral dudosa.

doubtfully [ˈdaʊtfʊlɪ] [daut-fu-li], *adv.* Dudosamente, ambiguamente; sin convicción (say); con reserva (agree).

doubtfulness [ˈdaʊtfʊlnɪs] [daut-ful-nes], *s.* Duda, ambigüedad; incertidumbre, irresolución.

doubting [ˈdaʊtɪŋ] [dautin], *s.* Duda, dubitación.

doubtingly [ˈdaʊtɪŋlɪ] [dau-tin-li], *adv.* Dudosamente.

doubtless [ˈdaʊtlɪs] [daut-les], *a.* Seguro, confiado. -*adv.* Indubitablemente, sin duda.

doubtlessly [ˈdaʊtlɪslɪ] [daut-les-li], *adv.* Indubitablemente.

douce [duːs] [dus], *a. (Esco.)* 1. Serio, reposado, no frívolo. 2. *(Des.)* Dulce.

doucet [ˈduːsɪt] [du-sit], *s.* Flan, una especie de manjar dulce.

douceur [duːˈsɜːʳ] [du-saʳ], *s.* Halago, señuelo; cohecho; premio, recompensa; gratificación.

douche [duːʃ] [dush], *s.* 1. Ducha, chorro de agua dirigido sobre una parte del cuerpo. Irrigación o ducha vaginal (jet of liquid) 2. *(Fr.)* Instrumento para administrar la ducha. Irrigador vaginal (syringe).

dough [dəʊ] [dau], *s.* 1. *(Culin.)* Masa, amasijo (para hacer pan, bollos, etc.). 2. Masa, mezcla pastosa, como de arcilla, etc. 3. *(Sl.)* Guita, lana, plata, pasta (money). **My cake is dough,** me he llevado chasco, mi empresa se ha frustrado.

doughnut [ˈdəʊnʌt] [do-not], *s.* Especie de rosquilla o buñuelo frito.

doughtiness [ˈdaʊtɪnɪs] [do-ti-nes], *s.* Valentía, esfuerzo.

doughty [ˈdaʊtɪ] [dau-ti], *a.* 1. Bravo, valeroso; esforzado; ilustre, noble. 2. Jactancioso, fanfarrón.

doghy [ˈdəʊɪ] [daui], *a.* Crudo, blando.

douse [daʊz] [daus], *va.* 1. Zambullir. *V.* DUCK 2. Dar, dar golpes. 3. *(Mar.)* Recoger; arriar. 4. (Ger. de marineros) Extinguir. Sofocar (flames). **He doused himself with petrol,** se roció con gasolina. -*vn.* Zambullirse, caer de repente dentro del agua.

dove [dʌv] [dav], *s.* Palomo o paloma.

dove's-foot [dʌvzˈfuːt] [davs-fut], *s.* *(Bot.)* Geranio columbino.

dove-cot [dʌvkɒt] [dav-kot], **dove-house** [dʌvˈhaʊs] [dav-jaus], *s.* Palomar.

dovelike [dʌv] [dav], *a.* Columbino.

dovetail [dʌvˈteɪl] [dav-teil], *s.* Cola de milano, o de pato. -*va.* Ensamblar a cola de pato o de milano, machihembrar.

dovetailed [dʌvˈteɪlɪd] [dav-tei-lid], *a.* Ensamblado.

dovish [ˈdʌvɪʃ] [da-vish], *a.* Columbino, inocente como el palomo.

dowable [ˈdaʊəbl] [daua-bol], *a.* Capaz de ser dotado.

dowager [ˈdaʊədʒəʳ] [daua-chaʳ], *s.* La viuda que goza el título de su marido. **Queen dowager,** la reina viuda.

dowdy [ˈdaʊdɪ] [dau-di], *a.* Zafio, desaliñado, sucio; mal vestido; sin gracia, sin estilo (woman). **She wears dowdy clothes,** se viste con poca gracia. -*s.* Maritornes, mujer desaliñada.

dowel [ˈdaʊəl] [dauel], *s.* 1. Botón, macho de madera, espiga de un pie derecho. 2. Trozo de madera introducido en una pared para clavar algo en él.

dower, dowery [ˈdaʊəʳ] [dau-aʳ] [ˈdaʊərɪ] [daua-ri], *s.* 1. Dote. 2. Viudedad, porción vitalicia de los bienes del marido (la tercera parte por regla general) que gozan las viudas en ciertos casos en Inglaterra. 3. Dotación, don.

dowered [ˈdaʊəd] [daued], *a.* Dotado.

dowerless [ˈdaʊəlɪs] [daua-les], *a.* Sin dote.

dowie [ˈdaʊɪ] [daui], *a. (Esco.)* Murrio, alicaído, triste.

dowlas [ˈdaʊləs] [dau-las], *s.* Lienzo basto que se usaba antiguamente.

down [daʊn] [daun], *s.* 1. Plumón (on bird); flojel. 2. Vello, lana fina o pelo suave, blando y corto (on face, body); pelusa (on plant, fruit). 3. Llanura. 4. *(Ingl.)* Cuesta que tiene la cima ancha, sin árboles y cubiertas de hierba; el espacio raso en su cima. 5. Duna, montecillo de arena en la costa. **Downs,** colinas.

down, *a.* 1. Que va hacia abajo (literal o figuradamente); pendiente. **The down escalator,** la escalera mecánica de bajada o para bajar. 2. Abatido; sombrío, melancólico, deprimido (depressed). -*prep.* Abajo (in downward direction). **We ran down the slope,** corrimos cuesta abajo. **To come down the stairs,** bajar por la escalera. **Halfway down the page,** hacia la mitad de la página (at lower level). **We drove on down the coast,** seguimos por la costa (along). **The library is just down the street,** la biblioteca está un poco más allá o más adelante (further along). **I saw her down the pub yesterday,** ayer la vi en el bar (to, in). **Down the centuries,** a través de los siglos (through).

down, *adv.* 1. Abajo, en la parte inferior, hacia abajo (in downward direction). **I ran all the way down to the bottom,** corrí hasta abajo. **Can you come down?,** ¿puedes bajar? (downstairs). 2. En tierra, por tierra; tendido a la larga. Abajo (on position). **Down in the valley,** abajo en el valle. **Two floors down,** dos pisos más abajo. 3. En sujeción, bajo la dependencia de. 4. Bajo el horizonte. 5. A un volumen menor. **With the volume down low,** con el volumen al mínimo. **Circulation is down,** la circulación ha bajado. 6. A precio o paso reducido. 7. Al contado. 8. En un papel (in writing). **She's down for tomorrow at ten,** está apuntada o anotada para mañana a las diez. **To jot down,** anotar en un papel. 9. *(Mar.)* A sotavento o hacia sotavento; **To put the helm down,** poner el timón a sotavento. 10. En aplicación fija; **To get down to work,** aplicarse resueltamente al trabajo. 11. Bajado (lowered, pointing downward). **With the blinds down,** con las persianas bajadas. **Face down,** boca abajo. **Down from,** desde. **To go down,** ir abajo, bajar, descender; *(Fig.)* Tragar, creer sin examen, aceptar. **To be downstairs,** estar abajo, haber bajado. **Down the river/stream,** río abajo, agua abajo. **Up and down,** de arriba abajo; acá y allá. **Upside down,** patas arriba, lo de arriba abajo. **To lie down,** echarse. **To sit down,** sentarse. **To set down,** sentar o notar en un papel. **He had his ups and downs,** tuvo sus altos y bajos. **This will not go down with me,** lo que es esa no la trago. -*inter.* ¡Abajo! ¡a tierra! **Down with him!,** ¡a tierra con él! **Down to,** hasta. **Down on your knees!,** ¡de rodillas!

down, *va.* 1. *(Fam.)* Derribar, echar por tierra (knock down/person); vencer, domar. 2. Beberse o tomarse rápidamente (drink). **To be down and out,** estar en la miseria.

down-bed [ˈdaʊnbed] [daun-bed], *s.* Cama de plumón.

downcast [ˈdaʊnkɑːst] [daun-kast], *a.* Alicaído, abatido (dejected); apesadumbrado, mustio, cabizbajo, encorvado. **With downcast eyes,** con la mirada baja (directed downward). -*s.* 1. (Poco us.) Tristeza, abatimiento. 2. (Minería) Galería descendente; pozo de entrada de aire.

downed [ˈdaʊnd] [dau-nd], *a.* Cubierto o henchido con plumón.

downer [ˈdaʊnəʳ] [dau-naʳ] *s. (Sl.)* Sedante (barbiturate); palo (depressing experience). **To be on a downer,** estar con la depre.

downfall [ˈdaʊnfɔːl] [daun-fol], *s.* Caída (of king, dictator); ruina, decadencia, perdición (of state).

downfallen [ˈdaʊnfɔːlən] [daun-fo-len], *a.* Caído, arruinado.

downgrade [ˈdaʊngreɪd] [daun-greid] *s.* 1. Bajada, cuesta abajo. **A downgrade of 1 in 40,** una pendiente del 2,5%. **To be on the downgrade,** ir cuesta abajo, ir de mal en peor. 2. Descenso a un grado inferior. *va.* Bajar de categoría (employee/hotel).

downhaul [ˈdaʊnhɔːl] [daun-jaul], *s. (Mar.)* Cargadera.

downhaul-tackle [ˌdaʊnhɔːlˈtækl] [daun-jol-ta-kel], *s. (Mar.)* Aparejo de cargadera.

down-hearted [ˈdaʊnhɑːtɪd] [daun-jar-ted], *a.* Abatido, desmayado, desanimado, alicaído, desmoralizado.

downhill [ˈdaʊnhɪl] [daun-jil], *a.* 1. Pendiente, inclinado, en declive; cuesta abajo (downward/path). **A downhill slope,**

una bajada, una pendiente. Dé descenso contra reloj (in skiing). 2. **It's all downhill from here,** de aquí en adelante todo va a marchar sobre ruedas o todo va a ser coser y cantar (easy, pleasant). -*s.* Declive o declivio, bajada, rampa. **The downhill,** el descenso contra reloj (in skiing). *adv.* Cuesta abajo (walk, run). **To go downhill,** ir cuesta abajo.

down-home [daʊnˈhəʊm] [daun-joum] *a.* Sureño (del sur de los EEUU) (entertainment, sound); casero (cooking); rústico (appearance); de las cosas sencillas (appeal).

Downing Street [ˌdaʊnɪŋˈstriːt] [dau-nin-strit] *s.* Downing Street (calle de Londres donde se encuentra la residencia oficial del primer ministro británico.

download [daʊnˈləʊd] [daun-loud] *va. (Inform.)* Trasvasar.

down-looking [daʊnˈluːkɪŋ] [daun-lu-kin], *a.* Cabizbajo, murrio, melancólico, triste, duro de genio.

down-lying [daʊnˈlaɪɪŋ] [daun-laiin], *a.* Parturienta. -*s.* 1. El tiempo de dormir o reposar. 2. Parto.

downmarket [daʊnˈmɑːkɪt] [daun-mar-ket] *adv.* **The paper has gone downmarket,** el diario ha perdido categoría; el diario se dirige ahora a un sector más popular del público (deliberately). *a.* Popular (newspaper); barato (store).

down payment [daʊnˈpeɪmənt] [daun-pei-ment], *s.* Pago oficial. *(Mex.)* Enganche. Cuota o entrada inicial, pie.

downpour [ˈdaʊnpɔːʳ] [daun-poʳ], *s.* Chaparrón, fuerte aguacero.

downright [ˈdaʊnraɪt] [daun-rait], *adv.* Perpendicularmente, a plomo; claramente, llanamente. **It was downright dangerous!,** ¡fue peligrosísimo! **He was downright rude!,** ¡estuvo de lo más grosero!. -*a.* 1. Abierto, manifiesto, patente, claro, palpable, evidente. 2. Descarado (lie, insolence); redomado, de tomo y lomo (crook, liar, rogue); total y absoluto (madness). 3. Derecho, perpendicular. 4. Franco, abierto, sincero. 5. Llano, liso. **Downright booby,** solemnísimo bobo.

downrightly [ˈdaʊnraɪtlɪ] [daun-rait-li], *adv.* Llanamente.

downriver [ˈdaʊnrɪvəʳ] [daun-ri-vaʳ] *adv.* Río abajo.

downside [ˈdaʊnˌsaɪd] [daun-said] *s.* Inconveniente, desventaja. **On the downside, it is expensive,** tiene el inconveniente de ser caro.

down's syndrome [ˈdaʊnˌsɪndrəʊm] [daun-sin-droum] *s.* Síndrome de Down; afectado por el síndrome de Down (child).

downstairs [ˈdaʊnˈstɛəz] [daun-stears], *s.* 1. Abajo. 2. Piso inferior, planta baja. *adv.* Abajo. **The kitchen's downstairs,** la cocina está abajo o en el piso de abajo. **He went downstairs to open the door,** bajó a abrir la puerta.

downstream [ˈdaʊnˈstriːm] [daun-strim], *adv.* Aguas abajo.

down-to-earth [ˈdaʊntʊˈɜːθ] [daun-tu-erz] *a.* Realista, práctico.

downtown [ˈdaʊntaʊn] [daun-taun], *s.* Centro, parte céntrica de una ciudad. **A downtown restaurant,** un restaurante céntrico o del centro. *adv.* **To go/live downtown,** ir al/vivir en el centro.

downtrod, downtrodden [ˈdaʊntrɒd] [daun-trod] [ˈdaʊntrɒdn] [daun-trodn] *a.* Pisado, pisoteado, oprimido.

downward [ˈdaʊnwɑːd] [daun-uard], **downwards** [ˈdaʊnwɑːdz] [daun-uards], *adv.* Hacia abajo.

downward, *a.* 1. Inclinado, pendiente; hacia abajo (direction, pressure). 2. Descendente, que va hacia abajo (movement, spiral). *(Fin.)* A la baja (tendency). **A downward path,** un camino en bajada o cuesta abajo.

downwind [ˈdaʊnˌwɪnd] [daun-uind] *adv.* En la dirección del viento.

downy [ˈdaʊnɪ] [dau-ni] *a.* Velloso, felpudo, blando, suave, dulce, tranquilo.

dowry [ˈdaʊrɪ] [dau-ri], *s.* 1. Dote. 2. Antiguamente, cantidad o recompensa pagada por una esposa. 3. Dotación, dádiva o posesión.

doxological [ˌdɒksəˈlɒdʒɪkl] [dok-so-lo-yi-kal], *a.* Lo que se refiere o pertenece a la alabanza de Dios.

doxology [dɒkˈsɒlədʒɪ] [dok-so-lo-yi], *s.* Himno de alabanza a Dios, el gloria patri.

doxy [ˈdɒksɪ] [dok-si], *s. (Ger.)* Querida, manceba; y a menudo, ramera, prostituta.

doze [dəʊz] [dous], *vn.* Dormitar, cabecear, estar medio dormido; vivir en la ociosidad o en la inacción. -*va.* Pasar sin darse cuenta de ello, o dormitado.

doze off Quedarse dormido, dormirse.

doze, *s.* Sueño ligero, sopor, adormecimiento.

dozen [ˈdʌzən] [dousen], *s.* Docena. **Baker's dozen,** docena de fraile, trece. **Four dollars a/per dozen,** cuatro dólares la docena. *a.* Docena de. **A dozen/two dozen eggs,** una docena/dos docenas de huevos.

doziness [ˈdəʊzɪnɪs] [dou-si-nes], *s.* Somnolencia, entorpecimiento, modorra.

dozing [ˈdəʊzɪŋ] [dou-sin], *s.* Somnolencia o soñolencia.

dozy [ˈdəʊzɪ] [dou-si], *a.* 1. Soñoliento, amodorrado, adormecido (sleepy). 2. Dormido (quiet). **A dozy village,** un pueblecito dormido. 3. *(Coloq.)* Tonto, abombado (stupid).

drab [dræb] [drab], *a.* 1. Pardo, de color pardo. 2. Soso, sin gracia (clothing, decor, appearance). **A drab green,** un verde apagado. 3. Gris, monótono (humdrum/life, occupation). -*s.* 1. Color entre gris y amarillento, color pardo. 2. *(Ant.)* Pelleja, mujercilla. 3. En las salinas, cajón para desaguar la sal; pipa de saladar.

drab, *va.* Acompañar a mujerzuelas.

drabbing [ˈdræbɪŋ] [dra-bin] *s.* El acto de asociarse con mujerzuelas.

drachm [dræm] [dram], *s. V.* DRAM.

drachma [ˈdrækmə] [drak-ma], *s.* 1. Dracma, moneda de plata entre los griegos. 2. Antigua medida de peso. 3. En el griego moderno, gramo.

draconian [drəˈkəʊnɪən] [dra-ko-nian], *a.* Draconiano, alusivo a Dracón; inexorable, cruel.

draff [drɑːf] [draf], *s.* Residuo de los granos que se emplean en las cervecerías y destilatorios, desperdicios, heces.

draft [drɑːft] [draft], *s.* 1. Giro, libranza, letra de cambio. **Sight draft,** giro a la vista. 2. Borrador, bosquejo. **A rough draft,** un borrador. 3. Diseño, plan; versión (formulation). **The final draft of my speech,** la versión final de mi discurso. 4. Corriente de aire (cold air). 5. *(Mil.)* El llamamiento o llamado a filas.

draft, *va.* 1. Bosquejar, delinear los contornos de, trazar, diseñar. 2. Bosquejar, hacer borrador, componer la primera forma (de un escrito) (formulate/document, contract, letter); preparar (speech). 3. *(Mil.)* Destacar, separar para cualquier servicio, reclutar; hacer alistamiento forzoso. 4. En tejeduría, hacer pasar entre los lizos del telar.

draft dodger [ˌdrɑːftˈdɒdʒəʳ] [draft-do-yaʳ] *s.* Prófugo, insumiso, remiso.

draftee [drɑːfˈtiː] [draf-ti], *s.* Conscripto, quinto, recluta.

draftsman, draughtsman [ˈdrɑːftsmən] [drafts-man], *s.* Diseñador, dibujador, delineante.

drafty, (GB) draughty [ˈdrɑːftɪ] [draf-ti] *a.* Con corrientes de aire.

drag [dræg] [drag], *va.* 1. Arrastrar, tirar, llevar a rastras (haul). **To drag somebody's name/reputation through the mud/dirt,** cubrir de fango/manchar el buen nombre de alguien. **To drag for an anchor,** *(Mar.)* rastrear un ancla. *(Coloq.)* **I dragged myself out of bed,** me forcé a salir de la cama (force). 2. Arrastrar (allow to trail/tail, garment, anchor). **I don't want to drag the kids around with me all day,** no quiero ir con los niños a cuestas todo el día. 3. Dragar (dredge/river, lake). -*vn.* 1. Arrastrar por el suelo. 2. Ir tirando, avanzar penosa o lentamente. 3. Garrar (trail, anchor); arrastrar (coat); rezagarse (lag). 4. Hacerse pesado (go on slowly/work, conversation); hacerse largo (film, play). 5. *(Coloq.)* Echarse un pique (race cars).

drag down Arrastrar (morally). **He tries to drag everyone down to his level,** quiere arrastrar a los demás a su nivel.

drag in Sacar a colación (subject, topic).

drag on Alargarse interminablemente.

drag out Alargar.

drag up Sacar a relucir (recall); críar (child).

drag, *s.* 1. Carretilla. 2. Instrumento con garfio o gancho. 3. **What a drag!,** ¡qué lata! (tiresome thing). 4. Resistencia al avance (resistant force). 5. *(Coloq.)* Pitada, calada (on cigarette). 6. **In drag,** vestido de mujer; de travestis o transformistas (act show). **Drag queen,** reinona. 7. *(Sl.)* **The main drag,** la calle principal.

drag chute [dræg't ʃuːt] [drag-chut], *s. (Aer.)* Paracaídas de frenado.

draggle ['drægl] [dra-guel], *va.* Emporcar alguna cosa arrastrándola por el suelo. -*vn.* Ensuciarse alguna cosa por llevarla arrastrando.

dragman [drægmən] [drag-man], *s.* Pescador con red barredera.

dragnet ['drægnet] [drag-net] *s.* 1. Red barredera (large net). 2. Operación u operativo policial de captura (police operation).

dragoman [drægəˈmæn] [dra-go-man], *s.* Dragomán, trujamán, intérprete que emplean los viajeros en Levante, en especial el intérprete de una embajada o consulado.

dragon ['drægən] [dra-gon], *s.* 1. Dragón. **Dragon's blood/gum dragon,** sangre de dragón/goma de India. 2. Hombre o mujer feroz. 3. *(Astr.)* Dragón, una de las constelaciones boreales.

dragonfly ['drægənflaɪ] [dra-gon-flai], *s. (Ent.)* Libélula, *(Fam.)* caballito del diablo, insecto volador neuróptero; tiene la cabeza grande y los ojos enormes.

dragonish ['drægənɪʃ] [dra-go-nish], *a.* Dragontino.

dragon-like ['drægənˌlaɪk] [dra-gon-laik], *a.* Fiero, furioso, violento.

dragonnade ['drægəneɪd] [dra-go-neid], *s.* 1. Dragonadas, persecuciones dirigidas contra los calvinistas franceses por los dragones de Luis XIV. 2. Cualquier persecución militar.

dragoon [drəˈguːn] [dra-gun], *s. (Mil.)* Dragón, soldado de a caballo; originalmente soldado que servía igualmente a pie que a caballo.

dragoon, *va.* Acosar o perseguir por medio de dragones; gobernar despóticamente, intimidar.

dragooning [drəˈguːnɪŋ] [dra-gu-nin], *s.* Saqueo, pillaje; asolamiento.

drain [dreɪn] [drein], *va.* 1. Desaguar. Vaciar (container, tank); drenar, avenar (land, swamp); drenar (blood); extraer (sap, water). 2. Desangrar, empobrecer o agotar poco a poco. 3. Agotar, secar, escurrir, enjugar. *(Culin.)* Escurrir, colar (vegetables, pasta). 4. Vaciar, apurar (drink up/glass, cup). 5. Agotar, consumir (consume, exhaust/ resources, strength. **Draining-trough,** *(Mar.)* Coladera. *vn.* Escurrirse (dry/dishes); **All the strength seemed to drain from my limbs,** los brazos y las piernas se me quedaron como sin fuerzas (disappear). Desaguar (discharge/pipes, river).

drain away Irse agotando (strength, resources). **The bathwater takes ages to drain away,** la bañera tarda mucho en vaciarse. **The rain gradually drains away into the soil,** la lluvia se va filtrando en la tierra.

drain off 1. Escurrirse (rainwater). 2. *(Culin.)* Escurrir. *(Tec.)* Extraer.

drain, *s.* 1. Desaguadero, canal de desagüe, sumidero (pipe). **The drains,** el alcantarillado (of town); las tuberías de desagüe (of building). Sumidero (grid). 2. Tajea, reguera. Fuga (outflow, loss). 3. Zanja de derivación para desecar un terreno. 4. *(Mar.)* Colador. 5. Desagüe (plughole). **That's money down the drain,** eso es tirar el dinero. 6. **A drain on the country's resources,** una sangría para el país. **The extra work is an enormous drain on my energy,** el trabajo extra me está agotando.

drainable ['dreɪnəbl] [drei-na-bol], *a.* Desaguable.

drainage ['dreɪnɪdʒ] [drei-nich], *s.* 1. La acción u operación de desaguar; drenaje, avenamiento (fields, marshes). 2. Desagüe (of household waste); canalización (of rainwater); desecación. **Drainage system,** alcantarillado. 3. Desecamiento, sistema de desecar las tierras por medio de zanjas y canales de desagüe. 4. Lo que está desaguado, derrame de agua. 5. La superficie desaguada, cuenca de un río.

drainboard [dreɪnˈbɔːd] [drein-bord] (GB) **draining board** [dreɪn] [drein] *s.* Escurridero.

drainpipe [dreɪnˈpaɪp] [drein-paip] *s.* Tubo o caño del desagüe.

drake [dreɪk] [dreik], *s.* 1. El ánade macho. 2. Piedra plana que se usa en el juego de *ducks and drakes* (= cabrillas). *V.* DUCK.

dram [dræm] [dram], *s.* 1. Dracma, la octava parte de una onza, sesenta gramos peso farmacéutico o 27.34 del peso comercial (setenta y dos en España). 2. *V.* DRACHMA. 3. *(Fam.)* Un trago, una copita de licor espirituoso. 4. Parte o porción pequeña de alguna cosa.

dram, *vn.* Beber aguardiente u otro licor destilado. **Dram-drinker** *s.* Bebedor de licores espirituosos.

drama ['drɑːmə] [dra-ma], *s.* 1. *(Teat.)* Obra dramática (play), drama; teatro, drama (plays collectively); arte dramático (dramatic art). 2. Dramatismo (excitement). **Hijack drama continues,** continúan los dramáticos sucesos en torno al secuestro (exciting event, story).

dramatic, dramatical [drəˈmætɪkl] [dra-ma-ti-kal], *a.* 1. *(Teat.)* Dramático, teatral; dramático, histriónico (exaggerated/pause, entrance). 2. Espectacular, drástico (striking/change, improvement); espectacular (increase); dramático (momentous/events, development).

dramatically [drəˈmætɪklɪ] [dra-ma-ti-ka-li], *adv.* Dramáticamente, de manera teatral o histriónica (exaggeratedly/pause, announce); de manera espectacular (strikingly/change, improve, increase).

dramatics [drəˈmætɪks] [dra-ma-tiks] *s. (Teat.)* **Amateur dramatics,** teatro amateur o de aficionados. **His dramatics are very wearing,** hace tanto teatro o es tan teatral que uno llega a cansarse (histrionics).

dramatist ['dræmətɪst] [dra-ma-tist], *s.* Dramático, el autor de composiciones dramáticas.

dramatization [ˌdræmətaɪˈzeɪʃən] [dra-ma-tai-sei-shon] *s. (Teat.)* Dramatización, adaptación teatral.

dramatize ['dræmətaɪz] [dra-ma-tais], *va.* 1. *(Teat.)* Dramatizar, dar un giro dramático; hacer drama de; hacer una adaptación teatral de (story, novel). *(Cin.)* Llevar al cine. 2. Referir o representar de una manera dramática; dramatizar, exagerar (exaggerate/situation, event).

dramaturge, dramaturgist ['dræmətɜːdʒ] [dra-ma-turch], *s.* Dramaturgo, autor o director de obras dramáticas.

drank ['dræŋk] [drank], *pret.* del verbo TO DRINK.

drap [dræp] [drap], *v.* y *s. (Esco.) V.* DROP.

drape [dreɪp] [dreip], *va.* 1. Cubrir con un ropaje, revestir con telas colgantes (cover). 2. Arreglar, disponer los pliegues de un vestido, de un cortinaje, o el ropaje de una estatua (arrange). Diseñar o arreglar colgaduras o ropajes. **They draped a flag over the tomb,** colocaron una bandera formando pliegues sobre la tumba.

drape, *s.* Cortina, colgadura. *V.* DRAPERY.

draper ['dreɪpəʳ] [drei-paʳ], *s.* Pañero, mercader de paños. **Linen-draper,** lencero, mercader de lienzos.

drapery ['dreɪpərɪ] [drei-pe-ri], *s.* 1. Paños o telas de lana. 2. *(Esc. y Pint.)* Ropaje, también cortinas, colgaduras, tapicería, etc. (covering). 3. Oficio y tráfico de un pañero; mercería, pañería (shop); mercería (merchandise).

drastic ['dræstɪk] [dras-tik], *a.* 1. *(Med.)* Drástico. 2. Drástico, radical (radical/solution, mesure). 3. Radical, drástico, espectacular (striking/change, effect).

drastically ['dræstɪkəlɪ] [dras-ti-ka-li] *adv.* Drásticamente.

draught [drɑːft] [draft] *s.* 1. Corriente de aire, aire colado. 2. Trago (of water, beer); la porción de cualquier licor que se bebe de una vez. **Beer on draught,** cerveza de barril (storage under pressure). 3. Poción, bebida medicinal, toma, dosis. **A sleeping draught,** una pócima para dormir (of drug). 4. Tiro, la acción de tirar o arrastrar carruajes. **Draught-horse,** caballo de tiro. 5. *(Pint.)* Dibujo, diseño. **Rough draught,** borrador. **Draught of a ship,** plano de un buque. 6. *(Mil.)* Destacamento. 7. *(Des.)* Sentina, albañal. 8. *(Mar.)* Cala o calado de un buque, o el fondo que necesita en el agua. 9. Libranza o letra de cambio. *V.* DRAFT, que es como se escribe siempre en los Estados Unidos. 10. **Draught-hooks,** *(Art.)* ganchos de telera. 11. **Draught-hook of a washer,** gancho de volandera. **Draughts,** tirantes, las cuerdas o correas que sirven para tirar de un carruaje; juego de damas. *Draft* tiene mucha aceptación, especialmente en los Estados Unidos.

draught, *va.* V. DRAFT.

daught-house [drɑːftˈhaʊs] [draft-jaus], *s.* Estercolero, sitio para arrojar las inmundicias.

draughtsman [ˈdrɑːftsmən] [drafts-man], *s.* 1. Dibujante, delineante. 2. Peón, pieza del juego de damas.

draw [drɔː] [dro], *va. (pret.* DREW, *pp.* DRAWN). 1. Tirar, traer hacia sí; atraer. **He drew her aside/to one side,** la llevó a un lado, la llevó aparte. **To draw one's chair up,** acercar o arrimar la silla a la mesa (in specified direction). 2. Atraer (attract/customers, crowd); ganar, persuadir; conseguir (ellicit, praise); provocar, suscitar (criticism, protest). **To draw tears/a smile from somebody,** hacer llorar/hacer sonreír a alguien. 3. Arrastrar, tirar de (pull along/cart, sled). 4. Chupar, mamar. 5. Aspirar, respirar, inspirar, el aliento. **To draw breath,** respirar (cause to flow). 6. Sacar, extraer, arrancar (pull out/tooth, cork); desenfundar, sacar (gun); desenvainar, sacar (sword). **To draw blood,** sacar sangre, hacer sangrar. *(Games)* Sacar, robar (card, domino). **Italy has been drawn to play France,** a Italia le ha tocado en el sorteo jugar contra Francia (in contest, tournament). 7. Poner de manifiesto, sacar a la luz; sacar de. 8. Correr las cortinas, abriéndolas o cerrándolas (move by pulling/curtains, bolt); descorrer (open), correr (shut); tensar (bow). 9. Dibujar, bosquejar, delinear, representar (sketch/flower, picture). 10. Deducir, inferir, sacar (derive/strength, lesson). **She drew comfort from the fact that…,** se consoló pensando que… 11. Escribir o extender. 12. Destripar, desentrañar. 13. Tirar, alargar, estirar; a menudo va seguido de *out.* 14. *(Fin.)* Librar, girar una letra de cambio (check); cobrar, percibir (salary, pension). **To draw money from/out of the bank,** retirar o sacar dinero del banco. 16. Tender (un arco). 17. Preparar por medio de infusión. 18. Establecer (establish/distintion, parallel). 19. *(Dep.)* Empatar. *—vn.* 1. Tirar, arrastrar como los animales que tiran de un carruaje. 2. Encogerse, arrugarse. 3. Adelantarse, moverse, acercarse (move). 4. *(Art.)* Dibujar, diseñar. 5. Sortear. 6. Calar una embarcación, hundirse en el agua hasta cierto punto. 7. Moverse libremente a fuerza de succión o atracción; tener libre corriente de aire. 8. Salir algo a fuerza de tirar de ello; ser extraído. Tirar (take in air/chimney, cigar). 9. Atraer la sangre o los humores a la superficie, como lo hace un vejigatorio. 10. Moverse como si tirasen de ello; venirse, irse; se usa con adverbios. 11. (GB) *(Jueg., Dep.)* Empatar; hacer tablas (in chess game). **To draw nigh,** acercarse. **To draw again,** volver a tirar. **To draw a bridge,** levantar un puente. **To draw along,** arrastrar. **To draw asunder,** separar, dividir. **To draw forward,** atraer. **To draw forth,** hacer salir, sacar. **To draw near to an end,** fenecer. **To draw to an issue,** acabar, concluir. **To draw over,** persuadir. **To draw so many feet of water,** *(Mar.)* calar (una embarcación) tantos pies de agua.

draw away, quitar, llevar; disuadir, divertir, distraer; enajenar. **To draw away from something,** alejarse de algo (move off). **To draw away from somebody,** alejarse o distanciarse de alguien (in competition, race).

draw back, retroceder, volver hacia atrás (recoil); perder terreno, retirarse (retreat); ceder, aflojar, desistir; volverse atrás; recular, cejar; hacer retroceder o retirarse; hacer cejar o volver hacia atrás.

draw down, bajar, tirar hacia abajo; hacer bajar (blind).

draw in 1. Atraer, seducir, inducir, granjear, ganar; arrastrar tras sí, involucrar (into quarrel, war); darle participación a (into conversation). 2. Esconder, retraer (retract/claws). 3. Llegar (arrive/train); hacerse más corto (days, nights).

draw off, sacar, extraer (drain/beer, sap); trasegar; distraer, disuadir, separar; retirarse; ganar a alguno a su partido

haciéndole abandonar el que seguía antes; confundir (divert/pursuers); quitarse (remove/glove, stocking).

draw on 1. Conducir; causar; incitar, empeñar a alguno, arrastrar a uno a que haga lo que no quiere, obligar; acercarse; estar en el último trance. 2. Ponerse (glove, stocking). 3. Recurrir a, hacer uso de (make use of/resources, reserves). **She drew on her own experiences,** se inspiró en sus propias experiencias. 4. **Night is drawing on,** está anocheciendo (approach, advance).

draw out 1. sacar, extraer, tirar (extract, remove/tooth, horn); sacar (wallet, handkerchief); sacar, sonsacar (information); arrancar (confession); sacar (withdraw/money). 2. Alargar, dilatar, diferir, extraer, extender, desarrollar, hacerse más largo (become longer). 3. **See if you can draw him out of himself,** a ver si logras que se muestre un poco más comunicativo.

draw together 1. Juntar, amontonar, apretar. 2. Reunirse, acercarse.

draw up 1. Tirar hacia arriba, acercar, arrimar (bring near/chair). Componer algún libro, discurso o informe; hacer o extender una escritura; redactar, preparar (prepare, draft/contract, treaty); hacer (list). Ordenar para el combate; alinear, formar (arrange in formation/troops, competitors). 2. Detenerse, parar (car). 3. **To draw oneself up,** erguirse (straighten oneself).

draw, *s.* 1. El acto de tirar, sacar o entresacar. **The fastest draw in Texas,** el pistolero más rápido de Texas. **To be quick on the draw,** ser rápido en desenfundar (with gun); pescarlas al vuelo (with reply). 2. Jugada, suerte o mano; sorteo (raffle). **The second draw,** a la segunda carta, jugada o sorteo. 3. Tablas; empate. 4. Gancho, atracción (attraction).

drawable [ˈdrɔːəbl] [droua-bol], *a.* Capaz de ser tirado, sacado o sorteado.

drawback [ˈdrɔːbæk] [drou-bak], *s.* 1. Rebaja o descuento, cierta cantidad de dinero que se abona al pagador por pagar al contado o antes del tiempo estipulado. 2. Rebaja o descuento de derechos de aduana, la rebaja que se hace al extraer las manufacturas del país o ciertas mercancías extranjeras que ya han pagado los derechos de entrada. 3. Desventaja, inconveniente, menoscabo, lo que detrae.

drawbridge [ˈdrɔːbrɪdʒ] [drou-brich], *s.* Puente levadizo.

drawee [drɔːˈiː] [droui], *s.* La persona a cuyo cargo está girada una letra de cambio.

drawer [drɔːʳ] [drouaʳ], *s.* 1. Gaveta, naveta, cajoncito de un escritorio (in furniture). 2. *(Com.)* Librador, el que libra o gira una letra de cambio (of check). 3. *(Ant.)* Aguador. 4. *(Des.)* Mozo de taberna. **Drawers,** calzoncilos (clothing). *(Prov.)* Paños menores. 5. *(Art)* Dibujante.

draw-head [ˈdrɔːhed] [dro-jed], *s.* (Ferrocarril) Cabeza de la barra de tracción.

drawing [ˈdrɔːɪŋ] [droin], *s.* 1. Dibujo. **Drawing board,** tablero, mesa de dibujo. 2. Tiro. 3. Sorteo (de una lotería).

drawing-room [ˈdrɔːɪŋrʊm] [droin-rum], *s.* 1. Salón o sala de estrado. 2. Sala principal de una casa.

drawl [drɔːl] [drol], *vn.* Pronunciar con pesadez y lentitud. **To drawl out,** arrastrar las palabras. **To drawl out his time,** haraganear. *va.* Decir arrastrando las palabras.

drawl, *s.* El acto de hablar como arrastrando las palabras; articulación tarda, falta de energía. **A Southern drawl,** un acento sureño.

drawn [drɔːn] [dron], *pp.* del verbo TO DRAW. *a.* 1. Desenvainado, destripado, desentrañado; demacrado (features, face). 2. Movido, inducido. 3. Tablas, juego nulo, sin resultado. *(Mil.)* Indeciso, hablando de un encuentro o batalla. 4. Abierto. 5. En estado de fusión, fundido, derretido. **Drawn butter,** manteca derretida. 6. Desenvainado, desnudo, fuera de.

drawn-out [drɔːnˈaʊt] [droun-aut] *a.* Larguísimo, interminable.

drawstring ['drɔːstrɪŋ] [drou-strin] s. Cordón del que se tira para cerrar algo. Fruncido con un cordón o una cinta (bag, waist).

draw-well ['drɔːwel] [dro-uel] s. Pozo.

dray, dray-cart [dreɪ] [drei], s. 1. Carro que sirve para llevar cargas; carromato, carretón; por lo común más bajo hacia atrás que al frente. 2. (Ingl.) Narria, rastra.

drayage ['dreɪədʒ] [dreiech], s. 1. Acarreo, carretaje, el acto de conducir por carretón. 2. Carretaje, lo que se paga por ese servicio.

dray-horse [dreɪˈhɔːz] [drei-jors], s. Caballo de carro.

drayman ['dreɪmən] [drei-man], s. Carromatero, carretero, el que guía los caballos que tiran de los carros.

dread [dred] [dred], s. Miedo, terror, espanto. -a. Terrible, espantoso, tremendo, formidable; augusto, respetable.

dread, va. Temer, tener miedo o temor a. **I dread to think what might have happened,** no quiero ni pensar en lo que podría haber pasado. -vn. Temer, recelar.

dreadable ['dredəbl] [dre-da-bol], a. Temible, temedero.

dreader ['dredər] [dre-dar], s. Temedor.

dreadful ['dredfʊl] [dred-ful], a. Terrible, espantoso (news, experience, weather); horroroso, formidable, espantador. **I feel dreadful about not having helped,** me siento muy mal por no haber ayudado. **You look dreadful,** tienes muy mala cara.

dreadfulness ['dredfʊlnɪs] [dred-ful-nes], s. Terribilidad, horror.

dreadfully ['dredfəlɪ] [dred-fu-li], adv. Terriblemente, enormemente (upset, late); espantosamente mal (write, sing). **I'm dreadfully sorry,** lo siento muchísimo o en el alma.

dreadless ['dredlɪs] [dred-les], a. Intrépido, arrojado.

dreadlessness ['dredlɪsnɪs] [dred-les-nes], s. Intrepidez, arrojo.

dreadlocks ['dredlɒks] [dred-loks] s. pl. Rizos al estilo de los rastafaris.

dreadnaught ['drednɔːt] [dred-not], s. 1. El que no teme nada. 2. Tela muy doble y el capote de capucha hecho con ella. (dread y naught, cero).

dream [driːm] [drim] s. 1. Sueño (while sleeping); ensueño, suceso o especie que se representa en la fantasía de uno mientras duerme. **A bad dream,** una pesadilla. **Sweet dreams!,** ¡que duermas bien!, ¡que sueñes con los angelitos! 2. Desvarío, cosa fantástica sin fundamento ni razón; sueño (fantasy, ideal, aspiration). **It was beyond my wildest dreams,** ni en sueños lo hubiera imaginado. **A dream come true,** un sueño hecho realidad. **Your dream home,** la casa de sus sueños. 3. Sueño, ensueño (daydream). **He goes around in a dream,** vive en las nubes. 4. (Coloq.) Sueño (something wonderful). **To go like a dream,** salir a las mil maravillas (event); funcionar de maravilla (car).

dream, vn. (pret. y pp. DREAMED y DREAMT). 1. Soñar (in sleep); desvariar, discurrir fantásticamente, estar en las nubes (daydream). 2. **I dreamed of going to live in the country,** soñaba con irme a vivir al campo (imagine). **I wouldn't dream of borrowing money,** ni se me ocurriría pedir dinero prestado (contemplate). -va. 1. Soñar, ver en sueños (in sleep). **I dreamed that I was drowning,** soñé que me ahogaba. 2. Imaginarse (imagine). **I never dreamed he'd be so rude,** nunca me imaginé que iba a ser tan grosero.

dream away Pasarse soñando.

dream up Idear (plan).

dreamer ['driːmər] [dri-mar], s. Soñador; visionario, iluso.

dreamful ['driːmfʊl] [drim-ful], a. El que sueña mucho.

dreamily, dreamingly ['driːmɪlɪ] [drim-mi-li] ['driːmɪŋlɪ] [drim-min-li], adv. Negligentemente, perezosamente, lentamente.

dreamland ['driːmlænd] [drim-land], s. El reino de los sueños.

dreamless ['driːmlɪs] [drim-les], a. Sin sueños; tranquilo (sleep).

dreamt ['driːmt] [dremt], pret. y pp. de TO DREAM.

dream-world ['driːmˌwɔːld] [drim-ueld], s. El mundo de las ilusiones.

dreamy ['driːmɪ] [dri-mi], a. 1. Desvariado, perteneciente a los ensueños; dado a soñar. 2. Peculiar de los sueños. 3. Soñador, fantasioso (abstracted/person); distraído (gaze); etéreo, sutil (music).

drear [drɪər] [dria^r], a. (Poét.) V. DRARY.

drearily ['drɪərɪlɪ] [dria-ri-li], adv. Funestamente, tristemente.

dreariness ['drɪərɪnɪs] [dria-ri-nes], s. Tristeza; melancolía; aspecto lúgubre o murrio.

dreary ['drɪərɪ] [dria-ri], a.

dredge [dredʒ] [drech], va. 1. Limpiar, excavar, labrar profundamente por medio de draga; dragar. 2. Rastrear, recoger por medio de la red barredera; pescar con dicha red. 3. Esparcir harina sobre alguna cosa al guisarla; enharinar, polvorear.

dredge up Dragar (mud, sand); desenterrar, sacar a relucir (story, scandal).

dredge, s. 1. Aparato para levantar o sacar algo que se halla debajo del agua: (a) draga, aparato para excavar los puertos, canales, etc; (b) red barredera. 2. V. DREDGER, 3ª acep. 3. (Ant.) Mezcla de cebada y avena sembradas juntamente.

dredger ['dredʒər] [dre-char] s. 1. El que draga o rastrea; pescador de ostras. 2. **Dredger/dredging-machine,** draga, máquina y el barco de fondo llano que la lleva para limpiar los puertos o ríos. 3. Cajita para espolvorear harina sobre las viandas.

dreen ['driːn] [drin], v. y s. (Dialecto) V. DRAIN.

dregginess ['dregɪnɪs] [dre-gui-nes], s. Posos, heces; feculencia.

dreggish ['dregɪʃ] [dre-guish], **dreggy** ['dregɪ] [dre-gui], a. Feculento, turbio.

dregs [dregz] [dregs], s. pl. 1. Heces. 2. Escoria, barreduras, morralla, zupia, desperdicio; posos, cunchos, conchos (sediment). **The dregs of the people,** el populacho, la gentuza, la canalla. (Mex.) Los léperos.

drench [drentʃ] [drench], va. 1. Empapar, humedecer completamente. **To get drenched,** empaparse. 2. (Vet.) Purgar con violencia. 3. Abrevar, bañar, embeber.

drench, s. 1. Tragantada. 2. (Vet.) Bebida purgante que se da a un animal. 3. Volumen de líquido suficiente para ahogar; diluvio. 4. Solución para empapar o remojar.

drencher ['drentʃər] [dren-cha^r], s. El que remoja alguna cosa.

drenching ['drentʃɪŋ] [dren-chin] s. **To get a drenching,** empaparse.

dress [dres] [dres], va. (pret. y pp. DRESSED y DREST) 1. Vestir (put clothes on); ataviar, adornar. **To get dressed,** vestirse. **He was dressed in white,** iba vestido de blanco. 2. (Med.) Curar las heridas; vendar (wound). 3. almohazar. 4. Componer; ajustar; arreglar, poner en orden. 5. Cocinar, guisar, adobar, aderezar, disponer las cosas para comer; aliñar (season/salad); preparar (prepare/chicken, fish). **Dressed crab,** cangrejo preparado. 6. Adobar y curtir pieles. 7. Preparar lino o cáñamo. 8. Arreglar o disponer una cosa de modo que sirva para un uso particular. (Albañ.) Allanar, aplanar. 9. Alinear, poner en línea recta, v. gr. a una compañía de soldados. -vn. 1. Vestirse (put on, wear clothes). **He always dresses in black,** siempre se viste de negro. **She dresses very well,** viste muy bien. **To dress for dinner,** cambiarse para cenar (dress formally) 2. (Mil.) Formar los soldados en hileras; alinearse. **To dress a child,** mudar de ropa a un niño. **To dress a dead body,** amortajar. **To dress a garden,** cultivar un jardín. **To dress a vine,** podar. **To dress a lady's hair,** peinar a una señora. (Mil.) **Dress left, right!,** ¡a la izquierada, a la derecha, alinearse!

dress up 1. Ponerse elegante (dress smartly). **All dressed up and no place/nowhere to go,** compuesta y sin novio. 2. Disfrazarse (in fancy dress). **To dress up as something,** disfrazarse de algo. 3. Disfrazar (idea, plan). **Criticism dressed up as advice,** críticas disfrazadas de consejos.

dress, s. 1. Vestido, traje (for woman, girl). 2. Atavío, tocado. 3. **They arrived in formal dressing,** llegaron vestidos de etiqueta (clothing, style of dressing). **Dress affair,** velada o reunión que requiere traje de gala. **Dress ball,** baile de gala.

Full dress, traje de etiqueta, uniforme completo. **Dress suit,** frac. **Dress parade,** *(Mil.)* parada con uniforme completo.

dressage ['drɛsɑːdʒ] [dre-sach] *s.* Método de adiestramiento de caballos para que ejecuten ciertas maniobras.

dresser ['drɛsər] [dre-sa^r], *s.* 1. Ayuda de cámara, moza de cámara. *(Teat.)* Ayudante de camerino. 2. Mesa de cocina. 3. Aparador (in kitchen); tocador (in bedroom. 4. Cocinero. 5. **He's a sloppy/stylish dresser,** se viste con mucho descuido/estilo.

dressing ['drɛsɪŋ] [dre-sin], *s.* 1. La acción de vestir, ataviar, adornar; adorno. 2. *(Culin.)* Aderezo, aliño (for salad); relleno (stuffing). Lo que se usa para aderezar, etc.: (a) cura, curación, hilas, vendajes, etc.; (b) aderezo (de las telas, de los manjares, de las pieles); (c) *(Agr.)* bina, renda, segunda labor de las viñas; (d) estercoladura, estercuelo; (e) corte, poda de los árboles; cultivo de tierra, labrantía; (f) encoladura de paños; (g) labrado, talla de los cantos. 3. *(Fam.)* Castigo o regaño. 4. *pl.* *(Arq.)* Molduras, adornos. 5. *(Med.)* Apósito, gasa, vendaje (bandage). **Dressing-case,** tocador. **Dressing-gown,** peinador, bata, albornoz.

dressing-room [,drɛsɪŋ'rʊm] [dre-sin-rum], *s.* Cámara o gabinete para vestirse.

dressmaker ['drɛsmeɪkər] [dres-mei-ka^r], *s.* Costurera, modista; la que hace vestidos para las mujeres y niños.

dressmaking ['drɛsmeɪkɪŋ] [dres-mei-kin], *s.* El arte de hacer vestidos, el oficio de costurera.

dressy ['drɛsɪ] [dre-si], 1. Acicalado, aficionado a ataviarse, amigo de compostura. 2. Elegante, distinguido en porte y aspecto.

drest [drɛst] [drest], *pp.* del verbo TO DRESS.

drew [druː] [dru], *pret.* de TO DRAW.

dribble ['drɪbl] [dri-bol], *vn.* 1. Gotear, caer gota a gota; destilar. 2. Babear (drool). **He dribbles,** se le cae la baba, babea. 3. *(Dep.)* Driblar, driblear. *-va.* 1. Hacer caer gota a gota. **To dribble saliva,** babear. 2. *(Dep.)* **He dribbled the ball past/around a defender,** dribló o dribleó o regateó a un defensa. *s.* Saliva.

dribbling ['drɪblɪŋ] [dri-blin], *s.* El acto de gotear.

driblet ['drɪblɪt] [dri-blit], *s.* 1. Pico, cantidad pequeña de dinero. 2. Quebrado o corto resto de alguna cantidad principal.

dried ['draɪd] [draid], *part.* de TO DRY. *a.* Seco (figs, flowers); salado, seco (fish); en polvo (milk, eggs).

drier ['draɪər] [draia^r], *s.* Desecante, lo que tiene la propiedad de desecar: (a) substancia añadida a un color para que se seque más rápidamente.; (b) aparato para secar (las frutas, etc.). V. DRYER. *Drier, Driest,* comp. y super. de DRY.

drift [drɪft] [drift] *s.* 1. Impulso, violencia. 2. Todo objeto arrastrado por las aguas o arrebatado por el viento. 3. Montón de alguna cosa que junta el viento (of sand); ventisquero (of snow). 4. Objeto o blanco de algún discurso. 5. Designio, intento. Sentido (meaning). **I didn't quite catch your drift,** no entendí o capté muy bien lo que querías decir. 6. Manejo, entremetimiento. 7. *(Mar.)* La dirección de una corriente; deriva; ángulo de deriva; cambio a sotavento. 8. *(Arq.)* Empuje de un arco. 9. *(Min.)* Socavón, galería, cañón de desagüe. 10. *(Art. y Of.)* Broca, punzón para taladrar palastro. 11. **The drift from the land,** el éxodo rural (movement). **The drift of public opinion,** el cambio en la opinión pública. **Drifts of ice,** hielos flotantes. **Drifts of sand,** arena movediza. **To go adrift,** fluctuar a merced de los vientos. **To set adrift,** echar o dejar a la ventura. **Drifts of dust,** nubes de polvo. **Drift-wood,** madera o tronco flotante o echado a tierra por las aguas.

drift, *va.* Impeler, apilar, amontonar. *-vn.* 1. Ser llevado como por una corriente (on water); moverse empujado por el viento (in air/balloon). Ir a la deriva (be adrift/boat, person). 2. Formar en montones, amontonarse (pile up/sand, snow); esparcir, salpicar, moverse en varias direcciones. 3. **He drifted from job to job,** iba sin rumbo de un trabajo a otro. **The crowd began to drift away,** la muchedumbre comenzó a dispersarse (proceed aimlessly).

drifter ['drɪftər] [drif-ta^r] *s.* 1. **He's a drifter,** va dando tumbos por la vida (person). 2. Trainera (boat).

drift-way ['drɪftweɪ] [drift-uei], *s.* Camino de ganado.

drift-wind ['drɪftwɪnd] [drift-uind], *s.* Viento que levanta o amontona alguna cosa.

driftwood ['drɪftwuːd] [drift-wud] *s.* Madera, tablas, etc. que flotan en el mar a la deriva o que arrastra el mar hasta la playa.

drill [drɪl] [dril], *va.* 1. Taladrar, barrenar, perforar (wood, metal); agujerear, perforar (hole); trabajar o limpiar con la fresa (tooth). 2. Sembrar, plantar, en hileras o surcos. 3. *(Mil.)* Disciplinar reclutas, enseñarles el ejercicio. *-vn.* 1. Estar ocupado en ejercicios militares u otros análogos. 2. Plantar en surcos. 3. Perforar, hacer perforaciones. **To drill for oil/water,** perforar en busca de petróleo/agua.

drill, *va.* y *vn.* Hacer salir gota a gota; fluir lentamente.

drill, *s.* 1. Taladro, instrumento de varios tamaños, para agujerear o taladrar, terraja, parauso, taladro que usan los cerrajeros. *(Dent)* Torno, fresa. *(Eng. Min.)* Perforadora, barreno; broca (drill head). 2. Máquina para plantar y cubrir semillas menudas en hileras, sembradora de granos. 3. Hilera de semillas sembradas o surcos hechos con esa máquina. 4. Una especie de mono. 5. *(Mil.)* Instrucción de reclutas. *(Educ.)* Ejercicio. **Fire drill,** simulacro de incendio (rehearsal). **Drill-plough,** arado sembrador, sementero. (GB) *(Coloq.)* **What's the drill?,** ¿qué se hace? (correct procedure).

drilling ['drɪlɪŋ] [dri-lin], 1. El acto de usar un taladro o de taladrar. 2. Instrucción de reclutas. 3. Material extraído o excavado por un talador. 4. Dril, tela fuerte y cruzada de algodón o hilo. **Drilling platform,** plataforma de perforación.

drily ['draɪlɪ] [dri-li] *adv.* Secamente, con sequedad.

drink [drɪŋk] [drink], *va.* y *vn.* (*pret.* DRANK, antiguamente DRUNK; *pp.* DRUNK, antig. DRUNKEN). 1. Beber, tomar (swallow); apagar la sed, embriagarse, emborrachar o emborracharse; beber, tomar (consume alcohol). **Give me something to drink,** dame algo de beber o para tomar. 2. Chupar, embeber, absorber. 3. Ser habitualmente un borracho. **To drink away,** beber a porfía. **To drink away one's time,** malgastar el tiempo bebiendo. **To drink down,** tragar; *(Fig.)* borrar el recuerdo de algo bebiendo, emborracharse. **To drink down sorrow,** ahogar las penas en vino. **To drink hard,** beber mucho. **To drink huge draughts,** beber a tragantadas. **To drink off/out/up,** beber hasta la última gota. **To drink one's health,** brindar, beber a la salud de alguno. **To drink to somebody,** brindar por alguien (toast). **I'll bring to that!,** ¡brindo por que así sea!

drink in, embeber, chupar. Empaparse de (scenery). **Plants drink in water through their roots,** las plantas absorben el agua a través de sus raíces. **We drank in the fresh air,** respiramos el aire puro.

drink up Bebérselo o tomárselo todo, terminar su copa.

drink, *s.* 1. Bebida (any liquid). 2. Licor, copa, trago (alcoholic). 3. Trago, la cantidad que se puede tragar de una vez (amount drunk, served, sold). **Have a drink of water/milk,** bebe o toma un poco de agua/leche. **To have a drink,** tomar una copa. **The drinks are on me!,** ¡yo invito!

drinkable ['drɪŋkəbl] [drin-ka-bol], *a.* Potable (water). **This is not drinkable!,** ¡ esto no se puede beber!.

drinker ['drɪŋkər] [drin-ka^r], *s.* Bebedor, borracho. **He's a heavy drinker,** es un gran bebedor o un bebedor empedernido. **I'm a beer drinker myself,** yo prefiero la cerveza.

drinking ['drɪŋkɪŋ] [drin-kin], *s.* La acción de beber (of liquid). **His drinking is causing concern,** lo mucho que bebe está causando preocupación (of alcohol). **Drinking-glass,** vaso, copa. **Drinking-horn,** vaso de cuerno. **Drinking-house,** taberna, tienda de vinos, vinatería. **Drinking-pot,** jarro. **Drinking water,** agua potable.

drink-money [drɪŋk'mʌnɪ] [drink-ma-ni], *s.* Dinero para beber.

drip [drɪp] [drip], *vn.* 1. Gotear, destilar. **Water was dripping from the ceiling,** el techo goteaba, caían gotas del techo. 2. Chorrear, gotear (let drops fall/washing, hair); gotear (faucet, tap). **I'm dripping with sweat,** estoy chorreando de sudor. 3. **She was dripping with diamonds,** iba cubierta de brillantes (display). *-va.* Despedir algún líquido a gotas, hacer gotear. **You're dripping coffee down your shirt,** te estás manchando la camisa de café, te estás chorreando la camisa con el café.

drip, *s.* 1. Lo que cae gota a gota; goteo (of rainwater, tap). **The steady drip/drip of the rain,** el continuo gotear de la lluvia. 2. *(Med.)* Suero, gota a gota. **He's on a drip,** le han puesto suero o el gota a gota. 3. *(Coloq.)* Soso (ineffectual person).

drip-dry ['drɪp'draɪ] [drip-drai] *a.* De lava y pon, de lavar y poner (fabric, garment).

dripping ['drɪpɪŋ] [dri-pin], *s.* Pringue, la grasa que chorrea de cualquier cosa crasa puesta al fuego. *a. (Coloq.)* Empapado. **To be dripping wet,** estar chorreando o empapado.

dripping-pan [drɪpɪŋ'pɑːn] [dri-pin-pan], *s.* Grasera, la cazuela en que se recoge el pringue.

drive [draɪv] [draiv], *va. y vn. (pret.* DROVE, *pp.* DRIVEN). 1. Impeler, empujar, arrojar; estimular, precisar. 2. Cochear; llevar en coche (convey in vehicle). **She drove me home/into town,** me llevó en coche a casa/into town. 3. Llevar, manejar, conducir (car, bus, train); pilotar, pilotear (racing car, power boat); inducir, forzar a, reducir a. 4. Enclavar, clavar (make penetrate/nail); hincar (stake). **He drove the nail through the plank,** atravesó la tabla con el clavo. 5. Ser impelido o empujado. 6. Andar o ir en coche. 7. Apuntar o asestar. 8. Secuestrar. 9. Conducir, llevar, guiar (un tiro de caballos, un carruaje, una manada, un rebaño, etc.). 10. Excavar horizontalmente, perforar, abrir (open up/tunnel, shaft). 11. Transferir la fuerza a otra acción mecánica. 12. **The Indians were driven off their lands,** los indios fueron expulsados de sus tierras (cause to move). *(Dep.)* Mandar, lanzar (ball); hacer funcionar, mover (provide power for, operate). 13. Volver (cause to become). **Imprisonment drove him insane,** la prisión lo volvió loco o lo llevó a la locura. **She drives herself too hard,** se exige demasiado a sí misma (overwork). **To drive along,** empujar, llevar hacia adelante. **To drive away,** echar fuera, ahuyentar, desterrar; *(Fig.)* Trabajar diligentemente y con persistencia. **To drive back,** rechazar. **To drive in/into,** hacer entrar por fuerza, meter o encajar a golpe de martillo, echar adentro o a lo hondo; entrar en alguna parte en coche. **To drive out of heart,** desanimar. **To drive to leeward,** *(Mar.)* sotaventear. **To be driven to the wall,** verse entre la espada y la pared. **To drive mad,** hacer perder la cabeza, enloquecer.

drive at, tener puesta la mira en; rematar, terminar. Querer, decir, insinuar. **What are you driving at?,** ¿qué quieres decir?, ¿qué (es lo que) estás insinuando?

drive off 1. Ahuyentar (repel); arrojar, hacer salir de una parte; silbar, mofar; diferir, dilatar. 2. Irse, partir (car, driver); salir (in golf).

drive on, 1. Tocar; empujar, apresurar la ejecución de una cosa (incite). 2. Salir (adelante).

drive out Arrojar, hacer salir, expeler, expulsar.

drive up 1. Llegar (vehicle, driver). 2. Hacer subir (prices, demand).

drive, *s.* 1. Accionamiento, impulsión. Golpe fuerte (in golf, tennis). 2. Paseo en coche o en automóvil. **To go for a drive,** ir a dar un paseo o una vuelta en coche. 3. Calzada, paseo, camino, avenida (leading to house); entrada para coches (in front of house. 4. Urgencia, presión. 5. Empuje, dinamismo (energy). *(Psych.)* Impulso, instinto (compulsion). **The sex drive,** el apetito sexual. 6. Campaña (organized effort). **A sales drive,** una campaña de ventas. *(Mil.)* Ofensiva, avanzada (attacking move). Ataque (in US football). 7. Transmisión, propulsión (propulsion system). **Front-**

wheel/rear-wheel drive, tracción delantera/trasera. **Four-wheel drive,** tracción en las cuatro ruedas. **Drive lever,** palanca de impulsión.

drive-in [draɪv'ɪn] [draiv-in], *a./s.* Accesible en automóvil. Se aplica a cines, restaurantes, bancos, etc., en que el automovilista ve o es atendido sin abandonar el vehículo.

drivel ['drɪvl] [dri-vel], *vn.* Babear, bobear, chochear, decir tonterías.

drivel, *s.* 1. Baba. 2. Cháchara necia, sandeces, vaciedades, tonterías, estupideces.

driveling ['drɪvlɪŋ] [dri-vlin], *a.* Baboso.

driveller ['drɪvələ^r] [dri-ve-la^r], *s.* Fatuo, simple.

driven ['drɪvn] [driven], *pp.* de TO DRIVE.

driver ['draɪvə^r] [drai-va^r], *s.* 1. Conductor, el que conduce o guía, chofer o chófer (of car, truck, bus); cochero, carretero, conductor de locomotora. Piloto (of racing car). **Drivers are asked to avoid this area,** se ruega a los automovilistas que eviten circular por esta zona. 2. Rueda o fuerza motriz. 3. *(Mar.)* Maricangalla o maría-cangalla, especie de vela latina que se pone en la mesana, cuando hay bonanza. **Driver-boom,** *(Mar.)* Botalón de maricangalla. 4. Arriero; porquero, vaquero o boyero.

driver's license [,draɪvəz'laɪsəns] [drai-vers-lai-sens] *s.* Licencia o permiso de conducción; carné o permiso de conducir, libreta, licencia o pase, registro, brevete (less formally).

driver's seat [,draɪvəz'siːt] [drai-vers-sit] *s.* Asiento del conductor. **To be in the driver's seat,** estar al frente, llevar las riendas.

driveway ['draɪvweɪ] [draiv-uei], *s.* Entrada para vehículos.

driving ['draɪvɪŋ] [drai-vin], *s.* 1. *(Mar.)* Garrar, se dice cuando el ancla no hace presa en el fondo. 2. Impulso, el acto de dar movimiento; tendencia a hacer alguna cosa. 3. *(Auto.)* Conducción. **I don't think much of his driving,** no me gusta mucho como maneja o conduce. *-a.* 1. Motor, motriz. 2. Impetuoso, violento. Torrencial (rain); azotador (wind). **She's the driving force behind the project,** es el alma-máter o la impulsora del proyecto. **Driving-whip,** látigo de cochero. **Driving-shaft,** árbol motor. **Driving-wheel,** rueda motriz.

driving license ['draɪvɪŋ,laɪsəns] [drai-vin-lai-sens], *s.* Licencia para manejar.

driving range ['draɪvɪŋ,reɪndʒ] [drai-vin-reinch] *s.* Campo de golf diseñado para practicar tiros de salida.

driving school ['draɪvɪŋskuːl] [drai-vin-skul], *s.* Autoescuela.

driving test ['draɪvɪŋtest] [drai-vin-test] *s.* Examen de conducir o de manejar.

drizzle ['drɪzl] [dri-sel], *vn.* Llovizar, gotear, caer a gotas. *-va.* Echar o despedir en gotas menudas, rociar. **Drizzling rain,** llovizna.

drizzle, *s.* Llovizna.

drizzly ['drɪzlɪ] [dris-li], *a.* Lloviznoso. **Drizzly weather,** tiempo brumoso, de llovizna.

droll [drəʊl] [droul], *a.* Festivo, chancero, jocoso, chistoso, gracioso, con chispa (comic), raro; curioso (quaint, curious). **Droll saying,** dicho gracioso. **Droll affair,** cosa rara. *-s.* 1. Bufón, bufonada. 2. Farsa.

droll, *vn.* Chocarrear, chancearse.

drollery ['drəʊlərɪ] [drou-le-ri], *s.* Chocarrería bufonería o bufonada.

drollish ['drəʊlɪʃ] [drou-lish], *a.* Divertido, chistoso o gracioso.

dromedary ['drɒmɪdərɪ] [dro-mi-da-ri], *s.* Dromedario, camello de una sola giba.

drone [drəʊn] [droun], *s.* 1. Zángano de colmena, el macho de la abeja (bee). 2. Zángano, zangandungo, haragán. 3. Roncón de gaita. 4. *(Aer.)* Avión radioguiado. 5. Zumbido (sound of bees, traffic, aircraft); cantinela, sonsonete (of voice). **Drone-fly,** abejorro.

drone, *vn.* 1. Zanganear, holgazanear. 2. Producir un sonido sordo; zumbar (bee, engine, plane).

drone on (*Fam.*) **She droned on for hours,** estuvo horas con la misma perorata.

dronish ['drəʊnɪʃ] [drou-nish], *a.* Ocioso, perezoso, lento, tardo, flojo.

drool [druːl] [drul], *vn.* Babear (dog, baby). **We drooled at the sight of the cakes,** se nos hizo la boca agua al ver los pasteles. *s.* Babas, baba (dribble). (*Sl.*) Bobadas (drivel).

droop [druːp] [drup], *vn.* 1. Inclinarse, doblarse hacia el suelo, bajarse como obligado por debilidad o flaqueza. 2. Descaecer, decaer, amilanarse, desanimarse, entristecerse, acabarse, penar, consumirse, marchitarse, ponerse mustio (sag/flowers); flaquear, decaer (flag/spirits); desfallecer, decaer (person). **His shoulders drooped,** se encorvó. *-va.* Permitir caer; inclinar, bajar.

drooping ['druːpɪŋ] [dru-pin], *s.* Languidez, tristeza, abatimiento. *-a.* Lánguido, triste, afligido. Gacho (head); mustio (flowers).

drop [drɒp] [drop], *s.* 1. Gota, glóbulo de un líquido cualquiera. **We haven't had a drop of rain for six weeks,** no ha caído una gota de agua en seis semanas. 2. Gota, pequeña porción de alguna cosa. **Can I have a drop?,** ¿me das una gotita?. **A drop in the ocean,** un grano de arena en el desierto, una insignificancia. 3. Pendiente con diamantes pequeños. 4. Caída, baja (fall/in prices), descenso (in temperature); pendiente, declive. Caída (a difference in height). **She had to take a drop in salary,** tuvo que aceptar un sueldo más bajo. **At the drop of a hat,** en cualquier momento. **A sheer drop,** una caída a plomo. 5. *-pl.* Medicamento líquido dado en gotas. **Ear/nose drops,** gotas para los oídos/la nariz. **Eye drops,** colirio. 6. Lanzamiento (of supplies). 7. Buzón (letter box); punto de recogida (collection point). **Drop-curtain,** telón de boca. **Drop-letter,** carta que ha de ser entregada al destinatario por la misma estafeta en que fué echada al correo. **Drop by drop,** gota a gota. **Drop of a sail,** (*Mar.*) caída de una vela.

drop, *va.* 1. Destilar. 2. Soltar, desprender, dejar caer de cualquier modo, literal o figuradamente (accidentally). Dejar caer, tirar (deliberately/cup, vase); lanzar (bomb, supplies). **Drop that gun!,** ¡suelta ese revólver! **I dropped the cup,** se me cayó la taza. **Don't drop it!,** ¡que no se te caiga! **To drop tears,** derramar lágrimas. 3. Soltar, proferir una palabra casualmente o como por incidencia (utter/hint, remark). **To let it drop that…,** dejar escapar que… (inadvertently); dejar caer que… (deliberately). 4. Dejar de hacer o cesar en lo que se estaba haciendo; abandonar, (give up, abandon/case). Retirar (charges); abandonar, renunciar a (plan, idea); dejar de ver a (friends, associate). Omitir (omit/letter, syllable, word); suprimir algo (chapter, scene, article). **Let's drop the subject,** cambiemos de tema. **Just drop everything and come,** déjalo todo y vente. **To drop somebody from a team,** sacar a alguien de un equipo. 5. Dejar o desprenderse de algún dependiente o compañero; despedir, echar. 6. Dejar, sufrir que una cosa se pierda o se olvide. 7. Parir los animales. 8. (*Fam.*) Hacer caer, como con un arma de fuego. 9. Alargar, bajar (lower/hem); bajar (eyes, voice). 10. Dejar (set down/passenger, cargo); pasar a dejar (deliver). **I can drop them there on my way home,** puedo pasar por allí a dejarlos de camino a casa. *-vn.* 1. Gotear, caer gota a gota; soltar gotas. 2. Caer (fall/object), bajar de un lugar alto a otro más bajo; caer sin ímpetu. Bajar, descender (plane). Desplomarse (collapse). **To be ready to drop,** estar cayéndose. **He dropped to the ground,** se tiró al suelo (deliberately); cayó de un golpe (fell). 3. Quedarse muerto o morir de repente. **To drop (down) dead,** caerse muerto. (*Coloq.*) **Drop dead!,** ¡vete al demonio! 4. Desvanecerse o disiparse alguna cosa. Amainar (decrease/wind); bajar, descender (temperature); bajar, experimentar un descenso (prices); bajar (voice); caer (in height/terrain). 5. Sobrevenir, venir de repente. **To drop a word unawares,** soltar alguna expresión incautamente; dejar escapar alguna palabra que no debía decirse. **To drop a courtesy,** hacer una cortesía. **To drop anchor,** anclar. **To drop in**

unexpectedly, entrar en alguna parte de improviso. **To drop the curtain,** correr el telón. (*Met.*) Encubrir, ocultar.

drop away 1. Morir. 2. Caer (ground); disminuir (support, interest).

drop back Rezagarse, quedarse atrás. **She dropped back to third place,** se rezagó quedando en el tercer puesto.

drop behind Rezagarse, quedarse atrás; rezagarse con respecto a, quedarse atrás (competitors, classmates).

drop by (*Coloq.*) Pasar; pasar por. **Why don't you drop by for a cup of coffee some time?,** ¿por qué no pasas un día a tomar un café?. **I have to drop by the office,** tengo que pasar por la oficina.

drop in 1. Entrar, introducirse, meterse de rondón. 2. (*Coloq.*) Pasar. **I'll drop in sometime tomorrow,** pasaré mañana en algún momento. **To drop in on somebody,** pasar a ver a alguien, caerle a alguien.

drop off 1. Decaer, ir en decadencia; perder un empleo o acomodo. 2. Caerse (fall); dormirse, quedarse dormido (fall asleep). Disminuir (decrease/sales, numbers). 3. Dejar (person, goods).

drop out 1. Desaparecer, disiparse algún líquido. 2. No presentarse a un concurso, una carrera (before event); abandonar un curso, una carrera (during event). **To drop out of politics,** dejar o abandonar la política. **To drop out (of society),** marginarse, convertirse en un marginado.

drop over, drop round (GB) (*Coloq.*). Pasar. **I'll drop over to her house,** pasaré por su casa.

dropcloth ['drɒpklɒθ] [drop-kloz] Cubierta para proteger muebles y suelos mientras se pinta.

drop-forge ['drɒpfɔːdʒ] [drop-forch], *va.* Forjar a martinete.

drop hammer ['drɒphæməʳ] [drop-ja-maʳ], *s.* Martinete.

drop kick ['drɒpkɪk] [drop-kik], *s.* 1. En el fútbol, puntapié que se da a la pelota al rebotar. 2. Botepronto (in rugby); patada voladora (in wrestling).

droplet ['drɒplɪt] [drop-let], *s.* Gotita.

dropout ['drɒpaʊt] [drop-aut] *s.* Marginado.

dropper ['drɒpəʳ] [dro-paʳ], *s.* Cuentagotas.

dropping ['drɒpɪŋ] [dro-pin], *s.* 1. Lo que cae gota a gota. **Droppings of the nose,** moquita. 2. El acto de caer en gotas. 3. *pl.* (*Fam.*) Excrementos de los animales domésticos.

droppingly ['drɒpɪŋlɪ] [dro-pin-li] *adv.* A gotas, gota a gota.

dropstone ['drɒpstəʊn] [drop-stoun], *s.* Espato en figura de gotas.

dropsy ['drɒpsɪ] [drop-si] *s.* Hidropesía.

drop zone ['drɒpzəʊn] [drop-soun] *s.* Zona de lanzamiento.

dross [drɒs] [dros], *s.* 1. Escoria de metales; borra; espuma; hez. 2. Orín, moho, herrumbre. 3. Impurezas, residuo, heces; basura (waste).

drossy ['drɒsɪ] [dro-si], *a.* 1. Lleno de escoria, espuma o heces. 2. Vil, despreciable; impuro, puerco; grosero.

drought, drouth [draʊt] [draft], *s.* 1. Seca, sequedad, sequía. 2. Sed.

droughtiness ['draʊtɪnɪs] [draf-ti-nes], *s.* Sequedad, sequía.

droughty, drouthy ['draʊtɪ] [draf-ti], *a.* Seco; sediento; árido.

drove [drəʊv] [drouv], *s.* 1. Manada (of animals); hato, rebaño de ganado lanar. 2. Cualquier conjunto de animales; gentío, multitud, muchedumbre. **They came in droves,** vino gente a montones.

drove, *pret.* de TO DRIVE.

drover ['drəʊvəʳ] [drou-vaʳ], *s.* Ganadero, criador de ganado mayor y traficante en él.

drown [draʊn] [draun], *va.* 1. Ahogar (person, animal). **To be drowned,** ahogarse, morir ahogado. 2. Anegar, cubrir (landscape, fields); sumergir. **He drowned his meal in gravy,** se puso un montonazo de salsa en la comida. 3. Inundar. 4. Sofocar alguna cosa. **To drown one's sorrow in wine,** ahogar sus pesares en vino, embriagarse. **To be drowned in tears,** estar anegado en lágrimas. **Drown out,** ahogar (make inaudible/noise, cries, screams). *-vn.* Anegarse, ahogarse; morir ahogado.

drowner ['draʊnəʳ] [drau-naʳ], s. Anegador, sofocador.

drowning ['draʊnɪŋ] [drau-nin], s. 1. Ahogamiento, acción de ahogar o ahogarse. 2. Sumersión, inundación. -pa. de TO DROWN.

drowse [draʊz] [draus], va. Adormecer, causar pesadez o sueño. -vn. 1. Adormecerse. 2. Tener murria, estar murrio o cabizbajo.

drowsily ['draʊzɪlɪ] [drau-si-li], adv. Soñolientamente; lentamente.

drowsiness ['draʊzɪnɪs] [drau-si-nes] s. Somnolencia, pereza, indolencia, adormecimiento, lentitud.

drowsy ['draʊzɪ] [drau-si], a. Soñoliento, soporífero, lerdo, estúpido; pesado, somnoliento, adormecido (sleepy/person, look). Somnoliento, perezoso (peaceful, inactive/atmosphere, afternoon). **Wine makes me drowsy,** el vino me da sueño o me amodorra.

drowsy-headed ['draʊzɪ'hedɪd] [drau-si-je-did], a. Lerdo, pesado, soñoliento.

drub [drʌb] [drab], s. Golpe, puñada.

drub, va. Apalear, sacudir, pegar.

drubbing ['drʌbɪŋ] [dra-bin], s. Paliza o zurra, tunda.

drudge ['drʌdʒ] [dradch], vn. 1. Afanarse, fatigarse, trabajar sin descanso. 2. Afanarse a trabajar en oficios u ocupaciones desagradables o viles, sin provecho ni honra. -va. Pasar el tiempo fastidiosamente o con trabajo.

drudge, s. 1. Ganapán; marmitón, grumete, galopín de cocina. 2. Esclavo.

drudgery ['drʌdʒərɪ] [drad-che-ri], s. Faena o trabajo vil, desagradable, ingrato. **This job is sheer drudgery,** este trabajo es una pesadez.

drudgingly ['drʌdʒɪŋlɪ] [drad-chin-li], adv. Laboriosamente, penosamente; desagradablemente.

drug [drʌg] [drag], s. 1. Droga, estupefaciente (narcotic). Medicamento, medicina, fármaco (medication). **To be on drug,** drogarse. **I don't do drugs,** yo no me drogo. **Drug dependence,** drogodependencia. (Coloq.) **Drug pusher,** camello, conecte, jíbaro. 2. Cualquier cosa de difícil salida, sin venta.

drug, va. 1. Mezclar con drogas, hacer narcótico por medio de drogas. 2. Jaropar, dar drogas o medicinas con exceso; sumir en torpor, entumecer. Drogar (person, animal). Adulterar con drogas (add drugs to/food, wine). **A drugged sleep,** un sueño pesado. -vn. Administrar o recetar drogas.

drug abuse ['drʌgə'bjuːs] [drag-a-bius] s. Consumo de drogas o estupefacientes.

drug addict ['drʌg'ædɪkt] [draga-dikt] s. Drogadicto, toxicómano. **Drug addiction,** drogadicción, toxicomanía.

druggist ['drʌgɪst] [dra-guist], s. Farmacéutico, boticario.

drugstore ['drʌgstɔːʳ] [drag-stoʳ] Establecimiento que vende medicamentos, cosméticos, periódicos y una gran variedad de artículos.

druid ['druːɪd] [druid], s. Druida, sacerdote de los antiugos bretones y celtas.

drum [drʌm] [dram], s. 1. (Mus.) Tambor, atambor. **Drums,** batería (in band). 2. Tambor, uno de los diversos objetos cilíndricos en figura de tambor: v. g. un aparato para difundir el calor, el cilindro que comunica movimiento a una máquina (machine part); un cuñete o barrilito de pescado, de higos u otros frutos, etc. (machine part). 3. Tímpano del oído.

drum, vn. 1. (Mus.) Tocar el tambor; dar golpecitos. tamborilear (beat, tap/person); repiquetear (rain, hail, hooves). 2. Tamborilear, golpetear (table, floor). **To drum one's fingers,** tamborilear con los dedos. -va. 1. Batir sobre el tambor, batir sin intermisión. 2. (Mil.) Expeler a toque de tambor: (seguido de out). 3. Reiterar; aturdir. 4. Atraer parroquianos. **To drum up,** congregar o juntar a toque de tambor.

drum into. To drum something into somebody/ somebody's head, hacerle aprender algo a alguien a fuerza de repetírselo o de machacárselo.

drum out of Expulsar de (of army, school).

drum up Conseguir, obtener (support).

drumble ['drʌmbl] [dram-bel], vn. 1. Sonar como un tambor. 2. Zanganear, golgazanear.

drum-major [drʌm'meɪdʒəʳ] [dram-mei-yaʳ], s. Tambor mayor.

drum-maker [drʌm'meɪkəʳ] [dram-mei-kaʳ], s. Tamborero.

drummer ['drʌməʳ] [dra-maʳ], s. 1. Tambor, el que toca el tambor. (Mil.) 2. Tamborilero. 3. (Com. Amer.) Agente vendedor de una casa de comercio. 4. Batería, baterista (pop, jazz). **To hear/move/march to a different drummer,** ir contra la corriente.

drummond light [drʌmən'laɪt] [dra-mon-lait], s. Luz de oxicalcio.

drumstick ['drʌmstɪk] [dram-stik], s. 1. Baqueta, palillo o bolillo de tambor. 2. (Fam.) Lo que se asemeja a una baqueta, como el hueso de la pierna de un pavo. 3. (Culin.) Muslo, pata.

drunk [drʌŋk] [drank], a. Embriagado, borracho, ebrio (intoxicated). **To be drunk,** estar borracho. (Law) **Drunk and disorderly,** en estado de embriaguez y alterando el orden público. **Drunk driver,** conductor en estado de embriaguez. **Drunk with success/power,** ebrio o borracho de gloria/poder (elated). s. Borracho.

drunkard ['drʌŋkəd] [dran-kard], s. Borrachón. (Met.) Cuero, el que bebe mucho.

drunk driving [drʌŋk'draɪvɪŋ] [drank-drai-vin] s. Delito de conducir bajo la influencia del alcohol.

drunken ['drʌŋkən] [dran-ken], a. Ebrio, borracho (person, mob); de borrachos (orgy, brawl). **In a drunken stupor,** en un sopor etílico.

drunkenly ['drʌŋkənlɪ] [dran-ken-li], adv. Ebriamente.

drunkenness ['drʌŋkənnɪs] [dran-ken-nes], s. Embriaguez; borrachera habitual (state); alcoholismo (alcoholism).

drupaceous ['druːpeɪʃəs] [dru-pei-shos], a. (Bot.) Drupáceo, que produce drupas o es parecida a ellas.

dry [draɪ] [drai], a. 1. Arido (dull, boring/lecture, book); seco; sin jugo. Seco (not wet/ground, washing). Seco (cough). **There wasn't a dry eye in the house,** no hubo quien no llorara. 2. Sediento. 3. Seco, estéril, frío (lacking natural moisture/leaves, skin, hair); 4. Duro, austero, satírico; mordaz, cáustico (ironic/humor, wit); seco (lacking warmth/ laugh, style). 5. Apretado, agarrado, mísero, avariento. 6. Taciturno. 7. Privado de dulzura; seco (not sweet/wine, sherry); brut, seco (champagne). 8. Que no da leche, v. gr. una vaca. 9. Seco (dried up/well, river). Seco (not rainy, not humid/climate, weather, heat). **Tomorrow will be dry,** mañana no lloverá. Seco (using no fluid/cell). **A piece of dry bread,** una rebanada de pan sin mantequilla. **He had a dry shave,** se afeitó en seco. 10. Seco donde está prohibida la venta de bebidas alcohólicas (prohibiting sale of alcohol/state, county). **Dry land,** tierra firme. **Dry goods,** tejidos, telas, lienzos, ropa, lencería; (Ingl.) artículos que se venden por medida de capacidad, áridos; y también, en general, especierías, pinturas (colores), etc., en contraposición a otras mercancías y a los tejidos. **Dry style,** estilo seco, insípido.

dry, va. 1. Secar, quitar o extraer la humedad (clothes, crockery). Secar (preserve/fish, fruit, meat). **To dry oneself,** secarse. 2. Enjugar. 3. Abrasar con sed. 4. Desangrar, desaguar. -vn. Secarse, enjugarse (washes, dishes, paint). **You wash and I'll dry,** tú lavas y yo seco. **To dry up,** enjugar, desecar, agotar, privar enteramente de la humedad.

dry off Secarse.

dry out Secarse, secar (soil, clothes). (Coloq.) Curarse de alcoholismo, hacerse una cura de desintoxicación (alcoholic).

dry up Secarse completamente (stream, pond); agotarse (funds, resources, inspiration). (Coloq.) Quedarse en blanco (actor). Secar los platos (dry dishes).

dryad ['draɪəd] [draiad] s. 1. Dríade, o dríade, ninfa de los bosques. 2. Lirón: Myoxus dryas.

dry battery [draɪ'bætərɪ] [drai-ba-te-ri], s. (Elec.) Pila o batería seca.

dry cell ['draɪ'sel] [drai-sel], s. (Elec.) Pila seca.

dry clean ['draɪˈkliːn] [drai-klin] *va.* Limpiar en seco. **I had my coat dry cleaned,** mandé el abrigo a la tintorería.

dry cleaner('s) ['draɪˈkliːnaᵣs] [drai-kli-naᵣs] *s.* Tintorería.

dry cleaning ['draɪˈkliːnɪŋ] [drai-kli-nin], *s.* Limpieza en seco (action); **I collected my dry cleaning,** recogí mi ropa de la tintorería (clothes).

dry dock ['draɪˈdɒk] [drai-dok], *s.* Dique de carena, dique seco, astillero.

dryer ['draɪəᵣ] [draiaᵣ], *s.* 1. Secante. 2. (*Quím.*) Desecativo, desecante. 3. Secadora (machine/for clothes); tendedor, tendedero (rack); secadora centrífuga (spin dryer); secadora de aire caliente (tumble dryer).

dry-eyed ['draɪˈaɪd] [drai-aid], *a.* Ojienjuto. *adv.* Sereno, sin una lágrima.

dry farming ['draɪˈfɑːmɪŋ] [drai-far-min], *s.* Cultivos de secano.

dry ice ['draɪˈaɪs] [drai-ais], *s.* Hielo seco, bióxido sólido de carbono.

dryly ['draɪlɪ] [drai-li], *adv.* Secamente, fríamente.

dryness ['draɪnɪs] [drai-nes], *s.* 1. Sequedad, aridez, cualidad o estado de lo que es seco (of ground, hair, skin, climate). 2. Sequedad, tibieza, aridez de estilo. Sequedad (of manner); lo mordaz o cáustico (of humor, wit). 3. Lo seco (of wine, sherry).

dry-nurse ['draɪˈnɜːs] [drai-ners], *s.* Ama que cría aun niño sin darle de mamar.

dry-rot ['draɪˈrɒt] [drai-rot], *s.* 1. Carcoma, enfermedad de la madera causada por los ataques de algunas especies de hongos. 2. Enfermedad de los tubérculos de la patata. 3. (*Fig.*) Corrupción interna y oculta, de las costumbres, de la moralidad, etc.

dry-rub ['draɪˈrʌb] [drai-rab], *va.* Estregar o limpiar una cosa sin humedecerla.

drysalter ['draɪˈsɑːltəᵣ] [drai-sal-taᵣ] *s.* Traficante en viandas saladas y secas, aceites, escabeches, materias de tinte, etc.

dry-shod ['draɪˈʃɒd] [drai-shod], *a.* A pie enjuto.

dry-wall ['draɪˈwɔː] [drai-uol], *a.* Con paredes de tipo seco. (Se aplica a construcción.)

dual ['djʊəl] [diual], *a.* 1. Doble (double/role, function); doble (nationality); compartido (joint/ownership, interest); **Dual carriageway,** autovía, carretera de doble pista. **Dual control,** doble mando, doble volante de mando (car, brakes). **Dual personality,** doble personalidad. 2. (*Gram.*) Dual, número dual.

dualism ['djʊəlɪzm] [diua-lism], *s.* 1. *V.* DUALITY. 2. Dualismo, todo sistema filosófico que admite en el universo dos principios activos, la materia y el espíritu, o el genio del bien y el del mal.

dualist ['djʊəlɪst] [diua-list], *s.* Dualista, sectario del dualismo.

duality ['djʊəlɪtɪ] [diua-li-ti], *s.* Dualidad, expresión del número dos; estado de ser dos; división, separación.

dual-purpose ['djʊəlˈpɜːpəs] [diual-per-pos] *a.* De doble uso (utensil); de doble acción (cleaner); de doble función o uso (furniture).

dub [dʌb] [dab], *va.* 1. (*Cin.*) Doblar (una película cinematográfica). (*Audio*) Mezclar. 2. **To dub somebody (a) knight,** armar a alguno caballero. 3. Conferir cualquier dignidad. 4. Titular, apodar, dar nombre (nickname). 5. Alisar, estregar, aderezar.

dub, *s.* 1. Golpe. 2. Lodazal.

dubbed ['dʌbɪd] [da-bid], *a.* *V.* BLUNT.

dubbing ['dʌbɪŋ] [da-bin] *s.* (*Cin.*) Doblaje. (*Audio*) Mezcla.

dubious ['dʌbɪəs] [da-bios], *a.* 1. Dudoso, discutible (questionable/honor, achievement); irresoluto, indeciso. 2. Dudoso, incierto, equívoco, problemático, oscuro, ambiguo; turbio (past); sospechoso (motives, person). **He seems a rather dubious character to me,** no me parece una persona de fiar.

dubiously ['dʌbɪəslɪ] [da-bios-li], *adv.* 1. Dudosamente. 2. Con recelo o desconfianza (doubtfully/look, say); sospechosamente (suspiciously/behave).

dubiousness ['dʌbɪəsnɪs] [da-bios-nes], *s.* Duda, incertidumbre.

dubitable ['dʊbɪəteɪbl] [du-biu-tei-bol], *a.* Dubitable, dudable.

dubitation ['dʊbɪˈteɪʃən] [du-bi-tei-shon], *s.* Dubitación, duda.

ducal ['djuːkəl] [diu-kal] *a.* Ducal.

ducat ['djuːkət] [diu-kat], *s.* Ducado, moneda de oro o plata y de diverso valor en los varios países en que se ha usado y se usa.

duchess ['dʌtʃɪs] [da-chis], *s.* Duquesa, la esposa o viuda de un duque; o la princesa soberana de un ducado.

duchy ['dʌtʃɪ] [da-chi], *s.* El territorio o estado sobre el que recae el título de duque.

duck [dʌk] [dak], *s.* 1. Anade, pato. También el pato hembra, en contraposición al *drake,* o macho. 2. Cabeceo, la acción de volver la cabeza a un lado y a otro. 3. Cabrillas, juego de muchachos. 4. Mona, querida; es voz de cariño. **A lame duck** (en la bolsa de Nueva York), el corredor, agiotista o especulador que no puede pagar sus pérdidas. **To make/to play at ducks and drakes,** cabrillear, jugar el juego de cabrillas; hacer saltar una piedra plana en el agua; (*Fig.*) gastar de una manera pródiga; comprometer inconsideradamente. Usado con *of* o *with.* **A dead duck,** un asunto acabado. **He took to skiing like a duck to water,** empezó a esquiar como si lo hubiera hecho toda la vida.

duck, *s.* Lienzo fuerte no cruzado de hilo o algodón, más ligero y fino que la lona. -*pl.* (*Fam.*) Pantalones hechos de este tejido.

duck *vn.* Agacharse (bow down). **I ducked behind a pillar,** me escondí rápidamente detrás de una columna (hide). *va.* 1. Agachar, bajar (lower, head). 2. Hundir (submerge). 3. Eludir, esquivar (dodge, question); eludir, evadir (responsibility). **To duck out of something,** escabullirse de algo, eludir algo.

duck-bill ['dʌkbɪl] [dak-bil], *s.* 1. (*Zool.*) Ornitorrinco, mamífero acuático y ovíparo de Australia. (Ornithorhynchus paradoxus). 2. Lo que tiene figura de pico de ánade.

ducker ['dʌkəᵣ] [da-kaᵣ], *s.* Buzo; quitapelillos, zalamero.

ducking ['dʌkɪŋ] [da-kin], *s.* 1. Zambullidura, zabullidura, chapuzón. 2. (*Mar.*) Zambullida, especie de castigo que se da a bordo.

ducking-stool ['dʌkɪŋstuːl] [da-kin-stul], *s.* Silla de madera, fuerte y tosca, a la que ataban a una mujer para sumergirla en el agua. Antiguo castigo que se daba a las mujeres pendencieras, murmuradoras y gruñonas.

duck-legged ['dʌkɪŋlegɪd] [da-kin-le-guid], *a.* Corto de piernas.

duckling ['dʌklɪŋ] [da-klin], *s.* 1. Anadeja. 2. Monina; voz cariñosa. 3. (*Zool.*) Patito, anadón. (*Culin.*) Pato joven.

duck-meat ['dʌkˈmiːt] [dak-mit], o **duck-weed** ['dʌkɪŋ] [da-kin], *s.* (*Bot.*) Lenteja acuática.

duck's-foot ['dʌkzfuːt] [daks-fut] *s.* (*Bot.*) Especie de serpentaria.

duct ['dʌkt] [dakt], *s.* (*Anat. Tech.*) Conducto, canal, tubo.

ductile ['dʌktɪl] [dak-til], *a.* 1. Dúctil, flexible, blando, correoso. 2. Tratable, obsequiso.

ductileness ['dʌktɪlnɪs] [dak-til-nes], **ductility** ['dʌktɪlɪtɪ] [dak-ti-li-ti] *s.* Ductilidad; docilidad.

dud [dʌd] [dad], *s.* 1. (*Mil.*) Bomba que no estalla (shell, bomb). 2. (*Vul.*) Persona o cosa que resulta un fracaso; birria, porquería (useless thing); calamidad, inútil (useless person). 3. **Duds,** *pl.* (*Vul.*) trapos, andrajos, ropa vieja. *a.* 1. (*Coloq.*) Falso (useless, valueless); sin fondos (check). **A dud battery,** una pila gastada o que no funciona. 2. (*Mil.*) Que no estalla (shell, bomb).

dude [djuːd] [diud] (*Sl.*) Petimetre, currutaco, tipo, tío.

dudgeon ['dʌdʒən] [dad-yon], *s.* 1. Ojeriza, desazón, enojo, cólera. **In high dudgeon,** indignadísimo, lleno de indignación. 2. La raíz de boj, cuya madera se usó antiguamente para los puños de las dagas; una madera cualquiera abigarrada o veteada.

due [djuː] [diu], *a.* 1. Debido, cumplido, devengado. **The rent is due,** hay que pagar el alquiler (payable). **The respect due to one's elders,** el respeto que se les debe a los mayores (owed). **It's all due to you,** todo gracias a ti, te lo debemos todo a ti. 2. Debido, apto, propio, conveniente, oportuno (consideration, regard); exacto, caído; merecido (deserved/reward). **Without due cause,** sin causa justificada. **In due course,** en su debido tiempo, a su debido momento. 3. Aguardado, algo cuya llegada está señalada o prevista (scheduled). **When is the next train/flight due?,** ¿cuándo llega el próximo tren/vuelo?. **When is the baby due?,** ¿para cuándo espera o tiene fecha?. **She's due for promotion,** le corresponde un ascenso. 4. Que se puede atribuir o achacar. **Due to,** debido a. **All flights were canceled due to bad weather,** se cancelaron todos los vuelos debido al mal tiempo. **Due west,** *(Mar.)* poniente derecho. *-adv.* Exactamente. **We headed due north,** nos dirigimos derecho hacia el norte. V. DULY. *-s.* Lo que da derecho pertenece a alguno, deuda u obligación; derecho; tributo, impuesto. **King's dues,** derechos del rey. **In due time,** a su tiempo; a propósito. **To give him his due, he is efficient,** tienes que reconocer que es eficiente. **Dues,** *s. pl.* Cuota (subscription).

due date ['djuːdeɪt] [diu-deit], *s.* Plazo; fecha de vencimiento. **When is your due date?,** ¿para cuándo esperas o tienes fecha? (of birth).

duel ['djuːəl] [diuel], *s.* Duelo. **To fight a duel,** batirse en duelo.

duel, *vn.* Combatir en duelo. *-va.* Acometer a otro en duelo o desafío.

dueller ['djuːələ*] [diue-la*], **duellist** ['djuːdeɪt] [daiu-deit], *s.* Duelista.

duelling ['djuːəlɪŋ] [diue-lin], *s.* Desafío.

dueness ['djuːənɪs] [diue-nes], *s.* Aptitud. V. FITNESS.

duenna ['djuːənɑː] [diue-na] *sf.* Dueña, mujer anciana encargada antiguamente de guardar doncellas.

duet ['djuːet] [diu-et], *s. (Mús.)* Dúo. **A violin duet,** un dúo de violín.

duff [dʌf] [daf] *a.* (GB) *(Coloq.)* Malo, chafa. *s. (Sl.)* Trasero, culo.

duff up, darle una paliza a.

duffel ['dʌfl] [da-fel], *s.* 1. Moletón, tejido velludo de lana. 2. Equipo, pertrechos. **Duffel bag,** talego, tula, bolso marinero.

duffer ['dʌfə*] [da-fa*] *s. (Coloq.)* Inútil, zoquete, chambón.

dug [dʌg] [dag], *s.,* Teta o pezón de teta de algún animal. *pret. y pp.* del verbo TO DIG.

dugong ['dʌgɒŋ] [da-gon], *s.* Mamífero acuático de la India y Australia. Muy parecido al manatí de la América tropical.

dugout ['dʌgaʊt] [dag-aut], *s.* 1. Piragua. 2. Cueva; dogaut, caseta (in baseball). 3. *(Mil.)* Refugio contra bombardeos.

duke [djuːk] [diuk], *s.* 1. Duque, título de los primeros entre la nobleza. 2. *(Ant.)* General, capitán.

dukedom ['djuːkdəm] [diuk-dom], *s.* Ducado.

dulcet ['dʌlsɪt] [dal-sit], *a.* 1. Dulce, agradable al paladar. 2. Dulce, suave, armonioso. 3 Agradable a la mente, lo que solaza o consuela. **I could hear her dulcet tones,** oía su dulce voz.

dulcification [dʌlsɪfɪˈkeɪʃən] [dal-si-fi-kei-shon], *s.* 1. Dulcificación. 2. *(Quím.)* Dulcificación, la combinación de algún ácido mineral con el alcohol.

dulcified ['dʌlsɪfaɪd] [dal-si-faid], *a.* Dulcificado.

dulcify ['dʌlsɪfaɪ] [dal-si-fai], *va.* Dulcificar, dulzurar, endulzar.

dulcimer ['dʌlsɪmə*] [dal-si-ma*], *s.* Tímpano, salterio, instrumento músico.

dulcinea [dʌlsɪnɪə] [dal-si-nia], *f.* Amada, dama y señora de los pensamientos de uno.

dulcoration ['dʌlkəˈreɪʃən] [dal-ko-rei-shon], *s.* Dulcificación.

dulia ['dʌlɪə] [da-lia], *s.* Dulía, culto que se da a los santos.

dull [dʌl] [dal], *a.* 1. Embotado, obtuso, romo, sin filo o corte (edge, blade). 2. No agudo o violento; v. g. **A dull pain,** un dolor sordo. 3. Lerdo, estúpido, torpe, negado, insípido (faculties); sordo (pain, ache); sordo, amortiguado (pain). 4.

Flojo, tardo, perezoso, pesado; lánguido, insensible. 5. Triste, melancólico, pensativo, murrio. 6. Opaco, oscuro, ofuscado; nebuloso, gris, feo (overcast/day, morning); apagado (not bright/color); sin brillo (eyes, complexion); pálido (light, glow); mate (not shiny/finish); sin brillo (hair). **It's rather dull out today,** hoy está bastante nublado. 7. Soñoliento; aburrido (boring/speech, person). **Dull of hearing,** algo sordo, tardo o duro de oído.

dull, *va.* 1. Embotar, engrosar los filos y puntas de instrumentos cortantes. 2. Entontecer, embotar (senses); entorpecer, obstruir; contristar. 3. Hacer menos agudo, aliviar, moderar, mitigar (make less sharp/pain). 4. Ofuscar, deslumbrar; empañar, deslustrar, deslucir; quitar el brillo a, opacar (make less bright/color, surface). *-vn.* 1. Embotarse, entontecerse. 2. Ofuscarse; entristecerse; mitigarse, entorpecerse.

dullard ['dʌləd] [da-lar *dʌlsɪt]* [dal-sit]d], *s.* Bestia, estólido; zopenco. *-a.* Estúpido.

dull-brained ['dʌlˈbreɪnd] [dal-breind], *a.* Estúpido, tonto.

dull-browed ['dʌlbraʊd] [dal-braud], *a.* El que tiene las cejas dispuestas de tal modo que atristan los ojos.

dulled ['dʌld] [dald], *a.* Oscurecido, no claro.

duller ['dʌlsə*] [da-la*], *s.* Lo que hace oscuro, lerdo o flojo.

dull-eyed ['dʌlˌaɪd] [dal-aid], *a.* El que tiene los ojos naturalmente apagados.

dull-head ['dʌlhed] [dal-jed], *s.* Zote, un hombre estúpido.

dull-witted ['dʌlwɪtɪd] [dal-uited], *a.* Lerdo, sin viveza.

dully ['dʌlɪ] [da-li], *adv.* Lentamente, torpemente, zafiamente, estúpidamente; débilmente, pálidamente (dimly/glow, shine); de manera aburrida (boringly/talk, write).

dulnes ['dʌlnɪs] [dal-nes], *s.* Estupidez, incapacidad, tontería, estolidez, torpeza, rudeza; somnolencia, negligencia, pereza, entorpecimiento, pesadez, deslustre; embotadura.

dulse ['dʌls] [dals], *s.* Alga marina abundante de color rojo claro, que se come en Escocia y en otros países.

duly ['djuːlɪ] [diu-li], *adv.* Debidamente (correctly, properly); regularmente, exactamente, puntualmente, a su tiempo. **Your comments have been duly noted,** se ha tomado debida nota de sus observaciones. **Permission was duly granted,** el permiso fue concedido, como era de esperar. **He duly arrived at four,** llegó a las cuatro, como estaba previsto (as expected, planned).

dumb [dʌm] [dam], *a.* 1. Mudo, privado del habla (unable to speak). **She's deaf and dumb,** es sordomuda. **To strike one dumb,** enmudecer a uno. 2. *(Coloq.)* Bobo (stupid). **To act dumb,** hacerse el tonto. **Dumb-bell,** halterio, pesas, aparato gimnástico, mancuerna. **Dumb creature,** bestia, bruto. **Dumb show,** pantomima por señas, signo, gesto. **Dumb motions,** señas mudas. **Dumb-waiter,** ascensor doméstico, montaplatos (elevator; estante giratorio para vajilla, mesa de servicio, mesita rodante (table).

dumb, *va.* Imponer silencio, mandar callar. **Dumbfound,** anonadar. **We were dumbfounded at the news,** la noticia nos dejó anonadados.

dumbly ['dʌmblɪ] [dam-bli], *adv.* Mudamente.

dumbness ['dʌmnɪs] [dam-nes], *s.* Mudez; silencio.

dumdum ['dʌmdʌm] [dam-dam] **dumdum bulet** *s. (Mil.)* Bala expansiva.

dumfound, dumbfound ['dʌmfaʊn] [dam-faun], *va. (Fam.)* Confundir, enmudecer a alguno.

dummy ['dʌmɪ] [da-mi], *s.* 1. *(Fest.)* Mudo. 2. *(Mec.)* Locomotora de calles, pequeña y poco ruidosa. También un carro cuya parte delantera es la locomotora y la trasera coche de pasajeros. 3. En el juego de naipes, cuando el juego debe hacerse entre cuatro personas y hay sólo tres, se ponen a un lado las cartas del que falta; a esto los ingleses llaman *dummy;* mano del muerto (in bridge, whist); muerto (player). 4. Maniquí para vestidos, cabeza para pelucas, etc., que sirven de anuncio en las tiendas (in window display, for dressmaker); muñeco (in tests, stunts). **Ventriloquist's dummy,** muñeco de ventrílocuo. 5. *(Coloq.)* Bobo (fool).

dummy, *a.* 1. Fingido, falseado, imitado, de juguete (gun, telephone). **A dummy package,** un paquete vacío. 2. *(Neg.)* Que actúa como testaferro (shareholder). **A dummy firm,** una empresa fantasma. (GB) *(Coloq.)* **Dummy run,** *s.* Ensayo, prueba.

dump [dʌ] [damp], *s. (Vul.)* 1. Murria, tristeza. En este sentido se usa sólo en plural. **To be in the dumps,** tener murria, esplín: estar triste, alicaído, malhumorado. 2. Arrebato, rapto. 3. Asombro, susto. 4. *(E.U.)* Lugar donde se echan y amontonan las basuras, cenizas, etc.; y también el montón mismo de basuras; vertedero, basural, tiradero (place for waste). *(Mil.)* Depósito (temporary store). 5. *(Coloq.)* Lugar de mala muerte (unpleasant place). **Dump truck,** volquete, camión volteador o de volteo, volqueta.

dump, *va.* 1. Vaciar de golpe; descargar, verter (set on ground/load, sand). **Where can I dump my things?,** ¿dónde puedo dejar o poner mis cosas?. *(Inform.)* Volcar (data, disks). 2. Tirar, botar (get rid of/waste, refuse). *(Neg.)* **To dump goods/products,** inundar el mercado con mercancías/productos a bajo precio. 3. *(Coloq.)* Plantar, botar, largar (boyfriend, girlfriend). *vn. (Inform.)* Volcar.

dump body [dʌmpˈbɒdɪ] [damp-bo-di], *s.* Caja de volteo (de un camión).

dumping [ˈdʌmpɪŋ] [dam-pin] *s.* 1. **The dumping of nuclear waste,** el vertido de residuos nucleares. **No dumping,** prohibido arrojar o tirar basura (of waste). **Dumping ground,** vertedero, basural, tiradero. 2. *(Neg.)* Dumping.

dumpish [ˈdʌmpɪʃ] [dam-pish], *s.* Murrio, mustio, triste, melancólico.

dumpishness [ˈdʌmpɪʃnɪs] [dam-pish-nes], *s.* Tristeza, descontento, melancolía.

dumpling [ˈdʌmplɪŋ] [dam-plin], *s.* 1. Pudín de pasta rellena de fruta o carne. 2. (Prov. Ingl.) Un enano. 3. Bola de masa que se come en sopas o guisos. **Apple dumpling,** manzana al horno, envuelta en masa.

dumpster [ˈdʌmpstəʳ] [damps-taʳ] *s.* Contenedor para escombros.

dumpy [ˈdʌmpɪ] [dam-pi], *a.* Gordo, regordete.

dun [dʌn] [dan], *va.* Importunar a un deudor. *(Vul.)* Moler, jorobar, fastidiar.

dun, *s.* 1. Acreedor importuno. 2. Altura; seto. *a.* Pardo.

dunce [dʌns] [dans], *s.* Zote, zopenco, bolo, tonto, burro. **Dunce cap,** (GB) **dunce's cap,** capirote, orejas de burro.

dunderhead, dunderpate [ˈdʌndəhed] [dan-der-jed], *s.* Zote, zopenco, tonto.

dune [djuːn] [diun], *s.* Duna, marisma, médano, montecillo de arena suelta y movediza que se forma en las cercanías del mar.

dung [dʌŋ] [dan], *s.* Estiércol, fiemo, excremento animal. **Cow-dung,** boñiga. **Dog-dung,** canina. **Goat, rat, mice, dung,** cagarruta. **Hen-dung,** gallinaza. **Horse-dung,** cagajón.

dung, *va.* Estercolar. *-vn.* Estercolar, echar de sí la bestia el excremento o estiércol.

dungarees [ˌdʌŋɡəˈriːz] [dan-ga-ris], *s. pl.* Pantalones o ropa de trabajo hechos de tela basta, overol (workman's); pantalon de peto (fashion).

dungcart [ˈdʌŋkɑːt] [dan-kart], *s.* Carro de basura.

dunged [ˈdʌŋɡɪd] [dan-gued], *a.* Estercolado, engrasado.

dungeon [ˈdʌndʒən] [dan-yon], *s.* Calabozo, mazmorra. *(Mex.)* Bartolina.

dungeon, *va.* Encalabozar.

dung-fork [ˈdʌŋfɔːk] [dan-fork], *s.* Horca o pala para el estiércol.

dungheap [ˈdʌŋhiːp] [dan-jip], **dunghill** [ˈdʌŋhɪl] [dan-jil], *s.* 1. Estercolero, muladar. 2. Vivienda vil y ordinaria; situación vil o baja. **To raise one from the dunghill,** sacar a alguno de la nada o de la miseria. *-a.* Bajo, vil, indigno.

dungy [ˈdʌŋɪ] [dan-gui], *a.* Lleno de estiércol; vil.

dungyard [ˈdʌŋjɑːd] [dan-yard], *s.* Corral de estiércol o para el estiércol.

dunner [ˈdʌnəʳ] [da-naʳ], *s.* Cobrador de deudas atrasadas.

dunno [dəˈnəʊ] [da-nou] *(Coloq.)* **(I) dunno,** no sé, ni idea.

duo [ˈdjuːəʊ] [diu-ou], *s.* Dúo, pieza que se canta o toca por dos voces o instrumentos. *V.* DUET.

duodecimal [ˌdjuːəʊˈdesɪməl] [diuou-de-si-mal], *a.* Duodecimal, se dice del sistema de numeración que emplea doce carácteres, y cuya base es el número doce.

duodecimo [ˈdjuːəʊˈdesɪməʊ] [diuou-de-si-mal], *s.* Libro en dozavo, cuya página es de unas 4 1/2 por 7 1/2 pulgadas.

duodenal [ˌdjuːəʊˈdiːnl] [diuou-di-nal], *a.* Duodenal. **Duodenal ulcer,** *(Med.)* Úlcera duodenal.

duodenum [ˌdjuːəʊˈdiːnəm] [diuou-di-nom], *s.* Duodeno.

duotype [ˈdjuːəʊtaɪp] [diuou-taip], *s.* Dos fotograbados a media tinta obtenidos del mismo negativo.

dupe [djuːp] [diup], *s.* Crédulo; víctima de engaño o dolo; inocentón, primo.

dupe, *va.* Engañar, embaucar.

duple [ˈdjuːpl] [diu-pal], *a.* Doble.

duplex [ˈdjuːpleks] [diu-pleks], *a.* 1. Duplo, doble, dúplice. **Duplex apartment,** dúplex. **Duplex house,** casa de dos viviendas adosadas. 2. *(Mec.)* Dúplice, dúplex, que opera o actúa en dos direcciones, especialmente en las transmisiones opuestas simultáneas; v. g. telégrafo, dúplex.

duplicate [ˈdjuːplɪkɪt] [diu-pli-keit], *va.* 1. Duplicar, hacer duplicado, reproducir exactamente: hacer copias de (copy/letter, document); repetir en forma innecesaria. (repeat/work, efforts). 2. *(Biol.)* Dividirse en dos partes espontáneamente.

duplicate, *s.* 1. Duplicado, copia. **In duplicate,** por duplicado. 2. El número doble de un mismo objeto en las colecciones de historia natural, minerales, monedas y otras. *-a.* Duplicado, doble, en pares. **A duplicate key,** un duplicado o una copia de llave.

duplication [ˌdjuːplɪˈkeɪʃən] [diu-pli-kei-shon], *s.* Duplicación, copia (of document); plegadura, pliegue, doblez. Repetición innecesaria (of work, effort).

duplicative [ˈdjuːplɪkətɪv] [diu-pli-ka-tiv], *a.* Que se refierre a la duplicación; que produce la duplicación o está producido por ella.

duplicature [ˈdjuːplɪkətʃəʳ] [diu-pli-ka-chaʳ], *s.* Plegadura, pliegue, doblez.

duplicity [ˈdjuːplɪsɪtɪ] [diu-pli-si-ti], *s.* Doblez, duplicidad, engaño.

dura mater [ˈdjuːrəˌmɑːtəʳ] [diu-ra-ma-taʳ], *s. (Anat.)* Duramáter, membrana que envuelve el cerebro.

durability [ˌdjʊərəˈbɪlɪtɪ] [diu-ra-bi-li-ti], *s.* Estabilidad, cualidad o estado de lo durable, duración.

durable [ˈdjʊərəbl] [diu-ra-bol], *a.* Durable, duradero. *(Neg.)* **Durable goods,** bienes (de consumo) duraderos.

durableness [ˈdjʊərəblnɪs] [diu-ra-bol-nes], *s.* Dura, duración.

durably [ˈdjʊərəblɪ] [diu-ra-bli], *adv.* Duraderamente.

durance [ˈdjʊərəns] [diu-rans], *s.* 1. Cautividad, encarcelación, sujeción personal.

durant [ˈdjʊərənt] [diu-rant], *s.* Sempiterna, tejido fuerte de lana.

duration [ˈdjʊəreɪʃən] [diu-rei-shon], *s.* Duración, continuación, perseverancia. *(Mil.)* **For the duration,** mientras dure la guerra.

duress [djʊəˈres] [diu-res], *s.* Compulsión, coacción, prisión. Encierro, maltrato. **Under duress,** bajo coacción.

durex [ˈdjʊəreks] [diu-reks] *s.* 1. (GB) Preservativo, condón (condom). 2. *(Austral.)* Scotch Tape.

durham [ˈdɜːhɑːm] [der-jam], *s.* 1. Res de una casta de ganado vacuno de cuernos cortos, notable por la excelencia de su carne. 2. Barca de carga con fondo plano que se impele por medio de largas pértigas.

during [ˈdjʊərɪŋ] [diu-rin], *prep.* Mientras, durante el tiempo que, entretanto, al mismo tiempo. **You never see them during the day,** nunca se los ve durante el día o de día. **She'll call during the week,** llamará durante la semana.

durst, *pret. irr.* del verbo TO DARE.

dusk [dʌsk] [dask], *a.* Oscurecido, fusco, oscuro. -*s.* 1. El anochecer o entre dos luces; crepúsculo vespertino. **At dusk,** al anochecer. 2. Principio de oscuridad, color fusco, color negruzco.

duskily [ˈdʌskɪlɪ] [das-ki-li], *adv.* Oscuramente.

duskiness [ˈdʌskɪnɪs] [das-ki-nes], *s.* Principio de la oscuridad.

duskish [ˈdʌskɪʃ] [das-kish], *a.* Fusco, oscuro, negruzco, sombrío.

duskishness [ˈdʌskɪʃnɪs] [das-kish-nes], *s.* Oscuridad.

dusknes [ˈdʌsknɪʃ] [dask-nes], *s.* Ofuscamiento.

dusky [ˈdʌskɪ] [das-ki], *a.* 1. Oscuro, falto de luz. 2. Fusco; oscuro (pink); moreno, de tez morena (complexion). 3. (Raro) Murrio, triste, melancólico.

dust [dʌst] [dast], *s.* 1. Polvo, toda substancia reducida a partes muy menudas (particles of matter). **Gold dust,** oro en polvo. 2. Polvo, parte menuda de la tierra muy seca. 3. Nube, multitud de palabras o argumentos que turba y confunde; confusión controversia. **To kick up a dust,** *(Fig.)* levantar polvareda o cantera, causar disensiones. 4. Restos mortales, cenizas. 5. *(Fig.)* La tierra, la sepultura; polvo, estado o condición vil. 6. Basura, barreduras, residuos. 7. *(Fam.)* Oro en polvo, de aquí, dinero en general y dinero contante. **Sawdust,** serrín o aserraduras. **Pindust,** limaduras de alfileres. **Dust of a house,** barreduras de una casa. **To kick up/to raise a dust,** *(Fam.)* levantar polvareda, hacer disturbio. **To bite the dust,** morder el polvo, morir combatiendo (person); irse a pique (project, plan).

dust, *va.* 1. Despolvorear, sacudir o quitar el polvo (remove dust from). **To dust the furniture,** quitarle el polvo a los muebles, sacudir los muebles. 2. Polvorear, llenar de polvo (sprinkle). **She dusted her feet with talcum powder,** se echó o se puso talco en los pies.

dust down Sacudirle el polvo a.

dust off Quitarle el polvo a, sacudir (table, shelf); quitar (dirt); desempolvar (revive).

dustbin [ˈdʌstbɪn] [dast-bin], *s.* Receptáculo para polvo o ceniza; cubo o tacho, tambo o caneca, tobo de la basura.

dust-born [ˈdʌstbɔːn] [dast-born], *s.* Nacido del polvo.

dust bowl [ˈdʌstbəʊl] [dast-boul] *s.* Terreno semidesértico expuesto a la erosión causada por el viento.

dust-brush [ˈdʌstbrʌʃ] [dast-brash], *s.* Plumero para quitar el polvo; cepillo.

dust cloth [ˈdʌstklɒθ] [dast-kloz] *s.* Trapo del polvo, trapo de sacudir, sacudidor.

dust cover [ˈdʌstˌkʌvəʳ] [dast-ko-vaʳ] *s.* Funda para proteger del polvo (for furniture); tapa (hard cover); funda (flexible cover); sobrecubierta (dust jacket).

duster [ˈdʌstəʳ] [das-taʳ], *s.* 1. El que quita el polvo. 2. Plumero, atado de plumas u otro utensilio que sirve para despolvorear; borrador (for blackboard). 3. *(Clothing)* Sobretodo largo de lienzo que protege contra el polvo; guardapolvo (housecoat). 4. Utensilio para espolvorear veneno sobre las plantas con objeto de matar los insectos.

dustiness [ˈdʌstɪnɪs] [das-ti-nes], *s.* El estado de lo que se halla cubierto de polvo.

dustman [ˈdʌstmən] [dast-man], *s.* Basurero.

dust-pan [ˈdʌstpæn] [dast-pan], *s.* Pala de recoger la basura.

dust storm [ˈdʌststɔːm] [dast-storm], *s.* Tolvanera; tormenta de polvo.

dustup [ˈdʌstʌp] [dast-ap] *s.* *(Coloq.)* Pelea. **To have a dustup,** pelearse.

dusty [ˈdʌstɪ] [das-ti], *a.* Polvoriento (road, plain); polvoroso, lleno de polvo (furniture). **To get dusty,** llenarse de polvo, empolvarse.

Dutch [dʌtʃ] [dach], *a./s.* Holandés; lo perteneciente a Holanda, idioma que se habla en Holanda. **Dutch cheese,** queso de Flandes. **Dutch oven,** asador de vuelta. **Dutch tiles,** azulejos. **To go Dutch,** pagar a escote, pagar o ir a la americana, pagar o ir a la inglesa.

dutch cap *s.* (GB) Diafragma.

dutch courage [ˌdʌtʃˈkʌrɪdʒ] [dach-ka-rich] *s.* *(Coloq.)* Valentía o arrojo que se debe a la ingestión de una bebida alcohólica.

dutchman [ˈdʌtʃmən] [dach-man], *s.* 1. Holandés, el natural de Holanda. 2. (Fam. E. U.) Alemán.

duteous [ˈdjuːtɪəs] [diu-tios], *a.* Obediente, obsequiso, respetuoso.

dutiable [ˈdjuːtɪəbl] [diu-tia-bol], *a.* (Der.) Sujeto al pago de impuestos, o a derechos arancelarios.

dutiful [ˈdjuːtɪfʊl] [diu-ti-ful], *a.* 1. Obediente, sumiso, rendido o humillado a cualquier superior. 2. Respetuoso, respetoso, reverente, sumiso, consciente de sus deberes.

dutifully [ˈdjuːtɪfəlɪ] [diu-ti-fa-li], *adv.* Obedientemente, respetuosamente; diligentemente.

dutifulness [ˈdjuːtɪfʊlnɪs] [diu-ti-ful-nes], *s.* Obediencia, respeto, sumisión.

duty [ˈdjuːtɪ] [diu-ti], *s.* 1. Deber, obligación (obligation), *(Ant.)* respeto, homenaje. **To do one's duty,** cumplir con su deber u obligación. **Duty call/visit,** visita de cumplido. 2. Obligación. 3. Obediencia, sumisión, acatamiento. 4. *(Mil.)* Facción, acto del servicio militar. 5. Impuesto, los derechos que se pagan por la introducción o extracción de géneros, derechos de aduana o de puertas. 6. *(Mec.)* Trabajo mecánico, el hecho por una máquina comparado con los combustibles consumidos; efecto útil. 7. Servicio (service). **To do night duty,** hacer el turno nocturno. **To be on/off duty,** estar/no estar de turno o guardia (nurse, doctor); estar/no estar de servicio (policeman/fireman). **Duty roster,** lista de guardias. **Duties,** *s. pl.* Funciones, responsabilidades (responsibilities). **Duty free,** libre de derechos, exento. **Duty free shop,** duty free, tienda libre de impuestos.

duumvirate [ˈdjuːəmˈvɪreɪt] [diu-um-vi-reit], *s.* Duunvirato.

duvet [ˈdjuːveɪ] [diu-vei] *s.* (GB) Edredón nórdico. **Duvet cover,** funda de edredón.

dwale [ˈdweɪl] [dueil], *s.* 1. (Bot.) Solano. 2. (Her.) Sable, negro.

dwarf [dwɔːf] [duorf], *s.* 1. Enano. 2. Cualquier animal o planta que no tiene su ordinario grandor. **Dwarfelder,** yezgo, especie de saúco.

dwarf, *va.* 1. Impedir que alguna cosa llegue a su tamaño natural. 2. Hacer aparecer pequeño en comparación con otra cosa (building). **Her achievements dwarf those of her rivals,** sus logros eclipsan los de sus rivales. -*vn.* Empequeñecerse, achicarse.

dwarfish [ˈdwɔːfɪʃ] [duor-fish], *a.* Enano, bajo, pequeño.

dwarfishly [ˈdwɔːfɪʃlɪ] [duor-fish-li], *adv.* Como un enano.

dwarfishness [ˈdwɔːfɪʃnɪs] [duor-fish-nes], *s.* Pequeñez de estatura.

dwell [dwel] [duel], *vn.* 1. Habitar, morar, residir, vivir en algún paraje. 2. Hallarse en algún estado o condición. 3. (Con *on* o *upon*) Pararse, detenerse, dilatarse, insistir hablando de cualquier asunto. -*va.* (Des.) Vivir, ocupar.

dwell on. Try not to dwell on the past, trata de no pensar demasiado en el pasado.

dweller [ˈdweləʳ] [due-laʳ], *s.* Morador, habitante. **City dwellers,** la gente que vive en la ciudad.

dwelling [ˈdwelɪŋ] [due-lin], *s.* Habitación, domicilio, vivienda, morada.

dwelling-house [ˈdwelɪŋhaʊs] [due-linjaus], *s.* Domicilio, morada; casa.

dwelling-place [ˈdwelɪŋpleɪs] [due-lin-pleis], *s.* Residencia, morada, domicilio.

dwindle [ˈdwɪndl] [duin-dol], *vn.* 1. Mermar, disminuirse, reducirse, menguar (numbers, population). **To dwindle away to nothing,** irse reduciendo hasta quedar en la nada. 2. Degenerar; descaecer, decaer. 3. Aniquilarse, consumire. **Dwindling resources,** recursos cada vez más limitados. -*va.* Disminuir, rebajar, romper; disipar.

dwindled [ˈdwɪndld] [duin-deld], *a.* Contraído, disminuído.

dye [daɪ] [dai], *va.* Teñir (clothes). **She dyes her hair blonde,** se tiñe el pelo de rubio.

dye, *s.* Tinte; materia colorante, o fluido que se usa para teñir. **Dye-house,** tintorería. **Dye-works,** taller de tintorero.

dyed-in-the-wool [daɪdɪn'θewuːl] [daid-in-de-wul], *a.* Fanático, ferviente, convencido; recalcitrante.

dyer ['daɪəʳ] [daiaʳ], *s.* Tintorero.

dyeing ['daɪɪŋ] [daiin], *s.* Tintorería, el arte de teñir; tinta, teñidura, tintura. -*a.* Colorante.

dyestuff ['daɪstʌf] [dai-staf], *s.* Materia de tinte, droga.

dyers'weed ['daɪswiːd] [dais-uid], *s.* (*Bot.*) Gualda.

dying ['daɪɪŋ] [daiin], *pa.* 1. Moribundo, agonizante (near death, extinction/person, animal). 2. Mortal, destinado a morir, en vías de extinción (race, art). 3. Mortal, que se refiere a la muerte; en el instante de morir; último, postrero (related to time of death/wish, words, breath). **To be in a dying state,** estar a la muerte. **The dying words of one,** las últimas palabras de alguno. **Dying eyes,** ojos lánguidos o angustiados, vista desfallecida o desmayada. -*s.* Muerte.

dyingly ['daɪɪŋlɪ] [daiin-li], *adv.* A manera de moribundo.

dyke ['daɪk] [daik], *s.* 1. V. DIKE. 2. (*Sl.*) Tortillera (lesbian).

dynamic, dynamical [daɪ'næmɪk] [dai-na-mik], *a.* 1. Dinámico, referente a la dinámica, opuesto a estática. 2. Referente a una fuerza mecánica de cualquier especie. 3. Motor, motriz, que causa actividad o movimiento, eficaz.

dynamics [daɪ'næmɪkz] [dai-na-miks], *s.* Dinámica, la ciencia que trata de la acción de las fuerzas motrices sobre los cuerpos sólidos.

dynamism ['daɪnəmɪzəm] [dai-na-misem] *s.* Dinamismo.

dynamite ['daɪnəmaɪt] [dai-na-mait], *s.* Dinamita, substancia de enorme fuerza explosiva, compuesta de una materia absorbente y nitroglicerina. **These latest disclosures are political dynamite,** estas nuevas revelaciones son políticamente explosivas. *va.* Dinamitar, volar con dinamita.

dynamo ['daɪnəməʊ] [dai-na-mou], *s.* Dinamo o dínamo, máquina para convertir la fuerza mecánica en fuerza eléctrica; abreviatura de *dynamo-electric machine,* máquina electrodinámica.

dynamo-electric ['daɪnəməʊr'lektrɪk] [dai-na-mou-i-lek-trik], *a.* Electrodinámico, que transforma la fuerza mecánica en eléctrica o viceversa.

dynamometer ['daɪnəməʊˌmiːtəʳ] [dai-na-mou-mi-taʳ], *s.*

dynamometric ['daɪnəməʊmetrɪk] [dai-na-mou-me-trik], *a.* Dinamométrico.

dynasty ['dɪnəstɪ] [di-nas-ti], *s.* Dinastía, serie de príncipes de una misma familia.

dyne ['dɪn] [din], *s.* (*Fís.*) Dina.

dyscrasia, dyscrasy ['dɪskreɪʒɪə] [dis-krei-sia], *s.* Discrasia, mal temperamento.

dysenteric ['dɪsntərɪk] [di-sen-te-rik], *a.* Disentérico.

dysentery ['dɪsntərɪ] [di-sen-te-ri], *s.* Disentería, flujo de vientre o cámaras de sangre.

dysfunction ['dɪsfʌŋkʃən] [dis-fank-shon] *s.* Disfunción.

dysfunctional ['dɪsfʌŋkʃənl] [dis-fank-sho-nal] *a.* Disfuncional.

dyslexia [dɪs'leksɪə] [dis-lek-sia] *s.* Dislexia.

dyslexic [dɪs'leksɪk] [dis-lek-sik] *a.* Disléxico.

dyspepsia, dyspepsy [dɪs'peksɪə] [dis-lep-sia], *s.* Dispepsia, digestión laboriosa e imperfecta, por lo general de carácter crónico.

dyspeptic [dɪs'peptɪk] [dis-pep-tik], *a./s.* 1. Dispéptico, relativo a la dispepsia. 2. Enfermo de dispepsia, mórbido, quejoso. 3. Que tiende a la dispepsia, indigestible.

dysphagia [dɪs'feɪdʒɪə] [dis-fei-chia], *s.* Disfagia, dificultad de tragar.

dysphonia, dysphony [dɪs'fəʊnɪə] [dis-fou-nia], *s.* Disfonía, dificultad de hablar.

dyspnoea ['dɪspnɪə] [disp-nia], *s.* Disnea, dificultad de respirar.

dispnoeal, dyspnoeic [dɪs'fəʊnɪəl] [dis-fou-nial], *a.* Disneico, relativo a la disnea.

dysuria, dysury [dɪʒjʊrɪə] [di-shiu-ria], *s.* Disuria, dificultad en la expulsión de la orina.

E

e [iː] [i], esta letra tiene tres sonidos en inglés; uno igual al de la letra *i* en castellano; v. g. en *each* [ɪtʃ] [ich], *eagle* ['iːgl] [i-guel], y otro como el de la *e* en español; v. g. *men, bed, ten.* El tercero no es más que una variación del segundo; v. g. *elegant* [iː] [i], *daughter* [iː] [i],. Es muda cuando finaliza alguna palabra, excepto en las monosílabas y en las derivadas inmediatamente del griego; y sólo sirve, cuando es final, para prolongar la vocal que precede, como en *mine, fate* [iː] [i], **e.** en la rosa náutica denota el este u oriente; en la música, mi. **E flat,** Mi bemol.

each [iːtʃ] [ich], *pron.* Cualquier o cualquiera, cada, cada uno. **Each other,** entrambos, mutuamente, unos a otros, el uno al otro; uno sí y otro no. **They hate each other,** se odian. **We read each other's book,** cada uno lee los libros del otro. **I'll have a little of each, please,** sírveme un poco de cada uno, por favor. *a.* Cada. **Each child received a gift,** cada niño recibió un regalo. *adv.* **The apples are 20 cents each,** las manzanas valen 20 centavos por pieza cada una.

eager ['iːgəʳ] [i-guaʳ], *a.* 1. Ansioso, impaciente (excited, impatient); entusiasta (keen); ahincado, deseoso. 2. Fogoso, ardiente, vehemente, impaciente. **She looked at their eager faces,** miró sus caras llenas de ilusión. **She's eager to learn,** tiene muchos deseos o muchas ganas de aprender. **He's eager to please,** está deseoso de complacer. 3. Vivo, pronto. 4. Acre, mordaz.

eagerly ['iːgəlɪ] [i-guer-li], *adv.* Ansiosamente, con ansiedad e impaciencia (await); con entusiasmo (accept, agree); con avidez (listen, read); vehementemente, ardientemente; acremente. **To be eagerly busied,** estar embebido en los negocios.

eagerness ['iːgənɪs] [i-guer-nes], *s.* 1. Ansia, anhelo, ahínco. 2. Vehemencia, violencia, ardor; apresuramiento. 3. Aspereza. 4. Entusiasmo; impaciencia (impatience). **Her eagerness to please,** su afán de agrado.

eagle ['iːgl] [i-guel], *s.* 1. (*Zool.*) Águila. 2. Águila, insignia de los romanos. 3. águila, moneda de oro de los Estados Unidos.

eagle-eyed ['iːgl'aɪd] [i-guel-aid], **eagle-sighted** ['iːgl'saɪtɪd] [i-guel-sai-tid], *a.* De vista de lince.

eagle-speed ['iːgl'spiːd] [i-guel-spid], *s.* Velocidad de águila.

eagless ['iːglɪs] [ig-les], *f.* La hembra del águila.

eagle-stone ['iːgl'stəʊn] [iguel-stoun], *s.* Etites, piedra de águila, hierro oxidado moreno.

eaglet ['iːglɪt] [ig-let], *s.* Aguilucho.

eagle-winged ['iːgl'wɪndʒ] [iguel-wingd], *a.* Alado como águila.

eagle-wood ['iːgl'wuːd] [iguel-wud], *s.* Madera de águila.

ean, *vn.* V. YEAN.

ear ['ɪəʳ] [iaʳ], *s.* 1. (*Anat.*) Oreja, órgano del oído; pabellón de la oreja. **To be all ears,** ser todo oídos. **To be wet behind the ears,** estar verde, no tener experiencia. **To fall on deaf ears,** caer en oídos sordos. 2. Oído, sentido del oír. 3. Oído para la música. **To have a good ear for music/languages,** tener oído para la música/los idiomas. **To play something by ear,** tocar algo de oído. 4. Oído, la atención que se presta a lo que dice una persona. 5. Asa, asidero. 6. (*Bot.*) Espiga. **Dog's ears,** (*Fam.*) Orejones, las puntas de las hojas de los libros dobladas o arrolladas. **By ear,** de, o por oídas; de oído.

ear, *vn.* Espigar, empezar las semillas a crecer y echar espigas. -*va.* (*Des.*) Arar. **To set by the ears,** reñir, pelear.

earache ['ɪəreɪk] [iar-eik], *s.* Dolor de oídos.

ear-bored ['ɪəʳbɔːd] [iar-bord], *a.* El o la que tiene las orejas horadadas.

ear-deafening ['ɪədfnɪŋ] [iar-def-nin], *a.* Lo que ensordece.

eardrop ['ɪədrɒp] [iar-drop], *s.* Pendiente, zarcillo. V. EARRING. **Eardrops,** *s. pl.* Gotas para los oídos.

ear-drum ['ɪədrʌm] [iar-dram], *s.* Tímpano del oído.

eared ['ɪəd] [iard], *a.* 1. Lo que tiene orejas u oídos. 2. Espigado, provisto de espigas. 3. (*Des.*) Arado. 4. De las orejas. **Long-eared**, orejudo, de orejas largas. **Lap-eared**, de orejas pendientes.

earful [ˈɪəfʊl] [iar-ful] s. *(Coloq.)* **My mother gave me an earful**, mi madre me echó un rapapolvo o me cafeteó.

earing [ˈɪərɪŋ] [iarin] s. *(Ant.)* La acción de arar la tierra. **Earing of a sail**, *(Mar.)* empuñidura de una vela. **Head-earings**, *(Mar.)* empuñiduras de grátil. **Reef-earings**, *(Mar.)* empuñiduras de rizos.

earl [ɜːl] [erl], s. Conde, título de nobleza, hoy el tercero en Inglaterra. **Earl-marshal**, dignidad en la corte de Inglaterra que tiene a su cargo la dirección de las solemnidades militares y todos los asuntos respectivos a las armas y honores de las familias.

earlap [ɜːl] [erl], s. La punta de la oreja.

earldom [ˈɜːldɒm] [erl-dom], s. Condado, señorío de conde.

earless [ˈɪəlɪs] [ia-les], a. Desorejado; el que no quiere oír.

earlier, earliest [ˈɜːlɪəʳ] [er-liaʳ], comparativo y superlativo de EARLY.

earliness [ˈɜːlɪnɪs] [er-li-nes], s. 1. Precocidad, anticipación. 2. Presteza, prontitud.

earlobe [ˈɪələʊb] [ia-loub] s. Lóbulo de la oreja.

earlock [ˈɪəlɒk] [ia-lok], s. Una especie de bucle o rizo. V. LOVE-LOCK.

early [ˈɜːlɪ] [er-li], a. 1. Primitivo, del principio (far back in time). **Early man**, el hombre primitivo. **His earliest memories**, sus primeros recuerdos. **From the earliest times**, desde los primeros tiempos. 2. Avanzado, precoz, anticipado (before expected time/arrival, elections). **To be early**, llegar temprano (person); adelantarse (baby). **The bus was early**, el autobús pasó o salió antes de la hora. 3. Temprano, matinal (before normal time); cercano, próximo a suceder o acontecer. Temprano, tempranero (crop, variety). **An early fruit**, un fruto temprano. **To rise early**, madrugar, levantarse temprano. **Early riser**, madrugador. **Early in the spring**, al principio de la primavera. **You are early**, es Ud. matinal. 4. Pronto (in near future). **At the earliest possible moment**, lo antes o lo más pronto posible. *adv.* 1. Temprano, de madrugada (before usual time). 2. Luego, tan pronto como (soon). **They won't be here till nine at the earliest**, por temprano que lleguen no estarán aquí antes de las nueve. 3. Al principio de. **Early in the morning**, muy de mañana, de madrugada. **As early as possible**, tan pronto como sea posible, a la mayor brevedad. 4. **Early in the morning/afternoon**, por la mañana/tarde temprano. **Early in the week/year**, a principios de semana/año (toward beginning of period).

ear-mark [ˈɜːmɑːk] [ia-mark], s. 1. Señal en la oreja. 2. Toda señal que sirve para identificar.

ear-mark, va. 1. Marcar el ganado en las orejas. 2. Destinar (money, funds).

earmuff [ˈɔːmʌf] [ia-maf], s. Orejera.

earn [ɜːn] [ern], va. 1. Ganar, adquirir caudal (money, wages); dar, devengar (interest); obtener, conseguir. 2. Merecer, hacer algo que merece recompensa. 3. Ganarse (respect, gratitude); ganar (promotion). vn. Trabajar, ganar dinero.

earner [ˈɜːnəʳ] [er-naʳ] s. **He's the major/sole earner in the family**, es el que más dinero gana de la familia/es el único que gana dinero en la familia. (GB) *(Coloq.)* **It's a nice little earner**, ese negocio me/te/le gana un buen dinerito (source of income).

earnest [ˈɜːnɪst] [er-nest], a. 1. Ardiente, fervoroso, ansioso, ferviente (wish). 2. Activo, diligente, atento, cuidadoso. 3. Serio, concienzudo (sincere/effort, attempt); importante; formal, de buena fe; serio (serious). **He's terribly earnest**, se lo toma todo muy en serio. -s. 1. Veras, seriedad, gravedad. 2. Buena fe, realidad. 3. Arras, el primer dinero que se recibe por lo que se vende. 4. Prenda segura, seguridad, señal, caparra, la parte de precio que se anticipa en cualquier concierto como prenda de seguridad. **To give earnest**, dar señal o arras. **In earnest**, de veras. **In good earnest**, de buena fe. *(Fam.)* Con formalidad, con seriedad.

earnestly [ˈɜːnɪstlɪ] [er-nest-li], adv. Seriamente, de veras; encarecidamente; ansiosamente. Con seriedad (speak, look); de todo corazón (desire, believe).

earnestness [ˈɜːnɪstnɪs] [er-nest-nes], s. 1. Ansia, anhelo, vehemencia, ardor, celo. 2. Gravedad, seriedad, formalidad. 3. Solicitud, cuidado, ahínco, diligencia.

earning [ˈɜːnɪŋ] [er-nin], s. Salario, jornal, paga. **Earnings**, s. pl. Ingresos. **Earnings-related**, a. (GB) proporcional al sueldo.

earphone [ˈɪəfəʊn] [ia-foun], s. Audífono.

ear-pick [ˈɪəpɪk] [iar-pik], s. Mondaorejas, escarbaoídos.

ear-piercing [ˈɪəpɪəsɪŋ] [iar-pir-sin], a. 1. Que penetra el oído (sonido agudo). s. Perforación del lóbulo de la oreja.

earplug [ˈɪəplʌg] [iar-plag] s. Tapón para el oído.

earring [ˈɪərɪŋ] [iar-ring], s. Zarcillo, pendiente, arracada. (Cuba y Méx.) Arete, aro, caravana.

earshot [ˈɪəʃɒt] [iar-shot], s. Alcance del oído.

ear specialist [ˈɪəˈspeʃəlɪst] [iar-es-pe-sha-list], s. Otólogo, especialista de oídos.

earsplitting [ˈɪəplɪtɪŋ] [iar-spli-tin] a. Estridente, que rompe los tímpanos (scream); ensordecedor (noise).

earth [ɜːθ] [erz], s. 1. Tierra, el globo terráqueo o terrestre. **The Earth**, la Tierra. **Nothing on earth would make me do it**, no lo haría por nada del mundo. (GB) *(Coloq.)* **To cost the earth**, costar un ojo de la cara. **To promise the earth**, prometer el oro y el moro. 2. Tierra, porción sólida de nuestro globo. 3. *(Quím.)* Tierra, substancia inorgánica y fósil; óxido metálico, como alúmina. **Fuller's earth**, tierra de batán, greda muy fina. 4. Tierra, espacio de terreno a propósito para el cultivo (land, the ground, soil). **To bring somebody down to earth**, hacer bajar de las nubes a alguien. 5. Mundo, los que habitan el globo. 6. Madriguera, la cuevecilla en que habitan ciertos animales (burrow, hole). **To go to earth**, esconderse (person) **Argillaceous earth**, tierra arcillosa, greda. **Run to earth**, cazado hasta la misma madriguera. **Why on earth didn't you warn me?**, ¿por qué diablos o demonios no me avisaste? **Who on earth would do that?**, ¿a quién puede ocurrírsele hacer eso? (as intensifier)

earth, va. Enterrar, cubrir con tierra. *(Elec.)* Conectar a tierra. -vn. Retirarse debajo de tierra.

earth-bank [ɜːθ] [erz], s. Especie de cercado de tierra para guardar los sembrados.

earth-board [ˈɜːθbɔːd] [erz-bord], s. Orejera, la parte del arado que abre el surco. (Se llama más comúnmente MOLD-BOARD).

earth-born [ˈɜːθbɔːn] [erz-born], a. 1. Terrestre, producido por la tierra. 2. El que es de bajo nacimiento.

earth-bound [ˈɜːθbaʊnd] [erz-baund], a. Comprimido o apretado con tierra.

earth-bred [ˈɜːθbred] [erz-bred] a. Vil, bajo.

earth-created [ˈɜːθkrɪˈeɪtɪd] [erz-kri-eitid], a. Formado o hecho de tierra.

earthen [ˈɜːθən] [er-zen], a. Térreo, terreno, terroso, de barro. **Earthenware**, loza de barro. **Glazed earthenware**, loza vidriada.

earth-fed [ˈɜːθfed] [erz-fed], a. Bajo, vil.

earth-flax [ˈɜːθflæks] [erz-flaks], s. Amianto, fósil; asbesto.

earthiness [ˈɜːθɪnɪs] [er-zi-nes], s. Terrenidad; grosería.

earthliness [ˈɜːθlɪnɪs] [erz-li-nes], s. Vanidad mundana.

earthly [ˈɜːθlɪ] [erz-li], a. 1. Terreno, térreo, terrenal, terrestre, mundano (worldly, life). **All her earthly possessions**, todo lo que poseía o posee en este mundo. 2. Temporal, sensual, terrenal. 3. Grosero, basto, tosco. **It's no earthly use asking her**, es inútil preguntarle (as intensifier). s. (GB) *(Coloq.)* **You don't have/stand an earthly against her**, no tienes ni la más remota posibilidad de ganarle (chance). **I haven't got an earthly**, no tengo ni la menor idea o ni la más remota idea (idea).

earthly-minded [ˌɜːθlɪˈmaɪndɪd] [erz-li-main-did], a. Mundano, sensual.

earthly-mindedness [ˌɜːθlɪˈmaɪndɪdnɪs] [erz-li-main-did-nes], s. Grosería; sensualidad.

earth-nut [ˈɜːθnʌt] [erz-nat], *s.* 1. Criadilla de tierra; especie de hongo sin raíz, comestible, que se cría debajo de tierra. 2. Cacahuete, maní.

earthquake [ˈɜːθkweɪk] [erz-kueik], *s.* Temblor de tierra, terremoto.

earth-shaking [ɜːθˈʃeɪkɪŋ] [erz-shei-kin], **earth-shattering** [ɜːθˈʃætərɪŋ] [erz-sha-te-rin] *a.* 1. Lo que tiene poder de mover la tierra. 2. Que causa conmoción (event, news).

earthwork [ˈɜːθwɜːk] [erz-uerk], *s.* 1. Fortificación hecha en gran parte de tierra; terraplén. 2. Obra de ingeniería que necesita el movimiento de tierras.

earthworm [ˈɜːθwɜːm] [erz-uerm] *s.* 1. Lombriz de tierra. 2. Gusano, hombre vil y abatido.

earthy [ˈɜːθɪ] [erzi] *a.* Terroso (shade); a tierra (taste, smell); llano, campechano (person); desenfadado, directo (humor).

ear-wax [ˈɪəwæks] [ia-uaks], *s.* Cerilla o cera de los oídos.

earwig [ˈɪəwɪɡ] [ia-uig], *s.* 1. Tijereta, gusano del oído. Forfícula. 2. Cuchicheador, el amigo de cuchichear.

ear-witness [ˈɪəwɪtnɪs] [ia-uit-nes], *s.* Testigo auricular o de oídas.

ease [iːz] [is], *s.* 1. Quietud, tranquilidad, ocio, reposo; conveniencia, descanso, comodidad. 2. Alivio, descanso, desahogo. **A life of ease**, una vida desahogada (leisure). 3. Facilidad (facility), disposición para entender y hacer las cosas sin trabajo, despejo, desembarazo, donaire. **For ease of access**, para facilitar el acceso. **At ease**, con desahogo, descansadamente; a gusto. **I don't feel at ease with her**, con ella no me siento a gusto. **With ease**, con facilidad. **At heart's ease**, a pedir de boca. *(Mil.)* **(stand) at ease!**, ¡descansen!

ease, *va.* 1. Aliviar, calmar (relieve/pain); hacer disminuir, aliviar (tension); aligerar (burden); ablandar, mitigar, templar, suavizar, moderar. Paliar, mejorar ˈ (make easier/situation); facilitar (transition). **To ease the way for something**, preparar el terreno para algo. **He did it to ease his conscience**, lo hizo para descargarse la conciencia. 2. Dar alivio y descanso de algún trabajo corporal. **To ease oneself**, hacer de cuerpo. 3. Desembarazar, quitar algún estorbo o embarazo; relajar (rules, restrictions); aflojar (belt, rope). **Ease the ship**, *(mar.)* orza todo. **To ease off/away**, *(Mar.)* lascar o arriar. **They eased them into the weelchair**, lo sentaron con cuidado en la silla de ruedas (move with care). *vn.* Aliviarse, calmarse (pain); disminuir (tension).

ease off Amainar (rain); aliviarse, calmarse (pain); disminuir (pressure, traffic).

ease up Tomarse las cosas con más calma (slacken pace/of life); bajar el ritmo (of work, activity).

easel [ˈiːzl] [isel], *s.* Caballete, bastidor que sirve a los pintores para colocar el lienzo en que pintan.

easeless [ˈiːzlɪs] [ise-les], *a.* Inquieto, sin reposo.

easement [ˈiːzmənt] [is-ment], *s.* 1. *(For.)* Derecho incorpóreo distinto de la propiedad del suelo, como el que se tiene a una corriente de agua o al aire libre. 2. Alivio, apoyo, ventaja.

easily [ˈiːzɪlɪ] [isi-li], *adv.* 1. Fácilmente; sin dificultad, esfuerzo ni trabajo; sin inquietud, pesar o fastidio; quietamente, sosegadamente; prontamente. Con facilidad (readily/break, stain, cry). **You gave up too easily**, te diste por vencido demasiado pronto. **He's easily fooled**, es fácil de engañar. **It's easily obtainable**, se consigue sin problemas. **Languages come easily to him**, tiene facilidad para los idiomas. 2. Con mucho, fácil, de lejos (by far). Por lo menos, fácil (at least). **It must have cost easily $100**, debe de haber costado por lo menos 100 dólares. **There is easily enough for everybody**, hay de sobra para todos. 3. Perfectamente, fácilmente (very conceivably).

easiness [ˈiːzɪnɪs] [isi-nes], *s.* 1. Facilidad, presteza, diligencia (of task). 2. Libertad, quietud. 3. Comodidad, bienestar. 4. Despejo, desembarazo, gracia, facilidad de maneras; soltura, naturalidad (of manner, movement).

easing [ˈiːzɪŋ] [isin] *s.* **An easing of tension between the two countries**, un relajamiento de la tensión entre los dos países. **The easing of traffic congestion**, la descongestión del tráfico.

east [iːst] [ist], *s.* 1. Oriente; este (point of the compass, direction). **To the east of the city**, al este de la ciudad. **East wind**, viento del este o de levante. 2. En el comercio se designan con el nombre de Oriente las regiones y los pueblos del Asia que baña el Océano, y con el de Levante los que están en el Mediterráneo. 3. **East**, este (in bridge). *-a.* Oriental, de Oriente; el Este (wind). *adv.* Al este. **It's east of Dallas**, está al este de Dallas. **Back east**, (in US) en el este, en los estados del Este.

eastbound [ˈiːstbaʊnd] [ist-baun] *a.* Que va hacia el este o en dirección este.

east End [ˈiːstˈend] [ist-end] *s.* **The East End of London**, barrio del este de Londres de tradición obrera. **Eastender**, persona que vive o ha nacido en el East End.

easter [ˈiːstər] [is-taʳ], *s.* Pascua de resurrección o florida. **Easter Eve**, sábado santo. **Easter Day**, día de Pascua. **Eastertide**, estación o época de la Pascua; tiempo que ésta dura. **Easter egg**, huevo de Pascua. **The Easter vacation**, las vacaciones de Semana Santa.

easterling [ˈiːstəlɪŋ] [is-ter-lin], *s.* Natural de algún país al oriente de otro.

easterly [ˈiːstəlɪ] [is-ter-li], *a.* Oriental, del este, hacia el este, situado al este, o viniendo de él. **Easterly wind**, aire de levante, solano.

eastern [ˈiːstən] [is-tern], *a.* 1. Oriental, de Oriente, o que habita el Oriente. **The eastern areas of the country**, las zonas orientales o este del país. **Eastern Europe**, europa oriental o del este. 2. *V.* EASTERLY. 3. Oriental (oriental/appearance, custom). **Easterner**, nativo o habitante del este del país o de la región.

easternmost [ˈiːstənməʊst] [is-tern-moust] *a.* Más al este (town, island). **The easternmost tip of the island**, el extremo este u oriental de la isla.

eastward [ˈiːstwɑːd] [ist-uard], *a.* Que se dirige o tiende hacia el este. *-adv.* Hacia el oriente, hacia el este (travel, turn).

easy [ˈiːzɪ] [isi], *a.* 1. Fácil (not difficult); cómodo, que no exige gran esfuerzo ni trabajo. **It's very easy to do**, es muy fácil de hacer. **To take the easy way out**, optar por el camino más fácil. **She was an easy winner**, ganó sin problemas. 2. Fácil, complaciente, condescendiente, cortés, sociable. 3. Libre, tranquilo; contento; aliviado, exento de penas, de cuidados. 4. Acomodado, en buena situación de fortuna. 5. Acomodado, liso, llano. 6. Fácil, natural, que no es forzado; fácil, desahogado (undemanding/life). *(Neg.)* **Easy terms**, facilidades de pago. **To be easy on the eye/ear**, ser agradable a la vista/al oído. 7. Condescendiente, suave (lenient). **To be easy on somebody**, ser poco exigente o severo con alguien. (GB) *(Coloq.)* **I'm easy**, me da igual o lo mismo (without strong opinion). 8. *(Com.)* No en gran demanda ni escaso; en libre circulación, como el dinero. **Easy sail**, *(Mar.)* poca vela. **Easy labor**, parto feliz. **Easy to be borne**, soportable, fácil, de soportar. **Easy-going**, inalterable, sereno; de trato fácil, sin complicaciones.

easy *adv.* 1. **Love/money doesn't come easy**, el amor/dinero no es fácil de conseguir. **Easy come, easy go**, así como viene se va (without difficulty). 2. Despacio, con calma (slowly, calmly). **Easy does it**, despacito. **To take it easy**, tomárselo con calma. **Go easy on/with the sugar**, no te pases o llévatela suave con el azúcar (sparingly). **Go easy on him**, no seas muy duro con él (leniently).

easy chair [iːzɪˈtʃeəʳ] [isi-cheaʳ], *s.* Silla poltrona, sillón, butaca.

eat [iːt] [it], *va.* *(pret.* ATE, *pp.* EATEN). 1. Comer (meal, food); masticar. **To eat one's breakfast/dinner/supper**, almorzar/comer/cenar. 2. Roer; consumir, usar, gastar.

What's eating her?, ¿a ésta qué le pica o qué bicho la picó? (upset, bother). 3. Retractar, desaprobar lo dicho o hecho desdiciéndose de ello. -vn. 1. Alimentarse, mantenerse, sustentarse; comer. **We usually eat at seven**, solemos cenar a las siete. 2. Desdecirse, retractarse; apacentarse el ganado. 3. (Fam.) Saber a, tener buen o mal gusto.

eat away, comer con ánimo; roer (rats, mice); carcomer, consumir; picar, comerse (moths); corroer (acid).

eat into Corroer (acid, rust); comerse (profits, savings).

eat up 1. Comer, devorar, hartarse; destruir, arruinar. 2. Comerse (finish/meal, food). **Eat it all up now!**, ¡cómetelo todo! 3. Terminar de comer (finish meal). 4. Consumir, gastar (fuel, electricity). 5. Consumir (curiosity, ambition). **She's eaten up with envy**, la envidia la carcome, la consume la envidia.

eatable [ˌiːtəbl] [i-ta-bol], a. Comestible, bueno de comer, que se puede comer. -s. Comestibles víveres, vituallas, todo género de alimentos.

eater [ˈiːtəʳ] [i-taʳ], s. Comedor (person). **A great eater**, tragón. **We're big meat eaters**, comemos mucha carne.

eating [ˈiːtɪŋ] [itin] s. (El) comer. **It is/makes very good eating**, es muy sabroso. De mesa (apple).

eating-house [ˈiːtɪŋhaʊs] [itin-jaus], s. Figón, bodegón, hostería.

eaves [ˈiːvz] [ivs], s. pl. Socarrén, alero o ala de tejado.

eavesdrop [ˈiːvzdrɒp] [ivs-drop], vn. Escuchar por la ventana lo que se habla dentro de la casa; escuchar a las puertas.

eavesdropper [ˈiːvzdrɒpəʳ] [ivs-dro-paʳ], s. Escuchador, el que se pone con curiosidad y ocultamente a escuchar lo que otros hablan.

ebb [eb] [eb] vn. 1. Menguar o retroceder la marea (tide). **To ebb and flow**, fluir y refluir, ir y venir. 2. Menguar, decaer, disminuir, irse consumiendo alguna cosa (dwindle).

ebb away, **His life was ebbing away**, se consumía poco a poco. **I felt my strength ebbing away**, sentí que me abandonaban las fuerzas.

ebb, s. 1. (Mar.) Menguante, reflujo de la marea. **The tide was at the ebb**, la marea estaba bajando. 2. Decadencia o decremento de alguna cosa. **Ebbtide**, (Mar.) marea menguante. **The ebb of life**, la vejez. **To be at a low ebb**, estar decaído (person); estar en un punto bajo (diplomatic relations). **His fortunes were at a low ebb**, atravesaba un mal momento.

ebionite [ˈebɪənaɪt] [e-bio-nait], s. Ebionita, hereje que negaba la divinidad de Jesucristo.

ebon [ˈebən] [e-bon], a. Hecho de ébano; negro, como el ébano.

ebonite [ˈebənaɪt] [e-bo-nait], s. Ebonita, caucho negro endurecido o vulcanizado.

ebonize [ˈebənaɪz] [e-bo-nais], va. Ebonizar, dar a la madera el color del ébano.

ebony [ˈebənɪ] [e-bo-ni], **ebon**, s. Ebano, madera dura, negra, pesada y de mucho valor (wood); color de ébano (color); negro como el ébano (hair, skin).

ebriety [ˈebrɪətɪ] [e-bri-e-ti], s. Ebriedad, embriaguez, borrachera.

ebullience, ebulliency [ɪˈbʌlɪəns] [i-ba-liens], s. Ebullición.

ebullient [ɪˈbʌlɪənt] [i-ba-lient], a. 1. Hirviente, lo que está hirviendo. 2. Vivaz, lleno de vida (person). **He was in an ebullient mood**, estaba lleno de energía.

ebullition [ebəlɪʃən] [e-ba-li-shon], s. 1. Ebullición, hervor, fermentación. 2. (Fig.) Emoción profunda, viva agitación o exaltación del ánimo.

eburnated [ɪˈbɜːneɪtɪd] [i-ber-nei-tid], a. Condensado y endurecido como el hueso.

eburnean [ɪˈbɜːnɪən] [i-ber-nian], a. Ebúrneo, de marfil o que se parece a él.

EC s. (=**European Community**) CE.

eccentric, eccentrical [ɪkˈsentrɪkl] [ik-sen-tri-kal], a. 1. Excéntrico, que está fuera del centro o tiene un centro diferente. 2. Extravagante, disparatado, particular, singular, estrafalario, raro. 3. Apartado o distante del centro nervioso.

eccentric, s. 1. (Mec.) Rueda excéntrica. 2. El desvío del centro; la persona que se desvía del modo común de obrar.

eccentricity, excentricity [ɪkˈsentrɪtɪ] [ik-sen-tri-si-ti] s. 1. Excentricidad. 2. Extravagancia, particularidad, singularidad, rareza, extravagancia.

ecchymosis [ɪkɪˈmɔːsɪs] [i-ki-mou-sis], s. Equimosis, mancha acardenalada de la piel.

ecclesiastes [ɪˈklɪsɪəstəs] [i-kli-sias-tes], s. Eclesiastés, uno de los libros de la sagrada Escritura.

ecclesiastic, ecclesiastical [ɪˈklɪsɪəstɪk] [i-kli-sias-tik], a. Eclesiástico, lo que pertenece a la iglesia.

ecclesiastic, s. Eclesiástico, el que está ordenado y dedicado al ministerio de la iglesia.

ecclesiastically [ɪˈklɪsɪəstɪklɪ] [i-kli-sias-ti-ka-li], adv. Eclesiásticamente.

echape [ˈekeɪp] [e-keip], s. Caballo hijo de caballo y yegua de diferentes castas.

echelon [ˈekəlɒn] [e-ke-lon], s. 1. (Mil.) Escalón. 2. **Echelons**, s. pl. (levels). **The upper echelons of the civil service**, los niveles más altos del funcionariado público.

echinites [ˈekɪnaɪtɪz] [e-ki-nai-tis], s. (Min.) Equino petrificado, botón de mar.

echin, echinc [ˈekɪn] [e-kin], formas de combinación.

echinoderm [ˈekɪnədɜːm] [e-ki-no-derm], a. Equinodermo.

echinodermatous [ˈekɪnədɜːmətəs] [e-ki-no-der-ma-tous], a. Equinodermo, que tiene la piel erizada de púas, espinas o tubérculos.

echinus [ˈekɪnəs] [e-ki-nos], s. 1. (Arq.) Cuarto bocel, miembro de moldura. 2. Erizo de mar; equino. 3. Erizo, animal cubierto de púas aguadas como espinas.

echo [ˈekəʊ] [e-kou], s. Eco.

echo, vn. Resonar, formar eco, repetir (footsteps, voices). **The room echoed with/to the sound of laughter**, la sala resonaba o retumbaba con risas. -va. 1. Repercutir la voz o rechazarla (repeat). **To echo somebody's words**, repetir las palabras de alguien. 2. Hacerse eco de (express agreement with/opinion, criticism).

echometer [ˈekəʊmiːtəʳ] [e-kou-mi-taʳ], s. Ecómetro, instrumento para conocer la duración del sonido y distinguir sus intervalos.

eclair [ˈeɪkleəʳ] [ei-kleaʳ] s. Pastel individual relleno de crema.

eclaircissement [ˈeɪklɪˈeəˈsɪsmənt] [ei-klea-sis-ment], s. Aclaración, explicación, ilustración; noticia.

eclat [ˈeɪklɑː] [ei-kla], s. 1. Esplendor, lustre, magnificencia. 2. Aclamación, aplauso: renombre, celebridad.

eclectic [ɪˈklektɪk] [i-klek-tik], a. 1. Ecléctico; que analiza, escoge y concilia; se aplica al filósofo que elige y admite las opiniones o sistemas más probables. 2. Tolerante en materias de gusto, amplio, liberal. -s. Ecléctico, miembro de una secta de filósofos y médicos.

eclecticism [ɪˈklektɪsɪzəm] [i-klek-ti-si-sem], s. Eclecticismo, elección de lo mejor de toda doctrina o sistema, especialmente en medicina y filosofía.

eclipse [ɪˈklɪps] [i-klips], s. Eclipse, obscurecimiento de un cuerpo celeste por la interposición de otro que impide verlo bien o disminuye su luz.

eclipse, va. 1. Eclipsar, causar un astro la ocultación transitoria y total o parcial de otro, o de su luz, interponiéndose entre él y nuestra vista. 2. Eclipsar, extinguir, anublar; hacer desaparecer.

ecliptic [ɪˈklɪptɪk] [i-klip-tik], s. Eclíptica, círculo máximo de la esfera. -a. Eclíptico, obscurecido.

eclogue [ˈeklɒg] [e-klog], s. Egloga, poema pastoral.

ecological [ˌiːkəʊˈlɒdʒɪkəl] [i-kou-lo-chi-kal], a. Ecológico.

ecologically [ˌiːkəʊˈlɒdʒɪklɪ] [i-kou-lo-chi-ka-li] adv. Ecológicamente; desde el punto de vista ecológico, ecológicamente hablando.

ecologist [ɪˈkɒlədʒɪst] [i-ko-lo-chist], s. Ecólogo (student of ecology); ecologista (conservationist).

ecology [ɪˈkɒlədʒɪ] [i-ko-lo-chi], s. Ecología.

econometrics [ˌɪkɒnəˈmetrɪks] [i-ko-no-me-triks], s. Econometría.

economic, economical [ˌiːkəˈnɒmɪk] [i-ko-no-mik], *a.* 1. Económico, frugal, parco, moderado (growth, policy, development); rentable (profitable, rent). 2. Económico, perteneciente o relativo a la ciencia de la economía.

economically [ˌiːkəˈnɒmɪkəlɪ] [i-ko-no-mi-ka-li], *adv.* Económicamente (sound, secure); desde el punto de vista económico (indep); de manera económica (thriftily).

economics [ˌiːkəˈnɒmɪks] [i-ko-no-miks], *s.* Economía, la ciencia que trata de la riqueza de las naciones, su producción y distribución, y de los medios y métodos de vivir bien, aplicable así al estado, como a la familia y al individuo; economía política.

economist [ɪˈkɒnəmɪst] [i-ko-no-mist], *s.* 1. Economista, el que maneja con economía sus bienes o rentas. 2. Economista, el que estudia o profesa la economía política.

economize [ɪˈkɒnəmaɪz] [i-ko-no-mais], *va.* Economizar, ahorrar, administrar o manejar con prudencia y discreción. *vn.* Economizar. **To economize on something**, economizar o ahorrar algo.

economy [ɪˈkɒnəmɪ] [i-ko-no-mi], *s.* 1. Economía, régimen y gobierno de una casa o familia (economic state or system of country). **A mixed/market economy**, una economía mixta/de mercado. 2. Economía, frugalidad, moderación en los gastos (savings). Economía, (thrift); familiar (pack, size). **Economy class**, clase turista. **We're on an economy drive**, estamos tratando de economizar. **To make economies**, economizar, hacer economías. 3. Economía, disposición, arreglo u orden sea en sentido moral o físico. **Moral, political/rural economy**, economía moral, política o rural. **Political economy**, V. ECONOMICS.

ecosystem [ˈiːkəʊˌsɪstəm] [i-ko-no-mist] *s.* Ecosistema.

ecraseur [ɪˈkrəsəʳ] [i-kra-saʳ], *s.* Instrumento quirúrgico para extirpar los tumores sin efusión de sangre.

ecstasy [ˈekstəsɪ] [eks-ta-si], *s.* 1. Extasi o éxtasis (state). **She was in ecstasy over Jane's new baby**, estaba embelesada con el bebé de Jane. 2. Gozo, alegría, entusiasmo. 3. Distracción. 4. Extasis, estado exaltado del ánimo que suele preceder inmediatamente a la muerte. 5. Extasis (drug).

ecstatic, ecstatical [ˈekstətɪk] [eks-ta-tik], *a.* Extático, arrobado, absorto, gozoso, extasiado (look, expression); clamoroso, frenético (applause).

ecstatically [ˈekstətɪkəlɪ] [eks-ta-ti-ka-li] *adv.* Con gran entusiasmo (applaud). **Ecstatically happy**, extático de felicidad.

ectoderm [ˈektədɜːm] [ek-to-derm], *s.* Ectoderma, la capa exterior del tegumento de un organismo.

ectropium [ˈektrəpɪəm] [eks-tro-piom], *s.* Ectropión, inversión del párpado.

ecuador [ˌekwəˈdɔːʳ] [e-kua-doʳ] *N. (Geogr.)* Ecuador.

ecuadorean [ˌekwəˈdɔːrɪən] [e-kua-do-rian] *a./s.* Ecuatoriano.

ecumenical [ˌiːkjʊˈmenɪkəl] [e-kiu-me-ni-kal], *a.* Ecuménico.

eczema [ˈeksɪmə] [ek-si-ma], *s.* Eccema o eczema, enfermedad inflamatoria del cutis, acompañada de picazón.

eczematous [ˈeksɪmətəs] [ek-si-ma-tos], *a.* Eccematoso o eczematoso.

edacious [ɪˈdeɪʃəs] [i-dei-shos], *a.* Voraz, comedor, glotón.

edaciousness [ɪˈdeɪʃəsnɪs] [i-dei-shos-nes], **edacity** *s.* Voracidad, glotonería.

eddish [ˈedɪʃ] [e-dish], *s.* (Prov. Ingl.) Heno tardío.

eddy [ˈedɪ] [e-di], *s.* 1. Reflujo de agua contra la corriente. 2. Remolino, olla de agua. **Eddy of a ship**, *(Mar.)* reveses de un buque. **Eddy of the tide**, *(Mar.)* reveses de la marea. *-a.* Remolinado. *vn.* Formar remolinos (water); arremolinarse (smoke, dust).

eddy-water [ˈedɪˌwɔːtəʳ] [e-di-uo-taʳ], *s. (Mar.)* Estela, agua muerta.

edelweiss [ˈeɪdlvaɪs] [ei-del-vais], *s. (Bot.)* Edelweiss, flor de los Alpes.

edema [ɪˈdiːmə] [i-di-ma], *s.* Edema, hidropesía, hinchazón blanda producida por la obstrucción de los vasos linfáticos.

edematous [ɪˈdiːmətəs] [li-di-ma-tos], *a.* Edematoso, hinchado, lleno de humor seroso.

eden [ˈiːdn] [i-den], *s.* Edén, paraíso.

edenized [ˈiːdənaɪst] [i-de-naist], *a.* Admitido en el paraíso.

edentata [ˌiːdənˈteɪtə] [i-den-ta-ta], *s. (Zool.)* Desdentados, orden de los mamíferos que carecen de dientes incisivos; comprende los hormigueros, perezosos, armadillos y pangolines.

edentate [ˈiːdənteɪt] [i-den-teit], *a.* 1. Desdentado. 2. Perteneciente a los desdentados.

edge [edʒ] [ech], *s.* 1. Filo, el corte de un instrumento cortante (cutting part). **To be on edge**, estar nervioso, tener los nervios de punta. **His voice had a menacing edge to it**, su voz tenía un tono amenazante. 2. Punta, el extremo de alguna cosa que remata formando ángulo. 3. Canto (of coin); borde (of plate, table, chair); esquina, ángulo, margen (of page); ribete; orilla (of river, lake). **At the water's edge**, a la orilla del agua. **Frayed at the edges**, deshilachado en los bordes. 4. Punta, acrimonía. **To set the teeth on edge**, aguzar los dientes, destemplar los dientes. **Edge of the water**, la flor del agua. **To take off the edge**, embotar. **To set on edge**, aguzar, afilar.

edge, *va.* 1. Afilar, aguzar, adelgazar el corte o punta de un instrumento cortante. 2. Ribetear, guarnecer con franjas alguna cosa (border). **The collar was edged with fur**, el cuello estaba ribeteado de piel. 3. Aguijonear, incitar, hacer vehemente. 4. Avanzar, mover poco a poco de filo o de canto (move cautiously). **He edged his chair closer to hers**, fue acercando su silla a la de ella. *-vn.* Resistir, oponerse. **The child edged closer to his mother**, el niño se fue arrimando a su madre. **To edge away**, *(Mar.)* inclinarse a sotavento. **To edge in**, hacer entrar. **Two-edged sword**, espada de dos filos.

edge out Ganarle por la mano a o de la mano a (rival, opponent).

edged [ˈedʒt] [echt], *a.* Afilado.

edgeless [ˈedʒlɪs] [ech-les], *a.* Embotado, obtuso.

edge-tool [ˈedʒtuːl] [ech-tul], *s.* Herramienta afilada, instrumento afilado.

edgewise [ˈedʒwaɪz] [ech-uais], *adv.* De filo o de canto, de lado o sesgo.

edging [ˈedʒɪŋ] [ed-chin], *s.* Orla, orilla, ribete; encaje angosto. **The collar had an edge of lace**, el cuello tenía puntilla alrededor.

edgy [ˈedʒɪ] [ed-chi] *a.* Tenso, con los nervios de punta.

edible [ˈedɪbl] [e-di-bol], *a.* Comestible (safe to eat); pasable, comible (eatable).

edict [ˈiːdɪkt] [i-dikt], *s.* Edicto, mandato, orden, decreto, ordenanza.

edificant [ˈedɪfɪkənt] [e-di-fi-kant], *a.* Edificador, fabricador.

edification [ˌedɪfɪˈkeɪʃən] [e-di-fi-kei-shon], *s.* Edificación, aprovechamiento, ilustración, instrucción. **Here's a copy of the boss's memo for your edification**, aquí tienes una copia del memorándum del jefe para que te instruyas.

edificatory [ˈedɪfɪkətərɪ] [e-di-fi-ka-to-ri] *a.* Edificatorio, instructivo.

edifice [ˈedɪfɪs] [e-di-fis], *s.* Edificio, fábrica u obra de casa, palacio o templo, etc.

edificial [ˈedɪfɪʃəl] [e-di-fi-shal], *a.* Lo perteneciente a algún edificio o a su apariencia.

edifier [ˈedɪfaɪəʳ] [e-di-faiaʳ], *s.* Edificador, edificante.

edify [ˈedɪfaɪ] [e-di-fai], *va.* Edificar, instruir, enseñar, mejorar, en materias de fe, religión y moral.

edifying [ˈedɪfaɪɪŋ] [e-di-fai-in], *s.* Edificación, buen ejemplo. *a.* Edificante.

edifyingly [ˈedɪfaɪɪŋlɪ] [e-di-fai-in-li], *adv.* Ejemplarmente.

edile [ˈiːdaɪl] i-dail], *s.* Edil, magistrado de Roma.

Edinburgh [ˈedɪnbərə] [e-din-ba-ra] *N. (Geogr.)* Edimburgo.

edit [ˈedɪt] [e-dit], *va.* 1. Redactar, poner en orden y por escrito alguna cosa; corregir, editar (manuscript, correct); recortar, editar (cut). 2. Preparar para la imprenta; dirigir (manage/newspaper, magazine). 3. Montar, editar (movie, tape).

edit out Suprimir, eliminar.

editing ['edɪtɪŋ] [e-di-tin] *s.* 1. (*Publ.*) Redacción, dirección (managing); corrección, revisión, edición (correction); recorte (cutting). 2. (*Cin., Tv, Audio*) Edición.

edition [ɪ'dɪʃən] [i-di-shon], *s.* Edición, publicación o impresión de un libro.

editor ['edɪtəʳ] [e-di-toʳ], *s.* 1. Editor, el que prepara, compila y revisa alguna obra para su publicación; redactor principal (of text). 2. La persona que redacta una publicación periódica; la que se encarga de su impresión y circulación (of newspaper, magazine). 3. Editor (of movie, radio, show).

editorial ['edɪtɔrɪəl] [e-di-to-rial], *a.* Editorial, lo que pertenece al cargo de redactor. De redactor (assistant, director). (*Journ.*) Editorial (comment, decision, freedom). - *s.* Editorial, la parte escrita por la redacción en un periódico, el artículo de fondo.

editorship ['edɪtəʃɪp] [e-di-tor-ship], *s.* El cargo de redactor. Dirección.

educate ['edjʊkeɪt] [e-diu-keit], *va.* 1. Educar, criar; enseñar, instruir (teach, school). **She was educated in France**, se educó en Francia. 2. Concientizar, concienciar (make aware).

educated ['edjʊkeɪtɪd] [e-diu-kei-tid] *a.* Culto (person). **To make an educated guess**, hacer una conjetura hecha con cierta base.

education [ˌedjʊ'keɪʃən] [e-diu-kei-shon], *s.* 1. Educación, la crianza y doctrina con que se educan los niños y jóvenes (schooling, instruction). Educativo (system, policy). **He didn't have a university education**, no tuvo o no cursó estudios universitarios. 2. Pedagogía, teoría de la educación (academic subject). 3. Cultura (knowledge, culture).

educational ['edjʊkeɪʃənl] [e-diu-kei-sho-nal], *a.* Educador, educadora, perteneciente a la educación; docente, de enseñanza (establishment); educativo, instructivo (toy); instructivo (instructive).

educationalist ['edjʊkeɪʃnləɪst] [e-diu-kei-sho-na-list] *s.* Pedagogo.

educationally ['edjʊkeɪʃnəlɪ] [e-diu-kei-sho-na-li] *adv.* **Such methods are educationally unsound**, tales métodos carecen de una sólida base pedagógica. **Educationally, it makes no sense**, desde un punto de vista pedagógico, no tiene sentido.

educator ['edjʊkeɪtəʳ] [e-diu-kei-toʳ], *s.* Educador, instructor.

educe [ɪ'djuːs] [i-dius], *va.* Educir, sacar una cosa de otra; sacar a luz, extraer de la obscuridad.

eduction [ɪ'dʌkʃən] [i-dak-shon], *s.* Educción.

edulcorate ['edʌlkərɪt] [e-diu-keit], *va.* Edulcorar, dulzurar, endulzar.

edulcoration [ˌedʌlkə'reɪʃən] [e-dal-ko-rei-shon], *s.* 1. Edulcoración, dulcificación. 2. (*Quím.*) Purificación de alguna substancia lavándola con agua.

edulcorative ['edʌlkərətɪv] [e-dal-ko-ra-tiv], *a.* Dulcificante.

EEC *s.* (= **European Economic Community**) CEE.

eek [iːl] [il], *va.* (*Des.*) v. EKE.

eel [iːl] [il], *s.* Anguila. **As slippery as an eel**, escurridizo como una anguila.

eel-pie ['iːlpaɪ] [il-pai], *s.* Empanada de anguilas.

eelpout ['iːlpaʊt] [il-paut], *s.* V. BURBOT.

eel-spear ['iːlspɪəʳ] [il-spiaʳ], *s.* Tridente o arpón para pescar anguilas.

een [iːn] [in], *s. pl.* (*Esco.*) Ojos.

e'en [iːn] [in], *adv.* Contracción de EVEN.

e'er [ɛəʳ] [eaʳ], *adv.* Contracción de EVER.

eery, eerie ['ɪərɪ] [ia-ri], *a.* 1. Que inspira miedo o temor; imponente. 2. Atemorizado, afectado por el miedo. 3. Inquietante, espeluznante (atmosphere, silence, cry); fantasmagórico (glow, place); inquietante, sobrecogedor (resemblance).

eff [ef] [ef] *vn.* (*Sl.*) **To eff and blind**, decir palabrotas, soltar tacos.

effable ['ɪfəbl] [i-fa-bol], *a.* (*Ant.*) Decible, explicable.

efface [ɪ'feɪs] [i-feis], *va.* Borrar, cancelar, destruir.

effaceable [ɪ'feɪsəbl] [i-fei-sa-bol], *a.* Deleble, que puede borrarse.

effacement [ɪ'feɪsmənt] [i-feis-ment], *s.* Canceladura.

effect [ɪ'fekt] [i-fekt], *s.* 1. Efecto, consecuencia (consequence); fin, mira, intento, designio. **To take effect**, surtir efecto. **To be of little/no effect**, dar poco/no dar resultado. 2. Fortuna, ventaja. 3. Efecto, realidad; impresión (impression). **He only did it for effect**, lo hizo sólo para llamar la atención. 4. Vigor, operación activa; ejecución. **To come into effect/to take effect**, entrar en vigor o en vigencia. **To put something into effect**, poner en práctica algo. 5. (*Mec.*) Efecto o trabajo útil de una máquina. **Effects**, *-pl.* efectos, los bienes que alguno posee, sean muebles o raíces; caudal; (*Cin., Tv*) Efectos especiales; efectos (belongings). **Personal effects**, efectos personales. **To take effect**, salir bien una cosa, producir su efecto; ser puesto en vigor, hacer efectivo (v. g. una ley, un itinerario de trenes), etc. **Of no effect**, vano, inútil. **To this effect**, con este intento. **In effect**, efectivo, en operación, efectivamente.

effect, *va.* Efectuar (repairs); poner por obra, ejecutar, producir. Lograr (reconciliation, cure); llevar a cabo (escape); efectuar (payment).

effecter, *s.* V. EFFECTOR.

effectible [ɪ'fektɪbl] [i-fek-ti-bol], *a.* Factible, practicable.

effection [ɪ'fekʃən] [i-fek-shon], *s.* (*Geom.*) Construcción, problema derivado de alguna proposición general.

effective [ɪ'fektɪv] [i-fek-tiv], *a.* 1. Eficiente; eficaz; operativo, efectivo (producing the desired result/method, treatment). 2. Pasmoso, que produce viva impresión. 3. De mucho o gran efecto (striking/design, contrast). 4. Efectivo, real (real/control leader).

effectively [ɪ'fektɪvlɪ] [i-fek-tiv-li], *adv.* Eficientemente, eficazmente (manage, spend). **The cure worked effectively**, el tratamiento logró muy buenos resultados. 2. Efectivamente, realmente, de hecho (in effect). 3. Con mucho o gran efecto (contrast, decorate); convincentemente (speak).

effectiveness [ɪ'fektɪvnɪs] [i-fek-tiv-nes], *s.* 1. Efectividad, eficacia (of cure, treatment). 2. Eficiencia, eficacia (of plan). 3. Gran efecto (of color, display).

effectless [ɪ'fektlɪs] [i-fek-les], *a.* Ineficaz, impotente.

effector [ɪ'fektəʳ] [i-fek-toʳ], *s.* Causador, criador, hacedor, autor.

effectual [ɪ'fektʃʊəl] [i-fek-chual], *a.* Eficiente; eficaz, activo.

effectually [ɪ'fektʃʊəlɪ] [i-fek-chua-li], *adv.* Eficientemente, eficazmente.

effectuate [ɪ'fektʃʊeɪt] [i-fek-chueit], *va.* Efectuar, poner por obra, hacer eficaz, ejecutar.

effeminacy [ɪ'femɪnəsɪ] [i-fe-mi-na-si], *s.* Afeminación, afeminamiento, molicie, delicadeza afeminada.

effeminate [ɪ'femɪnɪt] [i-fe-mi-neit], *a.* Afeminado, mujeril, adamado, enervado. *va.* Afeminar, enervar, debilitar. *vn.* Afeminarse, enervarse.

effeminately [ɪ'femɪnɪtlɪ] [i-fe-mi-neit-li], *adv.* Afeminadamente.

effeminateness [ɪ'femɪnɪtnɪʃ] [i-fe-mi-neit-nes], *s.* Afeminamiento, afeminación.

effendi [ɪ'fendɪ] [i-fen-di], *s.* Título de respeto entre los turcos; nombre con que honran a los letrados, a los hombres de ciencia, y a los funcionarios del orden civil; casi igual a Señor o Don.

effervesce [ˌefə'ves] [e-fer-ves], *vn.* Hervir, fermentar, estar en efervescencia, burbujear (liquid); estar eufórico (person).

effervescence [ˌefə'vesəns] [e-fer-ve-sens], *s.* Efervescencia.

effervescent [ˌefə'vesənt] [e-fer-ve-sent] *a.* Efervescente (liquid, personality). **To be effervescent**, estar eufórico (person)

effete [ɪ'fiːt] [i-fit], *a.* 1. Estéril, infructuoso. 2. Usado, gastado, consumido, cascado. 3. Amanerado, afectado (manners, person). 4. Decadente (civilization, institution).

efficacious [ˌefɪ'keɪʃəs] [e-fi-kei-shos], *a.* Eficaz, activo, poderoso para obrar.

efficaciously [ˌefɪˈkeɪʃəslɪ] [e-fi-kei-shos-li], *adv.* Eficazmente.

efficaciousness [ˌefɪˈkeɪʃənɪs] [e-fi-kei-shos-nes], *s.* Eficacia.

efficacy [ˈefɪkəsɪ] [e-fi-ka-si], *s.* Eficacia.

efficience, efficiency [ˈefɪʃəns] [e-fi-shens], *s.* Eficiencia (of person, system); actividad, rendimiento; virtud, influencia. **Efficiency apartment**, apartamento pequeño (gen. amueblado).

efficient [ˈefɪʃənt] [e-fi-shent], *a.* Eficiente, eficaz (person, system); de buen rendimiento (machine, engine). *-s.* Hacedor, causador.

efficiently [ˈefɪʃəntlɪ] [e-fi-shent-li], *adv.* Eficientemente, de manera eficiente.

effigies [ˈefɪdʒiːs] [e-fi-chis], **effigy** [ˈefɪdʒɪ] [e-fi-yi], *s.* Efigie, retrato, imagen.

efflation [eˈfleɪʃən] [e-flei-shon], *s.* Insuflación; soplo.

effloresce [ˈefləres] [e-flo-res], *vn. (Quím.)* Eflorescer, disolverse una sal en polvo al contacto del aire, o cubrirse un cuerpo de partículas salinas en forma de moho.

efflorescence, efflorescency [ˌefləˈresns] [e-flo-resens] [ˌefləˈresnsɪ] [e-flo-resen-si], *s.* 1. Eflorescencia: cristales salinos que se pulverizan expuestos al aire libre. 2. Roncha, erupción que sale en el cutis. 3. Florescencia, la acción de florecer las plantas. 4. Excrecencia en forma de flor que se nota en algunos cuerpos.

efflorescent [ˌefləˈresnt] [e-flo-resent], *a.* Eflorescente: que entra o se halla en eflorescencia; en flor.

effluence [ˈefluːəns] [e-fluens], *s.* 1. Emanación, efluvio; efusión. 2. *(Fís.)* Efluencia, emanación de los corpúsculos en los cuerpos eléctricos.

effluent [ˈefluːənt] [e-fluent], *a.* 1. Efluente. 2. Efluente: epíteto dado a la calentura inflamatoria. 3. Vertidos (liquid waste); aguas residuales (sewage).

effluvium [eˈfluːvɪəm] [e-flu-vium], *pl.* EFFLUVIA, *s.* Efluvio, exhalación, emanación de partículas imperceptibles; especialmente las nocivas o hediondas.

efflux [ˈefloks] [e-fluks], *s.* Efusión, emanación; flujo, derrame.

efflux, *vn.* Fluir.

effort [ˈefət] [e-fort], *s.* 1. Esfuerzo, conato, empeño (attempt). **To make an effort**, hacer un esfuerzo, esforzarse. **She made no effort to hide her displeasure**, no hizo ningún esfuerzo para disimular su descontento. Esfuerzo (exertion, strain). **They've put a lot of effort into it**, han trabajado o se han esforzado mucho en ello. 2. **The war effort**, campaña solidaria de la población civil durante una guerra. *(Coloq.)* **What do you think of my latest effort?**, ¿qué te parece mi última obra o creación? (achievement).

effortless [ˈefətlɪs] [e-fort-les], *a.* Natural (grace); fluido (prose, style).

effortlessly [ˈefətlɪslɪ] [e-fort-les-li], *adv.* Sin esfuerzo (move, accomplish); con gracia o donaire (gracefully).

effrontery [ɪˈfrʌntərɪ] [i-fron-te-ri], *s.* Descaro, desfachatez, desvergüenza, impudencia.

effulge [ɪˈfuːldʒ] [e-fulch], *vn.* Brillar, lucir, resplandecer.

effulgence [ɪˈfuːldʒəns] [e-ful-chens], *s.* Resplandor, lustre, esplendor, fulgor.

effulgent [ɪˈfuːldʒənt] [e-ful-chent], *a.* Resplandeciente, lustroso, brillante, luminoso, efulgente.

effuse [ɪˈfjuːz] [e-fius], *va.* Derramar, verter, esparcir, desparramar.

effuse, *a.* 1. *(Bot.)* Divergente; que se extiende mucho y a gran distancia. 2. *(Des.)* Disipado, extravagante.

effusion [ɪˈfjuːʒən] [e-fiu-shon], *s.* 1. Efusión, derramamiento, desperdicio. 2. Efusión, manifestación afectuosa y cordial. 3. Flujo de palabras.

effusive [ɪˈfjuːsɪv] [e-fiu-siv], *a.* 1. Lleno de sentimiento, de afectos, impetuoso; demostrativo. 2. Difusivo, que derrama.

effusively [ɪˈfjuːsɪvlɪ] [e-fiu-siv-li] *adv.* Efusivamente.

effusiveness [ɪˈfjuːsɪvnɪs] [e-fiu-siv-nes] *s.* Efusividad.

EFL *s.* (= **English as a foreign language**) inglés para extranjeros.

eft [eft] [eft], *s.* 1. Salamandra acuática. *V.* NEWT. 2. Lagartija.

eftsoon, eftsoons [ˈeftsʊns] [eft-suns], *adv.* Luego, después, prontamente; en seguida, de prisa.

e.g., eg p. ej. o vg. o e.g. (for example); por ejemplo (in speech).

egalitarian [ɪˌɡælɪˈtɛərɪən] [i-ga-li-ta-rian] *a.* Igualitario.

egg [eg] [eg], *s.* 1. Huevo. **He's a good egg**, es buena gente, es un tipo bien. **To be left with egg on one's face**, quedar mal. 2. Huevo, el cuerpecito que cría la hembra de los peces, los insectos y la mayor parte de los reptiles. **To lay an egg**, poner un huevo, aovar. **Yolk of an egg**, yema de huevo. **White of an egg**, clara de huevo. **New-laid egg**, huevo fresco. **Addle egg**, huevo huero. **Egg-glass**, ampolleta de arena de tres minutos para cocer huevos. **Poached eggs**, huevos hervidos, echados sin cáscara en agua hirviendo. **Fried eggs**, huevos fritos o estrellados. **Soft-boiled eggs**, huevos pasados por agua. **Hard-boiled eggs**, huevos duros o cocidos. **Egg-laying**, que pone huevos, ovípara. **Egg-shell**, cáscara de huevo. **Egg-nog**, bebida compuesta de leche, huevos, azúcar y un licor espirituoso.

egg, *va.* Hurgar, incitar, provocar; cebar, atraer. (Islandés, eggja: *V.* EDGE, 3ª acep.)

egg, *va.* 1. Mezclar o cubrir con huevo. 2. *(E. U.)* Arrojar huevos a una persona. *-vn.* Coleccionar huevos de aves.

egg on, Incitar, azuzar.

egg beater [ˈegˌbiːtər] [eg-bi-ta^r], *s.* Batidor de huevos.

egg cell [ˈegsel] [eg-sel], *s.* Célula embrionaria.

eggcup [ˈegkʌp] [eg-kap], *s.* Huevera.

egg custard [ˈegˈkʌstəd] [eg-kas-tard], *s.* Natillas.

egger [ˈegər] [e-ga^r], *s.* Incitador, instigador.

egghead [ˈeghed] [eg-jed], *s. (Coloq.)* Cerebro.

egging [ˈegɪn] [e-guin], *s.* Incitamiento.

eggnog [ˈegnɒg] [eg-nog], *s.* Ponche de huevo. (Mex. y C. A.) Rompope.

eggplant [ˈegplɑːnt] [eg-plant], *s.* Berenjena, planta y fruto.

eggroll [ˈegrəʊl] [eg-roul] *s.* Rollito de primavera.

eggshell [ˈegʃel] [eg-shel] *s.* Cáscara de huevo.

egg timer [ˈegˌtaɪmər] [eg-tai-ma^r] *s.* Reloj de arena (de tres minutos) (with sand); avisador (clockwork).

egg white [ˈegwaɪt] [eg-uait] *s.* Clara de huevo.

egg yolk [ˈegjəʊk] [eg-youlk] *s.* Yema de huevo.

egilops, *V.* AEGILOPS.

egis [ˈiːgɪs] [e-guis], *s.* Escudo, armadura defensiva; una influencia o poder protector cualquiera.

eglantine [ˈegləntaɪn] [e-glan-tain], *s. (Bot.)* 1. Eglantina, flor del escaramujo. 2. Agavanzo.

ego [ˈiːgəʊ] [i-gou] *s.* **The ego**, el yo, el ego. Amor propio, ego (self-regard). **To boost somebody's ego**, alimentar el ego de alguien.

egocentric [ˌegəʊˈsentrɪk] [e-gou-sen-trik] *a.* Egocéntrico.

egoism [ˈegəʊɪzəm] [e-gou-isem], *s.* 1. Egoísmo, el inmoderado y excesivo amor a sí mismo y al bien propio, sin atender al de los demás (selfishness). 2. Egoísmo, una especie de pirronismo o escepticismo que consiste en dudar de todo menos de la propia existencia.

egoist [ˈegəʊɪst] [e-gouist], *s.* Egoísta, el partidario del egoísmo en uno y otro sentido (selfish person).

egoistic [ˌegəʊˈɪstɪk] [e-gou-is-tik], *a.* 1. Egoísta, que sólo mira a su interés propio y no procura el de los demás (selfish). 2. Egotista. 3. Relativo al pirronismo o al idealismo subjetivo.

egotism [ˈegəʊtɪzəm] [e-gou-tisem], *s.* Egotismo, vanidad, prurito de hablar de sí mismo (self-importance).

egotist [ˈegəʊtɪst] [e-gou-tist], *s.* Egotista (self-important person).

egotistic, egotistical [ˌegəʊˈtɪstɪk] [e-gou-tis-tik] [ˌegəʊˈtɪstɪkl] [e-gou-tis-ti-kal], *a.* Vanaglorioso, uno que se alaba a sí mismo. Egotista (self-important).

egotize [ˈegəʊtaɪz] [e-gou-tais], *vn.* Hablar mucho de sí mismo.

egregious [ɪˈgriːdʒəs] [i-gri-chos], *a.* 1. Egregio, insigne, extraordinario; famoso. 2. Mayúsculo, atroz.

egregiousness [ɪˈgriːdʒəsnɪʃ] [i-gri-chos-nes], *s.* Eminencia.

egress [ˈiːgres] [i-gres], **egression** *s.* Salida.

egret [ˈiːgret] [i-gret], *s.* 1. (*Orn.*) Especie de garza. 2. Pluma o plumaje.

Egypt [ˈiːdʒɪpt] [i-yipt] *N.* (*Geogr.*) Egipto.

Egyptian [ɪˈdʒɪpʃən] [i-yip-shan], *a.* Egipcio, de Egipto. *-s.* 1. Egipcio: copto, a distinción del árabe. 2. Idioma de Egipto.

eh [eɪ] [eik], *inter.* ¿Qué? ¿he? interjección interrogativa. **So you went to Paris, eh?**, ah, ¿así que fuiste a París? (expressing interest). ¿eh?, ¿no? (inviting agreement). ¿eh?, ¿qué?, ¿cómo? (inviting repetition).

eider, eider-duck [ˈaɪdəʳ] [ai-daʳ] [ˈaɪdəkʌk] [ai-daʳ-dak], *s.* Eider, eidero, especie de ánade.

eider-down [ˈaɪdədaʊn] [ai-der-daun], *s.* Edredón, plumazón de varias aves del norte; almohadón, plumón, cubrepiés.

eidograph [ˈaɪdəgræf] [ei-do-graf], *s.* Eidógrafo, aparato para copiar y reducir dibujos.

eidolon [ˈaɪdəlɒn] [ei-do-lon], *s.* (*pl.* EIDOLA). 1. Representación, imagen. 2. Fantasma. (Gr. id. imagen).

eight [eɪt] [eit], *a.* Ocho. *-s.* 1. Isleta en un río. 2. El número ocho. (*Coloq.*) **To have had over the eight**, haber bebido de más.

eighteen [ˈeɪˈtiːn] [ei-tin], *a.* y *s.* Dieciocho.

eighteenth [ˈeɪˈtiːnθ] [ei-tinz], *a.* Décimoctavo. *adv.* En decimoctavo lugar. *s.* (*Mat.*) Dieciochoavo. Dieciochoava parte (part). **It's her eighteenth today**, hoy cumple dieciocho años (birthday).

eightfold [ˈeɪtfəʊld] [eit-fould], *a.* Ocho veces tanto.

eighth [eɪtθ] [eiz], *a.* Octavo. *adv.* En octavo lugar. *s.* (*Mat.*) Octavo. Octava parte (part). **Eighth note**, corchea.

eighthly [ˈeɪtθlɪ] [eiz-li], *adv.* En el octavo lugar.

eightieth [ˈeɪtɪɪθ] [ei-tiez], *a.* Octogésimo. *adv.* En octogésimo lugar. *s.* (*Mat.*) Ochentavo. Ochentava u octogésima parte (part).

eighty [ˈeɪtɪ] [ei-ti] *a./s.* Ochenta.

eire [ˈɛərə] [e-re] *N.* (*Geogr.*) Eire, Irlanda.

eirie [ˈeɪriː] [ei-ri] *s.* V. AERIE.

either [ˈaɪðəʳ] [ai-daʳ], *a.* Cualquiera, cada uno o cada una, uno de dos, cualquiera de los dos. **You can take either route**, puedes tomar cualquiera de las dos rutas (one or the other). **On either side of the path**, a ambos lados o a cada lado del camino (each). *pron.* Cualquiera; ninguno (with neg.); alguno (in questions). **Either (one) would be suitable**, cualquiera (de los dos) serviría. **I couldn't wear either of those dresses**, no podría ponerme ninguno de esos vestidos. *-conj.* 1. O, sea, ya. **He is either a knave or a fool**, o es pícaro o tonto. **You can have either tea or coffee**, puedes tomar (o) té o café. 2. (*Fam.*) Por cierto, en todo caso, también; (precedido de una negación) tampoco. **He can't speak either Spanish or Italian**, no sabe hablar (ni) español ni italiano. *adv.* Tampoco (with neg.). **She can't cook and he can't either**, ella no sabe cocinar y él tampoco.

ejaculate [ɪˈdʒækjʊleɪt] [i-ya-kiu-leit], *va.* 1. Exclamar, pronunciar súbitamente, proferir (cry out). 2. (*Des.* o *Med.*) Arrojar, despedir, eyacular. *vn.* (*Physiol.*) Eyacular.

ejaculation [ɪˌdʒækjʊˈleɪʃən] [i-ya-kiu-lei-shon], *s.* 1. Jaculatoria. 2. La acción de arrojar alguna cosa con fuerza. 3. Eyaculación, emisión.

eject [ɪˈdʒekt] [i-yekt], *va.* Arrojar, expeler, despedir, desechar. Expulsar (troublemaker, cassette). *vn.* (*Aviat.*) Eyectarse.

ejection [ɪˈdʒekʃən] [i-yek-shon], *s.* 1. Expulsión (of troublemaker), eyección (by pilot); evacuación. 2. Deyección, la materia desechada.

ejection seat [ɪˈdʒekʃənˈsiːt] [i-yek-shon-sit], *s.* (*Aer.*) Asiento expulsor.

ejectment [ɪˈdʒektmənt] [i-yekt-ment], *s.* Auto de desahucio; expulsión de una casa, posesión, etc.

ejector [ɪˈdʒektəʳ] [i-yek-taʳ], *s.* Eyector, expulsor, desposeedor; el que o lo que expele o desposee.

eke [iːk] [ik], *va.* 1. Aumentar, suplir, integrar, ensanchar o añadir ligeramente, de manera que algo sea apenas suficiente, seguido de *out.* 2. Obtener, mantener o producir con dificultad, apenas, escasamente.

eke out 1. Estirar, hacer alcanzar (make last/resources, funds). 2. **To eke out a living**, ganarse la vida a duras penas (barely obtain).

elaborate [ɪˈlæbərɪt] [i-la-bo-reit], *va.* Elaborar, trabajar con esmero y cuidado. *vn.* Dar más detalles, entrar en detalles o explicaciones.

elaborate, *a.* Elaborado, esmerado, acabado, limado (decoration, design, hairstyle); curioso, primoroso; de mucho trabajo (meal); minucioso, detallado (plan, arrangements). **In elaborate detail**, con todo detalle, muy minuciosamente

elaborately [ɪˈlæbərɪtlɪ] [i-la-bo-reit-li], *adv.* Cuidadosamente, con mucho trabajo; minuciosamente, detalladamente (planned); muy elaboradamente (decorated).

elaboration [ɪˈlæbəˈreɪʃən] [i-la-bo-rei-shon], *s.* 1. Elaboración, la acción de elaborar o producir con primor y perfección en sus detalles (of a theory, plan). 2. Obra acabada.

élan [eɪˈlɑːn] [ei-lan] *s.* Ímpetu, brío, elán.

elapse [ɪˈlæps] [i-laps], *vn.* Pasar, correr el tiempo, transcurrir.

elastic, elastical [ɪˈlæstɪk] [i-las-tik], *a.* Elástico (waistband, garter); elastizado, elástico (stocking); elástico (fiber, properties); elástico (rule, definition). **Elastic gum**, V. INDIARUBBER. **Elastic fluids**, fluidos elásticos; se llaman así los vapores y los gases. *s.* Elástico; liga (garter).

elasticated [ɪˈlæstɪkeɪtɪd] [i-las-ti-kei-tid] *a.* Con elástico.

elastic band [ɪˈlæstɪkˌbænd] [i-las-tik-band] *s.* Goma elástica, gomita, liga, caucho, elástico, banda elástica.

elasticity [ˌiːlæsˈtɪsɪtɪ] [i-las-ti-si-ti], *s.* Elasticidad, la propiedad de una cosa de recobrar su forma o posición original (después de haberse ejercido sobre ella presión, expansión o torcedura); elasticidad (of fiber, substance); flexibilidad (of rule, definition).

elasticized [ɪˈlæstɪsaɪz] [i-las-ti-sais] *a.* Con elástico.

elate [ɪˈleɪt] [i-leit], *a.* Exaltado de espíritu, triunfante, gozoso.

elate, *va.* Exaltar, elevar, engreír, ensoberbecer.

elated [ɪˈleɪtɪd] [i-lei-ted] *a.* Eufórico.

elatedly [ɪˈleɪtɪdlɪ] [i-lei-ted-li], *adv.* Exaltadamente, triunfantemente.

elation [ɪˈleɪʃən] [i-lei-shon], *s.* Júbilo, exaltación del ánimo, viva alegría.

elbow [ˈelbəʊ] [el-bou], *s.* 1. Codo (of person, in pipe); recodo (on river, road). **My sweater is going at the elbows**, se me están gastando los codos del suéter. **To give somebody the elbow**, deshacerse de alguien. 2. Codo, cualquier cosa que forma ángulo saliente. **To be at the elbow**, estar a la mano, estar muy cerca.

elbow *va.* Darle un codazo a. **They elbowed us out of the way**, nos apartaron a empujones.

elbow grease [ˈelbəʊgriːs] [el-bou-gris], *s.* (*Vul.*) Ejercicio o trabajo constante que excita la transpiración; trabajo manual, duro esfuerzo. **Put some elbow grease into it!**, ¡dale con más fuerza!

elbow-room [ˈelbəʊrʊm] [el-bou-rum], *s.* Espacio para el libre movimiento de los codos; (*Fig.*) anchura, alcance, desahogo.

elder [ˈeldəʳ] [el-daʳ], *a.* Mayor, más viejo, de más edad. *- Comp. irr.* es preferido a *older* cuando sólo se comparan dos objetos. *-s.* 1. Mayor, el que tiene más edad que otro. **She's my elder by two years**, me lleva dos años, es dos años mayor que yo (older person). 2. (*Ecle.*) Príncipe o jefe de una tribu o familia; en el Nuevo Testamento, dignatario de la Iglesia cristiana; en el uso moderno, funcionario eclesiástico de rango y funciones diversos; miembro del consejo. *-pl.* Ancianos, mayores, antepasados. **The village/tribal elders**, los ancianos del pueblo/de la tribu.

elder, *s.* 1. (*Bot.*) Saúco, arbusto del género Sambucus. 2. Uno de varios árboles o plantas parecidos al saúco.

Elderberry, la baya o grano del saúco. **Elder-blow**, la flor del saúco.

elderly ['eldəlɪ] [el-de-li], *a*. Mayor, el de edad ya madura, anciano. **An elderly lady**, una señora mayor o de edad, una anciana. **The elderly**, *s. pl.* los ancianos.

eldest ['eldɪst] [el-dest], *a*. Mayor (brother, sister, child). **The eldest**, el mayor, el de más edad. *V.* OLDEST.

elect [ɪ'lekt] [i-lekt], *va*. 1. Elegir, escoger, designar entre varios (choose). 2. Elegir, escoger por voto de la mayoría. **He was elected president**, lo eligieron o fue elegido presidente.

elect, *a*. Elegido, escogido, electo; predestinado. **The president elect**, el presidente electo.

election [ɪ'lekʃən] [i-lek-shon], *s*. 1. Elección (act); elecciones (event). **To call/hold an election**, convocar, celebrar elecciones. Electoral (campaign, speech); de las elecciones (day, results). 2. *(E. U.)* Nombramiento por votos. 3. Escogimiento, elección, en general. 4. En teología, predestinación.

electioneer [ɪ,lekʃə'nɪəʳ] [i-lek-sho-niaʳ] *vn*. Hacer campaña o propaganda electoral.

electioneering [ɪ,lekʃə'nɪərɪŋ] [i-lek-sho-nie-rin], *s*. El acto de solicitar personas para que voten por el individuo que el partido propone para un empleo; campaña electoral.

elective [ɪ'lektɪv] [i-lek-tiv], *a*. 1. Electivo (post, assembly). **Elective attraction**, atracción electiva o afinidad química. 2. Optativo (optional/course, subject). *s*. Optativa.

electively [ɪ'lektɪvlɪ] [i-lek-tiv-li], *adv*. Electivamente.

elector [ɪ'lektəʳ] [i-lek-toʳ], *s*. 1. Elector, el que tiene derecho de elegir. 2. Elector, antiguamente cualquiera de los príncipes del imperio germánico que tenía voto en la elección del emperador.

electoral [ɪ'lektərəl] [i-lek-to-ral], *a*. Electoral (system, reform). **Electoral college**, colegio electoral. **Electoral register/roll**, padrón o censo, registro o planilla electoral.

electorate [ɪ'lektərɪt] [i-lek-to-reit] *s*. Electorado.

electoress [ɪ'lektərɪs] [i-lek-to-res], **electress** *f*. Electriz, la mujer o viuda del elector.

electric, electrical [ɪ'lektrɪk] [i-lek-trik], *a*. 1. Eléctrico; electrificado (fence); electrizante (performance, atmosphere). **Electric bill**, cuenta o recibo de la luz o de la electricidad. 2. *(Fig.)* Vivo, fogoso, magnético. **Electric cable**, cable conductor. **Electric chair**, silla eléctrica. **Electric eye**, ojo eléctrico o fotocélula. **Electric fixtures**, dispositivos eléctricos de instalación fija. **Electric motor**, motor eléctrico. **Electric plant**, planta eléctrica. **Electrical engineering**, ingeniería eléctrica. **Electrical transcription**, grabación fonográfica eléctrica. **Electrical storm**, tormenta eléctrica.

electric blanket [ɪ'lektrɪk,blæŋkɪt] [i-lek-trik-blan-ket] Manta o cobija o frazada eléctrica.

electric eel [ɪ'lektrɪk,iːl] [i-lek-trik-il], *s*. *(Zool.)* Anguila eléctrica.

electrician [ɪlek'trɪʃən] [i-lek-tri-shan], *s*. 1. Electricista; individuo versado en la electricidad. 2. El que inventa, hace, abastece o tiene a su cargo aparatos eléctricos.

electricity [ɪlek'trɪsɪtɪ] [i-lek-tri-si-ti], *s*. Electricidad, agente natural imponderable, invisible y poderoso, que produce muy variadas manifestaciones de su fuerza. **It runs on electricity**, funciona con o a electricidad. **Electricity bill**, cuenta o recibo de la electricidad. **Electric shock**, descarga eléctrica.

electrification [ɪ'lektrɪfɪ'keɪʃən] [i-lek-tri-kei-shon], *s*. 1. Electrificación. 2. Electrización.

electrify [ɪ'lektrɪfaɪ] [i-lek-tri-fai], *va*. 1. Electrificar. 2. Electrizar (excite, thrill).

electrifying [ɪ'lektrɪfaɪɪŋ] [i-lek-tri-faiin] *a*. Electrizante.

electro-. Forma de combinación que representa la palabra *electric* en composición. Estas palabras son muy numerosas; sólo se insertan aquí algunas de las más usadas.

electrocardiogram [ɪ'lektrəʊkɑːdɪəgræm] [i-lek-tro-kar-dio-gram], *s*. Electrocardiograma.

electrocardiograph [ɪ'lektrəʊkɑːdɪəgræf] [i-lek-tro-kar-dio-graf], *s*. Electrocardiógrafo.

electro-chemical [ɪ'lektrəʊ'kemɪkəl] [i-lek-tro-ke-mi-kal], *a*. Electroquímico, relativo a la electroquímica.

electro-chemistry [ɪ,lektrəʊ'kemɪstrɪ] [i-lek-tro-ke-mis-tri], *s*. Electroquímica, el ramo de la química que trata de la producción de cambios químicos por medio de la electricidad.

electrocute [ɪ'lektrəʊkjuːt] [i-lek-tro-kiut], *va*. Electrocutar, matar por medio de una corriente eléctrica.

electrocution [ɪ,lektrəʊ'kjuːʃən] [i-lek-tro-kiu-shon], *s*. Electrocución.

electrode [ɪ'lektrəʊd] [i-lek-troud], *s*. Electrodo, cada uno de los polos de una batería galvánica o un dinamo; los extremos o cabos metálicos de los conductores que proceden de ambos polos eléctricos.

electro-deposit [ɪ,lektrəʊdɪ'pɒzɪt] [i-lek-trou-di-po-sit], *va*. Depositar químicamente por medio de una corriente eléctrica.

electro-dynamic [ɪ,lektrəʊdaɪ'næmɪk] [i-lek-trou-dai-na-mik], *a*. Electrodinámico, que puede producir una corriente eléctrica.

electrodynamics [ɪ,lektrəʊdaɪ'næmɪks] [i-lek-trou-dai-na-miks], *s*. Electrodinámica.

electrolysis [ɪlek'trɒlɪsɪs] [i-lek-tro-li-sis], *s*. Electrólisis, electrolización, análisis o descomposición de un cuerpo por medio de la electricidad.

electrolyte [ɪlek'trɒlaɪt] [i-lek-tro-lait], *s*. Electrolito, cuerpo que puede descomponerse por la electricidad.

electrolytic [ɪlek'trɒlɪtɪk] [i-lek-tro-li-tik], *a*. Electrolítico, relativo a la electrólisis o a un electrolito.

electrolyzation [ɪ,lektrəlaɪ'zeɪʃən] [i-lek-tro-lai-sei-shon], *s*. Electrolización.

electrolyze [ɪ'lektrəlaɪz] [i-lek-tro-lais], *va*. Electrolizar, analizar o descomponer un cuerpo por medio de la electricidad.

electromagnet [ɪ'lektrəʊ'mægnɪt] [i-lek-tro-mag-net], *s*. Electroimán, centro de hierro dulce, convertido en imán mediante una corriente eléctrica.

electromagnetic [ɪ'lektrəʊ'mægnetɪk] [i-lek-tro-mag-ne-tik], *a*. Electromagnético, relativo al electroimán o al electromagnetismo.

electromagnetism [ɪ'lektrəʊ'mægnetɪzəm] [i-lek-tro-mag-ne-tisem], *s*. Electromagnetismo; la imantación o el magnetismo producido por medio de la electricidad; el estudio de las relaciones entre la electricidad y el magnetismo.

electrometallurgy [ɪ,lektrəʊmɪ'tælədʒɪ] [i-lek-tro-mi-ta-lur-chi], *s*. Electrometalurgia.

electrometer [ɪlek'trɒmɪtəʳ] [i-lek-tro-mi-taʳ], *s*. Electrómetro, instrumento para medir la cantidad y determinar la calidad de la electricidad.

electro-motive [ɪ,lektrəʊ'məʊtɪv] [i-lek-tro-mo-tiv], *a*. Electromotor, electromotriz, que se refiere al movimiento de la electricidad o a las leyes que lo gobiernan. **Electro-motive force**, fuerza electromotriz, la que produce el movimiento de la electricidad por un conductor.

electro-motor [ɪ,lektrəʊ'məʊtəʳ] [i-lek-tro-mo-toʳ], *s*. 1. Motor eléctrico. 2. Todo aparato que desarrolla electricidad.

electron [ɪ'lektrɒn] [i-lek-tron], *s*. Electrón. **Electron microscope**, microscopio electrónico.

electronegative [ɪ'lektrɒnegatɪv] [i-lek-tro-né-ga-tiv], *s. y a*. Electronegativo.

electronic [ɪlek'trɒnɪk] [i-lek-tro-nik], *a*. Electrónico. **Electronic data processing**, procesamiento electrónico de datos. **Electronic publishing**, edición electrónica. **Electronic cash**, dinero electrónico. **Electronic engineer**, ingeniero electrónico. **Electronic mail**, correo electrónico.

electronics [ɪlek'trɒnɪks] [i-lek-tro-niks], *s. pl*. 1. Electrónica (subject); electrónico (industry). 2. Sistema electrónico (circuitry).

electron microscope [ɪ,lektrɒn'maɪkrəskəʊp] [i-lek-tron-mai-kros-koup] *s*. Microscopio electrónico.

electroplate [ɪˈlektrəʊpleɪt] [i-lek-tro-pleit], *va.* Plaquear un metal por medio del galvanismo o de un dínamo; galvanoplatear, platear mediante electrólisis (with silver); electrodorar, dorar mediante electrólisis (with gold).

electroplating [ɪˈlektrəʊpleɪtɪŋ] [i-lek-tro-plei-tin], *s.* Electrochapeado, electrodeposicion, electroplastia.

electropositive [ɪˈlektrəpɒsɪtɪv] [i-lek-tro-po-si-tiv], *s.* y *a.* Electropositivo.

electroscope [ɪˈlektrəskəʊp] [i-lek-tros-koup], *s.* Electroscopio, instrumento para determinar la presencia de la electricidad en un conductor.

electrostatics [ɪˌlektrəʊˈstætɪks] [i-lek-tros-ta-tiks], *s.* Electroestática, el ramo de la ciencia eléctrica que trata de los fenómenos de la electricidad en estado de reposo o la electricidad producida por fricción.

electrotechnics [ɪˈlektrəʊteknɪks] [i-lek-tro-tek-niks], *s.* Electrotecnia.

electro-telegraphy [ɪlekˈtrəʊtelɪˈɡræfɪ] [i-lek-tro-te-li-grafi], *s.* Telegrafía por medio de la electricidad.

electro-telegraphic [ɪlekˈtrəʊtelɪˈɡræfɪk] [i-lek-tro-te-li-gra-fik], *a.* Electrotelegráfico.

electro-therapeutic [ɪˌlektrəʊθerəˈpjuːtɪk] [i-lek-tro-ze-ra-piu-tik], *a.* Electroterapéutico, que se refiere a la electricidad considerada como medio terapéutico.

electro-therapeutics [ɪˌlektrəʊθerəˈpjuːtɪks] [i-lek-tro-ze-ra-piu-tiks], *s.* Electroterapéutica, la aplicación de la electricidad a la terapéutica.

electrotherapy [ɪˌlektrəʊˈθerəpɪ] [i-lek-tro-ze-ra-pi], *s.* Electroterapia.

electrotype [ɪˈlektrətaɪp] [i-lek-tro-taip], *s.* 1. Electrotipo, grabado tipográfico que se obtiene por medio de la electrotipia. 2. Impresión de dicho grabado. *-va.* Electrotipar, hacer un electrotipo; duplicar por medio de la electrotipia.

electrotypy [ɪˈlektrətɪpɪ] [i-lek-tro-ti-pi], *s.* Electrotipia, arte de cubrir de una capa metálica, por medio de la electroquímica, monedas u objetos semejantes.

electrum [ˈeləktrɒm] [e-lek-trum] *s.* 1. Plata alemana, liga de níquel, cinc y cobre; cualquier otra mezcla semejante. 2. Antiguamente, electro o ámbar.

electuary [eˈlektʊərɪ] [e-lek-tua-ri] *s.* Electuario, confección farmacéutica.

eleemosynary [ˈeliːməsɪˈnærɪ] [e-li-mo-si-na-ri] *a. s.* 1. Caritativo, de caridad, de limosna. 2. Mendicante, que vive de limosna.

elegance, elegancy [ˈelɪɡəns] [e-li-gans] *f.* Elegancia, hermosura, primor; buen gusto, garbo, aire.

elegant [ˈelɪɡənt] [e-li-gant] *a.* Elegante, fino, delicado, pulido.

elegantly [ˈelɪɡəntlɪ] [e-li-gant-li] *adv.* Elegantemente, pulidamente.

elegiac, elegiacal [elɪˈdʒaɪək] [e-li-chiak], [elɪˈdʒaɪəkl] [e-li-chi-kal] *a.* Elegíaco.

elegiast [ˈelɪdʒɪəst] [e-li-chiast] *s.* Elegíaco, escritor de elegías.

elegy [ˈelɪdʒɪ] [e-li-chi] *f.* Elegía, canto fúnebre o melancólico.

element [ˈelɪmənt] [e-li-ment] *f.* 1. Elemento. 2. Elemento, la esfera o situación propia de cualquier cosa. 3. Elemento, ingrediente. 4. *(Biol.)* Una de las unidades primitivas de un organismo; celdilla o unidad morfológica. 5. *(Elec.)* Elemento de pila o batería, par. 6. *(Chem.)* Cuerpo simple, aquella forma de la materia que no puede descomponerse por ninguno de los medios que conoce la ciencia. **Elements,** primeros principios o ideas fundamentales; rudimentos. **To be out of one's element,** estar fuera de su elemento, como pez fuera del agua. **It's the personal element that counts,** es el factor personal el que cuenta.

elemental [elɪˈmentl] [e-li-men-tal] *a.* Elemental, primordial.

elementary [ˈelɪməntərɪ] [e-li-men-ta-ri] *a.* Elemental, inicial, primitivo; incipiente. **Elementary schooling,** primera enseñanza.

elemi [ˈelɪmɪ] [e-li-mi] *s.* Elemí, resina usada para emplastos y barnices.

elephant [ˈelɪfənt] [e-li-fant] *s.* Elefante.

elephantiasis [ˈelɪfənˈtaɪəsɪs] [e-li-fan-tia-sis] *f.* Elefantiasis.

elephantine [ˈelɪfəntiːn] [e-li-fan-tin] *a.* Elefantino, mastodóntico.

elevate [ˈelɪveɪt] [e-li-veit] *va.* 1. Elevar, alzar, levantar (rise). 2. Elevar, exaltar; promover, hacer adelantar (develop). 3. Excitar, animar, alegrar; inspirar (inspire). 4. Alzar el tono o aumentar la resonancia de la voz o de un instrumento musical.

elevated [ˈelɪveɪtɪd] [e-li-vei-ted] *a.* 1. Elevado, alzado, sublime. 2. Exaltado. **Elevated railroad,** tren elevado.

elevation [elɪˈveɪʃən] [e-li-vei-shon] *f.* 1. Elevación. 2. Altura, encumbramiento. 3. Elevación de espíritu, grandeza de alma, alteza de pensamientos. 4. *(Arq.)* Alzado de un edificio. 5. *(Astr.)* Altura de algún cuerpo celeste.

elevator [ˈelɪveɪtər] [e-li-vei-tar] *s.* 1. Elevador, ascensor, aparato que sirve para conducir personas o carga de uno a otro piso de un edificio. 2. Máquina a manera de noria para transferir granos desde los buques o carros de ferrocarril a los depósitos o graneros. *(E.U.)* **Elevator car,** caja de ascensor. *(E.U.)* **Elevator shaft,** hueco del ascensor.

elevator hoist [ˈelɪveɪtəˈhɔɪst] [e-li-vei-tar-joist] *s.* Montacargas, malacate, ascensor para carga.

eleven [ɪˈlevn] [i-le-ven] *a. s.* Once.

eleventh [ɪˈlevnθ] [i-le-venz] *a.* Onceavo, onceno, undécimo. **At the eleventh hour,** a la última hora.

elf [elf] [elf] *s.* 1. Duende, trasgo o espíritu travieso. 2. Demonio, diablo. 3. Enano, elfo. En plural se escribe *elves.*

elf-arrow [ˈelfˈærəʊ] [elf-arou] *s.* Pedernal en forma de flecha.

elfin [ˈelfɪn] [el-fin] *a.* Perteneciente a los duendes; mágico, encantado. *-s.* Diablillo, niño pequeño, travieso y enredador.

elfish [ˈelfɪʃ] [el-fish] *a.* Aduendado, que pertenece a duendes o demonios; travieso, fantástico, mágico.

elf-looks [ˈelfˈlʊks] [elf-luks] *s. pl.* Greñas de duende, trenzas de pelo.

elicit [ɪˈlɪsɪt] [i-li-sit] *va.* Sacar de; atraer, sonsacar, obtener (obtain, achieve), hacer salir como por medio de la atracción; educir o extraer gradualmente y sin violencia.

elicit, *a. (Filos.)* Que resulta de la volición libre o del escogimiento.

elide [ɪˈlaɪd] [i-laid] *va.* Elidir, suprimir una vocal en una o más palabras, v.g. *don't* por *do not,* o *'tis* por *it is.*

eligibility [ˌelɪdʒəˈbɪlɪtɪ] [e-li-chi-bi-li-ti] *f.* Elegibilidad, reunión de cualidades para ser elegido.

eligible [ˈelɪdʒəbl] [e-li-yi-bol] *a.* 1. Elegible, preferible. 2. A propósito, digno de admisión o aceptación, deseable. **To be elegible for,** tener los requisitos para, tener derecho a.

eligibleness [ˈelɪdʒəblnɪs] [e-li-yi-bol-nes] *f.* Elegibilidad.

eliminate [ɪˈlɪmɪneɪt] [i-li-mi-neit] *va.* 1. rechazar, echar fuera, arrojar, especialmente como perjudicial, dañoso o inútil; eliminar, suprimir. 2. *(Alg.)* Eliminar, hacer desaparecer una cantidad de una ecuación.

elimination [ɪˌlɪmɪˈneɪʃən] [i-li-mi-nei-shon] *s.* Eliminación, acción de eliminar; excreción.

eliminator [ɪˌlɪmɪˈneɪtər] [i-li-mi-nei-tar] *sm. (Boxeo)* Combate eliminatorio.

eliquation [elɪˈkweɪʃən] [e-li-kuei-shon] *s.* Separación de dos metales por medio de un grado de calor que pueda derretir al uno y no al otro.

elision [ɪˈlɪʃən] [i-li-shon] *s.* 1. *(Gram.)* Elisión. 2. División.

elite [eɪˈliːt] [ei-lit] *s.* Lo mejor, lo escogido, lo selecto; la flor y nata.

elitism [ɪˈliːtɪzəm] [i-li-ti-sem] *sm.* Elitismo.

elitist [ɪˈliːtɪst] [i-li-tist] *a.* Elitista.

elixir [e'liksɪʳ] [e-lik-siʳ] *s.* 1. Elixir, medicamento o tintura compuesta y extraída de varios ingredientes; cordial. 2. Extracto o quinta esencia de alguna cosa.

elk [elk] [elk] *f.* Alce o anta, cuadrúpedo muy corpulento de la familia del ciervo: habita en los bosques de los países del norte.

ell [el] [el] *s.* Ana, medida de longitud hoy rara vez usada.

ellipse [ɪ'lɪps] [i-lips] *s. (Geom.)* Elipse, curva cerrada que resulta de cortar un cono con un plano oblicuo a la dirección de su eje; óvalo.

ellipsis [ɪ'lɪpsɪs] [i-lip-sis] *s. (Gram.)* Elipsis, la omisión de una o más palabras necesarias para la recta construcción gramatical, pero sin que por eso se obscurezca el sentido de la oración.

ellipsoid [ɪ'lɪpsɔɪd] [i-lip-soid] *a.* Elipsoide, sólido formado por la revolución de la elipse sobre uno de sus dos ejes.

elliptic, elliptical [ɪ'lɪptɪk] [i-lip-tik] *s.* Elíptico.

elm [elm] [elm] *s. (Bot.)* Olmo, árbol de gran altura, tronco recto y madera fuerte y sólida.

elocution [ˌelə'kjuːʃən] [e-lo-kiu-shon] *f.* Elocución; habla, manera de hacer uso de la palabra.

eloge [ɪ'lɒdʒ] [i-loch] *s.* Oración fúnebre, panegírico.

elogist [ɪ'lɒdʒ] [i-lo-chist] *s.* Elogiador. *V.* EULOGIST.

elogy [ɪ'lɒdʒɪ] [i-lo-chi] *f.* Elogio, oración fúnebre; relación biográfica; se usa impropiamente en el sentido de encomio, alabanza.

elongate ['iːlɒŋgeɪt] [i-lon-gueit] *va.* Alargar. -*vn.* 1. Volverse más largo; alargarse, aumentarse. 2. Alejarse, desviarse un astro.

elongation [ˌiːlɒŋ'geɪʃən] [i-lon-guei-shon] *f.* 1. Prolongación, extensión. 2. El acto de alargarse alguna cosa. 3. *(Astr.)* Elongación.

elope [ɪ'ləʊp] [i-loup] *vn.* 1. Escapar, huir, evadirse (escape, evade). 2. Fugarse, huir una mujer de su casa en compañía de un amante o seductor. **To elope with,** fugarse con.

elopement [ɪ'ləʊpmənt] [i-loup-ment] *s.* Fuga, huída; evasión, escapada: se usa para expresar que una mujer casada se ha escapado con un seductor, o que una joven ha dejado la casa de sus padres para irse con su amante.

eloquence ['eləkwəns] [e-lo-kuens] *f.* Elocuencia, propiedad, pureza, buen empleo y distribución de palabras y pensamientos al hablar y escribir.

eloquent ['eləkwənt] [e-lo-kuent] *a.* Elocuente.

eloquently ['eləkwəntlɪ] [e-lo-kuent-li] *adv.* Elocuentemente.

else [els] [els] *a.* Otro. **Nobody else, no one else,** ningún otro, nadie más. **Nothing else,** nada más. -*adv.* 1. Más, además; en vez de. 2. De otro modo o manera; en otro caso; a menudo va precedido de *or* (o); si no. **Everything else, all else,** todo lo demás. **Anyone else would do it,** cualquier otra persona lo haría. **Somewhere else,** en otra parte. **What else?,** ¿qué más? **There was little else to do,** apenas quedaba otra cosa que hacer.

elsewhere ['els'weəʳ] [els-ueaʳ] *adv.* En cualquier otra parte, a otra parte, de otra parte.

elucidate [ɪ'luːsɪdeɪt] [e-lu-si-deit] *va.* Dilucidar, explicar, aclarar, ilustrar (explain, show).

elucidation [ɪ'luːsɪdeɪʃən] [e-lu-si-dei-shon] *f.* Elucidación, explicación, aclaración (explanation).

elucidative, elucidatory [ɪ'luːsɪdətɪv] [e-lu-si-da-tiv] [ɪ'luːsɪdətərɪ] [e-lu-si-da-to-ri] *a.* Explicativo, que se puede dilucidar.

elude [ɪ'luːd] [e-lud] *va.* 1. Eludir, huir la dificultar. 2. Burlar a alguno huyendo de él. **The name eludes me,** se me escapa el nombre, no me acuerdo del nombre.

eludible [ɪ'luːdɪbl] [i-lu-di-bol] *a.* Evitable.

elusion [ɪ'luːʃən] [i-lu-shon] *f.* Escapatoria; artificio para eludir.

elusive [ɪ'luːsɪvɪs] [i-lu-siv-nes] *a.* Que tiende a huir o escaparse; falaz, tenue, difícil de asir o de tener.

elusiveness [ɪ'luːsɪvɪs] [i-lu-siv-nes] *m.* Carácter esquivo.

elusorines [ɪ'luːsərɪnɪs] [i-lu-so-ri-nes], *s.* Fraude, engaño; astucia.

elusory [ɪ'luːsərɪ] [i-lu-so-ri], *a.* Falaz, engañador; hábil en artificios y subterfugios. *V.* ELUSIVE.

elutriate [ɪ'luːtrɪeɪt] [i-lu-trieit], *va.* Decantar; colar.

elutriation [ɪ'luːtrɪ'eɪʃən] [i-lu-triei-shon], *s.* La acción de lavar o limpiar con agua los minerales pulverizados.

elver ['elvəʳ] [el-vaʳ], *f.* Angula.

elvish, *a. V.* ELFISH.

elysian [ɪ'liːʒən] [i-li-shan], *a.* Ameno, delicios. **Elisyan Fields,** Campos Elíseos.

elytron, elytrum [ɪ'liːtrəm] [i-li-trum], *s. (pl. ELYTRA).* Élitro, estuche, cada una de las alas anteriores endurecidas de los coleópteros y ortópteros; también se da este nombre a las anchas escamas dorsales de ciertos gusanos.

em [em] [em], *s.* 1. Nombre de la letra M, la decimotercera del alfabeto inglés. 2. *(Impr.)* Eme, el cuadrado del cuerpo de un tipo, usado como unidad de medida.

'em, *pron. (Fam.)* Elisión de **them,** caso objetivo del pronombre **they.**

EM *Abreviatura de* **Engineer of Mines.**

emaciate [ɪ'meɪsɪeɪt] [i-mei-sieit], *va.* Extenuar, adelgazar. - *vn.* Enflaquecer, ponerse flaco o perder peso.

emaciate, *a.* Enflaquecido, flaco 2. *(Med.)* Emaciado, extenuado.

emaciation [ɪ'meɪsɪeɪʃən] [i-mei-siei-shon], *s.* Extenuación, flaqueza, enflaquecimiento.

email, e-mail [ɪ'meɪl] [i-meil], *m.* Correo electrónico.

emanant ['emənənt] [i-ma-nant], *a.* Emanante.

emanate ['eməneɪt] [i-ma-neit] *vn.* Emanar, preceder, derivarse.

emanation [ˌeməneɪʃən] [i-ma-nei-shon], *f.* Emanación; efluvio, efluencia.

emanative ['emənətɪv] [i-ma-na-tiv], *a.* Emanante.

emancipate [ɪ'mænsɪpeɪt] [i-man-si-peit], *va.* Emancipar; dar libertad, manumitir, libertar.

emancipation [ɪ'mænsɪ'peɪʃən] [i-man-si-pei-shon], *s.* Emancipación.

emancipator [ɪ'mænsɪpeɪtəʳ] [i-man-si-pei-taʳ], *s.* Libertador, manumisor.

emarginate [ɪ'mɑːdʒɪneɪt] [i-mar-chi-neit], *va.* 1. Quitar el margen, recortar. 2. *(Bot.)* Hacer una escotadura en el ápice de una hoja u otro órgano plano de las plantas.

emarginate, *a. (Bot.)* Escotado, emarginado, que tiene el margen interrumpido o mellado.

emasculate [ɪ'mæskjʊleɪt] [i-mas-kiu-leit], *a.* Afeminado, viciado; castrado. -*vt.* Castrar, mutilar, emascular.

emasculation [ɪ'mæskjʊ'leɪʃən] [i-mas-kiu-lei-shon], *f.* Castradura, castración, capadura; afeminación, afeminamiento.

embale [ɪm'beɪl] [im-beil], *va.* Embalar, enfardar, liar, atar.

embalm [ɪm'bɑːm] [im-balm], *va.* 1. Embalsamar, impregnar un cadáver de sustancias que impidan la putrefacción. 2. Conservar, impedir el decaimiento de alguna cosa; guardar afectuosamente un recuerdo. 3. Embalsamar, llenar de fragancia, aromatizar, perfumar.

embalmer [ɪm'bɑːməʳ] [im-bal-maʳ], *s.* 1. Embalsamador. 2. Cualquier cosa que impide el decaimiento o menoscabo de otra.

embalment [ɪm'bɑːment] [im-bal-ment], *m.* Embalsamamiento, acción de embalsamar.

embalming [ɪm'bɑːmɪŋ] [im-bal-min], *m.* Embalsamamiento.

embank ['ɪmbæŋk] [im-bank], *va.* Represar o contener por medio de una presa o dique.

embankment [ɪm'bæŋkmənt] [im-bank-ment], *m.* Presa, dique; terraplén.

embar [ɪm'bɑːʳ] [im-baʳ], *va.* 1. *(Ant.)* Barrear, cercar, cerrar. 2. Bloquear.

embarcation [ɪmbɑː'keɪʃən] [im-bar-kei-shon], *s. (Mar.)* Embarco, embarque. *V.* EMBARKATION.

embargo [ɪm'bɑːgəʊ] [im-bar-gou], *s.* 1. Embargo, secuestro de géneros. 2. Embargo, detención de buques. **To be under**

an **embargo**, estar prohibido. **To lift an embargo**, levantar una prohibición.

embargo, va. Embargar, detener.

embark [ɪmˈbɑːk] [im-bark], va. (Mar.) Embarcar, poner los géneros o personas a bordo de un buque. -vn. 1. (Mar.) Embarcarse, ir a bordo de una embarcación. 2. Empeñarse en algún negocio, dar principio a alguna ocupación; invertir el tiempo o el caudal; aventurarse. **To embark upon**, emprender, lanzarse.

embarkation [ɪmbɑːˈkeɪʃən] [im-bar-kei-shon], s. 1. Embarco, acto de embarcar o embarcarse personas. 2. Embarque, acción de embarcar géneros, provisiones, etc. 3. Lo que está embarcado; cargamento, fleto, carga.

embarrass [ɪmˈbærəs] [im-ba-ras], va. 1. Avergonzar, aturdir, desconcertar (disarrange, disturb). 2. Embarazar, enredar.

embarrassed [ɪmˈbærəst] [im-ba-rast], a. Apenado, cortado, avergonzado.

embarrassment [ɪmˈbærəsmənt] [im-ba-ras-ment], s. 1. Aturdimiento, agitación de ánimo, desconcierto. 2. Embarazo, dificultad, perplejidad, enredo. 3. Embarazo, impedimento, estorbo, atascadero.

embassador [ɪmˈbæsədɔr] [im-ba-sa-dar], sm. Embajador. V. AMBASSADOR.

embassadress [ɪmˈbæsədres] [im-ba-sa-dres], f. Embajadora.

embassy [ˈembəsɪ] [em-ba-si], f. Embajada.

embattle [ɪmˈbætl] [im-ba-tel], va. 1. Formar en orden de batalla, preparar o equipar para la batalla. 2. Almenar, coronar con almenas. -vn. Ponerse en orden de batalla.

embattled [ɪmˈbætld] [im-ba-teld], a. 1. En orden de batalla. **Here the embattled farmers stood**, aquí se posicionaron los granjeros en orden de batalla. 2. Que es o ha sido campo de un combate (city). 3. Almenado; cortado, recortado: se usa en arquitectura y en heráldica.

embattlement [ɪmˈbætlmənt] [im-ba-tel-ment], s. Aspillera; parapeto aspillerado.

embay [ˈɪmbeɪ] [im-bei], va. 1. (Mar.) Empeñar en una bahía. 2. Encerrar, cerrar con brazos protectores de tierra, como en una bahía.

embed [ɪmˈbed] [im-bed], va. Poner, depositar en una cama o lecho; encajonar, encajar, incrustar (weapon); empotrar. Equivalente, **imbed**.

embellish [ˈembelɪʃ] [em-be-lish] va. 1. Hermosear, embellecer, adornar una cosa; ribetear, ataviar. 2. Exornar, añadir algo imaginario para realzar el interés, bordar un cuento.

embellishment [ˈembelɪʃmənt] [em-be-lish-ment], sm. Adorno, ornato.

embers [ˈembəz] [em-bers], s. pl. Rescoldo.

ember-week [ˈembəwiːk] [em-ber-uik], s. Semana de témporas. **Ember-days**, las cuatro témporas.

embezzle [ˈembezl] [em-be-zel], va. Hurtar, apropiar o apropiarse alguna cosa ilícitamente.

embezzlement [ˈembezlmənt] [em-be-zel-ment], s. 1. Hurto, robo, acto de ocultar a hurtadillas alguna cosa con intención de quedarse con ella. 2. La cosa hurtada o robada de esta manera. 3. (For.) Ocultación maliciosa de bienes pertenecientes a una herencia que aún no ha sido aceptada por el heredero; malversación, desfalco.

embezzler [ˈembezlər] [em-bez-lar], s. Malversador, estafador, desfalcador; el que se apropia de dinero o bienes que otro le ha confiado a su cuidado.

embitter [ˈembɪtər] [em-bi-tar], va. 1. Hacer amargo al gusto. 2. Agriar, llenar de amargura, agravar, envenenar (relations). V. IMBITTER, como también se escribe.

embittering [ɪmˈbɪtərɪŋ] [im-bi-te-rin], a. Amargo (experience).

emblaze [ˈembleɪz] [em-bleis], va. 1. Adornar con colores brillantes, esmaltar. 2. Proclamar, divulgar; celebrar, alabar. 3. Hacer resplandeciente o brillante.

emblazon [ˈemblæzən] [em-bla-son], va. 1. Blasonar, disponer el escudo de armas de alguna ciudad o familia según las reglas del arte. 2. Blasonar; esmaltar con colores brillantes, engalanar; adornar con blasones o piezas del escudo. 3. Blasonar, ensalzar, alabar, engrandecer.

emblazoner [ˈemblæzənər] [em-bla-so-nar], s. 1. Blasonador, el que divulga alguna cosa pomposamente. 2. Heraldo, rey de armas.

emblem [ˈembləm] [em-blem], s. 1. Emblema, símbolo, signo. 2. Divisa, signo distintivo de una familia, un oficio, etc. 3. Emblema, pintura que encierra una alegoría. 4. Esmalte, labor de varios colores que se hace sobre oro o plata sobredorada.

emblematic, emblematical [ˌembləˈmætɪk] [em-ble-ma-tik], a. Emblemático, alusivo, simbólico.

emblematically [ˌembləˈmætɪklɪ] [em-ble-ma-ti-ka-li], adv. Emblemáticamente, figuradamente.

emblematicize [ˈembləmətɪsaɪz] [em-ble-ma-ti-sais], va. Dar a alguna cosa carácter emblemático; alegorizar.

emblematist [ˈembləmətɪst] [em-ble-ma-tist], s. Escritor o inventor de emblemas.

emblematize [ˈembləmətaɪz] [em-ble-ma-tais], va. Representar o figurar por emblemas.

emblements [ˈembləmənts] [em-ble-ments], s. pl. (For.) Las rentas, utilidad o beneficio que dejan las tierras o su cultivo.

emblemize [ˈembləmaɪz] [em-ble-mais], va. Representar por medio de un emblema, signo o figura.

embodiment [ɪmˈbɒdɪmənt] [im-bo-di-ment], s. 1. Incorporación, el acto y efecto de incorporar. 2. Personificación, encarnación (personification, expression); expresión concreta.

embody [ɪmˈbɒdɪ] [im-bo-di], va. 1. Dar cuerpo, revestir de materia; expresar concretamente, plasmar, expresar (express/thought, idea); encarnar, personificar (personify). 2. Incorporar, formar un todo o cuerpo; reunir en colección. -vn. Unirse, incorporarse.

emboguing [ɪmˈbɒgɪŋ] [em-bo-guing], s. Desembocadura o desembocadero de un río, canal o pantano, o el paraje por donde desaguan en el mar.

embolden [ɪmˈbəʊldən] [im-boul-den], va. Animar, envalentonar.

embolism [ˈembəlɪzən] [em-bo-lisem], s. 1. (Astr.) Intercalación de ciertos días para igualar el calendario. 2. (Med.) Embolia, la obstrucción de un vaso sanguíneo por un coágulo arrastrado por la circulación de la sangre.

embolus [ˈembələs] [em-bo-los], s. 1. Émbolo. 2. Cualquier cosa que obra o funciona dentro de otra.

emborder [ˈembɔːdər] [em-bor-dar], va. Guarnecer con marco o borde.

embosom [ˈembəsʊm] [em-bo-som], va. 1. Poner o meter en el seno, medio o centro de alguna cosa; envolver, encerrar, abrigar. 2. Tomar o recibir en el seno; querer, proteger.

emboss [ɪmˈbɒs] [im-bos], va. 1. Relevar, formar o fabricar alguna cosa en realce o relieve; realzar, resaltar. 2. Grabar un realce, en hueco, o de relieve. Repujar (leather, metal). **Embossed**, con membrete en relieve (stationery); estampado en relieve (wallpaper).

embossment [ɪmˈbɒsmənt] [im-bos-ment], s. Realce, relieve, resalte; resalto.

embouchure [ˌɒmbuˈʃʊər] [om-bu-shuar], s. 1. Boca o embocadura de un instrumento músico. 2. Embocadura, la posición o ajuste de la boca y la lengua al tocar un instrumento de viento.

embowel [ɪmˈbɒwəl] [im-bo-uel], va. 1. Desentrañar, destripar, sacar las entrañas; hacer reventar. 2. Hundir alguna cosa en otra substancia.

emboweller [ɪmˈbɒwələr] [im-bo-ue-lar], s. Desentrañador.

embower [ɪmˈbɒwər] [im-bo-uar], va. Cubrir, encerrar o abrigar con una enramada, emparrado o follaje; emparrar.

embrace [ɪmˈbreɪs] [im-breis], va. 1. Abrazar, estrechar entre los brazos (hug). 2. Abrazar, rodear, ceñir, contener, comprender, abarcar (include/range, elements). 3. Admitir, recibir; aceptar de buena gana; asir o aprovechar (la ocasión, la oferta, etc.). Abrazar (idea, principle); adoptar, abrazar (lifestyle, religion), -vn. 1. Abrazarse con alguna cosa. 2. Abrazarse mutuamente (couple, friends).

embrace, va. (For.) Influir o tratar de influir por medio del cohecho o la amenaza en la decisión de un juez, tribunal, árbrito o jurado.

embrace, embracement [ɪmˈbreɪsmənt] [im-breis-ment], s. Abrazo, recepción; las caricias conyugales.

embracer [ɪmˈbreɪʒəʳ] [im-brei-saʳ], s. Abrazador.

embracery [ɪmˈbreɪsərɪ] [im-brei-se-ri], s. (For.) El delito de influir en el ánimo del jurado por medios ilegales.

embracing [ɪmˈbreɪsɪŋ] [im-brei-sin], s. Abrazo.

embrasure [ɪmˈbreɪʃəʳ] [im-brei-shaʳ], s. (Fort.) Tronera, abertura; cañonera.

embrocate [ˈembrəʊkeɪt] [em-brou-keit], va. Embrocar, derramar algo lentamente sobre la parte enferma y frotarla al mismo tiempo.

embrocation [ˈembrəʊkeɪʃən] [em-brou-kei-shon], s. (Med.) Embrocación, linimento.

embroider [ˈembrɔɪdəʳ] [em-broi-daʳ] va. Bordar, adornar y enriquecer formando con la aguja figuras o labores (cloth, design); adornar (story). vn. Bordar.

embroiderer, embroideress [ɪmˈbrɔɪdərəʳ] [im-broi-de-raʳ], s. Bordador, bordadora.

embroidery [ɪmˈbrɔɪdərɪ] [im-broi-de-ri], s. Bordado, bordadura.

embroil [ɪmˈbrɔɪl] [im-broil], va. Embrollar, enredar; confundir; dividir, desunir. **To be/become embroiled in something**, estar/verse envuelto o enredado en algo.

embroilment [ɪmˈbrɔɪlmənt] [im-broil-ment], s. Alboroto, confusión; embrollo.

embrown [ɪmˈbrəʊn] [em-broun], va. 1. Hacer moreno, castaño. 2. Obscurecer, ofuscar. -vn. Volverse moreno u obscuro.

embrue [ɪmˈbruː] [em-bru], va. V. IMBRUE.

embryo [ˈembrɪəʊ] [em-briou], s. 1. Embrión, el feto que empieza a formarse. 2. El primer rudimento del animal o de la planta. 3. Principio, todavía informe, de una cosa. -a. En embrión.

embryogeny [ˌembrɪˈɒdʒənɪ] [em-brio-che-ni], s. Embriogenia, la ciencia de la formación y desarrollo de los organismos; la generación de los organismos.

embryology [ˌembrɪˈɒlədʒɪ] [em-brio-lo-chi], s. Embriología, el ramo de la biología que trata de los embriones o del desarrollo de los organismos.

embryonal [ˈembrɪənəl] [em-brio-nal], a. Embrionario.

embryonic [ˌembrɪˈɒnɪk] [em-brio-nik], a. (Biol.) Embrionario, perteneciente a un embrión, o parecido a él; rudimentario, que no está desarrollado. En estado embrionario (plan, policy).

emcee [ˈemˈsiː] [em-si] s. (Coloq.) Presentador (of program); maestro de ceremonias (of function).

emend [ɪˈmend] [i-mend], va. Enmendar, corregir, emendar.

emendable [ɪˈmendəbl] [i-men-da-bol], a. Corregible.

emendation [ˌiːmenˈdeɪʃən] [i-men-dei-shon] s. Enmienda.

emendator [ɪˈmendeɪtəʳ] [i-men-dei-taʳ], s. Corrector.

emendatory [ɪˈmendətərɪ] [i-men-da-to-ri], a. Lo que contribuye a enmendar, corregir, etc.

emerald [ˈemərəld] [e-me-rald]. s. 1. Esmeralda, piedra preciosa de color verde (gem); variedad del berilo. 2. Color verde vivo y claro como el de la esmeralda (color). 3. Tipo de letra. -a. 1. Del color verde claro de la esmeralda. 2. Impreso en el tipo llamado *emerald*.

emerge [ɪˈmɜːdʒ] [i-merch], vn. 1. Salir, surgir como de un fluido; salir de un escondrijo; aparecer, asomarse, presenarse tarse a la vista (come out). 2. Salir de la opresión; salir de la obscuridad, salir a la luz (facts); revelarse (truth); dibujarse (pattern); surgir, aparecer (become evident, known/problem). 3. Surgir (come into being, evolve/idea, system). **Emerging**, emergente, joven (nation); naciente, incipiente (industries).

emergence [ɪˈmɜːdʒəns] [i-mer-chens], s. 1. Emersión, salida, aparición (coming out); el procedimiento o efecto de salir, aparición, emergencia (en sentido óptico); aparición, surgimiento (of movement, trend). 2. Emergencia (uso incorrecto). 3. Lo que sale o sobresale, excrecencia.

emergency [ɪˈmɜːdʒənsɪ] [i-mer-chen-si], s. 1. Emergencia, caso o incidente no previsto (serious situation). **It's an emergency**, es una situación de emergencia. (Med.) Urgencia; de urgencia (case, operation). 2. Aprieto, necesidad urgente. (Govt.) **A state of emergency was declared**, se declaró el estado de excepción. **Emergency exit**, salida de emergencia. **Emergency landing**, aterrizaje forzoso. **Emergency room**, sala de urgencias o de guardia. **Emergency stop**, parada de emergencia.

emergency outlet [ɪˈmɜːdʒənsɪˌaʊtlet] [i-mer-chen-si-aut-let], s. 1. Salida de emergencia. 2. Válvula de escape. 3. Aliviadero o vertedero.

emergent [ɪˈmɜːdʒənt] [i-mer-chent], a. Emergente, joven (nation); repentino, subitáneo. En vías de desarrollo (developing); incipiente, emergente (subculture, technology).

emeritus [ɪˈmerɪtəs] [i-mi-ri-tus], a. Emérito, jubilado, el que después de haber servido en un cargo o una profesión cierto número de años, se retira gozando los honores y parte del sueldo. **Professor emeritus** o **emeritus professor**, profesor emérito.

emerods, emeroids, V. HEMORRHOIDS.

emersion [ɪˈmɜːʃən] [i-mer-shon] s. 1. Emersión, el acto de salir de algún fluido o de atrás de alguna cosa. 2. (Astr.) Emersión, reaparición.

emery [ˈemərɪ] [e-me-ri], s. Esmeril, variedad de corindón, piedra muy dura; en polvo se usa para bruñir los metales. **Emery board**, lima de esmeril. **Emery paper**, papel de lija.

emetic, emetical [ɪˈmetɪk] [i-me-tik], a. Emético, vomitivo.

emetic, s. Emético, vomitivo.

emetically [ɪˈmetɪkəlɪ] [i-me-ti-ka-li], adv. A manera de vomitivo.

emeu o emew [ˈemjuː] [e-miu], s. (Orn.) Dromeo. V. EMU.

emication [ˌemɪˈkeɪʃən] [e-mi-kei-shon], s. (Poco us.) Chispeo.

emigrant [ˈemɪgrənt] [e-mi-grant], s. Emigrado, emigrante.

emigrate [ˈemɪgreɪt] [e-mi-greit], vn. Emigrar, transmigrar.

emigrate, a. Emigrado; vago, vagabundo.

emigration [ˌemɪˈgreɪʃən] [e-mi-grei-shon], s. 1. Emigración, el acto de emigrar. 2. Los emigrados colectivamente. 3. V. MIGRATION.

émigré [ˈemɪgreɪ] [e-mi-grei] s. Exiliado.

eminence, eminency [ˈemɪnəns] [e-mi-nens], s. 1. Altura, elevación. 2. Cima, cuesta, sumidad. 3. Eminencia, distinción, excelencia; prestigio, renombre (fame). 4. Altura. 5. Eminencia, título de honor peculiar de los cardenales.

eminent [ˈemɪnənt] [e-mi-nent], a. 1. Eminente, exaltado, conspicuo, notable, distinguido, ilustre. 2. Independiente de otra autoridad, supremo; v. g. **Eminent domain**, el dominio supremo. 3. (Ant.) Alto, elevado, levantado. **Most eminent**, eminentísimo.

eminently [ˈemɪnəntlɪ] [e-mi-nent-li], adv. Eminentemente, conspicuamente, sumamente.

emir [eˈmɪəʳ] [e-miaʳ], s. 1. Emir, título de dignidad en Turquía y el Oriente mahometano. 2. Fatimita, descendiente de Fátima, hija de Mahoma.

emirate [ˈemɪreɪt] [e-mi-reit] s. Emirato.

emissary [ˈemɪsərɪ] [e-mi-sa-ri], s. 1. Emisario, espía, agente secreto. 2. Canal, desaguadero como para el agua. 3. (Anat.) Conducto excretorio o de comunicación. -a. 1. Perteneciente al emisario. 2. Enviado por delante o afuera.

emission [ɪˈmɪʃən] [i-mi-shon], s. Emisión.

emissive [ˈemɪsɪv] [e-mi-siv], a. Emisivo, que lanza o emite; que echa rayos o centellas o despide calórico.

emissory [ˈemɪsərɪ] [e-mi-so-ri], a. Que emite o lanza; emisivo. -s. Desaguadero.

emit [ɪˈmɪt] [i-mit], va. 1. Emitir (heat, light, radiation, sound); echar de sí; arrojar, despedir (gas, smell, vapor);

exhalar. 2. Emitir, poner en circulación, dar a luz autorizadamente.

emmanuel, *s. V.* IMMANUEL.

emmenagogue ['emɪnəgɒg] [e-mi-na-gog] *s.* Emenagogo, medicamento para provocar la menstruación detenida.

emmet ['emet] [e-met] *s.* Hormiga.

emollient [ɪ'mɒlɪənt] [i-mo-lient], *a.* Emoliente, lo que ablanda. -*s.* Emolientes, una clase de medicamentos, mucilaginosos u oleosos.

emolument [ɪ'mɒljəmənt] [i-mo-liu-ment], *s.* Emolumento, gaje, utilidad, provecho.

emolumental [ɪ'mɒljəməntl] [i-mo-liu-men-tal], *a.* Util, provechoso.

emotion [ɪ'məʊʃən] [i-mou-shon], *s.* 1. Emoción, perturbación o agitación del ánimo, conmoción. 2. La facultad de sentir; sensibilidad; sentimiento racional (feeling); emoción (strength of feeling).

emotional [ɪ'məʊʃənl] [i-mou-sho-nal], *a.* 1. Sensible, impresionable, que fácilmente cede a las impresiones o al sentimiento. 2. Lo que expresa la emoción; emocional, afectivo (disorder). **Emotional blackmail**, chantaje afectivo. Emotivo (sensitive/person, nature); emocionado (upset). **To get emotional**, emocionarse. Emotivo, conmovedor (moving/speech, experience, scene).

emotionalism [ɪ'məʊʃnlɪzən] [i-mou-sho-na-lisem], *s.* 1. La manifestación oral o la expresión de las emociones, de cualquier manera que se haga. 2. La tendencia a desarrollar el influjo de las emociones, o a ceder fácilmente a ellas.

emotionally [ɪ'məʊʃnəlɪ] [i-mou-sho-na-li] *adv. (Psych.)* Emocionalmente. **Emotionally deprived**, con carencias afectivas o emocionales. Con gran emotividad (behave, react, speak).

emotive [ɪ'məʊtɪv] [i-mou-tiv] *a.* Emotivo, cargado de emotividad.

empale [ɪ'mpeɪl] [im-peil], *va.* 1. Empalar, espetar a uno en un palo como se espeta el ave en el asador. 2. Cercar; rodear, encerrar con una estacada o cerca. 3. Poner uno al lado de otro, como iguales (v.g.en el blasón).

empalement [ɪ'mpeɪlmənt] [im-peil-ment], *s.* 1. Empalamiento. 2. Junta de armas en el blasón.

empanel, *va. V.* IMPANEL.

emparadise, *va. V.* IMPARADISE.

empathize ['empəθaɪz] [em-pa-zaiz] *vn.* **To empathize with somebody**, identificarse con alguien.

empathy ['empəθɪ] [em-pa-zi] *s.* Empatía.

emperor ['empərə'] [em-pe-ra'], *s.* 1. Emperador, el soberano de un imperio 2. Nombre de ciertas especies de mariposas diurnas y nocturnas. **Emperor-moth**, mariposa nocturna grande.

empery ['empərɪ] [em-pe-ri], *s.* 1. Soberanía, dominio. 2. Mando, autoridad de un emperador; imperio.

emphasis ['emfəsɪs] [em-fa-sis], *s.* Enfasis. **To lay/place/put emphasis on something**, hacer hincapié o poner énfasis en la importancia de algo.

emphasize ['emfəsaɪz] [em-fa-sais], *va.* 1. Recalcar, acentuar, pronunciar con fuerza o intención, hacer hincapié en (fact, point, warning); enfatizar, poner énfasis en (phrase, word); poner de relieve (fault, value); resaltar, hacer resaltar (shape, feature). 2. Destacar, clara y fuertemente; hacer más distino, positivo o impresivo.

emphatic, emphatical ['emfətɪk] [em-fa-tik], *a.* Enfático; fuerte, enérgico (gesture, tone); categórico (assertion, refusal).

emphatically ['emfətɪklɪ] [em-fa-tik-li], *adv.* Enfáticamente, aparentemente. Enérgicamente (say, declare); categóricamente, rotundamente (deny).

emphysema ['emfɪ'siːmə] [em-fi-si-ma], *s. (Med.)* Enfisema, tumefacción producida por aire o gas en el tejido celular.

emphysematous ['emfɪ'siːmətəs] [em-fi-si-ma-tos], *a.* Enfisematoso, que ofrece o presenta los caracteres del enfisema.

emphyteutic ['emfɪ'tjɒtɪk] [em-fi-tiu-tik], *a. (For.)* Enfitéutico, que se da en enfiteusis o que pertenece a ella.

empire ['empaɪə'] [em-paia'], *s.* 1. Imperio. 2. Mando, autoridad, dominio.

empiric, empirical ['empɪrɪk] [em-pi-rik], *a.* Empírico; charlatán, medicastro, curandero.

empirically [em'pɪrɪkəlɪ] [em-pi-ri-ka-li], *adv.* Empíricamente.

empiricism ['empɪrɪsɪzəm] [em-pi-ri-sizem], *s.* Empirismo, charlatanería.

emplacement [ɪm'pleɪsmənt] [Im-pleis-ment], *s.* Emplazamiento, la posición destinada a los cañones o a una batería dentro de una fortificación.

emplastic ['ɪmplæstɪk] [em-plas-tik], *a.* Viscoso, glutinoso, pegajoso. -*s.* 1. Medicamento que estriñe el vientre. 2. Substancia adhesiva, pegajosa.

emplead, *va. V.* IMPLEAD.

employ [ɪm'plɔɪ] [im-ploi], *va.* 1. Emplear, contratar (person/take on), ocupar; emplear, dar empleo (have working). **He's employed as a nightwatchman**, trabaja de vigilante nocturno. 2. Comisionar. 3. Emplear, llenar de ocupaciones; emplear, valerse de (methods, tactics, tool).

employ, *s.* Empleo, ocupación, puesto, oficio público, cargo. **To be in somebody's employ** o **in the employ of somebody**, trabajar para alguien.

employable [ɪm'plɔɪəbl] [im-ploia-bol], *a.* Empleable. **He's no longer employable**, ya nadie le va a dar trabajo.

employee, employe [ˌemplɔɪˈiː] [em-ploi-yi], *s.* Empleado, el que está al empleo de otro.

employer [ɪm'plɔɪə'] [im-ploia'] *s.* Empleador, patrón, dueño, principal, amo. **Unions and employers**, los sindicatos y la patronal/los empresarios. **List your three most recent employers**, indique las tres últimas empresas para las que ha trabajado.

employment [ɪm'plɔɪmənt] [im-ploi-ment], *s.* Empleo (availability of work), ocupación, aplicación, cargo; trabajo (work); contratación (hiring, taking on); laboral (legislation). *(Fam.)* **You will not want employment**, no le faltará a Ud. qué hacer. **Employment agency**, agencia de trabajo o colocación.

empoison [em'pɔɪzən] [em-poi-son], *va. (Ant.)* Envenenar, atosigar, emponzoñar.

emporium [em'pɔːrɪəm] [em-po-rium], *s.* 1. Emporio, cualquier ciudad donde concurren muchos para el tráfico y comercio. 2. Bazar; emporio (comercial).

empoverish [em'pɒvərɪʃ] [em-po-ve-rish], *va.* Empobrecer, minorar la fertilidad de alguna cosa.

empoverisher, *s. V.* IMPOVERISHER.

empoverishment, *s. V.* IMPOVERISHMENT.

empower [ɪm'paʊə'] [im-paua'], *va.* Autorizar, comisionar, habilitar, dar poder; conferirle, otorgarle poderes a (authorize). **He's empowered to sign the contract on my behalf**, está autorizado a/para firmar el contrato en mi nombre. *(Pol., Social.)* **To empower somebody/oneself**, investir de poder a alguien/investirse de poder.

empress ['emprɪs] [em-pris], *f.* Emperatriz, emperadora.

emprise ['empraɪs] [em-prais], *s. (Ant.)* Empresa.

emprison, *va. V.* IMPRISON.

emptier ['emptɪə'] [emp-tia'], *s.* Vaciador, el que vacía o instrumento para vaciar.

emptiness ['emptɪnɪs] [emp-ti-nes], *s.* 1. Vaciedad. 2. Vacío o vacuo; vacuidad (meaninglessness). Ausencia de vegetación, habitantes, etc. (of landscape, region). 3. Futilidad.

emptins ['emptɪns] [emp-tins], *s.* (Dial. E. U.) *V.* EMPTYINGS.

empty ['emptɪ] [emp-ti], *a.* 1. Vacío (container, table); vacuo, hueco; desocupado, desalojado; vaco, vacante. Vacío (words, gestures, life). **Empty house**, una casa por alquilar. 2. Vano, inútil, infructuoso (threat, promise). 3. Corto, ignorante, falto de talento o conocimientos. 4. Hambriento. 5. Ligero, frívolo, superficial.

empty, *va.* Vaciar, evacuar, agotar, desocupar (container, warehouse). **She emptied the water down the sink**, tiró el agua por el fregadero (take or pour out). -*vn.* Vaciarse (room, street). **To empty into something**, desaguar en algo (river, stream).

empty out Vaciar (bag, drawer, pockets); tirar, botar (garbage).

empty *s. (Coloq.)* Envase vacío, casco (bottle). **Empty-handed** *adv.* Con las manos vacías.

empty-headed ['emptɪˌhedɪd] [emp-ti-je-ded] *a.* **He's so empty-headed**, es una cabeza hueca.

emptyings ['emptɪŋz] [emp-tins] *s. pl.* Heces de la cerveza usadas en vez de levadura.

empurple ['empɜ:pl] [em-per-pol], *va.* Purpurar, teñir de púrpura.

empyema ['empiimə] [em-piima] *s. (Med.)* Empiema, acumulación purulenta en la cavidad de la pleura.

empyreal ['empɪrɪəl] [em-pi-rial], *a.* Empíreo.

empyrean [ˌempɪˈriːən] [em-pi-rian], *s.* Empíreo, el cielo de los bienaventurados. -*a.* Empíreo.

empyreuma ['empɪrjuːmə] [em-pi-riu-ma], *s.* Empireuma, olor y sabor particulares y desagradables que toman las substancias animales y algunas vegetales sometidas a fuego violento.

emu ['iːmjuː] [i-miu], *s.* 1. Dromeo, ave grande de Australia parecida al avestruz. 2. *(Des.)* Casoar. V. CASSOWARY.

emulate ['emjʊleɪt] [e-miu-leit], *va.* Emular, competir, imitar.

emulation ['emjʊˌleɪʃən] [e-miu-lei-shon], *s.* Emulación, pasión que nos excita a imitar y aun a exceder o superar a otros.

emulative ['emjʊˌlətɪv] [e-miu-la-tiv], *a.* Emulativo, inclinado a la emulación.

emulator ['emjʊˌleɪtər] [e-miu-lei-tar], *s.* Emulo, rival, antagonista, competidor, emulador.

emulatress ['emjʊlətrɪs] [e-miu-la-tris], *f.* Emula, emuladora.

emulgent [eˈmʌldʒənt] [e-mal-yent], *a.* Emulgente, que cuela; antes se aplicaba a los vasos renales.

emulous ['emjʊləs] [e-miu-los], *a.* Emulo, competidor, rival. **To be emulous of**, rivalizar con.

emulously ['emjʊləslɪ] [e-miu-los-li], *adv.* Con emulación, a porfía, a competencia.

emulsifier [ɪˈmʌlsɪˌfaɪər] [e-mal-si-faiar], *s.* Emulsionante, emulsivo.

emulsify [ɪˈmʌlsɪfaɪ] [e-mal-si-fai], *va.* Hacer o convertir en emulsión.

emulsion [ɪˈmʌlʃən] [e-mal-shon] *s.* 1. Emulsión, medicamento líquido de color de leche preparado de las almendras o de las semillas de algunas frutas. 2. Cualquier líquido lechoso. **Emulsion paint**, pintura al agua.

emulsive [ɪˈmʌlsɪv] [e-mal-siv], *a.* 1. Emulsivo, capaz de hacer emulsión. 2. De la naturaleza de una emulsión; dulcificante.

emunctory [ɪˈmʌŋktərɪ] [e-mank-to-ri], *a. (Med.)* Excretorio, que sirve para descargar materias excrementicias. -*s.* Emuntorio, el conducto o canal excretorio, emuntorio.

en [en] [en], *s.* 1. Nombre de la letra N, la décimocuarta del alfabeto inglés. 2. *(Impr.)* La mitad de una eme; la mitad del cuadrado del tipo.

en, partícula inseparable derivada del latín, escríbese a veces *en* o *in* indiferentemente.

enable [ɪˈneɪbl] [i-nei-bol], *vn.* Habilitar, proporcionar, facilitar, permitir, posibilitar (make possible); poner en estado de, hacer que.

enact [ɪˈnækt] [i-nakt], *va.* 1. Establecer, decretar, ordenar, mandar; *(Govt., Law)* promulgar. 2. Efectuar, poner en ejecución. 3. Hacer papel de, representar (play, role). **The scene being enacted before us**, la escena que se desarrollaba ante nosotros.

enactable [ɪˈnæktəbl] [i-nak-ta-bol], *a.* Que puede ser establecido, efectuado o representado.

enactive [ɪˈnæktɪv] [i-nak-tiv], *a.* Lo que establece o manda.

enactment [ɪˈnæktmənt] [i-nakt-ment], *s.* 1. Ley establecida, estatuto. 2. El acto de decretar o establecer una ley.

enactor [ɪˈnæktər] [i-nak-ta\(^r\)], *s.* Legislador, ejecutor, establecedor.

enallage [ɪˈnælədʒ] [i-na-leich], *s. (Gram.)* Enálage, el uso de una parte de la oración por otra.

enambush [ɪˈnæmbʌʃ] [i-nam-bash], *va.* Emboscar, armar celada o trampa.

enamel [ɪˈnæməl] [i-na-mel], *va.* Esmaltar, labrar con esmalte de varios colores. **A meadow enamelled with flowers**, una pradera esmaltada de flores.

enamel, *s.* 1. Esmalte. 2. Labor que se hace con el esmalte sobre algún metal. 3. Lo que se parece al esmalte en la tersura, como el esmalte de los dientes, una capa de charol, de laca, etc.

enameler, enameller [ɪˈnæmələr] [i-na-me-la\(^r\)], *s.* Esmaltador.

enamelling [ɪˈnæməlɪŋ] [i-na-me-lin], *s.* El arte de esmaltar.

enamelware [ɪˈnæməlwɛər] [i-na-mel-uea\(^r\)], *s.* Vasijas esmaltadas.

enamor, enamour [ɪˈnæmər] [i-na-ma\(^r\)], *va.* Enamorar. Se usa raramente fuera del participio pasado, y con *of* o *with*; **He was enamoured of her**, estuvo enamorado de ella. **I'm not very enamored of/with the idea**, no estoy muy entusiasmado con la idea.

enarthrosis [ˌɪnɑːˈθrəʊsɪs] [i-nar-zrou-sis], *s. (Anat.)* Enártrosis, especie de articulación floja y móvil de una cabeza huesosa que encaja en un alvéolo.

encage ['ɪnkeɪdʒ] [in-keich], *va.* Enjaular, encarcelar.

encamp [ɪnˈkæmp] [in-kamp], *vn.* Acampar, alojarse un ejército en tiendas de campaña. -*va.* Acampar, alojar a un ejército o parte de él en tiendas de campaña.

encamping [ɪnˈkæmpɪŋ] [in-kam-pin], *s.* Campamento, acampamento.

encampment [ɪnˈkæmpmənt] [in-kamp-ment], *s.* Campamento, campo.

encapsulate [ɪnˈkæpsjʊleɪt] [in-kap-siu-leit] *va.* Condensar, compendiar (story, problem).

encase [ɪnˈkeɪs] [in-keis], *va.* 1. Encajar, encajonar. V. INCASE. 2. Revestir, recubrir. **Encased in something**, revestido o recubierto de algo.

encash [ɪnˈkæʃ] [in-kash] *va.* Hacer efectivo, cobrar.

encave [ɪnˈkeɪv] [in-keiv], *va.* Esconder en una cueva.

encaustic [ɪnˈkɔːstɪk] [in-kos-tik], *a.* 1. Encáustico, (pintura) hecha al encausto o con fuego. 2. Pintado con adustión, o por medio del fuego, con ceras de colores. -*s.* Encausto, adustión, combustión. **Encaustic painting**, pintura encáustica.

enceinte [ɪnˈsiːnt] [in-sint], *a.* Preñada, embarazada, encinta. Es voz francesa. -*s.* 1. Recinto, reunión de bastiones y cortinas de muralla de una plaza. 2. Cerca, cercado.

encenia [ɪnˈsiːnɪə] [in-si-nia], *s. pl.* Fiestas en aniversario de la consagración de algún templo.

encephalic [ensɪˈfælɪk] [en-si-fa-lik], *a.* Encefálico; del encéfalo o cerebro.

encephalitis [ˌensefəˈlaɪtɪs] [en-se-fa-lai-tis], *s. (Med.)* Encefalitis, inflamación del cerebro.

encephalogram [ɪnˈsefələɡræm] [in-se-fa-lo-gram], *s.* Encefalograma.

encephaloid ['ensɪfəlɔɪd] [en-si-fa-loid], *a.* Encefaloideo, que se parece al cerebro en la materia o en el aspecto. **Encephaloid cancer**, cáncer encefaloideo; encefaloidea.

encephalon ['ensɪfələn] [en-si-fa-lon], *s.* Encéfalo, el cerebro.

encephalous ['ensɪfələs] [en-si-fa-los], *a.* Que tiene cabeza, p.ej. ciertos moluscos.

enchain [ɪnˈtʃeɪn] [in-chein], *va.* Encadenar; aprisionar.

enchant [ɪnˈtʃɑːnt] [in-chant], *va.* 1. Encantar, practicar la hechicería, hacer cosas maravillosas en apariencia. 2. Encantar, deleitar en sumo grado; cautivar (delight, charm).

enchanted [ɪnˈtʃɑːntɪd] [in-chan-tid] *a.* Encantado (under a spell). **Enchanted with/at something**, encantado con algo (delighted).

enchanter [ɪnˈtʃɑːntəʳ] [in-chan-taʳ], *s.* Encantador, hechicero; mago.

enchantingly [ɪnˈtʃɑːntɪŋlɪ] [in-chan-tin-li], *adv.* Como por encanto.

enchantment [ɪnˈtʃɑːntmənt] [in-chant-ment], *s.* Encantación, encanto, magia, embeleso. Encanto, hechizo (charm); embeleso (delight); encantamiento, hechizo (spell).

enchantress [ɪnˈtʃɑːntrɪs] [in-chan-tres], *f.* 1. Encantadora; maga, hechicera. 2. Seductora.

encharge [ɪnˈtʃɑːdʒ] [in-charch], *va.* Fiar a, cargar con.

enchase [ɪnˈtʃeɪs] [in-cheis], *va.* 1. Engastar. 2. Adornar, incrustar, cincelar, adornar con relieves. 3. Grabar, retratar por medio de figuras grabadas o en relieve. 4. Empotrar.

enchiridion [ɪnˈkɪrɪdɪən] [in-ki-ri-dion], *s.* Enquiridión, manual, libro pequeño; en especial, manual de devoción.

enchorial [ɪnˈkəːrɪəl] [in-ko-rial], *a.* Propio de un país determinado. Demótico; endémico; indígena, autóctono.

encircle [ɪnˈsɜːkl] [in-ser-kel], *va.* Cercar, rodear (camp, house); ceñir (waist, wrist).

enclave [ɪnˈkleɪv] [in-kleiv] *s.* Enclave.

enclitic [ɪnˈklɪtɪk] [in-kli-tik], *a. (Gram.)* Enclítico; se dice de la partícula o del vocablo que se liga con el vocablo precedente, formando con él una sola palabra. *-s.* Partícula o voz enclítica.

encloister [ɪnˈklɔɪstəʳ] [in-klois-taʳ], *va.* Enclaustrar.

enclose [ɪnˈkləʊz] [in-klous], *va.* 1. Cercar o circunvalar algún terreno (fence in); rodear, circundar; encerrar (surround). **A valley enclosed by high mountains**, un valle circundado o rodeado de altas montañas. 2. Incluir, poner una cosa dentro de otra; adjuntar, acompañar (in letter). 3. Disfrutar o apropiarse un terreno como por derecho exclusivo. V. INCLOSE. **Enclosed**, cerrado (area, space).

encloser [ɪnˈkləʊzəʳ] [in-klou-saʳ], *s.* Cercador.

enclosure [ɪnˈkləʊʒəʳ] [in-klo-shaʳ], *s.* 1. Cercamiento (of land), cercado, vallado, tapia, corral, etc. 2. Cercado, espacio cerrado; el hurto, prado u otro lugar o espacio rodeado de una cerca; recinto (enclosed space). **A fenced enclosure**, un cercado. *(Dep.)* Recinto (for spectators). 3. La inclusa, lo incluso; se dice de las letras de cambio, cuentas, cartas, etc., contenidas en algún pliego o carta.

enclothe [ɪnˈkləʊð] [in-kloz], *va.* V. TO CLOTHE.

encode [ɪnˈkəʊd] [in-koud] *va.* Codificar, cifrar.

encoffin [ɪnˈkɒfɪn] [in-ko-fin], *va.* Meter en un ataúd.

encomiast [ɪnˈkəʊmɪæst] [in-ko-miast], *s.* Encomiasta, panegirista, elogiador, encomiador.

encomiastic, encomiastical [ɪnˈkəʊmɪæstɪk] [in-ko-mias-tik] *a.* Encomiástico, eulogístico.

encomium [ɪnˈkəʊmɪəm] [in-ko-mium], *s.* Encomio, elogio, alabanza, panegírico.

encompass [ɪnˈkʌmpəs] [in-kam-pas] *va.* 1. Cercar, circundar, sitiar, rodear. 2. Circuir, encerrar. **To encompass the globe**, dar la vuelta al mundo.

encore [ɒŋˈkɔːʳ] [an-koʳ], *adv.* Otra vez, de nuevo, aún, además. *-inter.* ¡Otra! ¡otra vez! ¡que se repita! (Fr. < Lat. hanc, *esta* + horam, *hora*).

encore, *s.* El acto de pedir el público la repetición de una escena dramática o lírica; y la repetición de la misma por los actores o cantantes.

encore, *va.* Pedir que un actor repita lo que ha recitado o cantado; gritar «*encore!*»

encounter [ɪnˈkaʊntəʳ] [in-kaun-taʳ], *s.* 1. Encuentro, choque; entrevista, particularmente cuando es casual e imprevista. 2. Encuentro hostil; escaramuza; duelo, desafío; combate, pelea, batalla, refriega.

encounter, *va.* 1. Encontrar; encontrarse con (be faced with/danger, difficulty, opposition). 2. Acometer o embestir al enemigo. 3. Tropezar con alguno, hallarle por casualidad (come across). *-vn.* Pelear, combatir; encontrarse cara a cara, venir a las manos; oponerse.

encounterer [ɪnˈkaʊntərəʳ] [in-kaun-te-raʳ], *s.* Antagonista, adversario.

encourage [ɪnˈkʌrɪdʒ] [in-ka-rich], *va.* 1. Animar, incitar, alentar (give hope, courage); favorecer. 2. Infundir ánimo y valor; inspirar confianza. 3. Fomentar (industry, competition, bad habit); fomentar, estimular (growth); intensificar (speculation). **She encouraged me to carry on**, me animó a seguir adelante (stimulate, inspire).

encouragement [ɪnˈkʌrɪdʒmənt] [in-ka-rich-ment], *s.* Estímulo, incentivo, patrocinio, amparo, fomento; ánimo (heartening). **She doesn't need any encouragement**, no (le) hace falta que la animen a hacerlo.

encourager [ɪnˈkʌrɪdʒəʳ] [in-ka-ri-chaʳ], *s.* Patrón, protector, favorecedor, incitador.

encouraging [ɪnˈkʌrɪdʒɪŋ] [in-ka-ri-chin], *pa. y a.* Estimulante, que estimula, que excita y anima. Alentador, esperanzador (news, progress). **She's very encouraging**, me alienta mucho o me da muchos ánimos.

encouragingly [ɪnˈkʌrɪdʒɪŋlɪ] [in-ka-ri-chin-li], *adv.* De una manera estimulante y animadora.

encradle [ɪnˈkreɪdl] [in-kra-del], *va.* Meter en la cuna.

encrimson [ɪnˈkrɪmsən] [in-krim-son], *va.* 1. Purpurar, teñir de púrpura. 2. Ruborizar, avergonzar, hacer salir los colores a la cara.

encrinite [ɪnˈkrɪnɪt] [in-kri-nit], *s.* Encrinita, encrino fósil.

encroach [ɪnˈkrəʊtʃ] [in-krouch], *va.* Usurpar, avanzar gradualmente, irse apoderando poco a poco, apropiarse lo ajeno. *-vn.* Pasar los límites de la confianza, etc. **To encroach upon kindness**, abusar de la bondad de alguno. **To encroach on/upon something**, invadir algo (on land); cercenar algo (on rights).

encroacher [ɪnˈkrəʊtʃəʳ] [in-krou-chaʳ], *s.* Usurpador.

encroachingly [ɪnˈkrəʊtʃɪŋlɪ] [in-krou-chin-li], *adv.* Por usurpación o intrusión.

encroachment [ɪnˈkrəʊtʃmənt] [in-krouch-ment], *s.* Usurpación, intrusión. Invasión (on land); intrusión (on rights).

encrust [ɪnˈkrʌst] [in-krast], *va.* V. INCRUST. Recubrir. **Encrusted with mud**, con una costra de barro. **Encrusted with jewels**, con incrustaciones de pedrería.

encumber [ɪnˈkʌmbəʳ] [in-kam-baʳ], *va.* Embarazar, cargar demasiado, abrumar con un peso (burden); estorbar, poner estorbos o impedimentos (hamper). **To be encumbered with something**, estar cargado o agobiado de algo (with debt, responsibility).

encumbrance [ɪnˈkʌmbrəns] [in-kam-brans], *s.* Embarazo, impedimento, cargo, estorbo (burden, hindrance); pensión, carga, gravamen. **Free from encumbrances**, libre de toda carga.

encyclical [ɛnˈsɪkɪkəl] [en-si-kli-kal], *a.* Encíclica, carta del Papa a los obispos.

encyclopaedia, encyclopedia [ɛnˌsɪkləʊˈpiːdɪə] [en-si-klou-pi-dia], *s.* Enciclopedia, colección de todas las ciencias; obra en que se trata de muchas ciencias; o tratado completo de un ramo especial de conocimientos. La distribución de las materias es sistemática y por lo general en orden alfabético.

encyclopedic, encyclopaedic [ɛnˌsɪkləʊˈpiːdɪk] [en-si-klou-pi-dik], *a.* Enciclopédico.

encyclopedist [ɛnˌsɪkləʊˈpiːdɪst] [en-si-klou-pi-dist], *s.* Enciclopedista; compilador de una enciclopedia o el que colabora en ella.

encysted [ɛnˈsɪstɪd] [en-kis-ted], *a. (Cir.)* Enquistado, metido en un quiste.

end [end] [end], *s.* 1. Fin, cabo, extremidad, remate; extremo, punta (extremity/of rope, stick); final (of street). **At the other/ far end of the garden**, al otro extremo/al fondo del jardín. **The top end of the range**, lo mejor de la gama. **To stand something on its end**, poner algo vertical, parar algo. 2. Fin, conclusión, cesación, término; fin, final (finish, close). **She read it to the very end**, lo leyó hasta el final. **That was the end of the story**, ahí se acabó la historia. **In the end**, al final. 3. Destino, muerte (death, destruction). **They met a violent end**, tuvieron un final o un fin violento. **To come to a sticky end**, acabar o terminar mal. 4. Resolución, determinación final. 5. Objeto, mira, intento; fin (purpose). **An end in itself**, un fin en sí mismo. **To this end**, con/a este fin. 6. Consecuencia inevitable o natural. 7. Pieza, fragmento. 8. Fondo, límite extremo de un objeto; final (outcome). **There were no end of people there**, había la mar o la tira de gente. **To the end that**, a fin de que, para que; con el objeto de. **To no end**, sin efecto, en vano. **On end**, de cabeza, en pie, erguido. *(Mar.)* En candela, a plomo. **End to end**, cabeza contra cabeza; topando. **End for end**, al revés. **End on**, *(Mar.)* flechado. **Fag end**, pestaña. **Gable end**, socarrén. **At loose ends**, en desorden, desarreglado. **At the end of the month, of next month**, a fines del corriente, del mes próximo. **My hair stands on end**, se me erizan los cabellos. **In the end**, en fin, al fin. **At the latter end**, a las últimas, al fin. **To make an end of**, acabar con. **To make both ends meet**, atar ambos cabos. *(Fig.)* Hacer que baste la renta propia, sin contraer deudas.

end, *va.* 1. Acabar o terminar con (gossip, speculation); terminar, concluir, dar o poner fin (stop/argument, discussion, fight); fenecer. Terminar, concluir (conclude). 2. Matar, quitar la vida. *-vn.* Acabarse, finalizarse, terminarse; morir, fenecer. Acabar, terminar. **It will all end in tears**, va a acabar o terminar mal.

end up Terminar, acabar. **I ended up doing it myself**, terminé o acabé haciéndolo yo mismo.

end-all [end'ɔːl] [end-ol], *s.* Último remate, conclusión final.

endanger [ɪn'deɪndʒəʳ] [in-dein-chaʳ], *va.* Poner en peligro, arriesgar (life); hacer peligrar (chances, reputation). **Endangered**, en peligro o en vías de extinción (species, wildlife).

endangerment [ɪn'deɪndʒəmənt] [in-dein-cheʳ-ment], *s.* Peligro, riesgo.

endear [ɪn'dɪəʳ] [in-diaʳ], *va.* 1. Hacer o hacerse amar, o querer. **To enderar oneself to somebody**, granjearse el cariño de alguien. 2. Encarecer.

endearing [ɪn'dɪərɪŋ] [in-dia-rin], *s.* Atractivo.

endearment [ɪn'dɪəmənt] [in-dia-ment], *s.* Encarecimiento. Expresión de cariño. **Terms/words of endearment**, palabras cariñosas o de cariño.

endeavor, endeavour [ɪn'devəʳ] [in-de-vaʳ], *s.* Esfuerzo, conato, empeño, intento. **He made every endeavor to help**, intentó ayudar por todos los medios.

endeavor, endeavour, *va.* Tentar, probar, experimentar, tratar de, procurar, hacer lo posible. (Por lo general con un infinitivo) *-vn.* Esforzarse, hacer un esfuerzo.

endeavorer [ɪn'devərəʳ] [in-de-vo-raʳ], *s.* El que procura el logro de una cosa o hace esfuerzos para conseguirla. En especial, miembro de la sociedad llamada **Christian Endeavor**, del Esfuerzo Cristiano.

endeavour, etc. Esta es la manera usual de escribir estas palabras en Inglaterra.

endecagon [en'dekəgɒn] [en-de-ka-gon], *s.* Endecágono. *V.* HENDECAGON.

endemial [en'demɪəl] [en-de-mial], *V.* ENDEMIC.

endemic, endemical [en'demɪk] [en-de-mik], *a.* Endémico: se aplica al mal o enfermedad propios de un clima determinado.

endenizen [en'denɪzən] [en-de-ni-sen], *va.* Naturalizar; franquear, hacer libre.

ender ['endəʳ] [en-daʳ], *s.* Acabador.

endermic [en'dɜːmɪk] [en-der-mik], *a.* Endérmico, que cura por medio de la aplicación del medicamento a la piel, sobre todo después de ampollarse ésta.

endictment [en'dɪktmənt] [en-dikt-ment], *s. (Des.)* Edicto, estatuto. *V.* INDICTMENT.

ending ['endɪŋ] [en-din], *s.* 1. Conclusión, cesación, final, desenlace (conclusion). **The story has a happy ending**, la historia tiene un final feliz. 2. Desinencia, terminación final de las palabras. **Verb endings**, desinencias verbales. 3. Fin de la vida.

endive ['endaɪv] [en-daiv], *s. (Bot.)* Escarola, endivia, endibia.

endless ['endlɪs] [end-les], *a.* Infinito, sin límites (plain, patience); interminable (journey, meeting); perpetuo, continuo, incesante (chatter, complaining). Innumerable (innumerable). **The possibilities are endless**, las posibilidades son infinitas.

endlessly ['endlɪslɪ] [end-les-li] *adv.* 1. Infinitamente, sin fin, perpetuamente (infinitely). **The plain/road stretched out endlessly before us**, la llanura/carretera se extendía interminablemente ante nosotros. 2. Constantemente, incesantemente, sin parar (incessantly/talk, chatter). 3. Hasta la saciedad (time and time again).

endlessness ['endlɪsnɪs] [end-lis-nes], *s.* Perpetuidad.

endlong ['endlɒŋ] [end-lon], *adv.* 1. A lo largo, extendido. 2. En línea recta, continuadamente. 3. De pie, en pie, a plomo.

endmost ['endmɒst] [end-most], *a.* Lo más lejos, remoto.

endo-, end-, Formato de combinación del griego *endon*, dentro.

endocardiac, endocardial ['endəkɑːdɪək] [en-do-kar-diak], *a.* Endocardíaco, perteneciente al endocardio; colocado o situado dentro del corazón

endocarditis ['endəkɑːˌdaɪtɪs] [en-do-kar-dai-tis], *s.* Endocarditis, inflamación aguda o crónica del endocardio.

endocardium [endəʊ'kɑːdɪəm] [en-dou-kar-dium], *s.* Endocardio, membrana que tapiza las cavidades del corazón.

endocrine ['endəʊkraɪn] [en-do-krain], *a.* Endocrino.

end-of-term ['endɒfˌtɜːm] [end-of-term] *a.* De final de trimestre.

endogen ['endɒdʒɪn] [en-do-chin], *s. (Bot.)* Vegetal cuyo crecimiento se verifica interiormente e irregularmente, en oposición a los exógenos; endógeno.

endogenous [en'dɒdʒɪnəs] [en-do-chi-nos], *a.* 1. *(Bot.)* Endógeno, endógena, monocotiledóneo; que crece interiormente. 2. Que crece en el interior de alguna cosa.

endorse [ɪn'dɔːs] [en-dors], *va.* 1. Rotular, refrendar, aprobar (approve/statement, decision); rubricar, autorizar. **I fully endorse that opinion**, comparto totalmente esa opinión. 2. Endosar o endorsar una letra de cambio (sign/check, bill). 3. *(Auto)* Anotar los detalles de una infracción de tráfico en el permiso de conducir.

endorsee [ɪnˌdɔː'siː] [en-dor-si], *s.* La persona a cuyo favor está endosada una letra de cambio. *V.* INDORSEE.

endorsement [ɪnˌdɔː'smənt] [en-dors-ment], *s.* 1. Sobrescrito, rótulo; endoso de una letra de cambio; ratificación. Aprobación, aval (approval). *(Pol.)* Refrendo. *(Marketing)* Promoción. 2. Anotación de una fracción de tráfico (on driving licence).

endorse [ɪn'dɔːs] [en-dors], *s.* Endosante o endosador.

endosmose [ɪn'dɒsməʊz] [en-dos-mous], *s.* Endósmosis, corriente de fuera a dentro, que se establece cuando dos líquidos de distinta densidad están separados por una membrana.

endothelium [ˌendʊ'θeliəm] [en-do-ze-lium], *s. (Anat.)* Endotelio, membrana compuesta de celdillas planas y delgadas, que tapiza los vasos sanguíneos, los linfáticos y las cavidades. Su adjetivo es **Endothelial**.

endothermic [en'dətɜːmɪk] [en-do-zer-mik] *a.* Endotérmico.

endow [ɪn'daʊ] [in-dau], *va.* 1. Dotar a una mujer. 2. Dotar a una iglesia, colegio, etc. (provide income for/college, school, hospital). 3. Dotar, dar la naturaleza prendas, talento o algún otro de sus dones.

endower [ɪn'daʊəʳ] [in-dauaʳ], *s.* Dotador.

endowment [ɪnˈdɔʊmənt] [in-dou-ment], *s.* 1. Dote, dotación. 2. Dotes, los dones que recibimos de la naturaleza; prendas, talentos, gracias. Atributo, dote (attribute). 3. *(Fin.)* Donación, legado. **Endowment mortgage**, hipoteca de inversión.

endue [ɪnˈdjuː] [in-diu] *va.* Dotar, privilegiar; investir.

endurable [ɪnˈdjʊərəbl] [in-diua-ra-bol], *a.* Sufrible, tolerable, soportable.

endurance [ɪnˈdjʊrəns] [in-diu-rens], *s.* 1. Duración, continuación; paciencia, sufrimiento. 2. Resistencia, aguante (physical); entereza, fortaleza (mental). **Powers of endurance**, capacidad de aguante. **Endurance test**, capacidad de aguante.

endure [ɪnˈdjʊəʳ] [in-diuaʳ], *va.* 1. Soportar, sufrir el peso o la presión; resistir a. 2. Aguantar, sufrir, tolerar, soportar. - *vn.* 1. Durar, perseverar, continuar; perdurar (fame, friendship, memories). 2. Sufrir, tener paciencia.

endurer [ɪnˈdjʊərəʳ] [in-diua-raʳ], *s.* Sufridor; continuador.

enduring [ɪnˈdjʊərɪŋ] [in-diua-rin], *pa.* 1. Que demuestra duración, duradero (peace, change); durable, permanente; constante; imperecedero, perdurable (fame, memory). 2. Tolerante, paciente, sufrido.

endwise [ˈendwaɪz] [end-uais], *adv.* De punta, derecho; con la extremidad anterior. De canto, de lado (with end forward); a lo largo (end to end).

enema [ˈenɪmə] [e-ni-ma], *s.* Enema, lavativa, ayuda, inyección.

enemy [ˈenɪmɪ] [e-ni-mi], *s.* 1. Enemigo (adversary); antagonista; el diablo; toda cosa dañina o peligrosa. **She's her worst enemy**, su peor enemigo es ella. 2. **The enemy**, el enemigo (opponent in war); enemigo (action, forces, territory).

energetic, energetical [ˌenəˈdʒetɪk] [e-ner-ye-tik], *a.* Enérgico (exercise); muy activo (vacation, day); vigoroso, lleno de energía (person); ardiente, activo. Enérgico (forceful/denial, protest).

energetically [ˌenəˈdʒetɪklɪ] [e-ner-ye-ti-ka-li], *adv.* Enérgicamente (argue, deny); con energía (work, dance).

energic [ˈenədʒɪk] [e-ner-yik], *a.* Enérgico; motor, activo.

energize [ˈenədʒaɪz] [e-ner-chais], *va.* Hacer obrar con energía, excitar o dar energía, dar vigor o actividad. -*vn.* Obrar con energía.

energizer [ˈenədʒaɪzəʳ] [e-ner-chai-saʳ], *s.* Confortante, excitante, lo que da energía y fuerza.

energumen [ˈenədʒʊmən] [e-ner-guiu-men], *s.* Energúmeno, energúmena, la persona que está poseída del demonio.

energy [ˈenədʒɪ] [e-ner-yi], *s.* Energía, fuerza, vigor, espíritu, resolución. Energías (power, effort). **Energy-saving**, de ahorro energético.

enervate [ˈenɜːveɪt] [e-ner-veit], *va.* 1. Enervar, debilitar, quitar las fuerzas. 2. Dejar sin efecto, hacer ineficaz. 3. Cortar los nervios o los tendones.

enervate, *a.* Debilitado, enervado.

enervating [ˈenɜːveɪtɪŋ] [e-ner-vei-tin] *a.* Debilitante.

enervation [ˈenɜːveɪʃən] [e-ner-vei-shon], *s.* Enervación; afeminación.

enfeeble [ɪnˈfiːbl] [in-fi-bol], *va.* Debilitar, enervar; efeminar.

enfeeblement [ɪnˈfiːbəlmənt] [in-fi-bol-ment], *s.* Debilidad, desfallecimiento, flojedad.

enfeoff [ˈenfrəf] [en-fiof], *va.* Enfeudar, dar en feudo algún estado.

enfetter [ˈenfiːtəʳ] [en-fi-taʳ], *va.* Encadenar.

enfilade [ˌenfɪˈleɪd] [en-fi-leid], *s.* 1. Fuego o tiro enfilado o de enfilada. 2. Ringlera, fila, hilera.

enfilade, *va.* Enfilar, batir por el costado; tirar a lo largo de un cuerpo de tropas, o en la dirección de proa a popa de un buque.

enfold [ɪnˈfəʊld] [in-fould] *va.* Envolver. V. INFOLD.

enforce [ɪnˈfɔːs] [in-fors], *va.* 1. Esforzar, dar fuerza o vigor; poner en ejecución por la fuerza, como se hace con las leyes. 2. Violentar, ejecutar alguna cosa con violencia; forzar, obtener por fuerza. 3. Esforzar, apretar. 4. Demostrar, presentar fuertemente o convincentemente. 5. *(Ant.)* Compeler, obligar. Hacer respetar o cumplir (law, regulation). Hacer valer (claim, right). **Enforced**, forzoso, impuesto (leisure, silence).

enforceable [ɪnˈfɔːsəbl] [in-for-sa-bol], *a.* Lo que es capaz de compeler u obligar.

enforcedly [ɪnˈfɔːstlɪ] [in-forst-li], *adv.* Por fuerza, forzosamente.

enforcement [ɪnˈfɔːsmənt] [in-fors-ment], *s.* Compulsión, coacción, fuerza; sanción; aprieto, estrecho. **They are responible for the enforcement of the law**, son responsables de hacer cumplir o respetar la ley. **Enforcement agencies**, departamentos de seguridad del estado. **Enforcement officers**, agentes de la ley.

enfranchise [ɪnˈfræntʃaɪz] [in-fran-chais], *va.* 1. Dar o conceder franquicia o privilegio político, como el derecho de votar; conceder los privilegios de la ciudadanía. 2. Poner en libertad, dar soltura al que estaba preso; manumitir, enfranquecer, emancipar. 3. Naturalizar, adoptar, v. g. palabras extranjeras.

enfranchisement [ɪnˈfræntʃɪzmənt] [in-fran-chis-ment], *s.* 1. Franquicia, privilegio de ciudadano. 2. Manumisión, emancipación. 3. Libertad dada a un preso.

enfranchiser [ɪnˈfræntʃaɪzəʳ] [in-fran-chai-saʳ], *s.* 1. Libertador, el que da libertad. 2. Manumisor.

engage [ɪnˈgeɪdʒ] [in-gueich], *va.* 1. Empeñar, comprometer, constituir a una persona en alguna obligación. Contratar (hire/staff, performer). 2. Atraer a otro a su partido; unir, traer a sí. Captar, atraer (attention, interest). **To engage somebody in conversation**, entablar una conversación con alguien. 3. Empeñar, obligar, precisar, hacer responsable. 4. Halagar, ganar con halagos. 5. Ocupar, emplear la atención. 6. Acometer, embestir. 7. *(Mec.)* Engranar, encajar los dientes de una rueda con otra (cog, wheel); engranar, meter (g e a r) 8. Empeñar, dar o dejar algo en prenda o seguridad del pago. 9. Apalabrar, mandar hacer, ajustar; alquilar (un cuarto, una casa); obtener promesa del uso de una cosa o de los servicios de una persona. -*vn.* 1. Empeñarse, obligarse, dar palabra, comprometerse a hacer alguna cosa. 2. Aventurarse o meterse en algún asunto o negocio. **To engage in politics**, dedicarse a la política. 3. Pelear, venir a las manos. 4. Engranar (cog, wheel). **She is engaged to Mr. N.**, ella ha dado palabra de matrimonio al Sr. N. **To be engaged**, estar ocupado, empeñado o comprometido; haber dado palabra de matrimonio, ser prometido o prometida de. **To engage deeply in an object**, empeñarse demasiado. *(Fam.)* Enfrascarse en.

engaged [ɪnˈgeɪdʒd] [in-gueichd] *a.* 1. Prometido, comprometido (betrothed). **To get engaged**, prometerse, comprometerse. 2. Ocupado (occupied). **I'm otherwise engaged**, tengo otro compromiso. **The work we are engaged on**, el trabajo que nos ocupa. (GB) Ocupado (toilet). *(Telec.)* Ocupado, comunicado. **The engaged tone/signal**, la señal de ocupado o de comunicando.

engagedly [ɪnˈgeɪdʒdlɪ] [in-gueichd-li], *adv.* Parcialmente; con empeño.

engagement [ɪnˈgeɪdʒmənt] [in-gueich-ment], *s.* 1. Empeño. 2. Empeño, comprometimiento, ajuste, contrato; en especial, promesa de casamiento, compromiso, noviazgo; esponsales. **They have broken off their engagement**, han roto su compromiso. **Engagement ring**, anillo de compromiso. **A new engagement**, nueva contrata. 3. Empleo de la atención hacia alguna cosa. 4. Batalla, combate, pelea. 5. Obligación, motivo; compromiso (appointment).

engager [ɪnˈgeɪdʒəʳ] [in-guei-chaʳ], *s.* El que se empeña en algún asunto, el que se compromete o constituye en algún empeño u obligación.

engaging [ɪnˈɡeɪdʒɪŋ] [in-guei-chin], *a.* Atractivo, encantador, agraciado, insinuante, halagüeño; simpático. **She's very engaging**, es muy simpática.

engagingly [ɪnˈɡeɪdʒɪŋlɪ] [in-guei-chin-li], *adv.* Atractivamente.

engarland [ɪnˈɡɑːlənd] [in-gar-land], *va.* Enguirnaldar, coronar con guirnalda.

engarrison [ɪnˈɡɑːrɪsən] [in-ga-ri-son], *va.* Guarnecer, poner guarnición en una plaza o fortaleza.

engender [ɪnˈdʒəndəʳ] [in-yen-daʳ], *va.* 1. Engendrar, procrear. 2. Producir, formar, dar origen. *-va.* Engendrarse, producirse, causarse.

engenderer [ɪnˈdʒəndərəʳ] [in-yen-de-raʳ], *s.* Engendrador.

engild [ɪnˈɡɪld] [in-guild], *va.* Aclarar, iluminar.

engine [ˈendʒɪn] [en-yin], *s.* 1. Ingenio, máquina; motor (motor); (f.c.) locomotora (locomotive). **To have engine trouble**, tener problemas con el motor. **Steam-engine**, máquina de vapor. **Fire-engine**, bomba de incendio, aguatocha. **Pile-engine**, martinete. 2. Máquina complicada y bien acabada para hacer trabajos difíciles y superiores. 3. Mecanismo o aparato de gran tamaño, especialmetne para destruir o desagregar. 4. Instrumento, agente. **Condensing engine**, máquina condensadora. **Beam-engine**, máquina de balancín. **Expansion engine**, máquina de expansión. **Portable engine**, locomóvil, máquina portátil. **Rotary engine**, máquina de rotación. **Stationary engine**, máquina fija. **Engine builder, maker**, fabricante, constructor de máquinas. **Engine-driver**, *(Ingl.)* conductor de locomotora. **Engine-turned work**, trabajo hecho a máquina.

engineer [ˌendʒɪˈnɪəʳ] [en-che-niaʳ], *s.* Ingeniero (graduate); maquinista (AmE Rail); oficial (in factory); técnico, ingeniero (for maintenance). *va.* Urdir, tramar (plan); fraguar (defeat, downfall). **Genetically engineered**, creado por la ingeniería genética.

engine room [ˈendʒɪnrʊm] [en-chin-rum], *s.* Cuarto de máquinas. **Engine-room log**, cuaderno de máquinas.

engird [ˈenɡɜːd] [en-guerd], **engirt** [ˈenɡɜːt] [en-guert], *va.* Ceñir, cercar.

engirdle [ˈenɡɜːdl] [en-guer-del], *va.* Circundar, rodear, ceñir.

englify [ˈenɡlɪfaɪ] [en-gli-fai], *va.* Hacer inglés; hacer que alguien o algo imite o se parezca a los ingleses en la figura o en los modales.

English [ˈɪŋɡlɪʃ] [in-glish], *a.* Inglés, lo perteneciente a Inglaterra. *-s.* Inglés, el natural de Inglaterra y la lengua inglesa. **The English**, los ingleses, la nación inglesa. De inglés (lesson, teacher).

English, *va.* Traducir al idioma inglés.

English horn [ˈɪŋɡlɪʃhɔːn] [in-glish-jorn], *s. (Mús.)* Corno inglés.

Englishman [ˈɪŋɡlɪʃmən] [in-glish-man], *s.* Inglés, el natural o ciudadano de Inglaterra; persona de sangre inglesa. **An Englishman's home is his castle**, frase que señala la importancia que el inglés atribuye a la privacidad del hogar.

Englishwoman [ˈɪŋɡlɪʃwʊmən] [in-glish-uo-man], *f.* Inglesa: la que es natural de Inglaterra o es de sangre inglesa.

englut [ɪnˈɡlʌt] [in-glat], *va.* 1. Engullir, tragar. 2. Atracar, llenar de comida, hartar.

engorge [ɪnˈɡɔːdʒ] [in-gorch], *va.* Atracar, engullir, devorar. *-vn.* Comer con ansia y voracidad.

engraft [ɪnˈɡrɑːft] [in-graft], *va. V.* INGRAFT.

engrafted [ɪnˈɡrɑːftɪd] [in-graf-ted], *a.* Injertado; plantado-

engrain [ɪnˈɡreɪn] [in-grein], *va.* Teñir, dar color subido a alguna cosa. *V.* INGRAIN.

engrave [ɪnˈɡreɪv] [in-greiv], *va.* 1. Grabar; esculpir; tallar. **She had the bracelet engraved with her name**, hizo grabar su nombre en la pulsera. 2. Grabar en el ánimo, causar impresión o sensación. 3. Enterrar, sepultar.

engravement [ɪnˈɡreɪvmənt] [in-greiv-ment], *s.* Grabado, acción de grabar.

engraver [ɪnˈɡreɪvəʳ] [in-grei-vaʳ], *s.* Grabador; escultor.

engraving [ɪnˈɡreɪvɪŋ] [in-grei-vin], *s.* 1. Grabado, el acto, efecto y arte de grabar. 2. Grabado, lámina estampa, pintura. **Copper-plate engraving**, grabado en cobre o en talla dulce. **Steel engraving**, grabado sobre acero. **Wood engraving**, grabado en madera. **Photo-engraving**, fotograbado: grabado fotomecánico o fotoquímico.

engross [ɪnˈɡrəʊs] [in-grous], *va.* 1. Escribir en caracteres grandes y de adorno; hacer transcripción formal de algo. 2. Absorber, ocupar o cautivar, tener posesión de. **To be engrossed in something**, estar absorto o enfrascado en algo. 3. Antiguamente monopolizar, agavillar. 4. *(Des.)* Condensar, espesar, abultar.

engrosser [ɪnˈɡrəʊsəʳ] [in-grou-saʳ], *s.* 1. Pendolista, el que copia en letras hermosas y de adorno. 2. *(Ant.)* Monopolista.

engrossing [ɪnˈɡrəʊsɪŋ] [in-grou-sin], *s.* 1. *(For.)* Compulsa, copia de un instrumento legal. 2. *(Com.)* Monopolio de algunos géneros para hacer subir su precio. **Engrossing clerk**, escribiente de letra grande y hermosa. *a.* Fascinante, apasionante.

engrossment [ɪnˈɡrəʊsmənt] [in-grous-ment], *s.* 1. Monopolio. 2. Copia de un instrumento escrito. 3. Absorción, embebcimiento, embelesamiento, abstracción.

engulf [ɪnˈɡʌlf] [in-galf] *va.* Engolfar. *V.* INGULF. Envolver (flames, fire, waves); sepultar (lava); asaltar (feeling). **War engulfed the country**, el país se sumió en la guerra.

enhance [ɪnˈhɑːns] [in-jans], *va.* Encarecer, aumentar la estimación de una cosa (value); levantar en alto; agravar; realzar, dar realce a (beauty, taste); mejorar (reputation, performance).

enhancement [ɪnˈhɑːnsmənt] [in-jans-ment], *s.* 1. Encarecimiento, subida de valor o estimación. 2. Agravación, el acto de agravar alguna cosa. 3. Mejora (of quality, performance); realce (of flavor, beauty); aumento (of value).

enhancer [ɪnˈhɑːnsəʳ] [in-jan-saʳ], *s.* Encarecedor.

enharmonic [ɪnˈhɑːmənɪk] [in-jar-mo-nik], *a.* Enarmónico, uno de los tres géneros del sistema músico.

enigma [ɪˈnɪɡmə] [i-nig-ma], *s.* 1. Enigma, dicho o frase cuyo sentido se encubre intencionadamente, haciéndolo obscuro y difícil de entender. 2. Suceso o acto de difícil explicación.

enigmatic, enigmatical [ˌenɪɡˈmætɪk] [i-nig-ma-tik], *a.* Enigmático.

enigmatically [ˌenɪɡˈmætɪkəlɪ] [i-nig-ma], *adv.* Enigmáticamente.

enigmatist [ˌenɪɡˈmætɪst] [i-nig-ma-tist], *s.* Enigmatista, el que habla con enigmas.

enigmatize [ˌenɪɡˈmætaɪz] [i-nig-ma-tais], *-vn.* Usar de enigmas.

enjoin [ɪnˈdʒɔɪn] [in-yoin], *va.* Mandar, ordenar, encargar, prescribir; advertir. **To enjoin something on somebody**, encarecerle algo a alguien (strongly urge).

enjoiner [ɪnˈdʒɔɪnəʳ] [in-yoi-naʳ], *s.* 1. Mandante. 2. El que da encargos, preceptos u órdenes.

enjoinment [ɪnˈdʒɔɪnmənt] [in-yoin-ment], *s. (Des.)* Mandato, precepto, orden; encargo.

enjoy [ɪnˈdʒɔɪ] [in-yoi], *va.* 1. Gozar, sentir o percibir alguna cosa con gusto, complacencia y alegría. **I enjoyed the book**, me gustó mucho el libro (like). **I enjoyed the party**, lo pasé bien en la fiesta. 2. Gozar, tener, poseer; disfrutar de, gozar de (have experience/good health). 3. Agradar, alegrar. **To enjoy oneself**, gozarse, vivir contento y alegre, divertirse. *-vn.* Vivir felizmente. **Enjoy!**, ¡buen provecho! (on serving food).

enjoyable [ɪnˈdʒɔɪəbl] [in-yoia-bol], *a.* Gozable, deleitable, encantador. Agradable, placentero (day, meal, vacation). **An enjoyable book**, un libro de lectura muy amena.

enjoyer [ɪnˈdʒɔɪəʳ] [in-yoia^r], *s.* Gozador.

enjoyment [ɪnˈdʒɔɪmənt] [in-yoi-ment], *s.* Goce, fruición, felicidad, gusto, placer (pleasure). **She gets a lot of enjoyment from/out of reading**, disfruta mucho leyendo, le encanta leer.

enkindle [enˈkɪndl] en-kin-del], *va.* 1. Encender, pegar fuego. 2. Inflamar, enardecer y avivar a uno. 3. Incitar, mover, estimular.

enlace [ɪnˈleɪs] [in-leis], *va.* Rodear, circundar con encaje o bordado; atar con un encaje; entrelazar, enredar.

enlarge [ɪnˈlɑːdʒ] [in-larch], *va.* 1. Agrandar (hole, area); engrandecer, aumentar, ensanchar. 2. Dilatar (gland, heart); extender, alargar; ampliar (room, office). 3. Ampliar, amplificar (print, photograph). 4. Soltar, desencarcelar, sacar de la prisión, poner en libertad a uno. *-vn.* Difundirse, extenderse; dilatarse en la narración o explicación de las cosas. **To enlarge on/upon something**, extenderse sobre algo.

enlargedly [ɪnˈlɑːdʒ] [in-larch], *adv.* Extensamente, ampliamente.

enlargement [ɪnˈlɑːdʒ] [in-larch], *s.* 1. Aumento, incremento, extensión, ampliación (of building). 2. Soltura, libertad, que se da al prisionero. 3. Dilatación, expansión; difusión. 4. Amplificación, plenitud de relación. 5. Ampliación, fotografía mayor que su prueba negativa. 6. Dilatación (of gland, heart).

enlarger [ɪnˈlɑːdʒəʳ] [in-lar-cha^r], *s.* Ampliador, amplificador.

enlarging [ɪnˈlɑːdʒɪŋ] [in-lar-chin], *s.* Extensión, ampliación. **Enlarging apparatus**, aparato para ampliar fotografías.

enlight [ɪnˈlaɪt] [in-lait], *va.* Alumbrar, iluminar.

enlighten [ɪnˈlaɪtn] [in-lai-ten], *va.* 1. *(Ant.)* Alumbrar, iluminar. 2. Iluminar, instruir, ilustrar (people, population); explicar, aclarar; comunicar o dar luz tanto en lo físico como en lo moral. **Would you care to enlighten me?**, ¿te importaría explicarme?

enlightened [ɪnˈlaɪtnd] [in-lai-tend] *a.* Progresista (person, view); inteligente (decision).

enlightener [ɪnˈlaɪtnəʳ] [in-lai-te-na^r], *s.* Alumbrador; instructor, ilustrador.

enlightening [ɪnˈlaɪtnɪŋ] [in-lai-te-nin] *a.* Esclarecedor, instructivo.

enlightenment [ɪnˈlaɪtnmənt] [in-lai-ten-ment], *s.* Ilustración, instrucción, iluminación. **I turned to her for enlightenment**, recurrí a ella en busca de una explicación o una aclaración. *(Hist.)* **The Age of Enlightenment**, la Ilustración, el Siglo de las Luces.

enlink [ɪnˈlɪŋk] [in-link], *va.* Encadenar, eslabonar, ligar.

enlist [ɪnˈlɪst] [in-list], *va.* 1. Alistar, sentar o poner a alguno en una lista. 2. Alistar, reclutar soldados (soldiers, helpers, members); enrolar (sailors); conseguir (support, aid). **Enlisted man**, soldado raso. 3. Ganar el interés y apoyo de otro; empeñar. *-vn.* 1. Alistarse, entrar voluntariamente en el servicio militar o naval. *(Mil.)* Sentar plaza. 2. Adherirse, tomar partido por, empeñarse en algo con interés.

enlistment [ɪnˈlɪstmənt] [in-list-ment] *s. (Mil.)* Alistamiento, reclutamiento.

enliven [ɪnˈlaɪvn] [in-lai-ven], *va.* 1. Vivificar, animar (conversation, person). 2. Alentar. 3. Avivar, alegrar, darle vida o alegría a (room, place); regocijar, causar alegría.

enlivener [ɪnˈlaɪvnəʳ] [in-liv-na^r], *s.* Vivificador, animador.

enlivening [ɪnˈlaɪvnɪŋ] [in-liv-nin], *s.* Lo que hace alegre, jovial o que causa placer.

en masse [əŋˈmæs] [en-mas] *adv.* En masa, en bloque.

enmesh [ɪnˈmeʃ] [in-mesh], *va.* Enredar, enmarañar, hacer caer en la red.

enmity [ˈenmɪtɪ] [en-mi-ti], *s.* Enemistad, odio, malevolencia; malicia; oposición.

enmoss [ˈenmɒs] [en-mous], *va.* Cubrir con musgo o con algo como musgo.

ennead [ɪnˈniːd] [in-nid], *s.* El número nueve; sistema o grupo de nueve objetos.

enneadic [ɪnˈniːdɪk] [in-ni-dik], *a.* Noveno, novena, relativo a nueve.

enneagon [ɪnˈnɪəgɒn] [in-nia-gon], *s. (Geom.)* Eneágono, polígono de nueve ángulos y nueve lados.

ennoble [ɪˈnəʊbl] [i-nou-bel], *va.* 1. Ennoblecer. 2. Ilustrar, engrandecer. 3. Elevar, levantar.

ennoblement [ɪˈnəʊblmənt] [i-nou-bel-ment], *s.* Ennoblecimiento.

ennui [əˈnwiː] [a-nui], *s.* Displicencia, aburrimiento, tedio, enfado, hastío.

enorm [ɪˈnɔːm] [i-norm], *a. (Ant.)* Irregular, enorme; perverso.

enormity [ɪˈnɔːmɪtɪ] [i-nor-mi-ti], *s.* Enormidad, exceso, demasía; atrocidad, delito enorme; fealdad, ruindad. **Enormities**, atrocidades horribles.

enormous [ɪˈnɔːməs] [i-nor-mos], *a.* 1. Enorme, inmenso, irregular, desmesurado; excesivo, demasiado. 2. Perverso, atroz, nefando. 3. Enorme (strength, courage).

enormously [ɪˈnɔːməslɪ] [i-nor-mos-li], *adv.* Enormemente (enjoy, benefit). **He's enormously fat/rich**, es gordísimo/riquísimo.

enormousness [ɪˈnɔːməsnɪʃ] [i-nor-mos-nes], *s.* Enormidad.

enough [ɪˈnʌf] [i-naf], *a.* Bastante, suficiente; bastantes, suficientes. **I don't have enough money to buy it**, no me alcanza el dinero para comprarlo. **I didn't get enough sleep**, no dormí bastante o lo suficiente. *pron.* **They don't pay us enough**, no nos pagan bastante o lo suficiente. **That's enough for me, thank you**, es suficiente, gracias. **Enough is enough!**, ¡ya basta! **I've had enough!**, ¡ya estoy harto! *-s.* Lo bastante, lo suficiente. *-adv.* Bastantemente, suficientemente. **You don't go out enough**, no sales lo suficiente (sufficiently). **Their house is more than big enough for three people**, su casa basta y sobra para tres personas. **Curiously enough**, curiosamente, aunque parezca curioso. **He seemed willing enough to help**, parecía muy dispuesto a ayudar (quite, very). **I like my job well enough but…**, mi trabajo me gusta pero… (tolerably, passably). *-inter.* ¡Basta!

enounce [ɪˈnəns] [i-nons], *va.* Declarar, publicar.

enow [ɪˈnəʊ] [i-no], *a., s.* y *adv.* (Ant. o Poét.) V. ENOUGH.

enquicken [ɪnˈkwɪkn] [in-kui-ken], *va. (Des.)* Avivar.

enquire [ɪnˈkwaɪəʳ] [in-kuaia^r], *va.* Inquirir. V. INQUIRE y sus derivados.

enquirer [ɪnˈkwaɪrəʳ] [in-kuai-ra^r], *s.* V. INQUIRER.

enrage [ɪnˈreɪdʒ] [in-reich], *va.* Enfurecer, irritar, provocar, encolerizar.

enraged [ɪnˈreɪdʒt] [in-reicht] *a.* Enfurecido. **He was enraged when he found out**, cuando se enteró se puso furioso, o se enfureció.

enrank [ɪnˈræŋk] [in-rank], *va.* Enfilar.

enrapt [ɪnˈræpt] [in-rapt], *a.* Arrebatado, entusiasmado: transportado, extasiado.

enrapture [ɪnˈræptʃəʳ] [in-rap-cha^r], *va.* Arrebatar, elevar, transportar, arrobar, extasiar.

enravish [ɪnˈrævɪʃ] [in-ra-vish], *va.* Arrebatar, extasiar, enajenar.

enravishment [ɪnˈrævɪʃmənt] [in-ra-vish-ment], *s.* Arrobamiento, rapto, enajenamiento, pasmo, alborozo, éxtasis.

enregister [ɪnˈrɪdʒɪstəʳ] [in-ri-chis-ta^r], *va.* Registrar, empadronar.

enrich [ɪnˈrɪtʃ] [in-rich], *va.* 1. Enriquecer, hacer rico y opulento. 2. Fecundar, fertilizar. 3. Mejorar la calidad de algo, hacerle adiciones de valor. 4. Enriquecer, adornar, embellecer, aumentar la hermosura de alguna cosa.

enrichment [ɪnˈrɪtʃmənt] [in-rich-ment], *s.* 1. Enriquecimiento; abono, beneficio que se da a las tierras. 2. Adorno, embellecimiento.

enridge [ɪnˈrɪdʒ] [in-rich], *va.* Formar protuberancias longitudinales; formar surcos.

enring [ɪnˈrɪŋ] [in-rin], *va.* Cercar, rodear con anillos.

enrobe [ɪnˈrəʊb] [in-roub], *va.* Vestir, adornar o cubrir con vestidos.

enroll [ɪnˈrəʊl] [in-roul], *va.* 1. Alistar, sentar o escribir en una lista. 2. Registrar; matricular, inscribir (parents). **The club enrolled 20 new members last year**, el año pasado 20 personas se hicieron socias del club. 3. Envolver, arrollar. **To enroll oneself a soldier**, sentar plaza de soldado. *vn.* Matricularse, inscribirse.

enroller [ɪnˈrəʊləʳ] [in-rou-laʳ], *s.* Registrador.

enrollment, enrolment [ɪnˈrəʊlmənt] [in-roul-ment], *s.* 1. Registro, protocolo. 2. Inscripción, matrícula.

enroot [ɪnˈruːt] [in-rut], *va.* Arraigar, radicar.

en route [ɪnˈruːt] [in-rut], *adv.* En el camino, en ruta. *(Gal.)* **We were en route to/for Cambridge**, íbamos camino a Cambridge.

ens [ens] [ens], *s.* Ente, ser; entidad.

ensample [anˈsæmpl] [an-sam-pel], *s.* *(Ant.)* V. EXAMPLE.

ensample, *va.* V. EXEMPLIFY.

ensanguine [ɪnˈsæŋɡwɪn] [in-san-guin], *va.* Ensangrentar.

ensate [ɪnˈseɪt] [in-seit], *a.* *(Biol.)* Ensiforme, en forma de espada.

enschedule [ɪnˈsledjuːl] [in-ske-dul], *va.* Insertar en algún escrito.

ensconce [ɪnˈskɒns] [in-skons], *va.* 1. Cubrir, resguardar, poner a cubierto, establecer cómodamente. **I was comfortably ensconced in an armchair**, estaba cómodamente arrellanado o instalado en un sillón. Se usa a menudo como reflexivo. **To ensconce oneself**, instalarse. 2. *(Ant.)* Defender, proteger con un fortín.

ensela [ɪnˈskalə] [in-se-la], *va.* *(Ant.)* Imprimir, señalar como con un sello.

enseam [ɪnˈsiːm] [in-sim], *va.* Coser o hacer costura.

ensemble [anˈsæmbl] [an-sam-bel], *s.* 1. El conjunto, el total, la apariencia y efecto generales (whole). 2. Vestido de mujer de más de una pieza, conjunto (clothing). 3. Conjunto (group of performers).

ensheathe [ɪnˈhiːθ] [ins-jiz], *va.* Envainar, meter en la vaina (sword); encerrar, incluir.

enshrine [enˈʃraɪn] [en-shrain], *va.* Guardar como reliquia.

enshroud [enˈʃraʊd] [en-shroud], *va.* Cubrir, proteger. Envolver, esconder.

ensiform [ˈensɪfɔːm] [en-si-form], *a.* Ensiforme, en forma de espada.

ensign [ɪnˈsaɪn] [in-sain], *s.* 1. *(Mil.)* Bandera, insignia de un regimiento. 2. *(Mar.)* Bandera de popa. 3. Insignia, divisa; enseña, pabellón (flag). 4. *(Mil.)* Abanderado, el oficial que lleva la bandera; alférez (in US navy).

ensign *va.* 1. Señalar con algún indicio o nota; distinguir por algún adorno o divisa.

ensign-bearer [ˌɪnsaɪnˈbɛərəʳ] [in-sain-bea-raʳ], *s.* Abanderado.

ensilage [ɪnˈsɪlædʒ] [in-si-lach] *s.* Ensilaje, acción y efecto de ensilar; forraje conservado en un silo subterráneo.

enskied [ɪnˈskaɪd] [in-skaid], *a.* *(ant. y poet.)* Celestial; encumbrado, puesto sobre las nubes.

enslave [ɪnˈsleɪv] [in-sleiv], *va.* Esclavizar, cautivar.

enslavement [ɪnˈsleɪvmənt] [in-sleiv-ment], *s.* Esclavitud, cautiverio, servidumbre.

enslaver [ɪnˈsleɪvəʳ] [in-skons], *s.* Esclavizador.

ensnare [ɪnˈsnɛəʳ] [in-snea], *va.* 1. Entrampar, hacer caer a algún animal en una trampa. 2. Engañar, tender un lazo.

ensphere [ɪnˈsfɪəʳ] [in-sfia], *va.* Colocar en esfera, redondear.

enstamp [ɪnˈstæmp] [in-stamp], *va.* Estampar o imprimir una señal.

ensue [ɪnˈsjuː] [in-siu], *-vn.* 1. Seguirse, inferirse. 2. Suceder o continuar una cosa a otra por turno o número. *-va. (Ant.)* Seguir, perseguir, ir en seguimiento de alguna cosa. **Seek peace and ensue it**, buscad la paz, y seguidla.

ensure [ɪnˈsʊəʳ] [in-sua], *va.* 1. Asegurar, dar seguridad y fianza de alguna cosa. 2. Asegurar, dar seguro. V. INSURE.

ensurer [ɪnˈsʊərəʳ] [in-sua-raʳ], *s.* Asegurador.

entablature [ɪnˈtæblətʃəʳ] [in-ta-bla-chaʳ], **entablement** [ɪnˈtæbləmənt] [in-ta-bla-ment], *s.* *(Arq.)* Entablamento.

entad [ˈɪntæd] [in-tad], *adv.* *(Anat. y Zool.)* Hacia el centro del cuerpo o de un órgano; opuesto a *ectad.*

entail [ɪnˈtaɪl] [in-teil], *s.* 1. Vínculo, mayorazgo. 2. Cualquier cosa transmitida como herencia inalienable.

entail, *va.* 1. Vincular, sujetar los bienes a vínculo. 2. Vincular, asegurar o fundar alguna cosa en otra; perpetuar, continuar, fincar, establecer. 3. Transmitir, legar; imponer, ocasionar. causar; traer sobre otro como consecuencia o legado.

ental [ɪnˈtəl] [in-tal], *a.* *(Anat. y Zool.)* De lo interior; opuesto a *ectal.*

entangle [ɪnˈtæŋɡl] [in-tan-gol], *va.* 1. Enredar, enmarañar, embrollar, embarazar, intrincar. 2. Multiplicar las dificultades de una obra.

entanglement [ɪnˈtæŋɡlmənt] [in-tan-guel-ment], *s.* Enredo, embarazo, confusión, perplejidad.

entangler [ɪnˈtæŋɡləʳ] [in-tan-glaʳ], *s.* Enredador, embrollón.

entender [ɪnˈtendəʳ] [in-ten-daʳ], *va.* *(Ant.)* Enternecer, ablandar, poner tierna y blanda una cosa.

enter [ˈentəʳ] [en-taʳ], *va.* 1. Entrar; penetrar. 2. Hacer empezar o emprender alguna cosa; introducir. 3. Asentar o poner por escrito, registrar. 4. Hacerse miembro de; unirse a; ser iniciado. 5. Ingerir, insertar. 6. *(Com.)* Declarar, hacer una declaración de géneros en la aduana. 7. *(For.)* Incoar (un procedimiento); notar, archivar. *-vn.* 1. Entrar, ir o venir adentro. 2. Penetrar, alcanzar con el discurso. 3. Meterse en algún asunto; dar principio a una cosa, empeñarse en algo.

enter, *prefijo.* V. INTER.

enterclose [ˈentəkləʊz] [en-ter-klous], *s.* *(Arq.)* Pasadizo, corredor, pasillo, comunicación entre dos piezas o cuartos.

enterer [ˈentərəʳ] [en-te-raʳ], *s.* El que entra o principia.

enteric [enˈterɪk] [en-te-rik], *a.* Entérico, perteneciente a los intestinos. **Enteric fever**, fiebre tifoidea.

entering [ˈentərɪŋ] [en-te-rin], *s.* Entrada, paso.

enteritis [ˌentəˈraɪtɪs] [en-te-rai-tis], *s.* Enteritis, inflamación de la mucosa de los intestinos.

enterocele [ˈentərəsiːl] [en-te-ro-sil], *s.* *(Cir.)* Enterocele, hernia inguinal o femoral.

enterocolitis [ˌentərəkəˈlaɪtɪs] [en-te-ro-ko-lai-tis], *s.* Enterocolitis, inflamación de los intestinos delgados y del colon.

entermphalos [ˈentɜːmfələs] [en-zerm-fa-los], *s.* *(Cir.)* Enterónfalo, hernia umbilical producida por los intestinos.

enterotome [ˈentərətəʊm] [en-te-ro-toum], *s.* *(Med.)* Enterótomo, instrumento quirúrgico que sirve para abrir los intestinos.

enterozoa [ˈentərəzə] [en-te-ro-so], *s. pl.* Los parásitos intestinales.

enterprise, enterprize [ˈentəpraɪz] [en-ter-prais], *s.* 1. Empresa, la determinación de emprender algún negocio arduo; tentativa difícil. 2. Resolución, energía e inventiva en los asuntos prácticos.

enterprise, *va.* Emprender.

enterpriser [ˈentəpraɪzəʳ] [en-ter-prai-saʳ], *s.* Emprendedor.

enterprising [ˈentəpraɪzɪŋ] [en-ter-prai-sin], *s.* Empresa. *-a.* Atrevido, enérgico, emprendedor.

entertain [ˌentəˈteɪn] [en-ter-tein], *va.* 1. Conversar, hablar, tener conversación con alguno. 2. Convidar; tratar, dar de comer a los que se convida. 3. Hospedar, festejar, agasajar. 4. Mantener, tener alguna persona a su servicio; asistir con o dar asistencias. 5. Concebir, pensar alguna cosa. 6. Entretener, divertir; admitir con satisfacción a alguno.

entertainable [ˌentəˈteɪnəbl] [en-ter-tei-na-bol], *a.* Abarcable o contenible en la mente, concebible (como opinión).

entertainer [ˌentəˈteɪnəʳ] [en-ter-tei-naʳ], *s.* 1. Anfitrión, el que convida a otro a comer. 2. El que alegra, regocija o divierte a otros. 3. El que alberga con cordialidad; huésped.

entertaining [ˌentəˈteɪnɪŋ] [en-ter-tei-nin], *a.* Entretenido, chistoso, alegre, divertido, agradable.

entertainingly [ˌentəˈteɪnɪŋlɪ] [en-ter-tei-nin-li], *adv.* Divertidamente, chistosamente.

entertainment [ˌentəˈteɪnmənt] [en-ter-tein-ment], s. 1. Conversación, plática familiar. 2. Convite, agasajo, festín, festejo; mantenimiento. **House of entertainment**, fonda, posada. 3. Hospedaje, acogida, recibimiento agradable. 4. Empleo, cargo, servicio. 5. Entretenimiento, diversión, pasatiempo en general. 6. Pensamiento, el acto de tener en la mente.

enthalpy [ˈenθəlfɪ] [en-zal-fi], s. Entalpía.

enthrall [ɪnˈθrɔːl] [in-zrol], va. 1. Poner bajo una influencia dominante: se dice del ánimo o de los sentidos. 2. Esclavizar, encadenar; sojuzgar.

enthrone [ɪnˈθrəʊn] [in-zroun], **enthronize** [ɪnˈθrənaɪz] [in-zro-nais], va. 1. Entronizar, colocar en el trono. 2. Elevar, instalar como obispo.

enthronization [ˌɪnθrənaɪˈzeɪʃən] [in-zro-nai-zei-shon], s. Entronización.

enthusiast [ɪnˈθuːzɪæst] [in-zu-siast], s. Entusiasta; fanático.

enthusiastic, enthusiastical [ɪnˈθuːzɪæstɪk] [in-zu-sias-tik], a. Entusiasmado; iluso, fanático, visionario; determinado.

enthymeme [ɪnˈzɪmem] [in-zi-mem], s. Entimema, silogismo que consta de dos proposiciones; silogismo imperfecto.

entice [ɪnˈtaɪs] [in-tais], va. Halagar, acariciar; atraer con halagos o esperanzas; excitar, inducir. **To entice a girl**, corromper a una doncella. **To entice away**, tentar, inducir al mal; sonsacar; robar a una doncella.

enticement [ɪnˈtaɪsmənt] [in-tais-ment], s. .1 Incitación, instigación, sugestión de hacer alguna cosa mala; seducción. 2. Incitamiento; encantos o atractivos que incitan o inducen al mal.

enticer [ɪnˈtaɪsər] [in-tai-sar], Incitador, instigador, seductor.

enticing [ɪnˈtaɪsɪŋ] [in-tai-sin], s. Incitamiento, a hacer algo malo.

enticingly [ɪnˈtaɪsɪŋlɪ] [in-tai-sin-li], adv. Halagüeñamente, seductoramente.

entire [ɪnˈtaɪər] [in-taiar], a. 1. Entero, cabal, cumplido, completo, perfecto. 2. Entero, robusto, sano, fuerte. 3. Entero, constante, firme, fiel, leal, adicto, afecto. 4. Íntegro, imparcial, sincero.

entirely [ɪnˈtaɪəlɪ] [in-taia-li], adv. Enteramente, totalmente, absolutamente, fielmente.

entireness [ɪnˈtaɪənɪs] [in-taia-nes], s. 1. Entereza, integridad, totalidad, estado completo. 2. (Ant.) Integridad, honradez.

entirety [ɪnˈtaɪətɪ] [in-taia-ti], s. Totalidad, integridad, entereza.

entitative [ɪnˈtɪtətɪv] [in-ti-ta-tiv], a. (Met.) Lo que se considera por sí mismo separadamente de todas las circunstancias accesorias.

entitatively [ɪnˈtɪtətɪvlɪ] [in-ti-ta-tiv-li], adv. Por sí mismo.

entitle [ɪnˈtaɪtl] [in-tai-tol], va. 1. Titular; intitular. 2. Tener derecho, habilitar, conceder o dar algún derecho, privilegio o pretexto; calificar; autorizar.

entity [ˈentɪtɪ] [in-ti-ti], s. Entidad, ente.

ento-, ent-. Formas de combinación: derivadas del griego *entos*, dentro de, interior.

entomb [ɪnˈtuːm] [in-tum], va. Enterrar, sepultar, colocar un cadáver en el sepulcro.

entombment [ɪnˈtuːmmənt] [in-tum-ment], s. Entierro, sepultura.

entomological, entomologic [ˌentəməˈlɒdʒɪkəl] [en-to-mo-lo-yi-kal], a. Entomológico, perteneciente a la entomología.

entomologist [ˌentəməˈlɒdʒɪkəl] [en-to-mo-lo-yi-kal], s. Entomólogo, naturalista consagrado a la entomología.

entomologize [ˌentəˈmɒlədʒɪst] [en-to-mo-lo-chist], -vn. Estudiar la entomología; coleccionar insectos para investigación científica.

entomology [ˌentəˈmɒlədʒɪ] [en-to-mo-lo-yi], s. 1. Entomología, la parte de la zoología que trata especialmente de los insectos. 2. Tratado sobre esta materia.

entomophagous [ˌentəˈmɒfəɡəs] [en-to-mo-fa-gos], a. Entomófago, insectívoro.

entozoa [ˈentəzuː] [en-to-su], s. pl. Entozoarios, los animales parásitos dentro de los cuerpos de otros.

entozoan [ˈentəzəʊn] [en-to-soun], a. V. ENTOZOIC. -s. Uno de los entozoarios.

entozoic [ˈentəzɔɪk] [en-to-soik], a. 1. Que vive dentro de otro animal; entozoico, de los entozoarios. 2. (Bot.) Que vive dentro de un animal.

entozoon [ˈentəzuːn] [en-to-sun], s. (pl. ZOA). Uno de los entozoarios.

entrails [ˈentreɪlz] [en-treils], s. pl. 1. Entrañas, las vísceras contenidas en las cavidades del cuerpo, y se da particularmente este nombre a las del vientre. 2. Lo más interior y oculto de alguna cosa. El singular *entrail* se usa rara vez.

entrammelled [ˈentræmlɪd] [en-tram-lid], a. Encrespado, enredado.

entrance [ˈentrəns] [en-trans], s. 1. Entrada, el acto de entrar, en cualquier sentido. 2. Entrada, el sitio por donde se entra a alguna parte (door, way). 3. Permiso o facultad de entrar. 4. Principio, el acto de empezar; conocimiento anticipado. 5. Toma de posesión de un empleo o dignidad.

entrance, va. Extasiar, transportar, suspender o arrebatar el ánimo.

entrant [ˈentrənt] [en-trant], a. Entrante, que entra; que admite. -s. Principiante, el que empieza alguna cosa; novicio.

entrap [ɪnˈtræp] [en-trap], va. Entrampar; enmarañar, enredar; ngañar.

entreat [ɪnˈtriːt] [en-trit], va. Rogar, pedir con instancia, suplicar; vencer o conseguir alguna cosa a fuerza de ruegos o instancias; tratar, comunicar. -vn. Hacer una súplica, pedir un favor.

entreatable [ɪnˈtriːtəbl] [en-tri-ta-bol], a. Tratable, accesible al ruego.

entreater [ɪnˈtriːtər] [en-tri-tar], s. Suplicante.

entreative [ɪnˈtriːtɪv] [en-tri-tiv], a. Suplicativo.

entreaty [ɪnˈtriːtɪ] [en-tri-ti], s. Petición, ruego, súplica, instancia, solicitud.

entree [ˈɒntreɪ] [an-trei], s. 1. Entrada, el acto de entrar. 2. Privilegio de entrar como visitante. 3. (Coc.) Cada uno de los principio o entradas, platos que se sirven en una mesa, entre la sopa y el asado.

entremets [ɪnˈtrɪmets] [in-tri-mets], s. pl. 1. Intermedios, platos que se sirven en una mesa entre el asado y los postres. 2. Entremés, intermedio, sainete, farsa. 3. V. INTERLUDE.

entrench [ɪnˈtrentʃ] [in-trench], va. 1. Atrincherar, proteger con trincheras. 2. Hacer trincheras en o sobre. -vn. Invadir, infringir. V. ENCROACH.

entrenchment [ɪnˈtrentʃmənt] [en-trench-ment], s. 1. Atrincheramiento, trinchera; parapeto de tierra. 2. Cualquier defensa o protección. 3. El acto y efecto de atrincherar. 4. Infracción, invasión, transgresión.

entrepot [ˈɒntrəpəʊ] [an-tre-pou], s. 1. Centro comercial de distribución. 2. Almacén. V. DEPOT.

entrepreneur [ˌɒntrəprəˈnɜːr] [an-tre-pre-nar], s. Empresario.

entropy [ˈentrəpɪ] [en-tro-pi], s. Entropía.

entrust [ɪnˈtrʌst] [en-trast], va. .1 Entregar con confianza, confiar, dar en fideicomiso. 2. Poner a cargo o al cuidado de. (Seguido de *with*). **To entrust one with a secret**, confiar un secreto a alguien.

entry [ˈentrɪ] [en-tri], s. 1. Entrada, vestíbulo, portal, pórtico por dondes se entra en alguna casa. 2. Entrada, el acto de entrar. 3. El acto de tomar posesión de una propiedad. 4. Asiento, anotación de alguna cosa por escrito. **A little entry**, el pasadizo, o el pasillo. 5. (Mar.) Registro, declaración de entrada de un barco. 6. (Com.) Partida. **Single entry, double entry**, partida simple, doble.

entwine [ɪnˈtwaɪn] [int-uain], va. Entrelazar, torciendo.

entwist [ˈentwɪst] [en-tuist], va. Torcer; enroscar.

enucleate [ˈenjuːklɪeɪt] [e-niu-kli-eit], va. 1. Descascarar, extraer el núcleo; en cirujía, extraer de un saco o bolsa, extraer de raíz, extirpar. 2. Desenvolver o desarrollar claramente, aclarar; explicar.

enucleation [ˈenjuːklɪˌeɪʃən] [e-niu-kli-ei-shon], *s.* Enucleación, acción de extirpar, de extraer un tumor en su totalidad.

enumerate [ɪˈnjuːməreɪt] [e-niu-me-reit], *va.* Énumerar, numerar.

enumeration [ɪˌnjuːməˈreɪʃən] [e-niu-me-rei-shon], *s.* 1. Enumeración, cómputo o cuenta numeral; y de aquí, catálogo. 2. *(Ret.)* Enumeración, recapitulación.

enumerative [ɪˌnjuːməˈrətɪv] [e-niu-me-ra-tiv], *a.* Enumerativo.

enunciate [ɪˈnʌnsɪeɪt] [i-nan-shiet], *va.* 1. Articular, pronunciar. 2. Enunciar, declarar, manifestar.

enunciation [ɪˌnʌnsɪˈeɪʃən] [i-nan-shie-shon], *s.* 1. Pronunciación, articulación de sonidos vocales; producción. 2. Enunciación, noticia, conocimiento, declaración pública; expresión en los escritos; prolación.

enunciative [ɪˈnʌnsɪətɪv] [i-nan-shia-tiv], *a.* Enunciativo, declarativo.

enunciatively [ɪˈnʌnsɪətɪvlɪ] [i-nan-shia-tiv-li], *adv.* Enunciativamente.

enunciatory [ɪˈnʌnsɪətərɪ] [i-nan-shia-to-ri], *a.* V. ENUNCIATIVE.

enure [ɪˈnjʊəʳ] [i-niuaʳ], *-vn.* Ponerse en operación; tener efecto; servir para el uso o provecho de. V. INURE.

envelop [ˈenvələʊp] [en-va-loup], *va.* Envolver, aforrar, esconder.

envelope [ˈenvələʊp] [en-va-loup], *s.* 1. Envoltura, envolvedor. 2. Sobre de carta, cubierta, sobrescrito.

envelopment [ˈenvələʊpmənt] [en-va-loup-ment], *s.* Envolvimiento; lo que envuelve, cubierta, envolvedor.

envenom [ɪnˈvenəm] [in-ve-nom], *va.* Envenenar, atosigar; enfurecer, irritar; hacer odioso.

enviable [ˈenvɪəbl] [en-via-bol], *a.* Envidiable.

envier [ˈenvaɪəʳ] [en-vaiaʳ], *s.* Envidiador, el que envidia.

envious [ˈenvɪəs] [en-vios], *a.* Envidioso, lleno de envidia.

enviously [ˈenvɪəslɪ] [en-vios-li], *adv.* Envidiosamente.

enviousness [ˈenvɪəsnɪs] [en-vios-nes], *s.* Envidia; carácter envidioso.

environ [ɪnˈvaɪərən] [in-vaia-ron], *va.* Rodear, cercar, bloquear, sitiar; envolver.

environment [ɪnˈvaɪərənmənt] [in-vaia-ron-ment], *s.* Ambiente, medio ambiente. Todo lo que cerca y rodea; todas las circunstancias externas de un organismo.

environmental [ɪnˌvaɪərənˈment] [in-vaia-ron-men-tal], *a.* Ambiental.

environs [ɪnˈvaɪərənz] [in-vaia-ronz], *s. pl.* Contornos, alrededores, cercanías o inmediaciones, el terreno o sitios de que está rodeado cualquier lugar o población; afueras, suburbios.

envoy [ˈenvɔɪ] [en-voi], *s.* Enviado, ministro público, inferior al embajador, mensajero.

envoyship [ˈenvɔɪʃɪp] [en-voi-ship], *s.* Legación, dignidad de enviado.

envy [ˈenvɪ] [en-vi], *va. y -vn.* 1. Envidiar, tener envidia, sentir el bien ajeno. 2. Envidiar, desear el goce del mismo bien que otro posee.

envy, *s.* Envidia; emulación; rencor.

envying [ˈenvɪɪŋ] [en-vi-in], *s.* Malicia, malignidad.

enwheel [ˈenwiːl] [en-uil], *va.* Rodear, circuir.

enwomb [ˈenwɒm] [en-wom], *va.* 1. *(Ant. y Poét.)* Sepultar o esconder en las entrañas o en lo más profundo de alguna cosa. 2. *(Des.)* Empreñar.

enwrap [ˈenwræp] [en-rap], *va.* Envolver.

enwrapment [ˈenwræpmənt] [en-rap-ment], *s.* Cubierta, envolvedor.

enwreathe [ˈenwriːθ] [en-vriz], *va.* Rodear como con una guirnalda.

enzymatic, enzymic [ˈenzɪmætɪk] [en-si-ma-tik], *a.* Enzimático.

enzyme [ˈenzaɪm] [en-saim], *s.* Enzima.

enzymology [ˈenzɪməlɒdʒɪ] [en-si-mo-lo-chi], *s.* Enzimología.

eocene [ˈiːəʊsiːn] [iou-sin], *a. (Geol.)* Eoceno, eocena; se dice de la capa más antigua de los terrenos terciarios. *-s.* Época eocena.

eolian [ˈiːəʊlɪən] [iou-lian], **eolic**, *a.* Eólico, uno de los cinco dialectos de la lengua griega. **Eolian harp**, arpa de Eolo, instrumento músico de cuerdas que suenan movidas por el viento.

eolipile [ˈiːəlɪpɪl] [io-li-pil], *s.* Eolípila, instrumento de física, esfera hueca de metal con un tubo, que sirve para hacer experimentos con el vapor.

eon o Aeon [ˈiːən] [ion], *s.* Eón, espacio incalculable de tiempo.

eosin [ˈiːəsɪn] [io-sin], *s.* Eosina, nombre de una materia colorante rojiza (CHBrO). Se obtiene del alquitrán de hulla.

epact [ˈɪpækt] [i-pakt] Epacta, el número de días en que el año solar excede al lunar común.

eparch [ˈɪpɑːtʃ] [i-parch], *s.* 1. Hiparcar, sátrapa, gobernador de una provincia griega. 2. Obispo ruso metropolitano u otro.

epaulet [ˈepɔːlet] [e-po-let], *s. (Mil.)* Charretera.

epaulement [ˈepɔːlmənt] [e-pol-ment], *s. (Fort.)* Espalda, espaldón.

epenetic [ˈepɪnətɪk] [e-pi-ne-tik], *a.* Laudatorio, panegírico.

epenthesis [ˈepɪnθɪsɪs] [e-pin-zi-sis], *s. (Gram.)* Epéntesis, interposición de una letra o sílaba en medio de una palabra.

epergne [ˈepɜːn] [e-pern], *s.* Centro de mesa, adorno para la mesa del comedor.

ephah [ˈefɑː] [e-fa], *s.* Efa, medida hebraica de una fanega.

ephemera [ɪˈfemərə] [i-fe-ma-ra], *s.* 1. Efémera o efímera, calentura que dura regularmente sólo un día. 2. Insecto efímero o que vive un solo día.

ephemeral [ɪˈfemərəl] [i-fe-me-ral], **ephemeric** [ɪˈfemərɪk] [i-fe-me-rik], *a.* Efímero, lo que empieza y acaba en un mismo día.

ephemerides [ɪˈfemərɪdɪs] [i-fe-me-ri-dis], *s. pl.* Efemérides o tablas astronómicas.

ephemeris [ɪˈfemərɪs] [i-fe-ma-ris], *s.* Efemérides, libro o comentario en que se refieren los hechos de cada día; diario.

ephemerist [ɪˈfemərɪst] [i-fe-ma-rist], *s.* Astrólogo.

ephemerous [ɪˈfemərəs] [i-fe-ma-ros], *a.* Efímero, efiemeral.

ephesian [ɪˈfemiːsɪən] [i-fi-sian], *a.* Efesino, efesina, de Efeso.

ephialtes [ɪˈfɪəltz] [i-fialts], *s.* Pesadilla, opresión nocturna. V. NIGHTMARE.

ephod [ˈefɒd] [e-fod], *s.* Efod, adorno de los sacerdotes hebreos.

ephor [ˈefɔːʳ] [e-foʳ], *s. (pl.* EPHORS y EFORI). Éforo, nombre que se daba en Esparta y otras ciudades dóricas a los cinco magistrados elegidos por el pueblo.

epi-. Preposición griega usada como prefijo. Quiere decir en, sobre, al lado de, etc. Delante de una vocal se convierte en ep- y en eph- delante de la inspiración fuerte.

epic [ˈepɪk] [e-pik], *a.* Épico, lo que pertenece a la epopeya o poesía heroica. *-s.* Poema épico o epopeya.

epicarp [ˈepɪkɑːp] [e-pi-karp], *s. (Bot.)* Epicarpo, la membrana que exteriormente cubre el pericarpio.

epicede, epicedium [ˈepɪsiːd] [e-pi-sid], *s.* Epicedio, elegía.

epicedian [ˈepɪsiːdɪən] [e-pi-si-dian], *a.* Elegíaco.

epicene [ˈepɪsiːn] [e-pi-sin], *a. (Gram.)* Epiceno; de género común.

epicenter [ˈepɪsentəʳ] [e-pi-sen-taʳ], *s.* 1. Epicentro. 2. Cualquier punto focal.

epicure [ˈepɪkjʊəʳ] [e-pi-kiuaʳ], *s.* Epicúreo.

epicurean [ˌepɪkjʊˈrɪən] [e-pi-kiu-rian], *a.* Epicúreo, el que se entrega a los placeres desordenadamente. *-s.* Sectario de Epicuro.

epicurism [ˈepɪkjʊərɪzm] [e-pi-kiua-ri-sem], *s.* Epicureísmo, sensualidad, la doctrina de Epicuro.

epicurize [ˈepɪkjʊraɪz] [e-pi-kiu-rais], *-vn.* Seguir la doctrina de Epicuro; deleitarse sensualmente; complacerse en el mal de otro.

epicycle [ˈepɪsaɪkl] [e-pi-sai-kol], *s.* Epiciclo, círculo cuyo centro se supone estar en la circunferencia de otro.

epicycloid ['epɪsɪklɔɪd] [e-pi-si-kloid], *s*. Epiciclode, curva descrita por el movimeinto de un círculo sobre la circunferencia de otro.

epidemic, epidemical [ˌepɪ'demɪk] [e-pi-de-mik], *a*. Epidémico, epidemial; general, universal. *-s*. Epidemia, enfermedad general, que se extiende a lo lejos.

epidemy ['epɪdemɪ] [e-pi-de-mi], *s*. Epidemia.

epidermal [ˌepɪ'dɜːməl] [e-pi-der-mal], *a*. Epidérmico, cuticular, de la epidermis.

epidermic, epidermical [ˌepɪ'dɜːmɪk] [e-pi-der-mik], *a*. Epidérmico, que cubre el cutis; semejante a la epidermis.

epidermis, epiderm [ˌepɪ'dɜːmɪs] [e-pi-der-mis], *s*. 1. Epidermis, cutícula. 2. *(Bot.)* Epidermis, capa exterior de celdillas que cubre la superficie de una planta.

epigastric [ˌepɪ'gæstrɪk] [e-pi-gas-trik], *a*. Epigástrico.

epigastrium [ˌepɪ'gæstrɪəm] [e-pi-gas-trium], *s*. Epigastrio, región superior del abdomen, especialmente la que queda sobre el estómago.

epigee ['epɪdʒiː] [e-pi-yi], *s*. Perigeo. *V.* PERIGEE.

epiglottis [ˌepɪ'glɒtɪs] [e-pi-glo-tis], *s*. Epiglotis, cartílago elástico, ovalado, que tapa la glotis al tiempo de la deglución.

epigram ['epɪgræm] [e-pi-gram], *s*. Epigrama.

epigrammatic, epigrammatical [ˌepɪɡrə'mætɪk] [e-pi-gra-ma-tik], *a*. Epigramático.

epigrammatist ['epɪgræmətɪst] [e-pi-gra-ma-tist], *s*. Epigramatista.

epigraph ['epɪgrɑːf] [e-pi-graf], *s*. 1. Epígrafe, título, inscripción. 2. Epígrafe, la sentencia que suelen poner los autores a la cabeza de una obra o de sus capítulos.

epilepsy ['epɪlepsɪ] [e-pi-lep-si], *s*. Epilepsia, gota coral, mal caduco.

epileptic, epileptical ['epɪleptɪk] [e-pi-lep-tik], *a*. Epiléptico.

epilogistic ['epɪlɒdʒɪstɪk] [e-pi-lo-chis-tik], *a*. Epiogal.

epilogize ['epɪlɒdʒaɪz] [e-pi-lo-chais], *va*. Dar epílogo; proveer de un epílogo. *-vn*. Epilogar; recitar un epílogo.

epilogue ['epɪlɒg] [e-pi-log], *s*. Epílogo, conclusión o peroración de un discurso, o de un poema dramático.

epinicion ['epɪnɪʃən] [e-pi-ni-shon], *s*. Himno de victoria.

epiphany [ɪ'pɪfənɪ] [i-pi-fa-ni], *s*. Epifanía, día de Reyes, festividad que celebra la Iglesia el seis de Enero, en conmemoración de la Adoración de los Reyes.

epiphonema [ˌepɪfə'nɪmə] [e-pi-fo-ni-ma], *s*. Epifonema, exclamación.

epiphora ['epɪfərə] [e-pi-fo-ra], *s*. Epifora, lagrimeo involuntario y repentino.

epiphyllospermous [ˌepɪfɪləs'pɜːməs] [e-pi-fi-los-per-mus], *a*. Epifilospermo o dorsífero; se dice de las plantas que tiene la semilla en el dorso de las hojas.

epiphysis [e'pɪfɪsɪs] [e-pi-fi-sis], *s*. *(Anat.)* Epífisis, eminencia huesosa, separada del cuerpo principal del hueso por una capa cartilaginosa.

epiphytal ['epɪfɪtəl] [e-pi-fi-tal], *a*. Epífito, que crece sobre otros vegetales sin que le sirvan de alimento.

epiphyte ['epɪfɪaɪt] [e-pi-fi-fait], *s*. Epífita, la planta no parásita que crece sobre otros vegetales.

episcopacy [ɪ'pɪskəpəsɪ] [i-pis-ko-pa-si], *s*. 1. Episcopado, el gobierno de una iglesia por obispos, especialmente por los órdenes de obispos, prebíteros y diáconos. 2. Episcopado, dignidad de obispo. 3. El conjunto de los obispos.

episcopal [ɪ'pɪskəpəl] [i-pis-ko-pal], *a*. 1. Episcopal, aquello cuyo gobierno se confía a los obispos. 2. Episcopal, perteneciente al obispo.

episcopalian [ɪ'pɪskəpəlɪən] [i-pis-ko-pa-lian], *a*. Episcopal, perteneciente a la Iglesia protestante episcopal, sus doctrinas, ceremonial, etc. *-s*. 1. Episcopal, el que no reconoce al Papa, y considera a cada obispo como cabeza de la iglesia. 2. Individuo de la Iglesia protestante episcopal.

episcopally [ɪ'pɪskəpəlɪ] [i-pis-ko-pa-li], *adv*. Episcopalmente.

episcopate [ɪ'pɪskəʊpət] [i-pis-kou-pat], *s*. Obispado.

episcopy [ɪ'pɪskəpɪ] [i-pis-ko-pi], *s*. Pesquisa, inspección.

episode ['epɪsɒd] [e-pi-soud], *s*. Episodio, digresión.

episodic, episodical ['epɪsəʊdɪk] [e-pi-sou-dik], *a*. Episódico.

epispastic ['epɪspæstɪk] [e-pis-pas-tik], *a*. y *s*. Epispástico; vejigatorio.

episperm ['epɪspɜːm] [e-pis-perm], *s*. *(Bot.)* Episperma, tegumento exterior que envuelve la semilla.

epistaxis ['epɪstæksɪs] [e-pis-tak-sis], *s*. Epistaxis, flujo de sangre por las narices.

epistemology [ɪˌpɪstə'mɒlədʒɪ] [i-pis-te-mo-lo-yi], *s*. Epistemología.

epistle [ɪ'pɪsl] [i-pisel], *s*. Epístola, carta. (Voz más formal que *letter*, y aplicada especialmente a las epístolas apostólicas).

epistler [ɪ'pɪslər] [i-pis-lar], *s*. Excritor de cartas; epistolero, el que lee o canta la epístola en el oficio divino.

epistolary [ɪ'pɪstələrɪ] [i-pis-to-la-ri], **epistolical** [ɪ'pɪstəlɪkl] [i-pis-to-li-kal], *a*. Epistolar.

epistrophe [ɪ'pɪstrəʊf] [i-pis-trouf], *s*. 1. *(Ret.)* Conversión. 2. *(Mús.)* Estribillo.

epistyle [ɪ'pɪstaɪl] [i-pis-tail], *s*. Epístilo, arquitrabe.

epitaph ['epɪtɑːf] [e-pi-taf], *s*. Epitafio.

epitaphian ['epɪtɑːfɪən] [e-pi-ta-fian], **epitaphic** ['epɪtɑːfɪk] [e-pi-ta-fik], *a*. Lo que pertenece al epitafio.

epitasis ['epɪtəsɪs] [e-pi-ta-sis], *s*. Epítasis, enredo, nudo, parte del poema dramático.

epithalamium ['epɪθələmɪəm] [e-pi-za-la-mium], *s*. Epitalamio, himno o canción nupcial.

epithelial ['epɪθelɪəl] [e-pi-ze-lial], *a*. Epitelial, relativo al epitelio.

epithelium ['epɪθelɪəm] [e-pi-ze-lium], *s*. *(Anat.)* Epitelio, capa o cubierta más superficial de las membranas mucosas; también la epidermis.

epithet ['epɪθet] [e-pi-zet], *s*. Epíteto.

epitome [ɪ'pɪtəmɪ] [i-pi-to-mi], *s*. Epítome, resumen, compendio.

epitomize [ɪ'pɪtəmaɪz] [i-pi-to-mais], *va*. Epitomar, abreviar, compendiar.

epitomizer [ɪ'pɪtəmaɪzər] [i-pi-to-mai-sar], **epitomist** [ɪ'pɪtəmɪst] [i-pi-to-mist], *s*. Abreviador, compendiador.

epitrope [ɪ'pɪtrəʊp] [i-pi-troup], *s*. *(Ret.)* Epítrope, concesón, figura por la que se concede una cosa, a fin de hacer admitir otra más importante.

epizootic [ɪ'pɪzuːtɪk] [i-pi-su-tik], *a*. Epizoótico. *-s*. Epizootia.

epizooty [ɪ'pɪzuːtɪ] [i-pi-su-ti], *s*. Epizootia, enfermedad contagiosa de los ganados.

epoch ['iːpɒk] [i-pok], **epocha**, *s*. Época, punto fijo y determinado de tiempo desde el cual se comienzan a numerar los años.

epode ['iːpəʊd] [i-poud], *s*. *(Poet.)* 1. Epodo, epoda, la última parte de la oda; y aunque sigue a la estrofa y antiestrofa. 2. Especie de composición lírica en la que un verso largo va seguido de uno corto.

epopee ['epəpɪ] [e-po-pi], *s*. Epopeya, poema épico

epsom salts ['epsəm'sɔːts] [ep-som-solts], *s, pl*. Epsomita, sal de Epsom, sal de Higuera, sulfato de magnesia.

epulotic [ɪ'pjʊlətɪk] [i-piu-lo-tik], *a*. Epulótico, cicatrizativo.

equability [ˌekwə'bɪlɪtɪ] [e-kua-bi-li-ti], *s*. Igualdad, uniformidad.

equable ['ekwəbl] [e-kua-bol], *a*. Igual, uniforme.

equableness ['ekwəblɪnɪs] [e-kua-bli-nes], *s*. *V.* EQUABILITY.

equably ['ekwəblɪ] [e-kua-bli], *adv*. Igualmente.

equal ['iːkwəl] [i-kual], *a*. 1. Igual, semejante. 2. Adecuado, propio para una cosa, en estado de. 3. Imparcial, justo, recto; neutral. 4. Indiferente. 5. Lo que es ventajoso a dos partes que tienen intereses contrarios. 6. *(Bot.)* Que tiene los dos lados semejantes, como las hojas; simétrico. *-s*. El que no es inferior ni superior a otro; igual.

equal, *va*. 1. Igualar, hacer igual una persona o cosa con otra. 2. Recompensar, compensar, satisfacer enteramente. **Not to be equalled**, sin igual.

equality [ɪˈkwɒlɪtɪ] [e-kua-li-ti], *s.* 1. Igualdad, uniformidad, semejanza perfecta. 2. Calidad de nivelado, nivel.

equalize, equalise [ˈiːkwəlaɪz] [i-kua-lais], *va. y vn.* Igualar.

equalization, equalisation [ˌiːkwəlaɪˈzeɪʃən] [i-kua-lai-sei-shon], *s.* Igualamiento.

equally [ˈiːkwəlɪ] [i-kua-li], *adv.* Igualmente; imparcialmente, uniformemente.

equalness [ˈiːkwəlnɪs] [i-kual-nes], *s.* Uniformidad, igualdad, ecuanimidad.

equanimity [ˌekwəˈnɪmɪtɪ] [e-kua-ni-mi-ti], *s.* Ecuanimidad, igualdad y serenidad de ánimo.

equanimous [ˈekwɒnɪməs] [e-kua-ni-mos], *a.* (Poco us.) Igual, constante.

equation [ɪˈkweɪʒən] [i-kuei-shon], *s.* Ecuación.

equator [ɪˈkweɪtər] [i-kuei-tar], *s.* Ecuador.

equatorial [ˌekwəˈtɔːrɪəl] [e-kua-to-rial], *a.* Ecuatorial, perteneciente al ecuador; relativo, cercano o determinado por un ecuador, especialmente el terrestre. -*s.* Ecuatorio, gran telescopio que gira sobre dos ejes en ángulo recto, uno de los cuales es paralelo al eje de la tierra; así se logra que un objeto dado permanezca constantemente en el campo del telescopio, a pesar del movimiento de rotación de la tierra.

equerry [ˈekwərɪ] [e-kua-ri], *s.* 1. Caballerizo del rey. 2. Establo, de un príncipe.

equestrian [ɪˈkwestrɪən] [i-kues-trian], *a.* Ecuestre.

equi- [ˈiːkwɪ] [i-kui], Forma de combinación.

equiangular [ˌiːkwɪˈæŋɡʊlər] [i-kui-an-gu-lar], *a.* Equiángulo.

equicrural [ˌiːkwɪˈkruərəl] [i-kui-krua-ral], *a.* Lo que tiene sus miembros o lados iguales; isósceles.

equidistance [ˈiːkwɪˈdɪstəns] [i-kui-dis-tans], *s.* Equidistancia.

equidistant [ˈiːkwɪˈdɪstənt] [i-kui-dis-tant], *a.* Equidistante.

equidistantly [ˈiːkwɪˈdɪstəntlɪ] [i-kui-dis-tant-li], *adv.* A la misma distancia.

equiformity [ˈiːkwɪˈfɔːmɪtɪ] [i-kui-for-mi-ti], *s.* Uniformidad.

equilateral [ˈiːkwɪˈlætərəl] [i-kui-la-te-ral], *a. y s.* Equilátero, de lados iguales.

equilibrate [ˈiːkwɪˈlɪbreɪt] [i-kui-li-breit], *va.* 1. Equilibrar. 2. Contrapesar.

equilibration [ˈiːkwɪˈlɪbreɪʃən] [i-kui-li-brei-shon], *s.* Equilibración; equilibrio.

equilibrious [ˈiːkwɪˈlɪbrɪəs] [i-kui-li-brios], *a.* Equilibre, que está equilibrado.

equilibriously [ˈiːkwɪˈlɪbrɪəslɪ] [i-kui-li-brios-li], *adv.* En equilibrio.

equilibrist [ˈiːkwɪˈlɪbrɪst] [i-kui-li-brist], *s.* El que equilibra.

equilibrity [ˈiːkwɪˈlɪbrɪtɪ] [i-kui-li-bri-ti], *s.* Equilibrio, igualdad de peso.

equilibrium [ˈiːkwɪˈlɪbrɪəm] [i-kui-li-briom], *s.* Equilibrio, la posición igual que guardan los dos extremos de una palanca o balanza; contrapeso.

equine [ˈekwaɪn] [ekuain], *a.* Caballuno, del caballo, que pertenece o se parece al caballo. -*s.* Caballo o animal parecido a él, como la cebra.

equinoctial [ˌiːkwɪˈnɒkʃəl] [i-kui-nok-shal], *a.* Equinoccial, lo perteneciente al equinoccio. -*s.* Línea equinoccial.

equinoctially [ˌiːkwɪˈnɒkʃəlɪ] [i-kui-nok-sha-li], *adv.* En dirección equinoccial.

equinox [ˈiːkwɪnɒks] [i-kui-dis-noks], *s.* Equinoccio, la entrada del sol en los puntos equinocciales.

equinumerant [ˈiːkwɪˈnjʊmərənt] [i-kui-niu-me-rant], *a.* Igual en número.

equip [ɪˈkwɪp] [i-kuip], *va.* Equipar, pertrechar, proveer de lo necesario. **To equip one with money**, dar a alguno el dinero que necesita. **To equip a ship**, aprestar un navío.

equipage [ɪˈkwɪpeɪdʒ] [i-kui-peich], *s.* 1. Equipaje, los artículos esenciales para un objeto o fin determinado, como el conjunto de ropas y objetos que se llevan en los viajes. V. EQUIPMENT, 3ª acep. 2. Carroza. 3. Tren, el aparato de criados, etc., que lleva un personaje en las funciones de pompa y ostentación.

equipaged [ɪˈkwɪpeɪdʒd] [i-kui-peichd], *a.* (*Ant.*) Equipado, aparejado; decorado espléndidamente.

equipendency [ɪˈkwɪpendənsɪ]w[i-kui-pen-den-si], *s.* Peso igual, equilibrio.

equipment [ɪˈkwɪpmənt] [i-kuip-ment], *s.* 1. Equipo, el acto de equipar. 2. Equipaje. 3. Apresto, hablando de buques; equipo o provisión para un objeto especial. 4. Fornitura, montura, uniformes.

equipoise [ˈiːkwɪpɔɪz] [i-kui-pois], *s.* 1. Equilibrio, igualdad de peso o de fuerza. 2. Contrapeso. V. COUNTERPOISE.

equipollence, equipollency [ɪˈkwɪpələns] [i-kui-po-lens], *s.* Equipolencia o equivalencia.

equipollent [ɪˈkwɪpələnt] [i-kui-po-lent], *a.* Equipolente o equivalente.

equipollently [ɪˈkwɪpələntlɪ] [i-kui-po-lent-li], *adv.* De un modo equivalente.

equiponderance, equiponderancy [ɪˈkwɪpɒndərəns] [i-kui-pon-de-rans], *s.* Igualdad de peso.

equiponderant [ɪˈkwɪpɒndərənt] [i-kui-pon-de-rant], *a.* Equiponderante.

equiponderate [ɪˈkwɪpɒndəreɪt] [i-kui-pon-de-reit], *vn.* Equiponderar, tener una cosa igual peso que otra.

equitable [ˈekwɪtəbl] [e-kui-ta-bol], *a.* Equitativo, justo, imparcial.

equitableness [ˈekwɪtəblnɪs] [e-kui-ta-bol-nes], *s.* Equidad, imparcialidad, justicia.

equitably [ˈekwɪtəblɪ] [e-kui-ta-bli], *adv.* Equitativamente.

equitancy [ˈekwɪtənsɪ] [e-kui-tan-si], *s.* Equitación.

equitant [ˈekwɪtənt] [e-kui-tant], *a.* (*Bot.*) Acaballado; se dice de la posición de las hojas de algunas plantas.

equitation [ˈekwɪteɪʃən] [e-kui-tei-shon], *s.* Equitación, el arte de montar a caballo; el manejo del caballo.

equity [ˈekwɪtɪ] [e-kui-ti], *s.* Equidad, justicia, rectitud, imparcialidad.

equivalence, equivalency [ɪˈkwɪvələns] [i-kui-va-lens], *s.* 1. Equivalencia. 2. (*Quím.*) V. ALENCE.

equivalent [ɪˈkwɪvələnt] [i-kui-va-lent], *a.* Equivalente. -*s.* Equivalente, lo que iguala a otra cosa.

equivalently [ɪˈkwɪvələntlɪ] [i-kui-va-lent-li], *adv.* Equivalentemente.

equivocal [ɪˈkwɪvəkəl] [i-kui-vo-kal], *a.* Equívoco, ambiguo, de doble sentido. -*s.* Equívoco.

equivocally [ɪˈkwɪvəkəlɪ] [i-kui-vo-ka-li], *adv.* Equivocadamente, ambiguamente.

equivocalness [ɪˈkwɪvəkəlnɪs] [i-kui-vo-kal-nes], *s.* Equívoco, voz o frase dudosa.

equivocate [ɪˈkwɪvəkeɪt] [i-kui-vo-keit], *vn.* Usar de palabras o frases equívocas o de expresiones ambiguas que pueden entenderse de dos maneras; prevaricar. -*va.* Equivocar.

equivocation [ɪˌkwɪvəˈkeɪʃən] [i-kui-vo-kei-shon], *s.* Equívoco, vocabo equívoco de que se usa para engañar o divertir; sentido equívoco, ambigüedad de una frase, anfibología.

equivocator [ɪˈkwɪvəkeɪtər] [i-kui-vo-kei-tor], *s.* El que usa de equívocos.

equivoke [ɪˈkwɪvəʊk] [i-kui-vouk], *s.* Equívoco.

-er [ər] [ar]. Sufijo usado (a) para formar nombres de cosa o persona agente, como -dor en español. **To do**, hacer; **doer**, hacedor. (b) Para formar el grado comparativo; *long*, largo; *longer*, más largo. (c) Para formar los verbos llamados en inglés frecuentativos y diminutivos. (d) Para denotar una persona (agente, etc.), sin derivación de un verbo, v. g. *pensioner*, pensionista.

era [ˈɪərə] [ia-ra], *s.* Era, época o fecha determinada desde la cual se empiezan a contar los años.

eradiate [ɪˈrædɪeɪt] [i-ra-dieit], *vn.* Radiar; centellar, relumbrar.

eradiation [ɪˈrædɪeɪʃən] [i-ra-diei-shon], *s.* Radiación; brillo, centelleo.

eradicate [ɪˈrædɪkeɪt] [i-ra-di-keit], *va.* Desarraigar, erradicar, destruir, extirpar.

eradication [ɪˌrædɪˈkeɪʃən] [i-ra-di-kei-shon], *s.* Erradicación, extirpación.

eradicative [ɪˈrədɪkətɪv] [i-ra-di-ka-tiv], *a.* Erradicativo, lo que tiene la virtud de desarraigar.

erasable, erasible [ɪˈreɪsəbl] [i-rei-sa-bol], *a.* Borrable, que se puede borrar, rayar, raspar, etc.

erase [ɪˈreɪz] [i-reis], *va.* 1. Cancelar, borrar, rayar, raspar, testar. 2. *(Des.) V.* RAZE.

erasement [ɪˈreɪzmənt] [i-reis-ment], *s. (Ant.)* Canceladura, testadura. *V.* ERASURE.

eraser [ɪˈreɪzəʳ] [i-rei-saʳ], *s.* 1. Borrador, goma de borrar. 2. Raspador.

erasion [ɪˈreɪʒən] [i-rei-shon], *s.* Raspadura, borradura, canceladura; acción de borrar.

erasure [ɪˈreɪʒəʳ] [i-rei-shaʳ], *s.* Raspadura, acción y efecto de raspar, o lo que se quita de la superficie raspando.

ere [eəʳ] [eaʳ], *adv.* Antes, más pronto, más presto, antes que, más bien que. *-prep.* Antes de.

erebus [ˈeəbʌs] [ea-bas], *s. (Mitol.)* Erebo, el infierno; obscuridad, tenebrosidad.

erect [ɪˈrekt] [i-rekt], *va.* 1. Erigir, levantar, poner a plomo. 2. Construir, edificar; establecer. 3. Exaltar, elevar, alzar a una posición determinada o más elevada. 4. Dibujar sobre una base o plan, como un diseño arquitectónico o una figura geométrica. *-vn.* Erigirse, enderezarse, ponerse derecho.

erect, *a.* 1. Derecho, levantado hacia arriba, erguido, vertical. 2. Audaz, osado; vigoroso; vigilante, atento. 3. Firme. **To sit erect**, sentarse derecho. **To stand erect**, estar en pie.

erectile [ɪˈrektaɪl] [i-rek-tail], *a.* Eréctil, capaz de enderezarse o ponerse en erección.

erection [ɪˈrekʃən] [i-rek-shon], *s.* Erección, elevación, el acto o procedimiento de edificar o construir; fundación, construcción; estructura.

erective [ɪˈrektɪv] [i-rek-tiv], *a.* Levantado, lo que está alzado.

erectness [ɪˈrektnɪs] [i-rekt-nes], *s.* Erección, postura derecha.

erector [ɪˈrektəʳ] [i-rek-toʳ], *s.* 1. Erector, el que o lo que erige, levanta o endereza, v. gr. un arquitecto, un músculo. 2. Lente de inversión.

erelong [ˈtəlɒŋ] [ia-lon], *adv.* Antes de mucho, dentro de poco tiempo.

eremite [ˈrɪmaɪt] [i-ri-mait], *s.* Ermitaño.

eremitage [ɪˈrɪmɪteɪdʒ] [i-ri-mi-teich], *s.* Ermita.

eremitic, eremitical [ɪˈrɪmɪtɪk] [i-ri-mi-tik], *a.* Eremítico, solitario.

erenow [ɪˈrɪnəʊ] [i-ri-nou], *adv.* Antes de ahora.

ereption [ɪˈrepʃən] [i-rep-shon], *s.* Arrebato; el acto de arrebatar alguna cosa.

erethism [ˈɪrɪθɪzm] [i-ri-zi-sem], *s. (Med.)* Eretismo, exaltación anormal de las propiedades vitales de un órgano.

erewhile, erewhiles [ˈɪrɪwaɪl] [i-ri-uails], *adv.* Rato ha, poco ha.

erg [ɜːg] [erg], *s. (Fís.)* Ergio, unidad medidora de trabajo y energía, que representa el esfuerzo necesario para mover un cuerpo del peso de dos gramos a razón de un centímetro por segundo.

ergo [ˈɜːgəʊ] [er-gou], *adv.* Consiguientemente, luego; la conclusión de un argumento. Es voz latina.

ergonomics [ˌɜːgəˈnɒmɪks] [er-go-no-miks] *s.* Ergonomía (field of study).

ergot [ˈɜːgət] [er-got], *s.* 1. Cornezuelo de centeno; honguillo parásito en forma de cuerno. 2. *(Vet.)* Especie de espolón en las patas de los caballos.

ergotism [ˈɜːgətɪʒm] [er-go-ti-sem], *s.* 1. *(Med.)* Ergotismo, estado de envenenamiento por el cornezuelo de centeno; enfermedad producida por cantidades excesivas del mismo. 2. Conclusión deducida silogísticamente.

eriach [ˈerɪək] [e-riak], **eric** [ˈerɪk] [e-rik], *s.* Multa pecuniaria.

erica [ˈerɪkə] [e-ri-ka], *s. (Bot.) V.* HEATH.

erinaceous [ˈerɪneɪʃəs] [e-ri-nei-shos], *a.* Del erizo o parecido a él.

eringo [ɪˈrɪŋɡəʊ] [i-rin-gou], *s. (Bot.)* Eringe, cardo corredor.

eristic [ɪˈrɪstɪk] [i-ris-tik], *a.* 1. Erístico, relativo a la controversia. 2. Pendenciero.

eritrea [erəˈtreɪə] [e-ri-tria] *N. (Geogr.)* Eritrea.

eritrean [errˈtreɪən] [e-ri-trian] *a.* Eritreo.

ermelin [ˈɜːməlɪn] [er-me-lin], *s. (Ant.) V.* ERMINE.

ermine [ˈɜːmɪn] [er-min], *s.* 1. Armiño, cuadrúpedo pequeño, de piel muy suave. 2. La piel de este animal. 3. Toga oficial o dignidad de un juez; pureza ideal del cargo judicial.

ermined [ˈɜːmɪnd] [er-mind], *a.* Armiñado.

erode [ɪˈrəʊd] [i-roud], *va.* 1. Corroer (acid, metal); roer; comer. Minar, socavar (confidence, faith). 2. *(Geol.)* Gastar, por medio de diversos agentes. Erosionar (water, wind, waves).

erodent [ɪˈrəʊdənt] [i-rou-dent], *a. (Med.)* Corrosivo, cáustico (hablando de un medicamento).

erogenous zone [ɪˈrɒdʒənəsˌzəʊn] [i-ro-chi-nos-soun] *a.* Zona erógena.

erosion [ɪˈrəʊʒən] [i-rou-shon], *s.* 1. Erosión (by water, wind, waves); corrosión (by acid); menoscabo, deterioro (of confidence, power, rights). 2. *(Geol.)* La acción de gastar o roer las rocas, como por medio del agua.

erosive [ɪˈrəʊzɪv] [i-rou-siv], *a.* Que obra por erosión, que tiene la facultad de roer o gastar; erosivo.

erotic, erotical [ɪˈrɒtɪk] [i-ro-tik], *a.* Erótico, amatorio.

erotica [ɪˈrɒtɪkə] [i-ro-ti-ka] *s.* Literatura erótica (literature); arte erótico (art).

eroticism [ɪˈrɒtɪsɪzəm] [i-ro-ti-si-zem] *s.* Erotismo.

eroticize [ɪˈrɒtɪsaɪz] [i-ro-ti-sais] *vt.* Erotizar.

erotomania [ɪˌrɒtəʊˈmeɪnɪə] [i-ro-to-mei-nia], *s.* Erotomanía, delirio causado por el amor.

erpetology [ˈɜːpəˈtələdʒɪ] [er-pe-to-lo-chi], *s. V.* HERPETOLOGY.

err [ɜːʳ] [aʳ], *vn.* 1. Vagar, errar; desviarse. 2. Extraviarse, apartarse del buen camino, pecar. 3. Errar, no dar en el blanco, no acertar. **To err on the side of caution**, pecar de cauteloso o por exceso de precaución. **To err is human**, errar es de humanos.

errable [ˈerəbl] [e-ra-bol], *a.* Falible, capaz de errar.

errand [ˈerənd] [e-rand], *s.* 1. Recado, mensaje, mandado (short mission). **To run an errand for somebody**, hacerle un mandado o un recado a alguien. **Errand-boy**, muchacho para hacer mandados. 2. Misión (task). **An errand of mercy**, una misión de caridad o auxilio. **What errand brings you here?**, ¿qué le trae por aquí?

errant [ˈerənt] [e-rant], *a.* 1. Errante, ambulante, vagabundo, vago. 2. Inconstante; vil, abandonado; descarriado (child); infiel (husband). **Knight-errant**, caballero andante.

errantry [ˈerəntrɪ] [e-ran-tri], *s.* Vida errante; caballería andante.

errata [eˈrɑːtə] [e-ra-ta], *s. pl. V.* ERRATUM.

erratic, erratical [ɪˈrætɪk] [i-ra-tik], *a.* Errático (course), errante, vagante, vagabundo; irregular, desigual (performance, work); imprevisible (person, moods). **Erratic**, *s. (Des.)* Pícaro.

erratically [ɪˈrætɪkəlɪ] [i-ra-ti-ka-li], *adv.* Erradamente; irregularmente.

erratum [ɪˈrætəm] [i-ra-tum], (*pl.* ERRATA), *s.* Errata, equivocación que se halla en lo impreso o escrito. *-pl.* Erratas, fe de erratas.

errhine [eˈriːn] [e-rin], *s.* Errino, remedio tomado por la nariz.

erring [eˈrɪŋ] [e-rin], *a.* Errado, errante.

erroneous [ɪˈrəʊnɪəs] [i-rou-nios], *a.* 1. Errado, falso, erróneo. 2. Irregular, no de acuerdo con la forma legal.

erroneously [ɪˈrəʊnɪəslɪ] [i-rou-nios-li], *adv.* Erróneamente.

erroneousness [ɪˈrəʊnɪəsnɪs] [i-rou-nios-nes], *s.* Error.

error [ˈerəʳ] [e-roʳ], *s.* Error, yerro, equivocación, engaño, descuido; pecado. **By error**, por error. **A clerical/printer's error**, un error administrativo/de imprenta. **To make an error**, cometer un error. **To see the error of one's ways**, darse cuenta de que se ha actuado mal. **Errors and omissions excepted**, salvo error u omisión.

ersatz [ˈɛəzæts] [ea-sachs], *a.* Sintético. **Ersatz fur**, imitación de piel, piel sintética. **Ersatz coffee**, sucedáneo o sustituto del café.

erse [ɜːs] [ers], *s.* Lenguaje de los montañeses de Escocia.

erst [ɜːst] [erst], *adv. (Ant. o Poét.)* Primero, primeramente, al principio, antiguamente, antes; hasta entonces, hasta ahora.

erstwhile [ˈɜːstwaɪl] [erst-uail], *adv.* Hasta entonces; en otro tiempo. *-a.* Antiguo.

erubescence, erubescency [ˈerjʊbəsəns] [e-riu-be-sens], *s.* Erubescencia, rubor.

erubescent [ˈerjʊbəsənt] [e-riu-be-sent], *a.* Colorado; sonrojado, abochornado.

eruct [ɪˈrʌkt] [i-rakt], *va.* Eructar, regoldar.

eructate [ˈɪrʌkteɪt] [i-rak-teit], *va. (Ant.)* Eructar; vomitar.

eructation [ˈɪrʌkteɪʃən] [i-rak-tei-shon], *s.* Eructación, eructo, regüeldo.

erudite [ˈerɪdaɪt] [e-riu-dait], *a.* Erudito, instruído, sabio.

erudition [ˌerʊˈdɪʃən] [e-riu-di-shon], *s.* Erudición, ciencia, doctrina.

eruginous [ˈerjʊdʒɪnəs] [e-riu-yi-nos], *a.* Ruginoso, de color de cardenillo, o parecido al moho del cobre; lo que participa del cobre.

erupt [ɪˈrʌpt] [i-rapt], *vn.* 1. Hacer erupción, entrar en erupción (volcano, geyser). 2. Salir o manar a chorros (water). 3. Estallar (break out/violence, fighting). **He erupted with anger at the news**, estalló en cólera al oír la noticia. **To erupt into a house**, irrumpir en una casa.

eruption [ɪˈrʌpʃən] [i-rap-shon], *s.* 1. Erupción (of volcano); emisión, salida. Brote (of violence); estallido (of anger). 2. Erupción cutánea. 3. Excursión hostil.

eruptive [ɪˈrʌptɪv] [i-rap-tiv], *a.* 1. Eruptivo, que estalla. 2. De, o perteneciente a, la acción volcánica. 3. *(Med.)* Eruptivo, que produce una erupción cutánea.

eryngo [ɪˈrɪŋɡəʊ] [i-rin-gou], *s. (Bot.)* Eringe, cardo corredor.

erysipelas [ˌerɪˈsɪpɪləs] [e-ri-si-pi-las], *s.* Erisipela, afección inflamatoria exantemática o de la piel.

erysipelatous [ˌerɪˈsɪpɪlətəs] [e-ri-si-pi-la-tos], *a.* Erisipelatoso, lo que tiene las calidades de la erisipela o se asemeja a ella.

erythrocyte [ɪˈrɪθrəʊˌsaɪt] [i-ri-si-zrou-sait], *s.* Eritrocito.

escadrille [ˈeskədriːl] [es-ka-dril], *s.* 1. Escuadrilla naval. 2. Escuadrilla aérea.

escalade [ˈeskəleɪd] [es-ka-leid], *s.* Escalada, la acción de escalar o poner escalas en los muros.

escalate [ˈeskəleɪt] [es-ka-leit], *va.* Intensificar (fighting, tension); aumentar (demands). *vn.* Intensificarse (fighting, violence, dispute). Aumentar (prices, claims). **The scuffles escalated into a riot**, las refriegas terminaron en serios disturbios callejeros. **Escalating**, creciente (dispute, tension).

escalation [ˈeskəleɪʃən] [es-ka-lei-shon], *s.* Intensificación (of dispute); aumento (of prices). Escalada (of war, violence).

escalator [ˈeskəleɪtəʳ] [es-ka-lei-toʳ], *s.* Escalera mecánica.

escalop [ˈeskəlɒp] [es-ka-lop], *s.* 1. *(Conq.)* Pechina, venera de peregrino. 2. Las desigualdades en forma de puntas o dientes en los bordes de alguna cosa. *V.* SCALLOP.

escalope [ˈeskəlɒp] [es-ka-lop] *sm.* Escalope.

escapade [ˌeskəˈpeɪd] [es-ka-peid], *s.* 1. Escapada, travesura, campanada, extravagancia, acción inconsiderada (strangeness, piece of mischief). 2. Escapada, salida oculta, fuga, huída (escape, flight). 3. Escapada, el acto de dar manotadas y brincos el caballo que caracolea.

escape [ɪsˈkeɪp] [is-keip], *va.* Huir, evitar; escapar; eludir. Escaparse o librarse de (pursuer, police); salvarse de, escapar a (capture); librarse de (responsibilities, consequences). **They escaped punishment/prosecution**, se libraron de ser castigados/juzgados. **The name escapes me**, no puedo recordar el nombre. *-vn.* 1. Escapar, salir de algún aprieto o peligro, sustraerse, evadirse, salvarse. Escaparse (flee); fugarse, escaparse (prisoner). **To escape from something**, escapar(se) o fugarse de algo (from prison); escaparse de algo (from cage/zoo); escapar de algo (from

danger, routine). 2. Salvarse (from accident, danger). **She escaped with minor injuries**, sólo sufrió heridas leves.

escape, *s.* 1. Escapada, huída, fuga (from prison). **To make one's escape**, escaparse. **Escape attempt**, intento de fuga. 2. Descuido, inadvertencia. 3. Avería, pérdida, merma de un líquido que sale por una abertura. Escape, fuga (of gas, water, air). **Escape valve**, válvula de escape. **Escape hatch**, escotilla de salvamento. 4. Escapatoria, los medios de fuga o de rescate. 5. Evasión (from reality). *(Inform.)* **Press escape**, pulse u oprima la tecla de escape. De escape (key, routine). **To have a narrow/miraculous escape**, salvarse o escaparse por muy poco/milagrosamente. **Escape chute**, rampa de emergencia. **There is no escape**, no hay escapatoria posible. **Escape artist**, escapista. **Escape clause**, cláusula de escape o evasión.

escape capsule [ˌɪskeɪpˈkæpsjɒ] [is-keip-kap-siul], *s. (Aer.)* Cápsula de emergencia.

escaped [ɪsˈkeɪpt] [is-keipt] *a.* Huído, fugado (from prison).

escapee [ɪskerˈpiː] [is-kei-pi] *s.* Fugitivo.

escapement [ɪsˈkeɪpmənt] [is-keip-ment], *s.* Escape, en relojería.

escaper [ɪsˈkeɪpəʳ] [is-kei-paʳ], *s.* El que escapa o evita.

escaping [ɪsˈkeɪpɪŋ] [is-kei-pin], *s.* Escape.

escapism [ɪsˈkeɪpɪzəm] [is-kei-pi-sem], *s.* Escapismo.

escapist [ɪsˈkeɪpɪst] [is-kei-pist], *s.* Soñador, fantaseador. *a.* Escapista.

escapologist [ˌeskəˈpɒlədʒɪst] [es-ka-po-lo-chist] *s.* Escapista.

escarp [ɪsˈkɑːp] [is-karp], *va. (Mil.)* Escarpar, hacer escarpa.

escarpment [ɪsˈkɑːpmənt] [is-karp-ment], *s.* Escarpa, el declive áspero de cualquier terreno.

eschar [ɪsˈkɑːʳ] [is-kaʳ], *s.* Escar, costra o postilla producida por la mortificación o la cauterización.

escharotic [ɪsˈkɑːrətɪk] [is-ka-ro-tik], *a.* Escarótico. *-s.* Cáustico.

eschatology [ˌeskəˈtɒlədʒɪ] [es-ka-to-lo-yi] *f. (Rel.)* Escatología.

escheat [ɪsˈkiːt] [is-kit], *s. (For.)* Derecho a la sucesión o herencia de una persona por caducidad, confiscación o falta de herederos legítimos.

escheat, *va.* 1. Confiscar, caducar a favor del fisco. *-vn.* 2. Adquirir el derecho a la sucesión o a la herencia de una propiedad, por confiscación, caducación o falta de herederos legítimos.

eschew [ɪsˈtʃuː] [is-chu], *va.* Huir, evitar, abstenerse de, evadir.

escort [ˈeskɔːt] [es-kort], *s.* 1. Escolta (guard); convoy. **Under police/naval escort**, escoltado por la policía/la armada. De escolta (vessel, carrier, fighter). 2. El que por cortesía acompaña a una mujer; acompañante, caballero (male companion); señorita de compañía (hired companion/woman); acompañante (man). **Escort agency**, agencia de acompañantes.

escort, *va.* 1. Escoltar, convoyar, resguardar (for protection/ politician, procession, ship). 2. Acompañar (accompany); llevar, conducir (prisoner, intruder).

escritoire [ˌeskrɪˈtʃwəʳ] [es-kri-tuaʳ], *s.* Escritorio, mesa para escribir.

escrow [ˈeskrəʊ] [es-krou], *s. (For.)* Plica, escrito sellado referente a alguna condición o requisito.

escudo [esˈkuːdəʊ] [es-ku-dou] *s.* Escudo.

esculapian [ɪsˈkjɒlæpɪən] [is-kiu-la-pian], *a.* Medicinal, referente a Esculapio, dios de la medicina o al arte de curar.

esculent [ɪsˈkjɒlənt] [is-kiu-lent], *a. y s.* Comestible; comedero.

escutcheon [ɪsˈkʌtʃən] [is-ka-chan], *s.* Escudo de armas.

escutcheoned [ɪsˈkʌtʃənd] [is-ka-chand], *a.* Blasonado.

eskimo, eskimau [ˈeskɪməʊ] [es-ki-mou], *s.* Esquimal, habitante de la región boreal de la América del Norte.

esophagus [ɪˈsɒfəɡəs] [i-so-fa-gus], *s.* Esófago, conducto por donde pasan la comida y bebida al estómago.

esopian [ɪˈsəʊpɪən] [i-sou-pian], *a.* Esópico, lo tocante a Esopo.

esoteric [ˌesəʊˈterɪk] [e-sou-te-rik], *a*. Esotérico, que se enseña a un número limitado de discípulos y es conocido solamente por ellos: de aquí, oculto, reservado; confidencial.

esoterism [ˌesɒtəˈrɪzəm] [e-so-te-ri-sem], *s*. Doctrinas o principios esotéricos; lo oculto.

espadrille [ˌespəˈdrɪl] [es-pa-dril] *s*. Alpargata.

espalier [ɪˈspælɪəʳ] [is-pa-liaʳ], *s*. 1. Espaldera, armazón de madera para servir de apoyo a ciertos árboles y plantas enredaderas. 2. Espaldera, cierta dirección dada a los árboles por medio de la poda.

espalier, *va*. (*Jard.*) Hacer o formar espalderas.

especial [ɪsˈpeʃəl] [is-pe-shal], *a*. Especial, particular; principal.

especially [ɪsˈpeʃəlɪ] [is-pe-sha-li], *adv*. Especialmente, principalmente, sobre todo. **Why did you choose that one especially?**, ¿por qué escogió ése precisamente o en particular? **Everyone was bored, especially me**, estaba todo el mundo aburrido, sobre todo yo o especialmente yo. **He especially ought to know**, él debería saberlo más que nadie.

esperanto [ˌespəˈræntəʊ] [es-pe-ran-tou] *s*. Esperanto.

espial [ɪsˈpaɪəl] [is-paial], *s*. Espía; observación, descubrimiento.

espier [ɪsˈpaɪəʳ] [is-paiaʳ], *s*. Espiador, espía, espiante.

espionage [ˌespɪəˈnɑːdʒ] [es-pio-nash], *s*. Espionaje, la acción de espiar; el empleo de espías.

esplanade [ˌespləˈneɪd] [es-pla-neid], *s*. 1. Espacio llano y abierto, en especial a los bordes del agua, para pasear a pie o en coche. 2. (*Fort.*) Explanada. 3. V. LAWN.

espousal [ɪˈspaʊzl] [is-pou-sal], *s*. 1. Desposorio. 2. Adopción, protección. -*a*. Esponsalicio. **Espousals**, -*pl*. esponsales.

espouse [ɪˈspaʊz] [is-pou-sa], *va*. y *vn*. 1. Desposar o desposarse, contraer esponsales (marry). 2. Casarse, contraer matrimonio (to get married). 3. Defender, sostener, adoptar; apoyar, propugnar (plan). 4. Adherirse a (cause).

espouser [ɪˈspaʊzəʳ] [is-pou-saʳ], *s*. Mantenedor, soportador, defensor de alguna causa.

espresso [esˈpresəʊ] [es-pre-sou] *s*. Café exprés, expreso.

esprit [ˈespriː] [es-pri], *s*. 1. Espíritu. 2. Chiste, agudeza, gracia. (*Gal.*)

espy [ɪsˈpaɪ] [is-pai], *va*. Divisar, acechar; averiguar, percibir, descubrir; espiar. -*vn*. (*Des.*) Velar, mirar alrededor.

esquimau (*pl.* ESQUIMAUX) *s*. V. ESKIMO.

esquire [ɪsˈkwaɪəʳ] [is-kuaiaʳ], *s*. 1. Escudero; título de honor en Inglaterra, como el de *Don* en España. 2. En Inglaterra, dueño de bienes raíces, propietario de provincia. V. SQUIRE.

esquire, *va*. Servir como escudero.

essay [ˈeseɪ] [e-sei], *va*. 1. Ensayar, tentar, intentar, probar, examinar (try, task). 2. Hacer prueba o ensayo de alguna cosa.

essay, *s*. 1. Conato, empeño, esfuerzo. 2. Ensayo, tentativa; obra suelta, ensayo (literary composition); obra o pieza irregular; trabajo, ensayo (academic composition); composición, redacción (language exercise). 3. Ensaye, prueba, experiencia.

essayer [ˈeseɪəʳ] [e-seiaʳ], *s*. Ensayista, escritor de ensayos u obras sueltas.

essayist [ˈeseɪɪst] [e-sei-ist] *s*. Ensayista.

essence [ˈesəns] [e-sens], *s*. 1. Esencia, el ser y naturaleza de las cosas (central feature, quality). **In essence**, en esencia, fundamentalmente, principalmente. **Of the essence**, de fundamental importancia **In essence**, principalmente, fundamentalmente. 2. Esencia, cierto licor espirituoso; perfume, aceite volátil. 3. Personificación (personification). **He's the very essence of a diplomat**, es la diplomacia personificada, es la personificación de la diplomacia. 4. (*Culin.*) **Vanilla essence o essence of vanilla**, esencia de vainilla.

essenes [ˈesiːnz] [e-sins], *s. pl.* Esenianos, una secta de judíos.

essential [ɪˈsenʃəl] [i-sen-shal], *s*. Esencia. Imperativo, elemento esencial (something indispensable). **She brought only the bare essentials**, trajo sólo lo imprescindible. **Essentials**, *pl*. puntos esenciales o fundamentales (fundamental features). -*a*. Esencial, substancial, principal, importante, notable; puro, rectificado. **It is essential that/to**, es necesario/imprescindible que. **The essential thing**, lo esencial.

essentiality [ɪˌsenʃəˈlɪtɪ] [i-sen-sha-li-ti], *s*. Esencialidad, naturaleza, los principios constituyentes.

essentially [ɪˈsenʃəlɪ] [i-sen-sha-li], *adv*. Esencialmente, fundamentalmente; en lo esencial, esencialmente (indep).

essoin [ɪˈsɔɪn] [i-soin], *s*. (Derecho inglés) Excusa, exención; alegación de una persona legalmente citada para no comparecer en juicio.

essoin, *va*. (*For.*) Excusar, disculpar.

essoiner [ɪˈsɔɪnəʳ] [i-soi-naʳ], *s*. (*For.*) Excusador, disculpador.

establish [ɪsˈtæblɪʃ] [is-ta-blish], *va*. 1. Establecer, fundar (colony, community, company); fijar, erigir; instituir, crear (committee, fund). 2. Afirmar, confirmar. 3. Probar, demostrar, establecer (prove/guilty, innocence); establecer (ascertain/motive, fact, identity). 4. Ratificar, sancionar. 5. Establecer (criteria, procedure, diplomatic relations). **To establish oneself**, establecerse (person). **To establish that**, comprobar, constatar que. **To establish itself**, consolidarse, arraigar.

established [ɪsˈtæblɪʃt] [is-ta-blisht] *a*. 1. De reconocido prestigio (expert, company, person); de renombre (star); sólido (reputation); establecido (practice); comprobado (fact). 2. Oficial (church, religion).

establisher [ɪsˈtæblɪʃəʳ] [is-ta-bli-shaʳ], *s*. Establecedor.

establishment [ɪsˈtæblɪʃmənt] [is-ta-blish-ment], *s*. 1. Establecimiento, ley, ordenanza, estatuto. **The literary establishment**, las figuras consagradas del mundo literario (ruling group). 2. Fundación (of colony, business); creación (of committee); establecimiento (of criteria, relations); erección, institución; algo establecido, como la iglesia de un estado, una organización militar o naval, etc. 3. Establecimiento, la colocación o suerte estable de una persona; asiento, domicilio. 4. Renta, salario, fortuna que se da o proporciona a una persona. 5. El modo como está constituída una familia. 6. Estableci-miento (club, hotel, shop). **Research establishment**, centro de investigación.

estafet [ɪsˈtæfɪt] [is-ta-fit], *s*. Estafeta, correo militar.

estate [ɪsˈteɪt] [is-teit], *s*. 1. Estado, el público, el interés general de alguna nación. 2. Estado, rango, la condición o calidad de una persona con respecto a sus circunstancias en general. 3. Caudal, bienes, propiedad, fortuna, hacienda, finca (land, property). **Man's estate**, la edad viril. **Personal estate**, bienes muebles. **She left a large estate**, dejó una gran fortuna. **Real estate**, bienes raíces o inmuebles. **Third estate**, el estado llano. **Fourth estate**, (jocoso), la prensa periódica; antiguamente la clase baja del estado llano. 4. (Law) Patrimonio; sucesión (of deceased person).

estate, *va*. Dotar, dar o señalar algún caudal o hacienda; establecer, fijar.

estate agent [ɪsˈteɪtˌeɪdʒənt] [is-teit-ei-yent] *s*. Agente de la propiedad inmobiliaria.

esteem [ɪsˈtiːm] [is-tim], *va*. 1. Estimar, valorar (quality); apreciar, considerar, honrar, reputar, contemplar, tener en gran estima (person). 2. Pensar, juzgar, ser de opinión. -*vn*. Apreciarse, reputarse, tenerse por.

esteem, *s*. Estimación, estima, aprecio. **I hold him in high/ great esteem**, lo aprecio mucho, lo tengo en gran estima. **He's gone down in my esteem since that incident**, desde que pasó aquello no le tengo la misma estima.

esteemable [ɪsˈtiːməbl] [is-ti-ma-bol], *a*. Estimable.

esteemed [ɪsˈtiːmd] [is-timd] *a*. Estimado.

esteemer [ɪsˈtiːməʳ] [is-ti-maʳ], *s*. Estimador.

ester [ˈestəʳ] [es-taʳ], *s*. (*Quím.*) Éster.

esthete, esthete [ˈiːsθiːt] [is-zit], *s*. Esteta, partidario o admirador del arte o de la estética.

esthetic, aesthetic ['iːsθiːtɪk] [is-zi-tik], *a.* Estético, estética, perteneciente a la ciencia de lo bello.

esthetical ['iːsθiːtɪkl] [is-zi-ti-kal], *a. V.* ESTHETIC.

esthetically, aesthetically ['iːsθiːtɪklɪ] [is-zi-ti-ka-li], *adv.* Estéticamente, de una manera estética.

esthetics, aesthetics ['iːsθiːtɪks] [is-zi-tiks], *s.* Estética, la ciencia que trata de la investigación y determinación de lo bello en la naturaleza y en el arte.

estimable ['estɪməbl] [es-ti-ma-bol], *a.* Estimable, digno de estimación, de aprecio.

estimableness ['estɪməblnɪs] [es-ti-ma-bol-nes], *s.* Estimabilidad, aprecio.

estimate ['estɪmɪt] [es-ti-meit], *va.* 1. Estimar, apreciar, tasar; calcular, computar (calculate aproximately/price, number, age). **The company estimates its losses at 7 million**, la compañía calcula que ha sufrido pérdidas del orden de 7 millones. 2. Juzgar, valorar (form judgment of/outcome, ability). 3. **Estimated**, aproximado (cost/speed). **Estimated time of arrival**, hora de llegada prevista.

estimate, *s.* 1. Estimación, tasa, aprecio. 2. Cálculo, cómputo (rough calculation); concierto; (*Neg.*) presupuesto (of costs). **At a rough estimate**, aproximadamente, haciendo un cálculo aproximado. 3. Opinión.

estimation [estɪ'meɪʃən] [es-ti-mei-shon], *s.* 1. Estimación, calculación, valuación; honra. 2. Estimación. **To go up/down in somebody's estimation**, ganarse o perder la estima de alguien (esteem). 3. Opinión, juicio (judgment, opinion). **In my estimation**, a mi juicio.

estimative ['estɪmətɪv] [es-ti-ma-tiv], *a.* 1. Estimativo. 2. Lo que compara el valor o la estimación que debe darse a cosas diferentes entre sí para hallar cuál es la más apreciable o de más valor.

estimator ['estɪmeɪtər] [es-ti-mei-tar], *s.* Estimador, computista.

estival ['estɪvəl] [es-ti-val], *a.* Estival, lo que pertenece al estío o verano; veraniego; estivo, lo que dura todo el estío.

estivate ['estɪveɪt] [es-ti-veit], *vn.* Veranear, pasar el verano.

estivation ['estɪveɪʃən] [es-ti-vei-shon], *s.* 1. El acto de pasar el tiempo de estío. 2. (*Zool.*) Descanso de ciertos animales durante el estío. 3. (*Bot.*) Prefloración, arreglo de las partes de una flor en la yema.

estonia [e'stəʊnɪə] [es-tou-nia] *N.* (*Geogr.*) Estonia.

estonian [e'stəʊnɪən] [es-tou-nian] *a./s.* Estonio (person/language).

estop [es'tɒp] [es-top], *va.* 1. (*For.*) Impedir en un procedimiento judicial la afirmación de lo que es contrario a los actos y admisiones hechos previamente. 2. Excluir o anular uno mismo su demanda en virtud del propio acto o declaración anterior.

estoppel [es'tɒpəl] [es-to-pel], *s.* 1. (*For.*) Impedimento, excepción, la acción o admisión que no puede ser negada legalmente. 2. Obstáculo, oposición.

estovers [es'tɒvəz] [es-to-vers], *s. pl.* (*Der. inglés*) Señalamiento o asignación de asistencias, alimentos, etc., por auto de un tribunal.

estrade [es'treɪd] [es-treid], *s.* 1. Estrado, tarima. *V.* DAIS. 2. (*Mil.*) Estrada.

estrange [ɪs'treɪndʒ] [is-treinch], *va.* Estrañar, apartar, enajenar (separate, divide). **She's estranged from her husband**, vive o está separada de su marido. **His estranged wife**, su mujer, de quien está separado.

estrangement [ɪs'treɪndʒmənt] [is-treinch-ment], *s.* Enajenamiento, extrañeza, distancia, separación voluntaria.

estray [ɪs'treɪ] [is-trei], *s.* (*For.*) Animal descarriado del rebaño o manada.

estreat [es'triːt] [es-trit], *va.* 1. (*Der. inglés*) Extraer, sacar traslado de un original. 2. Imponer una multa.

estrepement [es'triːpmənt] [es-trip-ment], *s.* Deterioración de tierras o bosques con perjuicio del propietario.

estrogen, (GB) oestrogen ['iːstrəʊdʒən] [is-trou-chen], *s.* (*Biol.*) Estrógeno.

estuary ['estjʊərɪ] [es-tiua-ri], *s.* Estuario, brazo de mar; ría, desembocadura de lago o río.

estuate ['estjʊeɪt] [es-tiu-eit], *va.* (*Des.*) Hervir, causar hervor.

estuation [estjʊ'eɪʃən] [es-tiu-ei-shon], *s.* (*Des.*) Hervor, ebullición.

ETA *s.* 1. (Basque separatist organization) ETA. 2. (*Transp.*) = **estimated time of arrival**.

etagère [eɪtə'dʒɛər] [ei-ta-yar], *s.* Estante, armario con anaqueles. (*Gal.*)

etc, &c. Contracción de las voces latinas *et cætera*, que significan lo mismo que, lo demás, lo que resta, lo que sigue.

et cetera [ɪt'setrə] [it-se-tra] *adv.* Etcétera.

etch [etʃ] [ech], *va.* 1. (*Art, Print.*) Grabar al agua fuerte. 2. Delinear, grabando las líneas por medio de un buril. **To be etched on somebody's mind/memory**, estar grabado en la memoria de alguien.

etcher ['etʃər] [e-char], *s.* Aguafuertista, el que graba al agua fuerte.

etching ['etʃɪŋ] [e-chin], *s.* Aguafuerte, grabado hecho al agua fuerte y el procedimiento por el cual se hace.

eternal [ɪ'tɜːnl] [i-ter-nal], *a.* Eterno, perpetuo, inmortal, inmutable. (*Coloq.*) Constante (noise, complaints). -*s.* El Eterno, Dios.

eternalist [ɪ'tɜːnlɪst] [i-ter-na-list], *s.* El que sostiene o defiende la eternidad del mundo.

eternalize [ɪ'tɜːnlaɪz] [i-ter-na-lais], *va.* Eternizar, perpetuar para siempre.

eternally [ɪ'tɜːnəlɪ] [i-ter-na-li], *adv.* Eternamente, perennemente; para siempre (forever). (*Coloq.*) Permanentemente, constantemente (continually, complain).

eternity [ɪ'tɜːnɪtɪ] [i-ter-ni-ti], *s.* Eternidad, duración sin fin. **The film seemed like an eternity**, parecía que la película no se iba a acabar nunca. **Eternity ring**, anillo o aro de brillantes (como símbolo de amor eterno).

eternize [ɪ'tɜːnaɪz] [i-ter-nais], *va.* Eternizar, inmortalizar, perpetuar.

etesian [ɪ'tiːzɪən] [i-ti-sian], *a.* Etesio, anualmente periódico; se dice de un viento.

ethane [i'θeɪn] [i-zein], *sm.* Etano.

ethanol ['eθənɒl] [i-za-nol], *sm.* Etanol.

ether ['iːθər] [e-zar], *s.* 1. Eter, las regiones superiores de la bóveda celeste. 2. (*Quím.*) Eter, licor volátil formado por la destilación del alcohol con algún ácido; en especial éter sulfúrico. 3. éter, fluido imponderable que llena el espacio, por el cual se propagan las vibraciones de la luz, del calor y de la electricidad.

ethereal [ɪ'θɪərɪəl] [i-zia-rial], **ethereous** [ɪ'θɪərɪəs] [i-zia-rios], *a.* 1. Etéreo, celeste. 2. De la naturaleza del éter o del aire; aéreo, ligero, fino, sutil, exquisito. 3. (*Quím.*) Etéreo, relativo a un éter.

etherealize [ɪ'θɪərɪəlaɪz] [i-zia-ria-lais], *va.* 1. Hacer etéreo, espiritualizar. 2. Convertir en éter. -*vn.* Hacerse etéreo.

etherification [ɪθɪərɪfaɪ'keɪʃən] [i-zia-ria-fi-kei-shon], *s.* Eterificación; la formación del éter.

etheriform [ɪ'θerɪfɔːm] [i-ze-ri-form], *a.* Eteriforme, que tiene el carácter del éter.

etherify [ɪ'θerɪfaɪ] [i-ze-ri-fai], *va.* Eterificar, convertir en éter.

etherization [ɪθerɪzeɪʃən] [i-ze-ri-zei-shon], *s.* Eterización, la administración del éter por las vías respiratorias para practicar una operación quirúrgica sin dolor.

etherize, etherise [ɪ'θeraɪz] [i-ze-rais], *va.* Eterizar, someter a la influencia del éter.

ethic ['eθɪk] [e-zik] *s.* Ética.

ethical ['eθɪkəl] [e-zi-kal], *a.* Ético, relativo a la moral (dilemma); de conducta (code).

ethically ['eθɪkəlɪ] [e-zi-ka-li], *adv.* Moralmente.

ethics ['eθɪks] [e-ziks], *s. pl.* Ética, la parte de la filosofía comúnmente llamada *filosofía moral*. **Professional ethics**, ética profesional.

Ethiop [ɪ'θɪəʊp] [i-zioup], *s.* Etíope, negro.

Ethiopia [iːθɪ'əʊpɪə] [i-ziou-pia] *N.* (*Geogr.*) Etiopía.

Ethiopian [i:θɪ' əʊpɪən] [i-ziou-pian], *a.* Etiópico, etíope, etiopio; propio o natural de Etiopía. -*s.* Etíope, el natural de Etiopía.

Ethiopic [ɪ'θɪəʊpɪk] [i-ziou-pik], *s.* Lengua etiópica.

ethiops mineral ['ɪθɪəʊps,mɪnərəl] [i-zioups-mi-ne-ral], *s.* Etíope mineral.

ethmoid ['eθmɔɪd] [ez-moid], *s.* Etmóides, uno de los huesos de la cabeza.

ethmoidal ['eθmɔɪdəl] [ez-moid-al], *a. (Anat.)* Etmoidal, etmoides, parecido a una criba.

ethnic, ethnical ['eθnɪk] [ez-nik], *a.* Etnico (origin; group); pagano, gentil. De las minorías étnicas (culture, art, vote). **An ethnic minority**, una minoría étnica. **Ethnic cleansing**, limpieza étnica.

ethnicity ['eθnɪsɪtɪ] [ez-ni-si-ti] *s.* Origen étnico (origin); identidad étnica (identity).

ethnicism ['eθnɪsɪzm] [ez-ni-si-zem], *s.* Paganismo, gentilismo.

ethnics ['eθnɪks] [ez-niks], *s. pl.* Etnicos, los gentiles.

ethnocentric [,eθnəʊ'sentrɪk] [ez-nou-sen-trik] *a.* Etnocéntrico.

ethnocentrism [,eθnəʊ'sentrɪzəm] [ez-nou-sen-tri-sem], *sm.* Etnocentrismo.

ethnogeny ['eθnɒdʒənɪ] [ez-no-ye-ni], *s.* Etnogenía, la parte de la etnología que trata del origen de las razas.

ethnographer [eθ'nɒgrəfəʳ] [ez-no-gra-faʳ], *s.* Etnógrafo.

ethnographic, ethnographical [,eθnəʊ'græfɪk] [ez-nou-gra-fik], *a.* Etnográfico, referente a la etnografía.

ethnography [eθ'nɒgrəfɪ] [ez-no-gra-fi], *s.* Etnografía, la parte de la antropología cuyo objeto es el estudio y descripción de los diferentes pueblos del orbe.

ethnologic, ethnological [eθ'nəʊ'lɒdʒɪk] [ez-no-lo-yik], *a.* Etnológico, perteneciente a la etnología.

ethnologist ['eθnɒlədʒɪst] [ez-no-lo-chist], *s.* Etnólogo.

ethnology ['eθnɒlədʒɪ] [ez-no-lo-yi], *s.* Etnología, ciencia que trata del conocimiento del origen, usos, costumbres, etc., de las naciones en general o en particular.

ethological ['eθɒlədʒɪkl] [ez-zo-lo-yi-kal], *a.* Etológico, moral.

ethology ['eθɒlədʒɪ] [ez-zo-lo-yi], *s.* Etología, la ciencia que trata de la formación del carácter humano.

ethos ['i:θɒs] [i-zos] *s.* **The middle class ethos**, los valores y las actitudes de la clase media. **The ethos of free enterprise**, el espíritu de la libre empresa.

ethyl ['i:θaɪl] [i-zail], *s.* y *a.* Etilo, elemento monoatómico (C2H5) de la serie de parafinas, que existe en el alcohol común.

ethylene ['eθɪli:n] [e-zi-lin] *s.* Etileno.

ethylic ['eθɪlɪk] [e-zi-lik], *a.* Etílico.

etiolate ['eθɪəleɪt] [e-zio-leit], *va.* y *vn.* hacer o hacerse blanco, blanquear o blanquearse, v. g. una planta o persona privada de la luz del sol.

etiolated ['eθɪəleɪtɪd] [e-zio-lei-tid] *a. (Bot.)* Decolorado.

etiology [,i:tɪ'ɒlədʒɪ] [e-zio-lo-yi], *s. (Med.)* Etiología, ciencia de las causas en general, y especialmente de las enfermedades.

etiquette ['etɪket] [e-ti-ket], *s.* Etiqueta, honor profesional; protocolo. **It is medical/professional etiquette**, es de protocolo o es lo acostumbrado entre los médicos/en la profesión.

ettle ['etl] [e-tel], *va.* Ganar.

ettle, *va.* 1. *(Esco.)* Intentar, designar. 2. Conjeturar, suponer. -*vn.* 1. Apuntar (con *at*). 2. Dirigirse. 3. Hacer conato de. 4. Ser ambicioso.

etui, etwee ['etwi:] [e-tui], *s.* Estuche; caja; bolsa; vaina. *(Fr.)*

etymological [,etɪmə'lɒdʒɪkəl] [e-ti-mo-lo-chi-kal], *a.* Etimológico.

etymologically [,etɪmə'lɒdʒɪkəlɪ] [e-ti-mo-lo-chi-ka-li], *adv.* Etimológicamente.

etymologist [,etɪmə'lɒdʒɪst] [e-ti-mo-lo-chist], *s.* Etimologista, etimólogo.

etymologize [,etɪmə'lɒdʒaɪz] [e-ti-mo-lo-chais], *va.* Etimologizar.

etymology [,etɪmə'lɒdʒɪ] [e-ti-mo-lo-chi], *s.* Etimología, el origen, raíz o principio de las voces.

etymon ['etɪmɒn] [e-ti-mon], *s.* Forma radical de una palabra, voz primitiva.

EU *s.* = European Union.

eucalyptus [,ju:kə'lɪptəs] [iu-ka-lip-tos], *s. (Bot.)* Eucalipto, género de árboles siempre verdes originarios de Australia. **Eucalyptus oil**, bálsamo de eucalipto.

eucharist ['ju:kərɪst] [yu-ka-rist], *s.* Eucaristía, la cena del Señor.

eucharistic, eucharistical ['ju:kərɪstɪk] [iu-ka-ris-tik], *a.* 1. Eucarístico. 2. Expresivo de gracias.

euchology ['ju:kələdʒɪ] [iu-ko-lo-chi], *s.* Eucologio, formulario del rezo.

euchre ['ju:kəʳ] [iu-kaʳ], *s.* Juego de naipes.

euclid ['ju:klɪd] [iu-klid], *N.* Euclides

euclidean ['ju:kli:dɪən] [iu-kli-dian], *a.* Euclidiano.

eucrasy, eucrasia ['ju:krəsɪ] [iu-kra-si], *s.* Eucrasia, buen temperamento del cuerpo humano.

euclase ['ju:kleɪs] [iu-kleis], *s. (Min.)* Euclasa, piedra verde y muy dura del Perú.

eudemonic [,juːdɪ'məʊnɪk] [iu-di-mou-nik], *a.* Perteneciente a la felicidad, o que tiende a producirla.

eudemonics [,juːdɪ'məʊnɪks] [iu-di-mou-niks], *s.* 1. El ramo de la ética que trata de la felicidad. 2. Los medios de obtener o producir comodidad o felicidad.

eudiometer [,juːdɪ'miːtəʳ] [iu-di-mi-taʳ], *s. (Quím.)* Eudiómetro, instrumento para determinar la pureza del aire o del gas.

eudiometry [,juːdɪ'ɒmɪtrɪ] [iu-dio-mi-tri], *s.* Eudiometría, el arte de medir o determinar la pureza o salubridad del aire.

Eugenics [juː'dʒenɪks] [iu-che-niks], *s.* Eugenesia.

eulogic ['juːlədʒɪk] [iu-lo-chik], *a. (Ant.)* Laudatorio.

eulogist ['juːlədʒɪst] [iu-lo-chist], *s.* Elogista, aplaudidor.

eulogistic ['juːlədʒɪstɪk] [iu-lo-chis-tik], *a.* Laudatorio, aprobador.

eulogize ['juːlədʒaɪz] [iu-lo-chais], *va.* Elogiar, ensalzar, aplaudir.

eulogy ['juːlədʒɪ] [iu-lo-chi], *s.* Elogio, loa, encomio, alabanza; panegírico.

eunomy ['juːnɒmɪ] [iu-no-mi], *s.* Eunomía, gobierno de buenas leyes.

eunuch ['juːnək] [iu-nuk], *s.* Eunuco, capón, hombre castrado; oficial de un palacio oriental.

eunuchism ['juːnəkɪzm] [iu-nu-ki-sem], *s.* Castradura, calidad y estado de eunuco.

euonymus ['juːənɪməs] [iuo-ni-mus], *s. (Bot.)* Bonetero, arbusto.

eupatorium ['juːpətərɪəm] [iu-pa-to-rium], *s. (Bot.)* Eupatorio, agrimonia; género extenso de plantas compuestas.

eupepsia ['juːpepsɪə] [iu-pep-sia], *s.* Sana digestión; opuesta a *dyspepsia*.

eupeptic ['juːpeptɪk] [iu-pep-tik], *a.* 1. Perteneciente a la buena digestión. 2. Que favorece la digestión.

euphemism ['juːfɪmɪzəm] [iu-fi-misem], *s.* Eufemismo, la descripción de una cosa ofensiva con expresiones decorosas; nombre con que se designa delicadamente una cosa desagradable.

euphemistic, euphemistical [,juːfɪ'mɪstɪk] [iu-fi-mis-tik], *a.* Caracterizado por el eufemismo.

euphone ['juːfɒn] [iu-fon], *s.* Registro melodioso de órgano.

euphonic, euphonical ['juːfɒnɪk] [iu-fo-nik], *a.* Eufónico, música, agradable al oído.

euphonious ['juːfɒnɪəs] [iu-fo-nios], *a.* Eufónico, agradable al oído, v. gr. una palabra o una frase.

euphoniously [ˈjuːfɒnɪəslɪ] [iu-fo-nios-li], *adv.* Eufónicamente, agradablemente al oído.

euphonium [ˈjuːfɒnɪəm] [iu-fo-nium], *s.* 1. Instrumento de viento de fuerte sonido. 2. Eufono, instrumento músico compuesto de 42 cilindros de vidrio.

euphony [ˈjuːfɒnɪ] [iu-fo-ni], *s.* Eufonía, sonido músico y agradable al oído.

euphorbium [ˈjuːfɔːbɪəm] [iu-for-bium], *s.* 1. (*Bot.*) Euforbio. 2. Una especie de goma resinosa.

euphoria [juːˈfɔːrɪə] [iu-fo-ria] *s.* Euforia.

euphoric [juːˈfɔːrɪk] [iu-fo-rik] *a.* Eufórico.

euphrasia, euphrasy [juːˈfreɪʃə] [iu-frei-sha], *s.* (*Bot.*) Eufrasia, hierba medicinal.

euphuism [juːˈfɔːrzəm] [iu-fui-sem], *s.* 1. Culteranismo, afectación de elegancia en el estilo; gongorismo. 2. Elegancia afectada en el vestir.

euphuistic [juːˈfɔːrslɪk] [iu-fuis-tik], *a.* Culterano, culterana.

Eurasia [jʊəˈreɪʃə] [iua-rei-sha] *N.* (*Geogr.*) Eurasia.

Eurasian [jʊəˈreɪʃn] [iua-rei-shan], *s.* y *a.* Así europeo como asiático. (Se dice de las plantas y de los animales). Eurasiático.

eureka [jʊəˈriːkə] [iua-ri-ka], *inter.* Lema del Estado de California: «¡Lo he hallado!» expresivo de la exultación que causa un descubrimiento.

euripus [jʊˈrɪpəs] [iua-ri-pus], *s.* Euripo, estrecho de mar.

euro [jʊˈrəʊ] [iu-rou], *m.* Euro (European currency).

eurobonds [ˈjʊərəbɒndʒ] [iua-ro-bonds] *sm. pl.* Eurobonos.

eurocentric [ˈjʊərəʊsentrɪk] [iua-rou-sen-trik], *a.* Eurocentrista.

eurocentrism [ˈjʊərəʊsentrɪzəm] [iua-rou-sen-tri-sem], *m.* Eurocentrismo.

eurocheque [ˈjʊərəʊtʃek] [iua-rou-chek] *s.* Eurocheque.

euroclydon [ˈjʊərəˈklaɪdən] [iua-rou-klai-don], *s.* Euroclidón, viento del nordeste peligroso en el Mediterráneo.

eurodollar [ˈjʊərəʊdɒlər] [iua-rou-do-laʳ] *s.* Eurodólar.

euro-MP [ˈjʊərəʊˌemˌpiː] [iua-rou-em-pi] *s.* Eurodiputado.

Europe [ˈjʊərəp] [iua-rop] *N.* (*Geogr.*) Europa.

European [ˌjʊəəˈpiːən] [iua-ro-pian], *s.* y *a.* Europeo. **European Commission**, Comisión Europea, Comisión de las Comunidades Europeas. **European Currency Unit**, unidad monetaria europea. **European (Economic) Community**, Comunidad (Económica) Europea. **European Union**, Unión Europea.

eurovision [ˈjʊərəvɪʒən] [iua-ro-vi-shon] *s.* Eurovisión. **The Eurovision Song Contest**, el festival de Eurovisión.

eurus [ˈjʊərəs] [iua-ros], *s.* Euro, viento o aire solano.

eurythmics [ˈjʊərɪθmɪks] [iua-riz-miks], *s.* Euritmia, majestad y elegancia en alguna obra de las bellas artes.

eustachian [juːˈsteɪʃən] [ius-tei-shan], *a.* De Eustaquio, anatomista italiano. **Eustachian tube**, trompa de Eustaquio, canal de comunicación entre la faringe y el tímpano del oído.

eustyle [ˈjʊstaɪl] [ius-tail], *s.* (*Arq.*) Intercolumnio.

euthanasia [ˌjuːθəˈneɪzɪə] [iu-za-nei-shia], **euthanasy** [ˌjuːθəˈneɪzɪ] [iu-za-nei-shi], *s.* Eutanasia, muerte tranquila.

eutychian [juːˈtɪkɪən] [yu-ti-kian], *a.* Eutiquiano.

evacuant [ɪˈvækʊənt] [i-va-kuant], *s.* (*Med.*) Evacuante.

evacuate [ɪˈvækjʊeɪt] [i-va-kueit], *va.* 1. Evacuar, desocupar, vaciar, desalojar (building, area); evacuar (residents, population). 2. Evacuar, desocupar, retirarse de. -*vn.* Vaciarse, fluir hacia afuera.

evacuation [ɪˌvækjʊˈeɪʃən] [i-va-kuei-shon], *s.* Evacuación, desalojo.

evacuative [ɪˈvækjʊətɪv] [i-va-kua-tiv], *a.* Purgativo, evacuativo.

evacuator [ɪˈvækʊeɪθəʳ] [i-va-kuei-taʳ], *s.* El o lo que desocupa, evacúa o se retira de algún lugar.

evacuee [ɪˌvækʊˈiː] [i-va-kui] *s.* Evacuado.

evade [ɪˈveɪd] [i-veid], *va.* y *vn.* 1. Evadir, huir, escapar, salvarse (arrest, enemy, responsibility). 2. Evadir, eludir, evitar (questions, issue). 3. Eludir, huir de la dificultad (regulations, military). Evadir (taxes).

evagation [ɪvəˈgeɪʃən] [i-va-guei-shon], *s.* Evagación; excursión.

evaluate [ɪˈvæljʊeɪt] [i-va-liueit], *va.* Evaluar (ability, data); valorar, tasar, avaluar (value).

evaluation [ɪˌvæljʊˈeɪʃən] [i-va-liuei-shon] *s.* Evaluación (of data); tasación, valoración (of monetary value).

evanesce [ɪˈvɒnes] [i-va-nes], *vn.* Desaparecer gradualmente; disiparse; desvanecerse.

evanescence [ˌiːvəˈnesns] [i-va-ne-sens], *s.* Desaparecimiento, desvanecimiento.

evanescent [ˌiːvəˈnesnt] [i-va-ne-sent], *a.* 1. Imperceptible, lo que se desvanece o desaparece de la vista. 2. A punto de desaparecer. 3. (*Mat.*) Que se aproxima al cero. 4. (*Biol.*) No permanente, instable.

evangel, evangelly [ɪˈvændʒəl] [i-van-chel], *s.* Buena nueva, evangelio.

evangelic, evangelical [ɪˈvændʒəlɪk] [i-van-che-lik], *a.* Evangélico.

evangelism [ɪˈvændʒəˌlɪzən] [i-van-che-li-sem], *s.* La promulgación del evangelio. Evangelismo.

evangelist [ɪˈvændʒəlɪst] [i-van-che-list], *s.* 1. Evangelista, cada uno de los cuatro escritores sagrados que escribieron el Evangelio. **The four Evangelists**, los cuatro evangelistas. 2. Predicador del Evangelio que va de un lugar a otro y trata de despertar el fervor religioso de sus oyentes (preacher); evangelista (member of an evangelical church).

evangelistary [ɪˈvændʒəlɪstərɪ] [i-van-che-lis-ta-ri], *s.* La colección de los evangelios que deben leerse o cantarse durante el oficio divino en las Iglesias griega y romana.

evangelize [ɪˈvændʒɪlaɪz] [i-van-che-lais], *va.* Evangelizar.

evaporable [ɪˈvæpərəbl] [i-va-po-rei-bol], *a.* Evaporable.

evaporate [ɪˈvæpəreɪt] [i-va-po-reit], *vn.* 1. Evaporarse, disiparse en vapor, despedir los cuerpos sus partes más sutiles o espirituosas (liquid). 2. Desvanecerse (fear). 3. Evaporarse, esfumarse (support, opposition). 4. Esfumarse (confidence). -*va.* 1. Evaporar, despedir vapores. 2. Evaporar, exhalar, dar salida a alguna cosa. 5. Evaporar, hacer despedir a los cuerpos sus partes más sutiles o espirituosas por medio del calor.

evaporated [ɪˈvæpəreɪtɪd] [i-va-po-rei-ted], *a.* Evaporado. **Evaporated milk**, leche evaporada, leche condensada.

evaporation [ɪˌvæpəˈreɪʃən] [i-va-po-rei-shon], *s.* 1. Evaporación ; exhalación del vapor. 2. Desaparición, desvanecimiento (of support, confidence).

evaporator [ɪˈvæpəreɪtəʳ] [i-va-po-rei-toʳ], *s.* Evaporador, aparato para desecar substancias por medio de la evaporación.

evasion [ɪˈveɪʒən] [i-vei-shon], *s.* 1. Evasiva (evasive statement); efugio, escapatoria, excusa; evasión (of responsibility). 2. (*Des.*) Evasión, salida, escape.

evasive [ɪˈveɪzɪv] [i-vei-siv], *a.* Evasivo (equivocal, reply); sofístico, ambiguo; engañoso. (*Mil.*) **To take evasive action**, realizar maniobras para eludir un ataque.

evasively [ɪˈveɪzɪvlɪ] [i-vei-siv-li], *adv.* Sofísticamente, evasivamente.

eve, even [iːv] [iv], *s.* Tardecita, la caída de la tarde, cerca del anochecer; vigilia, víspera (day, night before). **On the eve of**, la víspera de. **Christmas Eve**, víspera de Navidad. (La forma *Even* es poética o anticuada.)

evection [ɪˈviːkʃən] [i-vek-shon], *s.* 1. (*Astr.*) Evección, la mayor desigualdad periódica en el movimiento de la luna, por efecto de la atracción solar. 2. (*Des.*) Exaltación.

ev'n [iːvn] [iven]. Contracción de EVEN.

even [ˈiːvən] [i-ven], *a.* 1. Llano, liso, igual, raso, suave. Plano (flat, smooth/ground, surface); uniforme (coat of paint). **The floor isn't even**, el suelo no está nivelado. Uniforme, parejo (regular, uniform/color, lighting). Acompasado, regular (breathing). 2. Igual por ambos lados o partes; par. **To be even with**, estar en paz con, estar a mano, no deber nada. 3. Par, que se puede dividir exactamente por 2 (divisible by two). 4. Constante (temperature), firme; sereno, invariable en la disposición, acción o calidad. Equitativo, igual (equal/distribution).

After four rounds they're even, tras cuatro vueltas están o van igualados o empatados. **To get even with**, desquitarse, vengarse. **I'll get even with her**, me las pagará. 5. Al mismo nivel o en la misma línea. **Even with the ground**, al nivel de la tierra. **To lay even with the ground**, arrasar, demoler. **To be even with**, ir igualados (game); estar en paz (with somebody). **To get even with one**, ajustar cuentas con alguien; vengarse, pagar con la misma moneda. **To make even**, allanar, igualar.

even, *adv*. 1. Aun, hasta, incluso. **Even a child could do it**, hasta un niño lo podría hacer. **Even now, five years later**, incluso ahora, cuando ya han pasado cinco años. 2. Aun cuando, supuesto que. 3. No obstante, sin embargo. 4. Lisamente, llanamente, regularmente (v. g. los versos). 5. Aún, todavía (with comparatives). **The next day was even colder**, al día siguiente hizo aún o todavía más frío. **Even you**, tú también. **Even as**, como. **Even down**, hacia abajo. **Even now**, ahora mismo. **Even on**, derechamente. **Even so**, lo mismo, de veras, así es; cierto; es verdad. **Not even**, ni siquiera. **You're not even trying**, ni siquiera lo estás intentando.

even, *va*. 1. Igualar, allanar, enrasar, nivelar (level, surface); unir; desquitar, liquidar cuentas. **To even with the ground**, arrasar. 2. Igualar (make equal/score); equilibrar (contest, situation).

even out 1. Compensar, nivelar. 2. Compensarse, nivelarse.

even up 1. Equilibrar (balance/numbers, accounts). 2. *(Coloq.)* **To even up with somebody**, arreglar cuentas con alguien (repay).

evene [ɪˈviːn] [i-vin], *vn*. Acontecer, acaecer, suceder.

evener [ˈiːvənəʳ] [i-ve-naʳ], *s*. 1. Reconciliador. 2. *(Mec.)* Aplanador, igualador.

evenhand [ˈiːvənˈhænd] [i-ven-jand], *s*. Paridad de rango o grado.

even-handed [ˈiːvənˈhændɪd] [i-ven-jan-did], *a*. Imparcial, ecuánime.

evening [ˈiːvnɪŋ] [iv-nin], *s*. Tardecita, el anochecer, el principio de la noches (before dark); noche (after dark). Se usa frecuentemente en sentido figurado, para significar fin, término. **At ten in the evening**, a las 10 de la noche. **Good evening**, buenas tardes (early on); buenas noches (later). **Every Tuesday evening**, todos los martes por la tarde/noche. **Last evening**, ayer tarde. **Saturday evening**, el sábado por la tarde. *-a*. Vespertino. **Evening classes**, clases nocturnas. **Evening dress**, traje de noche (women), traje de etiqueta (men). **Evening party**, tertulia. **Evening performance**, función nocturna. **Evening service**, misa vespertina. **Evening-song**, *V.* EVENSONG. **Evening tide**, *V.* EVENTIDE. **Evening primrose**, *(Bot.)* enotera, onagra, planta americana de flores grandes y amarillas que se abren al caer la tarde.

evening-star [ˈiːvnɪŋstɑːʳ] [iv-nin-staʳ], *s*. Héspero, véspero, estrella vespertina.

evenly [ˈiːvənlɪ] [i-ven-li], *adv*. 1. Igualmente, llanamente; sin accidentes ni asperezas, de una manera igual, uniforme (spread). Equitativamente, en o a partes iguales (equally/distribute, divide). 2. Horizontalmente, a nivel. 3. Imparcialmente. 4. Sin alterar la voz (calmly/say, speak). Con regularidad (steadily/breathe).

evenness [ˈiːvənnɪs] [i-ven-nes], *s*. Igualdad, uniformidad, llanura, lisura (flatness), imparcialidad, serenidad de ánimo (temper).

evens [ˈiːvənz] [i-vens] *a*. Que paga la misma cantidad que se apuesta (favorite, bet).

even-song [ˈiːvənsɒŋ] [i-ven-son], *s*. 1. Vísperas, el oficio divino de la tarde o el tiempo de la tarde. 2. Canción vespertina, cantada por la tarde; himno de la tarde.

event [ɪˈvent] [i-vent], *s*. 1. Evento, acontecimiento (happening, incident), caso, suceso. **In the normal course of events**, en circunstancias normales. *(Dep.)* Prueba. 2. éxito, consecuencia, resulta. **At all events**, sea lo que fuere, o en todo caso, a todo trance; sobre todo. **Coming events**, sucesos futuros. **In the event of**, en caso de. **After the**

event, a posteriori. **In any event**, en todo caso. **The event will show**, ya veremos.

even-tempered [ˈiːvəntempəd] [i-ven-tem-perd] *a*. Ecuánime, sereno.

eventerate [ɪˈventəreɪt] [i-ven-te-reit], *va*. Destripar.

eventful [ɪˈventfʊl] [i-vent-ful], *a*. Lleno de acontecimientos, incidentes o sucesos (week); extraordinario, singular. Rico en experiencias (life). Crucial (momentous).

eventide [ɪˈvəntaɪd] [i-ven-taid], *s*. La tarde, la caída de la tarde; vigilia. **Eventide home**, hogar de ancianos.

eventual [ɪˈventʃʊəl] [i-ven-chual], *a*. 1. Consiguiente, último, final. 2. Eventual, fortuito. **The eventual outcome was…**, lo que sucedió finalmente fue… **The eventual winners**, el equipo que acabó alzándose con la victoria.

eventuality [ɪˌventʃʊˈælɪtɪ] [i-ven-chu-a-li-ti], *s*. Eventualidad, casualidad.

eventually [ɪˈventʃʊəlɪ] [i-ven-chua-li], *adv*. Eventualmente, finalmente, últimamente; con el tiempo. **Eventually people became used to the idea**, con el tiempo, la gente se acostumbró a la idea.

eventuate [ɪˈventʃʊeɪt] [i-ven-chueit], *vn*. 1. Tener desenlace, terminarse, concluir. 2. Acontecer, acaecer, suceder. **To eventuate in**, resultar en (EU).

ever [ˈevəʳ] [e-vaʳ], *adv*. 1. En cualquier tiempo (at any time). **Have you ever visited London?**, ¿has estado en Londres alguna vez? 2. Siempre; perpetuamente (always). **For ever and ever**, por siempre jamás, eternamente. **Forever**, perpetuamente, para siempre, de por vida. Se contrae muchas veces en *e'er*. **Ever since**, desde entonces, después. **Ever and anon** or **every now and then**, de cuando en cuando, de vez en cuando. **Did you ever see such a thing!**, ¡habráse visto cosa igual! (expressing incredulity, indignation). 3. En cualquier grado; en todo caso; generalmente. **I'm ever so grateful**, le estoy muy agradecido. **Be he ever so rich**, por rico que sea. **As ever**, tanto, tanto como, lo más. **Run as fast as ever you can**, corra Ud. lo más que pueda. **What ever do you want?**, ¿qué demonios quieres? (to emphasize). **Ever so**, en cualquier grado o extensión; muy. **He is ever so strong**, él es muy fuerte. **The patient is ever so much better**, el enfermo se halla muy mejorado. 4. Después de una voz negativa o limitativa, nunca, jamás. **Hardly/scarcely ever**, casi nunca. **I do not know if I shall ever see it**, no sé si jamás lo veré. **The situation is worst than ever**, la situación está peor que nunca (after comp. or superl.). **Ever so much**, muchísimo. **As quickly as ever you can**, lo antes que puedas. **They lived happily ever after**, vivieron felices y comieron perdices (in fairy tales). **When will you ever learn?**, ¿cuándo vas a aprender? **She's ever so beautiful**, es bellísima (as intensifier).

ever-burning [evəˈbɜːnɪŋ] [eva-ber-nin], *a*. Inextinguible.

ever-changing [evəˈtʃeɪndʒɪŋ] [eva-chein-yin], *a*. Infinitamente variable.

ever-during [evəˈdjuːrɪŋ] [eva-diu-rin], *a*. Eterno, sempiterno.

everglade [ˈevəgleɪd] [eva-gleid], *s*. Terreno bajo y pantanoso cubierto en su mayor parte por altas hierbas.

evergreen [ˈevəgriːn] [eva-grin], *a*. Siempre verde. De hoja perenne (tree/shrub). Favorito (story, song). Eterno, perenne (subject to conversation). *-s*. *(Bot.)* Siempreviva, planta que mantiene su verdor en todas las estaciones. Planta/árbol de hoja perenne (plant/tree). **Evergreen oak**, encina.

evergrowing [ˈevəɡrəʊɪŋ] [eva-grouin], *a*. Que crece o aumenta continuamente.

everlasting [evəˈlɑːstɪŋ] [eva-las-tin], *a*. Eterno, sempiterno, perpetuo, perdurable (eternal/peace, love, gratitude); imperecedero (fame, glory); continuo, eterno (constant). *-s*. 1. Eternidad; ser eterno. 2. Sempiterna, especie de tela de lana. 3. Cualquier planta cuyas flores conservan sus formas y colores después de recogidas y secadas. **Everlasting-pea**, *(Bot.)* siemprehuele, siempreviro.

everlastingly [evəˈlɑːstɪŋlɪ] [eva-las-tin-li], *adv*. Eternamente, perpetuamente, sin cesar.

everlastingness [ˌevəˈlɑːstɪŋnɪs] [eva-las-tin-nes], *s.* Eternidad.

everliving [ˌevəˈlɪvɪŋ] [e-vaʳ-li-vin], *a.* Inmortal, eterno, sempiterno.

evermore [ˈevəˈmɔːʳ] [e-vaʳ-moaʳ], *adv.* Eternamente, para siempre jamás. **For evermore**, por siempre jamás.

ever-open [evəˈɔʊpən] [e-vaʳ-ou-pen], *a.* Nunca cerrado, siempre abierto.

everpleasing [ˌevəˈpliːsɪŋ] [e-vaʳ-pli-sin], *a.* Lo que deleita siempre.

eversion [ɪˈvɜːʒən] [i-ver-shon], *s.* 1. El acto de volver lo de dentro afuera o hacia atrás. 2. Eversión, trastorno, subversión.

evert [ɪˈvɜːt] [i-vert], *va.* 1. Everter, volver de dentro afuera; volver hacia atrás o afuera. 2. *(Des.)* Subvertir, destruir, arruinar.

ever-watchful [evəˈwɔːθʃʊl] [eva-uoch-ful], *a.* Siempre vigilante.

every [ˈevrɪ] [e-vri], *a.* Cada uno o cada una; todo, todos. **Every room was searched**, se registraron todas las habitaciones, se registró cada una de las habitaciones (each). **Every now and again**, de vez en cuando. **Every one of you**, todos y cada uno de ustedes. **Every day**, todos los días, cada día (indicating recurrence). **Everywhere**, en o por todas partes. **Everybody**, todos, todo el mundo, cada uno. **Every other day**, cada dos días, día sí día no. **Everything**, todo, cada cosa. **Every so often**, cada cierto tiempo. **Every whit**, enteramente. **They have every confidence in us**, confían plenamente en nosotros (very great, all possible). **They gave me every assistance**, me ayudaron en todo lo que podían.

everybody [ˈevrɪbɒdɪ] [e-vri-bo-di] *pron.* Todos. **Is that everybody?**, ¿están todos?, ¿está todo el mundo?

everyday [ˈevrɪdeɪ] [e-vri-dei], *a.* Cotidiano, de todos los días, ordinario (occurrence, problems, activities); de diario (suit, clothes); corriente, de todos los días (expression). **Everyday life**, la vida diaria o cotidiana. **In everyday use**, de uso diario o corriente.

everyone [ˈevrɪwʌn] [e-vriuan] *pron.* V. EVERYBODY.

everyplace [ˈevrɪpleɪs] [e-vri-pleis] *adv.* V. EVERYWHERE.

ever-young [ˈevəjʌʊŋ] [e-vaʳ-yaun], *a.* Siempre joven; nunca decaído.

everything [ˈevrɪθɪŋ] [e-vri-zin] *pron.* Todo. **Everything possible has been done**, se ha hecho todo lo posible.

everywhere [ˈevrɪweəʳ] [e-vriueaʳ] *adv.* **I've looked everywhere for it**, lo he buscado por todas partes o por todos lados. **They go everywhere by car**, van a todos lados o a todas partes en coche.

evesdropper [ˈevzdrɒpəʳ] [evs-dro-paʳ], *s. (Des.)* V. EAVESDROPPER.

evict [ɪˈvɪkt] [i-vikt], *va.* 1. Desposeer o privar a alguno de sus bienes en virtud de una sentencia legal; echar fuera, expulsar, desalojar (demonstrators); deshauciar, desalojar (tenant, squatter). 2. Arrebatar, arrancar, alienar, v. g. los bienes.

eviction [ɪˈvɪkʃən] [i-vik-shon]. *s.* Desposesión de bienes por sentencia judicial. Desalojo, deshaucio (tenant, squatter). **Eviction order**, orden de desalojo.

evidence [ˈevɪdəns] [e-vi-dens], *s.* 1. Evidencia, certidumbre manifiesta; demostración. Indicio, señal (sign, indication). **He isn't much in evidence these days**, últimamente no se le ve mucho. 2. Testimonio (testimony); prueba (proof); pruebas (objects); deposición, declaración. **What evidence is there that …?**, ¿qué prueba(s) hay de que …? **To turn state's evidence**, descubrir, delatar a su cómplice. **On the evidence of those present**, según (el testimonio de) los que estaban presentes. 3. *(Des.)* Testigo. **Circumstancial evidence**, prueba circunstancial, indicios vehementes. **State's evidence**, el cómplice que, por librarse del castigo, declara contra los otros. **To give evidence**, dar testimonio; deponer, declarar. **To hold something in evidence**, llevar o citar algo como prueba. **To make evidence**, probar, patentizar, demostrar (prove).

evidence, *va.* Evidenciar, hacer patente, probar.

evidencer [ˈevɪdənsəʳ] [e-vi-den-saʳ], *s.* Testigo.

evident [ˈevɪdənt] [e-vi-dent], *a.* Evidente, claro, patente, notorio, manifiesto. **To be evident**, constar, ser evidente. **As is evident from his film**, como queda claro en su película.

evidential [ˈevɪdənʒəl] [e-vi-den-shal], *a.* Lo que produce evidencia o prueba.

evidently [ˈevɪdəntlɪ] [e-vi-dent-li], *adv.* Claramente, evidentemente, obviamente (embarrassed, unsuitable. Aparentemente, según parece. **Is she coming too?- evidently**, ¿ella también viene?-eso parece o según parece. **Evidently she can't join us**, por lo visto, no puede reunirse con nosotros.

evil [ˈiːvl] [i-vil], *a.* 1. Malo, maligno (wicked/demon, wizard) depravado, miserable, dañoso, pernicioso; de gran maldad (deeds, thoughts, character); maléfico, funesto (influence); diabólico, maléfico (plan, suggestion). **An evil spirit**, un espíritu maligno o maléfico. **The evil one**, el diablo, Satanás. **Evil communications corrupt good manners**, las malas conversaciones corrompen las buenas costumbres. 2. Asqueroso (unpleasant, smell). **To put off the evil day/ hour**, retrasar o posponer el día/momento fatídico o funesto. *-s.* 1. Maldad, acción malvada; mal (sin, wrong-doing), daño, injuria. **The lesser of two evils**, el menor de dos males. 2. Desgracia, infortunio, calamidad. 3. Enfermedad. **King's evil**, escrófula; en otro tiempo se suponía curable por el contacto de un rey. **The social evil**, impureza sexual, prostitución. *-adv.* Malamente, injuriosamente. **To do evil**, hacer el mal. **To speak evil of somebody**, hablar mal de alguien.

evil-affected [ˈiːvlˈəfektɪd] [i-vil-a-fek-ted], *a.* Desafecto, maligno.

evil-doer [ˈiːvlduːəʳ] [i-vil-doaʳ], *s.* Malhechor.

evil-eyed [ˈiːvlaɪd] [i-vil-aid], *a.* Lo que tiene la vista dañosa, que mira de mal ojo. **To put the evil eye on somebody**, echarle o hacerle mal de ojo a alguien.

evil-favored [ˈiːvlfeɪvəd] [i-vil-fei-vord], *a.* Disforme. V. ILL-FAVOURED.

evil-favoredness [ˈiːvlfeɪvədnɪs] [i-vil-fei-vord-nes], *s.* Deformidad.

evilly [ˈiːvɪlɪ] [i-vi-li], *adv.* Malamente.

evil-minded [ˈiːvlˈmaɪndɪd] [i-vil-main-ded], *a.* Malicioso, mal intencionado.

evilness [ˈiːvlnɪs] [i-vil-nes], *s.* Maldad.

evil-smelling [ˈiːvɪlɪ] [i-vi-li] *a.* Hediondo.

evil-speaking [ˈiːvlˈspiːkɪŋ] [i-vil-spi-kin], *s.* Maledicencia, murmuración, calumnia.

evil-tempered [ˈiːvlˈtempəd] [i-vil-tem-ped] *a.* Con un humor de perros.

evil-wishing [ˈiːvlˈwɪʃɪŋ] [i-vil-ui-shin], *a.* Malévolo, el que desea mal a otro.

evil-worker [ˈiːvlˈwɔːkəʳ] [i-vil-uor-kaʳ], *s.* Malhechor.

evince [ɪˈvɪns] [i-vins], *va.* Probar, justificar, demostrar, hacer patente y manifiesta alguna cosa (talent, qualities). Mostrar, manifestar (desire, astonishment). *-vn.* Probar.

evincible [ɪˈvɪnsɪbl] [i-vin-si-bol], *a.* Demostrable.

evincibly [ɪˈvɪnsɪblɪ] [i-vin-si-bli], *adv.* Evidentemente, indudablemente.

evincive [ɪˈvɪnsɪv] [i-vin-siv], *a.* Capaz de probar, convincente.

evirate [ɪˈvɪreɪt] [i-vi-reit], *va.* Castrar.

eviscerate [ɪˈvɪsəreɪt] [i-vi-sa-reit], *va.* Destripar, desentrañar, sacar las entrañas.

evitable [eˈvɪtəbl] [i-vi-ta-bol], *a.* Evitable.

eviternal [ɪˈvɪtɜːnəl] [i-vi-ter-nal], *a.* Eviterno, sempiterno.

evocation [ˌevəˈkeɪʃən] [e-vo-kei-shon], *s.* 1. Evocación. 2. *(For.)* Avocación, la transferencia de un litigio de un tribunal inferior a uno superior.

evocative [ˌevəˈkətɪv] [e-vo-ka-tiv] *a.* Evocador. **To be evocative of something**, evocar algo.

evoke [ɪˈvəʊk] [i-vouk], *va.* 1. Evocar, llamar a alguna para que dé favor o auxilio. 2. Avocar, remover a un tribunal diferente. 3. Provocar, suscitar (response, admiration, sympathy); evocar (memories, associations).

evolute [ɪˈvəluːt] [i-vo-lut] *s.* (Geom.) Evoluta, curva geométrica de muchos centros.

evolution [ˌiːvəˈluːʃən] [i-vo-lu-shon], *s.* 1. Desplegadura; evolución, desarrollo. 2. (Biol.) Evolución, desarrollo gradual, transformismo. 3. (Alg.) Extracción de una raíz. 4. (Mil. y Mar.) Evolución, movimientos que hacen las naves o los soldados para mudar de posición y tomar otra nueva.

evolutional [ˌiːvəˈluːʃənl] [i-vo-lu-sho-nal], *a.* De la evolución o que resulta de ella.

evolutionary [ˌiːvəˈluːʃnərɪ] [i-vo-lu-sho-na-ri], *a.* 1. Evolutivo, evolucionario, relativo a la evolución, en cualquier sentido. 2. Evolucionista (theory); evolutivo (development, process).

evolutionist [ˌiːvəˈluːʃənɪst] [i-vo-lu-sho-nist], *a.* Perteneciente a la evolución bilógica. -*s.* 1. Creyente en la evolución biológica o metafísica. 2. Jefe diestro en las evoluciones o maniobras militares.

evolve [ɪˈvɒlv] [i-volv], *va.* 1. Desenvolver, desplegar, desenredar, desarrollar (system, theory). 2. Producir por la evolución. 3. Echar fuera, v. gr. los gases. -*vn.* Abrirse, desplegarse, extenderse, desarrollarse (idea, system); evolucionar.

evolvement [ɪˈvɒlvmənt] [i-volv-ment], *s.* 1. Emanación, producción de gases. 2. Desplegadura, despliegue.

evolvent [ɪˈvɒlvənt] [i-vol-vent], *s.* (Geom.) Evolvente. V. INVOLUTE.

evulsion [ɪˈvʌlʃən] [i-val-shon], *s.* Arranque, la acción de arrancar alguna cosa, sea de raíz o de otra suerte.

ewe [juː] [iu], *f.* Oveja, la hembra del carnero.

ewer [ˈjuːər] [iuar], *s.* Aguamanil, jarro, cántaro de boca ancha para servir agua.

ewry [ˈjuːrɪ] [iu-ri], *s.* (Ant.) Sausería, un oficio de palacio.

ex [eks] [eks], Preposición latina que quiere decir fuera, fuera de, afuera, más allá. Se usa muchas veces con fuerza intensiva y también para expresar que una persona o cosa no goza o tiene el empleo u oficio que tenía; v. g. *Exalt, ex*-altar, *re*-alzar; **ex-general**, exgeneral, o general que fue. **Ex-captain**, capitán retirado.

exacerbate [eksˈæsəbeɪt] [ek-sa-ser-beit], *va.* Exacerbar, exasperar, irritar.

exacerbation [eksˌæsəˈbeɪʃən] [ek-sa-ser-bei-shon], *s.* Exacerbación, irritación; paroxismo, aumento momentáneo en la fuerza de la enfermedad.

exacervation [eksˌæsəˈveɪʃən] [ek-sa-ser-vei-shon], *s.* Amontonamiento.

exact [ɪɡˈzækt] [ik-sakt], *a.* Exacto (precise/number, size, time, date); cabal, metódico, puntual, esmerado, justo, estricto; preciso (accurate/description, definition). **The exact truth**, la estricta verdad. **Those were her exact words**, ésas fueron sus palabras textuales.

exact, *va.* Exigir; arrancar (promise). **The price they exacted from us**, el precio que nos hicieron pagar. -*vn.* Cometer exacciones, obtener por fuerza.

exacter [ɪɡˈzæktər] [ik-sak-tar], *s.* Exactor, opresor.

exacting [ɪɡˈzæktɪŋ] [ik-sak-tin] *a.* Que exige mucho (work, job); exigente (supervisor, employer); riguroso (standards, conditions).

exaction [ɪɡˈzækʃən] [ik-sak-shon], *s.* Exacción, extorsión.

exactitude [ɪɡˈzæktɪtjuːd] [ik-sak-ti-tiud], *s.* Exactitud, precisión, puntualidad y fidelidad.

exactly [ɪɡˈzæktlɪ] [ik-sakt-li], *adv.* Exactamente, cabalmente, con precisión (measure, calculate). **At six thirty exactly**, a las seis y media en punto.

exactness [ɪɡˈzæktnɪs] [ik-sakt-nes], *s.* Exactitud, precisión, puntualidad; conducta arreglada.

exactor [ɪɡˈzæktər] [ik-sak-tar], *s.* Exactor, opresor.

exactress [ɪɡˈzæktrɪs] [ik-sak-tres], *f.* Exactora.

exaggerate [ɪɡˈzædʒəreɪt] [ik-sa-che-reit], *va.* 1. Exagerar, encarecer, abultar, ponderar una cosa, dando de ella idea mayor de la que en realidad merece. 2. Aumentar

inmoderadamente; realzar el efecto, dibujo o diseño de una cosa.

exaggerated [ɪɡˈzædʒəreɪtɪd] [ik-sa-che-rei-tid] *a.* Exagerado.

exaggeration [ɪɡˌzædʒəreɪʃən] [ik-sa-che-rei-shon], *s.* Exageración.

exaggeratory [ɪɡˈzædʒərətərɪ] [ik-sa-che-ra-to-ri], *a.* Exageratorio.

exalt [ɪɡˈzɔːlt] [ik-solt], *va.* 1. Exaltar, elevar, levantar (elevate). 2. Alentar, alegrar (encourage). 3. Exaltar, alabar. 4. Exaltar, realzar, ilustrar, engrandecer (praise).

exaltation [ˌeɡzɔːlˈteɪʃən] [ik-sol-tei-shon], *s.* Exaltación, elevación; dignidad; júbilo (exaltation, joy).

exalted [ɪɡˈzɔːltɪd] [ik-sol-ted], *pp.* y *a.* Exaltado, elevado (position, person); de aquí, eminente, noble, grande, sublime.

exaltedness [ɪɡˈzɔːltɪdnɪs] [ik-sol-tid-nes], *s.* Exaltación, sublimidad.

exalter [ɪɡˈzɔːltər] [ik-sol-tar], *s.* Loador, exaltador, elevador.

exam [ɪɡˈzæm] [ik-sam] *s.* V. EXAMINATION.

examinable [ɪɡˈzæmɪnəbl] [ik-sa-mi-na-bol], *a.* Investigable, averiguable.

examinant [ɪɡˈzæmɪnənt] [ik-sa-mi-nant], *s.* 1. Examinador. 2. (Des.) Examinando, el que está para ser examinado.

examinate [ɪɡˈzæmɪneɪt] [ik-sa-mi-neit], *s.* Examinado.

examination [ɪɡˌzæmɪˈneɪʃən] [ik-sa-mi-nei-shon], *s.* 1. Examen, acción de examinar. **To take/sit an examination**, presentarse a, o dar, rendir o tomar un examen, examinarse. **To pass an examination**, aprobar o pasar un examen. **To fail an examination**, reprobar, suspender o perder un examen. 2. Examen interrogatorio (of witness); investigación, indagación, averiguación. 3. Revisión, inspección (inspection/of accounts); control (of passports); reconocimiento, examen, revisación (by doctor). Examen (study, investigation).

examine [ɪɡˈzæmɪn] [ik-sa-min], *va.* 1. Examinar (inspect), escudriñar, investigar críticamente; inspeccionar, revisar (accounts); registrar, revisar (baggage); examinar, estudiar (document, dossier). 2. Examinar, tomar declaración al reo; examinar a algún testigo. 3. Investigar, probar o tantear por medio de preguntas y ejercicios la idoneidad y suficiencia de alguien, p. ej. de un discípulo o candidato. 4. Hacer pruebas, ensayar; analizar. (Med., Dent.) Examinar, revisar. 5. Interrogar (witness, accused).

examinee [ɪɡˈzæmɪniː] [ik-sa-mi-ni] *s.* (Educ.) Examinando, alumno. Candidato, aspirante (for professional exam).

examiner [ɪɡˈzæmɪnər] [ik-sa-mi-nar], *s.* Examinador, escudriñador.

example [ɪɡˈzɑːmpl] [ik-sam-pol], *s.* 1. Ejemplar, original, prototipo, muestra. 2. Caso precedente semejante a otro posterior. 3. Ejemplar, ejemplo, pauta de lo que se debe seguir o imitar (model). **To follow somebody's example**, seguir el ejemplo de alguien. 4. Ejemplo, el que ha sufrido un castigo para escarmiento de los demás (warning). **To make an example of somebody**, darle un castigo ejemplar a alguien. 5. Ejemplo, símil o comparación de que se usa para aclarar o apoyar alguna cosa (specimen, sample). **To set an example**, dar ejemplo. **For example**, por ejemplo.

exanimate [ɪɡˈzænɪmeɪt] [ik-sa-ni-meit], *a.* 1. Exánime, muerto, sin vida, sin vigor. 2. Desmayado, acobardado, sin valor, sin ánimo.

exanimation [ɪɡˌzænɪˈmeɪʃən] [ik-sa-ni-mei-shon], *s.* Muerte, pasmo.

exanthem, exanthema, *pl.* EXANTHEMATA, *s.* (Med.) Exantema, erupción, sarpullido. V. RASH.

exanthematous [ɪɡˈzænθɪmətəs] [ik-san-zi-ma-tos], *a.* Eruptivo, exantemático.

exarch [ɪɡˈzɑːtʃ] [ik-sarch], *s.* 1. Exarca o exarco, antiguo oberñador de Italia delegado por los emperadores de Oriente. 2. Legado de un patriarca en la Iglesia griega.

exarchate [ɪɡˈzɑːtʃeɪt] [ik-sar-cheit], *s.* 1. Exarcado, distrito sujeto a un exarca. 2. La dignidad y el cargo de exarca.

exarticulate [ɪɡˈzɑːtɪkjʊleɪt] [ik-sar-ti-kiu-leit], *va*. 1. Dislocar, descoyuntar. 2. *(Cir.)* Desarticular, amputar por una coyuntura.

exarticulation [ɪɡˌzɑːtɪkjʊˈleɪʃən] [ik-sar-ti-kiu-lei-shon], *s*. 1. Dislocación, descoyuntamiento. 2. Desarticulación, amputación.

exasperate [ɪɡˈzɑːspəreɪt] [ik-sas-pe-reit], *va*. 1. Exasperar, irritar, enojar, provocar. 2. Exasperar, hacer más intenso, agravar, amargar.

exasperated [ɪɡˈzɑːspəreɪtɪd] [ik-sas-pe-rei-ted], *a*. Provocado, exasperado, irritado. *(Bot.)* Áspero.

exasperater [ɪɡˈzɑːspəreɪtəʳ] [ik-sas-pe-rei-taʳ], *s*. Provocador, provocante.

exasperating [ɪɡˈzɑːspəreɪtɪŋ] [ik-sas-pe-rei-tin] *a*. Exasperante. **It's so exasperating!**, es para volverse loco, es una locura.

exasperation [ɪɡˌzɑːspəˈreɪʃən] [ik-sas-pe-rei-shon], *s*. Exasperación, provocación, irritación; enojo; agravación, recargo.

excamb [ɪksˈkæm] [iks-kam], *va*. *(Der. esco.)* Cambiar, permutar, trocar, especialmente terrenos por terrenos.

excandescence, escandescency [eksˈkændəsəns] [eks-kan-de-sens], *s*. 1. *(Quím.)* Excandecencia. 2. *(Des.)* Excandecencia, irritación vehemente, ira. *V.* INCANDESCENCE.

excarnate [eksˈkɑːneɪt] [eks-kar-neit], *va*. Descarnar, despojar de carne.

excarnation, excarnification [eksˈkɑːneɪʃən] [eks-kar-nei-shon], *s*. Descarnadura.

excavate [ˈekskəveɪt] [eks-ka-veit], *va*. Excavar, ahondar.

excavation [ˈekskəveɪʃən] [eks-ka-vei-shon], *s*. 1. Excavación, cavidad. 2. *(Agr.)* Excava.

excavator [ˈekskəveɪtəʳ] [eks-ka-vei-taʳ], *s*. Excavador (person); excavadora (machine).

exceed [ɪkˈsiːd] [ik-sid], *va*. Exceder; sobrepujar, sobresalir; pasar los límites regulares o prescritos (be greater than); rebasar, sobrepasar (go beyond/limit, minimun); superar (expectations, fears, hopes); excederse en (powers). -*vn*. Excederse, propasarse; aventajarse.

exceeder [ɪkˈsiːdəʳ] [ik-si-daʳ], *s*. El que sobresale o excede.

exceeding [ɪkˈsiːdɪŋ] [ik-si-din], *a*. Excesivo. -*s*. Lo que sobrepuja los límites ordinarios. -*adv*. *(Ant.)* Eminentemente, en alto grado.

exceedingly [ɪkˈsiːdɪŋlɪ] [ik-si-din-li], *adv*. Excesivamente, sumamente, extremadamente.

exceedingness [ɪkˈsiːdɪŋnɪs] [ik-si-din-nes], *s*. Grandeza o tamaño excesivo, magnitud desmesurada; duración extraordinariamente larga; extensión muy grande.

excel [ɪkˈsel] [ik-sel], *vn*. Sobresalir, sobrepujar, aventajarse a, tener buenas propiedades o calidades en sumo grado. **To excel in/at something**, destacar en algo. **To excel oneself**, lucirse. -*va*. Sobresalir, exceder singularmente a otra persona o cosa en cuanto a las buenas propiedades o calidades.

excellence, excellency [ˈeksələns] [ek-se-lens], *s*. 1. Excelencia, dignidad, rango, preeminencia. 2. Excelencia, un título de honor. 3. Pureza, bondad.

excellent [ˈeksələnt] [ek-se-lent], *a*. Excelente, selecto, sobresaliente, primoroso.

excellently [ˈeksələntlɪ] [ek-se-lent-li], *adv*. Excelentemente, primorosamente.

excelsior [ekˈselzɪɔːʳ] [ek-sel-siaʳ], *a*. Aún más alto; siempre hacia arriba; lema del Estado de Nueva York. -*s*. Madera en hebras y virutas delgadas para empaquetar y rellenar colchones (EU).

excentric [ˈeksəntrɪk] [ek-sen-trik], *a*. *V.* ECCENTRIC.

except [ɪkˈsept] [ik-sept], *va*. Exceptuar, omitir, excluir; particularmente excluir la mención o consideración de alguien o algo (exclude). -*vn*. Excepcionar, poner excepciones a lo que se alega; recusar o declinar la jurisdicción de alguno.

except, *prep*. 1. Excepto, con exclusión de, a excepción de, fuera de, menos (apart from). **Except for**, si no fuera por (if

it weren't for). 2. Si no, a menos que. *Conj*. **Except that**, pero (if it weren't that).

excepting [ɪkˈseptɪŋ] [ik-sep-tin], *prep*. A excepción de, fuera de, salvo, excepto (except). **We must invite everyone, not excepting Sam**, tenemos que invitarlos a todos, incluyendo a Sam.

exception [ɪkˈsepʃən] [ik-sep-shon], *s*. 1. Excepción; la cosa exceptuada. **To make an exception**, hacer una excepción. **Without exception**, sin excepción. 2. Exclusión. 3. *(For.)* Excepción, recusación; objeción.

exceptionable [ɪkˈsepʃənəbl] [ik-sep-sho-na-bol], *a*. Recusable, tachable, expuesto o sujeto a reparos y contradicciones.

exceptional [ɪkˈsepʃənl] [ik-sep-sho-nal], *a*. Excepcional, que forma excepción a la regla común; poco común, no usual, superior.

exceptionally [ɪkˈsepʃənəlɪ] [ik-sep-sho-na-li] *a*. Excepcionalmente.

exceptionless [ɪkˈsepʃənlɪs] [ik-sep-shon-les], *s*. 1. Excepción; la cosa exceptuada. 2. Exclusión. 3. *(For.)* Excepción, recusación; objeción.

exceptious [ɪkˈsepʃəs] [ik-sep-shos], *a*. Impertinente, ridículo; litigioso; delicado, resentido.

exceptiousness [ɪkˈsepʃəsnɪs] [ik-sep-shos-nes], *s*. Impertinencia.

exceptive [ɪkˈseptɪv] [ik-sep-tiv], *a*. 1. Exceptivo, excepcional, de la naturaleza de una excepción. 2. Susceptible, quisquilloso, caviloso.

exceptor [ɪkˈseptəʳ] [ik-sep-toʳ], *s*. Exceptuador, el que pone excepciones.

excerpt [ˈeksɜːpt] [ik-serpt], *va*. Sacar, extraer, tomar, como se toma o cita de un libro (to take, to get). -*s*. Extracto, selección, cita de materia escrita o impresa. Pasaje.

excerption [ˈeksɜːpʃən] [ik-serp-shon], *s*. El acto de hacer extractos; selecciones, colecciones, extractos.

excerptive [ˈeksɜːptɪv] [ik-serp-tiv], *a*. Que extrae o entresaca.

excerptor [ˈeksɜːptəʳ] [ik-serp-taʳ], *s*. El que se aprovecha de los escritos de otros tomando trozos de ellos; plagiario.

excess [ɪkˈses] [ik-ses], *s*. 1. Exceso, excedente. 2. Exceso, la porción o parte que hay de más. Excedente (surplus). **In excess of**, superior a, por encima de. 3. Exceso, demasía en el comer o beber; destemplanza; transgresión de los límites debidos, desorden, desarreglo. **To eat and drink to excess**, comer y beber en exceso. **To carry something to excess**, llevar algo a la exageración. *a*. **Excess weight/profits**, exceso de peso/beneficios.

excess baggage [ˌɪksesˈbægɪdʒ] [ik-ses-ba-guich], *s*. Exceso de equipaje.

excess fare [ˈɪksesfɛəʳ] [ik-ses-feaʳ], *s*. Suplemento (pagado en el transporte público).

excessive [ɪkˈsesɪv] [ik-se-siv], *a*. Excesivo, vehemente, desarreglado, inmoderado, desmesurado.

excessively [ɪkˈsesɪvlɪ] [ik-se-siv-li], *adv*. Excesivamente, extremadamente.

excessiveness [ɪkˈsesɪvnɪs] [ik-se-siv-nes], *s*. Exceso, calidad de excesivo.

exchange [ɪksˈtʃeɪndʒ] [ik-cheinch], *va*. 1. Cambiar; canjear. 2. Cambiar, trocar, permutar. **To exchange words**, cambiar, decirse algunas palabras. **To exchange guns, pisotols, o shots**, darse o tirarse pistoletazos. **To exchange cards**, desafiarse. **To exchange prisoners**, canjear prisioneros de guerra. **To exchange signs**, hacerse señas.

exchange, *s*. 1. Cambio, trueque o permuta; canje. 2. La cosa que se da o recibe en cambio de otra. 3. *(Com.)* Bolsa, lonja, plaza o casa de contratación. **Exchange control**, control de divisas. 4. *(Com.)* Cambio, el giro o conmutación de dinero de una parte a otra. **Exchange rate**, tipo de cambio. 5. *(Com.)* Cambio, el aumento o disminución de valor que se da a la moneda al tiempo de la paga en los parajes adonde se la destina. 6. *(Com.)* Cambio, el interés que lleva el cambista o banquero. *(Mil.)* **Exchange of prisoners**, canje de prisioneros. **Exchange of shots**, tiroteo. 7. Despacho central de teléfonos.

exchangeable [ɪks'tʃeɪndʒəbl] [ik-chein-cha-bol], *a*. Lo que se puede cambiar.

exchanger [ɪks'tʃeɪndʒəʳ] [ik-chein-chaʳ], *s*. Cambista o cambiante de letras o moneda, banquero.

exchequer [ɪks'tʃekəʳ] [ik-che-kaʳ], *s*. Hacienda, fisco, tesorería. **Exchequer bills**, vales de la tesorería que se libran y se pagan cada año; vales reales.

exchequer, *va*. Procesar en el tribunal de la hacienda.

excipient [ɪks'sɪpɪənt] [ik-si-pient], *s*. *(Med.)* Excipiente, substancia que sirve para incorporar otras a un medicamento o disolverlas en él.

excisable [ek'saɪzəbl] [ek-sai-za-bol], *a*. Sujeto al derecho de sisa, tasable.

excise, *va*. 1. Cortar, extirpar. 2. Sisar; aforar, exigir tributo sobre algo.

exciseman ['eksaɪzmæn] [ek-saiz-man], *s*. Sisero, el oficial o guarda que registra los géneros que deben pagar el derecho de sisa.

excision [ek'sɪʒən] [ek-si-shon], *s*. 1. *(Cir.)* Separación, corte o remoción de una parte; excisión. 2. Extirpación.

excitability [ɪk'saɪtə'bɪlɪtɪ] [ik-sai-ta-bi-li-ti], *s*. Excitabilidad, la capacidad de excitarse o de ser excitado.

excitable [ɪk'saɪtəbl] [ik-sai-ta-bol], *a*. Excitable.

excitant [ɪk'saɪtənt] [ik-sai-tant], *s*. y *a*. Estimulante, excitante.

excitation [eksɪ'teɪʃən] [ek-si-tei-shon], *s*. Excitación; instigación, incitamiento.

excitative, excitator [ɪk'saɪtətɪv] [ik-sai-ta-tiv], *a*. Excitativo.

excite [ɪk'saɪt] [ik-sait], *va*. Excitar, mover, animar, estimular. **Exciting cause**, *(Med.)* causa ocasional o concausa.

excited [ɪk'saɪtɪv] [ik-sai-ted], *a*. Entusiasmado, emocionado. **To get excited**, ilusionarse, entusiasmarse; alborotarse (crowd).

excitement [ɪk'saɪtmənt] [ik-sait-mant], *s*. Estímulo, incitamiento, instigación, motivo, agitación, conmoción (upheaval, commotion). **To cause great excitement**, causar gran emoción. **Why all the excitement**, ¿a qué se debe tanta conmoción?

exciter [ɪk'saɪtəʳ] [ik-sai-taʳ], *s*. Motor, incitador, agitador, instigador.

exciting [ɪk'saɪtɪŋ] [ik-sai-tin], *a*. Estimulador, excitante, emocionante (moving, thrilling).

exclaim [ɪks'kleɪm] [iks-kleim], *vn*. Exclamar, dar gritos y voces, clamar mucho.

exclaim, *s*. Clamor, gritería.

exclamation [ˌeksklə'eɪʃən] [eks-kla-mei-shon], *s*. 1. Exclamación, grito, clamor. 2. Expresión precipitada o enfática del pensamiento o del sentido. 3. *(Gram.)* Interjección. 4. Admiración, el signo ortográfico!

exclamatory [eks'klæmətərɪ] [eks-kla-ma-to-ri], *a*. Exclamatorio.

exclude [ɪks'kluːd] [iks-klud], *va*. Excluir, echar fuera; exceptuar; rechazar; *(Biol.)* expeler, arrojar.

exclusion [ɪks'kluːʒən] [iks-klu-shon], *s*. Exclusión, exclusiva, excepción; emisión.

exclusionist [ɪks'kluːʒənɪst] [iks-klu-sho-nist], *s*. El que quiere excluir a otros.

exlusive [ɪks'kluːsɪv] [iks-klu-siv], *a*. Exclusivo, privativo; exceptuado. **Exclusive rights**, exclusiva.

exclusively [ɪks'kluːsɪvlɪ] [iks-klu-siv-li], *adv*. Exclusivamente, sin entrar en cuenta.

exclusiveness [ɪks'kluːsɪvnɪs] [iks-klu-siv-nes], *s*. Exclusiva, repulsa; calidad de exclusivo.

exclusivism [ɪks'kluːsɪvɪzm] [iks-klu-si-vi-sem], *s*. Sistema de exclusión.

exclusivity [ɪks'kluːsɪvɪtɪ] [iks-klu-si-vi-ti], *a*. Exclusividad.

excogitate [ɪks'kɒdʒɪteɪt] [iks-ko-chi-teit] *va*. Excogitar, pensar, imaginar, inventar. -*vn*. Pensar.

excogitation [ɪks'kɒdʒɪteɪʃən] [iks-ko-chi-tei-shon], *s*. Invención, pensamiento.

excommunicable [ˌekskə'mjuːnɪkəbl] [eks-ko-miu-ni-ka-bol], *a*. Digno de excomunión.

excommunicate [ˌekskə'mjuːnɪkeɪt] [eks-ko-miu-ni-keit], *va*. Excomulgar, descomulgar, anatematizar.

excommunicate, *a*. y *s*. Excomulgado, el que está apartado y excluído de la comunión de los fieles.

excommunication ['ekskə,mjuːnɪ'keɪʃən] [eks-ko-miu-ni-kei-shon], *s*. Excomunión, descomunión, anatema religioso.

excoriate [eks'kɔːrɪeɪt] [eks-ko-rieit], *va*. Desollar; y de aquí, excoriar, gastar, arrancar o corroer el cutis quedando la carne descubierta.

excoriation [eks'kɔːrɪeɪʃən] [eks-ko-riei-shon], *s*. Excoriación, desolladura.

excortication [eks'kɔːrtɪkeɪʃən] [eks-kor-ti-kei-shon], *s*. Descortezadura, el acto de descortezar.

excreate [eks'krɪeɪt] [eks-krieit], *va*. *(Des.)* Escupir, expectorar.

excrement ['ekskrɪment] [eks-kri-ment], *s*. Excremento.

excremental ['ekskrɪmentl] [eks-kri-men-tal], *a*. Excrementoso.

excrementitial, excrementitious [ˌekskrɪmen'tɪʃəl] [eks-kri-men-ti-shal], *a*. Excrementicio.

excrescence, excrescency [ɪks'kresns] [iks-kre-sens], *s*. Excrecencia, carnosidad o superfluidad que se cría en animales y plantas.

excrescent [ɪks'kresnt] [iks-kre-sent], *a*. Superfluo, lo que forma una excrecencia.

excrete [eks'kriːt] [eks-krit], *va*. Excretar, echar fuera, arrojar los humores o materias fecales.

excrete, *s*. Excreta, lo que se excreta; materia inútil.

excretion [eks'kriːʃən] [eks-kri-shon], *s*. 1. Excreción, la acción de excretar. 2. Excreta, la materia que se excreta.

excretive [eks'kriːtɪv] [eks-kri-tiv], *a*. Excretorio, lo que tiene virtud de preparar los fluidos destinados a ser expelidos del cuerpo.

excretory [eks'kriːtərɪ] [eks-kri-to-ri], *a*. Excretorio, perteneciente a la excreción; que lleva o conduce una materia excretada. -*s*. El órgano excretrio o que sirve para la excreción.

excruciable [ɪks'kruːʃəbl] [eks-kru-sha-bol], *a*. Sujeto o expuesto a tormentos.

excruciate [ɪks'kruːʃɪeɪt] [eks-kru-shieit], *va*. Atormentar, afligir o molestar corporalmente a otro.

excruciating [ɪks'kruːʃɪeɪtɪŋ] [eks-kru-shiei-tin], *a*. 1. Que atormenta agudamente, que causa el dolor más violento; extremamente doloroso. 2. *(Fam. E. U.)* Extremadamente remilgado, exigente o presuntuoso.

excruciation [ɪks'kruːʃɪeɪʃən] [eks-kru-shiei-shon], *s*. Tormento, molestia.

excubation [ɪks'kjʊbeɪʃən] [eks-kiu-bei-shon], *s*. *(Des.)* Vela, la acción de pasar toda la noche despierta.

exculpate ['ekskʌlpeɪt] [eks-kal-peit], *va*. Disculpar, excusar, justificar.

exculpation [ˌekskʌl'peɪʃən] [eks-kal-pei-shon], *s*. Disculpa.

exculpatory [ˌekskʌlpə'tərɪ] [eks-kal-pa-to-ri], *a*. Disculpador, justificativo.

excursion [ɪks'kɜːʃən] [iks-ker-shon], *s*. 1. Paseo, viaje corto o de poca duración. 2. Excursión, correría o entrada en país enemigo. 3. La acción de separarse del camino regular o trillado. 4. Digresión. 5. *(Fís.)* La mitad del movimiento de oscilación o vibración de un cuerpo. **Excursion ticket, train**, billete de ida y vuelta, tren de excursión.

excursionist [ɪks'kɜːʃənɪst] [iks-ker-sho-nist], *s*. El que hace una excursión; el que viaja por curiosidad y distracción.

excursive [ɪks'kɜːsɪv] [iks-ker-siv], *a*. 1. Errante, vagante, paseante. 2. *(Fig.)* Digresivo, errático, pasajero, mudable.

excursively [ɪks'kɜːsɪvlɪ] [iks-ker-siv-li], *adv*. De un modo vago, digresivo o errante.

excursiveness [ɪks'kɜːsɪvnɪs] [iks-ker-siv-nes], *s*. El acto de pasar los límites acostumbrados.

excusable [ɪks'kjuːzəbl] [iks-kiu-sa-bol], *a*. Excusable, disculpable.

excusableness [ɪksˈkjuːzəblnɪs] [iks-kiu-sa-bol-nes], *s.* Excusa, calidad de excusable.

excusatory [ɪksˈkjuːzətərɪ] [iks-kiu-sa-to-ri], *a.* Apologético, lo que excusa.

excuse [ɪksˈkjuːs] [iks-kius], *va.* 1. Excusar, disculpar, dar excusas. 2. Eximir, libertar, exentar, dispensar (exempt, free). 3. Perdonar, no exigir, remitir, tolerar (allow, bear). 4. Justificar, vindicar (justify). **Excuse me!**, con permiso, perdón, disculpe. **I must ask to be excused this time**, esta vez les ruego me dispensen.

excuse, *f.* Excusa, disculpa, justificación (justification); pretexto (no sincere). **To make excuses for somebody**, presentar excusas de alguien. **There is no excuse for this**, esto no tiene disculpa.

excuseless [ɪksˈkjuːslɪs] [iks-kius-les], *a.* Inexcusable.

excuser [ɪksˈkjuːsəʳ] [iks-kiu-saʳ], *s.* Excusador, intercesor; perdonador; apologista.

excuss [ɪksˈkʌs] [iks-kas], *va.* 1. (*Ant.*) Echar de sí, arrojar. 2. Embargar los bienes a alguno.

excussion [ɪksˈkʌʒən] [iks-ka-shon], *s.* (*Des.*) Ejecución, la aprehensión que se hace de la persona o bienes del que es deudor; embargo de bienes.

ex dividend [ˌeksˈdɪvɪdend] [eks-di-vi-dend], *a.* Sin dividendo.

execrable [ˈeksɪkrəbl] [ek-si-kra-bol], *a.* Execrable, abominable, detestable, aborrecible.

execrably [ˈeksɪkrəblɪ] [ek-si-kra-bli], *adv.* Execrablemente.

execrate [ˈeksɪkreɪt] [ek-si-kreit], *va.* Execrar, maldecir, abominar.

execration [ˌeksɪˈkreɪʃən] [ek-si-krei-shon], *s.* Execración, maldición, abominación.

execratory [ˈeksɪkrətərɪ] [ek-si-kra-to-ri], *s.* Juramento execratorio.

executable [ˈeksɪkjuːtəbl] [ek-si-kiu-ta-bol], *a.* Ejecutable. **Executable file**, fichero ejecutable (*Inform.*).

executant [ˈeksɪkjuːtənt] [ek-si-kiu-tant], *s.* El que ejecuta o pone por obra; en especial, ejecutante.

execute [ˈeksɪkjuːt] [ek-si-kiut], *va.* 1. Ejecutar, poner por obra lo que está ideado (plan). 2. Ejecutar, ajusticiar (crime). 3. Matar, asesinar (kill). -*vn.* 4. Ejecutar su deber. 5. Servir una cosa perfectamente para el fin a que se la destina. 6. Otorgar, conceder (document).

executer [ˈeksɪkjuːtəʳ] [ek-si-kiu-taʳ], *s.* Ejecutor, el que ejecuta o pone por obra alguna cosa.

execution [ˌeksɪˈkjuːʃən] [ek-si-kiu-shon], *s.* 1. Cumplimiento, ejecución, el acto de ejecutar. 2. Ejecución, embargo, la aprehensión que se hace en la persona o bienes del que es deudor por mandamiento de juez competente (distraint, seizure). **Writ of execution**, auto de ejecución. 3. Ejecución, justicia, el acto público de ejecutar en el reo la pena capital. 4. Destrucción, mortandad (destruction). 5. Agilidad, destreza para tocar un instrumento o cantar; de aquí, destreza técnica (performance). 6. Trabajo efectivo. 7. Comisión (act, crime).

executioner [ˌeksɪˈkjuːʃənəʳ] [ek-si-kiu-sho-naʳ], *s.* 1. Ejecutor, la persona que pone por obra alguna cosa; especialmente, verdugo (hangman). 2. El instrumento o la agencia que sirve para ejecutar algo.

executive [ɪɡˈzekjuːtɪv] [ik-se-kiu-tiv], *a.* Ejecutivo. -*s.* **The executive**, el poder ejecutivo, el gobierno; la corte; la autoridad suprema. **Executive car**, coche de ejecutivo. **Executive comittee**, junta directiva.

executor [ɪɡˈzekjuːtəʳ] [ik-se-kiu-taʳ], *s.* Albacea, testamentario.

executorship [ɪɡˈzekjuːtəʃɪp] [ik-se-kiu-tòr-ship], *s.* Albaceazgo.

executory [ɪɡˈzekjuːtərɪ] [ik-se-kiu-to-ri], *a.* 1. Ejecutorio, ejecutivo; administrativo. 2. Que se debe ejecutar o poner en vigor y efecto; que llega a tener fuerza y efecto en ocasión futura.

executress [ɪɡˈzekjuːtrɪs] [ik-se-kiu-tres], **executrix** [ɪɡˈzekjuːtrɪks] [ik-se-kiu-triks], *f.* Albacea, ejecutora, la mujer que ha sido nombrada testamentaria.

exegesis [ˌeksɪˈdʒiːsɪs] [ek-si-chi-sis], *s.* Explicación, exposición clara, exégesis; especialmente de la Sagrada Biblia.

exegetical [ˌeksɪˈdʒiːtɪkl] [ek-si-chi-ti-kal], *a.* Exegético, explicativo.

exegetically [ˌeksɪˈdʒiːtɪklɪ] [ek-si-chi-ti-ka-li], *adv.* Por vía de explicación.

exemplar [ˈɪɡzemplɑː] [ig-sem-plaʳ], *s.* Ejemplar, original, modelo (model, example).

exemplarily [ˈɪɡzemplərɪlɪ] [ig-sem-pla-ri-li], *adv.* Ejemplarmente; por ejemplo.

exemplariness [ˈɪɡzemplərɪnɪs] [ig-sem-pla-ri-nes], *s.* Estado, situación o calidad que debe servir de ejemplar o modelo.

exemplarity [ˈɪɡzemplərɪtɪ] [ig-sem-pla-ri-ti], *s.* Ejemplo digno de imitación.

exemplary [ˈɪɡzemplərɪ] [ig-sem-pla-ri], *a.* 1. Ejemplar, lo que merece ser imitado (model). 2. Que sirve como ejemplo de amonestación o escarmiento.

exemplification [ɪɡˌzemplɪfɪˈkeɪʃən] [ig-sem-pli-fi-kei-shon], *s.* 1. Ejemplar, traslado; ejemplificación, declaración o ilustración hecha con ejemplos. 2. (*For.*) Copia certificada.

exemplifier [ɪɡˈzemplɪfaɪəʳ] [ig-sem-pli-faiaʳ], *s.* El que da ejemplo; el que demuestra con ejemplos.

exemplify [ɪɡˈzemplɪfaɪ] [ig-sem-pli-fai], *va.* Ejemplificar, declarar, manifestar; trasladar, copiar.

exempt [ɪɡˈzempt] [ig-sempt], *va.* Exentar, libertar, eximir, privilegiar a alguna persona o cosa. **He's exempt from paying**, está exento de pagar.

exempt, *a.* Exento; no sujeto, no obligado.

exemptible [ɪɡˈzemptɪbl] [ig-semp-ti-bol], *a.* Exento, privilegiado, libre.

exemption [ɪɡˈzempʃən] [ig-semp-shon], *s.* Exención, franquicia, inmunidad.

exenterate [ɪɡˈzentəreɪt] [ig-sen-te-reit], *va.* Desentrañar, destripar.

exequatur [ɪɡˈzekwətʊʳ] [ig-se-kua-tuʳ], *s.* Exequátur, la autorización que se da a un cónsul extranjero para que pueda ejercer el cargo de que se halla revestido.

exequial [ɪɡˈzekwɪəl] [ig-se-kuial], *a.* Lo tocante a las exequias o funerales; antiguamente, exequial.

exequies [ɪɡˈzekwiːz] [ig-se-kuis], *s. pl.* Exequias, honras fúnebres.

exercisable [ˈeksəsaɪzəbl] [ek-ser-sai-sa-bol], *a.* Ejercitativo.

exercise [ˈeksəsaɪz] [ek-ser-sais], *s.* 1. Ejercicio, trabajo **In the exercise of my duties**, en el ejercicio de mi cargo. 2. Ejercicio, ensayo; el acto de ejercitar alguna cosa. 3. Tarea. 4. Práctica, empleo o ejercicio de alguna cosa para adquirir conocimiento habitual de ella. **Physical exercises**, gimnasia. 5. Acto de hablar, leer, declamar, etc., como en los actos públicos de las escuelas y en las reuniones religiosas; se usa generalmente en plural **Exercises**, ceremonias (EU). Recreación, recreo. 6. (*Ant.*) El acto de dar culto a Dios.

exercise, *vn.* Hacer ejercicio; ejercitarse. -*va.* 1. Ejercitar, formar, adiestrar o habituar (dog, horse, team, sport). 2. Atarear; ejercer (influence, power). 3. Emplear (patience, right). 4. Causar ansiedad de ánimo. 5. Comunicar como efecto; dar parte. -*vr.* Emplearse, adiestrarse, ejercitarse. **To be exercised about something**, estar preocupado por algo.

exerciser [ˈeksəsaɪzəʳ] [ek-ser-sai-saʳ], *s.* Ejercitante.

exercitation [ˌeksəsɪˈteɪʃən] [ek-ser-si-tei-shon], *s.* Ejercicio, ejercitación, práctica.

exergue [ɪɡˈzɜːɡ] [ik-serg], *s.* Exergo, la leyenda que está en las medallas debajo del emblema o figura del anverso.

exert [ɪɡˈzɜːt] [ik-sert], *va.* 1. Esforzar; ejecutar, poner por obra alguna cosa; poner en acción. 2. *vr.* **To exert oneself**, empeñarse, hacer esfuerzo, apurarse, darse trabajo (overdo).

exertion [ɪɡˈzɜːʃən] [ik-ser-shon], *s.* Esfuerzo, trabajo excesivo (effort). **Exertions**, *pl.* diligencias, pasos, medios.

exfoliant [eksˈfəʊlɪənt] [eks-fou-liant], *s.* Exfoliante.

exfoliate [eksˈfəʊlɪeɪt] [eks-fou-lieit], *vn.* 1. (*Cir.*) Exfoliarse, separarse de los huesos ciertas hojitas o láminas cariadas. 2.

Escamarse, separarse de la superficie en hojas o láminas. - *va*. Quitar láminas, hojas o esquirlas de alguna cosa.

exfoliation [eksˌfəʊlˈeɪʃən] [eks-fou-liei-shon], *s*. Exfoliación, separación por hojas o láminas, como de las partes cariadas de un hueso, de la corteza, de una lámina de mineral, o de la piel.

exfoliative [eksˈfəʊlɪətɪv] [eks-fou-lia-tiv], *a*. Exfoliativo: se dice de los remedios que pueden ayudar a la exfoliación.

ex-guardian [eksˈgɑːdɪən] [eks-gar-dian], *s*. Ex-guardián.

exhalable [ˌeksˈhæləbl] [eks-ja-la-bol], *a*. Exhalable, evaporable.

exhalation [ˌeksˈhælˈeɪʃən] [eks-ja-lei-shon], *s*. 1. Exhalación. 2. Exhalación, efluvio, vapor.

exhale [eksˈheɪl] [eks-jeil], *va*. 1. Exhalar, echar de sí vapor o vaho; emitir (fume). 2. Evaporar, hacer evaporarse (evaporate). -*vn*. Disiparse en vapor; desvanecerse (disappear).

exhalement [eksˈheɪlmənt] [eks-jeil-ment], *s*. (Des.) Exhalación, vapor o vaho.

exhaust [ɪgˈzɔːst] [ik-sost], *va*. 1. Apurar, consumir el agua u otro licor. 2. Agotar; gastar, consumir, disipar (finish, drain). 3. Empobrecer; debilitar, enflaquecer (weaken). 4. Cansar (get tired). **To be exhausted**, no poder más. **Exhausted receiver**, recipiente de que se ha extraído el aire. **Exhaust pipe**, tubo de escape.

exhaust, *s*. Escape, descarga, expulsión. **Exhaust chamber**, cámara de escape. **Exhaust pipe**, tubo de escape.

exhauster [ɪgˈzɔːstəʳ] [ik-sos-taʳ], *s*. Agotador.

exhaustible [ɪgˈzɔːstɪbl] [ik-sos-ti-bol], *a*. Agotable, capaz de ser apurado o agotado.

exhausting [ɪgˈzɔːstɪŋ] [ik-sos-tin], *a*. Exhaustivo, agotador.

exhaustion [ɪgˈzɔːsʃən] [ik-sos-shon], *s*. Agotamiento.

exhaustive [ɪgˈzɔːstɪv] [ik-sos-tiv], *a*. Apurador, que tiende a agotar; cabal, completo en su ejecución, detallado.

exhaustively [ɪgˈzɔːstɪvlɪ] [ik-sos-tiv-li], *adv*. Cabalmente, completamente.

exhaustiveness [ɪgˈzɔːstɪvnɪs] [ik-sos-tiv-nes], *s*. Calidad de completo, de cabal.

exhaustless [ɪgˈzɔːstlɪs] [ik-sost-les], *a*. Inagotable.

exheredate [eksˈherədeɪt] [eks-je-re-deit], *va*. Desheredar.

exheredation [eksherəˈdeɪʃən] [eks-je-re-dei-shon], *s*. (For.) Desheredamiento.

exhibit [ɪgˈzɪbɪt] [ik-si-bit], *va*. 1. Exhibir, manifestar (emotion), ofrecer, presentar (book, film), mostrar **To be on exhibit**, estar expuesto. 2. (Med.) Administrar, recetar un medicamento.

exhibit, *s*. 1. Cualquier objeto o colección de objetos expuestos a la vista pública. 2. Manifestación. 3. (For.) Documento fehaciente presentado en un tribunal de justicia.

exhibiter, exhibitor [ɪgˈzɪbɪtəʳ] [ik-si-bi-taʳ], *s*. 1. Exponente, el que exhibe, que muestra alguna cosa en público. 2. El que presenta documento fehaciente en un tribunal de justicia.

exhibition [ˌeksɪˈbɪʃən] [ik-si-bi-shon], *s*. 1. Exhibición, manifestación o presentación de alguna cosa; exposición. **An exhibition of cleverness**, una demostración de inteligencia. 2. Espectáculo, la acción de presentar alguna cosa en público (art, sport). 3. (Med.) Administración de un remedio. 4. (Ingl.) Beca (school).

exhibitioner [ˌeksɪˈbɪʃənəʳ] [ik-si-bi-sho-naʳ], *s*. Estudiante que disfruta en las universidades de Inglaterra de una pensión para su sostenimiento. Esta palabra equivale a *Beca de merced o pensionado*.

exhibitionism [ˌeksɪˈbɪʃənɪzəm] [ik-si-bi-sho-nisem], *sm*. Exhibicionismo.

exxhibitionist [ˌeksɪˈbɪʃənɪst] [ik-si-bi-sho-nist], *a*. Exhibicionista.

exhibitive [ekˈsɪbɪtɪv] [ik-si-bi-tiv], *a*. Representativo.

exhibitively [ekˈsɪbɪtɪvlɪ] [ik-si-bi-tiv-li], *adv*. Representativamente.

exhibitor [ˌeksɪˈbɪtəʳ] [ik-si-bi-taʳ], *s*. Expositor.

exhibitory [ˌeksɪˈbɪtərɪ] [ik-si-bi-to-ri], *a*. Exhibitorio, lo que exhibe o manifiesta.

exhilarant [ɪgˈzɪlærənt] [ik-si-la-rant], *a*. Alegrador, que causa regocijo o alegría.

exhilarate [ɪgˈzɪləreɪt] [ik-si-la-reit], *va*. Alegrar, causar alegría; causar sensación de viveza en; llenar de alegría (cheer up, gladden). -*vn*. Alegrarse.

exhilaration [ɪgˌzɪləˈreɪʃən] [ik-si-la-rei-shon], *s*. Alegría, buen humor, regocijo (joy).

exhort [ɪgˈzɔːt] [ik-sort], *va*. Exhortar, inducir y mover con razones; excitar.

exhortation [ˌegzɔːˈteɪʃən] [ek-sor-tei-shon], *s*. 1. Exhortación. 2. Aviso, consejo.

exhortative, exhortatory [ˌegzɔːˈtətɪv] [ek-sor-ta-tiv], *a*. Exhortatorio.

exhorter [ɪgˈzɔːtəʳ] [ik-sor-taʳ], *s*. Exhortador.

exhumate [ˈekshjuːmeɪt] [ek-siu-meit], *va*. (Fam.) V. EXHUME.

exhumation [ˌekshjuːˌeɪʃən] [ek-siu-mei-shon], *s*. Exhumación, desentierro de un cadáver.

exhume [eksˈhjuːm] [ek-sium], *va*. Exhumar, desenterrar.

ex-husband [ˌeksˈhʌzbənd] [eks-jas-band], *sm*. Ex-marido.

exiccate [ˈeksɪkeɪt] [ek-si-keit], *va*. Desecar, secar. V. EXSICCATE.

exiccation [ˌeksɪˈkeɪʃən] [ek-si-kei-shon], *s*. Desecación. V. EXSICCATION.

exiccative [ˈeksɪkətɪv] [ek-si-ka-tiv], *a*. Desecativo. V. EXSICCATIVE.

exigence, exigency [ˈeksɪdʒəns] [ek-si-yens], *s*. Exigencia, falta, necesidad (need), urgencia, aprieto (emergency), apuro, lance apretado; ocasión.

exigent [ˈeksɪdʒənt] [ek-si-yent], *a*. Exigente, urgente, que demanda acción inmediata (urgent); exigente, que pide demasiado. -*s*. Urgencia; embarazo, perplejidad; cabo, fin, remate.

exigible [ˈeksɪdʒɪbl] [ek-si-chi-bol], *a*. Exigible, que puede exigirse.

exiguity [ˈeksɪgʊɪtɪ] [ek-si-güi-ti], *s*. Pequeñez, parvedad, modicidad, exigüidad.-

exiguous [egˈzɪgjʊəs] [ek-si-guos], *a*. Exiguo, pequeño.

exile [ˈeksaɪl] [ek-sail], *s*. 1. Destierro. 2. Desterrado.

exile, *va*. Desterrar, deportar.

exiled [ˈeksaɪld] [ek-saild], *a*. Exiliado.

exility [ˈeksaɪlətɪ] [ek-sai-la-ti], *s*. (Ant.) Tenuidad, pequeñez.

eximious [ˈeksɪmɪəs] [ek-si-mios], *a*. Eximio, eminente, excelente.

exinanition [ˌeksɪnəˈnɪʃən] [ek-si-na-ni-shon], *s*. Exinanición, gran falta de vigor y fuerza.

exist [ɪgˈzɪst] [ik-sist], *vn*. Existir.

existence [ɪgˈzɪstəns] [ik-sis-tens], *s*. 1. Existencia. 2. Vida, continuación de ser. 3. Ente. **To come into existence**, nacer, fundarse, formarse.

existent [ɪgˈzɪstənt] [ik-sis-tent], *a*. Existente.

existential [ɪgˈzɪstənʃəl] [ik-sis-ten-shal], *a*. Lo que tiene existencia.

existentialism [ɪgˈzɪstənʃəlɪzm] [ik-sis-ten-sha-lisem], *s*. (Fil.) Existencialismo.

exit [ˈeksɪt] [ek-sit], *s*. 1. Sale: palabra que se pone en los argumentos de las comedias para indicar cuando el actor se retira de la escena. 2. Partida, muerte. 3. Salida, éxito. **To make one's exit**, marcharse, salir.

exitial [ˈeksɪʃəl] [ek-si-shal], **exitious** [ˈeksɪʃəs] [ek-si-shos], *a*. Destructivo, pernicioso.

exode [ˈeksɒd] [ek-sod], *s*. Exodo, una de las cuatro partes de la tragedia griega que contenía la conclusión trágica o catástrofe.

exodus [ˈeksədəs] [ek-so-dos], *s*. 1. Salida, emigración, éxodo. 2. Éxodo, el segundo libro del antiguo Testamento.

exogen [ˈeksədʒɪn] [ek-so-chin], *s*. (Bot.) Planta exógena, aquella cuyo tallo crece por la adición de capas externas concéntricas; dicotiledónea.

exogenous [ˈeksədʒɪnəs] [ek-so-chi-nos], *a*. Exógeno, exógena, que crece por la adición de capas externas.

exomphalos [ˈeksəmfələs] [ek-som-fa-los], *s*. (Cir.) Exónfalo, hernia umbilical.

exonerate [ɪɡ'zɒnəreɪt] [ik-so-ne-reit], *va.* 1. Vindicar de una acusación o censura. 2. Exonerar, descargar; aliviar del peso, cargo u obligación.

exoneration [ɪɡ,zɒnə'reɪʃən] [ik-so-ne-rei-shon], *s.* 1. Exoneración. 2. Vindicación de una censura o acusación.

exonerative [ɪɡ'zɒnərətɪv] [ik-so-ne-ra-tiv], *a.* Lo que puede exonerar.

exorable [ɪɡ'zɒnərəbl] [ik-so-ra-bol], *a.* Exorable, el que se mueve por ruegos.

exorbitance, exorbirtancy [ɪɡ'zɔ:bɪtəns] [ik-sor-bi-tans], *s.* Exorbitancia, exceso desorde, enormidad, extravagancia.

exorbitant [ɪɡ'zɔ:bɪtənt] [ik-sor-bi-tant], *a.* Exorbitante, excesivo, desproporcionado, enorme, extravagante.

exorbitantly [ɪɡ'zɔ:bɪtəntlɪ] [ik-sor-bi-tant-li], *dv.* Exorbitantemente.

exorcise ['ekzɔ:saɪz] [ek-sor-sais], *va.* Exorcizar, conjurar.

exorciser ['ekzɔ:saɪzəʳ] [ek-sor-sai-saʳ], **exorcist** ['ekzɔ:sɪst] [ek-sor-sist], *s.* Exorcista.

exorcism ['ekzɔ:sɪzəm]ek-sor-si-sem], *s.* Exorcismo, la acción de exorcizar los espíritus malignos; también conjuro ordenado por la Iglesia contra el espíritu maligno.

exorcist ['ekzɔ:sɪst] [ek-sor-sist], *s.* Exorcista.

exordium ['ekzɔ:dɪəm] [ek-sor-dium], *s.* Exordio, principio o introducción de un discurso.

exosmose ['ekzɒsməʊs] [ek-sos-mous], *s. (Fís.)* Exósmosis, corriente de dentro a fuera, que se establece al mismo tiempo que se contraria la endósmosis, cuando dos líquidos de distinta densidad están separados por una membrana.

exosmotic [,ekzɒs'məʊtɪk] [ek-sos-mou-tik], *a.* Exosmótico, relativo a la exósmosis.

exosseous ['ekzɒsɪəs] [eks-osious], *a.* Desosado, sin huesos.

exostosis ['ekzɒstəʊsɪs] [ek-sos-to-sis], *s.* Exóstosis, tumor del hueso.

exoteric, exoterical [,ɪɡzə'terɪk] [ik-so-te-rik], *a.* Exotérico, público, común a todos, lo contrario de esotérico.

exotic, exotical [ɪɡ'zɒtɪk] [ik-so-tik], *a.* Exótico, extranjero; advenedizo. -*s. (Bot.)* Planta exótica.

exotically [ɪɡ'zɒtɪklɪ] [ik-so-ti-kli], *adv.* De manera exótica (dress, design, name, meal, etc).

exotic fuel [ɪɡ'zɒtɪk,fju:l] [ik-so-tik-fiul], *s.* Combustible, inusual, combustible de alta potencia.

exoticism [ɪɡ'zɒtɪzɪzm] [ik-so-ti-si-zem], *s.* Exotismo.

expand [ɪks'pænd] [iks-pand], *va.* 1. Extender, dilatar, alargar, ensanchar la superficie. 2. Extender, desarrollar, esparcir; desplegar. -*vn.* Desarrollarse, dilatarse, ensancharse.

expanse [ɪks'pæns] [iks-pans], *s.* Extensión, espacio.

expansibility [,ɪkspænsɪ'bɪlɪtɪ] [iks-pan-si-bi-li-ti], *s.* Expansibilidad.

expansible [ɪks'pænsɪbl] [iks-pan-si-bol], *a.* Expansible, capaz de expansión.

expansion [ɪks'pænʃən] [iks-pan-shon], *s.* 1. Expansión. 2. Aumento de tamaño, dilatación; anchura, largura; desarrollo. 3. Extensión, inmensidad. 4. Aumento de volumen, como el del vapor. **Triple expansion engine**, máquina de vapor de triple expansión.

expansile [ɪks'pænsɪl] [iks-pan-sil], *a.* Capaz de extensión, que tiene poder de dilatarse.

expansive [ɪks'pænsɪv] [iks-pan-siv], *a.* Expansivo.

expansively [ɪks'pænsɪvlɪ] [iks-pan-siv-li], *adv.* 1. Ampliamente, extensamente (relate). 2. Calurosamente, cálidamente (welcome).

expansiveness [ɪks'pænsɪvnɪs] [iks-pan-siv-nes], *s.* Expansibilidad, propiedad de un cuerpo de ocupar mayor espacio.

ex parte [ɪks'pɑ:t] [iks-part]. *(For.)* De una parte, de una de las partes.

expatiate [ɪks'peɪʃɪeɪt] [iks-pei-shiet], *vn.* 1. Espaciarse, dilatarse, difundirse. 2. Extenderse, discurrir con muchas palabras (be discursive, linger over). -*va.* Dar libre curso o alcance; extender (spread, extend).

expatiation [ɪks,peɪʃɪ'eɪʃən] [iks-pei-shi-ei-shon], *s.* Digresión, difusión, prolijidad.

expatiator [ɪks'peɪʃɪeɪtəʳ] [iks-pei-shi-ei-toʳ], *s.* Amplificador, el que habla larga y profusamente sobre un asunto.

expatiatory [eks'pænʃɪətərɪ] [iks-pei-shia-to-ri], *a.* Difuso, prolijo.

expatriate [ɪks'pætrɪeɪt] [iks-pa-trieit], *va.* Expatriar, desterrar.

expatriation [eks,pætrɪ'eɪʃən] [eks-pa-tri-ei-shon], *s.* Expatriación, destierro.

expect [ɪks'pekt] [iks-pekt], *va.* 1. Esperar, aguardar (wait). 2. Fiarse, descansar en, contar con, como cosa debida (suppose). 3. *(Fam.)* Suponer, en este sentido es un solecismo familiar. 4. *(Ant.)* Quedar, esperar. **I expect she's here by now**, me imagino que habrá llegado. **Just what I expected**, lo que yo esperaba, ya me lo figuraba. **As one might expect**, como era de esperar. **Don't expect me till you see me**, no contéis conmigo hasta que me veáis llegar. **To be expecting**, estar embarazada, estar encinta.

expectable [ɪks'pektəbl] [iks-pek-ta-bol], *a.* Expectable, lo que es de esperar o temer.

expectance, expectancy [ɪks'pektəns] [iks-pek-tans], *s.* Expectación, expectativa, esperanza, espera.

expectant [ɪks'pektənt] [iks-pek-tant], *a.* Expectante; se dice del que está en expectación de alguna cosa. **Expectant treatment**, tratamiento expectante. -*s.* Esperador; el que está en expectación de alguna cosa.

expectation [,ekspek'teɪʃən] [eks-pek-tei-shon], *s.* Expectación, expectativa, esperanza (hope, life, state). **A prince of great expectation**, un príncipe de grandes esperanzas. **Expectation of life**, esperanza de vida. **It's beyond my expectations**, es mejor de lo que esperaba.

expectative [ɪks'pektətɪv] [iks-pek-ta-tiv], *a.* Expectativo. -*s. (Des.)* Objeto de expectación.

expecter [ɪks'pektəʳ] [iks-pek-taʳ], *s.* Esperador.

expectorant [ɪks'pektərənt] [iks-pek-to-rant], *s. (Med.)* Expectorante, que promueve la expectoración, que hace expectorar. -*s.* Medicamento expectorante.

expectorate [ɪks'pektəreɪt] [iks-pek-to-reit], *va.* Expectorar, arrancar del pecho y arrojar por la boca flemas y otras materias viscosas.

expectoration [ɪks,pektə'reɪʃən] [iks-pek-to-rei-shon], *s.* Expectoración; esputo, gargajo.

expectorative [ɪks'pektərətɪv] [iks-pek-to-ra-tiv], *a.* Expectorativo, expectorante.

expedience, expediency [ɪks'pi:dɪəns] [iks-pi-diens], *s.* Aptitud, propiedad; lo más practicable, o factible, o lo que más conviene hacer dadas las circunstancias, conveniencia, utilidad, oportunidad.

expedient [ɪks'pi:dɪənt] [iks-pi-dient], *a.* 1. Oportuno, conveniente; prudente, propio. 2. *(Des.)* Expedito, pronto. -*s.* Expediente, medio, corte, recurso.

expediently [ɪks'pi:dɪəntlɪ] [iks-pi-dient-li], *adv.* Aptamente, convenientemente.

expeditate [ɪks'pi:dɪteɪt] [iks-pi-di-teit], *va.* Cortar una especie de espolones agudos que cierta clase de perros tienen en las patas y con los cuales desgarran la caza.

expeditation [,ɪkspɪdɪ'teɪʃən] [iks-pi-di-tei-shon], *s.* La acción de cortar los espolones y las uñas de las patas de los perros.

expedite ['ekspɪdaɪt] [eks-pi-dait], *va.* 1. Desembarazar, facilitar. 2. Acelerar, apresurar, dar prisa. 3. Expedir, dar curso y despacho a las causas o negocios.

expedite, *a. V.* EXPEDITIOUS.

expeditely ['ekspɪdaɪtlɪ] [eks-pi-dait-li], *adv.* Expeditamente.

expedition [,ekspɪ'dɪʃən] [eks-pi-di-shon], *s.* 1. Expedición, prisa, diligencia, celeridad. 2. Caminata, jornada de muchas personas con un objeto determinado y la colectividad de personas que la emprende. 3. Expedición, empresa de guerra.

expeditious [ekspɪ'dɪʃəs] [eks-pi-di-shos], *a.* Pronto, veloz, expedito.

expeditiously [ˌekspɪˈdɪʃəslɪ] [eks-pi-di-shos-li], *adv.* Expeditamente, prontamente.

expel [ɪksˈpel] [iks-pel], *va.* Expeler, arrojar (things), expulsar (person), echar fuera por medio de la fuerza o autoridad; desterrar, excluir; despedir.

expellable [ɪksˈpeləbl] [iks-pe-la-bol], *a.* Expulsable, que puede ser expelido.

expeller [ɪksˈpeləʳ] [iks-pe-laʳ], *s.* El o lo que expele, expulsa, etc.

expend [ɪksˈpend] [iks-pend], *va.* Expender, gastar (money), emplear dinero, tiempo, palabras (words), esfuerzos (efforts), etc, en alguna cosa; desembolsar.

expendable [ɪksˈpendəbl] [iks-pen-da-bol], *s.* Que no es imprescindible. Sustituible, reemplazable.

expenditure [ɪksˈpendɪtʃəʳ] [iks-pen-di-chaʳ], *s.* Gasto, desembolso.

expense [ɪksˈpens] [iks-pens], *s.* Expensas, gasto, coste (spent). **At any expense**, a toda costa. **To be at expense, to go to expense**, meterse o ponerse en gastos. **At his expense**, a su costa. **With all expenses paid**, con todos los gastos pagados.

expenseless [ɪksˈpenslɪs] [iks-pens-les], *a.* Poco o nada costoso.

expensive [ɪksˈpensɪv] [iks-pen-siv], *a.* 1. Pródigo, gastador, manirroto, amigo de gastar; liberal, generoso. 2. Costoso; dispendioso, de mucho precio.

expensively [ɪksˈpensɪvlɪ] [iks-pen-siv-li], *adv.* Costosamente.

expensiveness [ɪksˈpensɪvnɪs] [iks-pen-siv-nes], *s.* Prodigalidad, profusión; costa, coste, costo (spendings).

experience [ɪksˈpɪərɪəns] [iks-pia-riens], *s.* 1. Experiencia, conocimiento, práctica. 2. Algo experimentado o gozado. 3. Ejercicio espiritual; conversión. **To learn by experience**, aprender por experiencia propia; hacer la prueba.

experience, *va.* Experimentar; conocer y reconocer por medio del uso.

experienced [ɪksˈpɪərɪənst] [iks-pia-rienst], *a.* Experimentado, perito; hábil.

experiencer [ɪksˈpɪərɪənsəʳ] [iks-pia-rien-saʳ], *s.* Experimentador.

experiment [ɪksˈperɪmənt] [iks-pe-ri-ment], *s.* 1. Experimento, prueba, ensayo (test, essay). 2. Lo que va pasando por una prueba práctica. **He would not try the experiment**, no quiso hacer prueba, no quiso exponerse.

experiment, *vn.* Experimentar, hacer una prueba, un experimento.

experimental [ɪksˈperɪmentl] [iks-pe-ri-men-tal], *a.* Experimental; sabido y conocido en virtud de repetidas pruebas y experiencias (well known).

experimentalist [ɪksˈperɪmentəlɪst] [eks-pe-ri-men-ta-list], *s.* Experimentador.

experimentally [eksˌperɪˈmentəlɪ] [eks-pe-ri-men-ta-li], *adv.* Experimentalmente.

experimentation [eksˌperɪmenˈteɪʃən] [iks-pe-ri-men-tei-shon], *s.* Experimento, la acción u operación de experimentar.

experimenter [ɪksˈperɪmentəʳ] [eks-pe-ri-men-taʳ], *s.* Experimentador.

experimentist [ɪksˈperɪmentɪst] [iks-pe-ri-men-tist], *s.* Experimentador.

expert [ˈekspɜːt] [eks-pert], *a.* Experimentado, experto, práctico, pronto, diestro, hábil.

expertly [ˈekspɜːtlɪ] [eks-pert-li], *adv.* Diestramente, hábilmente, mañosamente.

expertness [ˈekspɜːtnɪs] [eks-pert-nes], *s.* Maña, destreza, habilidad.

expiable [ˈekspɪəbl] [eks-pia-bol], *a.* Expiable, lo que se puede expiar.

expiate [ˈekspɪeɪt] [eks-pieit], *va.* Expiar, limpiar y borrar un delito; pagar las penas debidas por las culpas, reparar un daño, dar satisfacción.

expiation [ˌekspɪˈeɪʃən] [eks-pi-ei-shon], *s.* Expiación, el acto de expiar; reparación, resarcimiento de un daño cualquiera. *V.* ATONEMENT.

expiatist, expiator [ˈekspɪətɪst] [eks-pia-tist], *s.* El que expía o hace expiación.

expiatory [ˈekspɪətərɪ] [eks-pia-to-ri], *a.* Expiatorio.

expiration [ˌekspaɪəˈreɪʃən] [eks-paia-rei-shon], *s.* 1. Espiración, salida del aire, aspirado en los pulmones (exhalation). 2. Muerte, el último suspiro o aliento (death). 3. Remate, término (end), fin. 4. Vapor.

expire [ˈɪkspaɪəʳ] [iks-paiaʳ], *va.* 1. Exhalar, despedir exhalaciones o vapores (breath out). 2. Expirar, respirar; concluir, acabar (end). -*vn.* Expirar, morir, dar el último aliento (die). 2. Acabarse alguna cosa, caducar (ticket).

explain [ɪksˈpleɪn] [iks-plein], *va.* Explanar (plain), explicar, aclarar (speak clearly). **That explains it**, con eso queda todo aclarado. **Explain away**, explicar o razonar de manera convincente.

explainable [ɪksˈpleɪnəbl] [iks-plei-na-bol], *a.* Explicable.

explainer [ɪksˈpleɪnəʳ] [iks-plei-naʳ], *s.* Expositor, comentador, intérprete.

explanation [ˌekspləˈneɪʃən] [eks-pla-nei-shon], *s.* Explanación, explicación, interpretación (clarification). **There must be some explanation**, tiene que haber una explicación.

explanatory, explanative [ɪksˈplænətərɪ] [iks-pla-na-to-ri], *a.* Interpretativo, explicativo, que sirve para explicar o tiende a ello.

expletive [eksˈpliːtɪv] [eks-pli-tiv], *a.* Expletivo, que sirve para hacer más llena o armoniosa la locución, pero que no es necesario para el sentido de la frase. -*s.* 1. Interjección, a menudo profana. 2. Partícula expletiva. 3. Algo que sirve para hechir; añadidura.

expletory [eksˈpletərɪ] [eks-ple-to-ri], *a.* Que sirve para llenar o hechir.

explicable [eksˈplɪkəbl] [eks-pli-ka-bol], *a.* Explicable.

explicate [ˈeksplɪkeɪt] [eks-pli-keit], *va.* Explicar, aclarar, alguna cosa que está confusa; desenredar, interpretar.

explication [ˌeksplɪˈkeɪʃən] [eks-pli-kei-shon], *s.* Explicación, ilustración, interpretación.

explicative [ˈeksplɪkətɪv] [eks-pli-ka-tiv], *a.* Explicativo.

explicator [ˈeksplɪkeɪtəʳ] [eks-pli-kei-toʳ], *s.* Expositor, antiguamente, exponedor, el que explica; ilustrador.

explicatory [ˈeksplɪkətərɪ] [eks-pli-ka-to-ri], *a.* Explicativo.

explicit [ɪksˈplɪsɪt] [iks-pli-sit], *a.* Explícito, claro, formal, categórico (clear).

explicit. (Lat. en vez de *explicitus est*, está terminado) Antiguamente se ponía esta palabra a lo último de los libros en lugar de la voz *fin* que ahora se usa.

explicitly [ɪksˈplɪsɪtlɪ] [iks-pli-sit-li], *adv.* Explícitamente (clearly).

explicitness [ɪksˈplɪsɪtnɪs] [iks-pli-sit-nes], *s.* Claridad en el lenguaje; lucidez en las ideas (clear words).

explode [ɪksˈpləʊd] [iks-ploud], *va.* 1. Hacer explosión, estallar, disparar con estallido. 2. Desacreditar, demostrar la falsedad de algo, difamar (rumor, theory). 3. Expeler con violencia y estrépito. -*va.* 1. Estallar, dar un estallido, hacer explosión, abrirse con estrépito (burst). 2. Silbar, como la pólvora. 3. Reventar, tener súbito fin; desplomarse (come crashing down). 4. (*Fisiol.*) Salir o dejarse ver súbitamente.

exploder [ɪksˈpləʊdəʳ] [iks-plou-daʳ], *s.* Causa cualquiera de una explosión; el que o lo que hace explosión o estalla.

exploit [ˈeksplɔɪt] [eks-ploit], *s.* Hazaña, hecho heroico o famoso (achievement).

exploit, *va.* (*Neol.*) 1. Explotar, sacar todo el beneficio o producto posible de una cosa o persona; utilizar para su interés particular. 2. Buscar. 3. Referir con pormenores.

exploitable [eksˈplɔɪtəbl] [eks-ploi-ta-bol], *a.* Explotable, que puede ser explotado.

exploitation [ˌeksplɔɪˈteɪʃən] [eks-ploi-tei-shon], *s.* 1. Explotación, la acción de explotar, de hacer uso de recursos naturales desatendidos hasta entonces. 2. Utilización en interés particular de alguien.

exploitative [ˌeksˈplɔɪtətɪv] [eks-ploi-ta-tiv], *a.* Explotador.

exploiting [eksˈplɔɪtɪŋ] [eks-ploi-tin], *s.* Explotación.

exploration [ˌeksplɔːˈreɪʃən] [eks-plo-rei-shon], *s.* Exploración, examen; investigación científica, particularmente geográfica, en regiones poco conocidas.

explorator [ˌeksplɔˈreɪtəʳ] [eks-plo-rei-taʳ], *s.* Explorador, examinador.

exploratory [eksˈplɒretərɪ] [eks-plo-ra-to-ri], *a.* Exploratorio.

explore [ɪksˈplɔːʳ] [iks-ploʳ], *va.* Explorar, averiguar, examinar, sondear, profundizar, observar.

explorer [ɪksˈplɔːrəʳ] [iks-plo-raʳ], *s.* Explorador.

explosion [ɪksˈplɒʊʒən] [iks-plou-shon], *s.* Explosión.

explosive [ɪksˈplɒʊzɪv] [iks-plou-siv], *a.* Explosivo, lo que tiene capacidad de hacer explosión. -*s.* Cualquiera substancia que puede causar explosión por su repentina combustión o descomposición.

explosiveness [ɪksˈplɒʊzɪvnɪs] [iks-plou-siv-nes], *f.* Calidad de explosivo.

expoliation [eksˈpɒlɪˈeɪʃən] [eks-po-li-ei-shon], *s.* Despojo; gasto.

exponent [eksˈpɒʊnənt] [eks-pou-nent], *s.* 1. (*Mat.*) Exponente. 2. Representante.

exponential [ˌekspɒʊˈnenʃəl] [eks-pou-nen-shal], *a.* Exponencial.

export [ˈekspɔːt] [eks-port], *va.* Exportar, sacar o extraer géneros de un país para otro. **Export duty**, derechos de exportación. **Export trade**, comercio de exportación. **Export credit**, crédito a la exportación. *f.* Exportación.

exportable [ˈekspɔːtəbl] [eks-por-ta-bol], *a.* Exportable, lo que puede ser exportado.

exportation [ˌekspɔːˈteɪʃən] [eks-por-tei-shon], *s.* Exportación, extracción. **Bounty on exportation**, prima de exportación. **Channel of exportation**, punto de salida de géneros.

exporter [eksˈpɔːtəʳ] [eks-por-taʳ], *s.* Exportador, el que exporta.

exports [ˈekspɔːtz] [eks-ports], *s. pl.* Las mercancías o géneros de un país para otro.

expose [ɪksˈpɒʊz] [iks-pous], *va.* 1. Exponer, poner de manifiesto alguna cosa, mostrar, descubrir, publicar, manifestar. 2. Exponer, poner en peligro, arriesgar. 3. Manifestar las cualidades de alguna persona de modo que se la exponga a ser censurada, burlada o despreciada; comprometer; ponerse en ridículo; descubrirse, faltar a la decencia (ridicule, compromise). 4. Abandonar una persona o cosa a su suerte. 5. Poner a descubierto, desenmascarar, descubrir y divulgar un enredo, abuso o escándalo (fake). **To expose oneself to**, exponerse a (danger).

exposé [ekˈspɒʊzeɪ] [eks-pou-sei], *f.* Exposición.

exposed [ɪksˈpɒʊzd] [iks-pousd], *pp.* y *a.* 1. Expuesto, mostrado, etc. 2. Descubierto, no abrigado.

exposer [ɪksˈpɒʊzəʳ] [iks-pou-saʳ], *s.* Exponente, el que expone.

exposition [ˌekspɒʊˈzɪʃən] [iks-pou-si-shon], *s.* 1. Exposición, la acción de exponer a la vista; exhibición pública de productos industriales, agrícolas, artísticos, etc (showing). 2. Exposición, explicación, interpretación (explanation). 3. Análisis retórico. 4. Desenlace de un drama. 5. Riesgo, peligro (danger, risk).

expositive [ɪksˈpɒzɪtɪv] [iks-po-si-tiv], *a.* Expositivo.

expositor [ɪksˈpɒzɪtəʳ] [iks-po-si-taʳ], *s.* Expositor; comentador, intérprete.

expository [ɪksˈpɒsɪtərɪ] [iks-po-si-to-ri], *a.* Expositivo, explicativo.

ex post facto [eksˌpɒstˈfæktə] [eks-post-fak-to]. Expresión latina para calificar la resolución tomada acerca de una cosa que ha sucedido antes; v. gr. se llama una ley *ex post facto*, cuando se aplica a un caso o delito anterior a ella.

expostulate [ɪksˈpɒstjɒleɪt] [iks-pos-tju-leit], *vn.* Debatir seriamente, reconvenir a uno amigablemente; representar el error o los inconvenientes de un acto, una medida, etc.,

procurando hacer cambiar a otro de opinión: seguido de *with*. **Expostulate with**, Discutir con, intentar convencer a.

expostulation [ɪksˌpɒstjɒˈleɪʃən] [iks-pos-tju-lei-shon], *s.* Debate, reconvención, disuasión.

expostulator [ɪksˈpɒstjɒleɪtəʳ] [iks-pos-tju-lei-taʳ], *s.* El que ventila algún asunto con otro reconviniéndole amigablemente.

expostulatory [ɪksˌpɒsˈtjɒlətərɪ] [iks-pos-tju-la-to-ri], *a.* Lo que contiene cargos o reconvenciones amistosas.

exposure [ɪksˈpɒʊʒəʳ] [iks-pou-shaʳ], *s.* 1. Manifestación, el acto de exponer (exposition). 2. Situación arriesgada o peligrosa (risk). 3. Aspecto; situación o posición con respecto a uno de los puntos cardinales. **The house has a southern exposure**, la casa da o mira al sur. 4. Escándalo; revelación de algo oculto y escandaloso, exhibición (Sex). **To die from exposure**, morir de frío.

exposure meter [ɪksˈpɒʊʒəˈmiːtəʳ] [iks-pou-sha-mi-taʳ], *s.* En fotografía, medidor de exposición, fotómetro.

expound [ɪksˈpaʊnd] [iks-paund], *va.* Exponer, declarar, interpretar, comentar.

expounder [ɪksˈpaʊndəʳ] [iks-paun-daʳ], *s.* Expositor, comentador.

express [ɪksˈpres] [iks-pres], *va.* 1. Expresar; manifestar, dar a entender. 2. Representar, ser símbolo o imagen de alguna cosa. 3. Designar, denotar; declarar el pensamiento de uno, proferir, articular. 4. Exprimir, sacar o extraer el jugo de alguna cosa. 5. Enviar, expedir por expreso o mensajero.

express, *a.* 1. Expreso, claro, formal, explícito (clear). **Express warranty**, garantía escrita. 2. Pintiparado, copiado, parecido (similar). 3. Hecho o llevado por expreso; pronto, de prisa. **Express train**, (tren) rápido. -*s.* 1. Expreso, correo, mensajero, propio. 2. Expreso, el mensaje o aviso que lleva algún expreso o correo extraordinario. 3. Expreso, servicio organizado para el rápido transporte de mercancías y paquetes de un punto a otro. 4. Exprimir (juice). **To send a letter express**, enviar una carta urgente. **To express oneself**, expresarse.

expressage [ɪksˈpreseɪdʒ] [iks-pre-seich], *s.* 1. Porte, coste de llevar por expreso. 2. Todo lo que se envía por expreso.

express car, *s.* Vagón expreso.

express company, *s.* Empresa de transportes rápidos.

expressible [ɪksˈpresɪbl] [iks-pre-si-bol], *a.* 1. Decible; expresable. 2. Exprimible, que puede exprimirse para sacar el jugo.

expression [ɪksˈpreʃən] [iks-pre-shon], *s.* 1. Expresión; gesto, acción de expresarse; expresión de la fisonomía que manifiesta los sentimientos, las emociones, etc. 2. Expresión, locución, voz o palabra; modo de expresar o hacer extender lo que se quiere o piensa. 3. Verdad y viveza con que están expresados los efectos en las artes. 4. (*Fam.*) Expresión, el acto de exprimir con prensa el zumo o aceite de las plantas (juice, oil). **As an expression of thanks**, en señal de agradecimiento.

expressionism [eksˈpreʃənɪzəm] [eks-pre-sho-ni-sem], *s.* Expresionismo.

expressionist [ɪksˈpreʃənɪst] [iks-pre-sho-nist], *a.* y *s.* Expresionista.

expressive [ɪksˈpresɪv] [iks-pre-siv], *a.* Expresivo, significativo, enérgico, enfático.

expressively [ɪksˈpresɪvlɪ] [iks-pre-siv-li], *adv.* Expresivamente, enérgicamente.

expressiveness [ɪksˈpresɪvnɪs] [iks-pre-siv-nes], *s.* Energía.

expressly [ɪksˈpreslɪ] [iks-pres-li], *adv.* Expresamente.

expressman [ɪksˈpresmæn] [iks-pres-man], *s.* Mensajero, empleado de una compañía de expreso.

expressness [ɪksˈpresnɪs] [iks-pres-nes], *s.* Calidad de exacto, específico y determinado.

expresso [ɪkˈspresəʊ] [iks-pre-sou], *f.* Espresso, café exprés.

express train, *s.* Expreso, tren expreso.

express way [ɪksˈpreswer] [iks-pres-uei], *s.* Autopista (EU).

exprobrate [eksˈprəbreɪt] [eks-pro-breit], *va.* (*Ant.*) Vituperar, afear, echar en cara, dar en rostro.

expropriate [eks'prəʊprieit] [eks-pro-prieit], *va.* Enajenar, expropiar.

expropriation [eks͵prəʊpri'eiʃən] [eks-pro-priei-shon], *s.* Enajenamiento, expropiación, renuncia o privación de la propiedad de algo.

expugn [ɪks'pʊgn] [iks-pugn], *va.* Expugnar, tomar por fuerza o asalto una ciudad o plaza.

expugnable [ɪks'pʊgnəbl] [iks-pug-na-bol], *a.* Expugnable, que se puede expugnar.

expugnation [͵ɪkspʊg'neiʃən] [iks-pug-nei-shon], *s.* Expugnación, toma por asalto.

expugner [ɪks'pʊgnəʳ] [iks-pug-naʳ], *s.* Expugnador.

expulsion [ɪks'pʌlʃən] [iks-pal-shon], *s.* Expulsión.

expulsive [ɪks'pʌlsɪv] [iks-pal-siv], *a.* Expulsivo, que tiende a expulsar.

expunction [ɪks'pʊŋkʃən] [iks-punk-shon], *s.* Borradura, raspadura.

expunge [ɪks'pʌndʒ] [iks-punch], *va.* 1. Borrar, cancelar, rayar (cancel, score out). 2. Borrar, lavar las manchas o defectos. 3. Acabar, aniquilar.

expunging [ɪks'pʌndʒɪŋ] [eks-pun-chin], *s.* Cancelación, el acto de cancelar.

expurgate ['ekspɜ:geit] [eks-per-gueit], *va.* Expurgar, tachar u omitir las palabras o cláusulas censurables de un libro; limpiar, purificar de lo que es nocivo.

expurgation [͵ekspɜ:'geiʃən] [eks-per-guei-shon], *s.* Expurgación, purificación, expurgo.

expurgatory [͵ekspɜ:gətəri] [eks-per-ga-to-ri], *a.* Expurgatorio.

exquisite [eks'kwɪzɪt] [eks-kui-sit], *a.* 1. Exquisito, exquisitamente bello, de singular primor en su especie; consumado (delightful, excellent, precious). 2. Intenso, excesivo, atroz (intense, powerful). **Exquisite pain**, dolor excesivo, pena atroz. 3. Remilgado, exigente, quisquilloso, delicadamente sensible o impresionable. 4. Vivo, delicioso. **Exquisite pleasure**, vivo placer. -*s.* Elegante, petimetre, pisaverde.

exquisitely [eks'kwɪzɪtli] [eks-kui-sit-li], *adv.* Exquisitamente, completamente.

exquisiteness [eks'kwɪzɪtnɪs] [eks-kui-sit-nes], *s.* Primor, delicadeza, excelencia, perfección.

exsanguinate [eks'sæŋgineit] [eks-san-gui-neit], *va.* Desangrar, quitar la sangre.

exsanguine [eks'sæŋgi:n] [eks-san-guin], *a.* Que no tiene sangre; desangrado.

exscind [ek'sɪmd] [ek-sin], *va.* Cortar, extirpar.

exsect [ek'sekt] [ek-sekt], *va.* Cortar, extirpar, quitar.

exsection [ek'sekʃən] [ek-sek-shon], *s.* Cortadura, corte de una parte de un miembro o una corta extensión de hueso.

exserted [ek'sɜ:tɪd] [ek-ser-tid], *a.* (*Bot.*) Exserto, que proyecta o sobresale de las partes que lo rodean, como los estambres, sin cubierta.

exsiccant [ek'sɪkənt] [ek-si-kant], *a.* Desecativo, desecante.

exsiccate [ek'sɪkeit] [ek-si-keit], *va.* Desecar, secar.

exsiccation [ek'sɪkeiʃən] [ek-si-kei-shon], *s.* Desecación.

exsiccative [ek'sɪkətɪv] [ek-si-ka-tiv], *a.* Desecativo, desecante.

exspuition [eks'pʊiʃən] [eks-pui-shon], *s.* Esputo, saliva.

exstipulate [eks'tɪpju:leit] [eks-ti-piu-leit], *a.* (*Bot.*) Sin estípulas, que carece de estípulas.

exsuction [ek'sɒkʃən] [ek-suk-shon], *s.* Chupadura, chupetón.

extancy [eks'tænsi] [eks-tan-si], *s.* (*Ant.*) La parte que sobresale en alguna cosa.

extant [eks'tænt] [eks-tant], *a.* 1. Estante, existente; viviente (being)., 2. (*Ant.*) Sobresaliente, lo que sobresale sobre las demás partes de la misma especie.

extasy ['ekstæsi] [eks-ta-si], *s.* Extasis o éxtasis. V. ECSTASY.

extatic, extatical [eks'tætɪk] [eks-ta-tik], *a.* Extático, arrobado, fuera de sí. V. ECSTATIC.

extemporal [eks'tempərəl] [eks-tem-po-ral], *a.* (*Des.*) V. EXTEMPORANEOUS.

extemporaneous [eks'tempərəniəs] [eks-tem-po-ra-nios], **extemporary** [eks'tempərəri] [eks-tem-po-ra-ri], *a.* 1. Repentino, improviso, ejecutado o hecho sin mucha o ninguna preparación; ocasional. 2. Dado a hablar en público sin apuntes, improvisando.

extemporaneously [eks'tempərəniəsli] [eks-tem-po-ra-nios-li], *adv.* Repentinamente, de improviso.

extempore [eks'tempɔ:ʳ] [eks-tem-poʳ], *a.* Sin estudio previo, improvisado. -*adv.* Extemporáneamente, de improviso, de repente, in promptu.

extemporiness [eks'tempərinis] [eks-tem-po-ri-nes], *s.* Improvisación, la facultad de decir alguna cosa extemporáneamente.

extemporize [eks'tempəraiz] [eks-tem-po-rais], *va.* Improvisar, hablar, tocar o componer música extemporáneamente o de repente.

extend [ɪks'tend] [iks-tend], *va.* 1. Extender, tender, alargar; ensanchar, amplificar; prolongar el tiempo (increase). 2. Alargar el brazo, tender la mano (help). 3. Conceder, dar, comunicar (welcome, thanks). -*vn.* Alcanzar o extenderse a alguna distancia. **To extend the arm, the hand**, alargar el brazo; tender la mano. **To extend over**, abarcar, incluir. **To extend trade**, dar extensión al comercio. **To extend the time of payment**, dar prórroga, diferir la época del pago. **His power does not extend so far**, su poder no se extiende tan lejos, no llega a tanto.

extendable [ɪks'tendəbl] [iks-ten-da-bol], *a.* Extensible, alargable.

extended [ɪks'tendɪd] [iks-ten-did], *a. y. pp.* 1. Extenso, prolongado en el espacio, tiempo o alcance **Extended forecast**, pronóstico a largo plazo. 2. (*Tip.*) Tipo abierto, ancho con relación a su altura; v. g. letra abierta. **Extended-play**, maxi-single.

extendedly [ɪks'tendɪdli] [iks-ten-did-li], *adv.* Extensamente.

extender [ɪks'tendəʳ] [iks-ten-daʳ], *s.* Extendedor.

extendible [ɪks'tendɪbl] [iks-ten-di-bol], *a.* Extendedor.

extensibility [ɪks͵tensɪ'brlɪti] [iks-ten-si-bi-li-ti], **extensibleness** [ɪks'tend] [iks-tend], *s.* Extensibilidad.

extensible [ɪks'tensɪbl] [iks-ten-si-bol], *a.* Extensivo, extensible.

extension [ɪks'tenʃən] [iks-ten-shon], *s.* 1. Extensión; aumento, prolongación; despliegue, ampliación (increase, building, stay, roads, etc.). 2. Anexo; cosa agregada. 3. Extensión, espacio, propiedad de la materia. 4. (LAm) Interno. **Extensión cable**, alargador eléctrico. **Extension ladder**, escalera extensible.

extensional [ɪks'tenʃənl] [iks-ten-sho-nal], *a.* Muy extendido, lo que tiene mucha extensión.

extensive [ɪks'tensɪv] [iks-ten-siv], *a.* Extenso, dilatado, espacioso, vasto, grande, de mucha extensión (roomy, vaste).

extensively [ɪks'tensɪvli] [iks-ten-siv-li], *adv.* Extensivamente, comúnmente. **It is used extensively**, se utiliza commúnmente. **To travel extensively**, viajar por muchos lugares.

extensiveness [ɪks'tensɪvnis] [iks-ten-siv-nes], *s.* Extensión, anchura, capacidad, grandor; extensibilidad.

extensor [ɪks'tensəʳ] [iks-ten-soʳ], *s.* (*Anat.*) Extensor, músculo que sirve para extender.

extent [ɪks'tent] [iks-tent], *s.* 1. Extensión (space), grado, compás, término. 2. Tamaño, magnitud (size). 3. (*For.*) Ejecución; embargo. 4. (*Des.*) Comunicación, distribución. **To a certain extent**, hasta cierto punto. **To the full extent**, en toda su extensión. **To a great extent**, en sumo grado, grandemente. **To what extent?**, ¿hasta qué punto?

extenuate [eks'tenjoeit] [eks-te-nueit], *va.* 1. Disminuir, minorar, mitigar, atenuar, paliar (mitigate). 2. Extenuar, desengrosar, adelgazar.

extenuating [eks'tenjoeitiŋ] [eks-te-nuei-tin], *a.* Atenuante, paliativo (circumstance), excusador.

extenuation [eks'tenjoeiʃən] [eks-te-nuei-shon], *s.* Extenuación, mitigación, paliación, atenuación de una falta (mitigation, paliation); excusación.

exterior [eks'tɪərɪəʳ] [eks-te-rioʳ], a. 1. Exterior, de la parte de afuera. 2. Externo. 3. Disinguido o notado por los sentidos, manifiesto. -s. Lo exterior; la apariencia o aspecto de una persona o cosa.

exteriority [eksˈtɪərɪrɪtɪ] [eks-te-rio-ri-ti], s. (Poco us.) Exterioridad.

exteriorize [eksˈtɪərɪərɑɪz] [eks-te-ria-rais], vt. Exteriorizar.

exteriorly [eksˈtɪərɪəlɪ] [eks-te-rio-li], adv. Exteriormente.

exterminate [eksˈtɜːmɪneɪt] [eks-ter-mi-neit], va. 1. Exterminar, dessarraigar, destruir, extirpar. 2. (Alg.) Hacer desaparecer. V. ELIMINATE.

extermination [eksˌtɜːmɪˈneɪʃən] [eks-ter-mi-nei-shon], s. Exterminación, destrucción, desolación, extirpación.

exterminator [eksˈtɜːmɪneɪtəʳ] [eks-ter-mi-nei-toʳ], s. Exterminador.

exterminatory [eksˈtɜːmɪnətərɪ] [eks-ter-mi-na-to-ri], a. Lo que extermina.

extern [ˈekstɜːn] [eks-tern], a. (Ant.) Externo, exterior; extrínseco.

extern, externe, s. 1. Alumno externo de una escuela o colegio, el que no es pupilo. 2. Médico o practicante de un hospital que no habita en el edificio.

external [ˈekstɜːnl] [eks-ter-nal], a. 1. Externo, exterior. **External audit**, auditoría externa. 2. Extranjero, exterior. **External trade**, comercio exterior o extranjero. **For external use**, para uso externo. -s. Lo exterior, la parte externa; símbolo, ceremonia, rito externo, v. gr. los de una religión. **Externals**, aspecto externo.

externality [ˈekstɜːnəlɪtɪ] [eks-ter-na-li-ti], s. 1. Exterioridad, calidad de lo que es exterior. 2. Percepción externa. 3. Objeto externo; rito, símbolo.

externalize, externalise [ɪksˈtɜːnəlaɪz] [iks-ter-na-lais], va. 1. Dar figura, dar cuerpo, incorporar. 2. Hacer real de una manera exterior y visible.

externally [eksˈtɜːnəlɪ] [eks-ter-na-li], adv. Exteriormente.

extersion [ˈekstɜːʃən] [eks-ter-shon], s. Borradura, raspadura.

extinct [ɪksˈtɪŋkt] [iks-tinkt], a. 1. Extinto, extinguido, apagado (volcano); destruído, desaparecido (person, animal). 2. Extinto, sin sucesión. 3. Abolido, suprimido (law, etc.). **To become extinct**, extinguirse, apagarse; morir, desaparecer.

extinction [ɪksˈtɪŋkʃən] [iks-tink-shon], s. 1. Extinción, apagamiento. 2. Destrucción, supresión, aniquilación, abolición.

extinguish [ɪksˈtɪŋgwɪʃ] [iks-tin-güish], va. 1. Extinguir, apagar. 2. Suprimir, destruir; obscurecer.

extinguishable [ɪksˈtɪŋgwɪʃəbl] [iks-tin-güi-sha-bol], a. Extinguible.

extinguisher [ɪksˈtɪŋgwɪʃəʳ] [iks-tin-güi-shaʳ], s. Extinguidor, apagador, apagavelas (candle, fire). **Fire extinguisher**, extintor de incendios.

extinguishment [ɪksˈtɪŋgwɪʃmənt] [iks-tin-güish-ment], s. 1. Apagamiento, extinción; abolición, aniquilamiento. 2. Anulación; amortización, p. ej. de una deuda pública.

extirpable [ˈekstɜːpəbl] [eks-ter-pa-bol], a. Capaz de ser extirpado.

extirpate [ˈekstɜːpeɪt] [eks-tir-peit], va. Extirpar, desarraigar.

extirpation [ˌekstəˈpeɪʃən] [eks-ter-pei-shon], s. 1. Extirpación, exterminio. 2. (Cir.) Excisión, extirpación, la acción de separar o cortar por completo un órgano, tumor, excrecencia, etc.

extirpator [ˈekstɜːpeɪtəʳ] [eks-ter-pei-taʳ], s. Exterminador, extirpador.

extol [ɪksˈtɒl] [iks-tol], va. Engrandecer, ensalzar, aplaudir, magnificar.

extoller [ɪksˈtɒləʳ] [iks-to-laʳ], s. Ensalzador, alabador, loador.

extorsive [ɪksˈtɔːsɪv] [iks-tor-siv], a. Que causa extorsión, que sirve para violentar; inicuo, injusto.

extorsively [ɪksˈtɔːsɪvlɪ] [iks-tor-siv-li], adv. Con extorsión.

extort [ɪksˈtɔːt] [iks-tort], va. Sacar u obtener por fuerza alguna cosa; arrancar, adquirir por violencia u opresión. -vn. Practicar extorsión.

extorter [ɪksˈtɔːtəʳ] [iks-tor-taʳ], **extortioner** [ɪksˈtɔːʃənəʳ] [iks-tor-sho-naʳ], s. Opresor, el que causa extorsión; concusionario.

extortion [ɪksˈtɔːʃən] [iks-tor-shon], s. 1. Extorsión, el acto y efecto de obtener algo de otro por fuerza e indebidamente. 2. Lo que se ha obtenido por fuerza o violencia (violently obtained). 3. (Der.) Extorsión, el delito que comete un empleado público con exacciones injustas.

extortionary [ɪksˈtɔːʃənərɪ] [iks-tor-sho-na-ri], a. Lo que tiene el carácter o implica una extorsión o acto ilegal.

extortionate [ɪksˈtɔːʃəneɪt] [iks-tor-sho-neit], a. Opresivo, injusto, violento; excesivo (price).

extortionist [ɪksˈtɔːʃənɪst] [iks-tor-sho-nist], s. V. EXTORTIONER.

extra [ˈekstrə] [eks-tra], a. Extra, además, doble, de repuesto, adicional, suplementario. -s. Algo fuera de lo ordinario o lo exigido. Extra, edición suplementaria de un diario. **Extra charge**, recargo. **Extra work, extra pay**, trabajo, paga extraordinaria, sobresueldo. **Extra hand**, empleado supernumerario. **For extra security**, para mayor seguridad. **The coffe is extra**, el café no está incluído (price of a menu). adv. De manera extraordinaria, especialmente. **Extra beautiful**, más bello que de costumbre.

extra, prefijo Preposición latina que significa afuera, más allá, o exceso, y entra en composición de las voces.

extract [ˈekstrækt] [eks-trakt], va. 1. Extraer, sacar algo de un lugar, tirar. 2. Extraer, separar por medio de una operación química. 3. Extractar, compendiar, hacer extractos. 4. (Mat.) Buscar, hallar una raíz. **Many beautiful colours are extracted from coal-tar**, se sacan muchos colores hermosos del alquitrán de hulla.

extract, s. 1. Extracto, sustancia que se saca de una planta. 2. Cita, mención (Liter.).

extractable, extractible [ˈekstræktɪbl] [eks-trak-ti-bol], a. Extraíble, que puede ser extraído.

extraction [ˈekstrækʃən] [eks-trak-shon], s. 1. Extracción, origen, descendencia, linaje, alcurnia. 2. (Quím.) Extracción, acción de separar o extraer uno o varios de los diversos elementos que forman los cuerpos compuestos.

extractive [ˈekstræktɪv] [eks-trak-tiv], a. Extractivo, que puede extraer o ser extraído. -s. (Med.) Extractivo, la porción de un extracto que se hace insoluble.

extractor [ˈekstræktəʳ] [eks-trak-toʳ], s. 1. Extractor, extractador. 2. herramienta para extraer.

extradite [ˈekstrədaɪt] [eks-tra-dait], va. Extraditar, entregar un reo refugiado en un país a las autoridades de su propia nación.

extradition [ˌekstrəˈdɪʃən] [eks-tra-di-shon], s. Extradición, acción de entregar un reo, refugiado en país extranjero, al gobierno del suyo propio. **Extradition warrant**, orden de extradición.

extrados [ˈekstrədəs] [eks-tra-dos], s. (Arq.) Tradós, curva exterior de una bóveda.

extrafoliaceous [ˈekstrəfəˈlieɪʃəs] [eks-tra-fo-lia-shos], a. Extrafoliáceo, el órgano que tiene su asiento en cualquier parte distinta del sobaco o axila de las hojas.

extrajudicial [ˌekstrəˈdʒuːdɪʃəl] [eks-tra-yu-di-shal], a. Extrajudicial.

extrajudicially [ˌekstrəˈdʒuːdɪʃəlɪ] [eks-tra-yu-di-sha-li], adv. Extrajudicialmente.

extramarital [ˌekstrəˈmærɪtəl] [eks-tra-ma-ri-tal], s. Extramarital.

extramission [ˌekstrəˈmɪʃən] [eks-tra-mi-shon], s. El acto de echar hacia fuera alguna cosa; emisión.

extramundante [ˌekstrəˈmʌndənt] [eks-tra-mun-dant], a. Lo que está fuera del mundo.

extramural [ˈekstrəˈmjʊərəl] [eks-tra-mua-ral], a. Extramuros.

extraneous [eksˈtreɪnɪəs] [eks-trei-nios], a. Extraño, externo, extranjero, extrínseco.

extraordinarily [ɪksˈtrɔːdɪnərɪlɪ] [iks-tror-di-na-ri-li], adv. Extraordinariamente.

extraordinariness [ɪksˈtrɔːdɪnərɪnɪs] [iks-tror-di-na-ri-nes], *s.* Singularidad, estado o cosa extraordinaria.

extraordinary [ɪksˈtrɔːdɪnərɪ] [iks-tror-di-na-ri], *a.* 1. Extraordinario, singular, que no es nada común, que excede al tipo o uso común y normal. **It is that extraordinary that,** es increíble que. 2. Especial. *-s.* Cualquier cosa extraordinaria o no común: se usa igualmente en plural. - *adv.* Extraordinariamente.

extraparochial [ˈekstrəpəˈrɔʊkɪəl] [eks-tra-pa-ro-kial], *a.* Extraparroquial.

extrapolate [ɪksˈtrəpəleɪt] [iks-tra-po-leit], *va.* y *vn.* Extrapolar.

extrapolation [ɪksˌtræpəˈleɪʃən] [iks-tra-po-lei-shon], *f.* Extrapolación.

extraregular [ɪksˈtrərɪgjʊləʳ] [iks-tra-re-guiu-laʳ], *a.* Irregular.

extrasensory [ˈekstrəˈsensərɪ] [iks-tra-sen-so-ri], *a.* Extrasensorio. **Extrasensory perception,** percepción extrasensorial.

extraspecial [ˌekstrəˈspeʃəl] [iks-tras-pe-shal], *a.* Extremadamente especial.

extraterrestrial [ˌekstrətəˈrestrɪəl] [eks-tra-te-res-trial], *a.* Extraterrestre.

extraterritorial [ˈekstrəˌterɪˈtɔːrɪəl] [eks-tra-te-ri-to-rial], *a.* Extraterritorial.

extravagance, extravagancy [ɪksˈtrævəgəns] [iks-tra-va-gans], *s.* 1. Extravagancia, salida de los límites prescritos; disparate, locura, desarreglo, desorden, desbarro. 2. Disipación, profusión, prodigalidad, gastos excesivos.

extravagant [ɪksˈtrævəgənt] [iks-tra-va-gant], *a.* 1. Extravagante, singular, estrafalario (eccentric); exorbitante, disparatado. 2. Profuso, pródigo (lavish), manirroto, gastador, despilfarrador (wasteful). *-s.* 1. Estrafalario, el que comete extravagancias o es extravagante. 2. *pl.* Extravagantes, ciertas constituciones pontificias.

extravagantly [ɪksˈtrævəgəntlɪ] [iks-tra-va-gant-li], *adv.* Extravagantemente, profusamente, exorbitantemente, costosamente; locamente.

extravaganza [eksˌtrævəˈgænsə] [eks-tra-va-gan-sa], *s.* Pieza de música, o composición dramática, extravagante y fantástica (piece of art).

extravagate [ɪksˈtrævəgeɪt] [iks-tra-va-gueit], *vn.* Vaguear, andar a discreción o más allá de los límites debidos.

extravagation [ɪksˈtrævəgeɪʃən] [iks-tra-va-guei-shon], *s.* Vagancia.

extravasate [ɪksˈtrævəseɪt] [iks-tra-va-seit], *va.* y *vn.* Extravasarse, rebosar o derramarse fuera de los vasos naturales.

extravasate, *a.* Extravasado.

extravasation [ɪksˈtrævəseɪʃən] [iks-tra-va-sei-shon], *s.* (*Med.*) Extravasación.

extraversion [ˌekstrəˈvɜːʃən] [eks-tra-ver-shon], *s.* (*Des.*) El acto de arrojar fuera alguna cosa.

extravert [ˈekstrəvɜːt] [eks-tra-vert], *va.* Volver hacia afuera o a un lado.

extreme [ɪksˈtriːm] [iks-trim], *a.* 1. Extremo, excesivo, sumo. **In the extreme,** en sumo grado. 2. Último, extremo, postrero. 3. Riguroso, estricto, extremado (care); radical. *-s.* 1. Extremo, ápice; el grado más elevado de alguna cosa. 2. Fin, cabo (end).

extremely [ɪksˈtriːmlɪ] [iks-trim-li], *adv.* Extremamente, sumamente.

extremism [ɪksˈtriːmɪzəm] [iks-tri-mi-sem], *s.* Extremismo.

extremist [ɪksˈtriːmɪst] [iks-tri-mist], *s.* y *a.* Extremista.

extremity [ɪksˈtremɪtɪ] [iks-tre-mi-ti], *s.* 1. Extremidad. 2. Suma violencia, rigor; necesidad, apuro. *-pl.* 1. Medidas extremas. 2. (*Zool.*) Extremidades; mano, pie, órgano locomotor o un apéndice. **To drive one to extremities,** apurar a uno la paciencia; ponerle entre la espada y la pared. **In this extremity,** en tal apuro.

extricable [ˈekstrɪkəbl] [eks-tri-ka-bol], *a.* Capaz de ser desenredado, desembarazado; evitable.

extricate [ˈekstrɪkeɪt] [eks-tri-keit], *va.* Desembarazar, desenredar (disentangle), desembrollar; sacar de un peligro, dificultad o apuro.

extrication [ekstrɪˈkeɪʃən] [eks-tri-kei-shon], *s.* Desembarazo, desenredo.

extrinsic, extrinsical [ˈekstrɪnsɪk] [eks-trin-sik], *a.* Extrínseco, exterior, lo que viene de afuera.

extrinsically [ekstˈrɪnsɪkəlɪ] [eks-trin-si-ka-li], *adv.* Extrínsecamente.

extrorse, extrorsal [ɪksˈtrɔːs] [iks-trors], *a.* 1. (*Bot.*) Extrorso, que se abre al lado exterior de la flor; se dice de la antera. 2. (*Zool.*) Vuelto afuera del cuerpo.

extrovert [ˈekstrəʊvɜːt] [eks-trou-vert], *a.* Extravertido.

extroverted [ˈekstrəʊvɜːtɪd] [eks-trou-ver-tid], *a.* Extrovertido (EU).

extrude [eksˈtruːd] [eks-trud], *va.* Rechazar, expulsar (force out, move), resistir un cuerpo a otro forzándole a retroceder en su curso o movimiento; empujar, echar adelante.

extrusion [eksˈtruːʒən] [eks-tru-shon], *s.* Rechazo, empuje, expulsión.

extuberant [ɪgzˈtjuːbərənt] [iks-tiu-be-rant], *a.* (Poco us.) *V.* PROTUBERANT.

extuberance, exuberancy [ɪgsˈtjuːbərənt] [iks-tiu-be-rant], *s.* Exuberancia, extrema fecundidad, superabundancia.

exuberant [ɪgˈzuːbərənt] [ik-su-be-rant], *a.* Exuberante, eufórico (spirit), abundantísimo.

exuberantly [ɪgˈzuːbərəntlɪ] [ik-su-be-rant-li], *adv.* Abundantemente, eufóricamente.

exuberate [ɪgˈzuːbəreɪt] [ik-su-be-reit], *vn.* Sobreabundar.

exudation [ɪgzuːˈdeɪʃən] [ik-su-dei-shon], *s.* 1. Exudación, la acción y efecto de exudar o rezumarse. 2. Transpiración, sudor; lo exudado, lo rezumado.

exude [ɪgˈzuːd] [ik-sud], *vn.* Sudar, exhalar (sweat). *-va.* Transpirar, echar hacia fuera.

exulceration [ˌɪgzʌlsəˈreɪʃən] [ik-sal-se-rei-shon], *s.* (*Ant.*) Exulceración, enconamiento; corrosión.

exulceratory [ɪgˈzʌlsərətərɪ] [ik-sal-se-ra-to-ri], *s.* (*Ant.*) Exulceratorio.

exult [ɪgˈzʌlt] [ik-salt], *vn.* Triunfar, regocijarse sobremanera, alegrarse, hasta lo sumo. **To exult in/at,** regocijarse por.

exultance, exultancy [ɪgˈzʌltəns] [ik-sal-tans], *s.* Recogijo, triunfo, rapto de alegría.

exultant [ɪgˈzʌltənt] [ik-sal-tant], *a.* 1. Triunfante (winner). 2. Regocijado, regocijada, festivo, que indica o muestra gran alegría.

exultation [ˌegzʌlˈteɪʃən] [ek-sal-tei-shon], *s.* Triunfo; exultación, regocijo grande, sumo placer; transporte, demostración o expresión de alegría.

exulting [ɪgˈzʌltɪŋ] [ik-sal-tin], *a.* y *part. a.* Transportado, embriagado de alegría; triunfante.

exuveæ [ɪgˈzjuːvæ] [ik-siu-ve], *s. pl.* 1. Los despojos de los animales. 2. (*Geol.*) Los restos animales petrificados o fósiles.

exuviate [ɪgˈzjuːvɪeɪt] [ik-siu-vieit], *va.* Mudar, echar de sí alguna parte; como las plumas de las aves, el pelo, los cuernos, la concha o el carapacho de los crustáceos, etc.

exuviation [ɪgˈzjuːvɪeɪʃən] [ik-siu-viei-shon], *s.* La muda de las aves, de los crustáceos.

eyas [eɪəs] [eias], *s.* Halcón niego; halconcillo recién sacado del nido. *-a.* (*Des.*) Implume.

eye [aɪ] [ai], *s.* 1. Ojo. 2. Ojo: tómase por la misma vista o el modo de mirar; mirada. 3. Ojo, la atención y vigilancia que se pone en alguna cosa (care, watch). 4. Miramiento, acatamiento, atención, estimación (considerateness). 5. La vista; el aspecto, frente o cara (look). 6. Ojo, el agujero que tienen algunas cosas, como la aguja. 7. Ventana redonda hecha en algún edificio. 8. (*Bot.*) Yema o botón de las plantas (yolk). 9. Matiz ligero de algún color. **One-eyed, blind of one eye,**

tuerto. **Evil eyes**, ojos malos. **Red eyes**, ojos encarnizados. **Before one's eyes**, a la vista, en presencia de alguno. **With an eye to**, con la intención de, con miras a. **In the twinkling of an eye**, en un abrir y cerrar de ojos. **An eye for an eye**, ojo por ojo. **To catch the eye**, llamar la atención. **To have a thing in one's eyes**, aspirar a alguna cosa. **To keep a sharp eye on**, vigilar de cerca. **Black eye**, (a) ojo negro. (b) Ojo amoratado por un golpe. **Half an eye**, ojeada, mirada rápida y ligera. **To close one's eyes to**, (Fig.) hacer la vista gorda. **Eye of the anchor**, (Mar.) ojo, la parte de la caña del arganeo. **Eye of a strap**, (Mar.) ojo de gaza. **Eye of a stay**, (Mar.) ojo del estay. **An eye must be had to the laws of courtesy**, se han de observar las reglas de la cortesía. **To keep an eye out**, ir con cuidado, tener cuidado. **All in one's eye**, (Ger.) imaginario. **Eye-opener**, todo lo que sirve para abrir o hacer abrir los ojos, literal o figuradamente; cuento maravilloso, noticia increíble o inesperada. (Fam.) Lo que permite a uno comprender aquello de que antes no podía darse cuenta.

eye, va. 1. Ojear, echar los ojos y mirar con atención a una parte determinada; contemplar, observar (glance); velar. 2. Hacer un agujero en, como el de la aguja.

eye-ball [ˈaɪbɔːl] [ai-bol], s. Globo del ojo.

eye-beam [ˈaɪbiːm] [ai-bim], s. Ojeada.

eye-bolt [ˈaɪbɔːlt] [ai-bolt], s. (Mar.) Cáncamo del ojo.

eye-bright [ˈaɪbraɪt] [ai-brait], s. (Bot.) Eufrasia.

eye-brightening [aɪˈbraɪtnɪŋ] [ai-brait-nin], a. Lo que aclara la vista.

eye-brow [ˈaɪbrɔː] [ai-bro], s. Ceja.

eye-catching [ˈaɪkætʃɪŋ] [ai-ka-chin], s. Llamativo, vistoso.

eyecup [ˈaɪkʌp] [ai-kap], s. Lavaojos.

eyed [aɪd] [aid], a. Lo que tiene ojos. **Blue-eyed**, ojizarco, ojiazul, que tiene ojos azules. **Brown-eyed**, ojimoreno. **Blear-eyed**, lagañoso.

eye doctor [ˈaɪdɒktəʳ] [ai-dok-taʳ], s. Oculista (EU).

eye-drop [ˈaɪdrɒp] [ai-drop], s. Lágrima.

eye-dropper [ˈaɪdrɒpəʳ] [ai-dro-paʳ], sm. Cuentagotas.

eye-flap [ˈaɪflæp] [ai-flap], s. Anteojera, cada una de las piezas de vaqueta que caen junto a los ojos de las caballerías de tiro.

eyeful [ˈaɪfʊl] [ai-ful], s. Ojeada, vistazo. **To get an eyeful of**, echar un vistazo a.

eye-glance [ˈaɪɡlɑːns] [ai-glans], s. Ojeada, mirada pronta y ligera.

eye-glass [ˈaɪɡlɑːs] [ai-glas], s. 1. Ocular, cristal óptico de un anteojo, monóculo. 2. Ocular, la lente próxima al ojo en el microscopio o telescopio. 3. **Eye-glasses**, pl. lentes, quevedos.

eye-hole [ˈaɪhəʊl] [ai-joul], s. 1. Ojete, abertura pequeña y redonda por donde puede pasar un alfiler, un corchete o gancho, un cordón, etc. 2. Atisbadero, rendija o agujero por donde se puede atisbar.

eye-lash [ˈaɪlæʃ] [ai-lash], s. Pestaña.

eyeless [ˈaɪlɪs] [ai-les], a. Ciego; sin ojos o privado de la vista.

eyelet [ˈaɪlɪt] [ai-let], s. 1. Resquicio, cualquier abertura por donde entra la luz. 2. Ojete; y en especial un pequeño anillo metálico que protege los bordes de una agujero hecho en el lienzo, cañamazo, papel, etc. **Eyelet-holes of the reefs**, (Mar.) ollados de drizas.

eyeleteer [ˈaɪlɪtɪəʳ] [ai-le-tiaʳ], s. Punzón para abrir ojetes.

eyelid [ˈaɪlɪd] [ai-lid], s. Párpado.

eyeliner [ˈaɪlaɪnəʳ] [ai-lai-naʳ], s. Delineador de ojos.

eye-offending [ˈaɪɒfendɪŋ] [ai-o-fen-din], a. Lo que hiere u ofende la vista.

eye-opener [ˈaɪəʊpnəʳ] [ai-oup-naʳ], s. Sorpresa, revelación.

eye-pencil [ˈaɪpensl] [ai-pen-sil], s. Lápiz de ojos.

eye-piece [ˈaɪpiːs] [ai-pis], s. Ocular, lente o combinación de lentes que se halla más próxima al ojo en un anteojo o microscopio.

eye-pleasing [ˈaɪpliːsɪŋ] [ai-pli-sin], a. Agradable a la vista.

eyer [ˈaɪəʳ] [aiaʳ], s. Mirador, el que mira atentamente.

eye-salve [ˈaɪsɑːlv] [ai-salv], s. Ungüento para los males de los ojos.

eye-servant [ˈaɪsɜːvənt] [ai-ser-vant], s. El criado que sólo trabaja en presencia de su amo, o cuando sabe que lo vigilan.

eye-service [ˈaɪsɜːvɪs] [ai-ser-vis], s. Servicio hecho de mala gana y sólo cuando está presente quien lo manda.

eye-shade [ˈaɪʃeɪd] [ai-sheid], s. Visera, guardavista que sirve para proteger los ojos de una luz viva.

eyeshot [ˈaɪʃɒt] [ai-shot], s. Ojeada, alcance del ojo; la vista.

eyesight [ˈaɪsaɪt] [ai-sait], s. 1. Vista, el sentido de la vista. 2. Vista, alcance o extensión de la vista.

eye-sore [ˈaɪsɔːʳ] [ai-soʳ], s. 1. Mal de ojos. 2. Cosa que hiere, ofende u ofusca la vista; (Fig.) todo lo que disgusta o desagrada.

eyespot [ˈaɪspɒt] [ai-spot], s. 1. órgano visual rudimentario de algunos invertebrados. 2. Mancha en forma de ojo.

eye-spotted [ˈaɪspɒtɪd] [ai-spo-tid], a. Abigarrado con manchas como ojos.

eye-stone [ˈaɪstəʊn] [ai-stoun], s. Piedra llamada del ojo, gránulo calcáreo que colocado debajo del párpado en el ángulo interno del ojo, sirve para hacer salir de éste las substancias extrañas que lo irritan.

eyestrain [ˈaɪstreɪn] [ai-strein], s. Vista cansada o fatigada.

eye-string [ˈaɪstrɪŋ] [ai-strin], s. Fibra del ojo.

eye-tooth [ˈaɪtuːθ] [ai-tuz], s. Colmillo.

eye-wash [ˈaɪwɒʃ] [ai-uosh], s. Loción para los ojos.

eye-water [ˈaɪwɔːtəʳ] [ai-uo-taʳ], s. Colirio, loción para los ojos.

eye-wink [ˈaɪwɪŋk] [ai-uink], s. Guiñada.

eye-witness [ˈaɪwɪtnɪs] [ai-uit-nis], s. Testigo ocular o presencial.

eyre [ˈaɪəʳ] [aiaʳ], s. (Ant.) 1. Vuelta, circuito. 2. Especie de juzgado en Inglaterra compuesto de jueces que iban de un punto a otro.

eyry, eyrie [ˈaɪərɪ] [aia-ri], s. Nido de ve de rapiña; el paraje en que pone sus huevos y cría.

F

f [ef] [ef]. Esta letra tiene el mismo sonido que en castellano, bien que pronunciado con más fuerza. Por abreviatura la **F**. equivale a *fellow*, miembro, socio.

fa [fɑː] [fa]. Cuarta voz de la escala música.

FAA, s. Abrev. de **Federal Aviation Administration**. (EU).

Fabian [ˈfeɪbɪən] [fei-bian], a. Fabiano, relativo a Fabio; que recurre a la dilación y la astucia, como lo hizo Fabio con Aníbal en la segunda guerra púnica.

fable[ˈfeɪbl] [fei-bol], s. 1. Fábula, apólogo, ficción moral o histórica. 2. Fábula, la acción que sirve de asunto a los poemas épicos y dramáticos. 3. Ficción; fábula, mentira, cuento, falsedad.

fable, vn. Fingir, mentir, inventar una fábula. -va. Contar fábulas, mentiras o cuentos; fabular.

fabled [ˈfeɪbld] [fei-bold], a. Fabuloso, celebrado en fábulas.

fabler [ˈfeɪbləʳ] [fei-blaʳ], s. 1. Fabulista. 2. Cuentero, mentiroso.

fabric [ˈfæbrɪk] [fa-brik], s. 1. Fábrica, edificio (factory). 2. Material de uso o de adorno (material); tejido, tela, fieltro (cloth), etc. 3. Manufactura, fábrica; clase de construcción o fabricación. textura. **Fabric-lands**, tierras o rentas de fábrica, las que sirven para los reparos y gastos de la iglesia.

fabricate [ˈfæbrɪkeɪt] [fa-bri-keit], va. 1. Fabricar, edificar, construir por medio del trabajo manual o de una de las artes. 2. Forjar, fingir, inventar con falsedad (document).

fabrication [ˌfæbrɪˈkeɪʃən] [fa-bri-kei-shon], s. 1. Fabricación, fábrica, el arte de fabricar, y lo que ha sido fabricado o construido; construcción; edificio (building); tisú, tejido (cloth). 2. Ficción, mentira, fábula (fiction). **All that he says is a fabrication**, todo lo que dice es mentira.

fabricator [ˈfæbrɪkeɪtəʳ] [fa-bri-kei-taʳ], s. Fabricante, fabricador.

fabricature ['fæbrɪkətʃəʳ] [fa-bri-ka-chaʳ], *s.* V. FABRI-CATION.

fabrile ['fæbrɪl] [fa-bril], *a.* Fabril.

fabulist ['fæbjʊlɪst] [fa-biu-list], *s.* Fabulista, autor de fábulas.

fabulize, fabulise ['fæbjʊlaɪz] [fa-biu-lais], *va.* Componer o narrar fábulas.

fabulous ['fæbjʊləs] [fa-biu-los], *a.* Fabuloso.

fabulously ['fæbjʊləslɪ] [fa-biu-los-li], *adv.* Fabulosamente.

fabulousness ['fæbjʊləsnɪs] [fa-biu-los-nes], *s.* Invención de mentiras, cuentos o cosas fabulosas.

facade [fə'sɑːd] [fa-ad], *s.* Fachada, parte frontal de un edificio.

face [feɪs] [feis], *s.* 1. Cara, rostro, faz. 2. Cara, lado, haz, superficie de una cosa (side); facie (de un cristal). 3. Semblante o facciones de la cara. **To put on a new face**, mudar de semblante. **Brazen face**, cara de vaqueta, desfachatado. 4. Fachada, frontis de un edificio (of building). 5. (*Mil.*) Frente. 6. Aspecto, semblante, estado o disposición que toman las cosas. 7. Apariencia, aspecto, presencia (look); conocimiento inmediato, vista. 8. Descaro, atrevimiento, desfachatez. 9. Mueca, gesto. **To make wry faces**, hacer muecas. 10. Cara, lo que está formalmente declarado en un documento; el valor neto, excluyendo el interés y el descuento. 11. (*Tip.*) Ojo de la letra. **To fly in the face of**, (*Fig.*) oponerse rotundamente a. **Face to face**, cara a cara. **In face of the sun**, a la faz del sol, o de todo el mundo; públicamente. **In my face**, en mi presencia, en mis barbas. **Face-ache, face-ague**, neuragia facial. **Face-card**, figura en la baraja. **Face downstairs**, boca abajo. **Face-value**, valor nominal, el que está escrito o impreso en un documento. **To make/pull faces**, hacer muecas. **On the face of it**, a primera vista.

face, *va. y vn.* 1. Aparentar, engañar haciendo el hipócrita. 2. Encararse; hacer frente. 3. Cubrir, aforrar. **To face a cloak**, poner embozo a una capa. **To face about**, volver la cara. **To face one out**, sostener alguna cosa a presencia de una persona que la niega, o ponerse ante su vista para insultarla descaradamente; turbar a fuerza de descaro. **To face out a lie**, sostener una mentira con impudencia. **To face out**, arrostrar, hacer frente, salir del paso a fuerza de descaro. (*Mil.*) Volver las espaldas. **To face the music**, hacer frente intrépidamente a las consecuencias. **Let's face it!** ¡seamos realistas! **Face this way!**, ¡vuélvase hacia aquí! **To face in a direction**, estar orientado en una dirección.

face about, (*Fig.*) cambiar de parecer, cambiar de postura.

face down, intimidar con la mirada (EU).

face-cloth ['feɪsklɒθ] [feis-kloz], *s.* Sudario, lienzo con que se cubre el rostro de un cadáver.

facecream ['feɪskriːm] [feis-krim], *sf.* Crema de belleza.

faced [feɪst] [feist], *a.* Lo que tiene cara o semblante; se usa casi siempre en composición. **Ill-faced**, mal encarado o engestado.

facelift [feɪs] [feis], *s.* 1. Estiramiento facial (beauty). 2. (*Fig.*) Mejora, reforma, modernización.

face-guard ['feɪsgɑːd] [feis-gard], *s.* Careta, con que se cubre el rostro para protegerlo en ciertos experimentos de química u operaciones mecánicas; máscara que se usa en los ejercicios de esgrima.

faceless ['feɪslɪs] [feis-lis], *a.* Sin cara, sin facha.

facepack ['feɪspæk] [feis-pak], *m.* Tratamiento facial.

face-painter ['feɪspeɪntəʳ] [feis-pein-taʳ], *s.* Retratista.

face-painting [feɪs'peɪtɪŋ] [feis-pein-tin], *s.* 1. Dar colorete al rostro, usar afeites. 2. El arte de retratar.

facer ['feɪsəʳ] [fei-saʳ], *s.* Golpe dado en la cara, entre pugilistas. Problema, dificultad. **What a facer!**, ¡menudo problemón!

facet ['fæsɪt] [fa-sit], *va.* Labrar una faceta o facetas sobre algo. -*s.* 1. Faceta, cada uno de los lados labrados de una piedra preciosa. 2. (*Arq.*) Filete plano pero saliente entre las estrías de una columna. 3. (*Zool.*) Faceta, cada una de las pequeñas divisiones del ojo compuesto; también, la superficie o córnea de dicho ojo, v. gr. en los insectos.

faceted ['fæsɪtɪd] [fa-si-tid], *pp. y a.* 1. Labrado en facetas. 2. Que tiene facetas, p. ej. el ojo compuesto.

facetious [fə'siːʃəs] [fa-si-shos], *a.* Salado, chistoso, alegre, jocoso, gracioso (graceful, amusing, funny).

facetiously [fə'siːʃəslɪ] [fa-si-shos-li], *adv.* Chistosamente, alegremente.

facetiousness [fə'siːʃəsnɪs] [fa-si-shos-nes], *s.* Jocosidad, chiste, gracia, broma.

facial ['feɪʃəl] [fei-shal], *a.* Facial, que pertenece a la cara, que le afecta o que está cercano a ella. **Facial angle**, ángulo facial, el que sirve para medir la inclinación o depresión del cráneo, formado por dos líneas que van respectivamente desde los incisivos superiores a la parte media de la frente y al conducto auditivo.

facile ['fæsaɪl] [fa-sail], *a.* 1. Fácil (victory). 2. Obsequioso, obediente, dócil (animal, person). 3. Vivo, listo, diestro, hábil. 4. Accesible, afable. 5. Vulgar, común. 6. Ligero, superficial (expression).

facilely ['fæsaɪləlɪ] [fa-sai-le-li], *adv.* Fácilmente. V. EASILY.

facileness ['fæsaɪlnɪs] [fa-sail-nes], *s.* Docilidad.

facilitate [fə'sɪsɪteɪt] [fa-si-li-teit], *va.* Facilitar, allanar una dificultad, minorar el trabajo, posibilitar.

facilitation [fə'sɪsɪteɪʃən] [fa-si-li-tei-shon], *s.* Facilitación.

facility [fə'sɪsɪtɪ] [fa-si-li-ti], *s.* 1. Facilidad, destreza, habilidad (with languages); **credit facilities** facilidades (de pago); **public transport facilities** servicios de transporte público. 2. Docilidad, prontitud en someterse a una influencia cualquiera, ya sea buena o mala. 3. Afabilidad. 4. Lo que hace algo más fácil; ayuda, conveniencia.

facing ['feɪsɪŋ] [fei-sin], *s.* 1. Paramento (Arq.), revestimiento. 2. Cubierta. 3. *prep* de cara a, frente a. 4. *a.* Opuesto.

facsimile [fæk'sɪmɪlɪ] [fak-si-mi-li], *s.* Facsímile, copia exacta. Se usa también como adjetivo.

fact [fækt] [fakt], *s.* 1. Hecho, acción, suceso (information); lo que se ve como actualmente existente; lo concreto opuesto a lo abstracto. 2. Realidad, verdad (not fiction); una cosa cualquiera estrictamente verdadera. 3. Dato, motivo. **In fact**, en efecto, en verdad. **In the very fact**, en el mero hecho. **Facts are stubborn things**, no hay nada tan terco como un hecho. **Matter of fact**, hecho positivo, cierto; verdad. **As a matter of fact man**, un hombre positivo, no imaginativo. V. MATTER.

faction ['fækʃən] [fak-shon], *s.* 1. Facción, bando, liga, parcialidad. 2. Alboroto, tumulto. 3. Espíritu de partido, discordia, disensión.

factional ['fækʃənl] [fak-sho-nal], *a.* Faccionario, partidario.

factionist ['fækʃənɪst] [fak-sho-nist], *s.* El que excita facciones y discordias.

factious ['fækʃəs] [fak-shos], *a.* 1. Faccioso, sedicioso, revoltoso. 2. Partidista.

factiously ['fækʃəslɪ] [fak-shos-li], *adv.* Sediciosamente, facciosamente.

factiousness ['fækʃəsnɪs] [fak-shos-nes], *s.* Espíritu de partido o de facción.

factitious [fæk'tɪʃəs] [fak-ti-shos], *a.* Facticio; artificial, hecho por mano o arte del hombre.

factitive ['fæktɪtɪv] [fak-ti-tiv], *a.* Factitivo.

factor ['fæktəʳ] [fak-taʳ], *s.* 1. (*Com.*) Factor, agente comisionado. 2. (*Mat.*) Factor, el multiplicador y multiplicando. 3. Una de las causas que producen un resultado. 4. Administrador o depositario de bienes embargados.

factor *v.* (*Mat.*) Descomponer en factores.

factorage ['fæktəreɪdʒ] [fak-to-reich], *s.* 1. (*Com.*) Comisión o el tanto por ciento que se paga a los comisionistas. 2. Factoría, empleo y cargo de factor.

factoring ['fæktərɪŋ] [fak-to-rin] (*Mat.*) Descomposición en factores.

factorship ['fæktəʃɪp] [fak-tor-ship], *s.* 1. Agencia, factoría. 2. Factoraje.

factory ['fæktərɪ] [fak-to-ri], *s.* 1. Fábrica, manufactura, taller, establecimiento para fabricar alguna cosa. 2. Factoría, establecimiento de comercio, especialmente el instalado en país extranjero. **Factory inspector**, inspector de trabajo. **Factory ship**, buque factoría. **Factory worker**, obrero, industrial.

factotum [fæk'təʊtəm] [fak-tou-tom], *s.* 1. Criado que hace todo. 2. La persona que por su habilidad y circunstancia se hace necesaria en una familia o sociedad. 3. Factótum.

factual ['fæktʃʊəl] [fak-chual], *a.* actual, relativo a hechos precisos.

facture ['fæktʃəʳ] [fak-chaʳ], *s.* 1. (*Com.*) Factura. V. INVOICE. 2. (*Des.*) Hechura.

facultative [fæ'kjɔltətɪv] [fa-kiul-ta-tiv], *a.* 1. Facultativo, que produce o da facultad o poder. 2. Que otorga autoridad o poder. 3. (*For.*) Potestativo. 4. Contingente.

facula ['fækjɔlə] [fa-kiu-la], *s.* (*Astr*) Fácula, cada una de aquellas partes más brillantes que se observan en el disco del Sol.

faculty ['fækəltɪ] [fa-kul-ti], *s.* 1. Facultad, potencia o virtud para hacer alguna cosa. 2. Facultad, potencia o virtud natural. 3. Maña, talento, don, destreza, habilidad. 4. Propiedad, eficacia, fuerza. 5. Facultad, poder, autoridad, privilegio. 6. Facultad, el conjunto de doctores y profesores de las ciencias o facultades que se enseñan en las universidades.

facund ['fækənd] [fa-kund], *a.* Facundo, elocuente.

fad [fæd] [fad] *s.* Moda, novedad, manía afición pasajera.

faddist ['fædɪst] [fa-dist] *s.* persona caprichosa, con aficiones pasajeras.

faddle [fædl] [fa-del], *vn.* Juguetear, jugar, travesear.

fade [feɪd] [feid], *vn.* 1. Desaparecer gradualmente (eye sight, hearing, memory, hopes); palidecer, descolorarse. 2. Decaer, marchitarse (flower), acabarse poco a poco; durar poco. -*va.* 1. Marchitar, poner pálido, ofuscar; descolorar. 2. Debilitar, enflaquecer, desmejorar. **Day faded into twilight**, el día palideció hasta covertirse en crepúsculo. **To fade from sight**, perderse de vista.

fadeless ['feɪdlɪs] [feid-les], *a.* Que no palidece o se descolora; que no está mustio ni marchito, que no se pasa o decae.

fade out ['feɪdaʊt] [feid-aut], *s.* Desvanecimiento gradual de la imagen o escena (cine).

fadge ['feɪdʒ] [feich], *vn.* (*Ant.*) Adaptar; suceder; convenir.

fading ['feɪdɪŋ] [fei-din], *s.* 1. Decadencia, flojedad. 2. Desvanecimiento, pérdida gradual de color, intensidad. 3. Disminución o fluctuación de la intensidad de las señales (radio).

fadingness ['feɪdɪŋnɪs] [fei-din-nes], *s.* Tendencia a decaer o marchitarse.

fady ['fædɪ] [fa-di], *a.* Lo que decae o se marchita.

fæces ['fiːsiːz] [fi-sis], *s. pl.* Heces, excrementos.

fæcula, fecula ['fiːkjɔlə] [fi-kiu-la], *s.* (*Quím.*) Fécula, almidón que se saca de las plantas farináceas.

faerie, faery ['fɛərɪ] [fea-ri], *a.* (*Ant.*) V. FAIRY.

fag [fæg] [fag], *va.* 1. Fatigar, cansar. 2. Emplear como ganapán, galopín o marmitón, exigir de uno faenas groseras. -*vn.* 1. Desfallecer o desmayarse de cansancio. 2. Trabajar o hacer faenas groseras en lugar de otro.

fag, *s.* 1. Esclavo, trabajador; marmitón, ganapán. 2. Nudo en el paño. 3. Pitillo, cigarrillo.

fag-end ['fæg'end] [fag-end], *s.* 1. Cadillos, pestañas, los primeros hilos de lanurdimbre de la tela. 2. Desecho, sobra o desperdicio de alguna cosa. 3. (*Mar.*) Cordón. 4. Colilla.

fagot, faggot ['fægət] [fa-got], *s.* 1. Haz o gravilla de leña. 2. Haz de barras de hierro o acero (de 120 libras de peso). 3. Montón de hierro viejo para fundirlo. 4. El tormento de ser quemado vivo. 5. Montón de pescado acumulado para secarlo o para cubrirlo y protegerlo. 6. (*GB*) vieja, bruja.

fagot, *va.* 1. Liar, hacer líos o haces. 2. Recoger, recaudar.

Fahrenheit ['færənhaɪt] [fa-ren-jait], *a.* Que designa, pertenece o se refiere a la escala termométrica en que el punto de congelación se marca a los 32° y el de ebullición a los 212°; es la escala usual en la Gran Bretaña y los Estados Unidos.

faience ['faɪəns] [faaiens], *s.* Fayenza, una variedad de mayólica o loza, por lo general muy adornada.

fail [feɪl] [feil], *va.* Faltar a la obligación; abandonar, descuidar o no cumplir con lo que se debe; omitir, olvidar; engañar, chasquear. -*vn.* 1. Faltar, no existir alguna cosa, calidad o circunstancia que debiera haber. 2. Consumirse, acabar, fallecer, desvanecerse, decaer, menguar; perecer, perderse (crops). 3. No corresponder uno a lo que es, o una cosa o efecto a lo que se esperaba; tener mal éxito; salir mal una cosa. 4. Quebrar, hacer bancarrota (business). 5. **To fail in one's duty**, faltar, no cumplir con su obligación. **Not to fail**, no dejar de.

fail, *s.* Falta, omisión, en la locución. **Without fail**, sin falta u omisión.

failing ['feɪlɪŋ] [fei-lin], *s.* 1. Falta, desliz, defecto; decadencia, malogro. 2. El acto de hacer bancarrota; quiebra. -*prep.* a falta de, falto de.

failure ['feɪljəʳ] [fei-liaʳ], *s.* 1. Falta, culpa, omisión, descuido. 2. (*Com.*) Quiebra, bancarrota. 3. Concurso de acreedores. 4. Desliz. **It is a complete failure**, ha salido completamente mal. 5. Hablando de asuntos literarios, o cosas comunes, se dice: **It was a failure**, salió un disparate, quedó mal. (*Vul.*) Salió una plasta, se hizo un pastel. **Failure of issue**, carencia de descendientes a la muerte de la persona de que se trata.

fain [feɪn] [fein], *a.* 1. Alegre, contento. 2. Obligado, estrechado, precisado. 3. Dispuesto, conforme, resignado. -*adv.* Gustosamente, voluntariamente, de buena gana, alegremente, con gusto.

faint [feɪnt] [feint], *vn.* 1. Desmayarse, caer en síncope, pasmarse. 2. Acobardarse, extenuarse, desanimarse; dejarse abatir, desalentarse. 3. Descaecer, desvanecerse. **To faint with thirst, with hunger**, no poder aguantar la sed, el hambre.

faint, *a.* Lánguido, extenuado; indistinto o mal definido en color o sonido, opaco, oscuro; bajo, cobarde, abatido, perezoso. **Faint heart never won fair lady**, (*Prov.*) a los cobardes no los ayuda Dios, o Quien no se aventura no pasa la mar. **To grow faint**, desmayarse, sentirse mal de repente. **To be faint with hunger**, estar exánime, estar muerto de hambre.

faint-hearted ['feɪnt'hɑːtɪd] [feint-jar-tid], *a.* Cobarde, medroso, pusilánime, apocado.

faint-heartedly [feɪnt'hɑːtɪdlɪ] [feint-jar-tid-li], *adv.* Medrosamente.

faint-heartedness [feɪnt'hɑːtɪdnɪs] [feint-jar-tid-nes], *s.* Cobardía, miedo, pusilanimidad.

fainting ['feɪntɪŋ] [fein-tin], *s.* Deliquio, desmayo, desfallecimiento.

faintish ['feɪntɪʃ] [fein-tish], *a.* Flojo, débil, que empieza a ponerse malo. **Are you faintish?**, ¿va Ud. a sentirse mal?, ¿se siente Ud. mal? V. FAINT.

faintly ['feɪntlɪ] [fein-tli], *adv.* Desmayadamente, débilmente, obscuramente, lánguidamente.

faintness ['feɪntnɪs] [feint-nes], *s.* Languidez, flaqueza, abatimiento, timidez.

faintly ['feɪntlɪ] [fein-tli], *a.* Lánguido, débil. V. FAINTISH.

fair [fɛəʳ] [feaʳ], *a.* 1. Claro, sereno, no oscurecido por nubes, favorable, próspero. 2. Blanco, rubio; no moreno ni descolorido. **Fair complexion**, tez blanca. 3. Hermoso, perfecto, bello. 4. Recto, justo, bueno, natural, sincero, honrado, razonable, abierto, franco, ingenuo. 5. Suave, dulce, blando; cortés, liberal. 6. Favorable, propicio, en buen estado; medianamente bueno o grueso, corriente, pasable, ordinario. 7. Bien formado, distinto; legible. **To play fair**, jugar limpio. **If the weather holds fair**, si el tiempo se mantiene despejado. **The fair sex**, el bello sexo. **A fair wind**, un viento favorable. **A fair name**, un nombre honrado, sin tacha. **You will make a fair copy of it**, lo pondrá Ud. en limpio. **To give one a fair hearing**, oír, escuchar con imparcialidad. **To be in a fair way to succeed**, estar en buen camino de prosperar. **By fair means**, por medios rectos, honrados. **A fair man, a fair woman**, un hombre rubio, una mujer rubia. **Fair and square**, honrado a carta cabal. **Fair-haired**, de cabellos blondos o rubios. (Equivalente, **light-haired**). **Fair-complexioned**, de tez blanca. **Fair play**, buena conducta, proceder leal. -*adv.* Decentemente, cortésmente, felizmente.

fair, *s.* 1. (*Ant. y Poét.*) Belleza, beldad, hermosura; honradez. 2. Feria, la concurrencia de mercaderes y negociantes en un lugar y día señalados para vender y comprar. 3. Exposición ocasional o periódica de objetos de arte o de capricho; o de productos de la agricultura, aves, caballos, perros, etc.

fairground ['fɛəɡraʊnd] [fea-graund], *s.* 1. Campo donde se celebra una exposición o feria. 2. Parque de atracciones.

fairing ['fɛərɪŋ] [fea-rin], *s.* 1. Ferias, dádiva o agasajos que se hacen en tiempo de ferias. 2. (*Ingen.*) Miembro o estructura que da forma aerodinámica a un avion. etc.

fairish ['fɛərɪʃ] [fea-rish], *a.* 1. Razonablemente justo; así. 2. Bastante bueno o grande, regular.

fairly ['fɛəlɪ] [fea-li], *adv.* 1. Bellamente, con primor y perfección. 2. Cómodamente, suavemente. 3. Justamente. 4. Ingenuamente, claramente. 5. Cabalmente. 6. Medianamente. 7. Limpiamente (according to the rules).

fair-minded ['fɛəmaɪndɪd] [fea-main-did], *a.* Imparcial, justo, equitativo.

fairness ['fɛənɪs] [fea-nes], *s.* 1. Hermosura, belleza. 2. Honradez, candor. 3. Justicia, equidad. **In all fairness**, a decir verdad.

fair-spoken ['fɛəspəʊkn] [fea-spou-ken], *a.* Bien hablado, cortés.

fairway ['fɛəweɪ] [fea-uei], *s.* 1. (*Mar.*) Canalizo, paso expedito de un canal. **That vessel lies in the fairway**, ese buque está anclado al través, a lo ancho del canalizo. 2. Parte expedita de un campo de golf.

fair-weather ['fɛəˌwɛθəʳ] [fea-ue-daʳ], *a.* Se dice de lo que anuncia prosperidad o buen tiempo. **A fair-weather friend**, un amigo de los días prósperos.

fairy ['fɛərɪ] [fea-ri], *s.* 1. Duende, trasgo. 2. Hada, bruja, encantadora. -*a.* Lo que pertenece a los duendes. **The fairy land**, la tierra de los duendes. **Fairy tales**, cuentos de hadas o de encantadoras. **Fairy queen**, reina de las hadas.

fairylike ['fɛərɪˌlaɪk] [fea-ri-laik], *s.* Aduendado, de las hadas.

faith ['feɪθ] [feiz], *s.* 1. Fe, creencia. 2. Fe, confianza en Dios. 3. Fidelidad, sinceridad. 4. Fe, palabra que se da. 5. Exactitud en cumplir con su obligación. **To break faith with one**, faltar a la palabra dada a alguien. **Upon my faith**, a fe mía. -*adv.* En verdad.

faithful ['feɪθfʊl] [feiz-ful], *a.* Fiel, leal (friend, servant, spouse); justo, recto.

faithfully ['feɪθfəlɪ] [feiz-fu-li], *adv.* Fielmente, firmemente, exactamente.

faithfulness ['feɪθfʊlnɪs] [feiz-ful-nes], *s.* 1. Fidelidad, honradez, lealtad. 2. Exactitud. 3. Fe

faithless ['feɪθlɪs] [feiz-les], *a.* 1. Infiel, sin fe, pérfido, desleal. 2. Traidor.

faithlessness ['feɪθlɪsnɪs] [feiz-lis-nes], *s.* 1. Infidencia, traición, infidelidad, deslealtad. 2. Incredulidad.

faithworthy ['feɪθwɜːθɪ] [feiz-ue-zi], *a.* Fidedigno, veraz.

fake [feɪk] [feik], *s.* (*Mar.*) Aduja de cable; cada vuelta que forma el cable al recogerlo o arrollarlo.

fake, *va.* (*Ger.*) 1. Ocultar engañosamente los defectos de una cosa. 2. Fingir, inventar falsedades, fantasear. 3. Hurtar. -*s.* 1. Estafa; trampa, engaño; estafador. 2. Noticias ficticias, o inventadas.

faker ['feɪkəʳ] [fei-kaʳ], *s.* Imitador, falsificador, impostor.

fakir ['fɑːkɪəʳ] [fa-kiaʳ], *s.* 1. Alfaquí, religioso mendicante entre los mahometanos y en la India. 2. (*Vul.*) Buhonero.

falcade ['fɔːlkeɪd] [fol-keid], *s.* Falcada, especie de corveta del caballo. **To make falcades**, falcar, deslizarse un caballo repetidas veces sobre las ancas.

falcation [fɔːl'keɪʃən] [fol-kei-shon], *s.* Encorvadura en forma de hoz.

falchion ['fɔːlkɪən] [fol-kion], *s.* 1. Cimitarra. 2. (*Poem.*) Espada.

falciform ['fɔːlsɪfɔːm] [fol-si-form], *a.* Falciforme, que tiene la forma de una falce o de una hoz.

falcon ['fɔːlkən] [fol-kon], *s.* 1. (*Orn.*) Halcón. 2. (*Art.*) Falcón, un cañón del siglo XVI.

falconer ['fɔːlkənəʳ] [fol-ko-naʳ], *s.* Halconero, cetrero.

falconet ['fɔːlkənɪt] [fol-ko-nit], *s.* (*Art.*) Falconete, cañoncito del siglo XVI.

falconry ['fɔːlkənrɪ] [fol-kon-ri], *s.* Halconería, cetrería.

falderal ['fɔːldərəl] [fol-de-ral], *s.* 1. Chuchería, fruslería. 2. Estribillo de una canción sin sentido.

faldstool ['fɔːldsˌtuːl] [fold-stul], *s.* 1. Fascitol, atril desde el cual se lee la letanía. 2. Faldistorio, asiento pequeño que usan los obispos en ciertas ceremonias; banquillo sobre el cual se arrodillan los soberanos de Inglaterra en su coronación. 3. Silla de tijera.

fall [fɔːl] [fol], *vn.* (*pret.* FELL, *pp.* FALLEN). 1. Caer, caerse. 2. Apostatar, apartarse de la fe o de la virtud. 3. Morir repentinamente o de muerte violenta. 4. Caer, perder el poder, empleo o valimiento. 5. Caer, pasar del estado de prosperidad al de desgracia o a un estado peor que el que se tenía antes; disminuir. 6. Pasar el cuerpo o alma a un nuevo estado. **To fall asleep**, dormirse. **To fall sick**, enfermar. **To fall in love**, enamorarse. 7. Aparecerse por casualidad; llegar o hallarse casualmente en alguna parte. 8. Principiar alguna cosa con ardor. 9. Apoderarse de alguno una pasión de ánimo. 10. Tocarle a alguien una propiedad. 11. Bajar, minorarse el precio de alguna cosa. 12. Acontecer, acaecer, suceder, tocar. **To fall to one's lot**, caber o caer en suerte, tocar. -*va.* 1. Soltar, dejar caer. 2. Hundir, abatir, bajar. 3. Parir la oveja. 4. (*fam.*) Derribar, derrocar, echar por tierra, cortar.

fall away, enflaquecer; apostatar; perecer; marchitarse.

fall back, retroceder, retirarse; (*Fig.*) faltar a su palabra, retractarse. (*fam.*) Llamarse andana.

fall backward, caer de espaldas. **To fall back on** o **upon**, (a) (*Mil.*) retirarse hacia o a (una posición, cuerpo de tropas, etc.). (b) Recurrir *a*.

fall behind, quedarse atrás, perder terreno.

fall down, prosternarse, postrarse, caer al suelo. **To fall flat**, no corresponder a lo que se esperaba, tener mal éxito.

fall from, abandonar, renunciar a favor de uno, rebelarse.

fall in, concurrir, coincidir; acceder; acordarse, conceder; alinearse los soldados.

fall in with, encontrarse.

fall into, acceder, conceder, entrar en las ideas o proyectos de alguno.

fall off, enflaquecer, menguar; desaparecer, disolverse; perecer; separarse; apostatar, degenerar.

fall on, principiar alguna cosa con empeño; asaltar, embestir, acometer. (*fam.*) Echarse sobre, fajar sobre. **To fall on one's feet**, salir del vado.

fall out, reñir, querellar, disputar, desamistarse; acaecer, acontecer, suceder.

fall over, desertarse de un partido a otro.

fall to, principiar a comer con ansia, irarse sobre; someterse; ponerse a hacer algo.

fall under, hacerse el objeto de; estar sujeto a; colocarse en, ser del número de, ser considerado como. **To fall under one's displeasure**, incurrir en la indignación de alguno, caer en desgracia.

fall upon, atacar, invadir, asaltar, embestir. **To fall upon an expediente**, echar un corte. **To fall short**, faltar, no corresponder a lo que se esperaba. No conseguir, no lograr, no llegar a, no alcanzar. (*Vul.*) Quedar chasqueado, llevarse un petardo.

fall through, salir mal una cosa. **To fall aboard**, (*Mar.*) abordar, caer sobre un bajel. **To fall astern**, (*Mar.*) dejarse caer por la popa. **To fall calm**, (*Mar.*) calmar. **To fall to leeward**, (*Mar.*) dejarse caer a sotavento. **All the real**

property fell to the elder brother, todos los bienes raíces le tocaron al hermano mayor. **When the note fell due**, cuando venció el pagaré. **Falling star**, estrella errante.

fall, *s.* 1. Caída. 2. Muerte, destrucción, ruina, desolación. 3. Decadencia, declinación. 4. Baja o disminución de precio; caída, pérdida en los fondos públicos. 5. Declive. 6. Desembocadura de un río. 7. Catarata, cascada, salto. 8. Otoño. 9. Corta de leña. **Fall of a tackle**, *(Mar.)* tira de aparejo. 10. Cadencia, en la música y en la oratoria; caída o bajada de tono, o disminución del volumen del sonido. - *a. (E. U.)* Del otoño, relativo o perteneciente al otoño. **Fall wheat**, trigo sembrado en el otoño. **A fall overcoat**, un sobretodo de medio tiempo.

fallacious [fəˈleɪʃəs] [fa-lei-shos], *a.* Falaz, sofístico, ilógico, engañoso, vano, ilusorio.

fallaciously [fəˈleɪʃəslɪ] [fa-lei-shos-li], *adv.* Falazmente, engañosamente.

fallaciousness [fəˈleɪʃəsnɪs] [fa-lei-shos-nes], *s.* Falacia, engaño, fraude, sofisma.

fallacy [ˈfæləsɪ] [fa-la-si], *s.* falacia, sofistería, engaño, error. **To cherish a fallacy**, acariciar una ilusión; equivocarse, estar equivocado.

fallen [ˈfɔːlən] [fo-len], *pp.* y *a.* Caído, derribado, trastornado, disfamado, arruinado.

fallibility [ˌfælɪˈbɪlɪtɪ] [fa-li-bi-li-ti], *s.* Falibilidad, posibilidad de error.

fallible [ˈfæləbl] [fa-li-bol], *a.* Falible.

fallibly [ˈfælɪblɪ] [fa-li-bli], *adv.* Faliblemente.

falling [ˈfɔːlɪŋ] [fo-lin], *s.* y *ger.* de TO FALL. 1. Concavidad pequeña. 2. Caída y la cosa que cae. 3. *(Med.)* Caída, descenso; prolapso. **Falling away**, defección, apostasía; enflaquecimineto. **Falling down**, postración, prosternación; hundimiento, derrumbe. **Falling, in**, caída, desmoronamiento; hueco (de las mejillas). **Falling off**. caída, decadencia; apostasía, etc. *(Mar.)* **Falling tide**, reflujo, marea descendente. V. *To fall off* en FALL.

falling-sickness [ˈfɔːlɪŋsɪknɪs] [fo-lin-sik-nes], *s.* Epilepsia, gota coral, mal caduco.

fallout [ˈfɔːlaʊt] [fol-aut], *s.* 1. Descenso de partículas, frecuentemente radiactivas, excitadas o producidas por una explosión nuclear. 2. Conjunto de dichas partículas.

fallow [ˈfæləʊ] [fa-lou], *a.* 1. Flavo, leonado. **Fallow deer**, corzo. 2. Cultivable pero en descanso; no sembrado. 3. Barbechado, arado. 4. Desocupado, abandonado. -*s. (Agr.)* Barbecho; tierra que descansa. **To let lie fallow**, dejar en barbecho.

fallow, *va.* Barbechar.

fallow-finch [ˈfæləʊfɪntʃ] [fa-lou-finch], *s. (Orn.)* Triguero.

fallowness [ˈfæləʊnɪs] [fa-lou-nes], *s.* Esterilidad de algún terreno.

false [fɔːls] [fols], *a.* 1. Falso, contrario a la verdad o a los hechos. 2. Fingido, postizo, contrahecho, falseado. 3. No conforme a la regla, incorrecto, irregular, ilegal. 4. Mentiroso, falsificador. 5. Engañoso, falaz, pérfido, desleal, infiel, traidor, aleve. 6. *(Mec.)* Provisional, de sustitución, o imitado de; falso. 7. *(Bio.)* Cuasi, seudo; impropiamente nombrado o titulado; incompleto en su disposición o en sus funciones. 8. *(Mús.)* Falso, discordante, que hace violencia a las reglas de la armonía. -*adv.* Falsamente, infustamente. **False teeth**, dientes postizos. **A false claim**, una pretensión infundada. **False imprinment**, prisión, detención ilegal.

false bottom [ˈfɔːlsˈbɒtəm] [fols-bo-tom], *s.* Doble fondo.

false colors [ˈfɔːlsˈkʌləs] [fols-ka-lors], *s. pl.* 1. Bandera supuesta que se enarbola para engañar. 2. Fingimiento.

false-faced [ˈfɔːlsˈfeɪsɪd] [fols-fei-sid], *a.* Hipócrita, falso.

false-hearted [ˈfɔːlsˈhɑːtɪd] [fols-jar-tid], *a.* Traidor, pérfido, aleve, falso.

falsehood [ˈfɔːlshʊd] [fols-jud], *s.* Falsedad, mentira, engaño, perfidia.

falsely [ˈfɔːlslɪ] [fols-li], *adv.* Falsamente, alevosamente, pérfidamente.

falseness [ˈfɔːlsnɪs] [fols-nes], *s.* Perfidia, falsedad, engaño.

falsetto [fɔːlˈsetəʊ] [fol-se-tou], *s. (Mús.)* Falsete, voz de cabeza.

falsies [ˈfɔːlsiːz] [fol-sis], *s. pl. (Vul.)* Senos postizos.

falsifiable [ˌfɔːlsɪfaɪˈeɪbl] [fol-si-fai-ei-bol], *a.* Falsificable.

falsification [ˌfɔːlsɪfɪˈkeɪʃən] [fol-si-fi-kei-shon], *s.* Falsificación; confutación.

falsifier [ˈfɔːlsɪfaɪəʳ] [fol-si-faiaʳ], **falsificator** [ˌfɔːlsɪfɪˈkeɪtəʳ] [fol-si-fi-kei-taʳ], *s.* Falsificador, embustero, falsario.

falsify [ˈfɔːlsɪfaɪ] [fol-si-fai], *va.* 1. Falsificar, representar falsamente. 2. Confutar, refutar, desmentir. 3. Falsear, contrahacer, adulterar. 4. *(For.)* Falsificar, alterar. 5. Violar, ser falso a alguno. -*vn.* Mentir, decer falsedades, fábulas, etc.

falsity [ˈfɔːlsɪtɪ] [fol-si-ti], *s.* Falsedad, mentira.

falter [ˈfɔːltəʳ] [fol-taʳ], *va.* Balbucear, decir de una manera débil y balbuciente; se usa a menudo con la prep. *out.* -*vn.* Tartamudear; faltar; vacilar.

faltering [ˈfɔːltərɪŋ] [fol-te-rin], *s.* Debilidad, tartamudeo; vacilación.

falteringly [ˈfɔːltərɪŋlɪ] [fol-te-rin-li], *adv.* Vacilantemente, de una manera balbuciente.

fame [feɪm] [feim], *s.* 1. Fama, celebridad, renombre. 2. *(Ant.)* Fama, noticia o voz común.

fame, *va.* 1. Afamar; divulgar. 2. Hacer famoso; celebrar.

famed [feɪmd] [feimd], *a.* Afamado, celebrado, famoso, renombrado.

fameless [ˈfeɪmlɪs] [feim-les], *a.* Oscuro.

familiar [fəˈmɪljəʳ] [fa-mi-liaʳ], *a.* 1. Familiar, casero, común, ordinario. 2. Afable, agradable; no violento. 3. Acostumbrado, natural, fácil; versado, instruído (en este sentido va seguido de *with*). 4. Demasiado íntimo. -*s.* 1. Amigo íntimo. 2. Demonio familiar. 3. Familiar, criado o sirviente.

familiarity [fəmɪlɪˈærɪtɪ] [fa-mi-lia-ri-ti], *s.* Familaridad, llaneza, intimidad, confianza.

familiarize [fəˈmɪlɪəraɪz] [fa-mi-lia-rais], *va.* Familiarizar, acostumbrar.

familiarly [fəˈmɪlɪəlɪ] [fa-mi-liar-li], *adv.* Familiarmente, amistosamente.

family [ˈfæmɪlɪ] [fa-mi-li], *s.* 1. Familia (en todos sus sentidos); linaje, sangre, raza. 2. *(Bio.)* Familia, agrupación de géneros naturales que poseen gran número de caracteres comunes. -*a.* Familiar, de la familia, relativo o perteneciente a ella. **Family man**, padre de familia; un hombre de costumbres domésticas. **Family tree**, árbol genealógico. **Family-way**, *(Fam.)* embarazo de una mujer. **To be in the family-way**, estar encinta, embarazada. **In a family way**, familiarmente, sin cumplidos, sin ceremonia.

famine [ˈfæmɪn] [fa-min], *s.* Hambre, carestía.

famish [ˈfæmɪʃ] [fa-mish], *va.* Hambrear, matar de hambre. -*vn.* hambrear, morirse de hambre, sufrir tormento de hambre y sed.

famous [ˈfeɪməs] [fei-mos], *a.* Famoso, celebrado, afamado.

famously [ˈfeɪməslɪ] [fei-mos-li], *adv.* Famosamente.

fan [fæn] [fan], *s.* 1. Abanico. 2. *(Agr.)* Aventador, el bieldo con que se avienta la paja. 3. *(Mec.)* Ventilador, aparato para renovar el aire; también, volante que sirve para mantener las aspas de un molino en la dirección del viento. **Fan-blast**, la corriente de aire producida por el fuelle en los altos hornos. **Fan-blower**, aventador, soplador de abanico. **Fan-palm**, palmera en forma de abanico; particularmente la Corypha umbraculifera de Ceilán; la Sabal palmetto de Florida y la Chamærops humilis del sur de Europa. **Fan wheel**, rueda aventadora, rueda de paletas. **Fan window**, ventana en forma de abanico.

fan, *va.* 1. Abanicar. 2. Aventar, abalear, aechar, separar la paja del grano con el aventador o bieldo. 3. En beisbol, hacer perder el tanto, cuando el lanzador procura que un jugador falle tres veces consecutivas al tratar de golpear la pelota.

fanatic [fəˈnætɪk] [fa-na-tik], *s.* Fanático.

fanatic, fanatical [fəˈnætɪkəl] [fa-na-ti-kal], *a.* Fanático, entusiasta, visionario.

fanatically [fəˈnætɪklɪ] [fa-na-ti-ka-li], *adv.* Fanáticamente.

fanaticism [fəˈnætɪsɪzm] [fa-na-ti-si-zem], *s.* Fanatismo; celo, ardor, extravagante o furioso.

fancied [ˈfænsɪd] [fan-sid], *a.* 1. Imaginado, imaginario, concebido; no real. 2. Querido, preferido.

fancier [ˈfænsɪəʳ] [fan-siaʳ], *s.* 1. Aficionado a; criador y vendedor de aves y animales. 2. Apasionado por. 3. Visionario, soñador.

fanciful [ˈfænsɪfʊl] [fan-si-ful], *a.* Antojadizo, imaginativo, caprichoso.

fancifully [ˈfænsɪfʊlɪ] [fan-si-fu-li], *adv.* Caprichosamente.

fancifulness [ˈfænsɪfʊlnɪs] [fan-si-ful-nes], *s.* Antojo, capricho.

fancy [ˈfænsɪ] [fan-si], *s.* 1. Fantasía, imaginación. 2. Anteojo, capricho ventolera. 3. Imagen, idea, concepción. 4. Inclinación, afición, afecto, amor, gusto. **To take a fancy to a thing**, anotársele a uno alguna cosa, prendarse de ella. **Fancy ball**, baile de trajes o disfraces. *(Mex.)* Una Jamaica.

fancy, *a.* 1. Relativo a la fantasía o el capricho en cualquier sentido; v. g. (a). Adornador, que sirve para adorno u ornamento. (b) Ideal, imaginario; bello, elegante. 2. *(Com.)* De capricho o de gusto; caracterizado por la variedad, la delicadeza de la última mano, etc.; opuesto a *staple* (regular, normal). 3. Caprichoso, fantástico; extravagante. **Fancy-framed**, creado por la fantasía. **Fancy-free**, libre del poder del amor, sin amor. **Fancy-monger**, hombre fantástico. **Fancy-sick**, enfermo imaginario. **Fancy-goods**, géneros de capricho o de gusto.

fancy, *va.* 1. Creer o suponer sin fundamento; imaginar. 2. Gustar, tener complacencia en, querer. 3. Tener idea, concebir en la fantasía. -*vn.* 1. Apasionarse, aficionarse con exceso a alguna persona o cosa; imaginar, figurarse, fantasear. 2. *(Fam. Ingl.)* Suponer, creer.

fancy-dress [ˌfænsɪˈdres] [fan-si-dres], *a.* De disfraces, de trajes.

fancy-free [ˈfænsɪˈfriː] [fan-si-fri], *a.* Libre del poder del amor.

fancywork [ˈfænsɪwɜːk] [fan-si-uerk], *s.* Labores manuales.

fane [feɪn] [fein], *s.* Templo, antiguamente fano.

fanfare [ˈfænfɛəʳ] [fan-feaʳ], *s.* 1. Tocata o sonata de trompas. 2. Procesión o parada ruidosa u ostentosa. 3. Encuadernación vistosa. *(Fr.)*

fanfaronade [ˌfænfərəˈneɪd] [fan-fa-ro-neid], *s.* Fanfarronada, fanfarronería.

fang [fæŋ] [fang], *s.* 1. Colmillo. 2. Garra, uña. 3. *(Mec.)* Gancho, prolongación, ganchuda.

fang, *va. (Ant.)* Asir, agarrar.

fanged [ˈfæŋɪd] [fan-guid], *a.* Lo que tiene colmillos o garras.

fangled [ˈfæŋlɪd] [fan-glid], *a.* Poco usado, excepto cuando se une con la voz *new;* como, **new-fangled**, novelero, aficionado a novedades o a acosas nuevas.

fangless [ˈfæŋlɪs] [fan-gles], *a.* Descolmillado, desdentado.

fanion [ˈfænɪən] [fa-nion], *s.* Banderola, bandera pequeña como las que usan los agrimensores.

fanlight [ˈfænlaɪt] [fan-lait], *s. V.* FAN WINDOW en la voz *fan.*

fanlike [ˈfænlaɪk] [fan-laik], *a.* Parecido a un abanico; en forma de abanico.

fannel [ˈfænl] [fa-nel], *s.* Manípulo.

fanner [ˈfænəʳ] [fa-naʳ] *s. (Agr.)* Aventador, abanicador.

fanning [ˈfænɪŋ] [fa-nin], *s.* Ventilación.

fanon [ˈfænən] [fa-non], *s.* 1. Uno de los dos colgantes o caídas de la mitra episcopal. 2. *(Liturg.)* Manípulo.

fantail [ˈfænteɪl] [fan-tail], *s.* 1. Variedad de paloma que despliega la cola en forma de abanico. 2. Cola de abanico, pájaro, el matamoscas de Australia. 3. Mechero de abanico. 4. Ensambladura de cola de milano.

fantailed [ˈfænteɪld] [fan-taild], *a.* En forma de cola de abanico.

fantasia [fænˈteɪzɪə] [fan-tei-sia], *s. (Mús.)* Fantasía, composición música de forma irregular.

fantasied [ˈfæntəsɪd] [fan-ta-sid], *a.* Fantástico, quimérico, caprichoso, imaginario.

fantasm [ˈfæntəzm] [fan-tasm], *s.* Fantasma.

fantastic, fantastical [fænˈtæstɪk] [fan-tas-tik], *a.* 1. Fantástico, de apariencia caprichosa, grotesco. 2. Caprichoso, caprichudo. 3. Ilusorio, imaginario.

fantastic, *s.* Fantástico.

fantastically [fænˈtæstɪklɪ] [fan-tas-tik-li], *adv.* Fantásticamente.

fantasticalness [fænˈtæstɪklnɪs] [fan-tas-ti-kal-nes], *s.* Fantasía, humorada, capricho.

fantasy [ˈfæntəzɪ] [fan-ta-si], *s.* 1. Fantasía, imaginación, la facultad del ánimo de reproducir por medio de imágenes las cosas pasadas o lejanas. (En este sentido se escribe frecuentemente *phantasy*). 2. Idea fantástica, humorada, capricho. 3. Dibujo fantástico, como el de un bordado.

fantasy, *va.* Amar, tomar por fantasía un cariño extremado por alguno.

fantom, *s. V.* PHANTOM.

faquir [ˈfɑːkɪəʳ] [fa-kiaʳ], *s. V.* FAKIR.

far [fɑːʳ] [faʳ], *adv.* 1. Lejos, a lo lejos. 2. Lejos, a distancia, lejano de una época cualquiera. 3. En gran parte, en mucha proporción. 4. Desde lejos. **Far better**, mucho mejor. **Far be it from me**, lejos de mí, no permita Dios. **Far distant**, muy distante. **Far and wide**, por todas partes. **By far**, con mucho, en mucho. **So far**, tan lejos, hasta ahí, hasta ese punto. **Far beyond**, mucho más allá de. **Far off**, a gran distancia, a lo lejos. **As far as I see**, a lo que veo. **As far as, so far as**, *o* **in so far as**, en tanto que, tanto cuanto. **As far as I can**, en cuanto puedo o pueda. **Far from**, lejos de; muy lejos de eso, ni con mucho. **Are you happy? Far from it!**, ¿es Ud. feliz?, lejos de eso. **Far greater**, mucho mayor. **Far inferior**, mucho menor, muy inferior. **Far other**, muy diferente. **How far**, cuánto, cuán lejos, hasta dónde, hasta qué punto **How far is it?** *(thither)*, ¿cuánto hay de aquí a allí? **Thus far**, hasta aquí, hasta ahora; bastante. **Far too much**, demasiado, en demasía. **Far reaching**, de mucho alcance, que llega o se extiende a lo lejos. -*a.* 1. Lejano, distante, remoto. 2. Que se extiende a lo lejos; de gran alcance. 3. El más lejano de dos objetos. 4. Muy lejano del pensamiento o de la intención de uno.

far-about [ˈfærəbaʊt] [far-abaut], *s.* Rodeo; digresión.

far-away [ˈfɑːrəweɪ] [far-a-uei], *a.* 1. Lejano, alejado. 2. Abstraído, distraído.

farad [ˈfærəd] [fa-rad], *s. (Elect.)* Faradio, unidad de medida de la capacidad electromagnética de un cuerpo o de un sistema de cuerpos conductores, que con la carga de un culombio produce un voltio.

faradic [ˈfærədɪk] [fa-ra-dik], *a.* Farádico, de Faraday; relativo a las corrientes inducidas alternantes.

faradization [ˌfærədɪˈzeɪʃən] [fa-ra-di-sei-shon], *s.* Tratamiento de un nervio o músculo por una corriente farádica; faradización.

farce [fɑːs] [fars], *va.* 1. Embutir. 2. *(Des.)* Henchir, esparcir.

farce, *s.* 1. Farsa, entremés, sainete. 2. Ridiculez, cosa vana, éxito absurdo. 3. Albóndiga.

farcical [ˈfɑːsɪkəl] [far-si-kal], *a.* Entremesado, burlesco, ridículo.

farcing [ˈfɑːsɪŋ] [far-sin], *s.* Embutido.

farcy [ˈfɑːsɪ] [far-si], *s.* Muermo, una enfermedad de los caballos. *V.* GLANDERS.

fard [fɑːd] [fard], *va.* Pintar, colorar.

fardel [ˈfɑːdl] [far-del], *s.* Fardillo, lío o fardo pequeño.

fardel, *va.* Enfardelar.

fare [fɛəʳ] [feaʳ], *vn.* 1. Hallarse en cualquiera situación buena o mala; suceder, acontecer. 2. Comer, surtirse, tratarse en cuanto a la comida. 3. *(Ant. o Poét.)* Ir, andar, viajar. **He fares like a prince**, él se trata a cuerpo de rey.

fare, *s.* 1. Pasaje, precio que se paga por un viaje terrestre o marítimo. 2. Vianda, comida. 3. Viaje, pasaje. 4. Viajero. **Fare-box**, caja de depósito de pasajes (para carros urbanos). **Fare-indicator** *o* **register**, contador de pasajes.

farewell [fɛəˈwel] [fea-uel], *inter*, Adiós; páselo Ud. bien, quede Ud. con Dios. Locución que se usa sólo para despedirse. El verbo y el adverbio están muchas veces separados por el pronombre, v. g. **fare thee well** (FARE en imperativo y WELL). -*a.* Relativo a una partida, a una despedida o un adiós. **A farewell song**, una canción de despedida. -*s.* Despedida. **Last farewell**, el último adiós, la útlima despedida. **To bid one farewell o take farewel of**, despedirse de alguien.

far-famed [fɑːˈfeimd] [far-feimd], *a.* Célebre, famoso y conocido en luengas tierras; renombrado.

far-fetched [ˈfɑːˈfetʃt] [fa-fecht], *a.* 1. Traído de lejos. 2. Alambicado, apurado, refinado; no obvio. 3. Rebuscado, forzado.

farina [fæˈriːnə] [fa-ri-na], *s.* 1. (*E.U.*) Harina de maíz, preparada para comerla. 2. Harina de los cereales o raíces amiláceas. 3. (*Bot*) Almidón, y antiguamente polen.

farinaceous [ˌfærɪˈneɪʃəs] [fa-ri-nei-shos], *a.* Harinoso, farináceo.

farinose [ˈfærɪnəʊz] [fa-ri-nous], *a.* 1. Farináceo, que da harina. 2. Cubierto de una especie de sustancia blanca, parecida a la harina.

farm [fɑːm] [farm], *s.* 1. Heredad, finca de labranza; terreno destinado a la agricultura. 2. Sistema de arrendar las rentas o las contribuciones. **Farm-house**, alquería, cortijo, granja. (*Mex.*) Hacienda. **Grazing farm**, hacienda de ganados o de cría. (*Cuba*) Sitio. **Small farm**, una pequeña alquería o hacienda; un pequeño cortijo. (*Mex.*) Rancho. 3. (*Cuba*) Estancia.

farm, *va.* 1. Cultivar, dar a la tierra las labores que son necesarias para que fructifique. 2. Arrendar, tomar en arriendo. 3. Arrendar, dar en arrendamiento. 4. **To farm out**, dar a contrato a otros una parte del trabajo, etc., que uno tiene contratado.

farmable [ˈfɑːməbl] [far-ma-bol], *a.* 1. Arrendable. 2. Cultivable.

farmer [ˈfɑːməʳ] [far-maʳ], *s.* 1. Labrador, agricultor, hacendado. 2. Arrendatario; rentero; el recaudador de ciertas contribuciones, derechos, etc., mediante un tanto por ciento. **Small farmer**, labrador, labriego. (*Mex.*) Ranchero. (*Cuba*) Sitiero, estanciero. **Farmer-general**, arrendador o recaudador encargado de imponer ciertas contribuciones en Francia antes de 1789. **-Farmeress**, *sf.* Arrendadora, labradora; la que dirige una hacienda rural.

farmhand [ˈfɑːmhænd] [farm-jand], *s.* Mozo de labranza, gañán

farmhouse [ˈfɑːmhaʊs] [farm-jaus], *s.* 1. Granja, casa de labor. 2. Casa donde se mantiene y cuidan niños.

farming [ˈfɑːmɪŋ] [far-min], *s.* 1. Explotación, cultivo, beneficio de una heredad; agricultura. 2. Recaudación o arrendamiento de las contribuciones o rentas por un tanto por ciento.

farmost [ˈfɑːməʊst] [far-moust], *adv.* Lo más lejos o distante.

farmstead [ˈfɑːmsted] [farm-sted], *s.* Granja, alquería con sus dependencias.

farmyard [ˈfɑːmjɑːd] [farm-yard], *s.* Corral de una granja o casa de campo.

farness [ˈfɑːnɪs] [far-nes], *s.* Distancia, lejanía.

faro [ˈfɑːrəʊ] [fa-rou], *s.* Faraón, juego de naipes en el cual los jugadores apuestan contra el que da las cartas, acerca del orden en que irán saliendo éstas al tomarlas de la parte superior de la baraja.

far-piercing [fɑːˈpiːrsɪŋ] [far-pir-sin], *a.* Lo que penetra mucho.

farraginous [fəˈreɪdʒɪnəs] [fa-rei-yi-nos], *a.* Mezclado, abigarrado.

farrago [fəˈrɑːgəʊ] [fa-ra-gou], *s.* Fárrago, broza, mezcla.

far-reaching [fɑːˈriːtʃɪŋ] [far-ri-chin], *a.* De mucho alcance o trascendencia.

farreation, *s.* V. CONFARREATION.

farrier [ˈfærɪəʳ] [fa-riaʳ], *s.* 1. Herrador. 2. Albéitar, el que profesa el arte veterinaria o tiene por oficio curar las enfermedades de las bestias.

farriery [ˈfærɪərɪ] [fa-rie-ri], *s.* 1. Albeitería. 2. Taller de herrador, herrería.

farrow [ˈfærəʊ] [fa-rou], *s.* Lechigada de puercos; parto de la marrana. -*a.* Que no queda preñada en un año dado, horra; también machorra, que no ha parido nunca; se aplica a las vacas y las puercas.

farrow, *va.* Parir la puerca o marrana.

far-seeing [ˈfɑːsiːɪŋ] [far-siin], *a.* Que ve a gran distancia; previsor, precavido.

far-shooting [ˈfɑːʃuːtɪŋ] [far-shu-tin], *a.* Lo que es de largo alcance, tratándose de armas.

far-sighted [ˈfɑːsaɪtɪd] [far-sai-tid], *a.* 1. Que ve de lejos; présbita. 2. Dotado de vista penetrante; presciente. 3. Perspicaz, sagaz.

farther [ˈfɑːðəʳ] [far-daʳ], *adv.* Más lejos, a mayor distancia; más adelante, además de, demás de. -*a.* 1. Más lejos. 2. Ulterior, más alejado. 3. Más extenso.

farther, *va.* Adelantar, promover. V. FURTHER.

fartherance [ˈfɑːðərəns] [far-de-rans], *s.* Adelantamiento. V. FURTHERANCE.

farthermore [ˈfɑːðəmɔːʳ] [far-der-maʳ], *adv.* Además, a más de. V. FURTHERMORE.

farthermost [ˈfɑːðəməʊst] [far-der-moust], *a.* El más lejano o distante.

farthest [ˈfɑːðəst] [far-dest], *adv.* A lo más lejos.

farthest, *a.* Remotísimo. -*adv.* V. FURTHEST.

farthing [ˈfɑːθɪŋ] [far-din], *s.* 1. Cuarto de penique. 2. Ardite. (*fam.*) Un octavo. **I don't care a farthing about it**, no se me da un pito o un bledo; me importa muy poco.

farthingale [ˈfɑːθɪŋgeɪl] [far-din-gueil], *s.* Verdugado; guardainfante.

farthings-worth [ˈfɑːθɪŋzˌwɔːθ] [far-dins-uez], *s.* Lo que se vende por un ochavo.

fasces [ˈfæsɪs] [fa-sis], *s. pl.* Fasces, un hacecillo de varas.

fascet [ˈfæsɪt] [fa-sit], *s.* Vara de hierro con que se ponen las botellas en el horno para templarlas.

fascia [ˈfeɪʃə] [fei-sha], *s.* 1. (*Anat.*) Aponeurosis, membrana que cubre los músculos y los mantiene en su lugar. 2. (*Arq.*) Faja, banda de arquitrabe. 3. Faja, banda de arquitrabe. 3. Faja. venda, cinturón. 4. (*Astr.*) Nubecilla en forma de faja alrededor de un planeta.

fascial [ˈfeɪʃəl] [fei-shal], *a.* 1. (*Anat.*) Fascial, relativo o perteneciente a la.

fasciated [ˈfeɪʃɪeɪtɪd] [fei-shiei-tid], *a.* Fajado, vendado.

fascicle [ˈfæsɪkl] [fa-si-kol], *s.* 1. Racimo, manojo; hacecillo, haz pequeño. 2. (*Bot*) Glomérulo. 3. División de un libro publicado por entregas.

fascicled [ˈfæsɪklɪd] [fa-si-klid], *a.* Arracimado; fasciculado.

fascicular [fæˈsikjʊləʳ] [fa-si-kiu-laʳ], *a.* Fascicular; unido en forma de copa o racimo.

fasciculus [fæˈsiːkjʊləs] [fa-si-kiu-lus], *s.* (*Anat.*) Fascículo.

fascinate [ˈfæsɪneɪt] [fa-si-neit], *va.* 1. Fascinar, hechizar, encantar, aojar o hacer mal de ojo. 2. Atraer irresistiblemente.

fascinating [ˈfæsɪneɪtɪŋ] [fa-si-nei-tin], *a.* Fascinador, encantador.

fascination [ˌfæsɪˈneɪʃən] [fa-si-nei-shon], *s.* Fascinación, aojo, hechizo, encanto, alucinación.

fascine [fæˈsiːn] [fa-sin], *s.* Fagina.

fascism [ˈfæʃɪzəm] [fa-shi-sem], *s.* Fascismo.

fash [fɑːʃ] [fash], *va.* (*Scot.*) Enojar, irritar, enfadar. -*vn.* Irritarse, enfadarse.

fashion [ˈfæʃən] [fa-shon], *s.* 1. Forma, figura, hechura de alguna cosa. 2. Moda, uso, costumbre. 3. Rango, calidad, esfera, condición de nacimiento. **People of fashion**, gente de tono. (*Mex.*) Gente de sangre azul. **After o in a fashion**, a la manera de. **To be in fashion**, estar de moda. **It is out of fashion**, ya no es de moda. **I do not like the fashion of the coat**, no me gusta el corte de ese abrigo. **After the English**

fashion, a la inglesa. 4. **Fashion-pieces**, *(Mar.)* Aletas, piezas sujetas en los extremos de los yugos.

fashion, *va.* 1. Formar, amoldar. 2. Adaptar, ajustar. 3. Hacer o formar alguna cosa a la moda.

fashionable ['fæʃnəbl] [fa-sho-na-bol], *a.* 1. Establecido, usado, acostumbrado, practicado. 2. Hecho a la moda. **Fashionable hat**, sombrero a la moda. *-s.* Lechuguino, currutaco, petimetre. **The fashionables**, gente de porte o rango. *(Vul.)* La gente grande.

fashionableness ['fæʃnəblnɪs] [fa-sho-na-bol-nes], *s.* 1. Figura, forma y disposición de una cosa con respecto a su apariencia exterior. 2. Gentileza en el porte; la costumbre de ataviarse conforme a las modas predominantes. 3. Elegancia, buen tono.

fashionably ['fæʃnəblɪ] [fa-sho-na-bli], *adv.* A la moda, según la moda.

fashioner ['fæʃnəʳ] [fa-sho-naʳ], *s.* Hacedor.

fashionist ['fæʃnɪst] [fa-sho-nist], *s.* Lechuguino, petimetre.

fashion-monger ['fæʃənˌmʌŋgəʳ] [fa-shon-man-gaʳ], *s.* Modista.

fashion plate ['fæʃənˌpleɪt] [fa-shon-pleit], *s.* Figurín, persona que viste con elegancia.

fast [fɑːst] [fast], *vn.* Ayunar, hacer abstinencia.

fast, *s.* 1. Ayuno. **To break one's fast**, desayunarse. 2. Espacio de tiempo designado para el ayuno religioso. 3. De otra raíz, lazo, amarra. 4. Hielo fijo o inmóvil a lo largo de la ribera.

fast, *a.* 1. Firme, seguro, fuerte, inmoble, estable, apretado. 2. Constante, fiel. 3. Difícil de borrar o destruir; duradero. 4. Profundo. 5. Veloz, rápido, pronto, ágil, ligero. 6. Hecho o ejecutado rápidamente. 7. Adelantado, se dice de los relojes. **Your watch is three minutes fast**, su reloj adelanta tres minutos. 8. Gastador, derrochador; dado a la disipación, disoluto. **A fast friend**, un amigo seguro. **A fast color**, color sólido, de buen tinte, duradero. **A fast knot**, un nudo apretado, firme. **Fast and loose**, *(Prov.)* Anden y ténganse. *-adv.* 1. Fuertemente, firmemente. 2. Duraderamente; para siempre. 3. Profundamente. **Fast asleep**, profundamente dormido. 4. No lejos; cerca de. 5. Aprisa, de prisa. **To come fast on the heels of**, seguir muy de cerca.

fast-day ['fɑːstdeɪ] [fast-dei], *s.* Día de ayuno.

fasten ['fɑːsn] [fasen], *va.* 1. Afirmar, asegurar, atar, amarrar; trabar, unir. 2. Fijar, hacer pegarse. *-vn.* Fijarse, establecerse, pararse en alguna parte; agarrarse, asirse, pegarse a alguno. **To fasten a door**, cerrar una puerta. **To fasten one's eyes on**, fijar los ojos en. **To fasten in**, clavar, hincar, fijar, imprimir una cosa en otra. **To fasten upon**, unir o pegar una cosa a otra; imputar, cargar a alguno con obligaciones.

fastener ['fɑːsnəʳ] [fa-se-naʳ], *s.* El que afirma o asegura.

fastening ['fɑːstənɪŋ] [fas-te-nin], *s.* 1. *(Mar.)* Encapilladura. 2. Lo que asegura o sujeta: broche, cerradura, cierre, corchete, botón, etc. 3. Atadura, amarradura, amarra.

faster ['fɑːstəʳ] [fas-taʳ], *s.* Ayunador.

fast-handed ['fɑːstˈhændɪd] [fast-jan-did], *a.* Agarrado, apretado, mezquino, avariento.

fastidious [fæsˈtɪdɪəs] [fas-ti-dios], *a.* Fastidioso, desdeñoso, despreciador, melindroso, dengoso, descontentadizo.

fastidiously [fæsˈtɪdɪəslɪ] [fas-ti-dios-li], *adv.* Fastidiosamente, melindrosamente.

fastidiousness [fæsˈtɪdɪəsnɪs] [fas-ti-dios-nes], *s.* Escrupulosidad, delicadeza (en el vestir, etc.), exigencia, gusto exigente. 2. Desdén.

fastigiate [fæsˈtɪdʒɪeɪt] [fas-ti-yieit], *a.* *(Bot.)* Llano e igual en la cumbre o en el ápice.

fastigium [fæsˈtɪdʒɪəm] [fas-ti-yiom], *s.* Fastigio.

fasting ['fɑːstɪŋ] [fas-tin], *ger.* Ayunando, haciendo abstinencia. **To go out fasting**, salir en ayunas. *-s.* Ayuno, abs-

tinencia de alimentos. **Fasting and prayer**, el ayuno y la oración.

fasting-day ['fɑːstɪŋdeɪ] [fas-tin-dei], *s.* Día de ayuno.

fastness ['fɑːstnɪs] [fast-nes], *s.* 1. Firmeza, seguridad, solidez; fuerza. 2. Fortaleza o plaza naturalmente fuerte. 3. Celeridad, prontitud, diligencia; velocidad, rapidez. 4. Disipación, llujuria, libertinaje. 5. *(Biol)* Resistencia a la acción de ciertas sustancias.

fat [fæt] [fat], *a.* 1. Gordo, pingüe, corpulento. 2. Tosco, lerdo, grosero. 3. Opulento, rico; gananciaso, provechoso, lucrativo. 4. Grosero, tonto, estúpido. *-s.* 1. Gordo, el cebo o manteca de la carne del animal; enjundia. 2. La parte más rica o más deseable de alguna cosa. **To live on the fat of the land**, tener lo mejor de todo. 3. *(Ant.)* Tina. *V.* VAT.

fat, *va.* Engordar, nutrir. *-vn.* Engrosarse.

fatal [feɪtl] [fei-tal], *a.* 1. Fatal, mortal, funesto. 2. Inevitable, necesario.

fatalism ['feɪtəlɪzm] [fei-ta-lisem], *s.* Fatalismo.

fatalist ['feɪtəlɪst] [fei-ta-list], *s.* Fatalista.

fatality [fəˈtælɪtɪ] [fa-ta-li-ti], *s.* 1. Fatalidad, predestinación. 2. Desgracia, infortunio. 3. Acontecimiento final, muerte. 4. Decreto del destino.

fatally ['feɪtəlɪ] [fei-ta-li], *adv.* Fatalmente.

fatalness ['feɪtəlnɪs] [fei-tal-nes], *s.* Fatalidad; necesidad inevitable.

fat-brained [ˌfætˈbreɪnd] [fat-breind], **fat-headed** [fætˈhedɪd] [fat-je-did], *a.* Lerdo, tardo, torpe.

fat-cheeked [fætˈtʃiːkt] [fat-chikt], *a.* Cachetudo, molletudo, cachetón.

fate [feɪt] [feit], *s.* 1. Hado, destino, suerte, fortuna, providencia. 2. Hado, muerte, destrución. 3. *pl. (Mit)* las Parcas; los destinos.

fated ['feɪtɪd] [fei-tid], *a.* Lo que está dispuesto o decretado por los hados, antiguametne *hadado;* fatal, lo que necesariamente ha de suceder o cumplirse.

fateful ['feɪtfʊl] [feit-ful], *a.* 1. Determinado por el destino. 2. Fatal, funesto.

fatheaded ['feɪtˌhedɪd] [feit-je-did], *a.* Torpe, estúpido.

father ['fɑːðəʳ] [fa-daʳ], *s.* 1. Padre. 2. El principal y cabeza de una familia. 3. Padre, nombre que se da a un anciano o a un hombre respetable. 4. Confesor, padre de almas, padre espiritual. 5. Padre, la primera persona de la santísima Trinidad; Dios como criador. 6. Padre, título de los senadores romanos. 7. Creador, inventor, autor de algo. **Grandfather**, abuelo. **Our fore-fathers**, nuestro padres, abuelos o antepasados. **God-father**, padrino. **Foster-father**, padre adoptivo. **Father-like**, como si fuera padre, con afecto paternal. **Father in God**, un obispo.

father, *va.* 1. Prohijar, adoptar, declarar por hijo. 2. Achacar, imputar o atribuir a uno un hijo o un*'*escrito.

fatherhood ['fɑːðəhʊd] [fa-der-jud], *s.* Paternidad.

father-in-law ['fɑːðərɪnlɔː] [fa-der-in-lo], *s.* Suegro, el padre del marido respecto de la mujer, o el de la mujer respecto del marido.

fatherland ['fɑːðəlænd] [fa-der-land], *s.* Patria, tierra natal, madre patria.

fatherless ['fɑːðəlɪs] [fa-der-les], *a.* 1. Huérfano de padre. 2. Desautorizado, lo que no tiene autoridad bastante para ser creído o para merecer consideración.

fatherliness ['fɑːðəlɪnɪs] [fa-der-li-nes], *s.* Ternura o amor paternal.

fatherly ['fɑːðəlɪ] [fa-der-li], *adv.* Paternal, lo que es propio de un padre. *-adv.* Paternalmente.

fathom ['fæðəm] [fa-dom], *s.* 1. Braza, medida de seis pies de largo. 2. Alcance, penetración, profundidad.

fathom, *va.* 1. Sondar, sondear. 2. Sondear, rastrear, penetrar, profundizar, examinar a fondo, tantear. 3. *(Des.)* Abrazar, ceñir con los brazos.

fathomable ['fæðəməbl] [fa-do-ma-bol], *a.* Sondable, sondeable.

fathomer ['fæðəməʳ] [fa-do-maʳ], *s.* Sondeador.

fathomless [ˈfæðəmlɪs] [fa-dom-les], *a.* Insondable; impenetrable.

fatidical [fəˈtɪdɪkl] [fa-ti-di-kal], *a.* Fatídico, profético.

fatiferous [fəˈtɪfərəs] [fa-ti-fe-ros], *a.* Fatal, funesto.

fatigue [ˈfətɪg] [fa-tig], *s.* 1. Cansancio. 2. Fatiga, trabajo. 3. **Fatigue** o **fatigue-duty**, *(Mil.)* Faena, todo trabajo que hacen los militares distinto del manejo de las armas y demás ejercicios de su profesión. **Spent with fatigue**, rendido de cansancio; aspeado. **Fatigue-party**, los soldados que están de faena, limpieza, etc.

fatigue, *va.* Fatigar, cansar, con el trabajo corporal o del entendimiento.

fatigued [fəˈtiːɡd] [fa-tigd], *a.* Fatigado, cansado.

fatiguing [ˈfətɪgɪŋ] [fa-ti-guin], *ger.* y *a.* Cansado, pesado, que produce cansancio.

fatiscent [ˈfətɪsənt] [fa-ti-sent], *a.* Lo que puesto al aire se convierte en polvo.

fatling [ˈfətlɪŋ] [fa-tlin], *s.* Cebón, animal que se ceba para comerlo. *-a.* Gordo, grueso, regordete.

fatly [ˈfətlɪ] [fat-li], *adv.* Corpulentamente, toscamente.

fatness [ˈfətnɪs] [fat-nes], *s.* 1. Gordura. 2. Gordo, grasa. 3. Fertilidad, fecundidad.

fatten [ˈfætn] [fa-ten], *va.* 1. Engordar, nutrir, alimentar. 2. Cebar. 3. Fertilizar, fecundar o engrasar la tierra. *-vn.* Criar o echar carnes, engrasarse.

fattener [ˈfətnəʳ] [fat-naʳ], *s.* Cebo, lo que engorda.

fattiness [ˈfətɪnɪs] [fa-ti-nes], *s.* Gordura, pringue.

fattish [ˈfætɪʃ] [fa-tish], *a.* Gordiflón, algo gordo; pingüedinoso.

fatty [ˈfætɪ] [fa-ti], *a.* Untoso, craso, pingüe.

fatuitous [ˈfætɔɪtəs] [fa-tui-tos], *a.* 1. Necio, fatuo. 2. Vano, ilusorio.

fatuity [ˈfætɔɪtɪ] [fa-tui-ti], *s.* Fatuidad, simpleza.

fatuous [ˈfætʊəs] [fa-tuos], *a.* Fatuo, insensato, simple, tonto.

fat-witted [ˈfætˈwɪtɪd] [fat-ui-tid], *a.* Torpe, lerdo, pesado.

fauces [ˈfɔːsɪz] [fo-sis], *s. pl.* Fauces, la entrada del esófago; gaznate, garganta.

faucet [ˈfɔːsɪt] [fo-sit], *s.* Espita, canilla, llave, grifo; canilla con una válvula para regular la salida de un líquido.

faugh [fɔː] [fo], *inter.* Expresión de enfado o menosprecio: ¡puf! ¡bah!

fault [fɔːlt] [folt], *s.* 1. Falta, culpa, desliz o defecto en obrar. 2. Falta, defecto o privación de algo. 3. *(Geol.)* Falla, interrupción y dislocación de las capas que forman la corteza terrestre por sacudimientos interiores. 4. *(Elec.)* Avería accidental. **To find fault**, tachar, criticar; poner faltas. **I find no fault in their opinion**, no hallo nada reprensible en su modo de pensar. 5. Pérdida de la pista o del rastro; se dice de los perros cazadores.

fault, *va.* 1. *(Geol.)* Hacer una falla en. 2. (Raro o fam.) Acusar; echar a uno la culpa de alguna falta o delito. *-vn.* *(Des.)* Faltar; no tener razón; extraviarse.

fault-finder [ˈfɔːltˈfaɪndəʳ] [folt-fain-daʳ], *s.* Censurador, criticón, que todo lo encuentra mal.

faultily [ˈfɔːltɪlɪ] [fol-ti-li], *adv.* Defectuosamente, erradamente, culpablemente.

faultiness [ˈfɔːltɪnɪs] [fol-ti-nes], *s.* 1. Culpa, falta, vicio, defecto, ofensa. 2. Defectuosidad, imperfección.

faultless [ˈfɔːltlɪs] [fol-tles], *a.* Sin falta; sin tacha; perfecto, cumplido, acabado.

faultlessly [ˈfɔːltlɪslɪ] [fol-tles-li], *a.* Impecablemente, prefectamente, irreprochablemente.

faultlessness [ˈfɔːltlɪsnɪs] [fol-tles-nes], *s.* Perfección; inculpabilidad.

faulty [ˈfɔːltɪ] [fol-ti], *a.* Culpable, defectuoso, imperfecto.

faun [ˈfɔːn] [fon], *s.* Fauno, especie de dios de las selvas.

fauna [ˈfɔːnə] [fo-na], *s.* *(pl.* FAUNAE o FAUNAS). *(Zool.)* Fauna, conjunto de los animales de cada país o región (o su descripción científica).

faunist [ˈfɔːnɪst] [fo-nist], *s.* Naturalista que estudia una fauna.

fautor [ˈfɔːtəʳ] [fo-taʳ], *s.* *(Ant.)* Fautor, favorecedor.

fautress [ˈfɔːtrɪs] [fo-tris], *sf.* Fautora, fomentadora.

favillous [fəˈvɪləs] [fa-vi-los], *a.* Ceniciento.

favonian [fəˈvəʊnɪən] [fa-vou-nian], *a.* Que sopla del oeste; perteneciente al favonio; favorable, próspero.

favor o **favour** [ˈfeɪvəʳ] [fei-vaʳ], *va.* y *vn.* 1. Favorecer, patrocinar, proteger, ayudar, amparar, socorrer. **Favor me with that**, hágame usted el favor de eso, favorézcame Ud. con eso. 2. Favorecer, ayudar, asistir con ventajas o conveniencias. **To favor an opinion**, apoyar una opinión. 3. *(fam.)* Asemejarse, parecerse. **Everybody owns that this gentleman favors his father**, todo el mundo conviene en que este caballero se parece a su padre. 4. Favorecer, conducir, contribuir, convenir para algún fin. 5. Usar con precaución, v.g. un miembro lastimado; abstenerse de usar, guardar, reservar. 6. *(Art.)* Atenuar, paliar, mitigar.

favor, *s.* 1. Favor, fineza, beneficio. 2. Favor, socorro, patrocinio, amparo. 3. Mitigación, lenidad, blandura en el castigo. 4. Gracia, beneficio otorgado a uno con exclusión de otros; parcialidad. 5. Permiso, licencia. **By your favor**, con su permiso, licencia, venia. 6. Conveniencia para alguna cosa, facilidad. 7. Favor, cinta, adorno, flor, etc., recibida de una dama como agasajo; los lazos de cinta que se llevan en Inglaterra en algunas ocasiones en señal de regocijo o como signo de pertenecer a un partido, en particular, una fruslería dada en el cotillón. 8. En la correspondencia (esp. comercial), carta; grata, atenta. 9. *(Ant.)* Facción, semblante. **With your favor** o **by your favor**, con licencia o permiso de Ud. 10. *(Com.)* a favor de, pagadero a.

favorable [ˈfeɪvərəbl] [fei-va-ra-bol], *a.* 1. Favorable, propicio, benévolo. 2. Favorable, benigno. 3. Bien encarado, bien parecido.

favorableness [ˈfeɪvərəblnɪs] [fei-va-ra-bol-nes], *s.* Agrado, benignidad.

favorably [ˈfeɪvərəblɪ] [fei-va-ra-bli], *adv.* Favorablemente, benignamente.

favored [ˈfeɪvəd] [fei-vad], *a.* Favorecido, protegido, amparado. **Well-favored**, hermoso, bien parecido. **Ill-favored**, feo, mal carado.

favoredly [ˈfeɪvədlɪ] [fei-vad-li], *adv.* Sólo se usa unido a los siguientes adverbios: **Well** o **ill favoredly**, con buena o mala apariencia.

favoredness [ˈfeɪvədnɪs] [fei-vad-nes], *s.* *(Poco us.)* Apariencia, aspecto exterior. **Hard-favoredness**, dureza en la fisonomía; fealdad.

favorer [ˈfeɪvərəʳ] [fei-vo-raʳ], *s.* Favorecedor.

favorite, favourite [ˈfeɪvərɪt] [fei-vo-rit], *s.* Favorito, predilecto, privado, valido; confidente. *-a.* Amado, favorecido.

favoritism [ˈfeɪvərɪtɪzəm] [fei-vo-ri-tisem], *s.* Favoritismo, la influencia que el afecto por algún favorito o predilecto tiene en las acciones de una persona: se toma comúnmente en mal sentido.

favorless [ˈfeɪvəlɪs] [fei-vo-les], *a.* Desfavorecido, desamparado; adverso, contrario.

favose [ˈfeɪvəz] [fei-vos], *a.* Faveolado, guarnecido de celdillas como los alvéolos, del panal.

favour, favourable, favourite, etc. (es la forma común en Inglaterra). V. FAVOR, etc.

fawn [fɔːn] [fon], *s.* 1. Cervato, enodio, el macho pequeño de los ciervos; gamo o gama en su primer año. 2. *(Poco us.)* Lisonja o adulación servil y baja. 3. Color del cervato.

fawn, *vn.* 1. Parir la cierva. 2. Halagar o hacer fiestas como el perro a su amo; adular servilmente.

fawner [ˈfɔːnəʳ] [fo-naʳ], *s.* Lisonjero, zalamero, adulador, quitapelillos.

fawning [ˈfɔːnɪŋ] [fo-nin], *s.* Adulación o lisonja vil y baja; bajeza.

fawningly [ˈfɔːnɪŋlɪ] [fo-nin-li], *adv.* Lisonjeramente, zalameramente.

fay [feɪ] [fei], *s.* Duende. V. FAIRY.

fay, *va.* Empalmar, ajustar una pieza con otra. *-vn.* Cuadrar, venir bien una pieza con otra.

fealty [ˈfiːəltɪ] [fial-ti], *s.* Homenaje, fidelidad, lealtad.

fear [fɪəʳ] [fiaʳ], *s.* 1. Miedo, perturbación originada por la aprehensión de algún peligro. 2. Miedo, temor, recelo. 3.

Causa, motivo de temor; carácter alarmante. 4. Respeto, veneración con relación a la autoridad constituída. **Fear of the world**, respeto humano. **To be in fear**, tener miedo. **There is fear**, hay que temer. **For fear**, por temor de, por miedo de.

fear, *va*. 1. Temer, tener miedo. 2. Mirar con temor respetuoso y reverencia. 3. *(Ant. y Poét.)* Amedrentar, espantar. *-vn*. 1. Temer, tener horror a algo. 2. Temer, estar inquieto o receloso.

fearful ['fɪəfʊl] [fia-ful], *a*. 1. Medroso, miedoso, temeroso, pusilánime. 2. Tímido, encogido y corto de ánimo. 3. Tremendo, horrendo, espantoso, terrible; respetuoso. 4. Digno de respeto y reverencia.

fearfully ['fɪəfəlɪ] [fia-fu-li], *adv*. Medrosamente, temerosamente, con miedo y temor; de un modo digno de reverencia; de una manera espantosa, terriblemente.

fearfulness ['fɪəfʊlnɪs] [fia-ful-nes], *s*. 1. Timidez, temor, miedo, pusilanimidad, encogimiento. 2. Temor, miedo, pasión del ánimo que nos hace evitar las cosas dañosas o peligrosas.

fearless ['fɪəlɪs] [fia-les], *a*. Impertérrito, intrépido, arrojado, ardiente, bravo, atrevido, audaz.

fearlessly ['fɪəlɪslɪ] [fia-les-li], *adv*. Intrépidamente, sin miedo.

fearlessness ['fɪəlɪsnɪs] [fia-les-nes], *s*. Intrepidez, arrojo, bravura, valentía.

fearsome ['fɪəsəm] [fia-som], *a*. 1. Temible, espantoso, que infunde miedo. 2. Tímido, miedoso, asustado.

feasibility [ˌfiːzə'bɪlɪtɪ] [fi-sa-bi-li-ti], *s*. Posibilidad o capacidad de poderse ejecutar alguna cosa.

feasible ['fiːzɪbl] [fia-si-bol], *adv*. De un modo factible, practicable.

feasibly ['fiːzɪblɪ] [fia-si-bli], *adv*. de un modo factible.

feast [fiːst] [fist], *s*. 1. Banquete, festín, convite, comida o cena espléndida. *(fam.)* Comilitona, comilona. 2. Fiesta solemne, regocijo en día señalado. **Church feast**, fiesta religiosa 3. Cualquier cosa agradable al paladar.

feast, *va*. 1. Festejar, recibir con agasajo en su casa, regalar al que viene a ella a comer. 2. Atracar de comida y bebida. *-vn*. 1. Comer opíparamente. 2. Gozarse, entretenerse.

feaster ['fiːstər] [fis-ta'], *s*. 1. Comilitón, goloso. 2. Festejador, el que da banquetes, anfitrión, festejador.

feastful ['fiːstfʊl] [fist-ful], *a*. Festivo, placentero; suntuoso, voluptuoso.

feasting ['fiːstɪŋ] [fis-tin], *s*. Banquete; fiesta.

feast-rite ['fiːst'raɪt] [fist-rait], *s*. El ceremonial de los banquetes.

feat [fiːt] [fit], *s*. 1. Hecho, acción o hazaña notables. 2. Juego de manos, ligereza de manos. **Feats**, suertes. *-a. (Ant.)* 1. Apto, ingenioso. 2. Fino, pulido, galón; por ironía o desprecio. **To do feats**, hacer maravillas.

feat, *va. (Ds.)* Formar, amoldar.

feather ['feðər] [fe-da'], *s*. 1. Pluma. 2. Algo que se parece a una pluma o plumas; particularmente en la mecánica, lengüeta, cuña, rayo; refuerzo de eje. 3. Género, clase, naturaleza, especie. **Birds of a feather**, pájaros de una misma pluma, lobos de la misma camada. 4. Bagatela, fruslería. 5. Al remar, la acción de volver la pala del remo poniéndola casi horizontal. 6. Cacería de animales de pluma en general. **To cut a feather**, *(Mar.)* llevar buen viento, navegar con rapidez. **To show the white feather**, mostrarse cobarde, volverse atrás (se dice porque el verdadero gallo de pelea no tiene plumas blancas). **To pluck a bird's feather**s, desplumar. **A plume of feathers**, plumaje. **To laugh at a feather**, reírse de nada. **Feather-bed**, colchón de plumas, plumón. **Imitation feathers**, plumas de imitación, encrespadas para penachos. **Birds of a feather flock together**, *(Prov.)* Cada oveja con su pareja; o Dios los cría y ellos se juntan. **To be a feather in one's cap**, dar realce o importancia a alguna persona o cosa. **Feather-edged**, en bisel, en perfil. **Feather-brain**, imbécil, tonto, casquivano. **Feather-weight**, púgil o atleta de mínimo peso; persona de escasa importancia. **In high feather**, vivo, alegre.

feather, *va*. 1. Emplumar, poner o adornar con plumas. 2. Enriquecer, adornar, como con plumas. 3. Volver la pala del remo al sacarla del agua, poniéndola casi horizontal. 4. *(Mec.)* Ajustar una lengüeta o rayo en algo. 5. Estabilizar un avión por medio de una forma de rotación de hélices o motores. *-vn*. 1. Cubrirse con plumas. 2. Descomponerse en forma emplumada. **To feather one's nest**, enriquecerse, particularmente a expensas de otro, juntar mucho caudal, hacer su agosto.

featherbrain ['feðəbreɪn] [fe-da-brein], *s*. Persona de poco seso.

featherbedding ['feðəˌbedɪŋ] [fe-da-be-din], *s*. Imposición por parte de sindicatos de trabajadores innecesarios.

feather duster ['feðə'dʌstər] [fe-da-das-ta'], *s*. Plumero.

feathered ['feðəd] [fe-derd], *a*. 1. Plumado, emplumado. 2. Que tiene apéndices parecidos a plumas. 3. Alado; veloz como una flecha. **The feathered tribe**, los pájaros.

featheredged ['feðəredʒɪd] [fe-da-red-yid], *a*. 1. Achaflanado. 2. De borde muy delgado o afilado. 3. Cortado en cuña o bisel.

feathering ['feðərɪŋ] [fe-da-rin], *pa*. de TO FEATHER y *s*. (Se usa en composición.) **Feathering-wheel**, rueda de paletas movibles.

featherless ['feðəlɪs] [fe-da-lis], *a*. Desplumado, implume.

feather-seller ['feðəselər] [fe-da-se-la'], *s*. Plumajero, vendedor de plumajes.

featherweight ['feðəweɪt] [fe-da-ueit], *s. (Box)* Peso pluma.

feathery ['feðərɪ] [fe-da-ri], *a*. 1. Plumado, cubierto con plumas. 2. Ligero como una pluma, o parecido a las plumas.

featness ['fiːtnɪs] [fit-nes], *s*. Pulidez, destreza, gentileza.

feature ['fiːtʃər] [fi-cha'], *s*. 1. Semblante, rostro. 2. Facción del rostro, forma, figura. 3. Rasgo, carácter distintivo. *-pl*. Facciones, rostro, la cara entera.

feature, *va*. Asemejarse, parecerse en el semblante o cara.

featured ['fiːtʃəd] [fi-ched], *a*. 1. Lo que tiene buenas o malas facciones. 2. Se toma en sentido absoluto por el que tiene hermosas facciones. 3. Lo que se parece en el rostro o en las facciones. **Well-featured**, bien encarado, de facciones hermosas. **Ill-featured**, mal encarado o engestado.

featureless ['fiːtʃəlɪs] [fi-che-les], *a*. Que no tiene rasgos distinto ni fisonomía caracterizada; sin rasgos distintivos, poco interesante.

febricula ['febrɪkjʊlə] [fe-bri-kiu-la], *s. (Med)* Calenturilla, fiebre ligera.

febrific ['febrɪfɪk] [fe-bri-fik], *a*. Febrífico, febricitante, que causa fiebre.

febrifacient ['febrɪfeɪʃənt] [fe-bri-fei-shent], *a*. Febril, que causa o produce fiebre.

febrifugal ['febrɪfjʊgəl] [fe-bri-fiu-gal, *a*. Que tiene la cualidad de calmar la fiebre.

febrile ['fiːbraɪl] [fi-brail], *a. (Med.)* Febril, lo que indica o proviene de la fiebre.

February ['februərɪ] [fe-brua-ri], *s*. Febrero.

februation ['febru'eɪʃən] [fe-bru-ei-shon], *s*. Purificación o sacrificio entre los paganos.

fecal ['fiːkəl] [fi-kal], *a*. Fecal.

feces ['fiːsiːz] [fi-sis], *s. pl*. Excrementos; heces.

feck [fek] [fek], *a. (Esco.)* Endurecido, fuerte, robusto. *-s*. 1. Fuerza, poder, vigor. 2. Cantidad, número o valor. 3. La parte principal.

fecula ['fekjʊlə] [fe-kiu-la], *s*. 1. Almidón. 2. *V.* CHLOROPHYL.

feculence, feculency ['fekjʊləns] [fe-kiu-lens], *s*. 1. Feculencia; porquería debida a las heces; la calidad de hacer mucho poso o dejar muchas heces. 2. Posos, heces, sedimento.

feculent ['fekjʊlənt] [fe-kiu-lent], *a*. Feculento, heciento, puerco, fecal.

fecund ['fiːkənd] [fi-kond], *a*. Fecundo, fértil, prolífico.

fecundate ['fiːkəndeɪt] [fi-kon-deit], *va*. Fecundar.

fecundation [ˌfiːkən'deɪʃən] [fi-kon-dei-shon], *s*. Fecundación.

fecundify ['fiːkəndɪfaɪ] [fi-kon-di-fai], *va.* Fecunda, fecundizar.

fecundity ['fiːkʌndɪtɪ] [fi-kan-di-ti], *s.* Fecundidad, fertilidad, abundancia.

fed [fed] [fed], *pret.* y *pp.* del verbo TO FEED. **To be full fed**, tener el vientre lleno.

federal ['fedərəl] [fe-de-ral], *a.* 1. Federal, perteneciente a liga o contrato. 2. Relativo a una confederación de estados. 3. Partidario de la federación; en especial, partidario de la Unión en la guerra civil norteamericana de 1861-1865.

federalism ['fedərəlɪzm] [fe-de-ra-lisem], *s.* Federalismo; principios de los federales.

federalist ['fedərəlɪst] [fe-de-ra-list], *s.* Federalista, nombre dado en la América del Norte a los partidarios de la constitución de los Estados Unidos.

federalize, federalise ['fedərəlaɪz] [fe-de-ra-lais], *va.* Federalizar, formar una federación.

federate ['fedəreɪt] [fe-de-reit], *a.* Confederado, aliado. *-va.* V. FEDERALIZE.

federative ['fedərətɪv] [fe-de-ra-tiv], *a.* Federativo, unido por una liga.

federation ['fedəreɪʃən] [fe-de-rei-shon], *s.* Confederación, liga, federación.

fedora [fə'dɔːrə] [fe-do-ra], *s.* Sombrero de fieltro.

fee [fiː] [fi], *s.* 1. Recompensa o premio por algún trabajo. 2. Gratificación, paga extraordinaria que se da a las personas empleadas en los oficios públicos. 3. Derechos honorarios, salario, propina, estipendio que se da a los que ejercen alguna profesión por el ejercicio de ella. 4. *(Der.)* Bienes, hacienda de patrimonio. 5. *(For.)* Feudo. **Fee simple**, hacienda libre de condición.

fee, *va.* 1. Pagar, recompensar, premiar. 2. Alquilar, tener a sueldo. 3. Cohechar, sobornar. 4. Dar propina.

feeable ['fiːəbl] [fia-bol], *a.* Recompensable; se dice de la persona a quien se puede dar una retribución o propina, retribuible.

feeble ['fiːbl] [fi-bol], *a.* 1. Feble, débil, flaco, lánguido; enfermizo; debilitado por la edad o las desgracias. 2. Impotente, inválido. **To grow feeble**, debilitarse, enflaquecerse.

feeble, *va.* Debilitar. V. ENFEEBLE.

feeble-minded ['fiːbl'maɪndɪd] [fi-bol-main-ded], *a.* 1. Falto de inteligencia, imbécil. 2. Irresoluto, vacilante. **Feeble-mindedness**, debilidad de entendimiento, idiotez; irresolución.

feebleness ['fiːblnɪs] [fi-bol-nes], *s.* Debilidad, extenuación, flaqueza.

feebly ['fiːblɪ] [fi-bli], *adv.* Débilmente, flacamente, pobremente, escasamente.

feed [fiːd] [fid], *va.* 1. Dar de comer. 2. Pacer, apacentarse el ganado. 3. Nutrir, alimentar, v.g. una máquina; proveer, suplir lo que falta a alguna cosa. 4. Alimentar con esperanzas. 5. Deleitar, entretener. *-vn.* 1. Comer, alimentarse. 2. Pastar, comer la hierba del campo. 3. Engordar, cebar. **To feed on o upon**, alimentarse de.

feed, *s.* 1. Comida, alimento. 2. Pasto, hierba para alimentar los ganados. 3. *(Mec.)* Movimiento de empuje, y el material con que se alimenta una máquina; alimentación. **Feed-bag**, morral de pienso. **Feed-head**, *(Mec.)* depósito de agua para la alimentación de una máquina. **Feed-motion**, *(Mec.)* movimiento de alimentación. **Feed-pump**, bomba de alimentación para proveer de agua las máquinas de vapor.

feedback ['fiːdbæk] [fid-bak], *s. (Elect.)* Realimentación, regeneración.

feeder ['fiːdər] [fi-dar], *s.* 1. El que da de comer; particularmente persona o aparato para surtir de material a una máquina. 2. Comedor, el que come; también gorrista, dependiente, criado. 3. Una cosa cualquiera que suple las necesidades de otra o aumenta su importancia; v.g. el afluente de un río. 4. Atizador, incitador. **Nice feeder**, melindroso en los manjares. **High o greedy feeder**, comilón, glotón. **Dainty feeder**, goloso, lamerón.

feedback ['fiːdbæk] [fid-bak], *s. (Elect.)* Regeneración, realimentación.

feedhead ['fiːdhed] [fid-jed], *s.* Depósito de alimentación de la máquina de vapor.

feeding ['fiːdɪŋ] [fi-din], *s.* Herbaje, pastura, pasto; comida. **Feeding apparatus**, *(Mec.)* aparato de alimentación. **Feeding-bottle**, mamadera, biberón, botellita que sirve para la lactanacia artificial de los niños, corderos, etc.

fee-farm ['fiːfɑːm] [fid-farm], *s.* 1. *(For.)* Enfiteusis o propiamente arrendamiento de un terreno feudal. 2. Escritura de arrendamiento de tierras feudales.

feel [fiːl] [fil], *vn.* 1. Sentir, percibir por el tacto. 2. Tentar, examinar, sondear. 3. Tener sensibilidad pronta para percibir la impresión grata o desagradable que causan los objetos. 4. Producir una cosa impresión al tacto. 5. Palpar, tentar, manosear. 6. Tomar el pulso. 7. Sentir placer o pena física o moralmente. 8. Conocerse. **To feel for**, condolerse de. **To feel soft**, ser suave al tacto. **To feel coarse**, ser áspero al tacto. **To feel mortified**, abochornarse, correrse, mortificarse. **How do you feel?**, ¿cómo se siente Ud.?, ¿cómo se encuentra Ud.?

feel, *s.* Tacto, palpamiento.

feeler ['fiːlər] [fi-lar], *s.* 1. Tentador. 2. Un órgano del tacto; antena, cada una de las dos puntas que tienen en la cabeza algunos insectos; tentáculo. 3. Tentativa, acción con que se intenta experimentar, probar o tantear alguna cosa.

feeling ['fiːlɪŋ] [fi-lin], *s.* 1. Tacto, el sentido del tacto, palpamiento. V. FEEL. 2. Sensibilidad, ternura, compasión. 3. Sensación, percepción, sentimiento. **To touch one's feelings**, (a) conmover el ánimo; tocar en vivo. (b) herir el amor propio. **Good, proper feeling**, buen sentimiento. **Wrong, improper feeling**, mal sentimiento. *-part. a.* Sensible, tierno, conmovedor, patético.

feelingly ['fiːlɪŋlɪ] [fi-lin-li], *adv.* 1. Vivamente, con mucha expresión, con energía. **He spoke very feelingly**, habló al alma. 2. Sensiblemente, tiernamente; de un modo conmovedor. 3. Con compasión, tiernamente.

feet [fiːt] [fit], *s. pl.* de FOOT. Pies.

feetless ['fiːtlɪs] [fit-lis], *a.* Sin pies.

feeze [fiːz] [fis], *va. (Scot.)* Destorcer el chicote de un cabo, hacer pedazos. *-vn.* 1. Destorcerse, deshacerse. 2. *(Fam. E.U.)* Enfadarse, inquietarse.

feign [feɪn] [fein], *va.* 1. Inventar, fingir, idear o imaginar lo que no existe. 2. Pretextar, valerse de algún pretexto. 3. Fingir, disimular. *-vn.* Fingir, referir falsedades imaginarias. **A feigned treble**, *(Mús.)* Falsete. *(Fam.)* **To feign ignorance**, hacerse chiquito.

feignedly ['feɪnɪdlɪ] [fei-nid-li], *adv.* Fingidamente.

feignedness ['feɪnɪdnɪs] [fei-nid-nes], *s.* Ficción, fraude, engaño.

feigner ['feɪnər] [fei-nar], *s.* Fingidor.

feigning ['feɪnɪŋ] [fei-nin], *s.* Fingimiento, simulación, engaño.

feint [feɪnt] [feint], *s.* 1. Ficción, disimulación, artificio, treta. 2. Finta, movimiento con la espada para distraer o engañar al contrario. *-vn.* Hacer finta, fingir un golpe o estocada.

feldspar ['feldspɑːr] [feld-spar], *s.* Feldespato, silicato de alúmina y un álcali, que se encuentra en muchas rocas primitivas. (Escríbese también **Feldspath y Felspar**).

feldspathic [felds'pɑːθɪk] [feld-spa-zik], *a.* Del feldespato, que lo contiene o se le asemeja.

felicitate [fɪ'lɪsɪteɪt] [fi-li-si-teit], *va.* 1. Felicitar, dar el parabién o la enhorabuena, congratularse de algo con otro. 2. *(Des.)* Hacer feliz o dichoso a alguno.

felicitation [fɪlɪsɪ'teɪʃən] [fi-li-si-tei-shon], *s.* Felicitación, congratulación, parabién, enhorabuena.

felicitous [fɪ'lɪsɪtəs] [fi-li-si-tos], *a.* Feliz, dichoso; bienaventurado.

felicitously [fɪ'lɪsɪtəslɪ] [fi-li-si-tos-li], *adv.* Felizmente, dichosamente.

felicity [fɪ'lɪsɪtɪ] [fi-li-si-ti], *s.* Felicidad, dicha, bienaventuranza.

felidæ ['felɪdæ] [fe-li-da], *s. pl. (Zool.)* Félidos, familia de mamíferos carnívoros que comprende el león, tigre, gato, etc.

feline ['fiːlaɪn] [fi-lain], *a.* Gatuno, gatesco, que pertenece al género felino.

fell [fel] [fel], *a.* 1. Cruel, bárbaro, inhumano. 2. Fiero, sanguinario, feroz, sangriento.

fell, *s.* 1. Dobladillo, costura que tiene al lado una tira llana y lisa. 2. Remate del tejido. 3. Pelo, guedejas de pelo. 4. *(Ant.)* Cuero, piel, pellejo. 5. (Prov. Ingl.) Collado, sierra, peñasco.

fell, *pret.* de TO FALL.

fell, *va.* 1. Derrotar, derrocar, echar por tierra; acogotar (las reses). 2. Cortar para echar por tierra alguna cosa (heads, trees). **Felling of wood**, corta o corte de monte o leña. 3. Dobladillar, hacer un dobladillo.

fellah ['felə] (*pl.* FELLAHS o FELLAHEEN). En Egipto, Siria, etc., patán, labriego.

feller ['felər] [fe-lar], *s.* 1. Derribante. 2. Pieza accesoria de una máquina de coser para hacer dobladillos; sobrecosedor. 3. Cortador de árboles.

felling ['felɪŋ] [fe-lin], *s.* 1. Tala de árboles. 2. área talada o para ser talada.

fellmonger [fel'mɒŋər] [fel-mon-gar], *s. (Des.)* Pellejero, el que trata en pellejos.

fellness [fel] [fel, *s.* Crueldad, ferocidad, barbarie.

felloe ['feləʊ] [fe-lo], *s.* Pina de la rueda. V. FELLY.

fellow ['feləʊ] [fe-lou], *a.* Asociado; parecido, correspondiente. (Se usa frecuentemente para formar voces compuestas.) -*s.* 1. Persona, individuo. 2. Compañero, camarada, socio; igual. 3. Compañero, hermano, la cosa que hace juego con otra. **My cuff-buttons are not fellows**, mis gemelos no hacen juego o no son iguales. 4. Socio o individuo de algún colegio, sociedad o academia. 5. *(fam.)* Hombre, mozo, chico. A veces es expletivo cuando se une a los adjetivos, como, **a brave fellow**, un valiente. *(fam.)* Un buen chico, una buena alhaja. **A worthless fellow**, un inútil, un pícaro. **Dear little fellow**, querido, queridito mío. **A young fellow**, un joven, un mozo, un muchacho. **A clever fellow**, un mozo listo, entendido, de talento. 6. Pelafustán, hombre vulgar, persona inferior o desacreditada. **Fellow-being o creature**, el prójimo, nuestro semejante. V. F. Como abreviatura. **To be hail fellow, well met**, tratarse de igual a igual, como compañero.

fellow, *va.* 1. Hermanar, igualar una cosa con otra. 2. Convenir; hacer pareja; aparear.

fellow-citizen ['feləʊ'sɪtɪzən] [fe-lou-si-ti-sen], *s.* Conciudadano, compatriota.

fellow-commoner ['feləʊ'kʌmənər] [fe-lou-ka-mo-nar], *s.* El que tiene los mismos derechos que otro.

fellow-counsellor ['feləʊ'kʌnsələr] [fe-lou-kan-se-lar], *s.* Individuo del mismo consejo.

fellow-creature ['feləʊ'krɪətʃər] [fe-lou-kria-char], *s.* Criatura de la misma especie.

fellow-feeling ['feləʊ'fiːlɪŋ] [fe-lou-fi-lin], *s.* 1. Simpatía, compasión. 2. Interés común.

fellow-heir ['feləʊ'heər] [fe-lou-jea], *s.* Coheredero.

fellow-helper ['feləʊ'helpər] [fe-lou-jel-pa], *s.* Coadjutor, coadyuvador.

fellow-laborer ['feləʊ'læbərər] [fe-lou-la-bo-ra], *s.* Colaborador, compañero en algún trabajo.

fellow-maiden ['feləʊ'meɪdn] [fe-lou-mei-den], *sf.* Doncella que vive o está con otra.

fellow-member ['feləʊ'membər] [fe-lou-mem-ba], *s.* Individuo de la misma sociedad; miembro del mismo cuerpo; compañero.

fellow-minister ['feləʊ'mɪnɪstər] [fe-lou-mi-nis-ta], *s.* El que sirve el mismo oficio.

fellow-partner ['feləʊ'pɑːtnər] [fe-lou-part-na], *s.* Consocio con algún negocio o casa de comercio, donde hay más de dos compañeros.

fellow-peer ['feləʊ'pɪər] [fe-lou-pia], *s.* El que goza los mismos privilegios de nobleza, como sucede en Inglaterra,

donde los pares tienen títulos y precedencia diferentes, aunque son iguales en los demás privilegios.

fellow-prisoner ['feləʊ'prɪsnər] [fe-lou-pri-so-na], *s.* Preso en la misma cárcel o por la misma causa.

fellow-scholar ['feləʊ'skɒlər] [fe-lou-sko-la], *s.* Condiscípulo.

fellow-servant ['feləʊ'sɜːvənt] [fe-lou-ser-vant], *s.* Sirviente que tiene el mismo amo que otro.

fellowship ['feləʊʃɪp] [fe-lou-ship], *s.* 1. Intimidad, confraternidad, compañerismo; comunión. 2. Asociación, comunidad de intereses o de sentimientos; participación. 3. Compañía, cuerpo de individuos asociados. 4. Sociedad, compañía, reunión social. 5. *(Ingl.)* Beca, plaza de colegial en algún colegio: o *(E.U.)* fundación en las universidades para sostener a un estudiante que se dedica a una carrera universitaria. 6. *(Arit.)* Regla de compañía. **Good-fellowship**, espíritu de paz, de concordia. **Do it for good-fellowship**, hágalo Ud. en obsequio de la concordia. **The fellowship of the Holy Ghost**, la comunión del Espíritu Santo.

fellowship, *va.* y *vn.* Admitir, aceptar o unirse con otros en sociedad.

fellow-soldier ['feləʊ'səʊldɪər] [fe-lou-soul-dia], *s.* Comilitón.

fellow-student ['feləʊ'sjuːdənt] [fe-lou-stiu-dent], *s.* Condiscípulo.

fellow-subject ['feləʊ'sʌbdʒekt] [fe-lou-sab-yekt], *s.* El que vive bajo el mismo gobierno que otro.

fellow-sufferer ['feləʊ'sʌfərər] [fe-lou-sa-fe-ra], *s.* El que sufre por la misma causa o al propio tiempo que otro.

fellow-traveler ['feləʊ'trævlər] [fe-lou-tra-ve-la], *s.* 1. Compañero de viaje. 2. Comunisoide, simpatizador de los comunistas.

fellow-worker ['feləʊ'wɜːkər] [fe-lou-uer-ka], *s.* El que trabaja con el mismo propósito o en el mismo asunto que otro.

fellow-workman ['feləʊ'wɜːkmən] [fe-lou-uek-man], *s.* Artesano que trabaja en la misma obra que otro.

felly, fellow ['felɪ] [fe-li], *s.* Pina, cada uno de los trozos curvos de madera que forman en círculo la rueda de un coche o carro.

felly, *adv.* Cruelmente, bárbaramente, ferozmente.

felo-de-se ['feləʊ'deɪsɪ] [fe-lou-dei-si], *s. (For.)* Suicida.

felon ['felən] [fe-lon], *s.* 1. Reo de algún delito capital o grave. 2. Panadizo, panarizo, uñero. -*a.* 1. Adquirido por felonía. 2. Malvado, criminal; traidor.

felonious ['felənɪəs] [fe-lo-nios], *a.* Malvado, perverso, traidor, villano, maligno, pérfido.

feloniously ['felənɪəslɪ] [fe-lo-nios-li], *adv.* Traidoramente, alevosamente, malvadamente.

felonry ['felənrɪ] [fe-lon-ri], *s.* El conjunto de malhechores; toda la pillería.

felony ['felənɪ] [fe-lo-ni], *s.* Crimen o delito que tenía originalmente por pena el embargo de los bienes muebles e inmuebles, y hoy tiene pena capital o la encarcelación en una prisión de estado.

felsite ['felsaɪt] [fel-sait], *s.* Mezcla de cuarzo y feldespato. V. FELDSPAR.

felspar ['felspɑːr] [fel-spa], *s.* Feldespato. V. FELDSPAR. (Forma más usada en Inglaterra.)

felt [felt] [felt], *s.* Fieltro, lana no tejida, sino unida e incorporada a fuerza de agua caliente, lejía y goma. -*pret.* del verbo TO FEEL.

felt, *adv.* Trabajar el fieltro para los sombreros.

felting ['feltɪŋ] [fel-tin], *s.* 1. Materiales para hacer fieltro. 2. Fieltro en cantidad. 3. Acción de aserrar o cortar la madera en la dirección de la vena.

felt-maker [,felt'meɪkər] [felt-mei-ka], *s.* El oficial de sombrero que trabaja el fieltro.

felter ['feltər] [fel-ta], *adv.* Unir alguna cosa como si fuese fieltro.

felucca [felʊ'kə] [fe-liu-ka]. *s.* Falucho, falúa, embarcación menor y de remos con dos palos y velas latinas.

female ['fiːmeɪl] [fi-meil], *a.* 1. Femenino, del sexo femenino. 2. Femenino, propio y especial de las mujeres. 3. *(Bot.)*

Que tiene pistilos. *-s.* 1. Hembra, mujer o animal del sexo femenino. 2. Hembra, en las plantas, la que está provista de un pistilo, y que fecundada por el polen del estambre da fruto. **Female screw**, tuerca, hembra de tornillo. *Female* se aplica al sexo de la mujer, *femenine* a sus cualidades, particularmente a las más delicadas, a sus intereses, empleos u ocupaciones, etc. **Female voice**, voz de mujer. **Femenine voice**, voz femenina.

femalize ['feməlaɪz] [fe-ma-lais], *adv.* Afeminar, inclinar a uno a parecerse a las mujeres por sus gustos, modales y acciones.

feme covert [fiːmˈkʌvɜːt] [fim-ka-vert], *s. (For.)* Mujer casada. **Feme sole**, (a) soltera. (b) Mujer que comercia sola o sin auxilio de su marido.

feminality [ˌfemɪˈnælɪtɪ] [fe-mi-na-li-ti], *s.* Femineidad.

femineity [feˈmɪnɪtɪ] [fe-mi-ni-ti], *s.* V. FEMINALITY.

feminine ['femɪniːn] [fe-mi-nin], *a.* 1. Femenino, femíneo. 2. Femenil, tierno, delicado. 3. Mujeril, afeminado. 4. *(Gram.)* Del género femenino.

femininity [ˌfemɪˈnɪnɪtɪ] [fe-mi-ni-ni-ti], *s.* 1. Calidad, o estado de mujer. 2. El conjunto de las mujeres.

feminity, *s.* V. FEMINALITY.

feminize ['femɪnaɪz] [fe-mi-nais], *adv.* Afeminar.

femoral ['femərəl] [fe-mo-ral], *a.* Femoral, perteneciente al muslo.

femur ['fiːmər] [fi-mar], *s. (pl.* FEMURS o FEMORA). 1. *(Anat.)* Fémur, hueso del muslo. 2. *(Ento.)* Fémur, la tercera pieza o artejo de las patas de los insectos.

fen [fen] [fen], *s.* 1. Marjal, pantano. 2. Enfermedad mohosa del lúpulo. **Fen-berry**, especie de zarzamora. **Fen-born**, nacido en país pantanoso. **Fen-cress**, *(Bot.)* berro pantanoso. **Fen-cricket**, grillotalpa. **Fen-duck**, especie de ánade silvestre.

fence [fens] [fens], *s.* 1. Defensa, reparo, resguardo. 2. Cerca, palizada, vallado que se pone alrededor de un terreno para dividirlo de otro y resguardarlo. 3. Cercamiento, el acto de cercar. 4. Esgrima, el arte de manejar la espada. **Fence of pales o stakes**, empalizada, estacada. **A coat of fence o mail**, cota de malla. **Fence-month**, tiempo de veda, el en que se prohibe la caza. **Fence-keeper**, prendero comprador de efectos robados.

fence, *adv.* 1. Cercar, avallar un sitio o heredad. 2. Defender, preservar, guardar, custodiar. *-vn.* 1. Esgrimir, pelear. 2. Defenderse, luchar, v. gr. en una discusión.

fenceful ['fensfʊl] [fens-ful], *a.* Lo que da defensa o reparo.

fenceless ['fenslɪs] [fens-les], *a.* Abierto, lo que no está cercado.

fencer ['fensər] [fen-sar], *s.* 1. Esgrimidor, maestro de esgrima; tirador de florete. 2. Caballo ágil para saltar cercas.

fencible ['fensɪbl] [fen-si-bol], *a.* Defendible, capaz de defensa. **Fencibles**, *(Mil.)* Soldados destinados a la defensa particular del país o para algún servicio o tiempo señalado.

fencing ['fensɪŋ] [fen-sin], *s.* 1. Esgrima, ciencia de manejar la espada o el florete. 2. Los materiales para cercar o hacer vallados. 3. Conjunto de cercas o vallados.

fencing-master [ˌfensɪŋˈmɑːstər] [fen-sin-mas-tar], *s.* Esgrimidor, maestro de armas o de esgrima.

fencing-school [ˌfensɪŋˈskuːl] [fen-sin-skul], *s.* Escuela de esgrima.

fend [fend] [fend], *adv.* 1. Rechazar, reguardar; defenderse de. 2. Defender, preservar; parar. *-vn.* Esgrimir, defenderse, parar, rechazar los golpes del contrario.

fender ['fendər] [fen-dar], *s.* 1. Guardafango, guardafuegos (chimney) guardabarros (car). *(Mex.)* Salpicadera. 2. Enrejado de metal delante de la chimenea. 3. Defensas de trozos de cable al costado de un barco. **Fender-bnar 0 Fender-rail**, batayola de un buque por los costados. **Fender-board**, guardafangos, de escalera de carro. **Fender-pile**, estacada, empalizada.

fenestra ['fenɪstrə] [fe-nis-tra], *s. (Anat.)* Ventana del oído. Fenestra ovalis, ventana oval.

fenestral ['fenɪstrəl] [fe-nis-tral], *a.* Lo perteneciente a las ventanas.

fenestrate ['fenɪstreɪt] [fe-nis-treit], *a. (Ent.)* Se dice de las puntas trnasparentes en las alas de las mariposas.

fenian ['feniən] [fe-nian], *a.* Perteneciente o relativo a los fenianos. *-s.* 1. Individuo de una sociedad irlandesa llamada la Hermandad Feniana, establecida en Nueva York en 1857. 2. Persona que simpatiza con dicha sociedad.

fenland ['fenlənd] [fen-land], *s.* Tierra húmeda o pantanosa.

fennel ['fenl] [fe-nel], *s. (Bot.)* Hinojo. Fæniculum. **Fennel-seed**, la simiente de hinojo. **Giant fennel**, *(Bot.)* Cañaheja, férula.

fenny ['fenɪ] [fe-ni], *a.* 1. Palustre, pantanoso. 2. Empantanado.

fenugreek ['fenʊgriːk] [fe-nu-grik], *s. (Bot.)* Fenogreco, alholva.

feod, feodal, feodary, etc. V. FEUD, etc.

feoff ['fɪɒf] [fiof], *adv.* Enfeudar, investir, dar la investidura de un feudo.

feoff, *s.* Feudo. V. FIEF.

feoffee ['fɪɒfiː] [fio-fi], *s.* Feudatario, el que recibe la investidura de un feudo.

feoffer, feoffor ['fɪɒfər] [fio-far], *s.* El que da la investidura de un feudo.

feoffment ['fɪɒfmənt] [fiof-ment], *s.* Investidura, concesión y facultad que el señor da a su vasallo para obtener y poseer un feudo o dignidad. **Feoffment in trust**, *(For.)* Fide-icomiso.

feracious ['fɪreɪʃəs] [fi-rei-shos], *a.* Feraz, fértil.

feracity ['ferəsɪtɪ] [fe-ra-si-ti], *s.* Feracidad, fertilidad, fecundidad.

feral ['ferəl] [fe-ral], *a.* Feral, salvaje, no domesticado, feroz; también silvestre.

fere ['feər] [fear], *s.* Compañero; consorte.

ferial ['ferɪəl] [fe-rial], *a.* Ferial, lo que pertenece a todos los días de la semana a excepción del domingo.

ferine ['feriːn] [fe-rin], *a.* 1. Salvaje, no domesticado, silvestre, en estado natural. 2. Maligno: se dice de una enfermedad. *-s.* Fiera, animal feroz.

ferineness ['ferɪnnɪs] [fe-rin-nes], **ferity** ['ferɪtɪ] [fe-ri-ti], *s.* Barbaridad, fiereza, ferocidad, crueldad.

ferment ['fɜment] [fer-ment], *adv.* Hacer fermentar. *-vn.* 1. Fermentar, estar en fermentación. 2. Estar en conmoción, agitarse, estar excitado.

ferment, *s.* 1. Fermento. 2. Fermento, lo que hace fermentar a un cuerpo, como la levadura. 3. Fermentación, movimiento, agitación intestina; tumulto.

fermentable ['fɜːmentəbl] [fer-men-ta-bol], *a.* Fermentable, capaz de fermentación.

fermentation [ˌfɜːmenˈteɪʃən] [fer-men-tei-shon], *s.* 1. *(Quím.)* Fermentación. 2. *(Fig.)* Efervescencia, agitación de los ánimos.

fermentative ['fɜːmentətɪv] [fer-men-ta-tiv], *a.* Fermentativo, que hace fermentar, que pone en fermentación.

fermentativeness [ˌfɜːmentəˈtɪvnɪs] [fer-men-ta-tiv-nes], *s.* Capacidad de fermentar.

fermentescible ['fɜːmentəsɪbl] [fer-men-te-si-bol], *a.* Materia fermentable.

fermentible ['fɜːmentɪbl] [fer-men-ti-bol], *a.* Fermentable. V. FERMENTABLE.

fermillet ['fɜːmɪlɪt] [fer-mi-lit], *s.* Hebilla, broche.

fern [fɜːn] [fern], *s. (Bot.)* Helecho, planta criptógama, tipo de una familia muy numerosa, que en su mayor parte echa semillas en el envés de las hojas.

fernery ['fɜːnərɪ] [fer-ne-ri], *s.* Lugar donde se crían los helechos.

ferny ['fɜːnɪ] [fer-ni], *a.* Lleno de helechos, cubierto de helechos.

ferocious [fəˈrəʊʃəs] [fe-ro-shos], *a.* Feroz, fiero; salvaje, rapaz, voraz.

ferociously [fəˈrəʊʃəslɪ] [fe-ro-shos-li], *adv.* Ferozmente, fieramente.

ferociousness [fəˈrəʊʃəsnɪs] [fe-ro-shos-nes], *s.* Ferocidad, crueldad.

ferocity [fəˈrɒsɪtɪ] [fe-ro-si-ti], *s.* Ferocidad, fiereza.

ferreous, ferrean ['fɔerəʊs] [fe-rous], *a.* Férreo, lo que es de hierro; relativo al hierro, o parecido a él.

ferret ['ferɪt] [fe-rit], *s.* 1. Hurón, animal que sirve para cazar conejos. 2. Un hierro con que se prueba el metal derretido para ver si está en estado de trabajarlo. 3. Listón, especie de cinta angosta. **Ferret o ferret ribbon**, (a) Hiladillo, cinta de hiladillo, ribecillo, (*Prov.*) Esterilla, (b) Seda floja.

ferret, *adv.* 1. Rastrear, indagar, averiguar, hallar después de haber buscado con empeño y persistentemente; suele ir seguido de *out*. 2. Cazar con hurones.

ferreter ['ferɪtər] [fe-ri-tar], *s.* Hurón, el que averigua y descubre lo escondido y secreto.

ferriage, ferryage ['ferɪeɪdʒ] [fe-rieich], *s.* Barcaje, derecho por pasar en una barca.

ferric ['ferɪk] [fe-rik], *a.* 1. Perteneciente al hierro; férrico. 2. (*Quím.*) Férrico, relativo al hierro en sus más altas combinaciones.

ferricyanide ['ferɪsɪəˈnaɪd] [fe-ri-sia-nid], *s.* (*Quím.*) Ferrocianuro.

ferriferous ['ferɪfərəs] [fe-ri-fe-ros], *a.* (*Min.*) Ferrugiento, que produce hierro: se dice de las rocas.

ferrocalcite ['ferəkəlsaɪt] [fe-ro-kal-sait], *s.* Ferrocalcita, especie de tierra calcárea que contiene mucho hierro.

ferrocyanid, ferrocyanide ['ferəsɪəˈnaɪd] [fe-ro-sia-nid], *s.* Ferrocianuro, sal del ácido ferrociánico; ferrocianato. (A veces se escribe también **Ferrocyanate**).

ferrotype ['ferətaɪp] [fe-ro-taip], *s.* Ferrotipo; fotografía hecha sobre una placa delgada de hierro esmaltado. Se llama también *tintype*.

ferrous ['ferəs] [fe-ros], *a.* Ferroso, de hierro, relativo al hierro en sus más bajas combinaciones. **Ferrous sulphate**, caparrosa, sulfato de hierro.

ferruginous ['ferɒdʒɪnəs] [fe-ru-yi-nos], *a.* 1. Ferruginoso, lo que tiene propiedades o partículas de hierro. 2. Mohoso, enmohecido, es decir del color de la herrumbre.

ferrule ['feruːl] [fe-rul], *s.* 1. Regatón, virola, casquillo. 2. Zuncho o suncho. 3. Marco de una pizarra para escribir.

ferry ['ferɪ] [fe-ri], *adv.* 1. Sistema u organización para el transporte regular de pasajeros y mercancías por una extensión de agua de poca anchura. 2. El embarcadero. 3. (*Mar.*) Barco o vapor de transporte. **Ferry-boat**, barca de pasaje o vapor de río; por lo común con los dos extremos de igual forma.

ferryhouse ['ferɪhaʊs] [fe-ri-jaus], *s.* Embarcadero.

ferrying ['ferɪɪŋ] [fe-ri-in], *s.* Paso de un río, etc., en alguna embarcación.

ferryman ['ferɪmən] [fe-ri-man], *s.* 1. Barquero, el que gobierna una barca. 2. El que lleva géneros o pasajeros en un barco.

fertile ['fɜːtaɪl] [fer-tail], *a.* Fértil, fecundo, abundante.

fertilely ['fɜːtaɪlɪlɪ] [fer-tai-li-li], *adv.* Fértilmente, abundantemente.

fertileness ['fɜːtaɪlɪnɪs] [fer-tai-li-nes], **fertility** ['fɜːtaɪlɪtɪ] [fer-tai-li-ti], *s.* Fertilidad, fecundidad, copia, abundancia.

fertilization ['fɜːtɪlaɪˈzeɪʃən] [fer-ti-lai-sei-shon], *s.* Fertilización, la acción de fertilizar o hacer productivo.

fertilize ['fɜːtɪlaɪz] [fer-ti-lais], *adv.* Fertilizar, hacer fértil.

fertilizers ['fɜːtɪlaɪzəz] [fer-ti-lai-sers], *s. pl.* Fertilizantes, abonos.

ferula ['ferjʊlə] [fe-riu-la], *s.* 1. (*Bot.*) Férula, cañaheja; género de plantas umbelíferas que comprende la asafétida. 2. Cetro de los emperadores romanos de Oriente.

ferule ['ferjuːl] [fe-riul], *s.* Férula, palma, palmet. Castigar con la férula. *-vn.* Palmetear.

fervency ['fɜːvənsɪ] [fer-ven-si], *s.* 1. Fervor, ardor, calor. 2. Celo, devoción ardiente.

fervent ['fɜːvənt] [fer-vent], *a.* 1. Ferviente, hirvien-te. 2. Ardiente, fogoso, vehemente. **Fervent temper**, genio vivo. 3. Fervoroso, que tiene mucho fervor y devoción.

fervently ['fɜːvəntlɪ] [fer-vent-li], *adv.* 1. Angiosamente, vehementemente. 2. Fervorosamente, fervientemente.

ferventness ['fɜːvəntnɪs] [fer-vent-nes], *s.* Ardor, fervor, celo.

fervid ['fɜːvɪd] [fer-vid], *a.* 1. Ardiente, fogoso, vehemente. 2. Encendido, incandescente.

fervidity, fervidness, *s.* V. FERVENCY.

fervor ['fɜːvər] [fer-var], *s.* Fervor, celo, devoción ardiente; ardor, vehemencia.

fervour, *s.* (Es la forma preferida en Inglaterra.) V. FERVOR.

fescennine ['fesənɪn] [fe-se-nin], *a.* Obsceno, licencioso.

fescennine, *s.* 1. Un poema obsceno. 2. Fesceninos, versos obscenos que se cantaban en Roma en algunas fiestas.

fescue ['feskjuː] [fes-kiu], *s.* 1. Puntero, el palillo con que el maestro o el discípulo señalan las letras. 2. (*Bot.*) Festuca, género de plantas gramíneas. **Fescue-grass**, cualquier especie de festuca.

fesels ['fesəlz] [fe-sels], *s. pl.* Judías, habichuelas, frijoles, frisoles.

fess [fes] [fes], *s.* (*Her.*) Faja o lista que ocupa propiamente la tercera parte del escudo de armas.

festal ['festəl] [fes-tal], *a.* Festivo, alegre, juguetón.

fester ['festər] [fes-tar], *vn.* Enconarse, ulcerarse, ponerse de peor calidad la llaga, herida o parte dañada. *-va.* Enconar, emponzoñar. *-s.* Llaga pequeña o tumorcillo ulceroso.

festival ['festɪvəl] [fes-ti-val], *a.* Festivo, lo que pertenece a las fiestas.

festival, *s.* Fiesta, día festivo; a menudo es en celebración del aniversario de un suceso del orden civil o religioso.

festive ['festɪv] [fes-tiv], *a.* Festivo, alegre, regocijado, gozoso.

festivity [fesˈtɪvɪtɪ] [fes-ti-vi-ti], *s.* 1. Regocijo, festividad, animación (en un banquete), alegría. 2. Festividad, fiesta, celebración festiva.

festoon [fesˈtuːn] [fes-tun], *s.* 1. Festón. 2. (*Arq.*) Adorno en forma de festones.

festucine ['festɒsɪn] [fes-tu-sin], *a.* 1. Relativo a las hierbas festucas. 2. (*Des.*) Pajizo, de color de paja.

festucous ['festɒkəs] [fes-tu-kos], *a.* (*Des.*) Pajizo, pajoso.

fetal, fœtal ['fiːtl] [fi-tal], *a.* Fetal, relativo o perteneciente al feto.

fetch [fetʃ] [fech], *adv.* 1. Ir a traer algo, buscar y traer; también, traer o conducir de una manera cuaiquiera, literal o figuradamente. 2. Derivar, traer su origen, sacar, deducir. 3. (*fam.*) Traer a un arreglo, imponer condiciones *a.* 4. Herir desde lejos, pegar. 5. Ejecutar, hacer. 6. Obtener algo como precio; producir. *-vn.* Moverse, menearse; de aquí, (*Mar.*) arribar, llegar. **To fetch a com-pass**, hacer un rodeo, ir alrededor de.

fetch away, llevar, quitar; desatarse, v. g. a bordo.

fetch down, bajar; abatir; humillar; enflaquecer o debilitar.

fetch in o **within**, hacer entrar; llevar, traer o meter dentro.

fetch off, sacar, arrancar, llevarse, quitar; disuadir.

fetch out, sacar a luz, mostrar claramente; hacer salir, ir a tomar fuera alguna cosa.

fetch over, engañar, burlar.

fetch up, subir; recuperar, volver a ganar. **To fetch a walk**, dar un paseo. **To fetch one's breath**, tomar aliento, respirar. **To fetch a sigh**, dar un suspiro. **To fetch a leap blow**, tirar una estocada. **To fetch a circuit**, hacer un rodeo. **To fetch way**, (*Mar.*) Tener juego. **To fetch the pump**, (*Mar.*) Llamar la bomba.

fetch, *s.* 1. El acto de traer o de buscar y traer. 2. El espacio o la extensión de terreno por el cual se trae algo. 3. Estratagema, treta, artificio.

fetcher ['fetʃər] [fe-char], *s.* Llevador o traedor.

fetching ['fetʃɪŋ] [fe-chin], *a.* Atractivo, encantador.

fête [feɪt] [feit], *adv.* Festejar, honrar con regocijos. *-s.* Fiesta. (*Fr.*) **Fête-day**, día de fiesta, día del santo de alguno, o día de cumpleaños.

fetial ['feɪʃəl] [fei-shal], *a.* Fecial, perteneciente al heraldo que entre los romanos anunciaba la paz y la guerra.

fetich ['fetɪtʃ] [fe-tich], *s.* V. FETISH.

fetid ['fetɪd] [fe-tid], *a.* Fétido, hediondo, que huele mal.

fetidness ['fetɪdnɪs] [fe-tid-nes], *s.* Fetor, hedor, mal olor.

fetish ['fetɪʃ] [fe-tish], *s.* 1. Fetiche, ídolo o genio que, según los pueblos de África, puede producir el bien y el mal. 2. Objeto de devoción o de afición ciega.

fetishism ['fetɪʃɪzəm] [fe-ti-shi-sem], *s.* Fetichismo, culto de los fetiches.

fetlock ['fetlɒk] [fet-lok], *s.* Corneja, el manojo de cerdas que se cría en la cuartilla del caballo.

fetor ['fetəʳ] [fe-taʳ], *s.* Hedor, fetor.

fetter ['fetəʳ] [fe-taʳ], *adv.* Engrillar, encadenar.

fetters ['fetəz] [fe-ters], *s. pl.* Grillos, manijas, cierto género de prisiones con que aseguran a los reos. **Fetters for horses**, trabas para caballos.

fetterless ['fetəlɪs] [fe-ter-les], *a.* Desenfrenado, destrabado.

fettle ['fetl] [fe-tel], *adv.* Alisar, poner liso. -*vn.* 1. Poner en buen estado. 2. Hacer poco ó nada, emplearse en frioleras.

fettle, *s.* Buen reparo; condición vigorosa o próspera. **Fine fettle**, buena condición; buen humor, alegría.

fetus, fœtus ['fiːtəs] [fi-tus], *s.* Feto.

feud [fjuːd] [fiud], *s.* 1. Riña, contienda, desunión, guerra civil, disensión, enemistad. 2. Feudo, tierra que se entrega a la buena fe de otro con carga de homenaje, renta o servicio militar.

feudal ['fjuːdl] [fiu-dal], *a.* Feudal.

feudalism [ˌfjuːdəlɪzəm] [fiu-da-li-sem], *s.* Feudalismo, sistema feudal.

feudality [fjuːdælɪtɪ] [fiu-da-li-ti], *s.* Feudalidad.

feudalize ['fjuːdəlaɪz] [fiu-da-lais], *adv.* Enfeudar, constituir en feudo.

feudary ['fjuːdərɪ] [fiu-da-ri], *a.* Feudatario. -*s.* 1. Vasallo, sujeto a pagar un feudo. 2. Antiguamente, procurador del rey en los tribunales feudales.

feudatary, feudatory ['fjuːdətərɪ] [fiu-da-ta-ri], *a.* y *s.* 1. Feudo. 2. Feudatario.

feudist ['fjuːdɪst] [fiu-dist], *s.* Feudista.

feuilleton ['fjuːɪlətən] [fiui-le-ton], *s.* Folletín, la novela u otra lectura amena que se publica por lo regular en la parte inferior de los periódicos.

fever ['fiːvəʳ] [fi-vaʳ], *s.* 1. (*Med.*) Fiebre, calentura. 2. Agitación, sobreexcitación producida por una causa que influye en las pasiones. **To be in a fever**, estar con calentura; tener calentura. **Yellow fever**, fiebre amarilla o tifo icteroides. **Burning fever**, calentura ardiente. **Spotted fever**, tabardillo pintado. **Puerperal o child-bed fever**, fiebre puerperal. **That sets one's blood in a fever**, eso quema la sangre. **Fever-weakened**, debilitado por la fiebre.

fever, *adv.* Causar calentura.

fever-cooling ['fiːvəˈkuːlɪŋ] [fi-va-ku-lin], *s.* Lo que mitiga la calentura refrescando al que la padece.

feverfew [ˌfiːvəˈfkuː] [fi-va-fiu], *s.* (*Bot.*) Matricaria, planta estimada en otro tiempo por sus propiedades tónicas.

feverish ['fiːvərɪʃ] [fi-ve-rish], *a.* 1. Febricitante, calenturiento. 2. Lo que principia a presentar los síntomas de calentura. 3. Vario, incierto, inconstante; lo que está tan pronto frío como caliente. 4. Caliente, ardiente.

fevershness ['fiːvəʃnɪs] [fi-vesh-nes], *s.* Principio o amago de fiebre o calentura; desasosiego.

feverous ['fiːvərəs] [fi-ve-ros], *a.* Calenturiento.

fever-sick [ˌfiːvəˈsɪk] [fi-va-sik], *a.* Calenturiento, febricitante.

few [fjuː] [fiu], *a.* 1. Poco, en corto número. 2. Unos, algunos. **A few**, (a) un corto número, algunos. (b) En algún grado, algo. **No few**, no pocos, muchos. **The few**, la minoría. (*Few* se emplea siempre con un nombre en plural.) **In few**, en substancia, en una palabra.

fewel ['fjuːəl] [fiuel], *s.* Leña, carbón. V. FUEL.

fewer ['fjuːəʳ] [fiuaʳ], *a.* Comparativo de FEW; menos. **The fewer the better**, cuantos menos mejor.

fewness ['fjuːnɪs] [fiu-nes], *s.* 1. Pequeño o corto número de personas o cosas. 2. Brevedad, concisión, corto número de palabras.

fey [feɪ] [fei], *a.* (*Scot.*) Moribundo; predestinado a morir de repente. -*va.* (*Des.*) Limpiar una zanja de lodo.

fez [fez] [fez], *s.* Fez, especie de gorro de lana, sin borde, encarnado por lo común, que se usa en Oriente y en el norte de África.

fiancé, *m.* **fiancée**, [fɪˈɑːnseɪ] [fian-sei] *f.* Prometido, prometida, novio, novia. Desposado, desposada.

fiasco [fɪˈæskəʊ] [fi-as-kou], *s.* 1. Mal éxito de un espectáculo, etc. 2. Frasco, botella.

fiat ['faɪæt] [faiat], *s.* Fiat, orden, mandato absoluto.

fib [fɪb] [fib], *s.* Embuste, bola, falsedad, cuento, fábula; falsedad contada sin mala intención.

fib. *vn.* Mentir, contar mentiras, trapacear.

fibber ['fɪbəʳ] [fi-baʳ], *s.* Embustero, mentiroso, trapacero.

fiber, fibre, *s.* Fibra, hebra.

fibril ['faɪbrɪl] [fi-bril], *s.* Fibrita.

fibrin, fibrine ['faɪbrɪn] [fi-brin], *s.* Fibrina, la parte fibrosa de la sangre.

fibrinous ['fɪbrɪnəs] [fi-bri-nos], *a.* Fibrinoso, compuesto o de la anturaleza de la fibrina.

fibroid ['faɪbrɔɪd] [fi-broid], *a.* Fibroso, de la naturaleza o forma de la fibra. -*s.* (*Fibroid* o también **Fibroma**) Tumor, grosor, fibroso.

fibrous ['faɪbrəs] [fi-bros], **fibrose** ['faɪbrəʊs] [fi-brous], *a.* Fibroso, compuesto de fibras.

fibula ['fɪbjʊlə] [fi-biu-la], *s.* 1. (*Anat.*) Peroné, el hueso exterior y menor de la pierna. 2. (*Cir.*) Aguja empleada para coser las heridas. 3. (*Archeol.*) Corchete, broche; fíbula.

fibular ['fɪbjʊləʳ] [fi-biu-laʳ], *a.* Peroneo, que tiene relación con el peroné.

fichu ['fiːʃuː] [fi-shu], *s.* Pañoleta triangular llevada al cuello.

fickle ['fɪkl] [fi-kel], *a.* Voluble, variable, inconstante, mudable, veleidoso.

fickleness ['fɪklnɪs] [fi-kel-nes], *s.* Volubilidad, inconstancia, mutabilidad, veleidad.

fickly ['fɪklɪ] [fi-kli], *adv.* Inconstantemente.

fictile ['fɪktɪl] [fik-til], *a.* 1. Capaz de ser amoldado, plástico. 2. Cosa hecha de barro o por mano de alfarero.

fiction ['fɪkʃən] [fik-shon], *s.* 1. Ficción, invención. 2. Literatura novelesca. 3. Ficció, mentira, embuste, falsedad, fábula. 4. Ficción de derecho, acción de admitir o suponer lo que no es literalmente verdadero, a fin de poder pasar más rápidamente sobre lo que no se disputa y llegar a los puntos del litigio.

fictitious [fɪkˈtɪʃəs] [fik-ti-shos], *a.* Ficticio, contrahecho; fingido; fabuloso.

fictitiously [fɪkˈtɪʃəslɪ] [fik-ti-shos-li], *adv.* Fingidamente.

fictitiousness [fɪkˈtɪʃəsnɪs] [fik-ti-shos-nes], *s.* Representación fingida.

fictive ['fɪktɪv] [fik-tiv], *a.* Fingido, ficticio, imaginario.

fictor ['fɪktəʳ] [fik-taʳ], *s.* Artista que modela en cera, barro u otra material blanda.

ficus ['fɪkəs] [fik-tos], *s.* Higuera, extenso género de árboles y arbustos de la familia de las urticáceas.

fid [fɪd] [fid], *s.* 1. Barra atravesada que sirve de sostén. 2. (*Mar.*) Pasador o burel; tarugo grande de madera. **Fid of a topmast**, cuña de mastelero. **Fid-hole**, ojo de la cuña de mastelero.

fiddle ['fɪdl] [fi-del], *s.* 1. Violín. 2. Utensilio mecánico; los hay de varias clases. **Fiddle-bow**, arco de violín. **To play first fiddle**, llevar la batuta, ser el principal o la cabeza de una reunión, empresa, etc. **Fiddle-block**, montón de poleas diferenciales.

fiddle, *vn.* 1. Tocar el violín. 2. Enredar o jugar con las manos sin hacer nada. **Fiddling word**, trabajo en balde, tiempo perdido.

fiddle-de-dee ['fɪdldeɪˈdiː] [fi-del-dei-di], *inter.* ¡Quiá! ¡oiga! ¡qué simpleza! -*s.* Disparate, necedad.

fiddle-faddle ['fɪdlˈfædl] [fi-del-fa-del], *s.* (*fam.*) Bagatelas, frioleras.

fiddler ['fɪdləʳ] [fid-laʳ], *s.* Violinista.

fiddle-stick ['fɪdlstɪk] [fi-del-stik], *s.* 1. Arco de violín. 2. Bagatela.

fiddle-sticks! *inter.* ¡Oiga! ¡vaya! ¡vaya pues!

fiddle-string ['fɪdlstrɪŋ] [fi-del-strin], *s.* Cuerda de violín.

fidelity [fɪ'delɪtɪ] [fi-de-li-ti], *s.* Fidelidad, lealtad, veracidad.

fidget ['fɪdʒɪt] [fid-yit], *adv. (fam)* Molestar, inquietar. *-vn.* Moverse con impaciencia; mudar de posición frecuentemente; afanarse por nada.

fidget, *s.* Afán, agitación continua, ocupación inquieta e inútil.

fidgety ['fɪdʒɪtɪ] [fid-chi-ti], *a. (fam.)* Inquieto, agitado, impaciente.

fidicinal ['fɪdɪsɪnl] [fi-di-si-nal], *a.* Perteneciente o referente al arpa, a la viola o a un instrumento de cuerda parecido.

fiducial [fɪ'dju:ʃɪəl] [fi-du-shial], *a.* 1. Fiduciario, que depende del crédito y confianza que merezca; de confianza práctica. 2. Relativo o referente a un cargo depósito o cosa confiada; fiduciario. 3. Fiducial; se dice del punto fijo, línea u objeto, real o imaginario, desde el cual se mide o que sirve para determinar la posición de otros objectos. 4. *(Ant.)* Confiado, lleno de confianza.

fiducially [fɪ'dju:ʃɪəlɪ] [fi-du-shia-li], *adv.* Confiadamente; confidentemente.

fiduciary [fɪ'dju:ʃɪərɪ] [fi-du-shia-ri], *a.* 1. Fiduciario, perteneciente a un guardián o depositario, o a sus deberes como tal. 2. Confiado, resuelto, que no vacila. *-s.* 1. Fideicomisario. *(For.)* La persona a cuya buena fe y probidad se encomienda la ejecución de una cosa. V. TRUSTEE. 2. El que cree que basta la fe sin las obras para salvarse.

fie! [faɪ] [fai], *inter.* ¡Uf! ¡Quita allá! ¡Qué asco! Expresa impaciencia, desaprobación o repugnancia.

fief [fi:f] [fif], *s.* Feudo.

field [fi:ld] [fild], *s.* 1. Campo, campiña, campaña, llanura de tierra sin cerca ni población. 2. Campo, sembrado, trecho de terreno cultivado. 3. *(Mil.)* Campo de batalla. 4. C a m p a ñ a. 5. Campo, el sitio que ocupa un ejército. 6. Campo, en la pintura y grabado el espacio que no tiene figuras. 7. Campo, extensión o espacio en que cabe alguna cosa; el espacio en que se ve alguna cosa en un telescopio o microscopio. 8. Extensión o espacio en que se ejerce una fuerza. 9. La colectividad de los competidores en los juegos públicos, apuestas, carreras, etc. **To take the field**, entrar en o salir a campaña. **Fields of ice**, bancos de hielo. **Corn-field**, maizal. **Field-artillery**, artillería de campaña. **Field-glass**, (a) Anteojo de campaña. (b) Lente interior del ocular de un telescopio o microscopio. **Field-book**, manual, cuaderno de agrimensor. **Field-day**, día de ejercicios atléticos o militares; también, un día de exploración científica al aire libre. **Field-gun**, cañón de campaña. **Field-magnet**, el imán de una máquina magneto-eléctrica. **Field-basil**, *(Bot.)* clinopodio, albahaca silvestre. **Field-bed**, pabellón, cama de campaña colgada como pabellón. **Field-marshal**, (a) Feldmariscal, el grado más elevado del ejército en Inglaterra. (b) El general en jefe de un ejército. **Field-mouse**, turón, ratón silvestre. **Field-officer**, oficial de ejército cuyo mando puede extenderse a un regimiento, como el coronel y el teniente coronel. **Field-piece**, artillería de campaña, los cañones de pequeñoo calibre que se usan en los combates. **Field-preacher**, predicador en los campos o al raso. **Field-preaching**, el acto de predicar o arengar al aire libre. **Field-room**, espacio abierto. **Field-sports**, los entretenimientos o diversiones de la caza y de la carrera. **Field-works**, *(For.)* obras de campaña, las que levanta un ejército para sitiar una plaza, o los sitiados para defenderse.

fielded ['fi:ldɪd] [fil-did], *a.* 1. El que está en un campo de batalla. 2. Acampado.

fielder ['fi:ldəʳ] ['filda'], *s.* 1. En los juegos de *baseball* y *cricket*, el que están en pie en el campo para interceptar la pelota. 2. En las carreras de caballos, el que apuesta contra el favorito.

fieldfare ['fi:ldfɛəʳ] [fild-fea'], *s. (Orn.)* Zorzal, pájaro del mismo género que el tordo.

fieldy ['fi:ldɪ] [fil-di], *a.* Abierto, llano, como un campo.

fiend [fi:nd] [find], *s.* 1. Enemigo; por antonomasia, el demonio. 2. Ente infernal; furia. 3. Persona muy aficionada a una droga, un deporte, etc.

fiendful ['fi:ndfʊl] [find-ful], *a.* Endemoniado, perverso.

fiendish ['fi:ndɪʃ] [fin-dish], *a.* Diabólico; molo, perverso, malvado; semejante a un ente infernal.

fiendishness ['fi:ndɪʃnɪs] [fin-dish-nes], *s.* Maldad, perversidad, malicia infernal.

fiend-like [‚fi:nd'laɪk] [find-laik], *a.* Semejante al diablo o a un ente infernal; cruel, atroz, salvaje.

fierce [fɪəs] [fias], *a.* 1. Fiero, feroz, voraz. 2. Fiero, cruel, violento. 3. Fiero, furioso, vehemente, impetuoso, apasionado.

fiercely ['fɪəslɪ] [fias-li], *adv.* 1. Fieramente, furiosamente, ferozmente; con furia, con arrebato. 2. Vivamente, intensamente.

fierce-minded [‚fɪəs'maɪndɪd] [fias-main-did], *a.* Arrebatado, que tiene movimientos impetuosos de ira o anhela con ansia el hacer daño.

fierceness ['fɪəsnɪs] [fias-nes], *s.* 1. Fiereza, ferocidad. 2. Furia, violencia. 3. Vivencia, intensidad.

fieri-facias [‚fɪərɪ'feɪʃəs] [fie-ri-fei-shas], *s. (For.)* El auto jurídico que manda la ejecución de las decisiones de un tribunal.

fieriness ['fɪərɪnɪs] [fia-ri-nes], *s.* 1. Fuego, calor, ardor, arrebato, fogosidad, vehemencia, pasión. 2. Ardimiento y gran viveza de ánimo.

fiery ['fɪərɪ] [fie-ri], *a.* 1. Igneo, cosa de fuego o perteneciente a él. 2. Ardiente, caliente como el fuego; encendido. 3. Ardiente, vehemente, activo. 4. Fogoso, colérico, impaciente, vlvo. 5. Fiero, feroz, furibundo, indómito. 6. Que b r i l l a o echa chispas como el fuego. **A fiery furnace**, un horno ardiente. **A fiery disposition**, un genio iracundo o violento. **A fiery courser**, un caballo fogoso. **A fiery red face**, un rostro muy encendido.

fife [faɪf] [faif], *s.* Pífano, instrumento militar que suele acompañar a las cajas o tambores.

fif [fɪf] [fif], *adv.* y *vn.* Tocar el pífano.

fifer ['fɪfəʳ] [fi-fa'], *s.* Pífano, el que lo toca.

fifteen [fɪf'ti:n] [fif-tin], *a.* Quince. *-s.* Quince, número cardinal compuesto de diez y cinco, o el signo que lo representa. **She is fifteen**, ella tiene quince años.

fifteenth [fɪf'ti:nθ] [fif-tinz], *a.* 1. Décimoquinto, el ordinal de quince. 2. Quinceno; se dice de cada una de las quince partes iguales en que está dividida una cosa. *-s.* 1. Quincena; cada una de quince partes iguales; cociente de la unidad dividada por quince. 2. Quincena, registro del órgano. **The fifteenth century**, el siglo décimoquinto, el siglo quince.

fifth [fɪfθ] [fifz], *a.* Quinto, número ordinal de cinco. *-s.* El quinto, cada una de las cinco partes iguales de alguna cosa; cociente de la unidad dividida por cinco. **Charles the Fifth**, Carlos V.

fifth column [fɪfθ'kɒləm] [fifz-ko-lum], *s.* Quinta columna.

fifth columnist [fɪfθ'kɒləmnɪst] [fifz-ko-lum-nist], *s.* Quintacolumnista.

fifthly ['fɪfθlɪ] [fifz-li], *adv.* Lo quinto, en quinto lugar.

fiftieth ['fɪftɪɪθ] [fif-tiez], *a.* Quincuagésimo, lo que cumple el número de cincuenta.

fifty ['fɪftɪ] [fif-ti], *a.* y *s.* Cincuenta.

fig [fɪg] [fig], *s.* 1. Higuera, el árbol que produce higos. 2. Higo, la fruta que da la higuera. **A green fig**, higo fresco: breva. **A dry fig**, higo seco. 3. Berruga en la ranilla de un caballo. **Indian fig**, *(Bot.)* tuna, higo chumbo, fruto del nopal o higuera de Indias. **Infernal fig**, *(Bot.)* argémone, adormidera espinosa. **To give a fig for one**, dar una higa a alguno, hacer escarnio de él. **I do not care a fig for it**, no

fig 1374

me importa un bledo. **A fig for him**, ¡vaya enhoramala!
Figeater, (a) Escarabajo grande de color verde (allorhina nítida) y perjudicial a las frutas maduras. (b) Becafigo. **Figpecker**, becafigo.

fig, adv. (Ant.) Insultar o despreciar haciendo higas, -vn. (Des.) Moverse acelerada o repentinamente. **To fig up and down**, vagar.

figary ['fɪgərɪ] [fi-ga-ri], s. V. VAGARY.

fight [faɪt] [fait], adv. (pret. y pp. FOUGHT). 1. Pelear, guerrear, combatir, reñir. 2. Sostener con las armas; alcanzar por la fuerza de las armas; vencer. 3. Luchar, disputar, mantener sostener una contienda cualquiera. 4. Dirigir una batalla. 5. Hacer reñir (v.g. a los gallos). -vn. Batirse, defenderse, hacer la guerra. **To fight a battle**, dar batalla. **To fight another man's battles**, tomar la defensa de otro. **To fight it out**, terminar alguna contienda peleando. **To fight one's way**, hacerse o abrirse paso con las armas.

fight, s. Batalla, lid, combate, pelea. **Sea-fight**, batalla naval. **Running-fight**, retirada de las tropas peleando. **To pick a fight with**, meterse con, buscar camorra.

fighter ['faɪtəʳ] [fai-taʳ], s. Guerrero, combatiente; duelista. **He is a great fighter**, es un gran espadachín.

fighter plane [ˌfaɪtəˈpleɪn] [fai-tar-plein], s. 1. Caza. 2. Avión de combate o de caza.

fighting ['faɪtɪŋ] [fai-tin], a. 1. Aguerrido, apto para la guerra; combatiente. 2. Ocupado en guerrear. 3. **Fighting cock**, gallo de pelea. -s. Contención, combate, querella, riña.

fig-leaf ['fɪgliːf] [fig-lif], s. 1. Hoja de higuera. 2. Cobertura endeble y ligera.

figment ['fɪgmənt] [fig-ment], s. Ficción, invención.

figurable ['fɪgjʊrəbl] [fi-giu-ra-bol], a. Figurable, lo que se puede reducir a determinada forma o figura.

figural ['fɪgjʊrəl] [fi-ga-ral], a. Lo que pertenece a la figura.

figurant ['fɪgjʊrənt] [fi-giu-rant], s. Figurante de ópera.

figurante ['fɪgjʊræntɪ] [fi-giu-ran-ti], s. Bailarina de conjunto, figurante.

figurate ['fɪgjʊreɪt] [fi-giu-reit], a. 1. Figurado, que tiene cierta y determinada figura; parecido a un objeto de una forma determinada. 2. (Mús.) Figurado, embellecido.

figuration [ˌfɪgjʊreɪʃən] [fi-gu-rei-shon], s. 1. Figura, disposición de las partes de una cosa por la cual se diferencia de otras; el acto de dar forma determinada.

figurative ['fɪgjʊrətɪv] [fi-gu-ra-tiv], a. 1. Figurativo, que sirve de representación o figura de otra cosa. 2. Figurativo, que no es literal; metafórico. 3. Figurativo, escrito con expresiones retóricas figuradas.

figuratively ['fɪgjʊrətɪvlɪ] [fi-gu-ra-tiv-li], adv. Figuradamente.

figure ['fɪgəʳ] [fi-gaʳ], s. 1. Figura, forma exterior. 2. Figura, hechura, semejanza. 3. Figura, presencia, talle o disposición del cuerpo. 4. Figura, papel, viso. **To make a figure in the world**, hacer papel en el mundo. 5. Figura, estatua, imagen. 6. Figura, pintura que representa alguna cosa. 7. Cifra, guarismo o número. 8. (Ret.) Figura retórica. 9. (Gram.) Figura gramatical, desvío de las reglas de la analogía o sintaxis. 10. (Geom.) Figura que cierra un espacio con una o más líneas. 11. (Astrol.) Horóscopo. 12. (Teol.) Tipo, símbolo. 13. Impresión que produce una persona, facha. **To cut a poor figure**, hacer el ridículo, tener mala facha.

figure, adv. y vn. 1. Figurar, disponer, delinear y formar la figura de alguna cosa. 2. Figurar, cubrir o adornar con figuras alguna cosa. **Figured velvet**, terciopelo estampado. **Figured silk**, seda floreada. 3. Simbolizar, representar con semejanza simbólica o misteriosa. 4. Figurarse, pasar por la imaginación alguna cosa o formarla en ella. 5. Valerse de figuras retóricas; separarse del sentido literal. 6. Hacer papel.

figure-head ['fɪgəhed] [fi-ga-jed], s. 1. Figura o adorno que suelen tener los buques mercantes y de guerra en la roda, en lo más alto de la proa. 2. Caudillo o cabeza nominal, sin verdadera influencia o poder.

figuring ['fɪgərɪŋ] [fi-ga-rin], s. 1. Computación, acción de computar. 2. Acción de trazar figuras.

figurist ['fɪgərɪst] [fi-ga-rist], s. Figurista, el que emplea o explica las figuras de dicción.

figwort ['fɪgwɔːt] [fig-uort], s. (Bot.) Escrofularia, planta que da su nombre a la familia de las escrofulariáceas; cualquiera planta de esta familia.

fijian, feejeean ['fɪdʒɪən] [fi-yian], a. De Fijí, perteneciente a las islas de este nombre en el Océano Pacífico. -s. Habitante aborigen, o lengua aborigen de las Islas Fijí.

filaceous ['fɪləʃəs] [fi-le-shos], a. Hebroso, fibroso, filamentoso.

filament ['fɪləmənt] [fi-la-ment], s. 1. Hebra, fibra, filamento; hilo muy fino. 2. (Bot.) Filamento, tallo o sostén de la antera.

filamentous, filamentose ['fɪləməntəs] [fi-la-men-tos], a. Filamentoso, compuesto de hilos; semejante a un hilo; que tiene fibras o filamentos; parecido a una franja; fibroso.

filar ['fɪləʳ] [fi-laʳ], a. 1. Perteneciente al hilo, caracterizado por hilos; semejante a un hilo. 2. Con fibras o hilos muy finos que cruzan el campo de la visual, p. ej. en un microscopio.

filaria ['fɪlærɪə] [fi-la-ria], s. (Zool.) Filaria.

filariasis ['fɪlərɪəsɪs] [fi-la-ria-sis], s. (Med.) Filariosis.

filature ['fɪlətʃəʳ] [fi-la-chaʳ], s. 1. Hilandería, la acción o modo de hilar (la seda, etc.). 2. Hilandería, gran fábrica de hilados.

filbert ['fɪlbɜːt] [fil-bert], s. 1. Avellana de cáscara delgada. 2. Avellano, árbol. **Filbert-shaped**, de la forma de una avellana.

filch [fɪltʃ] [filch], vn. Ratear, sisar, hurtar con sutileza y destreza cosas de poca monta.

filcher ['fɪltʃəʳ] [fil-chaʳ], s. Ratero, ladrón que hurta cosas de poco valor, ladroncillo.

filchingly ['fɪltʃɪŋlɪ] [fil-chin-li], adv. Ladronamente, rateramente.

file [faɪl] [fail], s. 1. Lima, instrumento de acero para alisar y pulir los metales. **Half-round file**, lima de media caña. 2. Cualquier aparato destinado a guardar papeles y cartas en orden; punzón para ensartar papeles. 3. Legajo de papeles arreglado sistemáticamente para consultarlo; colección de periódicos dispuestos en orden cronológico. 4. (Mil.) Fila, hilera. 5. Catálogo, lista. 6. **Indian o single file**, fila india. File, -v. 1. Limar, pulir. 2. Ensartar, enhilar, arreglar sistemáticamente para servir de consulta. 3. Registrar, asentar, notar; archivar; presentar de la manera reglamentaria de modo que vaya en el acta o en la minuta de los procedimientos. 4. Ensuciar, manchar. -vn. (Mil.) Marchar en fila. **To file off**, cortar una cosa limándola. (Mil.) Desfilar.

file cas ['faɪlkɑːs] [fail-kas], s. Archivador.

file-cutter [faɪlˈkʌtəʳ] [fail-ka-taʳ], s. Picador de limas.

filefish ['faɪlfɪʃ] [fail-fish], s. Lija.

filemot ['faɪlmɒt] [fail-mot], s. (Ant.) De color leonado; color de hoja seca.

filer ['faɪləʳ] [fai-laʳ], s. Limador, el que lima los metales.

filial ['fɪlɪəl] [fi-lial], a. Filial, perteneciente al hijo; debido a los padres. **Filial duty**, deber filial. **Filial affection**, cariño filial.

filially ['fɪlɪəlɪ] [fi-lia-li], adv. Filialmente.

filiation [ˌfɪlɪˈeɪʃən] [fi-li-ei-shon], s. 1. Filiación, relación del hijo con el padre. 2. (Jur.) La determinación judicial del parentesco (padres).

filibuster ['fɪlɪbʌstəʳ] [fi-li-bas-taʳ], va. y vn. 1. Ser filibustero y conducirse como tal. 2. (E. U.) aplazar o impedir la aprobación de leyes, etc. por medio de proposiciones o discursos dilatorios. Obstruccionista. -s. Filibustero, pirata; aventurero que por la fuerza se apodera de territorio ajeno; el que procura impedir la legislación sobre una materia, poniéndole obstáculos.

filiform [ˈfɪlɪfɔːm] [fi-li-form], *a.* Filiforme, formado como hilo.

filigrane [ˈfɪlɪɡreɪn] [fi-li-grein], *s.* Filigrana.

filigreed [ˈfɪlɪɡriːd] [fi-li-grid], *a.* Afiligranado.

filings [ˈfɪlɪŋz] [fi-lins], *s. pl.* Limaduras.

fill [fɪl] [fil], *va.* 1. Llenar, rellenar, henchir. 2. Llenar, satisfacer, contentar. 3. Llenar, hartar. 4. Llenar una persona o cosa el hueco de otra, ocupar, empastar (teeth). **To fill the chair,** ocupar, desempeñar la cátedra. 5. Hinchar. 6. Terraplenar. *-vn.* 1. Echar de beber, dar de beber. 2. Llenarse, hartarse, atracarse. **To fill out,** echar algún líquido para beber; llenar. **To fill up,** colmar, llenar completamente, llenar a colmo; proveer un empleo vacante. **To fill one's place in his absence,** llenar u ocupar el puesto de alguno en su ausencia. **To fill up the time,** emplear el tiempo.

fill, *s.* 1. Lo que llena o es suficiente para llenar; terraplén; hartura, abundancia; satisfacción. 2. (Dialect) El hueco entre las varas de un carro o calesa. *V.* THILL.

filler [ˈfɪləʳ] [fi-laʳ], *s.* 1. Henchidor, llenador, el que o lo que llena; lo que se emplea para llenar. 2. Embudo. *V.* FUNNEL. **Fillers of tobacco,** tripas, relleno de tabaco.

fillet [ˈfɪlɪt] [fi-lit], *s.* 1. Venda, tira o faja, cinta puesta alrededor de alguna cosa. 2. Filete, solomillo; también, tajada de una pierna de ternera o carnero. 3. Carne arrollada y atada con bramante. 4. (Arq.) Filete, el adorno más delgado de una moldura. **Fillet of veal,** filete de ternera.

fillet, *va.* 1. Vendar, fajar, atar o ceñir con venda, faja o cinta. 2. (Arq.) Adornar con astrágalos.

filling [ˈfɪlɪŋ] [fi-lin], *s.* 1. Adición, suplemento, relleno. 2. Empastadura u orificación en los dientes.

filling station [ˈfɪlɪŋˌsteɪʃən] [fi-lin-stei-shon], *s.* Estación de gasolina.

fillip [ˈfɪlɪp] [fi-lip], *va.* 1. Dar un papirote. 2. Echar, arrojar, impeler, como un capirotazo; incitar, estimular.

fillip, *s.* 1. Papirote, el golpe que se da apoyando el dedo del corazón sobre el pulgar y soltando el del corazón con violencia. 2. Estímulo, aguijón.

filly [ˈfɪlɪ] [fi-li], *s.* 1. Potranca, la yegua que no pasa de tres años. 2. Doncellita o muchacha ligera y retozona: se usa despreciativamente.

film [fɪlm] [film], *s.* 1. Película, membrana o piel delgada. **A film on the eye,** tela o nube en el ojo. 2. (Foto.) Película, una capa muy delgada de materia sensibilizada; placa flexible, como de celuloide, para recibir una capa sensibilizada. **Film-carrier,** bastidor para mantener plana una película fotográfica.

film, *va.* Cubrir con una película.

filminess [ˈfɪlmɪnɪs] [fil-mi-nes], *s.* Calidad de membranoso; apariencia como de una película.

filmstrip [ˈfɪlmstrɪp] [film-strip], *s.* Tira de película. Película auxiliar de clases o conferencias.

filmy [ˈfɪlmɪ] [fil-mi], *a.* Membranoso, pelicular, compuesto de membranas o películas.

filose [ˈfɪləʊz] [fi-lous], *a.* (Anat.) Filiforme, que remata en hilillos.

filter [ˈfɪltəʳ] [fil-taʳ], *va.* Filtrar, depurar, hacer pasar los líquidos por entre los poros de un cuerpo sólido para purificarlos de las partes grasas o extrañas que contienen.

filter, *s.* 1. Filtro, la manga, lienzo o papel para filtrar. 2. Filtro, bebida con la cual se pretende excitar el amor. *V.* PHILTER.

filter-tip [ˌfɪltəˈtɪp] [fil-tar-tip], *a.* De filtro con boquilla. (Se aplica a los cigarrillos).

filth [fɪlθ] [filz], *s.* 1. Inmundicia, porquería; basura, suciedad, fango. 2. Corrupción, infección, impureza.

filthily [ˈfɪlθɪlɪ] [fil-zi-li], *adv.* Asquerosamente, suciamente.

filthiness [ˈfɪlθɪnɪs] [fil-zi-nes], *s.* Inmundicia, suciedad.

filthy [ˈfɪlθɪ] [fil-zi], *a.* 1. Sucio, puerco, asqueroso. 2. Poluto, inmundo, depravado o corrompido moralmente; obsceno, torpe.

filtrate [ˈfɪltreɪt] [fil-treit], *va.* Filtrar. *-s.* El líquido filtrado o separado por medio de la filtración.

filtration [fɪlˈtreɪʃən] [fil-trei-shon], *s.* (Quím.) Filtración, la acción de filtrar.

fimbriate [ˈfɪmbrɪeɪt] [fim-breit], *va.* Franjear; ribetear.

fin [fɪn] [fin], *s.* 1. Aleta que tienen los peces en varias partes del cuerpo y con las cuales se ayudan para nadar. 2. Parte saliente o apéndice de un utensilio. 3. Pescados, peces. 4. Barba (de ballena)

finable [ˈfaɪnəbl] [fai-na-bol], *a.* Multable, sujeto a multa.

final [ˈfaɪnl] [fai-nal], *a.* 1. Final, último. 2. Final, conclusivo, decisivo. 3. Final, mortal. 4. Lo que pertenece al fin, motivo u objeto con que se hace una cosa. **A final answer,** respuesta decisiva. **A final stroke,** golpe decisivo.

finale [fɪˈnɑːl] [fi-nal], *s.* 1. Acto último, escena última, final, fin. 2. (Mús.) Final, el último movimiento.

finality [faɪˈnælɪtɪ] [fai-na-li-ti], *s.* Finalidad, estado o calidad de final o completo; lo que es final, acto decisivo.

finally [ˈfaɪnəlɪ] [fai-na-li], *adv.* Finalmente, últimamente, en fin, en conclusión, por último.

finance [faɪˈnæns] [fai-nans], *s.* 1. Hacienda pública, la ciencia de los negocios monetarios; manejo pecuniario. 2. Renta, utilidad o beneficio que se saca anualmente de alguna posesión; en plural por lo común. *-va.* y *vn.* V. FINANCIER.

financial [faɪˈnænʃəl] [fai-nan-shal], *a.* Rentístico, monetario, que pertenece a la hacienda o rentas públicas.

financially [faɪˈnænʃəlɪ] [fai-nan-sha-li], *adv.* Rentísticamente, en materia de rentas.

financier [faɪˈnænsɪəʳ] [fai-nan-siaʳ], *va.* y *vn.* Manejar los negocios monetarios de; conducir operaciones rentísticas. *-s.* Recaudador de rentas públicas y el que las maneja, el cual puede llamarse rentista, hacendista o financiero.

financing [faɪˈnænsɪŋ] [fai-nan-sin], *s.* Financiamiento.

finary [ˈfaɪnərɪ] [fai-na-ri], *s.* V. FINERY, 2a.

fin-back [faʳˈbæk] [fain-bak], *s.* Ballena que tiene una aleta dorsal; se llama también, *rorqual y razor-back.*

finch [fɪntʃ] [finch], *s.* (Orn.) Pinzón, fringilino, pájaro de la familia de los fringílidos; picogordo, **goldfinch,** acanta. **Chaffinch,** pinzón. **Bull-finch,** pinzón real.

find [faɪnd] [faind], *va.* (*pret.* y *pp.* FOUND). 1. Encontrar, hallar, descubrir lo que se buscaba; tropezar o hallar por casualidad. 2. Encontrar una persona a otra. 3. Hallar una cosa perdida. 4. Hallar, conocer por experiencia, descubrir lo que estaba oculto, resolver, adquirir, saber, reconocer. 5. (For.) Juzgar, declarar, decidir según justicia; aprobar, admitir. 6. Surtir, abastecer, proveer, dar alguna cosa que se necesita. 7. Alimentar, mantener, *-vn.* (Der.) Fallar, dar sentencia. **Seek and ye shall find,** buscad y hallaréis. **To find fault** o **amiss,** desaprobar, criticar, hallar que decir. **To find in one's heart,** tener deseo de alguna cosa; estar de humor. **To find oneself,** hallarse, estar; mantenerse, alimentarse. **How do you find yourself!,** ¿cómo lo pasa Ud.?, ¿cómo se halla Ud.?, ¿cómo se siente Ud.? **To find one's way,** introducirse, conducirse. **To find out,** solver, desatar o resolver; hallar o descubrir; adivinar, imaginar, inventar, dar con, averiguar. **To find a person out,** llegar a saber quién es uno, o cual es su verdadero carácter. **To find a verdict for the plaintiff,** fallar o dar sentencia a favor del querellante o demandante. **To find a verdict for the defendant,** fallar o sentenciar a favor del demandado o acusado, o bien absolverle del cargo o de la demanda. **To find work for one,** dar ocupación a alguien.

find, *s.* Una cosa hallada, especialmente un descubrimiento útil.

finder [ˈfaɪndəʳ] [fain-daʳ], *s.* 1. Hallador; descubridor, inventor, el que hace algún nuevo descubrimiento. 2. (Opt.) Buscador, hallador, el pequeño telescopio que va al lado de uno mayor; buscador, lente suplementaria, con espejo, asegurado a una cámara fotográfica para ver el objeto en el campo de la visual: un portaobjetos para el microscopio, rayado con líneas muy finamente graduadas para colocar un objeto o un ejemplar de interés.

find-fault [ˈfaɪndfɔːlt] [faind-folt], *s.* Censurador, crítico.

finding [ˈfaɪndɪŋ] [fain-din], s. 1. Descubrimiento, invención. 2. Fallo, sentencia, decisión de un tribunal o árbitro, o de una comisión. 3. Gasto, mantenimiento. 4. *pl.* Herramientas y avíos de un obrero. y particularmente de un zapatero.

fine [faɪn] [fain], a. 1. Fino, refinado, puro; agudo, cortante; claro, transparente; delicado, primoroso; sagaz, astuto, diestro; galán, lindo; bello, elegante, hermoso, bien parecido; cortés, bien criado, instruído; vistoso, espléndido. 2. **Fine gold,** oro fino o de ley, **fine sand,** arena fina. -s. 1. Multa, pena pecuniaria. 2. (*Des.*) Fin conclusión. **In fine.** finalmente, en conclusión, por fin.

fine, *va.* 1. Afinar, refinar, perfeccionar, purificar; aclarar. 2. Lustrar, dar lustre, esplendor, brillantez o transparencia a alguna cosa. 3. **Multar.** -*vn.* Pagar una multa.

fine-draw [ˈfaɪndrɔː] [fain-dro], *va.* Zurcir o unir dos pedazos de cualquier tela cosiéndolos sutil y curiosamente.

fine-drawer [ˈfaɪndrəʊəʳ] [fain-droua'], s. Zurcidor.

fine-drawing [faɪndrɔɪŋ] [fain-droin], s. zurcidura, la acción de zurcir o la unión y costura de la cosa zurcida.

fine-fingered [ˈfaɪnˈfɪŋɡəd] [fain-fin-gued], a. Delicado, primoroso, el que es capaz de trabajar cosas primorosas o delicadas.

fineless [ˈfaɪnlɪs] [fain-les], a. Sin fin. *V.* ENDLESS.

finely [ˈfaɪnlɪ] [fain-li], *adv.* 1. Primorosamente, con elegancia; agudamente, sutilmente. 2. (*Irón.*) Miserablemente.

fine-looking [ˈfaɪnˈluːkɪŋ] [fain-lu-kin], a. Guapo, bien parecido.

fineness [ˈfaɪnnɪs] [fain-nes], s. Fineza, delicadeza, primor, lustre, hermosura, esplendor; agudeza, sutileza, ingenio, finura; pureza, perfección.

finer [ˈfaɪnəʳ] [fai-na'], s. Refinador de metales. -a. Comparativo de fine; más fino.

finery [ˈfaɪnərɪ] [fai-ne-ri], s. 1. Primor, vista, esplendor, elegancia; adorno, atavío, aderezo. 2. Antigua especie de fragua, hoy en desuso. **Finery cinder,** una especie de óxido negro de hierro en láminas pequeñas.

fine-spoken [ˈfaɪnspəʊkən] [fain-spou-ken], a. El que usa palabras o frases muy escogidas o afectadas. Se toma casi siempre irónicamente.

fine-spun [ˈfaɪnspʌn] [fain-span], a. Ingeniosamente ideado o delineado; inventado astutamente. (*fam.*) **Fine-spun,** tirado por los cabellos, alambicado.

finesse [fɪˈnes] [fi-nes], *vn.* Valerse de subterfugios y artificios. -s. 1. Artificio, treta, estratagema, astucia, sutileza. 2. Calidad de hábil, diestro o mafioso.

fin-footed [ˈfaɪnfuːtɪd] [fain-fu-tid], a. Palmeado; se aplica a las aves que tienen los dedos unidos por membranas.

finger [ˈfɪŋɡəʳ] [fin-ga'], s. 1. Dedo, miembro flexible de la mano. **Index finger,** dedo índice. **Middle finger,** dedo de en medio, dedo del corazón. **Ring finger,** dedo anular. **Little finger,** dedo meñique. 2. Parte parecida a un dedo; pequeña parte que sale o proyecta. 3. Medida de longitud, anchura del dedo, longitud del dedo medio. 4. Medida de profundidad, igual a la anchura del dedo. 5. Dedo, la mano, el instrumento de alguna obra. **Finger-stall,** dedal, apoyadedos. **Finger-ring,** anillo. **Finger-bowl, finger-glass,** enjuague, enjuagatorio, taza que se pone a cada convidado antes de alzar los manteles para limpiar los dedos y enjuagar la bota. **Finger-breadth,** anchura de un dedo; medida de longitud. **Finger-end,** punta del dedo. **Finger-mark,** marca, mancha hecha con el dedo; impresión del dedo pulgar que sirve para identificar las personas. **Finger-post,** poste indicador en el cual hay una mano o una flecha que indica el camino. **Finger-reading,** la lectura de letras en relieve por medio del tacto, con las puntas de los dedos, como lo hacen los ciegos. **His fingers are all thumbs,** usa de sus manos desmañadamente. **To have a finger in the pie,** meter la cuchara; tomar parte en un asunto.

finger, *va.* 1. Tocar, manosear; llegar a alguna cosa con la mano con ánimo de quitarla. 2. (*Mús.*) Tocar, pulsar, poner los dedos en algún instrumento de música; manejar, ejecutar alguna obra diestramente con las manos. **Light-fingered,** ligero de manos, dado al hurto.

finger-board [ˈfɪŋɡəbɔːd] [fin-ga'-bord], s. 1. La parte del mástil o mango del violín donde se ponen los dedos para tocar. 2. Teclado del órgano o pianoforte.

fingered [ˈfɪŋɡəd] [fin-gued], a. Que tiene dedos.

fingering [ˈfɪŋɡərɪŋ] [fin-gue-rin], s. 1. El acto de tocar ligeramente o de juguetear. 2. Modo de tocar o pulsar un instrumento de música; notación para indicar qué dedos han de emplearse. 3. La obra ejecutada primorosamente con los dedos. 4. Lana gruesa para medias.

fingerless [ˈfɪŋɡəlɪs] [fin-ga'-les], a. Sin dedos.

fingernail [ˈfɪŋɡəneɪl] [fin-ga'-neil], s. Uña del dedo de la mano. **Fingernail polish,** barniz para las uñas.

finger prints [ˈfɪŋɡəprɪntz] [fin-ga'-prints], s. *pl.* Huellas digitales.

finger wave [ˈfɪŋɡəweɪv] [fin-ga'-ueiv], s. Ondulado del cabello sin calor, ondulado al agua.

fingle-fangle [ˈfɪŋɡəfæŋl] [fin-ga'-fan-guel], s. Bujería, friolera.

finial [ˈfɪnɪəl] [fi-nial], s. (*Arq.*) Florón de pináculo; pináculo; remate que se dirige hacia arriba.

finical [ˈfɪnɪkl] [fi-ni-kal], a. Delicado, afectado, nimio en el vestir, en los modales, etc.

finically [ˈfɪnɪklɪ] [fi-ni-kli], *adv.* Afectadamente.

finicalness [ˈfɪnɪklnɪs] [fi-ni-kal-nes], s. Demasiada delicadeza, afectación propia de un petimetre.

finicking [ˈfɪnɪkɪŋ] [fi-ni-kin], a. Afectado, melindroso, meticuloso, nimio en el vestir, en los modales, en el lenguaje, etc. *V.* FINICAL. -s. Especie de paloma con cresta.

finish [ˈfɪnɪʃ] [fi-nish], *va.* 1. Acabar, terminar, concluir, poner fin. 2. Pulir, perfeccionar, dar la última mano. 3. Completar la educación de. 3. (*Fam.*) Matar o hacer impotente; vencer, aniquilar. -*vn.* Llegar al fin; cesar, **to finish doing, writting,** acabar de hacer, de escribir.

finish, s. 1. Final, fin, término, acabamiento, colmo. 2. Pulimento, la última mano.

finished [ˈfɪnɪʃt] [fi-nisht], a. 1. Acabado terminado, pulido. 2. Aniquilado, muerto.

finisher [ˈfɪnɪʃəʳ] [fi-ni-sha'], s. Consumador, el que consume, perfecciona o da la última mano a alguna cosa; lo que acaba o decide alguna cosa. **The finisher of the law,** el ejecutor de la justicia.

finishing [ˈfɪnɪʃɪŋ] [fi-ni-shin], s. Acabamiento, consumación; colmo, perfección; la última mano o pincelada. -a. Que acaba, concluye o consuma. **Finishing blow,** golpe de gracia. **To give the finishing stroke to,** dar la última mano a.

finite [ˈfaɪnaɪt] [fai-nait], a. Finito, lo que tiene fin; limitado.

finitely [ˈfaɪnaɪtlɪ] [fai-nait-li], *adv.* Limitadamente.

finiteness [ˈfaɪnaɪtnɪs] [fai-nait-nes], s. Limitación, restricción.

finless [ˈfɪnlɪs] [fin-les], a. Sin aletas, desaletado.

finlike [ˈfɪnlaɪk] [fin-laik], a. Aletado, que se parece a las aletas del pez.

Finn [fɪn] [fin], s. Finlandés, finlandesa, un miembro de la raza finlandesa; natural de Finlandia.

finned [ˈfɪnd] [find], a. Aletado, que tiene aletas como el pez.

finnic [ˈfɪnɪk] [fin-nik], a. Finés, perteneciente a los fineses, y a sus idiomas. -s. Lengua finesa.

finnish [ˈfɪnɪʃ] [fin-nish], a. Finlandés, perteneciente a Finlandia o a sus habitantes. -s. Idioma propio de los finlandeses.

finny [ˈfɪnɪ] [fi-ni], a. 1. Armado de aletas como los peces. 2. Abundante en peces.

fiord o **fjord** [fjɔːd] [fiord], s. Fiordo.

fir [fɜːʳ] [faʳ], s. Abeto, árbol semejante al pino. **Fir-tree,** el árbol llamado abeto. **Spruce-fir,** pinabete. **Scotch fir,** pino.

fire [faɪəʳ] [faiaʳ], s. 1. Fuego, lumbre; combustión; llama, toda materia combustible que está ardiendo. 2. Descarga de armas de fuego. 3. Fuego, incendio, de algún edificio. 4. Fuego, el ardor que excitan algunas pasiones de ánimo. 5. Fuego, ardor o viveza de la imaginación; actividad intelectual; fuerza de la expresión. 6. La tortura del fuego; los tormentos del infierno. 7. Cualquier desgracia o infortunio pesado; rabia. **Fire of love,** llama del amor. **Slow fire,** fuego lento. **Fire is a good servant, but a bad master,** (Prov.) sírvete del fuego, mas guardate de él. **Fire-alarm,** alarma o llamada de incendios, particularmente un sistema telegráfico. **Fire-annihilator.** v. FIRE-EXTINGUISHER. **Fire-back,** la pared posterior de un horno u hogar. **Fire-board,** delantera de chimenea: mampara o tabla con que se tapan las chimeneas en el verano. **Fire-box,** hogar, caja de fuego de una locomotora. **Fire-brick,** ladrillo refractario. **Fire-clay,** arcilla refractaria que resiste a la acción del fuego más intenso, con la cual se hacen los ladrillos refractarios. **Fire-damp,** fuego grisú, mofeta, hidrógeno carburado explosible en las minas. **Fire-dog,** morillo de hogar. **Fire-door,** puerta de horno u hornillo. **Fire-eater,** (a) Titiritero farsante que finge tragarse brasas ardiendo. (b). Jaque, matamoros, fierabrás; retador de profesión. **Fire-escape,** aparato de salvamento; escala de seguridad para bajar desde lo alto de un edificio incendiado. **Fire-extinguisher,** extinguidor o apagador portátil de incendios. (Amer.) Apagafuegos. **The fire of persecution,** la rabia, la violencia de la persecución. **To be on fire,** estar hecho un ascua, encendido, literal o figuradamente. **To put out the fire,** apagar el fuego. **To set fire to, to set on fire,** pegar fuego, quemar, incendiar. **By the fire,** a la lumbre, sentado junto al fuego. **To miss fire,** hacer fogonazo, no disparar. **He will never set the river on fire,** no inventó la pólvora; es decir, es de cortos alcances. **St. Anthony's fire,** erisipela. **Out of the frying-pan into the fire,** huir del fuego y dar en las brasas. **Under fire,** expuesto al fuego de fusil o de cañón; se usa también en sentido figurado. **Fire-arrow,** saeta incendiaria. **Fire-brush,** escobilla para barrer el hogar. **Fire-fan,** abanico de chimenea, pantalla que sirve para evitar que el calor de la lumbre dé en la cara. **Fire-fork,** hurgón. **Fire-insurance,** seguro contra incendios. **Fire-kiln,** hornillo. **Fire-lock,** fusil, carabina, escopeta. **Fire-maker,** cohetero. **Fire-master,** oficial de artillería que cuida de las obras de fuego. **Fire-new,** flamante, nuevo; recién salido de la fragua. **Fire-office,** oficina de seguros contra los incendios. **Fire-pan,** brasero, copa, chofeta para llevar fuego. **Fire-plug,** tapón de los encañados para apagar los incendios en las calles. **Fire-proof,** a prueba de incendio. **Fire-screen,** pantalla de chimenea, guardafuego. **Fire-ship,** (Mar.) brulote, bajel lleno de materias combustibles para quemar a otros. **Fire-shovel,** paleta, badil, badila. **Fire-stick,** tizón, tea. **Fire-stone,** pirita, piedra que puede resistir al fuego. **Fire-wood,** leña para la lumbre.

fire, va. 1. Encender, abrasar, quemar, inflamar, enardecer; avivar el fuego. 2. Encender, animar, excitar. 3. Cauterizar. **To set on fire o a-fire,** inflamar, incndiar. -vn. 1. Encenderse; dejarse dominar de alguna pasión, enojarse, enfadarse. 2. Tirar, disparar, descargar, hacer fuego.

fire-arm [ˈfaɪərɑːm] [faiararm], s. Arma de fuego.

fire-ball [ˈfaɪəbɔːl] [faia-bol], s. Granada real o de mano, globo lleno de pólvora, que revienta donde cae.

fireboat [ˈfaɪəbəʊt] [faia-bout], s. Embarcación para combatir incendios.

firebox [ˈfaɪəbɒks] [faia-boks], s. 1. Caja de fuegos, hogar (de caldera). 2. Caja que da la alarma de incendio.

firebrand [ˈfaɪəbrænd] [faia-brand], s. 1. Tizón o tea. 2. Incendiario, zizañero.

firebug [faɪəbʌg] [faia-bag], s. Incendiario.

firecracker [ˈfaɪəˌkrækəʳ] [faia-kra-kaʳ], s. Cohete.

fire-cross [ˈfaɪəkrɒs] [faia-kros], s. Símbolo de ataque o alarma en Escocia, que se figuraba con dos tizones encendidos y cruzados.

firedamp [ˈfaɪədæmp] [faia-damp], s. Grisú, mofeta.

fire department [ˈfaɪədɪˌpɑːtmənt] [faia-di-part-ment], s. Cuerpo de bomberos.

fire-drake [ˈfaɪədreɪk] [faia-dreik], s. Serpiente de fuego; especie de meteoro.

fire-eater [ˈfaɪɔiːtəʳ] [faia-itaʳ], s. 1. Titiritero que finge comer fuego. 2. Matamoros, jaque. 3. (E.U.) Los que estaban con los Estados del Sur antes de la guerra de secesión.

fire-engine [ˈfaɪəenʤɪn] [faia-en-yin], s. Bomba de apagar los incendios.

firefly [ˈfaɪəflaɪ] [faia-flai], s. Luciérnaga.

fireless cooker [ˈfaɪəlɪsˌkuːkəʳ] [faia-lis-ku-kaʳ], s. Vasija eléctrica para cocinar.

fireman [ˈfaɪəmən] [faia-man], s. 1. Bombero. 2. Fogonero.

fire-place [ˈfaɪəpleɪs] [faia-pleis], s. Hogar, la parte de la chimenea donde se enciende lumbre.

firer [ˈfaɪərəʳ] [faia-raʳ], s. Incendiario.

fire-side [ˈfaɪəsaɪd] [faia-said], s. Hogar, fogón de chimenea; la casa, el hogar doméstico.

fire truck [ˈfaɪətrʌk] [faia-trak], s. Autocamión de bomberos.

firewater [ˈfaɪəwɔːtəʳ] [faia-uo-taʳ], s. Aguardiente.

firewoods [ˈfaɪəwʊdz] [faia-wuds], s. Leña.

firework [ˈfaɪəwɜːk] [faia-uek], s. Fuego artificial, fiesta de pólvora.

fireworker [ˈfaɪəwɜːkəʳ] [faia-ue-kaʳ], s. Oficial de artillería inferior al maestro de fuegos.

firing [ˈfaɪərɪŋ] [faia-rin], s. 1. Leña, carbón, combustible. 2. Descarga.

firing-iron [ˈfaɪərɪŋˌaɪrɒn] [faia-rin-aion], s. Cauterio.

firing lever [ˈfaɪərɪŋˌlevəʳ] [faia-rin-li-vaʳ], s. Palanca del disparador.

firing party [ˈfaɪərɪŋˌpɑːtɪ] [faia-rin-par-ti], s. (Mil.) Piquete de salvas.

firkin [ˈfiːkɪn] [fir-kin], s. 1. Cuñete, barril pequeño, que puede contener unos 36 cuartillos. 2. Cuñete, o barrilete que se emplea para mantequilla y otros varios usos.

firm [fɜːm] [ferm], a. Firme, fuerte, estable, duro, constante, seguro. -s. (Com.) Firma, razón social, la denominación con que una casa de comercio hace sus negocios.

firmament [ˈfɜːməmənt] [fer-ma-ment], s. Firmamento.

firmly [ˈfɜːmlɪ] [ferm-li], adv. Firmemente, fuertemente.

firm name [ˈfɜːmˌneɪm] [ferm-neim], s. Razón social.

firmness [ˈfɜːmnɪs] [ferm-nes], s. Firmeza, dureza, consistencia, estabilidad, solidez; entereza, constancia, resolución.

first [fɜːst] [ferst], a. 1. Primero; temprano, delantero, primitivo. 2. Primero, excelente, grande, sobresaliente. -adv. Primero, en primer lugar, al principio, en el princi-pio. **At first, at the first,** desde luego, al principio. **First o last,** tarde o temprano, un día u otro. **At first blush,** a primera vista, sin madura consideración. **First-begotten, first-born,** primogénito, el hijo o hija que nace primero. **First-class,** de primera clase, de primer orden. **First-cousin,** primo hermano, prima hermana. **First-created,** se dice de la primera cosa criada o producida de su especie. **First-fruits,** primicia, fruto primero. **First-hand,** lo que viene directamente del orígen o del productor. **First floor,** (GB) primer piso, principal; (E.U.) bajos, planta baja. **First night,** (Teat.) noche de estreno. **First quarter,** cuarto creciente (moon).

first aid [ˈfɜːstˈeɪd] [ferst-eid], s. Primeros auxilios.

first-begotten [ˈfɜːstbeˈgɒtn] [ferst-be-to-ten], a. Primogénito.

firstling [ˈfɜːstlɪŋ] [ferst-lin], s. 1. Primogénito. 2. La cosa que ha sido producida antes que ninguna otra de su especie. -a. 1. Primogénito, se dice del hijo que nace primero y de lo que le pertenece. 2. Primerizo, lo que es primero o se anticipa a otro; lo primero que se hace o piensa.

firstly [ˈfɜːstlɪ] [ferst-li], adv. En primer lugar.

first mate [ˈfɜːstˈmeɪt] [ferst-meit], s. (Mar.) Piloto.

first-rate [ˈfɜːstˈreɪt] [ferst-reit], a. Preminente, de un mérito superior, de primera clase u orden.

firth [fɜːθ] [ferz], s. V. FRITH.

firwood [ˈfɜːwuːd] [fer-vud], s. Madera de abeto o pino.

fisc [fɪsk] [fisk], *s.* Fisco, el erario público, la tesorería, la real hacienda, la hacienda pública.

fiscal [ˈfɪskəl] [fis-kal], *s.* Ministro o Secretario de hacienda. *-a.* Fiscal, perteneciente al fisco, o al oficio del fiscal; rentístico.

fish [fɪʃ] [fish], *s.* 1. Pez. 2. Pescado: se dice de la carne de los peces como opuesta a la de los animales terrestres. 3. *(Mar.)* Jimelga. 4. gemelo, gaburón; *(Mec.)* refuerzo. **Food-fish,** pescado, pez comestible. **Sea-fish,** pez de mar. **Fresh-water fish,** pez de agua dulce. **Shell-fish,** pez de concha o testáceo. **Fish-car,** (a) Vivero, receptáculo sumergido en el agua, en el cual se pueden guardar los peces vivos. (b) Carro de ferrocarril para llevar pescado. **Fish-pond,** nansa, estanque de peces, vivero. **Flying fish,** pez volador. **A crawfish,** cangrejo de río o de agua dulce. **An odd fish,** un estrambótico, hombre raro. **Fish of an anchor,** *(Mar.)* Pescante de ancla. **To have other fish to fry,** tener que atender a cosas más importantes tener otras cosas en qué pensar.

fish, *va.* 1. Pescar. 2. Buscar en, y sacar a luz; intentar, obtener una cosa. 3. Aprovechar de (una cosa) para pescar: v. g. una red. 4. Componer o reforzar con una pieza de madera que se llama gemelo o gaburón; *(Fer.)* empalmar (los rieles, etc.) afirmando planchas a lo largo de ellos. **To fish in trouble waters,** pescar en río revuelto.

fish bait [ˈfɪʃbeɪt] [fish-beit], *s.* Carnada para pescar.

fish-bone [ˈfɪʃbəʊn] [fish-boun], *s.* Espina de pescado.

fish-culture [ˈfɪʃkʌltʃəʳ] [fish-kal-chaʳ], *s.* La crianza artificial de los peces.

fish-day [ˈfɪʃdeɪ] [fish-dei], *s.* Día de abstinencia de carnes.

fisher [ˈfɪʃəʳ] [fishaʳ], *s.* 1. Pescador. 2. El *pekan,* marta de América. *V.* PEKAN.

fisher-boat [ˈfɪʃəbəʊt] [fisher-bout], *s.* Barca pescadora.

fisherman [ˈfɪʃəmən] [fisher-man], *s.* 1. Pescador. 2. Barca pescadora.

fishery [ˈfɪʃərɪ] [fi-she-ri], *s.* Pesca, pesquera.

fish-garth [ˈfɪʃgɑːθ] [fish-garz], *s.* Pesquera o pesquería, paraje cerrado en un río para pescar.

fish-glue [ˈfɪʃgluː] [fish-glu], *s.* Cola de pescado, colapez.

fish-hook [ˈfɪʃhuːk] [fish-juk], *s.* Anzuelo, garfio para pescar.

fishing [ˈfɪʃɪŋ] [fishin], *s.* 1. Pesca, arte o práctica de pescar; pesquera, pesquería. 2. El derecho de pescar, o el paraje donde se concurre a pescar. 3. Amordazamiento, barrotaje de los carriles; acción de enganchar el pescador en la cruz del ancla e izarla. **Fishing-line,** cordel de pescar. **Fishing-fly,** mosca artificial para carnada. **Fishing-smack,** queche para pescar en el mar. **Fishing village,** pueblo de pescadores. **Fishing-tackle,** avíos de pescar, aparejo de pesca.

fishing-net [ˈfɪʃɪŋnet] [fishin-net], *s.* Red de pescar.

fishing-rod [ˈfɪʃɪŋrɒd] [fishin-rod], *s.* Caña de pescar.

fish-joint [ˈfɪʃdʒɔɪnt] [fish-yoint], *s.* En los ferrocarriles, junta de mordaza; dos planchas de hierro aseguradas con pernos a los rieles.

fish-kettle [ˈfɪʃketl] [fish-ke-tel], *s.* Caldera larga para cocer los peces enteros.

fishlike [ˈfɪʃlaɪk] [fish-laik], *a.* Semejante a pescado.

fishmarket [ˈfɪʃmɑːkɪt] [fish-mar-kit], *s.* Pescadería, el sitio donde se vende pescado.

fish-meal [ˈfɪʃmiːl] [fish-mil], *s.* Comida de pescado.

fishmonger [ˈfɪʃmʌŋgəʳ] [fish-mon-gaʳ], *s.* Pescadero, el que vende pescado.

fishplate [ˈfɪʃpleɪt] [fish-pleit], *s.* Mordaza, plancha de unión de dos rieles. *V.* FISH-JOINT.

fishspear [ˈfɪʃpɪəʳ] [fish-speaʳ], *s.* Arpón, dardo.

fishskin [ˈfɪʃskɪn] [fish-skin], *s.* 1. Piel de pescado. 2. Zapa, lija o piel de lija.

fish-story [ˈfɪʃstɔːrɪ] [fish-sto-ri], *s.* *(E.U.)* Fábula, cuento increíble.

fishtail [ˈfɪʃteɪl] [fish-teil], *s.* Cola de pez.

fishwife [ˈfɪʃwaɪf] [fish-uaif], **fish-woman** [ˈfɪʃwʊmən] [fish-vu-man], *sf.* Pescadera, mujer que vende pescado; mujer de plazuela, disputadora, marimacho.

fishworm [ˈfɪʃwɔːm] [fish-uerm], *s.* Lombriz que sirve de cebo en la pesca.

fishy [ˈfɪʃɪ] [fi-shi], *a.* 1. Lo que tiene las calidades o la figura de pescado. 2. Perteneciente o parecido al pescado; o habitado por pescados. 3. Abundante en pescado.

fisk [fɪsk] [fisk], *s.* Fisco.

fissate [ˈfɪseɪt] [fi-seit], *a.* Dividido, hendido.

fissile [ˈfɪsaɪl] [fi-sail], *a.* Hendible, rajadizo.

fission [ˈfɪʃən] [fi-shon], *s.* 1. Fisión, el acto de henderse, hendimiento. 2. *(Bio.)* La espontánea división de una celdilla o de un organismo en nuevas celdillas u organismos, a manera de reproducción.

fissionable [ˈfɪʃənəbl] [fi-sho-na-bol], *a.* Fisionable.

fissiparous [ˈfɪsɪpərəs] [fi-si-pa-ros], *s.* y *a.* Fisíparo, que se reproduce por la división de su propio cuerpo.

fissipedal [ˈfɪsɪpedl] [fi-si-pe-dal], *a.* *(Zool.)* Fisípedo, que tiene el pie dividido en muchos dedos.

fissure [ˈfɪʃəʳ] [fi-shaʳ], *s.* Grieta, hendedura, abertura.

fist [fɪst] [fist], *s.* Puño. **To strike with the fist,** dar puñetazos. **With clenched fist,** a puño cerrado.

fistic [ˈfɪstɪk] [fis-tik], *a.* Relativo al puño; de pugilato, riña a puñadas.

fisticuff [ˈfɪstɪkʌf] [fis-ti-kaf], *v.* Dar puñetazos. 2. Riña a puñetazos.

fistula [ˈfɪstjʊlə] [fis-tiu-la], *s.* *(Cir.)* Fístula.

fistular [ˈfɪstjʊləʳ] [fis-tiu-laʳ], *a.* Fistular, fistuloso, afistolado.

fistulate [ˈfɪstjʊleɪt] [fis-tiu-leit], *a.* Hueco como un tubo; afistolado, fistuloso.

fistulous [ˈfɪstjʊləs] [fis-tiu-los], *a.* Fistuloso, lo que tiene la forma de fístula o su semejanza.

fit [fɪt] [fit], *s.* 1. *(Med.)* Acceso, paroxismo o parasismo. 2. Mal, enfermedad; mal de madre; pasión histérica; convulsión. 3. Transportamiento, rebato o arrebatamiento pasajero; capricho, humor. 4. Ataque, acceso, ímpetu, rebato, acometimiento repentino de algún mal o de alguna pasión de ánimo. 5. *(Ant.)* Cantos de un poema o partes de una canción que se repiten. **Fainting-fit,** desmayo. **By fits, o by fits and starts,** a ratos perdidos, a tontas y a locas, al tuntún; espasmódicamente. **To give one fits,** *(E.U. Fam.)* Poner a uno como nuevo. **Cold fit,** escalofrío de una fiebre intermitente; temblor. **A melancholy fit,** un acceso de melancolía. **To be in fits of laughter,** destornillarse de risa. **If the fit takes me,** *(Fig.)* Si me parece, si me da la gana.

fit, *s.* 1. Forma, corte; ajuste; conveniencia, conformidad, adaptación. 2. Acción de alistar, preparación.

fit, *a.* 1. Apto, idóneo, a propósito para algo, conveniente, aprestado, dispuesto. 2. Hábil, capaz. 3. Cómodo, justo, juicioso, decente. 4. Listo, en estado de preparación. 5. **Fit to be tied,** loco de atar; muy impaciente o encolerizado. **To laugh fit to kill,** desternillarse de risa. 6. Como si, casi, cuasi; uso familiar adverbial. **If you think fit,** si a Ud. le parece. **He was not fit for it,** el no era propio para ello, o él no era a propósito para el caso.

fit, *va.* 1. Ajustar, acomodar, conformar; igualar, adaptar una cosa a otra. 2. Surtir, proveer lo que se necesita. 3. Poner en estado o disposición de. 4. Hacer acomodar una cosa a alguno; calzar, vestir. 5. Convenir, venir bien. *V.* BEFIT. *-vn.* Convenir, ser a propósito, venir, sentar o caer bien o mal. **That suit fits you very well,** ese vestido le sienta a Ud. bien, o le está bien. **To fit out,** proveer de todas las cosas necesarias, equipar a uno; tripular; armar. **To fit up,** ajustar una cosa con otra, acomodar, componer; alhajar, adornar, amueblar.

fitch [fɪtʃ] [fich], *s.* *(Zool.)* 1. Turón, veso. 2. Pincel de pelo de turón.

fitchet [ˈfɪtʃɪt] [fi-chet], **fitchew** [ˈfɪtʃuː] [fi-chiu], *s.* *(Engl.)* Veso, turón mamífero europeo.

fitful [ˈfɪtfʊl] [fit-ful], *a.* 1. Alternado con paroxismos, espasmódico; caprichoso; incierto, vacilante. 2. Caprichoso, impulsivo.

fitfully [ˈfɪtfəlɪ] [fit-fu-li], *adv.* Por intervalos; caprichosamente, de un modo vacilante.

fitly [ˈfɪtlɪ] [fit-li], *adv.* Aptamente, cómodamente, justamente.

fitment [ˈfɪtmənt] [fit-ment], *s.* 1. Apresto, equipo, provisión. 2. Lo que conviene o es a propósito. 3. Mueblaje, conjunto de muebles.

fitness [ˈfɪtnɪs] [fit-nes], *s.* Propiedad, aptitud, idoneidad, conveniencia, proporción. **Fitness of time,** oportunidad.

fittedness, *s.* V. SUITABLENESS.

fitter [ˈfɪtər] [fi-taʳ], *s.* Acoplador, disponedor, unidor, acomodador.

fitting [ˈfɪtɪŋ] [fi-tin], *a.* Propio para; adecuado, conveniente. -*s.* Guarnición; más usado en plural, herrajes; maniobras. **Fitting-shop,** taller de ajuste.

fittingly [ˈfɪtɪŋlɪ] [fi-tin-li], *adv.* Propiamente, aptamente.

fitty [ˈfɪtɪ] [fi-ti], *a.* Propenso a tener ataques o arrebatos.

fitz [fɪts] [fich], *s.* Hijo: usado solamente en los compuestos de nombres propios, como, **fitzhugh,** hijo de Hugo, **fitzroy,** hijo del rey.

five [faɪv] [faiv], *a.* Cinco. **He will tell you how many black beans make five,** el te dirá cuántas son cinco.

five-bar [ˈfaɪvbɑːʳ] [faiv-baʳ], **five-barred** [faɪvˈbærɪd] [faiv-ba-rid], *a.* Lo que tiene cinco barras o palenques.

five-finger [ˈfaɪvfɪŋɡəʳ] [faiv-fin-gaʳ], **five-leaf** [ˈfaɪvliːf] [faiv-lif], *s.* (Bot.) Cincoenrama.

fivefold [ˈfaɪvfəʊld] [faiv-fould], *a.* Quíntuplo.

fives [ˈfaɪvz] [faivs], *s.* Un juego de pelota.

fix [fɪks] [fiks], *va.* 1. Fijar, establecer; parar, detener. 2. Fijar, quitar la variedad que puede haber en alguna cosa. 3. Decidir definitivamente; señalar, determinar, establecer. 4. Tratar de suerte que se evite la acción de perder el color, de volatilizarse, o de deteriorarse. **To fix a negative,** fijar una prueba negativa fotográfica. 5. Dirigir con constancia hacia el mismo punto. 6. Arreglar el orden, poner en orden, ajustar. 7. (Fam. E.U.) Reparar, componer; colocar bien, de una manera conveniente. 8. Sobornar, cohechar, convencer. 9. Apretar las clavijas a alguien, ajustarle las cuentas. 10. Grabar en la mente, imprimir. 11. Atraer la atención, la mirada. -*vn.* 1. Fijarse, determinarse. 2. Fijarse, establecerse en alguna parte determinada. 3. Pasar un cuerpo del estado fluido al de sólido.

fix, *s.* (Fam.) Dificultad; aprieto, dilema. **To be in a bad fix,** hallarse en trance apurado.

fixable [ˈfɪksəbl] [fik-sa-bol], *a.* Fijable, que puede fijarse.

fixate [ˈfɪkseɪt] [fik-seit], *v.* fijar, fijarse.

fixation [fɪkˈseɪʃən] [fik-sei-shon], *s.* 1. Fijación, el acto de fijar. 2. Firmeza, estabilidad. 3. Sujeción, restricción. 4. Residencia fija en algún paraje. 5. Paso de un cuerpo fluido al estado de solidez.

fixative [ˈfɪksətɪv] [fik-sa-tiv], *a.* Que sirve para fijar o hacer permanente.

fixedly [ˈfɪksɪdlɪ] [fik-sid-li], *adv.* Fijamente, ciertamente.

fixedness [ˈfɪksɪdnɪs] [fik-sid-nes], *s.* Firmeza, estabilidad.

fixing [ˈfɪksɪŋ] [fik-sin], *s.* 1. La acción del verbo **to fix** en cualquier sentido. 2. (Foto.) La acción de tratar una plancha desarrollada de suerte que no se altere la imagen por la acción ulterior de la luz. 3. *pl.* Adornos, decoraciones o jaeces de cualquier clase; también, cosas preparadas para el uso. **Table-fixings,** accesorios de la mesa.

fixity [ˈfɪksɪtɪ] [fik-si-ti], *s.* 1. Firmeza y coherencia de las partes. 2. (Quím.) La calidad de los cuerpos por la cual pueden sostener mucho calor sin volatizarse.

fixture [ˈfɪkstʃəʳ] [fiks-chaʳ], *s.* 1. Cosa fija, instalación fija, accesorio. 2. Persona que no se mueve de un lugar. **Fixtures,** *s. pl.* Muebles fijos. **Light fixtures,** instalaciones fijas para las luces. **Electric light fixture,** lámpara, brazo, araña, etc, eléctrica. 3. Fecha fija para algunos actos. 4. Instalación de gas, electricidad, sanitaria, etc.

fizgig [ˈfɪzɡɪɡ] [fis-guig], *s.* 1. Arpón, dardo. 2. Especie de fuego artificial, cohete pequeño. 3. Gazmoña, coqueta, tontuela.

fizz, fizzle [fɪz] [fis], *vn.* Hacer un ruido sibilante; hacer un ruido sordo como la pólvora húmeda. **It is a fizzle,** ha hecho fiasco completo.

fizzle [fɪzl] [fi-sel], *s.* 1. (fam.) Estado acosado o cansado. 2. Mal éxito de alguna cosa.

fjord [fjɔːd] [fiord], *s.* V. FIORD.

flabbergast [ˈflæbəɡɑːst] [fla-ber-gast], *v.* Asombrar, dejar estupefacto.

flabby [ˈflæbɪ] [fla-bi], *a.* Blando, flojo, lacio.

• **flabellate** [ˈflæbɪleɪt] [fla-bi-leit], *a.* En forma de abanico.

flabelliform [ˈflæbɪlɪˈfɔːm] [fla-bi-li-form], *a.* V. FLABELLATE.

flaccid [ˈflæksɪd] [flak-sid], *a.* 1. Flojo, endeble, débil, flaco, lacio. 2. (Med.) Flácido.

flaccidity [ˈflæksɪdɪtɪ] [flak-si-di-ti], *s.* Flojedad, flaqueza, debilidad.

flag [ˈflæɡ] [flag], *vn.* 1. Pender, colgar. 2. Flaquear, amilanarse; debilitarse. -*va.* 1. Señalar por medio de una bandera, **To flag a car,** hacer señal de parada a un coche. 2. Poner una bandera sobre algo, por ejemplo encima de un edificio. 3. Enlosar, embaldosar.

flag, *s.* 1. Bandera; estandarte, insignia militar de los cuerpos de ejército. 2. Bandera o pabellón, insignia militar de las naves de guerra. 3. (Bot.) Gladiolo, espadaña. 4. Losa, baldosa. **Flag of truce, white flag.** Parlamentario, pabellón blanco, bandera de parlamento. **Green flag,** (F.C.) Banderín verde, señal de precaución. **Red flag.** (F.C.) Banderín encarnado, señal de peligro. **Black flag,** pabellón negro, el de los piratas. **Yellow flag,** bandera amarilla, insignia de cuarentena, o enfermedad contagiosa. **To strike** o **lower the flag.** Arriar la bandera.

flag-broom [ˈflæɡbruːm] [flag-brum], *s.* Escoba para barrer los enlosados.

flagellant [ˈflædʒələnt] [fla-che-lant], *a.* Flagelante. -*s. pl.* Flagelantes, secta religiosa.

flagellate [ˈɡlædʒəleɪt] [fla-che-leit], *va.* Azotar, flagelar.

flagellation [ˌflædʒəˈleɪʃən] [fla-che-lei-shon], *s.* Flagelación, disciplina.

flagellator [ˈflædʒəleɪtəʳ] [fla-che-lei-taʳ], *s.* Flagelador.

flagelliform [ˈflædʒəlɪfɔːm] [fla-che-li-form], *a.* Flageliforme, que tiene la forma de un látigo, o del renuevo de una planta.

flagellum [ˈflæɡələm] [fla-che-lum], *s.* 1. (Bio.) Apéndice parecido a un látigo; flagelo. 2. Azote. 3. (Bot.) Renuevo o vástago delgado de las plantas.

flageolet [ˈflædʒəlɪt] [fla-cheo-lit], *s.* Caramillo, flauta delgada; octavín.

flagginess [ˈflæɡɪnɪs] [fla-gui-nes], *s.* Flojedad, falta de tirantes o tensión.

flagging [ˈflæɡɪŋ] [fla-guin], *s.* 1. Enlosado, embaldosado. 2. Conjunto de baldosas. 3. La acción de embaldosar o enlosar. -*a.* Lánguido, flojo. -*pa.* de o **FLAG.**

flaggy [ˈflæɡɪ] [fla-gui], *a.* Flojo, lacio, endeble; insípido.

flagitious [ˈflædʒɪtɪəs] [fla-chi-tios], *a.* Facineroso, malvado; vicioso, corrompido; atroz, abominable.

flag-officer [ˈflæɡˈɒfɪsəʳ] [flag-o-fi-saʳ], *s.* (Mar.) Almirante, vicealmirante o contra-almirante; tiene el privilegio de desplegar un pabellón que indica su rango.

flagon [ˈflæɡən] [fla-gon], *s.* Frasco, garrafa, botella, jarro.

flagrance [ˈflæɡrəns] [fla-grans], *s.* Flagrancia, la actualidad de cometer algún delito, notoriedad, escándalo, atrocidad.

flagrancy [ˈflæɡrənsɪ] [fla-gran-si], *s.* 1. Incendio, abrasamiento, calor, ardor, fuego. 2. Impudencia descarada.

flagrant [ˈflæɡrənt] [fla-grant], *a.* 1. Ardiente, flagrante. 2. Colorado, encendido, con muchos colores en la cara. 3. Rojo. 4. Notorio, públicamente conocido; grande, insigne. 5. Notorio, escandaloso.

flagrantly [ˈflæɡrəntlɪ] [fla-grant-li], *adv.* Ardientemente; notoriamente.

flagship [ˈflæɡʃɪp] [flag-ship], *s.* (Mar.) Navío almirante, el buque que monta el que manda una escuadra, buque insignia.

flagstaff ['flægstɑːf] [flag-staf], *s. (Mar.)* El asta de la bandera o pabellón.

flagstone ['flægstəʊn] [flag-stoun], *s.* Losa o baldosa, piedra ancha y llana a propósito para enlosar.

flail ['fleɪl] [fleil], *va.* Golpear, azotar.

flake [fleɪk] [fleik], *s.* 1. Cualquier cosa que está en pedacitos sueltos y planos. 2. Copo (snow), vedija de lana, algodón o seda; y copo se dice también de la nieve cuando cae de lo alto. 3. Lámina, capa, tonga, tongada. 4. **Flake of fire,** centella, chispa. **Flake of ice,** carámbano. 5. Clavel que tiene rayas de un solo color sobre fondo blanco. **Flake white,** albayalde.

flake, *s.* 1. Cañizo, andamio ligero; en particular, secadero de pescado. 2. Faldón de silla para mantener la rodilla del jinete fuera del caballo.

flake, *va.* Reducir una cosa a copos. -*vn.* Romperse o quebrarse en láminas.

flaky ['fleɪkɪ] [flei-ki], *a.* 1. Vedijoso, vedijudo. 2. Lo que está colocado en capas o lechos. 3. Lo que está roto en pequeñas láminas.

flam ['flæm] [flam], *s.* 1. Falsedad, mentira, embuste; chasco. 2. Capricho, fantasía.

flam, *va.* Mentir, engañar mintiendo.

flambeau ['flæmbɪəʊ] [flam-biou], *s.* 1. Antorcha, hachón. 2. Candelabro grande adornado. 3. Gran caldera para azúcar. *(Gal.)*

flamboyant [flæm'bɔɪənt] [flam-boiant], *a.* 1. Extravagante y llamativo; retumbante. 2. Flamígero, flamante. 3. En forma de llamas.

flame [fleɪm] [fleim], *s.* 1. Llama, llamarada, fuego. 2. Impulso vehemente del ánimo, fuego de la animación, ardor del temperamento; fuego del amor. 3. *(fam.)* Enamorada, enamorado; persona armada.

flame, *vn.* 1. Arder, quemarse alguna cosa levantando llama; brillar. 2. Inflamarse en alguna pasión violenta. -*va. (Des.)* Inflamar, excitar.

flame-color [fleɪmˌkʌlər] [fleim-ka-laʳ], *s.* Color de llama.

flame-colored [fleɪmˌkʌləd] [fleim-ka-lord], *a.* Lo que tiene color de llama.

flame-eyed [fleɪmˌaɪd] [fleim-aid], *a.* El que tiene los ojos centellantes.

flameless ['fleɪmlɪs] [fleim-les], *a.* Sin llama.

flame thrower [fleɪmˌθrəʊər] [fleim-zrouaʳ], *s.* Lanzallamas.

flaming ['fleɪmɪŋ] [flei-min], *a.* 1. Flamante, que emite llamas. 2. Llamativo, faustoso. 3. Apasionado, que tiende a excitar.

flamingly ['fleɪmɪŋlɪ] [flei-min-li], *adv.* Espléndidamente, radiantemente.

flamingo [fləˈʃmɪŋɡəʊ] [fla-min-gou], *s. (Orn.)* Flamenco, ave palmípeda mayor que la cigüeña.

flanch, flanque ['flæntʃ] [flanch], *s. (Her.)* 1. Figura formada a cada lado del escudo por el segmento de un círculo. 2. Reborde, pestaña.

flange ['flændʒ] [flanch], *s.* 1. Realce, borde levantado para mantener alguna cosa en su lugar; repisa, borde saliente, reborde; reborde de una cañería o un tubo; pestaña de rueda de carro. 2. Plancha para cerrar la boca de un cañón.

flange, *va.* Proveer de realce o reborde.

flank ['flæŋk] [flank], *s.* 1. Ijada, delgado, vacío. 2. Lado, costado, porción lateral de cualquier cosa; ala, flanco de escuadra o ejército. 3. *(Fort.)* Flanco, la parte del baluarte que hace ángulo entrante con la cortina y saliente con la frente. 4. La parte delgada del pellejo que proviene de la ijada de un animal.

flank, *va.* 1. Lindar, confinar, estar inmediato a un límite; estar a un lado u otro de un confín o a ambos. 2. Atacar el flanco de un ejército o escuadra. 3. *(Fort.)* Flanquear. 4. Asegurar los flancos. -*vn.* Defender o atacar los flancos.

flanker ['flæŋkər] [flan-kaʳ], *s.* 1. *(Fort.)* Flanco. 2. Flanqueador.

flanker, *va.* 1. Guarnecer o defender los costados, alas o flancos de un cuerpo, campamento o muralla. 2. Atacar de flanco.

flannel ['flænl] [fla-nel], *s.* Franela o flanela. **Canton** o **cotton flannel,** moletón, franela de algodón.

flannelette [ˌflænəˈlet] [fla-na-let], *s.* Muletón, tela de franela para ropa interior.

flap [flæp] [flap], *s.* 1. Pieza o parte ancha, flexible y que cuelga sueltamente; como falda, faldilla, faldón; válvula; labio de una herida; oreja de zapato; ala de un sombrero. 2. Mosqueador. 3. Cachete; alazo; golpe ligero. 4. La acción de aletear, de agitar. 5. *(Aer.)* Aleta.

flap, *va.* 1. Golpear, pegar; agitar, columpiar; mosquear, espantar las moscas con el mosqueador. 2. Dejar caer, rebajar alguna cosa. 3. Despertar, hacer, recordar algo a otro por medio de un ligero golpe. **To flap the wings,** aletear, sacudir las alas. -*vn.* 1. Columpiarse, o moverse de arriba abajo, como oscilante al viento. 2. Agitarse, menearse, sacudirse.

flap-dragon [flæpˈdreɪɡən] [flap-drei-gon], *va. (Vul.)* Comer vorazmente.

flapdoodle ['flæpˌduːdl] [flap-du-del], *s. (Fam.)* Disparate, tontería.

flap-eared [flæpˈɪəd] [flap-iard], *a.* Orejudo, el que tiene las orejas grandes.

flapjack ['flæpdʒæk] [flap-yak], *s.* Especie de torta hecha a la sartén.

flap-mouthed [flæpˈmaʊθɪd] [flap-mauzd], *s.* Morrudo, bezudo, hocicudo.

flapper ['flæpər] [fla-paʳ], *s.* 1. Agitador, golpeador; el que o lo que sacude. 2. El que hace a otro acordarse de alguna cosa. 3. Avecilla que todavía no puede volar. 4. *(Fam.)* Jovencita, tobillera.

flapping ['flæpɪŋ] [fla-pin], *s.* La acción de aletear o de sacudirse.

flare [flɛər] [fleaʳ], *vn.* 1. Lucir, brillar, deslumbrar, relampaguear. 2. Brillar, lucir con colores muy vivos; vestirse de un modo faustoso y desagradable. 3. Abrirse o extenderse hacia fuera, como los bordes de un embudo. **To flare up,** encenderse; *(Fig.)* encolerizarse. **A flare up,** *(Fam.)* cólera, displicencia, incomodidad; jarana, disturbio.

flare, *s.* 1. Destello, resplandor, llamarada. 2. Señal luminosa, cohete de señales. 3. Arrebato de cólera. 4. Estruendo. 5. Ensanchamiento.

flash [flæʃ] [flash], *s.* 1. Relámpago, llamarada, rayo, ráfaga de luz, llama pronta y pasajera. 2. Llamarada, movimiento repentino del ánimo de corta duración. 3. Cualquier situación pasajera y corta; momento, instante, durante muy breve tiempo. 4. Borbollón, golpe de agua impelida con violencia. **Flash of the eye,** ojeada, vistazo. **Flash of wit,** agudeza, rasgo, dicho pronto y vivo. **Flash of hope,** rayo de esperanza. -*a.* 1. Que tiene relación con ladrones y su habla. **Flash language,** caló, jerigonza de gitanos. **Flash-house,** casa encubridora de hurtos, donde se acogen los ladrones. 2. Barato y de mal gusto.

flash, *vn.* 1. Relampaguear. 2. Brillar con un brillo pasajero. 3. Saltar, romper con violencia. 4. Prorrumpir en chistes o agudezas. -*vn.* 1. Cubrir el vidrio liso con una capa delgada de vidrio de color. 2. Despedir agua a borbollones.

flashback ['flæʃbæk] [flash-bak], *s.* Interrupción de la continuidad de un relato; por ej., en una película cinematográfica, para presentar escenas anteriores.

flashboard ['flæʃbɔːd] [flash-bord], *s.* Alza de presa.

flashbulb ['flæʃbʌlb] [flash-balb], *s.* Bombilla de destello, luz relámpago.

flasher ['flæʃər] [fla-shaʳ], *s.* 1. Luz intermitente, intermitente. 2. Interruptor intermitente. 3. **Flasher sign,** anuncio eléctrico intermitente.

flashily ['flæʃɪlɪ] [fla-shi-li], *adv.* Superficialmente, con vana ostentación.

flashing ['flæʃɪŋ] [fla-shin], *s.* 1. Producción de destellos. 2. Chorro fuerte de agua. 3. Tapajuntas (en la construcción de edificios).

flashlight ['flæʃlaɪt] [flash-lait], *s.* Linterna eléctrica de mano, lámpara portátil. **Flashlight photography,** fotografía instantánea con luz artificial.

flashy ['flæʃɪ] [fla-shi], *a.* 1. Superficial, aparente, presumido sin mérito. 2. Llamativo en apariencia, pero barato; de relumbrón.

flask [flɑːsk] [flask], *s.* 1. Frasco, redoma, botella. 2. Frasco, el recipiente en que se llevaba antes la pólvora.

flasket [flɑːskɪt] [flas-kit], *s.* Fuente o plato grande.

flat [flæt] [flat]. *s.* 1. Llanura, plano. 2. Plano, lo ancho de algún instrumento cortante. 3. Bajío, escollo. **Flat of an oar,** (*Mar.*) Pala de remo. **Flat of a floor-timber,** (*Mar.*) Plan de una varenga. 4. (*Mús.*) Bemol, el signo b que baja en un semitono la entonación natural de una nota. 5. Cualquier cosa de forma achatada o plana. como una barca, un techo plano, un carro de plataforma, etc. 6. (*fam.*) Mentecato, fácil de embaucar. 7. Habitación, conjunto de cuartos en un solo piso. -*a.* 1. Llano, liso, plano; raso (country); chato (nose), aplastado; **Flat food,** pie plano 2. Insulso, insípido. **Flat wine,** vino evaporado. 3. Triste, abatido. 4. Perentorio, absoluto. 5. Tendido, postrado en el suelo. **A flat lie,** una mentira premeditada. 6. En la lonja, sin interés. 7. (*Mús.*) (a) Debajo del diapasón; (b) menor, o disminuido. 8. Mate, sin lustre, como una superficie pintada.

flat, *va.* 1. (*Mús.*) Bajar, abajar un tono. 2. (*Mús.*) Hacer sonar (o cantar) una nota un poco más bajo de lo que está indicado o escrito (desafinar por bajo). 3. Allanar, poner llana la superficie de alguna cosa; aplastar, achatar. 4. Evaporar; desazonar. **To flat in,** (*Mar.*) Acuartelar, abroquelar. -*vn.* 1. (*Mús.*) Bajar el tono de lo que se canta o toca. 2. Aplastarse, aplanarse. 3. Atontarse.

flat back [flæt] [flat], *s.* y *a.* Lomo plano (encuadernación).

flatboat ['flætbəʊt] [flat-bout], *s.* Chalana, barcaza, barco o bote de fondo plano.

flat-bottomed ['flæt'bɒtəmd] [flat-bo-tomd], *a.* Lo que tiene el fondo plano: se dice de los botes y embarcaciones.

flatcar ['flætkɑːʳ] [flat-kaʳ], *s.* (*F.C.*) Plataforma.

flatfoot ['flætfʊt] [flat-fut], *s.* 1. Pie plano. 2. (*Fam.*) Resuelto, inflexible.

flat-footed ['flæt'fʊtɪd] [flat-fu-ted], *a.* 1. Que tiene los pies planos. 2. (*fam.*) Inflexible, resuelto, determinado.

flathead ['flæthed] [flat-jed] *s.* 1. Cabeza chata (de un perno, tornillo, etc). 2. Tornillo de cabeza chata. 3. Tonto, mentecato.

flatiron ['flæˌaɪən] [flat-aion], *s.* Plancha.

flatland ['flætlænd] [flat-land] *s.* Llano, llanura.

flatlong ['flætlɒŋ] [flat-lon], *adv.* De plano.

flatly ['flætlɪ] [flat-li], *adv.* 1. Horizontalmente, llanamente. 2. Fríamente. 3. Plano, absolutamente. **He flatly confessed it,** lo confesó de plano.

flatness ['flætnɪs] [flat-nes], *s.* 1. Llanura, lisura. 2. Desabrimiento, insipidez. 3. Abatimiento, apocamiento. 4. Insulsez, frialdad.

flat-nosed ['flætnəʊst] [flat-noust], *a.* Chato (nose), romo.

flatten ['flætn] [fla-ten], *va.* 1. Allanar, aplastar, achatar, poner chata una cosa. 2. Derribar, echar a tierra. 3. Evaporar; abatir. -*vn.* 1. Aplanarse, igualarse. 2. Atontarse, perder el espíritu y la viveza. 3. Hacerse plano o achatado en cualquier sentido. 4. Desbravarse, perder su espuma (champagne).

flatter ['flætəʳ] [fla-taʳ], *s.* Allanador, aplanador, laminador.

flatter, *va.* 1. Adular, lisonjear. 2. Agradar, causar gusto o placer. 3. Halagar o lisonjear a uno haciéndole formar esperanzas ilusorias. 4. Mimar. 5. Favorecer (portrait).

flatterer ['flætərəʳ] [fla-te-raʳ], *s.* Adulador, lisonjero, zalamero.

flattering ['flætərɪŋ] [fla-te-rin], *a.* Lisonjero, que lisonjea el amor propio; adulador que prodiga falsas alabanzas.

flatteringly ['flætərɪŋlɪ] [fla-te-rin-li], *adv.* Con zalamería, halagadoramente.

flattery ['flætərɪ] [fla-te-ri], *s.* Adulación, lisonja, carantoña, zalamería, halago.

flatting ['flætɪŋ] [fla-tin], *s.* 1. La acción del verbo *to flat* en sus varias acepciones, como el acto de bajar el tono de una nota musical, el aplanamiento o alisamiento de una cosa, etc. 2. Barniz mate, encoladura para preservar el dorado.

flat tire ['flæt'taɪəʳ] [flat-taiaʳ], *s.* Llanta desinflada, neumático desinflado, pinchazo.

flattish ['flætɪʃ] [fla-tish], *a.* 1. Chato, lo que está como aplastado. 2. Algo insípido.

flatting ['flætɪŋ] [fla-tin], *s.* Pintura sin brillo.

flattop ['flætɒp] [fla-top], *s.* Portaviones.

flatulency ['flætjʊlənsɪ] [fla-tiu-len-si], *s.* 1. Flatulencia, ventosidad. 2. Hinchazón, vanidad, presunción.

flatulent ['flætjʊlənt] [fla-tiu-lent], *a.* Flatulento; hinchado, vano.

flatuous ['flætjʊəs] [fla-tiuos], *a.* Ventoso, flatulento.

flatus ['flætəs] [fla-tus], *s.* 1. Flato, ventosidad en el cuerpo humano. 2. Soplo.

flatwise ['flætwaɪz] [flat-uais], *adv.* De llano; se dice del cuerpo que está descansando en el suelo por su parte más plana.

flatware ['flætwɛəʳ] [flat-uea], *s.* 1. Vajilla de plata. 2. Vajilla de porcelana.

flaunt ['flɔːnt] [flont], *vn.* Pavonearse, hacer ostentación de galas o vestidos.

flaunt, *s.* 1. Borla; cualquier cosa que cuelga airosamente. 2. Boato, ostentación, alarde.

flautist ['flɔːtɪst] [flo-tist], *s.* Flautista.

flavescent ['flɔːvəsnt] [flo-ve-sent], *a.* Que se vuelve amarillo; amarillento.

flavid ['flɔːnt] [flont] *a.* Amarillo de oro.

flavor, flavour ['fleɪvəʳ] [flei-vaʳ], *s.* 1. Sabor o gusto suave y delicado de alguna cosa. 2. Sainete, salsa o condimento apetitoso. 3. Calidad estética de una obra literaria.

flavor, flavour, *va.* 1. Saborear, comunicar buen sabor, añadir un sainete a un manjar. 2. Saber a, oler a. 3. (*Fig.*) Comunicar cualquier cualidad distintiva a una cosa.

flavored ['fleɪvəd] [flei-verd], *a.* Sabroso, gustoso.

flavoring ['fleɪvərɪŋ] [flei-vo-rin], *s.* Sainete, salsa que da buen sabor a los comestibles, condimento. También se usa en sentido figurado.

flavorless ['fleɪvəlɪs] [flei-va-les], *a.* Sin sabor, insípido, soso.

flavour, *s.* y *v.* V. FLAVOR. Manera usual de escribir esta palabra en Gran Bretaña.

flavous ['fleɪvəs] [flei-vos], *a.* (*Des.*) Flavo, amarillo.

flaw [flɔː] [flo], *s.* 1. Resquebradura, hendedura, grieta, pelo, paño, paja. 2. Falta, defecto, tacha. 3. (*Mar.*) Ráfaga, soplo repentino de viento. 4. (*Geol.*) Falla.

flaw, *va.* 1. Rajar, hender. 2. Hacer grietas en el cutis. 3. Causar defecto o vicio, estropear, afear

flawless ['flɔːlɪs] [flo-les], *a.* Sano, entero, exento de rajas, grietas u otro defecto.

flawy ['flɔːɪ] [floui] *a.* 1. Agrietado. 2. Defectuoso. 3. Propenso a ráfagas (wind).

flax [flæks] [flaks], *s.* Lino. **To brake flax.** Agramar lino. **To dress flax,** rastrillar lino. **Flaxseed,** grano de lino, linaza. **Flax-brake,** agramadera. **Flax-dressing,** rastrilleo del lino.

flax-comb [flæks'kɒm] [flaks-kom], *s.* Rastrillo.

flax-dresser [flæks'dresəʳ] [flaks-dre-saʳ], *s.* Rastrillador.

flaxen ['flæksn] [flak-sen], **flaxy** ['flæksɪ] [flak-si], *a.* 1. De lino. lo que está hecho de lino. 2. Blondo. **Flaxen-hai-red,** que tiene los cabellos rubios.

flaxseed ['flæksiːd] [flak-sid], *a.* (*Ento.*) Parecido a la linaza, como las ninfas del cecidomio. -*s.* Linaza.

flax-weed [flæks'wiːd] [flaks-uid], *s.* (*Bot.*) Linaria. V. TOADFLAX.

flay [fleɪ] [flei], *va.* 1. Desollar; descortezar. 2. (*Fig.*) Desollar vivo, robar. 3. Flagelar, fustigar.

flayer ['fleɪəʳ] [fleiaʳ], *s.* Desollador; descortezador.

flea [fliː] [fli], *s.* 1. Pulga, insecto parásito muy molesto. 2. Uno de ciertos escarabajos y crustáceos pequeños que saltan como las pulgas. **A flea in one's ear,** una amonestación; algunas veces, desaire, mala acogida. **To put a flea in one's ear,** decir algo que molesta.

flea, *va.* Espulgar, quitar las pulgas.

fleabane ['fliːbeɪn] [fli-bein], *s. (Bot.)* Coniza, pulguera.

flea-bite, flea-biting ['fliːbaɪt] [fli-bait] ['fliːbɪtɪŋ] [fli-bi-tin], *s.* 1. Picadura o picada de pulga. 2. *(Fig.)* Pequeña molestia.

flea-bitten ['fliːbɪtn] [fli-biten], *a.* 1. Picado de pulgas. 2. Vil, bajo, menospreciable.

fleam ['fliːm] [fli-m], *s.* 1. Fleme, especie de lanceta para sangrar las bestias. 2. *(Prov.Ingl.)* Zanja, arroyo.

fleawort ['fliːwɔːt] [fli-uort], *s. (Bot.)* Pulguera, zaragatona.

fleck o **flecker** [flek] [flek] ['flekəʳ] [fle-kaʳ], [fle-kaʳ], *va.* Abigarrar, varetear, señalar con rayas, manchas o lunares.

fleck, *s.* 1. Punto o lista; mancha, lunar, peca. 2. Copo, vedija de lana. 3. Lonja (de tocino).

fleckless ['fleklɪs] [flek-les], *a.* Sin mancha ni marca; inocente.

flection ['flekʃən] [flek-shon], *s.* 1. Flexión, la acción de doblar; inclinación. 2. La parte encorvada o torcida; corvadura, codo. 3. *(Gram.)* V. INFLECTION. 4. Ojeada o mirada.

flector, *s. V.* FLEXOR.

fled, *pret.* y *pp.* el verbo TO FLEE.

fledge [fledʒ] [fledch], *va. (Poco us.)* 1. Emplumar. 2. Criar (bird) hasta que puede volar. -*vn.* 1. Pelechar, emplumecer, emplumarse.

fledgling, fledgeling ['fledʒɪŋ] [fled-chin], *s.* Pajarito próximo a salir del nido. -*a.* Emplumecido hace poco; de aquí, novel, poco conocido, como un joven poeta o escritor.

flee [fliː] [fli], *va. (pret.* y *pp.* FLED). Huir, evitar, esquivar, escapar. -*vn.* 1. Huirse, apartarse de algún peligro, fugarse, escaparse. 2. No dejarse ver; cesar de ser visible; desaparecer. **He fled to Denmark,** huyó a Dinamarca.

fleece [fliːs] [flis], *s.* Vellón. **The order of the Golden Fleece,** la orden del Toisón de Oro. **Fleece-wool,** vellón, la lana cortada a las reses vivas.

fleece, *va.* 1. Esquilar la lana o pelo de los animales. 2. Desnudar, despojar a uno de lo que tiene. 3. Blanquear.

fleeced ['fliːst] [flist], *a.* 1. Velludo. 2. Esquilado.

fleecer ['fliːsəʳ] [fli-saʳ], *s.* 1. Despojador, ladrón. 2. Esquilador. 3. Desplumador.

fleecy ['fliːsɪ] [fli-si], *a.* Lanudo, cubierto de lana o parecido al vellón; pálido. **Fleecy clouds,** nubes aborregadas, a modo de vellones de lana.

fleer ['flɪəʳ] [fliaʳ], *vn.* Mofarse de alguno; hacer muecas o gestos. -*va.* Mofar, burlar.

fleer, *s.* 1. Burla, mueca; risa falsa. 2. El que huye.

fleet [fliːt] [flit], *s.* 1. Escuadra de navíos de guerra, armada; *(Mar.)* flota de buques mercantes. 2. Número cabal de buques que pertenecen a una compañía o a un gobierno. 3. *(Avia.)* Flota, escuadrilla de aviones. 4. Conjunto de coches, camiones etc., que pertenecen a una persona. 5. Caleta, ensenada.

fleet, *a.* Veloz, ligero. **Fleet-footed.** Dotado de pies ligeros; rápido. **Fleet-winged,** dotado de alas ligeras; que vuela velozmente.

fleet, *va.* y *vn.* 1. Volar, desvanecerse, apartarse alguna cosa repentinamente de la vista. 2. Pasar, ser una cosa pasajera, rozar. 3. Flotar. 4. Pasar el tiempo sin sentir. 5. Vivir o pasar el tiempo alegremente.

fleet-foot [fliːt'fuːt] [flit-fut], *a.* Veloz o ligero de pies; alípedo, alígero.

fleeting ['fliːtɪŋ] [fli-tin], *a.* Que pasa rápidamente, transitorio, momentáneo, pasajero.

fleeting-dish ['fliːtɪŋdɪʃ] [fli-tin-dish], *s.* Espumadera.

fleetly ['fliːtlɪ] [flit-li], *adv.* Velozmente, fugazmente.

fleetness ['fliːtnɪs] [flit-nes], *s.* Velocidad, ligereza, rapidez.

fleg [fleg] [fleg] *(Scot.),* *va.* Aterrar, espantar. -*s.* Choque.

fleming ['flemɪŋ] [fle-min], *s.* Flamenco, el natural de Flandes.

Flemish ['flemɪʃ] [fle-mish], *a.* Flamenco, el natural de Flandes y lo que pertenece a este país. **Flemish linen,** holanda, lienzo muy fino.

flense [flens] [flens], *va. (Mar.)* Despedazar una ballena o foca y sacarles la grasa.

flesh [fleʃ] [flesh], *s.* 1. Carne (person or animal alive). 2. Carnalidad, sensualidad; las pasiones groseras del hombre. 3. En teología y bíblica, la naturaleza pecaminosa del hombre. 4. La parte material del hombre; el cuerpo, a distinción del espíritu. 5. Carne, pulpa, la parte mollar de las frutas y vegetales. 6. *(Ant.)* Parentela, parientes cercanos. **After the flesh,** conforme a la carne, de una manera carnal. **Flesh any blood,** (a) Carne y sangre, la naturaleza carnal. (b) Hijos; progenie, casta; los hermanos y parientes cercanos. **One flesh,** una misma carne, una sola persona. **Proud flesh,** tejido granuloso parecido a la carne que se forma en las heridas o llagas que están en vías de curación.

flesh, *va.* 1. Hartar; saciar. 2. Endurecer, habituar, acostumbrar. 3. Dar muestra o pedazo de carne al halcón, al perro; dar ralea a, cebar; *(Fig.)* mojar en sangre. 4. En las tenerías, descarnar, pelambrar. 5. *(Fig.)* Hundir un arma en la carne. 6. Dar cuerpo o forma a algo.

flesh-broth ['fleʃbrɒθ] [flesh-broz], *s.* Caldo de carne o hecho con carne.

flesh-brush ['fleʃbrʌʃ] [flesh-brash], *s.* Cepillo para frotar la piel.

flesh-color [ˌfleʃ'kʌləʳ] [flesh-ka-laʳ], *s.* Color de carne; encarnación.

flesh-diet [flesh'daɪət] [flesh-daiet], *s.* Dieta de carne.

fleshed ['fleʃt] [flesht], *a.* Carnudo, carnoso; **hard-fleshed,** carne dura.

flesh-fly ['fleʃflaɪ] [flesh-flai], *s.* Mosca carnívora que deposita sus huevos en carne corrompida. Sarcophaga.

fleshful ['fleʃfʊl] [flesh-juk], *a.* Carnoso, gordo.

flesh-hook ['fleʃhʊk] [flesh-juk], *s.* Gancho o garabato para sacar la carne de la marmita.

fleshiness ['fleʃɪnɪs] [fle-shi-nes], *s.* Carnosidad.

fleshings ['fleʃɪŋz] [fle-shins], *s. pl.* 1. Calzón de punto muy ajustado que usan los bailarines, los acróbatas y lo actores en algunos papeles. 2. *(Ten.)* Descarnaduras, piltrafas.

fleshless ['fleʃlɪs] [flesh-les], *a.* Descarnado.

fleshliness ['fleʃlɪnɪs] [flesh-li-nes], *s.* Carnalidad.

fleshly ['fleʃlɪ] [flesh-li], *a.* 1. Carnoso, carnal, sensual, mundano. 2. Corporal. 3. Tierno, sensible.

flesh-meat ['fleʃmiːt] [flesh-mit], *s.* Carne, la de los animales o aves que se prepara para comer.

fleshment ['fleʃmənt] [flesh-ment], *s.* Ahínco, ardor, ufanía, por razón del buen éxito.

fleshmonger ['fleʃmɒŋgəʳ] [flesh-mon-gaʳ], *s.* 1. Carnicero. 2. Alcahuete.

fleshpot ['fleʃpɒt] [flesh-pot], *s.* 1. Marmita, olla. 2. **Fleshpots,** abundancia, vida regalada.

fleshy ['fleʃɪ] [fle-shi], *a.* 1. Gordo, grueso, corpulento. 2. Carnoso, mollar; pulposo; suculento. 3. Corporal; carnal, relativo a la naturaleza carnal.

fletch ['fletʃ] [flech], *va. (Des.)* Emplumar o empenachar una saeta.

fletcher ['fletʃəʳ] [fle-chaʳ], flechero, el que hace flechas y arcos.

fleur-de-lis ['flɜːdɪ'lɪs] [fler-di-lis], *s. sing.* y *pl.* Flor de lis, divisa heráldica de la casa de Borbón.

fleuron ['flʊərɒn] [flu-ron], *s. (Arq.)* Florón.

flew [fluː] [flu], *pret.* del verbo TO FLY.

flewed ['fluːəd] [flued], *a.* Boquihendido, que tiene belfos.

flews [fluːz] [flus], *s. pl.* Belfos, los labios grandes de un perro belfo.

flex [fleks] [fleks], *va.* Doblar, doblegar, encorvar. -*s.* Doblez.

flexibility [ˌfleksɪ'bɪlɪtɪ] [flek-si-bi-li-ti], *s.* 1. Flexibilidad. 2. Flexibilidad, docilidad de genio, condescendencia.

flexible ['fleksɪbl] [flek-si-bol] *a.* Flexible, correoso; dócil; dúctil; adaptable, conformado fácilmente, plástico; obediente; deferente.

flexibleness ['fleksɪblnɪs] [flek-si-bol-nes], *s.* Flexibilidad; docilidad.

flexile ['fleksɪl] [flek-sil], *a.* **Flexible.**

flexion ['flekʃən] [flek-shon], *s. V.* FLECTION.

flexor ['fleksəʳ] [flek-saʳ], *s. (Anat.)* Músculo flexor, el que sirve para doblar o encorvar ciertas partes del cuerpo.

flexuous ['fleksʊəs] [flek-suos], *a.* 1. Tortuoso, vario, inconstante. 2. *(Bot.)* Flexuoso, lo que muda de dirección en cada nudo.

flexure ['flekʒəʳ] [flek-shaʳ], *s.* Flexión, juntura, corvadura; zalamería.

flibbertigibbet ['flɪbətɪˈdʒɪbɪt] [fli-ba-ti-yi-bit], *s.* Veleta, persona voluble, casquivana. 2. Persona habladora.

flick [flɪk] [flik], *va.* Tocar o dar ligeramente con un látigo o dedo, etc. *-s.* Latigazo súbito y poco fuerte. 2. Sacudir la ceniza de un cigarro.

flicker ['flɪkəʳ] [fli-kaʳ], *vn.* 1. Vacilar una llama, reavivarse y luego morir. 2. Aletear, menear las alas; fluctuar. 3. Ir de un lado a otro, corretear, revolotear. **The candle flickers,** la vela pavesea, se está acabando. **Flickering flame,** llama vacilante. **Flickering fire,** fuego chispeante, trémulo.

flicker, *s.* 1. Vacilación, titilación, luz trémula. 2. Parpadeo, aleteo. 3. *(Orn.)* Pico del género Colaptes, común en el este de la América del Norte.

flicker-mouse ['flɪkəmaʊz] [fli-ker-maus], *s. (Zool.)* Murciélago.

flies, *s. pl.* de FLY. Moscas.

flier ['flaɪəʳ] [flaiaʳ], *s.* 1. Volador, lo que vuela; ave volatne, etc. 2. Volante de reloj o de otra máquina cualquiera. 3. Escalón; y en plural, escalones de una escalera que va siempre en línea recta, sin dar vueltas. 4. *(fam.)* Lo que se mueve con gran velocidad, como un tren expreso. 5. Rueda de molina, aspa. 6. Prospecto que se distribuye. 7. Operación arriesgada en bolsa, aventura.

flight [flaɪt] [flait], *s.* 1. Vuelo, el acto o la facultad de volar. 2. Bandada de pájaros; el conjunto de aves o de cosas que vuelan moviéndose juntas, como una descarga de flechas. 3. Rapidez, velocidad o movimiento veloz de cualquier manera que sea; también el espacio recorrido por un proyectil, por un ave en su vuelo, etc. 4. Arrebato, ímpetu, arranque; fuego o vuelo de la imaginación; elevación de ideas. 5. Escalera, serie continua de peldaños; tramo de escalera. **An arrow-flight,** vuelo de una flecha.

flight, *s.* 1. Huída, fuga. 2. *(For.)* Evasión, escape, el acto de huir de la justicia o de fugarse de una cárcel. **To betake oneself to flight,** escapar, huir, apelar a la fuga.

flightiness ['flaɪtɪnɪs] [flai-ti-nes], *s.* Irregularidad; travesura; ligero delirio.

flight pattern [ˌflaɪtˈpɑːtən] [flait-pa-tern], *s.* Esquema de vuelo.

flight plan ['flaɪtplæn] [flait-plan], *s.* Plan de vuelo, hoja de ruta.

flight-shot ['flaɪtʃɒt] [flait-shot], *s.* El alcance de una flecha o saeta.

flight strip ['flaɪtstrɪp] [flaitstrip], *s.* Pista para aterrizaje de emergencia al lado de una carretera.

flighty ['flaɪtɪ] [flai-ti], *a.* Veloz, acelerado, ligero, travieso, inconstante; delirante.

flimflam ['flɪmflæm] [flim-flam], *s. (Ger.)* 1. Embuste, ficcioncilla; superchería. 2. Engaño, necedad. *-va.* Engañar con astucia.

flimsiness ['flɪmsɪnɪs] [flim-si-nes], *s.* Textura débil y ligera; falta de solidez, fuerza o resistencia.

flimsy ['flɪmsɪ] [flim-si], *a.* Débil, endeble; fútil, insubstancial, poco sólido; ineficaz, frívolo. **A flimsy argument,** argumento frívolo. **Flimsies,** *s. pl.* Papel delgado de calcar; papel de tela de cebolla.

flinch [flɪntʃ] [flinch], *vn.* 1. Titubear, vacilar a causa de dolor o peligro; faltar a, echarse con la carga, desviar el cuerpo. 2. Echarse atrás, retroceder ante algo peligroso,

desagradable. *(Mex.)* Echarse con las petacas. **To flinch away,** huirse, retirarse. **To flinch back,** retroceder, volver hacia atrás, abandonar el campo; desdecirse. *(fam.)* Rebajarse, echar pie atrás. *(Vul.)* Llamarse andana. **Without flinching,** sin titubear, sin vacilar.

flincher ['flɪntʃəʳ] [flin-chaʳ], *s.* El que se echa con la carga; el que se vuelve atrás de lo que había dicho o de lo que había emprendido.

flinching ['flɪntʃɪŋ] [flin-chin], *s.* Vacilación, titubeo, retroceso.

flinder ['flɪndəʳ] [flin-daʳ], *s.* Astilla, pedacito, pequeño fragmento, tira. **Blown to flinders,** volado en pedazos menudos.

fling [flɪŋ] [flin], *va. (pret. y pp.* FLUNG). 1. Arrojar, tirar, lanzar, esparcir. 2. Empujar, demoler, arruinar; dar en rostro; despedir. 3. Echar en el suelo, como en la lucha a brazo partido; arrojar de la silla: de aquí, sobrepujar, vencer. *-vn.* 1. Lanzar un arma arrojadiza de cualquiera clase. 2. Escarnecer, mofarse, murmurar entre dientes. 3. Alborotarse, cocear, como el caballo; brincar, saltar. 4. Entregarse a movimientos violentos con impaciencia o pasión; saltar impetuosamente.

fling away, desperdiciar, descartar, desechar; exponer, prodigar; retirarse.

fling down, demoler, arruinar.

fling off, engañar en la caza.

fling out, (a) Arrojar por la fuerza. (b) Hablar violentamente, echar chispas. Alborotarse, cocear, hablando de caballos. **To fling out to one,** poner a la vista.

fling up, abandonar, dejar.

fling, *s.* 1. Tiro, el acto de tirar. 2. Mueca, gesto, burla, sarcasmo, chufleta, pulla. 3. Salto o coz. 4. Libertad de acción, oportunidad de obrar a discreción, sin trabas. 5. Fogosa libertad de movimiento; bravata, atrevimiento. 6. Baile escocés muy vivo. 7. Prueba, tentativa. 8. Brinco, coz. 7. **To go on a fling,** echar una cana al aire.

flinger ['flɪŋgəʳ] [flin-gaʳ], *s.* 1. Tirador, arrojador. 2. Mofador, escarnecedor.

flint [flɪnt] [flint], *s.* 1. Pedernal, piedra de chispa o lumbre. 2. Cualquiera cosa sumamente dura. **Flint glass,** cristal; vidrio que contiene plomo. **Flint stone,** pedernal.

flint-heart, flint-hearted ['flɪnthɑːt] [flint-jart], *a.* Empedernido, cruel, duro, insensible.

flintiness ['flɪntɪnɪs] [flin-ti-nes], *s.* La cualidad o naturaleza del pedernal; dureza excesiva.

flintlock ['flɪntlɒk] [flint-lok] *s.* Llave de fusil de chispa.

flinty ['flɪntɪ] [flin-ti], *a.* 1. Apedernalado, silicoso, de pedernal. 2. Empedernido, endurecido, inexorable, duro, cruel, inflexible.

flip [flɪp] [flip], *va.* 1. Lanzar ligera y rápidamente; chasquear. 2. Dar o golpear con un movimiento ligero y pronto; quitar por medio de un golpe ligero. *-s.* Papirotada; también *V.* FILLIP y FLICK.

flip, *s.* 1. Una bebida hecha con cerveza, ron y azúcar. 2. Golpe vivo, capirotazo. 3. Salto mortal.

flippancy ['flɪpənsɪ] [fli-pan-si], *s.* Petulancia, locuacidad, ligereza, impertinencia, ademanes reprensibles.

flippant ['flɪpənt] [fli-pant], *a.* Ligero, petulante, locuaz, impertinente.

flippantly ['flɪpəntlɪ] [fli-pant-li], *adv.* Locuazmente, impertinentemente.

flipper ['flɪpəʳ] [fli-paʳ], *s.* 1. Aleta o miembro ancho y plano que sirve para nadar; pata de tortuga o de foca. 2. *(Vul.)* La mano. 3. Paleta.

flirt [flɜːt] [flert], *vn.* 1. Coquetear, cocar; ser una mujer muy amiga de verse cortejada. 2. Proceder o portarse con ligereza. 3. Corretear, correr continuamente de una parte a otra. 4. Mofar, hacer mofa de alguno. *-va.* 1. Tirar o arrojar alguna cosa con ligereza. 2. Mofar, burlar. 3. Manejar o mover velozmente.

flirt, *s.* 1. Coqueta, cocadora. 2. Golpe o movimiento ligero; gesto, gesticulación; cualquier juego de manos ejecutado con ligereza y de repente. 3. Mueca, burla. *-a. (Des.)* Vivo, petulante; lascivo.

flirtation [flɜˈteɪʃən] [fler-tei-shon], s. 1. Coquetería. 2. (Poco us.) Movimiento ligero, ligereza.

flit [flɪt] [flit], vn. 1. Volar, revolotear, pasar rápidamente o lanzarse de un paraje a otro. 2. En Escocia, mudar de domicilio. -va. (Esco.) Desposeer; hacer mudar de domicilio.

flitch [flɪtʃ] [flich], s. 1. Hoja de tocino; el costado del cerdo salado y ahumado. 2. Lonja o tira cortada del lado de ciertos pescados, ahumada o a propósito para ahumar. 3. (Carp.) Costero, costanera.

flite [flaɪt] [flait], vn. Reñir, regañar. -s. Riña.

flitter [ˈflɪtəʳ] [fli-taʳ], s. 1. Harapo, andrajo. 2. V. FLINDER. 3. Lentejuela, pedacito de metal brillante que sirve de adorno.

flitter-mouse [ˌflɪtəˈmaʊz] [fli-ter-maus], s. Murciélago, murciégalo o murceguillo.

flitting [ˈflɪtɪŋ] [fli-tin], s. Fuga, vuelo rápido; la acción en general del verbo to flit. -a. Pasajero, fugitivo, ligero.

flivver [ˈflɪvəʳ] [fli-vaʳ] s. Automóvil o avión pequeño y barato. 2. Cosa sin valor. **3.** Fiasco.

flix [flɪks] [fliks], s. Borrilla, pelusilla; forro blando de pieles.

float [fləʊt] [flout], vn. 1. Flotar. 2. Fluctuar. 3. Cernerse las aves. 4. Nadar; ser sostenido o llevado por un líquido o gas. -va. 1. Hacer flotar o nadar, hacer sobrenadar. 2. Transportar siguiendo el curso del río. 3. (Com.) Poner en circulación; hallar venta o mercado para una cosa. 4. Estropear, enlucir o lavar una pared estucada. 5. Inundar, cubrir de agua.

float, s. 1. Cualquier cosa que flota sobre el agua; balsa, boya, masa flotante, alamadía. 2. Corcho de una caña de pescar. 3. Flotador de nivel de agua. 4. Regla para pulir o allanar una pared. 5. Boya, salvavidas, balsa. 5. Plataforma con ruedas que se usa en los espectáculos públicos. **Float-boards,** tableros de rodezno de agua.

floatable [ˈfləʊtəbl] [flou-ta-bol], a. Flotante, que puede flotar o ser llevado por la corriente.

floatage [ˈfləʊteɪdʒ] [flou-teich], s. V. FLOTAGE.

floater [ˈfləʊtəʳ] [flou-taʳ], s. Flotante.

floating [ˈfləʊtɪŋ] [flou-tin], a. 1. Flotante, boyante. 2. A flote, suelto, no anclado. 3. Movible, variable. 4. Flotante, no consolidado. 5. Plancha en natación. 6. Revestimiento. **Floating debt,** deuda flotante. **Floating dock,** dique flotante. **Floating policy,** póliza flotante. **Floating population,** población flotante. 7. Natillas adornadas con merengue.

floaty [ˈfləʊtɪ] [flou-ti], a. 1. Flotante. 2. El que cambia a menudo de ocupación, partido, residencia. 3. (E. U.) El que vota en unas elecciones fraudulentamente en varias secciones.

floccillation [ˌflɒksɪˈleɪʃən] [flok-si-lei-shon], s. Carfología, movimientos desordenados de las manos en el estado de delirio; síntoma grave.

floccose [ˈflɒkəʊz] [flo-kous], a. 1. (Bot.) Velludo, que tiene pelusa. 2. V. FLOCCULENT, 2a acep.

flocculence [ˈflɒkjʊləns] [flo-kiu-lens], s. 1. La calidad de ser velludo o lanudo. 2. (Ento.) Substancia blanda y semejante a la cera que excretan ciertos insectos, como los pulgones.

flocculent [ˈflɒkjʊlənt] [flo-kiu-lent], a. 1. Velludo, lanudo. 2. (Orn.) Parecido al plumón de las avecillas. 3. (Ento.) Cubierto con una substancia viscosa.

flocculose [ˈflɒkjʊləs] [flo-kiu-los], a. Que tiene pelusa, algo velludo.

flock [flɒk] [flok], s. 1. Manada, rebaño, grey. 2. Conjunto o concurrencia de muchas personas. 3. Vedija de lana. **A flock of birds,** bandada de aves. 4. Paño deshilado. **Flock-bed,** lecho de borra; colchón lleno de lana o crin muy desmenuzada. **Flock-paper,** papel aterciopelado para cubrir las paredes.

flock, vn. Congregarse, unirse en manadas, atroparse.

floe [fləʊ] [flou], s. Amontonamiento de hielos en el mar; masa de hielo flotante.

flog [flɒg] [flog], va. Azotar, vapulear, fustigar.

flogging [ˈflɒgɪŋ] [flo-guin], s. Tunda, felpa, zurra. (Prov.) Azotaina, pela. (Cuba) Monda. (Vul.) Bocabajo.

flood [flʌd] [flad], s. 1. Gran extensión o cantidad de agua, sea mar, río o laguna. 2. Diluvio, inundación. 3. Flujo o creciente de la mar en oposición al reflujo o menguante. 4. Menstruo excesivo. **Young flood,** marea baja. **High flood,** marea alta. **The Flood,** el Diluvio Universal.

flood, va. 1. Inundar, anegar. 2. Hacer subir el nivel del agua.

flood-gate [ˈflʌdgeɪt] [flad-gueit], s. Compuerta de esclusa.

flooding [ˈflʌdɪŋ] [fla-din], s. Inundación. (Met.) Hemorragia uterina.

floodlight [ˈflʌdlaɪt] [flad-lait], s. reflector, proyector de luz.

flood-mark [ˈflʌdmɑːk] [flad-mark], s. La señal que deja el mar en el sitio más alto adonde llega en la marea alta.

flook [fluːk] [fluk], s. (Mar.) V. FLUKE.

floor [flɔːʳ] [flaʳ], s. 1. Piso, suelo. 2. Piso de una casa. **The ground floor,** planta baja, primer piso. 3. **Fondo** (sea, swimming-pool). 4. Hemiciclo o lugar destinado a los diputados. **To ask for the floor,** pedir la palabra. 5. (E. U.) **Floor leader,** jefe de una fracción parlamentaria.

floor, va. 1. Solar, echar suelo o piso a una habitación. 2. Echar al suelo, tender en el suelo. 3. (Fig.) Vencer, superar (en un debate, etc.). (Fam.) Abrumar, dejar estupefacto.

floor-cloth [ˈflɔːklɒθ] [flor-kloz], s. Hule para cubrir el suelo.

flooring [ˈflɔːrɪŋ] [flo-rin], s. Suelo, piso, pavimento.

floorwalker [ˈflɔːˌwɔːkəʳ] [flor-uo-kaʳ], s. Dependiente mayor de departamento en las grandes tiendas.

flop [flɒp] [flop], va. 1. Dar un golpe, hacer golpear. 2. Moverse, aletear. -vn. 1. Caer, caerse inciertamente, agitarse. V. FLAP. 2. Desplomarse, hundirse. 3. (fam.) Fracaso. -s. (Fam.) Persona o cosa fracasada.

flora [ˈflɔːrə] [flo-ra], s. 1. Flora, conjunto de las plantas indígenas de un país o región. 2. Flora, la diosa de las flores. 3. Flora, uno de los asteroides.

floral [ˈflɔːrəl] [flo-ral], a. Floral, perteneciente a la diosa Flora o a las flores.

Florence [ˈflɒrəns] [flo-rens] s. Florencia.

florence [ˈflɒrəns] [flo-rens], s. 1. Especie de vino tinto que proviene de Toscana. 2. Moneda antigua de oro. 3. Tafetán delgado.

florentine [ˈflɒrəntiːn] [flo-ren-tin], s. 1. Florentina, o Florentín, especie de tela de seda. 2. Florentino, el natural de Florencia.

florescence [fləˈresns] [flo-re-sens] s. (Bot.) Florescencia.

florescent [fləˈresnt] [flo-re-sent] a. Florescente.

floret [ˈflɒrət] [flo-ret], s. 1. Florecilla, cada una de las que forman una flor compuesta. 2. Cadarzo; filoseda. 3. (Ant.) Florete de esgrima.

floriculture [ˈflɒrɪˌkʌltʃəʳ] [flo-ri-kal-chaʳ], s. Floricultura.

floriculturist [ˌflɒrɪˈkʌltʃərɪst] [flo-ri-kal-cha-rist], s. Floricultor.

florid [ˈflɒrɪd] [flo-rid], a. 1. Vivo, brillante; encarnado, de un rojo subido (face). 2. Embellecido con flores de retórica. 3. Sobrecargado de adornos. 4. Florido, lleno o adornado de flores. 5. Elegante, llamativo.

floridity [flɒˈrɪdɪtɪ] [flo-ri-di-ti], **floridness** [ˈflɒrɪdnɪs] [flo-rid-nes], s. 1. Frescura de color; estilo florido.

floridly [ˈflɒrɪdlɪ] [flo-rid-li], adv. Floridamente.

floriferous [flɒˈrɪfərəs] [flo-ri-re-ros], a. Florífero, florígero.

florin [ˈflɒrɪn] [flo-rin], s. Florín.

florist [ˈflɒrɪst] [flo-rist], s. Florista, el que cultiva flores y las cuida; el que las vende.

floscule [ˈflɒskjʊl] [flos-kiul], s. Flósculo, cada una de las florecitas que forman una flor compuesta, como en la del girasol.

flosculous [ˈflɒskjʊləs] [flos-kiu-los], a. Compuesto de flores.

floss [flɒs] [flos], s. 1. Seda floja; filoseda, la seda más fina, no torcida. 2. La borra o pelusa del maíz y de ciertas otras plantas. 3. (Fund.) Escorias que sobrenadan.

flossy [ˈflɒsɪ] [flo-si], a. 1. Ligero, suave. 2. Llamativo, cursi.

floss-silk [ˈflɒsˈsɪlk] [flos-silk], s. Seda floja, atanquía, borra de seda.

flota [ˈflɒtə] [flo-ta], s. (Mar.) Flota.

flotage [ˈfloʊteɪdʒ] [flou-teich], *s.* 1. Flotante, lo que flota sobre el agua. 2. Propiedad de una cosa de flotar o hacer flotar a otra. 3. Barcos que frecuentan un río o un puerto.

flotation [floʊˈteɪʃən] [flou-tei-shon], *s.* 1. La acción o el estado de flotar. 2. Teoría de los cuerpos flotantes. **Line of flotation,** línea de flotación.

flotilla [fləˈtɪlə] [flo-ti-la], *s.* Flotilla.

flotsam, flotson [ˈflɒtsəm] [flot-sam], *s.* 1. Los géneros lanzados o arrastrados al mar desde una embarcación y que se encuentran flotando. El dueño de esos efectos no pierde su derecho de propiedad. 2. Objetos de cualquier clase flotantes en el mar.

flounce [flaʊns] [flauns], *vn.* Pernear; saltar de enojo o enfado. -*va.* Guarnecer, adornar vestidos por las extremidades con algo que los embellezca. **To flounce out,** salir airadamente.

flounce, *s.* 1. Fleco, flueco, farfalá, cairel. 2. *(Cuba)* Vuelo. *(Mex.)* Olán. 3. Sacudida o movimiento rápido del cuerpo o de un miembro.

flounder [ˈflaʊndər] [flaun-da'], *s.* Lenguado, pez marino de cuerpo aplanado y comestible.

flounder, *vn.* Patear, revolcarse en agua o cieno; revolverse, tropezar, andar de una manera incierta; se usa muchas veces en sentido figurado. -*s.* Tumbo, tropiezo.

flour [ˈflaʊər] [flaua'], *s.* Harina. **Fine flour.** flor de harina o harina fina.

flourish [ˈflʌrɪʃ] [fla-rish], *vn.* 1. Florecer; gozar de prosperidad. 2. Jactarse, gloriarse, vanagloriarse. 3. Escribir haciendo rasgos y adornos con la pluma. 4. Usar un lenguaje florido; amplificar. 5. Agitar una cosa en el aire moviéndola irregularmente. 6. *(Mús.)* Florear, tocar sin regla determinada. -*va.* 1. Florear, blandir, mover alguna cosa con la mano con vibraciones aceleradas. 2. Exornar, embellecer. **To flourish a sword,** vibrar una espada.

flourish, *s.* 1. Muestra o señal de adorno; fausto, ostentación; cualquier cosa hecha exclusivamente por lucimiento y vano alarde, en especial los dibujos, rasgos o adornos que se hacen con la pluma. 2. *(Mús.)* Floreo, preludio. 3. La acción de blandir.

flourisher [ˈflʌrɪʃər] [fla-ri-sha'], *s.* 1. La persona que se halla en un estado floreciente o muy próspero. 2. El que hace rasgos de adorno con la pluma.

flourishing [ˈflʌrɪʃɪŋ] [fla-ri-shin], *a.* Floreciente, que florece; próspero.

flourishingly [ˈflʌrɪʃɪŋlɪ] [fla-ri-shin-li], *adv.* Pomposamente; floridamente; prósperamente.

floury [ˈflʌrɪ] [fla-ri], *a.* Harinoso; que se parece a la harina, o está cubierto de ella.

flout [flaʊt] [flaut], *va.* Rechazar con menosprecio; hacer burla, befar, escarnecer. -*vn.* Burlarse, mofarse.

flout, *s.* Mofa, burla, escarnio, desprecio, insulto.

flouter [ˈflaʊtər] [flau-ta'], *s.* Mofador; burlador.

floutingly [ˈflaʊtɪŋlɪ] [flau-tin-li], *adv.* Insolentemente.

flow [floʊ] [flou], *vn.* 1. Fluir, correr lo líquido; manar. 2. *(Mar.)* Crecer la marea. 3. Dimanar, proceder, provenir; seguir como consecuencia. 4. Ondear, flotar. 5. Abundar. 6. Descargar sangre, como en la menstruación. -*va.* Inundar. **The tide flows and ebbs,** sube y baja la marea. **To flow into,** desaguar. **To flow away,** deslizarse, pasar. **Tears flowed from her eyes,** las lágrimas corrían de sus ojos.

flow, *s.* 1. *(Mar.)* Creciente de la marea. 2. Copia, abundancia, muchedumbre. 3. Flujo de palabras; torrente de voces.

flower [ˈflaʊər] [flaua'], *s.* 1. Flor. 2. Flor, la parte primera y más floreciente, lo más puro, esmerado y perfecto de alguna cosa; figura retórica. 3. Flor, adorno, belleza. 4. Vigor de la edad viril. 5. *pl.* *(Quím.)* Flor, la parte más sutil de los cuerpos sólidos que se pega a la cabeza del aludel en forma de polvo fino al tiempo de sublimarlos. **Flower-stalk,** pedúnculo. **Flower of an hour,** hibisco. **Flower de luce,** flor de lis, iris. **Eternal flower,** perpetua. **Sun-flower,** girasol, perdiguera o flor del sol. **Sultan lower,** especie de centaura. **Trumpet-flower,** bignonia, arraigadora. **Wind-flower,** anémone. **Flower-bed,** cuadro de jardín. **Flower-**

bud, capullo, botón de flor. **Flower-girl,** florera, ramilletera. **Flower-pot,** tiesto, florero, maceta de flores. **Bed of flowers,** lecho de flores. **She was the flower of the family,** ella era la mejor, la más perfecta de la familia.

flower, *vn.* 1. Florecer, echar flor los árboles y plantas. 2. Florecer, crecer en prosperidad. 3. *(Ant.)* Fermentar, hervir. -*va.* Florear, adornar con flores artificiales. 4. Cultivar plantas de flor.

flower-gentle [ˈflaʊədʒəntl] [flauer-yen-tel], *s.* *(Bot.)* Especie de amaranto.

flower-inwoven [ˌflaʊənˈwəvn] [flauer-in-vouen], *a.* Adornado con flores.

flowerage [ˈflaʊəreɪdʒ] [floue-reich], *s.* 1. Acopio de flores, las flores colectivamente. 2. El acto o estado de florecer.

flowered [ˈflaʊəd] [flaued] *a.* Florido, floreado

floweret [ˈflaʊərɪt] [flaue-ret], *s.* Florecilla, florecita.

flower-garden [ˈflaʊəgɑːdn] [flaua-gar-den], *s.* Jardín de flores.

floweriness [ˈflaʊərɪnɪs] [flaua-ri-nes], *s.* Abundancia de flores; floreo de palabras.

flowering [ˈflaʊərɪŋ] [flaua-rin], *a.* Que tiene flores evidentes; fenógamo, opuesto a criptógamo. -*s.* Flor, o el conjunto de flores; también, eflorescencia, el acto o estado de florecer.

flowering-bush [ˈflaʊərɪŋblʌʃ] [flaua-rin-blash], *s.* *(Bot.)* Amaranto.

flowerless [ˈflaʊəlɪs] [flaua-les], *a.* Sin flores, que no tiene flores.

flowerpot [ˈflaʊəpɒt] [flaua-pot], *s.* Maceta, tiesto.

flowery [ˈflaʊərɪ] [flaua-ri], *a.* Florido, lleno de flores; florido, embellecido con figuras de retórica, poético.

flowing [ˈfloʊɪŋ] [flouin], *a.* 1. Corriente; fluctuante; que echa de sí. 2. Ondeante, movido por la brisa; colgante; pendiente, agitándose. 3. *(Fig.)* Fácil, suelto. -*s.* Derrame, escape de líquidos; flujo, creciente del agua.

flowingly [ˈfloʊɪŋlɪ] [flouin-li], *adv.* Abundantemente, copiosamente.

flowingness [ˈfloʊɪŋnɪs] [flouin-nes], *s.* Dicción fluida.

flown [floʊn] [floun], *pp.* del verbo *to fly.* 1. Huido, escapado. 2. Hinchado, engreído.

flu [fluː] [flu], influenza, gripe, resfriado.

fluctuate [ˈflʌktʃʊeɪt] [fluk-chueit], *vn.* 1. Fluctuar, ondear, undular; mover, o moverse como las olas. 2. Fluctuar, avanzar y retroceder; vacilar o dudar en la resolución de alguna cosa; estar indeciso.

fluctuation [ˌflʌktʃʊˈeɪʃən] [fluk-tu-ei-son], *s.* Fluctuación, irresolución, instabilidad, agitación, incertidumbre, duda.

flue [fluː] [flu], *s.* 1. Cañón o campana de chimenea, humero. 2. Cañón de órgano con efectos de flauta. 3. Flus, tubo de caldera.

flue, flew [fluː] [flu], *s.* Pelusa, borra, polvillo que se desprende de las telas en las fábricas de tejidos.

fluency [ˈfluːənsɪ] [fluen-si], *s.* Fluidez; afluencia, facundia; copia, abundancia; volubilidad.

fluent [ˈfluːənt] [fluent], *a.* 1. Flúido, líquido. 2. Fluente, corriente. 3. Copioso, abundante. 4. Fácil, fluido de palabra. -*s.* Arroyo, agua corriente.

fluently [ˈfluːəntlɪ] [fluent-li], *adv.* Con afluencia, facundia o abundancia de expresiones.

fluff [flʌf] [flaf], *va.* 1. Mullir. 2. Olvidar un pasaje en una representación en el teatro, radio, etc.

fluff, *s.* 1. Pelusa, vello, lanilla. 2. Plumón. 3. *(Teat.)* Papel mal aprendido.

fluffy [ˈflʌfɪ] [fla-fi], *a.* Que consta o está cubierto de plumón o vello; blando y suelto.

fluid [ˈfluːɪd] [fluid], *s.* 1. Fluido. 2. Fluido, suco, jugo, los humores del cuerpo humano. -*a.* Fluido.

fluidity [fluːˈɪdɪtɪ] [flui-di-ti], **fluidness** [ˈfluːɪd] [fluid], *s.* Fluidez.

fluke [fluːk] [fluk] 1. Lombriz que se halla en las entrañas del ganado lanar. 2. *(Ingl.)* Acedía, pez de forma aplanada. 3. Uña de ancla, de arpón. 5. Chiripa. **To arrive by a fluke,** llegar por chiripa.

fluke (to), *v.* Chiripear.

flume ['fluːm] [flum], *s.* 1. Caño, conducto por lo común de madera, para llevar agua al molino, etc.; caz, canal de esclusa. 2. Cañada o paso angosto por donde sale un torrente. 3. *V.* CHUTE.

flummery ['fluːmərɪ] [flu-me-ri], *s.* 1. Manjar blanco, plato ligero hecho con la harina o almidón de maíz. 2. Originalmente, jalea de harina de avena. 3. Lisonja grosera, hojarasca, patarata, cháchara.

flung, *pret.* y *pp.* del verbo TO FLING.

flunk [flʌŋk] [flank], *v. (vul. E.U.) va.* Faltar a la obligación; esquivar, evitar. *-vn.* Salir completamente mal; cejar, retroceder; cortarse, turbarse.

flunk, *s. (E.U.)* Fracaso, suspenso (examination), reprobación.

flunky, flunkey ['flʌŋkɪ] [flan-ki], *s.* 1. Lacayo. 2. *(Fig.)* Hombre rastrero, servil.

fluor [floəʳ] [fluaʳ], *s.* 1. Fluidez; fluido. 2. Menstruación. **Fluor-spar,** *(Min.)* Espato fluor.

fluorescence [floəˈresns] [fluo-re-sens], *s.* 1. Flourescencia, la cualidad que tienen algunos cuerpos transparentes, cuando están iluminados, de despedir una luz de color diferente del suyo propio y del de la luz que los ilumina.

fluorescent [floəˈresnt] [fluo-re-sent], *a.* Fluorescente. **Fluorescent light,** luz flourescente. **Fluorescent lighting,** alumbrado fluorescente.

fluoric acid [ˌfloərɪkˈæsɪd] [fluo-rik-asid], *s. (Quím.)* Acido fluórico.

fluorid, fluoride ['floəraɪd] [fluo-raid], *s. (Quím.)* Fluoruro.

fluoridation [ˌfloərɪˈdeɪʃən] [fluo-ri-dei-shon], *s.* Fluoruración.

fluorin, fluorine ['floəriːn] [fluo-rin], *s.* Fluor, elemento gaseoso de color verde pálido.

fluorit ['floərɪt] [fluo-rit], *s.* Fluorita.

fluoroscope ['floərəskəʊp] [fluo-ros-koup], *s.* Fluoróscopo.

flurry ['flʌrɪ] [fla-ri], *s.* 1. Ráfaga, soplo repentino de viento. 2. Prisa, precipitación; agitación, conmoción, perturbación. 3. Chubasco o nevada con viento. 4. Estertor de la ballena herida por el arpón.

flurry, *va.* Confundir, atropellar; alarmar, poner en agitación; agitar, avergonzar.

flush [flʌʃ] [flash], *vn.* 1. Fluir con violencia; venir precipitadamente. 2. Ponerse colorado. *-va.* 1. Abochornar, poner colorado, sonrojar. 2. Engreír, dar alas a uno para que se entone. 3. Ser causa de que la sangre se suba a la cabeza. 4. Igualar, nivelar, llenar hasta la superficie (se usa a menudo en este sentido con la palabra *up*). 5. Echar a volar (birds).

flush, *va.* Inundar con agua; echar gran cantidad de agua para limpiar las cloacas. *-vn.* 1. Salirse, arrojarse, derramarse repentinamente. 2. Llenarse de agua.

flush, *a.* 1. Fresco, robusto, lleno de vigor; afectado. 2. Copioso, abundante; opulento, abundante en riquezas. **Flush-deck,** *(Mar.)* Puente corrido. 3. Nivelado, a nivel. *-s.* 1. Flujo rápido o copioso. 2. Flux, reunión de cartas o naipes de un mismo palo. 3. Copia, abundancia, afluencia. 4. Bandada de aves espantadas. 5. Frescura, rubor, bochorno. 6. Flor, florescencia.

flushing ['flʌʃɪŋ] [fla-shin], *s.* 1. Rubor, bochorno o rubicundez de la cara. 2. Acción de echar agua para limpiar un pozo, un albañal, etc.

fluster ['flʌstəʳ] [flas-taʳ], *va.* 1. Poner a uno colorado a fuerza de beber. achispar. 2. Confundir, atropellar; aturdirle a uno la cabeza.

flustered ['flʌstəd] [flas-terd], *a.* Medio borracho, calamocano, a medio vino o a medios pelos.

flute [fluːt] [flut], *s.* 1. Flauta. 2. *(Arq.)* Estría. 3. Rizado, pliegue.

flute, *va.* 1. Estriar. 2. Alechugar, rizar, plegar. *(Mex.)* Encarrujar, *-vn.* Tocar la flauta.

fluting ['fluːtɪŋ] [flu-tin], *s.* 1. *(Arq.)* Estriadura, acanaladura. 2. Rizado, pliegue, como en ciertas prendas de vestir de las mujeres. 3. El acto de hacer una estría, como en una columna. 4. Conjunto de estrías.

flutist ['fluːtɪst] [flu-tist], *s.* Flautista.

flutter ['flʌtəʳ] [fla-taʳ], *vn.* 1. Revolotear. 2. Pavonearse, hacer ostentación del tren o vestidos. 3. Agitarse con movimientos o undulaciones ligeras. 4. Estar agitado; hallarse en un estado de incertidumbre; moverse sin objeto fijo o irregularmente. *-va.* 1. Desordenar o poner en desorden, como se espanta a una bandada de pájaros. 2. Cambiar sin orden alguno el sitio o lugar de una cosa. 3. Agitar, alterar el ánimo. 4. *(Mar.)* Flamear. 5. Crujir.

flutter, *s.* Alboroto, tumulto, baraúnda, confusión; agitación, vibración, undulación.

fluttering ['flʌtərɪŋ] [fla-te-rin], *s.* Agitación, perturbación; confusión.

fluvial ['fluːvɪəl] [flu-vial], *a.* Fluvial, perteneciente a los ríos o formado por ellos.

flux [flʌks] [flaks], *s.* 1. Flujo, el acto de fluir. 2. Cambio, mudanza. 3. Concurso, confluencia. 4. Flujo o cámaras de materia líquida; disentería. 5. Fundente, lo que mezclado con un cuerpo lo hace derretir o fundirse. 6. Derretimiento, fusión de metales. *-a. (Ant.)* Inconstante, mudable.

flux, *va.* 1. Fundir, derretir. 2. Mezclar con, fundente.

fluxation [flʌkˈseɪʃən] [flak-sei-shon], *s.* El acto de dejar de existir y dar lugar a otros; mudanza.

fluxibility [ˌflʌksɪˈbɪlɪtɪ] [flak-si-bi-li-ti], *s.* Fluxibilidad; fusibilidad.

fluxion ['flʌkʃən] [flak-shon], *s.* 1. *(Med.)* Fluxión, acumulación de los líquidos en alguna parte del cuerpo a consecuencia de la irritación; la hinchazón dolorosa de un órgano que no llega a supuración. 2. El acto de fluir. 3. *(Mat.)* Cálculo diferencial.

fluxional ['flʌkʃənl] [flak-sho-nal], *a.* 1. Que se refiere al cálculo diferencial. 2. Que se derrite o fluye fácilmente.

fluxionary ['flʌkʃənərɪ] [flak-sho-na-ri], *a.* Perteneciente al cálculo diferencial.

fluxionist ['flʌkʃənɪst] [flak-sho-nist], *a.* El matemático que es perito en la ciencia del cálculo diferencial.

fly [flaɪ] [flai], *va.* y *vn. (pret.* FLEW [fluː] [flu], *pp.* FLOWN [flən] [flon]). 1. Volar. 2. Volar, desaparecerse de la vista. 3. Pasar ligeramente, moverse con rapidez. 4. Separar con violencia; hacer caer una cosa separándola de otra. 5. Acometer o embestir de repente. 6. Saltar, reventar, romperse alguna cosa con estallido. 7. Huir, escapar. 8. Fluctuar, sostenerse o ser sostenido en los aires o en el agua; desplegarse. 9. Hacer volar una cometa.

fly abroad o **about,** derramarse; esparcirse, propagarse.

fly at, echarse encima de, arrojarse o lanzarse sobre alguno; cazar o coger pájaros con halcón. **The woman flew at his face like a tigress,** la mujer le saltó a la cara como una tigresa.

fly away, volar, escaparse; dejar, abandonar.

fly back, quedarse parado sin poder andar; pegar coces un caballo; refugiarse, huir de la justicia; volver la espalda, retroceder; desdecirse.

fly down, bajar volando.

fly from, huir, escapar, evitar. **To fly from a danger,** evitar un peligro. **To fly in the face,** obrar o hacer algo atrevidamente, insultar. **To fly into a passion,** encenderse en cólera.

fly off, tomar un vuelo; desaparecer, evaporarse. **To fly off the handle.** *(fam.)* Perder los estribos, los nervios.

fly on, acometer violentamente.

fly open, abrirse una cosa de repente o con violencia. **To fly to pieces,** romperse en mil pedazos; *(Fig.)* Echar chispas o venablos.

fly out, desenfrenarse, entrar en furor. **To fly to arms,** recurrir a las armas. **Flying camp,** campo volante. **Flying coach,** diligencia. **With flying colors,** con banderas desplegadas; triunfante. **To let fly,** dejar marchar o volar; descargar, tirar; desplegar la bandera. **To let fly the top gallant sheets,** *(Mar.)* Volar las escotas de los juanetes.

fly, *s.* 1. Mosca. 2. Volante. *V.* FLYER. 3. Mosca artificial, el anzuelo cubierto de plumas, etc., que imitan un insecto. Se usa para pescar con caña. 4. Cabriolé, calesín, una especie de coche, ligero. **Fly of an ensign,** *(Mar.)* Vuelo de bandera.

Vegetable fly, especie de hongo que se cría en las Indias. 5. Adulador. **6.** *(Fig.)* Algo insignificante que estropea una cosa agradable. 7. Brragueta. 8. Toldo que se pone por encima de una tienda de campaña. **Gad-fly,** tábano. **Day-fly,** mosca efímera. **Spanish-fly,** cantárida. **Fly-paper,** papel para coger o matar moscas. **To die like flies,** morir como moscas.

fly, *s.* 1. Uno de los varios objetos, herramientas o utensilio que se mueven rápidamente por el aire; como, (a) el sacapliegos de una prensa; (b) brazo de romana; (c) volante de un péndulo o de una máquina; (d) la parte de la veleta que indica de qué lado sopla el viento. 2. Braguita, trampilla (de los pantalones.) 3. Vuelo. **Flies,** *(Teat.)* Telar.

flyaway ['flaɪweɪ] [flai-uei], *a.* 1. Ondeante, flameante, suelto. 2. Inconstante. 3. Casquivano.

fly-bitten ['flaɪbɪtn] [flai-bi-ten], *a.* Manchado o descolorado por las moscas.

fly-blow ['flaɪbloː] [flai-blo], *s.* Cresa, huevo de mosca.

fly-blow, *va.* 1. Depositar la mosca sus huevos. 2. Corromper la carne llenándola de cresas, contaminar.

flyblown ['flaɪbloʊn] [flai-bloun], *a.* Lleno de cresa o huevos de mosca. 2. *(Fig.)* Contaminado, corrompido.

fly-boat ['flaɪboʊt] [flai-bout], *s. (Mar.)* Flibote, especie de embarcación velera.

fly-by-night ['flaɪbaɪnaɪt] [flai-bai-nait], *s.* 1. Persona poco fiable. 2. Noctámbulo. 2. El que se escapa por la noche.

fly-catcher ['flaɪˌkætʃə'] [flai-ka-cha'], *s.* Ave que atrapa insectos al vuelo; papamoscas; moscareta. Muscicapa.

flyer ['flaɪə'] [flaia'], *s.* 1. Volador. 2. Fugitivo, el que huye. 3. El volante de un torno de asar. V. FLIER.

fly-fishing ['flaɪfɪʃɪŋ] [flai-fi-shin], *s.* Pesca con moscas artificiales.

flyflap ['flaɪflæp] [flai-flap], *s.* Mosqueador, espantamoscas.

flying ['flaɪɪŋ] [flai-in], *pa.* 1. Volante; volador; apto para el movimiento veloz y fácil. **Flying artillery,** artillería volante. 2. Flotante, undulante; desplegado. **Flying banners,** banderas desplegadas o flotantes. 3. Que se extiende más allá de lo ordinario, extra. 4. Rápido, veloz. **Flying-jib,** petifoque, cuarto foque. **Flying bridge,** puente volante. **Flying buttress,** *(Arq.)* Botares, arbotante. **Flying squadron,** escuadra ligera. *-s.* Vuelo, el acto de volar. **To shoot flying,** tirar al vuelo. *(Zool.)* dragón, dragón volador. **Flying field,** aeropuerto, campo de aviación. **Flying saucer,** platillo volante. **Flying sickness,** mal de altura. **To come off with flying colours,** salir triunfante, tener un éxito completo.

flying-fish ['flaɪŋfɪʃ] [flai-in-fish], *s.* Pez volador.

flying fortress ['flaɪŋ'fɔːtrɪs] [flai-in-for-tres], *s.* Fortaleza volante o aérea.

flying saucer ['flaɪŋ'sɔːsə'] [flai-in-so-sa'], *s.* Plato volador, disco luminos volador.

fly-leaf ['flaɪliːf] [flai-lif], *s.* Guarda de un libro.

fly-net ['flaɪnet] [flai-net], *s.* 1. Red que llevan los caballos para librarlos de las moscas. 2. Mosquitero.

fly-speck ['flaɪspek] [flai-spek], *s.* Punto o mancha diminuta que hace el excremento de la mosca u otro insecto; cualquiera cosa insignificante.

flytrap ['flaɪtræp] [flai-trap], *s.* Atrapamoscas, trampa para moscas.

flyweight ['flaɪweɪt] [flai-ueit], *s. (Boxeo)* Peso mosca.

fly-wheel ['flaɪwiːl] [flai-uil], *s.* Rueda volante, voladora.

foal [foʊl] [foul], *s.* Potro; potrillo; buche, el borrico mientras mama. **To be in foal o with foal,** estar preñada la yegua, burra, o camella.

foal, *va.* y *vn.* Parir una yegua o una burra; dar crías, producir potrillo o buches; procrear.

foal-foot ['foʊlfuːt] [foul-fut], *s.* V. COLTSFOOT.

foam [foʊm] [foum], *s.* Espuma. **Foam rubber,** hule de espuma.

foam, *vn.* 1. Espumar, criar o echar espuma. 2. Echar espumarajos por la boca, estar colérico. *-va.* Arrojar espuma.

foamy ['foʊmɪ] [fou-mi], *a.* Espumajoso, espumoso.

fob [fɒb] [fob], *s.* 1. Faltriquera pequeña, como la del reloj. 2. Bolsillo de reloj. Fob chain, cadena de reloj. 3. Engaño.

fob, *va.* Engañar, defraudar, pegársela a uno; disimular.

F. O. B. (Abreviatura de Free on board) *a.* y *adv.* L.A.B. Libre a bordo.

focal ['foʊkəl] [fou-kal], *a.* Focal, que pertenece al foco; céntrico. **Focal distance o length,** distancia focal, punto donde convergen los rayos luminosos.

focus ['foʊkəs] [fou-kos], *s.* Foco, el punto céntrico en que se unen muchos rayos de luz en un espejo u otro cuerpo.

focus, *va.* Enfocar, afocar, acomodar en foco; poner en foco, hallar el foco. **Focusing-screen,** pantalla o visera para poner en foco una imagen.

fodder ['fɒdə'] [fo-da'], *s.* Forraje, alimento basto a propósito para los ganados, pienso.

fodder, *va.* Dar forraje a las bestias.

fodderer ['fɒdərə'] [fo-de-ra'], *s.* Forrajeador.

foe [foʊ] [fou], *s.* Enemigo, perseguidor, antagonista, adversario.

foelike ['foʊlaɪk] [fou-laik], *a.* Que obra o procede con enemistad; como un enemigo, hostil.

foeman ['foʊmən] [fou-man], *s.* Enemigo, antagonista.

fætus ['fiːtəs] [fi-tos], *s.* Feto, la criatura que está perfectamente formada en el vientre de su madre.

fog [fɒg] [fog], *s.* 1. Niebla, neblina, bruma, calina. 2. Extravío, confusión perplejidad. 3. *(Foto.)* Niebla o capa que obscurece una plancha revelada. **Fog-horn,** sirena.

fog, *va.* 1. Obscurecer; en sentido fotográfico, cubrir como con una niebla, empañar. *-vn.* 1. Hacerse brumoso, nebuloso. 2. *(Foto.)* Hacerse indistinto por una capa o película que oscurece. 3. En Escocia, criar musgo.

fog, fogge, foggage [ˈfɒgi:] [fo-gui], *s.* 1. La segunda cosecha de hierba de una estación; también, hierba seca que permanece en el campo durante el invierno. 2. *(Scot.)* Musgo.

fogbank ['fɒgbæŋk] [fog-bank], *s.* Neblina sobre el mar.

fogbound ['fɒgbaʊnd] [fog-baund], *a.* Envuelto en la niebla. 2. Inmovilizado o parado por la niebla.

foggily ['fɒgɪlɪ] [fo-gui-li], *adv.* Obscuramente, con nieblas; brumosamente.

fogginess ['fɒgɪnɪs] [fo-gui-nes], *s.* La oscuridad que produce la niebla.

foggy ['fɒgɪ] [fo-gui], *a.* 1. Nebuloso, brumoso, lleno de nieblas. 2. *(Bot.)* Mohoso, lleno de musgo. 3. *(Foto.)* Oscurecido como por niebla.

foghorn ['fɒghɔːn] [fog-jorn], *s. (Mar.)* Sirena, bocina.

fogram ['fɒgræm] [fo-gram], *a.* Anticuado, atrasado.

fogy ['fɒgɪ] [fo-gui], *a.* Vejestorio, persona de ideas anticuadas.

fogysm ['fɒgɪzm] [fo-guism], *s.* Obscurantimo, afición a las ideas anticuadas.

foh! [fɔː] [fo], *inter.* ¡Quita allá! expresión de enojo o disgusto.

foible ['fɔɪbl] [foi-bol], *s.* 1. Debilidad, el flaco; defecto leve de carácter. 2. La porción de una espada o de un florete desde el medio hasta la punta.

foil [fɔɪl] [foil], *va.* 1. Hacer nulo, vano; frustrar, deshacer al enemigo aunque sin ganar una completa victoria. 2. Embotar; adormecer. 3. Confundir, derrotar.

foil, *s.* 1. Hoja delgada de metal; pan, hoja de oro o plata para dorar o platear. 2. Hoja de estaño, la que se pone a un espejo por medio del azogue. 3. El fondo del diamante u otra piedra preciosa, la lentejuela puesta para aumentar el brillo; de aquí, contraste, todo lo que da realce a alguna cosa. 4. *(Arq.)* Hoja, lóbulo. 5. Florete, espada que se usa en la esgrima.

foil, *s.* 1. Huella, pista, rastro que deja la caza. 2. Caída imperfecta en la lucha cuerpo a cuerpo. 3. *(Des.)* Chasco, suceso contrario o adverso.

foilable ['fɔɪləbl] [foi-la-bol], *a.* Vencible; lo que se puede inutilizar o deshacer.

foiler ['fɔɪlə'] [foi-la'], *s.* Frustrador.

foiling ['fɔɪlɪŋ] [foi-lin], *s.* Rastro en la hierba.

foil-wrapped [fɔɪl'wræpt] [foil-rapt], *a.* Envuelto en papel estaño.

foin [fɔɪn] [foin], *vn.* Dar estocadas en la esgrima. *-va.* Punzar, aguijonear.

foin, *s.* 1. Garduña, fuina. 2. (*Des.*) Estocada, golpe dado con la punta de la espada o florete.

foist [fɔɪst] [foist], *va.* Insertar alguna voz o cláusula en un escrito; meterse, introducirse sin razón (seguido de *into* o *upon*). **To foist a candidate upon a party,** imponer injustamente un candidato a un partido.

foister ['fɔɪstə'] [fois-ta'], *s.* Falsificador, mentiroso.

fold [fəʊld] [fould], *s.* 1. Redil, el cercado o corral para encerrar ovejas; hato de ganado lanar; y (*Fig.*) una iglesia o la totalidad de la Iglesia cristiana. 2. Doblez, pliegue, plegadura, arruga. 3. Otro tanto. 4. (*Des.*) Límite, lindero. **Twofold,** duplo. **Fourfold,** cuádruplo.

fold, *va.* 1. Doblar, plegar. 2. Poner una cosa junto a otra, ajustar. 3. Abrazar, enlazar; cerrar, incluir. 4. Envolver, encerrar. 5. Encerrar ganado lanar en el redil; incluir. *-vn.* Doblarse o plegarse una cosa sobre otra, como las vidrieras y puertas plegadizas de dos hojas, ciertas persianas, etc. **To fold the arms,** cruzar los brazos. **To fold a letter,** doblar una carta.

folder ['fəʊldə'd] [foul-da'], *s.* 1. Plegador, doblador. 2. Plegadera. 3. Folleto, mapa, etc., plegadizo en forma compacta. 4. Carpeta (papers).

folderol ['fəʊldərəl] [foul-de-rol], *a.* Absurdo, desatinado. *-s.* Desatino, pampirolada, pampringada.

folding ['fəʊldɪŋ] [foul-din], *a.* Plegadizo, dobladizo. *-s.* 1. La acción de plegar o doblar. 2. El acto de cerrar ganado lanar en tierra labrantía. **Folding door,** puerta de dos hojas o plegadiza. **Folding camera, folding chair,** cámara, silla plegadiza. **Folding-machine,** máquina de plegar, plegadora mecánica. **Folding screen,** biombo.

fold-net ['fəʊldnet] [fould-net], *s.* Arañuelo, red muy delgada para coger pájaros por la noche.

foliaceous [ˌfəʊlɪ'eɪʃəs] [fou-li-ei-shos], *a.* 1. Foliáceo, de la naturaleza o forma de una hoja. 2. Laminado, que se presenta en láminas, como ciertos minerales.

foliage ['fəʊlɪɪdʒ] [fou-lieich], *s.* 1. Follaje, frondosidad. 2. Ramillete de hojas, flores y ramas. 3. Follaje, adorno de escultura y arquitectura.

foliate ['fəʊlɪeɪt] [fou-lieit], *va.* 1. Batir hojas de oro, plata u otro metal. 2. Azogar un espejo. 3. Follar (formar en hojas). 4. Adornar con follaje.

foliation [ˌfəʊlɪ'eɪʃən] [fou-liei-shon], *s.* 1. El acto de batir las hojas de oro, plata u otro metal. 2. (*Bot.*) Foliación, la disposición que guardan las hojas en las plantas. 3. El acto de desenvolverse, salir o apuntar las hojas. 4. Laminación.

foliature ['fəʊlɪətʃə'] [fou-lia-cha'], *s.* V. FOLIATION en todas sus acepciones.

folio ['fəʊlɪəʊ] [fou-liou], *s.* 1. Infolio, libro o tomo en folio. 2. (*Com.*) Hoja, folio, página numerada de un libro o registro. 3. Número de palabras que sirve como unidad para medir la extensión de un escrito.

foliole ['fəʊlɪəʊl] [fou-lioul], *s.* (*Bot.*) Folíolo.

foliose ['fəʊlɪəʊz] [fou-lios], *a.* Hojudo, fronduoso.

folk [fəʊk] [fouk], *s.* 1. (*Fam.*) Gente, personas, el género humano. 2. Nación, raza, tribu, pueblo (raramente usado en plural). 3. *pl.* La gente; (*fam. E.U.*) parentesco, parientes, los que son de la misma familia. **Old folks,** viejos o gente vieja. **I never saw such folks,** nunca he visto gente semejante. **What will folks say?** ¿Qué dirá la gente? **Folk tale,** cuento popular.

folklore ['fəʊkbɔː'] [fou-kla'], *s.* Folklore, conjunto de las tradiciones, creencias y costumbres populares.

folk music ['fəʊkˌmjuːzɪk] [fouk-miu-sik], *s.* Música folklórica.

folk song ['fəʊksɒŋ] [fouk-son], *s.* Canto folklórico, canción o balada folklórica.

folkway ['fəʊkweɪ] [fouk-uei], *s.* Costumbre tradicional de un pueblo o grupo social.

follicle ['fɒlɪkl] [fo-li-kol], *s.* 1. (*Anat.*) Folículo, un saquito o cuerpo pequeño membranoso cuyas paredes secretan un flúido que se derrama por la abertura diminuta que hay en uno de sus extremos. 2. (*Bot.*) Folículo, hollejo. 3. (*Ento.*) Capullo.

follicular ['fɒlɪkɪkjolə'] [fo-li-kiu-la'], *a.* Folicular; foliculoso, que tiene o produce folículos.

follow ['fɒləʊ] [fo-lou], *va.* 1. Seguir, ir detrás de alguien; moverse, andar detrás de alguno en la misma dirección; acompañar, escoltar, ir en compañía. 2. Seguir, venir después, suceder en orden o tiempo. 3. Perseguir. 4. Imitar; obedecer, copiar. 5. Obrar conforme a; ponerse de parte de; tener, sostener las mismas opiniones. 6. Aplicarse, dedicarse a ; cuidar sus asuntos; poner en práctica. 7. Observar, tener en vista o en la mente. 8. Resultar, ser consecuencia de algo. 9. Procurar obtener lo que se desea. *-vn.* 1. Seguir, venir una persona o cosa tras otra. 2. Seguirse, suceder y continuar una cosa a otra. 3. Seguirse, originarse, resultar, provenir. **To follow the law,** estudiar el derecho. **To follow one's business,** cuidar de sus negocios. **To follow one's pleasures,** abandonarse a los placeres. **To follow again,** volver a seguir. **It follows,** síguese, resulta, la consecuencia de eso es. **As follows,** como sigue. **To follow up,** continuar, proseguir. **To follow on,** continuar prosiguiendo, perseverar.

follower ['fɒləʊə'] [fo-loua'], *s.* 1. Seguidor; acompañante. 2. Dependiente, criado. 3. Discípulo; imitador, copiador; secuaz, partidario; obsequiante, amante; adherente, allegado, compañero. 3. Criado. 4. (*Mec.*) Parte de una máquina que recibe el movimiento de otra. **Followers,** *pl.* Comitiva, séquito.

following ['fɒləʊɪŋ] [fo-louin], *a.* Siguiente, próximo, subsiguiente. 2. Resultante, consiguiente. 3. Adherentes, partidarios, secuaces. 5. Profesión, carrera.

follow-up ['fɒləʊʌp] [fo-lou-ap], *s.* Recordatorio, continuidad. **Follow-up system,** sistema de cartas recordatorias para la correspondencia comercial, etc.

folly ['fɒlɪ] [fo-li], *s.* 1. Tontería, ignorancia, extravagancia, locura, patochada, bobería; disparate en lo que se hace o dice. 2. (*Des.*) Vicio, falta de rectitud. 3. Ligereza, debilidad, indiscreción, fragilidad.

foment [fəʊ'ment] [fou-ment], *va.* 1. Fomentar, dar calor natural o artificial; dar baños calientes. 2. Fomentar, proteger, patrocinar. 3. Provocar, excitar, instigar a la violencia.

fomentation [ˌfəʊmen'teɪʃən] [fou-men-tei-shon], *s.* 1. Fomentación, fomento. 2. Excitación, provocación, instigación.

fomenter ['fəʊmentə'] [fou-men-ta'], *s.* Fomentador, instigador.

fond [fɒnd] [fond], *a.* 1. Apasionado, demasiadamente indulgente; enloquecido, atontado o loco de contento. 2. Afectuoso, amoroso, cariñoso. 3. Loco, vano, imprudente, extravagante, frívolo. 4. Aficionado. 5. (*Ant.*) Disparatado, indiscreto. **To be fond of,** gustar extraordinariamente de alguna cosa, estar apasionado, enamorado o loco por ella. **A fond mother,** una madre cariñosa.

fondant ['fɒndənt] [fon-dant], *s.* Pasta de azúcar.

fondle ['fɒndl] [fon-del], *va.* Mimar, hacer caricias y halagos a alguno.

fondler ['fɒndlə'] [fond-la'], *s.* Mimador. (*fam.*) Mimón.

fondling ['fɒndlɪŋ] [fon-dlin], *s.* 1. Favorito, querido; niño mimado o mal criado. 2. Tonto.

fondly ['fɒndlɪ] [fon-dli], *adv.* Locamente, cariñosamente.

fondness ['fɒndnɪs] [fond-nes], *s.* 1. (*Ant.*) Tontería, locura, debilidad. 2. Terneza, pasión loca, apego poco racional; inclinación, afición, pasión por alguna cosa.

fonetic, *a.* V. PHONETIC.

font [fɒnt] [font], *s.* 1. Pila de bautismo. 2. Fuente o manantial. 3. Fundición, todo el surtido de caracteres de imprenta de un mismo grado.

fontanel [ˌfɒntəˈnel] [fon-ta-nel], s. 1. (*Anat.*) Fontanela, cada uno de los espacios que, en los niños recién nacidos median entre algunos huesos del cráneo hasta que se completa su osificación. 2. (*Ant.*) Fuente. V. ISSUE.

fonticulus [fɒnˈtɪkələs] [fon-ti-ko-los], s. Fontículo, hoyuela.

food [fuːd] [fud], s. 1. Alimento, comida; vituallas, víveres; pasto de los animales. 2. Lo que alimenta, mantiene activo o sostiene. **To give food for,** dar materia para.

foodful [ˈfuːdfʊl] [fud-ful], a. Fértil, fructífero.

foodless [ˈfuːdlɪs] [fud-les], a. Estéril, infructuoso.

foodstuffs [ˌfuːdsˈtʌfs] [fud-stafs], s. pl. Comestibles.

fool [fuːl] [ful], s. 1. Insensato, bobo, idiota, mentecato; tonto, necio. 2. Persona de pocos alcances, sin llegar a ser bobo o idiota. 3. Bufón, truhán, chocarrero. **To play the fool,** hacer el bobo. **To make a fool of one,** mofarse de alguno, hacer burla de él; frustrar. 4. (*Teol.*) Malvado. 5. Hazmerreír, el que es objeto de la irrisión de otros. **April fool,** inocente, inocentón.

fool, vn. Tontear, divertirse, chancear, juguetear diciendo o haciendo tonterías. -va. 1. Despreciar, chasquear; entontecer. 2. Engañar, defraudar, chupar. **To fool one with promises,** traer entretenido o embaucado a alguno con vanas esperanzas. **To fool one of his money,** pelar o desollar a uno, robarle el dinero.

foolery [ˈfuːləri] [fu-le-ri], s. Tontería, bobada, bobería.

fool-happy [ˈfuːlˈhæpi] [ful-ja-pi], a. Feliz por casualidad y sin haber puesto nada por su parte para serlo.

folhardiness [ˈfuːlˌhɑːdinɪs] [ful-jar-di-nes], s. Temeridad, locura.

foolhardy [ˈfuːlˌhɑːdi] [ful-jar-di], a. Arrojado, temerariamente audaz, locamente arriesgado.

fooling [ˈfuːlɪŋ] [fu-lin], s. Broma, engaño. **No fooling, without fooling,** en serio, hablando en serio.

foolish [ˈfuːlɪʃ] [fu-lish], a. 1. Fatuo, loco, escaso de juicio. 2. Bobo, tonto, indiscreto; malvado, necio. 3. Absurdo, ridículo.

foolishly [ˈfuːlɪʃli] [fu-lish-li], adv. Fatuamente, bobamente, sin juicio.

foolishness [ˈfuːlɪʃnɪs] [fu-lish-nes], s. Tontería, necedad, bobería, imprudencia.

foolproof [ˈfuːlpruːf] [ful-pruf], a. 1. Muy sencillo, fácil, a prueba de inexpertos. 2. Fuerte, resistente.

foolscap [ˈfuːlskæp] [ful-scap], s. 1. Papel ministro; papel de escribir plegado de modo que haga páginas de casi 13 por 8 pulgadas. 2. Gorro de bufón.

fool-trap [ˈfuːltræp] [ful-trap], s. Engañabobos.

foot [fʊt] [fut], s. (pl. FEET). 1. Pie; pata (of animal, chair). **Hind foot,** pata trasera. **From head to foot,** de pies a cabeza. 2. Pie, la parte inferior de alguna cosa; base. 3. (*Mil.*) Infantería; en este sentido no tiene plural. 4. Pie, fundamento, principio o escalón para adquirir otra cosa o ascender a ella. 5. Pie, medida de doce pulgadas, equivalente a 3,05 decímetros. 6. Paso, movimiento, acción. 7. Pie, cierto número de sílabas que constituyen parte de un verso. **On o by foot,** a pie. **The enemy disputed the ground foot by foot,** los enemigos disputaron el campo palmo a palmo. **On foot,** (a) De pie o a pie. (b) En estado de salud, activo. (c) Que va adelantando. **To be on foot,** estar haciendo alguna cosa; organizarse. **To know the length of one's foot,** conocer a uno, o comprenderle bien; saber los puntos que calza. **To put one's best foot foremost,** (fam.) esmerarse, hacer lo más que se pueda. **To put one's foot down,** (fam.) expresarse firmemente; tomar una resolución determinada. **To put one's foot in it,** meter la pata; hallarse en dificultades, por error o intervención oficiosa. **To set on foot,** poner en pie, empezar. **Under foot,** (a) Debajo de los pies. (b) (Fig.) En el camino (formando obstáculo); también, en poder de. **To trample** o **tread under foot,** pisotear.

foot, vn. 1. Bailar, saltar, brincar, andar a pie. 2. (fam.) Sumar, alcanzar un total de. -va. 1. Patear, tirar coces; pisar o pisotear. 2. Establecer, fijar; poner pies a alguna cosa. 3. (Fam. E.U.) Pagar una cuenta; pagar las costas; **To foot fhe**

bill, pagar la cuenta, los gastos, las consecuencias. 4. Sumar una columna de guarismos y poner la suma al pie.

footage [ˈfʊteɪdʒ] [fu-teich], s. 1. Longitud o distancia en pies. 2. (*Cine*) metraje.

foot-ball [ˈfʊtbɔːl] [fut-bol], s. 1. Pelota o balón para jugar con los pies. 2. Fútbol.

foot-band [ˈfʊtbænd] [fut-band], s. Destacamento de infantería.

footboard [ˈfʊtbɔːd] [fut-bord], s. 1. Pedal de una máquina; estribo (car). 2. Tabla del pescante, de la parte delantera de un coche donde se apoyan los pies. 3. Pie de la cama.

foot-boy [ˈfʊtbɔɪ] [fut-boi], s. Volante, lacayo.

foot-breadth [ˈfʊtbredθ] [fut-bredz], s. El espacio o lugar que puede cubrir un pie.

foot-bridge [ˈfʊtbrɪdʒ] [fut-brich], s. Puente angosto por el que pueden pasar solamente gentes a pie.

foot-cloth [ˈfʊtklɒθ] [fut-kloz], s. Gualdrapa, alfombrilla.

footfall [ˈfʊtɪd] [fu-tid], a. Formado como un pie.

footfall [ˈfʊtfɔːl] [fut-fol], s. El sonido de un paso; paso, pisada.

foot-fight [ˈfʊtfaɪt] [fut-fait], s. Batalla de a pie.

footgear [ˈfʊtɡɪəʳ] [fut-guiaʳ] s. Calzado; medias, calcetines.

foot-guards [ˈfʊtɡɑːdz] [fut-gards], s. pl. Guardias del rey que sirven a pie.

foothill [ˈfʊthɪl] [fut-jil], s. Cerro al pie de una montaña o colina.

foothold [ˈfʊthəʊld] [fut-jould], s. 1. Paraje o espacio en que cabe el pie; pie, fundamento seguro; posición establecida. **To lose one's foothold,** resbalar. 2. Chanclo de goma que no cubre el taión.

footing [ˈfʊtɪŋ] [fu-tin], s. 1. Pie, base, fundamento, lugar donde se pone el pie. 2. Piso, paso; baile, danza. 3. Establecimiento, estado, condición, posición fija. 4. Pie, fundamento, estribo, zócalo saliente. 5. Sumar de una columna. 6. El acto de añadir un pie a alguna cosa. **On a war footing,** bajo pie de guerra. **We are on equal footing,** en pie de igualdad, estamos en igualdad de condiciones. **To be on friendly footing with,** estar en relaciones amistosas con.

footless, a. V. FEETLESS. 1. Sin pie, sin base. 2. Torpe, desmañado.

foot-lights [ˈfʊtlaɪts] [fut-laits], s. pl. Candilejas, línea de luces en el proscenio del teatro.

foot-loose [ˈfʊtluːs] [fut-lus], a. Libre, sin restricciones, ni obligaciones.

footman [ˈfʊtmən] [fut-man], s. 1. Lacayo. 2. V. FOOT-SOLDIERS.

footmark [ˈfʊtmɑːk] [fut-mark], s. V. FOOTPRINT. Huella, pisada.

foot-note [ˈfʊtnəʊt] [fut-nout], s. Anotación debajo de un escrito, nota al pie.

foot-pace [ˈfʊtpeɪs] [fut-peis], s. Descanso de escalera; paso lento o corto.

foot-path [ˈfʊtpɑːθ] [fut-paz], s. Senda, vereda; acera.

foot-post [ˈfʊtpəʊst] [fut-poust], s. Correo de a pie.

footprint [ˈfʊtprɪnt] [fut-print], s. Huella, pisada, vestigio, impresión del pie.

footrest [ˈfʊtrest] [fut-rest], s. Escabel, banco para descansar los pies.

footrope [ˈfʊtrəʊp] [fut-roup], s. 1. Marchapié. 2. (Mar.) Relinga del pujamen.

foot-rule [ˈfʊtruːl] [fut-rul], s. Regla o medida de doce pulgadas.

foots [ˈfʊtz] [futs], s. Sedimiento, heces.

foot-soldier [ˈfʊtˌsəʊldʒəʳ] [fut-soul-diaʳ], s. Soldado que marcha y pelea a pie.

footsore [ˈfʊtsɔːʳ] [fut-saʳ], a. Que tiene los pies doloridos o lastimados de tanto andar.

foot-stalk [ˈfʊtstɔːk] [fut-stok], s. (Bot.) Pedúnculo, pezón.

foot-stall [ˈfʊtstɔːl] [fut-stol], s. Estribo de mujer para montar.

footstep [ˈfʊtstep] [fut-step], s. 1. Paso, la acción del pie al andar; sonido de un paso. 2. Paso, vestigio, señal, indicio, huella.

foot-stool [ˈfʊtstuːl] [fut-stul], *s.* Escabelo, escabel, tarimilla, banqueta.

footway [ˈfʊtweɪ] [fut-uei], *s.* 1. Sendero, senda, camino para peatones. 2. (*Ingl.*) Acera.

footwear [ˈfʊtweəˈ] [fut-uea'], *s.* Calzado.

footwork [ˈfʊtwɜːk] [fut-uek], *s.* 1. Movimiento de los pies en el boxeo, el baile, juego de futbol, etc. 2. (*Fam.*) Trabajo que se hace a pie para alguna investigación periodística.

footworn [ˈfʊtwɔːn] [fut-uorn], *a.* Estropeado por el paso de los pies. **Footworn carpet**, alfombra gastada por las pisadas. **Footworn traveler**, viajero cansado de caminar.

foozle [ˈfuːzl] [fu-sel], *v.* Hacer pifias. (Golf) Jugar mal. estropear la jugada.

foozler [ˈfuːzlə'] [fus-la'], *s.* Chafallón, chambón.

fop [fɒp] [fop], *s.* 1. Petimetre, pisaverde, currutaco, lechuguino. 2. Presumido, casquivano.

foppery [ˈfɒpəɪ] [fo-pe-ri], *s.* Perifollos, afectación en el vestir.

fopling [ˈfɒplɪŋ] [fo-plin], *s.* Petimetrillo.

foppish [ˈfɒpɪʃ] [fo-pish], *a.* Vano, ocioso; vanidoso, afectado, presumido.

for [fɔːˈ] [fa'], *prep.* (Palabra de muy amplia aplicación; indica por lo general la razón de un acto o el objeto que se procura o desea). 1. Por, a causa de. 2. En vista de, en consideración a; con respecto o con relación a; en cuanto a. 3. Para; lo que indica el objeto, el destino o la tendencia. 4. En busca de, según lo que, hacia; en favor o en provecho de; por motivo de; en honor o por el nombre de. 5. Con destino a. **Bound for Veracruz**, destinado a Veracruz. 6. Al grado, punto o número de. 7. A pesar de. 8. Mientras, durante; desde; por (en sentido futuro). *-conj.* 1. Porque, para que; pues. 2. Por cuanto, en atención a que. **As for me**, tocante a mí. **For as much**, respecto a, en cuanto a, por lo tocante a. **For why?** ¿por qué, para qué? ¿a qué? **For fear**, de miedo. **For pity**, de lástima. **For the present**, por ahora. **It is impossible for me to do it**, no puedo hacerlo, o me es imposible hacerlo. **For all that**, a pesar de eso; con todo eso. **For ever**, por o para siempre. **I took it for granted**, lo tomé por hecho, o por concedido. **To serve for**, servir de. **For the last five years of his life**, durante los últimos cinco años de su vida. **For the time to come**, en lo venidero, en lo futuro. **For aught**, en lo que, a lo que. **It is true for all that I know**, es verdad a lo que creo. **But for**, si no fuese por, a no ser por. **I should do it but for her**, lo haría, si no fuese por ella. **Thus much for**, esto por lo que a tal o cual cosa se refiere. **For shame!** ¡qué vergüenza! **For God's sake!** ¡por Dios, por amor de Dios! **Oh! for beter times!** ¡Oh! vengan tiempos mejores! **A remedy for headache**, un remedio para el dolor de cabeza.

for-. Prefijo que equivale a re- o muy. **Forbreak**, hacer añicos. **Forspend**, cansar al extremo, agotar. **Fordry**, reseco.

forage [ˈfɒrɪdʒ] [fo-reich], *vn.* 1. Forrajear, andar vagando en busca de forraje, particularmente en tiempo de guerra. 2. Proveer de forraje. *-va.* Recorrer una comarca para obtener forraje y víveres.

forage, *s.* 1. Forraje, pasto, toda especie de alimento para el ganado, particularmente para los caballos en tiempo de guerra. 2. (*Mil.*) **Forage cap**, gorra usada por la infantería.

forager [ˈfɒrɪdʒə'] [fo-rei-cha'], *s.* Forrajeador, (*ant.*) forrajero.

foraminifera [ˌfɒræmɪˈnɪfərə] [fo-ra-mi-ni-fe-ra], *s. pl.* Foraminíferos, protozoarios que forman el primer orden de la clase de los rizópodos. Son todos microscópicos y comprenden las especies primeras que aparecieron en el mundo.

foraminous [ˈfɒræmɪnəs] [fo-ra-mi-nos], *a.* Agujereado, lleno de agujeros.

foramuch [ˈfɒrəmʌtʃ] [fo-ra-mach], *conj.* **Foramuch as**, puesto que, ya que, visto que, por cuanto.

foray [ˈfɒreɪ] [fo-rei], *s.* Correría, irrupción; saqueo, pillaje. *-va.* Saquear, pillar, despojar.

forbade [fəˈbeɪd] [fo-beid], *pret.* del verbo FORBID.

forbear [fɔːˈbeəˈ] [fo-bea'], *vn.* (*pret.* FORBORE [ˈfɔːˈbɔːˈ] [fo-ba'], *pp.* FORBORNE [ˈfɔːˈbɔːn] [fo-born]. 1. Pararse, reprimirse, guardarse. 2. Abstenerse, dejar de reprimirse, guardarse. 3. (*Ant.*) Tener paciencia, contenerse. **I can not forbear laughing at it**, no puedo menos que reírme de ello. *-va.* 1. Omitir, dejar de hacer; evitar, abstenerse de; aguantar. 2. Tratar con dulzura.

forbearance [fɔːˈbeərəns] [fo-bea-rans], *s.* 1. El acto de evitar y precaver que suceda alguna cosa, antiguamente evitación. 2. Intermisión, interrupción. 3. Cachaza. 4. Dulzura, suavidad, paciencia, indulgencia, clemencia. 5. (*Com.*) Espera, prórroga.

forbearer [fɔːˈbeərə'] [fo-bea-ra'], *s.* El que interrumpe o evita.

forbearing [fɔːˈbeərɪŋ] [fo-bea-rin], *a.* Paciente, indulgente; dispuesto a abstenerse.

forbid [fəˈbɪd] [fo-bid], *va.* (*pret.* FORBADE, *pp.* FORBIDDEN, algunas veces también FORBID). 1. Prohibir, vedar; mandar que no se haga una cosa, o la abstención de ella. 2. Impedir, estorbar. **God forbid**, Dios no quiera, no permita Dios. *-vn.* Prohibir.

forbiddance [fəˈbɪdəns] [fo-bi-dans], *s.* (Poco us.) Prohibición.

forbiddenly [fəˈbɪdənlɪ] [fo-bi-den-li], *adv.* Ilícitamente.

forbiddenness [fəˈbɪdɪnnɪs] [fo-bi-den-nes], *s.* La calidad que hace a una cosa digna de prohibición.

forbidder [fəˈbɪdə'] [fo-bi-da'], *s.* El que prohibe.

forbidding [fəˈbɪdɪŋ] [fo-bi-din], *a.* Aborrecible, repugnante, prohibitivo, repusivo, desagradable. *-s.* Obstáculo, oposición.

forbore, *pret.* del verbo TO FORBEAR.

forby [ˈfɔːbɪ] [fo-bi], *adv.* y *prep.* (*Scot.*) 1. Además, a más de esto, fuera que. 2. (*Irel.*) Cerca de, más allá de.

force [fɔːs] [fors], *s.* 1. Fuerza, vigor, robustez, energía, virtud, poder, eficacia; firmeza de las leyes. 2. Fuerza, violencia, agravio. 3. Toda causa de movimiento. 4. Fuerzas, las armadas y ejércitos de un estado. 5. Necesidad, precisión, hado, destino. **Electromotive force**, fuerza electromotriz. **Main force**, fuerza mayor. **Motive, moving force**, fuerza motriz. **Forcepump**, bomba impelente. **Tensile force**, fuerza de tensión.

force, *va.* 1. Forzar, violentar; obligar o precisar por fuerza; coger alguna cosa a la fuerza. 2. Impeler, esforzar; constreñir. 3. Forzar, entrar y sujetar a fuerza de armas alguna plaza. 4. Forzar, dominar por la fuerza; violar, conocer a una mujer carnalmente contra su voluntad. 5. Mechar, rellenar, tratándose de guisados. 6. (*Hort.*) Forzar, apresurar, hacer madurar temprano. 7. Afinar, purificar los vinos. 8. (*Des.*) Reforzar un puesto, una guarnición, etc., con soldados. **To force along**, hacer avanzar o adelantar. **To force away**, obligar a alejarse. **To force back**, rechazar, hacer retroceder. **To force down**, obligar a bajar. **To force from**, obligar a salir, echar de alguna parte. **To force in**, clavar, meter un clavo, una espada, etc., romper, penetrar por un escuadrón o por un gentío; entrar por fuerza. **To force out**, arrancar, sacar u obtener por fuerza o con violencia; obligar a salir de alguna parte. **To force up**, hacer subir por fuerza.

forced [fɔːst] [forst], *pp./a.* Forzado, hecho con gran esfuerzo; afectado, exagerado, opuesto a lo natural. **Forced landing**, aterrizaje forzoso. **By forced marches**, a marchas forzadas.

forcedly [ˈfɔːsɪdlɪ] [for-sid-li], *adv.* Forzadamente, de una manera forzada; de un modo contrario a lo natural.

forcedness [ˈfɔːsɪdnɪs] [for-sid-nes], *s.* Constreñimiento, compulsión, apremio.

forceful [ˈfɔːsfʊl] [fors-ful], *a.* 1. Fuerte, potente, poderoso. 2. Dado o impelido por la violencia; violento.

forcefully [ˈfɔːsfʊlɪ] [fors-fu-li], *adv.* Forzosamente; violentamente.

forceless [ˈfɔːslɪs] [fors-les], *a.* Endeble, débil.

forcemeat [ˈfɔːsmiːt] [fors-mit], *s.* Relleno, embutido, salpicón. (Voz culinaria).

forceps [ˈfɔːseps] [for-seps], *s.* Fórceps, pinzas, tenaza. **Artery forceps,** *(Cir.)* Pinzas de torsión. **Bullet forceps,** sacabalas. **Dressing forceps,** pinzas de curación. **Obstetrical forceps,** fórceps de comadrón, muy usado en los partos laboriosos. **Stage forceps,** pinzas para la plataforma del microscopio.

forcer [ˈfɔːsəʳ] [for-saʳ], *s.* 1. Forzador; vencedor. 2. Lo que fuerza, impele o violenta. 3. Embolo, el macho de la bomba impelent

forcible [ˈfɔːsɪbl] [for-si-bol], *a.* 1. Fuerte, potente; eficaz, poderoso; violento. 2. Enérgico; de gran peso; concluyente; obligatorio.

forcibleness [ˈfɔːsɪblnɪs] [for-si-bol-nes], *s.* Fuerza, violencia.

forcibly [ˈfɔːsɪblɪ] [for-si-bli], *adv.* Fuertemente, forzadamente; violentamente, por fuerza.

forcing [ˈfɔːsɪŋ] [for-sin], *a. y gerundio* de FORCE. 1. Impelente. 2. Madurador; clarificador del vino por un procedimiento rápido. -*s.* La acción del verbo *to force* en cualquier sentido. **Forcing-bed,** *v.* HOT-BED. **Forcing-house,** invernadero para apresurar el desarrollo de las plantas o hacer salir las flores antes del tiempo natural.

forcipate [ˈfɔːsɪpeɪt] [for-si-peit], *a.* Lo que tiene figura de pinzas o tenazas.

forcipation [ˌfɔːsɪˈpeɪʃən] [for-si-pei-shon], *s.* El acto de atenacear o despedazar con tenazas; uno de los castigos que usaban antiguamente.

ford [fɔːd] [ford], *s.* 1. Vado. 2. *(Ant.)* Corriente de agua; embarcadero.

ford, *va.* Vadear.

fordable [ˈfɔːdəbl] [for-da-bol], *a.* Vadeable.

fordo [fɔːˈdəʊ] [for-dou], *va.* 1. *(Poét.)* Cansar. 2. *(Des.)* Arruinar.

fore [fɔːʳ] [faʳ], *a.* Anterior, delantero. **Fore foot,** pata delantera. -*adv.* 1. Anteriormente, delante, antes. 2. *(Mar.)* De proa. **Fore and aft,** de popa a proa.

fore. Prefijo que significa: (a) delante, ante, antes; (b) por, a causa de, en razón a; (c) en vez de.

foreallege [ˌfɔːrəˈledʒ] [foʳ-a-lech], *va.* Citar o mencionar antes.

foreappoint [ˌfɔːrəˈpɔɪnt] [foʳ-a-point], *vn.* Preordinar.

foreappointment [ˌfɔːrəˈpɔɪntmənt] [foʳ-a-point-ment], *s.* Preordinación, predestinación.

forearm [ˈfɔːrɑːm] [foʳ-arm], *s.* Antebrazo, la parte del brazo que media entre el codo y la mano.

forearm, *va.* Preparar, aparejar y disponer con anticipación armas y pertrechos. **Forewarned, forearmed,** hombre prevenido vale por dos.

forebay [ˈfɔːbeɪ] [for-bei], *s.* 1. Bocal, canalizo, abertura por donde sale el agua a una rueda hidráulica. 2. La enfermería de un buque.

forebode [fɔːˈbəʊd] [for-boud], *vn. y va.* Pronosticar, saber de antemano, particularmente lo malo, enojoso o desagradable; presentir, antever; presagiar, indicar. *(Fam.)* **My heart forebodes it,** me lo dice el corazón.

forebodement [fɔːˈbəʊdmənt] [for-boud-ment], *s.* Presentimiento, presagio.

foreboder [fɔːˈbəʊdəʳ] [for-bou-daʳ], *s.* Adivino o pronosticador, generalmente de mal agüero.

foreboding [fɔːˈbəʊdɪŋ] [for-bou-din], *s.* Presentimiento, presagio. *(Fam.)* Corazonada.

foreby [ˈfɔːbaɪ] [for-bai], *prep. V.* FORBY, 2ª.

forecast [ˈfɔːkɑːst] [for-kast], *va. y vn.* 1. Proyectar, formar o disponer proyectos; arreglar, preparar o trazar de antemano la ejecución de una cosa. 2. Prever, ver con anticipación, conocer o conjeturar de antemano. 3. Predecir, pronosticar.

forecast, *s.* 1. Previsión, penetración. 2. Proyecto, idea, plan trazado de antemano. 3. Pronóstico, pronosticación. *Weather forecast,* pronóstico del tiempo.

forecaster [ˈfɔːkɑːstəʳ] [for-kas-taʳ], *s.* 1. Previsor; en especial, el observador que predice las condiciones y los

fenómenos atmosféricos. 2. El que traza, proyecta o forma la idea de una cosa que se ha de ejecutar después.

forecastle [ˈfɔːkɑːsl] [for-ka-sel], *s. (Mar.)* Castillo de proa.

forechosen [fɔːˈtʃuːsn] [for-chu-sen], *pp.* Preelegido.

forecited [ˈfɔːsɪtɪd] [for-si-ted], *a.* Precitado, ya citado, arriba citado.

foreclose [fɔːˈkləʊz] [for-klous], *va.* Cerrar, impedir el paso, excluir; en especial, *(For.)* vender por orden judicial la cosa hipotecada o privar judicialmente del derecho de redimirla.

foreclosure [fɔːˈkləʊʒəʳ] [for-klo-shaʳ], *s. (For.)* Exclusión del derecho de redimir la cosa hipotecada.

foredate [ˈfɔːdeɪt] [for-deit], *va. V.* ANTEDATE.

foredeck [ˈfɔːdek] [for-dek], *s. (Mar.)* Proa, la parte delantera del navío.

foredesign [ˈfɔːdɪzaɪn] [for-di-sain], *va.* Prevenir, proyectar.

foredoom [ˈfɔːduːm] [for-dum], *va.* Predestinar, predeterminar, condenar de antemano.

fore end [ˈfɔːˈend] [for-end], *s.* Delantera, la parte anterior de alguna cosa.

forefather [ˈfɔːfɑːðəʳ] [for-fa-daʳ], *s.* Abuelo, ascendiente, antecesor.

forefinger [ˈfɔːfɪŋgəʳ] [for-fin-gaʳ], *s.* Índice, el dedo segundo de la mano.

forefoot [ˈfɔːfʊt] [for-fut], *s.* 1. Mano, pie delantero de cualquier cuadrúpedo. 2. *(Mar.)* Gorja, tajamar.

forefront [ˈfɔːfrʌnt] [for-front], *s.* La parte más adelantada; la primera fila, el primer puesto. **The forefront of a battle,** lo más recio de una batalla.

foreganger [ˈfɔːgændʒəʳ] [for-gan-chaʳ], *s.* 1. Predecesor. 2. Cuerda de arpón.

foreglimpse [ˈfɔːglɪmpz] [for-glimps], *s.* Vislumbre del futuro.

forego [fɔːˈgəʊ] [for-gou], *va. (pret.* FOREWENT, *pp.* FOREGONE). 1. Ceder, renunciar; hacer dimisión de algo. 2. Anteceder, preceder. 3. Descuidar, olvidarse de.

foregoer [ˈfɔːgəʊəʳ] [for-gouaʳ], *s.* Abuelo, progenitor; precursor; el que hace cesión.

foregoing [ˈfɔːgəʊɪŋ] [for-gouin], *s.* Precedente; el que va delante.

foregone [ˈfɔːgəʊn] [for-goun], *pp. y a.* Predeterminado, decidido de antemano.

foreground [ˈfɔːgraʊnd] [for-graund], *s.* Delantera, primer plano, la parte del campo de una pintura que parece estar próximo al que mira.

forehand [ˈfɔːhænd] [for-jand], *s.* 1. Cuarto delantero del caballo. 2. Posición ventajosa. 3. Adelantado, anticipado. -*a.* *(Scot.)* Delantero, hacia adelante.

forehanded [ˈfɔːhændɪd] [for-jan-did], *a.* 1. Temprano, lo que se hace o sucede antes del tiempo ordinario; hecho en tiempo oportuno. 2. *(E.U.)* Que tiene dinero ahorrado; poseedor de recursos o bienes.

forehead [ˈfɔːhed] [for-jed], *s.* 1. Frente, el espacio que hay en el rostro desde las cejas hasta el cabello. 2. Descaro, desvergüenza, insolencia.

forehew [ˈfɔːhjuː] [for-jiu], *va.* Cortar alguna cosa por la parte anterior o delantera.

forehorse [ˈfɔːhɔːs] [for-jors], *s. (Des.)* Caballo delantero.

foreign [ˈfɒrɪn] [fo-rein], *a.* 1. Extranjero, que pertenece a otra nación, o que tiene relación con otros países. 2. Exótico, exterior; que procede de otro país. 3. Extraño, advenedizo. 4. Ajeno, remoto; excluído. **Foreign trade,** comercio extranjero. **Foreign Office,** *(Ingl.)* Ministerio de Estado o de negocios extranjeros. **Foreign products,** productos exóticos.

foreign-built [ˈfɒrɪnˌbɪlt] [fo-rein-bilt], *a.* Construido en el extranjero.

foreigner [ˈfɒrɪnəʳ] [fo-ri-naʳ], *s.* Extranjero, forastero.

foreignism [ˈfɒrɪnɪzm] [fo-ri-nism], *s.* Extranjerismo.

foreignness [ˈfɒrɪnnɪs] [fo-rin-nes], *s.* Inconexión, extrañeza, falta de conexión entre las cosas.

forejudge, *va. V.* PREJUDGE.

forejudgment ['fɔːˈdʒʌdʒmənt] [for-yach-ment], *s.* Juicio formado con antelación al completo conocimiento de una cosa; prevención.

foreknow ['fɔːnəʊ] [for-nou], *va.* Prever, tener presciencia de alguna cosa, conocer de antemano.

foreknowable ['fɔːnəʊəbl] [for-noua-bol], *a.* Lo que se puede prever.

foreknower ['fɔːnəʊer] [for-noua'], *s.* Previsor, el que conoce o sabe lo que ha de acontecer.

foreknowledge ['fɔːnəʊlɪdʒ] [for-nou-lich], *s.* Presciencia, precognición.

foreland ['fɔːlænd] [for-land], *s.* Cabo, promontorio.

forelay ['fɔːleɪ] [for-lei], *va.* Poner asechanzas; prevenir.

foreleader ['fɔːliːdə'] [for-li-da'], *s.* El que guía a otros con su ejemplo.

foreleg ['fɔːleg] [for-leg], *s.* Brazo, pata delantera.

forelock ['fɔːlɒk] [for-lok], *s.* 1. Melena, mechón de pelo que cae sobre la frente. 2. *(Mar.)* Chaveta, cuñita de hierro que entra en el ojo del perno para afianzarlo. **Forelock bolts,** pernos de chaveta.

forelook ['fɔːluːk] [for-luk], *vn.* Mirar de antemano.

foreman ['fɔːmən] [for-man], *s.* 1. El presidente del jurado. 2. Capataz; regente de imprenta; jefe (de un taller, de una cuadrilla de trabajadores); dependiente principal de un establecimiento; oficial mayor en las oficinas públicas.

foremast ['fɔːmɑːst] [for-mast], *s. (Mar.)* Palo de trinquete.

forementioned ['fɔːmenʃənd] [for-men-shond], *a.* Ya citado, arriba citado.

foremost ['fɔːməʊst] [for-moust], *a.* Delantero; primero en situación o dignidad.

foremother ['fɔːmʌðə'] [for-ma-da'], *sf.* Abuela, ascendiente, antepasada.

forename ['fɔːneɪm] [for-neim], *s.* Prenombre, el nombre que precede al de familia, o apellido nombre de pila.

forenamed ['fɔːneɪmd] [for-neimd], *a.* Ya nombrado, susodicho.

forenoon ['fɔːnuːn] [for-nun], *s.* La mañana hasta mediodía.

forensic [fəˈrensɪk] [fo-ren-sik], *a.* Forense, lo que pertenece al foro; empleado en los pleitos o las formas judiciales.

foreordain ['fɔːrɔːˈdaɪn] [for-or-dain], *va.* Preordinar, predestinar.

foreordination ['fɔːrədaɪˈneɪʃən] [for-or-dai-nei-shon], *s.* Predeterminación.

forepart ['fɔːpɑːt] [for-part], *s.* Delantera; la primera parte. (Forma incorrecta; debe escribirse *Fore part.*)

forepromise ['fɔːprɒmɪs] [for-pro-mis], *va.* Prometer de antemano.

foreprize ['fɔːpraɪz] [for-prais], *va.* Apreciar o estimar de antemano.

foreran, *pret.* de FORERUN.

fore-rank ['fɔːræŋk] [for-rank], *s.* Primera fila; frente, hilera del frente.

forereach ['fɔːriːtʃ] [for-rich], *va. (Mar.)* Navegar delante de otro buque.

fore-remembered ['fɔːrɪˈmembəd] [for-ri-mem-berd], *a.* Ya acordado o mencionado.

forerun ['fɔːrʌn] [for-ran], *va. (pret.* FORERAN, *pp.* FORERUN, *ger.* FORERUNNING). 1. Preceder, ir delante como pronóstico o señal de lo que sigue. 2. Adelantarse, llegar antes que otro. 3. Anunciar.

forerunner ['fɔːrʌnə'] [for-ra-na'], *s.* 1. Precursor, el que va delante de otro; predecesor. 2. Presagio, pronóstico, anuncio, preludio. 3. Corredor, batidor. *(Mil.)* Explorador.

foresaid ['fɔːseɪd] [for-seid], *a.* Ya dicho, antedicho, susodicho.

foresail ['fɔːseɪl] [for-seil], *s.* Trinquete.

foresee ['fɔːsiː] [for-si], *va. (pret.* FORESAW, *pp.* FORESEEN). Prever, tener presciencia, anticipar.

foreseer ['fɔːsiːə'] [for-sia'], *s.* Previsor, el que prevé.

foreshadow [fɔːˈʃædəʊ] [for-sha-dou], *va.* Prefigurar, simbolizar.

foreship ['fɔːʃɪp] [for-ship], *s. (Mar.)* Proa, la parte delantera de una embarcación.

foreshorten [fɔːˈʃɔːtən] [for-shor-ten], *va. (Pint.)* Escorzar, degradar, reducir la longitud de un cuerpo u objeto, según las reglas de la perspectiva.

foreshow ['fɔːʃəʊ] [for-shou], *va.* Exhibir de antemano; predecir, pronosticar.

foreshower ['fɔːʃawə'] [for-sha-ua'], *s.* El que predice algún acontecimiento.

foreside ['fɔːsaɪd] [for-said], *s.* 1. Apariencia superficial. 2. El frente, la parte anterior de una cosa.

foresight ['fɔːsaɪt] [for-sait], *s.* 1. Previsión, providencia, prevención, cuidado por lo que puede suceder. 2. Presciencia. 3. Entre los agrimensores, croquis de nivel.

foresightful ['fɔːsaɪtfʊl] [for-sait-ful], *a.* Próvido, prevenido, cuidadoso.

foresignify ['fɔːsaɪnɪfaɪ] [for-sai-ni-fai], *va.* Prefigurar, presagiar, simbolizar.

foreskin ['fɔːrskɪn] [fors-kin], *s.* Prepucio.

foreskirt ['fɔːrskɜːt] [fors-kert], *s.* Parte delantera de una falda o de un faldón.

foreslow ['fɔːrsləʊ] [fors-lou], *va. (Des.)* Tardar, retardar, impedir; omitir. *-vn.* Descuidar; detenerse.

forespeak ['fɔːrspiːk] [fors-pik], *vn.* 1. *(Prov. Ingl.)* Predecir; prohibir; consagrar. 2. *(Scot.)* V. BESPEAK.

forespent ['fɔːrspent] [fors-pent], *a.* 1. *(Ant.)* Pasado, gastado, coonsumido. 2. Cansado, fatigado.

forespurrer ['fɔːrspʊərə'] [fors-pue-ra'], *s. (Des.)* Postillón, el que va a caballo delante de otro.

forest ['fɒrɪst] [fo-rist], *s.* Monte espeso, bosque, selva, foresta. **Forest-tree,** árbol del bosque, a diferencia de un árbol frutal. **Forest-born,** salvaje, nacido y criado en los bosques. **To thin a forest,** despejar o aclarar un bosque.

forest, *va.* Arbolar; formar un bosque.

forestaff ['fɔːstɑːf] [fors-taf], *s. (Mar.)* Ballestilla, instrumento que usaban los náuticos para tomar las alturas del sol, la luna y las estrellas.

forestage ['fɔːsteɪdʒ] [for-steich], *s.* Un tributo pagado antiguamente en Inglaterra por los que vivían en los montes.

forestal ['fɒrɪstəl] [fo-ris-tal], *a.* Forestal, relativo a las selvas o proveniente de ellas.

forestall [fɔːˈstɔːl] [fors-tol], *va.* 1. Anticipar. 2. Preocupar, prevenir. 3. Monopolizar, acaparar (los géneros de un mercado).

forestaller [fɔːˈstɔːlə'] [fors-to-la'], *s.* Monopolista; acopiador.

forestalling [fɔːˈstɔːlɪŋ] [fors-to-lin], *s.* Monopolio, acopio.

forestation [fɔːsteɪˈʃən] [fors-tei-shon], *s.* Forestación.

forestay [fɔːˈsteɪ] [fors-tei], *s. (Mar.)* Estay del trinquete. **Forestay-tackle,** *(Mar.)* Candeletón.

forested ['fɒrɪstɪd] [fo-ris-tid], *a.* Arbolado, poblado de árboles.

forester ['fɒrɪstə'] [fo-res-ta'], *s.* 1. Guardabosque. 2. Habitante de los bosques. 3. Árbol del bosque. 4. Mariposa del grupo de los cigénidos cuya oruga se alimenta de las hojas de la vid.

forestine ['fɒrɪstiːn] [fo-ris-tin], *a.* Natural de los bosques o hallado en ellos.

forestry ['fɒrɪstrɪ] [fo-ris-tri], *s.* Selvicultura, arte de plantar, cultivar y proteger las selvas.

foretackle ['fɔːtækl] [for-ta-kel], *s. (Mar.)* Aparejo del gancho del trinquete.

foretaste ['fɔːteɪst] [for-teist], *va.* 1. Tener presciencia o conocimiento previo de alguna cosa. 2. Catar o gustar antes que otro.

foretaste, *s.* Goce por anticipación.

foretaster ['fɔːteɪstə'] [for-teis-ta'], *s.* Catador, el que gusta o prueba alguna cosa antes que otro.

foretell [fɔːˈtel] [for-tel], *va.* Predecir, prenunciar, profetizar, presagiar. *-vn.* Profetizar o ser profeta.

foreteller [fɔːˈtelə'] [for-te-la'], *s.* Profeta.

foretelling [fɔːˈtelɪŋ] [for-te-lin], *s.* Predicción, profecía, presagio.

forethink ['fɔ:θɪŋk] [for-zink], *va. (Des.)* Premeditar, pensar o considerar anticipadamente. *-vn. (Des.)* Idear, proyectar, discurrir medios de antemano para el logro de algún intento.

forethought ['fɔ:θɔ:t] [for-zot], *s.* Prescriencia; providencia; prevención; premeditación. *-a.* Premeditado, previsto, pensado con anticipación.

foretoken [fɔ:'təʊkən] [for-tou-ken], *va.* Pronosticar; prefigurar.

foretoken, *s.* Pronóstico, presagio, señal anunciadora.

foretop ['fɔ:tɒp] [for-top], *s.* 1. *(Mar.)* Cofa de trinquete. 2. Tupé. 3. Copete (of horse).

forever [fɑr'evər] [for-eva'], *adv.* Siempre; para siempre (for always). (En Inglaterra se suele escribir en dos palabras, **for ever**). **Forevermore,** por siempre, para siempre. **Forever and a day o forever and ever,** para siempre jamás.

forewarn [fɔ:'wɔ:m] [for-uorn], *va.* 1. Prevenir o amonestar de antemano. 2. Advertir o avisar a alguno acerca de lo que ha de suceder. 3. Precautelar, precaver o prevenir contra alguna cosa. **Forewarned is forearmed,** persona prevenida vale por dos.

forewind [fɔ:'wɪnd] [for-uind], *s.* Viento favorable.

forewoman [fɔ:'wʊmən] [for-uo-man], *s.* Primera oficiala de un taller de mujeres; encargada.

foreword [fɔ:'wɜ:d] [for-ued], *s.* Preámbulo, prólogo, advertencia.

foreyard [fɔ:'jɑ:d] [for-yard], *s. (Mar.)* Verga del trinquete.

forfeit ['fɔ:fɪl] [for-fit], *s.* 1. Multa, pena (fine), la cosa perdida por su dueño como castigo de una falta o contravención; pérdida legal de un derecho; decomiso. **To pay the forfeit,** sufrir la pena de. 2. Prenda, gaje (en los juegos). **Game of forfeits,** juego de prendas. *-a.* 1. Sujeto a multa o confiscación. 2. Confiscado, perdido (lost).

forfeit, *va.* 1. Perder el título a una cosa o la posesión de ella por dejar de cumplir alguna obligación o condición. 2. Perder o exponerse a perder alguna cosa por falta, omisión, contravención, etc.; incurrir en la pena de embargo o confiscación.

forfeitable ['fɔ:fɪtəbl] [for-fi-ta-bol], *a.* Confiscable.

forfeiter ['fɔ:fɪtər] [for-fi-ta'], *s.* 1. El que pierde una cosa por faltar a alguna de las condiciones bajo las cuales la poseía. 2. El que incurre en una pena por dejar de cumplir con su obligación.

forfeiture ['fɔ:fɪtər] [for-fi-ta'], *s.* Confiscación; secuestro, decomiso, pérdida de bienes; multa (fine).

forfend ['fɔ:fend] [for-fend], *va. (Ant.)* Impedir; desviar. **Heaven forfend!,** ¡líbreme el cielo!

forficula [fɔ:'fɪkjʊlə] [for-fi-kiu-la], *s.* V. EARWIG.

forgather [fɔ:'gæðər] [for-ga-da'], *vi.* Reunirse.

forgave ['fɔ:'geɪv] [for-gueiv], *pret.* del verbo TO FORGIVE.

forge [fɔ:dʒ] [forch], *s.* 1. Fragua; fábrica de metales. 2. Forja, hornaza. **Forge-hearth,** atrio, hogar de fábrica.

forge, *va.* 1. Forjar, fraguar obras de herrería, cerrajería u otros metales. 2.Contrahacer, falsificar, falsear monedas, llaves, sellos, escritos, etc. 3. Forjar palabras, cuentos, etc. 4. Fraguar calumnias, falsedades, etc.; tramar, inventar. **To forge off,** *(Mar.)* franquear por encima de una roca o arrecife.

forger ['fɔ:dʒər] [for-ya'], *s.* Forjador, fraguador; falsificador, falsario.

forgery ['fɔ:dʒərɪ] [for-ye-ri], *s.* 1. Falsificación; alteración de lo escrito con intención de defraudar; el acto de hacer moneda falsa; falsedad. 2. Forjadura, lo que se forja en la fragua.

forget [fə'get] [fo-guet], *va. (pret.* FORGOT, *pp.* FORGOTTEN). 1. Olvidar. **Forget it,** no piense más en ello, no se preocupe. 2. Descuidar, dejar de atender. **Don't you forget it!,** ¡que no se te olvide! **I forgot all about it,** se me olvidó por completo.

forgetful [fə'getʊl] [fo-guet-ful], *a.* Olvidadizo, descuidado, desmemoriado.

fogetfulness [fə'getʊlnɪs] [fo-guet-ful-nes], *s.* Olvido, descuido, negligencia.

forget-me-not [fə'getmɪnɒt] [fo-guet-mi-not], *s.* Raspilla, miosota, planta y su flor, llamada comúnmente Nomeolvides.

forgetter [fə'getər] [fo-gue-ta'], *s.* Olvidadizo, el que es negligente o descuidado.

forgetting [fə'getɪŋ] [fo-gue-tin], *s.* Olvido, descuido, negligencia.

forgettingly [fə'getɪŋlɪ] [fo-gue-tin-li], *adv.* Descuidadamente.

forging [fə'gɪŋ] [fo-chin], *s.* 1. Defecto de algunas caballerías que golpean un pie con otro al andar o trotar. 2. Forja, forjadura; masa o trozo de metal al que se da forma martilleándolo.

forgivable [fə'gɪvəbl] [fe-gui-va-bol], *a.* Perdonable, remisible.

forgive [fə'gɪv] [fe-guiv], *va.* 1. Perdonar, remitir la injuria. 2. Perdonar, remitir una deuda o pena.

forgiven [gə'gɪvn] [fo-gui-ven], *pp.* del verbo TO FORGIVE.

forgiveness [fə'gɪvnɪs] [fo-gui-ven-nes], *s.* Perdón u olvido de alguna injuria; condonación, indulgencia, remisión de multa o pena; clemencia, misericordia, absolución.

forgiver [fə'gɪvər] [fo-gui-va'], *s.* Perdonador.

forgo [fɔ:'gəʊ] [fo-gou], *va.* y *vn. (pret.* FORWENT, *pp.* FORGONE). (Poco us.) V. FOREGO. Abandonar, renunciar a, privarse de.

forgot [fə'gɒt] [fo-got], *pret.* y *pp.* de TO FORGET.

forgot, forgotten, *pp.* de TO FORGET.

forisfamiliate [ʃəɹɪs'fæmɪlɪeɪt] [fo-ris-fa-mi-lieit], *va. (For.)* Dar al hijo la posesión de una parte de la herencia durante la vida de su padre.

fork [fɔ:k] [fork], *s.* 1. Tenedor (table). 2. Horca para aventar o hacinar heno, paja, estiércol, etc. 3. Cualquier cosa de figura ahorquillada: como la punta de una flecha; una púa, etc. 4. Bifurcación; paraje donde un camino se divide en dos; confluencia de un río. 5. *(Des.)* Horca, el patíbulo (gibbet).

fork, *va.* 1. Hacinar, echar, cargar con una horca; ahorquillar. 2. Hacer terminar en punta, o hacer dentado, como una rama. 3. (Chess) Atacar o amenazar dos piezas a la vez. *-vn.* 1. Ahorquillarse, bifurcarse. 2. Brotar en forma de horquillas.

forked [fɔ:kt] [forkt], *a.* Horcado, lo que tiene la forma de horca u horquilla, ahorquillado, hendido.

forkedly ['fɔ:ktlɪ] [forkt-li], *adv.* En figura de horquilla.

forkedness ['fɔ:kɪdnɪs] [for-kid-nes], *s.* Horcajadura, horcadura, horquilladura.

forkhead ['fɔ:khed] [fork-jed], *s.* Lengüeta de saeta o flecha.

forkiness ['fɔ:kɪnɪs] [for-ki-nes], *s.* Horcadura.

forklift truck [fɔ:'klɪft'trʌk] [fork-lift-trak], *s.* Carretilla elevadora.

forktail ['fɔ:kteɪl] [fork-teil], *s.* 1. Milano, ave de rapiña. 2. Tirano, pájaro de la América tropical. 3. Salmón en su carto año.

forlorn [fə'klɔ:n] [for-lorn], *a.* 1. Abandonado, destituído, perdido, olvidado, desamparado, desesperado (forgotten, lost). 2. Pequeño, ruin. **Forlorn hope,** destacamento militar encargado de un seervicio excepcional y en extremo peligroso; también, una empresa desesperada o con muy escasa esperanzas de éxito. *-s.* Hombre abandonado o desamparado.

forlornness [fə'klɔ:nnɪs] [for-lorn-nes], *s.* Desamparo, miseria; soledad, abandono.

form [fɔ:m] [form], *s.* 1. Forma, figura, modelo; modo. 2. Hermosura, elegancia exterior. 3. Ceremonia, formalidad, orden. 4. Método, práctica establecida (method). 5. Banco, asiento largo. 6. Forma, molde, patrón. 7. Cama de liebre, surco o ligera depresión en vez de madriguera. 8. Forma, molde que se pone en la prensa para imprimir. 9. La condición y el estado general, p. ej, de un caballo de carrera; de aquí, porte, conducta. 10. Lo que tiene figura o contorno sin cuerpo; aparición, sombra. **For form's sake,** por pura fórmula, para cumplir con las apariencias, por ceremonia. **In due form,** en toda forma, según las reglas, en debida forma.

Form in a school, clase de una escuela. 11. *(E.U.)* Esqueleto.

form, *va.* 1. Formar, hacer alguna cosa. 2. Formar, dar a las cosas una forma o figura; modelar, idear. 3. Poner en orden, juntar, colocar; asentar, componer, arreglar; hacer constituir. 4. Formar ideas, juicios. 5. *(Mil.)* Formar, poner en orden. *-vn.* Formarse, tomar una forma o figura.

formal ['fɔ:məl] [for-mal], *a.* 1. Formal, hecho o ejecutado según las regla; metódico, regular. 2. Exterior; en apariencia, pero sin substancia ni esencia. 3. Ceremonioso, formalista, etiquetero. 4. Formal, que se refiere a la forma, en oposición a la materia. 5. Esencial, constitutivo.

formaldehyde [fɔ:'mældɪhaɪd] [for-mal-di-jaid], *s. (Quím.)* Formaldehida, la aldehida del ácido fórmico (CH2O). Es un gas acre y un agente antiséptico de primer orden, muy usado hoy para desinfectar habitaciones, buques, etc.

formalin ['fɔ:məlɪn] [for-ma-lin], *s. (Quím.)* Formalina, nombre de una solución acuosa de la formaldehida.

formalism ['fɔ:məlɪzəm] [for-ma-lisem], *s.* Formalismo.

formalist ['fɔ:məlɪst] [for-ma-list], *s.* Ceremoniático, formalista.

formality [fɔ:'mælɪtɪ] [for-ma-li-ti], *s.* 1. Formalidad, ceremonia, etiqueta. 2. Formalidad, regla prescrita para proceder en juicio. 3. Esencia de una cosa.

formalize ['fɔ:məlaɪz] [for-ma-lais], *va.* Formalizar, dar forma.

formally ['fɔ:məlɪ] [for-ma-li], *adv.* Formalmente, con toda solemnidad; realmente. **Forma pauperis,** *(For.)* defendido por pobre.

format ['fɔ:mæt] [for-mat], *s.* Formato (de una publicación).

formate ['fɔ:meɪt] [for-meit], *s. (Quím.)* Formiato, sal formada de ácido fórmico con alguna base.

formation [fɔ:'meɪʃən] [for-mei-shon], *s.* 1. Formación, acción de formar; manera en que se forma una cosa; desarrollo. 2. Disposición de las partes para dar individualidad o forma característica. 3. Lo que está formado; *(Geol.)* formación.

formation flying [fɔ:'meɪʃən,flaɪɪŋ] [for-mei-shon-flai-in], *s.* Vuelo en formación.

formative ['fɔ:mətɪv] [for-ma-tiv], *a.* Formativo, que forma o da la forma.

former ['fɔ:məʳ] [for-maʳ], *a.* Anterior, primero; pasado; antecedente, precedente. *-s.* Formador; molde, matriz.

formerly ['fɔ:məlɪ] [for-mer-li], *adv.* Antiguamente, en tiempos pasados.

formic ['fɔ:mɪk] [for-mik], *a.* Fórmico, referente a lás hrmigas; derivado del ácido fórmico. **Formic acid,** acido fórmico o ácido de hormigas.

formication [fɔ:mɪ'keɪʃən] [for-mi-kei-shon], *s.* Hormigueo, sensación de comezón o picazón entre cuero y carne.

formicative ['fɔ:mɪkətɪv] [for-mi-ka-tiv], *a.* Formicante.

formidable ['fɔ:mɪdəbl] [for-mi-da-bol], *a.* Formidable, pavoroso, terrible, tremendo.

formidableness ['fɔ:mɪdəblnɪs] [for-mi-da-bol-nes], *s.* Calidad espantosa o formidable; horror.

formidably ['fɔ:mɪdəblɪ] [for-mi-da-bli], *adv.* Formidablemente, horriblemente.

formless ['fɔ:mlɪs] [form-les], *a.* Informe, disforme, deforme.

form letter ['fɔ:m'letəʳ] [form-le-taʳ], *s.* Carta circular.

formol ['fɔ:məl] [for-mol], *s. (Quím.)* Formol.

formula ['fɔ:mjələ] [for-miu-la], *s.* (*pl.* LAS ó LÆ). 1. Fórmula, forma prescrita. 2. Profesión de fe escrita. 3. *(Med.)* Receta médica, récipe. 4. Regla expresada en signos algebraicos. 5. *(Quím.)* Grupo de signos que expresan los elementos constitutivos de un cuerpo o de una substancia compuesta.

formulary ['fɔ:mjələrɪ] [for-miu-la-ri], *s.* Formulario, el libro o escrito que contiene las fórmulas que se han de observar para la ejecución de alguna cosa.

formulate ['fɔ:mjʊleɪt] [for-miu-leit], *va.* Formular, expresar en una fórmula; incluir en una forma exacta y metódica.

formulation ['fɔ:mjʊleɪʃən] [for-miu-lei-shon], *s.* Formulación.

formulism ['fɔ:mjʊlɪzm] [for-miu-li-sem], *s.* Formulismo.

formulist ['fɔ:mjʊlɪst] [for-miu-list], *s.* Formulista.

formulistic ['fɔ:mjʊlɪstɪk] [for-miu-lis-tik], *a.* Formulista.

formulize ['fɔ:mjʊlaɪz] [for-miu-lais], *va.* 1. Hacer formal, formalizar. 2. Formular. V. FORMULATE.

fornicate ['fɔ:nɪkeɪt] [for-ni-keit], *vn.* fornicar.

fornicate, *a.* Arqueado; abovedado, en forma de bóveda.

fornicated ['fɔ:nɪkeɪtɪd] [for-ni-kei-tid], *a.* Abovedado.

fornication [,fɔ:nɪ'keɪʃən] [for-ni-kei-shon], *s.* 1. Fornicación, cópula carnal entre dos personas que no están casadas. 2. *(Arq.)* Bóveda.

fornicator ['fɔ:nɪkeɪtəʳ] [for-ni-kei-taʳ], *s.* Fornicador, fornicario.

fornicatress ['fɔ:nɪkətrɪs] [for-ni-ka-tris], *sf.* Concubina; manceba.

fornix ['fɔ:nɪks] [for-niks], *s. (Anat.)* Superficie abovedada. La parte arqueada de una concha bivalva.

forsake ['fɔ:seɪk] [for-seik], *va.* (*pret.* FORSOOK, *pp.* FORSAKEN). Dejar, abandonar; faltar a, desertar; separarse de; alejarse de; renunciar.

forsaker ['fɔ:seɪkəʳ] [for-sei-kaʳ], *s.* Desertor; apóstata.

forsaking ['fɔ:seɪkɪŋ] [for-sei-kin], *s.* Abandono.

forsooth [fɔ:'su:θ] [for-suz], *adv.* Ciertamente. ¡De veras! ¡vaya! Se usa hoy generalmente en sentido irónico.

forswear ['fɔ:swɛəʳ] [fors-ueaʳ], *va.* (*pret.* FORSWORE, *pp.* FORSWORN). Renunciar con juramento; negar con juramento. **To foreswear oneself,** perjurarse. *-vn.* Perjurar, jurar falso.

forswearer ['fɔ:swɛərəʳ] [fors-uea-raʳ], *s.* Perjurador, perjuro.

forsworn, *pp.* de FORSWEAR.

fort [fɔ:t] [fort], *s.* Fuerte, castillo, fortaleza. **Little fort,** fortín.

fortalice ['fɔ:təlaɪz] [for-ta-lais], *s.* Fortín, obra pequeña en lo exterior de una fortificación.

forte [fɔ:t] [fort], *s.* El fuerte, el lado fuerte de alguno; talento o facultad particular en que uno se distingue o descuella.

forte, *s. (Mús.)* Forte, el trozo donde debe esforzarse el sonido. *-a.* De sonido fuerte.

forth [fɔ:θ] [forz], *adv.* 1. En adelante, hacia adelante, adelante; delante. 2. Fuera, afuera. 3. A la vista, públicamente. 4. Hasta lo último. **And so forth,** y así de lo demás; etcétera. **To go o come forth,** irse, salir fuera. **To step forth,** ir adelante, avanzar. **From that day forth,** desde aquel día en adelante, *-prep.* Fuera de.

forthcoming [fɔ:θ'kʌmɪŋ] [forz-ka-min], *a.* 1. Pronto a comparecer, que viene o está viniendo. 2. Próximo, venidero, disponible. **He is not forthcoming,** no viene; no es fácil que se presente o que venga. **Funds will not be forthcoming,** no habrá fondos disponibles.

forth-issuing [fɔ:θ'ɪsjuːɪŋ] [forz-isuin], *a.* Se dice de la persona o cosa que sale de donde estaba oculta.

forthputting [fɔ:θ'pʌtɪŋ] [forz-pa-tin], *a.* Atrevido, descarado.

forthright ['fɔ:θraɪt] [forz-rait], *adv.* Todo derecho, directamente, francamente, inmediatamente. *-s.* Senda angosta.

forthwith ['fɔ:θwɪθ] [forz-uiz], *adv.* Inmediatamente, sin dilación, sin tardanza.

forties ['fɔ:tiːz] [for-tis], *s. pl.* Los números desde el cuarenta al cuarenta y nueve.

fortieth ['fɔ:tɪɪθ] [for-tiez], *s.* Cuadragésimo.

fortifiable ['fɔ:tɪfɪəbl] [for-ti-fia-bol], *a.* Fortificable.

fortification [,fɔ:tɪfɪ'keɪʃən] [for-ti-fi-kei-shon], *s.* 1. Fortificación, arquitectura militar; acción de fortificar; obra construída para defenderse contra un ataque. 2. Plaza fuerte; fortaleza. 3. Aumento de fuerza.

fortifier [ˈfɔːtɪfaɪəʳ] [for-ti-faiaʳ], s. 1. Fortificador, ingeniero militar. 2. Fautor.

fortify [ˈfɔːtɪfaɪ] [for-ti-fai], va. 1. Fortificar. 2. Fortalecer, dar vigor o fuerzas a alguna cosa. 3. Corroborar, fijar, establecer, confirmar.

fortissimo [fɔːˈtɪːsɪməʊ] [for-ti-si-mou], a. y adv. (Ital.) Muy fuerte o fortísimo.

fortitude [ˈfɔːtɪtjuːd] [for-ti-tiud], s. 1. Fortaleza de ánimo para soportar el dolor o la adversidad con valor ó paciencia; resolución, firmeza, grandeza de alma. 2. Fuerza, vigor.

fortlet [ˈfɔːtlet] [fort-let], s. Fortín.

fortnight [ˈfɔːtnaɪt] [fort-nait], s. Quince días, dos semanas, quincena. **A fortnight hence,** de aquí a quince días. **A fortnight ago,** hace quince días.

fortnightly [ˈfɔːtnaɪtlɪ] [fort-nait-li], a. y adv. Una vez cada quince días; que sale a luz, ocurre o se publica cada quincena.

fortress [ˈfɔːtrɪs] [for-tris], s. Fortaleza, plaza fortificada, castillo, fuerte.

fortuitous [fɔːˈtjuːɪtəs] [for-tui-tos], a. Fortuito, impensado, casual, accidental.

fortuitously [fɔːˈtjuːɪtəslɪ] [for-tui-tos-li], adv. Fortuitamente, por casualidad, accidentalmente.

fortuitousness [fɔːˈtjuːɪtəsnɪs] [for-tui-tos-nes], s. Casualidad, acontecimiento impensado.

fortuity [fɔːˈtjuːɪtɪ] [for-tui-ti], s. Caso fortuito; accidente.

fortunate [ˈfɔːtʃənɪt] [for-chu-nit], a. Afortunado, feliz, dichoso.

fortunately [ˈfɔːtʃənɪtlɪ] [for-chu-na-tli], adv. Felizmente, dichosamente.

fortune [ˈfɔːtʃən] [for-chun], s. 1. Fortuna, suerte, buenaventura o mala. 2. Fortuna, el estado o condición en que uno vive. 3. Fortuna, suerte, destino, lo que ha de suceder a una persona. 4. Bienes de fortuna, sean raíces o muebles. **Man of fortune,** hombre rico. 5. Hacienda; dote, el caudal que lleva la mujer al tiempo de casarse. **To make one's fortune,** hacer su propia fortuna, enriquecerse. **A man of broken fortune,** un hombre arruinado. **Fortune-hunter,** buscador de dotes, el que anda en busca de esposa rica. **Fortuneteller,** sortílego, adivino, nigromante; gitano que dice la buenaventura.

fortuned [ˈfɔːtʃənd] [for-chund], a. Afortunado, dichoso.

fortune-book [ˈfɔːtʃənˌbʊk] [for-chun-buk], s. Libro de la buenaventura.

fortuneless [ˈfɔːtʃənlɪs] [for-chun-les], a. Sin fortuna, sin bienes.

fortuneller [ˈfɔːtʃənləʳ] [for-chun-laʳ], s. Adivino, el que dice la buenaventura.

forty [ˈfɔːtɪ] [for-ti], a. y s. 1. Cuarenta. 2. Cuarentena, número indeterminado. **He has turned forty,** ha cumplido la cuarentena, o los cuarenta. **He is forty,** tiene cuarenta años. **Forty winks,** siestecita.

forum [ˈfɔːrəm] [fo-rum], s. 1. Foro, plaza pública. 2. Tribunal, juzgado.

forward [ˈfɔːwəd] [for-uard], adv. Adelante, hacia adelante, más allá. **Hence forward,** de aquí en adelante. **From this time forward,** de aquí en adelante, en lo venidero. **From that time forward,** desde entonces, desde aquel instante. **To go, to move forward,** ir hacia adelante, adelantar. -a. 1. Delantero, que va delante o está al frente. 2. Precoz, adelantado, anterior. 3. Pronto, activo, que va adelante; apresurado, vivo, listo. 4. Audaz, osado, emprendedor, atrevido, avanzado. 5. (Pol.) Avanzado, progresista.

forward, va. 1. Adelantar; hacer crecer; promover, patrocinar. 2. Apresurar, activar, impeler. 3. Expedir, enviar, transmitir. 4. Impulsar, activar, apresurar.

forwarder [ˈfɔːwədəʳ] [for-uar-daʳ], s. Promotor; remitente, el que envía, agente expedidor, comisionista expedidor.

forwarding merchant [ˈfɔːwədɪŋˈmɜːtʃənt] [for-uar-din-mer-chant], s. Comisionista que recibe efectos para remitirlos a otros puntos.

forwardly [ˈfɔːwədlɪ] [for-uard-li], adv. 1. Anteriormente, en lugar delantero. 2. Con descaro o con muy poca vergüenza. 3. Prontamente.

forwardness [ˈfɔːwədnɪs] [for-uard-nes], s. 1. Adelantamiento, progreso. 2. Ansia, ahinco. 3. Prontitud, apresuramiento, ligereza. 4. Precocidad madurez anticipada. 5. Confianza excesiva; descaro, atrevimiento, audacia.

forwards [ˈfɔːwədz] [for-uards], adv. V. FORWARD. Adelante, hacia adelante, en la delantera.

foss, fosse [ˈfɒs] [fos], s. (Fort.) Foso.

fossa [ˈfɒsə] [fo-sa], s. (Anat.) Fosa.

fossil [ˈfɒsɪl] [fo-sil], a. Fósil, cavado o sacado de la tierra. -s. 1. Fósil, substancia orgánica y prehistórica, más o menos pretrificada, que se extrae de las capas terretres. 2. Persona o cosa anticuada, fuera de uso, antigualla, vejestorio. 3. (Des.) Fósil, cualquier substancia natural que se saca de las entrañas de la tierra.

fossiliferous [ˌfɒsɪˈlɪfərəs] [fo-si-li-fe-ros], a. Fosilífero, que contiene fósiles o restos orgánicos.

fossilist [ˈfɒsɪlɪst] [fo-si-list], s. Paleontólogo.

fossilization [ˈfɒsɪlaɪˈzeɪʃən] [fo-si-lai-sei-shon], s. Fosilización.

fossilize [ˈfɒsɪlaɪz] [fo-si-lais], va. Fosilizar, convertir en fósil; petrificar; hacer anticuado. -vn. Fosilizarse, petrificarse.

fossorial [ˈfɒsərɪəl] [fo-so-rial], a. 1. Cavador, el que cava. 2. Apto, a propósito para cavar. **Fossorial wasp,** avispa cavadora.

fossway [ˈfɒsweɪ] [fos-uei], s. Camino grande con fosos.

foster [ˈfɒstəʳ] [fos-taʳ], va. Criar, nutrir, mimar, dar alas; consolar. -vn. (Des.) Criarse con otros.

foster, a. De leche; adoptivo, de adopción. **Foster home,** hogar de adopción. **Foster nurse,** nodriza. **Foster father,** padre adoptivo.

fosterage [ˈfɒstərɪdʒ] [fos-te-rich], s. El cargo de criar niños, como el que tienen las amas de cría.

foster-brother [ˈfɒstəˌbrʌðəʳ] [fos-ter-bra-daʳ], s. Hermano de leche.

foster-child [ˈfɒstəˈtʃaɪld] [fos-ter-chaild], s. Hijo o hija de leche; también, alumno.

foster-dam [ˈfɒstəˈdæm] [fos-ter-dam], sf. Ama de cría o ama de leche, nodriza.

foster-earth [ˈfɒstəˈɜːθ] [fos-ter-erz], s. Tierra en que crecen las plantas que se han trasplantado de otra.

fosterer [ˈfɒstərəʳ] [fos-te-raʳ], s. El que cría al hijo de otro como si fuera suyo; promotor.

foster-father [ˈfɒstəˈfɑːðəʳ] [fos-ter-fa-daʳ], s. El que sirviendo de padre cría y enseña a un hijo ajeno.

fostering [ˈfɒstərɪŋ] [fos-te-rin], s. Alimento, nutrimento. -pa. de TO FOSTER.

fosterling, s. V. FOSTER-CHILD. Hijo de leche, hijo adoptivo.

foster-mother [ˈfɒstəˈmʌðəʳ] [fos-ter-ma-daʳ], sf. Ama de leche, la que cría hijos ajenos.

foster-nurse [ˈfɒstəˈnɜːs] [fos-ter-ners], s. Ama de leche. (Cuba) Criandera. (Mex.) Chichigua.

foster-son [ˈfɒstəsɒn] [fos-ter-son], s. Hijo de leche; alumno.

fostress, sf. V. NURSE.

fother [ˈfɒðəʳ] [fo-daʳ], s. Galápago de plomo que sirve de lastre; masa de plomo de ocho galápagos.

fother, va. (Mar.) Cerrar una abertura en el barco tapándola con estopa.

fought [fɔːt] [fot], pret. y pp. del verbo TO FIGHT.

foul [faʊl] [faul], a. 1. Sucio, puerco; impuro, inmundo, hediondo, ofensivo al sentido físico, a la moral o al pudor; obsceno. 2. Malvado, detestable, vil; injusto, sin derecho. 3. Enredado, atascado, que obstruye o daña, que sirve de obstáculo; infecto, pestífero. 4. (Des.) Feo, horrible. 5. (Imp.) Lleno de faltas. **Foul action,** bajeza, vileza, acción baja. **Foul dealing,** superchería, duplicidad, doblez, mala fe. **Foul copy,** borrador. **Foul language,** palabras injuriosas. **Foul means,** medios indignos, violencia, rigor. **Foul page,** página llena de faltas cuando se está imprimiendo. **Foul**

shame, infamia. **Foul stomach,** estómago sucio. **Foul weather,** mal tiempo. **Foul words,** palabras provocativas o injuriosas. **By fair means o foul,** a buenas o a malas. **Foul breath,** aliento fétido. -*s.* 1. La acción de ensuciar, enredarse una cosa en otra; violación de las reglas establecidas. 2. En el juego de **base-ball,** falta, golpe que lanza la pelota fuera de las líneas del juego. **To fall foul of,** chocar o abordar con un buque.

foul, *va.* 1. Ensuciar, emporcar, manchar; deshonrar. 2. Afear. 2. (*Mar.*) Abordar, chocar con, trabarse dos embarcaciones de modo que se impidan el paso. 3. Violar las reglas establecidas de un juego. -*vn.* 1. Ensuciarse. 2. Chocar, las embarcaciones.

foulard ['faʊləd] [fau-lard], *s.* 1. Fular, tela de seda fina y suave que se usa para vestidos de señora. 2. Pañuelo de fular.

foul brood [faʊl'bruːd] [faul-brud], *s.* Enfermedad muy contagiosa y destructiva de las larvas de las abejas.

foully ['faʊlɪ] [fau-li], *adv.* Asquerosamente, suciamente.

foul-mouthed ['faʊl'maʊðd] [faul-mau-ded], *a.* Obsceno, malhablado, deslenguado.

foulness ['faʊlnɪs] [faul-nes], *s.* 1. Asquerosidad, porquería, impureza. 2. Fealdad, deformidad. 3. Picardía, atrocidad, obscenidad. 4. Maldad, infamia.

foul play ['faʊl,pleɪ] [faul-plei], *s.* 1. Mala jugada. 2. Conducta deshonesta. 3. Engaño, perfidia. 4. Violencia, asesinato.

foul-spoken [faʊl'spəʊkn] [faul-spou-ken], *a.* Calumnioso, infamatorio, malhablado.

found [faʊnd] [faund], *va.* 1. Cimentar; apoyar. 2. Edificar, levantar algún edificio. 3. Fundar, establecer; dar principio a alguna cosa; fijar, asegurar. 4. Fundir, derretir o liquidar los metales.

found, *pret.* y *pp.* de TO FIND.

foundation [faʊn'deɪʃən] [faun-dei-shon], *s.* 1. Cimiento, fundación, fundamento. 2. Fundación, principio, origen, erección o establecimiento de alguna cosa, base. 3. Dotación o renta con que se funda alguna cosa. 4. Fundamento, la razón o motivo en que se funda alguna cosa. **Foundation school,** escuela dotada, que tiene dotación. **A scholar on the foundation,** un colegial pensionado, con beca.

foundationless [faʊn'deɪʃənlɪs] [faun-dei-shon-les], *a.* Sin fundamento.

founder ['faʊndə'] [faun-da'], *s.* 1. Fundador. 2. Fundidor.

founder, *vn.* 1. (*Mar.*) Irse a pique. 2. Salir mal de alguna empresa. 3. Desplomarse, hundirse. 4. Tropezar, caer. -*va.* Despear los pies del caballo.

foundering ['faʊndərɪŋ] [faun-de-rin], *s.* (*Mar.*) Hundimiento de un buque.

founderous ['faʊndərəs] [faun-de-ros], *a.* Arruinado, no practicable: se dice de los caminos.

foundery ['faʊndərɪ] [faun-de-ri], *s. V.* FOUNDRY.

founding ['faʊndɪŋ] [faun-din], *s.* 1. Fundación, establecimiento. 2. Fundición, arte de fundir los metales.

foundling ['faʊndlɪŋ] [faun-dlin], *s.* Hijo de la piedra, niño expósito, incluseno. **Founding hospital,** casa de niños expósitos. Inclusa. (*Mex.*) La cuna.

foundress ['faʊndrɪs] [faun-dris], *sf.* Fundadora.

foundry ['faʊndrɪ] [faun-dri], *s.* Fundición, fábrica en que se funde; el arte de fundir los metales.

fount [faʊnt] [faunt], *s.* 1. Fuente, manantial. 2. Depósito de una lámpara. 3. Fundición de caracteres de imprenta. 2. *V.* FONT.

fountain ['faʊntɪn] [faun-tin], *s.* 1. Fuente. 2. Nacimiento de un río. 3. Fuente, principio, fundamento, origen.

fountain-head ['faʊntɪnhɛd] [faun-tin-jed], *s.* Manantial de un río o arroyo; de aquí, origen de una cosa.

fountainless ['faʊntɪnlɪs] [faun-tin-les], *a.* Sin fuente.

fountain pen ['faʊntɪnpɛn] [faun-tin-pen], *s.* Pluma fuente, pluma estilográfica.

four [fɔː'] [fa'], *a.* y *s.* 1. Cuatro. **To go upon all fours,** gatear, andar a gatas. **A coach and four,** un coche con tiro de cuatro caballos, o con dos tiros. **Four-cornered, four-**

square, cuadrangular. **Four-footed,** cuadrúpedo. **Four-wheeled,** lo que tiene cuatro ruedas. 2. **Four hundred,** cuatrocientos. 3. (*E.U.*) **The four hundred,** la alta sociedad.

four-cornered [fɔː'kɔːnɪd] [for-kor-ned], *a.* Cuadrangular, cuatro ángulos.

four-cycle ['fɔː,saɪkl] [for-sai-kel], *a.* (*Mec.*) De cuatro tiempos.

four-flusher ['fɔː'flʌʃə'] [for-fla-sha'], *s.* En el juego de poker, lance con un flux de cuatro naipes. (*Fig.*) Fanfarrón.

fourfold ['fɔː'fəʊld] [for-fould], *a.* Cuádruplo, repetido cuatro veces.

four-footed ['fɔː'fuːtɪd] [for-fu-tid], *a.* De cuatro patas, cuádruplo.

four-in-hand ['fɔː'ɪnhænd] [for-in-jan], *s.* 1. Carruaje tirado por cuatro caballos. 2. Corbata larga, anudada de modo que las puntas cuelgan verticalmente.

four-o'clock [fɔː'əklɒk] [for-o-klok], *s.* 1. (*Bot.*) Dondiego de noche, planta originaria del Perú. 2. (*Zool.*) Pájaro de la Oceanía.

fourpence [fɔː'pens] [for-pens], *s.* Moneda de cuatro peniques.

fourscore [fɔːs'kɔː'] [for-ska'], *a.* 1. Ochenta. 2. Octogenario.

foursquare ['fɔːskɛə'] [for-skuea'], *a.* 1. Cuadrado, cuadrangular. 2. Firme, sincero. 3. Constante.

four-stage rocket [fɔː;steɪdʒ'rɒkɪt] [for-steich-ro-kit], *s.* Cohete de cuatro cuerpos.

fourteen [fɔː'tiːn] [for-tin], *a.* y *s.* Catorce.

fourteenth ['fɔː'tiːnθx] [for-tinz], *a.* Catorceno, décimocuarto. **Fourteenth of July,** el catorce de Julio, aniversario de la toma de la Bastilla, en 1789.

fourth [fɔːθ] [forz], *a.* Cuarto, la cuarta parte. **Fourth of July,** el cuatro de Julio, aniversario de la independencia de los Estados Unidos.

fourthly ['fɔːθlɪ] [forz-li], *adv.* En cuarto lugar.

four-way ['fɔːweɪ] [for-uei], *a.* De cuatro direcciones o pasos.

four-wheel ['fɔːwiːl] [for-uil], *a.* De cuatro ruedas.

fowl [faʊl] [faul], *s.* 1. Gallo, gallina; pollo. 2. *pl.* Aves domésticas o de corral. 3. Aves en general. 4. (Anticuado en singular) Ave. **Wild fowls,** aves silvestres.

fowl, *vn.* Cazar aves.

fowler ['faʊlə'] [fau-la'], *s.* Cazador de aves.

fowling ['faʊlɪŋ] [fau-lin], *s.* La caza de aves.

fox [fɒks] [foks], *s.* 1. Zorra, raposa; zorro. 2. Zorro, hombre astuto y engañoso. 3. (*Mar.*) Rebenque.

fox, *vn.* 1. Cazar zorras. 2. Hacer el papel de la zorra, disimular. 3. Agriarse, acedarse el vino, la cerveza u otro licor. 4. Ponerse rojizo, descolorarse; se dice de la madera de construcción, del papel, cuero, etc. -*va.* Atontar; emborrachar.

foxbane ['fɒksbeɪn] [foks-bein], *s.* (*Bot.*) Matalobos, acónico.

fox-case ['fɒkskeɪs] [foks-keis], *s.* Piel de zorra.

fox-chase ['fɒks'tʃeɪs] [foks-cheis], *s.* Caza de zorras.

fox-evil ['fɒksevɪl] [foks-e-vil], *s.* Enfermedad que hace caer el cabello.

foxery ['fɒksərɪ] [fok-se-ri], *s.* Astucia, zorrería.

foxglove ['fɒksglʌv] [foks-glav], *s.* (*Bot.*) Dedalera, digital purpúrea.

foxhole ['fɒkshəʊl] [foks-joul], *s.* Hoyo practicado en tierra para protegerse uno o dos soldados.

fox-hound ['fɒkshaʊnd] [foks-jaund], *s.* Perro zorrero o raposero, el adiestrado especialmente para la caza de zorras.

fox-hunter ['fɒkshʌntə'] [foks-jan-ta'], *s.* Cazador de zorras.

foxish ['fɒksɪʃ] [fok-sish], **fox-like** ['fɒkslaɪk] [foks-laik], *a.* Astuto o engañoso como el zorro.

fox-ship ['fɒkʃɪp] [fok-ship], *s.* Zorrería.

foxskin ['fɒkskɪn] [fok-skin], *s.* Piel de zorro.

foxtail ['fɒksteɪl] [foks-teil], *s.* Cola de zorra, planta gramínea; alopécuro.

fox-trap ['fɒkstræp] [foks-trap], *s.* La trampa para coger zorras.

fox trot ['fɒkstrɒt] [foks-trot], *s.* Fox-trot, ritmo y baile de E.U.

foxwood ['fɒkswuːd] [foks-wud], *s.* Madera deteriorada o descolorida; en especial, la que emite una luz fosforescente.

foxy ['fɒksɪ] [fok-si], *a.* 1. Raposuno, zorruno; astuto. 2. Rojizo, de color de zorro. **He is very foxy,** es muy astuto.

foxy, *a.* 1. Agriado, impropiamente fermentado, como el vino. 2. Descolorido, manchado, como una tela mal teñida.

foyer ['fɔɪəʳ] [foia'], *s. (Teat.)* Foyer, salón de descanso.

fracas ['frækɑː] [fra-ka], *s.* Contienda ruidosa, pelea, tumulto, batahola.

fract ['frækt] [frakt], *va.* Romper, quebrar.

fraction ['frækʃən] [frak-shon], *s.* 1. Rompimiento, rotura. 2. Fracción, número quebrado.

fractional ['frækʃənl] [frak-sho-nal], *a.* Fraccionario.

fractionate ['frækʃəneɪt] [frak-sho-neit], *v.* 1. Fraccionar. 2. *(Quím.)* Separar por destilación fraccionada.

fractious ['frækʃəs] [frak-shos], *a.* Quisquilloso, reacio, regañón.

fracture ['fræktʃəʳ] [frak-cha'], *s.* Fractura, rompimiento.

fracture, *va.* Fracturar, quebrar o romper un hueso; romper alguna cosa.

fragile ['frædʒaɪl] [fra-yail], *a.* 1. Frágil, quebradizo. 2. Frágil, caduco, perecedero. 3. Frágil, débil.

fragility [frə'dʒɪlɪtɪ] [fra-yi-li-ti], **fragileness** ['frədʒɪlnɪs] [fra-yil-nes], *s.* Fragilidad; instabilidad; debilidad, flaqueza.

fragment ['frægmənt] [frag-ment], *s.* Fragmento; trozo.

fragmentary ['fræg'məntərɪ] [frag-men-ta-ri], *a.* Fragmentario.

fragor ['frægəʳ] [fra-ga'], *s.* (Poco us.) Estallido, estampido.

fragrance, fragrancy ['freɪɡrəns] [fra-grans], *s.* Fragancia, buen olor, perfume natural.

fragrant ['freɪɡrənt] [fra-grant], *a.* Fragante, oloroso.

fragrantly ['freɪɡrəntlɪ] [fra-grant-li], *adv.* Con fragancia.

frail [freɪl] [freil], *a.* 1 Frágil, quebradizo. 2. Frágil, débil; propenso y expuesto a error o engaño. *-s.* Capacho, espuerta de juncos.

frailness ['freɪlnɪs] [freil-nes], **frailty** ['freɪltɪ] [freil-ti], *s.* Fragilidad, flaqueza, debilidad; instabilidad, inconstancia; caducidad.

frailty ['freɪltɪ] [freil-ti], *s.* Fragilidad, debilidad, flaqueza.

fraise ['freɪltɪ] [freis], *s.* Cuello alechugado.

framable ['freɪməbl] [frei-ma-bol], *a.* Componible; que puede ponerse en marco.

frame [freɪm] [freim], *va.* 1. Fabricar, formar, construir. 2. Fabricar, componer, ajustar; arreglar, dirigir. 3. Forjar, inventar, idear. 4. Colocar o encerrar en un marco o cerco. 5. Armar, montar. 6. Concebir, imaginar. 7. Expresar con palabras. **To frame up,** inventar algo contra alguien.

frame, *s.* 1. Figura, hechura, forma. 2. Forjadura, construcción mecánica; armazón, maderaje para la construcción de una casa, esqueleto. 3. Fábrica, marco, cerco. 4. Molde; bastidor. **Embroidery frame,** bastidor, o bastidor para bordar. 5. Arreglo general, orden, constitución de una cosa; condición o estado particular del ánimo. 6. *(Mar.)* Cuaderna. **Frame-timbers,** ligazones. **Midship-frame,** cuaderna maestra. **Stern-frame,** cuaderna del cuerpo popés. 7. Montura (glasses). 8. Cuadro (bicycle).

framer ['freɪməʳ] [frei-ma'], *s.* Fabricante de marcos; forjador; inventor, autor.

frame-up ['freɪmʌp] [freim-ap], *s.* Cosa preparada fraudulentamente, conspiración.

framework ['freɪmwɜːk] [freim-uek], *s.* 1. Armazón, esqueleto, entramado; sostén, lo que sostiene una cosa. 2. Obra de marco o cerco.

framing ['freɪmɪŋ] [frei-min], *s.* El acto de construir; la armazón de una cosa.

franc [fræŋk] [frank], *s.* Franco, moneda francesa.

France [frɑːns] [frans], *s. (Geog.)* Francia.

Frances ['frɑːnsɪs] [fran-sis], *n. pr.* Francisca.

franchise ['fræntʃaɪz] [fran-chais], *s.* 1. Franquicia, un derecho político o constitucional propio del pueblo. 2. Inmunidad, privilegio, exención, concedidos a una persona o un cuerpo. 3. Jurisdicción. 4. Asilo, santuario.

franchise, *va.* Franquear, conceder franquicias; exentar.

franchisement ['fræntʃaɪzmənt] [fran-chais-ment], *s.* Franqueza, libertad, exención; soltura.

Francis ['frɑːnsɪs] [fran-sis], *n. pr.* Francisco.

franciscan [fræ'sɪskən] [fran-sis-kan], *s. y a.* Franciscano, religioso de la orden de San Francisco.

frangible ['frændʒɪbl] [fran-chi-bol], *a.* Frangible, quebradizo, frágil; perecedero.

frangipani ['frændʒɪpənɪ] [fran-chi-pa-ni], *s.* Perfume que se obtiene del jazmín rojo de las Antillas.

Frank [fræŋk] [frank], *n. pr.* Franco. *(Dim.)* Francis.

frank [fræŋk] [frank], *a.* 1. Franco, abierto, natural en sus maneras; sincero, ingenuo. 2. Franco, privilegiado, exento de derechos. **Frank-hearted** Sincero, franco. **Frank-service,** trabajo libre, ejecutado por hombres libres. *-s.* 1. Franqueo; firma autorizada para exentar las cartas, etc., del pago de porte; también carta franca, la que no paga porte. 2. *(Des.)* Porqueriza, pocilga.

frank, *va.* 1. Franquear una carta. 2. *(Des.)* Encerrar en pocilga o zahurda. 3. *(Des.)* Cebar, engordar.

frank-chase ['fræŋktʃeɪs] [frank-cheis], *s.* Caza libre, privilegio de cazar.

frankfurter ['fræŋk.fɜːtəʳ] [frank-fer-ta'], *s.* Variedad de salchicha ahumada.

frankincense ['fræŋkɪnsəns] [fran-kin-sens], *s.* Incienso; goma aromática.

frankish ['fræŋkɪʃ] [fran-kish], *a.* Lo que pertenece a los antiguos franceses; en Levante, lo que se refiere o pertenece a los europeos en general.

franklin, *s. V.* FREEHOLDER. *(Eng.)* Labrador, propietario.

frankly ['fræŋklɪ] [fran-kli], *adv.* Francamente, abiertamente.

frankness ['fræŋknɪs] [frank-nes], *a.* Ingenuidad, sinceridad; franqueza, candor, lisura. 2. *(Ant.)* Generosidad.

frank-pledge ['fræŋkpledʒ] [frank-plech], *s.* Juramento de fidelidad al rey que se prestaba antiguamente en Inglaterra.

franks ['fræŋkz] [franks], *s. pl.* 1. Francos o galos. 2. Francos, nombre que dan los turcos o los moradores de la Europa occidental.

frantic ['fræntɪk] [fran-tik], *a.* Frenético, furioso, enfurecido.

frantically ['fræntɪkəlɪ] [fran-ti-kli], *a.* Frenéticamente, desesperadamente, furiosamente.

franticly ['fræntɪklɪ] [fran-ti-kli], *adv.* Frenéticamente, furiosamente.

franticness ['fræntɪknɪs] [fran-tik-nes], *s.* Frenesí, furor.

frap ['fræp] [frap], *va.* 1. Atar fuertemente. 2. *(Mar.)* Atortorar un buque.

fraternal [frə'tɜːnl] [fra-ter-nal], *a.* Fraternal. **Fraternal Society,** hermandad, mutualidad.

fraternally [frə'tɜːnəlɪ] [fra-ter-na-li] *adv.* Fraternalmente.

fraternity [frə'tɜːnɪtɪ] [fra-ter-ni-ti], *s.* Fraternidad, hermandad; sociedad, junta, gremio, compañía de ciertos artífices, traficantes o estudiantes.

fraternization [,frætɜːnaɪ'zeɪʃən] [fra-ter-nai-sei-shon], *s.* Hermandad, fraternidad.

fraternize ['frætɜːnaɪz] [fra-ter-nais], *vn.* Fraternizar, hermanarse, hermanar.

fratricidal ['frætrɪsaɪdl] [fra-tri-sai-dal], *a.* Relativo al fratricidio.

fratricide ['frætrɪsaɪd] [fra-tri-said], *s.* 1. Fratricidio, el asesinato de un hermano. 2. Fratricida, el que asesina a su hermano.

fraud [frɔːd] [frod], *s.* Fraude, engaño, superchería, artificio.

fraudful ['frɔ:dfʊl] [frod-ful], *a.* Pérfido, engañoso, astuto, artificioso, traidor, de mala fe, engañador; fraudulento.

fraudfully ['frɔ:dfʊlı] [frod-fu-li], *adv.* Engañosamente, pérfidamente.

fraudless ['frɔ:dlıs] [frod-les], *a.* Libre de todo fraude.

fraudulence, fraudulency ['frɔ:djʊləns] [fro-diu-lens], *s.* Fraudulencia, fraude, engaño.

fraudulent ['frɔ:djʊlənt] [fro-diu-lent], *a.* Fraudulento, engañoso.

fraudulently ['frɔ:djʊləntlı] [fro-diu-lent-li], *adv.* Fraudulentamente, fraudulosamente, traidoramente; artificiosamente.

fraught [frɔ:t] [frot], *va.* Cargar. V. FREIGT.

fraught, *a.* Cargado, lleno, atestado de, mezclado con. *(Vul.)* Preñado de. **Fraught with,** lleno o cargado de. -*s.* *(Des.)* Carga, cargazón.

fraxinella ['fræksɪ'nɪ:lə] [frak-si-ni-la], *s.* *(Bot.)* Fraxinela, fresnillo, dictamo blanco.

fray [freɪ] [frei], *s.* Refriega, combate, contienda; riña, disputa, querella. **To part the fray,** separar a los que riñen, ponerlos en paz.

fray, *va.* 1. Ludir, rozar la superficie, margen o borde de una cosa. 2. *(Ant.)* Espantar, ahuyentar. -*vn.* Deshilacharse, destejerse por el margen, deshilarse.

fraying ['freɪɪŋ] [frein], *s.* 1. Rozamiento, desgaste. 2. Deshiladura, acción y efecto de deshilarse.

freak [fri:k] [frik], *s.* Fantasía, capricho, visión; extravagancia. **Freak of nature,** cualquier producto raro, caprichoso o extravagante de la naturaleza.

freak, *va.* Varetear, formar listas de varios colores en los tejidos; abigarrar, gayar.

freakish ['fri:kɪʃ] [fri-kish], *a.* Caprichoso, fantástico, visionario, extravagante.

freakishly ['fri:kɪʃlı] [fri-kish-li], *adv.* Caprichosamente.

freakishness ['fri:kɪʃnɪs] [fri-kish-nes], *s.* La calidad de caprichoso o fantástico.

freckle ['frekl] [fre-kel], *s.* Peca, mota, pinta.

freckle, *vn.* Tener pecas, ponerse pecoso.

freckled ['frekld] [fre-kelt], *a.* Pecoso, moteado.

freckle-faced ['freklfæsɪd] [fre-kel-fa-sid], *a.* Pecoso, con cara pecosa.

freckly ['freklı] [fre-kli], *a.* Pecoso, lleno de pecas.

Fred [fred] [fred] *n. pr.* dim. Federiquito

Frederica ['fredrɪkə] [fre-dri-ka] *n. pr.* Federica.

Frederick ['fredrɪk] [fre-drik] *n.* Federico.

free [fri:] [fri], *a.* 1. Libre, independiente. 2. Libre, licencioso, insubordinado; disoluto, torpe, deshonesto; desenfrenado, atrevido. 3. Liberal, generoso, franco, abierto, ingenuo; familiar. 4. Exento, privilegiado, dispensado. 5. Libre, per mitido, voluntario. 6. Gratuito, lo que es de balde o gratis. 7. Inocente. 8. Cortés, airoso; vivo, activo. 9. *(Mar.)* zafo, flojo, suelto. **Free reed, lengüeta. Free and easy,** *(Fam.)* natural, despejado, no cohibido. **Free-board,** *(Mar.)* obra muerta. **Free-born,** nacido libre, no en esclavitud; libre por herencia. **Free goods,** mercancías exentas de derechos. **Free-handed.** (a) libre de manos, exento de trabas. (b) Liberal, dadivoso. **Free-liver,** comedor, comilón, el que come y bebe mucho. **To make free with,** usar con mucha o demasiada libertad; tomarse libertades con. **Free on board,** *(Com.)* libre de gastos a bordo; comúnmente se abrevia así: **f.o.b. Free port,** puerto franco. **This seat is free,** este asiento está vacante. **To ride a free horse to death,** *(Fig.)* abusar de la paciencia de alguno.

free, *va.* 1. Libertar, poner en libertad. 2. Librar, sacar o preservar a otro de algun riesgo. 3. Libertar, eximir. 4. Abrirse camino. 5. rescatar. **To free the ship,** achicar el agua del bajel.

freeboard ['fri:bɔ:d] [fri-bord] *s.* Obra muerta.

freebooter ['fri:bu:tər] [fri-bu-tar], *s.* 1. Ladrón, saqueador. 2. Filibustero, forbante.

freebooting ['fri:bu:tɪŋ] [fri-bu-tin], *s.* Saqueo, pillaje.

freeborn ['fri:bɔ:n] [fri-born], *a.* Nacido libre, digno de un pueblo libre.

freedman ['fredmən] [fred-man], *s.* Liberto, esclavo manumitido.

freedom ['fri:dəm] [fri-dom], *s.* 1. Libertad, independencia. 2. Libertad, falta de sujeción o subordinación; contravención desenfrenada a las leyes o buenas costumbres. 3. Libertad, licencia, franqueza o familiaridad atrevida: se usa muy comúnmente en plural en una y otra lengua para expresar una impudente o criminal llaneza o familiaridad. 4. Libertad, la facultad de hacer lo que no se oponga a las leyes ni a las buenas costumbres. 5. Libertad, facilidad, comodidad. 6. Libertad, soltura de presos y cautivos. 7. La posesión o concesión de inmunidades o privilegios particulares. **The freedom of a city,** la concesión de inmunidades y privilegios especiales en una ciudad. **The freedom of the press,** la libertad de imprenta. **Freedom of speech,** la libertad de palabra.

free flight ['fri:flaɪt] [fri-flait], *s.* *(Aer.)* Planeo, vuelo libre.

free-footed ['fri:fu:tɪd] [fri-fu-tid], *a.* El que puede andar sin ningún impedimento.

free-for-all ['fri:fə'rɔ:l] [fri-for-ol], *s.* *(Fam.)* Pelotera, lucha o contienda general.

freehand ['fri:hænd] [fri-jand], *a.* Hecho a pulso, sin ayuda de instrumentos. **Freehand drawing,** dibujo a pulso.

free-hearted ['fri:hɑ:tɪd] [fri-jar-tid], *s.* Liberal, generoso; franco, cordial.

freehold ['fri:həʊld] [fri-jould], *s.* Feudo franco, propiedad absoluta de una casa, hacienda, etc.

freeholder ['fri:həʊldər] [fri-joul-dar], *s.* Dueño, propietario absoluto de una casa, heredad, etc.

free-lance ['fri:lɑ:ns] [fri-lans], *a.* Independiente. **Free-lance writer, free-lance actor,** escritor o actor que trabajan independientemente de algún empleo regular.

freely ['fri:lı] [fri-li], *adv.* 1. Libremente, sin restricción, sin reserva; espontáneamente. 2. Desembarazadamente. 3. Francamente, generosamente, de buena gana.

freeman ['fri:mən] [fri-man], *s.* 1. Hombre libre, independiente. 2. Ciudadano, el que goza de los derechos civiles y políticos. 3. Propietario de tierras entre los antiguos anglosajones.

freemartin ['fri:mɑ:tɪn] [fri-mar-tin], *s.* Ternera nacida al mismo tiempo que un ternero y por lo general incapaz de reproducirse.

freemason ['fri:ˌmeɪsn] [fri-mei-son], *s.* Francmasón, masón.

freemasonry ['fri:ˌmeɪsnrı] [fri-mei-son-ri], *s.* Francmasonería.

free-minded ['fri:maɪndɪd] [fri-main-did], *a.* Desembarazado, sin cargas ni cuidados.

freeness ['fri:nɪs] [fri-nes], *s.* Libertad, franqueza; sinceridad; liberalidad.

free press ['fri:pres] [fri-pres], *s.* Libertad de imprenta.

freer ['fri:ər] [friar], *s.* Libertador. -*a.* Más libre; comparativo de **free**.

free-school ['fri:sku:l] [fri-skul], *s.* Escuela gratuita.

freesoiler ['fri:sɔɪlər] [fri-soi-lar], *s.* *(Amer.)* Abolicionista, partidario de la abolición de la esclavitud.

free-spoken ['fri:spəʊkən] [fri-spou-ken], *a.* Dicho sin reserva; franco.

freestone ['fri:stəʊn] [fri-stoun], *s.* 1. Piedra franca, piedra arenosa y blanda. 2. Abridero, durazno cuyo hueso se separa fácilmente de la carne. -*a.* Abridero, abridera, fruta cuyo hueso se desprende fácilmente de la carne.

free-thinker ['fri:ˈθɪŋkər] [fri-zin-kar], *s.* El que piensa con libertad, un filósofo. Esta palabra se toma generalmente en mal sentido, e indica un hombre que no cree la religión revelada, y también un libertino.

free-thinking [ˈfriːˈθɪŋkɪŋ] [fri-zin-kin], *s.* Libertad de pensar; filosofismo, libertinaje, irreligión. -*a.* Que piensa con libertad.

free trade [ˈfriːtreɪd] [fri-treid], *s.* Libre cambio; comercio exento de derechos arancelarios.

free-trader [ˈfriːtreɪdər] [fri-trei-daʳ], *s.* Libre cambista, partidario de la abolición de los derechos arancelarios.

free verse [ˈfriːvɜːs] [fri-vers], *s.* Verso libre.

freeway [ˈfriːweɪ] [fri-uei], *s.* Autopista sin cuota de peaje.

freewheeling [ˈfriːˌwiːlɪŋ] [fri-ui-lin], *s.* (*Mec.*) Marcha de rueda libre.

free-will [ˈfriːˈwɪl] [fri-uil], *s.* Libre albedrío, voluntariedad. -*a.* Hecho o ejecutado sin restricción; voluntario, de buena voluntad.

freewoman [ˈfriːˌwʊmən] [fri-uo-man], *sf.* Mujer libre, no esclava.

freezable [ˈfriːzəbl] [fri-sa-bol], *a.* Congelable.

freeze [friːz] [fris], *vn.* Helarse, helar, -*va.* 1. Congelar, helar de frío. 2. Pasmar de frío, matar de frío. **To freeze on to o to,** (*Ger.*) convertirse en sombra de otra persona; tomar posesión de una cosa. **To freeze out,** (*Fam. E.U.*) excluir, alejar a una persona tratándola con desvío o frialdad. 3. (*Com.*) congelar, inmovilizar fondos o créditos. 4. **To freeze over,** cubrir con una capa de hielo.

freeze-dry [ˌfriːzˈdraɪ] [fris-drai], *va.* Secar congelado, secar en estado de congelación.

freezer [ˈfriːzər] [fri-saʳ], *s.* Congelador, heladora, sorbetera. **Deep freezer,** congeladora.

freezing [ˈfriːzɪŋ] [fri-sin], *a.* Glacial, de hielo, refrigerante. **Freezing point,** punto que marca la congelación del agua en los termómetros. (O° C. y R.; 32° F.) -*s.* Congelamiento, hielo.

Freiburg [ˈfriːbɜːg] [fri-berg], *n. pr.* Friburgo.

freight [freɪt] [freit], *va.* 1. Fletar, dar y tomar a flete un buque. 2. Cargar. 3. Alquilar para el transporte. 4. Transportar por buque o tren.

freight, *s.* 1. Carga, el peso que lleva un buque de géneros u otra cosa; cargazón. 2. Flete, el precio que se paga por el transporte de las mercancías. **Freight outwards,** flete de ida. **Freight home o return freight,** flete de vuelta. **Freight out and in,** flete por viaje redondo. **Dead freight,** flete falso. **Freight free,** libre de flete. **To let to freight,** dejar a flete. **Freight-car,** furgón o carro de carga.

freightage [ˈfreɪtɪdʒ] [frei-tich], *s.* 1. Cargador, flete. 2. Transporte, porte.

freighter [ˈfreɪtər] [frei-tàʳ], *s.* Fletador, cargador, buque de carga.

freight house [ˈfreɪthaʊs] [freit-jaus], *s.* (*F.C. y Mar.*) Depósito de mercancías.

French [frentʃ] [french], *a.* y *s.* 1. Francés. **The French,** los franceses. **After the French fashion,** a la francesa. **A French girl o woman,** una joven o una mujer francesa. 2. El idioma francés. **In good o plain French,** en buen francés. **French leave,** despedida a la francesa, a la chita callando, como la del que ha cometido un hurto y toma soleta. To take French leave, tomar el pendingue. 3. **French horsepower,** caballo de fuerza, caballo de vapor. 4. **French window,** puerta vidriera de dos hojas.

french-bean [ˈfrentʃˈbiːn] [french-bin], *s.* Judía, habichuela, frisol o frijol.

french-chalk [ˈfrentʃˈtʃɔːk] [french-chok], *s.* Blanco de Meudón. V. CHALK.

french-horn [ˈfrentʃˈhɔːn] [french-jorn], *s.* Bocina, instrumento másico de viento. Corno. *V.* HORN.

frenchify [ˈfrentʃɪfaɪ] [fren-chi-fai], *va.* Afrancesarse, tomar o afectar las modas y costumbres de Francia.

french-like [ˈfrentʃlaɪk] [french-laik], *a.* Afrancesado, agabachado, el que imita o afecta las costumbres o modas francesas.

Frenchman [ˈfrentʃmən] [french-man], *s.* Francés, el natural de Francia.

frenetic [frɪˈnetɪk] [fri-ne-tik], *a.* Frenético, furioso.

frenum [ˈfriːnəm] [fre-num], *s.* (*Anat.*) Frenillo.

frenzied [ˈfrenzɪd] [fren-sid], *a.* Frenético, enloquecido.

frenzy [ˈfrenzɪ] [fren-si], *s.* Frenesí, enajenamiento furioso del juicio; locura, extravío, deaveno, desbarro.

frequency [ˈfriːkwənsɪ] [fri-kuen-si], *s.* Frecuencia; ocurrencia común. **Frequency modulation,** (Radio) modulación de frecuencia.

frequent [ˈfriːkwənt] [fri-kuent], *a.* 1. Frecuente; ordinario, común, usado. 2. (*Des.*) Frecuentado, lleno de gente.

frequent, *va.* Frecuentar o visitar a menudo algún lugar.

frequentation [ˈfriːkwənteɪʃən] [fri-kuen-tei-shon], *s.* Frecuentación, relación, trato.

frequentative [frɪˈkwentətɪv] [fri-kuen-ta-tiv], *a.* Frecuentativo.

frequenter [frɪˈkwentər] [fri-kuen-taʳ], *s.* Frecuentador, que tiene trato o relación.

frequently [ˈfriːkwəntlɪ] [fri-kuen-tli], *adv.* Frecuentemente.

fresco [ˈfreskəʊ] [fres-kou], *s.* 1. Pintura al fresco, la que se hace sobre estuco fresco o acabado de hacer; frescura. 2. Frescura, umbría; en la locución al fresco.

fresh [freʃ] [fresh], *a.* 1. Fresco, nuevo, reciente; recién llegado. 2. Refrescante; que reanima; refrigerante; que devuelve las fuerzas. 3. Fresco, sano, robusto, vivo, fuerte. 4. Dulce o nuevo, lo contrario de añejo o acecinado. 5. Inexperto. 6. Fresco, lo que no está caliente ni tibio; viento fresco o galeno. 7. Fresco, lo que no está salado ni mustio. 8. Presumido, oficioso, entremetido. 9. (*Esco.*) (a) Sobrio, no achispado; (b) sin helada; abierto. **Fresh way,** (*Mar.*) salida fresca. **Fresh wind,** (*Mar.*) viento fresco, el algo rápido y fuerte. **A fresh complexion,** una tez fresca. **Fresh horses,** caballos nuevos, de relevo. **A fresh hand,** un novicio. **Fresh from,** acabado de. -*s.* 1. Avenida, inundación. 2. Arroyo o manantial de agua dulce. 3. Mezcla de agua dulce y salada en los ríos y bahías; desbordamiento de un río.

fresh, *va. V.* REFRESH.

fresh-blown [ˈfreʃbloːn] [fresh-blon], *a.* Lo que acaba de echar flor.

freshen [ˈfreʃn] [fre-shen], *va.* Refrescar, desalar, refrigerar. **To freshen the hawse,** (*Mar.*) Refrescar los cables. -*vn.* Refrescarse. **The wind freshens,** (*Mar.*) Refresca el viento.

freshet [ˈfreʃɪt] [fre-shit] *s.* 1. Avenida, riada, inundación. 2. Corriente de agua dulce que entra en el mar.

freshly [ˈfreʃlɪ] [fresh-li], *adv.* Frescamente; hace poco, recientemente.

freshman [ˈfreʃmən] [fresh-man], *s.* 1. Estudiante de primer año. 2. (*Des.*) Novicio.

freshness [ˈfreʃnɪs] [fresh-nes], *s.* 1. Frescura, frescor, el fresco. 2. Frescura, viveza, hermosura, delicadeza, hablando de la tez o de los colores de las flores. 3. El estado de lo que no envejece o pierde fuerzas; renovación del vigor. 4. El estado de lo que es o está fresco, en oposición a lo salado. 5. Pureza. 6. Novedad. 7. Descaro, impertinencia.

fresh water [ˈfreʃˌwɔːtər] [fresh-uo-taʳ], *s.* Agua dulce. **Fresh-water,** *a.* De agua dulce.

fresh-watered [ˈfreʃˌwɔːtəd] [fresh-uoted], *a.* Provisto de agua dulce.

fret [fret] [fret], *s.* 1. Roce o rozamiento; la acción de gastar alguna cosa estregándola; raspadura. 2. Rozadura, el punto gastado o corroído. 3. Enojo, enfado, apuro 4. Hervor, agitación de la superficie de un líquido. 5. Empeine, herpes.

fret, *s.* 1. Traste de guitarra. 2. Obra hecha con cincel, o cualquier obra que forma realce o eminencias sobre un plano. 3. (*Arq.*) Greca, especie de adorno puesto por lo común cerca de las molduras. **Fret-saw,** sierra de calados. 4. Roce, rozamiento. 5. Rozadura, desgaste, roedura. 6. Impaciencia, irritación, preocupación. 7. Hervor, efervescencia. 8. Relieve, cinceladura.

fret, *va.* 1. Rozar, gastar o consumir alguna cosa a fuerza de restregarla. 2. Recamar, bordar en realce; varetear. 3. Agitar, enojar, enfadar. 4. Corroer. -*vn.* 1. Rozarse, gastarse o consumirse, apurarse, incomodarse, impacientarse. 2. Agitarse, enojarse, enfadarse. 3. Afligirse, entristecerse. 4. Fermentar. **Fretted columns,** columnas caladas o estriadas.

fretful ['fretfʊl] [fret-ful], *a*. Enojadizo, colérico, mohino, incómodo, molesto.

fretfully ['fretfəlɪ] [fret-fu-li], *adv*. Con mal humor; de mala gana.

fretfulness ['fretfʊlnɪs] [fret-ful-nes], *s*. Mal genio, mal humor.

fretter ['fretəʳ] [fre-taʳ], *s*. El que o lo que consume o enoja. **Vine-fretter,** pulgón de viña.

fretting ['fretɪŋ] [fre-tin], *s*. Agitación, conmoción; entristecimiento. -*pa*. de TO FRET.

fretty ['fretɪ] [fre-ti], *a*. 1. Realzado, bordado, cincelado. 2. *(Fam. E.U.)* Enojadizo, mohino; se aplica por lo común a las criaturas.

fretwork ['fretwɜ:k] [fret-uek], *s*. Greca, adorno; *(Carp.)* calado.

Freudian ['frɔɪdɪən] [froi-dian], *a*. Freudiano.

Freudianism ['frɔɪdɪənɪzm] [froi-dia-nism], *s*. Freudismo.

friability ['fraɪə'bɪlɪtɪ] [fraia-bi-li-ti], *s*. Friabilidad, la calidad de lo que se puede desmenuzar.

friable ['fraɪəbl] [fraia-bol], *a*. Friable, desmenuzable.

friar ['fraɪəʳ] [fraiaʳ], *s*. 1. Fraile, título que se da a los religiosos de algunas órdenes. **Austin friar,** fraile agustino. **Black friar,** dominicano. **Gray friar,** franciscano. **White friar,** carmelita. 2. **Friar o friarbird,** pájaro de Australia, el tropidorinco. **Friar's chicken,** *(Esco.)* Caldo de gallino y huevos. **Friar's lantern,** fuego fatuo, meteóro.

friar-like ['fraɪəlaɪk] [fraia-laik], *a*. Frailesco, frailero.

friary ['fraɪərɪ] [fraia-ri], *s*. Convento de frailes. -*a*. Frailero.

fribble ['frɪbl] [fri-bol], *vn*. Tontear, bobear; vacilar.

fribble, *a*. Vano, inútil, frívolo. -*s*. Pisaverde frívolo; hombre despreciable.

fribbler ['frɪbləʳ] [fri-blaʳ], *s*. Un hombre necio.

fricassee ['frɪkəsi:] [fri-ka-si], *s*. Fricasé, fritada, cochifrito.

fricassee, *va*. Hacer un fricasé o guisar algo a modo de fricasé.

fricative ['frɪkətɪv] [fri-ka-tiv], *a*. Caracterizado o producido por la fricción.

friction ['frɪkʃən] [frik-shon], *s*. 1. Fricción; frotación, frotadura. 2. Friega. **Friction clutch o coupling,** manguito de fricción. **Friction matches,** fósforos de fricción. **Friction gearing,** engranaje de fricción.

frictional ['frɪkʃənl] [frik-sho-nal] *a*. De fricción, de rozamiento; producido por el rozamiento. **Frictional resistence,** resistencia al rozamiento. **Frictional tape,** cinta aislante.

Friday ['fraɪdeɪ] [frai-dei], *s*. Viernes. **Good Friday,** viernes santo. **Black Friday,** cualquier viernes memorable por una calamidad pública.

fried [fraɪd] [fraid], *a*. Frito. **Fried egg,** huevo frito o estrellado.

friend [frend] [frend], *s*. 1. Amigo, amiga. 2. Compañero, favorecedor, persona propicia o favorable. 3. Adherente, partidario; aliado. 4. Cuáquero, miembro de la sociedad de los cuáqueros, secta religiosa. **A bosom friend,** amigo de corazón. **A friend at court,** amigo que tiene el poder de servir a otro. **To make friends with one,** reconciliarse, hacer las paces. **A friend in need is a friend indeed,** en la necesidad se conoce al verdadero amigo. **Short reckonings make long friends,** cuanto más amigos más claros; o las cuentas claras hacen los buenos amigos. **To make friends with,** trabar amistad con, hacerse amigo de; reconciliarse, hacer las amistades.

friendless ['frendlɪs] [frend-les], *a*. Desamparado, desvalido, sin protección ni amigos.

friend-like ['frendlaɪk] [frend-laik], **friendly** ['frendlɪ] [frend-li], *a*. 1. Amigable, amistoso, como amigo. 2. Servicial, favorable, benévolo, dispuesto a favorecer los intereses de otro. 3. Favorable, propicio.

friendliness ['frendlɪnɪs] [frend-li-nes], *s*. Amistad, amigabilidad, afabilidad, cordialidad.

friendship ['frendʃɪp] [frend-ship], *s*. Amistad, intimidad, afecto; favor, socorro, ayuda.

frieze [fri:z] [fris], *s*. 1. Frisa, tela de lana a modo de bayeta. 2. *(Arq.)* Friso.

frieze-like ['fri:zlaɪk] [fris-laik], *a*. Semejante a la frisa.

frigate ['frɪgɪt] [fri-guit], *s*. *(Mar.)* Fragata, antiguo bajel de guerra. **Frigate-bird,** fragata, ave acuática de los mares tropicales.

frigate-built ['frɪgɪt'bɪlt] [fri-guit-bilt], *a*. *(Mar.)* Construido a manera de fragata.

fright *(Poét.)*, **frighten** [fraɪt] [frait], *va*. Espantar, causar horror, miedo o espanto, asustar. **To frighten to death,** hacer, causar un miedo mortal. **To frighten away,** ahuyentar, espantar.

fright, *s*. 1. Susto, espanto, terror repentino. 2. Espantajo, esperpento, lo que causa espanto. **To take fright at,** asustarse de. **What a fright you have made of yourself!,** ¡está Ud. hecho un espantajo!

frighten ['fraɪtn] [frai-ten], *v*. Asustar, espantar aterrazar, atemorizar. **To frighten away,** ahuyentar.

frightful ['fraɪtfʊl] [frait-ful], *a*. Espantoso, horrible; feísimo, horroroso, espantable.

frightfully ['fraɪtəlɪ] [frait-fu-li], *adv*. Espantosamente, terriblemente.

frightfulness ['fraɪtfʊlnɪs] [frait-ful-nes], *s*. Horror, espanto.

frigid ['frɪdʒɪd] [fri-chid], *a*. 1. Frío, frígido. 2. Indiferente; impotente. 3. Frío, lo que no tiene brío, espíritu ni agudeza.

frigidity [frɪ'dʒɪdɪtɪ] [fri-chi-di-ti], *s*. 1. Frialdad, falta de calor. 2. Frialdad, flojedad, negligencia, lentitud. 3. Frialdad, despego, indiferencia, tibieza de afectos. 4. Impotencia.

frigidly ['frɪdʒɪdlɪ] [fri-chid-li], *adv*. Fríamente, con frialdad o despego.

frigorific ['frɪgərɪfɪk] [fri-go-ri-fik], *s*. Frigorífico.

frill [frɪl] [fril], *s*. 1. Escote, vuelo; chorrera, pechera. 2. Lechuga, pliegue. 3. Volante, chorrera. 4. *(Zool.)* Collar de plumas o de pelos. 5. *pl*. *(E.U. Fam.)* Aires, ademanes afectados.

frill, *s*. Tiritón que sufren los halcones y otras aves.

frill, *va*. 1. Hacer algo en forma de vuelo o chorrera. 2. Guarnecer con vuelos o pecheras. 3. Adornar con volantes. 4. Arrugar, escarolar. -*vn*. Formar o tener algo la forma de vuelo o chorrera.

fringe [frɪndʒ] [frinch], *s*. Franja; margen, borde, fleco, rodapié, orla, ribete, orilla, guarnición.

fringe, *va*. Ribetear, franjear, orillar.

fringe benefit ['frɪndʒ'benfɪt] [frinch-be-ne-fit], *s*. *(Com.)* Beneficio marginal o adicional.

fringeless ['frɪndʒlɪs] [frinch-les], *a*. Desprovisto de franjas; sin ribete.

fringe-maker ['frɪndʒ'meɪkəʳ] [frinch-mei-kaʳ], *s*. Fabricante de franjas, cordonero.

fringe-tree ['frɪndʒtri:] [frinch-tri], *s*. Árbol pequeño de los Estados Unidos del este.

fringy ['frɪndʒɪ] [frin-chi], *a*. Adornado con franjas; parecido a un ribete.

fripper, fripperer ['frɪpəʳ] [fri-paʳ], *s*. Ropavejero, baratillero; prendero.

frippery ['frɪpərɪ] [fri-pe-ri], *s*. 1. Ropavejería; baratillo. 2. Ropa vieja, vestidos viejos o desechos. 3. Fruslería, bobería. -*a*. Despreciable, frívolo.

friseur ['frɪsju:ʳ] [fri-siuʳ], *s*. Peluquero.

frisk [frɪsk] [frisk], *vn*. Saltar, brincar, cabriolar, estar en continuo movimiento; retozar.

frisk, *s*. Retozo; gambeta, brinco o salto.

frisker ['frɪskəʳ] [fris-kaʳ], *s*. El que es inconstante o voluble.

frisket ['frɪskɪt] [fris-kit], *s*. *(Impr.)* Frasqueta, bastidor de hierro que sujeta el papel en las prensas de mano.

friskiness ['frɪskɪnɪs] [fris-ki-nes], *s*. Viveza en el trato, alegría, vivacidad.

frisking ['frɪskɪŋ] [fris-kin], *s*. Alegría rústica, baile juguetón.

friskful ['frɪskfʊl] [frisk-ful], **frisky** ['frɪskɪ] [fris-ki], *a*. Juguetón, alegre, desparpajado, vivaracho, gallardo, vivo.

frit ['frɪt] [frit], *s*. 1. Frita; en las fábricas de vidrio, la mezcla destinada a fundirse en los crisoles. 2. Frita, el material o ingredientes de que se hacen ciertos artículos blandos y plásticos de alfarería.

frith o **firth** [frɪθ] [friz], *s*. 1. *(Esco.)* Estrecho o brazo de mar. 2. Nasa, especie de red.

frithy ['frɪθɪ] [fri-zi], *a*. *(Des.)* Leñoso, selvático.

fritillary ['frɪtɪlərɪ] [fri-ti-la-ri], *s*. *(Bot.)* Fritilaria, planta de las liliáceas.

fritter ['frɪtəʳ] [fri-taʳ], *s*. 1. Tajada, torrezno, fritilla. 2. Fragmento, parte pequeña de alguna cosa. 3. Quesadilla, torta de queso. 4. Buñuelo, hojaldre, fruta de sartén.

frivolity [frɪ'vɒlɪtɪ] [fri-vo-li-ti], *s*. Frivolidad.

frivolous ['frɪvələs] [fri-vo-los], *a*. Frívolo, vano, inútil.

frivolously ['frɪvələslɪ] [fri-vo-los-li], *adv*. Frívolamente, vanamente.

frivolousness ['frɪvələsnɪs] [fri-vo-los-nes], *s*. Frivolidad.

frizz, frizzle [frɪzl] [fri-sel], *va*. Frisar; rizar, encrespar, ensortijar.

frizzle, *s*. Rizo, bucle.

frizzler ['frɪzləʳ] [fris-laʳ], *s*. Rizador, frisador.

fro [frəʊ] [frou], *adv*. Atrás, hacia atrás. **To go to and fro,** ir y venir, ir de un lado a otro. **Goings to and fro,** idas y venidas.

frock [frɒk] [frok], *s*. 1. Bata de niño o de señora; túnica, vestido exterior de mujer. 2. Blusa. **Frock-coat,** levita. **Smock frock,** sayo, especie de camisa de lienzo ordinario, que se pone sobre el vestido para resguardarlo. 3. Hábito.

frog [frɒg] [frog], *s*. 1. Rana. Ranilla, hendidura del talón del caballo. 3. *(Ferro.)* Corazón de desvío; parte o sección de la vía en que un carril corta a otro o se separa de él, como sucede en los cambiavías o chuchos. **Frog-plate,** (a) Pieza que sirve para colocar la pata de una rana bajo el microscopio a fin de observar la circulación de la sangre. (b) Bastidor de cambio o de rana en los ferrocarriles. **Tree-frog,** calamite, sapo verde y pequeño.

frogbit ['frɒgbɪt] [frog-bit], *s*. *(Bot.)* Morena, planta acuática.

froggy ['frɒgɪ] [fro-gui], *a*. Lleno de ranas.

frogman ['frɒgmən] [frog-man], *s*. Hombre rana.

frolic ['frɒlɪk] [fro-lik], *s*. 1. Fantasía, capricho, extravagancia, jarana. 2. Juego, travesura. -*a*. Alegre, vivo, vivaracho, caprichoso.

frolic, *vn*. Loquear, juguetear, retozarse, estar de chacota, triscar, jaranear.

frolicsome ['frɒlɪksʌm] [fro-lik-sam], *a*. Juguetón, travieso.

frolicsomely ['frɒlɪksʌməlɪ] [fro-lik-sa-me-li], *adv*. Alegremente, con humorada o viveza.

frolicsomeness ['frɒlɪksʌmnɪs] [fro-lik-som-nes], *s*. Viveza, humorada, demasiada alegría.

from [frɒm] [from], *prep*. 1. De. **From my heart,** de lo íntimo de mi corazón. **From time to time,** de cuando en cuando. 2. Después, desde. **From that time,** desde entonces, desde aquel tiempo. 3. De, desde, hablando de lugar. **From top to toe,** de pies a cabeza. **From above,** desde arriba, de lo alto. **From afar,** de lejos. **From amidst,** del medio de. **From beneath.** De abajo, de lo hondo. **From behind,** desde atrás. **From beyond,** de más allá. **From far,** desde lejos, de lejos. **From without,** de fuera. **From among,** de entre. **From off,** lejos, fuera de. **From on high,** desde lo alto. **From out,** de, desde, del fondo de. **From under,** de debajo. 4. Por, a causa de, a fuerza de; debido *a*. **From an honorable motive,** por un motivo honroso. **Rather from policy than,** más bien por política que. **There is danger from ignorance,** hay peligro a causa de la ignorancia. 5. De, de parte de. **He came from the general.** 6. Según, conforme. **From what I hear,** según lo que oigo, o según oigo. **Painted from nature,** pintado del natural, conforme al natural. 7. Sobre; en; contra. **Men do not gather figs from thistles,** no se cogen higos en (o entre) los abrojos. **A revolt from the monarchy,** una rebelión contra la monarquía. 8. Con. **He made a supper from the remains of his dinner,** cenó con los restos de la comida. Esta preposición frecuentemente se invierte en el estilo familiar, como, **Where do you come from!,** ¿de dónde viene Ud.?

frond [frɒnd] [frond], *s*. *(Bot.)* 1. Fronda, la parte hojosa que sostiene la fructificación de los helechos y las algas. 2. Cualquier hoja grande de los trópicos, como la de la palmera.

frondas ['frɒndəs] [fron-das], *s*. *(Boot.)* Frondas, follaje.

frondent ['frɒndənt] [fron-dent], **frondose** ['frɒndəʊz] [frond-ous], *a*. *(Bot.)* Frondoso.

frondescent ['frɒnəsənt] [fron-de-sent], *a*. *(Bot.)* Frondescente; se dice de los vegetales cuando están desplegando sus hojas y de las plantas que llevan fronda.

frondiferous ['frɒndɪfərəs] [fron-di-fe-ros], *a*. *(Bot.)* Frondífero.

front [frɒnt] [front], *s*. 1. Frente. 2. Frente, la parte que está en frente de alguno. 3. Faz, cara; la manera de hacer frente a una persona o situación. **Put the best front you can on the matter,** ponga Ud. en este asunto la mejor cara que pueda. 4. Apariencia de grandeza y riqueza. **To put on a front,** aparentar, hacer ostentación. 5. Fachada, frontispicio. 6. Pechera de camisa. 7. *(Teat.)* Auditorio. 8. Paseo frente al mar. 9. **In the front of the book,** al principio del libro. **To stand front to front,** estar cara a cara. **In front of,** en frente de, cara a cara con. 4. Audacia, atrevimiento, descaro. 5. *(Arq.)* Frente, frontispicio, fachada; portal, como de una iglesia. 6. Pechera, delantera, camisolín; caña de una bota. **Front door,** puerta de entrada. **Front bolt,** pasador que asegura el fusil a la caja.

front, *a*. 1. Anterior, delantero, lo que está al frente. 2. Frontero, mirado del frente. 2. Frontero, mirado del frente. 3. Medido por el frente. 4. Frontal. **Front room,** cuarto de frente, cuarto a la calle o en la fachada principal de una casa. **Front view,** vista al frente.

front, *va*. 1. Hacer frente, oponerse cara a cara. 2. Estar en frente de alguna cosa. -*vn*. 1. Estar al frente. 2. Dar a, caer *a*. **This house fronts on the park,** esta casa da al parque.

frontage ['frɒntɪdʒ] [fran-tich], *s*. Extensión lineal de frente. **The lot has a frontage of seventy feet on North Street,** el solar tiene un frente de setenta pies en la calle Norte.

frontal ['frɒntl] [fran-tal], *a*. 1. Frontero, anterior. 2. Frontal, perteneciente a la frente. -*s*. 1. *(Arq.)* Tímpano pequeño. 2. Frontero, venda.

front curtain [frɒnt'kɑːtɪn] [front-kar-tin], *s*. *(Teat.)* Telón de boca.

frontier ['frɒntɪəʳ] [fron-tiaʳ], *s*. Frontera, la raya o término de un territorio. -*a*. Fronterizo, frontero. **Frontier town,** ciudad fronteriza.

frontiniac ['frɒntɪnɪək] [fron-ti-niak], *s*. Vino de Frontiñán en Francia.

frontispiece ['frɒntɪspiːs] [fron-tis-pis], *s*. 1. El frontis grabado de un libro. 2. Frontispicio.

frontless ['frɒntlɪs] [front-les], *a*. Descarado, desvergonzado, impudente.

frontlet ['frɒntlɪt] [front-let], *s*. 1. Venda para la frente. 2. *(Art.)* Frontón de mira. 3. *(Orn.)* Margen de la cabeza detrás del pico de las aves que está por lo común cubierto con cerdas.

front seat ['frɒntsiːt] [front-sit], *s*. Asiento delantero.

frost [frɒst] [frost], *s*. 1. Helada, hielo. **Hoar frost, white frost,** escarcha. **Frost bite,** congelación parcial de los dedos o las orejas. **Frost-nail,** clavo de gancho que se pone en las herraduras del caballo en tiempo de hielos para que no resbale. **Frost-nipped,** quemado por el hielo.

frost, *va*. 1. Helar. 2. Escarchar, cubrir un manjar con una composición azucarada, parecida a la escarcha. 3. Dañar por medio del frío o el hielo, quemar. 4. Deslustrar, despulir.

frosted ['frɒstɪd] [fros-tid], *pp*. y *a*. 1. Helado. 2. Deslustrado, despulido; que presenta una superficie áspera y sin brillo.

frost-bitten ['frɒstbɪtn] [frost-biten], *a*. Helado, quemado o marchitado por el hielo o la escarcha.

frostiness ['frɒstɪnɪs] [fros-ti-nes], *s*. Frío, helamiento.

frosting

frosting ['frɒstɪŋ] [fros-tin], *s.* 1. Clara de huevo batida con azúcar, que forma como una capa de nieve sobre ciertos pasteles. 2. Deslustre, aspereza en la superficie del metal, el cristal o la madera; cualquier superficie que imita la escarcha.

frost-work ['frɒst'wɜːk] [frost-uek], *s.* Garapiña, garapiñado.

frosty ['frɒstɪ] [fros-ti], *a.* 1. Helado, frío como el hielo. 2. Frío, indiferente, insensible. 3. Cano, canoso. 4. Glacial, escarchado.

froth [frɒθ] [froz], *s.* 1. Espuma que forma el hervor o agitación de algún líquido. 2. Bambolla, paja.

froth, *vn.* Espumar, criar espuma. -*va.* Hacer espuma.

frothily ['frɒθɪlɪ] [fro-zi-li], *adv.* Con espuma; frívolamente, sin sustancia.

frothiness ['frɒθɪnɪs] [fro-zi-nes], *s.* Vaciedad, frivolidad.

frothy ['frɒθɪ] [fro-zi], *a.* 1. Espumoso, lleno o cubierto de espuma. 2. Frívolo, vano, inútil.

frounce ['frɑʊns] [frouns], *va. (Ant.)* Rizar, encrespar o ensortijar el cabello. -*vn.* Ponerse ceñudo.

frouzy ['frɑʊsɪ] [frou-si], *a.* V. FROWZY.

frow [frɑʊ] [frou], *s. (Fam.)* Dama holandesa o alemana; mujer casada.

froward ['frɑʊəd] [frouard], *a.* Indómito, incorregible, díscolo, protervo; insolente, impertinente. **A froward child,** niño impertinente y difícil de contentar.

frowardly ['frɑʊədlɪ] [frouard-li], *adv.* Indócilmente, arrogantemente, insolentemente.

frowardness ['frɑʊədnɪs] [frouard-nes], *a.* Indocilidad.

frown [frɑʊn] [fraun], *va.* Mirar con ceño, poner mala cara. -*vn.* 1. Poner mal gesto, ponerse ceñudo, enfurruñarse. **To frown upon one,** mirar a alguno con malos ojos. **To frown anyone down,** avergonzar a uno, hacerle bajar los ojos, sonrojarle. 2. Rechazar a alguno con aspecto amenazador o severo. **He frowned them into silence,** su expresión amenazadora los redujo al silencio.

frown, *s.* Ceño, entrecejo, desagrado, enfado o enojo. **Frowns of fortune,** reveses de fortuna.

frowning ['frɑʊnɪŋ] [frau-nin], *a.* Ceñudo, hosco, malcarado.

frowningly ['frɑʊnɪŋlɪ] [frau-nin-li], *adv.* Enojadamente, con ceño, de mal ojo, hoscamente.

frowzy ['frɑʊzɪ] [frau-si], *a.* Desaliñado, desaseado, sucio; mal peinado.

froze [frɑʊz] [frous], *pret.* del verbo FREEZE.

frozen ['frɑʊzn] [frou-sen], *pp.* de TO FREEZE. 1. Helado, congelado; frío. 2. Fijo, inmóvil, invariable.

fructiferous [frʌk'tɪfərəs] [frak-ti-fe-ros], *a.* Fructífero, que da frutos.

fructification [ˌfrʌktɪfaɪ'keɪʃən] [frak-ti-fai-kei-shon], *s. (Bot.)* Fructificación; fecundación.

fructify ['frʌktɪfaɪ] [frak-ti-fai], *va.* Fertilizar, fecundar. -*vn.* Fructificar, dar o producir fruto.

fructivorous [frʌk'tɪvərəs] [frak-ti-vo-ros], *a. (Zool.)* Frugívoro.

fructose ['frʌktəʊs] [frak-tous], *s.* Fructosa.

fructuous ['frʌktɪəs] [frak-tos], *a.* Fructuoso, provechoso.

frugal ['fruːgəl] [fru-gal], *a.* Económico, frugal, sobrio, templado.

frugality [fruː'gælɪtɪ] [fru-ga-li-ti], *s.* Economía; frugalidad, moderación, sobriedad o templanza.

frugally ['fruːgəlɪ] [fru-ga-li], *adv.* Frugalmente, sobriamente.

frugiferous ['fruːdʒɪfərəs] [fru-chi-fe-ros], *a.* Fructífero.

frugivorous ['fruːdʒɪvərəs] [fru-chi-vo-ros], *a.* Frugívoro, que se alimenta de frutos.

fruit [fruːt] [frut], *s.* 1. Fruto. 2. Fruta. **Dry fruit,** fruta seca. **To live upon fruit,** mantenerse con fruta. 3. Fruto, producto, utilidad, provecho. 4. Prole. 5. Postres. **Fruit-basket,** cesta para fruta. **Fruit-knife,** cuchillo de postres. **Fruit-jar,** vaso o tarro para frutas, en especial el que puede cerrarse herméticamente. **Stone fruit,** fruta de hueso. **Fruit-bearing,** frutal, que produce fruta. **Fruit-dryer.** secadero de frutas. **Fruit-eating,** frugívoro. **Fruit press,** aparato para

prensar frutas. **Preserved fruit.** Fruta en almíbar. **Candied fruit,** fruta azucarada.

fruit, *vn.* Producir fruta, dar fruto, fructificar.

fruitage ['fruːtɪdʒ] [fru-tich], *s.* 1. Frutas, toda suerte de fruta general. 2. Fruto, resultado o efecto de alguna acción.

fruit-bearer [fruːt'bɛərəʳ] [frut-bea-raʳ], *s.* Frutal; lo que produce fruta.

fruit-bearing [fruːt'bɛərɪŋ] [frut-bea-rin], *a.* Fructífero; frutal.

fruit cake ['fruːtkeɪk] [frut-keik], *s.* Pastel de frutas.

fruiter ['fruːtəʳ] [fru-taʳ], *s.* Frutal, buque frutero.

fruiterer ['fruːtərəʳ] [fru-te-raʳ], *s.* Frutero (seller).

fruitery ['fruːtərɪ] [fru-te-ri], *s.* 1. Fruta. 2. Frutería, lugar destinado a guardar la fruta.

fruitful ['fruːtfʊl] [frut-ful], *a.* Fructífero, fértil, prolífico, abundante, copioso, fecundo; provechoso, útil, ventajoso.

fruitfully ['fruːtfəlɪ] [frut-fu-li], *adv.* Fértilmente, prolíficamente, provechosamente, fértilmente.

fruitfulness ['fruːtfʊlnɪs] [frut-ful-nes], *s.* Fertilidad, fecundidad.

fruit-groves ['fruːtgrəʊvz] [frut-grovs], *s. pl.* Vergel de frutales.

fruition [fruː'ɪʃən] [fru-ishon], *s.* 1. Fruición. 2. Fruición, gusto, complacencia.

fruit-piece ['fruːtpiːs] [frut-pis], *s.* Frutaje, frutero.

fruitless ['fruːtlɪs] [frut-les], *a.* Estéril, infructuoso; inútil, vano.

fruitlessly ['fruːtlɪslɪ] [frut-les-li], *adv.* Infructuosamente; inútilmente.

fruitlessness ['fruːtlɪsnɪs] [frut-les-nes], *s.* Esterilidad; infructuosidad.

fruit stand ['fruːtstænd] [frut-stand], *s.* Puesto de frutas.

fruit store ['fruːtstɔːʳ] [frut-staʳ], *s.* Frutería.

fruit-time ['fruːt'taɪm] [frut-taim], *s.* Otoño, cosecha, el tiempo de recoger los frutos.

fruit-tree ['fruːt'triː] [frut-tri], *s.* Frutal, árbol que produce fruta.

fruity ['fruːɪtɪ] [frui-ti], *a.* Semejante a la fruta en el sabor, el olor o las cualidades.

frumentaceous ['fruːmən'teɪʃəs] [fru-men-tei-shos], *a.* Frumenticio.

frumenty ['fruːməntɪ] [fru-men-ti], *s.* Manjar hecho de trigo cocido con leche.

frump [frʌmp] [framp], *s.* 1. Vieja que se viste a la antigua y es de genio áspero y regañón, regañona, chismosa. 2. Mujer desaliñada. 3. *(Des.)* Chiste, burla, mofa.

frumpish ['frʌmpɪʃ] [fram-pish], *a.* 1. Desaliñado. 2. Pasado de moda, anticuado (dress). 3. Malhumorado, regañón.

frush [frʌʃ] [frash], *va.* Romper, magullar, quebrar.

frush, *s. (Vet.)* Arestín.

frustrable ['frʌstrəbl] [fras-tra-bol], *a.* Capaz de ser frustrado.

frustrate ['frʌstreɪt] [fras-treit], *va.* 1. Frustrar, privar o defraudar a uno de lo que le tocaba o esperaba; burlar, dejar burlada la intención o esperanza de una persona. 2. Anular, hacer nula una cosa.

frustrate, *a.* 1. Frustrado, fallido, burlado. 2. Inútil, vano, nulo. 3. Desventajoso.

frustration [frʌs'treɪʃən] [fras-trei-shon], *s.* 1. Frustración, desbaratamiento, desconcierto. 2. Fracaso, contratiempo, chasco; privación.

frustrative ['frʌstrətɪv] [fras-tra-tiv], *a.* Falaz, engañoso.

frustratory ['frʌstrətərɪ] [fras-tra-to-ri], *a. (For.)* Frustratorio, lo que hace nula alguna cosa; frustráneo.

frustule ['frʌstjuːl] [fras-tiul], *s. (Bot.)* Frústula, el casco silíceo de un diátomo.

frustum ['frʌstrəm] [fras-trum], *s.* 1. Parte inferior de un cuerpo sólido que se forma cortando la cúspide por un plano paralelo a la base. 2. Trozo, pedazo.

frutescence ['fruːtəsəns] [fru-te-sens], *s. (Bot.)* Calidad de fruticoso.

frutescent [ˈfruːtəsənt] [fru-te-sent], *a. (Bot.)* Fruticoso; se dice de las plantas que se hacen arbustos o que se parecen a un arbusto.

fruticose [ˈfruːtɪkəʊz] [fru-ti-kous], *a.* Fruticoso, relativo a los arbustos o que se parecen a un arbusto.

fry [fraɪ] [frai], *s.* 1. El conjunto de pececillos que sale del desove o de las huevas. 2. Enjambre, la muchedumbre de cosas juntas o de personas, cuando unas y otras son de poca importancia. 3. Fritada, el conjunto de cosas fritas. 4. *(Fam.)* Aprieto, brete, estado de molestia o agitación.

fry, *va.* Freír. *-vn.* Freírse; derretirse de calor; estar agitado o acalorado. **To have other fish to fry,** tener otras cosas en que pensar.

frying-pan [ˈfraɪɪŋˌpæn] [frain-pan], *s.* Sartén. **To jump from the frying-pan into the fire,** saltar de la sartén y dar en las brasas.

fucate, fucated [ˈfjuːkeɪt] [fiu-keit], *a.* Pintado, disfrazado.

fuchsia [ˈfʌkʃə] [fak-sha], *s.* Fucsia, arbusto con flores rojas y purpúreas del mismo nombre, que cuelgan de las axilas; es planta de adorno originaria de la América del Sur.

fucoid [ˈfʊkɔɪd] [fu-koid], *a.* Fucóideo, que se parece a los fucus u ovas. *-s.* 1. Alga parecida al fuco. 2. Planta viva o fósil que se asemeja a las algas.

fucus [ˈfʌkəs] [fa-kos], *s.* 1. Afeite, aderezo y compostura del rostro; disfraz. 2. *(Bot.)* Fuco, ova. **Fuci,** *pl.* Fucos.

fuddle [fʌdl] [fa-del], *va.* Emborrachar. *-vn.* Emborracharse.

fudge [fʌdʒ] [fadch], *s.* 1. Embuste, cuento; se usa más como interjección. ¡Quita de ahí! ¡Quita allá! 2. Dulce de chocolate.

fudge, *v.* 1. Arreglar, amañar, inventar. 2. *(Impr.)* Insertar noticias de última hora.

fuel [fjʊəl] [fiuel], *s.* 1. Combustible, todo lo que sirve de alimento al fuego. 2. Pábulo, aliciente.

fuel, *va. (Ant.)* Servir material combustible al fuego; proveer con leña o materials para el fuego.

fueling [ˈfjʊəlɪŋ] [fiue-lin], *s.* Abastecimiento de combustible.

fugacious [ˈfəɡeɪʃəs] [fa-guei-shos], *a.* 1. Fugaz, volátil, instable; transitorio. 2. *(Bot.)* Fugaz, que se cae o que parece muy temprano.

fugaciously [ˈfəɡeɪʃəsli] [fa-guei-shos-li], *adv.* Fugazmente.

fugaciousness [ˈfəɡeɪʃəsnɪs] [fa-guei-shos-nes], **fugacity** [ˈfəɡæsɪti] [fa-gue-si-ti], *s.* Fugacidad, instabilidad, volatilidad.

fugh [fʌɡ] [fag], *inter.* ¡Fo! expresión de asco o enfado.

fugitive [ˈfjuːdʒɪtɪv] [fiu-yi-tiv], *a.* Fugitivo, desterrado, expulsado; fugaz, volátil, vagabundo, huidizo; pasajero, perecedero. *-s.* 1. Fugitivo, desertor, tránsfuga, apóstata. 2. Refugiado; contumaz, el que sustrae por la fuga a la acción de la justicia. **Fugitive pieces,** folletos sueltos.

fugitiveness [ˈfjuːdʒɪtɪvnɪs] [fiu-yi-tiv-nes], *s.* Fugacidad, instabilidad.

fugleman, fugelman [ˈfʌɡlmən] [fa-guel-man], *s.* 1. *(Mil.)* Jefe de fila; el que manda una hilera de soldados. 2. Guía, modelo.

fugue [ˈfjuːɡ] [fiug], *s. (Mús.)* Fuga, composición que gira sobre un tema y su imitación, repetidos con cierto artificio por diferentes tonos.

ful [fʊl] [ful], sufijo. 1. Lleno de; abundante en; que contiene. **Fruitful,** abundante en frutos. 2. Capacidad, cabida o medida; v. g. **spoonful,** cucharada; **a glassful,** un vaso lleno, el contenido de un vaso. Los nombres que tienen este sufijo forman el plural añadiendo la letra s: **cupful, cupfuls.**

fulcrum [ˈfʌlkrəm] [fal-krom], *s.* 1. *(Mec.)* Apoyo de palanca o alzaprima. 2. *(Bot.)* Accesorios, apéndice u órgano de las plantas, como pedúnculo, espina, aguijón, zarcillo, etc.

fulfil [fʊlˈfɪl] [ful-fil], *va.* 1. Colmar, llenar abundantemente, llenar hasta arriba. 2. Cumplir, ejecutar lo que se había prometido. 3. Observar con exactitud lo que está mandado. **To fulfil one's duty,** cumplir con su obligación.

fulfiller [fʊlˈfɪlər] [ful-fi-lar], *s.* El que cumple o llena.

fulfilling [fʊlˈfɪlɪŋ] [ful-fi-lin], *s.* Cumplimiento.

fulfilment [fʊlˈfɪlmənt] [ful-fil-ment], *s.* Ejecución completa de alguna cosa.

fulgency [ˈfʊldʒənsi] [ful-chen-si], **fulgidity** [fʊlˈdʒɪdɪti] [ful-chi-di-ti], **fulgor** [ˈfʊlɡər] [ful-gar], *s.* Fulgor, resplandor, esplendor.

fulgent [ˈfʊldʒənt] [ful-chent], **fulgid** [ˈfʊldʒɪd] [ful-chid], *a.* Fulgente, brillante, fúlgido.

fulgurate [ˈfʊlɡəreɪt] [ful-ga-reit], *vn.* Fulgurar.

fulguration [ˌfʊlɡəˈreɪʃən] [ful-ga-rei-shon] *s.* Fulguración, relámpago.

fulgurite [ˈfʊlɡərɪt] [ful-ga-rit] *s.* Fulgurita.

fuliginous [ˈfʊldʒɪnəs] [ful-chi-nos], *a.* Fuliginoso, denegrido, tiznado.

full [fʊl] [ful], *va.* Dar amplitud a una cosa, fruncir el borde de una tela; hacer espeso o grueso. *-vn.* 1. Hacerse lleno, grueso o espeso; llegar la luna a su plenilunio. 2. Fruncirse, plegarse; mostrar amplitud.

full, *va.* Abatanar o batanar el paño; hacerlo más espeso y compacto por medio de un procedimiento dado. *-vn.* Hacerse más espeso y compacto.

full, *a.* 1. Lleno, repleto, surtido de alguna cosa; gordo; amplio, pleno. 2. Harto, saciado; copioso, completo. 3. Maduro, perfecto; fuerte. **Full stop,** punto final. **Full of sorrow,** lleno de trabajos, consumido por los pesares. **Full of business,** abrumado de negocios. **Full of play,** amigo de retozar, alegre, juguetón. **Full moon,** plenilunio, luna llena. **Full sail,** vela llena. **Full sea,** mar bravío. **Full two years,** dos años bien cumplidos. **Full powers,** facultades amplias. **Full weight,** peso cabal. **Full and by,** *(Mar.)* A buen viento. **To keep the sails full,** *(Mar.)* andar a buena vela. *-s.* 1. Lleno, complemento; colmo; saciedad. 2. Tota, el todo que resulta de la unión de muchas cosas. *-adv.* 1. Enteramente, del todo, de lleno. **Full well,** muy bien. 2. Derechamente, rectamente, exactamente. **Full** se usa a menudo en la composición de algunas voces para denotar que una cosa ha llegado a su complemento o perfección. **Full-blooded,** (a) pletórico, que tiene plenitud de sangre. (b) De sangre pura; de sangre no mezclada. **Full blown,** (a) abierto, descogido o desplegado completamente; hablando de las flores. (b) Maduro, cabal; en todo su esplendor o desarrollo. (c) Hinchado completamente por el viento. **Full-butt,** *(Fam.)* con un choque súbito y violento. **Full-charged,** sobrecargado. **Full-cock,** montado, amartillado; se dice de un arma de fuego. **Full-dress,** gran gala; vestido de gran gala, de uniforme o como es preciso para presentarse de ceremonia en alguna función. **Full-drive,** a carrera tendida, a toda rienda, al galope. **Full-eared,** lo que tiene espigas llenas y grandes. **Full-faced,** (a) carrilleno, carigordo. (b) *(Impr.)* Letra negra; los mismos que **bold-face. Full-fed.** Bien alimentado, gordo, grueso. **Full-grown,** maduro; crecido completamente. **A full-grown man, woman,** un hombre hecho, una mujer hecha. **Full-hearted,** elevado, confiado; atrevido, valeroso. **Full length,** de grandor natural, de cuerpo entero. **Full-manned,** tripulado completamente. **Full-mouthed,** lo que tiene voz o sonido fuerte. **Full-orbed,** lo que tiene un orbe o una esfera completa; lo que está tan lleno como la luna durante el plenilunio. **Full-spread,** extendido a lo largo. **Full-summed,** completo en todas sus partes. **Full-winged,** lo que tiene alas grandes: alado.

fullage [ˈfʊlɪdʒ] [fu-lich], *s.* Lo que se paga por abatanar el paño.

full-aged [fʊlˈeɪdʒɪd] [ful-eichd], *a.* Mayor de edad.

fullback [ˈfʊlbæk] [ful-bak], *s.* Defensa (en el fútbol).

full-blooded [ˈfʊlˈblʌdɪd] [ful-bla-did], *a.* 1. De pura raza. 2. Pletórico.

full-blown [fʊlˈbləʊn] [ful-bloun], *a.* Maduro, desarrollado.

fuller [ˈfʊlər] [fu-lar], *s.* Batanero, el que abatana el paño.

fuller's earth [ˈfʊləzˈɜːθ] [fu-lers-erz], *s.* Tierra de batán, especie de greda que se emplea en los batanes para desengrasar los paños.

fuller's thistle [fʊlzˈθiːsl] [fuls-zisel], *s.* Capota, cardencha, dipsaco.

fullery [ˈfʊləri] [fu-le-ri], *s.* Batán y oficina del batanero.

full-fashioned [fʊlˈfæʃənd] [ful-fa-shond], *a.* Tejido o confeccionado para que ajuste bien (ropa interior, medias, etc.)

full-fledged [fʊlˈfledʒɪd] [ful-flecht], *a.* Completo, acabado. **A full-fledged doctor,** médico en todo el sentido de la palabra.

fulling-mill [fʊlɪŋˈmɪl] [fu-lin-mill], *s.* Batán.

full-length film [fʊlˈleŋθfɪlm] [ful-lenz-film], *s.* Película de largo metraje.

full swing [fʊlˈswɪŋ] [ful-suin], *adv.* En plena actividad, en todo su apogeo.

fully [ˈfʊlɪ] [fu-li], *adv.* Plenamente, completamente.

fulminant [ˈfʊlmɪnənt] [ful-mi-nant], *a.* Fulminante.

fulminate [ˈfʊlmɪneɪt] [ful-mi-neit], *va.* y *vn.* 1. Hacer explosión, estallar. 2. Tronar, dar un estallido, detonar. 3. Excomulgar, imponer una censura. 4. Fulminar. 5. Censurar, condenar.

fulminating [ˈfʊlmɪneɪtɪŋ] [ful-mi-nei-tin], *pa.* Fulminante. **Fulminating cap,** cápsula fulminante.

fulmination [ˌfʊlmɪˈneɪʃən] [ful-mi-nei-shon], *s.* Fulminación, el acto de fulminar y su efecto; trueno.

fulminatory [ˈfʊlmɪnətərɪ] [ful-mi-na-to-ri], *a.* Fulminante, fulmíneo, fulmíneo.

fulmine [ˈfʊlmɪn] [ful-min], *va.* Fulminar, lanzar con explosión, a manera de relámpago. -*vn.* Tronar; de aquí, hablar de una manera vehemente, con voz de trueno.

fulness o **fullness** [ˈfʊlnɪs] [ful-nes], *s.* 1. Plenitud, copia, llenura, abundancia, hartura, saciedad. 2. Complemento. 3. Fuerza o vigor del sonido. **Fullness of the heart,** abundancia de afecto; llenura del corazón.

fulsome [ˈfʊlsəm] [ful-som], *a.* Que ofende o disgusta por exceso de elogio; de aquí, grosero, bajo, repugnante.

fulsomely [ˈfʊlsəmlɪ] [ful-som-li], *adv.* Asquerosamente, indecentemente.

fulsomeness [ˈfʊlsəmnɪs] [ful-som-nes], *s.* Asquerosidad, insinceridad, bajeza.

fulvescent [ˈfʊlvəsənt] [ful-ve-sent], *a.* Algo leonado.

fulvid [ˈfʊlvɪd] [ful-vid], *a.* Leonado, amarillo rojizo.

fulvous [ˈfʊlvəs] [ful-vo], **fulvid,** *a.* Leonado, color leonado; amarillo obscuro con tinte rojizo.

fumarole [ˈfʊmərəʊl] [fu-ma-roul], *s.* Agujero pequeño por donde salen vapores volcánicos.

fumble [ˈfʌmbl] [fam-bel], *va.* 1. Chapucear, manosear desmañadamente o sin propósito. 2. Buscar a tientas, revolver buscando. 3. Titubear, balbucear. 4. Parar o coger una pelota desmañadamente, ocasionando una demora. -*vn.* Emplear las manos desmañadamente; ir a tientas. **To fumble along,** andar a tientas.

fumbler [ˈfʌmblər] [fam-blar], *s.* Chapucero, desmañado.

fumblingly [ˈfʌmblɪŋ] [fam-blin], *adv.* Chapuceramente.

fume [fjuːm] [fium], *s.* 1. El vapor que exhala alguna cosa que fermenta. 2. Vapor del estómago. 3. Cólera, acaloramiento. 4. Humo, vanidad, presunción. 5. (*Ant.*) Humo. **Fumes of wine,** vapores del vino.

fume, *vn.* 1. Humear, echar o arrojar humo. 2. Exhalar, despedir vapores. 3. Encolerizarse, enojarse. -*va.* 1. Ahumar; ahumar; exponer a los vapores del amoniaco, como en ciertas manipulaciones fotográficas. 2. Exhalar, despedir alguna cosa en vapores. **To fume away,** evaporarse alguna cosa.

fumet [ˈfjuːmɪt] [fiu-mit], *s.* (*Des.*) Freza, el estiércol de los venados. 2. Olor de un guisado, tufillo.

fumigate [ˈfjuːmɪɡeɪt] [fiu-mi-gueit], *va.* 1. Desinfectar por la acción del humo o del vapor. 2. Perfumar, sahumar. 3. Ahumar, curar por medio del humo.

fumigation [ˌfjuːmɪˈɡeɪʃən] [fiu-mi-guei-shon], *s.* 1. Sahumerio, sahumo. 2. (*Med.*) Fumigación.

fumigator [ˌfjuːmɪˈɡeɪtər] [fiu-mi-guei-tar], *s.* Fumigador, máquina fumigatoria.

fumigatory [ˈfjuːmɪɡətərɪ] [fiu-mi-ga-to-ri], *s.* Fumigatorio.

fuming [ˈfjuːmɪŋ] [fiu-min], *s.* El acto de humear; capricho vano. -*a.* 1. Humeante, fumante. 2. Encolerizado, furioso.

fumingly [ˈfjuːmɪŋlɪ] [fiu-min-li], *adv.* Coléricamente.

fumish [ˈfjuːmɪʃ] [fiu-mish], *a.* (*Bot.*) De color de humo.

fumitory [ˈfjuːmɪtərɪ] [fiu-mi-to-ri], *s.* (*Bot.*) Fumaria, hierba de sabor amargo. **Climbing fumitory,** fumaria trepadora.

fumy [ˈfjuːmɪ] [fiu-mi], *a.* Humoso, lleno de vapores.

fun [fʌn] [fan], *s.* Diversión, entretenimiento; chanza, chiste, chuscada, burla. **For fun** o **in fun,** en chanza, de burlas, por modo de fiesta, de chacota. **To have fun,** divertirse, pasar un buen rato. **To make fun of, to poke fun at,** burlarse de, reírse de.

fun, *v.* Bromear, divertirse.

funambulist [fjuːˈnæmbʊlɪst] [fiu-nam-bu-list], **funambulo** [ˈfjuːnæmbələʊ] [fiu-nam-bu-lou], *s.* Funámbulo, volatín.

function [ˈfʌŋkʃən] [fank-shon], *s.* 1. Función, el acto o ejercicio de algún empleo, facultad u oficio. 2. Desempeño o cumplimiento de un deber. 3. Ocupación, ejercicio. 4. Función, el ejercicio de los movimientos vitales de las diferentes partes del cuerpo animal. 5. Potencia, facultad. 6. (*Mat.*) Cantidad que depende de otra.

functional [ˈfʌŋkʃənəl] [fank-sho-nal] *a.* Funcional.

functionary [ˈfʌŋkʃənərɪ] [fank-sho-na-ri], *s.* Funcionario, empleado.

functionate [ˈfʌŋkʃəneɪt] [fank-sho-neit], *va.* Ejercer una función; tener oficio; obrar.

functioning [ˈfʌŋkʃənɪŋ] [fank-sho-nin], *s.* Funcionamiento.

fund [fʌnd] [fand], *s.* 1. Fondo, caudal de alguna cosa; acopio, reserva. **A great fund of humor,** un abundante fondo de buen humor. 2. Dinero contante, o capital convertible. 3. *pl.* Fondos públicos; (*Fam.*) dinero. **Sinking fund,** fondo de amortización.

fund, *va.* 1. Consolidar una deuda; destinar fondos al pago de los intereses de una deuda. 2. Poner dinero en los fondos públicos, o en los de una compañía o casa de comercio.

fundament [fʌnˈdəment] [fan-da-ment], *s.* 1. Fundamento, principio, cimiento. 2. Ancas, trasero; ano.

fundamental [fʌnˈdəmentl] [fan-da-men-tal], *a.* Fundamental. -*s.* Fundamento.

fundamentally [fʌnˈdəmentəlɪ] [fan-da-men-ta-li], *adv.* Fundamentalmente.

funded [ˈfʌndɪd] [fan-did], *pp.* y *a.* 1. Consolidado; convertido en préstamo permanente. **Funded debt,** deuda consolidada. 2. Acumulado e invertido, particularmente en los fondos públicos.

fundus [ˈfʌndəs] [fan-das], *s.* Fondo, base, la parte trasera o lo hondo de alguna cosa. (*Der.*) Fundo.

funeral [ˈfjuːnərəl] [fiu-ne-ral], *a.* Funeral, fúnebre, mortuorio. -*s.* Funeral, funerales, exequias, pompas fúnebres, entierro. **Funeral director,** director de pompas fúnebres. **Funeral parlor,** funeraria.

funereal [fjuːˈnɪərɪəl] [fiu-ni-rial], *a.* Fúnebre, triste, funesto, lúgubre.

funest [ˈfʌnɪst] [fa-nest], *a.* Lúgubre, lamentable.

fungi [ˈfʌnɡɪ] [fan-gui], *s.* (*Bot.*) Hongos.

fungicidal [ˈfʌnɡɪsaɪdl] [fan-gui-sai-dal], *a.* Que destruye los hongos, fungicida.

fungicide [ˈfʌnɡɪsaɪd] [fan-gui-said], *s.* Sustancia para destruir hongos, fungicida.

fungiform [ˈfʌnɡɪfɔːm] [fan-gui-form], *a.* Fungóideo, que tiene la forma de un hongo.

fungosity [ˈfʌnɡəsɪtɪ] [fan-go-si-ti], *s.* Fungosidad, excrecencia blanda.

fungous [ˈfʌnɡəs] [fan-gos], *a.* Fungoso, lo que se aproxima a la naturaleza del hongo; esponjoso, poroso.

fungus [ˈfʌnɡəs] [fan-gos], *s.* (*pl.* FUNGI o FUNGUSES). 1. (*Bot.*) Hongo, planta criptógama, de color vario pero nunca verde, que crece rápidamente; como el moho, el tizón, la seta y el agárico. Muchas especies son microscópicas. 2. (*Med.*) Excrecencia, carnosidad.

funicle [ˈfʌnɪkl] [fa-ni-kol], *s.* Cuerdecilla, fibra, ligamento pequeño.

funicular [fjuːˈnɪkələr] [fiu-ni-kiu-lar], *s.* Funicular. **Funicular railway,** ferrocarril funicular.

funk [fʌŋk] [fank], *s.* 1. (*Ger.*) Temor, miedo infundado. 2. (*Vulg.*) Hedor, mal olor.

funk, *va.* 1. *(Vulg.)* Emponzoñar con malos olores, apestar. 2. Espantar, atemorizar.

funnel ['fʌnl] [fa-nel], *s.* 1. Embudo. 2. Cañón, conducto por donde pasa aire, humo u otra cosa. **Funnel of a chimney,** cañón de chimenea.

funny ['fʌnɪ] [fa-ni], *a.* Cómico, alegre, burlesco, gracioso, chistoso; bufón, mono, chulo. -*s.* *(Vulg.)* Esquife. **Funny-bone,** *(Fam.)* Cóndilo interno del húmero.

fur [fɜːʳ] [faʳ], *s.* 1. Forro de pieles. 2. Pelo de las bestias. 3. Peletería. 4. Sedimento que se pega a la lengua o a las vasijas metálicas; la pelusa del durazno.

fur, *va.* 1. Aforrar con pieles finas. 2. Cubrir con alguna cosa blanda y suave. **To fur a ship,** forrar un navío.

furacious [fəˈreɪʃəs] [fa-rei-shos], *a.* Rapaz, inclinado a hurtar.

furacity ['fərædɪtɪ] [fa-ra-si-ti], *s.* Codicia; rapacidad.

furbelow ['fɜːbɪləʊ] [fer-bi-lou], *s.* Farfalá, vuelo.

furbelow, *va.* Adornar con farfalaes o vuelos.

furbish ['fɜːbɪʃ] [fer-bish], *va.* Acicalar, pulir, limpiar.

furbishable ['fɜːbɪʃəbl] [fer-bi-sha-bol], *a.* Capaz de ser pulido.

furbisher ['fɜːbɪʃəʳ] [fer-bi-shaʳ], *a.* Acicalador.

furcate ['fɜːkeɪt] [fer-keit], *a.* Ahorquillado, hendido.

furcation ['fɜːˈkeɪʃən] [fer-kei-shon], *s.* Horcajadura.

furcular ['fɜːkjoləʳ] [fer-kiu-laʳ], *a.* Horcado, que tiene la figura de una horquilla.

furfur ['fɜːfɜːʳ] [fer-faʳ], *s.* *(Med.)* Caspa; escamitas.

furious ['fjʊrɪəs] [fiu-rios], *a.* Furioso, frenético, furibundo, violento.

furiously ['fjʊrɪəslɪ] [fiu-rios-li], *adv.* Furiosamente, violentamente.

furiousness ['fjʊrɪəsnɪs] [fiu-rios-nes], *s.* Furia, frenesí.

furi ['fɜːrɪ] [fe-ri], *va.* Encoger, contraer. **To furi the sails,** *(Mar.)* Aferrar velas, recoger las velas y plegarlas encima de las vergas.

furl [fɜːrl] [ferl] *v.* Enrollar, plegar banderas. *(Mar.)* Aferrar, recoger velas.

furling-lines ['fɜːrlɪŋˈlaɪnz] [fer-lin-lains], *s.* *pl.* *(Mar.)* Aferravelas.

furlong ['fɜːrlɒŋ] [fer-lon], *s.* Estadio, la octava parte de una milla.

furlough ['fɜːlɔː] [fer-lo], *s.* *(Mil.)* Licencia o permiso que se da a un militar para ausentarse de su cuerpo o regimiento.

furmenty ['fɜːməntɪ] [fer-men-ti], *s.* V. FRUMENTY.

furnace ['fɜːnɪs] [fer-nis], *s.* 1. Horno, hornillo. **Blast-furnace,** horno u hornillo soplante; se usa en las herrerías. **Reverberatory furnace,** horno de reverbero. **Wind-furnace,** horno de aire. 2. Hogar de caldera; horno. **Furnace-hoist,** grúa o cabria de horno. **Furnace-rake,** limpiafuegos, utensilio de vidriería. **Furnace for silver ore,** buitrón, horno de manga para fundir minerales argentíferos. **Bloom reheating furnace,** horno de recocido. **Castilian furnace,** horno circular para plomo. **Muffle furnace,** horno de mufla, de copela. **Smelting furnace,** horno de fundición, alto horno. **To heat the furnace,** caldear el horno.

furnish ['fɜːnɪʃ] [fer-nish], *va.* 1. Surtir, suplir, proveer; aparejar, equipar; alhajar, decorar; adornar. **To furnish a house,** amueblar una casa. **To furnish with arms,** armar. 2. Proporcionar, procurar. **To furnish anyone with an opportunity,** proporcionar ocasión u oportunidad.

furnished ['fɜːnɪʃt] [fer-nisht], *a.* Amueblado. **Furnished apartment,** departamento o aposento amueblado. **Furnished room for rent,** se renta cuarto amueblado.

furnisher ['fɜːnɪʃəʳ] [fer-ni-shaʳ], *s.* 1. Equipador, decorador. 2. Aparejador, proveedor.

furnishing ['fɜːnɪʃɪŋ] [fer-ni-shin], *s.* 1. Habilitación, equipo, suministro. 2. Muestra. **Furnishings,** trastos, muebles fijos: (en las cuentas de sastres, etc.) avíos.

furnishment ['fɜːnɪʃmənt] [fer-nish-ment], *s.* Surtimiento, surtido, la acción de proveer, surtir o equipar de lo que se necesita.

furniture ['fɜːnɪtʃəʳ] [fer-ni-chaʳ], *s.* 1. Ajuar, los muebles de una casa, mueblaje. 2. Guarnición; adornos, decoraciones;

accesorios necesarios en las diversas aplicaciones de las artes. 3. *(Mar.)* Aparejo; obrajes de un arsenal. **Furniture dealer,** mueblista, comerciante en muebles.

furor, furore ['fjʊərəʳ] [fiua-raʳ], *s.* 1. Furia, rabia. 2. Furor, entusiasmo, fervor.

furred ['fʌrɪd] [fa-rid], *a.* 1. Cubierto de piel o de algo parecido a ella. *(Med.)* Cargado, tomado. 2. Forrado. **Furred tongue,** lengua cargada o sucia.

furrier ['fʌrɪəʳ] [fa-riaʳ] *s.* Peletero, el que trata en pieles finas.

furring ['fʌrɪŋ] [fa-rin], *s.* 1. Forro o guarnición de pieles. 2. Incrustación de una caldera y el procedimiento para limpiarla; sarro de la lengua. 3. *(Carp.)* Contrapar de armadura falsa; pedazos de madera para soportar latas o listones.

furrow ['fʌrəʊ] [fa-rou], *s.* 1. Surco; *(Fig.)* marca, señal. 2. Surco, cualquier canal largo y estrecho; encaje, muesca; estría, mediacaña; reguera, tajea, canaliza.

furrow, *va.* 1. Surcar, hacer surcos en la tierra. 2. Estriar. V. FLUTE.

furrow-faced ['fʌrəʊˌfeɪst] [fa-rou-feist], *a.* Cara surcada o arrugada.

furry ['fʌrɪ] [fa-ri], *a.* Hecho de pieles finas o guarnecido de ellas.

further ['fɜːðəʳ] [fer-daʳ], *a.* Ulterior, más distante, más separado. **Till further orders,** hasta nueva orden. -*adv.* Más lejos, más allá; además; aún; además de eso. **On the further side of the Pyrennees,** más allá, al otro lado de los Pirineos. **What further need have we of witnesses?,** ¿qué necesidad tenemos de más testigos?

further, *va.* Adelantar, promover, llevar adelante; asistir, ayudar, apoyar.

furtherance ['fɜːðərəns] [fer-de-rans], *s.* Adelantamiento, progreso, ayuda, socorro, asistencia, apoyo.

furtherer ['fɜːðərəʳ] [fer-de-raʳ], *s.* Promotor, fautor, patrón, protector.

furthermore ['fɜːðəˈmɔːʳ] [fer-der-maʳ], *adv.* Además, a más de esto o de aquello.

furthest ['fɜːðəst] [fer-dest], *a.* y *adv.* Lo más lejos, muy lejos, lo más remoto, apartado o separado.

furtive ['fɜːtɪv] [fer-tiv], *a.* Furtivo, oculto, secreto, hecho de tapadillo o a escondidas.

furuncle ['fʌrəŋkl] [fa-ran-kel], *s.* Furúnculo, divieso, grano.

fury ['fjʊərɪ] [fiu-ri], *s.* 1. Furor, locura confirmada. 2. Furia; ira, rabia, cólera. 3. Furor, arrebatamiento, entusiasmo. **Poetical fury,** furor o estro poético. 4. Furia, mujer furiosa y turbulenta.

fury-like ['fjʊərɪˌlaɪk] [fiua-ri-laik], *a.* Furibundo, rabioso, furioso.

furze [fɜːz] [fers], *s.* *(Bot.)* Tojo, hiniesta, espinosa; arbusto de las leguminosas.

furzy ['fɜːzɪ] [fer-si], *a.* Lleno de tojos o hiniestas espinosas.

fusain ['fjuːseɪn] [fiu-sein], *s.* Carboncillo.

fuscous ['fʌskəs] [fas-kos], *a.* 1. De color moreno que tira a gris. 2. Fusco.

fuse [fjuːz] [fius], *va.* Fundir, derretir. -*vn.* Fundirse, derretirse.

fuse, *s.* *(Elec.)* Fusible. **Fuse box,** caja de fusibles.

fusee [fjuːˈziː] [fiu-si], *s.* 1. Huso, cilindro pequeño alrededor del cual da vuelta la cuerda del reloj. 2. *(Art.)* Espoleta o espiga, el cañoncillo por donde se pega fuego a la bomba o granada. 3. V. FUSE. 1ª acep. 4. *(Des.)* Escopeta de pistón. V. FUSIL.

fuselage ['fjuːzələːdʒ] [fiu-se-lash], *s.* *(Aer.)* Fuselaje.

fusel-oil ['fjuːzlˈɔɪl] [fiu-sel-oil], *s.* Compuesto aceitoso y venenoso consistente en gran parte en alcohol amílico, que se obtiene rectificando el aguardiente de maíz o de uvas.

fusibility [ˌfjuːzɪˈbɪlɪtɪ] [fiu-si-bi-li-ti], *s.* Fusibilidad, calidad de fusible.

fusible ['fjuːzɪbl] [fiu-si-bol], *a.* Fusible, fundible.

fusiform ['fjuːzɪˈfɔːm] [fiu-si-form], *a.* Fusiforme, lo que remata en punta.

fusil ['fjuːzɪl] [fiu-sil], *a.* Fundible. -*s.* Escopeta de pistón.

fusileer o **fusilier** ['fjuːzɪlɪəʳ] [fiu-si-liaʳ], *s.* *(Mil.)* Fusilero.

fusillade ['fjuːzɪleɪd] [fiu-si-leid], s. Tiros de fusil, tiroteos a fusilazos.

fusing ['fjuːzɪŋ] [fiu-sin], a. Fundente; de fusión. **Fusing point,** punto de fusión.

fusion ['fjuːʒən] [fiu-shon], s. 1. Fundición, derretimiento. 2. Fusión, licuación de los metales.

fuss [fʌs] [fas], s. 1. Actividad injustificada y molesta; desasosiego; importancia exagerada que suele darse a lo que no la tiene. 2. Alboroto, ruido. 3. Persona exigente, demasiada preocupada, que se mete en todo.

fuss, va. 1. Molestar, perturbar con cosas sin importancia. -vn. 1. Agitarse; afligirse. 2. Preocuparse.

fussy ['fʌsɪ] [fa-si], a. Molesto, inquieto, remilgado, minucioso, exigente.

fust ['fʌst] [fast], s. 1. Fuste, el cuerpo de la columna. 2. Caballete del tejado.

fustian ['fʌstʃən] [fas-chan], s. 1. Fustán, tela de lino y algodón. 2. Palabras retumbantes; estilo altisonante. -a. 1. Hecho de fustán. 2. Altisonante, pomposo, retumbante, campanudo.

fustic ['fʌstɪk] [fas-tik], s. Fustoc, fustete, palo amarillo que sirve para los tintes.

fustigate ['fʌstɪgeɪt] [fas-ti-gueit], v. Fustigar, apalear.

fustigation [,fʌstɪ'geɪʃən] [fas-ti-guei-shon], s. Castigo o pena de azotes, palos o latigazos.

fustiness ['fʌstɪnɪs] [fas-ti-nes], s. 1. Enmohecimiento. 2. Hedor, hediondez.

fusty ['fʌstɪ] [fas-ti], **fusted** ['fʌstɪd] [fas-tid], a. 1. Mohoso. 2. Husmeador, fisgón, entrometido, oficioso.

futile ['fjuːtɪl] [fiu-til], a. Fútil, frívolo, vano, inútil.

futility [fjuː'tɪlɪtɪ] [fiu-ti-li-ti], s. 1. Futilidad, insubstancialidad. 2. Frivolidad. 3. Inutilidad.

futtock ['fjuːtɒk] [fiu-tok], s. (Mar.) Genol, ligazón, barraganete; arraigada. **Lower futtocks,** genoles o primeras ligazones. **Futtock-shrouds,** pernadas de las arraigadas.

future ['fjuːtʃər] [fiu-char], a. Futuro, venidero. -s. Lo futuro, lo porvenir. **In the near future,** en un futuro próximo, en fecha próxima.

futureless ['fjuːtʃəlɪs] [fiu-cha-les], a. Sin perspectivas para el futuro.

futurely ['fjuːtʃəlɪ] [fiu-til], adv. En lo venidero, para lo venidero.

futurism ['fjuːtʃərɪzəm] [fiu-cha-ri-sem], s. Futurismo.

futuristic [,fjuːtʃə'rɪstɪk] [fiu-cha-ris-tik], a. Futurista.

futurition ['fjuːtʃə'rɪʃən] [fiu-cha-ri-shon], s. Realización en lo futuro de algo profetizado o propuesto.

futurity ['fjuːtʃərɪtɪ] [fiu-cha-ri-ti], s. Futuro, el tiempo que ha de venir; sucesos venideros; porvenir. **Full of futurity,** preñado de consecuencias para lo venidero; lo que producirá sucesos importantes o de consecuencia en lo sucesivo.

fuzz [fʌz] [fas], vn. Deshilarse, deshilacharse, desflecarse, volar convertido en partículas, como vello o lanilla. -s. Lanilla, pelusa, hilacha menuda.

fuzz-ball ['fʌzbɔːl] [fas-bol], s. Bejín, hongo semejante a una bola.

fuzziness ['fʌzɪnɪs] [fa-si-nes], s. Calidad o estado de velloso.

fuzzy ['fʌzɪ] [fa-si], a. Provisto de una capa de pelusa o vello; parecido a lanilla.

fyke ['faɪk] [faik], s. Nasa, red de forma cónica; varias redes sucesivas, de forma cónica y con boca ancha.

fy [faɪ] [fai], inter. ¡Qué vergüenza!

fylfot ['faɪlfɔːt] [fail-fot], s. Svástica.

G

g [dʒiː] [yi], esta letra tiene dos sonidos en inglés; uno igual al de la misma letra en castellano antes de **a, o, u, l, r;** v. g. **gas, go, gun, grass, globe;** y otro más suave que el anterior antes de **e, i, y,** el cual equivale al de la **y consonante** en castellano, pronunciada con alguna más fuerza; v. g. **gem** (dyem), gibbet (dyibbet), dingy (dindyi), delante de las mismas letras, y de la **a** en muchos monosílabos y sus derivados, suena fuerte, y como si tuviese interpuesta una **u;** v. g. **get (guet), give (guiv), game (gueim).** En las palabras que comienzan con **gh,** sólo se pronuncia la primera; **v. g. ghost (gost);** en las que acaban con las mismas letras éstas se pronuncian como una **f;** v. g. **rough (raf);** bien que en algunas voces son mudas, como en **high (jái).** Antes de **n,** al principio o fin de dicción, es muda; v. g. **gnat (nat), reign (rein).**

gab [gæb] [gab], vn. (Fam.) Parlotear, picotear, charlar. -va. Decir; especialmente decir falsedades.

gab, s. 1. (Fam.) Locuacidad, cháchara. 2. Garabato, gancho, horquilla. **To have the gift of gab,** tener la lengua muy suelta. **Stop your gab!** ¡Cállese! **To have the gift of the gab,** ser locuaz.

gabardine [,gæbə'diːn] [ga-bar-din], **gaberdine,** s. Gabacha, gabardina.

gabble ['gæbl] [ga-bel], vn. 1. Charlar, parlar, parlotear, picotear, hablar mucho sin substancia y fuera de propósito. 2. Cacarear.

gabble, s. 1. Algarabía; charla. 2. Cacareo.

gabion ['gæbɪən] [ga-bion], s. (Fort.) Gavión, cestón de mimbres lleno de tierra.

gable ['gæbl] [ga-bol], s. Cabo angular o remate de tejado que está hecho con caballete y no aplanado.

gable-end ['gæbl'end] [ga-bel-end], s. Socarrén, alero.

gabbler ['gæblər] [ga-blar], s. Charlador, chacharero, parlador, hablador, charlante, picotero.

gablet ['gæblɪt] [ga-blit], s. Gablete.

Gabriel ['geɪbrɪəl] [guei-briel], n. pr. Gabriel.

gaby ['gæbɪ] [ga-bi], pl. bies. (Fam.) Necio, tonto.

gad [gæd] [gad], vn. Andorrear, corretear, callejear, pindonguear. **On the gad,** callejeando, correteando.

gad, s. 1. Cuña, punzón, aguja de minero. 2. Aguijón, vara con punta. 3. Clavo grande, cuña. 4. Barra, lingote.

gadabout ['gædəbaʊt] [gad-a-baut], a. Callejero, cantonero.

gadder ['gædər] [ga-dar], s. 1. Callejero o correteador. (Fam. Mex.) Cerero y aplanador. 2. Mujer cantonera, andorrera.

gadding ['gædɪŋ] [ga-din], s. Vagancia, briba; peregrinación; callejeo.

gaddingly ['gædɪŋlɪ] [ga-din-li], adv. Haraganamente, a la briba.

gadfly ['gædflaɪ] [gad-flai], s. Mosca de burro o de caballo, tábano; la hembra es grande y voraz.

gadget ['gædʒɪt] [gad-chit], s. Dispositivo o aparato que facilita las labores manuales.

Gaditanian ['gædɪ'teɪnɪən] [ga-di-tei-nian], a. Gaditano.

gadoid ['gædɔɪd] [ga-doid], a. De la familia de los peces cuyo tipo es el bacalao.

Gael ['geɪl] [gueil], s. Escocés, celta.

gaelic, galic ['geɪlɪk] [guei-lik], s. Gaélico o céltico, un dialecto de la lengua céltica. -a. Lo perteneciente a dicho dialecto.

gaeliscim ['geɪlɪsɪzm] [guei-li-si-sem], s. Gaelicismo, celtismo.

gaff [gæf] [gaf], s. 1. Arpón o garfio grande. 2. Espolón de gallo. V. GAFFLE. 3. (Mar.) Botavar, berlinga para extender el borde de ciertas velas. 4. Burla, engaño. 5. Gasto. 6. Charla. **To blow the gaff,** revelar un secreto.

gaff-boom ['gæfbom] [gaf-bum], s. (Mar.) Verga de cangreja.

gaff-sail ['gæfseɪl] [gaf-seil], s. (Mar.) Vela de cangreja.

gaffer ['gæfər] [ga-far], s. 1. Viejo, vejete; viene a significar casi lo mismo que tío, compadre. 2. Capataz.

gaffle ['gæfl] [ga-fel], s. Espolón de acero que se pone al gallo para pelear. (Mex.) Navaja de gallo.

gag [gæg] [gag], va. 1. Tapar la boca con mordaza; hacer callar a la fuerza. 2. Provocar bascas o náuseas. 3. Forzar, abrir por medio de una mordaza. -vn. Hacer esfuerzos para vomitar, tener náuseas.

gag, s. 1. Mordaza; cualquier limitación de la libertad de la palabra. 2. Asco; bocado que produce náuseas. 3. Broma, ridículo, engaño. 4. (Teat.) Episodio cómico. (Cir.)

Instrumento para mantener las mandíbulas separadas durante una operación.

gage ['geɪdʒ] [gueich], *s.* 1. Prenda, caución. 2. Variedad de ciruela. **Green gage,** ciruela verdal (o claudia).

gage, gauge, *s.* 1. Medida, regla de medir. 2. *(Mar.)* Barlovento.

gage, *va. (Ant.)* Empeñar una alhaja, darla en prenda.

gage, gauge, *va.* 1. Aforar, medir. 2. *(Mar.)* Arquear, medir una embarcación. 3. Comprometer.

gager ['geɪdʒəʳ] [guei-chaʳ], *s.* 1. Arqueador. 2. Empeño (de dar una prenda.). *V.* GAUGER.

gagger ['geɪgəʳ] [guei-gaʳ], *s.* 1. El que amordaza la boca de otro. 2. Trozo de hierro que se usa para mantener en su lugar el corazón de un molde. 3. Bromista.

gaggle ['gægl] [ga-guel], *vn.* Graznar, como el ánsar. *V.* GABBLE.

gaiety ['geɪɪtɪ] [guei-ti], *s. V.* GAYETY. 1. Alegría, jovialidad. 2. Viveza en los colores; lujo en el vestir, pompa.

gaily ['geɪlɪ] [guei-li], *adv. V.* GAYLY. Alegremente, jovialmente.

gain [geɪn] [guein], *s.* 1. Ganancia, ventaja, provecho, lucro. 2. *(Carp.)* Diminución, la que se hace en el espaldar del corte del cartabón. 3. El interés que una persona tiene en cualquiera cosa. 4. Ventaja o ganancia mal adquirida. **Net gain,** ganancia líquida, neta.

gain, *va.* 1. Ganar, adquirir caudal. 2. Ganar jugando o apostando; adquirir, llevar la palma; salir victorioso. 3. Ganar, conseguir, lograr, granjear. 4. Llegar a, alcanzar. 5. Conciliar; propiciar, apaciguar. **To gain the wind,** *(Mar.)* ganar el barlovento. -*vn.* 1. Enriquecerse. 2. Ganar tierra, adelantar poco a poco; obtener una ventaja, un provecho; prevalecer, sacar fruto; con **on** o **upon.** 3. Ganar, lograr, obtener influjo. 4. Aproximarse, acercarse, extenderse. **To gain credit,** acreditarse. **To gain one's end,** alcanzar lo que se desea, lograr su objeto. **To gain over,** conciliar, atraer al partido o parecer de uno. **The night is gaining upon us,** la noche nos sorprende o nos envuelve.

gainable ['geɪnəbl] [guei-na-bol], *a.* Capaz de ser adquirido, asequible.

gainer ['geɪnəʳ] [guei-naʳ], *s.* Ganador.

gainful ['geɪnfʊl] [guein-ful], *a.* Gananciosio, lucrativo, provechoso, ventajoso.

gainfully ['geɪnfʊlɪ] [guein-fu-li], *adv.* Ventajosamente.

gainfulness ['geɪnfʊlnɪs] [guein-ful-nes], *s.* Provecho, ganancia.

gainless ['geɪnlɪs] [guein-les], *a.* Desventajoso, infructuoso.

gainlessness ['geɪnlɪsnɪs] [guein-les-nes], *s.* Inutilidad, infructuosidad; falto de provecho.

gainsay [geɪn'seɪ] [guein-sei], *va.* *(pret. y pp.* GAINSAID). Contradecir; negar; contrariar.

gainsayer [geɪn'seɪəʳ] [guein-seiaʳ], *s.* Contradictor, adversario.

gainsaying [geɪn'seɪɪŋ] [guein-seiyin], *s.* Oposición, contradicción.

gainstand [geɪn'stænd] [guein-stand], *va. (Ant. y Poét.)* Resistir, oponer, combatir, reprimir.

gairish, *a. V.* GARISH.

gairishly, *adv. V.* GARISHLY.

gairishness ['geɪrɪʃnɪs] [guei-rish-nes], *s.* Pompa. *V.* GARISHNESS.

gait ['geɪt] [gueit], *s.* Marcha, paso, el modo de andar; porte, continente.

gaiter ['geɪtəʳ] [guei-taʳ], *s.* 1. Borceguí, polaina, calza de paño o cordobán. 2. Botín con elásticos, en lugar de botones o cordones.

gala ['gɑːlə] [ga-la], *s.* Gala, fiesta. **Gala day,** día de gala, de gran fiesta. **Gala dress,** traje de fiesta.

galactic [gə'læktɪk] [ga-lak-tik], *a.* 1. Relativo a la secreción de leche. 2. Relativo a la galaxia.

galactite [gə'læktaɪt] [ga-lak-tait] *s. (Min.)* Galactita.

galactometer, *s. V.* LACTOMETER.

galangal [gə'læŋgəl] [ga-lan-gal], *s. (Bot.)* Galanga.

galatian [gə'leɪʃən] [ga-lei-shan], *a.* y *s.* Gálata, de Galacia.

galaxy ['gæləksɪ] [ga-lak-si], *s.* 1. Galaxia, la vía láctea. 2. Reunión brillante de personas o cosas.

galbanum ['gælbənəm] [gal-ba-num], *s.* Gálbano, resina gomosa y medicinal.

galbulus ['gælbələs] [gal-bu-lus], *s. (Bot.)* Gálbula.

gale [geɪl] [gueil], *s.* 1. Viento fresco, muy fuerte, ventarrón; en especial un viento con velocidad de 40 a 70 millas por hora. **A fresh gale,** *(Mar.)* Temporal de viento. **A stiff gale,** fugada recia. 2. Diversión bulliciosa. 3. *(Bot.)* Galo o cerero de Luisiana, un arbusto oloroso.

galea ['geɪlɪə] [guei-lia], *s.* Yelmo, o lo que es de forma parecida a él.

galeate, galeated [gælɪ'eɪtɪd] [ga-li-ei-tid], *a.* 1. Cubierto como con yelmo. 2. *(Bot.)* Llámanse así las plantas que tienen flores en forma de yelmo, como el acónito.

Galen ['geɪlən] [guei-len], *n. pr.* Galeno.

galena [gə'lēnə] [ga-le-na], *s. (Min.)* Galena, sulfuro de plomo nativo, alquifol.

galenic, galenical [gə'lenɪk] [ga-le-nik], *a.* 1. Galénico, que contiene galena. 2. Galénico, relativo a Galeno o a los medicamentos que empleaba.

galenism [gə'lenɪzm] [ga-le-ni-sem], *s.* Galenismo, la doctrina de Galeno.

galenist [gə'lenɪst] [ga-le-nist], *s.* Galenista, el que sigue la doctrina de Galeno.

Galician [gə'lɪʃən] [ga-li-shian], *s.* Gallego.

Galilean [gælɪ'liːən] [ga-li-lian], *a.* 1. Galileo, natural de Galilea. 2. Galileo, el partidario de una secta entre los judío enemiga de los romanos.

galimatias [gə'lɪmeɪtɪəs] [ga-li-mei-tias], *s.* Galimatías.

galingange ['gælɪŋgædʒ] [ga-lin-ganch], *s. (Bot.)* Galanga.

galiot ['gælɪət] [ga-liot], *s. (Mar.)* Galeota.

galipot ['gælɪpɒt] [ga-li-pot], *s.* Galipodio, trementina solidificada en los pinos y abetos. Cuando está purificada recibe el nombre de **pez blanca** o de **Borgoña.**

galium ['gælɪəm] [ga-lium], *s. (Bot.)* Cuajaleche, galio, género numeroso de plantas rubiáceas.

gall [gɔːl] [gol], *s.* 1. Hiel, bilis recogida en una vejiga debajo del hígado. 2. Amargura, asperaza. 3. Hiel, odio, rencor, aversión; enfado; malicia, malignidad. 4. Rozadura o matadura de las caballerías. 5. Agalla, excrecencia dura redonda, debida a ciertos insectos, que se forma en el roble y otros árboles y arbustos. **Gall-apple** o **gall-nut,** agalla. **Gall-fly,** cinipo, insecto himenóptero que pica los árboles para depositar sus huevos y produce la agalla. **Gall-stones,** cálculos en la vejiga de la hiel.

gall, *va. y vn.* 1. Desollar, quitar, el pellejo o la piel; desollarse, rozarse, herirse ligeramente levantando un pedacito de pellejo. 2. Gastar, consumiendo poco a poco. 3. Acibarar; fatigar, hostigar; dañar.

gallant ['gælənt] [ga-lant], *a.* Galante, cortés; galanteador, cortejador de damas.

gallant, *a.* 1. Valeroso, animoso, valiente, intrépido, bizarro. 2. *(Ant.)* Garboso, bizarro, elegante en el vestir.

gallant, *s.* 1. Galán; galanteador; cortejo. 2. Galán, mancebo, majo; el favorecido por una mujer en el trato ilícito.

gallant, *va.* Galantear.

gallantly ['gæləntlɪ] [ga-lant-li], *adv.* Galanamente, valientemente.

gallantness ['gæləntnɪs] [ga-lant-nes], *s. (Ant.)* Elegancia, bizarría.

gallantry ['gæləntrɪ] [ga-lan-tri], *s.* 1. Espíritu heroico, valeroso; valor, heroísmo. 2. Galanteo, cortejo, obsequio y servicio a los débiles, y particularmente a las mujeres. 3. Amores, trato, amistad; atención excesiva dedicada a las mujeres; trato ilícito entre los dos sexos.

gallate ['gæleɪt] [ga-leit], *s. (Quím.)* Galato, sal formada por la combinación del ácido agálico con alguna base.

gall bladder ['gɔːlˌblædəʳ] [gol-bla-daʳ], *s.* Vesícula biliar.

galleas ['gælɪəs] [ga-lias], *s. (Mar.)* Galeaza.

galleon ['gælɪən] [ga-lion], *s.* Galeón, bajel grande usado antiguamente en España.

gallery ['gælərɪ] [ga-le-ri], *s.* 1. Galería, corredor. 2. *(Mar.)* Corredor de navío. **A quarter gallery,** jardine*s*. 3. *(Fort.)* Galería, corredor con que se ciega el foso. 4. El corredor más alto de un teatro. 5. Socavón, galería o pozo de una mina. **Drain-gallery,** *(Min.)* galería de desagüe. **Picture-gallery,** galería, coleccion de pinturas.

galley ['gælɪ] [ga-li], *s.* 1. *(Mar.)* Galera, embarcación de remo*s*. 2. El fogón de a bordo; cocina. 3. *(Impr.)* Galera, tabla con dos o tres bordes con sus muescas, en las que entra la volandera; se usa para poner la composición y formar las galerada*s*. **Galley-tiles,** azulejos.

galley proof ['gælɪpruːf] [ga-li-pruf], *s. (Impr.)* Galerada.

galley-slave ['gælɪsleɪv] [ga-li-sleiv], *s.* Galeote, el que remaba forzado en las galeras.

gallfly ['gɔːlflaɪ] [gol-flai], *s.* Cinípedo.

galliard ['gælɪəd] [ga-liard], *s.* Hombre gallardo, galán. -a. Vivo, alegre.

gallic acid ['gælɪkˌæsɪd] [ga-lik-a-sid], *s. (Quím.)* Ácido agálico o de agallas.

gallic ['gælɪk] [ga-lik], **gallican** ['gælɪkən] [ga-li-kan], *a.* Galicano.

gallicism ['gælɪsɪzəm] [ga-li-si-zem], *s.* Galicismo, modo de hablar privativo de la lengua francesa.

gallicize ['gælɪsaɪz] [ga-li-sais], *va.* Escribir o hablar de un modo conforme al estilo y giros de la lengua francesa.

Gallicus ['gælɪkəs] [ga-li-kos], *s.* Gálico.

galligaskins ['gælɪˌgɑːskɪnz] [ga-li-gas-kins], *s.* Botarga, calzacalzón.

gallimaufry ['gælɪməfrɪ] [ga-li-mo-fri], *s.* 1. Almodrote, jigote, picadillo, ropa vieja; mezcla ridícula de cosas contrarias. 2. Guisado de corazón, riñón, hígados; mezcolanza.

gallinaceous ['gælɪneɪʃəs] [ga-li-nei-shos], *a.* Lo que pertenece a las gallinas.

galling ['gælɪŋ] [ga-lin], *a.* Irritante, mortificante.

gallinule ['gælɪnjuːl] [ga-li-niul], *a. (Ornit.)* Gallineta.

galliot ['gælɪət] [ga-liot], *s.* Galiot.

gallipot ['gælɪpɒt] [ga-li-pot], *s.* Orza, vasija vidriada de barro.

gallium ['gælɪəm] [ga-liom], *s. (Quím.)* Galio.

gallivant (to) [ˌgælɪ ˈvænt] [ga-li-vant], *v.* 1. Callejear, viajar por placer. 2. Mariposear, andar entre las mujeres.

gall-less ['gɔːlˈlɪs] [gol-les], *a.* Sin hielo o amargura; apacible, sencillo, de genio suave.

gallnut ['gɔːlnʌt] [gol-nat], *s. (Bot.)* Agalla.

gallon ['gælən] [ga-lon], *s.* 1. Galón, medida de líquidos. 2. Medida inglesa de capacidad para áridos.

galloon ['gæluːn] [ga-lun], *s.* 1. Galón, género de tejido fuerte hecho de seda o hilo de oro o plata. 2. Ribecillo.

gallop ['gæləp] [ga-lop], *s.* Galope, movimiento del caballo más violento y acelerado que el paso y el trote. **Full gallop,** a galope tendido, a rienda suelta. **Hand-gallop,** a media rienda.

gallop, *vn.* Galopar.

gallopade ['gæləpeɪd] [ga-lo-peid], *s.* 1. Caracoleo, movimiento lateral del caballo. 2. Galope, baile de movimiento muy vivo, y la música del mismo.

galloper ['gæləpər] [ga-lo-par], *s.* Hombre o caballo que galopa.

galloping ['gæləpɪŋ] [ga-lo-pin], *a.* Galopante.

gallows ['gæləʊz] [ga-lous], *s.* 1. Horca, instrumento de suplicio en el cual mueren colgados los delincuentes condenados a la última pena. 2. Un aparato cualquiera del que se suspenden las cosas. **Gallows-bird,** el malvado que merece la pena de horca. 3. *pl. (Fam. E.U.)* Tirantes del pantalón.

gallows-free ['gæləʊzˌfriː] [ga-lous-fri], *a.* El que tiene la fortuna de no ser ahorcado mereciéndolo.

gally ['gælɪ] [ga-li], *a.* Amargo; lo que contiene hiel.

galore ['gælɔːr] [ga-lor], *a.* y *adv.* Muchísimo, abundante; sigue siempre al sustantivo.

galosh, galoche [gə'lɒʃ] [ga-losh], *s.* Chanclo, zueco, zapato fuerte que se lleva por lo común sobre otro, y por extensión se llama así algunas veces cualquier calzado; zapatón.

galvanic [gæl'vænɪk] [gal-va-nik], *a.* Galvánico, que pertenece al galvanismo.

galvanism ['gælvənɪzəm] [gal-va-ni-sem], *s.* Galvanismo, la electricidad puesta en acción por el contacto de dos substancias de diferente naturaleza.

galvanize ['gælvənaɪz] [gal-va-nais], *va.* 1. Galvanizar. 2. Dar, comunicar animación o energía ficticia. 3. *V.* ELECTROPLATE.

galvanometer [ˌgælvə'nɒmɪtər] [gal-va-no-mi-tar], *s.* Galvanómetro, aparato para medir la fuerza de una corriente eléctrica o la diferencia de la potencial.

gamma globuline [ˌgæmə'glɒbjoliːn] [ga-ma-glo-biu-lin], *s. (Med.)* Gama globulina.

gambade, gambado ['gæmbeɪd] [gam-beid], *s.* 1. Polaina para proteger contra el lodo. 2. *pl.* Cubiertas de cuero a manera de botas que protegen los pies y sirven de estribos.

gambit ['gæmbɪt] [gam-bit], *s.* 1. Gambito, lance en el juego de ajedrez. 2. Concesión para invitar a la discusión.

gamble ['gæmbl] [gam-bol], *vn.* 1. Jugar con exceso; jugar con trampas; garitear, frecuentar los garitos. 2. Jugar con dinero, especular, aventurarse.

gamble, *s.* Juego, empresa arriesgada.

gambler ['gæmblər] [gam-blar], *s.* Tahur, jugador.

gambling ['gæmblɪŋ] [gam-blin], *s.* Juego (with money), acción de jugar dinero. **Gambling table,** mesa de juego.

gamboge ['gæmbɒdʒ] [gam-boch], *s.* Gomaguta o gutagamba.

gambol ['gæmbəl] [gam-bol], *vn.* Brincar, saltar, caracolear.

gambol, *s.* Cabriola, brinco de alegría, caracoleo.

gambrel ['gæmbrɪl] [gam-bril], *s.* 1. Pierna trasera del caballo. 2. Palo en forma de cayado en que cuelgan la carne los carnicero*s*. 3. **Gambrel roof,** techo a la holandesa, de ángulo obtuso.

game [geɪm] [gueim], *s.* 1. Juego, entretenimiento, pasatiempo. 2. Chanza, burla, mofa. 3. Juego, partida o partido. **Low game cards,** cartas baja*s*. 4. Caza, lo que mata el cazador. 5. Juegos públicos. **Game-bag,** zurrón, morral. **The game is up,** (a) Se ha levantado la caza. (b) *(Fam.)* El proyecto ha salido mal; se acabó.

game, *vn.* Jugar, entretenerse con alguna especie de juego; jugar fuerte.

game-cock ['geɪmkɒk] [gueim-kok], *s.* Gallo inglés o de pelea.

game-keeper ['geɪmˌkiːpər] [gueim-ki-par], *s.* Guarda de coto, el que cuida de la caza.

game-leg ['geɪmleg] [gueim-leg], *s. (Ger.)* Pierna estropeada.

gameness ['geɪmnɪs] [gueim-nes], *s.* Valor, resolución.

gamesome ['geɪmsʌm] [gueim-sam], *a.* Juguetón, retozón.

gamesomeness ['geɪmsʌmnɪs] [gueim-sam-nes], *s.* Festividad, alegría, juguete.

gamesomely ['geɪmsʌmlɪ] [gueim-sam-li], *adv.* Alegremente.

gamester ['geɪmstər] [gueims-tar], *s.* 1. Tahur, jugador; garitero; fullero. 2. Chocarrero, bufón. 3. *(Ant.)* Ramera, mujer pública.

gamete ['gæmiːt] [ga-mit], *s. (Biol.)* Gameto.

gametophyte ['gæmɪtəˈfaɪt] [ga-mi-to-fait], *s.* Gametofia.

game warden ['geɪmwɑːdn] [gueim-uar-den], *s.* Guardabosque.

gaming ['geɪmɪŋ] [gui-min], **gambling** ['gæmblɪŋ] [gam-blin], *s.* Juego.

gaming-table ['geɪmɪŋˌteɪbl] [gui-min-tei-bol], *s.* Mesa de juego.

gamma ray ['gæmə'reɪ] [ga-ma-rei], *s.* Rayo gama.

gammer ['gæmər] [ga-mar], *sf.* Una vieja; comadre, tía.

gammon ['gæmən] [ga-mon], *s.* 1. Jamón, el pernil o nalgada del puerco salada y enjunta. 2. *V.* BACKGAMMON. **Gammoning of the bow-sprit,** *(Mar.)* Trincas del baupré*s*.

It is all gammon, *(Fam.)* Es una necedad o bobada, habladuría, jarabe de pico.

gammon, *va.* 1. Engañar, chasquear. 2. Ganar doble partida de chaquete.

gamopetalous ['gæmə'petələs] [ga-mo-pe-ta-los], *a. (Bot.)* Gamopétalo, monopétalo, se dice de las corolas de una sola pieza o de pétalos más o menos unidos.

gamp [gæmp] [gamp], *s.* Paraguas grande.

gamut ['gæmət] [ga-mot], *s. (Mús.)* Gama, escala.

gamy ['gæmɪ] [ga-mi], *a.* 1. Que tiene el tufillo o sabor de la caza. 2. *(Fam.)* Animoso, dispuesto a pelear.

ganch [gænt∫] [ganch], *va.* Arrojar a una persona desde lo alto sobre ganchos, especie de castigo bárbaro usado entre los turcos.

gander ['gændər] [gan-dar], *s.* Ansar, ganso, el macho de la gansa.

gang [gæŋ] [gang], *s.* 1. Cuadrilla, banda. **Gang of robbers,** cuadrilla de ladrones. 2. *(Mar.)* Partida. **Press-gang,** ronda de matrícula. 3. *(Min.)* V. GANGUE. **Gang-plank,** pasamano de un navío. **Gang-plough,** arado de reja múltiple. **Gang-saw,** sierra múltiple.

gangling ['gæŋglɪŋ] [gan-glin], *a.* Larguilucho, desgarbado.

ganglion ['gæŋglɪən] [gan-glion], *s.* 1. *(Anat.)* Ganglio, nudillo o tubérculo que se halla en el trayecto de los nervios y vasos linfáticos. 2. *(Cir.)* Ganglio, pequeño tumor enquistado que procede de un tendón.

gangplank ['gæŋplæŋk] [gang-plank], *s.* Plancha, pasarela.

gangrenate ['gæŋgrɪneɪt] [gan-gri-neit], **gangrene** ['gæŋgriːn] [gan-grin], *va.* Gangrenar. *-vn.* Gangrenarse. **gangrene,** *s.* Gangrena.

gangrenous ['gæŋgrɪnəs] [gan-gri-nos], *a.* Gangrenoso.

gang-board ['gæŋbɔːd] [gang-bord], *s. (Mar.)* Plancha, andamio.

gangster ['gæŋstər] [gans-tar], *s.* Pandillero, miembro de una organización de malhechores.

gangue ['gæŋg] [gang], *s. (Min.)* Ganga, materia no metálica que se halla en las venas de las minas.

gangway ['gæŋweɪ] [gang-uei], *s. (Mar.)* Pasamano de un buque, portalón.

gannet ['gænɪt] [ga-nit], *s.* Bubia, ave acuática de especie afín a la de los pelícanos.

ganoid ['gænɔɪd] [ga-noid], *a.* Perteneciente a los ganoideos, gran división de los peces.

gantlet, gauntlet ['gæntlɪt] [gan-tlit], *s.* Baquetas, castigo militar. **To run the gantlet,** pasar o correr baquetas.

gantry ['gæntrɪ] [gan-tri], *s.* 1. Poíno; caballete para barril. 2. Plataforma para grúas. 3. *(Ferro.)* Puente transversal para ferrocarriles.

gaol ['dʒeɪl] [yeil], *va.* Encarcelar.

gaol, *s.* Cárcel. V. JAIL.

gaoler ['dʒeɪlər] [yei-lar], *s.* Carcelero, el que guarda la cárcel.

gap ['gæp] [gap], *s.* 1. Boquete, portillo o abertura en un cercado. 2. Agujero, brecha, hueco. 3. Quebrada; barranca, hondonada. **To stand in the gap,** defender, exponerse por proteger a alguno que está en peligro.

gap, *v.* Abrir brecha o boquete.

gape [geɪp] [gueip], *vn.* 1. Bostezar, abrir involuntariamente la boca; boquear. 2. Anhelar, desear, ansiar. 3. Hendirse, rajarse, abrirse en grietas. 4. Estar con la boca abierta; admirarse neciamente de lo que uno ve y oye. **To gape after at** o **for,** ansiar alguna cosa. **To gape at,** embobarse, papar moscas.

gape, *s.* 1. Bostezo. 2. Abertura, hendedura; particularmente en zoología, anchura de la boca de un pájaro o de un pez, cuando la abre.

gaper ['geɪpər] [guei-par], *s.* El que bosteza, anhela o se emboba mirando u oyendo alguna cosa; papamoscas.

gar [gaːr] [ga], *va. (Esco.)* Causar, hacer; forzar.

gar, *s.* Sollo o belona. V. GARPIKE.

garage ['gærɑːʒ] [ga-rash], *s.* Garaje.

garage, *v.* Encerrar o dejar en el garage.

garb [gaːb] [garb], *s.* 1. Vestido, vestidura, traje; particularmente traje característico. 2. Apariencia, esterior, aspecto, aire.

garb, *v.* Vestir, ataviar.

garbage ['gaːbɪdʒ] [gar-bich], *s.* Tripas, desechos de un animal; basura, desperdicios de una casa.

garbel ['gaːbəl] [gar-bel], *s. (Mar.)* Aparadura, la primera traca que se dispone contra el alefrís de la quilla.

garble ['gaːbl] [gar-bel], *va.* 1. Alterar un escrito por supresión o elisión; pervertir, mutilar, falsificar. **A garble quotation,** citación mutilada. 2. Entresacar, apartar; antiguamente escoger lo bueno de lo malo. *-s. (Com.)* Desecho de especias y drogas.

garbler ['gaːblər] [gar-blar], *s.* 1. Alterador, falsificador. 2. El que separa lo bueno de lo malo.

garboard ['gaːbɔːd] [gar-bord], *s. (Mar.)* Tabla de la quilla.

garbure ['gaːjʊər] [gar-biua], *s.* Sopa de tocino y verduras.

garden ['gaːdn] [gar-den], *s.* 1. Huerta, huerto. 2. Jardín. **Nursery garden,** plantel, criadero, semillero. **Garden-balsam,** balsamina de jardín. **Garden-bed,** cuadro de un jardín. **Garden-mould,** tierra vegetal. **Garden-plot,** anco de tierra en un jardín o huerta. **Garden-stuff,** hortalizas, legumbres, frutas.

garden, *vn.* Cultivar un jardín o huerto. *-va.* Hacer jardines o huertos.

gardener ['gaːdnər] [gard-nar], *s.* Jardinero, hortelano.

gardenia [gaːˈdiːnɪə] [gar-di-nia], *s. (Bot.)* Gardenia.

gardening ['gaːdnɪŋ] [gard-nin], *s.* Jardinería.

gare ['geər] [guea], *s. (Prov. Ingl.)* Lana de caídas, lana burda que tienen en las piernas las reses de ganado lanar.

garfish ['gaːfɪʃ] [gar-fish], *s.* El pez aguja, belon.

gargarism ['gaːgərɪzm] [gar-ga-risem], *s.* Gargarismo.

gargarize ['gaːgəraɪz] [gar-ga-rais], *va.* Gargarizar, hacer gárgaras.

garget ['gaːgɪt] [gar-guit], *s.* 1. Enfermedad del ganado mayor caracterizada por hinchazón de la garganta. 2. Enfermedad de las ubres de las vacas.

gargle ['gaːgl] [gar-guel], *va.* 1. Gargarizar. 2. Gorgoritear, hacer quiebros cn la voz en la garganta.

gargle, *s.* Gargarismo, enjuague para hacer gárgaras.

gargoyle ['gaːgɔɪl] [gar-goil], *s. (Arq.)* Gárgola.

garish ['geərɪʃ] [guea-rish], *a.* 1. Deslumbrante, deslumbrador. 2. Pomposo, ostentoso; extravagante.

garishly ['geərɪʃlɪ] [guea-rish-li], *adv.* Ostentosamente, desatinadamente.

garishness ['geərɪʃnɪs] [guea-rish-nes], *s.* Pompa, oropel, ostentación; alegría desatinada.

garland ['gaːlənd] [gar-land], *s.* 1. Guirnalda, corona abierta tejida de flores, hojas, etc.; de aquí, señal de honor, dada como símbolo de la victoria o el buen éxito. 2. Colección de joyas literarias. 3. Cosa parecida a una guirnalda; corona, florón. *(Mar.)* Roñada.

garland, *va.* Enguirnaldar.

garlic ['gaːlɪk] [gar-lik], *s. (Bot.)* Ajo.

garlicky ['gaːlɪkɪ] [gar-li-ki], *a.* Parecido al ajo o que lo contiene; que huele a ajo.

garment ['gaːmənt] [gar-ment], *s.* Prenda de vestir.

garner ['gaːnər] [gar-na], *va.* Entrojar, almacenar el grano.

garner, *s.* Granero; acopio.

garnet ['gaːnɪt] [gar-nit], *s.* 1. Granate, silicato de varias especies, estimadas algunas como piedras preciosas. 2. Color rojo obscuro. 3. *(Mar.)* Palanca para levantar fardos, candeletón.

garnish ['gaːnɪʃ] [gar-nish], *va.* 1. Guarnecer, adorna, ataviar, componer. 2. Aderezar un plato o un manjar para la mesa. 3. *(Der.)* Prevenir, notificar. 4. Aprisionar con grillos.

garnish, *s.* 1. Guarnición, adorno. 2. Aderezo, de un plato o de un manjar.

garnishee ['gaːnɪʃiː] [gar-ni-shi], *s.* Persona cuyos bienes se embargan. *-va.* Embargar bienes.

garnisher ['gɑːnɪʃəʳ] [gar-ni-shaʳ], *s.* El que pone guarniciones o adornos.

garnishment ['gɑːnɪʃmənt] [gar-nish-ment], *s.* 1. Ornamento, adorno. 2. *(For.)* Orden judicial que prohibe a un tercero disponer de los fondos que tenga en su poder pertenecientes al demandado.

garniture ['gɑːnɪtsəʳ] [gar-ni-chaʳ], *s.* Guarnición, adorno.

garpike ['gɑːpaɪk] [gar-paik], *s.* 1 Pez americano de agua dulce, parecido al sollo. 2. *V.* GARFISH.

garret ['gærɪt] [ga-rit], *s.* Buhardilla, la habitación que está contigua al tejado; zaquizamí, desván.

garreteer ['gærɪtɪəʳ] [ga-ri-tiaʳ], *s.* El que vive en una buhardilla.

garrison ['gærɪsən] [ga-ri-son], *s. (Mil.)* 1. Guarnición, el conjunto de soldados para la defensa de una plaza. 2. Guarnición, plaza de armas guarnecida de tropas.

garrison, *va.* Guarnecer una plaza con las tropas necesarias para su defensa.

garrot ['gærɒt] [ga-rot], *s.* Torniquete.

garrote [gəˈrɒt] {ga-rot], *va.* 1. Ajusticiar por medio del garrote. 2. Agarrar por la garganta para ahogar y robar.

garrote, *s.* Garrote, estrangulación para robar.

garrulity [gəˈruːlɪtɪ] [ga-ru-li-ti], *s.* Garrulidad, locuacidad, charla.

garrulous ['gæroləs] [ga-ru-los], *a.* Gárrulo, locuaz, parlero.

garter ['gɑːtəʳ] [gar-taʳ], *s.* 1. Liga, cenojil, atadero con que se aseguran las medias; jarretera. 2. Jarretera, orden de este nombre, la más ilustre de Inglaterra. 3. Insignia de esta orden, la liga que llevan los caballeros en el jarrete de la pierna izquierda. **garter King-at-arms,** rey de armas. **Garter-fish,** lepidopo, género de peces.

garter, *va.* 1. Atar con liga o cenojil. 2. Investir con la orden de la Jarretera.

garth ['gærθ] [garz], *s.* 1. Obstrucción artificial de una corriente de agua para coger peces. 2. Patio de claustro.

gas [gæs] [gas], *s.* 1. *(Quím.)* Gas: nombre genérico para toda especie de fluido elástico permanente. 2. Gas para el alumbrado o la calefacción. 3. Mechero de gas. 4. Gas óxidonitroso. **Gas-fitter,** instalador de gas. **Gas-burner,** mechero, quemador de gas. **Gas-holder,** *V.* GASOMETER. **Gas-light,** (a) luz de gas. (b) Mechero de gas. **Gas-main,** cañería principal o maestra de gas. **Gas-meter,** gasómetro o contador de gas. **Gas-pipe,** tubo de gas. **Gas-works,** fábrica de gas. **Sewer gas,** emanaciones de las cloacas.

gas, *v.* 1. Abastecer o proveer de gas. 2. Exponer a la llama del gas. 3. *(Quím.)* Saturar de gas. 4. Asfixiar con gas. 5. Abastecer con gasolina. 6. Engañar, enlabiar, fanfarronear, charlar. 7. Funcionar con gasolina.

gascon ['gæskən] [gas-kon], *s.* Gascón.

gasconade ['gæskəneɪd] [gas-ko-neid], *s.* Gasconada, fanfarronada.

gasconade, *vn.* Jactarse, fanfarronear.

Gascony ['gækənɪ] [gas-ko-ni], *s. (Geogr.)* Gascuña.

gaseous ['gæsɪəs] [ga-sios], *a.* 1. Gaseoso, lo que tiene la naturaleza o la forma del gas; aeriforme. 2. Insubstancial.

gash [gæʃ] [gash], *va.* Dar una cuchillada, acuchillar; hacer un chirlo.

gash, *s.* 1. Cuchillada, herida larga y honda. 2. Cicatriz, la señal que queda de la herida.

gashful ['gæʃfol] [gash-ful], *a.* 1. Lleno de cuchilladas. 2. Terrible, horrendo, espantoso.

gasholder ['gæsˌhəoldəʳ] [gas-joul-daʳ], *s.* Gasómetro.

gasification [ˌgæsɪfɪˈkeɪʃn] [ga-si-fi-kei-shon], *s.* Gasificación.

gasiform ['gæsɪfɔːm] [ga-si-form], *a.* Gasiforme.

gasify ['gæsɪfaɪ] [ga-si-fai], *va.* Gasificar, convertir en gas.

gasket ['gæskɪt] [gas-kit], *s.* 1. *(Mec.)* Relleno, empaquetadura, sea de caucho, cuero, metal en planchas, cáñamo o plomo. 2. *pl. (Mar.)* Tomadore, unas cajetas largas con que se acaban de aforrar las velas. **Bunt-gaskets,** tomadores del batidero de una vela.

gaskins ['gæskɪnz] [gas-kins], *s. pl.* 1. Empaquetadura o empaque de cáñamo. 2. *(Des.)* Especie de medias anchas que se usaron en el siglo XVI.

gaslight ['gæslaɪt] [gas-lait], *s.* Mechero de gas; luz de gas.

gaslit ['gæslɪt] [gas-lit], *a.* Iluminado por gas.

gasman ['gæsmæn] [gas-man], *s.* Fabricante de gas, gasista.

gasolier ['gæsəlɪəʳ] [ga-so-liaʳ], *s.* Candelabro colgante de varios mecheros para gas.

gasoline ['gæsəliːn] [ga-so-lin], *s.* Gasoleno, gasolina, líquido incoloro, volátil, inflamable, que se obtiene destilando el petróleo crudo y se usa como combustible.

gasometer [gæˈsɒmɪtəʳ] [ga-so-mi-taʳ], *s.* 1. Gasómetro, aparato que en las fábricas de gas del alumbrado se emplea para que el flúido salga con unifomidad por efecto de una constante presión. 2. *(Quím.)* Aparato para acumular, conservar o mezclar gases.

gasp [gɑːsp] [gasp], *vn.* 1. Boquear, respirar convulsivamente, como por extenuación o temor. 2. Suspirar, anhelar, desear alguna cosa con ansia. **To gasp for breath,** jadear. -*va.* Hablar o emitir sonidos jadeando como lo hace una persona aterrorizada o moribunda.

gasp, *s.* La acción de respirar o echar el aliento convulsiva o entrecortadamente. **He is at the last gasp,** está dando la última boqueada.

gassing ['gæsɪŋ] [ga-sin], *s.* 1. Tratamiento con gas. 2. Ataque con gas.

gassy ['gæsɪ] [ga-si], *a.* Gaseoso.

gas-storage tank ['gæstərɪdʒˈtæŋk] [gas-torich-tank], *s.* Gasómetro.

gastric ['gæstrɪk] [gas-trik], *a.* Gástrico, perteneciente al estómago.

gastriloquous ['gæstrɪləkwəs] [gas-tri-lo-kuos], *a.* Ventrílocuo, el que cuando habla parece que saca la voz del vientre.

gastritis [gæsˈtraɪtɪs] [gas-trai-tis], *s.* Gastritis, inflamación del estómago.

gastronomer, gastronomist ['gæstrənəomeʳ] [gas-tro-nou-maʳ], *s.* Gastrónomo, persona aficionada a la buena mesa.

gastronomic [ˌgæstrəˈnɒmɪk] [gas-tro-no-mik], *a.* Gastronómico.

gastronomy [gæsˈtrɒnəmɪ] [gas-tro-no-mi], *s.* Gastronomía, arte de comer opíparamente.

gastropod ['gæstrəpɒd] [gas-tro-pod], *s.* Gastrópodo.

gastrorectomy [ˌgæstrəˈrektəmɪ] [gas-tro-rek-to-mi], *s.* Gastrotomia.

gastrotomy ['gæstrətəmɪ] [gas-tro-to-mi], *s.* Gastrotomía.

gat [gæɪ] [gat], *s.* Arma de fuego, pistola, revólver.

gate [geɪt] [gueit], *s.* 1. Puerta, la entrada de una ciudad o plaza. 2. Barrera, talanquera. 3. Puerta de cercado. 4. Vía, camino. 5. Compuertas de esclusa. **Flood-gate,** paradera, compuerta del caz de un molino. **Gate-keeper, gateward,** portero; guardabarrera de ferrocarril.

gate, *v.* 1. Poner puertas. 2. Castigar a un alumno haciéndole quedarse después de clase.

gated ['geɪtɪd] [guei-tid], *a.* Lo que tiene puertas.

gatekeeper ['geɪtˌkiːpəʳ] [gueit-ki-paʳ], *s.* Portero; guardabarrera.

gatepost ['geɪtpəost] [gueit-poust], *s.* Jamba de una puerta de cercado.

gateway ['geɪtweɪ] [gueit-uei], *s.* Entrada por las puertas de algún cercado.

gather ['gæðəʳ] [ga-daʳ], *va.* 1. Coger, recoger, amontonar. 2. Rebuscar, recoger los residuos de la viña vendimiada o de otros frutos. 3. Juntar, congregar, unir. 4. Fruncir, recoger la orilla del paño u otra tela. 5. Colegir, inferir. 6. Arrugar, plegar. -*vn.* Condensarse, aumentarse, unirse, juntarse. **To gather breath,** tomar aliento, descansar. **To gather dust,** cubrirse de polvo. **To gather flesh,** criar carnes, engordar. **To gather strength,** recuperarse, restablecerse, tomar fuerzas. **To gather o to come to a head,** llegar al estado de supuración, madurarse un tumor. **To gather corn,** hacer el verano, recoger la cosecha. **To gather grapes,** vendimiar. **To**

gather together, reunir, juntar, congregar. **To gather up,** alzar, recoger.

gather, s. 1. Pliegue. 2. Deslustre o deslucimiento del paño a fuerza de manosearlo o de hacerle pliegues.

gatherable ['gæðərəbl] [ga-ze-ra-bol], a. Deducible.

gatherer ['gæðərər] [ga-ze-raʳ], s. 1. Colector, segador, vendimiador. 2. Recaudador. 3. Avaro, tacaño.

gathering ['gæðəriŋ] [ga-ze-rin], s. 1. Asamblea; amontonamiento de gente. 2. Acumulación, amontonamiento de cosas. 3. Cuesta, demanda, colecta de limosnas o donativos para pobres u objetos piadosos. 4. Acumulación de pus o materia, absceso.

gauche [gəʊʃ] [gaush], a. 1. Zurdo. 2. Torpe, falta de tacto o de soltura.

gaucherie ['gəʊsəri:] [gau-she-ri], s. Torpeza, falta de tacto o de soltura.

gaud [gɔːd] [god], s. Adorno, joya, perifollo ostentoso.

gaudery ['gɔːdəri] [go-de-ri], s. Lujo ostentoso en el traje o modo de vestir. (Vul.) Charrada.

gaudily ['gɔːdɪlɪ] [go-di-li], adv. Ostentosamente, fastuosamente.

gaudiness ['gɔːdɪnɪs] [go-di-nes], s. Oropel, cosa de poco valor y mucho brillo; fausto, pompa; ostentación en el vestir.

gaudy ['gɔːdɪ] [go-di], a. 1. Brillante, lucido; de aquí, llamativo, charro.

gauge [geɪdʒ] [geich], va. 1. Aforar, medir y reconocer las vasijas que contienen vino o licores para saber su cabida. 2. Medir, tomar la medida de alguna cosa según su anchura, longitud o profundidad. 3. (Mar.) Medir o arquear los navíos.

gauge, s. La vara, sonda o escandallo con que se afora o mide. **Silver in sheets of suitable gauges,** plata en planchas de largo y grueso proporcionados. **Gauge-cock,** llave de prueba, de nivel, puesta en la parte anterior de una caldera. **Gauge-wheel,** (Mec.) Gálibo de contornear. **Axle-gauge,** ajustador de eje.

gauger ['geɪdʒəʳ] [gei-chaʳ], s. Aforador, arqueador.

gauging ['geɪdʒɪŋ] [gei-chin], s. El acto de aforar o medir. **Gauging-rod,** aforador, instrumento para aforar.

Gaul [gɔːl] [gol], s. Galia antigua, francia.

Gaulish ['gɔːlɪʃ] [gou-lish], a. Lo que pertenece a las Galias, galicano.

gaunt [gɔːnt] [gont], a. Flaco, delgado.

gauntlet ['gɔːntlɪt] [gont-lit], s. 1. Manopla, guantelete, armadura de hierro a modo de guante para la mano. 2. Guantelete, guante con prolongación de la muñeca.

gauntly ['gɔːntlɪ] [gon-tli], adv. Flacamente, flojamente.

gauze [gɔːz] [gos], s. Gasa, especie de tela a manera de red, muy menuda y transparente. **Silk-gauze,** gasa de seda. **Thread-gauze,** gasa de hilo. **Linen-gauze,** clarín.

gauziness ['gɔːzɪnɪs] [go-si-nes], s. Lo que es ligero o transparente como la gasa.

gauzy ['gɔːzɪ] [go-si], a. Delgado y diáfano como la gasa.

gave [geɪv] [gueiv], pret. de TO GIVE.

gavel ['gævl] [ga-vel], s. 1. Mazo de albañil. 2. Mazo que usa el presidente de una asamblea o reunión. 3. Gavilla, manojo de mieses. 4. (Hist.) Gabela, tributo.

gavelock ['gævlɒk] [ga-ve-lok], s. Barra o palanca de hierro.

gavial ['gævɪəl] [ga-vial], s. El cocodrilo del Ganges. Gavialis gangeticus.

gavot ['gævɒt] [ga-vot], s. Gavota, baile francés.

gawk [gɔːk] [gok], s. 1. Pápamo, bobo. 2. (Esco.) Cuclillo.

gawk, v. 1. Hacer el tonto. 2. Mirar embobado. 3. Mirar de forma impertinente.

gawky ['gɔːkɪ] [go-ki], s. Zote. -a. Bobo, tonto, rudo.

gay [geɪ] [guei], 1. Alegre, de buen humor, jovial. 2. Gayo, alegre, brillante, lucido; especioso. 3. Aficionado a los placeres, particularmente los vedados; inclinado a la lascivia. -s. (Des.) Adorno.

gayety, gaiety ['geɪətɪ] [gueie-ti], s. Alegría; muchachada; pompa, ostentación, fausto

gayly, gaily ['geɪlɪ] [guei-li], adv. Alegremente, jovialmente; espléndidamente.

gayness ['geɪnɪs] [guei-nes], s. Alegría, pompa.

gaze [geɪz] [gueis], vn. Contemplar, considerar. -va. Mirar de hito en hito.

gaze, s. 1. Contemplación, mirada, el acto de contemplar o mirar alguna cosa con atención. 2. El objeto que se mira o contempla con atención.

gaze-hound ['geɪz'haʊnd] [gueis-jaund], s. Perro que caza con la vista y no con el olfato; particularmente el galgo.

gazelle [gəˈzel] [ga-sel], s. Gacela.

gazer ['geɪzəʳ] [guei-saʳ], s. Mirón, el que mira con demasiada curiosidad.

gazette [gəˈzet] [ga-set], s. Gacet, papel periódico; en especial se designa con este nombre el órgano oficial del gobierno inglés.

gazette, va. Publicar, anunciar, en la Gaceta o diario oficial. **He was gazetted to a captaincy,** se publicó en la Gaceta su nombramiento de capitán.

gazetteer [ˌgæzɪˈtɪəʳ] [ga-si-tiaʳ], s. 1. Gacetero, el que compone la gaceta. 2. Nombre de un diccionario geográfico de todos los países, ciudades, ríos y lugares del mundo.

gazing-stock [ˌgeɪzɪŋˈstɒk] [guei-sin-stok], s. 1. Hazmerreír, la risa, el desprecio y burla de todos. 2. El objeto que llama mucho la atención de los que lo miran.

gear [gɪəʳ] [guiaʳ], s. 1. (Mec.) Engranaje, encaje de una rueda en otra; transmisión de movimiento; juego de piezas motrices. 2. (Mar.) Juego de drizas, cuadernales, etc., usado para manejar una verga, berlinga, o vela. 3. Rueda dentada. 4. Juego, manera como están relacionados dos o más cosas, de modo que sin separarlas tengan movimiento. 5. Lo que está preparado o sirve para la preparación de alguna cosa; de aquí, los vestidos, adornos o atavío, herramientas, aperos, utensilios caseros, arneses o aparejos de tiro. **Head-gear,** cofia, tocado de la cabeza. **Gears,** (Mar.) Drizas. **Main-gears,** drizas mayores. **Fore-gears,** drizas de la verga de trinquete. **Gear-block,** cuadernal de paloma. **In gear,** en juego, encajado. **Out of gear,** fuera de juego, desencajado; desengranado. **To put in gear,** relacionar, conexionar, engranar. **To throw into gear,** poner en juego. **To throw out of gear,** desencajar; desmontar. **Food gear,** calzado.

gear, va. 1. Aparejar, poner los aparejos, preparar. 2. (Mec.) Engranar, encajar, conectar. -vn. Venir o estar en juego.

gear box, gear case ['gɪəbɒks] [guia-boks], s. Caja de engranaje.

gearing ['gɪərɪŋ] [guia-rin], s. 1. (Mec.) Encaje, engranaje; piezas vivas colectivamente. 2. (Mar.) Sogas y aparejos.

gearshift ['gɪəʃɪft] [guia-shift], s. (Mec.) Cambio de velocidades. **Gearshift lever,** palanca de cambios o de velocidades.

gear wheel ['gɪəwiːl] [guia-uil], s. Rueda de engranaje, rueda dentada.

geat [giːt] [guit], s. El agujerito por donde entra en el molde el metal derretido.

gee [dʒiː] [yi], s. Nombre de la letra G.

gee, geeho [diːə] [yio], va. Hacer que un animal de tiro se dirija a la derecha, apartándose del carretero. -vn. Dirigirse un buey o una mula hacia la derecha, alejándose del carretero. En imperativo, ven, anda: voz de los carreteros para avivar y guiar a los caballos.

geese [giːs] [guis], s. pl. de GOOSE.

geiger counter ['gaɪgəˌkaʊntəʳ] [gai-ga-kaun-taʳ], s. Contador Geiger.

gelatin, gelatine ['dʒelətiːn] [ye-la-tin], s. Gelatina, substancia coherente, transparente, insípida, que se extrae de los huesos y cuernos o de las patas de los animales. Es soluble en agua caliente.

gelatinate, gelatinize ['dʒelətɪneɪt] [ye-la-ti-neit], va. yvn. Convertir o convertirse en substancia gelatinosa.

gelatinous ['dʒelətɪnəs] [ye-la-ti-nos], a. Gelatinoso, de la gelatina o de su naturaleza; semejante a la gelatina.

gelation ['dʒeleɪʃən] [ye-lei-shon], s. Congelación.

geld [geld] [gueld], va. 1. Castrar, capar (horse). 2. Castrar, quitar a las colmenas los panales con miel.

geld, s. Tributo antiguo; multa.

gelder ['geldəʳ] [guel-daʳ], s. Castrador, capador.

gelding ['geldɪŋ] [guel-din], s. Capón, cualquier animal capado, particularmente el caballo.

gelid ['dʒelɪd] [ye-lid], a. (Poét.) Sumamente frío, helado.

gelidity [dʒe'lɪdɪtɪ] [ye-li-di-ti], **gelidness** ['dʒelɪdnɪs] [ye-lid-nes], s. Frío extremo.

gem [dʒem] [yem], s. 1. Joya, presea. 2. Cosa preciosa, alhaja; objeto raro y cabal; obra literaria o de arte, corta y muy perfecta. 3. (Des.) Yema.

gem, va. Adornar con piedras preciosas. -vn. (Ant.) Abotonar, arrojar los árboles y plantas el botón.

gemel ['dʒeməl] [ye-mel], a. y s. Gemelo. **Gemel-ring,** sortija formada por dos o más anillos.

geminate ['dʒemɪneɪt] [ye-mi-neit], a. (Bot.) Que ocurre en pares; gemelo, de dos en dos. -va. Doblar, duplicar.

gemination [,dʒemɪ'neɪʃən] [ye-mi-nei-shon], s. Duplicación, repetición.

Gemini ['dʒemɪnɪ] [ye-mi-ni], s. Géminis, el tercer signo del zodíaco.

gemma ['dʒemɑː] [ye-ma], a. Botón, yema.

gemmation [dʒe'meɪʃən] [ye-mei-shon], s. 1. (Zool.) Gemación, reproducción asexual por medio de un cuerpo parecido a una yema, el cual llega a ser nuevo individuo. 2. (Bot.) El período del desarrollo de los botones; vernación.

gemmeous ['dʒemɪəs] [ye-mios], a. Lo que se asemeja a una piedra preciosa, o al botón o yema de las plantas.

gemmule ['dʒemjuːl] [ye-miul], s. Botón pequeño.

gemot ['dʒemɒt] [ye-mot], s. Antiguamente asamblea, reunión pública.

gender ['dʒendəʳ] [yen-daʳ], s. 1. Género, la división de los nombres según los diferentes sexos. 2. (Fam.) Sexo.

gender, va. Engendrar; producir, causar. -vn. (Ant.) Acción de copularse.

gene [dʒiːn] [yin], s. (Biol.) Gen. pl. **genes.**

genealogical [,dʒiːnɪə'lɒdʒɪkəl] [yi-nia-lo-yi-kal], a. Genealógico.

genealogist [,dʒiːnɪ'ælədʒɪst] [yi-nia-lo-yist], s. Genealogista.

genealogy [,dʒiːnɪ'ælədʒɪ] [yi-nia-lo-yi], s. Genealogía, la descripción de la estirpe de alguno.

generable ['dʒenərəbl] [ye-ne-ra-bol], a. Generable, que se puede producir por generación.

general ['dʒenərəl] [ye-ne-ral], a. 1. Genera, indeterminado, extensivo. 2. Público, ordinario, común, usual. 3. Visto como totalidad o conjunto. -s. 1. Lo general, la mayor parte; el público, el vulgo. **In general,** por la mayor parte, en general, por lo común. 2. General, oficial general. 3. Generala, un toque de tambor.

generalissimo [,dʒenərə'lɪsɪməʊ] [ye-ne-ra-li-si-mou], s. Generalísimo.

generality [,dʒenə'rælɪtɪ] [ye-ne-ra-li-ti], **generalty** ['dʒenərəl] [ye-ne-ral], s. Generalidad, la parte principal, la mayor parte, la multitud.

generalization [,dʒenərəlaɪ'zeɪʃən] [ye-ne-ra-lai-sei-shon], s. Generalización.

generalize ['dʒenərəlaɪz] [ye-ne-ra-lais], va. Generalizar.

generally ['dʒenərəlɪ] [ye-ne-ra-li], adv. Generalmente, comúnmente, por lo general, en general, extensivamente; por la mayor parte.

generalness ['dʒenərəlnɪs] [ye-ne-ral-nes], s. Frecuencia, extensión.

generalship ['dʒenərəlʃɪp] [ye-ne-ral-ship], s. Generalato.

generant ['dʒenərənt] [ye-ne-rant], a. Generativo. -s. 1. Generante, principio generativo. 2. V. GENERATRIX, 1ª.

generate ['dʒenəreɪt] [ye-ne-reit], va. 1. Engendrar, procrear, propagar. 2. Producir, ocasionar, causar. 3. (Mat.) Producir por el movimiento. **A generating line** o **Surface,** una línea o una superficie generatriz.

generation [,dʒenə'reɪʃən] [ye-ne-rei-shon], s. 1. Generación, el acto o la función de engendrar. 2. Generación, familia, linaje, prole, progenie. 3. Siglo, edad. 4. La formación de una figura o un cuerpo geométrico por el movimiento de un punto, de una línea o de una superficie.

generative ['dʒenərətɪv] [ye-ne-ra-tiv], a. Generativo, prolífico, fecundo.

generator ['dʒenəreɪtəʳ] [ye-ne-rei-toʳ], s. 1. Padre, procreador, engendrador. 2. La cosa que engendra, causa o produce. 3. Lo que origina o produce electricidad; máquina electrodinámica.

generatrix ['dʒenərətrɪks] [ye-ne-ra-triks], s. 1. (Mat.) Punto, línea o superficie que produce una figura por su movimiento. 2. Máquina electrodinámica. 3. Madre; la que produce.

generic, generical [dʒɪ'nerɪkəl] [yi-ne-ri-kal], a. Genérico, lo que comprende el género y es común a muchas especies.

generically [dʒɪ'nerɪkəlɪ] [yi-ne-ri-ka-li], adv. Genéricamente.

generosity [,dʒenə'rɒsɪtɪ] [ye-ne-ro-si-ti], s. Generosidad, liberalidad; garbo, bizarría.

generous ['dʒenərəs] [ye-ne-ros], a. 1. Liberal, bizarro, dadivoso; vigoroso; franco, abierto. 2. Generoso, noble, magnánimo. 3. Que tiene cualidades estimulantes, como el vino.

generously ['dʒenərəslɪ] [ye-ne-ros-li], adv. Magnánimamente, liberalmente, dadivosamente, bizarramente.

generousness ['dʒenərəsnɪs] [ye-ne-ros-nes], s. Generosidad, magnanimidad, nobleza, bizarría.

genesial ['dʒenɪzɪəl] [ye-ni-shial], a. Genésico.

genesis ['dʒenɪsɪs] [ye-ni-sis], s. 1. Creación, principio. 2. Relato o explicación del origen de alguna cosa. 3. Géneses, el primer libro del Antiguo Testamento. 4. (Geom.) V. GENERATION, 4ª acep.

genet ['dʒenɪt] [ye-nit], s. 1. Haca, jaca, de España. 2. (Zool.) Jineta, Gineta.

genet, s. 1. Gineta, mamífero que se parece mucho a la civeta, pero más pequeño. 2. La piel adobada de este animal.

genethliacs ['dʒenɪθlɪəks] [ye-niz-liaks], s. Genetlíaca, el arte de predecir la buena o mala ventura por el día y hora del nacimiento de una persona.

genetic [dʒɪ'netɪk] [yi-ne-tik], a. Genesiaco; relativo a la creación, la generación, o el origen de alguna cosa.

genetics [dʒɪ'netɪks] [yi-ne-tiks], s. (Biol.) Genética.

Geneva [dʒɪ'niːvə] [yi-ni-va], s. 1. Ginebra, ciudad de Suiza. V. GIN.

Genevan [dʒɪ'niːvən] [yi-ni-van], a. Ginebrino, de Ginebra. -s. 1. El natural de Ginebra. 2. Calvinista.

genial ['dʒiːnɪəl] [yi-nial], a. 1. Cordial, amistoso, de afables maneras, bondadoso. 2. Que comunica calor suave, da alivio o vida; consolador. 3. Nupcial; relativo al matrimonio; generativo.

genially ['dʒiːnɪəlɪ] [yi-nia-li], adv. Cordialmente; bondadosamente.

geniculate [dʒe'niːkjʊleɪt] [ye-ni-kiu-leit], a. En forma de ángulo, como la rodilla cuando está doblada.

geniculated [,dʒeniːkjʊ'leɪtɪd] [ye-ni-kiu-lei-tid], a. 1. Lo que tiene coyunturas o articulaciones. 2. (Bot.) Arrodillado, articulado.

geniculation [,dʒeniːkjʊ'leɪʃən] [ye-ni-kiu-lei-shon], s. 1. Genuflexión. 2. (Bot.) Articulación o nudo en las cañas de las plantas gramíneas; nudosidad.

genie ['dʒiːnɪ] [yi-ni], s. V. JINNEI.

genii ['dʒiːnɪ] [yi-ni], s. pl. Genios.

genista [dʒe'nɪstə] [ye-nis-ta], s. (Bot.) Genista, retama.

genital ['dʒenɪtl] [ye-ni-tal]. Genital perteneciente a la generación. **Genitals,** s. pl. Los órganos exteriores de la generación, en ambos sexos.

genitive ['dʒenɪtɪv] [ye-ni-tiv], *s. Gram.)* Genitivo, el segundo caso en la declinación de los nombre*s*. -*a.* Que indica, origen, posesión, etc.

genitor ['dʒenɪtə^r] [ye-ni-to^r], *s.* Padre, antiguamente genitor.

genius ['dʒiːnɪəs] [yi-nios], *s. (pl.* GENII). 1. Genio, numen o espíritu bueno o malo según el sistema del gentilismo. 2. Ingenio, talento inventivo, numen. 3. Genio, talento, don, prenda o disposición natural para alguna cossa. 4. Ingenio, la persona que posee grandes talentos. *(pl.* GENIUSES en este sentido.) 5. Genio, índole buena o mala; principio esencial de una cosa. 6. Tipo modelo y acabado de algo; personificación.

genocide ['dʒenəʊsaɪd] [ye-nou-said], *s.* Genocidio.

Genoese [ˌdʒenəʊˈiːz] [ye-nou-is], *a.* y *s.* Genovés, genovesa, el natural de Génova o lo que pertenece a esta ciudad.

genre [ʒɑːn^r] [yan^r], *s.* Género, estilo costumbrista.

genteel [dʒenˈtiːl] [yen-til], *a.* 1. Urbano, cortés, bien criado, señoril. 2. Gentil, lindo, gallardo, galán, airoso, decente, formal, caballeroso. 3. Vestido elegantemente, elegante, a la moda.

genteelly [dʒenˈtiːlɪ] [yen-ti-li], *adv.* Urbanamente, cortésmente, gentilmente.

genteelness [dʒenˈtiːlnɪs] [yen-til-nes], *s.* Gentileza, gracia, garbo, urbanidad, bizarría, gallardía, dulzura de genio, formalidad.

gentian ['dʒenʃɪən] [yen-shian], *s. (Bot.)* Genciana, cualquiera planta de la familia de las gencianas.

gentianella [ˌdʒenʃɪəˈniːlə] [yen-shia-ni-la], *s.* Especie de color azul.

gentile ['dʒentaɪl] [yen-tail], *a.* 1. Gentílico, perteneciente a un pueblo no judaico; pagano. 2. *(Gram.)* Gentilicio, nombre que indica la nación o patria. 3. Gentilicio, relativo a una tribu (**gens**) o **clan;** propio de las gentes. -*s.* 1. Gentil, el que no es judío. 2. Nombre gentilicio.

gentilic ['dʒentɪlɪk] [yen-ti-lik], *a.* 1. Gentílico. 2. Tribal, nacional, racial.

gentilism ['dʒentɪlɪzm] [yen-ti-li-sem], *s.* Gentilismo, gentilidad.

gentilitious [ˌdʒentɪlɪʃəs] [yen-ti-li-shos], *a.* Gentilicio, de una tribu; hereditario.

gentility [dʒenˈtɪlɪtɪ] [yen-ti-li-ti], *s.* 1. Nobleza de sangre, buen nacimiento. 2. Gentiliza, donosura, gracia, donaire. 3. Gente bien nacida. 4. Gentilidad, gentilismo.

gentle ['dʒentl] [yen-tel], *a.* 1. Suave, blando, apacible, dócil, manso, dulce, moderado, benévolo, tranquilo, benigno. 2. Bien nacido; de noble familia. -*s.* 1. *(Ant.)* V. GENTLEMAN. 2. Halcón adiestrado. 3. *(Ingl.)* Gusano, larva de mosca que sirve de cebo para pescar.

gentlefolk ['dʒentlfɔːlk] [yen-tel-folk], *s.* La gente bien nacida.

gentleman ['dʒentlmən] [yen-tel-man], *sm.* 1. Hombre superior al vulgo ya por su buen nacimiento, aunque no sea noble, ya por su carácter o circunstancias: corresponde en español unas veces a caballero y otras a señor, como términos de cortesía. 2. *(Fam.)* Hacendado, toda persona que vive de su hacienda o tiene rentas. **An independent gentleman,** una hacendado, propietario, rentista. **Well, gentlemen!,** ¡muy bien, señores! **A gentleman has asked for you,** un caballero ha preguntado por Ud. **Gentleman-farmer,** hacendado agricultor.

gentleman-like ['dʒentlmənˌlaɪk] [yen-tel-man-laik], **gentlemanly** ['dʒentlmənlɪ] [yen-tel-man-li], *a.* Caballeroso, galante, civil, urbano; lo que conviene a un hombre bien nacido o bien criado.

gentlemanliness ['dʒentlˌmənlɪnɪs] [yen-tel-man-li-nes], **gentlemanship** ['dʒentlmənʃɪp] [yen-tel-man-ship], *s.* Porte o calidad de caballero, urbanidad, corrección.

gentleman's agreement ['dʒentlmənzəˈgriːmənt] [yen-tel-mans-a-gri-ment], *s.* Pacto de caballeros.

gentleness ['dʒentlnɪs] [yen-tel-nes], *s.* 1. Dulzura, blandura, suavidad de carácter, mansedumbre, urbanidad. 2. Conducta caballerosa. 3. Nobleza.

gentlewoman ['dʒentlˌwʊmən] [yen-tel-uo-man], *sf.* Señora, dama. **The queen's gentlewomen,** las damas de honor de la reina.

gently ['dʒentlɪ] [yen-tli], 1. Dulcemente, suavemente. 2. Poco a poco, despacio, con tiento, con sentir.

gentoo ['dʒentuː] [yen-tu], *s.* El natural de la India oriental.

gentry ['dʒentrɪ] [yen-tri], *s.* 1. La clase de personas superiores al vulgo que no pertenecen a la nobleza: se usa también para expresar en general la clase, carácter o calidad de las familias distinguidas. 2. Cualquier clase de gente determinada; irónico, por lo común; como, **light-fingered gentry,** gente ladrona, rateros.

genuflect ['dʒejəʊflekt] [ye-niu-flekt], *v.* Doblar la rodilla, hacer una genuflexión.

genuflection [ˌdʒejəʊˈflekʃən] [ye-niu-flek-shon], *s.* Genuflexión.

genuine ['dʒejɔɪn] [ye-nuin], *a.* 1. Genuino, real, sin falsedad, ni falsificación. 2. Sincero, puro, propio; escrito por el autor cuyo nombre lleva. 3. *(Zool.)* Típico. 4. No afectado, franco, sincero; verdadero.

genuinely ['dʒejɔɪnlɪ] [ye-nuin-li], *adv.* Puramente, sinceramente, naturalmente.

genuineness ['dʒejɔɪnnɪs] [ye-nuin-nes], *s.* Pureza, la calidad que constituye alguna cosa pura y no adulterada.

genus ['dʒenəs] [ye-nos], *s.* 1. Género, lo que es común a varias especies y las comprende. 2. *(Biol.)* Género, conjunto de especies que poseen en común ciertos caracteres distintivos. 3. *(Mús.)* Clase, particularmente de escalas.

geocentric [ˌdʒiːəʊˈsentrɪk] [yiou-sen-trik], *a.* Geocéntrico; se dice de los planetas.

geochemical [ˌdʒiːəʊˈkemɪkəl] [yiou-ke-mi-kal], *s.* Geoquímico.

geochemistry [ˌdʒiːəʊˈkemɪstrɪ] [yiou-ke-mis-tri], *s.* Geoquímica.

geode [ˈdʒiːəʊd] [yioud], *s.* Geoda, piedra que tiene una cavidad tapizada de cristales; y el hueco mismo de dicha piedra.

geodesic [ˌdʒiːəʊˈdesɪk] [yiou-de-sik], *a.* Geodésico. **Geodesic dome,** cúpula geodésica.

geodesy [dʒiːˈɒdɪsɪ] [yi-o-di-si], *s.* Geodesia, topografía; a medición y representación gráfica de la tierra por medio de observaciones trigonométricas y astronómicas.

geodetic, geodetical [ˌdʒiːəʊˈdetɪk] [yiou-de-tik], *a.* V. GEODESIC.

geogenic [ˌdʒiːəʊˈdʒiːnɪk] [yiou-chi-nik], *a.* Geogénico.

geogeny [dʒiːˈɒdʒɪnɪ] [yiou-chi-ni], *s. (Geol.)* Geogenia.

geognosy [dʒiːˈɒgnəsɪ] [yi-og-no-si], *s. (Geol.)* Geognosia.

geographer [dʒɪˈɒgrəfə^r] [yio-gra-fa^r], *s.* Geógrafo, el que sabe o enseña la geografía.

geographical [dʒɪəˈgræfɪkəl] [yio-gra-fi-kal], *a.* Geográfico.

geographically [dʒɪəˈgræfɪkəlɪ] [yio-gra-fi-ka-li], Geográficamente.

geography [dʒɪˈɒgrəfɪ] [yio-gra-fi], *s.* 1. Geografía, descripción del globo terrestre. 2. Libro, particularmente el de texto, que contiene dicha descripción.

geoid [ˈdʒiːɔɪd] [yioid], *s. (Geol.)* Geoide.

geologic, geological [dʒɪəˈɒlɒdʒɪk] [yiou-lo-chik] [dʒɪəˈɒlɒdʒɪkəl] [yiou-lo-chi-kal], *a.* Geológico.

geologist [dʒɪˈɒlədʒɪst] [yiou-lo-chist], *s.* Geólogo, persona versada en geología.

geologize [dʒɪəˈɒlɒdʒaɪz] [yiou-lo-chais], *vn.* Estudiar la geología, particularmente sobre el terreno, en la sierra o en el campo.

geology [dʒɪˈɒlədʒɪ] [yi-o-lo-chi], *s.* 1. Geología, la ciencia que enseña y explica las propiedades de la tierra, su estructura y su historia. 2. Tratado sobre esta ciencia.

geomagnetic [ˌdʒiːəʊmægˈnetɪk] [yiou-mag-ne-tik], *a.* Geomagnético.

geometer [dʒɪˈɒmiːtə^r] [yiou-mi-ta^r], *s.* Geómetra, el que profesa el estudio de la geometría o está versado en ella.

geometric, geometrical [dʒɪəˈmetrɪk] [yiou-me-trik], *a.* Geométrico, lo que pertenece a la geometría.

geometrically [dʒɪəˈmetrɪkəlɪ] [yiou-me-tri-ka-li], *adv.* Geométricamente.

geometridæ [dʒɪəˈmetrɪdiː] [yiou-me-tri-di], *s. pl. (Ent.)* Geometrinos, suborden de insectos del orden de los lepidópteros o mariposas.

geometrize [dʒɪəˈmetraɪz] [yiou-me-trais], *vn.* Obrar conforme a las leyes de la geometría.

geometry [dʒɪˈɒmɪtrɪ] [yiou-mi-tri], *s.* Geometría, ciencia que trata de la extensión y de su medida.

geophysical [dʒiːəʊˈfɪzɪkəl] [yiou-fi-si-kal], *a.* Geofísico. **Geophysical year,** año geofísico.

geophysics [dʒiːəʊˈfɪzɪks] [yiou-fi-siks], *s. (Geol.)* Geofísica.

geopolitics [ˈdʒiːəʊpɒlɪtɪks] [yiou-po-li-tiks], *s.* Geopolítica.

geoponic, geoponical [ˌdʒiːəʊˈpɒnɪk] [yiou-po-nik], *a.* Geopónico, perteneciente a la agricultura.

geoponics [ˌdʒiːəʊˈpɒnɪks] [yiou-po-niks], *s.* Geopónica, la ciencia o arte de cultivar la tierra; agricultura; economía rural.

George [dʒɔːdʒ] [yorch], *n. pr.* Jorge.

george, *s.* 1. Figura adornada con piedras preciosas que representa a San Jorge en el acto de matar al dragón; una de las insignias del orden de la Jarretera. 2. Peluca grande del siglo XVIII.

georgette [dʒɔːˈdʒiːt] [yor-yit], *s.* Crespón de seda transparente.

Georgian [ˈdʒɔːdʒɪən] [yor-yian], *a.* 1. Perteneciente a los reinados de los cuatro Jorges de Inglaterra. 2. *a.* y *s.* Georgiano, natural del Estado norteamericano de Georgia o perteneciente a él. 3. Georgiano, lo perteneciente o relativo a la Georgia, país de la transcaucasia rusa, y a sus habitantes.

georgic [ˈdʒɔːdʒɪk] [yor-yik], *s.* Geórgica, poema rural tocante a la agricultura.

geoscopy [dʒɪˈɒskɒpɪ] [yi-ous-ko-pi], *s.* Geoscopia, especie de conocimiento de la naturaleza y calidad de un terreno, obtenido por la vista de él.

geotaxis [dʒɪəʊˈtæksɪs] [yiou-tak-sis], *s. (Biol.)* Geotaxia, geotactismo.

geotectonic [ˈdʒɪəʊtɒnɪk] [yiou-to-nik], *a.* Geotectónico.

geotectonics [ˈdʒɪəʊtɒnɪks] [yiou-tek-to-niks], *s.* Geotectónica.

geotropism [ˈdʒɪəʊtrəpɪzm] [yiou-tro-pi-sem], *s. (Bot.)* Geotropismo.

geraniaceae [dʒɪˈreɪnɪəsɪə] [yi-rei-nia-sia], *s. (Bot.)* Geraniáceas.

geranium [dʒɪˈreɪnɪəm] [yi-rei-niom], *s. (Bot.)* 1. Geranio, planta de jardín del género Pelargonium, con muchas especies y variedades procedentes en su mayor parte del África austral. 2. Geranio, pico de cigüeña, gran género de plantas de la familia de las geraniáceas.

Gerald [ˈdʒerəld] [ye-rald], *n. pr.* Gerardo.

gerent [ˈdʒerənt] [ye-rent], *s.* Gerente, director.

gerfalcon [ˈdʒɜːˈfælkən] [yer-fal-kon], *s.* 1. *(Ornit.)* Gerifalte. 2. *(Artill.)* Falconete.

geriatrician [dʒerɪəˈtrɪʃən] [ye-ria-tri-shan], *s.* Geriatra.

geriatrics [dʒerɪˈætrɪks] [ye-ria-triks], *s.* Geriatría.

germ [dʒɜːm] [yerm], *s.* 1. Germen, el elemento rudimenta de la vida. (a) *(Biol.)* La fase más primitiva de un organismo; embrión. (b) *(Bot.)* Brote, botón nuevo, germen; embrión; ovario, lo que contiene la semilla. 2. Principio, origen de alguna cosa. 3. Microbio, organismo microscópico. **Germ theory,** la teoría de que el tifo, la tisis y otras enfermedades en que entra el elemento de la fermentación, se deben al desarrollo y la multiplicación de microbios en el cuerpo.

german [ˈdʒɜːmən] [yer-man], *a.* Pariente, el que tiene relación de parentesco con otro. **Cousin german,** primo hermano, primo carnal.

German, *s.* y *a.* Alemán; germánico, tudesco. Idioma alemán. **To speak German,** hablar alemán. **German paste,** preparación especial para alimento de los pájaros cantores. **German silver,** plata alemana, alpaca, metal blanco. **German tinder,** yesca. V. AMADOU.

germane [ˈdʒɜːmeɪn] [yer-mein], *a.* Relacionado con, afín.

germanity [dʒɜːˈmænɪtɪ] [yer-ma-ni-ti], *s.* Hermandad.

german measles [ˈdʒɜːmənˌmiːzlz] [yer-man-mi-sels], *s. pl. (Med.)* Sarampión benigno.

germ cell [ˈdʒɜːmˈsel] [yerm-sel], *s.* Óvulo o espermatozoide, célula embrionaria.

germicidal [ˌdʒɜːmɪˈsaɪdl] [yer-mi-sai-dal], *a.* Germicida, que destruye gérmenes o microbios.

germicide [ˈdʒɜːmɪsaɪd] [yer-mi-said], *s.* Germicida, lo que destruye microbios o gérmenes o impide su desarrollo.

germinate [ˈdʒɜːmɪneɪt] [yer-mi-neit], *vn.* Brotar, desarrollarse. *-va.* Germinar.

germination [ˈdʒɜːmɪˈneɪʃən] [yer-mi-nei-shon], *s.* Germinación.

germinative [ˈdʒɜːmɪnətɪv] [yer-mi-na-tiv], *a.* Germinativo.

gerocomy [ˈdʒerəkəmɪ] [ye-ro-ko-mi], *s.* El régimen conveniente a la vejez.

gerontology [ˈdʒerɒnˈtɒlədʒɪ] [ye-ron-to-lo-yi], *s.* Gerontología.

gerrymander [ˈdʒerɪmændər] [ye-ri-man-dar], *s.* 1. *(E.U.)* División en distritos electorales hecha arbitrariamente con fines partidistas. 2. Tergiversación, argucia.

gerrymander, *v.* 1. *(E.U.)* Dividir arbitrariamente un estado en distritos electorales con fines partidistas. 2. Manejar injustamente resortes políticos. 3. Tergiversar.

gerund [ˈdʒerənd] [ye-rund], *s.* Gerundio.

gerundive [dʒəˈrʌndɪv] [ye-run-div], *s. (Gram.)* Gerundio adjetivado.

gest, geste [dʒest] [yest], *s.* Hecho, hazaña, gesta, romance.

gestation [dʒesˈteɪʃən] [yes-tei-shon], *s.* Preñez, preñado; el estado de la hembra preñada y el tiempo que está el feto en el vientre de la madre; embarazo en la mujer.

gestic [ˈdʒestɪk] [yes-tik], *a.* De movimiento y ademanes de baile.

gesticulate [dʒesˈtɪkjʊleɪt] [yes-ti-kiu-leit], *vn.* Gesticular, hacer gestos y ademanes; accionar. *-va.* Imitar, remedar.

gesticulation [dʒesˌtɪkjʊˈleɪʃən] [yes-ti-kiu-lei-shon], *s.* Gesticulación.

gesticulator [dʒesˈtɪkjʊleɪtər] [yes-ti-kiu-lei-tor], *s.* Gestero, el que hace gestos.

gesticulatory [dʒesˈtɪkjʊlətərɪ] [yes-ti-kiu-la-to-ri], *a.* Gesticular, perteneciente al gesto.

gesture [ˈdʒestʃər] [yes-char], *s.* Gesto, acción, movimiento expresivo.

gesture, *vn.* Accionar; gesticular.

get [get] [guet], *va. (pret.* GOT, *pp.* GOT o GOTTEN). 1. Ganar, adquirir, granjear alguna cosa con su trabajo; conseguir, obtener, alcanzar, llevar un premio, una ventaja, una victoria, etc.; recibir. **To get a letter,** recibir una carta. 2. Obtener o conseguir alguna ventaja a pesar de la oposición de otros; de aquí *(Fam.)* poseer, tener; también, estar obligado, haber de ser. **I have got to go,** tengo que marcharme. **It has got to be done,** hay que hacerlo, tiene que hacerse. 3. Aprender de memoria. **To get a lesson,** aprender una lección. **To get one's part,** aprender su papel. 4. Engendrar, procrear. 5. Hacer ser, hacer, mandar. **To get the work done,** disponer o hacer que se haga un trabajo. **To get oneself laughed at,** hacer que se rían de uno. **To get a carriage made,** mandar hacer un carruaje. 6. Persuadir, inducir, incitar, procurar, adquirir, conseguir, ganar, granjear, ir a buscar, traer. **Get him to come with us,** persuádale Ud. que venga con nosotros. **I can get him to do it,** puedo inducirle a que lo haga. **Get you gone!,** ¡váyase Ud.! ¡largo de aquí! *-vn.* 1. Alcanzar, lograr o conseguir alguna cosa poco a poco y con dificultad; prevalecer; adquirir caudal. 2. Pasar una persona o cosa de una situación o estado a otro diverso; llegar; llegar a ser, volverse, hallarse. **To get home,** llegar a casa. **To get better,** ponerse mejor, ir saliendo de una indisposición. **It gets cold early,** hace frío temprano. 3. Introducirse, meterse una persona o cosa entre otras. 4. *(Fam.)* Hallar el tiempo, los medios o la oportunidad.

get about, (a) V. **To get abroad.** (b) Poder moverse de un punto a otro, como lo hace un convaleciente.

get above one, vencer, sobrepujar a uno.

get along, hacer andar, adelantar; arrastrar; hallarse; ir siguiendo, adelantarse o mantenerse. *V.* FARE.

get among, hacerse uno de.

get at, ir a, alcanzar; embestir; descubrir, desenmascarar. **To get at the truth,** descubrir, alcanzar la verdad. **To get at the man,** alcanzar al hombre; también, embestirlo, atacarlo. **To get a fall,** caer. **To get a footing,** establecerse. **To get a wife** o **to get a husband,** casarse, tomar estado.

get away, quitar, sacar, apartar; huir, escaparse, poderse escapar, lograr irse.

get before, prevenir; adelantarse.

get back, recobrar; hacerse devolver; regresar, retroceder. **He got back his watch,** recobró su reloj.

get behind, (a) Penetrar; enterarse de los secretos de alguien. (b) Perder terreno; quedarse atrás. **To get by heart,** aprender de memoria. **To get children,** engendrar o procrear hijos. **To get clear,** salir bien de alguna dificultad o empeño. **To get clear of** o **quit of,** zafarse, libertarse de alguna cosa.

get down, bajar, descender; descolgar, desprender; tragar.

get forward, adelantarse, aprovechar.

get in, lograr entrar; hacer entrar, empeñar; cerrar, encerrar; insinuarse.

get off, deshacerse de algo, vender o despachar alguna cosa; salir de un asunto; escapar, huir; desprender; sacar de un mal paso; descender (from a horse).

get on, poner, meter; proceder, suceder, acertar; montar a caballo; entrar en un coche o carro; armonizarse. **To get on with,** vivir u obrar en concordancia con.

get out, salir; sacar, quitar, arrancar; lograr salir; desembarcar; hacerse público. **To get out of order,** descomponerse, desajustarse. **To get out of the way,** apartarse a un lado.

get over, pasar, pasar por encima; poner a un lado; atravesar, vencer o sobrepujar obstáculos; responder.

get ready, aparejarse; preparar, aprestar.

get rid of, deshacerse de, salir de.

get the better, salir vencedor, sobrepujar, sacar ventaja. *(Fam.)* Salir pujante. **To get the worse,** llevar lo peor o salir vencido. *(Fam.)* Salir con las manos en la cabeza. **To get there,** *(Ger.)* Llegar al fin que se desea, arribar.

get through, pasar por, salir de, pasar al través o de medio a medio.

get together, juntar, amontonar.

get up, levantar o levantarse, subir; montar a caballo; recurrir; preparar. **To get well again,** recuperarse, restablecerse. recobrar la salud. **To get wind of,** recibir un informe o una noticia casualmente. **To get with child,** poner encinta a una mujer. **To get money of one,** sacar a uno dinero. **To get the start of,** adelantarse a.

get, *s.* El acto de engendrar o lo engendrado; progenie, casta. **The get of a stallion,** lo engendrado por un caballo padre.

getaway ['getəweɪ] [guet-auei], *s.* 1. Partida, escape. 2. Comienzo, salida de una carrera. 3. Arranque (car).

gettable ['getəbl] [gue-ta-bol], *a.* Asequible, obtenible.

getter ['getə^r] [gue-ta^r], *s.* 1. El que procura, adquiere o consigue una cosa. 2. Engendrador, procreador.

getting ['getɪŋ] [gue-tin], *s.* Adquisición, ganancia, lucro, provecho.

get-up ['getʌp] [guet-ap], *s. (Fam.)* 1. Arreglo, disposición, presentación. 2. Traje, atavío.

gewgaw ['gjuːgɔː] [guiu-go], *s.* Chuchería, cosa de poca importancia, aunque pulida y delicada; miriñaque, juguete de niños.

geyser ['giːzə^r] [gui-sa^r], *s.* Geiser, manantial caliente que arroja agua o lodo en forma de columna y a veces a gran altura.

G-Force [dʒiːˈfɔːs] [yi-fors], *s. (Fís.)* Grado de aceleración producido por la gravedad.

ghastliness ['gɑːstlɪnɪs] [gas-tli-nes], *s.* Palidez, color o cara cadavérica, horror, espanto.

ghastly ['gɑːstlɪ] [gas-tli], *a.* 1. Lúgubre, parecido a la muerte; semejante a un espectro. 2. Horrible, espantoso.

gherkin ['gɜːkɪn] [guer-kin], *s.* Pepinillo en adobo; encurtido.

ghetto ['getəʊ] [gue-tou], *s.* 1. Ghetto, barrio judío. 2. Barrio de algún grupo racial.

ghost [gəʊst] [goust], *s.* 1. Aparecido, muerto aparecido, alma del otro mundo o ánima en pena; fantasma, duende, espectro. 2. Alma racional. 3. Sombra, imagen, traza leve. 4. *(Foto.* y *Opt.)* Imagen falsa o secundaria; mancha, línea o círculo debido a un defecto en la lente. **The ghosts,** los manes, las sombras. **To give up the ghost,** entregar el alma a Dios, morir. **The Holy Ghost,** el Espíritu Santo, la tercera persona de la Santísima Trinidad.

ghost-like ['gəʊstˈlaɪk] [goust-laik], *a.* Seco, marchito; con los ojos hundidos; espantoso, parecido a un espectro.

ghostliness ['gəʊstlɪnɪs] [goust-li-nes], *s.* Espiritualidad.

ghostly ['gəʊstlɪ] [gous-tli], *a.* 1. Espiritual, lo perteneciente al espíritu. 2. Espiritual, santo, bueno. 3. Lo perteneciente a los aparecidos.

ghostwrite ['gəʊstˌraɪt] [goust-rait], *v.* Escribir obras, artículos que firma otro.

ghost writer ['gəʊstˌraɪtə^r] [goust-rai-ta^r], *s.* Escritor que escribe bajo la firma de otra persona.

ghoul [guːl] [gul], *s.* Trasgo o demonio del que se supone que roba las tumbas y se come los cadáveres; ogro.

ghoulist ['guːlɪst] [gu-list], *a.* 1. Horrible, brutal, asqueroso. 2. Vampiresco.

ghurry ['guːrɪ] [gu-ri], *s. (Anglo-ind.)* 1. Clepsidra, reloj de agua, o su timbre; de aquí, cualquier reloj. 2. Hora; según la costumbre india, la sexagésima parte de un día o de una noche.

G.I., *s. (Fam.)* Soldado raso de ejército de E.U. *-a. (Fam.)* Relacionado con el ejército de E.U. (Las iniciales provienen de la Expresión **Government issue** y se originó en la segunda guerra mundial.)

giant ['dʒaɪənt] [yaiant], *s.* 1. Gigante. 2. Coloso; persona o cosa de gran tamaño, sea física, mental o figuradamente; fénix. **Giant- powder,** dinamita.

giantess ['dʒaɪəntnɪs] [yaiant-nes], *sf.* Giganta.

giant-like ['dʒaɪəntˈlaɪk] [yaiant-laik], *a.* Gigantesco, giganteo.

giantship ['dʒaɪəntʃɪp] [yaiant-ship], *s.* Calidad de gigante.

gib [dʒɪb] [yib], *s.* Chabeta, cuña, contraclavija; pieza de metal que mantiene a otra en su lugar. **Cotter (o key) and gib,** clavija y contraclavija.

gib, *vn.* Destrizar. *V.* GIP. Asegurar con chaveta, cuña.

gibber ['dʒɪbə^r] [yi-ba^r], *vn.* Hablar en jerigonza o en jerga.

gibberish ['dʒɪbərɪʃ] [yi-be-rish], *s.* Jerigonza, habladuría incoherente, ininteligible por ser muy rápida, confusa o simulada; guirigay. *-a.* Falto de sentido.

gibbet ['dʒɪbɪt] [yi-bit], *s.* Horca. *V.* GALLOWS.

gibbet, 1. Ahorcar. 2. Colgar un cuerpo muerto en la horca, o exponerle en ella. 3. Colgar alguna cosa en un travesaño.

gibbon ['gɪbən] [gui-bon], *s.* Mono de Asia.

gibbous ['gɪbəs] [gui-bos], *a.* 1. Gibado, convexo, encorvado. 2. Giboso, jorobado, corcovado.

gibbousness ['gɪbəsnɪs] [gui-bos-nes], *s.* Convexidad, corvadura.

gib-cat ['gɪbkæt] [guib-kat], *s.* Gato, particularmente el castrado.

gibe [dʒaɪb] [yaib], *vn.* Escarnecer, burlarse, mofar, hacer mofa o burla. *-va.* Improperar; burlar, chasquear, ridiculizar.

gibe, *s.* Escarnio, mofa, burla; pulla, chufleta.

giber ['dʒaɪbə^r] [yai-ba^r], *s.* Escarnecedor, mofador.

gibingly ['dʒaɪbɪŋlɪ] [yai-bin-li], desdeñadamente, de burlas, con desprecio.

giblet ['dʒaɪblɪt] [yai-blit], *s.* 1. Uno de los despojos y menudillos de un ave. 2. *pl.* Andrajos, guiñapos.

gid [gɪd] [guid], *s.* Torneo, modorra.

giddily ['gɪdɪlɪ] [gui-di-li], *adv.* Vertiginossamente; inconstantemente, negligentemente.

giddiness ['gɪdɪnɪs] [gui-di-nes], *s.* 1. Vértigo, vahido, atudimiento, atolondramiento de cabeza. 2. Instabilidad, inconstancia, veleidad. 3. Vaivén. 4. Devaneos, desvaríos.

giddy ['gɪdɪ] [gui-di], *a.* 1. Vertiginoso. 2. Veleidoso, voltario, voluble, ligero, inconstante. 3. Descuidado, enajenado, descabezado, desatinado, aturdido. 4. Bobo, necio, pelele. **A giddy girl,** una muchacha aturdida, casquivana. **Giddy fortune,** fortuna voluble, inconstante. **My head feels giddy,** se me va la cabeza; tengo vértigo. **Giddy-brained,** descuidado: ligero de cascos, con los cascos a la jineta. **Giddy-head, giddy-pate,** el hombre loco, fatuo o necio. **Giddy-headed, giddy-pated,** inconstante, voluble; imprudente.

gie [dʒiː] [yi], va. (pret. GA o GIED, pp. GIEN). (Esco.) V. GIVE.

gift [gɪft] [guift], s. 1. Don, dádiva, gracia, favor, presente, regalo; soborno (en lenguaje bíblico.) 2. Donación, el acto de donar. 3. Oblación, ofrenda. 4. Don, dote, prenda, el talento natural para hacer alguna cosa. **Christmas o New Year's gift,** aguinaldo. **Gift by will,** legado. **A deed of gift,** un instrumento o contrato de donación.

gift, dotar, adornar la naturaleza a alguno con dotes, prendas o talentos para alguna cosa.

gifted [ˈgɪftɪd] [guif-tid], a. Dotado, talentoso, hábil.

giftedness [ˈgɪftɪdnɪs] [guif-tid-nes], s. El estado de hallarse dotado de prendas o talentos sobresalientes.

gig [gɪg] [guig], s. 1. Calesa, birlocho, calesín, quitrín. 2. Máquina para tundir paño. 3. Esquife, bote de un navío en que los remeros se sientan en bancos alternados. 4. Trompo, peón, peonza, perinola. 5. V. FIZGIG. 6. Chacota; calaverada.

gig, v. Pescar con arpón.

gigantean [dʒaɪˈgæntɪən] [yai-gan-tian], a. Gigantesco; irresistible.

gigantic [dʒaɪˈgæntɪk] [yai-gan-tik], a. 1. Giganteo, gigantesco, enorme. 2. Terrible; excesivo, violento, extraordinario.

giggle [ˈgɪgl] [gui-guel], vn. Reírse tratando de suprimir u ocultar la risa, reírse sin motivo; reírse por nada.

giggle, s. Risa falsa, ahogada; risa convulsiva; acción de reírse sin motivo, tontamente.

gigolo [ˈʒɪgələ] [yi-go-lo], s. 1. Hombre que vive de las mujeres públicas. 2. Compañero de baile o acompañante de mujeres pagado por éstas.

gigot [ˈdʒɪgət] [yi-got], s. 1. Pierna de carnero. 2. (Mar.) Aurica, vela.

gild [gɪld] [guild], va. (pret. y pp. GILDED o GILT). 1. Dorar; dar una capa de oro; adornar con hojas de oro. 2. Dar un color amarillo, cubrir con reflejos dorados; iluminar. 3. Dar brillo o lustre; dar un barniz superficial y aparente.

gilder [ˈgɪldər] [guil-daʳ], s. 1. Dorador. 2. V. GUILDER.

gilding [ˈgɪldɪŋ] [guil-din], s. Doradura; dorado, adorno con objetos dorados.

gilia [ˈdʒɪlɪə] [yi-lia], s. Gilia, género de plantas americanas de numerosas especies, de la familia de las polemoniáceas.

gill [dʒɪl] [yil], s. 1. Medida de líquidos que contiene la cuarta parte de un cuartillo. 2. Moza; particularmente la que es lasciva; pelandusca. 3. (Bot.) Hiedra terrestre. 4. **Gill o gill-beer,** bebida medicinal hecha de cerveza con infusión de hiedra terrestre.

gill [gɪl] [guil], s. 1. Agalla, branquia, una de las aberturas que tienen los peces en el arranque de la cabeza. **Gill-cover,** membrana cartilaginosa que cubre las agallas. 2. Papada, la carne que crece debajo de la barba. 3. Barranco; rambla.

gillie [ˈgɪlɪ] [gui-li], s. (Esco.) Servidor, criado.

gillyflower, gilliflower [ˈgɪlɪˈflaʊəʳ] [gui-li-flauaʳ], s. (Bot.) Alelí.

gilt, pret. y pp. de TO GILD. -s. 1. Dorado, oro en hojuelas, el material usado para dorar. 2. Oropel; falso brillo; apariencaia ficticia, en oposición al verdadero mérito.

gilthead [ˈgɪlthed] [guilt-jed], s. (Zool.) Esparo o espátula.

gimbals [ˈdʒɪmbəlz] [yim-bals], s. pl. (Mar.) Balancines de la brújula.

gimcrack [ˈdʒɪmkræk] [yim-krak], s. Chuchería, obra mecánica de poco valor.

gimlet [ˈgɪmlɪt] [guim-lit], s. Barrena pequeña. GIMBLET.

gimmick [ˈgɪmɪk] [gui-mik], s. 1. Truco secreto de prestidigitador. 2. Dispositivo o ardid ingenioso para lograr algún fin.

gimp [gɪmp] [guimp], s. Bocadillo, alamar. **Gimp nail,** tachuela para tapicería. -a. (Des.) Lindo, precioso.

gin [dʒɪn] [yuin], s. 1. Una de varias máquinas; (a) almarrá, desmotadora de algodón; (b) cabria, o cabrestante portátil; (c) bomba movida por un molino de viento; (d) martinete. 2. Trampa, armadijo para cazar algún animal. (contracción de ENGINE.) 3. Ginebra, alcohol de semillas aromatizado con bayas de enebro. (Corrupción de GENEVA.) **Gin-mill,** (Ger. E.U.) despacho de licores. **Gin-palace,** tienda lujosa donde se venden licores. **Gin-shop,** despacho de ginebra, taberna.

gin, va. 1. Entrampar, coger en la trampa. 2. Alijar, desmotar el algodón.

ginger [ˈdʒɪndʒəʳ] [yin-chaʳ], s. (Bot.) Jengibre, ajengibre. **Ginger-ale, ginger-beer,** cerveza de jengibre. **Ginger-pop,** variedad inferior de cerveza de jengibre. **Ginger-snap,** galletica de jengibre.

ginger-bread [ˈdʒɪndʒəbred] [yin-ye-bred], s. Pan de jengibre. **Ginger-bread work,** chapuza, obra de adorno barata y de mal gusto.

gingerly [ˈdʒɪndʒəlɪ] [yin-cha-li], a. Cauteloso, escrupuloso o quisquilloso. -adv. Cautelosamente.

gingerness [ˈdʒɪndʒənɪs] [yin-cha-nes], s. Cautela, escrupulosidad.

gingersnap [ˈdʒɪndʒəsnæp] [yin-cha-snap], s. Galletita de jengibre.

gingery [ˈdʒɪndʒərɪ] [yin-cha-ri], a. El que sabe a jengibre, picante.

gingham [ˈgɪnəm] [gui-nam], s. Carranclán, guinga.

gingival [ˈdʒɪndʒɪvəl] [yin-chi-val], a. Lo perteneciente a las encías.

gingivitis [dʒɪndʒɪˈvaɪtɪs] [yin-yi-vai-tis], s. (Med.) Gingivitis.

gipsy [ˈdʒɪpsɪ] [yip-si], s. 1. Gitano. 2. Jerga, lengua de los gitanos, que llaman **Romani.** 3. Persona algo ruda y picaresca, especialmente una muchacha brusca y desparpajada. 4. Nombre despectivo que se aplica a las mujeres de piel muy morena. **Gipsy-winch,** grúa de soporte lateral. **Gipsy-moth,** ocneria, falena de los lipáridos, cuya oruga es muy dañina a los pinos. -a. Gitanesco, picarón. V. GYPSY.

giraffe [dʒɪˈrɑːf] [yi-raf], s. 1. (Zool.) Jirafa. 2. La constelación Camelopardalis. 3. (E.U.) Carro en forma de jaula que se usa en las minas y especialmente en las galería en declive; su armazón es más alta a un extremo que al otro.

girandole [ˈdʒɪrəndəʊl] [yi-ran-doul], s. Girándula, candelabro de muchos brazos.

girasol [ˈdʒɪrəsəl] [yi-ra-sol], s. Una especie de ópalo.

gird [gɜːd] [guerd], (pret. y pp. GIRDED o GIRT). 1. Ceñir, atar alguna cosa alrededor. 2. Cercar, rodear. 3. Vestir. 4. Investir. -vn. Mofarse, hace mofa. **To gird (o gird on) a sword,** ceñir espada.

gird, s. 1. Escarnio, mofa. 2. (Des.) Angustia, improperio.

girder [ˈgɜːdəʳ] [guer-daʳ], s. 1. (Arq.) Cuartón, madero grueso que sirve para las fábricas y otros usos. 2. Censor satírico.

girding [ˈgɜːdɪŋ] [guer-din], s. 1. Ceñidura. 2. Ceñidor.

girdle [ˈgɜːdl] [guer-del], s. 1. Cíngulo, cinturón, cinto, ceñidor que rodea la cintura. 2. Circunferencia, cerco, círculo. 3. Zodíaco. 4. (Anat.) La disposición anular de los huesos por medio de la cual se adhieren al tronco las extremidades de un animal vertebrado.

girdle, 1. Ceñir, cercar, rodear, circundar; atar con cinto. 2. Hacer una incisión circular en la corteza de un árbol.

girdle-belt [ˈgɜːdlbelt] [guer-del-belt], s. Ceñidor.

girl [gɜːl] [guerl], sf. 1. Muchacha, niña, doncellita; mujer joven, solterita. 2. (Fam.) Moza (de servicio), criada. 3. (Fam.) La joven a quien uno galantea. **Best girl,** la amada de uno, dulce amiga.

girlfriend [ˈgɜːlfrend] [guerl-frend], sf. Amiga, novia, compañera.

girl guide ['gɜːlgaɪd] [guerl-gaid], *s.* Guía, niña guía, niña exploradora.

girlhood ['gɜːlhʊd] [guerl-jud], *s.* Doncellez, soltería.

girlish ['gɜːlɪʃ] [guer-lish], *a.* Juvenil, como una muchacha, propio de una muchacha. **Girlish trick,** niñada.

girlishly ['gɜːlɪʃlɪ] [guer-lish-li], como una muchacha.

girl scout [ˌgɜːl'skaʊt] [guerl-skaut], *s.* Guía, niña guía, niña exploradora.

girondist ['dʒaɪrəndɪst] [yai-ron-dist], *s.* y *a.* Girondino, nombre de un partido político que se formó en Francia en tiempo de la Revolución.

girt [gɜːt] [guert], *pret.* de TO GIRD: *pp.* y *a.* 1. *(Mar.)* Amarrado de modo que se contrarreste la acción del viento o de la marea. 2. *(Ento.)* Braceado, sujetado, como una crisálida.

girt-line ['gɜːtlaɪn] [guert-lain], *s. (Mar.)* Andarivel.

girth [gɜːθ] [guerz], *s.* 1. Cincha, la faja con que se asegura la silla a la caballería; circunferencia. 2. Cinturón, faja. 3. Cintura, contorno.

girth, 1. Cinchar, asegurar con cincha. 2. Ceñir, rodear.

gist [dʒɪst] [yist], *s.* La clave, la substancia o el grano de un asunto; punto capital.

gitter ['gɪtəʳ] [gui-taʳ], *s. (Mús.)* Especie de laud medieval.

give [gɪv] [guiv], *va. (pret.* GAVE, *pp.* GIVEN). 1. Dar, donar. 2. Pagar, premiar, recompensar. 3. Conceder; ceder, renunciar; dar licencia. 4. Pronunciar, divulgar. 5. Mostrar, demostrar, explicar, exhibir material o mentalmente. 6. Habilitar, autorizar. 7. Entregarse, aplicarse, dedicarse, emplearse. 8. Rendirse (con **up**). V. Give up. 9. Conferir, remitir, entregar. 10. Ceder, dejar. 11. Presumir, suponer. 12. Ofrecer, presentar como producto o resultado. 13. Ser el autor, origen u ocasión de; suplir; conferir, excitar. *-vn.* 1. Dar libremente o de buena gana el título o la posesión de algo que tiene valor. 2. Dar de sí, aflojarse, ablandarse; cejar, recular. 3. Dar, mirar hacia una parte, tener vistas a (galicismo).

give again, volver a dar.

give away, enajenar, transferir, dar o traspasar a otro la posesión de alguna cosa, entregar, abandonar, dar libremente o de buena gana. *(Fam.)* Divulgar por descuido o tontería; vender una cosa de cualquier modo. **To give up for dead,** dar a uno por muerto o creerle muerto. **To give away for lost,** dar algo por perdido.

give back o **back again,** volver lo que se había recibido, restituir, devolver.

give forth, publicar, divulgar, sacar a luz, decir públicamente alguna cosa.

give in, ceder echar a huir, retroceder, retirarse, cejar, recular. **To give in to,** adoptar, abrazar una opinión, un partido, etc., inclinarse a una cosa con preferencia a otra. **To give it to one,** dar de palos; poner como nuevo a uno, o ponerle de oro y azul; zurrar o censurar de firme.

give off, arrojar de sí, emitir.

give out, publicar, proclamar, divulgar, relatar, extender la voz, esparcir, voces o rumores; faltar, consumirse, perderse; aparentar, fingirse uno lo que no es; darse por vencido, cesar en un intento o esfuerzo por agotamiento físico; repartir órdenes o trabajo; distribuir.

give over, cesar, dejar de ser o de hacer algo, parar, descontinuar, abandonar; detenerse, desistir; darse o entregarse completamente a la voluntad de otro o a alguna pasión vicio, etc.; desahuciar.

give up, dejar, ceder, renunciar, entregar, abandonar, dimitir, resignar, volver, restituir; desasirse; abandonar la esperanza respecto a. **To give a call,** llamar. **To give a description,** describir. **To give a fall,** caer. **To give a guess,** adivinar. **To give a look,** mirar. **To give a person his own,** dar a una persona su merecido o tratarla como se merece. **To give a portion,** dotar; también, entregar a uno su cuota. **To give content,** contentar. **To give credit,** dar fe o crédito, creer; prestar, dar fiado. **To give ear,**

escuchar, dar oídos. **To give evidence,** atestiguar. **To give fire,** disparar. **To give for lost,** dar por perdido. **To give ground,** retroceder, volver atrás. **To give heed,** advertir, reparar, hacer caso. **To give like for like,** pagar en la misma moneda. **To give joy,** dar el parabién, felicitar. **To give judgment,** juzgar. **To give leave,** permitir, dar licencia. **To give notice,** avisar, advertir, prevenir, hacer saber una cosa con anticipación. **To give oneself for lost,** darse por perdido, creerse perdido; no tener ninguna esperanza. **To give one's mind,** entregarse a una cosa, aplicarse, aficionarse. **To give place,** hacer lugar. **To give the hand,** dar la mano derecha; dar la preeminencia, reconocerse como inferior. **To give the lie,** desmentir. **To give the slip,** sustraerse, huirse. **To give trouble,** incomodar, dar que hacer. **To give warning,** advertir, poner sobre aviso.

give way, ceder, flaquear, rendirse; hacer lugar; cesar, desaparecer; empezar a bogar (por lo común en imperativo). **The ground gives way under my feet,** la tierra se hunde bajo mis pies. **He gave not a word,** no dijo una palabra. **To give one's respects,** dar memorias. **Given under my hand and seal,** *(For.)* Firmado y sellado de mi mano, o por mí. **To give birth to,** dar a luz, parir; ser causa de. **To give audience,** otorgar audiencia. **To give fire,** mandar tirar; tirar, descargar.

give, *s.* 1. Acción de dar de sí, de ceder. 2. Elasticidad.

give-and-take ['gɪvən'teɪk] [guiv-an-teik], *s.* 1. Toma y daca, concesiones mutuas. 2. Réplicas y observaciones agudas.

giveaway ['gɪvəweɪ] [guiv-auei], *s.* 1. Traición, denuncia. 2. Acción de venderse uno.

given ['gɪvn] [guiven], *pp.* 1. Dado, inclinado habitualmente, adicto. 2. Dado, fijado; concedido, convenido.

giver ['gɪvəʳ] [gui-vaʳ], *s.* Donador, dador; distribuyente.

giving ['gɪvɪŋ] [gi-vin], *s.* El acto de dar o conferir.

gizzard ['gɪzəd] [gi-sard], *s.* Molleja de ave. **He frets his gizzard,** *(Vul.)* se rompe los cascos, se devana los sesos.

glabrous ['glæbrəs] [gla-bros], *a.* Liso, calvo, llano; sin pelo ni pelusa.

glacé ['glæseɪ] [gla-sei], *a.* 1. De superficie lisa y lustrosa. (Se aplica a cuero, tela, etc.). 2. Garapiñado. (Se aplica a frutas, nueces, etc.

glacial ['gleɪsɪəl] [glei-sial], *a.* Glacial, helado.

glaciate ['gleɪsɪeɪt] [glei-sieit], 1. *(Geol.)* Cubrir con hielo glacial o de ventisquero. 2. *(Art. y Of.)* Producir sobre una superficie un efecto parecido al hielo. *-vn.* Helarse.

glaciation [ˌgleɪsɪ'eɪʃən] [glei-siei-shon], *s.* Helamiento, congelación.

glacier ['glæsɪəʳ] [gla-siaʳ], *s.* Glaciar, ventisquero.

glacis ['glæsɪʃ] [gla-sis], *s. (Fort.)* Glacis o explanada, declive que empieza desde el parapeto de la entrada cubierta y se pierde insensiblemente en el llano.

glad [glæd] [glad], *a.* 1. Alegre, contento, gozoso; agradable; agradecido. **To be glad,** alegrarse, celebrar. **I am glad to see you well,** me alegro de verlo (a UD.) bueno. **Glad tidings,** noticias alegres o agradables.

glad, *(Poét.)* **gladden** ['glædn] [gla-den], *va.* Alegrar, regocijar.

gladdon ['glædən] [gla-don], *s. (Bot.)* Lirio redondo; gladiolo, estoque.

glade [gleɪd] [gleid], *s.* 1. Claro, raso, sitio sin árboles en un bosque. 2. Extensión lisa de hielo descubierto; espacio abierto que no está helado. 3. V. EVERGLADE.

gladiator ['glædɪeɪtəʳ] [gla-diei-taʳ], *s.* Gladiador o gladiator, el que en los juegos públicos de los romano luchaba con otro hasta quitarle la vida o perderla.

gladiatorial [ˌglædɪə'tɔːrɪəl] [gla-dia-to-rial], **gladiatory** ['glædɪətərɪ] [gla-dia-to-ri], *a.* Gladiatorio.

gladiole, gladiolus ['glædɪəʊl] [gla-dioul], *s.* Planta del género gladiolo; gladio.

gladiolus ['glædɪələs] [gla-dio-lus], *s.* Espadaña, gladiolo, planta de adorno.

gladly ['glædlɪ] [glad-li], alegremente; de buena gana, con placer.

gladness ['glædnɪs] [glad-nes], s. Alegría, placer, buen humor.

gladsome ['glædsʌm] [glad-sam], a. Alegre, contento.

gladsomely ['glædsʌmlɪ] [glad-sam-li], alegremente.

gladsomeness ['glædsʌmnɪs] [glad-sam-nes], s. Alegría, buen humor, gracia, donaire.

glair ['glɛəʳ] [gleaʳ], s. 1. Clara de huevo: empleada en la encuadernación y en el dorado. 2. Cualquier substancia resbaladiza, viscosa y pegajosa.

glair, v. Dar o untar con clara de huevo.

glairy ['glɛərɪ] [glea-ri], a. Parecido a la clara de huevo; viscoso, pegajoso.

glaive ['gleɪv] [gleiv], s. Espada; especie de abalarda.

glamor ['glæməʳ] [gla-moʳ], s. 1. Encanto, hechizo; ilusión efectuada por el encanto. 2. Encanto, interés artificial, embeleso, fascinación, falsa apariencia.

glamorize ['glæməraɪz] [gla-mo-rais], embellecer, hermosear; hacer atrayente una persona, cosa o producto; dar encanto.

glance [glɑːns] [glans], s. 1. Vislumbre o replandor repentino; relámpago. 2. Ojeada, mirada: de aquí, pensamiento repentino o pasajero. 3. Desvío por herir de refilón u oblicuamente. 4. *(Min.)* Mineral lustroso. **Copper glance,** cobre sulfurado -vidrioso. **Glance-coal,** antracita. **At the first glance,** al primer aspecto, a primera vista.

glancing ['glɑːnsɪŋ] [glan-sin], s. 1. Censura por medio de indirectas. 2. Golpe de refilón. 3. Hecho o dicho de paso.

glancingly ['glɑːnsɪŋlɪ] [glan-sin-li], adv. De paso, oblicuamente.

gland [glænd] [gland], s. 1. *(Anat.)* Glándula, órgano destinado a secretar de la masa de la sangre un flúido determinado. 2. *(Bot.)* Glándula, órgano secretorio especial de las plantas. Segrega a menudo un flúido oloroso. 3. Bellota.

glandered ['glændəd] [glan-derd], a. Muermoso (horses).

glanders ['glændəz] [glan-ders], s. Muermo, enfermedad de los caballos.

glandiferous [glæn'dɪfərəs] [glan-di-fe-ros], a. Glandígero, lo que produce bellotas.

glandiform [glæn'dɪfɔːm] [glan-di-form], a. Glandiforme, de la figura de bellotas o glándulas.

glandular ['glændjʊləʳ] [glan-diu-laʳ], **glandulous** ['glændjʊləs] [glan-diu-los], a. Glanduloso, perteneciente a las glándulas.

glandule ['glændjʊl] [glan-diul], s. Glandulilla, glándula pequeña.

glans [glænz] [glans], s. *(pl.* GLANDES). Bellota, o una parte parecida a la bellota; (Anat) balano, extremidad del pene o del clítoris. *(Lat.)*

glare [glɛəʳ] [gleaʳ], vn. 1. Relumbrar, brillar. 2. Echar miradas de indignación. 3. Ser excesivamente brillante o charro en color. -va. Deslumbrar.

glare, s. 1. Deslumbramiento; mirada feroz y penetrante. 2. *(E.U.)* Superficie lisa y vidriosa. V. GLAIR, 2ª acep.

glareous, glaireous ['glɛərəs] [glea-ros], a. V. GLAIRY.

glaring ['glɛərɪŋ] [glea-rin], a. 1. Brillante, deslumbrador, deslumbrante. 2. Evidente, notorio. 3. Caracterizado por una mirada feroz y penetrante.

glaringly ['glɛərɪŋlɪ] [glea-rin-li], adv. Notoriamente, evidentemente.

glass [glɑːs] [glas], s. 1. Vidrio. 2. *(Quím.)* Substancia derretida que se asemeja al vidrio. **Glass of cobalt,** esmalte, safre, vidrio de cobalto. 3. Cualquier artículo hecho de vidrio, como un vaso para beber, una vidriera, u hoja de cristal o vidrio para ventanas, un espejo, una lente, un anteojo de teatro, etc.; y en plural, anteojos, lentes. 4. Vaso, la cantidad de líquido que contiene un vaso para beber. 5. Ampolleta, reloj de arena; de aquí, hilo o duración de la vida del hombre. 6. Termómetro o barómetro. **Crown-glass,** el vidrio que contiene cal; el vidrio más común. **Flint-glass,** cristal; el vidrio que contiene plomo. **Cut glass,** cristal tallado. **Burning glass,** lente de foco corto. **Glass bead,** abalorio, cuenta de vidrio, chaquira. **Focusing-glass,** lente

de enfocar. **Plate-glass,** vidrio cilindrado; grueso y muy pulido. **Perspective glass,** telescopio terrestre. **Drinking-glass,** vaso para beber. **Magnifying-glass,** vidrio de aumento. **Looking-glass,** espejo. **Cupping-glass,** ventosa. **Hour-glass,** reloj de una hora. **Window-glass,** cristal o vidrio para ventanas. **Wine-glass,** copa o copita de vino o para vino. **Pier-glass,** espejo grande que se coloca entre dos ventanas. **Spy-glass,** anteojo de larga vista. **Stained glass,** vidrio pintado al fundirlo, no exteriormente. **Weather-glass,** barómetro. **Glasses,** *(Mar.)* ampolletas. **To wear glasses,** usar gafas o lentes. *-a.* Vítreo, hecho de vidrio. **A glass bottle,** botella de vidrio.

glass-blower ['glɑːsˌbləʊəʳ] [glas-blauaʳ], s. Soplador de vidrio, vidriero.

glass case [glɑːskeɪs] [glas], s. Vitrina.

glassful [glɑːsfʊl] [glas-ful], s. Vaso, la cantidad de líquido que puede contener un vaso.

glass-furnace ['glɑːsˌfɜːneɪs] [glas-fer-neis], s. Horno de vidrio.

glass-grinder ['glɑːsˌgrɪndəʳ] [glas-grin-daʳ], s. Pulidor o bruñidor de cristales.

glass-house ['glɑːshaʊs] [glas-jaus], s. Vidriería fábrica de vidrio o cristal.

glassiness ['glɑːsɪnɪs] [gla-si-nes], s. Lisura, como la del vidrio; estado de vitrificación.

glass-like ['glɑːslaɪk] [glas-laik], a. Transparente como el vidrio.

glass-maker ['glɑːsˌmeɪkəʳ] [glas-mei-kaʳ], s. Vidriero, el que hace el vidrio.

glassman ['glɑːsmən] [glas-man], s. Vidriero, el que vende vidrio.

glass-metal ['glɑːsmetl] [glas-me-tal], s. El vidrio derretido.

glass-shop ['glɑːsʃɒp] [glas-shop], s. Vidriería, cristalería, tienda o almacén de cristales.

glassware ['glɑːswɛəʳ] [glas-ueaʳ], s. Vidriería, cristalería, todo género e vidrios y cristales.

glass-window [glɑːs'wɪndəʊ] [glas-uin-dou], s. Vidriera.

glasswork ['glɑːswɜːk] [glas-uerk], s. Fábrica de vidrio o cristales; cristalería, vidriería, todo género de vidrio y cristales.

glasswort ['glɑːswɜːt] [glas-uert], s. *(Bot.)* Sosa, barrilla.

glassy ['glɑːsɪ] [gla-si], a. Vítreo, cristalino, vidrioso.

glauber's salt ['glɔːbəzsɔːlt] [glo-bers-solt], s. *(Med.)* Sal de Glauber, sulfato de sosa.

glaucoma [glɔː'kəʊmə] [glo-ko-ma], s. *(Med.)* Glaucoma, enfermedad gravísima del globo del ojo, caracterizada por el aumento de los humores intraoculares, que acaba por producir la ceguera.

glaucous ['glɔːkəs] [glo-kos], a. 1. Verdemar, glauco. 2. *(Bot.)* Cubierto de una pelusa azulada y blanquecina.

glave, glaive ['gleɪv] [gleiv], s. 1. Arma cortante parecida a la alabarda. 2. *(Des.)* Espada ancha.

glaze [gleɪz] [gleis], va. 1. Poner cristales o vidrios en el bastidor de una ventana. 2. Vidriar, dar cierto género de barniz al barro u otros materiales; barnizar; dar una apariencia vidriosa. **Glazed linen,** lienzo lustroso o glaseado.

glaze, s. 1. Superficie lisa y lustrosa. 2. Barniz, lustre; cualquier substancia empleada para dar lustre.

glazed [gleɪzd] [gleist], a. 1. Vidriado. **Glazed tile,** azulejo. 2. Satinado, glaseado; **glaced paper,** papel satinado.

glazier ['gleɪzɪəʳ] [glei-siaʳ], s. Vidriero, el artífice que hace vidrieras para las ventanas.

glazing ['gleɪzɪŋ] [glei-sin], s. 1. El acto o arte de vidriar o barnizar; o de alisar un lienzo. 2. Barniz, lustre. 3. Vidriería, cristalería, conjunto de objectos de vidrio. 4. Vidriería, oficio del vidriero.

glazy ['gleɪzɪ] [glei-si], s. Brillante, lustroso.

gleam [gliːm] [glim], s. 1. Relámpago, cualquier fuego, resplandor o brillo muy fugaz. 2. Rayo, centelleo; toda cosa comparada al relámpago. **A gleam of wit,** agudeza chispeante.

gleam, vn. Relampaguear, brillar, lucir rápidamente.

gleaming ['gliːmɪŋ] [gli-min], *s.* Relámpago.

gleamy ['gliːmɪ] [gli-mi], *a.* Centelleante, fulgurante.

glean [gliːn] [glin], *va.* 1. Espigar, coger las espigas que los segadores han dejado en el campo después de segadas las mieses. 2. Recoger y juntar algunas cosas esparcidas.

glean, *s.* Rebusca, rebusco, colección hecha gradualmente.

gleaner ['gliːnəʳ] [gli-naʳ], *s.* Espigador, rebuscador, recogedor.

gleaning ['gliːnɪŋ] [gli-nin], *s.* Rebusca, rebusco.

glebe [gliːb] [glib], *s.* 1. (*Ant. o Poét.*) Gleba, césped, terrón. 2. (Gran Bretaña.) Tierras beneficiales, terreno anejo a algún beneficio o curato. 3. Extensión de tierra que contiene mineral.

glebous ['gliːbəs] [gli-bos], *a.* Gleboso; abundante en terrones o césped.

glede [gliːd] [glid], *s.* Milano, ave de rapiña; también, una de ciertas aves semejantes al milano.

gledge [gledʒ] [glech], *vn.* (*Esco.*) Mirar a hurtadillas, al soslayo.

glee [gliː] [gli], *s.* 1. Alegría, gozo, júbilo, jovialidad. 2. Una especie de canción para tres o más voces, sin acompañamiento.

glee club ['gliːklʌb] [gli-klab], *s.* Coro, club coral.

gleeful ['gliːfəl] [gli-ful], *a.* Alegre, gozoso, jovial.

gleeman ['gliːmən] [gli-man], *s.* Cantor ambulante.

gleesome ['gliːsʌm] [gli-sam], *a.* V. GLEEFUL.

gleet [gliːt] [glit], *s.* Gonorrea o blenorragia crónica.

gleety ['gliːtɪ] [gli-ti], *a.* Blenorrágico.

glen [glen] [glen], *s.* Valle, llanura de tierra entre montes o alturas; cañada.

glengarry ['glengərɪ] [glen-ga-ri], *s.* Gorra escocesa.

glenoid ['glenɔɪd] [gle-noid], *a.* Glenoideo.

glib [glɪb] [glib], *a.* 1. Voluble, corriente, suelto de la lengua. 2. (*Ant.*) Liso, resbaladizo.

glibly ['glɪblɪ] [gli-bli], *adv.* Corrientemente, volublemente.

glibness ['glɪbnɪs] [glib-nes], *s.* Volubilidad, fluidez, facundia.

glide [glaɪd] [glaid], *vn.* Manar suavemente y sin ruido; moverse con velocidad y suavidad; deslizarse, escurrirse.

glide, *s.* La acción de pasar suavemente de una parte a otra.

glider ['glaɪdəʳ] [glai-daʳ], *s.* (*Aer.*) Deslizador, planeador.

gliding ['glaɪdɪŋ] [glai-din], *s.* Deslizamiento, planeo.

gliff [glɪf] [glif], *s.* (*Esco.*) 1. Susto, espanto. 2. Ojeada rápida; momento.

glim [glɪm] [glim], *s.* (*Ger.*) Luz, candela. **To douse the glim,** (*Mar.*) Apagar la luz.

glimmer ['glɪməʳ] [gli-maʳ], *s.* 1. Vislumbre, resplandor tenue de la luz, luz débil e incierta. 2. Mirada ligera; aprehensión momentánea. 3. Mica laminar.

glimmer, *vn.* Vislumbrarse, alumbrar, brillar débilmetne y de una manera inconstante; alborear; de aquí, dar señales muy inciertas o ligeras de existencia.

glimmering ['glɪmərɪŋ] [gli-me-rin], *pa.* Vacilante, que brilla o alumbra débilmente. **The glimmering dawn,** el alba naciente. -*s.* Luz incierta, débil resplandor; vista imperfecta, aprehensión momentánea.

glimpse [glɪmps] [glimps], *s.* 1. Vislumbre, relámpago. 2. Lustre de poca duración; resplandor fugaz; reflejo, apariencia ligera. 3. Ojeada, mirada rápida y breve. **To catch a glimpse of,** entrever, vislumbrar.

glimpse, *va.* Ver con mirada rápida, como un relámpago. -*vn.* 1. Ojear, mirar de prisa. 2. Brillar a intervalos; aparecer por un momento.

glint [glɪnt] [glint], *s.* Brillo, rayo, destello.

glint, *v.* Brillar, destellar, lucir. 2. Rebotar. 3. **To glint the eye,** volver los ojos.

glisten ['glɪsn] [gli-sen], *vn.* Relucir, comúnmente por reflexión, brillar, resplandecer, relumbrar.

glisten, *s.* Brillo, centelleo.

glister ['glɪstəʳ] [glis-taʳ], *vn.* (*Ant.*) V. GLITTER.

glisteringly ['glɪstərɪŋlɪ] [glis-te-rin-li], *adv.* Espléndidamente, lustrosamente.

glitter ['glɪtəʳ] [gli-taʳ], *vn.* 1. Relucir, resplandecer; chispear, centellear. 2. Lucir, brillar, hacer figura brillante.

glitter, *s.* Lustre, esplendor, resplandor.

glittering ['glɪtərɪŋ] [gli-te-rin], *a.* Lustroso, resplandeciente, brillante. -*s.* Relámpago, lustre.

glitteringly ['glɪtərɪŋlɪ] [gli-te-rin-li], *adv.* Lustrosamente, con lustre.

gloam ['glɔm] [gloum], *va. y vn.* Obscurecer u obscurecerse, como sucede en el crepúsculo; anochecer.

gloaming ['glɔmɪŋ] [glou-min], *s.* Crepúsculo nocturno, la anochecida, el anochecer.

gloat [glɔt] [glout], *vn.* Mirar u ojear fijamente con satisfacción baja, mala o cruel; manifestar exultación maligna.

globate ['glɔbeɪt] [glo-beit], **globated** ['glɔbeɪtɪd] [glou-bei-tid], *a.* Esférico, hecho en forma de globo.

globe [glɔb] [glob], *s.* 1. Esfera. 2. Globo. 3. Bola. 4. Globo, receptáculo redondo, hueco; como una redoma para peces, o la bombilla de una lámpara. 5. La tierra, la esfera terrestre. **Globe-fish,** pez globo. **Globe-valve,** válvula esférica.

globetrotter ['glɔbˌtrɒtəʳ] [gloub-tro-taʳ], *s.* Trotamundos.

globose ['glɔbɔz] [glo-bous], **globous** (*Des.*) ['glɔbəs] [glo-bos], *a.* Globoso, redondo, casi esférico.

globular ['glɔbjɔləʳ] [glo-biu-laʳ], *a.* Globular.

globulariaceae [ˌglɔbjɔlərɪˈeɪsɪə] [glo-biu-la-riei-sia], *s.* (*Bot.*) Globulariáceas.

globulariaceous [ˌglɔbjɔlərɪˈeɪsɪəs] [glo-biu-la-riei-siss], *a.* (*Bot.*) Globulariáceo.

globule ['glɔbjuːl] [glo-biul], *s.* Glóbulo.

globulin ['glɔbjuːlɪn] [glo-biu-lin], *s.* (*Quím.*) Globulina.

globulous ['glɔbjuːləs] [glo-biu-los], *a.* Globuloso, en forma de globo o glóbulo.

glomerate ['glɔmereɪt] [glo-me-reit], *va.* Congomerar, aglomerar, formar cualquiera cosa a manera de ovillo o en forma de bola.

glomerate, *a.* Aglomerado, conglomerado; se dice de las glándulas que forman un ovillo.

glomeration ['glɔməˈreɪʃən] [glo-me-rei-shon], *s.* Conglobación.

glomerule ['glɔmərjuːl] [glo-me-riul], *s.* 1. (*Bot.*) Glomérula, gavilla o conjunto de flores en forma de cabeza compacta. 2. (*Anat.*) Masa redonda envuelta; particularmente el cuerpo malpigiano del riñón.

gloom [gluːm] [glum], *s.* 1. Tinieblas, oscuridad, lobreguez. 2. Melancolía, tristeza.

gloom, *vn.* 1. Lucir tenue o confusamente. 2. Encapotarse, oscurecerse. 3. Entristecerse, estar de mal humor. -*va.* Llenar de oscuridad o de tristeza.

gloomily ['gluːmɪlɪ] [glu-mi-li], *adv.* Obscuramente; tétricamente; tristemente, lúgubremente.

gloominess ['gluːmɪnɪs] [glu-mi-nes], *s.* Obscuridad, tinieblas; aspecto sombrío, nublado; melancolía, tristeza, abatimiento; adustez.

gloomy ['gluːmɪ] [glu-mi], *a.* 1. Tenebroso, sombrío, obscuro, lóbrego; nublado, cubierto de nubes. 2. Tétrico, triste, melancólico; abatido, desalentado; adusto.

gloria ['glɔːrɪə] [glo-ria], **s.** 1. (*Liturg.*) Gloria. 2. Gloria (tela). 3. Aureola.

gloried ['glɔːrɪd] [glo-riid], *a.* (*Des.*) Ilustre, lleno de gloria.

glorification ['glɔːrɪfɑɪˈkeɪʃən] [glo-ri-fai-kei-shon], *s.* Glorificación.

glorify ['glɔːrɪfɑɪ] [glo-ri-fai], *va.* Glorificar, honrar, alabar, exaltar, celebrar.

gloriole ['glɔːrɪɔl] [glo-rioul], *s.* Aureola, halo.

glorious ['glɔːrɪəs] [glo-rios], *a.* Glorioso, ilustre, digno de honor y alabanza; orgulloso, jactancioso, soberbio.

gloriously ['glɔːrɪəslɪ] [glo-rios-li], *adv.* Gloriosamente.

gloriousness ['glɔːrɪəsnɪs] [glo-rios-nes], *s.* Gloria, esplendor.

glory ['glɔːrɪ] [glo-ri], *s.* 1. Gloria, honra, alabanza, fama, renombre, celebridad; esplendor, magnificencia. 2. Aureola o círculo de luz que se pone sobre la cabeza de las imágenes de los santos. 3. Exaltación, adoración. 4. Calidad de resplandeciente; brillantez, resplandor, lustre. 5. Esplendor de la presencia de Dios; la gloria del Paraíso.

glory, *vn.* Gloriarse, jactarse, preciarse de alguna cosa, llenarse de orgullo.

gloss [glɒs] [glos], *s.* 1. Lustre, el viso luciente que despide alguna cosa; brillo. 2. Apariencia falaz.

gloss, *s.* 1. Glosa, escolio. 2. Disculpa o pretexto para ocultar o paliar una falta o un defecto.

gloss, *vn.* Glosar, comentar, interpretar, notar. -*va.* 1. Paliar, colorear, dar a alguna palabra, designio o acción mala o colorido que la haga parecer lo que no es; generalmente con la prep. **over.** 2. Barnizar, dar con barniz u otra cosa que produzca lustre.

glossaria [ˈglɒsərɪə] [glo-sa-ria], *a.* De glosa, glosario.

glossarist [ˈglɒsərɪst] [glo-sa-rist], *s.* Comentador.

glossary [ˈglɒsərɪ] [glo-sa-ri], *s.* Glosario, diccionario que sirve para explicar las palabras obscuras, extrajeras y antiguas de un libro: vocabulario explicativo de un dialecto o de una ciencia.

glossator [ˈglɒsətəʳ] [glo-sa-taʳ], **glossist** [ˈglɒsɪst] [glo-sist], *s.* Glosador, comentador.

glosser [ˈglɒsəʳ] [glo-saʳ], *s.* 1. Comentador. 2. Pulidor.

glossiness [ˈglɒsɪnɪs] [glo-si-nes], *s.* Pulimento, lustre superficial.

glossitis [ˈglɒsaɪtɪs] [glo-sai-tis], *s.* Glositis

glossographer [ˌglɒsəˈgræfəʳ] [glo-so-gra-faʳ], *s.* Glosógrafo, comentador.

glossography [ˈglɒsəgræfɪ] [glo-so-gra-fi], *s.* 1. El arte de escribir comentarios. 2. (*Anat.*) Descripción de la lengua.

glossology [ˈglɒsəlɒdʒɪ] [glo-so-lo-yi], *s.* Clasificación de las lenguas; filología comparada.

glossy [ˈglɒsɪ] [glo-si], *a.* 1. Lustroso, brillante como una superficie lisa que refleja el brillo. 2. Especioso, fino en apariencia, plausible.

glottis [ˈglɒtɪs] [glo-tis], *s.* Glotis, la abertura de laringe.

glove [glʌv] [glav], *s.* Guante. **To be hand and glove,** ser inseparables, ser uña y carne. **To handle without gloves,** tratar sin contemplaciones, severamente.

glove, *va.* Cubrir como con guante; enguantarse. **Glove compartment,** compartimento de guantes en un automóvil.

glover [ˈglʌvəʳ] [gla-vaʳ], *s.* Guantero.

glow [gləʊ] [glou], *vn.* 1. Estar encendida alguna cosa sin producir llama. 2. Arder, abrasarse, encenderse, inflamarse; cuando se habla de las pasiones del ánimo. 3. Lucir, relucir, resplandecer. -*va.* Calentar o encender alguna cosa.

glow, *s.* 1. Calor vivo, encendimiento; viveza de color; vehemencia de una pasión. 2. Luz, resplandor. **Glow lamp,** tubo de neón. 3. Ardor, animación, vehemencia. 4. Calor en el cuerpo, sensación de calor cuando se hace ejercicio.

glower [ˈglaʊəʳ] [glouaʳ], *vn.* Mirar con ceño, poner mala cara.

glowing [ˈgləʊɪŋ] [glauin], *pa.* Resplandeciente, que esparce luz o color excesivo; ardiente; colorado, entusiasta.

glowingly [ˈgləʊɪŋlɪ] [glauin-li], *adv.* De un modo resplandeciente.

glow-worm [ˈgləʊwɜːm] [glau-uerm], *s.* Luciérnaga.

gloxinia [glɒkˈsɪnɪə] [glok-si-nia], *s.* Flor hermosa de la familia de las escrofulariáceas.

gloze [gləʊz] [glous], *vn.* 1. Paliar, colorear, con una explicación especiosa. 2. (*Ant.*) Adular, lisonjear.

gloze [ˈgləʊzɪŋ] [glou-sin], *s.* 1. (*Ant.*) Adulación. 2. La explicación o interpretación artificiosa de un hecho, de una frase, etc.

glucin [ˈgluːsɪn] [glu-sin], **glucina** [ˈgluːsɪnə] [glu-si-na], *s.* (*Quím.*) Glucina, una de las tierras primitivas.

glucose [ˈgluːkəʊs] [glu-kous], *s.* Glucosa, azúcar de uvas o de almidón.

glue [gluː] [glu], *s.* Cola para pegar; liga; visco. **Fish-glue,** colapez, cola de pescado.

glue, *va.* Encolar, pegar, ligar, unir.

glue-boiler [gluːˈbɔɪləʳ] [glu-boi-laʳ], *s.* El fabricante de cola.

gluer [ˈgluːəʳ] [gluaʳ], *s.* El que encola.

gluey [ˈgluːɪ] [glui], *a.* Viscoso, pegajoso, glutinoso.

glueyness [ˈgluːɪnɪs] [glui-nes], *s.* Viscosidad, glutinosidad.

gluing [ˈgluːɪŋ] [gluin], *s.* Encoladura, pegadura.

gluish [ˈgluːɪʃ] [gluish], *a.* Viscoso, pegajoso.

glum [glʌm] [glam], *a.* De mal humor y callado; moroso, regañón, tétrico, triste.

glumaceous [gluːˈmeɪʃəs] [glu-mei-shos], *a.* (*Bot.*) Glumáceo, glumado; que tiene glumas o se refiere a ellas.

glume [gluːm] [glum], *s.* (*Bot.*) Gluma, cubierta floral de las plantas gramíneas.

glut [glʌt] [glat], *va.* 1. Atestar, hartar de bebida y comida; atracar, saciar; saturar. 2. Sobrellenar, llenar alguna cosa con más de lo que puede recibir. 3. Colmar, dar en abundancia, dar más de lo que se necesita. -*vn.* Devorar vorazmente, engullirse.

glut, *s.* 1. Lo que se engulle; hartura, hartazgo, plétora, superabundancia, llenura. 2. Cuña de madera. 3. (*Alb.*) Ripio de ladrillo.

gluten [ˈgluːtən] [glu-ten], *s.* (*Quím.*) Gluten.

glutinosity [ˌgluːtɪˈnɒsɪtɪ] [glu-ti-no-si-ti], **glutinousness** [ˈgluːtɪnəsnɪs] [glu-ti-nos-nes], *s.* Glutinosidad.

glutinous [ˈgluːtɪnəs] [glu-ti-nos], *a.* Glutinoso, viscoso, pegajoso.

glutted [ˈgluːtɪd] [glu-tid], *pp.* de GLUT. Harto, repleto.

glutton [ˈglʌtn] [gla-ton], *s.* 1. Glotón, tragón. 2. El que es voraz o insaciable. 3. Glotón, carcajú, wolverena, mamífero carnicero.

gluttonize [ˈglʌtənaɪz] [gla-to-nais], *vn.* Glotonear.

gluttonous [ˈglʌtənəs] [gla-to-nos], *a.* Glotón; goloso.

gluttonously [ˈglʌtənəslɪ] [gla-to-nos-li], *adv.* Vorazmente.

gluttony [ˈglʌtənɪ] [gla-to-ni], *s.* Glotonería.

glycerin, glycerine [ˈglɪsəriːn] [gli-se-rin], *s.* Glicerina, líquido incoloro, espeso y dulce, que se encuentra en los cuerpos grasos como base de su composición. Su adjetivo es **Glyceric** [ˈglɪsərɪk] [gli-se-rik].

glycogen [ˌglaɪkəʊdʒen] [glai-kou-yen], *s.* Glicógeno, compuesto blanco, farináceo, amorfo, que se halla en el hígado y en otros tejidos animales; se llama también «almidón animal».

glyph [glɪf] [glif], *s.* (*Arq.*) Glifo, media caña que sirve de adorno.

glyptic [ˈglɪptɪk] [glip-tik], *s.* Glíptica, el arte de grabar figuras en piedras preciosas.

glyptography [ˈglɪptəgrəfɪ] [glip-to-gra-fi], *s.* Gliptografía, conocimiento del grabado en hueco y relieve en las piedras preciosas.

gnarl [nɑːl] [narl], *vn.* 1. Refunfuñar, gruñir. 2. Torcer, retorcer.

gnarl, *s.* Nudo, protuberancia sobre un tronco o ramo; nudo duro en la madera.

gnarled [nɑːld] [narld], **gnarly** [ˈnɑːlɪ] [nar-li], *a.* Nudoso, lleno de nudos; retorcido. **A gnarled oak,** un roble retorcido.

gnash [næʃ] [nash], *va.* 1. (*Ant.*) Rechinar o crujir los dientes. 2. Rabiar de cólera rechinando los dientes.

gnashing [ˈnæʃɪŋ] [na-shin], *s.* Rechinamiento o crujido de los dientes.

gnat [næt] [nat], *s.* Mosquito, cínife; toda clase de mosquitos.

gnaw [nɔː] [nou], *va.* 1. Roer, comer poco a poco. 2. Morder, mordicar. 3. Corroer, gastar alguna cosa con los dientes.

gnawer [ˈnɔːəʳ] [nouaʳ], *s.* El que muerde, come o roe.

gneiss [naɪs] [nais], *s.* Gneis, roca de hojuelas planas y onduladas, compuesta de feldespato, cuarzo y mica u hornblenda. Se distingue del granito por su moderada tendencia a hendirse.

gneissoid [ˈnaɪsɔɪd] [nai-soid], *a.* Parecido al gneis.

gnome [nəʊm] [noum], *s.* 1. Máxima, aforismo. 2. Gnomo, una especie de genio, protector de las minas y de los mineros; trasgo, eneno. 3. (*Zool.*) Cierta especie de colibrí. 4. Máxima, sentencia, aforismo.

gnomical ['nəʊmɪkəl] [nou-mi-kal], *a.* Sentencioso, gnómico.

gnomology [nəʊ'mɒlɒdʒɪ] [nou-mo-lo-chi], *s.* Colección de aforismos.

gnomon ['nəʊmən] [nou-mon], *s.* Gnomón, el estilo o varita de hierro que señala las horas en los relojes de sol.

gnomonic, gnomonical ['nəʊmənɪk] [nou-mo-nik], *a.* Gnomónico.

gnomonics ['nəʊmənɪkz] [nou-mo-niks], *s.* Gnomónica, la ciencia que trata y enseña el modo de hacer los relojes de sol.

gnostic ['nɒstɪk] [nos-tik], *s.* Gnóstico, hereje de los primeros siglos.

gnosticism ['nɒstɪˌsɪzəm] [nos-ti-si-sem], *s.* Gnosticismo, sistema filosófico y religioso de los primeros siglos del cristianismo.

gnu [nuː] [nu], *s.* (*Zool.*) Bucéfalo, especie de antílope del sur de África, con cabeza aprecida a la del búfalo, crin como la del asno y cola de caballo.

go [gəʊ] [gou], *va.* (pret. WENT, pp. GONE). 1. (*Fam.*) Ir, tomar, como porción de algo, partir. **To go halves,** ir a medias. 2. Recibir con aprobación, asentir a, tolerar. 3. Apostar. –*vn.* 1. Ir, irse, moverse, pasar de un paraje a otro. 2. Andar, caminar, partir, partirse, marchar, pasear. 3. Ir en busca de, dirigirse a, acudir, recurrir. 4. Ir, estar o ser. 5. Salir, huir, escapar; ser libertado. 6. Pasar, acabarse una cosa. 7. Seguir, proseguir. 8. Cambiar, mudar de situación, opiniones, etc. 9. Pasar por, ser considerado como. 10. Ser aplicable, convenir; sentar, venir, ir, o caer bien; concernir, tocar a. 11. Estar encinta o preñada. 12. Influir, tener influencia. 13. Contribuir, concurrir, tender, tener por resultado, reunirse para componer alguna cosa. 14. Irse, morirse, estarse muriendo; decaer, debilitarse. 15. Ser desembolsado, vendido o cambiado. 16. Andar, como una máquina o un reloj.

go about, intentar, procurar, emprender, hacer todo lo posible, esforzarse por; rodear; desviarse; girar, rodar, andar o moverse alrededor o en torno, dar vueltar, andar rodando, andar de acá para allá. (*Mar.*) Virar de bordo. **Go about your business,** métase Ud. en lo que le importa: váyase Ud.

go abroad, salir, partir, marcharse; divulgarse o hacerse pública una cosa; correr alguna noticia.

go after, seguir a alguno.

go against, oponerse, contradecir, ir en contra de una persona. **The choice went against him,** no salió elegido.

go ahead, adelantar, proseguir.

go along, continuar, proseguir una cosa comenzada. **To go along with one,** acompañar a alguno.

go astray, descarriarse, descaminarse, perder el camino. (*Fig.*) Faltar a su deber, cometer una falta o delito. V ASTRAY.

go asunder, ir separadamente, marchar separados.

go away, salirse, marcharse. **To go away with a thing,** llevarse alguna cosa.

go back, retirarse, retroceder; ceder, desistir, volverse atrás de un empeño o designio; volver, volverse, ir otra vez al paraje donde se había estado antes. **To go back of,** mirar más allá de; poner en tela de juicio. **To go back from one's word,** desdecirse, retractarse.

go backwards, retroceder, volver hacia atrás.

go before, preceder, ir delante, adelantarse.

go behind, seguir a alguno, ir detrás de él; defraudar, engañar.

go between, interponerse, mediar, terciar.

go beyond, pasar o ir más allá de un punto determinado o limitado; sobrepujar, exceder.

go by, pasar por alto; escurrirse, escabullirse, pasar sin ser visto ni oído; sufrir con paciencia; observar alguna cosa como regla o principio o tomarla como regla, pauta o norma de conducta, arreglarse o ajustarse a algo; dirigirse por; pasar cerca. **To go by the worst,** llevar lo peor de una cosa.

go down, bajar, descender; ponerse el sol; (*Fam.*) ser bien recibida o aprobada alguna cosa; tragarse, persuadirse de o creer algo sin reflexión; tragar. **To go down the stream,** ir

con la corriente. **To go down the wind,** ir en decadencia, ir empobreciendo.

go far, valer mucho, tener gran influencia o alcance.

go for, ir por algo; ir a buscar o en busca de ; ser reputado o considerado por; declararse en favor de alguna persona o cosa; (*Ger.*) abrumar, embestir, atacar, particularmente con palabras.

go forth, salir, producir, parecer o aparecer, ser sacado a luz o al público.

go forward, adelantar, proseguir, hacer progresos, alguna cosa.

go from, dejar, partirse, separarse, faltar a alguna cosa convenida. **To go from the matter,** apartarse del asunto de que se trata. **To go from one's word,** desdecirse.

go hard, pasarlo mal, traer a mal traer.

go in, entrar. **To go in and out,** estar en libertad.

go in for, favorecer enérgicamente. **To go in to** o **unto,** (*Ant.*) Entrar a la presencia de; tener coito con.

go into, participar en (un asunto); investigar, discutir o ventilar.

go it, apresurarse inconsideramente; en imperativo, ¡prosiga Ud.!, ¡persista Ud.! ¡adelante!

go near, acercarse, tocar de cerca; correr algún peligro.

go off, morirse; irse, largarse, despedirse; dispararse o salir el tiro de un arma de fuego; seguir su curso, tener efecto, salir bien o mal (v.g. un concierto).

go on, continuar, seguir o proseguir lo comenzado; adelantarse, ir adelante; adelantar, progresar; atacar.

go over, pasar, atravesar; desertar, cambiar de casaca, pasarse a una religión, partido, etc., diverso del que se tenía o se profesaba antes. **To go out,** salir, ponerse en camino, salir a campaña, darse a la vela; apagarse, morirse la lumbre, la luz o el fuego; extinguirse, apagarse la vida, la imaginación, etc.

go out of the way, apartarse del camino, ponerse a un lado; descarriarse. **To go her time out,** acabarse el tiempo de la preñez, salir o estar fuera de cuenta; salir de cuidado.

go through, llevar a cabo alguna cosa, ejecutar o hacer ejecutar; pasar, examinar o recorrer completamente algo; determinar definitivamente; sufrir una operación quirúrgica; enhebrar, enhilar, ensartar; hender; pasar o atravesar algún camino; atravesar de parte a parte; salir al cabo de, salir con; conseguir alguna cosa.

Go to! (*Ant.*) ¡vaya!, ¡toma! **Go to grass, go to thunder,** interjecciones despectivas: ¡Vaya Ud. a paseo! ¡Mal rayo te parta! **Go-to-meeting,** (*Fam. E. U.*) Se dice del traje de los días de fiesta; la ropa dominguera.

go under, quebrar, hacer bancarrota; quedar arruinado, vencido o destruído; también pasar por, ser conocido por tal o cual nombre.

go up, subir. **To go up and down,** rodar, andorrear, corretear, ir de una parte a otra.

go upon, emprender, fundarse en algo. **To go upon sure grounds, estar bien fundado, ir sobre seguro. To go upon sure tick,** comprar fiado.

go with, acompañar. **To go with child,** estar preñada. **To go with the tide,** bajar con la marea.

go without, estar, arreglarse o pasarlo sin; no obtener una cosa a que se tenía derecho. **To go halves,** ir a medias con uno. **To go to the shade,** irse a la sombra. **To go to service,** ponerse a servir. **To go to the bottom,** ir o irse a pique. **The bell goes,** suena la campana. **To let go one's hold,** soltar la presa. **To go so far as,** ir hasta, llegar a. **To go the whole length,** llegar hasta; arriesgarlo todo.

go, *s.* (*Fam.*) 1. Moda, auge, furor. **It was all the go,** eso hacía furor. 2. Energía, actividad, empuje. 3. Giro, marcha, curso de los asuntos; predicamento. 4. Ajuste, pacto; buen éxito, esfuerzo dichoso. 5. Oportunidad, ensayo. 6. Marcha, curso, movimiento. **On the go,** en movimiento. 7. Tentativa. 8. **It is no go,** es inútil, es un fracaso.

goad [gəʊd] [goud], *s.* Aguijada, aijada, pincho, aguijón.

goad, *va.* 1. Aguijar, pinchar o herir con la aguijada. 2. Aguijonear, agarrochear, estimular, incitar. 3. Pinchar, irritar.

go-ahead ['gɔʊəhed] [gou-ajed], *a.* *(Fam.)* Emprendedor, activo, enérgico. **Go-ahead!** *inter.* ¡adelante!

goal [gɔʊl] [goul], *s.* 1. Meta, término. 2. Fin, objeto, motivo. 3. (Fútbol) gol, meta. **Goalkeeper,** guardameta, portero (en el fútbol).

goat [gɔʊt] [gout], *s.* Cabra, chiva, cabrón. **He-goat,** cabrón, macho de cabrío. **Young goat,** cabrito, chivo, choto. **Wild goat,** cabra montés. **To ride the goat,** *(Fest.)* Someterse a las ceremonias de iniciación en ciertas sociedades secretas.

goatbeard ['gɔʊtbɜːd] [gout-berd], *s.* *(Bot.)* Barba cabruna.

goatee [gɔʊ'tiː] [gou-ti], *s.* Perilla, mechón de pelos que se deja en la barba.

goatherd ['gɔʊthɜːd] [gout-jerd], *s.* Cabrero.

goatish ['gɔʊtɪʃ] [gou-tish], *a.* Cabruno, chotuno; lascivo.

goat-milker [ˌgɔʊt'mɪlkəʳ] [gout-mil-kaʳ], **goat-sucker** [ˌgɔʊt'sʌkəʳ] [gout-su-kaʳ], *s.* *(Orn.)* Caprimulga.

goat's-hair ['gɔʊtzheəʳ] [gouts-jeaʳ], *s.* Pelote.

goat-skin ['gɔʊtskɪn] [gout-skin], *s.* Piel de cabra.

goat's-rue ['gɔʊtzruː] [gouts-ru], *s.* *(Bot.)* Gálega, ruda cabruna.

goat's-thorn [ˌgɔʊtz'θɔːn] [gouts-zorn], *s.* *(Bot.)* Tragacanto.

gob [gɔb] [gob], *s.* 1. Una cantidad pequeña de cualquiera cosa; un bocado. 2. La boca.

gob, gobbin ['gɔbɪn] [go-bin], *s.* *(Min.)* Escombrera, explotación abandonada llena de escombros y desechos.

gobbet ['gɔbɪt] [go-bit], *s.* Bocado; pedacito.

gobble ['gɔbl] [go-bel], *va.* Engullir, tragar bocados enteros, tragar vorazmente. *-vn.* Hacer ruido en la garganta como los pavos.

gobbledygook ['gɔbldɪguːk] [go-bel-di-guk], *s.* Galimatías propio de ciertos funcionarios públicos.

gobbler ['gɔbləʳ] [go-blaʳ], *s.* 1. Engullidor, glotón, tragón, tragador. 2. *(Fam.)* El pavo, *(Méx.)* guajalote, (Cuba) guanajo.

go-between ['gɔʊbɪˌtwiːn] [gou-bi-tuin], *s.* 1. Mediador, medianero; entremetido. 2. Tercer, correvedile. 3. Alcahuete.

goblet ['gɔblɪt] [go-blit], *s.* Copa, vaso con pie para beber.

goblin ['gɔblɪn] [go-blin], *s.* Espíritu errante, duende.

go-by ['gɔʊbaɪ] [gou-bai], *s.* 1. Menosprecio, repulsa o desaire. 2. *(Des.)* Treta, trama, fraude. **To give one the go-by in a race,** adelantarse a otro, dejarlo atrás.

go-cart ['gɔʊkɑːt] [gou-kart], *s.* Carretilla o carretón para enseñar a andar a los niños. *(Méx.)* Andaderas.

God [gɔd] [god], *s.* 1. Dios, el ser supremo. 2. Dios, la persona o cosa que se adora con pasión desordenada. **God save the king,** Dios guarde al rey. **God forbid,** no quiera Dios. **Thank God,** gracias a Dios. **God's Day,** domingo; también la fiesta del Corpus Christi. **God's house,** iglesia o templo. **God-fearing,** reverente, temeroso de Dios y observador de sus leyes.

godchild ['gɔdtʃaɪld] [god-chaild], *s.* Ahijado, ahijada.

goddaughter ['gɔdˌdɔːtəʳ] [god-dau-taʳ], *sf.* Ahijada.

goddess ['gɔdɪs] [go-des], *sf.* Diosa.

goddess-like ['gɔdɪslaɪk] [go-des-laik], *a.* Semejante a una diosa, divina.

godfather ['gɔdˌfɑːðəʳ] [god-fa-daʳ], *s.* Padrino.

godhead ['gɔdhed] [god-jed], *s.* Deidad, divinidad.

godless ['gɔdlɪs] [god-les], *a.* Infiel, impío, sin Dios, ateo.

godlessness ['gɔdlɪsnɪs] [god-lis-nes], *s.* Estado de perdición.

godlike ['gɔdlaɪk] [god-laik], *a.* Divino, semejante a la divinidad.

godliness ['gɔdlɪnɪs] [god-li-nes], *s.* Piedad, devoción, santidad.

godling ['gɔdlɪŋ] [god-lin], *s.* Diosecillo, divinidad secundaria.

godly ['gɔdlɪ] [god-li], *a.* 1. Piadoso, devoto, religioso. 2. Recto, justificado. *-adv.* Piadosamente, justamente.

godmother ['gɔdˌmʌðəʳ] [god-ma-daʳ], *sf.* Madrina.

godown [gɔd] [god], *s.* Almacén chino o indio; (término angloindio.)

godsend ['gɔdsend] [god-send], *s.* Un milagro, un don particular de Dios. *(Fam.)* Ganga, chiripa.

godship ['gɔdʃɪp] [god-ship], *s.* Dignidad de un dios.

godson ['gɔdsʌn] [god-san], *sm.* Ahijado.

godspeed ['gɔdspiːd] [god-spid], *s.* Deseo de que Dios asista y guarde a alguien; ¡buena suerte! Se escribe a menudo en dos palabras.

godward ['gɔdwɔːd] [god-uord], *adv.* Hacia Dios.

godwit ['gɔdwɪt] [god-uit], *s.* *(Orn.)* Francolín.

goer ['gɔʊəʳ] [gouaʳ], *s.* 1. Andador, paseante, el que va de una parte a otra; vagabundo, ambulante. 2. *V.* GO-BETWEEN. **Goers and comers,** yentes y vinientes.

goggle ['gɔgl] [go-guel], *vn.* Entornar o hacer girar los ojos, mirar con los ojos muy abiertos o de soslayo.

goggle, *s.* Mirada entornada, vuelta afectada de los ojos. **Goggles,** anteojos de camino, para guardar la vista del polvo, o para el estrabismo; llámanse también así las anteojeras que se usan para los caballos espantadizos. *-a.* El que tiene los ojos muy abiertos o prominentes; ojos saltones.

goggle-eyed, *a. V.* GOGGLE, *a.*

going ['gɔʊɪŋ] [gouin], *s.* 1. El paso, el andar, el modo de andar. 2. Preñado, preñez. 3. Partida. 4. Paso, movimiento o acción en el modo de gobernarse y potarse. **The going of a horse,** andadura de un caballo. **Going forward,** progreso, lo que está pasando o sucediendo actualmente. **Going down,** puesta del sol, ocaso; baja de fondos, descenso de las aguas.

goiter, goitre ['gɔɪtəʳ] [goi-taʳ], *s.* *(Med.)* Papera, coto, bocio.

goitrous ['gɔɪtrəs] [goi-tros], *a.* Que se refiere a la papera; que la tiene o padece.

gola [gɔlə] [go-la], *s.* *(Arq.)* Gola, cimacio.

gold [gɔʊld] [gould], *s.* 1. Oro. 2. Oro, dinero, moneda de oro, riqueza. **Gold-leaf,** oro batido, pan de oro. **Crude mass of gold,** oro virgen, oro bruto. *(Prov.)* **It is not all gold that glitters,** no es oro todo lo que reluce.

gold, en composición; de oro. **Gold-bearing,** aurífero, productor de oro. **Gold-dust,** polvo de oro. *(Bot.)* Alisón, planta crucífera, con flores doradas. **Gold fever,** fiebre del oro, ansia de emprender la busca de oro. **Gold-field,** distrito o terreno aurífero. **Gold lace,** galón de oro. **Leaf-gold,** oro nativo en láminas u hojas.

gold-beater ['gɔʊldˌbiːtəʳ] [gould-bi-taʳ], *s.* Batihoja, batidor de oro.

gold brick ['gɔʊldbrɪk] [gould-brik], *s.* *(Vul.)* Engaño, estafa.

golden ['gɔʊldən] [goul-den], *a.* 1. Aureo, de oro, hecho de oro. 2. lustroso, brillante. 3. Excelente, de gran valor, precioso. 4. Feliz. 5. Amarillento, de color de oro. **Golden rule,** regla de oro.

golden mean ['gɔʊldən'miːn] [goul-den-min], *s.* Moderación, término medio.

golden-number ['gɔʊldən'nʌmbəʳ] [goul-den-nam-baʳ], *s.* Número áureo, el que indica el ciclo de la luna.

golden-thistle ['gɔʊldən'θɪzl] [goul-den-zi-sel], *s.* *(Bot.)* Cardillo.

golden wedding ['gɔʊldən'wedɪŋ] [goul-den-ue-din], *s.* Bodas de oro.

gold-filled ['gɔʊldˌfɪld] [gould-fil], *a.* Enchapado o revestido de oro.

goldfinch ['gɔʊldfɪntʃ] [gould-finch], *s.* *(Orn.)* Jilguero.

gold-fish ['gɔʊldfɪʃ] [gould-fish], *s.* Carpa pequeña de color rojo dorado, originaria de China y que hoy abunda en casi todos los países.

gold foil ['gɔʊldfɔɪl] [gould-foil], *s.* Hojuelas de oro.

gold-hilted ['gɔʊldhɪltɪd] [gould-jil-tid], *a.* Lo que tiene el puño de oro o dorado: se aplica comúnmente a las espadas.

gold-leaf ['gɔʊldliːf] [gould-lif], *s.* Pan u hoja de oro; oro en libritos, oro batido.

gold mine ['gɔʊldmaɪn] [gould-main], *s.* 1. Mina de oro. 2. *(Fig.)* Fuente de riqueza.

gold-proof ['gɔʊldpruːf] [gould-pruf], *a.* A prueba de oro, capaz de resistir las tentaciones del interés o la codicia.

gold-size ['gɔʊldsaɪz] [gould-sais], *s.* Cola o barniz de color de oro.

goldsmith ['gɔʊldsmɪθ] [gould-smiz], *s.* Orífice, platero de oro, el artífice que trabaja en oro.

gold standard ['gɔʊldsˈtændəd] [gould-stan-dard], *s.* Patrón oro.

gold-stone ['gəʊldstəʊn] [gould-stoun], *s.* Venturina.

gold-thread ['gəʊldθred] [gould-zred], *s.* Hilo de oro.

goldy-locks ['gəʊldɪlɒkz] [goul-di-loks], *s. (Bot.)* Crisocomo.

golf [gɒlf] [golf], *s.* Golf, juego de pelota que se juega con palos encorvados en los extremos y varios agujeros en la tierra. Golf club, 1. Palo que se emplea en este juego. 2. Club de golf. Golf links, campo de golf.

gondola ['gɒndələ] [gon-do-la], *s.* Góndola, barca con remos y toldo que se usa en Venecia.

gondolier ['gɒndəlɪəʳ] [gon-do-liaʳ], *s.* Gondolero.

gone [gɒn] [gon], *pp.* de TO GO. Ido; perdido, arruinado; pasado; muerto, fallecido; apagado.

gonfalon ['gɒnfələn] [gon-fa-lon], **gonfanon** ['gɒnfənən] [gon-fa-non], *s.* Confalón, gonfalón, estandarte o pendón llevado en la punta de una lanza.

gonfalonier ['gɒnfələnɪəʳ] [gon-fa-lo-niaʳ], *s.* Confalonero, nombre del jefe que llevaba el pendón o estandarte de algunas repúblicas de Italia.

gong [gɒŋ] [gong], *s.* Batintín, gongo, instrumento músico de percusión usado por los asiáticos.

goniometer [gɒnɪə'mi:təʳ] [go-nio-mi-taʳ], *s.* Goniómetro, medidor de ángulos.

goniometry ['gɒnɪə'mi:trɪ] [go-nio-mi-tri], *s.* Goniometría, el arte de medir los ángulos.

gonorrhæa [gɒnə'rɪə] [go-no-ria], *s.* Gonorrea, blenorragia.

goober ['gu:bəʳ] [gu-baʳ], *s. V.* PEANUT.

good [gʊd] [gud], *a.* Bueno, saludable; apto, conveniente, ventajoso, útil; completo; precioso; genuino, verdadero, válido; perfecto, virtuoso, religioso, justo; benévolo, bondadoso, clemente, misericordioso; de buena índole, cariñoso, alegre; dichoso, feliz; hábil, sobresaliente en su profesión; grande, considerable; legítimo, no fingido; digno. **My good sir,** mi buen señor. **A good turn,** un favor, una gracia. **In good time,** a tiempo, a propósito, con oportunidad. **It is a good as done,** es cosa hecha, es como si estuvies concluído. **It is a good way thither,** hay mucho camino de aquí a allá; está muy lejos. **In good earnest,** seriamente, de veras, de fijo. **To hold good,** subsistir, continuar en toda su fuerza. **To be as good as one's word; to make one's word good,** cumplir lo prometido. **Good Friday,** viernes Santo. **To make good,** probar o justificar alguna cosa; hacer bueno, abonar; completar, suplir, lo quefalta; indemnizar, reparar una falta o una pérdida; defender con buen éxito; acertar, lograr, salir bien en alguna empresa o empeño. **He made good his escape,** logró evadirse. **To see, to think good,** hallar bueno, juzgar a propósito. **A good deal,** bastante, mucho. **A good while,** un buen rato. **He is good for nothing,** no vale un comino, o un pito, o tres pepinos; no vale nada. **As good as,** tanto como, como, casi. **He is as good as ruined,** está casi arruinado. *-s.* Bien, lo que física o moralmente contribuye a la felicidad; prosperidad, adelantamiento, ventaja, realidad. *-pl.* Mercancías. *V.* GOODS. For good and all, seriamente, fuera de chanza, de seguro, sin miedo. Much good may it do you, buen provecho le haga. *-adv.* Bien, rectamente. *-inter.* ¡Bueno! ¡bien! **For good,** de una vez para siempre. **He comes for good,** viene para quedarse. **She is gone for good,** se ha ido de una vez, para no volver. **Good-conditioned,** bien acondicionado. **Good-day,** buenos días (saludo acostumbrado al encontrarse o al despedirse). **Good-morning,** buenos días. **Good-afternoon,** buenas tardes. **Good-night, good-evening,** buenas noches.

good-breeding [gʊd'bri:dɪŋ] [gud-bri-din], *s.* Buena crianza, finos modales.

good-bye ['gʊd'baɪ] [gud-bai], *adv.* Adiós, vaya Ud. con Dios. (Contracción de **God be with you.**)

good cheer [gʊd'tʃɪəʳ] [gud-chiaʳ], *s.* Alegría, buen humor, jovialidad.

good-fellow [gʊd'feləʊ] [gud-fe-lou], *s.* Socio o compañero festivo y jovial. *(Fam.)* Buen chico, buen muchacho.

good-fellowship [gʊd'feləʊʃɪp] [gud-fe-lou-ship], *s.* Compañía o sociedad alegre y festiva.

good-fortune [gʊd'fɔ:tju:n] [gud-for-tiun], *s.* Dicha, felicidad.

good-hearted [gʊd'hɑ:tɪd] [gud-jar-tid], *a.* De buen corazón, misericordioso.

good-humor [gʊd'hju:məʳ] [gud-jiu-moʳ], *s.* Buen humor, jovialidad.

good-humored [gʊd'hju:məd] [gud-jiu-mord], *a.* Jocoso, vivo, jovial.

good-humoredly [gʊd'hju:mədlɪ] [gud-jiu-mord-li], *adv.* Jocosamente, alegremente.

gooding ['gʊdɪŋ] [gu-din], *s.* Costumbre que hubo en Inglaterra de pedir regalos, limosnas o aguinaldos por Navidad.

goodish ['gʊdɪʃ] [gu-dish], *a.* 1. Algo bueno, no malo, ni dañoso. 2. Considerable, algo grande.

goodliness ['gʊdlɪnɪs] [gud-li-nes], *s.* Hermosura, gracia, elegancia.

good-looking ['gʊd'lʊkɪŋ] [gud-lu-kin], *a.* Bien parecido, bonito, de agradables facciones.

good-luck ['gʊdlʌk] [gud-lak], *s.* Suerte o buena suerte, dicha.

goodly ['gʊdlɪ] [gud-li], *a.* 1. Hermoso, bien parecido. 2. De calidad escogida; atractivo, agradable o vistoso. 3. Abultado; considerable; algo numeroso. **A goodly prospect,** hermosa perspectiva; buenas esperanzas.

good-manners ['gʊdmænəz] [gud-ma-ners], *s.* Cortesía, modales corteses, buena crianza.

good-nature ['gʊd'neɪtʃəʳ] [gud-nei-chaʳ], *s.* Bondad, benevolencia, buen natural, buen corazón.

good-natured ['gʊd'neɪtʃəd] [gud-nei-chad], *a.* Benévolo, cariñoso, de buen natural, afable.

good-naturedly ['gʊd'neɪtʃədlɪ] [gud-nei-chad-li], *adv.* Cariñosamente, afablemente.

goodness ['gʊdnɪs] [gud-nes], *s.* 1. Bondad, benevolencia, virtud. 2. Acto o expresión de bondad.

goods ['gʊdz] [guds], *s. pl.* 1. Bienes muebles, muebles de una casa; géneros, mercaderías. **Consignment of goods,** consignación de mercaderías. **Goods exported o exports,** géneros de exportación. **Goods imported o imports,** géneros importados. **Goods in demand,** géneros de buen despacho, muy solicitados. **Parcels of goods,** partidas de géneros. **Assortment of goods,** surtido de géneros. **Expediter of goods,** despachador de géneros. **Goods heavy of sale,** géneros difíciles de vender o poco buscados. **Green goods,** *(E.U.)* Papel moneda falso, billetes falsificados. 2. En composición, tiene en Inglaterra el mismo valor que **Freight** en los Estados Unidos. **Goods-shed,** almacén, depósito de mercancías. **Goods-train,** tren de mercancías. **Goods-wagon,** furgón, vagón de mercancías.

good-sense ['gʊdsens] [gud-sens], *s.* Juicio sano, buen sentido, perspicacia natural.

good-sized ['gʊdsaɪst] [gud-saist], *a.* Grande, de buen tamaño.

good-speed ['gʊdspi:d] [gud-spid], *s.* ¡Buena suerte! frase para mostrar a uno que se desea que logre su objeto.

good-turn ['gʊdtɜ:n] [gud-tern], *s.* Servicio en recompensa de un favor, asistencia, o buenos oficios recibidos.

good-wife ['gʊdwaɪf] [gud-uaif], *sf.* Ama de la casa.

good-will ['gʊdwɪl] [gud-uil], *s.* 1. Benevolencia, sinceridad, bondad. (En este sentido se escribe de ordinario en dos palabras.) 2. Parroquia y buen crédito de una tienda o establecimiento comercial; clientela.

good-woman ['gʊdwʊmən] [gud-vu-man], *sf.* Buena ama, mujer o señora; se usa entre rústicos.

goody ['gʊdɪ] [gu-di], *a.* Bonachón, pazguato, mojigato. *-s.* 1. Ama vieja y pobre, comadre. 2. Persona bonachona. 3. Confitura, golosina.

goose [gu:s] [gus], *s. (pl.* GEESE). 1. Ganso, ánsar, ocoa; la gansa, en oposición al ánsar macho o **gander. Wild goose,** ganso bravo, salvaje. 2. Plancha de sastre. 3. Persona inocente, ganso, bobo, necio. 4. Juego de la oca.

gooseberry ['gʊzbərɪ] [gus-be-ri], *s. (Bot.)* Uva espín o crespa.

goose-cap ['guːskæp] [gus-kap], *s.* Bobo, tonto, ganso, pazguato.

goose-flesh ['guːsfleʃ] [gus-flesh], *s.* Carne de gallina, los granitos que aparecen en la piel cuando uno tiene frío, miedo o terror.

goose-foot ['guːsfʊt] [gus-fut], *s. (Bot.)* Cualquier planta del género Chenopodiium; chual; llámase así por la figura de sus hojas.

goose-neck ['guːsnek] [gus-nek], *s. (Mar.)* Gancho de botalones; arbotante, cuello de cisne; pescante de bote.

goose-quill ['guːskɪl] [gus-kil], *s.* Pluma de ave, cañón, pluma para escribir hecha de los cañones de los gansos.

goose-wings ['guːswɪŋz] [gus-uings], *s. pl. (Mar.)* Calzones.

gopher ['gəʊfəʳ] [gou-faʳ], *s. (Zool.)* Geomís, roedor americano.

gopher-wood [gəʊfə'wʊd] [gu-fa-vud], *s. (Bot.)* 1. Árbol de Kentucky y Tennessee de madera amarilla. 2. Nombre que se da a la madera desconocida con que se construyó el arca de Noé.

gordian ['gɔːdɪən] [gor-dian], *a.* Intrincado, difícil; se dice por lo común **gordian-knot**, nudo gordiano, para ponderar alguna dificultad.

gore [gɔːʳ] [goʳ], *s.* Sangre, grumo de sangre, sangre cuajada; lodo.

gore, *s.* 1. Cuchillo, nesga; ensanche triangular del vestido para darle vuelo. 2. Pedazo de terreno de forma triangular.

gore, *va.* 1. Herir a uno con puñal u otra arma punzante. 2. Herir un animal con sus cuernos a otro. 3. Hacer una nesga o cuchillo; ajustar o ensanchar con cuchillos, como una vela o la falda de un vestido.

gorge [gɔːdʒ] [gorch], *s.* 1. Gorja, garganta, gaznate. 2. Garganta, desfiladero, cañada. 3. Cuello de una vestidura. 4. La acción de engullir; trago, bocado, lo que se ha tragado. 5. Apretujón, presión como la que hace el hielo.

gorge, *va.* Engullir, tragar con avidez; hartar, saciar. -*vn.* Hartarse, saciarse, atracarse.

gorged [gɔːdʒt] [gorcht], *a.* Lo que tiene garganta.

gorgeous ['gɔːdʒəs] [gor-yos], *a.* Primoroso, brillante, vistoso, esplendoroso, grandioso, magnífico.

gorgeously ['gɔːdʒəslɪ] [gor-yos-li], *adv.* Primorosamente, esplendorosamente, magnificencia,

gorgeousness ['gɔːdʒəsnɪs] [gor-yos-nes], *s.* Esplendor, magnificencia.

gorget ['gɔːdʒɪt] [gor-yit], *s.* 1. Gola, golilla. 2. Gorguera de la armadura antigua. 3. *(Orn.)* Lunar o mancha de color en la garganta de las aves. 4. Instrumento quirúrgico; conductor acanalado o cóncavo.

gorgon ['gɔːgən] [gor-gon], *s.* 1. Gorgona, monstruo fabuloso. 2. Alguna cosa muy fea y horrenda.

gorilla [gə'rɪlə] [go-ri-la], *s. (Zool.)* Gorila, mono de África, fuerte y fiero, de estatura igual a la del hombre.

gormand, gourmand ['gɔːmənd] [gor-mand], *s.* Glotón, gomia; goloso.

gormandize ['gɔːməndaɪz] [gor-man-dais], *vn.* Glotonea, comer con gula.

gormandizer ['gɔːmən'daɪzəʳ] [gor-man-dai-saʳ], *s.* Golosazo.

gorse [gɔːs] [gors], *s. (Bot.)* Especie de hiniesta espinosa. *V.* FURZE.

gory [gɔːrɪ] [go-ri], *a.* Cubierto de sangre grumosa; sangriento.

goshawk ['gɒshɔːk] [gos-jok], *s. (Orn.)* Azor, especie de halcón.

gosling ['gəslɪŋ] [gos-lin], *s. (Orn.)* Gansarón, el pollo del ganso.

gospel ['gɒspəl] [gos-pel], *s.* 1. Evangelio. 2. Lo que se considera como infaliblemente verdadero. -*va.* Instruir según el Evangelio; llenar de piedad.

gospeller ['gɒspələʳ] [gos-pe-laʳ], *s.* Evangelista; evangelistero.

gospellize ['gɒspəlaɪz] [gos-pe-lais], *va.* Evangelizar.

gossamer ['gɒsəməʳ] [go-sa-maʳ], *s.* 1. Hilo muy tenue de telaraña flotante en el aire; trama o tejido de dichos hilos. 2.

(Art. y *Of.)* Tela de araña, gasa muy sutil y suave, pero fuerte. 3. Impermeable, capa o sobretodo hecho con tela impermeable.

gossamer, *a.* Delgado, muy fino, sutil.

gossamery ['gɒsəmərɪ] [go-sa-me-ri], *a.* Ligero y delgado como la telaraña.

gossip ['gɒsɪp] [go-sip], *s.* 1. Compadre, comadre. 2. Compadre de taberna; un comadrero o comadrera. 3. Charla, charladuría, picotería, parlería, parla. 4. Chisme. 5. Padrino, madrina, persona que saca de pila a una criatura; este fué el sentido primitivo de la palabra.

gossip, *vn.* Charlar, hablar mucho y sin substancia, parlotear, picotear, chismear.

gossiping ['gɒsɪpɪŋ] [go-si-pin], *s.* La acción de pasar el tiempo charlando o parloteando; murmuración, chismografía.

got, *pret.* y *pp.* del verbo TO GET.

gothic ['gɒθɪk] [go-zik], *a.* Gótico, relativo a los godos. **Gothic type,** *(Impr.)* Letra gótica.

gothic, *s.* La lengua gótica o goda, el godo.

gothicism ['gɒθɪsɪzəm] [go-zi-si-sem], *s.* 1. El idioma gótico. 2. Rudeza de maneras; barbarie.

gothicize ['gɒθɪsaɪz] [go-zi-sais], *va.* Hacer alguna cosa como la hacían los godos.

gotten, *pp.* de TO GET.

gouge [gaʊdʒ] [gauch], *s.* Gubia, escoplo de media caña.

gouge, *va.* 1. Excavar o ahondar como con una gubia. 2. Sacar los ojos del enemigo con el dedo pulgar.

gouge-channel ['gaʊdʒ'ʃənəl] [gauch-cha-nel], *s. (Mar.)* Gubiadura.

goulash ['guːlæʃ] [gu-lash], *s.* Guiso de carne y verduras de origen húngaro.

gourd [gʊəd] [guard], *s. (Bot.)* Calabaza.

gourmand, *s. V.* GORMAND.

gourmandize, *V.* GORMANDIZE.

gourmet ['gʊəmeɪ] [gua-mei], *s.* Gastrónomo.

gout [gaʊt] [gaut], *s.* 1. Gota, inflamación del sistema fibroso y los ligamentos de las articulaciones. 2. *(Ant.)* Gota, grumo de sangre. **A fit of gout,** un ataque de gota. **Gout of o in the feet,** podagra.

gout, *s.* Gusto; inclinación.

goutiness ['gaʊtɪnɪs] [gau-ti-nes], *s.* El dolor de la gota y el estado del que la padece.

goutwort ['gaʊtwɔːt] [gaut-uort], *s. (Bot.)* Angélica.

gouty ['gaʊtɪ] [gau-ti], *a.* Gotoso. **Gouty land,** (Spenser) tierra pantanosa.

govern ['gʌvən] [ga-vern], *va.* 1. Gobernar, guiar, dirigir, regir. 2. Moderar, dominar, domar. 3. *Gram.)* Regir. 4. *(Mar.)* Dirigir los movimientos de la embarcación. -*vn.* Gobernar, tener dominio.

governable ['gʌvənəbl] [ga-ver-na-bol], *a.* Dócil, sumiso, sujeto, obediente, manejable.

governance ['gʌvənəns] [ga-ver-nans], *s.* Gobierno, ejercicio del poder, autoridad.

governess ['gʌvənɪs] [ga-ver-nes], *sf.* Gobernadora, aya, institutriz. **Daily governess,** maestra que va a dar lecciones a casa de las discípulas.

government ['gʌvənmənt] [ga-vern-ment], *s.* 1. Gobierno, ministerio, administración pública. 2. Gobierno, conducta, porte. 3. *(Gram.)* Régimen. 4. Dominio, gobierno, territorio sobre que tiene autoridad un gobierno. 5. El derecho de gobernar; autoridad. **For your government,** *(Com.)* para su gobierno.

governor ['gʌvənəʳ] [ga-ver-naʳ], *s.* 1. Gobernador, tutor, ayo. 2. *(Ant.)* Piloto. 3. *(Art.* y *Of.)* Regulador, moderador; mecanismo que en las máquinas, particularmente en las de vapor, sirve para regular la velocidad del movimiento.

gown [gaʊn] [gaun], *s.* 1. Vestido talar exterior de mujer; túnica. 2. Toga, vestidura talar que usan los estudiantes en algunas universidades.

gownman ['gaʊnmən] [gaun-man], **gownsman** [gaʊnzmən] [gauns-man], *s.* 1. Togado, individuo de una universidad, clérigo, magistrado u otro que por su estado lleva ropa talar. 2. Ciudadano, civil, en oposición al militar.

grab ['græb] [grab], *va.* 1. Arrebatar, apresar, agarrar, prender rudamente; asir con la mano. 2. Tomar posesión repentina, violenta o fraudulentamente; apresar. -*s.* 1. *(Fam.)* Toma, apresamiento; lo que está asido. 2. Gancho o aparato para asir.

grabble ['græbl] [gra-bel], *va.* Tentar, palpar, examinar y reconocer por medio del tacto. -*vn.* Postrarse.

grace [greɪs] [greis], *s.* 1. Gracia, influencia favorable de Dios en el alma humana. 2. Gracia, favor, merced, perdón, remisión. 3. Gracia, privilegio. 4. Gracia, garbo, donaire, agrado y despejo en la ejecución de alguna cosa. 5. Gracia, afabilidad en el trato común. 6. Gracia, don natural que hace agradable a quien lo posee. 7. Gracia, diosa del paganismo que se suponía otorgaba la hermosura; en este sentido se usa casi siempre en plural en las dos lenguas. 8. Gracia, atractivo o agrado adquirido. 9. Título de honor que se da en Inglaterra a los arzobispos y a los duques, y así equivale en unos casos al tratamiento de Excelencia y en otros al de Ilustrísima. 10. Gracias, las oraciones que se dicen antes y después de comer. **To say grace before a meal,** bendecir la mesa. **To say grace after a meal,** dar gracias después de comer o cenar. **Days of grace,** *(Com.)* Días de gracia, usualmente tres, el tiempo que se da para el pago de una letra de cambio después de su vencimiento.

grace, *va.* 1. Adornar, hermosear con adornos. 2. Agraciar, conceder alguna gracia, favorecer. 3. Dar gracia celestial.

grace-cup ['greɪskʌp] [greis-kap], *s.* El trago o brindis echado después de dar gracias.

graceful ['greɪsʃʊl] [greis-ful], *a.* 1. Gracioso, elegante, primoroso; fácil, natural. 2. Gracioso, decoroso, conveniente, cortés.

gracefully ['greɪsʃəlɪ] [greis-fu-li], *adv.* Elegantemente, con gracia.

gracefulness ['greɪsʃəlnɪs] [greis-ful-nes], *s.* Gracia, elegancia.

graceless ['greɪslɪs] [greis-les], *a.* Réprobo, malvado, abandonado, desesperado.

gracelessly ['greɪslɪslɪ] [greis-les-li], *adv.* Sin elegancia.

graces ['greɪsɪs] [grei-sis], *s. pl.* Gracias, tres divinidades mitológicas. **Good graces,** favor, amparo, patrocinio, valimiento.

gracile ['græsiːl] [gra-sil], *a.* Delgado, sutil, con gracia.

gracious ['greɪʃəs] [grei-shos], *a.* 1. Gracioso, benévolo, favorable, humano. 2. Virtuoso, bueno. **Our most gracious sovereign,** nuestro benignísimo soberano. 3. Primoroso, agradable, cortés.

graciously ['greɪʃəslɪ] [grei-shos-li], *adv.* Graciosamente, benignamente, agradablemente.

graciousness ['greɪʃəsnɪs] [grei-shos-nes], *s.* Gracia, afabilidad, bondad, dulzura, benignidad.

grackle ['grækl] [gra-kel], *s.* Especie de estornino; también, un mirlo americano.

gradation [grəˈdeɪʃən] [gra-dei-shon], *s.* 1. Graduación, el acto y efecto de graduar; paso gradual. 2. *(Mús.)* Gradación. 3. Grado, rango en una serie.

gradatory ['grædətərɪ] [gra-da-to-ri], *a.* 1. Graduado o gradual, lo que procede por grados. 2. A propósito para andar.

grade [greɪd] [greid], *s.* 1. Grado, graduación, rango, grado o división en cualquier serie o curso. 2. Inclinación respecto a la horizontal, declive de un camino, ferrocarril o superficie; también el grado de esa inclinación. 3. Animal o casta de animales producidos por el cruzamiento con los de una casta superior.

grade, *va.* 1. Colocar, clasificar por series o grados. 2. Nivelar, o igualar en declive. 3. Mejorar por medio del cruzamiento de castas.

grade crossing [ˌgreɪdˈkrɒsɪŋ] [greid-kro-sin], *s. (F.C.)* Paso a nivel.

grade scale ['greɪdskeɪl] [greid-skeil], *s.* Escalafón.

grade school ['greɪdskɒl] [greid-skul], *s.* Escuela primaria, escuela elemental.

gradient ['greɪdɪənt] [grei-dient], *a.* 1. Ambulante, lo que se mueve por grados o pasos. 2. Que baja o se levanta por grados regulares de inclinación. -*s.* 1. Pendiente o declive de un camino o ferrocarril, inclinación. 2. *(Meteor.)* Grado del aumento o disminución, p. ej. de la temperatura o de la presión atmosférica; o el diagrama que lo representa.

grading ['greɪdɪŋ] [grei-din], *s.* 1. Graduación, clasificación. 2. Nivelación.

gradual ['grædjʊəl] [gra-diual], *a.* Gradual, que procede por pasos o grados; regular y lento. -*s.* Un libro antiguo de himnos.

gradually ['grædjʊəlɪ] [gra-diua-li], *adv.* Gradualmente.

graduate ['grædjɔɪt] [gra-duet], *va.* 1. Graduar, conferir en una universidad el grado de doctor, licenciado o bachiller. 2. Graduar, dividir y señalar por grados. 3. Adelantar, subir o aumentar de grado en grado; graduar los colores de un cuadro; dar a los fluidos cierto grado de consistencia. -*vn.* 1. Graduarse, ganar un grado en un colegio o universidad (acepción muy usada, pero impropia). 2. Pasar por grados; cambiar gradualmente.

graduate, *s.* 1. Graduado, el que posee algún grado académico. 2. Vaso graduado para medir líquidos, componer recetas médicas, etc.

graduation [ˌgrædjɔˈeɪʃən] [gra-diu-ei-shon], *s.* 1. Graduación; acto de conferir u obtener grados académicos. 2. Acción y efecto de modificar o de dividir un espacio en partes regulares.

graft [græft] [graft], *s.* 1. Injerto. 2. *(Fam.)* Peculado, negocios ilícitos que se realizan al amparo de un puesto público.

graft, *va.* 2. Injertar, ingerir. 2. Incorporar, unir una cosa con otra de una manera vital. 3. *(Cir.)* Transferir, pasar de un animal a otro, *v. gr.* un trozo de piel. -*vn.* Hacer injertos.

grafter ['græftəʳ] [graf-taʳ], *s.* Injertador de árboles.

grafting ['græftɪŋ] [graf-tin], *s.* Injertación, injerto, el acto de infertar. **Cleft grafting,** injerto en púa. **Tangue, whip, grafting,** injerto de lengüeta.

graham bread ['greɪəmˌbred] [grei-am-bred], *s.* Acemita, pan de acemite.

grail [greɪl] [greil], *s.* Cáliz o taza ancha; en especial, **the Holy Grail,** el cáliz empleado por el Redentor en la última Cena. Según la leyenda, se disipa y desaparece cuando se acerca a él alguien que no es puro y santo.

grain [greɪn] [grein], *s.* 1. Grano, una sola semilla de cualquiera mies. 2. Grano, el fruto y semilla de las mieses. 3. Semilla de cualquier fruto. 4. Grano, porción o parte menuda de alguna cosa. 5. Grano, la parte mínima en que se divide el peso. 6. Veta, la lista o raya que se halla en la madera y otros cuerpos fibrosos. **Against the grain,** contra pelo, a repelo, con repugnancia. 7. Grana, cualquier cosa teñida con grana. 8. Genio, disposición, índole. 9. Grano, la suavidad o aspereza que existe en la superficie de alguna cosa. **A grain of allowance,** indulgencia. **A rogue in grain,** pícaro rematado. **Cross-grain,** a contrahilo. **Grain-fork,** bieldo. **Grain-moth,** mariposa cuya larva ataca los granos entrojados. **Grain-weevil,** gorgojo. **Grains of paradise,** cardamomo, grana del paraíso.

grain, *va.* 1. Granular, granear, formar en granos. 2. Agranelar, vetear o rayar; pintar o teñir para imitar la madera, el mármol, etc.

grain alcohol [greɪnˈælkəhɒl] [grein-al-ko-jol], *s.* Alcohol de granos, alcohol etílico.

grain elevator [ˌgreɪnˈelɪveɪtəʳ] [grein-e-li-vei-taʳ], *s.* Elevador de granos.

grainy ['greɪnɪ] [grei-ni], *a.* Granado; lleno de grano o semilla.

gram, gramme ['græm] [gram], *s.* Gramo, unidad de peso en el sistema métrico.

gramineous ['grəˈmiːnɪəs] [gra-mi-nios], *a.* Gramíneo.

graminivorous ['græmɪˈnɪvərəs] [gra-mi-ni-vo-ros], *a.* Graminívoro, que se alimenta de hierba.

grammar ['græmə^r] [gra-ma^r], *s.* 1. Gramática, el arte de hablar y escribir una lengua con propiedad. 2. Gramática, el libro que contiene las reglas de la gramática.

grammarian [grə'meɪrɪən] [gra-ma-rian], *s.* Gramático, maestro de gramática; dómine; autor de una gramática.

grammar school ['græmə'skol] [gra-mar-skul], *s.* Escuela primaria, escuela elemental.

grammatic, grammatical [grə'mætɪk] [gra-ma-tik] ['grə'mætɪkəl] [gra-ma-ti-kal], *a.* Gramatical.

grammatically [grə'mætɪkəlɪ] [gra-ma-ti-ka-li], *adv.* Gramaticalmente.

grammaticaster [grə'mætɪ'kɑ:stə^r] [gra-ma-ti-kas-ta^r], *s.* Gramaticuelo, pedante.

grammaticize [grə'mætɪsaɪz] [gra-ma-ti-sais], *va.* Ajustar a las reglas de la gramática.

grammatist, *s. V.* GRAMMARIAN.

gramophone [grə'mæfəʊn] [gra-mo-foun], *s.* Gramófono, tocadiscos.

grampus ['græmpəs] [gram-pos], *s. (Zool.)* Delfín, un pez.

granary ['grænərɪ] [gra-na-ri], *s.* Granero, el sitio o lugar donde se recogen los granos.

grand [grænd] [grand], *a.* Grande, ilustre, grandioso; sublime, magnífico, noble; elevado, espléndido, augusto, preeminente; comprensivo. **Grand jury,** *V.* JURY. **Grand-master,** gran maestre; dignidad en la francmasnería y otras asociaciones.

grandam, grandame ['grændəm] [gran-dam], *sf.* Abuela; una vieja arrugada.

grand-aunt [grænd'aʊnt] [grand-aunt], *sf.* La tía del padre o de la madre; la hermana del abuelo o la abuela.

grandchild ['grændtʃaɪld] [grand-chaild], *s.* Nieto o nieta.

grand-daughter ['grænˌdɔːtə^r] [grand-do-ta^r], *sf.* Nieta.

grandee ['grændiː] [gran-di], *s.* Grande, hombre de distinción, poder o dignidad. **Grandee of Spain,** grande de España.

grandeur ['grændjə^r] [gran-dia^r], *s.* Grandez, esplendor, fausto, pompa.

grandfather ['grænˌfɑ:ðə^r] [grand-fa-da^r], *sm.* Abuelo. **Great-grandfather,** bisabuelo. **Great-great-grandfather,** tatarabuelo.

grandiloquence [græn'dɪləkwəns] [gran-di-lo-kuens], *s.* Grandilocuencia.

grandiloquous [græn'dɪləkwəs] [gran-di-lo-kuos], *a.* Grandílocuo.

grand larceny [grænd'lɑ:sənɪ] [grand-lar-se-ni], *s.* Robo de consideración.

grandly ['grændlɪ] [grand-li], *adv.* Grandemente, sublimemente.

grandmother ['grænˌmʌðə^r] [gran-ma-da^r], *sf.* Abuela. **Great-grandmother,** bisabuela. **Great-great grandmother,** tatarabuela.

grandnephew [grænˈnefjuː] [gran-ne-fiu], *sm.* Sobrino nieto de un hermano o de una hermana.

grandness ['grænnɪs] [gran-nes], *s.* Grandor, grandeza.

grandniece ['grænniːs] [gran-nis], *sf.* Sobrina nieta de un hermano o de una hermana.

grand piano [grænˈpɪɑːnəʊ] [gran-pia-nou], *s.* Piano de cola.

grandsire [grænsaɪə^r] [gran-saia^r], *s.* Abuelo.

grandson ['grænsʌn] [gran-san], *s.* Nieto.

grandstand ['grændstænd] [grand-stand], *s.* Gradería principal para observar espectáculos o pasar revista.

grand-uncle [grænd'ʌŋkl] [gran-an-kel], *sm.* El tío del padre o de la madre; el hermano del abuelo o de la abuela.

grange [greɪndʒ] [greinch], *s.* 1. Granja, cortijo, alquería, hacienda, casa de labranza. 2. *(Ant.)* Granero.

granger ['greɪndʒə^r] [grein-cha^r], *s. (E.U.)* 1. Individuo de la sociedad llamada **Patrons of Husbandry** (Patronos de la Agricultura). 2. Patán, labrador despectivo.

granite ['grænɪt] [gra-nit], *s. (Min.)* Granito.

granitic, granitical [grə'nɪtɪk] [gra-ni-tik], *a.* Granítico, semejante al granito o formado de él.

granivorous [ˌgrænɪ'vərəs] [gra-ni-vo-ros], *a.* Granívoro, que se alimenta de granos.

granny ['grænɪ] [gra-ni], *sf. (Fest.)* Abuela; comadre, vieja.

grant [grɑ:nt] [grant], *va.* 1. Conceder, asentir o convenir en lo que otro dice o afirma. 2. Conceder, dar, otorgar, hacer merced y gracia de alguna cosa. 3. Conferir, transferir, transmitir el título de una propiedad, etc. **To take for granted,** presuponer, dar por supuesto. **To grant** o **allow for argument's** o **peace' sake,** dar de barato.

grant, *s.* 1. Concesión, don, dádiva, donación; permiso; privilegio. 2. Concesión, el acto de asentir o convenir en una cosa. 3. *(For.)* Documento que confiere un privilegio o transmite el título de una propiedad.

grantable ['grɑ:ntəbl] [gran-ta-bol], *a.* Capaz de ser concedido; dable, permisible.

grantee [grɑ:n'tiː] [gran-ti], *s.* Concesionario, donatario, el que recibe alguna concesión.

grantor [grɑ:n'tɔː^r] [gran-to^r], *s.* Cesionario, el que concede alguna cosa.

granular ['grænjʊlə^r] [gra-niu-la^r], **granulary** ['grænjʊlərɪ] [gra-niu-la-ri], *a.* Granular, granoso, granujoso.

granulate ['grænjʊleɪt] [gra-niu-leit], **n.** Granularse, formarse en granos pequeños. *-va.* Granular, granear, levantar grano en alguna cosa.

granulation ['grænjʊ'leɪʃən] [gra-niu-lei-shon], *s.* 1. Granulación, la acción de granular o granularse. 2. Superficie granulada. 3. *(Med.)* Encarnación, desarrollo de tejido en una herida en vías de curación.

granule ['grænjuːl] [gra-niul], *s.* Granillo, gránulo.

granulous ['grænjʊləs] [gra-niu-los], *a.* Granuloso, granilloso, granujoso.

grape [greɪp] [greip], *s.* 1. Uva. **Bunch of grapes,** racimo de uvas. 2. Vid, planta trepadora que produce las uvas. 3. *(Mil.)* V. GRAPE-SHOT. **To gather grapes,** vendimiar. **Grape-sugar,** glucosa, dextrosa. **Grape-vine,** vid, parra.

grapefruit ['greɪpfruːt] [greip-frut], *s.* Toronja.

grapeless ['greɪplɪs] [greip-les], *a.* Sin uva.

grapery ['greɪpərɪ] [grei-pe-ri], *s.* Invernadero o criadero de uvas.

grape-shot ['greɪpʃɒt] [greip-shot], *s.* Balas encadenadas, balas enramadas, metralla.

grape-stone ['greɪpstəʊn] [greip-stoun], *s.* Granuja, la simiente de la uva.

graph [grɑ:f] [graf], *s.* Gráfica, diagrama.

graphic ['græfɪk] [gra-fik], **graphical** ['græfɪkəl] [gra-fi-kal], *a.* 1. Gráfico, representado por medio de dibujos o figuras. 2. Delineado o descrito de un modo pintoresco. 3. Notado en letras; escrito, impreso o grabado; que pertenece al arte de escribir.

graphically ['græfɪkəlɪ] [gra-fi-ka-li], *adv.* Gráficamente, de un modo pintoresco.

graphite ['græfaɪt] [gra-fait], *s. (Min.)* Grafito, plombagina.

graphology [græ'fɒlədʒɪ] [gra-fo-lo-yi], *s.* Grafología, estudio psicológico de la escritura.

graphometer [græ'fɒmɪtə^r] [gra-fo-mi-ta^r], *s.* Grafómetro, instrumento para levantar planos.

grapline ['græplaɪn] [gra-plain], **grapnel** ['græpnəl] [grap-nel], *s. (Mar.)* 1. Anclote, ancla pequeña. 2. Arpeo, cloque, gancho para atracar y abordar.

grapple ['græpl] [gra-pel], *va.* Agarrar, asir; amarrar, tener firmemente. *-vn.* Agarrarse, venirse a las manos. **To grapple and board,** *(Mar.)* Atracarse, aferrarse o abordarse para pelear.

grapple, *s.* 1. Lucha, riña, pelea. 2. Arpeo, instrumento con que se asegura o agarra un buque a otro. 3. Cloque, rastra.

grappling ['græplɪŋ] [gra-plin], *s. (Mar.)* Rezón. **To warp with graplings,** *(Mar.)* Espiar con rezones. **Grapplingiron,** cloque, arpeo de abordaje.

grasp ['grɑ:sp] [grasp], *va.* 1. Empuñar, asir, agarrar. 2. Apoderarse, tomar y tener en posesión de uno. 3. Alcanzar, comprender, saber. *-vn.* Esforzarse por agarrar; asir. **To grasp at,** querer alcanzar, intentar, ambicionar. **Grasp all,**

lose all, quien mucho abarca poco aprieta; el que todo lo quiere todo lo pierde.

grasp, s. 1. Asimiento, agarro, la acción de agarrar. 2. Puño, puñado; garras.

grasper ['grɑːspəʳ] [gras-paʳ], s. Agarrador.

grass [grɑːs] [gras], s. 1. Hierba, herbaje, plantas con que se alimentan los ganados. 2. Césped, verde. 3. *(Bot.)* Cualquiera planta de las gramíneas. **Grass cloth,** batista de Cantón. **Canary grass,** alpiste. **Grass widow,** mujer separada temporalmente de su marido, o abandonada por él; también la mujer divorciada. **Grass-widower,** marido separado de su mujer. **To let the grass grow under one's feet,** perder el tiempo, haraganear.

grass, va. 1. Cubrir de hierba. 2. Extender sobre el césped; blanquear lino. 3. Apacentar los ganados. -vn. *(Des.)* Criar hierba.

grass-green ['grɑːsˌgriːn] [gras-grin], a. Verde como la hierba.

grass-grown ['grɑːsˌgrəʊn] [gras-groun], a. Cubierto con hierba o herbaje.

grasshopper ['grɑːsˌhɒpəʳ] [gras-jo-paʳ], s. 1. Langosta, saltamontes, saltón, insecto ortóptero. 2. Palanca de pianoforte.

grassless ['grɑːslɪs] [gras-les], a. Sin hierba.

grass-plot, grass-plat ['grɑːsplɒt] [gras-plot], s. 1. Prado, terreno cubierto de hierba; batey (Cuba). 2. *(Poét.)* La verde alfombra.

grassy ['grɑːsɪ] [gra-si], a. Herboso, abundante y lleno de hierba; herbáceo, parecido a la hierba.

grate [greɪt] [greit], s. 1. Reja, verja, rejilla, rejado o enrejado. 2. Fogón de rejas, brasero, enrejado de hierro; estufa.

grate, va. 2. Rallar, desmenuzar alguna cosa estregándola con el rallo. 2. Rallar, molestar, fastidiar. 3. Rechinar, formar o hacer ruido desapacible. **To grate the teeth,** rechinar los dientes. 4. Enrejar. -vn. 1. Rozarse o estregarse una cosa con otra de modo que se eche a perder. 2. Producir una impresión desagradable, causar irritación mental. **To grate up,** cerrar con rejas. **To grate,** *(Fam.)* Desollar, atormentar.

grateful ['greɪtfʊl] [greit-ful], a. 1. Grato, agradecido, reconocido. 2. Gustoso, agradable, bienvenido.

gratefully ['greɪtfəlɪ] [greit-fu-li], adv. Agradecidamente; gratamente.

gratefulness ['greɪtfʊlnɪs] [greit-ful-nes], s. 1. Gratitud, agradecimiento. 2. Agrado, gusto.

grater ['greɪtəʳ] [grei-taʳ], s. Rallo, especie de lima basta.

gratification [grætɪfɪˈkeɪʃən] [gra-ti-fi-kei-shon], s. 1. Gusto, placer, deleite. **For the gratification of,** por dar gusto a. 2. Agrado, gusto.

gratify ['grætɪfaɪ] [gra-ti-fai], va. 1. Satisfacer, cumplir; contentar, dar gusto, agradar. 2. Gratificar, premiar, recompensar.

grating ['greɪtɪŋ] [grei-tin], pa. Discordante, mal sonante; rudo, duro, penoso; ofensivo, áspero. **It must have been grating to his feelings,** eso ha debido de serle muy penoso.

gratings ['greɪtɪŋz] [grei-tins], s. pl. *(Mar.)* Ajedrez o jareta, red de cabos o enrejado de madera debajo del cual se pone la gente para pelear con más resguardo. **Gratings of the head,** *(Mar.)* enjaretado de proa. **Iron gratings,** enrejado de hierro.

gratingly ['greɪtɪŋlɪ] [grei-tin-li], adv. Ásperamente.

gratis ['grɑːtɪs] [gra-tis], adv. Gratis, de balde.

gratitude ['grætɪtjuːd] [gra-ti-tiud], s. Gratitud, agradecimiento, reconocimiento.

gratuitous [grəˈtjuːtəs] [gra-tui-tos], a. Gratuito, voluntario, sin prueba.

gratuitously [grəˈtjuːtəslɪ] [gra-tui-tos-li], .adv. Gratuitamente, de gracia; sin prueba.

gratuity [grəˈtjuːtɪ] [gra-tui-ti], s. Gratificación, recompensa, remuneración.

gratulate [grəˈtjuːleɪt] [gra-tu-leit], va. *(Ant.)* Congratular, dar el parabién, felicitar.

gratulation [grætjuːˈleɪʃən] [gra-tu-lei-shon], s. Congratulación, parabién, enhorabuena.

gratulatory [grəˈtjuːlətərɪ] [gra-tu-la-to-ri], a. Congratulatorio. **Gratulatory letters,** cartas de enhorabuena.

gravamen [grəˈveɪmen] [gra-vei-men], s. *(For.)* Agravio, la parte esencial de una queja.

grave [greɪv] [greiv], va. *(pret. GRAVED, pp. GRAVED o GRAVEN).* 1. Grabar, esculpir, imprimir alguna cosa. 2. *(Mar.)* Despalmar, limpiar la embarcación, embrearla y darle sebo. -vn. Grabar, dibujar o delinear en alguna cosa dura.

grave, s. 1. Sepultura, hoya, huesas donde se sepulta un cadáver; sepultero, tumba. 2. Cualquier sitio de destrucción y ruina. 3. Muerte; en la Biblia, el lugar de los muertos, hades.

grave, a. 1. Grave, serio, circunspecto. 2. Grave, importante, arduo, difícil. 3. Sencillo, modesto, honesto. 4. *(Mús.)* Grave, bajo, profundo en tono; de muy lento movimiento. 5. *(Gram.)* Grave, el acento opuesto al agudo.

grave-clothes ['greɪvklɒðs] [greiv-klozs], s. pl. Mortaja.

grave-digger ['greɪvˌdɪɡəʳ] [greiv-di-gaʳ], **grave-maker** ['greɪvˌmeɪkəʳ] [greiv-mei-kaʳ], s. Sepulturero, enterrador.

gravel ['grævəl] [gra-vel], s. 1. Cascajo, arena gruesa. 2. La arenilla que se forma en los riñones o en la vejiga; mal de piedra. **Gravel-pit,** arenaria, hoyo de donde se extrae el cascajo. **Gravel walk,** paseo arenoso, cubierto de arena gruesa.

gravel, va. 1. Llenar o cubrir alguna cosa con cascajo. 2. Enmarañar, confundir, inquietar, embarazar. 3. Lastimar el pie del caballo la arena metida entre la herradura.

graveless ['grævəlɪs] [gra-ve-les], a. Insepulto.

gravelly ['grævəlɪ] [gra-ve-li], a. Arenisco, cascajoso.

gravely ['greɪvlɪ] [greiv-li], adv. Seriamente, modestamente.

graven ['greɪvən] [grei-ven], pp. irr. de TO GRAVE. Esculpido, grabado.

graveness ['greɪvənɪs] [grei-ve-nes], s. Gravedad, seriedad, circunspección, compostura.

graver ['greɪvəʳ] [grei-vaʳ], s. 1. Grabador, escultor, cincelador. 2. Buril, instrumento de acero que usan los grabadores.

graves ['greɪvz] [greivs], s. pl. Residuo o sedimento del sebo derretido. (Var. de GREAVES).

gravestone ['greɪvstəʊn] [greiv-stoun], s. Lápida sepulcral; monumento fúnebre.

graveyard ['greɪvjɑːd] [greiv-yard], s. Cementerio, lugar descubierto destinado a enterrar cadáveres.

gravid ['grævɪd] [gra-vid], a. Preñada; embarazada, en cinta.

gravidity [græˈvɪdɪtɪ] [gra-vi-di-ti], s. Gravidez, embarazo, preñez.

gravimeter ['grævɪˌmiːtəʳ] [gra-vi-mi-taʳ], s. Gravímetro.

gravimetry ['grævɪmɪtrɪ] [gra-vi-mi-tri], s. Gravimetría, determinación de pesos y densidades.

graving ['greɪvɪŋ] [grei-vin], s. 1. Grabado. 2. Impresión profunda hecha en el ánimo por cualquiera cosa o suceso.

gravitate ['grævɪteɪt] [gra-vi-teit], vn. Gravitar, tender un cuerpo al centro de atracción.

gravitation [grævɪˈteɪʃən] [gra-vi-tei-shon], s. 1. Gravitación, la tendencia de los cuerpos a atraerse mutuamente; la fuerza con que todos los cuerpos se atraen. 2. Tendencia mental o moral hacia algún objeto o idea. 3. Gravedad.

gravity ['grævɪtɪ] [gra-vi-ti], s. 1. *(Fís.)* Gravedad, pesantez. 2. Gravedad, enormidad, seriedad. **Gravity feed,** alimentación a gravedad.

gravure ['grævjəʳ] [gra-viuaʳ], s. Clisé, plancha clisada para imprimir grabados.

gravy ['greɪvɪ] [gra-vi], s. 1. Salsa en general. 2. Jugo que despide de sí la carne cuando no está muy consumida por el fuego; pringue, caldillo, unto.

gray, grey [greɪ] [grei], s. 1. Gris, color que resulta de la mezcla del blanco y negro. 2. Animal gris; se aplica a los caballos, al tejón, a una especie de salmón, al pardillo, etc. -a. 1. Gris, pardo. **Gray cloth,** paño mezclilla. 2. Cano, encanecido. 3. Oscuro como cuando amanece o anochece. **Dark-gray,** gris oscuro. **Gray-eyed,** de ojos grises. **Gray-**

headed, canoso, encanecido, envejecido. **Gray horse,** caballo pardo.

graybeard ['greɪbɜːd] [grei-biad], *s.* Barbicano: hombre ya entrado en años.

grayfly ['greɪflaɪ] [grei-flai], *s.* Trompetilla, especie de mosca parda.

grayhound ['greɪhaɔnd] [grei-jaund], *s. V.* GREY-HOUND.

grayish ['greɪʃ] [greish], *a.* Pardusco; entrecano, grisáceo, gríseo.

grayling ['greɪlɪŋ] [grei-lin], *s.* (*Ict.*) Umbla.

grayness ['greɪnɪs] [grei-nes], *s.* La calidad de ser gris, encanecimiento.

graze [greɪz] [greis], *vn.* 1. Pacer, apacentarse el ganado (pasture). 2. Dar pasto o surtir de hierba. 3. Rozar, tocar ligeramente. *-va.* 1. Pastorear, llevar o conducir el ganado al campo o a pacer, apacentar. 2. Dar hierba a los animales; dar forraje a los caballos. 3. Tocar o herir ligeramente (touch lightly) y pasar o ir más allá. 4. Pasar volando, rasar la tierra.

graze, *s.* 1. Rozamiento, la acción de rozar (rub). 2. Roce o tocamiento ligero; raya ligera, raspadura. 3. Pasto, apacentamiento.

grazer ['greɪzəʳ] [grei-saʳ], *s.* Animal que pace o se apacienta.

grazier ['greɪzɪəʳ] [grei-siaʳ], *s.* Ganadero.

grazing ['greɪzɪŋ] [grei-sin], *s.* Apacentamiento; pasto, dehesa, tierra de pasto (grass, pasture).

grease [griːs] [gris], *va.* 1. Engrasar, pringar, untar, manchar con gordura o grasa (stain with grase). 2. Corromper o sobornar con dádivas o dinero: se dice familiarmente untar o untar las manos.

grease, *s.* 1. Grasa, manteca, sebo, pringue. 2. Soborno.

greaser ['griːsəʳ] [gri-saʳ], *s.* 1. El que o lo que unta con grasa. 2. (E.U. del Oeste) Mejicano o hispanoamericano; (despreciativamente).

greasily ['griːsɪlɪ] [gri-si-li], *adv.* Grasamente, untuosamente, pringosamente.

greasiness ['griːsɪnɪs] [gri-si-nes], *s.* Pringue, gordura, mugre, untuosidad (dirt, grime).

greasy ['griːsɪ] [gri-si], *a.* 1. Grasiento, craso, pringado, gordo (oily). 2. (*Vet.*) Atacado de las aguajas. 3. (*Des.*) Indecente, poco delicado, grosero.

great [greɪt] [greit], *a.* 1. De gran volumen, grueso, vasto, enorme, desmedido (vaste, huge). 2. Mucho, numeroso. 3. De larga duración, prolongado (long). 4. Gran, grande, considerable, importante (big). 5. Principal; poderoso, ilustre, eminente, noble, magnánimo (main, powerful). 6. Familiar, íntimo. 7. Adorable, admirable, maravilloso, sublime (marvelous). 8. Imponente, orgulloso, amenazador (tremendous, impressing). 9. Lleno, henchido; preñado. 10. Indica la tercera generación ascendente, o de los bisabuelos, y cada una de las que la preceden. **A great deal,** mucho, gran cantidad. **A great many,** muchos. **A great while,** largo tiempo. **To make greater,** agrandar, ensanchar o hacer mayor una cosa. **The great,** los grandes. **Great Dane,** el mastín danés, perro de gran tamaño y fuerza. **Great gun,** cañón de artillería. **Great-grandson,** biznieto. **Great-granddaughter,** biznieta. **Great-grandfather,** bisabuelo. **Great-grandmother,** bisabuela. **Great-great-grandfather,** tercer abuelo o tatarabuelo. **Great-great-grandmother,** tercera abuela o tatarabuela. *-s.* (*Des.*) Todo por junto, por entero. **By the great,** (*Des.*) por junto, por mayor.

great-bellied [greɪt'belɪd] [greit-be-lid], *a.* 1. Barrigudo. 2. Preñada.

great-coat ['greɪtkəɔt] [greit-kout], *s.* Levitón, sobretodo grueso.

greaten ['greɪtən] [grei-ten], *va.* Agrandar, engrandecer. *-vn.* Crecer, aumentarse.

great-hearted [greɪt'hɑːtɪd] [greit-jar-tid], *a.* Animado, osado, no abatido; de alma grande.

greatly ['greɪtlɪ] [greit-li], *adv.* 1. Muy, mucho. 2. Noblemente, ilustremente. 3. Grandemente, magnánimamente.

greatness ['greɪtnɪs] [greit-nes], *s.* 1. Grandeza, grandor, extensión. 2. Grandeza, majestad, nobleza, dignidad, poder.. 3. Magnanimidad, grandeza de alma. 4. Grandeza, fausto.

greaves ['griːvz] [grivs], *s. pl.* 1. Grebas, canilleras, piezas de armadura que cubrían las piernas. 2. Chicharrones, residuo de la grasa de cerdo derretida y del sebo.

grebe ['griːb] [grib], *s.* Colimbo, ave palmípeda con cuatro dedos y sin plumas en la cola.

Grecian ['griːʃən] [gri-shan], *s.* 1. Griego. 2. Helenista, judío que sabía la lengua griega. 3. Helenista, el que está bien instruido en el griego. *-a.* Griego.

grecianize ['griːʃənaɪz] [gri-sha-nais], *vn.* Grecizar, greguizar.

grecize ['griːʃaɪz] [gri-sais], *va.* Grecizar, dar a las palabras o frases forma griega; traducir en griego. *-vn.* Imitar a los griegos, llegar a parecerse a ellos.

grecism ['griːʃən] [gri-shan], *s.* Grecismo, helenismo, idiotismo de la lengua griega.

greed [griːd] [grid], *s.* 1. Codicia, avaricia, voracidad, gula (covetousness). 2. *V.* GREEDINESs.

greedily ['griːdɪlɪ] [gri-di-li], *adv.* Vorazmente, ansiosamente; vehementemente.

greediness ['griːdɪnɪs] [gri-di-nes], *s.* Voracidad, ansia; gula, hambre; codicia.

greedy ['griːdɪ] [gri-di], *a.* 1. Voraz, insaciable, goloso. 2. Ansioso, deseoso, apasionado, avaro (passioned, anxious). **Greedy-gut,** (*Vulg.*) Glotón.

Greek [griːk] [grik], *s.* 1. Griego, el natural de Grecia. 2. Griego, la lengua de los naturales de Grecia. 3. Helenista, literato versado en el idioma griego. 4. (*Fam.*) Lenguaje no inteligible. **It is all Greek to me,** para mí eso es griego o gringo. *-a.* Griego, lo que pertenece a Grecia y a sus habitantes.

greekess ['griːkɪs] [gri-kis], *sf.* Griega, mujer natural de Grecia.

greek-fire ['griːkfaɪəʳ] [grik-faiaʳ], *s.* Fuego griego, mixto incendiario que arde sobre el agua, inventado por los griegos para quemar las naves.

greekish ['griːkɪʃ] [gri-kish], *a.* Griego.

greekling ['griːklɪŋ] [gri-klin], *s.* Un autor griego de poco mérito: vocablo despectivo.

green [griːn] [grin], *a.* 1. Verde. 2. Verde, lo que aún no está maduro (immature, unripe). 3. Verde, floreciente, fresco, reciente, acabado de hacer (fresh). 4. Pálido, descolorido. 5. Crudo, lo que no está cocido. 6. Joven, tierno, novicio, inexperto. *-s.* 1. Verde, el color de las plantas. 2. Prado o pradera; lugar cubierto de hierba en un pueblo de campo. 3. Afeite, color o afeite verde o verdoso. **Bottle-green,** verde botella. **Sea-green,** verde mar. **Greens,** verduras, todo género de hortaliza. **Green corn,** maíz tierno; (*Mex.*) elote; (*Ingl.*) trigo en hierba. **Green hand,** novicio, principiante. **Green-laver o green-sloke,** alga marina comestible, de la familia de las ulváceas. Ulva lactuca. **Green vitriol,** caparrosa, vitriolo verde, sulfato de hierro. **Green ware,** loza cruda. **Green-cloth,** mayordomía, sección del servicio de la casa real inglesa, encargada principalmente del aprovisionamiento de palacio. **Green-colored,** pálido, enfermizo. **Green-eyed,** lo que tiene ojos verdes.

green. *va.* Teñir de verde, dar color verde a alguna cosa, verdear.

greenback ['griːnbæk] [grin-bak], *s.* Papel moneda del gobierno de los Estados Unidos, o de los bancos nacionales; se llama así por el color verde de la impresión en el reverso.

greenfinch ['griːnfɪntʃ] [grin-finch], *s.* (*Orn.*) Verdecillo, verderón o verderol.

greengage ['griːngeɪdʒ] [grin-gueich], *s.* Ciruela verdal.

greengrocer ['griːnˌgrəɔsəʳ] [grin-grou-saʳ], *s.* Verdulero.

greengrocery ['griːnˌgrəɔsərɪ] [grin-grou-se-ri], *s.* Verdulería, tienda de verduras y frutas.

greenheaded ['griːnhedɪd] [grin-je-did], *a.* Inexperto, ignorante.

greenhorn ['griːnhɔːn] [grin-jorn], *s.* (*Fam.*) 1. Persona sin experiecia, paleto. 2. Bobo, primo, incauto, persona fácil de engañar.

greenhouse ['gri:nhaʊs] [grin--jaus], *s.* Invernáculo para plantas tiernas.

greening ['gri:nɪŋ] [gri-nin], *s.* 1. El acto de volverse verde. 2. Manzana verde de diferentes variedades.

greenish ['gri:nɪʃ] [gri-nish], *a.* Verdoso, verdusco.

Greenland ['gri:nlənd] [grin-land], *s.* Groenlandia.

Greenlander ['gri:nləndər] [grin-lan-darʳ], *s.* Groelandés.

Greelandic ['gri:nləndɪk] [grin-lan-dik], *a.* Greolandés.

greenly ['gri:nlɪ] [grin-li], *adv.* 1. Nuevamente, recientemente. 2. Sin madurez, antes de madurar.

greenness ['gri:nnɪs] [grin-nes], *s.* Verdín, verdor, vigor, frescura; falta de experiencia; novedad.

greenroom ['gri:nrʊm] [grin-rum], *s.* 1. Hogar, salón general de un teatro donde esperan los actores que han de salir a la escena. 2. Cuarto destinado a contener loza cruda o tela acabada de hacer.

greensand ['gri:nsænd] [grin-sand], *s.* (*Geol.*) Arenisca verde; una de las capas del período cretáceo.

greensickness ['gri:nsɪknɪs] [grin-sik-nes], *s.* Clorosis, colores pálidos, una enfermedad de las jóvenes.

greenstall ['gri:nstɔ:l] [grin-stol], *s.* Puesto o tabla para vender frutas y verduras.

greenstone ['gri:nstəʊn] [grin-stoun], *s.* (*Geol.*) Diorita o dolerita.

greensward ['gri:nzwɔ:d] [grins-ued], *s.* El césped bien verde y tupido; alfombra de hierba.

greenwood ['gri:nwʊ:d] [grin-wud], *s.* Bosque verde; selva frondosa.

greet [gri:t] [grit], *va.* Saludar, hablar cortésmente a uno, llamarle. **Greet her in my name,** salúdela Ud. de mi parte. *-vn.* Encontrarse y saludarse.

greet, *vn.* (*Sco.*) Llorar, verter lágrimas, lamentarse.

greeter ['gri:tər] [gri-tarʳ], *s.* Saludador, el que saluda.

greeting ['gri:tɪŋ] [gri-tin], *s.* 1. Salutación, saludos. **Greetings!** ¡salud! 2. (*Sco.*) Lloro.

gregarian [grɪ'gæriən] [gri-ga-rian], *a.* Gregario, gregal.

gregarious [grɪ'gæriəs] [gri-ga-rios], *a.* Gregario, gregal, rebañego.

gregariously [grɪ'gæriəslɪ] [gri-ga-rios-li], *adv.* A manadas, gregariamente.

gregariousness [grɪ'gæriəsnɪs] [gri-ga-rios-nes], *s.* La propiedad de andar en manadas o rebaños.

gregorian [grɪ'gɔːriən] [gri-go-rian], *a.* Gregoriano.

gremial ['gremiəl] [gre-mial], *a.* 1. Lo que pertenece al regazo. 2. Perteneciente a gremios.

grenade [grɪ'neɪd] [gri-neid], *s.* Granada, granada real, granada de mano.

grenadier [ˌgrenə'dɪəʳ] [gre-na-diaʳ], *s.* Granadero.

grenadine ['grenədi:n] [gre-na-din], *s.* Granadina, tela delgada como la gasa que se usa para los vestidos de mujer.

grew [gru:] [gru], *pret.* de TO GROW.

grey [greɪ] [grei], *a.* Gris, V. GRAY.

greyhound ['greɪhaʊnd] [grei-jaund], *s.* 1. Galgo, galga; lebrel. 2. (*Neol.*) Vapor de alta mar muy veloz.

grice ['graɪs] [grais], *s.* Gorrino, lechón, cochinillo; osezno, cachorro.

grid [grɪd] [grid], *s.* 1. Parrilla, reja, rejilla serie de barras paralelas. 2. Criba grande de alambre para cerner el mineral.

griddle ['grɪdl] [gri-del], *s.* 1. Tartera para cocer pasteles. 2. Tapadera para el hornillo de una estufa de cocina. **Griddle-cake,** pastelillo cocido en una tartera; particularmente fritura ligera de trigo sarraceno.

gridiron ['grɪdˌaɪən] [gri-daion], *s.* 1. Parrillas. 2. (*Mar.*) Andamiada, basada de esqueleto, para reparar las embarcaciones.

grief [gri:f] [grif], *s.* 1. Pesar, pesadumbre, aflicción, pena (afflict, pain); dolor moral, como el causado por una desgracia. 2. Lo que causa pesar o perjuicio. *V.* GRIEVANCE.

griefless ['gri:flɪs] [grif-les], *a.* Exento de pesadumbres o penas; sin agravio.

griefshot ['gri:fʃɒt] [grif-shot], *a.* Traspasado de dolor, apesadumbrado.

griefstricken ['gri:fˌstrɪkən] [grif-stri-ken], *a.* Desolado, apesadumbrado, desconsolado.

grievance ['gri:vəns] [gri-vans], *s.* Pesar, molestia, agravio, injusticia, perjuicio, pesadumbre. **To redress grievances,** reparar agravios.

grieve [gri:v] [griv], *va.* Agraviar, afligir, oprimir; apesadumbrar (pain); herir la delicadeza de alguien. *-vn.* Apesadumbrarse, tomar pesadumbre, entristecerse, afligirse (sad). **It grieves me to hear it,** lo deploro, siento saberlo. **To grieve oneself to death,** morirse de pena.

griever ['gri:vəʳ] [gri-vaʳ], *s.* El que causa dolor.

grievingly ['gri:vɪŋlɪ] [gri-vin-li], *adv.* Apesaradamente.

grievous ['gri:vəs] [gri-vos], *a.* 1. Penoso, doloroso, lastimoso (painful). 2. Provocativo, ofensivo. 3. Grave, enorme; atroz, cruel (cruel).

grievously ['gri:vəslɪ] [gri-vos-li], *adv.* 1. Penosamente, con dolor y pena, molestamente. 2. Miserablemente, lastimosamente, tristemente.

grievousness ['gri:vəsnɪs] [gri-vos-nes], *s.* Dolor, pena, aflicción; atrocidad, calamidad, enormidad.

griffin ['grɪfɪn] [gri-fin], **griffon** ['grɪfən] [gri-fon], *s.* 1. Grifo. 2. (*Ornit.*) Buitre (vulture). 3. Dueña vigilante.

griffin-like ['grɪfɪnlaɪk] [gri-fin-laik], *a.* Rapaz.

griffon ['grɪfən] [gri-fon], *s.* (*Mit.*) Grifo. 2. Perro de cierta raza.

grig [grɪg] [grig], *s.* 1. Cigarra, grillo. **As merry as a grig,** alegre como un grillo. 2. Anguila pequeña. 3. Saltamontes.

grill [grɪl] [gril], *va.* 1. Asar en parrillas. 2. Atormentar, molestar.

grillade ['grɪlɑ:d] [gri-lad], *s.* Cualquier cosa asada en parrillas; carbonada.

grillage ['grɪleɪdʒ] [gri-leich], *s.* Emparrillado, zampeado. 2. Fondo de una blonda o encaje.

grille [grɪl] [gril], *s.* Enrejado, reja, calado de adorno.

grillroom ['grɪlrʊm] [gril-rum], *s.* Restaurante o comedor originalmente para alimentos asados.

grilse [grɪls] [grils], *s.* (*Esco.*) Esguín, salmón de poco tiempo, cuando por primera vez regresa del mar y sube por los ríos.

grim [grɪm] [grim], *a.* 1. Disforme, horrendo. 2. Torvo, ceñudo, severo, regañón. 3. Inflexible; formidable.

grimace [grɪ'meɪs] [gri-meis], *s.* Visaje, mueca, gesto.

grimalkin [grɪ'mælkɪn] [gri-mal-kin], *s.* Gatazo, gato viejo.

grime [graɪm] [graim], *s.* Tizne, mugre, porquería.

grime, *va.* Ensuciar, llenar de mugre.

grim-faced [grɪm'feɪst] [grim-feist], **grim-visaged,** *a.* Malcarado.

grimly ['grɪmlɪ] [grim-li], *a.* Espantoso, horrible (awful); ceñudo. *-adv.* Horriblemente, ásperamente.

grimness ['grɪmnɪs] [grim-nes], *s.* Grima, horror, espanto (displeasure, annoyance).

grimy ['graɪmɪ] [grai-mi], *a.* Tiznado, sucio, manchado, mugriento (dirty).

grin [grɪn] [grin], *vn.* Gestear, hacer gestos con la boca mostrando los dientes.

grin, *s.* Mueca de dolor, visaje (face); amplia y burlona sonrisa.

grind [graɪnd] [graind], *va.* (*pret.* y *pp.* GROUND). 1. Moler, pulverizar, quebrantar alguna cosa haciéndola polvo. 2. Amolar, afilar. 3. Estregar, refregar una cosa con otra. 4. Mascar. 5. Moler, molestar, agobiar, oprimir. 6. (*Fam.*) Estudiar con ahinco; también, burlar a alguno. *-vn.* 1. Hacer andar la rueda de un molino. 2. Moverse o andar alrededor como la rueda de un molino. 3. Pulirse, quedar alisado o afilado por el roce; deslustrar el vidrio. **Steel grinds easily,** el acero se afila (o se pule) fácilmente. **Ground glass,** vidrio deslustrado, opaco.

grind, *a.* 1. Molienda, trituración. 2. Rechinamiento de dientes. 3. (*Fam.*) Trabajo continuado. 4. Empollón.

grinder ['graɪndəʳ] [grain-daʳ], *s.* 1. Molinero, molendero. 2. Muela, piedra para moler y también la que sirve para afilar instrumentos cortantes. 3. Molino, molinillo. 4. Amolador. 5.

Muela, uno de los últimos dientes de la quijada. 6. Diente, en desprecio para denotar los de un tragón.

grindery ['graɪndərɪ] [grain-de-ri], *s.* Tienda de amolador, para afilar herramientas, navajas, etc.

grinding ['graɪndɪŋ] [grain-din], *s.* Pulverización, molienda; amoladura; bruñimiento, pulidura. -pa. de GRIND. **Grinding lathe,** torno de pulir. **Grinding plate,** disco pesado de hierro que gira sobre un eje vertical y se usa para pulir el vidrio.

grindstone ['graɪndstəʊn] [graind-stoun], *s.* 1. Amoladera. 2. Muela, la piedra en que se afilan los cuchillos, tijeras y otros instrumentos cortantes.

gringo ['grɪŋgəʊ] [grin-gou], *s. (Desp.)* Inglés o norteamericano.

grinner ['grɪnər] [gri-naʳ], *s.* El que se sonríe enseñando los dientes.

grinningly ['grɪnɪŋlɪ] [grai-nin-li], *adv.* Con sonrisa como una mueca, enseñando los dientes.

grip [grɪp] [grip], *s.* 1. Apretón de manos, acción de asir o aprehender. 2. Modo especial de tomar y oprimir la mano, para reconocerse los individuos de ciertas asociaciones. 3. *V.* GRIP-SACK. 4. Asidero, puño, la parte por donde se ase alguna cosa. 5. Garra (fiador, retén), aparato para agarrar el cable de tracción de un ferrocarril o soltarlo. 6. Capacidad de agarrar y retener, o de alcanzar, comprender. **Gripman,** empleado que maneja el fiador en un carro movido por cable. **Gripsack,** (Fam. E.U.) Saquillo, maleta ligera. 7. *(Med.)* Gripe. 8. **To come to grips with,** luchar cuerpo a cuerpo.

grip, *va.* Agarrar, empuñar, asir, cerrar. -*vn.* Tener firmemente, v. gr. una ancla.

gripe [graɪp] [graip], *va.* 1. Agarrar, asir, cerrar, empuñar; pellizcar, dar pellizcos. 2. Dar cólico o retortijones de tripas. 3. Afligir, acongojar el ánimo de alguno, apurarlo. -*vn.* 1. Padecer cólico. 2. Sisar, ganar dinero por medio de exacciones mezquinas.

gripe, *s.* 1. Toma, la acción de tomar; presa; apretón de la mano. 2. Agarro, la acción de agarrar o asir con la mano o con las garras. 3. Presión, la acción de apretar una cosa con otra. 4. Uña, garra, zarpa. 5. Agarradero, asidero, mango. 6. Opresión, aprieto, apuro. **Gripe of an anchor,** *(Mar.)* Tenedor de ancla. **Gripes,** *pl.* (a) Dolor cólico, retortijón de tripas. (b) *(Mar.)* Obenques o bozas de lancha.

griper ['graɪpər] [grai-paʳ], *s.* Usurero.

griping ['graɪpɪŋ] [grai-pin], *s.* Dolor o retortijón de tripas; aflicción.

gripingly ['graɪpɪŋ] [grai-pin], *adv.* Con dolor de tripas.

grippe, grip [graɪp] [graip], *s.* Gripe (flu), influenza, catarro epidémico, acompañado de serios trastornos del cuerpo y seguido de gran debilidad; se llama vulgarmente trancazo.

gripper ['grɪpər] [gri-paʳ], *s.* El que agarra o sujeta.

gripping ['grɪpɪŋ] [gri-pin], *a.* Muy conmovedor o interesante.

gripsack ['grɪpsæk] [grip-sak], *s.* Maletín, saco de mano.

griseous ['grɪʃəs] [gri-shos], *a.* Grisáceo, pardusco.

griskin ['grɪskɪn] [gris-kin], *s.* Costilla de cerdo.

grisly ['grɪzlɪ] [gris-li], *a.* Espantoso, horroroso, terrible.

grist [grɪst] [grist], *s.* 1. Molienda o grano para moler; de aquí, la harina que se saca de él. 2. Provisión, abasto, suministro. **Grist-mill,** molino harinero.

gristle ['grɪsl] [gri-sel], *s.* Cartílago, ternilla.

gristly ['grɪstlɪ] [grist-li], *a.* Cartilaginoso.

grit [grɪt] [grit], *s.* 1. Partículas ásperas y duras; arena, cascajo. 2. *(Geol.)* Variedad de arenisca de veta silícosa. 3. Firmeza de carácter, particularmente en peligro o contra obstáculos; valor, ánimo. 4. Moyuelo. 5. *pl.* Grano mondado y medio molido; sémola, farro.

grittiness ['grɪtɪnɪs] [gri-ti-nes], *s.* 1. Arenosidad. 2. Ánimo.

gritty ['grɪtɪ] [gri-ti], *a.* 1. Arenoso, lleno de partículas duras. 2. Valeroso, esforzado, animoso.

grizzle ['grɪzl] [gri-sel], *s.* Gris, color entre blanco y negro; mezclilla.

grizzled ['grɪzld] [gri-seld], *a.* Pardusco, mezclado con gris. -*s.* Criba grande para separar piedras gruesas y pequeñas en la explotación hidráulica. **Grizzly bear,** el oso pardo, grande y feroz, de la parte occidental de la América del norte.

grizzly ['grɪzlɪ] [gris-li], *a.* Grisáceo, pardusco.

groan ['grəʊn] [graun], *vn.* 1. Gemir, suspirar, quejarse. 2. Mugir el viento.

groan, *s.* 1. Gemido, suspiro, quejido. 2. Rumor de desaprobación. Mujido del viento.

groaning ['grəʊnɪŋ] [grau-nin], *s.* Lamentación, lamento, quejido (moan, wail); mugido.

groat ['grəʊt] [graut], *s.* Moneda de Inglaterra del valor de cuatro peniques: se usa también esta palabra para expresar una cantidad muy pequeña de dinero. **Groats,** avena o trigo mondado y medio molido.

groatsworth ['grəʊtswɔːθ] [grauts-uorz], *s.* El valor de un **groat,** cuatro peniques.

grocer ['grəʊsər] [grou-saʳ], *s.* Especiero, abacero, el lonjista que vende cacao, té, azúcar, especias, etc. *(Cuba)* Bodeguero. *(Amer.)* Pulpero. *(Mex.)* Tendero. **Grocer's shop,** lonja de especiero, especiería. *(Cuba)* Bodega. *(Amer.)* Pulpería, abacería. *(Mex.)* Tienda de abarrotes, o tienda.

grocery ['grəʊsərɪ] [grou-se-ri], *s.* 1. *(E.U.)* Tienda de comestibles, abacería, lonja. 2. *pl.* **Groceries,** especierías, todo género de comestibles que venden los especieros, víveres; *(Amer.)* abarrotes.

grog [grɒg] [grog], *s.* Grog, mezcla de aguardiente con agua.

groggy ['grɒgɪ] [gro-gui], *a.* 1. Medio borracho, a medios pelos. 2. Que anda irregularmente, v. gr. un caballo. 3. Vacilante: se dice de los púgiles.

grogram ['grəʊgræm] [grou-gram], *s.* Gorgorán, tejido basto de seda.

groin [grɔɪn] [groin], *s.* 1. Ingle. 2. *(Arq.)* Arista de encuentro, esquina viva.

groin, *va. (Arq.)* Formar aristas o esquinas vivas.

groining ['grɔɪnɪŋ] [groi-nin], *s. (Arq.)* Unos ornamentos en el techo interior de las iglesias y edificios llamados góticos.

grommet ['grɒmɪt] [gro-met], *s. (Mar.)* 1. Anillo de cuerda. 2. Roñado o anillo de las velas de estay. **Grommets of the eye-holes,** *(Mar.)* Roñadas de los sollados.

groom [gruːm] [grum], *s.* 1. Mozo de mulas o caballos; palafrenero; antiguamente cualquier criado. 2. Novio, el hombre recién casado. **Grooms-man,** padrino de boda. **Groom of the bedchamber,** ayuda de cámara del rey. **Groom in waiting,** camarero de semana. **Groom of the chamber,** caballerizo de cámara.

groom, *va.* Cuidar, almohazar los caballos.

groove [gruːv] [gruv], *s.* 1. Muesca, encaje, acanaladura, ranura, estría (snot). 2. Rutina, hábito fijo en los actos de la vida diaria (habit).

groove, *va.* Acanalar; hacer muescas, estrías o ranuras.

grope [grəʊp] [group], *vn.* Tentar, andar a tientas. -*va.* 1. Tentar, buscar alguna cosa a oscuras o en donde no se ve. 2. Buscar ciegamente en la oscuridad intelectual, sin guía seguro, ni medios de acierto.

groper ['grəʊpər] [grou-paʳ], *s.* El que tienta o busca a oscuras.

grosbeak ['grɒsbiːk] [gros-bik], *s.* 1. Picogordo, ave. 2. Cardenal, loxia, pájaro.

grosgrain ['grɒsgreɪn] [gros-grein], *s.* Gro. **Grosgrain ribbon,** cinta de gro.

gross [grɒs] [grous], *a.* 1. Grueso, corpulento, espeso, denso (burly, compact, dense). 2. Indecoroso, mal visto; vergonzoso, chocante (shameful); basto, tosco, craso, grosero, obsceno, descortés (rude, discourteous). 3. Lerdo, estúpido. **Gross amount,** importe total. -*s.* (*pl.* GROSS, lo mismo.) 1. Grueso, la parte principal de algún todo. 2. El conjunto, el todo. 3. Gruesa, el número de doce docenas. **To buy o sell by the gross,** vender o comprar al por mayor. **In**

gross, in the gross, en grueso, en conjunto. **Great gross,** doce gruesas o 144 docenas tomadas como unidad. **Small gross,** diez docenas, o 120.

grossly ['grəʊslɪ] [grous-li], *adv.* En bruto; toscamente, groseramente.

gross margin [ˌgrəʊs'mɑːdʒɪn] [grous-mar-chin], *s.* Margen bruto de ganancia.

grossness ['grəʊsnɪs] [grous-nes], *s.* 1. Rudez, grosería. 2. Grosura.

gross profit [ˌgrəʊs'prɒfɪt] [grous-pro-fit], *s.* Ganancia bruta.

grot [grɒt] [grot], *s.* Gruta. *(Poét.) V.* GROTTO.

grotesque [grəʊ'tesk] [grou-tesk], *a.* Grotesco o grutesco, incongruo, desproporcionado.

grotesquely [grəʊ'tesklɪ] [grou-tesk-li], *adv.* Fantásticamente.

grotto ['grɒtəʊ] [gro-tou], *s.* Gruta, caverna (cavern).

grouch ['graʊtʃ] [grauch], *s.* 1. Mal humor. 2. Persona malhumorada, cascarrabias. *-vi.* Refunfuñar, quejarse con mal humor.

groucher ['graʊtʃər] [grau-cha'], *s.* Persona gruñona.

grouchy ['graʊtʃɪ] [grau-chi], *a.* Gruñón, malhumorado.

ground [graʊnd] [graund], *s.* 1. Tierra, terreno, suelo, pavimento (land, terrain). 2. Tierra, país, región, territorio (country). 3. Tierra, heredad, posesión (herity). 4. Suelo, el asiento o poso que dejan los líquidos; en este sentido se usa en plural. 5. Baño, la primera mano del color que se da al lienzo que se ha de pintar. 6. Principio, fundamento, razón fundamental; pie, base, causa, motivo. 7. *(Mil.)* Campo de batalla, el sitio o terreno que ocupa un ejército mientras pelea. 8. Fondo o lo más hondo de alguna cosa. *(Mar.)* Tenedero. 11. Conexión de una corriente eléctrica con la tierra. **Rocky ground,** fondo de piedras. **On, upon the ground,** en tierra, en el suelo. **To break ground,** *(Fig.)* Empezar un trabajo o una empresa. **To be on one's own ground,** ocuparse en aquello en que está uno muy versado. **To fall to the ground,** caer al suelo; *(Fig.)* fracasar, no salir bien de un empeño. **To gain ground,** ganar terreno, adelantar en alguna cosa, hacer progresos. **To give o to lose ground,** perder terreno, retroceder, atrasar. **To stand o to keep one's ground,** mantenerse firme.

ground, *va.* 1. Fundar, zanjar, cimentar, apoyar. 2. Zanjar, establecer, fijar los principios o elementos de alguna ciencia. 3. Poner o sacar a tierra. *-vn. (Mar.)* Tocar, varar.

ground, *pp.* de TO GRIND.

groundage ['graʊndɪdʒ] [graun-dich], *s. (Mar.)* Derecho de puerto.

ground-breaking ['graʊndˌbreɪkɪŋ] [graund-brei-kin], *s.* Iniciación de una obra, colocación de la primera piedra.

ground-control approach, *s. (Aer.)* Acceso dirigido desde tierra.

grounder ['graʊndər] [graun-da'], *s.* En el beisbol, pelota que rueda después de golpeada.

ground-floor [graʊnd'flɔːr] [graund-floa'], *s.* El piso bajo de una casa.

ground hog ['graʊndhɒg] [graund-jog], *s. (Zool.)* Marmota americana.

grounding ['graʊndɪŋ] [graun-din], *s. (Mar.)* El acto de varar o dar en la costa.

ground installations [graʊndˌɪnstə'leɪʃənz] [graund-ins-ta-lei-shons], *s. pl. (Aer.)* Infraestructura.

ground-ivy [graʊnd'aɪvɪ] [graund-ai-vi], *s. (Bot.)* Hiedra terrestre.

groundless ['graʊndlɪs] [graund-les], *a.* Infundado, inmotivado, gratuito.

groundlessly ['graʊndlɪslɪ] [graund-les-li], *adv.* Infundadamente, sin razón, sin motivo.

groundling ['graʊndlɪŋ] [graund-lin], *s.* 1. Lo que habita sobre el suelo, animal terrestre. 2. *(Ict.)* Loche, loja, especie de espirenque de ríos. 3. Hombre vil y abatido.

groundnut ['graʊndnʌt] [graund-nat], *s.* Cacahuete, maní, chufa.

ground-pine [graʊnd'paɪn] [graund-pain], *s. (Bot.)* Camepitios, pinillo.

ground-plan ['graʊndplæn] [graund-plan], *s.* Plano horizontal; delineación del piso bajo de un edificio; bosquejo.

ground-plot ['graʊndplɒt] [graund-plot], *s.* 1. Solar, terreno o sitio en que se construye un edificio. 2. Icnografía o delineación de un edificio.

ground-rent ['graʊndrent] [graund-rent], *s.* La renta que se paga por el privilegio de levantar un edificio en el terreno de otra persona.

ground-room ['graʊndrʊm] [graund-rum], *s.* Cuarto bajo de una casa.

groundsel ['graʊndsɪl] [graund-sil] o **groundsil** ['graʊndsɪl] [graund-sil], *s.* 1. Umbral de puerta. 2. *(Bot.)* Hierba cana.

groundsill ['graʊndsɪl] [graund-sil], *s.* 1. *(Arq.)* Carrera inferior, solera de base. 2. Umbral de puerta.

groundswell ['graʊndswel] [graund-suel], *s.* Mar de leva o de fondo.

ground wire ['graʊndaɪər] [graund-uaia'], *s. (Elec.)* Alambre de tierra.

groundwork ['graʊndwɜːk] [graund-üek], *s.* 1. Base, fundamento, cimiento (foundation). 2. *(Arq.)* Infraestructura. 3. Principios, rudimentos. **To lay a groundwork for,** facilitar.

group ['gruːp] [grup], *s.* 1. Grupo, el conjunto de varias figuras que forman un todo. 2. Grupo, combinación, conjunto de figuras dispuestas en una obra de arte. 3. Grupo, serie, clase. **Group insurance,** seguro colectivo o de grupo.

group, *va.* Agrupar.

grouse [graʊs] [graus], *s.* 1. *(Orn.)* Gallina silvestre, urogallo, perdiz o faisán. 2. Queja, refunfuño (complaint).

grout [graʊt] [graut], *s.* 1. Mortero poco espeso mezclado con casacajo. 2. Harina basta; sémola, farro. 3. *(Bot.)* Especie de manzano. 4. *pl.* Heces, zurrapas, sedimento.

grout, *v.* Rellenar o recubrir con lechada o pasta clara de yeso.

grouty ['graʊtɪ] [grau-ti], *a.* 1. Turbio, fangoso. 2. Regañón, áspero, arisco, intratable.

grove [grəʊv] [grouv], *s.* Arboleda, bosquecillo, boscaje. **Oak grove,** robledal, robledo. **Pine grove,** pinar.

grovel ['grɒvl] [gro-vel], *vn.* 1. Serpear, arrastrarse, andar arrastrando por la tierra. 2. Envilecerse, bajarse.

groveler ['grɒvlər] [gro-ve-la'], *s.* Persona servil, rastrera.

groveling ['grɒvlɪŋ] [gro-vlin], *a.* Servil, rastrero.

grovelingly ['grɒvlɪŋlɪ] [gro-vlin-li], *adv.* Servilmente, rastreramente.

grovy ['grəʊvɪ] [grou-vi], *a.* (Poco us.) Arbolado, lleno de arboledas o perteneciente a ellas.

grow [grəʊ] [grou], *va. (pret.* GREW, *pp.* GROWN). Cultivar, hacer crecer o nacer algún vegetal (cultivate). *-vn.* 1. Crecer, aumentarse, tomar aumento, hacerse grandes así las cosas animadas como las inanimadas. 2. Nacer, vegetar, crecer y nutrirse los vegetales. 3. Adelantar, progresar, hacer progresos (develop). 4. Hacerse, ponerse o volverse diferente una cosa de lo que era; pasar de un estado o condición a otro. 5. Subir o llegar progresando sucesivamente a un estado superior al que antes se tenía. 6. Extenderse, dilatarse. 7. Nacer, proceder, provenir de una causa o razón cualquiera. 8. Pegarse, unirse; fijarse, echar raíces (con la **prep. to**).

grow into fashion, hacerse moda. **To grow into a proverb,** llegar a hacerse proverbial. **To grow into favor with one,** insinuarse en el favor de una persona, irse haciendo su favorito.

grow near o **on,** acercarse.

grow out of esteem, perder el crédito. **To grow out of favor,** perder la amistad. **To grow out of kind,** degenerar. **To grow out of use,** caer en desuso.

grow towards an end, ir acabándose. **To grow towards morning,** empezar a amanecer.

grow up, crecer, salir de la tierra las plantas, brotar, arrojar, apuntar los vegetales. **To grow less,** disminuir. **To grow hot,** acalorarse. **To grow old,** envejecer. **To grow tame,** domesticarse. **To grow well,** restablecerse. **To grow worse,** empeorar. **To grow weary,** cansarse. **To grow young again,**

remozarse. **To grow better,** ponerse mejor, enmendarse, corregirse. **To grow big,** engordar; aumentarse. **To grow childish,** chochear. **To grow cold,** enfriarse. **To grow dear,** encarecer. **To grow easy,** tranquilizarse. **To grow fat,** engordar, engruesar. **To grow late,** hacerse tarde. **It grows late,** se va haciendo tarde. **To grow poor,** empobrecerse. **To grow rich,** enriquecerse. **To grow strong,** ponerse fuerte, reponerse.

grower ['grəʊəʳ] [grouaʳ], s. 1. El que crece. 2. Arrendador, labrador, productor (farm laborer); cultivador. **Fruit-grower,** cultivador de frutas.

growing ['grəʊɪŋ] [grouin], s. 1. Crecimiento. 2. Vegetación o nacimiento de las plantas. 3. Extensión, progresión (del tiempo). -a. Creciente. **Growing children,** niños adolescentes.

growl [grəʊl] [groul], vn. 1. Regañar, gruñir, rezongar, refunfuñar. 2. Regañar el perro. -va. Indicar una cosa por gruñidos o regañando.

growl, s. 1. Regañamiento, refunfuño, gruñido de una persona descontenta. 2. Regañamiento de un perro.

growler ['grəʊləʳ] [grou-laʳ], s. 1. Perro arisco, muy gruñidor. 2. Regañón, persona que regaña o refunfuña habitualmente.

grown [grəʊn] [groun], a. y pp. 1. Cubierto o lleno de alguna cosa que está creciendo. **Grown with weeds,** cubierto de maleza. 2. Crecido, hecho, llegado a la estatura a que puede llegar. **A grown man,** hombre hecho. 3. Prevalente, dominante. **Grown up,** crecido, adulto.

growth [grəʊθ] [grouz], s. 1. Crecimiento, crecida, medro en la altura y corpulencia de los animales y plantas. 2. Producto, producción; el origen de las personas o cosas con relación al sitio donde fueron producidas. 3. Vegetación. 4. Crecimiento, acrecentamiento, aumento, subida en el número, tamaño, frecuencia o estatura. 5. Aumento, ampliación, extensión de una cosa. 6. Adelantamiento, aprovechamiento, mejora, progreso. 7. Estatura completa, altura. **This tree has not come to its full growth,** este árbol está creciendo aún.

grub [grʌb] [grab], va. Rozar o limpiar la tierra de las matas que cría arrancándolas; desarraigar; azadonar. -vn. 1. Cavar, labrando la tierra. 2. Emplearse en oficios bajos.

grup, s. 1. Gorgojo, larva. 2. (Vul.) Alimento, comestibles. 3. Hombre desaliñado (en desprecio). 4. (Amer.) Algo desarraigado, v. gr. una raíz. **Grub-ax,** azadón o legón para limpiar la tierra de las malas hierbas.

grudge [grʌdʒ] [grach], va. 1. Envidiar o apetecer secretamente el bien que otro goza. 2. Dar o tomar alguna cosa de mala gana. -vn. 1. Murmurar, mostrar disgusto. 2. Repugnar, hacer de mala gana, admitir con dificultad alguna cosa.

grudge, s. 1. Rencor, enemistad antigua, ira envejecida, refunfuño, tirria. **He owes him a grudge,** le debe una jugada, o una mala partida. 2. Ira, mala voluntad. 3. Envidia, odio, aborrecimiento. 4. Remordimiento de conciencia. 5. Cualquier síntoma que indica estar próxima alguna enfermedad.

grudging ['grʌdʒɪŋ] [grad-chin], s. 1. Envidia, descontento, sentimiento del bien ajeno; resentimiento, mala voluntad. 2. Refunfuñadura, refunfuño. 3. Repugnancia, aversión o resistencia a hacer o decir alguna cosa. 4. Deseo secreto de gozar el bien de los demás. 5. (Des.) Los síntomas precursores de un mal.

grudgingly ['grʌdʒɪŋlɪ] [grad-chin-li], adv. Con repugnancia, de mala gana, por pura necesidad.

gruel [grʊəl] [gruel], s. Especie de caldo espeso hecho de harina de trigo o maíz, bien hervida en agua. (Mex.) Atole.

gruesome, grewsome ['gruːsəm] [gru-som], a. Horrible, horrendo, que sugiere pensamientos horrorosos.

gruff [grʌf] [graf], a. Ceñudo, grosero, tosco, impolítico, mal engestado (rude).

gruffly ['grʌflɪ] [gra-fli], adv. Ásperamente, severamente.

gruffness ['grʌfnɪs] [graf-nes], s. Aspereza, severidad, dureza en la mirada; rudeza de modales, aspecto y lenguaje.

grum [grʌm] [gram], a. Áspero, severo.

grumble ['grʌmbl] [gram-bol], vn. Refunfuñar, gruñir, regañar, rezongar, murmurar, quejarse.

grumbler ['grʌmbləʳ] [gram-blaʳ], s. Refunfuñón, gruñidor, regañón, regañador, rezongador (grouchy).

grumbling ['grʌmblɪŋ] [gram-blin], s. Murmuración, queja, descontento, refunfuñadura.

grumblingly ['grʌmblɪŋlɪ] [gram-blin-li], adv. Agriamente, con queja o descontento.

grume ['gruːm] [grum], s. Grumo, cuajarón; masa espesa, viscosa y semifluida.

grumly ['grʌmlɪ] [gram-li], adv. Ásperamente.

grumous ['gruːməs] [gru-mos], a. 1. Grumoso, que forma cuajarones; espeso, coagulado. 2. (Bot.) Que consta de granos agrupados.

grump ['grʌmp] [gramp], s. Mal humor.

grumpy ['grʌmpɪ] [gram-pi], a. Gruñón, quejoso, áspero, rudo de modales, malhumorado.

Grundy (Mrs.) s. La gente, el qué dirán. **What will Mrs. Grundy say?,** ¿qué dirá la gente?

grunt [grʌnt] [grant], vn. 1. Grumpir, dar gruñidos, producir un sonido gutural. 2. Murmurar, quejarse, refunfuñar. 3. Nombre de un pez americano.

grunt, grunting ['grʌntɪŋ] [gran-tin], s. 1. Gruñido, la voz del cerdo o un sonido parecido a ella. 2. Hemulón, pogonia, pez comestible de los mares tropicales americanos.

grunter ['grʌntəʳ] [gran-taʳ], s. Gruñidor.

gruntingly ['grʌntɪŋlɪ] [gran-tin-li], adv. Regañando, refunfuñando.

gruntling ['grʌntlɪŋ] [gran-tlin], s. Cochinillo.

guacharo [gwə'tʃɑːrə] [gua-cha-ro], s. (Ornit.) Guácharo.

guaco ['gwɑːkə] [gua-ko], s. (Bot.) Guaco.

Guadeloupe [gwɑːdə'luːp] [gua-da-lup], n. pr. Guadalupe.

guaiac ['gwaɪək] [guaiak], s. Guayaco, resina o madera (palo santo).

guaiacum ['gwaɪəkəm] [guaia-kom], s. 1. Guayaco, árbol de la América tropical. 2. La resina que se obtiene de este árbol. **Guaiacum-wood,** palo santo.

guanaco ['gwɑːnəkə] [gua-na-ko], s. (Zool.) Guanaco, especie de llama.

guano ['gwɑːnəʊ] [gua-nou], s. Guano, huano, abono excelente compuesto principalmente de excrementos de aves marítimas. -va. Abonar la tierra con guano.

guarantee [gærən'tiː] [ga-ran-ti], s. 1. Lo mismo que GUARANTY, pero así en el sentido ordinario de la palabra como en el forense se prefiere la forma GUARANTY. 2. Fiado, caucionado, la persona por quien otro responde. 3. Común, pero incorrectamente, fiador, garante; lo opuesto a **guarantor.**

guarantee, va. 2. Garantir, afianzar, salir fiador o responsable; tomar sobre sí el cumplimiento de lo que se estipula. 2. Asegurar contra pérdida o daño.

guarantor [gærən'tɔːʳ] [ga-ran-taʳ], s. Garante, fiador, el que responde por otro.

guaranty ['gærəntɪ] [ga-ran-ti], s. 1. (For.) Garantía, caución, fianza. 2. El acto de hacer cierto y seguro, de afianzar.

guaranty, va. V. TO GUARANTEE.

guard [gɑːd] [gard], va. y vn. 1. Guardar, tener cuidado y vigilancia en defensa y seguridad de alguna cosa (watch over). 2. Guardar, defender, proteger, conservar (guard, protect). 3. Prevenirse, estar prevenido; estar sobre sí; conservar. 4. (Ant.) Guarnecer, adornar vestidos. 5. Guardarse, ponerse en estado de defensa.

guard, s. 1. Guarda, guardia; protección, custodia o defensa; reunión de gente para custodiar o defender algo o a alguien. 2. Precaución, prevención, cautela. 3. Posición o estado de defensa. 4. Guarnición de un vestido o de una espada; guarda, un expediente o medio cualquiera que sirve de protección o seguridad, v. g. **Dust-guard,** guardapolvo. **Watch-guard,** cordón para afianzar un reloj de bolsillo. 5. Conductor de ferrocarril o mayoral de diligencia. **To be on one's guard,** estar sobre sí; guardarse. **To be off one's guard,** estar desprevenido. **To mount guard,** montar la guardia. **To relieve the guard,** relevar la guardia. **To come**

off guard, salir de guardia. **Advanced guard,** guardia avanzada. **Rear-guard,** retaguardia. **Van-guard,** vanguardia. **On guard,** alerta. **Guard-chamber,** V. GUARD-ROOM. **Guard-rail,** (F.C.) Contracarril. (Mar.) Barandilla. **Guard-room,** (a) Cuarto de guardia. (b) Calabozo. **Guard-ship,** navío de guardia, de ronda o de estación; buque de guerra puesto en un puerto para su defensa.

guardable ['gɑːdəbl] [gar-da-bol], a. Capaz de ser guardado.

guarded ['gɑːdɪd] [gar-did], a. 1. Defendido, protegido. 2. Cauteloso, precapido, cauto.

guardedly ['gɑːdɪdlɪ] [gar-did-li], adv. Cautelosamente.

guardedness ['gɑːdɪdnɪs] [gar-did-nes], s. Cautela, precaución.

guardian ['gɑːdɪən] [gar-dian], s. 1. Guardián, el que guarda o cuida de alguna cosa (keeper). 2. Tutor o curador, la persona destinada a cuidar de la educación y administración de los bienes de otra. 3. Guardián, el prelado ordinario de los conventos de San Francisco. -a. 1. Lo que guarda. 2. Tutelar, lo que ampara o protege.

guardianship ['gɑːdɪənʃɪp] [gar-dian-ship], s. 1. Tutela, curaduría; de aquí, protección, amparo, guarda. 2. Guardianía.

guardless ['gɑːdlɪs] [gard-les], a. Desamparado, sin amparo ni defensa.

guardrail ['gɑːdreɪl] [gard-reil], s. Baranda, barandilla. 2. (Ferro.) Contracarril, carril de guía.

guardroom ['gɑːdrʊm] [gard-rum], s. Cuerpo de guardia.

guardsman ['gɑːdzmən] [gards-man], s. Centinela, oficial de guardia.

guava ['gwɑːvə] [gua-va], s. Guayabo, árbol; guayaba, su fruto. Psidium guaiava. **Guava-tree,** guayabo.

gubernatorial [ˌguːbənəˈtɔːrɪəl] [gu-bar-na-to-rial], a. (E. U.) Relativo a un gobernador o a la dignidad de gobernador.

gudgeon ['gʌdʒən] [gad-yon], s. 1. Gobio, pez pequeño de río. 2. Bobo, el que fácilmente se deja engañar; ganso, zote. (Cuba) Guanajo. 3. Algo que se puede obtener sin esfuerzo. **To swallow a gudgeon,** tragar una píldora, tener buenas tragaderas.

gudgeon, s. (Mec.) 1. Perno, luchadero o cuello de eje. 2. Pezón metálico en un eje de madera. 3. Cojinete de un eje; gorrón; peruete; (Mar.) hembra (del timón).

gudgeon, v. Engañar, estafar.

guelder-rose ['geldərəʊs] [gel-der-rous], s. (Bot.) Viburno, bola de nieve, mundillo.

guerdon ['gɜːdən] [guer-don], s. Recompensa, premio, galardón.

guerrilla [gəˈrɪlə] [gue-ri-la], s. Guerrilla.

guess [ges] [gues], va. y vn. 1. Conjeturar, suponer, aventurar una suposición acerca de alguna cosa (suppose). 2. Adivinar, acertar, descubrir lo oculto, atinar (read, prophesy). 3. (Fam.) Pensar, juzgar, imaginar, creer (judge, imagine). **You may guess the rest,** puede Ud. imaginarse lo demás.

guess, s. Conjetura; adivinación; suposición, sospecha.

guesser ['gesər] [gue-sar], s. Conjeturador, adivinador.

guessingly ['gesɪŋlɪ] [gue-sin-li], adv.

guestchamber [ges'tʃæmbər] [guest-cham-bar], s. Alcoba destinada a los huéspedes de la casa,

guestrope ['gestrəʊp] [gues-troup], s. (Mar.) Guía de falsa amarra.

guffaw [gʌˈfɔː] [ga-fo], s. Carcajada, risotada. (Imitativo.)

guffaw, v. Reír groseramente o a carcajadas.

guhr [gɜːr] [guar], s. (Geol.) Depósito de marga, ordinariamente calcárea, que deja el agua en el hueco de los peñascos. (Al.)

guidable ['gaɪdəbl] [gai-da-bol], a. Manejable.

guidance ['gaɪdəns] [gai-dans], s. Gobierno, dirección, conducta; la acción y efecto de guiar, de dirigir, de gobernar.

guidance beam ['gaɪdənsˌbiːm] [gai-dans-bim], s. (Aer.) Rayo electrónico orientador.

guide [gaɪd] [gaid], va. Guiar, dirigir, arreglar, gobernar (run, lead); influir, ajustar, poner en orden. **Guide-book,** guía del viajero.

guide, s. Guía, director, conductor, pauta, patrón.

guide-board ['gaɪdbɔːd] [gaid-bord], s. Tabla de guía en los caminos. V. GUIDE-POST.

guided missile ['gaɪdmɪsɪ] [gaid-mi-sil], s. Proyectil dirigido.

guideless ['gaɪdlɪs] [gaid-les], a. Sin guía ni director; sin gobierno.

guide-post ['gaɪdpəʊst] [gaid-poust], s. Hito, el poste de piedra o palo que hay donde se cruzan los caminos, con inscripciones para servir de guía a los caminantes.

guidon ['gɪdən] [gui-don], s. Guión, banderola de guía de los regimientos de caballería o de artillería montada; y el oficial que lo lleva.

guild [gɪld] [gild], s. 1. Gremio, cuerpo, comunidad, hermandad, corporación. 2. Hermandad, sociedad organizada para ayudar en el trabajo de una iglesia o feligresía. V. GILD.

guilder ['gɪldər] [guil-dar], s. Florín.

guildahall ['gɪldəhɔːl] [gil-da-jol], s. Casa consistorial, casa de ayuntamiento.

guile [gaɪl] [gail], s. Dolo, engaño, fraude, superchería; de aquí, estratagema, chasco.

guileful ['gaɪlfʊl] [gail-ful], a. Insidioso, traidor, aleve, engañoso, impostor. -s. Traidor.

guilefully ['gaɪlfəlɪ] [gail-fu-li], adv. Insidiosamente, alevosamente, engañosamente.

guileless ['gaɪlɪs] [gai-les], a. Sencillo, franco, sincero (simple, sincere); sin dolo ni doblez.

guilelessness ['gaɪlɪsnɪs] [gai-les-nes], s. Inocencia, franqueza, sencillez, sinceridad.

guilloche ['gaɪləʃ] [gai-losh], s. Guilloquis, adorno compuesto de franjas que se cruzan simétricamente.

guillotine [ɡɪləˈtiːn] [gui-lo-tin], s. 1. Guillotina. 2. Una forma de máquina para cortar papel. 3. Instrumento quirúrgico para cortar las amígdalas.

guillotine, va. Degollar, guillotinar.

guilt [gɪlt] [guilt], s. Delito, transgresión, culpa, crimen, falta (fault, crime); en teología, estado de condenación; maldad.

guiltily ['gɪltɪlɪ] [guil-ti-li], adv. Criminalmente.

guiltiness ['gɪltɪnɪs] [guil-ti-nes], s. Criminalidad, maldad, ruindad, malicia.

guiltless ['gɪltlɪs] [guilt-les], a. 1. Inocente, libre de culpa; puro, sin tacha. 2. Ignorante, inexperimentado; extraño a, virgen de. **Guiltless of the alphabet,** ignorante del abecedario. **The teeming earth yet guiltless of the plough,** la tierra fecunda aún virgen del arado.

guiltlessly ['gɪltlɪslɪ] [guilt-les-li], adv. Inocentemente.

guiltlessness ['gɪltlɪsnɪs] [guilt-les-nes], s. Inocencia, inculpabilidad.

guilty ['gɪltɪ] [guil-ti], a. 1. Reo, culpable, delincuente, malvado, vicioso, perverso (wicked, condemned). 2. (Ant.) Reo, sujeto a la pena (con la preposición of antes de pena). **Guilty of death,** reo de muerte. **To plead guilty,** confesarse culpable. **To be found guilty,** ser uno declarado reo del delito de que se le acusa.

guimpe [gɪmp] [guimp], s. Camisolín de mujer, que se usa con vestido descotado, canesú.

Guinea ['gɪnɪ] [gui-ni], s. 1. Guinea, unidad (moneda). **Guinea-fowl,** gallina de Guinea, pintada. **Guinea-hen,** (a) Pintada. (b) (Bot.) Fritilaria. **Guinea-pig,** conejillo de Indias; cobayo; (Cuba) curiel.

guinea-pepper [ˌɡɪnɪˈpepər] [gui-ni-pe-par], s. (Bot.) Pimiento de Guinea.

guise [gaɪz] [gais], s. 1. Modo, manera, modales (manners). 2. Continente, apariencia exterior, ya sea en el porte ya en el traje (look). 3. Práctica, costumbre (habit). 4. Máscara, capa, color, pretexto. **Under the guise of religion,** bajo capa, con la máscara de religión. **In this guise,** de este modo, bajo esta apariencia. 5. Aspecto, apariencia, disfraz.

guitar [gɪˈtɑːʳ] [gui-taʳ], *s.* Guitarra.

gulch [gʌlʃ] [galsh], *s. (Amer.)* Quebrada, rambla; valle estrecho y peñascoso.

gulden [ˈgʌldən] [gal-den], *s.* 1. Gulden (coin). 2. Florín holandés. 3. Florín austriaco.

gules [gʊlz] [guls], *s. (Her.)* Gules, el color rojo.

gulf [gʌlf] [galf], *s.* 1. Golfo, brazo de mar que avanza dentro de tierra. 2. Golfo, abismo, vorágine. 3. Olla, remolino de agua. 4. Sima, concavidad profunda. 5. Cualquier cosa insaciable.

Gulf Stream [gʌlfˈstriːm] [galf-strim], *s.* Gran corriente del Océano Atlántico que lleva sus aguas desde el Golfo de Méjico a lo largo de las costas de los Estados Unidos y después con dirección a la Gran Bretaña y la costa escandinava.

gulf-weed [ˈgʌlfwiːd] [galf-uid], *s.* Sargazo, gran alga marina de color aceitunado, provista de vejiuillas axiliares llenas de aire.

gull [gʌl] [gal], *va.* Engañar, defraudar; estafar, sisar.

gull, *s.* 1. *(Orn.)* Gaviota. 2. Engaño, fraude, petardo, estafa (fraud, trick). 3. El que es bobo, de poca capacidad o que con facilidad se deja engañar.

gull-catcher [gʌlˈkætʃəʳ] [gal-ka-chaʳ], *s.* Engañador, petardista, impostor.

gullery [ˈgʌləri] [ga-le-ri], *s.* Engaño, petardo, fraude, impostura.

gullet [ˈgʌlɪt] [ga-lit], *s.* 1. Gaznate, tragadero, gola. *(Anat.)* Esófago. 2. Zanja, trinchera profunda. V. GULLY y GUSSET.

gullibility [gʌlɪˈbɪlɪti] [ga-li-bi-li-ti], *s.* Tragadero, tragaderas, credulidad.

gullible [ˈgʌlɪbl] [ga-li-bol], *a.* Bobo, simple, crédulo, que se deja engañar fácilmente.

gully [ˈgʌli] [ga-li], *va.* Acanalar por la acción del agua corriente; cavar canalizas.

gully, *s.* Rambla, excavación causada por las aguas fluviales; barranca, hondonada; zanja honda.

gully-hole [ˈgʌlihəʊl] [ga-li-joul], *s.* Sumidero, albañal.

gulp [gʌlp] [galp], *va.* 1. Engullir, tragar con gula, engullir. 2. Reprimir las lágrimas, ahogar un sollozo. 3. Contener el aliento, no poder hablar por la emoción. Se usa frecuentemente con down. **To gulp up,** vomitar, vaciar.

gulp, *s.* Trago, engullida, esfuerzo para tragar.

gum [gʌm] [gam], *s.* 1. Goma. 2. Encía, la carne que cubre la quijada y guarnece la dentadura. **Gum-drop,** pastilla de goma. **Gum-elastic,** goma elástica, caucho. **Gum lac,** goma laca. **Resin,** gomorresina. **Gum-tree,** árbol que produce goma. **Gum-water,** agua de goma, goma arábiga disuelta en agua.

gum, *va.* Engomar, untar o unir con goma.

gum arabic [gʌmˈærəbɪk] [gam-a-ra-bik], *s.* Goma arábiga.

gumbo [ˈgʌmbə] [gam-bo], *s.* 1. Quingombó, quinbombó, hibisco comestible. V. OKRA. 2. Sopa de quingombó o guisado hecho con él. 3. Dialecto criollo en Luisiana.

gum-boil [ˈgʌmbɔɪl] [gam-boil], *s.* Flemón, tumor en las encías.

gumdrop [ˈgʌmdrop] [gam-drop], *s.* Pastilla de goma.

gummiferous [ˈgʌmɪfərəs] [ga-mi-fe-ros], *a.* Gomífero.

gumminess [ˈgʌmɪnɪs] [ga-mi-nes], *s.* Gomosidad.

gummy [ˈgʌmi] [ga-mi], gummous [ga-mos], *a.* 1. Gomoso, pegajoso, que se parece a la goma. 2. Engomado, cubierto de goma.

gump [gʌmp] [gamp], *s. (Fam.)* Páparo, simplón.

gumption [ˈgʌmpʃən] [gamp-shon], *s. (Fam.)* Conocimiento, habilidad.

gumshoe [ˈgʌmʃuː] [gam-shu], *s.* Chanclo de goma, zapato de lona con suela de goma. 2. (Pop) Polizonte, detective.

gumshoe, *v.* Andar sin hacer ruido; andar de forma furtiva o cautelosa.

gun [gʌn] [gan], *s.* 1. Arma o boca de fuego, como escopeta, fusil, pistola (riffle, weapon), etc. 2. Cañón, pieza de artillería (canyon). **Air-gun,** escopeta de viento. **Blow-gun,** cerbatana; pucuna (de los peruanos). **Breech-loading gun,** cañón, escopeta o rifle de retrocarga. **Double-barreled gun,** escopeta de dos cañones. **Field gun,** pieza de campaña. **Gatling gun,** ametralladora de Gatling. **Great gun,** (a) Cañón grueso. (b) *(Fam.)* Persona de consecuencia. **Greatguns!** Exclamación de sorpresa. **Swivel gun,** colisa, pedrero. **To spike a gun,** clavar un cañón. **Gun-barrel,** cañón de fusil. **Gun-carriage,** afuste, cureña de cañón. **Gundeck,** cubierta, principal, batería. **Gun-room,** *(Mar.)* Santa Bárbara, polvorín. **Gun-stock,** caja de escopeta.

gunboat [ˈgʌnbəʊt] [gan-bout], *s.* Cañonero, buque de guerra pequeño y de poco calado.

gun cotton [ˈgʌnˌkɒtn] [gan-ko-ton], *s.* Piroxilina, pólvora de algodón.

gun metal [ˈgʌnˌmetl] [gan-me-tal], *s.* 1. Metal para artillería. 2. Antiguo bronce de cañones. 3. Metal pavonado. 4. Color gris-pardo.

gunner [ˈgʌnəʳ] [ga-naʳ], *s.* 1. *(Mar.)* Condestable; artillero de un navío. 2. Escopetero, el que está armado con escopeta. **Gunner's mate,** *(Mar.)* artillero de segunda clase.

gunnery [ˈgʌnəri] [ga-ne-ri], *s.* Artillería.

gunning [ˈgʌnɪŋ] [ga-nin], *s.* Caza con escopeta.

gunny sack [ˈgʌnsæk] [gan-sak], *s.* 1. Saco de yute. 2. *(Fig.)* Traje estrecho y simple como un saco.

gunport-bars [ˈgʌnpɔːtˈbɑːz] [gan-port-bars], *s. pl. (Mar.)* Portas, las ventanas del navío donde se pone la artillería.

gunpowder [ˈgʌnpaʊdəʳ] [gan-pau-daʳ], *s.* Pólvora.

gunshot [ˈgʌnʃɒt] [gan-shot], *s.* 1. Tiro de escopeta, cañón u otra arma de fuego. 2. Tiro, la distancia a que alcanzan las armas disparadas. **Within gunshot,** a tiro, al alcance de fusil.

gunsmith [ˈgʌnsmɪθ] [gan-smiz], *s.* Armero, arcabucero.

gunstick [ˈgʌnstɪk] [gan-stik], *s.* Atacador, baqueta.

gunstock [ˈgʌnstək] [gan-stok], *s.* Caja de fusil.

gunwale [ˈgʌnweɪl] [gan-ueil], *s.* Regala de la borda del combés.

gurgitation [ˈgɜːgɪˈteɪʃən] [guer-gui-tei-shon], *s.* El movimiento de un líquido en una vorágine o en estado de ebullición; borbollón, borbotón.

gurgle [ˈgɜːgl] [guer-guel], *vn.* Manar o fluir haciendo un ruido semejante al que hace el agua que sale de una botella (run, flow); o murmurar como un arroyuelo en un lecho pedregoso. -*s.* 1. Salida de un líquido con dicho ruido; murmullo. 2. Borbolleo, borboteo, gorgoteo. **Death gurgle,** estertor.

gurnard [ˈgɜːnɑːd] [guer-nard], **gurnet** [ˈgɜːnɪt] [guernit], *s. (Ict.)* Trigla, golondrina.

gush [gʌʃ] [gash], *va.* Derramar con abundancia. -*vn.* 1. Brotar, fluir o manar con violencia; chorrear, fluir copiosamente. 2. Hacer demostraciones extravagantes de afecto o sentimiento.

gush, *s.* 1. Chorro, derrame repentino e impetuoso de un líquido. 2. Efusión, manifestación extravagante de sentimiento.

gusher [ˈgʌʃəʳ] [ga-shaʳ], *s.* Géiser, pozo brotante de petróleo.

gushing [ˈgʌʃɪŋ] [ga-shin], *a.* Que fluye, que mana, que sale a borbotones.

gust [gʌst] [gast], *s.* 1. Gusto, el sentido de paladar. 2. Deleite. 3. Inclinación, afición, amor (hobbie). 4. Soplo fuerte o bocanada de aire. 5. Transporte, acceso de pasión. 6. Gusto, discernimiento.

gustation [gʌsˈteɪʃən] [gas-tei-shon], *s.* Gustación, la acción y efecto de gustar.

gustatory, gustative [ˈgʌstətɔːri] [gas-ta-to-ri], *a.* Gustable, que pertence al gusto, que sirve para gustar, gustativo.

gusto [ˈgʌstəʊ] [gas-tou], *s.* Sabor, gusto, afición, placer.

gusty [ˈgʌsti] [gas-ti], *a.* Borrascoso, tempestuoso.

gut [gʌt] [gat], *s.* 1. Intestino: no se emplea entre personas bien habladas. 2. *pl. (Vulg.)* Estómago, el receptáculo de los alimentos; gula, glotonería. 3. Un paso estrecho. 4. Cuerda de tripa, sea de un animal, sea fibra de un gusano de seda cuando está a punto de hilar su capullo. La fibra del gusano de seda se emplea en la pesca y en cirugía.

gut, *va.* 1. Desventrar, destripar. 2. Desentrañar, sacar lo interior de alguna cosa.

gutta-percha [ˌgʌtəˈpɜːtʃə] [ga-ta-per-cha], *s.* Gutapercha, goma pardo rojiza.

gutter [ˈgʌtəʳ] [ga-taʳ], *s.* 1. Canalón, gotera; canal hecho por el agua o para que corra ésta. 2. Alcantarilla, cloaca para el desagüe; arroyo de calle. 3. Estría, canal de ebanistería. 4. Zanja, acequia.

gutter, *va.* -Acanalar, estriar. *-vn.* Caer en gotas.

guttle [gʌtl] [ga-tel], *v.* Comer, engullir.

guttural [ˈgʌtərəl] [ga-ta-ral], *a.* 1. Gutural, perteneciente a la garganta. 2. Gutural, lo que se pronuncia con la garganta.

gutturality [ˈgʌtərəlɪtɪ] [ga-ta-ra-li-ti], *s.* Calidad de gutural.

gutturally [ˈgʌtərəlɪ] [ga-ta-ra-li], *adv.* Guturalmente.

guy 1 [gaɪ] [gai], *s. (Mar.)* Retendia, el cabo que sirve para detener cualquiera cosa pesada a fin de que no golpee en el costado u otra parte del buque.

guy 2, *s.* 1. Individuo, tipo. 2. Persona mal vestida o de apariencia grotesca.

guy, *va.* 1. *(Mar.)* Sujetar o asegurar con una retenida. 2. *(Fam. E. U.)* Burlarse, mofarse de alguien.

guzzle [gʌzl] [ga-sel], *va.* y *vn.* 1. Beber mucho o repetidas veces. 2. Tragar vorazmente. *-vn.* Emborracharse.

guzzler [ˈgʌzləʳ] [gas-laʳ], *s.* Bebedor, discípulo de Baco; borracho; pellejo de vino.

gym [dʒɪm] [yim], *s.* **v.** GYMNASTICS

gymnasium [dʒɪmˈneɪzɪəm] [yim-nei-siom], *s.* 1. Gimnasio. 2. Liceo, escuela de latín o clásica, en oposición a una puramente técnica. 3. Gimnasio, edificio descubierto en que la juventud griega ejercitaba sus fuerzas.

gymnast [ˈdʒɪmnæst] [yim-nast], *s.* Gimnasta, el que es hábil en los ejercicios gimnásticos; atleta.

gymnastic, gymnastical [dʒɪmˈnæstɪk] [yim-nas-tik], *a.* Gimnástico, gímnico.

gymnastics [dʒɪmˈnæstɪks] [yim-nas-tiks], *s. pl.* Gimnasia, calisténica.

gymnosophist [ˈdʒɪmnəsəfɪst] [yim-no-so-fist], *s.* Gimnosofista, nombre de los brahmanes y alguna de sus sectas.

gymnosperm [ˈdʒɪmnəspɜːm] [yim-nos-perm], *s.* Planta gimnosperma, que tiene las semillas o gérmenes desnudos.

gymnospermous [ˈdʒɪmnəspɜːməs] [yim-nos-per-mos], *a.* *(Bot.)* Gimnospermo o que tiene la semilla desnuda.

gynarchy [ˈdʒɪnɑːkɪ] [yi-nar-ki], **gynaeocracy** [ˈdʒɪnækrəsɪ] [yi-na-kra-si], *s.* Ginecocracia, gobierno mujeril.

gynecologist [ˌgaɪnɪˈkɒlədʒɪst] [gai-ne-ko-lo-yist], *s.* Ginecólogo, persona versada en la ginecología.

gynecology [ˌgaɪnɪˈkɒlədʒɪ] [gai-ne-ko-lo-yi], *s.* Ginecología, la ciencia de las funciones y enfermedades propias de la mujer.

gyp [dʒɪp] [yip], *s.* 1. Criado en un colegio de Cambridge. 2. *(E. U.)* Estafa, timo; estafador, timador.

gyp, *v.* Timar, estafar.

gypseous [ˈdʒɪpsɪəs] [yip-sios], **gypsine** [ˈgɪpsaɪn] [guip-sain], *a.* Gipsoso o yesoso.

gypsum [ˈdʒɪpsəm] [yip-som], *s.* Yeso, sulfato de cal, aljez.

gypsy [ˈdʒɪpsɪ] [yip-si], *s.* **v.** GIPSY.

gypsidom [ˈdʒɪpsɪdəm] [yip-si-dom], *s.* Gitanería, los gitanos.

gypsyish [ˈdʒɪpsɪʃ] [yip-sish], *s.* Gitanismo.

gyral [ˈdʒaɪərəl] [yaia-ral], *a.* 1. Giratorio, que da vueltas o se mueve circularmente. 2. *(Anat.)* Que se refiere a las circunvoluciones del cerebro.

gyrate [dʒaɪˈreɪt] [yai-reit], *vn.* Girar, dar vueltas sobre un eje de rotación; revolver, ejecutar una revolución, particularmente en espiral o hélice.

gyration [dʒaɪˈreɪʃən] [yai-rei-shon], *s.* La acción y efecto de girar, giro; rotación.

gyratory [ˌdʒaɪˈreɪtərɪ] [yai-ra-to-ri], *a.* Giratorio, que gira alrededor.

gyre [ˈdʒaɪəʳ] [yaiaʳ], *s.* Giro, girada.

gyrfalcon [dʒaɪəˈfælkən] [yaia-fal-kon], *s.* Gerifalte.

gyrocompass [odʒaɪrəʊˈkʌmpəs] [yai-rou-kam-pas], *s.* Brújula giroscópica.

gyromancy [dʒaɪˈrəmænsɪ] [yai-ro-man-si], *s.* Giromancia, adivinación por medio del giro constante de una persona dentro de un círculo.

gyroscope [dʒaɪˈrəskəʊp] [yai-ros-koup], *s.* *(Fís.)* Giróscopo o giroscopio.

gyrostat [ˈdʒaɪrəstæt] [yai-ros-tat], *s.* Giróstato.

gyrostatics [dʒaɪrəsˈtætɪks] [yai-ros-ta-tiks], *s.* Girostática, conjunto de leyes que gobiernan la rotación de los cuerpos sólidos.

gyve [dʒaɪv] [yaiv], *va.* Encadenar, aprisionar con grillos.

gyves [dʒaɪvz] [yaivs], *s. pl.* Grillos, prisión con que aseguran a los reos en la cárcel.

H

h [eɪtʃ] [eich], esta letra tiene casi el sonido gutural de una J en español, aunque más suave, excepto en algunas voces en que es muda, como **hour, heir, honest,** etc.

ha [hɑː] [ja], *inter.* 1. Ah, interjección que sirve para expresar diversos afectos. 2. Expresión que repetida denota risa: ¡Ja, ja, ja! 3. Exclamación que indica duda, indecisión.

ha, *vn.* V. HAW.

habeas corpus [ˈheɪbɪəsˈkɔːpəs] [jei-bias-kor-pos], *s.* Habeas corpus. *(For.)* Fuero particular de las leyes inglesas y americanas.

haberdasher [ˈhæbədæʃəʳ] [ja-ba-da-shaʳ], *s.* 1. Tendero vendedor de artículos para caballeros: camisas, etc. 2. Mercero, el tendero que vende cintas, cofias y otros géneros de poco valor.

haberdashery [ˌhæbəˈdæʃərɪ] [ja-ba-da-she-ri], *s.* 1. Mercería, pasamanería; objetos pequeños. 2. Tienda de efectos para caballeros.

habergeon [ˈhəbɜːdʒən] [a-ber-yon], *s.* Corza pequeña.

habiliment [hæˈbɪlɪmənt] [a-bi-li-ment], *s.* Prenda de vestir, parte del vestido o traje (dress, cloth); en plural, vestido, traje, vestidura.

habilitate [ˈhæbɪlɪteɪθ] [a-bli-li-teit], *va.* *(E. U.)* Pertrechar, habilitar, **v.g.** para la explotación de una mina. *-vn.* Hacerse apto o idóneo para alguna cosa

habit [ˈhæbɪt] [ja-bit], *s.* 1. Hábito, uso, costumbre (custom). 2. Estado o disposición de alguna cosa; constitución, complexión o disposición particular de alguna persona. 3. Hábito (religioso), vestido, traje exterior. 4. En botánica, geología y mineralogía, modo característico del crecimiento o de otras modificaciones físicas. **Riding habit,** traje de montar. **To get in the habit,** *(Fam.)* Dar en la flor, tomar el tema, tomar la costumbre. **Bad habit,** mala costumbre. **To make a habit of something,** aficionarse a algo, tener afición por algo.

habit, *va.* Ataviar, adornar, vestir.

habitable [ˈhæbɪtəbl] [ja-bi-ta-bol], *a.* Habitable, que puede ser habitado.

habitableness [ˈhæbɪtəblˈnɪs] [ja-bi-ta-bol-nes], *s.* La posibilidad de ser habitado.

habitant [ˈhæbɪtənt] [ja-bi-tant], *s.* Habitante, morador.

habitat [ˈhæbɪtæt] [ja-bi-tat], *s.* Hábitat; en lenguaje científico se llama así al terreno o a la región donde se hallan o crecen naturalmente los individuos de una especie, animal o vegetal. *(Lat.)*

habitation [ˌhæbɪˈteɪʃən] [ja-bi-tei-shon], *s.* Habitación, el lugar o casa donde se mora o vive; domicilio, morada.

habited [ˈhæbɪtɪd] [ja-bi-tid], *a.* 1. Vestido, ataviado. 2. *(Ant.)* Habitado. 3. *(Des.)* Usual, acostumbrado.

habitual [ˈhæbɪtʃʊəl] [ja-bi-chual], *a.* Habitual, lo que se hace, se padece o se posee con continuación y por hábito.

habitually [ˈhæbɪtʃʊəlɪ] [ja-bi-chua-li], *adv.* Habitualmente.

habituate [ˈhæbɪtʃʊeɪt] [ja-bi-chueit], *va. y vn.* Habituar; habituarse, acostumbrarse a alguna cosa.

habituate, *a.* (Poco us.) Obstinado, inveterado.

habitude [ˈhæbɪtʃʊd] [ja-bi-chiud], *s.* Familiaridad, costumbre: trato o amistad en alguna cosa o con alguna persona.

habitué [həˈbɪtʃʊeɪ] [ja-bi-chuei], *s.* Parroquiano, cliente habitual.

hack [hæk] [jak], *s.* 1. Caballo de alquiler, rocín, cuartago; alquilón. 2. *(E. U.)* Un simón o coche de alquiler. 3. Peón, trabajador; *(Fig.)* escritor mercenario. 4. Pico, especie de azadón; azuela. 5. Muesca, corte, cuchillada, golpe con un instrumento cortante. 6. *(Fam.)* Tos corta y seca. **Hackman,** simón, cochero de alquiler.

hack, *va.* 1. Tajar, cortar, dividir una cosa en muchos pedazos pequeños, picar irregularmente. 2. Allanar piedras, picarlas como las amoladeras. 3. Hacer muescas, mellar. *-vn.* 1. Cortar, tajar irregularmente, repetidas veces o sin destreza. 2. Emitir una tos corta y seca. 3. Alquilarse, venderse, prostituirse; trabajar como escritor mercenario. **To hack into pieces,** hacer trizas.

hackamore [ˈhækəmɔːr] [ja-ka-maʳ], *s.* Cabezada o cabestro para domar potros.

hackberry [ˈhækberɪ] [jak-be-ri], *s.* Almez. *(Bot.)* Almeza.

hackle [hækl] [ja-kel], *va.* 1. Rastrillar. *V.* HATCHEL. 2. Hacer pedazos una cosa, tajar, estropear a tajos una cosa.

hackle, *s.* 1. Rastrillo. 2. Fibra no hilada, como la seda en rama. 3. Mosca para pescar.

hackmatack [ˈhækmətæk] [jak-ma-tak], *s.* El alerce o lárice americano. (Nombre indio.) *V.* TAMARACK.

hackney [ˈhæknɪ] [jak-ni], *s.* 1. Caballo de alquiler. 2. Rocín; cuartago; caballo pequeño que tiene buen paso. 3. Alquilón, lo que se alquila. *-a.* Alquilado: común; prostituido; cansado, gastado. **Hackney-coach,** coche de alquiler o simón. **Hackney writer,** escritor mercenario. **Hackney coachman,** cochero de alquiler o simón.

hackney, *va.* 1. Ejercitar, usar una cosa con continuación; vulgarizar una cosa, hacerla trivial y manoseada. 2. Llevar en coche de alquiler. **A hackneyed subject,** un asunto trillado, manoseado.

hack saw [ˈhæksɔː] [jak-so], *s.* Sierra de arco para trabajo de metales.

hacqueton [ˈhækɪtən] [ja-ki-ton], *s.* Especie de jubón antiguo.

had [hæd] [jad], *pret.* del verbo TO HAVE; se usa como auxiliar, equivalente a había o hubo.

haddock [ˈhædək] [ja-dok], *s.* Merluza, pescado de la familia de los gádidos.

hade [heɪd] [jeid], *s. (Min.)* Descenso escarpado en una mina, buzamiento.

Hades [ˈheɪdiːz] [jei-dis], *s.* 1. Hades, voz tomada del griego que significa el estado y la morada de las almas de los muertos; también, los infiernos. 2. Plutón o Dis, el señor del mundo inferior; el mundo inferior mismo.

Hadrian [ˈheɪdrɪən] [jei-drian], *n.pr.* Adriano.

haemal [ˈhæməl] [ja-mal], *a.* 1. De la sangre. 2. Situado en el lado del cuerpo donde se hallan el corazón y los vasos sanguíneos.

haematemesis [ˈhæmətɪˈmesɪs] [ja-ma-ti-me-sis], *s.* Hematemesis.

haemathermal [ˈhæməθɜːməl] [ja-ma-zer-mal], *a. (Zool.)* Hematermo.

haemorrhage [ˈhiːmɔːrɑːdʒ] [ji-mou-rach], *s.* Hemorragia.

haemorrhagic [ˈhiːmɔːrɑːdʒɪk] [ji-mou-ra-yik], *a.* Hemorrágico.

haemorrhoids [ˈhiːmɔːrɔɪdʒ] [ji-mou-roids], *s.* Hemorroides, almorranas.

haemostat [ˈhæməstæt] [ja-mos-tat], *s.* 1. Hemostático. 2. Instrumento para comprimir un vaso sanguíneo.

haemostatic [ˈhæməstætɪk] [ja-mos-ta-tik], *a.* Hemostático.

haft [hæft] [jaft], *s.* Mango, asa, agarradera; puño o guarnición de arma blanca.

hag [hæg] [jag], *s.* Vejancona, vejarrona fea; bruja, hechicera.

hag, *va.* Aterrar, infundir terror y espanto. **Hag-born,** nacido de bruja. **Hag-ridden,** cabalgado por brujas; de aquí, bajo el influjo de una pesadilla.

haggard [ˈhægəd] [ja-gard], *a.* 1. Consumido, desfigurado, flaco o macilento de aspecto (skinny); lleno de zozobra. 2. Zahareño, montaraz, intratable. *-s.* 1. Halcón, en especial, en cetrería, el halcón cogido cuando tiene ya todo su plumaje. 2. Fiera, el que es indómito o feroz. 3. *(Esco.)* Corral de niara; granero.

haggardly [ˈhægədlɪ] [ja-gard-li], *adv.* Fieramente; feamente.

haggish [ˈhægɪʃ] [ja-guish], *a.* Feo, horroroso.

haggle, *va.* Tajar, cortar en tajadas. *-vn.* Regatear, porfiar sobre el precio de alguna cosa.

haggler [ˈhæglər] [ja-glaʳ], *s.* 1. Tajador. 2. Regatón, regatero, el que regatea mucho.

hagiographal [ˌhægɪˈɒɡrəfəl] [ja-guio-gra-fal], *a.* Hagiógrafo, que pertenece a los libros o escritores hagiógrafos.

hagiographer [ˌhægɪˈɒɡrəfəʳ] [ja-guio-gra-faʳ], *s.* Hagiógrafo, autor que trata de los santos o de las cosas sagradas.

hagiography [ˌhægɪˈɒɡrəfɪ] [ja-guio-gra-fi], *s.* Hagiografía.

hagiolatry [ˌhægɪˈɒlətrɪ] [ja-guio-la-tri], *s.* Culto de los santos.

Hague (The) [heɪɡ] [jeig], *n. pr. (Geogr.)* La Haya.

hah [hɑːɡ] [ja], *inter. V.* HA.

ha-ha [ˈhɑːˈhɑː] [ja-ja], *s.* Cerca hundida; foso con escarpa.

haik [heɪk] [jeik], *s.* Jaique.

hail [heɪl] [jeil], *s.* 1. Granizo, la lluvia congelada en el aire. 2. Saludo; grito para llamar la atención. *-inter.* ¡Salve, dios te guarde! ¡Salud!

hail, *va. y vn.* 1. Granizar, arrojar las nubes granizo. 2. Saludar, hablar a otro cortésmente, llamar *a.* 3. Recibir, celebrar con aclamaciones. **To hail a ship,** *(Mar.)* Saludar a la voz, venir a voz. 4. *V.* POUR.

hail-fellow [ˈheɪlˈfeləʊ] [jeil-fe-lou], *s.* Compañero.

hailshot [ˈheɪlʃɒt] [jeil-shot], *s.* Perdigones, munición menuda.

hailstone [ˈheɪlstəʊn] [jeil-stoun], *s.* Piedra de granizo.

hailstorm [ˈheɪlstɔːm] [jeil-storm], *s.* Granizada.

haily [ˈheɪlɪ] [jei-li], *a.* Granujado, lleno de granizo.

hair [heəʳ] [jeaʳ], *s.* 1. Pelo, la hebra o hilo delgado que sale de los poros del cuerpo animal; se dice también del vello que cubre ciertas partes del cuerpo humano. 2. *(Biol.)* Filamentos del cuerpo y de las plantas. 3. Cabello, cabellera, pelo de la cabeza y de la cara. **Against the hair,** a contrapelo; de mala gana. **False hair,** pelo postizo. **Hair of the head,** cabellos. **To a hair,** exactamente, perfectamente. **A fine head of hair,** una cabellera hermosa. **Horse-hair,** crin. **To dress one's** hair, peinarse. **Hair-button,** botón de crin. **Hair-broom,** escoba de cerdas o crines. **Hair-brush,** cepillo, escobilla, para limpiar el cabello. **Hair-cloth,** (a) cilicio; (b) esterilla de cerda para sillas. **Hairdresser,** peluquero, peinador. **Hair-dye,** tinte para el pelo. **Hair-lace,** cinta para atar el pelo. **Hair-sieve,** tamiz de cerda para colar. **Hair-splitting,** quisquilla, distinción de poco momento. *-a.* Quisquilloso, que se para en quisquillas. **Hair-spring,** pelo, muelle (de reloj) muy fino en espiral.

hairbreadth [ˈheəbreθ] [jea-brez], *s.* Lo grueso de un pelo; poca cosa, casi nada, el negro de una uña. **To have a hairbreadth escape,** librarse de buena, salir de un apuro, librarse por un pelo.

haircloth [ˈheəklɒθ] [jea-kloz], *s.* 1. Tela de crin. 2. Cilicio.

haircut [ˈhɛəkʌt] [jea-kat], s. Corte de pelo.

hairdo [ˈhɛədu:] [jea-du], s. Peinado, tocado.

hairdresser [ˈhɛədresəʳ] [jea-dre-saʳ], s. Peluquero, peluquera, peinadora.

hairdressing [ˈhɛədresɪŋ] [jea-dre-sin], s. Peinados, peluquería, arte de peinar.

haired [hɛəd] [jead], a. peludo, cabelludo. **Black-haired,** pelinegro. **Curly-haired,** que tiene el pelo rizado o encrespado. **Gray-haired,** canoso.

hairhung [ˈhɛəhʌŋ] [jea-jang], a. Suspendido de un cabello.

hairiness [ˈhɛərɪnɪs] [jea-ri-nes], s. Calidad y estado de peludo o peloso.

hairless [ˈhɛəlɪs] [jea-les], a. Pelado, pelón, calvo.

hair net [hɛənet] [jea-net], s. Redecilla para el cabello.

hairpin [hɛəpɪn] [jea-pin], s. Horquilla, alfiler grande que usan las mujeres para sujetar el cabello.

hair-raising [ˈhɛəreɪzɪŋ] [jea-rei-sin], a. Espeluznante, horripilante.

hairsplitter [ˈhɛəsplɪtəʳ] [jea-spli-taʳ], s. Persona que hace distinciones demasiado sutiles.

hairsplitting [ˈhɛəsplɪtɪŋ] [jea-spli-tin], a. Demasiado sutil, que sutiliza demasiado.

hairy [ˈhɛərɪ] [jea-ri], a. Peludo, velludo, velloso, cabelludo, cubierto de pelo. **Hairy comet,** cometa crinito.

haitian, a. V. HAYTIAN.

hake [heɪk] [jeik], s. Merlango, pescado de la familia de los gádidos, semejante a la merluza.

halberd [ˈhɔːlbɜːd] [jol-berd], s. Alabarda.

halcyon [ˈhælsɪən] [jal-sion], a. Quieto, apacible, tranquilo, sereno, pacífico. **Halcyon days,** tiempo de paz y tranquilidad; veranillo de San Martín. -s. (Orn.) Alcedón, alción.

hale [heɪl] [jeil], a. Sano, robusto, fuerte, vigoroso; entero, ileso.

hale, va. Tirar con violencia: arrastrar, llevar a uno violentamente de una parte a otra.

half [hɑːf] [jaf], s. (pl. HALVES). Mitad, la parte media de un todo. -a. 1. Medio, lo que no está perfectamente concluido o es la mitad de una cosa. 2. Medio, formado por una mitad. **Half an hour,** media hora. **Half and half,** mitad de uno y mitad de otro: mezcla de cervezas u otros licores. **Half-seas over,** medio borracho, el que está calamocano. **Half** en composición significa semi, casi, cerca de o un poco.

halfback [ˈhɑːfbæk] [jaf-bak], s. Medio (football).

half-baked [ˈhɑːfbeɪkt] [jaf-beikt], a. 1. A medio asar. 2. (Vul.) Inmaturo, inexperto.

half-blood [ˈhɑːfblʌd] [jaf-blad], s. Medio hermano, media hermana.

half-breed [ˈhɑːfbriːd] [jaf-brid], a. y s. Mestizo, de sangre mezclada.

half-calf binding [ˌhɑːfkɑːˈfbaɪndɪŋ] [jaf-kaf-baindin], s. Encuadernación a media pasta, vitela.

half-caste [ˈhɑːfkɑːst] [jaf-kast], a. Mestizo, de sangre mezclada, en especial cuando el padre o la madre es de raza blanca.

half-cock [ˈhɑːfkɒk] [jaf-kok], a. En seguro; se dice de un arma de fuego a medio amartillar.

half-crown [ˈhɑːfkraʊn] [jaf-kraun], s. Antigua moneda inglesa de plata del valor de dos chelines y medio.

half-hearted [ˈhɑːfˈhɑːtɪd] [jaf-jar-tid], a. Sin ánimo, indiferente.

half holiday [ˈhɑːfˈhɒlɪdeɪ] [jaf-jo-li-dei], s. Medio día de fiesta.

half life [ˈhɑːflaɪf] [jaf-laif], s. Vida media, período medio.

half-mast [ˈhɑːfˈmɑːst] [jaf-mast], s. A media asta, posición de una bandera en el palo en señal de duelo. -va. Poner a media asta.

half-moon [ˈhɑːfˈmuːn] [jaf-mun], s. Semilunio; lo que tiene figura de media luna.

halfpenny [ˈhɑːfpenɪ] [jaf-pe-ni], s. (po. HALFPENCE [ˈhɑːfpens] [jaf-pens], o HALFPENNIES). Medio penique, moneda de cobre en Inglaterra.

half-tone [ˈhɑːftəʊn] [jaf-toun], a. Perteneciente o relativo a un procedimiento fotográfico para la obtención de láminas. -s. 1. Lámina obtenida por este procedimiento. 2. (Mús.) Semitono.

halibut [ˈhælɪbət] [ja-li-bat], s. Mero, pez de los mares septentrionales.

halitosis [ˌhælɪˈtəʊsɪs] [ja-li-tou-sis], s. Mal aliento.

hall [hɔːl] [jol], s. 1. Vestíbulo, zaguán; corredor. 2. Salón grande a la entrada de algunas casas; antecámara. 3. Sala, el paraje donde se reunen los magistrados de los tribunales superiores para ejercer su ministerio. 4. Casa de ayuntamiento. 5. Casa de un gremio o corporación. 6. Salón, el paraje donde se reunen los diputados del pueblo o los comisionados de un cuerpo para celebrar sus juntas. 7. Colegio en las universidades de Oxford y Cambridge. **Hall-mark,** sello o marca oficial del Gremio de Orífices y Plateros (Ingl.) que indica la ley de los artículos de oro y plata.

hallelujah [ˌhælɪˈluːjə] [ja-li-lu-ya], s. Aleluya, canto en acción de gracias que significa **alabad al Señor.**

hallo, halloa [hʌˈləʊ] [ja-lou], inter. Voz para llamar la atención o para saludar: ¡hola! ¡oye! ¡oiga! ¡eh!

halloo [həˈluː] [ja-lu], inter. ¡Sus! ¡Busca! Voz con que los cazadores azuzan a los perros.

halloo, va. y vn. 1. Gritar a los perros en la caza o azuzarlos con gritos. 2. Gritar a, dar grita, insultar con clamores y gritos. 3. Llamar a uno gritando o a gritos; avisar a uno o darle aviso por medio de un grito.

hallooing [həˈluːɪŋ] [ja-luin], s. Grito alto y vehemente.

hallow [ˈhæləʊ] [ja-lou], va. Consagrar, santificar; reverenciar.

Halloween [ˈhæləʊˈiːn] [ja-louin], s. Víspera del día de Todos los Santos. Lo celebran principalmente los niños en los E.U. con fiestas de disfraces.

Hallowmas [ˈhæləʊmæs] [ja-lou-mas], s. El día de Todos los Santos, y el de la conmemoración de los fieles difuntos, que son el uno y el dos de noviembre. **Hallow-eve,** la víspera del día de Todos los Santos; muy celebrada entre los irlandeses.

hallucinate [həˈluːsɪneɪt] [ja-lu-si-neit], vn. Alucinarse, confundirse, equivocarse.

hallucination [həˌluːsɪˈneɪʃən] [ja-lu-si-nei-shon], s. Alucinación, error, equivocación; disparate.

hallway [ˈhɔːlweɪ] [jol-uei], s. (E.U.) Vestíbulo, zaguán; pasillo, corredor.

halma [ˈhælmə] [jal-ma], s. Juego de salón, con tablero y piezas numerosas y en el que toman parte dos, tres o cuatro personas.

halo [ˈheɪləʊ] [jei-lou], s. 1. Halo o halón, corona, especie de metéoro que consiste en un círculo alrededor del sol y la luna. 2. Lauréola, auréola.

halogen [ˈheɪləʊdʒɪn] [jei-lou-yin], s. Halógeno.

halography [ˈheɪləʊgræfɪ] [jei-lou-gra-fi], s. Halografía.

haloid [ˈhælɔɪd] [ja-loid], a. Haloideo, parecido a la sal marina. -s. Sal haloidea.

halt [hɔːlt] [jolt], vn. 1. Cojear, andar cojo (limp). 2. Parar, hacer parada o alto en alguna marcha o viaje. 3. Vacilar, dudar, tartamudear (stammer).

halt, s. 1. Cojera, el acto de cojear. 2. Parada, alto (stop). -a. Encojado, cojo; estropeado, lisiado.

halter [ˈhɔːltəʳ] [jol-taʳ], s. 1. Cabestro, ronzal, ramal, jáquima. 2. Soga, cuerda con que se ahorca a los malhechores. 3. Cojo, el que cojea.

halter, va. 1. Poner el cabestro, echar el ronzal. 2. Encordar.

haltingly [ˈhɔːltɪŋlɪ] [jol-tin-li], adv. A cox cox, a cox, cojita, a la pata coja.

halve [hɑːv] [jav], va. Partir en dos mitades.

halves [hɑːvz] [javs], inter. A la parte me llamo: expresión con que alguno pide parte de lo que otro se ha encontrado o ha ganado. *-pl.* de HALF. **To go halves,** ir a medias tener una parte igual.

halyard [ˈhæljəd] [jal-yard], *s. (Mar.)* Driza. **Peak-halyard,** driza del pico. **Throat-halyards,** drizas del foque mayor.

ham [hæm] [jam], *s.* 1. Pernil, jamón, el anca y muslo del puerco salado. 2. *(Anat.)* Corva, la parte de la pierna opuesta a la rodilla. *-n. pr.* Cam, hijo de Noé.

hamate [ˈhæmeɪt] [ja-meit], *a.* Enredado, encorvado, ganchoso.

hamated [ˈhæmeɪtɪd] [ja-mei-tid], *a.* Garabateado; lo que está afirmado o clavado con ganchos o garabatos.

hamburger [ˈhæmbɜːgəʳ] [jam-ber-gaʳ], *s.* Hamburguesa, emparedado de carne molida.

hame [heɪm] [jeim], *s.* 1. Horcate, palo que se pone al pescuezo de las caballerías para el tiro. 2. *(Esco.) V.* HOME.

hamlet [ˈhæmlɪt] [jam-lit], *s.* Aldea, villorrio, población corta, aldehuela.

hammam [ˈhæməm] [ja-mam], *s.* En Turquía, casa de baño;: de aquí, en los países occidentales, baño turco.

hammer [ˈhæməʳ] [ja-maʳ], *s.* Martillo, herramienta de percusión, compuesta de una cabeza, por lo común de hierro, y un mango. **Sledge-hammer,** macho, mazo grande. **Clech-hammer,** martillo de presa, de oreja. **Claw-hammer,** martillo con pala hendida o de orejas. **Drop-hammer,** martinete. **Paving-hammer,** pico de cantero. **Peen hammer,** martillo de boca. **Piano hammer,** martinete de piano. **Tack-hammer,** martillo para puntillas. **To come under the hammer,** venderse en subasta. **Tuning-hammer,** templador de afinador. **Hammer-dressed,** escuadrado, labrado a escoda. **To be hammered,** recibir una paliza.

hammer, *va.* 1. Martillar, batir y dar golpes con el martillo. 2. Forjar, trabajar alguna cosa a martillo. 3. Forjar, idear, trabajar alguna cosa con el entendimiento. **To hammer one's brains,** devanarse los sesos. *-vn.* Trabajar, estar ocupado, agitarse, hallarse en agitación. **The player hammered the ball into the net,** el jugador clavó el balón en la red.

hammercloth [ˈhæməklɒθ] [ja-ma-kloz], *s.* Paño del pescante de un coche.

hammerer [ˈhæmərəʳ] [ja-ma-raʳ], *s.* Martillador.

hammerhead [ˈhæməhed] [ja-ma-jed], *s. (Zool.)* Cornudilla, pez martillo, especie de tiburón.

hammering [ˈhæmərɪŋ] [ja-ma-rin], *s.* 1. Martilleo; la acción de fraguar; el ruido que hacen los martillazos. 2. Batido a martillo: superficie repujada de un metal.

hammerman [ˈhæməmən] [ja-ma-man], *s.* Martillador.

hammock [ˈhæmɒk] [ja-mok], *s.* Hamaca, red gruesa y clara que sirve de cama o columpio; coy.

hamper [ˈhæmpəʳ] [jam-paʳ], *s.* 1. Cuévano, canasta, cesto grande y hondo que sirve para varios usos. 2. Aparejo, jarcias y motonería a bordo. 3. Traba, impedimento.

hamper, *va.* 1. Enmarañar, enredar, embarazar, estorbar. 2. Entrampar, persuadir con engaños o añagazas, embobar. 3. Encestar, recoger en una cesta.

hamstring [ˈhæmstrɪŋ] [jams-trin], *s.* Tendón de la corva.

hamstring, *va.* Desjarretar, cortar las piernas por el jarrete o por la corva.

hanaper [ˈhænəpəʳ] [ja-na-paʳ], *s.* 1. Canasta o cesta para documentos u objetos de valor. 2. Erario, tesorería.

hand [hænd] [jand], *s.* 1. Mano, parte del cuerpo humano que comienza en la muñeca y acaba en las puntas de los dedos. 2. Maña, destreza, habilidad (hability); también obra mecánica o manual, manos. 3. Mano derecha o izquierda, el lado derecho o izquierdo. 4. Operario, operaria, hombre o mujer que hace trabajo manual. 5. Una persona; gente; agente, instrumento; por lo común en plural. **All hands joined in the sport,** todos se pusieron a divertirse. 6. La mano como prenda de esponsales. 7. Manecilla o aguja de reloj. 8. Disciplina; influencia (influence); poder, posesión (possession). 9. Forma o carácter de escritura (writing). 10. Palmo, medida de cuatro pulgadas. 11. Mano, en el juego. 12. Acción, trabajo, agencia (action). **Clean hands,** manos limpias, es decir, honradez en asunto de interés. **Light hand,** dulzura, suavidad. **To bring up by hand,** dar de marmar artificialmente a un niño o un animalito. **To get one's hand in,** estar en vena, adquirir habilidad por medio de la práctica. **To get the upper hand,** llevar la ventaja, ganar la palmeta. **To come to hand,** estar o hallarse a la mano, ser recibido. **To have a hand in,** tener parte en, ser interesado o comprometido en. **To lay hands on,** echar mano (a alguno), acometer; ordenar por medio de la imposición de manos. **To lend a hand,** echar una mano, ayudar. **To set the hand to,** meter mano en, emprender, embarcarse en un negocio. **To stand one in hand,** concernir, importar a alguno. **To strike hands,** tocar la mano en señal de cerrar un contrato. **To shake hands,** apretar la mano (a alguno) en signo de amistad. **To wash one's hands of,** lavarse las manos, desentenderse, declinar toda responsabilidad. **To change hands,** cambiar de dueño. **Hands off!,** ¡manos quietas! **To lay violent hands on,** dar la muerte. **It is allowed on all hands,** todo el mundo conviene o todos confiesan. **In hand** De contado, desde luego, por de pronto, hablando de dinero que se recibe. **At hand o near at hand,** a la mano, cerca, al lado, junto. **To hold hand,** competir. **By the hand,** por medio de. **Under my hand,** firmado de mi puño y letra. **On the one hand,** por una parte o por un lado. **I have it from very good hands,** lo sé de buen origen. **Keep off your hands,** no me toques. **Hand in hand,** de concierto, de acuerdo, de inteligencia. **Short-hand,** abreviatura, taquigrafía. **Off-hand,** pronto sin detenerse. **On hand,** (a) a mano, en poder, en su legítima posesión; surtido. (b) a la mano, en su lugar, presente, puntual. **To buy at first hand,** comprar de primera mano. **A good hand at cards,** buen juego, buenas cartas. **They are hand and glove,** son uña y carne. **Out of hand,** luego, inmediatamente. **Hand over head,** inconsideradamente. **Minute hand,** minutero. **From hand to mouth,** de manos a boca, esto es, sin economía, sin previsión para el futuro. **First-rate hand,** *(Mec.)* un buen oficial, un excelente mecánico. **Second-hand clothes,** ropa usada. **Second-hand clothes shop,** ropavejería. **Second-hand bookseller,** librero de viejo, o de libros usados. **An off-hand sketch,** diseño improvisado. **To be short of hands,** carecer do brazos, de operarios. **All hands below!** ¡Abajo todo el mundo! **All hands on deck!** ¡Todo el mundo arriba! **Large hand,** letra grande. **Round hand,** letra redonda. **To be one's right hand,** ser la mano derecha de uno.

hand, *va.* 1. Alargar, alcanzar algo y darlo a otro. 2. Conducir, guiar por la mano (guide). 3. Agarrar, echar la mano. 4. Manejar una cosa o moverla con la mano. 5. Poner en manos de. *-vn.* Cooperar, concertarse, ir de acuerdo o inteligencia. **To hand down,** (a) transmitir, pasar sucesivamente de unos a otros. (b) bajar, entregar a un cuerpo inferior; pasar de arriba a abajo. **To hand in (o into),** dar la mano para entrar; ayudar a entrar en. **To hand round o around,** hacer pasar, hacer circular, pasar de uno a otro. **To hand the sails,** *(Mar.)* Aferrar las velas.

handbag [ˈhændbæg] [jand-bag], *s.* Bolsa de mano, saco de noche, maletín.

hand baggage [ˈhændbægɪdʒ] [jand-ba-guich], *s.* Equipaje de mano.

handball [ˈhændbɔːl] [jand-bol], *s.* 1. Pelota de mano. 2. Juego de ese nombre. 3. Bola hueca para rociar, etc.

handbarrow [ˈhændbærəʊ] [jand-ba-rou], *s.* Angarillas, parihuela.

hand-basket [ˈhændbɑːskɪt] [jand-bas-kit], *s.* Cestilla, cesta pequeña.

handbell [ˈhændbel] [jand-bel], *s.* Esquila, campanilla.

handbill [ˈhændbɪl] [jand-bil], *s.* Cartel, anuncio, prospecto.

handbook [ˈhændbʊk] [jand-buk], *s.* Manual, guía.

handbow [ˈhændbəʊ] [jand-bau], *s.* Arco de mano para disparar flechas.

handbreadth ['hændbreθ] [jand-brez], *s.* Palmo, lo ancho de la mano.

handcar ['hændkɑːʳ] [jand-ka'], *s. (Ferro.)* Vagón pequeño que se hace andar con unas palancas movidas a mano.

handcart ['hændkɑːt] [jand-kart], *s.* Carrito o carretilla de mano.

handcraft, *s. V.* HANDICRAFT.

handcuff ['hændkʌf] [jand-kaf], *s.* Manilla, esposas.

handcuff, *va.* Maniatar.

handed ['hændɪd] [jan-did], *a.* 1. Lo que tiene el uso de la mano. 2. *(Des.)* Con las manos juntas. En composición: **Right-handed,** que usa habitualmente de la mano derecha. **Left-handed,** zurdo, que usa con preferencia de la mano izquierda. *V.* también SCREW. **Four-handed,** a cuatro manos. **Empty-handed,** con las manos vacias. **Hard-handed,** de manos callosas; de mano pesada. **High-handed,** imperioso. **One-handed,** manco. **Open-handed,** generoso, liberal. **Single-handed,** con una sola mano; por sí solo.

hander ['hændəʳ] [jan-da'], *s.* El que transmite o envía.

handfast ['hændfɑːst] [jand-fast], *va.* 1. Desposar, casar a uno por palabras de presente. 2. Atar, boligar, precisar por deber.

handful ['hændfʊl] [jand-ful], *s.* 1. Puñado manojo, una mano llena. 2. *(Des.)* El ancho de la mano. **handful of flour,** puñado de harina. **Handful of people,** puñado de gente. **Double handful,** almuerzo.

hand-gallop ['hændgæləp] [jand-ga-lop], *s.* Galope fácil o corto.

hand grenade ['hændgrɪˌneɪd] [jand-gre-neid], *s.* Granada de mano.

hand-gun ['hændgʌn] [jand-gan], *s.* Escopeta de mano.

hand-glass ['hændglɑːs] [jand-glas], *s.* 1. Espejo de mano. 2. Lente para leer.

handicap ['hændɪkæp] [jan-di-kap], *va.* Imponer ciertos impedimentos o desventajas para contrapesar determinadas ventajas: de aquí, poner obstáculos, estorbar, detener (hamper, linder). -*s.* 1. Condición que se impone para igualar las probabilidades de éxito de los competidores, p. ej. llevar un exceso de peso o empezar una carrera después que los otros contendientes. 2. Carrera con caballos de peso igualado.

handicapped ['hændɪkæpt] [jan-di-kapt], *a.* Impedido, estorbado por algún inconveniente o desventaja.

handicraft ['hændɪkrɑːft] [jan-di-kraft], *s.* 1. Oficio, arte mecánica, obra manual. 2. Menestral, mecánico.

handicraftsman ['hændɪkrɑːftsˌmən] [jan-di-krafts-man], *s.* Artesano, menestral, mecánico, el que ejerce algún arte mecánica o manual.

handicuff ['hændɪkʌf] [jan-di-kaf], *s.* Manotada, revés, puñetazo.

handily ['hændɪlɪ] [jan-di-li], *adv.* Mañosamente, con destreza (skillfully).

handiness ['hændɪnɪs] [jan-di-nes], *s.* Maña, habilidad, destreza para hace alguna cosa.

handiwork ['hændɪwɜːk] [jan-di-uek], *s.* Obra mecánica o manual.

hardkerchief ['hæŋkətʃɪf] [jan-ker-chif], *s.* Pañuelo.

hand-language ['hændɪˌlæŋgwɪtʃ] [jan-di-lan-güich], *s.* El arte de entenderse por medio de las manos o de los dedos, por señas.

handle ['hændl] [jan-del], *va.* 1. Palpar, tocar con las manos (touch). 2. Manejar; hacer tratable (use, manipulate). 3. Tratar un asunto, una materia, una cuestión, etc (deal). 4. Practicar una profesión o arte. 5. Comerciar en, comprar y vender. 6. Tratar, portarse bien o mal con alguno. -*vn.* 1. Hacer uso de las manos, trabajar con ellas. 2. Ser manejado. **Handle with care,** frágil; con cuidado.

handle, *s.* 1. Mango, puño, asa, asidero, manija, cabo. **A fan with ivory handles,** abanico con varillas de marfil. 2. Cualquier cosa que se puede echar mano para usarla. 3. *(Fam.)* Tratamiento, título que da una profesión.

handle bar ['hændlbɑːʳ] [jan-del-ba'], *s.* Manubrio (de bicicleta, etc.)

handless ['hændlɪs] [jand-lis], *a.* Manco, sin mano.

handling ['hændlɪŋ] [jand-lin], *s.* 1. Manejo, el acto de manejar alguna cosa (use). 2. Toque, en la pintura o escultura. 3. Manejo, treta, astucia, ardid (trick).

hand-made ['hændmeɪd] [jand-meid], *a.* Hecho a mano.

handmaid ['hændmeɪd] [jand-meid], **handmaiden** ['hændmeɪdən] [jand-mei-den], *sf.* Criada, asistenta.

hand-me-down ['hændmɪdaɪn] [jand-mi-daun], *a.* Hecho, de confección; barato de segunda mano; poco elegante.

hand-mill ['hændmɪl] [jand-mil], *s.* Molinillo, molino que se mueve con la mano.

hand-organ ['hændɔːgən] [jand-or-gan], *s.* Organillo, órgano de cigüeña.

handout ['hændaʊt] [jand-aut], *s.* 1. *(Fam.)* Ropa o comestibles que se dan de limosna. 2. Volante de distribución gratuita. 3. Noticias o información distribuidas por una agencia de publicidad. 4. Declaración oficial proporcionada a la prensa.

hand-picked ['hændpɪkt] [jand-pikt], *a.* Escogido o seleccionado con cuidado.

handrail ['hændreɪl] [jand-reil], *s.* Barandal, pasamano.

hand-sails ['hændseɪlz] [jand-seils], *s. pl. (Mar.)* Velas manuales.

hand-saw ['hændsɔː] [jand-so], *s.* Sierra de mano, serrucho.

hand-screw ['hændskruː] [jand-skru], *s.* Gato de mano, cornaquí.

handsel, hansel ['hændsl] [jand-el], *s.* 1. Estrena, el primer dinero que se recibe por lo que se vende o la primera venta de algún objeto; regalo que se da como muestra de benevolencia. 2. Prenda que se da como garantía de una venta o contrato.

handsel, hansel, *va.* (Poco us.) Estrenar alguna cosa o estrenarse en ella; dar un regalo o aguinaldo; dar prenda en garantía.

handset ['hændset] [jand-set], *s.* Microteléfono (aparato con el micrófono y auricular en una sola pieza.)

handshake ['hændʃeɪk] [jand-sheik], *s.* Apretón de manos.

hands-off [ˌhændzˈɒf] [jands-of], *a.* De no intervención; **hands off policy,** política de no intervención.

handsome ['hænsəm] [jan-som], *a.* 1. Apuesto, perfecto, de buena figura, gentil, lindo, agradable a la vista. 2. Primoroso, excelente (excellent). 3. Amplio, liberal, dadivoso (generous). 4. Generoso, noble. 5. Honrado, honesto (honest). 6. Fino, distiguido, correcto. **It is not handsome for you to say so,** no está bien que Ud. hable así. **A handsome man,** un hombre apuesto.

handsomely ['hænsəmlɪ] [jan-som-li], *adv.* Hermosamente, primorosamente; generosamente.

handsomeness ['hænsəmnɪʃ] [jan-som-nes], *s.* Hermosura, gracia, elegancia; generosidad. «**Handsomeness is the more animal excellence, beauty the more imaginative**», la hermosura es la excelencia más corpórea, la belleza la más espiritual.

handspring ['hændsprɪŋ] [jand-sprin], *s.* Voltereta.

handstroke ['hændstrəʊk] [jand-strouk], *s.* Golpe dado con la mano; puñetazo.

handstaff ['hændstɑːf] [jand-staf], *s.* Jabalina, arma antigua.

handwheel ['hændwiːl] [jand-uil], *s. (Mec.)* Rueda o volante de mando o maniobra.

handwork ['hændwɜːk] [jand-uerk], *s.* Obra hecha a mano y no a máquina; obra manual.

handwriting ['hændwraɪtɪŋ] [jand-rai-tin], *s.* 1. Carácter de letra, la forma de letra que cada uno tiene, quirografía. 2. Escritura, algo escrito.

handy ['hændɪ] [jan-di], *a.* 1. Manual o ejecutado con la mano. 2. Socorrido, de uso conveniente; muy arrimado, junto, cerca, de fácil acceso. 3. Diestro, hábil, mañoso. 4. *(Mar.)* Manual, lo que es fácil de manejar.

handygripe ['hændɪgraɪp] [jan-di-graip], *s.* El acto de agarrar, ya sea con las manos o con las garras.

handy man ['hændɪmən] [jan-di-man], *s.* 1. Manitas. 2. Persona con facilidad para muchos oficios.

handywork ['hændɪwɜːk] [jan-di-uerk] *s.* Obra mecánica o manual.

hang [hæŋ] [jang], *va.* (*pret.* y pr. HUNG o HANGED). 1. Colgar, suspender alguna cosa en alto (put up). 2. Inclinar alguna cosa, ponerla más baja de lo que debía estar. 3. Desplegar alguna cosa colgándola. 4. Fijar algo de modo que pueda moverse en determinadas direcciones (fix). 5. Colgar, ahorcar. (En este sentido el participio pasado es **hanged** solamente). 6. Entapizar, adornar con tapices o telas. -*vn.* 1. Colgar, estar alguna cosa pendiente en el aire. 2. Fluctuar, vacilar (hesitate). 3. Ser ahorcado, sufirir la pena de horca. 4. Pegarse, agregarse alguno a otro importunamente y sin ser llamado. 5. Colgarse, abrazarse fuertemente al cuello de alguna persona. 6. Continuar en el mismo estado. 7. Quedarse suspenso al oír algo. 8. Depender de la voluntad o dictamen de otro. 9. Formar pendiente. 10. Tardar, dilatar. 11. (*E. U.*) No poder avenirse los pareceres, p. ej. en un jurado. **Cf.** núm. 6.

hang around, tardar, haraganear.

hang back, rehusar ir adelante, vacilar antes de adelantar.

hang down, bajar; colgar, estar pendiente.

hang out, enarbolar.

hang up, levantar, suspender en el aire. **To hang about one's neck,** abrazarse estrechamente con alguno. **To hang loose,** estar colgada una cosa de modo que se pueda mover con facilidad.

hang over, cabecear, inclinarse.

hang together, acordarse.

hang upon, mirar con afecto particular. (*Mar.*) Cargar sobre. **To hang the rudder,** (*Mar.*) Montar el timón. **To hang fire,** (*Mil.*) suspender el fuego; se dice también de las armas de fuego que no disparan al instante; de aquí, tardarse, no tener lugar, no hacerse al tiempo debido. **To hang a room with tapestry,** entapizar una pieza. **Hanging knees,** (*Mar.*) curvas de alto abajo. **Hang me, if it is not a fib all that he says,** (*Fam.*) que me emplumen si no es mentira todo lo que dice. **Hang-bird,** pájaro que fabrica un nido colgante, como la oropéndola y eloriol de Baltimore; a éste último se le llama también familiarmente **fiery hang-bird.**

hang, *s.* 1. La manera como cuelga o se cuelga una cosa. 2. (*Fam.*) Uso o conocimiento familiar, maña, destreza. 3. Idea, prevalente, conexión, aceptación general. 4. (*Mar.*) Curva, bajada rápida.

hangar ['hæŋəʳ] [jan-gaʳ], *s.* (*Aer.*) Hangar.

hangbird ['hæŋbɜːd] [jang-berd], *s.* Pájaro que fabrica un nido colgante.

hangby ['hæŋbaɪ] [jang-bai], (*Ant.*) **Hanger on,** *s.* 1. Dependiente; mogollón, gorrista, pegote, moscón, ladilla. 2. Familiar; paseante en corte.

hangdog ['hæŋdɒg] [jang-dog], *a.* De carácter o apariencia vil; bajo, tacaño. -*s.* Hombre vil, ruin e insidioso; mataperros.

hanger ['hæŋəʳ] [jan-gaʳ], *s.* Soporte colgante, barra, gancho. 2. Colgadero, percha. 3. Sable corto.

hanging ['hæŋɪŋ] [jan-guin], *s.* 1. Colgadura; tapices o telas con que se cubren y adornan las paredes interiores de las casas. 2. Muestra, exhibición. 3. Muerte en la horca. -*a.* Digno de ser ahorcado o digno de horca. **Hanging face,** cara de ahorcado.

hangman ['hæŋman] [jang-man], *s.* Verdugo, el ejecutor de las penas corporales y de la pena capital.

hangnail ['hæŋneɪl] [jang-neil], *s.* Padrastro, respigón, pedacito de pellejo que se levanta de la carne inmediata a las uñas de la mano.

hangout ['hæŋaʊt] [jang-aut], *s.* Morada, guarida; punto de reunión.

hangover ['hæŋəʊvəʳ] [jang-ou-vaʳ], *s.* 1. Cruda. (*Amer.*) Resaca, goma, guayabo. 2. Sobrante.

hank [hæŋk] [jank], *s.* 1. Madeja de hilo, ovillo. 2. (*Vulg.*) Lazo, freno; influencia, inclinación, poder. **Hanks,** (*Mar.*) Anillos o arcos de palo.

hank, *V.* 1. Hacer madejas. 2. Adujar.

hanker ['hæŋkəʳ] [jan-kaʳ], *vn.* Ansiar, apetecer.

hanker, *s.* Obrero que ata o empaqueta madejas.

hankering ['hæŋkərɪŋ] [jang-ka-rin], *s.* Ansia fuerte o vehemente, antojo, deseo; afición, inclinación, apetencia.

hanky ['hæŋkɪ] [jan-ki], *s.* Pañuelo (children).

hanky-panky ['hæŋkɪ'pæŋkɪ] [jan-ki-pan-ki], *s.* 1. Charlatanería de prestidigitador para distraer la atención. 2. Engaño. 3. Prestidigitación.

Hannah ['hɑːnə] [ja-na], *n. pr.* Ana.

Hannibal ['hænɪbəl] [ja-ni-bal], *n. pr.* Aníbal.

Hanover ['hænəvəʳ] [ja-no-vaʳ], (*Geog.*) Hannover.

Hanoverian [ˌhænəˈvɪərɪən] [ja-no-via-rian], *a.* Hannoveriano.

hanse ['hænz] [jans], *s.* 1. Gremio o unión mercantil. 2. Hansa, Ansa.

hap [hæp] [jap], *s.* 1. Caso, lance, acaso; casualidad, accidente. 2. Fortuna, buena suerte.

hap, *vn.* Acontecer, acaecer, suceder. -*va.* (*Esco.*) Cubrir; vestir.

haphazar ['hæp'hæzəd] [jap-ja-sard], *a.* 1. De casualidad. 2. Descuidado, a medias.

hapless ['hæplɪs] [ja-plis], *a.* Desgraciado, desventurado, desamparado, miserable.

haply ['hæplɪ] [ja-pli], *adv.* 1. Quizá o quizás. 2. Casualmente, por casualidad.

happen ['hæpən] [ja-pen], *vn.* 1. Acontecer, acaecer (occur, take place); suceder por casualidad; sobrevenir; llegar el caso de. 2. Hallarse en alguna parte. **Whatever happens,** suceda lo que quiera, venga lo que viniere. **I happened to be there,** por casualidad me hallaba allí. **It unfortunately happened that I was not there,** por desgracia no me hallé allí. **To happen in,** (*Fam.*) Hacer una visita por casualidad. **To happen on,** encontrar, hallar por acaso. **I happened on other things,** hallé o me encontré con otras materias. **He happened to be there,** estaba allí por casualidad. **Hi, what's happening?,** hola, ¿qué tal? (*Amer*). **These things happen,** son cosas que pasan.

happening ['hæpnɪŋ] [jap-nin], *s.* Acontecimiento, suceso.

happily ['hæpɪlɪ] [ja-pi-li], *adv.* Dichosamente, felizmente; graciosmente.

happiness ['hæpɪnɪs] [ja-pi-nes], *s.* Felicidad, prosperidad, dicha (joy); gracia natural o no estudiada.

happy ['hæpɪ] [ja-pi], *a.* 1. Feliz, bienaventurado, dichoso, afortunado. 2. Expedito, desembarazado. **To lead a happy life** Pasar una vida feliz o dichosa.

happy-go-lucky ['hæpɪgəʊˈlʌlɪ] [ja-pi-gou-la-ki], *a.* Despreocupado, contento de su suerte.

hara-kiri o **hari-kari** ['hærəˈkɪrɪ] [ja-ra-ki-ri], *s.* Procedimiento japonés de suicidio por medio del desentrañamiento.

harangue [həˈræŋ] [ja-rang], *s.* Arenga, oración.

harangue, *vn.* Arengar, decir en público, alguna arenga o discurso. -*va.* Hablar arengando.

haranguer [həˈræŋəʳ] [ja-ran-gaʳ], *s.* Orador.

harass ['hærəs] [ja-ras], *va.* 1. Cansar, causar cansancio, acosar, fatigar, hostigar, incomodar. (*Vulg.*) Moler, jorobar. 2. (*Mil.*) Hostigar, cansar al enemigo por medio de ataques repetidos.

harassment ['hærəsmənt] [ja-ras-ment], *s.* Cansancio, fatiga, hostigamiento.

harbinger ['hɑːbɪndʒəʳ] [jar-bin-chaʳ], *s.* Precursor, el que va delante de otro; aposentador; anuncio, presagio. -*va.* Presagiar, anunciar; ser precursor de.

harbor, harbour ['hɑːbəʳ] [jar-baʳ], *s.* 1. Puerto, ensenada. **Harbor-dues,** derechos de puerto. **Harbor-master,** capitán de puerto. 2. Asilo, lugar de refugio y descanso. 3. (*Des.*) Albergue, posada.

harbor, *va.* 1. Abrigar, amparar, defender, resguardar (defend). 2. Albergar, acoger, hospedar, dar albergue u hospedaje; concebir, recibir en la mente. 3. Dar abrigo o ser capa de ladrones. *-vn.* Recibir amparo o protección.

harborage [ˈhɑːbərɪdʒ] [jar-ba-reich], *s.* 1. Puerto, lugar de abrigo para las embarcaciones. 2. Amparo, asilo.

harborer [ˈhɑːbərəʳ] [jar-ba-raʳ], *s.* 1. Amparador, albergador, acogedor, el que hospeda a alguno, antiguamente huésped. 2. Encubridor de robos o ladrones.

hard [hɑːd] [jard], *a.* 1. Duro, sólido, firme, endurecido (tough). 2. Difícil, dificultoso, arduo, penoso, trabajoso (dificult). 3. Oscuro, difícil de entenderse. 4. Insensible, cruel, riguroso, severo, rígido. **A hard winter,** invierno riguroso. 5. Injusto, contrario a la razón, opresivo, ofensivo. 6. Áspero, bronco, grosero (rude). 7. Escaso; tosco y desagradable al gusto. 8. Mezquino, miserable. 9. Cruda, gorda, que contiene ciertas sales minerales disueltas: se dice del agua. **Hard of bearing,** medio sordo, teniente o duro de oído. **Hard of belief,** incrédulo. **Hard to deal with,** intratable, poco sociable. **Hard words,** palabras ásperas o palabras injuriosas. **Hard drinking,** borrachera, la condición de beber a pote. *-adv.* 1. Cerca, a la mano. **Hard by,** inmediato, arrimado, muy cerca. 2. Diligentemente, con ahinco. **To study hard,** estudiar con ahinco. 3. Inquietamente, con inquietud: con impaciencia, vejación o pesar. **To go hard,** traer a mal traer, causar apuros. 4. Aprisa, ligeramente. 5. Difícilmente, con dificultad. 6. Tempestuosamente. 7. Reciamente, con fuerza, con dureza. 8. *(Mar.)* Todo al límite extremo. **Hard a-port,** a babor todo. **To drink hard,** beber con exceso. **To grow hard,** endurecerse. **It rains hard,** llueve a cántaros. **Hard and fast,** de cal y canto, a macha martillo. **Hard cash,** moneda sonante, numerario; opuesto a papel moneda. **Things go hard with him,** sus asuntos se hallan en mal esado. **It will go hard with me if I cannot prevent him,** me irá mal si no logro impedírselo. **The poor fellow was hard put to it for a living,** el pobre hombre vivía con mucho trabajo. **To be hard up,** hallarse en apuros, estar a la cuarta pregunta. **Hard-pressed, hard-pushed,** escaso o falto de recursos, apurado, reducido a una situación angustiosa.

hard-and-fast [ˈhɑːdənˈfɑːst] [jard-an-fast], *a.* Rígido, estricto. **Hard-and-fast rule,** disposición inquebrantable.

hard-bitted [ˈhɑːdˈbɪtɪt] [jard-bi-tid], *a.* Boquiduro (horse).

hard-bitten [ˈhɑːdˈbɪtn] [jard-bi-ten], *a.* Duro, resistente en la lucha, terco, tenaz.

hard-boiled [ˈhɑːdˈbɔɪld] [jard-boild], *a.* 1. Duro (egg). 2. Duro, insensible, inflexible. 3. Terco.

hard-bound [ˈhɑːdˈbaʊnd] [jard-baund], *a.* Estreñido; estéril.

hard cider [ˈhɑːdˈsɪdəʳ] [jard-si-daʳ], *s.* Sidra, bebida alcohólica.

hard coal [ˈhɑːdkəʊl] [jard-koul], *s.* Antracita.

hard-earned [ˈhɑːdˈɜːnd] [jard-ernd], *a.* Ganado o adquirido con dificultad.

harden [ˈhɑːdn] [jar-den], *vn.* 1. Endurecer, poner dura y sólida alguna cosa. 2. Endurecer, robustecer, hacer a uno más apto para la fatiga o para el trabajo; curtir. 3. Endurecer; hacer duro, insensible, obstinado, descarado. 4. Hacer a uno firme y constante. *-vn.* Endurecerse, empedernirse.

hardener [ˈhɑːdnəʳ] [jard-naʳ], *s.* El que endurece.

hardening [ˈhɑːdnɪŋ] [jard-nin], *s.* Endurecimiento. Hardening the arteries, arteriosclerosis.

hard-favoredness [ˈhɑːdˈfeɪvədnɪs] [jard-fei-vord-nes], *s.* Fealdad; facciones irregulares o duras.

hard-fisted [ˈhɑːdˈfɪstɪd] [jard-fis-tid], *a.* 1. Con las manos callosas o endurecidas. 2. Avaro, miserable. *V.* CLOSE-FISTED.

hard-fought [ˈhɑːdˈfɔːt] [jard-fot], *a.* Fuertemente combatido.

hard-got, hard-gotten [ˈhɑːdgɒt] [jard-got], *a.* Adquirido con mucho trabajo.

hard-handed [ˈhɑːdˈhændɪd] [jard-jan-did], *a.* 1. Basto, el que tiene las manos encallecidas por el trabajo; menestral, trabajador. 2. Severo, despótico.

hard-headed [ˈhɑːdˈhedɪd] [jard-je-did], *a.* 1. Testarudo, terco. 2. Astuto, sagaz.

hard-hearted [ˈhɑːdˈhɑːtɪd] [jard-jar-tid], *a.* Cruel, severo, bárbaro, inhumano, salvaje, duro de corazón, insensible, inflexible, inexorable.

hard-heartedness [ˈhɑːdˈhɑːtɪdnɪs] [jard-jar-tid-nes], *s.* Crueldad, falta de ternura o compasión, insensibilidad, inhumanidad, dureza de corazón.

hardihood [ˈhɑːdɪhuːd] [jar-di-jud], *s.* 1. Atrevimiento, valor; atrevimiento inconsiderado, temeridad. 2. Descaro, impudencia, desvergüenza.

hardiness [ˈhɑːdɪnɪs] [jar-di-nes], *s.* 1. Ánimo, osadía, valor, intrepidez. 2. Robustez, vigor.

hard labor [ˈhɑːdˈleɪbəʳ] [jard-lei-baʳ], *s.* Trabajos forzados (en una prisión, etc.)

hard-labored [ˈhɑːdˈleɪbəd] [jard-lei-bord], *a.* Elaborado, trabajado.

hardly [ˈhɑːdlɪ] [jard-li], *adv.* 1. Difícilmente, con dificultad, apenas. 2. No totalmente, casi no, apenas: eufemismo en lugar de no. 3. De mala gana, a viva fuerza. 4. Rigurosamente, con rigor y opresión; ásperamente, con aspereza, duramente, severamente. 5. Improbablemente.

hard-mouthed [ˈhɑːdˈmaɪθɪd] [jard-mau-zid], *a.* Desobediente al freno: se dice de los caballos de boca dura.

hardness [ˈhɑːdnɪs] [jard-nes], *s.* 1. Dureza, firmeza, solidez. 2. Oscuridad, la dificultad en darse a entender. 3. *(Ant.)* Dificultad de ejecutarse alguna cosa; pena, trabajo. 4. Escasez, penuria. 5. Obstinación en el mal. 6. Ferocidad, fiereza, crueldad, inhumanidad, severidad, obduración. 7. Rigor o aspereza del frío. **Hardness of heart,** dureza de corazón.

hard-pan [ˈhɑːdpæn] [jard-pan], *s.* 1. *(Min.)* Capa sólida de detrito debajo de un terreno blando. 2. *(Fam. E. U.)* De aquí, fundamento firme; base sólida.

hard rubber, *s. V.* RUBBER.

hards [ˈhɑːdz] [jards], *s.* 1. Desperdicio o parte basta del lino. 2. Mezcla de alumbre y sal que usan los panaderos para blanquear el pan.

hard-set [ˈhɑːdset] [jard-set], *a.* Apurado, que está en un aprieto. 2. Obstinado, firme, resuelto.

hard-shell [ˈhɑːdʃel] [jard-shel], *a.* 1. Cáscara o caparazón duro. 2. *(E.U.)* Intransigente.

hardship [ˈhɑːdʃɪp] [jard-ship], *s.* 1. Injuria, opresión, gravamen, injusticia. 2. Penalidad, trabajo, molestia, fatiga, pena.

hardtack [ˈhɑːdtæk] [jard-tak], *s.* Galleta de munición.

hardtop [ˈhɑːdtɒp] [jard-top], *s.* Capota dura.

hardware [ˈhɑːdwɛəʳ] [jard-ueaʳ], *s.* Quincallería, ferretería, quinquillería, mercaderías menudas de hierro, acero, cobre y otros metales; también muchos instrumentos de agricultura. **Hardware trade,** quincallería.

hardwareman [ˈhɑːdˈwɛəmən] [jard-uea-man], *s.* Quincallero, buhonero.

hard-won [ˈhɑːdˈwʌn] [jard-uan], *a.* Ganado a pulso, con dificultad.

hardwood [ˈhɑːdwʊd] [jard-wud], *s.* Madera dura, es decir, la de los árboles que mudan sus hojas, en oposición a los de hojas perenes o en forma de aguja.

hardy [ˈhɑːdɪ] [jar-di], *a.* 1. Osado, atrevido, bravo, intrépido (encouraged). 2. Fuerte, robusto, endurecido. 3. *(Hort.)* Que sobrevive en invierno, al aire libre; que aguanta bien el frío.

hare [hɛəʳ] [jeaʳ], *s.* 1. Liebre, mamífero roedor con orejas muy largas, del género Lepus. 2. Fibras del cáñamo. **Young hare,** lebratillo.

harebell [ˈhɛəbel] [jea-bel], *s.* *(Bot.)* 1. Campanilla. 2. *(Esco.)* Jacinto silvestre.

hare-brained [ˈhɛəbreɪnd] [jea-breind], *a.* Inconstante, volátil, precipitado, ligero de cascos, aturdido.

harefoot [ˈhɛəfʊt] [jea-fut], s. 1. (Zool.) Lagópedo, especie de gallina silvestre, del género Lagopus. 2. (Poét.) Corredor ágil 3. V. HARE'S-FOOT.

hare-footed [ˈhɛəfʊtɪd] [jea-fu-tid], (Poét.) Ligero, ágil. **Mad as a March hare, extravagante,** loco, insensato.

hare-hearted [ˈhɛəˈhɑːtɪd] [jea-jar-tid], a. Alebrado, temeroso, medroso, tímido, cobarde.

harehound [ˈhɛəhaʊnd] [jea-jaund], s. Lebrel, galgo.

hare-hunter [ˈhɛəˈhʌntəʳ] [jea-jan-taʳ], s. Aficionado a la caza de liebres.

hare-hunting [ˈhɛəˈhʌntɪŋ] [jea-jan-tin], s. Montería o caza de liebres.

harelip [ˈhɛəˈlɪp] [jea-lip], s. Hendidura o abertura del labio superior, labio leporino.

harelipped [ˈhɛəˈlɪpt] [jea-lipt], a. Labihendido, el que tiene partido el labio superior.

harem [ˈhɑːriːm] [ja-rim], s. 1. Harén, harem, serrallo, la habitación de las mujeres mahometanas. 2. Conjunto de las mujeres del harén.

haremint [ˈhɛəmɪnt] [jea-mint], s. (Bot.) Yaro, manto de Santa María.

harenet [ˈhɛənet] [jea-net], s. Especie de red para coger liebres.

harepipe [ˈhɛəpaɪp] [jea-paip], s. Lazo para coger liebres.

hare's-ear [ˈhɛəzˈɛəʳ] [jeas-eaʳ], s. (Bot.) Oreja de liebre, hierba de Europa.

hareslettuce [ˈhɛəzˈletjuːs] [jeas-le-tius], s. (Bot.) Ajonjera.

harewort [ˈhɛəˈwɔːt] [jea-uort], s. (Bot.) Malva de huerta.

haricot [ˈhærɪkəʊ] [ja-ri-kau], s. 1. Especie de guisado de carne con habichuelas. 2. Frijol, judía o habichuela.

hark [hɑːk] [jark], inter. ¡Eh! ¡oye! ¡mira!

hark, vn. Escuchar, oír con atención, atender.

harken, hearken [ˈhɑːkən] [jar-ken], va. Oír con atención, escuchar. -vn. Escuchar, atender; seguir con atención lo que se dice para obedecer; tomar en consideración.

harl [ˈhɑːl] [jarl], s. Hebras de lino; filamento.

harlequin [ˈhɑːlɪkwɪn] [jar-li-kuin], s. Arlequín, gracioso, bufón.

harlequin, va. Bufonear, decir gracias, hacer monerías; chasquear.

harlequinade [ˈhɑːlɪkwɪneɪd] [jar-li-kui-neid], s. Arlequinada, suertes de arlequín; pantomina.

harlot [ˈhɑːlɒt] [jar-lot], s. Ramera, meretriz, prostituta. -a. Ruin, vil; metricio.

harlot, vn. Prostituirse, hacerse ramera.

harm [hɑːm] [jarm], s. 1. Detrimento, daño, peligro, desgracia, perjuicio, agravio (pain, risk). 2. Maldad, mal.

harm, va. Dañar, injuriar, agraviar, ofender.

harmful [ˈhɑːmfʊl] [jarm-ful], a. Dañoso, nocivo; peligroso, perjudicial.

harmfully [ˈhɑːmfʊlɪ] [jarm-fu-li], adv. Dañosamente.

harmfulness [ˈhɑːmfʊlnɪs] [jarm-ful-nes], s. Maldad, daño, acción o disposición nociva.

harmless [ˈhɑːmlɪs] [jarm-les], a. 1. Sencillo, inocente, que no es nocivo, ni perjudicial. 2. Ileso, libre de daño; sano y salvo. **To hold harmless,** librar de responsabilidad, conservar sano y salvo.

harmlessly [ˈhɑːmlɪslɪ] [jarm-les-li], adv. Inocentemente, sin daño.

harmlessness [ˈhɑːmlɪsnɪs] [jarm-lis-nes], s. Calidad de no ser nocivo; sencillez, inocencia.

harmonic, harmonical [hɑːˈmɒnɪk] [jar-mo-nik], a. Armónico, lo perteneciente a la armonía.

harmonic, s. 1. Armónico, tono secundario; sonido que acompaña a otro fundamental. 2. Tono producido en un instrumento de cuerda oprimiendo ligeramente una de las cuerdas. 3. pl. Teoría de los sonidos musicales.

harmonica [hɑːˈmɒnɪkə] [jar-mo-ni-ka], s. Uno de varios instrumentos de música: (a) Armonio con teclas de vidrio; vidrios armónicos. (b) armónica, pequeño instrumento que se toca soplándolo.

harmonically [hɑːˈmɒnɪkəlɪ] [jar-mo-ni-ka-li], adv. Armónicamente, con proporción armónica.

harmonicon [hɑːˈmɒnɪkən] [jar-mo-ní-kon], s. 1. Armónicon, instrumento de música parecido al organillo y que imita los sonidos de una orquesta. 2. Armónica, pequeño instrumento de viento.

harmonious [hɑːˈməʊnɪəs] [jar-mo-nios], a. 1. Armonioso, proporcionado. 2. Armonioso, que tiene armonía; musical.

harmoniosly [hɑːˈməʊnɪəslɪ] [jar-mo-nios-li], adv. Armoniosamente, con armonía musical.

harmoniousnes [hɑːˈməʊnɪəsnɪs] [jar-mo-nios-nes], s. Armonía, la consonancia en la música.

harmonist [hɑːˈməʊnɪst] [jar-mo-nist], s. 1. Armonista, músico. 2. V. HARMONIZER.

harmonize o harmonise [ˈhɑːmɒnaɪz] [jar-mo-nais], va. 1. Armonizar, ajustar, concertar, poner de acuerdo; hacer vivir en buena inteligencia. 2. Armonizar, poner en consonancia música. -vn. 1. Armonizarse, concordar, congeniar las personas; convenir, corresponder. 2. Estar en armonía musical.

harmonizer [hɑːˈmɒnaɪzəʳ] [jar-mo-nai-saʳ], s. 1. Conciliador, el que pone de acuerdo. 2. (Mús.) Armonista. 3. El que reune los pasajes de un libro o escrito que concuerdan entre sí.

harmony [ˈhɑːmənɪ] [jar-mo-ni], s. 1. Armonía, la conveniente proporción y correspondencia de una cosa con otra. 2. Armonía, la consonancia en la música que resulta de la variedad de sonidos puestos en debida proporción. 3. Armonía, concordia, uniformidad.

harness [ˈhɑːnɪs] [jar-nis], s. 1. Atelaje, guarniciones, jaeces, los arreos y paramentos que se ponen a los caballos para tirar de los coches y carrozas. 2. Arnés, el conjunto de armas defensivas con que se armaban antiguamente para pelear. **Harness-maker,** guarnicionero. 3. (Fig.) Equipo para cualquier empresa u objeto; también, los requisitos y exigencias de un negocio cualquiera; servicio activo. **To die in harness,** morir en servicio activo, antes de retirarse de los negocios.

harnesser [ˈhɑːnɪsəʳ] [jar-ni-saʳ], s. El que pone jaeces o arneses.

harp [hɑːp] [jarp], s. 1. Arpa, instrumento músico de cuerda tañido con los dedos. 2. (Astr.) Arpa, constelación.

harp, va. y vn. 1. Tocar o tañer el arpa. 2. Excitar o mover alguna pasión, mover los afectos del alma. 3. Machacar, cansar, porfiar con terquedad sobre una misma cosa (se usa con **on** o **upon**).

harper [ˈhɑːpəʳ] [jar-paʳ], s. Arpista, el que tiene por oficio tocar el arpa.

harpings [ˈhɑːpɪŋz] [jar-pins], s. Arpista el que toca el arpa.

harpoon [hɑːˈpuːn] [jar-pun], s. Arpón, especie de arma arrojadiza que sirve para pescar ballenas.

harpoon, va. Arponear. **Harpoon-gun,** cañón pequeño para lanzar el arpón.

harpooner [hɑːˈpuːnəʳ] [jar-pu-naʳ], **harpooneer** [hɑːˈpuːnɪəʳ] [jar-pu-niaʳ], s. Arponero, el que tira el arpón.

harpsichord [ˈhɑːpsɪkɔːd] [jar-psi-kord], s. Clave, clavicordio, dulzaina.

harpy [ˈhɑːpɪ] [jar-pi], s. 1. Arpía, ave monstruosa. 2. Arpía, el hombre o la mujer muy codiciosos. 3. **Harpy o harpyeagle,** águila muy grande, con copete, de la América tropical.

harquebuss [ˈhɑːkwɪbəs] [jar-kui-bos], s. Arcabuz, arma de fuego que precedió al mosquete.

harquebussier [ˈhɑːkwɪbəsɪəʳ] [jar-kui-ba-siaʳ], s. Arcabucero.

harridan [ˈhærɪdən] [ja-ri-dan], s. Mujer colérica, vieja y fea.

harrier [ˈhærɪəʳ] [ja-riaʳ], s. 1. Lebrel, sabueso pequeño adiestrado para cazar liebres. 2. Pillador, asolador; molestador. 3. Ave de rapiña parecida al milano.

harrow [ˈhærəʊ] [ja-rou], s. Grada, rastro, rastrillo.

harrow, va. 1. Gradar, desmenuzar la tierra con grada o rastro. 2. Inquietar, perturbar, atormentar.

harrower [ˈhærəʊəʳ] [ja-rouaʳ], s. 1. El que desmenuza la tierra. 2. V. HARRIER, 3a acepción.

harrrowing [ˈhærəʊɪŋ] [ja-rouin], a. Horripilante, desgarrador.

harry ['hærɪ] [ja-ri], *va.* 1. Pillar, asolar, saquear. 2. Molestar, inquietar, cansar.

harsh [hɑːʃ] [jarsh], *a.* 1. Áspero, agrio, bronco, rígido, duro, riguroso, austero, desagradable (rude, umpleasant). 2. Desapacible: áspero al tacto, tosco.

harshly ['hɑːʃlɪ] [jarsh-li], *adv.* Ásperamente, severamente, con violencia, desagradablemente, desapaciblemente. **To speak harshly to,** hablar con dureza, con lenguaje violento. **To treat** o **use harshly,** tratar con aspereza, con palabras demasiado duras.

harshness ['hɑːʃnɪs] [jarsh-nes], *s.* 1. Aspereza, rudeza, austeridad en el trato, genio o costumbres; rigor, severidad, mal humor. 2. Sonido desagradable al oído.

harslet, *s. V.* HASLET.

hart [hɑːt] [jart], *s.* Ciervo, particularmente después de su quinto año. (*Mar.*) Motón de vigota.

hartshorn ['hɑːtˈʃɔːn] [jart-shorn], *s.* 1. Amoníaco en cualquier forma de preparación; antiguamente lo obtenían de los cuernos de ciervo por medio de la destilación. 2. (*Bot.*) Especie de llantén.

hartstongue ['hɑːtstəŋ] [jart-stong], *s.* (*Bot.*) Escolopendra, lengua de ciervo, especie de helecho.

hartwort ['hɑːtwɔːt] [jart-uort], *s.* (*Bot.*) Tordilum.

harum-scarum ['hɛərəmˈskɛərəm] [jea-ram-skea-ram], *a.* 1. Atolondrado, precipitado, como espantado. 2. Al tuntún, boca o patas arriba, confuso, desordenado.

haruspex, haruspice ['hærʊspeks] [ja-rus-peks], *s.* Arúspice, sacerdote romano que examinaba las entrañas de las víctimas para adivinar los sucesos.

harvest ['hɑːvɪst] [jar-vist], *s.* 1. Cosecha, agosto, el tiempo que se emplea en la recolección de los granos. 2. Agosto, la misma cosecha de granos. 3. Agosto, el fruto de algún trabajo. **To make harvest,** hacer agosto. **The harvest is late this year,** la cosecha está atrasada este año. **Harvest-bug,** mita, arador, insecto que se pega a la piel **Harvest-fly,** cicada, cigarra. **Harvest-man,** insecto llamado vulgarmente **daddy-long-legs;** arácnido de los falángidos. **Harvest moon,** luna de la cosecha, el plenilunio más próximo al equinocio de otoño; porque la luna sale casi a la misma hora por varias noches consecutivas. **Harvest-mouse,** ratón silvestre.

harvest, *va.* Cosechar, recoger las mieses, recolectar; hacer agosto.

harvester ['hɑːvɪstəʳ] [jar-vis-taʳ], **harvest-man** ['hɑːvɪstmən] [jar-vist-man], *s.* 1. Agostero, cosechero. 2. (**Harvester** sólo). Segadora, máquina de segar. **Combined harvester,** segadora de combinación (es decir, que siega, trilla y acecha a la vez); máquina muy usada en los Estados Unidos del Oeste.

harvest-home ['hɑːvɪstˈhəʊm] [jar-vist-joum], *s.* 1. Fiesta inglesa con que se celebra el fin de la cosecha. 2. La canción de los segadores al tiempo de recoger las mieses.

harvest-lord ['hɑːvɪstlɔːd] [jar-vist-lord], *s.* El primer segador de una siega.

harvest-queen ['hɑːvɪstkwiːn] [jar-vist-kuin], *s.* Una figura que llevan los segadores al acabar la siega.

hash [hæʃ] [jash], *va.* Picar, hacer pedazos menudos alguna cosa, desmenuzar, hacer picadillo (shred, flake).

hash, *s.* Picadillo; sapicón, jigote.

hashish, hasheesh ['hæʃɪʃ] [ja-shish], *s.* Hachich, hachís.

haslet ['hæslɪt] [jas-lit], *s.* Asadura de puerco, conjunto de livianos, como el hígado, bazo, corazón, etc.

hasp [hɑːsp] [jasp], *s.* Aldaba de candado; broche.

hasp, *va.* Abrochar; cerrar con aldaba.

hassock ['hæsək] [ja-sok], *s.* Banqueta, escabel, cojín o estera muy gruesa para arrodillarse.

hastate ['hæsteɪt] [jas-teit], *a.* 1. (*Bot.*) Alabardado, en figura de alabarda. 2. De punta aguda.

haste [heɪst] [jeist], *s.* 1. Prisa, presteza, diligencia, velocidad, precipitación. 2. Precipitación, celeridad indecente o mal aconsejada. *V.* HURRY. 3. Necesidad de apresurarse, urgencia. **The more haste the less speed,** quien más corre menos vuela. **To make haste,** darse prisa, apresurarse, despacharse. **To be in haste,** estar de prisa, tener prisa.

haste, hasten ['heɪsn] [jei-sen], *vn.* Moverse con velocidad, ser pronto, apresurarse (hurry). *-va.* Acelerar, apresurar, precipitar, avivar. **Whither are you hastening?,** ¿adónde va Ud. tan aprisa?

hastily ['heɪstɪlɪ] [jeis-ti-li], *adv.* 1. Aceleradamente, apresuradamente. 2. Temerariamente, precipitadamente. 3. Airadamente.

hastiness ['heɪstɪnɪs] [jeis-ti-nes], *s.* 1. Precipitación, demasiada prisa (rush). 2. Prisa, presteza, prontitud, diligencia. 3. Movimiento repentino de ira o enfado: impaciencia.

hastings ['heɪstɪŋz] [jeis-tins], *s. pl.* 1. Guisantes tempranos. 2. Cualquier fruto temprano.

hasty ['heɪstɪ] [jeis-ti], *a.* 1. Pronto, apresurado, ligero. 2. Pronto, vivo de genio. 3. Violento, colérico, petulante, temerario, arrojado. 4. Temprano.

hasty-pudding ['heɪstɪˈpʌdɪŋ] [jeis-ti-pa-din], *s.* Especie de papilla hecha con agua hirviendo y harina (de maíz); gachas.

hat [hæt] [jat], *s.* 1. Sombrero. 2. (*Fig.*) Capelo, dignidad de cardenal. **Beaver hat,** sombrero de castor. **Panama hat,** sombrero de Panamá. **Round hat,** sombrero redondo. **Silk hat, high hat,** (vulg. **stovepipe hat),** sombrero de copa, o de copa alta; (*fest.*) chistera. **Three-cocked hat,** sombrero de tres picos, tricornio. **Three-cornered hat,** sombrero de tres candiles. **To put on one's hat,** ponerse el sombrero. **To take off one's hat,** quitarse el sombrero. **Hats off!** ¡fuera sombreros!

hatable ['hætəbl] [ja-ta-bol], *a.* Detestable, aborrecible, odioso.

hat-band ['hætbænd] [jat-band], *s.* Cinta del sombrero.

hat-box ['hætbɒks] [jat-boks], **hat-case** [jat-keis], *s.* Sombrerera. **Hat-money,** (*Mar.*) gratificación que se da al patrón de un buque por su cuidado del cargamento.

hatch [hætʃ] [jach], *va.* 1. Criar pollos. 2. Empollar, fomentar los huevos para sacar pollos. 3. Fraguar, idear, tramar, maquinar. 4. Sombrear, poner sombras en la pintura, o cruzar líneas en el grabado. *-vn.* Empollarse, salir del cascarón; madurarse. **The birds are just hatched,** los pájaros acaban de salir del nido, o del huevo. **To count one's chickens before they are hatched,** echar la cuenta de la lechera.

hatch, *s.* 1. Cría, pollada, nidada, pollazón. 2. Salida del cascarón. 3. Media puerta. 4. (*Mar.*) Cuartel, especie de portezuelas que sirven para cerrar las bocas de las escotillas. **To be under hatches,** andar a sombra de tejado; de aquí, estar en la miseria, en la cárcel, etc. 5. Paradera, presa, exclusa en una corriente para coger peces.

hatch-bar ['hætʃbɑːʳ] [jach-baʳ], *s.* (*Mar.*) Barra para cerrar las escotillas.

hatchel ['hætʃəl] [ja-chel], *s.* Rastrillo, instrumento con que se limpia el lino o cáñamo.

hatchel, *va.* 1. Rastrillar, limpiar el lino o cáñamo de la arista y estopa. **Hatchelled flax,** lino rastrillado. 2. Contrariar, impacientar, fastidiar a alguno.

hatcheller ['hætʃələʳ] [ja-che-laʳ], *s.* Rastrillador.

hatcher ['hætʃəʳ] [ja-chaʳ], *s.* Trazador, tramador.

hatchet ['hætʃɪt] [ja-chit], *s.* Destral, hacha pequeña. **To burry the hatchet,** hacer la paz, olvidar las injurias. **To dig up (o take up) the hatchet,** desenterrar el hacha, hacer la guerra.

hatchet-face ['hætʃɪtfeis] [ja-chit-feis], *s.* Cara delgada, enjuta. **Hatchet-faced,** de facciones enjutas.

hatchet-helve ['hætʃɪtˌhelv] [ja-chit-jelv], *s.* Ástil de hacha.

hatching ['hætʃɪŋ] [ja-chin], *s.* El acto de sombrear, o la sombra hecha en el grabado con líneas transversas. 2. Acción de empollar, incubación.

hatchement ['hætʃmənt] [jach-ment], *s.* El escudo de armas que se llevaba en los funerales y se solía colocar en las fachadas de las casas de los difuntos.

hatchway [ˈhætweɪ] [jach-uei], *s. (Mar.)* Escotilla, la puerta o abertura hecha en las cubiertas. **Main-hatchway,** escotilla mayor. **Fore-hatchway,** escotilla de proa. **Magazine-hatchway,** escotilla de popa.

hate [heɪt] [jeit], *va.* Detestar, aborrecer, odiar, abominar.

hate, *s.* Odio, aborrecimiento, aversión.

hateful [ˈheɪtfʊl] [jeit-ful], *a.* Aborrecible, maligno, malévolo, odioso, detestable.

hatefully [ˈheɪtfəlɪ] [jeit-fu-li], *adv.* Malignamente, detestablemente, con tirria, con mala voluntad.

hatefulness [ˈheɪtfəlnɪs] [jeit-ful-nes], *s.* Odiosidad.

hater [ˈheɪtəʳ] [jei-taʳ], *s.* Aborrecedor, el que detesta. **Woman-hater,** enemigo de las mujeres.

hath [hæθ] [jaz], Tiene, ha, tercera persona del singular, indicativo presente de *TO HAVE. (Ant.).*

hating [ˈheɪtɪŋ] [jei-tin], *s.* Aversión (hate).

hat-maker, *s.* V. HATTER.

hat-pin [ˈhætpɪn] [jat-pin], *s.* Alfiler largo que usan las mujeres para prender y asegurar el sombrero en el pelo.

hatrack [ˈhætræk] [ja-trak], *s.* Clavijero o percha para sombreros.

hatred [ˈheɪtrɪd] [jei-trid], *s.* Odio, malignidad, mala voluntad, aborrecimiento, aversión, enemistad.

hatted [ˈhætɪd] [ja-tid], *a.* El o la que lleva sombrero.

hatter [ˈhæəʳ] [ja-taʳ], *s.* Sombrerero, el que hace o vende sombreros.

hauberk [ˈhɔːbɜːk] [jo-berk], *s.* Coraza de la edad media, túnica de malla formada por anillos de acero entrelazados.

haughtily [ˈhɔːtɪlɪ] [jo-ti-li], *adv.* Arrogantemente, con arrogancia, fieramente, orgullosamente.

haughtiness [ˈhɔːtɪnɪs] [jo-ti-nes], *s.* Altanería, soberbia, orgullo, arrogancia, presunción, altivez.

haughty [ˈhɔːtɪ] [jo-ti], *a.* Soberbio, altanero, altivo, vanidoso, arrogante, presuntuoso, orgulloso, vano.

haul [hɔːl] [jol], *va.* 1. Tirar, arrastrar con violencia. 2. *(Mar.)* Halar. **To haul aft the sheets,** cazar las escotas. **To haul down the colors,** arriar la bandera. **Haul home,** caza y atraca. **To haul up the courses in the brails,** cargar los mayores sobre las candelizas. **To haul the wind,** abarloar, ceñir el viento.

haul, *s.* 1. Estirón, la acción de tirar con fuerza; también lo que se logra tirando de ello. 2. Redada, entre pescadores. 3. La distancia que se hace recorrer a una cosa tirando de ella.

haulage [ˈhɔːlɪdʒ] [jo-lich], *s.* Acarreo.

hauling [ˈhɔːlɪŋ] [jo-lin], *s.* Estirón, el acto de tirar.

haulm, haum [ˈhɔːtlm] [jolm], *s.* Paja, rastrojo.

haunch [hɔːntʃ] [jonch], *s.* 1. Anca, grupa, la parte trasera de un animal 2. *(Arq.)* Riñón de una bóveda. **Haunch of venison,** pierna de venado.

haunt [hɔːnt] [jont], *va.* 1. Frecuentar, acudir muy a menudo a algún paraje; visitar muy frecuentemente a alguna persona (pay a visit). 2. Molestar, perseguir recurriendo constantemente a la mente. 3. Rondar, andar alrededor de alguna persona o cosa con el objeto de conseguir algo; visitar con frecuencia, a la manera de los duendes; causar obsesión. 4. Rondar, dar vueltas alrededor de alguna cosa (round).

haunt, *s.* 1. Guarida, paraje a que concurre alguno con frecuencia. 2. Hábito, costumbre, querencia (habit).

haunted [ˈhɔːntɪd] [jon-tid], *pp.* Frecuentado, visitado con frecuencia, particularmente por duendes y apariciones.

haunter [ˈhɔːntəʳ] [jon-taʳ], *s.* Frecuentador, el que acude a algún paraje o visita a alguna persona muy a menudo; rondador.

haunting [ˈhɔːntɪŋ] [jon-tin], *s.* Frecuentación, trato, comunicación frecuente con una persona.

haustellum [ˈhɔːstələm] [jos-te-lom], *s. (pl.* HAUSTELLA). Nombre científico de la trompa u órgano de succión de las mariposas, las moscas y ciertos crustáceos.

hautboy [ˈhɔːtbɔɪ] [jot-boi], *s.* 1. Oboe, instrumento músico de viento. 2. Una especie de fresa.

Havana [həˈvænə] [ja-va-na], *n. pr. (Geog.)* La Habana.

havana cigar [ˌhəvænəˈsɪɡɑːʳ] [ja-va-na-si-gaʳ], *s.* Habano.

have [hæv] [jav], *va. (pret.* y *pp.* HAD, ger. HAVING). 1. Haber, tener; poseer. 2. Contener, comprender, incluir. 3. Traer, llevar, tomar. 4. Obtener, gozar. 5. Experimentar o sentir; padecer, sufrir o gozar. 6. Concebir, tener en la mente. 7. Poner por obra, efectuar. 8. Procurar, mandar hacer; mandar o hacer (con otro infinitivo). **To have a house built,** mandar construir una casa. 9. Haber de, tener que, deber; estar a punto de. **I have to go,** tengo que ir. 10. Parir; hablando del padre, engendrar. **She had a child last week,** parió la semana pasada. 11. Mirar, estimar, apreciar. 12. Saber. **Had like,** estuvo a punto de. **Have at,** *(Ant.)* Hacer cara, provocar a combate, desafiar. **Have at you sir!,** ¡le tengo a Ud. rencor, señor mío!

have about one, tener, llevar consigo.

have down, hacer bajar, bajar.

have from, saber por alguien.

have in, hacer entrar.

have on, *(Fam.)* Llevar (una prenda). **She had on a blue dress,** llevaba un vestido azul. **To have it out,** concluir, terminar un negocio; también, hablar sin reserva, decir las verdades. **To have it out of a person,** pagar en la misma moneda, desquitarse. **To have rather,** querer más, preferir. (Familiar, pero no elegante); **would rather** es muy preferible). **To have a foresight,** preveer. **To have a thing by heart,** saber una cosa de memoria. **What would you have?,** ¿qué quiere Ud.?, ¿qué pide Ud.? **I must have him up,** es necesario que le haga subir. **We will have a trial at him** o **at it,** lo experimentaremos o lo probaremos. **Have with you,** iré con Ud. **Have after you,** seguiré a Ud. **I will have it so,** así lo quiero. **As fortune would have it,** por fortuna. **To have better,** más vale. **To have a mind,** tener gana, deseo, pensamiento de hacer algo. **To have nothing to do with him,** no tener nada que ver con él. Este verbo **to have** sirve en la lengua inglesa, así como en otras europeas, de verbo auxiliar para formar los tiempos compuestos. V. POSSESS.

haven [ˈheɪvn] [jei-ven], *s.* Puerto, abra, abrigo, asilo, refugio (shelter).

haver [ˈhævəʳ] [ja-vaʳ], *s.* 1. Poseedor, tenedor. 2. *(Esco.)* Avena.

haversack [ˈhævəsæk] [ja-va-sak], *s.* Mochila, saco basto para llevar víveres.

having [ˈhævɪŋ] [ja-vin], *s.* Bienes, hacienda, haber; el acto o estado de poseer.

havoc, havock [ˈhævək] [ja-vok], *s.* Estrago, ruina, destrucción, desolación, asolamiento, tala. *-inter.* Exclamación de matanza o de no dar cuartel.

havoc, *va.* Estragar, asolar, destruir, talar.

haw [hɔː] [jok], *s.* 1. La baya y simiente del espino blanco. 2. Granizo o mancha en el ojo. 3. Cañada, cerca, cercado. 4. Dificultad en pronunciar las palabras, balbucencia.

haw, *va.* Volver o hacer volverse a la izquierda; se usa hablando de los bueyes o las caballerías. Lo opuesto a **gee. To have and gee,** ir de un lado a otro; vacilar, estar irresoluto. *-vn.* Tartamudear; tartalear; hablar muy despacio.

Hawaii [həˈwaɪiː] [ja-uaii], *n. pr. (Geog.)* Hawaii.

Hawaiian [həˈwaɪən] [ja-uaian], *a.* De Hawaii, archipiélago de Oceanía y nombre de la mayor de sus islas.

hawfinch [ˈhɔːfɪntʃ] [jo-finch], *s.* Cascapiñones.

hawhaw [ˈhɔːhɔː] [jau-jau], *s.* 1. V. GUFFAW. 2. Especie de zanja o cerca dispuesta de tal modo que no se puede percibir hasta estar sobre ella. 3. Risotada, carcajada. V. HA-HA.

haw-haw [ˈhɔːhɔː] [jau-jau], *v.* Reír a carcajadas.

hawk [hɔːk] [jok], *s.* 1. Halcón, gavilán, azor, ave de rapiña o falcónidas. Hawk nose, nariz aguileña. 2. *(Entom.)* Esfinge.

hawk, *va.* 1. Cazar con halcón. 2. Pregonar géneros por las calles para venderlos. 3. Hacer esfuerzo para arrojar los esputos; expectorar, gargajear.

hawker [ˈhɔːkəʳ] [jo-kaʳ], *s.* 1. Buhonero, mercachifle. 2. Halconero, cetrero. 3. El que caza con halcón.

hawk-eyed [ˌhɔːkˈaɪd] [jok-aid], *a.* Lince, el que tiene la vista penetrante.

hawking [ˈhɔːkɪŋ] [jo-kin], *s.* Cetrería, el acto de cazar con halcón.

hawk-nosed [ˈhɔːnəʊst] [jok-noust], **hook-nosed** [ˈhuːknəʊst] [jouk-noust], *a.* Aguileño, de nariz aguileña.

hawkmoth [ˈhɔːkmɒθ] [jok-moz], *s.* Esfinge, género de mariposas nocturnas.

hawk-owl [ˈhɔːkəʊl] [jok-oul], *s.* (*Orn.*) Ulula, autillo.

hawk's-bell [ˈhɔːkzbel] [joks-bel], *s.* Cascabel.

hawkweed [ˈhɔːkwiːd] [jok-uid], *s.* (*Bot.*) Hieracio o hierba del gavilán.

hawse [ˈhɔːz] [jos], *s.* 1. Proa del buque en que están los escobenes. 2. Situación de los cables al salir de los escobenes cuando un buque está amarrado con dos anclas; también distancia o longitud de un cable. **Hawse-hole,** escobén, el agujero de la proa por donde pasan los cables, cuando el bajel está anclado. **Hawse-pipes,** canales de plomo en los escobenes. **Wawse-plugs,** tacos de los escobenes.

hawser [ˈhɔːzəʳ] [jo-saʳ], *s.* (*Mar.*) Guindaleza.

hawthorn [ˈhɔːθɔːn] [jou-zorn], *s.* (*Bot.*) Espino blanco.

hay [heɪ] [jei], *s.* Heno, hierba segada y seca para forraje. **Hay-cold, hay-fever,** especie de fiebre intermitente, enfermedad catarral caracterizada por la repetición anual de sus síntomas. **Hay-spreader, hay-tedder,** heneador (*Amer.*) máquina con ruedas para cosechar el heno. **Make hay while the sun shines,** aprovecha mientras puedas.

hay (*Ant.*) *s.* 1. Red para cercar la guarida de un animal. 2. Seto, cercado, vallado. 3. Danza en círculo. **To dance the hay,** bailar en círculo, en redondo.

hay, *vn.* Poner lazos para cazar conejos.

haycock [ˈheɪkɒk] [jei-kok], *s.* Pila, montón o niara pequeña de heno.

hay fever [ˈheɪˌfiːvəʳ] [jei-fi-vaʳ], *s.* Fiebre del heno.

hayfield [ˈheɪfiːld] [jei-fild], *s.* Henar.

hayfork [ˈheɪfɔːk] [jei-fork], *s.* (*Agr.*) Horca.

hay-harvest [ˈheɪhɑːvɪst] [jei-jar-vist], *s.* La siega del heno.

hayloft [ˈheɪlɒft] [jei-loft], *s.* henil, el sitio donde se guarda el heno.

haymow [ˈheɪmɔː] [jei-mou], *s.* Henal o henil.

hayrack [ˈheɪræk] [jei-rak], *s.* 1. Pesebre. 2. Armazón de un carro debajo del cual se transporta heno.

hayrake [ˈheɪreɪk] [jei-reik], *s.* Rastrillo para el heno.

hayrick [ˈheɪrɪk] [jei-rik], **haystack** [ˈheɪstæk] [jei-stak], *s.* Niara, montón o pila de heno.

hayseed [ˈheɪsiːd] [jei-sid], *s.* 1. Simiente de heno o de hierbas. 2. (*Fam.*) Paleto, patán, rústico.

haytian [ˈheɪʃən] [jei-shan], *a.* Haitiano, de la república de Haití.

haywire [ˈheɪwaɪəʳ] [jei-uaiaʳ], *s.* 1. Alambre para embalar heno. 2. **To go haywire,** (*Fam.*) Volverse loco, perder la cabeza.

hazard [ˈhæzəd] [ja-sard], *s.* 1. Peligro, riesgo. 2. Casualidad, acaso, accidente, suceso imprevisto. 3. Juego de azar a los dados. 4. Tronera, en el juego inglés de billar.

hazard, *va.* Arriesgar, poner en riesgo o en peligro (risk). - *vn.* Arriesgarse, probar la suerte; aventurar.

hazardable [ˈhæzədəbl] [ja-sar-da-bol], *a.* Osado, peligroso, arriesgado (risky).

hazarder [ˈhæzədəʳ] [ja-sar-daʳ], *s.* 1. Jugador. 2. El que aventura o arriesga.

hazardous [ˈhæzədəs] [ja-sar-dos], *a.* Arriesgado, peligroso, expuesto a riesgos.

hazardously [ˈhæzədəslɪ] [ja-sar-dos-li], *adv.* Peligrosamente, arriesgadamente.

haze [heɪz] [jeis], *s.* 1. Tufo, conjunto de partículas muy finas suspendidas en el aire, a menudo con poca o ninguna humedad. 2. Ofuscamiento mental.

haze, *vn.* Hacer tufo; estar el tiempo nebuloso o humoso. *-va.* 1. Hacer a uno víctima de petardos, chanzas o chascos; se

dice de los estudiantes. 2. Cansar, extenuar a fuerza de trabajo; se dice de los marineros.

hazel [ˈheɪzl] [jei-sel], *s.* (*Bot.*) Avellano, el árbol que produce la avellana. **Hazel-nut,** avellana.

hazel, *a.* Castaño, del color de avellana.

haziness [ˈheɪzɪnɪs] [jei-si-nes], *s.* Tufo, oscuridad.

hazy [ˈheɪzɪ] [jei-si], *a.* 1. Anieblado, cargado de humo, nublado, nebuloso. 2. Falto de claridad; confuso, oscuro.

h-bomb [ˈeɪtʃbɒm] [eich-bom], *s.* Bomba H, bomba de hidrógeno.

he [hiː] [ji], *pron.* 1. Él, pronombre personal, masculino, de tercera persona del singular. 2. Alguien, una persona cualquiera, indefinidamente. **He is an honest man,** él es un hombre de bien. Algunas veces se usa para determinar el género masculino de un animal. **He-goat,** macho cabrío. **He-bear,** oso.

head [hed] [jed], *s.* 1. Cabeza, la parte superior del cuerpo y por extensión de otras muchas cosas. 2. Lo que es análogo a la cabeza de un animal por su figura, posición, etc. **Head of cabbage,** etc., repollo de col, etc. **Head of a bed,** cabecera de una cama. **Head of a book,** título de libro. **Head of a cane,** puño de bastón. **Head of a cask,** fondo de un barril **Head of an arrow,** punta de un dardo. 3. Jefe, cabeza, el superior que gobierna y a quien los demás están subordinados. 4. Primera fila, la posición o rango de un jefe; frente. 5. Res, cabeza de ganado; (en este sentido **head** es igualmente singular y plural). **Two hundred head of sheep,** doscientas reses de ganado lanar. 6. Progreso, prosperidad, adelantamiento. 7. Juicio, talento, capacidad. 8. Crisis, mutación crítica. 9. Astas de ciervo o venado; puntas, extremo. **To go ahead,** ir adelante, proseguir, adelantarse. **To fall headlong,** caer de cabeza, precipitarse. **From head to foot,** de pies a cabeza. **Two heads are better than one,** más ven cuatro ojos que dos. 10. (*Mar.*) Cabeza de la nave, la proa con el bauprés que sale de ella; alas de proa. **Too much by the head,** muy metido a proa. **Head-fast,** cabo de retenida de proa. **Head-rope,** relinga de gratil. **A-head,** por la proa. **Head-sails,** velas de proa. **Head of a sail,** gratil. 11. Fuente, manantial. **Head of a river,** nacimiento de un río. 12. Soltura del freno. **To give a horse his head,** dar rienda suelta a un caballo. 13. Cofia o cualquier adorno para la cabeza. **Hand over head,** inconsideradamente. **Head and shoulders,** (a) Por fuerza. (b) En mucho. **Head of a discourse,** punto principal de un discurso. **On this head,** sobre este punto, asunto o particular. **To hit the nail on the head,** dar en el clavo. **To be over head and ears in debt, in love,** estar comido de deudas; estar enamorado hasta las cachas. **To have neither head nor tail,** no tener pies ni cabeza, no tener sentido común. **To drag in by the head and shoulders,** tirar por los cabellos. **To draw to a head,** supurar; recapitular. **To bring a business to a head,** concluir un negocio. **To make head against one,** hacer frente a alguno o resistirle, oponerse abiertamente. *-a.* Principal.

head, *va.* 1. Mandar, gobernar, dirigir (lead). 2. Degollar. 3. Poner cabeza, puño, punta o una parte muy principal a alguna cosa. 4. Podar los árboles. 5. Avanzar y cortar la retirada. *-vn.* 1. Adelantarse en una dirección determinada. 2. Repollar, acogollarse (como un col); anudar, cuajar las flores o frutos. 3. Tomar su origen, provenir de.

headache [ˈhedeɪk] [je-deik], *s.* Dolor de cabeza. **Migraine headache,** jaqueca, fuerte dolor de cabeza.

head-band [ˈhedbænd] [jed-band], *s.* 1. Cabezada de libro. 2. Cinta con que se venda la cabeza.

head-board [ˈhedbɔːd] [jed-bord], *s.* Cabecera de cama.

head cheese [ˈhedˌtʃiːz] [jed-chis], *s.* Queso de cerdo.

head-dress [ˈhedres] [jed-dres], *s.* Cofia, tocado, redecilla o escofieta.

headed [ˈhedɪd] [je-did], *a.* Lo que tiene cabeza. **Clear** o **long-headed,** agudo o profundo. **Thick-headed,** de pocos alcances; mentecato.

header ['hedəʳ] [je-daʳ], *s.* 1. El que pone las cabezas de los clavos, alfileres o cosas semejantes. 2. Caída o zambullida de cabeza. 3. Cabezada, golpe en la cabeza. 4. Descabezador de las mieses. 5. Cabeza, el que dirige un cuerpo o reunión de personas. 6. El primer ladrillo en el ángulo de una pared.

headfirst ['hedfɜ:st] [jed-fest], *adv.* De cabeza.

head-gear ['hedgɪəʳ] [jed-guiaʳ], *s.* 1. Tocado o cofia de mujer. 2. Las piezas de los jueces que rodean la cabeza del caballo, cabezada. 3. *(Mar.)* Aparejo de las velas de proa.

headily ['hedɪlɪ] [je-di-li], *adv.* Obstinadamente, desatinadamente.

headiness ['hedɪnɪs] [je-di-nes], *s.* Destino, precipitación, obstinación; sacudida.

heading ['hedɪŋ] [je-din], *s.* 1. Título, encabezamiento, encabezado (de cartas, billetes, recibos, facturas, etc.); membrete. 2. Témpano, tapa de barril o cuba. 3. *(Min.)* Galería, socavón; frente.

headland ['hedlænd] [jed-land], *s.* 1. Cabo, promontorio, punta. 2. Tierra no arada inmediata a los setos o cercados.

headledge ['hedledʒ] [jed-lech], *s. (Mar.)* Contrabrazola.

headless ['hedlɪs] [jed-lis], *a.* 1. Descabezado, degollado; acéfalo. 2. Ignorante, terco, obstinado; inconsiderado.

headlight ['hedlaɪt] [jed-lait], *s.* 1. Faro. 2. Foco, luz. **The headlights,** las luces (cars).

headline ['hedlaɪn] [jed-lain], *s.* Título o encabezado (de un periódico, etc.)

headlong ['hedlɒŋ] [jed-lon], *a.* Temerario, inconsiderado, imprudente, precipitado (bold). *-adv.* 1. De cabeza, con la cabeza adelante. 2. Temerariamente, imprudentemente, precipitadamente; a toda prisa, de hoz y de coz, sin consideración o sin reparo; al tuntún. **To cast down headlong,** precipitar. **To fall headlong,** caer con la cabeza abajo, caer la cabeza.

headman ['hedmən] [jed-man], *s.* 1. Jefe, caudillo, capataz. 2. Verdugo

head-master ['hedmɑ:stəʳ] [jed-mas-taʳ], *s.* El director de una escuela.

head-money ['hedmʌnɪ] [jed-ma-ni], *s.* Capitación.

head off ['hedɒf] [jed-of], *va.* Alcanzar, adelantarse para prevenir.

headphone ['hedfəʊn] [jed-foun], *s.* Auricular.

headpiece ['hedpi:s] [jed-pis], *s.* 1. Casco, yelmo, armadura de la parte superior de la cabeza. 2. Ingenio, entendimiento, cabeza. 3. Auricular para el teléfono. 4. *(Impr.)* Viñeta.

head-post ['hedpəʊst] [jed-poust], *s.* Pilar de la cabecera de una cama, poste de establo.

head-quarters ['hedkɔ:təz] [jed-kor-ters], *s.* Cuartel general.

head-sail ['hedseɪl] [jed-seil], *s. (Mar.)* Vela delantera.

head-sea ['hedsi:] [jed-si], *s. (Mar.)* Mar o marejada de proa.

headset ['hedset] [jed-set], *s.* Receptor de cabeza, auricular de casco.

headship ['hedʃɪp] [jed-ship], *s.* Jefatura, el cargo de jefe o cabeza; autoridad, gobierno.

headsman ['hedzmən] [jeds-man], *s.* Verdugo, degollador.

head-spring ['hedsprɪŋ] [jed-sprin], *s.* Fuente, origen.

headstall ['hedstɔ:l] [jed-stol], *s.* Cabezada del freno, testera. *(Mex.)* Bozal.

head-stone ['hedstəʊn] [jed-stoun], *s.* Piedra fundamental; piedra sepulcral.

headstrong ['hedstrɒŋ] [jed-stron], *a.* Terco, testarudo, cabezudo, rehacio, indócil, obstinado, encalabrinado, aferrado.

headtire ['hedtaɪəʳ] [jed-taiaʳ], *s.* Escofieta, atavío de la cabeza.

head waiter ['hedweɪtəʳ] [jed-uei-taʳ], *s.* Mayordomo, jefe de los mozos de un restaurante.

headwaters ['hedwɔ:təz] [jed-uo-tas], *s. pl.* Cabecera o fuentes (of rivers)

headway ['hedweɪ] [jed-uei], *s.* 1. Adelantamiento de un buque, el camino que va haciendo; ímpetu; progreso. 2. El intervalo de tiempo que media entre dos trenes o dos vehículos consecutivos de una misma línea. **Trains running**

on ten minutes' headway, trenes que salen a intervalos de diez minutos.

head wind ['hedwɪnd] [jed-uind], *s. (Mar.)* Viento en contra.

head-work ['hedwɜ:k] [jed-uek], *s.* 1. Trabajo mental, obra intelectual. 2. *(Arq.)* Adorno semejante a la cabeza de un animal, puesto, por ejemplo, sobre la clave de un arco.

heady ['hedɪ] [je-di], *a.* 1. Temerario, arrojado. 2. Fuerte, el licor que se sube a la cabeza y hace daño. 3. Violento, impetuoso.

heal [hi:l] [jil], *va.* 1. Curar, sanar, librar de una dolencia. 2. Reconciliar, componer, ajustar. 3. Purificar, devolver la pureza *a. -vn.* Sanar, recobrar la salud; curar o cicatrizarse una herida o llaga. **To heal up,** cicatrizarse una herida o llaga.

healable ['hi:ləbl] [ji-la-bol], *a.* Sanable, curable.

healer ['hi:ləʳ] [ji-laʳ], *s.* Sanador, el que sana; curador, el que cura; el que hace profesión de curar las enfermedades.

healing ['hi:lɪŋ] [ji-lin], *s.* Sanativo, curativo, medicinal, saludable; emoliente; conciliador, pacífico. *-s.* 1. Curación. 2. El poder de dar la salud.

health [helθ] [jelz], *s.* 1. Salud, sanidad. 2. Sanidad de alma, sinceridad, pureza de intención. 3. Brindis, la acción de beber a la salud de otro. **Health officer,** oficial de sanidad o de cuarentena. **Health-lift,** máquina de alzar pesos, como ejercicio. **Bill of health,** patente de sanidad. **Certificate of health,** certificado de sanidad. **Health-giving,** salubre, saludable, que da la salud. **Your health, sir,** a su salud, caballero.

healthful ['helθfʊl] [jelz-ful], *a.* Sano, saludable, salubre.

healthfully ['helθfʊlɪ] [jelz-fu-li], *adv.* Saludablemente, en buena salud, con salud.

healthfulness ['helθfʊlnɪs] [jelz-ful-nes], *s.* 1. Salud, buena disposición del cuerpo. 2. Sanidad, bondad, salubridad, lo sano o saludable de alguna cosa.

health-giving ['helθgɪvɪŋ] [jelz-gui-vin], *a.* Saludable, que da salud.

healthily ['helθɪlɪ] [jel-zi-li], *adv.* Saludablemente con salud.

healthiness ['helθɪnɪs] [jel-zi-nes], *s.* Sanidad, estado sano, goce de buena salud.

health insurance ['helθɪnsʊərəns] [jelz-in-sua-rans], *s.* Seguro de enfermedad.

healthless ['helθlɪs] [jelz-les], *s.* Enfermo, débil, el que no goza salud.

health resort ['helθrɪsɔ:t] [jelz-ri-sort], *s.* Centro o lugar de curaciones.

healthy ['helθɪ] [jel-zi], *a.* Sano, libre de enfermedades o achaques; sanativo.

heap [hi:p] [jip], *s.* 1. Montón, agregado o junta de muchas cosas puestas en un lugar. 2. *(Fam.)* Turba, muchedumbre de gente. **In heaps,** a montones.

heap, *va.* 1. Amontonar, poner unas cosas sobre otras sin orden ni concierto (pile). 2. Acumular, juntar, colamar (accumulate).

heaper ['hi:pəʳ] [ji-paʳ], *s.* Amontonador.

heaping ['hi:pɪŋ] [ji-pin], *s.* Amontonamiento.

heapy ['hi:pɪ] [ji-pi], *a.* Amontonado, lleno de montones.

hear [hɪəʳ] [jiaʳ], *va. (pret. y pp.* HEARD). 1. Oír, percibir por el órgano del oído cualquier sonido. 2. Dar audiencia o permiso para hablar. 3. Oír, entender, escuchar; obedecer. 4. Oír en justicia o judicialmente. *-vn.* Oír, escuchar, saber por relación, tener noticia, estar informado. **I hear he is to come back,** tengo entendido que vuelve. **Pray let me hear from you now and then,** sírvase Ud. darme noticias suyas de cuando en cuando. **To hear out,** oír hasta el fin. **To hear tell of,** *(Fam.)* Oír o entender por la voz común.

heard [hɜ:d] [jerd], *pret. y pp.* de TO HEAR.

hearer ['hɪərəʳ] [jia-raʳ], *s.* Oyente.

hearing ['hɪərɪŋ] [jia-rin], *s.* 1. Oído, el sentido de oír. 2. Audiencia; averiguación jurídica de alguna cosa; examen de testigos. 3. La acción de oír. 4. El alcance del oído. **To be hard of hearing,** ser duro de oído, ser algo sordo. **To be within hearing,** estar al alcance del oído.

hearsay ['hɪɹəseɪ] [jia-sei], s. Rumor, voz común, fama, lo que se dice de público y notorio, lo que se sabe o cuenta por dicho de otros. **To know a thing by hearsay,** saber alguna cosa de oídas.

hearse [hɜːz] [jers], s. 1. Carro fúnebre. 2. Ataúd, féretro. 3. (Ant.) Cenotafio, monumento.

hearse, va. Encerrar en el féretro o ataúd, enterrar.

hearse-cloth ['hɜːzklɒθ] [jers-kloz], s. Cubierta o paño mortuorio.

hearse-like ['hɜːzlaɪk] [jers-laik], a. Lúgubre, fúnebre.

heart [hɑːt] [jart], s. 1. Corazón, músculo impar que es el órgano central de la circulación de la sangre. 2. Corazón, centro de las pasiones, afectos y sentimientos (love). 3. Corazón, lo interior, el fondo, el centro o lo fuerte de cualquier cosa; la parte vital o principal de un asunto. 4. Ánimo, valor, esfuerzo. 5. Voluntad, amor, benevolencia; simpatía, caridad, filantropía. 6. Figura de corazón en los naipes que equivale a la figura de copas en los naipes españoles. **He died of a broken heart** o **broken hearted,** murió de pesadumbre, o de tristeza. **With all my heart,** con toda mi alma. **The heart of a country,** el centro de un país o territorio. **At heart,** en el fondo, esencialmente; en verdad. **By heart,** de memoria. **To learn by heart,** aprender de memoria. **Heart and hand, heart and soul,** todo, de una manera entusiástica, con instancia y empeño. **To find in one's heart,** querer, desear. **To have at heart,** querer con ternura y predilección; fomentar con empeño. **to lay** o **take to heart,** desconsolarse, apesadumbrarse; estar inquieto acerca de algo. **To take the heart out of one,** (Fam.) Desalentar, desanimar a alguno. **to be sick at heart,** tener la muerte en el alma. **To wear one's heart on one's sleeve,** llevar el corazón en la mano. **To have the heart in the mouth,** tener el alma entre los dientes, o estar con el alma en un hilo; no llegarle a uno la camisa al cuerpo. **Heart-chilled,** el que tiene el corazón helado o sin acción. **Heart-clot,** cuajado o sin acción. **Heart-clover, heart-trefoil,** (Bot.) Especie de alfalfa. **Heart-consuming, heart-corroding,** lo que consume o corroe el corazón. **Heart-deep,** grabado en el corazón. **Heart-discouraging,** desconsolador, lo que desanima, amilana o acobarda. **Heart-disease,** enfermedad del corazón. **Heart-easing,** lo que serena, tranquiliza o causa reposo. **Heart-eating,** lo que corroe el corazón. **Heart-expanding,** lo que abre el corazón o da alegría y placer. **Heart-grief,** congoja de corazón, angustia. **Heart-hardened,** endurecido, impenitente. **Heart-quelling,** lo que atrae el corazón o causa afición o amor. **Heart-rending,** agudo, penetrante, lo que parte o despedaza el corazón. **Heart-shaped,** acorazonado, en forma de corazón. **Heart-sick,** dolorido, afligido, desconsolado, amilanado. **Heart-sickness,** mal de córazón. **heart-sore,** afligido, apesadumbrado, muy angustiosamente; abatido, agobiado. **Heart-sorrowing,** el que está lleno de angustia. **Heart-strings,** las fibras del corazón. **Heart-struck,** fijo en el corazón; desmayado.

heart, va. V. HEARTEN.

heartache ['hɑːteɪk] [jart-eik], s. Angustia, aflicción, congoja, pesar, pena, inquietud.

heart-appalling ['hɑːtəˈpɔːlɪŋ] [jarta-po-lin], a. Lo que abruma, oprime o hace desmayar el corazón.

heart attack ['hɑːtətæk] [jart-a-tak], s. Ataque al corazón.

heartbeat ['hɑːtbiːt] [jart-bit], s. Latido del corazón, gran emoción.

heart-blood ['hɑːtblʌd] [jart-blad], s. 1. Sangre del corazón. 2. La esencia de alguna cosa. 3. Vida.

heart-break ['hɑːtbreɪk] [jart-breik], s. Angustia, disgusto, aflicción, pesar.

heart-breaking ['hɑːtˌbreɪkɪŋ] [jart-brei-kin], a. Congojoso, doloroso, desolador, lo que causa u ocasiona pena o aflicción. -s. Congoja, angustia.

heart-broken ['hɑːtˌbrəʊkən] [jart-brou-ken], a. Penetrado de dolor, de angustia o de congoja.

heartburn ['hɑːtbɜːn] [jart-bern], s. Cardialgía, dolor que se siente en la boca del estómago.

heart-ease ['hɑːtiːz] [jart-is], s. tranquilidad, sosiego, reposo, quietud, serenidad.

hearted ['hɑːtɪd] [jar-tid], a. 1. Lo que está fijo o tiene su asiento en el corazón. 2. Lo que se emprende con ardor o con todo el corazón. **Faint-hearted,** tímido, pusilánime.

hearten ['hɑːtn] [jar-ten], va. 1. Animar, alentar, dar vigor o aliento, fortificar. 2. Abonar, engrasar, estercolar las tierras.

heartener ['hɑːtnəʳ] [jar-te-naʳ], s. Animador, alentador.

heartfelt ['hɑːtfelt] [jart-felt], a. De corazón, cordial, sincero, sentido en el alma o en el fondo del corazón.

heart-free ['hɑːtfriː] [jart-fri], a. Libre, sin ningún amor.

heartgrief ['hɑːtgriːf] [jart-grif], s. Congoja, angustia.

hearth [hɑːθ] [jarz], s. 1. Hogar, fogón; hogar de forja o de horno. 2. Anaquel delante de una estufa. 3. Hogar doméstico, la casa de uno.

hearth-money [ˌhɑːθˈmʌnɪ] [jarz-ma-ni], s. Fogaje, derecho o tributo que se pagaba por cada casa.

heartily ['hɑːtɪlɪ] [jar-ti-li], adv. 1. Sinceramente, cordialmente. **To laugh most heartily,** reírse a más no poder. 2. Ansiosamente, con ansia.

heartiness ['hɑːtɪnɪs] [jar-ti-nes], s. Sinceridad; vigor.

heartless ['hɑːtlɪs] [jart-les], a. 1. Falto de corazón; sin piedad ni cariño; falto de simpatía, cruel. 2. Cobarde, tímido, pusilánime, amilanado.

heartlessly ['hɑːtlɪslɪ] [jart-les-li], adv. 1. Cruelmente, sin piedad, inhumanamente. 2. Pusilánimemente, tímidamente, sin ánimo.

heartlessness ['hɑːtlɪsnɪs] [jart-les-nes], s. Falta de simpatía y piedad; falta de ánimo.

heart's-ease ['hɑːtzˈiːz] [jarts-is], s. (Bot.) Trinitaria. V. PANSY.

heart-to-heart ['hɑːttəˈhɑːt] [jart-tu-jart], a. Sincero, de corazón a corazón. **Heart-to-heart talk,** charla íntima y confidencial.

heart trouble ['hɑːttrʌbl] [jart-tra-bel], s. Enfermedad del corazón, mal cardíaco.

heart-whole ['hɑːthəʊl] [jart-joul], a. 1. Desamorado, el que no está enamorado. 2. Valiente, intrépido, valeroso. 3. Sincero.

heart-wounded ['hɑːtwuːndɪd] [jart-wun-did], a. 1. Lleno de angustia. 2. Enamorado.

hearty ['hɑːtɪ] [jar-ti], a. 1. Sincero, alegre, puro, sencillo. 2. Sano, robusto, vigoroso. 3. Nutritivo, abundante. **Hearty eaten,** gran tragón.

heat [hiːt] [jit], s. 1. Calor, la impresión que produce el fuego. 2. Calor, el estado de cualquier cuerpo sujeto a la acción del fuego. 3. Calor, lo más fuerte o vivo de alguna acción (passion, warm). 4. Carrera o corrida de un caballo o de muchos. 5. Grano que sale en la cara por efecto del calor. 6. Fogosidad, viveza demasiada; ardor, vehemencia; cólera, odio, animosidad. 7. Celo, apetito a la generación en los irracionales, principalmente en las hembras. 8. Una sola operación de calentar, encender, derretir o fundir metales. 9. Fermentación. **Heat-stroke,** insolación. V. SUNSTROKE. **Heat shield,** protector contra el calor. **Heat wave,** ola de calor. **Bottom heat,** calor artificial bajo las capas de tierra en los invernaderos. **Red heat,** calor llevado hasta el rojo; de aquí, emoción o pasión fuerte. **White heat,** candecia, incandescencia; pasión la más intensa. **Prickly heat,** salpullido. **In heat,** en celo, cachonda, salida.

heat, va. 1. Calentar, encender, causar ardor. 2. Hacer fermentar. -vn. 1. Fermentar, ponerse algún cuerpo en movimiento de fermentación. 2. Encolerizarse. 3. Arder o estar poseído de una pasión.

heater ['hiːtəʳ] [ji-taʳ], s. 1. Calentador. 2. Calorífero. **Hot-air heater,** calorífero de aire caliente.

heath [hiːθ] [jiz], s. 1. 1. (Bot.) Brezo, cualquier arbusto de los géneros Erica o Calluna. 2. Brezal, páramo, matorral.

heathcock ['hiːθkɒk] [jiz-kok], s. (Orn.) Gallo silvestre.

heathen ['hi:ðən] [ji-zen], s. 1. Gentil, pagano, idólatra. 2. Ateo, ateísta.

heathen, heathenish ['hi:ðənɪʃ] [ji-ze-nish], a. Gentílico, salvaje, bárbaro, feroz.

heathenishly ['hi:ðənɪʃlɪ] [ji-ze-nish-li], adv. A la manera de los gentiles o de los paganos.

heathenishness ['hi:ðənɪʃnɪs] [ji-ze-nish-nes], s. El estado de pagano; profanidad, irreligiosidad.

heathenize ['hi:ðənaɪz] [ji-ze-nais], va. Hacer a uno pagano o idólatra.

heather ['heðəʳ] [je-daʳ], s. 1. Brezo, urce. 2. Tejido de lana.

heathery ['heðərɪ] [je-de-ri], o **heathy** ['heðɪ] [je-di], a. Lleno de brezos, o parecido a ellos; o cubierto de brezos.

heating ['hi:tɪŋ] [ji-tin], s. Calefacción, caldeo, calda; la acción de calentar o calentarse.

heat lightning ['hi:t'laɪtnɪŋ] [jit-lait-nin], s. Relámpago sin truenos.

heat-resistant ['hi:rɪ'sɪstənt] [jit-ri-sis-tant], a. Calorífugo.

heat wave ['hi:tweɪv] [jit-ueiv], s. Onda cálida, onda de calor.

heave [hi:v] [jiv], va. (pret. y pp. HEAVED, HOVE. **Hove** está casi limitado al uso náutico. 1. Alzar, levantar alguna cosa pesada; (Mar.) izar. 2. Echar fuera, arrojar. 3. Exhalar, prorrumpir. **To heave the lead,** escandallar, echar el escandallo. **To heave a sigh,** exhalar un suspiro. 4. Inflar o hinchar alguna cosa. 5. (Geol.) Fracturar un filón y forzarlo fuera de su posición normal. -vn. 1. Levantarse y bajarse alternativa y pesadamente, V. gr. el pecho, el mar; suspirar dando grandes sollozos. 2. Palpitar, como el corazón; respirar trabajosamente. 3. Trabajar con mucha fuerza. 4. Tener náuseas. (Mar.) Virar. **To heave at the capstan,** (Mar.) Virar al cabrestante. **To heave down,** descubrir la quilla. **To heave ahead,** virar para proa. **to heave overboard,** echar a la mar.

heave, s. 1. Elevación; esfuerzo para levantarse o alzarse. 2. Suspiros de congoja. 3. Estertor, hinchazón o elevación del pecho causada por la dificultad de respirar. 4. Náusea; esfuerzo para vomitar. 5. (Geol.) El grado de desviación de las partes de una veta forzadas fuera de su posición normal.

heaven ['hevn] [je-ven], s. 1. Cielo, firmamento, región etérea. 2. Cielo, paraíso, la mansión de Dios. 3. Cielo, el poder supremo. 4. Cielo, elevación, sublimidad. **Heaven-aspiring,** el que aspira a ganar el cielo. **Heaven-banished,** desterrado del cielo. **Heaven-begot,** procreado por un poder celeste. **Heaven-born,** nacido descendido del cielo; celeste, divino, angélico. **Heaven-bred,** criado en los cielos. **Heaven-built,** construido por los dioses. **Heaven-directed,** dirigido o elevado hacia el cielo. **Heaven-fallen,** caído del cielo. **Heaven-gifted,** dotado por el cielo. **Heaven-inspired,** inspirado del cielo. **Heaven-instructed,** instruido por el cielo. **Heaven-kissing,** tocando al cielo: se dice de las montañas que esconden sus cumbres en las nubes. **Heaven-loved,** querido del cielo: favorecido de Dios. **Heaven-warring,** el que hace la guerra o lucha contra el cielo.

heavenliness ['hevnlɪnɪs] [je-ven-li-nes], s. Excelencia suprema.

heavenly ['hevnlɪ] [je-ven-li], a. Celeste, divino, celestial. - adv. Celestialmente, divinamente.

heavenward ['hevnwɔːd] [je-ven-uord], adv. hacia el cielo.

heaver ['hevəʳ] [je-vaʳ], s. 1. (Mar.) Alzaprima. 2. Cargador, el que levanta; esta voz se usa para formar palabras compuestas. **Coal-heaver,** cargador de carbón.

heaves ['hi:vz] [jivs], s. pl. Huérfago, enfermedad asmática que ataca a las caballerías; enfisema de los pulmones.

heavily ['hevɪlɪ] [je-vi-li], adv. Pesadamente, lentamente; melancólicamente, tristemente. **To complain heavily,** quejarse amargamente.

heaviness ['hevɪlɪ] [je-vi-li], s. 1. Pesadez, peso, gravedad. 2. Pesadez, tardanza, torpeza, languidez. 3. Abatimiento de ánimo, aflicción, tristeza, angustia. 4. Opresión, carga.

heaving ['hevɪŋ] [je-vin], s. 1. Palpitación, movimiento, irregular del corazón. 2. Hinchazón u oleada del mar.

heavy ['hevɪ] [je-vi], a. 1. Grave, pesado, ponderoso. 2. Grande, fuerte, poderoso, muy vivo, violento. 3. Duro, opresivo, importuno, penoso, molesto. 4. Pesaroso, triste, melancólico. 5. Considerable, importante; que compra o vende en grandes cantidades. 6. Frío, falto de espíritu; tarde, lento, soñoliento, lerdo, estúpido. 7. Pesado, difícil de digerirse. 8. Denso, espeso; fuerte; arcilloso. **Heavy beer, liquor,** cerveza, licor fuerte. **Heavy road,** camino pesado o arcilloso. -adv. V. HEAVILY.

heavy-hearted [ˌhevɪ'hɑːtɪd] [je-vi-jar-tid], a. Abatido, descorazonado.

heavy water ['hevɪ'wɔːtəʳ] [je-vi-uo-taʳ], s. (Quím.) Agua pesada.

heavyweight ['hevɪweɪt] [je-vi-ueit], s. (Boxeo). Peso completo.

heazy ['hevɪ] [je-vi], a. Jadeante, asmático; ronco. V. WHEEZY.

hebdomad ['hebdəmæd] [jeb-do-mad], s. Siete; siete cosas cualesquiera, particularmente hebdómada, semana.

hebdomadal ['hebdəmædl] [jeb-do-ma-dal], **hebdomadary** ['hebdəmædərɪ] [jeb-do-ma-da-ri], a. Hebdomadario, semanal.

hebetate ['hi:bɪteɪt] [ji-bi-teit], va. Atontar, entorpecer, embrutecer. -a. (Bot.) Que tiene punta obtusa y blanda.

hebetation [ˌhi:bɪ'teɪʃən] [ji-bi-tei-shon], s. Atontamiento, entorpecimiento, embrutecimiento.

hebete ['hi:bɪt] [ji-bit], a. Entorpecido, embrutecido, atontado.

hebetude ['hi:bɪtjuːd] [ji-bi-tiud], s. Embotamiento, torpeza de los sentidos.

hebraism ['hi:breɪzm] [ji-breism], s. Hebraísmo, giro hebreo en el lenguaje.

hebraist ['hi:breɪst] [ji-breist], **hebrician** [hɪ'breɪʃən] [ji-brei-shan], s. Hebraizante, el erudito en la lengua hebrea.

hebraize ['hi:braɪz] [ji-brais], va. Hebraizar, hacer hebreo; verter al hebreo. -vn. Adoptar las costumbres o la lengua hebreas; volverse hebreo.

hebrew ['hi:bruː] [ji-bru], s. 1. Hebreo, la lengua hebrea. 2. Hebreo, judío. -a. Hebraico.

hecatomb ['hekətɒm] [je-ka-tom], s. Hecatombe, antiguo sacrificio griego de cien reses; de aquí, gran carnicería, matanza enorme.

heck [hek] [jek], s. 1. Enrejado, verja. (a) Enrejado, especie de trampa para coger peces. (b) Recipiente a modo de enrejado, para forraje. (c) Puerta cuya parte superior está enrejada o se mueve independientemente de la puerta misma. 2. Volante de un torno de hilar.

heckle ['hekl] [je-kel], v. HATCHEL.

hectare ['hektɑːʳ] [jek-taʳ], s. Hectárea, medida de superficie que contiene cien áreas; equivale a 2.471 acres ingleses.

hectic, hectical ['hektɪk] [jek-tik], a. Hético, héctico, el que padece calentura hética. s. Hética, consunción, fiebre hética.

hectically ['hektɪklɪ] [jek-ti-kli], adv. Constitucionalmente, hablando de la constitución física; de ordinario denota consunción.

hecto (o **hect**) Prefijo tomado del griego que significa ciento, o cien veces. **Hectogram, hectogramme,** hectograma, cien gramos. **Hectoliter, hectolitre,** hectólitro, cien litros. **Hectometer, hectometre,** hectómetro, cien metros.

hector ['hektəʳ] [jek-taʳ], s. Matasiete, fanfarrón, fierabrás, perdonavidas.

hedera ['hɪdərə] [ji-da-ra], s. Hiedra.

hedge [hedʒ] [jedch], s. Seto, vallado de zarzas. **Quickset hedge,** seto vivo. **Stake hedge,** seto muerto.

hedge, va. 1. Cercar alguna heredad con un seto. 2. Obstruir, impedir, tapar (impede); defender, proteger, como con un seto o vallado (protect). 3. Circundar; rodear (surround). - vn. 1. Ponerse al abrigo, agacharse, esconderse (como detrás de un seto). 2. Apostar a fin de compensar o igualar una apuesta anterior; procurar los medios de evadir la responsabilidad por lo que antesse ha dicho o hecho. **Don't hedge with me!,** ¡dímelosin rodeos!

hedge-born [ˈhedʒbɔːn] [jedch-born], *a.* Oscuro, el que es de linaje bajo y no conocido.

hedge-creeper [ˈhedʒˌkriːpəʳ] [jedch-kri-paʳ], *s.* Vagamundo.

hedgehog [ˈhedʒhɒg] [jedch-jog], *s.* 1. Erizo, animal cubierto de púas. 2. Voz de improperio.

hedge-hyssop [ˈhedʒˌhɪsɒp] [jedch-ji-sop], *s.* (*Bot.*) Hierba del pobre.

hedge-mustard [ˈhedʒˌmʌstəd] [jedch-mas-tard], *s.* (*Bot.*) Erísimo, jaramago.

hedge-nettle [ˈhedʒnetl] [jedch-ne-tel], *s.* (*Bot.*) Galiopsis.

hedge-note [ˈhedʒnəʊt] [jedch-nout], *s.* Mamotreto, voz de desprecio que se aplica a los malos escritos.

hedge-priest [ˈhedʒpriːst] [jedch-prist], *s.* Clerizonte, clérigo iliterato y mal mirado.

hedger [ˈhedʒəʳ] [jed-chaʳ], *s.* 1. Cercador, el que hace cercados o setos de árboles y arbustos. 2. El que compensa o iguala sus apuestas.

hedgerow [ˈhedʒərəʊ] [jed-che-rou], *s.* La serie de árboles o arbustos en los cercados o setos.

hedge-sparrow [ˈhedʒˌspærəʊ] [jedch-spa-rou], *s.* (*Orn.*) Curruca, especie de gorrión.

hedging-bill [ˈhedʒɪŋbɪl] [jed-chin-bil], *s.* Podadera corva para cortar los setos vivos.

hedonism [ˈhiːdənɪzm] [ji-do-ni-sem], *s.* Hedonismo, la doctrina de ciertos filósofos griegos de que el placer es el único bien en la ética, egoísmo, interés personal, indulgencia para consigo mismo.

heed [hiːd] [jid], *va.* Atender, prestar atención, estar con cuidado y aplicación a lo que se mira u oye; observar, notar. -*vn.* Considerar.

heed, *s.* 1. Cuidado, atención, cautela, precaución (care, caution). 2. Observación, reparo, aprecio. 3. Seriedad, gravedad, sobriedad, regularidad. **Take heed what you do,** mire Ud. lo que hace. **To take no heed of,** no hacer caso de.

heedful [ˈhiːdfʊl] [jid-ful], *a.* Vigilante, atento, cauteloso, cuidadoso, exacto, prudente, circunspecto.

heedfully [ˈhiːdfəlɪ] [jid-fu-li], *adv.* Cautelosamente, atentamente, con circunspección.

heedfulness [ˈhiːdfəlnɪs] [jid-ful-nes], *s.* Vigilancia, cautela, atención, cuidado, circunspección.

heedless [ˈhiːdlɪs] [jid-les], *a.* Descuidado, negligente, omiso, imprudente, inconsiderado, distraído, atolondrado.

heedlessly [ˈhiːdlɪslɪ] [jid-les-li], *adv.* Negligentemente.

heedlessness [ˈhiːdlɪsnɪs] [jid-les-nes], *s.* Descuido, omisión, negligencia, inadvertencia, imprudencia, distracción.

heedy [ˈhiːdɪ] [ji-di], *a.* Cauteloso.

heel [hiːl] [jil], *s.* 1. Talón, la parte posterior del pie; la parte correspondiente del pie en los animales. 2. Talón de toda clase de calzado; tacón. 3. El pie visto por atrás. 4. Cosa colocada a manera de talón, parte inferior; coz o pie de palo. **To take to one's heels,** apretar los talones, poner pies en polvorosa, huir. 5. La última parte de algo o de alguna cosa. **To be at the heels of,** perseguir estrechamente. **From head to heel,** de pies a cabeza. **Heels over head,** patas arriba. **The heel of his shoe came down,** se le destalonó el zapato. **Down at the heels,** de aspecto desaliñado, descuidado. **Neck and heels,** (*Fam.*) De pies a cabeza del todo. **To cool one's heels,** (*Fam.*) Hacer antesala, consumirse, esperar largo tiempo. **To kick one's heels,** tascar el freno, esperar ocasión para hablar u obrar. **To lay by the heels,** poner grillos, encadenar. **To show the heels o a clean pair of heels,** huir; tomar la delantera, dejar atrás. **To throw up the heels of,** echar a tierra de una zancadilla: de aquí, frustrar, dejar burlada la intención de alguien.

heel, *va.* 1. Poner talón (stockings, etc.) 2. Asir, agarrar por los talones. 3. Poner espolones al gallo. 4. (Ger. E.U.) Proveer de dinero. -*vn.* (*Mar.*) Ladearse, inclinarse, tumbarse hacia un lado.

heeler [ˈhiːləʳ] [ji-laʳ], *s.* 1. El gallo que usa con destreza de los espolones contra su contrario. 2. (Ger. E.U.) Subalterno de mala ley de un cacique político secuaz poco escrupuloso, politicastro.

heel-maker [ˈhiːlˌmeɪkəʳ] [jil-mei-kar], *s.* Taconero.

heel-piece [ˈhiːlpiːs] [jil-pis], *s.* Tapa, la suela que se pone debajo del tacón del zapato.

heel-piece, *va.* Poner o echar tapas a los zapatos.

hegemonic [hɪˈgemənɪ] [ji-ye-mo-ni], *a.* Predominante, dominante.

hegemony [hɪˈgemənɪk] [ji-ye-mo-nik], *s.* Hegemonía, preeminencia; en particular la de Atenas, esparta y Tebas.

Hegira [heˈdʒaɪərə] [je-yaia-ra], *s.* Hégira, égira, la era de los mahometanos, que se cuenta desde el día en que Mahoma huyó de la Meca a Medina A.D. 622.

heifer [ˈhefəʳ] [je-faʳ], *s.* Vaca joven (que aún no ha parido), novilla. **Heifer calf,** ternera.

heigh-ho! [ˈheɪˈhəʊ] [jei-jau], *inter.* ¡Ay! Voz con que se expresa languidez o inquietud.

height, hight [haɪt] [jait], *s.* 1. Altura, elevación sobre alguna base, como la superficie de la tierra o el nivel del mar. 2. Estatura, talla. 3. Lo que es alto; altura, colina, montaña; cima o cumbre, eminencia. 4. Sumidad, el ápice o extremidad de alguna cosa; extremo. 5. Elevación, altura, dignidad encumbrada. 6. Sublimidad, colmo, el más alto grado de una cosa; excelencia. **In the height of his happiness,** en el colmo de su dicha. **Height between decks,** (*Mar.*) Altura de entrepuentes. **Mount Popocatepetl is 17,784 feet in height,** el Popocatepetl tiene 17,784 pies (5,425 metros) de altura. **He (she) is about muy height,** el (ella) es poco más o menos de mi estatura. **The height of folly,** el colmo de la locura. 7. Colina (hill) **The heights,** las cumbres.

heighten, highten [ˈhaɪtn] [jai-ten], *va.* 1. Realzar, levantar más o poner una cosa más elevada de lo que antes estaba. 2. Adelantar, perfeccionar, mejorar. 3. Agravar, abultar. 4. Realzar, ilustrar, adornar. **To heighten the spirirts,** exaltar la imaginación.

heightening [ˈhaɪtnɪŋ] [jait-nin], *s.* Adorno; se aplica comúnmente a los de la poesía y retórica; la acción del verbo **heighten** en todas sus acepciones.

heinous [ˈheɪnəs] [jei-nos], *a.* Atroz, grave, nefando, malvado en extremo.

heinously [ˈheɪnəslɪ] [jei-nos-li], *adv.* Atrozmente, malvadamente, nefandamente.

heinousness [ˈheɪnəsnɪs] [jei-nos-nes], *s.* Atrocidad, enormidad, exceso de malicia o suma malicia.

heir [eəʳ] [eaʳ], *s.* Heredero, el que hereda. **Heir-apparent o general,** heredero forzoso. **Heir presumptive,** heredero presuntivo. **Joint heir,** coheredero. **Heir at law,** heredero legal.

heir, *va.* Heredar. *V.* INHERIT.

heirdom [ˈeədɒm] [ea-dom], *s.* herencia, los bienes y derechos heredados.

heiress [ˈeəres] [ea-res], *sf.* Heredera, la mujer que hereda.

heirless [ˈeəlɪs] [ea-es], *a.* Sin heredero.

heirloom [ˈeəluːm] [ea-lum], *s.* 1. (*For.*) Bienes muebles vinculados que pasan al heredero con la propiedad inmueble. 2. Prenda que desciende de un antepasado.

heirship [ˈeəʃɪp] [ea-ship], *s.* Estado, carácter o privilegio de heredero; herencia.

heliacal [hɪˈlaɪəkəl] [ji-laia-kal], *a.* (*Ast.*) Helíaco, del sol o perteneciente a él.

helibus [ˈhelɪbʌs] [je-li-bas], *s.* Helicóptero de transporte de pasajeros.

helical [ˈhelɪkəl] [je-li-kal], *a.* Espiral. **Helical line,** hélice o espira.

helicoid [ˈhelɪkɔɪd] [je-li-koid], *a.* 1. Helicoide, parecido a una hélice o a la concha de un caracol. 2. Perteneciente a los caracoles. -*s.* (*Geom.*) Superficie parecida a la de un tornillo.

helicopter [ˈhelɪkɒptəʳ] [je-li-kop-taʳ], *s.* Helicóptero.

heliocentric [ˌheliəˈsentrɪk] [je-lio-sen-trik], *a.* Heliocéntrico, lo que pertenece al centro del sol.

heliograph [ˈhiːliəɡrɑːf] [ji-liou-graf], *s.* 1. Heliógrafo, instrumento para fotografiar el sol. 2. Lámina fotográfica tomada por la luz del sol. 3. Heliotropo, helióstato, instrumento que sirve para enviar un rayo solar a un observador colocado a gran distancia.

heliographic [ˈhiːlɪəˈɡræfɪk] [ji-liou-gra-fik], *a.* Heliográfico, relativo al heliógrafo o a la heliografía.

heliography [ˈhiːlɪəˈɡrɑːfɪ] [ji-liou-gra-fi], *s.* 1. Operación de transmitir señales por medio del helógrafo. 2. Fotografía, heliografía. 3. Descripción de la superficie del sol.

heliolatry [ˈhiːlɪəˈlætrɪ] [ji-liou-la-tri], *s.* Culto del sol, sabeísmo.

heliometer [ˈhiːlɪəˈmiːtəʳ] [ji-liou-mi-taʳ], *s.* Heliómetro, instrumento para medir el diámetro del sol.

helioscope [ˈhiːlɪəskəʊp] [ji-lios-koup], *s.* Helioscopio, anteojo para mirar al sol sin que su resplandor hiera la vista.

heliospherical [ˈhiːlɪəsˈferɪkəl] [ji-lios-fe-ri-kal], *a.* Esférico como el sol.

heliostat [ˈhiːlɪəstæt] [ji-lios-tat], *s.* helióstato, instrumento para proyectar de una manera invariable el rayo solar.

heliotherapy [ˈhiːlɪəˈθerəpɪ] [ji-lio-ze-ra-pi], *s.* Helioterapia.

heliotrope [ˈhiːlɪətrəʊp] [ji-lio-troup], *s.* 1. *(Bot.)* Heliotropo, planta de flor muy olorosa, de la familia de las borragíneas. 2. Color de esta flor. 3. *(Fís.)* Heliotropo, instrumento para enviar un rayo solar a un observador colocado a gran distancia. 4. *(Min.)* Heliotropio o heliotropo, variedad de calcedonia de color verde claro o de puerro, con manchas de jaspe rojo.

heliotype [ˈhiːlɪətaɪp] [ji-lio-taip], *s.* Heliotipo, especie de fotograbado en una superficie de gelatina, de la cual se imprime después; dicha superficie de impresión y la impresión misma.

heliport [ˈhiːlɪpɔːt] [ji-li-port], *s.* *(Aer.)* Aeropuerto para helicópteros.

helispheris, helispherical [ˈhiːlɪsˈferɪks] [ji-lis-fe-riks], *a.* Espiral, sobre una esfera.

helix [ˈhiːlɪks] [ji-liks], *s.* 1. Espira, voluta, hélice. 2. *(Anat.)* Hélix, borde del pabellón de la oreja en el hombre. 3. Caracol de tierra de la familia de los helícidos.

hell [hel] [jel], *s.* 1. Infierno, el lugar de los condenados; el invierno, los espíritus infernales. 2. Cualquier lugar o estado de tormento o miseria extrema. 3. Infierno, el limbo o seno de Abraham, llamado por los griegos Hades y por los hebreos Sheol. 4. El lugar en que se depositan los desperdicios deshechos (como en las imprentas, caja para letras inservibles). **Hell-bender,** gran salamandra del valle del río Ohio, de vida muy tenaz. **Hell-fire,** fuego o tormento del infierno. **Hell-gate,** la puerta, el umbral del infierno. **They had a hell of a time,** pasaron un mal rato. **It was as hot as hell,** hacía un calor infernal. **Go to hell!** ¡vete al diablo!

hell-born [ˈhelbɔːn] [jel-born], *a.* Nacido en el infierno, infernal.

hell-cat [ˈhelkæt] [jel-kat], *s.* Bruja.

hell-doomed [ˈhelduːmd] [jel-dumd], *a.* Réprobo.

hellebore [ˈhelɪbɔːʳ] [je-li-boʳ], *s.* *(Bot.)* Eléboro, verdegambre.

helleborism [ˈhelɪbɔːrɪzm] [je-li-bo-risem], *s.* Preparación medicinal del eléboro.

Hellenic [heˈliːnɪk] [je-li-nik], *a.* Helénico, heleno, greciano; gentílico.

Hellenism [ˌheliːˈnɪzm] [je-li-ni-sem], *s.* Helenismo.

hellenist [ˈheliːnɪst] [je-li-nist], *s.* 1. Judío greguizante. 2. Helenista, el erudito en la lengua griega.

hellenistical [ˌheliːˈnɪstɪkl] [je-li-nis-ti-kal], *a.* Lo que pertece a los judíos que hablan el griego.

hellenize [ˈheliːnaɪz] [je-li-nais], *vn.* Grecizar.

hellfire [ˈhelfaɪəʳ] [jel-faiaʳ], *s.* Fuego o tormento del infierno.

hellgrammite [ˈhelɡrəmaɪt] [jel-gra-mait], *s.* Gran larva de un insecto acuático (Corydalus cornutus), que se emplea como carnada en la pesca.

hell-hag [ˈhelhæɡ] [jel-jag], *s.* Bruja del infierno.

hell-hound [ˈhelhaʊnd] [jel-jaund], *s.* 1. Perro del infierno, el cancerbero. 2. Agente infernal; perseguidor fiero y cruel.

hellish [ˈhelɪʃ] [je-lish], **helly** [ˈhelɪ] [je-li], *a.* Infernal, malvado.

hellishly [ˈhelɪʃlɪ] [je-lish-li], *adv.* Malvadamente, detestablemente, diabólicamente.

hellishness [ˈhelɪʃnɪs] [je-lish-nes], *s.* Malicia infernal, diablura.

hello [hʌˈləʊ] [ja-lou], *interj.* 1. ¡Hola!, ¡haló!. 2. ¡Diga! (en el teléfono). *Hello girl,* muchacha telefonista.

hellward [ˈhelwɑːd] [jel-uard], *adv.* Hacia el infierno.

helm [helm] [jelm], *s.* 1. *(Mar.)* Timón, gobernalle, el conjunto de timón, su caña y rueda: en especial, la barra o caña del timón, gobernalle. **After-piece of the helm,** azafrán del timón. **Main-piece of the helm,** madre del timón. **To shift the helm,** cambiar el timón. **To hang the helm,** calar el timón. **Play of the helm,** juego del timón. **Helmsman,** timonero, timonel, el que gobierna el timón. **A ship which answers the helm readily,** un buque que obedece fácilmente al timón. 2. Timón, la dirección y gobierno de un negocio; el puesto de autoridad y responsabilidad. 3. *(Ant.)* V. HELMET.

helm, *va.* *(Poét.)* 1. Timonear, gobernar el timón; guar. 2. Cubrir con un yelmo o celada.

helmed [ˈhelmɪd] [jel-mid], **helmeted** [ˈhemɪtɪd] [jel-mi-tid], *a.* Lo que tiene o lleva yelmo o celada.

helmet [ˈhelmɪt] [jelmit], *s.* 1. Yelmo, celada, morrión. 2. Casco de bombero, guardia, soldado. 3. Careta de esgrima. 4. *(Bot.)* Parte superior de una corola labiada.

helmet-flower [ˈhelmɪtˈflaʊəʳ] [jel-mit-flauaʳ], *s.* *(Bot.)* Acónito, matalobos.

helminthic [helˈmɪnθɪk] [jel-min-zik], *a.* Helmíntico: se dice de los remedios contra las lombrices.

helminthlogy [ˈhelmɪnˌθɒlədʒɪ] [jel-min-zo-lo-yi], *s.* helmintología, tratado y estudio de las lombrices y de sus efectos; o de los gusanos, especialmente los parásitos.

helmport [ˈhelmpɔːt] [jelm-port], *(Mar.)* Limera del timón.

helmsman [ˈhelmzmən] [jelms-man], *s.* *(pl.* MEN) Timonero, el que gobierna el timón en las embarcaciones.

helot [ˈhelɒt] [je-lot], *s.* Ilota, nombre del esclavo en Lacedemonia.

helotism [ˈhelətɪzm] [je-lo-tism], *s.* Hilotismo, condición de los esclavos en la antigua Esparta, esclavitud.

helotry [ˈhelətrɪ] [je-lo-tri], *s.* 1. Los ilotras. 2. Servidumbre, esclavitud.

help [help] [jelp], *va.* y *vn.* 1. Ayudar, asistir, socorrer, amparar, favorecer, patrocinar, sostener (favour, protect). 2. Servir a la mesa. 3. Aliviar, librar de dolor o enfermedad; remediar, reparar. 4. Evitar, dejar de hacer, abstenerse, no poder en manos de. **How can I help it?,** ¿cómo evitarlo?, ¿qué quiere Ud. que yo haga? -*vn.* Ayudar, contribuir, concurrir. **It helped much to his reputation,** eso contribuyó mucho a su reputación.

help back, ayudar a retroceder.

help down, ayudar a alguno a bajar.

help forward, adelantar, activar, promover, ayudar a alguno para que adelante.

help out, ayudar a salir; sacar de algún peligro o mal paso. **To help one another,** favorecerse mutuamente. **I cannot help believing that,** no puedo menos de creerlo.

help to o **on,** (a) *va.* Servir, ofrecer, proporcionar, promover. (b) *vn.* Contribuir, ayudar, concurrir a la ejecución de una cosa.

help, *s.* 1. Ayuda, auxilio, asistencia, socorro, remedio, apoyo, arrimo, protección, amparo, favor. 2. Medio, recurso; lo que contribuye a hacer adelantar o mejorar una cosa. 3. *(E.U.)* Criada; jornalera. 4. *(Fam.)* Porción de comida tomada de una vez. **To cry out for help,** pedir socorro, llamar en auxilio. **By the help of,** con auxilio de, por medio de. **There is no help for it,** no tiene remedio.

helper [ˈhelpəʳ] [jel-paʳ], *s.* 1. Auxiliador, el que auxilia y ayuda. 2. Socorredor, el que socorre.

helpful [ˈhelpfʊl] [jelp-ful], *a.* Útil, provechoso, sano, saludable.

helpfulness [ˈhelpfʊlnɪs] [jelp-ful-nes], *s.* Asistencia, utilidad.

helpless [ˈhelplɪs] [jelp-les], *a.* 1. Desamparado, destituído, abandonado. 2. Irremediable. 3. Inerte, desmañado, desvalido. 4. Imposibilitado.

helplessly [ˈhelplɪslɪ] [jelp-les-li], *adv.* Irremediablemente, sin recurso, en el desamparo, en el abandono.

helplessness ['helplɪsnɪs] [jelp-les-nes], *s.* 1. Desamparo, falta de amparo. 2. falta de fuerzas, de energía; debilidad, impotencia.

helpmate ['helpmeɪt] [jelp-meit], *s.* 1. Compañero, asistente, auxiliar. 2. Esposa, mujer.

helter-skelter ['heltə'skeltəʳ] [jel-ta-skel-taʳ], *adv.* A trochemoche, a trompa y talega, al tuntún, atropelladaente, sin orden ni concierto, confusamente, en desorden.

helve [helv] [jelv], *s.* Astil de hacha o destral, mango. **To throw the helve after the hatchet,** echar la soga tras el caldero, abandonar una empresa.

helve, *va.* Echar mango o cabo a una cosa.

Helvetic ['helvetɪk] [jel-ve-tik], *a.* Helvético, helvecio, de Suiza.

hem [hem] [jem], *s.* 1. Ribete, borde de la ropa o vestido; repulgo, orilla. 2. Dobladillo, costura. 3. El ruido que causa la expiración repentina y violenta del aliento. -inter. ¡Eh!

hem, *va.* 1. Ribetear, echar ribetes; repulgar, poner repulgos a algún vestido, repulgar, orillar. 2. Cercar, rodear o encerrar en un recinto. -vn. Hacer ruido espirando con violencia; desahogar las fauces. 3. Fingir tos, o toser de fingido.

hemal, haemal ['hi:mæl] [ji-mal], *a.* 1. Perteneciente a la sangre o al sistema vascular; de la naturaleza de la sangre. 2. Relativo al lado del cuerpo que contiene el corazón.

hematin ['hi:mətɪn] [ji-ma-tin], *s. (Quím.)* Hematina, principio colorante derivado del de la sangre por la acción de los ácidos. *V.* HEMATOXYLIN.

hematite ['hi:mətaɪt] [ji-ma-tait], *s.* Hematita, (Fe2O3), mineral común de hierro.

hematoxylin [ˌhi:mə'tɒksɪn] [ji-ma-tok-sin], *s.* Hematoxilina.

hemerobaptist [ˌhi:mərə'bæpstɪst] [ji-me-ro-bap-tist], *s.* Sectario judío de los que practicaban diarias abluciones.

hemi ['hemɪ] [je-mi], *a.* Voz que entra en la composición de varias otras, y equivale a medio o semi.

hemicrania, hemicrany [ˌhemɪ'kræniə] [je-mi-kra-nia], *s.* Hemicránea, jaqueca, dolor en un lado o en una parte de la cabeza.

hemicycle ['hemɪsaɪkl] [je-mi-sai-kel], *s.* Semicírculo.

hemina ['heminə] [je-mi-na], *s.* Hemina, una medida antigua; medida usada a veces en la farmacia, que tiene unas diez onzas.

hemiplegia, hemiplegy ['hemɪ'pli:dʒiə] [je-mi-pli-yia], *s.* Hemiplejía, parálisis de todo un lado del cuerpo.

hemiplegic ['hemɪ'pli:dʒɪk] [je-mi-pli-yik], *a.* Hemipléjico, de la hemiplejía.

hemisphere ['hemɪsfɪəʳ] [je-mis-feaʳ], *s.* Hemisferio, la mitad de una esfera, dividida por un plano que pasa por su centro.

hemispheric, hemispherical ['hemɪsfɪərɪk] [je-mis-fia-rik], *a.* Hemisférico.

hemistich, hemestic ['hemɪstɪʃ] [je-mis-tich], *s.* Hemistiquio.

hemlock ['hemlɒk] [jem-lok], *s. (Bot.)* 1. Pinabete o abeto americano. 2. Cicuta, hierba umbelífera venenosa.

hemoglobin, haemoglobin ['hi:məʊ'gləbɪn] [ji-mou-glo-bin], *s.* Hemoglobina, la materia colorante de la sangre.

hemophilia ['hi:məʊ'fɪliə] [ji-mou-fi-lia], *s. (Med.)* Hemofilia.

hemorrhage ['hi:məʊrɑ:dʒ] [ji-mou-rach], *s.* Hemorragia, flujo de sangre.

hemorrhoides ['hi:məʊrɔɪdz] [ji-mou-roids], *s. pl.* Hemorroides almorranas.

hemorrhoidal ['hi:məʊrɔɪdl] [ji-mou-roi-dal], *a.* Hemorroidal.

hemostatic ['hi:məstætɪk] [ji-mos-ta-tik], *a. (Med.)* Hemostático.

hemp [hemp] [jemp], *s. (Bot.)* Cáñamo. **Bastard-hem,** cañamón, cáñamo bastardo. **Hemp agrimony,** *(Bot.)* Eupatorio vulgar. **Raw hemp,** cáñamo sin peinar. **Indian hemp,** canabina.

hemp-beater ['hempbi:təʳ] [jemp-bi-taʳ], *a.* Espadador o espadillador de cáñamo.

hemp-breaker [hemp'breɪkəʳ] [jemp-brei-kaʳ], *s.* Agramador de cáñamo.

hemp-close ['hempkləʊz] [jemp-klous], **hemp-field** ['hempfi:ld] [jemp-fild], *s.* Cañamar, el terreno sembrado de cáñamo.

hemp-comb ['hempkɒmb] [jemp-komb], *s.* Peine para pasar el cáñamo después de rastrillado.

hempen ['hempən] [jem-pen], *a.* Cañameño, lo que se hace del hilo del cáñamo.

hemp-seed ['hempsi:d] [jemp-sid], *s.* 1. Cañamón. 2. *(Fam.)* Carne de horca.

hemstitch ['hempstɪtʃ] [jemp-stich], *va.* Hacer vainica. -s. Vainica.

hempy ['hempɪ] [jem-pi], *a.* Semejante al cáñamo.

hen [hen] [jen], *sf.* 1. Gallina, la hembra del gallo. 2. Ave hembra de cualquier especie. 3. *pl.* Pollos, gallinas, aves domésticas en general sin distinción de sexo. **Brood-hen,** gallina clueca. **Guinea-hen,** gallina de Guinea o de Indias; pintada. **Turkey-hen,** pava. **Moor-hen,** zarceta, ave acuática.

henbane ['hebeɪn] [je-bein], *s. (Bot.)* Beleño, planta venenosa.

hence [hens] [jens], *adv.* 1. De aquí, desde aquí, a distancia, de aquí, fuera de aquí. 2. De aquí, por esto, en consecuencia de esto. **Hence it is that they are all rich,** de aquí es que todos son ricos. **Ten years hence,** de aquí a diez años. **Far hence,** lejos de aquí. **Not many days hence,** dentro de unos días. **From hence,** locución pleonástica y anticuada, lo mismo que HENCE, desde aquí, fuera de aquí. 3. Anda, fuera; voz de mando. **Hence with you,** quítese Ud. de delante, largo de aquí.

henceforth ['hensfɔ:θ] [jens-forz], *adv.* De aquí en adelante; en adelánte, en lo futuro.

henceforward ['hensfɔ:wəd] [jens-for-uard], *adv.* De aquí en adelante; en lo venidero; para siempre.

henchman ['hentʃmən] [jench-man], *s.* 1. Agente servil y subordinado. 2. *(Ant.)* Criado.

hencoop ['henˌku:p] [jen-kup], *s.* Gallinero.

hendecagon ['hendɪkgən] [jen-di-ka-gon], *s.* Endecágono, polígono de once lados y once ángulos.

hendecasyllabic ['hendekəsɪ'læbɪk] [jen-de-ka-si-la-bik], *a.* Endecasílabo.

hendecasyllable ['hendekəsɪləbl] [jen-de-ka-si-la-bol], *s.* Verso endecasílabo.

henequen ['henɪkwɪn] [je-ni-kuin], *s. (Bot.)* Henequén.

hen-harm ['henhɑ:m] [jen-jarm], **hen-harrier** ['henhɑ:m] [jen-jarm], *s. (Orn.)* Pigargo.

henhouse ['henhaʊs] [jen-jaus], *s.* Gallinero.

henna ['henə] [je-na], *s.* Arbusto o árbol pequeño de Oriente, llamado Lawsonia intermis; y una preparación cosmética de sus hojas que da un color anaranjado.

hennery ['henərɪ] [je-na-ri], *s.* Gallinero, lugar donde las gallinas se recogen a dormir.

henpeck ['henpek] [jen-pek], *va.* Dominar; molestar, fastidiar, importunar con triquiñuelas: se dice de una mujer que así trata y maneja a su marido.

henpecked ['henpekt] [jen-pekt], *a.* Gurrumino, el que está dominado por su mujer. **Henpecked husband,** el marido cuya mujer lleva los calzones, calzonazos

Henrietta ['henri:tə] [jen-rie-ta], *n. pr.* Enriqueta.

henroost ['henru:st] [jen-rust], *s.* Gallinero.

Henry ['henrɪ] [jen-ri], *n. pr.* Enrique. -s. *(Elec.)* Unidad práctica de autoinducción.

hep [hep] [jep], *s.* Fruto del agavanzo. *V.* HIP. **Hep-bramble, hep-brier, hep-tree,** escaramujo, agavanzo. *a.* Sabedor, enterado, que está al corriente de todo. **To put someone hep to,** poner al corriente de.

heparin ['hepəri:n] [je-pa-rin], *s.* (Anticoagulante) Heparina.

hepatic, hepatical ['hepətɪk] [je-pa-tik], *a.* 1. Hepático, que pertece al hígado. 2. De color de hígado.

hepatica ['hepətɪkə] [je-pa-ti-ka], *s. (Bot.)* Hepática, planta de la familia de las ranunculáceas, llamada también **liver-leaf** (hoja de hígado).

hepaticae ['hepətɪkæ] [je-pa-ti-ka], *s. pl. (Bot.)* Ciertas piantas parecidas a los musgos.

hepatite [ˈhepataɪt] [je-pa-tait], *s. (Min.)* Hepatita, variedad de barita; debe su nombre al olor fétido que despide al calentarla.

hepatitis [ˌhepəˈtaɪtɪs] [je-pa-tai-tis], *s. (Med.)* Hepatitis.

hepatize [ˈhepətaɪz] [je-pa-tais], *va.* 1. Cambiar o transformar en una sustancia semejante al hígado, se aplica en medicina particularmente a los pulmones. 2. *(Quím.)* Llenar de gas hidrógeno sulfurado.

heptachord [ˈheptəkɔːd] [jep-ta-kord], *s.* 1. *(Mús.)* Heptacordio. 2. Instrumento músico de siete cuerdas.

heptagon [ˈheptəgən] [jep-ta-gon], *s.* 1. Heptágono, figura de siete lados y otros tantos ángulos. 2. *(Fort.)* Heptágono, fortaleza guarnecida con siete bastiones.

heptagonal [hepˈtægənəl] [jep-ta-go-nal], *a.* Heptagonal, lo que tiene siete ángulos y lados.

heptameride [ˈheptəmeraɪd] [jep-ta-me-raid], *s.* Lo que divide o que consiste en siete partes.

heptarchy [ˈheptɑːkɪ] [jep-tar-ki], *s.* Heptarquía, gobierno de siete personas, reinos o provincias.

Heptateuch [ˈheptɔːtʃ] [jep-toch], *s.* Heptateuco, los siete primeros libros del Viejo Testamento.

her [hɜːʳ] [jaʳ], *pron.* 1. Caso objetivo o acusativo de SHE. La, ella, a ella. 2. Caso posesivo o genitivo de SHE; también se usa como adjetivo posesivo: su, de ella. **I have not seen her,** no la he visto. **I have not sent the book to her,** no le he enviado el libro. **Herish her,** ámela Ud. con ternura. (En inglés, los adjetivos posesivos concuerdan en género con el poseedor.) **Her book, her house,** su libro, su casa (de ella).

herald [ˈherəld] [je-rald], *s.* 1. Heraldo, rey de armas. 2. Precursor; publicador.

heraldic [heˈrəldɪk] [je-ral-dik], *a.* Heráldico, genealógico.

heraldist [ˈherəldɪst] [je-ral-dist], *s.* Heráldico.

heraldry [ˈherəldrɪ] [je-ral-dri], *s.* Heráldica, arte o ciencia que trata del blasón; registro de genealogías.

heraldship [ˈherəldʃɪp] [je-rald-ship], *s.* Oficio de heraldo.

herb [ˈhɜːb] [jerb], *s.* Hierba; nombre genérico que se da a todas las plantas menores cuyo tallo nace todos los años; legumbres. **Sweet herbs,** hierbas odoríferas, olorosas o de olor. **Physical herbs,** hierbas medicinales. **Salad-herbs,** hierbas para ensalada. **Pot-herbs,** hortalizas.

herbaceous [hɜːˈbeɪʃəs] [jer-bei-shos], *a.* Herbáceo.

herbage [ˈhɜːbeɪdʒ] [jer-beich], *s.* Herbaje; pasto.

herbaged [ˈhɜːbeɪdʒt] [jer-beicht], *a.* Cubierto de hierba o herbaje.

herbal [ˈhɜːbəl] [jer-bal], *s.* Herbario. *-a.* Lo que pertence al herbario.

herbalist [ˈhɜːbəlɪst] [jer-ba-list], **herbarist** [ˈhɜːbərɪst] [jer-ba-rist], **herbist** [ˈhɜːbɪst] [jer-bist], *s.* Herbolario, el que entiende de hierbas y plantas.

herbarious [hɜːˈbærɪəs] [jer-ba-rios], *a.* Herbario.

herbarium [hɜːˈbærɪəm] [jer-ba-riom], *s.* 1. Herbario, colección de plantas secas colocadas según arte. 2. Libro o estante para contener plantas secas. 3. Edificio en que conservan plantas secas.

herbarize [ˈhɜːbæraɪz] [jer-ba-rais], *vn.* Herborizar, ir al campo en busca de hierbas o plantas.

herbary [ˈhɜːbərɪ] [jer-ba-ri], *s.* Jardín que contiene solamente hierbas.

herbescent [hɜːˈbesənt] [jer-be-sent], *a.* Parecido a una hierba; que tiende a convertirse en hierba.

Herbert [ˈhɜːbət] [jer-bert], *n. pr.* Heriberto.

herbiferous [hɜːˈbɪfərəs] [jer-bi-fe-ros], *a.* Herbífero, que produce hierbas.

herbivorous [hɜːˈbɪvərəs] [jer-bi-vo-ros], *a.* Herbívoro, que se alimenta de hierbas.

herbless [ˈhɜːblɪs] [jerb-les], *a.* Sin hierbas, yermo.

herborization [ˈhɜːbəraɪˈzeɪʃən] [jer-ba-rai-sei-shon], *s.* Herborización.

herborize [ˈhɜːbəraɪz] [jer-bo-rais], *vn.* Herborizar, ir al campo en busca de hierbas o plantas. *-va.* Formar dibujos de plantas o árboles, *v.g.* en una sustancia mineral.

herborizer [ˈhɜːbəraɪzəʳ] [jer-bo-rai-saʳ], herborizador, herborizante.

herbose [ˈhɜːbəʊz] [jer-bous], **herbous** [ˈhɜːbəz] [jer-bos], **herby** [ˈhɜːbɪ] [jer-bi], *a.* Herboso, lo que abunda en hierbas.

herbwoman [ˈhɜːbˌwʊmən] [jerb-uo-man], *sf.* Herbolaría; verdulera, mujer que vende hierbas.

herculanean [ˈhɜːkjuˈliːnɪən] [jer-kiu-li-nian], *a.* De Herculano, antigua ciudad romana cerca de Nápoles.

herd [hɜːd] [jerd], *s.* 1. Hato, grey, manada, rebaño, ganado, número de animales de una especie que pacen o caminan juntos (flock). 2. Hato, junta o reunión de gente; de aquí gentuza, tropel, multitud, vulgo, chusma. 3. Guarda de ganado. V. HERDSMAN. **The common herd,** el vulgo, la gente ordinaria, la gentuza. **A herd of rogues,** un hato de tunantes. **Herd's grass,** *(E.U.)* (a) En algunas partes, la planta gramínea llamada **red-top** (Agrostis vulgaris). (b) (Nueva Ingl.) La planta gramínea llamada **timothy.** Phleum pratense. Ambas plantas dan buen forraje. **Cow-herd,** vaquero o boyero. **Goat-herd,** cabrero. **Shepherd,** pastor de ovejas. **Swine-herd,** porquero.

herd, *vn.* Ir en manadas o hatos; ir en compañía de otros; asociarse; pacer juntos. *-va.* Reunir el ganado en hatos o rebaños.

herdic [ˈhɜːdɪk] [jer-dik], *s.* Nombre de un carruaje de dos o cuatro ruedas.

herdsman [ˈhɜːdzmən] [jerds-man], *s.* Guarda de ganado, pastor, zagal.

here [hɪəʳ] [jiaʳ], *adv.* 1. Aquí, en este lugar o en este paraje. 2. Acá, a o hacia este lugar. 3. Por aquí, por allá; en este momento, o este período. **Here I must pause,** en este punto he de detenerme. 4. He aquí, **here I am,** heme aquí. **Here he is, she is, they are,** hele aquí, hela aquí, helos aquí. **Here he comes,** hele aquí que llega. 5. Aquí, en este mundo, en esta vida. **Here below,** en esta vida, en la tierra. **Here goes,** *(Fam.)* voy a empezar; ahora entro yo; va seguido a menudo de **for.** He aquí, (Fam. **here's**). He aquí. **Here's another strike,** he aquí otra huelga. **Here is John now,** he aquí a Juan. **Here's a pretty how-do-you do!** *(Fam.)* ¡Esta sí que es buena! ¡Ahora sí que la hemos hecho! **Here is to you,** a la salud de Ud. **Here and there,** aquí y allá, acá y acullá. **Here it is,** aquí está.

hereabouts [ˈhɪərəˌbaʊts] [jiar-a-bauts], *adv.* Aquí alrededor, en estas cercanías, en estas inmediaciones.

hereafter [ˈhɪəˈæftəʳ] [jia-af-taʳ], *adv.* En el tiempo venidero, en lo futuro. *-s.* Estado futuro.

hereat [ˈhɪəriːt] [jia-rit], *adv.* A esto o esta, por eso.

hereby [ˈhɪəbaɪ] [jia-bai], *adv.* Por esto; por este medio o por este camino; por la presente.

hereditable [ˈherɪdɪteɪbl] [je-ri-di-tei-bol], *a.* Lo que puede ser heredado, antiguamente hereditable.

hereditament [ˌherɪˈdɪtəmənt] [je-ri-di-ta-ment], *s.* Herencia, bienes heredados.

hereditarily [ˈherɪdɪtərɪlɪ] [je-ri-di-ta-ri-li], *adv.* Por herencia, hereditariamente.

hereditary [ˈherɪdɪtərɪ] [je-ri-di-ta-ri], *a.* Hereditario, en sus varias acepciones.

herefrom [ˈhɪəfrɒm] [jia-from], *adv.* De aquí, desde aquí; a causa de esto.

herein [ˌhɪəriːn] [jia-in], **hereinto** [ˌhɪəriːˈntu] [jia-in-tu], *adv.* En esto, aquí dentro.

hereinafter [ˌhɪəriːˈnɑːftəʳ] [jia-rin-af-taʳ], *adv.* Después, más abajo, como se verá o se dice más adelante (en este escrito, libro o documento).

hereof [ˈhɪərɒv] [jia-ov], *adv.* De esto, de eso, de aquí.

hereon [ˈhɪərɒn] [jia-on], *adv.* Sobre esto, sobre este punto.

heresiarch [ˈherəsɪɑːk] [je-ra-siark], *s.* Heresiarca.

heresiarchy [ˈherəsɪɑːkɪ] [je-ra-siar-ki], *s.* Gran herejía.

heresy [ˈherəsɪ] [je-re-si], *s.* Herejía.

heretic [ˈherətɪk] [je-re-tik], *s.* Hereje.

heretical [hɪˈretɪkəl] [ji-re-ti-kal], *a.* Herético, heretical.

heretically [ˈherətɪklɪ] [je-re-ti-kli], *adv.* Heréticamente.

hereto [ˌhɪəˈtuː] [jia-tu], *adv.* A esto, a este fin.

heretofore [ˌhɪətʊˈfɔːʳ] [jia-tu-foʳ], *adv.* En otro tiempo, antes, antiguamente, en tiempos pasados, hasta aquí, hasta ahora, hasta el día. -*s.* El tiempo pasado, antaño.

hereunder [ˈhɪəʳˌʌndəʳ] [jiar-an-daʳ], *adv.* Bajo esto, en virutd de esto.

hereunto [ˈhɪəʳˈʌntə] [jiar-an-to], *adv.* A esto, a eso.

hereupon [ˈhɪərəˈpɒn] [jia-ra-pon], *adv.* Sobre esto.

herewith [ˈhɪəˈwɪð] [jia-uiz], *adv.* Con esto, junto con esto.

heritable [ˈherɪtəbl] [je-ri-ta-bol], *a.* Que se puede heredar. V. HEREDITABLE.

heritage [ˈherɪtɪdʒ] [je-ri-tich], *s.* 1. Herencia, sucesión a todos o alguno de los derechos que el difunto tenía al tiempo de su muerte; bienes patrimoniales. 2. Porción, interés (interest). 3. Condición, suerte o estado heredado (herity).

hermaphrodeity [ˈhɜːməˈfrədɪti] [jer-ma-fro-di-ti], *s.* Estado de hermafrodita. V. HERMAPHRODITISM.

hermaphrodite [hɜːˈmæfrədaɪt] [jer-ma-fro-dait], *a.* 1. Hermafrodita, que presenta los caracteres distintivos de ambos sexos; en botánica, bisexual, que tiene pistilos y estambres. 2. (*Mar.*) Con aparejo de cruz hacia la proa y arboladura de goleta a popa. -*s.* 1. Hermafrodita, andrógino, ser que tiene los dos sexos a la vez; como ciertos moluscos y gusanos y la mayor parte de las plantas. 2. (*Mar.*) Bergantín, goleta.

hermaphroditic, hermaphroditical [hɜːˈmæfrədaɪtɪk] [jer-ma-fro-dai-tik], *a.* Que participa de los dos sexos.

hermaphroditically [hɜːˈmæfrədɪtɪkəlɪ] [jer-ma-fro-di-ti-ka-li], *adv.* Como hermafrodita.

hermaphroditism, hermaphrodism [hɜːˈmæfrədɪtɪzm] [jer-ma-fro-di-ti-sem], *s.* hermafrodismo, reunión de ambos sexos en el mismo individuo.

hermeneutics [hɜːˈmɪnjʊtɪks] [jer-mi-niu-tiks], *s.* Hermenéutica, el arte de interpretar textos, y en especial los textos sagrados.

hermetic, hermetical [hɜːˈmetɪk] [jer-me-tik], *a.* 1. Hermético, relativo al Hermes griego, dios de los secretos y de la filosofía oculta; o al Hermes egipcio (Thoth). 2. Hermético, hecho a prueba de aire u otros flúidos. v.g. por medio de la fusión. **Hermetic art,** alquimia; de aquí, q u í m i c a .

hermetically [hɜːˈmetɪkəlɪ] [jer-me-ti-ka-li], *adv.* Herméticamente.

hermit [ˈhɜːmɪt] [jer-mit], *s.* Ermitaño, eremita, anacoreta, solitario.

hermitage [ˈhɜːmɪtɪdʒ] [jer-mi-tich], *s.* 1. Ermita, la vivienda del ermitaño. 2. Cierta clase de vino francés.

hermitary [ˈhɜːmɪtərɪ] [jer-mi-ta-ri], *s.* Celda de ermitaño aneja a un monasterio.

hermitess [ˈhɜːmɪtɪs] [jer-mi-tis], *sf.* Ermitaña.

hermitical [ˈhɜːmɪtɪkl] [jer-mi-ti-kal], *a.* Eremítico.

hermodactyl [ˈhɜːməˈdæktɪl] [jer-mo-dak-til], *s.* (*Bot.*) Hermodáctilo, especie de iris o lirio.

herns, *s.* V. HERON.

hernia [ˈhɜːnɪə] [jer-nia], *s.* Hernia, quebradura; (*Fam.*) potra.

hernial [ˈhɜːnɪəl] [jer-nial], *a.* Herniario, relativo a la hernia; herniado, que forma hernia.

hernshaw [ˈhɜːnʃɔː] [jern-sho], *s.* 1. Garza. 2. (*Her.*) Figura de una garza u otra ave semejante.

hero [ˈhɪərəʊ] [jia-rou], *s.* 1. Héroe, hombre eminente por su valor; hombre ilustre y de extraordinario mérito. 2. Semidios, persona de fuerzas sobrehumanas, etc: personaje ilustre que los angituos divinizaban después de muerto. 3. Protagonista o personaje principal de un poema, drama, comedia o novela.

Herod [ˈherəd] [je-rod], *n. pr.* Herodes.

herodians [ˈherədɪənz] [je-ro-dians], *s. pl.* Herodianos, unos sectarios entre los judíos.

heroic, heroical [hɪˈrəʊɪk] [ji-rouik], *a.* 1. Heroico, lo que produce héroes. 2. Heroico, noble, grande, sublime, ilustre, valeroso, magnánimo. 3. Heroico, lo perteneciente a los héroes o lo que refiere sus hechos.

heroically [hɪˈrəʊɪkəlɪ] [ji-roui-ka-li], *adv.* Heroicamente.

heroicomic [hɪˈrəʊɪkəmɪk] [ji-roui-ko-mik], *a.* Jocoserio, lo que consta de una mezcla de serio y jocoso, comicoheroico.

heroics [hɪˈrəʊɪkz] [ji-rouiks], *s.* 1. Verso heroico. 2. Lenguaje rimbombante.

heroin [ˈherəʊɪn] [je-rouin], *s.* Heroína (narcótico).

heroine [ˈherəʊɪn] [je-rouin], *sf.* heroína.

heroism [ˈherəʊɪzm] [je-roui-sem], *s.* heroísmo, heroicidad, grandeza de alma, excelencia en el valor.

heron [ˈherən] [je-ron], *s.* (*Orn.*) Garza, ave de caza.

heronry [ˈherənrɪ] [je-ron-ri], *s.* El lugar en que se crían las garzas.

heron's-bill [ˈherənzbɪl] [je-rons-bil], *s.* (*Bot.*) Pico de garza.

heroship [ˈherəʃɪp] [je-ro-ship], *s.* Calidad de héroe.

herpes [ˈhɜːpiːz] [jer-pis], *s.* (*Med.*) Herpes, erupción, granitos rojizos y arracimados que salen en el cutis.

herpetic [hɜːˈpiːtɪk] [jer-pi-tik], *a.* Herpético.

herpetologist [ˈhɜːpəˈtɒlədʒɪst] [jer-pe-to-lo-chist], *s.* Persona versada en la herpetología.

herpetology [ˈhɜːpəˈtɒlədʒɪ] [jer-pe-to-lo-yi], *s.* Herpetología, el ramo de la zoología que trata de los reptiles.

herring [ˈherɪŋ] [je-rin], *s.* Arenque. Clupea. **Herring-casks,** barriles de arenques. **Herring-fishery,** pesca de arenques. **Red herring,** arenque ahumado.

herringbone [ˈherɪŋbəʊn] [je-rin-boun], *s.* Punto de espiguilla (en las telas).

hers [hɜːz] [jers], *pron. pos.* Suyo, suya, de ella; el suyo, la suya, los suyos, las suyas. **The child is hers,** el niño es suyo. **Is the house yours?** ¿Es de Ud. la casa? **No, it is hers,** no, es la suya (de ella). **I have no money of hers,** no tengo dinero de ella.

herse, *s.* 1. (*Fort.*) Especie de rastrillo; caballo de frisia. 2. Especie de enrejado. 3. (*Des.*) V. HEARSE.

herself [hɜːˈself] [jer-self], *pron.* Ella misma. **She spoke of herself,** ella habló de sí misma. Suyo, suya, suyos, suyas, de ella; el suyo, la suya, los suyos, las suyas; el, la, los, las, de ella. Con **of** se convierte en adjetivo: **a brother of hers,** un hermano suyo (de ella).

Heruli [ˈhəruːlɪ] [je-ru-li], *s.* Hérulos.

hersilion [ˈhɜːsɪlɪən] [jer-si-lion], *s.* (*Mil.*) Caballo de frisa.

hesitancy [ˈhezɪtənsɪ] [je-si-tan-si], *s.* Duda, hesitación, incertidumbre, irresolución.

hesitate [ˈhezɪteɪt] [je-si-teit], *vn.* 1. Dudar, vacilar, tardar, pasuar, titubear. 2. Hablar con lentitud o indecisión; balbucear, tartamudear.

hesitation [ˌhezɪˈteɪʃən] [je-si-tei-shon], *s.* 1. Hesitación, duda, irresolución, perplejidad, vacilación. 2. Dificultad de pronunciar las palabras, balbucencia.

hesper [ˈhespəʳ] [jes-paʳ], *s.* Héspero o Venus, la estrella vespertina.

hesperian [ˈhespərɪən] [jes-pe-rian], *a.* hespérido, del poniente o del oeste; occidental. -*s.* Habitante de un país occidental.

hessian [ˈhesɪən] [je-sian], *a.* Perteneciente al ducado de Hesse, o que se refiere a Hesse. -*s.* Natural o ciudadano de Hesse. **Hessian fly,** cecidomio, mosca pequeña negruzca. **Hessian crucible,** crisol de arcilla refractaria.

hest [hest] [jest], *s.* Orden, mandato, precepto. V. BEHEST.

heter-, hetero-, Formas de combinación, derivadas del griego **heteros,** otro, diferente.

heteroclite [ˈhetərəʊˈklaɪt] [je-te-rou-klait], *s. y a.* Heteróclito, irregular.

heterodox [ˈhetərədɒks] [je-te-ro-doks], *a.* Heterodoxo, lo que es contrario a la opinión aceptada generalmente y en particular a una doctrina teológica; herético.

heterodoxy [ˈhetərədɒksɪ] [je-te-ro-dok-si], *s.* Heterodoxia, oposición a las opiniones dominantes, por lo general en materias religiosas.

heterodyne [ˈhetərədaɪn] [je-te-ro-dain], *a.* Heterodino.

heterogamous [ˈhetərəˈgæməs] [je-te-ro-ga-mos], *a.* (*Bot.*) Heterógamo, que tiene flores monoicas, bioicas o polígamas.

heterogeneity [ˈhetərəˈdʒiːnɪtɪ] [je-te-rou-yi-ni-ti], **heterogeneousness** [ˈhetərəˈdʒiːnɪəsnɪs] [je-te-rou-yi-nios-nes], *s.* Heterogeneidad.

heterogeneous ['hetərəʊˈdʒi:nɪəs] [je-te-rou-yi-nios], **heterogeneal** ['hetərəʊˈdʒi:nɪəl] [je-te-rou-yi-nial], *a.* Heterogéneo, lo que es de diferente género; lo opuesto a **homogéneo.**

heteronomous ['hetərənəməs] [je-te-ro-no-mos], *a.* 1. (*Biol.*) Diferente del tipo común. 2. Sujeto a la ley o al dominio de otro.

heteronym ['hetərənɪm] [je-te-rou-nim], *s.* 1. Palabra que tiene la misma ortografía que otra, pero sonido y sentido diferentes, v.g. **wind** [wind], viento, y **wind** [waind], enrollar. 2. Uno de los dos o más nombres con que se designa una misma cosa. Su adjetivo es HETERONYMOUS.

heteroscian ['hetərəʃən] [je-te-rou-shian], *s.* Heteroscio, literalmente, que tiene diferentes sombras. **The Japanese and the Australians are heteroscians,** los japoneses y los australianos son heteroscios.

hew [hju:] [jiu], *va.* (*pret.* HEWED, *pp.* HEWN y HEWED). 1. Tajar, cortar, picar. 2. Cortar con hacha u otro instrumento cortante; hachear. 3. Efectuar laboriosamente; trabajar. **To hew a stone,** picar, trabajar una piedra. **To hew right and left,** acuchillar a diestro y siniestro. **To hew in pieces,** destrozar, destroncar. **To hew out,** hachear, cortar; modelar en bruto; abrir paso. **To hew out a passage sword in hand,** abrirse paso espada en mano. **To rough-hew,** descortezar; desbastar; modelar en bruto.

hewer ['hju:əʳ] [jiuaʳ], *s.* El que tiene por oficio labrar piedra o madera; cantero; cortador de madera.

hexachord ['heksəkɔːd] [jek-sa-kord], *s.* (*Mús.*) Hexacordo.

hexagon ['heksəgən] [jek-sa-gon], *s.* Hexágono, figura plana que consta de seis ángulos y seis lados.

hexagonal ['hekˈsægənəl] [jek-sa-go-nal], *a.* Perteneciente al hexágono.

hexahedron ['heksəhiːdrən] [jek-sa-ji-dron], *s.* Hexaedro.

hexameter ['heksəmiːtəʳ] [jek-sa-mi-taʳ], *s.* Hexámetro.

hexametric, hexametrical ['heksəmiːtrɪk] [jek-sa-mi-trik], *a.* Que se compone de hexámetros.

hexangular ['hekˈsæŋɡjələʳ] [jek-san-guiu-laʳ], *a.* Herángulo, que tiene seis ángulos.

hexapod ['heksəpɒd] [jek-sa-pod], *a.* Hexápodo, que tiene seis patas. -*s.* Hexápodo.

hexapodan, hexapode ['heksəpɒdən] [jek-sa-po-dan], *a.* y *s.* V. HEXAPOD.

hey [heɪ] [jei], *inter.* 1. ¡Eh! expresión de alegría y gozo. 2. Lo mismo que eh; interjección para preguntar, llamar, despreciar, reprender y advertir; equivale a arre, anda, para arrear a las caballerías, y sirve también para azuzar los perros.

heyday ['heɪdeɪ] [jei-dei], *s.* Colmo, apogeo de vitalidad y vigor. -*inter.* ¡Hola! (expresa alegría, sorpresa o asombro).

hiatus [haɪˈeɪtəs] [jai-ei-tos], *s.* 1. Grieta, abertura, raja, hendedura. 2. Hiato, sonido desagradable que resulta de la pronunciación de dos vocablos seguidos, cuando el primero acaba en vocal y el segundo empieza con la misma vocal acentuada.

hibernal [haɪˈbɜːnəl] [jai-ber-nal], *a.* Invernizo, hiemal, invernal, lo que pertenece al invierno.

hibernate [haɪˈbɜːneɪt] [jai-ber-neit], *vn.* 1. Invernar, pasar la estación del invierno en lugar abrigado y en torpor, como ciertos animales. 2. Pasar el tiempo en el retiro o la inacción.

hibernian [haɪˈbɜːnɪən] [jai-ber-nian], *s.* Irlandés, de Hibernia.

hibernianism, hibernicism [haɪˈbɜːnɪənɪzm] [jai-ber-nia-ni-sem], *s.* Idiotismo irlandés, giro o forma de expresión irlandesa.

hibiscus [hɪˈbɪskəs] [ji-bis-kos], *s.* Hibisco, género numeroso de plantas de la familia de las malváceas.

hiccough, hiccup, hickup ['hɪkʌp] [ji-kap], *s.* Hipo.

hiccough, hiccup, hickup, *vn.* Tener o padecer hipo.

hickory ['hɪkərɪ] [jai-ko-ri], *s.* 1. Árbol americano parecido al nogal, del género Carya. 2. Su madera. 3. Algo hecho de la madera de este nogal. (Nombre indio).

hick-wall ['hɪkwɔːl] [jik-uol], **hick-way** ['hɪkweɪ] [jik-uei], *s.* (*Orn.*) Especie de picamaderos.

hid [hɪd] [jid], *pret.* y *pp.* de TO HIDE. V. HIDDEN.

hidden ['hɪdn] [ji-den], *a.* y *pp.* Oculto, recóndito, escondido.

hiddenly ['hɪdnlɪ] [ji-den-li], *adv.* Escondidamente, secretamente.

hide [haɪd] [jaid], *s.* 1. Cuero, piel, el pellejo del animal adobado o por adobar. **To dress hides,** adobar y curtir cueros. **To warm, to tan one's hide for him,** zurrar, calentar el pellejo a alguien, pegarle una tunda. **Raw hide,** cuero crudo, sin curtir. **Neither hide nor hair,** ni rastro, ni vestigio. 2. Antiguamente una cantidad de tierra, bastante para mantener a una familia.

hide, *va.* (*pret.* HID, *pp.* HIDDEN o HID). 1. Esconder, ocultar, encubrir, guardar o retirar de la vista alguna cosa para que no se vea (conceal, guard). 2. Tapar, disimular (disguise). 3. Volver (la vista) a otra parte; apartar los ojos de. **Adam and his wife hid themselves from the presence of the Lord God,** escondiéndose Adán y su mujer de la presencia del Señor Dios. **To hide one's fears,** disimular, ocultar sus temores. **To hide the face from,** ocultar el rostro; volverse de espaldas, rechazar la presencia y las atenciones de alguno. -*vn.* Esconderse, ocultarse. **Hide and seek,** juego de escondite.

hide, *va.* Pegar a uno una tunda, castigar con un rebenque o vergajo.

hide-bound ['haɪdbaʊnd] [jaid-baund], *a.* 1. El que está muy extenuado y tiene la piel pegada a los huesos. 2. Obstinado, apocado, encogido, mojigato.

hideous ['haɪdɪəs] [jai-dios], *a.* Horrible, horrendo, espantoso, feo, deforme, repugnante.

hideously ['haɪdɪəslɪ] [jai-dios-li], *adv.* Horriblemente, espantosamente.

hideousness ['haɪdɪəsnɪs] [jai-dios-nes], *s.* Horror, espanto; fealdad deformidad.

hiding ['haɪdɪŋ] [jai-din], *s.* 1. Encubrimiento. 2. Retiro, retrete. **Hiding-plance,** sitio de retiro, retrete, escondite. 3. (*Fam.*) Zurra, paliza.

hie [haɪ] [jai], *vn.* Darse prisa, apresurarse. -*va.* 1. Activar, apresurar. 2. Correr, pasar con rapidez. **Hie thee,** date prisa. **Hie thee home,** apresúrate a volver a casa.

hierarch ['haɪərɑːk] [jaia-rark], *s.* Jerarca, prelado, pontífice.

hierarchal [ˌhaɪəˈrɑːkəl] [jaia-rar-kal], **hierarchical** [ˌhaɪəˈrɑːkɪkəl] [jaia-rar-ki-kal], *a.* Jerárquico.

hierarchism [ˌhaɪəˈrɑːkɪzm] [jaia-rar-ki-sem], *s.* Jerarquía, los principios y el dominio del gobierno eclesiástico; afecto a ese gobierno.

hierarchy ['haɪərɑːkɪ] [jaia-rar-ki], *s.* 1. Jerarquía, gobierno eclesiastico por orden y grados diversos; y el conjunto de los jerarcas. 2. (*Biol.*) Orden y diversos grados de seres vivos, como reino, clases, órdenes, familias, etc.

hieratic, hieratical [ˌhaɪəˈrætɪk] [jaia-ra-tik], *a.* Jerárquico, sacerdotal; consagrado. **Hieratic writing,** escritura de los antiguos egipcios, forma más compleja que la común.

hieroglyph ['haɪərəglɪf] [jaia-ra-glif], **hieroglyphic** ['haɪərəglɪfɪk] [jaia-ra-gli-fik], *s.* Jeroglífico, símbolo, emblema.

hieroglyphic, hieroglyphical ['haɪərəglɪfɪkəl] [jaia-ra-gli-fi-kal], *a.* Jeroglífico o hieroglífico.

hierogram ['haɪərəgræm] [jaia-ra-gram], *s.* Escritura sagrada, carácter o símbolo de significación sagrada.

hierogrammatic ['haɪərəgræmətɪk] [jaia-ra-gra-ma-tik], **hierographical** ['haɪərəgræfɪkəl] [jaia-ra-gra-fi-kal], *a.* Perteneciente a una especie de escritura sagrada.

hierography ['haɪərəgrəfɪ] [jaia-ra-gra-fi], *s.* Escritura sagrada.

hierologic ['haɪərəlɒdʒɪk] [jaia-ra-lo-chik], *a.* Hierológico, perteneciente a la hierología.

hierology [ˈhaɪərəlɒdʒɪ] [jaia-ra-lo-yi], *s.* 1. Hierología, la ciencia o el libro que trata de las escrituras e inscripciones sagradas del antigo Egipto. 2. Hierología, estudio y comparación científicos de todas las religiones del mundo.

hieromancy [ˈhaɪərəmənsɪ] [jaia-ra-man-si], *s.* Hieromancia, adivinación por medio de sacrificios.

hierophant [ˈhaɪərəfænt] [jaia-ra-fant], *s.* Hierofante, el que enseña las reglas de la religión.

hifalutin, *a.* y *s.* V. HICHFALUTIN.

hi-fi (High-fidelity) [ˈhaɪˈfaɪ] [jai-fai], *a.* (*Mús.*) De alta fidelidad. -*s.* Fonógrafo de alta fidelidad.

higgle [ˈhɪgl] [ji-guel], *vn.* Regatear, altercar, porfiar sobre el precio de alguna cosa puesta en venta.

higgledy-piggledy [ˈhɪgldɪˈpɪgldɪ] [jai-guel-di-pi-guel-di], *adv.* (*Fam.*) Confusamente.

higgler [ˈhɪglər] [ji-glar], *s.* Revendedor de comestibles de puerta en puerta.

high [haɪ] [jai], *a.* 1. Alto, levantado, elevado. 2. Difícil, dificultoso, arduo (difficult). 3. Altivo, jactancioso, orgulloso (arrogant). 4. Severo, opresivo. 5. Fuerte, poderoso. 6. Noble, ilustre, grande, sublime. 7. Violento o tempestuoso (wind), vehemente, impetuoso; ardiente, fogoso, vivo; borrascoso (sea). 8. Solemne. 9. Turbulento, indómito. 10. Lleno, cumplido. 11. Alto, grande, enorme. 12. Caro. 13. (*Mús.*) Alto, agudo. 14. Maleado, maloliente, corrompido: se dice de la carne. **High color,** color muy vivo o muy subido. **High sauces o spices,** salsas o especias muy fuertes o picantes. **High treason,** alta traición, delito de lesa majestad. **It was high time to do so,** Ya era hora de hacerlo. **High-water,** marea alta. **The Most High,** el Altísimo. **High road,** camino real. **High mass,** misa mayor. **A high look,** una mirada altanera. **A high hand,** audacia, befa del derecho y de la autoridad. **High and dry,** en seco, completamente fuera del agua. **High and mighty,** poderoso, arrogante. **A high day,** un gran día, un día solemne, o de fiesta. **A high compliment,** un gran cumplimiento, de alto carácter. **With a high hand,** despóticamente, tiránicamente. **High passions,** pasiones ardientes. **High words,** palabras altivas, arrogantes. **In high terms,** en términos lisonjeros. **At high noon,** en pleno mediodía. **High-aimed, High-aspiring,** el que tiene grandes designios o aspira a cosas grandes. **High-arched,** lo que consta de bóvedas alta. **High-blest** Supremamente feliz. **High-blown,** inflado, hinchado con aire. **High-born,** noble, ilustre de nacimiento. **High-built.** elevado: se dice de los edificios. **High-climbing,** que sube en alto. **High-colored,** subido de color. **High-day,** fino, primoroso. **High-designing,** el que tiene grandes proyectos. **High-embowed,** se dice del edificio cuyas bóvedas son muy elevadas. **High-engendered,** engendrado en el aire. **High-fed,** atracado. **High-flaming,** lo que echa llama muy alta. **High-flier,** el extravagante en sus opiniones o pretensiones. **High-flown,** altivo, orgulloso; hinchado; fiero, soberbio presuntuoso. **High-flushed,** elevado; henchido, lleno, colmado. **High-flying,** extravagante en alguna cosa. **High-grown,** muy crecido o alto. **High-heaped,** colmado, amontonado altamente. **High-hearted,** animoso, de pelo en pecho. **High-heeled,** de tacones altos. **high-hung,** suspendido en alto, colgado. **High mettled,** osado, atrevido. **High-placed,** elevado en situación, posición o grado. **High-principled,** extravagante en sus opiniones o sentimientos. **High-raised,** (a) De pensamientos elevados. (b) Muy alto o muy elevado. **High-reaching,** lo que se extiende hacia arriba: ambicioso. **High-reared,** de estructura alta. **High-resolved,** resuelto, determinado. **High-roofed** Que tiene el tejado alto (un edificio). **High-seasoned,** picante, demasiadamente sazonado con especias. **High-seated,** fijado o asentado arriba. **High-spirited,** osado, atrevido, valeroso. **High-stomached,** altivo, obstinado. **High-tasted,** picante. **High-towered,** lo que tiene torres altas. -*adv.* Arriba, sobre; alto; poderosamente, sumamente, profundamente. **On high,** arriba; a voces, en alto, particularmente en el cielo; sobre.

highball [ˈhaɪbɔːl] [jai-bol], *s.* Bebida hecha de un licor espiritoso, comúnmente **whiskey** y agua. (*Mex.*) Jaibol.

high beams [ˈhaɪbiːmz] [jai-bims], *s. pl.* Luces de carretera.

high blood pressure [ˌhaɪblʌdˈpreʃər] [jai-blad-pre-shar], *s.* Hipertensión arterial, alta presión arterial.

high energy physics [ˌhaɪˈenədʒɪˌfɪzɪks] [jaie-nar-yi-fi-siks], *s.* Física de altas energías.

highfalutin [ˈhaɪfəˈluːtɪn] [jai-fa-lu-tin], *a.* (*Ger.*) (*E.U.*) Hinchado, pomposo, retumbante. -*s.* Estilo altisonante, palabras retumbantes.

high fidelity [ˌhaɪfɪˈdelɪtɪ] [jai-fi-de-li-ti], *s.* (*Mús.*) Alta fidelidad.

high-frequency [ˌhaɪˈfriːkwənsɪ] [jai-fri-kuan-si], *a.* (*Elec.*) De alta frecuencia.

high-grade [ˈhaɪˈgreɪd] [jai-greid], *a.* Excelente, de muy buena calidad.

high-handed [ˈhaɪˈhændɪd] [jai-jan-did], *a.* Arbitrario soberbio, tiránico.

high-keyed [ˈhaɪkiːd] [jai-kid], *a.* 1. (*Mús.*) Agudo, de sonido alto. 2. Impresionable, de mucho corazón.

high jump [ˈhaɪdʒʌmp] [jai-yamp], *s.* Salto de altura.

highland [ˈhaɪlænd] [jai-land], *s.* País de montañas, tierras montañosas.

highlander [ˈhaɪlændər] [jai-lan-dar], *s.* 1. Montañés, el que vive en las montañas o es natural de ellas. 2. Montañés escocés.

high light [ˈhaɪlaɪt] [jai-lait], *s.* 1. Lo que más descuella en una pintura o dibujo. Lo más interesante.

highlight [ˈhaɪlaɪt] [jai-lait], *va.* Iluminar, llenar de luz, acentuar, destacar.

highly [ˈhaɪlɪ] [jai-li], *adv.* 1. Altamente, elevadamente. 2. Sumamente, en sumo grado, infinitamente. 3. Altivamente, arrogantemente, ambiciosamente. 4. Con aprecio, con estimación. **I am highly obliged to you,** le quedo a Ud. sumamente agradecido o reconocido. **To think highly of one,** estimar, altamente a alguno. **To think highly of oneself,** tener gran concepto de sí mismo.

high-minded [ˈhaɪˈmaɪndɪd] [jai-main-did], *a.* 1. De altos o de elevados pensamientos, magnánimo. 2. (*Ant.*) Altivo, arrogante, ambicioso, fiero.

highness [ˈhaɪnɪs] [jai-nes], *s.* 1. Altura, elevación. 2. Alteza, tratamiento que se da a los hijos de los reyes y a otros príncipes.

high-octane [ˈhaɪˌɒkteɪn] [jai-ok-tein], *a.* De alto octano.

high-pitched [ˈhaɪˈpɪtʃt] [jai-picht], *a.* Agudo. **High-pitched voice,** voz chillona.

high-powered [ˈhaɪpaʊəd] [jai-pauerd], *a.* De alta potencia.

high-pressure [ˈhaɪˈpreʃər] [jai-pre-shar], *a.* De alta presión. **High-pressure salesman,** vendedor insistente y tenaz.

high-priced [ˌhaɪˈpraɪst] [jai-praist], *a.* Caro, costoso.

high-priest [ˈhaɪpriːst] [jai-prist], *s.* Jerarca, papa; en especial jerarca del pueblo de Israel.

high school [ˈhaɪskuːl] [jai-skul], *s.* Escuela secundaria.

high seas [ˈhaɪsiːz] [jai-sis], *s. pl.* Alta mar.

high spirits [ˈhaɪˈspɪrɪts] [jai-spi-rits], *s. pl.* Animación, jovialidad.

high-strung [ˈhaɪstrʌŋ] [jai-strang], *a.* Excitable, nervioso.

high-test [ˈhaɪest] [jai-test], *a.* De alta graduación o volatilidad.

high-toned [ˈhaɪtəʊnd] [jai-tound], *a.* 1. Honrado, honroso, de nobles principios. 2. De tono o diapasón alto. 3. (*Fam. E.U.*) Aristocrático a la moda.

high-water, *s.* V. HIGH.

high-water mark [ˈhawɔːtəˈmɑːk] [jai-uo-ta-mark], *s.* 1. Marea alta. 2. Pináculo.

highway [ˈhaɪweɪ] [jai-uei], *s.* Camino real.

highwayman [ˈhaɪweɪmən] [jai-uei-man], *s.* Bandolero, ladrón, salteador de caminos.

hike [haɪk] [jaik], *s.* Excursión a pie, caminata. -*vn.* Ir de excursión a pie, caminar largo trecho.

hilarious [ˈhaɪlærɪəs] [jai-la-rios], *a.* Alegre, bullicioso.

hilarity [ˈhaɪlærɪtɪ] [jai-la-ri-ti], *s.* Alegría, júbilo y contento de ánimo, regocijo.

hill [hɪl] [jil], *s.* 1. Collado, altura de tierra que no llega a ser montaña; cuesta, cerro, monte, eminencia, altozano. 2. Montoncillo de tierra, hecho artificialmente, como por los animales o en el cultivo. **Hill of beans,** montoncillo de habas. **Ant-hill,** hormiguero. **Little hill,** colina. **Up-hill work,** cuesta arriba. **Down-hill,** cuesta abajo. **To write up-hill,** escribir torcido. **Up hill and down dale,** por montes y valles.

hill, *V.* 1. Amontonar. 2. Acogibar, aporcar.

hillbilly [ˈhɪlˌbɪlɪ] [jil-bi-li], *s.* Montañés, rústico.

hilling [ˈhɪlɪŋ] [jil-lin], *s.* Amontonamiento.

hillock [ˈhɪlɒk] [ji-lok], *s.* Colina, collado pequeño, lomo, montecillo; otero.

hillside [ˈhɪlsaɪd] [jil-said], *s.* Lado de una cuesta o de un collado; ladera.

hilltop [ˈhɪltɒp] [jil-top], *s.* Cima, cumbre de un collado o de una cuesta.

hilly [ˈhɪlɪ] [ji-li], *a.* Abundante en colinas, montuoso; pendiente de una cuesta.

hilt [hɪlt] [jilt], *s.* Puño, empuñadura de un arma.

him [hɪm] [jim], *pron.* Le, a él (hablando de un sustantivo masculino no personificado); es el caso acusativo. **I'll see him tomorrow,** le veré mañana. **As for him,** en cuanto a él. **He beats the dog and kills him,** pega al perro y lo mata. **What do you think of him?,** ¿qué piensas de él? **Give it to him,** déselo a él.

Himalayan [ˌhɪməˈlaɪən] [ji-ma-laian], *a.* Del Himalaya, relativo al Himalaya.

himself [ˌhɪmˈself] [jim-self], Pronombre que en los casos oblicuos tiene significación recíproca. Él, él mismo, se, sí. **He will go himself,** el mismo irá, irá en persona. **He thinks himself a great man,** se tiene por un gran hombre. **By himself,** por sí mismo, por sí solo. **It is himself,** es él mismo, hélo aquí.

hind [hɪnd] [jind], *a.* Trasero, zaguero, posterior. *-s.* 1. Cierva, la hembra del ciervo. 2. Criado, la persona que sirve por un salario. 3. Patán, zafio. **Hind wheels,** juego trasero del coche.

hinder [ˈhɪndər] [jin-dar], *va.* Impedir, embarazar, estorbar, detener, poner obstáculos. *-vn.* Causar impedimento, oponerse. *-a.* Posterior, trasero.

hinderance [ˈhɪndərəns] [jin-de-rans], *s.* Impedimento, obstáculo, embarazo, estorbo; perjuicio, daño.

hindermost [ˈhɪndəməʊst] [jin-da-moust], *a.* Postrero, último.

hindoo, hindu [ˈhɪndɔ] [jin-du], *s.* 1. Indostano, natural del Indostán. 2. El idioma indostánico, deriva del sánscrito. 3. El indostano que profesa el brahmanismo.

hindustani [hɪndəstənɪ] [jin-dus-ta-ni], *s.* El idioma oficial y común en la India; una forma del indostántico, mezclado con palabras persas y arábigas.

hinge [ˈhɪndʒ] [jinch], *s.* 1. Gozne, charnela, bisagra, eje principal, resore. **Butt-hinge,** quicio. **Dovetail hinges,** *(Mar.)* bisagras a cola de pato. 2. Los dos polos o ejes del mundo. 3. Principio, la razón principal sobre la cual se procede en cualquier asunto. **To be off the hinges,** salirse de sus casillas. **Hinge joint,** articulación móvil.

hinge, *va.* Engoznar, poner goznes a alguna cosa; fijar; encorvar. *-vn.* Dar vueltas como un gozne.

hinny, *vn. V.* TO NEIGH y TO WHINNY.

hinny [ˈhɪnɪ] [ji-ni], *s.* Burdégano.

hint [hɪnt] [jint], *va.* Apuntar, insinuar o tocar ligeramente alguna especie o cosa; sugerir indirectamente. *-vn.* Sugerir, echar una indirecta. **To hint at,** hacer una alusión velada, hacer entrever, dar a entender. **He never so much as hinted at it,** ni siquiera hizo alusión a ello.

hint, *s.* Indirecta, sugestión, alusión lejana o velada, aviso, idea, insinuación.

hip [hɪp] [jip], *s.* 1. Cadera; la parte del cuerpo que está sobre los muslos. 2. Escaramujo, el fruto de la planta llamada escaramujo; agavanzo. 3. *(Arq.)* Caballete, el ángulo exterior del techo. **To have o catch on the hip,** tener o llevar ventaja sobre alguno; por alusión a una astucia de los luchadores. **To smite hip and thigh,** derrotar

completamente. **Hip-bath,** baño de asiento, semicupio. **Hip-bone,** hueso de la cadera, hueso ilíaco.

hip, *va.* 1. Descaderar, lastimar o fracturar la cadera. 2. *(Arq.)* Construir un techo con cubierta a cuatro aguas. 3. Echar el luchador a su antagonista sobre la cadera.

hip, hipped, hippish; *s. V.* HYPOCHONDRIAC.

hip-gout [ˈhɪpgaʊt] [jip-gaut], *s.* ciática.

hippocampus [ˈhɪpəʊˈkæmpəs] [ji-pou-kam-pos], *s.* 1. Hipocampo, pez llamado también caballo marino. 2. Nombre de dos eminencias del cerebro.

hippocentaur [ˈhɪpəˈsentər] [ji-po-sen-to], *s.* Hipocentauro, monstruo fabuloso.

hippocras [ˈhɪpəkrɑːs] [ji-po-kras], *s.* Hipocrás, antigua bebida que se hacía de vino, azúcar, canela, clavo y otros ingredientes.

hippocrates's-sleeve [ˈhɪpəkrætzsliːv] [ji-po-krats-sliv], *s.* Manga o calza de lienzo, tela u otra cosa hecha en figura cónica, para colar líquidos.

hippocratism [ˈhɪpəkrætɪzm] [ji-po-kra-ti-sem], *s.* La doctrina médica de Hipócrates.

hippodrome [ˈhɪpədrəʊm] [ji-po-droum], *s.* 1. Hipódromo, circo. 2. Circo moderno.

hippogriff [ˈhɪpəgrɪf] [ji-po-grif], *s.* Hipogrifo, caballo con alas.

hippophagist [ˈhɪpəfægɪst] [ji-po-fa-guist], *s.* El que come carne de caballo.

hippophagous [ˈhɪpəfægəs] [ji-po-fa-gos], *a.* Hipófago, que se alimenta de carne de caballo.

hippophagy [ˈhɪpəfægɪ] [ji-po-fa-gui], *s.* Hipofagia, alimentación con carne de caballo.

hippopotamus [ˌhɪpəˈpɒtəməs] [ji-po-po-ta-mos], *s.* Hipopótamo.

hippuric [ˈhɪpjuːrɪk] [ji-piu-rik], *a.* Hipúrico, de la orina del caballo, o parecido a esa orina. **Hippuric acid,** ácido hipúrico.

hipshot [ˈhɪpʃʌt] [jip-shat], *a.* Descaderado, con las caderas lisiadas.

hipwort [ˈhɪpwɔːt] [jip-uort], *s. (Bot.)* Escaramujo.

hircine [ˈhaɪəsiːn] [jaia-sin], *a.* Cabrío; particularmente que tiene un olor semejante al de las cabras.

hire [ˈhaɪər] [jaia], *va.* 1. Alquilar, tomar en alquiler o arrendamiento alguna cosa. 2. Asalariar. 3. Cohechar, sobornar. 4. Alquilar, arrendar, dar en arriendo. **To hire out,** alquilar, dar en alquiler. **To hire out oneself,** alquilarse, ponerse a servir, servir a otro por un salario. Algunas veces se suprime el pronombre; *v.g.* **To hire out for a year,** ponerse a servir por un año.

hire, *s.* 1. Alquiler, el precio que se da por el uso de alguna cosa. 2. Salario, el estipendio que los amos dan a sus criados por su servicio y trabajo.

hireless [ˈhaɪəlɪs] [jaia-lis], *a.* Sin salario o recompensa.

hireling [ˈhaɪəlɪŋ] [jaia-lin], *s.* 1. Jornalero, el que sirve por jornal o salario. 2. Hombre mercenario; mujer prostituta. *-a.* Mercenario, venal.

hirer [ˈhaɪərər] [jaia-ra], *s.* Alquilador, arrendador, el que alquila o arrienda.

hirsute [ˈhɜːsjuːt] [jer-siut], *a.* 1. Hirsuto, velludo, guarnecido de cerdas o cubierto de pelos. 2. *(Ant.)* Áspero, grosero.

hirsuteness [ˈhɜːsjuːtnɪs] [jer-siut-nes], *s.* Vellosidad.

his [hɪz] [jis], *pron.* 1. Caso posesivo o genitivo de HE; de él. 2. *pron. pos.* **mas.** El suyo, la suya, los suyos, las suyas. 3. *adj. pos.* Su, sus (debe concordar con el género del poseedor y nunca con la cosa poseída). **This book is his,** este libro es suyo, o de él. **His daughter,** su hija (de él).

Hispanic [hɪsˈpænɪk] [jis-pa-nik], *a.* Hispánico, hispano.

Hispaniola [hɪsˈpænɪələ] [jis-pa-nio-la], *s.* Isla de Santo Domingo o Haití.

Hispanist [ˈhɪspənɪst] [jis-pa-nist], *s.* Hispanista.

Hispanophile [hɪsˈpænəʊfaɪl] [jis-pa-nou-fail], *a.* Hispanófilo.

hispid [ˈhɪspɪd] [jis-pid], *a.* Híspido.

hiss [hɪs] [jis], *vn.* Silbar; producir un silbo, como la serpiente y otros animales; burlarse, hacer burla. *-va.* 1. Silbar, reprobar alguna cosa, hacer burla de ella. Manifestar desagrado el público por medio de silbidos. 2. Producir un silbido cualquiera, hacer oír un sonido agudo.

hiss, *s.* 1. Silbido de serpiente. 2. Silbido, escarnio o burla que se hace en los teatros. 3. Chirrido.

hissing [ˈhɪsɪŋ] [ji-sin], *s.* 1. Silbido de serpiente. 2. Objeto de burla o escarnio.

hist [hɪst] [jist], **inter.** Chito o chitón, interjección de que se usa para imponer silencio o mandar callar.

histologic, histological [hɪsˈtɒlədʒɪk] [jis-to-lo-yik], *a.* Histológico, relativo a la histología.

histologist [hɪsˈtɒlədʒɪst] [jis-to-lo-yist], *s.* histólogo o histologista, persona versada en la histología.

histology [hɪsˈtɒlədʒɪ] [jis-to-lo-chi], *s.* Histología, parte de la anatomía que trata de los tejidos orgánicos; la anatomía microscópica.

historian [hɪsˈtɔːrɪən] [jis-to-rian], *s.* Historiador, el que escribe historia.

historic, historical [hɪsˈtɒrɪk] [jis-to-rik], *a.* Histórico, lo perteneciente a la historia.

historically [hɪsˈtɒrɪkəlɪ] [jis-to-ri-ka-li], *adv.* Históricamente.

historiographer [hɪsˌtɒrɪəˈɡrɑːfəʳ] [jis-to-rio-gra-faʳ], *s.* Historiógrafo, historiador, cronista, el que escribe historia o crónicas.

historiography [ˌhɪstɒrɪˈɒɡrəfɪ] [jis-to-rio-gra-fi], *s.* Historiografía, el arte de historiar.

historiology [ˌhɪstɒrɪˈɒlədʒɪ] [jis-to-ri-o-lo-yi], *s.* Conocimiento de la historia; comentarios sobre la historia.

history [ˈhɪstərɪ] [jis-to-ri], *s.* 1. Historia, narración de las cosas y de los hechos dignos de memoria. 2. Historia, el conocimiento de los hechos y sucesos que ella comprende.

history-pece [ˈhɪstərɪˈpes] [jis-to-ri-pes], *s.* Historia, los cuadros o tapices que contienen episodios históricos.

histrion, *s. V.* PLAYER.

histrionic, histrionical [ˌhɪstrɪˈɒnɪk] [jis-trio-nik], *a.* Histriónico, lo que pertenece al arte cómico o a los cómicos; teatral.

histrionically [ˌhɪstrɪˈɒnɪkəlɪ] [jis-trio-ni-ka-li], *adv.* Cómicamente, teatralmente.

histrionism [ˌhɪstrɪˈɒnɪzm] [jis-trio-ni-sem], *s.* Histrionismo, representación dramática; de aquí, afectación.

hit [hɪt] [jit], *va. (pret.* y *pp.* HIT). 1. Dar, pegar, golpear (knock). 2. Atinar, acertar, dar en el hito. **You hit the nail on the head,** Ud. lo acertó, o dio en el clavo. 3. Lograr, conseguir alguna cosa. 4. Tocarle a uno donde le duele. *-vn.* 1. Ludir o rozar una cosa con otra. 2. Acaecer o acontecer felizmente, tener buen éxito por casualidad; salir bien, no malograrse alguna cosa. 3. Tropezar, encontrar por casualidad. 4. Acertar, determinar felizmente. **To hit the mark,** dar en el blanco. **To hit in the teeth with,** dar en rostro. **To hit against,** dar contra alguna cosa; encallar un buque. **When we hit the main road,** cuando lleguemos a la carretera principal. **To hit together,** encontrarse por casualidad. **To hit upon,** hallar, encontrar; acordarse. **To hit off,** describir breve y hábilmente, expresar exactamente. **To hit out,** ejecutar. **You hit it right,** dio Ud. en ello.

hit, *s.* 1. Golpe, choque de dos cuerpos duros. 2. Suerte feliz, golpe de fortuna; chiste, chanza graciosa. 3. Alcance. **Hit or miss,** *(Fam.)* a todo riesgo, sea como fuere, salga pez o salga rana. **A lucky hit,** golpe de fortuna, ocurrencia feliz; éxito, buen suceso.

hitch [hɪtʃ] [jich], *va.* 1. Atar, ligar por un tiempo, enganchar, sujetar; *(Mar.)* Amarrar. 2. Mover a saltos, adelantar a brincos. *-vn.* 1. Saltar, moverse a saltos. 2. Rozarse, tropezar o golpear con los pies: se dice de los caballos. 3. Caer dentro, enredarse. 4. *(Fam.)* Obrar o vivir en concordancia con otro: ser compatible, estar de acuerdo y conformidad.

hitch, *s.* 1. Alto, parada; de aquí, tropiezo, dificultad, impedimento, obstáculo. 2. Acción de coger agarrar o colgar. 3. Acción de tirar de algo hacia arriba. 4. *(Mar.)* Vuelta de cabo.

hitchel [ˈhɪtʃəl] [ji-chel], *va.* Rastrillar.

hitchel, *s. V.* HATCHEL.

hitchhike [ˈhɪtʃhaɪk] [jich-jaik], *vn.* Avanzar, especialmente cuando se va a pie, consiguiendo ser llevado por tramos en automóviles que pasan.

hitchhiking [ˈhɪtʃhaɪkɪŋ] [jich-jai-kin], *s.* Auto-stop.

hither [ˈhɪðəʳ] [ji-zaʳ], *adv.* 1. Acá, desde otro paraje a este. **Come hither,** ven acá. 2. A este fin, para este intento. *-a.* Citerior, lo que está más cercano o de la parte de acá. **On the hither side of,** (a) Del lado de acá, hacia el que habla. (b) Más joven, de menos años. **She is on the hither side of sixty,** ella tiene menos de sesenta años.

hithermost [ˈhɪðəməʊst] [ji-za-moust], *a.* Lo más cercano o próximo.

hitherto [ˈhɪðəˈtuː] [ji-zar-tu], *adv.* Hasta ahora, hasta aquí.

hive [haɪv] [jaiv], *s.* 1. Colmena, especie de caja de corcho o de madera en que se crían las abejas. 2. Enjambre, las abejas que se juntan y pueblan una colmena.

hive, *va.* Enjambrar, encerrar las abejas en las colmenas. *-vn.* Acogerse o encerrarse en una parte muchas personas juntas; vivir o estar muchos en un mismo lugar.

hive-dross [ˈhaɪvdrɒs] [jaiv-dros], *s.* Cera cruda o áspera.

hiver [ˈhaɪvəʳ] [jai-vaʳ], *s.* Colmenero, el que enjambra.

hives [haɪvz] [jaivs], *s. (Med. Fam.)* Nombre familiar de la erupción llamada urticaria, y de otras erupciones ligeras.

ho, hoa! [həʊ] [jo], **inter.** 1. ¡Eh! ¡basta! ¡mira, hola! voz con la cual se llama o avisa a alguno. 2. *V.* WHOA!

hoar [hɔːʳ] [joʳ], *a.* Blanco, cano, canoso por la edad; mohoso; lo que aparece blanco por estar cubierto de nieve o de hielo; escarcha. *-s.* Antigüedad.

hoarfrost [ˈhɔːfrɒst] [jor-frost], *s.* Escarcha blanca.

hoard [hɔːd] [jord], *s.* 1. Provisión, montón, cantidad de una cosa acumulada y tenida de reserva (supply, provision). 2. Repuesto oculto de dinero u otra cosa; tesoro escondido.

hoard, *va.* y *vn.* 1. Atesorar, amontonar, acumular, recoger o guardar tesoros, riquezas u otra cosa. 2. Hacer repuesto o acopio.

hoarder [ˈhɔːdəʳ] [jor-daʳ], *s.* Atesorador, el que hace repuestos en secreto.

hoarding [ˈhɔːdɪŋ] [jor-din], *s.* 1. Amontonamiento, atesoramiento, ahorro. 2. Cerca o valla de construcción. 3. Cartelera.

hoarhound, horehound [ˈhɔːhaʊnd] [jor-jaund], *s. (Bot.)* Marrubio, hierba medicinal de la misma familia que la hierbabuena, el tomillo, etc., que produce tallos vellosos y blanquecinos.

hoariness [ˈhɔːrɪnɪs] [jo-ri-nes], *s.* 1. Blancura. 2. Moho. 3. Canas de viejo; y la vejez misma.

hoarse [hɔːs] [jors], *a.* Ronco, enronquecido, el que tiene ronquera, como uno que está resfriado. **To speak in a hoarse voice.** Hablar ronco.

hoarsely [ˈhɔːslɪ] [jors-li], *adv.* Roncamente, broncamente.

hoarseness [ˈhɔːsnɪs] [jors-nes], *s.* Ronquera, carraspera, bronquedad.

hoary [ˈhɔːrɪ] [jo-ri], *a.* 1. Blanco, blanquecino. 2. Cano, el que tiene el cabello blanco por la edad. 3. Escarchado, blanco con la escarcha. 4. *(Des.)* Mohoso, cubierto de moho.

hoast [həʊst] [joust], *s. (Esco.)* Tos. *V.* COUGH.

hoax [həʊks] [jouks], *s.* Engaño, burla, petardo, broma, mentira.

hoax, *va.* Engañar, burlar, dar un petardo.

hob [hɒb] [jb], *s.* 1. Antehogar, anaquel a un lado del hogar, donde se coloca lo que se quiere conservar caliente. 2. Cubo o maza de rueda. 3. Plancha de taladro, para cortar roscas de tornillo. 4. Juego con monedas en Inglaterra. 5. *(Des.)* Patán; duende. 6. *(Prov. Ingl.)* Error, paso en falso. **To play hob with,** trastornar, volver patas arriba, poner en confusión.

hobble [ˈhɒbl] [jo-bel], *va.* y *vn.* 1. Cojear, andar inclinando el cuerpo más a un lado que a otro, o cargar sobre una pierna más que sobre la otra; andar cojeando. 2. Hacer versos desiguales o irregulares. 3. Embarazar, enredar, confundir a uno.

hobble, *s.* 1. Dificultad, atolladero. **To get** o **thrust oneself into a hobble,** meterse en un atolladero, en un berengenal. 2. Cojera. 3. Traba, atadura puesta en los pies de los caballos. *V.* HOPPLE.

hobbledehoy [ˈhɒbldɪˈhɔɪ] [jo-bel-di-joi], *s.* Joven entre catorce y veintiún años de edad, adolescente, muchacho grandullón.

hobbler [ˈhɒbləʳ] [jo-blaʳ], *s.* En la edad media, soldado de caballería ligera.

hobblingly [ˈhɒblɪŋlɪ] [jo-blin-li], *adv.* Groseramente.

hobby [ˈhɒbɪ] [jo-bi], *s.* 1. *(Fam.)* La ocupación u objeto favorito de una persona. 2. Haca de Irlanda o de Escocia. 3. Caballico, caballito, la caña o palo con que juegan los niños, montándolo y corriendo sobre él. 4. Zoquete, hombre rudo y torpe. 5. Sacre, especie de halcón.

hobbyhorse [ˈhɒbɪhɔːs] [jo-bi-jors], *s.* 1. Objeto o empeño predilecto. 2. Caballito con que juegan los niños. 3. Zoquete, hombre tonto.

hobgoblin [ˈhɒbˌɡɒblɪn] [job-go-blin], *s.* Duende, espectro, espíritu.

hobit [ˈhɒbɪt] [jo-bit], *s. (Mil.)* Mortero pequeño.

hoblike [ˈhɒblaɪk] [job-laik], *a.* Rústico, grosero.

hobnail [ˈhɒbneɪl] [job-neil], *s.* Clavo de herradura.

hobnailed [ˈhɒbneɪld] [job-neild], *a.* Clavado con clavos de herradura.

hobnob [ˈhɒbnɒb] [job-nob], *v.* Beber juntos familiarmente. 2. Codearse, rozarse, tratarse familiarmente.

hobo [ˈhəʊbəʊ] [jou-bou], *s.* (E. U. del Oeste) Obrero holgazán, sin recursos, vagabundo.

hobson's choice [ˈhɒbsənˈtʃɔɪs] [job-son-chois], *s.* Expresión proverbial con que se designa una elección en que no hay alternativa.

hock [hɒk] [jok], *s.* 1. Vino añejo del Rin, originalmente de Hochheim. 2. Jarrete, corvejón de las bestias.

hock, *va.* Cortar los jarretes, desjarretar. *V.* HOUGH.

hockey [ˈhɒkɪ] [jo-ki], *s.* 1. Juego de pelota en el que se emplea un palo encorvado en uno de sus extremos. 2. *(Prov. Ingl.) V.* HARVEST-HOME.

hockle [ˈhɒkl] [jo-kel], *va.* 1. Desjarretar, cortar las piernas por el jarrete o por la corva. 2. Guadañar el rastrojo.

hocus [ˈhəʊkəs] [jou-kos], *va.* 1. Engañar, chasquear. 2. Dejar insensible a uno por medio de una bebida narcótica, para robarlo.

hocus-pocus [ˈhəʊkəsˈpəʊkəs] [jou-kos-pou-kos], *s.* 1. Jugador de manos, titiritero. 2. Pasapasa, juego de manos. **to do things by virtue of hocus-pocus,** hacer las cosas por arte de birlibirloque.

hod [hɒd] [jod], *s.* El artesón o artesa en que el peón lleva el mortero o los ladrillos al albañil.

hodge-podge [ˈhɒdʒpɒdʒ] [joch-poch], *s.* Almodrote, mezcla de ingredientes cocidos juntos.

hodiernal [ˈhɒdɪənəl] [jo-dia-nal], *a.* Lo que es de hoy o de este día.

hodman [ˈhɒdmən] [jod-man], *s.* Peón de albañil.

hoe [huː] [ju], *s.* Azada, azadón.

hoe, *va.* Cavar la tierra con azada o azadón.

hog [hɒɡ] [jog], *s.* 1. Puerco, cerdo (pig). 2. Nombre genérico de todo ganado de cerda. **Hog's bristle,** cerdas, setas. 3. *(Met.)* Persona grosera, sucia o avarienta; egoísta, indiferente a los derechos de otros. 4. *(Mar.)* Escoba. 5. *(Prov.)* Carnero o buey de un año. **Hog's pudding,** morcillas. **To go the whole hog,** ir al extremo, llegar hasta el último límite.

hog, *va.* 1. Limpiar el casco de un buque debajo del agua. 2. *(Mar.)* hender o partir una embarcación por el medio. 3. *(Fam. E.U.)* Tomar posesión de más de lo que a uno le corresponde. -*vn.* Arquearse, combarse, torcerse; se dice de una embarcación.

hogback [ˈhɒɡbæk] [jog-bak], *s.* Cuchilla, cerro escarpado.

hogcote, *s. V.* HOGSTY.

hoggerel [ˈhɒɡərəl] [jo-gue-rel], *s. (Prov.)* Oveja de dos años.

hoggish [ˈhɒɡɪʃ] [jo-guish], *a.* 1. Porcuno, porcino. 2. Egoísta. 3. Glotón, comilón. 4. Sucio, puerco.

hoggishly [ˈhɒɡɪʃlɪ] [jo-guish-li], *adv.* Puercamente, cochinamente; vorazmente, vilmente.

hoggishness [ˈhɒɡɪʃnɪs] [jo-guish-nes], *s.* 1. Brutalidad, voracidad; porquería, cochinada. 2. Glotonería. 3. Egoísmo.

hogherd [ˈhɒɡəd] [jo-guerd], *s.* Porquero, porquerizo, el que guarda puercos.

hogshead [ˈhɒɡzhed] [jogs-hed], *s.* 1. Medida inglesa de líquidos que contiene sesenta galones. 2. Barril grande.

hog-shearing [ˈhɒɡʃɪərɪŋ] [jog-shia-rin], *s.* Expresión que equivale a la de mucho ruido y pocas nueces.

hogsteer [ˈhɒɡstɪəʳ] [jogs-tiaʳ], *s.* Jabalí de tres años

hogsty [ˈhɒɡstɪ] [jogs-tai], *s.* Porqueriza, zahurda, el sitio donde se recogen los puercos.

hogwash [ˈhɒɡwɔːʃ] [jog-uosh], *s.* Bazofia.

hoiden [ˈhɔɪdn] [joi-den], *s.* 1. Paya, moza agreste, zafia e ignorante. 2. Payo, patán. -*a.* Rústico, grosero. Se escribe también **hoyden.**

hoiden, *vn.* Retozar, moverse, saltar o jugar con grosería o descompostura.

hoist [hɔɪst] [joist], *va.* 1. Guindar, alzar, levantar en alto. 2. *(Mar.)* Izar, tirar para levantar o subir en alto las vergas y los masteleros. **Hoist away,** ¡Iza, iza!

hoist, *s.* 1. Cabria, pescante, aparejo para izar o levantar fardos de mercancías u otros pesos. 2. El acto de levantar. 3. Altura perpendicular de un pabellón o una vela.

hoisting [ˈhɔɪstɪŋ] [jois-tin], *s.* Elevación, alzamiento. **Engine-hoisting equipment,** equipo de izar motores. **Hoisting machinery,** maquinaria elevadora. **Friction-hoisting machine,** máquina de fricción para izar. **Hoisting of the flag,** izamiento de la bandera.

hoity-toity [ˈhɔɪtɪˈtɔɪtɪ] [joi-ti-toi-ti], *a. (Vulg.)* Voluble, descuidado; juguetón. -*inter.* ¡Ola! ¡Tate!

hold [həʊld] [jould], *va. (pret.* y *pp.* HELD, *pp. (Ant.)* HOLDEN).* 1. Detener, contener (stop); restringir, estrechar, limitar (limit, restrict). 2. Contener en sí alguna cosa; caber. 3. Tener, asir, mantener asida alguna cosa; agarrar. 4. Tener, mantener, sostener. 5. Juzgar, reputar, entender (judge). 6. Tener, poseer, gozar. 7. Apostar, hacer alguna apuesta. 8. Continuar, proseguir; guardar, no infringir. -*vn.* 1. Valer, ser válido, tener fuerza y solidez. 2. Tenerse, mantenerse en su ser. 3. Durar, continuar. 4. Refrenarse, abstenerse. 5. Adherirse a alguna persona o partido. 6. Depender o estar dependiente de alguno. 7. Deducir.

hold back, retener, resistir. 8. Echarse atrás.

hold down, sujetar.

hold forth, sacar a la vista o al público, mostrar, descubrir; predicar, hablar en público, arengar.

hold in, tener en sujeción, refrenar; contenerse, refrenarse; continuar. **To hold in hand,** entretener con falsas esperanzas.

hold off, apartar, alejar, mantener o mantenerse separado o a cierta distancia; apartarse, alejarse, separarse.

hold on, seguir, proseguir, persistir; continuar, prolongar.

hold out, ofrecer, proponer; sostener; extender; mantenerse firme, no ceder, no rendirse; durar; alargar; ir aguantando o sufriendo alguna cosa, continuar haciendo algo o sufriendo algún mal; proferir.

hold up, levantar, alzar; apoyar, sostener, proteger; entretener con buenas palabras; sostenerse, tenerse firme, mantenerse. (a) (E.U. del Oeste) Mandar detenerse para robar; v.g. **To hold up a train,** parar un tren para robarlo. (b) Cesar, dejar de. **The rain will soon hold up,** pronto cesará la lluvia. **To hold a wager,** apostar, hacer una apuesta. **To hold fast to,** afirmarse en. **To hold one's peace** o **one's tongue,** callar. **to hold one's laughing,** contener la risa. **to hold together,** mantenerse o estar juntos o reunidos. **To hold with one,** ser del partido u opinión de alguna persona; declararse por alguno. **Hold your head up,** levanta la cabeza.

hold, inter. ¡Tente! ¡para! ¡quieto!

hold, *s.* 1. Presa, la acción de prender, asir o agarrar. 2. Agarradero, asidero, la parte por donde se agarra alguna cosa; mango, asa. 3. Cualquier cosa que agarra como garfio. 4. Prisión, cárcel; custodia. 5. *(Mar.)* Bodega, todo el espacio entre la sobrequilla y la cubierta (en este sentido se deriva de HOLE). **Afterhold,** bodega de popa. **Forehold** Bodega de proa. **To trim the hold,** abarrotar. **Depth** o **height of the hold,** puntal de la bodega. 6. Escondite, paraje oculto, propio para esconderse; fuerte, fortaleza, plaza fuerte. 7. Apresamiento, la acción de apresar; toma la acción de tomar. 8. Poder o influencia. 9. *(Mús.)* El signo que significa pausa. 10. Llave (en la lucha) **To lay hold of.** 1. Agarrar. 2. Apoderarse de. 3. Reunir, recoger. 4. Aprovecharse de.

holdback [ˈhəʊldbæk] [jould-bak], *s.* 1. Restricción, freno. 2. Cejadero, tirante para cejar los carruajes.

holder [ˈhəʊldəʳ] [joul-daʳ], *s.* 1. Tenedor, el que tiene alguna cosa en su mano. 2. Agarrador, el que agarra. 3. El que guarda o retiene alguna cosa. 4. Poseedor, el que posee algo. 5. Apoyo, el o lo que sostiene. 6. Arrendador; arrendatario, inquilino de una casa. 7. Asidero, mango, puño, asa. 8. Vasija que contiene algo. 9. *(Mar.)* Marinero de la bodega. (**Holder** se traduce a veces en español por la palabra **porta;** *V. gr.* **pen-holder,** porta-plumas; **plate-holder,** portaplacas (de una cámara fotográfica). **Holder of stock,** tenedor de acciones o valores. **Holder of a bill,** tenedor o portador de una letra. **Holder of a share,** accionista.

holdfast [ˈhəʊldfɑːst] [jould-fast], *s.* Cualquier cosa que agarra; barrilete, grapón, grapa, laña; apoyo, aquello en que está apoyada alguna persona o cosa; *(Fam.)* Hombre muy avaro.

holding [ˈhəʊldɪŋ] [joul-din], *s.* 1. Tenencia, posesión. 2. Arrendamiento. 3. Poder, influencia. 4. *(Des.)* Coro, estribillo. **Holding-ground,** *(Mar.)* buen fondo, fondo donde el áncora se conserva bien agarrada.

holding company [ˈhəʊldɪŋˈkɒmpənɪ] [joul-din-kom-pa-ni], *s.* Empresa tenedora (de acciones o valores de otras compañías).

hold-up [ˈhəʊldʌp] [jould-ap], *s.* Atraco. **Holdman,** atracador, salteador.

hole [həʊl] [joul], *s.* 1. Agujero, agujerito, cavidad, hueco. 2. Cueva, cavidad subterránea; hoyo. 3. Cabaña, choza, vivienda vil y mala. 4. *(Fam.)* Atolladero, dificultad grande, dilema. 5. **A hole to crawl out of,** escapatoria, excusa, refugio. **A hole in one's coat,** mancha en la reputación defecto en el carácter de alguno. **Armhole,** sobaco.

hole, *va.* 1. Cavar, agujerear, perforar (pierce). 2. En el juego de billar, meter la bola en la tronera. *-vn.* Entrar o meterse, deslizarse en un agujero; invernar.

holibut, *s. V.* HALIBUT.

holiday [ˈhəʊlɪdeɪ] [jou-li-dei], *s.* 1. Día festivo, de fiesta. 2. Día feriado, de descanso y suspensión del trabajo. 3. Aniversario, fiesta que se hace cada año en día señalado. **Holidays,** vacaciones. 4. *(Mar.)* Mancha, punto que queda sin que lo toque la brocha al pintar, alquitranar, etc. *-a.* Alegre, festivo, propio de un día de fiesta. **To be on holiday/vacation,** estar de vacaciones.

holily [ˈhəʊlɪlɪ] [jou-li-li], *adv.* Piadosamente: inviolablemente, santamente.

holiness [ˈhəʊlɪnɪs] [jou-li-nes], *s.* 1. Santidad, perfección e integridad de costumbres conforme a la ley y a la religión. 2. Santidad, beatitud; tratamiento que se da al sumo pontífice.

holing [ˈhəʊlɪŋ] [jou-lin], *s.* Perforación, taladro para introducir un clavo, perno, cabilla, etc (perforation).

Holland [ˈhɒlənd] [jo-land], *s.* Holanda, especie de lienzo fino. **Brown holland,** holanda cruda.

Hollander [ˈhɒləndəʳ] [jo-lan-daʳ], *s.* Holandés.

hollands, *s. V.* GIN.

hollen, *s. (Prov.) V.* HOLLY.

hollo, holloa [ˈhəʊlə] [jou-lo], **inter.** ¡Hola! voz usada para llamar a uno que está distante o lejos. *-s.* Grito, grita.

V. HALLO.

hollo, *vn.* Gritar altamente.

hollow [ˈhɒləʊ] [jo-lou], *a.* 1. Hueco, lo que es cóncavo o está vacío (empty). 2. El sonido que resulta de la percusión de un cuerpo hueco. 3. Disimulado, falso, insincero (false, disguised). 4. Hundido, empujado hacia adentro. **Hollow eyes,** ojos hundidos. **Hollow heart,** corazón doble, disimulado, traidor. *-s.* Cavidad, caverna, cueva, canal, paso; concavidad, hueco, valle, cañada. **Hollow ware,** ollas, pucheros y otros utensilios de cocina, hechos de hierro, vidriado o barnizado por dentro.

hollow, *va.* Excavar, ahondar, ahuecar; escotar.

hollowly [ˈhɒləʊlɪ] [jo-lou-li], *adv.* 1. Con cavidades. 2. Doblemente, traidoramente.

hollowness [ˈhɒləʊnɪs] [jo-lou-nes], *s.* 1. Cavidad, hueco. 2. Doblez, simulación, falacia, falta de sinceridad.

holly [ˈhɒlɪ] [jo-li], *s. (Bot.)* Acebo, árbol silvestre.

hollyhock [ˈhɒlɪhɒk] [jo-li-lok], *s. (Bot.)* Malva hortense.

holm [ˈhəʊm] [joum], *s.* 1. Isleta de río. 2. Terreno bajo y llano cerca de una corriente. 3. *(Bot.)* Encina. 4. Acebo. **Holm-oak,** encina.

holocaust [ˈhɒləkɔːst] [jo-lo-kost], *s.* 1. Holocausto, el sacrificio en que se quemaba toda la víctima; de aquí, sacrificio o renunciación completos de algo por causa de consagración. 2. Destrucción en masa a sangre y fuego.

holocephalan [ˈhɒləˈsɪfələn] [jo-l-si-fa-lan], *a.* Holocéfalo.

holograph [ˈhɒləgræf] [jo-lo-graf], *s.* El testamento escrito enteramente de la mano del testador.

holster [ˈhəʊlstəʳ] [jouls-taʳ], *s.* Funda de pistola, pistolera. **Holster-cap,** caperuza.

holt [ˈhəʊlt] [joult], *s.* Bosque; monte.

holy [ˈhəʊlɪ] [jou-li], *a.* 1. Santo, pío; puro, inmaculado. 2. Sagrado, consagrado, santificado. **Holy-cross** o **Holy-rod day,** día de la exaltación de la Santa Cruz, que es el 14 de Septiembre. **Holy day,** día de fiesta, día sagrado, como el domingo. **Holy Office,** el Santo Oficio o tribunal de la Inquisición. **Holy Rood,** la Santa Cruz. **Holy Ghost, Holy Spirit,** Espíritu Santo. **Holy One,** solo santo, nombre de Dios o Jesucristo. **Holy Thursday,** (a) Día de la ascensión de Nuestro Señor. (b) Jueves Santo. *V.* MAUNDY-THURSDAY. **Holy-water,** agua bendita. **Holy-water sprinkler,** hisopo.

holystone [ˈhəʊlɪstəʊn] [jou-lis-toun], *s. (Mar.)* Piedra bendita, trozo de arenisca que se usa para limpiar la cubierta de los buques. *-va.* Limpiar la cubierta con la piedra llamada **holystone.**

homage [ˈhɒmɪdʒ] [jo-mich], *s.* Homenaje, reverencia, respeto; sumisión que se muestra al superior. **To pay homage,** rendir homenaje.

homage, *va.* Reverenciar, honrar, profesar fidelidad.

homageable [ˈhɒmɪdʒəbl] [jo-mi-cha-bol], *a.* Sujeto a homenaje.

homager [ˈhɒmɪdʒəʳ] [jo-mi-chaʳ], *s.* 1. El que posee una cosa a título de homenaje. 2. Homenaje.

home [ˈhəʊm] [joum], *s.* 1. Hogar, casa propia, morada, mansión o habitación en que uno vive. 2. Patria, el país o tierra de donde uno es natural. 3. Domicilio, residencia. 4. Cualquier lugar de descanso y abrigo; asilo, hospedería, refugio; de aquí, sepulcro; muerte, estado futuro. **One's long home,** el sepulcro, el estado futuro. 5. En los juegos, meta, límite o término. **To come home,** regresar al hogar, volver a su país. **To take home,** llevar a casa, *(Fig.)* tomar para sí. **To hit** o **strike home,** dar en el blanco; herir en lo vivo, llegar al alma. **Home is home, be it never so homely,** mi casa y mi hogar cien doblas vale. *-a.* 1. Doméstico, de casa; de su país, natal; opuesto a extranjero, indígena. 2. Que da en lo vivo o en el hito. **A home-thrust,** gran golpe, que da en el blanco. 3. En los juegos, que llega al término. *-adv.* 1. A su propia casa o habitación. **He is gone home,** se ha ido a casa. 2. A su tierra o país. 3. Al propósito, al intento. 4. Intimamente, estrechamente; con fuerza, eficazmente. **At home,** (a) En casa, (en fechas de cartas) casa de Ud. (b) En su patria, en su propio país. (c) Libre, espontáneo, como si estuviese en la propia casa. **To be away from home,** estar fuera de casa, hallarse ausente.

home-born [ˈhəʊmbɔːn] [joum-born], *a.* Natural de; doméstico, indígena.

homebound [ˈhəʊmbaʊnd] [joum-baund], *a.* 1. Imposibilitado para salir de casa. 2. En dirección a su casa o país.

home-bred [ˈhəʊmbred] [joum-bred], *a.* 1. Nativo, natural. 2. Casero, lo que se cría o hace en casa y lo que pertenece a ella. 3. Rudo, agreste, inculto. 4. Doméstico, lo que es propio de la casa o pertenece a ella (homely).

home-brew [ˈhəʊmbruː] [joum-bru], *s.* Bebida fermentada en casa.

home econonomics [ˈhəʊmiːkəˈnɒmɪks] [joumi-ko-no-miks], *s.* Economía doméstica.

home-felt [ˈhəʊmfelt] [joum-felt], *a.* Privado, interno (private).

home-keeping [ˈhəʊmˈkiːpɪŋ] [joum-ki-pin], *a.* Persona de su casa, de gustos y costumbres caseros.

homeland [ˈhəʊmlænd] [joum-land], *s.* Patria, tierra natal.

homeless [ˈhəʊmlɪs] [joum-les], *a.* Destituído; sin casa ni hogar.

homelike [ˈhəʊmlaɪk] [joum-laik], *a.* Semejante al hogar doméstico; sosegado y cómodo, que procura bienestar.

homeliness [ˈhəʊmlɪnɪs] [joum-li-nes], *s.* Simpleza, sencillez, falta de cultivo; grosería; fealdad.

homely [ˈhəʊmlɪ] [joum-li], *a.* 1. Casero, doméstico, sencillo. 2. Liso, llano. 3. Feo, no hermoso. 4. Ignorante, rústico, inculto; grosero, vulgar, sin elegancia. -*adv.* Llanamente, simplemente; como de casa; groseramente.

home-made [ˈhəʊmˈmeɪd] [joum-meid], *a.* Hecho en casa, fabricado en el país.

homemaker [ˈhəʊmˈmeɪkəʳ] [joum-mei-kaʳ], *s.* Ama de casa, dueña de casa (housewife).

homeopathic, homoeopathic [ˈhəʊmɪəʊˈpæθɪk] [jou-mio-pa-zik], *a.* Homeopático, relativo a la homeopatía.

homeopathist, homoeopathist [ˈhəʊmɪəʊˈpæθɪst] [jou-mio-pa-zist], *s.* Homeópata, el partidario de la homeopatía o el que la practica.

homeopathy, homoeopathy [ˈhəʊmɪəʊˈpæθɪ] [jou-mio-pa-zi], *s.* homeopatía.

Homer [ˈhəʊməʳ] [jou-maʳ], *n. pr.* Homero.

homer [ˈhəʊməʳ] [jou-maʳ], *s.* 1. Homer, medida antigua de los judíos. 2. Paloma viajera, paloma correo.

Homeric [həʊˈmerɪk] [jou-me-rik], *a.* Homérico, que se refiere a Homero; que tiene el carácter de su poesía.

homesick [ˈhəʊmsɪk] [joum-sik]. *a.* Nostálgico, que experimenta la nostalgia; que siente vivamente estar separado de su hogar o de su país. **To be homesick for,** sentir nostalgia de.

homesickness [ˈhəʊmsɪknɪs] [joum-sik-nes], *s.* Nostalgia, mal del país, pena o trsiteza profunda de verse ausente de su patria o de su hogar.

homespun [ˈhəʊmspʌn] [joum-span], *a.* 1. Casero, lo que se hila o se hace en casa. 2. Liso, llano, basto, grosero. 3. Común, vulgar. 4. Tela hecha en casa.

homestall [ˈhəʊmstɔːl] [joum-stol], *a.* **homestead** [ˈhəʊmstiːd] [joum-stid], *s.* Sitio de la casa, casa propia.

homesteader [ˈhəʊmstiːdəʳ] [joum-sti-daʳ], *s.* 1. Dueño de una heredad que habita en ella y la cultiva. 2. (*E.U.*) Colono que recibe las tierras del Estado.

home stretch [ˈhəʊmstretʃ] [joum-strech], *s.* 1. Última parte de una carrera (especialmente de caballos). 2. (*Fig.*) Final de alguna actividad u operación.

homeward, homewards [ˈhəʊmwəd] [joum-uard], *adv.* Hacia casa, hacia su país; de vuelta. **Homeward bound,** de vuelta, que regresa al punto de donde salió.

homework [ˈhəʊmwɜːk] [joum-uek], *s.* Tarea, estudio hecho fuera de la clase.

homicidal [ˌhɒmɪˈsaɪdl] [jo-mi-sai-dal], *a.* 1. Sanguinario, matador; homicida (murderer).

homicide [ˈhɒmɪsaɪd] [jo-mi-said], *s.* 1. Homicidio, la muerte causada a una persona por otra (murder). 2. Homicida, el que comete homicidio.

homiletic, homiletical [ˈhɒmɪlektɪk] [jo-mi-lek-tik], *a.* 1. Homilético, referente a la homilética.

homilist [ˈhɒmɪlɪst] [jo-mi-list], *s.* Autor de homilías.

homily [ˈhɒmɪlɪ] [jo-mi-li], *s.* Homilía, sermón.

homing pigeon [ˈhəʊmɪŋˌpɪdʒən] [jou-min-pi-chon], *s.* Paloma mensajera.

hominy [ˈhɒmɪnɪ] [jo-mi-ni], *s.* Maíz machacado.

homocerc [ˈhəʊmaʊsɜːk] [jou-mou-serk], *a.* Homocerco.

homochlamydeous [ˌhɒmaʊkləˈmɪdɪəs] [jo-mou-kla-mi-dios], *a.* (*Bot.*) Homoclamídeo.

homodyne [ˈhɒmədaɪn] [jo-mo-dain], *a.* Homodino.

homogen [ˈhɒmədʒɪn] [jo-mo-yin], *s.* Estructura o parte homogénea.

homogeneal [ˈhɒmədʒɪnɪəl] [jo-mo-yi-nial], **homogeneous** [ˌhɒməˈdʒiːnɪəs] [jo-mo-yi-nios], *a.* Homogéneo, lo que es de la misma naturaleza o género que otra cosa.

homogenealness [ˌhɒməˈdʒiːnɪəlnɪs] [jo-mo-yi-ni-nial-nes], **homogeneity** [ˌhɒməʊdʒəˈniːɪtɪ] [jo-mo-yi-ni-ti], **homogeneousness** [ˌhɒməˈdʒiːnɪəsnɪs] [jo-mo-yi-nios-nes], *s.* Homogeneidad, uniformidad o semejanza de las partes de un todo comparadas entre sí.

homogenize [həˈmɒdʒənaɪz] [jo-mo-yi-nais], *va.* Homogeneizar (la leche, etc.)

homogenous [ˌhɒməˈdʒɪnəs] [jo-mo-yi-nos], *a.* (*Biol.*) Del mismo género; de una misma estructura.

homograph [ˈhɒməɡrɑːf] [jo-mo-graf], *s.* Homógrafo.

homographic [ˈhɒməɡræfɪk] [jo-mo-gra-fik], *a.* Homógrafo.

homologate [hɒˈmɒlədʒeɪt] [jo-mo-lo-gueit], *v.* Homologar.

homolog, homologue [ˈhɒmələɡ] [jo-mo-log], *s.* Parte homóloga o análoga a otra en posición, estructura, etc.

homologation [ˌhɒmələˈɡeɪʃən] [jo-mo-lo-guei-shon], *s.* Confirmación o publicación de un acto de justicia para darle más autoridad.

homologous [ˈhɒmələɡəs] [jo-mo-lo-gos], *a.* Homólogo, que tiene una estructura, proporción, valor o posición correspondientes o semejantes; proporcional entre sí.

homology [ˈhɒmələdʒɪ] [jo-mo-lo-yi], *s.* Homología.

homonym [ˈhɒmənɪm] [jo-mo-nim], *s.* Homónimo, palabra cuya pronunciación es igual a otra de una sentido diferente: *V. g.* **reed,** caña y **read,** leer; **sea,** el mar, see, ver; o en castellano, si y sí, mas y más, hora y ora.

homonymous [ˈhɒmənɪməs] [jo-mo-ni-mos], *a.* 1. Homónimo; se dice de las voces semejantes que tienen un sentido diferente. 2. Equívoco, ambiguo.

homonymy [ˈhɒmənɪmɪ] [jo-mo-ni-mi], *s.* Homonimia.

homophone [ˈhɒməfəʊn] [jo-mo-foun], *s.* Vocablo homófono.

homophonous [ˈhɒməfənəs] [jo-mo-fo-nos], *a.* Homófono.

homophony [ˈhɒməfəʊnɪ] [jo-mo-fou-ni], *s.* Homofonía.

homopterous [ˈhɒməptərəs] [jo-mop-te-ros], *a.* Homóptero.

homosexual [ˈhɒmədˈsekjʊəl] [jo-mou-sek-siual] *s. & a.* Homosexual.

Honduran [hɒnˈdjuərən] [jon-diua-ran], *s.* y *a.* Hondureño.

hone [həʊn] [joun], *s.* Piedra de afilar.

honest [ˈɒnɪst] [o-nist], *a.* 1. Honrado, recto, justo (honorable). 2. Honesto, casto, recatado (pure, decent). **A downright honest man,** hombre de bien a carta cabal. 3. Sincero, íntegro; fiel; leal, equitativo. **An honest judge,** un juez íntegro. **An honest confession,** una confesión sincera. **Honest people,** gente honrada. **Honest dealin,** proceder leal, buena fe.

honestly [ˈɒnɪstlɪ] [o-nist-li], *adv.* Honradamente, rectamente; honestamente, modestamente. **To deal honestly,** tratar con honradez; ser honrado en sus tratos.

honesty [ˈɒnɪstɪ] [o-nis-ti], *s.* 1. Honradez, justicia, integridad (justice). 2. Honestidad. 3. (*Bot.*) Lunaria.

honey [ˈhʌnɪ] [ja-ni], *s.* 1. Miel. 2. Dulzura, la calidad de las cosas dulces (sweets). 3. Voz de cariño. **Honey-ant,** hormiga pequeña. **Honey-bee,** abeja de miel.

honey, *va.* 1. Enmelar, cubrir con miel, enmelar. 2. Adular, alagar. -*vn.* Hablar con cariño.

honey-bag [ˈhʌnɪbæg] [ja-ni-bag], *s.* El órgano en que la abeja lleva a la colmena la parte que recoge de las flores, con la cual fabrica la miel.

honeybee [ˈhʌnɪbiː] [ja-ni-bi], *s.* Abeja melífera, abeja doméstica.

honey-colored [ˈhʌnɪˈkʌləd] [ja-ni-ka-lord], *a.* Melado, gilvo.

honey-comb [ˈhʌnɪkəʊm] [ja-ni-koum], *s.* 1. Panal, el cuerpo esponjoso de cera que forman las abejas y en el cual depositan la miel. 2. *(Art.)* Escarabajos, los huequecillos que quedan en la parte interior de los cañones por defecto del molde o del metal.

honey-combed [ˈhʌnɪkəʊmbɪd] [ja-ni-koum-bid], *a.* 1. Lleno de perforaciones o de celdillas, dispuesto a manera de panal. 2. Agujereado por gusanos.

honey-dew [ˈhʌnɪdjuː] [ja-ni-diu], *s.* 1. Rocío. 2. Sustancia dulce como la miel. 3. Tabaco humedecido con melaza. 4. Variedad de melón blanco y muy dulce.

honeyed [ˈhʌnɪd] [ja-nid], *a.* Dulce, meloso, enmelado, cubierto de miel.

honeyless [ˈhʌnɪlɪs] [ja-ni-les], *a.* Sin miel.

honey-mouthed [ˈhʌnɪˈmaʊθɪd] [ja-ni-mauzd], *a.* Adulador, melifluo.

honey-moon [ˈhʌnɪmuːn] [ja-ni-mun], **honey-month** [ˈhʌnɪmɒnθ] [ja-ni-monz], *s.* La luna de miel; el primer mes de casados el tiempo que supone dura el pan de la boda.

honey-stalk [ˈhʌnɪstɔːk] [ja-ni-stok], *s. (Bot.)* Trébol. V. CLOVER.

honey-suckle [ˈhʌnɪsʌkl] [ja-ni-sa-kel], *s. (Bot.)* Madreselva.

honey-sweet [ˈhʌnɪswiːt] [ja-ni-suit], *a.* Dulce como la miel.

honey-tongue [ˈhʌnɪtɒŋ] [ja-ni-tong], *s.* Lengua melosa.

honk [hɒŋk] [jonk], *v.* 1. Tocar la bocina. 2. Graznar.

honk, *s.* 1. Bocinazo. 2. Graznido.

honor, honour [ˈɒnəʳ] [o-naʳ], *s.* 1. Honra, reverencia, veneración (veneration). **I take it as a great honor,** lo tengo a mucha honra. 2. Fidelidad, rectitud, honradez, probidad, integridad (honesty). 3. Gloria, reputación, fama (fame). 4. Pudor, castidad, recato, vergüenza (shame, purity). 6. Honor, dignidad, cargo, empleo. **Act of honor,** *(Com.)* Acto o protesta de intervención. 6. Grandeza de alma, magnanimidad. 7. Dignidad en el porte o en las acciones. 8. Honor, obsequio público que se hace a alguna persona. 9. Honor, privilegio de clase o de nacimiento. En castellano se usa casi siempre en plural en las dos últimas acepciones. 10. Cortesía, civilidad. 11. Ornamento, decoración. 12. Señorío. 13. Se da el tratamiento de **your honor** al vicecanciller de Inglaterra y otros dignatarios. **-pl.** 14. Los cuatro naipes más altos en el juego de **whist. Honor bright,** bajo mi palabra de honor; o como interrogación, ¿de veras? ¿en realidad? **On** o **upon honor,** por mi honor, bajo mi palabra de honor. **Point of honor,** pundonor, punto de honor.

honor, honour, *va.* 1. Honrar, reverenciar, respetar, estimar, venerar; glorificar (glorify, respect). 2. Dar un empleo o cargo de brillo y estimación. 3. Dar honor, lustre o gloria. **To honor a bill of exchange,** aceptar, honrar una letra de cambio, pagarla. **On my honor!,** ¡palabra de honor! **To have the honor of,** tener el honor de.

honorable, honourable [ˈɒnərəbl] [o-no-ra-bol], *a.* 1. Ilustre, noble, esclarecido. 2. Grande, magnánimo, generoso. 3. Honrado, honorífico, honroso; equitativo, justo.

honorableness [ˈɒnərəblnɪs] [o-no-ra-bol-nes], *s.* Honradez; eminencia; honestidad.

honorably [ˈɒnərəblɪ] [o-no-ra-bli], *adv.* Honorablemente; honoríficamente; generosamente; descentemente.

honorarium [ˌɒnəˈrɛərɪəm] [o-no-rea-riom], *s.* 1. Honorarios, emolumentos que se dan a los que ejercen una profesión por el ejercicio de la misma. 2. Paga o recompensa voluntaria en cambio de servicios por los cuales la ley no da derecho a obtener remuneración.

honorary [ˈɒnərərɪ] [o-no-ra-ri], *a.* 1. Honorario, honorífico, que honra o da honor. 2. Honorario, que posee un título o un empleo sin desempeñar sus funciones ni cobrar los emolumentos. *-s. V.* HONORARIUM.

honorer [ˈɒnərəʳ] [o-no-raʳ], *s.* Honrador, el que honra.

honorless [ˈɒnəlɪs] [o-nor-les], *a.* Sin honra, deshonrado.

hood [hʊd] [jud], *s.* 1. Caperuza o toca de mujer; muceta de graduados; capilla o capucha de religioso. 2. *(Mar.)* Caperuza de palo. **Hood** or **companion,** *(Mar.)* Sombrero de la escalera. **Hood of the chimney,** sombrero de la chimenea. 3. Capota de coche. 4. Campana de hogar. *(Arq.)* Marquesina, colgadizo.

hood, sufijo que significa calidad, estado, condición o totalidad. Muchas veces equivale al sufijo castellano *-dad* o *-ez;* v.g. **Brotherhood,** fraternidad; **manhood,** virilidad (también, edad, viril; valor, bravura); **maindenhood,** virginidad, doncellez. **Childhood,** niñez, edad de los niños. **Sisterhood,** hermandad; congregación de mujeres.

hood, *va.* 1. Cubrir con caperuza o capirote. 2. Cubrir, tapar, cegar poniendo alguna cosa delante de los ojos.

hoodlum [ˈhuːdləm] [jud-lom], *s.* 1. Tunante, golfo, gorila, matón. 2. Pandillero.

hoodman-blind [ˌhʊdmənˈblaɪnd] [jud-man-blaind], *s.* Juego de la gallinita ciega.

hoodoc [ˈhʊdɒk] [ju-dok], *va. (Fam. E.U.)* Hacer a alguno mal de ojo, llevarle la mala suerte, particularmente por la presencia de una persona. *-s.* Causa de mala suerte; persona cuya presencia trae mala fortuna; lo opuesto a **mascot.**

hoodwink [ˈhʊdwɪŋk] [jud-uink], *va.* 1. Vendar a uno los ojos. 2. Encubrir, tapar, ocultar. 3. Engañar.

hoof [huːf] [juf], *s.* (**pl.** HOOFS, raramente HOOVES) 1. El casco de las bestias caballares, vacunas, etc. 2. Animal que tiene cascos.

hoof, *vn.* Andar, moverse muy despacio: se dice de las bestias.

hoof beat [ˌhuːfˈbɪːt] [juf-bit], *s.* Ruido de cascos de las bestias.

hoof-bound [ˈhuːfbaʊnd] [juf-baund], *a.* Estrecho de cascos: se dice de los caballos.

hoofed [huːft] [juft], *a.* Se dice del animal que tiene cascos.

hook [hʊk] [juk], *s.* 1. Gancho, garfio. 2. Anzuelo, arponcillo de hierro que sirve para pescar. 3. Atractivo, aliciente (bait). 4. *(Mús.)* El signo a manera de banderola que sale de una corchea o nota más corta. **By hook or by crook,** de un modo u otro, a tuertas o a derechas, a buenas o malas. **Off the hooks,** agitado, distraído; no tenerlas todas consigo. **To drop off the hooks,** estirar la pata, morir. **To get the hooks,** ser puesto de patitas en la calle. 5. Instrumento cortante y curvo, hoz. **To get someone off the hook,** sacar a alguien de apuros. **To take the phone off the hook,** descolgar el teléfono.

hook, *va.* 1. Enganchar, coger alguna cosa con gancho, garfio o anzuelo. 2. Enganchar, atraer a uno con arte, atrapar, engatusar; hacer caer en el garlito. 3. Embestir o lastimar con los cuernos; se dice de una vaca o un toro. 4. *(Ger.)* Ratear, hurtar cosas de poco valor. **To hook the cat to the anchor,** *(Mar.)* Enganchar la gata al ancla.

hook-and-eye [hʊk] [juk], *s.* Macho y hembra. (Se aplica a broches).

hooked [hʊkt] [jukt], *a.* Enganchado, encorvado, ganchoso.

hooked rug [ˈhʊktrʌg] [jukt-rag], *s.* Tapete tejido con gancho.

hooker [ˈhʊkəʳ] [ju-kaʳ], *a.* Enganchado, encorvado, ganchoso.

hook-nosed [ˌhʊkˈnəʊzd] [juk-nousd], *a.* El que tiene nariz aguileña álgo corva en el medio.

hookup [ˈhʊkʌp] [juk-ap], *s.* 1. (Radio) Radiotransmisión en circuito por una cadena de emisoras. 2. Cadena de estaciones radiotransmisoras. 3. *(Fam.)* Alianza entre dos gobiernos.

hookworm [ˈhʊkwɜːm] [juk-uerm], *s.* Lombriz intestinal.

hooky [ˈhʊkɪ] [ju-ki], *a.* Lleno de ganchos o perteneciente a ellos.

hooky, *s.* **To play hooky,** hacer novillos, irse de pinta, pintar venados.

hoop [huːp] [jup], *s.* 1. Aro, arco, cerco de barril o tonel. 2. Tontillo, especie de guardapiés ahuecado que usaban las señoras. 3. Arete, zarcillo. 4. Anillo, anilla, sortija.

hoop, *va.* 1. Poner arcos o cercos a una cosa. 2. Cercar, rodear. -*vn.* Gritar, vociferar; ojear. **Hoop-poles,** cujes. **Lining-hoop,** aro que refuerza la tapa.

hooper [ˈhuːpəʳ] [ju-paʳ], *s.* Tonelero.

hooping-cough, *s. V.* WHOOPING-COUGH.

hoot [huːt] [jut], *vn.* 1. Gritar, burlarse de alguno dando gritos. 2. Gritar como el buho. -*va.* Ojear, espantar los animales a fuerza de gritos.

hoot, inter, *(Esco.)* ¡Fuera! ¡vaya! ¡puf!

hoot, *s.* Grito, ruido, clamor.

hooting [ˈhuːtɪŋ] [ju-tin], *s.* Grito, el acto de dar voces.

hoove, hove, hooven [huːv] [juv], *s. (Vet.)* Enfermedad del ganado vacuno y lanar caracterizada por la distensión del abdomen.

hop [hɒp] [jop], *vn.* 1. Saltar, dar saltos (jump, vault). 2. Cojear de un pie. 3. Juguetear, brincar (play). 4. **To hop off,** despegar, alzar el vuelo de un avión. 5. Cruzar saltando. -*va.* Mezclar el lúpulo en la cerveza.

hop, *s.* 1. Salto, brinco. 2. *(Bot.)* Lúpulo, u hombrecillo. **Hop pillow,** almohada rellena de lúpulo para inducir el sueño. 3. *(Pop.)* Vuelo en avión. **On the hop,** en movimiento. 4. **To hope against,** esperar lo imposible. **In one hop,** de un salto, de un tirón, sin hacer escala *(Aer.)*. **To catch someone on the hop,** pillar a alguien desprevenido.

hope [həʊp] [joup], *s.* 1. Esperanza, confianza (expectation). 2. Apoyo, sostén (help); el que o lo que es la causa de esperanza o confianza. 3. La cosa esperada o ansiada. **Forlorn hope,** una empresa sin esperanza.

hope, *s. (Prov. Ingl.)* Cuesta, subida; declive. Se usa en composición en los nombres de lugares: como Stanhope.

hope, *vn.* Esperar, tener esperanza; confiar, poner la confianza en lo futuro o venidero. -*va.* Esperar con ansia.

hope chest [ˈhəʊptʃest] [joup-chest], *s.* Arca en que las solteras acumulan ropa y mantelería en anticipación a su matrimonio.

hopeful [ˈhəʊpfʊl] [joup-ful], *a.* 1. Lleno de buenas calidades; de grandes esperanzas o que da grandes esperanzas, que promete mucho. Esperanzado, lleno de esperanzas.

hopefully [ˈhəʊpfəlɪ] [joup-fa-li], *adv.* Con esperanza.

hopefulness [ˈhəʊpfəlnɪs] [joup-ful-nes], *s.* Buena disposición, apariencia o perspectiva de buenos resultados.

hopeless [ˈhəʊplɪs] [joup-les], *a.* Desesperado, desahuciado, desesperanzado.

hopelessly [ˈhəʊplɪslɪ] [joup-les-li], *adv.* Sin esperanza, desesperadamente, irremediablemente.

hoper [ˈhəʊpəʳ] [joup-paʳ], *s.* El que espera o tiene esperanza.

hop-garden [ˈhɒpgɑːdn] [jop-gar-den], **hop-yard** [ˈhɒpjɑːd] [jop-yard], *s.* Plantío de lúpulos.

hopingly [ˈhəʊpɪŋlɪ] [jou-pin-li], *adv.* Con esperanza.

hopper [ˈhɒpəʳ] [jou-paʳ], *s.* 1. El que da saltos o brincos sobre un pie. 2. Tolva, la caja que está colgada sobre la piedra del molino, donde se echa el grano para molerlo. 3. Sementero, el saco o costal en que se lleva el grano para sembrar. 4. Insecto que salta; saltamontes. 5. Tolva.

hoppers [ˈhɒpəz] [jou-pers], *s. pl. V.* HOPSCOTCH.

hop-picker [ˈhɒpˈpɪkəʳ] [jop-pi-kaʳ], *s.* El que hace la recolección de lúpulo.

hopple [ˈhɒpl] [jou-pel], *va.* 1. Atar las patas a un caballo para que no dé brincos. 2. Enredar, estorbar. -*s.* Traba, atadura que se pone en las patas de los caballos cuando se les pone a pastar.

hop-pole [ˈhɒpˌpəʊl] [jop-poul], *s.* Varal o palo para sostener el lúpulo.

hop-scotch [ˈhɒpskɒʃ] [jop-skoch], *s.* El juego llamado "a la pata coja". 2. Coxcojita, infernáculo, reina mora.

Horace [ˈhɒrɪs] [jo-ris], *n. pr.* Horacio.

horal [ˈhɒrəl] [jo-ral], **horary** [ˈhɒrərɪ] [jo-ra-ri], *a.* Horario.

horatian [hɒˈreɪʃən] [jo-rei-shan], *a.* De Horacio, que se refiere o se parece a Horacio o a su poesía.

horde [hɔːd] [jord], *s.* 1. Horda. 2. Multitud, enjambre, manada.

horde, *v.* Formar hordas.

hordeolum [hɔːˈdɪələm] [jor-dio-lom], *s.* Orzuelo, tumorcillo que sale en el borde de los párpados.

horizon [həˈraɪzn] [jo-rai-son], *s.* Horizonte.

horizontal [ˌhɒrɪˈzɒntl] [jo-ri-zon-tal], *a.* Horizontal.

horizontality [ˌhɒrɪˈzɒntælɪtɪ] [jo-ri-zon-ta-li-ti], *s.* Horizontalidad.

horizontally [ˌhɒrɪˈzɒntəklɪ] [jo-ri-zon-ta-li], *adv.* Horizontalmente.

hormonal [hɔːˈməʊnəl] [jor-mou-nal], *a.* Hormonal.

hormone [ˈhɔːməʊn] [jor-moun], *s.* Hormona.

horn [hɔːn] [jorn], *s.* 1. Cuerno, asta, el arma que tienen algunos animales en la cabeza. 2. Cuerna, el asta o cuerno del ciervo o venado (antler); cacho. 3. *(Zool.)* Tentáculo; palpo o antena. 4. Corneta de monte, trompa de caza; bocina. 5. Cuerno, vaso de cuerno para beber y otros usos. 6. Poder, honor; usado simbólicamente en la Sagrada Escritura. 7. *(Mús.)* Cuerno, trompa. *(Aut.)* Bocina, claxon. **To be on the horns of a dilemma,** estar entre la espada y la pared. **To wear the horns,** ser cornudo. **Ink-horn,** tintero. **Shoehorn,** calzador de cuerno. **To draw in one's horns,** recoger velas, hacer economías.

horn, *va.* 1. Poner cuernos, hacer a uno cornudo. 2. *(Mús.)* Tocar el cuerno. 3. *(E.U.)* Entrometerse.

hornbeak [ˈhɔːnbiːk] [jorn-bik], **hornfish** [ˈhɔːnfɪʃ] [jorn-fish], *s. (Ict.)* Aguja.

hornbeam [ˈhɔːnbiːm] [jorn-bim], *s. (Bot.)* Arpe u ojaranzo.

hornbill [ˈhɔːnbɪl] [jorn-bil], *s.* Cálao, ave de gran tamaño notable por lo enorme de su pico.

hornblende [ˈhɔːnblend] [jorn-blend], *s. (Min.)* Hornblenda.

hornblower [ˈhɔːnblaʊəʳ] [jorn-blauaʳ], *s.* El que toca la trompa, trompetero, bocinero.

hornbook [ˈhɔːnbʊk] [jorn-buk], *s.* Cartilla, el cuaderno que contiene los primeros rudimientos para aprender a leer.

horned [ˈhɔːnd] [jornd], *a.* 1. Astado, cornudo, enastado. **Horned cattle,** ganado vacuno. 2. Encornado. 3. En forma de cuerno. 4. *(Ornit.)* **Horned owl,** búho. 5. **Horned toad,** especie de lagarto cornudo de Norteamérica. 6. *(Zool.)* **Horder viper,** vívora cornuda.

hornedness [ˈhɔːndnɪs] [jornd-nes], *s.* La cosa que tiene semejanza a cuerno o que tiene puntas como las de los cuernos.

horner [ˈhɔːnəʳ] [jor-naʳ], *s.* El que trabaja el cuerno o lo vende.

hornet [ˈhɔːnɪt] [jor-nit], *s.* Avispón, avispa grande. **To stir up a hornet's nest,** meterse en un avispero; excitar la hostilidad de mucha gente.

hornfoot [ˈhɔːnfʊt] [jorn-fut], *s.* Lo que tiene cascos como los de los caballos.

hornify [ˈhɔːnɪfaɪ] [jor-ni-fai], *va.* Hacer semejante al cuerno.

horning [ˈhɔːnɪŋ] [jor-nin], *s.* El aspecto de la luna creciente.

hornish [ˈhɔːnɪʃ] [jor-nish], *a.* Duro, semejante a cuerno.

hornless [ˈhɔːnlɪs] [jorn-les], *a.* Lo que no tiene cuernos.

hornpipe [ˈhɔːnpaɪp] [jorn-paip], *s.* 1. Gaita. 2. Baile especial predilecto de los marineros.

hornsilver [ˈhɔːnsɪlvəʳ] [jorn-sil-vaʳ], *s. (Min.)* Cloruro de plata, cerargirita.

horn-spoon [ˈhɔːnspuːn] [jorn-spun], *s.* Cuchara de cuerno.

hornstone [ˈhɔːnstəʊn] [jorn-stoun], *s. (Min.)* Hornstenio o piedra de cuerno, especie de feldespato.

hornwork [ˈhɔːnwɜːk] [jorn-uerk], *s. (Fort.)* Hornabeque u obra a tenaza.

horny [ˈhɔːnɪ] [jor-ni], *a.* Hecho de cuerno; parecido al cuerno; calloso.

horography [hɒˈrɒɡræfɪ] [jo-ro-gra-fi], *s.* Gnomónica, el arte de construir relojes de sol.

horologe [hɒˈrɒləʊg] [jo-ro-loug], **horology** [hɒˈrɒlədʒɪ] [jo-ro-lo-yi], *s.* Reloj o cualquier instrumento que sirve para medir el tiempo.

horologic, horological [ˌhɒrɒˈlədʒɪk] [jo-ro-lo-yik], *a.* Que se refiere a la relojería o a la gnomónica.

horologiography [ˌhɒrɒləgɪəˈgræfɪ] [jo-ro-lo-guio-gra-fi], *s.* 1. El conocimiento de los instrumentos que sirven para señalar las horas. 2. Gnomónica, el arte de construir relojes de sol.

horometry [ˈhɒrəmiːtrɪ] [jo-ro-mi-tri], *s.* Horometría, el arte de medir y dividir las horas.

horopter [hɒˈrəptəʳ] [jo-rop-taʳ], *s. (Opt.).* Horopter, horoptero.

horopteric [ˌhɒrəpˈterɪk] [jo-rop-te-rik], *a.* Horoptérico.

horoscope [ˈhɒrəskəʊp] [jo-ros-koup], *s.* Horóscopo, observación supersticiosa que hacían los astrólogos en el nacimiento de alguno, para predecir la suerte y sucesos de su vida en vista de la posición de los astros.

horrendous [hɒˈrendəs] [jo-ren-dos], *a.* Horrendo, espantoso (awful).

horrent [ˈhɒrent] [jo-rrent], *a.* 1. Erizado, que tiene puntas hacia fuera. 2. Horrible, espantoso, que causa destestación.

horrible [ˈhɒrɪbl] [jo-ri-bol], *a.* Horrible, espantoso, terrible, horrendo; enorme (huge).

horribleness [ˈhɒrɪblnɪs] [jo-ri-bol-nes], *s.* Horribilidad.

horribly [ˈhɒrɪblɪ] [jo-ri-bli], *adv.* Horriblemente, espantosamente, enormemente, terriblemente.

horrid [ˈhɒrɪd] [jo-rid], *a.* Horrible, hórrido, espantoso, áspero; oscuro, tenebroso.

horridly [ˈhɒrɪdlɪ] [jo-rid-li], *adv.* Enormemente, horriblemente, espantosamente.

horridness [ˈhɒrɪdnɪs] [jo-rid-nes], *s.* Carácter o naturaleza horrible: aspecto horrendo, enormidad, horror.

horrific [ˈhɒrɪfɪk] [jo-ri-fik], *a.* Horrífico (terrific).

horrify [ˈhɒrɪfaɪ] [jo-ri-fai], *v.* Horrorizar (frighten).

horrifying [ˈhɒrɪfaɪɪŋ] [jo-ri-fain], *a.* Horroroso, horripilante (fright).

horripilate [ˈhɒrɪpɪleɪt] [jo-ri-pi-leit], *v.* Horripilar, hacer erizar los cabellos.

horripilation [ˈhɒrɪpɪˈleɪʃən] [jo-ri-pi-lei-shon], *s.* Horropilación.

horrisonant [ˈhɒrɪsənənt] [jo-ri-so-nant], *a.* Horrísono.

horror [ˈhɒrəʳ] [jo-raʳ], *s.* 1. Horror, consternación, terror, espanto (terror, dread): detestación. 2. Gran accidente, calamidad. **A railroad horror,** una catástrofe en la vía férrea. **The horrors.** *(Fam.)* Melancolía, hipocondría; también, delirium tremens.

horrorous [ˈhɒrərəs] [jo-ro-ros], *a.* Horroroso.

hors d'oeuvre [ɔːˈdɜːvr] [or-devr], *s.* Entremés, canapé.

horse [hɔːs] [jors], *s.* 1. Caballo, mamífero solípedo. **Saddle-horse,** caballo de silla. **Pack-horse,** caballo de carga. **Carriage-horse,** caballo de tiro. **Race-horse,** caballo de carrera. **Cart-horse,** caballo de carro. **White horse,** caballo blanco; *(Mex.)* tordillo. **Black horse,** caballo negro. **Fine, shining black horse,** caballo retinto. **Pie-bald horse,** caballo moro. **Pied horse,** caballo picazo. **Hestnut horse,** caballo castaño. **Bay horse,** caballo bayo. **Dapple horse,** tordo rodado. **Gray horse,** caballo pardo. **Duppled gray** (horse), pardo rodado. **Sorrel** (horse), alazán. **Brown sorrel** (horse) Alazán tostado. **Seed horse,** caballo desbocado. **To ride a horse,** montar a caballo. 2. Caballería. **Light horse,** caballería ligera. 3. Caballete para secar la ropa lavada; bastidor llamado también burro, borrico; tendedor, mesa de papel, etc. 4. Garatura o tabla de descarnar. 5. Caballo de palo o potro en que se castiga a los soldados. 6. Traducción, apuntes u otros medios de que se valen los alumnos para preparar sus lecciones. 7. Manía, tema predilecto. *V.* HOBBY. 8. Trabajo cuyo precio se pide antes de ejecutar aquél. **Horse of the bowsprit,** *(Mar.)* Guardamancebo del bauprés. **Horse of a yard,** *(Mar.)* Guardamancebo de una verga. **Horse of a sail,** *(Mar.)* Nervio de vela. **Hackney, livery horse,** caballo de alquiler. **Iron horse,** locomotora, **blood horse,** caballo de sangre, de pura raza. **Dark horse,** caballo del cual nadie espera que gane una carrera; de aquí, en política, competidor desconocido, inesperado. **To groom a horse,** cuidar, curar un caballo. **To clap spurs to one's horse,** espolear un caballo. **To put a horse to full speed,** poner un caballo a rienda suelta, a escape tendido. **As fast as his horse could carry.** A rienda suelta, a escape. **To get on** o **mount the high horse,** asumir un porte altivo, orgulloso, o arrogante. **To take horse,** (a) Cabalgar, pasear a caballo. (b) Permitir la yegua que la cubra el caballo. La voz **horse** se usa frecuentemente en composición para calificar a una cosa de grosera y grande.

horse, en composición: **Horse-ant,** la hormiga roja. Formica rufa. **Horse-bean,** *(Bot.)* Haba panosa o caballuna. **Horse-bot,** lombriz de caballo. **Horse-boy,** mozo de caballos, el que los cuida y limpia. **Horse-box,** (G.B.) *V.* HORSE-CAR, 2ª acepción, **horse-breaker,** picador o domador de caballos. **Horse-car,** *(E.U.)* carro para transportar caballos por ferrocarril **Horse-cloth,** mantilla de caballo. **Horse-colt,** potro. **Horse-com,** almohaza. **Horse-doctor,** veterinario. **Horse-drench,** toma de medicina para caballo, y el aparato para administrarla. **Horse-dung,** cagajón, estiércol de caballos. **Horse-faced,** que tiene la cara larga y de facciones groseras. **Horse-keeper,** establero, mozo de caballos, el que cuida de ellos. **Horse-laugh,** gran carcajada, risa grosera. **Horse-leech,** sanguijuela; albéitar. *(Fig.)* La persona que constantemente pordiosea o molesta. **Horse-litter,** litera de dos caballos. **Horse-load,** carga de caballo. **Horse-mackered,** caballa, haleche: atún, y varios otros peces. **Horse-mill,** molino de sangre, el que mueven hombres o caballerías. **Horse-milliner,** el que vende cintas y otros adornos para los caballos. **Horse-pond,** estanque para dar de beber o bañar a los caballos. **Horse-race,** carrera o corrida de caballos. **Horse-stealer,** cuatrero, ladrón de caballos. **Horse-tail,** *(Bot.)* Cola de caballo. **Horse-way,** camino de herradura.

horse, *va.* 1. Montar a caballo o llevar sobre él. 2. Proveer de caballos, proporcionar caballos. 3. Cabalgar, montar el caballo padre a la yegua o cubrirla. 4. *(Mar.)* mandar o hacer trabajar tiránicamente o cruelmente (a los marineros). 5. Azotar. 6. *(Mil.)* Remontar. *-vn.* 1. Cabalgar, andar a caballo. 2. Pedir el precio de un trabajo antes de ejecutarlo.

horse-aloes [ˌhɔːsəˈluːz] [jors-a-lus], *s.* Acíbar caballuno.

horseback [ˈhɔːsbæk] [jors-bak], *s.* Lomo de caballo o asiento del jinete. **to get on horseback,** montar a caballo.

horse-boat [ˈhɔːsbəʊt] [jors-bout], *s.* Barco para transportar caballos.

horse-block [ˈhɔːsblɒk] [jors-blok], *s.* Apeadero; montador o montadero, cualquier cosa que sirve para montar.

horsebreaker [ˈhɔːsˌbreɪkəʳ] [jors-brei-kaʳ], *s.* Picador, domador de caballos.

horse-chestnut [ˈhɔːsˈtʃesnʌt] [jors-ches-nat], *s. (Bot.)* Castaño de Indias.

horsefair [ˈhɔːsfɛəʳ] [jors-feaʳ], *s.* Feria de caballos. 2. *a.* Chalanesco, engañoso.

horse-flesh [ˈhɔːsfleʃ] [jors-flesh], *s.* 1. Carne de caballo. 2. Conjunto de caballos. 3. Variedad de caoba de las Bahamas.

horse-fly [ˈhɔːsflaɪ] [jors-flai], *s.* 1. Tábano, mosca de caballo. 2. *V.* BOT-FLY. 3. Moscarda, garrapata de caballo.

horse-guards [ˈhɔːsgɑːdz] [jors-gards], *s. pl.* 1. Guardias de a caballo. 2. Cuartel general del ejército de la Gran Bretaña.

horsehide [ˈhɔːshaɪd] [jors-jaid], *s.* Cuero de caballo.

horsekeeper [ˈhɔːsˌkiːpəʳ] [jors-ki-paʳ], *s.* Establero, mozo de cuadras.

horselaugh [ˈhɔːslɑːf] [jors-laf], *s.* Risa grosera, risotada.

horseleech [ˈhɔːsliːtʃ] [jors-lich], *s.* 1. *(Zool.)* Variedad de sanguijuela. 2. Pedigüeño.

horseload [ˈhɔːsləʊd] [jors-loud], *s.* Carga de un caballo. 2. *(Fig.)* De gran cantidad.

horseman [ˈhɔːsmən] [jors-man], *s.* 1. Jinete, el que sabe montar bien a caballo. 2. Soldado de a caballo. 3. Jinete, el que está montado a caballo.

horsemanship [ˈhɔːsmənʃɪp] [jors-man-ship], *s.* Manejo, el arte de manejar los caballos; equitación.

horsemint ['hɔːsmɪnt] [jors-mint], *s. (Bot.)* Mastranzo, planta herbácea de la familia de las labiadas. Monarda.

horse-play ['hɔːspleɪ] [jors-plei], *s.* Chanza pesada.

horsepond ['hɔːspɒnd] [jors-pond], *s.* Abrevadero, alberca para abrevar los caballos.

horsepower ['hɔːspaʋəʳ] [jors-paua'], *s.* 1. Caballo de fuerza, unidad teórica de la medida del trabajo. 2. Máquina o aparato mecánico para convertir el tiro de un caballo en fuerza mecánica. **Horsepower-hour,** caballo hora, caballo de fuerza hora.

horseradish ['hɔːsˌrædɪʃ] [jors-ra-dish], *s. (Bot.)* Rábano picante o rústico.

horseshoe ['hɔːsʃuː] [jors-shu], *s.* 1. Herradura de caballo. 2. Lo que se parece a una herradura, por ejemplo la curva que forma un río. 3. *(Zool.)* Límulo, cangrejo.

horsewhip ['hɔːswɪp] [jors-uip], *s.* Látigo. (Cuba) Chucho. (Mex. Cuarta, azote.

horsewhip, *va.* Azotar, castigar con látigo.

horsewoman ['hɔːsˌwʊmən] [jors-uo-man], *s.* Amazona, mujer que monta a caballo.

horsing ['hɔːsɪŋ] [jor-sin], *s.* 1. Tablilla sobre que se sienta, el amolador de cuchillos. 2. Tunda, zurra que se da a un muchacho llevado a cuestas por otro.

horsy, horsey ['hɔːsɪ] [jor-si], *a.* 1. Caballuno. 2. Aficionado a caballos.

hortation [hɔːsˈteɪʃən] [jor-tei-shon], *s.* Exhortación.

hortative ['hɔːtətɪv] [jor-ta-tiv], *a.* Exhortatorio, que tiende a excitar o animar; de la naturaleza de exhortación.

hortatory [ˌhɔːtəˈtɔːrɪ] [jor-ta-to-ri], *a.* Exhortatorio, que contiene o comunica exhortaciones.

hortensia ['hɔːtənsɪə] [jor-ten-sia], *n. pr.* 1. Hortensia. 2. *(Bot.)* Hortensia.

hortensial ['hɔːtənsɪəl] [jor-ten-sial], *a.* Exhortatorio, que contiene o comunica exhortaciones.

hortensial, *a.* Apto para jardín o huerta, relativo a un jardín.

horticultural [ˌhɔːtɪˈkʌltʃərəl] [jor-ti-kal-cha-ral], *a.* Horticultural, que pertenece al cultivo de los jardines y huertas. **Horticultural, society,** sociedad hortícola, la establecida para promover la introducción y el cultivo de árboles frutales, de legumbres, etc.

horticulture [ˌhɔːtɪˈkʌltʃəʳ] [jor-ti-kal-cha'], *s.* Horticultura, jardinería (gardening).

horticulturist [ˌhɔːtɪˈkʌltʃərɪst] [jor-ti-kal-cha-rist], *s.* Horticultor, hortelano, aficionado a cultivar los jardines y las huertas, o diestro en ese arte.

hortus siccus ['hɔːtəsˈsɪkəs] [jor-tos-si-kos], *s. (Bot.)* Herbario seco, conjunto de plantas secas y preservadas con orden.

hortyard ['hɔːtjɑːd] [jort-yard], *s. (Des.)* Huerto.

hosanna [ɒˈsɑːnə] [o-sa-na], *s.* Hosana, exclamación de alabanza a Dios. *(Heb.)*

hose [həʋz] [jous], *s.* 1. Medias, calcetines (stockings, socks); antiguamente bragas, calzones, 2. Manguera, tubo flexible de cuero, de hule, etc., para conducir líquidos; manguera de una bomba de incendios. **Great hose,** zaragüelles. **Hose nozzles,** boquereles de manguera. **Hose pipes,** tubos de manguera. **Lawn hose,** mangueras de regar prados.

Hosea ['həʋzɪə] [jou-sia], *n. pr.* Oseas.

hosier ['həʋzɪəʳ] [jou-sia'], *s.* Mediero, el que vende medias.

hosiery ['həʋzɪərɪ] [jou-sia-ri], *s.* 1. Medias, calcetines, los artículos que vende el mediero. 2. Comercio de medias, etc.

hospice ['hɒspɪs] [jos-pis], *s.* Hospicio, hospedería, particularmente en los Alpes.

hospitable [hɒsˈpɪtəbl] [jos-pi-ta-bol], *a.* Hospitalario, caritativo, benigno y afable con los huéspedes.

hospitableness [ˌhɒspɪˈtəblnɪs] [jos-pi-ta-bol-nes], *s.* Hospitalidad.

hospitably ['hɒspɪtəblɪ] [jos-pi-ta-bli], *adv.* Hospitalariamente.

hospital ['hɒspɪtl] [jos-pi-tal], *s.* Hospital, la casa donde recogen y curan a los enfermos o los heridos. 2. *(Des.)* Hospicio, fonda. **Hospital staff,** el personal, los empleados de un hospital.

hospitality [ˌhɒspɪˈtælɪtɪ] [jos-pi-ta-li-ti], *s.* Hospitalidad, el recibimiento caritativo de huéspedes, pasajeros o refugiados.

hospitalization [ˌhɒspɪtəlaɪˈzeɪʃən] [jos-pi-ta-lai-sei-shon], *s.* Hospitalización.

hospitalize ['hɒspɪtəlaɪz] [jos-pi-ta-lais], *va.* Hospitalizar.

hospital-ship ['hɒspɪtlˌʃɪp] [jos-pi-tal-ship], *s. (Mar.)* Barco hospital.

hospital ward ['hɒspɪtlˌwɑːd] [jos-pi-tal-uard], *s.* Sala de hospital.

hospodar ['hɒspəʋdəʳ] [jos-pou-da'], *s.* Título de dignidad que pertenecía antiguamente a varios príncipes europeos y hoy al emperador de Rusia.

host [həʋst] [joust], *s.* 1. Patrón, huésped, el que hospeda en su casa a alguno. 2. Mesonero, posadero, el amo de una posada. 3. Hueste, ejército, multitud. 4. Hostia. **To reckon without the host,** hacer la cuenta sin la huéspeda.

hostage ['hɒstɪdʒ] [jos-tich], *s.* Rehén, la persona que queda en poder del enemigo como prenda, prenda, gaje.

hostel ['hɒstəl] [jos-tel], *s.* 1. Posada, hostal. 2. En las universidades de Francia e Inglaterra, casa de huéspedes para estudiantes.

hostelery, hostelry ['hɒstəlrɪ] [jos-tel-ri], *s.* Posada, mesón, hostería (inn).

hostess ['həʋstɪs] [jous-tes], *sf.* Posadera, mesonera, patrona, huéspeda, ama.

hostess-ship [ˌhəʋstɪsˈʃɪp] [jous-tes-ship], *s.* Carácter u oficio de posadera o mesonera.

hostile ['hɒstaɪl] [jos-tail], *a.* Hostil.

hostilely ['hɒstaɪlɪlɪ] [jos-tai-le-li], *adv.* Hostilmente.

hostility [hɒsˈtɪlɪtɪ] [jos-ti-li-ti], *s.* Hostilidad.

hostilize ['hɒstɪlaɪz] [jos-ti-lais], *v.* Hostilizar.

hostler ['ɒsləʳ] [ost-la'], *s.* Mozo de paja y cebada, el que cuida de las caballerías en una posada.

hot [hɒt] [jot], *a.* 1. Cálido, caliente (warm). **Hot weather,** tiempo caluroso. 2. Ardiente, fogoso, impaciente, fervoroso (passioned). 3. Picante, acre. 4. Violento, furioso, colérico (violent). 5. *(Fam.)* Intolerable, que causa pena y apuros. **to grow hot,** calentarse, encenderse. **To make hot,** calentar. **To be burning hot,** quemarse; hacer mucho calor, asarse los pájaros. **The summer is now at its hottest,** estamos en los calores más fuertes del estío. **Hot mustard,** mostaza muy picante. **Hot blast,** corriente, tiro de aire caliente. **Hot and heavy,** *(Fam.)* Furioso, fiero y contundente. **Piping hot,** caliente hasta hervir o bullir. **To be in hot water,** estar en ascuas. **Hot-livered,** irascible, de carácter colérico, botafuego.

hot-air [hɒtˈeəʳ] [jot-ea'], *a.* De aire caliente; hot-air heating, calefacción de aire caliente.

hot-bed ['hɒtbed] [jot-bed], *s.* Era, cuadro de huerta cubierto con capas de estiércol y abrigado con vidrieras. *(Fig.)* Foco, plantel. **A hotbed of sedition,** un foco de sedición.

hot-blooded ['hɒtˈblʌdɪd] [jot-bla-did], *a.* Excitable, fogoso.

hot-brained ['hɒtbreɪnd] [jot-breind], *a.* Violento, furioso.

hotch-potch ['hɒtʃpɒtʃ] [joch-poch], *s.* Almodrote.

hot dog ['hɒtdɒg] [jot-dog], *s.* Emparedado de salchicha, perrito caliente.

hotel [həʋˈtel] [jou-tel], *s.* 1. Posada, hotel. 2. Palacio, residencia de altos personajes; también, ayuntamiento, como en Francia.

hotelkeeper [həʋtelˈkiːpəʳ] [jou-tel-ki-pa'], *s.* Hotelero.

hotfoot ['hɒtfʊt] [jot-fut], *adv.* Prontamente, a toda prisa, precipitadamente.

hot-headed ['hɒtˈhedɪd] [jot-je-did], *a.* Vehemente, violento, fogoso, colérico.

hot-house ['hɒthaʋs] [jot-jaus], *s.* 1. Invernadero o invernáculo con estufas para guardar las flores en invierno. 2. Estufa, aposento recogido para sudar u otros usos.

hotly ['hɒtlɪ] [jot-li], *adv.* 1. Con calor. 2. Vehementemente. 3. Lascivamente.

hot-press ['hɒtpres] [jot-pres], *s.* 1. Prensa recargada. 2. Calandra térmica para satinar.

hot press, *va.* Prensar papel o paños con láminas de hierro caliente.

hot rod [ˈhɒtrɒd] [jot-rod], *s.* Automóvil reconstruido para que alcance altas velocidades y rápida aceleración.

hot-roll [ˈhɒtrɒl] [jot-rol], *v.* Laminar en caliente.

hotspur [ˈhɒtzpɜːʳ] [jots-paʳ], *s.* 1. La persona colérica que con facilidad se enfada. 2. Especie de guisante que se cría en poco tiempo. *-a.* Violento.

hottentot [ˈhɒtəntɒt] [jo-ten-tot], *s.* 1. Hotentote, natural de la Hotentocia, en el sur de África. 2. Hotentote, salvaje, un hombre brutal o tosco.

hough [hɒʊ] [jau], *va.* Desjarretar, descuadrillar. *V.* HOCK.

hough, *s.* 1. Jarrete; corvejón de las bestias. *V.* HOCK. 2. *(Des.) V.* HOE.

hound [haʊnd] [jaund], *s.* 1. Sabueso, perro de montería. **Blood-hound,** sabueso ventor. **Greyhound,** galgo, lebrel. 2. Perro, collón, hombre vil 3. *(Mar.)* Cacholas. *V.* CHEEKS. **A pack of hounds,** una traílla de perros.

hound, *va.* 1. Cazar, perseguir con perros de caza. 2. Soltar los perros. 3. Seguir la pista. **Hound down,** perseguir. **To hound on,** incitar.

hound's-tongue [ˌhaʊndzˈtɒŋ] [jaunds-tong], *s.* *(Bot.)* Cinoglosa, viniebla, lengua de perro.

hound-tree [haʊ] [jau], *s. (Bot.)* Cornejo.

hour [aʊəʳ] [auaʳ], *s.* 1. Hora, sesenta minutos. 2. Hora, tiempo señalado o definido, como la hora de la muerte. 3. *pl.* Horas, rezos de la Iglesia católica que se dicen a ciertas horas del día, como las vísperas y maitines. 4. Jornada o camino de una hora; una legua, poco más o menos. **An hour ago, an hour since,** hace una hora. **It takes hours,** es cosa de mucho tiempo, de muchas horas. **About the eleventh hour,** a eso de las once. **To keep good hours,** retirarse o volver a la casa temprano. **To keep bad hours,** Volver a deshora. **Small hours,** primeras horas de la madrugada. **To strike the hour,** dar la hora. **After hours,** fuera de horas.

hourglass [ˈaʊəglɑːs] [aua-glas], *s.* Ampolleta o reloj de arena.

hourhand [ˈaʊəhænd] [aua-jand], *s.* Horario, la saetilla que indica la hora en el reloj.

houri [ˈaʊərɪ] [aua-ri], *s.* Hurí, ninfa del paraíso mahometano.

hourly [ˈaʊəlɪ] [aua-li], *adv.* A cada hora, frecuentemente (often). *-a.* Lo que sucede cada hora, frecuente.

hour-plate [ˈaʊəpleɪt] [aua-pleit], *s.* Muestra de reloj.

house [haʊs] [jaus], *s.* 1. Casa, edificio hecho para habitarlo; residencia, domicilio. **Country-house,** casa de campo. **To keep house,** tener casa. 2. Casa o comunidad. *V.* HOUSEHOLD. 3. Casa, familia, descendencia, linaje. 4. El género de vida, mesa o modo de tratarse con respecto a los alimentos. 5. Casa, razón social, establecimiento mercantil. 6. La gente que compone el concurso de oyentes, el auditorio. 7. Cámara de un cuerpo legislativo. **House of Lords,** cámara de los pares en Inglaterra. **House of Commons,** cámara baja o de los comunes. **House of Representatives,** cámara de los Representantes (en el Congreso de los Estados Unidos). **Ale-house,** cervecería. **Coffee-house,** café. **Pigeon-house,** palomar. **Workhouse,** (a) Hospicio. (b) Casa de corrección. **Ice-house,** nevera o nevería. **Town house,** casa consistorial o casa ayuntamiento. **House and home,** hogar. **Summer-house,** glorieta. **Engine-house, round-house,** casa de máquinas, rotonda. **Wheelhouse,** carroza, garita o mirador del timonel. **To bring down the house,** provocar aplauso general y ruidoso. **To keep open house,** recibir abiertamente, ser hospitalario. **It's on the house,** invita la casa. **House-duty,** *(G.B.)* Impuesto sobre las casas.

house, *va.* 1. Albergar, tener a uno en casa (put up, lodge); dar casa o habitación a alguna persona. 2. Entrojar; poner a cubierto. 3. *(Mar.)* Afianzar o cubrir cuando hay borrasca. 4. Almacenar, guardar, poner en seguridad (store). *-vn.* Residir.

houseboat [ˈhaʊsbaʊt] [jaus-bout], *s.* Barco vivienda, casa flotante.

house-breaker [ˈhaʊsˌbreɪkəʳ] [jaus-brei-kaʳ], *s.* El ladrón que fuerza de noche las puertas de una casa para robarla, caco.

house-breaking [ˈhaʊsˌbreɪkɪŋ] [jaus-brei-kin], *s.* robo de noche con quebrantamiento de puertas.

house-dog [ˈhaʊsdɒg] [jaus-dog], *s.* Mastín, perro de guarda.

housefather [ˈhaʊsfɑːðəʳ] [jaus-fa-daʳ], *s.* Cabeza de familia.

housefly [ˈhaʊsflaɪ] [jaus-flai], *s.* Mosca común o doméstica.

household [ˈhaʊshəʊld] [jaus-jould], *s.* 1. Casa, la familia que vive junta en una casa. **King's household,** la casa real. 2. Manejo doméstico, gobierno de casa. **Household furniture,** el ajuar o menaje de una casa. **Household bread,** pan casero o bazo.

householder [ˈhaʊsˌhəʊldəʳ] [jaus-joul-daʳ], *s.* Amo de casa, padre de familia.

household-stuff [ˈhaʊshəʊldˌstʌf] [jaus-jould-staf], *s.* Ajuar o muebles de una casa.

housekeeper [ˈhaʊsˌkiːpəʳ] [jaus-ki-paʳ], *s.* 1. Ama de gobierno o ama de llaves, la mujer que tiene el gobierno económico de una casa. 2. La persona casera o que está casi siempre en casa. 3. Amo de casa, padre de familia.

housekeeping [ˈhaʊsˌkiːpɪŋ] [jaus-ki-pin], *s.* El manejo de los asuntos domésticos, caseros; cuidado de la casa. *-a.* Doméstico, casero.

house-lamb [ˈhaʊslæmb] [jaus-lamb], *s.* Cordero criado y engordado en casa.

houseleek [ˈhaʊliːk] [jaus-lik], *s. (Bot.)* Siempreviva o hierba puntera.

houseless [ˈhaʊslɪs] [jaus-les], *a.* Sin habitación o sin casa.

house-maid [ˈhaʊsmeɪd] [jaus-meid], *s.* Criada de casa. **House-maid's knee,** *(Med.)* higroma, hidrartrosis.

housemother [ˈhaʊsˌmʌðəʳ] [jaus-ma-daʳ], *s.* 1. Madre de familia. 2. Mujer encargada de una residencia de estudiantes.

house of cards, *s.* Castillo de naipes, construcción frágil.

house of correction, *s.* Casa correccional, reformatorio.

house organ [ˈhaʊsˌɔːgən] [jaus-or-gan], *s.* Órgano de publicidad de una institución u organización.

house party [ˈhaʊsˌpɑːtɪ] [jaus-par-ti], *s.* 1. Fiesta (in a country house) en que los invitados permanecen más de un día. 2. Los invitados a una casa de campo por más de un día.

house-pigeon [ˈhaʊsˌpɪdʒən] [jaus-pi-chon], *s.* Paloma mansa o doméstica.

house-rent [ˈhaʊsrent] [jaus-rent], *s.* Alquiler de casa, lo que se paga por ella.

house-room [ˈhaʊsrʊm] [jaus-rum], *s.* Cabida de una casa.

house-stuff [ˈhaʊsstʌf] [jaus-staf], *s.* Menaje, alhajas.

housetop [ˈhaʊstɒp] [jaus-top], *s.* Techo, tejado, azotea. **To shout from the housetops,** pregonar a los cuatro vientos.

house-warming [ˈhaʊsˌwɔːmɪŋ] [jaus-uor-min], *s.* Recepción y convite que se dan al tiempo de estrenar una casa nueva.

housewife [ˈhaʊswaɪf] [jaus-uaif], *sf.* 1. Ama de una casa; madre de familia. 2. Ama de gobierno o de llaves. 3. Mujer casera y económica. 4. Costurero, cajita o saquito que contiene alfileres, agujas, tijeras, etc. *(Mex.)* Almohadilla.

housewifely [ˈhaʊswaɪflɪ] [jaus-uaif-li], *adv.* Con la economía de una mujer casera. *-a.* Lo que pertenece a la mujer que sabe gobernar bien una casa.

housework [ˈhaʊswɜːk] [jaus-uek], *s.* Quehaceres domésticos, labores caseras.

housing [ˈhaʊzɪŋ] [jau-sin], *s.* 1. Mantilla, el adorno que cubre las ancas del caballo, gualdrapa; comúnmente en plural. 2. Habitación, alojamiento; abrigo contra la intemperie (shelter). 3. *(Arq.)* Nicho para colocar una estatua. 4. *(Art. y Of.)* Muesca, encaje de una viqueta; hueco hecho en una pieza para recibir parte de otra. **Housing cooperative,** cooperativa de la vivienda. **Housing subsidy,** subsidio por vivienda. **Housing project,** proyecto para construir viviendas.

housing, *s. (Mar.)* Piola, cabito de tres filásticas que sirve para varios usos.

hove [həʊv] [jouv], *pret.* del verbo TO HEAVE.

hove, *s.* Enfermedad propia de la raza bovina. *V.* HOOVE.

hovel ['hɒvəl] [jo-vel], *s.* Cobertizo, choza, cabaña.

hovel, *va.* Abrigar en cabaña.

hover ['hɒvəʳ] [jo-vaʳ], *vn.* 1. Revolotear, aletear (flutter); rondar, dar vueltas alrededor de un mismo paraje (round). 2. Colgar, estar suspenso en el aire. 3. Dudar, estar suspenso, en la incertidumbre. 4. Estar durante algún tiempo entre la vida y la muerte. 5. Asomar una sonrisa o alguna expresión.

how [haʊ] [jau], *adv.* Como, de qué modo; cuan, cuánto; a qué precio; hasta qué punto; en qué extensión; por qué. **How far?,** ¿a qué distancia?, ¿cuánto dista? **How long?,** ¿cuánto tiempo? **How do you do?,** ¿cómo le va a Ud.? ¿cómo está Ud.? **How so?,** ¿por qué? ¿cómo así? **How great soever,** por grande que sea. **How d'ye do?,** ¿cómo lo pasa Ud.?, ¿qué tal? **How is it?** ¿cómo es? ¿cómo sucede? **How now?,** ¿pues qué?, ¿qué significa eso? **How do you sell apples?,** ¿a cómo vende Ud. las manzanas? **To know how,** saber. **To know how to write,** saber escribir.

howbeit ['haʊbeɪt] [jau-beit], *adv.* Sea como sea, sin embargo, de cualquier modo que.

howdah ['haʊdɑː] [jau-da], *s.* Castillo que se pone sobre el elefante.

howel ['haʊəl] [jauel], *s.* Doladera, azuela de tonelero.

however [haʊˈevəʳ] [jau-e-vaʳ], *adv.* 1. Sin embargo, como quiera que sea. 2. En todo caso, al menos, a lo menos. 3. No obstante, sin embargo. **However clever he is,** por muy listo que sea. **However that may be,** sea como sea.

howitzer ['haʊɪtsəʳ] [jaui-chaʳ], *s.* Obús, especie de mortero.

howl [haʊl] [jaul], *vn.* 1. Aullar: se dice del lobo y el perro. 2. Dar alaridos, quejarse tristemente. 3. Rugir, bramar, como el viento o la tempestad. -*va.* Gritar, chillar, hablar gritando.

howl, *s.* 1. Aullido (wolves, dogs). 2. Alarido. 3. Rugido.

howler ['haʊləʳ] [jau-laʳ], *s.* 1. Aullador, el que aúlla; gritador. 2. Mono de la América tropical de voz muy fuerte y penetrante.

howlet, *s. V.* OWL.

howling ['haʊlɪŋ] [jau-lin], *s.* Aullido; grito, lamento. *V.* HOWL.

howsoever [haʊsəˈevəʳ] [jau], *adv.* Como quiera; aunque.

hoy [hɔɪ] [joi], *s. (Mar.)* Buque de pasaje de una cubierta. -*inter. (Mar.)* ¡Hola!

hoyden ['hɔɪdn] [joi-den], *s.* Muchacha traviesa.

hub [hʌb] [jab], *s.* 1. Cubo, maza de la rueda. 2. Por extensión, cualquier cosa céntrica por su posición o importancia. 3. Clavo, perno a que se arroja el tejo. **The Hub,** (Jocoso) La ciudad de boston en Massachusetts.

hubbub ['hʌbʌb] [ja-bab], *s.* Grito, ruido; alboroto, tumulto, batahola, bulla, enredo.

hub cap, hub cover ['hʌbkæp] [jab-kap] ['hʌbkʌvəʳ] [jab-ka-vaʳ], *s.* Tapacubos.

Hubert ['hʌbɜːt] [ja-bert], *n. pr.* Huberto.

huckaback [ˌhʌkəˈbæk] [jak-a-bak], *s.* Alemanisco, lienzo basto adamascado para servilletas.

huckle, *s. V.* HIP.

huckle-backed ['hʌkl] [ja-kel], *a.* Jorobado.

huckleberry [ˌhʌklˈberi] [ja-kel-be-ri], *s. (Bot.)* Arándano, la baya comestible del género Gaylussacia.

hucklebone ['hʌklbəʊn] [ja-kel-baun], *s.* Cía, el hueso de la cadera.

huckster ['hʌkstəʳ] [jaks-taʳ], *s.* 1. Regatón, revendedor, el que revende géneros por menor. 2. Perillán, pícaro astuto y vagamundo.

huckster, *vn.* Regatonear.

hucksteress ['hʌkstərɪs] [jaks-te-res], *sf.* Regatona revendedora.

huddle ['hʌdl] [ja-del], *va.* 1. Tapujar, arrebujar, confundir, mezclar. 2. Hacer las cosas precipitada y confusamente. -*vn.* Venir en tropel o confusamente.

huddle, *s.* 1. Tropel, confusión, baraúnda, alboroto, desorden. 2. Reunión secreta.

huddler ['hʌdləʳ] [jad-laʳ], *s.* El que hace o pone las cosas confusamente; chapucero.

hue [hjuː] [jiu], *s.* 1. Color, tez del rostro; matiz de un color. 2. Clamor, alarma que se da contra un criminal. En esta última significación **hue** va casi siempre junto con **cry.**

huff [hʌf] [jaf], *s.* Bufido, gruñido (grunt); altivez. **In a huff,** encolerizado, enojado, ofendido.

huff, *va.* 1. Hinchar, inflar (swell). 2. Bufar, bravear; maltratar de palabra, tratar con aspereza o insolencia. 3. Soplar una dama en el juego. -*vn.* 1. Hincharse, engreírse. 2. Patear de enfado.

huffish ['hʌfɪʃ] [ja-fish], *a.* Arrogante, insolente, petulante, impertinente.

huffishness ['hʌfɪʃnɪs] [ja-fish-nes], *s.* Petulancia, arrogancia, insolencia (insolence), impertinencia.

huffy ['hʌfɪ] [ja-fi], *a.* 1. Arrogante, petulante, que se ofende fácilmente; malhumorado (bad tempered). 2. Hinchado, engreído.

hug [hʌg] [jag], *va.* 1. Abrazar (embrace), acariciar, halagar. 2. Abrazarse a alguna cosa fuertemente. 3. Aplaudirse o felicitarse de una ventaja supuesta. 4. *(Mar.)* Navegar muy cerca de la costa. **To hug the wind,** ceñir el viento.

hug, *s.* Abrazo apretado. *A cornish hug,* Una zancadilla.

huge [hjuːdʒ] [jiuch], *a.* Vasto (vast), inmenso, grande (big), enorme. **It was a huge success,** fue un éxito enorme.

hugely ['hjuːdʒlɪ] [jiuch-li], *adv.* Enormemente, extremadamente.

hugeness ['hjuːdʒnɪs] [jiuch-nes], *s.* Magnitud o grandeza enorme.

hugenot ['hjuːdʒnɒt] [jiuch-not], *s.* Hugonote: nombre que se dio en Francia a los protestantes.

huh ['hʌ] [ju], *interj.* ¿Qué?, ¡ja!, sí, sí.

hula-hula ['huːləˌhuːlə] [ju-la-ju-la], *s.* Baile típico de Hawaii.

hulk [hʌlk] [jalk], *s.* 1. *(Mar.)* Casco de la embarcación; particularmente uno viejo y en mal estado; casco abandonado de buque náufrago, restos (wreck). 2. Armatoste, cualquier cosa tosca y pesada; masa, cuerpo abultado.

hulk, *va.* Desentrañar.

hulking ['hʌlkɪŋ] [jal-kin], *a. (Coloq.)* Grandote, descomunal. **A hulking great brute,** una bestia de hombre.

hull [hʌl] [jal], *s.* 1. Cáscara, la corteza y cubierta de las frutas y de algunas otras cosas. **Hull of a bean,** vaina o vainilla de las habas. 2. *(Mar.)* Casco y cuerpo de la embarcación, el buque sin palos ni jarcias. **A-hull,** *(Mar.)* a palo seco.

hull, *vn. (Des.)* Navegar a palo seco. -*va.* 1. Mondar, pelar, quitar a los frutos su cáscara, vaina o vainilla. 2. Disparar cañonazos contra el casco de un buque.

hullabaloo [ˌhʌləbəˈluː] [ja-la-ba-lu], *s.* Alboroto, batahola, bulla, tumulto, jaleo (fuss).

huller ['hʌləʳ] [ja-laʳ], *s.* Descascarador.

hullo ['hʌlə] [ja-lo], *v. s.* e *inter.* Lo mismo que HALLOO.

hully ['hʌlɪ] [ja-li], *a.* Cascarudo.

hulver, *s. V.* HOLLY.

hum [hʌm] [jam], *va.* y *vn.* 1. Zumbar. 2. Hablar entre dientes, susurrar; decir *hum* al verse sorprendido o desconcertado. *V.* HEM. 3. Roncar; susurrar, hacer un ruido monótono como el zumbido de un moscón. 4. Cantar o hablar en voz baja; canturriar. 5. Engañar. 6. Apestar (stink), oler mal.

hum, *s.* 1. Zumbido, baraúnda; ruido suave. 2. Voz inarticulada (como *hem*) con que se expresa aprobación o disentimiento. 3. Burla, chasco. -*inter.* ¡Ya! interjección con que se da a entender duda o suspensión. **To make things hum** o **to keep things humming,** *(Fam. E. U.)* Ejecutar cosas de una manera viva y fogosa; ser muy activo.

human ['hjuːmən] [jiu-man], *a.* Humano. **I'm only human,** todos somos humanos. -*s.* Humano. **Human being,** ser humano. **A wonderful human being,** una persona estupenda.

humane [hjuːˈmeɪn] [jiu-mein], *a.* Humano, humanitario, apacible, compasivo, afable, benigno; cortés.

humanely [hjuːˈmeɪnlɪ] [jiu-mein-li], *adv.* Humanamente, benignamente.

humanism [ˈhjuːmənɪzəm] [jiu-ma-ni-sem], *s.* Humanismo, literatura castiza y elegante; cultura derivada de las letras humanas o clásicas.

humanist [ˈhjuːmənɪst] [jiu-ma-nist], *s.* Humanista, el que profesa las buenas letras o las humanidades.

humanitarian [hjuːˌmænɪˈtɛərɪən] [jiu-ma-ni-tea-rian], *a.* Humanitario. -s. 1. Filántropo. 2. El que cree que Jesucristo no fue más que un hombre. 3. El que profesa la doctrina de que los deberes del hombre se limitan a hacer bien a los demás y a procurar la mayor felicidad del género humano.

humanity [hjuːˈmænɪtɪ] [jiu-ma-ni-ti], *s.* 1. Humanidad. 2. El género humano colectivamente. **Crimes against humanity,** crímenes contra la humanidad. 3. Humanidad, benignidad, ternura, dulzura, benevolencia, 4. Humanidades o letras humanas.

humanize [hjuːˈmænɪtɪ] [jiu-ma-ni-ti], *va.* Humanar, humanizar, quitar la ferocidad, suavizar las costumbres.

humankind [ˈhjuːmənˈkaɪnd] [jiu-man-kaind], *s.* El linaje humano, la especie humana.

humanly [ˈhjuːmənlɪ] [jiu-man-li], *adv.* 1. Humanamente. 2. V. HUMANELY.

human nature [ˈhjuːmənˌneɪtʃər] [jiu-man-nei-chaʳ], *s.* Naturaleza humana.

human rights [ˈhjuːmənraɪts] [jiu-man-raits], *s.pl.* Derechos humanos

humble [ˈhʌmbl] [jam-bel], *a.* Humilde, modesto (modest), sumiso, bajo, casero. **In my humble opinion,** en mi modesta opinión.

humble, *va.* 1. Humillar (humiliate), postrar, abatir el orgullo y la soberbia. 2. Domar, aniquilar, abatir, confundir. **The battle of Waterloo humbled the power of Napoleon,** la batalla de Waterloo aniquiló el poder de Napoleón.

humble-bee [ˈhʌmblbiː] [jam-bel-bi], *s.* Abeja grande y silvestre. V. BUMBLE-BEE.

humble-mouthed [ˈhʌmblˈmaʊθɪd] [jam-bel-mau-zid], *a.* Manso, blando.

humbleness [ˈhʌmblnɪs] [jam-bel-nes], *s.* Humildad.

humble-pie [ˈhʌmblpaɪ] [jam-bel-pai], *s.* Empanada hecha de los despojos de venado, que solía servirse a los monteros y criados. **To eat humble-pie,** dar excusas, desdecirse, retractarse.

humbler [ˈhʌmbləʳ] [jam-blaʳ], *s.* Humillador.

humbles [ˈhʌmblz] [jam-bels], *s. pl.* Despojo o entrañas de venado.

humbling [ˈhʌmblɪŋ] [jam-blin], *s.* Humillación, abatimiento, rendimiento.

humbly [ˈhʌmblɪ] [jam-bli], *adv.* Humildemente, modestamente (modestly).

humbug [ˈhʌmbʌg] [jam-bag], *s.* 1. Trampantojo, bola, patraña (nonsense), engañifa, engaño, decepción, trampa, embuste, fraude, dolo. 2. Vaya, cantaleta, zumba.

humbug, *va.* Embaucar, engañar; chasquear.

humdinger [ˈhʌmdɪŋəʳ] [jam-din-gaʳ], *s. (Coloq.)* Maravilla, portento.

humdrum [ˈhʌmdrʌm] [jam-dram], *a.* Torpe, sin interés ni aliciente, monótono (monotonous), trivial. -vn. Pasar el tiempo torpe o monótonamente. -s. 1. Fastidio; enojo, fatiga. 2. Habla, dejo o tono fastidioso. 3. Pesadilla, persona cargante, fastidiosa.

humective [ˈhʌmɪktɪv] [jiu-mik-tiv], *a.* Humectativo, que humedece.

humeral [ˈhjuːmərəl] [jiu-me-ral], *a.* Humeral, lo que pertenece al hombro.

humerus [ˈhjuːmərəs] [jiu-me-ros], *s. (Anat.)* Húmero.

humid [ˈhjuːmɪd] [jiu-mid], *a.* Húmedo.

humidifier [hjuːˈmɪdɪfaɪəʳ] [jiu-mi-di-faiaʳ], *s.* Humedecedor, humectador, humidificador.

humidify [hjuːˈmɪdɪfaɪ] [jiu-mi-di-fai], *va.* Humedecer.

humidistat [hjuːˈmɪdɪstæt] [jiu-mi-dis-tat], *s.* Regulador de humedad.

humidity [hjuːˈmɪdɪtɪ] [jiu-mi-di-ti], *s.* Humedad.

humidor [ˈhjuːmɪdəʳ] [jiu-mi-daʳ], *s.* 1. Caja acondicionada para conservar el tabaco humedecido. 2. Dispositivo con esponjas mojadas para conservar el aire humedecido.

humiliate [hjuːˈmɪlɪeɪt] [jiu-mi-lieit], *vt.* Humillar.

humiliating [hjuːˈmɪlɪeɪtɪŋ] [jiu-mi-liei-tin], *a.* Humillante.

humiliation [hjuːˌmɪlɪˈeɪʃən] [jiu-mi-liei-shon], *s.* Humillación, mortificación.

humility [hjuːˈmɪlɪtɪ] [jiu-mi-li-ti], *s.* Humildad, sumisión, rendimiento.

hummer [ˈhʌməʳ] [ja-maʳ], *s.* Zumbón.

humming [ˈhʌmɪŋ] [ja-min], *s.* Zumbido.

hummingbird [ˈhʌmɪŋbɜːd] [ja-min-berd], *s.* Colibrí, pájaro mosca; *(Cent. Amer.)* guainambí.

humor, humour [ˈhjuːməʳ] [jiu-maʳ], *s.* 1. Humor, sustancia tenue y fluida del cuerpo animal. 2. Humor (mood), carácter, genio, índole, natural, humorada, fantasía, capricho. 3. Sal, agudeza, chanza de buen gusto, inofensiva. 4. Erupción cutánea que se supone debida al mal estado de la sangre. **Broad humor,** farsa, acción jocosa y burlesca. **Dry humor,** chiste socarrón, dicho agudo. **To be in humor,** estar de buen humor. **To take one in the humor,** llegarse a alguno en un momento favorable.

humor, *va.* 1. Satisfacer, agradar (please), complacer, dar gusto, acceder; consentir en; mimar. 2. Cumplir, ejecutar lo que a uno se le manda. 3. Adaptarse, acomodarse a; desempeñar bien. **A player who humors hispart,** un actor que desempeña bien su papel. **A good-humored man,** hombre de buen humor. **To humor a song,** dar alma y viveza a lo que se canta.

humoral [ˈhjuːmərəl] [jiu-mo-ral], *a. (Med.)* Humoral.

humoralism, humorism [ˈhjuːmərəlɪzm] [jiu-mo-ra-li-sem], *s.* 1. Humorismo, la doctrina médica que hace depender las enfermedades de los humores. 2. El ingenio y la gracia en el decir de un escritor festivo.

humorist [ˈhjuːmərɪst] [jiu-mo-rist], *s.* 1. Humorista, escritor festivo. 2. Chocarrero, bufón.

humorless [ˈhjuːmələs] [jiu-mo-les], *a.* Sin sentido del humor.

humorous [ˈhjuːmərəs] [jiu-mo-ros], *a.* 1. Grotesco (hideous), extravagante, voluntarioso, caprichoso, antojadizo, caprichudo. 2. Festivo, chistoso, juguetón, placentero.

humorously [ˈhjuːmərəslɪ] [jiu-mo-ros-li], *adv.* Jocosamente; caprichosamente.

humorousness [ˈhjuːmərəsnɪs] [jiu-mo-ros-nes], *s.* Inconstancia, antojo, impertinencia; humorada.

humorsome [ˈhjuːmərsəm] [jiu-mo-som], *a.* Petulante, enojoso, caprichoso, impertinencia; humorada.

humorsome, *a.* Petulante, enojoso, caprichoso, impertinente, voluntarioso.

hump [hʌmp] [jamp], *s.* Giba, joroba, corcova, -va. 1. Doblar, encorvar la espalda. 2. *vr. (Ger.)* Apurarse, hacer un esfuerzo, tomarse el trabajo.

humpbacked [ˈhʌmpbækt] [jamp-bakt], *a.* Jorobado (hunchback), corcovado, giboso.

humped [ˈhʌmpt] [jampt], *a.* Jorobado, corcovado.

humpy [ˈhʌmpɪ] [jam-pi], *a.* Giboso, marcado o caracterizado por protuberancias.

humus [ˈhjuːməs] [iu-mos], *s.* Humus, mantillo.

hun [hʌn] [jan], *s.* Huno, pueblo procedente de la Sarmacia asiática.

hunch [hʌntʃ] [janch], *va.* 1. Dar de puñadas o de codazos. 2. Hacer a uno giboso o corcovado.

hunch, *s.* 1. Golpe, puñado, codazo. 2. Giba, corcova. 3. *(Coloq.)* Presentimiento (premonition), pálpito, corazonada. **I have a hunch that you will pass the exam,** tengo el presentimiento de que aprobarás el examen.

hunchbacked [ˈhʌntʃbækt] [janch-bakt], *a.* V. HUMPBACKED.

hundred [ˈhʌndrɪd] [jan-drid], *a.* Ciento. -s. 1. Centena o centenar, un ciento. **Five hundred pages,** quinientas páginas. **By hundreds,** a centenares. **A hundred-weight,** quintal, el peso de cien libras o cuatro arrobas. **Hundred-fold,** céntuplo, cien veces una cantidad cualquiera. **To**

increase a hundredfold, centuplicar. 2. División de los contados en Inglaterra en ciertos distritos.

hundreder [ˈhʌndrəd] [jan-dred], *s.* 1. Un individuo del jurado, cuando éste se reúne para decidir sobre la adjudicación de posesiones situadas en el distrito donde se junta el jurado. 2. El que tiene la jurisdicción del distrito llamado en inglés *hundred.*

hundredth [ˈhʌndrɪθ] [jan-driz], *a.* Centésimo.

hung [hʌŋ] [jang], *pret. y pp.* del verbo TO HANG. **Hung beef,** cecina de vaca.

Hungarian [hʌŋˈɡɛərɪən] [jan-guea-rian], *a.* Húngaro, de Hungría. *-s.* Lengua húngara, húngaro. **Hungarian goulash,** guiso de carne y verduras de origen húngaro.

Hungary [ˈhʌŋɡərɪ] [jan-ga-ri], *s.* Hungría.

hungary-water [ˈhʌŋɡərɪˌwɔːtəʳ] [jan-ga-ri-uo-taʳ], *s.* Agua de la Reina de Hungría: nombre de un perfume.

hunger [ˈhʌŋɡəʳ] [jan-gaʳ], *s.* 1. Hambre, ganas de comer. **Pinched with hunger,** acosado de hambre. **Starved with hunger,** muerto de hambre. **Hunger strike,** huelga de hambre. 2. Hambre, sed, deseo grande de algo. **A hunger for learning,** ansia de aprender, hambre por aprender.

hunger, *vn.* Hambrear; desear con ansia. *-va. V.* FAMISH.

hungerbit, hungerbitten [ˈhʌŋɡəbɪt] [jan-ga-bit], *a.* Presa del hambre, atormentado por el hambre.

hungrily [ˈhʌŋɡrɪlɪ] [jan-gri-li], *adv.* Hambrientamente, ávidamente.

hungry [ˈhʌŋɡrɪ] [jan-gri], *a.* 1. Hambriento, acosado de hambre; voraz. 2. Estéril, infecundo, pobre. **To be hungry, to feel hungry,** tener hambre.

hunk [hʌŋk] [jank], *s. (Fam.)* Pedazo de buen tamaño, rebanada gruesa, trozo (chunk).

hunks [hʌŋks] [janks], *s.* Hombre sórdido y avaro.

hunt [hʌnt] [jant], *va.* 1. Montear, cazar, 2. Seguir, perseguir, 3. Buscar (search). 4. Guiar los perros en la caza. *-vn.* 1. Cazar; ir de caza. 2. Seguir la pista a, ir en busca de; correr tras de. **To hunt out,** buscar con empeño, descubrir. **To hunt after,** buscar, desear con ansia. **To hunt up and down,** buscar por todos lados. **To hunt after riches,** correr tras la fortuna, tras las riquezas.

hunt, *s.* 1. Jauría, cuadrilla de perros podencos para cazar. 2. Caza (chase), la acción y acto de cazar. 3. Perseguimiento, acosamiento. 4. Asociación de cazadores. 5. Búsqueda (search).

hunted [ˈhʌntɪd] [jan-tid], *a.* Atormentado, acorralado, perseguido (pursued).

hunter [ˈhʌntəʳ] [jan-taʳ], *s.* 1. Montero, cazador de monte. 2. Podenco, perro que olfatea la caza. 3. Caballo de caza. **Hunter's cap,** montera o gorra que usan los cazadores.

hunting [ˈhʌntɪŋ] [jan-tin], *s.* Montería, caza, cacería.

hunting, en composición: **Hunting-box, hunting-lodge,** pabellón de caza, punto de cita de los cazadores. **Hunting-case,** cubierta de saboneta. **Hunting-ground,** terreno favorable para la caza. **Happy hunting-grounds,** el cielo o paraíso de los indios norteamericanos. **Hunting-horn,** corneta de montería, trompa de caza. **Hunting-horse,** caballo de caza. **Hunting-match,** partida de caza. **Hunting-watch, hunting-case watch,** reloj de caza, saboneta.

huntress [ˈhʌntrɪs] [jan-tres], *sf.* Cazadora.

huntsman [ˈhʌntzmən] [jants-man], *s.* Montero, cazador de monte.

huntsmanship [ˈhʌntzmənˌʃɪp] [jants-man-ship], *s.* Calidades necesarias para ser buen cazador.

hunt's-up [ˈhʌntsʌp] [jants-ap], *s.* Toque matinal con la trompa de caza para despertar a los monteros; de aquí, cualquier cosa que despierta.

hurdies [ˈhɜːdɪz] [jer-dis], *s. pl. (Esco.)* Las nalgas.

hurdle [ˈhɜːdl] [jer-del], *s.* 1. Zarzo, tejido compuesto de varas o mimbres. *(Mil.)* Fagina, haz o cesto de mimbres que se usa para fortificar. 3. Especie de serón en que llevaban los reos a la horca o al suplicio. 4. Obstáculo (obstacle).

hurdle, *va.* Hacer cercas de palos y mimbres; defender con faginas.

hurdler [ˈhɜːdləʳ] [jer-dlaʳ], *s.* Corredor de vallas.

hurdles [ˈhɜːdlz] [jer-dels], *s.* 1. Carrera de vallas. 2. Vallas. **100 meters hurdles,** cien metros vallas.

hurl [hɜːl] [jerl], *va.* 1. Tirar, precipitar o impeler con violencia, arrojar (throw). 2. Gritar, llamar con vehemencia. *-vn.* 1. Moverse o lanzarse rápidamente. 2. Jugar al palocorvo. **To hurl oneself into ruin,** arruinarse, perderse. **To hurl out,** gritar, dar alaridos.

hurl, *s.* Tiro, el acto de tirar o arrojar; lanzamiento.

hurlbat [ˈhɜːlbæt] [jerl-bat], *s.* Especie de garrote o cachiporra.

hurler [ˈhɜːləʳ] [jer-laʳ], *s.* El que arroja o impele; el que juega a una especie de juego de pelota llamado *hurling.*

hurley [ˈhɜːlɪ] [jer-li], *s.* 1. El juego de aplocorvo. 2. Palo encorvado para este juego.

hurling [ˈhɜːlɪŋ] [jer-lin], *s.* 1. Antiguo juego de pelota semejante al de *football.* 2. En Irlanda, especie de juego de pelota, palocorvo.

hurly-burly [ˌhɜːlɪˈbɜːlɪ] [jer-li-ber-li], **Hurly,** *s.* Baraúnda, alboroto, tumulto, confusión.

hurrah, hurra [hʊˈrɑː] [ju-ra], *inter.* Exclamación de aplauso o alegría que corresponde casi siempre a ¡viva! *-va y vn.* Animar, alentar con vivas; vitorear, aplaudir. **Hurrah for!,** ¡viva!

hurricane [ˈhʌrɪkən] [ja-ri-ken], *s.* Huracán, gran tempestad; originalmente, ciclón.

hurricane lamp [ˈhʌrɪkənˌlæmp] [ja-ri-ken-lamp], *s.* Farol.

hurried [ˈhʌrɪd] [ja-rid], *a. y pp.* de TO HURRY. Precipitado, apresurado (rushed), hecho de prisa. **A hurried note,** un billete escrito a escape. **Hurried away,** llevado por la fuerza, arrastrado, arrebatado.

hurriedly [ˈhʌrɪdlɪ] [ja-rid-li], *adv.* Apresuradamente. **She left hurriedly,** se fue apresuradamente.

hurrier [ˈhʌrɪəʳ] [ja-riaʳ], *s.* 1. Acelerador, apresurador. 2. *(G.B.)* El trabajador que saca un carretón de hulla de una mina de carbón de piedra.

hurry [ˈhʌrɪ] [ja-ri], *va.* 1. Acelerar, apresurar, dar prisa. 2. Atropellar; precipitar (hasten), no dar respiro; confundir a fuerza de prisa. *-vn.* 1. Atropellarse, apresurarse. 2. (GB) Arrastrar un carretón en una mina de carbón de piedra.

hurry away, llevar, traer o salir precipitadamente.

hurry after, correr detrás o en pos de.

hurry back, volver (o hacer volver) de prisa; apresurarse a volver.

hurry in, hacer entrar deprisa; entrar con precipitación en.

hurry into, arrastrar, impeler hacia.

hurry off, huir, salir deprisa; hacer partir con precipitación.

hurry on, apresurar, precipitar; impulsar, empujar; apresurarse.

hurry over, hacer pasar rápidamente; despachar, expedir; pasar apresuradamente.

hurry up, darse prisa, apresurarse.

hurry, *s.* 1. Precipitación, demasiada prisa. 2. Confusión, desorden.

hurry-skurry, hurry-scurry [ˈhʌrɪˈskʌrɪ] [ja-ri-ska-ri], *adv.* Confusamente, con ruido y tumulto.

hurst [hɜːst] [jerst], *s.* Bosquecillo, montecillo poblado de árboles.

hurt [hɜːt] [jert], *va. (pret. y pp.* HURT) 1. Dañar, hacer mal o daño; herir; ofender. 2. Perjudicar a alguien en sus intereses; herir la delicadeza de alguno. **To hurt one's feelings,** dar que sentir, lastimar. **He has hurt his leg,** el se ha lastimado la pierna. **She hurt his head,** ella le hirió en la cabeza. **That does not hurt you,** eso no le hace a Ud. daño.

hurt, *a.* 1. Golpe, herida, contusión. 2. Mal. daño, perijuicio. **What hurt is there in that?,** ¿qué hay de malo en eso? I have done it to my hurt, lo he hecho en perjuicio mío. *- a.* Latimado, dolido en los sentimientos. **I feel hurt,** estoy dolido.

hurter [ˈhɜːtəʳ] [jer-taʳ], *s.* 1. Dañador, el que daña o hiere. 2. Viga que se pone frente a las ruedas de los cañones para proteger la muralla o parapeto.

hurtful [ˈhɜːtfʊl] [jert-ful], *a.* Pernicioso, dañoso, nocivo (harmful), funesto, dañino, hiriente.

hurtfully [ˈhɜːtfʊlɪ] [jert-fu-li], *adv.* Dañosamente, perniciosamente.

hurtle [hɜːtl] [jer-tel], *vn.* Encontrarse; rechinar; arrojarse con violencia hacia adelante; girar. *-va.* Menear, empujar con violencia; dar vueltas; blandir.

hurtleberry, *s. V.* HUCKLEBERRY y WHORTLEBERRY.

hurtless [ˈhɜːtlɪs] [jert-les], *a.* 1. Inocente que no hace daño. 2. Ileso (unharmed), intacto, que no ha recibido daño.

hurtlessly [ˈhɜːtlɪslɪ] [jert-les-li], *adv.* Inocentemente.

hurtlessness [ˈhɜːtlɪsnɪs] [jert-les-nes], *s.* Inocencia.

husband [ˈhʌzbənd] [jas-band], *s.* 1. Marido, esposo. **Husband and wife,** marido y mujer. 2. *(Ant.)* Hombre económico, comedido, frugal en sus gastos.

husband, *va.* 1. Gobernar con economía y frugalidad, ahorrar (save), economizar. 2. Procurar marido a alguna mujer. 3. Ser marido de; hacer el papel de marido; pasar por tal.

husbandless [ˈhʌzbəndlɪs] [jas-band-les], *a.* Soltera (single), viuda: se dice de la mujer sin marido.

husbandman [ˈhʌzbəndmən] [jas-band-man], *s.* Labrador, viñador.

husbandry [ˈhʌzbəndrɪ] [jas-ban-dri], *s.* 1. Labranza, agricultura. 2. Frugalidad, economía, parsimonia, ahorro. 3. El gobierno económico de la casa. **Animal husbandry,** cría de animales.

hush [hʌʃ] [jash], *interj.* ¡Chitón! *-s.* ¡Silencio! *-a.* Quieto, callado.

hush, *va.* 1. Apaciguar, aquietar, sosegar, acallar (quieten). 2. Mitigar, calmar. 3. Callar. **To hush up,** ocultar, mantener secreto. *-vn.* Estar quieto, estar callado.

hushaby [ˈhʌʃəbaɪ] [ja-sha-bai], *interj.* ¡A dormir! Voz que se usa para haçer dormir a los niños. *-a.* Propenso a amodorrar o apaciguar.

hushed [hʌʃt] [jash], *a.* Silencioso. **In hushed tones,** en voz muy baja.

hush money [ˈhʌʃˌmʌnɪ] [jash-ma-ni], *s.* El dinero que se da a alguno para comprar su silencio.

husk [hʌsk] [jask], *s.* 1. Cáscara, vaina, vainilla, pellejo, hollejo de frutos, legumbres, semillas, etc. 2. Alguna cosa de mínimo valor que cubre la parte útil o esencial; bagazo; desperdicio.

husk, *va.* Descansar, desvainar, mondar, despellejar, deshollejar.

husked [hʌskt] [jaskt], *a.* Lo que tiene cáscara, vaina o pellejo.

husker [ˈhʌskəʳ] [jas-kaʳ], *s.* El que o lo que descascara, desvaina, etc.; descascaradora, desgranadora, máquina para descascarar el maíz.

huskiness [ˈhʌskɪnɪs] [jas-ki-nes], *s.* 1. Ronquera. 2. El estado de tener cáscara, vaina o pellejo.

huskily [ˈhʌskɪlɪ] [jas-ki-li], *adv.* Roncamente, secamente.

husky [ˈhʌskɪ] [jas-ki], *a.* 1. Lo que abunda, en vainas o cáscaras. 2. Ronco; falto de claridad; seco. *-s.* Perro esquimal.

hussar [həˈzɑːʳ] [ja-saʳ], *s.* Húsar, soldado de caballería ligera.

hussy [ˈhʌsɪ] [ja-si], *s.* 1. Buena maula, buena alhaja, picudilla. 2. Una especie de estuche para poner agujas, hilo, etc. *V.* HOUSEWIFE.

hustings [ˈhʌstɪŋz] [jas-tins], *s.* 1. El tablado que se levanta para verificar la elección de los individuos de la cámara de los comunes. 2. Consejo o tribunal en la ciudad de Londres. Se usa algunas veces en singular. **The hustings,** la campaña electoral.

hustle [ˈhʌsl] [ja-sel], *va.* Escaramuzar; mezclar, confundir; empujar con fuerza, sacudir. *-vn.* 1. Moverse con dificultad en un tropel; apiñarse, adelantarse dando empujones. 2.

(Fam. E. U.) Moverse con prisa y prontitud; demostrar energía y perseverancia. *-s.* 1. Ajetreo (hurry). **The hustle and bustle of the big city,** el ajetreo y el bullicio de la gran ciudad. 2. Empuje (energy), garra. 3. *(Coloq.)* Chanchullo (swindle).

hustler [ˈhʌsləʳ] [jas-laʳ], *s.* 1. *(Fam. E. U.)* Hombre de gran energía y actividad. 2. Estafador (swindler).

huswife [ˈhʌswaɪf] [jas-uaif], *s. sf. 1. V.* HOUSEWIFE. 2. *V.* HUSSY. *-va.* Gobernar la casa con economía.

hut [hʌt] [jat], *s.* Choza, cabaña (cabin, shack), barraca.

hut, *va.* Acumular, almacenar o abrigar en una choza o chozas. *-vn.* Vivir en una choza o chozas; alojarse en chozas.

hutch [hʌtʃ] [jach], *s.* 1. Arca, cesto, cofre. 2. Trampa para coger ratones. 3. Caja para guardar y alimentar conejos.

hutch, *va.* Atesorar, recoger.

huzza [hʌˈzɑː] [ja-sa], *interj.* ¡Viva! voz con que se aclama y aplaude.

huzza, *vn.* Vitorear, victorear, aclamar (acclaim). *-va.* Recibir a alguno con vivas.

hyacinth [ˈhaɪəsɪnθ] [jaia-sinz], *s.* 1. *(Bot.)* Jacinto. 2. *(Min.)* Jacinto, piedra preciosa; variedad de zircón de varios colores.

hyacinthine [ˈhaɪəsɪnθiːn] [jaia-sin-zin], *s.* Jacintino, perteneciente al jacinto, o de color semejante al del jacinto.

hyaena, *s. V.* HYENA.

hyaline [ˈhaɪəlaɪn] [jaia-lain], *a.* Cristalino, vidrioso, transparente.

hybrid, hybridous [ˈhaɪbrɪd] [jai-brid], *a.* Mestizo, híbrido, de dos castas o géneros de animales o plantas.

hybridize [ˈhaɪbrɪdaɪz] [jai-bri-dais], *va.* Producir híbridos, asociar animales o plantas de diversas especies para obtener híbridos; hibridar. *-vn.* 1. Producir o generar híbridos. 2. Ser capaz de cruzamiento.

hydatid [ˈhaɪədætɪk] [jai-da-tid], *s.* 1. Hidátide, vejiguilla redonda y llena de agua. 2. Estado enquistado de la larva de una tenia.

hydra [ˈhaɪdrə] [jai-dra], *s.* 1. Hidra, monstruo fabuloso con muchas cabezas. 2. Mal de muchas formas y difícil de extirpar. 3. Pólipo de agua dulce del género Hydra.

hydragogue [ˈhaɪdrəgɒg] [jai-dra-gog], *s.* *(Med.)* Hidragogo, remedio para arrojar fuera del cuerpo la serosidad que en él se halla derramada o infiltrada.

hydrangea [haɪˈdrændʒiːə] [jai-dran-yia], *s.* *(Bot.)* Hortensia.

hydrant [ˈhaɪdrənt] [jai-drant], *s.* Boca de riego.

hydrate [ˈhaɪdreɪt] [jai-dreit], *s.* *(Quím.)* Hidrato.

hydraulic, hydraulical [ˈhaɪdrɔːlɪk] [jai-dro-lik], *a.* Hidráulico.

hydraulics [ˈhaɪdrɔːlɪks] [jai-dro-liks], *s. pl.* Hidráulica, la ciencia que trata de los líquidos en movimiento, y particularmente del agua.

hydrazine [ˈhaɪdrəzaɪn] [jai-dra-sain], *s.* Hidrazina (combustible).

hydric [ˈhaɪdrɪk] [jai-drik], *a.* *(Quím.)* Hídrico, perteneciente al hidrógeno en combinación, o al agua.

hydriodic [ˈhaɪdrɪədɪk] [jai-drio-dik], *a.* *(Quím.)* Iodohídrico.

hydrocarbon [ˈhaɪdrəʊˈkɑːbən] [jai-drou-kar-bon], *s.* *(Quím.)* Hidrocarburo.

hydrocephalus [ˈhaɪdrəʊˈsɛgələs] [jai-drou-se-fa-los], *s.* *(Med.)* Hidrocéfalo, hidropesía de la cabeza.

hydrochlorate [ˈhaɪdrəˈklɔreɪt] [jai-dro-klo-reit], *s.* *(Quím.)* Clorhidrato, hidroclorato.

hydrochloric [ˈhaɪdrəˈklɒrɪk] [jai-dro-klo-rik], *a.* Hidroclórico o clorhídrico. **Hydrochloric acid,** ácido clorhídrico.

hydrodynamics [ˈhaɪdrədaɪˈnæmɪks] [jai-dro-dai-na-miks], *s. pl.* Hidrodinámica, ciencia que aplica los principios de la dinámica para determinar el movimiento o el reposo de los flúidos.

hydroelectric [ˈhaɪdrərˈlektrɪk] [jai-dro-i-lek-trik], *a.* Hidroeléctrico.

hydrofoil [ˈhaɪdrəɔfɔɪl] [jai-drou-foil], *s.* Hidrodeslizador.

hydrogen [ˈhaɪdrədʒɪn] [jai-dro-yin], *s. (Quím.)* Hidrógeno. **Carbureted hydrogen,** hidrocarburo. **Hydrogen peroxide,** agua oxigenada, peróxido hidrogenado. **Hydrogen sulphide,** sulfhídrico.

hydrogenate [ˈhaɪdrədʒɪneɪt] [jai-dro-yi-neit], *va.* Hidrogenar.

hydrogenation [ˈhaɪdrədʒɪˌneɪʃən] [jai-dro-yi-nei-shon], *s.* Hidrogenación.

hydrogen bomb [ˈhaɪdrədʒɪn] [jai-dro-yin], *s.* Bomba de hidrógeno.

hydrographer [haɪˈdrɒgræfəʳ] [jai-dro-gra-faʳ], *s.* Hidrógrafo, el profesor de hidrografía.

hydrographical [haɪˈdrɒgræfɪkl] [jai-dro-gra-fi-kal], *a.* Hidrográfico.

hydrography [haɪˈdrɒgræfɪ] [jai-dro-gra-fi], *s.* Hidrografía, descripción de las aguas navegables.

hydrokinetic [ˈhaɪdrəkɪnɪtɪl] [jai-dro-ki-ni-tik], *a.* Hidromecánico, que se refiere al movimiento de los fluídos y a la energía desarrollada por ese movimiento.

hydrology [haɪˈdrɒlɒdʒɪ] [jai-dro-lo-yi], *s.* Hidrología, descripción de las aguas terrestres.

hydrolysis [haɪˈdrɒlɪsɪs] [jai-dro-li-sis], *s. (Quím.)* Hidrólisis.

hydrolyze [ˈhaɪdrəɔlaɪz] [jai-drou-lais], *va.* Hidrolizar.

hydromancy [haɪˈdrɒmænsɪ] [jai-dro-man-si], *s.* Hidromancia, adivinación por medio del agua.

hydromel [haɪˈdrɒmələ] [jai-dro-mel], *s.* Hidromel, aguamiel.

hydrometer [haɪˈdrɒmɪtəʳ] [jai-dro-mi-taʳ], *s.* 1. Hidrómetro, instrumento para medir la gravedad, densidad, etc., del agua u otros fluidos. 2. Instrumento para medir la corriente de agua en ríos, conductos, etc.; fluviómetro.

hydronics [haɪˈdrɒnɪks] [jai-dro-niks], *s.* Hidrónica.

hydropathy [haɪˈdrɒpæθɪ] [jai-dro-pa-zi], *s.* Hidropatía, método curativo por medio del agua.

hydrophobia [ˌhaɪdrəˈfəʊbɪə] [jai-dro-fou-bia],

hydrophoby [ˌhaɪdrəˈfəʊbɪ] [jai-dro-fou-bi], *s.* Hidrofobia, mal de rabia, sed ardiente con horror al agua.

hydropic, hydropical [ˈhaɪdrəpɪk] [jai-dro-pik], *a.* Hidrópico.

hydroplane [ˌhaɪdrəpleɪn] [jai-dro-plein], *s.* Hidroplano.

hydroponics [ˌhaɪdrəˈpɒnɪks] [jai-dro-po-niks], *s.* Hidroponia.

hydropsy [ˈhaɪdrəpsɪ] [jai-drop-si], *s.* Hidropesía.

hydrostat [ˈhaɪdrəstæt] [jai-dros-tat], *s.* Hidrostato, aparato para impedir la explosión de las calderas de vapor.

hydrostatic, hydrostatical [ˌhaɪdrəˈstætɪk] [jai-dros-ta-tik], *a.* Hidrostático.

hydrostatics [ˌhaɪdrəˈstætɪks] [jai-dros-ta-tiks], *s. pl.* Hidrostática, la ciencia que enseña y examina la gravedad o peso de los cuerpos líquidos.

hydrotherapy [ˌhaɪdrəʊˈθerəpɪ] [jai-drou-ze-ra-pi], *s.* Hidroterapia, método curativo por medio del agua.

hydroxide [haɪˈdrɒksaɪd] [jai-drok-said], *s. (Quím.)* Hidróxido.

hyena [haɪˈiːnə] [jai-ina], *s.* Hiena, mamífero carnicero.

hyetal [haɪˈɪtəl] [jai-ital], *a.* Perteneciente a la lluvia; lluvioso.

hygiene [ˈhaɪdʒiːn] [jai-yin], *s.* Higiene, la parte de la medicina que trata del modo de conservar la salud.

hygienic [haɪˈdʒiːnɪk] [jai-yi-nIk], *a.* Higiénico.

hygienist [ˈhaɪdʒiːnɪıst] [jai-yi-nist], *s.* Higienista.

hygrometer [ˈhaɪgrəmiːtəʳ] [jai-gro-mi-taʳ], **hygroscope** [ˈhaɪgrəskəʊp] [jai-gros-koup], *s.* Higrómetro, higroscopio, instrumento que sirve para apreciar la existencia del vapor acuoso en el aire o en un gas cualquiera.

hygroscopic [ˌhaɪgrəsˈkəʊpɪk] [jai-gros-kou-pik], *a.* Higroscópico, perteneciente o relativo al higroscopio.

hyla [ˈhaɪlə] [jai-la], *s.* Rubeta; rana del género Hyla.

hylozoic [ˈhaɪləzɔɪk] [jai-lo-soik], *s.* El partidario de una secta antigua que sostenía la animación de la materia.

hymen [ˈhaɪmen] [jai-men], *s.* 1. Himeneo, el dios de las bodas o casamientos. 2. Himen, la membrana virginal.

hymeneal [ˈhaɪmenɪəl] [jai-me-nial], **hymenean** [ˈhaɪmenɪən] [jai-me-nian], *s.* Himeneo. -*a.* Nupcial, que pertenece a las bodas.

hymn [hɪm] [jim], *s.* 1. Himno. 2. *(Relig.)* Cántico.

hymn, *va.* Alabar con himnos. -*vn.* Cantar himnos.

hymnal [ˈhɪmnəl] [jim-nal], *s.* Cantoral, himnario.

hymnbook [ˈhɪmbʊk] [jim-buk], *s.* Cantoral, himnario.

hymnology [ˈhɪmˈnəlɒdʒɪ] [jim-no-lo-yi], *s.* Colección de himnos.

hyp [haɪp] [jaip], *va.* Melancolizar, entristecer, desanimar.

hype [haɪp] [jaip], *s. (Coloq.)* Despliegue, bombo publicitario. -*vt. (Coloq.)* Promocionar a bombo y platillo.

hyper [ˈhaɪpəʳ] [jai-paʳ], *pref.* Hiper-, sobre; se usa en palabras compuestas.

hyperactive [ˌhaɪpərˈæktɪv] [jai-per-ak-tiv], *a.* Hiperactivo.

hyperbola [haɪˈpɜːbələ] [jai-per-bo-la], *s. (Geom.)* Hipérbola, curva geométrica que resulta de la intersección de un cono con un plano.

hyperbole [haɪˈpɜːbəlɪ] [jai-per-bo-li], *s.* Hipérbole, figura retórica que aumenta o disminuye excesivamente la verdad de lo que se habla; exageración.

hyperbolic, hyperbolical [haɪˈpɜːbəlɪk] [jai-per-bo-lik], *a.* 1. Hiperbólico. 2. Perteneciente a la hipérbole.

hyperbolically [haɪˈpɜːbəlɪkəlɪ] [jai-per-bo-li-ka-li], *adv.* Hiperbólicamente.

hyperbolist [haɪˈpɜːbəlɪst] [jai-per-bo-list], *s.* El que exagera o hace hipérboles; exagerador.

hyperbolize [haɪˈpɜːbəlaɪz] [jai-per-bo-lais], *vn.* Usar de hipérboles, antiguamente hiperbolizar. -*va.* Exagerar.

hyperborean [haɪˈpɜːbərɪən] [jai-per-bo-rian], *a.* Hiperbóreo, de las regiones septentrionales.

hypercritic [haɪˈpɜːkrɪtɪk] [jai-per-kri-tik], *s.* Crítico, inflexible. -*a.* Crítico.

hypercritical [haɪˈpɜːkrɪtɪkəl] [jai-per-kri-ti-kal], *a.* Crítico severo.

hyperdulia [haɪˈpɜːdʊlɪə] [jai-per-du-lia], **hyperduly** [haɪˈpɜːdʊlɪ] [jai-per-du-li], *s.* Hiperdulía.

hypergolic [haɪˈpɜːgɒlɪk] [jai-per-go-lik], *a.* Hipergólico, auto-inflamable al contacto de sus componentes.

hypericon [ˈhaɪpərɪkəɒn] [jai-pe-ri-koun], **hypericum** [ˈhaɪpɜːɪkəm] [jai-pe-ri-kom], *s. (Bot.)* Hipericón, hipérico, planta llamada más comúnmente *St. John's wort.*

hypermarket [ˈhaɪpəˌmɑːkɪt] [jai-per-mar-kit], *s.* Hipermercado.

hypermeter [ˈhaɪpəˌmiːtəʳ] [jai-per-mi-taʳ], *s.* Lo que excede a una medida determinada.

hypersarcoisis [ˌhaɪpəˈsɑːkəʊsɪs] [jai-per-sar-kou-sis], *s. (Cir.)* Hipersarcosis, excrecencia carnosa que se forma en las heridas.

hypersensitive [ˌhaɪpəˈsensɪtɪv] [jai-per-sen-si-tiv], *a.* Excesivamente impresionable, hipersensible.

hypersonic [ˈhaɪpəsɒnɪk] [jai-per-so-nik], *a.* Supersónico, hipersónico.

hypertension [ˈhaɪpəˈtenʃən] [jai-per-ten-shon], *s. (Med.)* Hipertensión.

hypertrophy [haɪˈpɜːtrəfɪ] [jai-per-tro-fi], *s.* 1. *(Med.)* Hipertrofia, aumento excesivo del volumen de un órgano o tejido sin alteración efectiva en su composición. 2. Cualquier aumento excesivo.

hyperventilate [ˌhaɪpəˈventɪleɪt] [jai-pa-ven-ti-leit], *vi.* Hiperventilarse.

hyphen [ˈhaɪfən] [jai-fen], *s.* Guión o guiones, signo que denota la unión de las partes de una voz.

hypnosis [hɪpˈnəʊsɪs] [jip-nou-sis], *s.* Hipnosis. **Under hypnosis,** hipnotizado, en estado de hipnosis.

hypnotic [hɪpˈnɒtɪk] [jip-no-tik], *s.* Hipnótico, medicamento que produce el sueño.

I

hypnotism [ˈhɪpnətɪzəm] [jip-no-ti-sem], *s.* Hipnotismo o hipnalismo; sueño artificial producido por el magnetismo o por la contemplación fija y reiterada de ciertos objetos; estado pasivo de la mente.

hypnotist [ˈhɪpnətɪst] [jip-no-tist], *s.* Hipnotizador.

hypnotize [ˈhɪpnətaɪz] [jip-no-tais], *va.* Hipnotizar.

hypoallergenic [ˌhaɪpəʊˈæləˈdʒenɪk] [jai-pou-a-ler-ye-nik], *a.* Hipoalergénico.

hypocaust [ˈhaɪpəʊˈkəʊst] [jai-pou-kaust], *s.* 1. Hipocausto, el lugar subterráneo donde ponían los griegos y romanos la lumbre para calentar los baños. 2. El sitio donde está la lumbre que mantiene caliente un invernáculo.

hypochondria [ˌhaɪpəʊˈkɒndrɪə] [jai-pou-kon-dria], **hypochondriasm** [ˌhaɪpəʊˈkɒndrɪæzm] [jai-pou-kon-dria-sem], *s.* Hipocondría, melancolía.

hypochondriac [ˌhaɪpəʊˈkɒndrɪæk] [jai-pou-kon-driak], *s.* Hipocondríaco.

hypocist [ˈhɪpɒsɪst] [ji-po-sist], *s.* (*Bot.*) Hipocístide o hipocisto, el retoño del cisto, planta.

hypocrisy [hɪˈpɒkrɪsɪ] [ji-po-kri-si], *s.* Hipocresía, disimulo.

hypocrite [ˈhɪpɒkrɪt] [ji-po-krit], *s.* Hipócrita.

hypocritic, hypocritical [ˌhɪpəˈkrɪtɪk] [ji-po-kri-tik], *a.* Hipócrita, falso (false, insincere), disimulado.

hypocritically [ˌhɪpɒˈkrɪtɪkəlɪ] [ji-po-kri-ti-ka-li], *adv.* Hipócritamente.

hypodermic [ˌhaɪpəˈdɜːmɪk] [jai-po-der-mik], *a.* Subcutáneo, hipodérmico; introducido o hallado debajo del cutis. -*s.* Aguja hipodérmica.

hypogastric [ˌhaɪpəˈgæstrɪk] [jai-po-gas-trik], *a.* hipogástrico: se dice de la región inferior del vientre.

hypogastrium [ˌhaɪpəˈgæstrɪəm] [jai-po-gas-triom], *s.* Hipogastro.

hypophosphate [ˌhaɪpəˈfɒsfeɪt] [jai-po-fos-feit], *s.* (*Quím.*) Hipofosfato.

hypophyge [ˌhaɪpəˈfaɪdʒɪ] [jai-po-fai-chi], *s.* (*Arq.*) Imóscapo, nacela, moldura cóncava; escocia.

hypostasis [haɪˈɒstəsɪs] [jai-pos-ta-sis], *s.* (*Teol.*) 1. Hipóstasis, supuesto o persona: se dice de la Santísima Trinidad. 2. (*Med.*) Sedimento de la orina.

hypostatic, hypostatical [ˌhaɪpəʊˈstætɪk] [jai-pos-ta-tik], *a.* Hipostático; constitutivo; personal.

hyposulphate [ˌhaɪpəˈsəlfeɪt] [jai-po-sul-feit], *s.* (*Quím.*) Hiposulfato.

hyposulphite [ˌhaɪpəˈsəlfaɪt] [jai-po-sul-fait], *s.* (*Quím.*) Hiposulfito.

hypotension [ˌhaɪpəˈtenʃən] [jai-po-ten-shon], *s.* Hipotensión.

hypotenuse, hypothenuse [haɪˈɒtɪnjʊz] [jai-po-ti-nius], *s.* Hipotenusa, el lado mayor de un triángulo rectángulo.

hypothecate [haɪˈpɒθɪkeɪt] [jai-po-zi-keit], *va.* Hipoiecar, empeñar (pawn). *V.* PLEDGE.

hypothesis [haɪˈpɒθɪsɪs] [jai-po-zi-sis], *s.* Hipótesis.

hypothesize [haɪˈpɒθɪsaɪz] [jai-po-zi-sais], *vi.* Hacer hipótesis

hypothetic, hypothetical [ˌhaɪpəʊˈθetɪk] [jai-pou-ze-tik], *a.* Hipotético.

hypothetically [ˌhaɪpəʊˈθetɪkəlɪ] [jai-pou-ze-ti-ka-li], *adv.* Condicionalmente, hipotéticamente.

hyssop [ˈhɪsəp] [ji-sop], *s.* (*Bot.*) Hisopo.

hysterectomy [ˌhɪstəˈrektəmɪ] [jis-te-rek-to-mi], *s.* Histerectomía, extirpación quirúrgica del útero.

hysteria [hɪsˈtɪərɪə] [jis-tia-ria], *s.* (*Med.*) Histeria. **Mass hysteria,** histeria colectiva.

hysteric, hysterical [hɪsˈterɪk] [jis-te-rik], *a.* Histérico, perteneciente al histerismo.

hysterically [hɪsˈterɪkəlɪ] [jis-tie-ri-ka-li], *adv.* Histéricamente.

hysterics [hɪsˈterɪks] [jis-te-riks], *s.* Histérico, paroxismo histérico.

hythe [haɪθ] [jaiz], *s.* Puerto pequeño.

i [aɪ] [ai], en inglés tiene varios sonidos; uno breve, que corresponde al de la *i* castellana, como en *pin, bid* y *lid;* y otro largo, muy semejante al del diptongo español *ai,* como en *sign, mild, find.* La *i* tiene también otro sonido entre la *e* y *o* españolas en *sir, bird, shirt,* y otras semejantes, y que se aproxima al diptongo oe alemán o eu en francés. En este volumen se indica este sonido por el signo ǝe. Ninguna voz puramente inglesa acaba en *i*.

i, *pron.* Yo: el pronombre *yo* se escribe siempre con letra mayúscula I.

iambic [aɪˈæmbɪk] [ai-am-bik], *a.* (*Poet.*) Yámbico, perteneciente al pie yambo o que lo emplea. -*s.* 1. Pie yámbico. *V.* IAMBUS. 2. Verso (line, stanza, strophe) compuesto de yambos.

iambus [aɪˈæmbəs] [ai-am-bos], *s.* Yambo, pie de verso compuesto de dos sílabas, la primera breve y la segunda larga; o en el día, la segunda acentuada.

i-beam [aɪˈbiːm] [ai-bim], *s.* Viga en I o viga doble.

iberia [aɪˈbɪərɪə] [ai-bia-ria], *s.* Iberia.

iberian [aɪˈbɪərɪən] [ai-bia-rian], *a.* y *s.* Ibérico, ibero. **The Iberian peninsula,** la península ibérica.

ibex [ˈaɪbeks] [ai-beks], *s.* Íbice, especie de cabra montés.

ibis [ˈaɪbɪs] [ai-bis], *s.* Ibis, ave del orden de las zancudas.

-ic, *suf.* Usado para formar adjetivos con la significación de «de» «perteneciente a», «parecido a», como en artistic, artístico; o como desinencia de substantivos, v. g. en logic, lógica.

ice [aɪs] [ais], *s.* 1. Hielo, agua congelada. **Flakes of ice,** bancos de hielo. **Ice-bound,** rodeado de hielos. **Ice-spurs,** patines. 2. Sorbete. 3. Azúcar garapiñado. *V.* FROSTING. **Ice-boat,** (a) Bote que anda sobre el hielo; casco o armazón con patines y velas que corre sobre el hielo. (b) Barco rompehielos; vapor con máquinas poderosas para romper el hielo en los canales navegables. **Ice-box, ice-chest,** nevera, caja para hielo. **Ice-blink,** resplandor o claridad producida cerca del horizonte por la reflexión lejana de masas de hielo. **Ice-field, ice-float, ice-floe,** témpano de hielo, flotante. **Ice-water,** (a) agua enfriada por el hielo, (b) hielo derretido o nieve derretida.

ice, *va.* Helar, cubrir de hielo. **To ice with sugar,** cuajar de azúcar, garapiñar, alfeñicar.

iceberg [ˈaɪsbɜːg] [ais-berg], *s.* Iceberg, gran masa o montaña de hielo que flota en los mares del norte. **Iceberg lettuce,** lechuga repollada.

icebuilt [ˈaɪsbɪlt] [ais-bilt], *a.* Formado de hielo.

ice cream [ˈaɪsˈkriːm] [ais-krim], *s.* Helado. **Ice-cream cone,** barquillo de helado. **Ice-cream parlor,** heladería, nevería. **Ice-cream soda,** helado con soda.

iced [ˈaɪst] [aist], *a.* Helado (chilled).

ice-house [ˈaɪshaʊs] [ais-jaus], *s.* Nevería.

iceland [ˈaɪslænd] [ais-land], *s.* Islandia.

icelander [ˈaɪslændər] [ais-lan-dar], *s.* Islandés.

iceland moss [ˈaɪslændˌmɒs] [ais-land-mos], *s.* (*Bot.*) Liquen o musgo de Islandia.

ice-pack [ˈaɪspæk] [ais-pak], *s.* Aplicaciones de hielo.

ice-pick [ˈaɪspɪk] [ais-pik], *s.* Punzón para hielo.

ice skates [ˈaɪsskeɪts] [ais-skeit], *s. pl.* Patines para hielo.

ichneumon [ˈaɪsnjuːmɒn] [ais-niu-mon], *s.* 1. Icneumon, mamífero carnicero, especie de fuína o garduña. 2. (*Ent.*) *V. Ichneumon-fly.* **Ichneumon-fly,** Icneumón, insecto himenóptero de la forma de una avispa pero sumamente pequeño.

ichnographical [ˈɪknəˈgræfɪkəl] [ik-no-gra-fi-kal], *a.* Icnográfico.

ichnography [ˈɪknəˈgræfɪ] [ik-no-gra-fi], *s.* Icnografía, delineación de la planta de un edificio.

ichor [ˈaɪkər] [ai-kor], *s.* Icor, serosidad acre de la sangre.

ichorous [ˈaɪkərəs] [ai-ko-ros], *a.* Icoroso.

ichthyocolla ['ɪkθɪə'kələ] [ik-zio-ko-la], *s.* Colapez o cola de pescado.

ichthyology [ˌɪkθɪ'ɒlədʒɪ] [ik-zio-lo-yi], *s.* Ictiología, el arte de la zoología que trata de los peces.

icicle ['aɪsɪkl] [ai-si-kol], *s.* Cerrión, carámbano.

icily ['aɪsɪlɪ] [ai-si-li], *adv.* Fríamente, con frialdad; de una manera frígida.

iciness, icyness ['aɪnɪs] [ai-si-nes], *s.* Congelación.

icing ['aɪsɪŋ] [ai-sin], *s.* Capa de azúcar garapiñado (para tortas, pasteles, etc.), glaseado.

icon ['aɪkɒn] [ai-kon], *s.* 1. Icono, imagen, representación; en la Iglesia griega, cuadro, mosaico sagrado, etc. 2. En los libros científicos, ilustración, grabado.

iconoclast ['aɪkɒnəklæst] [ai-ko-no-klast], *s.* Iconoclasta, hereje que niega el culto a las sagradas imágenes.

iconoclastic [aɪˌkɒnə'klæstɪk] [ai-ko-no-klas-tik], *a.* Iconoclástico, iconoclasta.

iconography [ˌaɪkɒ'nɒgrəfɪ] [ai-ko-no-gra-fi], *s.* Iconografía, descripción de imágenes o pinturas.

iconolater ['aɪkɒnɒlætə'] [ai-ko-no-la-ta'], *s.* Iconólatra, el que da culto a las imágenes.

iconology [ˌaɪkɒ'nələdʒɪ] [ai-ko-no-lo-yi], *s.* Iconología, representación de las virtudes, vicios u otras cosas morales o naturales, con la figura o apariencia de personas.

iconoscope ['aɪkɒnəskəʊp] [ai-ko-nos-koup], *s.* Iconoscopio.

icosahedron ['aɪkɒsə'hiːdrən] [ai-ko-sa-ji-dron], *s.* Icosaedro, sólido terminado por veinte caras.

-ics, Sufijo, de forma plural pero singular por su significación, derivado del plural griego neutro, *-ika* y que significa un arte o una ciencia.

icteric, icterical [ɪk'terɪk] [ik-te-rik], *a.* 1. Ictérico, que padece icterica. 2. Ictérico, remedio contra la icterica.

ictus ['ɪktəs] [ik-tos], *s.* 1. *(Med.)* Golpecito; como la pulsación de una arteria, o la picadura de un insecto. 2. Acento tónico o métrico en una sílaba o palabra.

icy ['aɪsɪ] [ai-si], *a.* 1. Helado (freezing), cubierto de hielo. 2. Frío, libre de pasiones. 3. Tardo, lento.

i'd [ɪd] [id], contracción de I WOULD o I HAD.

idea [aɪ'dɪə] [ai-dia], *s.* 1. Idea, imagen mental (impression). **That's not my idea of fun,** eso no es lo que yo entiendo por diversión. 2. Idea (plan, suggestion). **That's a good idea,** es una buena idea. 3. Idea, opinión (view).

ideal [aɪ'dɪəl] [ai-dial], *a.* Ideal, mental, intelectual. *-s.* Ideal, el sumo grado de perfección concebible; prototipo, modelo (archetype).

idealism [aɪ'dɪəlɪzəm] [ai-dia-li-sem], *s.* 1. Idealismo, sistema filosófico. 2. Idealismo, aptitud del artista, orador, poeta, etc., para elevar sobre la realidad sensible los objetos que describe o representa. 3. Esfuerzo para conseguir o lograr la perfección.

idealist [aɪ'dɪəlɪst] [ai-dia-list], *s.* Idealista, partidario del idealismo en todas sus acepciones.

idealistic [aɪ'dɪəlɪstɪk] [ai-dia-lis-tik], *a.* Idealista.

ideality [aɪ'dɪəlɪtɪ] [ai-dia-li-ti], *s.* 1. Idealidad, calidad de ideal. 2. Sentimiento de lo bello, de lo poético, de lo elocuente.

idealize, idealise [aɪ'dɪəlaɪz] [ai-dia-lais], *va.* Hacer ideal, idealizar: exaltar, espiritualizar: dar carácter ideal. *-vn.* Formarse ideales, tipos perfectos.

ideally [aɪ'dɪəlɪ] [ai-dia-li], *adv.* Idealmente, mentalmente, intelectualmente. **They are ideally suited,** están hechos el uno para el otro.

idem [aɪ'dem] [ai-dem], *pron.* y *a.* (abreviatura **Id**) Idem, lo mismo.

identical [aɪ'dentɪkəl] [ai-den-ti-kal], *a.* Idéntico, el mismo. **Identical twins,** gemelos idénticos.

identically [aɪ'dentɪkəlɪ] [ai-den-ti-ka-li], *adv.* Idénticamente. **They are identically priced,** tienen exactamente el mismo precio.

identicalness [aɪ'dentɪkəlnɪs] [ai-den-ti-kal-nes], *s. V.* IDENTITY.

identifiable [aɪˌdentɪ'faɪəbl] [ai-den-ti-fai-abol], *a.* Identificable.

identification [aɪˌdentɪfɪ'keɪʃən] [ai-den-ti-fi-kei-shon], *s.* Identificación, el acto de identificar. **Identification card,** tarjeta de identificación, comprobantes o documentos de identificación. **Identification parade,** rueda de reconocimiento.

identify [aɪ'dentɪfaɪ] [ai-den-ti-fai], *va.* 1. Identificar. 2. Establecer la identidad de alguien o algo, afirmar o probar ser lo mismo. 3. Asemejar; considerar como idéntico. 4. Identificarse con, unirse con. 5. Servir como señal por la cual se reconoce una cosa o persona.

identity [aɪ'dentɪtɪ] [ai-den-ti-ti], *s.* Identidad. **Identity card,** carné de identidad.

ideograph ['ɪdɪəgræf] [i-dio-graf], *s.* Jeroglífico; símbolo, pintura.

ideographic [ˌɪdɪə'græfɪk] [i-dio-gra-fik],` *a.* Ideográfico, perteneciente a la ideografía, o representación gráfica del pensamiento.

ideological [ˌaɪdɪə'lɒdʒɪkəl] [ai-dio-lo-yi-kal], *a.* Ideológico.

ideologist [aɪdɪ'ɒlədʒɪst] [ai-di-o-lo-yist], *s.* Ideólogo, el que profesa la ideología; idealista.

ideology [aɪdɪ'ɒlədʒɪ] [ai-di-o-lo-yi], *s.* Ideología, ciencia que trata de las ideas.

ides [aɪdz] [aids], *s.* Idus, el 15 de marzo, mayo, julio y octubre y el 13 de los demás meses entre los romanos.

idiocrasy, *s. V.* IDIOSYNCRASY.

idiocy ['ɪdɪəsɪ] [i-dio-si], *s.* Idiotez, necedad, falta de entendimiento.

idiom ['ɪdɪəm] [i-diom], *s.* 1. Idiotismo, el modo de hablar propio y peculiar de una lengua, modismo (expression). 2. Idioma, modo particular de hablar de algunos o en algunas ocasiones; jerigonza. 3. Genio, índole de una lengua.

idiomatic, idiomatical [ˌɪdɪə'mætɪk] [i-dio-ma-tik], *a.* Idiomático.

idiopathic ['ɪdɪəfætɪk] [i-dio-fa-tik], *a.* Idiopático, se dice de las enfermedades primitivas o esenciales.

idiopathy ['ɪdɪəfætɪ] [i-dio-fa-ti], *s.* 1. Idiopatía, afección o sensación particular. 2. *(Med.)* Enfermedad primitiva o peculiar.

idiosyncrasy [ˌɪdɪə'sɪŋkrəsɪ] [i-dio-sin-kra-si], *s.* Idiosincrasia, temperamento o disposición peculiar de una persona. **He has his little idiosyncrasies,** tiene sus pequeñas manías.

idiosyncratic [ˌɪdɪəsɪŋ'krætɪk] [i-dio-sin-kra-tik], *a.* Idiosincrásico.

idiot ['ɪdɪət] [i-diot], *s.* 1. Idiota, un hombre bobo e imbécil, en quien nunca se ha desarrollado la razón. 2. Necio (stupid), bobo, tonto.

idiotic, idiotical ['ɪdɪətɪk] [i-dio-tik], *a.* Tonto, bobo, necio; simple. **It was an idiotic thing to say,** fue una idiotez decir eso.

idiotism ['ɪdɪətɪzm] [i-dio-tism], *s.* 1. Idiotismo, necedad, ignorancia. 2. Idiotismo, modo de hablar peculiar a una lengua.

idiotize ['ɪdɪətaɪz] [i-dio-tais], *vn.* Volverse tonto o necio, embrutecerse.

idle ['aɪdl] [ai-del], *a.* 1. Ocioso, perezoso (lazy), desocupado, holgazán. 2. Inútil, vano, frívolo; estéril. 3. Futil, sin importancia; *(Mec.)* que produce movimiento sin fuerza efectiva. 4. Que proporciona tiempo desocupado (unoccupied), ocio. **An idle life,** una vida ociosa. **Idle hours,** horas desocupadas. **Idle efforts,** vanos esfuerzos. **An idle amusement,** una diversión frívola. **Idle story,** cuento de viejos. **An idle thing,** una bagatela, una cosa fútil. **Idle fellow,** azotacalles, callejero.

idle, *vn.* Holgazanear, haraganear, estar ocioso. *-va.* Gastar ociosamente, consumir sin provecho.

idle-headed ['aɪdlˌhedɪd] [ai-del-je-did], *a.* Tonto, desrazonable; infatuado.

idleness ['aɪdlnɪs] [ai-del-nes], s. 1. Ociosidad (inactivity), pereza (lazyness), holgazanería, negligencia. 2. Trivialidad, frivolidad, inutilidad; indignidad.

idle-pated ['aɪdlˌpætɪd] [ai-del-pa-tid], a. Tonto, estúpido; majadero.

idler ['aɪdlə^r] [aid-la^r], s. Haragán, holgazán, poltrón, vago (lazy).

idless, idlesse ['aɪdlɪs] [aid-les], s. (Poet.) V. IDLENESS.

idly ['aɪdlɪ] [aid-li], adv. Ociosamente, tontamente; inútilmente, vanamente.

idol ['aɪdl] [ai-dol], s. 1. Ídolo, imagen. 2. Idolo, el objeto excesivamente amado.

idolater [aɪ'dɒlətə^r] [ai-do-la-ta^r], s. Idólatra; amante, admirador.

idolatress [aɪ'dɒlətrɪs] [ai-do-la-tris], sf. 1. Idólatra, la que idolatra. 2. La mujer a quien se idolatra, adora o ama con exceso.

idolatrous [aɪ'dɒlətrəs] [ai-do-la-tros], a. 1. Idólatra, idolátrico, que adora ídolos o falsas deidades. 2. Idólatra, que ama desordenamdamente a una persona o cosa.

idolatry [aɪ'dɒlətrɪ] [ai-do-la-tri], s. Idolatría, adoración de los ídolos.

idolism [aɪ'dɒlɪzm] [ai-do-li-sem], s. Culto de idolatría y la defensa de este culto.

idolize ['aɪdəlaɪz] [ai-do-lais], va. Idolatrar; amar con exceso.

idolizer ['aɪdəlaɪzə^r] [ai-do-lai-sa^r], s. El que ama hasta la adoración.

idyll ['ɪdɪl] [i-dil], s. Idilio, por extensión, poema corto, descriptivo o narrativo, muy embellecido, de estilo artístico. V. PASTORAL.

idyllic [ɪ'dɪlɪk] [i-di-lik], a. Idílico, concerniente al idilio; parecido a él.

i. e. Contrac. de ID EST. Es decir; esto es.

if [ɪf] [if], conj. 1. Si, partícula o conjunción condicional. **If he comes, I'll stay,** si viene, me quedaré. 2. Si (whether). **He asked if she had left,** preguntó si se había ido. 3. Aunque (though), dado que, supuesto que, aun cuando. **As if,** como si; antes de una cláusula, cual si. **As if one should say,** como si dijéramos, como quien diría. **If so be,** con tal que, supuesto que. **If you but take my part,** con tal que Vd. se ponga de mi parte. **Without «ifs» o «buts»,** sin si ni pero, sin poner pegas.

iffy ['ɪfɪ] [i-fi], a. (Coloq.) Dudoso, incierto (uncertain).

igad ['ɪgæd] [i-gad], inter. V. EGAD.

igloo ['ɪglu:] [i-dlu], s. Iglú.

igneous ['ɪgnɪəs] [ig-nios], a. Ígneo.

igniferous ['ɪgnɪfərəs] [ig-ni-fe-ros], a. Ignífero, que produce fuego.

ignify ['ɪgnɪfaɪ] [ig-ni-fai], va. Encender (light).

ignipotent [ɪg'nɪpətent] [ig-ni-po-tent], a. (Poet.) Ignipotente.

ignis fatuus ['ɪgnɪʃˌfætəs] [ig-nis-fa-tus], s. (pl. IGNES FATUI). Fuego fátuo, helena, fuego de San Telmo.

ignite [ɪg'naɪt] [ig-nait], va. 1. Encender (light), pegar fuego. 2. Hacer luminoso, causar una apariencia luminosa. -vn. Encenderse, enrojecerse por el calor.

ignitible, ignitable [ɪg'naɪtəbl] [ig-nai-ter-bol], a. Inflamable, fácil de encender o de excitar.

ignition [ɪg'nɪʃən] [ig-ni-shon], s. 1. Ignición, el acto de encender o poner fuego. **Ignition key,** llave de contacto. 2. (Quím.) Ignición, el acto de poner los metales al fuego para que se hagan ascua.

ignobility [ˌɪgnəʊ'bɪlɪtɪ] [ig-no-bi-li-ti], s. Villanía, bajeza, la falta de magnanimidad, de grandeza o de elevación de ánimo.

ignoble [ɪg'nəʊbl] [ig-nou-bel], a. 1. Innoble, plebeyo (plebeian), villano; indigno, bajo, vil; cobarde. 2. De casta inferior, se aplica en cetrería a los halcones de alas cortas.

ignobleness [ɪg'nəʊblnɪs] [ig-nou-bel-nes], s. Bajeza, vileza (vileness). falta de dignidad en el porte; falta de nobleza en el nacimiento.

ignobly [ɪg'nəʊblɪ] [ig-nou-bli], adv. Vilmente, bajamente; villanamente.

ignominious [ˌɪgnəmɪnɪəs] [ig-no-mi-nios], a. Ignominioso.

ignominiously [ˌɪgnə'mɪnɪəslɪ] [ig-no-mi-nios-li], adv. Ignominiosamente, vilmente.

ignominy ['ɪgnəmɪnɪ] [ig-no-mi-ni], s. Ignominia, infamia, deshonra, oprobio.

ignoramus [ˌɪgnə'reɪməs] [ig-no-rei-mos], s. Ignorante (ignorant), tonto, simple, inculto.

ignorance ['ɪgnərəns] [ig-no-rans], s. Ignorancia; inadvertencia. **He answered in ignorance of the questions,** respondió ignorando las preguntas.

ignorant ['ɪgnərənt] [ig-no-rant], a. 1. Ignorante; el que carece de conocimientos o instrucción. **He's totally ignorant about politics,** no tiene ni idea de política. 2. Ignorado, no descubierto. 3. Maleducado (rude). -s. Ignorante, el que ignora.

ignorantly ['ɪgnərəntlɪ] [ig-no-rant-li], adv. Ignorantemente.

ignore [ɪg'nɔː^r] [ig-no^r], va. 1. Ignorar. **Just ignore him,** ignórale, no le hagas caso. 2. (For.) Rechazar, sobreseer; dar un fallo de «no ha lugar».

iguana [ɪ'gwɑːnə] [i-gua-na], s. (Zool.) Iguana, reptil de cuerpo semejante al del lagarto; lagarto grande.

il, Prefijo que reemplaza a *in* antes de la letra *l*.

ileum ['ɪlɪəm] [i-liom], s. Ileon, el tercer intestino delgado, comprende las tres quintas partes inferiores del intestino delgado.

ilex ['aɪleks] [ai-leks], s. (Bot.) 1. Nombre científico del acebo y de la familia a que pertenece. 2. Coscoja.

ilk [ɪlk] [ilk], a. (Ant. or Sco.) Lo mismo. **Kent of that ilk,** pájaros de la misma pluma. *kent* del lugar del mismo nombre. **And others of that ilk,** y otros de ese jaez. **People of that ilk,** gente de esa clase.

ill [ɪl] [il], a. y s. 1. Malo, enfermo, doliente. 2. Malo, contrario al bien; insalube, malsano. 3. De calidad inferior, grosero, ordinario. 4. Poco diestro, inhábil. 5. Desgraciado, funesto. **Ill-humor,** mal humor. **Ill weeds grow apace, la** mala hierba crece a la vista. **To put an ill construction,** tomar una cosa a mal, interpretarla en mal sentido. **Dangerously ill,** peligrosamente enfermo -s. 1. Mal, maldad. 2. Desgracia, infortunio. -adv. Mal, malamente, apenas (hardly). **He can ill afford it,** apenas puede permitírselo. **To take ill,** llevar a mal. *Ill* se usa frecuentemente en composición expresando su significación primitiva. **Ill-affected** o **disposed,** mal intencionado. **Ill-contrived,** mal pensado, mal dispuesto, mal arreglado; cruel, de malas entrañas, duro. **Ill-fated,** desgraciado, malaventurado, desdichado. **Ill-gotten,** mal adquirido o ganado. **Ill-grounded** o **founded,** mal fundado. **Ill-luck,** desgracia, desdicha. **Ill-winded,** maligno, malvado, mal intencionado. **Ill-pleased,** malcontento. **Ill spoken of,** el que tiene mala reputación. **Ill-advised,** no bien considerado, imprudente. **Ill-favored,** disforme, feo. **Ill-nature,** malevolencia, mala intención, mal genio. **Ill-natured,** duro o áspero de genio; malévolo, nocivo; descontentadizo. **Ill-stared,** desdichado, desgraciado. **Ill-temper,** aspereza de genio, irritabilidad, morosidad. **Ill-will,** mala voluntad tirria, aversión; tedio. **To bear** o **to owe a person ill-will,** tener, guardar rencor o temor a alguno.

I'll [aɪl] [ail], Contracción familiar de *I shall or I will;* formas del futuro.

illapese [ɪlə'piːz] [i-la-pis], s. 1. Entrada gradual de una cosa en otra. 2. Acceso; (flg.) Inspiración, descenso, como el del Espíritu Santo.

illation [ɪ'leɪʃən] [i-lei-shon], s. Ilación, consecuencia, inferencia.

illative ['ɪlətɪv] [i-la-tiv], a. Ilativo, conclusivo. -s. Lo que indica alguna ilación.

illatively [ɪlə'tɪvlɪ] [i-la-tiv-li], adv. Por ilación o conclusión.

illaudable ['ɪlɔːdəbl] [i-lo-da-bol], a. Indigno de alabanza.

illaudably ['ɪlɔːdəblɪ] [i-lo-da-bli], adv. Indignamente.

ill-bred ['ɪl'bred] [il-bred], a. Malcriado, mal educado.

illegal [ɪ'liːgəl] [i-li-gal], a. Ilegal (unlawful), contra ley. **illegal immigrant,** inmigrante ilegal.

illegality [ˌɪliːˈgælɪtɪ] [i-li-ga-li-ti], *s.* Ilegalidad, falta de legalidad.

illegalize [ɪˈliːgəlaɪz] [i-li-ga-lais], *va.* Hacer ilegal alguna cosa.

illegally [ɪˈliːgəlɪ] [i-li-ga-li], *adv.* Ilegalmente.

illegibility [ɪˈledʒɪˈbɪlɪtɪ] [i-le-yi-bi-li-ti], *s.* Condición o calidad de lo que no se puede leer.

illegible [ɪˈledʒəbl] [i-le-ya-bol], *a.* Ilegible, lo que no se puede leer o es muy difícil de leer.

illegibly [ɪˈledʒəblɪ] [i-le-ya-bli], *adv.* De un modo ilegible.

illegitimacy [ˌɪlɪˈdʒɪtɪˌəsɪ] [i-li-yi-ti-ma-si], *s.* Ilegitimidad.

illegitimate [ˌɪlɪˈdʒɪtɪmɪt] [i-li-yi-ti-mit], *a.* 1. Contrario a la ley, ilegal; especialmente, ilegítimo, bastardo, el nacido o procreado fuera de matrimonio legítimo. 2. Falso, erróneo, ilógico. 3. No autorizado por el uso.

illegitimate, *va.* Ilegitimar.

illegitimately [ˌɪlɪˈdʒɪtɪmɪtlɪ] [i-li-yi-ti-mit-li], *adv.* Ilegítimamente.

illegitimation [ˌɪlɪˈdʒɪtɪˌmeɪʃən] [i-li-yi-ti-mei-shon], *s.* 1. Bastardía, ilegitimidad. 2. Suposición, impostura, falsedad.

illeviable [ˌɪlɪˈvaɪəbl] [i-li-via-bol], *a.* Lo que no puede ser exigido.

ill-humored [ɪlˈhjuːməd] [il-jiu-mord], *a.* Malhumorado, de mal humor.

illiberal [ɪˈlɪbərəl] [i-li-be-ral], *a.* 1. Ruin, tacaño, mezquino, miserable. 2. Escaso de inteligencia, de entendimiento limitado. 3. Indigno de un hombre bien educado, innoble, el que carece de nobleza de alma o de dignidad.

illiberality [ɪˈlɪbərælɪtɪ] [i-li-be-ra-li-ti], *s.* 1. Tacañería, miseria (poverty), ruindad. 2. Poquedad, pusilanimidad, apocamiento, cortedad de ánimo.

illicit [ɪˈlɪsɪt] [i-li-sit], *a.* 1. Ilícito, que no es permitido, ilegal. 2. Que se relaciona con cosas o acciones ilícitas.

illicitly [ɪˈlɪsɪtlɪ] [i-li-sit-li], *adv.* Ilegalmente, ilícitamente.

illicitness [ɪˈlɪsɪtnɪs] [i-li-sit-nes], *s.* Carácter, naturaleza ilícta, ilegalidad.

illimitable [ɪˈlɪmɪtəbl] [i-li-mi-ter-bol], *a.* Ilimitable (boundless); infinito, indeterminado.

illimitably [ɪˈlɪmɪtəblɪ] [i-li-mi-ter-bli], *adv.* Ilimitadamente.

ill-informed [ˈɪlɪnˈfɔːmd] [il-in-formd], *a.* Mal informado.

illinois [ˈɪlɪnɔɪs] [i-li-nois], *s. pl.* Nombre genérico de ciertas tribus algonquinas, de los aborígenes norteamericanos, cuyo territorio comprendía el actual Estado de Illinois.

illiquation [ɪˈlɪkwɪʃən] [i-li-kei-shon], *s.* Acción de fundir una cosa en otra.

illision [ɪˈlɪʃən] [i-li-shon], *s.* Choque, golpe, colisión (crash).

illiteracy [ɪˈlɪtərəsɪ] [i-li-te-ra-si], *s.* 1. Analfabetismo. 2. Falta de instrucción, ignorancia.

illiterate [ɪˈlɪtərɪt] [i-li-te-reit], *a.* 1. Analfabeto. 2. Ignorante.

illiterateness [ɪˈlɪtərɪtnɪs] [i-li-te-reit-nes], *s.* La falta de conocimientos.

illiterature [ɪˈlɪtətʃəʳ] [i-li-ter-chaʳ], *s.* Falta de instrucción, ignorancia (ignorance).

ill-lived [ɪlˈlɪvd] [i-livd], *a.* Malvado.

ill-looking [ɪlˈluːkɪŋ] [il-lu-kin], *a.* Mal carado.

ill-mannered [ɪlˈmænəd] [il-ma-nerd], *a.* Descortés (impolite), malcriado.

ill-nature [ɪlˈneɪtʃəʳ] [il-nei-chaʳ], *s.* Malevolencia, mala intención, malicia, mal genio.

ill-natured [ɪlˈneɪtʃəd] [il-nei-chad], *a.* Malévolo, nocivo; duro o áspero de genio, indómito, indomable (indomitable), malicioso, descontentadizo.

ill-naturedly [ɪlˈneɪtʃədlɪ] [il-nei-chad-li], *adv.* De mala gana; con mala intención, con repugnancia.

ill-naturedness [ɪlˈneɪtʃədnɪs] [il-nei-chad-nes], *s.* Falta de cariño; malicia, mala intención.

illness [ˈɪlnɪs] [il-nes], *s.* 1. Mal, enfermedad (disease). 2. Maldad, depravación.

illogical [ɪˈlɒdʒɪkəl] [i-lo-yi-kal], *a.* Que no es conforme a las reglas de la lógica.

illogically [ɪˈlɒdʒɪkəlɪ] [i-lo-yi-ka-li], *adv.* En oposición a las reglas de la lógica.

ill-principled [ɪlˈprɪndɪpləd] [il-prin-si-peld], *a.* 1. Inmoral (immoral), sin principios. 2. Inicuo, sin creencias.

ill-satisfied [ˈɪlˈsætɪsfaɪd] [il-sa-tis-faid], *a.* No satisfecho, descontento (dissatisfied).

ill-shaped [ˈɪlˈʃeɪpt] [il-sheipt], *a.* Disforme, irregular (uneven), mal hecho, mal formado.

illsounding [ˈɪlˈsaʊndɪŋ] [il-saun-din], *a.* Mal sonante.

ill-starred [ɪlˈstɑːd] [il-stard], *a.* Malaventurdo, desdichado, desgraciado.

illtempered [ˈɪlˈtempəd] [il-tem-pard], *a.* De mal carácter, de mal genio.

ill-treated [ˈɪlˈtriːtɪd] [il-tri-tid], *a.* Maltratado, injuriado, agraviado.

illume [ɪˈluːm] [i-lum], *va. (Poet.)* Iluminar, aclarar.

illuminate [ɪˈluːmɪneɪt] [i-lu-mi-neit], *va.* 1. Iluminar (light), alumbrar con luces; dar luz. 2. Iluminar, ilustrar. 3. Iluminar, inspirar. 4. Adornar una cosa con pinturas o letras iniciales transparente o iluminadas.

illuminate, *a.* Iluminado; instruído. *-s.* El que procura ser mirado como un talento de orden superior. *Illuminati or Illuminates, s. pl.* Los iluminados, nombre que se dio a ciertos entusiastas del siglo XVIII.

illumination [ɪˌluːmɪˈneɪʃən] [i-lu-mi-nei-shon], *s.* 1. Iluminación (lighting), alumbrado, alumbramiento. 2. Iluminación, luminarias. 3. Brillo, esplendor. 4. Inspiración. 5. Alumbramiento, luces del cielo en nuestras almas.

illuminative [ɪˈluːmɪnətɪv] [i-lu-mi-na-tiv], *a.* Iluminativo.

illuminator [ɪˈluːmɪneɪtəʳ] [i-lu-mi-nei-toʳ], *s.* 1. Iluminador, el que o lo que ilumina o alumbra; lámpara, lente, etc., para concentrar la luz sobre objetos o lugares determinados. 2. Iluminador, el que tiene por oficio iluminar libros o manuscritos.

illumine [ɪˈluːmɪn] [i-lu-min], *va.* Iluminar. V. ILLUMINATE.

illusion [ɪˈluːʒən] [i-lu-shon], *s.* Ilusión, engaño, falsa apariencia (false appearance), aprensión, imaginación engañosa. **An optical illusion,** una ilusión óptica.

illusive [ɪˈluːsɪv] [i-lu-siv], *a.* Ilusivo, falso, engañoso.

illusively [ɪˈluːsɪvlɪ] [i-lu-siv-li], *adv.* Falsamente, aparentemente.

illusiveness [ɪˈluːsɪvnɪs] [i-lu-siv-nes], *s.* Ilusión, engaño, apariencia falsa.

illusory [ɪˈluːsərɪ] [i-lu-so-ri], *a.* Ilusorio, fantástico, aparente; engañoso, artificioso.

illustrate [ˈɪləstreɪt] [i-lus-treit], *va.* 1. Ilustrar, elucidar, aclarar por medio de figuras, comparaciones, ejemplos, etc. 2. Demostrar (show), poner de manifiesto. 3. Ilustrar una obra con pinturas, grabados, etc. 4. *(Ant.)* Engrandecer, ennoblecer. 4. *(Ant.)* V. ILLUMINATE, 1a acep.

illustration [ˌɪləˈstreɪʃən] [i-las-trei-shon], *s.* 1. Ilustración, elucidación. 2. Dibujo, grabado, cuadro. 3. Arte o acción de ilustrar. 4. Ejemplo (example).

illustrative [ˈɪləstrətɪv] [i-las-tra-tiv], *a.* Ilustrativo, explicativo.

illustratively [ˈɪləstrətɪvlɪ] [i-las-tra-tiv-li], *adv.* Explícitamente.

illustrator [ˈɪləstreɪtəʳ] [i-las-trei-taʳ], *s.* Ilustrador.

illustrious [ɪˈləstrɪəs] [i-las-trios], *a.* Ilustre (distinguished), conspicuo (eminent), esclarecido, insigne, célebre.

illustriously [ɪˈləstrɪəslɪ] [i-las-trios-li], *adv.* Ilustremente, esclarecidamente.

illustriousness [ɪˈləstrɪəsnɪs] [i-las-trios-nes], *s.* Eminencia, grandeza, nobleza (nobility).

ill-usage [ˈɪlˈjuːseɪdʒ] [il-iu-seich], *s.* Injusticia; crueldad; mal trato.

ill will [ˈɪlˈwɪl] [il-uil], *s.* Mala voluntad, malevolencia, tirria, aversión, rencor (spite).

I'm [aɪm] [aim], *contrac.* de I AM. Yo soy o estoy.

image [ˈɪmɪdʒ] [i-mich], *s.* 1. Imagen (picture), efigie, estatua, retrato, pintura. 2. Imagen, figura, representación, semejanza de una cosa con otra; apariencia. **Corporate image,** imagen de empresa. 3. *(Opt.)* Imagen, duplicado de un objeto, producido por medio de la reflexión o refracción. 4. Idea, representación de los objetos en el ánimo. 5. Personificación (embodiment).

image, va. 1. Figurar, formar una imagen de, reflejar. 2. Representar en la mente. 3. Parecer.

image-worship ['ɪmɪdʒˌwɜːkʃɪp] [i-mich-uerk-ship], s. El culto de las imágenes.

imagery ['ɪmɪdʒərɪ] [i-mi-che-ri], s. 1. Acción de formar imágenes, en cualquier sentido, conjunto de imágenes. 2. Exterioridad, apariencia. 3. Imaginación, aprehensión, vuelos de la fantasía, ideas falsas. 4. Forma o hechura exterior de las cosas 5. Tapicería con figuras o pinturas.

imaginable ['ɪmædʒməbl] [i-mi-chi-na-bol], a. Imaginable. **She's the most beautiful person imaginable**, es la persona más bella que se pueda imaginar.

imaginary [ɪ'mædʒɪnərɪ] [i-ma-chi-na-ri], a. Imaginario, fantástico.

imagination [ɪˌmædʒɪ'neɪʃən] [i-ma-chi-nei-shon], s. 1. Imaginación. **It's only your imagination**, son imaginaciones tuyas. 2. Imaginación, inventiva (inventiveness), pensamiento. 3. Imaginación, aprehensión, idea fantástica, visión.

imaginative [ɪ'mædʒnətɪv] [i-ma-chi-na-tiv], a. Imaginativo. **Elizabeth is very imaginative**, Elizabeth es muy imaginativa.

imagine [ɪ'mædʒɪn] [i-ma-chin], va. 1. Imaginar, representarse algo en la imaginación. 2. Imaginar, pensar, concebir, idear, inventar, discurrir alguna cosa. 3. Premeditar, formar de antemano un proyecto en el ánimo. -vn. Imaginarse, figurarse (believe). **I imagine you're very tired**, me figuro que estarás muy cansado.

imaginer [ɪ'mædʒɪnəʳ] [i-ma-chi-naʳ], s. El que imagina, idea o inventa.

imagining [ɪ'mædʒɪnɪŋ] [i-ma-chi-nin], s. Imaginación, fantasía.

imago [ɪ'mægə] [i-ma-go], s. (Lat.) Insecto adulto llegado a la perfección, desarrollado sexualmente.

Imam [ɪ'mɑːm] [i-mam], s. 1. Imán, ministro de la religión mahometana, que recita las oraciones. 2. Título de Mahoma y sus cuatro sucesores inmediatos.

imbalance [ɪm'bæləns] [im-ba-lans], s. Desequilibrio.

imbank [ɪm'bæŋk] [im-bank], va. Respecto de esta palabra y otras en im- que no se hallan aquí, véase em-.

imbarn [ɪm'bɑːn] [im-barn], va. Entrojar, encerrar en graneros.

imbecile ['ɪmbəsiːl] [im-be-sil], a. Imbécil, necio, débil, tonto (idiot).

imbecility [ˌɪmbɪ'sɪlɪtɪ] [im-bi-si-li-ti], s. Imbecilidad, debilidad; impotencia.

imbed ['ɪmbed] [im-bed], va. V. EMBED.

imbibe [ɪm'baɪb] [im-baib], va. 1. Embeber, atraer y recoger en sí alguna cosa líquida. 2. Empapar, chupar. 3. Embelesar el ánimo con alguna idea: en castellano sólo se usa en este sentido como neutro el verbo embeber, y se dice embeberse o embebecerse. 4. Beber (drink), ingerir.

imbiber [ɪm'baɪbəʳ] [im-bai-baʳ], s. Embebedor, la persona o cosa que embebe.

imbibiton [ɪm'bɪbɪtən] [im-bi-bi-ton], s. Imbibición.

imbitter [ɪm'bɪtəʳ] [im-bi-taʳ], va. V. EMBITTER.

imbosom [ɪm'bəsəm] [im-bo-som], va. V. EMBOSOM.

imbricate, imbricated [ɪm'brɪkeɪt] [im-bri-keit], a. Imbricado, puesto o colocado uno sobre otro como ripias o pizarras.

imbrication [ˌɪmbrɪ'keɪʃən] [im-bri-kei-shon], s. Desigualdad cóncava, como la de las conchas.

imbroglio [ɪm'brəʊliəʊ] [im-brou-liou], s. Embrollo, engaño. complicación de la cual resulta confusión.

imbrown [ɪm'braʊn] [im-braun], va. V. EMBROWN.

imbrue [ɪm'bruː] [im-bru], va. Remojar, embeber o empapar una cosa en algún líquido. **To imbure one's hands in blood**, teñir sus manos en sangre.

imbrute [ɪm'bruːt] [im-brut], va. Embrutecer, degradar a uno o reducirle al estado de los brutos. -vn. Reducirse al estado de bruto.

imbue [ɪm'bjuː] [im-biu], va. 1. Tinturar, teñir. 2. Imbuir, infundir (inspire), llenar o penetrar de una doctrina, una opinión, etc.

imitability [ˌɪmɪtə'bɪlɪtɪ] [i-mi-ter-bi-li-ti], s. La calidad de ser imitable.

imitable ['ɪmɪtəbl] [i-mi-ter-bol], a. Imitable, que se puede imitar.

imitate ['ɪmɪteɪt] [i-mi-teit], va. 1. Imitar, tomar por modelo, seguir el ejemplo. 2. Remedar, contrahacer. 3. Copiar.

imitation [ˌɪmɪ'teɪʃən] [i-mi-tei-shon], s. 1. Imitación (copying). **To learn by imitation**, aprender imitando. 2. Ejemplar, modelo; copia. 3. Método de traducir libremente un escrito o composición. -a. De imitación.

imitational [ˌɪmɪ'teɪʃənl] [i-mi-tei-sho-nal], a. Imitador, referente a la imitación.

imitative ['ɪmɪtətɪv] [i-mi-ter-tiv], a. Imitativo, imitado.

imitator ['ɪmɪteɪtəʳ] [i-mi-tei-taʳ], s. Imitador.

imitatorship ['ɪmɪteɪtəʃɪp] [i-mi-ter-ship], s. Imitación, calidad de ser imitador.

immaculate ['ɪmækjɒlɪt] [i-ma-kiu-lit], a. 1. Inmaculado, puro (pure). 2. Impecable.

inmaculately [ɪ'mækjɒlɪtlɪ] [i-ma-kiu-lit-li], adv. Inmaculadamente.

inmaculateness [ɪ'mækjɒlɪtnɪs] [i-ma-kiu-lit-nes], s. Pureza, inocencia.

immailed ['ɪmeɪld] [i-meild], a. Lo que tiene malla o armadura.

immalleable ['ɪmælɪəbl] [i-ma-lia-bol], a. No maleable.

immanacle ['ɪmænəkl] [i-ma-na-kol], va. 1. Aprisionar con esposas o grillos. 2. (Fam.) Echar o poner grillos o esposas.

immance ['ɪməns] [i-mans], a. (Ant.) Vasto, enorme (huge).

immanely ['ɪmænlɪ] [i-ma-ni-li], adv. Mostruosamente.

immanence, immanency ['ɪmənəns] [i-ma-nans], s. La calidad y el estado de inmanente; inherencia.

immanent ['ɪmənənt] [i-ma-nant], a. Inmanente, inherente, intrínseco, interno; lo que va unido de un modo inseparable a la esencia de un ser.

immanuel [ɪ'mænjɒəl] [i-ma-nuel], n. pr. Nombre bíblico de Jesucristo, que quiere decir Dios con nosotros.

immask ['ɪmɑːsk] [i-mask], va. Enmascarar, disfrazar.

immaterial [ˌɪmə'tɪərɪəl] [i-ma-tia-rial], a. 1. Inmaterial, incorpóreo. 2. Frívolo, fútil; indiferente; de ninguna importancia, irrelevante (unimportant).

immaterialism [ˌɪmə'tɪərɪəlɪzm] [i-ma-tia-ria-li-sem], s. 1. Espiritismo. 2. Inmaterialismo; idealismo.

immaterialist [ˌɪmə'tɪərɪəlɪst] [i-ma-tia-ria-list], s. Inmaterialista, nombre dado a unos sectarios que sostenían que todo es espíritu; los partidarios del espiritismo.

immateriality [ˌɪmə'tɪərɪˌælɪtɪ] [i-ma-tia-ria-li-ti], s. Inmaterialidad, espiritualidad.

immaterialized [ˌɪmə'tɪərɪəlaɪst] [i-ma-tia-ria-laist], a. Incorpóreo, espiritual.

immaterially [ˌɪmə'tɪərɪəlɪ] [i-ma-tia-ria-li], adv. Espiritualmente.

immaterialness [ˌɪmə'tɪərɪəlnɪs] [i-ma-tia-rial-nes], s. Inmaterialidad.

immature [ˌɪmə'tʃʊəʳ] [i-ma-chuaʳ], a. 1. Inmaturo, que no ha llegado a la perfección; imperfecto, no desarrollado. 2. Temprano, adelantado, prematuro, precoz.

immaturely [ˌɪmə'tʃʊəlɪ] [i-ma-chua-li], adv. Prematuramente, antes de tiempo o de la completa madurez; demasiado pronto.

immeasurability, immeasurableness [ɪ'meʒərə'bɪlɪtɪ] [i-me-sa-ra-bi-li-ti], s. Inmensidad, inmensurabilidad, calidad de lo que no puede medirse.

immeasurable [ɪ'meʒərəbl] [i-me-sa-ra-bol], a. Inmensurable, inmenso (vast).

immeasurably [ɪ'meʒərəblɪ] [i-me-sa-ra-bli], adv. Inmensamente.

immediacy [ɪˈmiːdɪəsɪ] [i-mi-dia-si], *s*. Independencia absoluta, facultad de obrar sin intervención de otro.

immediate [ɪˈmiːdɪət] [i-mi-diet], *a*. Inmediato (prompt), lo que se sigue próximamente; instánteneo, o que no admite dilación. 2. Inmediato, lo que obra por sí sin la mediación de otra cosa; directo. 3. Inmediato, lo que está cercano o contiguo a otra cosa. 4. Intuitivo, perteneciente a una concepción directa. **Immediate truths**, verdades intuitivas.

immediately [ɪˈmiːdɪətlɪ] [i-mi-diet-li], *adv*. 1. Inmediatamente, luego, al instante. **It's not immediately obvious**, no resulta obvio a primera vista. 2. Directamente (directly), sin intervención de otra causa; intuitivamente.

immediateness [ɪˈmiːdɪətnɪs] [i-mi-diet-nes], *s*. 1. Calidad o estado de inmediato. 2. Presencia inmediata.

immedicable [ɪˈmiːdɪkəbl] [i-mi-di-ka-bol], *a*. Incurable, irremediable.

immelodious [ɪˈmiːlədɪəs] [i-mi-lo-dios], *a*. Discorde; lo que carece de melodía.

immemorial [ɪˈmiːmərɪəl] [i-mi-mo-rial], *a*. Inmemorial o inmemorable, tan antiguo que no hay memoria de cuándo comenzó o sucedió.

immense [ɪˈmens] [i-mens], *a*. Inmenso, infinito, ilimitado; vasto; desmedido, que no tiene medida.

immensely [ɪˈmenslɪ] [i-mens-li], *adv*. Inmensamente, sin medida, ilimitadamente.

immenseness [ɪˈmensnɪs] [i-mensnes], *s*. Inmensidad, grandeza ilimitada.

immensity [ɪˈmensɪtɪ] [i-men-si-ti], *s*. Inmensidad, infinidad en extensión o medida.

immensurability [ɪˈmensərəˈbɪlɪtɪ] [i-men-su-ra-bi-li-ti], *s*. Inmensurabilidad.

immensurable [ɪˈmenśrəbl] [i-men-su-ra-bol], **immensurate** [ɪˈmensəreɪt] [i-men-su-reit], *a*. Inmensurable.

immerge [ɪˈmɜːdʒ] [i-merch], *va*. Sumergir, zambullir, meter alguna cosa dentro de un fluido. *-vn*. Ocultarse, perderse de vista, como una estrella ante la luz del sol.

immerse [ɪˈmɜːs] [i-mers], *va*. 1. Sumergir (submerge), zambullir, meter alguna cosa dentro del agua o cualquier otro fluido. 2. Meter alguna cosa en un sitio muy hondo o en algo muy espeso. 3. Sumergir o anegar en penas, dolor, miseria, etc. 4. Bautizar por medio de la inmersión.

immersed [ɪˈmɜːst] [i-merst], *a*. Hundido, sumido, sumergido, agobiado.

immersion [ɪˈmɜːʃən] [i-mer-shon], *s*. Inmersión, hundimiento, sumersión. **Immersion heater**, calentador eléctrico.

immersionist [ɪˈmɜːʃənɪst] [i-mer-sho-nist], *s*. Inmersionista, el que cree en la necesidad de la inmersión total del cuerpo en el bautismo.

immesh [ɪˈmeʃ] [i-mesh], *va*. *V*. ENMESH.

immethodical [ˌɪmeˈθədɪkl] [i-me-zo-di-kal], *adv*. Confusamente, de una manera falta de orden o método.

immethodicalness [ˌɪmeˈθədɪklnɪs] [i-me-zo-di-kal-nes], *s*. Confusión, falta de orden o método.

immigrant [ˈɪmɪɡrənt] [i-mi-grant], *s*. Inmigrante, el que llega a un país con ánimo de establecerse en él.

immigrate [ˈɪmɪɡreɪt] [i-mi-greit], *vn*. Inmigrar, trasladarse o llegar a un país para establecerse en él.

immigrate, *vn*. Inmigrar, trasladarse o llegar a un país para establecerse en él.

inmigration [ˌɪmɪˈɡreɪʃən] [i-mi-grei-shon], *s*. Inmigración.

imminence [ˈɪmɪnəns] [i-mi-nens], *s*. El peligro próximo, inminente o cercano.

imminent [ˈɪmɪnənt] [i-mi-nent], *a*. Inminente, lo que amenaza o está para suceder prontamente.

immingle [ɪˈmɪŋɡl] [i-min-guel], *va*. Mezclar (mix), trabar, unir.

immiscibility [ˌɪmɪsɪˈbɪlɪtɪ] [i-mi-si-bi-li-ti], *s*. (*Quím.*) Inmiscibilidad, calidad de lo que no es susceptible de mezcla.

immiscible [ˈɪmɪsɪbl] [i-mi-si-bol], *a*. Inmiscible, que no se puede mezclar homogéneamente con otra cosa, como el agua y el aceite.

immission [ˈɪmɪʃən] [i-mi-shon], *s*. Introducción, inyección, acto y efecto de inyectar o de hacer entrar, lo opuesto a *emission*.

immit [ˈɪmɪt] [i-mit], *va*. Introducir una cosa en otra, inyectar; opuesto a *emit*.

immitigable [ˈɪmɪtɪɡəbl] [i-mi-ti-ga-bol], *a*. Inmitigable, lo que no puede ser mitigado.

immobile [ɪˈməʊbaɪl] [i-mou-bail], *a*. 1. Inmóvil (motionless), inmoble, que no se puede mover. 2. Inmoble, que no se deja afectar por las emociones; constante en sus afectos.

immobility [ɪˈməʊbaɪlɪtɪ] [i-mou-bai-li-ti], *s*. Inmovilidad, falta de movimiento, resistencia al movimiento.

immobilize [ɪˈməʊbɪlaɪz] [i-mou-bi-lais], *vt*. Inmovilizar.

immoderacy [ɪˈmɒdɪrəsɪ] [i-mo-di-ra-si], *s*. Exceso, inmoderación.

immoderate [ɪˈmɒdərɪt] [i-mo-de-rit], *a*. Inmoderado, excesivo, irrazonable; intemperante, desarreglado, radical, extremista..

immoderately [ɪˈmɒdərɪtlɪ] [i-mo-de-rit-li], *adv*. Inmoderadamente.

immoderateness [ɪˈmɒdərɪtnɪs] [i-mo-de-rit-nes], *s*. Inmoderación.

immoderation [ˌɪmɒdəˈreɪʃən] [i-mo-de-rei-shon], *s*. Inmoderación, exceso, desarreglo.

immodest [ɪˈmɒdɪst] [i-mo-dist], *a*. 1. Falto de reserva, de decoro, de pudor; inmodesto, presuntuoso (conceited), impuro, indecente, deshonesto. 2. Impudente, atrevido, insolente. 3. (*Ant.*) Inmoderado, poco razonable.

immodestly [ɪˈmɒdɪstlɪ] [i-mo-dist-li], *adv*. Inmodestamente, de una manera indecorosa, deshonestamente.

immodesty [ɪˈmɒdɪstɪ] [i-mo-dis-ti], *s*. Inmodestia (conceit), falta de modestia; de decoro; indecencia (indecency), deshonestidad; profanidad.

immolate [ˈɪməʊleɪt] [i-mou-leit], *va*. Inmolar, sacrificar.

immolation [ˌɪməʊleɪʃən] [i-mou-lei-shon], *s*. Inmolación, sacrificio (cruento, por regla general).

immolator [ˈɪməʊleɪtəʳ] [i-mou-lei-taʳ], *s*. Inmolador, sacrificador.

immoral [ɪˈmɒrəl] [i-mo-ral], *a*. Inmoral, depravado, malvado; desarreglado, licencioso (dissolute), vicioso, corrompido.

immorality [ˌɪməˈrælɪtɪ] [i-mo-ra-li-ti], *s*. Inmoralidad, pravedad, iniquidad, perversidad, corrupción de costumbres, desarreglo, desorden.

immortal [ɪˈmɔːtl] [i-mor-tal], *a*. 1. Inmortal; perpetuo. 2. Inmortal, digno de eterna fama.

immortality [ˌɪmɔːˈtælɪtɪ] [i-mor-ter-li-ti], *s*. 1. Inmortalidad, calidad de inmortal. 2. Inmortalidad, eterna memoria o fama entre los hombres.

immortalization [ˌɪmɔːtələraɪzeɪʃən] [i-mor-ter-lai-sei-shon], *s*. El acto de inmortalizar; perpetuación.

immortalize [ɪˈmɔːtəlaɪz] [i-mor-ter-lais], *va*. Inmortalizar, eternizar.

immortally [ɪˈmɔːtəlɪ] [i-mor-ter-li], *adv*. Inmortalmente, sin fin, para siempre.

immotile [ɪˈmɒtɪl] [i-mo-til], *a*. (*Biol.*) Inmóvil, estacionario.

inmovability [ɪˈmuːvəˈbɪlɪtɪ] [i-mu-va-bi-li-ti], *s*. Inmovilidad, incapacidad o imposibilidad de moverse.

immovable [ɪˈmuːvəbl] [i-mu-va-bol], *a*. 1. Inmóvil, inamovible, fijo, inmoto. 2. Inmoble, inmutable (unchanging), firme, inflexible en un designio, inalterable. 3. Impasible, insensible, apático. **Immovables, immovable estate**, inmueble: se dice de los bienes raíces o fincas.

immovableness [ɪˈmuːvəblnɪs] [i-mu-va-bol-nes], *s*. Inmovilidad; inmutabilidad; inalterabilidad; insensibilidad.

immovably [ɪˈmuːvəblɪ] [i-mu-va-bli], *adv*. Inmóvilmente, inmutablemente, de un modo inalterable.

immune [ɪˈmjuːn] [i-miun], *a*. (*Med.*) Inmune, exento de una enfermedad; especialmente, protegido por la inoculación. **I've had measles, so I'm immune**, ya he tenido el sarampión, así que estoy inmunizado.

immunization [ˌɪmjuːnaɪˈzeɪʃən] [i-miu-nai-sei-shon], *s.* Inmunización.

immunize [ˈɪmjʊnaɪz] [i-miu-nais], *va.* Hacer inmune, proteger por la inoculación contra la infección.

immunity [ɪˈmjuːnɪtɪ] [i-miu-ni-ti], *s.* Inmunidad, libertad, privilegio, exención (exemption) de cargas, obligaciones, penas, etc.; franquicia. **Parliamentary immunity**, inmunidad parlamentaria.

immure [ɪˈmjʊəʳ] [i-miuaʳ], *va.* Emparedar, tapar o cercar con paredes o muros.

immutability [ɪˈmjʊtəˈbɪlɪtɪ] [i-miu-ter-bi-li-ti], *s.* Inmutabilidad, firmeza, constancia.

immutable [ɪˈmjʊtəbl] [i-miu-ter-bol], *a.* Inmutable, que no puede mudar; inalterable. **This law is immutable**, esta ley es inmutable.

immutableness [ɪˈmjʊtəblnɪs] [i-miu-ter-bol-nes], *s.* Inmutabilidad.

immutably [ɪˈmjʊtəblɪ] [i-miu-ter-bli], *adv.* Inmutablemente, inalterablemente.

imp [ɪmp] [imp], *s.* 1. Diablillo, duende, trasgo. 2. Diablillo, tunantuelo, muchacho travieso.

impact [ˈɪmpækt] [im-pakt], *va.* Empaquetar; unir varias cosas entre sí apretándolas mucho unas con otras.

impact, *s.* Acción de dar un golpe; choque, colisión de un cuerpo que está en movimiento con otro. **The bomb exploded on impact**, la bomba estalló al hacer impacto.

impacted [ɪmˈpæktɪd] [im-pak-tid], *a.* Impactado.

impaction [ɪmˈpækʃən] [im-pak-shon], *s. (Med.)* Atasco, impedimiento de un órgano, como el intestino; también, presión de una parte sobre otra.

impair [ɪmˈpɛəʳ] [im-peaʳ], *va.* Empeorar, disminuir en cantidad o en valor; alterar, deteriorar, echar a perder, debilitar. *-vn.* Empeorar, ir una cosa de mal en peor; enflaquecer; gastarse o echarse a perder alguna cosa.

impairer [ɪmˈpɛərəʳ] [im-pea-raʳ], *s.* Lo que disminuye o empeora.

impairing [ɪmˈpɛərɪŋ] [im-pea-rin], *s.* Diminución, alteración (disturbance).

impairment [ɪmˈpɛəmənt] [im-pea-ment], *s.* Empeoramiento, deterioración, deterioro.

impale, *va. V.* EMPALE.

impalpability [ɪmˌpælpəˈbɪlɪtɪ] [im-pal-pa-bi-li-ti], *s.* Impalpabilidad (intangibility), calidad de lo que es impalpable.

impalpable [ɪmˈpælpəbl] [im-pal-pa-bol], *a.* 1. Impalpable, que no se puede tocar o palpar. 2. Intangible (intangible), incomprensible, ininteligible, sin realidad.

impanate [ɪmˈpəneɪt] [im-pa-neit], *va. (Teol.)* Empanar; incorporar en el pan.

impanation [ˌɪmpəˈneɪʃən] [im-pa-nei-shon], *s.* Empanación, la subsistencia del pan con el cuerpo de Jesucristo después de la consagración, según los luteranos.

impanel [ɪmˈpənl] [im-pa-nel], *va.* 1. Inscribir en la lista de los jurados. 2. Formar la lista de los jurados; hacer prestar juramento, como lo prestan los miembros de un jurado.

imparadise [ɪmˈpærədaɪz] [im-pa-ra-dais], *va.* Colocar en un estado feliz semejante al del paraíso.

imparity [ɪmˈpærɪtɪ] [im-pa-ri-ti], *s.* 1. Desigualdad, desproporcion (disparity). 2. Indivisibilidad, calidad de impartible. 3. Disparidad, diferencia.

impark [ɪmˈpɑːk] [im-park], *va.* Encerrar o incluir en un parque; rodear, hacer un parque por medio de cercas.

impart [ɪmˈpɑːt] [im-part], *va.* 1. Dar (give), conceder, conferir. 2. Comunicar, dar parte, hacer saber.

impartial [ɪmˈpɑːʃəl] [im-par-shal], *a.* Imparcial.

impartiality [ɪmˌpɑːʃɪˈælɪtɪ] [im-par-shia-li-ti], *s.* Imparcialidad, equidad (fairness), desinterés.

impartially [ɪmˈpɑːʃəlɪ] [im-par-sha-li], *adv.* Imparcialmente, equitativamente.

impartible [ɪmˈpɑːtɪbl] [im-par-ti-bol], *a.* 1. Impartible, indivisible. 2. Comunicable; concedible.

impartment [ɪmˈpɑːtmənt] [im-part-ment], *s.* Acción de dar, de conferir; comunicación.

impassable [ɪmˈpɑːsəbl] [im-pa-sa-bol], *a.* Intransitable, impracticable.

impassableness [ɪmˈpɑːsəblnɪs] [im-pa-sa-bol-nes], *s.* Incapacidad de ser pasado o de admitir pasaje o paso.

impasse [ɪmˈpɑːs] [im-pas], *s.* 1. Camino intransitable. 2. *(Fig.)* Callejón sin salida, obstáculo insuperable, atolladero, atascadero, punto muerto.

impassibility [ˌɪmpɑːsəˈbɪlɪtɪ] [im-pa-sa-bi-li-ti], *s.* 1. Impasibilidad, incapacidad de padecer. 2. Inalterabilidad.

impassible [ɪmˈpɑːsɪbl] [im-pa-si-bol], *a.* 1. Impasible, incapaz de padecer. 2. Apático (apathetic), insensible, sin emoción.

impassibleness [ɪmˈpɑːsɪblnɪs] [im-pa-si-bol-nes], *s.* Impasibilidad.

impassion [ɪmˈpæʃən] [im-pa-shon], *va. (Poet.)* Mover las pasiones, excitar fuertemente el ánimo. *-vn.* Apasionarse (enthuse).

impassionable [ɪmˈpæʃənəl] [im-pa-sho-na-bol], *a.* Conmovible, susceptible de apasionamiento.

impassionate [ɪmˈpæʃəneɪt] [im-pa-sho-neit], *va.* Apasionar; conmover, afectar vivamente.

impassioned [ɪmˈpæʃənd] [im-pa-shond], *a.* Apasionado, vehemente; que expresa pasión, ardor, etc.

impassive [ɪmˈpæsɪv] [im-pa-siv], *a.* Lo que está exento de la influencia de las causas externas.

impassiveness [ɪmˈpæsɪvnɪs] [im-pa-siv-nes], *s.* El estado de hallarse exento de la influencia de las causas externas.

impastation [ɪmˈpæsteɪʃən] [im-pas-tei-shon], *s.* 1. Una mezcla se substancias de diversos colores y consistencia, unidas entre sí por un cemento y endurecidas por el aire o el fuego. 2. *(Pint.)* Empaste.

impaste [ɪmˈpeɪst] [im-peist], *va.* 1. Hacer pasta o poner una cosa en forma de pasta. 2. *(Pint.)* Empastar, sobrecargar de colores lo que se ha dibujado.

impatible [ɪmˈpætɪbl] [im-pa-ti-bol], *a.* Intolerable.

impatience [ɪmˈpeɪʃəns] [im-pei-shans], *s.* 1. Impaciencia, desasosiego. 2. Irritabilidad, intolerancia de toda oposición o sujeción; petulancia, ansia, apresuramiento.

impatient [ɪmˈpeɪʃənt] [im-pei-shant], *a.* 1. Impaciente. 2. Inquieto, irritable, intolerante; apresurado. *-s.* El que es impaciente, el que tiene pasiones fuertes.

impatiently [ɪmˈpeɪʃəntlɪ] [im-pei-shant-li], *adv.* Inquietamente, impacientemente.

impawn [ɪmˈpɔːn] [im-pon], *va.* Empeñar, dar o dejar alguna cosa en prenda.

impeach [ɪmˈpiːtʃ] [im-pich], *va.* 1. Acusar, denunciar o delatar en virtud de autoridad pública; imputar; dirigir una acusación a un personaje, encausarlo. 2. *(For.)* Tachar, hacer objeción a, poner tachas.

impeachable [ɪmˈpiːtʃəbl] [im-pi-cha-bol], *a.* Delatable, susceptible de acusación; censurable, cuestionable, expuesto a ser tachado.

impeacher [ɪmˈpiːtʃəʳ] [im-pi-chaʳ], *s.* Acusador, denunciador, delator.

impeachment [ɪmˈpiːtʃmənt] [im-pich-ment], *s.* 1. Reconvención, tacha; desdoro. 2. Acusación pública; la acción de pedir cuentas; en especial, acusación y proceso de un alto funcionario del orden civil. 3. Imputación, delación.

impearl [ɪmˈpɜːl] [im-perl], *va.* 1. Hacer alguna cosa ne figura de perlas. 2. Adornar con perlas.

impeccability [ɪmˈpekəˌbɪlɪtɪ] [im-pe-ka-bi-li-ti], *s.* Impecabilidad.

impeccable [ɪmˈpekəbl] [im-pe-ka-bol], *a.* Impecable, incapaz de pecar.

impeccancy [ɪmˈpekənsɪ] [im-pe-kan-si], *s.* Impecabilidad, incapacidad de epcar.

impeccant [ɪmˈpekənt] [im-pe-kant], *a.* Exento de pecar; sin tacha.

impecuniosity [ɪmˈpekjʊnɪˈɒsɪtɪ] [im-pe-kiu-nio-si-ti], *s.* Falta de dinero, de recursos.

impecunious [ˌɪmpɪˈkjuːnɪəs] [im-pi-kiu-nios], *a*. Falto de dinero; habitualmente pobre.

impede [ɪmˈpiːd] [im-pid], *va*. Impedir, imbarazar con obstáculos, o sser obstáculo; retadar, obstruir.

impediment [ɪmˈpedɪmənt] [im-pe-di-ment], *s*. Impedimento, embarazo, obstáculo; obstrucción.

impedimental [ɪmˈpedɪməntl] [im-pe-di-men-tal], *a*. Que impide, detiene o retarda; que sirve de obstáculo para la ejecución de una cosa.

impeditive [ɪmˈpedɪtɪv] [im-pe-di-tiv], *a*. Impeditivo.

impel [ɪmˈpel] [im-pel], *va*. 1. Impeler, excitar a obrar, poner en movimiento, hacer avanzar. 2. Impeler, incitar, apretar, apurar.

impellent [ɪmˈpelənt] [im-pe-lent], *a*. Impelente; impulsor; que tiende a impeler. -*s*. 1. Empuje o empujo. 2. Motor, móvil, autor.

impeller [ɪmˈpelə^r] [im-pe-la^r], *s*. Impulsor, el que empuja o impele hacia adelante.

impen [ɪmˈpen] [im-pen], *va*. V. IMPOUND.

impend [ɪmˈpend] [im-pend], *vn*. Amenazar, amagar, ser inminente.

impendence [ɪmˈpendəns] [im-pen-dans], **Impendency** [ɪmˈpendənsɪ] [im-pen-dan-si], *s*. El estado de lo que amenaza o está próximo a caer sobre uno.

impendent [ɪmˈpendənt] [im-pen-dant], **impending** [ɪmˈpendɪŋ] [im-pen-din], *a*. Inminente, pendiente, amenazante.

impenetrability [ɪmˌpenɪtrəˈbɪlɪtɪ] [im-pe-ni-tra-bi-li-ti], *s*. 1. Impenetrabilidad, calidad de lo impenetrable. 2. *(Fís.)* Impenetrabilidad, propiedad que impide la presencia de un cuerpo en el lugar que otro ocupa.

impenetrable [ɪmˈpenɪtrəbl] [im-pe-ni-tra-bol], *a*. 1. Impenetrable, intransitable, que no se puede penetrar; se dice de las cosas materiales. 2. Impenetrable, que no se puede penetrar con la vista ni con la mente; abstruso, difícil de comprender; denso, espeso. **Impenetrable darkness**, obscuridad densa, impenetrable. 3. *(Fís.)* que posee la propiedad física de la impenetrabilidad.

impenetrableness [ɪmˈpenɪtrəblnɪs] [im-pe-ni-tra-bol-nes], *s*. Impenetrabilidad.

impenetrably [ɪmˈpenɪtrəblɪ] [im-pe-ni-tra-bli], *adv*. Impenetrablemente.

impenitence [ɪmˈpenɪtəns] [im-pe-ni-tens], **impenitency** [ɪmˈpenɪtənsɪ] [im-pe-ni-ten-si], *s*. Impenitencia. endurecimiento de corazón, obstinación en el pecado.

impenitent [ɪmˈpenɪtənt] [im-pe-ni-tent], *a*. Impenitente, obstinado en la culpa. -*s*. El que es impenitente.

impenitently [ɪmˈpenɪtəntlɪ] [im-pe-ni-tent-li], *adv*. Sin penitencia o contrición, con endurecimiento de corazón.

impennate [ɪmˈpeneɪt] [im-pe-neit], *a*. Impennado, que tiene alas cortas y con plumar tan pequeñas que parecen escamas, como las alas de los pingüinos.

impennous [ɪmˈpenəs] [im-pe-nos], *a*. Sin alas.

imperate [ɪmˈpəreɪt] [im-pe-reit], *a*. Lo que nace de voluntad y se hace de buena gana, por una convicción interior de que debe hacerse.

imperative [ɪmˈperətɪv] [im-pe-ra-tiv], *a*. Imperativo, imperioso, que expresa un mandato positivo; perentorio. -*s*. 1. Mandato perentorio. 2. *(Gram.)* Modo imperativo.

imperatively [ɪmˈperətɪvlɪ] [im-pe-ra-tiv-li], *adv*. Imperativamente, por orden expresa.

imperceptible [ˌɪmpəˈseptəbl] [im-pa-sep-ter-bol], *a*. Imperceptible, que no se puede percibir. -*s*. Cosa imperceptible o pequeñísima.

imperceptibleness [ˌɪmpəˈseptəblnɪs] [im-pa-sep-ter-bol-nes], *s*. Imperceptibilidad.

imperceptibly [ˌɪmpəˈseptəblɪ] [im-pa-sep-ter-bli], *adv*. Imperceptiblemente.

imperception [ˌɪmpəˈsepʃən] [im-pa-sep-shon], *s*. Falta de percepción, impercepción.

imperceptive [ˌɪmpəˈseptɪv] [im-pa-sep-tiv], **impercipient** [ˌɪmpəˈsɪpɪənt] [im-pa-si-piant], *a*. Lo que no tiene poder de percibir o de percepción.

imperfect [ɪmˈpɜːfɪkt] [im-per-fikt], *a*. Imperfecto, incompleto, defectuoso.

imperfection [ˌɪmpəˈfekʃən] [im-pa-fek-shon], *s*. 1. Imperfección. 2. Imperfección, falta o defecto ligero en lo moral.

imperfectly [ɪmˈpɜːfɪktlɪ] [im-per-fikt-li], *adv*. Imperfectamente.

imperfectness [ɪmˈpɜːfɪktnɪs] [im-per-fikt-nes], *s*. Imperfección, defecto, falta.

imperforable [ɪmˈpɜːfərəbl] [im-per-fo-ra-bol], *a*. Imperforable, lo que no se puede agujerear.

imperforate, imperforated [ɪmˈpɜːfərɪt] [im-per-fo-rit], *a*. Imperforado, sin perforaciones, cerrado.

imperforation [ˌɪmpəfəˈreɪʃən] [im-per-fo-rei-shon], *s*. Imperforación, cerramiento, obstrucción de las partes que deben estar abiertas.

imperial [ɪmˈpɪərɪəl] [im-pi-rial], *a*. 1. Imperial, perteneciente a un imperio o a un emperador o emperatriz. 2. Soberano, predominante. 3. A propósito para un emperador, digno o en calidad. -*s*. 1. Pera, perilla, porción de barba que se deja crecer bajo el labio inferior. 2. *(Arq.)* Cúpula con perfil de cimacio, como las moriscas. 3. Cualquier cosa de tamaño o calidad superior en su clase.

imperialism [ɪmˈpɪərɪəlɪzəm] [im-pi-ria-li-sem], *s*. Imperialismo, estado, carácter o espíritu imperial; aspiración a formar un imperio; doctrino de los imperialistas.

imperialist [ɪmˈpɪərɪəlɪst] [im-pi-ria-list], *s*. Imperial, imperialista, partidario del gobierno imperial; en particular, (a) partidario del antiguo imperio de Alemania; (b) partidario del imperio francés, en oposición así a la república como a la monarquía; bonapartista.

imperialized [ɪmˈpɪərɪəlaɪst] [im-pi-ria-laist], *a*. El que es del partido de un emperador.

imperially [ɪmˈpɪərɪəlɪ] [im-pi-ria-li], *adv*. Imperialmente.

imperialty [ɪmˈpɪərɪəltɪ] [im-pi-rial-ti], *s*. El poder imperial.

imperil [ɪmˈpɪərɪl] [im-pi-ril], *va*. Poner en peligro, en riesgo; arriesgar.

imperious [ɪmˈpɪərɪəs] [im-pi-rios], *a*. 1. Imperioso, altivo, orgulloso, arrogante, fiero, despótico. 2. Urgente, perentorio, irresistible. **An imperious necessity**, una necesidad urgente, imperiosa.

imperiously [ɪmˈpɪərɪəslɪ] [im-pi-rios-li], *adv*. Imperiosamente, con altivez.

imperiousness [ɪmˈpɪərɪəsnɪs] [im-pi-rios-nes], *s*. Autoridad, mando; arrogancia, altivez.

imperishable [ɪmˈperɪʃəbl] [im-pe-ri-sha-bol], *a*. Imperecedero; indestructible; eterno.

impermanence [ɪmˈpɜːmənəns] [im-per-ma-nens], **impermanency** [ɪmˈpɜːmənənsɪ] [im-per-ma-nen-si], *s*. Inestabilidad.

impermanent [ɪmˈpɜːmənət] [im-per-ma-nent], *a*. Que no es permanente.

impermeability [ɪmˌpɜːmɪəˈbɪlɪtɪ] [im-per-mia-bi-li-ti], *s*. Impermeabilidad.

impermeable [ɪmˈpɜːmɪəbl] [im-per-mia-bol], *a*. Impermeable, impenetrable, que no puede ser penetrado por los fluidos.

impersonal [ɪmˈpɜːsnl] [im-per-so-nal], *a*. 1. Impersonal, que no tiene ni implica personalidad. 2. Que no se relaciona con una persona o cosa determinada. 3. *(Gram.)* Impersonal, que tiene o contiene sujeto indeterminado; en inglés, ese sujeto es generalmente el pronombre *it*. **It happened to me to be seated beside her at table**, me tocó sentarme a su lado en la mesa.

impersonally [ɪmˈpɜːsnəlɪ] [im-per-so-na-li], *adv.* Impersonalmente.

impersonate [ɪmˈpɜːsəneɪt] [im-per-so-neit], *va.* 1. Personificar. 2. Representar, hacer el papel de.

impersonation [ɪmˌpɜːsəˈneɪʃən] [im-per-so-nei-shon], *s.* Representación, papel; personificación.

imperspicuous [ɪmˈpɜːspɪkjʊəs] [im-pers-pi-kiuos], *a.* Oscuro, lo que no es perspicuo o claro.

impersuadable [ɪmˈpɜːsʊədəbl] [im-per-sua-da-bol], **impersuasible** [ɪmˈpɜːsɪəsɪbl] [im-per-sua-si-bol], *a.* Impersuasible, incapaz de ser persuadido.

impertinence [ɪmˈpɜːtɪnəns] [im-per-ti-nens], **impertinency** [ɪmˈpɜːtɪnənsɪ] [im-per-ti-nen-si], *s.* Impertinencia; absurdo; insolencia; extravagancia; importunidad; bagatela, cosa de poca o ninguna importancia.

impertinent [ɪmˈpɜːtɪnənt] [im-per-ti-nent], *a.* Impertinente, incómodo, importuno, cansado; frívolo; insolente; descortés. *-s.* Un impertinente, el que en todo se mete.

impertinently [ɪmˈpɜːtɪnəntlɪ] [im-per-ti-nent-li], *adv.* Impertinentemente, insolentemente.

imperturbability [ɪmˌpɜːtɜːbəˈbɪlɪtɪ] [im-per-ter-ba-bi-li-ti], *s.* Imperturbabilidad, serenidad.

imperturbable [ˌɪmpəˈtɜːbəbl] [im-per-ter-ba-bol], *a.* Imperturbable.

imperturbably [ˌɪmpəˈtɜːbəblɪ] [im-per-ter-ba-bli], *adv.* Imperturbablemente.

imperturbation [ˌɪmpəˈtɜːbeɪʃən] [im-per-ter-bei-shon], *s.* Tranquilidad, calma, serenidad, frialdad, sangre fría.

imperturbed [ˌɪmpəˈtɜːbd] [im-per-terbd], *a.* Sereno, quieto, tranquilo, sosegado.

impervious [ɪmˈpɜːvɪəs] [im-per-vios], *a.* Impenetrable, impermeable. **Impervious to air**, impenetrable al aire.

imperviously [ɪmˈpɜːvɪəslɪ] [im-per-vios-li], *adv.* Impenetrablemente.

imperviousness [ɪmˈpɜːvɪəsnɪs] [im-per-vios-nes], *s.* Impenetrabilidad.

impetiginous [ˌɪmpɪˈtɪdʒɪnəs] [im-pi-ti-chi-nos], *a.* Tiñoso, impetiginoso.

impetigo [ˌɪmpɪˈtaɪɡəʊ] [im-pi-tai-gou], *s.* Impétigo, afección cutánea contagiosa; tiña. Se llama familiarmente *crusted scall.*

impetrative [ɪmˈpɪtrətɪv] [im-pi-tra-tiv], *a.* Impetrador, que emplea ruegos, o que tiende a obtener (alguna cosa) por la impetración.

impetuosity [ɪmˌpetjʊˈɒsɪtɪ] [im-pe-tiu-o-si-ti], *s.* Impetuosidad, vehemencia: vivez extremada.

impetuous [ɪmˈpetjʊəs] [im-pe-tiuos], *a.* Impetuoso, violento, arrebatado, vehemente.

impetuously [ɪmˈpetjʊəslɪ] [im-pe-tiuos-li], *adv.* Impetuosamente.

impetuousness [ɪmˈpetjʊəsnɪs] [im-pe-tiuos-nes], *s.* Impetuosidad.

impetus [ˈɪmpɪtəs] [im-pi-tus], *s.* 1. Impetu, fuerza de impulsión, movimiento violento. 2. *(Fig.)* Impulso, incentivo.

impicture [ɪmˈpɪktʃər] [im-pik-cha'], *va.* Pintar, formar un cuadro sobre algo.

impiety [ɪmˈpaɪətɪ] [im-pai-ti], *s.* Impiedad, irreligión.

impignorate [ɪmˈpɪɡnəreɪt] [im-pig-no-reit], *va. (Ant.)* Empeñar, dar o dejar alguna cosa en prenda.

impinge [ɪmˈpɪndʒ] [im-pinch], *vn.* Tocar, caer o golpear contra una cosa después de moverse; tropezar.

impious [ˈɪmpɪəs] [im-pios], *a.* Impío, sacrílego, malvado, perverso, irreligioso, profano.

impiously [ˈɪmpɪəslɪ] [im-pios-li], *adv.* Impíamente.

impiousness [ˈɪmpɪəsnɪs] [im-pios-nes], *s.* Impiedad, desprecio de la religión.

impish [ˈɪmpɪʃ] [im-pish], *a.* Travieso, malicioso, parecido a un diablillo.

implacability [ɪmˌplækəˈbɪlɪtɪ] [im-pla-ka-bi-li-ti], *s.* Implacabilidad; perseverancia en el resentimiento; rencor, odio inveterado, intratable, inexorable, irreconciliable.

implacable [ɪmˈplækəbl] [im-pla-ka-bol], *a.* Implacable, irreconciliable; inexorable.

implacableness [ɪmˈplækəblnɪs] [im-pla-ka-bol-nes], *s.* Odio implacable.

implacably [ɪmˈplækəblɪ] [im-pla-ka-bli], *adv.* Implacablemente.

implacental, implacentate [ˌɪmpləˈsentəl] [im-pla-sen-tal] [ɪmˈplæsenteɪt] [im-pla-sen-teit], *a. (Biol.)* Que no tiene placenta. *-s.* Mamífero que no tiene placenta.

implant [ˈɪmplɑːnt] [im-plant], *va.* Fijar, plantar, ingerir; inculcar, sembrar.

implantation [ˌɪmplənˈteɪʃən] [im-plan-tei-shon], *s.* Injertación, plantación; inculcación.

implausible [ɪmˈplɔːzəbl] [im-plo-si-bol], *adv.* Sin apariencia o probabilidad.

implead [ɪmˈpliːd] [im-pled], *va.* Acusar, demandar ante la justicia; en especial, proceder contra dos o más personas a un tiempo; poner pleito.

impleader [ɪmˈpliːdər] [im-ple-da'], *s.* Acusador, demandante.

implement [ˈɪmplɪmənt] [im-pli-ment], *s.* 1. Herramienta, cualquier instrumento o cualquier útil de que usan los artífices para trabajar en sus obras y labores; utensilio, lo que sirve para comodidad de la vida; arma. 2. Originalmente, suplefaltas, el que llena algún hueco o socorre alguna necesidad; medios.

implete [ɪmˈpliːt] [im-plit], *va.* Llenar, colmar.

implicate [ˈɪmplɪkeɪt] [im-pli-keit], *va.* Implicar, envolver; enredar, embrollar.

implication [ˌɪmplɪˈkeɪʃən] [im-pli-kei-shon], *s.* 1. Implicación, la parte que tiene o se supone tener alguno en la perpetración de un delito. 2. Ilación, deducción; *(For.)* inducción implícita, la que no se expresa aunque tácitamente se comprende.

implicative [ɪmˈplɪkətɪv] [im-pli-ka-tiv], *a.* Implicativo, implicante.

implicatively [ɪmˈplɪkətɪvlɪ] [im-pli-ka-tiv-li], *adv.* Por implicación.

implicit [ɪmˈplɪsɪt] [im-pli-sit], *a.* 1. Implícito, lo que se da a entender sin expresarlo. 2. Fundado en la confianza o fe absolutas, sin reserva, que se tiene en otra persona. **With implicit faith**, con fe ciega, sin vacilación ni reserva.

implicitly [ɪmˈplɪsɪtlɪ] [im-pli-sit-li], *adv.* Implícitamente, tácitamente; sin reserva, sin dudas ni preguntas.

implicitness [ɪmˈplɪsɪtnes] [im-pli-sit-nes], *s.* Calidad de implícito.

implied [ɪmˈplaɪd] [im-plaid], *a. y pp.* de IMPLY. Contenido, incluído, aunque no formalmente expresado; implícito.

impliedly [ɪmˈplaɪdlɪ] [im-plaid-li], *adv.* Por implicación o ilación.

imploration [ˌɪmpləˈreɪʃən] [im-plo-rei-shon], *s.* Imploración, ruego humilde y ferviente.

implore [ɪmˈplɔːr] [im-plo'], *va.* Implorar, suplicar, rogar, pedir con instancia.

implorer [ɪmˈplɔːrər] [im-plo-ra'], *s.* Solicitador.

imploring [ɪmˈplɔːrɪŋ] [im-plo-rin], *a.* Implorante, suplicante.

imploringly [ɪmˈplɔːrɪŋlɪ] [im-plo-rin-li], *adv.* De un modo suplicante, implorante.

imply [ɪmˈplaɪ] [im-plai], *va.* 1. Dar a entender (una significación no expresada), querer decir; significar, denotar. 2. implicar, envolver, enredar. 3. Adscribir, atribuir.

impolicy [ɪmˈpɒlɪsɪ] [im-po-li-si], *s.* Imprudencia, poca maña; indiscreción, impolítica.

impolite [ˌɪmpəˈlaɪt] [im-po-lait], *a.* Descortés, grosero, impolítico.

impoliteness [ˌɪmpəˈlaɪtnɪs] [im-po-lait-nes], *s.* Impolítica, falta de cortesía.

impolitic [ɪmˈpɒlɪtɪk] [im-po-li-tik], *a*. 1. Imprudente, indiscreto, falto de prudencia y discreción. 2. Impolítico, perjudicial para los intereses pendientes.

impolitically [ɪmˈpɒlɪtɪklɪ] [im-po-li-ti-kli], *adv*. Sin previsión ni arte, impolíticamente, indiscretamente.

imponderability [ɪmˌpɒndərəˈbɪlɪtɪ] [im-pon-de-ra-bi-li-ti], *s*. Imponderabilidad, carencia de peso.

imponderable [ɪmˈpɒndərəbl] [im-pon-de-ra-bol], *a*. Imponderable, que no tiene peso perceptible; como el calor, la luz, la electricidad, etc.

imporosity [ˌɪmpəˈrɒsɪtɪ] [im-po-ro-si-ti], *s*. Falta de poros, densidad.

imporous [ɪmˈpɒrəs] [im-po-ros], *a*. Sólido, macizo, que no tiene poros.

import [ˈɪmpɔːt] [im-port], *va*. 1. Importar, introducir géneros extranjeros en un país. 2. Denotar, significar. 3. Importar, ser de entidad, tener importancia, interesar en alto grado. 4. Implicar, envolver; introducir en general. -*vn*. Convenir, importar, ser de entidad.

import, *s*. 1. Tendencia, sentido, significación; dirección. 2. Los géneros importados o que se introducen de un país extranjero; más usado en plural. 3. Importancia; momento, peso, consecuencia, entidad. *Import-duty*, Derechos de entrada.

importable [ɪmˈpɔːtəbl] [im-por-ta-bol], *a*. Importable.

importance [ɪmˈpɔːtəns] [im-por-tans], *s*. 1. Importancia, momento, consecuencia. 2. Autoridad, crédito, dignidad social. 3. Importunidad, vanidad, presunción.

important [ɪmˈpɔːtənt] [im-por-tant], *a*. 1. Importante, que es de importancia, consecuencia o valor. 2. De pretensiones, pomposo, afectado.

importantly [ɪmˈpɔːtəntlɪ] [im-por-tant-li], *adv*. Importantemente.

importation [ˌɪmpɔːˈteɪʃən] [im-por-tei-shon], *s*. 1. Importación, entrada o introducción de géneros extranjeros. 2. La persona o cosa importada.

importer [ɪmˈpɔːtəʳ] [im-por-taʳ], *s*. Introductor de géneros extranjeros.

importing [ɪmˈpɔːtɪŋ] [im-por-tin], *a*. Importador.

importunacy [ˌɪmpɔːtjʊnəsɪ] [im-por-tiu-na-si], *s*. Importunidad.

importunate [ɪmˈpɔːtjʊnɪt] [im-por-tiu-neit], *a*. Importuno, pesado, insistente; urgente, apremiante.

importunately [ˌɪmpɔːˈtjʊnɪtlɪ] [im-por-tiu-neit-li], *adv*. Importunamente.

importunateness [ˌɪmpɔːˈtjʊnɪtnɪs] [im-por-tiu-neit-nes], *s*. Importunidad, solicitación incesante.

importune [ˌɪmpɔːˈtjuːn] [im-por-tiun], *va*. Importunar, instar, pedir con instancia; cansar con frecuentes o incesantes solicitaciones.

importuner [ˌɪmpɔːˈtjuːnəʳ] [im-por-tiu-naʳ], *s*. Importunador.

importunity [ˌɪmpɔːˈtjuːnɪtɪ] [im-por-tiu-ni-ti], *s*. Importunación, importunidad.

imposable [ɪmˈpəʊzəbl] [im-pou-sa-bol], *a*. Pechero, imponible, sujeto a impuestos.

impose [ɪmˈpəʊz] [im-pous], *va*. 1. Imponer cargas, obligaciones, leyes, u otra cosa. 2. Colocar por influencia o fuerza; prescribir, infligir. 3. Imponer las manos el obispo. 4. (*Impr.*) Imponer, colocar en la rama. 5. Engañar, hacer creer y persuadir con engaños alguna falsedad. **To impose on** o **upon**, engañar, hacer creer una cosa falsa. **I have been imposed upon**, me han engañado.

imposer [ɪmˈpəʊzəʳ] [im-pou-saʳ], *s*. El que impone, manda o encarga.

imposing [ɪmˈpəʊzɪŋ] [im-pou-sin], *a*. *y pa*. Imponente, impresivo, que infunde respeto. -*s*. (*Impr.*) Imposición, la acción de colocar en su debido orden las páginas y los blancos. **Imposing-stone o -table**, piedra, o mesa, de imponer.

imposition [ˌɪmpəˈzɪʃən] [im-po-si-shon], *s*. 1. Imposición, la acción de poner una cosa sobre otra. 2. Imposición, la acción de imponer. 3. Imposición, carga, tributo u obligación que se impone. 4. Opresión, violencia. 5. Impostura, ficción, fraude, engaño. 6. La tarea extraordinaria que se da a los jóvenes por castigo. **To prevent imposition**, para precaverse de toda impostura. **The imposition of hands**, la imposición de las manos del obispo en la confirmación o la ordenación.

impossibility [ɪmˌpɒsəˈbɪlɪtɪ] [im-po-si-bi-li-ti], *s*. 1. Imposibilidad. 2. Imposible.

impossible [ɪmˈpɒsəbl] [im-po-si-bol], *a*. Imposible.

impossibly [ɪmˈpɒsəblɪ] [im-po-si-bli], *adv*. De forma imposible, imposiblemente. **The exam was impossibly difficult**, el examen fue de lo más difícil.

impost [ˈɪmpəʊst] [im-poust], *s*. 1. Impuesto, tributo, gabela, contribución. 2. (*Arq.*) Imposta, especie de cornisa sobre que asienta el arco, bóveda, etc.

impostor [ɪmˈpɒstəʳ] [im-pos-taʳ], *s*. Impostor, el que finge y engaña o el que atribuye a otro falsamente alguna cosa.

imposture [ɪmˈpɒstʃəʳ] [im-pos-chaʳ], *s*. Impostura, fraude, engaño, falsedad.

impotence [ɪmˈpɒtəns] [im-po-tans], *s*. 1. Impotencia, falta de fuerza física o intelectual; debilidad. 2. Impotencia, incapacidad de procrear. 3. Desenfreno, arrebato, desarreglo de alguna pasión.

impotent [ɪmˈpɒtənt] [im-po-tent], *a*. 1. Impotente, sin potencia, que carece de vigor o de fuerza; (*Ant.*) imposibililitado por naturaleza o por enfermedad; impedido, tullido o baldado de algún miembro. 2. Impotente, incapaz de engendrar o concebir; se aplica más generalmente al varón o al macho. 3. Desenfrenado, desarreglado, que carece de imperio sobre sí mismo. -*s*. 1. Alfeñique, persona delicada. 2. Hombre impotente, falto de vigor sexual.

impotently [ɪmˈpɒtəntlɪ] [im-po-tent-li], *adv*. Impotentemente.

impound [ɪmˈpaʊnd] [im-paund], *va*. 1. Encerrar, acorralar, meter los ganados en el corral; aprisionar, restringir. 2. (*For.*) Depositar, poner en la custodia de un tribunal de justicia.

impoverish [ɪmˈpɒvərɪʃ] [im-po-va-rish], *va*. 1. Empobrecer, reducir a alguno a la pobreza o la indigencia. 2. Minorar la calidad o la fertilidad de una cosa; deteriorar. **Impoverished blood**, sangre deteriorada, empobrecida.

impoverishment [ɪmˈpɒvərɪʃmənt] [im-po-va-rish-ment], *s*. Empobrecimiento.

impracticability [ɪmˌpræktɪkəˈbɪlɪtɪ] [im-prak-ti-ka-bi-li-ti], *s*. 1. Impracticabilidad, el estado o la cualidad de no ser hacedero. 2. Cosa no hacedera, no factible, impracticable.

impracticable [ɪmˈpræktɪkəbl] [im-prak-ti-ka-bol], *a*. 1. Impracticable, imposible, infactible, lo que no es hacedero. 2. No práctico, inútil, de ningún servicio. 3. Intratable, irrazonable, con quien no se puede vivir; terco; se dice de las personas que tienen mal genio.

impracticableness [ɪmˈpræktɪkəblnɪs] [im-prak-ti-ka-bol-nes], *s*. 1. Imposibilidad. 2. Terquedad, obstinación.

imprecate [ˈɪmprɪkeɪt] [im-pri-keit], *va*. Imprecar, maldecir, desear abiertamente algún mal para sí o para otro.

imprecation [ˌɪmprɪˈkeɪʃən] [im-pri-kei-shon], *s*. Imprecación, maldición.

imprecise [ˌɪmprɪˈsaɪs] [im-pri-sais], *a*. Impreciso, inexacto.

imprecision [ˌɪmprɪˈsɪʒən] [im-pri-si-shon], *s*. Imprecisión, inexactitud.

impregnable [ɪmˈpregnəbl] [im-preg-na-bol], *a*. 1. Inexpugnable, capaz de impregnación o de impregnarse.

impregnate [ˈɪmpregneɪt] [im-preg-neit], *va*. 1. Empreñar, hacer concebir a la hembra; fecundar. 2. Impregnar, comunicar las virtudes o calidades de una cosa a otra. 3. Fecundar, imbuir, penetrar con un principio o elemento activo.

impregnate, *a*. Impregnado; empreñado.

impregnation [ˌɪmpregˈneɪʃən] [im-preg-nei-shon], *s*. 1. Fecundación, impregnación; fertilización; infusión. 2. El principio o elemento con el cual se impregna una cosa.

impresario [ˌɪmpreˈsɑːrɪəu] [im-pre-sa-riou], *s*. Empresario.

imprescriptible [ɪmˈpreskrɪptɪbl] [im-pres-krip-ti-bol], *a*. Imprescriptible, que no se puede adquirir ni perder por el uso o la prescripción.

impress [ˈɪmpres] [im-pres], *va*. 1. Imprimir, estampar; formar o fijar por medio de la presión. 2. Impresionar, fijar en el ánimo. 3. Influir, v. g. para hacer tomar una determinación. 4. Marcar por medio de la presión; mellar. 5. Hacer una leva, reclutar soldados o marineros contra su voluntad.

impress, *s*. 1. Impresión, señal, marca, figura o imagen producida por medio de la presión. 2. Empresa, divisa, lema, mote. 3. Leva, recluta de soldados o marineros hecha contra su voluntad. 4. Impresión, efecto que causan las cosas espirituales en el ánimo.

impressibility [ˌɪmprɪsɪˈbɪlɪtɪ] [im-pri-si-bi-li-ti], *s*. La capacidad de ser impresionado o de recibir impresiones.

impressible [ɪmˈprɪsəbl] [im-pri-si-bol], *a*. Impresionable, capaz de recibir impresiones o de ser impresionado; que puede ser estampado, impreso, marcado (sobre un cuerpo o cosa).

impression [ɪmˈpreʃən] [im-pre-shon], *s*. 1. Impresión, la acción y efecto de imprimir. 2. Impresión, la marca señal o huella que una cosa deja sobre otra apretándola. 3. Impresión, el efecto visible o material producido por cualquier agencia. 4. Impresión, efecto que causan las cosas en el ánimo, en los sentidos o en la conciencia. 5. Recuerdo ligero o confuso; creencia que se tiene sin fundamentos suficientes. 6. Impresión, edición, todos los ejemplares de una obra ya impresa; también es la marca o señal del tipo, de los grabados, etc. **The enemy made no impression on the fort**, el enemigo no causó efecto material en el fuerte. **The impression of a seal, of type**, la marca o señal de un sello, del tipo. **I have an impression that the color was lilac**, creo (o me parece) que el color era lila.

impressionable [ɪmˈpreʃnəbl] [im-pre-sho-na-bol], *a*. Impresionable, susceptible de recibir impresiones; que se impresiona con facilidad. *V*. EMOTIONAL.

impressionism [ɪmˈpreʃənɪzəm] [im-pre-sho-ni-sem], *s*. (*Art. y Lit.*) Impresionismo.

impressive [ɪmˈpresɪv] [im-pre-siv], *a*. Impresivo, que produce impresión o tiene la facultad de producirla; que excita la admiración o la emoción, o que atrae la atención.

impressively [ɪmˈpresɪvlɪ] [im-pre-siv-li], *adv*. De un modo poderoso o eficaz.

impressiveness [ɪmˈpresɪvnɪs] [im-pre-siv-nes], *s*. La calidad de hacer impresión; carácter propio para impresionar, o causar admiración.

impressment [ɪmˈpresmənt] [im-pres-ment], *s*. Leva, el acto de reclutar forzosamente para la marina o de apropiar para el uso público.

imprest [ɪmˈprest] [im-prest], *s*. (GB.) Pago adelantado de dinero.

imprimatur [ˌɪmprɪˈmeɪtəʳ] [im-pri-mei-taʳ], *s*. 1. Voz latina que significa «Imprímase»: decreto que autoriza o permite imprimir un libro. 2. Cédula, permiso, licencia en general.

imprint [ˈɪmprɪnt] [im-print], *va*. 1. Imprimir, estampar, marcar por medio de presión. 2. Imprimir, señalar o estampar las letras en papel, pergamino o alguna tela. 3. Fijar, grabar en el ánimo o en la memoria.

imprint, *s*. 1. Impresión, la marca o señal que resulta de imprimir, estampar o apretar. 2. Impresión que deja o efecto que causa alguna cosa. 3. Nombre del impresor o del editor puesto en un libro u otra publicación.

imprison [ɪmˈprɪzn] [im-pri-son], *va*. Encerrar, encarcelar, poner preso, aprisionar.

imprisonment [ɪmˈprɪznmənt] [im-pri-son-ment], *s*. Reclusión, prisión, encierro, encarcelación. **False imprisonment**, prisión ilegal.

improbability [ɪmˌprɒbəˈbɪlɪtɪ] [im-pro-ba-bi-li-ti], *s*. Improbabilidad, inverosimilitud.

improbable [ɪmˈprɒbəbl] [im-pro-ba-bol], *a*. Improbable, lo que no tiene apariencia de verdad; inverisímil.

improbably [ɪmˈprɒbəblɪ] [im-pro-ba-bli], *adv*. Improbablemente.

improbation [ˌɪmprɒˈbeɪʃən] [im-pro-bei-shon], *s*. Desaprobación, reprobación.

improbity [ɪmˈprɒbɪtɪ] [im-pro-bi-ti], *s*. Falta de probidad, improbidad.

impromptu [ɪmˈprɒmptjuː] [im-promp-tiu], *a*. Hecho, efectuado o pronunciado sin premeditación; *adv*. de repente, en el acto. -*s*. Un repente, un ímpetu; composición u obra improvisada.

improper [ɪmˈprɒpəʳ] [im-pro-paʳ], *a*. 1. Impropio, inepto, no justo ni conveniente en vista de las circunstancias. 2. Contrario a las reglas establecidas o a las buenas costumbres; irregular, impolítico; indecente, grosero; incorrecto.

improperly [ɪmˈprɒpəlɪ] [im-pro-pa-li], *adv*. Impropiamente; imperfectamente.

impropriate [ɪmˈprəʊprɪeɪt] [im-pro-prieit], *va*. 1. Apropiarse, tomar para sí alguna cosa haciéndose dueño de ella. 2. Secularizar, enajenar la posesión de los bienes o réditos eclesiásticos dándola a los legos o seglares.

impropriate, *a*. Secularizado; se aplica a los bienes que habiendo pertenecido a la iglesia pasan a manos de seglares.

impropriation [ɪmˌprəʊprɪˈeɪʃən] [im-pro-priei-shon], *s*. 1. Posesión exclusiva. 2. Venta o secularización de los bienes eclesiásticos.

impropriety [ɪmˈprəʊprɪətɪ] [im-pro-prie-ti], *s*. Impropiedad, incongruencia, descortesía; cualquier cosa impropia.

improvable [ɪmˈpruːvəbl] [im-pru-va-bol], *a*. 1. Mejorable, perfectible; de aquí, laborable, capaz de cultivo y beneficio. 2. Que puede emplearse con ventaja o ser aprovechado.

improvably [ɪmˈpruːvəblɪ] [im-pru-va-bli], *adv*. De un modo que admite mejora, mejorablemente.

improve [ɪmˈpruːv] [im-pruv], *va. y vn*. 1. Mejorar, adelantar, aumentar o perfeccionar alguna cosa; beneficiar, abonar (lands), embellecer, hermosear; corregir, enmendar, rectificar; cultivar, poner en producción; explotar, trabajar, una mina, una hacienda, etc. 2. Mejorar, adelantar en perfección, aprovechar; utilizar, aprovecharse de, sacar partido de alguna cosa. -*vn*. 1. Mejorarse, adelantarse, hacer progresos. 2. (*Com.*) Subir, encarecer, aumentar de valor. **The price of wool has improved**, el precio de la lana ha subido. **The markets are improving**, los mercados están en alza. **To improve an opportunity**, aprovechar una oportunidad, una ocasión. **Some things improve by being kept**, hay cosas que se mejoran conservándolas. **We amend a bad, but improve a good thing**, se corrige lo que es malo, pero se mejora lo que es bueno.

improvement [ɪmˈpruːvmənt] [im-pruv-ment, *s*. Mejora, mejoría, medra, progreso, adelantamiento o aumento de alguna cosa. 2. Mejoramiento, mejora; empleo ventajoso, aplicación; cosa de que se saca partido. 3. Instrucción, edificación. 4. Cambios u obras útiles hechos en alguna cosa, como en una fábrica, en los ríos y puertos, etc.

improver [ɪmˈpruːvəʳ] [im-pru-vaʳ], *s*. 1. Adelantador, mejorador, enmendador. 2. Aprendiza de costurera o modista.

improvidence [ɪmˈprɒvɪdəns] [im-pro-vi-dans], *s*. Descuido, falta de previsión.

improvident [ɪmˈprɒvɪdənt] [im-pro-vi-dant], *a*. Imprévido, descuidado, inconsiderado, imprudente.

improvidently [ɪmˈprɒvɪdəntlɪ] [im-pro-vi-dant-li], *adv*. Imprévidamente.

improvisate [ɪmˈprɒvɪseɪt] [im-pro-vi-seit], *a*. Improvisado, no premeditado.

improvisation [ˌɪmprəvaɪˈseɪʃən] [im-pro-vi-sei-shon], *s*. 1. Improvisación, acción y efecto de improvisar, de hablar o componer sin preparación anterior. 2. Obra improvisada, particularmente una composición poética.

improvisator [ɪmˈprəvɪseɪtər] [im-pro-vi-sei-ta[r]], *s. V.* IMPROVISER.

improvisatory [ɪmˈprəvɪsətəri] [im-pro-vi-sa-to-ri], *a.* Improvisatorio, que se refiere a la improvisación.

improvise [ˈɪmprəvaɪz] [im-pro-vais], *va.* Improvisar, hablar o componer de repente, sin previo estudio ni preparación.

improviser [ˈɪmprəvaɪzə[r]] [im-pro-vai-sa[r]], *s.* Improvisador, el que compone o habla sin previo estudio.

imprudence [ɪmˈpruːdəns] [im-pru-dans], *s.* Imprudencia, indiscreción, inconsideración, irreflexión.

imprudent [ɪmˈpruːdənt] [im-pru-dant], *a.* Imprudente, inconsiderado, indiscreto, irreflexivo.

imprudently [ɪmˈpruːdəntli] [im-pru-dant-li], *adv.* Imprudentemente, indiscretamente.

impudence [ˈɪmpjʊdəns] [im-piu-dans], *s.* Impudencia, insolencia, inmodestia, desvergüenza, atrevimiento, descaro.

impudent [ˈɪmpjʊdənt] [im-piu-dant], *a.* 1. Impudente, descarado, audaz, insolente. 2. Impúdico, inmodesto, desvergonzado.

impudently [ˈɪmpjʊdəntli] [im-piu-dant-li], *adv.* 1. Descaradamente, impudentemente, insolentemente. 2. Impúdicamente, sin recato, inmodestamente.

impudicity [ˈɪmpjʊˈdɪsɪti] [im-piu-di-si-ti], *s.* Impudicia, inmodestia, deshonestidad.

impugn [ɪmˈpjuːn] [im-piun], *va.* Impugnar, oponerse a lo que otro dice o hace; poner en tela de juicio, contradecir, contrariar.

impugnable [ɪmˈpjuːnəbl] [im-piu-na-bol], *a.* Impugnable, que puede impugnarse.

impugner [ɪmˈpjuːnə[r]] [im-piu-na[r]], *s.* Impugnador.

impulse [ˈɪmpʌls] [im-pals], *s.* 1. Impulso, impulsión, movimiento comunicado de repente. 2. Impulso, ímpetu o estímulo, instigación, motivo. 3. Fuerza muy grande que obra o se ejerce en muy poco tiempo; ímpetu, momento mecánico, debido a una fuerza.

impulsion [ɪmˈpʌlʃən] [im-pal-shon], *s.* Impulsión, impulso, ímpetu.

impulsive [ɪmˈpʌlsɪv] [im-pal-siv], *a.* y *s.* 1. Impulsivo, que obra por impulso o emoción, más bien que por reflexión. 2. Impulsivo, que procede del impulso; que tiene fuerza impelente.

impulsively [ɪmˈpʌlsɪvli] [im-pal-siv-li], *adv.* Por impulso, impulsivamente.

impunity [ɪmˈpjuːnɪti] [im-piu-ni-ti], *s.* Impunidad, falta de castigo, exención de daño o perjuicio.

impure [ɪmˈpjʊə[r]] [im-piua[r]], *a.* 1. Impuro, sucio, poco limpio; adulterado, echado a perder por la mezcla de alguna cosa extraña y perjudicial. 2. Impuro, impúdico, deshonesto, inmundo; manchado por el pecado. 3. Que contiene tachas gramaticales o idiotismos extranjeros. 4. Profano, no apto para usos religiosos.

impurely [ɪmˈpjʊəli] [im-piua-li], *adv.* Impuramente.

impureness [ɪmˈpjʊənɪs] [im-piua-nes], **impurity** [ɪmˈpjʊərɪti] [im-piua-ri-ti], *s.* 1. Impureza; adulteración. 2. Impureza, liviandad, deshonestidad.

impurple [ɪmˈpɜːpl] [im-par-pel], *a.* Purpurar, teñir de púrpura.

imputable [ɪmˈpjʊtəbl] [im-piu-ta-bol], *a.* Imputable, que se puede imputar o atribuir a otro.

imputableness [ɪmˈpjʊtəblnɪs] [im-piu-ta-bol-nes], *s.* Imputabilidad.

imputation [ˌɪmpjʊˈteɪʃən] [im-piu-tei-shon], *s.* 1. Imputación, acción de imputar, achacar o atribuir a otro. 2. Acusación; reconvención, censura.

imputative [ɪmˈpjʊtətɪv] [im-piu-ta-tiv], *a.* Imputable, transferido por imputación.

impute [ɪmˈpjuːt] [im-piut], *va.* Imputar, atribuir, achacar.

imputer [ɪmˈpjʊtə[r]] [im-piu-ta[r]], *s.* Imputador.

in [ɪn] [in]. Preposición relativa al lugar, estado o disposición en que se hallan las cosas, al tiempo en que se hacen o sucedieron, al modo con que se hacen, etc.; y corresponde en castellano a *en, por, a, de, durante, bajo, con*. 1. En (indicando lugar), **He is in Spain**, está en España. 2. En, de, por, con (indicando estado presente). **In his sleep**, durante el sueño, o mientras dormía. **He is the best writer in England**, es el mejor escritor de Inglaterra. **Crippled in his hands**, baldado de manos. **In time**, a tiempo, con tiempo. **I am in the right**, tengo razón, estoy en mi derecho. **To be in great hopes**, abrigar grandes esperanzas. **In writing**, por escrito. 3. De, durante, por (indicando duración o espacio de tiempo). **In the night**, durante la noche, de noche. **In the daytime**, de día. **In the afternoon**, por la tarde o durante la tarde. **In a few years**, dentro de, o a la vuelta de pocos años. **In the reign of Elizabeth**, en el reinado o bajo el reinado, o reinando Isabel. **In the morning**, por la mañana o a la mañana. 4. Por, a fin de, con (indicando causa). **In obedience to you**, por obediencia a Ud. **In order to**, a fin de. **In order that**, a fin que. **In defiance of all right**, con menosprecio de toda justicia. *In* denota también el poder o aptitud de hacer una cosa, y en este caso se traduce generalmente cambiando el giro de la oración en castellano. **It is not in him to do it**, no puede hacerlo o no es capaz de hacerlo. También expresa la proporción que hay entre dos cosas, y entonces corresponde a en, de o entre. **Not one in a hundred will do it**, no hay uno en ciento o entre ciento que lo haga. **In as much as**, en cuanto, por cuanto; puesto que, en vista de. **In that**, *(Ant.)* porque, a causa de. **In the meantime o in the meanwhile**, entre tanto. **In so far**, hasta allí. *In so far as*, en cuanto a, a medida que, tocante a. *-adv.* 1. Dentro, adentro. 2. En casa, en su casa; ahí, aquí o allí. **Are you in?**, ¿está Ud. ahí? **To be in**, estar aquí o allí. 3. En poder de, en su lugar. **He drove the nail in**, clavó el clavo en su lugar. **When the tide was in**, en la bajamar. **To go in, to come in, o to walk in**, entrar. *In* está muy a menudo unido a los verbos y muda casi siempre su sentido recto. **Walk in**, entre Ud. o pase Ud. adelante. *In* se usa en composición, expresando generalmente negación o privación. **To be in for it**, (a) estar deseoso de algo en particular, o comprometido a seguir una conducta determinada. (b) *(Fam.)* al revés me la vestí, y ándese así; no tener medios de evitar una cosa, v. g. un castigo. **To be in it**, (Ger.) participar en una cosa, especialmente si es próspera o afortunada; por lo general con negación. **To be in with**, *(Fam.)* ser íntimo o estar en favor con alguien. **In-and-in**, *adv.* (a) de una misma casta o raza. (b) *(Fig.)* con un movimiento continuo recíproco. **To breed in-and-in**, aparear, juntar animales de la misma casta.

inability [ˌɪnəˈbɪlɪti] [i-na-bi-li-ti], *s.* Inhabilidad, incapacidad, ineptitud, insuficiencia; impotencia, falta de fuerza; falta de medios suficientes.

inaccessibility [ˈɪnækˌsesəˈbɪlɪti] [in-ak-se-si-bi-li-ti], *s.* Inaccesibilidad.

inaccessible [ˌɪnækˈsesəbl] [in-ak-se-si-bol], *a.* Inaccesible.

inaccessibly [ˌɪnækˈsesəbli] [in-ak-se-si-bli], *adv.* Inaccesiblemente.

inaccuracy [ɪnˈækjʊrəsi] [in-a-kiu-ra-si], *s.* 1. Inexactitud, falta de exactitud. 2. Falta, defecto, error; impropiedad de una expresión.

inaccurate [ɪnˈækjʊreɪt] [in-a-kiu-reit], *a.* Inexacto, erróneo, incorrecto.

inaccurately [ɪnˈækjʊrɪtli] [in-a-kiu-reit-li], *adv.* Incorrectamente; inexactamente.

inaction [ɪnˈækʃən] [in-ak-shon], *s.* Inacción, abstención de trabajo, descanso; holgazanería.

inactive [ɪnˈæktɪv] [in-ak-tiv], *a.* 1. Inactivo. 2. Indolente, flojo, negligente; perezoso. 3. Inerte; que no tiene la facultad de moverse.

inactively [ɪnˈæktɪvli] [in-ak-tiv-li], *adv.* Inactivamente, indolentemente; perezosamente; en estado de inercia.

inactivity [ˌɪnækˈtɪvɪti] [in-ak-ti-vi-ti], *s.* 1. Inactividad. 2. Ociosidad, desidia, flojedad.

inadequacy [ɪnˈædɪkwəsɪ] [in-a-de-kua-si], *s.* 1. Insuficiencia; desproporción. 2. Estado incompleto; imperfección.

inadequate [ɪnˈædɪkwɪt] [in-a-de-kuit], *a.* Inadecuado, insuficiente, desproporcionado, incompleto.

inadequately [ɪnˈædɪkwɪtlɪ] [in-a-de-kuit-li], *adv.* Inadecuadamente, incompletamente, sin medios suficientes.

inadequateness [ɪnˈædɪkwɪtnɪs] [in-a-de-kuit-nes], *s.* Defecto de proporción; imperfección.

inadmissible [ˌɪnədˈmɪsəbl] [in-ad-mi-si-bol], *a.* Inadmisible, que no puede admitirse, recibirse ni permitirse.

inadvertence [ˌɪnədˈvɜːtəns] [in-ad-ver-tens], *s.* Inadvertencia.

inadvertent [ˌɪnədˈvɜːtənt] [in-ad-ver-tent], *a.* 1. Inadvertido, hecho sin intención, sin designio, accidental. 2. Atolondrado, negligente, descuidado.

inadvertently [ˌɪnədˈvɜːtəntlɪ] [in-ad-ver-tent-li], *adv.* Inadvertidamente, por falta de atención, no hecho adrede; atolondradamente.

inadvisable [ˌɪnədˈvaɪzəbl] [in-ad-vai-sa-bol], *a.* Falto de prudencia, impropio, inconveniente.

inaffability [ˌɪnæfəˈbɪlɪtɪ] [in-a-fa-bi-li-ti], *s.* Reserva, cautela en la conversación.

inaffable [ɪnˈæfəbl] [in-a-fa-bol], *a.* Reservado; descortés; poco afable o cariñoso.

inalienable [ɪnˈeɪlɪənəbl] [in-ei-lia-na-bol], *a.* Inalienable o inajenable.

inalienably [ɪnˈɔɪlɪənəblɪ] [in-ei-lia-na-bli], *adv.* De un modo inalienable.

inalterable [ɪnˈæltərəbl] [in-al-te-ra-bol], *a.* Inalterable. V. UNALTERABLE.

inane [ɪˈneɪn] [i-nein], *a.* 1. Turulato, atontado, falto de inteligencia, mentecato. 2. Inane, lo que está vacío o desocupado. -*s.* Vacío, espacio desocupado.

inanimate [ɪnˈænɪmɪt] [in-a-ni-mit], *a.* 1. Desprovisto de vida animal. 2. Inanimado, falto de animación o de vida; exánime; sin alma ni espíritu.

inanimation [ˌɪnænɪˈmɪʃən] [in-a-ni-mi-shon], *s.* Falta de animación, de vida, de espíritu.

inanition [ˌɪnəˈnɪʃən] [in-a-ni-shon], *s.* Inanición, debilidad por falta de alimento; condición de hallarse vacío o desocupado.

inanity [ɪˈnænɪtɪ] [i-na-ni-ti], *s.* Vacuidad; vanidad; inutilidad, nulidad.

inappeasable [ˌɪnəˈpliːzəbl] [in-a-pli-sa-bol], *a.* Incapaz de apaciguarse o aplacarse; que no puede ser satisfecho.

inappetence [ɪnˈæpɪtəns] [in-a-pi-tens], *s.* Inapetencia.

inapplicability [ˌɪnəplɪkəˈbɪlɪtɪ] [in-a-pli-ka-bi-li-ti], *s.* Ineptitud para algún objeto particular.

inapplicable [ɪnˈæplɪkəbl] [in-a-pli-ka-bol], *a.* Inaplicable.

inapposite [ɪnˈæpəzɪt] [in-a-po-sit], *a.* No pertinente, fuera de propósito, no apropiado, poco conveniente.

inappreciable [ˌɪnəˈpriːʃəbl] [in-a-pri-sha-bol], *a.* Inapreciable, inestimable.

inapprehensible [ˌɪnəprɪˈhensɪbl] [in-a-pri-jen-si-bol], *a.* Ininteligible, incapaz de comprenderse.

inapprehension [ˌɪnəprɪˈhenʃən] [in-a-pri-jen-shon], *s.* Falta de aprensión.

inapprehensive [ˌɪnəprɪˈhensɪv] [in-a-pri-jen-siv], *a.* Negligente, descuidado, indolente.

inappropriate [ˌɪnəˈprəʊprɪɪt] [in-a-prou-preit], *a.* Poco apropiado, inadecuado, que no conviene a una cosa, impropio.

inappropriately [ˌɪnəˈprəʊprɪɪtlɪ] [in-a-prou-preit-li], *adv.* Impropiamente, fuera del caso.

inappropriateness [ˌɪnəˈprəʊprɪɪtnɪs] [in-a-prou-preit-nes], *s.* Impropiedad, falta de conveniencia.

inaptitude [ɪnˈæptɪtjuːd] [in-ap-ti-tiud], *s.* Ineptitud, insuficiencia.

inarch [ɪnˈɑːtʃ] [in-arch], *va.* Injertar o juntar dos ramas de árboles diferentes; injertar por aproximación.

inarticulate [ˌɪnɑːˈtɪkjʊlɪt] [in-ar-ti-ku-leit], *a.* 1. Inarticulado, articulado o pronunciado confusa o indistintamente; mudo, incapaz de hablar articuladamente. 2. (*Zool.*) Inarticulado, que no tiene articulaciones o segmentos.

inarticulately [ˌɪnɑːˈtɪkjʊlɪtlɪ] [in-ar-ti-ku-leit-li], *adv.* De un modo inarticulado.

inarticulateness [ˌɪnɑːˈtɪkjʊlɪtnɪs] [in-ar-ti-ku-leit-nes], *s.* Inarticulación.

inarticulation [ˌɪnɑːˈtɪkjʊlɪt] [in-ar-ti-ku-leit], *s.* Falta de claridad en la articulación de las palabras.

inartificial [ˌɪnɑːtɪˈfɪʃəl] [in-ar-ti-fi-shal], *a.* 1. Lo que es contrario a las reglas del arte; construido sin plan ni maña. 2. Natural, simple, sencillo, sin artificio.

inasmuch [ɪnəzˈmʌtʃ] [in-as-mach], *adv.* Visto, o puesto que, en vista de, ya que; en cuanto a, a medida que. Va siempre seguido de *as.*

inattention [ˌɪnəˈtenʃən] [in-a-ten-shon], *s.* Desatención, descuido, distracción, inadvertencia.

inattentive [ˌɪnəˈtentɪv] [in-a-ten-tiv], *a.* Desatento, descuidado, atolondrado.

inattentively [ˌɪnəˈtentɪvlɪ] [in-a-ten-tiv-li], *adv.* Descuidadamente, sin atención.

inaudible [ɪnˈɔːdəbl] [in-o-di-bol], *a.* Inaudible, no oíble, que no puede oírse, o que no se deja oír.

inaugural [ɪˈnɔːgjʊrəl] [in-o-guiu-ral], *a.* Inaugural, relativo a una inauguración.

inaugurate [ɪˈnɔːgjʊreɪt] [in-o-guiu-reit], *va.* 1. Inaugurar, consagrar, dedicar. 2. Investir de un cargo con las ceremonias acostumbradas; instalar. 3. Principiar, originar, poner en operación o en movimiento.

inauguration [ɪˌnɔːgjʊˈreɪʃən] [in-o-guiu-rei-shon], *s.* Inauguración, instalación, exaltación; el acto o la cermonia de inaugurar, de investir con un cargo, de poner en operación, etc., hecha con cierto aparato.

inauguratory [ɪˈnɔːgjʊrəˈtərɪ] [in-o-guiu-ra-to-ri], *a.* Inauguratorio, que pertenece a la inauguración.

inauspicious [ˌɪnɔːsˈpɪʃəs] [in-os-pi-shos], *a.* Poco propicio, desfavorable, que prognostica mal, infeliz.

inauspiciously [ˌɪnɔːsˈpɪʃəslɪ] [in-os-pi-shos-li], *adv.* Desgraciadamente, bajo malos auspicios.

inauspiciousness [ˌɪnɔːsˈpɪʃəsnɪs] [in-os-pi-shos-nes], *s.* Infelicidad, malos auspicios.

inbeing [ɪnˈbiːɪŋ] [in-biin], *s.* Inherencia, inseparabilidad.

inboard [ˈɪnbɔːd] [in-bord], *a. y adv.* 1. (*Mar.*) Interior al casco; dentro del casco. 2. (*Mec.*) Hacia el interior.

inborn [ˈɪnbɔːn] [in-born], *a.* Insito, innato, connatural, de nacimiento.

inbreathe [ɪnˈbreθ] [in-brez], *va.* Inspirar, infundir por inspiración.

inbred [ɪnˈbred] [in-bred], *a.* Insito, innato, natural, nacido dentro de nosotros mismos.

inbreed [ɪnˈbriːd] [in-brid], *vn.* Producir, crear.

inca [ˈɪŋkə] [in-ka], *s.* Inca, título de los soberanos que reinaron en el Perú hasta la conquista de Pizarro.

incage [ɪnˈkeɪdʒ] [in-keich], *va.* 1. Enjaular, encerrar, poner dentro de una jaula. 2. Encerrar dentro de un espacio muy estrecho.

incagement [ɪnˈkeɪdʒmənt] [in-keich-ment], *s.* El acto de enjaular.

incalculable [ɪnˈkælkjʊləbl] [in-kal-kiu-la-bol], *a.* Incalculable.

incalescence [ɪnˈkæləsəns] [in-ka-le-sens], *s.* Principio de calor, calor incipiente, progresivo.

incalescent [ɪnˈkæləsənt] [in-ka-le-sent], *a.* Cuyo calor va aumentando.

incandescence [ˌɪnkænˈdesns] [in-kan-de-sens], *s.* Incandescencia, candencia, el estado de un cuerpo hecho ascua.

incandescent [ˌɪnkænˈdesnt] [in-kan-de-sent], *a.* Incandescente, candente, hecho ascua. **Incandescent lamp**, lámpara eléctrica incandescente; también lámpara para gas cuya luz se aumenta mediante la incandescencia de una redecilla de material refractario.

incantation [ˌɪnkænˈteɪʃən] [in-kan-ten-shon], *s.* Encantamiento, encantación, encanto, arte mágica.

incantatory [ˌɪnkænˈtətərɪ] [in-kan-ta-to-ri], *a.* Mágico; lo que pertenece a los encantamientos.

incapability [ɪnˌkeɪpəˈbɪlɪtɪ] [in-kei-pa-bi-li-ti], *s.* Inhabilidad, incapacidad, falta de capacidad.

incapable [ɪnˈkeɪpəbl] [in-kei-pa-bol], *a.* 1. Incapaz, inhábil. 2. Incapaz, inepto, falto de talento, que no puede comprender o entender algo. 3. Incapaz de una acción baja, de mentir, de hurtar, etc. 4. Inhabilitado o declarado inhábil o incapaz de gozar algún derecho, prerrogativa, etc.

incapacious [ˌɪnkəˈpeɪʃəs] [in-ka-pei-shos], *a.* Estrecho, angosto, poco capaz.

incapaciousness [ˌɪnkəˈpeɪʃəsnɪs] [in-ka-pei-shos-nes], *s.* Estrechez, angostura.

incapable [ɪnˈkeɪpəbl] [in-kei-pa-bol], *a.* Incompetente, incapaz. **He is incapable of shame**, no tiene vergüenza.

incapacitate [ˌɪnkəˈpæsɪteɪt] [in-ka-pa-si-teit], *va.* 1. Inhabilitar, imposibilitar a uno para alguna cosa; debilitar. 2. Inhabilitar, declarar a uno incapaz de gozar alguna cosa.

incapacitation [ˈɪnkəˌpæsɪˈteɪʃən] [in-ka-pa-si-tei-shon], *s.* Inhabilitación, la acción y efecto de inhabilitar.

incapacity [ˌɪnkəˈpæsɪtɪ] [in-ka-pa-si-ti], *s.* Incapacidad, falta de capacidad, insuficiencia.

incarcerate [ɪnˈkɑːsəreɪt] [in-kar-se-reit], *va.* Encarcelar, aprisionar, meter o poner a uno en la cárcel.

incarcerate, *a.* Encarcelado, preso.

incarceration [ɪnˌkɑːsəˈreɪʃən] [in-kar-se-rei-shon], *s.* 1. Encarcelamiento, prisión. 2. *(Cir.)* Estrangulación, v. g. de una hernia.

incarnadine [ɪnˈkɑːnədɪn] [in-kar-na-din], *va.* Encarnar, dar color de carne. -*a.* Encarnadino, color encarnado claro; color de carne.

incarnate [ɪnˈkɑːnɪt] [in-kar-neit], *va.* Encarnar, vestir de carne.

incarnate, *a.* 1. Encarnado, vestido o incorporado con carne. 2. Encarnado, de color de carne.

incarnation [ˌɪnkɑːˈneɪʃən] [in-kar-nei-shon], *s.* 1. Encarnación, encarnadura. 2. *(Cir.)* Encarnación, desarrollo de tejido en una herida cuando está en vías de curación.

incarnative [ɪnˈkɑːnətɪv] [in-kar-na-tiv], *s.* Encarnativo, remedio que se usa con el objeto de apresurar la cicatrización de las heridas.

incase [ɪnˈkeɪs] [in-keis], *va.* Encajar, incluir, encerrar, encajonar. V. ENCASE.

incask [ɪnˈkɑːsk] [in-kask], *va.* Entonelar.

incautious [ɪnˈkɔːʃəs] [in-ko-shos], *a.* Incauto, descuidado, negligente, imprudente.

incautiously [ɪnˈkɔːʃəslɪ] [in-ko-shos-li], *adv.* Incautamente, descuidadamente.

incautiousness [ɪnˈkɔːʃəsnɪs] [in-ko-shos-nes], *s.* Falta de cautela, descuido, negligencia.

incendiarism [ɪnˈsendɪəˌrɪzm] [in-sen-dia-ri-sem], *s.* Acto de incendiar maliciosamente, de pegar fuego adrede.

incendiary [ɪnˈsendɪərɪ] [in-sen-dia-ri], *s.* Incendiario, el que maliciosamente incendia algún edificio, mieses, etc. -*a.* 1. Incendiario, relativo al incendio criminal. 2. Que sirve para pegar fuego. 3. Inflamatorio, que tiende a inflamar las pasiones o suscitar sediciones; cizañero, sedicioso, revoltoso.

incense [ɪnˈsens] [in-sens], *s.* 1. Incienso. 2. Incienso. alabanza lisonjera. 3. Cualquier perfume agradable.

incense, *va.* 1. Exaperar, irritar, sulfurar, encolerizar. 2. Incensar, perfumar con incienso.

incensement [ɪnˈsensˌmənt] [in-sens-ment], *s.* Rabia, ira, furia, cólera, arrebato.

incension [ɪnˈsenʃən] [in-sen-shon], *s.* (Poco us.) Encendimiento, el acto de encender, de pegar fuego, o el de estar ardiendo y abrasándose.

incensive [ɪnˈsensɪv] [in-sen-siv], *a.* Incitativo; que tiende a excitar o provocar.

incensor [ɪnˈsensəʳ] [in-sen-saʳ], *s.* Incitador, el que provoca la ira o inflama las pasiones.

incensory [ɪnˈsensərɪ] [in-sen-so-ri], *s.* Incensario, el braserillo en que se quema el incienso para incensar.

incentive [ɪnˈsentɪv] [in-sen-tiv], *s.* Incentivo, estímulo, impulso, motivo. -*a.* Incitativo, que anima o impele.

inception [ɪnˈsepʃən] [in-sep-shon], *s.* El principio de alguna cosa; período inicial; estreno.

inceptive [ɪnˈseptɪv] [in-sep-tiv], *a.* Incipiente, incoativo, que principia o comienza.

inceptor [ɪnˈseptəʳ] [in-sep-taʳ], *s.* 1. Principiante. 2. Nombre que se da en las universidades inglesas a la persona admitida a pasar el examen necesario para recibir el grado de maestro en artes.

inceration [ˌɪnseˈreɪʃən] [in-se-rei-shon], *s.* Enceramiento, la acción de cubrir alguna cosa con cera.

incerative [ɪnˈserətɪv] [in-se-ra-tiv], *a.* Lo que se pega como cera.

incertitude [ɪnˈsɜːtɪtjuːd] [in-ser-ti-tiud], *s.* 1. Incertidumbre, duda. 2. Obscuridad.

incessable [ɪnˈsesəbl] [in-se-sa-bol], *a.* Incesable, continuo, incesante, constante.

incessant [ɪnˈsesnt] [in-se-sant], *a.* Incesante, constante, incesable.

incessantly [ɪnˈsesntlɪ] [in-se-sant-li], *adv.* Incesantemente.

incest [ˈɪnsest] [in-sest], *s.* Incesto.

incestuous [ɪnˈsestjʊəs] [in-ses-tiuos], *a.* Incestuoso.

incestuously [ɪnˈsestjʊəslɪ] [in-ses-tiuos-li], *adv.* Incestuosamente.

incestuousness [ɪnˈsestjʊəsnɪs] [in-ses-tiuos-nes], *s.* El estado de ser incestuosa una persona o cosa.

inch [ɪntʃ] [inch], *s.* 1. Pulgada, la duodécima parte de un pie (= 25.4 milímetros). 2. Pizca, una porción mínima o muy pequeña de alguna cosa. **Within an inch**, poco más o menos. **Within an inch of**, a dos dedos de. **Inch by inch**, palmo a palmo o a pulgadas. **By inches** o **inch by inch**, (Fam.) a pedacitos. **Every inch**, cabalmente. **Every inch a man**, hombre hecho y derecho. **Miners' inch**, pulgada de fontanero. V. WATER-INCH. **Inch-pound**, el esfuerzo necesario para elevar una libra de peso a una pulgada de altura en el espacio de un segundo.

inch, *va.* Arrojar o echar a uno de donde estaba poco a poco o a palmos; hacer valer una cosa todo lo posible; medir por pulgadas. En general este verbo va unido en su significación activa con la preposición *out*. -*vn.* Avanzar o retirarse poco a poco y haciendo paradas.

inched [ˈɪntʃt] [incht], *a.* 1. Marcado o dividido en pulgadas. 2. De tantas pugadas. **A five-inched cable**, un cable de cinco pulgadas.

inchoate [ˈɪnkəʊeɪt] [in-koueit], *a.* Principiado, comenzado, incoado, empezado. -*va.* Incoar, principiar, empezar.

inchoately [ˈɪnkəʊeɪtlɪ] [in-koueit-li], *adv.* En el primer grado.

inchoation [ˈɪnkəʊeɪt] [in-koueit], *s.* Principio.

inchoative [ɪnˈkəʊətɪv] [in-koua-tiv], *a.* Incipiente, incoativo.

incidence [ˈɪnsɪdəns] [in-si-dens], *s.* 1. Incidencia, la dirección en que una línea, un plano o un cuerpo se encuentra con otro. 2. Carga, como la de una contribución, que recae o grava desigualmente.

incident [ˈɪnsɪdənt] [in-si-dent], *a.* 1. Incidente, que cae sobre o dentro de algo, que toca o choca desde afuera. 2. Probable, acontecedero. 3. Casual, fortuito; concomitante, dependiente de.

incident, *s.* 1. Incidente, casualidad, acontecimiento. 2. Episodio, digresión.

incidental [ˌɪnsɪˈdentl] [in-si-den-tal], *a*. 1. Contingente; concomitante, que sobreviene en el curso de otra cosa, que la acompaña. 2. Casual, que sobreviene o acontece irregularmente.

incidentally [ˌɪnsɪˈdentəlɪ] [in-si-den-ta-li], *adv*. Incidentemente.

incidently [ˌɪnsɪˈdentlɪ] [in-si-den-tli], *adv*. Ocasionalmente, casualmente.

incinerate [ɪnˈsɪnəreɪt] [in-si-ne-reit], *va*. Incinerar, reducir una cosa a cenizas, consumir por medio del fuego.

incineration [ɪnˌsɪnəˈreɪʃən] [in-si-ne-rei-shon], *s*. Incineración.

incipiency [ɪnˈsɪpɪənsɪ] [in-si-pien-si], *s*. Principio.

incipient [ɪnˈsɪpɪənt] [in-si-pient], *a*. Incipiente.

incircle [ɪnˈsɜːkl] [in-ser-kol], *va. V.* TO ENCIRCLE.

incise [ɪnˈsaɪz] [in-sais], *va*. Tajar, hacer incisión, cortar en, grabar, esculpir en hueco.

incised [ɪnˈsaɪzd] [in-saisd], *a*. Inciso, cortado.

incision [ɪnˈsɪʒən] [in-si-shon], *s*. Incisión; corte, recorte.

incisive [ɪnˈsaɪsɪv] [in-sai-siv], *a*. Incisivo, incisorio; agudo; mordaz. **An incisive style**, estilo agudo, mordaz.

incisor [ɪnˈsaɪzər] [in-sai-saʳ], *a*. Incisivo, apto para cortar. -*s*. Incisivos, los cuatro dientes delanteros en cada mandíbula, así llamados porque cortan los alimentos.

incitation [ˌɪnsɪˈteɪʃən] [in-si-tei-shon], *s*. Incitación, instigación.

incite [ɪnˈsaɪt] [in-sait], *va*. Incitar, mover, estimular, aguijonear.

incitement [ɪnˈsaɪtmənt] [in-sait-ment], *s*. Incitamento, incitamiento, estímulo, aguijón; lo que induce a ejecutar una cosa.

inciter [ɪnˈsaɪtər] [in-sai-taʳ], *s*. Incitador; instigador.

incitingly [ɪnˈsaɪtɪŋlɪ] [in-sai-tin-li], *adv*. De un modo estimulante o alentador; incitantemente.

incivility [ˌɪnsɪˈvɪlɪtɪ] [in-si-vi-li-ti], *s*. Incivilidad, inurbanidad, descortesía, desatención.

inclasp [ɪnˈklɑːsp] [in-klasp], *va*. Estrechar, abrazar; agarrar; abrochar.

inclavated [ɪnˈklæveɪtɪd] [in-kla-vei-tid], *a*. Enclavado, fijo.

inclemency [ɪnˈklemənsɪ] [in-kle-men-si], *s*. 1. Inclemencia, rigor de la estación; aprieto, aflicción, apuro. 2. Crueldad, severidad.

inclement [ɪnˈklemənt] [in-kle-ment], *a*. 1. Inclemente, severo, duro. 2. Inclemente, riguroso, borrascoso, tempestuoso. 3. Adverso, contrario, malandante; se dice de las circunstancias.

inclinable [ɪnˈklɪnəbl] [in-kli-na-bol], *a*. Favorable, inclinado a alguna cosa.

inclination [ˌɪnklɪˈneɪʃən] [in-kli-nei-shon], *s*. 1. Inclinación; tendencia mutua de dos líneas, superficies o cuerpos el uno hacia el otro. 2. La superficie inclinada; declive, declivio, descenso. 3. Inclinación, acatamiento, reverencia bajando la cabeza. 4. Inclinación, afición, amor, afecto. 5. Inclinación de la aguja magnética. *V.* DIP. 6. (*Fam.*) Descantación. *V.* DECANTATION.

inclinatory [ɪnˈklɪnətərɪ] [in-kli-na-to-ri], *a*. Ladeado.

incline [ɪnˈklaɪn] [in-klain], *va*. 1. Inclinar, enderezar alguna cosa hacia una parte determinada. 2. Ladear, torcer; doblar, doblegar. 3. Inclinar el cuerpo o la cabeza por respeto o reverencia. -*vn*. 1. Inclinarse, torcerse un poco hacia abajo alguna cosa. 2. Inclinarse, hacer reverencia o acatamiento. 3. Inclinarse, sentir disposición favorable hacia alguna persona o cosa; hablando de colores, tirar a. **A hue which inclines to green**, un matiz que tira al verde. **Inclined plane**, plano inclinado. -*s*. Declivio; declive de una vía férrea.

incloister [ɪnˈklɔɪstər] [in-klois-taʳ], *va*. Enclaustrar.

inclose [ɪnˈkləʊz] [in-klous], *va*. 1. Encerrar, cerrar; poner bajo sobre (a letter). 2. Cerrar, rodear, incluir, circuir. *V.* ENCLOSE.

inclosure [ɪnˈkləʊʒər] [in-klo-shaʳ], *s. V.* ENCLOSURE.

incloud [ɪnˈklaʊd] [in-klaud], *va*. Oscurecer, ocultar como con nubes.

include [ɪnˈkluːd] [in-klud], *va*. 1. Incluir, encerrar. 2. Comprender, como parte componente; abrazar, contener.

inclusion [ɪnˈkluːʒən] [in-klu-shon], *s*. 1. Inclusión, restricción, limitación. 2. Lo que está incluído o contenido; especialmente un gas o líquido contenido en un mineral.

inclusive [ɪnˈkluːsɪv] [in-klu-siv], *a*. Inclusivo.

inclusively [ɪnˈkluːsɪvlɪ] [in-klu-siv-li], *adv*. Inclusivamente, inclusive.

incoagulable [ɪnˈkəʤʊləbl] [in-ko-giu-lei-bol], *a*. Incoagulable.

incog [ɪnˈkɒg] [in-kog], *a., s.* y *adv. V.* INCOGNITO.

incogitable [ɪnˈkɒʤɪtəbl] [in-ko-chi-ta-bol], *a*. Inconcebible.

incogitancy [ɪnˈkɒʤɪtənsɪ] [in-ko-chi-tan-si], *s*. Irreflexión, falta de reflexión.

incogitantly [ɪnˈkɒʤɪtəntlɪ] [in-ko-chi-tant-li], *adv*. Inadvertidamente.

incognito [ɪnˈkɒgnɪtəʊ] [in-kog-ni-tou], *adv*. y *a*. Incógnito o de incógnito. -*s*. 1. La acción de asumir un nombre, papel, tipo o carácter fingidos. 2. Persona que vive, viaja o pasa de incógnito.

incognizable [ɪnˈkɒgnɪzəbl] [in-kog-ni-sa-bol], *a*. No cognoscible, que no puede reconocerse o distinguirse, particularmente por el hombre.

incoherence [ˌɪnkəʊˈhɪərəns] [in-kou-ia-rens], **incoherency** [ˌɪnkəʊˈhɪərənsɪ] [in-kou-ia-ran-si], *s*. Incoherencia; inconsecuencia.

incoherent [ˌɪnkəʊˈhɪərənt] [in-kou-ia-rent], *a*. Incoherente, inconsecuente, inconexo; no adherente, suelto.

incoherently [ˌɪnkəʊˈhɪərəntlɪ] [in-kou-ia-rent-li], *adv*. Con incoherencia, sin conexión.

incombustible [ˌɪnkəmˈbʌstəbl] [in-kom-bas-ta-bol], *a*. Incombustible.

income [ˈɪnkʌm] [in-kam], *s*. Renta, entrada, utilidad y beneficio que rinde una cosa anualmente (o en plazo determinado). **To live up to one's income**, gastar uno lo que gana.

incomer [ɪnˈkʌmər] [in-ka-maʳ], *s*. Recién llegado; el que entra o llega; inquilino o tendero que sucede a otro.

income tax [ˈɪnkʌmtæks] [in-kam-taks], *s*. Impuesto sobre la renta.

incoming [ˈɪnˌkʌmɪŋ] [in-ka-min], *a*. Entrante, que llega o está por llegar. **An incoming tenant**, inquilino entrante o que toma posesión. **Incoming steamer**, vapor que está por llegar.

incommensurability [ˌɪnkəmenʃərəˈbɪlɪtɪ] [in-ka-men-sha-ra-bi-li-ti], *s*. Inconmensurabilidad, la calidad de lo que no es mensurable.

incommensurable [ˌɪnkʌˈmenʃərəbl] [in-ka-men-sha-ra-bol], *a*. Inconmensurable, no conmensurable.

incommensurate [ˌɪnkʌˈmenʃərɪt] [in-ka-men-sha-reit], *a*. Desproporcionado, insuficiente, que no admite una medida común.

incommensurately [ˌɪnkʌˈmenʃərɪtlɪ] [in-ka-men-sha-reit-li], *adv*. Desproporcionadamente, de un modo desproporcionado.

incommode [ˌɪnkʌˈməʊd] [in-ko-moud], *va*. Incomodar, fastidiar, hacer mala obra, molestar.

incommodious [ˌɪnkʌˈməʊdɪəs] [in-ko-mou-dios], *a*. Incómodo, inconveniente, que no proporciona espacio o comodidad suficiente; estrecho.

incommodiously [ˌɪnkʌˈməʊdɪəslɪ] [in-ko-mou-dios-li], *adv*. Incómodamente.

incommodiousness [ˌɪnkʌˈməʊdɪəsnɪs] [in-ko-mou-dios-nes], *s*. Incomodidad, inconveniencia, molestia.

incommunicable [ˌɪnkʌˈmjɒnɪkəbl] [in-ko-miu-ni-ka-bol], *a*. Incomunicable, indecible.

incommunicably [ˌɪnkʌˈmjɒnɪkəblɪ] [in-ko-miu-ni-ka-bli], *adv*. Sin comunicación, de un modo incomunicable.

incommunicating [ˌɪnkʌˈmjɒnɪkeɪtɪŋ] [in-ko-miu-ni-kei-tin], *a*. Incomunicado, que no tiene comunicación.

incommutability [ˌɪnkʌmjʊtəˈbɪlɪtɪ] [in-ko-miu-ta-bi-li-ti], *s*. Inconmutabilidad.

incommutable [ˌɪnkʌˈmjʊtəbl] [in-ko-miu-ta-bol], *a.* Inconmutable.

incommutably [ˌɪnkʌˈmjʊtəblɪ] [in-ko-miu-ta-bli], *adv.* Inconmutablemente.

incomparable [ɪnˈkɒmpərəbl] [in-kom-pa-ra-bol], *a.* Incomparable, sin igual.

incomparableness [ɪnˈkɒmpərəblnɪs] [in-kom-pa-ra-bol-nes], *s.* Excelencia superior a toda comparación.

incomparably [ɪnˈkɒmpərəblɪ] [in-kom-pa-ra-bli], *adv.* Incomparablemente, sin comparación.

incompatibility [ˈɪnkəmpəˌbɪlɪtɪ] [in-kom-pa-bi-li-ti], *s.* Incompatibilidad, contrariedad.

incompatible [ˌɪnkəmˈpætəbl] [in-kom-pa-ti-bol], *a.* Incompatible.

incompatibly [ˌɪnkəmˈpætəblɪ] [in-kom-pa-ti-bli], *adv.* Incongruentemente, opuestamente.

incompetence [ɪnˈkɒmpɪtəns] [in-kom-pe-tens], *s.* Incompetencia, inhabilidad, insuficiencia.

incompetent [ɪnˈkɒmpɪtənt] [in-kom-pe-tent], *a.* 1. Incompetente, que no tiene las cualidades necesarias; insuficiente, que no basta. 2. *(For.)* Inadmisible, que no puede invocarse en derecho; incompetente.

incompetently [ɪnˈkɒmpɪtəntlɪ] [in-kom-pe-tent-li], *adv.* Incompetentemente.

incomplete [ˌɪnkəmˈpliːt] [in-kom-plit], *a.* Incompleto, falto, imperfecto.

incompleteness [ˌɪnkəmˈpliːtnɪs] [in-kom-plit-nes], *s.* Falta, imperfección.

incompliance [ˌɪnkəmˈplaɪəns] [in-kom-plaians], *s.* Contrariedad de genio; desobediencia, indocilidad.

incomprehensibility [ˈɪnˌkɒmprɪˈhensɪˈbɪlɪtɪ] [in-kom-prijen-si-bi-li-ti], *s.* Incomprensibilidad, obscuridad de una cosa que hace que no se pueda entender.

incomprehensible [ˈɪnˌkɒmprɪˈhensəbl] [in-kom-pri-jen-si-bol], *a.* Incomprensible.

incomprehensibleness [ˈɪnˌkɒmprɪˈhensəblnɪs] [in-kom-pri-jen-si-bol-nes], *s.* Incomprensibilidad.

incomprehensibly [ˈɪnˌkɒmprɪˈhensəblɪ] [in-kom-pri-jen-si-bli], *adv.* De un modo incomprensible, incomprensiblemente.

incomprehension [ˈɪnˌkɒmprɪˈhenʃən] [in-kom-pri-jen-shon], *s.* Falta de comprensión.

incomprehensive [ˈɪnˌkɒmprɪˈhensɪv] [in-kom-pri-jen-siv], *a.* Lo que no tiene la extensión necesaria o no comprende lo que debe.

incomprehensiveness [ˈɪnˌkɒmprɪˈhensɪvnɪs] [in-kom-pri-jen-siv-nes], *s.* Incomprensibilidad.

incompressible [ˈɪnˌkɒmprɪˈhensɪbl] [in-kom-pri-jen-si-bol], *a.* Incomprimible.

inconcealable [ˌɪnkənˈsiːləbl] [in-ko-si-la-bol], *a.* Lo que no se puede ocultar o encubrir.

inconceivable [ˌɪnkənˈsiːvəbl] [in-ko-si-va-bol], *a.* 1. Inconcebible, incomprensible. 2. Contradictor, que encierra una contradicción; inherentemente contradictorio.

inconceivableness [ˌɪnkənˈsiːvəblnɪs] [in-ko-si-va-bol-nes], *s.* Incomprensibilidad, calidad de lo que es inconcebible o que encierra una contradicción.

inconceivably [ˌɪnkənˈsiːvəblɪ] [in-ko-si-va-bli], *adv.* Incomprensiblemente, de un modo inconcebible.

inconclusive [ˌɪnkənˈkluːsɪv] [in-kon-klu-siv], *a.* Que no concluye ni hace fuerza, ineficaz; que no presenta razones concluyentes; indeciso, que no prueba.

inconclusively [ˌɪnkənˈkluːsɪvlɪ] [in-kon-klu-siv-li], *adv.* Sin conclusión o evidencia decisiva.

inconclusiveness [ˌɪnkənˈkluːsɪvnɪs] [in-kon-klu-siv-nes], *s.* Carencia de conclusión o decisión, calidad de lo que es poco concluyente.

incondite [ɪnˈkɒndaɪt] [in-kon-dait], *a.* Mal construido, irregular, no acabado.

incongealable [ˌɪnkənˈsʒiːləbl] [in-kon-chi-la-bol], *a.* Incapaz de congelarse.

incongruence [ɪnˈkɒŋgrʊəns] [in-kon-gruens], **incongruity** [ˌɪnkɒŋˈgruːɪtɪ] [in-kon-grui-ti], *s.* Incongruencia, incongruidad; desproporción, falta de relación, falta de conveniencia.

incongruent [ɪnˈkɒŋgrʊənt] [in-kon-gruent], *a.* Incongruente, falto de congruencia.

incongruous [ɪnˈkɒŋgrʊəs] [in-kon-gruos], *a.* Incongruo, desproporcionado, inconexo; compuesto de partes discordantes o heterogéneas.

incongruously [ɪnˈkɒŋgrʊəslɪ] [in-kon-gruos-li], *adv.* Incongruamente.

incongruousness [ɪnˈkɒŋgrʊəsnɪs] [in-kon-gruos-nes], *s.* Incongruencia.

inconsequence [ɪnˈkɒnsɪkəns] [in-kon-si-kuens], *s.* Inconsecuencia.

inconsequent [ɪnˈkɒnsɪkənt] [in-kon-si-kuent], *a.* 1. Inconsecuente, inconsiguiente, que no es consiguiente a otra cosa, que no resulta del modo acostumbrado. 2. Inconsecuente, inconsistente, ilógico, informal.

inconsequential [ˌɪnˌkɒnsɪˈkwenʃəl] [in-kon-si-kuen-shal], *a.* Inconsecuente, falto de consecuencia.

inconsiderable [ˌɪnkənˈsɪdərəbl] [in-kon-si-de-ra-bol], *a.* Inconsiderable, insignificante, de poca importancia o consideración; frívolo.

inconsiderableness [ˌɪnkənˈsɪdərəblnɪs] [in-kon-si-de-ra-bol-nes], *s.* Falta de importancia, frivolidad.

inconsiderate [ˌɪnkənˈsɪdərɪt] [in-kon-si-de-reit], *a.* Inconsiderado, inadvertido; irreflexivo, falto de miramiento y consideración.

inconsiderately [ˌɪnkənˈsɪdərɪtlɪ] [in-kon-si-de-reit-li], *adv.* Inconsideradamente, irreflexivamente.

inconsiderateness [ˌɪnkənˈsɪdərɪtnɪs] [in-kon-si-de-reit-nes], *s.* Inconsideración, inadvertencia.

inconsistence [ˌɪnkənˈsɪstəns] [in-kon-sis-tens], **inconsistency** [ˌɪnkənˈsɪstənsɪ] [in-kon-sis-ten-si], *s.* 1. Incompatibilidad, contradicción, incongruencia. 2. Inconsistencia, mutabilidad, volubilidad, inconsecuencia.

inconsistent [ˌɪnkənˈsɪstənt] [in-kon-sis-tent], *a.* 1. Inconsistente, incompatible, contradictorio. 2. Implicatorio, inconsecuente. 3. Inconstante, variable, mudable, veleidoso.

inconsistently [ˌɪnkənˈsɪstəntlɪ] [in-kon-sis-tent-li], *adv.* Incongruamente, contradictoriamente.

inconsolable [ˌɪnkənˈsəʊləbl] [in-kon-sou-la-bol], *a.* Inconsolable.

inconsonance [ˌɪnkənˈsənəns] [in-kon-so-nens], *s.* Falta de consonancia; también, falta de harmonía, disonancia de los sonidos entre sí; implicación en los términos o entre sí.

inconspicuous [ˌɪnkənˈspɪkjʊəs] [in-kons-pi-kuos], *a.* No conspicuo, poco visible; tan pequeño u obscuro que no puede fácilmente apreciarse con la vista; sin importancia.

inconstancy [ɪnˈkɒnstənsɪ] [in-kons-tan-si], *s.* Inconstancia; diversidad.

inconstant [ɪnˈkɒnstənt] [in-kons-tant], *a.* Inconstante, mudable, voluble, variable.

inconstantly [ɪnˈkɒnstəntlɪ] [in-kons-tant-li], *adv.* Inconstantemente.

inconsumable [ˌɪnkənˈsjɒməbl] [in-kon-siu-ma-bol], *a.* Que no se puede consumir.

incontestable [ˌɪnkɒnˈtestəbl] [in-kon-tes-ta-bol], *a.* Incontestable, indisputable, irrecusable, irrefragable.

incontestably [ˌɪnkɒnˈtestəblɪ] [in-kon-tes-ta-bli], *adv.* Incontestablemente, irrecusablemente.

incontiguous [ˌɪnkɒnˈtɪgjʊəs] [in-kon-ti-guiuos], *a.* Separado, que no está contiguo.

incontinence [ɪnˈkɒntɪnəns] [in-kon-ti-nens], *s.* 1. Incontinencia, falta de recato y dominio en las pasiones y particularmente en los apetitos carnales; lascivia. 2. Incontinencia, flujo no contenido (v. g. de palabras). 3. *(Med.)* Incontinencia, incapacidad de contener las evacuaciones naturales.

incontinent [ɪnˈkɒntɪnənt] [in-kon-ti-nent], *a.*
1. Incontinente, desenfrenado en las pasiones de la
carne. 2. *(Med.)* Incontinente, incapaz de retener una
evacuación natural. -*s.* Un incontinente, el que no
domina sus pasiones.

incontinently [ɪnˈkɒntɪnəntlɪ] [in-kon-ti-nent-li], *adv.* 1.
Incontinentemente. 2. Inmediatamente, al instante.

incontrollable [ɪnˈkɒntrələbl] [in-kon-tro-la-bol], *a.*
Irresistible, incontrastable.

incontrollably [ɪnˈkɒntrələblɪ] [in-kon-tro-la-bli], *adv.* Sin
restricción.

incontrovertible [ɪnˌkɒntrəˈvɜːtəbl] [in-kon-tro-ver-ti-
bol], *a.* Incontrovertible, incontrastable, irrefragable,
indisputable.

incontrovertibly [ɪnˌkɒntrəˈvɜːtəblɪ] [in-kon-tro-ver-ti-bli],
adv. Indisputablemente, sin disputa.

inconvenience [ˌɪnkənˈviːnɪəns] [in-kon-vi-niens], *s.* 1.
Inconveniencia, falta de conveniencia. 2. Inconveniente,
incomodidad, embarazo, estorbo, desventaja, dificultad.

inconvenience, *va.* Causar inconvenientes; embarazar,
incomodar, estorbar.

inconvenient [ˌɪnkənˈviːnɪənt] [in-kon-vi-nient], *a.*
1. Incómodo, embarazoso, molesto, fastidioso. 2.
Inconveniente, impropio; inoportuno, no a propósito.

inconveniently [ˌɪnkənˈviːnɪəntlɪ] [in-kon-vi-nient-li], *adv.*
Incómodamente, importunamente.

inconversable [ˌɪnkənˈvɜːsəbl] [in-kon-ver-si-bol], *a.*
Inconversable, intratable, insociable.

inconvertible [ˌɪnkənˈvɜːtəbl] [in-kon-ver-ti-bol], *a.*
Inconvertible.

inconvincible [ˌɪnkənˈvɪnsəbl] [in-kon-vin-si-bol], *a.*
Inconvencible.

incorporate [ɪnˈkɔːpəreɪt] [in-kor-po-reit], *va.* 1. Agregar,
unir dos o más cosas para que formen un todo. 2. Dar
cuerpo o forma material, revestir de materia. 3. Incorporar;
formar una corporación legal, un gremio o cuerpo político;
asociar. -*vn.* Incorporarse, agregarse o unirse para formar
un todo.

incorporate, *a.* 1. Incorporado, asociado, unido, mezclado.
2. Incorporal, inmaterial. 3. No constituido en corporación
o asociación.

incorporation [ɪnˌkɔːpəˈreɪʃən] [in-kor-po-rei-shon], *s.*
Incorporación, formación de un gremio o cuerpo político;
adopción, asociación.

incorporeal [ˌɪnkɔːˈpɔːrɪəl] [in-kor-po-rial], *a.* Incorpóreo.

incorporeally [ˌɪnkɔːˈpɔːrɪəlɪ] [in-kor-po-ria-li], *adv.*
Incorporalmente.

incorrect [ˌɪnkəˈrekt] [in-ko-rekt], *a.* Incorrecto, inexacto,
erróneo; inmoral.

incorrectly [ˌɪnkəˈrektlɪ] [in-ko-rekt-li], *adv.*
Incorrectamente, inexactamente.

incorrectness [ˌɪnkəˈrektnɪs] [in-ko-rekt-nes], *s.* Inexactitud;
incorrección; impropiedad, inconveniencia; descuido.

incorrigible [ɪnˈkɒrɪdʒəbl] [in-ko-ri-chi-bol], *a.*
Incorregible, indócil, obstinado, terco.

incorrigibility [ɪnˌkɒrɪdʒɪˈbɪlɪtɪ] [in-ko-ri-chi-bi-li-ti], *s.*
Incorregibilidad, indocilidad, terquedad de genio, dureza de
carácter.

incorrigibly [ɪnˈkɒrɪdʒəblɪ] [in-ko-ri-chi-bli], *adv.*
Incorregiblemente, obstinadamente.

incorrupt [ˌɪnkəˈrʌpt] [in-ko-rapt], *a.* 1. Incorrupto, libre de
corrupción, lo que no se corrompe o no padece corrupción.
2. Incorrupto, íntegro, recto.

incorruptible [ˌɪnkəˈrʌptəbl] [in-ko-rap-ti-bol], *a.*
1. Incorruptible, cosa no corruptible. 2. Incorruptible,
incorrupto, persona incapaz de dejarse corromper o cohechar.

incorruption [ˌɪnkəˈrʌpʃn] [in-ko-rap-shon], *s.*
Incorrupción.

incorruptive [ˌɪnkəˈrʌptɪv] [in-ko-rap-tiv], *s.* Incorrupto.

incorruptness [ˌɪnkəˈrʌptnɪs] [in-ko-rapt-nes], *s.* 1.
Incorrupción, pureza de vida o costumbres. 2. Incorrupción,

el estado de una cosa que no se corrompe o no puede
corromperse.

incrassate [ɪnˈkræsɪt] [in-kra-seit], *va.* Espesar, condensar,
encrasar, engrosa; en especial, espesar un fluido como por
medio de una mezcla o por evaporación. -*vn.* Espesarse,
condensarse, engrosarse.

incrassate, *a.* Encrasado, que se va aumentando hacia la
extremidad, como las antenas y los fémures de ciertos
insectos y las hojas de la hierba puntera.

incrassation [ˌɪnkrəˈseɪʃən] [in-kra-sei-shon], *s.* Espesura,
condensación: se dice de los líquidos y de los fluidos;
también, engrasación, hinchazón a causa de gordura.

incrassative [ɪnˈkræsətɪv] [in-kra-sa-tiv], *a.* Espesativo,
incrasante.

increasable [ɪnˈkriːsəbl] [in-kri-sa-bol], *a.* Aumentable.

increase [ˈɪnkriːs] [in-kris], *va.* Acrecentar, aumentar;
abultar, alargar. -*vn.* Crecer, tomar aumento, acrecentarse,
multiplicarse; engrandecer.

increase, *s.* 1. Aumento, acrecentamiento, adelantamiento,
incremento. 2. Producto, cosecha; provecho, ganancia,
interés. 3. Generación, progenie. 4. Creciente (moon);
crecida (waters).

increaser [ɪnˈkriːsəʳ] [in-kri-saʳ], *s.* Aumentador,
acrecentador; productor.

increasing [ɪnˈkriːsɪŋ] [in-kri-sin], *a.* Creciente.

increasingly [ɪnˈkriːsɪŋlɪ] [in-kri-sin-li], *adv.* En vías de
aumento; en creciente.

incredibility [ˌɪnkredəˈbɪlɪtɪ] [in-kre-di-bi-li-ti], *s.*
Incredibilidad.

incredible [ɪnˈkredəbl] [in-kre-di-bol], *a.* Increíble, lo que
no se puede creer.

incredibleness [ɪnˈkredəblnɪs] [in-kre-di-bol-nes], *s.*
Incredibilidad.

incredibly [ɪnˈkredəblɪ] [in-kre-di-bol], *adv.* Increíblemente.

incredulity [ɪnˈkredəbl] [in-kre-di-bli], *s.* Incredulidad,
repugnancia a, o dificultad en creer; escepticismo.

incredulous [ɪnˈkredjələs] [in-kre-diu-ls], *a.* Incrédulo, el
que cree con dificulta, o repugna creer lo que es creíble;
escético.

incredulousness [ɪnˈkredjələsnɪs] [in-kre-diu-los-nes], *s.*
Incredulidad.

incremate [ɪnˈkremeɪt] [in-kre-meit], *va.* V. CREMATE.

increment [ɪnˈkremənt] [in-kre-ment], *s.* 1. Incremento,
aumento en el crecer; producto. 2. Adición, añadidura,
agregación. 3. *(Mat.)* Cantidad diferencial. 4. *(Ret.)*
Gradación, clímax.

increpate [ɪnˈkrepeɪt] [in-kre-peit], *va.* *(Des.)* Increpar,
reprender con dureza y severidad.

increscent [ɪnˈkresənt] [in-kre-sent], *a.* Creciente; se dice de
la luna.

incriminate [ɪnˈkrɪmɪneɪt] [in-kri-mi-neit], *va.* Incriminar,
acusar de un crimen o delito; acriminar.

incrust [ɪnˈkrʌst] [in-krast], **incrustate** [ɪnˈkrʌsteɪt] [in-
kras-teit], *va.* Encostrar; incrustar, adornar con incrustaciones
o embutidos. **A vessel incrusted with salt,** una vasija
encostrada de sal. Se escribe *encrust* en sentido figurado y
poético, pero rara vez en las acepciones mecánica y literal.

incrustation [ˌɪnkrʌsˈteɪʃən] [in-kras-tei-shon], *s.*
Incrustación, embutido; encostradura.

incubate [ɪnˈkjobeɪt] [in-kiu-beit], *vn.* Empollar, ponerse las
aves sobre los huevos.

incubation [ˌɪnkjʊˈbeɪʃən] [in-kiu-bei-shon], *s.* 1.
Incubación, empolladura, la acción de empollar por
cualesquiera medios. 2. *(Med.)* Incubación, el tiempo que
media entre la impresión de las causas morbosas y la
invasión o principio de las enfermedades.

incubator [ˌɪnkjʊˈbeɪtəʳ] [in-kiu-bei-taʳ], *s.* Lo que incuba o
empolla; incubadora, aparato para efectuar la incubación
artficial.

incubus [ˈɪŋkjʊbəs] [in-kiu-bus], *s.* 1. Una cosa cualquiera
que tiende a sobrecargar u oprimir; carga, cuidado, aflicción;
desánimo. 2. Incubo, pesadilla. 3. *(Ant.)* Demonio íncubo.

inculcate [ɪnˈkʌlkeɪt] [in-kal-keit], *va*. Inculcar, introducir algo en la memoria o entendimiento a fuerza de repetirlo.

inculcation [ˌɪnkʌlˈkeɪʃən] [in-kal-kei-shon], *s*. Inculcación, el acto y efecto de inculcar.

inculcator [ˌɪnkʌlˈkeɪtəʳ] [in-kal-kei-taʳ], *s*. Inculcador, el que inculca.

inculcatory [ɪnˈkʌlkətərɪ] [in-kal-ka-to-ri], *a*. Inculcador, que inculca o sirve para inculcar.

inculpable [ˌɪnkʌlˈpəbl] [in-kal-pa-bol], *a*. Inculpable, irresprensible, exento de culpa; inocente.

inculpableness [ˌɪnkʌlˈpəblnɪs] [in-kal-pabl-nes], *s*. Inculpabilidad.

inculpably [ˌɪnkʌlˈpəblɪ] [in-kal-pa-bli], *adv*. Inculpablemente.

inculpate [ˌɪnkʌlˈpeɪt] [in-kal-peit], *va*. Culpar, imputar falta alguien; inculpar.

inculpation [ˌɪnkʌlˈpeɪʃən] [in-kal-pei-shon], *s*. Inculpación, acción de inculpar.

inculpatory [ˌɪnkʌlˈpətərɪ] [in-kal-pa-to-ri], *a*. Inculpador, imputador.

incumbency [ɪnˈkʌmbənsɪ] [in-kam-ben-si], *s*. 1. La posesión o goce de un cargo, particularmente de un beneficio eclesiástico; y el período durante el cual se ocupa o ejerce dicho cargo. 2. Incumbencia, obligación y cargo de hacer una cosa.

incumbent [ɪnˈkʌmbənt] [in-kam-bent], *a*. 1. Echado; obligatorio, precios, exigido, demandado. 2. Sostenido por; que se apoya en algo, como una antera en un filamento. **To serve God is incumbent on all men**, servir a Dios es deber de todos los hombres. -*s*. Beneficiado, el que está en actual posesión de algún empleo público o de un beneficio eclesiástico.

incumber [ɪnˈkʌmbəʳ] [in-kam-baʳ], *va*. V. ENCUMBER.

incumbrance [ɪnˈkʌmbrəns] [in-kam-brans], *s*. Impedimento, embarazo, obstáculo, carga, imposición. V. ENCUMBRANCE.

incur [ɪnˈkɜːʳ] [in-keʳ], *va*. Incurrir, merecer las penas señaladas por una ley; atraerse, causarse. **To incur a debt**, contraer una deuda.

incurability [ɪnˌkjʊərəˈbɪlɪtɪ] [in-kiu-ra-bi-li-ti], *s*. La calidad que constituye un mal incurable.

incurable [ɪnˈkjʊərəbl] [in-kiua-ra-bol], *a*. Incurable, irreparable, que no tiene remedio. -*s*. Incurable.

incurableness [ɪnˈkjʊərəblnɪs] [in-kiua-ra-bol-nes], *s*. El estado del cuerpo o alma que no admite remedio.

incurably [ɪnˈkjʊərəblɪ] [in-kiua-ra-bli], *adv*. De un modo incurable.

incurious [ɪnˈkjʊərɪəs] [in-kiua-rios], *a*. Incurioso, descuidado, negligente, dejado, omiso.

incuriously [ɪnˈkjʊərɪəslɪ] [in-kiua-rios-li], *adv*. Sin curiosidad, negligentemente.

incuriousness [ɪnˈkjʊərɪəsnɪs] [in-kiua-rios-nes], *s*. Negligencia, descuido, incuria, omisión.

incursion [ɪnˈkɜːʃən] [in-ker-shon], *s*. Incursión, correría; acometimiento.

incurvate [ɪnˈkɜːveɪt] [in-ker-veit], **incurve** [ɪnˈkɜːv] [in-kerv], *va*. Encorvar, doblar o torcer alguna cosa.

incurvate, *a*. Encorvado, doblado.

incus [ɪnˈkəs] [in-kus], *s*. Yunque, uno de los huesecillos del oído medio.

indebted [ɪnˈdetɪd] [in-de-ted], *a*. 1. Adeudado, endeudado, empeñado; el que tiene deudas. **He is indebted over head and ears**, está empeñado hasta los ojos. 2. Obligado, reconocido. **I am indebted to him for many favors**, le debo muchos favores.

indebtedness [ɪnˈdetɪdnɪs] [in-de-ted-nes], *s*. 1. Calidad y estado de deudor, de endeudado. 2. Deuda pasiva, importe o suma de las deudas de alguien.

indebtment [ɪnˈdetmənt] [in-det-ment], *s*. Estado de adeudado.

indecency [ɪnˈdiːsnsɪ] [in-di-sen-si], *s*. Indecencia, inmodestia; grosería, vulgaridad.

indecent [ɪnˈdiːsnt] [in-di-sent], *a*. 1. Indecente, grosero, torpe, obsceno. 2. Inconveniente, impropio.

indecently [ɪnˈdiːsntlɪ] [in-di-sent-li], *adv*. Indecentemente, torpemente.

indecision [ˌɪndɪˈsɪʒən] [in-di-si-shon], *s*. Indecisión, irresolución.

indecisive [ˌɪndɪˈsaɪsɪv] [in-di-sai-siv], *a*. 1. Indeciso, que no es decisivo. 2. Dudoso, indeterminado, irresoluto.

indecisiveness [ˌɪndɪˈsaɪsɪvnɪs] [in-di-sai-siv-nes], *s*. La calidad o el estado de indecisión o irresolución.

indeclinable [ˌɪndɪˈklaɪnəbl] [in-di-klai-na-bol], *a*. Indeclinable. -*s*. Nombre que no se declina.

indeclinably [ˌɪndɪˈklaɪnəblɪ] [in-di-klai-na-bli], *adv*. De un modo indeclinable, sin variación.

indecorous [ɪnˈdekərəs] [in-de-ko-ros], *a*. Indecoroso, vil, indigno, indecente.

indecorously [ɪnˈdekərəslɪ] [in-de-ko-ros-li], *adv*. Indecorosamnete.

indecorousness [ɪnˈdekərəsnɪs] [in-de-ko-ros-nes], *s*. Indecoro.

indecorum [ɪnˈdekərəm] [in-de-ko-rum], *s*. Indecoro, ignominia, indecencia.

indeed [ɪnˈdiːd] [in-did], *adv*. Verdaderamente, realmente, bien que, de veras, a la verdad, sí. ¿De veras? ¡De veras! ¡Vaya, vaya! **But indeed**, pero bien reflexionado. **Though indeed**, aunque considerado todo. **Then indeed**, entonces sí. **That indeed**, Eso sí. **Indeed** se usa muy a menudo de un modo expletivo para dar más fuerza al sentido de la frase o de la oración, y entonces corresponde casi siempre en castellano a «ciertamente, muy o verdaderamente. **Indeed? can you suppose it?** ¿De veras? ¿puede Vd. suponerlo?

indefatigable [ɪnˈdefætɪgəbl] [in-de-fa-ti-ga-bol], *a*. Infatigable, incansable.

indefatigableness [ɪnˌdefætɪˈgeɪbəlnɪs] [in-de-fa-ti-ga-bol-nes], *s*. La calidad de ser infatigable.

indefatigably [ɪnˈdefætɪgəblɪ] [in-de-fa-ti-ga-bli], *adv*. Infatigablemente, incansablemente, sin cansarse.

indefeasible [ɪnˈdefesɪbl] [in-de-fe-si-bol], *a*. (*For.*) Incapaz de ser abrogado o anulado; inabrogable, irrevocable.

indefectibility [ɪnˌdeektɪˈbɪlɪtɪ] [in-de-fek-ti-bi-li-ti], *s*. Indefectibilidad, imposibilidad de faltar o fenecer.

indefectible [ɪnˈdefektɪbl] [in-de-fek-ti-bol], *a*. Indefectible.

indefensible [ɪnˈdefensɪbl] [in-de-fen-si-bol], *a*. Indefendible, indefensible, que no puede ser defendido.

indefensive [ɪnˈdefensɪv] [in-de-fen-siv], *a*. Indefenso, que no tiene defensa o no se puede defender.

indefinable [ˌɪndɪˈfaɪnəbl] [in-di-fai-na-bol], *a*. Indefinible.

indefinite [ɪnˈdefɪnɪt] [in-de-fi-nit], *a*. Indefinido, indeterminado, incierto; sutil, imperceptible.

indefinitely [ɪnˈdefɪnɪtlɪ] [in-de-fi-nit-li], *adv*. Indefinidamente, por un tiempo o espacio indeterminado; de un modo incierto o vago.

indefiniteness [ɪnˈdefɪnɪtnɪs] [in-de-fi-nit-nes], *s*. Estado o calidad de lo que es indefinido.

indehiscence [ɪnˈdehɪsəns] [in-de-ji-sens], *s*. (*Bot.*) Indehiscencia, incapacidad de abrirse natural o espontáneamente.

indehiscent [ɪnˈdehɪsənt] [in-de-ji-sent], *a*. (*Bot.*) Indehiscente, que no se abre o hiende espontáneamente.

indeliberate [ˌɪndeˈlɪbɪrɪt] [in-de-li-bi-reit], *a*. No premeditado, hecho sin reflexión.

indelibility [ˌɪndelɪˈbɪlɪtɪ] [in-de-li-bi-li-ti], *s*. La calidad de ser indeleble.

indelible [ɪnˈdeləbl] [in-de-li-bol], *a*. 1. Indeleble, que no se puede borrar. 2. Irrevocable, que no se puede revocar o anular.

indelibly [ɪnˈdeləblɪ] [in-de-li-bi], *adv*. Indeleblemente, irrevocablemente.

indelicacy [ɪnˈdelɪkəsɪ] [in-de-li-ka-si], *s*. Falta de delicadeza, de decoro; grosería, inurbanidad.

indelicate [ɪnˈdelɪkeɪt] [in-de-li-keit], *a*. Falto de decoro, no delicado, inmodesto; grosero, inurbano.

indemnification [ɪnˌdemnɪfɪˈkeɪʃən] [in-dem-ni-fi-kei-shon], *s*. Indemnización, resarcimiento.

indemnify [ɪnˈdemnɪfaɪ] [in-dem-ni-fai], *va.* 1. Indemnizar, resarcir los daños y perjuicios sufridos. 2. Asegurar a alguno el resarcimiento de una pérdida o pena.

indemnity [ɪnˈdemnɪtɪ] [in-dem-ni-ti], *s.* 1. Indemnización, resarcimiento. 2. Indemnidad, contrafianza, garantía contra pérdidas.

indemonstrable [ɪnˈdemənstrəbl] [in-de-mons-tra-bol], *a.* Indemostrable, incapaz de demostración, que no es demostrable.

indenize [ɪnˈdenaɪz] [in-de-nais], *va.* Dar liberted. *V.* ENDENIZE y sus derivados.

indent [ˈɪndent] [in-dent], *va.* 1. Dentar, endentar, cortar en forma de una carrera de dientes; mellar el borde de. 2. *V.* INDENTURE, verbo. 3. En lo escrito o lo impreso, sangrar, empezar una línea más adentro que las otras. -*vn.* 1. Mellarse, hacerse o ponerse dentado. 2. *(Ant.)* Hacer un contrato, pactar.

indent, *s.* 1. Mella, diente, abertura parecida a una mella. 2. *V.* INDENTURE, substantivo. 3. *(Des.)* Desigualdad; impresión.

indentation [ɪndenˈteɪʃən] [in-den-tei-shon], *s.* 1. La acción de dentar o cortar en puntas. 2. Cortadura dentada, la que está hecha en figura de dientes de sierra; mella.

indented [ɪnˈdentɪd] [in-den-tid], *a. y pp.* Dentado; *(Bot.)* dentellado.

indention [ɪnˈdenʃən] [in-den-shon], *s.* 1. Abolladura, desigualdad. *V.* DENT. 2. Sangría de una línea en lo escrito o impreso.

indenture [ɪnˈdentʃəʳ] [in-den-chaʳ], *s.* 1. *(For.)* Carta partida, la escritura o contrato que se hace formando dos copias unidas y semejantes entre sí, cortándolas después por el medio para que la una sirva de contraseña a la otra. 2. Acción y efecto de dentar o cortar en forma de dientes.

indenture, *va.* Ligar, obligar, por medio de un contrato de aprendizaje hecho por duplicado.

independence [ˌɪndɪˈpendəns] [in-di-pen-dens], *s.* 1. Independencia, libertad de obrar, autonomía. 2. Situación económica desahogada, bienestar. Independencia, en las mismas acepciones que tiene en castellano. 3. Espíritu de confianza en sí mismo. **Independence Day**, en los Estados Unidos, el 4 de Julio.

independent [ˌɪndɪˈpendənt] [in-di-pen-dent], *a.* 1. Independiente, que no depende de otra peersona o cosa para su gobierno o sustento. 2. Que posee los medios de independencia o de libertad de acción; también, que vive de sus rentas. 3. Libre, fácil, cómodo; intrépido. 4. Separado, desunido (con la prep. *of*). **The soul may exist independent of matter**, el alma puede existir separada de la materia. **An independent gentleman**, propietario, rentista, hombre que vive de sus rentas. -*s.* Una clase de sectarios llamados independientes, que no reconocen autoridad eclesiástica alguna.

independently [ˌɪndɪˈpendəntlɪ] [in-di-pen-dent-li], *adv.* Independientemente.

indeprecable [ˌɪndɪˈprekəbl] [in-di-pre-ka-bol], *a.* Indeprecable, inexorable, que no puede ser deprecado.

indeprivable [ˌɪndɪˈprɪvəbl] [in-di-pri-va-bol], *a.* Aquello de que no se puede privar a uno.

indescribable [ˌɪndɪsˈkraɪbəbl] [in-dis-krai-ba-bol], *a.* Indescriptible.

indestructibility [ˌɪndɪstrʌktəˈbɪlɪtɪ] [in-des-trak-ti-bi-li-ti], *s.* Indestructibilidad.

indestructible [ˌɪndɪsˈtrʌktəbl] [in-dis-trak-ti-bol], *a.* Indestructible.

indeterminable [ˌɪndɪˈtɜːmɪnəbl] [in-di-ter-mi-na-bol], *a.* 1. Indeterminable, lo que no se puede determinar. 2. (Hist. Naut.) Que no admite clasificación ni nombre a causa de su mala o imperfecta condición.

indeterminate [ˌɪndɪˈtɜːmɪnɪt] [in-di-ter-mi-neit], *a.* Indeterminado, no exacto, indefinido.

indeterminately [ˌɪndɪˈtɜːmɪnɪtlɪ] [in-di-ter-mi-neit-li], *adv.* Indeterminadamente.

indeterminateness [ˌɪndɪˈtɜːmɪnɪtnɪs] [in-di-ter-mi-neit-nes], *s.* Indeterminación, duda, irresolución.

indetermination [ˈɪndɪˌtɜːmɪˈneɪʃən] [in-di-ter-mi-nei-shon], *s.* Indeterminación, irresolución.

indetermined [ˌɪndɪˈtɜːmaɪnd] [in-di-ter-mind], *a.* Indeterminado, vacilante, irresoluto, irresuelto.

index [ˈɪndeks] [in-deks], *s. (pl.* INDEXES, INDICES. 1. Indicio o señal de alguna cosa; una cosa cualquiera que marca o señala, o manifiesta. 2. Índice, el dedo segundo de la mano. 3. Índice o tabla de materias de un libro dispuestas en orden alfabético, indicando dónde se halla cada tema o asunto. 4. Manecilla de reloj; manecilla en la imprenta, el signo 5. Índice expurgatorio.

index, *va.* Poner un índice alfabético a un libro.

indexical [ˈɪndeksɪkl] [in-dek-si-kal], *a.* 1. Que tiene la forma de índice. 2. Que sirve para indicar, indicativo.

indexterity [ˌɪndeksˈterɪtɪ] [in-deks-te-ri-ti], *s.* Desmaña, falta de destreza.

India [ˈɪndɪə] [in-dia], *s.* India, Indias, vasta región del sur de Asia. **India-ink**, tinta de la China, o tinta China. **India-paper**, papel de China; papel delgado, absorbente, para imprimir; se emplea para obtener las pruebas más delicadas de planchas grabadas. *India-proof*, prueba original y escogida hecha en papel de China con una plancha grabada.

indian [ˈɪndɪən] [in-dian], *a.* 1. Indio, natural de la India (oriental u occidental) o relativo a ella. 2. *(E.U.A.)* Hecho de maíz. -*s.* 1. Indio, el natural de la India oriental. 2. Indio, el antiguo poblador o aborigen de todo el continente americano. 3. El natural de las Antillas o el naturalizado y residente en ellas. 4. El europeo que ha residido en la India; anglo-indiano. **Indian-berries**, cocas de Levante. **Indian-corn**, maíz, trigo de la América, trigo de Turquía. **Indian-meal**, harina de maíz.

indian-cress [ˈɪndɪənˌkres] [in-dian-kres], *s. (Bot.)* Capuchina; se llama más común y familiarmente *nasturtium*.

indian-rubber [ˈɪndɪənˌrʌbəʳ] [in-dian-ra-baʳ], *s.* Caucho, cauchuco, goma elástica. *(Mex.)* Hule.

indian-summer [ˈɪndɪənˌsʌməʳ] [in-dian-sa-maʳ], *s. (E.U.)* Veranillo de San Martín. Días de calor y calma en noviembre.

indicant [ˈɪndɪkənt] [in-di-kant], *a.* Indicante.

indicate [ˈɪndɪkeɪt] [in-di-keit], *va.* Indicar, señalar, designar, dar a entender, anunciar.

indication [ˌɪndɪˈkeɪʃən] [in-di-kei-shon], *s.* 1. Indicación, indicio; señal; signo. 2. Manifestación; *(Med.)* indicación que dan los síntomas de una enfermedad en lo relativo al tratamiento que ha de seguirse.

indicative [ɪnˈdɪkətɪv] [in-di-ka-tiv], *a.* Indicativo. **Indicative mode (o mood)**, modo indicativo.

indicatively [ɪnˈdɪkətɪvlɪ] [in-di-ka-tiv-li], *adv.* Indicativamente.

indicator [ˈɪndɪkeɪtəʳ] [in-di-kei-taʳ], *s.* Indicador, señalador, apuntador, el que o lo que indica. Indicador, manómetro; instrumento para recibir de un telégrafo de cuadrante.

indicatory [ɪnˈdɪkətərɪ] [in-di-ka-to-ri], *a.* Demostrativo, indicatorio.

indices [ˈɪndɪsiːz] [in-di-sis], *s.* Plural de *Index;* se usa especialmente en las ciencias y en las matemáticas.

indict [ɪnˈdaɪt] [in-dait], *va.* 1. Acusar por escrito ante el juez. *(For.)* Procesar, demandar judicialmente. 2. *(Ant.)* Componer, escribir o dictar.

indictable [ɪnˈdaɪtəbl] [in-dai-ta-bol], *a. (For.)* Procesable, denunciable; expuesto a ser denunciado o juzgado, sujeto a denuncia.

indictee [ɪnˈdaɪtiː] [in-dai-ti], *s.* La persona acusada de un delito o demandada en juicio.

indicter [ɪnˈdaɪtəʳ] [in-dai-taʳ], *s. (For.)* Denunciante, fiscal, acusador, denunciador.

indiction [ɪnˈdaɪʃən] [in-dai-shon], *s.* 1. Indicción, período de quince años, instituido por Constantino y adoptado por los papas, como parte de su sistema cronológico. 2. Dicho período o uno cualquiera de sus años.

indictment [ɪnˈdaɪtmənt] [in-dait-ment], *s. (For.)* Acusación de alguna ofensa criminal o delito; particularmente la formulada por el Gran Jurado bajo juramento y por escrito, como base para el procesamiento del acusado.

indifference [ɪnˈdɪfrəns] [in-di-fe-rens], s. 1. Indiferencia, imparcialidad. 2. Indiferencia, descuido, frialdad, tibieza. 3. Indiferencia, desinterés, desapego del ánimo a las cosas.

indifferent [ɪnˈdɪfrənt] [in-di-fe-rent], a. 1. Indiferente, que no interesa. 2. Indiferente, que no se toma interés por ninguna cosa, que no se mueve por nada. 3. Imparcial, desapasionado. 4. Pasadero, mediano, pasable, tal cual, ni bueno ni malo; ordinario.

indigence [ˈɪndɪdʒəns] [in-di-chens], **indigency** [ˈɪndɪdʒənsɪ] [in-di-chen-si], s. Indigencia, pobreza, necesidad.

indigene, a. y s. V. INDIGENOUS.

indigenous [ɪnˈdɪdʒɪnəs] [in-di-che-nos], a. 1. Indígena, el que es natural de un país o lugar determinado; lo opuesto a exótico; de aquí, innato. 2. (Geol.) Producido por deposición en la superficie de la tierra, como por un sedimento.

indigent [ˈɪndɪdʒənt] [in-di-chent], a. Indigente, pobre, necesitado; falto.

indigested [ˈɪndɪdʒestɪd] [in-di-ches-tid], a. 1. Indigesto, mal digerido; se dice de las obras escritas sin orden ni método. 2. Indigesto, mal digerido, crudo difícil de digerir.

indigestible [ˌɪndɪˈdʒestəbl] [in-di-ches-ti-bol], a. Indigestible, indigesto.

indigestion [ˌɪndɪˈdʒestʃən] [in-di-ches-shon], s. Indigestión.

indignance, indignancy, s. V. INDIGNATION.

indignant [ɪnˈdɪgnənt] [in-dig-nant], a. Indignado, conmovido a la vez por la cólera y el desdén.

indignantly [ɪnˈdɪgnəntlɪ] [in-dig-nant-li], adv. Con indignación.

indignation [ˌɪndɪgˈneɪʃən] [in-dig-nei-shon], s. Indignación, sentimiento de cólera y desprecio, excitado por la injusticia, la mezquindad, la inhumanidad, etc.; despecho, cólera.

indignity [ɪnˈdɪgnɪtɪ] [in-dig-ni-ti], s. Indignidad, ultraje, afrenta; aprobio.

indigo [ˈɪndɪgəʊ] [in-di-gou], s. 1. Añil, índigo, planta de cuyo jugo se hace una pasta que sirve para teñir, y que recibe el mismo nombre. 2. Color azul obscuro algo violado.

indirect [ˌɪndɪˈrekt] [in-dai-rekt], a. 1. Indirecto, oblicuo, torciod. 2. Torcido, doloso, inicuo, falto de rectitud y honradez.

indirection [ˌɪndɪˈrekʃən] [in-di-rek-shon], s. 1. Oblicuidad, rodeo, tortuosidad. 2. Efugio, medio tortuoso o siniestro; vía indirecta; segunda intención.

indirectly [ˌɪndɪˈrektlɪ] [in-dai-rekt-li], adv. Indirectamente, oblicuamente; siniestramente.

indirectness [ˌɪndɪˈrektnɪs] [in-dai-rekt-nes], s. 1. Oblicuidad, tortuosidad. 2. Rodeo, efugio o excusa falsa, doblez, manejo fraudulento.

indiscernible [ˌɪndɪˈsɜːnəbl] [in-di-ser-ni-bol], a. Indiscernible, imperceptible.

indiscernibleness [ˌɪndɪˈsɜːnəblnɪs] [in-di-ser-ni-bol-nes], s. La incapacidad de discernir; carácter de lo indiscernible.

indiscernibly [ˌɪndɪˈsɜːnəblɪ] [in-di-ser-ni-bli], adv. Imperceptiblemente.

indisciplinable [ˌɪndɪˈsɪpɪnəbl] [in-di-si-pi-na-bol], a. Indescubrible.

indiscoverable [ˌɪndɪsˈkʌvərəbl] [in-di-ko-ve-ra-bol], a. Indescubrible.

indiscreet [ˌɪndɪsˈkriːt] [in-dis-krit], a. Indiscreto, imprudente, inconsiderado, incauto.

indiscreetly [ˌɪndɪsˈkriːtlɪ] [in-dis-krit-li], adv. Indiscretamente, imprudentemente.

indiscrete [ˌɪndɪsˈkriːt] [in-dis-krit], a. Que no está separado o desunido.

indiscretion [ˌɪndɪsˈkreʃən] [in-dis-kre-shon], s. Indiscreción, inconsideración, imprudencia.

indiscriminate [ˌɪndɪsˈkrɪmɪnɪt] [in-dis-kri-mi-neit], a. 1. Que no hace distinciones. 2. Indistinto, confuso, promiscuo, general.

indiscriminately [ˌɪndɪsˈkrɪmɪnɪtlɪ] [in-dis-kri-mi-neit-li], adv. Indistintamente, promiscuamente.

indiscriminating [ˌɪndɪsˈkrɪmɪneɪtɪŋ] [in-dis-kri-mi-nei-tin], a. Indiscriminado; que no hace distinción alguna.

indiscrimination [ˌɪndɪsˈkrɪmɪneɪʃən] [in-dis-kri-mi-nei-shon], s. Falta de distinción o claridad.

indispensability [ˌɪndɪspensəˈbɪlɪtɪ] [in-dis-pen-sa-bi-li-ti], s. Indispensabilidad.

indispensable [ˌɪndɪsˈpensəbl] [in-dis-pen-sa-bol], a. Indispensable, imprescindible; preciso.

indispensableness [ˌɪndɪsˈpensəblnɪs] [in-dis-pen-sa-bol-nes], s. Indispensabilidad, necesidad.

indispensably [ˌɪndɪsˈpensəblɪ] [in-dis-pen-sa-bli], adv. Indispensablemente, precisamente.

indispose [ˌɪndɪsˈpəʊz] [in-dis-pous], va. 1. Indisponer, hacer a uno contrario o desfavorable a una cosa. 2. Hacer poco apto para o incapaz de. 3. Indisponer, poner a uno mal con otro. 4. Indisponer, causar algún ligero quebranto en la salud.

indisposedness [ˌɪndɪsˈpəʊzdnɪs] [in-dis-pousd-nes], s. Desazón, desavenencia, indisposición, repugnancia.

indisposition [ˌɪndɪspəˈzɪʃən] [in-dis-pou-si-shon], s. 1. Indisposición, desazón, falta de salud. 2. Desafecto, desavenencia; aborrecimiento.

indisputable [ˌɪndɪsˈpjuːtəbl] [in-dis-piu-ta-bol], a. Indisputable.

indisputableness [ˌɪndɪsˈpjuːtəblnɪs] [in-dis-piu-ta-bol-nes], s. Certeza.

indisputably [ˌɪndɪsˈpjuːtəblɪ] [in-dis-piu-ta-bli], adv. Indisputablemente, ciertamente.

indissolvable [ˌɪndɪˈsɒlvəbl] [in-di-sol-va-bol], a. Indisoluble; permanente, obligatorio.

indissolubility [ˌɪndɪsɒljʊˈbɪlɪtɪ] [in-di-so-liu-bi-li-ti], s. Indisolubilidad.

indissoluble [ˌɪndɪˈsɒljʊbl] [in-di-so-liu-bol], a. Indisoluble, firme, estable.

indissolubleness [ˌɪndɪˈsɒljʊblnɪs] [in-di-so-liu-bol-nes], s. Indisolubilidad.

indissolubly [ˌɪndɪˈsɒljʊblɪ] [in-di-so-liu-bli], adv. Indisolublemente.

indistinct [ˌɪndɪsˈtɪŋkt] [in-dis-tinkt], a. Indistinto, confuso; obscuro, vago.

indistinction [ˌɪndɪsˈtɪŋkʃən] [in-dis-tink-shon], s. 1. Indistinción; obscuridad, falta de claridad, confusión. 2. Igualdad de rango o condición.

indistinctly [ˌɪndɪsˈtɪŋktlɪ] [in-dis-tinkt-li], adv. Indistintamente confusamente, vagamente.

indistinctness [ˌɪndɪsˈtɪŋktnɪs] [in-dis-tinkt-nes], s. Confusión, oscuridad, incertidumbre.

indistinguishable [ˌɪndɪsˈtɪŋgwɪʃəbl] [in-dis-tin-güi-sha-bol], a. Indistinguible.

indite [ɪnˈdaɪt] [in-dait], va. 1. Poner por escrito; componer, escribir. 2. (Ant.) Dictar, dirigir. 3. (Des.) V. INDICT.

inditement [ɪnˈdaɪtmənt] [in-dait-ment], s. Composición; escritura.

inditer [ɪnˈdaɪtəʳ] [in-dai-taʳ], s. Autor.

indium [ɪnˈdɪəm] [in-dium], s. Indio, metal parecido al estaño, color de plata y maleable, descubierto en 1863.

individual [ˌɪndɪˈvɪdjʊəl] [in-di-vi-diual], a. 1. Solo, único. 2. Individual, particular, individuo, que pertenece a uno solo. **An individual soul**, un alma única. -s. 1. Individuo, el particular de su especie, una sola persona, cosa o animal; especialmente persona humana, la propia persona. 2. Particular, persona privada, en oposición a una sociedad o corporación.

individualism [ˌɪndɪˈvɪdjʊəlɪzəm] [in-di-vi-diua-li-sem], s. 1. Individualismo; sistema de refinado egoísmo, de aislamiento en los estudios, trabajos y existencia. 2. Sistema que no reconoce más realidad que la del individuo y en él cree encontrar el fundamento y fin de todas las leyes, etc. 3. Sistema que ensancha la esfera de acción y derecho del individuo a expensas de las funciones sociales.

individualistic ['ɪndɪˌvɪdjʊə'lɪstɪk] [in-di-vi-diua-lis-tik], *a.* Individualista.

individuality ['ɪndɪˌvɪdjʊ'ælɪtɪ] [in-di-vi-diua-li-ti], *s.* Individualidad.

individualize [ˌɪndɪ'vɪdjʊəlaɪz] [in-di-vi-diua-lais], *va.* Individualizar, particularizar.

individually [ˌɪndɪ'vɪdjʊəlɪ] [in-di-vi-diua-li], *adv.* Individualmente.

individuate [ˌɪndɪ'vɪdjʊeɪt] [in-di-vi-dueit], *va.* Individualizar, particularizar. -*a.* 1. Convertido en individuos. 2. Individual, que posee diferencia e identidad numéricas.

indivisibility ['ɪndɪˌvɪsɪ'bɪlɪtɪ] [in-di-vi-si-bi-li-ti], **indivisibleness** [ˌɪndɪ'vɪsɪblnɪs] [in-di-vi-si-bol-nes], *s.* Indivisibilidad.

indivisible [ˌɪndɪ'vɪzəbl] [in-di-vi-si-bol], *a.* Indivisible. -*s.* Incapaz de división.

indivisibly [ˌɪndɪ'vɪzəblɪ] [in-di-vi-si-bli], *adv.* Indivisiblemente.

indocile [ɪn'dəsɪl] [in-do-sil], *a.* Indócil, cerril.

indocility [ɪndə'sɪlɪtɪ] [in-do-si-li-ti], *s.* Indocilidad, pertinacia, dureza, aspereza.

indoctrinate [ɪn'dɒktrɪneɪt] [in-dok-tri-neit], *va.* Doctrinar, enseñar, disciplinar, instruir.

indoctrination [ɪnˌdɒktrɪ'neɪʃən] [in-dok-tri-nei-shon], *s.* Instrucción, enseñanza.

Indo-European ['ɪndəʊˌjʊərə'piːən] [in-do-iu-ro-pian], *a.* Indoeuropeo, indoeuropea; indogermánico, ario.

indolence ['ɪndələns] [in-do-lens], *s.* 1. Indolencia, pereza. 2. (*Med.*) Ausencia de dolor o sufrimiento.

indolent ['ɪndələnt] [in-do-lent], *a.* 1. Indolente, perezoso, indiferente a todo. 2. (*Med.*) Indolente, sin dolor, que no causa sufrimiento.

indolently ['ɪndələntlɪ] [in-do-lent-li], *adv.* Indolentemente, perezosamente, con indolencia.

indomitable [ɪn'dɒmɪtəbl] [in-do-mi-ta-bol], *a.* Indomable, que no se puede domar.

indoor ['ɪndɔːʳ] [in-doʳ], *a.* Interno, interior; de puertas adentro. **Indoor work**, trabajo interior.

indoors [ɪn'dɔːz] [in-dors], *adv.* Adentro; en el interior de un edificio; en casa, o en la habitación.

indorsable [ɪn'dɔːzəbl] [in-dor-sa-bol], *a.* Endosable, endorsable.

indorse [ɪn'dɔːs] [in-dors], *va.* 1. Endorsar, escribir en el dorso, respaldar un documento (para archivarlo). 2. Endosar, escribir al dorso de una letra de cambio, vale o libranza, para cederla a otro o para garantizar su pago. 3. Dar sanción a, aprobar, confirmar. *V.* ENDORSE.

indorsee [ɪn'dɔːsiː] [in-dor-si], *s.* Endosado, portador; la persona a cuya orden se ha endosado una libranza, pagaré, etc.

indorsement [ɪn'dɔːzmənt] [in-dors-ment], *s.* 1. Endoso de una letra de cambio, vale o libranza. 2. Traspaso de un vale o pagaré. 3. Rótulo, sobrescrito. 4. Sanción, aprobación, ratificación.

indorsor, indorsor [ɪn'dɔːsəʳ] [in-dor-saʳ], *s.* Endosante, endosador, el que endosa.

indraft, indraught [ɪn'drɑːft] [in-draft], *s.* Entrada, el acto de atraer o de inspirar, y lo que es atraído.

indrawn [ˌɪn'drɔːn] [in-dron], *a.* Atraído, inspirado; con voz ahogada; de aquí, abstraído, distraído.

indubitable [ɪn'djuːbɪtəbl] [in-diu-bi-ta-bol], *a.* Indubable, indubitable, lo que no se puede dudar.

indubitableness [ɪn'djuːbɪtəblnɪs] [in-diu-bi-ta-bol-nes], *s.* El estado de lo que es indubable.

indubitably [ɪn'djuːbɪtəblɪ] [in-diu-bi-ta-bli], *adv.* Indudablemente, indubitablemente.

induce [ɪn'djuːs] [in-dius], *va.* 1. Inducir, aconsejar o persuadir a uno a que ejecute alguna cosa; instigar, incitar. 2. Inferir, sacar consecuencias. 3. Producir, causar, ocasionar, efectuar gradualmente, inspirar. 4. (*Fís.*) Producir por la inducción eléctrica o magnética.

inducement [ɪn'djuːsmənt] [in-dius-ment], *s.* Incitamento, móvil, inducimiento, aliciente lo que induce o persuade a alguna cosa, persuasión.

inducer [ɪn'djuːsəʳ] [in-diu-saʳ], *s.* Inducidor, persuadidor, inspirador.

inducible [ɪn'djuːsəbl] [in-diu-si-bol], *a.* Deducible, que puede sacarse por inducción o ilación.

induct [ɪn'dʌkt] [in-dakt], *va.* 1. Introducir. 2. Instalar, dar posesión al que ha obtenido algún beneficio o empleo. 3. Obtener por inducción.

inductance [ɪn'dʌktəns] [in-dak-tans], *s.* Inductancia.

induction [ɪn'dʌkʃən] [in-dak-shon], *s.* Inducción (en todos sus significados). **Induction coil**, (*Elec.*) bobina de inducción. **Induction coefficient**, coeficiente de inducción. **Series-wound induction coil**, bobina de inducción en serie. **Vibrator-type induction coil**, bobina de inducción con temblador. **Cross induction**, inducción transversal.

inductive [ɪn'dʌktɪv] [in-dak-tiv], *a.* 1. Inductivo. 2. Ilativo. 3. (*Elec.*) Inductivo, capaz de inducción; producido por la inducción, o que obra por ella.

inductively [ɪn'dʌktɪvlɪ] [in-dak-tiv-li], *adv.* Inductivamente, por inducción, por ilación o inferencia.

inductor [ɪn'dʌktəʳ] [in-dak-taʳ], *s.* 1. El que instala o da posesión de algún beneficio eclesiástico. 2. (*Elec.*) Inductor, cualquier parte de un aparato eléctrico que obra sobre otra por inducción.

indue [ɪn'djuː] [in-diu], *va.* 1. Vestir, cubrir con vestido, investir. 2. Dotar a alguno con algún don o excelencia.

indulge [ɪn'dʌldʒ] [in-dalch], *va.* 1. Consentir, por lo común fuera de propósito o poco prudentemente; no oponerse a la ejecución de alguna cosa; condescender, gratificar, dar gusto, tolerar; contentar, satisfacer. 2. Conceder, dar gratuitamente; permitir. 3. Favorecer, animar. **To indulge to**, entregarse, darse a. **To indulge in**, lisonjearse. -*vn.* Entregarse a, abandonarse a; satisfacer un deseo sin restricción; se usa con la preposición *in*. **To indulge oneself**, darse gusto; obrar con toda comodidad; beber de codos.

indulgence [ɪn'dʌldʒəns] [in-dal-chens], **indulgency** [ɪn'dʌldʒənsɪ] [in-dal-chen-si], *s.* 1. Indulgencia, cariño, afecto, halago, condescendencia, gratificación, satisfacción, goce. 2. Abandono, acción de entregarse a sus pasiones. 3. Indulgencia, disimulo, inclinación a perdonar y sufrir; facilidad, placer, bondad. 4. Favor, gracia concedida, complacencia; (*Com.*) permiso para aplazar un pago. 5. Indulgencia, gracia concedida en la Iglesia romana por el Papa y los obispos, en remisión de las penitencias canónicas.

indulgent [ɪn'dʌldʒənt] [in-dal-chent], *a.* 1. Indulgente, tierno, clement, favorable. 2. Indulgente, condescendiente, complaciente, fácil.

indulgently [ɪn'dʌldʒəntlɪ] [in-dal-chent-li], *adv.* Indulgentemente.

indulger [ɪn'dʌldʒəʳ] [in-dal-chaʳ], *s.* Indulgente, el que es complaciente o fácil en acomodarse al gusto de los demás.

indult [ɪn'dʌlt] [in-dalt], *s.* Indulto, gracia, o privilegio concedido por el Papa; exención.

indurate [ɪn'djʊreɪt] [in-diu-reit], *va.* 1. Endurecer una cosa. 2. Endurecer a uno, hacer duro, insensible u obstinado. -*vn.* Endurecerse, empedernirse.

indurate, *a.* Impenitente, obstinado en la culpa o el mal; duro, endurecido.

induration [ɪn'djʊreɪʃən] [in-diu-rei-shon], *s.* 1. Endurecimiento, la acción, el acto de endurecer; estado de lo que se halla endurecido. 2. Dureza de corazón.

industrial [ɪn'dʌstrɪəl] [in-das-trial], *a.* Industrial, que pertenece a la industria. **Industrial exhibition**, exposición de la industria, fabril, etc. **Industrial psychology**, psicología industrial. **Industrial school**, escuela industrial, de artes y oficios.

industrialism [ɪn'dʌstrɪəlɪzm] [in-das-tria-li-sem], *s.* 1. Industrialismo, el sistema moderno industrial; sistema social que considera la industria como el más importante de los fines humanos. 2. Industria, trabajo.

industrialist [ɪnˈdʌstrɪəlɪst] [in-das-tria-list], *s.* Industrialista.

industrialization [ɪnˌdʌstrɪəlɪˈzeɪʃən] [in-das-tria-li-sei-shon], *s.* Industrialización.

industrialize [ɪnˈdʌstrɪəlaɪz] [in-das-tria-lais], *va.* Industrializar.

industrious [ɪnˈdʌstrɪəs] [in-das-trios], *a.* 1. Industrioso, diligente, laborioso, aplicado. 2. Industrioso, hecho con industria o mucho arte.

industriously [ɪnˈdʌstrɪəslɪ] [in-das-trios-li], *adv.* 1. Industriosamente. 2. Industriosamente, de industria, de propósito, de intento, adrede.

industry [ˈɪndəstrɪ] [in-das-tri], *s.* 1. Industria, esmero, diligencia, destreza. 2. Labor, trabajo útil en general (particularmente de la industria manufacturera). 3. Cualquier ramo aislado de la actividad productiva.

indwell [ˈɪndwel] [ind-wel], *va. y vn.* Existir interiormente; morar dentro, habitar; morar permanentemente en el alma.

inebriant [ɪˈniːbrɪənt] [in-i-briant], *a.* Embriagador, que embriaga. -*s.* Sustancia embriagadora.

inebriate [ɪˈniːbrɪɪt] [in-i-brieit], *va.* 1. Embriagar, emborrachar. 2. Infatuar, cegar, desvanecer. -*vn.* 1. Embriagarse o emborracharse. 2. Infatuarse. -*s.* Borracho.

inebriation [ɪˌniːbrɪˈeɪʃən] [in-i-bri-ei-shon], *s.* Embriaguez, borrachera.

inedited [ɪnˈedaɪtɪd] [in-i-dai-ted], *a.* 1. Inédito. 2. No redactado aún.

ineffable [ɪnˈefəbl] [in-e-fa-bol], *a.* 1. Inefable, que no se puede expresar con palabras. 2. Se aplica a aquellas cosas de que no se debe hablar, v. g. el nombre de Jehová.

ineffableness [ɪnˈefəblnɪs] [in-e-fa-bol-nes], *s.* Inefabilidad.

ineffably [ɪnˈefəblɪ] [in-e-fa-bli], *adv.* Inefablemente, indeciblemente.

ineffaceable [ˌɪnɪˈfeɪsəbl] [in-i-fei-sa-bol], *a.* Indeleble, imborrable, que no se puede borrar.

ineffaceably [ˌɪnɪˈfeɪsəblɪ] [in-i-fei-sa-bli], *adv.* Indeleblemente, imborrablemente.

ineffective [ˌɪnɪˈfektɪv] [in-i-fek-tiv], *a.* Ineficaz; vano, inútil; impotente.

ineffectual [ˌɪnɪˈfektʃʊəl] [in-i-fek-chual], *a.* Ineficaz; sin efecto, incapaz de producr el efecto deseado. **To prove ineffectual**, no tener resultado, quedar sin efecto.

ineffectually [ˌɪnɪˈfektʃʊəlɪ] [in-i-fek-chua-li], *adv.* Ineficazmente; sin resultado.

ineffectualness [ˌɪnɪˈfektʃʊəlnɪs] [in-e-fek-chual-nes], *s.* Ineficacia.

inefficacious [ˌɪnefɪˈkeɪʃəs] [in-e-fi-kei-shos], *a.* Ineficaz.

inefficaciousness [ˌɪnefɪˈkeɪʃəsnɪs] [in-e-fi-kei-shos-nes], *s.* Ineficacia.

inefficacy [ɪnˈefɪkəsɪ] [in-e-fi-ka-si], **inefficiency** [ˌɪnɪˈfɪʃənsɪ] [in-i-fi-shan-si], *s.* Ineficacia, falta de eficacia.

inefficient [ˌɪnɪˈfɪʃənt] [in-i-fi-shant], *a.* Ineficaz.

inelastic [ˌɪnɪˈlæstɪk] [in-i-las-tik], *a.* Falto de elasticidad.

inelasticity [ˌɪnɪləsˈtɪsɪtɪ] [in-i-las-ti-si-ti], *s.* Carencia de elasticidad.

inelegance [ɪnˈelɪɡəns] [in-e-li-gans], *s.* Inelegancia, falta de elegancia.

inelegant [ɪnˈelɪɡənt] [in-e-li-gant], *a.* Inelegante, falto de elegancia, de buen gusto.

inelegantly [ɪnˈelɪɡəntlɪ] [in-e-li-gant-li], *adv.* Sin elegancia, de un modo falto de elegancia.

ineligibility [ˌɪnelɪdʒɪˈbɪlɪtɪ] [in-e-li-chi-bi-li-ti], *s.* Estado o calidad de lo que no puede ser elegido.

inelegible [ɪnˈelɪdʒəbl] [in-e-li-cha-bol], *a.* 1. Excluido de elección, incapaz de ser elegido. 2. Que no conviene escoger; poco deseable.

ineluctable [ˌɪnɪˈlʌktəbl] [in-i-lak-ta-bol], *a.* Inevitable, irresistible, ineluctable.

inept [ɪˈnept] [i-nept], *a.* 1. Inepto; no idóneo. 2. Absurdo, tonto, inconsistente con la razón.

ineptitude [ɪˈneptɪtjuːd] [i-nep-ti-tiud], **ineptness** [ɪˈneptnɪs] [i-nept-nes], *s.* Ineptitud, incapacidad.

ineptly [ɪˈneptlɪ] [i-nept-li], *adv.* Ineptamente, neciamente.

inequal [ɪˈnɪkwəl] [i-ni-kual], *a. (Ento.)* Desigual; se dice de una superficie.

inequality [ˌɪnɪˈkwɒlɪtɪ] [i-ni-kuo-li-ti], *s.* 1. Desigualdad, diferencia en cosas de la misma clase; disparidad, desemejanza. 2. Desigualdad, falta de regularidad, o de proporción; superficie escabrosa. 3. Desigualdad, variedad o inconstancia; desviación en el movimiento de un astro. 4. Insuficiencia; incompetencia. 5. Injusticia.

inequitable [ɪˈnɪkwɪtəbl] [i-ni-kui-ta-bol], *a.* Que no es equitativo o justo.

ineradicable [ˌɪnɪˈrædɪkəbl] [i-ni-ra-di-ka-bol], *a.* Que no se puede erradicar.

inerrable [ɪˈnerəbl] [i-ne-ra-bol], *a.* Inerrable, libre de error.

inerrant [ɪˈnerənt] [i-ne-rant], *a.* Exento de error, infalible.

inert [ɪˈnɜːt] [i-nert], *a.* Inerte, flojo, que carece de fuerza inherente para moverse o resistir a una fuerza impulsante; inanimado, sin vida.

inertia [ɪˈnɜːʃə] [i-ner-sha], *s.* 1. Flojedad, inacción, desidia. 2. *(Fís.)* Inercia, propiedad que tienen los cuerpos de permanecer en el estado de movimiento o de reposo en que se encuentran, hasta que una acción exterior obra sobre ellos con suficiente energía.

inertly [ɪˈnɜːtlɪ] [i-nert-li], *adv.* Pesadamente, flojamente, indolentemente.

inertness [ɪˈnɜːtnɪs] [i-nert-nes], *s.* Flojedad, inacción.

inestimable [ɪnˈestɪməbl] [in-es-ti-ma-bol], *a.* Inestimable, inapreciable, lo que no se puede estimar dignamente.

inestimably [ɪnˈestɪməblɪ] [in-es-ti-ma-bli], *adv.* De un modo inestimable.

inevitable [ɪnˈevɪtəbl] [in-e-vi-ta-bol], Inevitable.

inevitability [ɪnˌevɪtəˈbɪlɪtɪ] [in-e-vi-ta-bi-li-ti], *s.* El estado o calidad de lo que es inevitable.

inevitably [ɪnˈevɪtəblɪ] [in-e-vi-ta-bli], *adv.* Inevitablemente.

inexact [ˌɪnɪɡˈzækt] [in-ik-sakt], *a.* Inexacto, falto de exactitud o de verdad; incorrecto.

inexactly [ˌɪnɪɡˈzæktlɪ] [in-ik-sakt-li], *adv.* De manera inexacta.

inexcusable [ˌɪnɪksˈkjuːzəbl] [in-iks-kiu-sa-bol], *a.* Inexcusable, injustificable, imperdonable.

inexcusableness [ˌɪnɪksˈkjuːzəblnɪs] [in-iks-kiu-sa-bol-nes], *s.* Enormidad o atrocidad que no merece excusa, disculpa o perdón.

inexcusably [ˌɪnɪksˈkjuːzəblɪ] [in-iks-kiu-sa-bli], *adv.* Inexcusablemente, sin excusa.

inexhaustible [ˌɪnɪɡˈzɔːstəbl] [in-iks-sos-ti-bol], **inexhaustive** [ˌɪnɪɡˈzɔːstɪv] [in-iks-sos-tiv], *a.* Inexhausto, inagotable.

inexhaustibleness [ˌɪnɪɡˈzɔːstəblnɪs] [in-iks-sos-ti-bol-nes], *s.* El estado o calidad de lo que es inagotable.

inexistence [ˌɪnɪɡˈzɪstəns] [in-ik-sis-tans], *s.* Inexistencia.

inexistent [ˌɪnɪɡˈzɪstənt] [in-ik-sis-tant], *a.* Inexistente.

inexorable [ɪnˈeksərəbl] [in-ek-so-ra-bol], *a.* Inexorable, duro, inflexible.

inexorability [ɪnˌeksərəˈbɪlɪtɪ] [in-ek-so-ra-bi-li-ti], **inexorableness** [ɪnˈeksərəblnɪs] [in-ek-so-ra-bol-nes], *s.* Inflexibilidad.

inexorably [ɪnˈeksərəblɪ] [in-ek-so-ra-bli], *adv.* Inflexiblemente.

inexpansible [ˌɪneksˈpænsɪbl] [in-eks-pan-si-bol], *a.* Poco expansible, incapaz de expansión.

inexpedience [ˌɪneksˈpɪdɪəns] [in-eks-pi-diens], *s.* Inoportunidad, impropiedad, falta de conveniencia en el orden, tiempo o circunstancias en que se hace o se proyecta hacer una cosa.

inexpedient [ˌɪneksˈpɪdɪənt] [in-eks-pi-dient], *a.* Impropio, inoportuno, que no viene al caso o está fuera de propósito.

inexpensive [ˌɪnɪksˈpensɪv] [in-iks-pen-siv], *a.* Poco costoso, que no exige grandes gastos; barato.

inexperience [ˌɪnɪksˈpɪərɪəns] [in-iks-pia-riens], *s.* Inexperiencia, impericia.

inexperienced [ˌɪnɪksˈpɪərɪənst] [in-iks-pia-rienst], *a.* Inexperimentado, falto de experiencia.

inexpert [ɪnˈekspɜːt] [in-iks-pert], *a.* Inexperto, poco mañoso, inhábil.

inexpiable [ˌɪnɪksˈpaɪəbl] [in-iks-paia-bol], *a.* Inexpiable, lo que no puede ser perdonado o satisfecho, expiado o lavado, hablando de culpas o delitos.

inexpiableness [ˌɪnɪksˈpaɪəblnɪs] [in-iks-paia-bol-nes], *s.* El estado o calidad de lo que es inexpiable o no se puede purgar o satisfacer.

inexpiably [ˌɪnɪksˈpaɪəblɪ] [in-iks-paia-bli], *adv.* De un modo inexpiable, en un grado que no admite expiación.

inexplicable [ˌɪnɪksˈplɪkəbl] [in-iks-pli-ka-bol], *a.* Inexplicable, que no se puede explicar.

inexplicably [ˌɪnɪksˈplɪkəblɪ] [in-iks-pli-ka-bli], *adv.* Inexplicablemente.

inexplorable [ˌɪnɪksˈplɔrəbl] [in-iks-plo-ra-bol], *a.* Que no se puede explorar.

inexpressible [ˌɪnɪksˈpresəbl] [in-iks-pre-si-bol], *a.* Indecible, lo que no se puede expresar. **-Inexpressibles,** *s. pl. (Fest.)* Los pantalones.

inexpressibly [ˌɪnɪksˈpresəblɪ] [in-iks-pre-si-bli], *adv.* Indeciblemente.

inexpressive [ˌɪnɪksˈpresɪv] [in-iks-pre-siv], *a.* 1. Falto de expresión en el hablar o en la fisonomía. 2. *(Poét.)* Indecible.

inextensible [ˌɪnɪksˈtensəbl] [in-iks-ten-si-bol], *a.* Incapaz de ser extendido; invariable en longitud o superficie.

inextinct [ˌɪnɪksˈtɪŋkt] [in-iks-tinkt], *a.* Que no está extinto o apagado.

inextinguishable [ˌɪnɪksˈtɪŋgwɪsəbl] [in-iks-tin-güi-sa-bol], *a.* Inextinguible, lo que no se puede extinguir; implacable, que no se puede apaciguar.

inextricable [ˌɪnɪksˈtrɪkəbl] [in-iks-tri-ka-bol], *a.* Intrincado, confuso, enmarañado.

inextricableness [ˌɪnɪksˈtrɪkəblnɪs] [in-iks-tri-ka-bol-nes], *s.* El estado de lo que es intrincado o confuso.

inextricably [ˌɪnɪksˈtrɪkəblɪ] [in-iks-tri-ka-bli], *adv.* Intrincadamente, enmarañadamente.

infallibility [ɪnˌfæləˈbɪlɪtɪ] [in-fa-bi-li-ti], **infallibleness** [ɪnˈfæləblɪs] [in-fa-li-bol-nes], *s.* Infabilidad, suma certeza, incapacidad de engañar o engañarse.

infallible [ɪnˈfæləbl] [in-fa-li-bol], *a.* 1. Infalible. 2. Infalible, seguro, cierto, indefectible.

infallibly [ɪnˈfæləblɪ] [in-fa-li-bli], *adv.* Infaliblemente, seguramente.

infamous [ˈɪnfəməs] [in-fei-mos], *a.* 1. Infame, ignominioso, desacreditado, vil, mal reputado; vergonzoso. 2. Infamante, infamatorio, que infama o que merece la infamia; odioso, aborrecible, notoriamente injusto o malvado.

infamously [ˈɪnfəməslɪ] [in-fei-mos-li], *adv.* Infamemente, ignominiosamente.

infamousness [ˈɪnfəməsnɪs] [in-fei-mos-nes], **infamy** [ˈɪnfəmɪ] [in-fa-mi], *s.* Infamia, descrédito, deshonra, oprobio, baldón.

infancy [ˈɪnfənsɪ] [in-fan-si], *s.* 1. Infancia, la edad del hombre hasta que tiene uso de razón. 2. Infancia, los primeros años. 3. Infancia, el principio u origen de alguna cosa. 4. *(Der.)* Menor edad, minoridad, período de la vida antes de la mayor edad (esto es, antes de la capacidad legal).

infant [ˈɪnfənt] [in-fant], *s.* 1. Infante, niño o niña de tierna edad; criatura. 2. Menor, la persona que aún no ha llegado a la edad que determinan las leyes en los diferentes países para gobernar su hacienda y disponer libremente de su persona. *-a.* 1. V. INFANTILE. 2. De menor edad. 3. *(Fig.)* Joven, naciente, que no ha llegado a la madurez. **Infant industries,** industrias nacientes.

infanticidal [ˌɪnfəntɪˈsaɪdə] [in-fan-ti-sai-dal], *a.* Que se refiere al infanticidio.

infanticide [ɪnˈfæntɪsaɪd] [in-fan-ti-said], *s.* 1. Infanticidio, homicidio de un niño o criatura. 2. Infanticida, la persona que comete este homicidio.

infantile [ˈɪnfəntaɪl] [in-fan-tail], *a.* Infantil, pueril. **Infantile paralysis,** parálisis infantil, poliomielitis.

infantine [ˈɪnfəntaɪn] [in-fan-tain], *a.* Infantil, propio de niño.

infant-like [ˈɪnfəntˌlaɪk] [in-fant-laik], *a.* Semejante a un niño.

infantry [ˈɪnfəntrɪ] [in-fan-tri], *s.* Infantería, peones, infantes.

infarct [ˈɪnfɑːkt] [in-farkt], *s.* Infarto, lo que forma una hinchazón u obstrucción en un órgano.

infarction [ɪnˈfɑːkʃən] [in-fark-shon], *s. (Med.)* Obstrucción por repleción; infartamiento, infartación.

infatuate [ɪnˈfætjʊeɪt] [in-fa-tiueit], *va.* Infatuar, embobar, privar del uso de razón, preocupar.

infatuate, infatuated [ɪnˈfætjʊeɪtd] [in-fa-tiueitd], *a.* Infatuado.

infatuating [ɪnˈfætjʊeɪtɪŋ] [in-fa-tiuei-tin], *a.* Que infatúa o entontece.

infatuation [ɪnˌfætjʊˈeɪʃən] [in-fa-tiuei-shon], *s.* Infatuación, preocupación ciega, encaprichamiento.

infeasible [ɪnˈfezɪbl] [in-fe-si-bol], *a.* Impracticable.

infect [ɪnˈfekt] [in-fekt], *va.* 1. Infectar, apestar, inficionar, corromper. 2. *(For.)* Tachar de ilegalidad.

infection [ɪnˈfekʃən] [in-fek-shon], *s.* 1. Infección, la acción de infectar; comunicación de una enfermedad por medio del contacto, del aire, del agua o de las ropas. 2. Lo que inficiona, materia morbífica e infecta, como los miasmas. 3. *(For.)* Acción de tachar de ilegalidad.

infectious [ɪnˈfekʃəs] [in-fek-shos], *a.* 1. Infecto, inficionado; corruptor. 2. *(Med.)* Pestilente, comunicable por vía de infección o indirectamente; distinto de contagioso. 3. *(For.)* Tachado de ilegalidad.

infectiously [ɪnˈfekʃəslɪ] [in-fek-shos-li], *adv.* Por infección.

infectiousness [ɪnˈfekʃəsnɪs] [in-fek-shos-nes], *s.* Calidad o propiedad de infectar.

infective [ɪnˈfektɪv] [in-fek-tiv], *a.* Infectivo, pestilente.

infecund [ɪnˈfekənd] [in-fe-kun], *a.* Infecundo, estéril.

infecundity [ˌɪnfeˈkəndɪtɪ] [in-fe-kun-di-ti], *s.* Infecundidad, esterilidad.

infelicitous [ˌɪnfɪˈlɪsɪtəs] [in-fi-li-si-tos], *a.* 1. Inepto, poco apropiado, poco conveniente. 2. Infeliz, desdichado, desgraciado.

infelicity [ˌɪnfɪˈlɪsɪtɪ] [in-fi-li-si-ti], *s.* 1. Infelicidad, desgracia, desdicha, infortunio. 2. Ineptitud, falta de idoneidad, de conveniencia. 3. Palabra o expresión fuera de propósito, poco conveniente.

infer [ɪnˈfɜːʳ] [in-feʳ], *va.* 1. Inferir, deducir, concluir. 2. Mostrar, implicar. *-vn.* Sacar una consecuencia.

inferable [ɪnˈferəbl] [in-fe-ra-bol], *a.* Deducible. V. INFERRIBLE.

inference [ˈɪnfərəns] [in-fe-rens], *s.* Inferencia, ilación, consecuencia, inducción.

inferential [ˌɪnfəˈrenʃəl] [in-fe-ren-shal], *a.* Ilativo: de la naturaleza de una inferencia.

inferior [ɪnˈfɪərɪəʳ] [in-fi-riaʳ], *a.* 1. Inferior, lo que es menos que otra cosa en cantidad o calidad. 2. Inferior, debajo de otra cosa o más bajo que ella. 3. *(Mús.)* De tono más bajo. 4. Inferior, el que está sujeto a otro o el que es menos que otra persona en saber, valer, poder, puesto o mando; subordinado, subalterno. 5. *(Impr.)* Inferior, que está debajo del nivel de la línea. *-s.* Inferior, el que está subordinado a un superior.

inferiority [ɪnˌfɪərɪˈɒrɪtɪ] [in-fi-rio-ri-ti], *s.* Inferioridad. **Inferiority complex,** complejo de inferioridad.

infernal [ɪnˈfɜːnl] [in-fer-nal], *a.* Infernal, cosa del infierno o perteneciente a él.

infernalness [ɪnˈfɜːnlnɪs] [in-fer-nal-nes], *s.* El estado de lo que es infernal.

inferrible [ɪnˈfɜːrɪbl] [in-fe-ri-bol], *a.* Que se puede deducir o inferir.

infertile [ɪnˈfɜːtaɪl] [in-fer-tail], *a.* Infecundo, infértil, estéril.

infertility [ˌɪnfɜːˈtɪlɪtɪ] [in-fer-ti-li-ti], *s.* Infecundidad, infertilidad, esterilidad.

infest [ɪn'fest] [in-fest], *va.* 1. Infestar, incomodar, trabajar; inficionar, apestar. 2. Infestar, causar el enemigo daños y estragos con hostilidades y correrías.

infestation [ˌɪnfes'teɪʃən] [in-fes-tei-shon], *s.* Infestación; molestia, disturbio.

infested [ɪn'festɪd] [in-fes-ted], *a.* Infestado; molestado, acosado.

infestive [ɪn'festɪv] [in-fes-tiv], *a.* Triste, melancólico.

infeudation [ˌɪnfjʊ'deɪʃən] [in-fiu-dei-shon], *s.* Enfeudación, el acto de enfeudar.

infidel ['ɪnfɪdəl], *s.* Infiel, gentil, pagano. -*a.* Infiel; desleal, fementido, pérfido.

infidelity [ˌɪnfɪ'delɪtɪ] [in-fi-de-li-ti], *s.* 1. Infidelidad, falta de fe, escepticismo respecto de la religión generalmente reconocida; falta de buena fe, infidelidad conyugal. 2. Deslealtad, alevosía, perfidia.

infiltrate ['ɪnfɪltreɪt] [in-fil-treit], *va.* Infiltrar, hacer que un líquido o gas penetre por los poros o intersticios. -*vn.* Infiltrarse, recalar, entrar penetrando por los poros.

infiltration [ˌɪnfɪl'treɪʃən] [in-fil-trei-shon], *s.* 1. Infiltración, el acto de infiltrar. 2. Lo que está infiltrado; *(Med.)* infarto blando.

infinite ['ɪnfɪnɪt] [in-fi-nit], *a.* 1. Infinito, lo que no tiene fin ni término; ilimitado (limitless). 2. Infinito, innumerable; muy grande. 3. Que lo contiene todo; cabal y perfecto; que comprende todas las perfecciones (perfect).

infinitely ['ɪnfɪnɪtlɪ] [in-fi-nit-li], *adv.* Infinitamente, ilimitadamente.

infiniteness ['ɪnfɪnɪtnɪs] [in-fi-nit-nes], *s.* Infinidad, cualidad de lo infinito.

infinitesimal [ˌɪnfɪnɪ'tesɪməl] [in-fi-ni-te-si-mal], *a. (Mat.)* Infinitesimal: se dice del cálculo o cantidad. -*s.* Infinitésima, parte infinitamente pequeña de cualquier cantidad.

infinitive [ɪn'fɪnɪtɪv] [in-fi-ni-tiv], *a.* Infinitivo. -*s.* Modo infinitivo.

infinitude [ɪn'fɪnɪtjuːd] [in-fi-ni-tiud], *s.* Infinidad; muchedumbre innumerable o infinita.

infinity [ɪn'fɪnɪtɪ] [in-fi-ni-ti], *s.* 1. Infinidad, extensión ilimitada; espacio sin límites, inmensidad. 2. Estado o cualidad de lo infinito; perfección.

infirm [ɪn'fɜːm] [in-ferm], *a.* 1. Enfermizo, inválido, doliente, achacoso. *(Fam.)* Enclenque. 2. Enfermo, frágil, débil. 3. Instable, poco firme y seguro; irresoluto. 4. *(For.)* Anulable; que se puede invalidar.

infirmary [ɪn'fɜːmərɪ] [in-fer-ma-ri], *s.* Enfermería (medical room); hospital.

infirmity [ɪn'fɜːmɪtɪ] [in-fer-mi-ti], *s.* 1. Flaqueza, fragilidad (weakness), falta cometida por la debilidad natural del sexo, de la edad, del genio, etc. 2. Falta, desliz, traspié. 3. Enfermedad, dolencia, achaque, mal, indisposición, padecimiento (pain, illness).

infirmness [ɪn'fɜːmnɪs] [in-ferm-nes], *s.* Debilidad, extenuación, flaqueza.

infix ['ɪnfɪks] [in-fiks], *va.* 1. Clavar, introducir alguna cosa puntiaguda en otra. 2. Imprimir, inculcar, grabar en el alma alguna cosa. -*s. (Gram.)* Partícula que va interpuesta en una palabra para modificar su significación. **Cf.** PREFIX y SUFFIX.

inflame [ɪn'fleɪm] [in-fleim], *va.* 1. Inflamar, encender, hacer arder (liter). 2. Inflamar, encender, enardecer (passion), acalorar, azuzar, provocar, irritar. 3. Exagerar, agravar. -*vn.* *(Med.)* Inflamarse, hincharse.

inflamed [ɪn'fleɪmd] [in-fleimd], *a.* Encendido, irritado, acalorado, enardecido.

inflamer [ɪn'fleɪmər] [in-flei-mar], *s.* Inflamador, enardecedor, el que inflama, lo que enciende o enardece.

inflaming [ɪn'fleɪmɪŋ] [in-flei-min], *s.* Inflamación, enardecimiento.

inflammability [ˌɪnflæmə'bɪlɪtɪ] [in-fla-ma-bi-li-ti], *s.* Inflamabilidad, calidad o propiedad de lo que es inflamable; aptitud o disposición a inflamarse.

inflammable [ɪn'flæməbl] [in-fla-ma-bol], *a.* Inflamable (thing, situation). **Inflammable air**, *(Des.)* aire inflamable o gas hidrógeno.

inflammableness [ˌɪnflæ'məblnɪs] [in-fla-ma-bol-nes], *s.* Inflamación, enardecimiento; la calidad de lo que es inflamable.

inflammation [ˌɪnflæ'meɪʃən] [in-fla-mei-shon], *s.* 1. Inflamación, encendimiento. 2. Inflamación, enardecimiento de las pasiones y de los afectos del ánimo. 3. *(Med.)* Inflamación, estado mórbido de alguna parte del cuerpo, que produce en ella rubicundez, tumefacción, calor y dolor.

inflammative [ɪn'flæmətɪv] [in-fla-ma-tiv], *a.* Inflamatorio, que produce o es propio para producir inflamación, tumulto, o sedición; incendiario. 2. Inflamatorio, que se relaciona con una inflamación.

inflammatory [ɪn'flæmətərɪ] [in-fla-ma-to-ri], *a.* Inflamatorio, incendiario.

inflatable [ɪn'fleɪtəbl] [in-flei-ter-bol], *a.* Hinchable, que se puede inflar.

inflate [ɪn'fleɪt] [in-fleit], *va.* 1. Inflar, hinchar (gas), entumecer. 2. Hinchar, engreír, envanecer. 3. Soplar (blow).

inflated [ɪn'fleɪtɪd] [in-flei-tid], *a.* Hinchado, inflado, entumecido, engreído, excesivo (price).

inflation [ɪn'fleɪʃən] [in-flei-shon], *s.* 1. Inflación, hinchazón (bump), entumecimiento. 2. Hinchazón, engreimiento, envanecimiento.

inflect [ɪn'flekt] [in-flekt], *va.* 1. Torcer, doblar (twist), encorvar, mudar, variar, modular (voice). 2. *(Gram.)* Declinar, conjugar.

inflection [ɪn'flekʃən] [in-flek-shon], *s.* 1. Inflexión, dobladura. 2. Inflexión, modulación de la voz. 3. *(Gram.)* Inflexión, la variación de las terminaciones en los nombres o verbos.

inflectional [ɪn'flekʃənl] [in-flek-sho-nal], *a.* Con inflexión.

inflective [ɪn'flektɪv] [in-flek-tiv], *a.* Lo que tiene virtud para doblar o torcer.

inflex [ɪn'fleks] [in-fleks], *va.* Encorvar, torcer, doblar.

inflexibility [ɪnˌfleksɪ'bɪlɪtɪ] [in-flek-si-bi-li-ti], **inflexibleness** [ɪnˌflek'sɪblnɪs] [in-flek-si-bol-nes], *s.* Inflexibilidad, dureza, pertinacia, obstinación.

inflexible [ɪn'fleksəbl] [in-flek-sa-bol], *a.* 1. Inexorable. 2. Inflexible. 3. Inalterable.

inflexibly [ɪn'fleksɪblɪ] [in-flek-si-bli], *adv.* Inflexiblemente; inexorablemente.

inflexion, *s. V.* INFLECTION.

inflict [ɪn'flɪkt] [in-flikt], *va.* 1. Castigar, infligir, imponer penas corporales (penalty). 2. Cubrir de. **To inflict disgrace**, cubrir de oprobio, de vergüenza.

inflicter [ɪn'flɪktər] [in-flik-tar], *s.* Castigador.

infliction [ɪn'flɪkʃən] [in-flik-shon], *s.* Imposición o castigo de una pena corporal (tax, penalty); inflicción.

inflictive [ɪn'flɪktɪv] [in-flik-tiv], *a.* Inflictiva, la pena que se impone al delincuente, o la que se ha de imponer.

inflorescence [ɪn'flɔːresns] [in-flo-re-sens], *s.* 1. *(Bot.)* Inflorescencia, disposición general de las flores en los vegetales. 2. Florescencia, acción de florecer; conjunto de las flores del mismo género.

inflow ['ɪnfləʊ] [in-flau], *s.* Afluencia.

influence ['ɪnflʊəns] [in-fluens], *s.* Influencia; influjo, valimiento. **To be under the influence of drugs**, estar bajo los efectos de las drogas, estar drogado. **To bring influence on somebody**, ejercer presión sobre alguien. **To have influence to get a job**, tener enchufe para conseguir un puesto de trabajo.

influence, *va.* Influir: (a) causar ciertos efectos unos cuerpos en otros. (b) Intervenir, tener parte en algún negocio. (c) Comunicar Dios algún efecto o don de su gracia. (d) Tener ascendiente o autoridad moral sobre alguien. (e) Modificar, cambiar la manera de ser.

influencing ['ɪnflʊənsɪŋ] [in-fluen-sin], *s.* Influencia, influjo.

influent ['ɪnflʊənt] [in-fluent], *a.* Que fluye hacia dentro.

influential [ˌɪnflʊ'enʃəl] [in-fluen-shal], *a.* Que influye, que tiene influencia, influyente.

influentially [ˌɪnfluˈenʃəlɪ] [in-fluen-sha-li], *adv*. Por medio de influencia o influjo.

influenza [ˌɪnfluˈenzə] [in-fluen-sa], *s*. Catarro, gripe, fluxión epidémica, acompañada de fiebre.

influx [ˈɪnflʌks] [in-flaks], *s*. 1. Influjo, el acto de influir en alguna cosa. 2. Afluencia, entrada (of people, goods, etc.) 3. Instilación, intromisión. 4. Desembocadura, paraje por donde desemboca un río, canal, etc.

influxion [ˈɪnflʌkʃən] [in-flak-shon], *s*. Infusión de alguna gracia o don divino.

infold [ˈɪnfold] [in-fold], *va*. 1. Envolver, arrollar. 2. Abrazar, apretar, estrechar entre los brazos (embrace).

inform [ɪnˈfɔːm] [in-form], *va*. 1. Informar, dar noticias a alguno; instruir, enseñar (teach, announce, tell). 2. Delatar, acusar ante el juez (accuse). 3. Dar forma a, animar, infundir vida o fuerza (encourage, liven up). -*vn*. Informar, dar parte. **To inform against one,** delatar a uno. **Well informed,** instruido, erudito. **To keep somebody informed about something,** tener a alguien al corriente de algo. **To be informed,** estar al corriente, estar avisado. **I'm reliably informed that,** me informan de buena fuente que, sé de buena tinta que.

informal [ɪnˈfɔːməl] [in-for-mal], *a*. 1. Informal, irregular, que no está conforme a lo establecido (person). 2. Informal, que carece de formas oficiales, sin ceremonia (occasion). 3. Íntimo, de confianza.

informality [ˌɪnfɔːˈmælɪtɪ] [in-for-ma-li-ti], *s*. 1. Informalidad, irregularidad, familiaridad, falta de la forma establecida, regular o legal. 2. Hecho o acción informal.

informally [ɪnˈfɔːməlɪ] [in-for-ma-li], *adv*. Irregularmente, sin ceremonia, de manera informal. **The king spoke informally to the journalists,** el rey habló en tono de confianza con los periodistas.

informant [ɪnˈfɔːmənt] [in-for-mant], *s*. Informante, denunciador, persona que informa o hace saber **Who was your informant?,** ¿quién te lo dijo? Se diferencia del **informer** o delator.

informatics [ˌɪnfɔːˈmætɪks] [in-for-ma-tiks], *sf*. Informática.

information [ˌɪnfəˈmeɪʃən] [in-for-mei-shon], *s*. 1. Informe, información, instrucción, aviso, noticia (news, notice); saber, conocimientos sacados del estudio, de la observación (knowing), etc. 2. Acusación, delación, denunciación (accusation). 3. Información, el acto de informar. **To gather information,** informarse, tomar informes. **A piece of information,** un dato, una noticia. **To lay information against,** delatar, acusar. **The information superhigh-way,** la autopista de la información. **For your information,** a título informativo, para su información. *(Amer.)* Servicio de información telefónica. **Information bureau,** oficina o centro de información.

informative [ɪnˈfɔːmətɪv] [in-for-ma-tiv], *a*. Informativo, didáctico.

informed [ɪnˈfɔːmd] [in-formd], *a*. 1. Instruído, informado, inteligente (clever). 2. Informe.

informer [ɪnˈfɔːməʳ] [in-for-maʳ], *s*. 1. Delator, denunciador (betrayer); espía, soplón (spy). 2. Informador, el que informa. *V.* INFORMANT. 3. El que forma, amolda o anima. **To turn informer,** hacerse delator.

infossous [ɪnˈfɒsəs] [in-fo-sos], *a*. *(Bot.)* Deprimido de manera que forma canal, v. gr. las venas en ciertas hojas.

infra-. Prefijo que significa bajo, debajo de; en la parte inferior.

infract [ɪnˈfrækt] [in-frakt], *va*. Romper, quebrantar.

infracted [ɪnˈfræktɪd] [in-frak-tid], *s*. Roto, quebrado, quebrantado.

infraction [ɪnˈfrækʃən] [in-frak-shon], *s*. 1. Quebrantamiento, rompimiento (infringement). 2. Infracción, quebrantamiento, transgresión, contravención de una ley, bando o edicto; violación de un tratado.

infractor [ɪnˈfræktəʳ] [in-frak-taʳ], *s*. Infractor, transgresor, contraventor.

infralapsarian [ˌɪnfrælæpˈsærɪən] [in-fra-lap-sa-rian], *a*. y *s*. *(Teol.)* Epíteto dado a ciertos calvinistas que pretenden

que Dios no proporciona a los hombres los medios de salvarse.

inframammary [ɪnˈfræməmərɪ] [in-fra-ma-ma-ri], *a*. Situado debajo de los pechos.

inframaxillary [ˌɪnfrəˈmɑːksɪlərɪ] [in-fra-mak-si-la-ri], *a*. Perteneciente a la quijada inferior. -*s*. Quijada inferior.

infrangible [ɪnˈfrændʒɪbl] [in-fran-chi-bol], *a*. Infrangible, inquebrantable.

infrangibleness [ɪnˈfrændʒɪblnɪs] [in-fran-chi-bol-nes], *s*. El estado de lo que es infrangible.

infraorbital [ˌɪnfrəˈɔːbɪtəl] [in-fra-or-bi-tal], *a*. Situado debajo de la órbita del ojo.

infrared [ɪnˈfrɑːd] [in-frard], *a*. Infrarrojo.

infrastructure [ˈɪnfrəˌstrʌktʃəʳ] [in-fras-trak-chaʳ], *sf*. Infraestructura.

infrequency [ɪnˈfriːkwənsɪ] [in-fri-kuen-si], **infrequence** [ɪnˈfriːkwəns] [in-fri-kuens], *s*. Rareza, raridad.

infrequent [ɪnˈfriːkwənt] [in-fri-kuent], *a*. Raro, infrecuente, poco común, que ocurre o acaece a largos intervalos.

infrequently [ɪnˈfriːkwəntlɪ] [in-fri-kuent-li], *adv*. Infrecuentemente, rara vez.

infringe [ɪnˈfrɪndʒ] [in-frinch], *va*. 1. Infringir, quebrantar, violar una ley o pacto, contravenir a (break, contravene); entrar sin derecho sobre. 2. Destruir, impedir, embarazar, estorbar, transgredir. -*vn*. Violar derechos y privilegios. **To infringe on a patent-right,** violar una patente, imitar o falsificar un artículo que tiene privilegio de invención.

infringement [ɪnˈfrɪndʒmənt] [in-frinch-ment], *s*. Infracción, violación, transgresión, contravención, quebrantamiento de la ley, de una obligación, de un privilegio o derecho (contravention, violation).

infringer [ɪnˈfrɪndʒəʳ] [in-frin-chaʳ], *s*. Violador, contraventor, quebrantador, infractor de una ley o convenio.

infumed [ɪnˈfjuːmd] [in-fiumd], *a*. Desecado al humo.

infundibular, infundibuliform [ˌɪnfənˈdɪbjʊləʳ] [in-fan-di-biu-laʳ], *a*. Infundibuliforme, en forma de embudo.

infuriate [ɪnˈfjʊərɪeɪt] [in-fiu-rieit], *a*. Enfurecido, furioso, rabioso.

infuriate, *va*. Enfurecer, irritar, enojar; hacer, volver o poner rabioso.

infuriating [ɪnˈfjʊərɪeɪtɪŋ] [in-fiua-riei-tin], *a*. Irritante, enloquecedor, exasperante.

infuscation [ˌɪnfʌsˈkeɪʃən] [in-fas-kei-shon], *s*. Obscurecimiento.

infuse [ɪnˈfjuːz] [in-fius], *va*. 1. Infundir, echar en infusión, poner un simple en algún licor por cierto tiempo para extraer sus virtudes. 2. Infundir, causar algún efecto en el ánimo o mover alguna pasión. 3. Echar un licor en alguna cosa que pueda contenerle. 4. Infundir, inculcar, instilar, como principios o calidades: con **into. To infuse zeal into his pupils,** infundir estímulo en sus discípulos.

infused [ɪnˈfjuːzt] [in-fiust], *a*. Infuso, infundido.

infuser [ɪnˈfjuːzəʳ] [in-fiu-saʳ], *s*. El que infunde o introduce en el ánimo.

infusible [ɪnˈfjuːzɪbl] [in-fiu-si-bol], *a*. 1. Infundible, lo que no se puede fundir, derretir o liquidar; lo que no sufre fusión. 2. Capaz de infusión.

infusion [ɪnˈfjuːʒən] [in-fiu-shon], *s*. 1. Infusión, la acción de infundir. 2. Infusión (Culin.). 3. El acto de embeber o empapar una cosa en un líquido. 4. Infusión, inspiración, gracia infusa en el alma.

infusive [ɪnˈfjuːzɪv] [in-fiu-siv], *a*. Lo que puede ser infundido o lo que es capaz e infundir.

infusoria [ɪnˈfjuːʒərɪə] [in-fiu-so-ria], *s*. Infusorios.

infusorial [ɪnˈfjuːʒərəl] [in-fiu-so-rial]], *a*. Infusorio, que contiene infusorio, o perteneciente a ellos. **Infusorial earth,** sustancia terrosa muy fina que consiste principalmente en esqueletos silíceos de diátomos.

infusorian [ɪnˈfjuːʒərɪən] [in-fiu-so-rian], *a*. *V.* INFUSORIAL. -*s*. Uno de los infusorios. Lo mismo (adjetivo y nombre) significa INFUSORY.

ingate [ɪnˈɡeɪt] [in-gueit], s. 1. En la fundición, bebedero, agujero por donde entra el metal derretido. 2. Entrada que comunica el pozo de la mina con una galería lateral.

ingathering [ɪnˈɡæθərɪŋ] [in-ga-ze-rin], s. Cosecha; el acto de recoger los productos de la tierra.

ingelable [ɪnˈdʒələbl] [in-ye-la-bol], a. Lo que no puede ser congelado.

ingeminate [ɪnˈdʒəmɪneɪt] [in-ye-mi-neit], a. Reduplicado, duplicado, repetido.

ingeminate, va. Reduplicar, duplicar, repetir.

ingemination [ˌɪndʒəmɪˈneɪʃən] [in-ye-mi-nei-shon], s. Reduplicación.

ingenerable [ɪnˈdʒenərəbl] [in-ye-ne-ra-bol], a. Ingenerable, que puede ser producido dentro, en el interior.

ingenerate [ɪnˈdʒenəreɪt] [in-ye-ne-reit], va. Procrear, producir, engendrar.

ingenerate, a. Innato; ingénito.

ingenious [ɪnˈdʒiːniəs] [in-yi-nios], a. 1. Ingenioso, hábil, sutil, que tiene facultad inventiva (resourceful, witty); apto para discurrir o inventar. 2. Apto; bien formado, bien concebido o proyectado; mañoso (capable).

ingeniously [ɪnˈdʒiːniəslɪ] [in-yi-nios-li], adv. Ingeniosamente.

ingeniousness [ɪnˈdʒiːniəsnɪs] [in-yi-nios-nes], s. Ingeniosidad, sutileza, industria, destreza.

ingenuity [ɪnˈdʒenɔɪtɪ] [in-ye-niu-ti], s. 1. Ingeniosidad, facultad inventiva (cleverness, wittiness). 2. Maña, habilidad, destreza para construir, idear o hacer algo (hability).

ingenuous [ɪnˈdʒenɔəs] [in-ye-nuos], a. Ingenuo, real, sincero, sin doblez, franco (candid, simple).

ingenuously [ɪnˈdʒenɔəslɪ] [in-ye-nuos-li], adv. Ingenuamente.

ingenuousness [ɪnˈdʒenɔəsnɪs] [in-ye-nuos-nes], s. Ingenuidad, sinceridad.

ingest [ɪnˈdʒest] [in-yest], va. Introducir o ingerir en el estómago alguna cosa.

ingesta [ɪnˈdʒestə] [in-yes-ta], s. pl. Alimentos tomados o tragados; (Fig.) cosas incorporadas.

ingestion [ɪnˈdʒestʃən] [in-yes-shon], s. Ingestión, introducción de una cosa en el estómago.

ingle [ɪŋl] [in-guel], s. (Esco.) Fuego, llama. **Ingleside,** hogar. **Inglenook,** rincón de la chimenea.

inglorious [ɪnˈɡlɔːriəs] [in-glo-rios], a. 1. Vil, afrentoso, ignominioso, bajo, deshonroso, vergonzoso (shameful). 2. Insensible al honor, a la ambición o a la gloria.

ingloriously [ɪnˈɡlɔːriəslɪ] [in-glo-rios-li], adv. Ignominiosamente.

ingloriousness [ɪnˈɡlɔːriəs] [in-glo-rios], s. 1. Ignominia, vileza, deshonra. 2. Insensibilidad o falta de ansia por adquirir fama, reputación o gloria.

ingluvies [ɪnˈɡluːvɪz] [in-glu-vis], s. El buche de las aves granívoras.

ingoing [ˈɪnɡəʊɪŋ] [in-gouin], a. Entrante, que entra. -s. Entrada.

ingot [ˈɪŋɡət] [in-got], s. 1. Riel, barra de oro, plata u otro metal en bruto; lingote. **Ingot of gold,** tejo de oro. **Ingot or copper,** galápago de cobre. 2. Cualquier barra o pedazo de metal sin labrar, y a veces se ha llamado así el molde donde se labra el metal.

ingraft [ɪnˈɡræft] [in-graft], va. 1. Injertar o enjertar. V. GRAFT. 2. Imprimir, grabar, inspirar o fijar profundamente en el ánimo ideas, sentimiento, máximas, etc.

ingrafting [ɪnˈɡræftɪŋ] [in-graf-tin], s. Injertación, enjertación, el acto de injertar o enjertar.

ingraftment [ɪnˈɡræftmənt] [in-graft-ment], s. Injerto o enjerto.

ingrain [ɪnˈɡreɪn] [in-grein], a. Teñido en rama; fijado, impreso o grabado profundamente en el alma. -s. Alfombra teñida en rama.

ingrain, va. 1. Teñir en rama; particularmente, teñir con grana o cochinilla. 2. Fijar o impregnar profundamente.

ingrate [ɪnˈɡreɪt] [in-greit], a. Ingrato, desagradecido; desapacible (ungrateful). -s. Una persona ingrata.

ingratiate [ɪnˈɡreɪʃɪeɪt] [in-grei-shiiet], vn. Insinuarse, captar, ganar la voluntad de alguno; congraciarse, solicitar la benevolencia de una persona o granjearse su favor. **To ingratiate oneself,** congraciarse.

ingratiating [ɪnˈɡreɪʃɪeɪtɪŋ] [in-grei-shiei-tin], s. El acto de granjearse el favor o la benevolencia de una persona. -a. Insinuante.

ingratitude [ɪnˈɡrætɪtjuːd] [in-gra-ti-tiud], s. Ingratitud, desagradecimiento.

ingredient [ɪnˈɡriːdɪənt] [in-gri-dient], s. Ingrediente, lo que entra en la composición de alguna cosa.

ingress [ɪnˈɡres] [in-gres], s. 1. Ingreso, entrada. 2. Acceso, facultad de entrar; también el lugar de entrada (access).

ingression [ɪnˈɡreʃən] [in-gre-shon], s. Ingreso, entrada.

ingrown [ɪnˈɡrəʊn] [in-graun], a. Que crece hacia adentro. **Ingrown toenail,** uñero.

inguinal [ˈɪŋɡwɪnl] [in-güi-nal], a. Inguinal, lo que pertenece a las ingles.

ingulf [ɪnˈɡʌlf] [in-galf], va. 1. Embocar, sumir, precipitar, hacer entrar violentamente una cosa en un boquete estrecho o sumidero. 2. Engolfar, hacer que alguno se arrebate con un pensamiento o afecto.

ingurgitate [ɪnˈɡɜːdʒɪteɪt] [in-guer-yi-teit], va. (Ant.) Tragar, beber, engullir, -vn. Beber o tragar copiosamente; hartarse.

ingurgitation [ˌɪnɡɜːdʒɪˈteɪʃən] [in-guer-yi-tei-shon], s. Voracidad, glotonería.

inhabit [ɪnˈhæbɪt] [in-ja-bit], va. Habitar, ocupar alguna habitación. -vn. (Ant.) Habitar, vivir, residir en algún paraje (region).

inhabitability [ˌɪnhæbɪtəˈbɪlɪtɪ] [in-ja-bi-ter-bi-li-ti], s. Habitabilidad, calidad de habitable.

inhabitable [ɪnˈhæbɪtəbl] [in-ja-bi-ter-bol], a. 1. Habitable.

inhabitance [ɪnˈhæbɪtəns] [in-ja-bi-tans], s. Habitación, morada permanente, residencia en un lugar.

inhabitant [ɪnˈhæbɪtənt] [in-ja-bi-tant], s. Habitador, habitante, vecino, morador.

inhabitation [ˌɪnhæbɪˈteɪʃən] [in-ja-bi-tei-shon], s. Habitación, domicilio, morada.

inhabited [ɪnˈhæbɪtɪd] [in-ja-bi-tid], a. Poblado, habitado.

inhabiter [ɪnˈhæbɪtəʳ] [in-ja-bi-taʳ], s. Habitador, habitante, morador, vecino.

inhabitress [ɪnˈhæbɪtrɪs] [in-ja-bi-tres], sf. Habitadora.

inhalant [ɪnˈheɪlənt] [in-jei-lant], a. Inhalante.

inhalation [ˌɪnhəˈleɪʃən] [in-ja-lei-shon], s. 1. Inspiración, el acto de inspirar. 2. (Med.) Inhalación, vapor medicamentoso para aspiraciones.

inhale [ɪnˈheɪl] [in-jeil], va. Inspirar, aspirar, introducir en el pulmón dilatando el pecho, como se hace con el aire exterior.

inhaler [ɪnˈheɪləʳ] [in-jei-laʳ], a. Inhalador.

inharmonic, inharmonical [ɪnhɑːˈməʊnɪk] [in-jar-mo-nik], a. Dísono o disonante, inarmónico.

inharmonious [ˌɪnhɑːˈməʊnɪəs] [in-jar-mou-nios], a. 1. Poco armonioso, falto de armonía; discordante. 2. Falto de concordancia, recíprocamente opuesto.

inhaul [ɪnˈhɔːl] [in-jol], s. (Mar.) Cabo o jarcia que sirve para halar el botalón de foque.

inhere [ɪnˈhɪəʳ] [in-jiaʳ], vn. Inherir, adherir, ser inherente, tener unión íntima con otra cosa.

inherence [ɪnˈhɪərəns] [in-jia-rans], **inherency** [ɪnˈhɪərənsɪ] [in-jia-ran-si], s. 1. Inherencia. 2. Cualidad de estar relacionado con otra cosa como elemento, atributo, propiedad o condición.

inherent [ɪnˈhɪərənt] [in-jia-rant], a. Inherente; innato, intrínseco.

inherently [ɪnˈhɪərəntlɪ] [in-ji-rant-li], adv. Inherentemente.

inherit [ɪn'herɪt] [in-je-rit], va. 1. Heredar, tener uno las cualidades físicas o mentales de sus antepasados. 2. Heredar, adquirir una herencia por disposición testamentaria o legal (to be heir to). -vn. Suceder como heredero o por derecho de sucesión.

inheritable [ɪn'herɪtəbl] [in-je-ri-ter-bol], a. Heredable, herditable.

inheritance [ɪn'herɪtəns] [in-je-ri-tans], s. 1. Herencia, patrimonio. 2. Herencia, la posesión de los bienes heredados. **Inheritance tax,** impuesto sobre la herencia.

inheritor [ɪn'herɪtəʳ] [in-je-ri-taʳ], s. Heredero.

inheritress [ɪn'herɪtrɪs] [in-je-ri-tres], **inheritrix** [ɪn'herɪtrɪks] [in-je-ri-triks], sf. Heredera.

inhibit [ɪn'hɪbɪt] [in-ji-bit], va. 1. Inhibir, contener, detener, impedir (impede, restrain). 2. Prohibir, vedar (prohibit). 3. Prohibir a un sacerdote que ejerza sus funciones espirituales.

inhibited [ɪn'hɪbɪtɪd] [in-ji-bi-tid], a. Cohibido, impedido, vedado.

inhibition [ˌɪnhɪ'bɪʃən] [in-ji-bi-shon], s. 1. Inhibición, prohibición, impedimento. 2. (For.) Inhibición, prohibición a un juez del conocimiento de alguna causa.

inhibitory [ɪn'hɪbɪtərɪ] [in-ji-bi-to-ri], **inhibitive** [ɪn'hɪbɪtɪv] [in-ji-bi-biv], a. Inhibitorio, que prohibe, restringe, o impide.

inhive [ɪn'hiːv] [in-jiv], va. Enjambrar, reunir las abejas que andan esparcidas y meterlas en colmenas.

inhospitable [ˌɪnhɒs'pɪtəbl] [in-jos-pi-ter-bol], a. Inhospitalario, inhospitable.

inhospitableness [ˌɪnhɒs'pɪtəblnɪs] [in-jos-pi-ter-bol-nes], **inhospitality** [ˌɪnhɒs'pɪtælɪtɪ] [in-jos-pi-ter-li-ti], s. Inhospitalidad, falta de hospitalidad, falta de hospitalidad o de caridad.

inhospitably [ˌɪnhɒs'pɪtəblɪ] [in-jos-pi-ter-bli], adv. Sin hospitalidad.

inhuman [ɪn'hjuːmən] [in-jiu-man], a. Inhumano, cruel, riguroso, despiadado (cruel, merciless).

inhumanity [ˌɪnhjuː'mænɪtɪ] [in-jiu-ma-ni-ti], s. Inhumanidad, suma crueldad, barbarie (cruelty, mercilessness).

inhumanly [ɪn'hjuːmənlɪ] [in-jiu-man-li], adv. Inhumanamente.

inhumation [ˌɪnhjuː'meɪʃən] [in-jiu-mei-shon], s. Entierro, sepultura.

inhume [ɪn'hjuːm] [in-jium], **inhumate** [ɪn'hjuːmeɪt] [in-jiu-meit], va. 1. Inhumar, enterrar, sepultar. 2. (Quím.) Exponer a un calor constante enterrando el recipiente en tierra o estiércol caliente.

inimaginable [ˌɪnɪ'mædʒɪnəbl] [in-i-ma-yi-na-bol], a. Inimaginable. V. UNIMAGINABLE.

inimical [ɪ'nɪmɪkəl] [i-ni-mi-kal], a. Enemigo, contrario, opuesto, dañoso, perjudicial (enemy, damaging). **Inimical to,** opuesto a, contrario a.

inimically [ɪ'nɪmɪkəlɪ] [i-ni-mi-ka-li], adv. Enemigamente, con enemistad, hostilmente; dañosamente.

inimitability [ˌɪnɪmɪtə'bɪlɪtɪ] [i-ni-mi-ter-bi-li-ti], s. Imposibilidad o incapacidad de ser imitado.

inimitable [ɪ'nɪmɪtəbl] [i-ni-mi-ter-bol], a. Inimitable.

inimitableness [ɪ'nɪmɪtəblnɪs] [i-ni-mi-ter-bol-nes], s. Calidad o estado de lo que es inimitable.

inimitably [ɪ'nɪmɪtəblɪ] [i-ni-mi-ter-bli], adv. Inimitablemente.

iniquitous [ɪ'nɪkwɪtəs] [i-ni-kui-tos], **iniquous** [ɪ'nɪkwɪtəs] [i-ni-kui-tos], a. Inicuo, malvado, facineroso, injusto (wrong, unjust).

iniquity [ɪ'nɪkwɪtɪ] [i-ni-kui-ti], s. Iniquidad, injusticia, perfidia, maldad, picardía. **Iniquities,** injusticias (of system), excesos (of person).

initial [ɪ'nɪʃəl] [i-ni-shal], a. 1. Inicial, lo que está al principio (start). 2. Incipiente. **Initials,** letras iniciales de un capítulo, verso, etc., particularmente cuando son de adorno. **Initial stage,** primeras etapa. **Initial reaction,** primera reacción.

initialize [ɪ'nɪʃəlaɪz] [i-ni-sha-lais], vt. Inicializar.

initially [ɪ'nɪʃəlɪ] [i-ni-sha-li], adv. De un modo incipiente, en un principio.

initiate [ɪ'nɪʃɪɪt] [i-ni-shieit], va. 1. Iniciar; instruir en los rudimentos o principios; introducir en una sociedad o culto religioso. 2. Tomar la iniciativa, poner en pie, empezar, dar origen (plan, reform). **To initiate someone into a company,** admitir a alguien en una compañía.

initiated [ɪ'nɪʃɪɪtɪd] [i-ni-shiei-tid], a. Iniciado, instruído, admitido a la participación, uso o conocimiento de alguna cosa.

initiating [ɪ'nɪʃɪɪtɪŋ] [i-ni-shiei-tin], a. Iniciativo. -s. 1. El acto de instruir a alguno en los elementos de un arte o ciencia. 2. La introducción de una persona en cualquiera parte.

initiation [ɪˌnɪʃɪ'eɪʃən] [i-ni-shi-ei-shon], sf. 1. Comienzo, iniciación, principio (beginning, start). 2. Estreno, principio, primer uso o el acto de ejercer o poner por obra alguna cosa. 3. Iniciación en los ritos o misterios.

initiative [ɪ'nɪʃɪətɪv] [i-ni-sha-tiv], a. Iniciativo, que sirve para iniciar. -s. 1. Primer paso o acción; acto introductivo (starting). 2. Facultad de poner en pie, de empezar, o de iniciar. 3. Iniciativa, derecho de proponer leyes, etc. **To take the initiative,** tomar la iniciativa.

initiator [ɪ'nɪʃɪeɪtəʳ] [i-ni-shiei-taʳ], sf. Iniciador.

initiatory [ɪ'nɪʃɪətərɪ] [i-ni-shia-to-ri], a. Iniciativo.

inject [ɪn'dʒekt] [in-yekt], va. 1. Inyectar alguna cosa por fuerza, y particularmente por medio de inyección. 2. Introducir sin razón o sin necesidad, injertar (graft). V. TO INTERJECT. 3. (Des.) Echar sobre, aglomerar.

injected [ɪn'dʒektɪd] [in-yek-tid], a. Inyectado, introducido por medio de inyección; también, demasiado cargado de sangre.

injection [ɪn'dʒekʃən] [in-yek-shon], s. 1. Inyección, acción y efecto de inyectar, y el líquido inyectado. 2. (Med.) Inyección, lavativa; ayuda, el acto de introducir algún líquido en el cuerpo por medio de jeringa u otro instrumento. 3. (Mec.) Inyección, acción de echar agua en el condensador de una máquina de vapor.

injection pump [ɪn'dʒekʃənˌpʌmp] [in-yek-shon-pamp], s. Bomba inyectora.

injector [ɪn'dʒektəʳ] [in-yek-taʳ], s. Inyector, el que o lo que inyecta; particularmente aparato de las máquinas de vapor.

injudicable [ɪn'dʒuːdɪkəbl] [in-yu-di-ka-bol], a. Ilegal, que no puede ser objeto del conocimiento de un juez.

injudicial [ˌɪndʒʊ'dɪʃəl] [in-yu-di-shal], a. Informal, informe, ilegal.

injudicious [ˌɪndʒʊ'dɪʃəs] [in-yu-di-shos], a. Indiscreto, sin discreción; poco juicioso, imprudente.

injudiciously [ˌɪndʒʊ'dɪʃəslɪ] [in-yu-di-shos-li], adv. Tontamente, sin juicio.

injudiciousness [ˌɪndʒʊ'dɪʃəsnɪs] [in-yu-di-shos-nes], s. Indiscreción, imprudencia.

injunction [ɪn'dʒʌŋkʃən] [in-yank-shon], s. 1. Mandato, precepto, mandamiento, orden expresa. 2. Auto interlocutorio del tribunal de equidad o Cancillería, en virtud del cual se ordena, y más generalmente se prohibe hacer una cosa determinada.

injure [ɪn'dʒɔʳ] [in-yaʳ], va. 1. Injuriar, agraviar, ofender (offend). 2. Molestar, hacer mala obra, perjudicar (chances, reputation).

injurer [ɪn'dʒɔrəʳ] [in-ya-raʳ], s. Injuriador, el que injuria a otro; ofensor, el que ofende.

injurious [ɪn'dʒʊərɪəs] [in-yu-rios], a. 1. Injurioso, injusto, dañoso, perjudicial (harmful). 2. (Ant.) Contumelioso, detractivo, ofensivo (insulting).

injuriously [ɪn'dʒʊərɪəslɪ] [in-yu-rios-li], adv. Injuriosamente.

injuriousness [ɪn'dʒʊərɪəsnɪs] [in-yu-rios-nes], s. Injuria, calidad de lo injurioso.

injury [ɪn'dʒərɪ] [in-ya-ri], s. 1. Injuria, daño, agravio sin razón, perjuicio, mal, detrimento, molestia (wound, bother, nuisance). 2. Injuria, afrenta, baldón, insulto (offense).

injustice [ɪn'dʒʌstɪs] [in-yas-tis], s. Injusticia, agravio.

ink [ɪŋk] [ink], s. 1. Tinta, líquido negro o de otro color, y en ciertos casos substancia viscosa, que se emplea para escribir, imprimir o dibujar. 2. El líquido opaco secretado por la jibia. **Indeleble ink** o **marking-ink,** tinta indeleble o de marcar.

ink, *va.* Entintar, teñir o tiznar con tinta; dar tinta. **To ink the forms,** dar tinta a los moldes; *(Impr.)* entintar la forma. **To ink one's fingers,** untarse de tinta los dedos. **To ink in,** entintar. **To ink out,** tachar con tinta.

ink blot ['ɪŋkblɒt] [ink-blot], *sm.* Borrón de tinta.

inkbottle ['ɪŋk'bɑtl] [ink-ba-tel], *s.* Botellita de tinta, que sirve de tintero.

inkhorn ['ɪŋkhɔːn] [ink-jorn], *s.* Tintero de bolsillo, hecho originalmente de cuerno. V. INKSTAND. -*a.* Pedantesco, pomposo.

inkiness ['ɪŋkɪnɪs] [in-ki-nis], *s.* Entintamiento; mancha de tinta.

inkle [ɪŋkl] [in-kel], *s.* Cinta angosta.

inkling ['ɪŋklɪŋ] [in-klin], *s.* Insinuación o aviso secreto de alguna cosa.

inkmaker ['ɪŋk'meɪkəʳ] [ink-mei-kaʳ], *s.* El que hace tinta para escribir o imprimir.

inknot ['ɪŋknɒt] [ink-not], *va.* Atar o anudar.

inkstand ['ɪŋkstænd] [ink-stand], *s.* Tintero.

inkwell ['ɪŋkwel] [ink-uel], *s.* Tintero.

inky ['ɪŋkɪ] [in-ki], *a.* Que se compone de tinta; semejante o parecido a la tinta; manchado de tinta (stained).

inlace [ɪn'leɪs] [in-leis], *va.* Adornar con cordones, encordonar o acordonar.

inlaid [ɪn'leɪd] [in-leid], **pret. y pp.** de INLAY.

inland ['ɪnlənd] [in-land], *a.* 1. Interior, lo que está tierra adentro o distante del mar. 2. No extranjero, doméstico; transportado de un punto a otro del mismo país. -*s.* El interior de un país. -*adv.* Tierra adentro.

inlander ['ɪnləndəʳ] [in-lan-daʳ], *s.* El que habita tierra adentro o lejos del mar. *(Amer.)* Tierradentreño.

in-laws ['ɪnˌlɔːz] [in-los], *pl.* Parientes políticos.

inlay ['ɪnleɪ] [in-lei], *va. (pret. y pp.* INLAID). Embutir, meter una cosa dentro de otra; en especial, ataracear, taracear, hacer embutidos de varios colores en madera u otra materia; formar mosaico; incrustar. **Inlaid work,** embutido, taracea, ataracea; incrustación, ataujía. **To inlay something with something,** hacer incrustaciones de algo en algo.

inlay, *s.* 1. Materia con que se ataracea o embute. 2. Ataracea, embutido; dibujo producido por el acto de embutir.

inlayer ['ɪnleɪəʳ] [in-leiaʳ], *s.* El que ataracea o embute; operario en embutidos o taracea.

inlaying ['ɪnleɪɪŋ] [in-lein], *s.* El arte o acto de ataracear o embutir.

inlet ['ɪnlet] [in-let], *s.* 1. *(Geog.)* Entrada, paso para entrar en un paraje cerrado. 2. Cuerpo pequeño de agua que da entrada a otro mayor: (a) abra, cala; (b) arroyo o río que alimenta a un lago. *(Mec.)* **Inlet valve,** válvula de entrada o admisión.

inlock ['ɪnlɒk] [in-lok], *va.* Cerrar, encajar, poner una cosa dentro de otra.

inly ['ɪnlɪ] [in-li], *adv.* Interiormente.

inmate ['ɪnmeɪt] [in-meit], *s.* Habitante, inquilino, el que vive en una casa con otro (inhabitant, tenant); huésped, persona alojada en una casa, fábrica u hospital; cualquier ocupante (occupant). Presidiario (prison).

inmost ['ɪnmɒʊst] [in-moust], *a.* 1. Íntimo, lo más interior o interno de alguna cosa; lo más lejano de la parte exterior, lo más profundo. 2. El más recóndito, secreto, oculto.

inn [ɪn] [in], *s.* Posada, fonda, mesón. **Inns of court,** (GB) colegios de abogados o jurisconsultos.

innate, innated [ɪ'neɪt] [i-neit], *a.* Innato, natural, propio (natural, own).

innately [ɪ'neɪtlɪ] [i-neit-li], *adv.* Naturalmente, de forma innata. **She's innately evil,** es mala de por sí.

innateness [ɪ'neɪtnɪs] [i-neit-nes], *s.* El estado o calidad de lo que es innato.

innavigable [ɪ'nævɪgəbl] [i-na-vi-ga-bol], *a.* Innavegable.

inner ['ɪnəʳ] [i-naʳ], *a.* Interior. **Inner tube,** cámara interior o neumática (de una llanta de automóvil). **Inner city,** zona centro de una ciudad. **The inner man,** el estómago.

innermost ['ɪnəmɒʊst] [i-na-moust], *a.* Íntimo. V. INMOST.

innervate ['ɪnəveɪt] [i-na-veit], *va.* Proveer de nervios; comunicar estímulo nervioso a.

innervation [ˌɪnəˈveɪʃən] [i-na-vei-shon], *s. (Fís.)* 1. Inervación, acción de dar estímulo nervioso a un órgano. 2. Disposición de los filamentos nerviosos en cualquier parte del cuerpo animal.

innerve [ɪ'nɜːv] [i-nerv], *va.* Dar vigor, nervio, fuerza.

inning ['ɪnɪŋ] [i-nin], *s.* 1. Turno de lanzamiento, entrada (baseball, cricket). 2. Los terrenos que un tiempo estuvieron cubiertos por las aguas del mar. *(Fig.)* Oportunidad, ocasión.

innkeeper ['ɪnkiːpəʳ] [in-ki-paʳ], *s.* Posadero, mesonero, fondista, huésped.

innocence ['ɪnəsns] [i-no-sens], **innocency** ['ɪnəsnsɪ] [i-no-sen-si], *s.* 1. Inocencia, pureza (kindness). 2. Inocencia, estado del que se halla inocente del delito que se le imputa. **In all innocence,** sin mala intención, sin malicia. 3. Sencillez, simplicidad (simpleness). 4. Cualidad de lo que no es nocivo, de lo innocuo.

innocent ['ɪnəsnt] [i-no-sent], *a.* 1. Inocente. 2. Inocente, simple, tonto, idiota. 3. No nocivo, innocuo. -*s.* 1. Inocente, el niño que no tiene uso de razón. 2. Inocente, el que está libre de culpa, absuelto (not guilty).

innocently ['ɪnəsntlɪ] [i-no-sent-li], *adv.* Inocentemente.

innocuous [ɪ'nɒkʊəs] [i-no-kuos], *a.* Innocuo, inofensivo (harmless), inocente, innocivo, que no hace daño; sencillo (simple).

innocuously [ɪ'nɒkʊəslɪ] [i-no-kuos-li], *adv.* Inocentemente.

innocuousness [ɪ'nɒkʊəsnɪs] [i-no-kuos-nes], *s.* Inocencia; estado y calidad de lo que no hace daño.

innominable [ɪ'nɒmɪnəbl] [i-no-mi-na-bol], *a. (Ant.)* Innominable, innombrable.

innominate [ɪ'nɒmɪneɪt] [i-no-mi-neit], *a.* 1. Innominado (nameless), que no tiene nombre especial: se emplea en anatomía; hueso innominado, arteria innominada. 2. Anónimo, sin autor conocido (anonymous).

innovate ['ɪnəʊveɪt] [i-nou-veit], *va.* Innovar, hacer innovaciones; introducir cosas nuevas.

innovating ['ɪnəʊveɪtɪŋ] [i-nou-vei-tin], *a.* Innovador; se toma comúnmente en mal sentido.

innovation [ˌɪnəʊˈveɪʃən] [i-nou-vei-shon], *s.* Innovación, novedad.

innovator ['ɪnəʊveɪtəʳ] [i-nou-vei-taʳ], *s.* Innovador, el que innova o introduce novedades y también el que hace esfuerzos para introducirlas. V. INNOVATING.

innovatory ['ɪnəʊvətərɪ] [i-nou-va-to-ri], *a.* Innovador.

innoxious [ɪ'nɒksɪəs] [i-nok-sios], *a.* 1. Innocivo, innocuo, que no es nocivo. 2. *(Ant.)* Inocente, libre, exento de culpa.

innoxiously [ɪ'nɒksɪəslɪ] [i-no-ksios-li], *adv.* Sin daño, innocuamente.

innoxiousness [ɪ'nɒksɪəsnɪs] [i-nok-sios-nes], *s.* Incapacidad de hacer daño.

innuendo [ˌɪnjʊ'endəʊ] [i-niu-en-dou], *s.* Indirecta, insinuación, pulla (insinuation).

innumerability [ˌɪnjʊmərə'bɪlɪtɪ] [i-niu-me-ra-bi-li-ti], *s.* Innumerabilidad.

innumerable [ɪ'njuːmərəbl] [i-niu-me-ra-bol], *a.* Innumerable.

innumerableness [ɪ'njuːmərəblnɪs] [i-niu-me-ra-bol-nes], *s.* Innumerabilidad, muchedumbre grande y excesiva.

innumerably [ɪ'njuːmərəblɪ] [i-niu-me-ra-bli], *adv.* Innumerablemente.

innumerous [ɪ'njuːmərəs] [i-niu-me-ros], *s.* Innumerable.

innutrition [ˌɪnjʊ'trɪʃən] [i-niu-tri-shon], *s.* Falta de nutrición.

innutritious [ˌɪnjʊ'trɪʃəs] [i-niu-tri-shos], *a.* No nutritivo, que carece de propiedades nutritivas.

inobservable [ɪˈnɒbsɜːˈvəbl] [in-ob-ser-va-bol], *a.* Inobservable.

inobservance [ɪˌnəbsɜːˈvəns] [in-ob-ser-vans], *s.* Inobservancia.

inobservation [ɪˌnəbsɜːˈveɪʃəm] [in-ob-ser-vei-shon], *s.* Inobservación.

inoculate [ɪˈnɒjʊleɪt] [i-no-kiu-leit], *va.* 1. Inocular, comunicar una enfermedad infecciosa por contacto o por medios artificiales. 2. Injertar un botón en un árbol para propagarlo. 3. *(Fig.)* Imbuir, infundir; infectar, inficionar. - *vn.* 1. Comunicar una enfermedad por medio de inoculación. 2. Inocular, injertar, propagar una planta por medio del injerto de un botón.

inoculation [ɪˌnɒjʊˈleɪʃən] [i-no-kiu-lei-shon], *s.* 1. Injertación, inoculación, el acto de injertar los árboles. 2. Inoculación, la inserción de un virus, como el de la viruela. 3. Contaminación, infección.

inoculator [ɪˈnɒjʊleɪtəʳ] [i-no-kiu-lei-taʳ], *s.* Inoculador, el que practica la inoculación.

inodorous [ɪˈnɒdərəs] [i-no-do-ros], *a.* Indoro, que carece de olor, que no despide olor.

inoffensive [ˌɪnəˈfensɪv] [i-no-fen-siv], *a.* Inofensivo.

inoffensively [ˌɪnəˈfensɪvlɪ] [i-no-fen-siv-li], *adv.* Inofensivamente, pacíficamente.

inoffensiveness [ˌɪnəˈfensɪvnɪs] [i-no-fen-siv-nes], *s.* La calidad de lo que no ofende, inocuidad; inocencia.

inofficial [ˌɪnəˈfɪʃəl] [i-no-fi-shal], *a.* V. UNOFFICIAL.

inoperable [ɪnˈɒpərəbl] [in-o-pe-ra-bol], *a. (Cir.)* Inoperable, que no puede ser operado.

inoperative [ɪnˈɒpərətɪv] [in-o-pe-ra-tiv], *a.* Falto de efecto, ineficaz.

inopportune [ɪnˈɒpətjuːn] [in-o-por-tiun], *a.* Inconveniente, inoportuno.

inopportunely [ɪnˈɒpətjuːnlɪ] [in-o-po-tiun-ni], *adv.* Inoportunamente.

inopportuneness [ɪnˈɒpətjuːnnɪs] [in-o-po-tiun-nes], *s.* Inoportunidad.

inordinacy [ɪˈnɔːdɪnəsɪ] [i-nor-di-na-si], *s.* Desarreglo, desorden; exceso más allá de lo razonable y lo derecho; naturaleza excesiva.

inordinate [ɪˈnɔːdɪnɪt] [i-nor-di-nit], *a.* Desordenado, irregular, desarreglado.

inordinately [ɪˈnɔːdɪnɪtlɪ] [i-nor-di-nit-li], *adv.* Desordenadamente.

inordinateness [ɪˈnɔːdɪnɪtnɪs] [i-nor-di-nit-nes], *s.* Desorden, exceso, demasía.

inorganic, inorganical [ˌɪnɔːˈgænɪk] [i-nor-ga-nik], *a.* Inorgánico.

inosculate [ɪˈnɒskjʊleɪt] [i-nos-kiu-leit], *va.* Unir una cosa con otra por contacto físico de aberturas; unir por anastomosis. -*vn.* Anastomarse; comunicar mutuamente.

inosculation [ɪˌnɒskjʊˈleɪʃən] [i-nos-kiu-lei-shon], *s.* Unión de una cosa con otra por algo parecido a un tubo o canal; anastomosis; unión que implica continuidad.

in-patient [ˈɪnˌpeɪʃənt] [in-pei-shant], *s.* Paciente interno.

input [ˈɪnpʊt] [in-put], *s.* 1. *(Elec. Mech.)* Entrada. 2. *(Fig.)* Gasto, inversión.

inquest [ˈɪnkwest] [in-kuest], *s.* 1. *(Jur.)* Indagación, averiguación, examen, información o pesquisa judicial con ayuda de un jurado (inquiry, investigation). 2. El jurado u otro cuerpo que hace dicha pesquisa. 3. Examen ante el juez para determinar valores o daños y perjuicios. 4. Escudriñamiento, examen diligente de alguna cosa. **Coroner's inquest,** la investigación o pesquisa que hace el jurado presidido por el empleado público llamado **Coroner,** para indagar la causa de las muertes repentinas y de las debidas a un acto de violencia.

inquietude [ɪnˈkwɪtjuːd] [in-kui-tud], *s.* Inquietud, desasosiego, descontento.

inquirable [ɪnˈkwaɪəbol] [in-kuaia-bol], *a.* Investigable, que puede ser inquirido o examinado.

inquire [ɪnˈkwaɪəʳ] [in-kuaiaʳ], *vn.* Inquirir, averiguar, examinar (investigate, exam); informarse, buscar información por medio de preguntas. -*va.* Preguntar alguna cosa. **To inquire about,** hacer preguntas sobre alguna cosa; preguntar por alguno **I was only inquiring,** sólo era una pregunta. **To inquire after** o **for,** preguntar por algo. **To inquire something of someone,** preguntar algo a alguien. **To inquire into,** investigar alguna cosa, tratar de saber algo con toda certidumbre.

inquirer [ɪnˈkwaɪərəʳ] [in-kuaia-raʳ], *s.* Inquiridor, investigador, examinador, preguntón.

inquiring [ɪnˈkwaɪərɪŋ] [in-kuaia-rin], *a.* Curioso, activo, interrogativo.

inquiry [ɪnˈkwaɪərɪ] [in-kuaia-ri], *s.* 1. Interrogación, examinación, indagación. 2. Pesquisa, escudriñamiento, información, investigación. 3. Pregunta (question).

inquisition [ˌɪnkwɪˈzɪʃən] [in-kui-si-shon], *s.* 1. Inquisición, escudriñamiento. 2. Inquisición, tribunal eclesiástico que inquiría y castigaba los delitos contra la fe católica; el Santo Oficio. 3. Investigación.

inquisitional [ˌɪnkwɪˈzɪʃənl] [in-kui-si-sho-nal], *a.* Inquisitorial, perteneciente a la inquisición.

inquisitive [ɪnˈkwɪzɪtɪv] [in-kui-si-tiv], *a.* Inquisitivo, preguntón, curioso, investigador. **An inquisitive mind,** una mente investigadora; un natural curioso.

inquisitively [ɪnˈkwɪzɪtɪvlɪ] [in-kui-si-tiv-li], *adv.* Inquisitivamente.

inquisitiveness [ɪnˈkwɪzɪtɪvnɪs] [in-kui-si-tiv-nes], *s.* Curiosidad, deseo de saber y averiguar alguna cosa.

inquisitor [ɪnˈkwɪzɪtəʳ] [in-kui-si-taʳ], *s.* 1. Inquisidor, el que inquiere; juez investigador. 2. Inquisidor, juez eclesiástico que entendía en las causas sobre asuntos de fe en algunos países católicos. 3. Persona curiosa.

inquisitorial [ɪnˌkwɪzɪˈtɔːrɪəl] [in-kui-si-to-rial], *a.* Inquisitorial, a la manera de un inquiridor o de un inquisidor.

inracinate [ɪnˈræsɪneɪt] [in-ra-si-neit], *va.* Arraigar, implantar; fijar.

inroad [ˈɪnrəʊd] [in-roud], *s.* Incursión, correría; invasión, irrupción, tala (invasion).

inrush [ˈɪnrʌʃ] [in-rash], *s.* Empuje, como el de la marea; invasión. Afluencia (people).

insalivate [ɪnˈsælɪveɪt] [in-sa-li-veit], *va.* Insalivar, mezclar (el alimento) con saliva.

insalivation [ˌɪnsælɪˈveɪʃən] [in-sa-li-vei-shon], *s.* Insalivación.

insalubrious [ˌɪnsəˈluːbrɪəs] [in-sa-lu-brios], *a.* Insalubre, malsano.

insalubrity [ˌɪnsəˈluːbrɪtɪ] [in-sa-lu-bri-ti], *s.* Insalubridad.

insane [ɪnˈseɪn] [in-sein], *a.* 1. Insano, loco, demente, que ha perdido la razón, acometido de enajenación mental; insensato (fool). 2. Usado o puesto aparte para los locos. **Insane asylum,** casa de locos, asilo para los locos. **To drive someone insane,** volver loco a alguien.

insanely [ɪnˈseɪnlɪ] [in-sein-li], *adv.* Locamente, terriblemente, como un loco (act, laugh).

insanity [ɪnˈsænɪtɪ] [in-sa-ni-ti], *s.* Locura, manía, demencia, enajenación mental.

insatiable [ɪnˈseɪʃəbl] [in-sei-sha-bol], *a.* Insaciable.

insatiableness [ɪnˈseɪʃəblnɪs] [in-sei-sha-bol-nes], *s.* Insaciabilidad.

insatiably [ɪnˈseɪʃəblɪ] [in-sei-sha-bli], *adv.* Insaciablemente.

insatiate [ɪnˈseɪʃɪeɪt] [in-sei-shieit], *a.* Insaciable.

insatiately [ɪnˈseɪʃɪeɪtlɪ] [in-sei-shieit-li], *adv.* Insaciablemente.

inscribe [ɪnˈskraɪb] [in-skraib], *va.* 1. Inscribir. 2. *(Geom.)* Inscribir, formar una figura dentro de otra. 3. Dedicar una composición o escrito a una persona (book).

inscriber [ɪnˈskraɪbəʳ] [in-skrai-baʳ], *s.* El que inscribe y dedica (book).

inscription [ɪnˈskrɪpʃən] [in-skrip-shon], *s.* 1. Inscripción; cualquier leyenda o letrero en caracteres permanentes. 2.

Inscripción, registro en una lista o rol. 3. La dedicatoria de un escrito hecha a alguna persona. 4. *(For.)* Obligación que contrae el acusador de sufrir la pena misma que la ley prescribe al delito de que acusa, si no puede probar que ha sido cometido.

inscriptive [ɪnˈskrɪptɪv] [in-skrip-tiv], *a.* De la naturaleza de una inscripción; inscrito, inscripto.

inscrutability [ɪnˌskruːtəˈbɪlɪtɪ] [in-skru-ter-bi-li-ti], *s.* Inescrutabilidad.

inscrutable [ɪnˈskruːtəbl] [in-skru-ter-bol], *a.* Inescrutable, inescudriñable, incomprensible.

inscrutably [ɪnˈskruːtəblɪ] [in-skru-ter-bli], *adv.* Inescrutablemente.

inseam [ˈɪnsiːm] [in-sim], *va.* Señalar o marcar con alguna señal, costura, filón o vena.

inseam, *s.* Costura interior: se dice de los zapatos o vestidos.

insect [ˈɪnsekt] [in-sekt], *s.* Insecto, nombre genérico de una clase de animales cuyo cuerpo está dividido en segmentos. **Insect-powder,** polvos insecticidas. **Insect bite,** picadura de insecto. **Insect spray,** insecticida.

insectean [ˈɪnsektɪən] [in-sek-tian], **insectile** [ˈɪnsektaɪl] [in-sek-tail], *a.* Que pertenece a la clase de insectos antiguamente insectil; **insectile** significa también, parecido a un insecto.

insecticide [ˈɪnsektɪsaɪd] [in-sek-ti-said], *s.* Insecticida, el que o lo que mata los insectos.

insectivorous [ˌɪnsekˈtɪvərəs] [in-sek-ti-vo-ros], *a.* Insectívoro, que come insectos o se alimenta de ellos.

insecure [ˌɪnsɪˈkjʊʳ] [in-si-kiuʳ], *a.* 1. Inseguro, que no está o no es seguro; lo que está en peligro; poco sólido, poco firme. 2. Expuesto a pérdida, daño o riesgo.

insecurely [ˌɪnsɪˈkʊəlɪ] [in-si-kiua-li], *adv.* Inseguramente.

insecurity [ˌɪnsɪˈkʊrɪtɪ] [in-si-kiu-ri-ti], *s.* Inseguridad, incertidumbre; peligro, riesgo.

inseminate [ɪnˈsemɪneɪt] [in-se-mi-neit], *va.* 1. Emitir el semen, inseminar; con menos exactitud se usa también en el sentido de engendrar, fecundar. 2. *(Des.)* Sembrar.

insensate [ɪnˈsenseɪt] [in-sen-seit], *a.* Insensato.

insensibility [ɪnˌsensəˈbɪlɪtɪ] [in-sen-sa-bi-li-ti], *s.* 1. Insensibilidad, falta de sentimiento. 2. Estupidez, insensatez, falta de comprensión. 3. Torpeza, adormecimiento de algún sentido corporal.

insensible [ɪnˈsensəbl] [in-sen-sa-bol], *a.* 1. Insensible, imperceptible. 2. Insensible, indiferente (unfeeling). 3. Insensible, duro de corazón.

insensibleness [ɪnˈsensəblnɪs] [in-sen-sa-bol-nes], *s.* Insensibilidad.

insensibly [ɪnˈsensəblɪ] [in-sen-sa-bli], *adv.* 1. Insensiblemente. 2. Gradualmente, lentamente, poco a poco.

insensitive [ɪnˈsensɪtɪv] [in-sen-si-tiv], *a.* Insensible.

insensitivity [ˌɪnsensɪˈtɪvɪtɪ] [in-sen-si-ti-vi-ti], *sf.* Insensibilidad, calidad de insensible.

insentient [ɪnˈsensənt] [in-sen-shant], *a.* Insensible, lo que no siente o percibe.

inseparability [ˌɪnsepərəˈbɪlɪtɪ] [in-se-pa-ra-bi-li-ti], **inseparableness** [ɪnˈsepərəblnɪs] [in-se-pa-ra-bol-nes], *s.* Inseparabilidad.

inseparable [ɪnˈsepərəbl] [in-se-pa-ra-bol], *a.* Inseparable, indisoluble.

inseparably [ɪnˈsepərəblɪ] [in-se-pa-ra-bli], *adv.* Inseparablemente.

inseparate [ɪnˈsepəreɪt] [in-se-pa-reit], *a.* No separado, unido.

insert [ɪnˈsɜːt] [in-sert], *va.* Insertar, ingerir una cosa entre otras, colocar en medio de: intercalar; hacer inserta. **To insert a notice in a newspaper,** insertar un anuncio en un periódico.

insertion [ɪnˈsɜːʃən] [in-ser-shon], *s.* 1. Inserción, la acción de ingerir o insertar; la cosa inserta o insertada. 2. Tira bordada o labrada. (Cuba) Antolar; entredós. 3. Paraje o modo de ligadura o inserción; inserción de una hoja en una

rama o inserción de un músculo. 4. Inserción, publicación (newspaper).

in-service [ɪnˈsɜːvɪs] [in-ser-vis], *a.* En funcionamiento.

inserviceable [ɪnˈsɜːvɪsəbl] [in-ser-vi-sa-bol], *a.* Inservible.

insessorial [ˌɪnseˈsɔːrɪəl] [in-se-so-rial], *a.* Perchador, a propósito para perchar; ave perchadora.

inset [ˈɪnset] [in-set], *va.* Meter en; fijar, plantar.

inshelter [ɪnˈʃeltəʳ] [in-shel-taʳ], *va.* Poner una cosa bajo la protección de otra.

inshore [ɪnˈʃɔːʳ] [in-shoʳ], *a.* 1. Que está o sucede cerca de la orilla. 2. En dirección a tierra. -*adv.* Hacia la orilla o cerca de ella.

inshrine, *va.* V. ENSHRINE.

insiccation [ˌɪnsɪˈkeɪʃən] [in-si-kei-shon], *s.* Desecación.

inside [ˈɪnsaɪd] [in-said], *s.* 1. Interior, lo que está en la parte de dentro (place). 2. Contenido, lo que está contenido. 3. Viajero, pasajero del interior. -*a.* Interior, de la parte de adentro. -*adv.* Dentro, adentro, en el interior. **Inside out,** de dentro afuera; al revés. **To be inside,** estar a la sombra, en la cárcel. **Inside 2 weeks,** en menos de 2 semanas (time). 4. Confidencial, secreto (information).

insider [ɪnˈsaɪdəʳ] [in-sai-daʳ], *s.* 1. Empleado de una casa. 2. Persona enterada, informada.

insides [ˈɪnsaɪdz] [in-saids], *s.* **pl.** Entrañas.

insidious [ˈɪnsɪdɪəs] [in-si-dios], *a.* Insidioso, engañoso.

insidiously [ˈɪnsɪdɪəslɪ] [in-si-dios-li], *adv.* Insidiosamente, engañosamente.

insidiousness [ˈɪnsɪdɪəsnɪs] [in-si-dios-nes], *s.* El estado o calidad de lo que es insidioso.

insight [ɪnˈsaɪt] [in-sait], *s.* 1. Conocimiento profundo de alguna cosa; discernimiento intelectual. 2. Percepción de la naturaleza interior de una cosa. 3. Intuición, perspicacia.

insignia [ɪnˈsɪgnɪə] [in-sig-nia], *s.* *pl.* Insignias, divisas honoríficas; estandartes.

insignificance [ˌɪnsɪgˈnɪfɪkəns] [in-sig-ni-fi-kans], **insignificancy** [ɪnˈsɪgnɪfɪkənsɪ] [in-sig-ni-fi-kan-si], *s.* 1. Falta de sentido o significación; insignificancia. 2. Friolera, poca importancia; nulidad.

insignicant [ˌɪnsɪgˈnɪfɪkənt] [in-sig-ni-fi-kant], *a.* Insignificante, frívolo, nulo.

insignificantly [ˌɪnsɪgˈnɪfɪkəntlɪ] [in-sig-ni-fi-kant-li], *adv.* Insignificantemente, frívolamente.

insignificative [ɪnˈsɪgnɪfɪkətɪv] [in-sig-ni-fi-ka-tiv], *a.* Insignificativo.

insincere [ˌɪnsɪnˈsɪəʳ] [in-sin-siaʳ], *a.* 1. Doble, hipócrita, poco sincero. 2. Turbado; corrompido; agitado.

insincerely [ˌɪnsɪnˈsɪəlɪ] [in-sin-sia-li], *adv.* Con doble, con segunda intención.

insincerity [ˌɪnsɪnˈserɪtɪ] [in-sin-se-ri-ti], *s.* Doblez, disimulación.

insinuate [ɪnˈsɪnjʊeɪt] [in-si-niu-eit], *va.* 1. Insinuar **To insinuate that,** dar a entender que, insinuar que. 2. Apuntar, insinuar, dar a entender alguna cosa. **To insinuate oneself,** insinuarse, introducirse con maña y habilidad en la amistad de alguno. -*vn.* Insinuarse, ganar la voluntad de otro poco a poco y con maña; envolver.

insinuating [ɪnˈsɪnjʊeɪtɪŋ] [in-si-niuei-tin], *a.* Insinuador; malintencionado, que va con segundas intenciones.

insinuation [ɪnˌsɪnjʊˈeɪʃən] [in-si-niuei-shon], *s.* 1. Insinuación, artificio con que alguno va suavemente atrayendo a sí la atención y benevolencia de otro. 2. Insinuación, indirecta.

insinuative [ɪnˈsɪnjʊətɪv] [in-si-nua-tiv], *a.* Insinuante, lo que se insinúa o granjea el afecto de alguien.

insinuator [ɪnˈsɪnjʊeɪtəʳ] [in-si-niuei-taʳ], *s.* Insinuador, insinuante, el que insinúa algo por medio de indirectas.

insipid [ɪnˈsɪpɪd] [in-si-pid], *a.* 1. Insípido, desabrido. 2. Insulso, soso.

insipidity [ˌɪnsɪˈpɪdɪtɪ] [in-si-pi-di-ti], **insipidness** [ɪnˈsɪpɪdnɪs] [in-si-pid-nes], *s.* 1. Insipidez, desabor. 2. Insulsez, sosería.

insipidly [ɪnˈsɪpɪdlɪ] [in-si-pid-li], *adv.* Insulsamente.

insist [ɪnˈsɪst] [in-sist], *vn.* 1. Insistir, instar o persistir en una cosa. 2. Descansar una cosa en otra; hallar apoyo. **Insist** se usa con **on** o **upon.**

insistence [ɪnˈsɪstəns] [in-sis-tans], **insistency** [ɪnˈsɪstənsɪ] [in-sis-tan-si], *s.* Insistencia.

insistent [ɪnˈsɪstənt] [in-sis-tant], *a.* 1. Insistente, que insiste, insta o persiste. 2. Conspicuo. 3. Que se apoya o descansa en alguna cosa.

insistently [ɪnˈsɪstəntlɪ] [in-sis-tant-li], *adv.* De manera insistente. Insistentemente, urgentemente.

insition [ɪnˈsɪʃən] [in-si-shon], *s.* Injertación, el acto de injertar.

in situ [ɪnˈsɪtjuː] [in-si-tiu], *adv.* En el sitio, in situ.

insnare [ɪnˈsneər] [ins-near], *va.* V. ENSNARE.

insnarl, *va.* V. SNARL y ENSNARL.

insobriety [ɪnsəˈbrɪətɪ] [in-so-brie-ti], *s.* Embriaguez, borrachera, falta de sobriedad.

insolate [ɪnˈsəleɪt] [in-so-leit], *va.* Insolar, secar al sol.

insolation [ˌɪnsəˈleɪʃən] [in-so-lei-shon], *s.* 1. Insolación, el acto de poner alguna cosa al sol para que se seque o fermente. 2. Insolación, una enfermedad. V. SUNSTROKE.

insole [ˈɪnsəʊl] [in-soul], *s.* Plantilla (del zapato).

insolence [ˈɪnsələns] [in-so-lens], **insolency** [ˈɪnsələnsɪ] [in-so-len-si], *s.* Insolencia, orgullo, desprecio, orgulloso, altanería; atrevimiento.

insolent [ˈɪnsələnt] [in-so-lent], *a.* Insolente, arrogante, atrevido, orgulloso.

insolently [ˈɪnsələntlɪ] [in-so-lent-li], *adv.* Insolentemente.

insoluble [ɪnˈsɒljʊbl] [in-so-liu-bol], *a.* 1. Insoluble; indisoluble. 2. Que no puede resolverse ni explicarse.

insolubleness [ɪnˈsɒljʊblnɪs] [in-so-liu-bol-nes], *s.* Indisolubilidad, la incapacidad de disolverse.

insolvable [ɪnˈsɒlvəbl] [in-sol-va-bol], *a.* 1. Inexplicable, que no admite explicación. 2. Indisoluble, que no se puede desatar o resolver. 3. Que no se puede pagar o saldar.

insolvency [ɪnˈsɒlvənsɪ] [in-sol-ven-si], *s.* Insolvencia, imposibilidad de pagar las deudas.

insolvent [ɪnˈsɒlvənt] [in-sol-vant], *a.* Insolvente, el que no tiene para pagar sus deudas. **Insolvent debtor,** el deudor que no tiene recursos con que pagar a sus acreedores.

insomnia [ɪnˈsɒmnɪə] [in-som-nia], *s.* Insomnio, desvelo, incapacidad crónica de dormir.

insomniac [ɪnˈsɒmnɪæk] [in-som-niak], *a.* Insomne.

insomnious [ɪnˈsɒmnɪəs] [in-som-nios], *a.* Insomne, que está desvelado, que no duerme.

insomnolence [ɪnˈsɒmnələns] [in-som-no-lens], *s.* Falta de sueño.

insomuch [ˌɪnsəʊˈmʌtʃ] [in-sou-mach], *conj.* De manera que, de suerte que, de modo que.

inspect [ɪnˈspekt] [ins-pekt], *va.* Reconocer, examinar, inspeccionar con cuidado; investigar y probar oficialmnte.

inspection [ɪnˈspekʃən] [ins-pek-shon], *s.* Inspección, la acción y efecto de reconocer y examinar atentamente alguna cosa; particularmente, examen oficial.

inspector [ɪnˈspektər] [ins-pek-tar], *s.* 1. Inspector, superintendente. 2. Oficial de la policía en muchas ciudades.

inspectorate [ɪnˈspektəreɪt] [ins-pek-to-reit], *s.* 1. El distrito que corresponde a un inspector. 2. Cargo o empleo de un inspector.

insphere [ɪnˈsfɪər] [ins-fia], *va.* Colocar en una esfera o globo.

inspiration [ˌɪnspəˈreɪʃən] [ins-pa-rei-shon], *s.* Inspiración. **To find inspiration in,** inspirarse en.

inspirationist [ˌɪnspəˈreɪʃənɪst] [ins-pa-rei-sho-nist], *s.* Defensor de la doctrina de la inspiración.

inspiratory [ˌɪnspɪrəˈtərɪ] [ins-pi-ra-to-ri], *a.* Inspirador, que aspira aire en los pulmones; inspiratorio, que sirve o concierne a la inspiración.

inspire [ɪnˈspaɪər] [ins-paia], *vn.* 1. Inspirar, introducir el aire exterior en los pulmones. 2. Soplar suavemente. -*va.* 1. Inspirar el aire. 2. Inspirar, sugerir, comunicar al ánimo algún movimiento o idea (suggest). 3. Inspirar, iluminar Dios el entendimiento o mover la voluntad.

inspirer [ɪnˈspaɪərər] [ins-paia-ra], *s.* Inspirador.

inspiring [ɪnˈspaɪərɪŋ] [ins-paia-rin], *a.* Inspirador.

inspirit [ɪnˈspɪrɪt] [ins-pi-rit], *va.* Alentar, animar, vigorizar, infundir espíritu.

inspissate [ɪnˈspɪseɪt] [ins-pi-seit], *va.* Espesar, condensar. -*adj.* Espeso.

inspissation [ˌɪnspɪˈseɪʃən] [ins-pi-sei-shon], *s.* Condensación, el acto de condensar o espesar alguna cosa líquida.

instabillity [ˌɪnstəˈbɪlɪtɪ] [ins-ter-bi-li-ti], *s.* Instabilidad, inestabilidad, inconstancia.

instable [ˈɪnsteɪbl] [ins-tei-bol], *a.* Inconstante, vario, variable, mudable

install [ɪnˈstɔːl] [ins-tol], *va.* Instalar, poner en posesión al que ha obtenido algún empleo, cargo o beneficio.

installation [ˌɪnstəˈleɪʃən] [ins-ter-lei-shon], *s.* 1. Instalación, el acto o la ceremonia de dar posesión de un cargo o destino. 2. Emplazamiento y montaje de máquinas o aparatos.

instalment, installment [ɪnˈstɔːlmənt] [ins-tol-ment], *s.* 1. Pago parcial; pago en plazos determinados; plazo. 2. Parte o porción de algo que se da, reparte o publica en plazos determinados. **An instalment of a story,** entrega, porción de una novela, etc., que se publica de una vez. 3. Instalación, acto de instalar.

instance [ˈɪnstəns] [ins-tans], *s.* 1. Ejemplo; suceso determinado, caso; prueba. 2. Instancia, ruego, solicitación. 3. Nueva razón u objeción con que se urge algún argumento, pleito o dificultad. 4. (*For.*) Instancia, expediente, el curso legal de la acción hasta la sentencia definitiva. **For instance,** por ejemplo. **In that instance,** en ese caso. **At the instance of,** a petición de, a instancia de. **We have no instance of it,** no hay ejemplo de ello. **In the first instance,** en primer lugar, primeramente (*Jur.*).

instance, *va.* Ofrecer como ejemplo; citar como ejemplo o prueba.

instanced [ˈɪnstənst] [ins-tanst], *a.* Presentado como prueba, dado como ejemplo.

instancy [ˈɪnstənsɪ] [ins-tan-si], *s.* Urgencia, instancia, insistencia, solicitación porfiada.

instant [ˈɪnstənt] [ins-tant], *a.* 1. Inminente, inmediato, al instante; pronto, presente; importuno. 2. (*Ant.*) Urgente, activo; importuno. -*s.* 1. Instante, momento, duración indivisible, tiempo señalado. 2. El mes corriente o presente. **The fifth instant,** el cinco del corriente. **Instant replay,** repetición de jugada. **On the instant, this instant,** en seguida, al instante, al momento.

instantaneity [ˌɪnstənˈteɪnɪːtɪ] [ins-tan-tei-ni-ti], *s.* Instantáneo, la calidad de ser instantáneo.

instantaneous [ˌɪnstənˈteɪnɪəs] [ins-tan-tei-nios], *a.* Instantáneo, o que dura un instante; hecho en un instante.

instantaneously [ˌɪnstənˈteɪnɪəslɪ] [ins-tan-tei-nios-li], *adv.* Instantáneamente.

instantaneousness, *s.* V. INSTANTANEITY.

instanter [ˌɪnstənˈtər] [ins-tan-tar], *adv.* Al instante, inmediatamente.

instantly [ˈɪnstəntlɪ] [ins-tant-li], *adv.* 1. Instantáneamente, en un momento. 2. (*Ant.*) Con instancia o porfía.

instate [ˈɪnsteɪt] [ins-teit], *va.* Colocar en algún orden o clase.

instead [ɪnˈsted] [ins-ted], *adv.* En lugar de, en vez de; originalmente dos palabras. **Instead of,** en vez de, en lugar de.

instep [ɪnˈstep] [ins-tep], *s.* 1. Empeine o garganta del pie. 2. La parte anterior de la pata de atrás de una caballería.

instigate [ɪnˈstɪɡeɪt] [ins-ti-gueit], *va.* Instigar, mover, excitar, incitar poner por obra mediante el incitamento.

instigation [ɪnˈstɪɡeɪʃən] [ins-ti-guei-shon], *s.* Instigación, sugestión, provocación a hacer daño.

instigator [ɪnˈstɪgeɪtəʳ] [ins-ti-guei-taʳ], s. Instigador, incitador.

instill [ɪnˈstɪl] [ins-til], va. 1. Instilar, echar poco a poco o gota a gota algún líquido. 2. Instilar, insinuar, introducir, inculcar, infundir en el ánimo algún afecto.

instillation [ˌɪnstɪˈleɪʃən] [ins-ti-lei-shon], s. 1. Instilación, el acto de echar los líquidos gota a gota o de introducir insensiblemente alguna cosa en el ánimo; insinuación. 2. La cosa instilada o introducida.

instiller [ɪnˈstɪləʳ] [ins-ti-laʳ], s. El que instila o insinúa; insinuante.

instilment, instillment [ɪnˈstɪlmənt] [ins-til-ment], s. Cualquier cosa instilada.

instinct [ɪnˈstɪŋkt] [ins-tinkt], a. Animado desde adentro; movido por impulso interior: se usa con **with. Instinct with pity,** movido por la piedad.

instinct, s. 1. Instinto, sagacidad natural de los animales. 2. Instinto, el movimiento natural que hace obrar a las personas sin que tenga parte la reflexión.

instinctive [ɪnˈstɪŋktɪv] [ins-tink-tiv], a. Instintivo, determinado por un impulso natural; espontáneo.

instinctively [ɪnˈstɪŋktɪvlɪ] [ins-tink-tiv-li], adv. Por instinto.

institute [ˈɪnstɪtjuːt] [ins-ti-tiut], va. 1. Instituir, establecer, fundar. 2. Poner por obra, poner en operación, empezar. 3. Conferir canónicamente un beneficio eclesiástico. 4. (Des.) Instruir, educar.

institute, s. 1. Instituto, establecimiento. 2. Regla, principio, máxima. **Institutes of Justinian,** instituto de Justiniano, libro que contiene los principios del derecho romano. **Teachers' institue,** (E. U. a.) Asamblea de maestros para instrucción y auxilio muto.

institution [ˌɪnstɪˈtjuːʃən] [ins-ti-tiu-shon], s. 1. Institución; establecimiento; tradición (custom). 2. Ley positiva, derecho positivo. 3. Instrucción, educación, enseñanza (education). 4. Institución canónica, el acto de poner a alguno en posesión de un beneficio eclesiástico.

institutional [ˌɪnstɪˈtjuːʃənl] [ins-ti-tiu-sho-nal], a. 1. Prescrito, instituido por la autoridad. 2. Elemental.

institutionalize [ˌɪnstɪˈtjuːʃənl] [ins-ti-tiu-sho-nal], va. Institucionalizar, establcer.

institutive [ˈɪnstɪtjuːtɪv] [ins-ti-tiu-tiv], a. 1. Instituente, instituidor, capaz de establecer o instituir. 2. Establecido, instituido.

institutor [ˈɪnstɪtjuːtəʳ] [ins-ti-tiu-taʳ], s. Instituidor, fundador, el que funda o pone por obra.

instruct [ɪnˈstrʌkt] [ins-trakt], va. 1. Instruir, enseñar, doctrinar (teach); modelar o formar el ánimo. 2. Instruir, dar a conocer a uno el estado de una cosa o informarle de ella. 3. Dar instrucciones, órdenes a; mandar (order).

instruction [ɪnˈstrʌkʃən] [ins-trak-shon], s. 1. Instrucción, enseñanza (teaching, training). 2. Instrucción, conocimiento o saber adquirido. 3. Instrucción, orden. **Instructions for use,** modo de empleo. **To give somebody instruction,** enseñar, instruir.

instructive [ɪnˈstrʌktɪv] [ins-trak-tiv], a. Instructivo.

instructively [ˌɪnstrʌkˈtɪvlɪ] [ins-trak-tiv-li], adv. Instructivamente.

instructiveness [ˌɪnstrʌkˈtɪvnɪs] [ins-trak-tiv-nes], s. El poder o la capacidad de instruir.

instructor [ɪnˈstrʌktəʳ] [ins-trak-taʳ], s. 1. Instructor, maestro. 2. En los colegios norteamericanos, instructor, maestro de categoría algo más baja que la de un profesor.

instructress [ɪnˈstrʌktrɪs] [ins-trak-tres], sf. Instructora, profesora.

instrument [ˈɪnstrəmənt] [ins-tru-ment], s. 1. Instrumento, aquello de que nos servimos para hacer una cosa, herramienta o máquina que se usa para trabajar. 2. Instrumento, agente, persona que obra según el dictado o el capricho de otra. 3. (For.) Escritura, acta, documento, instrumento con que se justifica alguna cosa o que contiene un contrato. V. DEED. **A wind instrument,** instrumento de viento. **A stringed instrument,** instrumento de cuerda. **Instrument approach,**

(Aer.) Aproximación por instrumentos. **Instrument board,** tablero de instrumentos. **Instrument flying,** (Aer.) Vuelo a ciegas, vuelo con instrumentos. **Instruments and supplies of war,** pertrechos. **Instrument panel,** (Aut.) salpicadero. **Set of instruments,** instrumental.

instrumental [ˌɪnstrʊˈmentl] [ins-tru-men-tal], a. 1. Instrumental, lo que conduce a la consecución de algún fin. 2. Instrumental, lo que pertenece a los instrumentos.

instrumentality [ˌɪnstrʊmenˈtælɪtɪ] [ins-tru-men-ter-li-ti], s. El acto de servir de instrumento para una cosa y la calidad de lo que sirve de instrumento.

instrumentally [ˌɪnstrʊˈmentəlɪ] [ins-tru-men-ter-li], adv. Instrumentalmente; con instrumentos de música.

instrumentalness [ˌɪnstrʊˈmentəlnɪs] [ins-tru-men-tal-nes], s. La utilidad de una cosa para servir de instrumento en el logro de un día.

instrumentation [ˌɪnstrʊmənˈteɪʃən] [ins-tru-men-tei-shon], s. Instrumentación.

insubjection [ˌɪnsəbˈʒekʃən] [in-sab-yek-shon], s. Inobediencia.

insubordinate [ˈɪnsəˌbɔːdɪnɪt] [in-sa-bor-di-nit], a. Insubordinado.

insubordination [ˈɪnsəˌbɔːdɪˈneɪʃən] [in-sa-bor-di-nei-shon], s. Insubordinación.

insufferable [ɪnˈsʌfərəbl] [in-sa-fe-ra-bol], a. Insufrible, insoportable, detestable (hateful, detestable).

insufferably [ɪnˈsʌfərəblɪ] [in-sa-fe-ra-bli], adv. Insufriblemente, insoportablemente.

insufficiency, insufficience [ˌɪnsəˈfɪʃənsɪ] [in-sa-fi-shan-si], s. Insuficiencia, incapacidad.

insufficient [ˌɪnsəˈfɪʃənt] [in-sa-fi-shant], a. Insuficiente; impotente; incapaz, inhabil; mal a propósito.

insufficiently [ˌɪnsəˈfɪʃəntlɪ] [in-sa-fi-shant-li], adv. Insuficientemente.

insufflate [ɪnˈsʌfleɪt] [in-sa-fleit], va. 1. Insuflar, soplar en o sobre; tratar por la insuflación. 2. Respirar sobre otra persona; acto simbólico en ciertas ceremonias religiosas. 3. (Med.) Insuflar, introducir a soplos en un órgano o en una cavidad un gas, un líquido o una sustancia pulverizada.

insufflation [ˌɪnsəˈfleɪʃən] [in-sa-flei-shon], s. 1. Soplo. 2. Insuflación, como ceremonia religiosa. 3. (Med.) Insuflación, operación por medio de la cual se introduce aire libre en los pulmones de los asfixiados, o una sustancia pulverizada en una cavidad.

insular [ˈɪnsjələʳ] [in-sha-laʳ], a. 1. Insular, isleño; aislado. 2. (Fig.) Estrecho de miras, iliberal; escaso.

insularity [ˌɪnsjʊˈlærɪtɪ] [in-siu-la-ri-ti], s. Estado de ser insular o isleño; de aquí, estrechez de miras.

insulate [ˈɪnsjʊleɪt] [in-siu-leit], va. 1. Aislar. 2. (Elec.) Aislar de otros cuerpos conductores, por medio de un soporte o de una cubierta de material mal conductor; impedir que se escape la electricidad.

insulated [ˈɪnsjʊleɪtɪd] [in-siu-lei-tid], a. Aislado, apartado; escueto, exento, solitario.

insulating [ˈɪnsjʊleɪtɪŋ] [in-siu-lei-tin], a. (Elec.) Aislante. **Insulating tape,** cinta aislante.

insulation [ˌɪnsjʊˈleɪʃən] [in-siu-lei-shon], s. 1. Aislamiento, acción de aislar estado de hallarse aislado. 2. Acción de rodear un cuerpo con otros no conductores. 3. (Elec.) Materias, materiales usados para aislar.

insulator [ˈɪnsjʊleɪtəʳ] [in-siu-lei-taʳ], s. Aislador, el cuerpo que aisla o interrumpe la comunicación de la electricidad con los cuerpos que le rodean.

insulin [ˈɪnsjʊlɪn] [in-siu-lin], s. Insulina.

insult [ˈɪnsʌlt] [in-salt], s. 1. Insulto, ultraje, denuesto; injuria. 2. (Des.) Salto, el acto de saltar sobre algo; de aquí, el acto de cubrir el macho a la hembra. Decíase del ganado vacuno y caballar.

insult, va. 1. Insultar, ultrajar, ajar, injuriar. 2. Despreciar, pisar.

insulter [ˈɪnsʌltəʳ] [in-sal-taʳ], s. Insultador, denostador.

insulting [ɪnˈsʌltɪŋ] [in-sal-tin], a. Insultante, ultrajante; insolente.

insultingly [ɪnˈsʌltɪŋlɪ] [in-sal-tin-li], *adv.* Insolentemente.

insuperability [ɪnˌsuːpərəˈbɪlɪtɪ] [in-su-pe-ra-bi-li-ti], *s.* La calidad de ser insuperable.

insuperable [ɪnˈsuːpərəbl] [in-su-pe-ra-bol], *a.* Insuperable, lo que no se puede superar.

insuperableness [ɪnˈsuːpərəblnɪs] [in-su-pe-ra-bol-nes], *s.* Invencibilidad.

insuperably [ɪnˈsuːpərəblɪ] [in-su-pe-ra-bli], *adv.* Invenciblemente. **Insuperably difficult,** dificilísimo.

insupportable [ˌɪnsəˈpɔːtəbl] [in-sa-par-ter-bol], *a.* 1. Insoportable, inaguantable. 2. Insufrible, intolerable.

insupportably [ˌɪnsəˈpɔːtəblɪ] [in-sa-par-ter-bli], *adv.* Insoportablemente.

insuppressible [ˌɪnsəˈpresɪbl] [in-sa-pre-si-bol], *a.* Lo que no puede ser ocultado o suprimido.

insurable [ɪnˈʃʊərəbl] [in-shua-ra-bol], *a.* Capaz de ser asegurado, contra pérdida de la vida, contra incendios, etc.

insurance [ɪnˈʃʊərəns] [in-shua-rans], *s.* 1. Seguro, contrato o escritura con que se asegura algo. 2. Sistema de seguros. 3. Prima del seguro, cantidad que paga el asegurado al asegurador. 4. Cantidad total que se obliga a pagar el asegurador al asegurado. **Insurance claim,** demanda de seguro. **Insurance company,** compañía de seguros. **Insurance surveyor,** tasador de seguros. **Endowment insurance,** seguro dotal. **Liability insurance,** contrato por el cual una compañía de seguros asume, mediante el pago de un premio, la responsabilidad legal de un individuo o una corporación. **Life insurance,** seguro de vida. **Fire insurance,** seguro contra incendio. **Accident insurance,** seguro contra accidentes o percances.

insurance policy [ɪnˈʃʊərənsˌpɒlɪsɪ] [in-shua-rans-po-li-si], *s.* Póliza.

insure [ɪnˈʃʊər] [in-shua], *va.* 1. Asegurar, responder el asegurador, mediante el precio convenido, de todos o de alguno de los daños que puedan sobrevenir a una cosa o persona. 2. Obtener seguros, hacer negocios de seguros, asegurar; garantizar, afianzar. -*vn.* 1. Asegurarse, tomar una póliza de seguro. 2. Tener por ocupación habitual la de hacer u obtener seguros.

insurer [ɪnˈʃʊərər] [in-shua-ra], *s.* Asegurador.

insurgent [ɪnˈsɜːdʒənt] [in-ser-yent], *s.* Insurgente, sublevado, insurrecto.

insurmountable [ˌɪnsəˈmaʊntəbl] [in-ser-mon-ter-bol], *a.* Insuperable, insalvable.

insurmountably [ˌɪnsəˈmaʊntəblɪ] [in-ser-mon-ter-bli], *adv.* Invenciblemente.

insurrection [ˌɪnsəˈrekʃən] [in-sa-rek-shon], *s.* Insurrección, levantamiento, conjuración, sedición, tumulto.

Insurrectional [ˌɪnsəˈrekʃənl] [in-sa-rek-sho-nal], **insurrectionary** [ˌɪnsəˈrekʃənərɪ] [in-sa-rek-sho-na-ri], *a.* Insurreccional, tumultuoso.

insusceptible [ˌɪnsəsˈseptɪbl] [in-sas-sep-ti-bol], *a.* No susceptible, insensible; incapaz de recibir modificación o impresión.

intact [ɪnˈtækt] [in-takt], *a.* Intacto, que no ha sufrido menoscabo; entero, íntegro (whole, complete).

intaglio [ɪnˈtægliəʊ] [in-ter-glio], *s.* Obra de entalladura.

intake [ˈɪnteɪk] [in-teik], *s.* 1. Acceso de aire. 2. Orificio de entrada o acceso de agua. 3. Canal de alimentación. 4. Válvula de aspiración. 5. Cosa tomada o cantidad de ella, toma, admisión. **Intake manifold,** válvula múltiple de admisión. 6. Consumo (food).

intangibility, intangibleness [ˈɪntændʒəˈbɪlɪtɪ] [in-tan-ya-bi-li-ti], *s.* Cualidad o estado de lo que es intangible.

intangible [ɪnˈtændʒəbl] [in-tan-yi-bol], *a.* Intangible, que no debe o no puede ser tocado; (*Fig.*) incomprensible a la mente.

integer [ˈɪntɪdʒər] [in-te-ga], *s.* Entero (number), un todo, total.

integral [ˈɪntɪgrəl] [in-ti-gral], *a.* 1. Íntegro, total, completo (whole). 2. Entero, perfecto; sano, lo que no está dividido en fracciones o quebrados. -*s.* El todo de una cosa considerado con relación a las partes que la componen.

integrally [ˈɪntɪgrəlɪ] [in-ti-gra-li], *adv.* Integralmente.

integrant [ˈɪntɪgrənt] [in-ti-grant], *a.* Integrante, integral, se aplica por lo común a las partes que entran en la composición de un todo. **Integrant molecule,** molécula integrante.

integrate [ˈɪntɪgreɪt] [in-ti-greit], *va.* 1. Integrar, formar un todo. 2. Indicar la suma. 3. (*Mat.*) Integrar. -*vn.* Integrarse, completarse, volverse entero.

integration [ˌɪntɪˈgreɪʃən] [in-ti-grei-shon], *s.* Reintegro, el acto de reintegrar.

integrator [ˈɪntɪgreɪtər] [in-ti-grei-ta], *s.* Integrador.

integrity [ɪnˈtɪgrɪtɪ] [in-ti-gri-ti], *s.* 1. Integridad, entereza. 2. Pureza, honradez (honesty).

integument [ɪnˈtegjʊmənt] [in-te-guiu-ment], *s.* Tegumento, integumento, cubierta natural de un animal o de una semilla.

integumentary, integumental [ɪnˈtegjʊməntərɪ] [in-te-guiu-men-ter-ri], *a.* Integumentario, que sirve de integumento o pertenece a él.

intellect [ˈɪntɪlekt] [in-ti-lekt], *s.* Entendimiento, inteligencia.

intellective [ˈɪntɪlektɪv] [in-ti-lek-tiv], *a.* Intelectivo, que tiene la facultad de entender; intelectual.

intellectual [ˌɪntɪˈlektjʊəl] [in-ti-lek-chual], *a.* Intelectual, mental, ideal. -*s.* (*Ant.*) Entendimiento.

intellectuality [ˌɪntɪˈlektjʊəlɪtɪ] [in-ti-lek-chua-li-ti], *s.* Entendimiento en la acepción de potencia, facultad intelectual; antiguamente, intelectualidad.

intelligence [ɪnˈtelɪdʒəns] [in-te-li-yens], *s.* 1. Inteligencia, conocimiento, comprensión, el acto de entender, penetración. 2. Informe, noticia, aviso. 3. Inteligencia, correspondencia mutua, armonía, amistad recíproca. 4. Un ser inteligente. 5. Servicio secreto, espionaje. **Intelligence quotient, I.Q.,** cociente Intelectual.

intelligencer [ɪnˈtelɪdʒənsər] [in-te-li-yen-se], *s.* El que comunica o envía avisos o noticias secretas o interesantes; noticiero, mensajero.

intelligence test [ɪnˈtelɪdʒənsˌtest] [in-te-li-yens-test], *s.* Prueba a examen para medir la inteligencia.

intelligent [ɪnˈtelɪdʒənt] [in-te-li-yent], *a.* 1. Inteligente, sabio, perito, instruído. 2. Sabio; distinguido por la inteligencia; bien informado. 3. Dotado de facultad intelectiva; que comprende y raciocina.

inteligently [ɪnˈtelɪdʒəntlɪ] [in-te-li-yent-li], *adv.* Inteligentemente.

intelligentsia [ɪnˈtelɪdʒəntsɪə] [in-te-li-yen-tsia], *s.* Círculo de los intelectuales, la clase intelectual.

intelligibility [ɪnˌtelɪdʒəˈbɪlɪtɪ] [in-te-li-yi-bi-li-ti], *s.* La posibilidad de ser comprendido o entendido; perspicuidad, claridad.

intelligible [ɪnˈtelɪdʒɪbl] [in-te-li-yi-bol], *a.* Inteligible.

intelligibleness [ɪnˈtelɪdʒɪblnɪs] [in-te-li-yi-bol-nes], *s.* Comprensiblidad, perspicuidad, claridad.

intelligibly [ɪnˈtelɪdʒɪblɪ] [in-te-li-yi-bli], *adv.* Inteligiblemente.

INTELSAT *Abreviatura de* **International Telecommunications Satellite Organization,** Organización Internacional de Telecomunicaciones por Satélite.

intemperance [ɪnˈtempərəns] [in-tem-pe-rans], *s.* Intemperancia, destemplanza, exceso, desarreglo; particularmente el uso inmoderado de las bebidas alcohólicas.

intemperate [ɪnˈtempəreɪt] [in-tem-pe-reit], *a.* 1. Destemplado; inmoderado, desenfrenado, desmandado, desarreglado (uncontrolled). 2. Intemperante, dado al uso excesivo de las bebidas alcohólicas. 3. Excesivo en carácter o grado (excessive).

intemperately [ɪnˈtempəreɪtlɪ] [in-tem-pe-reit-li], *adv.* Destempladamente, inmoderadamente, desarregladamente.

intend [ɪn'tend] [in-tend], *va*. 1. Intentar, tener ánimo o designio de ejecutar alguna cosa (try); destinar, aplicar, determinar, proyectar hacer, designar, proponerse (propose, design). **I did not intend it,** no era esa mi intención. 2. Dar a entender, significar, señalar. **What do you intend by that?,** ¿qué quiere decir con eso? 3. (*Ant.*) Fijar en un curso dado, dirigir; cuidar, mirar por.

intendancy [ɪn'tendənsɪ] [in-ten-dan-si], *s*. Intendencia, empleo de intendente.

intendant [ɪn'tendənt] [in-ten-dant], *s*. Intendente, el que tiene a su cargo la intendencia o dirección de algún ramo particular del servicio público. **Intendant of a province,** intendente o gobernador de una provincia o territorio.

intended [ɪn'tendɪd] [in-ten-did], *s*. (*Fam.*) 1. Desposado, novio; 2. Deseado.

intendedly [ɪn'tendɪdlɪ] [in-ten-did-li], *adv*. Adrede, con intención.

intendment [ɪn'tendmənt] [in-tend-ment], *s*. 1. (*For.*) El verdadero intento o la significación correcta de la ley. 2. (*Ant.*) Intento, designio, intención.

inteneration [ˌɪntenə'reɪʃən] [in-te-ne-rei-shon], *s*. Enternecimiento, el acto de enternecer.

intense [ɪn'tens] [in-tens], *a*. 1. Intenso, estirado, que tiene tensión, esforzado en alto grado (strong); vivo, ardiente, fogoso (ardent, vivid). 2. Excesivo, vehemente, violento, extremado, sumo. **Intense sufferings,** padecimientos excesivos violentos. 3. Intenso, que hace esfuerzos activos. 4. (*Foto.*) V. DENSE.

intensely [ɪn'tenslɪ] [in-tens-li], *adv*. Intensamente. **To speak intensely,** hablar con exageración.

intenseness [ɪn'tensnɪs] [in-tens-nes], *s*. Intensidad, vehemencia, fuerza, vigor; ardor; fogosidad. *V.* INTENSITY.

intensifier [ɪn'tensɪfaɪər] [in-ten-si-faiar], *s*. El que o lo que hace más intenso; disolución química usada en fotografía para hacer más intensas las imágenes negativas.

intensify [ɪn'tensɪfaɪ] [in-ten-si-fai], *va*. 1. Hacer o volver más intenso. 2. (*Foto.*) Aumentar la densidad de una película para obtener más marcados contrastes. -*vn*. Volverse intenso.

intension [ɪn'tenʃən] [in-ten-shon], *s*. 1. Intensión; grado. 2. Tensión. 3. (Lógica) El contenido.

intensity [ɪn'tensɪtɪ] [in-ten-si-ti], *s*. 1. Intensidad, exceso, fuerza, rigor (power). 2. Tensión, estado de lo que se halla tenso o estirado. 3. (*Fís.*) Intensidad, grado de actividad y fuerza de cualquier agente físico. 4. Fogosidad, ardor; aplicación constante del ánimo. 5. (*Foto.*) Contraste fuerte entre las luces y las sombras en una prueba negativa.

intensive [ɪn'tensɪv] [in-ten-siv], *a*. 1. Intensivo, que sirve para aumentar o hacer intenso; en gramática, que da énfasis. 2. Capaz de hacerse intenso. 3. Entero, completo, concentrado. 4. (Logic) Relativo al contenido.

intensively [ɪn'tensɪvlɪ] [in-ten-siv-li], *adv*. Intensivamente.

intent [ɪn'tent] [in-tent], *a*. Atento, cuidadoso, aplicado con ahinco (absorbed). -*s*. Intento, designio, deseo, intención, ánimo. **With intent to,** con el propósito de, con ánimo de. **To all intents and purposes,** en todos sentidos, para el caso. (*For.*) Para todos los casos y efectos que haya lugar. **To be intent on** o **upon,** estar absorto en, aplicado a. **To be wholly intent on,** pensar sólo en.

intention [ɪn'tenʃən] [in-ten-shon], *s*. 1. Intención, determinación de la voluntad, en un sentido determinado. 2. Intención, ánimo, designio, mira, fin. **With the best intentions,** con la mejor intención. **What are her intentions?,** ¿qué piensa hacer? 3. (*For.*) Propósito consciente de cometer una acción criminal. 4. (*Chyr.*) Curso o procedimiento natural. **Healing by first intention,** cura de primera intención, sin supuración. **Healing by second intention,** cura por cicatrización, después de la supuración.

intentional [ɪn'tenʃənl] [in-ten-sho-nal], *a*. Intencional, intencionado.

intentionally [ɪn'tenʃnəlɪ] [in-ten-sho-na-li], *adv*. Intencionalmente.

intently [ɪn'tentlɪ] [in-tent-li], *adv*. Ansiosamente; atentamente.

intentness [ɪn'tentnɪs] [in-tent-nes], *s*. Aplicación ansiosa, atención, afición.

inter ['ɪntər] [in-tar], *va*. Enterrar, soterrar, sepultar.

inter- ['ɪntər] [in-tar], prefijo, preposición latina que significa **entre, en medio** o **mutuamente;** entra en la composición de muchas voces.

interact [ˌɪntər'ækt] [in-te-rakt], *va*. Obrar entre sí, recíprocamente; afectar el uno al otro. (*Comput.*) Interactuar.

interact, *s*. Entreacto, intermedio, el espacio de tiempo entre los actos de las representaciones dramáticas.

interaction [ˌɪntər'ækʃən] [in-te-rak-shon], *s*. 1. Acción o influencia recíproca, interacción. 2. Acción intermedia.

interadditive [ˌɪntər'ædɪtɪv] [in-te-ra-di-tiv], *a*. Intercalar, ingerido o añadido a otra cosa, puesto entre paréntesis.

interamnian [ˌɪntər'æmnɪən] [in-te-ram-nian], *a*. Situado entre ríos.

interarticular [ˌɪntər'ɑːtɪkjʊlər] [in-te-rart-ti-kiu-lar], *a*. Interarticular, que está situado entre las articulaciones.

interbreed [ˌɪntə'briːd] [in-ter-brid], *va*. y *vn*. V. HYBRIDIZE.

intercalary [ɪn'tɜːkələrɪ] [in-ter-ka-la-ri], *a*. Intercalar, lo que se pone o introduce entre otras cosas.

intercalate [ɪn'tɜːkəleɪt] [in-ter-ka-leit], *va*. Intercalar, interponer.

intercalation [ɪnˌtɜːkə'leɪʃən] [in-ter-ka-lei-shon] *s*. Intercalación.

intercede ['ɪntəsiːd] [in-ter-sid], *vn*. 1. Interceder, mediar. 2. Interponerse, ponerse una cosa entre otras.

interceder [ˌɪntə'siːdər] [in-ter-si-dar], *s*. V. INTERCESSOR.

interceding [ˌɪntə'siːdɪŋ] [in-ter-si-din], *s*. Mediación, intercesión.

intercept [ˌɪntə'sept] [in-ter-sept], *va*. 1. Interceptar, coger, sorprender alguna carta o pliego antes de llegar a su destino. 2. Obstruir, cerrar el paso, impedir que vaya adelante alguna persona o cosa, o detenerla en su movimiento (stop). 3. Atajar (cut off).

interceptor [ˌɪntə'septər] [in-ter-sep-tar], *s*. Interceptor. **Interceptor missile,** (*Mil.*) Proyectil interceptor.

interception [ˌɪntə'sepʃən] [in-ter-sep-shon], *s*. Intercepción, interrupción de movimiento.

intercession [ˌɪntə'seʃən] [in-ter-se-shon], *s*. 1. Intercesión, mediación. 2. (Liturgy) Oración u oraciones para personas de diferente condición.

intercessory [ˌɪntə'seʃərɪ] [in-ter-se-so-ri], *s*. Intercesorio.

interchain [ˌɪntə'tʃeɪn] [in-ter-chein], *va*. Encadenar, entrelazar.

interchange ['ɪntə'tʃeɪndʒ] [in-ter-cheinch], *va*. 1. Alternar, variar una cosa repitiéndola sucesivamente. 2. Cambiar, trocar, permutar. -*vn*. Suceder alternativamente, con alternación.

interchange, *s*. 1. Comercio, negociación, tráfico, permuta de géneros (trade). 2. Sucesión mutua, vicisitud. 3. Donación recíproca o la acción de dar y recibir al mismo tiempo. 4. Intercambio. **Interchange of compliments,** Cortesías mutuas. **Interchange of gifts,** presentes o regalos recíprocos.

interchangeability [ˌɪntəˌtʃeɪndʒə'bɪlɪtɪ] [in-ter-chein-cha-bi-li-ti], *s*. Permutabilidad.

interchangeable [ˌɪntə'tʃeɪndʒəbl] [in-ter-chein-cha-bol], *a*. Permutable; sucesivo; mutuo, recíproco.

interchangeableness [ˌɪntə'tʃeɪndʒəblnɪs] [in-ter-chein-cha-bol-nes], *s*. Cambio, permuta, sucesión alternativa.

interchangeably [ˌɪntə'tʃeɪndʒəblɪ] [in-ter-chein-cha-bli], *adv*. Alternativamente, mutuamente, recíprocamente.

interchapter [ˌɪntə'tʃæptər] [in-ter-chap-tar], *s*. Capítulo interpuesto.

intercipient [ˌɪntə'sɪpɪənt] [in-ter-si-pient], *a*. Interceptador, que intercepta algo. -*s*. La cosa que intercepta.

inter-city ['ɪntə'sɪtɪ] [in-ter-si-ti], *s*. Tren intercity, tren de largo recorrido.

interclude [ˌɪntə'kluːd] [in-ter-klud], *va*. Obstruir o interceptar, ocultar a la vista.

interclusion [ˌɪntəˈkluːʃən] [in-ter-klu-shon], *s.* Intercepción, obstrucción.

intercollegiate [ˌɪntəkəˈliːdʒɪt] [in-ter-co-li-yeit], *a.* Interuniversitario.

intercolumnar [ˌɪntəˈkʌləmnəʳ] [in-ter-ka-lam-naʳ], *a.* Colocado entre columnas; intercolumnar.

intercom [ˈɪntəkɒm] [in-ter-kom], *s.* Interfono, intercomunicador.

intercommon [ˈɪntəkɒmən] [in-ter-ko-mon], *va.* (Hist. de GB) Proscribir a uno por sostener comunicación con malhechores o reos, o por albergarlos. -*vn.* 1. Tener unos mismos prados en común, cuando se habla de pueblos; alimentarse en los mismos prados, hablando de animales. 2. (Poc. us.) Comer en comunidad, a la misma mesa que otros, en mesa redonda.

intercommunicate [ˌɪntəkəˈmjuːnɪkeɪt] [in-ter-ko-miu-ni-keit], *vn.* Comunicar con otro; sostener comunicación.

intercommunication [ˈɪntəkəmjuːnɪˈkeɪʃən] [in-ter-ko-miu-ni-kei-shon], *s.* Comunicación mutua o recíproca.

intercontinental [ˌɪntəkɒnˈtɪnəntl] [in-ter-kon-ti-nen-tal], *a.* Intercontinental. **Intercontinental ballistic missile**, proyectil de alcance intercontinental.

intercostal [ˌɪntəˈkɒstl] [in-ter-kos-tal], *a.* Intercostal.

intercourse [ˌɪntəˈkɔːs] [in-ter-kors], *s.* 1. Comercio, tráfico, cambios comerciales entre varios países. 2. Comunicación, correspondencia, trato. **Intercourse of trade**, giro de comercio. **Sexual intercourse**, cópula, coito.

intercross [ˌɪntəˈkrɒs] [in-ter-kros], *va.* 1. Entrecruzar, cruzarse mutuamente, como las líneas. 2. Cruzar castas o razas de animales o de plantas; hibridar.

intercurrence [ˌɪntəˈkɜːrəns] [in-ter-ke-rens], *s.* Intercurrente, paso o tránsito entre dos parajes, intervención, ocurrencia.

intercurrent [ˌɪntəˈkɜːrənt] [in-ter-ke-rent], *a.* Lo que corre entre dos parajes, lo que interviene u ocurre mientras se está haciendo alguna cosa.

intercutaneous [ˌɪntəkʌˈteɪnɪəs] [in-ter-ka-tei-nios], *a.* Intercutáneo.

interdenominational [ˈɪntədɪˌnɒmɪˈneɪʃnl] [in-ter-di-no-mi-nei-sho-nal], *a.* Intersectario.

interdepartmental [ˈɪntədɪpɑːtˈmentl] [in-ter-di-par-men-tal], *a.* Interdepartamental.

interdependence [ˌɪntəˈdɪpəndəns] [in-ter-di-pen-dans], *s.* Dependencia mutua.

interdependent [ˌɪntəˈdɪpəndənt] [in-ter-di-pen-dant], *a.* Que depende recíprocamente.

interdict [ˈɪntədɪkt] [in-ter-dikt], *va.* 1. Prohibir, vedar (antiguamente, entredecir o interdecir). 2. Entredecir, poner entredicho.

interdict, *s.* 1. Prohibición, mandato prohibitiorio. 2. Interdicción, entredicho, censura eclesiástica.

interdiction [ˈɪntədɪkʃən] [in-ter-dik-shon], *s.* Interdicción, prohibición.

interdictive [ˈɪntədɪktɪv] [in-ter-dik-tiv], *a.* Lo que entredice o tiene poder de prohibir o de entredecir.

interdictory [ˈɪntədɪktərɪ] [in-ter-dik-to-ri], *a.* Lo que pertenece a prohibición o entredicho.

interdigital [ˌɪntəˈdɪdʒɪtəl] [in-ter-di-chi-tal], *a.* Interdigital, situado entre los dedos.

interdisciplinary [ˌɪntəˈdɪsɪplɪnərɪ] [in-ter-di-si-pli-na-ri], *a.* Interdisciplinario.

interest [ˈɪntrɪst] [in-te-rest], *va.* 1. Interesar, hacer tomar parte en alguna cosa (participate). 2. Interesar, empeñar, hacer tomar parte a la voluntad o al corazón en algo. -*vn.* Interesarse, tomar parte.

interest, *s.* 1. Interés, provecho, utilidad (profit, advantage). 2. Interés, la parte que se toma en el logro de alguna cosa; influjo, empeño (insistance). 3. Interés, la parte que se toma en alguna negociación lucrativa, lucro del capital, cantidad que se paga por el uso del dinero (benefit). 4. Propiedad parcial, porción o derecho copropietario. 5. Influencia, el poder de procurar favorable consideración, influjo. 6. Viva simpatía, curiosidad (curiosity). **To show interest**, mostrar interés, interesarse. **To take no further interest**, dejar de interesarse, perder interés. **Compound interest**, interés compuesto. **To put out on interest**, dar a interés. **To bear five per cent interest**, producir cinco por ciento de interés. **To act in someone's interests**, obrar en beneficio de alguien. **Interest rate**, tipo de interés.

interesting [ˈɪntrɪstɪŋ] [in-te-res-tin], *a.* Interesante, atractivo. **In an interesting condition**, en estado interesante, en cinta.

interface [ˈɪntəfeɪs] [in-ter-feis], *sf. (Comput.)* Interfaz.

interfere [ˌɪntəˈfɪəʳ] [in-ter-fiaʳ], *vn.* 1. Interponerse, meterse, mezclarse, intervenir; especialmente, embarazar, poner obstáculos, impedir; algunas veces, entremeterse. 2. Chocar, oponerse mutuamente. 3. (*Vet.*) Rozarse o herirse un pie con el otro al andar (horses).

interference [ˌɪntəˈfɪərəns] [in-ter-fia-rans], *s.* 1. Estorbo, obstáculo. 2. Ingerencia, entremetimiento. 3. Interposición, intervención. 4. Interferencia. 5. Ruidos parásitos. **Interference filter**, antiparásito.

interfering [ˌɪntəˈfɪərɪŋ] [in-ter-fia-rin], *a.* Entrometido, curioso.

interfluent [ˌɪntəˈfloənt] [in-ter-fluent], **interflueous** [ˌɪntəˈfloəs] [in-ter-fluos], *a.* Lo que fluye por medio de otra cosa.

interfulgent [ˌɪntəˈfʊldʒənt] [in-ter-ful-chent], *a.* Lo que luce o resplandece entre otras cosas.

interfuse [ˌɪntəˈfjuːz] [in-ter-fius], *va.* 1. Hacer fluir juntamente, como dos fluidos; hacer pasar a través de los poros. 2. Entremezclar, producir una mezcla. -*vn.* Fluir uno en otro, mezclarse.

intergalactic [ˌɪntəgəˈlæktɪk] [in-ter-ga-lak-tik], *a.* Intergaláctico.

interim [ˈɪntərɪm] [in-te-rim], *s.* Intermedio, interin, el espacio que hay entre un tiempo y otro. **In this interim**, en el interin, entretanto, mientras esto sucedía.

interior [ɪnˈtɪərɪəʳ] [in-te-riaʳ], *a.* Interior, interno, lo que está en la parte de dentro. -*s.* El interior.

interiorly [ɪnˈtɪərɪəlɪ] [in-te-riar-li], *adv.* Interiormente.

interjacent [ˌɪntəˈdʒəsənt] [in-ter-ya-sent], *a.* Interyacente, interpuesto, situado en medio de otras cosas.

interject [ˈɪntədʒekt] [in-ter-yekt], *va.* Poner en medio, insertar. -*vn.* Interponer, intervenir.

interjection [ˌɪntəˈdʒekʃən] [in-ter-yek-shon], *s.* 1. Interjección, una de las partes de la oración. 2. Intervención, interposición.

interjoin [ˌɪntəˈdʒɔɪn] [in-ter-yoin], *va.* Unir mutuamente, también, casar entre sí a cuatro o más personas de dos familias.

interlace [ˌɪntəˈleɪs] [in-ter-leis], *va.* Entrelazar, entremezclar.

interlard [ˈɪntəlɑːd] [in-ter-lard], *va.* 1. Mechar, introducir mechas o rajitas de tocino gordo en la carne de las aves u otras viandas. 2. Entreponer, insertar. 3. Entremezclar, entretejer.

interleave [ˌɪntəˈliːv] [in-ter-liv], *va.* Interpolar o interponer hojas blancas entre las escritas o impresas de un libro.

interline [ˌɪntəˈlaɪn] [in-ter-lain], *va.* Interlinear, entrerreglonar, insertar escribiendo entre renglones.

interlinear [ˌɪntəˈlaɪnəʳ] [in-ter-lai-naʳ], **interlineary** [ˌɪntəˈlaɪnərɪ] [in-ter-lai-na-ri], *a.* Interlineal.

interlineation [ˌɪntəˈlaɪnɪˈeɪʃən] [in-ter-lai-nei-shon], *s.* Interlineación, corrección interlineal.

interlining [ˌɪntəˈlaɪnɪŋ] [in-ter-lai-nin], *s.* 1. Entretela. 2. Interlineación, corrección interlineal.

interlink [ˌɪntəˈlɪŋk] [in-ter-link], *va.* Eslabonar, encadenar.

interlocation [ˌɪntələˈkeɪʃən] [in-ter-lo-kei-shon], *s.* Interposición.

interlock [ˌɪntəˈlɒk] [in-ter-lok], *va.* y *vn.* Trabar, unir uno con otro por mutua acción; unirse, entrelazarse una cosa con otra.

interlocution [ˌɪntəˈlɒkjʊʃən] [in-ter-lo-kiu-shon], *s.* 1. Interlocución, plática o conferencia alternada entre dos o más personas. 2. Auto interlocutorio.

interlocutor [ˌɪntəˈlɒkjʊtəʳ] [in-ter-lo-kiu-taʳ], *s.* Interlocutor.

interlocutory [ˌɪntəˈlɒkjʊtərɪ] [in-ter-lo-kiu-to-ri], *a.* 1. Dialogístico, que se compone de diálogos o conferencias entre dos o más personas. 2. Interlocutorio, auto o sentencia interlocutoria.

interlope [ˈɪntələʊp] [in-ter-loup], *vn.* Entremeterse sin derecho; mezclarse en partidos o bandos; traficar sin licencia.

interloper [ˈɪntələʊpəʳ] [in-ter-lou-paʳ], *s.* 1. Entremetido, el que se mete en asuntos que no le atañen. 2. El que trafica en un comercio que por derecho pertenece a otros, intérlope.

interlude [ˈɪntəluːd] [in-ter-lud], *s.* 1. Intermedio, baile, sainete, farsa, etc., representada entre los actos o jornadas de una pieza dramática. 2. Pasaje musical corto que se toca, como intervalo o transición, entre las partes de un himno, de una composición sagrada, etc. 3. *(Mús.)* Interludio.

interlunar [ˈɪntələʊnəʳ] [in-ter-lu-naʳ], **interlunary** [ˈɪntələnərɪ] [in-ter-lu-na-ri], *a.* Perteneciente al interlunio.

intermarriage [ˌɪntəˈmærɪdʒ] [in-ter-ma-rich], *s.* Matrimonio o casamiento mutuo que se celebra entre dos familias; v.g. dos hermanas con dos hermanas.

intermarry [ˌɪntəˈmærɪ] [in-ter-ma-ri], *vn.* Casarse mutuamente cuatro o más personas de dos familias.

intermeddle [ˌɪntəˈmedl] [in-ter-me-del], *vn.* Entremeterse, meterse uno o ingerirse donde no le llaman o mezclarse en lo que no le toca. -*va.* Entremezclar, mezclar (mix up).

intermeddler [ˌɪntəˈmedləʳ] [in-ter-med-laʳ], *s.* Entremetido.

intermedial [ˌɪntəˈmiːdɪəl] [in-ter-mi-dial], **intermediate** [ˌɪntəˈmiːdɪət] [in-ter-mi-diet], *s.* Intermedio, intermediado. -*s.* 1. Agente intermedio, algunas veces, medio o médium espiritista. 2. *V.* INTERMEDIATION.

intermediary [ˌɪntəˈmiːdɪərɪ] [in-ter-mi-dia-ri], *a.* Intermediario.

intermediate [ˌɪntəˈmiːdɪət] [in-ter-mi-diet], *a.* Intermedio, mediano. **Intermediate range ballistic missile,** *(Mil.)* Proyectil de alcance intermedio.

intermediation [ˈɪntəmiːdɪˈreɪʃən] [in-ter-mi-diei-shon], *s.* Intervención, mediación.

intermedium [ˌɪntəˈmiːdɪəm] [in-ter-mi-diom], *s.* Intermedio, agente intermedio.

interment [ɪnˈtɜːment] [in-ter-ment], *s.* Entierro, sepultura, funeral.

intermigration [ˌɪntəmɪˈɡreɪʃən] [in-ter-mi-grei-shon], *s.* Mudanza recíproca de una parte a otra.

interminable [ˌɪntəˈmɪnəbl] [in-ter-mi-na-bol], *a.* Interminable, ilimitado (endless). -*s.* El Ser infinito, Dios.

interminably [ˌɪntəˈmɪnəblɪ] [in-ter-mi-na-bli], *adv.* Interminablemente, como si no tuviera fin.

intermingle [ˌɪntəˈmɪŋl] [in-ter-min-guel], *va.* Entremezclar. -*vn.* Mezclarse.

intermission [ˌɪntəˈmɪʃən] [in-ter-mi-shon], *s.* 1. Intermisión, interrupción. 2. Intermisión, tiempo intermedio.

intermissive [ˌɪntəˈmɪsɪv] [in-ter-mi-siv], *a.* Intermitente.

intermit [ˈɪntəmɪt] [in-ter-mit], *va.* Intermitir. -*vn.* Descontinuar o cesar la calentura; cesar o parar un rato alguna acción o movimiento para principiar otra vez después; suspender.

intermittent [ˌɪntəˈmɪtənt] [in-ter-mi-tent], *a.* Intermitente.

intermittently [ˌɪntəˈmɪtəntlɪ] [in-ter-mi-tent-li], *adv.* A intervalos, intermitentemente.

intermix [ˌɪntəˈmɪks] [in-ter-miks], *va.* entremezclar, mezclar unas cosas con otras. -*vn.* Entremezclarse, mezclarse.

intermixture [ˌɪntəˈmɪkstʃəʳ] [in-ter-miks-chaʳ], *s.* 1. Mezcla de una cosa con otra. 2. Masa de ingredientes mezclados. 3. Un ingrediente adicional; mezcla, cantidad añadida.

intermundane [ˌɪntəˈmɪndeɪn] [in-ter-mun-dein], *a.* Entremundano, situado entre mundos, como el espacio.

intermural [ˌɪntəˈmɔərəl] [in-ter-miu-ral], *a.* Entremural, emparedado: colocado entre muros.

intern [ɪnˈtɜːn] [in-tern], *a.* (Poco us.) Interno, intestino. -*s.* Médico o cirujano residente en un hospital.

intern, *va.* Internar, encerrar en un lugar determinado, poner bajo vigilancia. -*vn.* Trabajar en un hospital como méidco interno.

internal [ɪnˈtɜːnl] [in-ter-nal], *a.* 1. Interno, interior, doméstico (interior). 2. Intrínseco, real, inherente (intrinsic), basado en las mismas cosas: derivado de lo interior o de la substancia: como **internal evidence**, prueba íntima, testimonio derivado de la cosa misma. 3. Interior, intestino, que se halla dentro del cuerpo social.

internally [ɪnˈtɜːnəlɪ] [in-ter-na-li], *adv.* Internamente; mentalmente, intelectualmente.

international [ˌɪntəˈnæʃnəl] [in-ter-nei-sho-nal], *a.* Internacional, lo concerniente a dos o más naciones entre sí. **International law,** derecho internacional.

internationalism [ˌɪntəˈnæʃnəlɪzəm] [in-ter-nei-sho-na-li-sem], *sm.* Internacionalismo.

internationalist [ˌɪntəˈnæʃnəlɪst] [in-ter-nei-sho-na-list], *a.* Internacionalista.

internationalize [ˌɪntəˈnæʃnəlaɪz] [in-ter-nei-sho-na-lais], *va.* Internacionalizar.

internecine [ˌɪntəˈniːsaɪn] [in-ter-ni-sain], *a.* Lo que es recíprocamente destructivo. **Internecine war,** guerra a muerte.

internet [ˈɪntənet] [in-ter-net], *s.* Internet. **To surf the internet,** navegar por Internet.

internode, internodium [ˈɪntənəʊd] [in-ter-noud], *s.* 1. *(Bot.)* Internodio, entrenudo, espacio o intervalo entre los nudos de las plantas o de los árboles. 2. *(Anat.)* Parte situada entre dos articulaciones.

internship [ˈɪntɜːnʃɪp] [in-tern-ship], *s.* Internado (en un hospital, etc.)

internuncio [ˌɪntəˈnʌnʃə] [in-ter-nan-sho], *s.* 1. Internuncio, el que habla por otro o lleva mensajes de una parte a otra. 2. Internuncio, ministro pontificio que hace veces de nuncio.

interpellate [ɪnˈtɜːpəleɪt] [in-ter-pe-leit], *va.* Interpelar; dirigir una excitación al gobierno para que dé explicaciones sobre un hecho o sobre su conducta en circunstancias especiales.

interpellation [ˌɪntɜːpəˈleɪʃən] [in-ter-pe-lei-shon], *s.* 1. Interpelación, acción de interpelar; excitación hecha a un gobierno o a una persona para que dé explicaciones. 2. Interrupción. 3. Ruego o súplica ardiente. 4. Interpelación, citación que se hace en justicia para que responda o comparezca un reo.

interpenetrate [ˌɪntɜːˈpenətreɪt] [in-ter-pe-ne-treit], *va. y vn.* Penetrar completamente; penetrarse mutuamente, formar unión por medio de la penetración.

interphone [ˈɪntəfəʊn] [in-ter-foun], *sm.* Interfono.

interplanetary [ˌɪntəˈplænɪtərɪ] [in-ter-pla-ne-ter-ri], *a.* Interplanetario.

interplay [ˈɪntəpleɪ] [in-ter-plei], *s.* 1. Acción o influencia mutuas. 2. Acción o efecto recíprocos, interacción.

interplead [ˈɪntəpliːd] [in-ter-plid], *vn.* (*For.*) Litigar entre sí dos o más demandantes, para que el tribunal resuelva sobre la propiedad de una cosa.

interpleader [ˈɪntəpliːdəʳ] [in-ter-pli-daʳ], *s.* (*For.*) Procedimiento para determinar cuál entre dos o más personas es el dueño legal de la cosa litigada.

interpledge [ˈɪntəpledʒ] [in-ter-pledch], *va.* Dar y tomar recíprocamente una cosa como prenda.

interpolate [ɪnˈtɜːpəleɪt] [in-ter-po-leit], *va.* 1. Interpolar, insertar una palabra, cláusula o frase en un escrito, sea para completar, sea para alterar el sentido; falsificar. 2. Interpolar, interponer una cosa entre otras.

interpolation [ɪnˌtɜːpəˈleɪʃən] [in-ter-po-lei-shon], *s.* Interpolación, añadidura o entrerrenglonadura de una palabra o frase en un manuscrito antiguo.

interpolator [ɪnˌtɜːpəˈleɪtəʳ] [in-ter-po-lei-taʳ], *s.* Interpolador, el que añade subrepticiamente alguna palabra o frase a un manuscrito antiguo.

interposal [ˌɪntəˈpəʊzl] [in-ter-pau-sal], *s.* 1. Interposición, mediación de alguna persona entre otras dos. 2. Intervención, asistencia.

interpose [ˌɪntəˈpəʊz] [in-ter-paus], *va.* 1. Interponer, entreponer (remark). 2. Interponer el favor, crédito, autoridad, etc., en beneficio de alguno. -*vn.* 1. Interponerse, mediar entre dos personas desavenidas para componerlas entre sí. 2. Intervenir; interponerse una cosa entre otras. 3. Interrumpir a alguno, hacer objeción.

interpret [ɪnˈtɜːprɪt] [in-ter-prit], *va.* 1. Interpretar, explicar o explanar el sentido de alguna cosa (show). 2. Dar sentido a lo que no lo tiene; descifrar (understand, decipher). 3. Representar, ilustrar (represent). 4. Traducir oralmente, como intérprete (translate).

interpretable [ɪnˈtɜːprɪtəbl] [in-ter-pri-ter-bol], *a.* Interpretable, que es capaz de interpretación o explanación.

interpretation [ɪnˌtɜːprɪˈteɪʃən] [in-ter-pri-tei-shon], *s.* 1. Interpretación, acción de interpretar (meaning). **What interpretation are we to place on his conduct?**, ¿cómo hemos de interpretar su conducta? 2. Explicación, exposición; el sentido dado por un intérprete o un expositor.

interpretative [ɪnˈtɜːprɪtətɪv] [in-ter-pri-ter-tiv], *a.* Interpretativo.

interpreter [ɪnˈtɜːprɪtəʳ] [in-ter-pri-taʳ], *s.* Intérprete, traductor, el que interpreta o traduce de un idioma a otro, en especial el que lo hace oralmente.

interpreting [ɪnˈtɜːprɪtɪŋ] [in-ter-pri-tin], *sf.* Interpretación.

interregnum, interreign [ˌɪntəˈreɪn] [in-ter-rein], *s.* Interregno, espacio de tiempo en que un trono está vacante. 2. Suspensión de la autoridad ejecutiva a causa de un cambio de gobierno. 3. Cualquier período de espera, transición o desorden.

interrelate [ˌɪntəˈrɪleɪt] [in-ter-ri-leit], *vt.* Interrelacionar.

interrelated [ˌɪntəˈrɪleɪtɪd] [in-ter-ri-lei-tid], *a.* Correlativo, con relación recíproca.

interrelation [ˌɪntəˈrɪleɪʃən] [in-ter-ri-lei-shon], *sf.* Interrelación.

interrogate [ɪnˈterəgeɪt] [in-te-ro-gueit], *va.* Interrogar, preguntar, examinar, -*vn.* Interrogar, hacer un interrogatorio.

interrogation [ɪnˌterəˈgeɪʃən] [in-te-ro-guei-shon], *s.* 1. Interrogación, pregunta, pesquisa. 2. Interrogación, signo interrogativo(?).

interrogative [ˌɪntəˈrɒgətɪv] [in-te-ro-ga-tiv], *s.* Pronombre interrogativo, que se usa cuando se pregunta alguna cosa, como **who? what?** ¿quién? ¿qué? -*a.* Interrogativo.

interrogatively [ˌɪntəˈrɒgətɪvlɪ] [in-te-ro-ga-tiv-li], *adv.* Interrogativamente.

interrogator [ɪnˈterəgeɪtəʳ] [in-te-ro-guei-taʳ], *s.* Interrogante.

interrogatory [ˌɪntəˈrɒgətərɪ] [in-te-ro-ga-to-ri], *s.* Interrogatorio, la serie de preguntas que se hacen al acusado o parte y a los testigos. -*a.* Interrogativo, que expresa una pregunta.

interrupt [ˌɪntəˈrʌpt] [in-te-rapt], *va.* 1. Interrumpir, estorbar, impedir la continuación de una cosa. 2. Dividir, separar, entrecortar, romper la continuidad o la sucesión de.

interruptedly [ˌɪntəˈrʌptɪdlɪ] [in-te-rap-tid-li], *adv.* Interrumpidamente.

interrupter [ˌɪntəˈrʌptəʳ] [in-te-rap-taʳ], *s.* Interruptor, el que interrumpe o impide alguna cosa; útil para interrumpir la corriente eléctrica.

interruption [ˌɪntəˈrʌpʃən] [in-te-rap-shon], *s.* Interrupción, embarazo, obstáculo; interposición; intermisión.

interscapular [ˌɪntəˈzkæpjələʳ] [in-ters-ka-piu-laʳ], *a.* Interescapular, que está situado entre ambas escápulas.

interscholastic [ˌɪntəskəˈlæstɪk] [in-ters-ko-las-tik], *a.* Interescolar.

intersect [ˌɪntəˈsekt] [in-ter-sekt], *va.* Entrecortar. -*vn.* (*Geom.*) Intersecarse, cortarse dos líneas.

intersection [ˌɪntəˈsekʃən] [in-ter-sek-shon], *s.* Intersección.

interspace [ˌɪntəˈspeɪs] [in-ter-speis], *s.* Intervalo, intersticio, espacio que media entre varios cuerpos.

interspace, *va.* Hacer intervalos entre dos o más cuerpos; ocupar los intersticios entre ellos.

intersperse [ˌɪntəˈspɜːs] [in-ter-spers], *va.* Esparcir una cosa entre otras; entremezclar; diseminar.

interspersion [ˌɪntəˈspɜːʃən] [in-ter-sper-shon], *s.* El acto de esparcir una cosa entre otras.

interspinal [ˌɪntəˈspɪnəl] [in-ter-spi-nal], **interspinous** [ˌɪntəˈspɪnəs] [in-ter-spi-nos], *a.* Interespinoso, interespinal, situado entre las apófisis de las vértebras.

interstate [ˌɪntəˈsteɪt] [in-ter-steit], *a.* Que se refiere a las relaciones y al tráfico entre diferentes estados, se aplica particularmente a los estados que forman la confederación norteamericana. **Interstate commerce**, comercio interior, entre los varios estados.

interstellar [ˌɪntəˈsteləʳ] [in-ter-ste-laʳ], *a.* Que está situado entre las estrellas: interestelar.

interstice [ˌɪntəˈstɪs] [in-ter-stis], *s.* 1. Intersticio, intervalo o espacio que hay de una cosa a otra. 2. Intersticio, intermedio, intervalo, el espacio de tiempo que media entre un acto y otro.

intertexture [ˌɪntəˈtekstʃəʳ] [in-ter-tek-chaʳ], *s.* El entretejido o enlazamiento de una cosa con otra.

intertwine [ˌɪntəˈtwaɪn] [in-ter-tuain], **intertwist** [ˌɪntəˈtwɪst] [in-ter-tuist], *va.* Entretejer, entrelazar o tejer una cosa con otra.

interurban [ˌɪntəˈɜːbən] [in-ter-er-ban], *a.* Interurbano.

interval [ˈɪntəvəl] [in-ter-val], *s.* 1. Intervalo, intersticio, distancia de un lugar a otro (distance). 2. Intervalo, el tiempo que pasa entre una cosa y otra (time). 3. (*Mús.*) Intervalo, distancia que media de un tomo a otro. 4. Remisión o intermisión de algún mal. **Lucid interval**, intervalo lúcido, el espacio de tiempo en que los delirantes gozan algún alivio en su mal. **An interval for meditation**, una pausa para la meditación. **Without an interval**, sin parar, sin interrupción.

interveined [ˌɪntəˈviːnd] [in-ter-veind], *a.* Interpolado o cortado como las venas.

intervene [ˌɪntəˈviːn] [in-ter-vin], *vn.* 1. Intervenir, mediar, ponerse por medio, interponerse (take part, contribute); ocurrir, sobrevenir (happen). 2. Interponer con algún fin. 3. Sobrevenir algo de manera que sirva de obstáculo o impedimento. **I shall come if nothing intervenes**, vendré si nada ocurre que lo impida.

intervenient [ˌɪntəˈviːnɪənt] [in-ter-vi-niant], *a.* Interpuesto; ocurrido.

intervention [ˌɪntəˈvenʃən] [in-ter-ven-shon], *s.* 1. Intervención, asistencia, concurrencia en algún negocio. 2. Interposición, mediación.

interventionism [ˌɪntəˈvenʃnɪzm] [in-ter-ven-sho-ni-sem], *sm.* Dirigismo.

intervertebral [ˌɪntəˈvɜːtəbrəl] [in-ter-ver-te-bral], *a.* Intervertebral, que se halla situado entre las vértebras.

interwee [ˌɪntəˈwiː] [in-ter-ui], *s.* Persona entrevistada.

interview [ˈɪntəvjuː] [in-ter-viu], *s.* 1. Vistas, entrevista, conferencia, el encuentro o concurrencia de personas citadas para verse y conferenciar. 2. Abocamiento, conferencia verbal, cita entre dos o más personas para conferenciar mutuamente; particularmente en el periodismo, conferencia con alguien cuya opinión o cuyos informes se solicitan para publicarlos; y el relato de lo dicho u ocurrido en esa conferencia.

interview, *va.* Celebrar una entrevista con alguno; en el periodismo, interrogar a una persona para obtener de ella informes destinados a la publicación.

interviewer [ˈɪntəvjuəʳ] [in-ter-viuaʳ], *s.* Periodista que se avista y conferencia con los hombres de Estado, artistas y otras personas que por cualquier concepto llaman la atención pública.

intervolve [ˌɪntəˈvɒlv] [in-ter-voulv], *va.* Envolver una cosa dentro de otra.

interweave [ˌɪntəˈwiːv] [in-ter-uiv], *va.* Entretejer, enlazar, entremeter o meter una cosa entre otra.

interweaving [ˌɪntəˈwiːvɪŋ] [in-ter-ui-vin], *s.* Entretejedura.

interwreathe [ˌɪntəˈwriːθ] [in-ter-vrez], *va.* Tejer en forma de guirnalda.

intestable [ɪnˈtestəbl] [in-tes-ta-bol], *a.* El que legalmente no puede testar o hacer testamento.

intestacy [ɪnˈtestəsɪ] [in-tes-ta-si], *s.* La falta de testamento.

intestate [ɪnˈtestɪt] [in-tes-teit], *a.* Intestado, el que muere sin hacer testamento.

intestinal [ˌɪntesˈtaɪnl] [in-tes-tai-nal], a. 1. Intestinal, perteneciente o relativo a intestinos. 2. Interior, intestino.

intestine [ɪnˈtestaɪn] [in-tes-tain], a. Interior, intestino, doméstico. -s. Intestino, tripa: se usa por lo común en plural.

intextured [ɪnˈteksʃəd] [in-teks-chad], a. Entretejido, labrado, adornado con labores.

inthrall [ɪnˈθrɔːl] [in-zrol], va. Esclavizar. V. ENTHRALL.

inthralment [ɪnˈθrɔːlmənt] [in-zrol-ment], s. Esclavitud.

inthrone, va. V. ENTHRONE, etc.

intimacy [ˈɪntɪməsɪ] [in-ti-ma-si], s. Intimidad, familiaridad, confianza.

intimate [ˈɪntɪmɪt] [in-ti-meit], a. 1. Íntimo, interior, cordial, familiar. 2. Que se adhiere estrechamente. 3. Interno, que procede de lo interior. -s. Amigo íntimo o de toda confianza.

intimate, va. Insinuar, dar a entender alguna cosa indirectamente o por medio de rodeos.

intimately [ˈɪntɪmɪtlɪ] [in-ti-mit-li], adv. 1. Íntimamente, estrechamente, familiarmente. 2. En el fondo del alma; con afecto particular.

intimation [ˌɪntɪˈmeɪʃən] [in-ti-mei-shon], s. Insinuación, indirecta, prevención; aviso indirecto.

intimidate [ɪnˈtɪmɪdeɪt] [in-ti-mi-deit], va. Intimidar, poner o causar miedo o temor; aterrar, espantar.

intimidation [ɪnˌtɪmɪˈdeɪʃən] [in-ti-mi-dei-shon], s. Intimidación.

intimidatory [ˈɪntɪmɪdətərɪ] [in-ti-mi-da-to-ri], a. Intimidador, que intimida.

into [ˈɪntʊ] [in-tu], prep. 1. En, dentro, adentro, hacia el interior de. Denota: (a) entrada en, (b) penetración a través de algo, (c) inserción, inclusión, (d) cambio de estado, (e) por, multiplicado por. 2. Además de. **What are you into?**, ¿a qué te dedicas? **Into the bargain**, además del trato, por demás, como adición. **To change something into something else**, convertir algo en otra cosa. **To go off into the desert**, adentrarse en el desierto. **To get into a plane**, subirse a un avión. **To walk into**, entrar en. **The lorry drove into the car**, el camión chocó contra el coche. **To be into something**, dedicarse a, apasionarse por.

intolerable [ɪnˈtɒlərəbl] [in-to-le-ra-bol], a. Intolerable, lo que no se puede sufrir o tolerar.

intolerableness [ɪnˈtɒlərəblnɪs] [in-to-le-ra-bol-nes], s. Intolerabilidad.

intolerably [ɪnˈtɒlərəblɪ] [in-to-le-ra-bli], adv. Intolerablemente.

intolerance [ɪnˈtɒlərəns] [in-to-le-rans], s. Intolerancia.

intolerant [ɪnˈtɒlərənt] [in-to-le-rant], a. Intolerante, falto de tolerancia. -s. El que no aguanta ni sufre; el que no puede aguantar o sufrir.

intolerated [ɪnˈtɒləreɪtɪd] [in-to-le-rei-tid], a. Lo que no es tolerado.

intoleration [ɪnˈtɒləˈreɪʃən] [in-to-le-rei-shon], s. Intolerantismo.

intomb [ɪnˈtomb] [in-tomb], va. Enterrar, sepultar, poner en un sepulcro.

intonate [ɪnˈtəʊneɪt] [in-tou-neit], vn. 1. Entonar, solfear, cantar. 2. (Des.) Tronar.

intonation [ɪnˈtəʊneɪʃən] [in-tou-nei-shon], s. 1. La modulación de la voz al hablar. 2. Entonación; la acción de entonar.

intone [ɪnˈtəʊn] [in-toun], va. y vn. 1. Entonar, dar tono a las voces. 2. Recitar monótonamente, salmodiar; cantar el oficio de la iglesia.

intorsion, s. V. INTORTION.

intoxicant [ɪnˈtɒksɪkənt] [in-tok-si-kant], s. Lo que emborracha o embriaga, como el alcohol y el opio.

intoxicate [ɪnˈtɒksɪkeɪt] [in-tok-si-keit], a. Emborrachado, borracho, embriagado.

intoxicated [ɪnˈtɒksɪkeɪtɪd] [in-tok-si-kei-tid], a. Ebrio, borracho (drunk). **Intoxidated with joy**, frenético de alegría.

intoxication [ɪnˌtɒksɪˈkeɪʃən] [in-tok-si-kei-shon], s. 1. Embriaguez, borrachera (drunkenness). 2. Trasportamiento, arrebatamiento, entusiasmo. 3. (Med.) Intoxicación, envenenamiento.

intra- [ˈɪntrə] [in-tra], prefijo; preposición latina que significa dentro.

intractable [ɪnˈtræktəbl] [in-trak-ter-bol], a. Intratable, áspero, terco (akward).

intractableness [ˌɪntrækˈtəblnɪs] [in-trak-ter-bol-nes], s. Obstinación, porfía, terquedad (akwardness).

intractably [ˌɪntrækˈtəblɪ] [in-trak-ter-bli], adv. Obstinadamente, porfiadamente.

intramural [ˌɪntrəˈmjʊərəl] [in-tra-miu-ral], a. Intramuros, que se halla dentro de los muros.

intranquility [ˌɪntrənˈkwɪlɪtɪ] [in-tran-kui-li-ti], s. Desasosiego, falta de tranquilidad; intranquilidad.

intransient [ɪnˈtrænsɪənt] [in-tran-sient], a. Permanente, que no se muda o cambia fácilmente; inmutable.

intransigent [ɪnˈtrænsɪdʒənt] [in-tran-si-yent], a. Intransigente.

intransitive [ɪnˈtrænsɪtɪv] [in-tran-si-tiv], a. Intransitivo.

intransitively [ɪnˌtrænsɪˈtɪvlɪ] [in-tran-si-tiv-li], adv. Intransitivamente.

intransmutability [ɪnˌtrænsmjʊtəˈbɪlɪtɪ] [in-trans-miu-ter-bi-li-ti], s. Intransmutabilidad.

intransmutable [ɪnˌtrænsˈmjʊtəbl] [in-trans-miu-ter-bol], a. Intransmutable, lo que no se puede mudar.

intrant [ɪnˈtrənt] [in-trant], a. Entrante, que entra.

intravenous [ˌɪntrəˈviːnəs] [in-tra-vi-nos], a. Intravenoso. **Intravenous shot**, inyección intravenosa.

intravenously [ˌɪntrəˈviːnəslɪ] [in-tra-vi-nos-li], adv. Por vía intravenosa.

intrench [ɪnˈtrentʃ] [in-trench], vn. Invadir, usurpar, quitar a otro lo que es suyo. -va. 1. Atrinchear. 2. Llenar de hoyos o cortes alguna cosa. V. ENTRENCH.

intrenchment [ɪnˈtrentʃmənt] [in-trench-ment], s. Atrincheramiento, trinchera.

intrepid [ɪnˈtrepɪd] [in-tre-pid], a. Intrépido, arrojado, osado.

intrepidity [ɪnˈtrepɪdɪtɪ] [in-tre-pi-di-ti], s. Intrepidez, arrojo, osadía.

intrepidly [ɪnˈtrepɪdlɪ] [in-tre-pid-li], adv. Intrépidamente.

intricacy [ˈɪntrɪkəsɪ] [in-tri-ka-si], s. Embrollo, confusión, embarazo, dificultad.

intricate [ˈɪntrɪkɪt] [in-tri-ket], a. Intrincado, confuso, enredado, complicado.

intricate, va. Intrincar, enredar, confundir, embrollar.

intricately [ˈɪntrɪkɪtlɪ] [in-tri-kit-li], adv. Intrincadamente.

intricateness [ˈɪntrɪkɪtnɪs] [in-tri-kit-nes], s. Embrollo, perplejidad, oscuridad.

intrigue [ɪnˈtriːg] [in-trig], s. 1. Intriga, manejo, trama (complot, scheme); arte o amaño secreto para lograr un fin. 2. Intriga amorosa, galanteo, trato secreto entre los amantes (love affair). 3. Embrollo, confusión (entanglement). 4. Enredo o maraña de una comedia.

intrigue, va. Intrigar: tramar, manejar o negociar secretamente un asunto; tramar galanteos secretos. -va. Embarazar, turbar, intrincar.

intriguer [ɪnˈtriːgəʳ] [in-tri-gaʳ], s. 1. Intrigante, embrollador, entremetido, zaramullo. 2. Amante, la persona que galantea en secreto a una mujer.

intriguingly [ɪnˈtriːgɪŋlɪ] [in-tri-guin-li], adv. Por medio de intrigas o manejos secretos.

intrinsic, intrinsical [ɪnˈtrɪnsɪk] [in-trin-sik], a. 1. Intrínseco, inherente, esencial, verdadero. 2. Intrínseco, interno, interior.

intrinsically [ɪnˈtrɪnsɪklɪ] [in-trin-si-kli], adv. Intrínsecamente, esencialmente, interiormente.

intrinsicalness [ɪnˈtrɪnsɪklnɪs] [in-trin-si-kal-nes], s. Realidad; mérito intrínseco.

introduce [ˌɪntrəˈdjuːs] [in-tro-dius], va. 1. Introducir, meter dentro o dar entrada a uno en algún lugar (get into) **I was**

introduced into the car, me hicieron entrar al coche. 2. Introducir, facilitar o porporcionar la gracia o amistad de alguno. 3. Introducir, insertar algo en un escrito o discurso. 4. Ocasionar, dar motivo (cause). 5. Empezar, establecer, poner en uso o noticia. 6. Proponer, presentar (offer). **To introduce a bill a friend**, presentar un proyecto de ley, presentar a un amigo. **To introduce a problem**, abordar un problema.

introducer [ˌɪntrəˈdjuːsəʳ] [in-tro-diu-saʳ], s. Introductor.

introduction [ˌɪntrəˈdʌkʃən] [in-tro-dak-shon], s. 1. Introducción. 2. Introducción, prólogo o proemio de un libro. 3. Presentación, el acto de presentar a dos o más personas para que se conozcan.

introductive [ˌɪntrəˈdʌktɪv] [in-tro-dak-tiv], a. Introductivo, lo que sirve de medio para hacer alguna cosa o de introducción.

introductor [ˌɪntrəˈdʌktəʳ] [in-tro-dak-taʳ], s. Introductor.

introductory [ˌɪntrəˈdʌktərɪ] [in-tro-dak-ter-ri], s. Preliminar, proemial, introductivo.

introgression [ˌɪntrəˈɡreʃən] [in-tro-gre-shon], s. Entrada.

introit [ˈɪntrɔɪt] [in-troit], s. Introito de la misa o del oficio divino.

intromission [ˌɪntrəˈmɪʃən] [in-tro-mi-shon], s. Introducción, admisión.

intromit [ɪnˈtrəmɪt] [in-tro-mit], va. Introducir o dar entrada a alguna cosa, admitir. -vn. Tomar posesión de los bienes de otro por fuerza; entremeterse, mezclarse uno en lo que no le atañe.

intromittent [ɪnˈtrəmɪtənt] [in-tro-mi-tent], a. 1. Que introduce o echa dentro. 2. Que se emplea en el coito.

introreception [ˌɪntrɔrɪˈsepʃən] [in-tro-ri-sep-shon], s. Recepción, el acto de recibir o admitir dentro, en lo interior.

introspect [ɪnˈtrəspekt] [in-tros-pekt], va. Mirar adentro, mirar lo interior de alguna cosa.

introspection [ˌɪntrəˈspekʃən] [in-trous-pek-shon], s. Examen del interior de alguna cosa.

introspective [ɪnˈtrəspekt] [in-tros-pekt]. Introspectivo.

introsusception [ˌɪntrəsʌsˈpekʃən] [in-tro-sas-pek-shon], s. 1. El acto de recibir dentro, en lo interior. 2. Intususcepción, invaginación. V. INTUSSUSCEPTION.

introversion [ˌɪntrəˈdvɜːʃən] [in-trou-ver-shon], s. El acto de volver o dirigir hacia dentro; introversión.

introvert [ˈɪntrədvɜːt] [in-trou-vert], s. y a. Introvertido. -va. 1. Volver hacia el interior. 2. V. INVERT.

intrude [ɪnˈtruːd] [in-trud], vn. Entrometerse, introducirse sin permiso en alguna parte; mezclarse en lo que a uno no le toca (meddle); entrar o aparecer intempestivamente, donde a uno no le llaman. **To intrude on something**, molestar, importunar. **Am I intruding?**, ¿molesto? -va. 1. Presentar o introducir indebidamente a alguna persona. **To intrude oneself into a company**, intrusarse, presentarse en una reunión o tertulia sin ser invitado. 2. Introducir alguna cosa a viva fuerza.

intruder [ɪnˈtruːdəʳ] [in-tru-daʳ], s. Intruso, entrometido, el que se entromete.

intrusion [ɪnˈtruːʒən] [in-tru-shon], s. 1. Intrusión, entrometimiento; la acción de intrusarse, de meterse en alguna parte sin ser llamado. **Pardon the intrusion**, perdone que le moleste, perdone la intrusión. 2. Intrusión en alguna dignidad u oficio. 3. (Geol.) Intrusión de rocas volcánicas entre otras preexistentes.

intrusional [ɪnˈtruːʒənl] [in-tru-sho-nal], a. Intruso, relativo a la intrusión.

intrusive [ɪnˈtruːsɪv] [in-tru-siv], a. Intruso, que viene sin licencia ni permiso; fuera de orden regular; importuno, fastidioso. V. OBTRUSIVE.

intrusiveness [ɪnˈtruːsɪvnɪs] [in-tru-siv-nes], s. Intrusión, importunidad, fastidio.

intrust [ɪnˈtrʌst] [in-trast], va. 1. Confiar o fiar, hacer confianza de otro. 2. Poner en depósito. 3. Confiar un negocio, dar una comisión secreta.

intuit [ɪnˈtjɔɪt] [in-tiuit], vt. Intuir.

intuition [ˌɪntjuːˈɪʃən] [in-tui-shon], s. Intuición: conocimiento infuso o no adquirido, íntimo.

intuitive [ɪnˈtjuːɪtɪv] [in-tui-tiv], a. Intuitivo, perteneciente a la intuición; que tiene la facultad de descubrir la verdad sin necesidad del raciocinio.

intuitively [ɪnˈtjuːɪtɪvlɪ] [in-tiui-tiv-li], adv. Intuitivamente.

intumesce [ˈɪntʊmes] [in-tu-mes], vn. Hincharse, entumercerse.

intumescence [ˈɪntʊmesəns] [in-tu-me-sens], **intumescency** [ˈɪntʊmesənsɪ] [in-tu-me-sen-si], s. Intumescencia, entumecimiento, levantamiento, la acción de entumecerse, hincharse o levantarse alguna cosa, tumor, hinchazón.

intumescent [ˈɪntʊmesənt] [in-tu-me-sent], a. Intumescente, hinchado.

intussuception [ˌɪntʊˈsʌsepʃən] [in-tu-sa-sep-shon], s. Calidad y estado de ser recibido dentro: (a) Intususcepción, inversión de una porción de intestino en otra inmediata. (b) Intususcepción, modo de aumentar y crecer los animales y vegetales por los elementos que toman interiormente.

intwine [ˈɪntwaɪn] [in-tuain], va. Entrelazar, enlazar, una cosa con otra torciéndolas. V. ENTWINE.

inula [ˈɪnjʊlə] [i-niu-la], s. (Bot.) Enula o énula campana, ínula.

inulin [ˈɪnjʊliːn] [i-niu-lin], s. Inulina, substancia parecida al almidón extraída de la raíz de la énula campana.

inumbrate [ɪˈnʌmbreɪt] [i-nam-breit], va. Sombrear, echar sombrea sobre.

inunction [ɪˈnʌnkʃən] [i-nank-shon], s. Untura, untadura, untamiento de un medicamento en la piel.

inundat [ɪˈnʌndæt] [i-nan-dat], a. (Poco us.) Inundante.

inundate [ˈɪnʌndeɪt] [i-nan-deit], va. Inundar; abrumar.

inundation [ˌɪnʌnˈdeɪʃən] [i-nan-dei-shon], s. 1. Inundación, avenida de aguas. 2. Inundación, multitud excesiva de cualquiera cosa.

inurbane [ɪˈnɜːbeɪn] [i-ner-bein], a. Inurbano, descortés, rudo.

inurbaneness, inurbanity [ɪˈnɜːbeɪnɪs] [i-ner-bei-nes], s. Inurbanidad.

inure [ɪnˈjʊəʳ] [i-niuaʳ], va. Endurecer por el uso, acostumbrar, habituar (custom). -vn. Tener efecto; ser aplicado a, servir para el provecho de alguno, devolver por la ley.

inurement [ɪnˈjʊəmənt] [i-niua-ment], s. Práctica, hábito, uso, costumbre (habit, use).

inurn [ɪˈnɜːn] [i-nern], va. Introducir o poner en una urna cineraria.

inutility [ˌɪnjʊˈtɪlɪtɪ] [i-na-ti-li-ti], s. Inutilidad.

invade [ɪnˈveɪd] [in-veid], va. Invadir, acometer, asaltar, embestir; violar **to invade one's rights**, violar los derechos de alguno. **The disease invades the lungs**, la enfermedad invade los pulmones.

invader [ɪnˈveɪdəʳ] [in-vei-daʳ], s. Invasor, asaltador; acometedor, agresor, violador.

invaginate [ɪnˈvæfʒɪneɪt] [in-va-yi-neit], va. Envainar, meter o recibir en una vaina, como una parte de un tubo en otra; invaginar. V. INTROVERT.

invagination [ɪnˈvædʒɪneɪt] [in-va-yi-neit], s. Invaginación; intususcepción; bolsa dormada por la inversión de una membrana.

invalid [ɪnˈvælɪd] [in-va-lid], a. Inválido, nulo.

invalid [ɪnˈvəlɪd] [in-va-lid], va. 1. Matricular en el registro de inválidos. 2. Invalidar, estropear a uno.

invalidate [ɪnˈvəlɪdeɪt] [in-va-li-deit], va. Invalidar, anular; particularmente, privar de valor legal.

invalidation [ˌɪnvəlɪˈdeɪʃən] [in-va-li-dei-shon], s. Invalidación.

invalidity [ˌɪnvəˈlɪdɪtɪ] [in-va-li-di-ti], s. **invalidness** [ɪnˈvælɪdnɪs] [in-va-lid-nes], s. 1, Invalidación, nulidad de un auto. 2. Debilidad falta de fuerzas corporales.

invaluable [ɪnˈvæljʊəbl] [in-va-liu-a-bol], a. Invaluable, inestimable, inapreciable.

invaluably [ɪnˈvæljʊəblɪ] [in-va-liu-a-bli], *adv.* Invaluablemente.

invariability [ˌɪnvɛərɪəˈbɪlɪtɪ] [in-va-ria-bi-li-ti], *s.* Invariabilidad, la subsistencia permanente y sin variación de alguna cosa.

invariable [ɪnˈvɛərɪəbl] [in-va-ria-bol], *a.* Invariable.

invariableness [ɪnˈvɛərɪəblnɪs] [in-va-ria-bol-nes], *s.* Inmutabilidad, constancia.

invariably [ɪnˈvɛərɪəblɪ] [in-va-ria-bli], *adv.* Invariablemente.

invasion [ɪnˈveɪʒən] [in-vei-shion], *s.* 1. Invasión, acometimiento, acción de invadir. 2. *(Med.)* Principio de una enfermedad, 3. Infracción, violación de derechos ajenos.

invasive [ɪnˈveɪsɪv] [in-vei-siv], *a.* Hostil; invasor, que invade.

invasor [ɪnˈveɪʃəʳ] [in-vei-saʳ], *a.* Invasor.

invective [ɪnˈvektɪv] [in-vek-tiv], *s.* Invectiva, escrito o discurso injurioso. *-a.* Ultrajante, abusivo, acre.

invectivly [ɪnˈvektɪvlɪ] [in-vek-tiv-li], *adv.* Injuriosamente, ultrajosamente.

inveigh [ɪnˈveɪ] [in-vei], *vn.* Prorrumpir en invectivas, desencadenarse contra alguno; antiguamente invehir (Con la **prep. against**).

inveigher [ɪnˈveɪgəʳ] [in-vei-gaʳ], *s.* Declamador vehemente; ultrajador.

inveigle [ɪnˈveɪgl] [in-vei-guel], *va.* Seducir, engañar con arte y maña, persuadir al mal con palabras seductoras.

inveiglement [ɪnˈveɪglmənt] [in-vei-guel-ment], *s.* Engañifa, seducción.

inveigler [ɪnˈveɪgləʳ] [in-vei-glaʳ], *s.* Seductor.

inveiled [ɪnˈveɪld] [in-veild], *a.* Cubierto como un velo.

invent [ɪnˈvent] [in-vent], *va.* 1. Inventar, descubrir. 2. Inventar, forjar, fraguar, fingir.

inventer [ɪnˈventəʳ] [in-ven-taʳ], *s. (Des.) V.* INVENTOR.

inventful [ɪnˈventfʊl] [in-vent-ful], *a. (Des.)* Inventivo, el que tiene disposición para inventar.

inventible [ɪnˈventɪbl] [in-ven-ti-bol], *a.* Lo que puede ser inventado.

invention [ɪnˈvenʃən] [in-ven-shon], *s.* 1. Invención, inventiva, maña o ingenio para inventar. 2. Invención, invento, la cosa inventada. 3. Invención, ficción, mentira, falsedad, etc. 4. *(Ant.)* Invención, descubrimiento, hallazgo.

inventive [ɪnˈventɪv] [in-ven-tiv], *a.* 1. Inventivo, hábil para inventar, fecundo en expedientes, ingenioso. 2. Inventivo, que demuestra invención o maña para inventar.

inventiveness [ɪnˈventɪv] [in-ven-tiv-nes], *s.* Inventiva, ingenio.

inventor [ɪnˈventəʳ] [in-ven-taʳ], *s.* 1. Inventor, el primero que discurre algún arte o secreto; también el que dedica su tiempo a la invención. 2. Inventor, invencionero, el que forja o finge alguna cosa.

inventorial [ɪnˈventərɪəl] [in-ven-to-rial], *a.* Lo perteneciente al inventario.

inventorially [ɪnˈventərɪəlɪ] [in-ven-to-ria-li], *adv.* Por o con inventario.

inventory [ɪnˈventərɪ] [in-ven-to-ri], *s.* Inventario, catálogo o lista de muebles, mercancías u otros objetos o bienes.

inventory, *va.* Inventariar, hacer un inventario.

inventress [ɪnˈventrɪs] [in-ven-tres], *f.* Inventora, la mujer que inventa.

inverse [ˈɪnˈvɜːs] [in-vers], *a.* Inverso, invertido, trastocado, trastornado.

inversely [ˈɪnˈvɜːslɪ] [in-vers-li], *adv.* Inversamente.

inversion [ˈɪnˈvɜːʃən] [in-ver-shon], *s.* Inversión, transmutación de orden o tiempo; cambio del orden natural de las cosas, sea de las palabras o los términos de una proporción o de la estructura molecular. *(Mús.)* Imitación que consiste en reproducir una melodía tomando las notas en orden opuesto.

invert [ˈɪnˈvɜːt] [in-vert], *va.* Invertir, poner al revés o en sentido inverso, trastornar, trastocar, mudar el orden de las cosas, transponer.

invertebral [ɪnˈvɜːtɪbrˈl] [in-ver-ti-bral], *a. V.* INVERTEBRATE.

invertebrate [ɪnˈvɜːtɪbrɪt] [in-ver-ti-brit], *a.* Invertebrado, que carece de columna vertebral. *-s.* Animal invertebrado

invertedly [ɪnˈvɜːtɪdlɪ] [in-ver-tid-li], *adv.* Al revés.

invest [ɪnˈvest] [in-vest], *va.* 1. Vestir, cubrir y adornar el cuerpo con el vestido (embellish). 2. Investir, dar la investidura de algún feudo, señorío o dignidad. 3. Conferir, dar (give). 4. Sitiar, cercar o cerrar con tropas una plaza fuerte, un puesto fortificado (besiege), etc. 5. Cercar o rodear a una persona (surround). 6. *(Com.)* Invertir, emplear o imponer dinero en valores o propiedades. 7. Adquirir, comprar (buy). 8. Confiar en, apoyar.

investigable [ɪnˈvestɪgəbl] [in-ves-ti-ga-bol], *a.* Averiguable, investigable.

investigate [ɪnˈvestɪgeɪt] [in-ves-ti-gueit], *va.* Investigar, indagar, buscar, averiguar; examinar con cuidado.

investigation [ɪnˌvestɪˈgeɪʃən] [in-ves-ti-guei-shon], *s.* 1. Investigación, pesquisa, averiguación. 2. Escrutinio, examen diligente o cuidadoso.

investigative [ɪnˈvestɪgeɪtɪv] [in-ves-ti-guei-tiv], *a.* Dispuesto a investigar, investigador.

investigator [ɪnˈvestɪgeɪtəʳ] [in-ves-ti-guei-taʳ], *s.* Investigador, indagador, averiguador.

investiture [ɪnˈvestɪtʃəʳ] [in-ves-ti-chaʳ], *s.* 1. Investidura, el acto solemne por el cual se confiere un feudo, señorío o dignidad. 2. Instalación. *V.* INSTALLATION.

investment [ɪnˈvestmənt] [in-vest-ment], *s.* 1. *(Com.)* Inversión, colocación o empleo de un capital; el dinero invertido y los bienes comprados. 2. Cerco, acción de cercar una plaza para sitiarla (besiegement). 3. Instalación, concesión de autoridad. 4. Cubierta; envoltura en su sentido biológico.

investor [ɪnˈvestəʳ] [in-ves-taʳ], *s.* Inversionista.

inveteracy [ɪnˈvetərəsɪ] [in-ve-te-ra-si], **inveterateness** [ɪnˈvetəreɪtnɪs] [in-ve-te-reit-nes], *s.* Perseverancia o continuación prolongada de un mal físico o moral.

inveterate [ɪnˈvetərɪt] [in-ve-te-reit], *a.* Inveterado, lo que se ha arraigado o ha tomado raíces: se dice de los males físicos o morales.

inveteration [ɪnˌvetəˈreɪʃən] [in-ve-te-rei-shon], *s. (Poco us.)* endurecimiento; estado inveterado.

invidious [ɪnˈvɪdɪəs] [in-vi-dios], *a.* Envidioso, odioso, aborrecible (hateful).

invidiousness [ɪnˈvɪdɪəsnɪs] [in-vi-dios-nes], *s.* Calidad o propiedad que excita la envidia o el odio (hate, envy).

invigorate [ɪnˈvɪgəreɪt] [in-vi-go-reit], *va.* Vigorizar, dar vigor.

invigoration [ɪnˌvɪgəˈreɪʃən] [in-vi-go-rei-shon], *s.* 1. El acto de vigorizar. 2. Corroboración, esfuerzo o vigor infundido por algún medio.

invincibility [ɪnˌvɪnsɪˈbɪlɪtɪ] [in-vin-si-bi-li-ti], *s.* La calidad que constituye invencible a alguno o alguna cosa.

invincible [ɪnˈvɪnsɪbl] [in-vin-si-bol], *a.* Invencible.

invincibly [ɪnˈvɪnsɪblɪ] [in-vin-si-bli], *adv.* Invenciblemente.

inviolability [ɪnˌvaɪələˈbɪlɪtɪ] [in-vaio-la-bi-li-ti], *s.* Inviolabilidad.

inviolable [ɪnˈvaɪələbl] [in-vaio-la-bol], *a.* Inviolable, que no se debe o no se puede violar ni profanar.

inviolableness [ɪnˈvaɪələblnɪs] [in-vaio-la-bol-nes], *s.* Inviolabilidad.

inviolably [ɪnˈvaɪələblɪ] [in-vaio-la-bli], *adv.* Inviolablemente.

inviolate [ɪnˈvaɪəleɪt] [in-vaio-leit], *a.* Inviolado, entero, incorrupto, íntegro.

inviolated [ɪnˈvaɪəleɪtɪd] [in-vaio-lei-tid], *a.* Inviolado, incorrupto.

inviscate [ɪnˈvɪskeɪt] [in-vis-keit], *va.* Encolar una cosa, hacerla viscosa.

invisibility [ɪnˌvɪzəˈbɪlɪtɪ] [in-vi-sa-bi-li-ti], **invisibleness** [ɪnˈvɪzɪblnɪs] [in-vi-si-bol-nes], *s.* Invisibilidad.

invisible [ɪnˈvɪzɪbl] [in-vi-si-bol], *a.* Invisible.

invisibly [ɪnˈvɪzɪblɪ] [in-vi-si-bli], *adv.* Invisiblemente.

invitation [ˌɪnvɪˈteɪʃən] [in-vi-tei-shon], *s.* Invitación, convite, llamamiento, instancia; cebo para atraer a alguno.

invitatory [ɪnˈvɪtətərɪ] [in-vi-ter-to-ri], *a.* Invitador, que invita. *-s.* Invitatorio.

invite [ɪnˈvaɪt] [in-vait], *va.* Convidar, invitar, mover, incitar, tentar (move, incite, rouse); llamar, instar, estimular a la ejecución de alguna cosa (encourage, estimulate).

inviter [ɪnˈvaɪtəʳ] [in-vai-taʳ], *s.* Convidador.

inviting [ɪnˈvaɪtɪŋ] [in-vai-tin], *a.* Halagador, seductivo, seductor, incitante (tempting, provoking). *-s.* Convite.

invitingly [ɪnˈvaɪtɪŋlɪ] [in-vai-tin-li], *adv.* Halagüeñamente, apetitosamente.

invitingness [ɪnˈvaɪtɪŋnɪs] [in-vai-tin-nes], *s.* El poder o la calidad de convidar, halagar o incitar.

invocate [ɪnˈvəʊkeɪt] [in-vou-keit], *va.* (*Ant.*) Invocar, implorar auxilio o ayuda.

invocation [ˌɪnvəʊˈkeɪʃən] [in-vou-kei-shon], *s.* 1. Invocación. 2. (*For.*) Citación, demanda u orden judicial.

invoice [ˈɪnvɔɪs] [in-vois], *s.* Factura, la nota con precios de los géneros que un comerciante envía a otro. **Invoice-book**, libro de facturas.

invoke [ɪnˈvəʊk] [in-vouk], *va.* Invocar, llamar, implorar, suplicar, rogar (implore).

involucel [ˌɪnvəˈljʊsəl] [in-vo-liu-sel], *s.* (*Bot.*) Involucrillo o involucro secundario.

involucral [ˈɪnvəlʊkrəl] [in-vo-lu-kral], *a.* Involucral, que pertenece al involucro; provisto de un involucro.

involucrate, involucred [ˈɪnvəlʊkreɪt] [in-vo-lu-kreit], *a.* Involucrado, provisto de un involucro; que forma involucor.

involucre [ˈɪnvəlʊkr] [in-vo-lukʳ], **involucrum** , *s.* 1. (*Bot.*) Involucro, verticilo de brácteas, situado en el arranque del conjunto de varias flores agrupadas, como en la zanahoria. 2. (*Anat.*) Envoltura, membrana que envuelve un órgano.

involuntarily [ɪnˈvɒləntərɪlɪ] [in-vo-lu-ta-ri-li], *adv.* Involuntariamente.

involuntariness [ɪnˈvɒləntərɪnɪs] [in-vo-lu-ta-ri-nes], *s.* Involuntariedad.

involuntary [ɪnˈvɒləntərɪ] [in-vo-lun-ta-ri], *a.* Involuntario.

involute [ˈɪnvəluːt] [in-vo-lut], *a.* Encorvado o torcido hacia dentro. *-s.* (*Geom.*) Envolvente, involuta, cierta curva.

involuted [ˌɪnvəˈluːtɪd] [in-vo-lu-tid], *a.* Intrincado.

involution [ɪnˈvəluːʃən] [in-vo-lu-shon], *s.* 1. Envolvimiento, la acción de envolver. 2. Complicación. 3. (*Med.*) Restitución de un órgano a su volumen normal después de haber sido ensanchado. 4. Envolvedero, envolvedor. 5. Enredo, embrollo, ebolismo.

involve [ɪnˈvɒlv] [in-volv], *va.* 1. Envolver, arrollar. 2. Envolver, implicar, comprometer. 3. Torcer, retorcer (twist). 4. Envolver, implicar, enredar (implicate). **To involve oneself in troubles**, meterse en embrollos. 5. Intrincar, enmarañar, complicar (entangle, complicate). 6. Revolver, mezclar (mix). 7. Multiplicar una cantidad por sí misma.

involvedness [ɪnˈvɒlvdnɪs] [in-vol-vid-nes], *s.* El estado o la calidad de envuelto, arrollado, etc.; envolvimiento.

invulnerability [ɪnˌvʌlnərəˈbɪlɪtɪ] [in-val-ne-ra-bi-li-ti], **invulnerableness** [ɪnˌvʌlnərəˈblnes] [in-val-ne-ra-bol-nes], *s.* Invulnerabilidad, el estado o la calidad que constituye invulnerable alguna cosa.

invulnerable [ɪnˈvʌlnərəbl] [in-val-ne-ra-bol], *a.* Invulnerable, que no puede ser herido.

inwall [ɪnˈwɔːl] [in-uol], *va.* (Poco us.) Emparedar, tapiar, cercar o rodear con pared, tapia o muro.

inward, inwards [ɪnˈwədz] [in-uods], *adv.* Hacia dentro, hacia lo interior, interiormente, adentro, en lo interior.

inward, *a.* 1. Interior, lo que está de la parte de adentro. 2. Interno, doméstico. 3. Secreto, oculto. *-s.* El interior; lo que está dentro; en plural, entrañas.

inwardly [ɪnˈwədlɪ] [in-uord-li], *adv.* Interiormente, internamente.

inwardness [ɪnˈwədnɪs] [in-uord-nes], *s.* 1. Calidad, naturaleza o estado interior. 2. Estado de ser interior, efectiva o figuradamente. 3. (*Des.*) Intimidad, familiaridad.

inweave [ɪnˈwiːv] [in-uiv], *va.* Entretejer, enlazar.

inwheel [ɪnˈwiːl] [in-uil], *va.* Circundar, cercar.

inwork [ɪnˈwɜːk] [in-uek], *va.* Labrar en o dentro, entretejer. *-vn.* Producir efecto en el interior, especialmente en el ánimo o en lamente.

inwrought [ɪnˈwrɔt] [in-rout], *a.* Labrado, adornado con labores.

iodic [aɪˈəʊdɪk] [ai-ou-dik], *a.* Yodado, que se refiere al yodo.

iodid, iodide [ˈaɪədɪd] [aia-did], *s.* Yoduro, combinación del yodo con un metaloide o metal

iodin, iodine [ˈaɪədiːm] [aia-din], *s.* (*Quím.*) Yodo, cuerpo simple de color azul negruzco y lustre metálico y que da vapores de color violado; se usa en medicina y en la fotografía.

iodism [ˈaɪədɪdɪzm] [aia-di-sem], *s.* (*Med.*) Yodismo, estado mórbido ocasionado por el uso prolongado del yodo.

iodize [ˈaɪədaɪz] [aia-dais], *va.* 1. (*Med.*) Someter a la influencia del yodo. 2. (*Foto.*) Echar yodo a; exponer a los vapores del yodo.

iodoform [aɪˈɒdəfɔːm] [aia-do-foʳ], *s.* Yodoformo, compuesto cristalizable de color amarillo claro y de olor característico. Se emplea en la cirugía.

ion [ˈaɪən] [aion], *s.* Substancia que resulta de la descomposición electroquímica, o uno de los componentes de dicha sustancia.

ionian [aɪˈəʊnɪən] [ai-ou-nian], *a.* Jónico.

ionic [aɪˈɒnɪk] [aio-nik], *a.* Jónico.

ionization [ˈaɪənaɪˈzeɪʃən] [aiou-nai-sei-shon], *s.* (*Elec.*) Ionización.

ionize [ˈaɪənaɪs] [aio-nais], *va.* Ionizar.

ionosphere [aɪˈɒnəsfɪəʳ] [aio-nos-fiaʳ], *s.* Ionosfera.

iota [aɪˈəʊtə] [ai-ou-ta], *s.* Jota, ápice, tilde, punto. **Not a single iota**, ni tan siquiera una tilde; ni siquiera un punto, ni miaja.

ipecac [ˈaɪpɪkæk] [ai-pi-kak], *s.* V. IPECACUANHA.

ipecacuanha [ˌaɪpɪkæˈkwənə] [ai-pi-ka-kua-na], *s.* Ipecacuana, raíz medicinal de América, llamada por otro nombre **bejuquillo**.

ipomoea [ˈaɪpəmiːə] [ai-po-mia], *s.* Ipomea, vasto género de plantas tropicales de la familia de las convolvuláceas. La batata, la jalapa y la patata silvestre son muy conocidas.

irak, Iraq [ɪˈrɑːk] [i-rak], *s.* Irak, Iraq.

iraki [ɪˈrɑːkɪ] [i-ra-ki], *a.* Iraquí.

iranian [ɪˈreɪnɪən] [i-rei-nian], *a.* Iraní, referente a Irán o Persia.

irascibility [ɪˌræsɪˈbɪlɪtɪ] [i-ras-si-bi-li-ti], *s.* Iracundia, irascibilidad.

irascible [ɪˈræsɪbl] [i-ra-si-bol], *a.* Irascible.

irate [aɪˈreɪt] [ai-reit], *a.* Encolerizado, enfurecido, airado.

ire [aɪəʳ] [aiaʳ], *s.* Ira, iracundia, enojo, enfado.

ireful [ˈaɪəfʊl] [aia-ful], *a.* Iracundo, colérico.

irefully [ˈaɪəfʊlɪ] [aia-fu-li], *adv.* Airadamente, enojadamente.

Ireland [ˈaɪələnd] [aia-land], *pr. n.* (*Geogr.*) Irlanda.

irenic, irenical [ˈaɪrɪnɪk] [ai-ri-nik], *a.* Pacífico, conciliador.

iridescence [ˌɪrɪˈdəsəns] [i-ri-de-sens], *s.* Iridación, estado de lo iridescente.

iridescent [ˌɪrɪˈdəsənt] [i-ri-de-sent], *a.* Iridescente, que refleja los colores del iris; irisado.

iridium [ɪˈrɪdɪəm] [i-ri-diom], *s.* (*Quím.*) Iridio, elemento metálico de color de plata.

iris [ˈaɪərɪs] [aia-ris], *s.* 1. (*Anat.*) Iris, ojo. 2. Iris o arco iris. 3. (*Bot.*) Lirio; flor de lis. **Arco Iris**, rainbow. *Pl.* Irises o irides.

Irish [ˈaɪərɪʃ] [aia-rish], *a.* Irlandés, natural de Irlanda, y lo perteneciente a esta isla. *-s.* 1. Irlandés, el natural de Irlanda. 2. Irlandés, la lengua nativa céltica de Irlanda. 3. Acento especial del idoma inglés en Irlanda, caracterizado por la pronunciación llamada «*brogue*» or «*broad*». **Irishman**, irlandés. **Irishgirl**, joven irlandesa. **Irish moss**, musgo de Irlanda. **The Irish**, los irlandeses. **Irish coffee**, café irlandés (café con whisky y nata). **Irish Sea** Mar de Irlanda.

irishism [ˈaɪərɪʃɪzm] [aia-ri-shi-sem], *s.* 1. Locución irlandesa. 2. Carácter o rasgos irlandeses colectivamente.

iritis ['aɪərɪtɪs] [aia-ri-tis], *s*. Iritis, inflamación del iris del ojo.

irk [ɜːk] [erk], *va*. Fastidiar, molestar. **It irks me**, me fastidia, estoy cansado de ello. Este verbo se usa casi siempre impersonalmente.

irksome ['ɜːksəm] [erk-som], *a*. Tedioso, fastidioso, enfadoso, cansado.

irksomeness ['ɜːksəmnɪs] [erk-som-nes], *s*. Tedio, fastidio, molestia, cansancio.

iron ['aɪən] [aion], *s*. 1. Hierro, metal duro que se funde y amartilla; el más importante de los elementos metálicos. Hierro candente (for branding). **Bar iron**, hierro en barras. **Cast iron**, hierro colado. **Forged o wrought iron**, hierro forjado. **Round iron**, hierro vergajón o cabilla. **Flat iron**, hierro en planchuela. **Wrought iron**, hierro forjado. **Smoothing-iron**, hierro de planchar; plancha de sastre. **Curling-irons**, hierros o tenacillas para rizar el pelo. **Old iron**, chatarra. **One-inch, square iron**, hierro cuadradillo. 2. Hierro, cualquier cosa hecha de hierro. 3. Plancha (for pressing clothes). 4. *Pl*. Hierros, grilletes (chains). **To put in irons**, aprisionar, encadenar. **Will of iron**, voluntad de hierro. -*a*. 1. Férreo, lo que es de hierro o tiene sus propiedades. **Iron chest**, arca o caja de hierro para guardar los libros de comercio o dinero. **Iron horse**, (Mar.) Batayora. **Iron-mill**, herrería o ferrería. **Iron-work**, herraje. **Iron-work of the rudder**, (Mar.) herraje del timón. 2. Duro, áspero, severo. 5. Férreo, duro, impenetrable. **Iron plate**, pletina, plancha de hierro batido. **Iron wire**, hilo de hierro. **Iron pot**, olla o marmita de hierro. **Iron ware**, trastos de hierro. **To have the iron enter into none's soul**, estar como en un potro. **To have too many irons in the fire**, tener demasiados asuntos entre manos (to be busy).

iron, *va*. 1. Aplanchar, alisar alguna cosa con plancha de hierro. (*Vulg.*) Planchar. **To iron linen**, planchar ropa blanca. 2. Aprisionar, poner en prisión. **Iron out**, hacer desaparecer, suprimir (remove).

iron, en composición: **Iron-bound**, (a) Rodeado de arcos de hierro. (b) Erizado o rodeado de rocas, (c) Difícil de alterar; inflexible. **Iron-clad**, (a) Blindado con armadura de hierro o de acero, como los buques de, guerra. (b) Riguroso, que no puede evadirse. (c) Capaz de resistir, fuerte. **Iron-founder**, fundidor de hierro. **Iron-rust**, V. RUST. **Iron-works**, fundición de hierro, establecimiento para la manufactura de artículos de hierro de gran peso y tamaño.

iron Age ['aɪənˌeɪdʒ] [aion-eich], (*Geol.*) Edad de Hierro.

ironclad ['aɪənklæd] [aion-klad], *a*. 1. Armado de hierro. 2. (*Fam.*) Rígido. **An ironclad alibi**, una coartada perfecta. -*s*. Buque de guerra blindado.

iron curtain ['aɪənˌkɜːtɪn] [aion-ker-tin], *s*. Telón de acero, cortina de hierro.

ironed ['aɪənd] [aiond], *a*. 1. Planchado, aplanchado. 2. Engrillado; armado.

ironer ['aɪənə] [aio-na^r], *s*. Planchadora, la persona o la máquina que plancha.

iron-hearted ['aɪənˌhɑːtɪd] [aion-jar-tid], *a*. Duro, áspero, severo.

ironic, ironical ['aɪənɪk] [ai-ro-nik], *a*. Irónico.

ironically ['aɪənɪklɪ] [ai-ro-ni-ka-li], *adv*. Irónicamente.

ironing board ['aɪənɪŋbɔːd] [ai-ro-nin-bord], *s*. Tabla de planchar.

iron lung ['aɪənlʌŋ] [ai-ron-lang], *s*. Pulmón de acero.

ironmonger ['aɪənˌmʌŋgə^r] [ai-ron-mon-ga^r], *s*. Mercader o traficante en hierro. (*Amer.*) Quinquillero, ferretero. **Ironmonger's shop**, tienda de hierro. (*Amer.*) Quinquillería, ferretería.

ironmongery ['aɪənˌmʌŋgərɪ] [ai-ron-man-ga-ri], *s*. Ferretería, cerrajería, el conjunto de los artículos de hierro.

iron-mould ['aɪənˌməʊld] [ai-ron-mould], *s*. Mancha de herrumbre o de orín de hierro en el lienzo o paño.

ironside, Ironsides ['aɪənsaɪd] [ai-ron-said], *a*. Lo que tiene un lado o lados de hierro; fuerte, enérgico, terrible en la guerra; soldado del ejército de Cromwell.

ironware ['aɪənweə^r] [ai-ron-uea^r], *s*. Artículos de ferretería.

iron-wood ['aɪənwʊd] [ai-ron-vud], *s* Madera de hierro, especie de madera muy dura y pesada. (*Amer.*) Palo hacha.

iron-work ['aɪənwɜːk] [ai-ron-uek], *s*. Herraje, obra u objeto de hierro. Carpintería metálica (Iron framework).

iron worker ['aɪənwɜːkə^r] [ai-ron-ue-ka^r], *s*. Herrero.

irony ['aɪərənɪ] [ai-ro-ni], *s*. Ironía, figura con que se quiere dar a entender que se siente lo contrario de lo que se dice. *a*. Férreo, de hierro.

irradiance, Irradiancy [ɪˈreɪdɪəns] [i-rei-dians], *s*. Irradiación; rayos de luz.

irradiate [ɪˈreɪdɪeɪt] [i-rei-dieit], *va*. Irradiar.

irradiate, *va*. 1. Irradiar, herir el sol u otro cuerpo luminoso con sus rayos alguna cosa iluminándola. 2. Iluminar, inspirar. 3. Animar con fuego, calor o luz. 4. Adornar con cosas que den brillo. -*vn*. Lucir sobre una cosa.

irradiate, *a*. (*Poét.*) Resplandeciente, iluminado.

irradiation [ɪˌreɪdɪˈeɪʃən] [i-rei-diei-shon], *s*. 1. Irradiación. 2. Iluminación. 3. (*Fís.*) Ampliación aparente de un objeto luminoso cuando se ve contra un fondo oscuro.

irradiative [ɪˈreɪdɪətɪv] [i-rei-dia-tiv], *a*. Radiante (irradiant). *Fig*. Que ilumina (for the soul).

irradicate [ɪˈrædɪkeɪt] [i-ra-di-keit], *va*. Arraigar firme o profundamente.

irrational [ɪˈræʃənl] [i-ra-sho-nal], *a*. 1. Irracional, que carece de razón o de inteligencia. 2. Irracional, absurdo. 3. (*Alg.*) Irracional, que no tiene medida conocida, ni número cierto.

irrationalism [ɪˈræʃənlɪzm] [i-ra-sho-na-li-sem], *s*. *m*. Irracionalismo.

irrationalist [ɪˈræʃənlɪst] [i-ra-sho-na-list], *a./s*. Irracionalista.

irrationality [ɪˈræʃənlɪtɪ] [i-ra-sho-na-li-ti], *s*. Irracionalidad.

irrationaly [ɪˈræʃənlɪ] [i-ra-sho-na-li], *adv*. Irracionalmente.

irreceivable [ɪˈresɪvəbl] [i-re-si-va-bol], *a*. Inadmisible.

irreclaimable [ɪˈreklaɪməbl] [i-re-klai-ma-bol], *a*. Indómito, incorregible, obstinado, que no se puede redimir.

irreclaimably [ɪˈreklaɪməblɪ] [i-re-klai-ma-bli], *adv*. Incorregiblemente.

irrecognizable [ɪˈrekəgnɪsəbl] [i-re-kog-ni-sa-bol], *a*. Irreconocible.

irreconciability [ɪˈrekənˌʃəbɪlɪtɪ] [i-re-kon-sha-bi-li-ti], *s*. Incompatibilidad (of opinions). Imposibilidad de reconciliarse (of enemies).

irreconcilable [ɪˌrekənˈsaɪləbl] [i-re-kon-sai-la-bol], *a*. Irreconciliable, incomponible, implacable; incompatible.

irreconcilableness [ɪˌrekənˈsaɪləblnɪs] [i-re-kon-sai-la-bol-nes], *s*. Imposibilidad de reconciliarse.

irreconcilably [ɪˌrekənˈsaɪləblɪ] [i-re-kon-sai-la-bli], *adv*. Irreconciliablemente.

irreconciled [ɪˌrekənˈsaɪld] [i-re-kon-saild], *a*. Se dice de la maldad, delito o culpa que no se ha expiado.

irreconcilement [ɪˌrekənˈsaɪlmˈnt] [i-re-kon-sail-ment], **Irreconciliation** [ɪˌrekənˈsaɪleɪʃən] [i-re-kon-sai-lei-shon], *s*. Falta de reconciliación, discordia.

irrecoverable [ɪrɪˈkʌvərəbl] [i-ri-ka-ve-ra-bol], *a*. Irreparable, perdido sin recurso; irrecuperable, irremediable; incobrable.

irrecoverableness [ɪrɪˈkʌvərəblnɪs] [i-ri-ka-ve-ra-bol-nes], *s*. El estado y la calidad de lo que no se puede recobrar o es irrecuperable.

irrecoverably [ɪrɪˈkʌvərəblɪ] [i-ri-ka-ve-ra-bli], *adv*. Irremediablemente, sin recurso, irreparablemente.

irrecuperable [ɪrɪˈkʌpərəbl] [i-ri-ka-pe-ra-bol], *a*. Irrecuperable, irremediable.

irrecusable [ɪrɪˈkjʊsəbl] [i-ri-kiu-sa-bol], *a*. Irrecusable.

irredeemable [ɪrɪˈdiːməbl] [i-ri-di-ma-bol], *a*. Irredimible (which cannot be bought back). Inconvertible (paper money). *Fig*. Incorregible (incorrigible) Irremediable. Irreparable (fault).

irredeemably [ˌɪrɪ'diːməblɪ] [i-ri-di-ma-bli], *adv.* De un modo irredimible.

irrendentism [ˌɪre'dentɪzm] [i-re-den-ti-sem], *s.* Irredentismo.

irrendentist [ˌɪre'dentɪst] [i-re-den-tist], *a.* Irredentista.

irreducibility [ˌɪrɪ'djʊsɪ'bɪltɪ] [i-ri-diu-si-bi-li-ti], *s.* Irreductibilidad.

irreducible [ˌɪ'djuːsəbl] [i-ri-diu-sa-bol], *a.* 1. Irreducible, que no se puede reducir; que no se puede llevar al estado, a la forma o al arreglo deseados. 2. *(Cir.)* Que no cede al tratamiento; se dice de una hernia o fractura.

irreflective [ˌɪrɪ'flektɪv] [i-ri-flek-tiv], *a.* Irreflexivo, que carece de reflexión.

irrefragability [ˌɪrɪ'flektɪv] [i-ri-flek-tiv], *s.* Incontestabilidad, indiscutibilidad.

irrefragable [ˌɪrɪ'frægəbl] [i-ri-fra-ga-bol], *a.* Irrefragable, que no se puede impugnar ni contradecir, incontestable.

irrefrangible [ˌɪrɪ'frændʒɪbl] [i-ri-fran-yi-bol], *a.* Inviolable (law).

irrefutable [ˌɪrɪ'fjuːtəbl] [i-ri-fiu-ter-bol], *a.* Irrefragable, indubitable, cierto, indisputable.

irregular [ɪ'regjʊləʳ] [i-re-guiu-laʳ], *a.* 1. Irregular, falto de regularidad (conduct, attendance). 2. Desordenado, que desdice de alguna virtud o se opone a ella, desarreglado. 3. Irregular, que no sigue regla, disciplina o sistema determinados. 4. *(Zool.)* Irregular, que se aparta de un tipo establecido. 5. Desigual (surface). *-s.* El que no sigue regla determinada; soldado de tropas irregulares, empírico, charlatán.

irregularity [ɪˌregju'lærɪtɪ] [i-re-guiu-la-ri-ti], *s.* 1. Irregularidad. 2. Desorden, demasía, exceso.

irregulary [ɪ'regjʊlərlɪ] [i-re-guiu-lar-li], *adv.* Irregularmente.

irrelative [ɪ'relətɪv] [i-re-la-tiv], *a.* Absoluto; inconexo, sin relación alguna; sin regla, sin orden.

irrelatively [ɪ'relətɪvlɪ] [i-re-la-tiv-li], *adv.* De un modo inconexo.

irrelevance [ɪ'reləvəns] [i-re-le-vans], *s.* Irrelevancia, impertinencia. 2. Observación fuera de lugar (irrelevant remark). Acto improcedente, improcedencia.

irrelevant [ɪ'reləvənt] [i-re-le-vant], *a.* Que no es aplicable o a propósito, que no prueba nada, no concluye o no es del caso. Ajeno, fuera de lugar (remark). Impertinente. Improcedente. **Irrelevant cuestion to the subject** Cuestión que no tiene nada que ver con el tema.

irrelevantly [ɪ'reləvəntlɪ] [i-re-le-vant-li], *adv.* Fuera de propósito.

irrelievable [ɪ'relaɪəbl] [i-re-laia-bol], *a.* Irremediable, irreparable.

irreligion [ˌɪrɪ'lɪdʒən] [i-ri-li-yon], *s.* Irreligión, ateísmo, impiedad.

irreligious [ˌɪrɪ'lɪdʒəs] [i-ri-li-yos], *a.* Irreligioso, que no tiene religión; contrario a la religión; impío, profano.

irreligiously [ˌɪrɪ'lɪdʒəslɪ] [i-ri-li-yos-li], *adv.* Irreligiosamente.

irreligiousness [ˌɪrɪ'lɪdʒəsnɪs] [i-ri-li-yos-nes], *s.* Irreligiosidad, falta de religión.

irremediable [ˌɪrɪ'miːdəbl] [i-ri-mi-da-bol], *a.* 1. Irremediable, irreparable. 2. Incurable; incorregible.

irremediableness [ˌɪrɪ'miːdəblnɪs] [i-ri-mi-da-bol-nes], *s.* El estado o la condición de lo que no tiene remedio.

irremissible [ˌɪrɪ'mɪsɪbl] [i-ri-mi-si-bol], *a.* Inevitable (unavoidable). Irremisible, imperdonable (unpardonable).

irremissibly [ˌɪrɪ'mɪsɪblɪ] [i-ri-mi-si-bli], *adv.* Irremisiblemente.

irremovable [ˌɪrɪ'muːvəbl] [i-ri-mu-va-bol], *a.* 1. Inamovible, que no puede ser removido, que no puede ser privado de su empleo, ni trasladado a otro. 2. Inmutable.

irremunerable [ɪrɪˌmjʊ'nerəbl] [i-ri-miu-ne-ra-bol], *a.* Incapaz de ser remunerado o premiado.

irreparability [ˌɪrepærə'bɪlɪtɪ] [i-re-pa-ra-bi-li-ti], *s.* El estado de lo que es irreparable.

irreparable [ɪ'repərəbl] [i-re-pa-ra-bol], *a.* Irreparable (cannot be repaired). Irremediable.

irreparably [ɪ'repərəblɪ] [i-re-pa-ra-bli], *adv.* Irreparablemente.

irrepealable [ˌɪrɪ'pɪələbl] [i-re-pa-lia-bol], *a.* Inabrogable, que no puede ser abrogado, anulado o revocado.

irreplaceable [ˌɪrɪ'pleɪsəbl] [i-re-plei-sa-bol], *a.* Irremplazable, insustituible.

irreprehensible [ˌɪrɪprɪ'hensɪbl] [i-ri-pri-jen-si-bol], *a.* Irreprensible.

irreprehensibly [ˌɪrɪprɪ'hensɪblɪ] [i-ri-pri-jen-si-bli], *adv.* Irreprensiblemente.

irrepresentable [ˌɪrɪprɪ'sentəbl] [i-ri-pri-sen-ter-bol], *a.* Lo que no se puede poner a la vista por medio de alguna representación o figura.

irrepressible [ˌɪrɪ'presəbl] [i-ri-pre-sa-bol], *a.* 1. Lo que no puede ser oprimido ni reprimido. 2. Incontrolable. **Irrepressible laughter** risa incontenible.

irreproachable [ˌɪrɪ'prəʊtʃəbl] [i-ri-prou-cha-bol], *a.* Intachable, incensurable.

irreproachably [ˌɪrɪ'prəʊtʃəblɪ] [i-ri-prou-cha-bli], *adv.* Irreprensiblemente.

irreprovable [ˌɪrɪ'pruːvəbl] [i-ri-pru-va-bol], *a.* Irreprensible.

irreprovably [ˌɪrɪ'pruːvəblɪ] [i-ri-pru-va-bli], *adv.* Sin tacha, sin cometer falta ninguna.

irresistance [ˌɪrɪ'zɪstəns] [i-ri-sis-tans], *s.* Falta de propensión a hacer oposición o resistir; paciencia para sufrir las injurias.

irresistibility ['ɪrɪˌzɪstɪ'bɪlɪtɪ] [i-ri-sis-ti-bi-li-ti], *s.* Fuerza o poder irresistible, lo que no se puede resistir o contrarrestar.

irresistible [ˌɪrɪ'zɪstɪbl] [i-ri-sis-ti-bol], *a.* Irresistible.

irresistibleness [ˌɪrɪ'zɪstɪblnɪs] [i-ri-sis-ti-bol-nes], *s.* Poder o calidad irresistibles.

irresistibly [ˌɪrɪ'zɪstɪblɪ] [i-ri-sis-ti-bli], *adv.* Irresistiblemente.

irresoluble [ɪ'rezəlʊbl] [i-re-so-lu-bol], *a.* Irresoluble, que no se puede resolver o determinar.

irresolubleness [ɪ'rezəlʊblnɪs] [i-re-so-lu-bol-nes], *s.* Solidez o resistencia de un cuerpo a la separación de sus partes.

irresolute [ɪ'rezəluːt] [i-re-so-lut], *a.* Irresoluto, vacilante, indeciso.

irresolutely [ɪ'rezəluːtlɪ] [i-re-so-lut-li], *adv.* Irresolutamente.

irresoluteness [ɪ'rezəluːtnɪs] [i-re-so-lut-nes], *s.* Irresolución.

irresolution [ɪ'rezəluːʒən] [i-re-so-lu-shon], *s.* Irresolución, vacilación, duda, indecisión.

irrespective [ˌɪrɪ'spektɪv] [i-ris-pek-tiv], *a.* Inconsiderado, independiente de condiciones; que carece de relación, que no hace al caso. Se usa por lo común con la prep. *of.* **Irrespective of ability**, independiente de la habilidad o capacidad.

irrespectively [ˌɪrɪ'spektɪvlɪ] [i-ris-pek-tiv-li], *adv.* Inconsideradamente.

irrespirable [ˌɪrɪs'paɪərəbl] [i-ris-pai-ra-bol], *a.* Irrespirable; impropio para la respiración.

irresponsibility ['ɪrɪsˌpɒnsɪ'bɪlɪtɪ] [i-ris-pon-sa-bi-li-ti], *s.* Irresponsabilidad, falta de responsabilidad.

irresponsible [ˌɪrɪs'pɒnsɪbl] [i-ris-pon-si-bol], *a.* Irresponsable, exento de responsabilidad. Irreflexivo. Falto de seriedad.

irresponsive [ˌɪrɪs'pɒnsɪv] [i-ris-pon-siv], *a.* 1. Frío, poco entusiasta. 2. Insensible (insensive).

irretraceable [ˌɪrɪ'træʃəbl] [i-ri-tra-sha-bol], *a.* Se aplica al camino por donde se va y no se puede volver; que no puede ser puesto de nuevo en su estado anterior.

irretrivable [ˌɪrɪ'triːvəbl] [i-ri-tri-va-bol], *a.* Irrecuperable, irreparable, incobrable.

irretrievably [ˌɪrɪ'triːvəblɪ] [i-ri-tri-va-bli], *adv.* Irreparablemente.

irreturnable [ˌɪrɪ'tɜːnəbl] [i-ri-ter-na-bol], *a.* Incapaz de volver o retornar.

irreverence [ɪ'revərəns] [i-re-ve-rans], *s.* Irreverencia, falta de reverencia, de veneración, particularmente hacia cosas sagradas.

irreverent [ɪˈrevərənt] [i-re-ve-rant], *a.* Irreverente, falto de reverencia, de veneración; irrespetuoso, desatento.

irreverently [ɪˈrevərəntlɪ] [i-re-ve-rant-li], *adv.* Irreverentemente.

irreversibility [ˈɪrɪˌvɜːsɪˈbɪlɪtɪ] [i-ri-ver-si-bi-li-ti], *a.* Irreversibilidad. Irrevocabilidad (of a decision).

irreversible [ˌɪrɪˈɜːsəbl] [i-ri-ver-sa-bol], *a.* 1. Que no se puede volver al revés; que no puede ser mudado o puesto en lugar de otra cosa. 2. Irrevocable.

irreversibleness [ˌɪrɪˈɜːsəblnɪs] [i-ri-ver-sa-bol-nes], *s.* El estado de lo que es irrevocable.

irreversibly [ˌɪrɪˈɜːsəblɪ] [i-ri-ver-sa-bli], *adv.* Sin poder ser revocado.

irrevocability [ˌɪrɪvəkəˈbɪlɪtɪ] [i-re-vo-ka-bi-li-ti], *s.* Irrevocabilidad.

irrevocable [ɪˈrevəkəbl] [i-re-vo-ka-bol], *a.* Irrevocable.

irrevocableness [ɪˈrevəkəblnɪs] [i-re-vo-ka-bol-nes], *s.* El estado o la calidad irrevocable de una cosa.

irrevocably [ɪˈrevəkəblɪ] [i-re-vo-ka-bli], *adv.* Irrevocablemente.

irrigable [ˈɪrɪgəbl] [i-ri-ga-bol]. Irrigable. **Irrigable lands**, tierras de regadío.

irrigant [ˈɪrɪgənt] [i-ri-gant], *a.* Regador, que sirve para regar.

irrigate [ˈɪrɪgeɪt] [i-ri-gueit], *va.* 1. Regar, conducir el agua por medio de acequias o canales para fertilizar la tierra. 2. Mojar, humedecer; irrigar una llaga.

irrigation [ˌɪrɪˈgeɪʃən] [i-ri-guei-shon], *s.* Riego, regamiento.

irrision [ɪˈrɪʃən] [i-ri-shon], *s.* Irrisión, desprecio, burla.

irritability [ˌɪrɪtəˈbɪlɪtɪ] [i-ri-ter-bi-li-ti], *s.* 1. Irritabilidad, una de las calidades exclusivamente propias de los cuerpos organizados; propiedad de responder a un estímulo. 2. Propensión a irritarse fácilmente.

irritable [ˈɪrɪtəbl] [i-ri-ter-bol], *a.* 1. Irritable, irascible, que es capaz de irritación. 2. Irritable, que está dotado de irritabilidad. **To get irritable**, enojarse, irritarse.

irritableness [ˈɪrɪtəblnɪs] [i-ri-ter-bol-nes], *s.* Iracundia, irritabilidad, con propensión a irritarse.

irritant [ˈɪrɪtənt] [i-ri-tant], *a.* 1. (*For.*) Irritante, irrito, lo que anula o invalida. 2. Irritante, lo que irrita. (*Fig.*) Molestia, fastidio.

irritate [ˈɪrɪteɪt] [i-ri-teit], *va.* 1. Irritar, exasperar. 2. Irritar, agitar.

irritating [ˈɪrɪteɪtɪŋ] [i-ri-tei-tin], *a.* 1. Molesto, fastidioso, 2. Pesado, tedioso (tedious).

irritation [ˌɪrɪˈteɪʃən] [i-ri-tei-shon], *s.* 1. Irritación, provocación, movimiento de cólera (act). 2. (*Med.*) Irritación, picor, conmoción violenta de algunos humores. 3. Enfado, mal humor (state).

irritative [ˈɪrɪtətɪv] [i-ri-ter-tiv], *a.* Irritador, irritante, que sirve para causar irritación; acompañado de irritación.

irruption [ɪˈrʌpʃən] [i-rap-shon], *s.* Irrupción, entrada violenta o forzada; invasión.

irruptive [ɪˈrʌptɪv] [i-rap-tiv], *a.* Invasor, que comete o hace alguna irrupción.

is [ɪz] [is], Es o está, tercera persona singular del presente de indicativo del verbo TO BE.

isagogical [ˌɪzəˈgɒdʒɪkl] [i-sa-go-yi-kal], *a.* Isagógico, que pertenece a la introducción de los libros de la Biblia, su historia literaria, inspiración, etc.

isagon [ˈɪzəgən] [i-sa-gon], *s.* (*Geom.*) Iságono, figura de ángulos iguales.

ISBN *s.* Abreviatura de **International Standard Book Number**.

ischiatic [ˈɪskɪətɪk] [is-kia-tik], *a.* Isquiático, perteneciente o relacionado con el hueso isquion.

ischury [ˈɪskərɪ] [is-ka-ri], *s.* Iscuria, retención de orina.

ischuretic [ˈɪskərɪtɪk] [is-ka-ri-tik], *s.* Cualquier remedio para hacer salir la orina detenida o suprimida.

iserine [ˈɪsəriːn] [i-sa-rin], *s.* (*Min.*) Iserina, especie de minera o quijo de titanio.

-ish [ɪʃ] [ish], Terminación inglesa que sirve para expresar diminución en la calidad del substantivo a que se añade, o para hacer adjetivos gentilicios o patronimicos, como

bluish, azulado, de **blue**, azul; **sickish**, enfermizo, **de sick**, enfermo; **Spanish**, español, de **Spain**, España.

isinglass [ˈaɪzɪŋglɑːs] [ai-sin-glas], *s.* Colapiscis, colapez, o cola de pescado.

islam [ˈɪzlɑːm] [is-lam], *s.* 1. Islam, islamismo, la religión de Mahoma. 2. Islam, conjunto de los hombres y pueblos que creen y aceptan esta religión.

islamic [ɪzˈlæmɪk] [is-la-mik], *a.* Islámico/a.

island [ˈaɪlənd] [ai-land], *s.* 1. Isla. 2. Isleño.

islander [ˈaɪləndəʳ] [ai-lan-daʳ], *s.* Isleño, el natural de alguna isla o el que vive en ella.

isle [aɪl] [ail], *s.* Isla pequeña (generalmente voz poética).

islet [ˈaɪlɪt] [ai-lit], *s.* Isleta.

isn't [ˈɪznt] [isent], **Is not**.

isobar [ˈaɪsəbɑːʳ] [ai-sou-baʳ], *s. f.* Isobara.

isobaric [ˈaɪsəʊˈbærɪk] [ai-sou-ba-rik], *a.* Isobárico.

isochromatic [ˈaɪsəkrəˈmætɪk] [ai-so-krou-ma-tik], *a.* 1. Isocromático, que tiene o denota el mismo color. 2. V. ORTHOCHROMATIC.

isochronal [ˈaɪsəkrɒml] [ai-so-krou-mal], **Isochronous** [ˈaɪsəˈkrɒnəs] [ai-so-kro-nos], *a.* Isócrono.

isogloss [ˈaɪsəglɒs] [ai-so-glos], *s.* Isoglos, Isoglos, línea de demarcación entre regiones de diferencias lingüísticas.

isolate [ˈaɪsəʊleɪt] [ai-so-leit], *va.* 1. Aislar, separar, apartar, poner solo. 2. (*Elec.*) Aislar. 3. (*Quím.*) Eliminar de una sustancia toda combinación.

isolated [ˈaɪsəʊleɪtɪd] [ai-so-lei-tid], *a.* Separado, apartado, aislado (place). **Isolated case**, caso único.

isolation [ˌaɪsəʊˈleɪʃən] [ai-so-lei-shon], *s.* Aislamiento, separación; estado de soledad. **In isolation**, por separado. **Isolation ward**, pabellón de aislamiento.

isolationism [ˌaɪsəʊˈleɪʃənɪzm] [ai-so-lei-sho-ni-sem], *s.* Aislacionismo.

isolationist [ˌaɪsəʊˈleɪʃənɪst] [ai-so-lei-sho-nist], *s.* Aislacionista, partidario del aislacionismo en las relaciones internacionales.

isomerism [ˌaɪsəˈmerɪzm] [ai-so-me-ri-sem], *s.* (*Quím.*) Isomerismo, identidad de elementos y proporciones con propiedades diferentes.

isometric [ˌaɪsəʊˈmetrɪk] [ai-sou-me-trik], *a.* Isométrico.

isometrics [ˌaɪsəʊˈmetrɪkz] [ai-sou-me-triks], *s.* Isometría.

isomorphic [ˌaɪsəʊˈmɔːfɪk] [ai-sou-mor-fik], *a.* Isomorfo.

isomorphism [ˌaɪsəʊˈmɔːfɪzm] [ai-sou-mor-fi-sem], *s.* (*Min.*) Isomorfismo, isomorfia, estado de los cuerpos que, difiriendo en su composición, presentan al cristalizar formas iguales.

isomorphous [ˌaɪsəʊˈmɔːfəs] [ai-sou-mor-fos], *a.* Isomorfo.

isoperimetrical [ˌaɪsəʊˌperɪˈmetrɪkl] [ai-sou-pe-ri-me-tri-kal], *a.* Isoperimétrico.

isosceles [aɪˈsɒsɪliːz] [ai-so-si-lis], *a.* Isósceles.

isotherm [ˈaɪsəʊθɜːm] [ai-sou-zerm], *s.* Línea isoterma, la que pasa por los puntos de la tierra en que es la misma la temperatura media.

isothermal [ˌaɪsəʊˈθɜːməl] [ai-sou-zer-mal], *a.* Isotermo, isotérmico.

isotope [ˈaɪsəʊtəʊp] [ai-sou-toup], *s.* (*Fís. y Quím.*) Isótopo.

Israeli [ɪzˈreɪlɪ] [is-ria-lait], *a. & s.* Israelí.

Israelite [ˈɪzrɪəlaɪt] [is-ria-lait], *s.* Israelita, descendiente de Israel (o Jacob); hebreo, judío.

iss Abreviatura de **issue**.

issuable [ˈɪʃʊəbl] [i-shua-bol], *a.* Lo que es capaz de llevar o conducir una cosa hasta su terminación.

issue [ˈɪʃʊː] [i-shu], *s.* 1. Salida, el acto de salir. 2. Salida, la parte por donde se sale fuera de algún sitio o lugar. 3. Lo que se produce, emite o publica: (a) edición, v.g. la de un periódico. **Back issue**, número atrasado (magazine); (b) prole, progenie, sucesión; (c) emisión de valores; (d) rentas, réditos. **He died without issue**, murió sin sucesión (offspring). 4. Evento, consecuencia, resultado, fin, término, conclusión. 5. Fuente, cauterio, una llaga pequeña que se mantiene abierta artificialmente con varios objetos. 6. Decisión, conclusión. **Issue of blood**, pérdida de sangre.

Issue a wall, cuarteadura. **A cause at issue**, una causa que está para verse o sentenciarse. **Feigned issue**, (*For.*)

expediente formado con el consentimiento de ambas partes para la decisión del punto en cuestión, sin pasar por los trámites judiciales. **Point at issue**, materia de que se trata, punto en cuestión; asunto, proceso. **To join issue**, tomar partes opuestas en una discusión o un pleito; tener pareceres contrarios sobre una proposición; contradecirse mutuamente. **To take issue with**, estar en desacuerdo, discrepar.

issue, *vn.* 1. Salir, pasar de la parte de adentro a la de afuera. 2. Prorrumpir, brotar. 3. Venir, proceder, traer su origen. 4. Provenir, salir o proceder de algún fondo. 5. Acabarse, terminarse, resolverse; esparcirse en líneas. **To issue something to somebody**, entregar algo a alguien. -*va.* 1. Echar, brotar, arrojar para afuera. 2. Expedir, despachar alguna cosa judicialmente (passports, warrant). 3. Emitir, poner en circulación (tickets, stamps). 4. Dar a la luz, publicar (books, newspapers, magazines).

issueless [ˈɪʃuːlɪs] [i-shu-lis], *a.* Sin sucesión.

issuing [ˈɪʃuːɪŋ] [i-shuin], *s.* Salida.

isthmus [ˈɪsθməs] [isz-mos], *s.* Istmo, lengua de tierra, entre dos mares que une dos continentes o una península a un continente.

iT *s.* **Income Tax** (Fin.).

it [ɪt] [it], Pronombre inglés que se pone en lugar de los nombres de cosas inanimadas, y aun de los animales cuyo sexo no puede determinarse; por consiguiente corresponde en español a *él, ella, ello, lo, la, le*, según los géneros y casos de las cosas a que se refiere: v.g. **He will not have it** (con referencia un *libro*), él no *lo* quiere; (con referencia a una *manzana*), él no *la* quiere. **She caught the butterfly, and preserved it**, ella cogió la mariposa, y la conservó. Cuando *it* es objeto de los verbos, se traduce por medio del pronombre *lo*, o se omite, según la frase; como, **He saw it**, él lo vió. **They know nothing of it**, Ellos no saben nada sobre ello. *It*, en las frases impersonales, y cuando se usa en lugar del sujeto que se pospone al verbo, no se traduce; v.g. **It is warm**, hace calor. **It is a matter of constant experience that bodily exercise is conducive to health**, es materia de constante experiencia, que el ejercicio corporal conduce a la salud. Tampoco se traduce en las preguntas o respuestas de la misma clase; v.g. **It was he who did it**, él fue quien lo hizo. *It* se usa para preguntar por el estado de una persona o cosa. **How is it with the boss?**, ¿cómo está el jefe? **Who is it?**, ¿quién es? **It's Peter**, soy Peter. **You're it!**, te toca (games). **That's it!**, ¡ya basta! (disaproval); ¡correcto!, ¡eso es! (aproval). Se usa algunas veces después de los verbos neutros para dar énfasis a su significación.

Italian [ɪˈtælɪən] [i-ter-lian], *s.* Italiano, el natural de Italia y la lengua de este país. -*a.* Italiano.

italianize [ɪˈtælɪənaɪz] [i-ter-lia-nais], *va.* 1. Hacer italiano; conformar al carácter, costumbres o lengua italianos. 2. Convertir abejas en la clase de las llamadas italianas, dándoles una reina italiana.

italic [ɪˈtælɪk] [i-ter-lik], *a.* Bastardilla, cursiva, carácter de letra. **It is printed in italics**, está impreso en letra bastardilla.

italicize [ɪˈtælɪsaɪz] [i-ter-li-sais], *va.* Distinguir con letras bastardillas; de aquí, dar énfasis.

itch [ɪtʃ] [ich], *s.* 1. Sarna, enfermedad cutánea. 2. Comezón, picazón. 3. Sarna, el deseo vehemente de conseguir alguna cosa; prurito, flujo. **Itch-insect**, (*Ent.*) Acaro, arador, insecto que se engendra en las postillas sarnosas.

itch, *vn.* 1. Picar, sentir picazón o comezón. **My arm itches**, me pica el brazo. 2. Antojarse, padecer antojo o deseo vehemente de alguna cosa, tener prurito por algo.

itchiness [ˈɪtʃɪnɪs] [i-chi-nes], *s.* 1. Escozor, picazón. 2. Sarnosidad.

itching [ˈɪtʃɪŋ] [i-chin], *s.* 1. Escozor, picazón; irritación de la piel. 2. Deseo ardiente, prurito. **To be itching to do something**, arder en deseos de hacer algo.

itchy [ˈɪtʃɪ] [i-chi], *a. Comp.* **Itchier**, *Superl.* **Itchiest.** 1. Sarnoso. 2. Lo que produce comezón o picazón; picante. **My leg is itchy**, tengo picor en la pierna.

it'd, It would; it had.

item [ˈaɪtəm] [ai-tem], *adv.* Item; otro sí, aun más: se usa para distinguir los diversos artículos en un escrito. -*s.* 1. Cada uno de los artículos separados por el adverbio item en algún escrito. 2. Partida, artículo, párrafo.

itemize [ˈaɪtəmaɪz] [ai-te-mais], *va.* Sentar alguna cosa por artículos; apuntar cada artículo.

iterable [ˈaɪtərəbl] [ai-te-ra-bol], *a.* Iterable, capaz de repetirse.

iterate [ˈaɪtəreɪt] [ai-te-reit], *va.* Iterar, repetir, reiterar; inculcar.

iteration [ˌaɪtəˈreɪʃən] [ai-te-rei-shon], *s.* Iteración, la repetición de un acto.

iterative [ˈaɪtərətɪv] [ai-te-ra-tiv], *a.* 1. Iterativo, que se reitera o repite. 2. (*Gram.*) Frecuentativo.

itinerant [ɪˈtɪnərənt] [i-ti-ne-rant], *a.* Itinerante, viandante; vago; ambulante, errante.

itinerary [ɪˈtɪnərərɪ] [i-ti-ne-ra-ri], *s.* 1. Itinerario, derrotero y dirección de un camino por donde se debe pasar haciendo un viaje. 2. Viaje de exploración, su plan o su relato. 3. Guía (book, guide). -*a.* Itinerario, hecho en viaje, perteneciente a él.

itinerate [ɪˈtɪnəreɪt] [i-ti-ne-reit], *vn.* Viajar.

-itis, Sufijo que denota inflamación.

it'll, It shall; it will.

ITO Abreviatura de **International Trade Organization**.

its [ɪtz] [its], El genitivo del pronombre *It*. Su (de él, de ella, de ello). **A house and its furniture**, una casa con sus muebles.

it's, Abreviatura de **it is**.

itself [ɪtˈself] [it-self], *pron.* El mismo, la misma, lo mismo; pronombre recíproco que se aplica solamente a las cosas, como *himself* y *herself* se aplican a las personas. **It moves by itself**, eso se mueve por sí mismo. **She is virtue itself**, es la virutd misma. **She did it herself**, lo hizo ella sola, por sí misma.

I. *V. s. m.* Gota a gota.

i.v. Abreviatura de **invoice value**.

i've [aɪv] [aiv], Contracción familiar de **I have**, yo tengo. **I've seen it!** ¡Lo he visto!

-ive [ɪv] [iv], Sufijo equivalente a -or o -ivo en español; que sirve para ejecutar la acción del verbo. **Expulsive**, expulsivo.

IVF Abreviatura de **In Vitro Fertilization** (FIV).

ivied [ˈɪviːd] [i-vid], *a.* Cubierto de hiedra.

ivory [ˈaɪvərɪ] [ai-vo-ri], *s.* 1. Marfil, el colmillo del elefante. 2. Sustancia que se parece al marfil. 3. *pl.* Cosas hechas de marfil. 4. (*Fest.*) *pl.* Dientes. -*a.* Ebúrneo, lo que está hecho de marfil, o se parece a él; blanco, duro.

ivy [ˈaɪvɪ] [ai-vi], *s.* 1. (*Bot.*) Hiedra. **Ground ivy**, hiedra terrestre.

iwis [ˈaɪwiːz] [ai-uis], *adv.* Ciertamente; a saber. *V.* YWIS.

-ize, -ise Sufijo usado en la formación de verbos que significan hacer, dar, practicar.

J

j [dʒeɪ] [yei], Esta letra tiene siempre en inglés un sonido semejante al de la *y* consonante castellana, aunque mucho más fuerte, igual al de la sílaba *gi* en italiano, como en *giorno, giocoso*. Puede representarse por *dy;* v.g. *jade* «[dyed]»; pero en este diccionario conserva su propia forma inglesa.

JA Abreviatura de **Judge Advocate**.

jab [dʒæb] [yab], *va.* (*Fam.*) Pinchar con violencia; golpear rudamente. -*s.* Punzada; golpe a manera de pinchazo.

jabber [ˈdʒæbər] [ya-baʳ], *vn.* 1. Charlar, hablar mucho y sin substancia. 2. Farfullar, parlar precipitadamente. 3. (*Fam.*) Hablar en jerigonza, hablar en griego, marmotear. 4. Mascar o farfullar las palabras.

jabberer [ˈdʒæbərəʳ] [ya-ba-raʳ], *s.* Farfullador, parlanchín.

jabberment [ˈdʒæbəˈmənt] [ya-ber-ment], *s.* Charla, farfulla, jerga, algarabía, guirigay.

jaborandi [ˌdʒæbəˈrændɪ] [ya-bo-ran-di], *s.* Jaborandi, pilocarpo, planta medicinal del Brasil.

jacent [ˈdʒæsənt] [ya-sent], *a.* Yacente, que está echado o tendido.

jacinth [ˈdʒæsɪnθ] [ya-sinz], *s.* 1. (*Bot.*) V. HYACINTH. 2. (*Min.*) V. ZIRCON.

Jack [dʒæk] [yak], *s.* 1. Juanito, Juanillo, diminutivo de *John*, Juan; hombre; marinero. 2. Martinete, el palillo del clavicordio que hiere las cuerdas. 3. Torno de asador. 4. Jarro o vaso de cuero negro encerado. 5. Cota de malla. 6. Boliche o bola pequeña que se echa en el juego de las bolas par que sirva de señal a los jugadores. 7. Macho, el animal del sexo masculino. 8. Burro, armazón con que los aserradores afianzan el madero que se ha de aserrar. 9. (*Mar.*) Bandera de proa. 10. (*Ic.*) Lucio o luso pequeño, un pez. 11. La sota entre los naipes. 12. Gato (cars). **Jacko'-lantern**, fuego fatuo o de San Telmo, helena. **Jack-boots**, botas grandes y fuertes. **Jack of the clock-house**, estatua de reloj que da la hora con un mazo. **Jack plug**, enchufe hembra (*Elec.*). **Jack sauce**, hombre descarado. **To be jack of all trades**, (a) aprendiz de todo y oficial de nada. (b) sabelotodo. **Jack-o'-lent, Jackalent**, maniquí, efigie de Judas Iscariote que solían llevar en las procesiones de cuaresma en Inglaterra y a la que se apedreaban después. **Jack-in-the-pulpit**, V. INDIAN TURNIP. **Jack-plane**, garlopa, cepillo grande de carpintero. **Jack-pudding**, arlequín, bufón, titiritero, payaso. **Jack-rabbit**, liebre americana de orejas y piernas muy largas. **Jack in** Dejar (*fam.*).

jackal [ˈdʒækəl] [ya-kal], *s.* Chacal, animal semejante al perro.

jackanapes [ˈdʒækəneɪps] [ya-ka-neips], *s.* 1. Pisaverde, mequetrefe, un impertinente. 2. Salvaje, necio, tonto. **Hatter's jack**, Carda.

jackass [ˈdʒækɑːs] [ya-kas], *s.* 1. Garañón, asno, borrico. 2. (*Fig.*) Asno, tonto, necio, imbécil.

jackboot [ˈdʒækbʊt] [yak-but], *s. f.* Bota de montar. Bota militar.

jackdaw [ˈdʒækdɔː] [yak-dou], *s.* (*orn.*) Corneja pequeña, ave parecida al cuervo y al grajo.

jacket [ˈdʒækɪt] [ya-kit], *s.* 1. Chaqueta, saco. 2. (*Mec.*) Chaqueta, cubierta del cilindro. **Jacket (of a book)**, forro de un libro.

jackhammer [ˈdʒækˌhæməʳ] [yak-ja-maʳ], *s.* Perforadora.

jack-in-the-box [lˈdʒekɪðəbɒks] [yak-in-de-boks], *s. f.* Caja sorpresa.

jack Ketch [ˌdʒækˈketʃ] [yak-kech], *s.* Verdugo.

jack-knife [ˈdʒæknaɪf] [yak-naif], *s.* Navaja sevillana, navaja fuerte de bolsillo.

jackpot [ˈdʒækpɒt] [yak-pot], *s. m.* Primer premio, premio gordo. **To hit the jackpot**, obtener el premio gordo. Ser un gran éxito (*Fig.*).

jackscrew [ˈdʒækˈskruː] [yak-skru], *s.* (*Mar.*) Gato cornaquí.

jacksmith [ˈdʒæksmɪθ] [yak-smiz], *s.* El que hace tornos de asador.

jackstaff [ˈdʒækstɑːf] [yak-staf], *s.* (*Mar.*) Asta de bandera.

jackstone [ˈdʒækstəʊn] [yak-stoun], *s.* Una de las piedrecitas o piezas de metal usadas en cierto juego de niños.

jackstraw [ˈdʒækstrɔː] [yak-stro], *s.* 1. Efigie de paja; de aquí, hombre insignificante, sin influencia. 2. *pl.* Juego con pajitas o astillas de madera, hueso, etc. En singular, una de esas pajas o astillas.

jack-tree [ˈdʒæktriː] [yak-tri], *s.* Artocarpo, árbol de cultivo, semejante al árbol del pan.

jacobean [ˌdʒækəˈbiːən] [ya-ko-bian], *a.* Que se refiere al tiempo de Jacobo I, rey de Inglaterra.

jacobin [ˌdʒækəˈbiːn] [ya-ko-bin], *s.* 1. Dominico o fraile dominicano. 2. Jacobino, demócrata, antimonárquico. 3. Irreligioso. 4. Pichón con copete.

jacobin, Jacobinical [ˌdʒækəˈbiːn] [ya-ko-bin] [ˌdʒækəˈbiːnɪkl] [ya-ko-bi-ni-kal], *a.* Jacobínico.

jaconibinism [ˌdʒækəˈbɪnɪzm] [ya-ko-bi-ni-sem], *s.* Jacobinismo.

jacobinize [ˌdʒækəˈbɪnaɪz] [ya-ko-bi-nais], *va.* Infundir o propagar los principios o máximas de los jacobinos.

jacobite [ˈdʒækəbaɪt] [ya-ko-bait], *s.* 1. Hereje. 2. Jacobita, el partidario del rey Jacobo II de Inglaterra.

jacob's-ladder [ˈdʒækəbzˈlædəʳ] [ya-kobs-la-daʳ], *s.* 1. (*Bot.*) Polemonio azul. 2. (*Mar.*) Escala de jarcias para subir a las cofas.

jacob's-staff [ˈdʒækəbzˈstɑːf] [ya-kobs-staf], *s.* 1. Bordón de peregrino; bastón con estoque. 2. (*Mar.*) Báculo de Jacob, astrolabio.

jaconet, Jacconet [ˈdʒækənɪt] [ya-ko-nit], *s.* Chaconá, chaconada, especie de tela de algodón muy fina que usan las mujeres para vestidos de verano.

jactitation [ˈdʒæktɪˈteɪʃən] [ya-ti-tei-shon], *s.* Agitación, inquietud.

jaculate [ˈdʒækjəleɪt] [ya-kiu-leit], *va.* Lanzar, arrojar.

jaculation [ˌdʒækjəˈleɪʃən] [ya-kiu-lei-shon], *s.* (*Ant.*) Lanzamiento.

jaculatory [ˈdʒækjələtərɪ] [ya-kiu-la-to-ri], *a.* 1. Arrojado o disparado de pronto. 2. Jacultorio, breve y fervoroso.

jacuzzi [dʒæˈkuːzɪ] [ya-ku-si], *s. m.* Jacuzzi, baño de burbujas.

jade [dʒeɪd] [yeid], *s.* 1. Rocín, caballo alquilón y de mala traza. 2. Mujercilla, picarona, buena alhaja: término de desprecio. 3. (*Min.*) Piedra nefrítica. 4. Jade, especie de esmeralda.

jade, *va.* Cansar, acosar; sujetar, maltratar, tiranizar. -*vn.* Desanimarse, desalentarse.

jaded [ˈdʒeɪdɪd] [yei-did], *a.* Harto, hastiado. **To feel jaded**, estar harto.

jadery [ˈdʒeɪderɪ] [yei-da-ri], *s.* Burla pesada.

jadish [ˈdʒeɪdɪʃ] [yei-dish], *a.* 1. Vicioso: se dice de las yeguas. 2. Incontinente; dícese de las mujeres.

jag [dʒæg] [yag], *va.* Dentar, formar dientes en alguna cosa.

jag, *s.* 1. Diente, las puntas que se hacen en ciertos instrumentos; punta saliente, púa. 2. Carga para un solo caballo; de aquí, licor fuerte en cantidad bastante para embriagar.

jagged [ˈdʒægɪd] [ya-guid], *a.* Dentado; recortado en los bordes de un modo desigual.

jaggedness [ˈdʒægɪdnɪs] [ya-guid-nes], *s.* El estado de lo que está dentellado o dentado.

jaggy [ˈdʒægɪ] [ya-gui], *a.* Dentado, dentellado.

jai Alai [ˈdʒaɪəˈlaɪ] [yai-alai], *s.* Jai Alai, frontón, juego de pelota vasca.

jail [dʒeɪl] [yeil], *s.* Cárcel, prisión. **Jail fever**, tifo, fiebre de las cárceles.

jail-bird [ˈdʒeɪlbɜːd] [yeil-berd], *s.* El que ha sido encarcelado, tal vez con frecuencia; criminal, presidiario.

jailbreak [ˈdʒeɪlbreɪk] [yeil-breik], *s. f.* Evasión, fuga.

jailer [ˈdʒeɪləʳ] [yei-laʳ], *s.* Carcelero, alcaide de una cárcel.

jalap [ˈdʒæləp] [ya-lap], *s.* Jalapa.

jalopy [dʒəˈlɒpɪ] [ya-lo-pi], *s.* Auto viejo y destartalado.

jam [dʒæm] [yam], *s.* 1. Conserva o mermelada de frutas. 2. Aprieto, apretura causada por mucha gente o por muchos objetos; apretadura, apiñadura. 3. Apuro, en cualquier situación.

jam, *va.* Apiñar; acuñar o apretar, estrechar, apachurrar. 2. Llenar y cerrar algo apretando o apiñando. 3. (*Rad.*) Enredar la difusión de una difusora. -*vn.* Quedarse inmóvil por efecto de apretadura o acumulación.

Jamaican [dʒəˈmeɪkə] [ya-mei-ka], *a.* Jamaicano, perteneciente a la isla de Jamaica.

jamaica pepper [dʒəˈmeɪkəˌpepəʳ] [ya-mei-ka-pe-paʳ], *s.* (*Bot.*) Pimienta.

jamaica wood [dʒəˈmeɪkəˌwʊd] [ya-mei-ka-wud], *s.* 1. Palo de Campeche. 2. Brasilete. 3. Caoba fina.

jamb [ˈdʒæmb] [yamb], *s.* Quicial, el madero que asegura y afianza las puertas y ventanas.

jamboree [ˌdʒæmbəˈriː] [yam-bo-ri], *s.* 1. (*Fam.*) Jolgorio, ruidoso festival. 2. Reunión nacional o internacional de muchachos exploradores.

jam-packed [ˈdʒæmˈpækt] [yam-pakt], *a.* Apiñado, apretujado (full of people). Atestado (full of things).

jam session [ˈdʒæmˈseʃən] [yam-se-shon], *s.* Reunión de músicos para improvisar música popular.

Jan Abreviatura de **January**, enero.

jangle [ˈdʒæŋgl] [yan-guel], *vn.* Reñir, altercar; charlar. *-va.* Hacer sonar desapaciblemente alguna cosa.

jangle, *s.* Sonido discordante; de aquí, disputa, querella, altercado.

jangler [ˈdʒæŋglər] [yan-glaʳ], *s.* Un charlatán; parlanchín, disputador.

jangling [ˈdʒæŋglɪŋ] [yan-blin], *s.* Sonido discordante; riña, pendencia; charla.

janitor [ˈdʒænɪtər] [ya-ni-taʳ], *s.* Portero (doorkeeper); bedel, en los colegios y universidades (caretaker).

jannock [ˈdʒænɒk] [ya-nok], *s.* Pan de avena.

jant, Janty, V. JAUNT, JAUNTY.

january [ˈdʒænʊərɪ] [ya-nua-ri], *s.* Enero, el primer mes del año.

jap [dʒæp] [yap], **Japanese** (fam: offensive).

japan [ˈdʒæpən] [ya-pan], *s.* Charol, obra charolada; barniz. **Japan earth**, tierra japónica.

japan, *va.* 1. Charolar, embarnizar. 2. Limpiar y dar lustre al calzado.

Japanese [ˌdʒæpəˈniːz] [ya-pa-nis], *a.* Japonés, natural del Japón o perteneciente a él. *-s.* 1. Natural del Japón. 2. Idioma japonés, lengua aglutinante.

japhetic [ˈdʒæfɪtɪk] [ya-fe-tik], *a.* Jafético, descendiente de Jafet, hijo de Noé, o que se refiere a él.

jar [dʒɑːʳ] [yaʳ], *vn.* 1. Chocar una cosa con otra. 2. (*Mús.*) Discordar, desentonar (clash). 3. Reñir, desavenirse, disputar, descompadrar, contender, cruzar (opinion). 4. Sonar alguna cosa con un sonido o vibración igual, como el tic-tac de un reloj. *-va.* 1. Hacer discordar o desentonar. 2. Agitar, sacudir (shake).

jar, *s.* 1. Jarro o jarra; tinaja, cántaro, tarro, orza, botija. **To have a jar**, tomar un trago. 2. Choque, pendencia, disensión, riña. 3. Sonido desapacible y repetido. 4. Balanceo, como el de una puerta sobre sus goznes; se emplea solamente en la locución **on a jar, on the jar**, entreabierto. V. AJAR. **To give somebody a jar**, dejar perplejo, dejar de piedra. **To jar on someone's nerves**, poner a alguien los nervios de punta.

jardinière [ˌdʒɑːdɪˈnɪəʳ] [yar-di-niaʳ], *s.* Jardinera, mueble para colocar en él macetas conplantas.

jargon [ˈdʒɑːgən] [yar-gon], *s.* 1. Jerga, jerigonza, guirigay, monserga. 2. Caló. V. CANT y LINGO.

jargon, Jargoon [ˈdʒɑːguːn] [yar-gun], *s.* (*Min.*) Jacinto, una especie de piedra preciosa. V. JACINTH.

jargonelle [ˌdʒɑːgəˈnil] [yar-go-nil], *s.* Especie de pera tempranera.

jarl [ˈdʒɑːl] [yarl], *s.* (Histo. escand.) 1. Noble, hidalgo. 2. Jefe, caudillo.

jarring [ˈdʒɑːrɪŋ] [ya-rin], *s.* Riña, contienda.

jashawk [ˈdʒɑːsɒk] [ya-sok], *s.* Halconcillo.

jasmine [ˈdʒæzmɪn] [yas-min], **jessamine** [ˈdʒɛsəmɪn] [yi-sa-min], *s.* (*Bot.*) Jazmín. **American jasmine**, Jazmín americano. **Carolina o yellow jasmine** (o **jessamine**), Jazmín amarillo, planta medicinal.

jasper, jasperite [ˈdʒæspəʳ] [yas-paʳ], *s.* 1. Jaspe, variedad opaca e impura de cuarzo, de uno o varios colores. 2. (Biblia) Piedra preciosa en el pectoral del gran sacerdote de los judíos.

jato [ˈdʒætə] [ya-to], *s.* (*Aer.*) Propulsión auxiliar para el despegue de aviones.

jaundice [ˈdʒɔːndɪs] [yon-dis], *s.* 1. Ictericia. (*Vulg.*) Tiricia, una enfermedad. 2. Celos, prevención, preocupación del ánimo. *-va.* Afectar con ictericia, de aquí, preocupar, predisponer el ánimo contra alguien o algo.

jaundiced [ˈdʒɔːndɪst] [yon-dist], *pp.* y *a.* Ictérico, ictericiado. Rencoroso, resentido (attitude).

jaunt [ˈdʒɔːnt] [yont], *vn.* Corretear, andar de una parte a otra, ir y venir.

jaunt, *s.* 1. Excursión, caminata. 2. Llanta, pina. *V.* FELLOES.

jauntiness [ˈdʒɔːntɪnɪs] [yon-ti-nes], *s.* Viveza, gentileza, garbo, ligereza.

jaunty [ˈdʒɔːntɪ] [yon-ti], *a.* Ostentoso, vistoso, delicado, gentil, galán, airoso.

javanese [ˌdʒɑːvəˈniːz] [ya-va-nis], *a.* Javanés, javo, de la isla de Java o perteneciente a ella. *-s.* 1. Natural o habitante de Java. 2. Lengua del centro de Java.

javelin [ˈdʒævlɪn] [ya-ve-lin], *s.* Jabalina, especie de media lanza.

jaw [dʒɔː] [yo], *s.* 1. Quijada, mandíbula; hueso maxilar; órgano análogo en los invertebrados. 2. (Art. y Of.) Boca, quijada. 3. Boca; (*fig.*) abismo, garras. **The jaws of death**, las garras de la muerte. 4. (*Vulg.*) Vituperio o insulto hecho con palabras groseras. **Jaw-teeth**, las muelas. **The jaws of hell**, la boca del infierno. **Jaw of a vise**, telera.

jawbone [ˈdʒɔːbəʊn] [yo-boun], *s. m.* Mandíbula (person).

jawbreaker [ˈdʒɔːˌbreɪkəʳ] [yo-brei-kaʳ], *s.* Trabalenguas, palabra kilométrica.

jawed [ˈdʒɔːd] [yod], *a.* Lo que tiene la apariencia de las quijadas o es semejante a ellas.

jay [dʒeɪ] [yei], *s.* (*Orn.*) Gayo, ave parecida al cuervo en su forma.

jaywalk [ˈdʒeɪwɔːk] [yei-uok], *vn.* Cruzar imprudentemente a pie calles de intenso tráfico.

jaywalker [ˈdʒeɪˌwɔːkəʳ] [yei-uo-kaʳ], *s. m./f.* Peatón/a imprudente.

jazz [dʒæz] [yas], *s.* Jazz, música popular sincopada originaria de E. U. A. **Progressive jazz**, Jazz progresivo. **... and all that jazz**,... y cosas por el estilo.

jazz up [ˈdʒæzʌp] [yas-ap], *v.* 1. Sincopar (music). 2. Avivar, animar (party).

KCS *s.* Abreviatura de **Joint Chiefs of Staff**.

jct. Abreviatura de **junction** (Rail).

JD *s.* Abreviatura de **Justice Department**, Ministerio de Justicia.

jealous [ˈdʒeləs] [ye-los], *a.* 1. Celoso. 2. Envidioso. 3. Receloso, el que teme. 4. Desconfiado, el que desconfía. 5. Suspicaz.

jealously [ˈdʒeləslɪ] [ye-los-li], *adv.* Celosamente, sospechosamente.

jealousy [ˈdʒeləsɪ] [ye-lo-si], *s.* 1. Celos, sospecha, inquietud, recelo, suspicacia. 2. Desconfianza; emulación.

jealousness [ˈdʒeləsnɪs] [ye-los-nes], *s.* Vigilancia, sospecha, celos.

jean [dʒiːn] [yin], *s.* Mezclilla, tela burda de algodón. **Jeans**, *pl.* Pantalones vaqueros.

jeep [dʒiːp] [yip], *s.* Jeep, automóvil pequeño de transporte.

jeer [dʒɪəʳ] [yiaʳ], *vn.* Befar, mofar, escarnecer. *-va.* Escarnecer, tratar con escarnio. Abuchear, gritar.

jeer, *s.* 1. Befa, mofa, escarnio, burla. 2. Abucheo (from crowd).

jeerer [ˈdʒɪərəʳ] [yia-raʳ], *s.* Mofador, escarnecedor, burlador.

jeering [ˈdʒɪərɪŋ] [yia-rin], *s.* 1. Insolente, mofador. Burlón, sarcástico. 2. Burlas (mockery), protestas, insultos (protests, insults).

jeering, *s.* Burla, escarnio.

jeeringly [ˈdʒɪərɪŋlɪ] [yia-rin-li], *adv.* Con escarnio.

jeez [dʒiːz] [yis], *interj.* ¡Santo Dios! (*fam.*).

Jehovah [dʒɪˈhəʊvə] [yi-jou-va], *s.* Jehová, nombre hebreo de Dios.

jehu [ˈdʒɪhuː] [yi-ju], *s.* 1. Aficionado a guiar caballos; cochero que guía veloz o furiosamente. 2. Cochero en general. **To drive like Jehu**, ir desempedrando las calles.

jejuneness, Jejunity [dʒɪˈdʒuːnɪs] [yi-yu-nes], *s.* Carestía, esterilidad; pobreza, tibieza, aridez de estilo.

jejunum [dʒɪˈdʒuːnəm] [yi-yu-num], *s.* (*Anat.*) Yeyuno, el segundo de los intestinos delgados.

jellied [ˈdʒelɪd] [ye-lid], *a.* Gelatinoso, convertido en jalea; dulce como una jalea.

jelly ['dʒelɪ] [ye-li], *s.* Jalea, jaletina. **Currant jelly**, Jalea de grosellas. **Jelly broth**, Consumado. **Baby jelly**, caramelo de goma, golosina.

jellyfish ['dʒelɪfɪʃ] [ye-li-fish], *s.* 1. Aguamar, medusa. 2. *(Fam.)* Calzonazos.

jemmy ['dʒemɪ] [ye-mi], *a.* V. SPRUCE. *-s.* Pie de cabra corto, palanqueta. V. JIMMY.

jennet ['dʒenɪt] [ye-net], *s.* Jaca.

jenny ['dʒenɪ] [ye-ni], *s.* 1. Torno, máquina para hilar. 2. Una hembra; particularmente, asna, burra, borrica. 3. *(Orn.)* Troglodita.

jeopard ['dʒepəd] [ye-pard], *va.* Arriesgar, exponer a pérdida o daño.

jeopardize ['dʒepədaɪz] [ye-par-dais], *va.* V. JEOPARD.

jeopardy ['dʒepədɪ] [ye-par-di], *s.* Riesgo, peligro.

jerboa [dʒɜː'bəʊ] [yer-bou], *s.* Gerbo, cuadrúpedo roedor.

jeremiad [,dʒerɪ'maɪəd] [ye-ri-maiad], *s.* Jeremiada, lamentación, a veces sarcástica, sobre la maldad o la depravación de otros.

jerk [dʒɜːk] [yerk], *s.* 1. Tirón o empellón repentino; sacudida, sobarbada, sacudimiento, vibración (shake). 2. La sacudida o golpe repentino que dan las cosas elásticas cuando se rompen o saltan. 3. Salto o brinco. 4. Tasajo, charqui. **She sat up with a jerk**, se puso de pie de un salto. 5. Pelma, pesado *(fam.)*. Pendejo.

jerk, *va.* 1. Tirar o arrojar con impulso violento y repentino, dar un tión repentino y brusco; mover a tirones; emitir de una manera convulsiva. 2. Tasajear, charquear, cortar la carne (de buey) en lonjas largas y secarlas al sol sin salarlas. **Jerked beef**, tasajo, charqui. *-vn.* Sacudir; vibrar.

jerker ['dʒɜːkəʳ] [yer-kaʳ], *s.* Sacudidor, tirador.

jerkin ['dʒɜːkɪn] [yer-kin], *s.* 1. Coleto de ante sin mangas. V. JACKET. 2. *(Orn.)* Especie de halcón.

jerk out ['dʒɜːkaʊt] [yerk-aut], *v.* Hablar con voz entrecortada (words).

jerky ['dʒɜːkɪ] [yer-ki], *a.* Vacilante (speech).

jerry-built ['dʒerɪbɪlt] [ye-ri-bilt], *a.* Mal edificado, construido con material deficiente.

jerry can ['dʒerɪkæn] [ye-ri-kan], *s. m.* Bidón.

jersey ['dʒɜːsɪ] [yer-si], *s.* 1. Estambre fino. 2. Camisa fuerte hecha de punto de lana fina. 3. Jubón o chaqueta elástica muy ajustada al cuerpo, hecha de lana o de seda. 4. Res de ganado mayor oriundo de la isla de Jersey, en el canal de la Mancha.

jerusalem artichoke [dʒɜ'ruːsələm,a:tɪtʃəʊk] [ye-ru-sa-lem-ar-ti-chouk], *s. (Bot.)* Pataca, aguaturma.

jess [dʒes] [yes], *s.* Grillos de halcón, correilla que se ataba a la pata del halcón.

jessamine ['dʒesəmiːn] [ye—sa-min], *s. (Bot.)* Jasmín. V. JASMINE.

jesse ['dʒesiː] [ye-si], *s.* 1. Arafia o candelero sin pie con muchos mecheros. 2. *(Ger.)* Represión, zaherimiento. **To give one (particular) Jesse**, ponerlo a uno como nuevo.

jest [dʒest] [yest], *vn.* Bufonearse, burlarse, chancearse, zumbar, chulear.

jest, *s.* 1. Chanza, burla, broma, zumba; chiste. 2. Hazmerreír. **A piercing jest**, Broma pesada, chasco.

jester ['dʒestəʳ] [yes-taʳ], *s.* Gracioso, mofador, bufón, burlón, chancero.

jesting ['dʒestɪŋ] [yes-tin], *s.* Mofadura, chanza, bufonería.

jestingly ['dʒestɪŋlɪ] [yes-tin-li], *adv.* De burlas.

jesuit ['dʒezʊɪt] [ye-suit], *s.* Jesuita.

jesuitic, Jesuitical ['dʒezʊɪtɪk] [yi-sui-tik], *a.* Jesuítico.

jesuits' bark ['dʒezʊɪtz,ba:ʳ] [ye-suits-baʳ], *s.* Quina, cascarilla.

jesus ['dʒiːsəs] [yi-sas], *s.* Jesús, el Hijo de Dios.

jesus Christ ['dʒiːsəsˌkraɪst] [yi-sas-kraist], *s.* Jesucristo.

jet [dʒet] [yet], *s.* 1. Azabache. 2. Surtidor; mechero para gas; tubo que sirve para dar salida a un fluido. 3. Objeto, blanco, antiguamente escopo. **Jet of water**, chorro de agua. 4. Avión (plane). V. JUT. **Jet-black**, negro como el azabache. **Jet engine**, reactor (plane).

jet, *vn.* Echar arrojar fuera, lanzar; contonearse, inflarse; traquear, vacilar; correr de una parte a otra. **To jet it along**, andar con orgullo. **To jet out**, sobresalir.

jet plane ['dʒetpleɪn] [yet-plein], *s.* Avión de retropropulsión, avión a chorro.

jet-propelled [,dʒetprə'pelt] [yet-pro-pelt], *a.* A reacción.

jet propulsion [,dʒetprə'pʌlʃən] [yet-pro-pal-shan], *s.* Propulsión a chorro, propulsión por reacción, retropropulsión.

jetsam ['dʒetsəm] [yet-sam], o **Jetson** ['dʒetsən] [yet-son], *s.* 1. *(Mar.)* Echazón. 2. Parte de la carga de un buque cuando hay necesidad de aligerarla; en derecho, los géneros echados al mar que quedan debajo del agua; en contraposición a **flotsam**, los que flotan.

jettee, *s.* V. JETTY.

jettison ['dʒetɪsən] [ye-ti-son], *va.* Arrojar al mar fardos de mercancías y otros objetos para aligerar un buque en peligro. *-s.* 1. Echazón. 2. V. JETSAM, 2ª acepción.

jetty ['dʒetɪ] [ye-ti] *a.* Hecho de azabache, azabachado, negro. *-s.* 1. Salidizo. 2. Muelle. V. JUTTY.

jew ['dʒuː] [yu], *s.* Judío.

jewel ['dʒuːəl] [yual], *s.* 1. Joya. 2. Piedra preciosa. *Jewels*, Pedrería. 3. Prenda, expresión de cariño.

jewel, *va.* Adornar con piedras preciosas.

jeweled ['dʒuːəld] [yuald], *a.* Enjoyado, adornado con piedras preciosas.

jewel-like ['dʒuːəlˌlaɪk] [yual-laik], *a.* Brillante como pedrería.

jeweler ['dʒuːələʳ] [yua-laʳ], *s.* Joyero, dimantista.

jewelry ['dʒuːəlrɪ] [yual-ri], *s. f. pl.* Alhajas, joyas. **A piece of jewelry**, una joya.

Jewess ['dʒuːɪs] [yuis], *sf.* Judía.

Jewish ['dʒuːɪʃ] [yuish], *a.* Judaico, judío.

jewishness ['dʒuːɪʃnɪs] [yuish-nes], *s.* Ritos religiosos de los judíos.

Jewry ['dʒʊərɪ] [yua-ri], *s.* 1. Judea. 2. Judería.

jews'-ears ['dʒuːz'ɪəz] [yus-ias], *s. (Bot.)* Orejas de Judas, especie de hongo.

jews'-harp ['dʒuː'hɑːp] [yus-jarp], *s.* Birimbao. *(Amer.)* Marímbula, trompa.

jezebel ['dʒezəbel] [ye-sa-bel], *s.* Mujer presumida, jamona e impertinente.

jib [dʒɪb] [yib], *s. (Mar.)* Maraguto o foque. **Flying-jib**, petifoque o cuarto foque. **Standing-jib**, contrafoque. **Middle-jib**, segundo foque. **Jib-boom**, botalón de foque. **Jib-iron**, arraca.

jibe [dʒaɪb] [yaib], *va. (Mar.)* Mudar un botavante.

jiffy ['dʒɪfɪ] [yi-fi], *s. (Fam.)* Instante, momento.

jig [dʒɪg] [yig], *s.* 1. Cualquier baile y música vivos y alegres. 2. Trampa, petardo. 3. *(Min.)* Criba. 4. Anzuelo que tiene el astil cargado de plomo. 5. *(Mec.)* Conductor o guía para fabricar piezas idénticas. **Jig-saw**, Sierra de vaivén.

jig, *va.* 1. Cantar o tocar música. 2. Sacudir de abajo hacia arriba; separar minerales con una criba. 3. Formar o adaptar por medio de guías. *-vn.* 1. Bailar sin maestro; bailar mal o con poca gracia. 2. Pescar con el anzuelo emplomado llamado *jig*.

jigger ['dʒɪgəʳ] [yi-gaʳ], *s.* 1. El que baila; lo que va y viene. 2. Cualquier utensilio que tiene movimiento de vaivén; v. g. criba para minerales; rueda de alfarero, *(Mar.)* aparejuelo, el palanquín de socaire.

jigger, *s.* 1. Nigua, insecto muy parecido a la pulga que se introduce bajo la epidermis de los pies (en el Perú, se llama *pique*). V. CHIGOE. 2. Pulga, garrapata u otra sabandija.

jiggered ['dʒɪgəd] [yi-gad], *a.* **I'm jiggered if I will**, que me cuelguen si lo hago.

jigjog ['dʒɪgjəg] [yig-yog], *s. (Vulg.)* Empujón, sacudimiento.

jigsaw ['dʒɪgsɔː] [yig-so], *s.* Sierra de vaivén o de calar.

jigsaw puzzle ['dʒɪgsɔːˌpʌzl] [yig-so-pa-sel], *s.* Rompecabezas que consiste en pedazos de cartón cortados con sierra de vaivén.

jill [dʒɪl] [yil], *s*. 1. Una joven; querida; a menudo significa manceba, concubina. 2. Hurón hembra. 3. Taza, jícarra. **Jill-flirt**, Mujer ligera y coqueta.

jilt [dʒɪlt] [yilt], *s*. La mujer que caprichosamente despide a un pretendiente; dícese también algunas veces del hombre que no corresponde al amor de una mujer.

jilt, *va*. Engañar una mujer a sus amantes; lisonjear una mujer a un hombre traidoramente dándole esperanzas falsas. *(Fam.)* Plantar, dejar colgado. **To jilt a man**, despedirle, darle calabazas. -*vn*. Hacer una mujer el papel de coqueta u ocuparse en intrigas amorosas.

jingle [ˈdʒɪŋɡl] [yin-guel], *vn*. 1. Retiñir, sonar o resonar. 2. Hacer eco; rimar. -*va*. Producir un sonido agudo, como de pequeños objetos metálicos.

jingle, *s*. 1. Retintín, sonido de campanas pequeñas o pedazos de metal. 2. Cualquier sucesión agradable de sonidos rítmicos; rima pueril, aleluya.

jingoism [ˈdʒɪŋɡəʊɪzəm] [yin-gou-isem], *s*. Jngoísmo, patriotería exaltada.

jingoist [ˈdʒɪŋɡəʊɪst] [yin-gouist], *s*. y *a*. Jingoísta.

jingoistic [ˌdʒɪŋɡəʊˈɪstɪk] [yin-gou-is-tik], *a*. Jingoísta, patriotero/a.

jinks [ˈdʒɪŋkz] [yinks], *s. pl*. **High jinks**, jolgorio, juerga. **To have high jinks**, pasárselo pipa.

jinx [ˈdʒɪnks] [yinks], *s*. Cenizo, portador de la mala suerte.

jippo [ˈdʒɪpəʊ] [yin-pou], *s*. Jubón, jaqueta o chaqueta sin mangas; una especie de cotilla.

jitterbug [ˈdʒɪtəbʌɡ] [yi-ta-bag], *s*. Bailador, en forma exagerada de música sincopada (jazz).

jitters [ˈdʒɪtəz] [yi-tars], *s. pl*. **To get the jitters**, ponerse nervioso. **To give the jitters**, asustar, causar miedo a alguien, poner nervioso a alguien *(fam.)*.

jittery [ˈdʒɪtərɪ] [yi-ta-ri], *a*. Muy nervioso, inquieto *(fam.)*.

jive [dʒaɪv] [yaiv], *s*. 1. Cierta música sincopada, swing. 2. Jerga de músicos. 3. Galimatías. 4. Tonterías, chorradas (nonsense). **Don't give me all that jive**, deja de decir tonterías.

job [dʒɒb] [yob], *s*. 1. Tarea: labor o trabajo hecho o que ha de hacerse como un todo; destajo, remiendo (job). 2. Negocio u ocupación lucrativa a expensas del público, engañifa; cucaña, ganga, el negocio o empleo que es muy lucrativo con poco trabajo. 3. *(Fam.)* Empleo, obtención de trabajo, puesto de trabajo. 4. *(Fam.)* Suceso, circunstancia; negocio. 5. La herida hecha con arma punzante. V. JAB. **Job-printing**, impresión de remiendos. **Odd job**, trabajo de poca monta, friolera, bagatela. **It was big job**, dio mucho trabajo. **Part-time/full-time job**, trabajo de media jornada/a jornada completa.

job, *va*. 1. Comprar en grueso al importador o fabricante y vender a los comerciantes. 2. Hacer al destajo, por ajuste; trabajar al destajo. 3. Dar una mojada o herir repentinamente con arma punzante. -*vn*. Negociar en los fondos públicos; cambalachear o chalanear.

jobber [ˈdʒɒbər] [yo-bar], *s*. 1. Agiotador, agiotista, el que negocia en los fondos públicos. 2. Destajero, destajista; *(Com.)* Corredor. V. MIDDLEMAN. 3. *(Fam.)* El que se emplea en negocios bajos. 4. Remendero, remendón, el que hace obras de poca monta.

jobbery [ˈdʒɒbərɪ] [yo-ba-ri], *s*. Engañifa, manejos bajos para fines políticos.

jobbing [ˈdʒɒbɪŋ] [yo-bin], *pa*. y *s*. Acción del verbo **to job**. **Jobbing house**, casa que compra a importadores o fabricantes y vende a detalladores. **Jobbing printer**, impresora de folletos.

jobless [ˈdʒɒblɪs] [yob-les], *a*. Cesante, sin empleo, sin trabajo.

job lot [ˈdʒɒblət] [yob-lot], *s*. Colección miscelánea de mercancías que se supone de calidad inferior.

job seeker [ˈdʒɒbˌsiːkər] [yob-si-kar], *s*. El que busca empleo.

jockey [ˈdʒɒkɪ] [yo-ki], *s*. 1. El jinete que corre a caballo en las carreras públicas. 2. Chalán, el que trata en caballos. 3. Engañabobos, el que usa de embustes y trampas. **To jockey somebody into**, convencer a alguien.

jockey, *va*. 1. Atropellar a uno con un caballo. 2. Trampear, engañar con trampas o fraudes.

jocose [dʒəˈkəʊs] [yo-kous], *a*. Jocoso, festivo, chancero, burlesco, jovial.

jocosely [dʒəˈkəʊslɪ] [yo-kous-li], *adv*. Jocosamente, en burla, en chanza.

jocoseness [dʒəˈkəʊsnɪs] [yo-kous-nes], **Jocosity** [dʒəˈkəʊsɪtɪ] [yo-kou-si-ti], *s*. Jocosidad, festividad, alegría, chanza.

jocular [ˈdʒɒkjʊlər] [yo-kiu-lar], *a*. Jocoso, chistoso, divertido; burlesco.

jocularity [ˌdʒɒkjʊˈlærɪtɪ] [yo-kiu-la-ri-ti], *s*. Festividad, jocosidad.

jocularly [ˈdʒɒkjʊləlɪ] [yo-kiu-lar-li], *adv*. Jocosamente.

joculatory [ˈdʒɒkʊlətərɪ] [yo-kiu-la-to-ri], *a*. Chistoso, gracioso, chancero, divertido.

jocund [ˈdʒɒkənd] [yo-kond], *a*. Alegre, festivo, plácido, agradable.

jodh-purs [ˈdʒɒdpɜːz] [yod-pers], *s. pl*. Pantalones de montar.

Joe [dʒəʊ] [you], *s*. **The average Joe**, el hombre de la calle. **Joe Soap**, fulano.

Joe Miller [ˈdʒəʊˌmɪlər] [you-mi-lar], *(Fam.)* Chanza muy sabida, chiste que data de mucho tiempo; libro de chistes.

jog [dʒɒɡ] [yog], *va*. 1. Empujar; dar un golpe suave a alguno para llamar su atención; sacudir con el codo o la mano. 2. *(Fig.)* Excitar suavemente, estimular. **To jog the memory**, estimular la memoria. -*vn*. Traquearse, bambolearse, moverse, suavemente. **To jog on**, empujar a alguno hacia adelante, moverse hacia adelante con un movimiento suave; andar a saltos.

jog, *s*. 1. Empellón, sacudimiento ligero, movimiento irregular. 2. Traqueo, zangoloteo, bazuqueo: dícese del movimiento de un coche o carruaje.

jogging [ˈdʒɒɡɪŋ] [yo-guin], *s*. Sacudimiento, traqueo.

joggle [ˈdʒɒɡl] [yo-guel], *vn*. 1. Moverse o agitarse con movimiento trémulo. 2. Vacilar. -*va*. Empujar.

John [dʒɒn] [yon], *n. pr*. Juan; muchacho; tipo nacional. **John Bull**, (a) apodo dado al inglés típico; de aquí, el pueblo inglés. Su traducción literal es Juan Toro. (b) Juego con peniques. **John Chinaman**, un chino, los chinos en general.

John-apple [ˈdʒɒnˌeɪpl] [yon-ei-pol], *s*. *(Bot.)* Especie de manzana tardía. **St. John's Gospel**, el evangelio de San Juan. **St. John's bread**, *(Bot.)* garrofa o algarroba, fruto del árbol llamado algarrobo. **St. John's bread tree**, algarrobo. **St. John's wort**, hipérico, corazoncillo. **John-dory**, dorado, fabro, pez de mar de forma comprimida.

john, *s. m*. Retrete, baño.

Johnny [ˈdʒɒnɪ] [yo-ni], *n. pr*. Juanito, dim. de Juan, apodo dado a los confederados por los soldados de los Estados Unidos del Norte durante la guerra civil.

Jonny-cake [ˈdʒɒnɪˌkeɪk] [yo-ni-keik], *s*. *(E. U.)* Torta de maíz.

join [dʒɔɪn] [yoin], *va*. 1. Juntar, unir, añadir, trabar. 2. Juntar, unir a una persona con otra en alianza o en matrimonio; asociar. 3. Juntarse o unirse a; empeñarse juntos, por lo general en sentido hostil contra otro u otros; chocar, embestir. **To join battle**, empezar la batalla. -*vn*. 1. Unirse, juntarse; ser contiguo o próximo a. 2. Unirse, aliarse, confederarse por alianza o por matrimonio. 3. Agregarse, asociarse. **To join with one**, asociarse a alguno o tener parte en lo que alguno ha hecho. **To join forces**, aliarse. **To join together**, juntarse, unirse. **Join in**, tomar parte, participar (game, protest). **I joined in the game**, me uní al juego. **Join on**, situarse al final de (queue). **Join up**, alistarse *(Mil.)*.

joinder [ˈdʒɔɪndər] [yoin-dar], *s*. *(For.)* Junta, unión, asociación.

joiner [ˈdʒɔɪnər] [yoi-nar], *s*. Ensamblador, carpintero de obra prima.

joinery [ˌdʒɔɪnərɪ] [yoi-na-ri], *s.* Ensambladura, juntura; el arte del ensamblador. Carpintería.

joint [ˈdʒɔɪnt] [yoint], *s.* Coyuntura, articulación. 2. Gozne, bisagra; charnela. 3. Cuarto, uno de los miembros de un animal cortado para aderezarlo y comerlo; uno de esos trozos de carne puesto sobre la mesa. 4. Ensambladura. 5. Nudo o articulación de una planta. **Out of joint**, lujado; desunido, despegado; desordenado, confuso, desconcertado, descoyuntado. *-a.* 1. Distribuído, dividido, repartido. 2. Participante, el que tiene parte en alguna cosa; común a muchos, solidario. **Joint heir**, coheredero. 3. Unido, combinado, indiviso. **With joint consent**, de común acuerdo. **Joint responsibility**, responsabilidad solidaria. **Joint property**, propiedad indivisa. **Joint-stock**, capital social, fondos en común. **Joint-stock company**, compañía por acciones. **Joint tenant**, inquilino en común con otro; terrateniente pro indiviso. **Joint account**, cuenta común.

joint, *va.* 1. Juntar, unir, agregar. 2. Formar nudos, articulaciones o coyunturas. 3. Descuartizar. 4. Confederar, hacer alianza.

jointed [ˈdʒɔɪntɪd] [yoin-tid], *a.* Nudoso, lo que está lleno de nudos o junturas; de o con coyunturas; de movimiento.

jointer [ˈdʒɔɪntəʳ] [yoin-taʳ], *s.* Juntera, instrumento de carpintería.

jointly [ˈdʒɔɪntlɪ] [yoint-li], *adv.* Juntamente, unidamente, mancomunadamente. **Jointly and severally**, Todos y cada uno de por sí.

jointress [ˈdʒɔɪntrɪs] [yoin-tris], *sf.* Mujer que posee alguna cosa por derecho de viudedad.

joint-stool [ˈdʒɔɪntstuːl] [yoint-stul], *s.* Asiento o banquillo plegadizo, silla de tijera.

jointure [ˈdʒɔɪntʃəʳ] [yoin-chaʳ], *s.* Viudedad, lo que ha de poseer la mujer después de la muerte de su marido, señalado ya en la vida de éste.

jointure, *va.* Asignar bienes o rentas a una mujer en las capitulaciones matrimoniales.

joist [ˈdʒɔɪst] [yoist], *s.* Viga o vigueta de bovedilla o suelo.

joke [dʒəʊk] [youk], *s.* Chanza, dicho o hecho burlesco, burla, chocarrería. **In joke**, en chanza, de burlas, en zumba. **A ready joke**, un dichito al caso. **A practical joke**, un bromazo, un petardo, una mala pasada. **A sorry joke**, una broma pesada. **A crack a joke**, decir un chiste, una agudeza; hacer el gracioso. **To play a joke on**, gastar una broma. **It's no joke**, no tiene ninguna gracia. **She can't take a joke**, no aguanta las bromas, no le gusta que le tomen el pelo ¡**You must be joking!**, ¡no lo dices en serio!

joke, *vn.* Chancear, chancearse, usar de chanzas.

joker [ˈdʒəʊkəʳ] [you-kaʳ], *s.* 1. Burlón, chancero, deudor. 2. En algunas formas del juego de naipes, el comodín.

joking [ˈdʒəʊkɪŋ] [you-kin], *s.* 1. Chanza, burla, chiste. 2. Burlón/ona, bromista (tone). **Apart joking**, bromas aparte, hablando en serio. **He's not in a joking mood**, no está para bromas.

jokingly [ˈdʒəʊkɪŋlɪ] [you-kin-li], *adv.* En broma, en chanza, chistosamente.

jollily [ˈdʒɒlɪlɪ] [yo-li-li], *adv.* Alegremente.

jolliness [ˈdʒɒlɪnɪs] [yo-li-nes], *s.* **Jollity** [yo-li-ti], *s.* Viveza; alegría, regocijo.

jolly [ˈdʒɒlɪ] [yo-li], *a.* 1. Alegre, festivo, airoso, gallardo, vivo, placentero, agradable. 2. Rollizo, lleno, robusto. **She was jolly glad**, se alegró muchísimo. **To jolly along**, dar ánimos. **Jolly good!** ¡estupendo, fabuloso!

jolly-boat [ˈdʒɒlɪbəʊt] [yo-li-bout], *s.* (*Mar.*) Botequín, serení.

jolt [dʒəʊlt] [yoult], *vn.* Traquearse, bambolearse. *-va.* Traquear, sacudir; menear repentinamente de arriba abajo.

jolt, *s.* Vaivén, traqueo, salto. **To give a bit of a jolt**, dar un buen susto.

jolter [ˈdʒəʊltəʳ] [youl-taʳ], *s.* Lo que traquea o sacude.

jolthead [ˈdʒəʊlthed] [yoult-jed], *s.* Cabeza redonda, zote, bolonio.

jonquil [ˈdʒɒŋkwɪl] [yon-kuil], *s.* (*Bot.*) Junquillo, planta de jardín de flores amarillas.

joss [dʒɒs] [yos], *s.* Ídolo o dios chino. **Joss-house**, templo o lugar para ídolos chinos. **Joss-paper**, papel dorado o plateado que queman los chinos en los funerales y en ciertos ejercicios religiosos. **Joss-stick**, pajuela perfumada, cubierta con polvos de maderas olorosas, que los chinos queman ante sus ídolos.

jostle [ˈdʒɒsl] [yo-sel], *va.* Rempujar, apretar, codear. *-vn.* Dar un tropezón con otro, empujarse. **To jostle against**, chocar, dar empujones.

jot [dʒɒt] [yot], *s.* Jota, ápice, tilde, punto, una cosa mínima. **Every jot**, todo. **There's not a jot of truth in it**, no tiene ni pizca de verdad. *V.* IOTA.

jot, *va.* **To jot down**, apuntar, tomar notas.

jotting [ˈdʒɒtɪŋ] [yo-tin], *s.* Apunte, nota.

joule [dʒuːl] [yul], *s.* Julio, unidad de medida del trabajo eléctrico, equivalente al producto de un voltio por un culombio; el esfuerzo necesario para mantener la resistencia de un amperio contra la de un ohmio durante un segundo.

jounce [dʒəʊns] [yauns], *va.* y *vn.* (*Fam.*) Sacudir o sacudirse, traquear. *-s.* Sacudimiento repentino o violento.

journal [ˈdʒɜːnl] [yer-nal], *s.* 1. Diario, relación de lo que sucede cada día. 2. Diario, papel periódico que se da al público cada día. 3. Jornal, libro en que los mercaderes hacen los asientos de sus operaciones o negocios por días, desde el borrador o diario, para anotarlos después en el libor mayor. 4. (*Mec.*) Luchadero, manga de eje, cilindro que termina un árbol de rotación, sostenido por un cojinete. **Journal-bearing**, cojinete.

journalism [ˈdʒɜːnəlɪzəm] [yer-na-li-sem], *s.* Periodismo, profesión y ocupación de periodista.

journalist [ˈdʒɜːnəlɪst] [yer-na-list], *s.* Diarista, periodista.

journalize [ˈdʒɜːnəlaɪz] [yer-na-lais], *va.* (*Com.*) Pasar al jornal, por vía de preparación para el libro mayor. *-vn.* Apuntar en el diario.

journey [ˈdʒɜːnɪ] [yer-ni], *s.* 1. Jornada. 2. Viaje, tramo, trayecto (trip). 3. Tránsito, el paso o acto de pasar de un paraje a otro. **To break one's journey**, hacer una parada. **Outward/return journey**, viaje de ida/de vuelta.

journey, *va.* Viajar, ir de viaje de una parte a otra.

journeyman [ˈdʒɜːnɪmən] [yer-n-mani], *s.* Jornalero, el que trabaja por un jornal. **Journeyman tailor**, oficial de sastre.

journey-work [ˈdʒɜːnɪwɜːk] [yer-ni-uerk], *s.* Jornal, trabajo del jornalero.

joust [dʒəʊst] [yaust], *s.* Justa, torneo, regocijo público entre los antiguos caballeros.

joust, *vn.* Justar, combatir en una justa.

jove [dʒəʊv] [youv], *s.* **By jove!** ¡caramba!

jovial [ˈdʒəʊvɪəl] [you-vial], *a.* Jovial, alegre, festivo.

joviality, **jovialness** [ˌdʒəʊvɪˈælɪtɪ] [you-via-li-ti], *s.* Jovialidad, festividad, buen humor, regocijo.

jovially [ˈdʒəʊvɪəlɪ] [you-via-li], *adv.* Alegremente, con alegría y jovialidad.

jowl [dʒəʊl] [yaul], *s.* Carrillo o quijada; de aquí, cabeza de pescado aderezada o cocida. Papada (cheek).

jowler [ˈdʒəʊləʳ] [yau-laʳ], *s.* Nombre dado a una especie de perros de caza.

joy [dʒɔɪ] [yoi], *s.* 1. Alegría, júbilo, alborozo, regocijo. 2. Gozo, gusto, complacencia, deleite, la cosa que causa deleite. **I wish you joy**, le doy a Vd. la enhorabuena. **To wish one joy**, desear prosperidad a alguno, dar la enhorabuena. **Joy, joy!** ¡albricias, albricias! **Joy-bells**, *s. pl.* campaneo en señal de regocijo.

joy, *vn.* (*Poét.*) Regocijarse, recrearse. *-va.* (*Des.*) 1. Congratular, felicitar, dar el parabién o la enhorabuena a otro por la felicidad que ha logrado. 2. Gozar, poseer. **To have joy in something**, tener éxito en algo. **I wish you joy of it!**, ¡enhorabuena!, ¡que lo disfrutes!

joyful [ˈdʒɔɪfʊl] [yoi-ful], *a.* Alegre, gozoso. **To be joy about**, alegrarse de.

joyfully [ˈdʒɔɪfəlɪ] [yoi-fa-li], *adv.* Alegremente.

joyfulness [ˈdʒɔɪfʊlnɪs] [yoi-ful-nes], *s.* Alegría, gozo, júbilo.

joyless [ˈdʒɔɪlɪs] [yoi-les], *a.* Triste, sin alegría, insulso.

joylessly [ˈdʒɔɪlɪslɪ] [yoi-les-li] *adv.* Tristemente, insulsamente.

joylessness [ˈdʒɔɪlɪsnɪs] [yoi-les-nes], *s.* Tristeza, melancolía.

joyous [ˈdʒɔɪəs] [yoios], *a.* Alegre, festivo, gozoso.

joyously [ˈdʒɔɪəslɪ] [yoios-li], *adv.* Alegremente, gozosamente.

joyousness [ˈdʒɔɪəsnɪs] [yoios-nes], *s.* Condición o estado de gozoso.

joyride [ˈdʒɔɪraɪd] [yoi-raid], *s. f.* Huida, escapada.

joystick [ˈdʒɔɪstɪk] [yoi-stik], *s. f.* Palanca de control (Computers). Palanca de mando (Aer).

JP Abreviatura de **Justice of the Peace**.

JTPA Abreviatura de **Job Training Partnership Act** (Programa gubernamental de formación profesional en US).

jubilant [ˈdʒuːbɪlənt] [yu-bi-lant], *a.* El que se regocija cantando himnos de alegría.

jubilate [ˈdʒuːbɪleɪt] [yu-bi-leit], *vn.* Alegrarse, proferir sonidos o voces de alegría.

jubilation [ˌdʒuːbɪˈleɪʃən] [yu-bi-lei-shon], *s.* Júbilo, regocijo, alegría.

jubilee [ˈdʒuːbɪliː] [yu-bi-li], *s.* 1. Jubileo, cierta fiesta que celebran los israelitas cada cincuenta años. 2. El quincuagésimo aniversario de cualquier evento y el año en que ocurre ese aniversario. 3. Jubileo, una solemnidad y ceremonia eclesiásticas de la Iglesia católica.

judaic, judaical [dʒuːˈdeɪk] [yu-deik], *a.* Judío, judaico.

judaically [dʒuːˈdeɪkəlɪ] [yu-dei-ka-li], *adv.* A manera de judío.

judaism [ˈdʒuːdeɪɪzəm] [yu-dei-isem], *s.* Judaísmo.

judaize [ˈdʒuːdeɪaɪz] [yu-dei-ais], *vn.* Judaizar, abrazar la religión de los judíos.

judaizer [ˈdʒuːdeɪaɪzəʳ] [yu-dei-aisaʳ], *s.* Judaizante, el que judaiza.

judas-tree [ˈdʒuːdəstriː] [yu-das-tri], *s. (Bot.)* Arbol del amor, árbol de Judas, algarrobo loco.

judean [ˈdʒuːdɪən] [yu-dian], *a.* Judaico, que se refiere a la Judea.

judge [dʒʌdʒ] [yadch], *s.* 1. Juez, magistrado revestido de autoridad para administrar justicia. 2. Juez árbitro, el que es designado para resolver una duda o contienda; el que es capaz de discernir el mérito de alguna cosa. **To be no judge of**, no ser juez en la materia, no entender de. **A good/bad judge of**, conocedor/poco conocedor de. **I'll be the judge of that**, yo mismo lo decidiré. **I judged the moment well**, escogí un buen momento, acerté, atiné. **To judge for oneself**, juzgar por sí mismo.

judge, *vn.* 1. Juzgar, sentenciar, fallar como juez. 2. Juzgar, hacer buen o mal juicio de alguna cosa. 3. Censurar, criticar. 4. Discernir, distinguir.

judgment, jdgement [ˈdʒʌdʒmənt] [yadch-ment], *s.* 1. Juicio, discernimiento. 2. Juicio, decisión, fallo; sentencia del juez. 3. Juicio, voto, sentir, opinión, dictamen. **Last Judgement**, juicio final. **A man of judgment**, hombre de discernimiento. **In my judgment he is greatly mistaken**, yo creo que se engaña mucho. **Judgment-seat**, tribunal. **To the best of on's judgment**, según el leal saber y entender de uno. **To pass judgement on**, dictar sentencia sobre, emitir un juicio crítico sobre *(Jur.)*. **She showed excellent judgement**, demostró tener muy buen gusto.

judgmental, judgemental [dʒʌdʒˈmentl] [yadch-men-tal], *a.* Crítico/a.

judger [ˈdʒʌdʒəʳ] [yad-chaʳ], *s.* Juez, el que juzga.

judgeship [ˈdʒʌdʒəʃɪp] [yad-cha-ship], *s.* Oficio o dignidad de juez; magistratura.

judicable [ˈdʒuːdɪkeɪbl] [yu-di-kei-bol], *a.* Que puede ser probado o juzgado.

judicative [dʒuːˈdɪkətɪv] [yu-di-ka-tiv], *a.* Judicativo, que tiene facultad para juzgar.

judicatory [ˈdʒuːdɪkeɪtərɪ] [yu-di-ka-to-ri], *s.* 1. Justicia. 2. Tribunal de justicia. *-a.* Judicial, que administra justicia.

judicature [ˈdʒuːdɪkətʃəʳ] [yu-di-ka-chaʳ], *s.* 1. Judicatura, magistratura. 2. Tribunal de justicia.

judicial [dʒuːˈdɪʃəl] [yu-di-shal], *a.* 1. Judicial, lo que pertenece al juicio o a la administración de jsuticia. 2. Penal, lo que se impone como pena o castigo por un delito. 3. Legal (separation). 4. Crítico (Mind).

judicially [dʒuːˈdɪʃəlɪ] [yu-di-sha-li], *adv.* Judicialmente.

judiciary [dʒuːˈdɪʃərɪ] [yu-di-sha-ri], *a.* 1. Judiciario; judicial. 2. Magistratura (judges). Poder judicial.

judicious [dʒuːˈdɪʃəs] [yu-di-shos], *a.* Juicioso, prudente, circunspecto, mirado.

judiciously [dʒuːˈdɪʃəslɪ] [yu-di-shos-li], *adv.* Juiciosamente, con juicio.

judiciousness [dʒuːˈdɪʃəsnɪs] [yu-di-shos-nes], *s.* El estado o la calidad que constituye a uno juicioso.

judo [ˈdʒuːdəʊ] [yu-dou], *s. m.* Judo.

jug [dʒʌg] [yag], *va.* 1. Introducir o cocer en una botija o cacharro. 2. *(Vulg.)* Encarcelar. *-vn.* Lanzar cierta nota especial, como lo hacen el ruiseñor y algunos otros pájaros. (Voz onomatopéyica). *-s.* 1. *(E. U.)* Jarro, cacharro, por lo general de barro y con tapón, de boca estrecha y cuerpo ancho, para conservar o conducir líquidos. 2. Jarro, botija, porrón.

juggernaut [ˈdʒʌgənɔːt] [ya-ga-naut] *s. m.* Camión de carga pesada (lorry).

juggle [ˈdʒʌgl] [ya-guel], *vn.* Hacer juegos de manos; engañar, fingir, hacer trampas.

juggle, *s.* 1. Juego de manos. 2. Impostura, engaño, truhanería.

juggler [ˈdʒʌgləʳ] [ya-glaʳ], *s.* 1. Juglar, truhán, titiritero. 2. Impostor, el que finge y engaña con apariencias de verdad. 3. Prestidigitador, jugador de manos, malabarista.

juggling [ˈdʒʌglɪŋ] [ya-glin], *s.* Engaño, impostura, trampa, truhanería.

jugglingly [ˈdʒʌglɪŋlɪ] [ya-glin-li], *adv.* Engañosamente.

jugular [ˈdʒʌgjʊləʳ] [ya-guiu-laʳ], *a.* 1. Yugular, perteneciente a la garganta. 2. Yugular, que se relaciona con la vena yugular. *-s.* 1. Vena yugular. 2. *(Ict.)* Yugular, orden de peces que tiene las aletas ventrales delante de las pectorales.

jugulate [ˈdʒʌgjʊleɪt] [ya-guiu-leit], *va.* Degollar, cortar la garganta.

jugulation [ˌdʒʌgjʊˈleɪʃən] [ya-guiu-lei-shon], *s.* Degollación, degüello.

juice [dʒuːs] [yus], *s.* 1. Zumo, el líquido que se saca de algunas plantas y frutas exprimiéndolas. 2. Jugo, la substancia que se saca de alguna cosa cociéndola. **Juice of the sugar-cane**, zumo de caña; (Cuba) guarapo. 3. Jugo, la substancia de las hierbas. 4. Suco, el humor de que se alimentan los animales y plantas. 5. Corriente (Electr.). **Expressed juice**, zumo, **Boiled juice**, jugo. *(Mex.)* **The unfermented juice of the maguey**, aguamiel.

juiceless [ˈdʒuːslɪs] [yus-les], *a.* Seco, sin zumo, sin jugo.

juiceness [ˈdʒuːsɪnɪs] [yu-si-nes], *s.* Jugosidad.

juicy [ˈdʒuːsɪ] [yu-si], *a.* Jugoso, zumoso, suculento.

jujitsu [dʒuːˈdʒɪtsʊ] [yu-yit-su], *s.* Jiu-jitsu, arte japonés de ucha sin armas.

juke box [ˈdʒuːkbɒks] [yuk-boks], *s.* Tocadiscos. *(Mex.)* Tragadieces, tragaveintes.

julep [ˈdʒuːlep] [yu-lep], *s.* 1. Bebida compuesta de aguardiente o whisky, azúcar, hielo y menta. 2. Julepe, bebida dulce que se usa para tomar en ella un medicamento.

julienne [ˈdʒuːlɪen] [yu-lien], *s.* Caldo claro de carne que contiene zanahorias y otras legumbre picadas; sopa de hierbas.

july [dʒuːˈlaɪ] [yu-lai], *s.* Julio, el séptimo mes del año.

jumble [ˈdʒʌmbl] [yam-bel], *va.* Mezclar y revolver confusamente unas cosas con otras. *-vn.* Mezclarse, revolverse, confundirse.

jumble, *s*. 1. Mezcla, revoltillo, bazuqueo, enredo, embrollo, confusión. 2. Bollito delgado y dulce.

jumbler [ˈdʒʌmbləʳ] [yam-blaʳ], *s*. Mezclador, embrollón, el que mezcla confusamente unas cosas con otras.

jument [ˈdʒʌmənt] [ya-ment], *s*. Acémila, jumento, cualquier bestia de carga.

jump [dʒʌmp] [yamp], *vn*. 1. Saltar, brincar, cruzar una distancia. 2. Traquearse, sacudirse; moverse a saltos. 3. Convenir, concordar. -*va*. 1. Arriesgar, aventurar inconsideradamente. 2. (*Ger., E. U. y Austral.*) Usurpar, tomar posesión por fuerza o en ausencia del propietario (v. g. de una mina). 3. Pasar por, omitir. 4. En el juego de damas, tomar o comer un peón del adversario. **To jump at**, aceptar algo con entusiasmo. **To jump on one**, (*Fam.*) poner a uno verde. **To jump over**, saltar de un lado a otro por encima de alguna cosa. **To jump to a conclusion**, apresurarse a deducir. **To be one jump ahead**, llevar la ventaja.

jump, *s*. 1. Salto, brinco. 2. Distancia o extensión de un salto. 3. (*Min.*) Falla de una vena. 4. Alza o subida en los precios. **On the jump**, (*E. U.*) a paso rápido; enérgicamente.

jumped-up [ˈdʒʌmptˈpl] [yampt-ap], *a*. Presumido/a.

jumper [ˈdʒʌmpəʳ] [yam-paʳ], *s*. 1. Saltador, brincador. 2. (*E. U.*) Especie de zamarra o camiseta fuerte exterior que llega hasta las caderas, hecha de algodón cruzado o de lienzo basto; la usan los marineros, estivadores, carreteros y otros. 3. (*Mec.*) Mecanismo que funciona con un movimiento como de salto.

jumpsuit [ˈdʒʌmpsʊt] [yamp-sut], *s. m.* Mono.

jumpy [ˈdʒʌmpɪ] [yam-pi], *a*. Inquieto, nervioso.

junction [ˈdʒʌŋkʃən] [yank-shon], *s*. 1. Junta, unión, agregación y adición de unas cosas a otras. 2. Paraje de unión: empalme, punto en que se unen dos ferrocarriles; estación de empalme.

juncture [ˈdʒʌŋktʃəʳ] [yank-chaʳ], *s*. 1. Juntura. 2. Juntura, coyuntura, articulación. 3. Unión, amistad. 4. Coyuntura, sazón, oportunidad; momento crítico.

june [dʒuːn] [yun], *s*. Junio, el sexto mes del año. **June-bug**, insecto coleóptero que empieza a volar a principios de junio.

jungle [ˈdʒʌŋgl] [yan-guel], *s*. Soto espeso tropical; matorral, zarzal; red de hierbas gigantescas (en África); pantano intransitable o impenetrable. **Jungle-fever**, fiebre intermitente característica de las selvas del Indostán y de África.

junior [ˈdʒuːnɪəʳ] [yu-niaʳ], *a*. 1. Más mozo, más joven que otro; hijo, el menor. 2. Menos antiguo; más bajo en grado. **A junior partner**, socio menos antiguo. **Samuel Adams, junior**, Samuel Adams, hijo. **Junior high school**, instituto de Enseñanza Media. **4 years his junior**, 4 años menor que él.

junior college [ˈdʒuːnɪəˌkʌlɪdʒ] [yu-nio-ko-lich], *s*. Los dos primeros años en un colegio universitario.

juniority [ˈdʒuːnɪərɪtɪ] [yu-nio-ri-ti], *s*. El estado de ser más joven que otro.

juniper [ˈdʒuːnɪpəʳ] [yu-ni-paʳ], *s*. (*Bot.*) Enebro, el árbol que produce las nebrinas o bayas de enebro. **Juniper-berries**, bayas de enebro.

junk [dʒʌŋk] [yank], *s*. 1. (*Mar.*) Junco, cierta embarcación del Oriente o de la China. 2. Trozada, trozos de cable viejo; desecho de cualquier clase que puede usarse de nuevo, como hierro viejo, botellas usadas, etc. **Junk dealer**, vendedor de objetos usados. **Junk mail**, buzoneo, propaganda de buzón, publicidad por correo.

junket [ˈdʒʌŋkɪt] [yan-kit], *s*. 1. Festín, comida a escote. 2. Golosina, manjar delicado hecho de cuajadas. 3. Dulce seco; cualquier género de cosa confitada en seco.

junket, *vn*. Tener o dar un convite, o una comida a escote (party). Festín.

junkie [ˈdʒʌŋkɪ] [yan-ki], *s*. Drogadicto, heroinómano (*Fam.*).

junkman [ˈdʒʌŋkmən] [yank-man], *s*. Chatarrero.

junta [ˈdʒʌntə] [yan-ta], *s*. Junta, asamblea o reunión de personas para tratar de algún negocio.

Jupiter [ˈdʒuːpɪtəʳ] [yu-pi-taʳ], *s*. (*Astr.*) 1. Júpiter, uno de los planetas. 2. Júpiter, dios de los antiguos griegos y romanos.

jupon [ˈdʒʊpən] [yu-pon], *s*. 1. Especie de casaca corta, jubón de los siglos XIV y XV. 2. Tela francesa de urdimbre de algodón, con trama de lana cardada.

jurat [ˈdʒʊrət] [yu-rat], *s*. 1. Jurado, magistrado de algunas poblaciones. 2. Cláusula de un certificado oficial que da fe de un juramento.

juratory [ˈdʒʊərətərɪ] [yua-ra-to-ri], *a*. Juratorio, lo que está acompañado, de juramento: se usa en la expresión *fianza juratoria*.

juridical [dʒuəˈrɪdɪkəl] [yua-ri-di-kal], *a*. Jurídico, judicial.

juridically [dʒʊəˈrɪdɪkəlɪ] [yua-ri-di-ka-li], *adv*. Jurídicamente.

jurisconsult [ˌdʒʊərɪsˈkɒnsʌlt] [yua-ris-kon-salt], *s*. Jurisconsulto, abogado.

jurisdiction [ˌdʒʊərɪsˈdɪkʃən] [yua-ris-dik-shon], *s*. 1. Jurisdicción, derecho o facultad legal de ejercer autoridad. 2. Límite, territorio en que puede ejercerse dicha autoridad.

jurisdictional [ˌdʒʊərɪsˈdɪkʃənl] [yua-ris-dik-sho-nal], *a*. Jurisdiccional.

jurisdictive [ˌdʒʊərɪsˈdɪktɪv] [yua-ris-dik-tiv], *a*. Que tiene jurisdicción.

jurisprudence [ˌdʒʊərɪsˈpruːdəns] [yua-ris-pru-dans], *s*. Jurisprudencia, la ciencia del derecho.

jurisprudent [ˌdʒʊərɪsˈpruːdənt] [yua-ris-pru-dant], *a*. Jurisperio, jurisprudente, abogado.

jurist [ˈdʒʊərɪst] [yua-rist], *s*. Jurista, legista, profesor de derecho, jurisperito.

juror [ˈdʒʊərəʳ] [yua-raʳ], *s*. 1. (*For.*) Jurado, cada uno de los miembros que componen la institución jurídica del mismo nombre. 2. Jurado, individuo de una comisión o junta encargada de adjudicar premios, decidir en las oposiciones o los certámenes, etc.

jury [ˈdʒʊərɪ] [yua-ri], *s*. Jurado, reunión de personas congregadas para decidir, bajo juramento, si de los hechos que se les representan resulta que se ha cometido un delito, o si es culpable de él la persona acusada. **Grand jury**, el gran jurado, jurado de acusación; consiste de doce a veintitres miembros, doce de los cuales por lo menos han de estar de acuerdo para que haya acusación con fuerza legal. **Petty o petit jury**, jurado de juicio, encargado de declarar y determinar el hecho. Entre los anglosajones lo componen doce individuos, cuyo fallo ha de ser unánime para que haya veredicto. **Jury-box**, lugar que ocupan los jurados en la sala del tribunal. **To be on a jury**, ser miembro de un jurado. **Jury duty, to do jury duty**, actuar como jurado. **Trial by jury**, proceso con jurado.

juryman, *s*. V. JUROR.

jurymast [ˈdʒʊərɪmɑːst] [yua-ri-mast], *s*. (*Mar.*) Bandola, palo que se arbola provisionalmente en alta mar en lugar de un mástil tronchado o perdido. **To pitch o set up a jurymast**, armar una bandola.

just [dʒʌst] [yast], *a*. 1. Justo, que es conforme a la justicia, equitativo, verdadero. 2. Recto, íntegro, honrado, virtuosos, puro, inocente. 3. Justo, exacto; cabal, aquello a que nada sobra ni falta. 4. Ordenado, colocado en orden; exactamente proporcionado. **A just judge**, un juez íntegro, recto. **Just dealing**, buena fe. **A just charge**, una acusación fundada; una admonición justa, imparcial. -*adv*. 1. Justamente, exactamente, cabalmente. 2. Apuradamente, tasadamente. 3. Casi o cuasi; a punto de. **He's just about finished his meal**, está a punto de terminar su comida. 4. No más que, apenas; en el mismo instante; sólo, solamente. 5. Poco ha o hace, dentro de un momento; nuevamente, de nuevo. **Just as**, al momento que, luego que, al tiempo que; cuando; no bien. **Just then**, en ese mismo instante. **Not just now**, hasta ahora no. **Just as** (like), lo mismo que, semejante a. **Just now**, ahora mismo, en este mismo instante, poco hace, recientemente, últimamente. **Just by**, aquí cerca. **Just as I came in**, en el momento mismo o al tiempo de entrar yo.

Just as you please, como Ud. guste. **Just beyond**, un poco más allá. **That will just do**, eso será conveniente. **To have but just time**, tener justamente el tiempo necesario. **It's just what I wanted**, es precisamente lo que quería. **Leave it just as it is**, déjalo tal y como está. **To have everything just so**, tener cada cosa en su sitio. **She'd just as soon not go**, ella prefiere no ir. **Just over/under 500 grs.**, poco más de 500 grs. **Just listen!** ¡escucha un poco! **Just shut up!** ¡Cállate ya! (Imperatives). **It's just perfect!**, ¡qué maravilla! (Emphatic). **Just in case**, por si acaso (phrases).

just, joust, *s*. Justa, combate singular a caballo y con lanza.

just, joust, *vn*. Justar, lidiar, combatir en una justa.

justice ['dʒʌstɪs] [yas-tis], *s*. 1. Justicia, virtud que consiste en dar a cada uno lo que le pertenece; equidad. 2. Justicia, el acto de ejecutar en el reo la pena impuesta por sentencia. 3. Justicia, razón, derecho. 4. Justicia, el ministro que por su autoridad la ejerce. **Justice of the Peace**, juez de paz, alcalde, magistrado de jurisdicción limitada. **To bring to justice**, llevar ante los tribunales. **To do justice to skills**, estar a la altura de su capacidad.

justiciable ['dʒʌstɪˈʃɪəbl] [yas-ti-shia-bol], *a*. Lo que debe examinarse en los tribunales de justicia.

justiciary ['dʒʌstɪˈʃɪərɪ] [yas-ti-shia-ri], *s*. Juez, el que administra justicia; alto magistrado.

justifiable ['dʒʌstɪˈfaɪəbl] [yas-ti-faia-bol], *a*. Justificable, conforme a la razón, según justicia.

justifiableness ['dʒʌstɪˈfaɪəblnɪs] [yas-ti-faia-bol-nes], *s*. Rectitud; la posibilidad de ser justificado.

justifiably ['dʒʌstɪˈfaɪəblɪ] [yas-ti-faia-bli], *adv*. Justificadamente.

justification [ˌdʒʌstɪfɪˈkeɪʃən] [yas-ti-fi-kei-shon], *s*. 1. Justificación. 2. Descargo, defensa, los motivos que expone el acusado en un tribunal para defenderse de los cargos que se le hacen.

justificative ['dʒʌstɪfɪkətɪv] [yas-ti-fi-ka-tiv], *a*. Justificativo.

justificator [ˌdʒʌstɪfɪˈkeɪtər] [yas-ti-fi-kei-tar], *s*. Defensor; justificador.

justificatory ['dʒʌstɪfɪkətərɪ] [yas-ti-fi-ka-to-ri], *a*. Justificativo, defensivo.

justifier ['dʒʌstɪfaɪər] [yas-ti-faia'], *s*. Justificador; justificante.

justify ['dʒʌstɪfaɪ] [yas-ti-fai], *va*. 1. Justificar, declarar a uno inocente del delito que se le imputa, o absolverle de la acusación. 2. Justificar, probar en justicia alguna cosa; defender: absolver. 3. *(Teol.)* Absolver, perdonar una falta, reinstalar en la gracia de Dios. 4. *(Impr.)* Justificar, espaciar bien, ajustar a una misma medida las líneas de una plana. Alinear, justificar (Comput., Typ.).

justle, *s. y v. V.* JOSTLE.

justly ['dʒʌstlɪ] [yast-li], *adv*. Justamente, rectamente; cabal y exactamente, precisamente.

justness ['dʒʌstnɪs] [yast-nes], *s*. 1. Justicia, equidad, precisión. 2. Exactitud, la propiedad con que está hecha alguna cosa; regularidad: primor.

jut [dʒʌt] [yat], *vn*. Sobresalir, extenderse más allá de la parte principal de alguna cosa; se usa frecuentemente con la prep. *out;* combarse. *-s*. Salidizo, vuelo, proyección. **To jut out**, sobresalir.

jute [dʒuːt] [yut], *s*. 1. Hierba asiática del género Corchorus, familia de las tiliáceas. 2. Yute, cáñamo chino o de las Indias, fibra textil obtenida de la corteza interior de dicha planta.

jut-window ['dʒʌtˈwɪndəʊ] [yut-uin-dou], *s*. Ventana saliente, mirador.

juvenescence ['dʒuːˈvənəsns] [yu-ve-ne-sens], *s*. Renovación de la juventud. *V.* REJUVENESCENCE.

juvenescent ['dʒuːˈvənəsnt] [yu-ve-ne-sent], *a*. Rejuveneciente, que se remoza.

juvenile ['dʒuːvənaɪl] [yu-ve-nail], *a*. 1. Juvenil (sports). Infantil *(pej.)*. 2. Joven, menor.

juvenility [ˌdʒuːvəˈnɪlɪtɪ] [yu-ve-ni-li-ti], *s*. 1. Mocedad, juventud. 2. Ligereza, ardor o fuego de la juventud.

juxtapose ['dʒʌkstəpəʊz] [yaks-ta-pous], *v*. Yuxtaponer.

juxtaposition [ˌdʒʌkstəpəˈzɪʃən] [yaks-ta-pou-si-shon], *s*. Yuxtaposición, el modo de aumentar de volumen los cuerpos por la incorporación de los elementos que se les agregan exteriormente.

K

k [keɪ] [kei], undécima letra del abecedario inglés; se pronuncia en inglés siempre como la *c* antes de *a* en castellano; v. g. *kali* (cáli), *ken* (quen). Antes de *n* no se pronuncia; v. g. *knight* (náit).

k., abreviatura significa potasio (kalio). K. o Kt., *knight*, Caballero.

kaaba ['kɑːbə] [ka-ba], *s*. Caaba, Caba, templo venerado en la Meca, que contiene una piedra sagrada.

kafir, kaffir ['kæfər] [ka-a'], *s*. 1. Cafre, miembro de una de las tribus bantus, del sur de África. 2. Idioma de los cafres sudafricanos. 3. Natural del Kafiristán, región del Afganistán. 4. Infiel, el que no profesa la fe mahometana.

kafta ['kæftə] [kaf-ta], *s*. Las hojas de un arbusto de Arabia usadas en sustitución del té y el café; artículo de comercio.

kaiak, kayak ['kaɪæək] [kaiak], Canoa de los esquimales.

kail o **kale** ['keɪl] [keil], *s. (Bot.)* Bretón, especie de berza; col rizada.

kaiser ['keɪzər] [kei-sa'], *s*. Káiser, antiguo emperador de Alemania.

kaleidoscope [kəˈleɪdəskəʊp] [ka-lei-dos-koup], *s*. Caleidoscopio, aparato óptico, con espejos inclinados que al menor movimiento presentan una nueva imagen.

kaleidoscopic [kəˈleɪdəskəʊpɪk] [ka-lei-dos-kou-pik], *a*. Caleidoscópico, perteneciente al caleidoscopio; de aquí, variado, pintoresco.

kali ['keɪlɪ] [kei-li], *s*. Barrilla, hierba.

kalmia ['kælmɪə] [kal-mia], *s. (Bot.)* Kalmia, un género norteamericano de plantas fruticosas siempre verdes, con umbelas de flores azules, purpúreas o blancas.

kalmuck ['kælmʌk] [kal-mak], *s*. 1. Calmuco, raza mongola del Asia central. 2. Su idioma.

kalsomine, v. y s. V. CALCIMINE.

kamikaze [ˌkæmɪˈkɑːzɪ] [ka-mi-ka-si], *s. m.* Kamikaze.

kana ['kænə] [ka-na], *s*. Escritura japonesa propia; tiene 48 caracteres.

kanaka ['kænəkə] [ka-na-ka], *s*. Natural de las islas de Hawai; por extensión, cualquier habitante de las islas del Pacífico.

kangaroo [ˌkæŋɡəˈruː] [kan-ga-ru], *s*. Canguro, mamífero del orden de los marsupiales.

kantianism [ˌkænʃəˈnɪzən] [kan-sha-ni-sem], *s*. Kantismo, doctrina del filósofo Kant.

kaolin ['keɪəlɪn] [keia-lin], *s*. Caolín, arcilla blanca muy pura con que se hace la porcelana fina.

kapellmeister ['kæpəlˈmeɪstər] [ka-pel-meis-ta'], *s*. Maestro de capilla; director de una orquesta o de un coro.

kaput ['kæpət] [ka-put], *a*. Estropeado, roto *(fam.)*.

karakul ['kærəkəl] [ka-ra-kul], *s*. Astracán, piel de astracán.

karate ['kærət] [ka-rat], *s. m.* Karate.

karma ['kɑːmə] [kar-ma], *s*. (Sánscrito) Efecto de cualquier acto, religioso u otro; retribución ineludible.

karn ['kɑːn] [karn], *s*. Montón de piedras. V. CAIRN. *(Ingl.)*

karting ['kɑːtɪŋ] [kar-tin], *s. m.* Kárting (Sports).

kat [kæt] [kat], *s.* V. KAFTA.

kata-, *prefijo. V.* CATA.

katydid ['kætɪdɪd] [ka-ti-did], *s*. Insecto arbóreo, verde y con largas antenas, del orden de los ortópteros.

kayak ['kaɪək] [kaiak], *s. m.* Kayac.

KB, *s*. Abreviatura de **kilobyte**.

kd Abreviatura de **knocked down**, desmontado (US).

kebboc [ˈkebɒk] [ke-bok], *s. (Esco.)* Un queso.

keck [ˈkek] [kek], *vn.* Querer vomitar, tener náuseas. *-s.* Tallo de cicuta.

keckle [ˈkekl] [ke-kel], *va. (Mar.)* Aforrar un cable.

kecksy, *s.* V. KEX.

kedge [kedʒ] [kedch], *s. (Mar.)* Anclote; ancla pequeña.

kedger [ˈkedʒəʳ] [ked-chaʳ], *s.* Anclote; pescadero.

keel [ˈkiːl] [kil], *s.* 1. *(Mar.)* Quilla, pieza de madera o hierro, que va de popa a proa por la parte inferior del barco. **False keel**, zapata de quilla. **Rabbit of the keel**, alefriz de quilla. **Searfs of the keel**, juntas de quilla. **Sheathing of the keel**, embón de quilla. 2. *(Bot.)* Quilla, pétalo inferior de una flor papilionácea que incluye los estambres y el pistilo. **Keel over**, volcar, zozobrar *(Mar.);* desmayarse, desplomarse *(Pers.).*

keel, *va.* Enfriar; refrescar. *-vn.* Resfriar, desanimar.

keelage [ˈkiːleɪdʒ] [ki-leich], *s. (Mar.)* Derechos de quilla.

keelfat [ˈkiːlfæt] [kil-fat], *s.* Garapiñera, vasija grande en que se pone a enfriar algún líquido.

keelhale [ˈkiːlheɪl] [kil-jeil], *va. (Mar.)* Pasar por la quilla.

keelhaul [ˈkiːlhəʊl] [kil-joul], *va.* Aplicar a los marineros el antiguo castigo que consistía en zambullir y sacar varias veces del mar a un delincuente, atado con una cuerda.

keeling [ˈkiːlɪŋ] [ki-lin], *s. (Ict.)* Especie de merluza.

keelrope [ˈkiːlrəʊp] [kil-roup], *s. (Mar.)* Cabo imbornalero de las varengas.

keelson [ˈkiːlsən] [kil-son], *s. (Mar.)* Sobrequilla, pieza de madera de casi todo el largo del buque, colocada directamente encima de la quilla.

keen [kiːn] [kin], *a.* 1. Afilado; aguzado. 2. Agudo, penetrante, sutil, vivo. 3. Ansioso, vehemente. 4. Acre, desabrido, mordaz, satírico, picante. **Keen-sighted**, el que tiene vista perspicaz. **Keen appetite**, gran apetito. **To be keen on something**, ser aficionado a algo. **Are you keen on cinema?**, ¿te gusta el cine?

keenly [ˈkiːnlɪ] [kin-li], *adv.* 1. Agudamente, sutilmente. 2. Intensamente, vivamente. Fijamente (look).

keenness [ˈkiːnnɪs] [kin-nes], *s.* 1. Agudeza, sutileza o delicadeza de filo. 2. Agudeza, perspicacia, viveza o sutileza de ingenio. 3. Rigor o aspereza del frío. 4. Ansia, anhelo, deseo vehemente. 5. Aspereza de genio, acrimonia.

keep [kiːp] [kip], *va. (pret.* y *pp.* KEPT). 1. Tener, mantener, retener (retain). 2. Preservar, librar, guardar (preserve). 3. Cuidar, proteger, defender (.4. Impedir, detener, entretener (detain). 5. Conservar, reservar, ocultar. 6. Poner por escrito o de otra manera para referencia; apuntar; llevar (los libros de comercio). 7. Mantener, proveer del alimento necesario. **To earn one's keep**, ganarse el sustento. 8. Sostener algo para que no se caiga. 9. Proseguir, voluntariamente en lo que se está haciendo; ser fiel *a.* 10. Observar, guardar o cumplir exactamente alguna cosa (agreement, promise). 11. Solemnizar. *-vn.* 1. Mantenerse, perseverar o subsistir en un mismo estado. 2. Acostumbrar, soler. 3. Mantenerse, proveerse del alimento necesario. 4. Continuar en alguna situación, quedar. 5. Vivir, residir. 6. Tener cuidado de alguna cosa.

keep along, continuar en la misma situación; seguir una senda.

keep aloof, apartarse, ponerse a un lado, no entremeterse.

keep asunder, tener separado o desunido; estar o vivir separado o desunido.

keep at it, *(Fam.)* perseverar, persistir. **To keep at home**, quedarse en casa.

keep away, tener o retener a alguno apartado o alejado; estar o vivir apartado o alejado; mantenerse ausente.

keep back, retener, detener, ocultar, impedir; preservar, guardar, reservar; restringir (put aside) **Where do you keep the salt?**, ¿dónde guardas la sal?

keep down, sujetar; tener humillado.

keep from, guardar o guardarse; defender; evitar; impedir.

keep in, reprimir, refrenar, moderar, contener, tener en sujeción; esconder, ocultar. **To keep in awe**, hacerse temer; darse a respetar o hacerse respetar.

keep off, impedir, desanimar; estar o mantenerse separado o alejado; mantener a distancia, no admitir a alguno.

keep on, ir adelante, proseguir, adelantar.

keep out, impedir a uno que entre; estar o mantenerse fuera de algún sitio; no querer entrar. **To keep out of sight**, esconder, quitar de delante; estar o mantenerse oculto.

keep to, adherirse estrictamente a alguna cosa; detenerse.

keep under, sujetar, tener debajo o en sujeción.

keep up, mantener, conservar, continuar; mantenerse con resolución en alguna situación o estado; no ceder, no cesar; estar de jarana. **He keeps up his usual retinue**, mantiene su tren acostumbrado. **To keep it up**, *(Fam.)* persistir en una acción. **To keep company**, acompañar o estar frecuentemente con alguno; tener trato familiar con una persona. **To keep books**, llevar los libros de comercio. **To keep cash**, tener o guardar la caja o el dinero de una casa de comercio, ser cajero. **To keep fit**, mantenerse en forma. **To keep holidays**, guardar las fiestas. **To keep Lent**, observar la cuaresma o los preceptos de la religión pertenecientes a los ayunos, etc., en tiempo de cuaresma. **To keep one's bed**, guardar cama. **To keep one at bay**, divertir a alguno; entretenerle con buenas palabras o promesas. **To keep one hungry**, hacer padecer hambre a alguno. **To keep one's ground**, mantenerse firme, defender sù terreno. **To keep one's temper**, tener calma, ser dueño de sí mismo, contenerse. **To keep somebody posted**, tener a alguien al corriente. **To keep the land aboard**, *(Mar.)* mantenerse inmediato a la tierra. **To keep off**, *(Mar.)* mantenerse distante de la tierra, no arrimarse. **To keep the sea**, *(Mar.)* mantenerse mar afuera. **How is she keeping?**, ¿qué tal está (ella)? **He's keeping better**, él está mejor. (health).

keep, *s.* 1. Mantenimiento, medios de subsistencia; guarda, guardia, custodia, cuidado. 2. Torre, la parte más fuerte de los castillos antiguos; torreón; de aquí, castillo, alcázar. 3. Construcción en que se conserva algo. **For keeps**, (Fam. E.U.) para guardar o retener, para siempre.

keeper [ˈkiːpəʳ] [ki-paʳ], *s.* 1. Defensor, defendedor. 2. Tenedor, el que tiene a su cargo alguna cosa, por lo regular en nombre de otro; guardián, guardador, el que guarda. 3. Carcelero. 4. Guardabosque. 5. Guarda, el que tiene a su cargo o cuidado la conservación de alguna cosa. **Book-keeper**, tenedor de libros. **Goal keeper**, portero, guardameta.

keepership [ˈkiːpəʃɪp] [ki-pa-ship], *s.* Oficio o empleo de guarda; alcaidía, oficio o empleo de carcelero.

keeping [ˈkiːpɪŋ] [ki-pin], *s.* 1. Cargo, custodia, mantenimiento; cuidado, preservación, defensa; guarda. 2. Congruencia; razón o relación justa o recta. **Not in keeping**, No congruente, mal avenido. **Book-keeping**, teneduría de libros.

keepsake [ˈkiːpseɪk] [kip-seik], *s.* Dádiva, recuerdo o presente hecho para que el que lo recibe lo conserve en memoria del que lo da.

keeve [kiːv] [kiv], *s.* Cuba o tina, vasija en que fermenta la cerveza antes de envasarla.

keever [ˈkiːvəʳ] [ki-vaʳ], *s.* Enfriadera de cerveza. *V.* BACK.

keg [keg] [keg], *s.* Cuñete, barrilito.

keir ó **kier** [kɛəʳ] [keaʳ], *s.* Cuba, tanque de blanquear.

kell [kel] [kel], *s.* Una membrana o telilla que sacan algunas criaturas en la cabeza al nacer. *V.* CAUL.

kelp [kelp] [kelp], *s.* 1. Las especies de alga marina cuyas cenizas sirven para hacer vidrio y contienen yodo; las grandes algas bastas, de cualquier especie, como las laminariáceas y las fucáceas. 2. Las cenizas de algas.

kelpie ó **kelpy** [ˈkelpɪ] [kel-pi], *s.* Un duende, fantasma o espectro que los escoceses suponen andan sobre el agua.

kelson [ˈkelsən] [kel-shon], *s. (Mar.)* Sobrequilla. *V.* KEELSON.

kelt, keltic [kelt] [kelt], *V.* CELT.

kelter [ˈkeltəʳ] [kel-taʳ], *s.* Buen orden o estado para trabajar. *V.* KILTER.

ken [ken] [ken], *va.* 1. (Ant. o esco.) Divisar, espiar o reconocer de lejos, ver a una gran distancia, ver de lejos (recognize). 2. Saber (fact), conocer, alcanzar, comprender. - *vn. (Des.)* Mirar alrededor.

ken, *s.* Vista, la distancia hasta donde se alcanza a ver alguna cosa.

kendal-green [ˈkendəlˈgriːn] [ken-dal-grin], *s.* Especie de paño verde.

kennel [kenl] [ke-nel], *s.* 1. Perrera, el lugar o sitio donde se guardan los perros. 2. Jauría; traílla, cuadrilla de perros podencos en una cacería. 3. Zorrera, la cueva de la zorra. 4. Habitación sórdida. 5. Conducto o canal para dar curso o salida a las aguas en las calles cuando llueve; arroyo.

kennel, *vn.* Encamarse, echarse o estar en la cama; se dice regularmente de los animales. y por desprecio algunas veces de los hombres. *-va.* Tener en perrera.

keno [ˈkenəʊ] [ke-nou], *s.* Quinterno en la lotería; juego de azar.

kentle [kentl] [ken-tel], *s. V.* QUINTAL.

kentledge [ˈkentledʒ] [ken-tel-edch], *s. (Mar.)* Lingotes de hierro para lastre, puestos permenentemente encima de la sobrequilla.

kept, *pret.* y *pp.* del verbo TO KEEP.

keramic, *a. V.* CERAMIC.

kerb [kɜːb] [kerb], *s. m.* Bordillo. **Kerb market,** mercado no oficial (después del cierre de la Bolsa).

kerb-stone [ˈkɜːbstəʊn] [kerb-stoun], *s.* 1. Brocal de pozo. 2. Guardacantón, piedra grande o poste puesto a las esquinas de las casas para resguardarlas de los golpes de los carros o carruajes. 3. *V.* CURB-STONE.

kerchief [ˈkɜːtʃɪf] [ker-chif], *s.* Cofia, tocado de mujer; pañuelo.

kerchiefed [ˈkɜːtʃɪfd] [ker-chifd], *a.* Adornado, vestido.

kerf [kɜːf] [kerf], *s.* 1. La abertura que hace la sierra en la madera. 2. La cortadura que hace una máquina de esquilar o tundir.

kerfuffle [ˈkɜːfʌfl] [ker-fa-fol], *s. m.* Follón, lío *(Fam.).*

kermes [ˈkɜːmɪs] [ker-mis], *s.* 1. Quermes, el gusanillo que se engendra dentro del coco de la grana. **Kermes oak,** coscoja. 2. Quermes mineral, hidro-sulfureto de antimonio, una preparación de antimonio.

kermess [ˈkɜːmɪs] [ker-mis], *s.* En algunos países, fiesta, romería fuera de casa; originalmente una fiesta religiosa.

kern [kɜːn] [kern], *s. (Esco. e Ingl. del Norte)* 1. La última gavilla del agosto, fin de cosecha, y la fiesta con que se celebra. 2. *(Impr.)* Hombro de una letra de imprenta que sobresale, como en una *f* bastardilla. 3. Patán. 4. Soldado irlandés. 3 y 4 se derivan de otra raíz. **Kern** o **corn baby,** una figura o muñeco que los agosteros conducen con gran regocijo al concluir el agosto.

kern, *vn.* 1. Granar, formarse completamente el grano cuando llega a madurar. 2. Formarse en granos.

kerned [ˈkɜːnd] [kernd], *a. (Impr.)* Se dice del tipo que tiene hombro.

kernel [ˈkɜːnl] [ker-nel], *s.* 1. Almendra, la pepita, simiente que se encuentra en las frutas de hueso, que se llama cuesco, grano, semilla, etc., según las frutas. **Kernel of an apple,** la pepita de la manzana. 2. La parte central de alguna cosa. 3. Haba, cierto género de roncha que sale en el cutis. 4. Concreción dura en la carne. 5. Meollo, núcleo *(Fig.).*

kernel, *vn.* Madurar las almendras, pepitas o cuescos de las frutas.

kernelly [ˈkɜːnəlɪ] [ker-na-li], *a.* Almendrado; que está lleno de almendras.

kernelwort [ˈkɜːnlˌwɔːt] [ker-nel-uort], *s. (Bot.)* Escrofularia, ruda canina.

kerosene [ˈkerəsiːn] [ke-ro-sin], *s.* Queroseno, petróleo, aceite destilado de nafta cruda.

kersey [ˈkɜːsɪ] [ker-si], *s.* Una especie de tela basta de lana.

kerseymere [ˈkɜːsɪmɪəʳ] [ker-si-miaʳ], o **cassimere** [ˈkəsɪmɪəʳ] [ka-si-miaʳ], *s.* Casimiro o casimira, tela de lana muy fina.

kestrel [ˈkəstrəl] [kes-trel], *s. (Orn.)* Cernícalo.

ketch [ketʃ] [kech], *s. (Mar.)* Quaiche o queche, especie de embarcación de dos palos o masteleros.

ketchup, *s. V.* CATCHUP.

kettle [ˈketl] [ke-tel], *s.* Caldera, vasija en que se cuece algún licor o cosa líquida. **A large kettle,** calderón. **A small kettle,** tetera. **That's a different kettle of fish,** eso es harina de otro costal *(Prov.).*

kettledrum [ˈketldrʌm] [ke-tel-dram], *s.* 1. Timbal, atabal. **Kettledrummer,** timbalero, atabalero. 2. Sarao, té, reunión informal de las señoras por la tarde.

kettlepins [ˈketlpɪnz] [ke-tel-pins], *s.* Juego de bolos.

kevel [ˈkevl] [ke-vel], *s.* 1. *(Mar.)* Manigueta o maniguetón, el extremo de los palos que están en la borda del alcázar. 2. *(Zool.)* Gacela, antílope de África. **Kevel-head,** Escalamote, abitón.

key [kiː] [ki], *va.* 1. Enchabetar, calzar, acuñar; sujetar con una llave. 2. Proveer con llaves. 3. Afinar, templar un instrumento de música con una llave.

key, *s.* 1. Llave, instrumento de metal que sirve para abrir y cerrar puertas, etc. 2. Llave, destornillador, cierto instrumento que se usa para quitar o poner tornillos. 3. Clave o llave de una cifra o de un enigma. 4. (Art. y Of.) Chabeta; cuña; clavija (en la encuadernación): sotrozo. 5. Llave, conmutador de una máquina telegráfica. 6. Tecla, cualquiera de las piezas para los dedos en las máquinas de escribir o en las de componer y distribuir tipos (of piano, typewriter). 7. *(Mús.)* Tecla. 8. *(Mús.)* Clave, conjunto o sistema de tonos relacionados entre sí. **To change key,** cambiar de tonalidad. 9. Cualidad, intensidad o diapasón del tono al hablar. **She spoke in a high key,** ella habló en tono alto. 10. *(Bot.)* La cáscara que contiene la simiente de algunas plantas. **To be under lock and key,** estar bajo llave o cerrado con llave; estar bien guardado. **Skeleton-key, pass-key,** ganzúa, llave maestra. **In key,** templado, de acuerdo, en harmonía. **Key-action,** el teclado de un órgano o piano y el mecanismo relacionado con él. **Natural key** *(Mús.)* (a) cualquier tecla blanca del teclado de un órgano o piano, (b) clave de C# tocada en las teclas blancas. **The key to success,** la clave del éxito.

key, *s.* Cayo, isleta particularmente de coral y cercana a la costa.

keyboard [ˈkiːbɔːd] [ki-bord], *s.* Teclado, como el de un piano o de una máquina para escribir.

keyed [ˈkiːɪd] [kiid], *a.* 1. Teclado, que tiene teclas; que tiene llave. **An eight-keyed flute,** una flauta con ocho llaves. 2. Estirado, puesto en estado de tensión, como una cuerda. 3. Templado, como un instrumento de música.

keyhole [ˈkiːhəʊl] [ki-joul], *s.* Agujero de la cerradura, la parte por donde entra en ella la llave.

key ring [ˈkiːrɪŋ] [ki-ring], *s.* Llavero.

keystone [ˈkiːstəʊn] [ki-stoun], *s.* Clave o llave de un arco o bóveda, la última piedra con que se cierra.

key-word [ˈkiːwɜːd] [ki-uerd], *s.* Palabra clave.

khaki [ˈkɑːkɪ] [ka-ki], *s.* y *a.* Color caqui.

khan [ˈkɑːn] [kan], *s.* 1. Kan o Khan, jefe o gobernador entre los tártaros; caballero, en la India. 2. Posada o mesón en Turquía.

kibitzer [ˈkɪbɪtʃəʳ] [ki-bi-chaʳ], *s.* 1. Mirón, espectador en un juego de naipes. 2. *(Fam.)* Camasquince, entremetido.

kick [kɪk] [kik], *va.* Acocear, cocear, dar o tirar coces. *-vn.* Patear, dar patadas o puntapiés. **To kick one out of the house,** echar a alguno a puntapiés. 2. Ofrecer resistencia como por medio de coces; oponerse, quejarse: es uso vulgar. **It was a kick in the teeth for her,** le sentó como una patada *(Fam.).* **To do something for kicks,** hacer algo por diversión *(Fam.).*

kick, *s.* 1. Puntapié, patada; coz. 2. *(Ger.)* Oposición, protesta.

kick about, around, *vt.* Dar patadas a alguien. Darle vueltas a (idea).

kick back, *vt.* Devolver (Ball).

kickback [ˈkɪbæk] [kik-bak], *s.* Retroceso, movimiento de retroceso cuando un motor o maquinaria da marcha atrás.

kick down, *vt.* Derribar a patadas.

kicker ['kɪkə^r] [ki-ka^r], *s.* Acoceador, coceador, el que da o tira coces; el que hace objeciones.

kick in, *vt.* Derribar o romper a patadas.

kicking ['kɪkɪŋ] [ki-kin], *s.* Coceadura, la acción y efecto de cocear; pateamiento, pateadura.

kick off ['kɪkɒf] [kik-of], *s. m.* Saque inicial (Football, etc.).

kick out, *vi.* Dar coces (animal). Echar a patadas.

kickshaw ['kɪkʃɔ:] [ki-sho], *s.* 1. Patarata, ridiculez, monada, fruslería, bagatela. 2. Almodrote, especie de guisado.

kick up, *vt.* **To kick up a row,** armar follón. **To kick up a fuss about something,** montar una escena por algo.

kid [kɪd] [kid], *s.* 1. Cabrito, la cría de la cabra. 2. Cabritillo. **Kid upper leathers,** capelladas de cabritilla. 3. La carne de cabrito. 4. *pl.* Guantes o zapatos hechos de cabritilla. 5. *(Ger.)* Niño, niña; muchachito, muchachita.

kid, *vn.* Parir cabritos.

kidded ['kɪdɪd] [ki-did], *a.* Nacido, hablando de cabritos.

kiddle ['kɪdl] [ki-del], *s.* Presa o represa en un río.

kiddow ['kɪdəʊ] [ki-dou], *s. (Orn.)* Especie de colimbo, ave marítima.

kiddy ['kɪdɪ] [ki-di], *s.* Niño, chiquillo *(Fam.).*

kidling ['kɪdlɪŋ] [kid-lin], *s.* Cabritillo.

kidnap ['kɪdnæp] [kid-nap], *va.* Secuestrar.

kidnaper ['kɪdnæpə^r] [kid-na-pa^r], *s.* Raptor, secuestrador. Plagiador *(Mex.).*

kidnaping ['kɪdnæpɪŋ] [kid-na-pin], *s. m.* Secuestro, rapto. Plagio *(Mex.).*

kidney ['kɪdnɪ] [kid-ni], *s.* 1. Riñón. 2. Calaña; índole, temperamento. **Kidney-vetch,** *(Bot.)* vulneraria. **Kidneywort,** *(Bot.)* ombligo.

kidney-bean ['kɪdnɪbi:n] [kid-ni-bin], *s.* Judía, habichuela, frijos; se usa generalmente en plural.

kilerg ['kɪlɜ:g] [ki-lerg], *s.* Unidad de trabajo o energía: 1000 *ergs.*

kill [kɪl] [kil], *va.* 1. Matar, quitar la vida. **To kill oneself,** matarse; tomarse mucho trabajo, fatigarse demasiado (animal o vegetal), por cualquier medio que sea; hacer morir. 2. Destruir, privar de vigor, de eficacia o de utilidad; amortiguar; neutralizar. 3. Descartar; suprimir. 4. Hacer una carnicería. 5. Apagar, parar (engine). **To kill two birds with one stone,** matar dos pájaros de un tiro *(Fig.).* **To kill time,** matar el tiempo.

kill, *s.* Riachuelo, arroyo, caleta.

killer ['kɪlə^r] [ki-la^r], *s.* Asesino, matador. **Killer question,** pregunta muy difícil. **Killer disease,** enfermedad mortal.

kill-joy ['kɪldʒɔɪ] [kil-yoi], *s.* Aguafiestas.

kill off, *vt.* Exterminar, acabar (lit). Echar por tierra (rumor).

killow ['kɪləʊ] [ki-lou], *s.* Tierra gallinera o negruzca.

kiln ['kɪln] [kiln], *s.* Horno, fábrica hecha en forma de bóveda que sirve para secar, quemar o calcinar alguna cosa. **Brick-kiln,** ladrillera o ladrillal. **Lime-kiln,** calera.

kilo ['ki:ləʊ] [ki-lou]. Prefijo y abreviatura de **kilogram.**

kilobyte ['kɪləʊbaɪt] [ki-lou-bait], *s. m.* Kilobyte.

kilocalorie ['kɪləʊkæləri:] [ki-lou-ka-lo-ri], *s. (Fis.)* Kilocaloría.

kilocycle ['kɪləʊsaɪkl] [ki-lou-sai-kol], *s.* (Elec. y Radio) Kilociclo.

kilogram, kilogramme ['kɪləʊgræm] [ki-lou-gram], *s.* Kilogramo, peso de mil gramos: = 2204 libras.

kilohertz ['kɪləʊhɜ:ts] [ki-lou-jerts], *s. m.* Kilohercio.

kiloliter ['kɪləʊlɪtə^r] [ki-lou-li-ta^r], *s.* Kilolitro, mil litros.

kilometer ['kɪləʊmi:tə^r] [ki-lou-mi-ta^r], *s.* Kilómetro, longitud de mil metros: = 0.621 o cinco octavas partes de una milla inglesa.

kilometric ['kɪləʊmetrɪk] [ki-lou-me-trik], *a.* Kilométrico.

kiloton ['kɪləʊtʌn] [ki-lou-tan], *s.* Kilotonelada, kilotón.

kilovolt ['kɪləʊvəʊlt] [ki-lou-voult], *s. (Elec.)* Kilovoltio.

kilowatt ['kɪləʊwɒt] [ki-lou-uat], *s. (Elec.)* Kilovatio. **Kilowatt-hour,** Kilovatio-hora.

kilt [kɪlt] [kilt], *s.* Túnica corta que usan los montañeses de Escocia.

kilter, kelter ['kɪltə^r] [kil-ta^r], *s. (Prov. E.U. e Ingl.)* Estado propio para trabajar; buena condición.

kimono [kɪ'məʊnəʊ] [ki-mou-nou], *s.* Quimono, túnica japonesa.

kin [kɪn] [kin], *s.* 1. Parentesco, vínculo, conexión. 2. Parientes, los que son de la misma familia o linaje. 3. Género, especie, clase. **They are all of a kin,** son todos de una misma especie, son lobos de una camada. 4. Terminación diminutiva, como **manikin,** Hombrezuelo. **Next of kin,** pariente próximo, el primero en el orden de parentesco. *-a.* Congenial; de la misma naturaleza.

kind [kaɪnd] [kaind], *a.* Benévolo, benigno, bondadoso, benéfico, favorable, afable, cariñoso. **She is very kind to me,** me trata con mucho cariño o es muy cariñosa conmigo. **You are very kind,** Ud. tiene mucha bondad, es muy amable. **Kind-hearted,** benévolo. *-s.* 1. Género, especie, clase. 2. Naturaleza, la esencia y propio ser de cada cosa. 3. Modo, manera; especie, calidad. **In such a kind,** de tal suerte, de tal manera. **This kind of men,** este linaje de hombres. **The human kind,** el género humano. **A different kind of plant,** una planta de especie diferente. **It's the only one of its kind,** es único en su especie. **A kind reception,** una acogida favorable, bondadosa. **Kind-hearted,** dotado de buen corazón. **Kind-heartedness,** bondad de corazón. **Kind of,** (Fam. E.U.) algo; de un modo, como si. **It's kind of difficult,** es bastante difícil.

kindergarten ['kɪndəgɑ:tn] [kin-da-gar-ten], *s.* Jardín infantil.

kindle ['kɪndl] [kin-del], *va.* 1. Encender, hacer que una cosa se inflame y arda. 2. Inflamar, enardecer y avivar a uno (emotion). 3. (Des. o Prov. Ingl.) Parir; se dice sólo de la liebre y algunos otros animales. *-vn.* Arder, quemarse alguna cosa levantando llama.

kindler ['kɪndlə^r] [kin-dla^r], *s.* Incendiario; incitador, agitador; el que fomenta disturbios o revoluciones.

kindliness ['kaɪndlɪnɪs] [kaind-li-nes], *s.* Amabilidad, favor, benevolencia; índole; curso natural de las estaciones, etc.

kindling wood ['kaɪndlɪŋwʊd] [kain-dlin-wud], *s.* Leña fácilmente inflamable.

kindly ['kaɪndlɪ] [kain-dli], *adv.* Benignamente, naturalmente, propiamente. *-a.* 1. Benigno, cariñoso, suave, tratable. 2. Beneficioso, provechoso. 3. *(Ant.)* Natural, idóneo, propio.

kindness ['kaɪndnɪs] [kaind-nes], *s.* 1. Benevolencia, beneficencia, buena voluntad, cariño, afecto, humanidad. 2. Favor, gracia, beneficio, atención, fineza.

kindred ['kaɪndrɪd] [kain-drid], *s.* 1. Parentesco, conexión por consanguinidad o afinidad. 2. Parentela, casta. *-a.* Emparentado, el que tiene parentesco con otro. **The stirrups are of no kindred,** los estribos no son parejos.

kinematics ['kɪnəmætɪks] [ki-ne-ma-tiks], *s. (Fís.)* Cenemática, parte de la mecánica que trata del movimiento sin considerar las fuerzas que lo producen.

kinescope ['kɪnəskəʊp] [ki-nes-koup], *s.* Cinescopio, kinoscopio.

kinetic [kɪ'netɪk] [ki-ne-tik], *a.* Cinético. **Kinetic energy,** energía cinética.

kinetics [kɪ'netɪkz] [ki-ne-tiks], *s.* Dinámica, ciencia que trata de las fuerzas que dan movimiento a los cuerpos o lo modifican.

king [kɪŋ] [king], *s.* 1. Rey, el soberano o monarca de un reino. **God save the king,** Dios guarde al rey. 2. Rey, la carta o naipe que tiene figura de rey. **King's yellow,** color amarillo hecho de oropimente.

king, en composición: **King-bolt,** perno, pinzote, perno real. **King-crab,** límulo, animal crustáceo. **King-cup,** *(Bot.)* botón de oro, especie de ranúnculo. **King James' version of Bible,** *V.* VERSION. **Kingpin,** (a) *V.* KING-BOLT. (b) En el juego de bolos, el que se coloca delante de los otros. (c) (Fam. E.U.) Persona de gran importancia. **An oil king,** un magnate del petróleo. **The king and queen,** los reyes.

king, *va.* 1. Dar un rey al reino que no le tenía: se usa casi siempre en sentido jocoso. 2. Elevar a alguno a la dignidad real. 3. Coronar un peón haciéndole dama, en el juego de las damas.

king-bird ['kɪŋbɜːd] [king-berd], *s.* *(Orn.)* Tirano, muscícapa.

kingcraft ['kɪŋkræft] [king-kraft], *s.* Arte de gobernar, arte de reinar o mandar como rey.

kingdom ['kɪŋdəm] [king-dom], *s.* 1. Reino, los territorios o dominios sujetos a un rey. 2. Reino, la clase u orden diferente de seres o cosas, especialmente en la historia natural. 3. Región, una extensión cualquiera de tierra.

kingfisher ['kɪŋfɪʃəʳ] [king-fi-shaʳ], *s.* Alción, íspida o martín pescador.

kinghood ['kɪŋhʊd] [king-jud], *s.* Soberanía, estado, oficio o dignidad de rey.

kinglet ['kɪŋlɪt] [kin-glet], *s.* 1. Reyezuelo, rey insignificante. 2. *(Orn.)* Abadejo, régulo.

kinglike ['kɪŋlaɪk] [king-laik], **kingly** ['kɪŋlɪ] [king-li], *a.* 1. Real, soberano, monárquico. 2. Regio, noble, augusto, pomposo, majestuoso.

kingly ['kɪŋlɪ] [king-li], *adv.* Majestuosamente, con majestad.

kingpin ['kɪŋpɪn] [king-pin], *s.* 1. En el juego de bolos, el bolo central. 2. *(Fam.)* Cabeza de un grupo o empresa. 3. Pivote.

kingship ['kɪŋʃɪp] [king-ship], *s.* Majestad, la dignidad real, y por metáfora el trono o cetro: monarquía.

king-size ['kɪŋsaɪz] [king-sais], *a.* De tamaño grande (cigarettes).

kingspear ['kɪŋspɪəʳ] [king-spiaʳ], *s.* *(Bot.)* Gamón.

kink [kɪŋk] [kink], *s.* 1. Torcedura, vuelta que forma un cabo o un hilo de metal al desdoblarse; ojal, coca. 2. (Fam. E.U.) Capricho infundado.

kink, *va.* y *vn.* 1. Formar cocas, como una soga. 2. Torcerse, enredarse.

kinky ['kɪŋkɪ] [kin-ki], *a.* 1. Que tiende a formar cocas u ojales. 2. Que tiene cocas u ojales; pasudo; se dice de la lana y de los cabellos lanosos. 3. Extraño, raro, extravagante.

kinkhaust ['kɪŋkhɔːst] [kink-jost], *s.* Tos violenta.

kino ['kɪnəʊ] [ki-nou], *s.* Quino, un extracto vegetal que se usa en la medicina como astringente.

kinsfolk ['kɪnzfəʊk] [kins-fouk], *s.* Parentela, parientes.

kinship ['kɪnʃɪp] [kin-ship], *s. m.* Afinidad *(Fam.)*. Parentesco.

kinsman ['kɪnzmən] [kins-man], *s.* Parentela, el que es de la misma familia que otro.

kinswoman ['kɪnzwʊmən] [kins-uo-man], *s. f.* Parienta.

kiosk ['kiːɒsk] [kiosk], *s.* Kiosko, cabina. **Telephone kiosk,** cabina telefónica.

kip [kɪp] [kip], *s.* 1. Pellejo no curtido de un ternero, o del ganado vacuno de talla menos que mediana. **Kip-leather, kip-skin,** becerro, pellejo curtido de dichos animales. 2. Alojamiento (lodging). 3. Sueño (sleep). **To have a kip,** echar una siesta, dormir un rato.

kipper ['kɪpəʳ] [ki-paʳ], *a.* 1. Término aplicado a los salmones cuando están desovando o poco después del tiempo del desove. 2. Arenque ahumado.

kirk [kɜːk] [kerk], *s.* Iglesia (Escocia).

kirtle ['kɜːtl] [ker-tel], *s.* Manto, capa; chupa larga.

kismet ['kɪsmɪt] [kis-met], *s.* Hado, destino.

kiss [kɪs] [kis], *va.* 1. Besar. 2. Acariciar, hacer caricias y halagos. 3. Besar, tocar suavemente, rozar. 4. Retrucar, hacer retruque en el juego de billar.

kiss, *s.* 1. Beso, ósculo. 2. Toque o rozamiento suaves. 3. Merengue dulce. 4. Retruco, retruque, en el juego de billar.

kisser ['kɪsəʳ] [ki-saʳ], *s.* Besucador, besador, amigo de besar.

kissing-crust ['kɪsɪŋˌkrʌst] [ki-sin-krast], *s.* Beso, la parte del pan que se toca con otro al cocerse en el horno.

kiss-off ['kɪsɒf] [kis-of], *s. m.* **To give the kiss-off,** tirar (something); echar a la calle, dejar plantado (somebody, employee).

kist [kɪst] [kist], *s.* (Ingl. del Norte y Esco.) Cofrecillo, caja.

kit [kɪt] [kit], *s.* 1. Vasija para salmón o caballa; colodra, como para mantequilla. 2. Violín pequeño de tres cuerdas. 3. Aparejo, apresto, conjunto de artículos y herramientas para un fin particular. 4. *(Foto.)* Marquito, un marco interior para sostener una placa más pequeña que la que corresponde al marco.

kit out, *vt.* Equipar, llevar puesto (clothing).

kitbag ['kɪtbæg] [kit-bag], *s. m.* Macuto.

kitcat ['kɪt] [kit], *a.* 1. Término que se aplica a una tertulia o junta de personas que hablan de política, y a los retratos de poco menos de medio cuerpo. 2. **Kitcat** o **kitcat-roll,** rodillo para las tierras de labranza, formado por dos conos unidos por sus bases.

kitchen ['kɪtʃɪn] [ki-chen], *s.* Cocina. **Kitchen furniture** o **utensils,** el ajuar de la cocina, que también se dice batería; el cobre o la espetera, cuando las piezas son de cobre o hierro. **Kitchen-garden,** huerta, el sitio o paraje donde se plantan hortalizas y legumbres. **Kitchen-maid,** criada que sirve en la cocina y ayuda a la cocinera. **Kitchen-stuff,** (a) material de cocina; también, hierbas de cocina, legumbres. (b) Grasa, la manteca o pringue que da de sí la carne cocida o asada. **Kitchen units,** muebles de cocina. **Kitchen-wench,** fregona, fregatriz.

kitchenette [kɪtʃɪˈnet] [ki-chi-net], *s.* Cocina pequeña que se combina con el comedor y la despensa. **Kitchenette apartment,** pequeño departamento en que una cocina diminuta se combina con el resto de la habitación.

kitchen police ['kɪtʃɪnpəˈliːs] [ki-chin-po-lis], *s.* *(Mil.)* 1. Trabajo de cocina en un campamento. 2. Soldados ayudantes de cocina.

kitchen range ['kɪtʃɪnˌreɪndʒ] [ki-chin-reinch], *s.* Estufa, cocina económica.

kite [kaɪt] [kait], *s.* 1. Milano, ave de rapiña. 2. Cometa, *(prov.)* barrilete, (Cuba) papalote, armazón de papel y cañas que se echa a volar. 3. *(Mar.)* Sobrejuanete, foque volante. **Kite-flying,** (a) acción de remontar una cometa. (b) *(Geor.)* Acción de poner en circulación pagarés sin valor.

kith [kɪθ] [kiz], *s.* Los conocidos o amigos de alguien; sólo se usa en la locución **kith and kin,** parientes y amigos.

kitten ['kɪtn] [ki-ten], **kitling** ['kɪtlɪŋ] [kit-lin], *s.* Gatito, gatico.

kitty ['kɪtɪ] [ki-ti], *s.* Gatito; voz de que se usa para llamar al gato, como miz y minino.

kleptomania [ˌkleptəʊˈmeɪnɪə] [klep-tou-mei-nia], *s.* Cleptomanía, aberración mental que se manifiesta por una tendencia irresistible al robo.

kleptomaniac [ˌkleptəʊˈmeɪnɪæk] [klep-tou-mei-niak], *s.* Cleptómano.

klick, *v.* y *s.* *V.* CLICK.

knack [næk] [nak], *s.* 1. Maña, destreza, habilidad, prontitud, gracia, arte para ejecutar alguna cosa; treta astuta. 2. Costumbre, hábito, uso. **To get the knack,** dar en la tecla. **To have a knack for,** tener el don de.

knack, *vn.* 1. Crujir, estallar, rechinar. 2. Hablar culto o con afectación; antiguamente, cultiparlar.

knaggy ['nægɪ] [na-gui], *a.* Nudoso; áspero.

knap [næp] [nap], *s.* (Des. o prov. Ingl.) Bulto que sobresale en alguna parte del cuerpo; cerro, montecillo, cumbre; cualquier eminencia pequeña que sobresale en una cosa llana.

knap, *va.* (Ant.) 1. Morder, romper con los dientes. 2. Golpear alguna cosa haciendo ruido. -*vn.* Crujir, estallar, rechinar; chasquear o dar chasquidos la madera.

knapsack ['næpsæk] [nap-sak], *s.* Mochila, la talega en que los soldados llevan su ropa y algunas provisiones.

knapweed ['næpwiːd] [nap-uid], *s.* *(Bot.)* Cabezuela; varias especies de centáurea.

knave [neɪv] [neiv], *s.* 1. Bribón, pícaro, bellaco. 2. La sota de los naipes castellanos. 3. *(Ant.)* Muchacho; criado; siervo.

knavery ['neɪvərɪ] [nei-va-ri], *s.* 1. Picardía, bellaquería, bribonada. 2. Travesura.

knavish ['neɪvɪʃ] [nei-vish], *a*. 1. Fraudulento, malicioso, ratero, pícaro. 2. Travieso.

knavishly ['neɪvɪʃlɪ] [nei-vish-li], *adv*. Fraudulentamente, pícaramente. **To look knavishly,** tener cara de ahorcado.

knavishness ['neɪvɪʃnɪs] [nei-vish-nis], *s*. El estado o la calidad que constituye a uno pícaro, ratero o travieso.

knaw, *v*. V. GNAW.

knead [niːd] [nid], *va*. Amasar, formar o hacer una masa como la del pan.

kneader ['niːdəʳ] [ni-daʳ], *s*. Panadero, amasador.

kneading ['niːdɪŋ] [ni-din], *s*. Amasadura, acción de amasar. **Kneading-trough,** amasadera, la artesa en que se amasa.

knee [niː] [ni], *s*. 1. Rodilla, la parte de la pierna que la une con el muslo. 2. *(Mar.)* Curva, pieza de madera o de metal que por la parte exterior forma un ángulo y por la interior una línea curva. **Knee of the head,** *(Mar.)* curva capuchina. **Upper part of the knee,** *(Mar.)* brazo superior de la curva. **Hanging-knees,** *(Mar.)* curvas de peralto o de abajo. **Wing-transom-knees,** *(Mar.)* curvas del yugo principal. **Deck-transom-knees,** *(Mar.)* curvas de la cubierta. **Small-knees,** *(Mar.)* curvatones. **Knee-crooking,** obsequioso. **Knee-deep,** metido hasta la rodilla, subido hasta las rodillas. **Knee-high,** hasta la rodilla. **Knee-high to a grasshopper,** (Fest. E.U.) muy corto, muy pequeño. **Knee-joint,** (a) juntura, articulación de la rodilla. (b) (Art. y Of.) Codo, ángulo, escuadra. (c) Junta de codillo. **Knee-jointed,** encorvado o angular como la rodilla. **Knee-timber,** madera a propósito para hacer piezas curvas o rodillas. **Knee-tribute,** genuflexión, la acción de ponerse de rodillas para mostrar obediencia o respeto. **To go down on one's knees,** arrodillarse.

knee, *va*. Suplicar algo de rodillas. *-vn*. Arrodillarse para pedir.

kneecap ['niːkæp] [ni-kap], *s*. Rótula, choquezuela.

kneeholly ['niːhɔlɪ] [ni-jo-li], **kneeholm** ['niːkhɔlm] [ni-joulm], *s*. *(Bot.)* Brusco.

knee-length ['niːleŋθ] [ni-lenz], *a*. **Knee-length sock,** media, calcetín de media.

kneel ['niːl] [nil], *vn*. Arrodillarse, hincar la rodilla, hincarse de rodillas, ponerse de hinojos.

kneeler ['niːləʳ] [ni-laʳ], *s*. El que se arrodilla.

kneepan ['niːpæn] [ni-pan], *s*. *(Anat.)* Rótula o choquezuela, el hueso en la parte anterior de la articulación de la tibia con el fémur. *V.* PATELLA.

knell [nel] [nel], *s*. Doble, tañido fúnebre, el sonido de las campnas cuando tocan a muerto; de aquí, mal agüero.

knell, *va*. y *vn*. 1. *(Poét.)* Doblar, tocar las campanas a muerto; convocar por medio de ese toque. 2. Dar un sonido lúgubre, o un toque de aviso.

knew [njuː] [niu], *pret*. de TO KNOW.

knickerbocker [nɪkəbɒkəʳ] [ni-ka-bo-kaʳ], *s*. 1. Descendiente de una de las primeras familias holandesas que se establecieron en Nueva York, E.U. 2. **Knickers, knickerbockers,** calzón corto y ancho, ceñido debajo de la rodilla, que antiguamente llevaban los muchachos y los ciclistas.

knickers ['nɪkəz] [ni-kars], *s. pl.* V. KNICKERBOCKER, *pl.*

knick-knack ['nɪknæk] [nik-nak], *s*. *(Fam.)* Bujería, juguete.

knife [naɪf] [naif], *s*. (*pl.* KNIVES [naɪvs] [naivs]). 1. Cuchillo, cuchilla, navaja. **Carving-knife,** trinchante, cuchillo de trinchar. **Chopping-knife,** cuchilla de carnicero. **Clasp-knife,** cuchillo grande que se cierra; cuchillo de caza. **Pocket-knife,** Navaja. **Table-knife,** cuchillo de mesa. **Dessert-knife,** cuchillo de postre. **Pruning-knife,** podadera. **Pen-knife, pocket knife,** cortaplumas. **Shoemaker's paring-knife,** trinchete de zapatero. **Flemish knife,** navaja flamenca. 2. Puñal, espada. 3. Cuchilla, hoja de cuchillo que forma parte de una herramienta o de una máquina.

knife, *va*. (Ger.) 1. Cortar o matar con un cuchillo. 2. *(E.U. Fig.)* Deshacer o arruinar por medio de oposición secreta.

knight [naɪt] [nait], *s*. 1. Caballero; campeón. **Knight-errant,** caballero andante. 2. Caballo, pieza del juego del ajedrez (Chess). **Knight of the shears,** *(Fest.)* sastre.

knight, *va*. Crear o hacer a uno caballero; armar caballero.

knight-errantry ['naɪt'erəntrɪ] [nait-e-ran-tri], *s*. Caballería andante.

knighthead ['naɪthed] [nait-jed], *s*. *(Mar.)* Tragante exterior del bauprés. **Knighthead of the windlass,** *(Mar.)* cepos o bitas del molinete. **Knightheads of the gears,** *(Mar.)* guindastes.

knighthood ['naɪthʊd] [nait-jud], *s*. Caballería, la dignidad de caballero; honor o grado de nobleza concedido para recompensar un mérito.

knightly ['naɪtlɪ] [nait-li], *a*. Propio o digno de caballero. *-adv*. Caballerosamente, caballerescamente.

knit [nɪt] [nit], *va*. y *vn*. 1. Enlazar, unir, entretejer; trabajar a punto de aguja; hilar, hacer malla. **To knit stockings,** hacer media o calceta con agujas. 2. Atar, juntar, anudar, unir; unirse. **The bones knit,** los huesos se unen. 3. Contraer. 4. Entretejer o tejer con las manos. 4. Entretejer o tejer con las manos. **To knit the eyebrows,** fruncir las cejas.

knit, *s*. Tejido o tela hecha a mano. **Knit stockings,** medias de punto.

knittable ['nɪtəbl] [ni-ta-bol], *a*. Capaz de ser tejido, unido o atado.

knitter ['nɪtəʳ] [ni-taʳ], *s*. Calcetero, mediero.

knitting ['nɪtɪŋ] [ni-tin], *s*. 1. Unión, junta. 2. Acción u ocupación de hacer calceta; trabajo de punto. **Knitting-machine,** máquina para hacer calceta. **Knitting-needle,** aguja de hacer medias de punto. **Knitting-work,** trabajo de punto.

knittle ['nɪtl] [ni-tel], *s*. 1. *(Mar.)* Sardineta. 2. Cordoncillo de bolsa.

knitwear [nɪtweəʳ] [nit-weaʳ], *s. m.* Géneros o tejidos de punto.

knives [naɪvz] [naivs], *s. pl.* de KNIFE.

knob [nɒb] [nob], *s*. 1. Prominencia, bulto o eminencia que sobresale en alguna cosa; nudo en la madera. 2. Borlita o borlilla que está unida a una cosa para adornarla. 3. Perilla, botón. 4. Manecilla o bola para tirar de una puerta y cerrarla, botón, gorrón 5. *(Arg.)* Abollón.

knobbed ['nɒbɪd] [no-bid], *a*. Lo que tiene bultos o eminencias.

knobbiness ['nɒbɪnɪs] [no-bi-nes], *s*. Calidad de lo que tiene bultos.

knobby ['nɒbɪ] [no-bi], *s*. Calidad de lo que tiene bultos.

knock [nɒk] [nok], *va*. y *vn*. 1. Chocar, encontrarse, tropezar una cosa con otra. 2. Golpear, tocar, llamar a una puerta. *V.* TO RAP. 3. Golpear, dar o pegar golpes. 4. Pegar, dar con una cosa contra otra causando estallido o ruido; aporrear, macear.

knock down, derribar, echar por tierra de un golpe.

knock in, martillar o amartillar; hacer entrar en una parte alguna cosa a fuerza de golpes.

knock off, (a) hacer saltar una cosa a fuerza de golpes. (b) Cesar, descontinuar, suspender el trabajo. (c) *(Fam.)* Hacer o ejecutar prontamente. (d) Rebajar, descontar.

knock out, dejar fuera de combate.

knock over, Atropellar, derribar, voltear.

knock together, construir algo toscamente o de prisa.

knock under, someterse, rendirse.

knock up, (a) hacer levantar a uno a golpes. (b) Cansar en extremo, extenuar con el excesivo trabajo.

knock, *s*. Choque, golpe; llamada.

knockabout ['nɒməbaʊt] [nok-a-baut], *a*. Ruidoso, bullicioso.

knockdown [nɒkdaʊn] [nok-daun], *a*. De saldo, rebajado.

knocker ['nɒkəʳ] [no-kaʳ], *s*. 1. Golpeador. 2. El que cae al suelo de un golpe. 3. Llamador, la aldaba o el aldabón con que se llamaba a las puertas y en lugar del cual se usa hoy el timbre o campanilla. **Knockers,** tetas *(Fam.).*

knocking ['nɒkɪŋ] [no-kin], *s*. Aldabazo, aldabonazo, toque de puerta; el acto de tocar o llamar a la puerta.

knock-kneed ['nɒk'niːd] [nok-nid], *a*. Patizambo.

knock-on ['nɒk'ɒn] [nok-on], *s. m.* Autopase (sports).

knockout ['nɒkaʊt] [nok-aut], *s*. 1. Golpe decisivo en una pelea. 2. *(Fam.)* Persona o cosa sumamente atractiva.

knock-up ['nɒkʌp] [nok-ap], *s. m.* Peloteo (Tennis).
knoll [nɒl] [nol], *va.* Doblar, tocar las campanas a muerto. -
vn. Sonar como campana.
knoll, *s.* 1. Colina o montecillo redondeado; también, cumbre
o cima de una colina. 2. El doblar de las campanas.
knop [nɒp] [nop], *s.* 1. *(Ant.) V.* KNOB. 2. *(Arq.)* Florón,
ramo de flores hecho de realce.
knot [nɒt] [not], *s.* 1. Nudo, atadura o ligadura que se hace en
cualquier hilo, cuerda o cinta. 2. Lazo, cualquier figura
cuyas líneas se cruzan mutuamente. 3. Nudo, vínculo, lazo,
del matrimonio, de la amistad, etc. 4. Nudo de la madera o
de los árboles y plantas. 5. Enredo, maraña, en las
composiciones dramáticas, antiguamente nudo. 6.
Confusión, embrollo, dificultad, intriga. 7. Asociación,
confederación, colección, reunión. 8. Nudo, el punto más
arduo y embarazoso de una cosa. 9. Milla náutica. **To sail
twelve knots an hour,** correr doce millas por hora. **Knots of
the log-line,** señales de la corredera. 10. *V.* SHOULDER-
KNOT. **Hard knot,** nudo apretado. **Loose knot,** nudo flojo.
Running knot, slip-knot, nudo corredizo. **To tie up in
knots,** meter o meterse en un aprieto *(Fig.).*
knot, *s.* Canuto, tríngido, ave de la familia de las escolopácidas.
knot, *va.* Anudar, enredar, juntar; intrincar, unir. -*vn.* 1. Echar
nudos las plantas. 2. Hacer nudos para adornar los vestidos.
knotgrass ['nɒtgrɑːs] [not-gras], *s.* 1. Centinodia. 2.
Polígono. 3. Grama, trigo rastrero.
knothole ['nɒθəʊl] [not-joul], *s.* Hoyo correspondiente a un
nudo de la madera.
knotless ['nɒtlɪs] [not-les], *a.* Sin nudos.
knotted ['nɒtɪd] [no-tid], *a.* Lleno de lazos; nudoso.
knottiness ['nɒtɪnɪs] [no-ti-nes], *s.* Abundancia de nudos;
desigualdad; dificultad; bulto.
knotty ['nɒtɪ] [no-ti], *a.* Nudoso; duro, áspero; intrincado,
difícil.
knout [naʊt] [naut], *s.* Instrumento de suplicio, azote hecho
de correas de cuero.
know [nəʊ] [nou], *va.* 1. Conocer, saber. 2. Distinguir,
discernir. 3. Reconocer, hacerse cargo, caer en algo. 4. Saber,
no ignorar, estar familiarizado con, estar al corriente de. 5.
(Ant.) Conocer carnalmente, tener acto carnal con persona de
otro sexo. **To know how many black beans make five,**
(prov.) saber cuántas son cinco. -*vn.* 1. Comprender, conocer,
saber de cierto; tener noticia de alguna cosa; estar informado,
informarse. 2. Tomar nota de; obtener experiencia o
instrucción. **He knows his own mind,** él sabe lo que quiere.
To know by sight, conocer de vista. **To know something
backwards,** saber algo de pe a pa.
knowable ['nəʊəbl] [noua-bol], *a.* Conocible.
know-all ['nəʊɔːl] [nou-ol], *a.* Sabelotodo, sabihondo.
knower ['nəʊəʳ] [nouaʳ], *s.* Sabio, el que tiene sabiduría;
conocedor, el que tiene mucho conocimiento.
know-how ['nəʊhaʊ] [nou-jau], *s.* Capacidad, habilidad,
conocimientos.
knowing ['nəʊɪŋ] [nouin], *a.* Instruído, inteligente, hábil,
entendido; diestro. -*s.* Conocimiento, inteligencia. **A thing
worth knowing,** una cosa digna de saberse.
knowingly ['nəʊɪŋlɪ] [nouin-li], *adv.* Hábilmente; a
sabiendas, de intento, adrede, a propósito.
know-it-all ['nəʊɪtɔːl] [nou-it-ol], *s. (Fam.)* Sabelotodo.
knowledge ['nɒlɪdʒ] [no-lich], *s.* 1. Conocimiento, erudición,
ciencia, saber, instrucción, noticia. 2. Inteligencia, destreza,
habilidad, experiencia práctica de alguna cosa. **To (the best
of) my knowledge,** que yo sepa. **Not to my knowledge,** no
que yo sepa. **Carnal knowledge,** acto carnal. **Without his
knowledge,** sin su conocimiento, sin saberlo. **To he best of
my knowledge,** según mi leal saber y entender. **To our
knowledge,** que nosotros sepamos.
knowledgeable ['nɒlɪdʒəbl] [no-lich-a-bol], *a.* Enterado
(person). Erudito (thesis, report, etc.).
known ['nəʊn] [naun], *pp.* de TO KNOW. Conocido, sabido,
reconocido, comprendido. **As is well known,** como es bien
sabido, como ya se sabe.

knuckle ['nʌkl] [na-kel], *s.* 1. Nudillo, artejo, juntura de
los dedos. 2. Jarrete de ternero. 3. Juntura o articulación
de las plantas.
knuckle, *vn.* Someterse, rendirse; abandonar la partida.
knuckled ['nʌkld] [na-keld], *a.* Nudoso; lo que tiene
articulaciones.
knuckle down, *vi.* To knuckle down to do something,
ponerse a hacer algo con ahínco.
knuckle under, *vi.* Someterse.
knur [nɜːʳ] [neʳ],
knurl [nɜːl] [nerl], *s.* 1. Nudo, protubernaica. 2.
Sustancia dura.
knurled [nɜːld] [nerld], **knurry** [ne-ri], *a.* Nudoso,
lleno de nudos.
K.O. Abreviatura de **Knock Out.**
koala [kəʊˈɑːlə] [kou-a-la], *s.* Koala.
kodak ['kɒdæk] [ko-dak], *s. (foto.)* Marca de fábrica. Se
aplica a cámaras portátiles para instantáneas y a otros
productos. -*va.* (foto) sacar una instantánea.
koran [kɒˈrɑːn] [ko-ran], *s.* Alcorán o Corán, el libro sagrado
de los mahometanos.
Korean [kəˈrɪən] [ko-rian], *a.* Coreano/a.
kosher ['kəʊʃəʳ] [kou-shaʳ], *a.* 1. Autorizado para los judíos.
(Se aplica a alimentos. 2. *(Fam.)* Genuino, legítimo, correcto.
kowtow ['kaʊtaʊ] [kau-tau], *s.* Reverencia que hacen los
chinos hincándose de rodillas y tocando el suelo con la
frente. -*vn.* Hacer esa clase de reverencia.
kraal ['krɑːl] [kral], *s.* 1. Población de hotentotes en el sur de
África; reunión de barracas. 2. Corral, redil.
kraft, kraft paper ['krɑːft] [kraft], *s.* Papel de estraza, papel
basto de envolver.
Kremlin ['kremlɪn] [krem-lin], *s.* Kremlin, fortaleza de una
ciudad rusa; en especial, la de Moscow.
kumiss o **koomiss** ['kʊmɪs] [ku-mis], *s.* Caracosmos, leche
fermentada de yegua.
KW, kw Abreviatura de **kilowatt.**
KW/h Abreviatura de **Kilowatt/hours.**
kyanize, kyanise ['kaɪənaɪz] [kaia-nais], *va.* Impedir que se
pudra la madera dándole un baño de sublimado corrosivo.
ky, kye, kie [kaɪ] [kai], *s. pl. (Sco.)* Vacas.

L

l [el] [el], La pronunciación de la *l* es la misma que en
castellano, excepto cuando está seguida de *f, k* o *m,* pues
entonces no se pronuncia; v. g. *palm.* En las voces
monosílabas se duplica al fin, como en *wall, mill,* si la *l* no
está después de un diptongo, pues en este caso no se duplica.
-La L. como abreviatura, quere decir libra esterlina; y
también 50 como número romano. LL.B. o D., Bachiller o
Doctor en ambos derechos.
la ↓ɑː] [la], *s.* La sexta voz de la escala musical en el solfeo.
la, *inter.* (Des. o bajo) He aquí, ved aquí, mirad, pues, ya; sí;
ya se ve; ¡vamos!
labarum ['læbərəm] [la-ba-rom], *s.* Lábaro, el estandarte
imperial en que Constantino hizo poner la cruz, y la cifra del
nombre de N. *s.* Jesucristo.
labdanum ['læbdənəm] [la-da-nom], *s.* Ládano. *V.*
LADANUM.
labefaction [ˌlæbɪˈfækʃən] [la-bi-fak-shon], *s.* Decadencia,
decaimiento; enflaquecimiento; declinación.
label ['leɪbl] [lei-bol], *s.* 1. Marbete, pedacito de papel pegado
al extremo de las piezas de tela o paño en el que está escrito
el número de varas que tiene la pieza, etc; rótulo, rotulata,
membrete, letrero. 2. El pedazo de papel y a veces de pergamino
pegado a un escrito, que contiene comúnmente el sello.
label, *va.* Rotular o señalar alguna cosa con un rótulo que
exprese lo que contiene, su dueño, etc.; de aquí, designar,
clasificar.

labellum [ˈlæbələm] [la-be-lom], *s.* 1. (*Bot.*) Pétalo inferior, a menudo ensanchado o de varias figuras, de una flor orquídea. 2. (*Ento.*) Parte de la trompa o probóscide de un insecto díptero.

labial [ˈleɪbɪəl] [lei-bial], *a.* 1. Labial, perteneciente a los labios; formado o modificado juntando los labios. 2. Que tiene labios o bordes, v. gr. un cañón de órgano. -*s.* 1. Letra labial, como p. b, v, w. 2. Cañón de órgano provisto de comisuras a manera de labios.

labiate [ˈleɪbɪeɪt] [lei-bieit], *a.* (*Bot.*) Labiado, en forma de labios. -*s.* Cualquier planta de la familia de las labiadas, de corolas gamopétalas.

labiated [ˈleɪbɪeɪtɪd] [lei-biei-tid], *a.* Dividido a modo de labios.

labiodental [ˌleɪbɪəʊˈdentəl] [lei-biou-den-tal], *a.* Labiodental, pronunciado por la cooperación de los labios y dientes.

labium [ˈleɪbɪəm] [lei-biom], *s.* (*pl.* LABIA). Labio, o algo en forma de labio; labio inferior de los insectos, o labio de una flor.

labor [ˈleɪbəʳ] [lei-baʳ], *s.* 1. Trabajo, labor, pena, fatiga. 2. Obra o trabajo que se tiene que hacer o está ya hecho. 3. Ejercicio, quehacer. 4. Dolores de parto. **His wife is in labor,** su mujer está de parto. 5. Violento balanceo y cabeceo de un buque. **Hard labor,** trabajo arduo, rudo; trabajo forzado en una prisión. **Labor-saving,** que ahorra trabajo; propio para disminuir un trabajo. **To have one's labor for one's pains,** trabajar en balde, trabajar para el Gran Turco.

labor, *vn.* 1. Trabajar, afanarse, esforzarse. 2. Hacer algo con dificultad o mediante esfuerzo doloroso; (*Des.*) tener algún mal o enfermedad. 3. Estar sufriendo agravios, injurias, persecuciones, etc. 4. Estar de parto. 5. (*Mar.*) Trabajar en mar y viento grandes. -*va.* 1. Elaborar, formar con trabajo y cuidado; pulir, perfeccionar. 2. Labrar, cultivar o arar la tierra. 3. Hacer trabajar, activar. 4. (*Des.*) Trabajar, zurrar, golpear, sacudir. **A ship that labors much,** un buque que balancea mucho.

laboratory [ˈlæbrəˌtɔːrɪ] [la-bo-ra-to-ri], *s.* 1. Laboratorio, la oficina en que se hacen las operaciones químicas o farmacéuticas, los experimentos físicos, etc. 2. (*Mil.*) Taller en un arsenal donde se hacen cebos fulminantes, cartuchos, torpedos, etc.

labored [ˈleɪbəd] [lei-bad], *a.* Fatigoso, cansado (breathing). Pesado (style).

laborer [ˈleɪbərəʳ] [lei-ba-raʳ], *s.* 1. Peón, gañán, jornalero.

laboring [ˈleɪbərɪŋ] [lei-ba-rin], *s.* Trabajó, esfuerzo. **A laboring beast,** una bestia de carga.

laborious [ˈleɪbərɪəs] [lei-ba-rios], *a.* Laborioso, trabajoso, penoso; difícil; diligente.

laboriously [ˈleɪbərɪəslɪ] [lei-ba-rios-li], *adv.* Laboriosamente.

laboriousness [ˈleɪbərɪəsnɪs] [lei-ba-rios-nes], *s.* Laboriosidad, afán, trabajo, diligencia, aplicación; dificultad.

laborsome [ˈleɪbəsʌm] [lei-bar-sam], *a.* Trabajoso, penoso.

labor union [ˈleɪbəjuːnɪən] [lei-bar-iu-nion], *s.* Sindicato obrero.

labour [ˈleɪbəʳ] , [lei-baʳ], *s.* V. LABOR. Forma usual en Inglaterra, y lo mismo con sus derivados, **labourer,** etc.

labra, *pl.* de LABRUM.

labradorite [ˈleɪbrədɔːrɪt] [lei-bra-do-rit], *s.* (*Min.*) Labradorita, feldespato laminar de color gris, translúcido, iridiscente, que entra en la composición de diferentes rocas.

labrum [ˈleɪbrəm] [lei-bram], *s.* (*Zool.*) Labro, labio exterior o superior (de los insectos). (Plural, LABRA o LABRUMS.)

laburnum [ˈleɪbɜːnəm] [lei-ber-nom], *s.* (*Bot.*) Codeso o ébano de los Alpes.

labyrinth [ˈlæbərɪnθ] [la-be-rinz], *s.* 1. Laberinto. 2. (*Anat.*) Laberinto, los canales sinuosos del oído interno.

labyrinthian [ˌlæbərɪnθɪən] [la-be-rin-zian], *a.* 1. Lo perteneciente al laberinto. 2. Intrincado, confuso, enmarañado.

lac [læk] [lak], *s.* 1. Laca, especie de resina dura, encarnada, transparente y quebradiza, que sirve para teñir y para hacer lacre y barnices. **Stick, seed o shell lac,** laca en palillos, en granos o en tablillas. 2. V. LACQUER.

lac, lakh [læk] [lak], *s.* 1. La suma de (100,000) cien mil; por sí solo, cien mil rupias. 2. Gran número o multitud.

lace [leis] [leis], *s.* 1. Encaje, randa, pasamano, galón de oro o plata. 2. Cuerda, cordón, cinta. 3. (*Des.*) Lazo, trampa. **Black silk lace,** cinta negra. **Thread-lace,** encaje de hilo, puntas de hilo. **Twisted** o **plaited laces,** cordones, torzales. **Lace-pillow,** almohadilla para hacer encajes. **Point-lace,** punta; encaje de origen italiano, costoso, y hecho completamente a mano, con aguja.

lace, *va.* 1. Abrochar, cerrar, unir y afianzar los vestidos a una otra cosa con lazos o cordones; atar; encordonar, enlazar. 2. Galonear, guarnecer y adornar los vestidos con galones. 3. V. INTERLACE. 4. Rayar con líneas muy finas. 5. (*Fam.*) V. TO LASH. **Lace-frame,** telar para encajes. **Lace-woman,** vendedora de encajes, randas, etc.; pasamanera. **Lace-man,** pasamanero, el que trata en encajes, galones, randas, etc. **Lace-winged,** provisto de alas como de gasa o encaje.

laced [leist] [leist], *a.* y *pp.* Atado con un lazo o cordón.

lacemaking [ˈleisˌmeɪkɪŋ] [leis-mei-kin], *s. f.* Labor de encaje.

lacerable [ˈlæsərəbl] [la-se-ra-bol], *a.* Que se puede lacerar.

lacerate [ˈlæsərət] [la-se-reit], *va.* Lacerar, rasgar, despedazar, hacer pedazos; lastimar.

laceration [ˌlæsəˈreɪʃən] [la-se-rei-shon], *s.* Laceración, desgarradura, desgarrón, rasgón.

lacertian [ˈlɒsɜːʃən] [la-ser-shan], *a.* Lacertídeo, parecido a un lagarto. -*s.* Lagarto, lacerto, reptil terrestre.

lacewing [ˈleiswɪŋ] [leis-uin], *s.* Crisopo, insecto neuróptero, con alas transparentes.

lachrymal [ˈlækrɪməl] [la-kri-mal], *a.* Lacrimal. V. LACRIMAL.

lachrymary, etc. V. LACRIMARY, etc.

lachrymose [ˈlækrɪməʊs] [la-kri-mous], *a.* Lacrimoso.

lacing [ˈleisɪŋ] [lei-sin], *s.* 1. Enlace, enlazamiento, la acción de enlazar o atar con un lazo; en particular el uso de corsés. 2. Cordón, cordoncillo, cuerda para atar con alguna cosa. 3. Algo que enlaza o refuerza, pieza de espaldar, como una curva de barco. 4. (*Fam.*) Zurra, tunda.

laciniate [ˈleisɪneɪt] [lei-si-neit], *a.* Serrado, dentado.

lack [læk] [lak], *va.* y *vn.* Carecer, necesitar, tener o padecer falta de alguna cosa, estar o hallarse necesitado, faltar algo.

lack, *s.* Falta, menester, carencia o necesidad de alguna cosa.

lackadaisical [ˌlækəˈdeɪzɪkəl] [la-ka-dei-si-kal], *a.* 1. Sentimental, pensativo con afectación, lánguido (distracted). 2. Flojo, perezoso (lazy).

lack-a-day [ˌlækəˈdeɪ] [lak-a-dei], *inter.* ¡Mal día!, ¡día aciago! exclamación de dolor, con la cual se expresa que el día en que ha sucedido una cosa, ha sido de mala ventura.

lackbrain [ˈlækbreɪn] [lak-brein], *s.* Un tonto, una persona falta de entendimiento.

lacker [ˈlækəʳ] [la-kaʳ], *s.* 1. El que hace falta. 2. V. LACQUER.

lacker, *va.* Barnizar.

lackey [ˈlækɪ] [la-ki], *s.* Lacayo.

lackey, *va.* Servir como criado; servir bajamente a alguna persona en cualquier negocio. -*vn.* Ser criado de alguien, andar en torno de una persona por interés.

lacklinen [ˈlæklɪnən] [lak-li-nen], *a.* Descamisado, falto de camisa.

lacklove [ˈlæklʌv] -[lak-lov], *s.* Desamorado.

lackluster [ˈlækˌlʌstəʳ] [lak-las-taʳ], *a.* Deslustrado, falto de brillo (dull). Apagado, sin brillo.

laconic, laconical [ləˈkɒnɪk] [la-ko-nik] [ləˈkɒnɪk] [la-ko-nik], *a.* Lacónico, breve, conciso, compendioso.

laconically [ləˈkɒnɪkəlɪ] [la-ko-ni-ka-li], *adv.* Lacónicamente, en breve.

laconism [ləˈkɒnɪzəm] [la-ko-ni-sem], *s.* Laconismo, estilo lacónico.

lacquer [ˈlækəʳ] [la-kaʳ], *va.* Barnizar; dar una capa de laca. -*s.* 1. Barniz. 2. **Lacquer o lacquer-work,** construcción de madera, particularmente china o japonesa, pulida con barniz duro y brillante y a menudo incrustada con oro, plata, marfil, etc.

lacquering [ˈlækərɪŋ] [la-ke-rin], *s*. 1. Arte o acción de barnizar con laca. 2. Adorno de barniz abrillantado; capa de barniz de laca.

lacrimal [ˈlækrɪməl] [la-kri-mal], *a*. Lacrimal. -*s*. Hueso lacrimal.

lacrimary [ˈlækrɪmərɪ] [la-kri-ma-ri], *a*. Que contiene lágrimas o está destinado a contenerlas.

lacrimation, lachrymation [ˌlækrɪˈmeɪʃən] [la-kri-mei-shon], *s*. Efusión o derramamiento de lágrimas.

lacrimatory [ˈlækrɪmətərɪ] [la-kri-ma-to-ri], *s*. Lacrimatorio, vaso en que los antiguos recogían las lágrimas que vertían por los difuntos.

lacrimose, lachrymose [ˈlækrɪməʊz] [la-kri-mous], *a*. Llorón, lloroso, plañidero; que hace llorar.

lacros [ləˈkrɒs] [la-kros], *s*. Cierto juego de pelota de origen indio, común en el Canadá; se juega con una especie de raqueta.

lactage [ˈlækteɪdʒl] [lak-teich], *s*. La cantidad de leche que dan los animales.

lactary [ˈlækərɪ] [lak-ta-ri], *a*. Lácteo, lactario. -*s*. Lechería.

lactate [ˈlækteɪt] [lak-teit], *s*. Lactato, sal formada de ácido láctico con alguna base.

lactation [lækˈteɪʃən] [lak-tei-shon], *s*. 1. Lactancia, acción de mamar, y el tiempo que dura la lactancia; lactación. 2. Secreción de la leche.

lacteal [ˈlæktɪəl] [lak-tial], *a*. 1. Lácteo, lo que es de leche o tiene sus propiedades. 2. Quilífero, lo que lleva el quilo o lo conduce; se aplica a los vasos linfáticos de los intestinos.

lacteous [ˈlæktɪəs] [lak-tios], *a*. Lácteo.

lactescence [ˈlæktesəns] [lak-te-sens], *s*. Semejanza con la leche.

lactescent [ˈlæktesənt] [lak-te-sent], *a*. Lácteo, lactario, lo que es semejante a la leche.

lactic [ˈlæktɪk] [lak-tik], *a*. Lácteo, perteneciente a la leche. **Lactic acid**, (*Quím.*) Ácido láctico.

lactiferous [ˈlæktɪferəs] [lak-ti-fe-ros], *a*. Lactífero, lo que da o tiene leche.

lactometer [ˈlæktəmɪtəʳ] [lak-to-mi-taʳ], *s*. Lactómetro, galactómetro, probeta graduada para determin la calidad de la leche.

lactose [ˈlæktəʊs] [lak-tous], *s*. Lactosa, azúcar de la leche.

lacuna [ləˈkjuːnə] [la-kiu-na], *s*. (*pl*. LACUNE). 1. Laguna, blanco, claro, falta (en un texto); abertura, espacio que carece de algo. 2. Hoyo o hueco pequeño; pequeña abertura, como en los huesos y en los vegetales.

lacunar, lacunal [ləˈkjuːnəʳ] [la-kiu-naʳ] [ləˈkjuːnəl] [la-kiu-nal], *a*. Que tiene lagunas u hoyos, o les pertenece.

lacunar, *s*. (*Arq.*) Lagunar, artesonado.

lacustrine, lacustral [ˈlækʌstraɪn] [la-kas-train], *a*. 1. Lacustre, perteneciente a los lagos o pantanos. 2. Hallado en los lagos o que se cría en ellos.

lacy [ˈleɪsɪ] [lei-si], *a*. Similar al encaje. **Lacy dress**, vestido de encaje.

lad [læd] [lad], *s*. Mozo, joven muchacho, mozalbete. **Come, my lads!.** ¡vamos, muchachos!, ¡vamos, compañeros!

ladanum [ˈlædənəm] [la-da-nom], *a*. Ládano, resina de color obscuro que destila la jara.

ladder [ˈlædəʳ] [la-daʳ], *s*. 1. Escala o escalera portátil. **Step of a ladder**, peldaño de escalera. **Accommodation-ladder**, (*Mar.*) escala de popa o de la toldilla. **Quarter-deck ladder**, (*Mar.*) escala de alcázar. 2. Escalón, grado que se sube en dignidad o el paso que se adelanta en las aspiraciones o pretensiones de uno. **To be at the top of the ladder**, estar en la cumbre de su carrera o profesión.

lade [leɪd][leid], *s*. 1. Desaguadero, canal de desagüe. 2. Embocadero, desembocadero.

lade, *va*. (*pp*. LADED o LADEN). 1. Cargar, poner una cosa sobre otra; cargar un macho, un burro, etc. *V*. TO LOAD. **Laden in bulk**, (*Mar.*) buque cargado con cosas echadas a granel en la bodega. 2. Sacar agua; sacar, o echar un

líquido con un cucharón, un jarro, un cubo, etc; vaciar; echar en. -*vn*. (*Mar.*) Hacer agua una embarcación, abrir agua.

lading [ˈleɪdɪŋ] [lei-din], *s*. Carga, cargamento, flete, cargazón. **Bill of lading**, conocimiento, póliza.

ladkin [ˈlədkɪn] [lad-kin], *s*. Jovencito, mozuelo.

ladle [ˈleɪdl] [lei-del], *s*. 1. Cucharón, cuchara grande. (*Culin.*). **Pitch-ladle**, (*Mar.*) Cucharón de brea. 2. Alabe, una de las paletas cóncavas de que se compone el rodezno de los molinos de agua. 3. Vertedor para achicar el agua de un bote. 4. (*Art.*) Cuchara, instrumento que sirve para sacar la carga de un cañón.

ladle, *va*. 1. Achicar, sacar, vaciar el agua u otro líquido con un cucharón. Servir con un cazo o cucharón. 2. Repartir generosamente (money).

ladleful [ˈleɪdlfʊl] [lei-del-ful], *s*. Cucharada.

lady [ˈleɪdɪ] [lei-di], *sf*. Señora, señorita, dama. **The lady of the house**, El ama o la señora de la casa. **My lady**, señora. **Lady love**, dama. (*Fam.*) querida, amante, cortejo. **Lady in waiting**, dama de una reina o princesa. **Lady's-mantle**, (*Bot.*) alquímila, pie de león. **Lady's-slipper**, zueco, planta orquídea, común en América; cualquier especie del género Cipripidio. **Lady's-smock**, (*Bot.*) cardamina. **Lady's-tresses**, (*Bot.*) planta orquídea; cualquier especie del género Spiranthus. **Our Lady**, Nuestra Señora (*Rel.*). **Ladies and Gentlemen**, Señoras y Señores. **Ladies' man**, mujeriego.

lady-bird [ˈleɪdɪbɜːd] [lei-di-berd], **lady-bug** [ˈleɪdɪbʌg] [lei-di-bag], **lady-cow** [↓eɪdɪkaʊ] [lei-di-kau], **lady-fly** [ˈleɪdɪflaɪ] [lei-di-flai], *s*. (*Ento.*) Coquito de San Antón, mariquita; coccinela, insecto coleóptero. Coccinella (beetle).

lady-day [ˈleɪdɪdeɪ] [lei-di-dei], *s*. El día de la Anunciación de Nuestra Señora.

lady-fern [ˈleɪdɪfɜːn] [lei-di-fern], *s*. Aspidio, helecho hembra.

lady-killer [ˈleɪdɪˌkɪləʳ] [lei-di-ki-laʳ], *s*. (*Fest.*) Un Don Juan, un Tenorio; galanteador de oficio, hombre de quien se supone que agrada a las mujeres.

lady-like [ˈleɪdɪlaɪk] [lei-di-laik], *a*. Delicado, afeminado; tierno, elegante, señoril, aseñorado, político; afectado.

lady-love [ˈleɪdɪlʌv] [lei-di-lav], *s*. Amada, la mujer querida.

ladyship [ˈleɪdɪʃɪp] [lei-di-ship], *sf*. Señoría, tratamiento de cortesía y respeto que se da a las mujeres e hijas de los marqueses, condes, vizcondes o barones en Inglaterra; corresponde en castellano unas veces a Excelencia y otras a Señoría.

lag [læg] [lag], *a*. Trasero, postrero, zaguero, último; posterior, lo que está o viene detrás.

lag, *vn*. 1. Remolonear, roncear, tardar en hacer lo que se debe, rezagarse; moverse lentamente. 2. Quedarse atrás, detenerse, tardar. -*s*. 1. (*Mec.*) Retardación de movimiento por cualquier causa y la medida de esa retardación. 2. Listón de madera; parte de una capa de cascajo.

la -r [ˈlægəʳ] [la-gaʳ], *s*. Especie de cerveza. *V*. BEER.

laggard [ˈlægəd] [la-gard], *a*. Tardío, perezoso, holgazán.

lagger [ˈlægəʳ] [la-gaʳ], *s*. Haragán, holgazán.

lagoon [ləˈguːn] [la-gun], *s*. 1. Laguna; agua poco profunda, como en la desembocadura de algunos ríos. 2. Laguna, el agua tranquila dentro de un atolón o isleta de coral. 3. Concavidad en las altas mesas de los E.U. del Oeste.

laic [laɪk] [laik], *s*. y *a*. Laico, lego, seglar.

laical [ˈlaɪkəl] [lai-kal], *a*. Laical, laico, lego, secular, seglar.

laid [leɪd] [leid], *pret*. y *pp*. del verbo TO LAY.

laidly [ˈleɪdlɪ] [leid-li], *a*. (*Esco.*) Feo, asqueroso.

lain [leɪn] [lein], *pp*. del verbo TO LIE.

lair [ˈlɛəʳ] [leaʳ], *s*. 1. Cubil, la cama en que se recogen las fieras y otros animales salvajes. 2. (*Esco.*) Espacio de terreno destinado a la inhumación de cadáveres.

laird [lɛəd] [leard], *s*. (*Esco.*) Lord; hacendado; a veces, un propietario.

laity [ˈleɪtɪ] [lei-ti], *s*. El estado seglar, en contraposición al estado eclesiástico.

lake [leɪk] [leik], *s*. 1. Lago, laguna. 2. Charco, pantano, depósito artificial de agua. 3. Color rojo obscuro preparado con grana o rubia para pintar.

lake, *vn. (Prov.)* Jugar.

lakelet ['leɪklɪt] [leik-lit], *s.* Lago pequeño -laguito.

lallation ['læleɪʃən] [la-lei-shon], *s.* Imperfección en la pronunciación que consiste en dar a la erre el sonido de ele.

laky ['leɪkɪ][lei-ki], *a.* (Poco us.) Lagunoso, perteneciente a lagos o lagunas.

lama ['lɑːmə] [la-ma], *s.* 1. Sacerdote, monje o monja budista de Tibet. *V.* LLAMA.

lamb [læm] [lam], *s.* 1. Cordero, el hijo de la oveja. *(Mex.)* Borrego. **A yearling lamb,** borrego, borrega; borro, borra. 2. El Salvador del mundo. 3. Persona apacible o inocente.

lamb, *vn.* Parir corderos.

lamb-ale [ˌlæmˈeɪl] [lam-eil], *s. (Ingl.)* Fiesta que se celebra al tiempo del esquileo de los corderos.

lambast(e) [læmˈbeɪst] [lam-beist], *vt.* Azotar.

lambative [læmˈbətɪv] [lam-ba-tiv], *a.* Lo que se lame. *-s.* Cualquier medicina que se toma lamiéndola.

lambdoidal [læmˈdɔɪdəl] [lam-doi-dal], *a.* Lo que está formado como la lamda griega, que tiene esta figura.

lambent ['læmbənt] [lam-bent], *a.* Ligero, undulante, que se mueve de una manera suave y lenta. **Lambent flame,** fuego fatuo, llama ligera.

lambkin ['læmkɪn], *s.* Corderito.

lamb-like ['læmlaɪk] [lam-laik], *a.* Manso, inocente, semejante a un cordero.

lambrequin [læmˈbrɪkwɪn] [lam-bri-kuin], *s.* 1. Guardamalleta, pieza de adorno que pende sobre el cortinaje por la parte superior y que permanece fija. 2. Cubierta de adorno de paño, etc., que se ponía al yelmo.

lamb's-wool ['læmzwuːl] [lams-wul], *s.* Lana de cordero. **Lambskin,** corderina. **Lamb's-lettuce,** *(Bot.)* macha, valerianilla; se llama también, **corn-salad. Lamb's-wool,** cerveza mezclada con manzanas asadas, nuez moscada y azúcar.

lame [leɪm] [leim], *a.* Lisiado, estropeado, defectuoso en algún miembro del cuerpo; cojo, renco; imperfecto. Débil, poco convincente (argument). **To go lame,** cojear, andar cojeando (temporarily). **Lame expression,** expresión manca. **Lame comparison,** comparación defectuosa. **Lame excuse,** disculpa frívola, poco convincente. **Lame verses,** versos cojos o defectuosos. **A lame account,** una relación imperfecta. **A lame excuse,** una mala excusa. **Lame duck,** especulador que no cumple sus compromisos, insolvente.

lame, *va.* Lisiar, estropear.

lamella ['læməkɑː] [la-me-la], *s. (pl.* LAMELLÆ). Laminilla; la hoja. lámina o concha muy delgada; hoja delgada de los hongos.

lamellar ['læmələʳ] [la-me-laʳ], *a.* Compuesto de láminas.

lamellate, lamellated ['læmələɪt] [la-me-leit], *a.* Laminado, hecho o compuesto de láminas; hojaldrado.

lamelliform [ˌlæməlɪˈfɔːm] [la-me-li-form], *a.* Lameliforme, en forma de láminas u hojas.

lamely ['leɪmlɪ] [leim-li], *adv.* Con cojera; imperfectamente, defectuosamente; débilmente.

lameness ['leɪmnɪs] [leim-nes], *s.* Cojera; falta, defecto, imperfección; el estado de una persona lisiada o estropeada.

lament [ləˈment] [la-ment], *va.* y *vn.* Lamentar o lamentarse, sentir con llanto o gemido alguna cosa; afligir y afligirse.

lament, *s.* Lamento, expresión de pesar.

lamentable ['læmentəbl] [la-men-ta-bol], *a.* Lamentable, lamentoso, deplorable, lastimoso.

lamentabl ['læmentəblɪ] [la-men-ta-bli], *adv.* Lamentablemente.

lamentation [ˌlæmenˈteɪʃən] [la-men-tei-shon], *s.* Lamentación, duelo, gemido, lamento.

lamenting [ləˈmentɪŋ] [la-men-tin], *s.* Lamentación, acto de lamentar.

lamia ['læmɪə] [la-mia], *s.* 1. Lamia, especie de demonio. 2. *(Zool.)* Género de coleópteros, de la familia de los cerambícidos.

lamina ['læmɪnə] [la-mi-na], *s.* Lámina, planchita, hoja o capa delgada que encaja en otra; en plural, LAMINÆ.

laminable ['læmɪnəbl] [la-mi-na-bol], *a.* Laminable, susceptible de ser reducido a láminas u hojas.

laminar ['læmɪnəʳ] [la-mi-naʳ], *a.* Laminar, compuesto de hojas o láminas.

laminate, laminated ['læmɪneɪt] [la-mi-neit], *a.* Laminado, dispuesto en láminas, reducido a láminas u hojas delgadas.

lammas ['læməs] [la-mas], *s.* El día primero de agosto.

lamp [læmp] [lamp], *s.* 1. Lámpara, y a veces farol o velón. **Argand lamp,** especie de lámpara en cuyo interior circula el aire; se conoce en España con el nombre de quinqué (de su primer fabricante francés). **Astral lamp,** lámpara de aceite o gas, que por medio de un globo de vidrio difunde la luz con más claridad. 2. Lo que esparce luz. **Lamp-chimney,** tubo de lámpara, bombillo. **Lamp-holder,** porta-lámparas. **Lamplighter,** (a) farolero, lamparero. (b) Lo que sirve para encender lámparas, como un fósforo de cartón o un aparato eléctrico. **Lamp-post,** peana, poste, pie de farol en la calle. **Lamp-shade,** pantalla de lámpara. **Lamp-wick,** mecha.

lampass, *s. V.* LAMPERS.

lampblack ['læmpblæk] [lamp-blak], *s.* Hollín de resina, humo de pez, negro de humo. *(Mex.)* Humo de ocote, que sirve para hacer la tinta que usan los impresores.

lampers ['læmpəz] [lam-pers], *s. (Vet.)* Bulto de carne, acompañado de inflamación, en la parte superior de la boca de los caballos.

lamplight ['læmplaɪt] [lamp-lait], *s.* Luz de una lámpara; luz artifical.

lampoon [læmˈpuːn] [lam-pun], *s.* Sátira o escrito insultante y denigrativo, libelo; pasquín.

lampoon, *va.* Satirizar, escribir sátiras o zaherir y motejar con ellas; hacer coplas contra alguno o coplearle.

lampooner [læmˈpuːnəʳ] [lam-pu-naʳ], *s.* Satirizante, escritor de sátiras personales.

lamprey ['læmprɪ] [lam-pri], *s. (Zool.)* Lampresa.

lampron ['læmprən] [lam-pron], *s.* 1. *(Zool.)* Especie de lamprea. 2. *(Zool.)* Especie de anguila larga.

lanary ['lænərɪ] [la-na-ri], *s.* Almacén para lana.

lanate, lanated ['læneɪt] [la-neit], *a.* Lanoso. *(Bot.)* Lanudo.

lance ['lɑːns] [lans], *s.* 1. Lanza, arma blanca. 2. Lanceta. 3. Lancetada, lancetazo, lanzada. 4. *-m.* Lanza, el que usa una lanza. 5. Llamarada.

lance, *va.* 1. Lancear, dar una lanzada; penetrar, cortar. 2. Abrir una apostema con lanceta o bisturí.

lanceolate ['lɑːnsɪəlɪt] [lan-sio-leit], *a.* Lanceolado, formado como lanza o lanceta.

lancer ['lɑːnsəʳ] [lan-saʳ], *s.* 1. El que lancea. 2. Lancero, soldado de a caballo armado de lanza. 3. *-pl. V.* LANCIERS.

lancet ['lɑːnsɪt] [lan-sit], *s.* 1. Lanceta. 2. *(Arq.)* Arco puntiagudo, bóveda gótica. 3. Trompetilla de los mosquitos, tábanos y otros dípteros.

lancewood ['lɑːnswʊd] [lans-vud], *s.* 1. Palo de lanza. 2. Cualquier árbol que produce esta madera, especie de chirimoyo; anona.

lanch ['lɑːntʃ] [lanch], *va.* Lanzar. *V.* LAUNCH.

lanciers ['lɑːnsɪəz] [lan-siars], *s. pl.* Lanceros.

lancinate ['lɑːnsɪneɪt] [lan-si-neit], *va.* Lacerar, despedazar.

lancination [ˌlɑːnsɪˈneɪʃən] [lan-si-nei-shon], *s.* Laceración; dolor agudo.

land [lænd] [land], *s.* 1. Tierra, en contraposición al agua; la porción sólida de nuestro globo. 2. Terreno, sitio de nuestro globo. 2. Terreno, sitio o espacio de tierra. 3. Suelo, terruño; bienes raíces, hacienda. 4. País, región, reino, provincia; territorio considerado como habitación del hombre; nación. **Native land,** patria. (country, nation). 5. Continente. **To travel by land,** viajar por tierra. **To go on land,** tomar tierra, ir a tierra, desembarcar. **Dry land,** tierra firme. **Law of the land,** ley nacional. **Arable land,** tierra labrantía o de labranza. **To make (the) land,** descubrir tierra, acercar la nave a la costa. **To see how the land lies,** sondar el terreno. **To know how the land lies,** *(Fig.)* estar al corriente de un asunto; saber a qué atenerse. **Land-agent,** corredor de fincas rurales. **Land-breeze,** brisa de tierra. **Land forces,** fuerzas terrestres, tropas de tierra. **Land-jobbing,** Especulación en la compra y venta de bienes raíces. **Land-hunger,** codicia de poseer tierras. **Land-office,** oficina del catastro. **Land-poor,**

a. poseedor de muchas tierras que dan rentas insuficientes para pagar los gastos. **Land Rover,** vehículo todo terreno *(Aut.).* **Land-surveying,** agrimensura.

land, *va.* 1. Desembarcar. 2. Coger (un pez). -*vn.* 1. *(Mar.)* Aterrarse, saltar en tierra, abordar. 2. *(Aer.)* Aterrizar. Posarse (birds). **To land on one's feet,** caer de pie; salir adelante *(Fig.).*

landed ['lændɪd] [lan-did], *a.* Hacendado, el que tiene hacienda o patrimonio en tierras. -*pp.* Desembarcado.

landfall ['lændfɔːl] [land-fol], *s.* 1. Herencia de tierras por muerte del anterior poseedor. 2. *(Mar.)* Recalada.

landgrave ['lændgreɪv] [land-greiv], *s.* Langrave, título de algunos príncipes de Alemania.

landgraviate [ˌlændgreɪˈvɪeɪt] [land-grei-vieit], *s.* Langraviado, título de algunos principados de Alemania.

landholder ['lændˌhəʊldər] [land-joul-dar], *s.* Hacendado, el que tiene hacienda en tierras.

landing ['lændɪŋ] [lan-d-], *s.* 1. Desembarco. 2. Aterrizaje de un avión. 3. Pasillo o descanso de escalera. **Landing craft,** equipo o aparato de aterrizaje (aircraft). **Landing field,** campo de aterrizaje. **Landing gear,** tren de aterrizaje. **Landing net,** red para pescado. **Landing place,** desembarcadero. **Landing stage,** desembarcadero *(Naut.).*

landjobber ['lændˈdʒɒbər] [land-yo-bar], *s.* Corredor de bienes raíces, el que compra o vende tierras por otro.

landlady ['lændˌleɪdɪ] [land-lei-di], *sf.* 1. Ama, casera, la mujer que arrienda o da alguna cosa en arrendamiento. 2. Huéspeda, mesonera, posadera, patrona.

landless ['lændlɪs] [land-les], *a.* Sin bienes o sin tierras; sin fortuna, pobre.

landlocked ['lændlɒkt] [land-lokt], *a.* Cercado de tierra, resguardado o abrigado de los vientos por la tierra.

landlord ['lændlɔːd] [land-lord], *s.* 1. El propietario o dueño de tierras o casas. 2. Amo, huésped posadero; casero, patrón.

landlordism [ˌlændlɔːˈdɪzəm] [land-lor-di-sem], *s.* 1. Acción, conducta u opiniones propias del propietario, huésped o casero; autoridad del propietario. 2. El conjunto de los propietarios en general.

landlubber ['lændˌlʌbər] [land-la-bar], *s.* Término de desprecio usado por los marinos para motejar a los que no son de su profesión.

landmark ['lændmɑːk] [land-mark], *s.* Mojón, marca, la señal que se pone para dividir los términos lindes y caminos. **Landmarks,** *(Mar.)* marcas.

landowner ['lændˌəʊnər] [land-ou-nar], *s.* Propietario, terrateniente.

landscape ['lændskeɪp] [land-skeip], *s.* 1. País, la extensión de terreno: todo lo referente a embellecer el paisaje por medios humanos, ya en pequeños jardines, ya en vastas extensiones.

landslide ['lændslaɪd] [land-slaid], **landslip** ['lændslɪp] [land-slip], *s.* 1. Derrumbamiento, derrumbe, desprendimiento de tierra; *(Méx.)* desliz. 2. La masa de tierra que se ha derrumbado.

landslide, *s.* En la política, abrumadora mayoría de votos.

land-surveyor [ˌlændsəˈveɪər] [land-sar-veia'], *s.* Agrimensor.

land-tax ['lændtæks] [land-taks], *s.* Tributo sobre tierras y sobre el terreno que ocupan las casas.

land-waiter [ˌlændˈweɪtər] [land-uei-ta'], *s.* Guarda de puerto, empleado de la aduana que vigila el desembarque de los géneros en los puertos.

landward ['lændwəd] [land-uord], *adv.* Hacia la tierra.

lane [leɪn] [lein], *s.* Senda, vereda, calle, el camino estrecho que hay entre dos setos. 2. Callejuela, calle angosta. 3. Calle o paso formado por dos hileras de personas.

language ['læŋgwɪdʒ] [lan-güich], *s.* 1. Habla, lenguaje. 2. Lengua, lenguaje, el idioma particular de cada nación o provincia. 3. Lenguaje, expresión por medio de signos, o por sonidos inarticulados, como los de las aves. 4. Vocabulario de una ciencia, lenguaje particular de algún ramo de negocio, etc. 5. V. LANGUET. **Language degree,** título en idiomas. **Bad language,** lenguaje indecente.

languaged ['læŋgwɪdʒt] [lan-güicht], *a.* Lengüetero, se dice del que sabe muchas lenguas.

languet ['læŋgwɪt] [lan-güit], *s.* 1. Lengüeta, cualquier cosa cortada en figura de lengua pequeña. 2. Orejeta, lengüeta de la guarnición de una arma.

languid ['læŋgwɪd] [lan-güid], *a.* Lánguido, débil, flaco; sin animación ni interés; descaecido.

languidly ['læŋgwɪdlɪ] [lan-güid-li], *a..* Lánguidamente.

languidness ['l. gwɪdnɪs] [lan-güid-n-es], *s.* Languidez, caimiento, falta de fuerza.

languish ['læŋgwɪʃ] [lan-güish], *va.* y *vn.* 1. Descaecer, enflaquecer, extenuarse, consumirse, penar o padecer lentamente; adolecer. 2. Agostarse, ponerse mustio. 3. Aflojar, entibiarse. 4. Mirar con ternura. 5. Debilitar, consumir.

languisher ['læŋgwɪʃər] [lan-güi-sha'], *s.* El que se consume o se aflige.

languishing ['læŋgwɪʃɪŋ] [lan-güi-shin], *s.* Languidez, flaqueza. -*a.* Lánguido, descaecido, afligido; enamorado o derretido, hablando de amantes.

languishingly ['læŋgwɪʃɪŋlɪ] [lan-güi-shin-li], *adv.* Lánguidamente.

languishment ['læŋgwɪʃmənt] [lan-güish-ment], *s.* 1. Languidez, debilidad. 2. Angustia.

languor ['læŋgər] [lan-go'], *s.* Desfallecimiento, disminución de ánimo, flojedad, descaecimiento.

languorous ['læŋgərəs] [lan-go-ros], *a.* Lánguido, flojo, que induce o sugiere descaecimiento.

laniard ['leɪnɪəd] [lei-niard], *s.* *(Mar.)* Acollador. V. LANYARD.

laniary ['leɪnɪərɪ] [lei-nia-ri], *a.* Propio para lacerar, como los dientes caninos. -*s.* Colmillo, diente canino.

lank [læŋk] [lank], *a.* 1. Flojo, flaco, descarnado, delgado, desfallecido. 2. Largo y recto. **Lank hair,** cabellos largos y lacios.

lankly ['læŋklɪ] [lan-kli], *adv.* Flojamente, sueltamente.

lankness ['læŋknɪs] [lank-nes], *s.* Flaqueza, flojedad.

lanky ['læŋkɪ] [lan-ki], *a.* *(Fam.)* Larguirucho, alto y delgado (persons).

lanner ['lænər] [la-na'], *s.* *(Orn.)* Alcotán. **Lanneret,** alcotanillo.

lanolin ['lænəlɪn] [la-nou-lin], *s.* Lanolina, manteca o gordura clarificada de oveja o de carnero; se usa en farmacia como base de ungüentos.

lantern ['læntən] [lan-tern], *s.* 1. Linterna, farol. **Dark-lantern,** farol de ronda, linterna sorda, que deja o no ver la luz a voluntad del que la lleva. **Poop-lantern,** *(Mar.)* farol de popa. **Top-lantern,** *(Mar.)* farol de la cofa. **Battle o hand lantern,** *(Mar.)* farol de combate. **Signal lanterns,** *(Mar.)* faroles de señales. **Lantern-maker,** linternero. 2. Faro, fanal, que sirve de guía a los marinos. 3. *(Arq.)* Linterna, fábrica de figura redonda con ventanas para dar entrada a la luz.

lantern-jaws ['læntənjɔːz] [lan-tern-yos], *s.* Quijadas de farol, chupado de cara.

lantern slide ['læntənslaɪd] [lan-tern-slaid], *s.* Diapositiva, fotografía positiva en cristal.

lanyard ['lænjəd] [lan-yard], *s.* *(Mar.)* Acollador, cabo delgado que sirve para tener tiesos y estirados los obenques, brandales y estays. **Lanyards of the stoppers,** *(Mar.)* mojeles de las hozas. **Lanyards of the buoy,** *(Mar.)* rebenques de cabeza de la boya.

lap [læp] [lap], *s.* 1. Faldas, regazo; faldón, faldones. 2. Rodillas; *(Fig.)* seno. 3. *(Mec.)* Longitud o extensión determinada. 4. Presilla, oreja de bolsillo, etc. 5. *(Mec.)* Rueda de metal blando, madera o cuero, que usan los lapidarios para labrar joyas y bruñir metales duros. **Lapstone,** Piedra sobre la cual baten el cuero los zapateros. **Lap-dog,** Perro de faldas, perrillo faldero.

lap, *s.* Salidizo, la parte saliente de un objeto o cuerpo que cubre a otro. 2. Pliegue, doblez; solapadura, avance. 3. Regazo. **Lap of honor,** vuelta de honor (sports, etc.).

lap, *va.* 1. Arrollar, envolver; plegar, hacer pliegues; doblar una cosa sobre sí misma. 2. Caer, recaer, replegarse sobre; cruzar; exceder, hacer salidizo. *-vn.* Doblarse alguna cosa torciéndose sobre sí misma; estar replegado; estar echado o tendido al lado de otra cosa.

lap, *va.* 1. Lamer, beber a lengüetadas, alimentarse o comer lamiendo los alimentos (milk, ice-cream, etc.). 2. Bañar, tocar el agua, o hacer ondulaciones en una orilla (waves). *-vn.* 1. Lamer. 2. Hacer un sonido como de lamido o toque suave.

laparotomy [ˌlæpəˈrɒtəmɪ] [la-pa-ro-to-mi], *s.* Laparotomía, operación quirúrgica, incisión abdominal hecha por el costado.

lapel [ˈlæpl] [la-pel], Solapa.

lapful [ˈlæpfʊl] [lap-ful], *s.* Lo que puede caber en el regazo o enfaldo.

lapidary [ˈlæpɪdərɪ] [la-pi-da-ri], *s.* Lapidario, el que trabaja y labra las piedras preciosas o comercia en ellas. *-a.* 1. Lapidario, perteneciente al arte de labrar las piedras preciosas. 2. Inscripto sobre piedra. 3. Lapídeo.

lapidate [ˈlæpɪdeɪt] [la-pi-deit], *va.* 1. Labrar las piedras finas y preciosas. 2. (Poco us.) Apedrear, matar a pedradas.

lapidation [ˌlæpɪˈdeɪʃən] [la-pi-dei-shon], *s.* Lapidación, apedreamiento.

lapidescence [ˈlæpɪdesəns] [la-pi-de-sens], *s.* Concreción de piedra.

lapidescent [ˈlæpɪdesənt] [la-pi-de-sent], *a.* Lo que se petrifica o vuelve piedra.

lapidification [ˌlæpɪdɪfaɪˈkeɪʃən] [la-pi-di-fai-kei-shon], *s.* Lapidificación.

lapidist [ˈlæpɪdɪst] [la-pi-dist], *s.* Lapidario.

lapis [ˈlæpɪs] [la-pis], *s.* 1. Procedimiento para estampar indianas con añil. 2. Piedra: se usa solamente en composición. **Lapis infernalis,** piedra infernal, nitrato de plata.

lapis lazuli [ˈlæpɪsˈlæzjʊlaɪ] [la-pis-la-ziu-lai], *s.* Lapislázuli, mineral exquisito de color azul, duro como el acero y acompañado frecuentemente por pirita de hierro.

laplander [ˈlæplændər] [lap-lan-dar], *s. V.* LAPP.

lappling [ˈlæplɪŋ] [la-plin], *s.* Apodo que se aplica al hombre que gusta mucho de los placeres sensuales; voz despectiva.

lapp, Lapp [læp] [lap], *s.* 1. Lapón, natural de Laponia. 2. Idioma de los lapones.

lapper [ˈlæpər] [la-par], *s.* El que lame, arrolla o pliega alguna cosa.

lappet [ˈlæpɪt] [la-pit], *s.* Caídas de toca o escofeta, aquellas partes de la misma que penden como adorno.

lapsable [ˈlæpsəbl] [lap-sa-bol], *a.* Prescriptible; que puede sufrir tra -ación de derecho; susceptible de caer o deslizarse.

lapse [læps] [laps], *s.* 1. Caída, la acción de caer; movimiento imperceptible hacia adelante o hacia abajo; de aquí, intervalo de tiempo. 2. Desliz, traspié, yerro, falta ligera. 3. (For.) Prescripción, traslación de derecho o dominio. **In the lapse of time,** con el transcurso del tiempo, o andando el tiempo. **To lapse into one's old ways,** volver a las andadas. **To lapse into unconciousness,** perder el conocimiento.

lapse, *vn.* 1. Escurrir, manar o fluir poco a poco. 2. Deslizarse, decir o hacer alguna cosa irreflexivamente. 3. Caer en algún defecto, desliz o error. 4. (For.) Prescribir, caducar. *-va.* 1. Dejar caer. 2. (Des.) Acusar; convencer.

lapsed [læpst] [lapst], *a.* Caído; deslizado; omitido; prescrito.

lapwing [ˈlæpwɪŋ] [lap-uin], *s. (Orn.)* Avefría, frailecillo.

lapwork [ˈlæpwɜːk] [lap-uek], *s.* Obra entrelazada o entretejida.

lar [lɑːr] [lar], *s.* Lar, dios doméstico: por lo común en plural. LARES.

larboard [ˈlɑːbɔːd] [lar-bord], *s. (Mar.)* Babor, el lado o costado izquierdo del buque mirando de popa a proa.

larcener, larcenist [ˈlɑːsənər] [lar-se-nar] [ˈlɑːsənɪst] [lar-se-nist], *s.* Ladrón, ratero.

larceny [ˈlɑːsənɪ] [lar-se-ni], *s. (For.)* Ratería, hurto de cosas de poca importancia; robo. **Petty larceny,** hurto cuyo monto sólo llega a un valor determinado. **Grand larceny,** el que pasa de dicho valor.

larch [lɑːtʃ] [larch], *s. (Bot.)* Alerce, lárice.

lard [lɑːd] [lard], *s.* Manteca de puerco o de cerdo; lardo, tocino gordo. **Lard-oil,** aceite espeso que se extrae del lardo.

lard, *va.* 1. Mechar. 2. Engordar. 3. Entreverar, mezclar alguna cosa con otra para mejorarla. **Larding-pin,** mechera, aguja de mechar.

lardaceous [ˈlɑːdeɪʃəs] [lar-dei-shos], *a.* 1. Lardoso, grasiento. 2. (Med.) Que indica degeneración crasa de un órgano.

larder [ˈlɑːdər] [lar-dar], *s.* Despensa.

larderer [ˈlɑːdərər] [lar-dei-shos], *s.* Despensero.

large [lɑːdʒ] [larch], *a.* 1. Grande, abultado, grueso. 2. Ancho, amplio, vasto, espacioso, extenso. 3. Largo, franco, liberal, espléndido. 4. Dilatado, difuso, copioso. **At large,** sin limitación; a lo largo; difusamente, por extenso; en general; en libertad, libre en sus movimiento. **As large as life,** de carne y hueso. *-adv.* 1. Con viento a la cuadra. 2. *(Fam.)* Con jactancia. **To sail large,** (Mar.) navegar con viento largo o con viento a la cuadra. **To talk large,** darse tono; presumir de gran señor.

large-heartedness [ˈlɑːdʒhɑːtɪdnɪs] [larch-jar-tid-nes], *s.* Liberalidad, largueza, generosidad.

largely [ˈlɑːdʒlɪ] [larch-li], *adv.* Largamente, latamente, liberalmente, ampliamente.

largeness [ˈlɑːdʒnɪs] [larch-nes], *s.* 1. Grandor, extensión, anchura, amplitud. 2. Liberalidad, generosidad. 3. Grandeza de ánimo.

larger [ˈlɑːdʒər] [lar-char], *a.* **It looked larger than life,** parecía más grande de lo que era realmente.

large-scale [ˈlɑːˈskeɪl] [larch-skeil], *a.* En gran escala.

largess [ˈlɑːdʒɪs] [lar-chis], *s.* Don, dádiva, liberal; presente. 2. (Ant.) Liberalidad.

larghetto [ˈlɑːgetəʊ] [lar-gue-tou], *a. (Mús.)* Lento, a compás algo menos lento que «largo». *-s.* Música en dicho compás. *(Ital.)*

largo [ˈlɑːgəʊ] [larg-gou], *adv. (Mús.)* Largo, lento.

lariat [ˈlærɪət] [la-riat], *s.* 1. Reata. 2. Lazo. *V.* LASSO.

lark [lɑːk] [lark], *s. (Orn.)* Alondra, calandria. **Meadowlark, tit-lark,** alondra de los prados.

lark, *s. (Fam.)* Calaverada, travesura. **To be on a lark,** hacer una travesura; hacer de las suyas, andar de picos pardos, andar de holgorio.

lark about, around, *vi.* Hacer el tonto, tontear, juguetear.

larker [ˈlɑːkər] [lar-ka], *s.* Cazador de alondras.

lark-like [ˈlɑːklaɪk] [lark-laik], *a.* Semejante a la alondra.

larksheel, *s. (Bot.) V.* NASTURTIUM.

larkspur [ˈlɑːkspɜːr] [lark-sper], *s. (Bot.)* Espuela de caballero, delfinio; planta y su flor.

larrup [ˈlærʌp] [la-rap], *va. (Fam.)* Zurrar, tundir, zurriagar.

larum [ˈlærəm] [la-ram], *s. (Des. o poét.)* Alarma, ruido que indica riesgo o peligro. *V.* ALARM.

larva [ˈlɑːvə] [lar-va], *s. (Zool.)* Larva u oruga; la primera forma de algunos animales.

larval [ˈlɑːvəl] [lar-val], *a.* Larval, que pertenece a la larva.

larvate, larvated [ˈlɑːveɪt] [lar-veit], *a.* Larval, encubierto, que tiene larva o máscara.

laryngeal [ˈlærɪndʒɪə] [la-rin-yial], *a.* Laríngeo, relativo a la laringe.

laryngitis [ˌlærɪnˈdʒaɪtɪs] [la-rin-yai-tis], *s. (Med.)* Laringitis.

laryngoscope [ˌlærɪnˈgəskəʊp] [la-rin-gos-koup], *s.* Laringoscopio, instrumento que sirve para explorar la laringe.

laryngoscopy [ˌlærɪnˈgəskəʊpɪ] [la-rin-gos-kou-pi], *s.* Laringoscopia.

laryngotomy [ˈlærɪngətəmɪ] [la-rin-go-to-mi], *s. (Cir.)* Laringotomía, la operación de cortar la traquiarteria a fin de dar paso al aire y evitar la asfixia.

larynx [ˈlærɪŋks] [la-rinks], *s.* Laringe, la cabeza o boca de la tráquea.

lascivious [ləˈsɪvɪəs] [la-si-vios], *a.* Lascivo, incontinente, lujurioso.

lasciviousness [ləˈsɪvɪəsnɪs] [la-si-vios-nes], *s.* Lascivia, incontinencia, lujuria.

laser [ˈleɪzəʳ] [lei-shaʳ], *s.* Laser, amplificación de luz por estímulo de emisiones de radiación.

lash [læʃ] [lash], *s.* 1. La punta del látigo, fusta, etc., con que se da un latigazo. 2. Latigazo, golpe dado con un látigo u otra cosa flexible. 3. Sarcasmo, invectiva, dicho satírico y picante. 4. Pestaña. **Drooping lashes,** pestañas caídas.

lash, *va.* 1. Dar latigazos; azotar (stroke). 2. Mover alguna cosa violentamente haciendo ruido. 3. Satirizar, zaherir con sátiras o invectivas. 4. *(Mar.)* Amarrar, ligar o trincar. -*vn.* Latiguear, andar chasqueando el látigo. **To lash out,** desenfrenarse, repartir golpes, hacerse extravagante en el trato o en las costumbres. **To lash out at/against,** saltar por. Gastar en demasía (spend).

lasher [ˈlæʃəʳ] [la-shaʳ], *s.* Azotador.

lash-free [ˈlæʃfriː] [lash-fri], *a.* Lo que está libre o no tiene peligro de que lo satiricen.

lashing [ˈlæʃɪŋ] [la-shin], *s.* 1. Ligadura, lazo, cabo de cuerda que sirve para atar una cosa con otra; *(Mar.)* amarra, amarradura. 2. Castigo de azotes; acción de satirizar o de lanzar invectivas. **Lashings of the long-boat,** *(Mar.)* obenques de la lancha. **Lashing-ringe,** *(Mar.)* argollas de amura. **Lashings of,** montones de.

lasket [ˈlæskɪt] [las-kit], *s. (Mar.)* Badaza de boneta.

lass [læs] [las], *s. f.* Doncella, mujer joven y soltera; moza, muchacha: aplícase comúnmente a las campesinas o aldeanas.

lassie [ˈlæsɪ] [la-si], *f.* Muchachita, mozuela.

lassitude [ˈlæsɪtjuːd] [la-si-tiud], *s.* Lasitud, cansancio, fatiga.

lasso [læˈsuː] [la-su], *va.* Coger con un lazo. -*s.* Lazo, larga tira de cuero trenzado que termina en un lazo corredizo; se usa para coger caballos y toros salvajes.

last [lɑːst] [last], *a.* Último, postrero, pasado. **At last,** Al fin, finalmente. **To the last,** hasta lo último. **Last week,** la semana pasada. **Last night,** anoche. **The last but one,** el penúltimo. **The last but two,** el antepenúltimo. **To be on one's last legs,** estar en apuros. **That is the last straw,** eso es el colmo. **That is the last thing I expected,** es lo menos que esperaba. **The last word,** la última palabra, lo mejor, la última moda. -*adv.* De último, al final. -*s.* Horma para zapatos.

last, *vn.* 1. Durar, permanecer, continuar existiendo. 2. Conservarse, guardarse, continuar en buen estado. 3. Sostenerse, no rendirse a los sitiadores. **Last out,** aguantar, resistir.

lastage [ˈlɑːstɪdʒ] [las-tich], *s.* 1. Espacio para el cargamento de un buque. 2. Lastre.

lasting [ˈlɑːstɪŋ] [las-tin], *a.* Duradero, perpetuo, perdurable, durable, permanente, constante. -*s.* 1. Sempiternas, tejido fuerte de lana y estambre. 2. Acción de ahormar las palas de un zapato.

lastingly [ˈlɑːstɪŋlɪ] [las-tin-li], *adv.* Perpetuamente, para siempre.

lastingness [ˈlɑːstɪŋnɪs] [las-tin-nes], *s.* Duración, continuación.

lastly [ˈlɑːstlɪ] [last-li], *adv.* Últimamente, en conclusión, por fin, finalmente. por último.

lastmaker [ˈlɑːstˌmeɪkəʳ] [last-mei-kaʳ], *s.* Hormero.

latch [lætʃ] [lach], *s.* Aldaba de puerta; pestillo, picaporte.

latchkey [ˈlætʃkiː] [lach-ki], *s. f.* Llavín.

latch-string, cordón de aldaba. **The latch-string is (always) out,** sea Ud. bienvenido; está Ud. en su casa.

latch, *va.* Cerrar con aldaba; ajustar, unir.

latchet [ˈlætʃɪt] [la-chit], *s.* Agujeta de zapato.

late [leɪt] [leit], *a.* 1. Tardío: remoto, lejano; tardo, lento. 2. Último, el postrero en algún oficio o empleo. 3. Difunto, la persona que acabó la vida temporal: o que ha ejercido una dignidad o cargo. **Late Professor of Latin,** profesor que ha

sido de lengua latina. **The late Mrs. Roberts,** la difunta Sra. Roberts. 4. Reciente, o comparativamente reciente. -*adv.* 1. Tarde, fuera de tiempo, pasado mucho tiempo. 2. Poco ha, últimamente, antes. **Of late,** de poco tiempo acá, de poco tiempo a esta parte. **Better late than never,** más vale tarde que nunca. **Late in the year,** al fin del año. **You are late,** llega Ud. tarde. **What made you so late?,** ¿qué le ha retardado a Ud.? **To keep late hours,** acostarse tarde, volver a deshora. **To make somebody late,** retrasar, entretener a alguien. **It was late in the season,** la estación estaba ya adelantada. **Too late,** demasiado tarde; después del tiempo señalado. **At a late stage,** a última hora. **Late in life,** a una edad avanzada.

latecomer [ˈleɪtkʌməʳ] [leit-ka-maʳ] *s.* Persona que se retrasa, que llega tarde a menudo. **A latecomer entreprise,** una empresa nueva.

lateen [ləˈtiːn] [la-tin], *a.* Latino, voz que significa un palo corto, percha larga y vela triangular. **Lateen-sail,** *(Mar.)* vela latina o de burro.

lately [ˈleɪtlɪ] [leit-li], *adv.* Poco ha, no ha muc, recientemente, poco tiempo hace.

latency [ˈleɪtənsɪ] [lei-tan-si], *s.* El estado de lo que se halla oculto, obscuridad, confusión.

lateness [ˈleɪtnɪs] [leit-nes], *s.* 1. Tiempo o edad avanzada. 2. Tiempo moderno en contraposición a otro más antiguo.

latent [ˈleɪtənt] [lei-tant], *a.* Latente, escondido, oculto.

later [ˈleɪtəʳ] [lei-taʳ], *adv.* y *a.* (comp. de LATE). Más tarde; más adelantado, posterior, subsecuente. **Sooner or later,** tarde o temprano. **A later development,** manifestación o suceso más reciente. **At a later stage,** más adelante.

lateral [ˈlætərəl] [la-te-ral], *a.* Lateral, ladeado.

laterally [ˈlætərəlɪ] [la-te-ra-li], *adv.* Lateralmente.

laterite [ˈlæteraɪt] [la-te-rit], *s.* Una arcilla roja y ferruginosa, muy abundante en algunos países tropicales.

latescent [lætəsənt] [la-te-sent], *a.* Que se va obscureciendo u ocultando.

latest [ˈleɪtɪst] [lei-tist], *a.* y *adv.* Superlativo de **late,** el último, últimamente. **At the latest,** a más tardar. **The latest in fashion,** el último grito en moda. **What's the latest on...?,** ¿qué noticias hay sobre...? **At the latest,** a más tardar, como muy tarde.

latex [ˈleɪteks] [lei-teks], *s. (Bot.)* Látex, jugo lechoso de algunas plantas, del que se obtiene caucho, resinas, etc.

lath [læθ] [laz], *s.* Lata, listón, palo que sirve para formar las techumbres y para colocar en ellas las tejas y pizarras. **Lath of a bed,** varilla de cama.

lath, *va.* Poner latas en los techos.

lathe [leɪð] [leid], *s.* 1. Torno, máquina que usa el tornero para tornear su obra. 2. Lecho, cama de telar. V. LAY.

lather [ˈleɪðəʳ] [lei-daʳ], *vn.* Espumar, hacer espuma, hacer o formar espuma como el jabón. -*va.* Bañar con espuma de jabón y agua.

lather, *s.* Jabonaduras, la espuma que se forma al jabonar o batir el agua con jabón.

lathwork [ˈlæθwɜːk] [laz-uek], *s.* Enlistonado (in carpentry).

lathy [ˈlæθɪ] [la-zi], *a.* Delgado como lata.

latidentate [ˌlætɪˈdenteɪt] [la-ti-den-teit], *a.* Latidentado, de dientes anchos.

Latin [ˈlætɪn] [la-tin], *a.* Latino. -*s.* El latín o la lengua latina.

Latin American [ˈlætɪnəˈmerɪkən] [la-tin-a-me-ri-kan], *s.* y *a.* Latinoamericano.

latinism [ˈlætɪnɪzəm] [la-ti-ni-sem], *s.* Latinismo.

latinist [ˈlætɪnɪst] [la-ti-nist], *s.* Latinista, persona que cultiva la lengua y literatura latinas.

latinity [ləˈtɪnɪtɪ] [la-ti-ni-ti], *s.* Latinidad: estilo latino, modo de emplear la lengua latina.

latinize [ˈlætɪnaɪz] [la-ti-nais], *va.* 1. Latinizar, traducir al latín. 2. Dar forma latina a las palabras de otra lengua. -*vn.* Servirse de palabras o locuciones sacadas del latín.

latish [ˈlætɪʃ] [la-tish], *a. (Fam.)* Algo tarde, retardado.

latirostrous [ˈlætɪˈrɑstrəs] [la-ti-ros-tros], *a.* Latirostro, que tiene el pico ancho (birds).

latitude [ˈlætɪtɪuːd] [la-ti-tiud], *s.* 1. Latitud, la distancia que hay desde cualquier lugar o paraje al ecuador. 2. Latitud, anchura, extensión, difusión. 3. Acepción ilimitada de una cosa; laxitud en las opiniones. 4. Latitud, exención de las reglas fijas o apartamiento de ellas.

latitudinal [ˌlætɪˈtjuːdɪnl] [la-ti-tiu-di-nal], *a.* Latitudinal, relativo o referente a la latitud.

latitudinarian [ˌlætɪtjuːdəˈnærɪən] [la-ti-tiu-dai-na-rian], *a.* 1. Libre, sin freno o regla; de vasto alcance o extensión; de aquí, no exacto ni preciso. 2. Libre en materias concernientes a las opiniones religiosas. -*s.* La persona que es libre en sus opiniones religiosas.

latria [ˈlætrɪə] [la-tria], *s.* Culto de latría, adoración debida sólo a Dios.

latten [ˈlætn] [la-ten], *s.* Latón, azófar, un metal cuando está en planchas u hojas, pues cuando está en masa se llama *brass*.

latter [ˈlætər] [la-tar], *a., pron.* 1. Posterior, más reciente, que viene después de otra cosa; moderno. 2. Este o esto, el último de quien se habla, si se trata de dos, a distinción de *former*, anterior, *aquél o aquello*. 3. *(Des.)* Último. **Latter-day**, del presente; de un período reciente. **Latter-day Saints**, el pueblo mormón. (Variedad de LATER).

latterly [ˈlætəlɪ] [la-ta-li], *adv.* Recientemente, poco ha, de poco tiempo acá.

lattermath [ˈlætəmɑːθ] [la-ta-maz], *s. (Agric.)* V. AFTERMATH.

lattice [ˈlætɪs] [la-tis], *s.* Celosía, rastel, enrejado de listoncillos de madera o hierro puesto en una ventana; cualquier cosa hecha con esa clase de enrejado, como una ventana o un biombo.

lattice, *va.* Enrejar, hacer un enrejado a manera de celosía.

laud [lɔːd] [lod], *s.* Alabanza, elogio.

laud, *va.* Alabar, celebrar, loar.

laudability [ˈlɔːdəˈbɪlɪtɪ] [lo-da-bi-li-ti], *s.* V. LAUDABLENNESS.

laudable [ˈlɔːdəbl] [lo-da-bol], *a.* Laudable, loable, digno de alabanza.

laudableness [ˈlɔːdəblnɪs] [lo-da-bol-nes], *s.* El estado de lo que merece alabanza; la propiedad o calidad laudable de una cosa.

laudably [ˈlɔːdəblɪ] [lo-da-bli], *adv.* Laudablemente, loablemente, con elogio.

laudanum [ˈlɔːdənəm] [lo-da-nom], *s.* Láudano, tintura de opio, una dicina.

laudative [ˈlɔːdətɪv] [lo-da-tiv], **laudatory** [ˈlɔːdətərɪ] [lo-da-to-ri], *a.* Laudatorio. -*s.* Panegírico.

lauder [ˈlɔːdər] [lo-dar], *s.* Loador.

laugh [lɑːf] [laf], *vn.* 1. Reír; estar contento. 2. Sonreír; mostrarse alegre, animado o retozón. -*va.* Mofar, burlar, escarnecer. **To laugh at,** reírse de, mofarse, ridiculizar, poner en ridículo, divertirse a costa ajena. **To laugh at one to his face,** reírsele a uno en las barbas. **To laugh at a feather,** reírse de nada o por nada. **To laugh out, to burst out laughing,** reírse a carcajadas; echarse a reír. **To laugh in one's sleeve,** reírse interiormente. **To laugh down,** ridiculizar, hacer desistir a otro de un plan o propósito por medio del ridículo; hacer callar a un orador a carcajadas. **To laugh out of the other side of the mouth,** llevarse chasco o petardo, particularmente después de jactarse de algo. **There is nothing to laugh at,** no hay motivo de risa. **She laughed till she cried,** se rió a mandíbula batiente.

laugh, *s.* Risa, risada. **Horse-laugh,** carcajada, risotada. **Laugh-and-lay-down,** un juego de naipes. **To carry off the laugh,** ser el último en reírse. **To turn off with a laugh,** hacer burla de una cosa, tomarla a broma.

laughable [ˈlɑːfəbl] [la-fa-bol], *a.* Risible, ridículo; divertido, que excita la risa.

laughing [ˈlɑːfɪŋ] [la-fin], *a.* Risueño; que ríe, reidor. -*s.* Risa, alegría. **Laughing eyes,** ojos alegres, reidores. **Laughing-gas,** gas hilarante, protóxido de ázoe. **To be no laughing**

matter, no ser cosa de risa. **To be the laughing stock of the family,** ser el hazmerreír de la familia.

laughingly [ˈlɑːfɪŋlɪ] [la-fin-li], *adv.* Alegremente, con risa.

laughing-stock [ˈlɑːfɪŋstɒk] [la-fin-stok] *s.* Hazmerreír, el que es objeto de la irrisión de otros, juguete de todos.

laughter [ˈlɑːftər] [laf-tar], *s.* Risa, risada.

launch [lɔːntʃ] [lonch], *vn.* 1. Arrojarse, echarse, tirarse al agua. 2. Extenderse, dilatarse; alargarse; vagar o andar vagando. 3. Lanzarse. -*va.* 1. Botar o echar al agua. 2. Llevar adelante, empezar una empresa o una profesión. 3. Lanzar o arrojar alguna cosa con ímpetu y violencia.

launch, *s.* 1. Lanzamiento. 2. Botadura al agua de un buque recién construido (ship). 3. *(Mar.)* Lancha, chalupa; el mayor de los botes de un buque de guerra. 4. Lancha de recreo (vessel).

launcher [ˈlɔːntʃər] [lon-char], *n. m.* Lanzacohetes.

launching pad [ˈlɔːntʃɪnˈpæd] [lon-chin-pad], *s. (Aer.)* Torre de lanzamiento, plataforma de lanzamiento.

launder [ˈlɔːndər] [lon-dar], *va.* Lavar la ropa.

launderer [ˈlɔːndərər] [lon-da-rar], *s.* Lavandero.

laundering [ˈlɔːndərɪŋ] [lon-da-rin], *n.* Colada, ropa lavada. Blanqueo *(Fam.)*.

laundromat [ˈlɔːndrəmæt] [lon-dro-mat], *s.* Lavandería automática.

laundry [ˈlɔːndrɪ] [lon-dri], *s.* 1. Lavandería. 2. Lavado de ropa. 3. Ropa sucia para lavar.

laundryman [ˈlɔːndrɪmən] [lon-dri-man], *s.* Lavandero.

laureate [ˈlɔːrɪɪt] -lo-riit], *a.* Laureado. **Poet-laureate,** poeta laureado.

laureation [ˌlɔːrɪˈeɪʃən] [lo-ri-ei-shon], *s.* El acto de recibir algún grado académico.

laurel [ˈlɒrəl] [lo-rel], *s.* 1. *(Bot.)* Laurel guindo o laurel regio. 2. *(E. U.)* Arbusto siempre verde. 3. Corona o guirnalda de laurel; honor, distinción.

laurelled [ˈlɒrəld] [lo-reld], *a.* Laureado.

laurentian [ˈlɒrənʃən] [lo-ren-shan], *a.* 1. *(Geol.)* Lorenziano, perteneciente al río San Lorenzo roca de las más antiguas. 2. Relativo a Lorenzo de Médicis o a la Laurentina.

lava [ˈlɑːvə] [la-va], *s.* Lava, la materia que arrojan los volcanes al tiempo de su erupción.

lavabo [ˈlɑːvəbəʊ] [la-va-bou], *s.* 1. Lavabo litúrgico. 2. Lavamanos.

lavaliere [ˈlɑːvəlɪər] [la-va-liar], *s.* Pendiente, medallón.

lavatory [ˈlɑːvətərɪ] [la-va-to-ri], *s.* Lavatorio, lavadero; loción.

lave [leɪv] [leiv], *va. y vn.* 1. Lavar, bañar. 2. Lavarse, bañarse. **To lave water,** sacar agua.

lavement [ˈleɪvmənt] [leiv-ment], *s.* 1. Lavado, acción de lavar. 2. Enema, lavativa, ayuda.

lavender [ˈlævɪndər] [la-vin-dar], *s. (Bot.)* Espliego, lavanda, lavándula. **Lavender cotton,** santolina.

laver [ˈleɪvər] [lei-var], *s.* Lavadero, aguamanil, vasija para lavarse.

laver, *s.* Ova, cualquier algoa comestible del género Porphyra, o un plato preparado con ella. **Green laver** (ova verde).

lavish [ˈlævɪʃ] [la-vish], *a.* Pródigo, profuso, descabellado, despilfarrado.

lavish, *va.* 1. Desparramar, disipar, malbaratar, malgastar, gastar con profusión. 2. Prodigar cumplimientos, alabanzas, etc. 3. Sacrificar, despreciar su sangre, su vida, etc.

lavishly [ˈlævɪʃlɪ][la-vish-li], *adv.* Pródigamente, profusamente.

lavishment [ˈlævɪʃmənt][la-vish-ment], **Lavishness** [la-vish-nes], *s.* (Poco us.) Despilfarro, prodigalidad, profusión, disipación.

law [lɔː], *s.* 1. Ley, regla y norma de conducta. 2. Ley, constitución o estatuto. 3. Ley, regla o principio convencional. 4. Derecho. **According to law,** según derecho. **Civil law,** derecho civil. 5. Litigio judicial entre partes. 6. Jurisprudencia. 7. *(Bib.)* Tora, libro de la ley judía. 8. Ley de la naturaleza, la ocurrencia uniforme de los fenómenos, naturales de un mismo modo, bajo las mismas condiciones. **To go to law with one,** poner pleito a uno. **To**

follow the law, estudiar las leyes. **Father, son, daughter** o **brother-in-law,** suegro, yerno, nuera o cuñado. *(Fam.)* Padre, hijo o hermano político, hija política. **In point of law,** desde el punto de vista legal. **Law of nations,** derecho internacional. **Law of gravity,** la ley de la gravedad. **To lay down the law,** hablar autoritariamente *(Fig.)* **To take the law in one's own hands,** tomar la justicia por su mano. **Law court,** tribunal de justicia.

law-abiding [ˈlɔːəˌbaɪdɪŋ][lo-a-bai-din], *a.* Persona que observa las leyes.

lawbreaker [ˈlɔːˌbreɪkəʳ][lo-brei-kaʳ], *s.* Transgresor, el que viola la ley.

law-day [ˈlɔːdeɪ][lo-dei], *s.* Día en que están abiertos los tribunales.

lawful [ˈlɔːfʊl][lo-ful], *a.* Legal, según derecho, conforme a la ley; permitido, legítimo, justo, válido, lícito. **A lawful prize,** una presa legítima. **Lawful goods,** géneros permitidos o lícitos.

lawfully [ˈlɔːfəlɪ][lo-fa-li], *adv.* Legalmente, legítimamente.

lawfulness [ˈlɔːfʊlnɪs][lo-ful-nes], *s.* Legalidad, legitimidad.

lawgiver [ˈlɔːˌgɪvəʳ][lo-gui-vaʳ], *s.* Legislad.

lawgiving [ˈlɔːˌgɪvɪŋ][lo-gui-vin], *a.* Legislativo.

lawless [ˈlɔːlɪs][lo-les], *a.* No sujeto a la ley; ilegal; desordenado, desarreglado.

lawlessly [ˈlɔːlɪslɪ][lo-les-li], *adv.* Ilegalmente, contra las leyes.

lawlessness [ˈlɔːlɪsnɪs][lo-les-nes], *s.* Desorden, desobediencia.

lawmaker [ˈlɔːˌmeɪkəʳ][lo-mei-kaʳ], *s.* Legislador.

lawn [lɔːn][lon], *s.* 1. Prado, campo abierto entre bosques o casas. 2. Linón. t -a fina de lino. **Long lawn,** estopilla. -a. Hecho de linón. **Lawn-mower,** segadora de mano para prados. **Lawn-sprinkler,** regadera para prados.

lawnmower [ˈlɔːnˌməʊəʳ][lon-mouaʳ], *s.* Cortacésped.

lawn tennis [ˈlɔːnˈtenɪs][lon-te-nis], *s.* Variedad del juego de tenis.

lawsuit [ˈlɔːsuːt][lo-sut], *s.* Pleito, proceso, litigio, causa. *(For.)* Lite.

lawyer [ˈlɔːjəʳ][lo-yaʳ], *s.* Abogado, jurista, jurisconsulto. (Mex. y C. *a.*) Licenciado. **Lawyer's office,** bufete de abogados.

lawyerly [ˈlɔːjəlɪ][lo-ya-li], *a.* Judicial.

lax [læks][laks], *a.* 1. Laxo, suelto, flojo, desatado. 2. Vago, indeterminado. 3. Corriente de vientre. -s. (Poco us.) Despeño, cámaras, flujo de vientre, diarrea. **To be lax about,** ser negligente.

laxation [lækˈseɪʃən][lak-sei-shon], *s.* Laxación.

laxative [ˈlæksətɪv][lak-sa-tiv], *a.* Laxativo, laxante. -s. Laxante, purgante.

laxity [ˈlæksɪtɪ][lak-si-ti], **laxness** [ˈlæksnɪs][laks-nes], *s.* 1. Aflojamiento, la acción y efecto de aflojar; laxitud, flojedad. 2. Relajamiento de nervios, etc.; relajación de costumbres, etc. 3. Anchura, soltura, desahogo. 4. Despeño, diarrea.

laxly [ˈlækslɪ][laks-li], *adv.* Flojamente, sueltamente.

lay [leɪ][lei], *pret.* del verbo TO LIE.

lay [leɪ][lei], *va.* (*pret.* y *pp.* LAID) 1. Poner, fijar, colocar alguna cosa. 2. Tender, extender o echar a lo largo en el suelo; echar o tumbar por tierra; impedir que se levante alguna cosa que está caída; hacer doblar las espigas o la hierba hacia el suelo. **To be laid low with flu,** mantenerse en cama por la gripe. 3. Matar el polvo 4. Enterrar. 5. Pintar, representar algo por medio de figuras. 6. Calmar, aquietar, sosegar, apaciguar. 7. Preparar las plantas enterrando sus vástagos. 8. Añadir, juntar. 9. Imponer cargas, obligaciones u otra cosa. 10. Proyectar, trazar, discurrrir. 11. Imputar. 12. Mandar, ordenar como una obligación. 13. Abatir, derrocar, derribar. 14. Apostar. 15. Exhibir, presentar, manifestar alguna cosa. -vn. 1. Poner huevos las hembras de las aves y otros animales. 2. Tramar, formar un plan. 3. *(Mar.)* Venir o ir como mandado; como **to lay aloft,** ir arriba. 4. Estar situado, formar.

lay about, hacer todos los esfuerzos posibles por el logro de algún objeto, mover cielo y tierra por conseguir alguna cosa; dar golpes a ciegas o sin concierto.

lay against, acusar.

lay aft, ir a popa.

lay apart, reservar, poner aparte.

lay aside, desechar, echar o poner a un lado, arrinconar, poner en olvido, despreciar, descuidar, omitir, abandonar; separar, reservar, poner aparte.

lay at, intentar, dar golpes, golpear.

lay away, dejar, echar a un lado.

lay before, exponer a la vista, desplegar, mostrar, manifestar; representar ante alguna autoridad exponiendo daños, quejas o agravios.

lay by, reservar, guardar, conservar alguna cosa para tiempo oportuno; deponer o apear de algún empleo o cargo; despedir, despachar, echar fuera; omitir, arrimar, arriconar.

lay down, sentar y sostener una opinión o parecer; apostar; poner en depósito como prenda o equivalente, pagar, devolver, restituir; perder; rendir las armas. **To lay down a garden,** Delinear un jardín.

lay for, *(Fam.)* Asechar, poner asechanzas.

lay forth, Extenderse: poner o colocar a un muerto de un modo decente.

lay hold of, asir, agarrar, coger; prender. **To lay in,** atesorar; comprar.

lay in for, hacer proposiciones con un objeto insidioso o doble.

lay on, aplicar con violencia alguna cosa; obrar con vehemencia; imponer cargas u obligaciones; extender una cosa sobre la superficie de otra.

lay open, descubrir, poner al descubierto, hacer ver, demostrar.

lay out, gastar, emplear, desembolsar, ajustar, hacer divisiones, disponer, esforzarse; desplegar; descartarse en el juego.

lay over, cubrir una cosa con otra; desembolsar.

lay to, acusar; acometer; aplicarse con energía a algo; sentar una proposición; empeñar, consignar o depositar alguna cosa; renunciar; reposar. **To lay to heart,** tomar a pecho, resentir vivamente.

lay under, someter, sojuzgar.

lay up, guardar, acumular, atesorar, amontonar, juntar, encerrar; cerrar, apretar; guardar cama por estar enfermo; prender o meter a uno en la cárcel o en paraje seguro.

lay upon, imponer, cargar; poner algo sobre otra cosa. **To lay a bet,** apostar, hacer una apuesta. **To lay eggs,** aovar, poner huevos las aves u otros animales ovíparos. **To lay claim,** reclamar, pretender. **To lay hands on one,** sentar la mano, pegar a alguien. **To lay hands on oneself,** Matarse, cometer suicidio. **To lay level,** igualar, allanar, destruir, arruinar. **To lay the blame on another,** echar la culpa a otro. **To lay ropes,** *(Mar.)* colchar cabos. **To lay waste,** asolar. **Laying on of hands,** imposición de manos.

lay, *s.* 1. Caída, la manera como está situada o colocada alguna cosa, dirección relativa, contorno. 2. Negocio particular. 3. Cantidad determinada de hilo. 4. Marco oscilante de telar. 5. Ganancia o parte de ganancia. 6. Lecho, tongada, capa o cama con que se ponen algunas cosas sobre otras. **Lay-days,** *(Mar.)* Días de demora o estadía. **Over-lay-days, demurrage,** *(Mar.)* sobreestalas, días de detención.

lay, *s.* Canción, balada, poema narrativo en estilo llano y sencillo.

lay, *a.* Secular, lego, seglar; no eclesiástico; no profesional. **A lay opinion,** opinión no profesional. **Lay brother,** hermano o fraile lego. **Lay clerk,** capiscol, sochantre de una iglesia. **Lay reader,** lego autorizado para leer las oraciones en una iglesia. **Lay land,** baldío, campo que está inculto. *V.* LEA.

lay-by [ˈleɪbaɪ][lei-bai], *n.* Área de aparcamiento (cars).

layer ['leɪəʳ][leiaʳ], *s.* 1. Lecho, capa, cama, tonga, tongada. 2. Vástago, pimpollo, renuevo de alguna planta; acodo. 3. Gallina que pone. **Layer out,** mayordomo. **Layer up,** tesorero.

layer, *va.* Acodar, propagar plantas por medio de acodos.

lay-figure ['leɪˈfɪgəʳ][lei-fi-gaʳ], *s.* Maniquí, figura movible que se puede poner en varias actitudes.

laying ['leɪɪŋ][lein], *s.* 1. El acto de colocar o poner alguna cosa. 2. Capa, costra. -*a.* Situado, colocado. *(Mar.)* Anclado.

layman ['leɪmən][lei-man], *s.* Lego, seglar.

lay-off ['leɪɒf][lei-of], *s.* Despedida del trabajo. -*va.* Cesar o despedir de un trabajo.

lay of the land ['leɪɒfðəˈlænd][lei-of-de-land], *s.* 1. Disposición o plano de un terreno. 2. Estado de algún asunto o circunstancias prevalecientes del mismo.

layout ['leɪaʊt][lei-aut], *s.* 1. Plan, esquema. 2. Disposición. distribución.

layover ['leɪəʊvəʳ][lei-ou-vaʳ], *s.* Permanencia de pasada en algún lugar.

lazar ['læzəd][lei-zard], *s.* Lázaro, leproso.

lazily ['leɪzɪlɪ][lei-si-li], *adv.* Perezosamente, pesadamente.

laziness ['leɪzɪnɪs][lei-si-nes], *s.* Pereza, desidia, ociosidad, haraganería.

lazuli, *s. V.* LAPIS LAZULI.

lazy ['leɪzɪ][lei-si], *a.* 1. Perezoso, ocioso, flojo, desidioso, haragán. 2. Tardo, pesado.

lea [liːʧ][li], *s.* Prado, pradera; llanura.

leach [liːʧ][lich], *va.* Lavar las cenizas de lejía para extraer el álcali; lixiviar. -*s.* 1. Cenizas de lejía y la disolución obtenida por la lixiviación. 2. Lixiviación. 3. **Leach o leach-tub,** cubo o tina donde se ponen las cenizas para hacer la colada.

lead ['liːd][lid], *s.* 1. Plomo, metal blanco, pesado, flexible y correoso (metal). **Leads,** Techo emplomado. **Lead-mine,** mina de plomo (pencil). **Black-lead,** lápiz-plomo, plombagina, grafito. **White-lead,** albayalde. **Red-lead,** almagra o almagre; también se da este nombre al minio o azarcón. **Yellow-lead,** albayalde calcinado. *V.* MASSICOT. **Lead-pencil,** lápiz. **Sugar of lead,** azúcar de plomo, acetato de plomo. 2. Interlínea, regleta. 3. *(Mar.)* Sondalesa, escandallo. **Deep-sea-lead,** escandallo mayor. **To heave the lead,** echar la sonda. **The lead constantly going,** sondeando constantemente. 4. Indicación, pista, señal (clue). **To play the lead,** interpretar el papel principal.

lead, *va. (pret.* y *pp.* LEADED). 1. Emplomar, forrar o guarnecer con plomo. 2. *(Impr.)* Interlinear, poner una regleta entre las líneas.

lead, *s.* 1. Primacía, primer lugar. **To take the lead,** llevarse la primacía; tomar la delantera. 2. Mano, el que juega primero en las partidas de naipes. 3. Salida, el palo que juega el que es mano en algunos juegos de naipes.

lead, *va. (pret.* y *pp.* LED). 1. Llevar de la mano. 2. Conducir, guiar o dirigir a otro. 3. Mandar, regir, gobernar. 4. Guiar, ir delante. 5. Enseñar, amaestrar. 6. Halagar, atraer, inducir, mover, motivar. 7. Gastar o emplear el tiempo en alguna cosa. -*vn.* 1. Mandar en jefe. 2. Guiar, enseñar el camino, conducir; dominar. 3. Ser mano en el juego de naipes.

lead along, conducir, acompañar.

lead astray, llevar fuera del camino recto, extraviar; seducir.

lead away, Llevar o traer de una parte a otra, hacer una persona que otra la acompañe.

lead back, acompañar de vuelta, volver a conducir a una persona al paraje de donde se la había traído antes. **To lead a horse to water,** llevar a abrevar un caballo.

lead in o **into,** introducir.

lead off o **out of,** desviar, estorbar, impedir; principiar. **To lead one a dance,** hacer dar a uno muchos pasos innecesarios. **To lead out of the way,** descarriar. **To lead a good life,** vivir bien. **To lead a new life,** enmendarse.

lead up to, conducir a, llevar a. **To lead the way,** mostrar el camino, tomar la delantera.

leaded ['ledɪd][le-did], *pp.* y *a.* 1. Interlineado. 2. Emplomado, plomado; guarnecido de plomo o engastado en plomo o grafito. **Leaded petrol,** gasolina con plomo.

leaden ['ledn][le-den], *a.* 1. Hecho de plomo. 2. Aplomado, de color de plomo. 3. Pesado, tardo, lento, estúpido. **Leaden-hearted,** duro, insensible, que tiene corazón de mármol. **Leaden-heeled,** lento, tardo.

leader ['liːdəʳ][li-daʳ], *s.* 1. Guía, conductor, la persona que encamina y enseña el camino. 2. Jefe, general, capitán, comandante, el superior que dirige un ejército o parte de él; caudillo, corifeo, cabeza, principal de una facción, reunión, etc. 3. Guión, el que va delante. **Leader of a dance,** guión, director de una danza o un baile. **Ringleader,** jefe de partido. *(Fam.)* Cabecilla, cabeza de bando.

leadership ['liːdəʃɪp][li-da-ship], *s.* Dirección, estado, liderazgo.

lead-in ['liːdɪn][lid-in], *s.* Introducción.

leading ['liːdɪŋ][li-din], *a.* Principal, primero; capital. **To have the leading hands at cards,** ser mano en el juego. **Leading, man,** jefe de partido. **Leading-strings,** (a) Andadores, los cordones o cintas con que se sostiene al niño que empieza a andar. (b) De aquí, dirección, refrenamiento, especialmente si es desagradable o estorba. **Leading word,** la primera palabra. -*s.* Guía, conducción.

leadsman ['liːdzmən][lids-man], *s. (Mar.)* Sondeador.

leady ['liːdɪ][li-di], *a.* Aplomado, parecido al plomo o que lo contiene.

leaf [liːf][lif], *s. (pl.* LEAVES). 1. *(Bot.)* Hoja. 2. Hoja, la parte de un libro que se compone de dos páginas o llanas (book). **To take the leaf of somebody's book,** seguir el ejemplo de alguien. 3. Hoja de puerta, o de mesa que se dobla (table). 4. Hoja, plancha batida y muy delgada. **A leaf of gold or silver,** hoja o pan de oro o plata. **Leaf brass,** oropel. **Over the leaf o turn the leaf,** a la vuelta. **Fly-leaf** *(Impr.)* guarda, hoja blanca. **To turn down a leaf,** hacer un pliegue a una hoja. **To turn over a new leaf,** doblar la hoja, enmendar uno su conducta o sus costumbres. **Leaf-bud,** yema, botón de una planta que se desarrolla en una rama frondosa. **Leaf-hopper,** insecto hemíptero saltador. **Leaf-lard,** manteca en rama. **Leaf question,** pregunta tendenciosa. **Leaf-stalk,** pecíolo, pezón.

leaf, *vn.* Echar hojas.

leafage ['liːfeɪdʒ][li-feich], *s.* Follaje, la abundancia de hoja.

leafed ['liːft][lift], **leafy** ['liːfɪ][li-fi], *a.* Frondoso, poblado de hoja: se dice de los árboles, hojoso.

leafiness ['liːfɪnɪs][li-fi-nes], *s.* Follaje, abundancia de hojas.

leaflet ['liːflɪt][lif-let], *s. dim.* Hojilla, hojuela, octavilla.

leaf tobacco ['lefˌtəbækəʊ][lift-to-ba-ko], *s.* Tabaco en rama.

league [liːg][lig], *s.* 1. Liga, alianza, confederación; unión, asociación entre dos o varias personas, partidos; estados, etc. 2. Legua, medida de tierra de tres millas geográficas. La legua marina es de tres millas náuticas. **League table,** clasificación. **They're not in the same league,** no hay comparación *(Fam.).*

league, *vn.* Confederarse, ligarse, aliarse, unirse.

leagued ['liːgɪd][li-guid], *a.* Confederado, ligado, aliado.

leaguer ['liːgəʳ][li-gaʳ], *s.* 1. Coligado, conjurado. 2. *(Mil.)* Campamento.

leak [liːk] [lik], *s.* 1. Rendija, grieta, raja por donde entra o se escapa el agua; *(Mar.)* vía de agua. 2. Goteo, filtración, paso de un flúido por una grieta, rendija o cualquier abertura. **To spring a leak,** *(Mar.)* hacer aguas, o abrir una vía de agua un barco (ship). **To fother a leak,** *(Mar.)* atajar una corriente, cegar una vía de agua.

leak, *vn.* Gotear, hacer agua; derramarse, rezumarse. **The ship leaks,** *(Mar.)* el navío hace agua. **A barrel that leaks,** barril que se rezuma. **Leak out,** escaparse, fugarse (gas, liquid).

leakage [ˈliːkɪdʒ] [li-keich], *s.* 1. Goteo, filtración. 2. Avería, pérdida, merma de un líquido que sale por una abertura. 3. Merma, derrame, la rebaja que se hace por lo que se rezuman las vasijas o medidas de los líquidos.

leakproof [ˈliːkpruːf] [lik-pruf], *a.* 1. Hermético. 2. A prueba de escape.

leaky [ˈliːkɪ] [li-ki], *a.* 1. Roto; haciendo agua; que se rezuma. 2. *(Fam.)* Locuaz, indiscreto, la persona propensa a revelar secretos.

leal [liːl] [lil], *a. (Poét. Prov. Ingl. y Esco.)* Leal, fiel, sincero. **The land of the leal,** la morada de los fieles, el cielo.

lean [liːn] [lin], *vn.* 1. Apoyarse, recostarse contra alguna cosa, reclinarse, repantigarse. 2. Inclinarse, torcerse un poco hacia abajo, encorvase. 3. Inclinarse, tener propensión a alguna cosa. *-va.* Inclinar, torcer algo hacia abajo, encorvar. **lean against,** apoyase en, arrimarse *a.*

lean back, reclinarse.

lean on, apoyarse (en alguien o contra algo).

lean out, asomarse.

lean over, adelantarse hacia alguna parte.

lean, *a.* Flaco, magro; mezquino, necesitado. *-s.* 1. Carne mollar, carne magra sin gordura. 2. **Lean** o **leaning,** inclinación, disposición, propensión.

leaning [ˈliːnɪŋ] [li-nin], *s.* 1. Inclinación. 2. *a.* Inclinado.

leanly [ˈliːnlɪ] [lin-li], *adv.* Pobremente; sin gordura.

leanness [ˈliːnnɪs] [lin-nes], *s.* Flaqueza, pobreza.

leant [lent] [lent], *pt., pp of* TO LEAN.

lean-to [ˈliːntuː] [lin-tu], *s.* Colgadizo.

lean-witted [ˈliːnwɪtɪd] [lin-ui-tid], *a.* Tonto, necio.

leap [liːp] [lip], *vn.* 1. Saltar, brincar. 2. Correr hacia alguna parte con precipitación y de repente. 3. Saltar, brotar, salir con ímpetu. 4. Palpitar el corazón. *-va.* 1. Saltar, brincar. 2. Cubrir, tener coito el macho cuadrúpedo con la hembra. **To leap again,** volver a saltar. **To leap at,** apresurarse a. **To leap for joy,** saltar de alegría de gozo. **To leap about,** dar saltos. **A leap in the dark,** un salto al vacío. **To leap out at somebody,** echarse encima de alguien. **To leap over,** saltar por encima. **To leap to one's feet,** incorporarse de un salto.

leap, *s.* 1. Salto, el acto de saltar. 2. Salto, el espacio de tierra que mide un salto. 3. Salto, tránsito desproporcionado de una cosa a otra, paso repentino o súbito. 4. Asalto o acometimiento de algún animal feroz. 5. El ayuntamiento o coito de los animales. 6. Salto o tránsito desproporcionado de una cosa a otra. 7. *(Prov. Ingl.)* Cestón para pescado.

leaper [ˈliːpəʳ] [li-paʳ], *s.* 1. Saltador, brincador. 2. El caballo que pasa saltando todos los obstáculos que encuentra en la carrera.

leapfrog [ˈliːpfrɒg] [lip-frot], *s.* Salto a la burra.

leaping [ˈliːpɪŋ] [li-pin], *s.* Salto, el acto de saltar.

leapingly [ˈliːpɪŋlɪ] [li-pin-li], *adv.* A brincos, a saltos.

leapt [ˈlept] [lept], *Pt, pp of* TO LEAP.

leap-year [ˈliːpjɪəʳ] [lip-yiaʳ], *s.* Año bisiesto o intercalar.

learn [lɜːn] [lern], *va. (pret. y pp.* LEARNED o LEARNT*).* 1. Aprender, adquirir el conocimiento de alguna cosa por medio del estudio; fijar en la mente. 2. *(Des.)* Instruir, enseñar: informar. *vn.* 1. Aprender siguiendo el ejemplo de otro; instruirse. 2. Saber, recibir una noticia. **We learnt that he is dead,** supimos, recibimos la noticia de que está muerto.

learnable [ˈlɜːnəbl] [ler-na-bol], *a.* Que puede aprenderse.

learned [ˈlɜːnɪd] [ler-nid], *a.* 1. Docto, erudito. 2. Sabio, inteligente. 3. Hábil, diestro; versado en, perito, experto. **The learned,** los doctos, los sabios, los literatos. **The learned world,** la república de las letras. **My learned brother,** mi ilustrado colega.

learnedly [ˈlɜːnɪdlɪ] [ler-nid-li], *adv.* Sabiamente, doctamente.

learner [ˈlɜːnəʳ] [ler-naʳ], *s.* Escolar, estudiante, aprendiz; discípulo, principiante.

learning [ˈlɜːnɪŋ] [ler-nin], *s.* 1. Literatura, el conocimiento y ciencia de las letras; saber, ciencia, erudición, estudio. 2. Conocimiento de alguna cosa. **To have learning difficulties,** ser retrasado, disminuido psíquico.

learnt [lɜːnt] [lernt], *Pt, pp of* TO LEARN.

leasable [ˈliːzəbl] [li-sa-bol], *a.* Arrendable.

lease [liːs] [lis], *s.* 1. Arriendo, escritura de arrendamiento, alquiler. 2. Posesión de una cosa cualquiera. 3. En los tejidos, paso, cruce. **To give a new lease of life,** dar nuevos bríos, nuevas fuerzas.

lease, *va.* Arrendar, dar en arriendo la posesión de casas o tierras por tiempo fijo de años. *-vn.* (Poco us.) Espigar, coger las espigas que han dejado de segar los segadores o las que han quedado en el campo. **Lease back,** subarrendar. **Leasehold,** derechos de arrendamiento. **Lease out,** arrendar, alquilar.

leaser [ˈliːsəʳ] [li-saʳ], *s.* 1. Espigador. 2. *(Des.)* Embustero.

leaseholder [ˈliːshəʊldəʳ] [lis-joul-daʳ], *s.* Arrendatario.

leash [liːʃ] [lish], *s.* 1. Cuerda, traílla, correa. 2. Tres, par y medio. **Leash of hares,** tres liebres. **Leash of partridges,** tres perdices. 3. Cualquier cosa con que está atada otra. 4. Lizo, entre los tejedores.

leash, *va.* Atar con cuerda o correa.

leasing [ˈliːsɪŋ] [li-sin], *s.* Mentira, falsedad.

least [liːst] [list], *a. (sup.* de LITTLE*).* Mínimo; el menor, el mínimo, el más pequeño. **The least space,** el menor espacio. **The least of the apostles,** el menor de los apóstoles. *-adv.* Lo menos. **The least you can do,** lo menos que puedes hacer. **At least,** por lo menos. **At the least o at leastwise,** en la menor cantidad posible. **Not in the least,** ni en lo más mínimo; de ninguna manera. **Be not in the least uneasy,** no tenga Ud. el menor cuidado. **Least of all me,** yo menos que nadie. **Not in the least!** ¡de ninguna manera!, ¡faltaría más!

leat [ˈliːt] [lit], *s. (Ant.)* El cauce o canal que conduce el agua a un molino o por donde sale de él.

leather [ˈleðəʳ] [le-daʳ], *s.* 1. Cuero, cordobán, pellejo. 2. Pieza, porción o artículo hecho de cuero. 3. Cuero, pellejo o piel de racional: en este último sentido se usa sólo hablando con ironía o desprecio. **Alum leather, tawed leather,** cuero blanco, curtido con alumbre y sal. **Patent leather, enamelled leather,** charol. **Sheep's leather,** badana. **Wash leather,** gamuza. **Alligator leather,** cuero de caimán (cocodrilo). **Russia leather,** V. RUSSIA. *-a.* V. LEATHERN. **Leather-winged,** que tiene alas como de cuero, se dice de algunos insectos.

leather, *va.* 1. Forrar, guarnecer con cuero. 2. Hacer cuero, cambiar en cuero. 3. Golpear, pegar, zurrar con una correa de cuero. *-vn.* Batir, sacudir; dar tundas.

leather-coat [ˈleðəkəʊt] [le-da-kout], *s.* Especie de manzana; una cosa cualquiera cubierta con una corteza correosa.

leather-cutter [ˈleðəkʌtəʳ] [le-da-ka-taʳ], *s.* El que vende cuero curtido por menor.

leather-dresser [ˈleðədresəʳ] [le-da-dre-saʳ], *s.* Curtidor, pellejero.

leatherette [ˌleðəˈret] [le-da-rit], *s.* Cuero artificial; imitación de cuero hecha con papel o tela.

leatherhead [ˈleðəhed] [le-da-jed], *s.* 1. Tropidorinco. *V.* FRIAR-BIRD. 2. Un tonto, un estúpido.

leathern [ˈleðən] [le-dern], *a.* De cuero, hecho de cuero o cordobán.

leathery [ˈleðərɪ] [le-da-ri], *a.* Lo que se parece al cuero, correoso.

leave [liːv] [liv], *s.* 1. Licencia, permiso, venia. **By your leave,** con el permiso de Ud., con licencia de Ud. **Give me leave to tell you,** permítame Ud. que le diga. 2. Despedida, la acción de despedirse; se dice también **Leave-taking. To take leave of one's friends,** despedirse de los amigos. **To be absent on leave,** hallarse ausente con permiso o licencia. **To take French leave,** despedirse a la francesa. *V.* FRENCH. **To leave the rails,** descarrilar (train).

leave, *va.* y *vn. (pret.* y *pp.* LEFT*).* 1. Dejar, permitir la permanencia; no alejar. 2. Dejar o legar alguna cosa después de muerto. **To leave issue,** dejar hijos o sucesión. 3. Dejar, desamparar, abandonar. 4. Dejar, separarse de una persona o lugar. 5. Dejar, dar, ceder o renunciar una cosa a favor de otro. 6. Dejar, despojarse, renunciar. 7. Dejar, cesar, desistir de un empeño, etc. 8. Referirse a alguien o a algo; entregar, confiar en depósito (give).

leave about, around, dejar tirado.

leave aside, dejar de lado.

leave behind, dejar atrás; dejar en pos de sí a su muerte.

leave in, dejar como está (passage, words).

leave off, cesar, parar, descontinuar. **To leave off a garment,** quitarse una prenda de ropa.

leave on, dejar puesto (hat).

leave out, omitir. olvidar (forget), descuidar, desatender; excluir. **Nothing was left out,** no se omitió nada.

leave over, aplazar (postpone). **To be left till called for,** en lista del correo.

leaved ['liːvd] [livd], *a.* Hojoso, hecho de hojas.

leaven ['levn] [le-ven], *s.* 1. Levadura, fermento. **Leavened bread,** pan de levadura. 2. Toda cosa que ejerciendo una influencia latente y poderosa, ocasiona un cambio general.

leaven, *va.* 1. Fermentar, leudar, poner en movimiento intestino las partículas de un cuerpo. 2. Corromper, contaminar, pervertir, viciar. 3. Imbuir buenas máximas, buenos principios, etc.

leavening ['levnɪn] [lev-nin], *s.* Fermento.

leavenous ['levənəs] [le-ve-nos], *a.* Lo que contiene fermento; corrompido.

leaver ['liːvəʳ] [li-vaʳ], *s.* El que abandona o deja.

leaves ['liːvz] [livs], *s. pl.* de LEAF, hoja. **Marbled leaves,** cortes jaspeados. **Gilt leaves,** cortes dorados, hablando de libros.

leaving ['liːvɪŋ] [li-vin], *s.* 1. Partida, acción de partir de un lugar. 2. *pl.* Sobras, relieves; desechos, desperdicios, residuo, sobra.

leavy, *a. (Ant.)* V. LEAFY.

lecher ['letʃəʳ] [le-chaʳ], *s.* Hombre putañero, disoluto, libertino.

lecherous ['letʃərəs] [le-che-ros], *a.* Lujurioso, impúdico, lascivo.

lecherousness ['letʃərəsnɪs] [le-che-ros-nes], **lechery** ['letʃərɪ] [le-che-ri], *s.* Lujuría, el apetito desordenado de los deleites carnales.

lectern ['lektɜːn] [lek-tern], *s.* Atril, facistol de iglesia.

lection ['lekʃən] [lek-shon], *s.* 1. Lección, lectura que se hace en la celebración del oficio divino. 2. Lección, la letra o texto de alguna obra.

lectionary ['lekʃənərɪ] [lek-sho-na-ri], *s.* Leccionario, libro que contine las lecciones del oficio divino.

lector ['lektɔːʳ] [lek-taʳ], *s.* Lector *(Univ.).*

lecture ['lektʃəʳ] [lek-chaʳ], *s.* 1. Discurso, razonamiento o plática razonada sobre alguna materia; discurso moral o religioso; particularmente explicación de los principios de alguna ciencia. 2. Fraterna, corrección, reprensión pedantesca.

lecture, *va.* 1. Enseñar, instruir, por medio de razonamientos. 2. Enseñar alguna cosa de un modo pedantesco. *-vn.* Dar explicaciones públicas sobre los principios de alguna ciencia.

lecturer ['lektʃərəʳ] [lek-cha-raʳ], *s.* Lector, instructor; teniente de cura de alguna parroquia.

lectureship ['lektʃəʳʃɪp] [lek-cha-ship], *s.* El empleo de quien da lecciones o explicaciones.

lecturn, *s.* V. LECTERN.

led, *pp.* y *pret.* del verbo TO LEAD.

ledge [ledʒ] [ledch], *s.* 1. Anaquel, moldura saliente, o parte parecida a un anaquel; capa, tonga, tongada; arrecife. **Ledge of rocks,** arrecife de piedras o peñas. 2. *(Mar.)* Latas de los baos. **Ledges of the gratings,** *(Mar.)* barrotes de los enjaretados.

ledger ['ledʒəʳ] [led-chaʳ], *s.* 1. Libro mayor, el libro principal en que los comerciantes asientan sus cuentas. **Alphabet of the ledger,** índice alfabético del libro mayor. 2. Alguna cosa, como una barra o piedra, que ha de yacer o tenderse llana o quedarse en una posición fija; como solera de emparrillado, traviesa de andamio. *-a.* Ligero. V. LEGER.

led-horse ['ledhɔːs] [led-jors], *s.* Caballo de mano.

lee [liː] [li], *s.* 1. *(Mar.)* Sotavento, el costado del navío opuesto a la parte por donde da el viento. 2. Paraje resguardado, al abrigo de los vientos. (No tiene plural). *-a.* 1. *(Mar.)* Sotaventado, expuesto al sotavento; opuesto a *weather* (barlovento). 2. *(Esco.)* Solitario. **Lee shore,** *(Mar.)* costa de sotavento. **Lee side,** *(Mar.)* banda de sotavento. **Leeway,** *(Mar.)* abatimiento o derriba. **Lee braces,** *(Mar.)* brazos de sotavento. **Under the lee** o **sea room,** tener buen sotavento. **Lee tide,** marca de donde viene el viento. **On the lee beam,** a la banda de sotavento.

leech [liːtʃ] [lich], *s.* 1. Sanguijuela. 2. *(Ant.)* Médico, el que sabe y profesa el arte de la medicina o de curar. **Horseleech,** albéitar. 3. Instrumento para sangrar, como escarificador, ventosa, etc., llamado **artificial leach.** 4. *(Mar.)* Caídas. **Leech-lines,** *(Mar.)* apagapenoles. **Leech-rope,** *(Mar.)* relinga de las caídas.

leech, *va.* 1. LEACH. 2. *(Ant.)* Curar, sanar.

leechcraft ['liːtʃkræft] [lich-kraft], *s. (Des.)* Arte de curar.

leek [liːk] [lik], *s. (Bot.)* Puerro.

leer [lɪəʳ] [liaʳ], *s.* 1. Ojeada, mirada de reojo, que puede ser maliciosa, amorosa o equívoca. 2. Templador, especie de horno que sirve para templar y enfriar el cristal y vidrio después de vaciado. *-a. (Des. o prov. Ingl.)* Vacío, frívolo, sin juicio.

leer, *vn.* Ojear o mirar de soslayo o de reojo. *-va.* Atraer con risa, engañar con miradas.

leeringly ['lɪərɪŋlɪ] [lia-rin-li], *adv.* Con risa engañosa o mirada de desprecio.

lees [liːz] [lis], *s. pl.* Heces, sedimento, poso. (Antiguamente se empleaba también en singular, *lee;* hez, zupia).

leet [liːt] [lit], o **Court-leet** ['kɔːtliːt] [kert-li], *s.* Un tribunal de justicia en tiempos antiguos, y el día en que se reunía.

leeward ['liːwəd] [li-uard], *a. (Mar.)* Sotavento. **Leeward ship,** *(Mar.)* navío sotaventeador. **Leeward Islands,** islas de sotavento. **Leeward-tide,** *(Mar.)* marca en la dirección del viento. **To leeward,** *(Mar.)* a sotavento.

leeway ['liːweɪ] [li-uei], *s.* 1. *(Mar.)* Deriva, abatimiento del rumbo; ángulo de deriva. 2. De aquí en general desviación de un rumbo fijo.

left [left] [left], *pp.* y *pret.* del verbo TO LEAVE. **This package is to be left at Mr. N's,** este paquete deberá entregarse o dejarse en casa del Sr. N. **Left-off,** puesto a un lado, desechado.

left, *a.* Siniestro, izquierdo, lo que no está a la mano derecha. **To the left,** a la izquierda. **Over the left,** *(Vulg.)* exactamente lo opuesto.

left-hand ['lefthænd] [left-jand], *a.* 1. zurdo, situado al lado izquierdo. 2. Que da vueltas, rueda, se abre o se mueve hacia la mano izquierda. **Left-handed,** (a) zurdo. (b) Poco diestro, desmañado. (c) Indirecto, insincero, malicioso. (d) Que da vueltas en sentido contrario al movimiento de las manecillas de un reloj; que gira el plano de polarización hacia la izquierda. (e) *(Des.)* Desgraciado, intempestivo. **Lefthanded** screw, tornillo zurdo. **Left-handedness,** el uso habitual de la mano izquierda. **Left-handiness,** costumbre zafia.

leftist ['leftɪst] [lef-tist], *a. & s.* Izquierdista.

leftovers ['left'əʊvəz] [left-ou-vars], *s. pl.* Sobras (de comida).

leg [leg] [leg], *s.* 1. Pierna; pata de las aves y animales. 2. Pie, la base sobre que se maniente el cuerpo de alguna cosa; pata. **Leg of a table,** pata de una mesa. 3. La parte de una prenda de ropa que cubre la pierna; caña sea media. 4. *(Mar.)* Espacio recorrido por un buque en una bordada. 5. Lado de un triángulo que no es su base. **Leg-bail,** *(Vulg.)* Huida, fuga de la cárcel o custodia. **To take leg-bail,** tomar las de Villadiego. **On one's last legs,** a la muerte, agonizante, literal y figuradamente; exhausto de recursos. **On** o **upon its legs,** en pie, firmemente establecido. **To get on one's legs,** (a) Levantarse para dirigir la palabra a una cámara o concurso. (b) Recobrar la salud. **To give a leg to,** ayudar a montar un caballo afirmando la pierna. **Not to have a leg to stand on,** hallarse enteramente sin recursos; no saber por qué lado echar. **Not to leave one a leg to stand on,** poner a uno entre la espada y la pared. **To pull one's leg,** obtener dinero o favores de una persona por engaño. **To pull someone's leg,** tomar el pelo a alguien.

legacy ['legəsɪ] [le-ga-si], *s.* Legado, manda.

legacy-hunter [ˈlegəsɪˌhʌntəʳ] [le-ga-si-jan-taʳ], *s.* El que anda a caza de herencias.

legal [ˈliːgəl] [li-gal], *a.* 1. Legal, jurídico, legítimo; lícito, permitido por la ley. 2. Definido, provisto por la ley, que puede remediarse apelando a la ley.

legalese [ˌliːgəˈliːz] [li-ga-lis], *s. f.* Jerga legal.

legality [lɪˈgælɪtɪ] [li-ga-li-ti], *s.* Legalidad, legitimidad.

legalize [ˈliːgəlaɪz] [li-ga-lais], *va.* Legalizar, autorizar, legitimar.

legally [ˈliːgəlɪ] [li-ga-li], *adv.* Legalmente. **Legally binding,** de obligatoriedad jurídica.

legal tender [ˈliːgəlˌtendəʳ] [li-gal-ten-daʳ], *s.* Moneda legal.

legate [ˈlegɪt] [le-guit], *s.* 1. Legado, diputado. 2. Legado, cardenal u obispo enviado por el Papa con una misión.

legatee [ˌlegəˈtiː] [le-ga-ti], *s.* Legatario, la persona a quien por testamento se deja algún legado.

legateship [ˈlegɪtʃɪp] [le-guit-ship], *s.* legacía, el empleo de legado.

legatine [ˈlegətiːn] [le-ga-tin], *a.* hecho por un legado o que pertenece a él.

legation [lɪˈgeɪʃən] [li-gei-shon], *s.* Legación, embajada.

legato [lɪˈgɑːtəʊ] [li-ga-tou], *adv. (Mús.)* Ligado, de un modo igual y conexo, lo opuesto a *staccato. (Ital.)*

legator [ˈlɪgeɪtəʳ] [li-guei-taʳ], *s.* El que hace testamento dejando legados.

legend [ˈledʒənd] [le-yend], *s.* 1. Leyenda o legenda, crónica o registro de las vidas de los santos. 2. Relación, narración. 3. Letrero, la inscripción que tienen las medallas o monedas. 4. Narrativa increíble y no auténtica, fábula.

legendary [ˈledʒəndərɪ] [le-yen-da-ri], *a.* Fabuloso, quijotesco. *-s.* 1. Legendario, el libro de las actas y vidas de los santos. 2. Hagiógrafo, el escritor de vidas de los santos.

leger [ˈledʒəʳ] [le-yaʳ], *a.* 1. Ligero y delicado, como una línea. 2. *(Des.)* Residente, permanente. **Leger-lines,** líneas adicionales para escribir notas de música. **Leger space,** espacio comprendido por una de esas líneas adicionales. *-s.* V. LEDGER.

legerdemain [ˈledʒədəˈmeɪn] [le-ya-da-mein], *s.* Ligereza de manos, juego de manos, engaños a ojos vista, el que usan los saltimbancos.

legged [ˈlegɪd] [le-guid], *a.* Lo que tiene piernas, empernado. Se usa en composición; como **three-legged stool,** banqueta, banquillo de tres patas.

legging [ˈlegɪn] [le-guin], *s.* Polaina larga que llega a la rodilla; guardapierna.

leggy [ˈlegɪ] [le-gui], *a.* Patilargo, zanquilargo.

leghorn [ˈlegɔːn] [leg-jorn], *s.* 1. Sombrero de paja de italia; y el tejido fino hecho con esta paja. 2. Casta o raza de gallinas.

legibility [ˌledʒɪˈbɪlɪtɪ] [le-yi-bi-li-ti], *s.* La calidad de lo que puede ser leído fácilmente.

legible [ˈledʒəbl] [le-yi-bol], *a.* Legible, patente, manifiesto.

legibleness [ˈledʒəblnɪs] [le-yi-bol-nes], *s.* El estado o calidad de lo que es legible.

legibly [ˈledʒɪblɪ] [le-yi-bli], *adv.* Legiblemente.

legion [ˈliːdʒən] [li-yon], *s.* 1. Legión, un cuerpo de tropas romanas, que según los tiempos se componía de tres a cuatro mil hombres de caballería e infantería. 2. Legión, un gran número; tropa, multitud.

legionary [ˈliːdʒənərɪ] [li-yo-na-ri], *a. y s.* Legionario.

legislate [ˈledʒɪsleɪt] [le-yis-leit], *vn.* Legislar, dar leyes.

legislation [ˌledʒɪsˈleɪʃən] [le-yis-lei-shon], *s.* Legislación, la facultad legislativa.

legislative [ˈledʒɪslətɪv] [le-yis-la-tiv], *a.* Legislativo.

legislator [ˈledʒɪsleɪtəʳ] [le-yis-lei-taʳ], *s.* Legislador.

legislatorial [ˌledʒɪsˈleɪtərɪəl] [le-yis-lei-to-rial], *a.* Perteneciente o relativo a la legislación o a una legislatura.

legislatorship [ˈledʒɪsleɪtəʃɪp] [le-yis-lei-ta-ship], *s.* El oficio o dignidad de legislador; el poder o facultad de hacer leyes.

legislatress [ˈledʒɪslətrɪs] [le-yis-la-tris], *sf.* Legisladora.

legislature [ˈledʒɪsleɪtʃəʳ] [le-yis-lei-chaʳ], *s.* Legislatura, cuerpo legislativo.

legist [ˈledʒɪst] [le-yist], *s.* Legista, jurisconsulto.

legitimacy [lɪˈdʒɪtɪməsɪ] [li-yi-ti-ma-si], *s.* 1. Legitimidad, conformidad con la ley o con la lógica; legalidad. 2. Nacimiento legítimo. 3. Pureza, estado exento de falsificación.

legitimate [lɪˈdʒɪtɪmɪt] [li-yi-ti-meit], *a.* 1. Legítimo; legal, lícito, permitido por la ley y costumbre. 2. Nacido legalmente durante el matrimonio. 3. Legítimo, justo, resultante de consecuencias naturales o regulares.

legitimate, *va.* Legitimar, hacer legítimo, conferir los derechos de hijo legítimo al que nació fuera del matrimonio.

legitimately [lɪˈdʒɪtɪmɪtlɪ] [li-yi-ti-mat-li], *adv.* Legítimamente.

legitimateness [ˌlɪdʒɪtɪˈmɪtnɪs] [li-yi-ti-mit-nes], *s.* Legitimidad, legalidad.

legitimation [ˌlɪdʒɪtɪˈmeɪʃən] [li-yi-ti-mei-shon], *s.* 1. Legitimación, el acto de legitimar a un hijo natural. 2. En Europa, legitimación (para residir, etc.).

legitimist [lɪˈdʒɪtɪmɪst] [li-yi-ti-mist], *s.* Legitimista, partidario de cierta autoridad como legítima.

legitimize [lɪˈdʒɪtɪmaɪz] [li-yi-ti-mais], *va.* V. TO LEGITIMATE.

legume [ˈlegjuːm] [le-guium], **legumen** [ˈlegjuːmn] [le-guiu-men], *s. (Bot.)* Legumbre, vaina, fruto bivalvo unicelular de la familia de las leguminosas (habas, fríjoles, guisantes, etc.).

leguminous [ˈlegjuːmɪnəs] [le-guiu-mi-nos], *a. (Bot.)* Leguminoso, lo que pertenece a la familia de las leguminosas.

leisurable [ˈleʒərəbl] [le-sha-ra-bol], *a.* Hecho o ejecutado despacio y sin precipitación.

leisure [ˈleʒəʳ] [le-shaʳ], *s.* 1. Ocio, tiempo desocupado y de descanso; desocupación, ociosidad. 2. Comodidad. **At leisure,** despacio, con comodidad o cómodamente, con sosiego. **To be at leisure,** estar desocupado. *-a.* Conveniente, libre de negocios o asuntos. **Leisure hours,** las horas desocupadas, o destinadas al descanso o al reposo. **Leisure suit,** chandal. **Leisure wear,** ropa de sport.

leisurely [ˈleʒəlɪ] [le-sha-li], *a.* Pausado, deliberado. *-adv.* Despacio, con cachaza; deliberadamente.

leman [ˈlemən] [le-man], *s.* Amante, galán; cortejo, concubina, manceba.

lemma [ˈlemə] [le-ma], *s.* 1. Lema, proposición que se suele poner para demostrar otras que se siguen. 2. *(Bot.)* Lentícula (lenteja de agua).

lemming [ˈlemɪn] [le-min], *s. (Zool.)* Turón de Noruega.

lemon [ˈlemən] [le-mon], *s.* Limón, el fruto del **Lemon-tree,** limonero. **Candied lemon,** acitrón, dulce hecho con las cáscaras del limón. **Pickled lemon,** limón encurtido o salado. **Lemon-peel,** corteza de cidra. **Lemon squash,** limonada. **Lemon-squeezer,** exprimidor de limón. *-a.* 1. Sazonado con limón o que contiene limón. 2. De color de limón.

lemonade [ˌleməˈneɪd] [le-mo-neid], *s.* Limonada, bebida compuesta de agua, azúcar y zumo de limón.

lemon drops [ˈlemən드rɒpz] [le-mon-drops], *s.pl.* Pastillas de limón.

lemur [ˈleməʳ] [le-maʳ], *s.* Lémur, animal parecido al mono, uno de los prosimios o lemúridos. Vive en Madagascar e islas vecinas.

lend [lend] [lend], *va.* 1. Prestar, dar alguna cosa con la obligación de que sea restituída. 2. Dar, conceder. **To lend aid,** dar ayuda o auxilio. **To lend a hand (to),** dar o echar una mano, ayudar. **To lend out,** prestar.

lendable [ˈlendəbl] [len-da-bol], *a.* Prestadizo, prestable.

lender [ˈlendəʳ] [len-daʳ], *s.* Prestador, prestamista.

lending [ˈlendɪn] [len-din], *s.* Empréstito, préstamo. **Lending rate,** tipo de interés.

lene [liːn] [lin], *a. (Gram.)* Suave, no aspirado. *-s.* Consonante no aspirada; aspiración suave.

length [lenθ] [lengz], *s.* 1. Longitud, largura, lo largo de alguna cosa (size). **A picture in full length,** retrato de cuerpo entero. **It's 10 meters in length,** tiene 10 metros de largo. 2. Espacio o duración de tiempo (duration). 3. Extensión, dilatación, distancia. 4. Alcance (shot), capacidad de llegar; punto, grado. 5. Pedazo, trozo (piece). **At length,** (a) Al fin, finalmente, en conclusión. (b) Extensamente, sin abreviación ni omisión. **At full length,** a lo largo, de todo el largo. **Length of days,** lo largo de la vida, la existencia prolongada. **To speak at length,** hablar largamente. **To explain at length,** explicar detalladamente.

lengthen ['leŋθən] [len-zen], *va.* Alargar, extender. prolongar, dilatar. -*vn.* Aumentarse, alargarse, prolongarse o dilatarse alguna cosa. **To lengthen out,** estirar, dilatar, alargar.

lengthening ['leŋθənɪŋ] [leng-ze-nin], *s.* Alargamiento, continuación, prolongación.

lengthwise ['leŋθwaɪz] [lengz-uais], *adv.* Longitudinalmente: según lo largo, a lo largo.

lengthy ['leŋθɪ] [leng-zi], Bastante largo, indebidamente largo, algo difuso (speech, sermon).

lenient ['li:nɪənt] [li-niant], *a.* y *s.* 1. Benigno, clemente, misericordioso. 2. Leniente, emoliente, laxativo, lenitivo.

lenify ['lenɪfaɪ] [le-ni-fai], *va.* Lenificar, suavizar, mitigar, ablandar.

lenitive ['lenɪtɪv] [le-ni-tiv], *a.* Lenitivo. -*s.* 1. Lenitivo, la medicina o remedio que ablanda. 2. Lenitivo, cualquier medio para suavizar o aplacar las pasiones del ánimo.

lenity ['lenɪtɪ] [le-ni-ti], *s.* Lenidad, blandura, suavidad.

lens [lenz] [lens], *s.* (*pl.* LENSES). 1. Lente, vidrio generalmente de forma circular, convexo o cóncavo, de que se usa en los instrumentos ópticos. 2. Cristalino, cuerpo transparente situado inmediatamente detrás del iris del ojo. 3. Objetivo.

lent [lent] [lent], *pret.* y *pp.* del verbo TO LEND. Prestado.

lent, *s.* Cuaresma, los cuarenta días seguidos de abstinencia en las iglesias anglicana, católica romana y otras. **Lent dinner,** comida de viernes.

lenten ['lentən] [len-ten], *a.* 1. Cuaresmal, cuadragesimal, lo que pertenece a la cuaresma. 2. Escaso.

lenticel ['lentɪsl] [len-ti-sel], *s.* (*Bot.*) Lentejuela, tuberculillo que pertenece a la capa de corcho de las plantas.

lenticula ['lentɪkjolə] [len-ti-kiu-la], *s.* 1. (*Opt.*) Lente pequeño. 2. (*Med.*) V. FRECKLE. 3. (*Bot.*) V. LENTICEL.

lenticular ['lentɪkjoləʳ] [len-ti-kiu-laʳ], **lentiform** ['lentɪfɔ:m] [len-ti-form], *a.* Lenticular, semejante a las lentejas.

lentiginous ['lentɪdʒɪnəs] [len-ti-yi-nos], *a.* (*Bot.* y *Zool.*) Pecoso; que presenta la apariencia de haber sido polvoreado como con granillos.

lentil ['lentɪl] [len-til], *s.* (*Bot.*) Lenteja.

lenticus ['lentɪkəs] [len-ti-kos], **lentisk** ['lentɪsk] [len-tisk], *s.* (*Bot.*) Lentisco.

leo ['li:əʊ] [liou], *s.* (*Astr.*) 1. León, el quinto signo del zodíaco. 2. Constelación que antiguamente se hallaba en este signo, pero que está hoy en el signo Virgo.

leonine ['li:ənaɪn] [lio-nain], *a.* 1. Leonino, lo que toca o pertence al león o participa de sus propiedades. 2. Leonino, clase de versos latinos.

leopard ['lepəd] [le-pard], *s.* Leopardo, mamífero carnicero. **The leopard cannot change its spots,** genio y figura hasta la sepultura (*prov.*).

leotard ['letəd] [le-tard], *s.* Malla.

leper ['lepəʳ] [le-paʳ], *s.* Un leproso, el que padece lepra.

leperous ['lepərəs] [le-pe-ras], *a.* V. LEPROUS.

lepidoptera ['lepɪ'dɒptərə] [le-pi-dop-te-ra], *s.* (*Ent.*) Lepidópteros, orden de insectos.

lepidopterous ['lepɪ'dɒptərəs] [le-pi-dop-te-ros], *a.* Lepidóptero, perteneciente a los insectos llamados lepidópteros.

leporine ['lepəri:n] [le-po-rin], *a.* Lebruno, lo que pertenece a la liebre.

leprose ['leprəs] [le-pros], *a.* (*Bot.*) Casposo, escamoso, cubierto de escamas delgadas.

leprosity ['leprəsɪtɪ] [le-pro-si-ti], *s.* La calidad de ser escamoso.

leprosy ['leprəsɪ] [le-pro-si], *s.* Lepra.

leprous ['leprəs] [le-pros], *a.* Leproso.

leprousness ['leprəsnɪs] [le-pros-nes], *s.* Leprosidad.

lepus ['lepəs] [le-pos], *s.* Liebre, una constelación del hemisferio austral.

lesbian ['lezbɪən] [les-bian], *a.* & *s.* Lesbiano, lesbio.

lese-majesty ['leɪz,mædʒəstɪ] [leis-ma-yes-ti], *s.* **Lesa** majestad.

lesion ['li:ʒən] [li-shon], *s.* Lesión, en sus acepciones médicas y forenses.

less [les] [les], *a.* (Comp. de LITTLE). Menor, menos, inferior. -*s.* Una cantidad más pequeña que otra. -*adv.* Menos, en grado más pequeño; en grado más bajo. **Much less,** mucho menos. **More or less,** más o menos. **Less and less,** de menos en menos. **To grow less,** disminuirse, achicarse. **To make less,** aminorar, disminuir, escatimar. **So much the less,** tanto menos cuanto. **So much the less,** tanto menso cuanto. **The less .... the less,** cuanto menos .... menos. **We eat less meat than before,** comemos menos carne que antes.

less, sufijo. terminación negativa o privativa, que expresa la privación o falta de una cosa; sin. **Childless,** sin hijos; **hopeless,** sin esperanza, etc. **Penniless,** sin un cuarto, sin un céntimo.

lessee [le'si:] [le-si], *s.* Arrendatario, el que toma en arrendamiento alguna cosa.

lessen ['lesn] [le-sen], *va.* 1. Minorar, achicar, disminuir, acortar, reducir a menos. 2. Degradar, privar a alguno de sus honores, grados o dignidad. -*vn.* 1. Mermar, disminuirse. 2. Degradarse, bajarse.

lesser ['lesəʳ] [le-saʳ], *a.* (comp. de LITTLE). Menor, más pequeño: se usa **lesser** con los nombres colectivos o en plural, y **less** con los nombres en singular. **The lesser prophets,** los profetas menores. **To a lesser degree,** en menor grado.

lesson ['lesn] [le-son], *s.* 1. Lección, enseñanza, instrucción, precepto, lectura. 2. Fraterna, corrección, reprensión. 3. Lección, pasaje de la Sagrada Escritura que se lee en los oficios divinos. 4. Lección, saber, conocimiento obtenido, v.g. por la experiencia.

lesson, *va.* (Poco us.) Enseñar, instruir.

lessor ['lesəʳ] [le-soʳ], *s.* Arrendador, el que da una cosa en arrendamiento.

lest [lest] [lest], *conj.* Para que no, por miedo de que.

let [let] [let], *va.* (*pret.* y *pp.* LET). 1. Dejar, conceder, permitir. 2. Arrendar, dar en arrendamiento alguna renta, casa, heredad o posesión; alquilar. **To let,** se alquila. 3. Dejar, no impedir. **Let me alone,** déjeme Ud. en paz. **Let me sit,** déjeme Ud. sentar o permita Ud. que me siente. **Let me go,** déjeme Ud. ir o permita Ud. que me vaya. 4. (*Ant.*) Impedir, estorbar. -*vn.* Ser alquilado o arrendado. **A house to let,** una casa por alquilar. **The house lets for forty dollars,** la casa se alquila por cuarenta dólares.

let alone, dejar solo, dejar a un lado; dejar hacer, abandonar.

let by, dejar pasar.

let down, dejar caer; desinflar: bajar, descender; defraudar, fallar (fail).

let in, dejar entrar, admitir, recibir, introducir, hacer entrar.

let into, dejar entrar en; dejar conocer, hacer entrar.

let off, disparar, descargar, tirar un tiro.

let out, dejar salir; poner en libertad, soltar; hacer salir; arrendar, alquilar. **To let out to use,** poner dinero a interés.

let up, dejar subir, (fam. E.U.) cesar, parar, disminuir en severidad. **To let be,** dejar que una cosa sea lo que es; no entremeterse en un sunto o negocio. **To let blood,** sangrar, hacerse sangrar. **To let fall a word,** soltar inadvertidamente una palabra. **To let fly,** (*Fam.*) Disparar, dejar salir el tiro de una arma de fuego; decir disparates. **To let go,** soltar. **To LET** tiene el pretérito y participio **let** en todas sus significaciones. *Let* es auxiliar del modo imperativo, como en **Let us go,** vámonos. **Let Peter, read,** que lea Pedro. **Let her alone,** déjala en paz. **To let know,** advertir, hacer presente, hacer saber, dar a conocer. **To let loose,** soltar, aflojar; desatar, desencadenar.

let, *s.* Estorbo, obstáculo, impedimento. De ordinario sólo se usa en la locución. **Without let or hindrance,** sin estorbo ni obstáculo.

letch [letʃ] [lech], *va. y s.* V. LEACH.

letdown [ˈletdaʊn] [let-daun], *s.* 1. Aflojamiento. 2. *(Fam.)* Decepción, abatimiento.

lethal [ˈliːθəl] [li-zal], *a.* Letal, mortal. **This tea is lethal!** ¡este té está asqueroso!

lethality [lɪˈθælɪtɪ] [li-za-li-ti], *s.* Mortalidad.

lethargic, lethargical [leˈθɑːdʒɪk] [le-zar-yik], *a.* Letárgico, lo que pertenece al estado de letargo.

lethargied [leˈθɑːdʒɪd] [le-zar-yid], *a.* Aletargado.

lethargize, lethargise [leˈθɑːdʒaɪs] [le-zar-yais], *va.* Aletargar.

lethargy [leˈtɑːdʒɪ] [le-tar-yi], *s.* 1. *(Med.)* Letargo. 2. Letargo, torpeza, enajenamiento del ánimo. 3. Entorpecimiento producido por la invernada.

lethean [ˈliːθɪən] [li-zian], **Letheed** [lɪˈθiːd] [li-zid], *a.* Léteo.

letter [ˈletər] [le-taʳ], *s.* Letra, carácter. **Letter o bill of exchange,** Letra de cambio. **Letter of license,** moratoriá, espera. **Letters of safe conduct,** guía, salvoconducto. **Letter of attorney,** poder, procuración. 3. Carta, carta misiva. **Letters inclosed,** cartas inclusas o adjuntas. **To frank letters,** franquear las cartas. **Direction of letters,** sobre o sobrescrito de cartas. **Letter of credit,** carta de crédito. **Letter rogatory,** *(For.)* Suplicatoria. 4. Letra, el sentido gramatical de una frase, sentencia o discurso. 5. *pl.* Letras, literatura, erudición. **Man of letters,** hombre de letras, hombre erudito, literato. **Letter-book,** copiador de cartas, el libro en que las conservan o copian los comerciantes. **Letter-box,** (a) buzón. (b) Caja de correspondencia; taquilla, caja cerrada para recibir cartas, en el correo o a la puerta de una casa. **Letter-carrier,** cartero, el que reparte las cartas. **Letter-case,** cartera; escribanía, portátil. **Letter-drop,** buzón, agujero por donde se echan las cartas en el correo. **Letter carrier,** cartero. **Letter-file,** guardacartas, cualquier mueble o aparato para archivar las cartas. **Letter-founder,** fundidor de letras. V. TYPE-FOUNDER. **Letter-founding,** fundición, acto de fundir letras. **Letter-paper,** papel de cartas, papel de escribir (mayor que el papel para esquelas). **Silent letters,** letras mudas o que no se pronuncian, como *ugh* en *though* y *k* en *knee.*

letter, *va.* Estampar con letras; escribir, poner un rótulo. **To letter a book,** rotular un libro.

lettered [ˈletəd] [le-tard], *a.* Letrado, instruido, erudito, literato, docto.

letterhead [ˈletəhed] [le-tar-jed], *s.* membrete.

lettering [ˈletərɪŋ] [le-ta-rin], *s.* 1. El acto u oficio de poner rótulos o de hacer letras. 2. Letrero, inscripción, rótulo; estampilla.

letter-perfect [ˈletəpɜːfekt] [le-tar-per-fekt], *a.* Preciso, que se sabe a la perfección.

letterpress [ˈletəpres] [le-tar-pres], *s.* Impresión, la obra impresa, en contraposición a la grabada; el texto de un libro, en oposición a los grabados.

lettuce [ˈletɪs] [le-tis], *s. (Bot.)* Lechuga.

let-up [ˈletʌp] [let-ap] *n.* Descanso, tregua *(Fig.).*

leucocyte [ˈluːkəˌsaɪt] [lu-ko-sait], *s.* Leucocito, corpúsculo blanco de la sangre y de la linfa.

leucoma [ˈluːkəʊmə] [lu-kou-ma], *s. (Med.)* Leucoma, mancha corneal.

leucorrhea [ˈluːkəˌrɪə] [lu-ko-ria], *s.* Leucorrea.

leukemia [ˈluːkɪmɪə] [lu-ki-mia], *s.* Leucemia.

levant [ˈlevənt] [le-vant], *s.* Levante, oriente, las costas del Mediterráneo. *-a.* Oriental. **Levanter,** viento de Levante. **Levant trade,** comercio de levante.

levantine [ˈlevəntaɪn] [le-van-tain], *a.* Levantino. **Levantines handkerchiefs,** pañuelos de Cantón.

levator [lɪˈveɪtəʳ] [li-vei-taʳ], *s.* 1. Músculo elevador. 2. Levantador, instrumento de cirugía.

levee [ˈleviː] [le-vi], *s.* 1. *(Des.)* El tiempo de levantarse por la mañana. 2. Corte, el concurso de gente que hace la corte a algún personaje. 3. Recepción sin ceremonia en las habitaciones particulares de una persona. 4. Dique para detener el agua.

level [ˈlevl] [le-vel], *a.* 1. Llano, igual, nivelado, a nivel, allanado. 2. Casi horizontal, no en declive. 3. Igual a otra cosa. 4. Apuntado o moviéndose en línea recta; de aquí, honrado, probo. 5. *(Fam.)* De buen juicio, avisado, bien equilibrado, **To be level,** estar el nivel; estar el alcance del entendimiento. **To make level,** allanar, nivelar. **Everything lies level to our wish,** todo va a medida de vuestros deseos.

level, *s.* 1. Llano, llanura. 2. Plano, superficie plana, ras, nivel. 3. Igualdad de rango, moralidad, educación, etc. 4. Nivel, instrumento de los agrimensores. 5. Nivel, la altura media de una cosa. **Sea level,** nivel del mar. 6. La línea de dirección de una bala o cualquier otra cosa disparada. 7. La línea de la vista. **A level spoonful,** una cucharada rasa *(Culin.).* **To be level pegging,** ir empatados. **To be on a level with,** estar al nivel.

level, *va.* 1. Igualar, aplanar, allanar. 2. Nivelar. 3. Arrasar, hacer caer, derribar. 4. Apuntar, asestar. 5. Dirigir, encaminar. 6. Proporcionar, adaptar, ajustar. 7. Igualar, hacer igual una cosa con otra. *-vn.* 1. Apuntar el cañón u otra arma. 2. Emplear el nivel en la agrimensura. 3. Acordar, concordar, conformar, convenir una cosa con otra. **To level at,** apuntar (gun), dirigir (blow).

leveler, leveller [ˈlevələʳ] [le-ve-laʳ], *s.* 1. Allanador, igualador, aplanador, nivelador. 2. El que quiere hacer a todos iguales sin distinción de personas ni de clases:

level-headed [ˈlevlhedɪd] [le-vel-je-did], *a.* Sensato, juicioso.

leveling, levelling [ˈlevlɪŋ] [lev-lin], *s.* 1. Nivelación, acción de nivelar. 2. Igualación de rangos o condiciones.

levelness [ˈlevlnɪs] [le-vel-nes], *s.* Igualdad, allanamiento, nivel.

lever [ˈlevəʳ] [le-vaʳ], *s.* 1. Palanca. 2. Escape de reloj.

leveret [ˈlevərɪt] [le-va-rit], *s.* Lebratillo, el hijuelo de la liebre.

leviable [lɪˈvaɪəbl] [li-vaia-bol], *a.* Exigible.

leviathan [lɪˈvaɪəθən] [li-vaia-zan], *s.* Leviatán, un animal enorme del mar; supuesto mostruo marino.

levigate [ˈlevɪgeɪt] [le-vi-gueit], *va.* 1. Reducir cualquier sustancia sólida a polvo impalpable. 2. *(Des.)* Pulir, alisar, acepillar.

levigate, *a.* Aligerado, alisado, reducido a polvo.

levigation [ˌlevɪˈteɪʃən] [le-vi-guei-shon], *s.* Reducción a polvo impalpable.

levitation [ˌlevɪˈteɪʃən] [le-vi-tei-shon], *s.* El acto o calidad de hacer ligera alguna cosa.

levite [ˈlevaɪt] [li-vait], *s.* Levita, de la tribu de Leví.

levitical [ˈlevɪtɪkəl] [le-vi-ti-kal], *a.* Levítico, lo perteneciente a los levitas o sacerdotes judíos.

levity [ˈlevɪtɪ] [le-vi-ti], *s.* 1. Levedad, ligereza. 2. Inconstancia, veleidad. 3. Vanidad. 4. Alegría loca o inconsiderada ligereza.

levulose [ˈlevjʊləʊs] [le-viu-lous], *s.* Levulosa, variedad de azúcar que se halla en la miel y en varias frutas.

levy [ˈlevɪ] [le-vi], *va.* Hacer leva, levantar gente; exigir tributos. *(For.)* Embargar y vender los bienes de un deudor para pagar al acreedor.

levy, *s.* 1. Leva, alistamiento de tropas. 2. Colecta, recaudación, exacción de tributos, impuesto. 3. Embargo de bienes.

lewd [luːd] [lud], *a.* 1. Lujurioso, lascivo, deshonesto, disoluto, libertino. 2. *(Ant.)* Malvado, perverso, depravado. 3. *(Des.)* Lego, ignorante.

lewdly [ˈluːdlɪ] [lud-li], *adv.* Malvadamente, lascivamente; tontamente, ignorantemente.

lewdness [ˈluːdnɪs] [lud-nes], *s.* Lascivia, incontinencia, relajación, licencia, disolución de vida o costumbres: libertinaje, desenfreno, prostitución, en las mujeres.

lewis o Lewisson [ˈluːɪs] [luis], *s.* Clavija para mover o alzar piedras, castañuela de cantera; grapa, retén.

lexical [ˈleksɪkəl] [lek-si-kal], *a.* 1. Relativo a las palabras de un idioma, y no a su construcción gramatical. 2. Lexicográfico.

lexicographer [ˌleksɪˈkɒgrəfəʳ] [lek-si-ko-gra-faʳ], *s.* Lexicógrafo, escritor de diccionarios.

lexicographic [ˌleksɪˈkɒgrəfɪk] [lek-si-ko-gra-fik], *a.* Lexicográfico.

lexicography [ˌleksɪˈkɒgrəfɪ] [lek-si-ko-gra-fi], *s.* Lexicografía.

lexicon [ˈleksɪkən] [lek-si-kon], *s.* Léxico o lexicón, diccionario del idioma latino, griego o hebreo.

liability [ˌlaɪəˈbɪlɪtɪ] [laia-bi-li-ti], *s.* 1. Condición de estar sujeto o expuesto, como a un accidente, daño, etc. 2. Responsabilidad; deuda pasiva; pasivo. **Legal liability insurance,** seguro por el cual se asume la responsabilidad legal de una persona o corporación. 3. Propensión. 4. Riesgo (risk).

liable [ˈlaɪəbl] [laia-bol], *a.* 1. Sujeto, expuesto a una pena, a las costas, al pago de daños y perjuicios, etc. 2. Responsable, deudor, justa o legalmente. 3. Propenso, con tendencia a (en sentido desfavorable).

liableness [ˈlaɪəblnɪs] [laia-bol-nes], *s.* 1. Propensión, inclinación a alguna cosa. 2. Responsabilidad.

liaison [lɪˈeɪzɒn] [li-ei-son], *s.* Enlace, coordinación (coordination). Relación.

liaison officer [lɪˈeɪzɒnˌɒfɪsəʳ] [li-ei-son-o-fi-saʳ], *s. (Mil.)* Oficial de intercomunicación.

liar [ˈlaɪəʳ] [laiaʳ], *s.* Embustero, mentiroso, el que dice una mentira.

lias [ˈlaɪəs] [laias], *s. (Geol.)* Lías, sistema de rocas calcáreas y arcillosas del terreno jurásico.

lib [lɪb] [lib], *va.* (Prov. Ingl. y Escocia) Castrar, capar.

libation [laɪˈbeɪʃən] [lai-bei-shon], *s.* Libación.

libel [ˈlaɪbəl] [lai-bol], *s.* 1. Libelo, el papel o escrito satírico y denigrativo. 2. *(For.)* Libelo, cargo que se hace por escrito y en derecho contra alguna persona.

libel, *va.* y *vn.* 1. Satirizar, escribir sátiras o zaherir y motejar con ellas. 2. Difamar, calumniar o quitar el crédito por medio de libelos infamatorios o de sátiras denigrativas.

libelant, libellant [ˈlaɪbələnt] [lai-be-lant], *s. (For.)* El actor o demandante en las acciones ante el tribunal.

libeler, libeller [ˈlaɪbələʳ] [lai-be-laʳ], *s.* Libelista, el autor de libelos; infamador.

libeling, libelling [ˈlaɪbəlɪŋ] [lai-be-lin], *s.* Difamación.

libellous [ˈlaɪbələs] [lai-be-las], *a.* Infamatorio, difamatorio.

liber [ˈlaɪbəʳ] [li-baʳ], *s.* 1. Libro, volumen de instrumentos auténticos, archivos o hipotecas. 2. *(Bot.)* Líber, corteza interior de los vegetales.

liberal [ˈlɪbərəl] [li-be-ral], *a.* 1. Liberal, generoso, dadivoso, bizarro; *(Fam.)* campechano, desprendido, que no es mezquino ni miserable. 2. Liberal, honorífico, caballeroso. 3. Liberal, libre; propenso a ideas democráticas o republicanas; libre de fanatismo o de sumisión a una autoridad o un dogma. 4. Abundante. 5. Libre, que no es estricto ni a la letra. 6. Noble, bien nacido.

liberal arts [ˈlɪbərəlˌɑːts] [li-be-ral-arts], *s.* Letras (humanas), humanidades, artes liberales.

liberalism [ˈlɪbərəlɪzən] [li-be-ra-li-sem], *s.* Liberalismo en los principios políticos y religiosos.

liberality [ˌlɪbəˈrælɪtɪ] [li-be-ra-li-ti], *s.* Liberalidad, generosidad, bizarría, munificencia.

liberalize [ˈlɪbərəlaɪz] [li-be-ra-lais], *va.* Liberalizar, hacer liberal, generoso, tolerante.

liberally [ˈlɪbərəlɪ] [li-be-ra-li], *adv.* Liberalmente, dadivosamente.

liberal-minded [ˈlɪbərəlˌmaɪndɪd] [li-be-ral-main-did], *a.* Liberal, de ideas tolerantes.

liberate [ˈlɪbəreɪt] [li-be-reit], *va.* Libertar, librar, manumitir.

liberation [ˌlɪbəˈreɪʃən] [li-be-rei-shon], *s.* El acto de libertar.

liberator [ˈlɪbəreɪtəʳ] [li-be-rei-taʳ], *s.* Libertador, librador.

libertarian [ˌlɪbəˈtɛərɪən] [li-ber-tea-rian], *a.* Libertario.

libertinage [ˈlɪbətɪnɪdʒ] [li-ber-ti-nich], *s. V.* LIBERTINISM.

libertine [ˈlɪbətiːn] [li-ber-tin], *s.* 1. Libertino, hombre disoluto. 2. *(For.)* En la historia romana, libertino, el hijo de liberto. -*a.* Libertino, disoluto.

liberty [ˈlɪbətɪ] [li-ber-ti], *s.* 1. Libertad, condición del que es o está libre. 2. Libertad, libre albedrío. 3. Exención, privilegio, prerrogativa, inmunidad, franquicia. 4. Libertad, poder de obrar conforme a las leyes. 5. Libertad, franqueza, llaneza demasiada de una persona. 6. Libertad, soltura de presos o cautivos. 7. Licencia, permiso. **To take liberties with,** tomarse demasiadas libertades con.

libidinist [ˈlɪbɪdɪnɪst] [li-bi-di-nist], *s.* (Poco us.) Mico, el que es libidinoso.

libidinous [lɪˈbɪdɪnəs] [li-bi-di-nos], *a.* Libidinoso, liviano, deshonesto, lascivo, lujurioso, disoluto, impúdico.

libidinously [lɪˈbɪdɪnəslɪ] [li-bi-di-nos-li], *adv.* Libidinosamente, lascivamente.

libido [lɪˈbiːdəʊ] [li-bi-dou], *s.* Libido.

libra [ˈliːbrə] [li-bra], *s. (Astr.)* Libra, un signo del zodíaco.

libral [ˈlɪbrəl] [li-bral], *a.* (Poco us.) Relativo a la libra romana.

librarian [laɪˈbrɛərɪən] [lai-brea-rian], *s.* 1. Bibliotecario. 2. *(Des.)* Copiante.

librarianship [laɪˈbrɛərɪənʃɪp] [lai-brea-rian-ship], *s.* El empleo u oficio de bibliotecario.

library [ˈlaɪbrərɪ] [lai-bra-ri], *s.* 1. Biblioteca, librería, conjunto de libros, folletos, etc. 2. El edificio o la pieza que contiene la biblioteca.

librate [ˈlaɪbreɪt] [lai-breit], *v.* Balancear, poner en equilibrio.

libration [laɪˈbreɪʃən] [lai-brei-shon], *s.* Libración, balance; equilibrio.

libratory [ˈlaɪbrətərɪ] [lai-bra-to-ri], *a.* Lo que balancea.

libretto [lɪˈbretəʊ] [lai-bre-tou], *s. (Mús.)* Libreto (de una ópera, etc.).

lice, *s. pl.* de LOUSE. Piojos.

licebane [ˈlaɪsbeɪn] [lais-bein], *s. (Bot.)* Albarraz, hierba piojera.

license, licence [ˈlaɪsəns] [lai-sens], *s.* 1. Licencia, permiso. 2. Despacho, cédula, título; diploma; certificado escrito o impreso que contiene un permiso, una autorización. 3. Licencia, libertinaje, libertad inmoderada o desordenada, desorden, desarreglo, desenfreno de costumbres.

license. *va.* 1. Licenciar, dar licencia o permiso; autorizar; dar cédula, despacho o privilegio. 2. Soltar, dar soltura.

licensee, licencee [ˈlaɪsəns] [lai-sens], *s.* Concesionario, el que obtiene una licencia.

licentiate [ˈlaɪsəns] [lai-sens], *s.* 1. El que usa de licencia. 2. Licenciado, el que ha recibido en alguna universidad el grado asíllamado. 3. Licenciado, el que tiene licencia para predicar o practicar una profesión.

licentious [laɪˈsenʃəs] [lai-sen-shos], *a.* Licencioso, desordenado, libertino, disoluto.

licentiously [laɪˈsenʃəslɪ] [lai-sen-shos-li], *adv.* Licenciosamente.

licentiousness [laɪˈsenʃəsnɪs] [lai-sen-shos-nes], *s.* Licencia, libertad inmoderada, disolución, desarreglo o desenfreno de vida o costumbres.

lich [lɪtʃ] [lich], *s. (Des.)* Cadáver, un cuerpo muerto. **Lich-gate,** sotechado que proyecta sobre la entrada de un Cementerio. **Lich-owl,** lechuza, especie de buho, del que se cree vulgarmente que pronostica la muerte.

lichen [ˈlɪtʃn] [li-chen], *s. (Bot.)* Liquen, empeine, planta criptógama.

licit [ˈlɪsɪt] [li-sit], *a.* Lícito, permitido.

licitly [ˈlɪsɪtlɪ] [li-sit-li], *adv.* Lícitamente.

licitness [ˈlɪsɪtnɪs] [li-sit-nes], *s.* Calidad o condición de lícito.

lick [lɪk] [lik], *va.* 1. Lamer, chupar. 2. *(Vulg.)* Cascar, aporrear, golpear; dar una tunda o felpa. 3. *(Vulg.)* Sobresalir, sobrepujar, vencer. **To lick up,** devorar, consumir. **To lick somebody's boots,** hacer la pelota a alguien *(Fam.)*.

lick, *s.* 1. Lamedura, lametada, lengüetada. 2. Lengüetada, la cantidad que se puede lamer de una vez. 3. *(E.U.)* Depósito de sal, al que acuden ciertos animales que la lamen. 4. *(Fam.)* Mojicón, cachete, bofetón. **A lick of paint,** una mano de pintura.

licker [ˈlɪkəʳ] [li-kaʳ], *s.* Lamedor, el que lame.

lickerish [ˈlɪkərɪʃ] [li-ka-rish], **lickerous** [ˈlɪkərəs] [li-ka-ros], *a.* Regalado, delicado, apetitoso, sabroso.

lickerishness [ˈlɪkərɪnɪs] [li-ke-rí-nes], *s.* Delicadeza de paladar, regalo.

lickerishly [ˈlɪkərɪʃlɪ] [li-ka-rish-li], *adv.* Deliciosamente.

lickspittle [ˈlɪkspɪtl] [lik-spitel], *s.* Quitapelillos, parásito, hombre servil.

licorice, liquorice [ˈlɪkərɪs] [li-ko-rish-li], *s.* (*Bot.*) Regaliz, regaliza, orozuz. **Licorice-juice** o **Spanish-licorice,** zumo de orozuz, regaliz en pasta.

lictor [ˈlɪktəʳ] [lik-taʳ], *s.* Lictor.

lid [lɪd] [lid], *s.* 1. Tapa, la parte superior que cierra las cajas, etc. 2. Párpado, el pellejo blando que cubre los ojos. **This puts the lid on it!** ¡Esto es el colmo! **She's flipped her lid,** se ha vuelto loca, ha perdido la cabeza (*Fam.*).

lido [ˈlɪsɪt] [li-sit], *s.* Piscina pública. (*Mex.*). Pileta pública.

lie [ˈlaɪ] [lai], *s.* 1. Mentira, ficción, embuste. 2. Desmentida, mentís. 3. Error, vanidad, lo que sirve para engañar o que crea una impresión falsa.

lie, *s.* 1. Posición en que está echada una cosa; caída. 2. Cubil, cama de un animal salvaje. **The lie of the land,** la caída, la situación relativa del terreno.

lie, *vn.* (*pret.* y *pp.* LIED, *pa.* LYING). Mentir, levantar falsos testimonios; decir o hacer falsedades con intento de engañar.

lie, *vn.* (*pret.* LAY, *pp.* LAIN). 1. Echarse, tumbarse, tenderse a la larga. **To lie sick,** guardar cama. 2. Descansar recostado, apoyarse. 3. Reposar, acostarse, estar acostado. 4. Yacer, estar echado o tendido, se usa comúnmente hablando de los muertos. 5. Yacer, existir de algún modo, estar alguna persona o cosa en algún paraje. 6. Residir, morar, habitar. 7. Apretarse, estrecharse. 8. Consistir, depender; estar en la mano alguna cosa; tocar o pertenecer a alguno la ejecución de un empleo, negocio, etc. 9. Costar. 10. Estar pendiente una acusación contra alguno.

lie at, importunar, molestar; estar expuesto. **To lie at heart,** tener clavada una cosa en el corazón; sentir mucho y por largo tiempo alguna desgracia o contratiempo. **To lie at the point of death,** estar expirando. **To lie at stake,** estar muy interesado en algo.

lie about, estar esparcido.

To lie along, (*Mar.*) Dar a la banda.

lie back, recostarse

lie by, reposar; estar tranquilo o quieto.

lie down, acostarse, reposar, yacer en el sepulcro.

lie in, estar de parto. **To lie in the way,** (a) Ser obstáculo o impedimento. (b) Presentarse convenientemente. **To lie in wait,** espiar, observar, reconocer y notar con disimulo y secreto; asechar. **To lie in one's way,** hallarse en el camino que otro lleva, presentarse a alguno, estar cómodo; ser un obstáculo, impedir.

lie on, (*Mar.*) Estar a la capa.

lie out, dormir fuera de casa. **To lie out at length,** tenderse a la larga.

lie under, estar sujeto a, hallarse expuesto, acusado o atacado; estar sumido.

lie up and down, estar en desorden.

lie upon, hacer alguna cosa un deber u obligación para alguno; ser un deber la ejecución de algo.

lie with, estar acostado con otro, hablar con alguno en la cama; tener coito, conocer carnalmente.

lie-down [ˈlaɪdaʊn] [lai-daun], *s.* Siesta, descanso.

lief [liːf] [lif], *adv.* De buena gana, de buena voluntad. -*a.* (*Des.*) 1. Agradable, querido. 2. Bien dispuesto; inclinado.

liege [ˈliːdʒ] [lidch], *s.* 1. Ligio, feudatario. 2. Soberano. 3. Vasallo, súbdito. -*s.* (*Des.*) Soberano, señor de vasallos.

lie-in, [ˌlaɪˈɪn] [lai-in] *s.* **To have a lie-in,** levantarse tarde.

lien [lɪən] [lian] *s.* 1. Derecho de retención. 2. De aquí, una demanda que ha de ser atendida.

lientery [ˈlɪəntərɪ] [lian-te-ri], *s.* Lientería, flujo de vientre en el cual se echan los alimentos a medio digerir.

lier [lɪəʳ] [liaʳ], *s.* (*Ant.*) El que descansa o yace, el que está oculto o escondido.

lieu [luː] [lu], *s.* Lugar, en la locución **In lieu of,** en lugar de, en vez de.

lieutenancy [lefˈtenənsɪ] [lef-te-nan-si], *s.* 1. Tenencia, lugartenencia, el cargo u oficio de teniente. 2. (*Des.*) El cuerpo de tenientes.

lieutenant [lefˈtenəntɪ] [lef-te-nant], *s.* 1. Teniente o lugarteniente. 2. (*Mil.*) Teniente, el que ocupa el puesto inmediato al de un superior.

lieutenantship [lefˈtenəntʃɪp] [lef-te-nant-ship], *s.* Tenencia, el cargo u oficio de teniente.

lieve [liːv] [liv], *adv.* (*Des.*) V. LIEF.

life [laɪf] [laif], *s.* 1. Vida. 2. Vida, el acto de vivir o la permanencia en la unión del alma y del cuerpo. 3. Vida, el principio de nutrición en los animales y vegetales. 4. Vida, el espacio de tiempo desde el nacimiento hasta la muerte. 5. Vida, conducta, el modo de vivir; el modo de pasar la vida con respecto a sus comodidades e incomodidades. 6. Vida, la relación o historia de las acciones de una persona. 7. Viveza, prontitud, vivacidad, fuego, ardor; espíritu. 8. Vida: expresión de cariño. 9. Semejanza exacta; la forma viva y exacta; el carácter real y verdadero. 10. Espíritu, la idea central y esencial. 11. Mundo, lo que pasa en él; el curso de los asuntos o sucesos humanos. 12. Vida, figuradamente se entiende de los seres organizados. **Life-annuity,** renta vitalicia. **Life-insurance** o **assurance,** seguro sobre la vida o de vida. **To depart this life,** morir. **To have life,** vivir. **For life,** por toda la vida. **A pension for life,** una pensión vitalicia. **To call one into question for his life,** acusar a una persona de un delito que merece pena capital. **I would lay my life upon it,** pondría mi cabeza a que es así. **Life-belt,** cinto de salvamento, para sostenerse en el agua. **Life-boat,** lancha salvavidas. **Life-buoy,** boya o guíndola salvavidas. **Life-interest,** renta o hacienda vitalicia. **Life-line,** cuerda salvavidas. **Life-preserver,** salvavidas, aparato, chaqueta o cinto flotante, etc., que sirve para sobrendar. **To bring back to life,** reanimar, resucitar. **To do life,** cumplir cadena perpetua (*Fam.*). **Not on your life!,** ¡ni hablar!, ¡Lo que faltaba! **True to life,** fiel a la realidad.

lifebelt [ˈlaɪfbelt] [laif-belt], *s.* Salvavidas.

life-blood [ˈlaɪfblʌd] [laif-blad], *s.* Sangre vital, alma, nervio, lo que constituye la fuerza o la energía.

lifeboat [ˈlaɪfbəʊt] [laif-bout], *s.* Bote de salvamento.

life-giving [ˈlaɪfɡɪvɪŋ] [laif-gui-vin], *a.* Vivificante, lo que da vida.

lifeguard [ˈlaɪfɡɑːd] [laif-gard], *s.* Vigilante de playa, guardia, salvavidas.

life insurance [ˌlaɪfɪnˈʃʊərəns] [laif-in-shu-rans], *s.* Seguro de vida.

life jacket [ˈlaɪfˌdʒækɪt] [laif-ya-ket], *s.* Chaleco salvavidas.

lifeless [ˈlaɪflɪs] [laif-les], *a.* 1. Muerto, inanimado, amortiguado. 2. Falto de fuerza, espíritu o vigor; flojo. 3. Inhabilitado por hombres y animales, sin vida aparente.

lifelessly [ˈlaɪflɪslɪ] [laif-les-li], *adv.* Sin vigor, sin espíritu.

life-like [ˈlaɪflaɪk] [laif-laik], *a.* Que parece estar vivo.

lifeline [ˈlaɪflaɪn] [laif-lain], *s.* Cuerda de salvamento. Cordón umbilical.

lifelong [ˈlaɪflɒŋ] [laif-long], *a.* Que dura toda la vida.

life raft [ˈlaɪfrɑːft] [laif-raft], *s.* Balsa salvavidas.

life-saving [ˈlaɪfseɪvɪŋ] [laif-sei-vin], *sn.* Salvamento.

life-size(d) [ˈlaɪfaɪz] [laif-sais], *a.* De tamaño natural (de una persona).

lifestring [ˈlaɪfstrɪŋ] [laif-strin], *s.* Nervio o cordón en el organismo humano por donde se suponía que los órganos recibían su vitalidad.

lifetime [ˈlaɪftaɪm] [laif-taim], *s.* Durante el tiempo de la vida. **In his lifetime,** en su vida.

life-weary [ˈlaɪfweərɪ] [laif-uea-ri], *a.* Infeliz, cansado de la vida.

lift [lɪft] [lift], *va.* 1. Alzar, elevar, levantar. 2. Exaltar, ensalzar, elevar, levantar. 3. Engreír, envanecer, ensoberbecer. 4. Quitar la presión de (alguna cosa). 5. (*Fam.*) Hurtar, quitar, llevarse. -*vn.* 1. Hacer fuerza o esforzarse para levantar alguna cosa. 2. Alzarse y disiparse en la atmósfera. **To lift up,** levantar o alzar alguna cosa. **To lift the hat,** quitarse el sombrero para saludar. **To lift the feet,** acudir presuroso al socorro de alguno. **To lift the eyes,**

levantar los ojos, fijar la atención en. **To lift the face,** levantar la cara como para suplicar. **To lift up the hand,** *(Fig.)* (a) Jurar. (b) Orar, suplicar. **To lift up the heel against,** tratar coninsolencia y desprecio. **To lift the horn,** (a) Tratar con insolencia, con desdén. (b) Establecer en autoridad. **To lift up the voice,** levantar la voz, gritar.

lift, *s.* 1. El esfuerzo que se hace para levantar alguna cosa pesada. 2. Alzamiento, la acción y efecto de alzar. 3. El modo de alzar alguna cosa. 4. El acto de levantar o hacer levantar algo. 5. Máquina o utensilio para alzar; *(Ingl.)* elevador, ascensor. 6. Alza. 7. (Prov. Ingl.) Cielo, atmósfera. **to give one a lift,** ayudar a uno a levantarse o hacer algo. **At one lift,** de un golpe. **Lifts,** *(Mar.)* Amantillos, cabos que sirven para levantar las vergas por una parte bajándolas por otra. **Topping-lifts,** *(Mar.)* Amantillos de la botavara. **Handing-lifts,** *(Mar.)* Mostachos. **Lift-down,** bajar. **Lift off,** levantar, quitar, despegar. **Lift out,** sacar. **Lift up,** levantar. **To give a lift,** llevar en coche.

lifter [ˈlɪftəʳ] [lif-taʳ], *s.* 1. El que levanta. 2. Ladrón. *V.* SHOPLIFTER.

lifting [ˈlɪftɪŋ] [lif-tin], *s.* El acto de levantar, la ayuda o auxilio que se da a uno para que se levante.

lift-off [ˈlɪftɒf] [lift-of], *s.* Despegue de un cohete.

ligament [ˈlɪgəmənt] [li-ga-ment], *s.* Ligamento; ligazón, ligadura.

ligation [lɪˈgeɪʃən] [li-guei-shon], *s.* Ligación, la acción y efecto de ligar.

ligature [ˈlɪgətʃəʳ] [li-ga-chaʳ], *s.* 1. Ligadura, en sus acepciones médica, musical y mecánica. 2. Ligación, la acción de ligar. 3. *(Impr.)* Ligadas como fi, fl, etc.

light [laɪt] [lait], *s.* 1. Luz; claridad, claro, resplandor. 2. Luz, vela, bujía, lámpara, farol; emisión de luz. 3. Vista, ventana o cuadro de vidrio. 4. Luz, ilustración, conocimiento; explicación de alguna cosa obscura. 5. Luz, noticia, aviso, estado de visibilidad; publicidad; aspecto, punto de vista. 6. Luz, el punto o centro desde donde se iluminan y alumbran los objetos pintados en un cuadro. 7. Vista, poder de visión; percepción; inteligencia. 8. Día; alba, amanecer. *-a.* 1. Ligero, leve. 2. Llevadero, lo que fácilmente se puede sufrir o aguantar. 3. Fácil de ejecutarse; fútil, de poco valor o consideración; frívolo, superficial 4. Ligero, ágil, desembarazado. 5. Leve, inconstante, mudable. 6. Alegre, vivo. 7. Liviano, incontinente. 8. Claro, resplandeciente, brillante, reluciente. 9. *(Mar.)* Boyante, la embarcación que no está cargada o no tiene lastre suficiente. 10. Claro, que no es de color muy subido; blondo, rubio: se dice del pelo o de la tez. **Light brown,** castaño claro. **Light complexión,** tez blonda. **Light supper,** colación. **Light of belief,** crédulo. **To make light of a thing,** burlarse de una cosa, tomarla en chanza. **Northern lights,** aurora boreal. *-adv. V.* LIGHTLY. **In the light of,** a la luz de. **To come to light,** salir a la luz.

light, *va.* 1. Encender. **To light a fire,** encender lumbre. 2. Alumbrar, dar luz, iluminar. **Light me home,** alúmbreme Ud. hasta mi casa. 3. *(Mar.)* Aligerar, hacer más ligera una embarcación. *-vn.* 1. Tropezar, hallar, encontrar por casualidad. 2. Desmontarse, apearse de la caballería o carruaje; desembarcar; salir del coche u otra parte. 3. Parar, descansar. **Light-wave,** onda u ondulación de luz. **Light-armed,** armado levemente o a la ligera. **Light-borne,** llevado, traído por la luz o en medio de la luz. **Light-fingered,** largo de uñas, ligero de dedos; el que tiene habilidad para hurtar.

light-brain [ˈlaɪtbreɪn] [lait-brein], *s.* Hombre frívolo e ignorante o con los cascos a la jineta.

lighten [ˈlaɪtn] [lai-ten], *vn.* 1. Relampaguear. 2. Brillar. 3. Hablar con vehemencia. 4. Caer, descender sobre. *-va.* 1. Iluminar, alumbrar. 2. Exonerar, descargar. 3. Aligerar, hacer menos pesada una cosa. **To lighten a ship,** *(Mar.)* Aligerar un bajel. 4. Alegrar, infundir alegría.

lighter [ˈlaɪtəʳ] [lai-taʳ], *s.* 1. *(Mar.)* Alijador, lanchón o gabarra. **Ballast-lighter,** lanchón de lastrar. 2. Cualquier

cosa que comunica luz o claridad. 3. Encendedor, utensilio para encender el gas; mecha, pedazo de papel torcido o antorcha para encender las luces.

lighterage [ˈlaɪtərɪdʒ] [lai-te-rich], *s.* Gabarraje, el flete de las gabarras.

lighterman [ˈlaɪtəmən] [lai-ter-man], *s. (Mar.)* Lanchonero, el que gobierna el alijador o lanchón.

light-faced type [ˈlaɪtfeɪstˌtaɪp] [lait-feist-taip], *s. (Impr.)* Letra o tipo delgado.

light-foot, Light-footed [ˈlaɪtfʊt] [lait-fut], *a.* Ligero de pies.

light-headed [ˈlaɪthedɪd] [lait-je-did], *a.* 1. Ligero de cascos, casquivano. 2. Delirante, el que delira, dice disparates o despropósitos. 3. Atolondrado, aturdido.

light-headedness [ˈlaɪthedɪdnɪs] [lait-je-did-nes], *s.* Delirio, atolondramiento, aturdimiento.

light-hearted [ˈlaɪthɑːtɪd] [lait-jar-tid], *a.* Alegre, festivo, jovial.

light heavyweight [ˈlaɪthevɪˌweɪt] [lait-je-vi-ueit], *s.* (Boxeo) Peso semipesado.

light-horse [ˈlaɪthɔːs] [lait-jors], *s.* Caballería ligera.

lighthouse [ˈlaɪthaʊs] [lait-jaus], *s. (Mar.)* Faro, fanal o torre de luces que sirve de guía a los navegantes.

lighting [ˈlaɪtɪŋ] [lai-tin], *s.* Iluminación artificial, alumbrado. **Electric lighting,** alumbrado eléctrico.

light-keeper [ˈlaɪtˌkiːpəʳ] [lait-ki-paʳ], *s.* Torrero; farolero.

lightless [ˈlaɪtlɪs] [lait-les], *a.* Oscuro, falto de luz, sin luz, sin claridad.

lightly [ˈlaɪtlɪ] [lait-li], *adv.* 1. Ligeramente, levemente. 2. Fácilmente; prontamente. 3. Sin razón, sin motivo. 4. Alegremente, con alegría, airosamente. 5. Deshonestamente, livianamente.

light-minded [ˈlaɪtˌmaɪndɪd] [lait-main-did], *a.* Voluble, inconstante, variable, atolondrado.

light-money [ˈlaɪtmʌnɪ] [lait-ma-ni], *s.* Derechos de faro o de fuego.

lightness [ˈlaɪtnɪs] [lait-nes], *s.* 1. Levedad, ligereza; agilidad, velocidad. 2. Inconstancia. 3. Liviandad, deshonestidad.

lightning [ˈlaɪtnɪŋ] [lait-nin], *s.* 1. Relámpago, rayo, la descarga eléctrica. 2. Aligeramiento. **As quick as lightning,** *(Fam.)* como un relámpago.

lightning bug [ˈlaɪtnɪŋˌbʌg] [lait-nin-bag], *s.* Luciérnaga.

lightning rod [ˈlaɪtnɪŋˌrɒd] [lait-nin-rod], *s.* Pararrayo.

light-room [ˈlaɪtrʊm] [lait-rum], *s. (Mar.)* Caja de faroles del pañol de pólvora o lampión.

lightship [ˈlaɪtʃɪp] [lait-ship], *s.* Buque fanal o buque faro.

lightsome [ˈlaɪtsʌm] [lait-sam], *a.* 1. Alegre, festivo, airoso. 2. *(Poét.)* Luminoso, claro.

lightweight [ˈlaɪtweɪt] [lait-ueit], *s.* (Boxeo) Peso ligero. *-a.* De poco peso, liviano.

light-year [ˈlaɪtjɪəʳ] [lait-yiaʳ], *s. (Astr.)* Año luz.

ligneous [ˈlɪgnɪəs] [lig-nios], **Lignous** [ˈlɪgnəs] [lig-nos], *a.* Le~oso, hecho de madera o semejante a ella.

ligniferous [lɪgˈnɪfərəs] [lig-ní-fe-ros], *a.* Leñífero, que produce madera.

lignify [ˈlɪgnɪfaɪ] [lig-ni-fai], *va.* y *vn.* Convertir o convertirse en madera.

lignite [ˈlɪgnaɪt] [lig-nait], *s.* Lignito, combustible fósil.

ligulate [ˈlɪgjʊleɪt] [li-giu-leit], *a. (Bot.)* Acintillada, semiflosculosa o ligulada: se dice de la flor compuesta que consta de cintillas o semiflósculos.

ligule [ˈlɪgjuːl] [li-guiul], *s. (Bot.)* Florecilla acintillada, lígula o semiflósculo.

ligure [ˈlɪgəʳ] [li-gaʳ], *s.* Ligurio, piedra preciosa mencionada en el Éxodo.

like [laɪk] [laik], *a.* 1. Semejante, parecido; igual lo mismo que. 2. Creíble, probable, verosímil. *-s.* Semejante, semejanza. *-adv.* 1. Como, del mismo modo que. 2. Verosímilmente, probablemente. Se usa muy a menudo esta voz en composición para expresar semejanza. **To give like for like,** pagar en la misma moneda. **He has not his like,** no tiene igual. **Like master, like man,** *(Prov.)* tal para cual. **To be of like force,** ser de la misma fuerza. **Unlike manner,** del mismo modo, que no se parece a nada. **To look like,** parecerse a, tener el aspecto de. **To be as like as two peas,** parecerse como dos gotas de agua. **He is well liked here,** se le quiere mucho aquí. **Likes and dislikes,** preferencias.

like, *va. y vn.* 1. Hallar agrado en, a su gusto; contentarse con; estar contento de. 2. Querer, amar; gustar, agradar alguna cosa. **As you like it,** como Ud. quiera, o como Ud. guste. **I should like to see,** yo quisiera ver, me gustaría ver. **Do you like this tea?,** ¿le gusta a Ud. este té? **How do you like her?** ¿cómo la halla Ud.?

likelihood [ˈlaɪklɪhʊd] [laik-li-jud], **Likeliness** [ˈlaɪklɪnɪs] [laik-li-nes], *s.* Probabilidad, versimilitud, posibilidad.

likely [ˈlaɪklɪ] [lai-ke-li], *a.* 1. Probable, verosímil; creíble, plausible. 2. Bien parecido; placentero; loable,; que da buenas esperanzas. 3. Apto, idóneo, a propósito. *-adv.* Probablemente según todas las apariencias. **Likely enough,** no sería extraño. **Most likely,** es regular. **The likely outcome,** el resultado más probable. **She is not likely to come,** no es probable que venga.

like-minded [ˈlaɪkˈmaɪndɪd] [laik-main-did], *a.* De la misma opinión o parecer.

liken [ˈlaɪkən] [lai-ken], *va.* Asemejar, comparar.

likeness [ˈlaɪknɪs] [laik-nes], *s.* 1. Semejanza, conformidad, igualdad. 2. Viso, forma, apariencia, aire. 3. Semejante, la cosa que se semeja a otra. 4. Retrato fiel o vivo de una persona.

likewise [ˈlaɪkwaɪz] [laik-uais], *adv.* También, asimismo, además, igualmente.

liking [ˈlaɪkɪŋ] [lai-kin], *s.* 1. Inclinación, gusto, agrado, deseo; aprobación, preferencia. 2. *(Ant.)* Semblante, apariencia, en lo que se refiere a la salud de una persona.

lilac [ˈlaɪlək] [lai-lak], *s. (Bot.)* Lila o lilas, arbusto. *-a.* Del color de la lila común.

liliaceous [ˌlɪlɪˈeɪʃəs] [li-li-eis-shos], *a. (Bot.)* Liliáceo, perteneciente a la familia de los lirios (las liliáceas).

lilt [lɪlt] [lilt], *vn.* 1. (Prov. Ingl.) Hacer alguna cosa diestramente. 2. Cantar, bailar, saltar alegremente.

lily [ˈlɪlɪ] [li-li], *s.* 1. Lirio, azucena, planta de adorno del género Lilium o su flor. 2. Planta o flor parecida a ésta;: como **water-lily,** ninfea, nenúfar; **day-lily,** hemerocálide; funkia. 3. Flor de lis. **Lily of the valley,** lirio de los valles, muguete. **White lily,** azucena.

lily-handed [ˈlɪlɪˌhændɪd] [li-li-jan-did], *a.* Manos de alabastro, el que tiene las manos muy blancas.

lily-livered [ˈlɪlɪˌlɪvəd] [li-li-li-vad], *a.* Cobarde; doble.

lilywort [ˈlɪlɪwɔːt] [li-li-uort], *s.* Una planta cualquiera de las liliáceas.

Lima [ˈliːmə] [li-ma], *n.pr.* Lima, capital del Perú. **Lima beans,** habas de Lima, grandes y aplastadas; variedad de haba trepadora. **Lima wood,** brasilete.

limaceous [ˈlɪmeɪʃəs] [li-mei-shos], *a.* Limáceo, parecido a la limaza o babosa.

limb [lɪm] [lim], *s.* 1. Miembro, parte del cuerpo, como un brazo, una pierna, un ala, etc. 2. Rama de árbol; vástago que brota del tallo o tronco principal. 3. Orilla, extremo o remate de una cosa. 4. *(Fam.)* Travieso, turbulento, enredador, malévolo.

limb, *s.* Limbo: se dice de la orilla o borde del disco del sol y de la luna.

limb, *va.* 1. Poner miembros o cosas que se les asemeje. 2. Desmembrar, despedazar, hacer pedazos.

limbed [ˈlɪmbɪd] [lim-bid], *a.* Membrudo, fornido.

limber [ˈlɪmbəʳ] [lim-baʳ], *a.* Manejable, flexible, blando. *-s.* 1. Avantrén de cureña, armón, juego delantero de un furgón de artillería. 2. *(Mar.)* Groera del canal del agua.

limber, *va.* 1. Poner flexible o manejable. 2. Poner o colocar el armón; poner el avantrén a una cureña; se usa con prep. *up.* **Limber up,** desentumecerse.

limber-boards [ˈlɪmbəbɔːz] [lim-ba-bors], *s. pl. (Mar.)* Panas imbornaleras de las varengas. **Limber-holes,** *(Mar.)*

imbornales de las varengas. **Limber-rope,** *(Mar.)* cabo imbornalero de las varengas.

limberness [ˈlɪmbənɪs] [lim-ba-nes], *s.* Flexibilidad.

limbless [ˈlɪmlɪs] [lim-les], *a.* Inmembre, que no tiene miembros.

limbo [ˈlɪmbəʊ] [lim-bou], *s.* 1. Limbo, el lugar a donde se dice que van las almas de los niños que mueren sin bautismo. 2. Cualquier paraje donde hay miseria y falta de libertad. *(Fest.)* **To be in limbo,** estar en Babia.

lime [laɪm] [laim], *s.* 1. Cal. **Quicklime,** cal viva. **Limelight,** luz de calcio. **Lime-kiln,** calera, horno de cal. **Limewater,** agua de cal. 2. Liga, materia viscosa y pegajosa que sirve para cazar pájaros, untando con ella unas varillas o espartos. *V.* BIRD-LIME. **Lime-twig,** vareta, varilla untada con liga. **Lime-twigged,** lo que tiene varetas o palitos untados con liga. 3. Agua de cal.

lime, *s.* 1. *(Bot.)* Lima, una especie de limón pequeño y redondo. **Lime-juice,** zumo de lima, remedio contra el escorbuto. 2. *V.* LINDEN.

lime, *va.* 1. Enredar, enmarañar. 2. Untar con liga. 3. Unir con betún, argamas, mortero o mezcla. 4. Abonar la tierra con cal.

lime-burner [ˈlaɪmbɜːnəʳ] [laim-ber-naʳ], *s.* Calero, el que hace cal.

limehound [ˈlaɪmhaʊnd] [laim-jaund], *s.* Perro grande para cazar jabalíes; sabueso.

limelight [ˈlaɪmlaɪt] [lim-lait], *s.* 1. Rayo de luz concentrada que se proyecta sobre el escenario. 2. Lugar que ilumina esta luz. 3. Posición brillante a los ojos del público. **To be in the limelight,** estar en el candelero.

limestone [ˈlaɪmstəʊn] [lim-stoun], *s.* Piedra de cal o piedra caliza.

limit [ˈlɪmɪt] [li-mit], *s.* 1. Límite, término, fin; lindero, linde; frontera, raya, confín. 2. Lo que impide o restriñe; obstáculo, impedimento, freno. 3. *(Mat.)* Una cantidad determinada.

limit, *va.* Limitar, fijar; restringir. **Limited, limited liability,** *V.* COMPANY.

limitation [ˌlɪmɪˈteɪʃən] [li-mi-tei-shon], *s.* Limitación, modificación, restricción.

limited [ˈlɪmɪtɪd] [li-mi-tid], *a.* Limitado, restringido.

limiter [ˈlɪmɪtəʳ] [li-mi-taʳ], *s.* Limitador.

limitless [ˈlɪmɪtlɪs] [li-mit-les], *a.* Ilimitado.

limn [lɪmn] [limn], *va. (Ant. o Poét.)* Pintar; dibujar; retratar.

limner [ˈlɪmnəʳ] [lim-naʳ], *s. (Ant. o Poét.)* Pintor; dibujador; retratista.

limning [ˈlɪmnɪŋ] [lim-nin], *s.* Pintura.

limo [ˈlɪməʊ] [li-mou], *s. V.* LIMOUSINE.

limous [ˈlɪməs] [li-mon], *a.* Cenagoso.

limousine [ˈlɪməsiːn] [li-mou-sin], *s.* Vehículo de lujo.

limp [lɪmp] [lImp], *s.* Cojera. *-a.* 1. Débil, flexible, falto de rigidez. 2. Insípido, falto de espíritu, sin firmeza de carácter.

limp, *vn.* 1. Cojear. 2. *(Mec.)* Cojear, agotar irregularmente.

limper [ˈlɪmpəʳ] [lim-paʳ], *s.* Cojo.

limpet [ˈlɪmpɪt] [lim-pit], *s.* Lepada o lepas, molusco común. **Like a limpet,** como una lapa.

limpid [ˈlɪmpɪd] [lim-pid], *a.* Limpio, claro, transparente.

limpidity, limpidness [lɪmˈpɪdɪtɪ] [lim-pi-di-ti], *s.* Claridad; limpieza.

limping [ˈlɪmpɪŋ] [lim-pin], *pa.* Cojera.

limpingly [ˈlɪmpɪŋlɪ] [lim-pin-li], *adv.* Con cojera.

limy [ˈlɪmɪ] [li-mi], *a.* 1. Viscoso, glutinoso, pegajoso. 2. Calizo.

linchpin [ˈlɪntʃpɪn] [linch-pin], *s.* Sotrozo, perno, pasador; *(Art.)* pezonero.

lincture [ˈlɪŋktʃəʳ] [link-chaʳ], **linctus** [ˈlɪŋktəs] [link-tos], *s.* Lamedor, jarabe.

lind [ˈlɪnd] [lind], *s. (Des.) V.* LINDEN.

linden, linden-tree [ˈlɪndən] [lin-dən], *s. (Bot.)* Tilo, teja.

line [laɪn] [lain], *s.* 1. *(Mat.)* Línea, longitud que se considera sin latitud o con una sola dimensión. 2. *(Mil.)*

Línea, las defensas que levanta y forma en el campo un ejército; línea de batalla. 3. Línea, vía (de ferrocarril o de vapores). 4. Línea, serie o sucesión de parientes de diferentes grados que descienden todos del mismo tronco. 5. Línea, raya; se dice de las señaladas en la palma de la mano y en la cara; rasgo, arruga; esquicio, contorno, trazo, croquis. 6. Línea o línea equinoccial, el ecuador. 7. Línea, renglón, raya, hablando de un manuscrito o impreso. **To send a line** o **a few lines**, enviar cuatro líneas o cuatro renglones; escribir una carta muy corta. 8. Línea, la duodécima parte de la pulgada. 9. Línea, término, límite. 10. Cualquier cordón muy delgado; cuerda, cordel; *(Mar.)* vaivén. 11. Ramo de negocios. 12. Surtido, cantidad de géneros de una clase particular. 13. Curso de pensamiento y acción. **Fishing-line,** sedal para pescar. **Tarred line,** *(Mar.)* vaivén alquitranado. **Lead-line,** *(Mar.)* sondalesa. **Leech-lines,** *(Mar.)* apagapenoles. **Log-line,** *(Mar.)* corredera. - **Lines,** *pl.* versos. **Lines drawn up and down on paper for accounts,** cajilleros. **Head-line,** encabezamiento, título corriente. **Branch line,** *(F.C.)* ramal, vía lateral. **Junction line,** *(F.C.)* línea de empalme. **Isothermal line,** línea isotérmica. **Tape-line,** lienza, cinta de medir. **Tow-line, towing-line,** remolque, estacha, sirga. **Hard lines,** *(Fam.)* apuro, situación angustiosa. **To draw a line under,** subrayar. **To learn one's line,** aprenderse el papel *(Teat.).* **Line drawing,** dibujo lineal.

line, *va.* 1. Linear, trazar líneas, hacer líneas sobre. 2. Alinear; poner en su propia relación, v. g. las partes de una máquina. 3. Leer en voz clara, línea por línea. 4. Hacer concebir; se usa comúnmente hablando de los animales. -*vn.* Estar en línea; colocarse en posición, como para jugar a la pelota.

line, *va.* 1. Forrar, aforrar; llenar lo interior de. 2. Revestir; cubrir o fortalecer la muralla o pared. 3. Colocar, disponer personas o cosas a lo largo, en hileras.

lineage ['laɪnɪɪdʒ] [lai-nich], *s.* Linaje, línea, descendencia de una familia.

lineal ['laɪnɪəl] [lai-nial], *a.* 1. Lineal, lo perteneciente a la línea; hecho con líneas. 2. Descendiente, emparentado; hereditario.

lineally ['laɪnɪəlɪ] [lai-nia-li], *adv.* En línea recta.

lineament ['laɪnɪəmənt] [lai-nia-ment], *s.* Lineamento, facción del rostro.

linear ['lɪnɪəʳ] [lai-niaʳ], *a.* Lineal, compuesto de líneas.

lineate ['laɪnɪət] [lai-niet], *a.* Señalado con líneas.

lineation [ˌlaɪnɪˈeɪʃ ən] [lai-ni-ei-shon], *s.* Dibujo de línea o líneas.

linebacker ['laɪnbækəʳ] [lain-ba-kaʳ], *s.* Defensa (American football).

lined ['laɪnd] [laind], *a.* Arrugado (face). Rayado (paper).

linefishing ['laɪnfɪʃɪŋ] [lain-fi-shin], *s.* Pesca con caña.

linejudge ['laɪndʒʌdʒ] [lain-yach], *s.* Juez de línea o fondo.

linen ['laɪnɪn] [lai-nin], *s.* Lienzo, lino; tela hecha de lino o cáñamo. **Linen,** ropa blanca. **Linen basket,** cesto de la ropa. **Linen cambric,** Olán batista, cambray. *(Méx.)* Cambray superfino. **Clean linen,** ropa limpia. **Bleached linen,** lienzo blanqueado. **Baby-linen,** pañales. **Table-linen,** mantelería. **A change of linen,** muda de ropa. **Linen collars, cuffs,** cuellos, puños de hilo. **Linen damask,** Damasco de hilo. **Linen hose,** manqueras de lienzo. **Linen hosiery,** medias de hilo. **Linen-prover,** cuentahilos.

linen-draper ['laɪnɪnˌdræpəʳ] [lai-nin-dra-paʳ], *s.* Lencero, mercader de lienzos.

linen trade ['laɪnɪnˌtreɪd] [lai-nin-treid], *s.* Lencería.

line-up ['laɪnʌp] [lain-ap], *s.* Alineación, formación (sports).

linen-weaver ['laɪnɪnˌwevəʳ] [lai-nin-ui-vaʳ], *s.* Tejedor de lienzos.

liner ['laɪnəʳ] [lai-naʳ], *s.* Trasatlántico (avión o barco).

linesman ['laɪnzmən] [lains-man], *s.* Linier.

ling [lɪŋ] [lin], *s.* 1. *(Bot.)* Brezo. 2. *(Zool.)* Molva, lota, merluza, pez de la familia de los gádidos.

-ling, *sufijo.* Se usa para formar diminutivos; v. g. **stripling,** mozuelo, jovencito; **duckling,** anadeja; **gosling,** gansarón, el pollo del ganso.

linger ['lɪŋgəʳ] [lin-gaʳ], *vn.* 1. Consumirse, penar, padecer poco a poco o lentamente. 2. Estar en expectación de alguna cosa por mucho tiempo. 3. Ir pasando, tardar mucho en llegar a alguna parte o en conseguir algún fin. 4. Estar parado, quedar o estar suspenso. -*va.* Prolongar, dilatar, pasar el tiempo en expectación; se usa con *out* o *away.*

lingerer ['lɪŋgərəʳ] [lin-gue-raʳ], *s.* El que tarda, prolonga o está suspenso.

lingerie ['lænʒəri:] [lan-che-ri], *s. f.* Ropa interior femenina.

lingering ['lɪŋgərɪŋ] [lin-che-rin], *a.* Lento, pesado, tardo, lánguido. -*s.* Tardanza, dilación; prolongación.

linget, *s.* V. LINGOT.

lingle ['lɪŋgəl] [lin-gol], *s.* Sedal o hilo de zapatero.

lingo ['lɪŋgəʊ] [lin-gou], *s.* *(Vulg.)* Algarabía, greguería, dialecto.

linguadental ['lɪŋgwəˈdentl] [lin-gua-den-tal], *a.* Linguodental, articulado con la lengua y los dientes.

lingual ['lɪŋgwəl] [lin-gual], *a.* 1. Lingual, que pertenece o se refiere a la lengua. 2. Pronunciado principalmente con la extremidad de la lengua. -*s.* Letra lingual, como la *l, t,* etc.

linguist ['lɪŋgwɪst] [lin-güist], *s.* Linguista, el que sabe y habla varias o muchas lenguas.

linguistic [lɪŋˈgwɪstɪk] [lin-güis-tik], *a.* Lingüístico.

Linguisticis [lɪŋˈgwɪstɪks] [lin-güis-tiks], *s.* Lingüística, la ciencia del lenguaje o estudio comparativo de los idiomas.

liniment ['lɪnɪmənt] [li-ni-ment], *s.* Linimento.

lining ['laɪnɪŋ] [lai-nin], *s.* 1. Forro, aforro. 2. Cualquier cosa que sirve para cubrir la parte interior de otra.

link [lɪŋk] [link], *s.* 1. Eslabón o anillo de cadena. 2. Cadena, enlace. 3. Hacha de viento. **Link-motion,** cuadrante de la corredería, el conjunto de las piezas que sirven para operar las válvulas de una locomotora u otra máquina semejante. **Rail link,** enlace ferroviario (train).

link, *va.* 1. Enlazar, unir y trabar una cosa con otra. 2. Juntar o reunir por confederación o contrato. 3. Ensartar, encadenar. -*vn.* Tener conexión una cosa con otra.

links ['lɪŋkz] [links], *s. pl.* Terreno dispuesto para el juego de golf.

linkup ['lɪŋkʌp] [link-ap], *s.* Enlace, conexión, unión.

linnet ['lɪnɪt] [li-nit], *s.* *(Orn.)* Pájaro de una de las especies de la familia de los fringílidos (pardillo, acanta).

linoleum ['laɪnəʊˌlɪəm] [lai-nou-liom], *s.* Linoleo, preparación de aceite de linaza endurecida por un procedimiento de oxidación.

linotype ['laɪnəʊtaɪp] [lai-nou-taip], *s.* 1. Linotipo, línea de tipos de molde fundida en una sola pieza. **Linotype machine,** linotipia. **Linotype operator,** linotipista.

linseed ['lɪnsi:d] [lin-sid], *s.* Linaza.

linstock, linstock ['lɪnstɒk] [lin-stok], *s.* Botafuego, disparador.

lint [lɪnt] [lint], *s.* 1. Lino. 2. Hila.

lintel ['lɪntl] [lin-tel], *s.* Lintel o dintel, tranquero.

lion ['laɪən] [laion], *s.* 1. León. 2. Hombre de valor. 3. Objeto de interés y curiosidad. 4. León, signo del zodíaco. **Lion's share,** la parte del león; el todo o la mayor parte. **Lion's-foot,** *(Bot.)* pie de león, alquemila. **Lion-leaf,** *(Bot.)* lóntice leontopétalo. **Lion's-tail,** *(Bot.)* leonuro.

lioness ['laɪənes] [laio-nes], *s. f.* Leona.

lion-like ['laɪənlaɪk] [laion-laik], **lionly** ['laɪənlɪ] [laion-li], *a.* Aleonado.

lip [lɪp] [lip], *s.* 1. Labio (mouth, wounds). 2. Los órganos del lenguaje; la boca; el habla. 3. Extremidad o borde de alguna cosa. 4. Pico o pezón de una ampolleta. **Great lip,** bezudo. **To make a lip,** bejar, hacer beja, hacer muecas, hacer gestos. **Lip-glue,** cola de boca. **Lip-devotion,** devoción de boca; devoto de boca. **Lip-good,** se dice del que tiene buenas palabras y malas obras, farisaico. **Lip-labor,** jarabe de pico, palabras vanas, cumplimientos de corte, vanas ofertas. **Lip-reading,** la comprensión o interpretación de lo que quiere expresar una persona observando el movimiento de sus labios, como sucede entre los sordomudos. **Lip-salve,** ungüento para los labios, manteca de cacao. **Lip-wisdom,** charla, habladuría sin sustancia.

liposuction [ˈlaɪpəˌsʌkʃən] [lai-po-sak-shon], *s. f.* Liposucción.

lipped [ˈlɪpt] [lipt], *a.* Que tiene labios. **Blubber-lipped,** belfo, morrudo, hocicudo.

lip-read [ˈlɪpred] [lip-red], *vt., vi.* Leer en los labios.

lipstick [ˈlɪpstɪk] [lip-stik], *s.* Lápiz de labios, lápiz labial, tubo de labios.

liquate [ˈlɪkwɪt] [li-kuit], *vn.* Derretirse, licuarse, liquidarse, fundirse.

liquation [ˈlɪkweɪʃən] [li-kuei-shon], *s.* 1. Licuación, licuefacción, liquidación; conversión de un cuerpo sólido en líquido. 2. La propiedad de derretirse o disolverse.

liquefaction [ˈlɪkwɪˌfækʃən] [li-kui-fak-shon], *s.* Licuación, liquidación, licuefacción.

liqueflable [ˈlɪkwɪfæbl] [li-kui-fa-bol], *a.* Liquidable, licuable.

liquefy [ˈlɪkwɪfaɪ] [li-kui-fai], *va.* Licuar, derretir o liquidar alguna cosa sólida. -*vn.* Liquidarse, derretirse.

liquescent [ˈlɪkwɪsənt] [li-kui-sent], *a. (Fís.)* Licuescente lo que es capaz de licuarse, derretirse o liquidarse.

liqueur [lɪˈkjʊəʳ] [li-kiuaʳ], *s.* Licor, bebida fuerte, dulce y aromática.

liquid [ˈlɪkwɪd] [li-kuid], *a.* 1. Líquido, fluido. 2. Claro, transparente. **Liquid air,** aire líquido o licuado (generalmente para refrigerantes). **Liquid fire,** *(Mil.)* fuego líquido (que se arroja de un lanzallamas). **Liquid hydrogen,** hidrógeno líquido. **Liquid measure,** medida para líquidos. -*s.* Líquido. **Liquid Paper,** Tipp-Ex, líquido corrector

liquidambar [ˈlɪkwɪdˌæmbəʳ] [li-kuid-am-baʳ], *s.* Liquidámbar, resina odorífera producida por un árbol del mismo nombre.

liquidate [ˈlɪkwɪdeɪt] [li-kui-deit], *va.* Liquidar, ajustar las cuentas.

liquidation [ˌlɪkwɪˈdeɪʃən] [li-kui-dei-shon], *s.* Liquidación, la acción y efecto de liquidar.

liquidator [ˈlɪkwɪdeɪtəʳ] [li-kui-dei-taʳ], *s.* Liquidador.

liquidity [lɪˈkwɪdɪtɪ] [li-kui-di-ti], *s.* Liquidez, fluidez. **Liquidity ratio,** relación de liquidez.

liquidize [ˈlɪkwɪdaɪz] [li-kui-dais], *vt.* Licuar *(Culin.).*

liquidizer [ˈlɪkwɪdaɪzəʳ] [li-kui-dai-saʳ], *s.* Licuadora.

liquidness [ˈlɪkwɪdnɪs] [li-kuid-nes], *s.* Liquidez; fluidez.

liquor [ˈlɪkɔːʳ] [li-kuoʳ], *s.* 1. Licor, el cuerpo líquido o fluido. 2. Licor, licor alcohólico, bebida fuerte. 3. Una de las diferentes disoluciones que se emplean en las artes y oficios; lico. **Tan liquor,** baño de casca. **Malt liquor,** cerveza. **Liquor-case,** cantina, frasquera.

liquor, *s.* En la farmacopea de los Estados Unidos, disolución acuosa de una sustancia no volátil.

liquorice [ˈlɪkwərɪz] [li-kuo-rais], *s. m.* Regaliz.

lira [ˈlaɪrə] [lai-ra], *s.* 1. Lira, nombre de una moneda italiana. 2. Moneda turca de oro.

Lisbon [ˈlɪsbən] [lis-bon], *s.* 1. Lisboa. 2. *(Des.)* Una especie de azúcar

lisle [laɪl] [lail], *s.* Hilo de algodón especial que se usa generalmente para calcetines.

lisp [lɪsp] [lisp], *vn.* Tartamudear, cecear. -*va.* Pronunciar las palabras ceceando.

lisp, *s.* Tartamudeo, ceceo.

lisper [ˈlɪspəʳ] [lis-paʳ], *s.* El que cecea o tartamudea.

lispingly [ˈlɪspɪŋlɪ] [lis-pin-li], *adv.* Con ceceo.

lissom, Lissome, *a.* V. LITHESOME.

list [lɪst] [list], *s.* 1. Lista, nómina, cédula de personas o cosas; catálogo. 2. *(Mar.)* Falsa banda, bandeo, inclinación de un buque sobre un costado. 3. *(Des.)* Deseo, gana; voluntad; elección. 4. El terreno cercado en que se tiene torneos. **List of topics,** temario. **To have a list,** dar a la banda. 5. Lista, tira o pedazo de cualquier tela; cenefa. 6. *(Arq.)* Filete, listelo, orla. 7. Listón, barandal. 8. *(Poét.)* Borde exterior, cabo, límite.

list, *vn.* 1. *(Mar.)* Inclinarse a la banda. 2. *(Ant.)* Querer, desear, inclinarse, gustar. -*va.* 1. Registrar, poner o inscribir en un registro o en una lista. 2. *(Mil.)* Alistar. 3. Cercar una liza para torneos. 4. Guarnecer con listones de diferentes

colores. 5. *(Poét.)* Escuchar. 6. *(Mec.)* Hacer disminuir la anchura de alguna cosa. 7. *(Mar.)* Dar carena al buque.

listed [ˈlɪstɪd] [lis-tid], *a.* Listado, listeado.

listel [ˈlɪstl] [lis-tel], *s. (Arq.)* Listel, flete.

listen [ˈlɪsn] [li-sen], *va.* y *vn.* 1. Escuchar, atender. 2. Seguir un consejo; obedecer, conformarse con una opinión. **To listen for,** estar atento.

listener [ˈlɪsnəʳ] [lise-naʳ], *s.* Escuchante, escuchador, espía, escucha.

listerism [ˈlɪstərɪzəm] [lis-ta-ri-sem], *s.* Listerismo, procedimiento quirúrgico antiséptico.

listing [ˈlɪstɪŋ] [lis-tin], *s.* 1. Orilla de paño, tira, cenefa. 2. *(E.U.)* Apuntar, acción de poner en un catálogo o lista.

listless [ˈlɪstlɪs] [list-les], *a.* Indiferente, descuidado, omiso, negligente.

listlessly [ˈlɪstlɪslɪ] [list-les-li], *adv.* Indiferentemente, negligentemente.

listlessness [ˈlɪstlɪsnɪs] [list-les-nes], *s.* Descuido, omisión, indiferencia, negligencia.

list price [ˈlɪstpraɪz] [list-prais], *s.* Precio de catálogo.

lit [lɪt] [lit], *pret.* y *pp.* del verbo TO LIGHT. Acontecido; alumbrado, encendido o inflamado.

litany [ˈlɪtənɪ] [li-ta-ni], *s.* Letanía.

liter [ˈlɪtəʳ] [lis-taʳ], *s.* Litro, medida de capacidad; decímetro cúbico.

literacy [ˈlɪtərəsɪ] [li-te-ra-si], *s. f.* Capacidad de leer y de escribir.

literal [ˈlɪtərəl] [li-te-ral], *a.* Literal. -*s.* Sentido literal.

literalist [ˈlɪtərəlɪst] [li-te-ra-list], *s.* El que se adhiere a la letra o al sentido literal.

literally [ˈlɪtərəlɪ] [li-te-ra-li], *adv.* Literalmente, conforme a la letra o al sentido literal.

literalness [ˈlɪtərəlnɪs] [li-te-ral-nes], *s.* Significación original, primaria o literal; conformidad con la letra, exactitud.

literary [ˈlɪtərərɪ] [li-te-ra-ri], *a.* Literario.

literate [ˈlɪtərɪt] [li-te-rit], *a.* Literato.

literati [ˌlɪtəˈrɑːtɪ] [li-te-ra-ti], *s. pl.* Literatos, sabios, doctos, eruditos.

literatim [ˌlɪtəˈrɑːtɪm] [li-te-ra-tim], *adv.* Letra por letra, a la letra; literalmente.

literator [ˈlɪtərətəʳ] [li-te-rei-taʳ], *a.* Maestro de escuela (despisefully).

literature [ˈlɪtərɪtʃəʳ] [li-te-ra-chaʳ], *s.* 1. Literatura. 2. Las obras literarias de una nación o época. 3. Trabajo literario. 4. Conocimiento de las letras o libros.

litharge [ˈlɪθɑːdʒ] [li-zarch], *s.* Litarigirio, litarge, almártaga.

lithate [ˈlɪθeɪt] [li-zeit], *s.* Urato. V. URATE.

lithe [laɪð] [laiz], *a.* Flexible, delgado, blando, manejable.

litheness [ˈlaɪðnɪs] [lai-nes], *s.* Flexibilidad, flojedad; blandura.

lither [ˈlɪðəʳ] [li-zaʳ], *a. (Prov. Ingl.)* Artificioso, malicioso; travieso, enredador. -*adv. (Des.)* Tardamente, perezosamente.

lithesome [ˈlaɪðsʌm] [laiz-sam], *a. (Poét.)* Flexible, que se dobla fácilmente; activo, ligero, listo.

lithia [ˈlɪθɪə] [li-zia], *s.* Litina, óxido alcalino de litio.

lithic [ˈlɪθɪk] [li-zik], *a.* Lítico, perteneciente a (a) cálculo de la vejiga; (b) a la piedra; (c) al litio.

lithium [ˈlɪθɪəm] [li-zium], *s. (Quím.)* Litio, elemento metálico, blando, blanco de plata, y tan ligero que flota sobre el agua.

lithocolla [ˈlɪθəˌkəʊlə] [li-zo-kou-la], *s.* Litocola, una especie de betún.

lithograph [ˈlɪθəgræf] [li-zo-graf], *va.* Litografiar. -*s.* Litografía, estampa de un dibujo en piedra.

lithographer [lɪˈθɒgræfəʳ] [li-zo-gra-faʳ], *s.* Litógrafo.

lithographic [ˌlɪθəʊˈgræfɪk] [li-zou-gra-fik], *a.* Litográfico, relativo a la litografía.

lithography [lɪˈθɒgræfɪ] [li-zo-gra-fi], *s.* Litografía, el arte de grabar sobre piedra.

lithoid, lithoidal [ˈlɪθɔɪd] [li-zoid], *a.* Litoideo, que tiene aspecto pétreo.

litholapaxy [ˈlɪθələpæksɪ] [li-zo-la-pak-si], *s.* Litolapaxia, la operación de pulverizar un cálculo dentro de la vejiga.

lithologic, lithological [ˌlɪθəˈlɒdʒɪk] [li-zo-lo-yik], *a.* Litológico, concerniente a la litología.

lithology [lɪˈθɒlədʒɪ] [li-zo-lo-yi], *s.* 1. Litología, historia natural de las piedras. 2. Tratado sobre los cálculos que se encuentran en el cuerpo humano y su curación.

lithophyte [ˈlɪθəʊfaɪt] [li-zou-fait], *s.* Litófito, especie de zoófito.

lithosphere [ˈlɪθəsfɪəʳ] [li-zous-fia], *s. (Geol.)* Litosfera.

lithotomist [lɪˈθɒtəmɪst] [li-zo-to-mist], *s.* *(Cir.)* Litotomista, el que extrae la piedra de la vejiga.

lithotomy [lɪˈθɒtəmɪ] [li-zo-to-mi], *s.* Litotomía, talla, la operación para extraer la piedra de la vejiga.

lithotrity [lɪˈθɒtrɪtɪ] [li-zo-tri-ti], *s.* Litotricia, operación de reducir a pedazos la piedra dentro de la vejiga.

lithotrite [ˈlɪθətraɪt] [li-zo-trait], *s.* Litotrictor, instrumento para hacer la operación de la litotricia.

Lithuanian [ˌlɪθjʊˈeɪnɪən] [li-ziu-ei-nian], *a.* Lituano, perteneciente a la Lituania.

litigant [ˈlɪtɪgənt] [li-ti-gant], *s.* y *a.* Litigante.

litigate [ˈlɪtɪgeɪt] [li-ti-gueit], *va.* Litigar o pleitear. *-vn.* Litigar, tener pleito pendiente.

litigation [ˌlɪtɪˈgeɪʃən] [li-ti-guei-shon], *s.* Litigio, pleito pendiente.

litigious [lɪˈtɪdʒəs] [li-ti-yos], *a.* Litigioso.

litigiously [lɪˈtɪdʒəslɪ] [li-ti-yos-li], *adv.* De un modo litigioso.

litre [ˈliːtəʳ] [li-ta], *s.* V. LITER.

litter [ˈlɪtəʳ] [li-ta], *s.* 1. Litera, cama portátil; antiguamente también vehículo llevado por dos caballerías. 2. Cama, la paja que se pone en las cuadras para que se echen las caballerías. 3. Lechigada, camada, ventregada, el número de animalillos que nacen de un parto. 4. Desechos, papeles, fragmentos esparcidos; estado de desorden. **Litter basket,** papelera.

litter, *va.* 1. Parir o dar a luz los animales. 2. Desordenar; cubrir algún sitio con cosas esparcidas sin orden ni concierto. 3. Cubrir de paja o con paja algún paraje. 4. Preparar algún sitio con paja para que descanse en él el ganado lanar. *-vn.* 1. Tenderse, echarse o dormir en la paja como el ganado. 2. Parir la puerca y otros animales.

litterbug [ˈlɪtəbʌg] [li-ta-bag], *s.* Persona que ensucia parques dejando tirados papeles, etc.

little [ˈlɪtl] [li-tel], *a. (comp.* LESS y a veces LESSER; *super.* LEAST). 1. Poco, escaso, limitado y corto en cantidad; pequeño, chico. 2. De poca importancia, insignificante; mediano, ligero; de aquí, despreciable, mezquino. **This has done me little or no service,** esto me ha servido de poco o nada. **A little one,** un niño. **By little and little,** poco a poco. **Be it ever so little,** por poco que sea. **Little** se traduce a menudo en español por una desinencia diminutiva: **a little house,** casita; **a little one,** chiquillo, chiquitín. *-s.* Poco, parte o porción pequeña de alguna cosa. **Little finger,** dedo meñique. **A little sleep,** un poco de sueño. *-adv.* Poco. **Sing a little,** cante Ud. un poco.

littleness [ˈlɪtlnɪs] [li-tel-nes], *s.* Pequeñez, bajeza, apocamiento de espíritu; falta de dignidad.

littoral [ˈlɪtərəl] [li-to-ral], *a.* Litoral, perteneciente a la ribera, costa o playa.

liturgic, liturgical [lɪˈtɜːdʒɪk] [li-ter-yik], *a.* Litúrgico.

liturgy [ˈlɪtədʒɪ] [li-tar-yi], *s.* Liturgia, el orden aprobado por la Iglesia para celebrar los oficios divinos.

livable [ˈlɪvəbl] [li-va-bol], *a.* 1. Digno de la vida; que vale la pena de vivir. 2. Aguantable, soportable.

live [lɪv] [liv], *va.* 1. Pasar, llevar; pasar la vida de cierto modo. 2. Conformarse habitualmente a alguna cosa. *-vn.* 1. Vivir. 2. Mantenerse, subsistir, sobrevivir (survive). 3. Morar, habitar (reside). 4. *(Mar.)* Estar, quedarse a flote; escapar a la destrucción. **To live at rest,** pasar tranquilamente la vida. **To live by oneself,** hacer corro o rancho aparte. **To live from hand to mouth,** vivir al día, de

un modo precario. **To live in,** ser interno. **To live off,** vivir de. **To live on,** vivir de (money). Seguir viviendo. **To live out,** ser externo. **To live together,** convivir. **To live up to,** vivir en conformidad con. **To live up to one's income,** comerse todas sus rentas. **To live down,** sobrevivir a; refutar una calumnia, borrar una falta. **They all lived happily ever after,** todos fueron felices y comieron perdices.

live [ˈlaɪv] [laiv], *a.* 1. Vivo, en vida. 2. Que manifiesta vida o energía: (a) listo, preparado para el uso, efectivo; (b) ardiente, abrasador, vivo, brillante; (c) útil para imprimir. **Live steam,** vapor efectivo. **A live coal,** una brasa, un carbón ardiente. 3. *(E.U.)* Vivo, fogoso, que tiene viveza, interés o animación. **Live-box,** (a) porta-animálculos, celdilla de vidrio para examinar los objetos vivos con el microscopio. **Live circuit** o **wire,** circuito o alambre por el cual está pasando una corriente eléctrica. **Live stock,** ganadería, conjunto de los animales domésticos de una finca o hacienda. **She is a real live wire!** ¡qué marcha tiene!

live broadcast [ˈlɪvˌbrɔːdkæst] [liv-broud-kast], *s.* Transmisión directa por radio o televisión, en contraste con las grabadas en cinta.

lived-in, [ˈlɪvdˌɪn] [livd-in], *a.* Acogedor/a.

livelihood [ˈlaɪvlɪhʊd] [laiv-li-jud], *s.* 1. Vida, modo de vivir o de ganar la vida; mantenimiento, subsistencia. 2. Apariencia de vida.

liveliness [ˈlaɪvlɪnɪs] [laiv-li-nes], *s.* Vida, viveza, prontitud, agilidad, vivacidad, actividad.

livelong [ˈlɪvlɒŋ] [liv-long], *a.* Tedioso, fastidioso, enfadoso, molesto, cansado; largo.

lively [ˈlaɪvlɪ] [laiv-li], *a.* 1. Vivo, vigoroso, brioso. 2. Gallardo, airoso, galán. 3. Animado, vivificado. 4. Eficaz. *-adv.* Vigorosamente; enérgicamente; vivamente, muy a lo vivo.

live-oak [ˈlaɪvˌəʊk] [laiv-ouk], *s.* Encina americana.

liver [ˈlaɪvəʳ] [lai-va], *s.* 1. Viviente. **Good liver,** el que se da buena vida. 2. Hígado.

livered [ˈlaɪvəd] [lai-verd], *a.* El que tiene hígado. **White-livered** o **lily-livered,** cobarde, bajo, mezquino, pérfido, que tiene malos hígados o mala voluntad.

liveried [ˈlaɪvərɪd] [lai-ve-rid], *a.* Que lleva una librea.

liverish [ˈlaɪvərɪʃ] [lai-ve-rish], *a.* **To feel liverish,** sentirse mal del hígado.

liverwort [ˈlaɪvəwɔːt] [lai-var-uez], *s. (Bot.)* Hepática.

livery [ˈlaɪvərɪ] [lai-ve-ri], *s.* 1. Librea, el vestido que se da a algunos criados. 2. Cualquier vestido que se lleva en señal de alguna cosa o a consecuencia de algún acontecimiento. **To keep horses at livery,** tener caballos de alquiler. 4. Entrega, el acto de dar o tomar posesión.

lives [laɪvz] [laivs], *pl.* de LIFE.

livestock [ˈlaɪvstɒk] [laiv-stok], *s.* Ganadería.

live wire [ˈlaɪvwaɪəʳ] [laiv-uaia], *s.* 1. Alambre cargado. 2. *(Fam.)* Persona muy activa y llena de vida. 3. Muchacho muy travieso.

livid [ˈlɪvɪd] [li-vid], *a.* Lívido, cárdeno, acardenalado, amoratado (color).

lividness [ˈlɪvɪdnɪs] [li-vid-nes], *s.* Lo cárdeno, lo amortado; el color lívido, cárdeno o amoratado.

living [ˈlɪvɪŋ] [li-vin], *s.* 1. Modo de vivir o de ganar la vida, subsistencia, mantenimiento. 2. Vida. 3. Beneficio eclesiástico. *-a.* Vivo, vigoroso; que tiene movimiento y vida. **Living coals,** brasas. **Standard of living,** nivel de vida.

livingly [ˈlɪvɪŋlɪ] [li-vin-li], *adv.* En estado de vida, vivo.

living room [ˈlɪvɪŋˌrʊm] [li-vin-rum], *s.* Sala, estancia.

living wage [ˈlɪvɪŋweɪdʒ] [li-vin-ueich], *s.* Jornal adecuado para la subsistencia.

lixivial [ˈlɪksɪvɪəl] [lik-si-vial], *a.* Lejivial.

lixivium [ˈlɪksɪvɪəm] [lik-si-viom], *s.* Lejía, agua impregnada de sales alcalinas.

lizard [ˈlɪzəd] [li-zard], *s.* Lagarto. *(Mex.)* Lagartija.

llama [ˈlɑːmɑː] [la-ma], *s.* Llama del Perú, animal rumiante.

LL. D. Abrev. de *legum doctor,* o doctor en ambos derechos.

lo [ləʊ] [lou], *inter.* He aquí, ved aquí, mirad.

load [ləʊd] [loud], *s.* 1. Carga; medida; peso. 2. Carga, gravamen; de aquí, opresión. 3. Fardo. 4. La resistencia que una máquina opone al motor que la impele. 5. Peso, presión hacia abajo sobre una construcción. **Ship-load,** cargamento de un buque. **Load-line, load-water line,** línea de flotación. **Cart-load,** carretada. **Boat-load,** barcada. **A load of,** un montón de. **That's a load off my mind!** ¡eso me quita un peso de encima!

load, *va.* 1. Cargar, poner o echar algún peso sobre el hombre, sobre las bestias, etc. 2. Embarazar, impedir. 3. Cargar un arma de fuego. 4. Colmar; llenar, agobiar. 5. Falsificar, adulterar. 6. Hacer pesado, cargar (como un plomo). **A loaded whip,** látigo emplomado. *-vn.* Tomar una carga o cargamento; a veces con la prep. *up.* **To load with favors,** colmar de favores. **To load with reproaches,** llenar de reconvenciones. **To load up,** cargar.

loaded [ˈləʊdɪd] [lou-did], *a.* Cargado (dice). **The dice are against him,** todo está en su contra. **A loaded question,** una pregunta tendenciosa.

loader [ˈləʊdəʳ] [lou-daʳ], *s.* Cargador, embarcador.

loadstone [ˈləʊdstəʊn] [loud-stoun], *s.* Imán. V. LODESTONE.

loaf [ləʊf] [louf], *s.* Pan, la masa de harina que se forma para cocer en el horno. **A large loaf,** hogaza. **A small loaf,** panecillo. **A loaf of sugar,** pilón de azúcar. **Loaf sugar,** azúcar de pilón. **Penny loaf,** rollo, bollo.

loaf, *va.* Pasar en la ociosidad; se usa con la prep. *away.* **To loaf one's time away,** pasar su tiempo en la ociosidad. *-vn.* Haraganear, holgazanear.

loafer [ˈləʊfəʳ] [lou-faʳ], *s.* Haragán, holgazán, tunante, pelafustán.

loam [ləʊm] [loum], *s.* 1. Marga, mezcla no cohesiva de arena y arcilla. 2. En fundición, tierra de moldeo.

loamy [ˈləʊmɪ] [lou-mi], *a.* Terroso, margoso.

loan [ləʊn] [loun], *s.* 1. Préstamo; empréstito. 2. Permiso para usar.

loath [ləʊθ] [louz], *a.* Repugnante, desinclinado, disgustado, poco dispuesto a. **I was loath to come away,** estaba poco dispuesta a irme.

loathe [ləʊð] [loudz], *va.* 1. Aborrecer, detestar. 2. Tener hastío, aborrecer alguna cosa por estar harto de ella. *-vn.* Fastidiar, causar o sentir fastidio, disgusto o aborrecimiento.

loather [ˈləʊðəʳ] [lou-zaʳ], *s.* El que está disgustado, fastidiado o lleno de tedio.

loathful [ˈləʊðʊl] [louz-ful], *a.* Fastidiado, lleno de tedio; aborrecido, odiado.

loathing [ˈləʊðɪŋ] [lou-zin], *s.* Disgusto, aversión, asco, repugnancia.

loathingly [ˈləʊðɪŋlɪ] [lou-zin-li], *adv.* De mala gana, con disgusto.

loathsome [ˈləʊðsəm] [louz-sam], *a.* Aborrecible, destestable, fastidioso, asqueroso.

loathsomeness [ˈləʊðsəmnɪs] [louz-sam-nes], *s.* La calidad o propiedad de lo que causa asco o fastidio.

loaves [ləʊvz] [louvs], *pl.* de LOAF.

lob [lɒb] [lob], *s.* 1. Lombriz grande. V. LOBWORM. 2. Masa, mezcla blanda y espesa. 3. Meta, término de los juegos de pelota. 4 *(Ant.)* Pelmazo, el sujeto tardo y pesado en sus acciones.

lob, *va.* Soltar o dejar caer alguna cosa por torpeza o falta de maña.

lobar [ˈlɒbəʳ] [lo-baʳ], *a.* Lobular. **Lobar pneumonia,** Neumonía de un lóbulo entero.

lobate, lobated [ˈlɒbeɪt] [lo-beit], *a.* Lobulado, en forma de lóbulo, o provisto de lóbulos.

lobby [ˈlɒbɪ] [lo-bi], *s.* Paso, pasillo o corredor que hay delante de la puerta de una sala u otra pieza de una casa; antecámara, vestíbulo, pórtico, galería, crujía.

lobby, *va.* y *vn. (E.U.)* Procurar la aprobación de una medida o proyecto de ley, tratando de obtener en su favor los votos de los legisladores.

lobbying [ˈlɒbɪɪŋ] [lo-biin], *s.* Cabildeo. *(Mex. col.)* Coyoteo.

lobe [ləʊb] [loub], *s.* 1. *(Zool. y Bot.)* Lóbulo; lobo. 2. Lóbulo, parte más marcada del esquema de señales que aparece en la pantalla.

lobelia [ləʊˈbiːlɪə] [lou-bi-lia], *s.* Lobelia, extenso género de plantas con flores muy vistosas; planta de este género.

lobster [ˈlɒbstəʳ] [lobs-taʳ], *s.* Langosta de mar, crustáceo comestible.

lobule [ˈlɒbjɒl] [lo-biul], *s.* dim. Lobulillo.

local [ˈləʊkəl] [lou-kal], *a.* Local, relativo a determinado lugar. **Local remedies,** remedios externos, tópicos. *-s.* 1. *(Fam. E.U.)* Noticia de interés local. 2. *(E.U.)* Tren de escala; *(Ingl.)* tren suburbano. 3. Batería o circuito local. **Local authority,** ayuntamiento, municipio. **Local time,** hora local.

localism [ˈləʊkəlɪzəm] [lou-ka-li-sem], *s.* 1. Costumbre o idiotismo particular de un lugar; locución local. 2. Provincialismo; estado local.

locality [ləʊˈkælɪtɪ] [lou-ka-li-ti], *s.* 1. Localidad, paraje determinado; posición, situación topográfica. 2. Particularidad o circunstancia local.

localize [ˈləʊkəlaɪz] [lou-ka-lais], *va.* Localizar, orientar.

locally [ˈləʊkəlɪ] [lou-ka-li], *adv.* Localmente.

local option [ˈləʊkəlɒpʃən] [lou-kal-op-shon], *s.* Derecho de una ciudad, distrito, etc. a permitir o no la venta de bebidas alcohólicas.

locate [ləʊˈkeɪt] [lou-keit], *va.* Poner, colocar, situar; trazar la línea de un ferrocarril.

location [ləʊˈkeɪʃən] [lou-kei-shon], *s.* Colocación, localidad, situación, ubicación.

loch [lɒx] [loj] *s. (Esco.)* Lago; también ensenada marina.

lochia [ˈlɒkɪə] [lou-kia], *s. pl.* Loquios, líquido que sale por los órganos de la mujer durante el puerperio.

lock [lɒk] [lok], *s.* 1. Cerradura, cerraja (box, door, etc). **Spring-lock,** cerradura de muelle. **Padlock,** candado. 2. Llave, la parte de las armas de fuego que sirve para dispararlas. 3. Abrazo estrecho y apretado. 4. Cercado, cerca, vallado. 5. Vedija de lana; bucle, rizo, trenza, guedeja (hair); ramillete, borla. 6. Exclusa, represa de río o canal navegable; compuerta. 7. Trabas, maniotas, para las manos de los caballos. 8. Tope, meta *(Aut.)* **Under lock and key,** bajo llave.

lock, *va.* 1. Cerrar. 2. Tener debajo de llave. 3. Abrazar, coger alguna cosa entre los brazos. *-vn.* 1. Estar una cosa cerrada; tener alguna cosa bajo llave. **The door does not lock,** la puerta no se cierra. 2. Unirse o entrelazarse una cosa con otra. **To lock away,** guardar bajo llave. Encerrar (criminal). **To lock in,** encerrar, poner bajo llave; abrazar. **To lock up,** cerrar, encerrar, dejar bajo llave (object). **To lock one out,** cerrar la puerta a uno para que no entre. Encarcelar (criminal). Cerrar (house).

lockage [ˈlɒkɪdʒ] [lo-kich], *s.* 1. Materiales para la construcción de una esclusa. 2. Diferencia de nivel en un canal de esclusas. 3. Portazgo de esclusa, derecho que se paga por pasar.

locked [ˈlɒkt] [lokt], *a.* 1. Cerrado con llave. 2. Entrelazado, enganchado.

locker [ˈlɒkəʳ] [lo-kaʳ], *s.* 1. Cajón, gaveta o cosa semejante cerrada con llave; armario. 2. *(Mar.)* Cajón o alacena de cámara. **Shot-locker,** *(Mar.)* chillera.

locket [ˈlɒkɪt] [lo-kit], *s.* Guardapelo, medallón pequeño.

lockjaw [ˈlɒkdʒɔː] [lok-yo], *s. (Med.)* Trismo, tétanos.

lockout [ˈlɒkaʊt] [lok-aut], *s. (Econ. polit.)* Cierre patronal.

lockram [ˈlɒkræm] [lok-ram], *s.* Estopa, especie de lienzo basto o tela grosera.

locksmith [ˈlɒksmɪθ] [lok-smiz], *s.* Cerrajero.

lockstitch [ˈlɒkstɪtʃ] [lok-stich], *s.* Punto de cadeneta.

locomotion [ˌləʊkəˈməʊʃən] [lou-ko-mou-shon], *s.* Locomoción, mudanza de lugar; potencia locomotriz.

locomotive [ˌləʊkəˈməʊtɪv] [lou-ko-mou-tiv], *a.* Locomotivo, capaz de moverse y de mudarse de lugar. *-s.* Locomotora, máquina motriz de los ferrocarriles.

locomotor [ˌləʊkəˌməʊtəʳ] [lou-ko-mou-taʳ], *a.* Locomotor, locomotriz, perteneciente a la locomoción.

locust ['ləʊkəst] [lou-kost], *s. (Ent.)* 1. Langosta, saltamontes. 2. *(E.U.)* Cigarra, cicada. 3. **Locust o locust-tree,** se llaman así vulgarmente el algarrobo, la acacia y otros árboles.

locution [ləˈkjuːʃən] [lo-kiu-shon], *s.* Locución, modo de hablar; frase.

locular [ləˈkjʊləʳ] [lo-kiu-laʳ], *a. (Bot.)* Locular, loculado, dividido en celdillas.

lode [ləʊd] [loud], *s.* 1. Filón, vena metálica (metalífera). 2. Extensión de agua detenida, como en una acequia.

lodestar ['ləʊdstɑːʳ] [loud-staʳ], *s.* Cinosura, estrella del norte, estrella de guía.

lodestone ['ləʊdstəʊn] [loud-stoun], *s.* Imán natural, piedra imán.

lodge [lɒdʒ] [lodch], *va.* 1. Alojar, aposentar, poner en alojamiento. 2. Colocar, poner alguna cosa en paraje determinado. 3. Dar hospedaje o alojamiento por breve tiempo. 4. Fijar alguna cosa en la memoria. 5. Abrigar, cubrir. 6. Derribar, echar abajo. -*vn.* 1. Residir, habitar, vivir, morar en algún lugar o casa. **Where do you lodge?,** ¿dónde vive Ud.? 2. Alojarse u hospedarse de noche. 3. Tenderse, echarse. 4. Alojarse, meterse. **The bullet lodged in the lung,** la bala se alojó en el pulmón. **Lodging-knees,** *(Mar.)* curvas valonas. **To lodge a complaint against somebody,** dar una queja contra alguien.

lodge, *s.* 1. Casa de guarda en el bosque o monte. 2. Cualquier casita pequeña pegada a otra mayor y formando parte de ella. **Porter's lodge,** covacha o cuarto del portero. 3. Logia, la reunión o subdivisión local de ciertas sociedades secretas y la casa en que se juntan (Freemasonry).

lodgment ['lɒdʒmənt] [lodch-ment], *s.* 1. Amontonamiento. 2. *(Mil.)* Atrincheramiento, trinchera.

lodger ['lɒdʒəʳ] [lod-chaʳ], *s.* Huésped, inquilino, morador.

lodging ['lɒdʒɪŋ] [lod-chin], *s.* 1. Posada, habitación, vivienda; cuartos alquilados. 2. Alojamiento, cuando se habla de tropas. 3. Morada, residencia temporal. **Private lodging,** habitación o cuarto en una casa particular. **Board and lodging,** mesa y habitación; casa de huéspedes. **Lodging-house,** casa de huéspedes amueblada, pensión.

loft [lɒft] [loft], *s.* 1. Suelo, piso. 2. Sobrado, desván. **Hayloft,** henil, pajar.

loftily ['lɒftɪlɪ] [lof-ti-li], *adv.* 1. En alto. 2. Altivamente, pomposamente.

loftiness ['lɒftɪnɪs] [lof-ti-nes], *s.* 1. Altura, elevacion. 2. Sublimidad o elevación. 3. Altivez, soberbia, orgullo; majestad.

lofty ['lɒftɪ] [lof-ti], *s.* 1. Alto, elevado, levantado. 2. Sublime, grande, excelso. 3. Altivo, orgulloso, soberbio.

log [lɒg] [log], *s.* 1. Leño, tronco, trozo de árbol o madera sin figura particular. **A log of mahogany,** una toza de caoba. 2. *(Mar.)* Barquilla, cierto palito en figura de barca que sirve para obrar con la corredera y carretel. **Logboard,** *(Mar.)* tableta de bitácora. **Log-line,** *(Mar.)* corredera. **Log-book,** *(Mar.)* diario de navegación. **Log-reel,** *(Mar.)* carretel. **Log-cabin, log-hut,** cabaña hecha con maderos o troncos de árboles. **Log in,** acceder, entrar en un sistema *(Inform.).* **Log off, = Log out. Log on, = log in. Log out,** salir de un sistema *(Inform.).*

log, *Abreviatura de* **logarithm.**

loganberry ['ləʊgənbərɪ] [lou-gan-be-ri], *s. (Bot.)* Variedad de zarzamora.

logarithm ['lɒgərɪθəm] [lo-ga-ri-zem], *s.* Logaritmo.

logarithmic, logarithmical ['lɒgərɪθmɪk] [lo-ga-riz-mik], *a.* Logarítmico.

loggerhead ['lɒgəhed] [lo-ga-jed], *s.* 1. Zote, necio. 2. Cierta tortuga marina de gran tamaño. 3. Pegareborda de los Estados Unidos. **To fall o to go to loggerheads,** reñir sin armas, estar de cuernos con uno. **To be at loggerheads with somebody,** estar picado/enfadado con alguien.

loggerheaded ['lɒgəhedɪd] [lo-ga-je-did], *a.* Necio, tonto, zote.

logic ['lɒdʒɪk] [lo-yik], *s.* Lógica, la ciencia que enseña a discurrir con exactitud.

logical ['lɒdʒɪkəl] [lo-yi-kal], *a.* Lógico, perteneciente a la lógica.

logically ['lɒdʒɪkəlɪ] [lo-yi-ka-li], *adv.* Lógicamente.

logician [lɒˈdʒɪʃən] [lo-yi-shan], *s.* Lógico, el que profesa o enseña la lógica.

logistics [lɒˈdʒɪstɪkz] [lo-yis-tiks], *s. pl. (Mil.)* Logística, ramo del arte militar que trata de los movimientos y el abastecimiento de tropas y de la dirección general de una campaña.

logo ['ləʊgəʊ] [lou-gou], *s. m.* Logo, logotipo.

logogram ['lɒgəʊgræm] [lou-gou-gram], *s.* 1. Abreviatura u otro signo que indica una palabra, como *lb.* por libra, $ por peso o dólar. 2. Logogrifo, enigma en verso.

logograph ['lɒgəʊgræf] [lou-gou-graf], *s.* Palabra escrita.

logogriph ['lɒgəʊgrɪf] [lou-gou-grif], *s.* Logogrifo, enigma.

logomachy ['lɒgəʊmækɪ] [lou-gou-ma-ki], *s.* 1. Logomaquia, altercación sobre voces o palabras. 2. Juego que consiste en formar nuevos vocablos con las letras de una palabra dada.

logwood ['lɒgwʊd] [log-wud], *s.* Palo de Campeche o de tinte.

loin [lɔɪn] [loin], *s.* Ijada, ijar, la parte del cuerpo situada entre las costillas falsas y los huesos de las caderas. **Loin chop,** chuleta de lomo. **Loins,** Lomos.

loincloth ['lɔɪnklɒθ] [loin-kloz], *s. m.* Taparrabo.

loiter ['lɔɪtəʳ] [loi-taʳ], *vn.* Haraganear, perder el tiempo, tardar. -*va.* Malgastar el tiempo.

loiterer ['lɔɪtərəʳ] [loi-ta-raʳ], *s.* Haragán, el holgazán, perezoso o negligente.

loll [lɒl] [lol], *vn.* 1. Apoyarse, recostarse o tenderse con dejadez y flojedad en alguna cosa. 2. Colgar hacia fuera. -*va.* Sacar la lengua de la boca. **To loll about/around,** repantigarse. **To loll against,** recostarse en.

lollipop ['lɒlɪpɒp] [lo-li-pop], *s.* Chupete, pirulí, polo (iced).

lolly ['lɒlɪ] [lo-li], *a.* = Lollipop. Lana *(Fam.).*

loment ['lɒmənt] [lo-ment], *s. (Bot.)* Lomento.

London ['lʌndən] [lan-don], *n. pr.* Londres.

Londoner ['lʌndənəʳ] [lan-do-naʳ], *s.* Londinense, el natural o habitante de Londres.

londonism ['lʌndənɪzəm] [lan-do-ni-sem], *s.* Londonismo; costumbre, locución o giro propios de los habitantes de Londres.

lone [ləʊn] [loun], *a.* 1. Solitario, solo, aislado. 2. Soltero o soltera. 3. *(Ant.)* No frecuentado.

loneliness ['ləʊnlɪnɪs] [loun-li-nes], *s.* Soledad.

lonely ['ləʊnlɪ] [loun-li], *a.* 1. Solitario; solo (solitary); abandonado. 2. Amante de la soledad. Aislado, solitario (isolated).

loneness ['ləʊnnɪs] [loun-nes], *s.* Soledad, retiro y poca afición a estar en compañía.

loner ['ləʊnəʳ] [lou-naʳ], *s.* Solitario.

lonesome ['ləʊn] [loun], *a.* Solitario, desierto.

lonesomely ['ləʊnsəmlɪ] [loun-sam-li], *adv.* Solitariamente.

lonesomeness ['ləʊnsəmnɪs] [loun-sam-nes], *s.* Estado o calidad del que está solo.

long [lɒŋ] [long], *a.* 1. Largo, extenso en espacio o en duración; de largo, de longitud. **Longer,** más largo. **Longest,** el más largo. **Longest liver,** sobreviviente. **A long way about,** un gran rodeo. **A piece of timber seventy feet long,** un madero de setenta pies de largo. **Two inches long,** dos pulgadas de largo o de longitud. **Long measure,** medida de longitud. 2. Dilatorio, tardo, lento; enfadoso, afectadamente, circunspecto. 3. Extenso, prolongado; continuo. 4. *(Com.)* Que retiene acciones o valores esperando un alza en los precios. -*adv.* 1. A una gran distancia; mucho. **Long after,** mucho después. **Long ago, long since,** hace tiempo. **Ere long,** antes de mucho. **As long as I live,** mientras viva. **At long last,** por fin. **So long as,** mientras que, en tanto que. **All my life long,** toda mi vida. **How long is it since?,** ¿cuánto hace o cuánto tiempo hace? **Not long before,** poco antes o poco tiempo antes. **Longer,** más tiempo. 2. En consecuencia de, debido a. -*s.* Longa, una antigua nota de música. **The long and the short,** lo largo y lo corto, es decir, el todo; la sustancia, el resumen. **She left before long,** se marchó muy pronto. **Long clothes,** las primeras ropas de una criatura, vestido largo que se extiende más allá de los pies. **Long-**

drawn, prolongado; fastidioso. **Long-headed,** astuto, sagaz, prudente. **Long staple,** de fibra larga (algodón).

long, *vn.* 1. Desear con vehemencia alguna cosa, anhelar, ansiar, suspirar por algo. **To long for something,** desear, anhelar algo. **To long for somebody,** añorar a alguien. **I long to see him,** tengo mucho deseo de verlo. 2. Antojarse; *(fam.)* pirrarse.

longanimity [ˌlɒŋəˈnɪmɪtɪ] [lon-ga-ni-mi-ti], *s.* Longanimidad, constancia de ánimo en las adversidades.

long-awaited [ˈlɒŋəˈweɪtɪd] [long-a-uei-tid], *a.* Largamente añorado o esperado.

long-boat [ˈlɒŋbəʊt] [long-bout], *s. (Mar.)* Lancha, falúa o faluca.

long-distance [ˈlɒŋˈdɪstəns] [long-dis-tans], *a.* De larga distancia. **Long-distance call,** llamada telefónica de larga distancia.

long-drawn-out [ˈlɒŋdrɔːnˈaʊt] [long-dron-aut], *a.* Interminable, que no tiene fin.

longe [ˈlɒŋ] [long], *s.* 1. Estocada, golpe. 2. Terreno en que se trabajan y adiestran los caballos para las carreras.

longevity [lɒnˈdʒevɪtɪ] [lon-ye-vi-ti], *s.* Longevidad, ancianidad, duración larga de la vida.

long-haired [ˈlɒŋˈheəd] [long-jead], *a.* De pelo largo.

longhand [ˈlɒŋhænd] [long-jand], *s.* La escritura ordinaria, sin abreviación de las palabras, a diferencia de la estenografía o taquigrafía.

long-haul [ˈlɒŋhɔːl] [long-jol], *a.* De larga distancia.

longhorn [ˈlɒŋhɔːn] [long-jorn], *s.* Animal de cuernos largos.

longicorn [ˈlɒŋɪkɔːn] [lon-gui-korn], *a.* y *s.* Longicornio, de largas antenas.

longimetry [ˈlɒŋɪmɪtrɪ] [lon-gui-mi-tri], *s.* Longimetría, arte de medir las distancias.

longing [ˈlɒŋɪŋ] [lon-guin], *s.* Antojo, deseo vehemente, anhelo, ansia. **A woman's longing,** un capricho de mujer.

longingly [ˈlɒŋɪŋlɪ] [lon-guin-li], *adv.* Vehementemente; impacientemente.

longish [ˈlɒŋɪʃ] [lon-guish], *a.* Algo largo, un poco largo.

longitude [ˈlɒŋgɪtjuːd] [lon-gui-tiud], *s.* 1. Longitud. 2. *(Geog.)* Longitud, la distancia que hay de un lugar cualquiera del globo al primer meridiano.

longitudinal [ˌlɒŋgɪˈtjuːdɪnl] [lon-gui-tiu-di-nal], *a.* Longitudinal, perteneciente a la longitud o hecho con arreglo a ella.

long-lasting [ˈlɒŋˈlɑːstɪŋ] [long-las-tin], *a.* 1. Largo, duradero (material, memory). 2. Duro (tough).

long-legged [ˈlɒŋˈlegɪd] [lon-le-guid], **long-shanked** [ˈlɒŋˈʃæŋkt] [long-shankt], *a.* Zanquilargo.

long-life [ˈlɒŋˈlaɪf] [long-laif], *a.* De larga duración.

long-lived [ˈlɒŋˈlɪvd] [long-livd], *a.* Longevo, de larga vida; de mucha vida.

longly [ˈlɒŋlɪ] [long-li], *adv.* 1. Por mucho tiempo. 2. *(Des.)* Ansiosamente, acuciantemente.

longness [ˈlɒŋnɪs] [long-nes], *s.* Largura.

long-pepper [ˈlɒŋˈpepəʳ] [long-pe-paʳ], *s.* Pimienta larga.

long-playing [ˈlɒŋˈpleɪɪŋ] [long-plein], *a.* De larga duración (record).

long-range [ˈlɒŋˈreɪdʒ] [long-reinch], *a.* De largo alcance (gun): de larga distancia (aircraft).

long-running [ˈlɒŋˈrʌnɪŋ] [long-ra-nin], *a.* Largo, duradero, taquillero, que dura mucho tiempo en cartelera (play, movies).

longshoreman [ˈlɒŋˈʃɔːmən] [long-shor-man], *s.* 1. Estivador, trabajador de muelle. 2. El hombre que vive a orillas del mar y subsiste de la pesca, o como remero, etc.

long-sighted [ˈlɒŋˈsaɪtɪd] [long-sai-tid], *a.* 1. Que ve a gran distancia; de aquí, sagaz, previsor, precavido. 2. Présbite, que ve mejor de lejos que de cerca.

long-sleeved [ˈlɒŋˈsliːvd] [long-slivd], *a.* De manga larga (clothes).

longspun [ˈlɒŋˈspʌn] [long-span], *a.* Prolijo, dilatado. *(Fam.)* Tirado por fuerza, o por los cabellos.

long-standing [ˈlɒŋˈstændɪŋ] [long-stan-din], *a.* De larga duración.

long-suffering [ˈlɒŋˈsʌfərɪŋ] [long-sa-fe-rin], *a.* Paciente, sufrido.

long-term [ˈlɒŋˈtɜːm] [long-term], *a.* De largo plazo, de larga duración.

longways [ˈlɒŋweɪz] [long-ueis], *adv. (Fam.)* V. LENGTHWISE.

long-winded [ˈlɒŋˈwɪndɪd] [long-uin-did], *a.* Largo, pesado, prolijo (person). Interminable (speech).

loo [luː] [lu], *s.* Baño, retrete *(Fam.)*.

loo, lu, *s.* Juego de naipes, en el que puede participar un número cualquiera de jugadores, con tres o cinco naipes cada uno.

loo, *va.* Ganar todas las bazas en el juego de naipes; dar capote; dar bola.

loof [luːf] [luf], *s. (Mar.)* Lof, la parte circular de la proa desde las amuras hasta la roda.

look [lʊk] [luk], *va.* y *vn.* 1. Mirar, dirigir la vista hacia algún objeto o poner la vista en él. 2. Mirar, considerar, pensar, contemplar; esperar. 3. Mirar, poner cuidado, tener cuidado. 4. Mirar, dar, caer, estar situada una cosa frente de otra. **The front of the house looks on o toward the garden,** la fachada de la casa mira el jardín, o hacia el jardín. 5. Parecerse a alguno, darse un aire, parecer, tener apariencia o traza de. 6. Mirar, buscar. 7. Mirar, dar una mirada.

look about one, estar alerta, tener vigilancia.

look after, cuidar; tener cuidado; prestar atención; buscar, inquirir, investigar alguna cosa.

look ahead, mirar hacia delante, hacer proyectos para el futuro.

look around, echar un vistazo alrededor.

look at, mirar a; considerar; atender.

look away, apartar la mirada, mirar hacia otro lado.

look back, reflexionar.

look down on/upon, despreciar.

look down upon one with scorn, mirar a alguno de arriba abajo, con desprecio.

look for, esperar, buscar.

look forward for, esperar algo ansiosamente.

look into, examinar, considerar; tomar conocimiento de una cosa, inspeccionar atentamente. **To look nine ways,** ser bisojo, torcer la vista. **To look on,** considerar, concebir, pensar, imaginarse; mirar, ver; dar, caer; ser espectador indiferente; estimar. **These windows look on the river,** estas ventanas dan al río.

look out, buscar; cuidar de (take care); estar alerta; mirar por; descubrir alguna cosa a fuerza de investigaciones o encontrarla a fuerza de buscarla. **Look out!,** ¡cuidado!

look over, examinar, echar un vistazo.

look round, mirar, recorrer con la vista; volver la cabeza (turn).

look to, cuidar de, velar, guardar; observar, considerar, contemplar.

look through, registrar (search), examinar cuidadosamente: hojear (leaf through), mirar por. **Look to it,** esté Ud. con cuidado, esté Ud. sobre sí.

look up to, esperar o tener esperanza en la protección de alguno. **To look black,** tener ceño, estar ceñudo, tener mala cara por estar enfadado. **To look big,** entonarse. **To look ill,** tener malas trazas o tener mala cara por presentar la apariencia de enfermo. **To look like,** semejarse. **To look sharp,** (a) *(Fam.)* estar muy alerta, tener mucho cuidado. (b) Apresurarse, ser muy pronto y despierto. **To look well,** tener buenas trazas o buena cara por tener la apariencia de salud. **To look out after a fleet of ships,** *(Mar.)* vigilar una escuadra. **Look before you leap,** *(prov.)* antes que te cases, mira lo que haces. **They went away looking daggers,** *(Fam.)* se fueron echando chispas. **To have a look,** echar un vistazo. **It looks good on her,** le sienta bien. **You look tired,** pareces cansado (seem). **To look one's best,** arreglarse, acicalarse, ponerse guapo. **Look where you're going!,** ¡fíjate por donde vas! **He was not looking himself,** no parecía el mismo, parecía otro.

look, *s.* 1. Aspecto, semblante, cara, aire, ademán. 2. Mirada. **The look-out,** *(Mar.)* vigía. *-inter.* Mira, atiende; he aquí, ¡cuidado!

lookalike [ˈlʊkəlaɪk] [luk-a-laik], *s.* Parecido, similar.

looker [ˈlʊkəʳ] [lu-kaʳ], *s.* 1. Mirador, el que mira; mirón, el que está mirando alguna cosa. 2. Guapa *(Fam.).* **Looker-on,** espectador/a.

look-in [ˈlʊkɪn] [luk-in], *s.* **To get a look-in,** tener una oportunidad *(Fam.).*

looking [ˈlʊkɪŋ] [lu-kin], *s.* 1. Miramiento, el acto de mirar, o considerar alguna cosa; mirada. 2. Expectación, el anhelo con que se espera alguna cosa.

looking-glass [ˈlʊkɪŋglɑːs] [lu-kin-glas], *s.* Espejo. **Paper looking-glasses,** tocadores, espejitos de cartón.

lookout [ˈlʊkaʊt] [luk-aut], *s.* 1. Vigía, atenta vigilancia. 2. Mirador, garita, torrecilla de observación, atalaya; la persona que vigila, guardia. 3. Toda cosa que ha de ser bien cuidada y guardada. **To keep a lookout,** estar al acecho. **That's her lookout,** eso es asunto suyo.

look-up [ˈlʊkʌp] [luk-ap], *s.* Consulta.

loom [luːm] [lum], *s.* 1. Telar. **Stocking-loom,** telar de medias. 2. Guión del remo. **Loom-gale,** *(Mar.)* fugada bonancible.

loom, *vn.* 1. Asomar, ir apareciendo o alzándose gradualmente, surgir. **The car loomed (up) out of the mist,** el vehículo surgió de la niebla. 2. Lucir, relucir.

looming [ˈluːmɪŋ] [lu-min], *s.* Ilusión óptica que parece elevar y prolongar la imagen de un objeto cualquiera, particularmente a través del agua.

loon [luːn] [lun], *s.* 1. Bobo, necio, estúpido. 2. *(Orn.)* Somorgujo, ave acuática palmípeda.

loony [ˈluːnɪ] [lu-ni], *a.* Chiflado, ido, loco *(Fam.).* **Loony bin,** manicomio.

loop [luːp] [lup], *s.* 1. Anillo, gaza, lazo; ojal, presilla. 2. Curva, comba de cualquier clase. 3. *(Mec.)* Abrazadera, anilla.

loop, *va.* 1. Atar o asegurar con una presilla. 2. Hacer gazas, enlazar, formar curvas. *-vn.* Andar haciendo curvas, como ciertas larvas (orugas). **To loop the loop,** rizar el rizo *(Aer.).* **To loop round,** dar vuelta a.

looped [ˈluːpt] [lupt], *a.* Ojalado, lleno de ojales.

loophole [ˈluːphəʊl] [lup-joul], *s.* 1. Abertura, mirador, tronera; una especie de cornisa ancha. 2. Escapatoria, refugio, excusa. 3. *(Mar.)* Tronera. **Every law has a loophole,** hecha la ley hecha la trampa.

loopholed [ˈluːphəʊld] [lup-jould], *a.* Lo que tiene muchos agujeros o cavidades.

loop-lace [ˈluːpleɪs] [lup-leis], *s.* Los adornos puestos alrededor de los ojales.

loop-maker [ˈluːpˌmeɪkəʳ] [lup-mei-kaʳ], *s.* Ojaladero, presillero.

loopy [ˈluːpɪ] [lu-pi], *a.* Ido, chiflado *(Fam.).*

loose [luːs] [lus], *va.* 1. Desatar, desprender y desenlazar una cosa de otra, desliar. 2. Desapretar, alojar. 3. Aliviar, dar alivio o descanso. 4. Soltar al que estaba preso. 5. Libertar de alguna obligación o riesgo; sacar de algún mal paso, desenredar; desocupar. **To loose one's hold,** abandonar, soltar lo que se había tomado.

loose, *a.* 1. Suelto, desatado, desconectado. 2. Flojo (clothing), movible, lo que no está bien apretado. 3. Vago, indeterminado, falto de precisión. 4. Suelto de vientre. 5. Libre, movible. 6. Suelto, puesto en libertad. 7. Disoluto. 8. Desenredado. 9. Descuidado, negligente. **To grow loose,** desbandarse. **To break loose,** ponerse en libertad; recobrar la libertad venciendo obstáculos; desencadenarse, desatarse. **To get loose from one,** desembarazarse de alguno. **To hang loose,** colgar, flotar. **To let loose,** liberar, poner en libertad. *-s.* Libertad; soltura. **A loose gown,** un vestido flotante. **Loose morals,** moral relajada. **Loose reasoning,** raciocinio vago. **A loose liver,** un libertino. **To be loose in the bowels,** andar suelto de vientre. **To give loose to,** dar rienda suelta. **To tie up loose ends,** no dejar ningún cabo suelto *(Fig.).* **To turn/let loose,** liberar, poner en libertad. **Loose off,** disparar, soltar.

loose-fitting [ˈluːsˈfɪtɪŋ] [lus-fi-tin], *a.* Suelto.

loose-leaf [ˈluːsˈliːf] [lus-lif], *a.* De hojas sueltas o insertables.

loosely [ˈluːslɪ] [lus-li], *adv.* Sueltamente, con desenvoltura, negligentemente.

loosen [ˈluːsn] [lu-sen], *vn.* Desunirse, desatarse, separarse. *-va.* 1. Aflojar, laxar, soltar, desliar. **To loosen the sails,** *(Mar.)* largar o descargar las velas. 2. Librar, libertar, desatar. 3. Soltar el vientre. **Loosen up,** desentumecerse, relajarse, soltarse.

looseness [ˈluːsnɪs] [lus-nes], *s.* 1. Aflojamiento, flojedad. 2. Relajación de costumbres, libertad, licencia, desgarro. 3. Soltura. 4. Flujo de vientre, diarrea, cursos.

loosening [ˈluːsnɪŋ] [lus-nin], *a.* Laxante.

loot [luːt] [lut], *va.* Saquear, pillar; llevarse como botín. *-s.* Botín, pillaje de un ejército vencedor.

looter [ˈluːtəʳ] [lu-taʳ], *s.* Saqueador.

looting [ˈluːtɪŋ] [lu-tin], *s.* Saqueo, pillaje.

lop [lɒp] [lop], *va.* Desmochar, podar. **To lop vines,** podar viñas.

lop, *s.* 1. La rama podada. 2. Pulga.

lope [ˈləʊp] [loup], *vi.* **To lope along,** andar con paso largo.

lopper [ˈləʊpəʳ] [lou-paʳ], *s.* Podador de árboles.

loppered [ˈləʊpəd] [lou-ped], *a.* Coagulado.

loppings [ˈləʊpɪŋz] [lou-pins], *s. pl.* Ramas cortadas.

lopsided [lɒpˈsaɪdɪd] [lop-sai-did], *a.* 1. Que se inclina demasiado a un lado; más pesado de un lado que de otro. 2. De aquí, maniático, lleno de temas o rarezas.

loquacious [ləˈkweɪʃəs] [lo-kuei-shos], *a.* Locuaz, charlatán, parlador o hablador.

loquaciousness [ləˈkweɪʃəsnɪs] [lo-kuei-shos-nes], **loquacity** [ləˈkwæsɪtɪ] [lo-kua-si-ti], *s.* Locuacidad, habladuría, flujo de habla, charla, parla.

loran [ˈlɒrən] [lo-ran], *s.* Loran. (Contracción de Long Range Navigation, sistema electrónico de navegación.)

lord [lɔːd] [lord], *s.* 1. Señor, monarca. 2. Dios, el Ser Supremo; también, Nuestro Señor Jesucristo. 3. Señor, amo, dueño. 4. Marido. 5. Lord, nombre genérico que se da a los pares de Inglaterra. 6. Barón, para distinguir a los que gozan este título en Inglaterra, de los duques, marqueses, condes o vizcondes. 7. Título que se añade a la denominación de algunos empleos de palacio que regularmente están servidos por pares. **My Lord,** Ilustrísima (bishop); señor (noble, judge). **Lord Chamberlain,** camarero mayor. **Lord High Steward,** mayordomo mayor. También se añade este título a las denominaciones de otros empleos, como **Lord Chief Justice,** el Presidente del tribunal supremo de Inglaterra; **Lord Mayor,** el Alcalde o Corregidor de Londres. **Lord's day,** domingo, el día del Señor. **Lord's Supper,** la Ultima Cena, el Sacramento de la Eucaristía. **Lord's table,** altar de la sagrada comunión; la misma comunión, Eucaristía. **Good Lord!** ¡Dios mío!

lord, *vn.* Señorear, dominar, mandar despóticamente. *-va.* Investir a uno con la dignidad y privilegios de par de Inglaterra.

lording [ˈlɔːdɪŋ] [lor-din], *s.* Hidalguillo, hidalgo de gotera, señor de poco más o menos.

lord-like [ˈlɔːdlaɪk] [lord-laik], *a.* 1. Como un lord o semejante a un lord. 2. Altivo, orgulloso, insolente.

lordliness [ˈlɔːdlɪnɪs] [lord-li-nes], *s.* 1. Dignidad, señorío. 2. Altivez, orgullo.

lordling [ˈlɔːdlɪŋ] [lord-lin], *s.* Un lord pequeño (término de desprecio).

lordly [ˈlɔːdlɪ] [lord-li], *a.* 1. Cosa perteneciente a un lord; señorial. 2. Altivo, orgulloso, imperioso. *-adv.* Imperiosamente, altivamente.

lordship [ˈlɔːdʃɪp] [lord-ship], *s.* 1. Señorío, dominio, poder. 2. Señoría.

lore [lɔːʳ] [loʳ], *s.* 1. Erudición, saber, ciencia; la erudición o cultura propia de un pueblo o de un siglo. 2. *(Ant.)* Lección, doctrina, enseñanza, instrucción.

loricate [ˈlɒrɪkeɪt] [lo-ri-keit], *va.* Planchear, cubrir alguna cosa con hojas o planchas protectoras.

loricate, *a.* Plancheado, cubierto con hojas o planchas.

lorication [ˌləɾɪˈkeɪʃən] [lo-ri-kei-shon], *s.* Superficie cubierta con alguna cosa.

loriot [ˈlɔːɾɪət] [lo-riot], *s.* (*Orn.*) Oropéndola de Europa.

loris [ˈlɒɾɪs] [lo-ris] *s.* (*Zool.*) Loris, animal pequeño y arbóreo, de la familia de los lemúridos.

lorn [ˈlɔːn] [lorn], *a.* Dejado, abandonado, sin parentesco ni amigos: (*ant.*) perdido.

lorry [ˈlɒɾɪ] [lo-ri], *s.* Camión. **Lorry load,** carga.

lory [ˈlɒɾɪ] [lo-ri], *s.* Loro, papagayo de color escarlata.

losable, loseable [ˈlɒsəbl] [lo-sa-bol], *a.* Que se puede perder.

lose [luːz] [lus], *va.* 1. Perder. 2. Perder, no conseguir lo que se deseaba. 3. Perder, desperdiciar, disipar, malgastar. 4. Exponer a la pérdida de. 5. Entregar a la ignominia o a la ruina. 6. Hacer perder. -*vn.* 1. Perderse, errar el camino que se llevaba o no encontrarle. 2. Declinar, decaer. **To lose ground,** perder terreno. **To lose one's way,** perderse, no acertar con el camino que se quiere llevar. **To lose out,** salir perdiendo. **To lose sight of,** perder de vista. **That stroke lost him many friends,** esa acción le hizo perder muchos amigos. **This watch loses 2 minutes,** este reloj está 2 minutos atrasado. **To lose to somebody,** perder contra alguien.

loser [ˈluːzəʳ] [lu-saʳ], *s.* Perdedor, el que pierde. **To be a born loser,** ser un perdedor nato. **To come off the loser,** salir perdiendo. **You shall be no loser by it,** nada perderá Ud. en ello.

losing [ˈluːzɪŋ] [lu-sin], *s.* Pérdida, disminución. **To fight a losing battle,** luchar por una causa perdida.

loss [lɒs] [los], *s.* 1. Pérdida, daño, menoscabo; privación, destrucción; mal éxito. 2. Desperdicio, disipación, mal uso de algo. **To be at a loss,** desatinar, perder el rastro, la huella o el rumbo; no atinar, no acertar; no saber qué hacer. **To cut one's losses,** cortar por lo sano. **She's a great loss,** es un desastre. **This ship is a total loss,** este buque es una pérdida total. **To make a loss on,** perder dinero con (products). **Loss leader,** producto o artículo de lanzamiento.

loss-making [lɒsˌmeɪkɪŋ] [los-mei-kin], deficitario, que tiene déficit (enterprise).

lost [lɒst] [lost], *pp.* y *pret.* de TO LOSE. 1. Perdido. 2. Perdido, no obtenido; malgastado, desperdiciado. 3. Desorientado, perplejo, confuso, embarazado; incapaz de hallar el buen camino. 4. Arruinado, perdido; sin remedio; perdido en sentido espiritual. **Like to be lost,** en peligro de perderse. (*Fam.*) **He lost his heart to her,** él se enamoró de ella, le entregó su corazón. **This remark was not lost upon Mr. N.,** el Sr. N. no dejó de advertir esta observación. **To be lost,** perderse. **Lost property office,** oficina de objetos perdidos. **Get lost!** ¡Vete al cuerno!, ¡Piérdete! **To give up for lost,** dar por perdido. **To make up for lost time,** recuperar el tiempo perdido.

lot [lɒt] [lot], *s.* 1. Suerte, el estado o modo de vivir que a cada uno le toca. 2. Lote, suerte, fortuna, el dado u otra cosa que se usa para determinar si uno ha de perder o ganar. **To cast/draw lots,** echar suertes. 3. Cuota, la cantidad que a alguno le toca de una contribución, repartimiento, gasto, etc.; partida, parte, porción. 4. Solar, extensión de terreno medido y destinado a la venta o a edificar en él. 5. (*Fam.*) Gran cantidad; mucho. **A lot of money,** gran cantidad de dinero. **Lots of trouble,** (*Fam.*) muchas molestias, angustias o penas. **The lot,** todo (everything).

lot, *va.* Asignar, destinar, repartir, distribuir en cuotas.

loth [lɒθ] [loz], *a.* *V.* LOATH.

lothario [ˈlɒtərɪə] [lo-za-rio], *s.* Libertino, tuno.

lotion [ˈləʊʃən] [lou-shon], *s.* Loción, ablución.

lotos o lotus [ˈləʊtəs] [lou-tos], *s.* 1. (*Bot.*) Loto, planta acuática. 2. Loto, almez. 3. Azufaifo.

lottery [ˈlɒtəɾɪ] [lo-te-ri], *s.* Lotería, rifa.

lotto [ˈlɒtəʊ] [lo-tou], *s.* Lotería, juego casero.

loud [laʊd] [laud], *a.* 1. Ruidoso, alto, fuerte (sound). **To speak loud,** hablar alto. 2. Clamoroso, turbulento, estrepitoso, alborotado (behavior, party). 3. (*Fam.*) Urgente. 4. (*Fam.*) Ostentoso sin gusto ni esmero; llamativo (color, clothes). **A loud laugh,** una risa estrepitosa. **A**

loud voice, una voz fuerte, alta. -*adv.* Ruidosamente, en alta voz, con ruido.

loudly [ˈlaʊdlɪ] [laud-li], *adv.* Ruidosamente, alborotadamente; con mucho ruido. Fuerte, en voz alta.

loudhailer [ˈlaʊdheɪləʳ] [laud-jei-laʳ], *s.* Bocina, megáfono.

loudmouth [ˈlaʊdmaʊθ] [laud-mauz], *s.* Bocazas (*Fam.*).

loudness [ˈlaʊdnɪs] [laud-nes], *s.* Ruido, mucho volumen de sonido, retumbo; alboroto, turbulencia.

loudspeaker [ˈlaʊdˈspiːkəʳ] [laud-spi-kaʳ], *s.* Altoparlante, altavoz.

lough [laʊ] [lau], *s.* Lago, laguna.

lounge [ˈlaʊdʒ] [launch], *vn.* 1. Haraganear, holgazanear, corretear, callejear; andar acá y acullá sin objeto fijo. 2. Repantigarse; ponerse uno a sus anchas. 3. Sala de estar, salón. **Lounge about,** haraganear, holgazanear. **Lounge bar,** salón-bar. *V.* LOLL.

lounge, *s.* 1. Haraganería, holgazanería; acción de repantigarse o tenderse. 2. Lugar que se escoge para descansar. 3. Canapé, sofá.

lounger [ˈlaʊdʒəʳ] [launchaʳ], *s.* Haragán, holgazán, ocioso.

lounging room [ˈlaʊdʒɪŋˌrom] [laun-chin-rum], *s.* Sala de espera, sala de descanso y esparcimiento.

lourdan, *s.* *V.* LURDAN.

louse [laʊs] [laus], *s.* *pl.* LICE [lais]. 1. Piojo. **Crab-louse,** ladilla. **Plant-louse,** pulgón, áfido. 2. Canalla, sinvergüenza (person). **Louse up,** echar a perder.

lousewort [ˈlaʊswɔːt] [laus-uort], *s.* (*Bot.*) Hierba piojera.

lousily [ˈlaʊzɪlɪ] [lau-si-li], *adv.* Con piojería, de un modo vil y bajo, mezquinamente.

lousiness [ˈlaʊzɪnɪs] [lau-si-nes], *s.* Piojería. (*Mex.*) Zicatería.

lousy [ˈlaʊzɪ] [lau-si], *a.* 1. Piojoso, piojento. 2. Piojoso, miserable, mezquino, apocado, soez, vil, bajo. 3. Desgraciado. **To have a lousy time,** pasarlo fatal. (*Mex.*) Zicatero.

lout [ˈlaʊt] [laut], *s.* Patán, rústico, zafio.

lout, *vn.* 1. Tardar, perder el tiempo, callejear. 2. (*Ant.*) Doblarse, encorvarse, someterse, hacer reverencia.

loutish [ˈlaʊtɪʃ] [lau-tish], *a.* Rudo, rústico, tosco, grosero.

louver [ˈluːvəʳ] [lu-vaʳ], *s.* Abertura en el cielo de un edificio, lumbrera, tronera, provista de tejadillos inclinados para impedir que entre la lluvia. **Louver-boards,** tejadillos.

lovable [ˈlʌvəbl] [la-va-bol], *a.* Amable, agradable, adorable.

love [lʌv] [lav], *va.* 1. Amar, tener gusto de. 2. Amar, querer, tener cariño (person). 3. Gustar, tener inclinación a alguna cosa que agrada. -*vn.* Deleitarse, tener gusto en. **To love one another,** amarse unos a otros. **To love to see,** gustar de ver. **To send one's love to somebody,** dar recuerdos a alguien.

love, *s.* 1. Amor. 2. Amor, el objeto amado. 3. Amor, expresión de cariño, inclinación o afecto a alguna persona o cosa; amistad. 5. Galanteo. **To make love,** galantear, cortejar. 6. Afición, pasión. **To be in love with one,** estar enamorado de alguno. **To fall in love,** enamorarse. **Self-love,** amor propio. **(Not) for love or money,** ni por amor ni por dinero. **Labor of love,** lo que se hace por amor a otro, sin esperanza de recompensa. **To marry for love,** casarse por amor. **To be out of love with a thing,** tener despego, repugnancia por una cosa. **Love thirty,** cero a treinta (tennis). **She loves going to the cinema,** le encanta ir al cine. **Love affair,** amorío.

lovebird [ˈlʌvbɜːd] [lav-berd], *s.* Periquito.

love-favor [ˈlʌvˌfeɪvəʳ] [lav-fei-vaʳ], *s.* Favor, expresión de agrado hecha por una dama.

love-feast [ˈlʌvfiːst] [lav-fist], *s.* Agapas, comidas de los primeros cristianos en las iglesias.

love-fit [ˈlʌvfɪt] [lav-fit], *s.* Transporte o arrebato de amor.

love-knot [ˈlʌvnɒt] [lav-not], *s.* Nudo o lazo de amor.

love-lass [ˈlʌvlæs] [lav-las], *f.* Cortejo, amada.

loveless [ˈlʌvlɪs] [lav-les], *a.* Desamorado, falto de amor, sin cariño, insensible, hurón.

love-letter [ˈlʌvˌletəʳ] [lav-le-taʳ], *s.* Esquela, billete o carta amorosa.

love-lies-bleeding [ˈlʌvlaɪzˌbriːdɪŋ] [lav-lais-bli-din], *s.* (*Bot.*) Una especie de amaranto.

loveliness [ˈlʌvlɪnɪs] [lav-li-nes], *s.* Amabilidad, agrado; belleza.

love-lock [ˈlʌvlɒk] [lav-lok], *s*. Rizo largo con lazo de cinta en su extremo que se usaba en el siglo XVII.

lovelorn [ˈlʌvlɔːn] [lav-lorn], *a*. Abandonado o desamparado por su amante.

lovely [ˈlʌvlɪ] [lav-li], *a*. 1. Amable, agradable, cariñoso. 2. *(Fam.)* Atractivo, precioso, bello, hermoso (beautiful). 3. *(Fam.)* Ameno, deleitoso. **A lovely dinner,** una cena deliciosa. *-adv*. Hermosamente, con agrado, con cariño, con alegría.

lovemaking [ˈlʌˌmeɪkɪŋ] [lav-mei-kin], *s*. 1. Enamoramiento, galanteo. 2. Relaciones sexuales.

love-potion [ˈlʌvpɒʃən] [lav-po-shon], *s*. Filtro.

lover [ˈlʌvəʳ] [lo-vaʳ], *s*. 1. Amante, galán, cortejo. 2. Amante, el que tiene afición a alguna cosa; amigo. **Lover of,** aficionado de (hobby, drink).

love-secret [ˈlʌvsiːkrɪt] [lav-si-krit], *s*. Secreto entre amantes.

love-shaft [ˈlʌvʃɑːft] [lav-shaft], *s*. Flecha de Cupido.

love-sick [ˈlʌvsɪk] [lav-sik], *a*. Enamorado, enamoricado, herido de amor.

lovesome [ˈlʌvsəm] [lav-sam], *a*. Amable.

love-song [ˈlʌvsɒŋ] [lav-song], *s*. Canción amorosa.

love-suit [ˈlʌvsuːt] [lav-sut], *s*. Cortejo, galanteo, enamoramiento, trato amoroso.

love-tale [ˈlʌvteɪl] [lav-teil], *s*. Cuentos de amor o de enamorados; requiebros.

love-thought [ˈlʌvθɔːt] [lav-zot], *s*. Pensamiento amoroso.

love-token [ˈlʌvˌtəʊkən] [lav-tou-ken], *s*. Regalo en señal de amor.

love-tricks [ˈlʌvtrɪks] [lav-triks], *s. pl*. Tretas de amantes o enamorados.

loving [ˈlʌvɪŋ] [la-vin], *pa*. 1. Amante. 2. Afectuoso, amoroso, cariñoso, aficionado. 3. Benigno, apacible, tierno.

loving-kindness [ˈlʌvɪŋˌkɑɪnɪs] [la-vin-kain-nes], *s*. Cariño, favor; misericordia.

lovingly [ˈlʌvɪŋlɪ] [la-vin-li], *adv*. Afectuosamente, amorosamente.

lovingness [ˈlʌvɪŋnɪs] [la-vin-nes], *s*. Afección, cariño, afecto, terneza, afabilidad.

low [ləʊ] [lau], *a*. 1. Bajo, pequeño, reducido (income, price). 2. Hondo, poco elevado. **Low-water,** *(Mar.)* bajamar, marea menguante o vaciante. 3. Bajo, lo que no mete ruido. 4. Abatido, débil, desanimado, amilanado. 5. Bajo, menospreciable, vil, ruin. 6. Bajo, lo que no es sublime ni elevado, humilde *(rank)*. 7. Pobre, falto de bienes. 8. Último, hablando de tiempo. 9. Deshonroso. 10. Reverente, sumiso. **Low latitude,** latitud cercana a la línea. **In a low tone,** en tono bajo. **The patient is very low,** el enfermo está muy débil. **A low fever,** una calentura lenta. **You seem in low spirits,** parece que está Ud. abatido. **A low trick,** una mala partida. **Low expressions,** expresiones vulgares, bajas. **Low-lived,** de modales groseros, innoble. **Low-necked,** escotado; se dice de los vestidos de mujer. **On low ground,** a nivel del mar. **Low pressure,** baja presión. **In low gear,** en primera *(Aut.)*. **Low season,** temporada baja. **low tide,** marea baja. *-adv*. 1. Abajo, cerca del suelo, en la parte inferior. 2. Barato, a precio bajo. 3. Bajamente; vilmente; sumisamente. 4. En voz baja; también en tono profundo.

low, *vn*. Mugir, dar mugidos al toro, la vaca o el buey. *-va*. *(Des.)* Bajar, poner una cosa más baja de lo que estaba.

low, *s*. *(Prov.)* Llama, fuego.

low beams [ˈləʊbiːms] [lau-bims], *s. pl*. Luces de cruce.

lowbrow [ˈləʊbrəʊ] [lau-brau], *a*. Poco culto.

low-cost [ˈləʊˈkɒst] [lau-kost], *a*. Barato, económico.

lower [ˈləʊəʳ] [lauaʳ], *va*. 1. Abajar, humillar, abatir. 2. Bajar, poner en lugar inferior lo que estaba en alto. 3. Bajar, minorar, disminuir. **To lower the sails,** *(Mar.)* arriar las velas. **To lower away gradually,** *(Mar.)* arriar poco a poco. *-vn*. Bajar, minorarse, disminuirse alguna cosa.

lower, *vn*. 1. Encapotarse o encubrirse el cielo. 2. Mirar con ceño, poner mala cara, fruncir el ceño.

lower, *vn*. *a*. Comp. de **Low,** más bajo. **Lower berth,** cama o litera baja (en un tren, etc.). **Lower case,** 1. Caja baja, la que contiene las letras minúsculas. 2. Letras minúsculas.

lower-case [ˈləʊəleɪs] [laua-keis], *a*. Diminuto, minúsculo.

lowering [ˈləʊərɪŋ] [laua-rin], *a*. Sombrío, nebuloso; amenazador.

lowermost [ˈləʊəˈməʊst] [laua-moust], o **lowest** [ˈləʊ] [lau], *a*. El más bajo, bajísimo, ínfimo.

low-fat [ˈləʊˈfæt] [lau-fat], *a*. **Low-fat milk,** leche desnatada. **Low-fat food,** alimento bajo en calorías.

low-grade [ˈləʊˌgreɪd] [lau-greid], *a*. De baja calidad.

low-heeled [ˈləʊˈhiːld] [lau-jild], *a*. de tacón bajo (shoes).

lowing [ˈləʊɪŋ] [lauin], *s*. Mugido, bramido.

lowland [ˈləʊlənd] [lau-land], *s*. Tierra baja. **The Lowlands,** las tierras bajas en el sur y el oeste de Escocia.

lowlander [ˈləʊləndəʳ] [lau-lan-daʳ], *s*. Habitante de la parte baja de un país, particularmente de las tierras bajas de Escocia.

low-level [ˈləʊˈlevl] [lau-le-vel], *a*. De bajo nivel.

lowlily [ˈləʊlɪlɪ] [lau-li-li], *adv*. Bajamente; vilmente.

lowliness [ˈləʊlɪnɪs] [lau-li-nes], *s*. 1. Humildad. 2. Bajeza, vileza, ruindad.

lowly [ˈləʊlɪ] [lau-li], *a*. 1. Humilde, sumiso. 2. Vil, bajo, ruin, despreciable. 3. Bajo, humilde, rastrero, hablando del estilo o de los modales. *-adv*. Humildemente, modestamente; vilmente.

lown [ˈləʊn] [laun], *s*. Pícaro, bobo, el que es tonto o necio.

low-necked [ˈləʊˈnekt] [lau-nekt], *a*. Escotado.

lowness [ˈləʊnɪs] [lau-nes], *s*. 1. Pequeñez. 2. Bajeza de condición o de carácter. 3. Bajeza de ánimo, apocamiento o poquedad de ánimo, abatimiento. 4. Humildad, sencillez en el estilo o pensamiento. 5. Sumisión. **Lowness of spirits,** abatimiento o caimiento de ánimo; tristeza. 6. Disminución de precio o de valor. 7. Gravedad del sonido o tono; suavidad, debilidad del sonido.

low-spirited [ˈləʊˈspɪrɪtɪd] [lau-spi-ri-tid], *a*. Abatido, amilanado, desanimado, acobardado, descorazonado.

lox [ˈlɒks] [loks], *s*. Oxígeno líquido.

loxodrome [ˈlɒksədrʊm] [lok-so-drom], *s*. Línea loxodrómica.

loxodromic [ˈlɒksədrʊm] [lok-so-dro-mik], *a*. Loxodrómico, que se refiere a la loxodromía. **Loxodromic line,** línea loxodrómica, curva que forma un mismo ángulo en su intersección con todos los meridianos y sirve para navegar con rumbo constante.

loyal [ˈlɔɪəl] [loial], *a*. Leal, constante, fiel.

loyalist [ˈlɔɪəlɪst] [loia-list], *s*. Realista, partidario del rey.

loyally [ˈlɔɪəlɪ] [loia-li], *adv*. Lealmente.

loyalty [ˈlɔɪəltɪ] [loial-ti], *s*. Lealtad.

lozenge [ˈlɒzɪndʒ] [lo-sinch], *s*. 1. *(Geom.)* Rombo. 2. Pastilla. 3. *(Her.)* Losanje, lisonja, la figura de rombo.

lozenged [ˈlɒzɪndʒɪd] [lo-sin-yid], *a*. Que tiene forma de losanje o rombo.

lozengy [ˈlɒzɪndʒɪ] [lo-sin-yi], *a*. Lisonjado, el escudo blasonado en forma de losanjes.

LP *Abreviatura de* **Long Playing record** *(Mús.)*.

LSD *Abreviatura de* **Lysergic Acid Diethylamide,** LSD.

lu, *s*. V. LOO.

lubber [ˈlʌbəʳ] [lu-baʳ], *s*. Tomajón, haragán, persona gorda y perezosa, un bobo; en especial, marinero de agua dulce; joven sin experiencia.

lubberly [ˈlʌbəlɪ] [lu-bar-li], *a*. Poltrón, perezoso, haragán, holgazán. *-adv*. Toscamente, zafiamente.

lube [ˈljuːb] [liub], *s*. *(Mec.)* Aceite lubricante.

lubricant [ˈluːbrɪkənt] [lu-bri-kant], *s*. Lubricante, como aceite, grasa, etc., para la maquinaria.

lubricate [ˈluːbrɪkeɪt] [lu-bri-keit], *va*. Hacer lúbrica o resbaladiza alguna cosa, lubricar o lubrificar; untar con alguna materia crasa.

lubricating [ˈluːbrɪkeɪtɪŋ] [lu-bri-kei-tin], *a*. Lubricante.

lubrication [ˈluːbrɪkeɪʃən] [lu-bri-kei-shon], *s*. Lubricación.

lubricator [ˈluːbrɪkeɪtəʳ] [lu-bri-kei-taʳ], *s*. Lubricador.

lubricity [ˈluːbrɪsɪtɪ] [lu-bri-si-ti], *s*. 1. Lubricidad, la lisura de alguna superficie. 2. Inconstancia, incertidumbre, ligereza, instabilidad. 3. Lubricidad, lujuria, lascivia, incontinencia.

lubrifaction [ˈluːbrɪˈfækʃən] [lu-bri-fak-shon], o **lubrification** [ˌluːbrɪfaɪˈkeɪʃən] [lu-bri-fi-kei-shon], s. El acto de hacer más tersa o lúbrica alguna cosa.

luce [ˈljuːs] [lus], s. (Ict.) Lucio.

lucern [ˈluːˈsɜːn] [lu-sern], s. (Bot.) Alfalfa, mielga, especie de trébol.

lucid [ˈluːsɪd] [lu-sid], a. 1. Luciente, diáfano, transparente, brillante, luminoso. 2. Lúcido, se aplica al intervalo de tiempo en que los locos hablan con alguna razón.

lucidity [ˈluːsɪd] [lu-sid], s. Perspicuidad, claridad en materias intelectuales.

lucidness [ˈluːsɪdnɪs] [lu-sid]-nes, s. Claridad, transparencia; esplendor, resplandor.

Lucifer [ˈluːsɪfəʳ] [lu-si-faʳ], s. 1. Lucero, la estrella del alba. 2. Lucifer, el príncipe de las tinieblas. 3. **Lucifer o lucifermatch,** fósforo de fricción.

luciferian [ˈluːsɪfɪrɪən] [lu-si-fi-rian], a. 1. Luciferino, diabólico, endiablado. 2. Lo perteneciente a la herejía de Lucífero, obispo de Cerdeña.

luciferous [ˈluːsɪfərəs] [lu-si-fe-ros], a. Luminoso, lucífero, resplandeciente.

lucific [ˈluːsɪfɪk] [lu-si-fik], a. Luciente, lúcido, lucífero.

luciform [ˈluːsɪfɔːm] [lu-si-form] a. Luciforme.

luck [lʌk] [lak], s. Acaso, casualidad, accidente o suceso feliz o infeliz, fortuna, suerte. **Good luck,** fortuna, dicha, feliz casualidad. **I wish you good luck,** le deseo a Ud. toda felicidad. **To be out of luck,** tener mala suerte. **To be in luck,** tener suerte, estar de suerte/racha. **To bring one luck,** traerle a uno la fortuna. **To take pot luck,** comer lo que haya, sin ceremonia. **It's the luck of the draw,** es cuestión de suerte (Fig.).

luckily [ˈlʌkɪlɪ] [la-ki-li], adv. Por fortuna, por dicha, dichosamente.

luckiness [ˈlʌkɪnɪs] [la-ki-nes], s. Dicha, buena fortuna o suerte, felicidad.

luckless [ˈlʌklɪs] [lak-les], a. Malaventurado, infeliz, desgraciado, desdichado, desventurado.

lucky [ˈlʌkɪ] [la-ki], a. Afortunado, feliz, dichoso, venturoso; propicio, favorable. **A lucky man,** un hombre feliz. **It was very lucky for you that…,** menos mal que… **Third time lucky!,** ¡a la tercera va la vencida! **Lucky dip,** caja de sorpresas.

lucrative [ˈluːkrətɪv] [lu-kra-tiv], a. Lucrativo, ganancioso.

lucre [ˈluːkəʳ] [la-kaʳ], s. Lucro; ganancia; usura.

lucubrate [ˈluːkjʊbreɪt] [lu-kiu-breit], va. Lucubrar, trabajar velando y con aplicacion en obras de ingenio.

luculent [ˈluːkjʊlənt] [lu-kiu-lent], a. Luciente, claro; evidente, cierto, indubitable.

ludicrous [ˈluːdɪkrəs] [lu-di-kros], a. Burlesco, jocoso, alegre, ridículo, cómico, risible.

ludicrously [ˈluːdɪkrəslɪ] [lu-di-kros-li], adv. Jocosamente, en chanza.

ludicrousness [ˈluːdɪkrəsnɪs] [lu-di-kros-nes], s. Ridiculez, extravagancia.

luff [lʌf] [laf], s. 1. Gratil. 2. Acción de orzar, orzada. 3. Cachete de proa. **Luff-tackle,** (Mar.) Aparejo de bolinear.

luff, va. (Mar.) Ceñir el viento, orzar, bolinear. **Keep your luff,** (Mar.) orza. **To luff round,** (Mar.) Meter todo a lof. **To loff up,** (Mar.) Tomar por avante. **To spring the luff,** (Mar.) Partir el puño.

lug [lʌg] [lag], s. (Fam.) 1. Tirón, estirón, el acto de tirar; la cosa tirada, una cosa lenta y pesada. 2. (Mar.) Vela al tercio.

lug, s. 1. Oreja, lóbulo de la oreja. 2. De aquí, prominencia parecida a veces a la oreja: (a) agarradera, asa; (b) jamba de chimenea; (c) correa de las varas de un carruaje. 3. (Prov. Ingl.) Pértiga, vara larga.

lug, va. 1. Tirar alguna cosa hacia sí. 2. (Mar.) Halar, tirar de los cabos. **To lug away, to lug off,** arrastrar, arrebatar. **To lug in o into,** arrastrar hacia dentro; (fam.) introducir, v. g. alguna cosa no pedida. **To lug out,** (Vulg.) desenvainar una espada, sacar la espada.

luggage [ˈlʌɡɪdʒ] [la-guich], s. 1. Originalmente, cualquier cosa pesada y embarazosa que hay que conducir de una parte a otra. 2. Equipaje. **Luggage checkroom,** consigna. **Luggage rack,** red (train); baca, portaequipajes (Aut).

lugger [ˈlʌɡəʳ] [la-gaʳ], s. (Mar.) Lugre, especie de embarcación pesada con vela cuadrada.

lughole [ˈlʌɡhəʊl] [lag-joul], s. Oreja (Fam.). Oído (inner ear).

lug-sail [ˈlʌɡseɪl] [lag-seil], s. (Mar.) Vela al tercio.

lugubrious [luːˈɡuːbrɪəs] [lu-gu-brios], a. Lúgubre, triste, funesto, melancólico.

lugworm [ˈlʌɡwɔːm] [lag-uem], s. Arenícola, lombriz de las riberas y costas, que sirve de cebo para pescar. Se llama también **lobworm y lugbait.**

lukewarm [ˈluːkwɔːm] [luk-uem], a. 1. Tibio, templado. 2. Tibio, indiferente, falto de celo y fervor, frío.

lukewarmly [ˈluːkwɔːmlɪ] [luk-uom-li], adv. Tibiamente, indiferentemente.

lukewarmness [ˈluːkwɔːmnɪs] [luk-uom-nes], s. 1. Calor moderado. 2. Indiferencia, tibieza, frialdad.

lull [lʌl] [lal], va. 1. Arrullar, cantar a los niños, para que se duerman. 2. Adormecer, aquietar, sosegar, calmar, mitigar.

lull, s. La calidad o el poder de calmar.

lullaby [ˈlʌləbaɪ] [la-la-bai], s. Arrullo, la cantilena con que el ama adormece al niño.

luller [ˈlʌləʳ] [la-laʳ], s. Niñero, el que mima a los niños.

lumbago [lʌmˈbeɪɡəʊ] [lam-bei-gou], s. Lumbago.

lumbar [ˈlʌmbəʳ] [lam-baʳ], a. Lumbar, lo que pertenece a los lomos.

lumber [ˈlʌmbəʳ] [lam-baʳ], s. 1. Tablazón, maderaje, madera, tablas, tablones, y otras maderas de construcción. 2. Armatoste, cualquier mueble inútil o engorroso. 3. (Fam.) Trastos o muebles inútiles o de poco uso. **Lumber-room,** camaranchón, cuarto de trastos, o muebles inútiles. **Lumber-yard,** depósito de maderas de construcción. **Lumber room,** trastero.

lumber, va. Amontonar trastos inútiles unos sobre otros sin orden ni método. -vn. 1. Andar pesadamente. 2. Avanzar con ruido sordo. **Lumber about/along,** moverse pesadamente.

lumbering [ˈlʌmbərɪŋ] [lam-ba-rin], s. Embarazado por su propio volumen o bulto; pesado y enorme; también, que produce un ruido sordo y prolongado.

lumberjack [ˈlʌmbədʒæk] [lam-ba-yak], s. 1. Hachero, leñador. 2. Maderero, comerciante en maderas.

lumber jacket [ˈlʌmbədʒækɪt] [lam-ba-ya-kit], s. Chamarra.

lumberman [ˈlʌmbəmən] [lam-ba-man], s. Maderero.

lumbrical [ˈlʌmbrɪkəl] [lam-bri-kal], a. Se dice de algunos músculos pequeños de las manos o pies.

luminary [ˈluːmɪnərɪ] [lu-mi-na-ri], s. 1. Luminar, lumbrera, cualquiera de los astros que despide luz o claridad; cualquier cuerpo que da luz o es luminoso. 2. Lumbrera, el hombre insigne que edifica e instruye al mundo con sus virtudes o sus doctrinas.

luminosity [ˌluːmɪˈnɒsɪtɪ] [lu-mi-no-si-ti], s. 1. Cualidad de lo luminoso. 2. Intensidad de la luz en un color, medida por la fotometría.

luminous [ˈluːmɪnəs] [lu-mi-nos], a. 1. Luminoso, resplandeciente. 2. Iluminado, luciente. 3. Perspicuo, lúcido, de fácil inteligencia.

luminously [ˈluːmɪnəslɪ] [lu-mi-nos-li], adv. De un modo luminoso.

luminousness [ˈluːmɪnəsnɪs] [lu-mi-nos-nes], s. Resplandor, brillo, brillantez.

lump [lʌmp] [lamp], s. 1. Masa informe de alguna cosa, particularmente pedazo, o masa pequeña. 2. El conjunto de cosas diversas que forman una masa. 3. Protuberancia, hinchazón. **To sell o buy by the lump,** vender o comprar por grueso o por junto; vender o comprar alguna cosa a ojo, sin medir o pesar. **Lump sugar,** azúcar de terrón o en terrones. **A lump of sugar,** un terrón de azúcar. **Lump sum,** cantidad total.

lump, va. 1. Amontonar sin orden ni método. 2. Tomar alguna cosa por junto o por mayor. -vn. 1. Trabajar como estivador. 2. Tomar una forma desigual, con protuberancias.

lump-fish [ˈlʌmpfɪʃ] [lamp-fish], s. (Ict.) Lumpo jibado.

lumping [ˈlʌmpɪŋ] [lam-pin], a. (Vulg.) Grande, pesado, largo.

lumpish [ˈlʌmpɪʃ] [lam-pish], a. Pesado, tardo, lento, torpe, lerdo, grosero; grave, macizo; tosco.

lumpishly [ˈlʌmpɪʃlɪ] [lam-pish-li], adv. Lerdamente, estúpidamente, pesadamente, groseramente.

lumpishness [ˈlʌmpɪʃnɪs] [lam-pish-nes], s. Pesadez, tardanza; majadería, tontería.

lumpy [ˈlʌmpɪ] [lam-pi], a. Lleno de terrones o de masas endurecidas.

lunacy [ˈluːnəsɪ] [lu-na-si], s. Locura intermitente, frenesí; trastorno de las facultades intelectuales.

lunar [ˈluːnəʳ] [lu-naʳ], a. 1. Lunar, perteneciente a la luna, o medido por las revoluciones de la luna. 2. Luniforme. V. LUNATE. 3. Causado por la luna o atribuido a ella; lunático. 4. En alquimia y medicina, relativo a la plata. **Lunar caustic,** lunar cáustico, nitrato de plata. **Lunar year,** año lunar, doce meses lunares, o 354 1/3 días.

lunar landing [ˈluːnəˌlændɪŋ] [lu-na-lan-din], s. Alunizaje.

lunary [ˈluːnərɪ] [lu-na-ri], a. Lunar, que se refiere a la luna. -s. (Bot.) Hierba de la plata, lunaria anual.

lunate [ˈluːneɪt] [lu-neit], a. Lunar, luniforme, en forma de media luna.

lunatic [ˈluːnətɪk] [lu-na-tik], a. Lunático, frenético, alunado. -s. Un lunático, un loco. **Lunatic asylum,** manicomio.

lunation [luːˈneɪʃən] [lu-nei-shon], s. Lunación, intervalo entre dos lunas nuevas, es decir 291/2 días.

lunch [lʌntʃ] [lanch], **luncheon** [ˈlʌntʃɪən] [lan-chion], s. Almuerzo, comida del mediodía. **To take a luncheon,** tomar un bocado, comer (meal).

lunch, va. Comer (midday).

lunchbox [ˈlʌntʃˈbɒks] [lanch-boks], s. Fiambrera.

lune [ˈljuːn] [liun], s. 1. Lúnula, figura limitada por dos arcos de círculo. 2. La luna.

lunette [ˈljuːnet] [liu-net], s. Una cosa en forma de media luna, como la luneta de una fortificación, un lente cóncavo-convexo, etc.

lung [lʌŋ] [lang], s. Pulmón, cada uno de los órganos situados en el pecho que son los principales agentes de la respiración; se llaman también bofes o livianos, principalmente cuando se habla de los animales. **To sing at the top of one's lungs,** (Fam.) cantar a grito pelado, a todo gritar.

lunge [lʌndʒ] [lanch], s. 1. Estocada. 2. (Fam.) Arremetida, movimiento brusco hacia adelante.

lunge, vn. 1. Dar un bote, un empuje. 2. Arrojarse, echarse hacia adelante.

lung-grown [ˈlʌŋɡraʊn] [lang-graun], a. Que tiene los pulmones pegados al pecho.

lungwort [ˈlʌŋwɔːt] [lang-uort], s. (Bot.) Pulmonaria oficinal.

lunisolar [ˈluːnɪsələʳ] [lu-ni-so-laʳ], a. Lunisolar, compuesto de la revolución del sol y de la luna.

lunt [lʌnt] [lant], s. 1. (Esco.) Bocanada de humo. 2. (Des.) Mecha de cañón.

lunulate [ˈlʌnjʊleɪt] [la-niu-leit], a. Lunado, formado como una media luna.

lunule [ˈlʌnjuːl] [lu-niul], s. 1. Figura o construcción en forma de luna creciente. 2. (Geom.) Lúnula. V. LUNE.

lupine [ˈluːpɪn] [lu-pin], s. (Bot.) Altramuz, lupino. -a. 1. Lupino, de lobo; como un lobo, voraz. 2. (Zool.) Perteneciete a la familia que comprende los perros y los lobos.

lupuline [ˈluːpʊliːn] [lu-pu-lin], s. Lupulino, polvo resinoso y amarillo que se halla en los frutos del lúpulo, y se emplea en medicina.

lupus [ˈlʌpəs] [la-pus], s. 1. (Astr.) El Lobo, una constelación austral. 2. (Med.) Lupia, lobanillo.

lurch [lɜːtʃ] [lerch], s. 1. Abandono. **To leave one in the lurch,** abandonar a uno; dejarle en la estacada, o en las astas del toro. 2. Partida doble en algunos juegos. 3. Vaivén o balance brusco (ship, train).

lurch, va. 1. (Ant.) Privar a uno de lo que esperaba, dar chasco, engañar. 2. Ganar una partida doble.

lurch, vn. Torcerse, dar un vaivén o balance repentino hacia un lado como un buque en mar alborotado; balancearse.

lurcher [ˈlɜːtʃəʳ] [ler-chaʳ], s. 1. El que está en acecho o espía la ocasión favorable para cometer una mala acción. 2. Perro de caza. 3. (Des.) Glotón.

lurching [ˈlɜːtʃɪŋ] [ler-chin], s. Celada.

lurdan [ˈlɜːdən] [ler-dan], a. (Ant.) Estúpido, incapaz. -s. (Des.) Patán.

lure [ljʊəʳ] [liuaʳ], s. 1. Señuelo, añagaza, armadijo para engañar y cazar pájaros. 2. Añagaza, cebo, engaño, para atraer a uno y engañarle. **To lure somebody into a trap,** hacer que alguien caiga en una trampa.

lure, vn. Llamar a los halcones con señuelo. -va. Atraer, persuadir, inducir. **To lure away from,** apartar de.

lurid [ˈljʊərɪd] [liua-rid], a. Lóbrego, triste; pálido, cárdeno.

lurk [lɜːk] [lerk], vn. 1. Espiar, acechar, ponerse en emboscada para hacer algo malo. 2. Ocultarse, esconderse.

lurker [ˈlɜːkəʳ] [ler-kaʳ], s. Acechador, espía, el que está en acecho para hacer daño.

lurking-place [ˈlɜːkɪŋˌpleɪs] [ler-kin-pleis], s. Escondite, escondrijo guarida, rincón; emboscada.

lurry [ˈlʌrɪ] [la-ri], s. 1. (Min.) Carretón especial que se usa en las minas. 2. (Ant.) Sonido confuso, inarticulado.

luscious [ˈlʌʃəs] [la-shos], a. 1. Dulzaino, empalagoso. 2. Azucarado, almibarado, meloso. 3. Grato, agradable, delicioso, exquisito.

lusciously [ˈlʌʃəslɪ] [la-shos-li], adv. Dulcemente, melosamente.

lusciousness [ˈlʌʃəsnɪs] [la-shos-nes], s. Dulzura que empalaga, melosidad.

lush [lʌʃ] [lash], a. 1. Suculento, jugoso; fresco y lozano. 2. Fácil de arar, poco duro, pulverizado, como el terreno.

lust [lʌst] [last], s. 1. Deseo, inclinación y voluntad, vehementes, vivos, desordenados. **The lust of conquest,** deseo ciego de conquistas. 2. Lujuria, sensualidad, incontinencia, concupiscencia, lascivia, impudicia, deshonestidad.

lust, vn. 1. Lujuriar, cometer el pecado de lujuria. 2. Codiciar, desear con ansia alguna cosa. 3. Desordenarse, desarreglarse.

luster [ˈlʌstəʳ] [las-taʳ], s. 1. Lustre, brillantez. 2. Araña de cristal. 3. Lucimiento, esplendor. 4. Lustro, el espacio de cinco años.

lusterless [ˈlʌstəlɪst] [las-ta-les], a. Sin brillo.

lustful [ˈlʌstfʊl] [last-ful], a. 1. Lujurioso, sensual, voluptuoso. 2. Deshonesto, impúdico, lascivo, incontinente.

lustfully [ˈlʌstfʊl] [last-fu-li], adv. Lujuriosamente, lascivamente, sensualmente.

lustfulness [ˈlʌstfʊlnɪs] [last-ful-nes], s. Lascivia, incontinencia, deshonestidad, impudicicia, lubricidad.

lustily [ˈlʌstɪlɪ] [las-ti-li], adv. Fuertemente, vigorosamente, con fuerza.

lustiness [ˈlʌstɪnɪs] [las-ti-nes], s. Lozanía, vigor, robustez.

lustral [ˈlʌstrəl] [las-tral], a. Lustral, lo que se usa en las purificaciones.

lustrate [ˈlʌstreɪt] [las-treit], va. (Des.) Lustrar, purificar.

lustration [ˈlʌstreɪʃən] [las-trei-shon], s. Lustración.

lustre [ˈlʌstəʳ] [las-taʳ], s. V. LUSTER.

lustring [ˈlʌstrɪŋ] [las-trin], s. Lustrina, tela de mucho lustre.

lustrous [ˈlʌstrəs] [las-tros], a. Lustroso, brillante.

lustrum [ˈlʌstrəm] [las-trom], s. 1. Lustro, período de cinco años. 2. Lustración, ceremonia de purificación.

lustwort [ˈlʌstwɜːt] [last-uert], s. (Bot.) Rocío del sol. V. SUN-DEW.

lusty [ˈlʌstɪ] [las-ti], a. 1. Lozano, fornido, fuerte, robusto, vigoroso. 2. (Des.) Hermoso; deleitoso.

lutanist [ˈlʊtənɪst] [lu-ta-nist], s. El que toca el laúd.

lutation [lʊˈteɪʃən] [lu-tei-shon], s. Lutación, el acto de tapar o embarrar las vasijas con el luten.

lute [luːt] [lut], *s.* 1. Laúd, instrumento músico de cuerdas. 2. Luten.

lute, *va.* Tapar, enlodar o embarrar con luten.

luter [ˈluːtəʳ] [lu-taʳ], **Lutist** [ˈluːtɪst] [lu-tist], *s.* El que tañe el laúd.

lutestring [loˈtɪstrɪŋ] [lu-tis-trin], *s.* 1. Cuerda de laúd. 2. *(Ento.)* Mariposa nocturna, cuyas alas tienen líneas semejantes a las cuerdas de un laúd. 3. Lustrina, especie de tela de seda (corrupción de *lustring*).

Lutheran [ˈluːθərən] [lu-ze-ran], *s.* y *a.* Luterano, que sigue la doctrina de Lutero.

Lutheranism [ˈluːθərənɪzəm] [lu-ze-ra-ni-sem], *s.* Luteranismo.

luthern [ˈluːθɜːn] [lu-zern], *s. (Arq.)* Especie de lumbrera o ventanilla de guardilla o desván.

lutose [ˈluːtəʊs] [lu-tous], *a.* Cubierto con arcilla, lodoso, cenagoso.

lux, *va. (Des.) V.* LUXATE.

luxate [ˈlʌkseɪt] [lak-seit], *va.* Dislocar, desencajar, desconcertar, descoyuntar.

luxation [ˈlʌkseɪʃən] [lak-sei-shon], *s.* Luxación, dislocación, descoyuntamiento.

luxuriance [lʌgˈzjʊərɪəns] [lak-siua-rians], **luxuriancy** [lʌgˈzjʊərɪənsɪ] [lak-siua-rian-si], *s.* Exuberancia, lozanía, suma abundancia, superabundancia, frondosidad, vicio.

luxuriant [lʌgˈzjʊərɪənt] [lak-su-riant], *a.* Exuberante, lozano, superabundante, sobreabundante; muy fértil; frondoso, vicioso.

luxuriantly [lʌgˈzjʊərɪəntlɪ] [lak-su-riant-li], *adv.* Abundantemente, con mucha fecundidad, con profusión.

luxuriate [lʌgˈzjʊərɪeɪt] [lak-su-rieit], *vn.* 1. Lozanear, ostentar lozanía o brillar con ella. 2. Crecer o brotar con exuberancia. 3. Vivir con lujo. 4. *(Fig.)* Gloriarse, jactarse, complacerse.

luxurious [lʌgˈzjʊərɪəs] [lak-su-rios], *a.* 1. Un glotón o regalón. 2. Exuberante, sobreabundante; frondoso; faustoso. 3. *(Des.)* Lujurioso, impúdico, libidinoso.

luxuriously [lʌgˈzjʊərɪəslɪ] [lak-su-rios-li], *adv.* Con lozanía o exuberancia; frondosamente; lozanamente; con lujo o fausto.

luxuriousness [lʌgˈzjʊərɪəsnɪs] [lak-su-rios-nes], *s.* El estado que constituye a una persona lujuriosa o voluptuosa; nimiedad excesiva en la elección de manjares.

luxury [ˈlʌkʃərɪ] [lak-su-ri], *s.* 1. Lujo, exceso y demasía en la pompa o regalo; fausto, molicie; gasto superfluos. 2. Manjar delicioso; una cosa cualquiera que procura placer y gusto, pero es innecesaria en realidad. 3. *(Des.)* Exuberancia, suma abundancia. 4. *(Des.)* Lujuria, lascivia, sensualidad, incontinencia, voluptuosidad.

-ly [lɪ] [li]. Sufijo que se emplea para formar (a) adjetivos que expressan semejanza; parecido a; como *manly*, de *man*, hombre; viril, varonil (como un varón). (b) Adverbios de modo, y en tales casos equivale a -mente. *Clear*, claro; *clearly*, claramente.

lycanthropy [laɪˈkænθrəpɪ] [lai-kan-zro-pi], *s.* Licantropía, un género de melancolía o manía en el cual el enfermo se cree transformado en lobo.

lyceum [laɪˈsiːəm] [lai-siom], *s.* Liceo, paraje situado cerca de Atenas en el que Aristóteles enseñaba la filosofía. 2. *(E.U.)* Liceo, asociación para la instrucción por medio de lecturas, discusiones o cursos públicos; y su edificio. 3. Escuela de segunda enseñanza.

lychnis [ˈlaɪknɪs] [laik-nis], *s. (Bot.)* Licnide, nombre genérico de plantas cariofileas.

lycopodium [ˌlaɪkəˈpɒdɪəm] [lai-ko-po-diom], *s.* Licopodio, polvo de una especie de musgo que es muy inflamable.

lydian [ˈlɪdɪən] [li-dian], *a.* Lidio, que se refiere a la antigua Lidia, famosa por su riqueza y su cultivo de la música.

lye [laɪ] [lai], *s.* 1. Lejía. 2. *(Ingl.)* Ramal, empalme lateral de un ferrocarril.

lying [ˈlaɪɪŋ] [lai-in], *a.* 1. Echado. **A ship lying along,** *(Mar.)* bajel tendido sobre la banda. **Lying to,** *(Mar.)* al pairo o en facha. **Lying-in hospital,** hospital de parturientes, casa refugio. *(Amer.)* Casa de maternidad. **Lying-in woman,** mujer parida. 2. Mentiroso, embustero, -s. La práctica o costumbre de mentir; mentira, embuste.

lyingly [ˈlaɪɪŋlɪ] [lai-in-li], *adv.* Mentirosamente, falsamente.

lymph [lɪmf] [limf], *s.* 1. Linfa, humor acuoso que se halla en varias partes del cuerpo. 2. Exudación coagulable de los vasos en las inflamaciones. 3. Virus, o cultura del virus de una enfermedad, que se emplea en la vacunación o inoculación. **Lymph-duct,** vaso linfático. **Lymph gland,** ganglio linfático.

lymphatic [ˈlɪmfætɪk] [lim-fa-tik], *s.* Linfático: se dice de los vasos que conducen la linfa. -*a.* 1. Linfático. 2. Flemático.

lymphoid [ˈlɪmfɔɪd] [lim-foid], *a.* Parecido a la linfa o a una glándula linfática.

lynch [lɪntʃ] [linch], *va.* Linchar, ahorcar.

lynching [ˈlɪntʃɪŋ] [lin-chin], *s.* Linchamiento.

lynx [lɪŋks] [links], *s. (Zool.)* Lince, mamífero carnicero.

lyrate [ˈlaɪreɪt] [lai-reit], *a.* Formado como la lira antigua.

lyre [ˈlaɪəʳ] [laiaʳ], *s.* Lira, instrumento músico de cuerdas que se usaba en lo antiguo; arpa.

lyre-bird [ˈlaɪəbɜːd] [laia-berd], *s. (Orn.)* Menura o menura-lira, ave de Australia cuya cola tiene la forma de una lira antigua.

lyric, lyrical [ˈlɪrɪk] [li-rik], *a.* 1. Lírico, lo que pertenece a la lira, o se compone para cantar al son de la lira. 2. Perteneciente o relativo a la poesía lírica.

lyric, *s.* 1. Poema lírico. 2. Poeta lírico.

lyrical [ˈlɪrɪkəl] [li-ri-kal], *a.* Lírico. Entusiasta, elocuente *(Fig.)*.

lyricist [ˈlɪrɪsɪst] [li-ri-sist], *s.* Letrista.

lyrist [ˈlɪrɪst] [li-rist], *s.* 1. El que toca la lira. 2. Poeta lírico.

lysin [ˈliːsɪn] [li-sin], *s.* Lisina.

lysis [ˈlaɪsɪs] [lai-sis], *s. (Med.)* Lisis, cesación gradual de una enferemdad, en contraposición a crisis.

lysozyme [ˈlɪsəzaɪm] [li-so-saim], *s.* Lisozima.

lyssa [ˈlɪsə] [li-sa], *s.* Rabia canina.

M

m [em] [em], nunca es muda en inglés, y se pronuncia como en español, aunque con más fuerza. No va nunca seguida de otra consonante al principio de las voces o sílabas en las palabras puramente inglesas; y cuando está seguida de *n* al fin de algunas voces, hace muda a esta última letra. *M* como numeral romano equivale a mil. Como abreviatura, M.A. es Maestro en Artes; M.B., Bachiller en medicina; M.C., Miembro del Congreso o de la Cámara de los Representantes; M.P., Miembro del Parlamento; M.S., Manuscrito, y MSS. Manuscritos.

ma [mɑː] [ma] *s. f.* Mamá.

ma'am [mæm] [mam], *s.* Contracción de *madam,* señora.

mac Prefijo, que en los nombres de origen escocés o irlandés significa «hijo de». (Se abrevia a menudo tomando la forma de Mc.)

macabre [məˈkɑːbr] [ma-kabaʳ], *a.* Macabro.

macadam [məˈkædəm] [ma-ka-dam], *s.* Piedras trituradas para macadamizar; calzada empedrada con ellas.

macaroni [ˌmækəˈrəʊnɪ] [ma-ka-rou-ni], *s.* 1. Macarrones, pasta alimenticia, en figura de canuto largo. 2. Una especie de muñeca. 3. Pisaverde; gracioso.

macaronic [ˌmækəˈrəʊnɪk] [ma-ka-rou-nik], *s.* Montón confuso o mezcla de muchas cosas. -*a.* 1. Macarrónico, consistente en una mezcla confusa de palabras de diferentes idiomas; mezclado. 2. Macarrónico, referente a los macarrones.

macaroon [ˌmækəˈruːn] [ma-ka-run], *s.* Almendrado, especie de pasta hecha de harina, almendras, huevos y azúcar; mostachón de almendras.

macassar [ˌmækəˈsɑːʳ] [ma-ka-saʳ], *s.* Macasar, aceite perfumado para el cabello.

macaw [məˈkɔː] [ma-kou], *s. (Orn.)* Guacamayo, papagayo de cola larga.

mace [meɪs] [meis], *s.* 1. Maza, la insignia que llevan los maceros delante de los magistrados y otras personas de autoridad en los actos públicos. 2. Maza, clava o porra de metal. 3. Macis o macías, la corteza sutil y olorosa que cubre la nuez moscada (spice).

macebearer [ˈmeɪsˌbɛərəʳ] [meis-bea-raʳ], *s.* Macero.

macerate [ˈmæsəreɪt] [ma-se-reit], *va.* 1. Macerar, poner en infusión algún cuerpo y prepararlo para la disolución o destilación. 2. *(Ant.)* Enflaquecer, debilitar, mortificar el cuerpo.

maceration [ˌmæsəreɪʃən] [ma-se-rei-shon], *s.* Maceración, el acto de macerar o infundir una cosa sólida en algún líquido para ablandarla.

machete [məˈʃiːt] [ma-shit], *s.* Machete.

Machiavellian, Machiavelian [ˌmækɪəˈvelɪən] [ma-kia-ve-lian], *s.* Maquiavelista, partidario del maquiavelismo, -a. Maquiavélico.

machiavelism [ˌmækɪəˈvelɪzm] [ma-kia-ve-li-sem], *s.* Maquiavelismo, sistema político de Maquiavelo; tiranía astuta; engaño, fraude, astucia; conducta zorrastrona.

machicolation [ˌməkɪkəʊˈleɪʃən] [ma-ki-kou-lei-shon], *s. (Arq.)* Matacán o ladronera, abertura entre un muro y un parapeto.

machinate [ˈmækɪneɪt] [ma-ki-neit], *vn.* Maquinar, tramar, fraguar, trazar, discurrir o idear medios para lograr algún fin, particularmente con avieso designio.

machination [ˌmækɪˈneɪʃən] [ma-ki-nei-shon], *s.* Maquinación, conjuración, trama, asechanza oculta.

machinator [ˈmækɪneɪtəʳ] [ma-ki-nei-toʳ], *s.* Maquinador, maquinante.

machine [məˈʃiːn] [ma-shin], *s.* 1. Máquina con que se da juego o movimiento a alguna cosa. 2. El que obra sin intención o de un modo meramente mecánico. 3. La organización de los poderes de un cuerpo complexo. 4. La parte que los entes sobrenaturales tiene en la acción de un poema. 5. *(E.U.)* Organización dentro de un partido político a fin de apropiarse y dirigir el repartimiento de cargos y destinos. **Machine-shop,** taller de maquinaria. **Machine-tool,** herramienta de máquina; máquina para operar con herramientas cortantes, o para modelar. **Machine translation,** traducción automática.

machine gun [məˈʃiːnɡʌn] [ma-shin-gan], *s.* Ametralladora. *va.* Ametrallar.

machinery [məˈʃiːnərɪ] [ma-shi-ne-ri], archivo sl-ie-ll.p65 10-06-98aria, mecánica; las piezas de una máquina, o el conjunto de máquinas y sus útiles y herramientas colectivamente. 2. *(Ant.)* El conjunto de entes sobrenaturales introducidos en un poema.

machinist [məˈkɪnɪst] [ma-ki-nist], *s.* Maquinista; mecánico, operario *(Tech).*

mach-number [ˈmətʃnʌmbəʳ] [mach-nam-baʳ], *s.* Número Mach; relación de la velocidad de un cuerpo con la del sonido.

mackerel [ˈmækərəl] [ma-ke-rel], *s. (Zool.)* Escombro. **Horse-mackerel,** *(Zool.)* Caballa, haleche. **Mackerel sky,** cielo aborregado.

mackinaw [ˈmɔkɪnɔː] [ma-ki-no], *s.* Chamarra.

mackintosh [ˈmækɪntɒʃ] [ma-kin-tosh], *s.* 1. Traje, levitón o sobretodo impermeables. 2. Tela delgada forrada interiormente de caucho.

mackle [ˈmækl] [ma-kel], *va. (Impr.)* Repintar, macular. -*s.* Maculatura.

macrobian [mæˈkrəʊbɪən] [ma-kro-bian], *s.* Macrobiano, persona de muy larga vida, particulamrente de más de cien años.

macrobiotic [ˌmækrəʊbaɪˈɒtɪk] [ma-kro-bai-o-tik], *s.* Macrobiótico.

macrobiotics [ˌmækrəʊbaɪˈɒtɪks] [ma-kro-bai-o-tiks], *s.* Macrobiótica.

macrocosm [ˈmækrəʊkɒzəm] [ma-kro-kosm], *s.* Macrocosmo, el mundo entero.

macroeconomics [ˈmækrəʊɪːkəˈnɒmɪks] [ma-kro-i-ko-no-miks], *s.* Macroeconomía.

macromolecule [ˈmækrəˈmɒlekjuːl] [ma-kro-mo-le-kiul], *s.* Macromolécula.

macula [ˈmækjʊlə] [ma-kiu-la], **macule** [ˈmækjuːl] [ma-kiul], *s.* Mácula, mancha, tacha, lunar. **Solar macula,** mácula del sol.

maculate [ˈmækjuːleɪt] [ma-kiu-leit], *va.* Macular, manchar.

maculate, *a.* Manchado, maculado.

mad [mæd] [mad], *a.* 1. Loco, demente, perturbado. 2. Furioso, rabioso, insensato, desesperado, furibundo *(Fam: angry)* **She's hopping mad,** está que muerde. 3. Precipitado (gallop, rush). **Mad-apple,** berengena. **Madbrain, madbrained,** loco, insensato, furioso; aturdido. **Madcap,** alocado, orate, el sujeto de poco juicio. **He's as mad as a hatter, he's a March hare,** está loco de atar, está como una cabra. **To be mad about something/somebody,** estar loco por algo/alguien.

mad, *va.* Enloquecer, enfurecer. -*vn.* Enloquecerse; estar loco.

madam [ˈmædəm] [ma-dam], *s.* Madama, señora: tratamiento de cortesía. Niña precoz *(fam).*

madcap [ˈmædkæp] [mad-kap] *a.* Alocado, ido, disparatado.

madden [ˈmædn] [ma-den], *va.* Enloquecer, hacer que uno se vuelva loco. -*vn.* Enloquecerse, volverse loco.

maddening [ˈmædnɪŋ] [ma-de-nin] *a.* Enloquecedor. **To be maddening,** ser enloquecedor, sacar de quicio. **It's maddening!** ¡es para volverse loco!

madder [ˈmædəʳ] [ma-daʳ], *s. (Bot.)* Rubia, una planta cuya raíz sirve para teñir de rojo. **Madder-roots,** rubia en raíz o graneada.

made [meɪd] [meid], *pret.* y *pp.* del verbo TO MAKE. 1. Fabricado; producido, particularmente con arte. 2. En posición desahogada, próspero. **Made-up,** (a) artificial, ficticio. (b) Completo, acabado.

Madeira Wine [məˈdɪərəˌwaɪn] [ma-dei-ra-uain], *s.* Vino de Madera.

made-to-measure [ˈmeɪdtəˈmeəʒəʳ] [meid-to-me-shaʳ] *a.* Hecho a medida.

made-to-order [ˈmeɪdtɔːˈɔːdəʳ] [meid-to-or-deʳ], *a.* Hecho a la orden, hecho a la medida.

made-up [ˈmeɪdʌp] [meid-ap] *a.* Hecho, confeccionado (dress). Ficticio (story).

mad-headed [ˈmædˈhedɪd] [mad-je-did], *a.* Fogoso, antojadizo.

madhouse [ˈmædhaʊs] [mad-jaus], *s.* Manicomio, casa de locos o de orates, el hospital donde se curan o encierran los locos.

madly [ˈmædlɪ] [mad-li], *adv.* Furiosamente, locamente.

madman [ˈmædmən] [mad-man], *s.* Loco, maniático, orate.

madness [ˈmædnɪs] [mad-nes], *s.* 1. Locura, demencia, manía, extravagancia. 2. Furor, arrebato de ira o cólera, enajenación mental; rabia.

madonna [məˈdɒnə] [ma-do-na], *s.* 1. Señora, madama; antigua voz italiana de tratamiento. 2. Dícese de las imágenes de la Virgen.

madras [ˈmædrəs] [ma-dras], *s.* 1. Madrás, tela fina de algodón que se usa generalmente para camisas de hombre. 2. Pañoleta de seda o de algodón de colores vivos.

madrepore [ˈmædrɪpɔːʳ] [ma-dri-poʳ], *s. (Zool.)* Madrépora, pólipo de los mares intertropicales, y su polipero, que llega a formar escollos e islas.

madrigal [ˈmædrɪɡəl] [ma-dri-gal], *s.* 1. Madrigal, una composición poética. 2. Canción pastoral. 3. Canto amoroso.

madwoman [ˈmædwʊmən] [mad-vu-man] *s. f.* Loca, alocada.

madwort [ˈmædwɔːt] [mad-uort], *s. (Bot.)* Marrubio, aliso.

maelstrom [ˈmeɪlstrəʊm] [meil-stroum], *s.* 1. Malstrom, peligroso remolino que forman las aguas junto a la costa de Noruega. 2. Cualquier fuerza o influencia poderosa que arruina y destruye.

magazine [ˌmægəˈziːn] [ma-ga-sin], s. 1. Revista, publicación ilustrada (journal). 2. Almacén para guardar géneros o cosas vendibles. 3. Cámara para cartuchos en un rifle de repetición. 4. Pañol de pólvora o Santabárbara.

Magdalen [ˈmægdəlɪn] [mag-da-lin], s. Ramera arrepentida. -n.pr. Magdalena.

mage [meɪg] [meig], s. Mago. V. MAGICIAN.

magenta [məˈdʒentə] [ma-yen-ta], s. Nombre de una materia de tinte obtenida de la anilina y de un rico color purpúreo rojizo.

maggot [ˈmægət] [ma-got], s. 1. Gusano, larva de una mosca. 2. (Vulg.) Capricho, fantasía, antojo.

maggoty [ˈmægətɪ] [ma-go-ti], a. 1. Lleno de gusanos. 2. (Vulg.) Caprichoso, fantástico.

Magi [ˈmeɪdʒaɪ] [mei-yai], s. pl. **The Magi,** los Reyes Magos o sabios de oriente.

magian [ˈmeɪdʒɪən] [ma-yian], a. Lo perteneciente a los magos o sabios del oriente.

magic [ˈmædʒɪk] [ma-yik], s. Magia. **Natural magic,** magia blanca. -a. Mágico, encantador. **Magic carpet,** alfombra voladora. **Magic lantern,** linterna mágica u óptica.

magical [ˈmædʒɪkəl] [ma-yi-kal], a. Mágico; encantado.

magically [ˈmædʒɪkəlɪ] [ma-yi-ka-li], adv. Mágicamente, por magia, por arte de encantamiento.

magician [ˈmædʒɪʃən] [ma-yi-shan], s. Mago, mágico, nigromante. Brujo, hechicero (witch).

magilp, megilp [ˈmægɪlp] [ma-guilp], s. Secante, aceite secante, compuesto de que se sirven los artistas para secar pronto los colores.

magisterial [ˌmædʒɪsˈtɪərɪəl] [ma-yis-tia-rial], a. Magistral, magisterial; imperioso, arrogante, absoluto.

magisterially [ˌmædʒɪsˈtɪərɪəlɪ] [ma-yis-tia-ria-li], adv. Magistralmente.

magistery [ˈmædʒɪstərɪ] [ma-yis-te-ri], s. 1. Decreto magisterial. 2. Panacea. 3. (Quím.) Magisterio, precipitado de composición no conocida.

magistracy [ˌmædʒɪsˈtrəsɪ] [ma-yis-tra-si], s. Magistratura.

magistral [ˌmædʒɪsˈtrəl] [ma-yis-tral], a. Magistral, magisterial.

magistrate [ˈmædʒɪstreɪt] [ma-yis-treit], s. 1. Magistrado. 2. Juez de paz.

magistratic [ˌmædʒɪsˈtrətɪk] [ma-yis-tra-tik], a. Lo que pertenece a la autoridad de magistrado.

magma [ˈmægmə] [mag-ma], s. Cualquier masa blanda, como la de harina.

magnanimity [ˌmægnəˈnɪmɪtɪ] [mag-na-ni-mi-ti], s. Magnanimidad.

magnanimous [mægˈnænɪməs] [mag-na-ni-mos], a. Magnánimo.

magnanimously [mægˈnænɪməslɪ] [mag-na-ni-mos-li], adv. Magnánimamente.

magnate [ˈmægneɪt] [mag-neit], s. 1. Magnate, noble. 2. Grande del reino de Hungría.

magnesia [mægˈniːʃə] [mag-ni-sha], s. Magnesia, tierra muy fina y blanca, usada en medicina; óxido de magnesia.

magnesian [mægˈniːʃən] [mag-ni-shan], a. Magnésico, que contiene magnesia.

magnesium [mægˈniːʃəm] [mag-ni-sham], s. Magnesio, metal blanco y maleable, que se usa a menudo en la fotografía para procurar una luz brillante.

magnet [ˈmægnɪt] [mag-nit], s. 1. Imán, piedra imán; particularmente un imán artificial. 2. Persona o cosa muy atractiva.

magnetic, magnetical [mægˈnetɪkəl] [mag-ne-ti-kal], a. 1. Magnético. 2. Dotado de magnetismo personal; que ejerce una fuerza moral atractiva.

magnetically [mægˈnetɪkəlɪ] [mag-ne-ti-ka-li], adv. De un modo atractivo.

magneticalness [mægˈnetɪkəlnɪs] [mag-ne-ti-kal-nes], **magneticness** [mægˈnetɪknɪs] [mag-ne-tik-nes], s. La calidad de lo que es magnético.

magnetism [ˈmægnetɪzəm] [mag-ne-ti-sem], s. Magnetismo.

magnetizable [ˌmægnɪˈtaɪzəbl] [mag-ni-ta-sai-bol], a. Magnetizable.

magnetize [ˈmægnɪtaɪz] [mag-ni-tais], va. 1. Magnetizar, imantar o imanar. 2. Atraer por medio de la simpatía e influencia personales. 3. Someter al hipnotismo. -vn. Imanarse, adquirir propiedades magnéticas.

magneto-electric [mægˈnɪtərˈlektrɪk] [mag-ni-to-i-lek-trik], a. Magneto-eléctrico.

magneto-electricity [ˌmægnɪtəɪlekˈtrɪsɪtɪ] [mag-ni-to-i-lek-tri-si-ti], s. Electromagnetismo.

magnetohydrodynamics [mægnɪtəˈhaɪdrədaɪˌnæmɪks] [mag-ni-to-hai-dro-dai-na-miks], s. Magneto-hidrodinámica.

magnetometer [ˌmægnɪtəmiːtər] [mag-ni-to-mi-te'], s. Magnetómetro, instrumento para medir la fuerza magnética por medio de una balanza de torsión.

magnetron [ˈmægnɪtrən] [mag-ni-tron], s. Magnetrón.

magnifiable [ˈmægnɪfaɪˈeɪbl] [mag-ni-fai-ei-bol], a. Capaz de ser engrandecido.

magnification [ˈmægnɪfaɪˈkeɪʃən] [mag-ni-fai-kei-shon], s. 1. Amplificación, aumento, poder de aumento de una lente. 2. Alabanza, glorificación; exageración.

magnificence [ˈmægnɪfɪsəns] [mag-ni-fi-sens], s. Magnificencia, grandeza, esplendor.

magnificent [ˈmægnɪfɪsənt] [mag-ni-fi-sent], a. Magnífico, espléndido, lucido.

magnificently [ˈmægnɪfɪsəntlɪ] [mag-ni-fi-sent-li], adv. Magníficamente.

magnifier [ˈmægnɪfaɪər] [mag-ni-faia'], s. 1. Microscopio, vidrio de aumento, lente. 2. El que magnifica, ensalza o alaba con exageración; panegirista.

magnify [ˈmægnɪfaɪ] [mag-ni-fai], va. 1. Aumentar la magnitud de los objetos a la vista. 2. Magnificar, exaltar, exagerar (exagerate). **Magnifying-glass,** lupa, vidrio de aumento, lente.

magniloquence [ˈmægnɪləˈkwəns] [mag-ni-lo-kuens], s. Altilocuencia; fanfarronada.

magnitude [ˈmægnɪtjuːd] [mag-ni-tiud], s. 1. Magnitud, grandeza, tamaño, grandor, envergadura, importancia. 2. Extensión en altura, anchura y espesor o profundidad.

magnolia [mægˈnəʊlɪə] [mag-nou-lia], s. (Bot.) Magnolia.

magnum [ˈmægnəm] [mag-num] sf. 1. Botella doble. 2. -a. **Magnum opus,** obra maestra.

magpie [ˈmægpaɪ] [mag-pai], s. Marica, urraca, picaza; pega.

maguey [ˈmægeɪ] [ma-guei], s. (Bot.) Maguey.

magyar [ˈmægɪər] [ma-guei], s. Magiar o Magyar; se dice de la raza predominate en Hungría y Transilvania y de su lengua.

maharajah [ˌmɑːhərˈɑːdʒə] [ma-ja-ra-ja], s. Maharajá.

mahaut [ˈmæhɔːt] [ma-jot], s. Guarda y guía de un elefante.

mahlstick, maulstick [ˈmælstɪk] [mals-tik], s. Tiento, bastoncillo en que el pintor apoya la mano derecha.

mahogany [məˈhɒgənɪ] [ma-o-ga-ni], s. Caoba o caobana.

Mahometan, Mahomedan, etc. V. MOHAMMEDAN, etc.

maid [meɪd] [meid], **maiden** [ˈmeɪdn] [mei-den], sf. 1. Doncella, soltera; virgen. **Oldmaid,** solterona, doncella jamona. 2. Hembra. 3. Criada. **Maid of honor in waiting,** dama de honor de una reina o princesa. 4. (Ict.) Especie de lija.

maiden, a. 1. Virgíneo, virginal, lo que pertenece a las vírgenes o doncellas; soltero, soltera. **A maiden aunt,** una tía soltera. 2. Nuevo, inicial, intacto, no se ha usado o no se ha tocado. **Maiden speech,** el primer discurso público hecho por un nuevo representante o miembro de una asamblea.

maidenhair [ˈmeɪdnheər] [mei-den-jea'], s. (Bot.) Culantrillo.

maidenhead [ˈmeɪdnhed] [mei-den-jed], **maidenhood** [ˈmeɪdnhʊd] [mei-den-jud], sf. Doncellez, virginidad; el estado de alguna cosa intacta.

maidenliness [ˈmeɪdnlɪnɪs] [mei-den-li-nes], s. Modestia, dulzura y conducta como la que debe tener una doncella.

maidenly ['meɪdnlɪ] [mei-den-li], **maiden-like** ['meɪdnlaɪk] [mei-den-laik], *a.* Virginal, modesto, púdico, reservado. - *adv.* Modestamente.

maidhood ['meɪdhʊd] [meid-jud], *s.* Virginidad.

maid-marian ['meɪdmærɪən] [meid-ma-rian], *s.* Maritornes, marimacho, o mujer impúdica.

maid-servant ['meɪdsɜːvənt] [meid-ser-vant], *sf.* Doncella de servicio, criada.

mail [meɪl] [meil], *s.* 1. Correo, servicio público para la conducción de la correspondencia; y también, correo, valija, el conjunto de cartas, etc., que se reciben o se despachan. 2. Maleta, valija a propósito para guardar o llevar ropas, etc. 3. Cota de malla, jacerina. 4. Renta; mancha. V. BLACKMAIL. **Mail-bag,** valija del correo. **Mail-catcher,** garra para asir los sacos del correo y depositarlos en un carro o vagón en movimiento. **Mail merge,** fusión del correo electrónico. **Mail order,** venta por correo. **Mail-sack,** saco de lona para periódicos y paquetes.

mail, *va.* 1. Armar con cota de malla, antiguamente mallar. 2. *(E. U.)* Depositar en un buzón para cartas; echar al correo. 3. *(Ant.)* Atar las alas.

mailable ['meɪləbl] [mei-la-bol], *a.* Que puede ser enviado por el correo.

mail box ['meɪlbɒks] [meil-boks], *s.* Buzón para el correo.

mailed ['meɪld] [mei-lid], *a.* Cubierto con cota de malla. -*pp.* del verbo TO *MAIL.*

mailman ['meɪlmæn] [meil-man], *s.* Cartero.

mail order ['meɪlɔːdəʳ] [meil-or-daʳ], *s.* Pedido postal. **Mail-order house,** casa que vende mediante pedidos postales.

mailplane ['meɪlpleɪn] [meil-plein], *s.* Avión postal.

mailshot ['meɪlʃɒt] [meil-shot], *s. f.* Circular, mailing.

maim [meɪm] [meim], *va.* Mutilar, cortar, cercenar alguna parte del cuerpo; estropear, lisiar.

maim, *s.* Mutilación, manquera, daño, defecto.

maimedness ['meɪmɪdnɪs] [mei-mid-nes], *s.* Mutilación, mancamiento, defecto.

main [meɪn] [mein], *a.* 1. Principal. 2. Violento, fuerte. 3. Mayor, lo que tiene la parte principal. 4. Importante, esencial, lo que importa. **Main hatchway,** *(Mar.)* escotilla mayor. **Main braces,** *(Mar.)* brazos mayores. **Main-top braces,** *(Mar.)* brazos de gavia. **Main-top-gallant braces,** *(Mar.)* brazos de juanete mayor. **Main course,** plato fuerte, principal *(Culin.).* **Main street,** calle mayor. **Main yard,** verga mayor. -*s.* 1. Océano o alta mar; del aquí, continente, porción principal de la tierra. 3. Fuerza, violencia. 4. Partida o pareja de gallos. 5. *(Ant.)* Grueso, la mayor parte o la más principal y fuerte de alguna cosa. **With might and main,** con todas sus fuerzas. **Upon the main,** al fin.

mainland ['meɪnlənd] [mein-land], *s.* Continente, tierra firme.

mainly ['meɪnlɪ] [mein-li], *adv.* Principalmente, primeramente; poderosamente.

mainmast ['meɪnmɑːst] [mein-mast], *s. (Mar.)* Palo mayor de un bajel.

main office [ˌmeɪnˈɒfɪs] [mein-o-fis], *s.* Casa matriz, oficina principal.

mainsail ['meɪnsl] [mein-seil], *s. (Mar.)* Vela mayor. **Main-top-gallant sail,** vela de juanete mayor. **Main-top-gallant-royal,** vela de sobrejuanete mayor.

main-sheet ['meɪnʃiːt] [mein-shit], *s. (Mar.)* Escota mayor.

mainspring ['meɪnsprɪŋ] [mein-spring], *s.* Muelle real (de reloj, etc.).

mainstay ['meɪnsteɪ] [mein-stei], *s. (Mar.)* 1. Estay mayor. 2. Sostén principal.

mainstream ['meɪnstriːm] [mein-strim], *s. f.* Corriente principal, línea central *(Fig.).*

maintain [meɪnˈteɪn] [mein-tein], *va.* 1. Tener, guardar, conservar (keep up). 2. Mantener, sostener alguna opinión (support); reivindicar, defender. 3. Mantener, hacer el gasto de alguna cosa. 4. Mantener, proveer a alguno de lo necesario para la vida. **To maintain secrecy,** observar el secreto.

maintainable [meɪnˈteɪnəbl] [mein-tei-na-bol], *a.* Defendible, sostenible.

maintainer [meɪnˈteɪnəʳ] [mein-tei-naʳ], *s.* Mantenedor; defensor, patrón.

maintenance ['meɪntɪnəns] [mein-ti-nans], *s.* Mantenimiento, apoyo, protección; sustento; continuación. **Maintenance agreement,** contrato de mantenimiento. **Maintenance staff,** personal de servicios.

main-top [meɪnˈtɒp] [mein-top], *s. (Mar.)* Cofa mayor o de gavia. **Main-top-mast,** mastelero mayor. **Main-top gallant,** mastelero de juanete mayor. **Main-top yard,** verga de gavia. **Main-top-gallant yard,** verga de juanete mayor. **Main-top-gallant-royal yard,** verga de sobrejuanete mayor.

maize [meɪz] [meis], *s.* Maíz (y maiza, la planta). Por lo general en los Estados Unidos se llama solamente *corn.* **Ear of maize,** elote, choclo *(Mex.).*

majestic, majestical [məˈdʒestɪk] [ma-yes-tik], *a.* Majestuoso, augusto; pomposo, elevado, sublime, grande.

majestically [məˈdʒestɪkəlɪ] [ma-yes-ti-ka-li], *adv.* Majestuosamente.

majesty [məˈdʒestɪ] [ma-yes-ti], *s.* 1. Majestad, poder, soberanía. 2. Majestad, título que se da a reyes y emperadores. **His/Her Majesty,** Su Majestad.

majolica, maiolica [məˈdʒɒlɪkə] [ma-you-li-ka], *s.* Mayólica, variedad de loza con esmalte metálico.

major ['meɪdʒəʳ] [mei-yoʳ], *a.* 1. Mayor; más grande en número, en cantidad, en extensión. 2. Mayor, más grande en dignidad o importancia; de primera consideración; principal. **Of major interest,** de máximo interés. 3. *(Mús.)* Mayor, normal; que contiene la tercera, la sexta y la séptima mayores. -*s.* 1. *(Mil.)* Sargento mayor de regimietno, comandante, jefe de batallón, oficial de rango inmediatamente superior al de capitán. 2. *(For.)* El mayor de edad. 3. Mayor, la primera proposición de un silogismo. 4. Asignatura principal *(E. U.).*

Major-General [ˌmeɪdʒəˈdʒenərəl] [mei-yor-ye-ne-ral], *s. (Mil.)* Mariscal de campo.

majority [məˈdʒɒrɪtɪ] [ma-yo-ri-ti], *s.* 1. Mayoría, la ventaja en que una cosa excede a otra. 2. Pluralidad, el mayor número. 3. Mayoría, mayor edad. 4. Sargentía mayor de un regimiento.

make [meɪk] [meik], *va. (pret.* y *pp.* MADE). 1. Hacer, crear, producir; causar, ocasionar; formar, fabricar; componer, trabajar; hablar, pronunciar, relatar. 2. Hacer, ejecutar, practicar, efectuar. 3. Hacer, disponer, aderezar. 4. Obtener, procurar, adquirir, ganar; granjear, proporcionar. 5. Hacer, dar el ser intelectual o formar algo con la imaginación. 6. Obligar, forzar, compeler. 7. Contribuir, constituir; disponer o inclinar a; alcanzar. 8. Atravesar, pasar por, cruzar. 9. *(Mar.)* Descubrir, avistar, llegar a, alcanzar. 10. Contar por, mirar como, decidir a otro. 11. Poner en estado o forma conveniente, arreglar. **To make a bed,** arreglar, hacer una cama. 12. Poner fin a, completar, acabar. 13. Hacer fortuna. 14. Inferir por raciocinio, concluir; pensar. 15. *(Ant.)* Intentar, tener intención de; estar a puno de. -*vn.* 1. Hacerse, volverse. 2. Ir, dirigirse o encaminarse a algún paraje determinado; tender. 3. Tener efecto, contribuir, servir; corresponder, concordar, venir bien una cosa con otra. 4. Hacer de o hacer él o la, fingir alguna cosa, aparentar ser una cosa diferente de la realidad. 5. Fluir o levantarse como la marea.

make after, tratar de coger, perseguir.

make again, rehacer, hacer de nuevo.

make against, estar en oposición a, ser contrario a; ser nocivo.

make at, arremeter.

make away, huir; gastar; tranferir el dominio de una cosa; matar, destruir; derrochar, disipar. **To make away with,** derrochar; hurtar; matar.

make for, dirigirse a; aprovecharse, tener utilidad, sacar ventaja o provecho de una cosa. **To make for a place,** ir hacia una parte, tomar rumbo hacia un lugar determinado.

make of, sacar utilidad o ventaja, aprovecharse; considerar, estimar, hacer caso; entender algo en. **I knew not what to make of,** no pude entenderlo.

make off, irse, huir, tomar las de Villadiego. **To make off with,** llevarse, quitar de delante; arrebatar.

make out, llegar a comprender, descifrar, descubrir, entender (get on); congeniar (person); establecer por testimonio, probar, justificar con pruebas; suplir, abastecer de lleno, completar; componer, redactar, o completar (los documentos legales, expedientes, etc.); estar o ser próspero, tener éxito. **We will make out the deeds at once,** redactaremos las actas auténticas en seguida. **To make out a case,** probar su pleito, justificar uno su demanda; llegar a comprender.

make over, (a) rehacer, hacer de nuevo; (b) ceder, traspasar o transferir el dominio de una cosa; depositar alguna cosa en poder de personas abonadas; confiar.

make towards, arrimarse a uno para cogerle.

make up, acabar, concluir; completar; juntar hasta el completo de una cosa; reparar, suplir; colmar; recompensar; formar; ajustar una cuenta; recuperarse de una pérdida; indemnizar, resarcir; conciliar, apaciguar; fabricar, contar fábulas o mentiras; prepararse como un actor; compaginar, arreglar en columnas o páginas (término de imprenta); enumerar, contar. **To make up a lip,** estar de hocico, amohinarse. **To make up to one,** acercarse a uno. **To make up for,** compensar, poner una cosa en lugar de otra perdida. **To make up for lost time,** recuperar el tiempo perdido. **To make up one's mind,** resolverse, hacer ánimo, tener determinado. **To make a doubt,** dudar. **To make a fool of,** burlarse o reírse de uno; dar chasco; divertirse a costa de alguna persona. **To make a jest of,** poner en ridículo. **To make a litter,** ensuciar, desordenar. **To make a man,** hacer la fortuna o la suerte de una persona. **To make a mistake,** equivocarse, engañarse. **To make a pen,** tajar una pluma. **To make a wonder,** admirar, admirarse. **To make account,** calcular; creer; echar la cuenta. **To make account of,** estimar, tener consideración o tratar con consideración, hacer caso. **To make angry,** enfadar, sulfurar. **To make as if,** aparentar, fingir, hacer como. **To make believe,** fingir, pretender. **To make little (o nothing) of,** hacer poco o ningún caso de, despreciar; hacer con facilidad; comprender poco, o no comprender nada. **To make much of,** hacer mucho caso de; acariciar, halagar, mostrar amistad o cariño; regalar, festejar; economizar, sacar de una cosa toda la utilidad posible; estimar, apreciar. **To make no difference o no matter,** ser indiferente, no importar. **That makes no difference,** eso no importa. **To make merry,** divertirse; comer opíparamente. **To make one's way,** (a) avanzar, progresar, abrirse paso. (b) Obtener buen éxito; salir bien. **To make amends,** indemnizar, resarcir, reparar, compensar. **To make clean,** limpiar. **To make fast,** (Mar.) amarrar, afianzar. **To make free,** libertar, poner en libertad. **To make free with,** tratar sin ceremonia; no gastar cumplimientos; estar como en su casa; coger una cosa sin pedirla. **To make gain of,** ganar. **To make good,** mantener, defender; hacer bueno, probar; mejorar, cumplir; garantizar, responder de; lograr. **To make good one's word or promise,** cumplir su palabra, promesa o empeño. **To make good a loss,** reparar, ressarcir una pérdida. **He made good his escape,** logró escaparse. **To make haste,** apresurarse, darse prisa. **To make head against,** hacer frente a, resistir. **To make hot,** acalorar. **To make interest,** empeñar. **To make it good to one,** indemnizar, resarcir, reparar. **To make it up,** hacer las amistades, hacer las paces. (Fam.) Contentarse, volver a ser amigos, olvidar lo pasado. **To make known,** publicar, hacer saber, notificar. **To make lean,** poner flaco. **To make less,** minorar, adelgazar, hacer más pequeña o delgada alguna cosa. **To make level,** allanar. **To make liable,** hacer responsable; sujetar. **To make light of,** menospreciar, tratar con desprecio, no hacer caso. **To make love,** enamorar, hacer el amor, cortejar, galantear. **To make many words,** altercar, disputar, porfiar sobre una cosa. **To make merry,** divertirse, regalarse, pasarlo alegremente. **To make money,** ganar dinero. **There is money to be made,** hay dinero que ganar. **To make no doubt,** no dudar. **To make one out of his wits,**

sacar de quicio, hacer perder la paciencia, poner a una persona fuera de sí o sacarla de sus casillas. **To make one's escape,** escaparse, huirse, evadirse, salvarse huyendo. **To make one's fortune,** hacer hombre, hacer rico o enriquecer a alguno. **To make oneself known,** darse a conocer. **To make oneself miserable,** hacerse infeliz, entristecerse, afligirse. **To make ready,** preparar, tener pronta alguna cosa. **To make sail,** dar a la vela. **To make sense of,** hallar sentido a. **To make no sense of,** no hallar sentido a, hallar confuso u obscuro un escrito, lenguaje, etc. **To make shift with,** sacar el mejor partido de una cosa poco favorable. **To make speed,** apresurarse, darse prisa. **To make sure of,** estar seguro, tener por cierto, asegurarse, en la posesión de una cosa; contar con una cosa; considerar como seguro y cierto. **To make the most of it,** aprovecharlo todo; sacar todas las ventajas posibles. **To make use,** servirse de una cosa o hacer uso de ella. **To make water,** (a) (Mar.) hacer agua o abrir una vía de agua. (b) Hacer aguas, mear, orinar. **Make yourself easy,** pierda Ud. cuidado. **He will make nothing of it at last,** al cabo nada sacará de ello. **To make more sail,** (Mar.) largar las velas. **To make sternway,** (Mar.) hacer camino para popa. **To make headway,** (Mar.) hacer camino para avante. **To make the land,** (Mar.) tomar tierra, descubrir la tierra. **That's made my day!** ¡eso me ha alegrado el día! **I made just in time,** llegué justo a tiempo. **What do you make of her?,** ¿qué piensas de ella?

make, s. 1. Hechura, forma, figura; estructura. 2. Fábrica, producción, manufactura. 3. Producto.

makeble ['meɪkəbl] [mei-e-bolk], a. Factible, practicable.

make-believe ['meɪkbɪˌliːv] [meik-bi-liv], a. Fingido, falso, imaginado; no real. -s. Ficción, cosa imaginada; pretexto.

make-peace ['meɪkˌpiːs] [meik-pis], s. Pacificador, conciliador.

maker ['meɪkəʳ] [mei-kaʳ], s. 1. Criador, hacedor supremo. 2. Artífice, fabricante (manufacturer). 3. Hacedor, el que hace alguna cosa. 4. Poeta; autor.

makeshift ['meɪkʃɪft] [meik-shift], a. Provisional; improvisado.

make-up ['meɪkʌp] [meik-ap], s. 1. Combinación de las partes de que consiste un todo. 2. (imptr.) Imposición de los tipos. 3. Carácter, modo de ser. 4. Maquillaje.

makeweight ['meɪkweɪt] [meik-ueit], s. Cualquier cosa pequeña que se pone en una balanza para igualar el peso.

making ['meɪkɪŋ] [mei-kin], s. 1. Composición, estructura, forma, hechura, trabajo. 2. (Des.) Poema.

making-iron [ˌmeɪkɪŋˈaɪən] [mei-kin-aion], s. (Mar.) Hierro de sentar.

mal-. Prefijo que significa malo o falto, defectuoso. **Maladjustment,** ajuste malo, defectuoso. **Maladministration,** mala administración.

malachite ['mæləˌkaɪt] [ma-la-kait], s. Malaquita, piedra de color verde.

malacology ['mæləˌkɒlədʒɪ] [ma-la-ko-lo-yi], s. Malacología, la parte de la zoología que trata de los moluscos.

maladdress ['mælədrɪs] [ma-la-dris], s. Grosería, poca maña o descortesía en el habla o en los modales; falta de finura.

maladjusted ['mæləˈdʒʌstɪd] [mal-ad-yas-tid] a. Inadaptado.

maladjustment ['mæləˈdʒʌstmənt] [mal-ad-yast-ment], s. 1. Mal ajuste. 2. Inadaptación.

maladroit ['mæləˈdrɔɪt] [ma-la-droit], a. Desmañado, torpe.

malady ['mælədɪ] [ma-la-di], s. 1. Mal, enfermedad, dolencia. 2. Mal mental; cualquier condición de desarreglo.

Malaga ['mæləgɑː] [ma-la-ga], s. Vino o uva de Málaga.

malaise [mæˈleɪz] [ma-leis], s. Indisposición, enfermedad ligera o pasajera.

malanders ['mæləndəʳz] [ma-lan-ders], s. (Vet.) Ajuagas, esparavanes.

malapert ['mæləpɜːt] [ma-la-pert], *a.* Desvergonzado, descomedido, descarado.

malapertness ['mæləpɜːtnɪs] [ma-la-pert-nes], *s.* Insolencia, atrevimiento, impudencia.

malapropism ['mæləprɒpɪzm] [ma-la-pro-pi-sem], *s.* Despropósito lingüístico.

malapropos ['mæləprɒpəs] [ma-la-pro-pos], *a.* Mal a propósito, fuera de propósito.

malar ['mælɑːʳ] [ma-laʳ], *a.* Malar, perteneciente a la mejilla. **Malar bone,** hueso malar, pómulo.

malaria [məˈlɛərɪə] [ma-la-ria], *s.* 1. Aire malsano, exhalación nociva; en especial las emanaciones de los pantanos o de materias animales o vegetales en estado de descomposición. 2. Enfermedad producida por dicho aire malsano o emanaciones nocivas; fiebre intermitente; calentura maligna.

malarial [məˈlɛərɪəl] [ma-la-rial], *a.* Afectado por la malaria o fiebre intermitente o causado por ella; de la naturaleza de una calentura intermitente o maligna; malsano, palúdico.

malarious [məˈlɛərɪəs] [ma-la-rios], *a.* Que contiene aire malsano o malaria; que produce calenturas intermitentes o malignas.

malate ['mæleɪt] [ma-leit], *s. (Quím.)* Malato, sal formada por la combinación de ácido málico con alguna base.

Malay, Malayan ['mæleɪ] [ma-lei] ['mæleɪən] [ma-leian], *a.* Malayo.

malaysian ['mæleɪʒɪən] [ma-lei-shian] *a.* Malasio.

malcontent ['mælkənˈtent] [mal-kon-tent], *a.* Malcontento; perturbador del orden público.

male [meɪl] [meil], *a.* 1. Masculino; varón, macho. **Male issue,** hijos varones, sucesión masculina. **Male nurse,** enfermero. 2. Compuesto de varones. **A male quartet,** cuarteto de varones. 3. *(Bot.)* Estaminado, provisto de estambres. 4. Que denota un útil, instrumento u objeto que tiene un correlativo conocido con el nombre de hembra: **male screw,** tornillo; **female screw,** hembra del tornillo, tuerca. *-s.* Macho, animal del sexo masculino o viril *(Zool., Bot.).*

malediction [ˌmælɪˈdɪkʃən] [ma-li-dik-shon], *s.* Maldición.

malefaction [ˌmælɪˈfækʃən] [ma-li-fak-shon], *s.* Delito, culpa.

malefactor ['mælɪfæktəʳ] [ma-li-fak-toʳ], *s.* Malhechor.

malefic ['mælɪfɪk] [ma-li-fik], *a.* Maléfico, dañoso.

maleficent [məˈlɪfɪʃənt] [ma-li-fi-shent], *a.* Maléfico, maligno.

maleficiation [ˌmælɪfɪʃɪˈeɪʃən] [ma-li-fi-shi-ei-shon], *s.* Hechicería.

malepractice ['mælɪˈpræktɪk] [ma-li-prak-tik], *s. (Des.)* V. MALPRACTICE.

malevolence [məˈlevələns] [ma-le-vo-lens], *s.* Malevolencia, aversión, mala voluntad, odio, tirria.

malevolent [məˈlevələnt] [ma-le-vo-lent], **malevolous** [məˈlevələs] [ma-le-vo-los], *a.* Malévolo, maligno; mal intencionado.

malevolently [məˈlevələntlɪ] [ma-le-vo-lent-li], *adv.* Malignamente.

malfeasance [məlˈfiəsəns] [mal-fia-sans], *s.* 1. Comisión de un acto malo y contrario a la ley. 2. Malhecho; acto ilegal; malversación.

malformation [ˌmælfɔːˈmeɪʃən] [mal-for-mei-shon], *s.* Hechura o formación defectuosa; cualquier irregularidad congénita de un organismo.

malformed [ˌmælˈfɔːmd] [mal-formd], *a.* Mal formado, malhecho, contrahecho.

malic ['mælɪk] [ma-lik], *a.* Málico, concerniente a las manzanas. **Malic acid,** ácido málico.

malice ['mælɪs] [ma-lis], *s.* Malicia, mala intención, malignidad, maldad, ruindad.

malicious [məˈlɪʃəs] [ma-li-shos], *a.* Malicioso, maligno.

maliciously [məˈlɪʃəslɪ] [ma-li-shos-li], *adv.* Maliciosamente.

maliciousness [məˈlɪʃəsnɪs] [ma-li-shos-nes], *s.* Mala intención, malicia.

malign [məˈlaɪn] [ma-lain], *a.* 1. Maligno, malicioso, mal inclinado. 2. Maligno, contagioso; se dice de las enfermedades.

malign, *va.* Envidiar, dañar, perjudicar; censurar. *-vn. (Des.)* Tener malicia.

malignancy [məˈlɪɡnənsɪ] [ma-lig-nan-si], *s.* Malignidad, malicia, malevolencia.

malignant [məˈlɪɡnənt] [ma-lig-nant], *a.* Maligno, malicioso; nocivo; envidioso. **Malignant fever,** calentura maligna. *-s.* Hombre maligno, mal intencionado o envidioso.

malignantly [məˈlɪɡnəntlɪ] [ma-lig-nant-li], *adv.* Malignamente.

maligner [məˈlɪɡnəʳ] [ma-lig-neʳ], *s.* Hombre mordaz, maligno o mal intencionado; detractor; difamador.

malignity [məˈlɪɡnɪtɪ] [ma-lig-ni-ti], *s.* Maliginidad, perversidad.

malignly [məˈlɪnlɪ] [ma-lin-li], *adv.* Malignamente.

malinger [məˈlɪŋɡəʳ] [ma-lin-gaʳ], *vn.* Fingirse enfermo para evitarse algún trabajo o servicio.

malingerer [məˈlɪŋɡərəʳ] [ma-lin-ga-raʳ], *s.* Maula, el que se finge enfermo para que se le dispense de algún servicio. Fingido.

malison ['mælɪsən] [ma-li-son], *s. (Poét.)* Maldición.

malkin ['mælkɪn] [mal-kin], *s.* 1. Aljofifa; deshollinador de horno. 2. Gorrona, mujer soez y vil, criada sucia. 3. Espantajo en figura de mujer. 4. Gato. V. GRIMALKIN.

mall [mɔːl] [mol], *s.* 1. Mazo, mallo. 2. *(Des.)* Bote, golpe. **Shopping mall,** centro comercial.

mall, *va.* V. MAUL.

mallard ['mæləd] [mo-lard], *s. (Orn.)* Lavanco, ánade silvestre.

malleability [ˌmælɪəˈbɪlɪtɪ] [ma-lia-bi-li-ti], **malleableness** ['mælɪəblnɪs] [ma-lia-bol-nes], *s.* Maleabilidad.

malleable ['mælɪəbl] [ma-lia-bol], *a.* Maleable, lo que se puede extender a golpe de martillo.

malleate ['mælɪt] [ma-lieit], *va.* Martillar, trabajar a martillo, y formar en planchas.

mallet ['mælɪt] [ma-lit], *s.* Mazo, mallo; mallete, martillo ligero. **Serving-mallet,** *(Mar.)* maceta de aforrar. **Calking-mallet,** maceta de calafate. **Driving-mallet,** maceta de ajustar.

malleus ['mæləs] [ma-los], *s.* Martillo, uno de los huesecillos del oído, contenidos en la caja del tímpano.

mallow, mallows ['mæləʊ] [ma-lou], *s. (Bot.)* Malva, malvas.

malmsey ['mælmseɪ] [malm-sei], *s.* Malvasía, cierta especie de uva y el vino que se saca de ella.

malnourished [ˌmælˈnʌrɪʃt] [mal-nu-risht], *a.* Desnutrido.

malnutrition ['mælnjʊˈtrɪʃən] [mal-niu-tri-shon], *s.* Desnutrición, mala nutrición.

malodorous [mæˈləʊdərəs] [mal-o-do-rous], *a.* Fétido, mal oliente.

malpractise, malpractice ['mælˈpræktɪs] [mal-prak-tis], *s.* 1. En medicina y cirugía, tratamiento erróneo, perjudicial o ilegal. 2. Mala conducta, mala dirección.

malt [mɔːlt] [molt], *s.* 1. Cebada preparada para hacer cerveza. 2. v. MALT-LIQUOR. **Malt-dust,** polvo que despide la cebada preparada al molerla para hacer cerveza. **Malt-floor,** suelo para germinar y secar cebada. **Malt-horse,** zote: voz de desprecio. **Malt-house,** la casa o paraje en donde se prepara y guarda la cebada para hacer cerveza. **Malt-kiln,** horno para secar la cebada germinada. **Malt-liquor,** cerveza, cualquier bebida preparada con cebada. V. ALE, BEER, PORTER. **Malt-mill,** molino para moler la cebada germinada.

malt, *va.* Hacer germinar la cebada, prepararla para hacer cerveza. *-vn.* Germinar la cebada para convertirse en cerveza.

maltha ['mɔːlθə] [mol-za], *s.* Especie de betún hecho con pez y cera.

maltman ['mɔːltmən] [molt-man], **maltster** ['mɔːltstəʳ] [molts-taʳ], *s.* El que prepara y dispone la cebada para hacer cerveza.

maltose ['mæltəʊz] [mal-tous], *s.* Maltosa, azúcar cristalizable.

maltreat [mæl'triːt] [mal-trit], *va.* Maltratar.

malvaceous [mæl'veɪʃəs] [mal-vei-shos], *a.* Malváceo, que pertenece a la malva.

malversation [ˌmælvɜːˈseɪʃən] [mal-ver-sei-shon], *s.* Malversación, mala administración, falta de fidelidad, particularmente en las funciones públicas.

mameluke o mamaluke [məmɪˈljuːk] [ma-mi-liuk], *s.* Mameluco.

mama, mamma ['mæmə] [ma-ma], *s.* Mamá, madre.

mamma ['mæmə] [ma-ma], *s.* Mama de los mamíferos; teta.

mammal ['mæməl] [ma-mal], *s.* Mamífero, animal que tiene mamas y da de mamar a sus pequeñuelos.

mammalia ['mæməlɪə] [ma-ma-lia], *s.* Mamífero, la clase primera de los animales cuyas hembras tienen tetas.

mammalian ['mæməlɪən] [ma-ma-lian], *a.* Mamífero.

mammalogy ['mæmələdʒɪ] [ma-ma-lo-yi], *s.* Mamalogía, el ramo de la zoología que trata de los mamíferos.

mammary ['mæmərɪ] [ma-mi-ri], *a.* Mamario, perteneciente a la teta o mama, o de la naturaleza de ella.

mamme-tree ['mæmɪˈtriː] [ma-mi-tri], *s.* (*Bot.*) Mamey, árbol de América cuya fruta tiene el mismo nombre.

mammet ['mæmɪt] [ma-mit], *s.* V. MAUMET.

mammiform ['mæmɪfɔːm] [ma-mi-form], *a.* Mamiforme, que tiene la figura de mamilas o tetas.

mammillary ['mæmɪlærɪ] [ma-mi-la-ri], *a.* Mamilar.

mammillate, mammillated ['mæmɪleɪt] [ma-mi-leit] ['mæmɪleɪtɪd] [ma-mi-lei-tid], *a.* Lo que tiene tetas.

mammography ['mæməfrəfɪ] [ma-mo-gra-fi] *s. f.* Mamografía.

mammon ['mæmən] [ma-mon], *s.* 1. El espíritu de la codicia. 2. El dios siríaco de las riquezas.

mammonist ['mæmənɪst] [ma-mo-nist], *s.* Mundano, avaro.

mammoth ['mæməθ] [ma-moz], *a.* Enorme, gigantesco. *-s.* Mamut, elefante fósil primitivo, ahora desaparecido.

mammy ['mæmɪ] [ma-mi], *s.* 1. (*Fam.*) Madre, mamá. 2. (*E.U. del Sur*) Negra, ama de leche para los niños blancos. 3. (*Ingl.*) Abuela.

man [mæn] [man], *s.* 1. Hombre, animal racional, acepción genérica bajo la cual se comprende toda la especie humana (Humanity). 2. Hombre, varón, respecto de la mujer o hembra y respecto también de un muchacho o joven. 3. Hombre: voz muy familiar con que se dirige la palabra a alguno. 4. Criado, servidor (varón). 5. Peón, una de las piezas delanteras del juego del ajedrez, o la pieza movible con que se juega a las damas. 6. Alguien; cualquiera. 7. (*Mar.* y *solamente en composición*) Buque, navío: **man-of-war,** buque de guerra; **merchant-man,** buque mercante. **A man in an instant may discover it,** cualquiera puede descubrirlo en un instante. **He is not his own man,** está fuera de sí o no está en sus sentidos. **To be one's own man,** no depender más que de sí, ser independiente. **The creditors went against it to a man,** los acreedores, sin faltar uno solo, se opusieron a ello. **So much a man,** tanto por cabeza o tanto por barba. **Man and wife,** marido y mujer. **Best man,** padrino de boda. **Man's estate,** edad viril. **Man-eater,** antropófago, caribe. **Man-hater,** misántropo; también el que o la que aborrece al sexo masculino. **Man-milliner,** hombre que comercia en artículos de modista. **To a man,** hasta el último, como un solo hombre, de acuerdo unánime. **Man-killer,** homicida, asesino. **Man-midwife,** partero, comadrón. **Man of straw,** testaferro, maniquí que no figura más que de nombre en una cosa. **That man Robert,** aquel (llamado) Robert.

man, *va.* 1. (*Mar.*) Tripular, poner gente en; armar. **To man the capstan,** (*Mar.*) armar o guarnir el cabrestante. 2. Guarnecer o fortalecer con gente una plaza o fortaleza. 3. (Poco us.) Amaestrar, adiestrar un halcón. **To want the yards,** disponer la gente sobre las vergas para poder maniobrar con las velas.

manacle [ˈmænəkl] [ma-na-kol], *s.* Manilla, el anillo de hierro que por prisión se echa a la muñeca. **Manacles,** pl, esposas, las dos manillas emparejadas con que se aseguran ambas manos.

manacle, *va.* Maniatar, atar las manos con esposas o manillas; atar las manos de las bestias con maniotas.

manage ['mænɪdʒ] [ma-nich], *va.* y *vn.* 1. Manejar, conducir, gobernar, dirigir, administrar o disponer de alguna cosa. 2. Manejar, usar o traer entre manos una cosa. 3. Manejar, dirigir o llevar bien un asunto o una dependencia. 4. Manejar, hablando de caballos, es gobernarlos. 5. Amansar, domar. *-vn.* Ingeniarse para, darse maña para alcanzar o conseguir alguna cosa; usar de medios prudentes; arreglarse para.

manage, *s.* 1. Manejo. 2. *V.* BEHAVIOR. 3. *V.* MANEGE.

manageable ['mænɪdʒəbl] [ma-ni-ya-bol], *a.* Manejable; dócil, tratable.

manageableness ['mænɪdʒəblnɪs] [ma-ni-ya-bol-nes], *s.* Docilidad; flexibilidad, mansedumbre.

management ['mænɪdʒmənt] [ma-nich-ment], *s.* Manejo, administración, negociación; prudencia, destreza; directores o empresarios colectivamente. **Management committee,** consejo de administración (enterprise). **Management studies,** administración de empresas (*Univ.*).

manager ['mænɪdʒəʳ] [ma-ni-chaʳ], *s.* 1. Administrador, director; empresario. 2. Hombre económico, el que sabe manejar su hacienda; buen padre de familia. 3. Proyectista diestro, intrigante. **Sales manager,** jefe de ventas.

manageress ['mænɪdʒəˈres] [ma-ni-che-res], *s. f.* Encargada (of a restaurant or a shop, etc.).

managerial [ˌmænəˈdʒɪərɪəl] [ma-ni-yia-rial] *a.* Administrativo. **Managerial staff,** personal de dirección (enterprise). **Managing director,** director gerente. **Managing editor,** subdirector (de una publicación, etc.).

manatee ['mænətiː] [ma-na-ti], *s.* (*Zool.*) Manatí, vaca marina, mamífero pisciforme de la familia de los sirenios.

manchineel ['mæntʃiniːl] [man-chi-nil], *s.* (*Bot.*) Manzanillo.

mancipation ['mænsɪpeɪʃən] [man-si-pei-shon], *s.* (*Der. rom.*) 1. Enajenación de bienes por venta. 2. Emancipación, acto por el cual daba un padre libertad a su hijo. 3. (*Des.*) Esclavitud.

manciple ['mænsɪpl] [man-si-pol], *s.* El mayordomo o administrador de un colegio o comunidad de cualquier clase.

Mancunian [mænˈkjuːnɪən] [man-kiu-nian], *a.* De Manchester.

mandamus ['mændəməs] [man-da-mus], *s.* (*For.*) Mandamiento, orden de un tribunal superior a otro inferior, o a una corporación o persona particular, para que hagan alguna cosa que están obligados a ejecutar.

mandarin ['mændərɪn] [man-da-rin], *s.* 1. Mandarín, título de dignidad en la china, funcionario civil o militar. 2. Mandarina, lengua sabia y oficial de la China. 3. Amarillo de mandarín. 4. Mandarina (fruit).

mandatary ['mændətərɪ] [man-da-ta-ri], *s.* 1. Mandatario, el sujeto que por encargo o mandato de otro entiende en algún asunto. 2. Mandante.

mandate ['mændeɪt] [man-deit], *s.* 1. Mandato, orden, precepto. 2. Encargo, poder que da uno a otro, comisión.

mandator ['mændeɪtəʳ] , [man-dei-toʳ], *s.* Director.

mandatory ['mændətərɪ] [man-da-to-ri], *a.* (*For.*) Preceptivo, que expresa un mandato positivo y no un permiso. *-s.* Mandatario.

mandible ['mændɪbl] [man-di-bol], *s.* Mandíbula, quijada o su equivalente en los pájaros y en los insectos.

mandibular ['mændɪbjɒləʳ] [man-di-biu-laʳ], *a.* Mandibular.

mandolin, mandoline ['mændəlɪn] [man-do-lin], *s.* Bandolín o mandolina, instrumento músico de cuerdas metálicas, y cuya caja es de forma parecida a la almendra.

mandragora ['mændrægərə] [man-dra-go-ra], **mandrake** ['mændreɪk] [man-dreik], *s.* (*Bot.*) 1. Mandrágora. 2. **Mandrake,** (*E.U.*) planta común de los bosques, llamada también **May-apple** (manzana de mayo), notable por sus grandes hojas. Se emplea en medicina.

mandrel ['mændrəl] [man-drel], *s.* Polea de madera de que usan los torneros en sus tornos, mandril; y el parahuso o taladro de los cerrajeros.

mandrill ['mændrɪl] [man-dril], *s. (Zool.)* Mandril.

manducate ['mændjʊkeɪt] [man-diu-keit], *va.* Comer, mascar, manducar.

manducation ['mændjʊ'keɪʃən] [man-diu-kei-shon], *s.* Manducación, mascadura.

mane [meɪn] [mein], *s.* Crin o clin de caballo; melena.

man-eater ['mæn,i:tə'] [man-ita'], *s.* Antropófago.

maned ['meɪnd] [meind], *a.* Crinado, crinito.

manège ['mɑːneʒ] [ma-nech], *s.* 1. Picadero, el lugar o sitio donde los picadores adiestran los caballos. 2. Escuela de equitación, lugar donde se enseña a montar a caballo.

manequin ['mænɪkɪn] [ma-ni-kin], *s. V.* MANIKIN.

manes ['meɪnz] [meins], *s.* Manes, las sombras o almas de los muertos.

maneuver, manœuvre [mə'nu:və'] [ma-nu-va'], *va.* 1. Maniobrar, hacer maniobras de tropas o de buques. 2. Llevar a un paraje determinado por medio de maniobras. *-vn.* 1. Maniobrar las tropas o una flota. 2. Intrigar, tramar, negociar artificiosamente.

maneuverable ['mænu:vrəbl] [ma-nu-vra-bol], *a.* Manejable.

manful ['mænfʊl] [man-ful], *a.* Bravo, valiente, animoso, esforzado, atrevido.

manfully ['mænfʊlɪ] [man-fu-li], *adv.* Valerosamente, valientemente.

manfulness ['mænfʊlnɪs] [man-ful-nes], *s.* Valentía, esfuerzo, aliento, valor, ánimo.

manganate ['mæŋɡəneɪt] [man-ga-neit], *s.* Manganato.

manganese [,mæŋɡə'ni:z] [man-ga-nis], *s.* Manganeso, metal duro de color gris, blanquecino y quebradizo.

manganic [mæŋɡənɪk] [man-ga-nik], *a.* Mangánico, relativo al manganeso, particularmente en su grado más alto de oxidación.

manganous ['mæŋɡənəs] [man-ga-nos], *a.* Manganoso, relativo al manganeso en su más bajo grado de oxidación.

mange [meɪndʒ] [meinch], *s.* Roña, sarna perruna, especie de sarna que da a los animales.

manger ['meɪndʒə'] [mein-cha'], *s.* 1. Pesebre. 2. *(Mar.)* Caja de agua.

manginess ['mændʒɪnɪs] [man-chi-nes], *s.* Sarnazo, roña, infección roñosa; comezón.

mangle ['mæŋɡl] [man-guel], *va.* 1. Mutilar, estropear; desfigurar, desgarrar cortando, lacerar. 2. *(Fig.)* Chafallar, hacer algo indivisiblemente; arruinar. 3. Lustrar, dar prensa y lustre a las telas, alisarlas, darles calandria o psarlas por la calandria.

mangle, *s.* Planchadora eléctrica.

mangler ['mæŋɡlə'] [man-gla'], *s.* 1. Destrozador, despedazador. 2. El que prensa y da lustre a las telas por medio de la calandria.

mangling ['mæŋɡlɪŋ] [man-glin], *s.* 1. Despedazamiento. 2. El acto de prensar y dar lustre a las telas con la calandria.

mango ['mæŋɡəʊ] [man-gou], *s.* Mango, árbol originario de la India, de fruta muy estimada y abundante en las Antillas.

mangonel ['mæŋɡənəl] [man-go-nel], *s.* Máquina para arrojar piedras grandes; catapulta de la edad media.

mangrove ['mæŋɡrəʊv] [man-grouv], *s. (Bot.)* Mangle, árbol que se cría en agua salada.

mangy ['meɪndʒɪ] [mein-yi], *a.* Sarnoso, el que padece de sarna.

manhandle ['mænhændl] [man-jan-del], *va.* Maltratar *(Fig.)*. Manipular *(Tech.)*.

manhole ['mænhəʊl] [man-joul], *s.* Entrada de pozo, abertura por donde puede se entrar en una caldera, tanque, alcantarilla, etc.

manhood ['mænhʊd] [man-jud], *s.* 1. Naturaleza humana. 2. Virilidad o edad viril. 3. *(For.)* Masculinidad. 4. Fortaleza, valor, valentía, espíritu, resolución.

mania ['meɪnɪə] [mei-nia], *s.* 1. Manía, locura furiosa. 2. Frenesí, acción disparatada, manía.

maniac ['meɪnɪæk] [mei-niak], *a.* Maniático, maníaco.

maniac, *s.* Loco, maniático o maníaco.

manic-depressive ['mænɪkdɪ'presɪv] [ma-nik-di-pre-siv] *a.* Maníacodepresivo *(Psych)*.

manicheism ['mænɪkɪzm] [ma-ni-kizm], *s.* Maniqueísmo.

manichord ['mænɪkɔ:d] [ma-ni-kord], *s.* Manicordio, instrumento músico parecido al clavicordio.

manicure ['mænɪkjʊə'] [ma-ni-kiua'], *s. (Neol.)* El cuidado y tratamiento de las manos y uñas; manicuro, manicura, la persona que se dedica a esa profesión. *-va.* Cuidar, curar y hermosear un manicuro las manos y las uñas de sus clientes.

manicurist ['mænɪkjʊərɪst] [ma-ni-kiuarist], *s.* Manicuro, manicurista.

manifest ['mænɪfest] [ma-ni-fest], *a.* Manifiesto, descubierto, patente, aparente, evidente. *-s.* 1. Manifiesto, declaración; la exhibición que un capitán hace en la aduana de todos los géneros y mercaderías que trae a bordo. 2. Por extensión, conocimiento, hoja de ruta.

manifest, *va.* Manifestar, hacer patente, hacer ver; declarar; demostrar, revelar.

manifestable ['mænɪfestəbl] [ma-ni-fes-ta-bol], *a.* Mostrable, demostrable.

manifestation ['mænɪfes'teɪʃən] [ma-ni-fes-tei-shon], *s.* Manifestación, acción de hacer patente; demostración evidente, ostensión, revelación.

manifestly ['mænɪfestlɪ] [ma-ni-fest-li], *adv.* Manifiestamente, evidentemente.

manifestness ['mænɪfestnɪs] [ma-ni-fest-nes], *s.* Evidencia clara o patente; perspicuidad.

manifesto ['mænɪfestəʊ] [ma-ni-fes-tou], *s.* Manifiesto, el escrito en que se justifica y declara al público alguna cosa.

manifold ['mænɪfəʊld] [ma-ni-fould], *a.* 1. Múltiple, multíplice, vario, de diversos géneros; numeroso. 2. Manifestado de muchos modos.

manifold, *va.* Sacar más de una copia a un tiempo.

manifoldly ['mænɪfəʊldlɪ] [ma-ni-fould-li], *adv.* De muchos modos, de diferentes maneras.

manifoldness ['mænɪfəʊldnɪs] [ma-ni-fould-nes], *s.* Multiplicidad.

maniglious ['mænɪɡlɪəs] [ma-ni-glios], *s. pl. (Art.)* Mangos de un cañón de artillería.

manihot ['mænɪhɒt] [ma-ni-jot], **manioc** ['mænɪɒk] [ma-nok], *s. (Bot.)* Yuca.

manikin ['mænɪkɪn] [ma-ni-kin], *s.* 1. Maniquí, figura artificial del cuerpo humano para hacer ver al estructura anatómica, etc. 2. Maniquí, modelo de la figura humana para uso de los artistas. 3. Hombrecillo, hombre pequeño.

manila [mə'nɪlə] [ma-ni-la], *s.* 1. Filipino, especie de cigarro que viene de Manila. 2. Abacá, cáñamo de Manila.

manille ['mænɪl] [ma-nil], **manilic** ['mænɪlɪk] [ma-ni-lik], *s.* 1. Manilla, especie de anillo o ajorca para adornar brazos y piernas. 2. Malilla, juego de naipes.

manioc ['mænɪɒk] [ma-niok], *s.* Mandioca, yuca.

maniple ['mænɪpl] [ma-ni-pel], *s.* 1. Manípulo, ornamento sacerdotal que se ciñe al brazo izquierdo. 2. Manípulo, la compañía de soldados en las cohortes romanas. 3. *(Raro)* Puñado.

manipular [mə'nɪpjʊlə'] [ma-ni-piu-la'], *a.* Lo que pertenece al manípulo.

manipulate [mə'nɪpjʊleɪt] [ma-ni-piu-leit], *va.* Manipular operar con las manos; de aquí, manejar, influir artificiosamente. *-vn.* Trabajar con las manos.

manipulation [mə,nɪpjʊ'leɪʃən] [ma-ni-piu-lei-shon], *s.* Manipulación, acción y efecto de operar con las manos o manipular.

manipulative [mə'nɪpjʊlətɪv] [ma-ni-piu-la-tiv], **manipulatory** [mə'nɪpjʊ,lətərɪ] [ma-ni-piu-la-to-ri], *a.* Manipulante, perteneciente a la manipulación; que se lleva a cabo por medio de la manipulación o es a propósito para ella.

manipulator [mə'nɪpjʊˌleɪtəʳ] [ma-ni-piu-lei-toʳ], _s._ Manipulador, el que manipula.

mankind [mæn'kaɪnd] [man-kaind], _s._ 1. El género humano, la especie humana. 2. Los hombres, en contraposición a las mujeres.

manless ['mænlɪs] [man-les], _a._ Sin hombres, sin gente.

manlike ['mænlaɪk] [man-laik], _a._ Varonil, de hombre, animoso.

manliness ['mælɪnɪs] [man-li-nes], _s._ hombrada, valentía, valor, brío, ánimo, fuerza, bravura.

manly ['mænlɪ] [man-li], _a._ Varonil, valiente, valeroso, lleno de dignidad. _-adv._ Varonilmente.

man-made [mæn'meɪd] [man-meid], _a._ Artificial, sintético. **Man-made satellite,** satélite artificial.

manna ['mænə] [ma-na], _s._ 1. Maná, mangla, licor o goma que se usa como purgante. 2. Maná.

manned flight ['mænd'flaɪt] [mand-flait], _s._ Vuelo tripulado.

mannequin ['mænɪkɪn] [ma-ni-kin], _s._ Maniquí.

manner ['mænəʳ] [ma-naʳ], _s._ 1. Manera, modo, método. 2. Maña, costumbre, hábito, moda. 3. Manera, porte o modales de una persona. 4. Suerte, género, especie. 6. Traza, aire, además, modo o manera de mirar. 6. _pl._ Modales, urbanidad, crianza. **In a manner of speaking,** hasta cierto punto, en cierto sentido. **In the same manner as,** del mismo modo que, así como. **After o in this manner,** así, de este modo. **Paul, as his manner was,** Pablo, como tenía por costumbre. **By all manner of means,** de todos modos; en todo caso; de cualquier modo posible. **To take in o with the manner,** coger o atrapar en el acto de cometer el delito; ser cogido en fragante o en el hecho. **Good manners,** buena crianza, buenas maneras, modales. **He has no manners,** es un mal educado, no tiene educación. **I shall teach you better manners,** yo te enseñaré a portarte mejor.

mannered ['mænəd] [ma-nerd], _a._ Bien educado, de buenos modales. **Ill-mannered,** descortés, brusco.

mannerism ['mænərɪzəm] [ma-ne-ri-sem], _s._ Adhesión pronunciada a una manera o a un estilo (literario o artístico); estilo amanerado, modismo.

mannerliness ['mænəlɪnɪs] [ma-ner-li-nes], _s._ Urbanidad, cortesía, política, cortesanía.

mannerly ['mænəlɪ] [ma-ner-li], _a._ Cortés, urbano, atento. _-adv._ Urbanamente.

mannikin ['mænɪkɪn] [ma-ni-kin], _s. V._ MANIKIN.

mannish ['mænɪʃ] [ma-nish], _a._ 1. Masculino, que tiene trazas de hombre, que remeda a los hombres. **A mannish woman,** marimacho. 2. _(Des.)_ Hombruno, varonil.

manoeuvable, [man-li] _a._ = **maneuverable** _(E.U.)_

manoeuvre, _s. f._ = **maneuver** _(E.U.)_

manometer [mə'nɒmiːtəʳ] [ma-no-mi-taʳ], _s._ Manómetro, instrumento para hacer ver o medir la fuerza elástica de los gases.

manor ['mænəʳ] [ma-noʳ], _s._ 1. Señorío o jurisdicción territorial, feudo. 2. **Manor-house, manorseat,** casa solariega, mansión o morada del señor de una jurisdicción o del poseedor de un señorío.

manorial [mə'nɔːrɪəl] [ma-no-rial], _a._ Señorial, perteneciente al señor de vasallos o de un feudo.

manpower ['mænpaʊəʳ] [man-pauaʳ], _s._ 1. Brazos de que se dispone. 2. Conjunto de elementos humanos de que dispone una nación para su defensa.

mansard (roof) ['mænsɑːd] [man-sard], _s._ Techo de boardilla, aboardillado.

manse [mæns] [mans], _s._ 1. Cortijo, granja, quinta, alquería. _(Mex.)_ Hacienda. 2. Casa rectoral, la morada del párroco, abadía en algunas provincias.

mansion ['mænʃən] [man-shon], _s._ Mansión, morada, residencia. **Mansion-house,** casa grande que sirve de habitación; palacio del Lord Mayor o alcalde de Londres.

manslaughter ['mænˌslɔːtəʳ] [man-slo-taʳ], _s._ Homicidio casual, involuntario.

man-slayer ['mænsleɪəʳ] [man-sleiaʳ], _s._ Homicida.

man-stealer ['mænstiːləʳ] [man-sti-laʳ], _s._ El que hurta y vende hombres.

man-stealing ['mænˈstiːlɪŋ] [man-sti-lin], _s._ La acción de hurtar hombres para venderlos.

mansuetude [ˌmænswəˈtjuːd] [man-sue-tiud], _s._ mansedumbre.

mantel ['mæntl] [man-tel], _s._ Manto, frente de la campana de una chimenea. **Mantel-piece,** repisa de chimenea, la parte que sobresale de la campana encima del hogar.

mantelet ['mæntəlɪt] [man-te-let], _s._ 1. Capotillo, manteleta de mujer. 2. _(Mil.)_ Mantelete, parapeto portátil cubierto para que sirva de defensa a los minadores.

mantilla [mæn'tɪlə] [man-tila], _s._ mantilla.

mantis ['mæntɪs] [man-tis], _s._ Mántide (f.), mantis, insecto ortóptero de muy rara figura; se llama vulgarmente rezadora.

mantle ['mæntl] [man-tel], _s._ 1. Manto, manteo, capa, manteleta, mantilla, mantelina. 2. _(Zool.)_ Manto, palio, capa, lo que encubre u oculta un órgano. 3. Caperuza.

mantle, _va._ y _vn._ 1. Cubrir, tapar, ocultar, disfrazar. 2. Extender las alas. 3. Extenderse mucho por la superficie; bañar, desparramarse.

mantling ['mæntlɪŋ] [man-tlin], _s._ _(Blas.)_ Mantelete, manto o ropaje alrededor de un escudo de armas.

mantua ['mæntʊə] [man-tua], _s._ Manto de señora.

manual ['mænjʊəl] [ma-niual], _a._ Manual. **Manual work,** trabajo, obra manual. **Sign manual,** firma. _-s._ 1. Manual, libro compendioso. 2. Teclado de órgano para las manos. 3. _(Mil.)_ Ejercicio sistemático en el manejo de algún arma.

manual training ['mænjʊəlˌtreɪnɪŋ] [ma-niual-trei-nin], _s._ Instrucción en trabajo o labores manuales. Enseñanza de artes y oficios.

manubrium ['mænjʊbrɪəm] [ma-niu-brium], _s._ 1. Manubrio, la empuñadura o mango de un instrumento. 2. _(Biol.)_ Manubrio, una parte o eminencia comparable a un mango.

manuductor [mænjʊˈdʌktəʳ] [ma-niu-dak-taʳ], _s._ Guía, guiador, conductor.

manufactory [ˌmænjʊˈfæktərɪ] [ma-niu-fak-to-ri], _s._ Fábrica, manufactura, edificio o lugar donde se fabrican mercancías.

manufacture [ˌmænjʊˈfæktəʳ] [ma-nu-fak-chaʳ], _s._ 1. Fabricación, el acto de fabricar. 2. Manufactura, fábrica, artefacto, obra, una cosa cualquiera manufacturada.

manufacture, _va._ Fabricar, manufacturar; hacer una cosa por medios mecánicos. Inventar _(Fig.)._ _-vn._ Estar ocupado en alguna manufactura.

manufacturer [ˌmænjʊˈfæktərəʳ] [ma-nu-fak-chu-raʳ], _s._ Fabricante, el que trabaja la materia prima; el propietario de una fábrica o manufactura.

manufacturing [ˌmænjʊˈfæktərɪŋ] [ma-nu-fak-chu-rin], _pa._ Fabricante, manufacturero, que se refiere a la manufactura; fabril. **Manufacturing costs,** costes de fabricación.

manumise, _va. V._ TO MANUMIT.

manumission [ˌmænjʊˈmɪʃən] [ma-niu-mi-shon], _s._ Manumisión, el acto de libertar al esclavo.

manumit ['mænjʊmɪt] [ma-niu-mit], _va._ Manumitir, dar libertad al esclavo.

manumotor [ˌmænjʊˈmɒtəʳ] [ma-niu-mo-toʳ], _s._ Cochecito movido a mano por el que va en él; lo usan los inválidos.

manurable ['mænjʊrəbl] [ma-niu-ra-bol], _a._ 1. Que puede ser fertilizado con abono. 2. _(Des.)_ Labrantío, de labor, cultivable.

manure [mə'njʊəʳ] [ma-niuaʳ], _va._ 1. Abonar, engrasar, estercolar. 2. _(Des.)_ Cultivar, labrar la tierra.

manure, _s._ Abono, el estiércol o cosa equivalente que se echa a las tierras para beneficiarlas; fiemo, basura. **Manure heap,** estercolero.

manus ['mænəs] [ma-nus], _s._ La mano, o la parte correspondiente terminal del miembro torácico.

manuscript ['mænjʊskrɪpt] [ma-nius-kript], _s._ Manuscrito. _a._ Manuscrito, que está escrito con la mano.

manutyper [ˌmænjʊˈtaɪpəʳ] [ma-niu-tai-paʳ], _s._ El o la que imprime a mano por medio de una máquina de escribir; y la máquina de escribir misma.

manx {mæŋks} [manks], *a.* y *s.* De la isla inglesa de Man.

many ['menɪ] [me-ni], *a.* (comp. MORE, sup. MOST). Muchos, muchas; varios, diversos. **Many a, an, o another.** Significa gran número pero como un todo aislado, y va seguido de nombre en singular. **Many a man,** muchos hombres. **Many a time,** muchas veces. **Many times,** muchas veces, frecuentemente. **Too many,** demasiados. **They were too many for us,** eran demasiado fuertes para nosotros. **One too many,** uno de más o de sobra. **Twice as many, el** doble, dos veces tantos. **How many?** ¿Cuántos, cuántas? **A great many,** un gran número, muchos. **So many,** tantos. **Many-colored,** de muchos colores, abigarrado. **Many-cornered,** polígono, que tiene muchos lados. **Many-headed,** que tiene muchas cabezas. **Many-languaged,** que tiene muchas lenguas o idiomas. **Many minded,** de mudable, parecer; voluble, versátil. **Not many people,** poca gente. **Many-peopled,** numeroso, populoso. **Many-sided,** multilátero. -*s.* Muchedumbre, multitud, gente; familia, criados; servidumbre, hablando de reyes.

manyplies ['menɪplaɪs] [me-ni-plais], *s.* Omaso, salterio, el tercer estómago de los rumiantes.

manzanita ['mænzənɪtə] [man-sa-ni-ta], *s.* Manzanita.

maoism ['maʊɪzən] [mau-isem], *s.* Maoísmo.

map [mæp] [map], *s.* Mapa, plano topográfico. **It's right off the map,** está en el quinto pino, en el quinto infierno (*Fig.*). **Map maker,** cartógrafo.

map, *va.* Delinear mapas, sean geográficos o topográficos. **Map out,** indicar en un mapa.

maple [mæpl] [ma-pel], *s.* (*Bot.*) Arce, plátano falso; cualquier árbol del género Acer.

mapmaking ['mæp,meɪkɪŋ] [map-mei-kin], *s.* Cartografía.

mappery ['mæpərɪ] [ma-pe-ri], *s.* Dibujo de mapas.

mapping, *s. f.* = **Mapmaking.**

mar [mɑːʳ] [maʳ], *va.* Echar a perder alguna cosa, dañar, desfigurar, corromper.

mar, *s.* Mancha, borrón, injuria.

marabou ['mærəbuː] [ma-ra-bu], *s.* (*Zool.*) Marabú, ave del género cigüeña, originaria de África, que tiene en las alas unas plumas muy hermosas y delicadas del mismo nombre, muy apreciadas para adorno.

marabout ['mærəbaʊt] [ma-ra-baut], *s.* Morabito, ermita, santón mahometano entre los bereberes.

maranatha ['mærənəθə] [ma-ra-na-za], *s.* Maranata, fórmula de excomunión entre los judíos.

maraschino [,mærəs'kiːnəʊ] [ma-ras-ki-nou], *s.* Licor marrasquino. **Maraschino cherries,** cerezas conservadas en licor marrasquino.

marasmus ['mærəsməs] [ma-ras-mus], *s.* (*Med.*) Marasmo, flaqueza y consunción de la sustancia del cuerpo.

marathon ['mærəθən] [ma-ra-zon], *s. m.* 1. Maratón. 2. *a.* Interminable, excesivamente largo.

maraud [məˈrɔːd] [ma-rod], *va.* Merodear, pillar, robar.

marauder [məˈrɔːdəʳ] [ma-ro-daʳ], *s.* Merodeador, soldado que sale a robar en el campo enemigo; pillador.

marauding [məˈrɔːdɪŋ] [ma-ro-din], *a.* Se dice del soldado que merodea. -*s.* Merodeo, pecorea, pillaje.

maravedi ['mærəvedɪ] [ma-ra-ve-di], *s.* Maravedí.

marble ['mɑːbl] [mar-bel], *s.* 1. Mármol. 2. **Marbles,** *pl.* Canicas, bolillas de mármol, de barro cocido, de vidrio o porcelana con que juegan los niños. -*a.* Marmóreo, de mármol. **Marble-cutter,** marmolista, obrero que trabaja en mármol. **Marble works,** marmolería. **To lose one's marbles,** perder la cabeza (*Fig.*).

marble, *va.* Jaspear, pintar imitando los colores del jaspe o mármol.

marble-hearted ['mɑːbl,hɑːtɪd] [mar-bel-jar-tid], *a.* Duro, insensible, que tiene corazón de mármol.

marbleize ['mɑːblaɪz] [mar-blais], *va.* Jaspear.

marc ['mɑːk] [mark], *s.* Orujo, el hollejo de la uva después de exprimida.

marcasite ['mɑːkəsaɪt] [mar-ka-sait], *s.* Marquesita, marcasita, pirita blanca.

march [mɑːtʃ] [march], *vn.* Marchar, caminar; andar con aire de majestad; limitar. -*va.* Poner en marcha, hacer marchar. **To march back,** volverse atrás; hacer volver. **To march in,** entrar, seguir. **To march off,** irse, partirse, retirarse; desalojar. **To march on,** marchar, caminar. **To march out,** salir o hacer salir. **To march up,** avanzar, adelantar; hacer avanzar, adelantar.

march, *a.* 1. Marzo, el tercer mes del año. 2. (*Mil.*) Marcha, la acción de marchar los soldados de un paraje a otro; la acción de marchar, modo de andar con cierta dignidad. 3. (*Mil.*) Marcha, el son que toca el tambor o el clarín para que se pongan en marcha los soldados. 4. Marcha, pieza de música que sirve para regularizar el paso de los que marchan. **To strike up a march,** tocar una marcha. 5. Adelanto, progreso. **Marches,** *pl.* Frontera, raya, límite, témino.

marcher ['mɑːtʃəʳ] [mar-chaʳ], *s.* Jefe militar o señor que antiguamente defendía los límites de una frontera.

marching ['mɑːtʃɪŋ] [mar-chin], *s.* Marcha, movimiento militar, paso de tropas. -*pa.* Marchando, dispuesto a caminar; de marcha. **Marching order,** orden de marcha. **To give somebody his marching orders,** despedir a alguien (*Fam.*).

marchioness ['mɑːʃənɪs] [mar-sha-nis], *sf.* Marquesa.

marchpane ['mɑːtpeɪn] [march-pein], *s.* Mazapán.

marcid ['mɑːsɪd] [mar-sid], *a.* macilento, magro, flaco: extenuado, descarnado.

mare ['meəʳ] [meaʳ], *sf.* Yegua, la hembra del caballo. **Mare's nest,** agua de cerrajas, algo que al principio pareció ser importante, y que resulta ser inútil, menguado o falso.

mare's-tail ['meəzteɪl] [meas-teil], *s.* (*Bot.*) Cola de caballo; planta acuática.

margaric ['mɑːtgærɪk] [mar-ga-rik], *a.* Margárico, perteneciente a la perla. **Margaric acid,** ácido margárico.

margaric, margarine ['mɑːdʒəˈriːn] [mar-ya-rin], *s.* (*Quím.*) Margarina.

margarite ['mɑːgərɪt] [mar-ga-rit], *s.* Margarita, perla.

marge [mɑːdʒ] [mardch], *s.* (*Poét.*) V. MARGIN. (*Fr.*)

margin ['mɑːdʒɪn] [mar-yin], *s.* 1. Margen, borde, orilla o extremidad de alguna cosa. 2. Margen, la porción del papel que se deja en blanco a una y otra parte de los escrito o impreso. 3. Provisión o reserva que se hace para atender a futuras contingencias o cambios. 4. Alcance. 5. (*Com.*) La diferencia entre el precio de compra y el de venta de las mercancías.

margin, *va.* 1. Marginar, margenar, escribir algo en el margen de un escrito o impreso. 2. Lindar, poner borde o margen; formar el borde de. -*vn.* Depositar fondos de reserva en manos de un agente de cambio.

marginal ['mɑːdʒɪnl] [mar-yi-nal], *a.* Marginal; escrito o anotado al margen.

marginally ['mɑːdʒɪnəlɪ] [mar-yi-na-li], *adv.* Al margen.

marginate, marginated ['mɑːdʒɪneɪt] [mar-yi-neit], *a.* Marginado.

Marguerite [,mɑːgəˈriːt] [mar-ga-rit], *s. f.* Margarita.

mariet ['mɑːrɪɪt] [mar-riet], *s.* (*Bot.*) Especie de campanilla.

marigold ['mærɪgəʊld] [ma-ri-gould], *s.* (*Bot.*) Caléndula, flamenquilla.

marihuana, marijuana [,mærɪˈhwɑːnə] [ma-ri-jua-na], *s.* Mariguana o marihuana.

marimba [məˈrɪmbə] [ma-rim-ba], *s.* (*Mús.*) Marimba.

marina [məˈriːnə] [ma-ri-na], *s.* 1. Estación de gasolina para los botes. 2. Puerto deportivo; dársena abrigada para embarcaciones con servicio de verdadero o grúas para izarlas.

marinate ['mærɪneɪt] [me-ri-neit], *va.* Escabechar pescado.

marine [məˈriːn] [ma-rin], *a.* Marino, de mar; oceánico; náutico; naval. **Marine engine,** máquina de vapor marina. -*s.* 1. Marino, soldado de marina. 2. Marina, fuerza naval; buques o bajeles en general. 3. Marina, pintura o cuadro que representa el mar.

mariner ['mærɪnəʳ] [ma-ri-naʳ], *s.* Marinero. **Mariner's compass,** brújula, compás para la navegación.

marionette [ˌmærɪə'net] [ma-rio-net], *s.* Marioneta, títere.

marish ['mærɪʃ] [ma-rish], *s.* V. MARSH. *-a. (Des.)* Pantanoso. V. MARSHY.

marital ['mærɪtl] [ma-ri-tal], *a.* Marital.

maritime ['mærɪtaɪm] [ma-ri-taim], *a.* Marítimo, naval, cercano al mar; que pertenece al mar, marino.

marjoram ['mɑːdʒərəm] [mar-yo-ram], *s. (Bot.)* Mejorana, almoradux.

mark [mɑːk] [mark], *s.* 1. Marca, señal, nota, impresión, huella. 2. Prueba, evidencia; observación, nota. 3. Blanco, señal fija y determinada a que se tira. **To hit the mark,** dar en el blanco, alcanzar el objetivo. 4. La cruz u otra señal que hace en lugar de firma el que no sabe escribir. 5. Marco, moneda de plata, unidad monetaria de Alemania. 6. La señal por la cual se sabe la edad de un caballo. 7. Señal característica. 8. Eminencia, distinción. 9. Regia, norma. 10. V. MARQUE. **St. Mark's gospel,** evangelio de S. Marcos. **Open marks,** señales evidentes. **To be up to the mark,** estar a la altura de las circunstancias. **To get high marks,** obtener buenas notas *(exams)*. **To get no marks at all as a musician,** ser un pésimo músico, ser un desastre como músico.

mark, *va.* Marcar, señalar; notar, advertir observar; mirar como válido o importante. *-vn.* Advertir, notar, reparar. **To mark down,** anotar, poner por escrito, marcar a un precio más bajo. **To mark off,** dividir, separar; diferenciar, distinguir. **To mark out,** mostrar, señalar; elegir, escoger; cancelar, borrar. **To mark up,** apuntar; sobrecargar (price).

markdown ['mɑːkdaʊn] [mark-daun], *s.* Subprecio.

marked ['mɑːkt] [markt], *a.* Acusado, marcado.

markedly ['mɑːkɪdlɪ] [mar-kid-li], *adv.* Apreciablemente, marcadamente, notablemente.

marked man ['mɑːkɪdmən] [mar-kid-man], *s.* Individuo sentenciado por sus enemigos.

marker ['mɑːkəʳ] [mar-kaʳ], *s.* 1. Marcador. 2. Marcador (games). 3. Rotulador.

market ['mɑːkɪt] [mar-kit], *s.* 1. Mercado, plaza de mercado o gran edificio en que se ponen a la venta los víveres o provisiones de boca y otros géneros. 2. Venta, tráfico, estado del comercio en cuanto a los precios o a la oferta y la demanda; precio, curso. 3. Localidad o país en que se puede comprar o vender alguna cosa. 4. Mercado, concurrencia de gente en un paraje determinado para comprar y vender géneros. **Market analysis,** análisis de mercado. **Market garden,** huerto. **Market rate,** tipo del mercado. **The market price of silver,** el precio corriente de la plata. **The cotton market is firm,** los precios del algodón se mantienen firmes. **Money market,** mercado monetario. **Markets are cheaper,** han bajado los precios. **Market-garden,** huerto o huerta, terreno donde se cultivan legumbres y frutas menores. **Market price, market rate,** el precio del mercado, precio corriente de las mercancías. **Market-town,** pueblo de mercado. **Market-man,** placero, el que va al mercado a vender o comprar. **Market-day,** día de mercado, o de plaza. **To be in the market for something** estar dispuesto a comprar algo.

market, *va.* Mercar, comprar o vender en mercado.

marketable ['mɑːkɪtəbl] [mar-ki-ta-bol], *a.* Vendible, corriente, pedido de venta.

marketing ['mɑːkɪtɪŋ] [mar-ki-tin], *s.* 1. Compra. 2. Venta. 3. Mercadotecnia. **Marketing research,** Análisis de mercados, mercadotecnia.

market-led ['mɑːkɪtˌled] [mar-kit-led], *a.* Generado por el mercado.

market-place ['mɑːkɪtpleɪs] [mar-kit-pleis], *s.* Mercado o plaza de mercado, el sitio donde se celebra el mercado.

marking ['mɑːkɪŋ] [mar-kin], *s. y pa.* Marcación, la acción de marcar. **Marking-ink,** tinta de marcar. **Marking-iron,** hierro de marcar. **Marking-machine,** máquina de marcar, de acordonar monedas. **Marking-nut,** agalla de caoba; su jugo mezclado con cal viva hace una tinta indeble.

marksman ['mɑːksmən] [marks-man], *s.* 1. Tirador, el que tira con acierto al blanco. 2. El que no sabe escribir su nombre y hace una señal.

marksmanship ['mɑːksmənʃɪp] [marks-man-ship], *s.* Puntería.

mark time ['mɑːktaɪm] [mark-taim], *vn.* 1. Llevar el compás de la música. 2. Quedar inactivo en espera de alguna actividad futura.

markup ['mɑːkʌp] [mark-ap], *s.* Sobreprecio.

marl [mɑːl] [marl], *s.* Marga, depósito de carbonato de cal, arcilla y arena que sirve para abonar los terrenos. **Marl-pit,** Marguera, gredal, margal.

marl, *va.* 1. Margar, abonar la tierra con marga. 2. *(Mar.)* Trincafiar, envolver con merlín anudado a cada vuelta.

marlaceous ['mɑːleɪʃəs] [mar-lei-shos], *a.* Margoso.

marline ['mɑːlɪn] [mar-lin], *s. (Mar.)* Merlín, cuerdas delgadas de cáñamo sin retorcer que se empapan en pez y sirven para liarlas alrededor de los cables.

marmalade ['mɑːmələɪd] [mar-ma-leid], *s.* Mermelada, conserva de frutas ácidas o amargas hecha con azúcar.

marmoration [ˌmɑːmə'reɪʃən] [mar-mo-rei-shon], *s.* Incrustación de mármol.

marmoreal [mɑː'mɔːrɪəl] [mar-mo-rial], **Marmorean** [mɑː'mɔːrɪən] [mar-mo-rian], *a.* Marmóreo.

marmoset ['mɑːməzet] [mar-mo-set], *s.* Mono muy pequeño de la América del Sur.

marmot ['mɑːmət] [mar-mot], *s.* Marmota, animal roedor.

maroon [mə'ruːn] [ma-run], *va.* Abandonar, castigar a un marinero dejándolo en una costa desierta.

maroon, *a.* De color purpúreo o rojo obscuro. *-s.* 1. Color rojo obscuro. 2. Materia de tinte obtenida del alquitrán de hulla.

maroon, *v.t.* Abandonar en una isla desierta, aislar.

maroon, *s.* 1. Cimarrón, negro esclavo de las Antillas que se refugiaba en los bosques. 2. Persona abandonada en una isla.

marplot ['mɑːplət] [mar-plot], *s.* Cizañero, revolvedor, el que con su intervención e intrigas hace malograr un proyecto.

marque [mɑːk] [mark], *s.* Licencia para tomar represalias. **Letter of marque,** patente de corso.

marquee [mɑː'kiː] [mar-ki], *s.* 1. Marquesina. 2. Gran tienda de campaña. 3. Toldo para una ventana.

marquess, *s.* V. MARQUIS.

marquetry ['mɑːkwɪtrɪ] [mar-kui-tri], *s.* Marquetería, ataracea.

marquis ['mɑːkwɪs] [mar-kuis], *s.* Marqués, título de dignidad.

marquisate ['mɑːkwɪseɪt] [mar-kui-seit], *s.* Marquesado.

marquisette ['mɑːkwɪsɪt] [mar-kui-sit], *s.* Tejido fino de malla.

marrer ['mɑːrəʳ] [ma-raʳ], *s.* El que echa a perder o el que daña a alguna persona o cosa.

marriage ['mærɪdʒ] [ma-rich], *s.* 1. Matrimonio, maridaje. 2. Casamiento (el estado y el acto), matrimonio. 3. Boda. 4. *(Fig.)* Enlace, íntima unión. **The marriage articles,** el contrato matrimonial o los contratos esponsalicios. **Mariage bonds,** lazos matrimoniales. **Marriage-song,** epitalamio. **The marriage-bed,** el lecho nupcial. **The marriage-day,** el día de la boda. **Marriage-bell,** toque de campanas con motivo de una boda. **Marriage-license,** licencia para casarse; cédula oficial concedida según la ley para que se casen las personas nombradas en ella. **Marriage-portion,** dote.

marriageable ['mærɪdʒəbl] [ma-ri-cha-bol], *a.* Casadero, núbil, capaz de contraer matrimonio. **She is not yet marriageable,** no ha llegado aún a la edad de tomar estado, o a la edad de matrimonio.

married ['mærɪd] [ma-rid], *a.* Casado, matrimonial, conyugal, connubial. **A married couple,** cónyuges, matrimonio, casados. **To get married,** casarse. **The married state,** el estado matrimonial.

marron ['mærən] [ma-ron], *s.* 1. Petardo pirotécnico. 2. Color castaño. 3. Gran castaña dulce del sur de Europa; se usa como alimento y para confitura.

marrow ['mærəʊ] [ma-rou], *s.* 1. Tuétano, médula. 2. Meollo, médula, la sustancia interior de alguna cosa; la esencia. **Vegetable marrow,** médula vegetal, calabacín.

marrowbone ['mærəʊbəʊn] [ma-rou-boun], *s.* Caña o hueso medular. **Marrowbones,** (*Fest.*) Las rodillas.

marrowfat ['mærəʊfæt] [ma-rou-fat], *s.* (*Bot.*) Guisante, especie de legumbre.

marrowish ['mærəʊɪʃ] [ma-rouish], *a.* Meduloso.

marrowless ['mærəʊlɪs] [ma-rou-lis], *a.* Falto de médula o tuétano.

marrowy ['mærəʊɪ] [ma-roui], *a.* Lleno de tuétano, meduloso; medular, de tuétano.

marry ['mærɪ] [ma-ri], *va.* 1. Casar, unir en matrimonio a un hombre y una mujer. 2. Casar, dar por esposo o esposa. 3. Tomar por marido o por mujer; desposar. 4. Casar, disponer algunas cosas de modo que hagan juego; (*Mar.*) ajustar los cabos sin aumentar el diámetro. -*vn.* Casar o casarse, contraer matrimonio. **To marry again,** volverse a casar, casarse de nuevo. **Marry in haste and repent at leisure,** tal se casa de prisa y se arrepiente despacio.

Mars [mɑːz] [mars], *s.* 1. Marte, uno de los planetas. 2. El dios romano de la guerra y de la fertilidad. 3. (*Des.*) Hierro.

marseilles [mɑːˈseɪlz] [mar-seils], *s.* Tela tupida de algodón con un dibujo en relieve.

marsh ['mɑːʃ] [marsh], *s.* Pantano, tremedal, ciénaga, marjal. **Marsh-elder,** (*Bot.*) Especie de guelde. **Marsh-mallow,** (a) (*Bot.*) Malvavisco, altea. (b) Confite hecho con altea. **Marsh-marigold,** (*Bot.*) Hierba centella. **Marsh-rocket,** (*Bot.*) Especie de berro.

marshal ['mɑːʃəl] [mar-shal], *s.* 1. Mariscal. 2. Bastonero o maestro de ceremonias. 3. Mariscal de campo, militar del más alto rango. 4. (*E. U.*) (a) Oficial de los tribunales de justicia de los Estados Unidos. (b) Jefe de la policía o del departamento de incendios en algunas ciudades. 5. Precursor, aposentador de camino.

marshal, *va.* Ordenar, poner en orden; guiar como director de alguna función, disciplinar. -*vn.* Juntarse y ordenarse (army).

marshaller ['mɑːʃələʳ] [mar-sha-laʳ], *s.* El que arregla, ordena y pone en orden alguna cosa: ordenador.

marshalship ['mɑːʃəlʃɪp] [mar-shal-ship], *s.* Mariscalía, mariscalato.

marshy ['mɑːʃɪ] [mar-shi], *a.* Pantanoso, cenagoso.

marsupial [mɑːˈsuːpɪəl] [mar-su-pial], *a.* Marsupial, que tiene una bolsa para llevar sus pequeñuelos. -*s.* Animal marsupial que tiene dicha bolsa.

mart [mɑːt] [mart], *s.* 1. Emporio, lugar donde concurren para comerciar gentes de diversas naciones; mercado público. 2. (*Des.*) Tráfico, compra y venta.

martel ['mɑːtl] [mar-tel], *s.* (*Her.*) Martillo, maza de armas.

marten ['mɑːtɪn] [mar-tin], *s.* 1. Marta, fuina, garduña, animal carnívoro cuya piel es muy estimada. 2. Piel de fuina. 3. (*Orn.*) Avión, vencejo.

martial ['mɑːʃəl] [mar-shal], *a.* 1. Marcial, belicoso, guerrero. 2. Marcial, militar. **Court-martial,** consejo de guerra. **Martial music,** música marcial. **Martial array,** orden de batalla.

martialism ['mɑːʃəlɪzm] [mar-sha-li-sem], *s.* Marcialidad; valentía.

martialist ['mɑːʃəlɪst] [mar-sha-list], *s.* Guerreador, guerrero.

martian ['mɑːʃən] [mar-shan], *a.* De Marte. (el planeta o el dios mitológico).

martin ['mɑːtɪn] [mar-tin], **martinet** [ˌmɑːtɪˈnet] [mar-ti-net], **martlet** ['mɑːtlɪt] [mart-let], *s.* Especie de golondrina; vencejo.

martinet [ˌmɑːtɪˈnet] [mar-ti-net], *s.* 1. El militar muy riguroso en la disciplina. 2. (*Mar.*) Apagapeoles.

martingale ['mɑːtɪŋgeɪl] [mar-tin-gueil], *s.* 1. Martingala; gamarra. 2. (*Mar.*) Moco del bauprés.

martini [mɑːˈtiːnɪ] [mar-ti-ni], *s.* Martini, vermú, bebida alcohólica compuesta.

martyr ['mɑːtəʳ] [mar-taʳ], *s.* 1. Mártir, el que padece muerte por la verdad o en defensa de la religión. 2. Mártir, el que

sufre muerte o persecución. 3. El que padece mucho tiempo (health).

martyrdom ['mɑːtədəm] [mar-ta-dom], *s.* Martirio.

martyrize ['mɑːtɪraɪz] [mar-ti-rais], *va.* Martirizar.

martyrological [ˌmɑːtɪrəˈlɒdʒɪkəl] [mar-ti-ro-lo-yi-kal], *a.* Lo perteneciente al martirologio.

martyrologist [ˌmɑːtɪˈrɒlɒdʒɪst] [mar-ti-ro-lo-yist], *s.* Escritor de martirologios.

martyrology [ˌmɑːtɪˈrɒlɒdʒɪ] [mar-ti-ro-lo-yi], *s.* Martirologio.

marvel ['mɑːvəl] [mar-vel], *s.* Maravilla, prodigio, lo que causa admiración. **Marvel of Peru,** (*Bot.*) maravilla del Perú. V. FOUR-O'CLOCK.

marvel, *vn.* Maravillar, maravillarse, admirar, admirarse, llenarse de admiración, pasmarse de alguna cosa.

marvelous ['mɑːvələs] [mar-ve-los], *a.* Maravilloso, pasmoso, admirable, prodigioso, asombroso, estupendo.

marvelously ['mɑːvələslɪ] [mar-ve-los-li], *adv.* Maravillosamente, pasmosamente.

marvelousness ['mɑːvələsnɪs] [mar-ve-los-nes], *s.* Maravilla, extrañeza, singularidad; lo maravilloso, lo extraordinario.

marxianism, marxism ['mɑːksɪənɪzm] [mark-sia-ni-sem], *s.* Marxismo, doctrina de Carlos Marx.

marxist ['mɑːksɪst] [mark-sist], *s.* Marxista, partidario de la doctrina de Carlos Marx.

marzipan [ˌmɑːzɪˈpæn] [mar-si-pan], *s.* Mazapán.

mascara [mæsˈkɑːrə] [mas-ka-ra], *s.* Tinte para obscurecer las pestañas, rimel.

mascot ['mæskət] [mas-kot], *s.* (*Fam.*) Alguna cosa de la que se supone que trae buena fortuna a su dueño.

masculine ['mæskjʊlɪn] [mas-kiu-lin], *a.* 1. Masculino, varonil. 2. (*Gram.*) Del género masculino (por su sexo o en sentido gramatical). **Masculine woman,** marimacho, mujer varonil.

masculineness ['mæskjʊlɪnnɪs] [mas-kiu-lin-nes], *s.* Masculinidad; virilidad.

maser ['mæsəʳ] [ma-saʳ], *s.* Maser, amplificación de microondas.

mash [mæʃ] [mash], *s.* 1. Amasijo, masa de alguna cosa ablandada, como afrecho amasado con agua. 2. Malta, el grano machacado o molido e infundido en agua caliente para hacer cerveza. 3. (*Des.*) Baturrillo, fárrago. **Mash o mashing-tub,** tina, vaso grande para mezclar cebada y agua.

mash, *va.* 1. Amasar, magullar, majar, poner blanda una cosa machacándola. 2. Amasar o mezclar la cebada molida con agua hirviendo para hacer cerveza. 3. (*Ger.*) Hacer cocos, cocar con persona del otro sexo.

mashy ['mæʃɪ] [ma-shi], *a.* Producido por magullación: magullado, abollado.

mask [mɑːsk] [mask], *s.* 1. Máscara, carátula, disfraz, carantoña, careta, mascarilla; mojiganga. 2. Velo, capa, pretexto, disimulación, disimulo, apariencia, color. **To put on a mask,** ponerse una máscara o careta. **Face mask,** mascarilla. **To take off the mask,** quitarse la máscara. 3. Molde que se obtiene de las facciones de una persona muerta. 4. Mascarada. V. MASQUERADE. 5. Representación dramática antigua en la que los actores asumían el papel de deidades mitológicas. 6. Máscara, persona que se disfraza. 7. (*Mil.*) Cubierta de ramaje para ocultar una batería.

mask, *va.* 1. Enmascarar, disfrazar y cubrir el rostro con máscara. **To mask a ship,** (*Mar.*) Disfrazar la bandera. 2. Encubrir, disimular, enmascarar, ocultar. -*vn.* Andar enmascarado. **Mask-ball o masked ball,** baile de máscaras, en que los concurrentes están disfrazados.

masker ['mɑːskəʳ] [mas-kaʳ], *s.* Máscara, el que se enmascara.

masking ['mɑːskɪŋ] [mas-kin], *s.* El acto de llevar máscara. -*pa.* de MASK.

masochism ['mæzəʊkɪzəm] [ma-sou-ki-sem], *s.* Masoquismo.

masochist ['mæzəʊkɪst] [ma-sou-kist], *a.* Masoquista.

masochistic [ˌmæzəʊˈkɪstɪk] [ma-sou-kis-tik], *a.* Masoquista.

mason, *s.* 1. Albañil. 2. Francmasón. **Mason-wasp,** Avispa albañila.

masonic [məˈsɒnɪk] [ma-so-nik], *a.* 1. Masónico, lo que pertenece a la sociedad de los francmasones. 2. Albañil, relativo a la albañilería.

masonry [ˈmeɪsnrɪ] [mei-shon-ri], *s.* 1. Albañilería, el arte u oficio del albañil. 2. Construcción de albañilería. 3. Francmasonería.

masorite [ˈmæzəraɪt] [ma-so-rait], *s.* Escritor del Masora.

masque [mɑːsk] [mask], *s.* MASK.

masquerade [ˌmæskəˈreɪd] [mas-ke-reid], *s.* 1. Mascarada, máscara, sarao de personas que se disfrazan con máscaras. 2. Mojiganga, disfraz, artificio para disimular. 3. Fiesta de cañas.

masquerade, *va.* Enmascararse, disfrazarse, ir disfrazado; asistir a algún sarao con máscara.

masquerader [ˌmɑːskəˈreɪdəʳ] [mas-ke-rei-daᶻ], *s.* Máscara, bufón.

mass [mæs] [mas], *s.* 1. Masa, montón, congerie, mole, conjunto de cosas que forman colectivamente un solo cuerpo. 2. Cuerpo informe; masa de materia concreta. 3. La parte principal de alguna cosa. 4. Bulto, volumen. **In mass** o **in the mass,** como un todo, en conjunto. **The masses,** el vulgo, la plebe, la gente con exclusión de los ricos y de las clases privilegiadas.

mass, *s.* 1. Misa, en la Iglesia católica. 2. Misa, la música que se compone para una misa solemne. **High mass,** misa mayor. **Low mass,** misa rezada. **A mass for the dead,** misa de réquiem o de ánima. **Mass-book,** misal, libro de misa. 3. Masa, multitud (of people).

massacre [ˈmæsəkəʳ] [ma-sa-kraʳ], *s.* Carnicería, matanza, mortandad grande.

massacre, *va.* Matar atrozmente, hacer una carnicería, destrozar.

massacrer [ˈmæsəkəʳ] [ma-sa-kraʳ], *s.* Matador, asesino.

massage [ˈmæsɑːdʒ] [ma-sach], *s.* Masaje. *-va.* Dar masajes, sobar el cuerpo.

masseter [ˈmæsətəʳ] [ma-sa-taʳ], *s.* Masetero, músculo masticatorio poderoso de la quijada inferior.

masseur [mæˈsɜːʳ] [ma-saʳ], *s.* Masajista (hombre).

masseuse [mæˈsɜːz] [ma-sesh], *s.* Masajista (mujer).

massicot [ˈmæsɪkət] [ma-si-kot], *s.* Albayalde calcinado, el óxido amarillo de plomo.

massiness [ˈmæsɪnɪs] [ma-si-nes], **Massiveness** [ˈmæsɪvnɪs] [ma-siv-nes], *s.* Peso, bulto, mole; solidez.

massive [ˈmæsɪv] [ma-siv], *a.* 1. Macizo, pesado, abultado, sólido. 2. *(Min.)* Sin forma definida de cristalización.

mass-media [ˈmæsmiːdɪə] [mas-mi-dia], *s.* Medios de comunicación de masas.

mass-meeting [ˈmæsˌmiːtɪŋ] [mas-mi-tin], *s.* Asamblea en masa; reunión pública a la que todos pueden concurrir.

mass-produce [ˈmæsprəˈdjuːs] [mas-pro-dius], *vt.* Producir en masa o en cadena.

mass production [ˈmæsprəˌdʌkʃən] [mas-pro-dak-shon], *s.* Fabricación en serie o en gran escala.

massy [ˈmæsɪ] [ma-si], *a.* Abultado, pesado, ponderoso, grueso, grande.

mast [mɑːst] [mast], *s.* 1. Palo de una embarcación; másitol. **Lower o standing mast,** *(Mar.)* Palos principales. **Top-masts,** *(Mar.)* Masteleros. **Mainmast,** palo mayor. **Foremast,** palo de trinquete. **Mizzen-mast,** palo de mesana. **Main-topmast,** mastelero mayor o de gavia. **Fore-top mast,** mastelero de proa. **Pole-mast,** palo de una pieza. **Made mast,** palo compuesto. **Fished mast,** palo reforzado. **Mast sprung,** palo rendido. **To spend a mast,** *(Mar.)* Perder un palo. 2. Bellota, fabuco, el fruto del roble y de la haya; avellana; en este sentido no tiene plural.

mast, *va.* 1. *(Mar.)* Arbolar un palo. 2. Cebar con bellotas, fabucos, etc., como a los cerdos.

master [ˈmɑːstəʳ] [mas-taʳ], *s.* 1. Amo. 2. Amo, dueño, señor, el poseedor de una cosa. 3. Maestro, en contraposición a discípulo o aprendiz. 4. Director, gobernador, jefe. 5.

Término de respeto que se usa como nombre genérico para designar a los señoritos muy jóvenes, o delante de los apellidos de estos mismos señoritos, como **Master Laight,** el señorito Laight. 6. Hombre entendido y diestro en alguna cosa. **Dancing-master,** maestro de baile. **Fencing-master,** maestro de esgrima. **Master of the horse,** caballerizo mayor. **Master of the ordnance,** director general de artillería o ingenieros. **Master-warden of the mint,** el director de la casa de moneda. **Master of arts,** maestro en artes o doctor en filosofía. **Master of a merchant vesel,** *(Mar.)* Capitán, maestre o patrón. **Past master,** (a) En muchas sociedades benéficas, el que ha tenido el oficio de director. (b) De aquí, el que es muy experto o hábil en alguna cosa. **Master-hand,** mano maestra, maestría. **Master-key,** llave maestra. **Master-stroke,** golpe maestro, golpe diestro. *-a.* Magistral, superior, principal. **To be master of the situation,** controlar la situación. **Master builder,** constructor principal, jefe de construcción. **Master workman,** maestro, capataz. **To be master of one's fate,** decidir su propio destino. **Master copy,** original (paper, book).

master, *va.* 1. Vencer, sujetar, domar; gobernar, dominar. 2. Ejecutar alguna cosa con maestría o destreza; comprender en todos sus detalles. *-vn.* Ser superior en alguna cosa. **To master the piano,** dominar el piano.

masterdom [ˈmɑːstədɒm] [mas-ta-dom], *s.* Dominio, mando.

masterful [ˈmɑːstəfʊl] [mas-ta-ful], *a.* 1. Imperioso, dominante; violento. 2. Hábil; diestro, capaz.

masterliness [ˈmɑːstəˌlɪnɪs] [mas-ta-li-nes], *s.* Maestría, destreza.

masterly [ˈmɑːstəlɪ] [mas-ter-li], *a.* 1. Magistral, que se ejecuta con maestría; digno de un maestro, hecho como por un maestro. 2. Ufano, imperioso, dominante. *-adv.* Magistralmente, con maestría.

master of ceremonies [ˈmɑːstəˈɒfˌserɪmənɪːz] [mas-ta-of-se-ri-mo-nis], *s.* Maestro de ceremonias.

masterpiece [ˈmɑːstəpiːs] [mas-ta-pis], *s.* Obra o pieza maestra, obra magistral.

mastership [ˈmɑːstəʃɪp] [mas-ta-ship], *s.* 1. Dominio, poder, gobierno. 2. Maestría, destreza. 3. Superioridad, preeminencia, conocimiento. 4. Magisterio, rectoría de un colegio u hospicio; la dignidad de ser el superior de un establecimiento público. 5. Tratamiento irónico de respeto.

masterwork [ˈmɑːstəwɜːk] [mas-ter-uerk], *s.* V. MASTERPIECE.

masterwort [ˈmɑːstəwɔːt] [ˈmɑː] [mas-ta-uort], *s.* *(Bot.)* Imperatoria.

mastery [ˈmɑːstərɪ] [mas-ta-ri], *s.* 1. Magisterio. 2. Dominio, poder, gobierno. 3. Preeminencia, superioridad. 4. Maestría, destreza, habilidad. 5. Adquisición de conocimientos, de superioridad o de poder.

mastful [ˈmɑːstfʊl] [mast-ful], *a.* Lo que abunda en bellotas, fabucos o castañas.

masthead [ˈmɑːsthed] [mast-jed], *s.* 1. *(Mar.)* Tope o remate del mástil. 2. Vigía, el marinero que vigila desde el mástil. 2. Enviar a un marinero al tope del mástil por castigo.

mastic [ˈmæstɪk] [mas-tik], *s.* Almáciga o almástiga, resina que destila el lentisco; materia pegajosa o betún.

masticate [ˈmæstɪkeɪt] [mas-ti-keit], *va.* Masticar, mascar, desmenuzar con los dientes.

mastication [ˌmæstɪˈkeɪʃən] [mas-ti-kei-shon], *s.* Masticación.

masticator [ˈmæstɪkeɪtəʳ] [mas-ti-kei-taʳ], *s.* 1. Mascador, el que masca. 2. Masticador, una máquina para preparar el caucho curdo o la gutaperpcha.

masticatory [ˈmæstɪkətərɪ] [mas-ti-ka-to-ri], *s.* Masticatorio, especie de medicamento.

mastiff [ˈmæstɪf] [mas-tif], *s.* Mastín.

mastitis [mæsˈtaɪtɪs] [mas-tai-tis], *s.* Mastitis, inflamación de la mama en las mujeres embarazadas.

mastless [ˈmæstlɪs] [mast-les], *a.* 1. Lo que no produce bellotas, fabucos o castañas. 2. *(Mar.)* Desarbolado, sin palo o árbol.

mastodon ['mæstədən] [mas-to-don], *s.* Mastodonte.

mastoid ['mæstɔɪd] [mas-toid], *a.* Mastoideo, que tiene forma de teta o pezón.

mastology ['mæstəlɒdʒɪ] [mas-to-lo-yi], *s. V.* MAMMALOGY.

masturbate ['mæstəbeɪt] [mas-ta-beit], *vn.* Practicar la masturbación.

mastubation ['mæstə'beɪʃən] [mas-ta-bei-shon], *s.* Masturbación, onanismo.

mat [mæt] [mat], *s.* 1. Estera, esterilla, petate, ruedo, felpufo hecho de esparto o de otra materia. **Sheep-skin mat,** zalca. 2. *(Mar.)* Palleta o pallete, empalletado, para impedir el roce. 3. Borde de cartón puesto alrededor de un cuadro, grabado, etc. **Chafed-mat,** *(Mar.)* Palleta afelpada.

mat, *va.* Esterar, cubrir con esteras; tejer.

mat, *va.* Producir (en los metales) una superficie mate, no pulida. *-a.* Mate, no pulido. *-s.* Herramienta para producir una superficie sin brillo. *V.* MATT.

matador ['mætədɔːʳ] [ma-ta-doʳ], *s.* Matador, espada (en las corridas de toros).

match ['mætʃ] [mach], *s.* 1. Mecha, pajuela, cualquier cosa a que se pega fuego con facilidad. 2. *(Art.)* Mecha, cuerdamecha, cuerdacalada. 3. Cerilla, fósforo. **Match-box,** fosforera, caja de cerillas.

match, *s.* 1. Compañero, pareja, una de las personas o cosas que forman un par. 2. Contrincante, el que compite con otro; igual, semejante. 3. Partido. 4. Juego, contienda, lucha de agilidad o fuerza. 5. Casamiento, alianza, boda. **Tennis match,** partido de tenis. **Match point,** punto de partido *(Tennis).* **He has met with his match,** ha encontrado la horma de su zapato. **A rich match,** alianza rica o ventajosa. **A running match,** una partida igual. **To be a bad match,** ir mal juntos, no emparejar.

match, *va.* 1. Igualar a, hacer conveniente, proporcionar. 2. Competir, entrar en competencia con otro. 3. Hermanar, aparear. **To match a pair of buckles,** hermanar un par de hebillas. **To match horses,** aparejar caballos. 4. Casar, dar en matrimonio. *-vn.* 1. Casar contraer matrimonio. *-vn.* 1. Casar, contraer matrimonio. 2. Hermanarse, ser una cosa igual a otra. **His stockings do not match,** sus medidas no son parejas o iguales. **Match up,** corresponder, hacer juego.

matchable ['mætʃəbl] [ma-cha-bol], *a.* Adaptable, igual, correspondiente, proporcionado.

matchbook ['mætʃbʊk] [mach-buk], *s.* Pequeño paquete de fósforos.

matching ['mætʃɪŋ] [ma-chin], *a.* Que hace juego.

matchless ['mætʃlɪs] [mach-les], *a.* Incomparable, sin igual, sin par.

matchlessly ['mætʃlɪslɪ] [mach-les-li], *adv.* Incomparablemente.

matchlessness ['mætʃlɪsnɪs] [mach-les-nes], *s.* El estado, calidad o propiedad de lo que no tiene igual.

matchlock ['mætʃlɒk] [mach-lok], *s.* Llave de los mosquetes antiugos que tenía una mecha.

match-maker ['mætʃmeɪkəʳ] [mach-mei-kaʳ], *s.* 1. Casamentero. 2. Pajuelero, fabricante de pajuelas o fósforos.

match-making ['mætʃmeɪkɪŋ] [mach-mei-kin], *s.* 1. Acción de meterse en hacer bodas. 2. Fabricación de pajuelas o fósforos.

mate [meɪt] [meit], *s.* 1. Consorte, marido o mujer. 2. Compañero, compañera; camarada. 3. Macho o hembra entre los animales. 4. Comensal, el que come a la mesa con otro. 5. Mate, en el juego del ajedrez. 6. *(Mar.)* Contramaestre, oficial de rango inferior al del capitán. **Boat-swain's mate** *(Mar.)* guardián del contramaestre. **Steward's mate,** *(Mar.)* Ayudante del despensero.

mate, *va.* 1. Casar, desposar, unir. 2. Igualar; aparar. 3. Competir; asombrar, asustar. 4. En el juego de ajedrez, dar jaque mate. 5. *(Des.)* Abrumar, confundir; vencer. 5. Acoplarse, aparearse *(Zool.).*

mateless ['meɪtlɪs] [meit-les], *a.* Solo, sin compañero, falto de consorte.

material [mə'tərɪəl] [ma-te-rial], *a.* 1. Material; corpóreo, físico. 2. Importante, que es de consecuencia o entidad,

principal, esencial, potente; serio, grave. **Nothing material,** nada de interesante o de importancia. 3. Material, lo contrapuesto a formal. **Most material to,** de la mayor importancia para. *-s.* 1. Material, ingrediente. 2. El material de que se compone una obra. **Building materials,** materiales de construcción.

materialism [mə'tərɪəlɪzəm] [ma-te-ria-li-sem], *s.* Materialismo.

materialist [mə'tərɪəlɪst] [ma-te-ria-list], *s.* Materialista, el sectario del materialismo; el que admite como unica sustancia la materia, negando la espiritualidad.

materialistic [mə'tərɪəlɪs'tɪk] [ma-te-ria-lis-tik], *a.* Materialista.

materiality [mə'tərɪəlɪtɪ] [ma-te-ria-li-ti], *s.* Materialidad, corporeidad, existencia meramente material.

materialize [mə'tərɪəlaɪz] [ma-te-ria-lais], *va.* 1. Hacer material alguna cosa; reducir a materia: considerar como materia. 2. Realizar, materializar, hacer visible y real. 3. Hacer común o vulgar. *-vn.* Realizarse, llegar a ser objeto de observación, tomar forma perceptible.

materially [mə'tərɪəlɪ] [ma-te-ria-li], *adv.* 1. Materialmente. 2. Esencialmente, de una manera importante. 3. Desde el punto de vista físico.

materialness [mə'tərɪəlnɪs] [ma-te-rial-nes], *s.* Materialidad, importancia.

maternal [mə'tɜːnl] [ma-ter-nal], *a.* Maternal, materno.

maternity [mə'tɜːnɪtɪ] [ma-ter-ni-ti], *s.* 1. Maternidad. 2. Hospital de parturientas: *(Amer.)* casa de maternidad.

mateship ['meɪtʃɪp] [meit-ship], *s.* Compañerismo.

math [mæθ] [maz], *s.* La siega del heno: se usa en composición, como **After-math,** retoño del heno.

mathematic, mathematical [ˌmæθə'mætɪk] [ma-ze-ma-tik], *a.* Matemático.

mathematically [ˌmæθə'mætɪkəlɪ] [ma-ze-ma-ti-ka-li], *adv.* Matemáticamente.

mathematics [ˌmæθə'mætɪkz] [ma-ze-ma-tiks], *s. pl.* Matemática, matemáticas, ciencia que trata de la cantidad.

mathesis ['mæθiːsɪs] [ma-zi-sis], *s. (Ant.)* Matemática, la doctrina o ciencia matemática.

matin ['mætɪn] [ma-tin], *s.* Mañana. *-a.* Matutino.

matinée ['mætɪneɪ] [ma-ti-nei], *s.* Matiné, función de la tarde. **Matinée idol,** actor que goza temporalmente de la adoración femenina.

mating ['meɪtɪŋ] [mei-tin], *s.* Apareamiento *(Zool.).* **Mating season,** época de celo.

matins ['mætɪnz] [ma-tins], *s. pl.* Maitines.

matrass ['mætrəs] [ma-tras], *s. (Quím.)* Matraz, una especie de retorta.

matriarch ['meɪtrɪɑːk] [mei-triark], *s.* Madre que gobierna a su familia.

matrices ['mætrɪsɪs] [ma-tri-sis], *s. pl.* de MATRIX.

matricidal ['mætrɪsɪdl] [ma-tri-si-dal], *a.* Que se refiere al matricidio.

matricide ['mætrɪsaɪd] [ma-tri-said], *s.* Matricidio; matricida.

matricula ['mætrɪkjʊlə] [ma-tri-kiu-leit], *s.* Matrícula, lista, catálogo, de un colegio o universidad.

matriculate [mə'trɪkjʊleɪt] [ma-tri-kiu-leit], *va. y vn.* Matricular, sentar en la matrícula; admitir o ser admitido en un colegio o en una universidad.

matriculate, *s. y a.* Matriculado.

matriculation [mə'trɪkjʊ'leɪʃən] [ma-tri-kiu-lei-shon], *s.* Matriculación, el acto de matricular en algún colegio o universidad.

matrimonial [ˌmætrɪ'məʊnɪəl] [ma-tri-mou-nial], *a.* Matrimonial, conyugal; marital.

matrimonially [ˌmætrɪ'məʊnɪəlɪ] [ma-tri-mou-nia-li], *adv.* Matrimonialmente.

matrimony [ˌmætrɪ'məʊnɪ] [ma-tri-mou-ni], *s.* 1. Matrimonio, el estado de los casados. 2. Casamiento, nupcias.

matrix ['meɪtrɪks] [mei-triks], *s.* 1. *(Anat.)* Matriz, útero. 2. *(Biol.)* Sustancia intercelular. 3. Matriz, molde. 4. Quijo, la piedra sólida en que se cría el metal en las minas.

matron ['meɪtrən] [mei-tron], *sf.* 1. Matrona, mujer casada, madre de familia; mujer de edad y respetable. 2. Ama de llaves o directora de un instituto o corporación.

matronal ['meɪtrənl] [mei-tro-nal], *a.* Matronal, lo perteneciente a la matrona.

matronize ['meɪtrənaɪz] [mei-tro-nais], *va.* 1. Dar la apariencia o las cualidades de matrona. 2. Acompañar a una joven a las tertulias o reuniones públicas.

matron-like ['meɪtrənlaɪk] [mei-tron-laik], *a.* Semejante a una matrona; grave, modesta.

matronly ['meɪtrənlɪ] [mei-tron-li], *a.* Como matrona, seria, grave.

matronymic ['meɪtrənɪmɪl] [mei-tro-ni-mik], *a.* Perteneciente al nombre de la madre o derivado de él. -*s.* Nombre así derivado.

matt [mæt] [mat], *a.* Mate, sin brillo, sin pulimento. **A matt surface,** Superficie, mate, sin brillo. -*s.* Superficie no bruñida.

matte [mæt] [mat], *s.* Mate, producto metálico sin purificar que contiene azufre; se obtiene especialmente del cobre.

matter ['mætər] [ma-tar], *s.* 1. Materia, cuerpo. 2. Materia o material con que se hace alguna cosa. 3. Materia, asunto, objeto de que se habla o de que se trata. 4. Cosas, asuntos, negocios, quehacer, dependencia. 5. Cuestión, proposición sobre que se disputa o trata. 6. Importancia, consecuencia, entidad. 7. Cualquier cosa o razón por la cual se siente alguna inquietud o cuidado. 8. Materia, pus. **What is the matter with you?** ¿qué le ocurre? **It is no matter,** no importa. **What is the matter?** ¿de qué se trata? ¿qué ocurre? **What is the matter that you are so sad?** ¿Por qué está Ud. tan triste? **Nothing is the matter,** no pasa nada. **I make no matter of it,** no hago caso de ello: familiarmente, maldito el caso que hago de tal cosa. **A matter of course,** una cosa de cajón. -*a.* Natural, que ha de esperarse. **It is a matter of fact,** es un hecho; cosa positiva, realidad. **A matter of fact man,** la persona que se atiene esprtictamente a lo que resulta de los hechos. **He only believes what he sees,** *(Vulg.)* Santo Tomás, ver y creer. **Off-hand matters,** cosas o asuntos de cada día. **No matter what she says,** diga lo que diga.

matter, *va.* 1. Importar, convenir o hacer al caso alguna cosa: se usa solamente después de *it, this, that o what.* **It matters not,** no importa, y familiarmente, no vale la pena. **What matters it?** ¿qué importa eso? **It matters much,** importa mucho. 2. Supurar, formarse materia o pus en una úlcera o llaga. -*va.* Hacer caso.

matterless ['mætəlɪs] [ma-ta-les], *a.* Fútil, falto de interés, de importancia o de objeto.

matting ['mætɪŋ] [ma-tin], *s.* 1. Esterado, tejido de juncos para entapizar. 2. *V.* MAT, 3ª acep. 3. Empalletado para impedir el roce.

mattock ['mætək] [ma-tok], *s.* Azadón de peto; zapapico, piqueta.

mattress ['mætrɪs] [ma-tris], *s.* 1. Colchón, cojín grande para descansar o dormir sobre él. 2. Empalletado, enlazado de ramaje, pértigas, etc., para proteger los diques y escolleras.

maturation [mætjʊəˈreɪʃən] [ma-chu-rei-shon], *s.* 1. Maduración, progreso hacia la madurez. 2. *(Med.)* Supuración.

mature [məˈtjʊər] [ma-chuar], *a.* 1. Maduro, sazonado. 2. Maduro, prudente, juicioso, sesudo. **Upon a more mature deliberation,** después de haberlo reflexionado detenidamente. 3. Acabado, elaborado. 4. *(Com.)* Vencido, pagadero. **To grow mature,** madurarse. **Mature years,** edad madura.

mature, *va.* 1. Madurar, disponer los medios para facilitar el logro de algún fin; adelantar hacia la conclusión. 2. Madurar, sazonar las frutas, etc. -*vn.* 1. Madurar o madurarse. 2. Ir madurando, tomando asiento o entrando en seso. 3. *(Com.)* Vencer, cumplirse un plazo.

maturely ['mætjʊəlɪ] [ma-chua-li], *adv.* Maduramente; con anticipación, con mucha reflexión.

matureness ['mætʃʊənɪs] [ma-chua-nes], *s.* Madurez, estado de perfección.

maturity [məˈtʃʊərɪtɪ] [ma-chua-ri-ti], *s.* 1. Madurez; edad madura. 2. Estado de perfección; a veces, la pubertad. 3. *(Com.)* Vencimiento (de un pagaré).

matutinal [ˌmætjʊˈtɪnəl] [ma-tu-ti-nal], *a.* Matutino, lo que pertenece a la mañana.

maudlin ['mɔːdlɪn] [mod-lin], *a.* 1. Entontecido por la embriaguez. 2. Lloroso y calamocano, que tiene el vino triste. -*s. V.* YARROW.

maugre ['mɔːgər] [mo- gar], *adv.* A pesar de, no obstante.

maukin ['mɔːkɪn] [mo-kin], *s.* Trapo; espantajo. *V.* MALKIN.

maul [mɔːl] [mol], *va.* 1. Apalear, maltratar a golpes, aporrear; tratar rudamente, abusar, vapulear. 2. Hender por medio de un mazo y cuñas.

maul, *s.* 1. Mazo o martillo grande de madera. 2. *(Mar.)* Bandarria, mandarria.

maul-stick ['mɔːlstɪk] [mol-stik], *s.* MAHLSTICK.

maunder ['mɔːndər] [mon-dar], *vn.* 1. Gruñir, murmurar, rezongar, refunfuñar. 2. *(Des.)* Mendigar.

maunderer ['mɔːndərər] [mon-de-rar], *s.* Gruñidor, murmurador.

maundering ['mɔːndərɪŋ] [mon-de-rin], *s.* Queja, quejido, gruñido, murmuración.

maundy ['mɔːndɪ] [mon-di], *s.* Mandato, la ceremonia eclesiástica de lavar los pies a doce personas. **Maundy Thursday,** Jueves santo, o jueves del mandato, la víspera del Viernes Santo.

mausolean [ˌmɔːsəˈlɪən] [mo-so-lian], *a.* Sepulcral, lo que pertenece al sepulcro o al mausoleo.

mausoleum [ˌmɔːsəˈlɪəm] [mo-so-liam], *s.* Mausoleo, sepulcro magnífico y suntuoso.

mauve [məʊv] [mouv], *s.* Color purpúreo delicado o lila; sustancia purpúrea de tinte.

maverick ['məvərɪk] [ma-ve-rik], *s.* 1. Animal sin marca de hierro. 2. Becerro sin madre. 3. *(Fam.)* Disidente.

mavis ['mævɪs] [ma-vis], *s. (Orn.)* Malvís, zorzal.

maw [mɔː] [mo], *s.* 1. Buche o molleja de las aves. 2. Cuajar, la parte del animal que corresponde al estómago en el hombre. 3. Vejiga de aire en los peces.

mawk ['mɔːk] [mok], *s.* (Prov. Ingl.) 1. Gusano. *V.* MAGGOT. 2. Mujer desaliñada; también se llama **mawks.** *V.* SLATTERN.

mawkish ['mɔːkɪʃ] [mo-kish], *a.* Fastidioso, empalagoso, desagradable al paladar; insípido o asqueroso.

mawkishness ['mɔːkɪʃnɪs] [mo-kish-nes], *s.* La calidad o propiedad de causar hastío o repugnancia; asquerosidad.

mawky ['mɔːkɪ] [mo-ki], *a.* Gusaniento.

maw-worm ['mɔːwɔːm] [mo-uorm], *s.* 1. Lombriz. 2. *V.* BOT.

max. *Abreviatura de* **maximum.**

maxi ['mæksɪ] [mak-si], *a.* Maxi *(Fam.).*

maxilla [mækˈsɪlə] [mak-si-la], *s.* Hueso maxilar, uno de los huesos de la quijada, particularmente de la superior.

maxillar [ˌmækˈsɪlər] [mak-si-lar], **maxilary** [ˌmæksɪˈlərɪ] [mak-si-la-ri], *a.* Maxilar, perteneciente a las mejillas o quijadas.

maxim ['mæksɪm] [mak-sim], *s.* 1. Máxima, sentencia, o dicho sentencioso, aforismo, regla. 2. Principio aceptado, teórico o práctico. 3. *(Ant.)* Axioma.

maximum ['mæksɪməm] [mak-si-mom], *s.* Lo sumo, lo más alto, lo último a que puede subir alguna cosa.

may [meɪ] [mei], *vr. irr. y def. (pret.* MIGHT*).* 1. Tener licencia, libertad, facultad o permiso, tener el poder moral; ser lícito, permitido. **If it may be,** si puede ser. **If I may say so,** si me es permitido decirlo o si puedo decirlo. 2. Ser posible dadas ciertas circunstancias; poderse. **As much as may be,** tanto como se pueda. **As soon as may be,** lo más pronto posible. **It may be,** puede ser. 3. Suceder, sea lo que sea: se usa elípticamente. **Be the pain what it may,** cualquiera que sea el dolor. 4. Denota deseo vivo, y se traduce por ojalá, Dios quiera, o se omite, y el verbo se pone en el modo optativo inglés, correspondiente al subjuntivo en castellano. **May I live long enough to see my country,** ojalá que yo viva hasta que pueda ver mi patria. **May you live long and happy,** viva Ud. largos y felices años. **May it please the court,** dígnese el tribunal (o el consejo) atender a mi súplica o solicitud. **I hope she may succeed,** espero que tenga suerte. **Be that as it may,** sea como sea. **May you have a happy life together!** ¡que sean felices! (wishes).

may ['meɪ] [mei], s. 1. Mayo, el quinto mes del año. 2. Primavera de la vida. 3. *(Des.)* Virgen, doncella. 4. *V.* HAWTHORN. **May-apple,** podófilo, la planta y su fruto. *V.* MANDRAKE, 2ª acep. **May-bloom,** *(Bot.)* Maya, espina blanca. **May-bug,** *(Ent.)* Especie de escarabajo. **May-lady, May-queen,** maya, la joven que sus compañeras elijen para que presida la fiesta de mayo. **May-lily,** *(Bot.)* Lirio de los valles. **May-pole,** mayo, el árbol cortado y adornado que se pone en los pueblos en algún lugar público para bailar alrededor de él en el primer día de mayo. **May-weed,** *(Bot.)* Manzanilla loca.

may, *vn.* Coger flores la mañana del día primero de mayo.

Maya ['maɪjə] [mai-ya], *a.* y *s.* Maya, Quiché.

maybe ['meɪbiː] [mei-bi], *adv.* Acaso, quizá, por ventura.

mayday ['meɪ] [mei], *s.* 1. SOS, socorro (distress call). 2. El día primero de mayo.

may-duke ['meɪdjɔːk] [mei-diuk], variedad de la cereza ordinaria (corrupción de Médoc.)

may-flower ['meɪflaʊəʳ] [mei-flauaʳ], *s. (Bot.)* 1. Maya; las flores que se hallan en mayo. 2. *(E. U.)* Planta rastrera primaveral.

may-fly ['meɪflaɪ] [mei-flai], *s. (Ent.)* Mosca de mayo o de pescadores; mosca de un día, insecto efímero.

may-game ['meɪɡeɪm] [mei-gueim], *s.* Juego, fiesta o diversión del día primero de mayo.

mayhem ['meɪhem] [mei-jem], *s.* 1. *(For.)* Mutilación. 2. Alboroto.

maying ['meɪɪŋ] [meiin], *s.* El acto de celebrar la antigua festividad del primero de mayo con guirnaldas, flores, bailes, etc.

mayo ['meɪəʊ] [meiou], *s.* = Mayonnaise *(E. U. fam.)*

mayonnaise [meɪə'neɪz] [meiou-neis], *s.* Mayonesa, salsa fría de yemas de huevo y aceite, batidos y sazonados a voluntad.

mayor ['meəʳ] [meiaʳ], *s.* Alcalde, corregidor, el magistrado principal de una ciudad.

mayoralty ['meərəltɪ] [mea-ral-ti], *s.* Corregimiento, el empleo y oficio del corregidor.

mayoress ['meərɪs] [mea-res], *sf.* Corregidora, la mujer del corregidor.

mazarine ['mæzəriːn] [ma-sa-rin], *s.* 1. Color azul subido. 2. Un modo particular de guisar aves. 3. Plato pequeño puesto dentro de otro mayor. **Mazarine blue,** color azul subido.

mazda lamp [ˌmæzdə'kæmp] [maz-da-lamp], *s.* Lámpara de tungsteno.

maze [meɪz] [meis], *s.* 1. Laberinto, lugar compuesto de varias calles o encrucijadas de difícil salida. 2. Laberinto, embolismo, enredo, duda, perplejidad, confusión. **To be in a maze,** estar perplejo, dudoso, confuso o sorprendido, estar metido en un laberinto.

maze, *s.* Taza de arce u otra madera.

maziness ['meɪznɪs] [meis-nes], *s.* Perplejidad, enredo.

mazurka ['mæzɜːkə] [ma-ser-ka], *s.* Mazurca, especie de polca y su música.

mazy ['meɪzɪ] [mei-si], *a.* Confuso, perplejo, asombrado, embrollado, enredado, confundido.

me [miː] [mi], *pron.* Me, el caso acusativo de **I,** yo; mí, después de una preposición. **As for me,** en cuanto a mí. **For me,** para mí, en mi sentir. **With me,** conmigo. **Do me the favor,** hágame Ud. el favor.

mead [miːd] [mid], *s.* Aguamiel, licor fermentado compuesto de miel y agua, aromatizado con especias.

mead *(Poét.)* **meadow** ['medəʊ] [me-dou], *s.* Pradera, pradería, vega, prado, por lo común produce el heno. **Meadowlark,** alondra de los prados.

meadow-saffron [ˌmedəʊ'sæfrən] [me-dou-sa-fron], *s. (Bot.)* Villorita, quitameriendas.

meadowy ['medəʊɪ] [me-doui], *a.* De pradera; parecido a un prado; lleno de prados.

meager, meagre ['miːɡəʳ] [mi-gaʳ], *a.* 1. Magro, flaco, enjuto; insuficiente. 2. Pobre, hambriento, falto de fertilidad o de riqueza. 3. Cuaresmal, propio de la cuaresma. **Meager soup,** sopa de viernes.

meagerly, meagrely ['miːɡəlɪ] [mi-ga-li], *adv.* Pobremente, flacamente.

meagerness, meagreness ['miːɡənɪs] [mi-ga-nes], *s.* Flaqueza, falta de carnes; escasez.

meal [miːl] [mil], *s.* 1. Comida, el sustento que se toma de una vez. 2. Harina, el grano comestible no muy molido.

mealman ['miːlmən] [mil-man], *s.* Harinero, el que comercia en harina.

mealtime ['miːltaɪm] [mil-taim], *s. f.* Hora de comer.

mealy ['miːlɪ] [mi-li], *a.* Harinoso, farináceo.

mealy-mouthed ['miːlɪmaʊðd] [mi-li-mauzd], *a.* Tímido y modesto en apariencia, doble, falso, hipócrita.

mealy-mouthedness ['miːlɪmaʊðnɪs] [mi-li-mauzd-nes], *s.* Melosidad, hipocresía en el hablar.

mean [miːn] [min], *a.* 1. Humilde, mediano; basto, inferior, pobre. 2. Bajo, vil, ruin, indigno, tacaño, obscuro, despreciable, abatido. **A mean action,** bajeza, bastardía, vileza, ruindad. **That was mean,** fue una vileza. 3. Mezquino, sórdido; pobre. 4. De poco valor o eficacia. **No mean foes,** no despreciables enemigos. 5. *(E.U.)* Formidable. **She played a mean game,** jugó estupendamente.

mean, *a.* 1. Medio, del medio. 2. Intermedio, en cuanto al volumen, al grado, a la calidad o al tiempo. **In the meantime, meanwhile,** entretanto, mientras tanto. **Mean time,** *(Astr.)* Tiempo medio.

mean, *s.* 1. Medio, lo que está entre los extremos; de aquí, mediocridad, medianidad, medianía. 2. Medio, manera, modo, forma, instrumento, expediente, diligencia o acción conveniente para el logro de alguna cosa. 3. *pl.* Medios, instrumento; lo que sirve para hacer una cosa; se usa a menudo con el verbo en singular. 4. *pl.* Medios, caudal, rentas, recursos, riquezas. 5. Término medio de un silogismo. **Private means,** rentas particulares. **By all means,** positivamente, sin duda, por supuesto. **By no means,** de ningún modo, de ninguna manera. **By fair means,** por medios lícitos; a buenas, por buenos modos, por dulzura. **By foul means,** por malos medios, por medios injustos, por la fuerza. **By no manner of means,** en absoluto. **By this means,** por este medio. **By some means or other,** de una manera u otra. **To live on one's means,** vivir de sus rentas. **He has no means to do it,** le faltan recursos para hacerlo. **To live within/beyond one's means,** vivir por debajo/encima de sus posibilidades.

mean, *vn.* (*pret.* y *pp.* MEANT). Hacer intención, hacer ánimo, pensar, proponerse o tener propósito de hacer alguna cosa (intend). **I mean to go by daybreak,** me propongo partir al romper el día. **I mean to go tomorrow,** estoy en ir mañana. - *va.* 1. Significar, querer decir, dar a entender. 2. Intentar, pretender. **What do you mean by that?** ¿qué quiere Ud. decir con eso? *What do you mean to do?* ¿qué pretende Ud. hacer? **He is a little rough, but he means well,** es un poco tosco, pero tiene buen corazón, o buenas intenciones. **What do you mean!** ¡Cómo se entiende! **What do you mean by taking it?** ¿cómo se atreve Ud. a coger eso? **Do you mean me?** ¿te refieres a mí? **To mean what one says,** pensar lo que se dice. **He did not mean to do it,** lo hizo sin querer, sin pensar. **She is meant to do it,** se supone que lo tiene que hacer ella. **He means well,** tiene buenas intenciones. **A well-meaning man,** un hombre de buena fe o buenos sentimientos; sincero, cándido, bien intencionado. **I mean what I say,** lo digo en serio. **Mean it!** ¡vaya! **The teacher means to be obeyed,** el profesor insiste en que se le obedezca.

meander [mɪ'ændəʳ] [min-daʳ], *s.* Laberinto, camino tortuoso y lleno de vueltas y revueltas.

meander, *va.* Rodear, hacer una cosa tortuosa o intrincada. - *vn.* Serpentear, voltear, tornar.

meandering ['mɪ'ændərɪŋ] [min-da-rin], *adj.* Serpenteante (road). Con meandros (river).

meandrian ['miːndrɪən] [min-drian], **meandry** ['miːndrɪ] [min-dr], *a.* Serpentino, tortuoso.

meandrous ['miːndrəs] [min-dros], *a.* Tortuoso, serpentino.

meaning ['miːnɪŋ] [mi-nin], *s.* 1. Ánimo, intención, voluntad, designio. 2. Sentido, significado, acepción, significación de una palabra o sentencia. **Double meaning,** ambigüedad, equívoco, doble sentido. *(Vulg.)* Retruécano. **There is no meaning in what he says,** es cháchara todo lo que dice; no tiene el menor fundamento cuanto dice. **Do you get his meaning?** ¿Le entiendes?

meaningful ['miːnɪŋfʊl] [mi-nin-ful], *a.* Significativo.

meaningless ['miːnɪŋlɪs] [mi-nin-les], *a.* Vacío de sentido, sin objeto ni importancia.

meaningly ['miːnɪŋlɪ] [mi-nin-li], *adv.* De una manera significativa, con intención.

meanly ['miːnlɪ] [min-li], *adv.* 1. Sin dignidad. **Meanly, born,** nacido de baja estofa. 2. Mediocremente. 3. Bajamente, vilmente. 4. Con desprecio; pobremente, miserablemente. **To think meanly of,** despreciar, hacer poco caso de.

meanness ['miːnnɪs] [min-nes], *s.* 1. Bajeza, pobreza. 2. Bajeza, vileza, villanía, infamia, maldad (nastiness). 3. Tacañería, miseria, ruindad, roñería, mezquindad (money).

meant [ment] [ment], *pret.* y *pp.* del verbo TO MEAN.

meantime, meanwhile ['miːn'taɪm] [min-taim] ['miːn'waɪl] [min-uail], *adv.* Mientas tanto, entretanto, en el intervalo. *-s.* Interin.

mease ['miːz] [mis], *s.* (Prov. Ingl.) La cantidad de quinientos. **A mease of herrings,** quinientos arenques.

measled ['miːzled] [mis-les], **Measly** ['miːzlɪ] [mis-li], *a.* 1. Atacado del sarampión o que tiene sarampión. 2. Roñoso (dícese de los cerdos). 3. *(Bajo)* Despreciable, vil; que no debe tocarse.

measles ['miːzlz] [mis-lis], *s.* 1. Sarampión, una fiebre eruptiva del cuerpo humano. 2. Roña de los cerdos y otros naimales, enfermedad causada por la lombriz solitaria. 2. Cáncer, enfermedad de los árboles.

measurable ['meʒərəbl] [me-sa-ra-bol], *a.* Mensurable; limitado y corto en cantidad.

measurableness ['meʒərəblnɪs] [me-sa-ra-bol-nes], *s.* Mensurabilidad.

measurably ['meʒərəblɪ] [me-sa-ra-bli], *adv.* Mesuradamente.

measure ['meʒəʳ] [me-saʳ], *s.* 1. Medida. 2. Unidad de medida; tipo, modelo. **Dry measure,** medida para áridos. **Liquid measure,** medida para líquidos. 3. Medida, proporción, correspondencia que guarda una cosa con otra. 4. Medida, la cantidad de sílabas de los versos. 5. Compás, metro, cadencia. 6. Modo, grado, cantidad. 7. Moderación. 8. Medida, disposición, providencia; medios, expediente que se toma para conseguir algún fin. 9. Acto o procedimiento determinado; en especial, propuesta de ley. 10. *(Mat.)* Cantidad que se toma como unidad para expresar las relaciones con otras cantidades. 11. *(Mús.)* Porción de música, entre dos barras de la pauta, compás. 12. *pl. (Geol.)* Serie de capas relacionadas que tiene algún rasgo común entre sí. **To have hard measure,** ser tratado con rigor. **In some measure,** de algún modo, hasta cierto punto. **In a great measure,** en gran manera, en mucha parte. **In large measure,** en gran medida. **Beyond measure, out of measure,** sin límite, con exceso. **Common measure,** compás ordinario. **To take measures,** tomar las medidas necesarias.

measure, *va.* 1. Medir. 2. Ajustar, proporcionar. 3. Medir, señalar, distribuir. 4. Formar juicio de la cantidad o extensión de una cosa. 5. Estimar, juzgar; valuar. 6. Atravesar midiendo. *-vn.* 1. Tomar la medida de alguna cosa. 2. Tener ciertas dimensiones. **Measure your desires by your fortune,** proporcionad vuestros deseos a vuestra fortuna. **Measure off,** medir. **Measure up,** ser capaz, estar a la altura de.

measured ['meʒəd] [me-sad], *pp.* y *a.* 1. Medido, calculado, determinado por un tipo o una regla. 2. Uniforme, lento, rítmico. 3. Limitado, restringido.

measureless ['meʒəlɪs] [me-sa-les], *a.* Inmenso, inmensurable.

measurement ['meʒəmənt] [me-sa-ment], *s.* Medida, la acción de medir. **Measurement-bill,** *(Mar.)* Certificación del porte de los buques.

measurer ['meʒərəʳ] [me-sa-raʳ], *s.* Medidor.

measuring ['meʒərɪŋ] [me-sa-rin], *s.* Medición, medida, el acto de medir. *-pa.* of MEASURE. **Measuring spoon,** cuchara para medir. **Measuring tape,** cinta métrica. **Measuring-worm,** cualquier oruga que se encoge y alarga alternativamente al andar; geómetra, oruga nociva.

meat [miːt] [mit], *s.* 1. Carne, la parte de los animales a propósito para comerse. 2. Vianda, la comida y sustento de los racionales. **Boiled meat,** cocido. **Stewed meat,** estofado. **Minced meat,** picadillo. **Roast meat,** asado. **Baked meat,** carne asada al horno. **Fried meat,** carne frita. **Broiled meat,** carne asada en parrilllas. **Cold meat,** carne fiambre. **Hashed meat,** guisado. **Preserved meats,** viandas conservadas. **One man's meat is another man's poison,** *(prov.)* Lo que a uno cura a otro mata. **Meat-fly,** mosca de carne: V. FISH-FLY.

meatball ['miːtbɔːl] [mit-bol], *s.* Pelota de carne picada, albóndiga.

meated ['miːtɪd] [mi-tid], *a.* Alimentado, comido, sustentado.

meatless ['miːtlɪs] [mit-les], *a.* Sin carne (diet).

meat market ['miːtmɑːkɪt] [mit-mar-kit], *s.* Carnicería.

meatus ['miːtəs] [mi-tos], *s.* Meato, cada uno de ciertos orificios o conductos del cuerpo humano.

meaty ['miːtɪ] [mi-ti], *a.* Carnoso, sustancioso *(Fig.).*

meazling ['mezlɪŋ] [mes-lin], *a.* Lo que cae o se destila a modo de llovizna. V. MIZZLING.

mechanic [mɪ'kænɪk] [mi-ka-nik], *a.* 1. Mecánico, perteneciente a la ciencia mecánica, que está hecho o construido según las leyes y reglas de la mecánica. 2. Materialista, atomístico.

mechanic, *s.* Mecánico, artesano.

mechanical [mɪ'kænɪkəl] [mi-ka-ni-kal], *a.* 1. Mecánico, que se refiere a las máquinas; producido por una máquina o por maquinaria. 2. Materialista. 3. Mecánico, que pertence a los oficios y obras de los menestrales; de artesano. 4. Que tiene talento inventivo o para la construcción. 5. Maquinal, que obra por una fuerza mecánica, o sin reflexión; hecho por costumbre. **Mechanical engineering,** ingeniería mecánica. **A mechanical motion,** un movimiento maquinal.

mechanically [mɪ'kænɪkəlɪ] [mi-ka-ni-ka-li], *adv.* Mecánicamente.

mechanicalness [mɪ'kænɪkəlnɪs] [mi-ka-ni-kal-nes], *s.* 1. Conformidad con las leyes de la mecánica. 2. Bajeza.

mechanician [ˌmɪkə'nɪʃən] [mi-ka-ni-shan], *s.* Mecánico, maquinista; persona hábil en mecánica.

mechanics [mɪ'kænɪkz] [mi-ka-nisk], *s.* Mecánica, la mecánica o la maquinaría.

mechanism ['mekənɪzəm] [me-ka-ni-sem], *s.* 1. Máquina. 2. Mecanismo. 3. Dispositivo. 4. *(Fil.)* Mecanicismo.

mechanist ['mekənɪst] [me-ka-nist], *s.* Mecanista.

mechanization [ˌmekənaɪ'zeɪʃən] [me-ka-nai-sei-shon], *s.* Mecanización.

mechanize ['mekənaɪz] [me-ka-nais], *va.* Mecanizar, hacer maquinal, convertir en máquina.

mechlin ['meklɪn] [mek-lin], *a.* Encaje o puntas de Malinas.

mechoacan ['mekʊəkən] [me-kua-kan], *s. (Bot.)* Mechoacán.

meconic ['mekənɪk] [me-ko-nik], *a.* Mecónico.

meconium ['mekənɪəm] [me-ko-niom], *s.* 1. Meconio. 2. *(Des.)* Meconio, opio.

MED *Abreviatura de* **Master of Education.**

medal ['medl] [me-dal], *s.* 1. Medalla. 2. Medalla o moneda antigua. **Medal, without a title,** medalla anepígrafa, la que no tiene título ni inscripción.

medallic ['medælɪk] [me-da-lik], *a.* Numismático, que pertenece a las medallas.

medallion [mɪ'dælɪən] [mi-da-lion], *s.* 1. Medallón, medalla grande. 2. Medallón, caja pequeña y de forma comprimida, donde se colocan retratos, rizos u otros objetos. 3. *(Arq.)* Medallón, cierto relieve bajo de forma redonda u ovalada.

medallist ['medəlɪst] [me-da-list], *s.* 1. Numismático, el inteligente en medallas o monedas antiguas; el colector de medallas; el que ha escrito un tratado sobre numismática. 2. Grabador de medallas. 3. El que ha obtenido una medalla como recompensa.

meddle ['medl] [me-del], *vn.* 1. Meterse, entremeterse, ingerirse uno donde no le llaman; tocar o manosar una cosa sin permiso o sin derecho. 2. *(Des.)* Tener que hacer en alguna cosa. -va. *(Des.)* Mezclar o trabar una cosa con otra.

meddler ['medlər] [med-laʳ], *s.* Entrometido, intrigante.

meddlesome ['medlsəm] [me-del-som], *a.* Entrometido, oficioso, intruso.

meddlesomeness ['medlsəmnɪs] [me-del-som-nes], *s.* Entrometimiento.

meddling ['medlɪŋ] [med-lin], *s.* Interposición impertinente y oficiosa.

media ['miːdɪə] [mi-dia], *s.* 1. *(Anat.)* La túnica media de un vaso. 2. *pl.* de MEDIUM: medios. **Media studies,** *(Univ.)* periodismo.

medial ['miːdɪəl] [mi-dial], *a.* Medio del centro.

median ['miːdɪən] [mi-dian], *a.* Mediano. *(E.U.)* mediana. *(Math)* Número medio.

mediastinum [ˌmiːdɪəsˈtɪnəm] [mi-dias-ti-nom], *s. (Anat.)* Mediastino, espacio comprendido entre las pleuras.

mediate ['miːdɪeɪt] [mi-dieit], *vn.* 1. Mediar, interponerse entre dos o más personas que contienden, procurando reconciliarlas. 2. Mediar, existir o estar una cosa en medio de otras. -va. 1. Procurar o facilitar por medio de la mediación. 2. Diligenciar, poner los medios o las diligencias.

mediate, *a.* Mediato, lo que en tiempo y lugar está en conexión con alguna cosa, mediando otra entre 1(Fam.). 2. Medio entre dos extremos. 3. Interpuesto.

mediately ['miːdɪeɪtlɪ] [mi-dieit-li], *adv.* Mediatamente.

mediation [ˌmiːdɪˈeɪʃən] [mi-diei-shon], *s.* Mediación, intercesión; interposición, intervención.

mediator ['miːdɪeɪtəʳ] [mi-diei-taʳ], *s.* Mediator, intercesor, medianero; tercero.

mediatorial [ˌmiːdɪəˈtɔːrɪəl] [mi-dia-ta-rial], **mediatory** ['miːdɪətərɪ] [mi-dia-ta-ri], *a.* Medianero.

mediatorship ['miːdɪətəʃɪp] [mi-dia-to-ship], *s.* El oficio de mediador.

medic ['medɪk] [me-dik], *s. (Bot.)* Alfalfa, mielga. Medicago.

medicable ['medɪkəbl] [me-di-ka-bol], *a.* Medicable, no incurable.

medicaid ['medɪˌkeɪd] [me-di-keid], *s. m. (E. U.)* Seguro de Enfermedad.

medical ['medɪkəl] [me-di-kal], *a.* 1. Médico, medical, que pertenece a la medicina; de medicina. 2. Medicinal, que tiene propiedades curativas. **Medical school,** escuela de medicina. **Medical services,** servicios médicos. **Medical transplant,** injerto, transplante de órganos en medicina.

medically ['medɪkəlɪ] [me-di-ka-li], *adv.* Médicamente.

medicament [meˈdɪkəmənt] [me-di-ka-ment], *s.* 1. Medicamento. 2. Agencia, tendencia o poder para sanar.

medicamental [ˌmedɪkəˈmentl] [me-di-ka-men-tal], *a.* Medicamentoso, sanador; que tiene propiedades curativas.

medicamentally [ˌmedɪkəˈmentəlɪ] [me-di-ka-men-ta-li], *adv.* Como medicamento o en calidad de medicina.

medicare ['medɪkeəʳ] [me-di-keaʳ], *s. m. (E. U.)* Seguro médico estatal.

medicaser ['medɪkeɪsəʳ] [me-di-kei-saʳ], *s.* Medicastro, empírico, curandero, charlatán.

medicate ['medɪkeɪt] [me-di-keit], *va.* 1. Medicinar, tratar con medicamentos. 2. Hacer medicinal alguna cosa.

medicated ['medɪkeɪtɪd] [me-di-kei-tid], *a.* Medicinal.

medication [ˌmedɪˈkeɪʃən] [me-di-kei-shon], *s.* 1. El acto de hacer alguna cosa medicinal. 2. El acto de medicinar, medicación.

medicative ['medɪkətɪv] [me-di-ka-tiv], *a. (Med.)* Medicinal.

medicinal [meˈdɪsɪnl] [me-di-si-nal], *a.* 1. Medicinal, que tiene virtud curativa. 2. *(Ant.)* Médico, lo perteneciente a la medicina.

medicinally [meˈdɪsɪnəlɪ] [me-di-si-na-li], *adv.* Médicamente, según el método y reglas de la medicina.

medicine ['medsɪn] [me-di-sin], *s.* 1. Medicina, medicamento, pócima, remedio. 2. Medicina, el arte o ciencia de conservar la salud y curar las enfermedades. **Medicine cabinet,** botiquín. **Medicine-chest,** botiquín, caja para medicamentos; farmacia portátil. **Medicine-lodge,** casilla o tienda cónica destinada a ciertas ceremonias místicas en un pueblo indio. **Medicine-man,** entre los salvajes, exorcista, hechicero. **Patent medicines,** remedios de patente, con privilegio. **To take one's medicine,** asumir las consecuencias.

medicine ball, *s.* Pelota grande de cuero usada en los gimnasios.

medicolegal [ˌmedɪkəˈliːgəl] [me-di-ko-li-gal], *a.* Médicolegal, que se refiere a la ciencia de la medicina en sus relaciones con los preceptos legales.

medieval, mediaeval [ˌmedɪˈiːvəl] [me-dii-val], *a.* De la edad media; relativo a o descriptivo de la edad media.

medievalism [ˌmedɪˈiːvəlɪzəm] [me-di-va-lism], *s.* El espíritu o los usos de la edad media.

mediocre [ˌmiːdɪˈəʊkəʳ] [mi-diou-kaʳ], *a.* Mediano, mediocre; ordinario, vulgar, trivial.

mediocrist [ˌmiːdɪˈɒkrɪst] [mi-dio-krist], *s.* El de mediano talento.

mediocrity [ˌmiːdɪˈɒkrɪtɪ] [mi-dio-kri-ti], *s.* Mediocridad; moderación, templanza.

meditate ['medɪteɪt] [me-di-teit], *va.* Meditar, idear, proyectar, premeditar, tramar, pensar. -vn. 1. Contemplar, meditar sobre una cosa. 2. Reflexionar, rumiar; proponerse, tener en vista una cosa.

meditation [ˌmedɪˈteɪʃən] [me-di-tei-shon], *s.* Meditación; discurso, reflexión.

meditative ['medɪtətɪv] [me-di-ta-tiv], *a.* 1. Meditativo, contemplativo. 2. Que procede de la meditación, o que la expresa.

Mediterranean [ˌmedɪtəˈreɪnɪən] [me-di-ta-rei-nian], **Mediterraneous** [ˌmedɪtəˈreɪnɪəs] [me-di-ta-rei-nios], *a.* Mediterráneo. **The Med,** *(Fam.)* el Mediterráneo.

medium ['miːdɪəm] [mi-diom], *s. (pl.* MEDIUMS o MEDIA). 1. Medio; expediente; lo que sirve de instrumento intermedio. 2. *(Fís.)* El éter a través del cual pasan la luz y el calor; también medio, cualquier sustancia a través de la cual o en la cual puede moverse, vivir, o ser llevada alguna cosa. 3. *(Pint.)* Vehículo líquido, como el aceite. 4. Objeto o estado intermedio. 5. Medium, persona a propósito para que en ella se manifiesten los fenómenos del magnetismo, o para comunicar con los espíritus. -a. mediano, intermedio; mediocre. **Medium-dry,** semi-seco (drink). **Medium-sized,** de grandor o talla medianos. **Medium wave,** onda media (Radio). **Circulating medium,** moneda corriente. **At a medium,** uno con otro.

medlar ['medləʳ] [med-laʳ], *s.* 1. *(Bot.)* Níspero, árbol. 2. Níspero, níspera o níspola, el fruto del níspero.

medley ['medlɪ] [med-li], *s.* Miscelánea, la mezcla, unión y entretejimiento de unas cosas con otras. -a. Mixto, mezclado, confuso. *(Fam.)* Mescolanza.

medullar ['medʌləʳ] [me-da-laʳ], **medullary** ['medʌlərɪ] [me-da-la-ri], *a.* Medular, tocante o perteneciente a la médula o tuétano.

medusa ['medjuːsə] [me-diu-sa], *s.* 1. Medusa, hechicera fabulosa, una de las tres Gorgonas. 2. (Zool. *pl.* MEDUSAE) medusa, aguamar. V. JELLY-FISH.

meed [miːd] [mid], *s.* Premio, recompensa dada al mérito.

meek [miːk] [mik], *a.* 1. Apacible, manso, tratable, halagüeño, dulce; que sufre pacientemente las injurias. 2. Humilde, sumiso; que no es orgulloso.

meek, meeken ['miːkən] [mi-ken], *va.* Amansar, suavizar.

meekly ['miːklɪ] [mik-li], *adv.* Mansamente, suavemente, modestamente.

meekness ['miːknɪs] [mik-nes], *s.* Mansedumbre, suavidad; modestia; dulzura.

meer, *a. y s. V.* MERE.

meerschaum ['mɪəskəm] [mia-skom], *s.* 1. Espuma de mar, un hidrosilicato blando y ligero de magnesia. 2. Pipa de espuma de mar.

meet [miːt] [mit], *va. (pret. y pp.* MET) 1. Encontrar, hallar; llegar donde está alguno (que viene en dirección diferente). 2. Tropezar, hallar casualmente. 3. Tocar una cosa a otra. 4. Hacer frente, refutar, destruir con argumentos. **To arrange to meet somebody,** quedar con alguien, citarse. **To meet expenses,** hacer frente a los gastos. **To meet a charge,** refutar, responder a una acusación. 5. Estar, hacer, o tener lugar en conformidad con. **That will meet my wishes,** eso se conformará a mis deseos. 6. Satisfacer, saldar una cuenta. 7. Batirse, pelear con. **When Greek meets Greek,** cuando un griego se bate con otro. 8. Verse, empezar a conocer, entrar en trato. **I met her at the seaside,** hice conocimiento con ella a orillas del mar. *-vn.* 1. Encontrar, tropezar una persona con otra. 2. Encontrarse, hallarse y concurrir juntas en un mismo lugar dos o más personas, abocarse con alguno, tener una entrevista con él. 3. Encontrarse, oponerse, enemistarse; chocar, pelear, combatir. 4. Unirse, juntarse, congregarse. 5. Adelantarse un sujeto a medio camino para encontrar otro que viene a buscarle. 6. Confluir. **To meet with,** encontrar lo que se buscaba; hallar lo que no se buscaba; juntarse, unirse; encontrarse inesperadamente con algún mal, combatir, venir a las manos; obviar, evitar, huir, apartar o quitar del medio lo que puede ser contrario: (en este último sentido es latinismo). **To meet with one,** desquitarse, corresponder, hacer otro tanto, pagar con la misma moneda. **To meet one full in the face,** encararse con. **Pleased to meet you!** ¡Encantado de conocerle! **Till we meet again,** hasta más ver. **Have we met?** ¿Nos conocemos? **Meet up,** encontrarse. **Meet with,** experimentar, pasar, sufrir (experience, difficulties), entrevistarse con.

meet, *a.* Apto, idóneo, propio, a propósito, conveniente.

meet, *s.* 1. Reunión de cazadores para una cacería. 2. Conjunto de personas que se reunen. 3. Cita, lugar de reunión.

meeting ['miːtɪŋ] [mi-tin], *s.* 1. Junta, asamblea o congreso de varias pesonas. **Meeting of creditors,** concurso de acreedores. **To call a meeting,** llamar a junta o convocar una junta. 2. Reunión; cita, compromiso; sesión. 3. Confluencia o concurrencia de dos ríos. 4. Encuentro, duelo. **Take measures to prevent their meeting,** tome Ud. medidas para impedir que se encuentren. **Meeting place,** lugar de reunión.

meeting-house ['miːtɪŋˌhaʊs] [mi-tin-jaus], *s.* Capilla o iglesia de los noconformistas y particularmente de los cuáqueros.

meetly ['miːtlɪ] [mit-li], *adv.* Convenientemente.

meetness ['miːtnɪs] [mit-nes], *s.* Aptitud, propiedad, conveniencia.

mega-, megalo-, Formas de combinación, derivadas de la griega *megas,* grande.

megabyte ['megəˌbaɪt] [me-ga-bait], *s. m. (Inform.)* Megabyte, megaocteto.

megacosm ['megəˌkɔzm] [me-ga-kosm], *s.* Megacosmo, el mundo grande, el universo.

megacycle ['megəˌsaɪkl] [me-ga-sai-kel], *s.* Megaciclo.

megalith ['megəlɪθ] [me-ga-liz], *s.* Monumento megalítico, piedra grande, de remota antigüedad. Cf. CROMLECH y DOLMEN.

megalithic [ˌmegə'lɪθɪk] [me-ga-li-zik], *a.* Megalítico.

megalomania ['megələʊˈmeɪnɪə] [me-ga-lou-mei-nia], *s.* Megalomanía, delirio de grandeza.

megalomaniac [megələʊˈmeɪnɪək] [me-ga-lou-mei-niak], *a.* Megalómano/a.

megaphone ['megəfəʊn] [me-ga-foun], *s.* Megáfono, instrumento que sirve para llevar la voz a larga distancia.

megascope ['megəskəʊp] [me-gas-koup], *s.* Megascopio, una modificación del microscopio solar, que permite ver cuerpos de grandes dimensiones.

megaton ['megətʌn] [me-ga-tan], *s.* Megatonelada, megatón.

megawatt ['megəwɒt] [me-ga-uot], *s. m.* Megavatio.

megrim ['megrɪm] [me-grim], *s.* Hemicránea, especie de jaqueca.

meikle, *a. y s.* V. MICKLE.

meiny ['meɪnɪ] [mei-ni], *s.* Familia, tren, criados domésticos.

melancholic [ˌmelən'kɒlɪk] [me-lan-kou-lik], *a.* Melancólico, abatido, que siente tristeza; hipocondríaco; triste, lúgubre, infeliz, desgraciado. *-s.* Melancólico, hipocondríaco.

melancholically [ˌmelən'kɒlɪkəlɪ] [me-lan-kou-li-ka-li], *adv.* De una manera melancólica.

melancholiness [ˌmelən'kɒlɪnɪs] [me-lan-kou-li-nes], *s.* Melancolía, hipocondría.

melancholy ['melənkəlɪ] [me-lan-ko-li], *s.* Melancolía, hipocondría, delirio; tristeza. *-a.* Melancólico, triste, hipocondríaco, tétrico.

melange [me'lɑːndʒ] [me-lansh], *s.* Mezcla. V. MEDLEY.

melanin ['melənɪn] [me-la-nin], *s. f.* Melanina.

melanoma [melə'nəʊmə] [me-la-nou-ma], *s. m.* Melanoma.

melanosis [ˌmelə'nəʊsɪs] [me-la-nou-sis], *s. (Med.)* Melanosis, cáncer negro.

melanospermous [ˌmelənəs'pɜːməs] [me-la-nos-per-mos], *a.* Melanospermo, de frutos negros.

melee ['meleɪ] [me-lei], *s.* Pelotera, revuelta.

melic ['melɪk] [me-lik], *a.* Mélico, lírico, propio para el canto: dícese de la poesía.

meliceris ['melɪsərɪs] [me-li-se-ris], *s. (Cir.)* Melíceris, nombre de una especie de lupia o tumor enquistado.

melilot ['melɪlɒt] [me-li-lot], *s. (Bot.)* Meliloto, trébol dulce.

meliorate ['melɪəreɪt] [me-lio-reit], *va.* Mejorar; hacer más soportable o menos penoso; adelantar; bonificar. *-vn.* Mejorarse.

melioration [ˌmelɪə'reɪʃən] [me-lio-rei-shon], *s.* Mejoramiento, medra, mejora, adelanto.

melissa ['melɪsə] [me-li-sa], *s. (Bot.)* Melisa, abejera, toronjil; planta herbácea medicinal.

melliferous ['melɪfərəs] [me-li-fe-ros], *a.* Melífero, que produce miel.

mellification [ˌmelɪfar'keɪʃən] [me-li-fai-kei-shon], *s. (Poco us.)* El acto o arte de melificar.

mellifluence [me'lɪflʊəns] [me-li-fluens], *s.* Melifluidad, dulzura, suavidad y delicadeza.

mellifluent [me'lɪflʊənt] [me-li-fluent], **mellifluous** [me'lɪflʊəs] [me-li-fluos], *a.* 1. Melífluo, que mana miel. 2. Melífluo, dulce y tierno en su expresión.

mellow ['meləʊ] [me-lou], *a.* 1. Maduro, sazonado. 2. Meloso; tierno, blando, suave. 3. Suave, agradable a los sentidos, armonioso. 4. Blando, poco duro, como ciertos terrenos. 5. Medio borracho, alegrado por la bebida. **To be mellow,** estar achispado, medio borracho.

mellow, *va.* Sazonar, madurar, ablandar. *-vn.* Madurar, madurarse.

mellowness ['meləʊnɪs] [me-lou-nes], *s.* 1. Madurez de los frutos. 2. Madurez de la edad. 3. Habla melosa, melosidad.

mellowy ['meləɪ] [me-loui], *a.* Blando, suave; untuoso.

melocoton, melacotoon ['meləkətuːn] [me-lo-ko-tun], *s.* 1. Membrillo o membrillero. 2. Melocotón. V. PEACH.

melodic [mɪ'lɒdɪk] [mi-lo-dik], *a.* Melódico, perteneciente a la melodía o que la contiene.

melodious [mɪ'ləʊdɪəs] [mi-lou-dios], *a.* Melodioso, dulce y suave al oído; musical.

melodiously [mɪ'ləʊdɪəslɪ] [mi-lou-dios-li], *adv.* Melodiosamente.

melodiousness [mɪ'ləʊdɪəsnɪs] [mi-lou-dios-nes], *s.* Melodía; calidad de lo que es agradable al oído por una sucesión suave de sonidos.

melodist [mɪ'ləʊdɪst] [mi-lou-dist], *s.* 1. Melodista, compositor o cantor de melodías. 2. Colección de melodías.

melodize [mɪ'ləʊdaɪz] [mi-lou-dais], *va.* Hacer melodioso. *-vn.* Hacer melodía o melodías.

melodrama ['meləʊˌdrɑːmə] [me-lou-dra-ma], **melodrame** ['meləʊdrəm] [me-lou-dram], *s.* Melodrama, representación dramática mezclada con canciones.

melodramatic [ˌmeləʊdrə'mætɪk] [me-lou-dra-ma-tik], *a.* Melodramático, propio del melodrama.

melodramatist [ˌmeləʊdrəˈmætɪst] [me-lou-dra-ma-tist], *s.* Autor de melodramas.

melody [ˈmelədɪ] [me-lo-di], *s.* 1. Melodía, cualidad del canto agradable. 2. Canción o poema armonioso, puesto en música. 3. Aire, la parte vocal principal. 4. Dulzura al hablar.

melon [ˈmelən] [me-lon], *s.* (*Bot.*) Melón, planta herbácea anual de la familia de las cucurbitáceas, y su fruto. **Watermelon,** sandía o zandía, melón de agua. **Musk-melon,** melón almizcleño. (Caracas) Patilla. **Melon-beetle,** diabrótico, insecto coleóptero muy nocivo a las hojas del melón y de plantas semejantes.

melrose [ˈmelrəʊz] [mel-rous], *s.* Miel de rosas.

melt [melt] [melt], *va.* 1. Derretir, fundir, liquidar; disolver. 2. Ablandar, enternecer, mover con cariño, aplacar. 3. Consumir, gastar, disolver, evaporar. *-vn.* 1. Derretirse, liquidarse. 2. Ablandarse, moverse a compasión. 3. Llenarse de aflicción, amilanarse; estar abatido. **To melt into tears,** deshacerse en lágrimas; llorar a lágrima viva. 4. Confundirse, mezclarse, unirse con otra cosa; disiparse. **Melt away,** derretirse, desvanecerse. **Melt down,** fundir.

melt, *s.* V. MILT.

melter [ˈmeltər] [mel-tar], *s.* 1. Fundidor. 2. Crisol.

melting [ˈmeltɪŋ] [mel-tin], *a.* Lo que se derrite o enternece, fundente. *-s.* Derretimiento, fundición, fusión; enternecimiento, cariño; el acto de ablandar o enternecer. **Melting-cone,** cono fusorio, vasija de figura cónica, para recibir y precipitar los metales fundidos. **Melting-point,** punto de fusión. **Melting-pot,** crisol.

meltingly [ˈmeltɪŋlɪ] [mel-tin-li], *adv.* Tiernamente, derretidamente.

melton [ˈmeltən] [mel-ton], *s.* Paño Melton, paño tupido de lana; se usa particularmente para sobretodos.

member [ˈmembər] [mem-bar], *s.* 1. Miembro, parte del cuerpo. 2. Miembro, cláusula o parte de un discurso, parte o elemento de un todo. 3. Miembro, individuo, de algún cuerpo o comunidad.

membered [ˈmembəd] [mem-bard], *a.* 1. Membrudo, fortachón, fornido de miembros. 2. (*Her.*) Membrado, se dice de las patas de los animales cuando son de diferente color que el cuerpo.

membership [ˈmembəʃɪp] [mem-ba-ship], *s.* 1. Personal de socios, miembros. 2. Número o nómina de socios.

membranaceous [ˈmembrəneɪʃəs] [mem-bra-nei-shos], **Membranous** [memˈbreɪnəs] [mem-brei-nos], *a.* Membranoso.

membrane [ˈmembreɪn] [mem-brein], *s.* 1. Membrana. 2. Trozo de pergamino.

membraniform [memˈbrænɪfɔːm] [mem-bra-ni-form], *a.* Membraniforme.

memento [məˈmentəʊ] [me-men-tou], *s.* Recuerdo, memento; memoria que se da de alguna cosa.

memo [ˈmeməʊ] [me-mou], *Abreviatura de* **memorandum. Memo pad,** bloc de notas.

memoir [ˈmemwɑːr] [me-muar], *s.* 1. Memoria, relación, narrativa. 2. *pl.* Memorias, recuerdos de una persona publicados juntos, en general o con relación a una época particular. 3. Memorial, relación biográfica.

memorabilia [ˌmemərəˈbiːlɪə] [me-mo-ra-bi-lia], *s. pl.* Cosas notables y dignas de recuerdo.

memorable [ˈmemərəbl] [me-mo-ra-bol], *a.* Memorable, memorando, digno de memoria.

memorably [ˈmemərəblɪ] [me-mo-ra-bli], *adv.* Memorablemente.

memorandum [ˈmemərəndəm] [me-mo-ran-dom], *s.* Memoria, nota, apuntes de una cosa para recuerdo y gobierno de alguno. **Memorandum-book,** libro de memoria.

memorative [ˈmemərətɪv] [me-mo-ra-tiv], *a.* Conmemorativo.

memorial [mɪˈmɔːrɪəl] [mi-mo-rial], *a.* Conmemorador de una persona fallecida o de un suceso. **A memorial window,** ventana conmemorativa en un templo u otro edificio, en recuerdo de una persona fallecida, o de un acontecimiento. *-s.* 1. Memoria; monumento, recuerdo. 2. Nota diplomática de carácter semioficial. 3. Memorial, petición, papel o escrito pidiendo alguna gracia o justicia. 4. (*For.*) Nota, apuntamiento que se archiva como protocolo.

memorialist [mɪˈmɔːrɪəlɪst] [mi-mo-ria-list], *s.* Memorialista, el que escribe o presenta un memorial; pretendiente.

memorialize [mɪˈmɔːrɪəlaɪz] [mi-mo-ria-lais], *va.* 1. Presentar una petición, un memorial. 2. Conmemorar.

memorize [ˈmemɪˈmɔːraɪz] [mi-mo-rais], *va.* 1. Aprender de memoria, confiar a la memoria. 2. Recordar, conservar memoria de.

memory [ˈmemərɪ] [me-mo-ri], *s.* 1. Memoria. **To call to memory,** traer a la memoria. **Weak memory,** memoria de gallo o de grillo, mala memoria. 2. Memoria, fama, gloria, lo que liberta del olvido. 3. Memoria, recuerdo, reminiscencia. **To commit to memory,** confiar a la memoria, aprender de memoria. **Of sound and disposing mind and memory,** (*For.*) en el goce pleno y cabal de sus facultades mentales; legalmente apto para testar. **To the memory of,** en memoria de.

men, *s. pl.* de MAN.

men-pleaser [ˈmenˌpliːsər] [men-pli-sar], *s.* La persona que pone demasiado cuidado en agradar a otras.

menace [ˈmenɪs] [me-nis], *va.* 1 Amenazar, intimidar con amenazas. 2. Mostrar o pronosticar algún mal. *-vn.* Hacerse amenazador.

menace, menacing [ˈmenɪsɪŋ] [me-ni-sin], *s.* Amenaza; presagio o pronóstico de un mal venidero.

menacer [ˈmenɪsər] [me-ni-sar], *s.* Amenazador.

ménage [meˈnɑːdʒ] [me-nash], *s.* 1. Familia de una casa. 2. Manejo de una familia; economía doméstica. 3. (*Des.*) V. MENAGERIE. (*Fr.*)

menagerie [mɪˈnædʒərɪ] [mi-na-che-ri], *s.* Colección de animales salvajes; casa de fieras, de animales raros.

mend [mend] [mend], *va.* 1. Recomponer, reparar, remendar. 2. Mejorar, reparar una cosa, darle nueva o mejor forma. 3. Corregir, enmendar, reformar las costumbres, hábitos, etc. 4. Adelantar, aprovechar, aumentar. *-vn.* 1. Corregirse, enmendarse, reformarse. 2. Restablecerse, curarse; mejorar de salud. **To mend one's pace,** apresurar el paso. *-s.* El acto de curarse, de enmendarse.

mendable [ˈmendəbl] [men-da-bol], *a.* Reparable, componible.

mendacious [menˈdeɪʃəs] [men-dei-shos], *a.* Mentiroso, embustero, falso.

mendacity [menˈdæsɪtɪ] [men-da-si-ti], *s.* Falsedad, mentira; carácter y mentiroso.

mender [ˈmendər] [men-dar], *s.* Enmendador, reformador; reparador; remendón. **Mender of old clothes,** sastre remendón, el que compone vestidos viejos.

mendicancy [ˈmendɪkənsɪ] [men-di-kan-si], *s.* Mendiguez, mendicidad.

mendicant [ˈmendɪkənt] [men-di-kant], *a.* Mendicante. *-s.* Mendicante, mendigo.

mendicity [menˈdɪsɪtɪ] [men-di-si-ti], *s.* Mendicidad, mendiguez.

mending [ˈmendɪŋ] [men-din], *s. f.* Compostura, reparación, remiendo.

menhaden [ˈmendheɪdən] [men-jei-dan], *s.* Pez marino parecido al sábalo (whitefish).

menial [ˈmiːnɪəl] [mi-nial], *a.* 1. Doméstico, de criado. 2. Servil, bajo. *-s.* Criado, doméstico, lacayo.

meningeal [menɪndʒɪəl] [me-nin-yial], *a.* Perteneciente a las meninges o situado cerca de ellas.

meninges [ˈmenɪndʒɪz] [me-nin-yis], *s. pl.* de MENINX. Meninges, tres membranas que envuelven el cerebro y la médula espinal.

meningitis [ˌmenɪnˈdʒaɪtɪs] [me-nin-yai-tis], *s.* Meningitis, inflamación de las meninges.

meninx [ˈmenɪnks] [me-ninks], *s.* Meninge, membrana que envuelve el cerebro y la médula espinal.

meniscus [məˈnɪskəs] [me-nis-kus], *s.* 1. Lúnula. 2. Menisco, un vidrio o lente convexo por un lado y cóncavo por el otro. 3. La superficie de una columna líquida hecha convexa o cóncava por la capilaridad.

menology ['menɒlədʒɪ] [me-no-lo-yi], *s.* Menologio, el martirologio de los griegos.

menopause ['menɒpɔːz] [me-no-pos], *s. (Med.)* menopausa, cesación del menstruo en las mujeres.

menow ['menɒʊ] [me-nou], *s.* V. MINNOW.

mensal ['mensl] [men-sal], *a.* 1. Lo perteneciente a la mesa. 2. Mensual, de cada mes.

mense ['mens] [mens], *s. (Esco. y prov. Ingl.)* Decoro, buena crianza, decencia.

menseful ['mensfʊl] [mens-ful], *a. (Esco. y prov. Ingl.)* Primoroso, gracioso, cortés, urbano.

menses ['mensɪz] [men-sis], *s. pl.* Menstruo, reglas; flujo periódico de la matriz de las mujeres y de las hembras de ciertos animales.

menstrual ['menstrʊəl] [mens-trual], *a.* Menstrual; mensual.

menstruate ['menstrʊeɪt] [mens-trueit], *vn.* Menstruar, tener la hembra la evacuación menstrual.

menstruation [ˌmenstrʊˈeɪʃən] [mens-truei-shon], *s.* Menstruación.

menstrucus ['menstrʊkəs] [mens-tru-kos], *a.* 1. Menstruo, menstruoso, menstruosa. 2. *(Bot.)* Que dura un mes.

menstruum ['menstrʊəm] [mens-truom], *s. (pl.* MENSTRUUMS o MENSTRUA). *(Quím.)* Menstruo, disolvente.

mensurability [ˌmenʒərəˈbɪlɪtɪ] [men-sa-ra-bi-li-ti], *s.* Mensurabilidad.

mensurable ['menʒərəbl] [men-sha-ra-bol], *a.* mensurable, que se puede medir.

mensural ['menʒərəl] [men-sha-ral], *a.* 1. Perteneciente a la medida. 2. Relativo a la primera forma de la música.

mensuration [ˌmenʒʊəˈreɪʃən] [men-siua-rei-shon], *s.* 1. Medición, acción de medir. 2. Medida; mensura, ramo de las matemáticas.

menswear ['menzweəʳ] [mens-uea], *s.* Ropa de caballero.

-ment. Sufijo de los substantivos verbales que denota el efecto, la condición, la acción o la agencia, equivalente al castellano -mento o miento, y algunas veces a -ción. **Acknowledgment,** reconocimiento. **Atonement,** expiación. **Movement,** movimiento.

mental ['mentl] [men-tal], *a.* 1. Mental, intelectual. 2. Efectuado por la mente, en especial sin el auxilio de símbolos escritos.

mentality ['mentælɪtɪ] [men-ta-li-ti], *s. f.* Mentalidad.

mentally ['mentəlɪ] [men-ta-li]. *adv.* mentalmente; con el pensamiento.

mentha ['menθə] [men-za], *s.* menta, género de hierbas odoríferas.

menthol ['menθɒl] [men-zol], *s.* Mentol.

mentholated [ˌmenθɒˈleɪtɪd] [men-zo-lei-tid], *a.* Que contiene mentol.

mention ['menʃən] [men-shon], *s.* Mención, recuerdo, alusión.

mention, *va.* Mencionar, hacer mención de; aludir, nombrar sin describir, hablar de.

mentionable ['menʃənəbl] [men-sho-na-bol], *a.* Mencionable, que se puede mencionar.

mentor ['mentəʳ] [men-ta], *s.* mentor, guía, consejero y amigo sabio, honrado y prudente.

menu ['menjuː] [me-niu], *s.* Lista de los platos de una comida; por extensión, la comida misma.

meow [mɪˈaʊ] [miau], *s.* y *vn.* MEW.

mephitic, mephitical ['mefɪtɪk] [me-fi-tik], *a.* Mefítico, infecto, pestífero, pestilente, nocivo a la vida; se usa a menudo en sentido figurado.

mephitis ['mefaɪtɪz] [me-fai-tis], *s.* Mefitis, vapor fétido, cualquier gas pestilente o destructivo; mofeta de una mina, etc.

mercantile ['mɜːkəntaɪl] [mer-kan-tail], *a.* Mercantil, de comercio.

mercenariness ['mɜːsmærɪnɪs] [mer-se-na-ri-nes], *s.* Venalidad, calidad de ser una cosa vendible o expuesta a la venta; vicio de la persona que se deja sobornar con dádivas.

mercenary ['mɜːmnərɪ] [mer-si-na-ri], *a.* Mercenario, venal. A *mercenary man,* hombre venal. -*s.* 1. Mercenario, el que trabaja por un estipendio; jornalero, el que trabaja a jornal o por un tanto. 2. Mercenario, interesado, el que obra sólo por interés.

mercer ['mɜːsəʳ] [mer-sa], *s.* Sedero, mercero, mercader de sedas, cintas, etc.

mercerized ['mɜːsəraɪst] [mer-se-raist], *a.* Mercerizado.

mercership ['mɜːsəʃɪp] [mer-sa-ship], *s.* Sedería, mediería, el trato o comercio en sedas y artículos menores.

mercery ['mɜːsərɪ] [mer-sa-ri], *s.* 1. Mercería, mercaderías y artículos en que tratan los merceros. 2. Sedería, mediería.

merchandise ['mɜːtʃəndaɪz] [mer-chan-dais], *s.* Mercadería, mercancía; todo género vendible.

merchandise, *vn.* Traficar, comerciar, negociar.

merchandiser ['mɜːtʃəndaɪzəʳ] [mer-chan-dai-sa], *s.* Negociante, comerciante.

merchant ['mɜːtʃənt] [mer-chant], *a.* Mercante, mercantil; apto para el comercio o empleado en él. -*s.* Mercader, comerciante, negociante. **Merchant captain,** capitán de un buque mercante. **Merchant navy,** marina mercante. **Merchant service,** marina mercante. **Merchant tailor,** sastre mercader, sastre que vende y pone el paño de los trajes que hace.

merchantable ['mɜːtʃəntəbl] [mer-chan-ta-bol], *a.* Comercializable.

merchant-like ['mɜːtʃəntlaɪk] [mer-chant-laik], *a.* Mercantil, como negociante.

merchantman ['mɜːtʃəntmən] [mer-chant-man], *s.* Barco o buque mercantil, embarcación de comercio o mercante.

merciful ['mɜːsɪfʊl] [mer-si-ful], *a.* Misericordioso, piadoso, benigno, clemente, humano.

mercifully ['mɜːsɪfəlɪ] [mer-si-fu-li], *adv.* Misericordiosamente, piadosamente.

merciless ['mɜːsɪlɪs] [mer-si-les], *a.* Cruel, inhumano, desalmado; sin misericordia, sin clemencia.

mercilessly ['mɜːsɪlɪslɪ] [mer-si-les-li], *adv.* Cruelmente, inhumanamente.

mercilessness ['mɜːsɪlɪsnɪs] [mer-si-les-nes], *s.* Crueldad, inhumanidad.

mercurial [mɜːˈkjʊərɪəl] [mer-kiua-rial], *a.* 1. Mercurial, perteneciente al dios Mercurio; de aquí, vivo, activo, jovial; volátil. 2. Mercurial, relativo al azogue. 3. Lo que sirve de dirección el alguna cosa. -*s.* 1. *(Des.)* Hombre vivo, alegre, activo e inconstante. 2. *(Med.)* Preparación química de azogue.

mercurialist [mɜːˈkjʊərɪəlɪst] [mer-kiua-ria-list], *s.* Persona, voluble, voltaria, versátil, activa, alegre e inconstante.

mercurialize [mɜːˈkjʊərɪəlaɪz] [mer-kiua-ria-lais], *va.* 1. *(Med.)* Someter a un tratamiento mercurial; salivar. 2. *(Foto.)* Emplear azogue en el desarrollo de las pruebas negativas. -*vn.* Ser chistoso, festivo o inconstante.

mercurification [ˌmɜːkjʊərɪfaɪˈkeɪʃən] [mer-kiua-ri-fai-kei-shon], *s. (Poco us.)* Mezcla de mercurio con otras cosas; la operación de extraer el mercurio de los minerales.

mercurochrome [mɜːˈkjʊərəkrəʊm] [mer-kiua-rou-kroum], *s. (Med.)* Mercurocromo.

mercury ['mɜːkjʊrɪ] [mer-kiu-ri], *s.* 1. Mercurio, azogue, metal fluido. 2. Viveza, vivacidad, desparpajo, desembarazo. 3. Gaceta o papel periódico. 4. Mensajero, gacetero; corredor de oreja. 5. *(Bot.)* Mercurial. 6. Mercurio, uno de los dioses del paganismo. 7. Mercurio, el menor de los planetas principales, más próximo al sol. **Mercury's wand,** caduceo.

mercy ['mɜːsɪ] [mer-si], *s.* 1. Misericordia, clemencia, piedad; merced, remisión de una falta, gracia, perdón. 2. Arbitrio, discreción, poder, capricho, voluntad. **For mercy, for mercy's sake,** por gracia, por dios; ¡ten misericordia! **to cry mercy,** pedir gracia, misericordia. **To show mercy,** mostrar misericordia. **Sisters of Mercy,** las monjas de la Merced, en la Iglesia católica, comunidad de religiosas que se dedican a obras de piedad.

mercy-seat ['mɜːsɪˌsiːt] [mer-si-sit], s. Propiciatorio, lámina de oro que según la antigua ley se colocaba sobre el arca del Testamento.

merd ['mɜːd] [merd], s. Estiércol, mierda.

mere [mɪəʳ] [miaʳ], a. Mero, puro, simple; solo, no más que (lo mencionado). -s. 1. (Raro en los E. U.) Lago, laguna grande. 2. (Esco.) El mar. 3. (Ingl.) Lindero, límite.

merely ['mɪəlɪ] [mia-li], adv. Solamente, meramente, simplemente; puramente.

meretricious [ˌmerɪ'trɪʃəs] [me-ri-tri-shos], a. 1. Meretricio. 2. Subido, chillón, de mal gusto, artificiosamente atractivo.

meretriciousness [ˌmerɪ'trɪʃəsnɪs] [me-ri-tri-shos-nes], s. Calidad o condición de meretricio o chillón, putería, putañería.

merganser ['mɜːgənsəʳ] [mer-gan-saʳ], s. (Orn.) Mergo, mergánsar, cuervo marino que tiene la parte superior del pico dentada en sus bordes.

merge [mɜːdʒ] [merch], va. Sumergir la identidad o la individualidad de. -vn. Estar sumergido, hundirse, perderse, absorberse.

merger ['mɜːdʒəʳ] [mer-chaʳ], s. Consolidación, fusión de empresas comerciales o industriales.

meridian [mə'rɪdɪən] [me-ri-dian], s. 1. Mediodía. 2. Meridiano, círculo máximo que pasa por los polos del mundo, dividiendo la esfera en dos hemisferios; meridiana. 3. Cenit, auge, el punto más elevado de gloria o poder. -a. 1. Meridiano, que está al mediodía; que se refiere al meridiano geográfico. 2. Elevado a lo sumo.

meridional [mə'rɪdɪənl] [me-ri-dio-nal], a. 1. Meridional, situado en el meridiano, en lo más elevado. 2. Meridional, del mediodía, del sur.

meridionality [mə'rɪdɪənælɪtɪ] [me-ri-dio-na-li-ti], s. Situación meridional.

meridionally [mə'rɪdɪənəlɪ] [me-ri-dio-na-li], adv. Hacia el mediodía.

meringue [mə'ræŋ] [me-rang], s. Merengue, dulce.

merino [mə'riːnəʊ] [me-ri-nou], a. Merino. -s. Paño merino.

merit ['merɪt] [me-rit], s. 1. Mérito, virtud, excelencia. 2. Mérito, merecimiento, lo que hace nuestras obras dignas de premio o castigo. 3. Premio.

merit, va. Merecer, ser digno de, tener derecho a, ya sea como premio o como castigo.

meritable ['merɪtəbl] [me-ri-ta-bol], **meritorious** ['merɪtərɪəs] [me-ri-to-rios], a. Meritorio, digno de recompensa.

merited ['merɪtɪd] [me-ri-tid], a. Meritorio, merecido.

meritoriousness ['merɪtərɪəsnɪs] [me-ri-to-rios-nes], s. Merecimiento, mérito.

meritory ['merɪtərɪ] [me-ri-to-ri], a. Meritorio.

merle ['mɜːl] [merl], s. (Orn.) Merla, mirlo.

merlin ['mɜːlɪn] [mer-lin], s. (Orn.) Esmerejón.

merlon ['mɜːlən] [mer-lon], s. (Fort.) Merlón, trozo de parapeto entre tronera y tronera.

mermaid ['mɜːmeɪd] [mer-meid], s. Sirena, ser fabuloso con hermosas facciones y busto de mujer, terminando en cola de pez.

merman ['mɜːmən] [mer-man], s. El macho de la sirena, ser fabuloso mitad hombre y mitad pez.

merops ['merəpz] [me-rops], s. Abejarruco, ave que persigue a las abejas.

merovinglian [ˌmerəʊ'vɪŋglɪən] [me-rou-vin-glian], a. Merovingio, perteneciente a la dinastía de los primeros reyes de Francia.

merrily ['merɪlɪ] [me-ri-li], adv. Alegremente, jovialmente.

merrimake ['merɪmeɪk] [me-ri-meik], s. Gaudeamus, concurso de algunas personas para comer, beber y divertirse; fiesta, regocijo.

merrimake, vn. Alegrarse, divertirse.

merriment ['merɪmənt] [me-ri-ment], s. Alegría, júbilo, diversión; fiesta, regocijo.

merriness ['merɪnɪs] [me-ri-nes], s. La disposición a alegrarse o regocijarse.

merry ['merɪ] [me-ri], a. 1. Alegre, apacible. 2. Risueño, placentero, agradable, jovial, festivo, divertido. **To make merry,** divertirse, recrearse. **To be a little merry,** estar alegre por haber bebido con algún exceso. **To live a merry life,** vivir alegremente. **Merry-Andrew,** bufón, truhán, chocarrero. **Merry-go-round,** tío vivo, caballitos, diversión consistente en figuras de caballos y otros animales de madera que giran alrededor de un eje y sirven de montura al público, y en especial a los niños. **Merry-making, merry-meeting,** fiesta, reunión jovial, jarana. (Amer.) Holgorio. **Merry-thought,** hueso de la pechuga de las aves. **To get merry,** achisparse (Fam.).

mersion ['mɜːʃən] [mer-shon], s. Inmersión.

mesentery ['mezəntrɪ] [me-san-tri], s. (Anat.) Mesenterio, entresijo.

meseraic ['mezəraɪk] [me-se-raik], a. Meseraico o mesentérico.

mesh [meʃ] [mesh], s. 1. Malla, la abertura que tiene la red entre nudo y nudo. 2. Obra de malla; randa, particularmente en plural. 3. Una cosa cualquiera que enreda o envuelve; trampa, lazo. 4. (Mec.) Engranaje.

mesh, va. Enredar, meter o coger en la red.

meshy ['meʃɪ] [me-shi], a. Reticular, hecho de malla como red.

mesial ['meʃɪəl] [me-shial], a. Mediano, del medio, dirigido hacia el medio. **Mesial plane,** plano mediano del cuerpo.

meslin ['meslɪn] [mes-lin], s. Tranquillón, la mezcla de granos cereales.

mesmeric [mez'merɪk] [mes-me-rik], a. Mesmeriano, relativo al mesmerismo.

mesmerism [mez'merɪzm] [mes-me-ri-sem], s. Mesmerismo, magnetismo animal, sugestión hipnótica.

mesmerist [mez'merɪst] [mes-me-rist], s. 1. Partidario del mesmerismo, mesmeriano. 2. Magnetizador.

mesmerize [mez'meraɪz] [mes-me-rais], va. 1. Influir o dirigir por el mesmerismo; practicar el hipnotismo. 2. Fascinar, hechizar.

meso-. Forma de combinación que significa del medio.

mesocolon [ˌmesə'kəʊlən] [me-so-kou-lon], s. (Anat.) Mesocolon.

mesoderm ['mesəʊdɜːm] [me-sou-derm], s. (Zool.) Mesodermo.

mesologarithm [ˌmesəʊlɒgəʳɪθəm] [me-sou-lo-ga-rizm], s. Mesologaritmo, logaritmo de la tangente.

meson ['miːzɒn] [mi-son], s. (Phys. and Chem.) Mesón.

mesozoic [ˌmesəʊ'zəʊɪk] [me-sou-zouik], a. (Geol.) Mesozoico, de la edad media; secundario.

mesquit ['mezkwɪt] [mes-kuit], s. Mezquite, algarrobo, árbol de América.

mess [mes] [mes], s. 1. Plato, la cantidad de vianda o manjar que se sirve de una vez en la mesa. 2. Rancho, reunión de varias personas que comen juntas. **Steward of the mess,** (Mar.) Ranchero. 3. Ración, porción.

mess, s. (Fam.) Estado de desorden, desorden sucio.

mess, vn. Comer en rancho o hacer rancho, comer a escote. -va. Dar de comer, proveer comidas para.

mess, va. 1. Mezclar en confusión, desordenar. 2. Hacer sucio, ensuciar. -vn. Formar desorden sucio o mezcla. **Mess about/around,** molestar, fastidiar. Macanear. **To mess about/around with something,** entretenerse con algo. **Mess up,** echar a perder (Fig.); desordenar. **What a mess-up!,** ¡vaya lío!

message ['mesɪdʒ] [me-sich], s. 1. Mensaje, el recado que envía una persona a otra de palabra o por escrito; parte, anuncio. 2. Comunicación oficial del que ejerce el poder ejecutivo a una asamblea legislativa.

messenger ['mesɪndʒəʳ] [me-sin-yaʳ], s. 1. Mensajero. 2. Portero, en los tribunales. 3. (Mar.) Aparejo para levar el ancla. *to clap a messenger on the cable,* (Mar.) Coser un aparejo al cable.

mess hall, mess room ['meshɔːl] [mes-jol] ['mesrɒm] [mes-rum], s. Comedor para soldados, marineros, etc.

Messiah [mɪ'saɪə] [mi-saia], s. Mesías, Cristo.

messieurs ['mesəz] [me-ses], *s. pl.* Señores: es palabra de cortesía en el trato civil, y se usa como plural de *mister;* se escribe por lo común *Messrs,* en abreviatura.

messmate ['mesmeɪt] [mes-meit], *s.* Comensal, el que come con otro a una misma mesa.

messuage ['mesʊədʒ] [me-suach], *s.* Menaje, ajuar de casa.

mestizo, mestino ['mɪs'tiːzəʊ] [mis-ti-sou], *s.* Mestizo; en América, persona de raza española e india.

met, *pret.* y *pp.* del verbo MEET.

metabola ['metəbɒlə] [me-ta-bo-la], *s. (Med.)* Mudanza de tiempo, aire o enfermedad.

metabolic [ˌmetə'bɒlɪk] [me-ta-bo-lik], *a.* Metabólico, que se refiere al metabolismo.

metabolism [me'tæbəlɪzəm] [me-ta-bo-li-sem], *s.* 1. *(Biol.)* Metabolismo, procedimiento de asimilación de los alimentos. 2. *(Ento.)* Metabología, metamorfosis. 3. Cambio de un metro poético a otro.

metacarpal [ˌmetə'kɑːpl] [me-ta-kar-pal], *a.* Metacarpiano, que pertenece al metacarpo.

metacarpus [ˌmetə'kɑːpəs] [me-ta-kar-pos], *s. (Anat.)* Metacarpo, parte de la mano comprendida entre el carpo y los dedos.

metachronism [ˌmetəkrə'nɪzəm] [me-ta-kro-ni-sem], *s.* Metacronismo, anacronismo en poner un hecho antes o después del tiempo en que sucedió.

metage ['metɑːdʒ] [me-tach], *s.* Medida o el acto de medir el carbón de piedra.

metagrammatism [ˌmetəgræ'mətɪzm] [me-ta-gra-ma-ti-sem], *s.* El arte o la práctica de hacer anagramas.

metal ['metl] [me-tal], *s.* 1. Metal. 2. Algo compuesto de uno o más elementos metálicos, o que se parece a ellos; liga, mezcla; piedra triturada que se emplea en la superficie de los caminos o para el terraplenaje. (c) Vidrio en fusión. 3. Sustancia constitutiva, cualidad esencial. **Babbitt metal,** metal blando y blanco resistente a la fricción. **Metal detector,** detector de metales.

metalepsis ['metəlɪpsɪs] [me-ta-lip-sis], *s.* Metalepsis, figura retórica, conjunción de dos o más tropos en la misma palabra.

metaleptically [ˌmetə'lɪptɪkəlɪ] [me-ta-lip-ti-ka-li], *adv.* Por transposición.

metalled ['metəld] [me-tald], *a.* Macadamizado; terraplenado, afirmado (se dice de una vía férrea).

metallic [mɪ'tælɪk] [mi-ta-lik], *a.* Metálico.

metalliferous ['metəlɪfərəs] [me-ta-li-fe-ros], *a.* Metalífero.

metalline ['metəlɪn] [me-ta-lin], *a.* Metálico.

metallist ['metəlɪst] [me-ta-list], *s.* 1. Metalario, el artífice que tiene conocimiento de los metales. 2. Partidario del uso de la moneda en metálico, en contraposición al papel moneda.

metallize ['metəlaɪz] [me-ta-lais], *va.* Metalizar, transformar en metal.

metallography ['metələgræfɪ] [me-ta-lo-gra-fi], *s.* Metalografía.

metalloid ['metəlɔɪd] [me-ta-loid], *a. (Quím.)* Metaloide, semejante a un metal. -*s.* Metaloide, cuerpo simple sin brillo metálico y mal conductor del calórico y de la electricidad, como el arsénico y el antimonio.

metallurgic, metallurgical [ˌmetə'lɜːdʒɪk] [me-ta-ler-yik], *a.* Metalúrgico.

metallurgist [ˌmetə'lɜːdʒɪst] [me-ta-ler-yist], *s.* Metalario, metalúrgico.

metallurgy [ˌmetə'lɜːdʒɪ] [me-ta-ler-yi], *s.* Metalurgia, el arte de beneficiar los minerales y de extraer económicamente los metales que contienen.

metalman ['metəlmən] [me-tal-man], *s.* El que trabaja los metales; calderero, hojalatero, estañero.

metal shears ['metəlʃɪəz] [me-tal-shiars], *s. pl.* Cizalla.

metalwork ['metəlwɜːk] [me-tal-uek], *s.* Metalistería.

metameric ['metəmerɪk] [me-ta-me-rik], *a.* 1. *(Quím.)* Metamérico. 2. *(Zool.)* Perteneciente a uno de la serie de segmentos homólogos que forman el cuerpo de un animal vertebrado o articulado.

metamorphic [ˌmetə'mɔːfɪk] [me-ta-mor-fik], *a.* 1. Metamórfico, que produce el metamorfismo. 2. Metamórfico, que presenta metamorfismo o se refiere a el.

metamorphism [ˌmetə'mɔːfɪzm] [me-ta-mor-fi-sem], *s.* 1. *(Geol.)* Metamorfismo, transformación natural ocurrida en las rocas mediante una nueva cristalización de sus elementos constitutivos, con cambio químico o sin él. 2. Cualquier metamorfosis.

metamorphize [ˌmetə'mɔːfaɪz] [me-ta-mor-fais], *va. V.* METAMORPHOSE.

metamorphose [ˌmetə'mɔːfəʊz] [me-ta-mor-fous], *va.* 1. Metamorfosear, transformar, cambiar la forma de una cosa; hacerle asumir un carácter diferente. 2. *(Geol.)* Cambiar por medio del metamorfismo.

metamorphosis [ˌmetə'mɔːfəʊzɪs] [me-ta-mor-fou-sis], *s.* Metamorfosis o metamorfosi, transformación, cambio de forma o de estructura.

metaphor ['metəfəʳ] [me-ta-foʳ], *s.* Metáfora, figura retórica.

metaphoric, metaphorical ['metəfɔːrɪk] [me-ta-fo-rik] [ˌmetə'fɒrɪkəl] [me-ta-fo-ri-kal], *a.* Metafórico.

metaphorically [ˌmetə'fɒrɪklɪ] [me-ta-fo-ri-ka-li], *adv.* Metafóricamente.

metaphorist ['metəfɔːrɪst] [me-ta-fo-rist], *s.* Metaforista.

metaphrase ['metəfreɪz] [me-ta-freis], *s.* Metafrasis, traducción literal.

metaphysic, metaphysical [ˌmetə'fɪzɪk] [me-ta-fi-sik] [ˌmetə'fɪzɪkəl] [me-ta-fi-si-kal], *a.* 1. Metafísico. 2. Sobrenatural.

metaphysically [ˌmetə'fɪzɪklɪ] [me-ta-fi-si-ka-li], *adv.* Metafísicamente.

metaphysician [ˌmetə'fɪzɪʃən] [me-ta-fi-si-shan], *s.* Metafísico.

metaphysics [ˌmetə'fɪzɪkz] [me-ta-fi-siks], *s.* Metafísica, la ciencia que trata de los primeros principios del conocimiento humano, de las ideas universales y de los seres espirituales; ontología.

metaplasm ['metəplæzm] [me-ta-plasm], *s. (Gram.)* Metaplasmo, cambio operado en una palabra por el aumento, la disminución o sustitución de una letra o sílaba.

metastasis ['metæstəsɪs] [me-tas-ta-sis], *s. (Med.)* Metástasis, mudanza del sitio de una enfermedad.

metastasize ['metætəsaɪz] [me-tas-ta-sais], *vn.* Metasticizar, diseminarse por metastasis.

metatarsal [ˌmetə'tɑːsl] [me-ta-tar-sal], *a.* Metatársico, metatarsiano, perteneciente al metatarso.

metatarsus [ˌmetə'tɑːsəs] [me-ta-tar-sos], *s. (Anat.)* Metatarso, parte del pie situada entre el tarso y los dedos.

metathesis [me'tæθəsɪs] [me-ta-zi-sis], *s. (Ret.)* Metátesis, transposición.

mete [miːt] [mit], *va.* 1. Distribuir conforme a medida; prorratear. 2. *(Ant.)* 2. Medida.

metempsychosis [ˌmetəmsaɪ'kəʊsɪs] [me-tam-sai-kou-sis], *s.* Metempsícosis, transmigración de las almas de un cuerpo a otro.

meteor ['miːtɪəʳ] [mi-tiaʳ], *s.* Meteoro, fenómeno repentino y luminoso, como una estrella por los aires; estrella errante. En sentido técnico significa cualquier fenómeno atmosférico.

meteoric [miː'tɪɒrɪk] [mi-tio-rik], *a.* 1. Meteórico; perteneciente a los meteoros, compuesto de meteoros. 2. Atmosférico, meteorológico. 3. Brillante temporalmente. **Meteoric iron,** hierro meteórico. *V.* METEORITE. **Meteoric showers,** lluvia de estrellas errantes.

meteorite, meteorolite ['miːtɪəraɪt] [mi-tio-rait], *s.* Aerolito, meteorito, masa pétrea o metálica que cae sobre la tierra desde las regiones planetarias, acompañada de fenómenos luminosos o de alguna detonación.

meteoroid ['miːtɪərɔɪd] [mi-tio-roid], *s.* Meteoroide.

meteorological [ˌmiːtɪərə'lɒdʒɪkəl] [mi-tio-ro-lo-yi-kal], *a.* Meteorológico, que pertenece a la atmósfera o a la ciencia de la meteorología.

meteorology [ˌmiːtɪərə'lɒdʒɪ] [mi-tio-ro-lo-yi], *s.* Meteorología, ciencia que trata de los meteoros, es decir, de los fenómenos de la atmósfera con espeical relación al clima y la temperautra y estado del aire (tiempo).

meteorous ['miːtɪərəs] [mi-tio-ros], *a.* Meteórico, lo que pertenece a los meteoros.

meter ['miːtəʳ] [mi-taʳ], *s.* 1. Medidor, el que mide. 2. Contador, instrumento para medir. **Gas-meter,** contador de gas. **Parking meter,** parquímetro. **Water-meter,** medidor mecánico del agua.

meter, *s.* 1. Metro, la medida del verso; el verso. 2. Metro, unidad de medida longitudinal del sistema métrico-decimal; palabra de origen francés. Equivale a la diez millonésima parte del arco del meridiano terrestre comprendido entre el polo y el ecuador.

methane ['miːθeɪn] [mi-zein], *s.* Metano.

methinks [miˈθɪnks] [mi-zinks], *v.impers.* Me parece, soy de parecer, creo, pienso.

method ['meθəd] [me-zod], *s.* 1. Método, el modo de obrar o proceder. 2. Orden, regla, regularidad. 3. Método, el orden que se sigue en las ciencias para hallar la verdad y enseñarla. 4. La clasificación de los cuerpos según sus cualidades comunes características. 5. Sistema de instrucción musical, libro para el estudio de un arte, una lengua, etc.; (*Mús.*) manera o estilo de ejecución; técnica.

methodic, methodical [mɪˈθɒdɪk] [mi-zo-dik] [mɪˈθɒdɪkəl] [mi-zo-di-kal], *a.* Metódico, dispuesto y arreglado con método; que usa de orden y método.

methodically [mɪˈθɒdɪkəlɪ] [mi-zo-di-ka-li], *adv.* Metódicamente, con método.

methodism ['meθɒdɪzəm] [me-zo-di-sem], *s.* Metodismo, la doctrina de la secta metodista.

methodist ['meθədɪst] [me-zo-dist], *s.* 1. Metodista, la persona que es metódica o procede con arte y método. 2. Metodista, el médico que pertenecía a la secta del metodismo. 3. Metodista, los individuos de una secta religiosa llamada metodismo.

methodistical ['meθədɪstɪkəl] [me-zo-dis-ti-kal], *a.* Metodístico.

methodize ['meθədaɪz] [me-zo-dais], *va.* Metodizar, regularizar, arreglar metódicamente.

methodology [ˌmeθəˈdɒlədʒɪ] [me-zo-do-lo-yi], *s. f.* Metodología.

methought, *pret.* del verbo METHINKS.

methyl ['meθɪl] [me-zil], *s.* (*Quím.*) Metilo.

methylene ['meθɪliːn] [me-zi-lin], *s.* Metileno, carburo de hidrógeno. **Methylene blue,** material de tinte.

meticulous ['meθɪkələs] [me-zi-ko-los] *a.* Meticuloso.

métier ['metɪeɪ] [me-tiei], *s. m.* Oficio.

metonymical [ˌmetəˈnɪmɪkəl] [me-to-ni-mi-kal], *s. adv.* Metonímicamente, por metonimia.

metonymically [ˌmetəˈnɪmɪkəlɪ] [me-to-ni-mi-ka-li], *adv.* Metonímicamente, por metonimia.

metonymy ['metənɪmɪ] [me-to-ni-mi], *s.* Metonimia.

metope ['metəp] [me-top], *s.* (*Arq.*) Metopa, distancia entre los triglifos del friso en el orden dórico.

metoposcopy ['metəpəskəʊpɪ] [me-to-pos-kou-pi], *s.* Metoposcopia, arte de adivinar el porvenir o las inclinaciones del hombre por las líneas del rostro.

metre ['miːtəʳ] [mi-taʳ], *s.* V. METER.

metric, metrical ['miːtrɪk] [mi-trik] ['miːtrɪkəl] [mi-tri-kal], *a.* Métrico, que consta de versos, perteneciente al metro, a la medida.

metrician ['miːtrɪʃən] [mi-tri-shan], **metrist** ['miːtrɪst] [mi-trist], *s.* Versificador, metrista.

metromania [ˌmetrəˈneɪmɪə] [me-tro-mei-nia], *s.* Metromanía, manía de hacer versos.

metronome ['metrənəʊm] [me-tro-noum], *s.* Metrónomo, máquina a manera de reloj con péndulo cronométirco, para marcar el compás de la música.

metropolis [mɪˈtrɒpəlɪs] [mi-tro-po-lis], *s.* Metrópoli, ciudad principal de algún país; a menudo es la capital.

metropolitan [ˌmetrəˈpɒlɪtən] [me-tro-po-li-tan], *a.* Metropolitano, perteneciente a la metrópoli o al arzobispo. -

s. 1. Metropolitano, el arzobispo respecto de sus obispos sufragáneos. 2. Ciudadano de una metrópoli, en contraposición al colono.

metropolitical [ˌmetrəpəˈlɪtɪkəl] [me-tro-po-li-ti-kal], *a.* Metroplitano.

-metry ['metrɪ] [me-tri], Sufijo que denota la acción, la ciencia o el arte de medir.

mettle ['metl] [me-tel], *s.* Materia de que se compone una cosa, en especial, disposición constitutiva, brío, bizarría, valor, coraje, firmeza, vivacidad, fuego. **To put one on (o to) his mettle,** picar el amor propio de alguno, estimularle.

mettled ['metld] [me-teld], **Mettlesome** ['metlsəm] [me-tel-som], *a.* Brioso, vivo, fogoso, ardiente.

mettlesomely ['metlsəmlɪ] [me-tel-som-li], *adv.* Briosamente, vivamente.

mettlesomeness ['metlsəmnɪs] [me-tel-som-nes], *s.* Brío, fuego, vivacidad.

mew [mjuː] [miu], *s.* 1. Jaula, encierro para las aves cuando mudan las plumas; cualqueir cercado o corral. 2. *pl.* Establo, caballeriza. 3. Maullido, maúllo, maído, la voz natural del gato. 4. (*Orn.*) Gaviota, ave marina de la familia de los láridos.

mew, *va.* 1. Enjaular, encerrar, encarcelar. 2. (*Des.*) Mudar las aves sus plumas. -*vn.* 1. Maullar o miar como el gato. 2. (*Des.*) Mudar o estar de muda los animales.

mewing ['mjuːɪŋ] [miuin], *s.* 1. Maullido, maído de los gatos. 2. (*Des.*) Muda, el acto de mudar las aves sus plumas.

mewl ['mjuːl] [miul], *vn.* Chillar, gritar o llorar como un niño.

mews [mjuːz] [miuz], *s. pl.* Las caballerizas reales de Londres; de aquí, cualquier caballeriza urbana.

Mexican ['meksɪkən] [mek-si-kan], *a.* Mejicano, perteneciente a Méjico. -*s.* Natural o ciudadano de los Estados Unidos Mejicanos.

mezereon [meˈziːrɪən] [me-si-rion], *s.* (*Bot.*) Mecereón, laurel hembra.

mezzanine ['mezəniːn] [me-sa-nin], *s.* Mezanina, entresuelo.

mezzo-rilievo ['metsərɪˈliːvə] [met-so-ri-li-vo], *s.* Medio relieve.

mezzotint, mezzotinto ['metsəʊtɪnt] [met-sou-tin], *s.* Estampa de humo, media tinta.

MFA *s. Abreviatura de* **Master of Fine Arts.** (*E.U*)

mg *Abreviatura de* **miligramme(s).**

MHz *Abreviatura de* **megahertz,** megahercio.

mi [miː] [mi], *s.* 1. Mi, la tercera nota de la escala musical; se usa en el solfeo. 2. La nota E.

MIA *Abreviatura de* **Missing In Action.**

miaow [miːˈaʊ] [miau], *s.* Maullido, miau. *v.* Maullar.

miasm ['mɪæzm] [miasm], **miasma** [mɪˈæzmə] [mias-ma], *s.* Miasma, exhalación morbífica de las materias animales o vegetales en estado de putrefacción; el virus de la malaria.

miasmal [mɪˈæzməl] [mias-mal], *a.* Abundante en miasmas.

miasmatic [mɪəsˈmætɪk] [mias-ma-tik], *a.* Miasmático, infecto, relativo a los miasmas o a la malaria, o producido por ellos. *V.* MALARIOUS.

mica ['maɪkə] [mai-ka], *s.* (*Min.*) Mica, mineral escamoso, lustroso, folicular, que se puede dividir en hojuelas muy delgadas. Las micas son silicatos de composición complicada, principalmente de alúmina con un álcali. **Micaschist,** Micasquisto, micacito, roca compuesta de mica con algún cuarzo.

micaceous ['maɪkeɪʃəs] [mai-kei-shos], *a.* Micáceo, que es de mica o pertenece a ella.

mice ['maɪs] [mais], *s. pl.* de MOUSE.

michaelmas ['maɪkəlməs] [mai-kal-mas], *s.* Día de San Miguel, fiesta que se celebra el veinte y nueve de septiembre.

mickle ['maɪkl] [mai-kel], *a.* (*Ant. o Esco.*) Mucho, grande.

microampere ['maɪkrəʊəmˈpeəʳ] [mai-krou-am-peaʳ], *s.* Microamperio.

microbalance [ˌmaɪkrəˈbæləns] [mai-kro-ba-lans], *s.* Microbalanza.

microbe ['maɪkrəʊb] [mai-kroub], *s.* Microbio.

microbial [maɪˈkrəʊbɪəl] [mai-krou-bial], **Microbic** [maɪˈkrəʊbɪk] [mai-krou-bik], *a.* Micróbico.

microbicide [ˌmaɪˈkrəʊbɪsaɪd] [mai-krou-bi-said], *s.* Microbicida.

microbiology [ˌmaɪkrəʊbaɪˈɒlədʒɪ] [mai-krou-baio-lo-yi], *s.* Microbiología.

microbus [ˈmaɪkrəʊbʌs] [mai-krou-bas], *s.* Microómnibus, microbús.

microchip [ˈmaɪkrəʊtʃɪp] [mai-krou-chip], *s.* Microplaqueta.

microcircuit [ˈmaɪkrəʊsɜːkɪt] [mai-krou-ser-kit], *s.* Microcircuito.

micrococcus [ˈmaɪkrəʊkɒkəs] [mai-krou-ko-kos], *s.* Micrococo, microbio de forma esférica.

microcomputer [ˌmaɪkrəʊkəmˈpjuːtəʳ] [mai-krou-kom-piu-taʳ], *s.* Microordenador, microcomputadora.

microcosm [ˈmaɪkrəʊkɒzəm] [mai-krou-kosm], *s.* Microcosmo, el mundo en pequeño; llámase así el hombre.

microeconomics [ˌmaɪkrəʊiːkəˈnɒmɪkz] [mai-kroi-e-ko-no-miks], *s. f.* Microeconomía.

microelectronics [ˈmaɪkrəʊiːlekˈtrɒnɪks] [mai-kroui-lek-tro-niks], *s. f.* Microelectrónica.

microfilm [ˈmaɪkrəʊfɪlm] [mai-krou-film], *s.* Microfilm, rollo de película fotográfica con reproducciones en tamaño muy reducido.

micrography [maɪˈkrəʊgræfɪ] [mai-krou-gra-fi], *s.* Micrografía, la descripción de los objetos pequeños que sólo se pueden distinguir con el microscopio.

microgroove [ˈmaɪkrəʊgruːv] [mai-krou-gruv], *s.* Microsurco, microestría.

microlight [ˈmaɪkrəʊlaɪt] [mai-krou-lait], *a.* Ultraligero.

micrometer [maɪˈkrɒmiːtəʳ] [mai-kro-mi-taʳ], *s.* Micrómetro, instrumento que se aplica al telescopio y al microscopio para medir las dimensiones o ángulos pequeños.

micrometric, micrometrical [maɪˈkrɒmiːtrɪk] [mai-kro-mi-trik], *a.* Micrométrico, relativo al micrómetro o hecho con él.

micrometry [maɪˈkrɒmiːtrɪ] [mai-kro-mi-tri], *s.* Micrometría, el arte de medir dimensiones pequeñas con el micrómetro.

micron [ˈmaɪkrən] [mai-kron], *s.* Micra, la millonésima parte de un metro.

microorganism [ˈmaɪkrəʊˈɔːgənɪzəm] [mai-krou-or-ga-ni-sem], *s.* Microorganismo.

microphone [ˈmaɪkrəfəʊn] [mai-kro-foun], *s.* Micrófono.

microphotograph [ˌmaɪkrəˈfəʊtəgræf] [mai-kro-fou-to-graf], **microphotography** [ˌmaɪkrəˈfəʊtəgræfɪ] [mai-kro-fou-to-gra-fi], *s.* Microfotografía.

microphysics [ˌmaɪkrəˈfɪzɪks] [mai-kro-fi-siks], *s.* Microfísica.

microprocessor [ˌmaɪkrəʊˈprəʊsesəʳ] [mai-krou-pro-se-saʳ], *s. f.* Microprocesador.

microprogramming [ˈmaɪkrəˈprəʊgræmɪŋ] [mai-kro-prou-gra-ming], *s. f.* Microprogamación.

micropyle [ˈmaɪkrəpaɪl] [mai-kro-pail], *s.* Micrópilo.

microscope [ˈmaɪkrəskəʊp] [mai-kros-koup], *s.* Microscopio, instrumento dióptrico que sirve para hacer perceptible lo que no lo es a la simple vista.

microscopic, microscopical [ˈmaɪkrəskəʊpɪk] [mai-kros-kou-pik] [ˈmaɪkrəskəʊpɪkl] [mai-kros-kou-pi-kal], *a.* Microscópico, relativo al microscopio, hecho o como hecho con el microscopio; extremamente pequeño, que no se puede ver sino con el microscopio.

microscopist [ˈmaɪkrəskəʊpɪst] [mai-kros-kou-pist], *s.* Microscopista, la persona versada en el uso del microscopio.

microscopy [ˈmaɪkrəskəʊpɪ] [mai-kros-kou-pi], *s.* Microscopia, microscópica, el arte de servirse del microscopio.

microsurgery [ˌmaɪkrəʊˈsɜːdʒərɪ] [mai-krou-ser-che-ri], *s. f.* Microcirugía.

microwave [ˈmaɪkrəʊweɪv] [mai-krou-ueiv], *s.* Microonda.

micturition [ˈmɪktjʊərɪʃən] [mik-chua-ri-shon], *s.* Micturición, micción, acción de orinar (frecuentemente).

mid [mɪd] [mid], *a.* Medio: se usa en composición. -*prep.* (*Poét.*) Entre, en medio de. V. AMID. **Mid-age,** la edad media de la vida. **Mid-course,** media carrera o medio camno. **Mid-heaven,** el medio del cielo, meridiano superior. **Mid-lent,** media cuaresma. **Mid-week,** que está en medio de la semana.

mida [ˈmɪdə] [mi-da], *s.* Mida, saltón o gusanillo que se halla en la flor del haba.

midday [ˈmɪddeɪ] [mid-dei], *s.* Mediodía. -*a.* Meridional, del mediodía.

middle [ˈmɪdl] [mi-del], *a.* Medio, intermedio. **Middle finger,** dedo de en medio o dedo del corazón. -*s.* Medio, intermedio, centro. **About the middle of June,** a mediados de junio. **In the middle of the way,** a medio camino. **Middle class,** la clase media, burguesía. **Middle Kingdom,** el imperio chino. **Middle voice,** voz media, se dice en griego de la clase de verbos que en las demás lenguas se llaman reflexivos. **Middle-aged,** de mediana edad. **Middle-distance race,** carrera de medio fondo. **Middle-sized,** de mediana estatura o tamaño. **To cut through the middle,** cortar por la mitad.

middle-class [ˈmɪdlˈklɑːs] [mi-del-klas], *s. f.* Clase media.

middle ear [ˈmɪdlˈɪəʳ] [mi-del-iaʳ], *s.* Tímpano del oído.

middleman [ˈmɪdlmæn] [mi-del-man], *s.* 1. (*Com.*) Agente de negocios; corredor. 2. Burgués, ciudadano de la clase media.

middlemost [ˈmɪdlməʊst] [mi-del-moust], *a.* Colocado en el medio, lo más céntrico.

middleweight [ˈmɪdlweɪt] [mi-del-ueit], *s.* (*Boxeo*) Peso medio.

middling [ˈmɪdlɪŋ] [mi-dlin], *a.* 1. Mediano, mediocre, pasadero. 2. De salud pasadera, pero no buena; (*Fam.*) no muy católico. -*s. pl.* Salvado.

middy (blouse) [ˈmɪdɪ] [mi-di], *s.* Blusa marinera.

midge [mɪdʒ] [midch], *s.* 1. Mosquito, o más bien, una mosca pequeña que no pica y tiene larvas acuáticas. 2. Enano.

midget [ˈmɪdʒɪt] [mid-chit], *s.* 1. Pequeña mosca. 2. Enano, pequeño. 3. Niño activo o inquieto.

midi [ˈmɪdɪ] [mi-di], *a.* **Midi system,** cadena musical compacta.

midland [ˈmɪdlənd] [mid-land], *a.* 1. Mediterráneo, rodeado de tierras. 2. Lo que está tierra adentro o en lo interior de un país.

midmost [ˈmɪdməʊst] [mid-moust], *a.* En el medio, del medio.

midnight [ˈmɪdnaɪt] [mid-nait], *s.* Media noche, las doce de la noche. -*a.* Lo que pasa o se hace a media noche.

midriff [ˈmɪdrɪf] [mid-rif], *s.* Diafragma, músculo que separa la cavidad del pecho de la del vientre.

midship [ˈmɪdʃɪp] [mid-ship], *a.* Que está en medio del buque. -*s. pl.* Bao o cuaderna maestra. **Midship beam,** bao maestro.

midshipman [ˈmɪdʃɪpmən] [mid-ship-man], *s.* (*Mar.*) Guardia marina.

midst [ˈmɪdst] [midst], *s.* Medio, la parte central; (*Fig.*) lo crudo, lo fuerte. **In the midst of winter,** en el rigor, en lo crudo del invierno. -*adv.* En medio. -*prep.* V. AMIDST.

midstream [ˈmɪdstriːm] [mid-strim], *s.* El medio de una corriente.

midsummer [ˈmɪdsʌməʳ] [mid-sa-maʳ], *s.* Solsticio estival, la época del solsticio o el 21 de junio; el rigor del estío. **Midsummer day,** el día de San Juan, el 24 de junio.

midway [ˈmɪdweɪ] [mid-uei], *s.* Medio camino, la mitad del camino. -*a.* Que está en el medio, a mitad del camino. -*adv.* En medio del camino, a medio camino.

midweek [ˈmɪdwiːk] [mid-uik], *a.* De entre semana. *adv.* Entre semana.

midwife [ˈmɪdwaɪf] [mid-uaif], *sf.* (*pl.* MIDWIVES [ˈmɪdwaɪvs] [mid-uaivs]) Comadre, partera. **Man-midwife,** comadrón, partero. -*va.* Partear. -*vn.* Hacer o ejercer el ofico de partera o comadrón.

midwifery [ˈmɪdˌwɪfərɪ] [mid-ui-fa-ri], *s.* 1. Obstetricia, el arte de partear. 2. El acto de producir o sacar a luz.

midwinter ['mɪd'wɪntəʳ] [mid-uin-taʳ], *s.* Solsticio hiemal; lo recio del invierno.

mien [mi:n] [min], *s.* Semblante, aire, porte.

miff [mɪf] [mif], *s.* (*Fam.*) Disgusto, mal humor, descontento. -*va.* Desagradar, ofender ligeramente, enojar; se usa por lo común en pasiva. **To be a little miffed,** (*Fam.*) enojarse o incomodarse un poco; amoscarse.

might [maɪt] [mait], *s.* Poder, fuerza. **With all my might,** con todas mis fuerzas. **With might and main,** con todas sus fuerzas(Fam.)ás no poder.

might, *pret.* de MAY. **He died that we might live,** murió para que pudiéramos vivir. **If it might be,** si eso pudiera ser. **There might be a hundred persons in the room,** podía haber unas cien personas en la habitación.

mightily ['maɪtɪlɪ] [mai-ti-li], *adv.* Poderosamente.

mightiness ['maɪtɪnɪs] [mai-ti-nes], *s.* Poder, potencia, fuerza; grandeza.

mighty ['maɪtɪ] [mai-ti], *a.* Fuerte, valiente, potente, poderoso, vigoroso; grande; violento; enorme; excelente; eficaz, importante. -*adv.* (*Irón.*) Extremadamente, sumamente.

mignonette [,mɪnjə'net] [mi-ño-net], *s.* Reseda, clavellina, planta cultivada por su fragancia.

migraine, migraine headache ['mi:greɪn] [mi-grein], *s.* Jaqueca.

migrant ['maɪgrənt] [mai-grant], *a.* Migratorio.

migrate [maɪ'greɪt] [mai-greit], *vn.* Emigrar, pasar de un país a otro, especialmente en grupos o familias.

migration [maɪ'greɪʃən] [mai-grei-shon], *s.* Emigración, acción de pasar de un país a otro en grupos; cambio de morada, viaje periódico de ciertos animales, aves o insectos.

migratory [maɪ'greɪtərɪ] [mai-grei-to-ri], *a.* Migratorio, que se muda de una parte a otra.

mikado ['mɪkədɔɪ] [mi-ka-dou], *s.* Micado, nombre del emperador del Japón.

mike [maɪk] [maik], *s.* *Abreviatura de* **microphone,** micro.

milch [mɪltʃ] [milch], *a.* Lactífera, lechera, que da leche. **Milch-cow,** vaca de leche.

mild [maɪld] [maild], *a.* 1. Moderado, indulgente, blando, dulce, apacible, suave, tierno, de buen genio. 2. Nuevo (beers); suave, no fuerte. **Mild tobacco,** tabaco suave.

mildew ['mɪldju:] [mil-diu], *s.* Añublo, moho, pelusilla, borra; tizón, tizoncillo.

mildew, *va.* y *vn.* Atizonarse el trigo o los otros granos.

mildewed ['mɪldju:d] [mil-diud], *a.* Mohoso.

mildly ['maɪldlɪ] [maild-li], *adv.* Suavemente, dulcemente; con indulgencia.

mildness ['maɪldnɪs] [maild-nes], *s.* Benignidad, clemencia, dulzura, blandura, bondad, indulgencia.

mile ['maɪl] [mail], *s.* Milla, medida de distancia que comprende mil pasos geométricos o 5,280 pies ingleses = 1,609.3 metros. **Geographical o nautical mile,** la sexagésima parte de un grado, o 1.852 metros.

mileage ['maɪlɪdʒ] [mai-lich], *s.* 1. Kilometraje, la longitud de alguna cosa en millas (o en kilómetros). 2. Derecho de peaje por milla. 3. Gastos de viaje proporcinados según el número de millas recorridas.

mile-post ['maɪlpəʊst] [mail-poust], **Mile-stone** ['maɪlstəʊn] [mail-stoun], *s.* Mijero, piedra millera, el poste que señala las millas en los caminos.

milesian ['maɪli:ʒən] [mai-li-shan], *a.* 1. Milesiano. 2. Irlandés, hibernés, hibérnico.

milestone ['maɪlstəʊn] [mail-stoun], *s. m.* Mojón (road). Hito (*Fig.*).

miliary ['mɪlɪərɪ] [mi-lia-ri], *a.* Miliar, semejante a los granos de mijo; dícese de una fiebre eruptiva y de algunas glándulas.

militancy ['mɪlɪtənsɪ] [mi-li-tan-si], *s.* Combate, guerra; se dice en contraposición a *industrialism.*

militant ['mɪlɪtənt] [mi-li-tant], *a.* 1. Militante, combatiente; v. g. **The Church militant,** la iglesia militante. 2. De un temperamento belicoso o guerrero.

militarism ['mɪlɪtərɪzəm] [mi-li-ta-ri-sem], *s.* Militarismo, predominio del elemento militar en el gobierno del Estado; el sistema de mantener grandes ejércitos permanente.

militarization ['mɪlɪtəraɪ'zeɪʃən] [mi-li-tan-rai-se-shon], *s.* Militarización.

militarize ['mɪlɪtəraɪz] [mi-li-ta-rais], *va.* Militarizar.

military ['mɪlɪtərɪ] [mi-li-ta-ri], *a.* Militar, soldadesco, belicoso, guerrero. **A military man,** un militar. **Military stores,** municiones de guerra. -*s.* Soldadesca, el conjunto de los soldados; la gente de guerra, la milicia.

military police, *s.* Policía militar.

military staff, *s.* Estado mayor.

militate ['mɪlɪteɪt] [mi-li-teit], *vn.* 1. Militar, haber o concurrir en cualquiera cosa alguna razón o circunstancia particular. 2. (*Ant.*) Combatir. **To militate against,** obrar en oposición a, ponerse *a.*

militia [mɪ'lɪʃə] [mi-li-sha], *s.* Milicia, el ejército o la guardia nacional, en oposición al ejército regular y permanente. **Militiaman,** miliciano, el que forma parte de la milicia.

milk [mɪlk] [milk], *s.* 1. Leche. **Cow's milk,** leche de vaca. **Ass's milk,** leche de burra. **Skimmed milk,** leche desnatada. 2. Leche, licor que se saca de algunas pepitas o semillas machacándolas; o el jugo blanco o lechoso de ciertas plantas. **Milk-abscess,** absceso del pecho. **Milk-and-water,** (*Fam.*) Vacilante y débil; incierto. **Milk diet,** régimen lácteo. **Milk-duct,** conducto de leche, vaso lactífero. **Milk-fever,** fiebre láctea. **Milk-food,** lacticinio. **Milk-leg,** inflamación de las extremidades inferiores que suelen sufrir las mujeres parturientas. **Milk-livered,** cobarde, mezquino. **Milk-maid,** lechera; mantequera. **Milk-man,** lechero, el que vende leche. **Milk-pail,** colodra. **Milk-pan,** lechera, vasija en que se guarda la leche para hacer queso y manteca. **Milk-pottage,** sopa de leche. **Milk-room,** lechería, cuarto o casa donde se conserva la leche. **Milk-thistle,** (*Bot.*) Titímalo, cardo lechero o sílibo. **Milk-tooth,** diente de leche. **Milk-vetch,** astrágalo, regaliz silvestre. **Milk-warm,** tibio, caliente como la leche que se acaba de ordeñar. **It's no good crying over spilt milk,** a lo hecho pecho (*Prov.*).

milk, *va.* 1. Ordeñar, exprimir las tetas de la hembra para sacar leche. 2. (*Fam.*) Desaguar, apurar, agotar, extraer de.

milker ['mɪlkəʳ] [mil-kaʳ], *s.* Ordeñador.

milkiness ['mɪlkɪnɪs] [mil-ki-nes], *s.* 1. Dulzura, suavidad. 2. Calidad o propiedad láctea.

milking machine ['mɪlkɪŋmə,ʃi:n] [mil-kin-ma-shin], *s.* Ordeñadora mecánica.

milk shake ['mɪlk'ʃeɪk] [milk-sheik], *s.* Batido de leche.

milksop ['mɪlsɒp] [milk-sop], *s.* Marica, el hombre afeminado y de pocos bríos.

milkweed ['mɪlkwi:d] [milk-uid], *s.* (*Bot.*) Asclepias, planta vivaz de América; llámase así por su jugo lechoso. Las semillas tiene filamentos sedosos, circunstancia que da origen a otro nombre, *silkweed.*

milk-white ['mɪlkwaɪt] [milk-uait], *a.* Blanco como la leche.

milkwort ['mɪlkwɔːt] [milk-uort], *s.* (*Bot.*) Cualquier planta del género polígala.

milky ['mɪlkɪ] [mil-ki], *a.* 1. Lácteo, lactífero. 2. Lechoso. 3. Lacticinoso, lechal. 4. Blando, tierno, suave, dulce; tímido.

Milky Way ['mɪlkɪ'weɪ] [mil-ki-uei], *s.* (*Astr.*) Galaxia, vía láctea, vulgarmente Camino de Santiago.

mill [mɪl] [mil], *s.* 1. Molino. 2. Taller, fábrica, edificio provisto de maquinaria para fabricar o manufacturar. **Cotton-mill,** hilandería de algodón. 3. Máquina que funciona con movimiento de rotación, como la rueda de un lapidario. 4. (*Vulg.*) Lucha a puñetazos. **Water-mill,** molino de agua, aceña. **Wind-mill,** molino de viento. **Horse-mill,** tahona. **Fulling o tuck mill,** batán. **A forge-mill,** molino de herrería o fragua. **Hand-mill,** molino de herrería o fragua. **Hand-mill,** molino de mano, molinete o molinillo. **Paper-mill,** molino de papel. **Rolling-mill,** laminador. **Stamping-mill,** molino de estampar. **Tan o bark-mill,** molino de corteza de roble. **Pepper-mill,** molinillo para moler la pimienta. **Coffee-mill,** molinillo de café. **Copper o lead-mill,** molino de cobre o plomo. **Sugar-mill,** trapiche o ingenio de azúcar. **Sawing-mill,** molino de aserrar. **Mill-board,** cartón muy grueso que usan los encuadernadores de libros. **Mill-clack,** taravilla, cítola. **Mill-course,** canal o cañal de agua de un molino. **Mill-dam,** esclusa o represa de molino; dique. **Mill-dust,** harija. **Mill-hopper,** tolva de molino. **Mill-horse,** caballo de tahona. **Mill-hand,** obrero u obrera en una fábrica. **Mill-race,** canal o conducto de molino de agua. **Mill-work,** maquinaria de molino; construcción de un molino. **To go through the mill,** saber por completo una cosa.

mill, s. La milésima parte; en los Estados Unidos, la décima parte de un centavo.

mill, va. 1. Moler, desmenuzar. 2. Batir el chocolate con el molinillo. 3. Acordonar, labrar el canto o cordoncillo de las monedas. **Mill about/around,** arremolinarse.

milled [mɪld] [mild], a. Molido (grain).

millenarian [ˌmɪləˈneərɪən] [mi-le-nea-rian], **millenist** [ˈmɪlənɪst] [mi-le-nist], a. Milenario, perteneciente al millar o al número mil. -s. Milenario, sectario.

millenary [ˈmɪlenərɪ] [mi-le-na-ri], s. Milenario; el espacio de mil años. -a. Milenario. V. MILLENARIAN.

millennial [mɪˈlenɪəl] [mi-le-nial], a. Milenario, perteneciente a un milenario o a un período de mil años.

millennium [mɪˈlenɪəm] [mi-le-niam], s. 1. Mileño, el espacio de mil años. 2. Los mil años del reino de Jesucristo en la tierra, con relación al Apocalipsis XX, 1-5.

milleped [ˈmɪlped] [mil-ped], s. Ciempiés, cientopiés, escolopendra, miriápodo con numerosos segmento y patas.

millepore [ˈmɪlpɔːʳ] [mil-po'], s. Milépore, género de políperos pétreos cuya superficie tiene una multitud de poros.

miller [ˈmɪləʳ] [mi-la'], s. 1. Molinero. 2. Mariposa nocturna, generalmente blanquizca y de alas empolvadas como con harina. llámase comúnmente **moth-miller. Miller's Thumb,** *(Ict.)* cota.

millerite [ˈmɪlərɪt] [mi-le-rit], s. Milerita, níquel sulfurado nativo (NiS) que cristaliza en el sistema hexagonal.

millesimal [mɪˈlesɪməl] [mi-le-si-mal], a. Milésimo.

millet [ˈmɪlɪt] [mi-lit], s. *(Bot.)* Mijo.

milliard [ˈmɪlɪɑːd] [mi-liard], s. Mil millones; mil millones de francos. *(Fr.)*

milligram, milligramme [ˈmɪlɪɡræm] [mi-li-gram], s. Miligramo, milésima parte de un grano.

milliliter [ˈmɪlɪˌliːtəʳ] [mi-li-li-ta'], s. Mililitro.

millimeter [ˈmɪlɪˌmiːtəʳ] [mi-li-mi-ta'], s. Milímetro, milésima parte de un metro.

milliner [ˈmɪlɪnəʳ] [mi-li-na'], s. Modista, mujer que confecciona y vende sombreros, gorros, etc., para señoras; en Inglaterra, la persona que vende o hace vestidos o adornos para las señoras.

millinery [ˈmɪlɪnərɪ] [mi-li-na-ri], s. 1. Los géneros que se emplean para hacer o adornar los sombreros, gorros, etc., de las señoras; cintas, lazos, flores artificiales, etc. 2. La ocupación o la tienda de una modista.

milling [ˈmɪlɪŋ] [mi-lin], s. 1. Molienda, acción de moler o machacar, de convertir el grano en harina. 2. Acción de acordonar las monedas, y el cordoncillo mismo.

million [ˈmɪljən] [mi-lion], s. 1. Millón, mil veces mil, un millar de millares. 2. Un número muy grande indeterminado. -a. Que consta de un millón.

millionaire [ˌmɪljəˈneəʳ] [mi-lio-nea'], s. Millonario, la persona cuyas riquezas se valúan en un millón o más.

millioned [ˈmɪljənd] [mi-liond], a. Multiplicado por millones.

millionth [ˈmɪljənθ] [mi-lionz], a. Millonésimo, que completa un millón o es una parte de él.

millipede [ˈmɪlɪpiːd] [mi-li-pid], s. Milpiés.

millisecond [ˈmɪlɪˌsekənd] [mi-li-se-kond], s. Milisegundo.

mill-pond [ˈmɪlpɒnd] [mil-pond], s. Alcubilla, alberca de agua para mover un molino.

millstone [ˈmɪlstəʊn] [mil-stoun], s. Muela, piedra de molino; molar, piedra molar. **To see into** o **through a millstone,** ver al través de una pared; tener mucha penetración.

millwright [ˈmɪlraɪt] [mil-rait], s. Constructor de molinos.

milt [mɪlt] [milt], s. 1. Bazo, parte del cuerpo que está en el hipocondrio izquierdo. 2. Lechecillas de los peces, la parte de los peces machos en que se contiene el semen.

milt, va. Impregnar las huevas de los peces.

milter [ˈmɪltəʳ] [mil-ta'], s. Pez macho. **Milter and spawner,** pez macho y hembra.

miltwaste [ˈmɪltweɪst] [milt-ueist], s. *(Bot.)* Doradilla.

mime [maɪm] [maim], s. 1. Mimo, truhán, bufón, gracioso, pantomimo, farsante. 2. Pantomima, farsa; mimo, especie de farse entre los antiguos.

mime, vn. 1. Bufonearse. 2. Remedar, representar una pantomima.

mimeograph [ˈmɪmɪəɡrɑːf] [mi-mio-graf], s. Mimeógrafo.

mimetical [mɪˈmetɪkl] [mi-me-ti-kal], a. Imitativo, mímico.

mimic [ˈmɪmɪk] [mi-mik], va. 1. Remedar, imitar burlescamente. 2. Imitar exactamente, contrahacer. 3. *(Biol.)* Asumir la forma o el color de algo, por vía de protección.

mimic, s. 1. Mimo, imitador, truhán, bufón. 2. Remedo servil o bajo. -a. Mímico, imitativo; chancer, burlesco.

mimical [ˈmɪmɪkəl] [mi-mi-kal], a. Burlesco.

mimically [ˈmɪmɪkəlɪ] [mi-mi-ka-li], adv. Burlescamente, mímicamente.

mimicry [ˈmɪmɪkrɪ] [mi-mi-kri], s. 1. Bufonada, bufonería, remedo o imitación burlesca. 2. *(Zool.)* Parecido, semejanza imitativa de un animal a otro o a un objeto inanimado.

mimosa [mɪˈməʊzə] [mi-mou-sa], s. *(Bot.)* Mimosa, sensitiva.

mimulus [ˈmɪmələs] [mi-mo-los], s. *(Bot.)* Mímulo.

min. *Abreviatura de* **minute(s)** o **minimum.**

minaret [mɪnəˈret] [mi-na-ret], s. *(Arq.)* Minarete, torre de las mezquitas mahometanas.

minatory [ˈmɪnətərɪ] [mi-na-to-ri], a. Amenazante, lo que amenaza.

mince [mɪns] [mins], va. 1. Desmenuzar; picar la carne. 2. Decir una cosa muy poco a poco y por partes. 3. Paliar, atenuar. 4. Afectar, hablar con afectación. -vn. 1. Andar a pasitos cortos, afectadamente. 2. Hablar con dengue o con melindre. Afectación en el andar o hablar. **Mince-meat,** carne picada, jigote, mezcla de carne, manzanas, grasa, frutas secas y especias picadas, para rellenar el pastel llamado **mince-pie.**

mince-meat [ˈmɪnsmiːt] [mins-mit], s. f. Picadillo, carne picada *(Culin.)*.

mincer [ˈmɪnsəʳ] [min-sa'], s. f. Máquina para picar carne.

mincingly [ˈmɪnsɪŋlɪ] [min-sin-li], adv. A pedacitos; con afectación; ligeramente, superficialmente.

mind [maɪnd] [maind], s. 1. Mente, entendimiento (intellect). 2. Gusto, propensión, elección, inclinación, afición, afecto. 3. Voluntad, gana, designio, intención, resolución, deseo (intention). 4. Pensamiento, opinión, parecer, dictamen (opinion). 5. Memoria, recuerdo (memory). 6. Espíritu, ánimo. **Of one mind,** unánimes. **With one mind,** unánimemente. **He has half a mind to do it,** está tentado de hacerlo. **I have a good mind to go,** ganas de ir no me faltan. **I have made up my mind,** estoy resuelto o decidido; he tomado una decisión. **To call to mind,** traer a la memoria. **To have something/somebody in mind,** tener algo/a alguien en mente. **To his mind,** a su parecer, según su opinión. **Out of mind,** olvidado. **Time out of mind,** tiempo inmemorial. **It will not be out of my mind,** no lo podré olvidar. **To put in mind,** acordar, recordar. **To speak one's mind,** decir su parecer. **To be out of one's mind,** haber perdido el juicio. **To be easy in one's mind,** tener el espíritu tranquilo. **To have half a mind to,** tener ligera inclinación, estar dispuesto a hacer una cosa. **Mind-reading,** adivinación del pensamiento de otra persona, sin intervención de los sentidos y a menudo desde gran distancia.

mind, va. 1. Notar, observar, considerar, atender, prestar atención (Pay attention to). 2. Cuidar; vigilar sobre (Take care). 3. Obedecer (Rules). 4. Estar alerta, resguardarse contra. 5. *(Fam.)* Recordar, acordar, refrescar la memoria. **Mind your business,** métase Ud. en lo que le importa; no se meta Ud. donde no le llaman. **Mind him,** ten cuidado con él. **Never mind,** no haga Ud. caso; no importa. -vn. 1. Inclinarse o tener inclinación a una cosa; estar dispuesto. 2. Ser obediente. 3. Acordarse. **To have a mind to,** darle a uno la gana. *(Fam.)* Pedírselo el cuerpo. **To mind one's p's and q's,** poner los puntos sobre las íes, tener mucho cuidado con lo que se hace o dice. **Not to mind a thing,** no hacer caso de una cosa. **Mind out!** ¡Cuidado!

mind-bending ['maɪnd,bendɪŋ] [maind-ben-din], **mind-boggling** ['maɪnd,bɔəglɪŋ] [maind-bo-glin], *a.* Increíble *(Fam.)*.

minded ['maɪnd] [maind], *a.* Inclinado, dispuesto, propenso. **High-minded,** de pensamientos elevados. **Evil-minded,** mal intencionado. **Low-minded,** de bajos pensamientos.

mindful ['maɪnd͡ful] [maind-ful], *a.* Atento, cuidadoso, diligente, vigilante, el que tiene presente alguna cosa. **To be mindful,** tener presente, no olvidar, acordarse.

mindfully ['maɪnd͡fulɪ] [maind-fu-li], *adv.* Atentamente, cuidadosamente, con diligencia.

mindfulness ['maɪnd͡fulnɪs] [maind-ful-nes], *s.* Atención, cuidado.

mindless ['maɪndlɪs] [maind-les], *a.* Descuidado, negligente; necio, insensato.

mind reading ['maɪnd,ri:dɪŋ] [maind-ri-din], *s.* Lectura del pensamiento.

mine [maɪn] [main], *pron. pos.* Mío, mía, lo mío; *(Ant.)* mí. **This pen is mine,** esta pluma es mía. **It is mine to search,** a mí me toca buscar. **Your faith and mine,** su fe y la mía. **Mine eye,** *(Ant.)* mi ojo.

mine, *s. (Min.)* 1. Mina. **A copper mine,** una mina de cobre. **Shaft of a mine,** pozo de una mina. 2. *(Mil.)* Mina. **Mine field,** campo minado. **Mine layer,** *(Mar.)* plantaminas. **Mine sweeper,** *(Mar.)* dragaminas.

mine, *vn.* 1. Minar, cavar o hacer minas. 2. Zapar, arruinar, hacer algún daño por medios ocultos. *-va.* 1. Minar, obtener cavando; explotar una mina. 2. Zapar, destruir; *(Fig.)* poco a poco, por medio de minas. 3. Dañar secretamente.

miner ['maɪnəʳ] [mai-naʳ], *s.* 1. Minador, el que hace minas en las fortificaciones. 2. Minero, el que trabaja en las minas para sacar los metales o minerales. *(mex.)* Barretero. **Miner's pick,** pico de hoja de salvia. **Corps of sappers and miners,** cuerpo de zapadores-minadores.

mineral ['mɪnərəl] [mi-ne-ral], *a.* Mineral, inorgánico. **Mineral kingdom,** reino mineral. **Mineral oil,** aceite mineral. **Mineral water,** agua mineral. *-s.* 1. Mineral. 2. Roca, fósil.

mineralization [,mɪnərəlaɪ'zeɪʃən] [mi-ne-ra-lai-se-shon], *s.* Mineralización.

mineralize ['mɪnərəlaɪz] [mi-ne-ra-lais], *va.* Mineralizar, reducir un metal a forma de mineral.

mineralizer ['mɪnərəlaɪzəʳ] [mi-ne-ra-lai-saʳ], *s.* Cuerpo simple que puede formar combinación con los metales.

mineralogical, mineralogic [,mɪnəˈrælədʒɪkəl] [mi-ne-ra-lo-yi-kal], *a.* Mineralógico, perteneciente a la mineralogía.

mineralogist [,mɪnəˈrælədʒɪst] [mi-ne-ra-lo-chist], *s.* Mineralogista, el que está versado en el conocimiento de los minerales.

mineralogize [,mɪnəˈrælədʒaɪz] [mi-ne-ra-lo-yais], *va.* Estudiar y recoger minerales; hacer excursiones mineralógicas.

mineralogy [,mɪnəˈrælədʒɪ] [mi-ne-ra-lo-yi], *s.* Mineralogía, la ciencia que trata de los minerales.

mineshaft ['maɪnʃɑːft] [main-shaft], *s.* Pozo de mina.

minever ['mɪnəvəʳ] [mi-ne-vaʳ], *s.* Forro de pieles blancas con manchas negras.

mingle ['mɪŋgl] [min-guel], *va.* 1. Mezclar, unir, incorporar; juntar cosas diversas. 2. Confundir. *-vn.* Mezclarse, juntarse, unirse, formar una mezcla.

mingle-mangle ['mɪŋglˌmæŋgl] [min-guel-man-guel], *s.* Miscelánea, almodrote.

mingledly ['mɪŋgldlɪ] [min-gueld-li], *adv.* Confusamente.

mingler ['mɪŋgləʳ] [min-glaʳ], *s.* Mezclador, el que mezcla.

miniate ['mɪnɪeɪt] [mi-nieit], *a.* Del color de bermellón. *-va. (Des.)* Pintar con bermellón.

miniature ['mɪnɪtʃəʳ] [mi-ni-chaʳ], *a.* De tamaño mucho menor que el natural o normal; en miniatura. *-s.* 1.

Miniatura, pintura en pequeño. 2. Dibujo en pequeño; cosa de tamaño reducido. 3. *(Des.)* Rúbrica.

miniaturization [,mɪnɪətʃəri'zeɪʃən] [mi-nia-cha-ri-zei-shon], *s.* Miniaturización.

minify ['mɪnɪfaɪ] [mi-ni-fai], *va.* 1. Empequeñecer, disminuir. 2. Disminuir el valor de; despreciar, denigrar.

minikin ['mɪnɪkɪn] [mi-ni-kin], *a. (Ant.)* Pequeño, menudo. *-s.* Cosa muy menuda o delgada; alfilerito.

minim ['mɪnɪm] [mi-nim], *s.* 1. Medida usada en farmacia que equivale a 0.95 grano de agua; casi una gota. 2. *(Mús.)* Mínima, mitad de la semibreve o compasillo. 3. Enano, hombre pequeño. 4. Mínimo, religioso de la orden de los mínimos.

minimal ['mɪnɪml] [mi-ni-mal], *a.* Mínimo, lo menor.

minimalist ['mɪnɪməlɪst] [mi-ni-ma-list], *a.* Minimalista.

minimarket ['mɪnɪˌmɑːkɪt] [mi-ni-mar-kit], *s. m.* Autoservicio.

minimize ['mɪnɪmaɪz] [mi-ni-mais], *va.* Reducir al mínimo; menospreciar, no hacer caso alguno de.

minimum ['mɪnɪməm] [mi-ni-mom], *s.* Lo mínimo, el último grado a que se puede reducir una cantidad. *-a.* Mínimo, lo menos posible. **Minimum wage,** salario o jornal mínimo.

mining ['mɪnɪŋ] [mi-nin], *s.* Minería, trabajo del minero, arte de explotar las minas. *-a.* De mina. **Mining-camp,** minería; reunión temporal de los que explotan una mina. **Gold-mining,** minería de oro.

minion ['mɪnjən] [mi-nion], *s.* 1. Privado, válido, favorito, el predilecto. 2. *(Impr.)* Miñona, glosilla, letra de siete puntos; (la de esta línea).

minion-like ['mɪnjənˌlaɪk] [mi-nion-laik], **minionly** ['mɪnɪən] [mi-nion], *adv.* Regaladamente, afectadamente.

miniseries ['mɪnɪˌsərɪz] [mi-ni-se-ris], *s. pl.* Miniserie *(TV)*.

minish ['mɪnɪʃ] [mi-nish], *va.* Disminuir, minorar.

miniskirt ['mɪnɪskɜːt] [mi-nis-kert], *s. f.* Minifalda.

minister ['mɪnɪstəʳ] [mi-nis-taʳ], *s.* 1. Ministro, ejecutor, instrumento que sirve para ejecutar lo que otro le manda. 2. Ministro de estado o del despacho. 3. Sacerdote, párroco, cura. 4. Delegado, agente, substituto. 5. Ministro, el agente de una potencia extranjera.

minister, *va. y vn.* 1. Dar, ministrar, administrar, surtir, proveer, socorrer, dar socorros. 2. Ministrar, servir o ejercitar algún oficio. 3. Oficiar, celebrar los oficios divinos. 4. Ministrar o administrar medicinas.

ministerial [,mɪnɪsˈtɪərɪəl] [mi-nis-tia-rial], *a.* Ministerial, perteneciente a los secretarios de estado o del despacho; subalterno, subordinado; eclesiástico; sacerdotal, parroquial. **The ministerial benches,** en Inglaterra, España y otros países los bancos del Parlamento, del Congreso de los Diputados, etc.

ministerially [,mɪnɪsˈtɪərɪəlɪ] [mi-nis-tia-ria-li], *adv.* Ministerialmente.

ministrant ['mɪnɪstrənt] [mi-nis-trant], *a.* Subordinado, subalterno.

ministration [,mɪnɪsˈtreɪʃən] [mi-nis-trei-shon], *s.* 1. El acto de cumplir un servicio como ministro o subordinado; servicio, agencia, comisión. 2. Ministerio u oficio eclesiástico.

ministress ['mɪnɪstrɪs] [mi-nis-tris], *sf.* Ministra.

ministry ['mɪnɪstrɪ] [mi-nis-tri], *s.* 1. Ministerio, cargo, incumbencia, oficio, servicio. 2. Ministerio eclesiástico, el clero. 3. Ayuda, intervención. 4. Ministerio, el gobierno de un ministro de estado.

minium ['mɪnɪəm] [mi-niom], *s. (Quím.)* Minio, azarcón, óxido rojo de plomo.

miniver ['mɪnɪvəʳ] [mi-ni-vaʳ], *s.* 1. Ardilla de Siberia y su piel. 2. Piel de abrigo blanca con motas negras.

mink [mɪŋk] [mink], *s.* Visón, mamífero de los mustélidos, cuya piel es muy estimada.

minnesinger ['mɪnɪˌsɪŋəʳ] [mi-ni-sin-gaʳ], *s.* Poeta lírico de Alemania en la edad media. *Cf.* TROUBADOUR.

minnow ['mɪnoʊ] [mi-nou], *s.* Vario, un pez pequeño de río. Se le llama también, **minnie.**

minor ['maɪnəʳ] [mi-naʳ], *a.* 1. Menor, más pequeño, menor de edad. 2. Secundario, inferior. 3. *(Mús.)* Menor, del tono cuya tercera es menos; medio tono más bajo. -*s.* 1. Menor o menor de edad. 2. Menor, la proposición segunda de un silogismo. 3. Fanciscano, menor, el fraile de la orden de San Francisco. *V.* MINORITE. 4. Menor, tono cuya tercera es menor; se usa en las composiciones solemnes o fúnebres. La tercera menor consta de un tono y un semitono. **Minor key,** tono menor.

minorite ['maɪnərɪt] [mi-no-rit], *s.* Menor, mínimo, fraile franciscano.

minority ['maɪ'nɒrɪtɪ] [mai-no-ri-ti], *s.* 1. Minoridad o menor edad. 2. Minoría, el menor número, los menos.

minotaur ['maɪnətɔːʳ] [mi-no-toʳ], *s.* Minotauro, monstruo fabuloso.

minster ['mɪnstəʳ] [mins-taʳ], *s.* Monasterio; iglesia catedral.

minstrel ['mɪnstrəl] [mins-tral], *s.* 1. Ministril, músico ambulante que en la edad media componía versos y se acompañaba con el arpa; trovador. 2. Originalmente, persona que tenía por oficio tocar instrumentos músicos para recreo de su señor. 3. *(E.U.)* Miembro de una compañía de cómicos que hacen papeles de negros, cantan las canciones de esa raza y dicen chistes y cuchufletas. 4. *(Poét.)* Bardo, poeta lírico.

minstrelsy ['mɪnstrəslɪ] [mins-tras-li], *s.* Música de instrumentos; orquesta o reunión de músicos que tocan instrumentos según las reglas del arte.

mint [mɪnt] [mint], *s.* 1. Casa de moneda. 2. Mina, tesoro; manantial, provisión abundante de cualquier cosa. **Master of the mint,** director de la casa de moneda. 3. *(Bot.)* Menta, hierbabuena, sándalo; ejemplar de una de las varias hierbas aromáticas de la familia de la labiadas.

mint, *va.* 1. Acuñar, batir, fabricar monedas. 2. Inventar, forjar, falsificar.

mintage ['mɪntədʒ] [min-tadch], *s.* Moneda acuñada; braceaje, derechos de cuño.

minter ['mɪntəʳ] [min-taʳ], *s.* Acuñador; inventor.

mint-master ['mɪntˌmɑːstəʳ] [mint-mas-taʳ], *s.* 1. Superintendente de una casa de moneda. 2. *(Ant.)* Inventor, fabricador.

minuend ['mɪnjʊend] [mi-niuend], *s.* Minuendo, cantidad mayor de que ha de restarse otra.

minuet [mɪnjʊ'et] [mi-niuet], *s.* Minué, minuete, antiguo baile de origen francés.

minus ['maɪnəs] [mai-nos], *a.* 1. Menos (una cantidad determinada); indicado por el signo -; negativo. 2. Desprovisto de, sin, falto de; sin valor positivo. **A knife minus an edge,** un cuchillo sin filo.

minuscule ['mɪnjəskjuːl] [mi-nas-kiul], *a.* Minúsculo.

minute ['mɪnɪt] [mi-nit], *a.* 1. Menudo, pequeño, dinimuto. 2. Muy exacto, minucioso.

minute, *s.* 1. Minuto, la sexagésima parte de una hora o de un grado geográfico. 2. Momento, minuto, instante. 3. Minuta, nota apuntamiento, un extracto sucinto de alguna cosa. **Minutes,** minutas, actas de un cuerpo deliberante; memoria auténtica. **Up to the minute news,** noticias de última hora. **Minute-book,** libro de minutas. **Minute-glass,** ampolleta o reloj de arena que dura un minuto. **Minute-hand,** minutero. **Minute-man,** soldado de la guardia nacional pronto para prestar servicio en el acto. **Minute-watch,** reloj de minutos, el que señala los minutos. **Wait a minute!** ¡espera un momento! **Every minute counts,** no hay tiempo que perder.

minute, *va.* Minutar, hacer la minuta de algún instrumento o contrato.

minutely ['mɪnɪtlɪ] [mi-niut-li], *adv.* Por menor; a cada minuto.

minutely, *adv.* A intervalos de un minuto.

minuteness ['mɪnɪtnɪs] [mi-niut-nes], *s.* Minucia, menudencia, cortedad, pequeñez.

minutia [mɪnjuːtɪə] [mi-niu-tia], *s.* *(pl.* MINUTIÆ). Minucia, particularidad pequeñísima; detalle minucioso; más usado en plural.

minx [mɪŋks] [minks], *s.* Moza atrevida y libre.

miny ['mɪnɪ] [mi-ni], *a.* Subterráneo, lo perteneciente a las minas o cavernas.

miocene ['maɪəsiːn] [maia-sin], *a.* *(Geol.)* Mioceno; se dice de la división media de las capas terciarias.

miracle ['mɪrəkl] [mi-ra-kol], *s.* 1. Milagro, maravilla; prodigio. 2. *(Teol.)* Acontecimiento en el orden natural, pero fuera del orden establecido; obra divina, hecho sobrenatural. 3. Espectáculo teatral de la edad media en el que se representaban escenas de las vidas de los santos. **Miracle-monger,** el que finge que puede hacer milagros, impostor, embustero. **Miracle cure,** remedio milagroso.

miraculous [mɪ'rækjʊləs] [mi-ra-kiu-los], *a.* 1. Sobrenatural, efectuado por agencia o poder divinos. 2. Milagroso, maravilloso.

miraculously [mɪ'rækjʊləslɪ] [mi-ra-kiu-los-li], *adv.* Por milagro, sobrenaturalmente; milagrosamente.

miraculousness [mɪ'rækjʊləsnɪs] [mi-ra-kiu-los-nes], *s.* Lo maravilloso; lo extraordinario.

mirage ['mɪrɑːdʒ] [mi-rach], *s.* Espejismo por el cual los objetos distantes dan una imagen en lo alto de la atmósfera, y por lo regular invertida. Es frecuente en las llanuras de los países cálidos y en el mar. *(Fr.)*

mire ['maɪəʳ] [maiaʳ], *s.* Cieno, lodo, fango, limo; lodazal, lugar lleno de cieno, cenagal.

mire, *va.* Encenagar, enlodar.

miriness ['maɪərɪnɪs] [maia-ri-nes], *s.* Cualidad de fangoso o condición de estar cubierto de lodo.

mirk, mirky ['mɜːkɪ] [mer-ki], *a. V.* MURKY.

mirk ['mɜːk] [merk], *a.* *(Esco.)* Tenebroso, lóbrego.

mirror ['mɪrəʳ] [mi-roʳ], *s.* 1. Espejo (de vidrio azogado posteriormente o de metal pulimentado). 2. Ejemplar, modelo; lo que refleja o representa claramente.

mirror, *va.* Reflejar, espejear.

mirth [mɜːθ] [merz], *s.* Alegría, regocijo, gozo, júbilo, contento.

mirthful ['mɜːθfʊl] [merz-ful], *a.* Alegre, jovial, gozoso, contento.

mirthfully ['mɜːθfʊlɪ] [merz-fu-li], *adv.* Alegremente, jovialmente.

mirthless ['mɜːθlɪs] [merz-les], *a.* Triste, melancólico.

miry ['maɪrɪ] [mai-ri], *a.* Canagoso, lodoso, que contiene cieno.

mis- [mɪs] [mis]. Prefijo que indica culpa, sin razón; mal; también, partícula inseparable negativa o despreciativa.

misacceptation [ˌmɪsəsep'teɪʃən] [mis-a-sep-tei-shon], *s.* Mala inteligencia, el acto de entender alguna cosa al revés; de echar algo a mala parte.

misadventure [ˌmɪsəd'ventʃəʳ] [mis-ad-ven-chaʳ], *s.* Desgracia, desventura, revés, infortunio.

misalliance [ˌmɪsə'laɪəns] [mis-a-laians], *s.* Asociación, unión o alianza impropias o fuera del orden regular.

misallied [ˌmɪsə'laɪd] [mis-a-laid], *a.* Lo que forma una unión o asociaicón impropia e irregular con otra cosa.

misanthrope ['mɪzənθrəʊp] [mi-san-zroup], o **misanthropist** [mɪ'zænθrɒpɪst] [mi-san-zro-pist], *s.* Misántropo, el que huye y aborrece el trato y compañía de los hombres.

misanthropic, misanthropical [ˌmɪzən'θrɒpɪk] [mi-san-zro-pik], *a.* Misantrópico, lo que pertenece a la misantropía.

misanthropy [mɪ'zænθrɒpɪ] [mi-san-zro-pist], *s.* Misantropía, aborrecimiento del género humano o aversión al trato humano.

misapplication ['mɪsˌæplɪ'keɪʃən] [mis-a-pli-kei-shon], *s.* Mala aplicación o mal uso de una cosa.

misapply ['mɪsə'plaɪ] [mis-a-plai], *va.* Usar de alguna cosa impropiamente o hacer mal uso de ella.

misapprehend [ˌmɪsˌæprɪ'hend] [mis-a-pri-jend], *va.* Entender mal o no comprender alguna cosa como se debe.

misapprehension ['mɪsˌæprɪ'henʃən] [mis-a-pri-jen-shon], *s.* Error, equivocación, yerro, engaño, aprehensión o falso concepto formado de alguna cosa en la imaginación.

misappropriate ['mɪsə'prəʊprɪeɪt] [mis-a-prou-prieit], *va.* Invertir, malamente, v. g. los fondos públicos; malversar.

misbecome ['mɪsbɪkʌm] [mis-bi-kam], *vn.* Desconvenir, no convenir; no estar bien o no sentar una cosa; no sentar bien; ser poco conveniente. **Levity misbecomes his years,** la levedad no conviene a sus años. **That has misbecomes her,** ese sombrero no le está bien, no le sienta, le cae mal.

misbecoming ['mɪsbɪkʌmɪŋ] [mis-bi-ka-min], *a.* Desproporcionado; indecoroso, impropio, indecente.

misbecomingness [ˌmɪsbɪ'kʌmɪŋnɪs] [mis-bi-ka-min-nes], *s.* Desproporción; impropiedad, indecencia.

misbegot, misbegotten ['mɪsbɪgɒt] [mis-bi-got], *a.* Ilegítimo, nacido fuera de matrimonio, bastardo.

misbehave ['mɪsbɪ'heɪv] [mis-bi-jeiv], *va.* Obrar o proceder mal. *-vn.* Portarse mal, conducirse mal.

misbehaved ['mɪsbɪ'heɪvd] [mis-bi-jeivd], *a.* Descortés, malcriado, impolítico.

misbehavior ['mɪsbɪ'heɪvɪɔʳ] [mis-bi-jei-vioʳ], *s.* Mala conducta, mal modo de portarse, mal paso o mala acción.

misbelief ['mɪsbɪli:f] [mis-bi-lif], *s.* 1. Error, opinión falsa o equivocada. 2. Heterodoxia, incredulidad, irreligión.

misbelieve ['mɪsbɪli:v] [mis-bi-liv], *vn.* Estar en error, tener opiniones falsas en cualquier asunto y principalmente en materias de religión.

misbeliever ['mɪsbɪli:vəʳ] [mis-bi-li-vaʳ], *s.* Incrédulo, el que duda en materias de religión.

misbelieving ['mɪsbɪli:vɪŋ] [mis-bi-li-vin], *pa.* Heterodoxo; infiel.

misbeseem ['mɪsbɪsi:m] [mis-bi-sim], *vn.* Venir mal alguna cosa; no convenir una cosa, no ser decente o propia.

misbode ['mɪsbɒd] [mis-bod], *va.* Venir mal alguna cosa; no convenir una cosa, no ser decente o propia.

miscalculate ['mɪs'kælkjʊleɪt] [mis-kal-kiu-leit], *va.* Calcular mal.

miscalculation ['mɪsˌkælkjʊ'leɪʃən] [mis-kal-kiu-lei-shon], *s.* Mal cálculo; cuenta errada.

miscall ['mɪs'kɔ:l] [mis-kol], *va.* 1. Nombrar erradamente o dar un nombre impropio *a.* 2. Ultrajar, difamar.

miscarriage ['mɪs'kærɪdʒ] [mis-ka-rich], *s.* 1. El éxito infeliz o desgraciado de alguna empresa; mala conducta o mal porte; falta. 2. Aborto, parto prematuro, malparto. 3. Extravío.

miscarry ['mɪs'kærɪ] [mis-ka-ri], *vn.* 1. Frustrarse, malograrse alguna cosa, salir mal de un empeño. 2. Abortar, malparir. 3. Extraviarse.

miscast [ˌmɪs'kɑ:st] [mis-kast], *va.* Tomar mal la cuenta de alguna cosa, contar mal.

miscegenation [ˌmɪsɪdʒɪ'neɪʃən] [mi-si-yi-nei-shon], *s.* Mezcla de razas, particularmente de las razas negra y blanca.

miscellanea [ˌmɪsɪ'leɪnɪə] [mi-si-lei-nia], *s. pl.* Miscelánea, en especial las misceláneas literarias.

miscellaneous [ˌmɪsɪ'leɪnɪəs] [mi-si-lei-nios], *a.* Misceláneo, mixto, mezclado o compuesto de varios géneros; diverso.

miscellany [mɪ'selənɪ] [mi-se-la-ni], **miscellaneousness** [ˌmɪsɪ'leɪnɪəsnɪs] [mi-si-lei-nios-nes], *s.* 1. Colección de composiciones literarias sobre diversas materias. 2. Miscelánea.

mischance [mɪs'tʃɑ:ns] [mis-chans], *s.* Desgracia, desdicha, desventura, infortunio, desastre, fatalidad.

mischarge [mɪs'tʃɑ:dʒ] [mis-charch], *va.* Cargar o poner en una cuenta lo que no debía ponerse.

mischief ['mɪstʃɪf] [mis-chif], *s.* 1. Mal, daño, perjuicio, pérdida, agravio; mala consecuencia, mala resulta. 2. Travesura, diablura. 3. La persona que molesta o veja. **To play the mischief,** causar daño. **He did it from downright mischief,** él lo hizo por pura maldad. **To get into mischief,** hacer travesuras.

mischief-maker ['mɪstʃɪfˌmeɪkəʳ] [mis-chif-mei-kaʳ], *s.* Dañador, el que causa daño o perjuicio a otro.

mischief-making ['mɪstʃɪfˌmeɪkɪŋ] [mis-chif-mei-kin], *a.* Que causa daño, dañino.

mischievous ['mɪstʃɪvəs] [mis-chi-vos], *a.* 1. Dañino, dañoso, perjudicial; perverso. 2. Malicioso, malévolo; enredador, travieso, juguetón.

mischievously ['mɪstʃɪvəslɪ] [mis-chi-vos-li], *adv.* Perversamente, de una manera traviesa, juguetona; perjudicialmente, dañosamente.

mischievousness ['mɪstˌφɑm.ˌɪs] [mis-chi-vos-nes], *s.* Malicia, malignidad, maldad, perversidad; picardía, travesura; carácter juguetón; carácter pernicioso y dañino.

mischna ['mɪskna] [misk-na], *s.* V. MISHNA.

miscibility [ˌmɪsɪ'bɪlɪtɪ] [mi-si-bi-li-ti], *s.* Cualidad de lo que se puede mezclar o incorporar con otra cosa.

miscible ['mɪsɪbl] [mi-si-bol], *a.* Mezclable, incorporable.

miscitation [ˌmɪsɪ'teɪʃən] [mi-si-tei-shon], *s.* Cita falsa o errónea.

miscite ['mɪsaɪt] [mi-sait], *va.* Citar falsa o equivocadamente.

misclaim ['mɪskleɪm] [mis-kleim], *s.* Pretensión mal fundada o sin justicia.

miscomputation [ˌmɪskəmpjʊ'teɪʃən] [mis-kom-piu-tei-shon], *s.* Cómputo falso.

misconceit ['mɪskənsi:t] [mis-kon-sit], **Misconception** ['mɪskən'sepʃən] [mis-kon-sep-shon], *s.* Concepto equivocado, idea falsa, error, equivocación, engaño; mala inteligencia.

misconceive ['mɪskən'si:v] [mis-kon-siv], *va.* y *vn.* 1. Formar concepto erróneo, juzgar mal. 2. Concebir una idea falsa.

misconduct [mɪs'kɒndʌkt] [mis-kon-dakt], *s.* Mala conducta, mal manejo, mal porte.

misconduct, *va.* Desacertar, obrar sin acierto, conducirse o portarse mal en algún asunto.

misconstruction ['mɪskəns'trʌkʃən] [mis-kon-trak-shon], *s.* Mala construcción, interpretación siniestra de palabras o acciones; mal sentido.

misconstrue ['mɪskən'stru:] [mis-kons-tru], *va.* Interpretar siniestramente, dar mal sentido o mal color a alguna acción o palabra.

misconstruer ['mɪskən'stru:əʳ] [mis-kons-truaʳ], *s.* El que interpreta siniestramente alguna cosa.

miscount ['mɪs'kaʊnt] [mis-kaunt], *va.* Contar mal. *-vn.* Equivocarse en la cuenta.

miscreancy ['mɪskrɪənsɪ] [mis-krian-si], *s.* Infidelidad, incredulidad, irreligión, adhesión a una religión falsa.

miscreant ['mɪskrɪənt] [mis-kriant], *s.* Descreído, infiel, mal creyente, incrédulo, impío; hombre malvado o perverso; hombre despreciable.

miscreate, miscreated ['mɪskrɪeɪt] [mis-krieit], *a.* Mal formado, contrahecho.

miscue ['mɪskju:] [mis-kiu], *s.* En el juego de billar, jugada en falso o desacertada por haberse deslizado el taco.

misdate ['mɪsdeɪt] [mis-deit], *va.* Fechar falsamente, o poner fecha equivocada a un escrito o documento.

misdeed ['mɪs'di:d] [mis-did], *s.* Mala acción, mal hecho, crimen, delito, iniquidad; transgresión, violación o quebrantamiento de un deber.

misdeem ['mɪs'di:m] [mis-dim], *va.* Formar malos juicios; juzgar mal; tener mala opinión de aglono; equivocar.

misdemean ['mɪs'dimi:n] [mis-di-min], *vn.* Portarse o conducirse mal, tener mala conducta.

misdemeanor ['mɪs'dimi:nɔʳ] [mis-di-mi-noʳ], *s.* 1. Mal proceder, mala conducta. 2. *(For.)* Delito, crimen de menor cuantía; transgresión de una ley no comprendida entre las que la jurisprudencia inglesa llama *felony.*

misdirect ['mɪsdɪ'rekt] [mis-di-rekt], *va.* Dirigir erradamente.

misdirection ['mɪsdɪ'rekʃən] [mis-di-rek-shon], *s.* 1. Mala dirección; informe falso; acción de guiar por una vía equivocada. 2. Error que comete un juez en el resumen del juicio o proceso que hace para información de los miembros del jurado.

misdisposition ['mɪsdɪspəʊ'sɪʃən] [mis-dis-po-si-shon], *s.* *(Poco us.)* La inclinación al mal.

misdo ['mɪsdu:] [mis-du], *va.* Errar, obrar mal a propósito, delinquir. *-vn.* Errar, cometer faltas y yerros.

misdoer ['mɪsdu:əʳ] [mis-duaʳ], *s.* Malhechor, criminal.

misdoing ['mɪsdu:ɪŋ] [mis-duin], *s.* Ofensa, yerro, falta, mala acción.

misdoubt ['mɪsdaʊt] [mis-daut], *va.* *(Ant.)* Recelar, temer, sospechar; dudar sin razón o sin fundamento.

misdoubt, *s.* *(Ant.)* Recelo, duda, irresolución, perplejidad, vacilación.

misemploy ['mɪsˈɪmplɔɪ] [mis-im-ploi], *va.* Abusar; emplear o dar a una cosa un destino que no le conviene.

misemployment ['mɪsˈɪmplɔɪmənt] [mis-im-ploi-ment], *s.* Abuso.

miser ['mɪsəʳ] [mi-saʳ], *s.* Tacaño, avariento, hombre sórdidamente interesado.

miser, mizer, *s.* Aparato tubular para abrir pozos; tiene una válvula y un tornillo de rosca para empujar la tierra hacia arriba.

miserable ['mɪzərəbl] [mi-sa-ra-bol], *a.* 1. Miserable, desdichado, infeliz, pobre. 2. Sin valor; despreciable. 3. Digno de lástima. 4. *(Ant.) V.* MISERLY.

miserableness ['mɪzərəblnɪs] [mi-sa-ra-bol-nes], *s.* Miseria; desesperación.

miserably ['mɪzərəblɪ] [mi-sa-ra-bli], *adv.* Miserablemente, mezquinamente.

misery ['mɪzərɪ] [mi-se-ri], *s.* 1. Miseria, infelicidad, desdicha. 2. Calamidad, infortunio, desventura. 3. Sufrimiento, padecimiento; *(E.U. del Sur)* dolor continuo.

miserere [mɪˈzɛrɛʳ] [mi-sa-reaʳ], *s.* 1. Miserere, el salmo penitencial que comienza con dicha palabra. 2. *(Arq.)* Repisa en algunas iglesias de la edad media.

misericorde ['mɪzərɪkɔːd] [mi-sa-ri-kord], *s.* Puñal pequeño que se usó en la edad media para dar muerte a un caballero caído.

misery ['mɪzərɪ] [mi-se-ri], *s. f.* 1. Pena, miseria, tristeza (sadness). 2. Desgracia (misfortune). **To put somebody out of his misery,** sacar a alguien de la incertidumbre *(Fig.).*

misfashion ['mɪsˈfæʃən] [mis-fa-shon], *va.* Hacer alguna cosa al revés de lo que debería ser; ejecutar algo fuera de orden.

misfeasance ['mɪsfɪəsəns] [mis-fia-sans], *s. (For.)* 1. La ejecución de un hecho legal de una manera ilegal, especialmente cuando media negligencia. 2. Infidencia.

misfit ['mɪsfɪt] [mis-fit], *va.* 1. Hacer que algo no siente bien; ajustar mal. 2. No sentar bien, no ser a propósito, ni propio para el caso. -*s.* Lo que no sienta bien.

misform ['mɪsfɔːm] [mis-form], *va.* Desfigurar.

misfortune [mɪsˈfɔːtʃən] [mis-for-chun], *s.* 1. Desgracia, infortunio, desventura, desdicha. 2. Desastre, calamidad.

misgive ['mɪsgɪv] [mis-giv], *va.* Llenar de deudas o recelos; hacer temer o dudar. -*vn.* 1. Ser receloso, tímido. 2. Faltar a. **My heart misgives me,** me falta corazón.

misgiving ['mɪsgɪvɪŋ] [mis-gi-vin], *s.* Recelo, duda, presentimiento; desconfianza, temor.

misgotten ['mɪsgɒtn] [mis-go-ten], *a.* Mal ganado, mal adquirido o adquirido injustamente.

misgovern ['mɪsˈgʌvən] [mis-go-vern], *va.* Desgobernar, gobernado mal; administrar deslealmente.

misgoverned ['mɪsˈgʌvənd] [mis-ga-vernd], *a.* 1. Mal gobernado, mal administrado. 2. Rudo, rústico, tosco, grosero.

misgovernment ['mɪsˈgʌvənmənt] [mis-ga-vern-ment], *s.* 1. Desgobierno, mala administración o mala dirección, particularmente de los negocios públicos. 2. Desbarato, mala conducta.

misgraft ['mɪsˈgræft] [mis-graft], *va.* Ingerir o injertar mal.

misgrowth ['mɪsgraʊθ] [mis-grauz], *s.* Crecimiento anormal; desarrollo defectuoso.

misguidance ['mɪsgɪdəns] [mis-gui-dans], *s.* Dirección errada o falsa; extravío, error.

misguide ['mɪsgaɪd] [mis-gaid], *va.* 1. Descaminar, descarriar, extraviar. 2. Inducir en error; tratar mal.

misguided ['mɪsgaɪdɪd] [mis-gai-did], *a.* Equivocado.

mishap ['mɪshæp] [mis-jap], *s.* Desgracia, desventura, calamidad, desastre.

mishappen ['mɪshæpn] [mis-ja-pen], *vn.* Acontecer en mala hora alguna cosa; llegar fuera de tiempo.

mishear ['mɪshɪəʳ] [mis-jiaʳ], *va. y vn.* Oír mal, entender mal o imperfectamente.

mishna ['mɪsnə] [mis-na], *s.* 1. Misna, la primera parte del Talmud, colección de tradiciones rabínicas. 2. Párrafo de esta colección.

misinform ['mɪsɪnˈfɔːm] [mis-in-form], *va. y vn.* 1. Informar o enterar mal, dar alguna información o informe falso. 2. Engañar u ofuscar a alguno dándole falsos informes o falsas noticias sobre alguna cosa.

misinformation [ˌmɪsɪnfəˈmeɪʃən] [mis-in-for-mei-shon], *s.* Aviso erróneo, noticia falsa.

misinformer, misinformant ['mɪsɪnˈfɔːməʳ] [mis-in-for-maʳ], *s.* El que engaña dando noticias o informes falsos.

misinterpret ['mɪsɪnˈtɜːprɪt] [mis-in-ter-prit], *va.* Interpretar mal o siniestramente; entender mal, tomar en sentido erróneo.

misinterpretation ['mɪsɪnˌtɜːprɪˈteɪʃən] [mis-in-ter-pri-tei-shon], *s.* Mala o falsa interpretación; contrasentido.

misinterpreter ['mɪsɪnˈtɜːprɪtəʳ] [mis-in-ter-pri-taʳ], *s.* El que interpreta falsa o erradamente.

misjoin ['mɪsˈdʒɔɪn] [mis-yoin], *va.* Unir mal o impropiamente una cosa a otra; adecuar, acomodar o ajustar mal unas cosas con otras.

misjudge ['mɪsˈdʒʌdʒ] [mis-yach], *vn.* Juzgar mal, formar conceptos erróneos. -*va.* Errar, juzgar mal.

misjudgment ['mɪsˈdʒʌdʒmənt] [mis-yach-ment], *s.* Juicio o determinación injusta; opinión o parecer errado.

mislay [mɪsˈleɪ] [mis-lei], *va.* Colocar mal, extraviar, poner una cosa fuera de su lugar o en donde no debe estar. **To mislay papers,** extraviar papeles.

mislayer [mɪsˈleɪəʳ] [mis-leiaʳ], *s.* El que pone o deja alguna cosa fuera de su lugar.

misle ['mɪsl] [mi-sel], *vn. V.* MIZZLE.

mislead [mɪsˈliːd] [mis-lid], *va.* Extraviar, descaminar, descarriar; alucinar, engañar, seducir; hacer ejecutar lo que no es justo ni bien hecho.

misleader [mɪsˈliːdəʳ] [mis-li-daʳ], *s.* Seductor, corruptor.

misled [mɪsˈled] [mis-led], *pt, pp of* **mislead.**

mislen ['mɪsln] [mis-len], *s.* Tranquillón, la mezcla de granos, como de trigo y avena.

misletoe [mɪsˈlɪtuː] [mis-li-tu], *s. V.* MISTLETOE.

mislike [mɪsˈlaɪk] [mis-laik], *va. (Poco us.)* Desasprobar. -*vn. (Des.)* No gustar o no tener afición a alguna cosa.

mismanage [mɪsˈmænɪdʒ] [mis-ma-nich], *va.* Manejar o conducir mal alguna cosa.

mismanagement [mɪsˈmænɪdʒmənt] [mis-ma-nich-ment], *s.* Mala conducta, desarreglo, despilfarro; mala administración.

mismanager [mɪsˈmænɪdʒəʳ] [mis-ma-ni-chaʳ], *s.* Mal administrador, mal gerente; persona que dirige mal.

mismatch ['mɪsˈmætʃ] [mis-mach], *va.* Desigualar; deshermanar, desajustar.

mismate ['mɪsˈmeɪt] [mis-meit], *va.* Aparecer, juntar o casar de una manera poco acertada o conveniente.

misname [mɪsˈneɪm] [mis-neim], *va.* Trasnombrar, dar un nombre equivocado o falso a alguna cosa.

misnomer [mɪsˈnəʊməʳ] [mis-nou-maʳ], *s.* Nombre aplicado sin razón, designación inaplicable; el acto de poner a una persona un nombre equivocado en un documento legal.

misogamist [mɪˈsɒgəmɪst] [mi-so-ga-mist], *s.* Misogamia, aborrecimiento del matrimonio.

misogamy [mɪˈsɒgəmɪ] [mi-so-ga-mi], *s.* Misogamia, aborrecimiento del matrimonio.

misogynist [mɪˈsɒdʒɪnɪst] [mi-so-chi-nist], *s.* Misógino, aborrecedor de las mujeres.

misogyny [mɪˈsɒdʒɪnɪ] [mi-so-yi-ni], *s.* Misoginia, aborrecimiento de las mujeres.

misperception [ˌmɪspəˈsepʃən] [mis-per-sep-shon], *s.* Percepción errónea.

mispickel ['mɪspɪkl] [mis-pi-kel], *s. (Min.)* Mispiquelio, hierro sulfurado.

misplace ['mɪspleɪs] [mis-pleis], *va.* Traspapelar, extraviar, colocar mal, poner algo fuera de su lugar.

misplacement [mɪsˈpleɪsmənt] [mis-pleis-ment], *s.* Extravío.

mispoint ['mɪspɔɪnt] [mis-point], *va.* Puntuar mal algún escrito.

misprint ['mɪsprɪnt] [mis-print], *va.* Imprimir mal, cometer erratas en la impresión.

misprint, *s.* Errata de un libro.

misprise, misprize ['mɪspraɪs] [mis-prais], *va.* 1. Errar, equivocar. 2. Menospreciar, no hacer caso.

mispronounce ['mɪsprə'naʊns] [mis-pra-nouns], *vn.* Pronunciar mal, hablar sin exactitud. *-va.* Pronunciar impropiamente.

misproportion ['mɪsprə'pɔːʃən] [mis-pro-por-shon], *va.* Desproporcionar, proporcionar mal una cosa con otra.

misquotation ['mɪskwəʊ'teɪʃən] [mis-kuou-tei-shon], *s.* Cita falsa o equivocada.

misquote ['mɪs'kwəʊt] [mis-kuout], *va.* Citar en falso o equivocadamente.

misrate ['mɪsreɪt] [mis-reit], *va.* Valuar erradamente, dar una estimación o valor mayor o menor del que en realidad tiene una cosa.

misrelate ['mɪsrɪleɪt] [mis-ri-leit], *va.* Referir o relatar inexactamente una cosa.

misremember ['mɪsrɪ'membəʳ] [mis-ri-mem-baʳ], *va.* Acordarse mal de algo.

misreport ['mɪsrɪpɔːt] [mis-ri-port], *va.* Esparcir una noticia falsa o faltar a la verdad al referir o describir una cosa; propagar chismes.

misreport, *s.* Informe falso, relación inexacta, errónea, falsa.

misrepresent ['mɪsˌreprɪ'zent] [mis-re-pri-sent], *va.* Representar mal o falsamente, o presentar una cosa bajo falsos colores; disfrazar, falsificar.

misrepresentation ['mɪsˌreprɪzen'teɪʃən] [mis-re-pri-sen-tei-shon], *s.* Falsedad, representación falsa, noticiar o relación falsa y maliciosa; chisme.

misrule ['mɪs'ruːl] [mis-rul], *s.* Tumulto, desorden, desarreglo, desgobierno, confusión.

miss [mɪs] [mis], *sf.* 1. Señorita; término de cortesía que precede al nombre o apellido de una jóven o de una mujer soltera. 2. Muchacha, joven; una señorita. 3. *(Des.)* Manceba. Cuando este término de cortesía se aplica a dos o más personas del mismo nombre, se pone en plural el título o el nombre, a discreción. **The Misses Brown o the Miss Browns,** las Señoritas Brown. La primera forma es preferible a la última.

miss, *va.* 1. Errar, no acertar, equivocar. 2. Errar el tiro, errar el golpe; no dar en el blanco. 3. Perder; no conseguir o no obtener lo que se desea; no hallar lo que se busca. 4. Echar de menos alguna cosa; echar de ver que falta algo. 5. Pasar sin alguna cosa o abstenerse de ella; carecer. 6. Omitir, dejar de hacer. *-vn.* 1. Frustrarse, desgraciarse, salir mal un negocio, un empeño, etc. 2. Faltar, caer en falta. 3. Acertar con algo por casualidad. **We cannot miss of it,** no podemos dejar de saberlo o de hallarlo. **To miss one's mark,** errar el blanco. **To miss fire,** errar, faltar el tiro. **I missed money from the cash-box,** noté que faltaba dinero en la caja, o de la caja. **She missed a glove,** ella perdió un guante. **Miss out,** saltarse, pasar por alto. **To miss stays,** *(Mar.)* faltar la virada, no virar. **Three volumes are missing,** faltan tres volúmenes.

miss, *s.* 1. El acto de no acertar, de no hallar, o no obtener, de echar de menos, etc. 2. *(Des.)* Pérdida, falta. 3. Señorita.

missal ['mɪsəl] [mi-sal], *s.* Misal, el libro que contiene el orden y modo de celebrar la misa.

missel, misselden, misseldine, *s. (Bot.)* V. MISTLETOE.

missel-thrush ['mɪsəlθrʌst] [mi-sel-zrast], *s.* Tordo grande de Europa que se alimenta mucho de las bayas de muérdago.

missend ['mɪsənd] [mi-send], *va. (pret.* y *pp.* MISSENT). Enviar en dirección equivocada; dirigir mal una carta, un paquete, etc.

misshape ['mɪʃeɪp] [mis-sheip], *va.* Deformar, desfigurar, afear.

missile ['mɪsaɪl] [mi-sail], *a.* Arrojadizo. **Missile weapons,** armas arrojadizas.

missing ['mɪsɪŋ] [mi-sin], *s.* El acto de omitir o echar de menos alguna cosa; el estado de lo que se halla ausente o de lo que falta. *-a.* Extraviado, perdido; ausente, que falta.

mission ['mɪʃən] [mi-shon], *s.* 1. Envío, acción de enviar. 2. Misión, comisión. 3. Misión, cierto número de eclesiásticos enviados para instruir a los fieles o convertir a los infieles, y

el sitio o paraje donde se establecen. 4. El destino voluntario o forzoso de una persona; la meta de sus esfuerzos. 5. Embajada, el cargo y la comisión de un representante diplomático en el extranjero.

missionary ['mɪʃənərɪ] [mi-sho-na-ri], *s.* 1. Misionero. 2. Persona enviada con un encargo o misión. *-a.* Misioner, perteneciente a las misiones.

missis, missus ['mɪsɪz] [mi-sis], *s.* 1. Señora; modo usual de pronunciar la palabra **Mistress,** cuya abreviatura es *Mrs.* 2. *(Fam. y dial.)* Mujer, esposa, parienta.

missive ['mɪsɪv] [mi-siv], *a.* Misivo, que se puede enviar o se destina a ser enviado. *-s.* Carta, misiva, comunicación escrita.

misspell ['mɪspel] [mis-pel], *va.* Deletrear mal, escribir con mala ortografía.

misspelling ['mɪspelɪŋ] [mis-pe-lin], *s.* Ortografía incorrecta, viciosa.

misspend ['mɪs'pend] [mis-pend], *va.* Malgastar, derrochar, disipar; hacer mal uso, emplear mal.

misspender ['mɪs'pendəʳ] [mis-pen-daʳ], *s.* Malbaratador, disipador.

misstate ['mɪs'teɪt] [mis-teit], *va.* Establecer o sentar mal una cuestión, una tesis; representar o relatar falsamente.

misstatement ['mɪs'teɪtmənt] [mis-teit-ment], *s.* Relación equivocada o falsa, error.

misstep ['mɪs'tep] [mis-tep], *vn.* Dar un paso en falso, tropezar. *-s.* Paso falso o erróneo, real o figuradamente; tropiezo; falta, culpa.

missy ['mɪsɪ] [mi-si], *s. (Ingl. y E.U. del Sur)* Señorita.

mist [mɪst] [mist], *s.* 1. Niebla, neblina, vapor espeso, llovizna. 2. Velo o venda que tapa los ojos del cuerpo o de la razón; niebla, confusión u oscuridad que no deja formar juicio recto de las cosas. **To be in a mist,** estar desconcertado. **A Scotch mist,** neblina muy espesa como las del oeste de Escocia; de aquí, *(fest.)* lluvia.

mist, *va.* Anieblar, anublar, oscurecer. *-vn.* Lloviznar, caer en gotas muy menudas.

mistakable [mɪs'teɪkəbl] [mis-tei-ka-bol], *a.* Suceptible de error; que se puede entender o interpretar mal; que puede ser equivocado.

mistake [mɪs'teɪk] [mis-teik], *va. (pret.* MISTOOK, *pp.* MISTAKEN). Equivocar, comprender mal; tomar una cosa por otra. **You mistake me,** Ud. no me comprende bien. *-vn.* Equivocarse, engañarse. **To mistake one's way,** descarriarse. **To be mistaken,** estar engañado, haberse equivocado. **My opinion is mistaken,** no han comprendido bien cuál es mi parecer. **You are mistaken,** Ud. se engaña.

mistake, *s.* Equivocación, yerro, engaño. **Book full of mistakes,** libro lleno de yerros o de erratas. **To make a mistake,** fallar, cometer un error.

mistaken [mɪs'teɪkən] [mis-tei-ken], *pp.* de TO MISTAKE. 1. Erróneo, incorrecto. 2. Errado, engañado, en error. 3. Comprendido mal, tomado en sentido erróneo.

mistakenly [mɪs'teɪkənlɪ] [mis-tei-ken-li], *adv.* Equivocadamente.

mistaking [mɪs'teɪkɪŋ] [mis-tei-lin], *s.* Yerro, equivocación, engaño.

mistakingly [mɪs'teɪkɪŋlɪ] [mis-tei-lin-li], *adv.* Erróneamente, equivocadamente.

mistaught, *pret.* y *pp.* de TO MISTEACH.

misteach [mɪs'tiːtʃ] [mis-tich], *va. (pret.* y *pp.* de MISTAUGHT). Enseñar o instruir mal.

mistemper [mɪs'tempəʳ] [mis-tem-paʳ], *va.* Destemplar, templar mal; desordenar.

mister ['mɪstəʳ] [mis-taʳ], *s.* Señor, término de cortesía que se antepone al apellido y corresponde unas veces a *Señor* y otras a *Don* o al *Señor Don* en castellano. Se escribe por lo general en abreviatura, *Mr.*

misterm ['mɪs'tɜːm] [mis-term], *va.* Nombrar o dar a una persona o cosa un nombre que no le conviene.

mistful ['mɪstfʊl] [mist-ful], *a.* Oscuro, nebuloso, anublado.

misthink ['mɪsθɪŋk] [mis-zink], *va.* Pensar mal o erróneamente.

mistily [mɪs'tɪlɪ] [mis-ti-li], *adv.* Oscuramente, anubladamente.

mistime [mɪs'taɪm] [mis-taim], *va.* Hacer alguna cosa fuera de tiempo; dejar pasar el tiempo oportuno o la ocasión favorable.

mistimed [mɪs'taɪmd] [mis-taimd], *pp. y a.* Inoportuno; fuera de tiempo.

mistiness [mɪs'tɪnɪs] [mis-ti-nes], *s.* Vapor; el estado de lo que se halla en forma de niebla o vapor.

mistletoe [mɪsltəʊ] [mi-sel-tou], *s. (Bot.)* Muérdaga, liga, visco; planta que los antiguos celtas tenían en gran veneración. **Mistletoe-berry,** baya de muérdago.

mist-like [mɪs'laɪk] [mis-laik], *a.* Nebuloso.

mistold, *pret. y pp.* de TO MISTELL.

mistook [mɪs'tʊk] [mis-tuk], *pret. y pp.* de TO MISTAKE.

mistrain [mɪs'treɪn] [mis-trein], *va.* Educar o criar mal.

mistral [mɪ'strɑːl] [mis-tral], *s.* Nombre de un viento frío, seco y violento que sopla del nordeste en el golfo de Lión.

mistranslate [mɪstræns'leɪt] [mis-trans-leit], *va.* Traducir mal.

mistranslation [mɪstræns'leɪʃən] [mis-trans-lei-shon], *s.* Traducción mal hecha o infiel.

mistreat [mɪs'triːt] [mis-trit], *vt.* Maltratar.

mistress [mɪstrɪs] [mis-tris], *sf.* 1. Ama, dueña, señora de la casa. 2. Señora, término de cortesía que se da a las casadas o viudas y equivale en español a Señora, a Doña, o a Señora Doña. 3. Mujer diestra en alguna cosa. **She is mistress of the English language,** domina la lengua inglesa. **Mistress of the Robes,** camarera mayor de una reina o princesa. 4. Maestra. 5. Cortejo, la mujer cortejada. 6. Concubina, amiga, querida. **Kept-mistress,** manceba. **She is mistress of herself,** ella es dueña de sus acciones, es independiente.

mistrial [mɪs'trɪəl] [mis-trial], *s.* Pleito viciado de nulidad por causa de error o por empate o desacuerdo del jurado.

mistrust [mɪs'trʌst] [mis-trast], *s.* Desconfianza, sospecha, recelo.

mistrust, *va.* 1. Desconfiar, recelar, sospechar. 2. Sospechar como probable, imaginarse, conjeturar; tener aprensión o sospecha de.

mistrustful [mɪs'trʌstfʊl] [mis-trast-ful], *a.* Desconfiado, receloso, sospechoso.

mistrustfully [mɪs'trʌstfəlɪ] [mis-trast-fu-li], *adv.* Desconfiadamente.

mistrustfulness [mɪs'trʌstfəlnɪs] [mis-trast-ful-nes], *s.* Desconfianza.

mistrustingly [mɪs'trʌstɪŋlɪ] [mis-tras-tin-li], *adv.* Con desconfianza.

mistune [mɪs'tjuːn] [mis-tiun], *va.* Desentonar.

misty [mɪstɪ] [mis-ti], *a.* Nebuloso, nublado.

misunderstand [mɪsʌndə'stænd] [mis-an-der-stand], *va.* Entender mal, comprender mal una cosa, equivocarse; tomar en sentido erróneo.

misunderstanding [mɪsʌndə'stændɪŋ] [mis-an-der-standin], *s.* 1. Concepto falso, idea equivocada, equivocación, engaño, error, mala inteligencia. 2. Desavenencia, disensión; tibieza, frialdad en el amor y la amistad.

misusage [mɪs'juːseɪdʒ] [mis-iu-seich], *s.* 1. Abuso, mal uso. 2. Uso erróneo o impropio, mala aplicación.

misuse [mɪs'juːs] [mis-ius], *va.* Maltratar, tratar mal; abusar de algo.

misword [mɪsw3ːd] [mis-uerd], *va.* Expresar en palabras o términos erróneos. **The telegram was misworded,** el telegrama estaba equivocado.

miswrought [mɪsraʊt] [mis-raut], *a.* Mal trabajado.

misyoke [mɪs'jəʊk] [mis-youk], *va.* Unir o juntar mal. *-vr.* Unirse o juntarse mal.

mit, *s. V.* MITT.

mite [maɪt] [mait], *s.* Ácaro, insecto aracnoide muy diminuto, como el ácaro del queso o el arador.

mite, *s.* 1. Pizca, la porción mínima de alguna cosa; blanca, ardite; nada o casi nada. 2. Antigua moneda muy pequeña de Palestina: cualquier moneda muy diminuta o pequeña cantidad de dinero.

miter, mitre [maɪtər] [mai-tar], *s.* 1. Mitra, toca alta y apuntada que usan los arzobispos y obispos en ocasiones solemnes; de aquí, dignidad de obispo, etc. 2. *(Mec.)* Unión de dos cuerpos en un ángulo dividido igualmente; inglete. 3. Obturador para chimenea. **Miter-box, miter-block,** caja de ingletes. **Miter-joint,** inglete, ensambladura a hebra. **Miter-shell,** concha univalva mitriforme muy hermosa.

miter, mitre, *va.* 1. Conferir una mitra. 2. Adornar como mitra. 3. Hacer o juntar con inglete.

mithridate [mɪθrɪdeɪt] [miz-ri-deit], *s.* Mitridato, antídoto y composición de varias drogas.

mitigable [mɪtɪgəbl] [mi-ti-ga-bol], *a.* Capaz de ser mitigado.

mitigant [mɪtɪgənt] [mi-ti-gant], *a.* Mitigante, lenitivo.

mitigate [mɪtɪgeɪt] [mi-ti-gueit], *va.* 1. Mitigar, moderar, hacer menos riguroso; suavizar. 2. Aplacar, calmar.

mitigation [mɪtɪ'geɪʃən] [mi-ti-guei-shon], *s.* Mitigación de los dolores, rebaja de las cargas o impuestos, minoración de cualquier trabajo o penalidad.

mitigative, mitigatory [mɪtɪgətɪv] [mi-ti-ga-tiv], *a.* Mitigativo.

mitigator [mɪtɪgeɪtər] [mi-ti-guei-tar], *s.* Mitigador.

mitochondrion [mɪtəkɒndrɪən] [mi-to-kon-drion], *s.* Mitocondrio.

mitosis [mɪtəʊsɪs] [mi-tou-sis], *s. (Biol.)* Mitosis.

mitre [mɪtər] [mi-tar], *V.* MITTER, *v. y s.*

mitred [mɪtrɪd] [mi-trid], *a.* Mitrado.

mitt [mɪt] [mit], *s.* 1. Mitón confortante, especie de guante sin dedos. 2. *V.* MITTEN.

mitten [mɪtn] [mi-ten], *s.* 1. Puño, mitón, guante con dedo para el pulgar, pero sin separaciones para los otros cuatro dedos. 2. Confortante. *V.* MITT. 3. *(Fam.)* Calabazas, repulsa de un amante. **To get o to give the mitten,** ser despedido un pretendiente, darle calabazas.

mittimus [mɪtɪməs] [mi-ti-mos], *s. (For.)* Auto o decreto de prisión.

mix [mɪks] [miks], *va.* 1. Mezclar, juntar o incorporar una cosa con otra. 2. Asociar, unir con. 3. Confundir; producir mezclando. *-vn.* 1. Unirse promiscuamente. 2. Mezclarse; tomar parte. **Mix in,** añadir. **Mix up,** confundir, preparar, mezclar.

mixed [mɪkst] [mikst], *a.* Variado, surtido (assorted, varied). **Mixed doubles,** mixtos (Sports). **Mixed weather,** tiempo variable. **Mixed-up,** confuso, revuelto.

mixer [mɪksər] [mik-sar], *s.* 1. Mezclador. 2. Mezcladora (máquina). **Concrete mixer,** mezcladora de hormigón. **A good mixer,** persona sociable que congenia fácilmente con otra.

mixt [mɪkst] [mikst], *pp. irr.* de TO Mix. Mezclado, mixto.

mixtion [mɪkʃən] [mik-shon], *s.* Mixtión, mezcla.

mixture [mɪkstʃər] [miks-cha-r], *s.* Mistura, mezcla, unión y enlace de una cosa con otra.

mizen o mizzen [mɪzn] [mi-sen], *s. (Mar.)* Mesana. **Mizzen-shrouds,** jarcia de mesana. **To change the mizzen,** cambiar la mesana. **To balance the mizzen,** tomar rizos en la mesana.

mizmaze [mɪzmeɪz] [mis-meis], *s.* 1. Laberinto. 2. Laberinto, confusión.

mizzle [mɪzl] [mi-sel], *vn.* Lloviznar, molliznar.

mizzling [mɪzlɪŋ] [mis-lin], *pa.* Lloviznando ligeramente.

MM *Abreviatura de* **Messieurs,** señores.

mm *Abreviatura de* **millimetre.**

mnemonic [nɪ'mɒnɪkz] [ni-mo-nik], *a.* Mnemotécnico, relativo a la memoria, que ayuda a la memoria.

mnemonics [nɪ'mɒnɪk] [ni-mo-niks], *s.* Mnemónica, el arte de la memoria; conjunto de preceptos y reglas para ayudar a la memoria.

moan [məʊn] [moun], *s.* Lamento, quejido, gemido, queja.

moan, *va.* Lamentar, gemir. *-vn.* Lamentarse, afligirse, quejarse; producir un sonido sordo y lúgubre; se dice de los objetos inanimados.

moaner [məʊnər] [mou-nar], *s.* Protestón, quejica *(Fam.)*.

moanful [məʊnfʊl] [moun-ful], *a.* Lamentable, triste, lúgubre.

moanfully ['mɔʊnfʊlɪ] [moun-fu-li], *a.* Lamentablemente.

moat [mɔʊt] [mout], *s.* Mota, ribazo de tierra para contener el agua o cerrar un campo; foso o canal que rodea una casa o castillo para su defensa. **Dry moat,** foso seco.

moat, *va.* Rodear con fosos o canales de agua.

mob [mɒb] [mob], *s.* 1. Populacho, gentuza, canalla, la gente baja y ruin. 2. Moño, cofia, toca o tocado o mujer. 3. Tumulto, desorden.

mob, *va.* 1. Tumultuar, levantar algún tumulto, motín o desorden, incitar a la plebe a que cometa excesos. 2. Atropellar, correr a alguno.

mobbish ['mɒbɪʃ] [mo-bish], *a.* Vil, bajo, ruin, tumultuoso.

mobile ['mɔʊbaɪl] [mou-bail], *a.* 1. Movible, móvil. **Mobile kitchen,** cocina ambulante. 2. Inconstante, variable.

mobility [mɔʊˈbɪlɪtɪ] [mou-bi-li-ti], *s.* 1. Movilidad, agilidad. 2. Inconstancia, volubilidad, instabilidad, ligereza.

mobilization [ˌmɔʊbɪlaɪˈzeɪʃən] [mou-bi-lai-sei-shon], *s.* Movilización.

mobilize ['mɔʊbɪlaɪz] [mou-bi-lais], *va.* Movilizar, poner en acción, en movimiento, v. g. un ejército.

mobster ['mɒbstəʳ] [mobs-taʳ], *s.* Pandillero, pandillista.

moccasin ['mɒkəsɪn] [mo-ka-sin], *s.* 1. Mocasín, calzado hecho de cuero flexible o de piel de gamo que usaban los indios de la América del Norte. 2. Mocasín, serpiente venenosa de la familia de los crotálidos que se halla en los Estados Unidos del Sur.

mocha ['mɔʊkə] [mo-ka], *s.* 1. Moca, especie de café muy estimado; estrictamente el traído de Moca, en Arabia. 2. Un peso de Abisinia, equivalente a una onza de los metales preciosos. **Mocha-stone,** *V.* MOSSAGATE.

mock [mɒk] [mok], *va.* 1. Mofar, escarnecer, hacer mofa o burla de otro. 2. Remedar. 3. Imitar de una manera despreciativa, poner en ridículo. 4. Frustrar, dejar sin efecto algún intento; engañar, burlar. -*vn.* Burlarse de, reírse de (con at). **They mocked at him,** se burlaron de él.

mock, *s.* Mofa, escarnio, burla; risa, mímica. -*a.* Ficticio, falso, fingido, cómico, burlesco. **Mock exam,** examen de prueba. **Mock praise,** alabanza irónica. **Mock prophet,** profeta falso.

mocker ['mɒkəʳ] [mo-kaʳ], *s.* 1. Mofador, escarnecedor, burlador. 2. Cerción, sinsonte, censontli. *V.* MOCKING-BIRD.

mockery ['mɒkərɪ] [mo-ka-ri], *s.* 1. Mofa, burla, irrisión, ridículo; zumba. 2. Remedo.

mocking ['mɒkɪŋ] [mo-kin], *a.* Burlón.

mocking-bird ['mɒkɪŋbɜːd] [mo-kin-berd], **mock-bird** ['mɒkbɜːd] [mok-berd], *s. (Orn.)* Cerción, pájaro americano del género Mimus.

mockingly ['mɒkɪŋlɪ] [mo-kin-li], *adv.* Con mofa, con burla.

mocking-stock ['mɒkɪŋstɒk] [mo-kin-stok], *s.* Juguete.

mocking-thrush ['mɒkɪŋtrʌʃ] [mo-kin-trash], *s.* Mirlo burlón.

mock-orange ['mɒkˈɒrɪndʒ] [mok-o-ranch], *s.* Arbusto de la familia de las saxífragas que tiene flores parecidas a las del naranjo.

mock-privet ['mɒkˈpraɪvɪt] [mok-prai-vit], **Mock-willow** ['mɒkˈwɪləʊ] [mok-ui-lou], *s. (Bot.)* Ladierno, labiérnago.

mock-up ['mɒkʌp] [mok-ap], *s. f.* Modelo, maqueta.

mod cons [ˌmɒdˈkɒnz] [mod-kons], *s. pl. Abreviatura de* **modern conveniences.**

modal ['mɔʊdl] [mou-dal], *a.* Modal, perteneciente al modo o la manera, particularmente a un modo gramatical o lógico. -*s.* Proposición que contiene algunas condiciones o restricciones.

modality [mɔʊˈdælɪtɪ] [mou-da-li-ti], *s.* Diferencia accidental.

mode [mɔʊd] [moud], *s.* 1. Modo, forma, accidente, diferencia accidental. 2. Manera, método. 3. Moda, uso o costumbre general. 4. Graduación, grado. 5. *(Gram.)* Modo, cada una de las maneras generales de manifestarse la significación del verbo en la conjugación. 6. *(Fil.)* Modo,

manera de ser en cuanto no es esencial; estado, cualidad accidental o contingente. 7. *(Mús.)* Disposición de los sonidos en la escala determinada por el lugar del semitono. **Major mode,** modo mayor. **Minor mode,** modo menor; equivalente al modo cólico griego y gregoriano. 8. Variedad de seda. *V.* ALAMODE.

model ['mɒdl] [mo-del], *s.* 1. Modelo. 2. Modelo o patrón que sirve de original. 3. Modelo, patrón, dechado para imitar o trabajar sobre él. 4. Molde, pieza hueca que da su figura a lo que en sí encierra. 5. Pauta. -*a.* Modelo, que se puede copiar o imitar. **A model school,** una escuela modelo. **Make models,** modelar.

model, *va.* 1. Modelar, formar según modelo; dar forma a, moldear. 2. Dibujar en relieve. -*vn.* Modelar, hacer un patrón (Art., Phot.).

modeling ['mɒdlɪŋ] [mo-de-lin], *s.* 1. Acción de trazar un modelo según el cual se ha de ejecutar una obra. 2. Arte de construir en cera o en arcilla un modelo que ha de hacerse después en piedra o metal.

modeller ['mɒdləʳ] [mo-de-laʳ], *s.* Modelador, trazador, dibujador, dibujante, diseñador.

modena ['mɒdiːnə] [mo-di-na], *s.* Color que se asemeja al carmesí.

moderate ['mɒdərɪt] [mo-de-rit], *a.* Moderado, templado, parco; pacato, quieto, tranquilo; mediano, mediocre; razonable no extremo, no radical, sobrio; apacible, suave; módico (en precio); *(Fam.)* habitualmente lento o pausado en el pensar, hablar o accionar.

moderate, *va.* 1. Moderar, limitar, restringir, reprimir; mantener en ciertos límites. 2. Moderar, templar, modificar, calmar. -*vn.* 1. Moderarse, hacerse menos intenso, menos violento; calmarse, apaciguarse. 2. Presidir, ejercer las funciones de presidente en una reunión.

moderately ['mɒdərɪtlɪ] [mo-de-rit-li], *adv.* Moderadamente; con moderación, con suavidad; sin exceso; razonablemente; módicamente; medianamente.

moderateness ['mɒdərɪtnɪs] [mo-de-rit-nes], *s.* Moderación, templanza; modicidad (de precio).

moderation [ˌmɒdəˈreɪʃən] [mo-de-rei-shon], *s.* 1. Moderación, ecuanimidad, calma, templanza en los afectos o pasiones.

moderato ['mɒdərətəʊ] [mo-de-ra-tou], *adv. (Mús.)* Palabra italiana que indica un tiempo entre el andante y el allegro.

moderator ['mɒdəreɪtəʳ] [mo-de-rei-taʳ], *s.* 1. Moderador, el que gobierna, árbitro. 2. Presidente de una reunión o asamblea; hoy sólo se emplea este término en las iglesias presbiteriana y congregacional. 3. Examinador en las universidades inglesas. 4. Moderador, pantalla translúcida que sirve para moderar y esparcir la luz que pasa a un objeto en el microscopio.

modern ['mɒdən] [mo-dern], *a.* Moderno, nuevo, reciente; que no es antiguo ni desusado. **Moderns,** *s. pl.* Modernos, los que viven o han vivido en nuestros tiempos, en contraposición a los antiguos.

modernism ['mɒdənɪzəm] [mo-der-ni-sem], *s.* 1. Modernismo, uso moderno, práctica moderna. 2. Neologismo.

modernist ['mɒdənɪst] [mo-der-nist], *s.* El que gusta de las cosas modernas.

modernity [mɒˈdɜːnɪtɪ] [mo-der-ni-ti], *s.* La condición o calidad de lo moderno; uso moderno o cosa moderna.

modernization [ˌmɒdənaɪˈzeɪʃən] [mo-der-nai-sei-shon], *s.* Modernización.

modernize ['mɒdənaɪz] [mo-der-nais], *va.* Modernizar, hacer moderna una cosa; poner en lenguaje moderno algo que está en lenguaje antiguo; arreglar al gusto del día.

modernness ['mɒdənɪs] [mo-der-nes], *s.* Novedad, el estado de las cosas recién hechas u ocurridas.

modest ['mɒdɪst] [mo-dist], *a.* 1. Modesto, contenido, recatado, casto, púdico. 2. Moderado; sencillo, sin presunción. **A modest estimate,** un cálculo moderado. **A modest woman,** una mujer modesta, púdica.

modestly ['mɒdɪstlɪ] [mo-dist-li], *adv.* Modestamente, con modestia, con recato, con pudor; humildemente, sin presunción.

modesty ['mɒdɪstɪ] [mo-dis-ti], *s.* Modestia, decencia, pudor; reserva; humildad; castidad y pureza de costumbres.

modicum ['mɒdɪkəm] [mo-dis-kom], *s.* Pitanza, bocado, porción pequeña; poco.

modifiable ['mɒdɪfaɪ'eɪbl] [mo-di-faiei-bol], **modificable** ['mɒdɪfɪkəbl] [mo-difi-ka-bol], *a.* Lo que se puede modificar o lo que es susceptible de modificación; modificable.

modification ['mɒdɪfɪ'keɪʃən] [mo-di-fi-kei-shon], *s.* Modificación: forma o manera particular.

modificative ['mɒdɪfɪkətɪv] [mo-di-fi-ka-tiv], *a.* Modificativo.

modify ['mɒdɪfaɪ] [mo-di-fai], *va.* 1. Modificar, hacer algo diferente; cambiar más o menos (Change). 2. Modificar, reducir las cosas a términos justos; moderar, templar.

modish ['mɒdɪʃ] [mo-dish], *a.* (*Ant.*) Hecho a la moda; conforme a la moda.

modishly ['mɒdɪʃlɪ] [mo-dish-li], *adv.* A la moda, según la moda.

modishness ['mɒdɪʃnɪs] [mo-dish-nes], *s.* Inclinación a seguir la moda, culto de la moda.

modular ['mɒdjʊləʳ] [mo-diu-laʳ], *a.* Modular, perteneciente a un modo o a una modulación.

modulate ['mɒdjʊleɪt] [mo-diu-leit], *va.* 1. Modular, cambiar de tono, diapasón o inflexión del sonido. 2. (*Mús.*) Cambiar a otra clave o escala.

modulation [ˌmɒdjʊ'leɪʃən] [mo-diu-lei-shon], *s.* 1. (*Mús.*) (*Fís.*) Modulación. 2. Modificación; adaptación.

modulator ['mɒdjʊleɪtəʳ] [mo-diu-lei-taʳ], *s.* Modulador.

module ['mɒdjuːl] [mo-diul], *s.* 1. (*Arq.*) Módulo. 2. (*Des.*) Molde, modelo.

modus ['məʊdəs] [mo-dus], *s.* El acto de pagar un tanto o cantidad alzada como equivalente del diezmo. **Modus operandi,** procedimiento.

mogul ['məʊgəl] [mou-gol], *s.* 1. Mogol. 2. Naipe de la mejor calidad. 3. Nombre de una clase de locomotoras de gran tamaño.

mohair ['məʊhɛəʳ] [mou-jeaʳ], *s.* Pelo de camello, hilo o tela hechos de pelo de camello.

Mohammed ['məʊhæmed] [mou-ja-med], *s.* Mahoma.

Mohammedan ['məʊhæmɪdən] [mou-ja-mi-dan], *s.* Mahometano.

Mohammedanism ['məʊhæmɪdənɪzəm] [mou-ja-mi-da-ni-zem], **Mohammedism** ['məʊhæmɪzəm] [mou-ja-me-di-sem], *s.* Mahometismo.

mohammedanize ['məʊhæmɪdənaɪz] [mou-ja-mi-da-nais], *va.* Hacer conforme al mahometismo o convertir a esa religión.

moil ['mɔɪl] [moil], *va.* 1. Enlodar, ensuciar. 2. Cansar, fatigar. *-vn.* Afanarse, fatigarse, inquietarse, desasosegarse.

moire, moiré ['mwɑːreɪ] [mua-rei], *s.* Moaré, muaré, seda con aguas o visos.

moist [mɔɪst] [moist], *a.* 1. Húmedo, que contiene humedad o está algo mojado. 2. Jugoso, suculento.

moisten ['mɔɪsn] [moi-sen], *va.* Humedecer; mojar ligeramente.

moistener ['mɔɪsnəʳ] [moi-se-naʳ], *s.* Humedecedor; antiguamente, humectante.

moistful ['mɔɪstfʊl] [moist-ful], *a.* Húmedo, muy húmedo.

moistness ['mɔɪstnɪs] [moist-nes], **moisture** ['mɔɪstʃəʳ] [mois-chaʳ], *s.* Humedad. **The moisture of plants,** los jugos de las plantas.

moisturize ['mɔɪstʃəraɪz] [mois-cha-rais], *vt.* Humedecer. **Moisturizing cream,** crema hidratante.

molar ['məʊləʳ] [mou-laʳ], *a.* Molar. **Molar teeth,** muelas, dientes molares.

molary ['məʊlərɪ] [mou-la-ri], *a.* V. MOLAR.

molasses [məˈlæsɪz] [mo-la-sis], *s.* Melaza, melote, miel.

mold ['məʊld] [mould], *s.* Molde; tierra; moho. V. MOULD.

mold, mould, *va.* V. MOULD.

moldboard ['məʊldbɔːd] [mould-bord], *s.* Vertedera del arado.

mole [məʊl] [moul], *s.* 1. Mola, pedazo de carne informe que se engendra en el útero de la mujer. 2. Lunar. 3. Muelle, dique. 4. Topo, roedor semejante al ratón y que habita debajo de tierra. **Mole furs** o **skins,** la peletería o pieles de topo. (*Amer.*) Piel de tusa. 5. Entre los romanos, mausoleo de grandes proporciones en forma de torre. **Mole-cast,** motoncillo de tierra. *V.* **Mole-hill. Mole-catcher,** cazador de topos. **Mole-cricket,** grillotalpa o topogrillo. **Mole-hill,** los montoncillos de tierra que levantan los topos escarbando. **Mole-eyed,** cegato, que tiene ojos de topo, de vista muy débil. **Mole-rat,** ratón-topo.

molecular [mə'lekjuːləʳ] [mo-li-kiu-laʳ], *a.* ´1. Molecular, perteneciente a la molécula (*Quím.*). 2. Resultante de la acción de las moléculas. **Molecular changes,** cambios moleculares, los que resultan de la acción de las moléculas. **Molecular biology,** biología molecular (*Quím.*).

molecularity [ˌmɒlɪkjuːˈlærɪtɪ] [mo-li-kiu-la-ri-ti], *s.* Estado o cualidad de molecular.

molecule ['mɒlɪkjuːl] [mo-li-kiul], *s.* Molécula, corpúsculo, parte pequeña de un cuerpo.

molehill ['məʊlhɪl] [moul-jil] *s. f.* Topera.

moleskin ['məʊlskɪn] [moul-skin], *s.* 1. Piel de topo. 2. Ratina, especie de paño de frisa.

molest [məʊ'lest] [mou-lest], *va.* Molestar, inquietar, atormentar, vejar, hostigar, perseguir, oprimir.

molestation [ˌməʊles'teɪʃən] [mou-les-tei-shon], *s.* Molestia, incomodidad, enfado, enojo, pena; persecución, importunidad, vejación, hostigamiento.

moletrack ['məʊltræk] [moul-trak], *s.* Topera, la excavación que hacen los topos por debajo de tierra.

molewarp ['məʊlwɑːp] [moul-uarp], *s.* Topo. V. MOLE.

molinism ['məʊlɪnɪzm] [mou-li-ni-sem], *s.* Molinismo, doctrina teológica de Molina, jesuita español.

mollah ['mɒlɑː] [mou-la], *s.* Título de cortesía que dan los mahometanos a los altos dignatarios de su religión.

mollient ['məʊlɪənt] [mou-lient], *a.* (*Poco us.*) Emoliente, lo que ablanda.

mollifiable [ˌmɒlɪfaɪ'eɪbl] [mo-li-fai-ei-bol], *a.* Molificable, que se puede ablandar.

mollification [ˌmɒlɪfaɪ'keɪʃən] [mo-li-fai-kei-shon], *s.* Molificación, ablandamiento; suavización, mitigación, alivio.

mollifier ['mɒlɪfaɪəʳ] [mo-li-faiaʳ], *s.* 1. Molificador, mitigador, pacificador. 2. Emoliente, lo que ablanda.

mollify ['mɒlɪfaɪ] [mo-li-fai], *va.* 1. Molificar; ablandar; apaciguar, aquietar. 2. Aliviar, aligerar el peso o pena de alguna cosa; suavizar, mitigar.

mollusca ['mɒləskə] [mo-lus-ka], *s. pl.* (*Zool.*) Moluscos.

molluscan ['mɒləskən] [mo-lus-kan], *a.* y *s.* Molusco.

mollusk ['mɒləsk] [mo-lusk], *s. m.* Molusco.

molluso, *s.* V. MOLLUSK.

mollycoddle ['mɒlɪkɒdl] [mo-li-ko-del], *s.* (*Vulg.*) Hombre afeminado; niño mimado; se abrevia a veces en **moll o molly.** *vt.* Mimar, proteger demasiado.

moloch ['mɒlək] [mo-lok], *s.* Nombre de un dios de los fenicios al que sacrificaban víctimas humanas, niños principalmente.

molossus ['mɒləsəs] [mo-lo-sos], *s.* Molos, pie de verso que consta de tres sílabas largas.

molt [məʊlt] [moult], *v.* y *s.* V. MOULT.

molten ['məʊltn] [moul-ten], *a.* y *pp. irr.* de TO MELT.

molting ['məʊltɪŋ] [moul-tin], *s.* V. MOULTING.

moly ['mɒlɪ] [mo-li], *s.* (*Bot.*) 1. Planta fabulosa de mágicas virtudes, citada por Homero. 2. Moli, especie de ajo silvestre.

molybdate ['mɒlɪbdeɪt] [mo-lib-deit], *s.* Molibdato, sal del ácido molíbdico.

molybdenum, Molybdena [mɒ'lɪbdenəm] [mo-lib-de-nom], *s.* (*Min.*) Molibdena, metal duro, blanco como la plata e infusible.

molybdenous ['mɒlɪbdɛnəs] [mo-lib-de-nos], *a.* Molibdoso, perteneciente a la molibdena, especialmente en su menor equivalencia.

mome [məʊm] [moum], *a. (Ingl. del Norte)* Blando, liso.

moment ['məʊmənt] [mou-ment], *s.* 1. Momento, minuto, instante, espacio brevísimo de tiempo. **A moment later,** al rato, poco después. **Any moment now,** de un momento a otro. **At the moment,** de momento. **For a moment,** por de pronto. 2. El tiempo presente. 3. Momento, importancia, consecuencia, entidad. 4. Fuerza, impulso. 5. La cosa que origina o causa; principio de movimiento o de desarrollo. **The moment of truth,** la hora de la verdad. **It won't take a moment,** no tardará mucho.

momental ['məʊməntəl] [mou-men-tal], *a.* Relativo al ímpetu.

momentarily ['məʊməntərɪlɪ] [mou-men-ta-ri-li], *adv.* Momentáneamente.

momentariness ['məʊməntərɪnɪs] [mou-men-ta-ri-nes], *s.* Momentaneidad.

momentous ['məʊməntəs] [mou-men-tos], *a.* Importante, de mucha importancia; grave, de consecuencia.

momentously [məʊ'məntəslɪ] [mou-men-tos-li], *adv.* Con importancia, con gravedad.

momentousness ['məʊməntəsnɪs] [mou-men-tos-nes], *s.* Importancia.

momentum ['məʊməntəm] [mou-men-tom, *s.* 1. Momento, la propensión que tiene un cuerpo grave a bajar hacia el centro. 2. Ímpetu, fuerza o cantidad de movimiento.

Mon. *Abreviatura de* **Monday.**

mon [mɒn] [mon], *s. (Esco. y prov. Ingl.)* Hombre.

mon-. Prefijo. *V.* MONO-.

monachal ['mɒnəkəl] [mo-na-kal], *a.* Monacal, monástico.

monachism ['mɒnəkɪzəm] [mo-na-ki-sem], *s.* Monaquismo, monacato.

monad ['mɒnæd] [mo-nad], *s.* 1. Mónada o mónade, ente simple y sin partes. 2. *(Biol.)* Organismo, muy pequeño de una sola celdilla; infusorio flagelado. 3. *(Quím.)* Átomo, radical o elemento con facultad de combinación que vale uno. 4. El espíritu, ser uno e indivisible, cuya totalidad constituye el universo (doctrina de Leibnitz). -*a.* Que se refiere o consta de una mónada; en química, que tiene facultad de combinación equivalente a uno.

monarch ['mɒnək] [mo-nark], *s.* Monarca, potentado; originalmente el único jefe de una nación, como rey, reina, o emperador; hoy es en general soberano hereditario constitucional.

monarchal ['mɒnəkəl] [mo-nar-kal], *a.* Monárquico, real, imperial.

monarchical, monarchial [mɒ'nɑːkɪkəl] [mo-nar-ki-kal], *a.* Monárquico.

monarchism ['mɒnəkɪzəm] [mo-nar-ki-sem], *s.* Monarquismo, los principios monárquicos; la adhesión que se profesa a la monarquía.

monarchist ['mɒnəkɪst] [mo-nar-kist], *s.* Monarquista.

monarchy ['mɒnəkɪ] [mo-nar-ki], *s.* 1. Monarquía, el gobierno monárquico. 2. Monarquía, el reino o imperio gobernado por un monarca.

monastery ['mɒnəstrɪ] [mo-nas-tri], *s.* Monasterio, la casa donde viven los monjes.

monastic, monastical [mə'næstɪkəl] [mo-nas-ti-kal], *a.* Monástico, perteneciente al estado de los monjes.

monastic [mə'næstɪk] [mo-nas-tik], *s.* Monje.

monastically [mə'næstɪkəlɪ] [mo-nas-ti-ka-li], *adv.* Monásticamente, monacalmente.

Monday ['mʌndɪ] [man-di], *s.* Lunes.

monetary ['mʌnɪtərɪ] [ma-ni-ta-ri], *a.* Monetario, perteneciente a la moneda; que consta de dinero; pecuniario.

monetize ['mʌnɪtaɪz] [ma-ni-tais], *va.* 1. Monetizar, legalizar como moneda. 2. Acuñar (un metal) en moneda.

money ['mʌnɪ] [ma-ni], *s.* 1. Moneda, dinero, metal acuñado para comerciar con él; moneda legal, papel moneda; cualquier medio de cambio o medida del valor. 2. Propiedad vendible, caudal, riqueza. 3. Sistema de acuñación. 4. *pl.* Pagos o recibos al contado. **Ready money,** dinero contante o dinero al contado. **Money talks,** el dinero manda, poderoso caballero es don Dinero. **Money governs the world,** quien tiene dineros pinta panderos. **To advance money,** adelantar dinero. **Bank-money,** billete de banco. **Paper-money,** papel moneda. **To get one's money's worth,** sacar el máximo provecho. **To put out money,** poner dinero a interés o a ganancia. **To take up money,** tomar prestado. **Hard money,** numerario, efectivo, moneda acuñada. **Earnest money,** prenda, arras, señal. **Copper money,** calderilla, moneda de cobre o de vellón. **Money makes the mare go,** *(prov.)* por dinero baila el perro. **Money back guarantee,** garantía de devolver el dinero. **Money-bag,** talega para guardar dinero. **Money-bags,** *(ger.)* un hombre rico, de muchas talegas. **Money-bill,** ley de hacienda. **Money-box,** caja, hucha para dinero. **Money-broker,** corredor de cambios. **Money-changer,** cambista de dinero. **Money-drawer,** gaveta, particularmente en las tiendas, que sirve para recibir el dinero de las ventas y para hacer cambio. **Money-lender,** prestamista. **Money-making,** *a.* (a) Resuelto a enriquecerse, que se complace en amontonar riquezas. (b) Ganancioso, lucrativo, provechoso. -*s.* El acto de acumular riquezas. **Money-matters,** cuentas de débito y crédito; negocio de dinero. **Money-order,** libranza o giro postal. **Money-scrivener,** corredor de dinero. **Money's-worth,** (a) cualquier cosa que vale dinero. (b) El valor cabal del dinero que se paga por una cosa.

money, *va.* Acuñar, hacer moneda, convertir en moneda.

moneyed ['mʌnɪd] [ma-nid], *a.* Adinerado, el que tiene mucho dinero. **A moneyed man,** un capitalista.

moneyer ['mʌnɪjəʳ] [ma-ni-yaʳ], *s. (Poco us.)* 1. Monedero, el que fabrica, forma y acuña la moneda. 2. Banquero, cambista.

money-grubbing ['mʌnɪˌgrʌbɪŋ] [ma-ni-gra-bin], *a.* Avaro.

moneyless ['mʌnɪlɪs] [ma-ni-les], *a.* Falto de dinero, pobre.

moneywort ['mʌnɪwɔːt] [ma-ni-uort], *s. (Bot.)* Lisimaquia numularia, hierba de la moneda.

monger ['mʌŋgəʳ] [man-gaʳ], *s.* Tratante, traficante. **Fishmonger,** pescadero. **Newsmonger,** novelero, el que anda a caza de noticias. **Whoremonger,** alcahuete. **Ironmonger,** ferretero, quincallero.

mongol ['mɒŋgəl] [mon-gol], *a.* Mongol, mongólico de la Mongolia china. -*s.* 1. Mongol; también, chino. 2. Idioma mongólico.

mongolian [mɒŋ'gəʊlɪən] [mon-gou-lian], *a.* 1. *V.* MONGOL. 2. Perteneciente a las razas amarillas de Asia. -*s.* 1. Mongol; también, chino. 2. Idioma mongólico.

mongoos, mongoose ['mɒŋguːs] [mon-gus], *s.* 1. Mangosta. 2. Un lemúrido blanco.

mongrel ['mɒŋgrəl] [mon-grel], *a. y s.* Mestizo, nacido de padre y madre de diferentes castas. Híbrido.

monism ['mɒnɪzm] [mo-ni-sem], *s.* 1. Monismo, teoría que pretende explicar todos los fenómenos cosmológicos, refiriéndolos a un solo principio. 2. *(Biol.)* Unidad de origen. *V.* MONOGENESIS.

monition ['mɒnɪʃən] [mo-ni-shon], *s.* Amonestación, consejo, aviso, prevención, advertencia, exhortación.

monitor ['mɒnɪtəʳ] [mo-ni-taʳ], *s.* 1. Amonestador, instructor, monitor, admonitor. 2. Tipo de buque blindado de mucho calado y bajo de borda, con una o dos torres que contienen cañones de gran calibre.

monitor, *va.* Controlar, vigilar, detectar.

monitory ['mɒnɪtərɪ] [mo-ni-to-ri], *a.* Instructivo, monitorio. -*s.* Amonestación, aviso eclesiástico.

monk [mʌŋk] [monk], *s.* Monje, fraile.

monkey ['mʌŋkɪ] [man-ki], *s.* 1. Mono. 2. Cualquier animal cuadrumano, sea mono, cinocéfalo, marmoseto o lemúrido. 3. Mono o mona: voz de desprecio unas veces, y otras de cariño. 4. Cada uno de varios artículos pequeños, como un fiador del martinete o un pequeño crisol para fundir el vidrio. **To play the monkey,** hacer monadas. **Monkey tricks,** monerías, travesuras. **Monkey-flower,** mímulo. *V.* MIMULUS. **Monkey-jacket,** capote o capotón de piloto. **Monkey-wrench,** llave inglesa. **I don't give a monkey's,** me importa un bledo *(Fam.).* **To monkey about/around,** hacer tonterías.

monkfish ['mʌŋkfɪʃ] [monk-fish], *s. m.* Pejesapo.

monkhood ['mʌŋkhʊd] [monk-jud], *s.* Monacato, el estado de los monjes.

monk's-hood ['mʌŋkzhʊd] [monks-jud], *s. (Bot.)* 1. Acónito, nombre genérico de plantas. 2. Napelo, acónito napelo.

mono- ['mɒnəʊ] [mo-nou], Prefijo que se deriva del griego *monos,* sólo, único, uno.

monoceros ['mɒnəserəs] [mo-no-se-ros], *s.* El unicornio, monoceronte.

monochlamydeous ['mɒnəklæ'mɪdɪəs] [mo-no-kla-mi-dios], *a. (Bot.)* Monoclamídeo, que tiene una sola cubierta floral.

monochord ['mɒnəkɔːd] [mo-no-kord], *s.* Monacordio, instrumento antiguo de música.

monochromatic [,mɒnəkrəʊ'mætɪk] [mo-no-krou-ma-tik], *a.* Monocromático, de un solo color.

monochrome ['mɒnəkrəm] [mo-no-krom], *s.* Monócromo, pintura de un solo color.

monocle ['mɒnʌkl] [mo-na-kel], *s.* Monóculo, lente para un solo ojo.

monoclinal ['mɒnəʊklɪnəl] [mo-nou-kli-nal], *a. (Geol.)* Que se inclina solamente en una dirección.

monoclinic ['mɒnəʊklɪnɪk] [mo-nou-kli-nik], *a. (Min.)* Monoclínico, caracterizado por tres ejes oblicuos sobrepuestos, dos iguales y uno desigual.

monocotyledon [,mɒnəkɒ'tɪlɪdən] [mo-no-ko-ti-li-don], *s. (Bot.)* Monocotiledón o planta monocotiledónea.

monocotyledonous [,mɒnəkɒ'tɪlɪdənəs] [mo-no-ko-ti-li-do-nos], *a. (Bot.)* Monocotiledóneo, monocotiledón.

monocular ['mɒnəkju:lə'] [mo-no-kiu-la'], **monoculous** ['mɒnəkjʊləs] [mo-no-kiu-los], *a.* 1. Monóculo, que no tiene más que un dedo.

monodactylous ['mɒnədæktɪləs] [mo-no-dak-ti-los], *a.* Monodáctilo, que no tiene más que un dedo.

monody ['mɒnədɪ] [mo-no-di], *s.* 1. Monodia, poema griego de carácter triste. 2. Composición literaria y triste, con un solo tema. 3. Canto en que una sola voz tiene la parte principal.

monogamist [mɒ'nɒgəmɪst] [mo-no-ga-mist], *s.* Monógamo, el casado con una sola mujer, o casado una vez solamente; el que desaprueba las segundas nupcias.

monogamous [mɒ'nɒgəməs] [mo-no-ga-mos], *a.* 1. Monógamo, casado una vez solamente. 2. *(Bot.)* Monógamo, de flores que tienen los estambres unidos.

monogamy [mɒ'nɒgəmɪ] [mo-no-ga-mi], *s.* Monogamia, el estado de los que se han casado una sola vez.

monogenesis [,mɒnɒ'dʒɪnɪsɪs] [mo-no-yi-ni-sis], *s.* 1. Unidad de origen: la doctrina de la descendencia de todos los seres vivos de una sola celdilla. 2. Reproducción asexual.

monogenism [,mɒnɒ'dʒɪnɪzəm] [mo-no-ye-ni-sem], *s.* La doctrina de que toda la raza humana es de una misma sangre o especie.

monogram ['mɒnəgræm] [mo-no-gram], *s.* 1. Monograma, cifra que contiene las letras, generalmente las iniciales, del nombre de una persona o cosa. 2. Una sola señal o carácter escrito que representa una palabra.

monograph ['mɒnəgræf] [mo-no-graf], *s.* Monográfico, dibujado de un rasgo; relativo a una monografía; dibujado con líneas sin colores.

monographic ['mɒnəgræfɪk] [mo-no-gra-fik], *a.* Monográfico, dibujado de un rasgo; relativo a una monografía; dibujado con líneas sin colores.

monography ['mɒnəgræfɪ] [mo-no-gra-fi], *s.* 1. Figura hecha con líneas, sin colores. 2. *(Des.)* Monografía, descripción de un solo asunto. *V.* MONOGRAPH.

monolith ['mɒnəlɪθ] [mo-no-liz], *s.* Monolito, monumento de piedra de una sola pieza.

monolithic ['mɒnəlɪθɪk] [mo-no-li-zik], *a.* Monolítico.

monologian ['mɒnələdʒɪən] [mo-no-lo-yian], **monologist** ['mɒnələdʒɪst] [mo-no-lo-yist], *s.* Monologista, el que recita monólogos o soliloquios.

monologue ['mɒnəlɒg] [mo-no-log], *s.* Monólogo, soliloquio.

monomachy ['mɒnəmækɪ] [mo-no-ma-ki], *s.* Monomaquia, desafío o duelo singular de uno a uno.

monomania [,mɒnəʊ'meɪnɪə] [mo-nou-mei-nia], *s.* 1. Monomanía, idea fija, forma de locura. 2. Manía, insensatez.

monomaniac [,mɒnəʊ'meɪnɪək] [mo-nou-mei-niak], *a.* Monomaniaco, monomaniático. *-s.* Monómano.

monome ['mɒnəʊm] [mo-noum], *s.* Monomio. *V.* MONOMIAL.

monomial ['mɒnəʊmɪəl] [mo-nou-mial], *a. (Alg.)* Que consta de un solo término. *-s.* Monomio, expresión algebraica de un solo término.

monopetalous [,mɒnə'petələs] [mo-no-pe-ta-lus], *a.* Monopétalo, flor que tiene un solo pétalo. *V.* GAMOPETALOUS.

monoplane ['mɒnəpleɪn] [mo-no-plein], *s.* Monoplano.

monopolist [mə'nɒpəlɪst] [mo-no-po-list], *s.* Monopolista, agavillador.

monopolize [mə'nɒpəlaɪz] [mo-no-po-lais], *va.* 1. Monopolizar, hacer monopolios. 2. Agavillar, tomarlo todo para sí. **To monopolize the conversation,** monopolizar la conversación, no dejar hablar a los demás.

monopolizer [mə'nɒpəlaɪzə'] [mo-no-po-lai-sa'], *s.* Monopolista.

monopoly [mə'nɒpəlɪ] [mo-no-po-li], *s.* 1. Monopolio, aprovechamiento en exclusiva de alguna industria o comercio. 2. Compañía en posesión de un monopolio. 3. Estanco.

monopteron [mə'nɒptərən] [mo-nop-te-ron], *s. (Arq.)* Monopterio.

monoptic [mə'nɒptɪk] [mo-nop-tik], *s.* El que ve con un solo ojo.

monopyrenous [mə'nəpɪrɪnəs] [mo-no-pi-re-nus], *a. (Bot.)* Monopireno o de una sola semilla o cuesco.

monosepalous [,mɒnə'sepələs] [mo-no-se-pa-los], *a. (Bot.)* Monosépalo, de sépalos unidos por el borde. *V.* GAMOSEPALOUS.

monospermous [mə'nəspɜːməs] [mo-nos-per-mos], *a. (Bot.)* Monospermo, flor que tiene una sola simiente.

monospherical [,mɒnəs'ferɪkəl] [mo-nos-fe-ri-kal], *a.* Que consta de una esfera.

monostich ['mɒnəstɪk] [mo-nos-tik], *s.* Monóstico, monostiquio, composición poético de un solo verso.

monostichous ['mɒnəstɪkəs] [mo-nos-ti-kos], *a. (Bot.)* Monóstico, dispuesto en una sola fila o hilera vertical.

monosyllabic, monosyllabical ['mɒnəʊsɪ'læbɪk] [mo-nou-si-la-bik] ['mɒnəʊsɪ'læbɪkəl] [mo-nou-si-la-bi-kal], *a.* Monosilábico, monosílabo.

monosyllable ['mɒnəsɪlæbl] [mo-nou-si-la-bol], *a.* Monosílabo, la voz de una sola sílaba.

monotheism ['mɒnəʊθiːɪzəm] [mo-nou-zi-isem], *s.* Monoteísmo, doctrina teológica de los que reconocen un solo Dios.

monotheist ['mɒnæʊθiːɪst] [mo-nou-zi-ist], *s.* Monoteísta, el que cree en un Dios único.

monotheistic ['mɒnəʊθiːɪstɪk] [mo-nou-zi-is-tik], *a.* Monoteísta, partidario del monoteísmo.

monotone ['mɒnətəʊn] [mo-no-toun], *s.* Monotonía, ya en la expresión y tono de la voz, ya en la música, la forma de composición, el estilo, etc.

monotonic, monotonical ['mɒnətəʊnɪk] [mo-no-tou-nik], *a.* Monótono.

monotonous [mə'nɒtənəs] [mo-no-to-nos], *a.* Monótono, uniforme en el tono.

monotony [mə'nɒtənɪ] [mo-no-to-ni], *s.* Monotonía, el estado o la cualidad de lo monótono; uniformidad fastidiosa del tono; falta de variedad en la cadencia o en la dicción.

monotriglyph [məˈnɒtrɪɡlɪf] [mo-no-tri-glif], *s. (Arq.)* Monotriglifo, espacio de triglifo entre dos columnas o pilastras.

monotype, monotyping [ˈmɒnəʊtaɪp] [mo-nou-taip], *s. (Impr.)* Monotinia.

monoxide, monoxid [mɒˈnɒskaɪd] [mo-nok-said], *s.* Compuesto que contiene un solo átomo de oxígeno.

monsoon [mɒnˈsuːn] [mon-sun], *s.* Monzón, viento periódico y general que corre hacia una misma parte en determinado tiempo.

monster [ˈmɒnstəʳ] [mons-taʳ], *s.* 1. Monstruo, animal fabuloso, parto o producción contra el orden regular de la naturaleza. 2. Monstruo, lo que es sumamente feo y también el que es sumamente, perverso. -*a.* Enorme, prodigioso, extraordinario. **A monster meeting,** una reunión numerosísima, enorme.

monstrance [ˈmɒnstrəns] [mons-trans], *a. (Ecle.)* Custodia, viril.

monstrosity [mɒnˈstrɒsɪtɪ] [mons-tro-si-ti], *s.* Monstruosidad, suma fealdad.

monstrous [ˈmɒnstrəs] [mons-tros], *a.* 1. Monstruoso, contrario al orden de la naturaleza. 2. Extraño, prodigioso, maravilloso. 3. Monstruoso, disforme, horrendo (dreadful). -*adv. (Fam.)* Excesivamente.

monstrously [ˈmɒnstrəslɪ] [mons-tros-li], *adv.* Monstruosamente, prodigiosamente.

monstrousness [ˈmɒnstrəsnɪs] [mons-tros-nes], *s.* Monstruosidad, enormidad.

montage [mɒnˈtɑːdʒ] [mon-tash], *s.* Montaje, arte de montaje.

montanic [ˈmɒntænɪk] [mon-ta-nik], *a.* Montañoso.

montanist [ˈmɒntænɪst] [mon-ta-nist], *s.* Montanista, hereje sectario de Montano.

montant [ˈmɒntənt] [mon-tant], *s.* Montante, término de esgrima y de carpintería.

monteith [ˈmɒnteɪθ] [mon-teiz], *s.* Una ponchera de adorno, se llama así del nombre de su inventor.

month [mʌnθ] [manz], *s.* Mes, originalmente un mes lunar, hoy una de las doce partes en que se divide el año. **A month ago,** hace un mes. **Once a month,** una vez al mes. **What day of the month is it?,** ¿Qué día del mes es hoy? **Lunar month, solar month,** mes lunar, mes solar. **A month of Sundays,** literalmente, un mes de domingos; tiempo que parece muy largo, como si cada día fuese una semana.

monthly [ˈmʌnθlɪ] [manz-li], *a.* Mensual, que continúa durante un mes o que acontece una vez al mes. -*s.* 1. Publicación que sale a luz regularmente una vez al mes. 2. *pl.* Las reglas, la indisposición periódica de las mujeres. -*adv.* Mensualmente.

monticle [ˈmʌntɪkl] [man-ti-kel], *s. (Poco us.)* Montecillo.

monticulous [mʌnˈtɪkjələs] [man-ti-kiu-los], *a. (Poco us.)* Lo que tiene muchos montecillos.

monument [ˈmɒnjʊmənt] [mo-niu-ment], *s.* 1. Monumento conmemorativo; columna, pilar, estatua, puestos encima de una tumba. 2. Monumento, memoria, recuerdo. 3. Piedra u otra señal permanente puesta por los agrimensores para marcar un límite o un ángulo.

monumental [ˈmɒnjʊməntl] [mo-niu-men-tal], *a.* Monumental, hecho en memoria o para conservar la memoria de alguna persona o acontecimiento; conmemorativo.

monumentally [ˌmɒnjʊˈməntəlɪ] [mo-niu-men-ta-li], *adv.* 1. Como recuerdo. 2. Por medio de monumentos.

moo [muː] [mu], 1. *vi.* Mugir. 2. *s. m.* Mugido.

mooch [muːtʃ] [much], *vi.* **To mooch about/around,** vagar *(Fam.)*.

mood [muːd] [mud], *s.* 1. Disposición de ánimo, genio o natural; humor, capricho. 2. Modo silogístico, la debida disposición de las varias proposiciones de un silogismo. 3. *(Gram.)* Modo en la conjugación de los verbos. *V.* MODE. Esta forma es preferible. **To be in a cheerful mood,** estar de buen humor. **To be in the mood to do,** estar de humor para hacer algo.

moodily [ˈmuːdɪlɪ] [mu-di-li], *adv.* Caprichosamente.

moodiness [ˈmuːdɪnɪs] [mu-di-nes], *s.* Capricho, extravagancia; mal humor; tristeza, cavilación, melancolía.

moody [ˈmuːdɪ] [mu-di], *a.* Fantástico, caprichoso, raro, extravagante; irritable, de mal humor; caviloso, triste, melancólico, taciturno.

moon [muːn] [mun], *s.* 1. Luna, satélite de la tierra. 2. Satélite de cualquier planeta. 3. Mes lunar. **To bay the moon,** ladrar a la luna, meter la mar en un pozo. **Moonbeam,** rayo lunar. **Moon-blind,** cegato, corto de vista. **Moon-blasted,** echado a perder por la influencia de la luna. **Moon-calf,** mola, monstruo; bobo, tonto. **Moon-dial,** reloj lunar. **Moon-fern,** *(Bot.)* botriquio.

mooned [ˈmuːnɪd] [mu-nid], *a.* Lunado, lo que tiene figura de media luna.

moon-eyed [ˈmuːnaɪd] [mun-aid], *a.* Ojizaino; bizco, bisojo; de ojos lunáticos.

moonflower [ˈmuːnflaʊəʳ] [mun-flauaʳ], *s.* Especie de ipomea con grandes y blancas flores que se abren por la noche.

moonless [ˈmuːnlɪs] [mun-les], *a.* Falto de la luz de la luna.

moonlight [ˈmuːnlaɪt] [mun-lait], *s.* Luz de la luna. -*a.* Iluminado por la luna.

moonlit [ˈmuːnlɪt] [mun-lit], *a.* Iluminado por la luna.

moonseed [ˈmuːnsiːd] [mun-sid], *s.* Cualquier planta del género Minespermo.

moonshine [ˈmuːnʃaɪn] [mun-shain], *s.* 1. Claridad de la luna. 2. Falta de realidad, ficción; disparate. 3. *(Prov.)* Licores fuertes matuteados o destilados ilegalmente. -*a.* o **Moonwhiny,** claro, lo que participa de la claridad de la luna.

moonshiner [ˈmuːnʃaɪnəʳ] [mun-shai-naʳ], *s. (E.U.)* El que destila los licores espirituosos ilícitamente; contrabandista, matutero, particularmente de licores espirituosos.

moonstruck [ˈmuːnstrʌkt] [muns-trakt], *a.* Lunático, loco.

moonwort [ˈmuːnwɔːt] [mun-uort], *s. (Bot.)* 1. Lunaria, especie de flor. 2. Botriquio.

moony [ˈmuːnɪ] [mu-ni], *a.* 1. *V.* MOONSTRUCK. 2. Parecido a la claridad de la luna. 3. *(Her. des.)* Lunado. -*s.* Bobo, simplón.

moor [mʊəʳ] [muaʳ], *s.* 1. *(Gran Bret.)* Páramo, a veces cubierto de brezos, a menudo elevado, pantanoso y abundante en turba; frezal, marjal. 2. Moro, sarraceno, árabe.

moor, *va.* Amarrar, atar con anclas, cables u otra cosa. **To moor by the stern,** amarrar con una reguera. **To moor by the head,** amarrar con las amarras de proa. **To moor with a spring,** amarrar con codera sobre el cable. -*vn.* Situarse en algún paraje. **Where the ship moored,** en donde estaba anclado el barco.

moor-buzzard [ˈmʊəbʌːzəd] [mua-bu-sard], *s. (Orn.)* Especie de halcón.

moor-hen [ˈmʊəhen] [mua-jen], *sf. (Orn.)* Cerceta, zarceta, gallineta o gallina de río.

mooring [ˈmʊərɪŋ] [mua-rin], *s. (Mar.)* Amarra, amarre, amarradura. **Mooring mast,** *(Mar.)* poste de amarre. **Mooring rings,** *(Mar.)* argollas de amarrar.

moorish [ˈmʊərɪʃ] [mua-rish], *a.* 1. Pantanoso, charcoso, cenagoso. 2. Morisco, moro.

moorland [ˈmʊəlænd] [mua-land], *s.* Marjal; brezal; erial, tierra arenisca y ligera.

moorstone [ˈmʊəstəʊn] [mua-stoun], *s.* Especie de granito.

moory [ˈmʊərɪ] [mua-ri], *a.* Que pertenece al marjal; pantanoso: se dice también de la tierra llana y abierta que contiene turba, brezo o hiniesta espinosa.

moose [muːs] [muus], *s.* Mosa, anta, la forma americana del alce.

moot [muːt] [mut], *va.* Disputar acerca de materias legales; ejercitarse en el arte de defender cualquier punto relacionado con los pleitos o causas criminales; discutir judicialmente.

moot, *s.* Una proposición o caso de jurisprudencia que los legistas sientan para discutir o disputar sobre él. **Moot**

case o **moot point,** el caso o proposición legal que sirve como tema de discusón; pleito fingido. **Moot-court,** conferencia en las escuelas de derecho; supuesto tribunal en el que los estudiantes de jurisprudencia se ejercitan en la práctica forense.

mooter [ˈmuːtəʳ] [mu-taʳ], *s.* 1. El que se ejercita o ensaya en defender pleitos. 2. *(Mar.)* El que hace los toletes o escálamos.

mop [mɒp] [mop], *s.* 1. Aljofifa, estropajo, rodilla para limpiar con agua estregando, o para sacudir el polvo. 2. Mechón, copete, puñado de cabellos, cerdas, hilachas, etc.

mop, *s.* 1. Mueca. 2. Una joven; una muchacha mimada o ceñuda.

mop, *va.* Aljofifar, limpiar alguna cosa estregándola con una aljofifa o un estropajo empapado en agua, o sacudir el polvo con rodilla, estropajo o aljofifa. *-vn. (Prov. Ingl.)* Hacer muecas.

mopboard [ˈmɒpbɔːd] [mop-bord], *s.* Banda de madera en la parte baja de las paredes de un cuarto.

mope [məʊp] [moup], *s.* El hombre abatido, atontado o estúpido.

mope, *vn.* Dormitar, entontecerse, estar triste y pensativo, estar melancólico. *-va.* Atontar, privar de las potencia naturales; poner estúpido a uno; desanimar.

moped [ˈməʊped] [mou-ped], *s. f.* Ciclomotor, moto.

mope-eyed [ˈməʊpaɪd] [moup-aid], *a.* Tuerto, falto de un ojo; cegato.

mopish [ˈmɒpɪʃ] [mo-pish], *a.* Atontado, estúpido, adormecido, medio dormido; distraído, que no presta atención.

mopishness [ˈmɒpɪʃnɪs] [mo-pish-nes], *s.* Abatimiento, adormecimiento.

moppet [ˈmɒpɪt] [mo-pit], *s.* 1. Muñeca, figura de muchacho o muchacha hecha de trapos. 2. *(Fam.)* Gachona: voz de cariño que se da a una niña. 3. Mueca.

mopsical [ˈmɒpsɪkəl] [mop-si-kal], *a.* Cegato. *V.* MOPE-EYED.

mopstick [ˈmɒpstɪk] [mop-stik], *s.* Mango de estropajo o aljofifa.

moquette [məˈket] [mo-ket], *s.* Moqueta, alfombra con trama de cáñamo.

moral [ˈmɒrəl] [mo-ral], *a.* 1. Moral, perteneciente a las buenas costumbres y acciones lícitas; ético. 2. Conforme a razón, virtuoso; particularmente casto, púdico; honrado. 3. Que obra según los dictados de la razón od el derecho en el hombre. 4. *(Lóg.)* Probable, como opuesto a demostrativo; v. g. **Moral certainty,** certidumbre moral. *-s.* 1. Moralidad, moraleja, deducción o enseñanza moral contenida en una fábula o narración. 2. *pl.* 1. Costumbres, práctica de los deberes de la vida; conducta, manera de vivir con referencia al bien y al mal; en especial, honestidad, castidad. 2. Ética, los principios de la moral y obligaciones del hombre.

morale [mɒˈrɑːl] [mo-ral], *s.* Moral, animación, entusiasmo.

moralist [ˈmɒrəlɪst] [mo-ra-list], *s.* Moralista.

morality [məˈrælɪtɪ] [mo-ra-li-ti], *s.* 1. Ética, moralidad, doctrina o enseñanza acerca de las buenas costumbres o del arreglo de vida. 2. Moralidad, reflexión o sentencia moral. 3. Moralidad de las acciones humanas, la cualidad de lo moral. 4. Moralidad, el sentido moral de una cosa. 5. Un antiguo drama legórico del siglo XIV.

moralization [ˌmɒrəlaɪˈzeɪʃən] [mo-ra-lai-sei-shon], *s.* Moralización.

moralize, Moralise [ˈmɒrəlaɪz] [mo-ra-lais], *va.* y *vn.* 1. Moralizar, discurrir acerca de las buenas costumbres y del arreglo de vida. 2. Moralizar, hablar o escribir sobre asuntos morales. 3. Hacer moral o virtuoso.

moralizer [ˈmɒrəlaɪzəʳ] [mo-ra-lai-saʳ], *s.* Moralizador.

morally [ˈmɒrəlɪ] [mo-ra-li], *adv.* 1. Moralmente, en sentido moral, conforme a las reglas de la moral. 2. Virtuosamente, honradamente. 3. Según las reglas de la razón y del juicio práctico; prácticamente.

moral support [ˈmɒrəlsəˈpɔːt] [mo-ral-so-port], *s.* Apoyo moral.

morass [məˈræs] [mo-ras], *s.* Cenagal, ciénaga, tremedal, pantano.

morat [məˈræt] [mo-rat], *s.* Bebida hecha de miel con el jugo de moras.

moratorium [ˌmɒrəˈtɔːrɪəm] [mo-ra-to-riom], *s.* Moratoria, plazo para pagar una deuda vencida.

moravian [mɒˈreɪvɪən] [mo-rei-vian], *a.* Moravo, relativo a la Moravia o a sus habitantes. *-s.* Moravo, natural de Moravia.

morbid [ˈmɔːbɪd] [mor-bid], *a.* 1. Mórbido, morboso, que no está sano. 2. Causado por enfermedad o que denota un estado insano del cuerpo o de la mente; patológico.

morbidness [ˈmɔːbɪdnɪs] [mor-bid-nes], **morbidity** [ˈmɔːbɪdɪtɪ] [mor-bi-di-ti], *s.* Estado de enfermedad o la situación del que se halla enfermo; estado mórbido.

morbific, morbifical [ˈmɔːbɪfɪk] [mor-bi-fik], *a.* Morbífico, que causa enfermedades o que lleva consigo el germen de las enfermedades.

morbose [ˈmɔːbəʊz] [mor-bous], *a.* *(Des.)* Morboso, malsano, enfermizo.

morceau [ˈmɔːsə] [mor-so], *s.* Pedacito; en música y en literatura, una composición corta.

morchella [ˈmɔːkiːlə] [mor-ki-la], *s.* Morilla, múrgura, hongo de sabor agradable.

mordacious [ˈmɔːdɪʃəs] [mor-dei-shos], *a.* *(Ant.)* Mordaz, maldiciente, satírico.

mordant [ˈmɔːdənt] [mor-dant], *s.* Mordiente, mordente, sustancia para preparar telas o maderas que se quieren teñir. *-a.* 1. Mordiente, que muerde, acre, mordaz. 2. Mordiente, que sirve para fijar los colores. *-va.* Aplicar un mordiente para fijar los colores.

mordent [ˈmɔːdənt] [mor-dent], *s.* *(Mús.)* Mordente, alteración rápida de dos notas contiguas, especie de trino.

more [ˈmɔːʳ] [moʳ], *a. (comp.* de MUCH, MANY). Mayor, más, más numeroso, adicional. *-adv.* 1. Más, con mayor exceso o intensión. 2. Más, término comparativo. **Never more,** nunca más o jamás. **Once more,** una vez más, otra vez. **More and more,** de más o de cada vez más. **So much the more,** tanto más, cuanto más, tanto mejor. **To make more of a thing than it is,** exagerar una cosa. 3. Más, antes bien. **No more,** no más; lo que no existe o ya se acabó. **He fell ill and is no more,** le sobrevino una enfermedad y se murió. **More** sirve para formar el comparativo de los adjetivos. **The more he spends the less he saves,** cuanto más gasta, menos ahorra. **The more he spends the less he saves,** cuanto más gasta, menos ahorra. **The more, the merrier,** cuanto más locos hay, más se ríe. *-s.* La cantidad o grado mayor de alguna cosa; otra cosa.

moreen [ˈmɔːriːn] [mo-rin], *s.* Filipichím; tela de lana para cortinas.

moreish [ˈmɔːrɪʃ] [mo-rish], *a.* Apetitoso.

moreland [ˈmɔːlænd] [mor-land], *s.* Tierra montuosa. *V.* MOORLAND.

morelle [ˈmɔːriːl] [mo-ril], *s.* Hierba mora, especie de solano.

morello [ˈmɔːliːlə] [mo-ri-lo], *s.* *(Bot.)* Especie de cereza de la que se hacen cerezas pasas.

moreover [mɔːˈrəʊvəʳ] [mo-rou-vaʳ], *adv.* Además, además de eso, por otra parte, a más de lo que se ha dicho. *-conj.* También.

moresk [ˈmɔːresk] [mo-resk], **Morisco** [ˈmɔːrɪskəʊ] [mo-ris-kou], *s.* Arabesco. *V.* MORESQUE.

moresque [ˈmɔːresk] [mo-resk], *s.* Arabesco: dícese de ciertas labores de escultura, dibujos y pinturas al estilo de los moros.

morganatic [ˌmɔːgəˈnætɪk] [mor-ga-na-tik], *a.* Morganático; dícese del matrimonio por que un hombre se casa con una mujer de rango inferior al suyo.

morgue [mɔːg] [morg], *s.* Depósito de cadáveres no identificados.

moribund ['mɒrɪbʌnd] [mo-ri-band], *a.* Moribundo.

morion ['mɔːrɪən] [mo-rion], *s.* 1. Morrión, antigua armadura de la cabeza. 2. Variedad de cuarzo humoso, casi negro.

morisco ['mɔːrɪskəʊ] [mo-ris-kou], *s.* 1. Morisco. 2. Arábigo, la lengua de los moros. 3. Danza morisca. 4. Arabesco.

mormon ['mɔːmən] [mor-mon], *s.* Mormón.

mormonism ['mɔːmənɪzəm] [mor-mo-ni-sem], *s.* Mormonismo, las doctrinas y sistema de gobierno de los mormones.

morn [mɔːn] [morn], **morning** ['mɔːnɪŋ] [mor-nin], *s.* 1. Mañana, la parte del día desde que amanece hasta las doce del mediodía; la primera parte del día. 2. Cualquier parte temprana. **I wish you a good morning,** tenga Ud. buenos días. **Early in the morning,** temprano, muy de mañana. **Tomorrow morning,** mañana por la mañana. **Every morning,** todas las mañanas. **Morning-dress,** traje de mañana. **Morning-glory,** dondiego de día, planta enredadera. **Morning-gown,** bata. **Morning-star,** (*Astr.*) el lucero de la mañana. *-a.* Matutino, matinal.

Moroccan [məˈrɒkən] [mo-ro-kan], *s.* y *a.* Marroquí.

morocco [məˈrɒkəʊ] [mo-ro-kau], *s.* 1. Marroquí, tafilete. 2. *n. p.* Marruecos.

moron ['mɔːrɒn] [mo-ron], *s.* Retrasado mental.

morose [məˈrəʊs] [mo-rous], *a.* Moroso; áspero de genio; bronco, cabezudo; fantástico; triste.

morosely [məˈrəʊslɪ] [mo-rous-li], *adv.* Broncamente; morosamente.

moroseness [məˈrəʊsnɪs] [mo-rous-nes], *s.* Morosidad; mal humor o aspereza de genio; capricho.

Morpheus ['mɔːfɪəs] [mor-fios], *s.* (*Mitol.*) Morfeo, dios del sueño.

morphia, morphin, morphine ['mɔːfɪə] [mor-fia] ['mɔːfɪn] [mor-fin], *s.* Morfina, alcaloide vegetal, amargo, cristalizble, que se extrae del opio; es el principal de sus alcaloides y se emplea en medicina.

morpho-. Forma que se usa en la composición de palabras, y significa forma, figura.

morphological [ˌmɔːfəˈlɒdʒɪkəl] [mor-fo-lo-yi-kal], *a.* Morfológico, referente a la morfología.

morphology [mɔːˈfɒlədʒɪ] [mor-fo-lo-yi], *s.* 1. Morfología, la parte de la biología que trata de la forma y estructura de los animales y de las plantas. 2. La ciencia de las formas o estructura del lenguaje.

morphosis [mɔːˈfəʊsɪs] [mor-fou-sis], *s.* (*Biol.*) Morfosis, el orden o modo de formación de un órgano o de un organismo.

morris chair [ˌmɒrɪsˈtʃɛər] [mo-ris-chea'], *s.* Potrona.

morris-dance [ˌmɒrɪsˈdɑːns] [mo-ris-dans], *s.* Danza morisca, baile de los moros; moniganga.

morrow ['mɒrəʊ] [mo-rou], *s.* Mañana, el día que sigue al de hoy. **On the morrow,** en el día de mañana. **After tomorrow,** pasado mañana.

morse code ['mɔːskəʊd] [mors-koud], *s.* Clave telgráfica de Morse.

morsel ['mɔːsl] [mor-sel], *s.* Bocado, la porción de alimento que cabe de una vez en la boca.

mort [mɔːt] [mort], *s.* 1. Muerte. 2. El toque de la trompa de caza al morir la res en las cacerías.

mortal ['mɔːtl] [mor-tal], *a.* 1. Mortal. 2. Mortal, que ocasiona o puede ocasionar la muerte, fatal. 3. Mortal, humano, lo que es propio de la especie humana. 4. Mortal, que no es venial. 5. (*Fam.*) Mortal, extremo, violento. 6. Prolijo, fastidioso. *-s.* Mortal, un ser sujeto a la muerte, particularmente un ser humano.

mortality [mɔːˈtælɪtɪ] [mor-ta-li-ti], *s.* 1. Mortalidad, capacidad de morir o padecer la muerte. 2. Muerte, la separación del alma del cuerpo. 3. Mortandad, proporción en que ocurren los fallecimientos con relación al número de habitantes. 4. Especie humana; naturaleza mortal.

mortally ['mɔːtəlɪ] [mor-ta-li], *adv.* 1. Mortalmente. 2. (*Vulg.*) Extremamente, sumamente.

mortar ['mɔːtəʳ] [mor-ta'], *s.* 1. Mortero, almirez. 2. Mortero, máquina de artillería de gran calibre, para disparar bombas. 3. Argamasa, mezcla, mortero, la cal y arena amasadas para unir piedras o ladrillos.

mortarboard ['mɔːtəbɔːd] [mor-ta-bord], *s.* 1. Esparavel de los albañiles. 2. Birrete o bonete académico.

mortar-piece ['mɔːtəpiːs] [mor-ta-pis], *s.* Mortero para disparar bombas.

mortgage ['mɔːtgɪdʒ] [mor-guich], *s.* 1. Hipoteca, gravamen que se impone sobre bienes inmuebles u otra clase de propiedad, para responder del cumplimiento de una obligación o del pago de una deuda. 2. El acta o instrumento legal en que consta dicho gravamen. **Covered by a mortgage,** gravado con una hipoteca. **To pay off a mortgage,** redimir o levantar una hipoteca.

mortgage, *va.* Hipotecar, asegurar un pago dando en fianza o hipoteca alguna finca o bienes raíces.

mortgagee ['mɔːtgɪdʒiː] [mor-gui-chi], *s.* Acreedor hipotecario, aquél a quien se le ha hipotecado un inmueble.

mortgager, mortgagor ['mɔːtgədʒəʳ] [mor-ga-cha'], *s.* Deudor hipotecario, el que hipoteca una propiedad.

mortician [mɔːˈtɪʃən] [mor-ti-shan], *s.* Agente funerario, director de pompas fúnebres. (*Cuba*) Zacateca.

mortiferous [mɔːˈtɪfərəs] [mor-ti-fe-ros], *a.* Mortífero, mortal.

mortification [ˌmɔːtɪfaɪˈkeɪʃən] [mor-ti-fai-kei-shon], *s.* 1. Mortificación, gangrena, la muerte de una de las partes del cuerpo, continuando vivas las restantes. 2. Maceración, mortificación, el acto de castigar al cuerpo con aspereza y rigor; humillación. 3. Mortificación, aflicción.

mortify ['mɔːtɪfaɪ] [mor-ti-fai], *va.* 1. Mortificar, humillar, herir el orgullo o amor propio; afligir, desazonar o causar pesadumbre o molestia. 2. Mortificar, macerar o castigar la carne; subyugar, domar las pasiones o los apetitos por la abstinencia o la elevación del espíritu. 3. Mortificar, destruir el tejido orgánico y las funciones vitales de una parte de un animal vivo. *-vn.* 1. Mortificarse una parte del cuerpo perdiendo su vitalidad; gangrenarse, corromperse. 2. Estar domado, subyugado.

mortise ['mɔːtaɪs] [mor-tais], *s.* Cotana o muesca. **Mortise-lock,** cerradura embutida.

mortise, *va.* Encajar un madero en la cotana o muesca que se ha hecho en otro.

mortmain ['mɔːtmeɪn] [mort-mein], *s.* Manos muertas; dícese de los cuerpos eclesiásticos y obras pías cuyas posesiones no se pueden enajenar.

mortuary ['mɔːtʊərɪ] [mor-tua-ri], *a.* Mortuario, que se refiere a la sepultura de los muertos. *-s.* 1. Manda o legado que hace alguno en compensación de los diezmos que ha dejado de pagar. 2. Depósito de cadáveres; lugar para recibirlos provisionalmente. 3. Cementerio.

mosaic [məˈzeɪɪk] [mou-seik], *a.* y *s.* Mosaico, obra taraceada de vidrio, esmalte o piedras de varios colores que parece pintura. *-a.* Mosaico, lo que pertenece a Moisés.

mosey ['məʊzɪ] [mou-si], *vi.* **To mosey about,** pasearse.

moslem ['mɒzlem] [mos-lem], *a.* Muslime, mahometano. *-s.* Musulmán, mahometano. Muslim.

mosque [mɒsk] [mosk], *s.* Mezquita, templo de los mahometanos.

mosquito [mɒsˈkiːtəʊ] [mos-ki-tou], *s.* Mosquito. **Mosquito net,** mosquitero.

moss [mɒs] [mos], *s.* (*Bot.*) 1. Musgo, musco, moho. 2. Especie de heno o acate que sirve para llenar colchones, cojines, etc. 3. Tremedal, terreno pantanoso que produce la turba. **A rolling stone gathers no moss,** (*prov.*) Piedra movediza nunca moho la cobija. **Iceland moss,** liquen de Islandia, musgo comestible. **Irish moss,** V. CARRAGEEN. **Moss-agate,** agata musgosa. **Moss-rose,** rosa musgosa. **Moss-trooper,** bandido, bandolero.

moss, *va.* Cubrir de musgo, moho.

moss-grown ['mɒsgraʊn] [mos-groun], *a.* Mohoso; cubierto de musgo.

mossiness ['mɒsɪnɪs] [mo-si-nes], *s.* El estado de lo que se halla cubierto de musgo o de moho.

mossy ['mɒsɪ] [mo-si], *a.* Mohoso; cubierto de musgo. **Mossy ground,** terreno cubierto de hierba menuda y fina.

most [məʊst] [moust], *a.* superl. Lo más, los más, la mayor parte de. **Most of the arts and sciences,** las más de las artes y ciencias. **Most of his money,** la mayor parte de su dinero, o casi todo su dinero. *-adv.* Sumamente, en sumo grado, muy. *-s.* 1. Los más, el mayor número. 2. Lo o el más, el mayor valor. **At most,** a lo más.

mostly ['məʊstlɪ] [moust-li], *adv.* Por la mayor parte, por lo común, ordinariamente.

mote [məʊt] [mout], *s.* 1. Mota, átomo; punto. 2. Se usa en composición con la significación de junta, asamblea o tribunal.; v. g. **folkmote.**

motel [məʊ'tel] [mou-tel], *s.* Motel.

motet [məʊ'tet] [mou-tet], *s. (Mús.)* Motete.

moth [mɒθ] [moz], *s.* 1. Mariposa nocturna. **Hawk-moth,** esfinge. **Silkworm-moth,** bombix, mariposa del gusano de seda. 2. Polilla, insecto que se cría en la ropa y la destruye. **Moth-miller,** noctuela blanquecina, polilla.

moth ball ['mɒθbɔːl] [moz-bol], *s.* Bola de naftalina contra la polilla.

moth-eaten ['mɒθˌiːtn] [moz-iten], *a.* Apolillado.

mother ['mʌðəʳ] [ma-daʳ], *sf.* 1. Madre; también animal hembra que ha parido. **Mother-in-law,** suegra. **Grandmother,** abuela. **Step-mother,** madrastra. 2. Causa, origen, lo que produce algo; también, la persona que cuida de las más jóvenes y débiles. 3. Religiosa, abadesa. 4. Madre, tía, mujer vieja; término de aprecio. 5. Instinto, sensibilidad de la madre. 6. Madre, la materia más crasa del mosto u otro licor que queda en el fondo de las vasijas. *-a.* 1. Natural, nativo, natal, materno; vernáculo. **Mother board,** placa madre *(Inform.).* **Mother-tongue,** lengua madre o vernácula. 2. Materno, nacional, metropolitano. **Mother church,** iglesia metropolitana.

mother, *va.* Servir de madre a. *-vn.* Criar madre, como el vino u otro licor.

mother-country ['mʌðəˈkʌntrɪ] [ma-dar-ken-tri], *s.* Patria, el país en que uno ha nacido.

motherhood ['mʌðəhʊd] [ma-dar-jud], *s.* Maternidad; estado o calidad de madre.

motherless ['mʌðəlɪs] [ma-da-les], *a.* Sin madre, **Motherless child,** huérfano o huérfana de madre.

motherliness ['mʌðəlɪnɪs] [ma-da-li-nes], *s.* Maternidad, la calidad de madre.

motherly ['mʌðəlɪ] [ma-da-li], *a.* Maternal, materno. *-adv.* Maternalmente.

mother-of-pearl ['mʌðərəv'pɜːl] [ma-dar-ov-perl], *s.* Madreperla, la cubierta interior de la concha en que se engendra la perla. **Mother of thyme,** *(Bot.)* Sérpol.

mother-to-be ['mʌðətə'biː] [ma-da-tu-bi], *s. f.* Futura madre.

motif [məʊ'tiːf] [mou-tif], *s.* Motivo, asunto, tema.

motile [məʊ'tɪl] [mou-til], *a.* Movible, que puede moverse espontáneamente.

motion ['məʊʃən] [mou-shon], *s.* 1. Movimiento. 2. Movimiento, moción, vitalidad. 3. Aire, ademán, modo de andar o moverse. 4. Movimiento, el que hace un ejército o un cuerpo de tropas mudando de posición. 5. Movimiento, ímpetu, agitación o impulso del ánimo. 6. Movimiento, impulso o dirección dada a una cosa para que mude de situación o de estado. 7. Proposición o propuesta que se hace para que se decida o resuelva alguna cosa. 8. Ocurrencia, especie que se presenta de repente a la imaginación. 9. Evacuación del vientre. **To put in motion,** agitar, mover, poner en movimiento. **To make a motion,** proponer, hacer una proposición en alguna junta o congreso para que se acuerde sobre ella, o bien hacer una propuesta a alguno.

Dumb motions, señas. **Reciprocating motion,** movimiento recíproco, alternativo o de vaivén. **To do a thing of one's own motion,** hacer alguna cosa por inspiración o impulso propio.

motion, *va.* 1. Proponer, presentar una moción, hacer una proposición o propuesta. 2. *(Raro)* Aconsejar, proponer planes o medios para conseguir un fin. *-vn.* Hacer una señal, hacer señas significativas para dirigir o para indicar algo.

motionless ['məʊʃənlɪs] [mou-shon-les], *a.* Inmóvil, inmoble, inmovible.

motion picture ['məʊʃənˌpɪktʃəʳ] [mou-shon-pik-chaʳ], *s.* Película, cinematográfica. *-s. pl.* Cine, cinematógrafo. **Motion picture camera,** tomavistas.

motivate ['məʊtɪveɪt] [mou-ti-veit], *va.* Motivar.

motive ['məʊtɪv] [mou-tiv], *a.* Motor, motriz, que mueve o tiene eficacia o virtud para mover. *-s.* 1. Motivo, causa o razón que mueve a hacer alguna cosa; aguijón, estímulo. 2. Idea, concepción predominante; sujeto, tema, designio; motivo músico.

motivity ['məʊtɪvɪtɪ] [mou-ti-vi-ti], *s.* Potencia motriz.

motley ['mɒtlɪ] [mot-li], *a.* 1. Abigarrado, gayado, pintado de colores varios o extraños, pintorreado, pintarrajado. 2. Mezclado, variado, diverso; que consta de elementos heterogéneos o incongruentes.

motor ['məʊtəʳ] [mou-taʳ], *s.* Motor, movedor, móvil, lo que mueve o que imprime movimiento; particularmente una máquina motriz. **Electric motor,** motor eléctrico; aparato que convierte la fuerza eléctrica en fuerza mecánica; lo contrario del dínamo. *-a.* Motor, móvil, que da o imprime movimiento. **Motor nerve,** nervio motor.

motorbike ['məʊtəbaɪk] [mou-to-baik], *s.* Ciclomotor.

motor boat ['məʊtəbəʊt] [mou-to-bout], **Motor launch,** gasolinera, lancha de motor.

motorbus ['məʊtəbʌs] [mou-to-bas], *s.* Autobús.

motorcade ['məʊtəkeɪd] [mou-to-keid], *s.* Automóvil.

motorcoach ['məʊtəkəʊtʃ] [mou-to-kouch], *s. m.* Autocar, camión *(Mex.).* Micro *(Argent.).*

motorcycle ['məʊtəsaɪkl] [mou-to-sai-kel], *s.* Motocicleta.

motorcyclist ['məʊtəˌsaɪklɪst] [mou-to-sai-klist], *s.* Motociclista.

motoring ['məʊtərɪŋ] [mou-to-rin], *s. f.* **School of motoring,** autoescuela.

motorist ['məʊtərɪst] [mou-to-rist], *s.* Automovilista.

motorization [ˌməʊtəraɪ'zeɪʃən] [mou-to-rai-sei-shon], *s.* Motorización.

motorize ['məʊtəraɪz] [mou-to-rais], *va.* Motorizar.

motorman ['məʊtəmən] [mou-to-man], *s.* Motorista (ship).

motor ship ['məʊtəʃɪp] [mou-to-ship], *s.* Motonave.

motor truck ['məʊtətrʌk] [mou-to-trak], *s.* Autocamión, camión.

mottle ['mɒtl] [mo-tel], *va.* Marcar con manchas diferentes colores, o con diversos matices; variegar, abigarrar.

mottled ['mɒtld] [mo-teld], *a.* Moteado, jaspeado.

motto ['mɒtəʊ] [mo-tou], *s.* Mote, sentencia notable que se pone en alguna inscripción; lema, divisa.

mould, mold [məʊld] [mauld], *s.* 1. Moho, el vello que se cría en el pan y otras cosas por estar mucho tiempo en lugares húmedos. 2. Tierra vegetal, suelo, el terreno en que nace alguna cosa. 3. Molde, matriz *(Mex.)* En los trapiches o ingenios de azúcar, formas. 4. La materia de que está hecha alguna cosa.

mould, mold, *va.* 1. Enmohecer, cubrir con moho alguna cosa. 2. Cubrir con tierra. 3. Moldar, amoldar, moldear. 4. Amasar, formar masa de alguna cosa. 5. *(Mar.)* Galivar. *-vn.* Enmohecerse, llenarse de moho o criar moho. *(Obs.)* En Inglaterra se escribe comúnmente con u y sin ella en los Estados Unidos. Lo mismo sucede con sus derivados.

moulder, molder ['məʊldəʳ] [maul-daʳ], *vn.* Convertirse en polvo, reducirse a polvo; consumirse, irse disminuyendo o consumiendo. *-va.* Convertir en polvo, consumir, destruir.

mouldiness ['məʊldɪnɪs] [maul-di-nes], *s.* Moho, el estado de lo que se halla mohoso.

moulding, molding ['məʊldɪŋ] [maul-din], s. Moldura. -pa. Lo que forma o modela; lo que causa moho o enmohece.

mouldy, moldy ['məʊldɪ] [maul-di] a. Mohoso.

moult, molt ['məʊlt] [mault], vn. Mudar la pluma como las aves; mudar o echar el integumento exterior, como la piel, las plumas o los cuernos.

moulting, molting ['məʊltɪŋ] [maul-tin], s. Muda, el acto de mudar el integumento exterior o sus pertenencias.

mound [maʊnd] [maund], s. 1. Montón de tierra, artificial o natural; terraplén, baluarte. 2. (Her.) Mundo, esfera que, como el cetro, forma parte de los atributos de un monarca.

mound, va. Atrincherar, fortalecer.

mount [maʊnt] [maunt], s. 1. Monte, montaña, cuesta. 2. Baluarte, terraplén de una fortificación.

mount, s. 1. Montadura, objeto que sirve para preparar una cosa o para exhibirla; v. g. e. cartón sobre que está colocado un dibujo. 2. Caballería. 3. Apeadero. 4. Monta, toque de clarín para montar a caballo.

mount, vn. 1. Subir, subirse o ascender. 2. Subir, elevarse a una altura considerable. 3. Subir o montar a caballo. 4. Subir, montar, importar, ascender a, hablando de una cuenta, una renta, etc. -va. 1. Subir, levantar, hacer una cosa más alta de lo que era, como cuando se habla de una pared, torre, etc.; o aumentar su fuerza, como cuando se habla de la voz. 2. Subir, llevar las cosas arriba. 3. Subir una escalera, una cuesta, etc. 4. Proveer de caballos; poner a caballo. 5. Montar o engastar las piedras preciosas; preparar una cosa para usarla, hacerla servir de adorno, mostrarla, examinarla o conservarla. 6. Alzar, elevar; exaltar. 7. Llevar, portar, ir equipado con. **This ship mounts sixteen guns,** este navío porta diez y seis cañones. **To mount a fan,** montar un abanico. **To mount guard,** (Mil.) Montar la guardia. **To mount a cannon,** (Art.) Montar un cañón.

mountable ['maʊntəbl] [maun-ta-bol], a. Que se puede montar o subir.

mountain ['maʊntɪn] [maun-ten], s. 1. Monte, sierra, montaña. 2. Montón, masa enorme. **Mountain chain,** sierra, cadena de montañas. **Mountain road,** camino por país montañoso. -a. Montés.

mountain-ash ['maʊntɪnˌæʃ] [maun-tin-ash], s. (Bot.) Mostajo, serbal de cazadores.

mountaineer ['maʊntɪ'nɪəʳ] [maun-ti-niaʳ], s. 1. Montañés, el que vive en las montañas. 2. Salteador de caminos, bandido. 3. Salvaje, el que es montaraz, o tiene genio y propiedades agrestes y groseras.

mountainous ['maʊntɪnəs] [maun-ti-nos], a. 1. Montañoso, país o tierra de montañas. 2. Montuoso, grande, abultado como una montaña. 3. Montaraz, el habitante de las montañas.

mountebank ['maʊntɪbæŋk] [maun-ti-bank], s. 1. Charlatán, el que vende supuestos medicamentos infalibles. 2. De aquí, saltimbanco, juglar, truhán.

mounting ['maʊntɪŋ] [maun-tin], s. 1. Subida; lo que sirve para subir alguna parte. 2. Montura, engaste, los ornamentos que hermosean y adornan una obra. V. MOUNT. 3. El acto o el arte de preparar una cosa para usarla o exhibirla.

mourn [mɔːn] [morn], vn. 1. Lamentarse, quejarse, apesadumbrarse, afligirse; plañir; hacer duelo y sentimiento. 2. Vestirse de luto o llevar luto. -va. Deplorar, lamentar, llorar. **To mourn for one,** llorar a alguno; llevar luto por alguien.

mourner ['mɔːnəʳ] [mor-naʳ], s. 1. Lamentador, el que lamenta. 2. Llorón. 3. El que hace el duelo en algún entierro, vestido de luto; plañidera. **Chief mourner,** dolorido, el que recibe los pésames y guía el duelo en un entierro. (Amer.) Doliente. -a. Lo que se usa en los entierros o lo que sirve para expresar duelo o tristeza.

mournful ['mɔːnfʊl] [morn-ful], a. 1. Triste, melancólico. 2. Funesto, deplorable. 3. Apesadumbrado; lúgubre, triste.

mournfully ['mɔːnfəlɪ] [morn-fu-li], adv. Tristemente, melancólicamente.

mournfulness ['mɔːnfʊlnɪs] [morn-ful-nes], s. 1. Pesar. 2. Tristeza, melancolía, aflicción, desconsuelo, duelo, sentimiento.

mourning ['mɔːnɪŋ] [mor-nin], a. Lamentoso, deplorable. -s. 1. Lamento, llanto, gemido, aflicción, tristeza. 2. Duelo; plañido. 3. Luto, el vestido que usan en señal de dolor los parientes o amigos de un difunto. **In mourning,** de luto. **Half mourning,** medio luto. **Mourning-bride, mourning-window,** escabiosa, planta herbácea y su flor. Scabiosa. **Mourning-dove,** paloma de la Carolina.

mouse [maʊs] [maus], s. 1. Ratón. 2. (Mar.) Barrilete.

mouse, vn. Cazar o coger ratones. -va. 1. Cazar a hurtadillas y con paciencia, como el gato al ratón. 2. Desgarrar, hacer trizas, hacer trizas, como un gato. 3. (Mar.) Amarrar, abarbetar, hacer barriletes. **To mouse a hook,** amarrar un gancho.

mouse-ear ['maʊsˌɪəʳ] [maus-iaʳ], s. (Bot.) Velosilla, pelosilla oficinal; miosotis.

mouse-hole ['maʊshəʊl] [maus-joul], s. Agujero pequeño.

mouse-hunt ['maʊshʌnt] [maus-jant], s. Caza de ratones.

mouser ['maʊsəʳ] [mau-saʳ], s. Cazador de ratones.

mouse-tail ['maʊsteɪl] [maus-teil], s. (Bot.) Miosuro, cola de ratón, nombre genérico de plantas.

mouse-trap ['maʊstræp] [maus-trap], s. Ratonera.

mous(e)y ['maʊsɪ] [mau-si], a. Pardusco (color). Tímido (person).

mousseline ['maʊsəliːn] [mau-se-lin], s. 1. Muselina fina francesa. 2. Vidrio de muselina, un vidrio muy delgado que imita los dibujos del encaje.

moustache, s. V. MUSTACHE.

mouth [maʊθ] [mauz], s. 1. Boca. 2. Boca, entrada; abertura, agujero. 3. Orificio, abertura de un vaso. 4. Embarcadero, embocadura o desembocadura de un río. 5. Boca, lengua, tomadas como instrumentos de la voz. 6. Gesto o mueca que se hace con la boca. **Down in the mouth,** cabizbajo, melancólico. **To make one's mouth water,** hacer la boca agua. **To stop the mouth,** cerar la boca; (Fig.) imponer silencio, quitar el habla. **To keep one's mouth shut,** permanecer callado, no decir ni pío (Fam.) **To be born with a silver spoon in one's mouth,** nacer de pies, nacer rico. **Shut your mouth!** ¡Cállate de una vez!

mouth, vn. Vocifera, hablar a gritos. -va. 1. Pronunciar de una manera extravagante; vocear, hablar alto. 2. Mascar, comer. 3. Agarrar con la boca o en la boca. 4. Insultar con palabras descomedidas.

mouthed [maʊðd] [mauzd], a. Lo que tiene boca. **Wide-mouthed,** bocudo o que tiene la boca grande. **Wry-mouthed,** el que tiene la boca torcida. **Foul-mouthed,** mal hablada, maldiciente. **Mealy-mouthed,** dulce, melifluo; tímido.

mouthful ['maʊθfʊl] [mauz-ful], s. 1. Bocado. 2. Miaja o migaja, parte o porción pequeña de alguna cosa.

mouthing ['maʊθɪŋ] [mauz-zin], a. El que está vociferando, hablando alto o haciendo ademanes.

mouthless ['maʊθlɪs] [mauz-les], a. Desbocado, sin boca.

mouth organ ['maʊθˌɔːɡən] [mauz-or-gan], s. Armónica.

mouthpiece ['maʊθpiːs] [mauz-pis], s. 1. Boquilla, embocadura de un instrumento de música; boquilla de cualquier herramienta o instrumento. 2. Portavoz.

mouthwash ['maʊθwɒʃ] [mauz-uosh], s. Lavado bucal.

mouthwatering ['maʊθˈwɔːtərɪŋ] [mauz-uo-ta-rin], a. Exquisito, apetitoso, que hace la boca agua.

movable, moveable ['muːvəbl] [mu-va-bol], a. Movible, movedizo, que puede moverse; que puede cambiar de un tiempo a otro.

movables ['muːvəblz] [mu-va-bols], s. pl. Muebles, los bienes que se pueden mover y llevar de una parte a otra, a distinción de los bienes raíces.

move [muːv] [muv], s. 1. Movimiento, acción de mover (movement). 2. Paso, acto en la prosecución de un plan o en la ejecución de algo (action). 3. En varios juegos, suerte, jugada, mano, el derecho de cambiar el lugar de una pieza (game). **To miss a move,** errar una jugada, una suerte. **Masterly move,** jugada maestra. **It is your move,** te toca jugar. **A wise move,** una acción, un paso acertado. **To make a move,** ponerse en marcha. **To get a move on,** darse prisa.

move, va. 1. Mover. 2. Mover o menear una parte del cuerpo; hacer mudar de postura. 3. Mover, impeler, dar o causar movimiento o impulso. 4. Proponer, hacer una proposición o propuesta; recomendar o pedir a uno que se encargue del cuidado de algún asunto. 5. Mover, excitar, incitar o disponr el ánimo para alguna cosa; persuadir, inclinar. 6. Mover a piedad, a lágrimas, etc., conmover, causar u ocasionar una pasión de ánimo. 7. Hacer mover el vientre. -vn. 1. Moverse, menearse, mudar de lugar, de postura. 2. Andar, ponerse en movimiento, en camino. 3. Marchar un ejército o cuerpo militar. 4. Entrar en acción, empezar a obrar. 5. Mudar de residencia, marchar, partir. 6. Avanzar, progresar de cierto modo. 7. Exonerarse el vientre.

move about/around, cambiar de sitio o posición, trasladarse.

move along, adelantar, circular, avanzar.

move away, alejarse; irse, marcharse; mudar de casa.

move back, regresar.

move forward, adelantarse, avanzar. **To move the clock forward,** adelantar el reloj.

move in, entrar; entrar a habitar una casa, instalarse.

move off, decampar; poner pies en polvorosa, tomar las de Villadiego, tomar viento.

move out, retirar, sacar, mudarse.

move round, 1. Dar vueltas a. 2. Recorrer.

move up, 1. Anticipar (una fecha). 2. Ascender, adelantar.

To move to laughter, hacer reír, causar o excitar la risa. **To move to anger,** enojar, irritar, conmover, provocar.

moveless ['mu:vlɪs] [muv-les], a. Inmóvil.

movement ['mu:vmənt] [muv-ment], s. 1. Movimiento, moción; meneo; marcha. 2. Serie de actos o incidentes que tienden a algún fin. **The temperance movement,** la propaganda o cruzada en favor de la templanza. 3. En literatura, acción, incidente. 4. Movimiento, conjunto de las piezas que hacen andar un reloj u otra acción mecánica. 5. (*Mús.*) Movimiento, el compás o tiempo en que mejor efecto produce una composición musical; como *allegretto,* etc. 6. Cámara, evacuación del vientre, cagada.

mover ['mu:vər] [mu-var], s. Motor, movedor, móvil; el autor de una proposición o propuesta. **Prime mover,** principio motor, motor primordial; fuerza motriz; agencia de la naturaleza.

movie ['mu:vi:] [mu-vi], s. (*Fam.*) Película cinematográfica. **Movie star,** estrella de cine.

movies ['mu:vi:z] [mu-vis], s. pl. (*Fam.*) Cine, cinematógrafo.

moving ['mu:vɪŋ] [mu-vin], s. 1. Movimiento. 2. Motivo, impulso. -a. Patético, tierno, persuasivo, sensible, afectuoso, lastimero.

movingly ['mu:vɪŋlɪ] [mu-vin-li], adv. Patéticamente.

movingness ['mu:vɪŋnɪs] [mu-vin-nes], s. El poder de excitar los afectos del ánimo; ternura, persuasión, unción.

moving picture ['mu:vɪŋˌpɪktʃər] [mu-vin-pik-char], s. Película cinematográfica. -pl. Cipe, cinematógrafo.

moving theater ['mu:vɪŋˌθɪətər] [mu-vin-zia-tar], s. Cine.

mow [məʊ] [mou], s. Granero, hórreo, troj, cámara; henil, el sitio donde se guarda el heno. -va. Entrojar, encerar el heno, etc., en las trojes, paneras o graneros.

mow, va. (pp. MOWED y MOWN). 1. Guadañar. 2. Segar, cortar con prisa y violencia, o sin distinción.

mow, vn. Hacer muecas; burlarse de. -s. Mueca.

mowburn ['məʊbɜ:n] [mou-bern], vn. Calentarse o fermentar el grano o heno por no estar bien seco al tiempo de entrojarlo.

mower ['məʊər] [moua], s. Dallador, guadañero, guadaña; máquina de cortar hierba.

mowing ['məʊɪŋ] [mouin], s. 1. Siega. 2. Gesto, mueca. 3. (*Des.*) Habilidad. **Mowing-machine,** máquina para cortar la hierba, guadañadora.

mown ['məʊn] [moun], pp. irr. de MOW. Guadañado, cortado.

moxa ['məʊksə] [mouk-sa], s. (*Med.*) 1. Moxa, cilindro de algodón que se quema encima de la piel. 2. (*Bot.*) Moxa, ajenjo de la India oriental que queman sobre la piel después de seco para curar varias enfermedades.

mpg *Abreviatura de* **miles per gallon.**

mph *Abreviatura de* **miles per hour.**

MRP *Abreviatura de* **Manufacturer's Recommended Price,** precio recomendado por el fabricante.

Mrs(.) ['mɪsɪz] [mi-sis], s. *Abreviatura de* **Mistress,** señora.

Ms(s) ['mɪsɪz] [mi-sis], s. *Abreviatura de* **Miss** o **Mrs.**

MS-DOS [ˌem'esdɒs] [em-es-dos] s. *Abreviatura de* **Microsoft Disk Operating System.**

Mt (*Geol.*). *Abreviatura de* **Mount, Mountain.**

much [mʌtʃ] [mach], a. 1. Mucho, abundante, excesivo; largo de duración. -adv. 1. Mucho, excesivamente, en gran manera, con mucho. **As much,** tanto, tan, otro tanto. **As much as,** tanto como. **How much?,** ¿cuánto? **So much,** tanto. **So much the better,** tanto mejor. **So much the worse,** tanto peor. **Too much,** demasiado, excesivo. **Very much,** mucho, extremamente. **For as much as,** por cuanto. **As much more,** otro tanto más. 2. Casi, cuasi, poco más o menos. **It is much the same,** es o está casi lo mismo; poco más o menos lo mismo. 3. Muy. **He is much afflicted,** está muy afligido. 4. Muchas veces; por largo tiempo. -s. 1. Muchedumbre, copia, abundancia, multitud. 2. Cosa extraña o poco común. **To make much of,** festejar, tratar a uno con cariño y estimación, acariciarle, tenerle en mucho. **He is much of a gentleman,** es todo un caballero. **I am much of your opinion,** soy casi de la misma opinión que Ud. **We don't see much of each other,** nos vemos poco. **Much ado about nothing,** mucho jaleo para nada; mucho ruido y pocas nueces. **Much at one,** casi de igual valor o influencia. **Much about,** alrededor, por ahí. **Much of a muchness,** (*Fam.*) Casi lo mismo; poco más o menos lo mismo. **I couldn't make much of the film,** no pude seguir la película (*Fam.*). **I hardly know him much less his brother,** apenas lo conozco, y mucho menos a su hermano. **Much the biggest,** el más grande con mucho (by far). **We are much the same size,** tenemos más o menos la misma talla.

muchness ['mʌtʃnɪs] [mach-nes], s. Cantidad, y vulgarmente calidad.

muchwhat ['mʌtʃwɒt] [mach-uot], adv. Casi, poco más o menos.

mucid ['mju:sɪd] [miu-sid], a. Viscoso, mohoso, glutinoso; mucilaginoso.

mucidness ['mju:sɪdnɪs] [miu-sid-nes], s. (*Poco us.*) Viscosidad, mucosidad.

mucilage ['mju:lɪdʒ] [miu-si-lich], s. Mucílago.

mucilaginous [ˌmju:sɪ'lædʒɪnəs] [miu-si-li-yi-nos], a. Mucilaginoso, viscoso.

mucin ['mju:sɪn] [miu-sin], s. Mucina, sustancia mucilaginosa secretada por las membranas mucosas.

mucivorcus [ˌmju:'vɔ:kəs] [miu-si-vor-kos], a. Mucívoro, que se alimenta de mucosidades, de los jugos de plantas.

muck [mʌk] [mak], s. 1. Abono, el estiércol que se echa a las tierras para beneficiarlas. 2. Tierra vegetal, despojos vegetales corrompidos y mezclados con tierra. 3. Porquería, basura, cualquiera cosa baja, vil y asquerosa. 4. Dinero: en sentido despreciativo. **To run a muck,** atropellar por todo sin consideración. V. AMUCK. **Muck-fork,** horquilla para estiércol.

muck, va. Estercolar, echar estiércol en la tierra. **Muck about/around,** fastidiar, hacer tonterías, incordiar. **Muck in,** arrimar el hombro, compartir (*Fam.*). **Muck out,** limpiar. **Muck up,** ensuciar, manchar.

muckender ['mʌkəndər] [ma-kan-dar], s. Mocador, moquero, pañuelo para los mocos.

muckhill ['mʌkhɪl] [mak-jil], s. Estercolero.

muckiness ['mʌkɪnɪs] [ma-ki-nes], s. Suciedad, porquería, inmundicia.

mucking ['mʌkɪŋ] [ma-kin], *s.* El acto de abonar con estiércol.

muckle, *s.* V. MICKLE.

muckraking ['mʌkrækɪŋ] [mak-ra-kin], *s. m.* Periodismo amarillo.

muck-sweat ['mʌkswiːt] [mak-suit], *s. (Med.)* Sudor copioso.

muck-worm ['mʌkwɔːm] [mak-uorm], *s.* 1. Gusano de estercolero o muladar. 2. Cicatero, ruin, miserable, mezquino.

mucky ['mʌkɪ] [ma-ki], *a.* Puerco, sucio, asqueroso.

muccid ['mʌksɪd] [mak-sid], *a.* Mucoso, semejante a mucosidad.

mucor ['mʌkəʳ] [ma-kaʳ], *s.* 1. Moco, mucosidad de los animales. 2. Estado de lo que se halla enmohecido. 3. Nombre de un género de hongos.

mucous ['mʌkəs] [ma-kos], *a.* Mocoso, viscoso, glutinoso, pegajoso.

mucousness ['mʌkəsnɪs] [ma-kos-nes], *s.* Mucosidad, viscosidad.

mucro ['mʌkrə] [ma-kro], *s.* Punta.

mucronate, mucronated ['mʌkrəneɪt] [ma-kro-neit], *a.* Puntiagudo, mucronato.

mucus ['mjuːkəs] [miu-kos], *s.* 1. Mucosidad, sustancia parecida al mucílago vegetal, secretador por las membranas mucosas; mocos de las narices. 2. Mucosidad.

mud [mʌd] [mad], *s.* 1. Fango, limo, légamo del mar, de un estanque, de un charco, etc. 2. Cieno, lodo. 3. Barro, la masa que resulta de la unión de la tierra con el agua. **To stick in the mud,** atolarse, enfangarse; estar en un cenagal. **Mud bank,** banco de arena. **Mud-dauber,** pelopeo, matador de arañas, avispa que construye para sus larvas celdas de barro a las cuales lleva arañas u orugas para alimento de las larvas. **Mud-lighter,** gánguil, lancha de draga. **Mud-bath,** baño de cieno en ciertos manantiales medicinales, en que se sumergen los neumáticos hasta el cuello. **Mud-sucker,** somormujo, ave acuática. **Mud-volcano,** cono volcánico que arroja cieno. *(Mex.)* Hornito.

mud, *va.* 1. Encenagar, meter o meterse en cieno. 2. Enturbiar, ensuciar. **To throw mud at somebody,** poner a alguien por los suelos, enturbiar el nombre de alguien.

muddily ['mʌdɪlɪ] [ma-di-li], *adv.* Turbiamente.

muddiness ['mʌdɪnɪs] [ma-di-nes], *s.* 1. Turbiedad, suciedad. 2. Confusión de ideas.

muddle ['mʌdl] [ma-del], *va.* 1. Enturbiar. 2. Embriagar, atontar, entontecer, embotar. *-vn.* Estar algo atontado; estar confuso.

muddleheaded ['mʌdkhedɪd] [ma-del-je-did], *a.* Confuso, despistado (person).

muddy ['mʌdɪ] [ma-di], *a.* 1. Cenagoso, lodoso, sucio, enturbiado, turbio. 2. Grosero, compuesto de tierra o barro, impuro. 3. Tonto, estúpido, confuso.

muddy, *va.* 1. Enturbiar, ensuciar. 2. Entontecer, obscurecer, turbar.

muddy-headed ['mʌdɪhedɪd] [ma-di-je-did], *a.* Turbio o torpe de entendimiento.

mudguard ['mʌdɡɑːd] [mad-gard], *s.* Guardafango, guardabarros.

mudpack ['mʌdpæk] [mad-pak], *s. f.* Mascarilla de barro.

mud-scow ['mʌdskəʊ] [mad-skou], *s.* Pontón con que se limpia el río.

mudsill ['mʌdsɪl] [mad-sil], *s.* 1. Madero de construcción puesto inmediatamente sobre el suelo. 2. *(E. U.)* Persona de baja condición social.

mud-wall ['mʌdwɔːl] [mad-wol], *s.* Tapia, pared formada de tierra sola.

mud-walled ['mʌdwɔːld] [mad-uold], *a.* Tapiado, hecho de tapias.

mudwort ['mʌdwɔːt] [mad-uort], *s. (Bot.)* Limosela, nombre genérico de plantas. **Common mudwort,** limosela acuática.

muesli ['mjuːzlɪ] [mius-li], *s. m.* Muesli.

muff [mʌf] [maf], *s.* Manguito; estufilla.

muff, Acción poco diestra; en el juego de la pelota, falta, dejar escapar o caer la pelota en vez de cogerla. *-va.* Hacer algo poco diestramente; dejar escapar la pelota en vez de cogerla. **To muff a chance,** desperdiciar una oportunidad.

muffin ['mʌfɪn] [ma-fin], *s.* Mollete, bodigo, panecillo.

muffle ['mʌfl] [ma-fel], *s.* 1. *(Quím.)* Mufla, cubierta de barro que se pone encima de los hornillos, copelas, etc. 2. Horno de esmaltar, horno de arcilla para cocer la alfarería; también horno de copela.

muffle, *va.* 1. Embozar, encubrir el rostro y defenderlo del frío. 2. Vendar a uno los ojos. 3. Envolver, encubrir, ocultar, tapar, para disminuir el sonido. **To muffle a drum,** enfundar, enclutar un tambor. **Muffled oars,** remos cubiertos de tela o trapos para apagar su ruido. *-vn.* Hablar confusamente.

muffler ['mʌfləʳ] [ma-flaʳ], *s.* 1. Bufanda. 2. Sordina. 3. Silenciador (car).

mufti ['mʌftɪ] [maf-ti], *s.* Mufti, el sumo sacerdote de los mahometanos.

mug [mʌɡ] [mag], *s.* 1. Cubilete, vasito sin pie y con asa para beber; pichel. 2. (Bajo) La cara o la boca; mueca. **Mug up,** empollar. **Mug's game,** cosa de bobos.

mugger ['mʌɡəʳ] [ma-gaʳ], *s.* Atracador, asaltante.

mugging ['mʌɡɪŋ] [ma-guin], *s. m.* Asalto callejero, atraco.

muggy ['mʌɡɪ] [ma-gui], **mugish** ['mʌɡɪʃ] [ma-guish], *a.* Húmedo, caluroso y sofocante (del tiempo); húmedo y mohoso (v.g. el heno).

mug-house ['mʌɡhaʊs] [mag-jaus], *s. (Vulg.)* Cervecería, el sitio o casa donde se vende cerveza.

mugweed ['mʌɡwiːd] [mag-uid], *s. (Bot.)* Cuajaleche cruzado, una planta británica.

mugwort ['mʌɡwɔːt] [mag-uort], *s. (Bot.)* Artemisa o artemisa vulgar.

mugwump ['mʌɡwʌmp] [mag-vamp], *s. (Política de los E. U.)* Elector que de ordinario vota con un partido, pero que se reserva el derecho de votar con entera independencia, llegado el caso.

mulatto [mjuːˈlætəʊ] [miu-la-tou], *s.* Mulato, la persona que ha nacido de negra y blanco o al contrario.

mulberry ['mʌlberɪ] [mal-be-ri], *s.* Mora, el fruto de la morera. **Mulberry-tree,** morera o moral, el árbol que produce las moras.

mulch [mʌltʃ] [malch], *va.* Cubrir (las plantas, hierbas, etc.) con paja y estiércol. *-s.* El estiércol y la paja, que se echa alrededor de los tallos de las plantas para abrigar sus raíces.

mulct [mʌlkt] [malkt], *s.* Multa, pena pecuniaria.

mulct, *va.* Multar, cargar e imponer alguna pena pecuniaria.

mulctuary ['mʌlktjʊərɪ] [malk-tiua-ri], *a.* Lo que pertenece a multa.

mule [mjuːl] [miul], *s.* 1. Mulo, macho, mula, animal engendrado de caballo y burra o de burro y yegua. **She mule,** mula. 2. Una planta cualquiera proveniente de una semilla fecundada por el polen de otra especie, cualquier híbrido. 3. Telar que tira del hilo, lo pone tenso y lo tuerce en una sola operación. **Mule-jenny,** telar para tejer algodón. V. 3ª acep. **Mule-twist,** algodón tejido con el telar llamado «mule-jenny». **To be as stubborn as a mule,** ser terco como una mula.

muleteer [ˌmjuːlɪˈtɪəʳ] [miu-li-tiaʳ], **Mule-driver** ['mjuːldraɪvəʳ] [miul-drai-vaʳ], *s.* Mulero, muletero o mulatero; mozo de mulas.

muliebrity ['mjuːlɪbrɪtɪ] [miu-li-bri-ti], *s.* Las costumbres, carácter y demás cualidades propias de las mujeres.

mulier ['mjuːlɪəʳ] [miu-liaʳ], *s.* 1. *(Der. civil.)* Mujer casada. 2. *(For.)* El hijo que ha nacido después que sus padres contrajeron matrimonio, a distinción del que ha nacido anteriormente, de los mismos padres.

mulish ['mjuːlɪʃ] [miu-lish], *a.* Obstinado o terco como una mula.

mull [mʌl] [mal], *s.* 1. *(Ingl.)* Estado confuso, enredo, desorden. 2. Muselina, clara, tela delgada y suave de algodón.

mull, *s.* 1. *(Esco.)* Cabo, promontorio. 2. Tabaquera de cuerno.

mull, *va.* Calentar cualquier licor sazonándolo al mismo tiempo con sustancias aromáticas. *-vn.* 1. Afanarse mucho y efectuar poco.

mull, *va.* 1. Moler, desmenuzar, reducir a polvo. 2. Confundir, aturrullar.

muller ['mʌlə^r] [ma-la^r], *s.* 1. Moleta (de los pintores). 2. Una piedra que usan varios artífices para moler con la mano y reducir a polvo alguna cosa sobre otra piedra horizontal.

mullet ['mʌlɪt] [ma-lit], *s.* 1. *(Ict.)* Múgil, mújol. 2. Barbo de mar. 3. *(Her.)* Estrellita de espuela, espolín.

mulligrubs ['mʌlɪgrʌbz] [ma-li-grabs], *s.* 1. *(Vulg.)* Retortijón de tripas; mal humor. 2. Pasión ilíaca; cólico.

mullion ['mʌlɪən] [ma-lion], *s. (Arq.)* Columna o pie derecho que divide el bastidor de una ventana.

mullion, *va.* Dividir (una ventana) por medio de una columna o pie derecho.

mulse ['mʌlz] [mals], *s.* Clarea, bebida que se hace de vino cocido con miel o azúcar.

multangular [mʌl'tæŋjʊlə^r] [mal-tan-guiu-la^r], *a.* Polígono, lo que consta de muchos lados o muchos ángulos.

multangularly [mʌl'tæŋjʊləlɪ] [mal-tan-guiu-la-li], *adv.* En figura de polígono.

multangularness [mʌl'tæŋjʊlənɪs] [mal-tan-guiu-la-nes], *s.* La propiedad de tener un cuerpo muchos lados o muchos ángulos.

multicapsular [,mʌltɪ'kæpsjʊlə^r] [mal-ti-kap-siu-la^r], *a.* Repartido en muchas cápsulas o celdillas.

multicultural [,mʌltɪ'kʌtʃərəl] [mal-ti-kal-cha-ral], *a.* Multicultural.

multidentate [,mʌltɪ'denteɪt] [mal-ti-den-teit], *a.* Multidentado, provisto de muchos dientes.

multifarious [,mʌltɪ'feərɪəs] [mal-ti-fea-rios], *a.* 1. Multifario, vario, diverso, multiplicado, diferente. 2. *(Bot. y Zool.)* Dispuesto en varias filas o líneas verticales.

multifariousness [,mʌltɪ'feərɪəsnɪs] [mal-ti-fea-rios-nes], *s.* Diversidad; variedad, desemejanza, diferencia.

multifid, multifidious ['mʌltɪfɪd] [mal-ti-fid], *a.* Dividido en muchas .partes, abierto o hendido en muchos lóbulos o porciones.

multiflorous ['mʌltɪ'flɔrəs] [mal-ti-flo-rous], *a.* Multífloro, de muchas flores.

multiform [,mʌltɪ'færɪəs] [mal-ti-fa-rios], *a.* Multiforme.

multiformity [,mʌltɪ'fɔ:mɪtɪ] [mal-ti-for-mi-ti], *s.* Multiformidad, diversidad en las figuras, formas, cualidades o propiedades de una cosa.

multifunctional [,mʌltɪ'fʌŋkʃnəl] [mal-ti-fank-sho-nal], *a.* Multifuncional.

multigenerous [,mʌltɪ'dʒɪnərəs] [mal-ti-yi-ne-ros], *a.* Lo que es de muchos géneros.

multigraph ['mʌltɪgræf] [mal-ti-graf], *s.* Multígrafo.

multigym ['mʌltɪdʒɪm] [mal-ti-yim], *s. m.* Gimnasio múltiple.

multilateral [,mʌltɪ'lætərəl] [mal-ti-la-ti-ral], *a. (Geom.)* Multilátero, que consta de más de cuatro lados.

multilineal [,mʌltɪ'lɪnɪəl] [mal-ti-li-nial], *a.* Que tiene muchas líneas.

multilocular [,mʌltɪ'lɔkjuːlə^r] [mal-ti-lo-kiu-la^r], *a.* Multilocular, de muchas celdillas.

multimillionaire [,mʌltɪmɪljə'neə^r] [mal-ti-mi-lio-nea^r], *s.* Multimillonario.

multinodous [,mʌltɪ'nɒdəs] [mal-ti-no-dos], *a.* Nudoso, que tiene muchos nudos.

multinomial [,mʌltɪ'nəʊmɪəl] [mal-ti-nou-mial], *a.* 1. Lo que tiene muchos nombres. 2. Multinomio: dícese en álgebra de la cantidad que tiene muchos términos.

multiparous [,mʌltɪ'pærəs] [mal-ti-pa-ros], *a.* Multípara, la hembra que pare muchos hijos a la vez.

multipartite [,mʌltɪ'pɑːtɪt] [mal-ti-par-tit], *a.* Que consta de muchas partes.

multiped ['mʌltɪpɪd] [mal-ti-pid], *a.* Multípedo, que tiene muchas patas. *-s.* Ciempiés, escolopendra, animalillo articulado que tiene numerosas patas.

multiple ['mʌltɪpl] [mal-ti-pel], *a.* Múltiple, que contiene más de uno; repetido más de una vez. *-s.* Multíplice o múltiplo. **Multiple choice question,** pregunta de varias posibles respuestas (test). **Multiple sclerosis,** *(Med.)* Esclerosis múltiple.

multiplex ['mʌltɪ,pleks] [mal-ti-pleks], *a.* 1. Multíplice, que consta de muchas partes. 2. V. MULTIPLICATE, 2ª acep.

multipiable ['mʌltɪplaɪəbl] [mal-ti-plai-ei-bol], **Multiplicable** ['mʌltɪplɪkeɪbl] [mal-ti-pli-kei-bol], *a.* Multiplicable.

multipliableness ['mʌltɪplaɪəblnɪs] [mal-ti-plai-ei-bol-nes], *s.* La capacidad de ser multiplicado o la calidad de ser multiplicable.

multiplicand ['mʌltɪplɪkænd] [mal-ti-pli-kand], *s.* Multiplicando.

multiplicate ['mʌltɪplɪkeɪt] [mal-ti-pli-keit], *a.* 1. Multiplicado, aumentado en cantidad o en número. 2. *(Bot.)* Plegado en muchos pliegues.

multiplication [,mʌltɪplɪ'keɪʃən] [mal-ti-pli-kei-shon], *s.* 1. Multiplicación. 2. *(Arit.)* Multiplicación, la regla que enseña a multiplicar un número por otro.

multiplicative ['mʌltɪplɪkətɪv] [mal-ti-pli-ka-tiv], *a.* Multiplicador, multiplicativo.

multiplicator ['mʌltɪplɪkeɪtə^r] [mal-ti-pli-kei-ta^r], *s.* Multiplicador.

multiplicity [,mʌltɪ'plɪsɪtɪ] [mal-ti-pli-si-ti], *s.* Multiplicidad, muchedumbre.

multiplier ['mʌltɪplaɪə^r] [mal-ti-plaia^r], *s.* 1. Multiplicador. 2. Multiplicador, espiral plana de alambre conductor que sirve para aumentar el efecto de una corriente eléctrica sobre una aguja. 3. Máquina que sirve para multiplicar.

multiply ['mʌltɪplaɪ] [mal-ti-plai], *va.* 1. Multiplicar. 2. Multiplicar un número por otro. *-vn.* 1. Multiplicar o multiplicarse, aumentarse por medio de la generación. 2. Cundir, propagarse.

multiplying-glass ['mʌltɪplaɪɪŋglɑːs] [mal-ti-plain-glas], *s.* Disposición especial de espejos diminutos, que multiplica el número de las imágenes. **Multiplying-lens,** lente de muchas facetas, lente multiplicadora.

multipolar ['mʌltɪpəʊlə^r] [mal-ti-po-la^r], *a.* Multipolar, que tiene más de dos polos; se dice de ciertas celdillas de nervio y de aparatos eléctricos.

multipresence ['mʌltɪ,presns] [mal-ti-pre-sens], *s.* La facultad de hallarse presente en varios parajes a un mismo tiempo.

multisiliquous ['mʌltɪ,sɪlɪkwəs] [mal-ti-si-li-kuos], *a. (Bot.)* Multisilicuoso, que tiene muchas vainas.

multisonous ['mʌltɪsənəs] [mal-ti-so-nos], *a.* Que tiene muchos sonidos.

multi-stage rocket ['mʌltɪsteɪdʒ,rɒkɪt] [mal-ti-steich-ro-kit], *s. (Aer.)* Cohete de ignición múltiple.

multisyllable ['mʌltɪ,saɪləbl] [mal-ti-sai-la-bol], *s.* Multisílabo, palabra compuesta de más de tres sílabas. V. POLYSYLLABLE.

multitude ['mʌltɪtjuːd] [mal-ti-tiud], *s.* 1. Multitud, muchedumbre, gran número de personas o cosas juntas. 2. Muchedumbre, pueblo, vulgo, turba, el común de la gente.

multitudinous ['mʌltɪtjuːdɪnəs] [mal-ti-tiu-di-nos], *a.* Numeroso: muchos; varios.

multivalve ['mʌltɪvaːlv] [mal-ti-valv], *a.* Multivalvo; dícese de las conchas que resultan de la reunión de más de dos valvas. *-s.* Multivalva, género de conchas de muchas almejas.

multocular ['mʌltɒkjuːlə^r] [mal-to-kiu-la^r], *a.* Que tiene muchos ojos.

multure ['mʌltʃə^r] [mal-cha^r], *s.* 1. Maquila, la porción de grano que corresponde al molinero por la molienda; molienda, el grano que se ha molido de una vez. 2. Tanto por ciento que se paga al dueño de un pulverizador de minerales.

mum [mʌm] [mam], *inter.* ¡Chito! ¡chitón! ¡silencio! Interjección de que se usa para imponer silencio. *-s.* Cerveza muy fuerte de trigo. *-a.* Callado, silencioso.

mum, *va.* y *vn.* Enmascarar, enmascararse; disfrazarse.

mumble ['mʌmbl] [mam-bel], *vn.* 1. Gruñir, murmullar entre dientes mostrando disgusto. 2. Murmurar, decir alguna cosa entre dientes, muy quedo. 3. Farfullar, hablar precipitadamente. 4. Mascar o comer poco a poco y con los labios cerrados. *-va.* 1. Musitar, barbotar, hablar entre dientes; barbullar. 2. Agarrar con la boca.

mumbler ['mʌmblər] [mam-blar], *s.* Farfulla, farfullador; gruñidor.

mumbling ['mʌmblɪŋ] [mam-blin], *s.* El acto de farfullar; mascadura con los labios cerrados.

mumblingly ['mʌmblɪŋlɪ] [mam-blin-li], *adv.* Con pronunciación mal articulada; farfullando.

mumbo jumbo ['mʌmbəʊ'dʒʌmbəʊ] [mam-bou-yam-bou], *s. m.* Galimatías.

mum-chance ['mʌmtʃɑːns] [mam-chans], *s.* 1. Silencio. 2. *(Des.)* Un juego de dados.

mummer ['mʌmər] [ma-mar], *s.* Máscara, el que está enmascarado o disfrazado.

mummery ['mʌmərɪ] [ma-ma-ri], **mumming** ['mʌmɪŋ] [ma-min], *s.* Momería, mojiganga, trampantojo, disfraz.

mummification ['mʌmɪfaɪ'keɪʃən] [ma-mi-fai-kei-shon], *s.* Momificación, conversión en momia.

mummiform ['mʌmɪfɔːm] [ma-mi-form], *a.* Momiforme, que se parece a una momia.

mummify ['mʌmɪfaɪ] [ma-mi-fai], *va.* Momificar, convertir en momia un cadáver; embalsamar; preservar secando.

mummy ['mʌmɪ] [ma-mi], *s.* 1. Momia, cuerpo embalsamado por los egipcios de un modo particular. **To beat to a mummy,** moler a palos. 2. Especie de cera o betún que usan los jardineros para plantar o injertar árboles.

mump [mʌmp] [mamp], *va.* 1. Mordiscar, morder o mascar. 2. Farfullar, hablar precipitadamente. 3. *(Vulg.)* Mendigar, pedir limosna de puerta en puerta.

mumper ['mʌmpər] [mam-par], *s.* Mendigo.

mumping ['mʌmpɪŋ] [mam-pin], *s.* El acto de mascar con la boca cerrada; mendiguez.

mumpish ['mʌmpɪʃ] [mam-pish], *a.* Moroso, intratable, malcontento, malhumorado.

mumpishness ['mʌmpɪʃnɪs] [mam-pish-nes], *s.* Ceño, morosidad; insociablilidad.

mumps ['mʌmpz] [mamps], *s.* 1. Tumores glandulosos del cuello; paperas, parótidas. 2. (Raro) Murria, mal humor.

munch ['mʌntʃ] [manch], *va.* Mascar despacio y con ruido; mascar a dos carrillos.

muncher ['mʌntʃər] [man-char], *s.* Tragón, comilón.

mundane ['mʌndeɪn] [man-dein], *a.* Mundano, rutinario.

mundic ['mʌndɪk] [man-dik], *s.* Especie de marquesita que se halla en las minas de estaño.

mundify ['mʌndɪfaɪ] [man-di-fai], *va.* Mundificar, limpiar, purgar, purificar.

mundivagant ['mʌndɪ'vəgənt] [man-di-va-gant], *a.* Vagamundo o vagabundo.

munerary ['mʌnərərɪ] [ma-ne-ra-ri], *a. (Poco us.)* De la naturaleza de un regalo o dádiva.

mungoose ['mʌnguːz] [man-gus], *s. V.* MONGOOSE.

mungrel ['mʌngrəl] [man-grel], *a.* y *s. V.* MONGREL.

municipal [mjuː'nɪsɪpəl] [miu-ni-si-pal], *a.* Municipal, lo que toca o pertenece a los derechos o costumbres de un pueblo o país.

municipality [mjuː'nɪsɪpæltɪ] [miu-ni-si-pal-ti], *s.* El partido o distrito de la jurisdicción del ayuntamiento de un pueblo.

muniferous [mjuː'nɪfərəs] [miu-ni-fe-ros], *a.* Dadivoso, liberal, generoso.

munificence [mjuː'nɪfɪsns] [miu-ni-fi-sens], *s.* Munificencia, liberalidad, generosidad, largueza.

munificent [mjuː'nɪfɪsnt] [miu-ni-fi-sent], *a.* Munífico, liberal, generoso.

munificently [mjuː'nɪfɪsntlɪ] [miu-ni-fi-sent-li], *adv.* Liberalmente, muníficamente.

muniment ['mjuːnɪmənt] [miu-ni-ni-ment], *s.* 1. Fortaleza; apoyo, defensa. 2. Títulos, documentos, papeles o escritos que se guardan en un archivo.

munition [mjuː'nɪʃən] [miu-ni-shon], *s.* 1. Fortificación, fortaleza. 2. Municiones, los pertrechos y bastimentos necesarios para la manutención de un ejército o plaza. **Munition-bread,** plan de munición. **Munition-ship,** navío almacén.

munitions [mjuː'nɪʃənz] [miu-ni-shons], *s. pl.* Municiones.

munnion ['mjuːnɪən] [miu-nion], *s. (Arq. Des.) V.* MULLION.

muntjack, muntjak [mʌnt'dʒæk] [mant-yakt], *s.* Animal de la familia del ciervo que se encuentra en la isla de Java.

murage ['mjʊərɪdʒ] [miua-ridch], *s.* Un tributo que antiguamente se pagaba para el reparo de los muros.

mural ['mjʊərəl] [miua-ral], *a.* **Mural,** lo que se refiere a los muros o paredes; apoyado en una pared. 2. Que se asemeja a una pared; escarpado, vertical. **Mural crown,** corona mural. **Mural circle,** *(Ast.)* Círculo mural. *V.* CIRCLE. **Mural tablet,** tablilla fijada en una pared.

murc [mɜːk] [merk], *s.* Orujo, hollejo de la uva y otras frutas después de exprimidas.

murder ['mɜːdər] [mer-dar], *s.* Asesinato, homicidio con premeditación.

murder, *va.* 1. Asesinar, matar alevosamente. 2. *(Fig.)* Mutilar, desfigurar, echar a perder, arruinar. 3. Destruir, exterminar, acabar con alguien o algo.

murderer ['mɜːdərər] [mer-da-rar], *s.* Asesino.

murderess ['mɜːdərɪs] [mer-da-res], *sf.* La mujer que comete un asesinato.

murderous ['mɜːdərəs] [mer-da-ros], *a.* 1. Homicida, matador. 2. Sanguinario, cruel, bárbaro: asesino.

murderously ['mɜːdərəslɪ] [mer-da-ros-li], *adv.* Sanguinariamente.

mure ['mjuːr] [miur], *va.* Murar, cercar con murallas.

murex ['mjuːrɪks] [miu-riks], *s. (Zool.)* Múrice, nombre genérico de unos caracoles de mar.

muriate ['mjuːrɪeɪt] [miu-rieit], *s.* Muriato.

muriatic ['mjuːrɪətɪk] [miu-ria-tik], *a.* Muriático; hidroclórico; nombre antiguo.

muricate o muricated ['mjuːrɪkeɪt] [miu-ri-keit], *a.* Punzante, espinoso.

muricide ['mjuːrɪsaɪd] [miu-ri-said], *s.* Matador de ratones.

muridae ['mjuːrɪdiː] [miu-ri-di], *s. pl.* Múridos, familia del orden de los roedores.

muriform ['mjuːrɪfɔːm] [miu-ri-form], *a. (Bot.)* Dispuesto del mismo modo que los ladrillos de un muro o papel; dícese de las celdillas de las plantas.

murk [mɜːk] [merk], *a. V.* MURKY. *-s.* 1. *(Ant.)* Oscuridad, lobreguez. 2. *V.* MURC.

murky ['mɜːkɪ] [mer-ki], *a.* Obscuro, lóbrego.

murmur ['mɜːmər] [mar-mar], *s.* 1. Murmullo, murmurio, susurro. 2. Murmullo, rumor. 3. Murmuración, queja, descontento.

murmur, *vn.* 1. Murmurar, susurrar, hablando de arroyos, hojas, abejas, etc. En este último sentido se usa con *at* delante de cosas, y *against* delante de personas. **Murmur not at your sickness,** no te quejes de tu enfermedad. **Murmur not against government,** no te quejes del gobierno.

murmurer ['mɜːmərər] [mar-ma-rar], *s.* Gruñidor, murmurador.

murmuring ['mɜːmərɪŋ] [mar-ma-rin], *s.* Murmullo; murmuración.

murmuringly ['mɜːmərɪŋlɪ] [mar-ma-rin-li], *adv.* Con murmullo; con queja.

murrain ['məreɪn] [ma-rein], *s.* Morriña, enfermedad epidémica que causa mucha mortandad en el ganado.

murre, murr ['mɜːʳ] [meʳ], *s.* 1. Ave marina, particularmente la uria. 2. Ave del género Alca. *V.* AUK.

murrey ['mɜːrɪ] [me-ri], *a.* Morado, color mezcla de rojo y negro.

murther, *s. V.* MURDER.

musa ['mjuːsə] [miu-sa], *s.* Nombre latino del bananero o plátano y de otras plantas musáceas.

MusBac *Abreviatura de* **Bachelor of Music.**

muscadel [ˌmʌskəˈdel] [mas-ka-del], **muscat** ['mʌskæt] [mas-kat], **muscatel** [ˌmʌskəˈtel] [mas-ka-tel], *s.* Moscatel especie de uva, de vino y de pera dulces.

muscadine [ˌmʌskəˈdiːn] [mas-ka-din], *s. (E. U.)* La vid silvestre de los Estados Unidos del Sur.

muscardine [ˌmʌskəˈdiːn] [mas-ka-din], *s.* Muscardina, enfermedad de los gusanos de seda.

muscle ['mʌsl] [ma-sel], *s.* 1. Músculo. 2. La fuerza de los músculos. 3. *V.* MUSSEL.

muscle-bound ['mʌslbaʊnd] [ma-sel-baund], *a.* Con los músculos rígidos (debido a excesiva actividad en los deportes).

muscoid ['mʌskɔɪd] [mas-koid], *a.* Parecido al musgo. -*s.* Planta que se asemeja al musgo.

muscosity ['mʌskəsɪtɪ] [mas-ko-si-ti], *s.* El estado de lo que se halla cubierto de moho o de musgo.

muscovado [ˌmʌskəˈveɪdəʊ] [mas-ko-vei-dou], *s.* Mascabado.

Muscovite ['mʌskəvaɪt] [mas-ko-vait], *a.* Moscovita, (of Moscow).

muscovy ['mʌskəvɪ] [mas-ko-vi], *s.* Anade americano mayor que el ánade ordinario. Se domestica mucho.

muscular ['mʌskjʊləʳ] [mas-kiu-laʳ], *a.* 1. Muscular. 2. Poderoso, vigoroso. **Muscular dystrophy,** distrofia muscular.

muscularity ['mʌskjʊˈlærɪtɪ] [mas-kiu-la-ri-ti], *s.* El estado de lo que tiene músculos.

musculature ['mʌskjʊkətʃəʳ] [mas-kiu-la-chaʳ], *s.* Musculatura, el conjunto o la disposición de los músculos.

MusDoc *Abreviatura de* **Doctor of Music.**

muse [mjuːz] [mius], *s.* 1. Musa, nombre de las nueve deidades del Parnaso. 2. Meditación profunda, atención intensa. 3. Musa. 4. Senda de liebres o conejos.

muse, *vn.* 1. Meditar, aplicar el pensamiento con intensidad a la consideración de alguna cosa, pensar o reflexionar profundamente. 2. Pasmarse, quedar suspenso o admirado. 3. Distraerse, dejarse llevar de la fantasía; estar meditando o ideando; estar distraído o pensativo.

museful ['mjuːzfʊl] [mius-ful], *a.* Cogitabundo, muy pensativo, muy distraído.

museless ['mjuːzlɪs] [mius-les], *a.* Que es insensible a los halagos de la poesía.

muser ['mjuːzəʳ] [miu-saʳ], *s.* El que está muy pensativo y absorto.

muset ['mjuːzɪt] [miu-sit], *s.* Senda de conejos, y de la caza en general.

museum [mjuːˈzɪəm] [miu-siom], *s.* Museo, gabinete de historia natural, de obras de arte, de las de la antigüedad o de curiosidades instructivas; y el edificio que contiene dicha colección.

mush [mʌʃ] [mash], *s. (E. U.)* 1. Potaje espeso o pudín que se hace cociendo harina de maíz en agua o leche. 2. Una cosa cualquiera blanda y mollar. 3. Mineral de hierro de primera calidad.

mushroom ['mʌʃrʊm] [mash-rum], *s.* 1. *(Bot.)* Seta, hongo, champiñón. 2. Persona que surge de la noche a la mañana. -*vn.* Crecer rápidamente, surgir de repente.

mushy ['mʌʃɪ] [ma-shi], *a.* Mollar, pulposo.

music ['mjuːzɪk] [miu-sik], *s.* 1. Música, el arte de combinar los sonidos armoniosos de la voz humana, de los instrumentos, o de una y otros, que comprende la melodía y la armonía. 2. Composición musical. 3. Sonido acorde y modulado o sucesión de dichos sonidos. 4. *(Zool.)* Estridor de varios insectos. **Music of the spheres,** la armonía de las esferas celestes que según la teoría de Platón podían oír sólo los dioses. **Music-book,** libro de música; libro o cuaderno que contiene trozos de música. **Music-box** o **musical box,** caja de música. **Music-hall,** salón de conciertos. **Music-stand,** (a) Pupitre para papeles de música. (b) Tablado para una orquesta. **Music-stool,** taburete o banqueta de piano. **Music-rack,** atril para música.

musical ['mjuːzɪkəl] [miu-si-kal], *a.* 1. Musical, que pertenece a la música. 2. Armonioso, melodioso.

musical comedy ['mjuːzɪkəlˌkʌmɪdɪ] [miu-si-kal-ko-mi-di], *s.* Comedia o revista musical.

musicale [ˌmjuːzɪˈkɑːl] [miu-si-kal], *s.* Velada musical.

musically ['mjuːzɪkəlɪ] [miu-si-ka-li], *adv.* Con armonía y consonancia.

musicalness ['mjuːzɪkəlnɪs] [miu-si-kal-nes], *s.* Armonía, melodía.

musician [mjuːˈzɪʃən] [miu-si-shan], *s.* Músico.

music-master ['mjuːzɪkˌmɑːstəʳ] [miu-sik-mas-taʳ], *s.* Maestro de música.

musing ['mjuːzɪŋ] [miu-sin], *a.* Contemplativo, pensativo, absorto en la meditación. -*s.* Reflexión profunda, meditación, ensueño.

musk [mʌsk] [mask], *s.* 1. Musco, almizcle, sustancia muy odorífera que se saca de la bolsa que el almizclero tiene en el vientre. 2. *(Bot.)* Almizcleña. 3. El olor de almizcle o una sustancia de parecido olor. 4. *V.* **Musk-deer, musk-apple,** camuesa o manzana almizcleña. **Musk-cat,** desmán. *V.* CIVET. **Musk-cherry,** *(Bot.)* Cereza almizcleña. **Musk-deer,** almizclero, animal rumiante muy parecido al corzo. Habita en casi toda el Asia. **Musk-grape,** moscatel. **Musk-pear,** mosqueruela, pera amizcleña. **Musk-rose,** rosa amizcleña. **Musk-seed,** grano de ambarilla. **Musk-thistle,** *(Bot.)* Cardo.

musk, *va.* Almizclar, perfumar con almizcle.

musked ['mʌskɪd] [mas-kid], *a.* Almizclado.

musket ['mʌskɪt] [mas-kit], *s.* 1. Mosquete. 2. Gavilán macho.

musketeer ['mʌskɪtɪəʳ] [mas-ki-tiaʳ], *s.* Mosquetero, el soldado que sirve con mosquete.

musketoon ['mʌskɪtuːn] [mas-ki-tun], *s.* Trabuco, una especie de escopeta que tiene la boca muy ancha.

muskiness ['mʌskɪnɪs] [mas-ki-nes], *s.* Olor de almizcle.

muskmelon ['mʌskmelən] [mask-me-lon], *s.* Melón almizcleño, muy fragante. *(Prov. Esp.)* Melón de Castilla.

muskrat ['mʌskræt] [mask-rat], *s.* Rata almizclada o almizclera, especie de roedor americano que se parece a la rata y que despide un olor como el del almizcle. Su piel es muy estimada para abrigos.

musky ['mʌskɪ] [mas-ki], *a.* Almizcleño, lo que huele a almizcle; almizclado.

muslim, *s. V.* MOSLEM.

muslin ['mʌslɪn] [mas-lin], *s.* 1. Muselina, tela fina hecha de algodón, llamada también bengala. 2. Tela de algodón propia para ropa interior y sábanas. -*a.* Hecho de muselina.

musquash ['mʌskwɑːʃ] [mas-kuash], *s.* Almizclera. *V.* MUSKRAT.

musqueteer, *s. V.* MUSKETEER.

muss [mʌs] [mas], *s.* 1. (Fam. E. U.) Estado de desorden, confusión. 2. *(Vulg.)* Arrebatiña, sarracina, riña. -*va. (Fam. E. U.)* 1. Poner en confusión, desarreglar, arrugar. 2. Ensuciar. *V.* MESS.

mussel ['mʌsl] [ma-sel], *s.* Mejillón, pequeño marisco comestible.

mussing ['mʌsɪŋ] [ma-sin], *s.* 1. Manoseo. 2. Desarreglo.

mussulman ['mjuːsəlmən] [miu-sul-man], *s.* Musulmán.

must [mʌst] [mast], *v. imp.* Deber; ser o estar obligado o precisado; ser preciso, ser menester, ser necesario, convenir, haber de hacerse alguna cosa. **He must have done it already,** él debe haberlo hecho ya. **It must be,** debe ser. **I must go and see it,** es preciso que yo vaya a verlo. **You must take the air oftener,** debe Ud. de tomar el aire más a menudo. **Do it if you must,** hazlo si es necesario. **You must have seen her,** debes haberla visto.

must, *s.* 1. Mosto, el zumo exprimido de la uva antes de hacerse vino. 2. La pulpa de patatas preparada para la fermentación.

must, *s.* V. MUSTINESS.

must, *va.* Enmohecer. *-vn.* Enmohecerse.

mustache ['mʌstæʃ] [mas-tash], *s.* 1. Mostachos, bigotes. 2. Mono llamado cercopiteco que habita en el oeste de África. 3. Soldado.

mustang ['mʌstæŋ] [mas-tang], *s.* Caballo medio salvaje de las llanuras americanas, de raza española.

mustard ['mʌstəd] [mas-tard], *s.* Mostaza. **Mustard gas,** gas de mostaza. **Mustard plaster,** cataplasma de mostaza. **Mustar-pot,** mostacera, salsera para la mostaza.

musteline, musteloid ['mʌstəliːn] [mas-ta-lin], *a.* Mustelino, parecido a la comadreja.

muster ['mʌstəʳ] [mas-taʳ], *vn.* (Mil.) Juntarse o unirse para formar un ejército; pasar lista. *-va.* 1. (Mil.) Pasar revista de tropas. 2. Agregar, congregar; recobrar o mostrar (courage).

muster, *s.* (Mil.) Revista; reseña. **To pass muster,** pasar revista; valer algo o servir de algo, ser aceptado. **Such excuses will not pass muster with God,** semejantes disculpas nada valdrán para con Dios.

muster-book ['mʌstəbʊk] [mas-ta-buk], *s.* Libro de revistas.

muster-master ['mʌstəˌmɑːstəʳ] [mas-ta-mas-taʳ], *s.* Comisario de revistas.

muster-roll ['mʌstərɒl] [mas-ta-rol], *s.* 1. Matrícula de revista. 2. (Mar.) Rol de la tripulación.

mustily ['mʌstɪlɪ] [mas-ti-li], *adv.* Con moho.

mustiness ['mʌstɪnɪs] [mas-ti-nes], *s.* Moho.

musty ['mʌstɪ] [mas-ti], *a.* 1. Mohoso, enmohecido. 2. Añejo, añejado. 3. Mustio, triste.

mutability [ˌmjuːtəˈbɪlɪtɪ] [miu-ta-bi-li-ti], *s.* Mutabilidad, inconstancia, instabilidad.

mutable ['mjuːtəbl] [miu-ta-bol], *a.* Mudable, alterable, inconstante, instable.

mutableness ['mjuːtəblnɪs] [miu-ta-bol-nes], *s.* Mutabilidad, inconstancia.

mutably ['mjuːtəblɪ] [miu-ta-bli], *adv.* Instablemente.

mutation [mjuːˈteɪʃən] [miu-tei-shon], *s.* Mudanza, alteración; mutación.

mutch ['mʌtʃ] [mach], *s.* (Esco.) Gorra con muchos pliegues, para mujer.

mute [mjuːt] [miut], *a.* 1. Mudo, silencioso, que no habla; en derecho, que se niega a responder ante la justicia. 2. Mudo, privado de la facultad de hablar. 3. (Gram.) Mudo, que no se pronuncia. *-s.* 1. Mudo, el que no puede hablar. 2. Letra muda. 3. (Mús.) Sordina, tablita de madera que se pone sobre los puentecillos de los instrumentos de cuerda para ensordecerlos.

mute, *vn.* (Des. o Prov.) Tullir, arrojar las aves los excrementos.

muted ['mjuːtɪd] [miu-tid], *a.* 1. Callado, silencioso. 2. Sordo (noise).

mutely ['mjuːtɪlɪ] [miu-ti-li], *adv.* Mudamente, sin hablar palabra.

muteness ['mjuːtnɪs] [miu-ti-nes], *s.* Silencio, aversión a hablar.

mutilate ['mjuːtɪleɪt] [miu-ti-leit], *va.* 1. Mutilar. 2. Mutilar, cortar o separar una parte esencial.

mutilation [ˌmjuːtɪˈleɪʃən] [miu-ti-lei-shon], *s.* Mutilación.

mutilator ['mjuːtɪleɪtəʳ] [miu-ti-lei-taʳ], *s.* Mutilador.

mutineer [ˌmjuːtɪˈnɪəʳ] [miu-ti-niaʳ], *s.* Amotinador, amotinado, sedicioso.

muting ['mjuːtɪŋ] [miu-tin], *s.* 1. Acción de poner sordina a un instrumento de música. 2. (Des.) Tullidura, el estiércol de ave.

mutinous ['mjuːtɪnəs] [miu-ti-nos], *a.* Amotinado, sedicioso, turbulento, faccioso.

mutinously ['mjuːtɪnəslɪ] [miu-ti-nos-li], *adv.* Amotinadamente.

mutinousness ['mjuːtɪnəsnɪs] [miu-ti-nos-nes], *s.* Amotinamiento, sedición, rebelión.

mutiny ['mjuːtɪnɪ] [miu-ti-ni], *vn.* Amotinarse, rebelarse.

mutiny, *s.* 1. Motín, amotinamiento, insurrección de soldados o de marineros contra sus jefes. 2. (Gran Bret.) Rebelión, sedición. 3. *vi.* Amotinarse, sublevarse.

mutism ['mjuːtɪzəm] [miu-ti-sem], *s.* Mudez, impedimiento en el habla, imposibilidad de hablar.

mutt [mʌt] [mat], *s.* 1. Bobo, necio (fam). 2. Chucho (EU).

mutter ['mʌtəʳ] [ma-taʳ], *vn.* 1. Pronunciar palabras en voz baja y con la boca casi cerrada, o con tono de mal humor o de queja. 2. Gruñir, refunfuñar, rezongar, murmurar. *-va.* Musitar, hablar entre dientes, hablar en voz baja e indistinta.

mutter, *s.* 1. Murmuración, queja, regañamiento. 2. El acto de musitar o hablar entre dientes.

mutterer ['mʌtərəʳ] [ma-ta-raʳ], *s.* Rezongador, gruñón.

muttering ['mʌtərɪŋ] [ma-ta-rin], *s.* Refunfuño.

mutteringly ['mʌtərɪŋlɪ] [ma-ta-rin-li], *adv.* En voz baja, inarticuladamente.

mutton ['mʌtn] [ma-ton], *s.* 1. Carnero, la carne del animal así llamado. 2. (Fest.) Carnero, el mismo animal.

mutton-broth ['mʌtn'brɒθ] [ma-ton-broz], *s.* Caldo de carnero.

mutton-chop ['mʌtnt'ʃɒp] [ma-ton-chop], *s.* Costilla de carnero, chuleta.

mutton-pie ['mʌtn'paɪ] [ma-ton-pai], *s.* Empanada de carnero.

mutual ['mjuːtkʊəl] [miu-chual], *a.* Mutuo, recíproco. **Mutal aid,** apoyo mutuo, ayuda mutua. **Mutual aid association.** 1. Asociación de ayuda mutua. 2. Mutualidad.

mutuality [ˌmjuːtjʊˈælɪtɪ] [miu-chua-li-ti], *s.* Reciprocidad, reciprocación.

mutually ['mjuːtkʊəlɪ] [miu-chua-li], *adv.* Mutuamente, recíprocamente.

muzzle ['mʌzl] [ma-sel], *s.* 1. Boca, entrada o abertura de alguna cosa. 2. Bozal, frenillo. 3. Boca de una persona, en desprecio; hocico, jeta de los animales. **Muzzle-loader,** escopeta o cañón, que se carga por la boca; lo opuesto a *breech-loader.* **Muzzle-loading,** *a.* que se carga por la boca. **Muzzle-moulding,** adornos de las bocas de los cañones. **Muzzle-ring,** anillo de las bocas de los cañones. **Muzzle-velocity,** velocidad inicial.

muzzle, *va.* 1. Embozar, abozalar, poner bozal a algún animal. 2. Imponer silencio, impedir que uno publique o arengue. 3. Se aplica figuradamente a las cosas con la significación de impedir que una cosa haga daño. *-vn.* Acercar el hocico los animales o ponerlo cerca de algo para oler.

muzzy ['mʌzɪ] [ma-si], *a.* (Vulg.) Distraído, olvidadizo, enajenado, descuidado, negligente; borracho.

MVP *Abreviatura de* **Most Valuable Player** (EU).

MW *Abreviatura de* **Medium Wave,** onda media (Radio).

my [maɪ] [mai], *adj. posses. y pron.* Caso posesivo o genitivo de *I,* yo; mi, mis, lo que es mío o me pertenece. **My house,** mi casa; **my houses,** mis casas. **My children,** mis hijos. **My own,** mío propio. **My own book,** mi propio libro. *Cf.* MINE.

myalgic [maɪˈældʒɪk] [mai-al-yik], *a.* Miálgico.

mycelium [maɪˈsiːlɪəm] [mai-se-liom], *s.* (Bot.) Micelión.

mycology [maɪˈkɒlədʒɪ] [mai-ko-lo-yi], *s.* Micetología, micología, tratado sobre los hongos.

myocarditis [ˌmaɪəkɑːˈdaɪtɪs] [maio-kar-dai-tis], *s.* (Med.) Miocarditis.

myocardium [ˌmaɪəˈkɑːdɪəm] [maio-kar-diom], *s.* Miocardio.

myography ['maɪəʊgræfɪ] [maiou-gra-fi], **myology** ['maɪʲɒlədʒɪ] [maio-lo-yi], *s.* Miografía o miología, descripción científica de los músculos.

myopathy ['maɪəpəθɪ] [mai-o-pa-zi], *s.* Enfermedad de los músculos.

myope ['maɪəʊp] [maioup], **myops** ['maɪəʊpz] [maioups], *s.* Miope, el que es corto de vista.

myopia, myopy ['maɪʲəʊpɪə] [mai-oupia], *s.* Miopía, cortedad de vista.

myriad ['mɪrɪəd] [mi-riad], *s.* 1. El número de diez mil entre los anticuarios. 2. Millares, se usa proverbialmente para expresar un gran número.

myosotis ['maɪəsətɪs] [maio-so-tis], *s.* Miosotis o miosótide.

myriarch ['mɪrɪɑːk] [mi-riark], *s.* El jefe de diez mil hombres.

myrmidon ['mɜːmɪdən] [mer-mi-don], *s.* Esbirro, rufián.

myrobalan ['mɑɪrəʊ'bælən] [mai-rou-ba-lan], *s.* Mirabolanos, especie de fruta parecida al dátil.

myropolist ['maɪrəpəlɪst] [mai-ro-po-list], *s.* Vendedor de ungüentos y perfumes.

myrrh ['mɜːʳ] [meʳ], *s.* Mirra, goma resinosa.

myrrhic ['mɜːrɪk] [me-rik], *a.* Mirrado, perteneciente a la mirra.

myrrhin ['mɜːrɪn] [me-rin], *s.* Principio resinoso contenido en la mirra.

myrtiform ['mɜːtɪfɔːm] [mer-ti-form], *a.* Mirtiforme, en figura de bayas de mirto.

myrtle ['mɜːrtl] [mer-tel], *s. (Bot.)* Mirto, arrayán.

myrtle-berry ['mɜːrtlˌberɪ] [mer-tel-be-ri], *s.* Murtón, la baya o fruto del mirto.

myself [maɪ'self] [mai-self], *pron.* Yo mismo; me, a mí, mí mismo. **I could not direct myself,** no podía dirigirme a mí mismo.

mystagogical ['mɪstə'gədʒɪkəl] [mis-ta-go-chi-kal], *a.* Lo que pertenece al intérprete de los misterios de la religión.

mystagogue ['mɪstəgəg] [mis-ta-gog], *s.* Mistagoga, sacerdote griego.

mysterious [mɪs'tɪərɪəs] [mis-tia-rios], **mysterial** [mɪs'tɪərɪəl] [mis-tia-rial], *a.* 1. Misterioso, impenetrable al entendimiento. 2. Misterioso, el que hace misterio de alguna cosa.

mysteriously [mɪs'tɪərɪəslɪ] [mis-tia-rios-li], *adv.* Misteriosamente.

mysteriousness [mɪs'tɪərɪəsnɪs] [mis-tia-rios-nes], *s.* 1. Impenetrabilidad de la cosas sagradas. 2. El acto de hacer misterio de alguna cosa.

mystery ['mɪstərɪ] [mis-te-ri], *s.* 1. Misterio: se dice de los de la religión. 2. Misterio, lo que está oculto y es muy difícil de comprender. 3. Enigma. 4. Autos sacramentales. 5. *(Ant.)* Oficio, profesión, ejercicio.

mystic, mystical ['mɪstɪkəl] [mis-ti-kal], *a.* Místico, misterioso, emblemático.

mystic ['mɪstɪk] [mis-tik], *s.* Místico, el que pretende recibir inspiración divina directa; partidario del misticismo.

mystically ['mɪstɪkəlɪ] [mis-ti-ka-li], *adv.* Místicamente, en sentido místico.

mysticalness ['mɪstɪkəlnɪs] [mis-ti-kal-nes], *s.* Mística, calidad de místico.

mysticism ['mɪstɪsɪzəm] [mis-ti-si-zem], *s.* 1. Misticismo, calidad de místico. 2. Misticismo, doctrina de los místicos que pretenden estar en relación directa con la divinidad.

mystification ['mɪstɪfaɪ'keɪʃən] [mis-ti-fai-kei-shon], *s.* El acto de hacer obscura una cosa; el de desconcertar intencionalmente a alguien.

mystify ['mɪstɪfaɪ] [mis-ti-fai], *va.* 1. Confundir intencionalmente, desconcertar a una persona. 2. Hacer obscuro, o tratar algo obscuramente.

myth [mɪθ] [miz], *s.* Mito, fábula, ficción alegórica, principalmente en asuntos religiosos.

mythical ['mɪθɪkəl] [mi-zi-kal], *a.* Mítico; fabuloso, imaginario.

mythological [ˌmɪθəʊ'lɒdʒɪkəl] [mi-zo-lo-yi-kal], *a.* Mitológico, relativo a la mitología.

mythologically [ˌmɪθəʊ'lɒdʒɪkəlɪ] [mi-zo-lo-yi-ka-li], *adv.* Mitológicamente.

mythologist [ˌmɪθəʊ'lɒdʒɪst] [mi-zo-lo-yist], *s.* Mitologista, el autor de una obra mitológica; el versado en mitología.

mythology [mɪ'θɒlədʒɪ] [mi-zo-lo-yi], *s.* 1. Mitología, la historia de los dioses y héroes fabulosos del gentilismo. 2. Estudio crítico de los diversos mitos y religiones.

myxomycetes [ˌmɪksəʊmaɪ'sɪtɪs] [mik-sou-mai-si-tis], *s. pl.* Mixomicetes, seres considerados ya como animales, ya como plantas, parecidos a los hongos microscópicos.

N

n [en] [en]. Letra décimacuarta del alfabeto inglés. Se pronuncia como en español, aunque en general un poco más fuerte, excepto delante de la *g*, pues en este caso ambas letras pierden algo de su fuerza. -La *n* final es muda cuando la precede una *m* o una *l*. -Al principio de las voces o sílabas las únicas consonantes que pueden seguirla o precederla inmediatamente son la *g, k,* y *s*, como en *gnaw, know, snow.*

nab [næb].[nab], *va. (Fam.)* Prender o coger de repente, atrapar.

nabob ['neɪbɒb] [nei-bob], *s.* 1. Nabab o nabob, título de los príncipes y gobernadores de las provincias mahometanas de la India. 2. Persona muy rica y fastuosa; indiano.

nacelle [næ'sel] [na-sel], *s. (Aer.)* 1. Cabina. 2. Navecilla. 3. Cápsula que recubre el motor.

nacre ['neɪkəʳ] [nei-kaʳ], *s.* Nácar, madreperla, sustancia con reflejos irisados que tapiza la superficie interior de varias conchas.

nacreous ['neɪkrɪəs] [nei-krios], *a.* Nacarado; nacarino.

nadir ['neɪdɪəʳ] [nei-diaʳ], *s.* Nadir, el punto de la esfera celeste opuesto al cenit.

naevose ['niːvəʊs] [ni-vous], *a.* Manchado, pecoso.

naevus ['niːvəs] [ni-vos], *s.* Lunar, mancha natural en alguna parte del cuerpo.

naff [næf] [naf] *a.* Inferior *(Fam.).*

nag [næg] [nag], 1. *s.* Haca, jaca, caballo pequeño. 2. *vt.* Regañar, molestar, fastidiar. **Nag get my doubts,** preocupado por las dudas. 3. *vi.* Quejarse. 4. *s.* Quejica.

naiad ['naɪæd] [naiad], *s. (Mitol.)* Náyade, ninfa de los ríos y fuentes.

naif [naɪf] [naif], *a.* 1. La forma masculina de *Naive.* V. 2. Lustroso antes de haber sido tallado o cortado.

nail [neɪl] [neil], *s.* 1. Uña. **To bite one's nails,** morderse las uñas. 2. Uña, pezuña; garra de los animales carniceros y de las aves. 3. Clavo, pedazo de hierro largo y delgado con cabeza y punta. **To hit the nail on the head,** dar en el clavo. 4. Medida de dos pulgadas y cuarto, o la dieciseisava parte de una vara. 5. Tachón, roblón. **Clut-nails,** *(Mar.)* Clavos sin cabeza. **Brass-headed nails,** clavos con cabeza de latón. **Clasp-nails,** *(Mar.)* clavos de ala de mosca. **Sheathing-nails,** *(Mar.)* Clavos de entablar. **Clincher-nails,** *(Mar.)* Clavos de tinglar. **Pump-nails,** *(Mar.)* Clavos de bomba. **On the nail,** luego, al instante, sobre la marcha. **Nail-brush,** cepillo para las uñas. **Nail-extractor, nail-puller,** arrancaclavos, desclavador. **Nail-file,** lima para las uñas. **Nail-plate,** metal en plancha para clavos.

nail, *va.* 1. Clavar. **To nail to the wall,** clavar en la pared. 2. Clavetear, guarnecer o adornar con clavos. **To nail a lie,** demostrar que una cosa es mentira, poner término a la circulación de un embuste. **To nail down** o **nail up,** sujetar con clavos; condenar una ventana, puerta, etc., clavándola.

nailer ['neɪləʳ] [nei-laʳ],, *s.* Chapucero, el fabricante de clavos.

nailery ['neɪlərɪ] [nei-la-ri], *s.* Fábrica de clavos.

nailing ['neɪlɪŋ] [nei-lin], *s.* Clavadura, el acto de clavar.

nainsook ['neɪnsʊk] [nein-suk], *s.* Nansú, nanzué, muselina de India, rayado a lo largo o lisa.

naissant ['neɪsent] [nei-sant], *a.* (*Her.*) Naciente: se dice del animal cuya cabeza y cuello salen por encima de una pieza del escudo.

naive [naɪ'iːv] [nai-iv], *a.* Ingenuo, candoroso, sencillo, natural, sin arte ni afectación.

naiveté [naɪ'iːvtɪ] [nai-ivti], *s.* Simplicidad; ingenuidad; gracia.

naked ['neɪkɪd] [nei-kid], *a.* 1. Desnudo, en cueros; también, en lo antiguo, insuficientemente vestido. 2. Desarmado, sin defensa. 3. Expuesto a la vista; patente, claro, evidente, mero. 4. Puro, simple. **The naked truth,** la verdad pura o desnuda. 5. (*Zool.*) Desnudo, privado de cubiertas epidérmicas, como de pelo, escamas, plumas, etc. **Stark naked,** completamente desnudo, en cueros. **A naked sword,** una espada desnuda, desenvainada.

nakedly ['neɪkɪdlɪ] [nei-kid-li], *adv.* Desnudamente, meramente, claramente.

nakedness ['neɪkɪdnɪs] [nei-kid-nes], *s.* 1. Desnudez; desabrigo; falta de defensa. 2. Claridad, evidencia; simplicidad.

namable, nameable ['næmbəbl] [na-ma-bol], *a.* Que puede recibir un nombre.

namby-pamby ['næmbɪ'pæmbɪ] [nam-bi-pam-bi], *a.* Insípido, afectado. *-s.* Pamplina; se dice hablando de versos para expresar que no son buenos.

name [neɪm] [neim], *s.* 1. Nombre. 2. Nombre, el título de alguna cosa por el cual es conocida. **Christian name,** nombre de bautismo, de pila. **In God's name,** en nombre de Dios, por el amor de Dios. 3. Nombre, nombradía, fama, opinión, reputación, crédito. **To get a good name,** tener buena reputación. 4. Nombre, autoridad, poder o virtud con que se ejecuta alguna cosa. 5. Apodo, mal nombre. **To call one names,** poner apodos a uno. 6. Pretexto. **By the name of,** bajo el nombre de. **An inventor, Marconi by name,** un inventor llamado Marconi. **Name-plate,** plancha con un nombre grabado o pintado; suele ser de metal para las puertas, de vidrio para las ventanas.

name, *va.* 1. Nombrar, poner nombre, bautizar. 2. Mencionar, hacer mención; proferir (Mention). 3. Especificar, elegir, señalar, designar, distinguir a una persona o cosa por su nombre. **Do not name it,** no vale la pena de hablar de ello; no hay de que. 4. Nominar.

nameless ['neɪmlɪs] [neim-les], *a.* Innominado, anónimo; desconocido.

namely ['neɪmlɪ] [neim-li], *adv.* Señaladamente, particularmente, especialmente; a saber.

name plate ['neɪmpleɪt] [neim-pleit], *s.* Placa con el nombre de una persona. (Generalmente se coloca en los escritorios de oficina).

namesake ['neɪmseɪk] [neim-seik], *s.* Tocayo.

naming ['neɪmɪŋ] [nei-min], *s.* 1. Nombramiento, el acto de nombrar. 2. El documento o título del nombramiento.

nankeen ['nænkiːn] [nan-kin], **Nankin** ['nænkiːn] [nan-kin], *s.* Mahón, manquín, tela de algodón, de color anteado, que viene de la China.

nanny ['nænɪ] [na-ni], *s. f.* Niñera.

nap [næp] [nap], *s.* 1. Sueño ligero, sueño de corta duración; siesta. **To take an afternnon nap,** dormir la siesta. 2. Vello de las plantas; lanilla, la pelusa que queda en las telas o tejidos de lana por la haz. 3. Golpecito, toque ligero. 4. (*Prov. Ingl.*) Cima, pico o punta de una roca.

nap, *vn.* Dormitar, tener sueño. *-va.* Hacer lanillas en el paño.

NAPA *Abreviatura de* **National Association of Performing Artists** (*EU*).

nape ['neɪp] [neip], *s.* Nuca, la parte superior de la cerviz, unión del espinazo con la cabeza.

napery ['neɪpərɪ] [nei-pa-ri], *s.* Ropa blanca, artículo de lienzo; mantelería.

naphtha ['næfθə] [naf-za], *s.* Nafta, aceite ligero.

naphtalene ['næftəliːn] [naf-ta-lin], *s.* (*Quím.*) Naftalina.

napiform ['næpɪfɔːm] [na-pi-form], *a.* Que tiene forma de nabo.

napkin ['næpkɪn] [nap-kin], *s.* 1. Servilleta (Table). 2. Pañal (Baby). 3. Compresa higiénica (Sanitary towel).

napless ['neɪplɪs] [neip-les], *a.* Raído, que no tiene pelusa, vello o lanilla.

napoleon [nə'pəʊlɪən] [na-pou-lion], *s.* Antigua moneda francesa de oro.

nappiness ['næpɪnɪs] [na-pi-nes], *s.* La propiedad de tener pelusa, vello o lanilla.

nappy ['næpɪ] [na-pi], *a.* 1. Espumoso. 2. Velloso.

narcissine [nɑː'sɪsaɪn] [nar-si-sain], *a.* Perteneceinte a la planta llamada narciso, o parecido al narciso.

narcissus [nɑː'sɪsəs] [nar-si-sos], *s.* (*Bot.*) Narciso, planta herbácea de flores olorosas.

narcosis [nɑː'kəʊsɪs] [nar-kou-sis], *s.* (*Med.*) Narcotismo, conjunto de los efectos producidos por los narcóticos.

narcotic [nɑː'kəʊtɪk] [nar-kou-tik], *a.* Narcótico, que adormece o entorpece los sentidos. Soporífero, soporífico. -*s.* Narcótico. *-s. pl.* Estupefacientes.

nard [nɑːd] [nard], *s.* (*Bot.*) 1. Nardo, dícese de la planta, el aceite o el ungüento. 2. Especie de valeriana empleada antiguamente en medicina.

nardine ['nɑːdiːn] [nar-din], *s.* Nardino, compuesto con nardo o que participa de sus cualidades.

nares [nɛəz] [nears], *s. pl.* de NARIS. Las ventanas de la nariz; narices.

narrate [nə'reɪt] [na-reit], *va.* Narrar, relacionar, relatar.

narrating [nə'reɪtɪŋ] [na-rei-tin], *s.* El acto de narrar, contar o relatar.

narration [nə'reɪʃən] [na-rei-shon], *s.* Narración, relación de alguna cosa.

narrative ['nærətɪv] [na-ra-tiv], *a.* Narrativo. -*s.* Narrativa, relato.

narratively ['nærətɪvlɪ] [na-ra-tiv-li], *adv.* Narrativamente.

narrator [nə'reɪtəʳ] [na-rei-taʳ], *s.* Relator, narrador, el que narra o relata.

narrow ['nærəʊ] [na-rou], *a.* 1. Angosto, estrecho, corto. 2. Apretado, ruin, avariento. 3. Estrecho, limitado. 4. Próximo, inmediato. 5. Vigilante, atento, escrupuloso. 6. De cerca, apenas suficiente para librarse de un daño o peligro. **A narrow escape,** una escapada difícil. **By a narow plurality,** por escasa mayoría. **A narrow-minded man,** un hombre de ideas mezquinas, avariento, de entendimiento limitado, de pocos alcances o de poco talento. **A narrow-spirited** o a **narrow-souled man,** un hombre apocado o encogido, de poca resolución o de cortos alcances; innoble, mezquino, bajo. **To bring into a narrow compass,** compendiar. **Narrow circumstances,** escasez pecuniaria. **Narrow-gauge,** ferrocarril de la vía estrecha. **Narrow-minded,** apocado, encogido, mezquino; intolerante. -*s.* Estrecho, pasaje angosto; desfiladero.

narrow, *va.* 1. Estrechar, angostar, encoger. 2. Bajar, humillar. 3. Disminuir, limitar. *-vn.* Andar los caballos con las patas muy juntas. **Narrow down,** reducirse.

narrow-gauge ['nærəʊˌɡeɪdʒ] [na-rou-gueich], *a.* De vía estrecha.

narrow-hearted ['nærəʊˌhɑːtɪd] [na-rou-jar-tid], *a.* Corto de ánimo, mezquino, cobarde, poquito.

narrowing ['nærəʊɪŋ] [na-rouin], *s.* Estrechamiento, estrechura.

narrowly ['nærəʊlɪ] [na-rou-li], *adv.* 1. Estrechamente. 2. Exactamente. 3. Por poco. **We narrowly escaped being drowned,** por poco nos ahogamos. 4. Escasamente, mezquinamente.

narrowness ['nærəʊnɪs] [na-rou-nes], *s.* 1. Angostura. 2. Estrechez, falta de capacidad; apretura. 3. Pobreza, miseria, bajeza.

narwhal ['nɑːwəl] [nar-ual], *s.* Narval, unicornio marino.

NAS *Abreviatura de* **National Academy of Sciences** (*EU*).

NASA ['næsə] [na-sa], s. *Abreviatura de* **National Aeronautics and Space Administration** (*EU*).

nasal ['neɪzəl] [nei-sal], *a.* Nasal, lo que pertenece a la nariz. -*s.* 1. Errinos, los remedios que se usan para el interior de la nariz; los medicamentos que se toman por la nariz. 2. Letra nasal.

nasalize ['neɪzəlaɪz] [nei-sa-lais], *va.* Ganguear, pronunicar con sonido nasal.

nasally ['neɪzəlɪ] [nei-sa-li], *adv.* Con gangueo, con sonido nasal.

nascent ['næsənt] [na-sent], *a.* Naciente, creciente.

nastily ['nɑːstɪlɪ] [nas-ti-li], *adv.* Suciamente.

nastiness ['nɑːstɪnɪs] [nas-ti-nes], *s.* Suciedad, porquería, obscenidad.

nasturtion [nəs'tɜːʃəm] [nas-ter-shon], *s.* (*Bot.*) Capuchina. *V.* NASTURTIUM.

nasturtium [nəs'tɜːʃəm] [nas-ter-shom], *s.* (*Bot.*) 1. Nasturcio. 2. Capuchina, planta geraniácea trepadora o baja.

nasty ['nɑːstɪ] [nas-ti], *a.* 1. Sucio, puerco. 2. Sucio, obsceno, deshonesto, hablando de acciones o palabras. 3. Impuro, sórdido. 4. (*Fam.*) Desagradable; de aquí, tempestuoso; lodoso, cenagoso.

natal [nə'tæl] [na-tal], *a.* Nativo; natal.

natalitial [nə'tælɪʃəl] [na-ta-li-shal], **natalitious** [nə'tælɪʃəs] [na-ta-li-shos], *a.* Natalicio, natal, lo que pertenece al día o fiesta del nacimiento.

natant ['neɪtənt] [nei-tant], *a.* 1. (*Bot.*) Nadando, flotando en la superficie del agua. 2. (*Her.*) Dícese de un pez representado en el escudo de armas horizontalmente o de través.

natation [nə'teɪʃən] [na-tei-shon], *s.* Nadadura, el acto de nadar.

natatorial [ˌneɪtə'tɔːrɪəl] [nei-ta-to-rial], *a.* Nadador, natátil, o apto para nadar.

natatory ['neɪtətɔːrɪ] [nei-ta-to-ri], *a.* Natatorio, que sirve para nadar.

nates ['neɪtz] [neits], *s. pl.* Nalgas, trasero.

nation ['neɪʃən] [nei-shon], *s.* 1. Nación. 2. Se usa enfáticamente para expresar un gran número o muchedumbre.

national ['næʃənl] [na-sho-nal], *a.* 1. Nacional; general, público. 2. Aficionado a su propio país, idioma o costumbres; patriótico. 3. Autorizado por un gobierno nacional. **The national debt,** la deuda pública.

nationalism ['næʃənəlɪzəm] [na-sho-na-li-sem], *s.* 1. Nacionalismo, devoción a toda la nación más bien que a una parte de ella. 2. Deseo de obtener o de mantener la independencia nacional. 4. Idiotismo, costumbre, rasgo característico nacional.

nationality [ˌnæʃə'nælɪtɪ] [na-sho-na-li-ti], *s.* Nacionalidad.

nationalization [ˌnæʃənəlaɪ'zeɪʃən] [na-sho-na-lai-sei-shon], *s.* Nacionalización.

nationalize ['næʃənəlaɪz] [na-sho-na-lais], *va.* Nacionalizar, hacer nacional.

nationally ['næʃənəlɪ] [na-sho-na-li], *adv.* Nacionalmente.

nation-state ['neɪʃən'steɪʃən] [nei-shon-stei-shon], *s. m.* Estado-nación.

nationwide ['neɪʃən'waɪd] [nei-shon-uaid] *a.* A escala nacional.

native ['neɪtɪv] [nei-tiv], *a.* 1. Nativo. 2. Nativo, lo perteneciente al nacimiento de cada uno; natural, originario de algún país. 3. Lo que ha nacido al mismo tiempo que otra cosa o tiene conexión íntima con ella. 4. Original, originario. -*s.* 1. Natural. 2. La consecuencia o resultado de alguna causa. **Native place,** lugar natal. **Native inhabitants,** habitantes indígenas.

natively ['neɪtɪvlɪ] [nei-tiv-li], *adv.* Naturalmente, originalmente, originariamente.

nativeness [nə'tɪvnɪs] [nei-tiv-nes], *s.* El estado de la cosa producida por la naturaleza.

nativity [nə'tɪvɪtɪ] [nei-ti-vi-ti], *s.* 1. Nacimiento, el acto de nacer. 2. Nacimiento, el origen o principio desde donde empezó a existir una cosa. 3. Horóscopo.

NATO ['neɪtəʊ] [nei-tou], *s. Abreviatura de* **North Atlantic Treaty Organization,** OTAN.

natron ['neɪtrən] [nei-tron], *s.* (*Quím.*) Natrón, carbonato de sosa usado en las fábricas de jabón, vidrio y tintes.

natty ['nætɪ] [na-ti], *a.* (*Fam.*) Elegante, fino; vestido con esmero.

natural ['nætʃrəl] [na-chral], *a.* 1. Natural, producido o causado por la naturaleza. 2. Conforme al orden establecido. 3. Afectuoso, cariñoso, tierno, humano. 4. Natural, hecho sin artificio. 5. Natural, sencillo (simple). 6. Natural, verdadero (true). 7. Natural, ilegítimo. 8. (*Mús.*) Natural, sin sostenido ni bemoles. -*s.* 1. (*Mús.*) Becuadro. 2. Tecla blanca; tecla natural. 3. Idiota, simplón (idiot). **Natural gas,** gas natural.

naturalism ['nætʃrəlɪzəm] [na-chra-li-sem], *s.* Naturalismo, el sistema de religión en que todo se atribuye a la naturaleza.

naturalist ['nætʃrəlɪst] [na-chra-list], *s.* Naturalista.

naturalization [ˌnætʃrəlaɪ'zeɪʃən] [na-chra-lai-sei-shon], *s.* Naturalización.

naturalize ['nætʃrəlaɪz] [na-chu-ra-lais], *va.* 1. Naturalizar, conceder o dar a los extranjeros el privilegio de la naturalización. 2. Naturalizar, habituar; aclimatar hombres, animales o plantas.

naturally ['nætʃrəlɪ] [na-chu-ra-li], *adv.* Naturalmente.

naturalness ['nætʃrəlnɪs] [na-chu-ral-nes], *s.* 1. Naturalidad. 2. Ingenuidad, sencillez.

natural science ['nætʃrəlˌsaɪəns] [na-chu-ral-saiens], *s.* Ciencias naturales.

nature ['neɪtʃər] [nei-chaʳ], *s.* 1. Naturaleza. 2. Naturaleza, la propiedad esencial de cada cosa. 3. Natural, índole, genio, inclinación de cada uno. 4. Naturaleza, el orden de las cosas criadas. 5. Naturaleza, especie, género, clase. 6. Naturaleza, la constitución de un cuerpo animado; complexión. **Good nature,** mansedumbre, benignidad, benevolencia, humanidad, afabilidad. **In the nature of,** algo así como. **By nature,** por naturaleza.

natured ['neɪtʃəd] [nei-chad], *a.* Se usa sólo en la formación de palabras compuestas. **Good-natured,** de buen natural. **Ill-natured,** de mal carácter, mal intencionado.

naturism ['neɪtʃərɪzəm] [nei-cha-ri-sem], *s. m.* Naturismo.

naturist ['neɪtʃərɪst] [nei-cha-rist], *s.* Naturista.

naturopathy [ˌneɪtʃə'rɒpəθɪ] [nei-chu-ro-pa-zi], *s. f.* Naturopatía.

naught [nɔːt] [not], *s.* Nada; cero, la cifra 0. **To set at naught,** hacer poco caso de, tener en poco; desdeñar, despreciar. -*a.* 1. De ningún valor. 2. (*Des.*) Malo, perverso, indigno, inicuo.

naughtily ['nɔːtɪlɪ] [no-ti-li], *adv.* Malvadamente, perversamente, inicuamente.

naughtiness ['nɔːtɪnɪs] [no-ti-nes], *s.* Maldad, iniquidad, perversidad, malignidad.

naughty ['nɔːtɪ] [no-ti], *a.* 1. Perverso, desobediente, díscolo, pícaro. 2. (*Ant.*) Malo, malvado, inicuo. **A naughty fellow,** un malvado. **A naughty boy,** un picarón o picaruelo; pillo, pillastrón. **A naughty trick,** una pillada, una gatada.

nausea ['nɔːsɪə] [no-sia], *s.* Náusea, bascas, gana de vomitar.

nauseant ['nɔːsɪənt] [no-siant], *a.* Nauseabundo. -*s.* Sustancia nauseabunda.

nauseate ['nɔːsɪeɪt] [no-sieit], *vn.* Nausear, tener bascas, tener asco; sentir disgusto, aversión o antipatía. -*va.* Dar asco o disgusto; causar aversión o antipatía.

nauseating ['nɔːsɪeɪtɪŋ] [no-sia-tin], *a.* Nauseabundo, repugnante.

nauseative ['nɔːsɪətɪv] [no-sia-tiv], *a.* Nauseativo, nauseoso.

nauseous ['nɔːsɪəs] [no-sios], *a.* Fastidioso, asqueroso.

nauseously ['nɔːsɪəslɪ] [no-sios-li], *adv.* Fastidiosamente.

nauseousness ['nɔːsɪəsnɪs] [no-sios-nes], *s.* Náusea.

nautch [nɔːtʃ] [noch], *s.* Baile de la India. **Nautch-girl,** bailarina india.

nautical ['nɔːtɪkəl] [no-ti-kal], *a.* Náutico, lo que pertenece a la navegación.

nautilus ['nɔːtɪləs] [no-ti-los], *s.* 1. Nautilo, nauclero, caracol hermoso de mar de concha univalva. 2. Argonauta, molusco cefalópodo. 3. Fisalia.

naval ['neɪvəl] [nei-val], *a.* Naval. **Naval officer,** oficial de marina; capitán de puerto. **Naval stores,** alquitrán, trementina, y otras resinas. **Naval tactics,** táctica naval, evoluciones marítimas.

navarchy ['nævɑːkɪ] [na-var-ki], *s.* Pilotaje.

nave ['neɪv] [neiv], *s.* 1. Cubo, maza, pieza guresa de madera en el centro de las ruedas de los carruajes. 2. Nave, parte principal del cuerpo de la iglesia.

navel ['neɪvəl] [nei-val], *s.* 1. Ombligo. 2. Centro, medio, la parte más interior de una cosa. 3. Nombre de una variedad de naranja procedente de Bahía en Brasil. **Navel-gall,** *(Vet.)* Matadura. **Navel-ill,** *(Vet.)* Inflamación del ombligo en los becerros y corderos. **Navel-string,** cordón umbilical.

naveled ['neɪvəld] [nei-veld], *a.* Que tiene ombligo; a manera de ombligo.

nave-line ['neɪvəl] [nei-val], *s. (Mar.)* Perigallo de racamento.

navelwort ['neɪvəlwɔːt] [nei-val-uort], *s. (Bot.)* Oreja de monje.

navigable ['nævɪgəbl] [na-vi-ga-bol], *a.* Navegable.

navigableness ['nævɪgəblnɪs] [na-vi-ga-bol-nes], *s.* El estado navegable de una extensión de agua, sea mar, río o lago.

navigate ['nævɪgeɪt] [na-vi-gueit], *vn.* Navegar, viajar por el agua. -*va.* Navegar, pasar el agua en barco.

navigation [ˌnævɪ'geɪʃən] [na-vi-guei-shon], *s.* 1. Navegación, náutica, el arte de navegar. 2. Navegación, la acción de navegar y el viaje que hace la embarcación. 3. *(Poét.)* Marina, las embarcaciones en general. **Navigation lights,** luces de posición.

navigator ['nævɪgeɪtəʳ] [na-vi-guei-taʳ], *s.* Navegador, navegante, marino hábil en el arte de navegar.

navvy ['nævɪ] [na-vi], *s. (Ingl.)* Peón, que trabaja en obras de canales, ferrocarriles, etc.

navy ['neɪvɪ] [nei-vi], *s.* Marina, se dice en general del cuerpo de oficiales, tropa, marineros, y aun de los buques que forman la fuerza naval de un estado; armada de una potencia. **The royal navy,** la real armada. **Navy-office,** almirantazgo. **Navy-yard,** arsenal de puerto.

navy bean ['neɪvɪbiːn] [nei-vi-bin]», *s.* Frijol blanco.

navy-blue ['neɪvɪbluː] [nei-vi-blu], *a.* Azul marino.

nawab ['næwəb] [na-uab], *s.* Babab, gobernador mahometano de una provincia en la India.

nay [neɪ] [nei], *adv.* 1. No, no sólo, sino; no sólo eso; pero o sino; también; aun más, además, y aun. **Nay verily,** no ciertamente. 2. Sirve para exagerar y dar énfasis, y corresponde en castellano a aun, aun más, también. **He has enough, nay, too much,** tiene bastante y aun demasiado. -*s.* 1. El que hace oposición votando en contra, y el mismo voto negativo. 2. Denegación, exclusión, repulsa.

Nazarene [ˌnæzə'riːn] [na-sa-rin], *a.* y *s.* Nazareno, y de aquí, cristiano.

nazarite ['næzəraɪt] [na-sa-rait], *s.* Nazareísta, nazareno, o nazareno, el hebreo que se consagraba al culto divino de un modo particular; los nazarenos, no tomaban bebidas alcohólicas y no se cortaban el cabello ni la barba.

naze ['neɪz] [neiw], *s.* Cabo, promontorio; roca escarpada.

nazi ['nɑːtsɪ] [na-tsi], *s.* y *a.* Nazi (del partido nacionalsocialista alemán).

nazism ['nɑːtsɪzəm] [na-si-sem], *s. m.* Nazismo.

NBA *Abreviatura de* **National Basketball Association** *(EU).*

NBC *Abreviatura de* **National Broadcasting Company** *(EU).*

NBS *Abreviatura de* **National Bureau of Standards** *(EU).*

NCO *Abreviatura de* **Non-Commissioned Officer.**

NEA *Abreviatura de* **National Educational Association** *(EU).*

neaf [niːf] [nif], *s. (Esco. y Prov. Ingl.)* Puño, la mano cerrada.

neal [niːl] [nil], *va. (Des.)* Templar, dar temple a alguna cosa por medio de un calor gradual. *V.* TO ANNEAL. -*vn.* Templarse al fuego.

Neanderthal [nɪ'ændətɑːl] [nan-da-tal], *a.* **Neanderthal man,** hombre de Neanderthal.

neap [niːp] [nip], *a.* Bajo, lo más bajo, ínfimo. -*s.* 1. Bajo, menguante. **Neap tide,** marea la más baja. 2. En algunas partes de los Estados Unidos, lanza de carretón.

neapolitan [nɪə'pɒlɪtən] [nia-po-li-tan], *a.* y *s.* Napolitano, de Nápoles.

near [nɪəʳ] [niaʳ], *prep.* Cerca de, inmediato a, junto a, próximo a. -*adv.* 1. Casi o cuasi. 2. Cerca, próxima, o inmediatamente. 3. Cerca de. **Near five thousand,** cerca de cinco mil o unos cinco mil. -*a.* 1. Cercano, próximo, inmediato. 2. Cercano, allegado, el que tiene parentesco inmediato con otro. **A near relation,** pariente cercano. 3. Íntimo, cordial, estrecho, hablando de amigos o parientes. 4. Interesante, que afecta o se refiere a la felicidad o al bienestar de uno mismo. 5. Cicatero, tacaño, mezquino. 6. Conforme en un todo al original, exacto, literal. 7. A la izquierda, de la izquierda. **The near ox,** el buey de la izquierda. 8. Corto, directo. **Come near me,** acércate, ven cerca de mí. **Near at hand,** a la mano, cerca, al primer golpe o de primer golpe, inmediatamente. **A near concern,** un interés que toca de cerca. **Near Quito,** cerca de Quito. **To come, to draw near,** acercar, acercarse. **Quite near,** muy cerca, contiguo. **That's near enough,** es suficiente. **The nearest way,** el camino más corto.

near, *va.* Acercar. -*vn.* Acercarse.

nearby ['nɪəbaɪ] [nia-bai], 1. *a.* Cercano. 2. *adv.* Cerca.

nearly ['nɪəlɪ] [nia-li], *adv.* 1. Cercanamente, a poca distancia. 2. Estrechamente. 3. Miserablemente, mezquinamente. 4. Casi, poco más o menos. 5. Íntimamente, de cerca. **That nearly concerns you,** eso te toca a Ud. de cerca. 6. Muy aproximadamente, casi literalmente.

nearness ['nɪənɪs] [nia-nes], *s.* 1. Proximidad, propincuidad, cercanía. 2. Proximidad, parentesco, cercano. 3. Amistad estrecha. 4. Tacañería, ruindad, mezquindad.

near-sighted ['nɪəsaɪtɪd] [nia-sai-tid], *a.* Corto de vista, miope.

neat [niːt] [nit], *a.* 1. Limpio, aseado, primoroso. 2. Bonito, pulido, lindo. 3. Puro, casto, natural, sin mezcla. 4. Gallardo, esmerado, de buenas proporciones, de forma graciosa. 5. *(Com.)* Neto. *V.* NET. -*s.* Ganado vacuno; vaca o buey. **Neat's leather,** cuero de ganado vacuno. **Neat's tongue,** lengua de vaca. **Neat's oil,** aceite de manitas. **Neat-cattle,** ganado mayor.

neat-handed ['niːθændɪd] [nit-jan-did], *a.* Limpio, diestro.

'neath ['niːθ] [niz], *prep.* Debajo de. *V.* BENEATH.

neatherd ['niːðəd] [ni-zerd], *s.* Vaquero, el pastor de ganado vacuno.

neatly ['niːtlɪ] [nit-li], *adv.* Pálidamente, con primor; limpiamente; aseadamente; elegantemente; diestramente, claramente.

neatness ['niːtnɪs] [nit-nes], *s.* 1. Hermosura, elegancia. 2. Limpieza, aseo. 3. Delicadeza.

neb [neb] [neb], *s.* 1. Nariz, pico, boca. 2. Pico, punta, cabo. *V.* NIB.

nebula ['nebjələ] [ne-biu-la], *s.* 1. *(Ast.)* Nebulosa, mancha blanquecina formada por una aglomeración de estrellas. 2. Nube en los ojos.

nebular ['nebjələʳ] [ne-biu-laʳ], *a.* Nebuloso, perteneciente a una nebulosa.

nebulizer ['nebjʊˌlaɪzəʳ] [ne-biu-lai-saʳ], *s.* Rociador (spray).

nebulosity ['nebjʊˌlɒsɪtɪ] [ne-biu-lo-si-ti], *s.* 1. Estado nebuloso de la atmósfera. 2. Nebulosidad, apariencia como de nebulosa.

nebulous ['nebjʊləs] [ne-biu-los], *a.* 1. Nebuloso, parecido a una nebulosa. (de estrellas). 2. Que tiene sus diversas partes confundidas o mezcladas.

necessaries ['nesɪsərɪɪz] [ne-si-sa-ris], *s. pl.* Necesario. **The necessaries of life,** lo necesario para vivir.

necessarily ['nesɪsərɪlɪ] [ne-si-sa-ri-li], *adv.* Necesariamente, indispensablemente.

necessariness ['nesɪsərɪnɪs] [ne-si-sa-ri-nes], *s.* Necesidad.

necessary ['nesɪsərɪ] [ne-si-sa-ri], *a.* 1. Necesario: decisivo, conclusivo; preciso; forzoso; menester. 2. Esencial, inevitable como conclusión. 3. Intuitivo. -*s.* 1. Lo necesario. 2. Necesaria, letrina.

necessitate [nɪ'sesɪteɪt] [ni-se-si-teit], *va.* Necesitar, obligar, precisar.

necessitous [nɪˈsesɪtəs] [ni-se-si-tos], *a.* Necesitado, indigente, pobre.

necessitousness [nɪˈsesɪtəsnɪs] [ni-se-si-tos-nes], *s.* Necesidad, pobreza, indigencia.

necessity [nɪˈsesɪtɪ] [ni-se-si-ti], *s.* 1. Necesidad; fatalidad. 2. Necesidad. **Necessity knows no law,** la necesidad carece de ley. *(Fam.)* La necesidad tiene cara de hereje. 3. Consecuencia necesaria e inevitable. 4. Violencia, compulsión; exigencia. 5. Pobreza, indigencia, penuria.

neck [nek] [nek], *s.* 1. Cuello. 2. Parte de un órgano que está oprimida o constreñida; cosa parecida a un cuello; cuello, gollete (bottle); clavijero (guitar, violin); degüello; collarino de una columna; la parte de un vestido que cubre el cuello y el seno. 3. Istmo, desfiladero, península. **To breathe down somebody's neck,** no dejar a alguien ni a sol ni a sombra *(fam).* **Neck of mutton,** pescuezo de carnero. **Neck of land,** lengua de tierra. **On the neck,** luego, inmediatamente, después. **To break the neck,** *(Met.)* Tener una cosa medio acabada; impedir la ejecución de alguna cosa. **Low-necked,** muy escotado (hablando de un vestido de mujer). **Neck and crop,** todo junto y a un tiempo; al momento. **To harden the neck,** obstinarse en una cosa. **Neck and neck,** con igual rapidez en una carrera. **Neck or nothing,** a todo correr; cueste lo que cueste. **On the neck of, over the neck of,** luego, inmediatamente después.

neckband [ˈnekbænd] [nek-band], *s.* Cabezón o cuello de camisa.

neck-beef [ˈnekbiːf] [nek-bif], *s.* Carne de pescuezo.

neckcloth [ˈneklɒθ] [nek-kloz], *s.* Corbata, corbatín.

neckerchief [ˈnekətʃiːf] [ne-ka-chif], **neck-handkerchief** [ˈnekˈhænkətʃiːf] [nek-jan-ker-chif], *s.* 1. Corbata. corbatín, pañuelo de cuello. 2. Bobillo, encaje que llevaban las mujeres prendido alrededor del escote.

necklace [ˈneklɪs] [nek-lis] *s.* Collar, gargantilla.

neckline [ˈneklaɪn] [nek-lain], *s. m.* Escote. **A dress with a low neckline,** un vestido escotado.

necktie [ˈnektaɪ] [nek-tai], *s.* Corbata.

neckwear [ˈnekwɛəʳ] [nek-ueaʳ], *s.* Corbatas, cuellos, bufandas, etc.

necro- [ˈnekrəʊ] [ne-krou]. Forma de combinación derivada del griego y que significa *muerto, cadáver.*

necrologic, necrological [ˌnekrəʊˈlɒdʒɪk] [ne-krou-lo-yik], *a.* Necrológico, que se refiere a los muertos.

necrologist [ˌnekrəʊˈlɒdʒɪst] [ne-krou-lo-yist], *s.* Necrologista, registrador de defunciones; también, el que escribe noticias obituarias.

necrology [ˌnekrəʊˈlɒdʒɪ] [ne-krou-lo-yi], *s.* Necrología, registro o lista de muertos.

necromancer [ˌnekrəʊˈmænsəʳ] [ne-krou-man-saʳ], *s.* Nigromante. *(Vulg.)* Brujo.

necromancy [ˌnekrəʊˈmænsɪ] [ne-krou-man-si], *s.* Nigromancia, magia negra. *(Vulg.)* Brujería.

necromantic [ˌnekrəʊˈmæntɪk] [ne-krou-man-tik], *a.* Nigromántico.

necropolis [neˈkrɒpəlɪs] [ne-kro-po-lis], *s.* Necrópolis, ciudad de los muertos; particularmente, cementerio antiguo.

necrosis [neˈkrɒsɪs] [ne-kro-sis, *s.* Necrosis, gangrena o mortificación del tejido óseo.

nectar [ˈnektəʳ] [nek-taʳ], *s.* Néctar, en sus varios sentidos.

nectarean [nekˈtɛrɪən] [nek-ta-rian], **Nectareous** [nekˈtɛrɪəs] [nek-ta-rios], **Nectarine** [nekˈtɛrɪn] [nek-ta-rin], *a.* Nectáreo, dulce como el néctar.

nectarial [nekˈtɛrɪəl] [nek-ta-rial], *a. (Bot.)* Que se refiere al nectario; nectáreo.

nectarine [ˈnektərɪn] [nek-ta-rin], *s.* Nectarina, abridor.

nectarine-tree [ˈnektərɪnˌtriː] [nek-ta-rin-tri], *s. (Bot.)* Abridor.

nectary [ˈnektərɪ] [nek-ta-ri], *s.* 1. Nectario, la parte que en algunas plantas contiene el néctar o la miel. 2. *(Ento.)* Tubo para miel.

née [neɪ] [nei], *a.* Nacida; se usa para designar el apellido de una mujer antes de casarse.

need [niːd] [nid], *s.* 1. Necesidad, urgencia. 2. Necesidad, pobreza, miseria. 3. Necesidad, falta de alguna cosa. **If need be,** si hubiese necesidad o si fuese necesario. **In case of need,** en caso de necesidad. **I stand much in need of your advice,** me hace mucha falta el consejo de Ud. **Her needs are few,** es poco lo que necesita.

need, *va.* Pedir, requerir lo que es necesario y conveniente; necesitar. -*vn.* 1. Necesitar, haber menester o tener necesidad o precisión de alguna cosa, hacer falta; carecer. 2. Tener que, haber de. **They need not fear,** nada tienen que temer. **He said: «we need but rise»,** dijo, «no tenemos más que levantarnos».» (El verbo neutro **need** se emplea a veces, quedando invariable. **She need not go,** ella no tiene necesidad de ir. **Just what I needed,** justo lo que necesitaba. **It need not follow that…,** lo que no significa necesariamente que…

needer [ˈniːdəʳ] [ni-daʳ], *s.* Necesitado.

needful [ˈniːdfʊl] [nid-ful], *a.* Necesario, indispensable, preciso.

needfully [ˈniːdfəlɪ] [nid-fu-li], *adv.* Necesariamente, indispensablemente.

needfulness [ˈniːdfəlnɪs] [nid-ful-nes], *s.* Pobreza, falta, necesidad.

needily [ˈniːdɪlɪ] [ni-di-li], *adv.* Pobremente.

neediness [ˈniːdɪnɪs] [ni-di-nes], *s.* 1. Indigencia, pobreza, necesidad. 2. Falta, vacío.

needle [ˈniːdl] [ni-del], *s.* 1. Aguja. 2. Palillo (bone, wood) para hacer medias. **Pack-needle,** aguja de ensalmar. **Needle of a dial,** estilo de un reloj de sol: mano, índice. **Needle,** *(Mar.)* Aguja de marear, brújula. **Sail-needle,** *(Mar.)* Aguja capotera. **Bolt-rope-needle,** *(Mar.)* Aguja de relinga. **Knitting-needle,** aguja de hacer medias, o de malla. **Shepherd's needle,** *(Bot.)* Aguja de pastor. **Needle of a balance,** lengüita, fiel de la balanza. **Crochet, darning needle,** aguja de crochet, de zurcir. **Sewing-machine needle,** aguja de máquina de coser. **Needle-gun,** fusil de aguja. **Needle-holder,** porta-agujas. **Needle-shaped,** *a.* acicular, de la forma de una aguja.

needle-case [ˈniːdlkeɪs] [ni-del-keis], *s.* Alfiletero, cañuto para guardar las agujas.

needleful [ˈniːdlfʊl] [ni-del-ful], *s.* Hebra de hilo.

needle-maker [ˈniːdlˌmeɪkəʳ] [ni-del-mei-kaʳ], **Needler** [ˈniːdləʳ] [ni-dlaʳ], *s.* Agujero, el que hace agujas.

needle point [ˈniːdlpɔɪnt] [ni-del-point], *s.* Punto de cruz, bordado de tapicería.

needless [ˈniːdlɪs] [nid-les], *a.* Superfluo, inútil. **Needless to say,** huelga decir que.

needlessly [ˈniːdlɪslɪ] [nid-les-li], *adv.* En balde; inútilmente.

needlessness [ˈniːdlɪsnɪs] [nid-les-nes], *s.* Superfluidad, inutilidad.

needlewoman [ˈniːdlwʊmən] [ni-del-uo-man], *sf.* La que hace labores de aguja; costurera.

needlework [ˈniːdlwɜːk] [ni-del-uek], *s.* Costura; bordado de aguja; obra de punto.

needs [ˈniːdz] [nids], *adv.* Necesariamente, indispensablemente. Se usa a menudo con *must:* **If it must needs be, we will go,** si es absolutamente necesario, iremos.

needy [ˈniːdɪ] [ni-di], *a.* Indigente, necesitado, pobre.

ne'er [ˈnɛəʳ] [neaʳ], *adv.* V. NEVER.

nefarious [nɪˈfɛərɪəs] [ni-fea-rios], *a.* Nefario, sumamente malo, atroz.

negation [nɪˈgeɪʃən] [ni-guei-shon], *s.* 1. Negación, la acción de negar. 2. *(Lóg.)* Negación, carencia de una calidad en un objeto que es incapaz de ella.

negative [ˈnegətɪv] [ne-ga-tiv], *a.* 1. Negativo. 2. *(Foto.)* Negativo, que presenta los claros y los obscuros invertidos. 3. *(Elec.)* Negativo, de potencia o fuerza relativamente baja. -*s.* 1. Negativa, una partícula en la gramática y una proposición en la lógica. 2. Negación, denegación, repulsa de lo que se pide. 3. Veto, derecho de rehusar. 4. Negativo, prueba negativa en fotografía. 5. Electricidad negativa.

negative, *va.* 1. Denegar, desaprobar, negar. 2. Oponerse a, votar en contra; poner su veto a.

negatively [ˈnegətɪvlɪ] [ne-ga-tiv-li], *adv.* Negativamente.

neglect [nɪˈglekt] [ni-glekt], *s.* 1. Descuido, dejadez, negligencia, olvido. 2. Desprecio, menosprecio, desdén, frialdad, indiferencia. 3. Desuso. **To fall into neglect,** caer en desuso.

neglect, *va.* 1. Descuidar, desatender. 2. Descuidar, olvidar, dejar de hacer lo que se debe; diferir; dilatar. 3. Menospreciar, desdeñar, no hacer caso, desdeñar, tener en menos. **To neglect one's duties,** descuidar sus deberes, faltar a su obligación.

neglecter [nɪˈglektəʳ] [ni-glek-taʳ], *s.* 1. Descuidado, negligente. 2. Despreciador.

neglectful [nɪˈglektfʊl] [ni-glekt-ful], *a.* Negligente, descuidado, omiso.

neglectfully [nɪˈglektfəlɪ] [ni-glekt-fa-li], *adv.* Negligentemente, descuidadamente.

neglectfulness [nɪˈglektfəlnɪs] [ni-glekt-fal-nes], *s.* Descuido, negligencia.

negligee [ˈneglɪdʒeɪ] [ne-gli-yi], *s.* Negligencia, descuido, omisión, incuria; dejadez, flojedad.

negligent [ˈneglɪdʒənt] [ne-gli-chent], *a.* Negligente, descuidado, dejado, flojo, perezoso.

negligently [ˈneglɪdʒəntlɪ] [ne-gli-yent-li], *adv.* Descuidadamente, negligentemente.

negligible [ˈneglɪdʒəbl] [ne-gli-chi-bol], *a.* Desatendible, lo que se puede desatender, descuidar, omitir o pasar por alto.

negotiable [nɪˈgəʊʃɪəbl] [ni-gou-shia-bol], *a.* Capaz de ser negociado.

negotiate [nɪˈgəʊʃɪeɪt] [ni-gou-shieit], *vn.* 1. Negociar, tratar y comerciar comprando, vendiendo o cambiando géneros, mercaderías o dinero. 2. Negociar, ajustar o manejar políticamente las pretensiones o negocios. *-va.* Negociar letras, vales u otros efectos comerciales. **To negotiate a bill,** negociar una letra de cambio.

negotiating [nɪˈgəʊʃɪeɪtɪŋ] [ni-gou-shiei-tin], *a.* Negociante, contratante. **A busy negotiating woman,** una mujer entremetida o trafagona.

negotiation [nɪˈgəʊʃɪeɪʃən] [ni-gou-shiei-shon], *s.* Negociación, negocio.

negotiator [nɪˈgəʊʃɪeɪtəʳ] [ni-gou-shiei-taʳ], *s.* Negociador.

negotiatrix [nɪˈgəʊʃɪətrɪks] [ni-gou-shia-triks], *s. f.* Negociadora.

negress [ˈniːgres] [ni-gres], *sf.* negra, mujer negra.

negro [ˈniːgrəʊ] [ni-grou] *s.* Negro, colored man.

negus [ˈniːgəs] [ni-gos], *s.* Carraspada, bebida, hecha con vino, agua, azúcar, canela y nuez de especia.

neigh [neɪ] [nei], *vn.* Relinchar.

neigh, *s.* Relincho, la voz del caballo o la yegua.

neighbor [ˈneɪbəʳ] [nei-boʳ], *s.* 1. Vecino. 2. Confidente, familiar. 3. Prójimo. *-a. (Ant.)* V. NEIGHBORING.

neighbor, *va.* Confinar, estar vecino o cercano; ser vecino de alguien, vivir cerca de otro.

neighborhood [ˈneɪbəhʊd] [nei-ba-jud], *s.* 1. Vecindad. 2. Vecindario, los que viven cerca unos de otros. 3. Cercanía, inmediación, proximidad.

neighboring [ˈneɪbərɪŋ] [nei-ba-rin], *a.* Vecino, cercano a, próximo, adyacente.

neighborliness [ˈneɪbəlɪnɪs] [nei-ba-li-nes], *s.* Urbanidad, cortesía de vecindad; buena vecina.

neighborly [ˈneɪbəlɪ] [nei-ba-li], *a.* Urbano, atento. *-adv.* Civilmente.

neighing [ˈneɪɪŋ] [nei-guin], *s.* Relincho.

neither [ˈnaɪðəʳ] [nai-daʳ], *conj.* 1. Ni; correlativo ordinario de *nor,* ni. **Neither one nor the other,** ni uno ni otro, ni el uno ni el otro. 2. Tampoco, aun no, nada de eso; después de una negación se reemplaza por *either,* excepto en el uso vulgar. **Neither will I do it,** yo tampoco lo haré. **Nor then either (neither),** ni entonces tampoco. *-pron.* Ninguno, ni uno ni otro. **To be on neither side,** ser o permanecer neutral; no tomar parte a favor de uno ni de otro. *-a.*

Ninguno, na. **Neither girl sings well,** ninguna de las dos chicas canta bien. **She neither smokes nor drinks,** ni fuma ni bebe.

nelly *s.* **Not on your nelly!** ¡ni hablar! *(Fam.).*

nemesis [ˈnemǝsɪs] [ne-me-sis], *s.* 1. Nemesis, diosa de la venganza. 2. Justicia retributiva.

neo- [ˈniːǝʊ] [niou]. Prefijo del griego que significa nuevo o reciente.

Neo-Catholic [ˈniːǝʊkǝθɒlɪk] [niou-ka-zo-lik], *a.* Neocatólico.

neoclassical [ˈniːǝʊˈlæsɪkǝl] [niou-kla-si-kal], *a.* Neoclásico.

neogamist [niːˈɒgæmɪst] [niou-ga-mist], *s.* Novio, el recién casado.

neolithic [ˌniːǝʊˈlɪθɪk] [niou-li-zik], *a.* Neolítico, de la segunda edad de piedra.

neological, neologic [nɪǝˈlɒdʒɪkǝl] [nio-lo-yi-kal], *a.* Neológico, lo que pertenece a las voces o locuciones de piedra.

neologism [nɪˈɒlǝdʒɪzǝm] [nio-lo-chi-sem], *s.* 1. Neologismo, vocablo o giro nuevo en una lengua. 2. Uso de estos vocablos o giros nuevos. 3. Nueva doctrina.

neology [nɪˈɒlǝdʒɪ] [nio-lo-chi], *s.* Neología, la invención o creación de voces nuevas en una lengua.

neomenia [ˌnɪǝʊˈmiːnɪǝ] [niou-mi-nia], *s.* neomenia, el primer día de la luna.

neon [ˈniːɒn] [nion], *s.* Neón. **Neon lamp,** lámpara de neón. **Neon sign,** anuncio luminoso de neón.

neophyte [ˈniːǝʊfaɪt] [niou-fait], *s.* Neófito, el recién convertido a la verdadera religión.

neoplatonism [nɪǝʊˈpleɪtǝnɪzǝm] [niou-plei-to-ni-sem], *s.* Neoplatonicismo, escuela filosófica cuya doctrina combinaba las ideas de Platón con las del misticismo oriental.

neoteric [ˌnɪǝʊˈterɪk] [niou-te-rik], *a.* Neotérico, moderno.

neozoic [ˌniːǝʊˈzǝʊɪk] [niou-zouik], *a. (Geol.)* Neozoico.

nepaulese [ˌnepɔːˈliːz] [ne-po-lis], *s.* Natural de Nepal, en el Indostán.

nephew [ˈnevjuː] [ne-fiu], *s.* Sobrino.

nephology [ˌnɪˈfɒlǝdʒɪ] [ni-fo-lo-yi], *s.* La parte de la meteorología que trata de las nubes.

nephoscope [ˈnɪfǝskǝʊp] [ni-fos-koup], *s.* Instrumento que indica la dirección, elevación, etc., de las nubes.

nephrite [ˈnefraɪt] [ne-frait], *s.* Nefrita, *(ant.)* ceraunita, variedad de jade.

nephritic [neˈfrɪtɪk] [ne-fri-tik], *a.* 1. Nefrítico: referente a los riñones. 2. Atacado de nefritis. **Nephritic wood,** palo nefrítico.

nephritis [neˈfraɪtɪs] [ne-frai-tis], *s.* Nefritis, inflamación de los riñones.

nephrotomy [neˈfrɒtǝmɪ] [ne-fro-to-mi], *s.* Nefrotomía, incisión de un riñón para extraer los cálculos o dar salida a un depósito purulento.

nepotism [ˈnepǝtɪzǝm] [ne-po-ti-sem], *s.* Nepotismo, desmedida preferencia dada a los parientes en la distribución de gracias y empleos.

neptune [ˈneptjuːn] [nep-tiun], *s.* 1. Neptuno, dios del mar; de aquí, océano. 2. Neptuno, el planeta más distante del sol, y que con mayor lentitud se mueve alrededor de este luminar.

neptunian [nepˈtjuːnɪǝn] [nep-tiu-nian], *a.* 1. Neptuniano, referente a Neptuno, o al océano. 2. *(Geol.)* Formado por el agua.

nereid [ˈnɪǝrɪɪd] [nia-rid], *s.* Nereida, ninfa que vivía en el mar.

nerval [ˈnɜːvǝl] [ner-val], *a.* Nervioso, referente a los nervios.

nervate [ˈnɜːveɪt] [ner-veit], *a. (Bot.)* Nervado.

nervation, nervature [ˈnɜːveɪʃǝn] [ner-vei-shon], *s.* Nervadura, distribución de las fibras de las hojas o de las ramificaciones en las alas de los insectos.

nerve [nɜːv] [nerv], *s.* 1. Nervio. 2. Nervio, fortaleza, vigor. 3. Tendón o cuerda. 4. *(Bot.)* Nervio, vena, fibra muy tenue que corre a lo largo de las hojas de las plantas. 5. Vena del ala de un insecto. 6. *pl.* Excitabilidad nerviosa. **Nerve cell,** neurona. **Nerve center,** centro nervioso.; punto neurálgico *(Fig)*.

nerve, *va.* Vigorizar, dar fuerza; animar, alentar.

nerved [nɜːvd] [nervd], *a.* Nervudo; venoso, marcado con venas.

nerviduct [ˈnɜːvɪdʌkt] [ner-vi-dakt], *s.* Conducto óseo para dar paso a un nervio.

nervine [ˈnɜːvɪn] [ner-vin], *a.* 1. Nervioso, nervoso. 2. Nervino, que fortifica y suaviza los nervios. -*s.* Medicamento que afecta los nervios.

nerveless [ˈnɜːvlɪs] [nerv-les], *a.* Enervado, débil, falto de fuerzas.

nervous [ˈnɜːvəs] [ner-vos], *a.* 1. Nervioso, nervoso; nervudo. 2. Que se agita o altera fácilmente. 3. Nervioso, que muestra vigor en las ideas, escritos, discursos, etc.

nervously [ˈnɜːvəslɪ] [ner-vos-li], *adv.* Nerviosamente.

nervousness [ˈnɜːvəsnɪs] [ner-vos-nes], *s.* Nerviosidad, nervosidad, vigor, fuerza; estado nervioso, irritable.

nervure [ˈnɜːvjʊəʳ] [ner-viuaʳ], *s.* 1. *(Arq.)* Costilla. 2. *(Bot.)* Nervura, conjunto de las venas más gruesas de las hojas. 3. *(Ento.)* Vena, nervadura de las alas de un insecto.

nervy [ˈnɜːvɪ] [ner-vi], *a.* Descarado, caradura (cheeky).

nescience [ˈnesəns] [ne-sans], *s.* Ignorancia, nesciencia, necedad.

-ness. Sufijo de origen anglosajón que expresa una cualidad o el estado de una cosa; como **darkness,** obscuridad, **greatness,** grandeza, **humaneness,** mansedumbre, benignidad.

ness [nes] [nes], *s.* Promontorio, cabo; se emplea como terminación en ciertos nombres de lugares, como Sheerness, Inverness.

nest [nest] [nest], *s.* 1. Nido. **Nest of birds,** nidada. 2. *(Vulg.)* Nido, lugar donde se reune gente de mala conducta. **Nest of thieves,** nido o guarida de ladrones. 3. Casa, habitación, morada, residencia, generalmente en mal sentido. 4. El conjunto de nichos de un escritorio en que encajan las gavetas; anaquel, gaveta. 5. Juego, serie; particularmente en mecánica, engranaje, conexión de pequeñas ruedas dentadas, resortes, etc. 6. *(Geol.)* Depósito aislado de mineral en una roca. **To make a nest,** hacer un nido, anidar. **A mare's nest,** descubrimiento fraudulento o embuste.

nest, *vn.* 1. Nidificar, anidar, hacerse un nido. 2. Buscar nidos. -*va.* 1. Anidar; alojar, fijar como en un nido. 2. Anidarse, establecerse, proveer de nido. 3. Colocar una serie de objetos uno dentro del otro.

nest-egg [ˈnesteg] [nest-eg], *s.* 1. Nidal, el huevo que se deja en el nido para que la gallina ponga en él. 2. Ahorros *(Fig.)*.

nestle [ˈnesl] [ne-sel], *vn.* 1. Anidarse, enjaular, enjaularse, alojándose en algún cuarto, vivienda o paraje estrecho. 2. Estar abrigado, como en un nido; apiñarse. -*va.* 1. Abrigar, poner como en un nido. 2. Acariciar, mimar, abrazar estrechamente.

nestling [ˈneslɪŋ] [nes-lin], *s.* Pollo, el ave recién salida del nido.

nestorian [ˈnestərɪən] [nes-to-rian], *s.* Nestoriano, nombre de unos herejes.

net [net] [net], *s.* Red; malla.

net, *va.* 1. Neto. 2. Limpio, líquido. **Net income,** ingreso neto. **Net profit,** utilidad neta. **Net weight,** peso neto. -*s.* Cantidad neta. -*vn.* Hacer redes. -*va.* 1. Enredar, prender o coger con red. 2. *(Com.)* Sacar el producto neto de alguna cosa.

nether [ˈneðəʳ] [ne-daʳ], *a.* Inferior, lo que está más bajo en situación. **The Netherlands,** los Países Bajos.

nethermost [ˈneðəmɔʊst] [ne-da-moust], *a.* Lo más inferior o más bajo.

netmaker [ˈnetmeɪkəʳ] [net-mei-kaʳ], *s.* Redero, el que hace redes.

netted [ˈnetɪd] [ne-tid], *a.* 1. Cubierto o protegido por una red. 2. Hecho en forma de red o redecilla.

netting [ˈnetɪŋ] [ne-tin], *s.* 1. Randa, obra de malla. 2. El acto o la operación de hacer redes o redecillas. **Nettings,** *pl. (Mar.)* Enjaretados, especie de enrejado. **Quarter-nettings,** *(Mar.)* Redes de combate.

nettle [ˈnetl] [ne-tel], *s.* *(Bot.)* Ortiga. **Great nettle,** ortiga mayor u ortiga dioica. **Roman nettle,** ortiga ilulífera. **Small nettle,** ortiga menor o picante. **Dead nettle,** ortiga muerta o lamio blanco. **Red dead nettle,** lamio purpúreo. **Nettle-fever, nettle-rash,** urticaria, erupción de la piel que causa gran comezón.

nettle, *va.* Picar como ortiga; irritar, provocar.

nettle-tree [ˈnetltriː] [ne-tel-tri], *s. (Bot.)* Almez, almezo.

nettling [ˈnetlɪŋ] [ne-tlin], *s.* Provocación, irritación.

network [ˈnetwɜːk] [net-uek], *s.* 1. Malla, randa. 2. Red de estaciones radiodifusoras. 3. Red, cadena de ferrocarriles.

neural [ˈnjʊərəl] [niua-ral], *a.* 1. Nervioso, referente al sistema nervioso. 2. Colocado en el lado que contiene el eje del sistema nervioso central; perteneciente a la medula espinal. 3. Red *(Inform.)*.

neuralgia [njʊəˈrældʒɪə] [niua-ral-yia], *s.* Neuralgia, dolor vivo a lo largo de un nervio, sin calentura.

neuralgic [njʊəˈrældʒɪk] [niua-ral-yik], *a.* Neurálgico, relativo a la neuralgia.

neurasthenia [ˌnjʊərəsˈθiːnɪə] [niua-ras-zi-nia], *s. (Med.)* Neurastenia.

neuritis [njʊəˈraɪtɪs] [niua-rai-tis], *s. (Med.)* Neuritis.

neurologist [njʊəˈrɒlədʒɪst] [niua-ro-lo-yist], *s.* Neurólogo.

neurology [njʊəˈrɒlədʒɪ] [niua-ro-lo-yi], *s.* Neurología, tratado o discurso sobre los nervios.

neuron, neurone [ˈnjʊərɒn] [niua-ron], *s. (Anat.)* Neurona, célula nerviosa.

neuropterous, neuropteral [njʊəˈrɒptərəs] [niua-rop-te-ros], *a.* Neuróptero, perteneciente al orden de los neurópteros.

neurosis [njʊəˈrəʊsɪs] [niua-rou-sis], *s.* Neurosis, enfermedad de los nervios (sin lesión).

neurotic [njʊəˈrəʊtɪk] [niua-rou-tik], *a. (Med.)* Neurótico, que influye principalmente sobre los nervios.

neuter [ˈnjuːtəʳ] [niu-taʳ], *a.* 1. *(Gram.)* neutro, ni masculino, ni femenino; sin sexo; verbo intransitivo. 2. *(Bot. y Zool.)* Sin sexo, o sin sexo determinado, como las hormigas obreras. 3. *(Ant.)* Ni uno ni otro; neutral.

neutral [ˈnjuːtrəl] [niu-tral], *a.* 1. Neutral, neutro; ni bueno ni malo, indiferente, inactivo. 2. Indefinido, mediano; sin síntoma característico ni color predominante; pardusco o azulado. 3. *(Biol.)* Neutro, asexual, sin estambres ni pistilos; sin sexo. 4. Neutro, ni ácido ni alcalino. -*s.* Neutral, el que se mantiene indiferente entre dos partidos opuestos.

neutrality [njuːˈtrælɪtɪ] [niu-tra-li-ti], *s.* 1. Neutralidad, indiferencia, el acto de no tomar partido por algo. 2. Calidad de neutro, ni ácido ni alcalino.

neutralize [ˈnjuːtrəlaɪz] [niu-tra-lais], *adv.* Neutralmente.

neutrino [ˈnjuːtriːnəʊ] [niu-tri-nou], *s. (Fís. y Quím.)* Neutrino.

neutron [ˈnjuːtrən] [niu-tron], *s.* (Phys. y Chem.) Neutrón.

never [ˈnevəʳ] [ne-vaʳ], *adv.* 1. Nunca, jamás, en ningún tiempo; de ningún modo. **I shall never be the better of it,** nada adelantaré con eso. **Never a one,** ni siquiera uno. **Never a whit,** nada absolutamente, ni pizca. 2. No. **Never mind,** no importa, no haga Ud. caso. **Never fear,** no hay cuiddo, no hay miedo. 3. Por; por más que. **Well I never!** ¡no me digas! ¡anda ya! **Were the world never so unfriendly,** por más hostil que fuese el mundo. **Never so great o little,** por grande o pequeño que sea.

never-ceasing [ˈnevəˈsiːsɪŋ] [ne-va-si-sin], *a.* Continuo, perpetuo.

never-ending [ˈnevəʳˈendɪŋ] [ne-var-en-din], *a.* Perpetuo, sin fin, eterno.

never-erring [ˈnevəʳˈerɪŋ] [ne-var-erin], *a.* Infalible.

never-fading [ˈnevəˈfeɪdɪŋ] [ne-va-fei-din], *a.* Inmarcesible.

never-failing [ˈnevəˈfeɪlɪŋ] [ne-va-fei-lin], *a.* Inagotable, infalible.

nevermore ['nevə'mɔːʳ] [ne-va-mo'], *adv.* Jamás, nunca.

neverteless [ˌnevəðə'les] [ne-va-de-les], *adv.* No obstante que, con todo eso, sin embargo, todavía, a pesar de eso.

new [njuː] [niu], *a.* 1. Nuevo, fresco, reciente, moderno. 2. Nuevo, no acostumbrado, no habituado, tierno. 3. Moderno; renovado. *-adv.* Nuevamente, recientemente. **The New-year,** el año nuevo, el primer día del año. **New bread,** pan fresco, tierno. **Bran new, spick and span new,** flamante, nuevecito. **This is something new for me,** esto es nuevo para mí, esto me sorprende. **To put on the new man,** transformarse en otro hombre. **The New World,** el Nuevo Mundo, el hemisferio occidental. **New Age music,** música de la Nueva Era.

new-blown ['njuː'blaʊn] [niu-blaun], *a.* Lo que acaba de florecer o echar flor.

new-born ['njuː'bɔːn] [niu-born], *a.* Recién nacido.

newcomer ['njuː'kʌməʳ] [niu-ka-ma'], *s.* Recién llegado.

new-created ['njuː'krɪ'eɪtɪd] [niu-kri-ei-tid], *a.* Recién criado.

new-delivered ['njuːˌdelɪvəd] [niu-de-li-ved], *a.* Recién parida.

newel ['njuːəl] [niuel], *s.* 1. Pilar de escalera de caracol. 2. Poste o pilar en la parte superior e inferior de una escalera, que sostiene el pasamano.

new-fallen ['njuː'fɔːlən] [niu-fo-len], *a.* Recién caído.

new-fangled ['njuːˌfæŋgld] [niu-fan-gueld], *a.* Novel, recién inventado.

new-fashion ['njuːˌfæʃən] [niu-fa-shon], *s.* La última moda.

new-fashioned ['njuːˌfæʃənd] [niu-fa-shond], *a.* Hecho a la última moda.

new-formed ['njuː'fɔːmd] [niu-formd], *a.* Reformado, formado de nuevo.

new-found ['njuːˌfaʊnd] [niu-faund], *a.* Recién hallado, recién descubierto. **New-foundland,** (a) Terranova. (b) Perro grande originario de Terranova. **Newfoundland fish,** bacalao o bacallao, abadejo.

new-grown ['njuː'grəʊn] [niu-groun], *a.* Recién crecido, recién salido.

new-healed ['njuː'hiːld] [niu-jild], *a.* Dícese del que acaba de salir de una enfermedad.

newish ['njuːɪʃ] [niuish], *a.* Nuevo, reciente.

new-hindled ['njuː'hɪndld] [niu-jin-deld], *a.* Encendido de nuevo.

new-laid ['njuː'leɪd] [niu-leid], *a.* Recién puesto o tendido.

newly ['njuːlɪ] [niu-li], *adv.* Nuevamente, recientemente, hace poco. **Newly come,** recién venido.

newlywed ['njuːlɪwɪd] [niu-liuid], *s.* y a. Recién casado.

new-made ['njuː'meɪd] [niu-meid], *a.* Nuevo.

new-married ['njuː'mærɪd] [niu-ma-rid], *a.* Novio, recién casado.

new-moulded ['njuː'maʊldɪd] [niu-maul-did], *a.* Amoldado de nuevo, recién hecho.

newness ['njuːnɪs] [niu-nes], *s.* 1. La cualidad de lo que es nuevo o reciente, novedad, cosa moderna; innovación. 2. Falta de práctica; la situación del que tiene que hacer por primera vez alguna cosa.

news [njuːz] [nius], *s.* 1. Noticias, novedades, nuevas. 2. Noticia, aviso que se da de alguna cosa; informe. En este sentido es siempre singular aunque tiene forma plural. **What is the news?** ¿Qué hay de nuevo? ¿qué noticias hay? **This was news to me,** me cogió de nuevo. **No news is good news,** falta de noticias, buena señal. **News agent,** vendedor de periódicos. **News-room,** gabinete de lectura. *-va.* (E. U. y Prov. Ingl.) Dar a luz, divulgar, publicar como noticia.

newscast ['njuː'zkɑːst] [nius-kast], *s.* Noticiario, *(Mex.)* Noticiero.

newsdealer ['njuːz'diːlə'] [nius-di-la'], *s.* Vendedor de periódicos.

news-monger ['njuːz'mʌŋgəʳ] [nius-mon-ga'], *s.* Novelero, amigo de noticias.

newspaper ['njuːsˌpeɪpəʳ] [nius-pei-pa'], *s.* Diario, periódico (por lo general cotidiano o semanal), gaceta. **Newspaper clipping,** recorte de periódico.

newsprint ['njuːzprɪnt] [nius-print], *s.* Papel para periódicos.

newsreel ['njuːzriːl] [nius-ril], *s.* Noticiario. *(Mex.)* Noticiero.

newsroom ['njuːzrʊm] [nius-rum], *s. f.* Sala de redacción.

newsstand ['njuːztænd] [nius-tand], *s.* Puesto de periódicos, revistas, etc.

newsworthy ['njuːzˌwɜːθɪ] [nius-uor-zi], *a.* De interés periodístico.

news-writer ['njuːzˌraɪtəʳ] [nius-rai-ta'], *s.* Gacetero.

newsy ['njuːzɪ] [ni-si], *a.* Abundante en noticias.

newt ['njuːt] [niut], *s.* Tritón, batracio pequeño.

newtonian [njuː'təʊnɪən] [niu-tou-nian], *a.* Neutoniano, lo perteneciente a la filosofía de Newton.

new-year's gift ['njuːˌjɪəzgɪft] [niu-yias-guift], *s.* Aguinaldo, regalo que se da el día de Año Nuevo.

New Yorker ['njuːˌjɔːkəʳ] [niu-yor-ka'], *s.* y a. Neoyorquino.

next ['nekst] [nekst], *a.* 1. Inmediato, contiguo. **The next house,** la casa vecina. 2. Próximo, lo más cercano. 3. Siguiente; sucesivo, que sigue inmediatamente en tiempo u orden. **The next day,** el día siguiente. **I'll do better next time,** lo haré mejor en el futuro. **Next to,** (a) casi. **He is next to the president,** es el primero después del presidente. (b) Casi, poco más o menos. **Next to impossible,** casi imposible. **What next?,** ¿y luego, qué? **What will you do next?,** ¿qué harás después? **Next year,** el año que viene, el año próximo venidero. **Next Sunday,** el domingo que viene. **The next life,** la otra vida, la vida venidera. **That is a difficulty next to impossible,** esa es una dificultad casi imposible o que raya en lo imposible. *-adv.* Luego, inmediatamente después.

next-door ['nekstdɔːʳ] [nekst-do'], *a.* **Next-door flat,** piso de al lado.

next-of-kin ['nekstɒvˌkɪn] [nekst-ov-kin], *s.* Pariente más cercano.

nexus ['neksəs] [nek-sus], *s.* Nexo, lazo o vínculo de una cosa con otra.

NGO *Abreviatura de* **Non-Governmental Organization** *(EU).*

NH *Abreviatura de* **Natural Health.**

niacin ['naɪəsɪn] [naia-sin], *s.* Niacina.

nib [nɪb] [nib], *s.* 1. Pico, el extremo de la cabeza del ave. 2. Pico, punta, el extremo de cualquiera cosa; punto de la pluma de acero, o tajo de la ave.

nib, *va.* Hacer punta; aguzar, afilar la punta de.

nibble ['nɪbl] [ni-bel], *va.* Picar, morder pedacitos de, roer, comer a bocaditos, morder, como muerde el pez el anzuelo, rozar, pacer. *-vn.* 1. Morder, mordiscar. 2. Satirizar, criticar; (con la prep. *at*).

nibble, *s.* 1. Roedura, la acción de roer, de comer poco a pcoo, a pedacitos menudos, el acto de morder algo con cautela. 2. Pedacito roído casi todo o en parte.

nibbler ['nɪbləʳ] [ni-bla'], *s.* El que pica o come poco a la vez; criticastro.

niccolite ['nɪkəlaɪt] [ni-ko-lait], *s.* Niquelina, arseniuro de níquel. Se llama también *copper-nickel* por su color rojizo.

nice [naɪs] [nais], *a.* 1. Delicado, mirado, exacto, diligente, solícito. 2. Circunspecto, cauto en extremo. 3. Tierno, delicado, lo que con facilidad se aja o deteriora. 4. Fino, primoroso, refinado, elegante, esmerado. 5. Fastidioso, escrupuloso, fácil de resentirse, vidrioso. 6. *(Fam.)* Gustoso, agradable de cualquier modo, delicioso, exquisito, bueno; gentil, amable. **To be nice,** hacer melindres. **Have a nice time!** ¡que lo pases bien! **To make nice,** ser escrupuloso o delicado. **A nice point,** un punto delicado. **A nice distinction,** una distinción exacta, sutil. **She is a nice girl,** es una muchacha gentil, amable. **A nice bit,** un buen bocado; un trozo escogido. **To be nice with somebody,** ser amable con alguien. **A nice mess!** ¡Vaya lío!

nice-looking [naɪsˈlʊkɪŋ] [nais-lu-kin], *a.* Guapo, lindo, mono.

nicely [ˈnaɪslɪ] [nais-li], *adv.* 1. Exactamente, con esmero. 2. Delicadamente. 3. Primorosamente.

niceness [ˈnaɪsnɪs] [nais-nes], *s.* 1. Exactitud, esmero. 2. Delicadeza, nimiedad.

nicety [ˈnaɪsɪtɪ] [nai-si-ti], *s.* 1. Cualidad de lo que es delicado, agradable, primoroso, exactitud, esmero en la ejecución de alguna cosa. 2. Delicadeza, sutileza, afeminación. 3. Circunspección, discreción, discernimiento; refinamiento, argucia, carácter prolijo de una observación o distinción. **Niceties,** detalles. **The niceties of logic, of politics,** las sutilezas de la lógica, las argucias de la política. **Nicety of honor,** la delicadeza del honor, el pundonor. **Meat done to a nicely,** carne, manjar guisado a punto. **To a nicely,** con la mayor precisión. **The niceties of a woman,** los melindres o arrumacos de una mujer. **Niceties,** golosinas, manjares delicados.

niche [niːʃ] [nish], *s.* Nicho, concavidad formada para colocar en ella una estatua, urna, florero, etc.

nick [nɪk] [nik], *s.* 1. Punto crítico, ocasión oportuna, tiempo preciso. 2. Muesca. 3. Escote. 4. Tarja. **In the nick of time,** al tiempo preciso, a buen tiempo a punto fijo. **In good nick,** en buenas condiciones *(fam).*

nick, *n. pr.* (abreviatura de Nicholas). **Old Nick,** el diablo.

nick, *va.* 1. Acertar, dar en el clavo; llegar a tiempo. 2. Cortar en muecas. 3. Tarjar, señalar números en tarjas. 4. *(Des.)* Engañar, pegársela a uno. 5. Arrestar, trincar (arrest). **You're nicked!** ¡queda detenido!

nickel [ˈnɪkl] [ni-kel], *s.* 1. *(Quím.)* Níquel, metal duro, maleable, blanco argentino, magnético, difícil de fundir y oxidar. 2. *(Fam.)* Moneda de cinco centavos de los Estados Unidos, hecha de una aleación de níquel y cobre. **Nickel-plated,** niquelado, que tiene una capa galvánica de níquel. **Nickel-plate,** *va.* Niquelar, cubrir otro metal con una capa de níquel, por medio de la galvanoplastia.

nicknack [ˈnɪknæk] [nik-nak], *s.* Friolera, cosa de poco valor. **Sundry nicknacks,** varias chucherías.

nickname [ˈnɪkneɪm] [nik-neim], *s.* Apodo, mote, mal nombre.

nickname, *va.* Motejar, poner apodos.

nicotin, nicotine [ˈnɪkətiːn] [ni-ko-tin], *s.* Nicotina.

nictitate [ˈnɪktɪteɪt] [nik-ti-teit], *vn.* Pestañear, parpadear. **Nictitating membrane,** membrana de pestañeo, el tercer párpado, o párpado lateral de las aves, de los cocodrilos, etc.

nictitation [ˌnɪktɪˈteɪʃən] [nik-ti-tei-shon], *s.* Pestañeo; en patología, pestañeo rápido e involuntario, debido a un desarreglo nervioso.

nidificant [ˈnɪdɪfɪkənt] [ni-di-fi-kant], *a.* Que hace nidos, como un ave.

nidification [ˌnɪdɪfɪˈkeɪʃən] [ni-di-fi-kei-shon], *s.* Nidificación, el acto de hacer nidos las aves.

nidify [ˈnɪdɪfaɪ] [ni-di-fai], *vn.* Nidificar, anidar.

nidor [ˈnaɪdɔːr] [nai-doᵉ], *s.* Olor, sabor, como de manjar cocido o a socarrado.

nidorosity [ˌnaɪdəˈrɒsɪtɪ] [nai-do-ro-si-ti], *s.* Eructo o regüeldo.

nidorous [ˈnaɪdərəs] [nai-do-ros], *a.* Lo que huele a carne o grasa asada; y en medicina lo que huele o sabe a huevo podrido.

nidulate [ˈnɪdjuːleɪt] [ni-diu-leit], *va.* V. NIDIFY.

nidulation [ˌnɪdjuːˈleɪʃən] [ni-diu-lei-shon], *s.* El tiempo de quedar en el nido.

niece [niːs] [nis], *sf.* Sobrina.

niello [ˈnɪeləʊ] [nie-lou], *s.* Niel, labor que se hace con el buril o el cincel en los metales. *-va.* Nielar, entallar o abrir a buril varias labores en metal, rellenando los huecos con otro metal diferente, o con una aleación negra.

nig [nɪɡ] [nig], *va.* 1. Cortar el borde de algo, v. g. de una moneda. 2. Labrar a pico (hablando de piedra).

nigella [ˈnɪɡelə] [ni-gue-la], *s.* *(Bot.)* Neguilla.

niggard [ˈnɪɡɑːd] [ni-gard], *s.* Tacaño, avaro y mezquino. *-a.* 1. Avariento, avaro, miserable, ruin. 2. Escaso, económico, mezquino.

niggard, *va.* *(Poco us.)* Escasear.

niggardish [ˈnɪɡɑːdɪʃ] [ni-gar-dish], *a.* Avariento, ruin, mezquino.

niggardliness [ˈnɪɡɑːdlɪnɪs] [ni-gard-li-nes], **niggardness** [ˈnɪɡɑːdnɪs] [ni-gard-nes], *s.* Tacañería, miseria, ruindad.

niggardly [ˈnɪɡɑːlɪ] [ni-gard-li], *adv.* Tacañamente, ruinmente.

nigger [ˈnɪɡɑːr] [ni-gaʳ], *s.* Negro *(Fam.).*

niggle [ˈnɪɡl] [ni-guel], *vn.* Jugar, travesear o retozar; burlarse de.

niggling [ˈnɪɡlɪŋ] [ni-glin], *a.* 1. Constante (doubt). 2. Insignificante (detail). 3. Meticuloso, quisquilloso (person).

nigh [naɪ] [nai], *prep.* Cerca, no lejos, a proximidad. **Nigh at hand,** cerca a la mano. **Nigh to death,** próximo a morir. *-adv.* Cerca, inmediato, junto a; casi, cuasi. **Draw nigh,** acérquese Ud. *-a.* 1. Cercano, próximo, vecino, poco lejano. 2. A la izquierda, de la izquierda; se dice de una yunta de bueyes o caballos. 3. *(E. U. y Prov. Ingl.)* Apretado, mezquino. 4. Allegado, pariente; íntimo.

nighness [ˈnaɪnɪs] [nai-nes], *s.* Cercanía, proximidad.

night [naɪt] [nait], *s.* 1. Noche, todo el tiempo que el sol permanece fuera de nuestro horizonte. 2. Caída de la tarde, término del día. 3. Noche, tinieblas, oscuridad; ceguedad física; falta de inteligencia; tristeza, aflicción. 4. La muerte, la sepultura, o la vejez muy avanzada. **By night,** de noche. **To wish one a good-night,** darle a uno las buenas noches. **Wednesday night,** miércoles por la noche. **Tonight,** esta noche, a la noche. **Last night,** la noche pasada, ayer noche. **To morrow night,** mañana por la noche. **Night,** en composición; **Night-bell,** campanilla para llamar por la noche. **Night-bird,** pájaro nocturno. **Night-blindness,** defecto del nervio óptico que sólo permite ver los objetos durante el día. **Night-brawler,** alborotador nocturno. **Night-clothes,** camisa de dormir, traje de dormir. **Night-chair,** V. **Night-stool. Night-dew,** sereno de noche. **Night-dog,** perro que caza de noche. **Night-dress,** vestido de noche. **Night-fire,** fuego fatuo, helena, santelmo. **Night-fly,** polilla que vuela de noche. **Night-glass,** anteojo para observaciones nocturnas. **Night-hag,** bruja nocturna. **Night-hawk,** chotacabras, pájaro nocturno. **Night-jar,** chotacabras europea. **Night-lamp, night-light,** mariposa, candelilla para conservar luz de noche. **Night-piece,** la pintura en que se representa la noche o una escena nocturna. **Night-raven,** *(Orn.)* Ave de mal agüero que canta de noche. **Night-rest,** el reposo de la noche. **Night-robber,** ladrón nocturno. **Night-robe,** camisa de dormir. **Night-school,** escuela nocturna; por lo común, escuela gratis para los que trabajan durante el día. **Night-shining,** que reluce o da resplandor de noche. **Night-shriek,** chillido que se oye de noche. **Night-spell,** encanto para librarse de percances por la noche. **Night-stool,** sillico; la silla agujereada bajo la cual se pone el sillico. **Night sweat,** sudor nocturno. **Night-time,** noche, el tiempo que media desde el anochecer hasta el alba. **Night-tripping,** lo que vaga de noche. **Night-vision,** sueño, visión nocturna. **Night-walk,** paseo de noche. **Night-walker,** sonámbulo. **Night-walking,** paseante de noche; sonámbulo. *-s.* Sonambulismo; paseo nocturno; solicitación de prostituta. **Night-wanderer,** el que vaga de noche. **Night-wandering,** noctívago. **Night-warbling,** el que canta por la noche. **Night-watch,** centinela o ronda de noche. **Night-work,** trabajo nocturno.

nightcap [ˈnaɪtkæp] [nait-kap], *s.* 1. Gorro de dormir. 2. *(Fam.)* Bebida que se toma antes de acostarse.

nighted [ˈnaɪtɪd] [nai-tid], *a.* Negro, obscuro.

nightfall [ˈnaɪtfɔːl] [nait-fol], *s.* El anochecer.

nightfaring ['naɪt'fɛərɪŋ] [nait-fea-rin], *a.* Que viaja de noche.

nightgown ['naɪtgaʊn] [nait-gaun], *s.* Bata que se usa de noche; traje de dormir.

nightingale ['naɪtɪŋgeɪl] [nai-tin-gueil], *s. (Orn.)* Ruiseñor.

night letter ['naɪtletəʳ] [nait-le-taʳ], *s.* Carta telegráfica nocturna.

nightly ['naɪtlɪ] [nait-li], *adv.* Por las noches, todas las noches. -*a.* Nocturno, de noche; que ocurre o aparece durante la noche.

nightman ['naɪtmən] [nait-man], *s.* Empleado que trabaja de noche.

nightmare ['naɪtmɛəʳ] [nait-meaʳ], *s.* Pesadilla.

night school ['naɪtskuːl] [nait-skul], *s.* Escuela nocturna.

night service ['naɪtsɜːvɪs] [nait-ser-vis], *s.* Servicio nocturno.

nightward ['naɪtwɔːd] [nait-uard], *a.* Lo que suele hacerse al acercarse la noche.

nigrescence ['nɪgrəsəns] [ni-gre-sens], *s.* La acción de ennegrecer y la negura producida.

nigrescent ['nɪgrəsənt] [ni-gre-sent], *a.* Ennegrecido, negruzco.

nigrification [ˌnɪgrɪfaɪ'keɪʃən] [ni-gri-fai-kei-shon], *s.* Ennegrecimiento.

nigrify ['nɪgrɪfaɪ] [ni-gri-fai], *va.* Hacer negro, ennegrecer.

nihil ['naɪɪl] [nail], *s. (Lat.)* Nada.

nihilism ['naɪɪlɪzəm] [nai-li-sem], *s.* 1. Nihilismo, negación de toda creencia. 2. Nihilismo.

nihilist ['naɪɪlɪst] [naii-list], *s.* 1. Nihilista.

nihility ['naɪɪlɪtɪ] [naii-li-ti], *s.* Estado de lo que no existe; la nada.

nil, nill [nɪl] [nil], *s.* Nada.

nilgau, nighau ['nɪlgəʊ] [nil-gou], *s.* Tragélafo, rumiante parecido al antílope.

nill [nɪl] [nil], *va.* Rehusar, no querer. **Will he, nill he,** a buenas o a malas, que quiera que no quiera.

nill, *s.* Chispa de bronce fundido.

nimbiferous [nɪm'bɪfərəs] [nim-bi-fe-ros], *a.* Que trae nubes, lluvia o tempestades.

nimble ['nɪmbl] [nim-bel], *a.* Ligero, vivo, activo, listo, ágil.

nimble-footed ['nɪmbl ˌfuːtɪd] [nim-bel-fu-tid], *a.* Ligero de pies.

nimbleness ['nɪmblnɪs] [nim-bel-nes], *s.* Ligereza, velocidad, actividad, agilidad, celeridad; expedición, destreza.

nimble-witted ['nɪmbl ˌwɪtɪd] [nim-bel-ui-tid], *a.* Pronto en hablar; penetrante, de inteligencia viva.

nimbly ['nɪmblɪ] [nim-bli], *adv.* Prontamente, ágilmente.

nimbosity ['nɪmbəsɪtɪ] [nim-bo-si-ti], *s.* Tormenta.

nimbus ['nɪmbəs] [nim-bos], *s.* 1. Nimbo, nube obscura y espesa. 2. Aureola, diadema o círculo de luz que se pone sobre la cabeza de los santos.

nincompoop ['nɪŋkəmpuːp] [nin-kom-pup], *s. (Fam.)* Badulaque, simplón, tonto.

nine [naɪn] [nain], *a.* Nueve. -*s.* 1. Nueve. 2. *(Poét.)* Las musas, las nueve hermanas. **Nine men's morris,** v. MORRIS.

ninefold ['naɪnfəʊld] [nain-fould], *a. y adv.* Nueve veces.

ninepins ['naɪnpɪnz] [nain-pins], *s.* Juego de bolos.

ninescore ['naɪnskɔːʳ] [nain-skoʳ], *a. y s.* Nueve veces veinte.

nineteen ['naɪn'tiːn] [nain-tin], *a. y s.* Diez y nueve.

nineteenth ['naɪn'tiːnθ] [nain-tinz], *a.* Décimonono.

ninetieth ['naɪntɪɪθ] [nain-tiez], *a.* Nonagésimo.

ninety ['naɪntɪ] [nain-ti], *a. y s.* Noventa.

ninth [naɪnθ] [nainz], *a.* Nono, noveno.

ninthly ['naɪnθlɪ] [nainz-li], *adv.* Noveno o en nono lugar.

Nip [nɪp] [nip], *a.* Japonés, nipón.

ninny, ninnyhammer ['nɪnɪ] [ni-ni] ['nɪnɪ'hæməʳ] [nin-ni-ja-maʳ], *s.* Un simple, un mentecato, un nene, un imbécil, un bobo, zote.

nip, *va.* 1. Arañar, rasguñar de repente, pellizcar; morder, cortar con las uñas o los dientes. 2. Quebrar, pellizcar, o desgarrar la superficie o extremo de. 3. Helar o secar los frutos antes de madurarse; marchitar, hacer perecer en germen. **To nip in the bud o blossom,** destruir en germen, en el principio. 4. Tocar de cerca, interesar. **To nip off,** cortar alguna cosa fácil de separarse de donde estaba unida.

nip, *s.* 1. Pellizco, acción y efecto de pellizcar; porción pequeña, pedacito; trago, traguito; uñada, dentellada. 2. Helada, escarcha. 3. Cogida; la situación de lo que está cogido entre los hielos o encerrado en ellos. 4. Daño repentino que sufren las plantas o los sembrados. **Nip and tuck,** *(Fam. E. U.)* Caso de igualdad, de empate. 5. *(Des.)* Sátira, dicho picante y mordaz.

nipper ['nɪpəʳ] [ni-paʳ], *s.* Lo que pellizca o muerde: pinza; la garra grande de un cangrejo; pala, diente delantero del caballo. V. NIPPERS.

nippers ['nɪpəz] [ni-pars], *s. pl.* 1. Alicates, tenazas. 2. *(Mar.)* Mojelas, badernas.

nipping ['nɪpɪŋ] [ni-pin], *s.* Arañazo, rasguño, mordedura. **Nipping jest,** Chanza pesada, dicho picante, sátira mordaz.

nippingly ['nɪpɪŋlɪ] [ni-pin-li], *adv.* Mordazmente.

nipple ['nɪpl] [ni-pel], *s.* 1. Pezón, la punta que sobresale en los pechos o tetas. 2. Chimenea de un arma de fuego de percusión. 3. Pezón artificial que se emplea con un biberón o para proteger un pezón lastimado. **Nipple shield,** pezonera.

nipplewort ['nɪplwɔːt] [ni-pel-uort], *s. (Bot.)* Lapsana común.

nirvana [nɪə'vaːnə] [nia-va-na], *s.* Nirvana.

nit [nɪt] [nit], *s.* 1. Liendre, el huevo del piojo. 2. Punto pequeño. 3. *a.* Tonto, imbécil *(Fam.)*.

nitency ['nɪtənsɪ] [ni-tan-si], *s.* Lustre, esplendor, brillantez.

niter, nitre ['nɪtəʳ] [ni-taʳ], *s.* Nitro, salitre, nitrato de potasa.

nitrate ['nɪtreɪt] [ni-treit], *s. (Quím.)* Nitrato, sal formada de ácido nítrico con alguna base.

nitre ['nɪtəʳ] [ni-taʳ], *s.* V. NITER.

nitric ['naɪtrɪk] [nai-trik], *a.* Nítrico, azoico.

nitrite ['naɪtrɪt] [nai-trit], *s.* Nitrito, sal formada del ácido nitroso con alguna base.

nitrogen ['naɪtrədʒɪn] [nai-tro-yin], *s.* Nitrógeno.

nitrogenize ['naɪtrədʒɪnaɪz] [nai-tro-yi-nais], *va.* Tratar por el nitrógeno o combinar con él.

nitrogenous ['naɪtrədʒɪnəs] [nai-tro-yi-nos], *a.* Nitrogenado, que pertenece o contiene nitrógeno, le pertenece o se relaciona con él.

nitroglycerin ['naɪtrəˌglɪsərɪn] [nai-tro-gli-se-rin], *s.* Nitroglicerina, líquido aceitoso, amarillo claro, de tremenda fuerza explosiva; se mezcla comúnmente con una sustancia neutra para formar la dinamita.

nitrous ['naɪtrəs] [nai-tros], **nitry** ['naɪtrɪ] [nai-tri], *a.* Nitroso.

nitrous oxide ['naɪtrəsˌɒksɪd] [nai-tros-ok-sid], *s.* Óxido nitroso, gas hilarante.

nitty ['nɪtɪ] [ni-ti], *a.* Lendroso, lleno de liendres. **To get down to the nitty-gritty,** ir directamente al grano.

nitwit ['nɪtwɪt] [nit-uit], *s.* Necio, bruto, imbécil.

nival ['nɪvəl] [ni-val], *a.* 1. Nevoso. 2. Que crece debajo de la nieve.

niveous ['nɪvɪəs] [ni-vios], *a.* Blanco como la nieve o lo que se parece a la nieve.

nix ['nɪks] [niks], **nixie** [nik-si], *s.* Genio de las aguas en la mitología alemana.

nix, *s. (Germ. E. U.)* Nada.

NNE *Abreviatura de* **North-North-East.**

NNW *Abreviatura de* **North-North-West.**

no [nəʊ] [nou], *adv.* No. **Whether or no,** sea o no sea; que ... no. **No more of this,** basta, bastante, no hablemos más de eso. -*a.* Ningún, ninguno. **By no means,** de ninguna manera, de ningún modo. **No matter, it is no matter,** no importa. **To no purpose,** sin razón alguna., sin objeto, en vano, inútilmente. **You shall come to no harm,** no le sucederá a Ud. nada de malo. **No one,** nadie. **To wrong no one,** no hacer daño a nadie. **No-account,** sin valor, despreciable, vil bajo.

Noah's Ark ['nəʋəsɑːk] [nous-ark], s. Arca de Noé; cajón de sastre.

noachian ['nəʋəkɪən] [noua-kian], a. Relativo a Noé.

nob ['nɒb] [nob], s. 1. *(Fest.)* La cabeza. 2. V. KNOB. 3. *(Germ.)* Persona de distinción social, de buen tono.

nobby ['nɒbɪ] [no-bi], a. *(Germ.)* Llamativo; ostentoso, a la moda.

Nobel prize ['nɒblpraɪs] [no-bel-prais], s. Premio Nobel.

nobiliary ['nɒbɪlɪərɪ] [no-bi-lia-ri], a. Nobiliario.

nobility [nəʋ'bɪlɪtɪ] [nou-bi-li-ti], s. 1. Nobleza. 2. Nobleza, se toma colectivamente por el brazo o cuerpo de nobles. 3. Nobleza, dignidad, grandeza, sublimidad de alma, de sentimientos, de estilo, etc.

noble ['nəʋbl] [nou-bel], a. 1. Noble, hidalgo, que pertenece al cuerpo de la nobleza. 2. Noble, insigne, esclarecido, majestuoso. 3. Noble, elevado, sublime. 4. Magnífico, generoso. 5. Liberal. -s. Noble, la persona que pertenece a la nobleza. **They are of noble extraction,** son de noble alcurnia, o de sangre azul. **To make noble,** ennoblecer. **Noble metals,** metales nobles, es decir, el oro, la plata y el platino.

nobleman ['nəʋblmən] [nou-bel-man], s. Noble, hidalgo. V. NOBLE, 1ª acep.

nobleness ['nəʋblnɪs] [nou-bel-nes], s. 1. Nobleza, dignidad, grandeza. 2. Lustre, esplendor.

noblesse ['nəʋbliːs] [nou-blis], s. 1. Nobleza, el conjunto o cuerpo de los nobles. 2. *(Ant.)* Nobleza, alcurnia noble.

noblewoman ['nəʋblwʊmən] [nou-bel-uo-man], s. Mujer noble, hidalga.

nobly ['nəʋblɪ] [nou-bli], adv. Noblemente. **Nobly born,** noble de nacimiento.

nobody ['nəʋbədɪ] [nou-ba-di], s. 1. Nadie, ninguna persona, ninguno. 2. Persona de ninguna estimación, un Don Nadie, un cero a la izquierda. **A mere nobody,** un Don Nadie. **To be nobody at all,** no ser nada absolutamente. **Nobody else,** nadie más, ningún otro.

nock [nɒk] [nok], s. 1. *(Mar.)* Puño de la boca (de una vela). 2. *(Des.)* Muesca, abertura. V. NOTCH.

noctiluca ['nɒktɪljuːkə] [nok-ti-liu-ka], s. Noctiluco, animalillo marino microscópico: es la causa ordinaria de la fosforescencia del mar.

noctivagant ['nɒktɪvəgənt] [nok-ti-va-gant], a. *(Poco us.)* Noctívago, el que anda vagando por la noche.

noctivagation [ˌnɒktɪvə'geɪʃən] [nok-ti-va-guei-shon], s. El acto de vagar de noche.

noctuary ['nɒktʊərɪ] [nok-tua-ri], s. Relación de lo que sucede por la noche.

noctuidæ ['nɒktʊdiː] [nok-tui-di], s. pl. Noctuinos, mariposas nocturnas.

nocturn ['nɒktɜːn] [nok-tern], s. Nocturno.

nocturnal [nɒk'tɜːnl] [nok-ter-nal], a. 1. Nocturnal, nocturno; hecho o sucedido de noche. 2. Activo de noche, que busca su alimento por la noche, como los buhos, los noctuinos, etc.

nocturnal, s. Nocturlabio, antiguo instrumento para medir de noche la latitud por la altura de las estrellas.

nocturne ['nɒktɜːn] [nok-tern], s. 1. Cuadro, pintura que representa una escena nocturna. 2. *(Mús.)* Nocturno, composición música de melodía dulce y sentimental.

nod [nɒd] [nod], vn. 1. Cabecear. 2. Hacer un movimiento con la cabeza inclinándola hacia abajo, en señal de respeto o de afecto. 3. Hacer una señal con la cabeza. 4. Amodorrarse, adormecerse. -va. 1. Mover la cabeza, dar cabezadas. 2. Indicar, hacer saber, con una inclinación de la cabeza. 3. Inclinar la cima o parte superior, como de una flor o de un árbol. **Nod off,** quedarse dormido. **Nod through,** dejar pasar (inclinando la cabeza). **She nodded his head,** asintió con la cabeza. **To go through on the nod,** ser aprobado sin discusión o votación.

nod, s. 1. Cabeceo. 2. Cabezada, el movimiento de la cabeza cuando uno se duerme. 3. Reverencia, mocha, inclinación de la cabeza en señal de cortesín. 4. Cualquiera señal hecha con la cabeza.

nodal ['nɒdəl] [no-dal], a. 1. Nodal, que se refiere a los nodos de una superficie vibrante. 2. Nudoso, referente a uno o varios nudos.

nodder ['nɒdəʳ] [no-daʳ], s. El que cabecea o da cabezadas.

nodding ['nɒdɪŋ] [no-din], pa. *(Bot.)* Nutante, cuya parte superior se inclina o cuelga parte superior se inclina o cuelga hacia abajo. -s. 1. Cabeceo. 2. Dormitación.

noddle ['nɒdl] [no-del], s. Mollera, cabeza: se usa despectivamente.

noddy ['nɒdɪ] [no-di], s. 1. Un simple, un tonto, zote. 2. Carruaje ligero de dos ruedas. 3. Ave de una de las varias especies de pájaros bobos.

node ['nəʋd] [noud], s. 1. Nudo. 2. *(Cir.)* Nodo, nudo, un tumor o dureza de los huesos. 3. *(Astr.)* Nodo, cualquiera de los dos puntos opuestos en que la órbita de un planeta corta la eclíptica. 4. *(Bot.)* Nudo, punto del tallo por donde frotan las ramas o de donde nacen las hojas. 5. Nodo, el punto en que una curva se corta a sí misma. 6. Enredo, nudo, intriga de una novela o drama.

nodose ['nəʋdəs] [nou-dos], a. Nudoso, que tiene nudoso o junturas salientes.

nodosity ['nəʋdəsɪtɪ] [nou-do-si-ti], s. Nudosidad, complicación o abundancia de nudos.

nodular ['nɒdjɒləʳ] [no-diu-laʳ],, a. Parecido a un nudo; que tiene nudos, nodular.

nodule ['nɒdjuːl] [no-diul], s. Nudillo, nódulo; bulto o elevación pequeña de cualquier especie.

noduled ['nɒdjuːld] [no-diuld], a. Lo que tiene nudillos o elevaciones.

noetic ['nəʋiːtɪk] [noui-tik], a. Mental, concebido por la mente; intuitivo.

nog [nɒg] [nog], s. 1. Baldosa cuadrada de madera. 2. *(Mar.)* Cabilla para escotas; clavija de madera.

nog, s. *(Prov. Ing.)* 1. Pucherito, cantarito. 2. Una cerveza fuerte. **Egg-nog,** bebida que se hace con leche, huevos, azúcar y algún licor espirituoso.

noggin ['nɒgɪn] [no-guin], s. *(Prov.)* Vasija de madera; también, jarro y su contenido. V. MUG.

nogging ['nɒgɪn] [no-guin], s. Tabique.

no-good [nəʋ'guːd] [nou-gud], *(EU)* Malvado, perverso.

no-hoper [nəʋ'həʋpəʳ] [nou-jo-paʳ], s. f. Nulidad.

noise [nɔɪz] [nois], s. 1. Ruido, sonido, estruendo. 2. Bulla, clamor, gritería. 3. ruido, rumor, y por extensión fama, nombre, noticia o novedad. **Noise in one's ears,** zumbido de oídos. **Noise pollution,** contaminación auditiva. **To make a noise,** hacer ruido. **To make noises about doing something,** manifestar intención de hacer algo. **Big noise,** pez gordo *(fig. person)*.

noise, va. 1. Esparcir, divulgar o extender alguna noticia. 2. Turbar con gritos o con estruendo.

noiseful ['nɔɪzfʊl] [nois-ful], a. Ruidoso.

noiseless ['nɔɪzlɪs] [nois-les], a. Quedo, sin ruido, tranquilo, callado.

noiselessly ['nɔɪzlɪslɪ] [nois-les-li], adv. En silencio.

noisemaker [nɔɪz,meɪkəʳ] [nois-mei-kaʳ], *(EU)* Matraca.

noisily ['nɔɪzɪlɪ] [noi-si-li], adv. De manera escandalosa, ruidosamente, con estrépito.

noisiness ['nɔɪzɪnɪs] [noi-si-nes], s. Estrépito, ruido, tumulto, alboroto.

noisome ['nɔɪsəm] [nois-som], a. 1. Ofensivo, asqueroso, desagradable, repugnante, particularmente al sentido del olfato. 2. *(Ant.)* Dañoso, nocivo, malsano.

noisomely ['nɔɪsəmlɪ] [noi-som-li], adv. Fétido, asqueroso, infeccionable.

noisomeness ['nɔɪsəmnɪs] [noi-som-nes], s. 1. Fastidio, náusea. 2. Malsano, repugnante; asquerosidad, infección.

noisy ['nɔɪzɪ] [noi-si], a. Ruidoso, clamoroso, turbulento, estrepitoso.

no-jump [nəʋ'dʒʌmp] [nou-yamp], s. m. Salto nulo.

nolition [ˈnɒlɪʃən] [no-li-shon], *a.* (*Teol.*) Nolición, el acto de la voluntad con que no se quiere alguna cosa.

nomad, nomadic [ˈnəʊmæd] [nou-mad], [nəʊˈmædɪk] [nou-ma-dik], *a.* Nómada, errante, que no tiene asiento ni habitación fija. *-s.* Nómada, miembro de una tribu errante.

nomancy [ˈnəʊmænsɪ] [nou-man-si], *s.* Supuesta adivinación por las letras del nombre de alguna persona.

nomarch [ˈnəʊmɑːk] [nou-mark], *s.* Nomarca, gobernador de un nomo en el antiguo Egipto y en la Grecia moderna.

nome [ˈnəʊm] [noum], *s.* 1. Provincia, nomo, prefectura del antiguo Egipto o de la Grecia moderna. 2. Expresión, cantidad algebraica.

nomenclator [nəʊˈmenklətə^r] [nou-men-kla-to^r], *s.* 1. Nomenclator, el que pone nombres propios a personas o cosas. 2. Lista de nombres.

nomenclature [nəʊˈmenklətʃə^r] [nou-men-kla-char, *s.* Nomenclatura, sistema o procedimiento para nombrar; el conjunto de las voces técnicas de una facultad o ciencia.

nominal [ˈnɒmɪnl] [no-mi-nal], *a.* 1. Nominal, que existe más en el nombre que en realidad. **A nominal king,** Rey de nombre. 2. Nominal, que pertenece a un nombre.

nominalism [ˈnɒmɪnəlɪzəm] [no-mi-na-li-sem], *s.* Nominalismo, antiguo sistema que negaba toda realidad a los términos genéricos y consideraba los nombres individuales y particulares como los únicos verdaderamente reales.

nominalist [ˈnɒmɪnəlɪst] [no-mi-na-list], *s.* Nominales, escolásticos opuestos a los realistas.

nominalization [ˈnɒmɪnəlaɪzeɪʃən] [no-mi-na-lai-sei-shon] *s. f.* Nominalización.

nominalize [ˈnɒmɪnəlaɪz] [no-mi-na-lais], *vt.* Nominalizar.

nominally [ˈnɒmɪnəlɪ] [no-mi-na-li], *adv.* Nominalmente.

nominate [ˈnɒmɪneɪt] [no-mi-neit], *va.* Nombrar, elegir, señalar.

nomination [ˈnɒmɪneɪʃən] [no-mi-nei-shon], *s.* Nombramiento, nominación.

nominative [ˈnɒmɪnətɪv] [no-mi-na-tiv], *s.* (*Gram.*) Nominativo, el primer caso del nombre; sujeto.

nominator [ˈnɒmɪneɪtə^r] [no-mi-nei-ta^r], *s.* Nominador, nombrador.

nominee [ˌnɒmɪˈniː] [no-mi-ni], *s.* Candidato, nombrado, provisto, el que es nombrado para algún empleo u oficio.

nominor [ˈnɒmɪnə^r] [no-mi-no^r], *s.* Electo, el nombrado para alguna dignidad o empleo.

nomography [ˈnɒməgræfɪ] [no-mo-gra-fi], *s.* Nomografía, tratado de jurisprudencia.

nomothetical [ˈnɒməθetɪkəl] [no-mo-ze-ti-kal], *a.* Legislativo.

-nomy. Sufijo que indica una ciencia y corresponde a *-nomía* en español. **Astronomy,** astronomía.

non- [nɒn] [non]. Partícula negativa que corresponde a los prefijos españoles *in, no:* se pone un guión a la palabra siguiente: **Non-ability,** inhabilidad, excepción legal. **Non-academic,** no docente. **Non-acceptance,** falta de aceptación; repulsa. **Non-acid,** no ácido, que no tiene las propiedades de un ácido. **Non-actinic,** no actínico, que no efectúa cambios químicos: dícese de ciertos rayos de luz. **Non-admission,** denegación, falta de admisión. **Non-appearance,** (*For.*) contumacia, rebeldía, no comparecencia en juicio; falta. **Non-arrival,** falta de llegada o arribo. **Non-assumpsit,** (*For.*) la alegación de que una persona no ha hecho alguna promesa. **Non-attendance,** falta de asistencia. **Non-attention,** desatención. **Non-commisioned,** sin título, sin despacho. **Non-commissioned officer,** clase; sargento o cabo. **Non-concurrence,** falta de unión o combinación. **Non-conducting,** no conductivo. **Non-conductor,** no conductor, sustancia que se opone al paso de una fuerza cualquiera, como el calórico y la electricidad. **Non-contagious,** no contagioso. **Non-content,** oponente; en la cámara británica de los pares se llama así al lord que vota en contra. **Non-delivery,** falta de remisión, descuido en hacer un envío o una entrega. **Non-essential,** no esencial. **Non-**

exportation, falta o suspensión de la extracción de géneros. **Non-importation,** falta o suspensión de la entrada de géneros. **Non-juring,** no juramentado, que rehusa prestar juramento de fidelidad. V. NONJUROR. **Non-natural,** (*Med.*) no natural. **Non-payment,** falta de pago. **Non-perfomance,** falta de ejecución. **Non-residence,** ausencia, falta de residencia en el que tiene obligación de residir en alguna parte. **Non-resident,** ausente, no residente. **Non-resistance,** obediencia pasiva. **Non-sensitive,** falto de percepción o de sensibilidad. **Non-solution,** insolvencia. **Non-tenure,** (*For.*) alegación de estar exento de una jurisdicción.

nonage [ˈnɒneɪdʒ] [non-eich], *s.* Minoridad, edad menor.

nonagenarian [ˌnɒnədʒɪˈneərɪən] [no-na-chi-nea-rian], *a. y s.* Nonagenario, de noventa o más años de edad.

nonagesimal [ˈnɒnədʒesɪml] [no-na-che-si-mal], *a.* Nonagésimo.

nonagon [ˈnɒnəgən] [no-na-gon], *s.* Nonágono, la figura de nueve ángulos.

nonce [ˈnɒns] [nons], *s.* Hogaño, el tiempo o la ocasión presente; la actualidad. **For the nonce,** al presente, actualmente, hoy día.

nonchalance [ˈnɒnˈtʃæləns] [non-cha-lans], *s.* Estado de indiferencia; descuido.

nonchalant [ˈnɒnˈtʃælənt] [non-cha-lant], *a.* Descuidado, incurioso, negligente.

nonchalantly [ˈnɒnˈtʃæləntlɪ] [non-cha-lan-tli], *adv.* 1. Con aplomo, tranquilamente. 2. Indiferentemente, negligentemente.

non-combatant [ˈnɒnkˈkɒmbətənt] [non-kom-ba-tant], *s.* 1. No combatiente, como el médico militar y el capellán castrense. 2. En tiempo de guerra, el que no pertenece al ejército; como las mujeres, los niños y otros no combatientes.

non-commital [ˈnɒnkˈkɒmɪtl] [non-ko-mi-tal], *adj.* Evasivo, que no se compromete a nada.

non-completion [ˈnɒnkˈkɒmpleʃən] [non-kom-ple-shon], *s. m.* Incumplimiento.

non-conductor [ˈnɒnkˈkɒndʌktə^r] [non-kon-dak-ta^r], *s. m.* Mal conductor, aislante (*Elec.*).

non-conformism [ˈnɒnˈkɒmfɔːmɪzəm] [non-kom-for-mi-sem], *s. m.* Inconformismo.

non-conformist [ˈnɒnˈkɒmfɔːmɪst] [non-kom-for-mist], *s.* No conformista o disidente, el que no se conforma con los ritos de la Iglesia anglicana.

non-conformity [ˈnɒnˈkɒmfɔːmɪtɪ] [non-kom-for-mi-ti], *s.* Desconformidad, disidencia, oposición, repugnancia a conformarse con los ritos de la Iglesia anglicana.

non-cooperation [ˌnɒnkəʊˌɒpəˈreɪʃən] [non-kouo-pa-rei-shon], *s. f.* No cooperación.

nondescript [ˈnɒndɪskrɪpt] [non-dis-kript], *a.* Que no está descrito; indeterminado; fantástico. V. ODD. Se usa también como substantivo para designar un objeto de historia natural que no ha sido nunca descrito.

non-drinker [ˈnɒnˈdrɪŋkə^r] [non-drin-ka^r], *a.* No bebedor, abstemio.

non-durable [ˈnɒnˈdjʊərəbl] [non-diu-ra-bol], *a.* Perecedero.

none [nʌn] [nan], *pron.* 1. Nadie, ninguno (person, thing). **None will be excepted,** no se exceptuará a nadie. **He has none,** no tiene ninguno. 2. Nada, nada de; fuera. **None of that,** nada de eso. **Non of them,** ninguno de ellos. **Come now, none of your mischief,** vamos, dejarse de travesuras. 3. *adv.* No. **He was none the worse,** no se hallaba peor. **We have none,** no tenemos ninguno. **None other than the king,** el rey en persona, el mismo rey. **There are none left,** no queda ninguno. **None-so-pretty,** (*Bot.*) V. LONDON PRIDE. Saxífraga.

nonentity [nɒˈnentɪtɪ] [non-en-ti-ti], **Non-existence** [ˈnɒnɪgˈsɪstəns] [non-ik-sis-tans], *s.* Nada, la nada; la falta de existencia.

nones [nɒnz] [nanz], *s. pl.* 1. Nonas; en el calendario romano el noveno día antes de los idus: el séptimo día de marzo, mayo, julio, y octubre y el quinto de los demás meses. 2.

Nona, hora menor del rezo eclesiástico (entre las doce y las tres).

nonesuch ['nʌnsʌk] [nan-sak], *s.* Sin igual, sin par.

nonetheless [ˌnʌnðə'les] [nan-de-les], *adv.* Nevertheless.

non-event [ˌnɒnɪ'vent] [non-ivent], *s. m.* Fracaso, acto fallido.

non-fattening [ˌnɒn'fætnɪŋ] [non-fat-nin], *a.* Que no engorda.

non-fulfillment [ˌnɒnfʊl'fɪlmənt] [non-ful-fil-ment], *s. m.* Incumplimiento.

non-governmental ['nɒnˌgʌvn'mentl] [non-go-vern-men-tal], *a.* No gubernamental.

nonillion ['nʌnɪlɪən] [na-ni-lion], *s.* Nonilión.

non-intervention ['nɒnˌɪntə'venʃən] [non-in-ta-ven-shon], *s. f.* No intervención.

non-iron ['nɒnˌaɪən] [non-aion], *a.* Que no se plancha, que no necesita ser planchado.

non-negotiable [ˌnɒnnɪ'gəʃɪəbl] [non-ni-gou-shia-bol], *a.* No negociable.

no-nonsense [ˌnəʊ'nɒnsns] [nou-non-sens], *a.* Sensato.

nonpareil ['nɒnpəreɪl] [non-pa-reil], *s.* 1. Sin par, bondad sin igual. 2. Especie de camuesa. 3. *(Impr.)* Nomparel, un grado de letra muy pequeña que usan los impresores. 4. Nombre de varias clases de pájaros; variedades de pinzón y de loro. *-a.* Sin igual, sobresaliente, que no tiene par.

non-partisan ['nɒnˌpɑːtɪ'zæn] [non-par-ti-san], *a.* Imparcial, independiente.

nonplus ['nɒn'plʌs] [non-plas], *s.* Embarazo, perplejidad, estado de no poder decidir ni avanzar; dificultad inquietante. **He was left at a nonplus,** no supo qué responder, se quedó cortado, perplejo.

nonplus, *va.* Confundir, atascar, cortar, arrinconar, estrechar en una disputa.

non-political [ˌnɒnpə'lɪtɪkəl] [non-po-li-kal], *a.* Apolítico.

non-polluting [ˌnɒnpə'juːtɪŋ] [non-po-liu-tin], *a.* No contaminante.

non-profit [ˌnɒn'prɒfɪt] [non-pro-fit], *a.* No lucrativo.

non-recurring ['nɒnrɪ'kɜːrɪŋ] [non-ri-ke-rin], *a.* Ocasional, único.

non-resident ['nɒn'rezɪdənt] [non-re-si-dent], *a.* No residente, transeúnte, huésped.

nonsense ['nɒnsəns] [non-sens], *s.* 1. Disparate, desatino, absurdo, necedad. 2. *(Fam.)* Bagatelas, fruslerías, cosas sin importancia, jerigonza. **Nonsense verses,** versos de buena forma, pero de sentido desatinado y absurdo.

nonsensical [nɒn'sensɪkəl] [non-sen-si-kal], *a.* Absurdo, dessatinado, impertinente.

nonsensically [nɒn'sensɪkəlɪ] [non-sen-si-ka-li], *adv.* Disparatadamente.

nonsensicalness [nɒn'sensɪkəlnɪs] [non-sen-si-kal-nes], *s.* Absurdidad; disparate.

non seq. *Abreviatura de* **non sequitur,** falta de lógica, incongruencia.

nonskid ['nɒn'skɪd] [non-skid], *a.* Antideslizante.

non-smoker ['nɒn'sməʊkər] [non-smou-kar], *s.* 1. No fumador (person). 2. Sección o departamento de no fumadores.

non-stick [ˌnɒn'stɪk] [non-stik], *a.* Antiadherente.

non-stop ['nɒn'stɒp] [non-stop], *adv.* 1. Sin parar, incesantemente. 2. Directo, sin paradas (rail).

nonsuit ['nɒnsuːt] [non-sut], *s. (For.)* 1. El abandono de un pleito por el demandante. 2. El acto de declarar que el demandante en un juicio ha perdido el derecho de continuar en su demanda por no haber cumplido lo que prescriben las leyes.

nonsuit, *va. (For.)* Absolver de la instancia, declarar que un demandante en juicio ha perdido el derecho de seguir en su demanda por no haber cumplido lo que prescriben las leyes.

non-toxic ['nɒn'tɒksɪk] [non-tok-sik], *a.* No tóxico.

non-verbal ['nɒn'vɜːbl] [non-ver-bal], *a.* Sin palabras.

non-yielding ['nɒn'jiːldɪŋ] [non-yil-din], *a.* Improductivo.

noodle ['nuːdl] [nu-del], *s.* Simplón, mentecato, idiota.

noodle, *s.* Tallarín; fideo.

nook [nʊl] [nuk], *s.* 1. Rincón, lugar estrecho y retirado, escondrijo.

noon [nuːn] [nun], *s.* 1. Mediodía, hora en que está el sol en el meridiano. 2. Culminación, apogeo. **High noon,** el mediodía en punto, las doce en punto.

noonday ['nuːndeɪ] [nund-ei], *s.* Mediodía. *-a.* Meridional.

no-one ['nəʊwʌn] [nou-uan], *pr.* **Nobody.**

nooning ['nuːnɪŋ] [nu-nin], *s.* Siesta, el descanso de mediodía.

noontide ['nuːntaɪd] [nun-taid], *a.* Meridional. *-a.* 1. La hora de mediodía. 2. Período de apogeo o culminación.

noose [nuːs] [nus], *s.* Lazo corredizo. **Noose snare,** trampa.

noose, *va.* 1. Enlazar, apretar con lazo corredizo. 2. Entrampar, hacer caer en la trampa.

nor [nɔːr] [nor], *conj.* Ni, no, tampoco; partícula correlativa de *neither* o *not,* pero en el uso poético o retórico, estas últimas palabras se omiten algunas veces. **I did not go, nor did I intend it,** no fui ni tuve intención de ir. **I neither love nor fear thee,** ni te amo ni te temo. **Neither A nor B,** ni A ni B. **Nor was this all,** pero esto no fue todo.

nordic ['nɔːdɪk] [nor-dik], *a.* Nórdico.

norm [nɔːm] [norm], *s.* 1. Norma, pauta, regla, tipo normal o modelo. 2. *(Biol.)* Unidad típica de conformación o estructura.

normal ['nɔːməl] [nor-mal], *a. (Geom.)* 1. Perpendicular, lo que forma un ángulo recto. 2. Normal, según las reglas o principios; que enseña las reglas o principios; conforme a un tipo o regla. **Normal-schools,** escuelas para enseñar a los maestros cómo han de desempeñar su obligación.

normalize ['nɔːməlaɪz] [nor-ma-lais], *vt.* Normalizar.

normally ['nɔːməlɪ] [nor-ma-li], *adv.* Normalmente.

norman ['nɔːmən] [nor-man], *a.* Normando, perteneciente a Normandía. *-s.* 1. Normando, el natural de Normandía. 2. *(Mar.)* Burel de molinete.

normative ['nɔːmətɪv] [nor-ma-tiv], *a.* Normativo.

norse [nɔːs] [nors], *a.* Escandinavo, perteneciente a los países o a los idiomas escandinavos. *-s.* Idiomas escandinavos, particularmente el de Islandia.

norseman ['nɔːsmən] [nors-man], *s.* Hombre del Norte, el antiguo escandinavo.

north [nɔːθ] [norz], *s.* 1. Norte, punto cardinal opuesto al Sur; septentrión. 2. Región o distrito al norte de un punto dado; particularmente en los Estados Unidos, la región que se halla al norte de los estados donde existió la esclavitud. *-a.* Septentrional, del Norte. **North African,** norteafricano. **North American,** norteamericano. **The North Pole,** el Polo Norte, Polo Ártico. **North by east,** Norte, cuarto nordeste. **North by west,** norte, cuarto noroeste. **North star,** estrella polar, estrella del norte.

northeast [nɔːθ'iːst] [norz-ist], *s. y a.* Nordeste.

northeaster ['nɔːθ'iːstər] [norz-is-tar], *s.* Temporal, ventarrón del nordeste.

northeasterly ['nɔːθ'iːstəlɪ] [norz-is-ter-li], *a.* Dirigido hacia al nordeste o que viene del nordeste.

northeastern ['nɔːθ'iːstən] [norz-is-tern], *a.* Situado en el nordeste, perteneciente a esta dirección.

norther ['nɔːðər] [nor-zar], *s.* Viento fuerte del norte; suele ser frío en Texas; en California a veces muy cálido y seco.

northerly ['nɔːθəlɪ] [nor-zer-li], **northern** ['nɔːθən] [nor-zern], *a.* Septentrional. **Northerly winds,** vientos del norte. **Northern lights,** aurora boreal.

northerner ['nɔːθənər] [nor-zer-na'], *a.* Del Norte, norteño, septentrional.

northing ['nɔːθɪŋ] [nor-zin], *s. (Mar.)* La diferencia de latitud de un buque en su rumbo.

northland ['nɔːθlənd] [norz-land], *s. (EU)* Tierra o región septentrional.

northman ['nɔːθmən] [norz-man], *s.* Escandinavo. V. NORSEMAN.

northward, northwards ['nɔːθwəd] [norz-uard], *adv.* Hacia el norte.

northwest ['nɔːθ'west] [norz-uest], *s.* y *a.* Noroeste, noroeste, norueste.

northwesterly ['nɔːθ'westəlı] [noz-ues-ter-li], *a.* Dirigido hacia el noroeste o que viene del noroeste.

northwestern ['nɔːθ'westən] [noz-ues-tern], *a.* Perteneciente o situado al noroeste.

north wind ['nɔːθ'wɪnd] [noz-uind], *s.* Norte, el viento septentrional.

norwegian [nɔː'wiːdʒən] [nor-vi-yan], *s.* y *a.* Noruego, perteneciente a Noruega, natural de Noruega.

no-score ['nəʊˌskɔːʳ] [nou-skoʳ], *a.* **No-score draw,** empate a cero.

nose [nəʊz] [nous], *s.* 1. Nariz, órgano del olfato y de la respiración; hocico de ciertos animales. 2. Olfato, sagacidad. 3. Lo que se asemeja a una nariz: (a) la proa de un buque; (b) tobera, cañuto de fuelle; pico, boca (de cafetera o de cántaro). **A flat nose,** nariz chata, roma o aplastada. **To blow one's nose,** sonarse la nariz. **To get one's nose in front,** llevar o conseguir una ligera ventaja. **To lead by the nose,** arrastrar como por fuerza; llevar tras sí, atraer ciegamente uno a otro a su dictamen o voluntad. **To thrust the nose into,** entremeterse. **To put the nose out of joint,** suplantar, desquiciar. **Pug nose,** nariz, rama, achatada. **To bleed at the nose,** echar sangre por las narices. **To blow one's nose,** sonarse las narices. **To pick one's nose,** hurgarse las narices. **To speak through the nose,** ganguear. **To turn up one's nose at something/somebody,** torcer el morro ante algo/alguien. **Under one's nose,** a las barbas de uno, en su presencia. **Nose-bag,** morral de hocico; cebadera.

nose, *va.* 1. Oler, olfatear. 2. Descubrir espiando o acechando; se usa con la prep. *out.* 3. Encararse; oponerse, hacer frente. **Nose about/around,** curiosear, cotillear. **Nose out,** husmear u olfatear algo.

nosebleed ['nəʊzbliːd] [nous-blid], *s.* 1. Sangre que sale por las narices, hemorragia nasal. 2. *(Bot.)* Milenrama.

nosegay ['nəʊzgeɪ] [nous-guei], *s.* Ramillete; manojo de flores.

nosel ['nəʊzl] [nou-sel], *s. V.* NOZLE.

noseless ['nəʊzlɪs] [nous-les], *a.* Desnarigado.

nose-piece ['nəʊzpiːs] [nous-pis], *s.* 1. Sobarba, muserola. 2. Remate del microscopio al cual se asegura el objetivo; porta-objetivos, anillo que sirve a este objeto. 3. Extremo, boquerel de manguera o de tubo.

nosey ['nəʊzı] [nou-si], *a.* Fisgón, entrometido.

nosology ['nəʊzələdʒı] [nou-so-lo-yi], *s.* Nosología, la descripción y clasificación de las enfermedades. Su adjetivo es *nosological,* nosológico.

nostalgia [nɒs'tældʒıə] [nous-tal-chia], *s.* Nostalgia.

nostalgic [nɒs'tældʒık] [nous-tal-chik], *a.* Nostálgico.

nostoc ['nɒstək] [nos-tok], *s.* Nostoc, género de algas de agua dulce. Forma masas gelatinosas o membranosas de color verde.

nostologic [nɒs'tələdʒık] [nos-to-lo-yik], *a.* Senil, relativo a la vejez avanzada o segunda niñez.

nostril ['nɒstrɪl] [nos-tril], *s.* Ventana de la nariz.

nostrum ['nɒstrəm] [nos-trom], *s.* 1. Secreto, remedio o medicina secreta. 2. Proyecto de charlatán o politicastro. 3. Remedio predilecto.

nosy ['nəʊzı] [nou-si], *a.* **Nosey.**

not [nɒt] [not], *adv.* No, partícula con que se niega o rehusa alguna cosa. **Not at all,** de ningún modo. **Not but, not that,** no que, no es (decir) que. **Not but that I shall go,** no es decir que no iré. **No that I say,** no es que yo lo diga. **Not to say,** por no decir. **Not so much as,** ni siquiera. **They had not so much as heard,** ni siquiera habían oído. **I think not,** no lo creo; creo que no. **Does it not?,** ¿no es verdad? **She sings well does she not?,** ella canta bien, ¿no es así?

notability [nəʊtə'bılıtı] [nou-ta-bi-li-ti], *s.* 1. Notabilidad, carácter notable. 2. Notabilidad, persona de consecuencia, notable.

notable ['nəʊtəbl] [nou-ta-bol], *a.* Notable, digno de nota, reparo o atención; memorable. **A notable example,** ejemplo notable, memorable.

notable, *a.* Eminentemente cuidadoso o arreglado en sus gastos; hábil. **A notable housewife,** una cuidadosa ama de casa.

notableness ['nəʊtəblnıs] [nou-ta-bol-nes], *s.* Notabilidad, cualidad de lo que es notable; carácter notable.

notably ['nəʊtəblı] [nou-ta-bli], *adv.* Notablemente, importantemente.

notarial [nəʊ'teərıəl] [nou-ta-rial], *a.* Perteneciente a un notario; ejecutado o hecho ante notario.

notarize ['nəʊtəraız] [nou-ta-rais], *vt. (EU)* Autenticar.

notary ['nəʊtərı] [nou-ta-ri], **notary-public** ['nəʊtərıˌpʌblık] [nou-ta-ri-pa-blik], *s.* Notario, escribano público, funcionario autorizado para dar fe en los instrumentos auténticos y otros actos extrajudiciales.

notation [nəʊ'teıʃən] [nou-tei-shon], *s.* 1. Notación, anotación; sentido, significación. 2. Notación, numeración escrita; sistema de signos, cifras o abreviaturas empleado en una ciencia o arte. Notación aritmética, musical, química, lógica.

notch [nɒtʃ] [noch], *s.* Muesca, abertura o corte que se hace en alguna cosa; ranura, mortaja, tajadura; hendidura; malla.

notch, *va.* Hacer muescas; dentar, ranurar, ruñar.

note [nəʊt] [nout], *s.* 1. Nota, marca, señal. 2. Caso, aprecio. 3. Nota, censura o reparo de las acciones de alguno. 4. Nota, tacha o defecto grave y reparable. 5. Nota, apuntación, apunte. 6. Nota, reparo o explicación que se hace sobre lo contenido en algún libro o escrito. 7. Carácter, reputación, consecuencia. 8. Aviso, noticia, advertencia. 9. *(Mús.)* Nota, la señal del tono que se hace; un sonido musical cualquiera; también una tecla. **The note F,** la tecla F. 10. Sonido melodioso o vocal, tono, voz, acento; modo de hablar; canto de las aves. 11. Nota, el estado de ser o poder ser observado. 12. Indirecta. 13. Esquela, billete. 14. Vale, pagaré, papel que se da en reconocimiento de alguna deuda. **Bank-note,** billete de banco. **Note of hand o promissory note,** pagaré. **Nothing of note,** sin novedad. **To take note,** hacer cargo; tomar nota, hacer apuntes, anotar; notar, advertir algo. **Foot-note,** nota al pie (de la página). **Half note,** *(Mús.)* mínima, la mitad de la semibreve. **Whole note,** semibreve, nota que vale un compás menor. **Note-book,** libro de memoria o de apuntaciones. **Leading note,** nota o tecla subtónica, la séptima de la escala. **Worthy of note,** digno de atención.

note, *va.* 1. Notar, marcar, distinguir. 2. Reparar, observar, advertir. 3. Anotar, notar, apuntar brevemente alguna cosa; poner por escrito, registrar. **To note a bill of exchange,** anotar una letra de cambio. 4. Censurar, imputar alguna culpa o delito. 5. Componer, hacer composiciónes musicales notando los tonos.

noted ['nəʊtıd] [nou-tid], *a.* Afamado, célebre, insigne, eminente.

notedly ['nəʊtıdlı] [nou-tid-li], *adv.* Notablemente; con nota.

notedness ['nəʊtıdnıs] [nou-tid-nes], *s.* Celebridad, fama, reputación.

noteless ['nəʊtlıs] [nout-les], *a.* Oscuro, sin celebridad, reputación o fama.

noter ['nəʊtəʳ] [nou-taʳ], *s.* Notador, observador.

noteworthy ['nəʊtˌwɜːðı] [nout-ue-zi], *a.* Notable, digno de nota, de atención, de observación.

nothing ['nʌθıŋ] [na-zin], *s.* 1. Nada, ninguna cosa. 2. Nadería, cosa de poca entidad, friolera. 3. Estado de lo que no tiene existencia; la nada. 4. La cifra 0; cero. **That is nothing to me,** eso nada me importa. **It is good for nothing,** para nada sirve. **Nothing much,** poca cosa. **Next to nothing,** casi nada. **He had nothing to live upon,** no tenía nada con que mantenerse. **It signifies nothing,** eso no significa nada, nada quiere decir. **He made nothing of his labor,** nada sacó de su trabajo. **To make nothing of,** (a) no hacer caso de, despreciar, tomar una cosa a burla. (b) No comprender, no poder entender. **I could make nothing of his talk,** no pude entender su charla. **To come to nothing,** anonadarse, aniquilarse. **To reduce to nothing,** reducir a la nada. **For nothing,** de balde, por nada, grauitamente. **Nothing else,**

nada más. **A multiplication of nothings,** un montón de bagatelas. **Thin, nothing of it!** ¡no hay de qué! **A good-for-nothing fellow,** un para nada. *-adv.* De ningún grado o medida. **You have nothing on him,** no le llegas ni a la suela del zapato.

nothingness [ˈnʌθɪŋnɪs] [na-zin-nes], *s.* Nonada, nadería, cosa de poca entidad; nada.

notice [ˈnəʊtɪs] [nou-tis], *s.* 1. Nota, reparo, observación; atención. **Worthy of notice,** digno de observación, de atención. 2. Aviso, noticia, informe. 3. Noticia, tratamiento respetuoso; corta noticia literaria. 4. Notificación, orden que se comunica a alguien. **To give notice,** advertir, hacer saber, avisar, dar aviso, informar. **Take no notice of it,** no haga Ud. caso de ello; haga Ud. como si no viese nada. **To take notice of,** hacer caso, atender, tener cuidado; notar, observar; cuidarse de. **To give short notice,** conceder un corto plazo. **To give out a notice,** dar una noticia, anunciar algo. **To avoid notice,** intentar pasar inadvertido. **He has had notice of it by letter,** ha sido advertido o informado por carta. **Notice to quit,** aviso de despedida. **At the shortest notice,** al momento, tan pronto como sea posible.

notice, *va.* 1. Notar, observar, mirar, reparar. 2. Hacerse cargo de, atender a, cuidar de; apercibirse de. 3. Mentar, hacer mención de. 4. Tener miramientos, tratar con atención, con finura. **The children were much noticed,** a los niños se les dedicó mucha atención.

noticeable [ˈnəʊtɪsəbl] [nou-ti-sa-bol], *a.* Digno de atención, notable; perceptible.

noticeably [ˈnəʊtɪsəblɪ] [nou-ti-sa-bli], *adv.* Notablemente, de un modo notable o perceptible.

notification [ˌnəʊtɪfɪˈkeɪʃən] [nou-ti-fi-kei-shon], *s.* 1. Notificación, el acto de notificar o hacer saber alguna cosa. 2. Aviso, advertencia, citación, cita.

notify [ˈnəʊtɪfaɪ] [nou-ti-fai], *va.* 1. Notificar, advertir, avisar; dar a conocer, informar por cualesquiera medios. 2. Dar a luz, dar noticias de, publicar.

noting [ˈnəʊtɪŋ] [no-tin], *s.* Notificación, aviso, el acto de notar o tomar notas; el acto de anotar una letra de cambio.

notion [ˈnəʊʃən] [nou-shon], *s.* 1. Noción; concepción mental, idea, pensamiento. 2. Parecer, voto, dictamen, opinión. 3. Entendimiento, sentido. 4. *(Fam.)* Intención, inclinación, designio. 5. *(Fam.)* Novedad, artículo vendible de poca monta. **I have a notion that…,** tengo la idea de que… **You have no notion!** ¡Ni te lo puedes imaginar!

notional [ˈnəʊʃənl] [nou-sho-nal], *a.* 1. Imaginario, ideal. 2. Quimérico, fantástico; que se recrea con quimeras; caprichudo, afectado, demasiado aficionado a pequeñeces. **A notional old bachelor,** un solterón viejo y maniático.

notionality [ˌnəʊʃəˈnælɪtɪ] [nou-sho-na-li-ti], *s.* La opinión o parecer que no tiene fundamento o nada en que fundarse.

notionally [ˈnəʊʃənəlɪ] [nou-sho-na-li], *adv.* Idealmente.

notoriety [ˌnəʊtəˈraɪətɪ] [no-to-rie-ti], *s.* Notoriedad, noticia pública; conocimiento que todos tienen de una cosa.

notorious [ˈnəʊtərɪəs] [no-to-rios], *a.* Notorio, público, conocido, manifiesto, aparente, evidente.

notoriously [ˈnəʊtərɪəslɪ] [no-to-rios-li], *adv.* Notoriamente.

notoriousness [ˈnəʊtərɪəsnɪs] [no-to-rios-nes], *s.* Notoriedad, noticia pública.

notus [ˈnəʊtəs] [no-tos], *s.* Noto, austro.

not-wheat [ˈnɒtwiːt] [not-uit], *s. (Bot.)* Trigo chamorro, trigo cuya espiga no tiene raspas.

notwithstanding [ˌnɒtwɪθˈstændɪŋ] [not-uit-stan-din], *conj.* No obstante, sin embargo, aunque, con todo, bien que; por más que. *-adv.* A despecho, sin relación a, a pesar de.

nougat [ˈnuːɡɑ] [nu-ga], *s. m.* Turrón.

nought [nɔːt] [not], *s.* Nada. V. NAUGHT.

noun [naʊn] [naun], *s. (Gram.)* Nombre, substantivo.

nourish [ˈnʌrɪʃ] [na-rish], *va.* 1. Nutrir. 2. Alimentar, sustentar, mantener. 3. Alentar, fomentar. 4. Criar, educar. *-vn.* Favorecer el crecimiento o desarrollo de.

nourishable [ˈnʌrɪʃəbl] [na-ri-sha-bol], *a.* 1. Que se puede alimentar, sustentar o fomentar. 2. *(Des.)* Nutricio.

nourisher [ˈnʌrɪʃər] [na-ri-shaʳ], *s.* Nutridor, nutriente, alimentador.

nourishment [ˈnʌrɪʃmnt] [na-rish-ment], *s.* 1. Nutrimento, alimento, sustento; lo que sustenta o promueve el crecimiento de una manera cualquiera. 2. La acción de nutrir. 3. Lo que favorece el desarrollo de una cosa.

nous [naʊs] [naus], *s.* Inteligencia, conocimiento, penetración, sentido.

novation [nɒˈveɪʃən] [no-vei-shon], *s. (For.)* Novación, renovación de una obligación contraída anteriormente.

novel [ˈnɒvəl] [no-vel], *a.* Novel, nuevo, moderno. *-s.* 1. Novel, historia fingida. 2. *(For.)* Novela, cualquier ley de los emperadores añadida al código de Justiniano.

novelette [ˈnɒvəleɪ] [no-ve-lei], *s.* Novela corta.

novelettish [ˌnɒvəˈletɪʃ] [no-ve-le-tish], *a.* Romántico, sentimental.

novelist [ˈnɒvəlɪst] [no-ve-list], *s.* 1. Novelista, novelador, el que escribe novelas. 2. *(Des.)* Novator, inventor de novedades.

novelistic [ˌnɒvəˈlɪstɪk] [no-ve-lis-tik], *a.* Novelesco, propio de una novela.

novelize [ˈnɒvəlaɪz] [no-ve-lais], *va.* 1. Poner en forma de novela. 2. *(Des.)* Innovar.

novelty [ˈnɒvəltɪ] [no-vel-ti], *s.* 1. Novedad, cosa nueva, extraña o poco común. 2. Calidad de nuevo. 3. Innovación.

November [ˈnɒvembər] [no-vem-baʳ], *s.* Noviembre.

novenary [ˈnɒvenərɪ] [no-ve-na-ri], *a.* Novenario, el número de nueve.

novennial [nɒˈviːnɪəl] [no-vi-nial], *a.* Que ocurre cada noveno año o que dura nueve años.

novercal [ˈnɒvɜːkl] [no-ver-kal], *a. (Ant.)* Propio de madrastra.

novice [ˈnɒvɪs] [no-vis], *s.* 1. Novicio, el principiante en cualquier arte o facultad. 2. Novicio, el que en la religión no ha hecho aún profesión de sus reglas o votos.

noviceship [ˈnɒvɪsʃɪp] [no-vis-ship], *s.* 1. Noviciado, aprendizaje de algún arte, oficio, etc. 2. Noviciado, el tiempo destinado para la probación antes de profesar en las órdenes religiosas.

novitiate [nɒvɪʃɪeɪt] [no-vi-shieit], *s.* 1. *V.* NOVICESHIP, 2ª acep. 2. El novicio mismo.

novocaine [ˈnɒvəkeɪn] [no-vo-kein], *s.* Novocaína, procaína.

now [naʊ] [nau], *adv.* 1. Ahora, en el tiempo o momento presente, actualmente. 2. Ahora, poco ha. 3. Después de esto, de aquí a poco. 4. Ahora bien, esto supuesto; ¡vamos! **Now and then,** de vez en cuando, de cuando en cuando, algunas veces; aquí y allá. **Just now,** ahora mismo, inmediatamente. **Just now** se expresa en español a menudo por el verbo *acabar de;* v. gr. **I have just now received a telegram,** acabo de recibir un telegrama. **How now?,** ¿cómo? ¿qué tal? **Before now,** antes de ahora. 5. Aún, todavía: ya, en otro tiempo. **It has happened before now,** ha sucedido ya, o en otro tiempo. **Until** o **till now,** hasta ahora, hasta este momento. **King Albert is now living,** el rey Alberto vive todavía. **Now…now…,** ya…ya; ora…ora, alternativamente. **Now soft, now loud,** ya suave, ya estrepitoso. **Now rich, now poor,** alternativamente rico y pobre; ora rico, ora pobre. **Now! what do you think?,** ¡vamos! ¿qué piensa Ud.?, ¿qué le parece a Ud.? *-conj.* Más, pero, pues. **Now it is true,** pues bien verdad es. *-s.* Actualidad, el momento presente.

nowadays [ˈnaʊədeɪz] [naua-deis], *adv.* En nuestros días, en nuestros tiempos, hoy día.

noway [ˈnaʊweɪ] [nauei], **noways** [ˈnaʊweɪz] [naueis], *adv.* De ningún modo.

nowhere [ˈnaʊweər] [noueaʳ], *adv.* En ninguna parte. **Nowhere else,** en ninguna otra parte. **It's nowhere you know,** no es ningún sitio que conoces. **It's nowhere near as good,** no es tan bueno ni con mucho.

nowhither [ˈnaʊwɪðər] [naui-zaʳ], *adv.* Hacia ningún lugar determinado; hacia ninguna parte.

nowise [ˈnaʊwaɪz] [nauais], *adv.* De ningún modo, de ninguna manera, de modo alguno.

noxious ['nɒkʃəs] [nok-shios], *a.* 1. Nocivo, dañoso, pernicioso. 2. *(Poco us.)* Culpable, delincuente.

noxiously ['nɒkʃəslɪ] [nok-shios-li], *adv.* Perniciosamente.

noxiousness ['nɒkʃəsnɪs] [nok-shios-nes], *s.* La calidad que constituye a una cosa perniciosa, dañosa o perjudicial; daño.

nozle, nozzle ['nɒzl] [no-sel], *s.* 1. Boquerel (de manguera); boquilla, gollete rígido al extremo de un tubo, para desaguar; canuto, tobera.

NP *Abreviatura de* **Notary Public.**

n.p. *Abreviatura de* **New paragraph,** punto y aparte.

NT *Abreviatura de* **New Testament.**

nuance ['njuːɑːns] [niuans], *s.* Ligera diferencia; matiz.

nub [nʌb] [nab], *s. m.* 1. Pedazo, protuberancia. 2. *(Fig.)* Parte esencial.

nubbin ['njuːbɪn] [niu-bin], *s. (Fam. E. U.)* Espiga de maíz imperfectamente desarrollada.

nubian ['njuːbɪən] [niu-bian], *a.* Nubio, que pertenece a la Nubia.

nubile ['njuːbaɪl] [niu-bail], *a.* Nubil, persona que por su edad es apta para contraer matrimonio; doncella casadera.

nubilous ['njuːbɪləs] [niu-bi-los], **nubilose** ['njuːbɪləz] [niu-bi-lous], *a.* Nubloso, nubiloso.

nuclear ['njuːklɪər] [niu-kliaʳ], *a.* Nuclear, nucleario. **Nuclear physics,** física nuclear. **Nuclear fission,** fisión nuclear, fisura nuclear. **Nuclear fusion,** fusión nuclear. **Nuclear reactor,** *(Fís.)* reactor nuclear. **Nuclear war,** guerra nuclear. **Nuclear waste,** vertidos nucleares. **Nuclear-free,** no nuclear.

nucleate ['njuːbɪləs] [niu-bi-los], *va. y vn.* Formar un núcleo; juntarse formando núcleo.

nucleic ['njuːkleɪk] [niu-kleik], *a.* Nucleico.

nucleon ['njuːʃɪən] [niu-klion], *s.* Nucleón.

nucleus ['njuːklɪəs] [niu-klios], *s.* 1. Núcleo, punto céntrico del desarrollo. 2. *(Biol.)* Cuerpo redondo u ovalado, de carácter determinado, encerrado en una celdilla o bien, masa de bioplasma; núcleo. 3. Punto parecido a una estrella que se ve a la cabeza de un cometa.

nudation [nəˈdeɪʃən] [nu-dei-shon], *s.* El acto de desnudar, de poner algo desnudo.

nude [njuːd] [niud], *a.* 1. Desnudo, nudo. 2. *(Der.)* Hecho sin compensación; nulo.

nudge [nʌdʒ] [nadch], *va.* Tocar ligeramente para advertir, como se hace con el codo. -*s.* Toque ligero dado con el codo para llamar la atención.

nudism ['njuːdɪzəm] [niu-di-sem], *s. m.* Nudismo.

nudist ['njuːdɪst] [niu-dist], *a.* Nudista.

nudity ['njuːdɪtɪ] [niu-di-ti], *s.* Desnudez.

nugation [njuːˈgeɪʃən] [niu-guei-shon], *s.* Fruslería, nonada.

nugatory ['njuːgətərɪ] [niu-ga-to-ri], *a.* Nugatorio, frustráneo, fútil, frívolo, fruslero.

nugget ['nʌgɪt] [na-guit], *s.* Pedazo; en especial, pepita de oro o de otro metal precioso.

nuggety ['nʌgɪtɪ] [na-gui-ti], *a.* Hallado en forma de pepitas; de la figura de una pepita.

nuisance ['njuːsns] [niu-sans], *s.* 1. Lo que molesta, enoja u ofende; persona o cosa cansada, fastidiosa; incomodidad, molestia, estorbo. 2. Indecencia, porquería. **Nuisance** como término legal es el perjuicio o daño que se causa ilegalmente a la propiedad de uno o más individuos. 3. *(Fig.)* Suplicio, fastidio, tormento, peste. **What a nuisance!** ¡Qué fastidio! ¡qué suplicio!

null [nʌl] [nal], *vn.* 1. Tornear algo en forma de rosario. 2. Torcerse como una soga. **Nulled work,** madera trabajada en la forma de las cuentas de un rosario.

null, *a.* Nulo, inválido, sin fuerza legal. -*s.* 1. Cosa que no tiene fuerza ni sentido alguno; nonada, cero. 2. Pieza de madera que sale del torno en la forma de las cuentas de un rosario.

nullification [nʌlɪfɪˈkeɪʃən] [na-li-fi-kei-shon], *s. f.* Anulación.

nullifidian ['nʌlɪfɪdɪən] [na-li-fi-dian], *s. (Ant.)* Persona sin fe, religión o creencia; nulo en todo.

nullify ['nʌlɪfaɪ] [na-li-fai], *va.* Anular, invalidar, abrogar.

nullity ['nʌlɪtɪ] [na-li-ti], *s.* Nulidad; falta de existencia.

numb [nʌm] [nam], *a.* Entorpecido, adormecido, privado de sensibilidad; entumecido de frío; aturdido.

numb, *va.* Entorpecer, causar torpor.

numbed ['nʌmd] [namd], *a.* Entumecido.

numbedness ['nʌmdnɪs] [namd-nes], *s.* V. NUMBNESS.

number ['nʌmbəʳ] [nam-baʳ], *va.* 1. Numerar, contar; computar. 2. Estimar, contar como uno en una reunión o colección. 3. Numerar, dar o poner número a una cosa. **Numbering machine,** máquina numeradora.

number, *s.* 1. Número, cantidad, multitud. 2. Armonía: poesía, versos; cadencia. 3. *(Gram.)* Número, en los nombres y verbos. **Numbers,** números, un libro del Antiguo Testamento. 4. La ciencia de los números o guarismos. 5. Entrega, cada uno de los cuadernos de un libro o periódico que se publica por partes. **A number of,** algunos, varios. **Any number of times,** muchas veces. **Back number,** ejemplar no muy reciente de un periódico; de aquí, persona o cosa atrasada, avejentada, que no está al día. **Broken number,** quebrado, fracción. **Number one,** *(Fam.)* Uno mismo, sí mismo. **To look out for number one,** cuidar de sí mismo. **Round numbers,** números redondos o pares. **I've got his number now,** le tengo calado (pillado) ya *(Fig.).* **A good number,** un buen chollo *(Fig: work).* **Numbers,** versos *(Poet.).*

numberer ['nʌmbərəʳ] [nam-ba-raʳ], *s.* Numerador, contador.

numberless ['nʌmbəlɪs] [nam-ba-les], *a.* Innumerable, sin número.

numbfish ['nʌmfɪʃ] [nam-fish], *s.* Torpedo.

numbles ['nʌmlz] [nam-bels], *s.* Entrañas de venado.

numbness ['nʌmbnɪs] [nam-nes], *s.* Torpor, entorpecimiento, adormecimiento.

numerable ['njuːmərəbl] [niu-me-ra-bol], *a.* Nu merable.

numeral ['njuːmərəl] [niu-me-ral], *a.* Numeral; numérico. -*s.* Guarismo. **Arabic numerals,** guarismo arábigos.

numerally ['njuːmərəlɪ] [niu-me-ra-li], *adv.* Numéricamente.

numerary ['njuːmərərɪ] [niu-me-ra-ri], *a.* Numerario.

numerate ['njuːməreɪt] [niu-me-reit], *va.* Numerar, contar.

numeration ['njuːməreɪʃən] [niu-me-rei-shon], *s.* Numeración.

numerator ['njuːməreɪtəʳ] [niu-me-rei-taʳ], *s.* Contador; numerador.

numeric [njuːˈmerɪk] [niu-me-rik], *a.* Numérico.

numerical [njuːˈmerɪkəl] [niu-me-ri-kal], *a.* Numérico.

numerically [njuːˈmerɪkəlɪ] [niu-me-ri-ka-li], *adv.* Numéricamente.

numerological ['njuːmer@'lʌdʒɪk@l] [niu-me-ro-lo-yi-kal], *a.* Numerológico.

numerology ['njuːmə'rɒlɒdʒɪ] [niu-me-ro-lo-yi], *s. f.* Numerología.

numerosity [,njuːmə'rɒsɪtɪ] [niu-me-ro-si-ti], *s.* 1. Numerosidad, multitud. 2. *(Ant.)* Cadencia o armonía en las cláusulas, períodos o versos.

numerous ['njuːmərəs] [niu-me-ros], *a.* 1. Numeroso; muchos, muchas. 2. *(Des.)* Numeroso, armonioso, rítmico. **Numerous things to do,** *(Fam.)* muchas cosas que hacer.

numerousness ['njuːmərəsnɪs] [niu-me-ros-nes], *s.* Numerosidad, muchedumbre.

numismatic ['njuːmɪz'mætɪk] [niu-mis-ma-tik], *a.* Numismático, que se refiere a las monedas o medallas.

numismatics ['njuːmɪz'mætɪkz] [niu-mis-ma-tiks], *s.* Numismática, la ciencia que trata de las medallas y monedas desde el punto de vista histórico. Se llama también Numismatology.

numismatography ['njuːmɪzmə'tɒgræfɪ] [niu-mis-ma-to-gra-fi], *s.* Numismática, el conocimiento de monedas y medallas antiguas.

nummary ['njuːmərɪ] [niu-ma-ri], *a.* V. NUMMULAR.

nummular ['nju:mələ^r] [niu-ma-la^r], *a.* 1. Pecuniario. 2. *(Med.)* Numuláceo, parecido a una moneda. **Nummular sputa,** esputos numuláceos.

numskull ['nju:mskɒl] [niums-kal], *s.* Zote, bobote.

numskulled ['nju:mskɒld] [niums-kald], *a.* Lerdo, zote, bobo.

nun [nʌn] [nan], *s.* 1. Monja, religiosa, mujer que habita en un convento. 2. Una de varias clases de aves; paro, variedad blanca de pichón doméstico con moño o copete, etc. **Nun-buoy,** boya de barrilete, en figura de dos conos unidos por sus bases. **Nun's veiling,** velo de monja, tejido de lana muy suave y delgado; se usa para velos y también para trajes.

nuncio ['nʌnʃɪəɪ] [nan-shiou], *s.* 1. Nuncio, enviado. 2. Nuncio, el embajador que envía el Papa.

nuncupate ['nʌnkəpeɪt] [nan-ka-peit], *va.* Declarar abiertamente.

nuncupative ['nʌnkəpətɪv] [nan-ka-pa-tiv], **nuncupatory** ['nʌnkəpətərɪ] [nan-ka-pa-to-ri], *a.* Nuncupativo, verbal, hecho de viva voz; dícese especialmente de un testamento.

nundinal ['nʌndɪnl] [nan-di-nal], **nundinary** ['nʌndɪnərɪ] [nan-di-na-ri], *a.* Lo que pertenece a los mercados o ferias.

nunnery ['nʌnərɪ] [na-na-ri], *s.* Convento o monasterio de monjas.

nunnish ['nʌnɪʃ] [na-nish], *a.* Monjil, perteneciente o parecido a las monjas; característico de ellas.

nuptial ['nʌpʃəl] [nap-shal], *a.* Nupcial, que pertenece a las bodas. **Nuptial song,** epitalamio. **Nuptial plumaje,** plumaje de un ave en la estación de la cría.

nuptials ['nʌpʃəlz] [nap-shals], *s. pl.* Nupcias, boda.

nurl [nɜːl] [nerl], *va.* Acordonar una moneda; hacerle el cordoncillo. **Nurling-tool,** en tonelería, porta-moleta.

nurse [nɜːs] [ners], *s.* 1. Ama de cría, nodriza; niñera, la persona encargada de cuidar niños. **Wet nurse,** ama de leche. *(Mex.)* Chichigua. *(Cuba)* Criandera. **Nurse-child,** niño de teta. 2. Enfermera, enfermero, la mujer u hombre que cuida de un enfermo. 3. La persona o cosa que cría, educa o protege; lo que favorece el crecimiento. 4. Una especie de tiburón. **Monthly nurse,** enfermera que por un estipendio se encarga de cuidar a una mujer parida. **Nurse-bee,** abeja de menos de dieciseis días.

nurse, *va.* 1. Criar criaturas o animales; dar de mamar. 2. Criar, alimentar, mantener. 3. Cuidar enfermos o asistirlos. 4. Fomentar, dar alas. **To nurse a business along,** promover un negocio. *-vn.* 1. Cuidar de un enfermo; dar de mamar a un niño. 2. Mamar, chupar la leche de los pechos.

nurse-maid ['nɜːsmeɪd] [ners-meid], **nursery-maid** ['nɜːmeɪd] [ners-meid], *sf.* La criada que cuida de los niños; niñera; criandera, ama.

nurser ['nɜːsə^r] [ner-sa^r], *s.* La persona que cría; promotor.

nursery ['nɜːsərɪ] [ner-se-ri], *s.* 1. Crianza. 2. Plantel, almáciga. 3. El jardín o huerta donde se crían flores o plantas para trasplantarlas, que casi siempre corresponde a lo que se llama en castellano criadero o semillero. 4. Plantel, semillero; un estado cualquiera que favorece el crecimiento. **The nursery of arts,** el plantel de las artes. **From the nursery,** desde la niñez. 5. El cuarto o habitación de los niños pequeños. 6. Asistencia a los enfermos o el acto de asistirlos y cuidarlos. **Nursery education,** educación preescolar. **Nursery-man,** jardinero que cuida de los planteles, criaderos o semilleros. **Nursery-tales,** cuentos de niños. **Nursery school,** guardería.

nursing ['nɜːsɪŋ] [ner-sin], *s.* El acto de criar niños o el de mamar los niños. **Nursing-bottle,** mamadera, biberón.

nursling ['nɜːslɪŋ] [ners-lin], *s.* Niño criado o acabado de criarse.

nurture ['nɜːtʃə^r] [ner-cha^r], *s.* 1. El acto de nutrir, de alimentar, de promover el crecimiento. 2. Nutrimento. 3. Educación, crianza.

nurture, *va.* Criar, educar, enseñar, promover.

nut [nʌt] [nat], *s.* 1. Nuez. **Hazelnut,** avellana. **Walnut,** nuez de nogal. 2. Piñón o rueda punteada. 3. Tuerca, matriz, hembra de tornillo. 4. El extremo movible del arco de violín por medio del cual se aflojan o se aprietan las cuerdas. 5. Puente, tablilla colocada en la parte superior de los instrumentos de cuerda, que sirve para levantar las cuerdas. **Nut of an anchor,** *(Mar.)* oreja de ancla. **A hard nut,** *(Fam.)* persona dura, áspera, no impresionable. **To give a hard nut to crack,** *(Fig.)* dar que roer, que hacer. **Brazil-nut, Paranut,** nuez del Brasil. **Cashew nut,** anacardo (el fruto). **Gallnut,** agalla. **Hickory nuts,** nueces de Carya, fruto del nogal de América. **Pecan nuts,** pecanas o pacanas. **Checknut, jam-nut,** contratuerca. **Finger-nut, thumb-nut, wing-nut,** tuerca con orejetas. **Nut-oil,** aceite de nueces. **To be nuts on** *(Fam.)* estar enamorado o ser admirador de una persona o cosa.

nut, *vn.* Coger nueces.

nutant ['nʌtənt] [na-tant], *a.* Nutante; dícese particularmente de las flores. *V.* NODDING.

nutation ['nʌteɪʃən] [na-tei-shon], *s.* Nutación, movimiento del eje de la tierra por el que se inclina más o menos sobre el plano de la eclíptica.

nutbrown ['nʌtbraʊn] [nat-braun], *a.* Avellanado, del color de la cáscara de una avellana madura.

nutcracker ['nʌtbraʊnkrækə^r] [nat-kra-ka^r], *s.* Cascanueces, partidor.

nutgall ['nʌtgɔːl] [nat-gol], *s.* Agalla de monte.

nuthatch ['nʌθætʃ] [na-zach], **nutpecker** ['nʌtpekə^r] [nat-pe-ka^r], *s. (Orn.)* Picamadero.

nuthook ['nʌthɒk] [nat-juk], *s.* Horquilla para hacer caer las nueces de los árboles.

nutmeg ['nʌtmeg] [nat-meg], *s.* Nuez mosacada.

nutria ['nju:trɪə] [niu-tria], *s. (Zool.)* Coipú, mamífero roedor de la América del Sur, y su piel.

nutrient ['nju:trɪənt] [niu-trient], *a.* 1. Nutricio, nutritivo. 2. Nutriente, que sirve para conducir el alimento o nutrición; v. g. una arteria. *-s.* Alimento nutritivo; lo que alimenta.

nutriment ['nju:trɪmənt] [niu-tri-ment], *s.* Nutrimento, alimento.

nutrimental ['nju:trɪmentl] [niu-tri-men-tal], *a.* Nutrimental.

nutrition ['nju:trɪʃən] [niu-tri-shon], *s.* Nutrición; nutrimento.

nutritious ['nju:trɪʃəs] [niu-tri-shos], **nutritive** ['nju:trɪtɪv] [niu-tri-tiv], *a.* Nutritivo, nutricio, alimentos.

nutshell ['nʌtʃel] [nat-shel], *s.* 1. Cáscara de nuez o avellana. 2. Alguna cosa de muy pequeño volumen, que contiene muy poco. **In a nutshell,** en pocas palabras, en resumidas cuentas.

nut-tree ['nʌt'triː] [nat-tri], *s. (Bot.)* Avellano.

nutty ['nʌtɪ] [na-ti], *a.* 1. Abundante en nueces. 2. Que tiene sabor de nueces, o se parece a ellas. 3. *(Fig.).* Loco, ido. **To be nutty about something,** estar loco por algo.

nux-vomica ['nɒks‚vɒmɪkə] [naks-vo-mi-ka, *s.* Nuez vómica, semilla muy venenosa; se emplea en medicina.

nuzzle ['nʌzl] [na-sel], *va.* 1. *(Prov. o des.)* Criar, fomentar; acariciar. 2. Anidarse; esconderse. *-vn.* Andar con el hocico hacia abajo. **To nuzzle in the blankets,** meterse o esconderse debajo de las sábanas.

NY *Abreviatura de* **New York** (Post).

nyctalopy ['nɪktæləpɪ] [nik-ta-lo-pi], *s.* Nictalopia, defecto de la vista que consiste en ver de noche mejor que de día.

nyctalops ['nɪktæləps] [nik-ta-lops], *s.* Nictálope, el que ve mejor de noche que de día.

nylon ['naɪlən] [nai-lon], *s.* Nylon o nilón (fibra sintética de carbón, aire y agua). **Nylon fabric,** tela de nylon o nilón.

nymph [nɪmf] [nimf], *s.* 1. Ninfa, deidad fabulosa. 2. Mujer hormosa, dama; aldeana. 3. Ninfa, palomilla, crisálida de los insectos.

nympha ['nɪmfə] [nim-fa], *s.* 1. *(Anat.)* Labio pequeño de la vulva. 2. *(Zool.)* Ninfa, crisálida, insecto no completamente desarrollado.

nymphæa ['nɪmfɪə] [nim-fia], *s.* Ninfea, nenúfar, lirio acuático.

nymphean ['nɪmfɪən] [nim-fian], *a.* Lo perteneciente a las ninfas.

nymphomania, nymphomany [‚nɪmfəʊ'meɪnɪə] [nim-fou-mei-nia], *s. (Med.)* Ninfomanía, furor uterino.

nyssa ['nɪsə] [ni-sa], *s. (Bot.)* Nisa.

O

o [əʊ] [ou]. 1. Decimoquinta letra del alfabeto inglés. Tiene diversos sonidos: uno en que se pronuncia lo mismo que la *o* española muy breve, como en *not, got, lot;* otro en que su pronunciación tira algo al diptongo *ou* español, como en *no, note, bone, alone;* otro cuando se pronuncia lo mismo que la *u* española muy breve, como en *wolf.* 2. Óvalo o círculo; punto, lentejuela. 1. Oh! interjección para exclamar, exhortar, etc. 2. Ojalá. **O! That morning would come!** ¡Ojalá que apuntara el día!

o/a *Abreviatura de* **on account,** a cuenta.

oaf [əʊf] [ouf], *s.* 1. Patán. 2. Idiota, zoquete, zote.

oafish [ˈəʊfɪʃ] [ou-fish], *a.* Lerdo, estúpido, tonto.

oafishness [ˈəʊfɪʃnɪs] [ou-fish-nes], *s. (Poco us.)* Torpeza, rudeza, estupidez.

oak [əʊk] [ouk], *s.* 1. *(Bot.)* Roble. **Evergreen oak, holm-oak,** *(Bot.)* encina. **Scarlet oak,** *(Bot.)* coscoja. 2. Roble, la madera del árbol así llamado. **Live-oak, holly-leaved oak,** encina siempre verde de California y Méjico. **Cork-oak,** roble de corcho, alcornoque. **Spanish oak, Turkey oak,** roble español, la **Quercus falcata,** de los Estados Unidos del Sur. **Italian oak,** roble de bellotas dulces: Quercus æsculus del sur de Europa. **White oak,** roble blanco, gran árbol americano de madera muy estimada. **Turkey oak,** en Europa, roble de Borgoña, Quercus cerris; en los Estados Unidos, la Quercus falacata. *V.* **Spanish oak. Oak-apple,** especie de agalla (de roble). **Oak-bark,** corteza de roble. **Oak-grove,** robledo, robledal, bosque de robles. **Oak-leaf,** hoja de roble. **Oak-leather,** (a) cuero curtido con cáscara de roble. (b) Hongo duro y correoso que se cría en las grietas de los robles viejos y se parece a la cabritilla blanca. **Oak-tanned,** curtido con corteza de roble. **Quartered oak,** *V.* QUARTER. **Oak-wood,** madera de roble. **Oak-tree,** *(Bot.)* roble. **Oak timber,** madera de roble para construcciones.

oaken [ˈəʊkən] [ou-ken], *a.* Hecho de roble; compuesto de robles o de las hojas y ramas del roble. **An oaken garland,** guirnalda de hojas de roble.

oakling [ˈəʊklɪŋ] [ou-klin], *s.* Roble tierno o de poco tiempo.

oakum [ˈəʊkəm] [ou-kom], *s. (Mar.)* Estopa, para calafatear.

oaky [ˈəʊkɪ] [ou-ki], *a.* Parecido a un roble; duro, fuerte.

oar [ɔːʳ] [oʳ], *s.* 1. Remo, instrumento de madera que sirve para impulsar las embarcaciones, haciendo fuerza en el agua. 2. Remero. 3. Entre ciertas lombrices, apéndice natatorio que se asemeja a un remo. **Oar-lock,** chumacera, escalamera. **Flat of an oar,** pala de remo. **To ship the oars,** armar los remos. **Hold on your oars,** alza los remos. **To lie on the oars,** cesar de remar, aguantar los remos; de aquí, familiarmente, descansar del trabajo.

oar, *vn.* Remar. *-va.* Bogar, conducir a remo.

oarage [ˈəʊrɪdʒ] [ou-rich] *s.* El conjunto de remos de una lancha o un bote.

oared [ɔːd] [ord], *a.* 1. Provisto de remos (por lo común, en composición): **Eight-oared,** de ocho remos. 2. *(Zool.)* Que tiene pies parecidos a remos, o apéndices natatorios.

oar-finned [ɔːˈfɪnd] [or-find], *a.* Lo que tiene remos.

oarsman [ˈɔːzmən] [ors-man], *s.* Remero.

oarsmanship [ˈɔːzmənʃɪp] [ors-man-ship], *s. m.* Arte de remar.

oary [ˈəʊrɪ] [ou-ri], *a.* Formado como remo; remado.

oasis [əʊˈeɪsɪs] [ouei-sis], *s.* Oasis, espacio de tierra fértil en un desierto arenoso. (*pl.* OASES.)

oast [əʊst] [oust], *s.* Horno para lúpulo.

oat, oats [əʊt] [out], *s.* Avena. **Wild oat,** avena loca o silvestre. Avena fatua. **Wild oats,** (a) avena silvestre. (b) Excesos de la juventud. **To sow one's wild oats,** pasar las mocedades, correrla. **Off one's oats,** indispuesto, desganado. **Oat-bran,** salvado de avena. **Rolled oats,** avena, descortezada, cilindrada y sometida a la acción del vapor y que sirve de alimento.

Oats-peas-beans, juego de niños que bailan y cantan en corro. **Potato oat,** avena geórgica. **Tartarian oat,** avena oriental. *Oat* se usa muy rara vez en singular excepto en composición; como **oat-straw,** paja de avena.

oat-cake [ˈəʊtkeɪk] [out-keik], *s.* Torta de harina de avena.

oaten [ˈəʊtn] [ou-ten], *a.* Aveníceo, hecho de avena; lo que produce avena.

oatfield [ˈəʊtfiːld] [out-fild], *s. m.* Avenal.

oath [əʊθ] [ouz], *s.* 1. Juramento, afirmación o declaración solemne poniendo por testigo a Dios, en sí mismo o en sus criaturas. 2. Juramento, blasfemia, uso frívolo del nombre de Dios o de algún objeto sagrado. **To put upon oath,** hacer prestar juramento. **To take an oath,** prestar juramento. **On o upon oath,** bajo juramento. **Oath-breaking,** violación de juramento, perjurio.

oatmeal [ˈəʊtmiːl] [out-mil], *s.* Harina de avena; gachas, puches de ella.

obconical, obconic [ɒbˈkɒnɪkl] [ob-ko-ni-kal], *a. (Bot.)* Obcónico, que tiene la forma de un cono invertido.

obcordate, obcordiform [ˌɒbˈkɔːkədeɪt] [ob-kor-kor-deit], *a. (Biol.)* Obcordado, que tiene la forma de un corazón invertido.

obduce [ɒbˈdjuːs] [ob-dius], *va. (Des.)* Cubrir, tapar.

obduracy [ˈɒbdjʊrəsɪ] [ob-diu-ra-si], *s.* Obduración, obcecación; obstinación; endurecimietno, dureza de corazón.

obdurate [ˈɒbdjʊrɪt] [ob-diu-rit], *a.* Endurecido, terco, áspero, duro, insensible, obstinado.

obdurately [ˈɒbdjʊrɪtlɪ] [ob-diu-rit-li], *adv.* Tercamente, obstinadamente.

obdurateness [ˈɒbdjʊrɪtnɪs] [ob-diu-rit-nes], **obduration** [ˌɒbdjʊˈreɪʃən] [ob-diu-rei-shon], *s.* Impenitencia, endurecimiento, obstinación, dureza de corazón.

obedience [əˈbiːdɪəns] [o-bi-diens], *s.* Obediencia, sujeción, sumisión a una orden; prohibición, ley conocida, deber o regla de conducta.

obedient [əˈbiːdɪənt] [o-bi-dient], *a.* Obediente, sumiso.

obediently [əˈbiːdɪəntlɪ] [o-bi-dient-li], *adv.* Obedientemente.

obeisance [əʊˈbeɪsəns] [ou-bei-sans], *s.* Cortesía, reverencia, saludo respetuoso.

obeliscal [ˈɒbɪlɪskl] [o-bi-lis-kal], *a.* De la forma de un obelisco.

obelisk [ˈɒbɪlɪsk] [o-bi-lisk], *s.* Obelisco.

obelus [ˈɒbɪləs] [o-bi-los], *s.* Obelisco.

obese [əˈbiːs] [ou-bis], *a.* Obeso, gordo, muy corpulento.

obeseness [əˈbiːsnɪs] [ou-bis-nes], **obesity** [əˈbiːsɪtɪ] [ou-bi-si-ti], *s.* Obesidad, crasitud.

obey [əˈbeɪ] [o-bei], *va.* 1. Obedecer, someterse a las órdenes de otro; hacer uno lo que se le ha mandado. 2. Obedecer, estar sujeto a, estar bajo el dominio de. 3. Ser gobernado por, ceder a. **The ship obeys the helm,** el navío obedece al timón.

obfuscate [ˈɒbfəskeɪt] [ob-fas-keit], *va.* Confundir la mente, ofuscar el entendimiento.

obit [ˈɒbɪt] [o-bit], *s.* 1. El fallecimiento, o fecha de la muerte de una persona. 2. Exequias, las honras que se celebran en el aniversario de un fallecimiento.

obituary [əˈbɪtjʊərɪ] [o-bi-chua-ri], *a.* Mortuorio, relativo a la muerte. *-s.* 1. Necrología, noticia biográfica de una persona recién fallecida. 2. En la Iglesia católica romana, obituario, libro de partidas de entierros.

object [ˈɒbdʒɪkt] [ob-yikt], *s.* 1. Objeto, lo que se percibe con alguno de los sentidos, o por las facultades mentales. 2. Objeto, término o fin de los actos de las potencias. 3. Objeto, fin, intento; blanco, punto. 4. *(Gram.)* Complemento, régimen directo. **To be an object of pity,** dar lástima. **With the object of,** con el propósito de.

object, *va.* 1. Objetar, presentar en oposición, poner reparos a alguna opinión, poner reparos a alguna opinión o razón para refutarla. 2. Hacer cargos. *-vn.* Dar en rostro, echar en cara, poner tachas o reparos. **No one objected to his title,** nadie discutió su derecho. **I object most strongly!** ¡me opongo rotundamente! **Do you object my smoking?** ¿Le molesta que fume?

objectable ['ɒbdʒɪktəbl] [ob-yik-ta-bol], *a.* V. OBJECTIONABLE.

object-glass ['ɒbdʒɪkt,glɑːs] [ob-yikt-glas], *s. (Opt.)* Objetivo, la lente o la combinación de lentes en los telescopios, microscopios y otros instrumentos ópticos.

objection [əb'dʒekʃən] [ob-yek-shon], *s.* Objeción, oposición, reparo, réplica; tacha. **I have no objection,** no tengo inconveniente en ello, o no tengo nada que decir a eso. **To meet an objection,** hacer frente a una objeción. **To raise an objection,** hacer una objeción.

objectionable [əb'dʒekʃnəbl] [ob-yek-sho-na-bol], *a.* Reparable, susceptible de objeción, censurable, reprensible; perjudicial.

objectionableness [əb'dʒekʃnəblnɪs] [ob-yek-sho-na-bol-nes], *s.* El estado de lo que está expuesto a objeciones o reparos.

objective [əb'dʒektɪv] [ob-yek-tiv], *a.* 1. Objetivo, perteneciente a un objeto. 2. Dirigido hacia los objetos y que corresponde a ellos. 3. Existente por sí mismo, independiente por su propia autoridad; lo opuesto a subjetivo. 4. *(Gram.)* Acusativo; se dice del caso que expresa el complemento de los verbos. *-s.* 1. El caso acusativo. 2. Objetivo. V. OBJECT-GLASS. 3. Punto objetivo, destinación.

objectively [əb'ʒektɪvlɪ] [ob-yek-tiv-li], *adv.* Objetivamente.

objectiveness [əb'dʒektɪvnɪs] [ob-yek-tiv-nes], *s.* Calidad de objeto, de lo que puede percibirse por los sentidos.

objectivism [əb'dʒektɪvɪzəm] [ob-yek-ti-vi-sem], *s. m.* Objetivismo.

objectivity [əb'dʒektɪvɪtɪ] [ob-yek-ti-vi-ti], *s. f.* Objetividad.

objectless [əb'dʒektlɪs] [ob-yekt-les], *a.* Sin objeto, sin fin.

objector [əb'dʒektəʳ] [ob-yek-taʳ], *s.* Impugnador, el que objeta, replica, o presenta objeciones.

objurgate ['ɒbdʒɜːgeɪt] [ob-yer-gueit], *va.* Reprender, censurar, desaprobar.

objurgation [,ɒbdʒɜː'geɪʃən] [ob-yer-guei-shon], *s.* Reprensión, censura, desaprobación.

objurgatory ['ɒbdʒɜːgətərɪ] [ob-yer-ga-to-ri], *a.* Reprobatorio.

oblate ['ɒbleɪt] [o-bleit], *a.* Achatado por los polos; dícese de un esferoide.

oblation ['ɒbleɪʃən] [o-blei-shon], *s.* 1. Oblación, ofrenda y sacrificio que se hace a Dios: la eucaristía. 2. En la antigua Iglesia cristiana, don u ofrenda para el clero y los pobres, o para los gastos de la Cena.

obligate ['ɒblɪgeɪt] [o-bli-gueit], *va.* 1. Obligar, ligar por contrato en sentido legal o moral. 2. Obligar a cumplir con un deber.

obligation [,ɒblɪ'geɪʃən] [o-bli-guei-shon], *s.* 1. Obligación, vínculo; contrato que lleva una condición y penalidad en caso de no cumplirse. 2. La fuerza coercitiva de la conciencia que impele a uno a cumplir un voto, promesa, juramento o ley. 3. Obligación, la correspondencia que uno debe manifestar por los beneficios, favores, mercedes o gracias, etc., que ha recibido. **I am under many obligations to him,** le debo muchos favores. 4. Obligación, la escritura en que uno se obliga a cumplir lo que ofrece.

obligatoriness [ɒ'blɪgətərɪnɪs] [o-bli-ga-to-ri-nes], *s.* El estado o calidad de lo que impone obligación.

obligatory [ɒ'blɪgətərɪ] [o-bli-ga-to-ri], *a.* Obligatorio.

oblige [ə'blaɪdʒ] [o-blaidch], *va.* 1. Obligar, precisar, ligar, imponer la obligación de hacer alguna cosa. 2. Complacer, agradar, servir, favorecer, hacer favor o merced a alguno. **You will greatly oblige me by writing to me,** le agradeceré mucho que me escriba. **I am much obliged to you,** le estoy muy reconocido. **I did it to oblige him,** lo hice por favorecerle.

obligee [,ɒblɪ'dʒiː] [o-bli-yi], *s. (For.)* Obligado.

obliger [ə'blaɪdʒəʳ] [o-blai-yaʳ], *s.* El que obliga por contrato.

obliging [ə'blaɪdʒɪŋ] [o-blai-yin], *a.* Servicial, servidor, favorecedor, galante; obsequioso, cortesano, oficioso, comedido.

obligingly [ə'blaɪdʒɪŋlɪ] [o-blai-yin-li], *adv.* Cortésmente, atentamente.

obligingness [ə'blaɪdʒɪŋnɪs] [o-blai-yin-nes], *s.* Obligación, cortesía, obsequio.

obligor [ə'blɪgəʳ] [o-bli-gaʳ], *s. (For.)* Deudor, el que contrae una obligación para con otro.

oblique [ə'bliːk] [o-blik], *a.* 1. Oblicuo, sesgado, torcido, atravesado. 2. *(Gram.)* Oblicuo; cualquiera de los casos excepto el nominativo y el vocativo. 3. Torcido, indirecto, doloso, siniestro. 4. Colateral, el pariente que no lo es por línea recta.

obliquely [ə'bliːklɪ] [o-blik-li], *adv.* 1. Oblicuamente, al sesgo. 2. Indirectamente, por rodeos.

obliqueness [ə'bliːknɪs] [o-blik-nes], **obliquity** [ə'blɪktɪ] [o-blik-ti], *s.* 1. Oblicuidad, desvío de la línea horizontal o perpendicular. 2. Desvío o declinación de lo recto y justo.

obliterate [ə'blɪtəreɪt] [o-bli-te-reit], *va.* 1. Borrar, testar o tachar lo escrito. 2. Consumir, destruir, arrasar; borrar insensiblemente la memoria de alguna cosa, irla olvidando; hacer imperceptible. **To become obliterated,** borrarse, apagarse.

obliteration [ə'blɪtəreɪʃən] [o-bli-te-rei-shon], *s.* Obliteración, canceladura, el acto de borrar un escrito o de borrar de la memoria o abolir; extinción.

oblivion [ə'blɪvɪən] [o-bli-vion], *s.* Olvido. **Act of oblivion,** amnistía, olvido general. **To cast into oblivion,** echar al olvido.

oblivious [ə'blɪvɪəs] [o-bli-vios], *a.* 1. Olvidadizo, desmemoriado. 2. Abstraído, absorto. 3. Que causa olvido. **To be oblivious of/to,** estar inconsciente de.

oblong ['ɒblɒŋ] [o-blong], *a.* Oblongo, más largo que ancho. *-s.* Rectángulo que tiene los lados contiguos desiguales.

oblongly ['ɒblɒŋlɪ] [o-blong-li], *adv.* En figura oblonga.

oblongness ['ɒblɒŋnɪs] [o-blong-nes], *s.* El estado de lo que es oblongo o más largo que ancho.

obloquy ['ɒbləkwɪ] [o-blo-kui], *s.* 1. Murmuración, detracción, maledicencia. 2. Infamia, deshonra, tacha o nota de acción fea. **He scorns the public obloquy,** se burla del qué dirán.

obmutescence [ɒb'mjuːtəsəns] [ob-miu-te-sens], *s.* Mudez, pérdida de la facultad de hablar; taciturnidad.

obnoxious [əb'nɒkʃəs] [ob-nok-sios], *a.* 1. Ofensivo, aborrecible, detestable, que causa aversión. **A law obnoxious to the people,** una ley detestable para el pueblo. 2. Sujeto, expuesto a; delincuente, culpable, responsable.

obnoxiously [əb'nɒkʃəslɪ] [ob-nok-sios-li], *adv.* En estado de sujeción; o en el de uno que está expuesto a ser castigado; odiosamente.

obnoxiousness [əb'nɒkʃəsnɪs] [ob-nok-sios-nes], *s.* El estado del que está expuesto a contingencias o castigos; carácter ofensivo o aborrecible.

obnubilation [,ɒbnəbɪ'leɪʃən] [ob-no-bi-lei-shon], *s.* 1. *(Med.)* Ofuscamiento de la vista; estado de confusión, como de vértigo o vahido. 2. *(Des.)* Oscurecimiento.

o.b.o *(EU) Abreviatura de* **or best offer,** abierto ofertas.

oboe ['əʊbəʊ] [ou-bou], *s.* Oboe, instrumento músico de viento con lengüeta doble.

oboist ['əʊbəʊɪst] [ou-bouist], *s.* Oboe (person).

obovate ['ɒbəveɪt] [o-bo-veit], *a.* Obovoide, inversamente aovado.

obreption ['ɒrepʃən] [o-brep-shon], *s.* Obrepción; introducción en alguna parte por sorpresa y secretamente.

obreptitious ['ɒbreptɪʃəs] [o-brep-ti-shos], *a.* Obrepticio, hecho por obrepción.

obscene [əb'si:n] [ob-sin], *a.* 1. Obsceno, impúdico, sucio, torpe, indecente. 2. (*Poét.*) Asqueroso; (*des.*) de mal agüero, siniestro.

obscenely [əb'si:nlɪ] [ob-sin-li], *adv.* Obscenamente.

obsceneness [əb'si:nnɪs] [ob-sin-nes], **obscenity** [əb'si:nɪtɪ] [ob-si-ni-ti], *s.* Obscenidad, impureza, suciedad, torpeza.

obscurantism [ˌɒbskjʊəˈræntɪzəm] [obs-kiua-ran-ti-sem], *s. m.* Oscurantismo.

obscurantist [ˌɒbskjʊəˈræntɪst] [obs-kiua-ran-tist], *a.* Oscurantista.

obscuration [ˌɒbskjʊəˈreɪʃən] [obs-kiua-rei-shon], *s.* Oscurecimiento, acción y efecto de oscurecer.

obscure [əbˈskjʊər] [obs-kiuaʳ], *a.* 1. Oscuro, lóbrego; tenebroso. 2. Oscuro, abstruso, ininteligible. 3. Oscuro, desconocido, humilde, retirado. 4. Oscuramente señalado; meramente indicado.

obscure, *va.* 1. Oscurecer, privar de la luz, hacer menos visible; cubrir de nubes. 2. Oscurecer, ofuscar la razón alterando y confundiendo la verdad o realidad de las cosas. 3. Oscurecer, deslustrar, empañar la fama, reputación, nombre o gloria. **Time has obscured the writing,** el tiempo ha hecho menos legible lo escrito. **To obscure the matter further,** complicar más el asunto.

obscurely [əbˈskjʊəlɪ] [ob-skiure-li], *adv.* 1. Oscuramente. 2. Oscuramente, sin hacer papel en el mundo. 3. Confusamente, entre sombras.

obscureness [əbˈskjʊənɪs] [ob-skiure-nes], **obscurity** [əbˈskjʊərɪtɪ] [ob-skiua-ri-ti], *s.* 1. Oscuridad, lobreguez, falta de luz y claridad. 2. Oscuridad, confusión, sombras. 3. Oscuridad, humildad o bajeza de nacimiento, estado o situación. 4. Oscuridad, falta de claridad en lo que se habla o escribe.

obsecrate [əbˈsɪkreɪt] [ob-si-kreit, *va.* Suplicar, ansiosamente; obsecrar.

obsecration [əbˈsɪkreɪʃən] [ob-si-krei-shon, *s.* 1. Obsecración. 2. Ruego, súplica.

obsequial ['ɒbsɪkwɪəl] [ob-si-kuial], *a.* Funeral, fúnebre, que se refiere a exequias o funerales.

obsequies ['ɒbsɪkwɪz] [ob-si-kuis], *s. pl.* Exequias, funeral, ritos fúnebres.

obsequious ['ɒbsɪkwɪəs] [ob-si-kuios], *a.* 1. Zalamero, empalagoso. 2. (*Ant.*) Obsequioso, rendido, sujeto a hacer la voluntad de otro.

obsequiously [əbˈsɪkwɪəslɪ] [ob-si-kuios-li], *adv.* Zalameramente; obsequiosamente.

obsequiousness [əbˈsɪkwɪəsnɪs] [ob-si-kuios-nes], *s.* 1. Complacencia baja o excesiva, zalamería. 2. (*Ant.*) Obsequio, obediencia, rendimiento.

observable [əbˈzɜːvəbl] [ob-ser-va-bol], *a.* 1. Observable, que se puede observar; perceptible a la vista o por medio de la observación. 2. Notable, conspicuo, eminente. 3. Acostumbrado, ordinario, de observancia usual.

observableness [əbˈzɜːvəblnɪs] [ob-ser-va-bol-nes], *s.* Calidad de notable.

observably [əbˈzɜːvəblɪ] [ob-ser-va-bli], *adv.* Notablemente, conspicuamente, visiblemente.

observance [əbˈzɜːvəns] [ob-ser-vans], *s.* 1. Observancia, reverencia, acatamietno, honor. 2. Observancia, cumplimiento exacto y puntual de un deber. 3. Rito o ceremonia religiosa; costumbre, práctica, uso (custom). 4. Observación, atención; respeto, cuidado, exacto.

observancy [əbˈzɜːvənsɪ] [ob-ser-van-si], *s.* Atención.

observant [əbˈzɜːvənt] [ob-ser-vant], *a.* 1. Observador, vigilante, atento, exacto. 2. Observador de las reglas y leyes, respetuoso, obsequioso, sumiso.

observation [ˌɒbzəˈveɪʃən] [ob-ser-vei-shon], *s.* 1. Observación, la acción de observar, de advertir con atención.

2. Escrutinio, examen científico de un fenómeno natural; observación astronómica o meteorológica. 3. Reflexión, experiencia adquirida por la observación. 4. Observación, nota o reparo crítico sobre alguna cosa. 5. Observancia, el cumplimiento de alguna orden, ley o precepto. **To escape observation,** pasar inadvertido. **To be under observation,** estar vigilado.

observatory [əbˈzɜːvətrɪ] [ob-ser-va-tri], *s.* 1. Observatorio, cúpula o edificio elevado propio para las observaciones astronómicas. 2. Atalaya, torre edificada para observar desde ella una gran extensión de terreno; cualquier punto desde el cual se decubre mucho espacio de tierra o mar.

observe [əbˈzɜːv] [ob-serv], *va.* 1. Observar, mirar, advertir con atención. 2. Observar, notar, reparar. 3. Observar, guardar y cumplir exactamente lo que se ejecuta y ordena. 4. Notar, expresar (una opinión, etc.) incidentalmente. -*vn.* 1. (*Des.*) Ser mirado o circunspecto. 2. Hacer observaciones o poner reparos. **It is to be observed,** es de notar.

observer [əbˈzɜːvəʳ] [ob-ser-vaʳ], *s.* 1. Observador, el que observa, particularmente con instrumentos de precisión. 2. Observador, observante, el que guarda y cumple lo que es de su obligación o se le manda.

observing [əbˈzɜːvɪŋ] [ob-ser-vin], *a.* Observador, cuidadoso, pronto a percibir; que presta atención particular a una cosa.

observingly [əbˈzɜːvɪŋlɪ] [ob-ser-vin-li], *adv.* Cuidadosamente, atentamente.

obsess [əbˈzes] [ob-ses], *vt.* Causar o provocar obsesión, obsesionar.

obsession [əbˈseʃən] [ob-se-shon], *s.* 1. Sitio, el acto de sitiar alguna plaza. 2. Obsesión.

obsessive [əbˈzesɪv] [ob-se-siv], *a.* Obsesionante.

obsidian [əbˈsɪdɪən] [ob-si-dian], *s.* (*Min.*) Obsidiana, mineral volcánico y vítreo.

obsidional [əbˈsɪdɪənl] [ob-si-dio-nal], *a.* Obsidional, lo que pertenece al sitio de una plaza.

obsolesce ['ɒbsəles] [ob-so-les], *vn.* Caer en desuso.

obsolescence [ˌɒbsəˈlesens] [ob-so-le-sens], *s.* Estado o acto de caer en desuso.

obsolescent [ˌɒbsəˈlesnt] [ob-so-le-sent], *a.* Lo que va quedándose anticuado o fuera de uso.

obsolete ['ɒbsəliːt] [ob-so-lit], *a.* 1. Obsoleto, desusado, fuera de uso. 2. (*Biol.*) Atrofiado, imperfectamente desarrollado, oscuro o suprimido.

obsoleteness ['ɒbsəliːtnɪs] [ob-so-lit-nes], *s.* 1. Desuso, el estado de haber caído en desuso. 2. (*Biol.*) Falta de desarrollo.

obstacle ['ɒbstəkl] [obs-ta-kol], *s.* Obstáculo, impedimento, embarazo, inconveniente. **Obstacle race,** carrera de obstáculos.

obstetric, obstetrical ['ɒbstɪtrɪk] [obs-ti-trik], *a.* Obstétrico, referente a la obstetricia.

obstetrician ['ɒbstɪtrɪʃən] [obs-ti-tri-shan], *s.* Partero, comadrón.

obstetrics ['ɒbstɪtrɪks] [obs-ti-triks], *s.* Obsteetricia, parte de la medicina que trata de la gestación, el parto y el puerperio. V. MIDWIFERY.

obstinacy ['ɒbstɪnəsɪ] [obs-ti-na-si], *s.* 1. Obstinación, pertinacia, porfía, terquedad; apego firme y por lo regular infundado a la propia opinión o proyecto. 2. (*Med.*) Carácter obstinado, resistencia.

obstinate ['ɒbstɪnɪt] [obs-ti-neit], *a.* 1. Obstinado, terco, porfiado, temoso, tenaz. 2. Difícil de subyugar o curar, rebelde.

obstinately ['ɒbstɪneɪtlɪ] [obs-ti-neit-li], *adv.* Obstinadamente, tercamente.

obstinateness ['ɒbstɪneɪtnɪs] [obs-ti-neit-nes], *s.* Obstinación, terquedad.

obstreperous ['əbstrepərəs] [obs-tre-pe-ros], *a.* Estrepitoso, ruidoso, turbulento, que hace mucho ruido.

obstreperously ['əbstrepərəslɪ] [obs-tre-pe-ros-li], *adv.* Estrepitosamente.

obstreperousness ['əbstrepərəsnɪs] [obs-tre-pe-ros-nes], *s.* Estrépito, bulla.

obstriction ['ɒbstrɪksən] [obs-trik-shon], *s.* *(Ant.)* Obligación, constreñimiento.

obstruct ['ɒbstrʌkt] [obs-trakt], *va.* 1. Obstruir, llenar de obstáculos; cerrar. 2. Impedir, retardar, estorbar; detener, no dejar pasar. **Plowing (o ploughing) was obstructed by rain,** la lluvia retardó la aradura.

obstructer ['ɒbstrʌktər] [obs-trak-taʳ], *s.* Estorbador.

obstruction ['ɒbstrʌkʃən] [obs-trak-shon], *s.* 1. Obstrucción de alguna vía natural. 2. Estorbo, obstáculo, impedimento, dificultad.

obstructionism [əb'strʌkʃənɪzəm] [obs-trak-sho-ni-sem], *s. m.* Obstruccionismo.

obstructionist ['ɒbstrʌkʃənɪst] [obs-trak-sho-nist], *s.* Estorbador, el que pone obstáculos, particularmente en asunto legislativos.

obstructive ['ɒbstrʌktɪv] [obs-trak-tiv], *a.* Obstructivo. -*s.* Embarazo. **You're being obstructive,** nos estás estorbando.

obstructiveness ['ɒbstrʌktɪvnɪs] [obs-trak-tiv-nes], *s.* La calidad que hace a una cosa obstructiva o capaz de causar obstrucciones.

obstruent ['ɒbstrʊənt] [obs-truent], *a.* Obstructivo; se emplea particularmente en medicina.

obtain [əb'teɪn] [ob-tein], *va.* 1. Obtener, adquirir, conseguir. 2. *(Ant.)* Alcanzar, lograr. -*vn.* 1. Estar establecido, mantenerse en uso o en práctica; existir alguna ley, calidad o condición en una cosa. 2. Prevalecer, tener ventaja. **This model didn't obtain in my day,** este modelo no existía en mis tiempos.

obtainable [əb'teɪnəbl] [ob-tei-na-bol], *a.* Asequible.

obtainer [əb'teɪnəʳ] [ob-tei-naʳ], *s.* El que obtiene.

obtainment [əb'teɪnmənt] [ob-tein-ment], *s.* Obtención, consecución.

obtemper [əb'tempəʳ] [ob-tem-paʳ], *va.* Obedecer, sujetarse a los preceptos de otro.

obtend [əb'tend] [ob-tend], *va.* 1. Pretender, alegar como razón. 2. Oponer.

obtest [əb'test] [ob-test], *va.* Rogar, suplicar, conjurar; encarecer; implorar.

obtestation [ˌɒbtes'teɪʃən] [ob-tes-tei-shon], *s.* Encarecimiento; ruego, súplica.

obtrude [əb'truːd] [ob-trud], *va.* Imponer, establecer o introducir a una persona o cosa con violencia o fraude en alguna aprte; colocar en posición prominente no debida. **To obtrude oneself,** entrometerse, meterse uno donde no le llaman. -*vn.* Entrometerse; ser importuno.

obtruder [əb'truːdəʳ] [ob-tru-daʳ], *s.* Un entremetido, un intruso.

obtruncate [əb'trʌnkeɪt] [ob-tran-keit], *va.* Cortar un miembro; podar o desmochar un árbol.

obtruncation [ˌɒbtʌn'keɪʃən] [ob-trun-kei-shon], *s.* Desmoche.

obtrusion [əb'truːʒən] [ob-tru-shon], *s.* Intrusión, entrometimiento.

obtrusive [əb'truːsɪv] [ob-tru-siv], *a.* Intruso, entrometido; importuno.

obtrusively [əb'truːsɪvlɪ] [ob-tru-siv-li], *adv.* Importunamente, de manera indiscreta.

obtund [əb'tʌnd] [ob-tand], *va.* Embotar, entorpecer, amortiguar.

obturation [ˌɒbtuː'reɪʃən] [ob-tu-rei-shon], *s.* El acto de cerrar o tapar alguna cosa con otra puesta encima de ella.

obturator [ˌɒbtuː'reɪtəʳ] [ob-tu-rei-taʳ], *s.* 1. *(Anat.)* Obturador; el órgano, membrana, vaso, etc., que cierra o tapa una cavidad o un conducto. 2. Obturador, instrumento para cerrar las aberturas producidas por una llaga o enfermedad.

obtusangular [ˌɒbtʊ'sæŋgjʊləʳ] [ob-tu-san-guiu-laʳ], *a.* Obtusángulo.

obtuse [əb'tjuːs] [ob-tius], *a.* 1. Obtuso, mayor que un ángulo recto; más de 90°. 2. Obtuso, romo, sin punta, embotado en la extremidad. 3. Obtuso, lerdo, torpe, tardo. 4. Sordo, hablando de ruido. **Obtuse-angled,** obtusángulo, que tiene ángulos obtusos.

obtusely [əb'tjuːslɪ] [ob-tius-li], *adv.* Obtusamente; lerdamente.

obtuseness [əb'tjuːsnɪs] [ob-tius-nes], *s.* Embotadura, embotamiento, torpeza.

obtusion [əb'tjuːʒən] [ob-tiu-shon], *s.* Embotamiento.

obvervant [əb'vɜːvənt] [ob-ver-vant], *a.* Familiar.

obverse ['ɒbvɜːs] [ob-vers], *s.* Anverso, en las medallas o cuños la cara en que está el busto. -*a.* Del anverso, que denota la cara de una medalla o moneda.

obvert ['ɒbvɜːt] [ob-vert], *va.* Volver hacia o dirigir alguna cosa a paraje determinado.

obviate ['ɒbvɪeɪt] [ob-vieit], *va.* Obviar, evitar o apartar inconvenientes o dificultades.

obvious ['ɒbvɪəs] [ob-vios], *a.* Obvio, evitar o apartar inconvenientes o dificultades.

obviously ['ɒbvɪəslɪ] [ob-vios-li], *adv.* Obviamente, patentemente, claramente.

obviousness ['ɒbvɪəsnɪs] [ob-vios-nes], *s.* Claridad, evidencia.

o/c *Abreviatura de* **overcharge.**

oc-. Prefijo, la forma de *ob,* antes de *c.*

oca ['ɒkə] [oka], *s.* Oca, planta indígena del Perú.

occasion [ə'keɪʒən] [o-kei-shon], *s.* 1. Ocasión, ocurrencia, casualidad; acaecimiento, acontecimiento (event). 2. Ocasión, sazón, coyuntura, tiempo oportuno. 3. Ocasión, motivo, causa, origen, razón. 4. Necesidad, falta (need). **To have occasion,** ofrecerse, tener que. **Upon occasion,** cuando se ofrece ocasionalmente. **To take occasion,** valerse de la ocasión, aprovechar la oportunidad. **By occasion of,** a consecuencia de. **On occasion,** en su oporutnidad, su debido tiempo. **As occasion requires,** en caso necesario, para cuando llegue la ocasión. **If you have occasion to use it,** si te ves en el caso de utilizarlo. **There was no further occasion for his services,** no hubo más necesidad de sus servicios.

occasion, *va.* Ocasionar, causar, excitar.

occasionable [ə'keɪʒənəbl] [o-kei-sho-na-bol], *a.* Lo que puede ser causado, producido u ocasionado.

occasional [ə'keɪʒənl] [o-kei-sho-nal], *a.* 1. Que ocurre más o menos frecuentemente, pero no a intervalos fijos y regulares; de circunstancia. 2. Ocasional, casual, contingente, fortuito, accidental, circunstancial. **Occasional visits,** visitas que sólo se hacen de vez en cuando. **Occasional worker,** trabajador temporal.

occasionally [ə'keɪʒənlɪ] [o-kei-sho-na-li], *adv.* Ocasionalmente, por contingencia; de vez en cuando.

occasioner [ə'keɪʒənəʳ] [o-kei-sho-naʳ], *s.* Motor, causador, causa, motivo.

occident ['ɒksɪdənt] [ok-si-dent], *s.* 1. Occidente, la Europa occidental. 2. Occidente, oeste.

occidental [ˌɒksɪ'dentl] [ok-si-den-tal], **occiduous** ['ɒksɪdʊəs] [ok-si-duos], *a.* Occidental.

occipital [ɒk'sɪpɪtəl]] [ok-si-pi-tal], *a.* Occipital, perteneciente al occipucio. **Occipital bone,** el hueso occipital.

occiput ['ɒksɪpʌt] [ok-si-pat], *s.* Colodrillo, occipucio, la parte posterior e inferior de la cabeza.

occlude [ɒ'kluːd] [o-klud], *va.* 1. Cerrar, tapar. 2. Absorber, como un metal absorbe un gas.

occlusion [ɒ'kluːʒən] [o-klu-shon], *s.* 1. *(Med.)* Cerradura, cerramiento, obstrucción de un poro, conducto o cavidad. 2. Absorción de gases por los metales.

occlusive [ɒ'kluːsɪv] [o-klu-siv], *a.* Oclusivo.

occult [ɒ'kʌlt] [o-kalt], *a.* 1. Oculto, escondido, ignorado; misterioso. 2. No conocido inmediata ni fácilmente. 3. Visible sólo para los que tienen visión espiritual; término de teosofía.

occultation [ɒ'kʌlteɪʃən] [o-kal-tei-shon], *s.* *(Astr.)* Ocultación, desaparición pasajera de una estrella o planeta ocultado por la luna.

occultism ['ɒkəltɪzəm] [o-kal-ti-sem], *s.* 1. La investigación de las cosas misteriosas, particularmente de lo sobrenatural.

2. Pretensión de poseer un poder sobrenatural; astrología. 3. Teosofía moderna.

occultist [ˈɒkəltɪst] [o-kal-tist], *a.* Ocultista.

occultness [ˈɒkəlnɪs] [o-kalt-nes], *s.* 1. Ocultación. 2. Ocultación, secreto por el cual se calla una cosa que se sabe, debiendo decirla.

occupancy [ˈɒkjʊpənsɪ] [o-kiu-pan-si], *s.* Ocupación, toma de posesión.

occupant [ˈɒkjʊpənt] [o-kiu-pant], *s.* Ocupador, ocupante, la persona que ocupa; en especial, inquilino que tiene posesión, a distinción del dueño.

occupation [ˌɒkjʊˈpeɪʃən] [o-kiu-pei-shon], *s.* 1. Ocupación, el acto de tomar posesión de un país o de otra cosa. 2. Manera o tiempo de poseer. V. TENURE. 3. Ocupación, trabajo, oficio, empleo, profesión.

occupational [ˌɒkjʊˈpeɪʃənl] [o-kiu-pei-sho-nal], *a.* Laboral, ocupacional, relativo al oficio.

occupier [ˈɒkjʊpaɪəʳ] [o-kiu-paiaʳ], *s.* 1. Ocupador. 2. El que está empleado en algún destino, arte u oficio.

occupy [ˈɒkjʊpaɪ] [o-kiu-pai], *va.* 1. Ocupar; ocuparse en; llenar el espacio, el tiempo o la capacidad de; usar de una manera exclusiva. 2. Ocupar, tomar posesión de, apoderarse de. 3. Emplear, dar empleo o trabajo *a.* **To be occupied with a thing,** ocuparse en alguna cosa, dedicarse a. -*vn.* (*Des.*) Traficar.

occur [əˈkɜːʳ] [o-keʳ], *vn.* 1. Encontrarse o hallarse aquí y allí; aparecer; de aquí, suceder, acaecer, acontecer (happen). 2. Ocurrir, venir a la imaginación o a la memoria (come to mind). **The thought did not occur to him,** no se le ocurrió tal idea. **The word glass occurs but once in the Old Testament,** la palabra vidrio se encuentra una sola vez en el Antiguo Testamento.

occurrence [əˈkʌrəns] [o-ka-rans], *s.* Ocurrencia, incidente, suceso casual; acontecimiento, acaecimiento, lance. **To be of actual occurrence,** haber sucedido realmente. **To be of frequent occurrence,** suceder a menudo.

ocean [ˈəʊʃən] [ou-shan], *s.* 1. Océano, el mar que rodea la tierra. 2. Océano, piélago, una de las partes del océano, como el Atlántico, el Pacífico, etc. 3. inmensidad, expansión sin límites.

oceanarium [ˌəʊʃəˈnɛərɪəm] [ou-sha—nea-riom], *s. m.* Oceanario.

oceanic [ˌəʊʃɪˈænɪk] [ou-shia-nik], *a.* 1. Oceánico, que pertenece al océano. 2. Inmenso. 3. (*Zool.*) Pelágico, que vive en el océano.

ocean liner [ˈəʊʃənˌlaɪnəʳ] [ou-shan-lai-naʳ], *s.* Transatlántico o trasatlántico.

oceanographer [ˌəʊʃəˈnɒgrəfəʳ] [ou-sha-no-gra-faʳ], *s.* Oceanógrafo.

oceanography [ˌəʊʃəˈnɒgrəfɪ] [ou-sha-no-gra-fi], *s.* Oceanografía.

ocellated, ocellatee [ˈɒsɪleɪtɪd] [o-si-lei-tid], *a.* 1. Ojoso, que tiene manchas que se parecen a ojos. 2. Que tiene una mancha de un color dentro de un círculo de otro. 3. Manchado.

ocelot [ˈəʊsɪlɒt] [ou-si-lot], *s.* Ocelote, leopardo o tigre de Méjico.

ochlocracy [əʊˈklɒkrəsɪ] [ou-klo-kra-si], *s.* Oclocracia.

ochra [ˈəʊkrə] [ou-kra], *s.* V. OKRA y GUMBO.

ochre, ocher [ˈəʊkəʳ] [ou-kaʳ], *s.* 1. Ocre, cierta tierra para pintar de amarillo. 2. Cualquier óxido de metal que se encuentra en forma de tierra o polvo. **Yellow ocher,** ocre amarillo. **Brown ocher,** ocre carmelita. **Red ocher,** ocre rojo o encarnado, ocre quemado, almagre, almazarrón.

ocherous, ochreous [ˈəʊkərəs] [ou-ke-ros] [ˈəʊkrɪəs] [ou-krios], **ochery** [ˈəʊkərɪ] [ou-ke-ri], *a.* Ocroso, de la naturaleza o del color del ocre o que lo contiene.

o'clock [əˈklɒk] [o-klok], *loc.* Contracción de **of the clock,** que significa (la hora) según el reloj. **At one o'clock,** a la una. **It is eight o'clock,** son las ocho.

OCR *Abreviatura de* **Optical Character Reader,** lector óptico de caracteres.

octagon [ˈɒktəgən] [ok-ta-gon], *s.* Octágono, la figura que consta de ocho lados y ocho ángulos.

octagonal [ɒkˈtægənl] [ok-ta-go-nal], *a.* Octagonal.

octahedral [ˈɒktəˈhiːdrəl] [ok-tai-dral], *a.* Octaédrico, que tiene los caracteres del octaedro.

octahedron [ˈɒktəˈhiːdrən] [ok-tai-dron], *s.* Octaedro.

octandria [ɒkˈtændrɪə] [ok-tan-dria], *s.* Octandria.

octane [ˈɒkteɪn] [ok-tein], *s.* Octano.

octangular [ɒkˈtæŋgjʊləʳ] [ok-tan-guiu-laʳ], *a.* Octangular.

octant [ˈɒktənt] [ok-tant], *a. y s.* 1. La octava parte de un círculo; la medida de cuarenta y cinco grados. 2. (*Astr.*) Octante, instrumento astronómico para tomar la altura del sol.

octateuch [ˈɒktətʊk] [ok-ta-teuk], *s.* Octateuco, los ocho primeros libros del Viejo Testamento.

octave [ˈɒkteɪv] [ok-teiv], *s.* 1. Octava, el día octavo de alguna festividad; los ocho días que inmediatamente se siguen a alguna festividad. 2. (*Mús.*) Octava, intervalo de ocho tonos, o de siete grados; una nota o tecla a este intervalo sobre o debajo de otra. **Octave coupler,** doblemano, mecanismo de los órganos modernos, para hacer que con la tecla baje la de la octava superior.

octave, *a.* Octavo, perteneciente al número ocho.

octavo [ɒkˈteɪvəʊ] [ok-tei-vou], *a.* 1. En octavo, la forma que tienen los libros cuando el pliego de impresión tiene ocho hojas. 2. Que denota cierto tamaño de la página, comúnmente pulgadas. -*s.* Libro, folleto, etc., en que un pliego está doblado en ocho hojas.

octennial [ɒkˈtɪnɪəl] [ok-ti-nial], *a.* Que dura ocho años.

octet [ɒkˈtet] [ok-tet], *s.* 1. Composición musical, compuesta para ocho ejecutantes. 2. Coro de ocho voces u orquesta de ocho ejecutantes.

octillion [ɒkˈtɪlɪən] [ok-ti-lion], *s.* Octillón.

October [ɒkˈtəʊbəʳ] [ok-tou-baʳ], *s.* Octubre, el décimo mes del año.

octoedrical [ˈɒktəˈhiːdrɪkəl] [ok-toi-dri-kal], *a.* Octoédrico, que tiene ocho lados. V. OCTAHEDRAL.

octogenarian [ˌɒktəʊdʒɪˈnɛərɪən] [ok-tou-yi-nea-rian], **octogenary** [ˈɒktəʊdʒɪnərɪ] [ok-tou-yi-nea-ri], *a. y s.* Octogenario, que tiene ochenta años.

octonocular [ɒkˈtɒnəkjʊləʳ] [ok-to-no-kiu-laʳ], *a.* Que tiene ocho ojos.

octopetalous [ˈɒktəpetələs] [ok-to-pe-ta-los], *a.* Octopétala, flor que tiene ocho hojas.

octopus [ˈɒktəpəs] [ok-to-pos], *s.* Pulpo, molusco cefalópodo octópodo; jibia octópoda.

octostyle [ˈɒktəstaɪl] [ok-tos-tail], *s.* (*Arq.*) Octóstilo, el edificio que tiene ocho columnas en su frontispicio.

octosyllabic [ˈɒktəʊsaɪˈlæbɪk] [ok-tou-sai-la-bik], *a.* Octosílabo, que está compuesto de ocho sílabas.

octuple [ˈɒktəpl] [ok-ta-pel], *a.* Octuplo, lo que contiene ocho veces tanto.

ocular [ˈɒkjʊləʳ] [o-kiu-laʳ], *a.* Ocular, perteneciente al ojo; derivado del ojo o que se refiere a él; visual. -*s.* Ocular, la combinación de lentes en un instrumento óptico por medio de la cual se ve aumentada la imagen.

ocularly [ˈɒkjʊlərlɪ] [o-kiu-lar-li], *adv.* Ocularmente, visiblemente.

oculate [ˈɒkjʊleɪt] [o-kiu-leit], *a.* Ocular, que tiene ojos.

oculist [ˈɒkjʊlɪs] [o-kiu-list], *s.* Oculista, oftalmólogo.

odalisk, odalisque [ˈəʊdəlɪsk] [ou-da-lisk], *s.* Odalisca, esclava o concubina del sultán que forma parte del harem.

odd [ɒd] [od], *a.* 1. Impar, que no puede dividirse en dos porciones sin fracción. 2. Marcado con un número impar. 3. Lo que queda de un número dado o lo que falta para completarlo. 4. Tanto, pico; número indeterminado que excede o sobra después del definido. **An odd card,** una carta sobrante, o de más. 5. Particular, extraordinario, singular, raro, extraño; fantástico. **To play at odd and even,** jugar a pares y nones. **Odd apparel,** traje fantástico, singular. **It is an odd affair,** es una cosa rara. **An odd character,** un ente singular; (*Fam.*) Pájaro, pajarraco. **Three hundred and**

odd pounds, trescientas y tantas libras. **To be odd man out,** estar de más, sobrar (surplus); quedar excluido (left out). **This town has two hundred thousand odd inhabitants,** esta ciudad tiene doscientos mil y pico de habitantes. 6. Solo, único, singular; que pertenece a un par o a una serie de la que falta el resto; desemparejado. **An odd glove,** un guante sin pareja; un solo guante. **An odd volume,** tomo suelto, un solo libro. 7. (*Ant.*) Desviado; lejano. **Odds and ends,** picos y cabos pendientes. **It is very odd that it was not thought of sooner,** es muy extraño que no se haya pensado antes en ello.

oddball ['ɒdbɔːl] [od-bol] *a.* Excéntrico, raro.

oddity ['ɒdɪtɪ] [o-di-ti], *s.* 1. Singularidad, particularidad, rareza. 2. Ente singular; (*Fam.*) pajarraco.

oddly ['ɒdlɪ] [od-li], *adv.* Desigualmente, extrañamente, singularmente; de un modo extraño; en número impar.

oddness ['ɒdnɪs] [od-nes], *s.* 1. Disparidad, desigualdad. 2. Singularidad, extravagancia, rareza en el obrar, hablar, vestir, etc.

odds ['ɒdz] [ods], *s. pl.* (y a veces *singular*) 1. Desigualdad, diferencia, disparidad. **That does not make any odds,** eso no hace diferencia alguna; eso no importa. **The odds were against me,** tuve que vérmelas con uno más fuerte que yo. **There are odds against it,** es poco probable. **To lay the odds with one,** hacer una apuesta desigual. 2. Partido desigual, apuesta desigual. 3. Ventaja, superioridad, exceso. 4. Riña, pendencia, disputa. **They are at odds,** están siempre riñendo. (*Fam.*) Están de cuernos, están de punta. **To set at odds,** desunir, descomponer, malquistar. **To fight against odds,** luchar contra una fuerza superior. **What's the odds?,** ¿qué más da? **To be odds of 5 to 1,** ofrecer 5 puntos de ventaja a 1. **The odds are that,** lo más probable es que. **All the odds and sods,** todo el mundo.

ode [əʊd] [oud], *s.* Oda, poema lírico; poema corto de gran elevación de tema y forma particular.

odeon ['ɒdɪən] [o-dion], *s.* 1. En la antigua Grecia, teatro con techo. 2. Teatro o salón de música.

odic ['ɒdɪk] [o-dik], *a.* Odico, perteneciente a una oda.

odious ['əʊdɪəs] [ou-dios], *a.* 1. Odioso, abominable, aborrecible. 2. Asqueroso, detestable, aborrecido.

odiously ['əʊdɪəslɪ] [ou-dios-li], *adv.* Odiosamente, abominablemente.

odiousness ['əʊdɪəsnɪs] [ou-dios-nes], *s.* 1. Odiosidad. 2. Odio; carácter odioso.

odometer [ɒ'dɒmɪtəʳ] [o-do-mi-taʳ], *s.* Odómetro, cuentakilómetros.

odometrical ['ɒdɒ'miːtrɪkl] [o-do-mi-tri-kal], *a.* Odométrico, relativo a un odómetro o hecho por él.

odontalgia [ˌɒdɒn'tældʒɪə] [o-don-tal-yia], *s.* Odontalgia, dolor de dientes o muelas.

odontalgic [ˌɒdɒn'tældʒɪk] [o-don-tal-chik], *a.* Odontálgico, que pertenece al dolor de dientes.

odontograph ['ɒdɒntəgræf] [o-don-to-graf], *s.* Odontógrafo, instrumento para formar los dientes de las ruedas.

odontoid ['ɒdɒntɔɪd] [o-don-toid], *a.* Odontóideo, que tiene la forma de un diente.

odontologist [ˌɒdɒn'tələdʒɪst] [o-don-to-lo-chist], *s.* Odontólogo, dentista.

odor ['əʊdəʳ] [ou-daʳ], *s.* Olor; fragancia, olor suave; aroma.

odoriferous [ˌəʊdə'rɪfərəs] [ou-do-ri-fe-ros], *a.* Odorífero, fragante, perfumado.

odorless, odourless ['əʊdəlɪs] [ou-da-les], *a.* Inodoro, que carece de olor.

odorous ['əʊdərəs] [ou-do-ros], *s.* Oloroso, fragante.

odour, etc. V. ODOR, etc. Manera usual de escribir estas palabras en Inglaterra.

odyl ['əʊdɪl] [ou-dil], *s.* Fuerza hipotética de la que se supone que explica los fenómenos del magnetismo animal.

odyssey ['ɒdɪsɪ] [o-di-si], *s.* Odisea o Ulixea, poema épico de Homero.

oe [ɪ] [i]. Para las palabras que comienzan por este diptongo y no se hallan aquí, véase la letra E.

oeconomics ['ɪkɒnɒmɪks] [i-ko-no-miks], *s.* Economía política.

oecumenical, ecumenical [ˌiːkjuː'mɪnɪkəl] [i-kiu-me-ni-kal], *a.* Ecuménico, universal.

oedema [ɪ'diːmə] [i-di-ma], *s.* Edema, hidorpoesía.

oedematous [ɪ'diːmətəs] [i-di-ma-tos], *a.* Edematoso, perteneciente al edema.

oenologist [ɪ'nɒlədʒɪst] [i-no-lo-yist], *a.* Enólogo.

oenology [ɪ'nɒlədʒɪ] [i-no-lo-yi], *s.* Enología.

o'er ['əʊəʳ] [aua]. Contracción poética de OVER.

oesophagus [iː'sɒfəgəs] [i-so-fa-gos], *s.* Esófago, tragadero.

oestrogen, estrogen ['iːstrɒdʒən] [is-trou-yen], *s. m.* Estrógeno.

oestrus ['iːstrəs] [is-tros], *s.* Estro, tábano.

of [ɒv] [ov], *prep.* 1. De, asociado con; expresa una causa. **Of the,** del, de la, de los, de las. **The value of land,** el precio o el valor de las tierras. 2. Desde, fuera de, proveniente de; expresa relación de instrumento, movimiento, separación o efecto. **To rid the town of a villain,** echar de la población a un malvado. 3. Tocante. **All entertain this opinion of the war,** todos son de esta opinión tocante o con respecto a la guerra. 4. De, según. **Of custom,** de costumbre o según costumbre. 5. Por; (pocas veces para). **Of his great mercy,** por su gran misericordia. 6. En, entre; sobre. **Of old,** en otro tiempo, antiguamente. **A doctor of law or divinity,** doctor en leyes o en teología. **Of all things,** entre o ante todas las cosas; sobre todas las cosas. **I shall think of it,** pensaré en ello. **It is well done of him,** ha hecho bien o ha obrado como debía. **Of himself,** de por sí, espontáneamente. **A friend of mine,** un amigo mío, uno de mis amigos. **Of necessity,** por necesidad. **Of old,** antiguamente, en otro tiempo, antaño. **A friend of old,** un amigo antiguo. **Of course,** por supuesto, bien entendido. **Of late,** últimamente, desde hace poco. **That was very unkind of her,** eso fue una descortesía por parte de ella. **The best of singers,** el mejor cantante. **The city of Havana,** la ciudad de la Habana. **By the name of Owens,** llamado Owens. **It was fine of an evening,** al anochecer hacía buen tiempo. **A smell of roses,** un olor a rosas.

off [ɒf] [of]. Adverbio y preposición que generalmente se une a los verbos para modificar o cambiar su significación, y ya unido, ya separado, sirve para expresar separación, ausencia, privación o distancia; lejos, a distancia, fuera de aquí. A veces corresponde al prefijo español *des.* **West of this forest scarcely off a mile,** escasamente una milla al oeste de este bosque. **A great way off,** muy lejos. **How far is it off?,** ¿Cuánto hay desde aquí a allí? o de aquí allá? **Far off,** lejos. **The match is off,** se ha cancelado el partido. **He is off,** se va, se marcha. **I saw him off,** le ví marcharse. **Either off or on,** ni en pro ni en contra. **The child had his stockings off,** el niño tenía quitadas las medias. **The locomotive ran off the track,** la locomotora descarriló. **The lock is off,** está quitada la cerradura. **The water is turned off,** el agua no corre; han cortado el agua. **Two per cent off for cash,** descuento de dos por ciento por pago al contado. **Off and on,** de vez en cuando, algunas veces; a intervalos; ya bien ya mal; dentro o fuera. **To be well off,** salir bien de alguna dificultad; estar bien o tener con qué pasarlo bien; (*Fam.*) tener el riñón bien cubierto. **Well off, badly off,** bien, mal en sus negocios. **We are no worse off than before,** no estamos peor que antes. **To be off from one,** reñir con alguno, abandonarle o separarse de él. **I am off,** lo dejo; me desdigo; me marcho. **Noises of,** ruido de fondo. **A voice off,** voz en off (Cinema). **Off-hand,** de repente, de improviso, sin pensarlo. (*Mar.*) **To be off Cadiz,** estar sobre Cádiz o a la altura de Cádiz. **Off color,** (a) de color poco satisfactorio; se dice de una joya. (b) (*Ger.*) Malo, indecente, verde. -*inter.* ¡Fuera! **Off from hence,** fuera de aquí. **Off with your hat,** quítese Ud. el sombrero o fuera ese sombrero. **Off with his head!** ¡Que le corten la cabeza!

off , *a.* 1. Más distante, a mayor distancia, más lejano; el lado derecho de una yunta o una pareja de animales; a la derecha, lo opuesto a *nigh o near.* 2. Desviado del camino principal. 3. De descanso, que denota una interrupción. **A day off,** un día de descanso. **To take a day off,** tomarse un día libre. **To**

be off sick, estar de baja. 4. *(Fam.)* En desacuerdo con la realidad; falso, incorrecto. **Off in his calculations,** errado en sus cálculos. **Off side,** (a) el lado derecho. (b) En el juego de pelota, falta, mala jugada. **The game is off,** el partido ha sido cancelado. **Right off, straight off,** ininterrumpidamente, sin parar. **To be off,** estar pasado, cortado (milk, food). **To be well off,** tener dinero, estar bien acomodado (financial). **To alow 10 % off the price,** rebajar un 10% el precio. **To dine off soup,** cenar sopa. **To be off-center,** estar descentrado.

offal ['ɒfəl] [o-fal], *s.* 1. Asadura, despojos de las reses muertas. 2. Desecho, desperdicio de alguna cosa. Se emplea también como adjetivo.

offbeat ['ɒf,biːt] [of-bit], *a.* Raro, excéntrico, no convencional.

offence, offenceless. *V.* OFFENSE.

offend [ə'fend] [o-fend], *va. y vn.* 1. Ofender, enfadar, irritar, provocar. 2. Acometer, embestir. 3. Violar, quebrantar alguna ley o precepto; pecar. 4. Ofender, agraviar, injuriar; desagradar, causar disgusto. 5. Delinquir, quebrantar la ley de Dios o sus preceptos.

offender [ə'fendər] [o-fen-daʳ], *s.* Delincuente, transgresor, ofensor.

offending [ə'fendɪŋ] [o-fen-din], *a.* Culpable, delincuente; ofensivo.

offendress [ə'fendrɪs] [o-fen-dres], *s. f.* Ofensora; pecadora.

offense [ə'fens] [o-fens], *s.* 1. Ofensa, quebrantamiento de la ley divina o humana; pecado; cualquier delito o culpa; crimen, agresión. 2. Ofensa, injuria, agravio hecho a alguno. 3. Ofensa, ataque, acometimiento. **To take offense,** ofenderse de alguna cosa, darse por sentido. **No offense,** sin ofender a Ud.

offenseless [ə'fenslɪs] [o-fens-les], *a.* Inofensivo, que no ofende.

offensive [ə'fensɪv] [o-fen-siv], *a.* 1. Ofensivo, injurioso, ultrajante. 2. Desagradable, que causa disgusto. 3. Perjudicial. **Offensive warfare,** guerra ofensiva. **An offensive odor,** un olor desagradable. -*s.* Ofensiva, ataque.

offensively [ə'fensɪvlɪ] [o-fen-siv-li], *adv.* Ofensivamente.

offensiveness [ə'fensɪvnɪs] [o-fen-siv-nes], *s.* Ofensa, desazón; cualidad perjudicial; causa de asco.

offer ['ɒfər] [o-faʳ], *va.* 1. Ofrecer; hacer patente, dar a conocer, poner en conocimiento del público. 2. Sacrificar, inmolar. 3. Ofrecer, prometer alguna cosa voluntariamente. 4. Atentar. 5. Ofrecer, proponer. -*vn.* 1. Ofrecerse, ocurrir o sobrevenir. 2. Intentar, tratar de. **Do not offer to do it,** guárdese Ud. de hacerlo. **Offer up,** ofrecer, rezar, hacer una ofrenda.

offer, *s.* 1. Oferta, ofrecimiento, palabra, promesa. 2. Propuesta; declaración de amor; primeras proposiciones o preliminares para un convenio. 3. Oferta, el precio que se ofrece por una cosa. 4. Esfuerzo. 5. Donativo, don, que se hace por vía de gratificación. **To close with an offer,** aceptar una oferta. **She has received many offers of marriage,** han pedido su mano muchas veces.

offering ['ɒfərɪŋ] [o-fa-rin], *s.* 1. Ofrecimiento, el acto de ofrecer. 2. Sacrificio, ofrenda, oblación. 3. Ofrenda, ofertorio, lo que se ofrece, lo que es presentado en el culto divino. **Peace-offering,** sacrificio propiciatorio. **Burnt-offering,** holocausto. **Votive offering,** exvoto, presentalla.

offertory ['ɒfətərɪ] [o-fa-to-ri], *s.* 1. Ofertorio, ofrecimiento, el acto de ofrecer alguna cosa. 2. Ofrenda, lo que se ofrece en el culto divino. 3. Ofertorio, parte de la misa; y la antífona cantada o pieza compuesta para órgano y ejecutada entre el *Credo* y el *Sanctus.*

offhand ['ɒf'hænd] [of-jand], *a.* 1. Hecho o ejecutado sin preparación. 2. No ceremonioso, informal. -*adv.* 1. Sin premeditación, sobre la marcha; sin estudio ni vacilación. 2. Sin apoyo artificial. **To shoot offhand,** tirar sin apoyo artificial. **She was very offhand about it,** lo discutió sin darle importancia.

offhandedly ['ɒf'hændɪdlɪ] [of-jan-did-li], *adv.* Descortésmente, sin miramientos.

offhandedness ['ɒf'hændɪdnɪs] [of-jan-did-nes], *s. f.* Informalidad, falta de cortesía.

office ['ɒfɪs] [o-fis], *s.* 1. Oficio, la obligación en que cada uno está constituido según su clase y estado. 2. Oficio, empleo, ejercicio, cargo público. 3. Oficio, operación o función. 4. Oficio, servicio que uno hace a otro. 5. Oficios, las funciones solemnes pertenecientes al altar; oficio, rezo. 6. Oficina, despacho, cuarto destinado al despacho de asuntos particulares. 7. La gente de oficina colectivamente. **Good-office,** favor. **Office-seeker,** pretendiente. **To be in office,** tener un empleo, estar colocado, estar en el poder. **To do the office of,** hacer el oficio de, servir de, hacer el papel de. **Booking office,** oficina de registro. **Ticket office,** despacho de billetes o papeletas. **Printing office,** imprenta. **The office of a lawyer, or an attorney,** el bufete, el estudio de un abogado, de un procurador. **Post-office,** administración de correos, estafeta, casa de correo. **Office-holder,** empleado público, funcionario. **Office automation,** ofimática. **Office boy,** ordenanza, chico de los recados. **Office staff,** personal de oficina.

officer ['ɒfɪsər] [o-fi-saʳ], *s.* 1. Oficial, el que tiene cualquier cargo público. 2. Oficial, empleado, dependiente en cualquier oficina. 3. Oficial, en la milicia desde alférez arriba. **Half-pay officer,** oficial retirado, a media paga. 4. Alguacil o ministro inferior de justicia. **Police officer,** agente de policía. **Commissioned officer,** oficial nombrado por el Gobierno. **Officer of the guard,** oficial de guardia. **Non-commissioned officer,** oficial nombrado por el jefe de un cuerpo. **Flag officer,** oficial general de marina. **Staff officer,** oficina de estado mayor.

officer, *va.* 1. Mandar. 2. Proveer de oficiales. **An army well offered,** un ejército con buena oficialidad.

official [ə'fɪʃəl] [o-fi-shal], *a.* 1. Oficial, perteneciente a algún cargo o empleo público. 2: Oficial, hecho o comunicado en virtud de autoridad. 3. Propio, autorizado para usarlo en medicina. **Official letters,** pliegos de oficio. -*s.* 1. Oficial público; funcionario.

officialism [ə'fɪʃəlɪzəm] [o-fi-sha-li-sem], *s.* 1. Estado, condición, costumbres oficiales. 2. Formalismo, apego a las formas oficiales.

officially [ə'fɪʃəlɪ] [o-fi-sha-li], *adv.* De oficio, oficialmente.

office supplies [ɒfɪs'səplaɪs] [o-fis-sa-plais], *s. pl.* Enseres de oficina.

officiate [ə'fɪʃɪeɪt] [o-fi-shieit], *va.* Hacer alguna cosa de oficio. -*vn.* 1. Oficiar, celebrar la misa y demás servicios divinos. 2. Sustituir a otro.

officinal [ə'fɪsɪnəl] [o-fi-si-nal], *a.* 1. Oficinal, hecho en la botica; preparado y en almacén. 2. *(Bot.)* Empleado en las artes o como medicamento.

officious [ə'fɪʃəs] [o-fi-shos], *a.* 1. Oficioso, entremetido. 2. Oficioso, obsequioso, agasajador.

officiously [ə'fɪʃəslɪ] [o-fi-shos-li], *adv.* Oficiosamente.

officiousness [ə'fɪʃəsnɪs] [o-fi-shos-nes], *s.* Oficiosidad, obsequio voluntario y muchas veces excesivo.

offing [ə'fɪŋ] [o-fin], *s.* Largo, aquella parte del mar visible que está lejana de la costa y más allá del lugar de anclaje: ensenada. **To gain the offing,** tomar el largo. **To stand for the offing,** *(Mar.)* correr a lo largo.

offish [ə'fɪʃ] [o-fish], *a.* Intratable, poco sociable, de maneras reservadas.

off-key [ɒf'kiː] [of-ki], *a.* Desafinado.

off-limits [ɒf'lɪmɪts] [of-li-mits], *a., adv.* Fuera de los límites.

off ramp ['ɒfræmp] [of-ramp], *s. (EU)* Vía de salida.

offscouring ['ɒfskɔrɪŋ] [of-sko-rin], *s.* Hez, excremento, desecho, basura, lavaduras.

offscum ['ɒfskəm] [of-skom], *s. y a.* Dejado; vil, bajísimo.

offset ['ɒfset] [of-set], *s.* 1. Balance, compensación, suma o valor puesto como equivalente. 2. Pimpollo, el vástago o tallo nuevo que echa la planta. 3. En agrimensura, cierta línea auxiliar que sirve en la medición y división de los terrenos. 4. *(Impr.)* Offset. **Offset printing**, impresión con máquina Offset.

offset, *va.* 1. Balancear, compensar; comparar una suma o valor con otro. 2. Medir la tierra por el procedimiento de ordenadas. 3. Hacer un voladizo.

offshoot ['ɒfʃuːt] [of-shut], *s.* Ramo, vástago; cosa secundaria o accesoria.

offshore ['ɒf'ʃɔːʳ] [of-shoʳ], *a.* Costanero. *-adv.* En la cercanía de la costa.

offspring ['ɒfsprɪŋ] [of-spring], *s.* 1. Prole, linaje, hijos, descendencia, casta. 2. Producción de cualquier especie, renuevo. 3. Cauce, venero.

off stage ['ɒfs'tɔɪdʒ] [of-steich], *a.* y *adv.* *(Teat.)* Entre bastidores, que sucede fuera del escenario.

off-the cuff [ɒfðəˈkʌf] [of-de-kaf], *a.* Dicho espontáneamente, improvisado (speech, remark).

offward ['ɒfwɔːd] [of-uord], *adv.* *(Mar.)* Al largo de la costa.

oft ['ɒfwɔːd] [of-uord], *a.* *(Poét.)* Frecuente. *-adv.* Muchas veces, a menudo.

often ['ɒfən] [o-fen], **oftimes** ['ɒftaɪmz] [of-taims], **oftentimes** ['ɒfənˈtaɪmz] [o-fen-taims], *adv.* Frecuentemente, muchas veces, a menudo. **As often as**, siempre que. **How often**, cuántas veces. **So often**, tantas veces. **Not often**, rara vez. **Too often**, demasiado a menudo. **It is no often that**, no es frecuente que. **Every so often**, cada cierto tiempo/distancia.

ogee ['ɒdʒiː] [o-yi], *s.* *(Arq.)* Cimacio, moldura o bóveda en forma de *s.*

ogival [ɒ'dʒaɪvəl] [ou-yai-val], *a.* Ojival.

ogive ['ɒdʒaɪv] [ou-yaiv], *s.* *(Arq.)* 1. Ojiva, curva saliente de una bóveda gótica. 2. Ojiva, arco apuntado.

ogle ['ɒgl] [ou-guel], *va.* Guiñar, mirar de reojo.

ogle, *s.* Guiñada, mirada al soslayo, ojeada.

ogler ['ɒgləʳ] [ou-glaʳ], *s.* Guiñador, el que mira al soslayo.

ogling ['ɒglɪŋ] [ou-glin], *s.* el acto de guiñar el ojo.

oglio ['ɒglɪəʊ] [ou-gliou, *s.* V. OLIO.

ogre ['ɒgəʳ] [ou-gaʳ], *s.* Ogro, monstruo imaginario del que se suponía que se alimentaba de carne humana.

ogress ['ɒgrɪs] [ou-gres], *f.* Ogro hembra.

oh! [ɒ] [ou], *inter.* ¡Oh! exclamación.

ohm [ɒm] [oum], *s.* Ohmio, unidad de resistencia eléctrica.

oho ['ɒhɒ] [ou-jou], *inter.* ¡Ajá! interjección.

oil [ɒɪl] [oil], *s.* Aceite; óleo. **Linseed-oil**, aceite de linaza. **Nut-oil**, aceite de nueces. **Salad-oil**, aceite de comer. **Palm-oil**, aceite del Senegal. **Neat's-foot oil**, aceite de manitas. **Olive-oil**, aceite de oliva. **Cod-liver oil**, aceite de hígado de bacalao. **Castor-oil**, aceite de ricino. **Rapeseed oil**, aceite de colza. **Kerosene-oil**, petroleum, kerosina, petróleo refinado. **Oil-colors**, colores al óleo. **Oil cars**, carros de tanque para petróleo. **Oil-bag**, glándula oleífera. **Oil-based product**, producto derivado del petróleo. **Oil-beetle**, méloe, insecto coleóptero que se emplea como vejigatorio. **Oil-painting**, pintura al óleo, cuadro pintado con colores al óleo. **To burn the midnight oil**, quemarse las cejas. **To strike oil**, encontrar una capa de petróleo; de aquí, *(E.U.)* hacerse rico de súbito. **Oil-bottle**, aceitera, vasija para el aceite. **Oil-cake**, los asientos de la linaza después de exprimido el aceite. **Oil-cloth**, encerado, hule. **Oil-color**, color molido con aceite. **Oil-mill, oil-press**, molino de aceite. **Oil-shop**, aceitería tienda de aceite.

oil, *va.* 1. Aceitar, engrasar; untar con aceite; de aquí, hacer liso, suave y agradable. 2. Ungir, olear, lubricar.

oil-can ['ɒɪlkæn] [oil-kan], *s.* Aceitera.

oildrum ['ɒɪldrʌm] [oil-dram], *s.* Bidón de aceite.

oiler ['ɒɪləʳ] [oi-laʳ], *s.* 1. El o lo que engrasa o aceita; obrero que unta la maquinaria con aceite. 2. Aceitera, aceitador; utensilio para untar con aceite. 3. Aceitera, vasija en que se tiene el aceite para llevarlo de un punto a otro; alcuza.

oilet ['ɒɪl-lit] [oi-lit], **oilet-hole** ['ɒɪlɪtˌhəʊl] [oi-lit-joul], *s.* 1. *(Arq.)* Tronera, mirador. 2. *(Des.)* Ojete.

oilfield ['ɒɪlfiːld] [oil-fild], *s.* Yacimiento petrolífero.

oiliness ['ɒɪlɪnɪs] [oi-li-nes], *s.* Oleaginosidad, untuosidad.

oilman ['ɒɪlmən] [oil-man], *s.* Aceitero.

oil paper ['ɒɪlpeɪpəʳ] [oil-pei-paʳ], *s.* Papel encerado.

oil platform ['ɒɪlˌplætfɔːm] [oil-plat-form], *s.* Plataforma petrolífera.

oil-refinery ['ɒɪlrɪˌfaɪnərɪ] [oil-ri-fai-ne-ri], *s.* Refinería de petróleo.

oilwell ['ɒɪlwel] [oil-uel, *s.* Pozo de petróleo.

oily ['ɒɪlɪ] [oi-li], *a.* aceitoso, oleoso, oleaginoso.

oily-grain ['ɒɪlɪˌgreɪn] [oi-li-grein], *s.* *(Bot.)* Ajonjolí, alegría, sésamo oriental.

oink [ɔɪŋk] [oink], *vi.* Gruñir.

ointment ['ɔɪntmənt] [oint-ment], *s.* Ungüento.

O.K. ['əʊ'keɪ] [ou-kei], 1. *interj.* ¡sí!, ¡está bien". 2. *adj.* Aprobado, de acuerdo, satisfactorio (agreed).

okay ['əʊ'keɪ] [ou-kei], = O.K.

okra ['əʊkrə] [ou-kra], *s.* Abelmosco, hibisco.

old [əʊld] [ould], *a.* 1. Viejo. **An old man**, hombre anciano. 2. Viejo, antiguo; anticuado. **Old age**, vejez. **How old are you?** ¿Cuántos años tiene Ud.? **I am twenty years old**, tengo veinte años. **To grow old**, envejecer. **Of old**, antiguamente, hace mucho tiempo. **To be old enough**, tener bastante edad; no ser niño. 3. Usado, gastado con el tiempo; que no es nuevo o que ya no está en uso; conocido desde hace mucho tiempo. 4. De costumbre, familiar; lo que hace mucho tiempo se produjo; del año anterior. **Old wine, old wheat**, vino añejo, trigo añejo. **Old shoes**, zapatos usados. **Old clothes**, ropa vieja, usada. **An old castle**, un castillo antiguo. **Old bachelor**, solterón. **Old maid**, (a) solterona. (b) La mona, cierto juego de naipes. **Old-maidish**, solterona. **Old-style**, *(Impr.)* estilo antiguo; tipo de forma antigua. Este es estilo antiguo. **Old world**, del viejo mundo; también del prehistórico.

olden ['əʊldən] [oul-den], *a.* *(Poét.)* Viejo, antiguo. **The olden time**, los tiempos pasados o antiguos. *-vn.* Envejecer, hacerse viejo.

old-fashioned ['əʊld'fæʃnd] [ould-fa-shond], *a.* Hecho a la antigua; del tiempo de Maricastaña.

old hand ['əʊldhænd] [ould-jand], *s.* Experto, perito.

oldie ['əʊldɪ] [ould-di], *s.* Melodía de ayer *(Music).*

oldish ['əʊldɪʃ] [oul-dish], *a.* Algo viejo o anciano; avejentado.

old-line ['əʊl'laɪn] [ould-lain], *a.* Conservador, anticuado.

oldness ['əʊldnɪs] [ould-nes], *s.* Ancianidad, vejez, antigüedad.

old school ['əʊldskʊl] [ould-skul], *s.* Grupo conservador de ideas anticuadas.

old-time ['əʊldtaɪm] [ould-taim], *a.* De antaño.

old wife ['əʊldwaɪf] [ould-uaif], *s.* Vieja.

oleaceous ['əʊlɪˈæʃəs] [ou-lia-shos], *a.* Oleáceo.

oleaginous ['əʊlɪˈæʒɪnəs] [ou-lia-yi-nos], *a.* Oleaginoso, aceitoso.

oleander [əʊlɪˈændəʳ] [ou-lian-daʳ], *s.* *(Bot.)* Adelfa, baladre.

oleaster [əʊlɪˈæstəʳ] [ou-lias-taʳ], *s.* *(Bot.)* Olivo silvestre o acebuche.

oleate ['əʊlɪeɪt] [ou-lieit], *s.* Oleato, sal formada por la combinación del ácido oleico con una base.

oleafiant ['əʊlɪˈæʃɪənt] [ou-lia-fiant], *a.* Olefiante.

oleic ['əʊleɪk] [ou-leik], *a.* Oleico; derivado del aceite, o perteneciente a él.

olein ['əʊlɪn] [ou-lin], *s.* Oleína.

oleomargarine ['əʊlɪəʊˌmɑːgərɪn] [ou-liou-mar-ga-rin], *s.* Oleomargarina.

oleose ['əʊlɪəʊs] [ou-lious], **Oleous** ['əʊlɪəʊs] [ou-lious], *a.* Oleoso.

oleraceous ['əʊlɪˈreɪʃəs] [ou-li-rei-shos], *a.* Semejante a hortaliza.

olfactory [ɒlˈfæktərɪ] [ol-fak-to-ri], *a.* Olfatorio, perteneciente al olfato.

olibanum ['ɒlɪbænəm] [o-li-ba-nom], *s.* Olíbano, goma aromática, incienso.

oligarchy ['ɒlɪɡɑːkɪ] [o-li-gar-ki], *s.* Oligarquía, gobierno de pocos.

olio ['əʊlɪəʊ] (ou-liou), *s.* 1. Mezcla, miscelánea. 2. Olla podrida.

olitory ['ɒlɪtərɪ] [o-li-to-ri], *s.* Huerta de hortalizas.

olivaceous [ˌɒlɪ'veɪʃəs] [o-li-vei-shos], *a.* Oliváceo, aceitunado.

olivary ['ɒlɪvərɪ] [o-li-va-ri], *a.* Oliviforme, de la forma de una oliva; parecido a una aceituna.

olive ['ɒlɪv] [o-liv], *s.* 1. *(Bot.)* Olivo, el árbol que produce las aceitunas. 2. Aceituna, oliva. *-a.* Aceitunado, que tiene color de aceituna.

olive-bearing ['ɒlɪvˌbɪərɪŋ] [o-liv-bia-rin], *a.* Olivífero.

olive branch ['ɒlɪvbrɑːntʃ] [o-liv-branch], *s.* Rama de olivo; emblema de paz.

olive-color ['ɒlɪvˌkʌləʳ] [o-liv-ka-la_], *s.* Aceitunado.

olive-drab ['ɒlɪvdræb] [o-liv-drab], *a.* De color aceitunado (de los uniformes militares de E.U.)

olive-green ['ɒlɪv'griːn] [o-liv-grin], *s.* Verde oliva.

olive-grove ['ɒlɪvɡrəʊv] [o-liv-grouv], **olive-yard** ['ɒlɪvjɑːd] [o-liv-yard], *s.* Olivar.

olive-oil ['ɒlɪv'ɔɪl] [o-liv-oil], *s.* El aceite de oliva o de mesa.

olive-tree ['ɒlɪvtriː] [o-liv-tri], *s.* Olivo.

olla ['ɒlə] (ou-la), *s.* 1. Olla. 2. Marmita, olla.

olympiad [əʊˈlɪmpɪæd] [o-lim-piad], *s.* Olimpiada, período de cuatro años entre los antiguos griegos.

olympian [əʊˈlɪmpɪən] [o-lim-pian], *a.* 1. Perteneciente a los dioses del Olimpo, y especialmente a Zeus (Júpiter); olímpico. 2. Referente a los juegos olímpicos.

olympic [əʊˈlɪmpk] [o-lim-pik], *a.* Olímpico.

olympus [əʊˈlɪmpəs] [o-lim-pos], *s.* Olimpo; el cielo.

Om [ɒm] [om], *s.* Nombre solemne del Ser Supremo entre los bracmanes.

omasum ['ɒməsəm] [o-ma-som], *s.* Omaso, ventrículo o tercer estómago de los rumiantes.

ombrometer [ˌɒmbə'miːtəʳ] [om-bro-mi-ta_], *s.* Un instrumento que sirve para medir la cantidad de lluvia que cae.

omega ['əʊmɪɡə] (ou-mi-ga), *s.* Omega, la letra vigésima cuarta y última del alfabeto griego; fin.

omelet(te) ['ɒmlɪt] [om-lit], *s.* Tortilla de huevos; fritada de huevos.

omen ['əʊmen] (ou-men), *s.* Agüero, pronóstico, presagio o anuncio de un mal o de un bien.

omentum [əʊˈmentəm] (ou-men-tum), *s.* Omento, el redaño que cubre las entrañas.

Omer ['əʊməʳ] (ou-me_), *s.* Homer.

ominous ['ɒmɪnəs] [o-mi-nos], *a.* 1. Ominoso, azaroso, siniestro, fatal. 2. De buen agüero, pronosticador en general.

ominously ['ɒmɪnəslɪ] [o-mi-nos-li], *adv.* Ominosamente; por vía de presagio.

ominousness ['ɒmɪnəsnɪs] [o-mi-nos-nes], *s.* La calidad que constituye a una cosa ominosa o de mal agüero.

omissible ['ɒmɪsɪbl] [o-mi-si-bol], *a.* Que se puede omitir o excluir.

omission [əʊˈmɪʃən] (ou-mi-shon), *s.* 1. Omisión; flojedad, descuido. 2. Alguna cosa omitida o que queda por hacer; olvido de insertar omencionar. **Errors and omissions excepted,** salvo error u omisión.

omissive ['əʊmɪsɪv] (ou-mi-siv), *a.* Que omite, excluye, o descuida insertar o mencionar.

omit [əʊˈmɪt] (ou-mit), *va.* 1. Omitir, dejar de hacer o usar alguna cosa; descuidar, excluir, desechar. 2. Omitir, pasar en silencio, olvidar la inserción o mención de.

omnibus ['ɒmnɪbəs] [om-ni-bos], *s.* Omnibus. *-a.* Que comprende muchos casos diferentes o una gran variedad de objetos. **An omnibus bill,** estatuto que comprende muchos asuntos diferentes.

omnifarious ['ɒmnɪˈfeərɪəs] [om-ni-fea-rios], *a.* De todo género y especie.

omniferous ['ɒmnɪfərəs] [om-ni-fe-ros], *a.* Que puede producir todas las cosas.

omniform ['ɒmnɪfɔːm] [om-ni-form], *a.* Omniforme, que tiene todas las formas o figuras.

omniformity ['ɒmnɪˌfɔːmɪtɪ] [om-ni-for-mi-ti], *s.* Omniformidad, la calidad de lo que tiene todas las formas o figuras.

omnigenous ['ɒmnɪdʒɪnəs] [om-ni-yi-nos], *a.* Omnígeno, que consta de todos los géneros.

omniparient ['ɒmnɪˌpærɪənt] [om-ni-pa-rient], **omniparous** ['ɒmnɪpərəs] [om-ni-pa-ros], *a.* Omníparo, que produce todas las cosas.

omnipercipiency [ˌɒmnɪpɜːˈpɪʃənsɪ] [om-ni-per-pi-shen-si], *s.* Percepción de todas las cosas.

omnipotence [ˈɒmnɪpətəns] [om-ni-po-tens], **omnipotency** [ˈɒmnɪpətənsɪ] [om-ni-po-ten-si], *s.* Omnipotencia.

omnipotent [ˈɒmnɪpətənt] [om-ni-po-tent], *a. y s.* Omnipotente, todopoderoso.

omnipresence [ˈɒmnɪ'prezəns] [om-ni-pre-sens], *a.* Omnipresente, presente en todas partes; ubicuo, en todas partes a la vez.

omniscience [ɒmˈnɪsɪəns] [om-ni-sians], **omnisciency** [ɒmˈnɪsənsɪ] [om-ni-sian-si], *s.* Omnisciencia.

omniscient [ɒmˈnɪsɪənt] [om-ni-siant], *a.* Omniscio, infinitamente sabio, que todo lo sabe, omnisapiente.

omnium ['ɒmnɪəm] [om-niom], *s.* 1. *(Ing.)* El agregado de diversas acciones en los fonods públicos. 2. Estante para bric-a-brac. **Omnium gatherum,** *(Fam.)* Miscelánea, mezcla confusa, mare mágnum.

omnivorous [ɒmˈnɪvərəs] [om-ni-vo-ros], *a.* 1. Omnívoro, que todo lo devora; que se alimenta indistintamente de toda clase de sustancias. 2. *(Zool.)* Omnívoro, que se alimenta de sustancias animales y vegetales (bears). 3. *(Fig.)* Que toda clase de libros. **Omnivorous reader,** "devora-libros".

omoplate ['ɒməpleɪt] [o-mo-pleit], *s.* *(Anat.)* Omoplato, espaldilla.

omphalic ['ɒmfælɪk] [om-fa-lik], *a.* Umbilical, que se refiere al ombligo.

on [ɒn] [on], *prep.* Sobre, encima, en; de; *a.* 1. Sobre, en contacto con la superficie superior de una cosa; suspendido de o soportado por; por medio de; además de; por la autoridad de. 2. En seguida, después de; tras, detrás de; con motivo de, por razón de; al cargo de; en conformidad con, según. 3. Con dirección a, hacia, a, al lado de, cerca. 4. En el acto de; bajo la influencia de; bajo. 5. En; en interés o favor de; en, se emplea con el participio presente; en el momento de; *on* no se traduce en castellano delante del nombre de un día o de una fecha. **On the fifth of May,** el cinco de mayo. 6. Por lo concerniente, respecto a, tocante a, acerca. 7. En estado o calidad de; como. **On record,** en calidad de archivado, registrado. \ 8. Por; y a veces para. **On an average,** por término medio. **It lies on the table,** está sobre o encima de la mesa. **On the right hand,** a la mano derecha. **On pain of death,** so pena de muerte. **On his arrival,** a su llegada. **On my return,** a mi vuelta. **On horseback,** a caballo. **On foot,** a pie. **On purpose,** de intento, adrede, a propósito, expresamente. **On high,** en alto. **On the contrary,** por el contrario. **On my part,** de mi parte o por mi parte; en cuanto a mí. **On condition that you come,** con tal que Ud. venga. **To be off and on,** estar indeciso. **To play on the violin,** tocar el violín. **To be on,** estar encendido, estar conectado. **On a sudden,** de golpe, de repente, de improviso. **My shoes are on,** estoy calzado. **On account of,** a causa de. **On no account o consideration,** por ningún concepto, por nada en el mundo. **On second thoughts,** bien pensado el caso, pensándolo bien. **On returning from the theater I went to my room,** al regresar del teatro fui a mi habitación. **On leaving the harbour of San Francisco,** al salir de San Francisco. **From that time on,** desde entonces. **Well on in years,** entrado en años, mayor. **To be on guard,** estar de guardia. **On every side,** por todas partes. *-inter.* ¡Vamos! ¡adelante! ¡marchen!

on, *adv.* 1. En contacto con una cosa que sirve de apoyo y sostén; encima, sobre; en posición o condición de adherencia. 2. En la misma dirección o manera, adelante; sin cesar, a lo largo. 3. En o hacia el propio y debido lugar de acción. 4. En existencia u operación. Frecuentemente *on* sirve para modificar el sentido de un verbo. **Go on,** prosiga Ud.; continúe Ud.; ¡marchen! ¡adelante! **To have on,** tener, llevar, puesto. **To have one's hat on,** tener puesto el sombrero, tener la cabeza cubierta. **To have one's clothes on,** tener puesto el vestido, estar vestido. **To look on,** mirar, considerar. **Lead on,** enséñal el camino. **Play on,** continuad jugando. **On and off,** a intervalos, de vez en cuando. **And so on,** y así sucesivamente, y así de lo demás; *(Fam.)* y otras hierbas. **To talk on and on,** hablar sin parar. **To go on, to run on, to read on,** seguir adelante, seguir corriendo, seguir leyendo (continuation).

onager ['ɒnədʒəʳ] [o-na-yaʳ], *s.* Onagro, asno salvaje.

onanism ['əʊnənizəm] [ou-na-ni-sem], *s. (Med.)* Onanismo, masturbación.

once [wʌns] [uans], *adv.* 1. Una vez. **Once for all,** una vez para siempre. **At once,** a un tiempo, de una vez, de un golpe. **All at once,** de repente. **Once more,** más todavía, otra vez. 2. En otro tiempo, otras veces, antiguamente. **For once,** una vez siquiera; últimamente, al fin. **Once in a way,** *(Fam.)* una vez siquiera. **Once upon a time,** en otro tiempo; hace mucho tiempo, érase una vez.

oncoming ['ɒnˌkʌmɪŋ] [on-ka-min], *a.* Venidero, próximo.

one [wʌn] [uan], *a.* 1. Un, uno; solo, único; uno solo, una sola. **One boy,** un muchacho. **One girl,** una muchacha. **One hundred and forty dollars,** ciento cuarenta pesos. **One while he laughs and another he cries,** ora ríe, ora llora. **One-horse,** de un caballo, tirado por un caballo; de aquí, de escasa capacidad, de poca importancia, pequeño, inferior. **One-story,** de un solo piso. 2. Mismo. **All in one direction,** todos en la misma dirección. **It is all one to me,** lo mismo me da; me es lo mismo. **One or other,** uno u otro. **With one accord,** de común acuerdo, unánimemente. *-pro.* Uno, una persona; el uno, la una; él, la; se, sí. **Every one,** cada uno. **This one,** éste, ésta. **One by one,** uno a uno, uno por uno. **Such a one,** uno, cierto sujeto o cierta persona, fulano. **The last but one,** el penúltimo. **Every one of them,** todos. **One** se usa frecuentemente en inglés como nombre general e indefinido, que se une con los adjetivos que no tienen substantivo expreso con que concierta, y en este caso casi nunca es necesario traducirlo en español. **This is a good one,** éste es bueno. **My little one,** mi niño, mi hijo, mi chiquito. **They are but little ones,** son pequeños, son chiquitos. **One's,** su, sus. **To live according to one's estate,** vivir arreglado a lo que se tiene. **One another,** el uno al otro. **To love one another,** amarse unos a otros. **One knows that,** sabido es que. **Ones sees how,** se ve cómo. **How shall one do it?** ¿cómo se ha de hacer? **Any one who says so is mistaken,** quienquiera que lo diga se equivoca.

one-eyed ['wʌn'aɪd] [uan-aid], *a.* Tuerto.

one-handed ['wʌn'hændɪd] [uan-jan-did], *a.* Manco.

oneness ['wʌnnɪs] [uan-nes], *s.* Unidad, singularidad de número, o la calidad que constituye el número uno como singular e indivisible.

onerary ['ɒnərərɪ] [o-ne-ra-ri], *a.* Propio para carga o conducción.

onerous ['ɒnərəs] [o-ne-ros], *a.* Oneroso, opresivo, pesado, molesto, gravoso.

oneself [wʌn'self] [uan-self], *pro.* Se, sí, sí mismo. **To come to oneself,** volver en sí.

one-sided ['wʌn'saɪdɪd] [uan-sai-ded], *a.* 1. De un solo lado; parcial, injusto; incompleto. 2. *(Bot.)* De lados desiguales inclinado a un lado.

one-step ['wʌnstep] [uan-step], *s.* 1. Variedad de baile de salón. 2. Ritmo musical de dicho baile.

one-time ['wʌntaɪm] [uan-taim], *a.* Antiguo, anterior. *-adv.* En otros tiempos.

one-track ['wʌntræk] [uan-trak], *a. (F.C.)* De una sola vía. **One-track mind,** mente estrecha, que sólo puede percibir una cosa a la vez.

one-way ['wʌnweɪ] [uan-uei], *a.* De una sola vía. **One-way street,** tránsito en un solo sentido.

onion ['ʌnjən] [a-nion], *s. (Bot.)* Cebolla. **Onion porridge o broth,** sopa, potaje o caldo de cebollas. **Bunch of onions,** ristra de cebollas. **Onion-bed,** cebollar.

onionskin ['ʌnjənˌskɪn] [a-nion-skin], *s.* Papel transparente satinado para copias.

onloocker ['ɒnˌlʊkəʳ] [on-lu-kaʳ], *s.* Espectador, asistente.

only ['əʊnlɪ] [oun-li], *a.* Único, solo; singular, raro. *-adv.* Solamente, únicamente, sino, no más que. **Only to think of it!** ¡sólo pensar en ello! **Only just,** apenas. **If only I could!** ¡ojalá pudiera!

onomantic, onomantical ['ɒnəʊmæntɪk] [o-no-man-tik], *a. (Poco us.)* Onomántico.

onomastic ['ɒnəʊmæstɪk] [o-no-mas-tik], *a.* Onomástico.

onomatechny ['ɒnəʊmæteknɪ] [o-no-ma-tek-ni], *s.* Onomancia, el arte de adivinar algo por las letras del nombre de alguna persona.

onomatopæia [ˌɒnəʊmætəʊˈpiːə] [o-no-ma-to-pia], *s.* 1. Onomatopeya, imitación del sonido de una cosa en el vocablo que se forma para significarla, p. ej. *Whizz,* chirrido, chisporroteo. 2. El mismo vocablo que imita el sonido de la cosa nombrada con él. 3. Figura retórica de este nombre.

onrush ['ɒnrʌʃ] [on-rash], *s. V.* ONSET.

onset ['ɒnset] [on-set], *s.* 1. Embestida, primer ímpetu, ataque. **To give a fresh onset,** volver a la carga. 2. Primer acceso de una enfermedad; estreno; principio de una pasión.

onslaught ['ɒnslɔːt] [ons-lot], *s.* Ataque furioso, embestida violenta, asalto.

onto ['ɒntʊ] [on-tu], *prep.* Por encima de, sobre; uso incorrecto en vez de *on.*

ontologist [ɒnˈtɒlədʒɪst] [on-to-lo-yist], *s.* Ontologista, metafísico.

ontology [ɒnˈtɒlədʒɪ] [on-to-lo-yi], *s.* Ontología, ciencia o tratado del ser en general.

onus ['əʊnəs] [ou-nos], *s. f.* Carga, responsabilidad. **The onus is upon her to,** le incumbe a ella.

onward ['ɒnwəd] [on-uard], *a.* Avanzado, progresivo, aumentado, adelantado.

onward, onwards, *adv.* 1. Adelante, hacia el frente, progresivamente. 2. En adelante, en lo venidero. **To come onward,** acercarse.

onyx ['ɒnɪks] [o-niks], *s.* 1. Onice, ónique u ónix, piedra preciosa con fajas blanquecinas sobre fondo azulado. 2. Uña. 3. Una especie de absceso en el ojo.

oolite ['əʊəlaɪt] [u-lait], *s. (Min.)* Oolita, piedra calcárea compuesta de pequeñas concreciones en forma de huevos de pescado.

oolitic [ˌəʊəˈlɪtɪk] [u-li-tik], *a.* Oolítico.

oology ['əʊəlɒdʒɪ] [u-lo-chi], *s.* Oología, la parte de la ornitología que trata de los huevos y de la nidificación de las aves.

oolong ['əʊəlɒŋ] [u-lon], *s.* Nombre de una variedad de té negro.

oops [ʊps] ups], *Excl.* ¡ay!

ooze [uːz] [us], *s.* 1. Fango, limo, cieno, légamo, cama de un estanque, de un río, etc.; tierra muy mojada o esponjosa. 2. Chorro suave de agua u otro líquido. 3. Adobe o adobo de curtidor.

ooze, *vn.* Manar o correr algún líquido suavemente; pasar lentamente como al través de poros o intersticios; filtrar. **Ooze away,** agotarse poco a poco, rezumarse.

oozy ['uːzɪ] [u-si], *a.* Cenagoso. **Oozy ground,** *(Mar.)* Baza.

opacity [əʊˈpæsɪtɪ] [o-pa-si-ti], *s.* Opacidad, cualidad de lo opaco, falta de transparencia; oscuridad.

opal ['əʊpəl] [ou-pal], *s.* Ópalo. **Fire opal,** ópalo de fuego. **Precious opal,** ópalo noble, precioso.

opalesce ['əʊpələs] [ou-pa-les], *vn.* Emitir reflejos como los colores del ópalo.

opalescence [ˌəʊpəˈlesns] [ou-pa-le-sens], *s.* Opalescencia, reflexión y refracción de la luz de color perla, como la del ópalo.

opalescent [ˌəʊpəˈlesnt] [ou-pa-le-sent], *a.* Opalino, que tiene reflejos de ópalo.

opaline ['əʊpəlɪn] [ou-pa-lin], *a.* Opalino, de color lechoso y azulado, con reflejos de ópalo.

opaque [əʊ'peɪk] [ou-peik], *a.* 1. Opaco, impenetrable a la luz; no diáfano ni transparente. 2. *(Bot. y Ento.)* Que no tiene brillo, oscuro, mate.

ope ['əʊp] [oup], *va. (Poét.) V.* TO OPEN. *vn.* Abrirse; ladrar.

OPEC *Abreviatura de* **Organization of Petroleum Exporting Countries,** Organización de Países Exportadores de Petróleo (OPEP).

open ['əʊpən] [ou-pen], *va.* 1. Abrir, descubrir o destapar lo que estaba cerrado, tapado o unido; deshacer, desempaquetar, quitar alguna cosa que cubre a otra. 2. Abrir, desprender, alejar, dar paso a, remover obstáculos. 3. Hacer público o de libre acceso. 4. Descubrir, hallar. 5. Abrir, hender, rajar; romper. 6. Abrir, empezar, dar principio a alguna cosa. **To open a campaign,** abrir una campaña, dar principio a ella. 7. Descubrir, revelar, manifestar lo que estaba secreto; mostrar, hacer saber; interpretar, explicar. 8. Ensanchar, aumentar. *-vn.* 1. Abrirse lo que estaba cerrado. 2. Abrirse, descubrirse, declararse con alguno. 3. Dividirse, entreabrirse. 4. Aparecer, hacerse visible, asomar. 5. Desarrollarse, llegar a ser receptivo, abrirse a la mente de un niño. 6. Comenzar, estrenar; comenzar a ladrar a la caza. **The shares opened at par,** las acciones comenzaron (a venderse) a la par. 7. Dar. **To open a little,** entreabrir, medio abrir, no abrir bien o del todo. **Her windows open upon a garden,** sus ventanas caen, dan o miran a un jardín. **That room opens into the kitchen,** esa habitación da a (comunica con) la cocina. **Open out,** abrirse, extenderse. **Open up,** desplegar, extender, abrir (map, box), inaugurar (business). **Open up!** ¡abran fuego!

open, *a.* 1. Abierto, extendido, desplegado; que no está cercado; sin sellar; desempaquetado, sin atar; destapado; descubierto; raso; libre, que no está obstruído, libre para todos los que vienen; abierto, que no está protegido, expuesto a un ataque; desnudo, a la vista. 2. Receptivo, dispuesto a recibir o a ser modificado o influido por lo que se acerca o se envía; listo, aparejado, preparado, dispuesto para los negocios, para la ocupación, etc.; dispuesto a escuchar y acoger lo que se dice; *(Com.)* abierto, sin arreglar, sin haberse hecho el saldo; no decidido, pendiente. 3. Patente, manifiesto, claro, evidente; sincero, franco, declarado. 4. Suave; más caliente que lo ordinario; abierto, libre de hielo. 5. Abierto, que tiene aberturas o agujeros; no tupido. 6. *(Mús.)* No pulsada con el dedo; se dice de una cuerda cuyo remate superior está abierto; se dice de un cañón de órgano. 7. Pronunciado con los órganos vocales sin obstrucción; que no termina en consonante. **A little open,** entreabierto. **In the open field,** a campo raso. **In the open street,** en medio de la calle. **To lie in the open air,** dormir o quedarse al raso, dormir en el mesón de la estrella. **To set, to throw open,** abrir. **With open force,** a mano armada, a viva fuerza. **An open winter,** un invierno templado, sin heladas. **An open and shut case,** un asunto (case) clarísimo. **Open shame,** vergüenza pública. **An open look,** una mirada franca, abierta. **In open court,** en pleno tribunal. **To fling (throw) a door open,** abrir una puerta de par en par. **To keep open house,** tener casa abierta para todos. **To keep the bowels open,** tener el vientre libre. **To cut open,** abrir, cortar. **An open question,** una cuestión pendiente. **Open-eyed,** alerta, vigilante, cuidadoso, activo. **Open-handed,** generoso, dadivoso, liberal, benéfico. **Open-hearted,** ingenuo, franco, sincero, abierto, sencillo. **Open-mouthed,** voraz, ávido; con la boca abierta. **Open prison,** prisión en régimen abierto.

open-air ['əʊpən,ɛəʳ] [ou-pen-eaʳ], *a.* Abierto, al aire libre.

opener ['əʊpnəʳ] [oup-naʳ], *s.* Abridor, el que abre; intérprete. **Can-opener,** abridor de cajas de lata.

open-handed ['əʊpn'hændɪd] [ou-pen-jan-did], *a.* Generoso, liberal.

open-heartedness ['əʊpn'hɑːtɪdnɪs] [ou-pen-jar-tid-nes], *s.* Liberalidad, generosidad, franqueza, ingenuidad.

opening ['əʊpnɪŋ] [ou-pe-nin], *s.* 1. Abertura, hendedura; camino abierto. 2. Vislumbre, conjetura, sospecha, indicio,

noticia remota o dudosa. 3. Entrada, tronera, abertura. *-a.* Aperitivo.

open letter ['əʊpn'letəʳ] [ou-pen-le-taʳ], *s.* Carta abierta (en un periódico o publicación) generalmente de súplica o protesta.

openly ['əʊpnlɪ] [ou-pen-li], *adv.* Abiertamente.

open-minded ['əʊpn'maɪndɪd] [ou-pen-main-did], *a.* Imparcial, que no tiene prejuicios.

open-mouthed ['əʊpn'məʊðd] [ou-pen-mauzd], *a.* Boquiabierto.

openness ['əʊpnnɪs] [ou-pen-nes], *s.* 1. Claridad. 2. Franqueza, sinceridad, ingenuidad, candor. **Openness of weather,** blandura del tiempo.

open question ['əʊpn'kwestʃən] [ou-pen-kues-chon], *s.* Asunto discutible.

open secret ['əʊpn'sɪkrɪt] [ou-pen-si-krit], *s.* Secreto a voces.

open-sesame ['əʊpn'sesəm] [ou-pen-se-sam], *s.* Ábrete, sésamo.

open shop ['əʊpn'ʃɒp] [ou-pen-shop], *s.* Contrato de trabajo según el cual pueden ocuparse obreros sindicalizados o no.

open-top ['əʊpntɒp] [ou-pen-top], *a.* Descubierto (car).

openwork ['əʊpnwɜːk] [ou-pen-uek], *s.* Calado, cualquier obra manual que contiene numerosas aberturas pequeñas.

opera ['ɒpərə] [o-pe-ra], *s.* Ópera, pieza dramática en música, y también el teatro en que se representa. **Opera-glass,** gemelos de teatro. **Opera-house,** sala o teatro de la ópera. **Opera bouffe,** ópera cómica o bufa.

operable ['ɒpərəbl] [o-pe-ra-bol], *a.* Operable.

operate ['ɒpəreɪt] [o-pe-reit], *va.* 1. Poner en acción y gobernar el movimiento de (machine); hacer funcionar. 2. Dirigir, manejar los negocios de. 3. Efectuar. *-vn.* 1. Obrar, operar. 2. Obtener un resultado determinado. 3. Producir el efecto propio o propuesto (v.g. un medicamento). 4. Exonerar, descarga el vientre, hacer de cuerpo. 5. Operar, hacer una operación quirúrgica con el fin de curar. 6. Especular en valores.

operatic, operatical [ˌɒpəˈrætɪk] [o-pe-ra-tik], *a.* De ópera, que pertenece a la ópera.

operating ['ɒpəreɪtɪŋ] [o-pe-rei-tin], *a.* 1. *(Cir.)* Operatorio. 2. *(Mil.)* Operacional. **Operating room,** quirófano, sala de operaciones. **Operating surgeon,** operador. **Operating table,** mesa de operaciones.

operation [ˌɒpəˈreɪʃən] [o-pe-rei-shon], *s.* 1. Operación, la acción y el efecto de operar. 2. *(Cir.)* Operación, el acto de cortar, abrir o separar una parte del cuerpo, con el fin de curar una enfermedad o de prevenir algún mal inminente. 3. Operación, acción, efecto; procedimiento, manipulación, movimiento. **To be in full operation,** estar en pleno rendimiento. **To undergo an operation,** ser operado.

operational [ˌɒpəˈreɪʃənl] [o-pe-rei-sho-nal] *a.* Operacional, de operaciones.

operative ['ɒpərətɪv] [o-pe-ra-tiv], *a.* Operativo, eficaz, activo. *-s.* Operario, trabajador, obrero.

operator ['ɒpəreɪtəʳ] [o-pe-rei-taʳ], *s.* 1. Operario, el que trabaja en alguna cosa. 2. *(Cir.)* Operador, el que ejecuta las operaciones quirúrgicas. 3. Agente, corredor de cambios o valores.

opercular ['ɒpɜːkjʊləʳ] [o-per-kiu-laʳ], *a.* Opercular, que cierra una cavidad a manera de tapa.

operculate ['ɒpɜːkjʊleɪt] [o-per-kiu-leit], *a.* Operculado, que cierra o cubre un opérculo; operculífero, que tiene un opérculo.

operculum ['ɒpɜːkjʊləm] [o-per-kiu-lum], *(Biol.)* Opérculo.

operetta [ˌɒpəˈretə] [o-pe-re-ta], *s.* Opereta, ópera corta con diálogo; zarzuela.

ophicleide ['ɒfɪklɪd] [o-fi-klid], *s. (Mús.)* Instrumento músico de viento, parecido a la corneta pero con mayor número de llaves.

ophidian ['ɒfɪdɪən] [o-fi-dian], *a. y s.* Ofidiano, perteneciente a los ofidios o serpientes; la serpiente misma, ofidio, un orden de reptiles.

ophthalmia [ɒfˈθælmɪə] [of-zal-mia], **ophthalmy** [ˈɒfθælmɪ] [of-zal-mi], s. Oftalmia, la inflamación de los ojos.

ophthalmic [ɒfˈθælmɪk] [of-zal-mik], a. Oftálmico, referente al ojo.

ophthalmology [ˌɒfθælˈmɒlədʒɪ] [of-zal-mo-lo-yi], s. Oftalmología, parte de la patología que trata de las enfermedades de los ojos.

opiate [ˈɒpɪeɪt] [o-pieit], s. Opiata, medicamento que contiene opio; bebida para hacer dormir. -a. Narcótico, soporífico.

opiate, va. 1. Hacer dormir por medio del opio. 2. Mezclar, o componer con opio.

opinable [əʊˈpaɪnəbl] [ou-pai-na-bol], a. Opinable, que se puede defender en uno y otro sentido.

opine [əʊˈpaɪn] [ou-pain], vn. (Ant.) Opinar, pensar, ser de parecer.

opinion [əˈpɪnjən] [o-pi-nion], s. 1. Opinión, dictamen, sentir o juicio que se forma de alguna cosa; pensamiento, idea. **This is my opinion,** esto es lo que yo pienso. **He has a high opinion of himself,** está muy pagado de sí mismo. 2. Opinión, fama o concepto que se forma con relación a personas o cosas. 3. Estimación, reputación; buena opinión, juicio favorable. **To share an opinion,** compartir una opinión.

opinionate, opinionated [əˈpɪnjəneɪt] [o-pi-nio-neit] [əˈpɪnjəneɪtɪd] [o-pi-nio-nei-tid], a. Porfiado, obstinado, terco, pertinaz.

opinionately [əˈpɪnjəneɪtlɪ] [o-pi-nio-neit-li], adv. Porfiadamente.

opinionative [əˈpɪnjənətɪv] [o-pi-nio-na-tiv], a. (Ant.) Terco, obstinado, porfiado, pertinaz.

opinionatively [əˈpɪnjənətɪvlɪ] [o-pi-nio-na-tiv-li], adv. Tercamente.

opinionativeness [əˈpɪnjənətɪvnɪs] [o-pi-nio-na-tiv-nes], s. Porfía, terquedad, obstinación.

opinioned [əˈpɪnjənd] [o-pi-niond], a. Presumido, pagado de sí mismo; obstinado.

opinionist [əˈpɪnjənɪst] [o-pi-nio-nist], s. 1. Opinante. 2. El que está adherido a su propia opinión o muy pagado de sí mismo.

opium [ˈəʊpɪəm] [o-piom], s. Opio, el zumo de las adormideras; narcótico.

opobalsam [ˌəʊpəˈbælsəm] [o-po-bal-sam], s. Opobálsamo, resina astringente y medicinal.

opossum [əˈpɒsəm] [o-po-som], s. Zorra mochilera, cuadrúpedo carnívoro de ambas Américas.

oppidan [əˈpɪdən] [o-pi-dan], a. Relativo a una ciudad, cívico.

oppilation [ˌɒpɪˈleɪʃən] [o-pi-lei-shon], s. Opilación, obstrucción.

opponency [əˈpəʊnənsɪ] [ou-po-nen-si], s. Oposición; ejercicio para recibir un grado académico; exposición de los argumentos en contra de una proposición.

opponent [əˈpəʊnənt] [ou-po-nent], s. Antagonista; contrincante, arguyente contrario; lo opuesto a *respondent o defendant;* parte adversa. -a. 1. Opuesto, contrario. 2. (Anat.) Oponente, que sirve para contraponer una parte en frente de otra.

opportune [ˈɒpətjuːn] [o-por-tiun], a. Oportuno, conveniente, hecho a tiempo o cuando conviene.

opportunely [ˈɒpətjuːnlɪ] [o-por-tiun-li], adv. Oportunamente, cómodamente, a tiempo.

opportuneness [ˌɒpəˈtjuːnnɪs] [o-por-tiun-nes], s. El estado de lo que es oportuno, oportunidad.

opportunism [ˌɒpəˈtjuːnɪzəm] [o-por-tiu-ni-sem], s. Oportunismo (generalmente en la política).

opportunist [ˌɒpəˈtjuːnɪst] [o-por-tiu-nist], a. Oportunista.

opportunity [ˌɒpəˈtjuːnɪtɪ] [o-por-tiu-ni-ti], s. Oportunidad, comodidad, sazón; ocasión, circunstancia favorable. **Opportunity makes the thief,** la ocasión hace al ladrón.

opposable [əˈpəʊzəbl] [o-pou-sa-bol], a. Oponible; (a) que se puede oponer a otra cosa; (b) que puede ser objeto de oposición.

oppose [əˈpəʊz] [o-pous], va. 1. Oponer, poner impedimento a una cosa, obrar en oposición a, resistir a, combatir. 2. Oponer, contraponer, poner una cosa enfrente de otra; colocar opuestamente o en contraste. 3. Oponer, objetar una razón, un argumento, etc. -vn. 1. Oponer u oponerse, contrariar, resistir. 2. Argüir, oponerse u objetar por medio de argumentos a lo que otro dice.

opposed [əˈpəʊzt] [o-poust], a. Opuesto, en contra.

opposeless [əˈpəʊzlɪs] [o-pous-lis], a. Irresistible.

opposer [əˈpəʊzəʳ] [o-pou-saʳ], s. Opositor, antagonista, rival.

opposing [əˈpəʊzɪŋ] [o-pou-sin], a. Opuesto, adversario, contrario.

opposite [əˈpəʊzɪt] [o-pou-sit], a. 1. Fronterizo, opuesto, lo que está en frente de otra cosa. 2. Opuesto, adverso, repugnante, contrario, antagónico; otro, diferente. **In the opposite direction,** en sentido contrario. **Opposite leaves,** hojas opuestas. **The opposite sex,** el otro sexo, el sexo opuesto. -s. 1. Antagonista, adversario. 2. Lo opuesto, lo contrario. -adv. En frente. **Opposite the theater,** frente al teatro.

oppositely [əˈpəʊzɪtlɪ] [o-pou-sit-li], adv. Enfrente, opuestamente.

oppositeness [əˈpəʊzɪtnɪs] [o-pou-sit-nes], s. Contrariedad, estado contrario.

opposition [ˌɒpəˈzɪʃən] [o-po-si-shon], s. 1. Oposición, la disposición de algunas cosas de modo que estén enfrente de otras. 2. Oposición, contrariedad. 3. Oposición, resistencia, contradicción. 4. Oposición, óbice, impedimento. 5. Oposición, el partido antiministerial o los individuos de un cuerpo legislativo que se oponen generalmente a las medidas del gobierno. 6. (Astr.) Situación relativa de dos cuerpos celestes cuando distan 180° uno de otro. **To meet with opposition,** encontrar, oposición.

oppositional [ˌɒpəˈzɪʃənl] [o-po-si-sho-nal], a. De la naturaleza de oposición; perteneciente a un partido antiministerial.

oppositionist [ˌɒpəˈzɪʃənɪst] [o-po-si-sho-nist], s. Miembro de la oposición.

oppositive [ˌɒpəˈzɪtɪv] [o-po-si-tiv], a. Capaz de ser puesto en oposición.

oppress [əˈpres] [o-pres], va. 1. Oprimir, apretar, aquejar o afligir a uno; sobrecargar; agobiar con impuestos excesivos; tratar con dureza injusta. 2. Oprimir, apretar o comprimir una cosa.

oppression [əˈpreʃən] [o-pre-shon], s. 1. Opresión, crueldad, tiranía; acción de oprimir. 2. Miseria, calamidad; calidad de oprimido, sobrecargado, afligido o aquejado. 3. Opresión de ánimo; fatiga; opresión o apretura de una parte del cuerpo; sensación de pesadez o de constricción.

oppressive [əˈpresɪv] [o-pre-siv], a. 1. Opresivo, cruel, inhumano, tirano. 2. Pesado, molesto.

oppressively [əˈpresɪvlɪ] [o-pre-siv-li], adv. Opresivamente.

oppressiveness [əˈpresɪvnɪs] [o-pre-siv-nes], s. Opresión.

oppressor [əˈpresəʳ] [o-pre-saʳ], s. Opresor.

opprobrious [əˈprəʊbɪəs] [o-prou-bios], a. 1. Oprobioso, ignominioso, infamante. 2. Injurioso, ultrajante.

opprobriously [əˈprəʊbɪəslɪ] [o-prou-bios-li], adv. Ignominiosamente.

opprobriousness [əˈprəʊbɪəsnɪs] [o-prou-bios-nes], s. Oprobio, ignominia.

opprobrium [əˈprəʊbɪəm] [o-prou-biom], s. Oprobio, ignominia.

oppugn [əˈpʌgn] [o-pagn], va. Opugnar, hacer resistencia; contrariar, combatir.

oppugnancy [əˈpʌgnənsɪ] [o-pag-nan-si], s. Opugnación, oposición, contradicción.

oppugnation [ˌəpʌgˈneɪʃən] [o-pag-nei-shon], s. Resistencia.

oppugner [əˈpʌgnəʳ] [o-pag-naʳ], s. Opugnador, resistidor.

opt [ɒpt] [opt], vi. Optar. **Opt out,** decidir no tomar parte, optar por no participar.

optative [ˈɒptətɪv] [op-ta-tiv], a. Optativo. -s. Optativo; modo optativo o subjuntivo.

optic, optical ['ɒptɪk] [op-tik], *a.* 1. Optico, de la vista, que pertenece a los órganos de la visión. 2. Optico, que pertenece a la óptica: *optical* significa además lo que ayuda a la visión. **Optic nerve,** nervio óptico. **Optical instruments,** instrumentos ópticos. -s. Cualquier órgano que sirve para ver.

optician ['ɒptɪʃən] [op-ti-shan], *s.* 1. Óptico, el que fabrica o vende anteojos y otros instrumentos ópticos. 2. El que es versado en la óptica.

optics ['ɒptɪks] [op-tiks], *s.* Óptica, ciencia físico-matemática que trata de la luz y de las leyes de la visión.

optimacy ['ɒptɪməsɪ] [op-ti-ma-si], *s.* Nobleza, el conjunto o cuerpo de los nobles.

optimism ['ɒptɪmɪzəm] [op-ti-mi-sem], *s.* 1. Optimismo. 2. Disposición a considerar las cosas bajo su aspecto más favorable.

optimist ['ɒptɪmɪst] [op-ti-mist], *s.* 1. Optimista, el que sigue y defiende el optimismo. 2. El que espera que sucederá lo mejor y más favorable que pueda ocurrir; el que lo ve todo de color de rosa.

optimist, optimistic ['ɒptɪmɪstɪk] [op-ti-mis-tik], *a.* Optimista.

optimization [ˌɒptɪmaɪˈzeɪʃən] [op-ti-mai-sei-shon], *s. f.* Optimización.

optimize ['ɒptɪmaɪz] [op-ti-mais], *vt.* Optimizar.

optimum ['ɒptɪməm] [op-ti-mom], *a. pl.* **optima** ['ɒptɪmə] [op-ti-ma], Mejor, óptimo. **In optimum conditions,** en las condiciones más favorables.

option ['ɒpʃən] [op-shon], *s.* 1. Opción, la facultad de elegir; preferencia, escogimiento. 2. *(Com.)* El derecho que se adquiere por un tanto y razón de comprar o vender una cosa por un precio dado, dentro de un plazo determinado. **You have no option,** no tienes más remedio.

optional ['ɒpʃənl] [op-sho-nal], *a.* Que tiene o da la facultad de elegir, que proviene de la elección. **To be optional with,** tener la elección de.

optometrist [ɒpˈtɒmətrɪst] [op-to-me-trist], *s.* Optometrista.

optometry [ɒpˈtɒmətrɪ] [op-to-me-tri], *s.* Optometría, medición de la vista.

opulence ['ɒpjʊləns] [o-piu-lens], **opulency** ['ɒpjʊlənsɪ] [o-piu-len-si], *s.* Opulencia, abundancia de bienes, riqueza; lozanía, copia.

opulent ['ɒpjʊlənt] [o-piu-lent], *a.* Opulento.

opulently ['ɒpjʊləntlɪ] [o-piu-lent-li], *adv.* Opulentamente.

opus ['əʊpəs] [ou-pus], *s.* (*pl.* OPERA. Obra o composición literaria o música.

opuscle ['əʊpəskl] [ou-pus-kl], *s.* Opúsculo.

or [ɔːr] [o^r], *conj.* 1. O, partícula disyuntiva que denota distribución u oposición y que se cambia en *u* cuando la palabra que sigue empieza con *o* u *ho.* Es a menudo correlativa de *whether o either.* Si la precede una negación, ni. 2. O, alias, por otro nombre. **I could not see either justice or reason in it,** no pude ver en ello ni justicia ni razón. **Either...or,** o...o, ya...ya; sea...sea; ni...ni. **Either by land or by sea,** o por tierra o por mar. **Either misery or opulence,** o pobreza u opulencia. **He must either fall or fly,** o ha de perecer o ha de huir. -*adv.* Antes. **Or ever,** antes de todo.

or, *s.* (*Her.*) Color de oro.

-or. Sufijo que sirve para formar; (a) los nombres que indican agencia, como **actor,** actor; **competitor,** competidor; (b) los comparativos de origen latino, como **junior,** menor, más joven; **major,** mayor; (c) substantivo abstractos y concretos de origen latino: **honor,** honor; **terror,** terror.

oracle ['ɒrəkl] [o-ra-kel], *s.* 1. Oráculo.

oracular [ɒˈrækjʊlər] [o-ra-kiu-la^r], **oraculous** [ɒˈrækjʊləs] [o-ra-kiu-los], *a.* 1. Lo que revela oráculos. 2. Positivo, magistral, dogmático. 3. Oscuro, ambiguo.

oraculously [ɒˈrækjʊləslɪ] [o-ra-kiu-los-li], *adv.* A modo de oráculo.

oral ['ɔːrəl] [o-ral], *a.* 1. Oral, verbal, hablado, no escrito. 2. Oral, perteneciente a la boca; cercano de, o alrededor de la boca, o en ella. **Oral contraceptive,** contraceptivo bucal u oral.

orally ['ɔːrəlɪ] [o-ra-li], *adv.* Verbalmente, de palabra.

orange ['ɒrɪndʒ] [o-rindch], *s.* 1. (*Bot.*) Naranjo, el árbol que produce las naranjas. 2. Naranja. **China oranges,** naranjas chinas. 3. Color de naranja. **Seville** o **bitter orange,** naranja amarga. **Washington** o **navel orange,** naranja navel. **Orange-blossom,** azahar, flor del naranjo. **Orange-dog,** oruga de la mariposa. **Orange-scale,** insecto cóccido que se cría en el naranjo. **Orange-color,** color de naranja. **Orange-dew,** rocío de naranja. **Orange-grove,** naranjal. **Orange-juice,** zumo de naranja. **Orange-musk,** pera anaranjada, especie de pera. **Orange-peel,** cáscara de naranja. **Orange-wife, orange-woman,** naranjera, vendedora de naranjas. -*a.* Lo perteneciente a las naranjas; anaranjado.

orangeade ['ɒrɪndʒˈeɪd] [o-rind-cheid], *s.* Naranjada, agua de naranja.

orangery ['ɒrɪndʒərɪ] [o-rind-cha-ri], *s.* Naranjal.

orang-outang, orang-utan ['ɔːræŋˈuːtæn] [o-rang-u-tan], *s.* Orangután, especie de mono grande.

orate [ɒˈreɪt] [o-reit], *vn.* (*Fest.*) Pronunciar una oración en público, arengar.

oration [ɒˈreɪʃən] [o-rei-shon], *s.* Oración, razonamiento, locución, arenga, declamación.

orator [ɒˈreɪtər] [o-rei-ta^r], *s.* 1. Orador. 2. Suplicante en el tribunal del Canciller de Inglaterra.

oratorial [ɒːˈrətɔːrɪəl] [o-ra-to-rial], **oratorious** [ɒˈrətɔːrɪəs] [o-ra-to-rios], *a.* Retórico, oratorio.

oratorian [ɒˈrətɔːrɪən] [o-ra-to-rian], *s.* Sacerdote que pertenece a un oratorio.

oratorical [ˌɒrəˈtɔːrɪkəl] [o-ra-to-ri-kal], *s.* 1. Oratorio, representación teatral de asuntos sagrados, con música. 2. Concierto de música sacra.

oratorio [ˌɒrəˈtɔːrɪəʊ] [o-ra-to-riou], *s.* 1. Oratorio, representación teatral de asuntos sagrados, con música. 2. Concierto de música seria dado en domingo.

oratory ['ɒrətərɪ] [o-ra-to-ri], *s.* 1. Oratoria, el arte que enseña a hacer oraciones retóricas; elocuencia, ejercicio de elocuencia. 2. Oratorio, lugar destinado para retirarse a hacer oración. 3. Oratorio, congregación de personas devotas.

oratress ['ɒrətrɪs] [o-ra-tris], **oratrix** ['ɒrətrɪks] [o-ra-triks], *s. f.* Oradora.

orb [ɔːb] [orb], *s.* 1. Orbe, esfera, globo, cuerpo esférico; astro. 2. Círculo, rueda. 3. Período de tiempo.

orb, *va.* Formar en, cercar o encerrar en círculo.

orbed ['ɔːbɪd] [or-bid], *a.* 1. Redondo, circular; esférico; en forma de órbita. 2. Redondeado; lleno. 3. Que tiene ojos; se usa en composición. **A bright-orbed maid,** una doncella de ojos vivos.

orbicular ['ɔːbɪkjʊlər] [or-bi-kiu-la^r], *a.* Orbicular, redondo.

orbit ['ɔːbɪt] [or-bit], *s.* 1. Órbita, la línea que describe un planeta en su movimiento de traslación. 2. Órbita, la cuenca del ojo.

orbit, *vn.* Describir órbitas.

orbital ['ɔːbɪtl] [or-bi-tal], *a.* Orbital, referente a una órbita en todas sus acepciones, orbitario, que se refiere a la órbita del ojo.

orbiter ['ɔːbɪtər] [or-bi-ta^r], *s.* Orbitador (space).

orc [ɔːk] [ork], *s.* Orca, orco, especie de cetáceo.

orchard ['ɔːtʃəd] [or-chard], *s.* Huerto, huerta, colección o plantío de árboles frutales; verjel.

orchardist ['ɔːtʃədɪst] [or-char-dist], *s.* Hortelano, cultivador de árboles frutales.

orchesis ['ɔːkɪsɪs] [or-ki-sis], *s.* Orquesis.

orchestra ['ɔːkɪstrə] [or-kis-tra], *s.* 1. Orquesta. 2. En los teatros griegos y romanos, espacio semicircular, reservado en los griegos para el coro, y en los romanos para los asientos de los senadores y otros personajes.

orchestral [ɔːˈkestrəl] [or-kes-tral], *a.* De orquesta, perteneciente a la orquesta; compuesto para, o ejecutado por una orquesta.

orchestra seat [ˈɔːkɪstrəˌsiːt] [or-kis-tra-sit], *s.* *(Teat.)* Luneta.

orchestrate [ˈɔːkɪstreɪt] [or-kis-treit], *vt.* Instrumentar, orquestar.

orchestration [ˌɔːkɪsˈtreɪʃən] [or-kis-trei-shon], *s.* *(Mús.)* Orquestación.

orchid [ˈɔːkɪd] [or-kid], *s.* Orquídea.

orchidaceous [ˈɔːkɪdeɪʃəs] [or-ki-dei-shos], *a.* Orquídeo, relativo o semejante a las plantas orquídeas.

orchis [ˈɔːkɪs] [or-kis], *s.* *(Bot.)* Orquídea. V. ORCHID. Satirión abejera o hierba de la abejera.

orchotomy [ɔːˈkɒtəmɪ] [or-ko-to-mi], *s.* *(Cir.)* Orcotomía, la amputación de los testículos.

orcin, orcine [ˈɔːsɪn] [or-sin], *s.* Orcina.

ord [ɔːd] [ord], *s.* 1. Filo, corte. 2. Principio.

ordain [ɔːˈdeɪn] [or-dein], *va.* 1. Ordenar, mandar, prescribir; decretar, establecer, instituir. 2. Ordenar, conferir las órdenes sagradas a alguno.

ordainability [ˌɔːdeɪnəˈbɪlɪtɪ] [or-dei-na-bi-li-ti], *s.* La calidad de lo que puede ser ordenado o arreglado para que llene un objeto.

ordainable [ˈɔːdeɪnəbl] [or-dei-na-bol], *a.* Que es capaz de ser ordenado o decretado.

ordainer [ˈɔːdeɪnəʳ]] [or-dei-naʳ], *s.* Ordenador.

ordeal [ɔːˈdɪːl] [or-dil], *s.* 1. Prueba rigurosa del valor de una persona, de su paciencia, conciencia, etc.; experiencia penosa, o una serie de ellas. 2. Ordalía. **A terrible ordeal,** una experiencia terrible.

order [ˈɔːdəʳ] [or-daʳ], *s.* 1. Orden, regla, método, arreglo. 2. Orden, mandato. 3. Orden, serie, clase, estado. 4. Medida, medio que se toma para conseguir alguna cosa. 5. *(Com.)* Pedido, encargo de una partida de mercancías; comisión de surtir, comprar o vender una cosa. 6. Orden, en botánica, la subdivisión de una clase. 7. Uso establecido, procedimiento regular; el estado existente de las cosas. 8. Orden, condecoración honorífica. 9. Orden o posición social. 10. Instituto religioso; rito, sacramento; orden. 11. Orden, de arquitectura. 12. **Orders,** *pl.* la jerarquía eclesiástica; el oficio de clérigo. **To confer holy orders,** ordenar, conferir a alguno las órdenes sagradas. **To put out of order,** poner en confusión, desordenar, descomponer. **In order to,** para, a fin de, con intención de, para que. **In order to do it,** para hacerlo, con el fin o con el objeto de hacerlo, a fin de hacerlo. **Out of order,** en mal estado, descompuesto, que anda o funciona mal. **To be out of order,** descomponerse, desarreglarse una cosa; no atenerse a los reglamentos, no tener derecho a hablar en una reunión o asamblea. **The order of the day,** la orden del día. **Till further orders,** hasta nueva orden. **Order-book,** libro de pedidos. **To give an order,** hacer un pedido. **Sailing orders,** últimas instrucciones dadas al capitán de un buque. **Higher orders,** las clases altas o elevadas. **Order of the Garter,** la orden de la Jarretera. **In holy orders,** revestido de funciones sacerdotales.

order, *va.* 1. Ordenar, poner en orden, disponer, arreglar, dar método u orden a alguna cosa. 2. ordenar, mandar. 3. Ordenar, conferir las órdenes sagradas. 4. Ordenar, encaminar y dirigir a algún fin. 5. *(Com.)* Mandar, pedir, mandarse hacer. **To order one's life,** arreglar su vida. **To order a bill of goods,** pedir una factura de géneros. **To order about/around,** mangonear, mandar a alguien de aquí para allá. **To order arms,** *(Mil.)* poner el fusil perpendicularmente contra el lado derecho, descansando la culata en el suelo. **To order away,** despedir a uno, decirle que se vaya. **To order in,** mandar entrar, mandar traer. **To order out,** mandar salir; mandar llevar; poner de patitas en la calle.

ordered [ˈɔːdəd] [or-derd], *a.* Disciplinado, metódico.

orderer [ˈɔːdərəʳ] [or-de-raʳ], *s.* Ordenador.

ordering [ˈɔːdərɪŋ] [or-de-rin], *s.* Manejo, dirección, disposición.

orderless [ˈɔːdəlɪs] [or-der-les], *s. a.* Desordenado, confuso, sin orden; irregular.

orderliness [ˈɔːdəlɪnɪs] [or-der-li-nes], *s.* Regularidad, orden, método, buena dirección o buena conducta.

orderly [ˈɔːdəlɪ] [or-der-li], *a.* 1. Ordenado, metódico, regular. 2. Bien arreglado, quieto, tranquilo. **Orderly,** (a) *(Mil.)* Asistente, ordenanza, el soldado que se halla al servicio inmediato de un superior. (b) Practicante, asistente en un hospital. *-adv.* Ordenadamente, regularmente, metódicamente, en orden. **Orderly officer,** oficial del día.

orders [ˈɔːdəz] [or-dars], o **holy Orders,** *s. pl.* V. ORDER.

ordinal [ˈɔːdɪnl] [or-di-nal], *a.* 1. Ordinal, lo que señala el orden de las cosas. 2. Perteneciente a un orden de animales o plantas. *-s.* 1. Número ordinal, el que indica el orden en que están puestas las cosas. 2. Ritual que contiene y enseña el modo de rezar y hacer los divinos oficios.

ordinance [ˈɔːdɪnəns] [or-di-nans], *s.* 1. Ordenanza, ley, mandato, reglamento, estatuto. 2. Rito, ceremonia del culto. 3. *(Arq.)* Sistema de arreglo, disposición.

ordinarily [ˈɔːdɪˈnɛərɪlɪ] [or-di-nea-ri-li] *adv.* Ordinariamente, regularmente.

ordinary [ˈɔːdnrɪ] [or-din-ri], *a.* 1. Ordinario, común, usual, regular. 2. Ordenado, metódico, normal. 3. Ordinario, bajo, vulgar, mediano, de bajo nacimiento. 4. Feo; de mala disposición. *-s.* 1. Ordinario, juez eclesiástico; juez (civil) que tiene autoridad para tomar conocimiento de las causas por derecho propio y no por delegación. 2. Fonda a precio fijo; mesa redonda. 3. *(Her.)* Figura ordinaria del escudo. 4. Capellán. **In ordinary,** (a) en actual servicio, con ejercicio. (b) *(Mar.)* Puesto en lugar seguro; fuera de uso, desarmado. **Ordinary people,** gente modesta. **Painter in ordinary to the king,** pintor de cámara del rey. **Vessels in ordinary,** *(Mar.)* buques desarmados.

ordinate [ˈɔːdɪneɪt] [or-di-neit], *a.* Ordenado, metódico. *-s.* *(Geom.)* Ordenada o aplicada, distancia entre un punto dado y el eje de abscisas.

ordination [ˌɔːdɪˈneɪʃən] [or-di-nei-shon], *s.* 1. Ordenación, disposición. 2. Ordenación, el acto de conferir orden sacerdotal.

ordnance [ˈɔːdnəns] [ord-nans], *s.* Nombre genérico de todas las armas de guerra; en especial, artillería, cañones. **The master general of the ordnance,** el director general de artillería. **Ordnance supplies u ordnance stores,** todas las armas de guerra, con las municiones y el conjunto de los equipos militares.

ordonnance [ˈɔːdənəns] [or-do-nans], *s.* 1. La disposición de las figuras y demás piezas de que se compone una pintura. 2. Ley, ordenanza, estatuo.

ordure [ˈɔːdjɔəʳ] [or-diuaʳ], *s.* Basura, porquería, excremento.

ore [ɔːʳ] [oʳ], *s.* Quijo, ganga, mineral, el metal conforme se saca de la mina.

oread [ˈɔːrɪəd] [or-riad], *s.* Oréade, ninfa de los bosques.

oregano [ˌɒrɪˈgɑːnəʊ] [o-ri-ga-nou], *s.* Orégano.

oreweed [ˈɔːwiːd] [or-uid], **orewood** [ˈɔːwʊd] [or-vud], *s.* Alga.

orfrays [ˈɔːfreɪs] [or-freis], *s.* V. ORPHREY.

orgal [ˈɔːgəl] [or-gal], *s.* Las heces secas de vino. V. ARGAL.

organ [ˈɔːgən] [or-gan], *s.* 1. Órgano, cualquiera de las partes constitutivas del animal o vegetal que ejercen alguna función. 2. Órgano, instrumento músico de viento. 3. Sistema de cañones de un órgano que tiene su propio teclado. **The ear is the organ of hearing,** la oreja es el órgano del oído. **Great organ,** gran órgano. **Organ-grinder,** el que toca un organillo.

organ-builder [ˈɔːgənˌbɪldəʳ] [or-gan-bil-daʳ], *s.* Organero.

organdy [ˈɔːgəndɪ] [or-gan-di], *s.* Organdí, especie de muselina muy fina, a menudo con dibujos.

organic, organical [ɔːˈgænɪk] [or-ga-nik], *a.* 1. Orgánico. 2. *(Quím.)* Que contiene carbón como parte constitutiva esencial. 3. Organizado, que se compone de órganos; sistematizado. 4. Constitutivo, fundamental. **Organic**

remains, restos orgánicos. **Organic chemistry,** química orgánica. **Organic laws,** leyes orgánicas fundamentales.

organically [ɔ:'gænɪkəlɪ] [or-ga-ni-ka-li], *adv.* Orgánicamente.

organicalness [ɔ:'gænɪkəlnɪs] [or-ga-ni-kal-nes], *s.* El estado de lo que es orgánico.

organism ['ɔ:gænɪzəm] [or-ga-ni-sem], *s.* 1. Organismo, un ser organizado o viviente; un animal o una planta. 2. Estructura orgánica; también, un órgano cualquiera. 3. Organismo, cualquier cosa análoga al organismo físico.

organist ['ɔ:gənɪst] [or-ga-nist], *s.* Organista, el que toca el órgano.

organization [ˌɔ:gənaɪ'zeɪʃən] [or-ga-nai-sei-shon], *s.* 1. Organización, la acción de organizar, o el estado de un cuerpo organizado. 2. Lo que está organizado; (a) un organismo animal o vegetal; (b) sociedad, unión de varias personas para un mismo fin. 3. Cualquier combinación o correpsondencia de partes o de fuerzas. **Organization chart,** organigrama.

organizational [ˌɔ:gənaɪ'seɪʃənl] [or-ga-nai-sei-sho-nal], *a.* Organizativo.

organize ['ɔ:gənaɪz] [or-ga-nais], *va.* 1. Organizar, poner en correspondencia las diversas partes de un todo; disponer, arreglar de tal manera que una parte pueda cooperar con otra. 2. Prepararse una asamblea deliberante para empezar sus trabajos. 3. (*Biol.*) Organizar, proveer de órganos. -*vn.* Organizarse, unirse en compañía o sociedad. **To get organized,** arreglárselas.

organized ['ɔ:gənaɪzd] [or-ga-naisd], *a.* Organizado, ordenado, metódico.

organizer ['ɔ:gənaɪzəʳ] [or-ga-nai-saʳ], *s.* Organizador.

organ-loft ['ɔ:genlɒft] [or-gan-loft], *s.* Tribuno para el órgano, sitio donde se coloca el órgano.

organography ['ɔ:gənəˌgræfɪ] [or-ga-no-gra-fi], *s.* (*Biol.*) Organografía, la descripción científica de los órganos de un ser viviente.

organology ['ɔ:gənələdʒɪ] [or-ga-no-lo-yi], *s.* Organología, parte de la biología que trata de los órganos del cuerpo.

organ-pipe ['ɔ:gənpaɪp] [or-gan-paip], *s.* Cañón o tubo de órgano.

organ stop ['ɔ:gənstɒp] [or-ga-stop], *s.* Registro de órgano.

organzine, organzin ['ɔ:gənzi:n] [or-gan-sin], *s.* 1. Hilo de seda hecho con varios otros hilos torcidos. 2. Tela que se hace con ese hilo.

orgasm ['ɔ:gæzəm] [or-ga-sem], *s.* 1. Excitación excesiva o conducta inmoderada. 2. (*Med.*) Orgasmo, tensión violenta y pasajera del tejido eréctil (particularmente en el coito).

orgeat ['ɔ:dʒi:t] [or-yit], *s.* Jarabe de horchata, que se hace con almendras, agua de azahar y azúcar.

orgies ['ɔ:dʒi:z] [or-yis], *s. pl.* Orgías, fiestas bacanales. -*sing.* orgy, orgía.

orgy ['ɔ:dʒɪ] [or-yi], *s. f.* Orgía.

orichalch ['ɔ:rɪkalk] [o-ri-kalk], **orichalcum** ['ɔ:rɪkælkəm] [o-ri-kal-kum], *s.* Latón, oricalco.

oriel ['ɔ:rɪəl] [o-riel], *s.* 1. Ventana circular. 2. Alcoba cerca de la sala principal.

orient ['ɔ:rɪənt] [o-rient], *a.* 1. Naciente como el sol. 2. Oriental. 3. Brillante, resplandeciente. -*s.* Oriente, Este.

orient, *va.* 1. Orientar, determinar la posición de una cosa con respecto al este. 2. Colocar algo de tal manera que el frente mire al este.

oriental [ˌɔ:rɪ'entəl] [o-rien-tal], *a.* Oriental, que pertenece al oriente. -*s.* Oriental; habitante de Asia.

orientalism [ˌɔ:rɪ'entəlɪzm] [o-rien-ta-li-sem], *s.* Estilo oriental, orientalismo.

orientalist [ˌɔ:rɪ'entəlɪst] [o-rien-ta-list], *s.* 1. Habitador o natural del oriente. 2. El que sabe las lenguas orientales.

orientalize [ˌɔ:rɪ'entəlaɪz] [o-rien-ta-lais], *va.* Orientalizar, conformar a las costumbres y al carácter del oriente.

orientate ['ɔ:rɪenteɪt] [o-rien-teit], *va.* 1. Orientar, colocar de modo que el frente esté hacia el este. 2. Colocar un cristal en

posición tal que presente simetría. -*vn.* Caer, mirar, hacia el este.

orientation [ˌɔ:rɪen'teɪʃən] [o-rien-tei-shon], *s.* 1. Orientación, dirección al este. 2. Colocación con relación a los puntos cardinales. 3. Cualquier procedimiento de agrimensura para determinar la dirección. 4. (*Zool.*) El instinto de dirigirse hacia el lugar nativo, como lo hacen las palomas.

orienteering [ˌɔ:rɪen'tɪərɪŋ] [o-rien-tia-rin], *s. f.* Orientación.

orifice ['ɒrɪfɪs] [o-ri-fis], *s.* Orificio, boca de alguna cosa; abertura de un conducto.

origan ['ɔ:rɪgən] [o-ri-gan], **origanum** ['ɔ:rɪgænəm] [o-ri-ga-nom], *s.* (*Bot.*) Orégano, mejorana silvestre, planta labiada.

origin ['ɒrɪdʒɪn] [o-ri-yin], *s.* 1. Origen, primera existencia. 2. Origen, principio, manantial, causa moral, nacimiento de alguna cosa. 3. Origen, ascendencia, familia.

original [ə'rɪdʒɪnl] [o-ri-yi-nal], *a.* Original, primitivo, primero. -*s.* 1. Original, prototipo o primera forma de alguna cosa; primer escrito, composición o invención que se hace de una cosa para que de ella se saquen las demás. 2. Original, el idioma en que un documento o libro se escribió primeramente. 3. Persona de carácter o índole como no hay otros.

originality [əˌrɪdʒɪ'nælɪtɪ] [o-ri-yi-na-li-ti], *s.* Originalidad; facultad de inventar.

originally [ə'rɪdʒənəlɪ] [o-ri-yi-na-li], *adv.* Originalmente, originariamente.

originary [ə'rɪdʒɪnərɪ] [o-ri-yi-na-ri], *a.* Productivo; originario, primitivo.

originate [ə'rɪdʒɪneɪt] [o-ri-yi-neit], *va.* Originar, causar, inventar, ser principio y origen de alguna cosa. -*vn.* Originarse, traer su origen, emanar de.

origination [əˌrɪdʒɪ'neɪʃən] [o-ri-yi-nei-shon], *s.* 1. Origen, primera producción de alguna cosa. 2. Modo de propagar o de producir.

originator [ə'rɪdʒɪneɪtəʳ] [o-ri-yi-nei-taʳ], *s.* Autor, inventor.

orillon ['ɒrɪlən] [o-ri-lon], *s.* (*Fort.*) Orejón, obra que se hace sobre el tercio del flanco del baluarte.

oriole ['ɔ:rɪəʊl] [o-rioul], *s.* 1. Oriol, oropéndola. **Baltimore oriole,** la oropéndola americana.

orion ['ɔ:rɪən] [o-rion], *s.* (*Astr.*) Orión.

orison ['ɒrɪzən] [o-rai-son], *s.* Oración, petición, súplica devota.

orle [ɔ:l] [orl], *s.* 1. (*Arq.*) Oria, filete o listón. 2. (*Her.*) Orla, alrededor dle escudo.

orlon ['ɔ:lɒn] [or-lon], *s.* Orlón.

orlop ['ɔ:ləʊp] [or-loup], *s.* (*Mar.*) Sollado o entarimado de una embarcación. **Orlop-beam,** (*Mar.*) bao vacío o bao del sollado.

ormolu ['ɔ:məʊlʊ] [or-mou-lu], *s.* 1. Aleación de cobre, cinc y estaño. 2. Oro molido, para dorar bronce. 3. Mercadería metálica, dorada o bronceada.

ornament ['ɔ:nəmənt] [or-na-ment], *s.* 1. Ornamento, adorno, ornato, compostura o atavío de alguna cosa. 2. Ornamento, las prendas que recomiendan a una persona. 3. Decoración, señal de distinción.

ornament, *va.* Ornamentar, adornar; embellecer.

ornamental [ˌɔ:nə'mentl] [or-na-men-tal], *a.* Que sirve de adorno; de la naturaleza de adorno.

ornamentally [ˌɔ:nə'mentəlɪ] [or-na-men-ta-li], *adv.* Ornadamente.

ornamentation [ˌɔ:nəmən'teɪʃən] [or-na-men-tei-shon], *s.* Ornamentación; conjunto de cosas que sirven de adorno.

ornamented ['ɔ:nəməntɪd] [or-na-men-tid], **ornate** [ɔ:'neɪt] [or-neit], *a.* Ornado, ornamentado, adornado, ataviado.

ornately [ɔ:'neɪtlɪ] [or-neit-li], *adv.* Vistosamente.

ornateness [ɔ:'neɪtnɪs] [or-neit-nes], *s.* Ornato, ornamento, adorno, atavío, aparato.

ornithological [ˌɔ:nɪθə'lɒdʒɪkəl] [or-ni-zo-lo-yi-kal], *a.* Ornitológico, concerniente a la ornitología.

ornithologist [ˌɔːnɪθəˈlɒdʒɪst] [or-ni-zo-lo-yist], s. Ornitólogo, el que se dedica al estudio y conocimiento de las aves.

ornithomancy [ˈɔːnɪθəˈmænsɪ] [or-ni-zo-man-si], s. Ornitomancia, adivinación por medio de las aves.

orographic [ˈɔːrəʊɡræfɪk] [o-rou-gra-fik], a. Orográfico, perteneciente a la orografía.

orography [ˈɔːrəʊɡræfɪ] [o-rou-gra-fi], s. Orografía, descripción del desarrollo y relaciones de las montañas.

oroide [ˈɒrɔɪd] [o-roid], s. Oroide, aleación de cobre, cinc, estaño y otros metales que tiene apariencia de oro.

orology [ˈɔːrəlɒdʒɪ] [o-ro-lo-yi], s. Orología, el estudio y conocimiento de las montañas; tratado sobre ellas.

orphan [ˈɔːfən] [or-fan], s. Huérfano, hijo o hija que carece de padre o madre o de ambos. -a. Huérfano, destituido de padres, niño desamparado.

orphan, va. Privar a uno de sus padres. **Orphaned,** pp. huérfano; sin padres.

orphanage [ˈɔːfənɪdʒ] [or-fa-nich], s. 1. Orfandad; los huérfanos colectivamente. 2. Asilo para huérfanos.

orphanhood [ˈɔːfənhʊd] [or-fan-jud], s. Orfandad.

orphean [ˈɔːfɪən] [or-fian], a. Lo que pertenece a Orfeo; poético o músico.

orpiment [ˈɔːpɪmənt] [or-pi-ment], s. Oropimente.

orpine [ˈɔːpɪn] [or-pin], s. 1. (Bot.) Telefio, fabacrasa. V. STONECROP. 2. Color de pintura, rojo o amarillo.

orrery [ˈɔːrərɪ] [o-re-ri], s. Planetario.

orris [ˈɒrɪs] [o-ris], s. 1. (Bot.) Lirio de Florencia. **Orris-root,** raíz de lirio. 2. Bocadillo y galón; y (des.) especie de encaje de oro y plata.

orthochromatic [ˈɔːθəʊkrəʊˈmætɪk] [or-zo-krou-ma-tik], a. Ortocromático.

orthodontist [ˈɔːθəʊˈdɒntɪst] [or-zou-don-tist], s. Ortodóntico.

orthodox [ˈɔːθədɒks] [or-zo-doks], a. 1. Ortodoxo, libre de herejía. 2. Perteneciente a la Iglesia Griega. 3. Aprobado; recibido; convencional.

orthodoxy [ˈɔːθədɒksɪ] [or-zo-dok-si], s. Ortodoxia.

orthodromics [ˈɔːθədrəmɪks] [or-zo-dro-miks], **orthodromy** [ˈɔːθədrəmɪ] [or-zo-dro-mi], s. (Mar.) Ortodromía, navegación en línea recta, en contraposición a la loxodromía.

orthoepic, orthoepical [ˈɔːθəʊɪpɪk] [or-zoi-pik], a. Ortológico, perteneciente a la ortología, propio de ella.

orthoepist [ˈɔːθəʊɪpɪst] [or-zoi-pist], s. Ortólogo, el que es versado en el arte de pronunciar correctamente.

orthoepy [ˈɔːθəʊɪpɪ] [or-zoi-pi], s. Ortología, el arte de pronunciar bien.

orthogon [ˈɔːθəɡən] [or-zo-gon], s. Ortogonio, figura rectangular.

orthogonal [ˈɔːθəɡənl] [or-zo-go-nal], a. Rectángulo.

orthographer [ˈɔːθəɡræfər] [or-zo-gra-faʳ], s. Ortógrafo, el que sigue las reglas de la ortografía.

orthographic, orthographical [ˈɔːθəˈɡræfɪk] [or-zo-gra-fik], a. Ortográfico, que pertenece a la ortografía.

orthographically [ˈɔːθəˈɡræfɪkəlɪ] [or-zo-gra-fi-ka-li], adv. Ortográficamente.

orthographist [ˈɔːθəɡræfɪst] [or-zo-gra-fist], s. Ortógrafo, autor que trata de la ortografía.

orthography [ˈɔːθəɡræfɪ] [or-zo-gra-fi], s. Ortografía, la parte de la gramática que enseña cómo se ha de escribir correctamente.

orthology [ˈɔːθəlɒdʒɪ] [or-zo-lo-yi], s. (Ant.) Ortología, descripción verdadera de las cosas.

orthometry [ˈɔːθəmiːtrɪ] [or-zo-me-tri], s. Ortometría, leyes y reglas para componer versos.

orthopedia, orthopædia, orthopedy [ˈɔːθəʊpiːdɪə] [or-zou-pi-dia], s. Ortopedia, el arte de corregir las deformidades del cuerpo, principalmente en los niños.

orthopedic, orthopædic [ˈɔːθəʊpiːdɪk] [or-zou-pi-dik], a. Ortopédico.

orthopedist [ˈɔːθəʊpiːdɪst] [or-zou-pi-dist], s. Ortopedista.

orthopnæa [ˈɔːθəpnɪə] [or-zop-nia], s. (Med.) Ortopnea, opresión de pecho que impide la respiración a no ser que el enfermo esté en pie.

orthoptera [ˈɔːθəptərə] [or-zop-te-ra], s. pl. Ortópteros.

orthopterous [ˈɔːθəptərəs] [or-zop-te-ros], a. Ortóptero.

ortive [ˈɔːtɪv] [or-tiv], a. (Astr.) Ortivo, que equivale a oriental.

ortolan [ˈɔːtələn] [or-to-lan], s. (Orn.) Hortelano; verderol de los cañaverales.

oryx [ˈɒrɪks] [o-riks], s. (Zool.) Orix, antílope abisinio.

oscillate [ˈɒsɪleɪt] [o-si-leit], va. Hacer oscilar. -vn. Oscilar, vibrar; moverse alternativamente en dos sentidos contrarios.

oscillating [ˈɒsɪleɪtɪŋ] [o-si-lei-tin], a. Oscilante.

oscillation [ˌɒsɪˈleɪʃən] [o-si-lei-shon], s. Oscilación, vibración, balanceo.

oscillatory [ˌɒsɪˈleɪtərɪ] [o-si-lei-to-ri], a. Oscilatorio, oscilante.

oscitancy [ˈɒsɪtænsɪ] [o-si-tan-si], s. (Ant.) 1. Bostezo. 2. Descuido, negligencia.

oscitant [ˈɒsɪtænt] [o-si-tant], a. (Ant.) Bostezante, soñoliento; pesado, negligente.

oscitate [ˈɒsɪteɪt] [o-si-teit], vn. (Ant.) Bostezar.

osculant [ˈɒskjʊlənt] [os-kiu-lant], a. 1. En biología, de carácter intermedio entre dos grupos. 2. Que se adhiere fuertemente; que se aferra, como ciertas orugas.

osculation [ˌɒskjʊˈleɪʃən] [os-kiu-lei-shon], s. 1. Beso, el acto de besar; ósculo. 2. (Geom.) Osculación.

osculatory [ˈɒskjʊlətərɪ] [os-kiu-la-to-ri], a. 1. Relativo a la acción de besar. 2. Osculatorio, perteneciente a la osculación.

osier [ˈəʊʒəʳ] [ou-shaʳ], s. (Bot.) Mimbrera, el arbusto cuyas ramas tiernas cortadas se usan como mimbres. **Common osier,** sauce mimbrero o mimbrera propiamente dicha. **Golden osier,** sauce vitelino, mimbrera ama.

osmazome [ˈɒsməzəʊm] [os-ma-soum], s. Osmazoma u osmazomo, sustancia contenida en la carne que da olor y sabor a los caldos.

osmic [ˈɒzmɪk] [os-mik], a. Ósmico, perteneciente al osmio o que lo contiene. **Osmic acid,** ácido ósmico, un óxido de osmio.

osmium [ˈɒzmɪəm] [os-miom], s. (Min.) Osmio, un metal que se halla mezclado con el platino y el iridio.

osmose [ˈɒzməʊz] [os-mous], **osmosis** [ɒzˈməʊsɪs] [os-mou-sis], s. Osmosis.

osmotic [ɒzˈmɒtɪk] [os-mo-tik], a. Osmótico, que se refiere a la osmosis.

osprey [ˈɒzprɪː] [os-pri], s. (Orn.) Águila marina, halieto, osífraga.

osseous [ˈɒsɪəs] [o-sios], a. Huesoso, óseo, ososo.

ossicle [ˈɒzɪkl] [o-si-kel], s. Huesecillo, hueso pequeño.

ossiferous [ˈɒsɪfərəs] [o-si-fe-ros], a. Osífero, que contiene huesos.

ossific [ˈɒsɪfɪk] [o-si-fik], a. Osífico, que convierte en hueso o que forma hueso.

ossification [ˌɒsɪfɪˈkeɪʃən] [o-si-fi-kei-shon], s. Osificación, la conversión insensible de las partes ternillosas en hueso.

ossified [ˈɒsɪfaɪd] [o-si-faid], a. Osificado.

ossifrage [ˈɒsɪfreɪdʒ] [o-si-freich], s. (Orn.) Osífraga, quebrantahuesos.

ossify [ˈɒsɪfaɪ] [o-si-fai], va. Osificar, convertir en hueso.

ossivorous [ˈɒsɪvərəs] [o-si-vo-ros], a. Osívoro, que come huesos.

ossuary [ˈɒsʊərɪ] [o-sua-ri], s. Osario, osar.

ostensible [ɒsˈtensəbl] [os-ten-sa-bol], a. 1. Profesado u ofrecido como verdadero; aparente, disfrazado. 2. Ostensible, manifestable. **Ostensible purpose,** designio aparente, que puede ser verdadero o fingido.

ostensibly [ɒsˈtensəblɪ] [os-ten-sa-bli], adv. Ostensiblemente; aparentemente.

ostensive [ɒsˈtensɪv] [os-ten-siv], a. Ostensivo, que muestra.

ostentation [ˌɒstenˈteɪʃən] [os-ten-tei-shon], s. Ostentación, gala, jactancia, fausto.

ostentatious [ˌɒstenˈteɪʃəs] [os-ten-tei-shos], *a.* Ostentador, lleno de ostentación, ostentoso, jactancioso, vanaglorioso, fastuoso.

ostentatiously [ˌɒstenˈteɪʃəslɪ] [os-ten-tei-shos-li], *adv.* Pomposamente.

ostentatiousness [ˌɒstenˈteɪʃənɪs] [os-ten-tei-shos-nes], *s.* Ostentación, vanidad, vanagloria, jactancia.

osteocolla [ˌɒstɪəʊˈkɒʊlə] [os-tiou-kou-la], *s.* Osteocola, cal carbonatada, incrustante, que se deposita sobre los vegetales.

osteocope [ˌɒstɪəʊˈkəʊp] [os-tiou-koup], *s.* Dolor osteócopo o dolor fijo y muy violento en los huesos.

osteocopic [ˌɒstɪəˈkəʊpɪ] [os-tiou-kou-pi], *a.* (*Med.*) Osteócopo.

osteography [ˌɒstɪəˈɡræfɪ] [os-tiou-gra-fi], *s.* Osteografía, descripción de los huesos.

osteologist [ˈɒstɪəʊˈlɒdʒɪst] [os-tiou-lo-yist], *s.* Osteólogo, el que sabe o profesa la osteología.

osteology [ˌɒstɪəʊˈlɒdʒɪ] [os-tiou-lo-yi], *s.* Osteología, la parte de la anatomía que trata de los huesos.

osteopathy [ˌɒstɪˈɒpəθɪ] [os-tiou-pa-zi], *s.* (*Med.*) Osteopatía.

ostiary [ˈɒstɪərɪ] [os-tia-ri], *s.* 1. Ostiario, el que tiene uno de los grados eclesiásticos así llamado. 2. Ostial, la boca de un río o canal, o el sitio de su desembocadura.

ostler [ˈɒslər] [os-la^r], *s. V.* HOSTLER.

ostosis [ˈɒstəʊsɪs] [os-tou-sis], *s.* Una formación de hueso; osificación.

ostracean [ˈɒstreɪʃən] [os-trei-shan], *a.* Ostráceo, referente a la ostra. *-s.* Ostra.

ostraceous [ˈɒstreɪʃəs] [os-trei-shos], *a.* Ostráceo, perteneciente a las ostras.

ostracism [ˈɒstrəsɪzəm] [os-tra-si-sem], *s.* 1. Exclusión del trato o favor (expulsion). 2. Ostracismo, destierro político entre los griegos.

ostracite [ˈɒstrəsɪt] [os-tra-sit], *s.* Ostracita, concha de ostra petrificada o parecida a ella.

ostracize [ˈɒstrəsaɪz] [os-tra-sais], *va.* Desterrar por voto del pueblo.

ostrich [ˈɒstrɪtʃ] [os-trich], *s.* (*Orn.*) Avestruz, la mayor de las aves existentes. **Ostrich plume, feather,** pluma de avestruz.

ostrogoth [ˈɒstrəgɒθ] [os-tro-goz], *s.* Ostrogodo.

otacoustic [ˈɒtəkʌstɪk] [o-ta-kas-tik], *a.* Otacústico, propio para perfeccionar el sentido del oído. *-s.* Trompetilla, instrumento a modo de trompeta para ayudar al sentido del oído.

otalgia [ˈɒtældʒɪə] [o-tal-yia], *s.* Otalgia, dolor de oído.

OTC *Abreviatura de* **Over The Counter,** al contado (Com).

other [ˈʌðər] [a-da^r], *pron.* 1. Otro, la persona o cosa diferente o distinta de aquella de que se habla. 2. El segundo de dos; el opuesto. **This book or the other,** este libro o el otro. **Every other day,** un día sí y otro no; cada dos días. **On the other side,** otro lado. *-s.* Otra persona o cosa. **Others,** *pl.* Los otros, los demás. **Among others,** entre otros. **Somebody or other,** alguno, alguien. *-a.* 1. Otro, diferente, no el mismo. 2. Adicional, además de. 3. Segundo; opuesto, contrario. **The other side,** el otro lado, el partido opuesto. **The other day,** el otro día; hace poco, recientemente.

otherness [ˈʌðənɪs] [a-da-nes], *s.* Alteridad.

otherwise [ˈʌðəwaɪz] [a-da-uais], *adv.* De otra manera, de otro modo, por otra parte. *-a.* Otro, diferente.

otic [ˈɒtɪk] [o-tik], *a.* Ótico, que se refiere a la oreja, o que está situado cerca de la oreja.

otiose [ˈəʊtɪəʊs] [ou-tious], *a.* Ocioso, que está en reposo; también perezoso, holgazán.

otolith [ˈɒtəlɪθ] [o-to-liz], *s.* Otolito.

otologist [ˈɒtəlɒdʒɪst] [o-to-lo-yist], *s.* Otólogo, el que es versado en otología; aurista.

otology [ˈɒtəlɒdʒɪ] [o-to-lo-yi], *s.* (*Med.*) Otología, la ciencia que trata del oído y sus enfermedades.

otorrhea, otorrhæa [ˈɒtərɪə] [o-to-ria], *s.* Otorrea, flujo por el oído.

OTT *Abreviatura de* **over the top.**

ottar [ˈɒtər] [o-ta^r], **otto** [ˈɒtəʊ] [o-tou], *s.* Aceite esencial. **Ottar of roses,** aceite esencial de rosas. *V.* ATTAR.

otter [ˈɒtər] [o-ta^r], *s.* 1. Nutra, o nutria, mamífero carnicero y anfibio. **Otter-skin,** piel de nutria. 2. Nutria de mar. 3. Oruga de una mariposa nocturna.

otter-hunting [ˈɒtəˌhʌntɪŋ] [o-ta-jan-tin], *s.* Caza de nutrias.

otter-pike [ˈɒtəpaɪk] [o-ta-paik], *s.* (*Ict.*) Dragón marino.

ottoman [ˈɒtəmən] [o-to-man], *a.* Otomano, nombre que se da al imperio de los turcos. *-s.* 1. Otomano, turco. 2. Escaño con cojín y sin respaldo. 3. Escabel movible cubierto con alfombra.

ouch [əʊtʃ] [ouch], *s.* 1. Engaste de una piedra preciosa. 2. Adorno de oro, particularmente un broche o corchete.

ouch, *inter.* ¡Huy! interjección.

ought [ɔːt] [ot], *s. y adv.* Algo, alguna cosa. **For ought I know,** por lo que yo puede comprender; en cuanto yo alcanzo o sé. Con más propiedad se escribe *aught. V.* AUGHT.

ought, *s.* Nada; corrupción de *naught.*

ought, *v. def. y auxiliar.* 1. Deber, tener la obligación moral de satisfacer alguna cosa. 2. Ser menester, necesario; convenir, ser conveniente. **You ought to remember that,** Ud. debería acordarse de eso. **It ought to be so,** conviene que sea así, o así debería ser. **I ought to,** es menester que yo; debería. **You ought to have come sooner,** Ud. debería haber venido antes. *-ought* tiene más fuerza que *should.* **That player ought to win,** ese jugador tiene más probabilidades de ganar. **You ought to go and see it,** deberías ir a verlo.

ounce [aʊns] [auns], *s.* 1. Onza, la décimosexta parte de una libra común. 2. Onza, mamífero carnicero de la India y Persia. 3. Felino semejante al jaguar. 4. Onza, antigua moneda de oro española. **If he had an ounce of common sense,** si tuviera una pizca de sentido común.

-our. Sufijo, lo mismo que -or.

our, ours [aʊər] [aua^r], *a. y pron. poss.* Nuestro, lo que a nosotros pertenece. **Our parents,** nuestros padres. **Our country,** nuestro país. **Our church,** nuestra iglesia. **Your house is larger than ours,** la casa de Ud. es mayor que la nuestra. **This is ours,** esto es nuestro o de nosotros.

ouranography [ˌaʊrəˈnɒɡræfɪ] [ou-ra-no-gra-fi], *s.* Uranografía, descripción de los cielos.

ourself [ˈaʊəself] [aua-self], *pron.* Yo mismo, yo misma; se usa solamente en el estilo oficial o regio.

ourselves [ˌaʊəˈsevz] [aua-sevs], *pron. recip.* Nosotros mismos.

-ous [ˈaʊz] [aus], Sufijo que corresponde a las desinencias castellanas oso, osa, uoso, uosa.

ousel [ˈaʊəsl] [aua-sel], *s.* (*Orn.*) Mirlo, mirla. *V.* OUZEL.

oust [ˈaʊst] [aust], *va.* Desposeer, desalojar; echar fuera, despedir.

ouster [ˈaʊstər] [aus-ta^r], *s.* (*For.*) Desposeimiento, despojo.

out [aʊt] [aut], *adv.* 1. Fuera, afuera, a la parte exterior. 2. En lo exterior, en condición de haber salido, ausente. 3. No conforme, no de moda o de uso; destituido, que no tiene ya empleo, que ha perdido el poder; en error, que no tiene razón. 4. Descubierto, que ya no está oculto; publicado, aparecido; en condición de haber perdido, faltado, de haber salido mal; extinguido, agotado, acabado; con pérdida (de tanto). 5. De una manera libre, abierta, franca; completamente, enteramente. 6. Libre de algo que obstruye, molesta o sirve de obstáculo. 7. Hasta el cabo, de cabo a cabo; hasta la extinción o el agotamiento; hasta obtener buen éxito. 8. En alta voz, distintamente, de un modo claro. **Right out, straight out,** sin rodeos, al grano. **Throw it out,** échelo Ud. afuera. **To go out,** salir, partir, marcharse. **He is out,** está fuera de casa. **Out at the elbows,** agujereado, roto por los codos. **Out at the heels,** con zapatos rotos. **To set out,** (a) partir; (b) plantar, introducir en la tierra. *V.* SET. **A way out,** salida, lugar por donde se sale. **The story is out,** se acabó, se concluyó el cuento. **The book has just come out,** el libro acaba de publicarse. **To be out at interest,** estar puesto a interés. **He was out one hundred francs,** perdió cien francos. **The soup was out,** se había acabado la sopa. **The time is out,** el tiempo ha pasado; el plazo ha expirado. **To be out,** estar fuera de su propio lugar o ausente; no estar en casa; no estar de moda o en boga; verse despedido de un cargo o empleo; sin poder jugar en ciertos juegos, por haber perdido; cortarse, quedarse cortado; haber perdido una suma de dinero; estar apagado, apagarse; acabar de publicarse, etc. **Out of,** (a) fuera de. (b) Más allá, además de; de; en, sobre. (c) Sin. (d) Por (indicando la causa). **Out of sight,** (a) fuera del alcance de la vista; (b) de calidad superior, muy excelente, notable. **Out of breath,** sin aliento. **Out of character,** impropio, fuera de carácter, no conveniente o poco a propósito. **To copy out of an author,** copiar de un autor. **Out of sorts,** (a) indispuesto, no muy bien de salud. (b) Descontento, poco satisfecho. (c) *(Impr.)* Falto de ejemplarse suficientes de un tipo o letra. **Out of spit,** por despecho. **Out of the woods,** fuera del vado, libre de dudas y dificultades; seguro. -En numerosos verbos compuestos, *out* añade el sentido de ir más allá, de sobrepujar o exceder. **Out of danger,** a salvo, fuera de peligro. **Out of doubt,** indudable. **Let him out,** déjele Ud. salir. **Out of place,** desacomodado. **Out of fashion,** no usado, anticuado. **Time out of mind,** tiempo inmemorial. **To be out of patience,** perder la paciencia. **He is much out in this point,** está muy equivocado, acerca de esto. **The candle is out,** la vela está apagada. **To be out of trim,** estar de mal humor; no tenerlas todas consigo. **Out of trim,** *(mar.)* mal estivado. **Out of tune,** desentonado; destemplado. **To fall out with one,** reñir con uno. **Out of hand,** luego, al punto. **Out of friendship,** por amistad. **Out of spite,** por despecho. **Out of pity,** por compasión. **Out of order,** desordenado, descompuesto; desarreglado. **To drink out of a glass,** beber de un vaso o con un vaso. **Out of hope,** desesperanzado, sin esperanza. **Out of humor,** de mal humor, enojado. **Out of measure,** desmesurado. **Out of his wits,** fuera de sí, insensato. **A book out of print,** un libro descatalogado. **Out of favor,** desvalido, desgraciado. **Pray, hear me out,** sírvase Ud. escucharme hasta que concluya. **Speak out,** hable Ud. cuanto tenga que decir. **It will out,** ello dirá; allá se verá; se descubrirá. **Murder will out,** el asesinato se descubirá. **A voyage out and home,** viaje redondo. **Out** se usa en inglés muy frecuentemente para modificar o cambiar la significación primitiva de los verbos. *-inter.* Fuera. **Out with it,** fuera con ella. Hable Ud. francamente, sin rodeos. **Out upon thee!** ¡maldito seas!

out, *s.* 1. El exterior o la parte exterior de alguna cosa; esquina, lugar exterior; también, el aspecto exterior de un asunto. 2. El que no tiene ya un empleo; en plural, los que han perdido el poder, la oposición. 3. Olvido, omisión que comete el cajista en la composición. 4. En algunos juegos, como el de *base-ball,* el efecto de echar a un jugador del lugar que ocupaba.

out, *va.* Expeler, desposeer, despojar.

outact ['aʊtækt] [aut-akt], *va.* Propasar, pasar más adelante de lo que se debía; ir más allá.

out-and-out ['aʊtən'aʊt] [aut-an-aut], *a.* Cabal, entero, sin calificación; verdadero. Completamente, verdaderamente.

outargue ['aʊtɑːg] [aut-arg], *va.* Sobresalir en la argumentación; imponer por la razón.

outbalance ['aʊt'bæləns] [aut-ba-lans], *va.* Preponderar, exceder en algo.

outbid ['aʊtbɪd] [aut-bid], *va.* Pujar, aumentar el precio puesto a alguna cosa que se vende o arrienda; sobrepujar.

outbidder ['aʊtbɪdəʳ] [aut-bi-daʳ], *s.* Pujador, el que hace puja en lo que se vende o arrienda.

outboard ['aʊtbɔːd] [aut-bord], *a. y adv.* Fuera de la borda del barco.

outbound ['aʊtbaʊnd] [aut-baund], *a.* Destinado a un viaje distante o a algún país extranjero.

outbrag ['aʊtbræg] [aut-brag], *va.* Exceder, sobrepujar en fanfarronadas.

outbrave ['aʊtbreɪv] [aut-breiv], *va.* 1. Exceder, ser superior en valentía o audacia. 2. Arrostrar los peligros. 3. Exceder en magnificencia o garbo.

outbreak ['aʊtbreɪk] [aut-breik], *s.* Erupción; ataque violento, pasión, tumulto.

outbreathe ['aʊtbriːð] [aut-briz], *va.* 1. Exhalar, emitir, echar el aliento. 2. Exhalar, echar de sí. 3. *(Poco us.)* Exceder a alguno en la carrera o en otro género de fatiga por poder sufrir la falta de aliento mejor que él.

outbuilding ['aʊtˌbiːldɪŋ] [aut-bil-din], *s.* Dependencia, construcción exterior.

outburst ['aʊtbɜːrst] [aut-berst], *s.* Explosión, erupción. *-vn.* *(Ant.)* Prorrumpir, brotar.

outcast ['aʊtkɑːst] [aut-kast], *a.* 1. Desechado, arrojado, inútil. 2. Desterrado, expulso, proscripto; perdido. *-s.* Un desterrado.

outclass [aʊt'klɑːs] [aut-klas], *va.* Exceder en habilidad, en calidad o en facultades.

outcome ['aʊtkʌm] [aut-kam], *s.* Éxito, resultado visible, consecuencia.

outcrop ['aʊtkrɒp] [aut-krop], *vn.* Asomar; en geología, aparecer en la superficie o encima de la superficie del terreno (rock).

outcrop, *s.* Aparición, porción visible de un estrato sobre la superficie de un terreno.

outcry ['aʊtkraɪ] [aut-krai], *s.* Clamor, voz lastimosa que indica aflicción o pasión de ánimo; ruido, alboroto, gritería, vocería.

outdare ['aʊtdɛəʳ] [aut-deaʳ], *va.* Osar, emprender alguna cosa con atrevimiento, atreverse demasiado o más que otro.

out-dated ['aʊt'deɪtɪd] [aut-dei-tid], *a.* Anticuado, pasado de moda.

outdo [aʊt'duː] [aut-du], *va.* Exceder a otro en alguna cosa; sobrepujar, eclipsar, dejar deslucido.

outdoor ['aʊtdɔːʳ] [aut-do'], *a.* 1. Externo, que está al raso, hecho al aire libre; fuera de la casa, de lo exterior. 2. Externo de ciertas instituciones públicas, como un hospital u hospicio. **Outdoor exercise,** ejercicio al aire libre. **Outdoor sports,** juegos al aire libre, en campo abierto.

outdoors ['aʊt'dɔːz] [aut-dors], *s.* El raso, el mundo de puertas afuera. *-adv.* Fuera de casa, al raso.

outdrink ['aʊtdrɪŋk] [aut-drink], *va.* Beber más que otro.

outer ['aʊtəʳ] [au-taʳ], *a.* Exterior, externo. **Outer space,** espacio interastral.

outerly ['aʊtəlɪ] [au-ter-li], *adv.* Hacia fuera, exteriormente.

outermost ['aʊtəməʊst] [au-ta-moust], *a.* Extremo; lo más exterior.

outface ['aʊtfeɪs] [aut-feis], *va.* Humillar a otro haciendo de generoso o magnánimo; mantener cara a cara.

outfall ['aʊtfɔːl] [aut-fol], *s.* 1. Canal para regar; desembocadura. 2. Riña, disensión.

outfit ['aʊtfɪt] [aut-fit], *s.* 1. Equipo, apresto. 2. Habilitación, desembolso; el gasto hecho para equipar un barco, o dar principio o fomento a una empresa, particularmente a un viaje. 3. Pertrechos, avíos, menesteres de alguna ocupación.

outfitter ['aʊtfɪtəʳ] [aut-fi-taʳ], *s.* Armador de una embarcación; abastecedor, proveedor, habilitador de todo lo necesario para un viaje, empresa o negocio.

outflank ['aʊt'flæŋk] [aut-flank], *va.* Franquear, extenderse un ejército o cuerpo de ejército más que las alas o flancos del enemigo.

outflow ['aʊtflaʊ] [aut-flau], *s.* Efusión, derrame, flujo; salida. *-vn. (Poét.)* Correr, manar hacia afuera.

outfly ['aʊtflaɪ] [aut-flai], *va.* Exceder en el vuelo, volar más o mejor.

outfox ['aʊt'fɒks] [aut-foks], *vt.* Ser más listo que.

outgate ['aʊtgeɪt] [aut-gueit], *s.* Salida, puerta exterior.

outgeneral [aʊt'dʒenərəl] [aut-ye-ne-ral], *va.* Exceder a uno en táctica militar.

outgive ['aʊtgɪv] [aut-guiv], *va.* Dar más que otro, exceder en generosidad.

outgo ['aʊtgəʊ] [aut-gou], *va.* Exceder, vencer; adelantarse, tomar la delantera.

outgo, *s.* Gasto, lo que se ha gastado; expendio, costas, lo opuesto a *income.*

outgoing [ˈaʊtˌɡəʊɪŋ] [aut-goin], s. Salida; la acción de partir. -a. Que sale o se retira de un empleo; saliente, aquel cuyo cargo termina.

outgrow [aʊtˈɡraʊ] [aut-grou], va. 1. Sobrecrecer, crecer más que otro. 2. Hacerse demasiado grande o viejo para algo. **The boy has outgrown his clothes,** el muchacho ha crecido tanto que la ropa le está corta.

outgrowth [ˈaʊtˌɡraʊθ] [aut-grouz], s. 1. Excrecencia, lo que crece en el exterior de otra cosa. 2. Resultado o efecto natural; consecuencia.

outguard [aʊtˈɡɑːd] [aut-gard], s. *(Mil.)* Guardia avanzada.

outhouse [aʊtˈhaʊs] [aut-jaus], s. 1. Casa pequeña de los criados o dependientes de una alquería, hacienda u otra posesión rural. 2. Retrete.

outing [ˈaʊtɪŋ] [au-tin], s. Salida; paseo, viaje corto para divertirse, excursión.

outland [aʊtˈlænd] [aut-land], s. Terreno situado más allá de los límites de ocupación o cultivación.

outlandish [aʊtˈlændɪʃ] [aut-lan-dish], a. 1. Extranjero, remoto. 2. Grosero, rústico, bárbaro en aspecto o acciones.

outlast [aʊtˈlɑːst] [aut-last], va. Durar más que otra cosa, excederla en duración; sobrevivir a.

outlaw [ˈaʊtlɔː] [aut-lo], s. 1. Proscripto. 2. Bandido, bandolero.

outlaw, va. Proscribir, privar a uno de la protección de las leyes; sentencia en rebeldía.

outlawry [ˈaʊtlɔːrɪ] [aut-lo-ri], s. Proscripción, la sentencia con que se condena a una o muchas personas, privándolas de la protección de las leyes.

outlay [ˈaʊtleɪ] [aut-lei], s. Desembolso, gasto; expendio.

outleap [ˈaʊtliːp] [aut-lip], va. Pasar saltando, saltar más allá del término señalado.

outlearn [ˈaʊtlɜːn] [aut-lern], va. Adelantar a otro en lo que se aprende.

outlet [ˈaʊtlet] [aut-let], s. Salida, orificio de salida, desagüe; desaguadero; portillo. **Outlets,** *(Des.)* contornos.

outlie [ˈaʊtlaɪ] [aut-lai], va. Mentir más que otro, excederle en decir o inventar mentiras. -vn. Dormir al raso, acampar en tiendas.

outlier [ˈaʊtlaɪəʳ] [aut-laiaʳ], s. Aquel cuya residencia no está en el mismo lugar en que se hallan su oficina o sus negocios.

outline [ˈaʊtlaɪn] [aut-lain], s. Contorno, perfil, diseño, bosquejo, traza, recorte; plan general.

outlive [aʊtˈlɪv] [aut-liv], va. Sobrevivir a; exceder en duración.

outlock [ˈaʊtlɒl] [aut-lok], s. 1. Vista, perspectiva, lo que se alcanza a ver desde un balcón, ventana o punto elevado; de aquí, la condición o aspecto de alguna cosa, la perspectiva de un negocio o empresa. 2. Vigilancia, previsión. 3. Atalaya, vigía; garita. 4. Centinela, guardia.

outlock, va. 1. Desconcertar, turbar por medio de conducta atrevida o descarada. 2. Ver más lejos, alcanzar a mayor distancia con la vista.

outlook [ˈaʊtlɒk] [aut-luk], s. Perspectiva, panorama.

outluster, outlustre [ˈaʊtlʌstəʳ] [aut-las-taʳ], va. Exceder en brillantez.

outlying [ˈaʊtlaɪɪŋ] [aut-lain], a. 1. Distante de, lejos de alguna cosa; extrínseco. 2. Exterior, fuera de límites o fronteras, forastero.

outmaneuver [ˌaʊtməˈnuːvəʳ] [aut-ma-nu-vaʳ], va. Mostrarse superior en táctica militar.

outmarch [ˈaʊtmɑːk] [aut-mark], va. Dejar atrás a otro en un paseo, viaje o marcha.

outmatch [ˈaʊtmætʃ] [aut-mach], va. Mostrarse superior a otro en alguna actividad.

outmeasure [ˈaʊtmeʒəʳ] [aut-me-shaʳ], va. Exceder en medida.

outmoded [aʊtˈməʊdɪd] [aut-mou-did], a. Anticuado, pasado de moda.

outmost [ˈaʊtməʊst] [aut-moust], a. Lo más exterior; lo más lejano.

outnumber [aʊtˈnʌmbəʳ] [aut-nam-baʳ], va. Excede en número.

out-of-door(s) [ˈaʊtɒvˈdɔːz] [aut-ov-dors], a. y adv. Al aire libre, afuera.

out-of-print [ˈaʊtɒvˈprɪnt] [aut-ov-print], a. Agotado (el libro, la edición, etc.)

out-of-stock [ˌaʊtɒvˈstɒk] [aut-ov-stok], a. Agotada (la existencia).

out-of-the-way [ˈaʊtɒvðəˈweɪ] [aut-ov-de-uei], a. 1. Lejano, de difícil acceso, apartado, desviado. 2. Fuera de lo ordinario, singular, extraño, particular.

outpace [aʊtˈpeɪs] [aut-peis], vt. Dejar atrás.

outparish [ˈaʊtˈpærɪʃ] [aut-pa-rish], s. Parroquia situada extramuros.

outpart [ˈaʊtpɑːt] [aut-part], s. Parte exterior; extremidad.

outpatient [ˈaʊtˌpeɪʃənt] [aut-pei-shant], s. Enfermo, paciente externo, no residente en un hospital o casa de salud.

outpensioner [ˈaʊtˌpenʃənəʳ] [aut-pen-sho-naʳ], s. Pensionista externo.

outporch [ˈaʊtpɔːtʃ] [aut-porch], s. Pórtico exterior.

outport [ˈaʊtpɔːt] [aut-port], s. 1. Un puerto de mar algo distante de la aduana principal. 2. Punto de exportación; puerto de mar.

outpost [ˈaʊtpəʊst] [aut-poust], s. Avanzada, guardia o puesto avanzado.

outpour [ˈaʊtpɔːʳ] [aut-poʳ], va. Chorrear, verter, despedir un líquido a chorros. -s. Chorreo, efusión libre.

outpouring [ˈaʊtˌpɔːrɪŋ] [aut-po-rin], s. Efusión abundante, chorro; emanación.

output [ˈaʊtpʊt] [aut-put], s. 1. Producción total de algo, cantidad obtenida o producida y pronta para venderse o distribuirse en fecha determinada. 2. Lo que se expele por los pulmones, los riñones o la piel. 3. La fuerza eléctrica de un dínamo; se expresa comúnmente en vatios.

outrage [ˈaʊtreɪdʒ] [aut-reich], va. Ultrajar, ajar o injuriar; maltratar, violentar, violar, abusar atrozmente; cometer rapto.

outrage, s. Ultraje, afrenta, violencia, tropelía; barbarie, tiranía.

outrageous [aʊtˈreɪdʒəs] [aut-rei-chos], a. 1. Violento. 2. Ultrajoso, de porte chocante, ofensivo. 3. Atroz, desenfrenado, desaforado.

outrageously [aʊtˈreɪdʒəslɪ] [aut-rei-chos-li], adv. Violentamente, atrozmente.

outrageousness [aʊtˈreɪdʒəsnɪs] [aut-rei-chos-nes], s. Furia, violencia.

outrank [aʊtˈræŋk] [aut-rank], va. Exceder en rango o posición.

outreach [aʊtˈriːtʃ] [aut-rich], va. Pasar más adelante que otro o tomarle la delantera; pasar más allá de lo que se debe.

outreason [aʊtˈriːʒən] [aut-ri-son], va. Discurrir mejor que otro.

outride [aʊtˈraɪd] [aut-raid], va. Ganar la delantera a caballo, andar a caballo más que otro. -vn. Andar a caballo o en carruaje de una parte a otra.

outrider [aʊdˈraɪdəʳ] [aut-rai-daʳ], s. 1. Volante, el lacayo que va a pie o a caballo delante del coche. 2. Batidor, el soldado o criado que va a caballo delante del coche de su jefe o amo. 3. *(Des.)* Receptor, oficial comisionado por un tribunal para ciertas diligencias.

outrigger [ˈaʊtˌrɪɡəʳ] [aut-ri-gaʳ], s. 1. Horqueta, vuelo, parte de una embarcación o máquina que sobresale y sirve de apoyo o punto de enganche. 2. Batanga, refuerzo de cañas gruesas de bambú, amadrinadas a lo largo de las canoas filipinas y de otras islas del Pacífico. 3. *(Mar.)* Pescante de banda para carenar; puntal de tope. **Outriggers of the tops,** *(Mar.)* pescantes de las cofas.

outright [aʊtˈraɪt] [aut-rait], a. Sincero, franco, sin segunda intención. -adv. 1. Sin reserva ni limitación; completamente, abiertamente. 2. Sin tardanza, al momento, luego, cumplidamente. **To laugh outright,** reír a carcajadas, desternillarse de risa, morirse de risa.

outrival [aʊtˈraɪvəl] [aut-rai-val], *va.* Sobrepujar en excelencia.

outroot [aʊtˈrʊt] [aut-rut], *va.* 1. Arraigar más y mejor que otra cosa. 2. *(Ant.)* Desarraigar, extirpar, arrancar de raíz.

outrun [aʊtˈrʌn] [aut-ran], *va.* 1. Correr más que otro, ganarle a correr. 2. Ganar, exceder. **To outrun the constable,** gastar más de lo que uno tiene, comerse los frutos antes de la cosecha.

outs [aʊtz] [auts], *s. pl.* **To be on the outs,** *(Fam.)* estar de monos.

outsell [ˈaʊtsel] [aut-sel], *va.* Vender a mayor precio o más caro que otro; vender más rápidamente.

outset [ˈaʊtset] [aut-set], *s.* Principio; estreno.

outshine [ˈaʊtʃaɪn] [aut-shain], *va.* 1. Brillar, resplandecer. 2. Exceder en brillantez, dejar deslucido, eclipsar.

outshoot [ˈaʊtʃʌt] [aut-shut], *va.* Ganar a uno a tirar; tirar más lejos que otro.

outside [ˈaʊtˈsaɪd] [aut-said], *a.* 1. Exterior, superficial. 2. Extraño, extrínseco. 3. Extremo, que alcanza al límite. 4. Ajeno, neutral, que no tiene parte ni interés. *-s.* 1. Superficie, parte externa o exterior. **Outside shutter,** contraventana. 2. Extremidad, la parte más remota del centro; lo último, lo extremo. 3. Exterior. 4. Apariencia superficial. 5. Costera, en las resmas de papel. *-adv.* Afuera, fuera. *-prep.* Fuera de, más allá de.

outsider [ˈaʊtˈsaɪdəʳ] [aut-sai-daʳ], *s.* El que está fuera; entremetido, intruso, el que no tiene parte ni interés en alguna cosa.

outsit [ˈaʊtsɪt] [aut-sit], *va.* Estar sentado más tiempo que lo preciso.

outskirt [ˈaʊtskɜːt] [aut-skert], *s.* Parte exterior; borde, linde, orilla; lugar cercano al confín; arrabal de una población; suburbio.

outsleep [ˈaʊtsliːp] [aut-slip], *va.* Dormir más tiempo del que se ha fijado, o más de lo que se debe.

outspeak [ˈaʊtˈspiːk] [aut-spik], *va.* 1. Hablar en alta voz; explicarse claramente. 2. Hablar mejor o más tiempo que otro. *-vn.* Hablar atrevidamente, osar hablar.

outspread [ˈaʊtˈspred] [aut-spred], *va.* Extender, difundir.

outstand [ˈaʊtˈstænd] [aut-stand], *va.* Sostener, resistir. *-vn.* 1. Hacer barriga o comba. 2. Salir fuera de la línea señalada. 3. subsistir en una parte más de lo regular.

outstanding [ˈaʊtˈstændɪŋ] [aut-stan-din], *a.* 1. Salidizo, saliente. 2. Sobresaliente, extraordinario, fuera de lo común. 3. Pendiente, no pagado. **Outstanding account,** cuenta pendiente por pagar.

outstare [ˈaʊtˈsteəʳ] [aut-steaʳ], *va.* Mirar a uno de hito en hito; desconcertar a una persona; mantener una cosa a la cara o en presencia de otro que la niega.

outstay [ˈaʊtsteɪ] [aut-stei], *va.* 1. Permanecer más tiempo que otros. 2. Resistir más que otros.

outstretch [ˈaʊtˈstretʃ] [aut-strech], *va.* Extenderse, alargar.

outstrip [ˈaʊtstrɪp] [aut-strip], *va.* Avanzar más que otro, dejar atrás; rezagar, sobrepujar, aventajar, ganar.

outtalk [ˈaʊtˈtʃɔːk] [aut-tok], *va.* **outtongue** [ˈaʊtˈtɒŋ] [aut-tong], *va.* Aturdir con voces; hablar más que otro.

outvalue [ˈaʊtˈvæljuː] [aut-va-liu], *va.* Subir de precio, exceder en valor.

outvote [aʊtˈvəʊt] [aut-vout], *va.* Ganar a uno en el número de votos.

outwalk [ˈaʊtˈwɔːk] [aut-uok], *va.* Andar más que otro, dejarle atrás; cansar a uno, rendirle a fuerza de andar.

outwall [ˈaʊtˈwɔːl] [aut-uol], *s.* 1. Pared exterior; antemural. 2. Lo exterior, la parte externa; apariencia.

outward [ˈaʊtwəd] [aut-uod], *a.* 1. Exterior, externo, visible. **An outward friendship,** una amistad superficial. 2. Extranjero, extraño. 3. Exterior, extrínseco. 4. *(Teol.)* Carnal, corpóreo. *-adv.* 1. Fuera, afuera, exteriormente. 2. Sobre la superficie, superficialmente. 3. Desde el puerto, hacia otro país, para el extranjero. **A ship bound outward,** embarcación destinada a otro país. *-s. (Poco us.)* La figura exterior.

outwardly [ˈaʊtwədlɪ] [aut-uod-li], *adv.* Exteriormente, extrínsecamente; en apariencia superficialmente.

outwards [ˈaʊtwədz] [aut-uods], *adv.* Hacia fuera, por fuera. V. OUTWARD.

outwatch [ˈaʊtwɒtʃ] [aut-uoch], *va.* Vigilar o velar más que otro.

outwear [ˈaʊtweəʳ] [aut-ueaʳ], *va.* 1. Durar más tiempo que. 2. Gastar, consumir, usar hasta el fin.

outweight [ˈaʊtweɪt] [aut-ueit], *va.* 1. Preponderar; pesar más que. 2. Sobrepujar, exceder en valor, en influjo, en excelencia.

outwit [ˈaʊtwɪt] [aut-uit], *va.* Engañar a uno a fuerza de tretas; sobrepujar con astucia.

outwork [ˈaʊtwɜːk] [aut-uek], *va.* Trabajar más que otro.

outwork, *s. (Fort.)* Obra de una plaza fuerte situada fuera de las murallas; *(ant.)* obra avanzada, obra exterior.

outworn [ˈaʊtwɔːn] [aut-uorn], *a.* Ajado, gastado, desgastado.

oval [ˈəʊvəl] [ou-val], *s.* Óvalo, figura plana muy parecida a la elipse. *-a.* Oval, ovalado.

ovally [ˈəʊvəlɪ] [ou-va-li], *adv.* En figura de óvalo.

ovarian, ovarial [əʊˈveərɪən] [ou-va-rian], *a.* Ovárico, perteneciente o relativo al ovario.

ovariotomy [ˌəʊvərɪˈɒtəmɪ] [ou-va-rio-to-mi], *s.* Ovariotomía, operación quirúrgica para extraer un ovario enfermo.

ovarious [ˈəʊvərɪəs] [ou-va-rios], *a.* Lo que se compone de huevos.

ovary [ˈəʊvərɪ] [ou-va-ri], *s.* 1. Ovario, órgano interno de la fecundación en las hembras; overa de los animales ovíparos. 2. *(Bot.)* Ovario, parte inferior del pistilo que contiene el rudimento de la semilla.

ovate, ovated [ˈəʊveɪt] [ou-veit], *a.* Ovado, formado de manera de huevo, con una extremidad más dilatada que la otra.

ovation [əʊˈveɪʃən] [ou-vei-shon], *s.* 1. Manifestación espontánea del entusiasmo público hacia una persona. 2. Ovación, uno de los triunfos menores entre los romanos.

oven [ˈʌvn] [a-ven], *s.* Horno para cocer pan o pastelería, para templar y secar ciertas sustancias. **Oven-fork,** hurgón. **Oven-full,** hornada. **Oven-peel,** pala de horno.

over [ˈəʊvəʳ] [ou-vaʳ], *prep.* 1. Sobre, encima por encima de; expresa superioridad de lugar; lo contrario de *under,* debajo, bajo de. **Over the gate was an inscription,** había una inscripción encima de la puerta. 2. Expresa superioridad en dignidad, poder estado; sobre. 3. A pesar de. **The bill was passed over the veto,** el proyecto de ley fue aprobado a pesar del veto. 4. Por encima, cubriendo o cubierto de; moviéndose sobre la superficie de; de un lado a otro; al otro lado de. 5. Más de. **Over five hundred dollars,** más de quinientos dólares. 6. Mientras, durante. **The ice kept over the summer,** el hielo se conservó durante todo el verano. 7. Por, en. **To be over head and ears in debt,** estar endeudado hasta los ojos; deber mucho. **Over the way,** al otro lado de la calle. **Over the hills,** más allá, al otro lado de las colinas o collados. **Over in Spain,** allá en España. **All over,** por todas pates, por todos lados. **All the world over,** por todo el mundo. *-adv.* 1. De un lado a otro, al lado opuesto. **She trembles all over,** está toda temblorosa. **We are over for the weekend,** hemos venido a pasar el fin de semana. **It happens all over,** ocurre en todas partes. **He was completely won over,** fue atraído al lado contrario, se pasó al enemigo; quedó persuadido. 2. De ancho, a lo ancho. 3. De arriba abajo, al revés, patas arriba, trastocado. 4. Encima, sobre. 5. Más, demás; completamente, desde el principio al fin. 6. Otra vez. 7. Demasiado, excesivamente. 8. En estado de hecho, al fin. **It is all over,** se acabó. **Over the last few months,** durante los últimos meses. **Over and above,** además de, por demás. **Over against,** enfrente. **Over and**

over, repetidas veces, una y otra vez. **Over again,** otra vez, segunda vez. **That's her all over,** eso es muy típico de ella. **To be over,** cesar, pasar, concluirse, acabar. **To bend over,** inclinarse, doblarse. **To run over,** rebosar, derramarse por encima; recorrer, registrar a la ligera, al paso; pasar por encima (car, train); aplastar. **Over** se une con mucha frecuencia a los verbos para modificar su significación, y se usa también en composición delante de los nombres y verbos.

overabound [ˌəʊvərəˈbaʊnd] [ou-ver-a-baund], *vn.* Superabundar, abundar con exceso.

overabundance [ˈəʊvərəˈbʌndəns] [ou-var-a-ban-dans], *s.* Superabundancia.

overact [ˈəʊvərækt] [ou-ver-akt], *va.* Llevar una cosa al extremo o más allá de lo justo y razonable.

overacting [ˈəʊvəræktɪŋ] [ou-var-ak-tin], *s. f.* Exageración, sobreactuación.

overalls [ˈəʊvərɔːlz] [ou-var-ols], *s. pl.* Zaragüelles, pantalones que se ponen sobre los otros para resguardarlos.

overanxious [ˈəʊvərˈæŋkʃəs] [ou-vank-shos], *a.* Demasiado ansioso.

overarch [ˌəʊvərɑːtʃ] [ou-var-arch], *va.* Cubrir con una bóveda o arco, abovedar; formar una bóveda encima de.

overawe [ˌəʊvərˈɔː] [ou-var-o], *va.* Tener bajo freno; imponer respeto; intimidar, sobrecoger.

overbalance [ˌəʊvəˈbæləns] [ou-va-ba-lans], *va. y vn.* Preponderar; echar más peso a un lado que a otro; llevar ventaja.

overbalance, *s.* Preponderancia, exceso de peso o de valor.

overbear [ˌəʊvəˈbeər] [ou-va-bea'], *va. (pret.* OVERBORE, *pp.* OVERBORNE). 1. Sojuzgar, sujetar, reprimir. 2. Subyugar, oprimir, abrumar, agobiar. *-vn.* Llevar demasiado fruto.

overbearing [ˌəʊvəˈbeərɪŋ] [ou-va-bea-rin], *a.* Ultrajoso, despótico; insufrible; insuperable.

overbid [ˈəʊvəbɪd] [ou-va-bid], *va.* 1. Ofrecer más, pujar. 2. Ofrecer demasiado por algo, pagar excesivamente.

overbidding [ˈəʊvəbɪdɪŋ] [ou-va-bi-din], *s.* Puja.

overbig [ˈəʊvəbɪg] [ou-va-big], *a.* Demasiado grande o grueso.

overblow [ˈəʊvəblaʊ] [ou-va-blau], *vn.* 1. *(Mar.)* Soplar con violencia excesiva. 2. *(Des.)* Pasar la borrasca; calmar el viento. *-va.* 1. Disipar soplando, como el aire disipa las nubes. 2. *(Ant.)* Cubrir con flores; esparcir flores sobre algo.

overblown [ˈəʊvəˈblaʊn] [ou-va-bloun], *a.* Pasado, marchito.

overboard [ˈəʊvəbɔːd] [ou-va-bord], *adv. (Mar.)* Al mar, fuera del barco. **To heave overboard,** *(Mar.)* echar a la mar. **To fall overboard,** caer al agua desde una embarcación.

overboil [ˈəʊvəbɔɪl] [ou-va-boil], *va.* Hervir o cocer demasiado.

overborne [ˈəʊvəbɔːn] [ou-va-born], *a. y pp.* Abatido o sujetado por alguna influencia superior. V. OVERBEAR.

overburden [ˌəʊvəˈbɜːdn] [ou-va-ber-den], *va.* Sobrecargar; oprimir.

overcapitalization [ˌəʊvəˌkæpɪtəlaɪˈzeɪʃən] [ou-va-ka-pi-ta-lai-sei-shon], *s.* 1. Capitalización excesiva. 2. Cálculo exagerado del capital de una corporación.

overcare [ˈəʊvəˈkeər] [ou-va-kea'], *s.* Solicitud, demasiado cuidado.

overcareful [ˈəʊvəkeəfʊl] [ou-va-kea-ful], *a.* Demasiado cuidadoso.

overcarry [ˈəʊvəkæri] [ou-va-ka-ri], *va.* Precipitar a una persona o instigarla a que obre sin precaución o precipitadamente; llevar alguna cosa más allá de lo regular.

overcast [ˈəʊvəkɑːst] [ou-va-kast], *va.* 1. Anublar, oscurecer; entristecer. 2. Cubrir. 3. Hilvanar; coser la orilla de una tela con puntadas envolventes, en forma espiral.

overcautious [ˈəʊvəˈkɔːʃəs] [ou-va-ko-shos], *a.* Demasiado circunspecto o precavido.

overcharge [ˈəʊvətʃɑːdʒ] [ou-va-charch], *va.* 1. Poner alguna cosa a precio muy subido. 2. Sobrecargar (un arma de

fuego). 3. Oprimir. 4. Exagerar. 5. Hacer una acusación exagerada o fantástica contra alguien.

overcheck [ˈəʊvətʃek] [ou-va-chek], *s.* Falsarrienda que pasa por encima de la cabeza del caballo, entre las orejas.

overcloud [ˈəʊvəklaʊd] [ou-va-klaud], *va.* Cubrir de nubes.

overcloy [ˈəʊvəklɔɪ] [ou-va-kloi], *va.* Saciar o llenar demasiado.

overcoat [ˈəʊvəkəʊt] [ou-va-kaut], *s.* Sobretodo, gabán, levitón, abrigo.

overcome [ˌəʊvəˈkʌm] [ou-va-kam], *va.* 1. Vencer, rendir, sujetar, domar, sojuzgar, conquistar, triunfar de. 2. Superar, vencer. *-vn.* Alcanzar superioridad sobre alguno; sobreponerse; hacerse superior a alguna cosa.

overcomer [ˌəʊvəˈkʌmər] [ou-va-ka-ma'], *s.* Vencedor.

overconfidence [ˌəʊvəˈkɒnfɪdəns] [ou-va-kon-fi-dans], *s.* Presunción, demasiada confianza.

overconfident [ˌəʊvəˈkɒnfɪdənt] [ou-va-kon-fi-dent], *a.* Demasiado confiado, confiado fuera de razón.

overcount [ˌəʊvəˈkaʊnt] [ou-va-kaunt], *va.* Tasar o apreciar alguna cosa en más de lo que vale.

overcredulous [ˌəʊvəˈkredjʊləs] [ou-va-kre-diu-los], *a.* Demasiado crédulo.

overcrowd [ˌəʊvəˈkraʊd] [ou-va-kraud], *s.* Excedente (people). *-va.* Apiñar, atestar, llenar demasiado (room).

overcurious [ˌəʊvəˈkɜːriəs] [ou-va-ka-rios], *a.* Demasiado curioso, nimio o delicado.

overdiligent [ˌəʊvəˈdɪlɪdʒənt] [ou-va-di-li-yent], *a.* Diligente en exceso.

overdo [ˌəʊvəˈduː] [ou-va-du], *vn. (pret.* OVERBID, *pp.* OVERDONE). Hacer más de lo necesario. *-va.* 1. Llevar al exceso; fatigar excesivamente, agobiar, abrumar de trabajo. 2. Exagerar. 3. Cocer, asar demasiado; socarrar. 4. *(Poét.)* Eclipsar, dejar deslucido. **To overdo oneself,** atarearse, perjudicarse a puro trabajar. **That meat is overdone,** esa carne está muy asada o cocida. **To overdo things,** cansarse, fatigarse, trabajar en exceso.

overdone [ˌəʊvəˈdʌn] [ou-va-dan], *pp.* 1. Pasado, demasiado asado o cocido. 2. Rendido, cansado.

overdose [ˈəʊvədəʊs] [ou-va-dous], *va.* Dar una dosis excesiva. *-s.* Dosis excesiva o tóxica.

overdraft [ˈəʊvədrɑːft] [ou-va-draft], *s. (Com.)* Giro, libranza en exceso de los fondos o el crédito disponibles; y el acto de hacer ese giro.

overdraw [ˈəʊvəˈdrɔː] [ou-va-dro], *va. (pret.* OVERDREW, *pp.* OVERDRAWN). 1. *(Com.)* Exceder, en un giro, del crédito disponible. 2. Estirar, tirar excesivamente. 3. Exagerar, ya sea en la escritura, narración, dibujo, ademanes o acciones.

overdress [ˌəʊvəˈdres] [ou-va-dres], *va. y vr.* Adornar con demasía, engalanar con exceso.

overdrink [ˌəʊvəˈdrɪŋk] [ou-va-drink], *vn.* Beber con exceso. *To* overdrink oneself, emborracharse.

overdrive [ˈəʊvədraɪv] [ou-va-draiv], *s.* Sobremarcha de un automóvil, capacidad adicional de propulsión. *-va.* Arrear demasiado, fatigar a los animales.

overdue [ˈəʊvədjuː] [ou-va-diu], *a.* Que ha pasado del tiempo debido; (a) no pagado al vencimiento; (b) no llegado al tiempo debido.

overeager [ˌəʊvərˈiːgər] [ou-va-i-ga'], *a.* Demasiado ansioso o celoso.

overearnest [ˌəʊvərˈɜːnəst] [ou-va-er-nest], *a.* Demasiado ardiente.

overeat [ˌəʊvərˈiːt] [ou-var-it], *vn.* Tupirse, hartarse de algún manjar o bebida, comer o beber demasiado.

overemphasize [ˌəʊvərˈemfəsaɪz] [ou-var-em-fa-sais],] *vt.* Sobreenfatizar.

overemployment [ˈəʊvərɪmˈplɔɪmənt] [ou-var-im-ploi-ment], *s.* Superempleo.

overestimate [ˈəʊvərˈestɪmɪt] [ou-var-es-ti-mit], *va.* Estimar en valor excesivo; tener opinión demasiado alta de alguien o algo.

overexcite [ˈəʊvərɪkˈsaɪt] [ou-var-ik-sait], *vt.* Sobreexcitar.

overexpose [ˈəʊvərɪksˈpəʊz] [ou-var-iks-pous], *vt.* Sobreexponer.

overexposure [ˈəʊvərɪksˈpəʊʒəʳ] [ou-var-iks-pou-shaʳ], *s.* Exposición excesiva.

overfatigue [ˈəʊvəˈfætɪg] [ou-va-fa-tig], *va.* Fatigar demasiado.

overfeed [ˈəʊvəˈfiːd] [ou-va-fid], *va.* Dar de comer en demasía.

overfeeding [ˈəʊvəˈfiːndɪŋ] [ou-va-fin-din], *s. f.* Sobrealimentación.

overfierce [ˈəʊvəˈfiːs] [ou-va-firs], *a.* Demasiado atrevido o soberbio; temerario.

overfill [ˈəʊvəfɪl] [ou-va-fil], *va.* Sobrellenar, llenar con exceso.

overflight [ˈəʊvəflaɪt] [ou-va-flait], *s.* Sobrevuelo.

overflourish [ˈəʊvəˈfləʊrɪʃ] [ou-va-flau-rish], *va.* Adornar, florear o engalanar alguna cosa en demasía.

overflow [ˈəʊvəfləʊ] [ou-va-flau], *vn.* Salir de madre; rebosar. -*va.* 1. Sobrellenar, llenar alguna cosa hasta que se vierta. 2. Inundar.

overflow, *s.* Inundación, diluvio; exceso, superabundancia.

overflowing [ˈəʊvəˈfləʊɪŋ] [ou-va-flauin], *s.* Superabundancia, inundación.

overflowingly [ˈəʊvəˈfləʊɪŋlɪ] [ou-va-flauin-li], *adv.* Superabundantemente.

overfly [ˈəʊvəˈflaɪ] [ou-va-flai], *va.* Pasar a vuelo, alcanzar mayores alturas que otra cosa.

overfond [ˌəʊvəˈfɒnd] [ou-va-fond], *a.* El que quiere o gusta excesivamente de alguna cosa.

overforward [ˈəʊvəˈfɔːwəd] [ou-va-for-uad], *a.* Demasiado ardiente o apresurado; muy vivo.

overfraught [ˈəʊvəˈfrɔːt] [ou-va-frot], *a.* Sobrecargado.

overfree [ˈəʊvəˈfriː] [ou-va-fri], *a.* Demasiado libre.

overfreight [ˈəʊvəˈfraɪt] [ou-va-frait], *a.* Sobrecargado.

overfruitful [ˈəʊvəˈfruːtfʊl] [ou-va-frut-ful], *a.* Demasiado rico; prolífico en demasía.

overgild [ˈəʊvəgɪld] [ou-va-guild], *va.* Sobredorar.

overgird [ˈəʊvəgɜːd] [ou-va-guerd], *va.* Atar muy apretado.

overgo [ˈəʊvəgəʊ] [ou-va-gou], *va.* Sobrepujar, exceder, sobresalir.

overgreedy [ˈəʊvəˈgriːdɪ] [ou-va-gri-di], *a.* Codicioso en demasía.

overgrow [ˈəʊvəgrəʊ] [ou-va-grou], *va.* (*pret.* OVERGREW, *pp.* OVERGROWN). 1. Cubrir con plantas o hierba; entapizar; remontarse sobre. 2. Crecer demasiado, hacerse demasiado grande para. *V.* OUTGROW. -*vn.* Crecer o desarrollarse con exceso. Se usa más en el participio pasado, **overgrown: A garden overgrown with weeds,** un jardín cubierto o lleno de mala hierba. **An overgrown child,** un niño que se ha desarrollado demasiado, o muy rápidamente.

overgrowth [ˈəʊvəgrəʊθ] [ou-va-grouz], *s.* 1. Vegetación exuberante. 2. Crecimiento, producción sobre o encima de alguna cosa.

overhang [ˈəʊvəhæŋ] [ou-va-jang], *va.* 1. Sobresalir por encima de alguna cosa; estar pendiente o colgando sobre ella; salir algo fuera del nivel de un edificio. 2. Mirar a, dar a, caer *a.* **This window overhangs the street,** esta ventana da a la calle. 3. Ser inminente, amenazar. 4. Poner demasiadas colgaduras. **The wall were overhung,** las paredes tenían demasiadas colgaduras.

overhanging [ˈəʊvəˈhæŋɪŋ] [ou-va-jan-guing], *a.* Sobresaliente.

overhard [ˈəʊvəhɑːd] [ou-va-jard], *a.* Duro en demasía.

overharden [ˈəʊvəˈhɑːdn] [ou-va-jar-den], *va.* Endurecer excesivamente.

overhasty [ˌəʊvəˈheɪstɪ] [ou-va-jeis-ti], *a.* Demasiado apresurado.

overhaul [ˈəʊvəhɔːl] [ou-va-jol], *va.* 1. Desparramar alguna cosa; registrar, examinar; volver las cosas de arriba abajo. 2. (*Mar.*) Alcanzar, o ir ganando un barco en la persecución de otro. 3. (*Mar.*) Recorrer, registrar, tiramollar. **To overhaul the tacks and sheets,** (*Mar.*) tiramollar las amuras y escotas. **To overhaul accounts,** reexaminar o revisar las cuentas.

overhead [ˌəʊvəˈhed] [ou-va-jed], *adv.* Encima, arriba, en lo alto, sobre la cabeza. **Overhead expense,** gastos generales (de un negocio, etc.).

overhear [ˌəʊvəˈhɪəʳ] [ou-va-jiaʳ], *va.* Oír por casualidad y de paso; escuchar palabras no destinadas a quien las oye.

overheat [ˌəʊvəˈhiːt] [ou-va-jit], *va.* Acalorar.

overhours [ˈəʊvəˈaʊəz] [ou-va-auars], *s. pl.* 1. Horas extraordinarias, horas de trabajo además de las de reglamento. 2. Horas de trabajo demasiado largas.

overindulge [ˌəʊvərˈɪndʌldʒ] [ou-var-in-daldch], *va.* 1. Mimar demasiado. 2. Darse uno demasiado gusto. 3. Excederse (drinks, food).

overjoy [ˌəʊvəˈdʒɔɪ] [ou-va-yoi], *va.* Arrebatar o enajenar de alegría, alegrar demasiado.

overjoyed [ˌəʊvəˈdʒɔɪd] [ou-va-yoid], *a.* Lleno de alegría.

overkind [ˈəʊvəkɪnd] [ou-va-kind], *a.* Excesivamente cariñoso o bondadoso.

overland [ˈəʊvəlænd] [ou-va-land], *a. y adv.* Que pasa o se ejecuta por tierra. **Overland route,** ruta, camino, rumbo, por tierra.

overlap [ˈəʊvəlæp] [ou-va-lap], *va.* 1. Tapar o cubrir en parte, extenderse sobre. 2. Hacer doblar o plegarse sobre. -*vn.* Extenderse de manera que descanse en parte sobre lo que está inmediato.

overlap, *s.* Estado o condición de extenderse sobre, de cubrir en parte; también la parte que cubre o descansa sobre lo que está inmediato.

overlarge [ˈəʊvəlɑːdʒ] [ou-va-larch], *a.* Demasiado grande.

overlay [ˈəʊvəleɪ] [ou-va-lei], *va.* 1. Echar encima, colocar sobre, cubrir de. 2. Calzar, aplicar pedacitos de papel llamados **overlays** al tímpano para corregir un hueco en el cuadro. 3. Anublar, oscurecer. 4. Echar un puente sobre. **To overlay ivory with gold,** incrustar, cubrir el marfil con oro.

overlaying [ˈəʊvəleɪɪŋ] [ou-va-lein], *s.* Capa o cubierta superficial de una sustancia, colocada de modo que cubra enteramente otro cuerpo de diferente material.

overleap [ˈəʊvəliːp] [ou-va-lip], *va.* Pasar de un salto de una parte a otra.

overlie [ˈəʊvəˈlaɪ] [ou-va-lai], *va.* Descansar o extenderse encima de o sobre.

overlive [ˈəʊvəˈlɪv] [ou-va-liv], *va.* Sobrevivir. -*va.* Vivir demasiado.

overload [ˈəʊvələʊd] [ou-va-loud], *s.* Sobrecarga, recargo. -*va.* Sobrecargar.

overlong [ˌəʊvəˈlɒŋ] [ou-va-long], *a.* Demasiado largo.

overlook [ˈəʊvəˈlʊk] [ou-va-luk], *va.* 1. Mirar desde lo alto; tener vista a, dominar con la vista una extensión de terreno. 2. Examinar una cosa. 3. Rever, volver a ver o examinar con cuidado; repasar. 4. Celar, dirigir, tener la dirección de. 5. Pasar por alto, disimular, tolerar; juzgar con indulgencia, hacer la vista gorda. 6. Descuidar, no hacer caso; desdeñar, mirar con desdén, menospreciar. 7. Mirar, dar, caer a. **The window overlooks the river,** la ventana mira al río. **To overlook a slight,** perdonar un desaire, pasarlo por alto. **To overlook the construction of a building,** celar, dirigir la construcción de un edificio.

overlook, *s.* 1. Mirada desde lo alto. 2. Altura, punto de vista elevado, como una montaña. 3. Planta trepadora de las leguminosas, con tres hojuelas.

overlooker [ˈəʊvəˈlʊkəʳ] [ou-va-lu-kaʳ], *s.* Sobrestante, celador, inspector, veedor.

overlying [ˈəʊvəlaɪɪŋ] [ou-va-lain], *a.* Que está colocado encima, que yace sobre algo.

overmaster [ˈəʊvəˈmɑːstəʳ] [ou-va-mas-taʳ], *va.* Señorear, dominar o gobernar con mucho imperio y autoridad.

overmatch [ˈəʊvəmɑːtʃ] [ou-va-mach], *va.* Sobrepujar, vencer o superar a otro.

overmeasure [ˈəʊvəˈmeʒəʳ] [ou-va-mea-shaʳ], *s.* Colmo, la porción que sobresale de la medida justa.

overmeasure, *va.* Dar demasiada importancia, estimación o valor a alguna cosa.

overmuch [ˈəʊvəˈmʌtʃ] [ou-va-mach], *a.* y *adv.* Demasiado, más de lo suficiente; en demasía.

overnight [ˈəʊvəˈnaɪt] [ou-va-nait], *a.* Que permanece en la noche. **Overnight guests,** invitados que se quedan a dormir.

overofficious [ˈəʊvərɒˈfɪʃəs] [ou-var-o-fi-shos], *a.* Demasiado entremetido, muy oficioso.

overpass [ˈəʊvəpɑːs] [ou-va-pas], *s.* Paso superior (roads).

overpay [ˈəʊvəpeɪ] [ou-va-pei], *va.* Pagar o premiar demasiado.

overpeople [ˈəʊvəˈpiːpl] [ou-va-pi-pol], *va.* Atestar de habitantes; poblar demasiado.

overpersuade [ˈəʊvəpəˈsweɪd] [ou-va-per-sueid], *va.* Persuadir a alguno a despecho de sus opiniones e inclinaciones.

overplus [ˈəʊvəpləs] [ou-va-plas], *s.* Sobrante.

overply [ˈəʊvəplaɪ] [ou-va-plai], *va.* Cargar de trabajo.

overpopulated [ˈəʊvəˈpɒpjʊleɪtɪd] [ou-va-po-piu-lei-tid], *a.* Superpoblado.

overpower [ˌəʊvəˈpaʊəʳ] [ou-va-pauaʳ], *va.* Predominar, subyugar, vencer, superar, sobrepujar; supeditar, oprimir, abrumar; colmar.

overpoweringly [ˈəʊvəˈpaʊərɪŋlɪ] [ou-va-paua-rin-li], *adv.* Con fuerza superior; de una manera incontrastable.

overpraise [ˈəʊvəpreɪz] [ou-va-preis], *vt.* Elogiar en exceso.

overpress [ˈəʊvəpres] [ou-va-pres], *va.* Oprimir, abrumar.

overprize [ˈəʊvəpraɪz] [ou-va-prais], *va.* Sobrestimar.

overproduce [ˌəʊvəprəˈdjuːs] [ou-va-pro-dius], *vt.* Producir demasiado.

overproduction [ˈəʊvəprəˈdʌkʃən] [ou-va-pro-dak-shon], *s.* Sobreproducción, superproducción.

overpromptness [ˈəʊvəˈprɒmptnɪs] [ou-va-prompt-nes], *s.* Precipitación.

overprotect [ˌəʊvəprəˈtekt] [ou-va-pro-tekt], *vt.* Proteger en exceso.

overrake [ˈəʊvəreɪk] [ou-va-reik], *va. (Mar.)* Barrer de popa a proa un buque al ancla, como lo hacen las olas.

overrate [ˈəʊvəreɪt] [ou-va-reit], *va.* Encarecer, apreciar o valuar alguna cosa en más de lo que vale.

overreach [ˌəʊvəˈriːt] [ou-va-rich], *va.* 1. Estafar, trampear, engañar astutamente. 2. Extender, alargar demasiado una de las extremidades o el cuerpo entero). 3. Ir, pasar, extenderse más allá. 4. Extenderse sobre, de manera que cubra. -*vn.* 1. Golpear con el pie de atrás contra el pie delantero; dícese de las caballerías. 2. *(Mar.)* Dar una virada más allá de lo necesario.

overreach, *s.* Coz, rozadura que ha recibido una caballería sobre el casco.

overreckon [ˈəʊvəˈrekn] [ou-va-re-kon], *va.* Calcular en más de la cuenta, hacer cálculos exagerados.

override [ˌəʊvəˈraɪd] [ou-va-raid], *va.* 1. Pasar por encima del cuerpo de; vencer. 2. Poner a un lado, rechazar arbitrariamente; anular. 3. Fatigar un caballo con exceso.

overripe [ˌəʊvəˈraɪp] [ou-va-raip], *a.* Demasiado maduro.

overripen [ˈəʊvəˈrɪpn] [ou-va-ri-pen], *va.* Madurar demasiado.

overroast [ˈəʊvərəʊst] [ou-va-roust], *va.* Tostar, asar demasiado.

overrule [ˌəʊvəˈruːl] [ou-va-rul], *va.* 1. Predominar, dominar; ganar, alcanzar superioridad sobre alguno. 2. *(For.)* Denegar, no admitir un alegato. 3. Gobernar, dirigir, regir, **There is an overruling Providence,** hay una Providencia que todo lo dirige.

overruler [ˌəʊvəˈruːləʳ] [ou-va-ru-laʳ], *s.* Director, gobernador.

overrun [ˈəʊvərʌn] [ou-va-ran], *va.* 1. Invadir, hacer correrías en algún territorio. 2. Adelantarse, tomar o ganar la delantera; ir o pasar más allá de los límites debidos, de cualquier clase que sean. 3. Cubrir enteramente alguna cosa. 4. Infestar, plagarse de, llenarse de. 5. Retocar o repasar los caracteres con que se imprime. 6. *V.* TO OUTRUN. 7. *(Des.)*

Injuriar alguna cosa pisándola. -*vn.* Rebosar; inundar; estar muy abundante.

overscrupulous [ˈəʊvəˈskruːpjʊləs] [ou-va-skru-piu-los], *a.* Demasiado escrupuloso.

overseas [ˈəʊvəˈsiːz] [ou-va-sis], *a.* De ultramar. -*adv.* Allende el mar.

oversee [ˈəʊvəˈsiː] [ou-va-si], *va. (pret.* OVERSAW, *pp.* OVERSEEN). 1. Inspeccionar, revistar, vigilar, celar, tener la inspección o superintendencia de alguna cosa. 2. Pasar, omitir, no reparar en alguna cosa, pasarla por alto. 3. Ver demasiado bien o claramente.

overseen [ˈəʊvəˈsiːn] [ou-va-sin], *pp.* Engañado, cegado, equivocado.

overseer [ˈəʊvəsɪəʳ] [ou-va-siaʳ], *s.* Sobrestante, superintendente, celador; director. *(Amer.)* Mayoral, administrador.

overseership [ˈəʊvəsɪəʃɪp] [ou-va-sia-ship], *s.* Cargo, oficio de superintendente.

overset [ˈəʊvəˈset] [ou-va-set], *va.* 1. Volcar, derribar, torcer ot trastornar alguna cosa hacia un lado de modo que caiga. 2. Trastornar; invertir el orden de alguna cosa; subvertir, arruinar. -*vn.* Volcarse, caerse.

overshade [ˈəʊvəˈʃeɪd] [ou-va-sheid], *va.* Oscurecer, echar sombra sobre algo; hacer sombra desde lo alto.

overshadow [ˌəʊvəˈʃædəʊ] [ou-va-sha-dou], *va.* 1. Asombrar, hacer sombra una cosa a otra. 2. Eclipsar, hacer insignificante por comparación. 3. *(Ant.)* Abrigar, amparar, patrocinar, proteger.

overshoe [ˈəʊvəʃuː] [ou-va-shu], *s.* Chanclo, calzado (shoe) que se lleva sobre otro.

overshoot [ˈəʊvəˈʃuːt] [ou-va-shut], *va. (pp.* y *pret.* OVERSHOT). 1. Tirar más allá del blanco. 2. Ir más allá de, exceder. 3. Pasar rápidamente por encima. -*vn.* Pasar de raya, llegar más allá del término que estaba señalado.

overshot [ˈəʊvəˈʃʌt] [ou-va-shat], *pa.* 1. Excedido, de cualquier manera que sea. 2. Que se hace pasando por encima de algo. **Overshot wheel,** rueda hidráulica de arcaduces o artesas.

oversight [ˈəʊvəsaɪt] [ou-va-sait], *s.* 1. Yerro, equivocación, inadvertencia, olvido, omisión. 2. Vigilancia, inspección; dirección atenta; superintendencia.

oversized [ˌəʊvəˈsaɪzd] [ou-va-saisd], *a.* Inmenso, descomunal, demasiado grande.

overskip [ˈəʊvəskɪp] [ou-va-skip], *va.* 1. Pasar saltando. 2. Pasar alguna cosa sin reparar; omitir, saltar; evitar.

overskirt [ˈəʊvəskəːt] [ou-va-skert], *s.* sobrefalda, saya que se lleva sobre la falda del vestido (de mujer).

oversleep [ˈəʊvəsliːp] [ou-va-slip], *vn.* Dormir demasiado.

oversoon [ˈəʊvəsuːn] [ou-va-sun], *adv.* Demasiado pronto.

overspent [ˈəʊvəˈspent] [ou-va-spent], *a.* Agotado, apurado.

overspread [ˈəʊvəˈspred] [ou-va-spred], *va.* 1. Desparramar, extender alguna cosa por el suelo, cubrir. 2. Estar echado sobre.

overstate [ˈəʊvəˈsteɪt] [ou-va-steit], *vn.* Exagerar, referir o relatar usando términos demasiado fuertes.

overstatement [ˈəʊvəˈsteɪtmənt] [ou-va-steit-ment], *s.* Exageración en lo dicho, declaración exagerada.

overstep [ˈəʊvəˈstep] [ou-va-step], *va.* Propasar, pasar de los límites, ir más allá; exceder.

overstock [ˈəʊvəˈstɒk] [ou-va-stok], *va.* Atestar, colmar, llenar alguna cosa con exceso.

overstore [ˈəʊvəˈstɔːʳ] [ou-va-stoʳ], *va.* Surtir o proveer en demasía.

overstrain [ˈəʊvəˈstreɪn] [ou-va-strein], *vn.* Esforzarse demasiado, hacer grandes esfuerzos. -*va.* Apretar o estirar demasiado.

overstretch [ˈəʊvəˈstretʃ] [ou-va-strech], *va.* Estirar demasiado.

overstrew, overstrow [ˈəʊvəˈstruː] [ou-va-stru], *va.* Esparcir, derramar sobre.

overstrung [ˈəʊvəˈstrʌŋ] [ou-va-strang], *a.* 1. Templado con exceso; demasiado excitable, muy sensible. 2. Que tiene dos juegos de cuerdas cruzadas oblicuamente.

overstuff [ˈəʊvəˈstʌf] [ou-va-staf], *va.* 1. Llenar en exceso. 2. Tapizar completamente (furniture).

oversway [ˈəʊvəzweɪ] [ou-vas-uei], *va.* Predominar, dominar, mandar con tiranía.

overswell [ˈəʊvəzwel] [ou-vas-uel], *va.* Hincharse por arriba.

overt [əˈvɜːt] [ou-vert], *a.* Abierto, público, manifiesto, claro, patente.

overtly [əˈvɜːtlɪ] [ou-vert-li], *adv.* Abiertamente, manifiestamente.

overtake [əʊvəˈteɪk] [ou-va-teik], *va.* 1. Alcanzar, seguir a alguna persona o cosa hasta encontrarla. 2. Coger o pillar.

overtaking [ˌəʊvəˈteɪkɪŋ] [ou-vas-tei-kin], *s. m.* Adelantamiento.

overtask [ˈəʊvəˈtæsk] [ou-va-task], *va.* Atarear demasiado.

overtax [ˈəʊvəˈtæks] [ou-va-taks], *va.* Oprimir con tributos.

overthrow [ˈəʊvəθrəʊ] [ou-va-zrou], *va.* 1. Trastornar, volver alguna cosa de arriba abajo. 2. Demoler, derribar, echar por tierra. 3. Vencer, ganar la victoria. 4. Destruir, aniquilar.

overthrow, *s.* 1. Trastornamiento, transtornadura. 2. Trastorno; ruina, destrucción, derrota. 3. Degradación.

overthrower [ˈəʊvəˈθrəʊəʳ] [ou-va-zrouaʳ], *s.* Trastornador; derrocador.

overthwart [ˈəʊvəθwɔːt] [ou-vaz-uort], *a. (Ant.)* 1. Fronterizo, opuesto. 2. Contrario, adverso. 3. Terco, porfiado. 4. Lo que cruza otra cosa. *-prep.* Por encima.

overtime [ˈəʊvətaɪm] [ou-va-taim], *s.* Horas extras. *-adv.* Fuera del tiempo estipulado.

overtire [əʊvəˈtaɪəʳ] [ou-va-taiaʳ], *va.* Fatigar demasiado.

overtired [əʊvəˈtaɪəd] [ou-va-taied], *a.* Muy fatigado, muerto de cansancio.

overtop [ˈəʊvəˈtɒp] [ou-va-top], *va.* 1. Elevarse sobre otra cosa, estar más elevado, dominar, mirar desde lo alto. 2. Sobresalir, exceder.

overtrade [əʊvəˈtreɪd] [ou-va-treid], *vn.* Hacer un comercio demasiado grande; emprender especulaciones comerciales demasiado arriesgadas.

overtrip [ˈəʊvətrɪp] [ou-va-trip], *va.* Pasar ligeramente por encima de alguna cosa.

overture [ˈəʊvətjʊəʳ] [ou-va-tiuaʳ], *s.* 1. Insinuación, declaración, proposición, propuesta. 2. *(Mús.)* La introducción musical de una ópera u oratorio. 3. Revelación, descubrimiento. 4. *(Des.)* Abertura, hendedura.

overturn [əʊvəˈtɜːn] [ou-va-tern], *va.* 1. Subvertir, trastornar; trastrocar, volver al revés, mudar de arriba abajo. 2. Sobrepujar, vencer.

overvalue [əʊvəˈvæljuː] [ou-va-va-liu], *va.* 1. Apreciar o estimar demasiado alguna cosa. 2. Encarecer, ponderar o exagerar el valor de una cosa.

overview [ˈəʊvəvjuː] [ou-ya-viu], *s. f.* Visión de conjunto.

overviolent [ˌəʊvəˈvaɪələnt] [ou-vaio-lent], *a.* Muy violento.

overwatch [əʊvəˈwɔːtʃ] [ou-va-uoch], *vn.* Cansar a fuerza de vigilias.

overweak [ˌəʊvəˈwiːk] [ou-va-uik], *a.* Demasiado endeble.

overweary [əʊvəˈweərɪ] [ou-va-ueari], *va.* Domar por la fatiga.

overweening [əʊvəˈwiːnɪŋ] [ou-va-ui-nin], *s.* Presunción. *-a.* Presuntuoso, arrogante, altanero.

overweeningly [əʊvəˈwiːnɪŋlɪ] [ou-va-ui-nin-li], *adv.* Presuntuosamente, con arrogancia.

overweight [əʊvəˈweɪt] [ou-va-ueit], *s.* 1. Preponderancia, exceso en el peso. 2. Superioridad, crédito.

overwhelm [əʊvəˈwelm] [ou-va-uelm], *va.* Abrumar, oprimir, abatir; sumergir; soterrar.

overwhelming [əʊvəˈwelmɪŋ] [ou-va-uel-min], *a. y a. part.* Abrumador, opresor; irresistible, dominante.

overwhelmingly [əʊvəˈwelmɪŋlɪ] [ou-va-uel-min-li], *adv.* Opresivamente; irresistiblemente.

overwise [əʊvəˈwaɪz] [ou-va-uais], *a.* Sabihondo, sabio con afectación. *-s. (Fam.)* Un sábelo todo, un pedante.

overwiseness [ˌəʊvəˈʃwaɪznɪz] [ou-va-uais-nes], *s.* Sabiduría afectada; pedantería.

overwork [əʊvəˈwɜːk] [ou-va-uek], *va.* 1. Hacer trabajar con exceso; fatigar, cansar con el trabajo; exigir esfuerzo superior a las facultades de uno. 2. Elaborar la superficie de (una cosa). *-vn.* Trabajar más allá de lo que permiten las fuerzas.

overwork, *s.* 1. Trabajo excesivo. 2. Trabajo hecho a dehora, fuera de las horas reglamentarias.

overworn [əʊvəˈwɜːn] [ou-va-uorn], *a.* Gastado por el trabajo; abrumado de fatiga.

overwrite [əʊvəˈraɪt] [ou-va-rait], *vt.* 1. Exagerar, cargar en efectos literarios. 2. Sobreescribir (Comput).

overwrought [əʊvəˈrɔːt] [ou-va-rot], *a.* 1. Excitado, estimulado, conmovido, excesivamente. 2. Elaborado, labrado por todas partes, como con calados y encajes. 3. Demasiadamente trabajado, demasiado esmerado. 4. Cansado, fatigado por el exceso de trabajo.

overzealous [ˈəʊvəˈzeləs] [ou-va-si-los], *a.* Demasiado celoso o ardiente.

ovicular [ˈəʊvɪkjʊləʳ] [ou-vi-kiu-laʳ], *a.* Ovicular, oval, perteneciente a un huevo.

oviduct [ˈəʊvɪdʌkt] [ou-vi-dakt], *s.* Oviducto, el conducto por el cual pasa el huevo fecundado del ovario al útero, o al exterior de un animal.

oviferous [ˈəʊvəferəs] [ou-vi-fe-ros], **ovigerous** [ˈeəvɪdʒərəs] [ou-vi-ye-ros], *a.* Ovífero, que contiene huevos.

oviform [ˈəʊvɪfɔːm] [ou-vi-form], *a.* Aovado, que tiene forma o figura de huevo.

ovine [ˈəʊvaɪn] [ou-vain], *a.* Lanar, ovejuno, cabruno, relativo a las ovejas o a las cabras.

oviparous [əˈvɪpərəs] [ou-vi-pe-ros], *a.* Ovíparo, dícese de los animales cuyas hembras ponen huevos.

oviposit [ˈəʊvɪpɒzɪt] [ou-vi-po-sit], *va.* Poner huevos, particularmente entre ciertos insectos por medio del órgano que termina el abdomen de las hembras y forma un taladro o un aguijón.

ovoid, ovoidal [ˈəʊvɔɪd] [ou-void], *a.* Ovoide, aovado, que tiene la figura o forma de un huevo.

ovolo [ˈəʊvələʊ] [ou-vo-lou], *s. (Arq.)* Ovol, equino, cuarto bocel.

ovulate [ˈɒvjɒleɪt] [o-viu-leit], *vi.* Ovular.

ovulation [ˌɒvjʊˈleɪʃən] [ou-viu-lei-shon], *s. f.* Ovulación.

ovule [ˈɒvjuːl] [ou-viul], *s.* Óvulo, germen contenido en el ovario antes de la fecundación; en botánica, rudimento de la semilla.

ovum [ˈəʊvəm] [ou-vom], *s. (pl.* OVA). 1. Celdilla con núcleo formada en el ovario de la hembra; huevo en su más amplio sentido. 2. *(Arq.)* Óvolo, equino, ornamento en forma de huevo.

owe [əʊ] [ou], *va. (pa.* OWING, *pp.* OWED; antiguamente OWN u OUGHT). 1. Deber, estar endeudado, tener deudas. 2. Deber, estar obligado; ser debido a; ser causado por. **I owe him many favors,** le debo muchos favores. **To be owing,** ser debido, que se debe; resultado, que es efecto de; imputable, atribuible a; por causa de, por. **To pay what is owing,** pagar lo que es debido. **To what is it owing?** ¿A qué se le debe atribuir o imputar?

owl [aʊl] [oul], *s. (Orn.)* Lechuza, búho, mochuelo, ave nocturna de rapiña de la familia de las estrígidas. **Barn-owl,** lechuza. **Screech-owl,** buho, zumaya, autillo. **Long-eared owl,** mochuelo común. **Snowy owl,** harfango.

owl, *vn. (For.)* Hacer contrabando.

owlet [ˈaʊlɪt] [au-lit], *s.* 1. Buho, lechuza pequeña. 2. Hijuelo del buho. 3. V. **Owlet-moth. Owlet-moth,** insecto de varias clases de mariposas nocturnas.

owl-light [ˈaʊllaɪt] [aul-lait], *s.* Crepúsculo.

owlish [ˈaʊlɪʃ] [au-lish], **owl-like** [ˈaʊlˈlaɪk] [aul-laik], *a.* Semejante a la lechuza.

own [əʊn] [oun], *a.* 1. Propio, lo que pertenece a uno propio, particular. 2. Del grado más cercano, real. **He wrote it with his own hand,** lo escribió de su propio puño. **To be one's own man,** ser dueño de sí mismo, no depender de nadie. **My own-self,** yo mismo. **Own cousin,** primo hermano, prima hermana. **My own brother,** mi propio hermano. **This is his own fault,** es culpa suya. **Own** sirve para dar énfasis y acompaña a los adjetivos y pronombres posesivos. **I do not want your hat, I want my own,** no quiero su sombrero de Ud., sino el mío propio. **He has nothing of his own,** no tiene nada que pueda llamar suyo. **He came to his own, and his own received him not,** lo suyo vino y los suyos no le recibieron. **On one's own,** solo, a solas. **Each to his own,** cada cual a lo suyo. **He owned his mistake,** reconoció su error.

own, *va.* 1. Poseer, ser dueño legítimo de alguna cosa. **Who owns this house?** ¿De quién es esta casa? 2. Reconocer, dar por suyo o confesar que una cosa es suya o le pertenece. **He owned the child as his,** reconoció al niño como suyo. 3. Confesar, aseverar.

owner [ˈəʊnəʳ] [ou-naʳ], *s.* Dueño, poseedor, propietario, el que tiene el título legal. **Owner of a ship,** naviero.

ownership [ˈəʊnəʃɪp] [ou-na-ship], *s.* Dominio, propiedad, posesión legítima.

owning [ˈəʊnɪŋ] [ou-nin], *s.* Confesión, reconocimiento.

ox [ɒks] [oks], *s.* Buey. -*pl.* OXEN. Bueyes. **Ox-eye,** *(Mar. y Bot.)* Ojo de buey. *(Orn.)* Pajarito. **Ox-bow,** yugo de buey, **Ox-cheek,** quijada de buey. **Ox-eyed,** que tiene ojos grandes, como los del buey. **Ox-fly,** tábano. **Ox-goad,** aguijada de bueyes. **Ox-house, ox-stall,** boyera, boyeriza, establo para los bueyes. **Ox-like,** semejante al buey. **Ox-tongue,** *(Bot.)* buglosa.

oxalate [ɒkˈsæleɪt] [ok-sa-leit], *s. (Quím.)* Oxalato, sal formada de ácido oxálico con alguna base.

oxalic [ɒkˈsælɪk] [ok-sa-lik], *a.* Oxálico.

oxen, *s. pl.* de OX.

oxidate [ˈɒksɪdeɪt] [ok-si-deit], *va.* V. OXIDIZE.

oxidation [ˌɒksɪˈdeɪʃən] [ok-si-dei-shon], *s.* Oxidación, acción y efecto de oxidar u oxidarse.

oxide [ˈɒksaɪd] [ok-said], *s. (Quím.)* Óxido.

oxidize [ˈɒksɪdaɪz] [ok-si-dais], *va.* Oxidar.

oxidizement [ˈɒksɪdaɪzmənt] [ok-si-dais-ment], *s.* Oxidación.

oxlip [ˈɒkslɪp] [oks-lip], *s. (Bot.)* Prímula descollada.

oxychloride [ˈɒksɪˌklɔːraɪd] [ok-si-klo-raid], *s.* Oxicloruro.

oxygen [ˈɒksɪdʒən] [ok-si-yen], *s. (Quím.)* Oxígeno.

oxygenate [ɒkˈsɪdʒəneɪt] [ok-si-ye-neit], *va.* Oxigenar, combinar con el oxígeno, oxidar.

oxygenation [ˌɒksɪdʒəˈneɪʃən] [ok-si-ye-nei-shon], *s.* Oxigenación, oxidación, el acto o procedimiento de oxigenar.

oxygenic, oxygenous [ɒkˈsɪdʒənɪk] [ok-si-ye-nik], *a.* De oxígeno, perteneciente al oxígeno o que lo contiene.

oxygenize [ɒkˈsɪdʒənaɪz] [ok-si-ye-nais], *va.* Oxigenar.

oxygen tent [ˈɒksɪdʒənˌtent] [ok-si-yen-tent], *s.* Tienda de oxígeno.

oxygon [ˈɒksɪɡən] [ok-si-gon], *s. (Geom.)* Oxigonio, acutángulo.

oxygonal [ɒkˈsɪɡənl] [ok-si-go-nal], **oxygonial** [ɒkˈsɪɡənɪəl] [ok-si-go-nial], *a.* Que pertenece o se refiere al oxigonio.

oxymel [ˈɒksɪmel] [ok-si-mel], *s.* Ojimiel, composición que se hace de miel y vinagre.

oxytone [ˈɒksɪtəʊn] [ok-si-toun], *a.* 1. Que tiene acento agudo en la última sílaba. 2. Que hace que una palabra precedente tome el acento agudo. -*s.* Palabra que lleva dicho acento, vocablo agudo.

oyer [ˈɔɪjəʳ] [ou-yaʳ], *s. (For.)* Audición, vista de un pleito o una causa. Audiencia o tribunal en donde se oyen y determinan causas. **Oyer and terminer,** tribunal de más alta jurisdicción criminal.

oyes, oyez [ˈəʊjez] [ou-yes], *inter. (For.)* Oíd, escuchad; voz de los ujieres de los tribunales para llamar la atención.

oylet, *s.* V. EYELET.

oyster [ˈɔɪstəʳ] [ois-taʳ], *s.* Ostra, marisco que se cría en una concha bivalva, muy estimado como alimento. **Pickled oysters,** ostras escabechadas. **Oyster-shells,** conchas de ostra. **Oyster-bed,** banco de ostras. **Oyster-farm,** espacio en el fondo de una bahía donde se cultivan las ostras. **Oyster-cocktail,** cóctel de ostras. **Oyster-fishery,** pesquería de ostras. **Oyster-plant,** salsifí. **Oyster-green,** ulva verde, alga marina.

oyster-woman [ˈɔɪstəˌwʊmən] [ois-ta-uo-man], *sf.* Ostrera, la mujer que vende ostras.

ozæna [əʊˈziːnə] [ou-si-na], *s.* Ocena, úlcera fétida en la nariz.

ozone [ˈəʊzəʊn] [ou-soun], *s. (Quím.)* Ozono.

ozonic, ozonous [əʊˈzəʊnɪk] [ou-sou-nik] [ˈəʊzəʊnəs] [ou-sou-nos], *a.* Ozónico, perteneciente al ozono, o que lo contiene.

ozonosphere [əʊˈzəʊnəsfɪəʳ] [ou-sou-nos-fiaʳ], *s. f.* Ozonosfera.

P

p [piː] [pi]. Décimasexta letra del alfabeto inglés, que se pronuncia en inglés como en español. Es muda, cuando precede a la *s* y a la *t* al principio de una palabra, como en *psalm, ptisan.* Cuando la *p* está antes de la *h* pierde su sonido, y se pronuncian las dos letras como *f,* según sucedía antiguamente en español. *P., p.,* es abreviatura de *page,* página.

pa [pɑː] [pa], *s.* Papá (dad).

pabular [ˈpæbjʊləʳ] [pa-biu-laʳ], *a.* Alimentoso, que alimenta o puede alimentar; nutritivo, que sustenta.

pabulum [ˈpæbjʊləm] [pa-biu-lom], *s.* 1. Pábulo, alimento, pasto para la subsistencia o conservación. 2. Pábulo, sustento, mantenimiento, hablando de las cosas inmateriales.

paca [ˈpækə] [pa-ka], *s.* Paca, mamífero roedor de América.

pacated [ˈpækeɪtɪd] [pa-kei-tid], *a.* Pacato, pacífico, tranquilo.

pace [peɪs] [peis], *s.* 1. Paso. 2. Paso, modo de andar; grado de celeridad. 3. Paso, la diligencia que se usa en la prosecución de algún negocio. 4. Paso, el movimiento regular con que caminan las caballerías. 5. Portante, paso especial del caballo, en el cual mueve a un tiempo la mano y el pie del mismo lado. 6. Medida de tres o 3.3 pies. 7. *(Arq.)* Estrado, tablado, parte del suelo algo elevado sobre el nivel general. **To keep pace with,** andar al mismo paso que otro; ir, seguir a un paso igual, llevar el mismo paso.

pace, *vn.* 1. Pasear, andar poco a poco, a pasos regulares. 2. Ir a paso de andadura las caballerías; andar el caballo alzando a la vez el pie y la mano del mismo lado. -*va.* 1. Andar a pasos medidos. 2. Medir a pasos. 3. Enseñar a andar.

pacemaker [ˈpeɪsˌmeɪkəʳ] [peis-mei-kaʳ], *s.* El que establece el paso o la marcha (en las carreras).

pacer [ˈpeɪsəʳ] [pei-saʳ], *s.* 1. El que mide a pasos. 2. Caballo de paso de andadura; caballería que va alzando a la vez la mano y el pie del mismo lado.

pacha [ˈpɑːʃə] [pa-sha], *s.* V. PASHA.

pachyderm [ˈpækɪdɜːm] [pa-ki-derm], *a.* Paquidermo, de piel gruesa y dura.

pachydermatous, pachydermous [ˌpækɪdəˈmætəs] [pa-ki-der-ma-tous], *a.* Paquidermo.

pacific [ˈpæsɪfɪk] [pa-si-fik], **pacifical** [ˈpæsɪfɪkl] [pa-si-fi-kal], **pacificatory** [ˈpæsɪfɪkəri] [pa-si-fi-ka-to-ri], *a.* 1. Pacífico, pacificador, dispuesto a hacer o a restablecer la paz. 2. Quieto, sosegado, tranquilo.

pacifically [pəˈsɪfɪkəli] [pa-si-fi-ka-li], *adv.* Pacíficamente.

pacificate [pəˈsɪfɪkeɪt] [pa-si-fi-keit], *va.* Pacificar, apaciguar.

pacification [ˌpəsɪfɪˈkeɪʃən] [pa-si-fi-kei-shon], *s.* Pacificación, apaciguamiento.

pacificator [ˌpəsɪfɪˈkeɪtəʳ] [pa-si-fi-kei-taʳ], **pacifier** [ˈpəsɪfaɪəʳ] [pa-si-faiaʳ], *s.* Pacificador.

pacificator, *s.* Pacificador, el que restablece la paz o pacifica los que están opuestos y enemistados.

pacifism ['pəsɪfɪzəm] [pa-si-fi-sem], *s. m.* Pacifismo.

pacifist ['pəsɪfɪst] [pa-si-fist], *s.* Pacifista.

pacify ['pəsɪfɪaɪ] [pa-si-fai], *va.* Pacificar, poner paz, sosegar, aquietar, calmar, tranquilizar.

pacing ['peɪsɪŋ] [pei-sin], *s.* Paso, andadura.

pack [pæk] [pak], *s.* 1. Lío, fardo, carta. 2. Baraja de naipes. 3. Muta, jauría, conjunto de perros de caza. 4. Conjunto de hombre o animales que van en compañía; vuelo de perdices; hatajo o cuadrilla de malhechores, mangantes, pícaros, **Pack of robbers,** cuadrilla de ladrones. 5. Gran extensión de hielos flotantes. 6. Cubierta de sábanas mojadas, que se usa en ciertos casos de enfermedad.

pack, *va.* 1. Enfardelar, embalar, envasar; encajonar, poner en cajas; disponer en buen orden para llevar. 2. Meter en cualquier receptáculo. 3. Apretar, juntar algo apretando; colmar. 4. Despachar, enviar de prisa. 5. Cargar, poner la carga a una acémila. 6. Llevar sobre la espalda o el lomo. 7. Envolver a un enfermo en sábanas mojadas con cubiertas secas al exterior. 8. Empandillar el naipe o poner un naipe junto con otros para hacer alguna trampa. 9. Juntar o unir personas escogidas para algún mal fin. *-vn.* 1. Empaquetar; hacer el baúl, arreglar el equipaje. 2. Reunirse en una masa firme. **Ground packs after a rain,** el terreno se consolida después de la lluvia. 3. Enfardelarse, empaquetarse, encajonarse. 4. Marcharse o irse corriendo.

pack away, off o **one's tools,** largarse, huir, tomar las de Villadiego.

pack down, apretar, comprimir.

pack off, despedir, despachar; poner de patitas en la calle. **To send one packing,** enviar a uno a pasear. **Can you pack in three more?,** ¿caben tres más?

package ['pækɪdʒ] [pa-kich], *s.* Fardo, paquete; embalaje, gasto de embalar o empaquetar géneros o mercancías.

packaging ['pækɪdʒɪŋ] [pa-ki-chin], *s. m.* Embalaje, envasado.

pack animal ['pækˌænɪməl] [pak-a-ni-mal], *s.* Acémila, animal de carga.

pack-cloth ['pækklɒθ] [pak-kloz], *s.* Arpillera.

packer ['pækəʳ] [pa-kaʳ], *s.* Embalador, empaquetador.

packet ['pækɪt] [pa-kit], *s.* 1. Paquete, fardo pequeño. 2. Paquete de cartas; la valija del correo de posta. 3. *(Mar.)* Paquebote, correo marítimo o buque que sirve de correo.

packet, *va.* Empaquetar, enfardelar.

packet-boat ['pækɪtˌbəʊt] [pa-kit-bout], *s.* Paquebot o paquebote, correo marítimo, embarcación que sirve para llevar los correos de una parte a otra.

pack-horse ['pækhɔːs] [pak-jors], *s.* Caballo de carga.

packing ['pækɪŋ] [pa-kin], *s.* 1. Embalaje, envase, enfardeladura. 2. Empaque, empaquetadura, relleno de estopa, grasa, etc., para hacer impermeable al agua u otro fluido, v. g. a un émbolo; o para llenar un espacio vacío. 3. *(Alb.)* Relleno, enripiado, cascajo. 4. *(Des.)* Fraude, engaño. **Packing-box, packing-case,** caja de embalaje; envase. **Packing leather,** cuero para empaquetadura.

packing house ['pækɪŋˌhaʊs] [pa-kin-jaus], *s.* 1. Empacadora. 2. Frigorífico.

packman ['pækmən] [pak-man], *s.* Buhonero, vendedor ambulante.

pack-saddle ['pækˌsædl] [pak-sa-del], *s.* Albarda, una de las piezas que componen el aparejo de las bestias de carga.

packstaff ['pækstɑːf] [pak-staf], *s.* Palo de buhonero.

packthread ['pækθred] [pak-zred], *s.* Bramante, hilo de acarreto, guita, hilo gordo o cordel muy delgado hecho de cáñamo.

pack train ['pæktreɪn] [pak-trein], *s.* Rueca (de animales de carga).

pact [pækt] [pakt]; **paction** ['pækŋən] [pak-shon], *s.* Pacto, contrato, convenio, tratado, composición, convención, ajuste, trato.

pad [pæd] [pad], *s.* 1. Cojín, almohadilla, colchoncillo lleno de alguna sustancia elástica para evitar la vibración o el roce; peto, coraza acolchada (para la esgrima); útil que sirve para aplicar tinta. 2. Cuaderno, conjunto de pliegos de papel engomados por dos cantos, que forman como un libro. 3. Hoja grande y flotante de una planta acuática.

pad, *va.* 1. Poner una almohada para que está más blando el asiento; forrar, rellenar de pelote o paja. 2. Aumentar (book) con material superfluo. 3. Encolar, pegar pliegos de papel por los cantos, de manera que formen cuadernos.

padded ['pædɪd] [pa-did], *a.* Acojinado, rellenado (with straw)

padder ['pædəʳ] [pa-daʳ], *s.* Rellenador; el que hace almohadillas.

padding ['pædɪŋ] [pa-din], *s.* 1. El acto de rellenar, de formar un colchoncillo o almohadilla. 2. Guata, (Amer. huata) lo que sirve para rellenar, o para hacer una almohadilla. 3. Lo que se inserta o introduce únicamente para aumentar el volumen de algo.

paddle ['pædl] [pa-del], *v.* 1. Remar. 2. Chapotear, golpear el agua con los pies o las manos de modo que salpique. *-va.* 1. Impeler con un canalete. 2. Manosear, tentar y tocar con las manos alguna cosa, dar repetidas palmaditas. 3. *(Fam.)* Golpear con un canalete.

paddle, *s.* Canalete, especie de remo; paleta. **Paddle-board, paddle-float,** paleta de rueda hidráulica. **Paddle-wheel,** rueda de paleta. **Paddle-wheel steamer,** vapor de ruedas. **To have a paddle,** chapotear en el agua.

paddle, paddlestaff ['pædlstɑːf] [pa-del-staf], *s.* Cualquier palo con un extremo de hierro puntiagudo; béstola o arrejada, instrumento que se usa para desbrozar el arado.

paddler ['pædləʳ] [pad-laʳ], *s.* Remero.

paddock ['pædɒk] [pa-dok], *s.* 1. Dehesa, cercado para ejercitar los caballos. 2. *(Prov. y Esco.)* Escuerzo, sapo. **Paddock-stool,** especie de hongo.

paddy ['pædɪ] [pa-di], *s.* 1. Un irlandés; apodo derivado del nombre propio **Patrick,** muy común entre los irlandeses. 2. Un ánade de la América del Norte. 3. Taladro para pozos con perforadores de expansión. **Paddywhack,** rabieta. **Paddy wagon,** coche celular *(EU).*

paddy, *s.* Arroz en cáscara, palay (nombre angloindio). **Paddy-field,** arrozal, campo de arroz.

padesoy ['pædsɔɪ] [pad-soi], *s. V.* PADUASOY.

padlock ['pædlɒk] [pad-lok], *s.* Candado.

padlock, *va.* Echar el candado, cerrar con candado.

pæan ['piːən] [pian], *s.* Canto o himno de triunfo.

pædobaptism ['piːdəbæpˌtɪzəm] [pi-do-bap-ti-sem], *s.* Bautismo de niños.

pagan ['peɪgən] [pei-gan], *s.* Pagano, gentil. *-a.* Pagano, gentil, étnico.

paganish ['peɪgənɪʃəm] [pei-ga-ni-sem], *a.* Pagano, idólatra.

paganism ['peɪgənɪzəm] [pei-ga-ni-sem], *s.* Paganismo, idolatría.

paganize ['peɪgənaɪz] [pei-ga-nais], *va. y vn.* Hacer o hacerse pagano.

page [peɪdʒ] [peich], *s.* 1. Página. 2. Libro, escrito; cualquier fuente de conocimientos. 3. Paje, criado, asistente; jovencito al servicio de algún alto personaje. **Page break,** *(Inform.)* límite de la página. **On the front page,** (news) en primera plana.

page, *va.* Foliar, paginar.

pageant ['pɒdʒənt] [pa-chant], *s.* 1. Espectáculo público (show); carro o arco triunfal; trofeo (trophy). 2. Apariencia, exterioridad (look). *-s.* Ostentoso, vistoso, pomposo; superficial.

pageantry ['pædʒəntrɪ] [pa-chan-tri], *s.* 1. Fasto, fausto, pompa. 2. Exterioridad.

pageboy ['peɪdʒbɔɪ] [peich-boi], *s. m.* Paje.

pagehood ['peɪdʒhʊd] [peich-jud], s. Estado o servicio de paje.

page proof ['peɪdʒpruf] [peich-pruf], s. (Impr.) Prueba de plana.

pager ['peɪdʒəʳ] [pei-chaʳ], s. m. Busca, aparato para localizar.

paginal ['pædʒɪnəl] [pa-yi-nal], a. Compuesto de páginas.

paginate ['pædʒɪneɪt] [pa-yi-neit], va. Paginar (book, magazine, etc.).

paging ['peɪdʒɪŋ] [pei-yin], s. Paginación, acción y efecto de numerar las páginas de un libro; el orden de las páginas. **Paging-machine**, máquina para numerar páginas.

pagoda [pəˈgəʊdə] [pa-gou-da], s. Pagoda, templo de la India oriental; una moneda del mismo país.

paid [peɪd] [peid], pret. y pp. de TO PAY.

paidology ['peɪdɒlədʒɪ] [pei-do-lo-yi], s. (Neolog.). Estudio científico del niño por especialistas instruidos al efecto.

paid-up ['peɪdˈʌp] [peid-ap], **paid in,** ['peɪdˈɪn] [peid-in], a. Acabado de pagar. **Paid-up policy,** póliza (de seguros) pagada.

pail [peɪl] [peil], s. Cubo, coldra; pozal, cubeta. (Mar.) Balde.

pailful ['peɪlfʊl] [peil-ful], s. Cubada o cubetada, la cantidad que cabe en un cubo.

pain [peɪn] [pein], va. 1. Causar dolor, atormentar, hacer padecer físicamente (Med.). 2. Acongojar, causar una pena, un daño moral, angustiar, afligir, inquietar, doler. **My eye pains me,** me duele el ojo. (Fig.) **You pain me!,** ¡me das lástima!

pain, s. 1. Pena, castigo. **On pain of death,** bajo pena de muerte. 2. Pena, dolor, tormento, trabajo. 3. Inquietud, pesadumbre, sentimiento. **Pains,** pl. (a) trabajo, incomodidad, fatiga (effort). (b) Ansiedad, inquietud, solicitud. (c) Dolores de parto. **A pain in the knee,** un dolor de rodilla. **To be in pain,** estar con mucho cuidado, estar inquieto; doler, padecer. **To be in pain all over,** dolerle a uno todo el cuerpo. **To feel pain,** sentir dolor. **Where do you feel pain?,** ¿dónde le duele a Ud.? **To be at the pains of,** tomarse el trabajo de, poner cuidado, aplicarse, cuidar. **To take great pains,** afanarse, empeñarse, esmerarse en algo. **No gains without pains,** no hay ganancia sin trabajo. **It gives pain to see,** duele verlo.

painful ['peɪnfʊl] [pein-ful], a. 1. Dolorido, afligido, desconsolado, atormentado. 2. Doloroso, aflictivo. 3. Penoso, difícil, laborioso, trabajoso. 4. Industrioso, aplicado.

painfully ['peɪnfʊlɪ] [pein-fu-li], adv. 1. Dolorosamente. 2. Penosamente. 3. Laboriosamente.

painfulness ['peɪnfʊlnɪs] [pein-ful-nes], s. Dolor, aflicción, pena, trabajo, fatiga; industria.

painim, a. y s. V. PAYNIM.

painkiller ['peɪnkɪləʳ] [pein-ki-laʳ], s. m. Analgésico.

painless ['peɪnlɪs] [pein-les], a. Sin pena o trabajo; libre de dolor.

painlessly ['peɪnlɪslɪ] [pein-les-li], adv. Fácilmente, sin dolor, sin esfuerzo (easily).

painlessness ['peɪnlɪsnɪs] [pein-les-nes], s. Ausencia de dolor.

painstaker ['peɪnzteɪkəʳ] [peins-tei-kaʳ], s. Trabajador, afanador.

painstaking ['peɪnzteɪkɪŋ] [peins-tei-kin], a. Cuidadoso, industrioso; afanoso, fiel en ejecución.

paint [peɪnt] [peint], va. 1. Pintar, cubrir de colores; en sentido más amplio, dar una capa delgada de algún líquido. 2. Pintar, representar o delinear una figura con colores. 3. Pintar, describir por escrito o de palabra alguna cosa. -vn. Afeitarse, aderezarse o componerse con afeites. **To paint the town red,** (Germ. E.U.) cometer diabluras, divertirse de una manera turbulenta, correr la tuna como embriagado, alborotar. **Paint in,** añadir (con pintura), pintar. **Paint out/over,** tachar con pintura, tapar.

paint, s. 1. Pintura, el color con que se pinta; material preparado para pintar o dar capas sobre otro, ya seco, ya mezclado con aceite, agua, etc. 2. Pintura, descripción o narración de alguna cosa. 3. Afeite, colorete. **Wet paint,** recién pintado. **Paint-box,** caja de colores o pinturas. **Paint-brush,** brocha, pincel. **Oil paints,** pinturas, colores al óleo. **Paint-roller,** rodillo (para pintar). **Paint-spray,** pistola de pintura.

painter ['peɪntəʳ] [pein-taʳ], s. 1. Pintor. 2. (Mar.) Amarra del bote o de la lancha. **House-painter,** pintor de casas. **Ornamental painter,** pintor decorador. **Sign-painter,** pintor de muestras.

painting ['peɪntɪŋ] [pein-tin], s. 1. Pintura, el arte de pintar; también, el acto u oficio de dar capas de colores con una brocha. 2. Pintura, el cuadro pintado. 3. Pintura, la narración o descripción que se hace de alguna cosa por escrito o de palabra.

paintress ['peɪntrɪs] [pein-tris], sf. Pintora.

pair [peəʳ] [peaʳ], s. 1. Par, el conjunto de dos cosas de una misma especie; dos personas o animales unidos o asociados. 2. Una sola cosa que tiene dos partes semejantes dependientes una de otra. **A pair of scissors, of spectacles,** un par de tijeras, de anteojos. 3. Par, pareja. 4. Juego de cosas semejantes que forman un todo; escalera. **To arrange in pairs,** colocar de dos en dos, por parejas.

pair, vn. 1. Aparearse, hacer pareja. 2. Hermanarse, igualarse una cosa con otra. -va. 1. Parear. 2. Hermanar; igualar una cosa con otra. **To pair off,** Aparearse; retirarse de una reunión en parejas. **To pair with,** hacer pareja dos personas.

paisley ['peɪzlɪ] [peis-li], s. f. Cachemira (desing, fabric).

pajamas, o **pyjamas** [pəˈdʒɑːməs] [pa-ya-mas], s. pl. Pijama.

Pakistani [ˌpɑːkɪsˈtɑːnɪ] [pa-kis-ta-ni], a. Paquistaní, pakistaní.

pal [pæl] [pal], s. (Vulg.) Compañero, confederado, camarada.

palace ['pælɪs] [pa-lis], s. Palacio; edificio suntuoso.

palacious [pəˈleɪnəs] [pa-lei-shos], V. PALATIAL.

paladin ['pælədɪn] [pa-la-din], s. Paladín, uno de los doce pares de Carlomagno; de aquí, modelo de caballería.

palæography, palæontology, s. V. PALEOGRAPHY, PALEONTOLOGY.

palanquin ['pælənkwɪn] [pa-lan-kuin], s. Palanquín, especie de litera cubierta.

palatable ['pælətəbl] [pa-la-ta-bol], a. Sabroso, gustoso al paladar.

palatal ['pælətl] [pa-la-tal], a. y s. Palatal, que se refiere al paladar; (consonante) pronunciada con el auxilio del paladar como la k, la ñ, la y.

palatalize ['pælətəlaɪz] [pa-la-ta-lais], vt. Palatalizar.

palate ['pælɪt] [pa-lit], s. 1. Paladar, el órgano del sentido del gusto. 2. Paladar, el apetito o deseo de cualquier cosa inmaterial o espiritual.

palatial [pəˈleɪʃəl] [pa-lei-shal], a. Palaciego, palatino, que pertenece a palacio; magnífico, suntuoso.

palatinate [pəˈlætɪnɪt] [pa-la-ti-nit], s. Palatinado, provincia o dominios de un príncipe palatino.

palatine ['pælətiːn] [pa-la-tin], a. 1. Palatino, dotado de privilegios reales. **A count palatine,** conde palatino. **A county palatine,** palatinado. 2. Paladial, perteneciente al paladar.

palaver [pəˈlɑːvəʳ] [pa-la-vaʳ], s. 1. Charla frívola, palabrería, particularmente zalamería, lisonja; embustes (wordiness). 2. Plática larga; conferencia o discusión pública (conference). -va. y vn. 1. Adular, lisonjear, usar de zalamerías, engatusar. 2. Charlar, hablar mucho sin sustancia (chat).

pale [peɪl] [peil], a. 1. Pálido, descolorido. 2. Claro o que no es de muy subido color (light). **Pale wine,** vino clarete. **Pale green,** verde claro. 3. Pálido, lo que no brilla ni tiene lustre. **To grow/turn pale,** volverse pálido, palidecer.

pale, s. 1. Estaca, palo puntiagudo para clavarlo en tierra (stake). 2. Palizada, empalizada, defensa de estacas (palisade). 3. Palizada, el sitio cercado de estacas. 4. Distrito, territorio limitado; mojón, límite (limit). **Outside the pale of,** fuera de los límites de. 5. Espacio cerrado, literal o figuradamente; esfera, seno, gremio, sociedad. 6. (Her.) Palo de escudo. **Pale of the church,** gremio de la iglesia, bajo la protección o autoridad de la iglesia.

pale, *va.* 1. Empalizar. 2. Cercar, rodear. 3. Poner pálido, hacer empalidecer a una persona. 4. Descolorar, quitar o amortiguar el color de una cosa.

palea ['peɪliːə] [pei-lia], *s.* (*Bot.*) Glumilla, arista, cubierta floral de las gramíneas. (*Lat.*)

paleaceous ['pælɪeɪʃəs] [pa-liei-shos], *a.* Aristoso, que tiene aristas o pajas.

pale-eyed ['peɪlaɪd] [peil-aid], *a.* Que tiene la vista turbia o los ojos pálidos.

paleface ['peɪlfeɪs] [peil-feis], *s.* Persona blanca o caucásica; nombre que dan los indios a los blancos, rostropálido.

pale-faced ['peɪlfeɪst] [peil-feist], *a.* Pálido, descolorido de cara.

palely ['peɪlˌlɪ] [peil-li], *adv.* Con palidez.

paleness ['peɪlnɪs] [peil-nes], *s.* Palidez.

paleograph [ˌpælɪˈɒɡrəf] [pa-lio-graf], *s.* Paleografía, conocimiento de las escrituras antiguas.

paleographer [ˌpælɪˈɒɡrəfəʳ] [pa-lio-gra-faʳ], *s.* Paleógrafo.

paleography [ˌpælɪˈɒɡrəfɪ] [pa-lio-gra-fi], *s. f.* Paleografía.

paleolithic [ˌpælɪəʊˈlɪθɪk] [pa-liou-li-zik], *a.* (*Geol.*) Paleolítico, relativo a la primera edad de la piedra.

paleologist [ˌpælɪˈɒlədʒɪst] [pa-lio-lo-yist], *s.* Paleólogo, el que es versado en paleología.

paleology [ˌpælɪˈɒlədʒɪ] [pa-lio-lo-yi], *s.* Paleología, arqueología, el estudio de la antigüedad o antigüedades.

paleontologist [ˌpælɪɒnˈtɒlədʒɪst] [pa-lion-to-lo-yist], *s.* Paleontologista, paleontólogo.

paleontology [ˌpælɪɒnˈtɒlədʒɪ] [pa-lion-to-lo-yi], *s.* Paleontología, ciencia que trata de los restos orgánicos fósiles y de cuanto tuvo vida en la superficie del globo en las épocas geológicas.

paleozoic ['pælɪəzɔɪk] [pa-lio-soik], *a.* Paleozoico, perteneciente a la época geológica más antigua.

Palestinian [ˌpæləsˈtɪnɪən] [pa-lis-ti-nian], *a.* Palestino.

palette ['pælɪt] [pa-lit], *s.* Paleta, tabla pequeña en que el pintor tiene los colores dispuestos para pintar. **Palette knife,** espátula.

palfrey ['pɔːlfrɪ] [pol-fri], *s.* Palafrén, caballo pequeño y manso para señoras.

palfreyed ['pɔːlfraɪd] [pol-fraid], *a.* Se dice de las señoras que tienen palafrén o van a caballo en él.

palindrome ['pælɪndrəʊm] [pa-lin-droum], *s.* Palindromia, palabra o sentencia que dice lo mismo leída al revés que al derecho.

paling ['peɪlɪŋ] [pei-lin], *s.* Estacada, palizada.

palingenesis, palingenesia [ˌpælɪnˈdʒɛnɪsɪs] [pa-lin-ye-ni-sis], *s.* Regeneración, renacimiento.

palinode ['pælɪnəʊd] [pa-li-noud], **palinody** ['pælɪnɒdɪ] [pa-li-no-di], *s.* Palinodia, retractación pública de lo que antes se había dicho. **To sing a palinode o to make his palinode,** cantar la palinodia.

palisade [ˌpælɪˈseɪd] [pa-li-seid], **palisado** [ˌpælɪˈseɪdə] [pa-li-sei-do], *s.* 1. Palizada, empalizada. 2. *pl.* Peñasco largo, precipicio de rocas. Extensa serie de rocas que forman precipicio, por lo general a orillas de un río.

palish ['pælɪʃ] [pa-lish], *a.* Algo pálido, paliducho.

pall [pɔːl] [pol], *s.* 1. Paño de ataúd, paño mortuorio; (*Fig.*) lo que ocasiona aflicción o tristeza. 2. Cubierta de cáliz; también, palio de arzobispo. 3. Manto, capa. **Pall-bearers,** los que en un funeral acompañan y rodean el cadáver en calidad de principales dolientes. **A pall of smoke,** una capa de humo.

pall, *vn.* Hacerse insípido o sin sabor; cesar de producir interés o dar placer. -*va.* 1. Evaporar, desvirtuar. 2. Desalentar, desanimar. 3. Saciar, ahitar, hartar.

palladium [pəˈleɪdɪəm] [pa-lei-diom], *s.* 1. Paladión; en Troya, imagen de Palas o Minerva, a la que se consideraba como garantía de la salud pública; de aquí, cualquier garantía o prenda de seguridad, salvaguardia. 2. (*Min.*) Paladio, metal raro que se halla mezclado con la platina.

pallet ['pælɪt] [pa-lit], *s.* 1. Paleta de reloj, fiador de rueda, retén, linguete. *V.* PAWL. 2. Uno de los discos en la cadena sin fin de una bomba de cadena. 3. (*Mar.*) Caja de lastre. 4. Torno de alfarero; también, paleta, instrumento de albañilería (platform). 5. Paleta de pintor. 6. Herramienta empleada para dorar o inscribir los lomos de los libros. 7. Válvula de cañón de órgano. 8. Jergón, camilla, cama pequeña y pobre (bed).

palletization [pælɪtaɪˈzeɪʃən] [pa-li-tai-sei-shon], *s. f.* Paletización.

pallial ['pælɪəl] [pa-lial], *a.* Que se refiere al palio o manto de los moluscos.

palliate ['pælɪeɪt] [pa-lieit], *va.* 1. Excusar, disculpar, extenuar o minorar una falta con disculpas (excuse). 2. Paliar un mal, no curarle de raíz, mitigar, reducir la severidad de algo, v. g. de una enfermedad (mitigate).

palliation [ˌpælɪˈeɪʃən] [pa-liei-shon], *s.* 1. Paliación, mitigación, alivio. 2. Cura paliativa o imperfecta.

palliative ['pælɪətɪv] [pa-lia-tiv], *a.* Paliativo, paliatorio, mitigador; aliviador. -*s.* Paliativo, lo que mitiga.

pallid ['pælɪd] [pa-lid], *a.* Pálido, descolorido.

pallidity [ˈpælɪdɪtɪ] [pa-li-di-ti], *s.* Palidez.

pallidness ['pælɪdnɪs] [pa-lid-nes], *s. f.* Palidez.

pallium ['pælɪəm] [pa-liom], *s.* 1. Palio. 2. Palio, clámide, de los antiguos griegos y romanos. 3. Palio, manto, de un molusco o de una gaviota.

pall-mall ['pɔːlmɔːl] [pal-mol], *s.* Mallo, un juego; el mallo con que se empuja la bola en este juego y el sitio donde se juega.

pallor ['pæləʳ] [pa-laʳ], *s.* Palidez, disminución del color natural; falta de color.

pally ['pælɪ] [pa-li], *a.* Afable, amigable. **They're very pally,** son muy amigos. **To be a pally sort,** ser una persona afable.

palm [pɑːm] [pam], *s.* 1. (*Bot.*) Palma, palmera, familia de plantas endógenas, que crecen principalmente en las regiones cálidas. **Palm-Sunday,** Domingo de Ramos. **Palm-oil,** aceite de palma. 2. Palma, rama de la palmera. 3. Palma, victoria. **To bear o carry away the palm,** alcanzar la palma, la victoria. 4. Palma, la parte interior y cóncava de la mano. 5. Palma, el ancho de la mano, medida de tres y a veces cuatro pulgadas. 6. (*Mar.*) Rempujo, especie de dedal que se usa para coser las velas. **palm-bird,** pájaro que habita en las palmeras; en especial, el llamado tejedor. Ploceus. **Palm-cabbage,** hojas tiernas comestibles que crecen en la cima de ciertas especies de palmeras. **Palm-tree,** palmera, palma, cualquier árbol de esta familia. **Palm-wine,** vino de palmera, la savia fermentada del cocotero, etc.

palm, *va.* 1. Escamotar, esconder en la mano como hacen los prestidigitadores. 2. Escamotar, engañar, defraudar a alguno con destreza. 3. Manejar, tomar en la mano; manosear, tentar y tocar con la mano. 4. (*Fam.*) Encajar, dar como verdadero lo que no lo es. 5. Cubrir de ramas de palmera. **Palm off,** encargar algo a alguien. **I asked Jim to palm the visitor off,** pedí a Jim que se encargara de la visita.

palmar ['pɑːməʳ] [pa-maʳ], *a.* Palmar, colocado cerca de la palma de la mano.

palmary ['pɑːmərɪ] [pa-ma-ri], *a.* Principal, palmario, claro, palmar.

palmate, palmated ['pɑːmeɪt] [pa-meit], *a.* Palmeado, parecido a una mano abierta; palmado, que tiene lóbulos (cinco por lo común) que divergen como los dedos de una mano.

palmately ['pɑːmeɪtlɪ] [pa-meit-li], *adv.* De un modo palmado o palmeado.

palmcorder ['pɑːmkɔːdəʳ] [pam-kor-daʳ], *s.* Videocámara portátil, minicámara.

palmer ['pɑːməʳ] [pa-maʳ], *s.* Palmero, peregrino, romero.

palmer-worm ['pɑːməwɔːm] [pa-ma-uorm], *s.* 1. Oruga velluda que es una plaga destructora. 2. Larva de cualquier coleóptero destructivo, como el gorgojo.

palmetto ['pɑːmiːtəʊ] [pa-mi-tou], *s.* 1. Palmera de la Carolina, cualquiera de las varias palmeras de copa en forma de abanico, especialmente la Sabal palmetto de los Estados Unidos. 2. Sombrero hecho de las hojas de esta palmera. **Palmetto State,** Carolina del Sur.

palmiferous [ˈpɑːmɪfərəs] [pa-mi-fe-ros], *a.* Palmífero, que produce palmas.

palmiped [ˈpɑːmɪpɪd] [pa-mi-pid], *a.* Palmeado, palmípedo, que tiene los dedos de los pies unidos con una membrana, como las aves acuáticas.

palmister [ˈpɑːmɪstəʳ] [pa-mis-taʳ], *s.* Quiromántico, el que pretende adivinar por la inspección de las palmas de las manos.

palmistry [ˈpɑːmɪstrɪ] [pa-mis-tri], *s.* Quiromancia, pretendida adivinación por la inspección de las palmas de las manos.

palmitic [ˈpɑːmɪtɪk] [pa-mi-tik], *a.* Palmítico, de la palmera, sacado de la palmera. **Palmitic acid,** ácido palmítico.

palmtop [ˈpɑːmtɒp] [pam-top], *s.* Ordenador de bolsillo *(Inform.).*

palmy [ˈpɑːmɪ] [pa-mi], *a.* 1. Próspero, floreciente; triunfal, de triunfo. 2. Palmar, lleno de palmas o palmeras.

palp, palpus [ˈpælp] [papl] [ˈpælpəs] [pal-pos], *s.* Palpo, órgano del tacto colocado en la parte inferior de la boca de ciertos insectos; apéndice oral de moluscos bivalvos.

palpability [ˌpælpəˈbɪlɪtɪ] [pal-pa-bi-li-ti], *s.* Palpabilidad, evidencia.

palpable [ˈpælpəbl] [pal-pa-bol], *a.* 1. Palpable. 2. Palpable, evidente, patente, obvio.

palpableness [ˈpælpəblnɪs] [pal-pa-bol-nes], *s.* El estado de lo que es palpable.

palpably [ˈpælpəblɪ] [pal-pa-bli], *adv.* Palpablemente, claramente.

palpation [ˈpælpeɪʃən] [pal-pei-shon], *s.* Palpamiento, palpadura; *(Med.)* exploración por medio de las manos.

palpebra [ˈpælpɪbrə] [pal-pi-bra] *a.* Pálpebra, párpado.

palpebral [ˈpælpɪbrəl] [pal-pi-bral], *a.* Palpebral, perteneciente a los párpados.

palpitate [ˈpælpɪteɪt] [pal-pi-teit], *vn.* Palpitar, latir, agitarse el corazón; agitarse o moverse irregularmente.

palpitating [ˈpælpɪteɪtɪŋ] [pal-pi-tei-tin], *a.* Palpitante.

palpitation [ˌpælpɪˈteɪən] [pal-pi-tei-shon], *s.* Palpitación, latido.

palsied [ˈpɔːlzɪd] [pol-sid], *a.* Paralítico.

palsy [ˈpɔːlzɪ] [pol-si], *s.* 1. Parálisis, perlesía. 2. Flaqueza de acción, ineficacia.

palsy, *va.* 1. Paralizar, afectar con parálisis. 2. Paralizar, impedir la acción moral de alguna cosa.

palter [ˈpɔːltəʳ] [pol-taʳ], *vn.* Jugar o burlarse de alguno, pegar petardos; usar de rodeos y circunlocuciones. *-va. (Des.)* Desperdiciar, malgastar.

palter, *s.* Petardista, engañador; el que usa de rodeos para lograr un fin.

paltriness [ˈpɔːltrɪnɪs] [pol-tri-nes], *s.* Vileza, bajeza, mezquindad.

paltry [ˈpɔːltrɪ] [pol-tri], *a.* Vil, despreciable, miserable, mezquino.

paludal [ˈpæljodəl] [pa-liu-dal], **palustral** [ˈpæləstrəl] [pa-lus-tral], *a.* Palúdico, palustre, perteneciente a lagunas o pantanos; también se dice de la fiebre que suelen ocasionar los miasmas de los pantanos.

paly [ˈpɔːlɪ] [po-li], *a.* 1. *(Poét.)* Pálido, marchito, que carece de colores y frescura. 2. *(Her.)* Dividido en partes iguales por medio de líneas o barras verticales.

pampas [ˈpæmpəs] [pam-pas], *s. pl.* Pampas, llanuras. **The Pampas,** la Pampa.

pamper [ˈpæmpəʳ] [pam-paʳ], *va.* Atracar, llenar de comida, engordar; tratar con mucho regalo, mimar, acariciar (spoil).

pampered [ˈpæmpəd] [pam-pad], *a.* 1. Consentido, mimado (child). 2. Fácil, regalado.

pamperer [ˈpæmpərəʳ] [pam-pa-raʳ], *s.* Acariciador.

pamphlet [ˈpæmflɪt] [pam-flit], *s.* Folleto; papelucho.

pamphleteer [ˌpæmflɪˈtɪəʳ] [pam-fli-tiaʳ], *s.* Folletista.

pan [pæn] [pan], *s.* 1. Cualquier vasija de metal o de barro ancha y honda destinada a componer o guardar la comida (utensil); paila de cerero; cazo, cuenco. 2. Gamella, cazo de hierro para ensayar arenas auríferas. 3. Cazoleta de un arma de fuego. 4. *(Mec.)* Quicio, rangua. 5. Cráneo. 6. Subsuelo muy duro, capa de arcilla. **Stewing-pan,** cazuela. **Frying-pan,** sartén. **Warming-pan,** calentador. **Baking-pan,** tartera. **Sauce-pan,** cazo, cacerola. **Perfuming-pan,** perfumador. **Dripping-pan,** grasera. **Earthen pan,** cazuela de barro, barreño pequeño, lebrillo, cuenco. **Snuffer-pan,** platillo para las despabiladeras. **Pan-pudding,** una especie de pudín cocido en el horno. **Brain-pan,** el cráneo. **Knee-pan,** rótula, choquezuela. **Pan of a gunlock,** cazoleta de escopeta. **A flash in the pan,** una chiripa.

pan, *va.* 1. Separar el oro sacudiendo la tierra o arena que lo contiene con agua en un cazo metálico. 2. *(Fam.)* Alcanzar, ensacar, enredar, lograr de cualquier modo. 3. Cocer y servir en una cazuela. *-vn.* 1. Con **out,** dar oro la tierra o arena; aparecer oro en un cazo; de aquí, *(Fam.)* dar buen resultado o provecho. Repartir. 2. Procurar obtener oro usando del cazo. 3. Girar la cámara fotográfica.

panacea [ˌpænəˈɪə] [pa-na-shia], *s.* 1. Panacea. 2. *(Bot.)* Pánace, planta medicinal.

panache [pəˈnæʃ] [pa-nash], *s. m.* Brío, garbo, aire.

panama hat [ˌpænəmɑːˈhɑːt] [pa-na-ma-jat], *s.* Sombrero panamá o de jipijapa.

Panamanian [ˌpænəˈmeɪnɪən] [pa-na-mei-nian], *a.* Panameño.

Pan-American [ˈpænəˈmerɪkən] [pa-na-me-ri-kan], *a.* Panamericano, perteneciente a ambas Américas del Norte y del Sur.

Pan-Americanism [ˈpænəˈmerɪkənɪzəm] [pan-a-me-ri-ka-ni-sem], *s.* Panamericanismo.

panary [ˈpænərɪ] [pa-na-ri], *a.* Lo que pertenece al pan, panado.

pancake [ˈpænkeɪk] [pan-keik], *s.* Fruta de sartén; buñuelo.

panchromatic [ˈpænkreɪmætɪk] [pan-kro-ma-tik], *a.* Pancromático (en fotografía).

pancratic, pancratical [ˈpænkrətɪk] [pan-kra-tik], *a.* Pancracial, que pertenece a ciertos ejercicios gimnásticos de los griegos; muy atlético, muy fuerte en los ejercicios gimnásticos.

pancreas [ˈpæŋkrɪəs] [pan-krias], *s. (Anat.)* Páncreas.

pancreatic [ˈpæŋkrɪətɪk] [pan-kria-tik], *a.* Pancreático, que pertenece al pancreas.

pandean [ˈpændɪən] [pan-dian], *a.* Que se refiere al dios Pan.

pandect [ˈpændekt] [pan-dekt], *s.* 1. El tratado que comprende todo lo que se sabe en alguna ciencia. 2. **Pandects,** *pl.* pandectas, la recopilación de varias obras. 3. La recopilación de las leyes del derecho civil hecha por Justiniano.

pandemic [pænˈdemɪk] [pan-de-mik], *a.* Pandémico, que ataca a todo un pueblo, muy epidémico.

pandemonium [ˌpændɪˈməʊnɪəm] [pan-di-mou-niom], *s.* 1. Pandemonio, el lugar de reunión de los demonios. 2. Tumulto, batahola diabólica.

pander [ˈpændəʳ] [pan-daʳ], *s.* 1. Alcahuete.

pander, *va.* 1. Alcahuetear. **To pander to,** consentir, mimar.

panderism [ˈpændərɪzəm] [pan-de-ri-sem], *s.* Alcahuetería.

pandiculated [ˈpændɪkjoleɪtɪd] [pan-di-kiu-lei-tid], *a.* Extendido, abierto.

pandore [ˈpændɔːʳ] [pan-doʳ], *s.* Bandola, instrumento músico de cuerdas de alambre.

pane [peɪn] [pein], *s.* 1. Cristal, hoja de vidrio. 2. Cuadro, cada una de las piezas de ciertas obras hechas de pedazos cuadrados. 3. Una superficie plana o llana en un objeto que tiene varios lados. *V.* PANEL.

paned, *a.* Se dice de la obra que contiene pedacitos cuadrados de diversos géneros.

panegyric [ˌpænɪˈdʒɪrɪk] [pa-ni-yi-rik], *s.* Panegírico, discurso en alabanza de alguno. *-a.* Panegírico, perteneciente a la alabanza o elogio.

panegyrical [ˌpænɪˈdʒɪrɪk] [pa-ni-yi-ri-kal], *a.* Panegírico.

panegyrist [ˌpænɪˈdʒɪrɪst] [pa-ni-yi-rist], *s.* Panegirista.

panel [ˈpænl] [pa-nel], *s.* 1. Entrepaño, tablero, pieza rectangular puesta en un bastidor (sew). 2. Tabla preparada para hacer un cuadro (art). 3. Superficie llana, cara de la piedra labrada (of wall). 4. Paño de otra tela insertado a lo largo de un vestido de mujer. **Panel-beater,** chapista.

panel, *s.* Panel, grupo de personas seleccionadas para un fin especial; jurados, oradores, especialistas, etc. **Panel discussion,** discusión a cargo de un panel. **Panel game,** concurso por equipos.

panel, *va.* Hacer alguna cosa en forma de tableros o cuarterones; labrar en artesones.

paneless ['pænlɪs] [pein-les], *a.* Se dice de las cosas hechas en cuadritos, cuarterones o pedazos de diversa figura cuando les faltan uno o más de ellos. **A paneless window,** una vidriera a la que le faltan algunos vidrios o cristales, ventana sin cristal.

paneling ['pænəlɪŋ] [pa-ne-lin], *s.* Artesón, artesonado; conjunto de entrepaños.

panful ['pænfʊl] [pan-ful], *s.* Cazada, el contenido de un cazo.

pang [pæŋ] [pang], *s.* Angustia, dolor, congoja, tormento, pena (pain). **The pangs of death,** las ansias de la muerte, la agonía. **The pangs of childbirth,** los dolores de parto.

pang, *va.* Atormentar, afligir, angustiar, acongojar.

panhandle ['pænhændl] [pan-jan-del], *vi.* Mendigar.

panhandler ['pænhændlə'] [pan-jand-la'], *s.* Limosnero, pordiosero.

panic ['pænɪk] [pa-nik], 1. *a.* Pánico. 2. *vt.* Aterrar, asustar. 3. *vi.* Aterrarse, ser presa del pánico.

panic, *s.* 1. Miedo o terror ciego, cobardía extrema. 2. Pánico comercial, que suele producir quiebras y desastres en el mundo de los negocios, precipitando bancarrotas. **Panic button,** botón de alarma. **It was panic stations,** reinaba el pánico. **Panic-stricken, panic-struck,** sobrecogido de terror.

panic, panic-grass, *s. (Bot.)* Panizo, nombre dado a un género de plantas gramíneas.

panicle ['pænɪkl] [pa-ni-kel], *s. (Bot.)* Panículo, panoja, variedad de inflorescencia compuesta.

paniculate, paniculated ['pænɪkjʊleɪt] [pa-ni-kiu-leit], *a. (Bot.)* Apanojado: se dice de las plantas cuyo tallo o flores están dispuestos en forma de panoja.

panier, *s. V.* PANNIER.

panniculus, pannicle ['pænɪkjʊləs] [pa-ni-kiu-los], *s. (Biol.)* Panículo, membrana delgada.

pannier ['pænɪə'] [pa-nia'], *s.* 1. Cuévano, uno de los dos canastos que llevan las acémilas. 2. Cesto grande, canasto, canastón. 3. Cestón, gabión. 4. *(Arq.) V.* CORBEL.

panoply ['pænəplɪ] [pa-no-pli], *s.* Panoplia, armadura completa.

panorama [,pænə'rɑːmə] [pa-no-ra-ma], *s.* Panorama, pintura en que se ven los objetos como si fuesen reales.

panoramic [,pænə'rɑːmɪk] [pa-no-ra-mik], *a.* Panorámico. **Panoramic view,** visión panorámica.

pansy ['pænzɪ] [pan-si], *s. (Bot.)* Trinitaria o violeta tricolor.

pant [pænt] [pant], *vn.* 1. Jadear, anhelar, respirar con vehemencia y congoja (gasp). 2. Anhelar, desear vivamente, estar ansioso por. 3. Palpitar, moverse y agitarse el pecho (heart). **To pant for** o **after,** suspirar por, desear con ansia. 4. *(Poét.)* Moverse lánguidamente. **The breeze pant on the leaves,** *(Poét.)* el céfiro juguetea con las hojas.

pant, *s.* Palpitación.

pantalets ['pæntəlɪts] [pan-ta-lits], *s. pl.* Pantalón, perniles largos que llevaban en otro tiempo las mujeres y los niños.

pantaloon ['pæntəluːn] [pan-ta-lun], *s.* 1. Arlequín, gracioso, bufón en las pantomimas o comedias. 2. *pl.* Pantalones, calzones. **A pair of pantaloons,** unos pantalones, un par de pantalones, bombachos. **Pantaloon stripes,** listado para pantalones.

pantelegraph ['pæntelɪgræf] [pan-ti-li-graf], *s.* Pantelégrafo, instrumento para transmitir por telégrafo autógrafos, dibujos, etc., en facsímile.

panter ['pæntə'] [pan-ta'], *s.* 1. Anheloso, el que respira con dificultad; jadeante; persona que desea con ansia. 2. *(Des.)* Red para ciervos; trampa.

pantheism ['pænθiːɪzəm] [pan-zii-sem], *s. m.* Panteísmo.

pantheist ['pænθiɪst] [pan-ziist], *a.* Panteísta.

pantheology ['pænɪˈɒlədʒɪ] [pan-zio-lo-yi], *s.* Panteología, sistema completo acerca de la divinidad.

pantheon ['pænθɪən] [pan-zion], *s.* Panteón, templo dedicado al culto de todos los dioses.

panther ['pænθə'] [pan-za'], *s.* 1. Pantera, leopardo. 2. Puma de América.

pantherine ['pænθərɪn] [pan-za-rin], *a.* Panterino.

panties ['pæntɪz] [pan-tis], *s. pl.* Pantaletas, breve pantalón íntimo de mujer. **A pair of panties,** unas bragas.

pantile ['pæntaɪl] [pan-tail], *s.* Teja, canalón.

panting ['pæntɪŋ] [pan-tin], *a.* Sin aliento, sin respiración. *-s.* Palpitación.

pantingly ['pæntɪŋlɪ] [pan-tin-li], *adv.* Con palpitación, anhelantemente.

pantofle ['pæntəfl] [pan-to-fel], *s.* Chinela, pantuflo.

pantograph ['pæntəgræf] [pan-to-graf], *s.* 1. Pantógrafo, instrumento para reducir un dibujo. 2. Compás de proporción.

pantographic, pantagraphic [,pæntəgræfɪk] [pan-to-gra-fik], *a.* Pantográfico, relativo al pantógrafo.

pantometer [pænˈtɒmiːtə'] [pan-to-mi-ta'], *s.* Pantómetro, instrumento para medir toda clase de ángulos.

pantomime ['pæntəmaɪm] [pan-to-maim], *s.* 1. Serie de gestos y ademanes que se hacen para darse a entender; lenguaje de signos. 2. Pantomima, representación teatral que se reduce a gestos y remedos.

pantomimic ['pæntəmɪmɪk] [pan-to-mi-mik], *a.* Pantomímico, perteneciente a la pantomima.

pantomimist ['pæntəmɪmɪst] [pan-to-mi-mist], *s.* Pantomimo, actor mudo.

pantry ['pæntrɪ] [pan-tri], *s.* Despensa, el lugar o sitio en donde se guardan los comestibles.

pants ['pæntz] [pants], *s. pl.* Pantalones.

pantsuit ['pæntsuːt] [pant-sut], *s. m. (EU)* Traje de chaqueta y pantalón.

panty ['pæntɪ] [pan-ti], *s. f.* Faja pantalón. *f. pl.* Medias.

panzer ['pænzə'] [pan-sa'], *s.* Ejército motorizado.

pap [pæp] [pap], *s.* 1. Pezón, la punta que sobresale en los pechos o tetas de los animales por donde los hijos chupan la leche. 2. Papas, papilla, las sopas blandas que se dan a los niños. 3. Carne, la parte mollar de la fruta.

papa ['pæpə] [pa-pa], *s.* Papá.

papacy ['pæpəsɪ] [pa-pa-si], *s.* Papado, la dignidad de Papa.

papal ['pæpəl] [pa-pal], *a.* Papal, relativo o perteneciente al Papa, pontificio.

paparazzi [pæpəˈrætsiː] [pa-pa-ra-chi], *s. pl.* Paparazzi.

papaverous ['pæpəvərəs] [pa-pa-ve-ros], *a.* Amapolado, papaveráceo, de la naturaleza de la adormidera.

papaw ['pæpɔː] [pa-pou], *s.* 1. Papayo, árbol tropical. 2. Papaya, su fruta. 3. Asimina.

papaya [pæˈpeɪə] [pa-paia], *s. f.* Papaya (fruit).

paper ['peɪpə'] [pei-pa'], *s.* 1. Papel (material). 2. Hoja de papel. 3. Papel auténtico, documento, relato formal, escrito o impreso; en plural, cartas de valor, papeles, apuntes; autos. 4. Diario, periódico. *V.* NEWSPAPER. 5. Ensayo literario, escrito, disertación. 6. Valor, vale comercial. 7. Paquete envuelto en papel, que contiene una cantidad, número limitado de algo. **A paper of tacks,** un paquete de tachuelas. **Leaf of paper,** hoja de papel. **Piece of paper,** hoja de papel, trozo de papel. **Sheet of paper,** pliego de papel. **Quire of paper,** mano de papel. **Ream of paper,** resma de papel. **Brown paper,** papel de estraza. **Stamped paper,** papel sellado. **Blotting-paper,** teleta, papel secante. **Fly-paper,** papel para coger moscas. **Marbled paper,** papel jaspeado. **Outside quires of paper,** costeras, papel quebrado. **Large paper,** papel marquillo o papel grande con relación al ordinario en que se tira casi el todo de una edición. **Vellum paper,** papel avitelado. **Waste paper,** papel viejo, el que se destina por inútil a envolver y otros usos semejantes. **Cap paper,** papel de escribir de varios tamaños. **Demy paper,** papel de unas 16 por 21 pulgadas. **Filter-paper,** papel de filtrar. **Emery-paper,** papel de lija o esmeril. **Music-paper,** papel pautado para música. **Laid paper,** papel acanillado. **Litmus paper,** papel de tornasol. **India paper,** papel de China. **Tissue-paper,** papel de seda, papel muy delgado y de varios colores. **Toilet-paper,** papel higiénico. **Unsized paper,** papel sin cola. **Wall-paper,** papel de empapelar. **Wove paper,** papel avitelado. **Wrapping-paper,** papel de envolver. **Paper bag,** saco de papel. **Paper-case,** papelera. **Paper-clip,** abrazadera para papeles. **Paper-cutter,** (a) cortapapel, cuchillo para abrir libros. (b) Máquina usada por los impresores para cortar papel. **Paper currency,** papel moneda. **Paper-folder,** plegadera. **Paper-hanger,** empapelador. **Paper kite,** cometa de papel. **Paper-knife,** cuchillo de palo, hueso o metal, para cortar papel; cortapapel. **Paper-machine, paper-making machine,** máquina para hacer papel continuo. **Paper-pulp,** pulpa, pasta de que se hace el papel. **Paper shop,** kiosko. **Paper-stainer,** fabricante de papeles pintados. **Paper-wasp,** avispa, particularmente la que fabrica una substancia parecida al papel. **Paper weight,** pisapapel, prensapapeles. **Paper work,** trabajo administrativo, de oficina. **On paper,** escrito o impreso. -*a.* Hecho de papel; delgado como un pliego de papel. **A paper wheet,** rueda hecha de papel prensado.

paper, *va.* Empapelar una pieza, forrarla con papel. **Paper over,** disimular.

paper chain ['peɪpətʃeɪn] [pei-pa-chein], *s.* Cadeneta de papel.

paper fastener ['peɪpəfɑːsnəʳ] [pei-pa-fas-naʳ], *s.* Grapa.

paper-hangings ['peɪpəˌhæŋɪŋz] [pei-pa-jan-gins], *s. pl.* 1. Colgaduras de papel pintado. 2. Papel pintado para empapelar.

paper-maker ['peɪpəˌmeɪkəʳ] [pei-pa-mei-kaʳ], *s.* Papelero, el que fabrica papel.

paper-mill ['peɪpəmɪl] [pei-pa-mil], *s.* Molino de papel.

paper money ['peɪpəmʌnɪ] [pei-pa-ma-ni], *s.* Papel moneda.

paper-office ['peɪpəˌɒfɪs] [pei-pa-o-fis], *s.* El archivo u oficina donde se guardan los documentos o papeles concernientes a algún negociado.

paper-staining ['peɪpəsteɪnɪŋ] [pei-pa-stei-nin], *s.* El acto de pintar papel; mercadería de papel pintado o jaspeado.

papery ['peɪpərɪ] [pei-pa-ri], *a.* Parecido al papel, de la naturaleza del papel; papiráceo.

papescent ['peɪpəsnt] [pei-pasnt], *a.* Pulposo, carnoso.

papier-maché ['pæpɪeɪˈmæʃeɪ] [pa-pie-ma-shei], *s.* Papel majado, subtancia plástica hecha de pasta de papel con goma, aceite, resina, etc.

papilio ['pæpɪlɪə] [pa-pi-lio], *s.* Mariposa; un género de mariposas.

papilla ['pæpɪlə] [pa-pi-la], *s.* 1. Teta, pezón. 2. Papila, los pezoncillos que se levantan sobre la lengua.

papillary ['pæpɪlərɪ] [pa-pi-la-ri], **papillous** ['pæpɪləs] [pa-pi-los], *a.* Papilar, mamilar.

papism, papistry. *V.* POPERY.

papist ['peɪpɪst] [pei-pist], *s.* Papista, nombre que los protestantes dan a los católicos romanos.

papistic, papistical ['peɪpɪstɪk] [pei-pis-til], *a.* Papal, papístico.

papoose, pappoose [pəˈpuːs] [pa-pus], *s.* Niño de los indios norteamericanos (baby).

pappose ['pæpəs] [pa-pos], **pappous** ['pæpəs] [pa-pos], *a.* Velloso, velludo.

pappus ['pæpəs] [pa-pos], *s.* (*Bot.*) Vilano, apéndice de filamentos que tienen las semillas de muchas plantas compuestas, y les sirve para ser transportadas por el aire.

pappy ['peɪpɪ] [pei-pi], *a.* Mollar, jugoso.

paprika ['pæprɪkə] [pa-pri-ka], *s.* Pimentón.

Papua New Guinea ['pæpjʊənjuːˈɡɪnɪə] [pa-piua-niu-gui-nia], *sf.* Papúa Nueva Guinea.

papula, papule ['pæpjʊlə] [pa-piu-la], *s.* 1. Pápula, especie de erupción en la piel, caracterizada por un tumorcillo sin serosidad ni pus. 2. Papila.

papular ['pæpjʊləʳ] [pa-piu-laʳ], *a.* Papuloso, cubierto de pápulas.

papulous ['pæpjʊləs] [pa-piu-los], *a.* Lleno de pápulas.

papyrus ['pæpɪrəs] [pa-pi-ros], *s.* 1. El papel de escribir de los antiguos egipcios, hecho de papiro. 2. Lo escrito sobre el papiro. 3. Papiro.

par [pɑːʳ] [paʳ], *s.* 1. Equivalencia, paridad, nivel. 2. Igualdad de cambio; equivalente sin prima ni descuento. **It's about par of the course,** es más o menos normal, lo que cabía esperar. **To be at par with one,** hallarse en situación igual a la de otro. **At par,** a la par, término del cambio mercantil. **On a par,** igual, de cantidad o valor iguales. 3. (*Golf.*) Par.

parable ['pærəbl] [pa-ra-bol], *s.* Parábola, instrucción alegórica.

parabola [pəˈræbələ] [pa-ra-bo-la], *s.* (*Geom.*) Parábola, sección cónica.

parabolic, parabolical [ˌpærəˈbɒlɪk] [pa-ra-bo-lik], *a.* 1. Parabólico, que incluye parábolas. 2. Perteneciente a la parábola geométrica. **Parabolic aerial,** antena parabólica.

parabolically [ˌpærəˈbɒlɪkəlɪ] [pa-ra-bo-li-ka-li], *adv.* Parabólicamente.

paraboloid ['pærəbəlɔɪd] [pa-ra-bo-loid], *s.* Paraboloide, sólido engendrado por la rotación de una parábola alrededor de su eje.

paracentric, paracentrical ['pærəsentrɪk] [pa-ra-sen-trik], *a.* Paracéntrico, lo que se desvía del centro.

paracetamol [pærəˈsiːtəmɒl] [pa-ra-si-ta-mol], *s.* Paracetamol.

parachronism ['pærəkrənɪzm] [pa-ra-kro-ni-sem], *s.* Paracronismo, error cronológio, que comete poniendo un suceso después del tiempo en que acaeció.

parachute ['pærəʃuːt] [pa-ra-shut], *s.* Paracaídas. **Parachute drop,** lanzamiento en paracaídas. **Parachute jumper,** paracaidista. -*vt.* Lanzar en paracaídas. -*vi.* Lanzarse en paracaídas.

parachutist ['pærəʃuːtɪst] [pa-ra-shu-tist], *s.* Paracaidista.

paraclete ['pærəkliːt] [pa-ra-klit], *s.* Paráclito o parácleto, nombre del Espíritu Santo, como consolador de los fieles.

parade [pəˈreɪd] [pa-reid], *s.* 1. (*Mil.*) Parada, muestra o revista de tropas. 2. Ostentación, pompa, alarde, gala, fachenda. 3. Procesión. (*Esg.*) Parada, repulsa. **Parade-ground,** plaza de armas, lugar de ejercicio para las tropas.

parade, *vn.* 1. Marchar la tropa en orden militar (troops). 2. Reunirse la tropa ya sea para formar en parada, para que la revisten o para hacer el ejercicio. 3. Fachedear, hacer gala, pasear, alardear. 4. Recorrer, pasear. (streets). -*va.* 1. Convocar a una revista. 2. Poner o arreglar como en orden militar. **To make a parade of,** ostentar, alardear. **Parade about/around,** pavonearse. **Parade-ground,** plaza de armas.

paradigm ['pærədɪm] [pa-ra-dim], *s.* Paradigma, modelo gramatical; ejemplo, ejemplar.

paradise ['pærədaɪs] [pa-ra-dais], *s.* 1. Paraíso terrenal. 2. Cielo. 3. Paraíso, cualquier sitio o lugar ameno.

paradisiac, paradisiacal [ˌpærədɪˈseɪk] [pa-ra-di-seik] [ˌpærədɪˈsaɪəkəl] [pa-ra-di-sia-kal], *a.* Paradisiaco, perteneciente al paraíso.

paradox ['pærədɒks] [pa-ra-doks], *s.* Paradoja, especie que está fuera de la común opinión y sentir de los hombres; aserción que parece estar en contradicción consigo misma.

paradoxical ['pærəˈdɒksɪkəl] [pa-ra-dok-si-kal], *a.* Paradójico.

paradoxically [ˌpærəˈdɒksɪkəlɪ] [pa-ra-dok-si-ka-li], *adv.* Paradójicamente.

paraffin, paraffine ['pærəfɪn] [pa-ra-fin], *s.* Parafina.

parage ['pæreɪdʒ] [pa-reich], *s.* 1. Igualdad de sangre, de dignidad o terreno (entre los coherederos). 2. (*For.*) Ser coheredero, heredero con otro.

paragoge ['pærəgɒɡ] [pa-ra-gog], *s.* Paragoge, adición de una letra o sonido al fin de una palabra.

paragogic ['pærəgɒdʒɪk] [pa-ra-go-yik], *a.* Paragógico, relativo a la paragoge.

paragon ['pærəgən] [pa-ra-gon], *s.* 1. Modelo, muestra de excelencia. 2. (Impr.) Paragona, grado de letra la mayor después de gran canon y de casi 20 puntos. 3. (Ant.) Par, compañero, rival. **Paragon of beauty,** hermosura sin par, modelo de hermosura.

paragraph ['pærəgrɑːf] [pa-ra-graf], *va.* Dividir en párrafos.

paragraph, *s.* 1. Párrafo, división de un capítulo o discurso que comienza con una nueva línea. 2. Párrafo, artículo corto en un diario. 3. Párrafo, el signo de esta forma que sirve para denotar la división de los párrafos, o como signo de referencia.

paragraphic, paragraphically ['pærəgrɑːfɪk] [pa-ra-gra-fik], *a.* Perteneciente a los párrafos, que consiste en, o es abundante en párrafos.

paraguayan [ˌpærəˈgwɑɪən] [pa-ra-guaian], *a.* y *s.* Paraguayo, paraguayano.

parakeet ['pærəkiːt] [pa-ra-kit], *s. m.* Periquito, perico.

paralegal [ˌpærəˈliːɡəl] [pa-ra-li-gal], *s.* Ayudante de abogado.

paraleipsis ['pærəlɪpsɪs] [pa-ra-lip-sis], **paralepsis** ['pærəlɪpsɪs] [pa-ra-lip-sis], *s.* (Ret.) Paralipse, supuesta omisión de lo que realmente se dice.

paralinguistic [ˌpærəlɪŋˈɡwɪstɪk] [pa-ra-lin-güis-tik], *a.* Paralingüístico.

parallactic, parallactical ['pærəlæktɪk] [pa-ra-lak-tik], *a.* Paraláctico, que pertenece a la paralaje.

parallax ['pærəlæks] [pa-ra-laks], *s.* Paralaje o paralaxis, la diferencia entre el lugar verdadero y el aparente del un astro.

parallel ['pærəlel] [pa-ra-lel], *a.* Paralelo; análogo, igual, semejante. *-s.* 1. Líneas paralelas, dirección paralela. 2. Paralelo, grado de latitud sobre el globo. 3. Paralelo, cotejo. 4. Conformidad, semejanza. 5. Par, igual, contraparte, copia. 6. (Mil.) Paralela, línea de comunicación de una trinchera a otra en el ataque de una plaza. 7. (Impr.) Signo de esta forma que sirve como señal de referencia. **Parallel ruler,** regla para trazar líneas paralelas. **To run parallel,** guardar una distancia igual, andar en línea paralela. **Parallel bars,** paralelas, barras paralelas (gym.). **In parallel,** en paralelo (Elect.).

parallel, *va.* 1. Paralelizar, hacer paralelas. 2. Parangonar, cotejar, poner en paralelo.

parallelable ['pærəlɪləbl] [pa-ra-li-la-bol], *a.* Que puede se igualado o puesto en paralelo.

parallelepiped ['pærəlˌeləˈpaɪped] [pa-ra-le-la-pai-ped], *s. m.* Paralelepípedo, cuerpo sólido terminado por seis paralelogramos, siendo iguales y paralelos cada dos opuestos entre sí.

parallelism ['pærəlelɪzəm] [pa-ra-le-li-sem], *s.* Paralelismo.

parllelogram [ˌpærəˈleləʊɡræm] [pa-ra-le-lou-gram], *s.* Paralelogramo, una figura de cuatro lados en la que los dos opuestos son paralelos.

parallelogramic, parallelogramical ['pærəˈleləʊɡræmɪk] [pa-ra-le-lou-gra-mik], *a.* Perteneciente al paralelogramo.

parallely ['pærəlelɪ] [pa-ra-le-li], *adv.* Con paralelismo.

paralogism ['pærəlɒdʒɪzəm] [pa-ra-lo-yi-sem], **paralogy** ['pærəlɒdʒɪ] [pa-ra-lo-yi], *s.* (Lógic.) Paralogismo, discurso falaz o conclusión falsa.

paralysis [pəˈræləsɪs] [pa-ra-lai-sis], *s.* 1. (Med.) Parálisis, privación o disminución notable del movimiento voluntario y algunas veces de la sensibilidad. 2. (Fig.) Cesación de las funciones normales. (Mex. Fam.) Insulto.

paralytic, paralytical [ˌpærəˈlɪtɪk] [pa-ra-li-tik], *a.* Paralítico, perlático.

paralytic, *s.* El que padece parálisis; paralítico, perlático. (Mex. Fam.) Insultado. **Paralyze, paralyse** ['pærəlaɪz] [pa-ra-lais], *va.* 1. Paralizar, causar parálisis. 2. Privar de la facultad de obrar.

paramagnetic [ˌpærəˈmæɡnetɪk] [pa-ra-mag-ne-tik], *a.* Paramagnético, que exhibe la polaridad magnética en la misma dirección que la fuerza magnetizante.

paramedic [ˌpærəˈmiːdɪk] [pa-ra-mi-dik], *s.* Paramédico.

parameter [pəˈræmiːtəʳ] [pa-ra-mi-tar], *s.* (Mat.) Parámetro, línea invariable que entra en la ecuación y formación de una curva.

paramilitary [ˌpærəˈmɪlɪtərɪ] [pa-ra-mi-li-ta-ri], *a.* Paramilitar.

paramorphism [ˌpærəˈmɔːfɪzəm] [pa-ra-mor-fi-sem], *s.* La transformación de un mineral en otro que tiene la misma composición química, pero diferente estructura molecular y otras propiedades físicas.

paramount ['pærəmaʊnt] [pa-ra-mount], *a.* Superior a los demás, supremo, eminente; de primer orden, en primera línea. **Our paramount duty,** nuestro primer deber. *-s.* Jefe, el superior.

paramour ['pærəmʊəʳ] [pa-ra-mua'], *s.* Amante, querido o querida; la persona con quien se tienen relaciones amorosas ilícitas.

paranoia ['pærənɔɪə] [pa-ra-noia], *s.* Paranoia, monomanía.

paranoiac ['pærənɔɪk] [pa-ra-noiik], *s.* Paranoico.

paranormal [ˌpærəˈnɔːməl] [pa-ra-nor-mal], *a.* Paranormal.

paranymph ['pærənɪmf] [pa-ra-nimf], *s.* 1. Paraninfo, el padrino de la boda. 2. El que ayuda, favorece o sostiene a otro.

parapet ['pærəpɪt] [pa-ra-pit], *s.* 1. (Arq.) Baranda, barandilla, parapeto. 2. Parapeto, baluarte o elevación de tierra para poner a los soldados a cubierto del fuego del enemigo.

paraphernalia ['pærəfəˈneɪlɪə] [pa-ra-fe-na-lia], *s. pl.* 1. Atavís, adornos accesorios. 2. Insignias. V. REGALIA. 3. (For.) Bienes parafernales, los que lleva la mujer al matrimonio fuera de la dote.

paraphrase ['pærəfreɪz] [pa-ra-freis], *s.* 1. Paráfrasis, la explicación de un texto más clara y difusa por lo general que el texto mismo; traducción libre. 2. En las iglesias escocesas, versión poética de un pasaje de la Sagrada Escritura.

paraphrase, *va.* Parafrasear, explicar un texto, traducir libremente.

paraphrast ['pærəfræst] [pa-ra-frast], *s.* Parafraste, autor de paráfrasis.

paraphrastic, paraphrastical ['pærəfræstɪk] [pa-ra-fras-tik], *a.* Parafrástico.

paraphrastically [ˌpærəˈfræstɪkəlɪ] [pa-ra-fras-ti-ka-li], *adv.* Parafrásticamente.

paraphrenitis ['pærəfrənɪtɪs] [pa-ra-fre-ni-tis], *s.* Parafrenitis.

paraplegia ['pærəpledʒɪə] [pa-ra-ple-yia], *s.* Paraplejia, parálisis de la mitad inferior del cuerpo, debida a enfermedad o lesión de la médula espinal.

paraplegic ['pærəpledʒɪk] [pa-ra-ple-yik], *s.* (Med.) Parapléjico.

parapsichological [ˌpærəsaɪkəˈlɒdʒɪkəl] [pa-ra-sai-ko-lo-yi-kal], *a.* Parapsicológico.

parapsichologist [ˌpærəsaɪkəˈlɒdʒɪst] [pa-ra-sai-ko-lo-yist], *s.* Parapsicólogo.

parapsychology [ˌpærəsaɪkəˈlɒdʒɪ] [pa-ra-sai-ko-lo-yi], *s.* Parapsicología.

parasite ['pærəsaɪt] [pa-ra-sait], *s.* 1. Parásito, animal o vegetal que vive asido a otro o dentro de él y del cual saca su alimento. 2. Pájaro que pone sus huevos en el nido de otro. 3. Parásito, gorrista.

parasitic, parasitical ['pærəsaɪtɪk] [pa-ra-sai-tik], *a.* 1. Parásito, que vive en otro organismo y que se alimenta de él. 2. Adulatorio, lisonjero, gorrístico. 3. (Med.) Parásítico, perteneciente a los parásitos, causado por ellos; de la naturaleza del parásito.

parasitically [ˌpærəˈsaɪtɪkəlɪ] [pa-ra-sai-ti-ka-li], *adv.* Lisonjeramente.

parasitism ['pærəsɪtɪzəm] [pa-ra-si-ti-sem], s. Parasitismo, la manera de ser de un parásito; estado o condición de un ser organizado que vive en otro cuerpo vivo a expensas de él.

parasitologist [ˌpærəsaɪˈtɒlədʒɪst] [pa-ra-sai-to-lo-yist], s. Parasitólogo.

parasitology [ˌpærəsaɪˈtɒlədʒɪ] [pa-ra-sai-to-lo-yi], s. Parasitología.

parasitosis [ˌpærəsaɪˈtəʊsɪs] [pa-ra-sai-tou-sis], s. Parsitosis.

parasol [ˌpærəˈsɒl] [pa-ra-sol], s. Parasol, quitasol, sombrilla.

paratrooper ['pærətruːpəʳ] [pa-ra-tru-paʳ], s. Paracaidista.

paratyphoid [pærəˈtaɪfɔɪd] [pa-ra-tai-foid], s. (Med.) Paratifoidea.

parboil ['pɑːbɔɪl] [par-boil], va. 1. Medio cocer, salcochar, cocer ligeramente. 2. Formar, producir vejiguillas o vesículas en la piel por medio del calor.

parbuckle ['pɑːbʌkl] [par-ba-kel], s. Tiravira, cuerda fuerte que sirve para hacer subir o bajar objetos pesados por un plano inclinado. -va. Levantar o bajar por medio de una tiravira.

parcel ['pɑːsl] [par-sel], s. 1. Paquete, lío o atado pequeño. 2. Un conjunto indeterminado de personas. **A parcel of rascals,** una cuadrilla de tunantes. 3. Porción, cantidad. **Parcel of ground,** lote de terreno, solar. 4. (Amer.) Paño de tierra. **Part and parcel,** carne y hueso. **Parcel-bomb,** paquete-bomba.

parcel, va. 1. Partir, dividir. 2. Empaquetar, formar un paquete de alguna cosa. **Parcel out,** parcelar (land). Repartir. **Parcel up,** embalar, empaquetar.

parcenary ['pɑːsənərɪ] [par-se-na-ri], s. La herencia que corresponde a muchos herederos y no está aún dividida.

parcener ['pɑːsnəʳ] [pars-naʳ], s. Coheredero.

parch [pɑːtʃ] [parch], va. 1. Desear, enjugar, agotar. 2. Tostar, quemar, abrasar. -vn. Tostarse, quemarse, abrasarse. **I am parched with thirst,** me muero de sed.

parcheesi [pɑːˈtʃiːsɪ] [par-chi-si], s. Especie de juego de chaquete.

parching ['pɑːtʃɪŋ] [par-chin], a. Abrasador, ardiente, secante. **A parching wind,** un viento abrasador.

parchment ['pɑːtʃmənt] [parch-ment], s. 1. Pergamino. 2. Lo escrito en pergamino. **Parchment-maker,** pergaminero.

pard [pɑːd] [pard], s. 1. (Ant.) Leopardo. 2. (Germ. E. U.) Socio, compañero, asociado. V. PARTNER.

pardon ['pɑːdn] [par-don], va. 1. Perdonar, absolver; hacer gracia de la pena correspondiente a un pecado, falta o delito. 2. Disculpar, dispensar, excusar. **Pardon me,** perdone Ud., Ud. dispense. **To pardon a criminal,** conceder gracia a un criminal.

pardon, s. Perdón, remisión de injuria, delito, pecado, deuda u otra cosa. **I beg your pardon,** Ud. dispense, perdone Ud. (cortesy). **General pardon,** amnistía. **To beg somebody's pardon,** pedir perdón a alguien.

pardonable ['pɑːdnəbl] [par-do-na-bol], a. Perdonable, excusable; venial.

pardonably ['pɑːdnəblɪ] [par-do-na-bli], adv. Venialmente.

pardoner ['pɑːdnəʳ] [par-do-naʳ], s. Perdonador.

pardoning ['pɑːdnənɪŋ] [par-do-nin], a. Indulgente.

pare [peəʳ] [peaʳ], va. 1. Recortar, cortar o cercenar alguna cosa. 2. Mondar, quitar la cáscara a las frutas, papas o patatas, etc. 3. Cercenar, escatimar, reducir disminuyendo poco a poco. **To pare the nails,** cortar las uñas. **To pare a horse's foot,** despalmar el casco de una caballería para que siente la herradura. **To pare bread,** raspar la corteza del pan. **To pare an apple,** mondar una manzana, **To pare away/down,** reducir (Fig.).

paregoric [ˌpeəˈgɒrɪk] [pea-go-rik], a. Paregórico, calmante. - s. Elixir paregórico, tintura alcanforada de opio; abreviación de **paregoric elixir.**

parenchyma ['pɛrəŋkɪmə] [pa-ren-ki-ma], s. 1. (Anat.) Parénquima, tejido propio de los órganos glandulosos en los animales. 2. (Bot.) La substancia blanda y esponjosa de las plantas.

parenchymal ['pərəŋkɪməl] [pa-ren-ki-mal], a. Parenquimal, que es de naturaleza del parénquima.

parenchymous ['pərəŋkɪməs] [pa-ren-ki-mos], a. Parenquimatoso.

parenesis ['pərɪnɪsɪs] [pa-ri-ni-sis], s. Parénesis, discurso moral, exhortación o amonestación.

parenetic [ˌpərɪˈnɪtɪk] [pa-ri-ni-tik], a. Parenético, persuasivo.

parent ['peərənt] [pea-rent], s. 1. El padre o la madre. **Parents,** pl. padres. 2. Cualquier ser organizado que engendra a otro. 3. Autor, productor, causa, origen. -a. Que tiene la relación de autor u origen. **Parent speech,** lengua madre, aquella de que han nacido o se han derivado otras.

parentage ['peərəntɪdʒ] [pea-ren-tich], s. Parentela, nacimiento, origen y descendencia de una persona.

parental [pəˈrentl] [pa-ren-tal], a. Paternal, lo que pertenece a los padres.

parenthesis [pəˈrenθɪsɪs] [pa-ren-zi-sis], s. Paréntesis.

parenthetical, parenthetic [ˌpærənˈθetɪkəl] [pa-ren-ze-ti-kal], a. Que pertenece al paréntesis, de la naturaleza de un paréntesis; entre o por paréntesis.

parenthood ['peərənthʊd] [pe-rent-jud], s. Calidad de padre o madre.

parenticide ['peərəntɪsaɪd] [pe-ren-ti-said], s. Parricidio.

parentless ['peərəntlɪs] [pe-rent-les], a. Huérfano.

parer ['peərəʳ] [pea-raʳ], s. Instrumento para recortar o mondar. **A smith's o frarrier's parer,** pujavante. **Apple-parer,** mondador de manzanas.

paresis ['peərɪsɪs] [pea-ri-sis], s. Paresia, parálisis parcial.

par excellence [pɑːˈreksələːns] [par-ek-se-lans], adv. Por excelencia.

parget ['pɑːdʒɪt] [par-yit], va. Enyesar, cubrir o decorar con yeso; dar lechada. -s. 1. Yeso. V. GYMPSUM. 2. Mortero, argamasa, para cubrir el interior de las chimeneas. 3. Enlucido. V. PARGETING.

pargeting ['pɑːdʒɪtɪŋ] [par-yi-tin], s. 1. Enlucido; obra de yeso; en particular, trabajo en estuco, escayola, adorno de estuco en relieve. 2. Argamasa. V. PARGET, 2ª acep.

parhelion [pəˈrɪlɪən] [pa-ri-lion], s. Parelia, o parelio, una especie de meteoro.

pariah ['pɑːrɪə] [pa-ria], s. 1. Paria, natural del Indostán, de la casta ínfima, que sirve de criado o peón. 2. Un proscrito de la India oriental; de aquí, cualquier persona rechazada, expulsada de todas partes.

parietal [pəˈraɪtl] [pa-rai-tal], s. (Anat.) Parietal, un hueso del cráneo. -a. 1. Paredaño, que está pared por medio; que forma las paredes de cualquier cavidad del cuerpo o pertenece a ellas. 2. Parietal, perteneciente o relativo a la pared; relativo a la residencia dentro de paredes, v. g. en un colegio; residencial. 3. (Bot.) Parietal.

parietes ['pærɪɪtɪs] [pa-rii-tis], s. pl. (Anat.) Los lados de la cabeza.

paring ['peərɪŋ] [pea-rin], s. Raedura, peladura, mondadura, pellejo, corteza. -a. Para cortar o pelar. **Paring knife,** cuchillo para pelar legumbres.

paris green ['pærɪsˌgriːn] [pa-ris-grin], s. Cardenillo, verde de París.

parish ['pærɪʃ] [pa-rish], s. 1. Parroquia, feligresía, curato. 2. Parroquia, el conjunto de los fieles que están gobernados en lo espiritual por un párroco. 3. En el Estado de Luisiana, división civil correspondiente a un condado (county). -a. Parroquial. **Parish clerk,** sacristán de parroquia. **Parish priest,** párroco.

parishioner [pəˈrɪʃənəʳ] [pa-ri-sho-naʳ], s. Parroquiano.

parisian [pəˈrɪzɪən] [pa-ri-sian], a. Parisiense, perteneciente a París. -s. Natural o habitante de París.

parity ['pærɪtɪ] [pa-ri-ti], s. Paridad, semejanza, igualdad.

park [pɑːk] [park], s. 1. Parque, bosque cerrado, lugar público de recreo en las ciudades. 2. Campiña, campo abierto. 3. En las Montañas Roqueñas, valle o llano pintoresco, escaso de árboles. **Park keeper,** guardabosques, guarda.

park, *va.* 1. Estacionar. 2. Aparcar, parquear. *(Esp. Am.)* 3. *(Mil.)* Aparcar.

parka ['pɑːk] [park], *s. f.* Anorak.

parking ['pɑːkɪŋ] [par-kin], *s.* Estacionamiento, aparcamiento. **Parking bay,** área de estacionamiento. **Parking lights,** luces de población. **Parking place/space,** aparcamiento. **Parking lot,** estacionamiento de automóviles. **Parking ticket,** multa por aparcamiento.

parkland ['pɑːklænd] [park-land], *s.* Zonas verdes.

parkway ['pɑːkweɪ] [park-uei], *s.* 1. Avenida, alameda, carretera, o avenida principal arbolada. 2. Calzada arbolada.

parlance ['pɑːləns] [par-lans], *s.* Modo de hablar, locución, habla; conversación.

parley ['pɑːlɪ] [par-li], *vn.* Parlamentar; discutir, conversar unos con otros; conferenciar verbalmente con un enemigo.

parley, *s.* 1. Conferencia, plática, como con un enemigo en el campo de batalla. 2. Parlamento, la acción de parlamentar. **To beat o sound a parley,** hacer oír el toque de parlamento.

parliament ['pɑːləmənt] [par-la-ment], *s.* Parlamento, el cuerpo legislativo de la Gran Bretaña, compuesto del rey, pares del reino y diputados nombrados por el pueblo; cuerpo legislativo en general.

parliamentarian [ˌpɑːləmenˈtɛərɪən] [par-la-men-tearian], *s.* Parlamentario, el que es versado en la ley parlamentaria.

parliamentary [ˌpɑːləˈmentərɪ] [par-la-men-ta-ri], *a.* 1. Parlamentario, perteneciente al parlamento, o hecho por el parlamento. 2. Conforme a las reglas y usos de las asambleas legislativas.

parliament-house ['pɑːləməntˌhaʊs] [par-la-ment-jaus], *s.* El sitio donde el parlamento celebra sus sesiones.

parliament-man ['pɑːləməntˌmən] [par-la-ment-man], *s.* Diputado, individuo del parlamento.

parlor ['pɑːləʳ] [par-laʳ], *s.* 1. Sala de recibo. 2. Parlatorio, locutorio. **Parlor game,** juego de salón.

parlor car ['pɑːləkaʳ] [par-la-kaʳ], *s. (F. C.)* Vagón-salón.

parlous ['pɑːləs] [par-los], *a.* 1. *(Ant.)* Peligroso, medroso, que infunde temor de un peligro. 2. *(Des.)* Astuto, chocarrero.

Parnassian ['pɑːneɪʃæn] [par-nei-shan], *a.* Parnáside, que pertenece o se refiere al Parnaso.

Parnassus [pɑːˈnæsəs] [par-na-sos], *s.* Parnaso, el monte de la Fócide, morada principal de las musas.

parochial [pəˈrəʊkɪəl] [pa-rou-kial], *a.* 1. Parroquial. 2. Sostenido por una parroquia o limitado a ella; estrecho.

parochialism [pəˈrəʊkɪəlɪzəm] [pa-rou-kia-li-sem], *s. m.* Estrechez, mentalidad estrecha *(Fig.).*

parochially [pəˈrəʊkɪəlɪ] [pa-rou-kia-li], *adv.* Por parroquias.

parodic [pəˈrɒdɪk] [pa-ro-dik], *a.* Paródico.

parody ['pærədɪ] [pa-ro-di], *s.* 1. Parodia. 2. Trova burlesca, imitativa. 3. *(Des.)* Refrán.

parody, *va.* Parodiar; trovar, convertir una obra seria en burlesca.

parol ['pærəl] [pa-rol], *a. (For.)* 1. Verbal, dado de vida voz, oral. 2. Escrito, pero no bajo sello.

parole [pəˈrəʊl] [pa-roul], *s.* 1. *(Mil.)* Palabra, promesa de honor de un prisionero de guerra de no intentar escaparse o no infundar o tomar armas contra sus captores hasta después de canjeado. 2. Libertad bajo caución, libertad condicional. **To be on parole,** estar en libertad bajo palabra. 3. Promesa, palabra de honor (promise).

parolee [pəˈrəʊliː] [pa-rou-li], *s.* 1. *(Mil.)* Prisionero libre bajo su palabra de honor. 2. Preso libre bajo caución.

paronomasia [ˌpærənəˈmeɪzɪə] [pa-ro-no-mei-sia], *s.* Paronomasia, figura retórica en que se emplean los parónimos.

paronomastic [ˌpærənəˈmæstɪk] [pa-ro-no-mas-tik], *a.* Paronímico.

paronym ['pærənɪm] [pa-ro-nim], *s.* 1. Parónimo, voz de igual etimología que otra. 2. Parónimo, palabra que se asemeja a otra en el sonido, pero que tiene otra significación

y se escribe de modo diferente, v. g. *ale,* cerveza, y *ail,* sufrir, o indisposición.

paronymous, paronymic ['pærənɪməs] [pa-ro-ni-mos] ['pærənɪmɪk] [pa-ro-ni-mik], *a.* Paronímico, relativo al parónimo: (a) derivado de la misma raíz, como *civil* del latin *civilis;* (b) semejante en sonido, pero escrito de diferente modo y con sentido, también diferente, como *fair,* rubio, bello, y *fare,* precio de pasaje, manjares.

paroquet, *s. V.* PARRAKEET.

parotid ['pærətɪd] [pa-ro-tid], *a.* Parótido, situado cerca de la oreja. *-s.* Parótida, glándula salival situada debajo del oído.

paroxysm ['pærəksɪzəm] [pa-rok-si-sem], *s.* Paroxismo o parasismo.

paroxysmal ['pærəksɪzməl] [pa-rok-sis-mal], *a.* 1. Paroxismal, que pertenece o procede del paroxismo. 2. *(Geol.)* Que resulta de una convulsión de las fuerzas naturales.

parquet ['pɑːkeɪ] [par-kei], *s. (Teat.)* Piso de las lunetas. **Parquet, parquet floor,** piso de parqué (mosaico de madera).

parquetry ['pɑːkɪtrɪ] [par-ki-tri], *s.* Entarimado, mosaico de madera, para suelos o muebles.

parrakeet ['pærəkiːt] [pa-ra-kit], *s.* Periquito, papagayo pequeño, cotorra, particularmente el que tiene la cola en forma de cuña.

parrel ['pærl] [pa-rel], *s.* 1. Manto de chimenea. 2. *(Mar.)* Racamento, el compuesto de vertellos, liebres y bastardo que pasa por ellos, y que se une y atraca la verga con el palo. **Parrel-rope,** bastardo. **Ribs of the parrel,** liebres del racamento. **Parrel-trucks,** *(Mar.)* vertellos del racamento.

parrhesia ['pærɪːzɪə] [pa-ri-sia], *s.* Libertad u osadía en el uso de la palabra.

parricidal ['pærɪsaɪdəl] [pa-ri-sai-dal], *a.* Parricida.

parricide ['pærɪsaɪd] [pa-ri-said], *s.* 1. Parricida, el que mata a su padre o madre. 2. Parricidio, el delito cometido por el parricida.

parrot ['pærət] [pa-rot], *s.* 1. Papagayo, loro. 2. El que repite o imita sin comprender. **Parrot cry,** eslogan. **Parrot-fish, parrot-wrasse,** escaro, pez cubierto de grandes escamas de color más o menos rojo.

parroted ['pærətɪd] [pa-ro-ted], *a.* Se dice de la persona a quien han enseñado a repetir las palabras como un papagayo.

parry ['pærɪ] [pa-ri], *vn.* 1. Esgrimir. 2. Parar, desviar los golpes del contrario.

parrying ['pærɪŋ] [pa-riin], *s.* El acto de parar, evitar o desviar los golpes del contrario.

parse ['pɑːs] [pars], *va.* Analizar alguna sentencia.

parsee, parsi ['pɑːsiː] [par-sii], *s.* 1. Parsi adorador del fuego, que profesa la religión de Zoroastro. 2. Idioma primitivo de los persas: parsi.

parseeism, parsism ['pɑːsiːzəm] [par-sii-sem], *s.* Parsismo, religión de Zoroastro.

parsimonious [ˌpɑːsɪˈməʊnɪəs] [par-si-mou-nios], *a.* Ahorrativo, avaro, mezquino, sumamente o indebidamente económico en sus gastos.

parsimoniously [ˌpɑːsɪˈməʊnɪəslɪ] [par-si-mou-nios-li], *adv.* Parcamente.

parsimoniousness ['pɑːsɪˈməʊnɪəsnɪs] [par-si-mou-nios-nes], *s.* Parcidad, miseria.

parsimony ['pɑːsɪmənɪ] [par-si-mo-ni], *s.* Parsimonia, tacañería, mezquindad.

parsing ['pɑːzɪŋ] [par-sin], *s.* Análisis de alguna oración o frase.

parsley ['pɑːslɪ] [pars-li], *s. (Bot.)* Perejil, planta hortense.

parsnip ['pɑːsnɪp] [pars-nip], *s. (Bot.)* Chirivía, planta hortense de raíz comestible.

parson ['pɑːsn] [par-son], *s.* 1. Clérigo. 2. Párroco, cura, rector.

parsonage ['pɑːsnɪdʒ] [par-so-nidch], *s.* 1. Curato. 2. Beneficio curado. 3. Curato o casa del cura. **Parsonage-house,** la casa del párroco.

part [pɑːt] [part], *s.* 1. Parte, porción, cantidad especial o determinada de una cosa o de un todo. 2. Parte esencial de un cuerpo u organismo; miembro (body). 3. Parte, región, lugar, sitio (place, region). **What part are you from?,** ¿de qué lugar es Ud.? 4. Parte, la porción que corresponde a alguna en un reparto; papel que representa un actor. **He acted the part of an emperor,** hizo el papel de emperador. 5. Interés, cuidado, lo que concierne o atañe. 6. Parte, partido, el lado a que alguno se inclina. 7. Obligación, deber. 8. *(Mús.)* Parte, melodía o música escrita para una sola voz o instrumento. **A 3 part song,** una canción a 3 voces. 9. Entrega de un libro o periódico. 10. Raya del cabello. 11. Pieza (Mech.) 12. Fascículo, tomo (book, journal). **Parts,** *pl.* Partes, las prendas, calidades y dotes naturales que adornan a alguno; talentos. **A man of parts,** hombre de talento. **For my part,** por lo que a mí toca, por mi parte, en cuanto a mí. **The funny part of it is that...,** lo gracioso es que... **To take part,** tomar parte en, participar. **To take part with one,** tomar la defensa o el partido de una persona. **Part and parcel,** uña y carne. **Part author,** co-autor. **Foreign parts,** parajes, países extranjeros. **Do your part,** cumpla Ud. con su obligación. **The part of a wise man is to,** es obligación de un hombre cuerdo. **Three parts,** tres cuartos. **To play a part,** representar un papel, hacer el papel. **Part owner,** condueño, propietario de una parte. **In good o ill part,** en buena o mala parte, por bien o por mal.

part, *va.* 1. Partir, repartir, distribuir. 2. Separar, desunir, dividir. 3. Partir, romper (break). 4. Apartar a dos que riñen. 5. Rayar, disponer con una línea de, división entre dos partes; tener o llevar en dos porciones. **To part the hair,** partir el pelo, hacerse la raya. -*vn.* 1. Partirse, desunirse, separarse, apartarse (crowd, etc.). 2. Despedirse. 3. Partir, irse. 4. Tener parte en alguna cosa; ir a la parte. 5. *(Mar.)* Apartarse del ancla. **To part with,** deshacerse de alguna cosa, ceder, dejar, vender, enajenar. **He parted with his house and lot,** enajenó, se deshizo de su casa y solar. **To part from,** despedirse, decir adiós. **He parted from his wife and children,** se despidió de su esposa e hijos.

partable ['pɑːtəbl] [par-ta-bol], *a.* Partible.

partage [pɑː'teɪdʒ] [par-teich], *s.* Repartimiento.

partake [pɑː'teɪk] [par-teik], *va.* (*pret.* PARTOOK, *pp.* PARTAKEN). Repartir, tener parte en. -*vn.* 1. Participar; tomar parte en. 2. Tener, poseer algo de la naturaleza, propiedad o función de.

partaken [pɑː'teɪkn] [par-tei-ken], *pp.* de TO PARTAKE.

partaker [pɑː'teɪkəʳ] [par-tei-kaʳ], *s.* Participante; cómplice.

parter ['pɑːtəʳ] [par-taʳ], *s.* Partidor.

parterre [pɑː'teə] [par-tea], *s.* 1. Era de un huerto, cuadro de jardín, división de tierra completamente igual y por lo común adornada con flores puestas con orden. 2. En los Estados Unidos el patio de un teatro, el área y los asientos que quedan debajo de las galerías y detrás de las lunetas o butacas.

parthenogenesis ['pɑːθɪnəʊ'dʒenɪsɪs] [par-zi-no-ye-ni-sis], *s.* Partenogénesis, reproducción sin unión sexual, como por medio de huevos, semillas o esporos no fertilizados.

Parthenon ['pɑːθənɒn] [par-za-non], *s.* Partenón, templo de Minerva en Atenas.

partial ['pɑːʃəl] [par-shal], *a.* 1. Parcial, que pertenece a la parte de un todo. 2. Parcial, el que sigue el partido de otro (biassed). 3. Parcial, que tiene parcialidad o demasiado afecto a alguna persona o cosa; aficionado a, amante de. 4. Particular, individual, no general. **To be partial to,** ser aficionado a.

partialist ['pɑːʃəlɪst] [par-sha-list], *s.* Partidario; muy apasionado.

partiality [ˌpɑːʃɪ'ælɪtɪ] [par-shia-li-ti], *s.* 1. Parcialidad; afecto excesivo. 2. Prevención, falta de equidad. 3. Predilección, gusto más pronunciado por una cosa que por otra; gusto particular.

partially ['pɑːʃəlɪ] [par-sha-li], *adv.* 1. Parcialmente, en parte, no del todo. 2. Parcialmente, con parcialidad.

partibility [ˌpɑːtɪ'bɪlɪtɪ] [par-ti-bi-li-ti], *s.* Divisibilidad.

partible ['pɑːtɪbl] [par-ti-bol], *a.* Partible, divisible.

participable [pɑː'tɪsɪpəbl] [par-ti-si-pa-bol], *a.* Participable.

participant [pɑː'tɪsɪpənt] [par-ti-si-pant], *a.* Participante, partícipe.

participate [pɑː'tɪsɪpeɪt] [par-ti-si-peit], *va.* y *vn.* Participar, recibir o tomar parte de alguna cosa.

participation [pɑːˌtɪsɪ'peɪʃən] [par-ti-si-pei-shon], *s.* Participación; distribución, repartimiento.

participatory [pɑːtɪsɪ'peɪtərɪ] [par-ti-si-pei-to-ri], *a.* Participativo (sports).

participial [ˌpɑːtɪ'sɪpɪəl] [par-ti-si-pial], *a.* Participial.

participially [ˌpɑːtɪ'sɪpɪəlɪ] [par-ti-si-pia-li], *adv.* Particialmente.

participle ['pɑːtɪsɪpl] [par-ti-si-pel], *s.* *(Gram.)* Participio, cierta forma del verbo que participa de la índole del verbo y del adjetivo. El participio presente del idioma inglés corresponde al gerundio español, y expresa el tiempo presente. Su desinencia es -**ing. The leaves are falling,** las hojas están cayendo. El participio pasado termina en *d, ed, en, n, o t,* y expresa tiempo pretérito. **Chafed,** estregado, rozando; **parted,** separado; **risen,** levantado, subido; **hurt,** herido, lastimado.

particle ['pɑːtɪkl] [par-ti-kel], *s.* 1. Partícula, parte o porción pequeña de alguna cosa; cantidad o grado pequeño (dust, etc.). *(Gram.)* Partícula, la palabra o voz de pocas sílabas que no se declina ni conjuga. 3. *(Mec.)* Cantidad de alguna subtancia tan pequeña que se la considera como un punto, aunque tiene todavía inercia y atracción.

parti-colored ['pɑːtɪˌkʌləd] [par-ti-ka-lad], *a.* Multicolor, de varios colores.

particular [pə'tɪkjʊləʳ] [par-ti-kiu-laʳ], *a.* 1. Particular, peculiar. 2. Particular, singular, extraordinario, poco común; notable (special). 3. Preciso, exacto, delicado o escrupuloso en el examen de alguna cosa. **A particular friend,** un amigo íntimo. 4. Particular, detallado, circunstanciado. 5. Exigente, quisquilloso, delicado en sus gustos. **A particular thing,** una cosa determinada. **She was most particular about it,** insistió mucho sobre esto. **A particular account,** relación circunstanciada o con todas sus menudencias. 6. Extravagante, extraño. -*s.* 1. Particular, el punto o materia de que se está tratando. 2. Particularidad, circunstancia o detalle particular; una persona o cosa determinada entre otras muchas. 3. Relación circunstanciada, dato, artículo. 4. Interés propio. **In particular,** particularmente. **Particular care,** cuidados especiales. **In every particular,** en todos los detalles. **To give particulars,** dar los detalles.

particularity [ˌpɑːtɪkjʊ'lærɪtɪ] [par-ti-kiu-la-ri-ti], *s.* Particularidad, cualidad o estado de lo particular, lo especial.

particularize [pə'tɪkjʊləraɪz] [par-ti-kiu-la-rais], *va.* Particularizar.

particularly [pə'tɪkʊləlɪ] [par-ti-kiu-lar-li], *adv.* Particularmente.

parting ['pɑːtɪŋ] [par-tin], *s.* 1. Separación, división, reparto: *(Quím.)* la acción de separar el oro de la plata. 2. Separación, partida, despedida, adiós. 3. Ruptura, v. g. la de un cable. 4. Paraje, línea o superficie de separación o división. -*pa.* 1. Que se refiere a una despedida, partida o separación. 2. Que se acaba, que se va. 3. Divisible, partible. **The parting hour,** la hora de la despedida. **A parting kiss,** un beso de despedida. **The knell of parting day,** el toque del día que declina. **Parting present,** regalo de despedida.

partisan, *a.* y *s.* V. PARTIZAN.

partition [pɑː'tɪʃən] [par-ti-shon], *s.* 1. Partición, repartimiento, división, la acción de dividir. 2. Separación, distinción, división; linde, línea de división. 3. Tabique, pared, *(Mar.)* mampara. 4. *(Bot.)* Pared interior que separa células o cavidades. **Partition-wall,** tabique, pared medianera. **Partition,** *va.* Partir, dividir o separar.

partitive ['pɑːtɪtɪv] [par-ti-tiv], *a.* 1. Partitivo, que separa en partes o divisiones. 2. *(Gram.)* Partitivo, que significa una de las aprtes en que se puede dividir un todo; también, distributivo. *-s.* Palabra o caso partitivo.

partizan, partisan [ˌpɑːtɪˈzæn] [par-ti-san], *a.* 1. Partidario, que se refiere o adhiere a un partido. **A partizan vote,** una votación de partido. 2. Que se refiere a guerrilleros o partidarios; llevado adelante por ellos.

partizan, partisan, *s.* 1. Partesana, especie de pica o alabarda; soldado que la lleva. 2. Bastón de mando.

partizanship, partisanship [ˌpɑːtɪˈzænːʃɪp] [par-ti-san-ship], *s.* Calidad de partidario; adhesión ciega a un partido.

parthly [ˈpɑːθlɪ] [parz-li], *adv.* En parte, en cierto modo.

partner [ˈpɑːtnəʳ] [part-naʳ], *s.* 1. Socio, compañero, compañera (business, games); socio, asociado, copropietario en una empresa. **Sleeping partner,** socio comanditario. 2. Pareja, se llama en los bailes el par de personas que bailan juntas. 3. *(Mar.)* Malletes o fogonaduras. **Partners of the main-mast,** *(Mar.)* fogonaduras del palo mayor. **Partners of the capstan,** *(Mar.)* malletes del cabrestante.

partner, *va.* Asociarse con otro; acompañar.

partnership [ˈpɑːtnəːʃɪp] [part-na-ship], *s.* 1. Sociedad, interés social, propiedad común a varias personas. 2. Asociación de dos o más personas para neegocios, fundada en un contrato; sociedad.

partook, *pret.* de TO PARTAKE.

part-owner [ˈpɑːtˈəʊnəʳ] [part-ou-naʳ], *s.* Copropietario.

partridge [ˈpɑːtrɪdʒ] [par-trich], *s. (Orn.)* Perdiz. **A young partridge,** perdigón. **A covey of partridge,** perdigón. **A covey of partridges,** un vuelo de perdices.

parturient [ˈpɑːtjɔrɪənt] [par-tiu-rient], *a.* Parturiente, que está de parto; que se refiere al parto.

parturition [ˌpɑːtjʊəˈtɪʃən] [par-tua-ri-shon], *s.* Parto, el acto de parir; alumbramiento; el estado de la hembra que está con los dolores de parto.

party [ˈpɑːtɪ] [par-ti], *s.* 1. Partido, el conjunto de personas que siguen una misma facción u opinión. 2. Partido, parcialidad o coligación; facción. **Party politics,** política de partidos. 3. Parte, cualquiera de los litigantes en un pleito. 4. Interesado. **He, too, was a party to the affair,** él tomó también parte en el asunto, o estuvo interesado en él. 5. Partida, función, convite, tertulia, reunión escogida de personas para comer juntas o divertirse. **Party of pleasure,** día de campo. *(Amer.)* Día de jarana o de diversión. **A hunting, fishing,** o **riding party,** una partida de caza, de pesca, una cabalgata. **To go (out) to a party,** ir de tertulia. **Party dress,** vestido de fiesta. **Party-goer,** asiduo, aficionado a las fiestas. **To join the party,** agregarse a la partida; también, afiliarse a un partido. 6. Partida, cierto número de soldados. 7. *(Fam. o bajo)* Persona, individuo.

party-colored [ˈpɑːtɪˌkʌləd] [par-ti-ka-lad], *a.* Abigarrado.

party-jury [ˈpɑːtɪˌdʒʊərɪ] [par-ti-yu-ri], *s.* Jurado compuesto por mitad de ingleses y de personas de cualquier otra nación.

party line [ˈpɑːtɪlaɪn] [par-ti-lain], *s.* 1. Línea telefónica que sirve a varios suscriptores. 2. Linde. 3. Política y normas fijadas por un partido político.

party-man [ˈpɑːtɪmən] [par-ti-man], *s.* Partidario, parcial, hombre de partido.

party-wall [ˈpɑːtɪwɔːl] [par-ti-uol], *s.* Pared medianera.

parvenu [ˈpɑːvənjuː] [par-ve-niu], *s.* y *a.* Medrado, el que desde condición oscura ha hecho gran fortuna o ha obtenido posición y honores superiores a sus méritos.

parvis [ˈpɑːvɪz] [par-vis], *s.* 1. *(Arq.)* El atrio delante de la puerta principal de una iglesia; el espacio alrededor del tabernáculo de los judíos. 2. Controversia académica.

pas [ˈpæs] [pas], *s.* 1. Paso. 2. Baile. 3. Precedencia. *V.* PRECEDENCE.

Paschal [ˈpɑːskəl] [pas-kal], *a.* Pascual.

pash [ˈpæʃ] [pash], *va.* Herir, golpear.

pasha [ˈpæʃə] [pa-sha], *s.* Bajá, gobernador, general o almirante turco o egipcio; funcionario de alta clase.

pasquinade [ˈpɑːskɪneɪd] [pas-kui-neid], **pasquil** [ˈpæskwɪl] [pas-kuil], **pasquin** [ˈpæskwɪn] [pas-kuin], *s.* Pasquín, pasquinada.

pass [pɑːs] [pas], *va.* 1. Pasar, llevar o conducir de un lugar a otro. 2. Pasar, ir más allá del punto determinado. 3. Pasar, atravesar, traspasar, cruzar. 4. Pasar, aprobar un cuerpo deliberante algún proyecto de ley, decreto u otra cosa. 5. Pasar la vida, el tiempo, las horas, etc. 6. Pasar, transferir o trasladar una cosa de un sujeto a otro. 7. Pasar, colar, cener. 8. Pasar, exceder, aventajar, superar. 9. Pasar, no poner reparo, censura o tacha en alguna cosa. 10. Pasar, hacer tener una cosa por otra. 11. Pasar, enviar. *-vn.* 1. Pasar, ir a alguna parte y transitar caminando por ella. 2. Pasar, cesar, disiparse, desvanecerse o acabarse alguna cosa; morir. 3. Pasar de un estado o situación a otro diverso. 4. Propasarse o excederse. 5. Pasar, ocurrir, suceder. 6. Pasar, ser admitida sin reparo la moneda, y por extensión se dice de otras muchas cosas; obtener aceptación general. 7. Pasar, admitirse o aprobarse alguna opinión, hecho, etc. 8. Omitir, dejar de hacer una cosa. 9. Pasar, vivir con alguna comodidad. 10. Pasar, salir con una exoneración del vientre. 11. Pasar, dar una estocada, hacer un pase en la esgrima. 12. En los juegos de naipes, dar al próximo jugador el derecho de elegir entre dos jugadas. 13. Arrojar una pelota a otro, como ejercicio.

pass about/around, pasar de mano en mano.

pass along, pasar a lo largo. **As I passed along,** al pasar yo.

pass away, gastar, desperdiciar; consumir, desvanecer, disipar; pasarse, irse consumiendo una cosa; fallecer.

pass by, pasar, excusar, olvidar, perdonar; omitir pasar por o cerca de alguna cosa; ir más allá de un punto determinado. **To pass by in silence,** pasar en silencio, pasar por alto.

pass for, pasar por, ser tenido o reputado.

pass off, dar o circular como legítimo lo que no es; pasar, seguir su curso; disiparse.

pass on o **upon,** entregar al próximo; engañar o abusar de alguien; formar juicio sobre, examinar y decidir sobre; *(Des.)* pasar su camino.

pass out, salir, perder el sentido.

pass over, atravesar, cruzar; pasar por alto; excusar, perdonar; no hacer caso; olvidar.

pass through, aguantar, pasar por; desvanecerse.

pass up, subir, volver o subir. **To pass a trick,** jugar una pieza. **To pass censures,** censurar. **To pass compliments,** hacer cumplimienots; dirigir alabanzas o elogios. **To pass sentence** o **judgment,** pronunciar sentencia. **To pass one's word for another,** empeñar su palabra por otro. **To come to pass,** suceder, acontecer. **To let pass,** dejar pasar, permitir; conceder entrada; excusar, no hacer caso, olvidar, perdonar. **To make a pass to,** tirar una puñalada a uno. **To bring to pass,** tracer a efecto, hacer suceder, efectuar.

pass, *s.* 1. Pasillo; paso, pasaje, lugar por donde se pasa; desfiladero, garganta, desembocadero; curso de las aguas. 2. Pase, licencia o permiso para pasar, o para ir y venir; billete de favor; a veces, pasaporte. 3. Estado, condición; crisis. 4. Salida feliz de un examen, prueba o inspección. 5. Gesto que hacen con la mano o con una varilla los magnetizadores. 6. Estocada. **Pass-book,** libro de cuenta y razón. **Pass-key,** llave maestra, ganzúa. **Pass-parole,** *(Mil.)* circule el santo y seña.

passable [ˈpɑːsəbl] [pa-sa-bol], *a.* 1. Pasadero, transitable. 2. Pasadero, que se puede tolerar. 3. Pasadero, que es medianamente bueno.

passably [ˈpɑːsəblɪ] [pa-sa-bli], *adv.* Tolerablemente, medianamente.

passage [ˈpæsɪdʒ] [pa-sich], *s.* 1. Pasaje; travesía. 2. Pasadizo; callejón, corredor. 3. Pasaje, paso, sitio o lugar por donde se pasa, camino. 4. Pasaje, porción corta de algún libro, escrito o discurso. 5. Ocurrencia, acontecimiento. **Passage-boat,** bote de pasaje. 6. Derecho de pasaje; libertad o facultad de pasar; entrada, salida, o tránsito libres. 7. Adopción de una ley. 8. Encuentro personal, pelea, disputa. 9. Migración, viaje periódico, particularmente de las aves. 10. Cámara, cagada, exoneración del vientre. **In the passage of time,** con el paso del tiempo.

passageway ['pæsɪdʒweɪ] [pa-sich-uei], *s.* Pasadizo, pasillo.

passe ['pæs] [pas], *pp.* y *a.* 1. Que ha pasado un examen para el ascenso. 2. Anterior, de otro tiempo. 3. Decretado, promulgado. *V.* PASS.

passé ['pæseɪ] [pa-sei], *a.* Pasado de moda.

passenger ['pæsndʒər] [pa-san-yaʳ], *s.* Pasajero, transeúnte; viajero.

passer ['pæsəʳ], [pa-saʳ], *s.* El que pasa; viandante.

passer-by ['pæsə'baɪ] [pa-sa-bai], *s.* Transeúnte.

passerine ['pæsərɪn] [pa-sa-rin], *a.* Paserino, parecido a los gorriones, o propio de ellos.

passibility [ˌpæsɪ'bɪlɪtɪ] [pa-si-bi-li-ti], **passibleness** ['pæsɪblnɪs] [pa-si-bol-nes], *s.* Pasibilidad, la capacidad de recibir impresiones de los agentes externos.

passim ['pæsɪm] [pa-sim], *adv.* Aquí y allá, repetidas veces, en varios pasajes de un libro o escrito.

passing ['pɑːsɪŋ] [pa-sin], *a.* 1. Pasajero, transitorio, momentáneo. 2. Pasando, sucediendo, ocurriendo. 3. *(Ant.)* Sobresaliente, eminente. *-adv.* Eminentemente, perfectamente. *-s.* 1. Paso, pasaje; salida; de aquí, muerte. 2. Adopción de un proyecto de ley; dictado de una sentencia. **Passing-place,** desviadero de los ferrocarriles. **Passing shot,** tiro pasado (sports).

passing-bell ['pɑːsɪŋbel] [pa-sin-bel], *s.* La campana que toca a muerto.

passion ['pæʃən] [pa-shon], *s.* 1. Pasión. 2. Impresión, el efecto o alteración que causa en un cuerpo otro extraño. 3. Ira, cólera, enojo. **To put into a passion,** encolerizar, irritar, sacar de sus casillas. 4. Pasión, fuerte afición a una cosa con preferencia a las demás; amor, afecto; celo, ardor. 5. Pasión, los últimos tormentos y muerte que padeció el Redentor del mundo. **Passion-week,** semana de pasión. **To burst into a passion,** irritarse, montar en cólera.

passionate ['pæʃənɪt] [pa-sho-nit], *a.* Apasionado; colérico; arrebatado, mohino; ardiente; vivo, impetuoso, intenso. **A passionate lover,** un amante apasionado, ardiente. **Passionate longing,** antojo, anhelo vivo o intenso.

passionately ['pæʃənɪtlɪ] [pa-sho-nit-li], *adv.* Apasionadamente; ardientemente; impetuosamente; coléricamente, enojosamente. **To be passionately in love,** amar perdidamente.

passionateness ['pæʃənɪtnɪs] [pa-sho-nit-nes], *s.* La disposición a encolerizarse; vehemencia de afectos; impetuosidad.

passionfruit ['pæʃənfruːt] [pa-shon-frut], *s.* Fruta de la pasión.

passionless ['pæʃənlɪs] [pa-shon-les], *a.* Frío, soso, desamorado; insensible, sin pasiones.

passive ['pæsɪv] [pa-siv], *a.* 1. Pasivo, que es objeto de una acción sin cooperar en ella. 2. Quieto; inactivo, inerte. 3. Pasivo, que recibe o padece sin resistencia. 4. En sentido pasivo. *-s.* La voz pasiva.

passively ['pæsɪvlɪ] [pa-siv-li], *adv.* Pasivamente.

passiveness ['pæsɪvnɪs] [pa-siv-nes], **passivity** ['pæsɪvɪtɪ] [pa-si-vi-ti], *s.* 1. Pasividad. 2. Sensibilidad. 3. Calma, paciencia.

passkey ['pæskɪ] [pas-ki], *s. f.* Llave maestra.

Passover ['pɑːsəʊvəʳ] [pa-sou-vaʳ], *s.* Pascua de los hebreos.

passport ['pɑːspɔːt] [pas-port], *s.* Pasaporte.

password ['pɑːswɜːd] [pas-ued], *s.* Palabra de pase, santo y seña, contraseña.

past [pɑːst] [past], *a.* 1. Pasado, transcurrido, último. **These six days past,** estos seis últimos días. **At half-past five o'clock,** a las cinco y media dadas. 2. Concluído, terminado; consumado. *-s.* 1. Lo pasado, el tiempo que pasó; antecedentes, historia. 2. *(Gram.)* Pretérito. 3. Los antecedentes, la historia de alguien o de una nación. *-pp.* 1. Más de, después (time). 2. Más allá de, fuera de (place). 3. Fuera de alcance, sin. *adv.* Por delante. **To march past,** desfilar. **To fly past,** pasar volando. **It is past four,** son más de las cuatro. **He is past recovery,** no hay esperanzas de que se cure. **Past the strait,** más allá del estrecho. **Past feeling,** fuera de sentido, sin sentido. **Past a doubt,** fuera de duba. **Past bearing,** insoportable; infecundo. **Past president,** presidente que fue, ex-presidente. **Past cure,** incurable. **Past dispute,** incontestable, fuera de duda. **Past** con referencia a empleos, se traduce *ex*, o *que fué*.

pasta ['pæstə] [pas-ta], *s.* Pasta alimenticia.

paste [peɪst] [peist], *s.* 1. Pasta, masa formada y unida de manera que forme un cuerpo viscoso (for sticking). 2. Engrudo, la masa que se hace de harina para pegar una cosa. 3. Pasta, la masa de que se hacen fideos, tallarines y otras cosas que sirven para sopa. 4. Una mezcla artificial hecha a imitación de las piedras preciosas. 5. Pasta, confección hecha de azúcar, goma, etc., con los zumos de frutas.

paste, *va.* Engrudar, pegar alguna cosa con engrudo.

pasteboard ['peɪstbɔːd] [peist-bord], *s.* Cartón fuerte. **Pasteboard binding,** encuadernación en cartoné.

pastel ['pætəl] [pas-tal], *s.* 1. Pastel, especie de dibujo hecho con lápices especiales de varios colores (drawing). 2. Lápiz de arcilla dura, de varios colores, clarioncillo (crayon). 3. *(Bot.)* Hierba pastel o glasto, planta; o su tinte azul.

pastern ['pæstɜːn] [pas-tern], *s.* 1. Cuartilla del caballo. 2. Atadura para los pies de un caballo.

pasteurize ['pæstəraɪz] [pas-ta-rais], *v.* Pasterizar (milk, etc.).

pasteurization [ˌpæstərɑɪ'zeɪʃən] [pas-ta-rai-sei-shon], *s.* Pasterización (of milk, etc.).

pastiche [pæs'tiːʃ] [pas-tish], *s. m.* Imitación, pastiche.

pastil ['pæstɪl] [pas-til], *s.* 1. Pastilla de olor, pasta para sahumerios. 2. Pastilla de boca. 3. En pirotecnia, el tubo de papel donde se contiene la pólvora que hace girar las ruedas y otros fuegos de artificio. 4. Pastel. *V.* PASTEL.

pastime ['pæstaɪm] [pas-taim], *s.* Pasatiempo, diversión, recreación.

past master ['pæstmɑːstəʳ] [pas-tai-maʳ], *s.* 1. Exfuncionario de una logia masónica. 2. Autoridad o experto (en alguna materia).

pastor ['pɑːstəʳ] [pas-toʳ], *s.* 1. Pastor espiritual, ministro del Evangelio que tiene a su cargo una iglesia, congregación o cura de almas. 2. Estornino. 3. *(Des.)* Pastor, zagal.

pastoral ['pɑːstərəl] [pas-to-ral], *a.* 1. Pastoril, que pertenece a los pastores de ganado. 2. Pastoral, que se refiere a un pastor o a la cura de almas. *-s.* 1. Pastoral, pastoril, bucólica; idilio. 2. Obra de arte que representa escenas campestres. 3. Pastoral, carta pastoral. 4. Pastorela.

pastorate ['pæstəreɪt] [pas-to-reit], *s.* 1. Oficio, estado o dignidad de un pastor; la cura de almas. 2. Tiempo que dura su cargo o curato.

pastorship ['pæstəʃɪp] [pas-tor-ship], *s. V.* PASTORATE.

pastry ['peɪstrɪ] [peis-tri], *s.* Pastelería, pasteles, pastas. **Pastry brush,** cepillo para repostería. **Pastrycase,** cobertura de pasta. **Pastry cutter,** cortador de pasta. **Pastry shop,** pastelería, confitería, repostería.

pastry-cook ['peɪstrɪkʊk] [peis-tri-kuk], *s.* Pastelero.

pasturable ['pɑːstjʊrəbl] [pas-tiu-ra-bol], *a.* Bueno para pasto.

pasturage ['pɑːstjʊrɪdʒ] [pas-tiu-rich], *s.* 1. Pastos, las hierbas que sirven para alimenatar a los animales. 2. Pasturaje, el lugar de pasto abierto o común. 3. Ganadería, el tráfico en ganados.

pasture ['pɑːstʃəʳ] [pas-chaʳ], *s.* 1. Apacentadero, dehesa (land). 2. Pastura, pasto; apacentamiento (grass). **Pasture-ground,** dehesa, pradera, apacentadero; pasturaje. *(Fig.)* **She's gone to pastures new,** ha pasado a mejor vida.

pasture, *va.* Pastar, apacentar. *-vn.* Pastar, pacer o comer la hierba del campo los ganados.

pasty ['peɪstɪ] [peis-ti], *a.* Pastoso, semejante a la pasta, o de la consistencia de ésta. *-s.* Pastel de carne. **Pasty-faced,** pálido.

Pat [pæt] [pat], *n. Diminutivo de* **Patrick** o **Patricia.**

pat, *a.* Apto, conveniente, propio, bueno, cómodo. *-s.* 1. Pasagonzalo, golpecillo ligero y acariciador dado con la mano o con los dedos. 2. Pastilla, masa pequeña moldeada o formada con los dedos; pastellino. *-adv.* Aptamente, convenientemente. 3. Pequeño golpe, palmadita (with hand). Caricia (caress). **To know something off pat,** saberse algo al dedillo. **To stand pat,** mantenerse firme, en sus trece *(EU).*

pat, *va.* Dar golpecillos, tocar ligeramente con la mano, de una manera suave y cariñosa. *vt.* Dar una palmada, tocar (touch).

patch [pætʃ] [pach], *va.* 1. Remendar, apedazar, echar remiendos o pedazos a alguna cosa rota (cloths, etc.). 2. Adornar el rostro con lunares o parches de tafetán negro. 3. Chafallar, hacer o remendar alguna cosa sin arte ni aseo. 4. Componer una cosa con retazos de diversos géneros; se usa generalmente con **up** (denotando el resultado) o **together** (indicando los materiales). *-vn.* Echar remiendos, hacer labor de retazos. **To patch up a quarrel,** hacer las paces.

patch, *s.* 1. Remiendo. 2. Pieza embutida en obra mosaica. 3. Lunar, parche de tafetán negro con el cual las señoras solían adornar sus rostros (spot). 4. Terreno, pedazo de tierra. **Patch of land** o **ground,** pedazo de terreno. **A patch of chocolate,** una mancha de chocolate. **It's not a patch on the other one,** no se puede comparar con el otro

patcher [ˈpætʃər] [pa-char], *s.* Chafallón; remendón.

patchwork [ˈpætʃwɜːk] [pach-uek], *s.* Obra o labor de retacitos; taracea de paño o lienzo, mosaico.

patchy [ˈpætʃɪ] [pa-chi], *a.* No uniforme, desigual.

pate [peɪt] [peit], *s. (Fest)* 1. La cabeza. 2. *(Fort.)* Especie de media luna.

pâté [ˈpɑːteɪ] [pa-tei], *s. m.* Paté, pastel.

pated [ˈpeɪtɪd] [pei-tid], *a.* Lo que tiene cabeza. **Long-pated man,** hombre de entendimiento, hombre de gran cabeza.

patella [pəˈtelə] [pa-te-la], *s.* 1. Rótula o choquezuela de la rodilla. 2. *(Zool.)* Parte semejante a una copa. 3. Vasija o cazo pequeño.

paten [ˈpætən] [pa-ten], *s.* Plato; en especial, patena, el platillo en donde se pone la hostia en la misa.

patent [ˈpeɪtənt] [pei-tent], *a.* Patente, manifiesto, visible (obvious); público. *-s.* 1. Patente, privilegio exclusivo; privilegio de invención, documento que garantiza al inventor, durante cierto número de años, el derecho exclusivo de explotar un invento nuevo. 2. Cédula oficial, como de tierras, de privilegio, título o franquicia. **Patent leather,** charol. **Patent Office,** oficina de los privilegios de invención, o de patentes.

patent, *va.* 1. Obtener una patente o privilegio exclusivo. 2. Conceder por cartas patentes, por privilegio.

patentable [ˈpeɪtəntəbl] [pei-ten-ta-bol], *a.* Que puede ser objeto de privilegio exclusivo.

patentee [ˌpeɪtənˈtiː] [pei-ten-ti], *s.* Privilegiado, el que tiene una patente, que disfruta un privilegio exclusivo.

patent leather [ˈpeɪtəntˌleðər] [pei-tent-le-daʳ], *s.* Charol.

patent medicine [ˈpeɪtəntˌmedsɪn] [pei-tent-med-sin], *s.* Medicina de patente.

paternal [pəˈtɜːnl] [pa-ter-nal], *a.* Paternal, paterno.

paternalism [pəˈtɜːnəlɪzəm] [pa-ter-na-li-sem], *s.* Paternalismo.

paternalist [pəˈtɜːnəlɪst] [pa-ter-na-list], *a.* Paternalista.

paternally [pəˈtɜːnəlɪ] [pa-ter-na-li], *adv.* Paternalmente.

paternity [pəˈtɜːnɪtɪ] [pa-ter-ni-ti], *s.* 1. Paternidad, cualidad de padre. 2. Linaje, alcurnia por parte de padre. 3. Origen en general.

pater-noster [ˈpætəˌnɒstər] [pa-ta-nos-taʳ], *s.* Paternóster, "padre nuestro", la oración dominical; *(Arq.)* contera.

path [pɑːθ] [paz], *s.* 1. Senda, sendero, vereda; camino estrecho para personas o animales (road, way). 2. Por extensión, camino, vía. 3. Paso, huella, curso, espacio, rastro, pista, trayectoria; de aquí, método de vida o de conducta. **To cross somebody's path,** crear dificultades a alguien, tropezar con alguien.

pathetic, pathetical [pəˈθetɪk] [pa-ze-tik], *a.* 1. Patético, tierno, conmovedor, que mueve a compasión y simpatía; que excita las emociones tiernas. 2. Apasionado, animado. **Pathetic fallacy,** engaño sentimental.

pathetically [pəˈθetɪkəlɪ] [pa-ze-ti-ka-li], *adv.* Patéticamente, tiernamente.

pathfinder [ˈpæθˌfaɪndər] [paz-fain-daʳ], *s.* Explorador que descubre un nuevo sendero.

pathless [ˈpæθlɪs] [paz-les], *a.* Intransitable, sin senda.

pathogenic [ˌpæθəˈdʒenɪk] [pa-zo-ye-nik], *a.* 1. Patógeno. 2. Patogénico.

pathological, pathologic [ˌpæθəˈlɒdʒɪkəl] [pa-zo-lo-yi-kal], *a.* Patológico.

pathologist [pəˈθɒlədʒɪst] [pa-zo-lo-yist], *s. (Med.)* Patólogo.

pathology [pəˈθɒlədʒɪ] [pa-zo-lo-yi], *s.* Patología, la parte de la medicina que trata de las enfermedades y de su naturaleza, causas y síntomas.

pathos [ˈpeɪθɒs] [pei-zos], *s.* Lo patético, lo tierno; lo que excita las pasiones y las emociones tiernas; lástima.

pathway [ˈpɑːθweɪ] [paz-uei], *s.* Senda, vereda, camino estrecho. *V.* PATH.

patience [ˈpeɪʃəns] [pei-shans], *s.* 1. Paciencia, resignación y tolerancia en los trabajos. 2. Paciencia, reposo, sosiego en lo que se desea. 3. *(Bot.)* Romaza, planta. **To be out of patience,** perder la paciencia, perder los estribos, salirse de sus casillas. **His patience is exhausted,** se le ha agotado la paciencia. **You wear out my patience,** Ud. pone a prueba mi paciencia. *(Fam.)* Me fastidias o eres muy majadero.

patient [ˈpeɪʃənt] [pei-shant], *a.* 1. Paciente, sufrido, asiduo, constante, que sufre con calma los males, injusticias y ofensas. 2. Constante, perseverante en sus esfuerzos. 3. tolerante, tierno, y que no se desalienta al ayudar a otros. 4. Que espera con calma, tranquilamente. 5. Sufrido, paciente en cuanto a las fatigas del cuerpo. *-s.* 1. Paciente, sujeto pasivo; persona o cosa que recibe impresiones externas. 2. Paciente, enfermo, el que padece alguna enfermedad o dolencia.

patiently [ˈpeɪʃəntlɪ] [pei-shant-li], *adv.* Pacientemente.

patina [ˈpætɪnə] [pa-ti-na], *s.* Pátina.

patio [ˈpætɪəʊ] [pa-tiou], *s.* Patio estilo español.

patness [ˈpætnɪs] [pat-nes], *s.* Aptitud, conveniencia.

patois [ˈpætwɑː] [pa-tua], *s.* Jerga, lenguaje corrompido y provincial.

patriarch [ˈpeɪtrɪɑːk] [pei-triak], *s.* 1. Patriarca, jefe de una familia, el que gobierna por derecho paterno. 2. Hombre anciano y venerable; de aquí, cualquier objeto digno de veneración.

patriarchal [ˌpeɪtrɪˈɑːkəl] [pei-tria-kal], *a.* Patriarcal.

patriarchate [ˌpeɪtrɪˈɑːkeɪt] [pei-tria-keit], **patriarchship** [ˈpeɪtrɪɑːkʃɪp] [pei-triak-ship], **patriarchy** [ˈpeɪtrɪɑːkɪ] [pei-tria-ki], *s.* Patriarcado.

patrician [pəˈtrɪʃən] [pa-tri-shan], *a.* Patricio, noble, de alcurnia aristocrática. *-s.* 1. Patricio, miembro de la nobleza de Roma. 2. Persona de alta clase. 3. Título de honor.

patricide [ˈpætrɪsaɪd] [pa-tri-said], *s. V.* PARRICIDE.

patrimonial [ˈpætrɪmənɪəl] [pa-tri-mo-nial], *a.* Patrimonial.

patrimony [ˈpætrɪmənɪ] [pa-tri-mo-ni], *s.* Patrimonio, lo bienes y hacienda que el hijo tiene heredados de su padre.

patriot [ˈpeɪtrɪət] [pei-triot], *s.* Patriota. *-a.* Patriótico.

patriotic [ˈpætrɪɒtɪk] [pa-trio-tik], *a.* Patriótico, inspirado por el amor al país natal a la patria, que tiene en mira el bien de su país.

patriotism [ˈpætrɪətɪzəm] [pa-trio-ti-sem], *s.* Patriotismo, celo patriótico, amor a la patria.

patrol [pəˈtrəʊl] [pa-troul], *s.* 1. El acto de patrullar. 2. Patrulla, el número de soldados que con un cabo salen a rondar. 3. Ronda del resguardo o de la policía. **Patrol car,** coche patrulla. **Patrol boat,** lancha patrullera.

patrol, *va.* y *vn.* Patrullar, rondar; hacer la ronda.

patrolman [pəˈtrəʊlmən] [pa-troul-man], *s.* Policía o vigilante rondador.

patrol wagon [pəˈtrəʊlˌwægən] [pa-troul-va-gon], *s.* Camión de policía.

patron [ˈpeɪtrən] [pei-tron], *s.* 1. Patrón, patrono, protector, defensor, amparador. 2. Patrón, el santo que se elige como especial protector. 3. Abogado, defensor. 4. Patrono, el que tiene el derecho del patronato eclesiástico.

patronage ['peɪtrənɪdʒ] [pei-tro-nich], *s.* 1. Patrocinio, amparo, protección. 2. Patronato, patronazgo, el derecho de presentar personas idóneas para empleos civiles o eclesiásticos. 3. El patrocinio de un santo.

patroness ['peɪtrənɪs] [pei-tro-nes], *s.f.* Patrona, protectora; señora, patrona de una obra de caridad o de una función social.

patronize ['pætrənaɪz] [pa-tro-nais], *va.* 1. Patrocinar, proteger (protect); apoyar, favorecer, alentar una empresa (promote). 2. Condescender con arrogancia. 3. *(Fam.)* Hacerse parroquiano de una tienda. **A patronizing manner,** aires o maneras condescendientes. **To be well patronized,** tener mucha clientela, estar acreditado (shop, etc.).

patronizer ['pætrənaɪzəʳ] [pa-tro-nai-saʳ], *s.* Patrón, patrocinador.

patronizing ['pætrənaɪzɪŋ] [pa-tro-nai-sin], *a.* Altivo, paternalista, superior.

patronless ['pætrənlɪs] [pa-tron-les], *a.* Desamparado, despatronado.

patronymic [ˌpætrəˈnɪmɪk] [pa-tro-ni-mik], *s.* y *a.* Patronímico, nombre de familia.

patsy ['pætsɪ] [pat-si], *a.* *(EU)* Bobo, estúpido, "primo".

patted ['pætɪd] [pa-tid], *a.* Golpeado ligeramente con la mano.

patten ['pætn] [pa-ten], *s.* 1. Galocha, zueco, especie de calzado de madera con la parte inferior muy gruesa. 2. Base de columna; cimiento, fundamento de una pared o muro.

patter ['pætəʳ] [pa-taʳ], *vn.* 1. Hacer ruido con una rápida sucesión de sonidos ligeros, como la lluvia. 2. **To patter with the feet,** patalear, patear; hacer ruido dando patadas. **To patter about,** amdar con pasos ligeros.

patter, *s.* 1. Sucesión de golpecitos o palmaditas. 2. Habla rápida y voluble. 3. Charla, habladuría, parlería (chat). 4. *(Bajo)* Dialecto, jerga.

pattern ['pætən] [pa-tern], *s.* 1. Model, dechado, norma. 2. Ejemplar, caso, suceso o hecho que se pone por modelo. 3. Muestra, la porción corta de alguna mercadería que se da para reconocer su calidad. 4. Patrón, dechado, cualquier cosa cortada en papel o en paño para imitar o trabajar sobre ella. **Goods of good patterns,** géneros de gusto o de moda.

pattern, *va.* Copiar, imitar; servir de ejemplo.

patterned ['pætənd] [pa-tend], *a.* Estampado (material).

patty ['pætɪ] [pa-ti], *s.* Pastelillo, pastel pequeño. **Patty-pan,** tortera o tartera.

patulous ['pætjʊləs] [pa-tiu-los], *a.* Abierto, extendido, un poco divergente.

paucity ['pɔːsɪtɪ] [po-si-ti], *s.* Poquedad, escasez, pequeño número, pequeña cantidad.

pauline ['pɔːlaɪn] [po-lain], *a.* Paulista, que se refiere a San Pablo.

paunch ['pɔːntʃ] [ponch], *s.* 1. Panza, barriga, vientre. 2. El *rumen* o primer estómago de los rumiantes. 3. Borde de una campana. 4. *(Mar.)* Pallete, jimelga de frente.

paunch *va.* Desbarrigar, romper o herir el vientre.

pauper ['pɔːpəʳ] [po-paʳ], *s.* Pobre, indigente, el que depende de la caridad, que no tiene para vivir más que los socorros de la parroquia o de la ciudad.

pauperism ['pɔːpərɪzəm] [po-pa-ri-sem], *s.* Pauperismo, indigencia, mucha pobreza, falta de medios de existencia.

pauperization [ˌpɔːpəraɪˈzeɪʃən] [po-pa-rai-sei-shon], *s.* Empobrecimiento.

pauperize, pauperise ['pɔːpəraɪz] [po-pa-rais], *va.* Reducir a la indigencia.

pause [pɔːz] [pos], *s.* 1. Pausa; duda, suspensión, interrupción del movimiento, acción o ejercicio. 2. Intervalo, tiempo de parada; interrupción o fin de párrafo. 3. Hesitación, irresolución, vacilación. 4. Signo que indica una pausa en música o puntuación. **I only require some pause,** no pido más que un poco de reposo. **To give somebody pause,** vacilar a alguien, dar que pensar a alguien. **Without pause,** sin descanso, sin interrupción.

pause, *-vn.* 1. Pausar, cesar, detenerse, interrumpirse, hacer una pausa (speaker); cesar de hablar por cualquier causa. 2. Tardar, pausar; vacilar. 3. Aguardar, estar en expectación. 4. Deliberar. **Pause a day or two,** aguarde Ud. uno o dos días. **Pause before you act,** piensa antes de actuar.

pauser ['pɔːzəʳ] [po-saʳ], *s.* El que se detiene; el que reflexiona o delibera.

pave [peɪv] [peiv], *va.* 1. Pavimentar, enladrillar, empedrar, enlosar, embaldosar. 2. Allanar el camino. **To pave the way for,** facilitar o allanar el camino para. **Paved road,** camino pavimentado.

pavement ['peɪvmənt] [peiv-ment], *s.* 1. Pavimento, suelo de losas o baldosas; empedrado de calle. 2. Camino o sendero empedrado. 3. El material con que está empedrada una superficie; pavimento. **Mosaic, tessellated pavement,** pavimento de mosaico.

paver ['peɪvəʳ] [pei-vaʳ], **pavier** ['peɪvɪəʳ] [pei-viaʳ], *s.* Empedrador; solador.

pavilion [pəˈvɪlɪən] [pa-vi-lion], *s.* 1. Pabellón, tienda de campaña; habitación movible y temporal; cenador de jardín. 2. *(Arq.)* Pabellón, construcción que forma parte del edificio principal. 3. Dosel, pabellón. 4. La oreja, el oído externo. 5. Pabellón, bandera.

paving ['peɪvɪŋ] [pei-vin], *s.* Empedrado, acción de empedrar; y empedrado, pavimento, la superficie empedrada. **Paving-stone,** adoquín. **Paving-tile,** loseta.

pavonine ['pævənaɪn] [pa-vo-nain], *a.* Relativo o que pertenece al pavo real; (Poco us.) irisado.

paw [pɔː] [po], *s.* 1. Garra, pata de un animal. 2. *(Fest.)* Garra, mano tosca del hombre; manaza.

paw, *-vn.* Patear el caballo o escarbar la tierra con un pie delantero. **To pat the ground,** piafar (horse). *-va.* 1. Herir con el pie delantero. 2. Manosear alguna cosa con poca maña o ajándola.

pawed ['pɔːd] [pod], *a.* Armado de garras; patiancho.

pawl ['pɔːl] [pol], *s.* Linguete, fiador de rueda, paleta de reloj, diente de encaje, retén, seguro. **Pawl of the capstan,** linguete del cabrestante. **Supporter of the pawl,** *(Mar.)* descanso del linguete. **Hanging pawls,** *(Mar.)* linguete de por alto.

pawn ['pɔːn] [pon], *va.* Empeñar, dar o dejar alguna cosa en prenda.

pawn, *s.* 1. Prenda, la alhaja que se entrega para la seguridad de alguna deuda o contrato. 2. Prenda, la condición de ser tenido como garantía del dinero prestado. **In pawn,** en prenda. 3. Peón, pieza del juego de ajedrez.

pawnbroker ['pɔːnˌbrəʊkəʳ] [pon-brou-kaʳ], *s.* 1. Prestamista, prendero, el que presta dinero y recibe prendas en seguridad de la deuda. 2. *(For.)* Comodatario.

pawnee ['pɔːniː] [po-ni], *s.* 1. Prestador, prestamista sobre prendas. 2. Nombre de una tribu de indios norteamericanos.

pawnshop ['pɔːnʃɒp] [pon-shop], *s.* Montepío, monte de piedad, casa de empeño.

pawpaw ['pɔːpɔː] [po-po], *s.f.* Papaya.

pax ['pæks] [paks], *s.* Paz, en la misa.

pay [peɪ] [pei], *va.* (*pret.* y *pp.* PAID). 1. Pagar; remunerar, recompensar. 2. Gastar, desembolsar; cubrir o pagar los gastos de; distribuir en pagos. 3. Dar tributo, ofrecer algo a uno; dar, hacer. 4. Ser provechoso a, aprovechar. 5. Pagar, sufrir el castigo o la pena por alguna falta, culpa, olvido, etc. 6. Pagar, corresponder a los beneficios que se reciben. *-vn.* 1. Pagar, satisfacer una deuda (bill, debt). 2. Producir adecuada ganancia, dar provecho. **To pay in full,** pagar por completo.

pay away, desembolsar, pagar.

pay back, pagar; devolver lo que se ha recibido; restituir.

pay down, pagar en dinero contante o al contado.

pay for, pagar una cosa que se compra; espiar, satisfacer, purgar culpas, pecados o yerros.

pay in, ingresar.

pay off, (a) pagar el sueldo completo. (b) Despedir, despachar. (c) Retornar, desquitar, pagar en la misma moneda.

pay out a cable, *(Mar.)* arriar el cable.

pay over, entregar, pagar.

pay up, pagar (de mala gana).

pay attention to, (a) dar, prestar atención a. (b) Dedicar atenciones a una mujer, cortejarla, galantearla. **To pay one's addresses to,** cortejar, pretender en matrimonio a una mujer. **To pay due honor to,** tributar a uno los honores que le son debidos. **Pay him my respects,** hágale Ud. presentes mis respetos. **He will get paid,** hará que le paguen. **He must be paid,** es menester pagarle. **To rob Peter to pay Paul,** ganar el cielo con rosario ajeno; literalmente, robar a Pedro para pagar a Pablo. **To pay a visit,** hacer una visita. **To pay on account,** pagar a cuenta. **To pay oneself,** tomarse la paga por su mano. **To pay cash,** pagar al contado. **To pay by instalments,** pagar a plazos.

pay, *va.* Embrear. **To pay a ship's bottom,** *(Mar.)* despalmar, embrear y alquitranar la embarcación. **To pay the seams,** *(Mar.)* embrear las costuras.

pay, *s.* 1. Paga; sueldo, salario. **Equal pay,** igualdad de salario. *(Mil.)* la paga diaria del soldado. 2. Compensación, recompensa; equivalente. 3. Recompensa, merecido, pena. **Half-pay,** medio sueldo. **Half-pay officer,** oficial retirado. **Pay-clerk,** empleado pagador. **Pay-dirt, pay-gravel,** tierra o arena que da cantidad provechosa de oro. **Pay increase,** incremento salarial. **To get one's pay,** cobrar. **Pay TV,** televisión de pago.

payable ['perəbl] [peia-bol], *a.* Pagadero. **Bill payable in March,** letra que vence en marzo.

paycheck ['pertʃek] [pei-chek], *s. m.* Pago, sueldo *(EU)*.

payday ['pertder] [pei-dei], *s.* Día de paga.

payee [peɹi:] [peii], *s. (For.)* La persona a quien se paga una letra de cambio; aquél a quien hacerse un pago.

payer ['peɪəʳ] [peiaʳ], *s.* Pagador. **Bad/slow payer,** moroso.

paying ['peɪɪŋ] [pei-yin], *s.* 1. El acto de despedir a alguno. 2. El acto de alquitranar o embrear. 3. Sacudimiento, apaleamiento. **Paying away** o **out,** *(Mar.)* el acto de arriar un cabo. **Paying guest,** pensionista, huésped de pago. **Paying off,** el acto de pagar a alguno. **Paying teller,** empleado pagador de un banco.

payload ['peɪləʊd] [pei-loud], *s.* Carga útil.

paymaster ['peɪmɑːstəʳ] [pei-mas-taʳ], *s.* Pagador. *(Mil.)* Habilitado.

payment ['peɪmənt] [pei-ment], *s.* 1. Pago, paga, pagamento. 2. Pago, recompensa, premio. 3. Paliza, zurra. **To take goods in payment,** tomar mercancías en pago. **To stop payment,** suspender los pagos, dar punto a los negocios. **Cash payment,** pago al contado, en especie. **Payment in instalments,** pago a plazos. **Payment in full (of all demands),** saldo de cuenta. **To delay, to defer the payment,** diferir, aplazar el pago. **To sue for payment,** perseguir el pago. **To meet a payment,** hacer frente a un pago. **On the payment of,** mediante el pago de. **Payment on invoice,** pago al presentar la factura. **Payment terms,** condiciones de pago.

paynim, painim ['peɪnɪm] [pei-nim], *a. y s. (Ant.)* Pagano, gentílico; mahometano. Paganismo, gentilismo.

payoff ['peɪɒf] [pei-of], *s.* 1. Acto de pagar salarios o sueldos. 2. Retribución. 3. *(Fam.)* Desenlace.

pay pause ['peɪpɔːz] [pei-pos], *s.* Congelación de salarios.

payroll ['peɪrəʊl] [pei-roul], *s.* Nómina de sueldos. *(Mex.)* Lista de raya.

PBS *(EU) Abreviatura de* **Public Broadcasting Service.**

PD *(EU) Abreviatura de* **Police Department.**

pea [piː] [pi], *s. (pl.* PEAS o PEASE). Guisante. Pisum sativum. **Canned peas,** guisantes en latas. **Chick-pea,** garbanzo. **Pea-chafer,** *V.* **Pea-weevil. Pea-green,** verde claro, color de guisante tierno. **Pea-gun,** cerbatana. **Peapod, pea-shell,** vaina de guisante. **Pea-weevil,** gorgojo. **Sweet pea,** látiro oloroso, guisante de olor.

peace [piːs] [pis], *s.* 1. Paz. 2. Paz, reposo, tranquilidad, sosiego. 3. Paz, descanso eterno. 4. Silencio, quietud. 5.

Estado de reconciliación, concordia, buena inteligencia, armonía. *-inter.* ¡Paz! ¡silencio! **To break the peace,** perturbar la paz. **To keep the peace,** no turbar la paz pública. **To hold one's peace,** guardar silencio, no hablar, callarse. **Peace establishment** o **footing,** *(Mil.)* pie de paz. **Peace Movement,** movimiento por la paz. **Justice of the peace,** juez de paz. alcalde. *V.* JUSTICE. **Peace-offering,** sacrificio propiciatorio. **Peace-officer,** el ministro de justicia que está encargado de la tranquilidad pública; guardia civil. **Peace talks,** negociaciones para la paz.

peaceable ['piːsəbl] [pi-sa-bol], *a.* Tranquilo, sosegado, pacífico, apacible.

peaceableness ['piːsəblnɪs] [pi-sa-bol-nes], *s.* Quietud, tranquilidad; carácter pacífico.

peaceably ['piːsəblɪ] [pi-sa-bli], *adv.* Pacíficamente, apaciblemente.

peaceful ['piːsfʊl] [pis-ful], *a.* Tranquilo, quieto, sosegado, pacífico.

peacefully ['piːsfʊlɪ] [pis-fu-li], *adv.* Tranquilamente, apaciblemente.

peacefulness ['piːsfʊlnɪs] [pis-ful-nes], *s.* Quietud, calma, tranquilidad, sosiego.

peace-keeper ['piːskiːpəʳ] [pis-ki-paʳ], *s.* Pacificador *(Mil.).*

peace-maker ['piːsmeɪkəʳ] [pis-mei-kaʳ], *s.* Pacificador.

peace pipe ['piːspaɪp] [pis-paip], *s.* Pipa de paz de las ceremonias de los indios de E.U.

peach [piːtʃ] [pich], *s. (Bot.)* Melocotón, durazno, pérsico, albérchigo (fruit); también melocotonero, durazon, pérsico, el árbol que produce estas frutas. **Freestone peach,** abridero; pérsico cuya carne no está adherida al hueso. **Clingstone peach,** albérchigo o pavía. **Dried peaches,** orejones. **Peach-borer,** mariposa nocturna azul. **She is a peach,** es un bombón, es una preciosidad. **Peach-yellows,** una enfermedad de los melocotoneros que causa la madurez prematura del fruto y poner amarillas las hojas.

peach, *-vn. (Fam.)* Hacerse delator de un cómplice.

peach-colored ['piːtʃkʌləd] [pich-ka-lad], *a.* Que tiene color de melocotón.

peach-tree ['piːtʃtriː] [pich-tri], *s.* Melocotonero, pérsico, un árbol.

peacock, peafowl ['piːkɒk] [pi-kok], *s.* Pavón o pavo real.

peahen ['piːhen] [pi-jen], *sf.* Pava real, la hembra del pavón.

peak [piːk] [pik], *s.* 1. Cima o cumbre, pico, montaña que termina en punta y sobresale de las otras. 2. Pico, cualquier cosa que remata en punta. 3. *(Mar.)* Pena o penol, pico, espiga de vela. **Peak-halliards,** *(Mar.)* drizas de la pena. **Peak hours,** hora punta. **Peak period,** periodo de gran o máxima actividad.

peak, *-vn.* Tener apariencia de enfermo. *-va. (Mar.)* Amantillar el pico. levantar una verga contra el mástil.

peaked ['piːkt] [pikt], *a.* 1. Puntiagudo; con caballete, como un tejado. 2. *(Fam.)* Enfermizo o flaco en apariencia. **Peaked cap,** gorra de visera.

peaking ['piːkɪŋ] [pi-kin], *a.* 1. Enfermizo, flaco, lánguido; ignoble. 2. *(Fam.)* Enfermizo, malucho.

peakish ['piːkɪʃ] [pi-kish], *a.* Perteneciente a la cima o cumbre de una montaña o a cualquier cosa que termina en pico.

peaky ['piːkɪ] [pi-ki], *a.* 1. Abundante en picos o cumbres. 2. *(Fam.)* De apariencia enfermiza.

peal [piːl] [pil], *s.* 1. Repique de campanas (bells). 2. Estruendo como el de los truenos o cañones; estrépito. **To ring the bells in a peal,** tocar las campanas a vuelo. **The last peal,** el último repique o toque, la última llamada. **Peal of laughter,** carcajada, risotada.

peal, *-vn.* Tocar con mucho ruido. *-va.* 1. Aturdir haciendo ruido muy grande. 2. Moverse alguna cosa con mucha agitación.

peanut ['piːnʌt] [pi-nat], *s.* Cacahué, cacahuete. *(Mex.)* Cacahuate. *(Cuba)* Maní. **Peanut brittle,** crocante de cacahuate o de maní. *(Mex.)* Pepitoria. **Peanut butter,** mantequilla de cacahuate o de maní.

peapod ['piːpɒd] [pi-pod], *s.* Vaina de guisante.

pear [pɛəʳ] [peaʳ], *s.* Pera, el fruto del peral (fruit); también el peral mismo (tree). **Pear-blight,** tizón, enfermedad de los perales. **Pear-shaped,** piriforme, en forma de pera. **Pear-tree,** peral.

pearl [pəːl] [parl], *s.* 1. Perla, concreción depositada en las conchas de varios moluscos, muy estimada en joyería. 2. Perla. alguna cosa parecida a una perla, como una gota de rocío, una lágrima; cosa preciosa, o exquisita en su clase; también, madreperla, nacar. 3. (*Impr.*) Perla, tipo o letra de 5 puntos. **Mother-of-pearl,** nácar, madreperla. **Pearl seed** o **seed pearl,** aljofar, rostrillo. **Pearl buttons,** botones de madreperla. **Puste pearl,** perla de papelillo. 4. Nube o catarata en el ojo. 5. (*Her.*) Perla, blanco o plata. **Pearl-ash,** potasa purificada, álcali vegetal refinado. **Pearl-barley,** cebada mondada, perlada. **Pearl-eyed,** el que tiene una nube en el ojo. **Pearl-grass, pearl-plant, pearlwort,** (*Bot.*) especie de saginia. **Pearl grey,** gris perla. **Pearl-oyster,** molusco parecido a la ostra que produce perlas; la Meleagrina margaritífera. **Pearl-powder, pearl-white,** blanco de perla, oxicloruro de bismuto.

pearled [pəːlɪd] [par-lid], *a.* Alfoforado; guarnecido de perlas.

pearly [pəːlɪ] [per-li], *a.* Que consta de perlas o es semejante a ellas.

peart [pəːt] [pert], *a.* (*Fam.*) Jovial, en buena salud y buen humor; alegre; vivaracho, activo.

peasant [pezənt] [pe-sant], *s.* Labriego, patán, el aldeano y labrador rústico. -*a.* Aldeano, campesino, rústico, agreste. **Peasan-like,** campesino, agreste.

peasantry [pezəntrɪ] [pe-san-tri], *s.* La gente del campo, lo aldeanos, los lugareños.

peascod [piːzkɒd] [peis-kod], **pea-shell** [piːʃel] [pi-shel], *s.* La vaina de los guisantes.

pease [piːz] [pis], *s. pl.* Guisantes, chícharos, en cantidad o colectivamente.

peat [piːt] [pit], *s.* 1. Turba, tierra bituminosa, que sirve de combustible. 2. Turba o césped de tierra de que se hace carbón. **Peat-bog,** pantano turboso. **Peat-charcoal,** carbón de turba. **Peat-moss,** (a) musgo de pantano. (b) (*Prov.*) Pantano turboso.

peaty [piːtɪ] [pi-ti], *a.* Turboso; parecido a la turba o que la contiene.

pebble, pebble-stone [pebl] [pe-bel], *s.* 1. Guija, china; piedra redondeada por las aguas, de tamaño menor que un guijarro. **She's not the only pebble on the beach,** no es la única en el mundo. 2. Cuero abollonado. 3. Pólvora gruesa. 4. Lente de cristal de roca.

pebble, *va.* y -*vn.* Granular, abollonar la superficie del cuero; presentar apariencia áspera.

pebbled [pebld] [pe-beld], *a.* Lleno de guijas.

pebble-ground [peblˈgraʊnd] [pe-bel-graund], *s.* (*Mar.*) Fondo de cascajo.

pebbly [peblɪ] [pe-blI], *a.* Abundante en guijas o chinas; guijoso.

pecan [piːkæn] [pi-kan], *s.* Pacana, pecana, árbol americano parecido al nogal y su fruto.

peccability [pekəˈbɪlɪtɪ] [pe-ka-bi-li-ti], *s.* Fragilidad, disposición a pecar.

peccable [pekəbl] [pe-ka-bol], *a.* Pecable, capaz de pecar.

peccadillo [pekəˈdɪləʊ] [pe-ka-di-lou], *s.* Pecadillo, pecado leve o venial.

peccancy [pekənsɪ] [pe-kan-si], *s.* 1. Vicio, la mala calidad o el defecto y daño físico en las cosas. 2. Vicio, el defecto moral en las accioens.

peccant [pekənt] [pe-kant], *a.* 1. Pecador, culpable de pecado, que peca. 2. Corrompido, ofensivo, dañoso, física o moralmente; mórbido, enfermizo. 3. Delincuente, vicioso, defectuoso.

peccary [pekərɪ] [pe-ka-ri], *s.* Pecarí, especie de cerdo silvestre que se encuentra desde Méjico hasta el Paraguay. Tiene en el dorso una glándula almizcleña.

peck [pek] [pek], *s.* 1. Medida de áridos en Inglaterra que es la cuarta parte de la medida llamada *bushel,* y equivale a 9.08 litros o poco menos de dos celemines; celemín, en general. 2. (*Fest.*) Montón, gran cantidad. **To get into a peck of troubles,** encontrarse con mil dificultades. 3. Picotazo, picotada, golpe con el pico. 4. Besito (kiss).

peck, *va.* 1. Picotear, golpear o herir con el pico. 2. Picar, herir con algún instrumento punzante. **To peck at,** regañar de continuo. 3. Recoger (alimento) con el pico. -*vn.* Picotear, dar golpes con el pico. **To peck at,** picotear (birds, people in eating).

pecker [pekəʳ] [pe-kaʳ], *s.* 1. El que pica o picotea. 2. (*Orn.*) Picoverde, un ave.

peckish [pekɪʃ] [pe-kish], *a.* 1. Hambriento. 2. Irritable (*EU*).

pecs [peks] [peks], *s. Abreviatura de* **pectorals,** pectorales.

pecten [pektən] [pek-tan], *s.* (pl. PECTINES [pek-tins]). 1. Peine, o algo parecido a él; en las aves, membrana vascular y colorida del globo del ojo. 2. Festón de una colcha.

pectin, pectine [pektɪn] [pek-tin], *s.* Pectina, substancia blanca que se extrae de las peras y otras muchas frutas.

pectinate, pectinated [pektɪneɪt] [pek-ti-neit], *a.* Dentado como un peine, parecido a las púas de un peine.

pectination [ˌpektɪˈneɪʃən] [pek-ti-nei-shon], *s.* El estado de lo que tiene dientes o púas como los peines.

pectoral [pektərəl] [pek-to-ral], *a.* Pectoral, que pertenece al pecho. -*s.* 1. Pectoral, la insignia que llevan al pecho los prelados eclesiásticos. 2. Peto, armadura del pecho. 3. Medicamento pectoral o que se emplea en las enfermedades del pecho.

peculate [pekjʊleɪt] [pe-kiu-leit], -*vn.* 1. Apropiarse los caudales públicos, cometer peculado. 2. Ratear, hurtar, robar.

peculation [ˌpekjʊˈleɪʃən] [pe-kiu-lei-shon], *s.* Peculado, la acción o delito de dedicar los caudales públicos al uso propio; malversación.

peculator [ˌpekjʊˈleɪtəʳ] [pe-kiu-lei-taʳ], *s.* Peculador, el que comete peculado; malversador.

peculiar [pɪˈkjuːlɪəʳ] [pi-kiu-liaʳ], *a.* 1. Peculiar, particular, singular, propio; que pertenece a una cosa con singularidad (belonging). 2. Escogido, especial, separado, distinguido (distinguish, especial). 3. Singular, raro, extraordinario (strange). **A style peculiar to oneself,** estilo propio de uno mismo. **A peculiar man,** un hombre singular, raro. -*s.* 1. La propiedad particular de cada uno. 2. (Der. canónico) La parroquia que no está sujeta a la jurisdicción del ordinario.

peculiarity [pɪˌkjɒlɪˈæritɪ] [pi-kiu-la-ri-ti], **peculiarness** [pɪˈkjɒlɪənɪs] [pi-kiu-la-nes], *s.* 1. Particularidad, singularidad; rasgo característico, lo que singulariza a una persona o cosa, haciéndola digna de atención o reparo; individualidad. **A peculiarity of speech,** una particularidad en el modo de hablar, y también en el idioma, idiotismo. **Special peculiarities,** sepas particulares (address). 2. Manía. **It's a peculiarity I have,** es una manía que tengo.

peculiarize [pɪˈkjɒləraɪz] [pi-kiu-la-rais], *va.* Particularizar, apropiar.

peculiarly [pɪˈkjɒlɪlɪ] [pi-kiu-la-li], *adv.* Peculiarmente, particularmente; separadamente; en particular, especialmente.

peculium [pɪˈkjɒlɪəm] [pi-kiu-liom], *s.* Peculio.

pecuniarily [pɪˌkjɒnɪˈærɪlɪ] [pi-kiu-nia-ri-li], *adv.* Pecuniariamente; con referencia al dinero.

pecuniary [pɪˈkjuːnɪərɪ] [pi-kiu-nia-ri], *a.* Pecuniario, que consta de dinero; referente al dinero monetario.

pecunious [pɪˈkjuːnɪəs] [pi-kiu-nios], *a.* Rico, adinerado.

pedagogic, pedagogical [ˌpedəˈgɒdʒɪk] [pe-da-go-yik], *a.* Pedagógico, perteneciente a la enseñanza de los niños, y lo que es propio de un pedagogo.

pedagogics [ˌpedəˈgɒdʒɪkz] [pe-da-go-yiks], *s.* Pedagogía, el arte y la ciencia de enseñar o educar.

pedagogism [ˌpedəˈgɒdʒɪʒəm] [pe-da-go-yi-sem], *s.* Pedagogismo, la naturaleza o el oficio de un pedagogo y particularmente de un pedante.

pedagogue ['pedəgɒg] [pe-da-gog], *s.* 1. Pedagogo, el que cuida de los niños y los enseña. 2. Maestro de escuela. 3. Pedante.

pedagogy [,pedə'gɒdʒi] [pe-da-go-yi], *s.* 1. Pedagogía. 2. Pedagogismo.

pedal ['pedl] [pe-dal], *a.* Perteneciente la pie o a una parte semejante al pie; del pie; relativo a un pedal. **Pedal pipe,** cañón del órgano de grueso calibre cuyas teclas se mueven con los pies.

pedal, *s.* 1. Pedal, palanca para el pie, aplicada sólo a ciertos instrumentos músicos, bicicletas o biciclos, triciclos, máquinas de coser y a la maquinaria ligera. **Pedal boat,** pedaló. 2. Bajo fijo, en la música. **Pedal pushers,** pantalones cortos de mujer que ajustan debajo de la rodilla.

pedant ['pedənt] [pe-dant], *s.* 1. Pedante, el que hace vano alarde de erudición y el que se precia de sabio teniendo escasos conocimientos. 2. (*Des.*) Dómine, maestro de niños.

pedantic, pedantical [pɪ'dæntɪk] [pi-dan-tik], *a.* Pedantesco, que hace vano alarde de su erudición.

pedantically [pɪ'dæntɪkəli] [pi-dan-ti-ka-li], *adv.* Con pedantería.

pedantism ['pedəntɪzəm] [pe-dan-ti-sem], **pedantry** ['pedənt] [pe-dant], *s.* Pedantería, pedantismo.

pedantize ['pedəntaɪz] [pe-dan-tais], -*vn.* Regentear, hacer de maestro, doctorear, pedantear, hablar magistralmente.

pedate ['pedeɪt] [pe-deit], *a.* 1. (*Zool.*) Parecido a un pie o que tiene sus funciones. 2. (*Bot.*) Que se divide o parte en forma palmar; se dice particularmente de las hojas.

peddle ['pedl] [pe-del], *va.* 1. Vender géneros en cortas cantidades, llevándolos de casa en casa. 2. Distribuir poco a poco. -*vn.* Recorrer los países vendiendo chucherías; ocuparse en frioleras.

peddler ['pedlər] [ped-lar], *s. V.* PEDLER.

pederast ['pedəræst] [pe-da-rast], *s.* Pederasta.

pederasty ['pedəræsti] [pe-da-ras-ti], *s. f.* Pederastia.

pedesis ['pedɪsɪs] [pe-di-sis], *s.* Pédesis, agitación de las partículas microscópicas contenidas en un líquido.

pedestal ['pedɪstl] [pe-dis-tal], *s.* Pedestal, peana.

pedestrian [pɪ'destrɪən] [pi-des-trian], *s.* Andador, peón, el que anda a pie; paseador, paseante. -*a.* Pedestre.

pediatrician [pedɪətrɪʃən] [pe-dia-tri-shan], *s.* (*Med.*) Pediatra, médico especialista de niños.

pediatrics [pedɪætrɪks] [pe-dia-triks], *s.* (*Med.*) Pediatría.

pedicel ['pedɪs] [pe-di-sel], *s.* Pedúnculo, pedicel, cabillo de una sola flor; pedúnculo de un animal.

pedicellate ['pedɪseleɪt] [pe-di-se-leit], *a.* Pedicelado, con pedicelo; sostenido por un pedicelo.

pedicle ['pedɪkl] [pe-di-kol], *s.* 1. (*Bot.*) Pedúnculo o el cabillo de la flor. 2. (*Med.*) Pedículo, la base angosta y reducida de un tumor.

pedicular ['pedɪkjələr] [pe-di-kiu-lar], **pediculous** ['pedɪkjələs] [pe-di-kiu-los], *a.* Pedicular; se aplica a la enfermedad en que el enfermo se plaga de piojos.

pedicure ['pedɪkjʊər] [pe-di-kiua], *s. f.* Pedicura.

pedigree ['pedɪgriː] [pe-di-gri], *s.* 1. Genealogía, la descripción de la estirpe de alguno; árbol genealógico (lineage). Pedigrí. 2. De raza, de pura sangre.

pediluvium ['pedɪlʊvɪəm] [pe-di-lu-viom], *s.* Pediluvio, baño de pies.

pediment ['pedɪmənt] [pe-di-ment], *s.* (*Arq.*) 1. Frontón, tímpano. 2. Adorno de molduras en forma triangular que se pone encima de las puertas o ventanas.

pedlar ['pedlər] [ped-lar], *s.* Buhonero, vendedor ambulante, que lleva sus mercancías de casa en casa. (*Amer.*) Baratilero, el que lleva y vende cosas de buhonería.

pedlery ['pedlərɪ] [ped-la-ri], *s.* Buhonería, la tienda portátil que el buhonero lleva colgada de los hombros y las baratijas que hay en ella.

pedling ['pedlɪŋ] [ped-lin], *a.* Frívolo, que es de poca monta.

pedological [,pedəʃlɒdʒɪk] [pi-do-lo-yi-kal], *a.* (*EU*) Pedológico.

pedology [pɪ'dɒlədʒɪ] [pi-do-lo-yi], *s. f.* (*EU*) Pedología.

pedometer [pɪ'dɒmɪtər] [pi-do-mi-ta], *s.* Podómetro, instrumento en forma de reloj que nota cada paso del que anda.

pedophile ['piːdəʊfaɪl] [pi-dou-fail], *s.* (*EU*) Pedófilo.

pedophilia ['piːdəʊ'fɪlɪə] [pi-dou-fi-lia], *s. f.* (*EU*) Pedofilia.

peduncle ['pedʌŋkl] [pe-dan-kel], *s.* 1. (*Bot.*) Pedúnculo, parte de la planta que sostiene una flor o muchas. 2. (*Anat.*) Pedúnculo, tallo o apéndice de un órgano por el cual se adhiere al cuerpo principal; parte del animal que le sirve de pie.

peduncular ['pedʌŋkjələr] [pe-dan-kiu-lar], *a.* Peduncular, perteneciente a un pedúnculo.

pedunculate, pedunculated ['pedʌŋkjʊleɪt] [pe-dan-kiu-leit], *a.* (*Bot.*) Pedunculado, que tiene un pedúnculo o sostén.

peek [piːk] [pik], -*vn.* (*Fam.*) Mirar por una hendidura, mirar a hurtadillas. *V.* PEEP.

peel [piːl] [pil], *va.* 1. Descortezar, pelar, mondar, descascarar, deshollejar (skin, covering). **To peel an orange,** mondar una naranja. 2. (*Ant.*) Pillar, hurtar, robar. **Peel away,** mondar, pelar. **Peel back,** despegar (covering). **Peel off,** desvestirse rápidamente, quitarse rápidamente (dress). Separarse, desviarse (separate from).

peel, *s.* 1. Corteza, cáscara, pellejo de lagunas frutas; hollejo de uvas, telilla de cebolla. 2. Pala de horno. 3. (*Mar.*) Palo del remo. 4. (*Des.*) Espito, colgador, instrumento para extender las hojas impresas.

peeler ['piːlər] [pi-lar], *s.* Pelador, mondador, el que pela, monda o descorteza.

peeling ['piːlɪŋ] [pi-lin], *s.* Peladura, mondadura, los pellejos de las frutas que se pelan o mondan.

peen [piːn] [pin], *s.* Extremo del martillo opuesto a la cara del mismo, cuando es de forma redondeada, cónica o a modo de cuña. **Peen-hammer,** martillo de punta.

peep [piːp] [pip], -*vn.* 1. Asomar, empezar a mostrarse alguna cosa. 2. Atisbar, mirar por un agujero sin ser visto; mirar a escondidas, furtivamente. **To peep in,** atisbar lo que pasa dentro de alguna parte. **To peep out,** atisbar lo que pasa fuera; mirar hacia fuera; asomar, salir. 3. Piar los pollos o los pájaros; chirriar.

peep, *s.* 1. Asomo, indicio o señal, de alguna cosa. **At the peep of day,** al romper del alba. 2. Ojeada, mirada furtiva. 3. Piada de las aves.

peeper ['piːpər] [pi-par], *s.* 1. Atisbador, el que atisba. 2. El pollito que empieza a romper la cáscara. **Peepshow,** espectáculo deshonesto.

peep-hole ['piːphəʊl] [pip-joul], **peeping-hole** ['piːpɪŋhəʊl] [pi-pin-joul], *s.* Atisbadero, agujero por donde uno puede ver sin ser visto.

peeping ['piːpɪŋ] [pi-pin], *s.* 1. Atisbadura; ojeada. 2. Piada, chirrido.

peeping, *a.* Que atisba. **Peeping Tom,** fisgón, atisbador. -*s.* 1. Atisbadura, ojeada. 2. Piada, chirrido.

peeptoe ['piːptəʊ] [pip-tou], *s.* **Peeptoe shoe,** zapato abierto.

peer [pɪər] [pia], -*vn.* 1. Atisbar, mirar con cuidado, como indagando o investigando. 2. (*Poét.*) Asomar, empezar a mostrarse, aparecer.

peer, *s.* 1. Par, igual, uno de la misma clase (equal); compañero (friend). 2. Par, grande, noble.

peerage ['pɪərɪdʒ] [pia-rich], *s.* La dignidad de par; el conjunto o cuerpo de los pares.

peeress ['pɪərɪs] [pia-ris], *s. f.* 1. La mujer de un par. 2. La que tiene uno de los títulos que pueden ser heredados por mujeres en Inglaterra.

peerless ['pɪərlɪs] [pia-les], *a.* Sin par, incomparable, que no admite comparación, que no tiene igual.

peerlessly ['pɪərlɪslɪ] [pia-les-li], *adv.* Incomparablemente, sin igual, sin par.

peerlessness ['pɪərlɪsnɪs] [pia-les-nes], *s.* Superioridad o excelencia incomparable o el estado de lo que no tiene igual.

peeve [piːv] [piv], *vt.* Enfadar, enojar, irritar.

peevish ['piːvɪʃ] [pi-vish], *a.* Impertinente, enfadoso, regañón, de mal humor; enojadizo, enojoso.

peevishly ['piːvɪʃlɪ] [pi-vish-li], *adv.* Con impertinencia.

peevishness ['piːvɪʃnɪs] [pi-vish-nes], *s.* Petulancia, impertinencia, mal humor, mal genio.

peewee ['piːwiː] [pi-ui], *s.* Chiquito, diminuto.

peg [peg] [peg], *s.* 1. Clavija, estaca, estaquilla; pedacito de madera que pasa por un agujero para asegurar alguna cosa; en un instrumento, clavija en que se aseguran y arrollan las cuerdas para templarlas. 2. Escarpia, colgador, clavija introducida parcialmente en una pared o una tabla y que sirve para colgar de ella alguna cosa (spike). 3. Pretexto o excusa (plea, pretext). 4. *(Fam.)* Grado en la posición social de una persona. 5. Broche, pinza (clothes). **To take one down a peg,** bajarle a uno los humos. **Peg-top,** peonza hecha de madera con punta de hierro; juguete al que se hace dar vueltas por medio de un bramante.

peg, *va.* Estaquillar, clavar, asegurar alguna cosa con clavijas o estaquillas. **Peg away,** machacar, afanarse en/por algo. **Peg down,** sujetar con estacas. **Peg out,** tender (clothes); señalar con estacas. *(Fig.).* Estirar la pata.

Pegasus ['pegəsəs] [pe-ga-sos], *s.* Pegaso.

pegleg ['pegleg] [peg-leg], *s.* Pata de palo.

pejorative [prɪ'dʒɒrɪtɪv] [pi-yo-ri-tiv], *a.* Que empeora el efecto o la significación.

pekan ['pekn] [pe-kan], *s.* Especie de mustela de la América del Norte, algo parecida a la zorra.

pekinese ['pekɪniːz] [pe-ki-nis], *s.* Pequinés.

pekoe ['pekuː] [pe-ku], *s. (Com.)* Una especie de té negro.

pelagic, pelagian [prɪ'lædʒɪk] [pi-la-yik] [prɪ'lædʒɪən] [pi-la-yian], *a.* 1. Pelágico, oceánico, que vive en el mar lejos de la tierra. 2. Flotante en la superficie del mar.

pelerine ['pelərɪn] [pe-la-rin], *s.* Esclavina, prenda de vestir que llevan las mujeres al cuello y sobre los hombros y suele terminar en punta por delante.

pelf [pelf] [pelf], *s.* Dinero, riquezas; significa a menudo riquezas mal adquiridas.

pelican ['pelɪkən] [pe-li-kan], *s.* 1. *(Orn.)* Pelícano, alcatraz, ave acuática del orden de las palmípedas que se alimenta de peces. 2. Alambique, vasija de vidrio con doble tubo de que se sirven los químicos para purificar los licores. 3. Pulicán, un instrumento para sacar muelas. **Pelican crossing,** semáforo sonoro.

pelisse ['peliːz] [pe-lis], *s.* Ropón, capote forrado en pieles; en Inglaterra se llama así un vestido muy usado en Rusia.

pell [pel] [pel], *s.* Pellejo, cuero; de aquí, rollo de pergamino. V. PELT. **Pell-rolls,** rollos de pergamino en que se asientan los gastos y recibos de la real hacienda en Inglaterra.

pellagra [pə'lægrə] [pe-la-gra], *s. (Med.)* Pelagra, cierta inflamación escamosa en las partes del cuerpo expuestas al sol y al aire.

pellet ['pelɪt] [pe-lit], *s.* Pelotilla; bala, perdigón (shot); bolita; píldora (pill).

pelleted ['pelɪtɪd] [pe-li-tid], *a.* Compuesto de balas.

pellicle ['pelɪkl] [pe-li-kel], *s.* 1. Película, piel o membrana delgada y delicada; hollejo. 2. Lapa, la telilla que se forma en la superficie del vino y otros licores.

pellitory ['pelətərɪ] [pe-li-to-ri], *s.* Cualquier especie de parietaria, planta urticácea. **Common wal pellitory,** parietaria oficinal. **Pellitory of Sapin,** pelitre.

pellmell ['pel'mel] [pel-mel], *adv.* Confusamente, atropelladamente, a atrochemoche, al tuntún.

pellucid [pe'luːsɪd] [pe-lu-sid], *a.* Transparente, diáfano.

pellucidity [ˌpeluːˈsɪdɪtɪ] [pe-lu-si-di-ti], **pellucidness** [pe'luːsɪdnɪs] [pe-lu-sid-nes], *s.* Transparencia, diafanidad.

pelota [prɪ'lɔʊtə] [pi-lou-ta], *s.* Pelota vasca (sport). **Pelota player,** pelotari.

pelt [pelt] [pelt], *s.* 1. Pellejo, cuero, zalea; también, pelada (skin). 2. Un golpe dado por una cosa arrojada.

pelt, *va.* Atacar, acometer arrojando piedras a otras cosas, tirar, arrojar (throw). *-vn.* Arrojar alguna cosa; descender violentamente, como el granizo. **To pelt with rain,** llover a cántaros. **To go pelting past,** ir como un rayo. **To go full pelt,** ir a máxima velocidad.

peltate, peltated ['peltɪt] [pel-teit], *a.* Peltado, en forma de pelta o escudo; *(Bot.)* que tiene su pecíolo inserto casi en medio del disco.

pelting ['peltɪŋ] [pel-tin], *s.* Acometimiento, violencia.

peltry ['peltrɪ] [pel-tri], *s.* Peletería, pieles, pellejos.

pelvic ['pelvɪk] [pel-vik], *a.* Pélvico, referente a la pelvis.

pelvis ['pelvɪs] [pel-vis], *s.* 1. Pelvis, cavidad del cuerpo en la parte inferior del tronco, o en la parte posterior del tronco en los irracionales; parte del esqueleto. 2. Pelvis, receptáculo membranoso en forma de embudo que se halla en cada riñón, y es el principio del uréter.

pen [pen] [pen], *s.* 1. Pluma; en otro tiempo cañón para escribir; hoy día, instrumento casi siempre de metal que sirve para escribir con una tinta flúida. 2. Pluma, estilo o habilidad y destreza en escribir. 3. Pluma, escritor. 4. Jaula, caponera, alcahaz, corral (enclosure). 5. Cisne hembra *(Orn.).* **Gold pen, quill pen, steel pen,** pluma de oro, de ave, de acero. **Ball-point pen,** bolígrafo. **Slip of the pen,** error de pluma. **Fountain pen,** pluma estilográfica. Pluma fuente. **Pen-and-ink drawing,** dibujo a pluma.

pen, *va.* 1. Enjaular, alchazar, encerrar, poner dentro de la jaula o del alcahaz. 2. Escribir, poner por escrito, componer. Este verbo tiene el pretérito y participio pasado *pent,* además de la forma regular, *penned.*

penal ['piːnl] [pi-nal], *a.* 1. Penal, que toca y pertenece a la pena o la incluye. 2. Que castiga. 3. Penal, provisto por la ley penal; que señala penas. **Penal code,** código penal. **Penal servitude,** presidio, pena de trabajos forzados.

penalization [ˌpiːnəlaɪˈzeɪʃən] [pi-na-lai-sei-shon], *s.* Castigo.

penalize ['piːnəlaɪz] [pi-na-lais], *vt.* Castigar, penar, sancionar (punish).

penalty ['penltɪ] [pe-nal-ti], *s.* 1. Pena, castigo (punishment). 2. Multa, pena pecuniaria (fine). 3. Penalti. **Penalty shoot-out,** tanda de penaltis. **Penalty spot,** punto de penalty (footbal).

penance ['penəns] [pe-nans], *s.* Penitencia, la pena que se impone en satisfacción del pecado.

pencase ['penkeɪz] [pen-keis], *s.* Estuche.

pence ['pens] [pens], *s. pl.* de PENNY.

pencil ['pensl] [pen-sil], *s.* 1. Lápiz. 2. Pincel, instrumento con que el pintor asienta los colores en el lienzo. **Pencil-case,** lapicero. **Pencil drawing,** dibujo a lápiz. **Black-lead pencil,** lápiz negro. **Red-lead pencil,** lápiz rojo. 3. Hacecillo de rayos de luz. **Pencil-box,** caja de lápices. **Pencil case,** plumier.

pencil, *va.* Marcar, dibujar, escribir con un lápiz.

pencil sharpener ['penslˌʃɑːpnər] [pen-sil-sharp-nar], *s.* Sacapuntas.

pendant ['pendənt] [pen-dant], *s.* 1. Pendiente, lo que está pendiente o cuelga de otra cosa para adorno o uso (earrings). 2. *(Arq.)* Adorno que cuelga de un techo. 3. Uno de los objetos que forman un par; cuadro u objeto de arte que se coloca de manera que corresponda con otro. 4. *(Mar.)* (a) Amante, maroma corta; (b) gallardete, cierto género de banderilla partida que se pone en lo alto de los masteleros de un navío. **Broad pendant,** *(Mar.)* corneta o gallardetón. **Brace pendants,** *(Mar.)* brazalotes. **Reeftackle-pendants,** *(Mar.)* amantes de aparejuelos de rizos. **Rudder-pendants,** *(Mar.)* barones del timón.

pendency ['pendənsɪ] [pen-dan-si], *s.* Suspensión, dilación, demora.

pendent ['pendənt] [pen-dant], *a.* 1. Pendiente, colgante. 2. Sobresaliente, que proyecta. 3. *(Bot.)* Pendiente, que cuelga con el ápice hacia abajo.

pendicle ['pendɪk] [pen-di-kol], *s.* 1. Miembro o porción inferior, accesorio; adjunto.

pending ['pendɪŋ] [pen-din], *a.* Pendiente, indeciso. *-prep.* 1. Durante. 2. Hasta; mientras, en el intervalo. **To be pending,** estar en trámite.

pendular ['pendjʊlər] [pen-diu-lar], *a.* Péndulo, perteneciente a un péndulo o a una péndola.

pendulosity [ˌpendjʊˈlɒsɪtɪ] [pen-diu-lo-si-ti], **pendulousness** [ˈpendjʊləsnɪs] [pen-diu-los-nes], _s._ Suspensión, el estado de lo que no está fijado en otra cosa.

pendulous [ˈpendjʊləs] [pen-diu-los], _a._ Péndulo, pendiente.

pendulum [ˈpendjʊləm] [pen-diu-lom], _s._ Péndulo, cuerpo suspendido de un punto fijo que puede moverse libremente con vaivenes u oscilaciones; péndulo o péndola de reloj. **Compensated** o **compensation pendulum,** péndulo de compensación. **Mercurial pendulum,** péndulo compensador de mercurio.

penetrability [ˌpenɪtrəˈbɪlɪtɪ] [pe-ni-tra-bi-li-ti], **penetrableness** [ˈpenɪtrəblnɪs] [pe-ni-tra-bol-nes], _s._ Penetrabilidad.

penetrable [ˈpenɪtrəbl] [pe-ni-tra-bol], _a._ Penetrable, que se puede penetrar, por una fuerza física, moral o intelectual.

penetrant [ˈpenɪtrənt] [pe-ni-trant], _a._ Penetrante, penetrativo, sutil; persuasivo.

penetrate [ˈpenɪtreɪt] [pe-ni-treit], _va._ 1. Penetrar, introducir un cuerpo en otro; horadar, entrar; atravesar, pasar al través. 2. Penetrar, comprender. 3. Penetrar el ánimo, llegar al corazón los sentimientos, afectar vivamente. _-vn._ Introducirse, penetrar.

penetrating [ˈpenɪtreɪlɪŋ] [pe-ni-trei-tin], _a._ Penetrativo, penetrante; agudo, astuto, sagaz, penetrador.

penetration [ˌpenɪˈtreɪʃən] [pe-ni-trei-shon], _s._ 1. Penetración, el acto o la propiedad de penetrar físicamente. 2. Penetración, inteligencia cabal de una cosa difícil; agudeza, sagacidad, perspicacia de ingenio.

penetrative [ˈpenɪtrətɪv] [pe-ni-tra-tiv], _a._ Penetrante.

penetrativeness [ˈpenɪtrətɪvnɪs] [pe-ni-tra-tiv-nes], _s._ La aptitud de penetrar.

penguin [ˈpeŋgwɪn] [pen-güin], _s._ 1. _(Orn.)_ Penguín, pingüino o pájaro bobo. V. PINGUIN.

penholder [ˈpenhəʊldər] [pen-joul-dar], _s._ Portapluma, mango o cabo de pluma.

penicillate [ˌpenɪˈsɪleɪt] [pe-ni-si-leit], _a._ _(Biol.)_ Penicilado, en forma de pincel; guarnecido de hebras finas.

penicillin [ˌpenɪˈsɪlɪn] [pe-ni-si-lin], _s._ _(Med.)_ Penicilina.

peninsula [pɪˈnɪnsjʊlə] [pi-nin-siu-la], _s._ Península. **The Peninsula** o **the Iberian Peninsula,** Iberia; España y Portugal.

peninsular [pɪˈnɪnsjʊlər] [pi-nin-siu-lar], _a._ Peninsular, lo concerniente a una península.

penis [ˈpiːnɪs] [pi-nis], _s._ Pene, el miembro viril.

penitence [ˈpenɪtəns] [pe-ni-tans], _s._ Penitencia.

penitent [ˈpenɪtənt] [pe-ni-tent], _a._ Penitente, arrepentido, contrito. _-s._ Penitente, la persona que se arrepiente de sus faltas o pecados.

penitential [ˌpenɪˈtenʃəl] [pe-ni-ten-shal], _a._ Penitencial, de arrepentimiento; que pertenece a la penitencia o la incluye; que se refiere a la penitencia como castigo. **The seven penitential psalms,** los siete salmos penitenciales. _-s._ Libro de penitencias.

penitentiary [ˌpenɪˈtenʃərɪ] [pe-ni-ten-sha-ri], _a._ 1. Penitenciario, que expresa el arrepentimiento; de penitencia, de castigo. 2. Penitenciario, referente al castigo y a la disciplina de los prisioneros. _-s._ 1. Penitenciaría, casa de corrección, cárcel. 2. Penitenciario, en sentido eclesiástico, confesor.

penitently [ˈpenɪtəntlɪ] [pe-ni-tent-li], _adv._ Con arrepentimiento, con penitencia.

penknife [ˈpennaɪf] [pen-naif], _s._ Cortaplumas, navaja pequeña; se llama así porque en otro tiempo se empleaba para cortar o tajar las plumas.

penman [ˈpenmən] [pen-man], _s._ Pendolista, calígrafo; maestro de escritura; el que tiene por oficio escribir.

penmanship [ˈpenmənʃɪp] [pen-man-ship], _s._ Escritura, el acto de escribir, el arte de escribir; caligrafía.

pen name [ˈpenneɪm] [pen-neim], _s._ Seudónimo, nombre ficticio de un escritor.

pennant [ˈpennənt] [pen-nant], _s._ 1. Flámula, gallardete. V. STREAMER. 2. _(Mar.)_ Amante, maroma corta. V. PENDANT.

pennate, pennated [ˈpenneɪt] [pen-neit], _a._ 1. Alado, que tiene alas. 2. _(Bot.)_ Lo que tiene la figura de pluma. V. PINNATE.

penned [ˈpenɪd] [pe-nid], _a._ Escrito; enjaulado.

penner [ˈpenər] [pe-nar], _s._ 1. Autor, escritor, el que escribe. 2. Plumero, estuche o vaso en que se guardaban antiguamente las plumas de escribir.

pen-nib [ˈpennɪb] [pen-nib], _s. f._ Punta de pluma, plumilla, plumín.

penniferous, [ˈpennɪfərəs] [pen-ni-fe-ros], _a._ Penígero, que tiene plumas.

penniform [ˈpennɪfɔːm] [pen-ni-form], _a._ Peniforme, parecido a una pluma.

penniless [ˈpenɪlɪs] [pen-ni-les], _a._ Sin dinero, sin un ochavo o sin blanca; muy pobre.

pennon [ˈpennən] [pen-non], _s._ Pendocito, flámula, bandera pequeña acabada en punta; pendón.

penny [ˈpenɪ] [pe-ni], _s._ _(pl._ PENNIES, para designar el número de las piezas, y PENCE, cuando se trata de su valor monetario). 1. Penique, antigua moneda de cobre de Inglaterra que valía la duodécima parte de un chelín. **I have not a single penny,** no tengo un cuarto. 2. _(Fam. E. U.)_ Centavo. 3. Dinero, hablando en general. 4. Coste; se emplea en composición, como **sixpenny. Two pennies,** dos piezas de dos cuartos. **Twopence,** cuatro cuartos, veinte céntimos. **A halfpenny,** un medio penique, un cuarto, cinco céntimos. **To turn an honest penny,** _(Fam.)_ Ganar el dinero honradamente. **A pretty penny,** _(Fam.)_ Bastante dinero, regular suma de dinero. **Like a bad penny,** como la falsa moneda _(expr.)_ **Penny-in-the-slot machine,** máquina tragaperras. **Penny-whistle,** flauta metálica.

penny-pinching [ˈpenɪˌpɪntʃɪŋ] [pe-ni-pin-chin], _s._ 1. Racanería, tacañería. _a._ 2. Avaro, tacaño (person.

penny-post [ˈpenɪpəʊst] [pe-ni-poust], _s._ Cartero, correo interior.

pennyroyal [ˈpenɪrɔɪəl] [pe-ni-roial], _s._ _(Bot.)_ Poleo.

pennyweight [ˈpenɪweɪt] [pe-ni-ueit], _s._ 1. Escrúpulo español.

penny-wise [ˈpenɪwaɪz] [pe-ni-uais], _a._ Se dice del que por ahorrar poco se expone a perder mucho. **Penny-wise and pound-foolish,** que escatima en los gastos pequeños y derrocha sumas cuantiosas.

pennyworth [ˈpenɪwɜːθ] [pe-ni-uez], _s._ 1. El valor de un penique o la cosa que se compra por un penique. 2. Cualquier cosa que se compra por dinero. 3. Una cantidad pequeña de cualquier cosa.

penological [ˌpiːnəˈlɒdʒɪkəl] [pi-no-lo-yi-kal], _a._ Penológico, referente a la ciencia de la penología.

penologist [piːˈnɒlədʒɪst] [pi-no-lo-yist], _s._ Criminólogo, penalista.

penology [piːˈnɒlədʒɪ] [pi-no-lo-yi], _s._ Penología.

pensile [ˈpensiːl] [pen-sil], _a._ Pensil, colgado, suspenso, pendiente en el aire.

pensileness [ˈpensɪlnɪs] [pen-sil-nes], _s._ El estado de lo que se halla suspenso o colgado.

pension [ˈpenʃən] [pen-shon], _s._ Pensión, cantidad que se concede periódicamente por un acto o servicio meritorio, particularmente por un gobierno; pensión de retiro. **To retire on a pension,** jubilarse. **Pension scheme,** plan de pensiones.

pension, _va._ Dar una pensión, pensionar. **To pension somebody off,** jubilar a alguien.

pensionary [ˈpenʃənərɪ] [pen-sho-na-ri], _a._ Pensionado, se dice del que goza de alguna pensión. _-s._ Pensionado, pensionista.

pensioner [ˈpenʃənər] [pen-sho-nar], _s._ 1. Pensionista, pensionado; _(Mil. y Mar.)_ inválido. 2. El que depende de la liberalidad de otro. 3. Estudiante ordinario en Cambridge; corresponde a _commoner_ en Oxford.

pensive [ˈpensɪv] [pen-siv], _a._ Pensativo, meditabundo; melancólico, triste.

pensively ['pensɪvlɪ] [pen-siv-li], *adv.* Pensativamente, melancólicamente, tristemente.

pensiveness ['pensɪvnɪs] [pen-siv-nes], *s.* Melancolía, tristeza; meditación profunda.

penstock ['penstɒk] [pens-tok], *s.* 1. La esclusa de la represa de los molinos. 2. Paradera (del caz). 3. Portapluma.

pent ['pent] [pent], *a. y pp.* de PEN. Acorralado, enjaulado, encerrado. **Here in the body pent,** aquí, encerrado en el cuerpo.

penta-, pent-, Formas derivadas del griego *pente,* cinco.

pentacapsular ['pentəˌkæpsjʊləʳ] [pen-ta-kap-siu-laʳ], *a. (Bot.)* Pentacapsular, de cinco cápsulas.

pentachord ['pentəkɔːd] [pen-ta-kord], *s.* Pentacordio, lira de cinco cuerdas.

pentad ['pentəd] [pen-tad], *s.* 1. El número cinco; grupo de cinco cosas. 2. Lustro, espacio de cinco años. 3. *(Quím.)* Átomo, radical, o elemento que tiene fuerza de combinación de cinco.

pentagon ['pentəgən] [pen-ta-gon], *s.* Pentágono, polígono de cinco ángulos y de cinco lados.

pentagonal [pen'tægənl] [pen-ta-go-nal], *a.* Pentagonal, pentangular.

pentagram ['pentəgræm] [pen-ta-gram], *s. f.* Estrella de cinco puntas.

pentagraph ['pentəgræf] [pen-ta-graf], *s.* Pentágrafo, instrumento para copiar diseños y pinturas en cualquier proporción.

pentahedron [ˌpentə'hiːdrən] [pen-ta-ji-dron], *s.* Pentaedro.

pentameter [ˌpen'tæmɪtəʳ] [pen-ta-mi-taʳ], *s.* Pentámetro.

pentangle [ˌpen'tæŋgl] [pen-tan-guel], *s.* Pentángulo.

pentangular [ˌpen'tæŋgjʊləʳ] [pen-tan-guiu-laʳ], *a.* Pentangular.

pentapetalous [ˌpentə'petələs] [pen-ta-pe-ta-los], *a.* Pentapétalo, que tiene cinco pétalos u hojas.

pentaphyllous [ˌpentə'fɪləs] [pen-ta-fi-los], *a.* Pentáfilo, que tiene cinco hojas.

pentateuch ['pentətjuːk] [pen-tan-tiuk], *s.* Pentateuco, los cinco libros de Moisés, que son los primeros del Antiguo Testamento.

Pentecost ['pentɪkɒst] [pen-ti-kost], *s.* 1. Pentecostés, fiesta de los judíos, que se celebraba el quincuagésimo día después de Pascua. 2. Pentecostés, la festividad de la venida del Espíritu Santo sobre los Apóstoles.

pentescostal [ˌpentɪ'kɒstl] [pen-ti-kos-tal], *a.* Perteneciente a la pascua de Pentecostés.

penthouse ['penthaʊs] [pent-jaus], *s.* 1. Tejaroz, tejadillo, colgadizo o cobertizo que sale de una pared con caída hacia fuera. 2. *(Mil.)* Mantelete. 3. Alguna cosa que se parece a un cobertizo.

pentice ['pentɪs] [pen-tis], *s.* Cualquier techo inclinado; tejado, tejadillo, sotechado.

Pentium processor [ˌpentɪəm'prəʊsesəʳ] [pen-tium-pro-se-saʳ], *s. (marca registrada)* Procesador Pentium.

pent-up ['pentʌp] [pent-ap], *a.* Cerrado, encerrado, contenido dentro de una cosa.

penult [pɪ'nʌlt] [pi-nalt], *s.* V. PENULTIMA.

penultima [pɪ'nʌltɪmə] [pi-nal-ti-ma], *s. (Gram.)* Penúltima, la sílaba anterior a la última en una palabra.

penultimate [pɪ'nʌltɪmɪt] [pi-nal-ti-mit], *a.* Penúltimo.

penumbra [pɪ'nʌmbrə] [pi-nam-bra], *s.* 1. *(Astr.)* Penumbra, sombra parcial en los eclipses entre lo iluminado y la parte obscurecida. 2. *(Pint.)* El punto o línea de un cuadro en que se confunde la sombra con la luz. 3. La franja obscura alrededor del punto céntrico de una mácula del sol.

penurious [pɪ'njʊərɪəs] [pi-niua-rios], *a.* 1. Tacaño, ruin, avaro, miserable. 2. Escaso; indigente.

penuriously [pɪ'njʊərɪəslɪ] [pi-niua-rios-li], *adv.* Escasamente, con escasez, miserablemente.

penuriousness [pɪ'njʊərɪəsnɪs] [pi-niua-rios-nes], *s.* Tacañería, ruindad, miseria; cortedad de ánimo; escasez.

penury ['penjʊrɪ] [pe-niu-ri], *s.* Penuria, pobreza, carestía, falta de alguna cosa muy necesaria.

pen-wiper ['penˌwaɪpəʳ] [pen-uai-paʳ], *s.* Limpiaplumas.

peon ['piːən] [pion], *s.* Criado, peón.

peony ['piːənɪ] [pio-ni], *s. (Bot.)* Peonía, cualquier planta del género *Pxonia,* de la familia de las ranunculáceas, y su flor.

people ['piːpl] [pi-pol], *s.* 1. Pueblo, nación, todas las personas que se hallan bajo el mismo gobierno, que hablan el mismo idioma, o que son de la misma sangre. 2. Población, habitantes (inhabitants). 3. Populacho, la gente común, el vulgo. 4. Gente, pluralidad de personas; tomando el verbo en el plural. **What will people say?** ¿Qué dirá la gente? ¿qué dirán? **Common people,** gentualla, gentuza. **15 people,** 15 personas. **The people of Mexico,** los habitantes de México; la nación mejicana. **Country people,** la gente del campo, los campesinos. **How are your people?,** ¿cómo están los tuyos? **Young people,** los jóvenes. **People think that,** se cree que, piensan que. **People mover,** cinta transportadora, pasillo móvil *(EU).*

people, *va.* Poblar.

pep [pep] [pep], *s. (Fam.)* Energía, vigor, entusiasmo, espíritu. *vt.* Animar, fortalecer, estimular.

pepper ['pepəʳ] [pe-paʳ], *s.* 1. Pimienta, fruto del pimentero (spice). 2. Pimentero, arbusto que da la pimienta. 3. Pimiento, ají, chile; cualquier planta del género Capsicum o su fruto. **Black pepper,** pimienta negra. **Long pepper,** pimienta larga. **Red** o **Cayenne pepper,** pimiento. *(Amer.)* Ají, guindilla. *(Mex.)* Chile. **Peppermill,** molinillo de pimienta. **Pepperpot,** pimentero, recipiente para pimienta. **Pepper steak,** filete a la pimienta. **The small red pepper,** chiltipiquín.

pepper, *va.* 1. Rociar o sazonar con pimienta o ají (spice). 2. Golpear; herir a uno con un tiro de perdigones u otra munición menuda.

Pepper-box, pepper-pot ['pepəbɒks] [pe-pa-boks], *s.* Pimentero.

pepper-corn ['pepəkɔːn] [pe-pa-korn], *s.* Bagatela, niñería, chuchería.

peppering ['pepərɪŋ] [pe-pa-rin], *a.* Caliente, fogoso, colérico. *-s.* Perdigonada, tiro de perdigones.

peppermint ['pepəmɪnt] [pe-pa-mint], *s. (Bot.)* Menta piperita, hierbabuena. **Peppermint drop,** pastilla de menta.

pepperwort ['pepəwɔːt] [pe-pa-wuort], *s. (Bot.)* Lepidio.

peppery ['pepərɪ] [pe-pa-ri], *a.* Picante. *(Fig)* De malas pulgas, enojadizo.

pepsin, pepsine ['pepsɪn] [pep-sin], *s.* Pepsina.

peptic ['peptɪk] [pep-tik], *a.* Digestivo.

peptone ['peptəʊn] [pep-toun], *s.* Peptona.

peptonize ['peptəʊnaɪz] [pep-tou-nais], *va.* Peptonizar, convertir en peptona.

peptonic ['peptəʊnɪk] [pep-tou-nik], *a.* Peptónico, perteneciente a la peptona o derivado de ella.

per [pɜːʳ] [peʳ], *prep.* Por. **As per invoice,** según factura. **Per annum,** al año. **Per capita,** por cabeza, por persona. **Per cent,** por ciento. **Per se,** por sí mismo, por su propia naturaleza.

peradventure [ˌpərædˈvəntʃəʳ] [pe-rad-ven-chaʳ], *adv.* Quizá, acaso, por acaso, por ventura. *-s.* Posibilidad de error; duda, cuestión.

perambulate [pəˈræmbjʊleɪt] [pe-ram-biu-leit], *va.* Pasar por alguna parte, transitar, recorrer algún territorio; ver, visitar. *-vn.* Ir paseando, andar.

perambulation [pəˌræmbjʊˈleɪʃən] [pe-ram-biu-lei-shon], *s.* La acción de caminar o transitar por alguna parte.

perambulator ['pəˈræmbjʊleɪtəʳ] [pe-ram-biu-lei-taʳ], *s.* 1. Cochecillo de niño. 2. Odómetro, máquina o rueda para medir caminos.

perborate [pəˈbɔːreɪt] [per-bo-reit], *s.* Perborato.

percale ['pəːkeɪl] [per-keil], *s.* Percal, cierta tela de algodón, blanca o pintada, que sirve para vestidos de mujer.

perceivable [pəˈsiːvəbl] [per-si-va-bol], *a.* Perceptible, que se puede percibir.

perceivably ['pəsiːvəblɪ] [per-si-va-bli], *adv.* Perceptiblemente.

perceive [pə'siːv] [per-siv], *va.* 1. Percibir, comprender, entender; conocer. 2. Percibir, recibir por alguno de los sentidos las impresiones de los objetos. 3. Recibir una cosa la impresión de otra. **To perceive before-hand,** presentir.

percentage [pə'sentɪdʒ] [per-sen-tich], *s.* 1. Porcentaje. 2. Tanto por ciento, interés por ciento.

perceptibility [ˌpəseptə'bɪlɪtɪ] [per-sep-ti-bi-li-ti], *s.* Perceptibilidad, facultad de ser percibido; raramente, la facultad de percibir.

perceptible [pə'septəbl] [per-sep-ti-bol], *a.* Perceptible, sensible; que puede percibirse.

perceptibly [pə'septəblɪ] [per-sep-ti-bli], *adv.* Perceptiblemente, sensiblemente, visiblemente.

perception [pə'sepʃən] [per-sep-shon], *s.* 1. Percepción, acción y efecto de percibir; conocimiento de las cosas exteriores obtenido por las impresiones sobre los sentidos; aprehensión, saber. 2. Facultad de percibir, de adquirir conocimiento de algo. 3. *(For.)* Toma, recibimiento, de cosechas o de ganancias.

perceptive [pə'septɪv] [per-sep-tiv], *a.* Perceptivo, que tiene la facultad de percibir.

perceptivity [ˌpəsep'tɪvɪtɪ] [per-sep-ti-vi-ti], *s.* Perceptibilidad.

perch [pɜːtʃ] [perch], *s.* 1. Perca, pez de agua dulce. 2. Pértica, medida de tierra de cinco varas y media. 3. Alcándara, percha.

perch, *vn.* Posarse, sentarse, pararse, empingorotarse, encaramarse; descansar las aves, ponerse en percha. *-va.* Emperchar, empingorotar.

perchance [pə'tʃɑːns] [per-chans], *adv.* Acaso, quizá, por ventura.

percher [pə'tʃəʳ] [per-chaʳ], *s.* 1. El ave que se pone en percha. 2. *(Des.)* Vela grande, cirio.

percheron [pə'tʃərən] [per-che-ron], *a.* y *s.* Percherón, caballo de tiro.

perchloric [pə'klɒrɪk] [per-klo-rik], *a. (Quím.)* Perclórico. **Perchloric acid,** ácido perclórico.

perchlorid, perchloride [pə'klɒrɪd] [per-klo-rid], *s.* Percloruro, combinación del cloro con los demás cuerpos en toda intensidad de que es susceptible aquél.

percipient [pə'sɪpɪənt] [per-si-pient], *a.* Percipiente, lo que tiene la virtud de percibir. *-s.* Percipiente, el ser que tiene la facultad de percibir.

perclose [pə'kləʊz] [per-klous], *s. (Arq.)* Barandilla o enverjado que encierra un lugar u objeto, como un altar o una capilla.

percoid ['pəkɔɪd] [per-koid], *a.* Percoide, que se parece a la perca.

percolate ['pɜːkəleɪt] [per-ko-leit], *va.* y *vn.* Colar, filtrar.

percolation ['pɜːkəleɪʃən] [per-ko-lei-shon], *s.* Coladura, filtración.

percolator ['pɜːkəleɪtəʳ] [per-ko-lei-taʳ], *s.* 1. Filtro, colador. 2. Cafetera, filtradora.

percuss ['pɜːkəs] [per-kas], *va.* Herir, golpear rápidamente; percutir, emplear la percusión como medio de exploración médica.

percussion [pɜː'kʌʃən] [per-ka-shan], *s.* 1. Percusión, golpe. 2. Resonación, el sonido causado por la repercusión; el choque producido por el encuentro de dos cuerpos. 3. *(Med.)* Percusión. **Percussion caps,** cebo de golpe o fulminante para las armas de fuego; pistón, cápsula.

percussionist [pɜː'kʌʃənɪst] [per-ka-sho-nist], *s.* Percusionista.

percussive [pɜː'kʌsɪv] [per-ka-siv], *a.* Que golpea contra otra cosa.

percutient [pɜː'kʌʃənt] [per-ka-shent], *a.* Percuciente; se dice de lo que hiere o causa impresión en otra cosa.

perdition [pɜː'dɪʃən] [per-di-shon], *s.* Perdición, destrucción, pérdida, ruina.

perdurable [pɜː'djʊərəbl] [per-diua-ra-bol], *a.* Perdurable, muy duradero.

perdurably [pɜː'djʊərəblɪ] [per-diua-ra-bli], *adv.* Perdurablemente.

peregrinate ['perɪɡrɪneɪt] [pe-ri-gri-neit], *va.* 1. Peregrinar, viajar de un país o de lugar a otro. 2. *(Des.)* Vivir en países extranjeros.

peregrination [ˌperɪɡrɪ'neɪʃən] [pe-ri-gri-nei-shon], *s.* Peregrinación, viaje por países extranjeros, o de un lugar a otro.

peregrine ['perɪɡrɪn] [pe-ri-grin], *a.* 1. Peregrino, migratorio, pasajero, como las aves. 2. Extranjero, que no es indígena.

peremptorily [ˌperemp'tərɪlɪ] [pe-remp-to-ri-li], *adv.* Perentoriamente; absolutamente.

peremptoriness [ˌperemp'tərɪnɪs] [pe-remp-to-ri-nes], *s.* Tono dogmático o magistral, juicio o decisión absolutos o decisivos; obstinación.

peremptory [pə'remptərɪ] [pe-remp-to-ri], *a.* Perentorio; absoluto, decisivo, definitivo; dogmático, magistral. **Peremptory orders,** órdenes perentorias. **Peremptory sale,** venta forzosa.

perennial [pə'renɪəl] [pe-re-nial], *a.* 1. Perenne, perennal; continuo, incesante, permanente, perpetuo. 2. *(Biol.)* Que crece continuamente: (a) *(Bot.)* Perenne, que sobrevive más de dos años; *(Ento.)* que sobrevive más de un año, o que forma colonias que duran varios años. *-s. (Bot.)* Planta perenne, que dura varios años, produciendo comúnmente flores y frutos cada año.

perennially [pə'renɪəlɪ] [pe-re-nia-li], *adv.* Constantemente, perennemente.

perfect ['pɜːfɪkt] [per-fekt], *a.* 1. Perfecto, acabado, que no tiene defecto ni falta; hábil, diestro, cabal, consumado. 2. *(Bot.)* Completo, provisto de estambres y pistilos. 3. *(Gram.)* Perfecto, que expresa un acto cumplido. 4. *(Fam.)* Puro, muy grande, excesivo. **She has a perfect horror of spiders,** ella tiene horror ciego a las arañas. *-s.* Tiempo perfecto.

perfect, *va.* 1. Perfeccionar, hacer perfecto; acabar enteramente. 2. Perfeccionar, instruir enteramente.

perfecter ['pɜːfɪktəʳ] [per-fik-taʳ], *s.* Perfeccionador.

perfectibility [pəˌfektɪ'bɪlɪtɪ] [per-fek-ti-bi-li-ti], *s.* Perfectibilidad, cualidad de lo perfectible.

perfectible [pə'fektəbl] [per-fek-ti-bol], *a.* Perfectible, que puede ser perfeccionado.

perfection [pə'fekʃən] [per-fek-shon], *s.* 1. Perfección, estado de lo perfecto, suprema excelencia. 2. El grado más alto de una cosa; lo extremo, lo supremo.

perfectionism [pə'fekʃənɪzm] [per-fek-sho-ni-sem], *s.* Perfeccionismo.

perfectionist [pə'fekʃənɪst] [per-fek-sho-nist], *a.* Perfeccionista.

perfective [pə'fektɪv] [per-fek-tiv], *a.* Perfectivo, que da o puede dar perfección.

perfectively [pə'fektɪvlɪ] [per-fek-tiv-li], *adv.* Con perfección.

perfectly ['pɜːfɪktlɪ] [per-fikt-li], *adv.* Perfectamente, cabalmente. **It's perfectly ridiculous,** es completamente absurdo.

perfectness ['pɜːfɪktnɪs] [per-fekt-nes], *s.* Pefección, habilidad, capacidad; excelencia.

perfidious [pɜː'fɪdɪəs] [per-fi-dios], *a.* Pérfido, desleal, traidor, fementido; infiel, que viola la fe.

perfidiously [pɜː'fɪdɪəslɪ] [per-fi-dios-li], *adv.* Traidoramente, pérfidamente.

perfidiousness [pɜː'fɪdɪəsnɪs] [per-fi-dios-nes], *s.* Perfidia, deslealtad, traición.

perfidy ['pɜːfɪdɪ] [per-fi-di], *s.* Perfidia.

perfoliate, perfoliated [pɜː'fəlɪeɪt] [per-fo-lieit], *a. (Bot.)* Perfoliado; se dice de una hoja que rodea el tallo y parece estar perforada por él.

perforate ['pɜːfəreɪt] [per-fo-reit], *va.* Perforar, horadar, penetrar alguna cosa agujereándola de una parte a otra; calar.

perforation [ˌpɜːfə'reɪʃən] [per-fo-rei-shon], *s.* 1. Perforación, el acto de horadar, taladrar o barrenar. 2. Cala.

perforator ['pɜːfəreɪtəʳ] [per-fo-rei-taʳ], *s.* Perforador, el que o lo que perfora; (a) barrena, taladro; (b) perforador, instrumento de obstetricia.

perforce [pəˈfɔːs] [per-fors], *adv.* Por fuerza, por necesidad. - *s.* Compulsión, apremio.

perform [pəˈfɔːm] [per-form], *va.* 1. Ejecutar, hacer, poner por obra alguna cosa; efectuar. 2. Desempeñar, llenar. **To perform one's promise,** cumplir con su palabra. **To perform one's duties,** cumplir con su obligación. -*vn.* 1. Representar, hacer papel; cantar; tocar un instrumento musical (play); salir bien en una empresa o empeño. **To perform the piano,** tocar el piano.

performable [pəˈfɔːməbl] [per-for-ma-bol], *a.* Ejecutable, practicable.

performance [pəˈfɔːməns] [per-for-mans], *s.* 1. Ejecución; cumplimiento (fulfilment). 2. Composición, obra (work). 3. Acción, hecho, hazaña (act). 4. Representación teatral. 5. Comportamiento, funcionamiento, rendimiento.

performer [pəˈfɔːməʳ] [per-for-maʳ], *s.* 1. Ejecutor, el que ejecuta o pone por obra alguna cosa. 2. El que ejecuta alguna habilidad en público; actor, representante, músico, sinfonista, acróbata.

performing [pəˈfɔːmɪŋ] [per-for-min], *a.* Amaestrado (animal).

perfume ['pɜːfjuːm] [per-fium], *va.* Pefumar, aromatizar alguna cosa; incensar. *s.* Perfume.

perfumer [pəˈfjuːməʳ] [per-fiu-maʳ], *s.* Perfumador, perfumero, perfumista.

perfumery [pəˈfjuːmərɪ] [per-fiu-ma-ri], *s.* Los perfumes en general; perfumería, la preparación de los perfumes.

perfunctorily [pəˈfʌŋktərɪlɪ] [per-fank-to-ri-li], *adv.* Descuidadamente, sin interés, superficialmente, por encima.

perfunctoriness [pəˈfʌŋktərɪnɪs] [per-fank-to-ri-nes], *s.* Descuido, negligencia.

perfunctory [pəˈfʌŋktərɪ] [per-fank-to-ri], *a.* Perfunctorio, superficial, indolente, negligente.

perfuse [pəˈfjuːz] [per-fius], *va.* (*Poco us.*) Tinturar; colmar, llenar demasiado; difundir, extender sobre.

perfusion [pəˈfjuːʒən] [per-fiu-shon], *s.* Tintura, el acto de difundir o derramar.

pergola ['pɜːgələ] [per-go-la], *s.* Pérgola, emparrado.

perhaps [pəˈhæps] [per-japs], *adv.* Puede ser, quizá, quizás, acaso, por ventura. **Perhaps so,** tal vez sea así, **Perhaps not,** puede que no.

peri ['perɪ] [pe-ri], *s.* Peri, hada de la mitología persa.

peri. Prefijo griego que significa cerca de, alrededor.

pericardial, pericardiac [ˌperɪˈkɑːdɪəl] [pe-ri-kar-dial] [ˌperɪˈkɑːdɪək] [pe-ri-kar-diak], **pericardian** [ˌperɪˈkɑːdɪən] [pe-ri-kar-dian], *a.* Pericardino, referente al pericardio.

pericarditis [ˌperɪˈkɑːdaɪtɪs] [pe-ri-kar-dai-tis], *s.* Pericarditis, inflamación del pericardio.

pericardium [ˌperɪˈkɑːdɪəm] [pe-ri-kar-diom], *s.* Pericardio, bolsa membranosa que rodea y protege el corazón.

pericarp, ['perɪkɑːp] [pe-ri-karp], *s.* Pericarpio, película que cubre el fruto de las semillas.

pericarpial, [ˌperɪˈkɑːpɪəl] [pe-ri-kar-pial], *a.* Pericarpial, que pertenece al pericarpio.

peridrome ['perɪdrəʊm] [pe-ri-droum], *s.* (*Arq.*) Peridromo, galería entre las columnas y la pared.

perigee ['perɪdʒiː] [pe-ri-yi], **perigeum** ['perɪdʒɪəm] [pe-ri-yiom], *s.* (*Astr.*) Perigeo, punto en la órbita de la luna (rara vez en la de un planeta) en que se halla más próxima a la tierra.

perihelion, perihelium [ˌperɪˈhiːlɪən] [pe-ri-ji-lion], *s.* (*Astr.*) Perihelio, punto en que un planeta se halla más inmediato al sol.

peril ['perɪl] [pe-ril], *s.* Peligro, riesgo, contingencia, acaso.

peril, *va.* Exponer al peligro, poner en peligro; arriesgar. -*vn.* Peligrar; estar en peligro.

perilous ['perɪləs] [pe-ri-los], *a.* Peligroso, aventurado.

perilously ['perɪləslɪ] [pe-ri-los-li], *adv.* Peligrosamente, arriesgadamente.

perilousness ['perɪləsnɪs] [pe-ri-los-nes], *s.* La situación peligrosa o arriesgada de una cosa.

perimeter ['perɪmɪtəʳ] [pe-ri-mi-taʳ], *s.* Perímetro, el ámbito o circunferencia de algún espacio, figura o lugar.

perinatal ['perɪnætl] [pe-ri-na-tal], *a.* Perinatal.

perineal ['perɪnɪəl] [pe-ri-nial], *a.* Perineal, relativo al perineo.

perineum ['perɪnɪəm] [pe-ri-niom], *s.* (*Anat.*) Perineo, el espacio entre el ano y los órganos de la generación.

period ['pɪərɪəd] [pi-riod], *s.* 1. Período, circuito, revolución. 2. Período, ciclo., época. **At that period,** en aquel entonces. 3. Período, cierto y determinado número de años, meses, días, etc. 4. Fin, conclusión; el último punto a que puede llegar alguna cosa. 5. (*Gram.*) Período, cláusula entera. 6. (*Méd.*) Período, fase particular de una enfermedad. 7. (*Mús.*) Período, frase de cierto número de compases uniformes y regulares. 8. Período, punto final, signo de puntuación. 9. **The period,** el día de hoy, el presente tiempo. -*pl.* La regla, la menstruación. **My early period,** mi juventud.

periodic, periodical ['pɪərɪədɪk] [pia-rio-dik] [ˌpɪərɪˈɒdɪkəl] [pia-rio-di-kal], *a.* Periódico.

periodically [ˌpɪərɪˈɒdɪkəlɪ] [pia-rio-di-ka-li], *adv.* Periódicamente.

periodicalness [ˌpɪərɪˈɒdɪkəlnɪs] [pia-rio-di-kal-nes], *s.* Periodicidad, calidad de periódico.

periodicity [ˌpɪərɪəˈdɪsɪtɪ] [pia-rio-di-si-ti], *s.* Periodicidad.

periodontal [ˌperɪˈdɒntl] [pe-ri-don-tal], *a.* Periodontal.

periosteum [ˌpɪərɪˈɒstɪəm] [pia-rios-tiom], *s.* Periostio, membrana vascular y nerviosa que cubre los huesos.

peripatetic [ˌperɪpəˈtetɪk] [pe-ri-pa-te-tik], *a.* 1. El que anda a pie desde un lugar a otro. 2. Peripatético, el secuaz de Aristóteles. **Peripatetic philosophy,** peripatetismo.

peripetia ['perɪpeʃə] [pe-ri-pe-sha], *s.* Peripecia, desenredo, desenlace de una pieza dramática.

peripheral [pəˈrɪfərəl] [pe-ri-fe-ral], *a.* 1. Periférico, periferal, perteneciente a una periferia. 2. Distante de un centro. *V.* DISTAL.

peripheric, peripherical [pəˈrɪfərəl] [pe-ri-fe-ral], *a. V.* PERIPHERAL.

periphery [pəˈrɪfərɪ] [pe-ri-fe-ri], *s.* 1. La superficie exterior. 2. Periferia, circunferencia.

periphrase [pəˈrɪfreɪs] [pe-ri-freis], *va.* Perifrasear, hacer circunlocuciones.

periphrasis, periphrase [pəˈrɪfrəsɪs] [pe-ri-fra-sis], *s.* Perífrasis, circunlocución.

periphrastic, periphrastical [ˌperɪˈfræstɪk] [pe-ri-fras-tik], *a.* Perifraseado.

periphrastically [ˌperɪˈfræstɪkəlɪ] [pe-ri-fras-ti-ka-li], *adv.* Con perífrasis.

periscope ['perɪskəʊp] [pe-ris-koup], *s.* Periscopio.

periscopic ['perɪskəʊpɪk] [pe-ris-kou-pik], *a.* Periscópico, que tiene vista a todos lados. **Periscopic lens,** lente periscópico, que por todos sus puntos transmite las imágenes de los objetos.

perish ['perɪʃ] [pe-rish], *vn.* Perecer, acabar, fenecer, morir: marchitarse, pasarse. **To perish with hunger,** perecer de hambre. **Perish the thought!** ¡Dios me libre!

perishable ['perɪʃəbl] [pe-ri-sha-bol], *a.* Perecedero.

perishableness ['perɪʃəblnɪs] [pe-ri-sha-bol-nes], *s.* La calidad de perecedero.

perishing ['perɪʃɪŋ] [pe-ri-shin], *a.* **It's cold perishing,** hace un frío glacial.

perisperm ['perɪspɜːm] [pe-ris-perm], *s.* (*Bot.*) Perispermo, envoltura de un óvulo o semilla rudimentaria.

peristalsis [ˌperɪˈstælsɪs] [pe-ris-tal-sis], *s.* Movimiento peristáltico o vermicular de un órgano hueco del cuerpo, particularmente del intestino.

peristaltic [ˌperɪˈstæltɪk] [pe-ris-tal-tik], *a.* Peristáltico, vermicular.

peristerion [ˌperɪˈstɪrɪən] [pe-ris-ti-rion], *s.* (*Bot.*) Verbena.

peristome [ˌperɪˈstəom] [pe-ris-toum], *s.* 1. *(Bot.)* Perístomo, franja de dientes menudos, generalmente un múltiplo de cuatro, que rodea el orificio de la cápsula de los musgos. 2. *(Zool.)* Las partes que rodean la boca de un marisco univalvo, un zoófilo o un insecto díptero.

peristyle [ˈperɪstɑɪl] [pe-ris-tail], *s. (Arq.)* Peristilo, galería de columnas que rodea un edificio o parte de él.

perisystole [ˈperɪstəol] [pe-ris-toul], *s. (Med.)* Perisístole, el intervalo entre la sístole y la diástole.

peritoneal [ˌperɪtəˈniːəl] [pe-ris-to-nial], *a.* Peritoneal, perteneciente o relativo al peritoneo.

peritoneum [ˌperɪtəˈniːəm] [pe-ris-to-niom], *s. (Anat.)* Peritoneo, membrana serosa que cubre interiormente la cavidad abdominal.

peritonitis [ˌperɪtəˈnɑɪtɪs] [pe-ris-to-nai-tis], *s.* Peritonitis, inflamación del peritoneo.

periwig [ˈperɪwɪg] [pe-ri-uig], *s.* Peluca, peluquín; cabellera postiza.

periwinkle [ˈperɪˌwɪŋkl] [pe-ri-uin-kel], *s.* 1. Litorina, bígaro, género de moluscos gasterópodos. 2. *(Bot.)* Pervenca, pervinca.

perjure [ˈpɜːdʒəʳ] [per-yaʳ], *va. y vn.* Perjurar, jurar en falso.

perjurer [ˈpɜːdʒərəʳ] [per-ya-raʳ], *s.* Perjurador, perjuro.

perjury [ˈpɜːdʒərɪ] [per-ya-ri], *s.* Perjurio. **To commit perjury,** jurar en falso.

perk [pɜːk] [perk], *vn.* Erguirse, levantar la cabeza con afectación de viveza. *-va.* 1. Adornar, decorar, vestir. 2. Erguir, levantar la oreja o la cabeza.

perk, perky [ˈpɜːkɪ] [per-ki], *a.* Que tiene la cabeza erguida con gentileza; gallardo.

perm [pɜːm] [perm], *sf.* Permanente. **To have a perm, to have one's hair permed,** hacerse una permanente (hairdressers').

permanence [ˈpɜːmənəns] [per-ma-nens], *s.* Permanencia, duración firme, continuación del mismo estado, fijeza.

permanency [ˈpɜːmənənsɪ] [per-ma-nen-si], *s.* 1. Permanencia. 2. Alguna cosa permanente, muy duradera, o indestructible.

permanent [ˈpɜːmənənt] [per-ma-nent], *a.* Permanente, que permanece estable, duradero, que continúa sin cambio.

permanently [ˈpɜːmənəntlɪ] [per-ma-nent-li], *adv.* Permanentemente.

permanent wave [ˈpɜːmənəntˌweɪv] [per-ma-nent-ueiv], *s.* Ondulado permanente (hair).

permanganate [pɜːˈmæŋgənɪt] [per-man-ga-neit], *s. (Quím.)* Permanganato, compuesto del ácido permangánico con una base salificable.

permeability [ˌpɜːmɪəˈbɪlɪtɪ] [per-mia-bi-li-ti], *s.* Permeabilidad, calidad o condición de permeable.

permeable [ˈpɜːmɪəbl] [per-mia-bol], *a. (Fís.)* Permeable, se dice de todo cuerpo por donde puede penetrar fácilmente el aire, la luz o cualquier otro fluido rezumable; penetrable.

permeant [ˈpɜːmɪənt] [per-miant], *a.* V. PERMEATIVE.

permeate [ˈpɜːmɪeɪt] [per-mieit], *va.* Penetrar, atravesar, calar, pasar por medio. Impregnar. **The pessimism permeates his work,** el pesimismo se evidencia en su obra.

permeation [ˈpɜːmɪeɪʃən] [per-miei-shon], *s.* Pasaje o penetración al través de los intersticios o poros de un cuerpo.

permeative [ˈpɜːmɪətɪv] [per-mia-tiv], *a.* Penetrativo, permeativo, que penetra por entre los poros.

permissible [pəˈmɪsəbl] [per-mi-sa-bol], *a.* Permisible, que se puede permitir o consentir.

permission [pəˈmɪʃən] [per-mi-shon], *s.* Permisión, permiso, licencia (licence, permit). **My mother gave me permission,** mi madre me dio permiso.

permissive [pəˈmɪsɪv] [per-mi-siv], *a.* Permisivo, permitido, tolerado, consentido.

permissively [pəˈmɪsɪvlɪ] [per-mi-siv-li], *adv.* Permisivamente.

permissiveness [pəˈmɪsɪvnɪs] [per-mi-siv-nes], *s.* Permisividad.

permit [ˈpɜːmɪt] [per-mit], *va.* 1. Permitir, consentir, tolerar, autorizar tácitamente o no poniendo obstáculos (authorize, allow). 2. Permitir, conceder permiso o libertad de hacer, autorizar. **Photographies are not permitted,** no se permiten fotografías.

permit, *s.* Permiso, licencia. **Work permit,** permiso de trabajo.

permittance [ˈpɜːmɪtəns] [per-mi-tans], *s.* 1. Capacidad electroestática. 2. Permisión, el acto de permitir.

permutation [ˌpɜːmjʊˈteɪʃən] [per-miu-tei-shon], *s.* 1. Permutación, permuta, cambio recíproco. 2. *(Mat.)* Permutación, combinación en que se atiende al número y términos que se comparan y a la diferencia resultante de los lugares en que se colocan.

permute [pəˈmjuːt] [per-miut], *va.* Permutar, trocar, cambiar entre sí.

permuter [pəˈmjuːtəʳ] [per-miu-taʳ], *s.* La persona que permuta, cambia o trueca.

pern [pɜːn] [pern], *s. (Orn.)* Buaro del género Pernis.

pernicious [pɜːˈnɪʃəs] [per-ni-shos], *a.* 1. Pernicioso, gravemente dañoso o perjudicial, funesto, fatal. 2. *(Des.)* Veloz.

perniciously [pɜːˈnɪʃəslɪ] [per-ni-shos-li], *adv.* Perniciosamente, perjudicialmente.

perniciousness [pɜːˈnɪʃəsnɪs] [per-ni-shos-nes], *s.* Malignidad, la calidad maligna o perniciosa de alguna cosa.

pernoctation [ˌpɜːnɒkˈteɪʃən] [per-nok-tei-shon], *s.* Pernoctación, el acto de dormir al raso; el acto de pasar en vela toda la noche.

peroration [ˌperəˈreɪʃən] [pe-ro-rei-shon], *s.* Peroración, la conclusión de alguna oración o discurso.

peroxid, peroxide [pəˈrɒksaɪd] [pe-rok-said], *s.* Peróxido, grado mayor de oxidación. **A peroxide blonde,** una rubia teñida.

perpend [pɜːˈpend] [per-pend], *va. (Ant.)* Reflexionar, pensar cuidadosamente, examinar o pesar las razones en que se funda una opinión.

Perpendicle [pɜːˈpendɪkl] [per-pen-di-kol], *s.* Cualquier cosa que cuelga perpendicularmente.

perpendicular [ˌpɜːpənˈdɪkjʊləʳ] [per-pen-di-kiu-laʳ], *a.* Perpendicular, se dice de la línea o plano que cae sobre otro plano o línea formando ángulos rectos. *-s.* Línea perpendicular.

perpendicularly [ˌpɜːpenˈdɪkjʊlərlɪ] [per-pen-di-kiu-lar-li], *adv.* Perpendicularmente.

perpetrate [ˈpɜːpɪtreɪt] [per-pi-treit], *va.* Perpetrar, cometer algún delito o culpa grave (commit); hacer, ejecutar (do); se usa también en sentido festivo.

perpetration [ˌpɜːpɪˈtreɪʃən] [per-pi-trei-shon], *s.* Perpetración, el acto de cometer algún delito.

perpetrator [ˈpɜːpɪtreɪtəʳ] [per-pi-trei-taʳ], *s.* Perpetrador.

perpetual [pəˈpetjʊəl] [par-pe-tiual], *a.* Perpetuo, continuo, incesante, eterno (endless, eternal); vitalicio. **Perpetual motion,** movimiento continuo, perpetuo, eterno.

perpetually [pəˈpetjʊəlɪ] [par-pe-tiua-li], *adv.* Perpetuamente, continuamente.

perpetuate [pəˈpetjʊeɪt] [par-pe-tiueit], *va.* Perpetuar, eternizar, proseguir sin intermisión.

perpetuation [pəˌpetjʊˈeɪʃən] [par-pe-tiu-ei-shon], *s.* Perpetuación, la acción de perpetuar.

perpetuity [ˌpɜːpɪˈtjuːɪtɪ] [par-pi-tui-ti], *s.* Perpetuidad, duración sin fin. *(Law)* **In perpetuity,** a perpetuidad

perplex [pəˈpleks] [par-pleks], *va.* 1. Confundir, perturbar, dejar a uno perplejo y lleno de dudas. 2. Intrincar, embrollar, enredar, enmarañar alguna cosa. 3. Atormentar. *-a.* Intrincado, enredado.

perplexed [pəˈplekst] [par-plekst], *s.* Perplejo, dudoso, irresoluto, confuso.

perplexedly [pəˈpleksɪdlɪ] [par-plek-sid-li], *adv.* Perplejamente, confusamente.

perplexedness [peˈpleksɪdnɪs] [par-plek-sid-nes], **perplexity** [pəˈpleksɪtɪ] [par-plek-si-ti], *s.* Perplejidad, duda, irresolución: confusión, inquietud.

perquisite ['pɜːkwɪzɪt] [per-kui-sit], *s.* Percance, gajes, buscas, propinas, los emolumentos o utilidades que se adquieren por algún empleo u ocupación además del salario o sueldo señalado.

perquisition [,pɜːkwɪ'zɪʃən] [per-kui-si-shon], *s.* Pesquisa, indagación, investigación.

perron ['pərən] [pe-ron], *s. (Arq.)* Grada o escalera abierta en la parte exterior de un edificio.

perry ['perɪ] [pe-ri], *s.* Sidra de peras.

persecute ['pɜːsɪkjuːt] [per-si-kiut], *va.* 1. Perseguir, molestar, hostigar, vejar (follow, bother); particularmente perseguir o afligir por motivo de las creencias religiosas de uno. 2. Molestar, fatigar, importunar (annoy).

persecution [,pɜːsɪ'kjuːʃən] [per-si-kiu-shon], *s.* Persecución, vejación; molestia.

persecutive ['pɜːsɪkjuːtɪv] [per-si-kiu-tiv], *a.* Perseguidor, que persigue.

persecutor ['pɜːsɪkjuːtəʳ] [per-si-kiu-taʳ], *s.* Perseguidor, dañador.

perseverance [,pɜːsɪ'vɪərəns] [per-si-vi-rans], *s.* Perseverancia, el acto o la costumbre de perseverar; persistencia, constancia.

perseverant [,pɜːsɪ'vɪərənt] [per-si-vi-rant], *a.* Perseverante, constante, firme.

persevere [,pɜːsɪ'vɪəʳ] [per-si-viaʳ], *vn.* Perseverar, persistir. **We persevered and it worked,** insistimos y funcionó.

persevering [,pɜːsɪ'vɪərɪŋ] [per-si-via-rin], *pa.* Perseverante, persistente, tenaz.

perseveringly [,pɜːsɪ'vɪərɪŋlɪ] [per-si-via-rin-li], *adv.* Perseverantemente, constantemente.

Persia ['pɜːʃə] [per-sha], *s.* Persia.

Persian ['pɜːʃən] [per-shan], *a.* Persa, persiano, perteneciente a Persia. *-s.* 1. Persa, persiano, el natural de Persia. 2. Persiana, tela delgada de seda. 2. Persa, persinao, la lengua de Persia. **Persian blinds,** celosías. **Persian Gulf,** el Golfo Pérsico. **Persian wheel,** azuda, máquina con que se saca agua de los ríos para regar los campos. **Persian carpet,** alfombra persa.

persic ['pɜːsɪk] [per-sik], *a.* Pérsico, persa. *-s.* Idioma persa.

persiflage [,pɜːsɪ'flɑːʒ] [per-si-flash], *s.* Choteo, guasa, pitorreo.

persimmon [pɜː'sɪmən] [per-si-mon], *s.* 1. Fruto globular, anaranjado, que se parece a una ciruela, del dióspiro. 2. Dióspiro, árbol que da este fruto. Diospyros Virginiana. **Japanese persimon,** Fruto muy estimado en el Oriente.

persist [pə'sɪst] [per-sist], *vn.* Persistir, permanecer; empeñarse, insitir.

persistence [pə'sɪstəns] [per-sis-tans], **persistency** [pə'sɪstənsɪ] [per-sis-tan-si], *s.* 1. Persistencia, permanencia o firmeza en la ejecución de alguna cosa, constancia. 2. Obstinación, contumacia. 3. Continuación, duración.

persistent [pə'sɪstənt] [per-sis-tant], *a.* 1. Persistente, firme, determinado, resuelto. 2. Permanente, invariable, continuo. 3. *(Biol.)* Persistente, que no cae o no se marchita.

persnickety [pə'snɪkɪtɪ] [pers-ni-ki-ti], *a.* (E.U.) Puntilloso, chinche.

person ['pɜːsn] [per-son], *s.* 1. Persona, individuo o sujeto de la naturaleza humana. **He is a wonderful person,** es una persona maravillosa. 2. Persona. 3. Persona de la Trinidad. 4. *(Gram.)* Persona, el nombre o pronombre que rige a un verbo o es regido por él. 5. *(Biol.)* Individuo. 6. *(Ant.)* Papel de un actor; por extensión, el sujeto que tiene alguna representación por cualquier concepto. **In person,** personalmente o en persona.

personable ['pɜːsnəbl] [per-so-na-bol], *a.* 1. Hermoso, de buena presencia. 2. *(Der. ant.)* Capaz de mantener una alegación en los tribunales.

personage ['pɜːsnɪdʒ] [per-so-nich], *s.* 1. Personaje, hombre o mujer de distinción o calidad. 2. Personaje, papel, carácter.

personal ['pɜːsnl] [per-so-nal], *a.* Personal; directo en persona; corporal; exterior. **Personal estate,** bienes muebles. **Personal property,** propiedad mueble. **Personal**

appearance, (a) Aspecto, apariencia personal. (b) Comparecencia en persona. **Personal computer,** ordenador personal.

personality [,pɜːsə'nælɪtɪ] [per-so-na-li-ti], *s.* 1. Personalidad, lo que constituye a una persona distinta de otra; también lo que constituye un individuo. 2. Personalidad, lo que se dice tocante a una persona determinada, particularmente una expresión injuriosa. 3. Personalidad, figura (public figure).

personalize ['pɜːsənəlaɪz] [per-so-na-lais], *va.* 1. Personalizar, hacer personal. 2. *(Ret.)* Personificar.

personally ['pɜːsnəlɪ] [per-so-na-li], *adv.* Personalmente. **Do you know them personally?,** ¿los conoces personalmente? (in person).

personate ['pɜːsəneɪt] [per-so-neit], *va.* 1. Representar, subrogarse en los derechos, autoridad o bienes de otro. 2. Contrahacer, remedar. 3. Representar, fingir, hacer el papel de alguna cosa o persona. *-vn.* Representar, ser actor en una pieza dramática.

personation [,pɜːsə'neɪʃən] [per-so-nei-shon], *s.* Disfraz, artificio con que una persona pasa por otra.

personator [,pɜːsə'neɪtəʳ] [per-so-nei-taʳ], *s.* 1. El que representa a otra persona. 2. Ejecutor, el que hace o ejecuta alguna cosa.

personification [pɜːsɒnɪfɪ'keɪʃən] [per-so-ni-fi-kei-shon], *s.* Personificación, prosopopeya, figura por la cual se hace hablar o accionar a personas fingidas o cosas inanimadas.

personify [pɜː'sɒnɪfaɪ] [per-so-ni-fai], *va.* Personificar, atribuir a las cosas inanimadas o abstractas las pasiones o afectos de las personas.

personnel [,pɜːsə'nel] [per-so-nel], *s.* Personal, cuerpo de empleados. **Personnel manager,** jefe de personal.

perspective [pə'spektɪv] [pers-pek-tiv], *s.* 1. Perspectiva, vista o aspecto de diversos objetos juntos mirados de lejos. 2. Vista, importancia relativa de sucesos o materias desde un punto de vista especial. **From a historical perspective,** desde una perspectiva histórica. *-a. (Pint.)* Perspectivo, perteneciente al arte de la perspectiva; que representa un objeto en perspectiva.

perspectively [pə'spektɪvlɪ] [pers-pek-tiv-li], *adv.* Por representación.

perspicacious [,pɜːspɪ'keɪʃəs] [pers-pi-kei-shos], *a.* Perspicaz, penetrante.

perspicaciousness [,pɜːspɪ'keɪʃəsnɪs] [pers-pi-kei-shos], **perspicacity** [,pɜːspɪ'kæsɪtɪ] [pers-pi-ka-si-ti], *s.* 1. Perspicacia; penetración o viveza de ingenio. 2. *(Ant.)* Agudeza de vista.

perspicuity [,pɜːspɪ'kjʊɪtɪ] [pers-pi-kui-ti], *s.* Perspicuidad, claridad, transparencia.

perspicuous [pə'spɪkjʊəs] [pers-pi-kuos], *a.* 1. Perspicuo, claramente expresado, inteligible. 2. *(Des.)* Perspicuo, claro, transparente.

perspicuously [,pɜːspɪ'kjʊəslɪ] [pers-pi-kuos-li], *adv.* Perspicuamente, claramente.

perspicuousness [,pɜːspɪ'kjʊəsnɪs] [pers-pi-kuos-nes], *s.* Perspicuidad, claridad de estilo.

perspirable [,pɜːs'paɪərəbl] [pers-paia-ra-bol], *a.* Transpirable.

perspiration [,pɜːspaɪə'reɪʃən] [pers-pai-rei-shon], *s.* 1. Transpiración, exhalación de un fluido acuoso por las glándulas excretorias de la piel. 2. Sudor, transpiración, serosidad que se exhala por los poros de los animales.

perspirative [,pɜːs'paɪərətɪv] [pers-paia-ra-tiv], *a.* Lo que transpira.

perspiratory [,pɜːs'paɪərətərɪ] [pers-paia-ra-to-ri], *a.* Transpiratorio, lo que pertenece a la transpiración.

perspire [,pɜːs'paɪəʳ] [pers-paia-raʳ], *vn.* Transpiar, evaporar los humores insensiblemente; exhalar fluido por los poros. *-va.* Exhalar, excretar. **A firtree perspires balsam,** un abeto excreta el bálsamo.

persuadable [pə'sweɪdəbl] [per-suei-da-bol], *a.* Persuasible.

persuade [pə'sweɪd] [per-sueid], *va.* Persuadir, convencer, atraer a uno con razones; excitar, mover a alguno a la ejecución de una cosa. **I'm easily persuaded,** me dejo convencer fácilmente.

persuader [pəˈsweɪdəʳ] [per-suei-daʳ], s. Persuasor, persuadidor.

persuasible [pəˈsweɪsɪbl] [per-suei-si-bol], s. Persuasible.

persuasion [pəˈsweɪʒən] [per-suei-shon], s. 1. Persuasión, acción y efecto de persuadir. 2. Persuasión, la idea o el juicio que se forma en virtd de algún fundamento. 3. Creencia, opinión religiosa, creencia fija; de aquí, partido, secta, o denominación. **People of all persuasions,** gente de todas las creencias. 4. Persuasiva, facultad de persuadir.

persuasive [pəˈsweɪsɪv] [per-suei-siv], a. Persuasivo, convincente (convincing). -s. Persuasiva, eficacia y destreza en persuadir.

persuasory [pəˈsweɪsərɪ] [per-sua-so-ri], a. Persuasivo.

pert [pɜːt] [pert], a. Petulante, atrevido, descocado (daring). 2. *(Des.)* Listo, vivo (clever).

pertain [pɜːˈteɪn] [per-tein], vn. 1. Pertenecer, tocar a alguno como atributo, derecho, deber, propiedad, cualidad o adjunto (belong to). 2. Concernir, referirse a.

pertinacious [ˌpɜːtɪˈneɪʃəs] [per-ti-nei-shos], a. 1. Pertinaz, obstinado, terco, tenaz. 2. Constante, incesante, continuo.

pertinaciously [ˌpɜːtɪˈneɪʃəslɪ] [per-ti-nei-shos-li], adv. Pertinazmente, obstinadamente.

pertinacity [ˌpɜːtɪˈnæsɪtɪ] [per-ti-na-si-ti], s. 1. Pertinacia, obstinación, terquedad, tenacidad (stubborness). 2. Perseverancia, constancia, resolución, firmeza (resolution).

pertinence [ˈpɜːtɪnəns] [per-ti-nens], **pertinency** [ˈpɜːtɪnəns] [per-ti-nans], s. Pertinencia, conexión, relación de una cosa con otra.

pertinent [ˈpɜːtɪnənt] [per-ti-nant], a. 1. Pertinente, que viene a propósito. 2. Perteneciente, pertinente (belonging).

pertinently [ˈpɜːtɪnəntlɪ] [per-ti-nant-li], adv. Pertinentemente, oportunamente.

pertly [ˈpɜːtlɪ] [per-tli], adv. 1. Insolentemente, descaradamente, descocadamente. 2. *(Des.)* Vivamente, prontamente.

pertness [ˈpɜːtnɪs] [pert-nes], s. Petulancia, descaro, atrevimiento, impertinencia (shamelessness).

perturb [pəˈtɜːb] [per-terb], va. Perturbar, inquietar, poner en desorden.

perturbable [pəˈtɜːbəbl] [per-ter-ba-bol], a. Perturbable, que se puede perturbar.

perturbation, perturbance [ˌpɜːtɜːˈbeɪʃən] [per-ter-bei-shon], [pəˈtɜːbəns] [per-ter-bans] s. 1. Perturbación, desorden, agitación de ánimo; efecto de perturbar. 2. Perturbación, desviación en el movimiento de un cuerpo celeste.

perturbator [ˌpɜːtɜːˈbeɪtəʳ] [per-ter-bei-taʳ], s. Perturbador, agitador.

perturber [pəˈtɜːbəʳ] [per-ter-baʳ], s. Perturbador, agitador.

pertuse [pəˈtjuːz] [per-tius], a. 1. Horadado con punzón, agujereado. 2. *(Bot.)* Perforado.

pertusion [pəˈtjuːʒən] [per-tiu-shon], s. 1. El acto de taladrar. 2. Taladro, el agujero hecho con el taladro o la barrena.

Peru [pəˈruː] [pa-ru], s. Perú.

peruke [pəˈruːk] [pa-ruk], s. Peluca, cabello postizo. **Peruke-maker,** peluquero.

perusal [pəˈruːzəl] [pa-ru-shal], s. Lectura, lección, acción de leer. **I enclose the dossier for your perusal,** le adjunto el documento para que lo examine.

peruse [pəˈruːz] [pa-rus], va. 1. Leer; leer con atención, leer hasta el fin. 2. *(Ant.)* Observar, examinar atentamente.

peruser [pəˈruːzəʳ] [pa-ru-shaʳ], s. Lector; revisor, examinador.

peruvian [pəˈruːvɪən] [pa-ru-vian], a. Peruano, del Perú. **Peruvian bark,** quina, cascarilla.

pervade [pɜːˈveɪd] [per-veid], va. Atravesar, esparcirse por todas partes, penetrar, ocupar, llenar (occupy, fill).

pervasion [pɜːˈveɪʃən] [per-vei-shon], s. Esparoimiento, el acto de esparcirse alguna cosa por todas partes.

pervasive [pɜːˈveɪsɪv] [per-vei-siv], a. Que se esparce por todas partes, penetrativo, penetrante.

perverse [pəˈvɜːs] [per-vers], a. 1. Perverso, depravado, malo, intratable. 2. Contrario, refractario, obstinado, terco (stubborn). 3. Enfadoso, molesto, vejador.

perversely [pəˈvɜːslɪ] [per-vers-li], adv. Perversamente, con obstinación.

perverseness [pəˈvɜːsnɪs] [per-vers-nes], s. Perversidad, maldad, terquedad, obstinación.

perversion [pəˈvɜːʃən] [per-ver-shon], s. Perversión, pervertimiento, depravación.

perversity [pəˈvɜːsɪtɪ] [per-ver-si-ti], s. Perversidad, conducta o naturaleza perversa, obstinación, terquedad.

perversive [pəˈvɜːsɪv] [per-ver-siv], a. Perversivo.

pervert [pəˈvɜːt] [per-vert], va. 1. Pervertir, corromper (corrupt). 2. Pervertir, falsear, viciar, dirigir mal o interpretar mal, desnaturalizar. -vn. 1. Apartarse, desviarse del camino recto. 2. Hacerse renegado, apostatar. **To pervert manners,** echar a perder las maneras. **To pervert the meaning,** desnaturalizar el sentido.

pervert, s. Renegado, apóstata; pervertido en oposición a convertido.

perverted [pəˈvɜːtɪd] [per-ver-tid], a. Pervertido (all senses).

perverter [pəˈvɜːtəʳ] [per-ver-taʳ], s. Pervertidor.

pervertible [pəˈvɜːtɪbl] [per-ver-ti-bol], a. Pervertible, lo que es fácil de corromper o pervertir.

pervious [ˈpɜːvɪəs] [per-vios], a. Penetrable; permeable. **Pervious to light,** que permite el paso a la luz.

perviousness [ˈpɜːvɪəsnɪs] [per-vios-nes], s. Penetrabilidad, permeabilidad.

peseta [pəˈsetə] [pe-se-ta], s. Peseta.

pesky [ˈpeskɪ] [pes-ki], a. *(Fam. E. U.)* Molesto, incómodo, también, apestado, excesivo.

pessary [ˈpesərɪ] [pe-sa-ri], s. *(Cir.)* Pesario.

pessimism [ˈpesɪmɪzəm] [pe-si-mi-sem], s. 1. Pesimismo, propensión a verlo todo bajo el aspecto más siniestro. 2. Cinismo, la tendencia a despreciar lo bueno y suponer lo malo. 3. Pesimismo, sistema de filosofía que considera la existencia como un mal.

pessimist [ˈpesɪmɪst] [pe-si-mist], s. Pesimista, persona que todo lo ve bajo el aspecto más desfavorable; partidario del pesimismo, o que desea el exceso del mal como medio de ilegar al bien.

pessimistic [ˌpesɪˈmɪstɪk] [pe-si-mis-tik], a. Pesimista.

pessimistically [ˌpesɪˈmɪstɪkəlɪ] [pe-si-mis-ti-ka-li], adv. En tono pesimista, de forma pesimista.

pest [pest] [pest], s. 1. Peste, pestilencia (stench, foul smell). 2. Peste, se dice de las personas o cosas muy dañosas a las buenas costumbres. **Pest-house,** lazareto. **Pest-control,** lucha contra las plagas de insectos.

pester [ˈpestəʳ] [pes-taʳ], va. Moler, molestar, vejar, cansar, atormentar, importunar (annoy). *(Fam.)* Jorobar. **He pesters me with his letters,** me muele a cartas.

pesterable [ˈpestərəbl] [pes-te-ra-bol], a. Molesto.

pesterer [ˈpestərəʳ] [pes-te-raʳ], s. Moledor. *(Vulg.)* Majadero, joroba, moscón, pejiguera.

pesticide [ˈpestɪsaɪd] [pes-ti-said], s. Pesticida.

pestiferous [pesˈtɪfərəs] [pes-ti-fe-ros], a. Pestífero, pestilente, pernicioso.

pestilence [ˈpestɪləns] [pes-ti-lens], s. Pestilencia, peste, enfermedad contagiosa; también en este sentido figurado.

pestilent [ˈpestɪlənt] [pes-ti-lent], a. 1. Pestilente, pestífero, que produce una enfermedad contagiosa. 2. Pernicioso, de influencia maligna, de efecto perjudicial. 3. Inoportuno, atormentador.

pestilential [ˌpestɪˈlenʃəl] [pes-ti-len-shal], a. Pestilencial, pernicioso, dañoso en sumo grado (damaging).

pestilentialness [ˌpestɪˈlenʃəlnɪs] [pes-ti-len-shal-nes], s. Calidad de pestilente.

pestilently [ˈpestɪləntlɪ] [pes-ti-lent-li], adv. Pestilencialmente.

pestle ['pestl] [pes-tel], *s.* Mano de almirez, majador de mortero. *-va.* Majar, moler o mezclar en un mortero.

pet [pet] [pet], *a.* Acariciado, mimado (spoiled); favorito; domesticado (tame). **Pet name,** nombre cariñoso, a menudo un diminutivo. **Pet lamb,** cordero criado en la casa, sin madre. **Pet food,** comida para animales. *-s.* 1. Enojo, enfado, despecho, acceso de mal humor. 2. Cualquier animal domesticado y acariciado. 3. Favorito. **He is a great pet,** es el favorito, el mimado, el querido. *(Mex.)* Chiqueado, amamantado. **To go away in a pet,** irse enojado o enfadado. **To get in a pet,** atufarse, enojarse. **He is in a great pet,** toma el cielo con las manos.

pet, *va.* Mimar, echar a perder con mimos (spoil).

petal ['petl] [pe-tal], *s. (Bot.)* Pétalo, cada una de las hojas que forman la corola de la flor.

petaled, petalous ['petəld] [pe-tald], *a. (Bot.)* Provisto de pétalos.

petaliferous [ˌpetə'lɪfərəs] [pe-ta-li-fe-ros], *a.* Que tiene pétalos.

petaloid ['petəlɔɪd] [pe-ta-loid], *a.* Petaloideo, semejante a los pétalos o que consta de ellos.

petard [pə'tɑːd] [pe-tard], *s.* Petardo, antigua máquina militar.

petardeer [pe'tɑːdɪəʳ] [pe-tar-diaʳ], *s.* Petardero.

Peter ['piːtəʳ] [pi-taʳd], *s.* Pedro. *-vn.* Disminuir, desaparecer una veta o filón en una mina. **The line finally peters out,** la línea finalmente desaparece.

petiole [pe'ʃɪəʊl] [pe-shioul], *s. (Bot.)* Pecíolo, pezón o rabillo de la hoja.

petit ['petɪ] [pe-ti], *a.* Pequeño; menor. (Desusado a no ser en frases forenses o tomadas del francés). V. PETTY.

petit bourgeois [ˌpetɪˌbʊəʒwɑː] [pe-ti-bua-ya], *a.* Pequeño burgués.

petite [pə'tiːt] [pa-tit], *a.* Chiquita, menuda.

petition [pə'tɪʃən] [pe-ti-shon], *s.* 1. Memorial, presentación. 2. Pedimento, petición, demanda. 3. Petición súplica dirigida al Ser Supremo.

petition, *va.* Suplicar, orar, rogar (pray); dirigir una petición. **To petition for divorce,** presentar una demanda de divorcio.

petitionary [pə'tɪʃənərɪ] [pe-ti-sho-na-ri], *a.* 1. Demandante, la parte que demanda en justicia. 2. Suplicante, el que pide o suplica.

petitioner [pə'tɪʃənəʳ] [pe-ti-sho-naʳ], *s.* Suplicante; memorialista, representante.

pet name ['petneɪm] [pet-neim], *s.* Apodo, nombre cariñoso.

petrean [pə'trɪən] [pe-trian], *a.* Pétreo, de roca, de la naturaleza de la roca.

petrel ['petrəl] [pe-trel], *s.* Procelario, petrel, ave de mar llamada también ave de San Pedro o de las tempestades.

petrescence ['petrəsəns] [pe-tre-sens], *s.* Petrificación, acción de convertirse en piedra.

petrescent ['petrəsənt] [pe-tre-sent], *a.* Que se petrifica.

petrifaction [ˌpetrɪ'fækʃən] [pe-tri-fak-shon], *s.* 1. Petrificación. 2. Petrificación, el cuerpo petrificado.

petrifactive ['petrɪfæktɪv] [pe-tri-fak-tiv], *a.*, **petrific** ['petrɪfɪk] [pe-tri-fik], *a.* Petrífico, petrificante.

petrification [ˌpetrɪfaɪ'keɪʃən] [pe-tri-fai-kei-shon], *s.* 1. Petrificación, el cuerpo petrificado. 2. Endurecimiento del corazón.

petrified ['petrɪfaɪd] [pe-tri-faid], *a.* 1. Muerto de miedo (terrified). 2. *(Geol.)* Petrificado.

petrify ['petrɪfaɪ] [pe-tri-fai], *va.* 1. Petrificar, transformar en piedra. 2. Endurecer el corazón, hacer a alguno sordo a los remordimientos. *-vn.* Petrificar, endurecerse alguna cosa de modo que parezca piedra.

petrine ['petrɪn] [pe-trin], *a.* Referente a San Pedro apóstol.

petrochemical [ˌpetrəʊ'kemɪkəl] [pe-trou-ke-mi-kal], *s.* Producto petroquímico.

petrochemistry [ˌpetrəʊ'kemɪstrɪ] [pe-trou-ke-mis-tri], *s.* Petroquímica.

petrol ['petrəl] [pe-trol], *s.* Gasolina. **Petrol station,** gasolinera.

petroleum [pə'trəʊlɪəm] [pe-tro-liom], *s.* Petróleo, carburo de hidrógeno, principio líquido de los betunes blandos y viscosos. **Petroleum jelly,** vaselina.

petrology [pə'trɒlədʒɪ] [pe-tro-lo-yi], *s.* Petrología, petrognosia, la ciencia de las rocas, su origen y distribución.

petronel ['petrənl] [pe-tro-nel], *s.* V. PISTOL.

petrous ['petrəs] [pe-tros], *a.* Petroso, pétreo, endurecido como la piedra.

petticoat ['petɪkəʊt] [pe-ti-kout], *s.* Guardapiés, zagalejo; enaguas, basquiña. **Quitted o embrothered petticoat,** zagalejo picado. *-a.* Lo que pertenece a las mujeres o es propio de ellas. **Petticoat government,** se usa para expresar la influencia de las mujeres en el gobierno o dirección de una cosa o negocio.

pettifog ['petɪfɒg] [pe-ti-fog], *vn.* Ejercer malamente la abogacía.

pettifogger ['petɪfɒgəʳ] [pe-ti-fo-gaʳ], *s.* 1. Abogado de guardilla. 2. Picapleitos.

pettifoggery ['petɪfɒgərɪ] [pe-ti-fo-ga-ri], *s.* Los embrollos y enredos de los malos abogados.

pettiness ['petɪnɪs] [pe-ti-nes], *s.* Pequeñez, mezquindad (triviality).

pettish ['petɪʃ] [pe-tish], *a.* Enojadizo, bronco, áspero, insociable, caprichudo, regañón.

pettishly ['petɪʃlɪ] [pe-tish-li], *adv.* Caprichosamente, ásperamente, broncamente.

pettishness ['petɪʃnɪs] [pe-tish-nes], *s.* Enojo, aspereza de genio, capricho.

petto ['petəʊ] [pe-tou], *s.* Pecho. *(Ital.)* **In petto,** en lo interior del pecho.

petty ['petɪ] [pe-ti], *a.* 1. Pequeño, corto, menudo (little, small). 2. Despreciable, mezquino (wretch). **Petty cash,** efectivo para gastos menores. **Petty king,** reyezuelo. **Petty larnecy,** robo de cosas de poco valor. **Petty jury,** V. JURY.

petulance ['petjʊləns] [pe-tiu-lans], *s.*, **petulancy** ['petjʊlənsɪ] [pe-tiu-lan-si], *s.* Mal humor, mal genio, enfado pasajero, impaciencia, despego en el trato.

petulant ['petjʊlənt] [pe-tiu-lant], *a.* 1. Enojadizo, de mal humor, que muestra impaciencia caprichuda o despego en el trato. 2. *(Des.)* Petulante, descarado.

petulantly ['petjʊləntlɪ] [pe-tiu-lant-li], *adv.* Con impaciencia, con aspereza, de mal humor.

petunia [pɪ'tjuːnɪə] [pi-tiu-nia], *s. (Bot.)* Petunia.

pew [pjuː] [piu], *s.* Banco, asiento, de iglesia; antiguamente un lugar cerrado a manera de cajón. *-pl.* Los dueños o arrendadores de los bancos de iglesia; la congregación.

pew, *va.* Proporcionar asientos o bancos particulares en las iglesias. *(Fam.)* **Take a pew!,** ¡toma asiento!

pewit, peewit ['piːwɪt] [pi-uit], *s.* Una de varias aves: (a) V. PEWEE. (b) Avefría, frailecillo. (c) Laro de cabeza negra, el pájaro reidor.

pew-opener [ˌpjuːˈəʊpnəʳ] [piu-oup-naʳ], *s. (G.B.)* El que abre o guarda los asientos en la iglesia.

pewter ['pjuːtəʳ] [piu-taʳ], *s.* 1. Peltre, especie de metal compuesto de estaño y plomo. 2. Peltre, el conjunto de platos, fuentes y otras vasijas de dicho metal.

pewterer ['pjuːtərəʳ] [piu-ta-raʳ], *s.* Peltrero, el que trabaja en objetos de peltre, estañador.

phaenogam ['fænəgæm] [fa-no-gam], *s.* Planta que tiene flores; planta fanerógama. V. PHANEROGAM.

phagocytes ['fægəsaɪts] [fa-go-saits], *s. pl.* Fagocitos, tipo de glóbulos blancos.

phalangean ['fæləndʒɪən] [fa-lan-yian], *a.* Falangético, falángido, que pertenece a la falange.

phalanges ['fæləndʒɪs] [fa-lan-yis], *s. pl.* de PHALANX.

phalanx ['fælæŋks] [fa-lanks], *s. (pl.* PHALANGES o PHALANXES, excepto en anatomía y botánica). 1. Falange, cuerpo de infantería de la antigua Grecia. 2. Cualquier cuerpo compacto y numeroso de personas unidas con un mismo fin. 3. Falange, cada uno de los huesos que hay en los dedos de la mano y el pie. 4. Coyuntura del tarso de los insectos.

phallic ['fælɪk] [fa-lik], a. Fálico. **Phallic symbol,** símbolo fálico.

phallus ['fæləs] [fa-los], s. Falo.

phanerogam ['fænɪrəʊgæm] [fa-ni-ro-gam], s. Planta fanerógama, que produce flores, es decir que tiene estambres y pistilos.

phantasm ['fæntæzəm] [fan-tasm], s. Fantasma (ghost).

phantasmagoria [ˌfæntæzməˈgɔːrɪə] [fan-tas-ma-go-ria], s. 1. Fantasmas incoherentes de un sueño 2. Fantasmagoría, arte de representar fantasmas por medio de una ilusión óptica; y la misma linterna empleada para ese objeto.

phantasmagoric [ˌfæntæzməˈgɔːrɪk] [fan-tas-ma-go-rik], a. Fantasmagórico.

phantasy ['fæntəzɪ] [fan-ta-si], s. V. FANTASY, y todas las voces que se derivan de ella.

phantom ['fæntəm] [fan-tom], s. Fantasma, espectro horrible, V. FANTOM.

pharaonic ['fɛərəʊnɪk] [fea-ra-ou-nik], a. Faraónico, concerniente a los Faraones.

pharisaic, pharisaical [ˌfærɪˈseɪk] [fa-ri-seik] [ˌfærɪˈseɪkəl] [fa-ri-sei-kal], a. Farisaico.

pharisaically [ˌfærɪˈseɪkəlɪ] [fa-ri-sei-ka-li], adv. De un modo farisaico.

pharisee ['færɪsiː] [fa-ri-si], s. Fariseo.

pharmaceutic, pharmaceutical [ˌfɑːməˈsjuːtɪk] [far-ma-siu-tik] [ˌfɑːməˈsjuːtɪkəlɪ] [far-ma-siu-ti-ka-li], a. Farmacéutico.

pharmacist ['fɑːməsɪst] [far-ma-sist], s. Farmacéutico, boticario.

pharmacology [ˌfɑːməˈkɒlədʒɪ] [far-ma-ko-lo-yi], s. Farmacología, conocimiento de los medicamentos.

pharmacopoeia [ˌfɑːməkəˈpiːə] [far-ma-ko-pia], s. Farmacopea, el libro que contiene las reglas para la composición de las medicinas.

pharmacy ['fɑːməsɪ] [far-ma-si], s. 1. Farmacia, el arte de preparar los medicamentos. 2. Botica.

pharyngeal ['færɪndʒəl] [fa-rin-yial], a. Faríngeo, perteneciente a la faringe.

pharyngitis [ˌfærɪnˈdʒaɪtɪs] [fa-rin-yai-tis], s. (Med.) Faringitis.

pharyngotomy [ˌfærɪnˈgɒtəmɪ] [fa-rin-go-to-mi], s. Faringotomía, incisión de la faringe.

pharynx ['færɪŋks] [fa-rinks], s. Faringe, la parte superior del esófago.

phase [feɪz] [feis], s. 1. Fase, aspecto, cada uno de los cambios que se notan en ciertos objetos (change). 2. (Astr.) Fase, cada una de las diversas figuras en que vemos la luna y los planetas.

phase, vt. 1. Escalonar, realizar por etapas. 2. Sincronizar (coordinate). **Phase in,** introducir paulatinamente. **Phase out,** retirar paulatinamente.

phasis ['feɪzɪz] [fei-sis], s. (Astr.) Fase.

pheasant ['feznt] [fe-sant], s. (Orn.) Faisán, ave del orden de las gallináceas, muy hermosa y de carne apreciada.

phenix ['fenɪks] [fe-niks], s. 1. Fénix, ave fabulosa, que se creía ser única y que renacía de sus cenizas; emblema de la inmortalidad. 2. Cosa extraordinaria, prodigio. 3. Constelación austral.

phenogam, etc. V. PHAENOGAM, etc.

phenol ['fiːnɒl] [fi-nol], s. 1. Cada uno de una serie de cuerpos derivados de la benzola. 2. Fenol.

phenomenal [fɪˈnɒmɪnl] [fi-no-mi-nal], a. Fenomenal.

phenomenon [fɪˈnɒmɪnəm] [fi-no-mi-nom], s. 1. Fenómeno. 2. Fenómeno, todo lo que admira por su novedad o rareza. Se escribe en plural PHENOMENA.

pheromone ['ferəməʊn] [fe-ro-moun], s. Feromona.

phial ['faɪəl] [faial], s. Redomilla, ampolla. Lo mismo que VIAL.

Philadelphia [ˌfɪləˈdelfɪə] [fi-la-del-fia], a. Filadelfia.

philander [fɪˈlændəʳ] [fi-lan-daʳ], vn. Hacer cocos, divertirse en galantear a una mujer. -s. Amante, pretendiente.

philanthropic, philanthropical [ˌfɪlənˈθrɒpɪk] [fi-lan-zro-pik], a. Filantrópico.

philanthropist [fɪˈlænθrɒpɪst] [fi-lan-zro-pist], s. Filántropo, amigo de los hombres; el que se ocupa en hacerles bien.

philanthropy [fɪˈlænθrɒpɪ] [fi-lan-zro-pi], s. Filantropía, humanidad, amor natural del género humano (charitableness).

philatelic [ˌfɪləˈtelɪk] [fi-la-te-lik], a. Filatélico.

philately [fɪˈlætəlɪ] [fi-la-te-li], s. Filatelia, ocupación o tarea de coleccionar sellos de franqueo de diversos países, para estudiarlos o formar colecciones.

philharmonic [ˌfɪlɑːˈmɒnɪk] [fi-lar-mo-nik], a. Filarmónico, apasionado por la música.

Philippine ['fɪlɪpiːn] [fi-li-pin], a. Filipino.

Philistine ['fɪlɪstaɪn] [fi-lis-tain], s. y a. 1. Filisteo. 2. Partidario a las ideas generalmente admitidas; personal venal, de ideas mezquinas.

philologist [fɪˈlɒlədʒɪst] [fi-lo-lo-yist], o **philologer** ['fɪlɒlədʒəʳ] [fi-lo-lo-gaʳ], s. Filólogo, el que estudia y profesa la filología.

philologic, philological ['fɪlələɒdʒɪk] [fi-lo-lo-yik] [ˌfɪlələɒdʒɪkəl] [fi-lo-lo-yi-kal], a. Filológico.

philologize [fɪˈlɒlədʒaɪz] [fi-lo-lo-yais], vn. Practicar la crítica y la filología.

philology [fɪˈlɒlədʒɪ] [fi-lo-lo-yi], s. Filología, erudición en las letras humanas.

philosophaster [ˌfɪlɒsəˈfæstəʳ] [fi-lo-so-fas-tar], s. Filosofastro.

philosopher [fɪˈlɒsəfəʳ] [fi-lo-so-faʳ], s. Filósofo. **Philosopher's stone,** piedra filosofal.

philosophic, philosophical [ˌfɪləˈsɒfɪk] [fi-lo-so-fik] [ˌfɪləˈsɒfɪkəl] [fi-lo-so-fi-kal], a. 1. Filosófico, relativo a la filosofía. 2. Filosófico, racional, sereno, calmoso.

philosophically [ˌfɪləˈsɒfɪkəlɪ] [fi-lo-so-fi-ka-li], adv. Filosóficamente.

philosophism [fɪləˈsɒfɪk] [fi-lo-so-fik], s. Filosofismo, secta o doctrina de los falsos filósofos.

philosophize [fɪˈlɒsəfaɪz] [fi-lo-so-fais], vn. Filosofar.

philosophy [fɪˈlɒsəfɪ] [fi-lo-so-fi], s. 1. Filosofía, ciencia natural o moral; amor a la ciencia. 2. Filosofía, estudio de los principios y de las causas; sistema de principios científicos; sistema particular de filosofía; razonamiento, discurso. 3. Filosofía, fortaleza de ánimo. 4. Tratado sobre algún sistema de filosofía.

philotechnic [ˌfɪləˈteknɪk] [fi-lo-tek-nik], a. Aficionado a las artes.

philter ['fɪltəʳ] [fil-taʳ], s. Filtro, hechizo amatorio.

philter, va. Hechizar con filtro.

phiz ['fɪz] [fis], s. (Vulg.) Facha, cara, jeta.

phlebitis [flɪˈbaɪtɪs] [fli-bai-tis], s. Flebitis.

phlebotomize [ˌfleˈbɒtəmaɪz] [fle-bo-to-mais], va. Sangrar, abrir una vena como medio curativo.

phlegm [flem] [flem], s. 1. Flema, mucosidad pegajosa que se arroja por la boca. 2. Flema, tardanza y lentitud en las operaciones; apatía indiferencia, genio cachazudo.

phlegmatic, [fleɡˈmætɪk] [fleg-ma-tik], a. 1. Flegmático o flemático. 2. Cachazudo, lento, indiferente, linfático.

phlegmon ['flegmən] [fleg-mon], s. (Med.) Flemón, inflamación del tejido celular, con tendencia a formar pus.

phlox [flɒks] [floks], s. (Bot.) Flox, género de plantas y de flores norteamericanas, tipo de la familia de las polemoniáceas.

phobia ['fəʊbɪə] [fou-bia], s. Fobia.

phoebe, phoebe-bird [fiːbˈbɜːd] [fib-berd], s. Febe, pájaro pequeño de los Estados Unidos del Este.

phoenix ['fiːnɪks] [fi-niks], s. 1. (Orn.) Fénix. 2. (Bot.) Palma.

phonation ['fəʊneɪʃən] [fou-nei-shon], s. Fonación, emisión de la voz o palabra.

phone ['fəʊn] [foun], s. (Fam.) Abreviatura familiar de **telephone,** teléfono. **Phone-card,** tarjeta de teléfono. **Phone-box,** cabina telefónica.

phone, *vt.* Telefonear. **Phone around,** llamar a varias personas. **Phone in,** llamar por teléfono. **Phone up,** telefonear.

phonetics [fəʊnɪtɪks] [fou-ne-tiks], *s.* Fonología, fonética, estudio de los sonidos de la voz humana.

phonic [ˈfɒnɪk] [fo-nik], *a.* Fónico, concerniente al sonido, o de la naturaleza del sonido.

phonogram [ˈfəʊnəgræm] [fou-no-gram], *s.* 1. Carácter, tipo que simboliza un sonido. 2. Fonograma, el trazo producido por un fonógrafo y por medio del cual se reproducen los sonidos articulados.

phonograph [ˈfəʊnəgrɑːf] [fou-no-graf], *s.* Fonógrafo. **Phonograph record,** disco fonográfico.

phonographer [ˈfəʊnəgrɑːfəʳ] [fou-no-gra-faʳ], *s.* 1. Taquígrafo fonético, persona versada en la fonografía. 2. Persona versada en el uso del fonógrafo.

phonographic [ˈfəʊnəgrɑːfɪk] [fou-no-gra-fik], *a.* Fonográfico, relativo a la fonografía o al fonógrafo.

phonography [ˈfəʊnəgrɑːfɪ] [fou-no-gra-fi], *s.* 1. Fonografía, el arte o la ciencia de escribir según los sonidos; una forma de la taquigrafía. 2. Fonografía, representación de los sonidos por medio de signos. 3. El arte de construir o de usar los fonógrafos.

phonologic, phonological [ˌfəʊnəˈlɒdʒɪk] [fou-no-lo-yik] [ˌfəʊnəˈlɒdʒɪkəl] [fou-no-lo-yi-kal], *a.* Fonológico, referente a la fonología.

phonology [fəʊnəlɒdʒɪ] [fou-no-lo-yi], *s.* Fonología.

phonometer [fəʊnəmɪtəʳ] [fou-no-mi-taʳ], *s.* Fonómetro, instrumento para medir la intensidad de la voz o del sonido.

phonometric [fəʊˈnəmɪtrɪk] [fou-no-mi-trik], *a.* Fonométrico, que se refiere al fonómetro.

phonotype [fəʊnətaɪp] [fou-no-taip], *s.* Fonotipo, carácter empleado en la impresión fonotípica.

phonotypy [fəʊnətaɪpɪ] [fou-no-tai-pi], *s.* Fonotipia, sistema de impresión en que cada sonido de la voz está representado por una letra o un carácter distinto.

phosphate [ˈfɒsfeɪt] [fos-feit], *s.* (*Quím.*) Fosfato, sal formada con ácido fosfórico y alguna base.

phosphatic [ˈfɒsfætɪk] [fos-fa-tik], *a.* Fosfático, que contiene algún fosfato.

phosphid, phosphide [ˈfɒsfaɪd] [fos-faid], *s.* Fosfuro, nombre genérico de las combinaciones del fósforo, no ácidas. con otro cuerpo simple.

phosphite [ˈfɒsfaɪt] [fos-fait], *s.* (*Quím.*) Fosfito, sal formada de ácido fosforoso con alguna base.

phosphor [ˈfɒsfəʳ] [fos-faʳ], *s.* 1. Fósforo, la estrella matutina. 2. *V.* PHOSPHORUS.

phosphorate [ˈfɒsfəreɪt] [fos-fo-reit], *va.* Combinar con el fósforo, impregnar de fósforo. **Phosphorated oil,** aceite fosforado.

phosphoresce [ˌfɒsfəˈres] [fos-fo-res], *vn.* Ser fosforescente, fosforescer, despedir luz en la oscuridad como hace el fósforo.

phosphorescence [ˌfɒsfəˈresns] [fos-fo-re-sens], *s.* Fosforescencia.

phosphorescent [ˌfɒsfəˈresnt] [fos-fo-re-sent], *a.* Fosforescente.

phosphoric [ˈfɒsfɒrɪk] [fos-fo-rik], *a.* 1. Fosfórico. 2. Fosforescente.

phosphorous [ˈfɒsfərəs] [fos-fo-ros], *a.* Fosforoso, sacado del fósforo en sus más bajas combinaciones. **Phosphorous acid,** ácido fosforoso.

phosphorus [ˈfɒsfərəs] [fos-fo-ros], *s.* Fósforo, metaloide muy combustible, de color blanco amarillento, que luce en la oscuridad cuando se pone en contacto con el aire, y se inflama fácilmente.

photic [ˈfɒtɪk] [fo-tik], *a.* Relativo a la luz y a la producción de la luz.

photo [ˈfəʊtəʊ] [fou-tou], *s.* (*Fam.*) Estampa fotográfica.

photocopy [ˈfəʊtəʊkɒpɪ] [fou-tou-ko-pi], *s.* Fotocopia.

photoelectric [ˈfəʊtəʊɪˈlektrɪk] [fou-toui-lek-trik], *a.* Fotoeléctrico.

photoengrave [ˌfəʊtəʊɪnˈgreɪv] [fou-touin-greiv] *vt.* Fotograbar.

photoengraving [ˈfəʊtəʊenˈgreɪvɪŋ] [fou-touen-grei-vin], *s.* Fotograbado.

photofinish [ˈfəʊtəʊˈfɪnɪʃ] [fou-tou-fi-nish], *s.* 1. En carreras de caballos, el triunfo reñidísimo que hay que decidir mediante fotografía tomada al efecto. 2. Esta fotografía.

photoflash [ˈfəʊtəʊflæʃ] [fou-tou-flash], *s.* Destello, relámpago, flash.

photogenic [ˌfəʊtəʊˈdʒenɪk] [fou-tou-ye-nik], *a.* Fotogénico, que favorece la acción química de la luz; producido por la acción de la luz.

photograph [ˈfəʊtəʊgræf] [fou-tou-graf], *va.* Fotografiar, reproducir por medio de la fotografía; también en sentido figurado. *vi.* **To photograph well,** salir bien en las fotos. -*s.* Fotografía, estampa obtenida por el arte fotográfico.

photographer [ˈfəʊtəʊgrəfəʳ] [fou-tou-gra-faʳ], *s.* Fotógrafo, el que ejerce la fotografía. **Press photographer,** reportero gráfico.

photographic, photographical [ˌfəʊtəʊˈgræfɪk] [fou-tou-gra-fik], *a.* 1. Fotográfico, relativo a la fotografía, o producido por este arte. 2. Semejante a una imagen fotográfica; representado con vigor y fidelidad.

photography [ˈfəˈtɒgræfɪ] [fo-to-gra-fi], *s.* Fotografía, arte o procedimiento de fijar las imágenes de la cámara obscura sobre una placa sensible a la acción de la luz.

photogravure [ˌfəʊtəʊgrəˈvjʊəʳ] [fou-tou-gra-viuaʳ], *s.* Fotograbado.

photometer [fəˈtɒmɪtəʳ] [fo-to-mi-tar], *s.* Fotómetro, instrumento para medir la intensidad de la luz.

photometric [ˌfəʊtəˈmetrɪk] [fou-to-me-trik], *a.* Fotométrico, relativo a la fotometría.

photon [ˈfəʊtɒn] [fou-ton], *s.* Fotón.

photoplay [ˈfəʊtəpleɪ] [fou-to-plei], *s.* Comedia cinematográfica.

photosphere [ˈfəʊtəsfɪəʳ] [fou-tos-fiaʳ], *s.* Fotosfera, la atmósfera luminosa del sol, o (rara vez) de una estrella fija.

photostatic [ˌfəʊtəʊˈstætɪk] [fou-tou-sta-tik], *a.* Fotostático.

photosynthesis [ˌfəʊtəʊˈsɪnθəsɪs] [fou-tou-sin-sis], *s.* Fotosíntesis.

phototype [ˌfəʊtəʊtaɪp] [fou-tou-taip], *s.* Fototipia.

phrasal [ˈfreɪzəl] [frei-sal], *a.* Frasal. **Phrasal verb,** verbo con preposición o adverbio, verbo frasal.

phrase [freɪz] [freis], *s.* 1. Frase, la construcción de algunas palabras que forman un sentido perfecto. 2. Frase, estilo, el modo particular con que expresa sus pensamientos cada escritor y la índole y forma especial de las oraciones en cada lengua. **As the phrase goes,** (*Fam.*) como suele decirse; vamos a decir.

phrase, *va.* Llamar, nombrar, intitular.

phrase-book [ˈfreɪzbʊk] [freis-buk], *s.* Libro de frases o modismos peculiares de cada lengua.

phraseless [ˈfreɪzlɪs] [freis-les], *a.* Indescriptible.

phraseologist [ˌfreɪzɪəˈlɒdʒɪst] [frei-sio-lo-yist], *s.* Fraseologista, el que habla en frases hechas, con afectación.

phraseology [ˌfreɪzɪˈɒlədʒɪ] [frei-sio-lo-yi], *s.* 1. Fraseología, dicción, construcción, estilo. 2. Libro de frases hechas.

phrenetic [frɪˈnetɪk] [fri-ne-tik], *a.* Frenético, loco.

phrenologist [frɪˈnɒlədʒɪst] [fri-no-lo-yist], *s.* Frenólogo, el que profesa la frenología.

phrenology [frɪˈnɒlədʒɪ] [fri-no-lo-yi], *s.* Frenología, sistema que atribuye a cada porción del cerebro diversa facultad intelectual, instinto, pasión o afecto.

phrensy, *s. V.* FRENZY.

phthisic [ˈθaɪsɪk] [zai-sik], *a.* 1. Tísico, bético, que padece de tisis. 2. Asmático.

phthisis [ˈθaɪsɪs] [zai-sis], *s.* Tisis, tuberculosis pulmonar.

phycology [ˌfaɪˈkɒlədʒɪ] [fai-ko-lo-yi], *s.* Algología, ciencia de las algas marinas.

phyllotaxis [ˌfaɪləˈtæksɪs] [fai-lo-tak-sis], *s. (Bot.)* Filotaxia, arreglo o disposición de las hojas sobre el tallo, y las reglas a que obedece.

phylloxera [ˌfɪlɒkˈsɪərə] [fai-lok-si-ra], *s.* 1. Filoxera. 2. Enfermedad de la viña, causada por dicho insecto.

physic [ˈfɪzɪk] [fi-sik], *va.* Medicinar y particularmente purgar.

physic, *s.* 1. Medicina, la ciencia que enseña a precaver y curar las enfermedades del cuerpo humano. 2. Medicamentos, remedios (medicine). 3. Purgante o purga.

physical [ˈfɪzɪkəl] [fi-si-kal], *a.* 1. Físico, perteneciente al universo material o a la ciencia de la física. 2. Material; corporal, corpóreo. 3. Físico, perteneciente a los fenómenos de que trata la física; obvio a los sentidos, externo. **Physical chemistry,** fisicoquímica. **Physical education,** educación física. **Physical examination,** reconocimiento médico. **Physical science,** ciencias físicas.

physically [ˈfɪzɪkəlɪ] [fi-si-ka-li], *adv.* Físicamente; naturalmente; materialmente; corporalmente; externamente.

physician [ˈfɪzɪʃən] [fi-si-shan], *s.* Médico, el que profesa la medicina.

physicist [ˈfɪzɪsɪst] [fi-si-sist], *s.* 1. Físico, persona versada en la física. 2. Partidario de la doctrina de que los fenómenos vitales son puramente físicos y químicos.

physics [ˈfɪzɪks] [fi-siks], *s. pl.* Física, la ciencia que estudia y enseña la naturaleza y las propiedades de los cuerpos.

physiognomist [ˌfɪzɪˈɒnəmɪst] [fi-sio-no-mist], *s.* Fisonomista, fisónomo, la persona dedicada al estudio de la fisonomía y sabe juzgar por ella a las personas.

physiognomy [ˌfɪzɪˈɒnəmɪ] [fi-sio-no-mi], *s.* 1. Fisonomía, el arte que da reglas para conjeturar por las facciones del rostro el temperamento y las buenas o malas inclinaciones de una persona. 2. Fisonomía, rostro, semblante, aspecto particular de cada persona.

physiologic, physiological [ˌfɪzɪˈɒlədʒɪk] [fi-sio-lo-yik], *a.* Fisiológico, perteneciente a la fisiología.

physiologist [ˌfɪzɪˈɒlədʒɪst] [fi-sio-lo-yist], *s.* Fisiologista, fisiólogo, el que estudia la fisiología.

physiology [ˌfɪzɪˈɒlədʒɪ] [fi-sio-lo-yi], *s.* Fisiología, la ciencia que trata de las funciones orgánicas de los seres vivientes, sean animales o vegetales.

physiotherapy [ˌfɪzɪəˈθerəpɪ] [fi-sio-ze-ra-pi], *s.* Fisioterapia.

physique [fɪˈziːk] [fi-sik], *s.* Físico, constitución, complexión.

phytology [faɪˈtɒlədʒɪ] [fai-to-lo-yi], *s.* Botánica, la ciencia que trata de las plantas y sus propiedades.

phytophagous [faɪˈtɒfəgəs] [fai-to-fa-gos], *a.* Fitófago, que se alimenta de plantas.

pi, pie [paɪ] [pai], *va.* Mezclar confusamente letras de imprenta. -*s.* Pastel, mezcla confusa de tipos de imprenta.

pianissimo [pɪəˈniːsɪmə] [pia-ni-si-mo], *adv.* y *a. (Mús.)* Muy suavemente; pianísimo, con fuerza apenas perceptible. En abreviatura, *pp.*

pianist [ˈpɪənɪst] [pia-nist], *s.* Pianista, el que toca el piano.

piano [ˈpjɑːnəʊ] [pia-nou], *a.* y *adv. (Mús.)* Dulcemente; piano, bajo, con sonido débil.

piano, *s. (Fam.)* Piano. V. PIANOFORTE.

pianoforte [ˌpjɑːnəˈfɪrtɪ] [pia-no-for-ti], *s.* Pianoforte, piano, instrumento músico de teclado y percusión. **Cabinet, upright, piano (forte),** piano vertical. **Grand piano (forte),** piano de cola. **Square piano,** piano de mesa.

pianola [pɪəˈnəʊlə] [pia-nou-la], *s.* Pianola, piano mecánico.

piazza [prˈætsə] [pia-cha], *s.* 1. Pórtico o columnata. 2. Galería, corredor cubierto.

pica [ˈpaɪkə] [pai-ka], *s.* 1. Lectura, cícero, letra de doce puntos. **Small pica,** lecturita, letra de unos diez u once puntos. 2. *(Med.)* Depravación del apetito, afición a comer arcilla, yeso, etc.

picador [ˈpɪkəˈdɔː] [pi-ka-dor], *s.* Picador, torero de a caballo.

picaresque [ˌpɪkəˈresk] [pi-ka-resk], *a.* Picaresco.

picaroon [ˌpɪkəˈruːn] [pi-ka-run], *s.* Picarón, ladrón, el que roba o hurta.

picayune [ˌpɪkəˈjuːn] [pi-ka-yu-ni], **Picayunish** [ˌpɪkəˈjuːnɪʃ] [pi-ka-yu-nish], *a.* De poco valor, mezquino. **Picayunish business,** negocio de chucherías.

piccaninny [ˌpɪkəˈnɪnɪ] [pi-ka-ni-ni], *s.* Niñito, particularmente el de raza negra.

piccolo [ˈpɪkələʊ] [pi-ko-lou], *s. (Mús.)* Flautín.

pick [pɪk] [pik], *va.* 1. Escoger, elegir (choose). 2. Coger, recoger (collect, take). 3. Mondar, limpiar (clean). **To pick one's teeth,** mondarse o limpiarse los dientes. **To pick a bone,** roer un hueso. **To pick a fowl,** descañonar un ave. 4. Picar, agujerear o penetrar en alguna cosa con un instrumento punzante. 5. Picotear. 6. Robar, birlar o soplar con ligereza alguna cosa. 7. Forzar o abrir por fuerza alguna cerradura con una herramienta. -*vn.* 1. Picar, comer alguna porción pequeña de comida. 2. Hacer alguna cosa con exagerada nimiedad o delicadeza.

pick off, (a) Arrancar, quitar. (b) Tirar con arma de fuego, apuntando cuidadosamente a un blanco determinado.

pick out, escoger o elegir una cosa entre otras; coger o atrapar algo con cuidado; separar, quitar o arrancar con violencia.

pick up, coger, recoger o alzar lo que estaba caído; juntar lo esparcido; sacar de un apuro; recobrar la salud. **To pick a hole in one's coat,** sacar a relucir una falta de otra persona; buscar camorra. **I have a bone to pick with him,** tengo que ajustar cuentas con él, o tengo con él una cuenta pendiente. **To pick a quarrel,** buscar pendencia sin provocación.

pick, *s.* 1. Herramienta de escultor y de cantero (tool); pico, instrumento de hierro puntiagudo para excavar en tierras duras, caminos, etc. 2. Escogimiento, derecho de elección. 3. Cantidad de ciertas mieses que se recogen con las manos. 4. En el arte de tejer, el golpe que empuja la lanzadera del telar. 5. Hilo; el número de los hilos en una pulgada determina el valor relativo de la tela de algodón. 6. *(Impr.)* mancha en un pliego impreso. **A pick of hops,** cosecha de lúpulo u hombrecillo. **Pick and pick,** variedad simétrica de matices producida por la alteración de hilos de diferentes colores (cloths). **Ear-pick,** limpiaoídos o escarbaoídos. **The pick of books,** el mejor de los libros.

pickaback, pickapack [ˈpɪkəbæk] [pi-ka-bak], *adv. (Fam.)* Sobre los hombros; a modo de fardo o del mismo modo que si fuera un fardo.

pickax, pickaxe [ˈpɪkæks] [pi-kaks], *s.* Pico, especie de azadón.

picked [pɪkt] [pikt], *a.* 1. Espinoso, que tiene espinas o púas. 2. Puntiagudo.

picked, *pp.* y *a.* Escogido con cuidado o para un fin especial; de la mejor calidad. **Picked fruit,** frutas de la mejor calidad. **Picked men,** hombres o soldados escogidos.

picker [ˈpɪkər] [pi-kar], *s.* 1. Escogedor. 2. El que con facilidad toma parte en algún negocio. 3. Escardador. 4. (En los telares) Recibidor. **A picker of quarrels,** camorrista, pendenciero.

pickerel [ˈpɪkərəl] [pi-ke-rel], *s.* 1. Lucio pequeño, pez de agua dulce. Esox. 2. Sollo pequeño.

picket [ˈpɪkɪt] [pi-kit], *s.* 1. Estaca puntiaguda, piquete. 2. *(Mil.)* Piquete.

picket, *va.* 1. Cercar con estacas o piquetes. 2. Poner o colocar de guardia. 3. Atar un caballo a la estaca. 4. Castigar a los soldados con el servicio de piquete.

picket-guard [ˈpɪkɪtˌgɑːd] [pi-kit-gard], *s. (Mil.)* Piquete, centinelas avanzados.

picking [ˈpɪkɪŋ] [pi-kin], *s.* La acción y el efecto del verbo **pick** en todas sus acepciones; por ejemplo, recolección, cosecha (de frutos, etc.); quite, arrancamiento; picadura, roedura; limpia, monda, elección, escogimiento; hurto, robo. En plural, desperdicios, residuos, desechos; también hurtos, arrebañaduras, raterías.

pickle [ˈpɪkl] [pi-kel], *s.* 1. Salmuera, escabeche, adobo. 2. Cualquier cosa puesta en escabeche o adobo. 3. Fruta o legumbre conservada en vinagre. 4. *(Fam.)* Estado, condición, situación; se usa en este último sentido para expresar desprecio. **Mixed pickles** (a) Varias legumbres, como pepinos, cebollas y coliflor, adobados en vinagre. (b) Mezcla, cosas o personas inconguras. **To have a rod in pickle,** tenérsela guardada a uno.

pickle, *va.* Escabechar, adobar, conservar en vinagre, adobo, salmuera o escabeche. **Pickled cucumbers,** pepinillos encurtidos. **Pickled herrings,** arenques salados. **Pickled fish,** pescado en escabeche. **Pickled salmon,** salmón escabechado.

picklock ['pɪklɒk] [pik-lok], *s.* 1. Ganzúa, alambre fuerte y encorvado para abrir una cerradura; llave falsa. 2. Ladrón nocturno. 3. La lana más fina, escogida.

pickpocket ['pɪkˌpɒkɪt] [pik-po-kit], *s.* Ratero, raterillo, el que hurta de los bolsillos de otros.

pickthank ['pɪkθæŋk] [pik-zank], *s.* Entremetido.

pick-up (of an auto) ['pɪkʌp] [pik-ap], *a.* 1. Aceleración, desarrollo de velocidad (car). 2. Pequeño camión de carga. 3. Fonocaptor.

picnic ['pɪknɪk] [pik-nik], *s.* 1. Partida de campo, merienda al aire libre en la que cada cual contribuye parte de las provisiones. 2. *(Ger. E. U.)* Ocupación o deber fácil y agradable. *-vn.* Tener una partida de campo, merienda o romería, o concurrir a ella.

picnicker ['pɪknɪkə^r] [pik-ni-ka^r], *s.* Excursionista.

picotee ['pɪkəʊtiː] [pi-kou-ti], *s.* Variedad de clavel doble.

pictography ['pɪktəgræfɪ] [pik-to-gra-fi], *s.* Pictografía, escritura ideográfica.

pictorial [pɪk'tɔːrɪəl] [pik-to-rial], *a.* 1. Pictórico, que pertenece a la pintura. 2. Gráfico.

picturable ['pɪktʃərəbl] [pik-cha-ra-bol], *a.* Que puede dibujarse o pintarse.

picture ['pɪktʃə^r] [pik-cha^r], *s.* 1. Pintura, retrato, cuadro, fotografía (painting, portrait). 2. Descripción, delineación verbal. 3. Imagen, retrato, semejanza (image); lo que se asemeja a alguna cosa o la sugiere; escena. 4. Panorama (situation). **That's the whole picture,** ésa es la situación, ése es el asunto.

picture, *va.* 1. Pintar, dibujar; hacer un cuadro (paint). 2. Figurar, describir (describe). 3. Imaginar, formar una imagen en la mente (image).

picture gallery ['pɪktʃəˈgælərɪ] [pik-cha-ga-la-ri], *s.* Museo de pinturas.

picture-like ['pɪktʃəlaɪk] [pik-cha-laik], *a.* Semejante a una pintura.

picturesque [ˌpɪktʃəˈresk] [pik-cha-resk], *a.* Pintoresco.

picturesqueness [ˌpɪktʃəˈresknɪs] [pik-cha-res-nes], *s.* Calidad de pintoresco.

piddle ['pɪdl] [pi-del], *vn.* 1. Pellizcar la comida, comer muy poco a poco y como con desgana. 2. Emplearse en bagatelas. 3. Orinar: voz que usan los niños.

piddler ['pɪdlə^r] [pid-la^r], *s.* El que come sin ganas.

pidgin-english ['pɪdʒɪŋˌeŋglɪʃ] [pid-yin-en-glish], *s.* Inglés chapurreado, mezcla de inglés con vocablos chinos, portugueses y malayos.

pie [paɪ] [pai], *s.* 1. Pastel, empanada. **Veal pie,** empanada de ternera. **Mince pie,** pastel de picadillo o de carne. **He intends to have his finger in the pie,** él se propone meter también cuchara. 2. *(Orn.)* Marica. 3. *(Impr.)* V. PI.

piebald ['paɪbɔːld] [pai-bold], *a.* Manchado de varios colores.

piece [piːs] [pis], *s.* 1. Remiendo, fragmento, pedazo, pieza (bit, fragment). 2. Pintura, retrato (painting). 3. Pieza, un cañón de artillería. 4. Pieza, cualquier especie de moneda. 5. Fusil. 6. Composición, obra, escrito; cualquier artefacto. **A piece of music,** una pieza musical. 7. Pieza, la porción de un tejido que se fabrica de una vez en el telar. 8. Trozo, pedazo de una pieza mayor cortada y rota; retal, retazo. **A piece of wit,** una gracia, una agudeza. **Of a piece (with),** de la misma clase o calidad; enterizo, de una sola pieza, de un solo pedazo. **To give one a piece of one's mind,** soltarle a uno cuatro frescas, decirle las verdades del barquero, ponerlo como un trapo o como nuevo. **A piece of news,** una noticia,

un informe. **A piece of advice,** un consejo. **A piece of folly,** un acto de locura. **A piece of furniture,** un mueble. **A piece of ground,** un solar, una porción de tierra. **A piece of paper, of wood,** un pedazo de papel, de madera. **To come to pieces,** desarmarse, deshacerse, separarse las piezas o fragmentos de una cosa. **To cut to pieces** o **in pieces,** cortar en pedazos; destrozar (army). **To tear to** o **in pieces,** romper en pedazos, rasgar, desgarrar en tiras. **To pull to pieces,** despedazar, desgarrar, hacer trizas. **A foling-piece,** una escopeta. **A (broken) piece of a bottle,** un tiesto o casco de botella.

piece, *va.* 1. Aumentar alguna cosa añadiéndole una pieza o pedazo de lo mismo. 2. Juntar, unir. 3. Remendar. *-vn.* Juntase, unirse una cosa con otra. **To piece out,** alargar, aumentar o engrandecer añadiendo retazos; *(Fig.)* aumentar, prolongar. **To piece up,** remendar, reparar.

pieceless ['piːslɪs] [pis-les], *a.* Que es todo de una pieza o que no está dividido en pedazos.

piecemeal ['piːsmiːl] [pis-mil], *adv.* En pedazos. *-a.* Dividido. *-s.* Fragmento, pedazo. **By piecemeal,** a pedacitos, a bocaditos.

piecer ['piːsə^r] [pi-sa^r], *s.* El que añade o remienda.

pied [paɪd] [paid], *a.* De varios colores, manchado, abigarrado.

piedness ['paɪdnɪs] [paid-nes], *s.* Variedad o diversidad de colores.

pie-plant [paɪ'plænt] [pai-plant], *s.* Ruipóntico, rapóntico, planta de huerta.

pier ['paɪə^r] [paiar], *s.* 1. Estribo de puente. 2. Pilar, pilón, estribo, sostén de obra de albañilería, de madera o de hierro. 3. Entrepaño de pared. 4. Muelle, malecón, desembarcadero; muelle, escollera, espolón. **Pier-glass,** espejo largo colocado en el entrepaño de una sala. **Pier-table,** consola, mueble que se coloca entre dos ventanas.

pierce [pɪəs] [pirs], *va.* 1. Penetrar, agujerear, taladrar, introducir algún cuerpo en otro. 2. Excitar o mover las pasiones, traspasar el corazón, conmover. 3. Abrir camino por medio de la fuerza. *-vn.* 1. Penetrar, llegar al interior de un cuerpo rompiendo o dividiendo su unión física. 2. Ser afectuoso, patético, atractivo o persuasivo. 3. Alcanzar o comprender alguna cosa dificultosa. 4. Llegar lo agudo del dolor o sentimiento al interior del alma. **Pierced with sorrow,** traspasado de dolor. **Pierced with holes,** acribillado, hecho una criba.

piercer ['pɪəsə^r] [pir-sa^r], *s.* Taladro; aguijón.

piercing ['pɪəsɪŋ] [pir-sin], *a.* Penetrante.

piercingly ['pɪəsɪŋlɪ] [pir-sin-li], *adv.* Agudamente.

pierrot ['pɪərəʊ] [pia-rou], *sm.* Pierrot.

pietism ['paɪətɪzəm] [pie-ti-sem], *s.* 1. Pietismo, doctrina de los pietistas. 2. Piedad, mística afectada.

pietist ['paɪətɪst] [pie-tist], *s.* 1. Pietista, partidario del pietismo luterano. 2. Misticón, beato.

piety ['paɪətɪ] [pie-ti], *s.* 1. Piedad, devoción, reverencia, hacia Dios; religiosidad (en general). 2. *(Ant.)* Piedad, atención, respeto y reverencia que se debe a los padres, a los mayores o a la patria.

piezometer ['paɪəzəʊˌmɪtə^r] [pie-sou-mi-ta^r], *s.* Piezómetro.

piffle ['pɪfl] [pi-fel], *s. (Fam.)* Estupideces.

pig [pɪg] [pig], *s.* 1. Cochino, cerdo, marrano, puerco, cochinillo, lechón (pork). **Sucking-pig,** lechoncillo. **Pig-sty,** zahurda, la pocilga en que se encierraan los puercos. 2. Masa oblonga de metal después de fundida en un molde basto, como de arena; tejo, lingote, pigote, galápago o barra; v. g. **Pig-lead,** un lingote de plomo. **To buy a pig in a poke,** cerrar un trato a ciegas sin saber bien lo que se hace. **Pig-iron,** hierro en lingotes; barra, masa de hierro colado. **Pig-pen,** pocilga.

pig, *vn.* 1. Parir la puerca. 2. Conducirse o vivir como cochinos. **Pig out,** darse un atracón.

pigeon ['pɪdʒən] [pid-chon], *s.* Pichón, aplomo, paloma. **Pigeon-hearted,** tímido, cobarde. **Pigeonhole,** (a) División que hay en los escritorios para guardar cartas y papeles. (b) *pl.* Un juego antiguo. **Pigeon-house, pigeon-loft,** palomar. **Pigeon-pie,** pastel de pichones. **Pigeon-toed,** (a) Que tiene los pies parecidos a los de un pichón; peristerópodo. (b) Que tiene los dedos del pie dirigidos hacia dentro.

pigeon-breast ['pɪdʒən,brest] [pid-chon-brest], *s.* Deformidad causada por la raquitis, que deprime la caja del pecho por ambos lados y hace sobresalir el esternón. **Pigeon-breasted,** que padece dicha deformidad.

pigeonfoot ['pɪdʒənfʊt] [pid-chon-fut], *s. (Bot.)* Pie de milano.

pigeon-livered ['pɪdʒən,li:vəd] [pid-chon-li-vad], *a.* Apacible, quieto; medroso.

pigeonry ['pɪdʒənrɪ] [pid-chon-ri], *s.* Palomar, paraje donde se recogen y crían las palomas.

piggery ['pɪgərɪ] [pi-ga-ri], *s.* Zahurda, lugar para criar cochinos.

piggin ['pɪgɪn] [pi-guin], *s.* 1. Cubeta, vasija pequeña de madera, con reborde saliente para servir como mango; también, cucharón con mango largo y vasija poco profunda. 2. Cántaro, cacharro, vasija de barro.

piggish ['pɪgɪʃ] [pi-guish], *a.* Que se porta como un cochino; voraz, puerco, sucio.

piggishness ['pɪgɪʃnɪs] [pi-guish-nes], *s.* Voracidad; porquería, suciedad.

piggyback ['pɪgɪbæk] [pi-gui-bak], *s. (F. C.)* Servicio de remolques en plataformas de ferrocarril. -*a.* Sobre los hombros.

pig-headed ['pɪghedɪd] [pig-je-did], *a.* Terco, obstinado, perverso.

piglet ['pɪglɪt] [pi-glit], *s.* Cochinillo.

pigmean, *a. V.* PIGMEAN.

pigment ['pɪgmənt] [pig-ment], *s.* Colores, los materiales de varios colores preparados para pintar; afeite; pigmento, cualquier substancia que da color a los tejidos animales o vegetales. 2. Vino ricamente aromátizado con especias y endulzado con miel.

pigmentation [,pɪgmən'teɪʃən] [pig-men-tei-shon], *s.* Pigmentación.

pigmy ['pɪgmɪ] [pig-mi], *s.* Pigmeo. *V.* PYGMY.

pignoration [,pɪgnə'reɪʃən] [pig-no-rei-shon], *s.* Empeño, pignoración.

pig-nut ['pɪgnʌt] [pig-nat], *s. (Bot.) (E.U.)* Nuez de un nogal de América y el árbol que la produce.

pike [paɪk] [paik], *s.* 1. Lucio, pez de agua dulce. 2. Pica, especie de lanza larga. 3. *V.* SPIKE.

pike, *s.* 1. Camino de barrera, camino real, calzada. 2. Barrera de portazgo. (Abrev. de TURNPIKE)

piked ['paɪkt] [paikt], *a.* Puntiagudo.

pikeman ['paɪkmən] [paik-man], *s.* Piquero, el soldado armado con pica.

piker ['paɪkəʳ] [pai-kaʳ], *s. (Fam.)* Agarrado, roñoso (stingy person).

pikestaff ['paɪkstɑːf] [paik-staf], *s.* Asta de pica.

pilaster [pɪ'læstəʳ] [pi-las-taʳ], *s.* Pilastra, columna cuadrada.

pilau ['paɪləʊ] [pai-lou], *s.* Pilau.

pilchard ['pɪltʃəd] [pil-chard], **pilcher** ['pɪltʃəʳ] [pil-chaʳ], *s.* Arenque menor, sardina arenque.

pile [paɪl] [pail], *s.* 1. Pila, montón, rimero (heap). 2. Pira, hoguera, montón de combustibles. 3. Estaca, pilote, madero fuerte que se hinca en el suelo para afianzar un cimiento (stick). *V.* SPILE. 4. Edificio grande y macizo (building). 5. Pelo de los animales. 6. *(Ar.)* Montón de balas. 7. Pelillo en las telas de lana; pelo, pelusilla, parte fina y aterciopelada del paño y varias telas. 8. Pila galvánica. **Piles,** almorranas. **Pile-drawer,** aparato para sacar o arrancar pilotes. **Pile-driver,** martinete, máquina para clavar pilotes. **Pile-hoop,** vilorta, loriga, anillo de hierro que se pone alrededor de la cabeza de un pilote para impedir que se hienda. **Pile-shoe,** zueco, guarda de metal puesta al extremo de un pilote. **He has made his pile,** *(Ger.)* Ha hecho su agosto, se ha enriquecido.

pile, *va.* 1. Amontonar, apilar (heap up). 2. Clavar, empujar pilotes. 3. Poner pelo o pelusa a una tela. **Pile in,** meterse.

Pile into, meterse en, arremeter contra, estrellarse contra. **Pile on,** exagerar en algo. **Pile up,** acumularse.

piler ['paɪləʳ] [pai-laʳ], *s.* Amontonador.

pilework ['paɪlwɜːk] [pail-uek], *s.* Pilotaje, estructura de pilotes.

pilfer ['pɪlfəʳ] [pil-faʳ], *va.* y *vn.* Ratear, hurtar cosas de poco valor con destreza y sutileza.

pilferer ['pɪlfərəʳ] [pil-fa-raʳ], *s.* Ratero (small-time thief).

pilfering ['pɪlfərɪŋ] [pil-fa-rin], *s.* Raterías, robos.

pilferingly ['pɪlfərɪŋlɪ] [pil-fa-rin-li], *adv.* Con ratería, rateramente.

pilfery ['pɪlfərɪ] [pil-fa-ri], *s. (Poco us.)* Ratería, el hurto de cosas de poco valor.

pilgrim ['pɪlgrɪm] [pil-grim], *s.* Peregrino, romero. **The Pilgrim Fathers,** los primeros colonizadores de Nueva Inglaterra.

pilgrim, *vn.* Peregrinar.

pilgrimage ['pɪlgrɪmɪdʒ] [pil-gri-mich], *s.* Peregrinación. **They will go on a pilgrimage,** van a ir de peregrinación.

piliferous, piligerous ['pɪlɪfərəs] [pi-li-fe-ros], *a. (Zool.)* Peludo, que tiene pelo, pelusa o borra.

piling ['paɪlɪŋ] [pai-lin], *s.* 1. Acto o procedimiento de preparar y de clavar pilotes. 2. Pilotes colectivamente; estructura de pilotes.

pill [pɪl] [pil], *s.* 1. Píldora. 2. Cualquier cosa que produce náuseas o que no es fácil de evitar. 3. *(Ger.)* Pesadilla, persona muy fastidiosa.

pillage ['pɪlɪdʒ] [pi-lich], *s.* Pillaje, botín, saqueo, latrocinio, rapiña.

pillage, *va.* Pillar, hurtar, robar.

pillager ['pɪlɪdʒəʳ] [pi-la-chaʳ], *s.* Pillador, saqueador.

pillar ['pɪləʳ] [pi-laʳ], *s.* 1. Columna, pilar. 2. Masa columnar, v. g. de carbón en una mina. 3. *(Biol.)* Columela, columna. 4. *(Fig.)* Soporte, sostén. **He was a pillar of the church,** era firme sostén de la iglesia. **From pillar to post,** de la ceca a la Meca.

pillar-box ['pɪləbɒks] [pi-la-boks], *s. (G. B.)* Buzón.

pillared ['pɪləd] [pi-lad], *a.* Sostenido por columnas.

pillbox ['pɪlbɒks] [pil-boks], *s.* 1. Pildorera, estuche para píldoras. 2. Sombrero chico de mujer, con copa redonda, sin ala. 3. *(Mil.)* Fortín con ametralladoras.

pillion ['pɪlɪən] [pi-lion], *s.* Albarda, sillón, la parte de la silla en que se sientan las mujeres a caballo detrás del jinete.

pilloried ['pɪlərɪd] [pi-lo-ried], *a.* Empicotado.

pillory ['pɪlərɪ] [pi-lo-ri], *s.* Picota, cepo, tabla con agujeros para las manos y cabeza, en donde se ponía a los malhechores a la vergüenza.

pillory, *va.* Empicotar, poner a un malhechor en una picota o argolla.

pillow ['pɪləʊ] [pi-lou], *s.* 1. Almohada. 2. **Pillow of the bowsprit,** *(Mar.)* Tragante o descanso del bauprés. **Pillows of the mast-heads,** *(Mar.)* Almohadas de las jarcias. **Pillow-case, pillow-slip,** funda de almohada. **Pillow-sham,** cubierta de adorno para almohada.

pillow, *va.* Poner alguna cosa sobre la almohada.

pilose ['pɪləʊz] [pi-lous], *a.* Peludo, velloso, con pelo o vello (hairy, shaggy).

pilosity ['pɪləsɪtɪ] [pi-lo-si-ti], *s.* Abundancia de pelo.

pilot ['paɪlət] [pai-lot], *va.* 1. Guiar, conducir (drive). 2. Pilotar, pilotear.

pilot, *s.* 1. Piloto. **Coast-pilot,** piloto práctico de costa. **Sea-pilot,** piloto de altura. 2. Carta de marear. 3. Instrumento para corregir la desviación de una brújula. 4. Guía, consejero. **Pilot-bird,** pájaro-piloto, ave que en el mar de las Antillas indica a los navegantes la proximidad de la tierra. **Pilot-boat,** bote del piloto, embarcación en que salen los pilotos al encuentro de los buques para guiarlos al entrar en puerto; lleva un número en la vela mayor. **Pilot-bread,** galleta. **Pilot-fish,** piloto, pez de mar, que se ve a menudo en latitudes cálidas en compañía de los tiburones. **Pilot-house,** garita o mirador de timonel, en que se pone el pilot cuando está de guardia.

pilotage ['paɪlətɪdʒ] [pai-lo-tich], *s.* 1. Pilotaje. **Book of pilotage,** derrotero. **Rates of pilotage,** timonaje. 2. Pilotaje, el sueldo del piloto.

pilot light ['paɪlət‚laɪt] [pai-lot-lait], *s.* Luz piloto.

pilous, pileous ['paɪləs] [pai-los], *a.* Piloso, peludo.

pimenta [pɪˈmentə] [pi-men-ta], o **pimento** [pɪˈmentəʊ] [pi-men-tou], *s.* Pimienta de Jamaica.

pimp [pɪmp] [pimp], *s.* Alcahuete, proxeneta.

pimp, *vn.* Alcahuetear.

pimpernel ['pɪmpənel] [pim-pa-nel], *s. (Bot.)* Anagálida.

pimpinel ['pɪmpɪnel] [pim-pi-nel], *s. (Bot.)* Pimpinela. Pimpinella saxifraga.

pimping ['pɪmpɪŋ] [pim-pin], *a. (Fam.)* Pequeño, fútil, mezquino, miserable.

pimple ['pɪmpl] [pim-pel], *s.* Grano, tumorcillo; botón, postilla, pupa, buba; barrillos.

pimpled ['pɪmpəld] [pim-peld], *a.* Engranujado, granujiento.

pin [pɪn] [pin], *s.* 1. Alfiler. **Hair-ins,** alfileres de gancho, horquillas para el cabello. 2. Bagatela, cosa de poco valor. **I don't care a pin,** no se me da un bledo, un pito, un ardite o tres pepinos. 3. Prendedor, broche. 4. Clavo, perno, chaveta; clavija, pasador. 5. Bolo, trozo de palo aguzado para que se tenga derecho en el suelo. **Pin of wood,** clavija, cabilla, saetín, perno. **Linch-pin of a wheel,** pezonera. **Larding-pin,** aguja de mechar. **Rolling-pin,** rodillo. **Block-pins** *(Mar.)* Pernos de mtoones. **Belaying-pins,** *(Mar.)* Cabillas de probados y jarcias. **Pin-clover,** *(Bot.)* Alfilerilla. **Pin-feather,** pluma que empieza a salir, pluma rudimentaria. **Pin-feathered,** que no tiene todavía plumas. **Pin-head,** cabeza de alfiler; objeto muy pequeño. **Pin-maker,** afilerero, fabricante de alfileres. **Pin-point,** punta de alfiler; minuciosidad, nimiedad.

pin, *va.* 1. Prender con alfileres. 2. Asegurar alguna cosa, fijar o unir una cosa a otra; asir y tener firmemente de cualquier manera. 3. *(Germ.)* Coger, tomar furtivamente, hurtar. **To pin up a gown,** arremangar, recoger o levantar un vestido asegurándolo con alfileres. **To pin one's reason to a woman's petticoat,** ser esclavo de los caprichos de una mujer. **To pin one's faith to upon,** confiar absolutamente en. **To pin one's opinion upon another's sleeve,** adherirse al parecer de alguien, identificarse con su opinión. **Pin back,** sujetar, fijar.

pin, *va.* Encerrar, enjaular. V. PEN.

pinafore ['pɪnəfɔːʳ] [pi-na-foʳ], *s.* Delantal (sin mangas) para niño.

pinaster ['pɪnəstəʳ] [pi-nas-taʳ], *s.* Pinastro.

pincase ['pɪnkeɪs] [pin-keis], *s.* Alfiletero, cajita para alfileres.

pincers ['pɪnsəz] [pin-sars], *s. pl.* 1. Pinzas, tenacillas. 2. *(Zool.)* Pinza. 3. *(Mil.)* Movimiento de pinzas.

pinch [pɪntʃ] [pinch], *va.* 1. Pellizcar, comprimir o apretar una cosa entre un dedo y el pulgar o entre los cantos de dos cuerpos duros (nip). 2. Apretar con pinzas o tenazas. 3. Apretar, oprimir, perseguir, estrechar a alguno persiguiéndole (press, squeeze). 4. Limitar mucho los gastos. 5. Examinar una cosa desentrañándola. -*vn.* 1. Apretar, acosar, hacerse sentir mucho alguna cosa. 2. Ahorrar, ser frugal, excusar gastos. **To pinch off,** arrebatar, aferrar, llevarse violentamente una cosa. **He who wears the shoe knows where it pinches,** cada uno sabe dónde le aprieta el zapato. **To pinch oneself,** privarse de lo necesario. **My shoe pinches,** me aprieta el zapato.

pinch, *s.* 1. Pellizco. 2. Polvo o pulgarada, la porción de cualquier cosa menuda que puede tomarse con las yemas de los dedos. 3. Dolor, tormento, pena, angustia; opresión, aprieto, apuro, extrema necesidad. **He is o he finds himself in a pinch,** se halla en un apuro. **A pinch of snuff,** un polvo de rapé. **Upon a pinch,** cuando fuere menester, llegado el caso. **To be a pinch,** estar en pena. 4. Esquina, pico. 5. Abolladura.

pinchbeck ['pɪntʃbek] [pinch-bek], *s.* Similor o similoro.

pincher ['pɪntʃəʳ] [pin-chaʳ], *s.* Pellizcador. -*pl.* Tenacillas.

pinchfist ['pɪntʃfɪst] [pinch-fist], *s.* Hombre tacaño, ruin o miserable.

pinch-hit ['pɪntʃhɪt] [pinch-jit], *vn.* 1. En el juego de beisbol, batear en lugar de otro. 2. Substituir a otro en una emergencia.

pinching-tongs ['pɪntʃɪŋtɒŋz] [pin-chin-tons], *s.* Tenazuelas que forman un molde en la fabricación del vidrio.

pincushion ['pɪŋkʊʃən] [pin-ku-shon], *s.* Acerico, almohadilla pequeña en que se clavan los alfileres.

pine [paɪn] [pain], *s.* 1. *(Bot.)* Pino, cualquier árbol del género Pinus de la familia de las coníferas. 2. Madera de cualquier pino. 3. Piña, anana. *V.* PINEAPPLE. 4. *(Des.)* Miseria. padecimiento. **Cluster pine,** *V.* PINASTER. **Scoth pine,** pino de Escocia, pino silvestre. **Pine-barren,** terreno estéril y arenoso cubierto de pinos. **Pine-marten,** marta cibelina. **Pine-needle,** hoja acicular de pino. **Pine-tree,** pino, árbol. **Pine-tree State,** el Estado norteamericano de Maine, llamado así por sus bosques de pinos.

pine, *vn.* 1. Desfallecer, estar lánguido, decaer perdiendo el vigor y las fuerzas (faint). Se emplea a menudo con la prep. **AWAY. She pined away after her husband's death,** ella decayó después de la muerte de su marido 2. Desear con vehemencia (seguido por la prep. **for). To pine for a new world,** anhelar, desear vivamente una nueva vida. -*va.* 1. Hacer debilitarse a alguno, causarle languidez, hacerle consumir a fuerza de sentimientos. 2. Lamentar en silencio, sentir interiormente algún mal. **To pine oneself to death,** morirse de pena.

pineal ['paɪnɪəl] [pai-nial], *a.* Que tiene figura de piña. **Pineal gland,** glándula pineal en el cerebro.

pineapple ['paɪnæpl] [pain-a-pol], *s.* Piña, anana. **The kerned of a pine-apple,** el corazón de la anana.

pine-branch ['paɪnbræntʃ] [pain-branch], *s.* Rama de pino.

pinery ['paɪnərɪ] [pai-ne-ri], *s.* 1. Inverandero para criar ananas. 2. Pinar, bosque de pinos.

piney ['paɪnɪ] [pai-ni], *a. V.* PINY.

ping-pong ['pɪŋpɒŋ] [ping-pong], *s.* Ping-pong, juego parecido al tenis.

pinguid ['pɪŋgwɪd] [pin-güid], *a.* Pingüe, craso, gordo, pingüedinoso.

pinghead ['pɪŋhed] [ping-jed], *s.* 1. Cabeza de un alfiler. 2. Algo pequeñísimo 3. Persona de muy poca inteligencia.

pinghole ['pɪŋhəʊl] [ping-joul], *s.* 1. El agujero que hace el afiler. 2. Punto diminuto transparente en una prueba negativa fotográfica.

pining ['pɪnɪŋ] [pi-ning], *a.* Lánguido. **Pining away,** *s.* Languidez.

pinion ['pɪnɪən] [pi-nion], *s.* 1. Piñón, el huesecillo último de las alas del ave. 2. Ala, y a veces también una pluma de la misma ala y el alón. 3. Piñón de reloj. 4. Esposas, prisiones para atar las manos.

pinion, *va.* 1. Atar las alas. 2. Maniatar, atar y ligar las manos a uno.

pinioned ['pɪnɪənd] [pi-niond], *a.* Alado, que tiene alas; maniatado.

pink [pɪŋk] [pink], *s.* 1. *(Bot.)* Clavel, dianto, planta y su flor del género Dianthus. 2. Cualquier flor parecida al clavel. 3. Color de rosa, rojo muy claro. **To be in the pink,** estar en plena forma (in top form). 4. Tipo de excelencia o de perfección, dechado, modelo. **The pink of politeness,** dechado, de cortesía. 5. Pez pequeño de color rojizo. -*a.* Rojizo claro, de color de clavel. **Pink eyes,** ojos pequeños.

pink, *va.* 1. Ojetear, hacer ojetes en la ropa. 2. Picar, adornar una tela con calados.

pinker ['pɪŋkəʳ] [pin-kaʳ], *s.* El que pica las telas de seda.

pinkeye ['pɪŋkaɪ] [pink-ai], *s.* 1. Catarro epidémico, contagioso y febril de los caballos, acompañado de oftalmia. 2. *(Med.)* Oftalmia contagiosa de las personas, caracterizada por el enrojecimiento de los ojos.

pink-eyed ['pɪŋkaɪd] [pink-aid], *a.* Ojialegre.

pinking ['pɪŋkɪŋ] [pin-kin], *s.* Picado, recortado; guiñadura. **Pinking-iron,** instrumento de hierro para picar las telas en forma de festones. **Pinking shears,** tijeras dentadas.

pink slip ['pɪŋkslɪp] [pink-slip], *s.* Notificación de despido.

pinky ['pɪŋkɪ] [pin-ki], *a.* Rosado, de color rojizo claro.

pinna ['pɪnə] [pi-na], *s.* 1. *(Bot.)* Una hoja pinada. 2. Oreja, pabellón externo del oído. 3. *(Zool.)* Ala, aleta, u órgano semejante.

pinnace ['pɪnɪs] [pi-nis], *s.* *(Mar.)* Pinaza, embarcación pequeña de remo y vela.

pinnacle ['pɪnəkl] [pi-na-kol], *s.* Pináculo, chapitel, la parte superior y más alta de algún edificio: cima, cumbre. **The pinacle of fame,** el pináculo de la fama.

pinnacle, *va.* Edificar con pináculos o chapiteles.

pinnate ['pɪneɪt] [pi-neit], **pinnated** ['pɪneɪtɪd] [pi-nei-tid], *a.* 1. *(Bot.)* Pinado, que tiene la figura de una pluma hablando de las hojas compuestas de las plantas. 2. Que tiene partes o apéndices parecidos a alas.

pinner ['pɪnər] [pi-na'], *s.* 1. El que asegura con alfileres, pernos, clavijas, etc. 2. V. PINAFORE. 3. Una especie de toca de mujer.

pinnule ['pɪnjuːl] [pi-niul], *s.* 1. *(Zool.)* Aleta pequeña. 2. *(Bot.)* Pínula, hojuela de una hoja pinada.

pinochle ['pɪnəkl] [pi-no-kel], *s.* Pinocle, juego de naipes.

pinpoint ['pɪnpɔɪnt] [pin-point], *s.* Punta de alfiler. *-va.* Precisar, determinar con gran precisión.

pint [paɪnt] [paint], *s.* Pinta, medida de áridos y líquidos.

pintail ['pɪnteɪl] [pin-teil], *s.* 1. Especie de ánade de cola larga. 2. Gallo silvestre.

pinwheel ['pɪnwiːl] [pin-uil], *s.* 1. Fuego artificial construido de manera que cuando se enciende gira rápidamente alrededor de un eje, formando una rueda de fuego. 2. Rueda de espigas. 3. Molino de viento, hecho de papel; juguete de los niños.

piny ['pɪnɪ] [pi-ni], *a.* Pinoso, referente o relativo a los pinos y abetos; cubierto o coronado de pinos. **Piny tallow,** sebo vegetal.

pioneer [ˌpaɪənɪər] [paio-nia'], *s.* 1. Explorador de un país; el que va delante apartando obstáculos y preparando el camino. 2. *(Mil.)* Gastador, zapador. *-va. y vn.* Explorar, ir delante preparando el camino; abrir un camino; guiar; ser explorador.

piony ['paɪənɪ] [paio-ni], *s.* *(Dial.)* Ponía.

pious ['paɪəs] [paios], *a.* 1. Pío, piadoso, devoto, religioso (religious, devout). 2. Que demuestra un espíritu reverente. 3. Practicado bajo pretexto de religión. 4. *(Ant.)* Que profesa a sus padres respeto y cariño. **A pious deed,** una obra piadosa. **A pious fraud,** un mojigato malvado.

piously ['paɪəslɪ] [paios-li], *adv.* Religiosamente, piadosamente.

pip [pɪp] [pip], *s.* 1. Pepita, enfermedad que padecen las aves en la lengua. 2. La semilla de una manzana, naranja, etc. 3. Punto de un naipe, dado o dominó. 4. Pitido. **Wait for the pips,** espere a oír la señal.

pip, *va.* Romper el cascarón, se dice de los polluelos. *-vn.* Piar ciertas aves. V. PEEP.

pipe ['paɪp] [paip], *s.* 1. Tubo, cañón, conducto, caño (tube). 2. Pipa para fumar. 3. Caramillo, churumbela, instrumento músico; pito o silbo del contramaestre. **Pipes of an organ,** cañones de órgano. **Bagpipe,** gaita. **Clyster-pipe,** cañoncito de jeringa. **Windpipe,** gaznate, tráquea. 4. Silbo, silbido, nota o llamada aguda y penetrante. 5. Pipa, medida de líquidos. **Pipe-staves,** duelas, las costillas de las pipas y cubas. **Elbow-pipe,** tubo acodillado. **Gas-pipe,** tubo, cañería de gas. **Water-pipe,** cañería, conducto de agua. **Stopped pipe,** cañón de órgano que tiene su extremo superior cubierto; tubo tapado. **Suction pipe,** tubo de aspiración, tubo aspirante de succión. **The bowl of a pipe,** el hogar o fogón de una pipa. **To smoke the pipe of peace,** fumar la pipa de la paz.

pipe, *va.* 1. Tocar la flauta u otro instrumento semejante. 2. Articular, proferir en tono alto. 3. Llamar por medio del pito de contramaestre. 4. Proveer de caños o tubos; conducir por cañería. **To pipe water from a spring,** conducir aguar por cañería desde un manantial. 5. Entre las costureras, hacer en

cordoncillo. *-vn.* 1. Tocar el caramillo o la gaita. 2. Silbar, producir un sonido penetrante.

pipe-clay ['paɪpkleɪ] [paip-klei], *s.* Tierra de pipa, especie de arcilla. *-va.* Blanquear con tierra de pipa.

pipeline ['paɪplaɪn] [paip-lain], *s.* Cañería, conducto.

pipe organ ['paɪpɔːgən] [paip-or-gan], *s.* *(Mús.)* Órgano.

piper ['paɪpər] [pai-pa'], *s.* Flautista, gaitero. **To pay the piper,** sufrir las consecuencias de una mala acción; pagar los platos rotos.

piperine ['paɪpərɪn] [pai-pa-rin], *a.* Pimentoso. *s.* Piperina, substancia incolora y cristalina que se halla en la pimienta.

pipe-tree ['paɪptriː] [paip-tri], *s.* *(Bot.)* Lila.

pipette ['paɪpet] [pai-pet], *va.* Gotear, sacar o desviar un líquido por medio de un gotero. *-s.* Gotero, pipeta, tubo pequeño, a menudo graduado, que se emplea para trasladar pequeñas cantidades de líquido de una vasija a otra.

piping ['paɪpɪŋ] [pi-pin], *a.* 1. Tocando el caramillo. 2. Hirviente, herviente, muy caliente; silbador, que silba. 3. Propio de la música no marcial, o caracterizado por ella.

pipit ['pɪpɪt] [pi-pit], *s.* Pajarito parecido a la alondra.

pipkin ['pɪpkɪn] [pip-kin], *s.* Pucherito.

pippin ['pɪpɪn] [pi-pin], *s.* *(Bot.)* Esperiega, una variedad de manzana.

piquancy ['piːkənsɪ] [pi-kan-si], *s.* Picante, acrimonia.

piquant ['piːkənt] [pi-kant], *a.* Punzante, picante (spicy); áspero, mordaz (sharp).

piquantly ['piːkəntlɪ] [pi-kant-li], *adv.* Agriamente; mordazmente.

pique [piːk] [pik], *s.* 1. Pique, desazón, desabrimiento, desavenencia, ligera. **I have no pique against him,** no le tengo ojeriza. 2. Pundonor, delicadez, puntillo.

pique, *va. y vn.* 1. Picar, enojar, provocar (anger)). 2. Ofender, irritar (irritate). 3. Picarse, preciarse de alguna cosa haciendo de ella punto de honor; jactarse. 4. Picarse, ofenderse, enojarse.

piquet [pɪˈket] [pi-ket], *s.* 1. Juego de los cientos. **To play at piquet,** jugar a los cientos. 2. *(Mil.)* Piquete, guardia avanzada.

piracy ['paɪərəsɪ] [paia-ra-si], *s.* Piratería.

piranha [pɪˈrɑːnjə] [pi-ra-ña], *s.* Piraña.

pirate ['paɪərɪt] [pai-rit], *s.* 1. Pirata. 2. Pirata, el que roba la propiedad de otro, y particularmente el impresor que sin derecho imprime obras ajenas.

pirate, *vn.* Piratear. *-va.* 1. Apropiarse sin derecho una propiedad literaria. 2. Pillar, hurtar, robar (steel).

piratical [paɪˈrætɪkəl] [pai-ra-ti-kal], *a.* Pirático.

pirogue ['pɪrɒg] [pi-rog], *s.* 1. Piragua, canoa de una pieza. 2. Barco grande sin quilla, que tiene el fondo plano para navegar por ríos poco profundos.

pirouette [ˌpɪruˈet] [pi-ruet], *s.* 1. Pirueta, vuelta que da el caballo sin mudar terreno. 2. Pirueta en el baile.

piscatory ['pɪskətərɪ] [pis-ka-to-ri], *a.* Piscatorio, que pertenece a la pesca o pesquería.

pisces ['paɪsiːz] [pai-sis], *s. pl.* 1. Los peces, una clase de los vertebrados. 2. *(Astr.)* Piscis, duodécimo signo del zodíaco.

pisciculture [ˌpɪsɪˈkʌltʃər] [pi-si-kal-cha'], *s.* Piscicultura, arte de repoblar de pesca los ríos y estanques.

piscivorous ['pɪsɪvərəs] [pi-si-vo-ros], *a.* Ictiófago, que se mantiene de pescado.

pish [pɪʃ] [pish], *inter.* ¡Bah! ¡Quita allá! Exclamación de desprecio.

pismire ['pɪsmaɪər] [pis-maia'], *s.* Hormiga (ant).

piss [pɪs] [pis], *vn.* *(Vulg.)* Orinar. **Piss off!,** ¡vete a la mierda! **That pisses me off,** ésto me cabrea, me molesta. *-s.* Orina.

pissed [pɪst] [pist], *a.* *(Fam.)* Cabreado.

pistachio [pɪsˈtɑːnɪəʊ] [pis-ta-shiou], *s.* *(Bot.)* Alfóncigo o pistacho, fruta de un árbol del mismo nombre.

piste [piːst] [pist], *s.* Pista.

pistil ['pɪstɪl] [pis-til], *s.* *(Bot.)* Pistilo, el órgano femenino de las flores.

pistillary ['pɪstɪlərɪ] [pis-ti-la-ri], *a.* Perteneciente al pistilo.

pistillate ['pɪstɪleɪt] [pis-ti-leit], *a.* Pistilado, que tiene pistilo; particularmente, que tiene pistilos, y no estambres.

pistol ['pɪstl] [pis-tol], *s.* Pistola, arma de fuego pequeña y corta. **Pocket-pistol,** pistolete, cachorro. **Pistol-shot,** pistoletazo, tiro de pistola. **Case o brace of pistols,** par de pistolas. **Two or three-barrelled pistol,** pistola de dos o tres cañones o tiros.

pistol, *va.* Tirar con pistola; matar a uno de un pistoletazo.

pistole ['pɪstəʊl] [pis-toul], *s.* Doblón.

pistolet ['pɪstəlɪt] [pis-to-lit], *s.* Pistolete, cachorro o cachorrillo.

piston ['pɪstən] [pis-ton], *s.* *(Mec.)* Émbolo, macho. **Piston ring,** aro o anillo de émbolo o de pistón. **Piston rod,** vástago sujetador del émbolo.

pit [pɪt] [pit], *s.* 1. Hoyo, el hueco o concavidad que queda después de sacada la tierra. 2. Abismo, profundidad sin término. 3. Hoyo, sepultura. 4. Area de un teatro ocupada por las lunetas o butacas. **The arm-pit,** el sobaco. **The pit of the stomach,** la boca del estómago. **Coal-pit,** mina de carbón de piedra. **Sand-pit,** mina de arena que se saca para hacer argamasa. **Gravel-pit,** cascajal o cascajar. **Turf-pit,** hornaguero. **To be at the pit's brink,** estar al borde del precipicio, estar con un pie en la sepultura. **Pit-coal,** hulla, carbón mineral. **Pit-head,** pozo de mina. **Pit-saw,** sierra larga para aserrar maderos sobre un hoyo o foso; sierra que se maneja entre dos.

pit, *va.* 1. Poner alguna cosa en un agujero. 2. Comprimir una cosa haciendo que forme hoyos. 3. Formar agujeritos en alguna cosa. 4. Incitar a uno a reñir. **Pit against,** enfrentar a.

pitapat ['pɪtəpæt] [pi-ta-pat], *s.* Palpitación de corazón (heartbeat); paso ligero y apresurado. *-adv.* Con una rápida sucesión de golpecitos; *(Fam.)* pit, pat; tictac.

pitch [pɪtʃ] [pich], *s.* 1. Punto, grado de elevación (height); punto extremo. 2. Grado de inclinación de una pendiente; declive, bajada (pent); inclinación con respecto al horizonte. 3. Declive, de un tejado. 4. *(Mec.)* Trecho que adelanta una rosca a cada vuelta; también, paso de un diente de encaje. 5. *(Mús.)* Grado más o menos alto de un tono, diapasón; el diapasón con referencia a un tipo. 6. En los juegos, lanzamiento, el acto de lanzar, o la distancia a que llega el objeto lanzado. **Pitch-pipe,** diapasón de voz, instrumento que sirve para entonar la voz o un instrumento músico. **He came to that pitch,** llegó a ese extremo. **The highest pitch of glory,** la cumbre, el pináculo, el más alto punto de gloria.

pitch, *s.* 1. Pez, la resina del pino espesada por medio del fuego; brea, alquitrán. **Pitch-brush,** escopero. **Pitch-kettle,** caldero de brea. **Pitch-pine,** pino de tea. 2. Jugo resinoso que exudan los pinos.

pitch, *va.* 1. Tirar, arrojar, lanzar al aire (moviendo el brazo como un péndulo); en el juego de **base-ball** Empujar, meter algo, arrojar la pelota al jugador que tiene la maza o **bat.** 2. Empujar, meter algo en la tierra, v. g. estacas de aquí, colocar, ordenar. **A pitched battle,** batalla campal. 3. Fijar, plantar. **To pitch a tent,** plantar una tienda de campaña. 4. Embrear. dar con brea, empegar. 5. *(Mús.)* Graduar el tono, dar el diapasón. *-vn.* 1. Arrojar por bajo mano; arrojar de una manera cualquiera. 2. Caerse alguna cosa hacia abajo. 3. Caer de cabeza. 4. Escoger. 5. Instalarse, fijarse, establecerse. 6. Arfar, cabecear el buque de popa a proa. **To pitch into,** *(Fam.)* acometer, embestir. **To pitch in,** *(Fam.)* empezar algo con decisión y energía.

pitcher ['pɪtʃər] [pi-char], *s.* 1. Cántaro, bocal, vasija de barro para llevar o traer agua (jug). 2. Piqueta, herramienta para abrir la tierra: una forma de pie de cabra. 3. Arrojador, el que arroja o lanza; en el juego de **base-ball,** el que tira la pelota al que tiene el bate. 4. *(Bot.)* Forma de hoja muy particular parecida a un cántaro.

pitchfork ['pɪtʃfɔːk] [pich-fork], *s.* 1. Horca o percha que usan los labradores. 2. Diapasón, instrumento de dos brazos paralelos para graduar el tono de un instrumento músico o de la voz.

pitchiness ['pɪtʃɪnɪs] [pi-chi-nes], *s.* Obscuridad; negrura, color de pez.

pitching ['pɪtʃɪŋ] [pi-chin], *a.* Inclinado, en declive. *-s.* 1. Arfada, cabezada de un buque. 2. Lanzamiento, la acción de lanzar o arrojar. **Pitching-pence,** *(GB)* contribución que se paga por poner en venta las mercancías en las ferias.

pitchstone ['pɪtʃstəʊn] [pich-stoun], *s.* Un vidrio volcánico.

pitchy ['pɪtʃɪ] [pi-chi], *a.* 1. Embreado, dado con brea o pez; que tiene las propiedades de la pez. 2. Negro, obscuro, triste.

piteous ['pɪtɪəs] [pi-tios], *a.* 1. Lastimoso, que mueve a compasión o excita simpatía. 2. Compasivo, tierno.

piteously ['pɪtɪəslɪ] [pi-tios-li], *adv.* Lastimosamente.

piteousness ['pɪtɪəsnɪs] [pi-tios-nes], *s.* Compasión, ternura.

pitfall ['pɪtfɔːl] [pit-fol], *s.* Trampa, hoya ligeramente cubierta para ocultarla; añagaza, peligro latente.

pith [pɪθ] [piz], *s.* 1. Meollo de planta o árbol. 2. Tuétano. 3. Fuerza, robustez. 4. Médula, energía, vigor de pensamiento y estilo (energy, power). 5. Médula, la parte esencial de alguna cosa. **The pith of life,** lo mejor de la vida.

pith, *va.* 1. Matar, destruyendo la médula espinal. 2. Quitar el meollo a una planta.

pithead ['pɪthed] [pit-jed], *s.* Bocamina.

pithily ['pɪθɪlɪ] [pi-zi-li], *adv.* Enérgicamente, fuertemente.

pithiness ['pɪθɪnɪs] [pi-zi-nes], *s.* Energía, eficacia.

pithless ['pɪθlɪs] [piz-les], *a.* Falto de meollo; endeble, sin fuerza, sin energía, necio.

pithy ['pɪθɪ] [pi-zi], *a.* 1. Enérgico, eficaz; meduloso. 2. Que contiene la parte esencial de un asunto; expresivo, lacónico, efectivo. **A pithy saying,** un dicho enérgico y expresivo, de mucha miga.

pitiable ['pɪtɪəbl] [pi-tia-bol], *a.* 1. Lastimoso, sensible, patético, digno de compasión. 2. Despreciable, desestimado.

pitiful ['pɪtɪfʊl] [pi-ti-ful], *a.* 1. Lastimoso, sensible (sentient, tender). 2. Despreciable, detestable (despicable). **He's pitiful!,** ¡da pena!

pitifully ['pɪtɪfəlɪ] [pi-ti-fu-li], *adv.* Lastimosamente; despreciablemente.

pitifulness ['pɪtɪfəlnɪs] [pi-ti-ful-nes], *s.* 1. Ternura, compasión, piedad, misericordia (pity, compasion). 2. Ruindad (meanness).

pitiless ['pɪtɪlɪs] [pi-ti-les], *a.* Despiadado, cruel, inhumano, duro de corazón.

pitilessly ['pɪtɪlɪslɪ] [pi-ti-les-li], *adv.* Cruelmente, inhumanamente.

pitilessness ['pɪtɪlɪsnɪs] [pi-ti-les-nes], *s.* Inhumanidad, dureza de corazón.

pitman ['pɪtmən] [pit-man], *s.* *(pl.* PITMEN). 1. Aserrador de foso; y particularmente, pocero, el minero que tiene a su cargo la maquinaria subterránea. 2. *(pl.* PITMANS) *(Mec.)* Barra de conexión; vara que conecta una pieza giratoria con otra que tiene movimiento de vavién.

pittance ['pɪtəns] [pi-tans], *s.* 1. Pitanza o ración, originalmente la porción de comida que se repartía a cada uno. v. g. en los conventos; pequeño donativo que se hace por caridad. 2. Porcioncilla, porción pequeña de alguna cosa. 3. Miseria.

pitted ['pɪtɪd] [pi-tid], *a.* Cavado, picado. **Pitted with the small-pox,** picado de viruelas.

pitter-patter ['pɪtəpætər] [pi-ta-pa-tar], *s.* Golpeteo, repiqueteo. *-adv.* **The stones went pitter-patter on the window,** las piedras golpeteaban en la ventana.

pituitary [pɪ'tjuːɪtərɪ] [pi-tui-ta-ri], *a.* Pituitario. *-s.* **Pituitary gland,** glándula pituitaria.

pity ['pɪtɪ] [pi-ti], *s.* 1. Piedad, misericordia, lástima, compasión (mercy, compassion). **I feel no pity for him,** no le tengo lástima. 2. Lástima, el objeto que excita la compasión; en este sentido tiene plural. **It is a pity that his book is lost,** es lástima que se haya perdido su libro. **It is a thousand pities,** es muchísima lástima. **For pity's sake, from pity,** por piedad.

pity, *va.* Compadecer, tener lástima. -*vn.* Lastimarse, apiadarse, tener piedad, enternecerse. **He is greatly to be pitied,** es muy digno de lástima.

pivot ['pɪvət] [pi-vot], *s.* 1. Espigón, gorrón, quicio, pivote. 2. Eje, polo, alma. 3. *V.* **Pivot-man. Pivo-gun,** cañón giratorio, colisa. **Pivot-hole** o **collar,** rangua, buje o quicio de eje. **Pivot-man,** guía, el soldado que se halla en el flanco sobre el cual se opera una conversión.

pivot, *va.* Colocar sobre un eje; proveer de un gorrón o espigón. -*vn.* Girar sobre un eje o pivote.

pivotal ['pɪvətl] [pi-vo-tal], *a.* Capital, fundamental. De la naturaleza de un gorrón o eje; se aplica al punto sobre el cual gira un asunto, una conversación, etc.

pixy ['pɪksɪ] [pik-si], *s. (pl.* PIXIES). Especie de hada o duende.

pizza ['piːtsə] [pi-cha], *s.* Pizza, torta muy condimentada de la cocina italiana.

pizzeria [ˌpiːtsəˈrɪə] [pi-cha-ria], *s.* Pizzería.

placability [ˌplækəˈbɪlɪtɪ] [pla-ka-bi-li-ti], *s.* Placabilidad; dulzura, clemencia.

placable ['plækəbl] [pla-ka-bol], *a.* Placable, aplacable.

placard ['plækɑːd] [pla-kard], *s.* 1. Cartel, anuncio; la proclama que se fija en las esquinas para noticia del público. 2. Herrete o plancha que lleva el nombre del dueño.

placard, *va.* Publicar o hacer manifiesta alguna cosa; fijar en las esquinas algún cartel o noticia al público.

placate ['plækeɪt] [pla-keit], *va.* Aplacar, apaciguar, conciliar, sosegar.

placatory ['plækətərɪ] [pla-ka-to-ri], *a.* Conciliatorio, apaciguador.

place ['pleɪs] [pleis], *s.* 1. Lugar, sitio, paraje, espacio en que está colocado un objeto (position, spot). **In all places,** en todas partes. 2. *(Mil.)* Plaza, fortaleza, puesto militar. 3. Residencia, mansión. 4. Lugar, texto, pasaje de un escrito o de un libro. **I've lose my place,** he perdido la página, por donde iba. 5. Colocación, orden de prioridad, posición; punto, grado en orden de precedencia. 6. Empleo, dignidad, oficio público, plaza (employment). 7. Lugar, camino (path); lugar, asiento (sit); recepción, buena acogida (reception). **Could you save me a place?,** ¿podrías guardarme un sitio? 8. Plaza en una ciudad, espacio abierto cuadrado; también callejón sin salida, o una calle corta y estrecha. **A place of refuge,** asilo. **In the first place,** en primer lugar. **To give place,** dar la preeminencia, ceder el paso. **In the next place,** luego, después. **In place of,** en lugar de, en vez de. **In no place,** en ninguna parte. **A watering-place,** (a) aguadero, abrevadero; (b) estación balnearia, punto de baños. **To take place,** verificarse, tener efecto, sobrevenir, suceder, pasar, ocurrir un suceso.

place, *va.* 1. Colocar, poner alguna cosa en un paraje determinado (put). 2. Fijar, establecer, plantar (fix). 3. Prestar a interés, poner dinero a ganancia. **To place in order,** arreglar, poner en orden. 4. Señalar, asignar, destinar a un deber. **I have placed (out) my son,** he colocado a mi hijo.

placebo [pləˈsiːbəʊ] [pla-si-bou], *s. (Med.)* Placebo.

placeman ['pleɪsmən] [pleis-man], *s.* Empleado público, oficinista.

placement ['pleɪsmənt] [pleis-ment], *s.* Colocación, empleo. **Placement test,** prueba de aptitud.

place name ['pleɪsneɪm] [pleis-neim], *s.* Topónimo, nombre geográfico.

placenta [pləˈsentə] [pla-sen-ta], *s.* 1. *(Bot.)* Placenta, la parte del fruto a la que están prendidas las semillas. 2. *(Anat.)* Placenta.

placer ['pleɪsər] [plei-sar], *s.* Colocador, el que coloca.

placid ['plæsɪd] [pla-sid], *a.* Plácido, quieto, sosegado, benigno, apacible.

placidity [pləˈsɪdɪtɪ] [pla-si-di-ti], **placidness** ['plæsɪdnɪs] [pla-sid-nes], *s.* Apacibilidad, afabilidad, dulzura, suavidad.

placidly ['plæsɪdlɪ] [pla-sid-li], *adv.* Apaciblemente, suavemente, dulcemente.

placit ['plæsɪt] [pla-sit], *s.* Decreto, resolución, orden.

plagal ['pleɪgəl] [plei-gal], *a. (Mús.)* Plagal, se dice de un modo musical en que la quinta es aguda y la cuarta grave.

plagiarism ['pleɪdʒɪərɪzəm] [plei-yia-ri-sem], *s.* Plagio, usurpación de los pensamientos u obras literarias de otro.

plagiarist ['pleɪdʒɪərɪst] [plei-yia-rist], *s.* Plagiario, el que roba los pensamientos u obras literarias de otro.

plagiarize, plagiarise ['pleɪdʒɪəraɪz] [plei-yia-rais], *va.* En las obras literarias o artísticas, plagiar, apropiarse los pensamientos de otros y darlos por suyos. -*vn.* Cometer o hacer plagios.

plague [pleɪg] [pleig], *s.* 1. Peste, enfermedad contagiosa y muy destructiva. 2. Plaga, miseria, calamidad. 3. Peste, majadero, majadería, joroba, cualquier cosa muy enfadosa o molesta. **I avoid Peter like the plague,** huyo de Peter como de la peste.

plague, *va.* 1. Atormentar, afligir, molestar, inquietar, vejar, importunar. 2. Jorobar, infestar, apestar, plagar. **My company is plagued with problems,** mi empresa está plagada de problemas.

plaguily ['pleɪgɪlɪ] [pla-gui-li], *adv. (Fam.)* Molestamente.

plaguey ['pleɪgɪ] [plei-gui], *a. (Fam.)* Enfadoso, molesto; apestado.

plaice [pleɪs] [pleis], *s.* Platija.

plaid [plæd] [pld], *s.* 1. Capa suelta que usan los montañeses de Escocia. 2. Listados en cuadro, o a lo ancho y a lo largo. 1. Que tiene un dibujo cuadriculado, de rayas que se cruzan en ángulos rectos. 2. En cuadros de varios colores.

plain [pleɪn] [plein], *a.* 1. Llano, raso, igual, sin tropiezo ni embarazo alguno (flat, smooth). 2. Liso, que no tiene adorno; sencillo (simple). 3. Ingenuo, llano, abierto; liso, sincero (sincere). 4. Puro, simple, común; simple, sencillo, modesto, que no tiene lujo ni riquezas. 5. Llano, claro, evidente, distinto. **In plain Spanish,** en buen castellano. **Plain people,** (a) gente sencilla. (b) gente humilde, común, de origen obscuro. 6. Verdadero, puro; acabado, rematado. 7. Falto de belleza personal, ordinario, feo. **A very plain girl,** una joven o muchacha más bien fea que bonita, sin belleza alguna. **Plain food,** alimento simple, sencillo. **Plain-chant, plain-song,** canto llano, canto plano, o de iglesia. **Plain work,** costura sencilla, lisa, a diferencia de la que tiene algún adorno. **Plain truth,** la pura verdad o sin disfraz alguno. **Plain man,** (a) hombre sincero. *(Fam.)* Hombre a la pata la llana. (b) El hombre que no es bien parecido. **In plain terms,** en términos claros. **To be plain with one,** hablar claro a uno, decirle francamente lo que se siente. -*adv.* 1. Claramente, distintamente. 2. Llanamente, sinceramente, con lisura o tersura y verdad. -*s.* 1. Llano, llanura, el campo o terreno igual, llanada. **The Great Plains,** las Grandes Llanuras. 2. *(Des.)* Campo de batalla. **Plain-dealer,** hombre de buena fe, hombre de bien, hombre sincero. **Plain-dealing,** buena fe, sinceridad en el trato, honradez. **Plain-hearted,** sencillo, sincero, bueno, sin doblez. **Plain-heartedness,** sinceridad. **Plain-spoken,** sencillo, claro y sincero en sus palabras.

plain, *va.* Allanar, hacer llana alguna cosa.

plain-clothes ['pleɪnˈkləʊðz] [plein-klouzs], *s.* De paisano, no uniformado (police).

plaining ['pleɪnɪŋ] [plei-nin], *s. (Poét.)* Queja, lamento.

plainly ['pleɪnlɪ] [plein-li], *adv.* 1. Llanamente. 2. Llanamente, con ingenuidad. 3. De veras. **I tell you plainly I cannot,** le digo a Ud. de veras que no puedo. 4. Claramente, sencillamente, francamente.

plainness ['pleɪnnɪs] [plein-nes], *s.* 1. Llanura, igualdad (equality). 2. Sencillez (simplicity). 3. Sinceridad, franqueza (bluntness). 4. Claridad.

plainsman ['pleɪnzmən] [pleins-man], *s.* Llanero.

plainspoken ['pleɪnˈpəʊkən] [plein-spou-ken], *a.* Franco, sincero (blunt).

plaint [pleɪnt] [pleint], *s.* Quejido, queja, lamento.

plaintful ['pleɪntfʊl] [pleint-ful], *a.* Quejoso; lloroso, doliente, dolorido.

plaintiff ['pleɪntɪf] [plein-tif], *s.* Demandante, el actor litigante que demanda en juicio.

plaintive ['pleɪntɪv] [plein-tiv], *a.* Lamentoso, lastimoso, dolorido.

plaintively ['pleɪntɪvlɪ] [plein-tiv-li], *adv.* De un modo lastimoso.

plait [plæt] [plat], *s.* 1. Pliegue, el doblez que se hace en la ropa. 2. Trenza, cordoncillo. *V.* BRAID. **Plait of hair,** trenza de cabellos. **Plait,** *va.* 1. Plegar, hacer dobleces o pliegues. 2. Alechugar, rizar, encarrujar. 3. Tejer, trenzar.

plaiter ['pleɪtəʳ] [plei-taʳ], *s.* Plegador.

plaiting ['pleɪtɪŋ] [plei-tin], *s.* Plegadura, pliegue.

plan [plæn] [plan], *s.* 1. Plan, designio, proyecto formulado para alcanzar algún resultado (intention, project). 2. Plan o modelo de alguna cosa (model); plano. 3. Icnografía, delineación de la planta de un edificio o buque; plano, proyección. 4. Diseño, esbozo, bosquejo, de una obra literaria o artística. 5. Método, hábito, modo usual, costumbre. **According to the plan,** de acuerdo con lo planeado.

plan, *va.* 1. Trazar, delinear algún plan; proyectar. 2. Urdir, tramar, fraguar. **I'm planning a surprise for his birthday,** estoy planeando una sorpresa para su cumpleaños. **Plan on,** pensar, tener intención.

planch ['plæntʃ] [planch], *va. (Des.)* Entarimar, entablar.

plancher ['plɑ:ntʃəʳ] [plan-chaʳ], *s.* 1. Entarimado, suelo o techo entarimado de una habitación. 2. Tabla de madera.

planchet ['plæntʃɪt] [plan-chit], *s.* Tejuelo, pieza de metal preparada para estampar el cuño sobre ella.

planchette [plɑ:n'ʃet] [plan-shet], *s.* 1. Grafómetro. *V.* CIRCUMFERENTOR. 2. Plancheta, tablita provista de un lápiz y dos ruedas.

plane [pleɪn] [plein], *a.* Llano (flat); *(Bot.)* que tiene una superficie llana. *-s.* 1. Plano, superficie plana. 2. Cepillo, instrumento de carpintería (brush). 3. *V.* PLANE-TREE. **Plane-table,** (a) plancheta, instrumento topográfico de los agrimensores. (b) Tablilla inclinada para disponer los minerales. **Bench-plane,** garlopa, cepillo de banco. **Jack-plane,** garlopa de alisar. **Robbet-plane,** cepillo de ranurar. **Dovetail-plane,** guillame de ensamblar.

plane, *va.* 1. Allanar. 2. Acepillar, alisar.

plane, *s.* Aeroplano, avión. Plano. Nivel. **This book is on a different plane,** este libro está a otro nivel, es de otra categoría (level).

planer ['pleɪnəʳ] [pla-naʳ], *s.* 1. Acepillador. 2. Cepillo mecánico, acepilladora, máquina de acepillar para madera o para metal.

planet ['plænɪt] [pla-nit], *s. (Astr.)* Planeta, astro opaco que gira con movimiento propio y periódico alrededor del sol.

planetarium [ˌplænɪt'teəriən] [pla-ni-tia-riom], *s.* Planetario, máquina que representa los movimientos de los planetas.

planetary ['plænɪtərɪ] [pla-ni-ta-ri], *a.* Planetario, que pertenece a los planetas.

planetoid ['plænɪtɔɪd] [pla-ni-toid], *s.* Planeta menor.

planet-struck ['plænɪtˌstrʌk] [pla-nit-strak], *a.* Asombrado, atolondrado, atónito, confundido.

planing ['pleɪnɪŋ] [pla-nin], *s.* Acepilladura, acción de acepillar. **Planing-machine,** máquina de acepillar (for wood or metal), cepillo mecánico; acepilladora.

planish ['plænɪʃ] [pla-nish], *va.* Alisar, allanar, pulir, aplanar.

planisher ['plænɪʃəʳ] [pla-ni-shaʳ], *s.* Planador.

plank ['plæŋk] [plank], *s.* Tablón, tabla gruesa. **Plank of ship,** *(Mar.)* tablaje, tablazón.

plank, *va.* Entablar, entarimar, cubrir con tablas alguna cosa. **To plank the deck,** *(Mar.)* entablar la cubierta.

plankton ['plæŋktən] [plank-ton], *s.* Plancton.

planned [plænd] [pland], *a.* Planeado. **Planned parenthood,** planificación familiar.

planner ['plænəʳ] [pla-naʳ], *s.* Trazador, persona que forma un plan, un proyecto.

planning ['plænɪŋ] [pla-nin], *s.* Planificación.

plant ['plænt] [plant], *s.* 1. Planta, nombre genérico de todo vegetal. 2. Planta, se llama así particularmente toda mata o hierba. 3. Planta, el asiento del pie. 4. Planta, plantel, instalación completa de maquinaria, herramientas, edificios, etc., necesarios para alguna empresa mecánica. **Plant-food,** lo que sirve para fomentar el crecimiento de las plantas. **Plant-louse,** pulgón, cualquier insecto áfido. **A perennial plant,** una planta perenne, la que vive más de dos años. **Plant pot,** maceta.

plant, *va.* 1. Plantar, meter en la tierra el vástago de un árbol o de otra planta para que vegete y crezca. 2. Colocar, poner, sentar una cosa fijamente. 3. Plantar, clavar en la tierra una cosa. 4. Plantar, fundar, establecer, engendrar. 5. Adornar un lugar poniendo plantas en él. **To plant a cannon,** sentar, colocar un cañón. **Plant out,** trasplantar.

plantain ['plæntɪn] [plan-tein], *s. (Bot.)* 1. Plátano, planta cuya fruta se come, hierba tropical perenne. 2. Llantén, planta; tipo de la familia de las plantagíneas.

plantar ['plæntəʳ] [plan-taʳ], *a.* Plantar, perteneciente a la planta del pie.

plantation [plæn'teɪʃən] [plan-tei-shon], *s.* 1. Plantación, planta, el acto de plantar. 2. Plantío, el lugar o sitio plantado. 3. Colonia, un establecimiento de nuevos pobladores. 4. Ostral, ostrera, criadero de ostras. 5. Finca de cultivo mayor. **Sugar plantation,** *(Amer.)* ingenio, trapiche, hacienda de azúcar. **Coffee plantation,** cafetal. **Plantation hoes,** azadones.

planter ['plæntəʳ] [plan-taʳ], *s.* 1. Plantador, cultivador. 2. Colono, el que cultiva la tierra en las colonias americanas.

plantigrade ['plæntɪgrəd] [plan-ti-greid], *a.* Plantígrado, que anda apoyado en la planta de los pies, como el hombre, los osos, etc. *-s.* Animal plantígrado.

planting ['plæntɪŋ] [plan-tin], *s.* Plantación, plantel.

plaque [plæk] [plak], *s.* 1. Plancha, chapa, o disco de metal, de porcelana u otro material embellecido artísticamente, v. g. para adornar las paredes. 2. Broche, o cosa semejante. 3. *(Zool.)* Disco o estructura parecido a un plato. 4. *(Dent.)* Placa, sarro.

plash [plæʃ] [plash], *s.* 1. Charquillo, charco pequeño, aguazar, lagunajo, 2. La rama cortada y entrejida con otras.

plash, *va.* 1. Enramar, entretejer ramas. 2. Hacer ruido moviendo o turbando el agua.

plashing ['plæʃɪŋ] [pla-shin], *s.* La entretejedura de ramas para hacer una empalizada o cerca.

plashy ['plæʃɪ] [pla-shi], *a.* Pantanoso.

plasm ['plæzəm] [pla-sem], *s.* 1. Molde, matriz. 2. La forma de **plasma** en las voces compuestas, como **bioplasm.**

plasma ['plæsmə] [plas-ma], *s.* 1. Plasma, la parte líquida de la sangre. 2. *(Min.)* Plasma (plasma), variedad verdusca de calcedonia.

plasmic ['plæzmɪk] [plas-mik], *a.* Plasmal, que se refiere al plasma; protoplásmico, formativo.

plaster ['plɑ:stəʳ] [plas-taʳ], *s.* 1. Yeso, sulfato de cal, para cubrir o lavar las paredes. **Plaster of Paris,** yeso, sulfato calcinado de cal. 2. Argamasa, mezcla de arena y cal para obras de albañilería; estuco. 3. Emplasto, medicamento. **Blister-plaster,** vejigatorio, cantárida. **Mustard plaster,** sinapismo. **Healing plaster** o **salve,** disecativo, ungüento.

plaster, *va.* 1. Enyesar, enlucir revocar o cubrir con yeso; sacar a plana. 2. Emplastar, poner emplastos sobre una parte enferma. **I have my left leg in plaster,** tengo mi pierna izquierda escayolada.

plasterer ['plɑ:stərəʳ] [plas-ta-raʳ], *s.* 1. Enjalbegador, revocador. 2. Plasmante, el que hace figuras de yeso o barro.

plastic ['plæstɪk] [plas-tik], *a.* 1. Plástico, perteneciente a la plástica. 2. Que da forma a una cosa, formativo. 3. Plástico, que puede ser modelado en una forma cualquiera. 4. *(Cir.)* Eficaz para renovar las partes perdidas, o para modificar las mal formadas.

plasticity [plæs'tɪsɪtɪ] [plas-ti-si-ti], *s.* Plasticidad, calidad de plástico; capacidad de ser modelado; facultad o propiedad formativa.

plastic surgery ['plæstɪkˌsɜ:dʒərɪ] [plas-tik-ser-ye-ri], *s.* Cirugía plástica, autoplastia, anaplastia.

plastron ['plæstrən] [plas-tron], *s.* 1. Peto, pecher, porción de una prenda de vestir, de un escudo, etc., que cubre el pecho. 2. (*Zool.*) Concha inferior de las tortugas; parte semejante de los anfibios.

plat ['plæt] [plat], *s.* 1. (*Mar.*) Baderna. 2. Pedazo de tierra señalado a un uso particular. V. PLOT. 3. Mapa o plano de un terreno medido o partido. 4. Especie de cintilla de paja o junco para hacer sombreros de mujer.

plat, *va.* 1. Entretejer, trenzar. 2. Trazar, delinear un plano o un mapa; disponer un terreno para usos particulares.

platband ['plætbænd] [plat-band], *s.* 1. (*Agr.*) Acirate, espacio que se dispone algo elevado en los jardines para plantar flores. 2. Tablas, el espacio entre dos hileras de árboles. 3. (*Arq.*) Faja de la cornisa.

plate [pleɪt] [pleit], *s.* 1. Plancha o lámina de metal o vidrio (sheet). 2. Plata labrada (silver). **Gold and silver plate,** vajilla. 3. Plato, vasija baja y redonda con una concavidad en medio. 4. Plato, porción de comida servida a la mesa (dish). 5. Palio, el premio que se señalaba en las corridas de caballos al que llegaba primero. 6. Plancha (print); estereotipo, clisé; electrotipo. 7. Placa o plancha, lámina de vidrio o de celuloide, sobre la cual se ha tomado una prueba negativa o se ha hecho alguna otra imagen o cuadro. 8. Vidrio cilindrado. 9. Pedazo de gutapercha, etc., en la cual se insertan uno o varios dientes artificiales. 10. (*Dent.*) Dentadura postiza (denture). 11. *V.* **Plate armor. Plate-brass,** latón en planchas. **Copper-plate engraver,** grabador en dulce o de láminas. **Unsilvered plates,** láminas de cristal sin azogue o desazogadas. **Dry plates,** placas secas de fotografía. **Wet plates,** placas húmedas de fotografía. **Plate armor,** blindaje, planchas de armadura. **Plate-culture,** cultivación de las bacterias en gelatina o en otros medios nutritivos extendidos en capas muy tenues, v. g. sobre láminas de vidrio. **Plate-holder,** portaplaca fotográfico; bastidor ligero impenetrable a la luz que lleva una o más comúnmente dos placas fotográficas. Se llama también **dark slide. Plate-glass,** vidrio cilindrado. **Plate-mark,** (a) prueba, marca (de las monedas de plata u oro); (b) marca de contraste (en el borde de una estampa). **Plate-paper,** papel de primera calidad para estampas. **Plate-matter,** material para periódicos fundido en clisés estereotípicos, para venderlo a varios periódicos que lo usan simultáneamente. **Plate-powder,** polvos para pulir la vajilla. **Plate-rack,** (a) vasar en el que se ponen los platos para que goteen; (b) bastidor para sostener las placas fotográficas mientras se secan. **Plate-warmer,** estufa para calentar los platos. **Plates,** (*Mar.*) chapas. **Back-stay-plates,** (*Mar.*) cadenas de los brandales.

plate, *va.* 1. Planchear, cubrir alguna cosa con planchas de metal; platear, dorar, niquelar por medio de la galvanoplastia. 2. Batir hoja, labrar el oro u otro metal reduciéndolo a hojas o planchas.

plateau ['plætəʊ] [pla-tou], *s.* (*pl.* PLATEAUX o PLATEAUS). 1. Altillanura, altiplanicie, mesa que se extiende sobre una altura. 2. Fuente ancha para el centro de la mesa.

plateful ['pleɪtfʊl] [pleit-ful], *s.* La cantidad contenida en un plato.

platen ['plætən] [pla-ten], *s.* 1. (*Impr.*) Platina, cuadro, en ciertas máquinas de imprimir y de escribir. 2. En maquinaria, platina, mesa que sostiene el material que se trabaja.

platform ['plætfɔːm] [plat-form] *-s.* 1. Plataforma, especie de tablado o andamio; terraplén. **Platform shoe,** zapato de plataforma. 2. Tribuna, lugar elevado desde donde se dirige la palabra a una asamblea. 3. Andén de ferrocarrril. 4. Plataforma al extremo de un carro urbano, ómnibus, etc. 5. Programa, declaración formal de principios, hecha por un cuerpo político, religioso u otro.

platina ['plætɪnə] [pla-ti-na], *s.* 1. Platino, metal blanquizco. *V.* PLATINUM. 2. Alambre torcido de plata.

platinum ['plætɪnəm] [pla-ti-nom], *s.* Platino, el más pesado de todos los metales.

platitude ['plætɪtjuːd] [pla-ti-tiud], *s.* 1. Perogrullada, verdad de Perogrullo; verdad trivial; lugar común, tópico. 2. Calidad de trivial, vulgar.

platonic [pləˈtɒnɪk] [pla-to-nik], *a.* Platónico, que pertenece o se refiere a Platón.

platonism ['pleɪtənɪzəm] [plei-to-ni-sem], *s.* Platonismo, sistema filosófico de Platón, y su doctrina.

platoon [pləˈtuːn] [pla-tun], *s.* (*Mil.*) Pelotón, un pequeño cuerpo de soldados.

platter ['plætəʳ] [pla-taʳ], *s.* Fuente, plato grande, por lo común de loza; antiguamente se hacía de peltre.

platting ['plætɪŋ] [pla-tin], *s.* Especie de cintillo de paja, junco o astilla para hacer sombreros de mujer.

plaudit ['plɔːdɪt] [plo-dit], *s.* Aplauso, aclamación.

plausibility [plɔːzəˈbɪlɪtɪ] [plo-si-bi-li-ti], **plausibleness** ['plɔːzəblnɪs] [plo-si-bol-nes], *s.* Plausibilidad.

plausible ['plɔːzɪbl] [plo-si-bol], *a.* Plausible, especioso, aparente.

plausibly ['plɔːzɪblɪ] [plo-si-bli], *adv.* Plausiblemente, con plausibilidad, de forma verosímil.

play [pleɪ] [plei], *vn.* 1. Jugar, entretenerse, divertirse, recrearse (enjoy). 2. Jugar, juguetear, travesear, enredar, retozar. 3. Jugar, burlarse unos con otros o unos de otros. 4. Jugar, competir con otro en algún juego (compete). **To play at cards,** jugar a los naipes. 5. Tocar, tañer, hablando de instrumentos músicos o de alguna orquesta (music instrument). 6. Jugar, ponerse alguna cosa compuesta de varias piezas en movimiento y ejercicio; estar corriente o franco, hablando de los muelles, llaves o piezas que juegan en las máquinas. 7. Flotar, ondular, ondear. 8. Representar en público. *-va.* 1. Disparar, tirar. 2. Hacer andar una máquina o ponerla en movimiento. 3. Remedar, hacer el papel de. 4. Representar una comedia, un papel. 5. Tocar un instrumento músico, una pieza, etc. 6. Jugar una partida de cualquier juego. 7. Burlar o chasquear a alguno.

play along, hacer el juego, cooperar.

play away one's money, jugar o perder al juego el dinero que se posee. **To play back,** poner una grabación.

play down, minimizar, restarle importancia.

play off, hacer alarde, desplegar; pretender, ostentar; hacer jugar; poner en oposición o contraposición. **To play the fool,** hacerse el tonto. **To play the knave,** engañar. **To play (the) truant,** hacer novillos, no asistir a la escuela, al aula, etc.

play on a musical instrument, tocar o tañer un instrumento músico, como el violín, piano, etc.

play up, molestar, dar guerra, dar la lata.

play upon, hacer equívoco de vocablos. **To play upon one,** burlarse de uno, hacer mofar de. **To play a set o game,** jugar un partido o una partida. **To play false,** engañar. **To play one a trick,** engañar a uno, hacerle una mala jugada, pegarle un petardo.

play, *s.* 1. Juego; divertimiento y ejercicio de recreación. 2. Representación de una pieza dramática y la misma pieza dramática. 3. Juego, la acción de jugar a un juego sujeto a reglas. 4. Juego, la disposición en que se hallan unidas algunas cosas entre sí, de modo que sin desunirse o separarse puedan ponerse en acción y movimiento, ya a la vez, ya de por sí. **To come in play,** entrar en juego, hacer uno su parte en una cosa ejecutada entre muchos. 5. Juego. *V.* GAMBLING. 6. El modo de tocar un instrumento o de representar una pieza dramática. 7. Libertad para obrar; vuelo, remonte, hablando de las pasiones de la imaginación, etc. 8. Movimiento ligero y rápido; reflejo de colores o de luces. **A child full of play,** un muchacho travieso o enredador. **To play fair lay,** jugar limpio, obrar con sinceridad, sin trastienda, de veras. **To play foul play,** entrampar en el juego; engañar. **By fair play,** sinceramente, con pureza. **In play,** en chanza, de burlas. **A play upon words,** equívoco de vocablos. **Foul play,** mala jugada, perfidia. **Play actor,** actor, cómico.

playback ['pleɪbæk] [plei-bak], *s.* Reproducción en magnetófono.

playbill ['pleɪbɪl] [plei-bil], *s.* Cartel de teatro, programa de una función teatral.

playboy ['pleɪbɔɪ] [plei-boi], *s.* Muchacho travieso, calavera, hombre de mundo.

play-day ['pleɪdeɪ] [plei-dei], *s.* Día de huelga, día de descanso.

play-debt ['pleɪdebt] [plei-debt], *s.* Deuda contraída en el juego.

player ['pleɪə͡r] [pleia͡r], *s.* 1. Jugador. 2. Holgazán, haragán. 3. Comediante, cómico, actor. **Strolling player,** cómico de la lengua. 4. Tocador, músico, tañedor, instrumentista. **Piano player,** pianista.

playfellow ['pleɪfeləʊ] [plei-fe-lou], *s.* Compañero de juego.

playful ['pleɪfʊl] [plei-ful], *a.* Juguetón, travieso.

playfully ['pleɪfəlɪ] [plei-fu-li], *adv.* Juguetonamente, alegremente.

playgame ['pleɪgeɪm] [plei-gueim], *s.* Juego de niños.

playgoer ['pleɪˌgəʊə͡r] [plei-goua͡r], *s.* Persona que frecuenta los teatros.

playground ['pleɪgraʊnd] [plei-graund], *s.* Patio de recreo.

playhouse ['pleɪhaʊs] [plei-jaus], *s.* 1. Teatro, casa de comedias; sala de espectáculos. 2. Casita de juguete para niños.

playing-card ['pleɪɪŋkɑːd] [plein-kard], *s.* Naipe, baraja, carta.

playlet ['pleɪlɪt] [plei-lit], *s.* Entremés teatral, comedia corta.

playmate, *s.* V. PLAYFELLOW.

plaything ['pleɪθɪŋ] [plei-zin], *s.* Juguete.

playtime ['pleɪtaɪm] [plei-taim], *s.* Recreo.

playwright ['pleɪraɪt] [plei-rait], *s.* Compositor de comedias, tragedias u óperas.

plaza ['plɑːzə] [pla-sa], *s.* Plaza (square).

plea [pliː] [pli], *s.* 1. El acto o forma de abogar. 2. Alegación, alegato, defensa que hace un abogado ante un tribunal. 3. Apología, disculpa, excusa, pretexto. 4. Súplica, instancia. **A plausible plea,** una excusa, disculpa plausible. **Plea in abatement,** instancia de nulidad.

pleach [pliːtʃ] [plich], *va.* Entretejer ramas.

plead [pliːd] [plid], *vn.* 1. Orar, argüir en un tribunal de justicia. 2. Raciocinar o argüir con otro alegando razones. 3. Abogar, defender en juicio, la causa de un reo. *-va.* 1. Defender en juicio. 2. Alegar o exponer razones. 3. Disculpar, excusar, interceder. **To plead guilty,** confesar que se ha cometido el delito de que se va a juzgar al reo. **To plead not guilty,** negar la acusación. **To plead for,** militar o argüir en favor de.

pleadable ['pliːdəbl] [pli-da-bol], *a.* Que se puede alegar en un pleito, o en defensa de alguna cosa.

pleader ['pliːdə͡r] [pli-da͡r], *s.* 1. Abogado, el que aboga en un tribunal de justicia. 2. Abogado, defensor; todo el que sostiene el pro o contra de alguna opinión.

pleading ['pliːdɪŋ] [pli-din], *s.* 1. Súplica. 2. *(Law)* Alegación, defensa. *-a.* Suplicante. *-pl. (For.)* Debates, litigios; alegaciones.

pleasant ['pleznt] [ple-sant], *a.* 1. Delicioso, agradable (nice). 2. Placentero, alegre, vivo (joyful, agreeble), 3. Divertido. **Pleasant dreams!,** ¡felices sueños!

pleasantly ['plezntlɪ] [ple-sant-li], *adv.* Deliciosamente, alegremente, de una manera grata.

pleasantness ['plezntnɪs] [ple-sant-nes], *s.* Delicia, alegría, gusto, agrado, placer, satisfacción, recreo.

pleasantry ['plezntrɪ] [ple-san-tri], *s.* 1. Gusto. 2. Agudeza, dicho agudo; chocarrería, chanza (joking remark).

please [pliːz] [plis], *va.* 1. Deleitar, agradar, dar gusto (delight). 2. Contentar, complacer. *-vn.* 1. Placer, agradar, gustar, gozar (like). 2. Querer, gustar, tener a bien, hallar por bueno. **To be pleased,** complacerse, recrearse, deleitarse. **Do as you please,** haga Ud. lo que guste. **Please God, o if God please, o if it please God,** ¡Dios lo quiera! ¡plegue a Dios! **Hard to please,** difícil de contentar. **Ill pleased,** malcontento. **Please come as soon as you can,** sírvase Ud. venir lo más pronto que pueda. **Please go in,** sírvase Ud.

entrar. **Please, sir, if you please,** con permiso de Ud. *-interj.* **Yes, please,** sí, gracias. **Please sit down,** siéntese, por favor.

pleased ['pliːzd] [plisd], *a.* Satisfecho, contento. **I'm very pleased with your exam results,** estoy muy contento con los resultados de tus exámenes.

pleaser ['pliːzə͡r] [pli-sa͡r], *s.* El hombre agradable que hace la corte a alguna persona para ganar su afecto o su favor.

pleasing ['pliːzɪŋ] [pli-sin], *a.* Agradable, placentero, jovial, alegre.

pleasingly ['pliːzɪŋlɪ] [pli-sin-li], *adv.* Agradablemente.

pleasurable ['pleʒərəbl] [ple-sa-ra-bol], *a.* Deleitante, divertido, festivo.

pleasure ['pleʒə͡r] [ple-sha͡r], *s.* 1. Gusto, placer, deleite, agrado, satisfacción, complacencia (liking), **What is your pleasure, madam?** ¿Qué quiere Ud., señora? ¿Qué es lo que Ud. desea? ¿en qué puedo complacer a Ud.? **It gives me great pleasure to see you,** me alegro mucho de ver a Ud. **I shall do it with great pleasure,** lo haré con mucho gusto. 2. Deleite sensual. **Woman of pleasure,** cortesana. 3. Arbitrio, propia voluntad (choice). **At his own pleasure,** como él quiera, como le plazca.

pleasure, *va.* Complacer, dar gusto a otro; servir, favorecer, hacer favor a uno.

pleasure boat ['pleʒəbəʊt] [ple-sha-bout], *s.* Barco de recreo.

pleasure-ground ['pleʒəgraʊnd] [ple-sha-graund], *s.* El jardín o praderas dispuestos con orden y hermosura; parque, jardín de recreo.

pleat [pliːt] [plit], *va. (Fam.)* Plegar, hacer dobleces o pliegues. *-s.* Pliegue, doblez, plegadura en la ropa. V. PLAIT.

pleb [pleb] [pleb], *s. (Fam.)* Ordinario.

plebeian [plɪˈbiːən] [pli-bian], *a.* y *s.* Plebeyo, pechero; vulgar, bajo, común.

plebeianism [plɪˈbiːənɪzəm] [pli-bia-ni-sem], *s.* 1. Condición de plebeyo, estado de la plebe. 2. Vulgaridad, la conducta de los plebeyos.

plebiscite ['plebɪsɪt] [ple-bi-sit], *s.* 1. Plebiscito, resolución tomada por todo un pueblo a pluralidad de votos. 2. Plebiscito, ley romana votada por los plebeyos a propuesta del tribuno.

plectrum ['plektrəm] [plek-tram], *s.* Plectro, instrumento pequeño para tocar las cuerdas de la lira, cítara, etc. Púa.

pledge [pledʒ] [plech], *s.* 1. Prenda, la alhaja que se da en seguridad de una deuda o contrato. 2. Fianza; rehén. 3. Promesa. **Election pledge,** promesa electoral.

pledge, *va.* 1. Empeñar, dar o dejar alguna cosa en prenda, dar fianza. 2. Corresponder uno al brindis que se le hace. 3. Comprometerse. **Your father pledged his word,** tu padre dio su palabra.

pledgee ['pledʒiː] [ple-chi], *s. (For.)* Depositario, la persona en quien se deposita alguna prenda.

pledgeless ['pledʒɪlɪs] [plech-les], *a.* Desprovisto de fianza, de garantía.

pledger ['pledʒə͡r] [ple-cha͡r], *s.* 1. Depositante, el que deposita alguna cosa. 2. El que corresponde al brindis que se le dirige.

pledget ['pledʒɪt] [ple-chit], *s.* Planchuela, plancha de hilas que se pone sobre una llaga o herida.

pleiades ['plaɪədiːz] [plaia-dis], *s. (Astr.)* Pléyadas o pléyades, grupo de estrellas en la constelación de Tauro.

pleiocene, *a.* V. PLIOCENE.

pleistocene ['plaɪstəsiːn] [plis-to-sin], *s.* El período cuaternario, la época más reciente de la historia geológica.

plenary ['pliːnərɪ] [pli-na-ri], *a.* 1. Plenario, lleno, entero (entire, complete). **Plenary powers,** plenos poderes. 2. *(For.)* Plenario, que ha cumplido con todas las formalidades que previenen las leyes.

plenipotential [ˌplenɪpəˈtenʃəl] [ple-ni-po-ten-shal], *a.* Autorizado con poder pleno.

plenipotentiary [ˌplenɪpəˈtenʃərɪ] [ple-ni-po-ten-sha-ri], *s.* y *a.* Plenipotenciario (representante diplomático), revestido de plenos poderes.

plenish ['plenɪʃ] [ple-nish], *va.* Llenar, rellenar.

plenist ['plenɪst] [ple-nist], *s.* El filósofo que niega que hay vacuo o vacío en la naturaleza.

plenitude ['plenɪtjuːd] [ple-ni-tiud], *s.* Plenitud, abundancia.

plenteous ['plentɪəs] [plen-tios], *a.* Copioso, fructífero, fértil, abundante (copious, abundant).

plenteously ['plentɪəslɪ] [plen-tios-li], *adv.* Copiosamente, abundantemente.

plentiful ['plentɪfʊl] [plen-ti-ful], *a.* Copioso, abundante, fértil.

plentifully ['plentɪfəlɪ] [plen-ti-fa-li], *adv.* Abundantemente.

plentifulness ['plentɪfəlnɪs] [plen-ti-fal-nes], *s.* Copia, fertilidad.

plenty ['plentɪ] [plen-ti], *s.* 1. Copia, abundancia (abundance). 2. Profusión, demasía. *-pron.* Muchos-as. **Plenty of balloons,** muchos libros.

plenum ['plenəm] [ple-nom], *s.* Pleno, plenitud de la materia en el espacio; espacio, lo opuesto a vacuo.

pleonasm ['pliːənæzəm] [plio-na-sem], *s.* 1. Pleonasmo. 2. *(Med.)* Exceso en el volumen o número.

pleonast ['pliːənæzəm] [plio-na-sem], *s.* El que acostumbra usar palabras superfluas.

pleonastic. pleonastical ['pliːənæstɪk] [plio-nas-tik], *a.* Redundante, pleonástico.

plethora ['pleθərə] [ple-zo-ra], **plethory** ['pleθərɪ] [ple-zo-ri], *s.* Plétora, repleción, superabundancia, exceso.

plethoric ['pleθərɪk] [ple-zo-rik], *a.* Pletórico, repleto.

pleurisy ['plʊərɪsɪ] [plua-ri-si], *s.* Pleuritis, pleuresía, inflamación de la pleura.

pleuron ['plʊːrən] [plu-ron], *s.* *(Zool.)* Parte o prominencia de un lado.

plexus ['pleksəs] [plek-sos], *s.* 1. Enlace, entrelazamiento de partes en forma de redecilla. 2. *(Anat.)* Plexo, tejido de varios nervios.

pliability [ˌplaɪəˈbɪlɪtɪ] [plaia-bi-li-ti], *s.* Flexibilidad, docilidad, cualidad de doblarse sin romperse.

pliable ['plaɪəbl] [plaia-bol], *a.* 1. Flexible, que se puede doblar o torcer fácilmente. 2. Dócil, manejable de disposición flexible, que cede fácilmente a un influjo moral (meek).

pliableness ['plaɪəblnɪs] [plaia-bol-nes], **pliancy** ['plaɪənsɪ] [plaian-si], *s.* Flexibilidad, blandura, docilidad.

pliant ['plaɪənt] [plaiant], *a.* 1. Flexible, dócil, blando, fácil de doblarse sin romperse (tender, soft, flexible). 2. Dócil, manejable, que cede fácilmente a un influjo moral, de disposición flexible.

pliantness ['plaɪəntnɪs] [plaiant-nes], *s.* Docilidad o flexibilidad de carácter.

plication ['plɪkeɪʃən] [pli-kei-shon], *s.* Plegadura, pliegue.

pliers ['plaɪəz] [plaiars], *s. pl.* Alicates, especie de tenazas. **Flat-pointed pliers,** tenacillas de boca. **Sharp-pointed pliers,** tenacillas de punta.

plight [plaɪt] [plait], *va.* 1. Empeñar, dar o dejar en prenda. **Plight** nunca se aplica a una propiedad, y en esto difiere de **pledge.** 2. Prometer en matrimonio, contraer esponsales.

plight, *s.* 1. Promesa, empeño, compromiso solemne (promise); esponsales, promesa de matrimonio. 2. Estado, condición; comúnmente, un estado apurado, embarazo, perplejidad. 3. *(Des.)* Pliegue. V. PLAIT. **A sorry (o woeful-plight,** un estado lastimoso.

plighter ['plaɪtəʳ] [plai-taʳ], *s.* Prometedor; el que empeña; la persona que contrae esponsales.

plimsoll ['plɪmsəl] [plim-sol], *s.* Zapatilla de lona, playera.

plinth [plɪnθ] [plinz], *s.* Plinto.

plod [plɒd] [plod], *vn.* 1. Afanarse, trabajar mucho; trajinar, andar de una parte a otra con trabajo. 2. Estudiar con aplicación y constancia; trabajar con perseverancia, trabajar de un tirón (familiar expression).

plodder ['plɒdəʳ] [plo-daʳ], *s.* El que se aplica mucho a un estudio, aunque sea sin utilidad.

plodding ['plɒdɪŋ] [plo-din], *s.* El acto de estudiar con aplicación.

plonket ['plɒŋkɪt] [plon-kit], *s.* Especie de tela de lana gruesa.

plot [plɒt] [plot], *s.* 1. Espacio pequeño de terreno destinado a un uso particular. V. PLAT. **Grass-plot,** césped. **Garden-plot,** jardincito, cuadro de flores. **Ground-plot,** terreno, solar de un edificio. 2. Plano, la delineación que se saca de un terreno, mapa. 3. Conspiración, conjuración, trama (conspiracy). 4. Enredo, nudo, intriga (mess, tangle). *(Fam.)* Entruchada. 5. Plan, proyecto, idea. 6. Estratagema, astucia, fingimiento y enredo artificioso.

plot, *va.* 1. Delinear, formar la planta de algún edificio o plaza. 2. Trazar, idear. *-vn.* 1. Conspirar. 2. Urdir, tramar.

plotful ['plɒtfʊl] [plot-ful], *a.* Abundante en tramas, enredos o maquinaciones; lleno de intrigas.

plotter ['plɒtəʳ] [plo-taʳ], *s.* 1. Conspirador, conjurado; tramador. 2. *(Inform.)* Trazador de gráficos.

plotting ['plɒtɪŋ] [plo-tin], *s.* 1. La delineación de algún terreno. 2. Conspiración, trama.

plotting-scale ['plɒtɪŋskeɪl] [plo-tin-skeil], *s.* Instrumento para levantar planos de terrenos.

plough, plow [plaʊ] [plau], *s.* 1. Arado, instrumento para arar la tierra. 2. Lengüeta, instrumento con que el encuadernador recorta las hojas de los libros. 3. Instrumento para apartar o desviar obstáculos o para pasar a través de ellos, v. g. la máquina que se emplea para apartar la nieve.

plough, plow, *vn.* Arar, labrar la tierra. *-va.* Arar. **To plough in,** cubrir arando. **To plough up,** (a) romper, partir, como con un arado. (b) Remover, arrancar del suelo, arándolo. **To plough with one's heifer,** (a) arar con la novilla, es decir, tratar con la mujer para alcanzar alguna cosa del marido. (b) Usar los bienes de otro en provecho propio. **To put one's hand to the plough,** empezar a hacer una cosa. **Gang-plough,** arado de reja múltiple. **Snow-plough,** quitanieves (in railway). **Plough-plane,** guillame, acanalador, especie de cepillo.

ploughboy ['plaʊbɔɪ] [plau-boi], *s.* Muchacho empleado en la labranza.

plougher ['plaʊəʳ] [plauaʳ], *s.* Arador, surcador.

ploughing ['plaʊɪŋ] [plauin], *s.* Aradura, labranza.

ploughland ['plaʊlænd] [plau-land], *s.* Tierra labrantía.

ploughman, plowman ['plaʊmən] [plau-man], *s.* 1. Arador, el que ara y cultiva la tierra. 2. Patán, campesino, rústico. 3. El hombre de campo que es muy fuerte y trabajador.

plough-monday ['plaʊmʌndɪ] [plau-man-di], *s.* El primer lunes después de la Epifanía.

ploughshare, plowsock ['plaʊʃɛəʳ] [plau-sheaʳ], *s.* Reja de arado. **Ploughstaff,** enrejada.

ploughwright ['plaʊraɪt] [plau-rait], *s.* El que hace arados.

plover ['plʌvəʳ] [plo-vaʳ], *s.* 1. Avefría, ave de las costas del género Charadrias. 2. Algún ave semejante. **Bastard plover,** frailecillo. V. LAPWING.

plow [plaʊ] [plau], *s.* V. PLOUGH.

ploy [plɔɪ] [ploi], *s.* Treta, ardid.

pluck [plʌk] [plak], *va.* 1. Tirar o traer hacia sí alguna cosa con fuerza; arrancar; derribar, derrocar, echar por tierra (pull down); en estas significaciones este verbo lleva tras sí regularmente **off, on, away, up o into.** 2. Desplumar, pelar, quitar las plumas al ave. **To pluck up heart o spirit,** hacer de tripas corazón.

pluck, *s.* 1. Valor, ánimo, resolución ante el peligro. 2. Arranque, tirón. 3. Asadura; hígado, corazón y bofes (animal).

plucker ['plʌkəʳ] [pla-kaʳ], *s.* Arrancador.

plucky ['plʌkɪ] [pla-ki], *a.* Animoso, valeroso, valiente.

plug ['plʌg] [plag], *s.* 1. Tapón, tarugo o llave de puente, émbolo. **Fire-plug,** llave o caño que abastece de agua en un incendio. 2. Porción de tabaco torcido. **Plug tobacco,** tabaco curado o torcido. 3. *(Fam.)* Cualquier artículo que no sirve para nada; rocín, penco, caballo de poco valor. 4. *(Ger.)* Sombrero de copa.

plug, *va.* 1. Atarugar, tapar con tapón o tarugo. **To plug melons o other fruits,** *(Fam.)* calar melones, etc. 2. Orificar, rellenar la picadura de una muela o de un diente. *(Fam.)* **He**

keeps plugging away his French, sigue dándole duro a su francés. **Plug in,** enchufar. **Plug up,** tapar.

plugger [ˈplʌgəʳ] [pla-gaʳ], s. Orificador, instrumento que sirve para orificar.

plughole [ˈplʌghəʊl] [plag-joul], s. Desagüe.

plum [plʌm] [plam], s. 1. Ciruela, fruto del ciruelo; el árbol mismo que da las ciruelas. 2. Pasas, la uva seca y puesta en cajas, particularmente las que se usan para guisar. 3. (Fam. Ingl.) La cantidad de cien mil libras esterlinas; riquezas, muchos bienes de fortuna. 4. La parte óptima de alguna cosa, lo mejor. **Dried plums,** ciruelas pasas. **Green gage plum,** ciruela claudia. **Plum-cake,** bollo o bizcocho con pasas de Corinto y pasas comunes. **Plum-curculio,** curculio, gorgojo, muy destructivo para las frutas del ciruelo, del melocotonero y del peral. **Plum-pudding,** pudín. **Plum-pie,** torta, pastel de ciruelas. **Plum-tree,** ciruelo.

plumage [ˈplʌmɪdʒ] [pla-mich], s. Plumaje, conjunto de plumas del ave.

plumb [plʌm] [plam], s. Plomada. -adv. A plomo, perpendicularmente.

plumb, va. 1. Sondar, sondear. 2. Aplomar, examinar con la plomada. 3. Instalar (in a building) cañerías para gas, agua y albañales.

plumbaginous [plʌmˈbeɪdʒɪnəs] [plam-bei-yi-nos], a. Plombaginoso, de plombagina o grafito; parecido a la dentelaria.

plumbago [plʌmˈbeɪgəʊ] [plam-bei-gou], s. 1. Lápiz, plomo, grafito, plombagina; se emplea para fabricar lápices y crisoles y para lubricar. 2. (Bot.) Dentelaria, plumbago, género de plantas con flores color de plomo.

plumbean [ˈplʌmbɪən] [plam-bian], **plumbeous** [ˈplʌmɪəs] [plam-bios], a. Plúmbeo, plomizo, plomado.

plumber [ˈplʌməʳ] [plam-baʳ], s. Fontanero.

plumbing [ˈplʌmɪŋ] [pla-min], s. 1. Arte u oficio del plomero; instalación de cañerías en un edificio. 2. Emplomadura, tubería, sistema de tubos para dichos usos, cañerías.

plumbline [ˈplʌmlaɪn] [plam-lain], s. Cuerda de plomada o sonda; nivel, instrumento para examinar si está igual un plano.

plume [pluːm] [plum], s. 1. Pluma, plumaje, penacho de plumas. 2. Orgullo, altivez. 3. (Bot.) V. PLUMULE.

plume, va. 1. Ajustar o componer las plumas. 2. Desplumar, pelar, quitar las plumas. 3. Adornar con plumas. **To plume oneself upon,** vanagloriarse de alguna cosa. 4. Pelar, desollar, desplumar, sacar el dinero a alguno. -vn. Emplumar o emplumecer.

plumeless [ˈpluːmlɪs] [plum-les], a. Implume.

plumigerous [pluːˈmɪdʒərəs] [plu-mi-ye-ros], a. Plumoso o plumado.

plummet [ˈplʌmɪt] [pla-mit], s. Plomada; sonda, sondaleza de los marineros. -vn. Caer en picado.

plumose [ˈpluːməʊz] [plu-mous], a. Plúmeo, plumoso.

plump [plʌmp] [plamp], a. 1. Gordo, rollizo, regordete, gordinflón (fatty). **Plump man,** hombre rechoncho. **Plump face,** cara llena. 2. Brusco, claro, sin reserva (rude). -adv. De golpe, de repente. -s. Grupo apretado; bandada de aves, espesura de árboles.

plump, va. Engordar, hinchar. -vn. Caer a plomo; hincharse, ponerse gordo y corpulento. **Plump for,** decidirse, optar por. **Plump up,** ahuecar una almohada, sacudir.

plumpness [ˈplʌmpnɪs] [plamp-nes], s. Gordura, corpulencia.

plumpy [ˈplʌmpɪ] [plam-pi], a. Gordo, lleno, rollizo.

plumula [ˈpluːmjʊlə] [plu-miu-la], s. (Orn.) Plúmula, plumón, pluma muy delgada y sedosa.

plumule [ˈpluːmjʊl] [plu-miul], s. 1. (Orn.) Plúmula, pluma blanda. 2. (Bot.) Plúmula, la parte del verdadero embrión de las simientes que sale fuera de la tierra.

plumy [ˈplʌmɪ] [pla-mi], a. Plumado, plumoso.

plunder [ˈplʌndəʳ] [plan-daʳ], va. 1. Pillar, tomar a viva fuerza lo que pertenece a un enemigo; despojar. 2. Saquear, pillar, hurtar, robar (steal).

plunder, s. 1. Pillaje, saqueo, despojo, lo que se toma por fuerza a un enemigo; despojar. 2. Pillaje, robo, botín.

plunderer [ˈplʌndərəʳ] [plan-da-raʳ], s. Saqueador, ladrón (thief).

plundering [ˈplʌndərɪŋ] [plan-de-rin], sm. Saqueo.

plunge [plʌndʒ] [planch], va. 1. Zambullir, zampuzar, somorgujar, sumergir, chapuzar, meter en el agua (dip, submerge). 2. Anegar, sumergir a uno en penas, en miseria, etc. 3. Precipitar, exponer a uno a alguna ruina. 4. Rempujar, meter alguna cosa a rempujones. -vn. 1. Sumergirse, meterse de repente debajo del agua. 2. Precipitarse, arrojarse. 3. Dar manotadas o coces como hacen los potros no domados.

plunge, s. 1. Sumersión, zambullida. 2. Movimiento repentino y violento. **Shares are taking a plunge,** las acciones están cayendo en picado. 3. (Des.) Estrecho, aprieto, apuro. **Plunge-bath,** baño suficientemente grande para zambullirse en él.

plungeon [ˈplʌndʒɪən] [plan-yion], s. (Orn.) Somorgujo, mergo.

plunger [ˈplʌndʒəʳ] [plan-yaʳ], s. 1. Buzo, somorgujador. 2. (Mec.) Émbolo de bomba, desatascador.

plunging [ˈplʌndʒɪŋ] [plan-yin], s. El acto de dar manotadas y brincos los caballos sin domar. -a. muy profundo.

pluperfect [pluːˈpɜːfɪkt] [plu-per-fikt], a. (Gram.) Pluscuamperfecto. -s. Pluscuamperfecto.

plural [ˈplʊərəl] [plua-ral], a. Plural, más de uno. **The plural number,** el número plural. -s. Plurar, el número que designa la pluralidad. **In the plural,** en plural.

pluralism [ˈplʊərəlɪzəm] [plu-ra-li-sem], s. 1. Pluralidad, pluralismo, calidad de ser más de uno. 2. Pluralidad de los beneficios, posesión de más de un beneficio eclesiástico a la vez.

pluralistic [plʊərəˈlɪstɪk] [plu-ra-lis-tik], a. Pluralista.

plurality [plʊəˈrælɪtɪ] [plua-ra-li-ti], s. 1. Pluralidad, multitud. 2. Pluralidad, mayoría, el mayor número.

plurally [ˈplʊərəlɪ] [plua-ra-li], adv. En sentido plural, en el número plural.

plus [plʌs] [plas], adv. 1. Más: es voz latina. 2. Más de cero; positivo. -s. 1. Signo de más. 2. Ventaja (advantage, bonus). -conj. Además de que.

plush [plʌʃ] [plash], s. Tripe, felpilla, tela felpada. **Silk plush,** felpa de seda, especialmente para sombreros. -a. Lujoso.

plushy [ˈplʌʃɪ] [pla-shi], a. Elegante, lujoso.

plutarchy [ˈpluːtɑːkɪ] [plu-tar-ki], s. Gobierno por los ricos, forma de la oligarquía.

plutocracy [pluːˈtɒkrəsɪ] [plu-to-kra-si], s. Plutocracia, poder, reino del dinero.

plutocrat [ˈpluːtəʊkræt] [plu-to-krat], s. Plutócrata, acaudalado político.

plutonian [pluːˈtəʊnɪən] [plu-tou-nian], a. Plutónico. V. PLUTONIC. -s. Plutonista, partidario del plutonismo. V. **Plutonic theory.**

plutonic [pluːˈtəʊnɪk] [plu-tou-nik], a. 1. Plutómano, perteneciente a Plutón, dios de los infiernos entre los antiguos. 2. Plutónico, ígneo, debido a la acción del fuego. **Plutonic rocks,** rocas plutónicas. **Plutonic theory,** plutonismo, doctrina que atribuye la formación de las capas del globo a la acción del fuego interior.

plutonist [pluːˈtəʊnɪst] [plu-tou-nist], s. Plutonista, partidario del plutonismo, de la teoría plutónica.

plutonium [pluːˈtəʊnɪəm] [plu-tou-niom], s. Plutonio.

pluvial [ˈpluːvɪəl] [plu-vial], a. Pluvial, que proviene de la lluvia o se refiere a ella; lluvioso. -s. Capa pluvial.

pluviometer [pluːvɪˈɒmɪtəʳ] [plu-vio-mi-taʳ], s. Pluvímetro, pluviómetro, instrumento para medir la lluvia que cae en lugar y tiempo dados.

ply [plaɪ] [plai], va. 1. Trabajar con ahínco, formar, disponer o ejecutar alguna cosa. 2. Ocupar, dar que hacer, usar con diligencia; manejar (needle, oar). 3. Instar, solicitar con importunidad. -vn. 1. Ir y venir entre dos puntos; hacer viajecitos. **The ferry which plies between San Francisco and Tiburon,** el vapor de puerto que hace viajes entre San Francisco y Tiburón. 2. Afanarse por hacer algo con exactitud y presteza. 3. Ir de prisa. 4. Barloventar.

ply, *s.* 1. Pliegue, doble, hoja o capa de una tela, de una alfombra o manguera, etc. 2. Propensión, inclinación. **Three-ply,** de tres dobleces o capas.

plying ['plaɪɪŋ] [plain], *s.* 1. Solicitación importuna. 2. *(Mar.)* Esfuerzo de vela contra el viento.

plywood ['plaɪwʊd] [plai-wud], *s.* Madera terciada, contrachapado.

pneumatic [njuːˈmætɪk] [niu-ma-tik], *s.* Neumático. **Pneumatic drill,** martillo neumático.

pneumatics [njuːˈmætɪks] [niu-ma-tiks], *s.* Neumática (science).

pneumatology [ˌnjuːməˈtɒlədʒɪ] [niu-ma-to-lo-yi], *s.* Neumatología, tratado sobre las cosas espirituales.

pneumonia [njuːˈməʊnɪə] [niu-mou-nia], *s.* *(Med.)* Neumonía, inflamación del pulmón, que se llama perineumonía o pulmonía.

poach [pəʊtʃ] [pouch], *va.* 1. Cocer, dar un hervor ligero a alguna cosa (boil). **To poach eggs,** pasar huevos por agua rompiéndolos. 2. Pillar, robar, hurtar. 3. *(Des.)* Herir con un instrumento aguzado. *-vn.* Cazar furtivamente en tierras vedadas con el objeto de hurtar la caza.

poachard ['pəʊtʃəd] [pou-chard], *s.* Pato de mar.

poacher ['pəʊtʃəʳ] [pou-chaʳ], *s.* El que caza en tierras vedadas para hurtar lo cazado, cazador furtivo.

poachiness ['pəʊtʃɪnɪs] [pou-chi-nes], *s.* Humedad.

poaching ['pəʊtʃɪŋ] [pou-chin], *s.* El acto de cazar sin licencia para hurtar la caza.

poachy ['pəʊtʃɪ] [pou-chi], *a.* Se dice del terreno que forma hoyos al pisarlo el ganado; húmedo, pantanoso.

POB *Abreviatura de* **Post Office Box,** apartado de correos.

pock [pɒk] [pok], *s.* Viruela, pústula, postilla. **Pock-marked,** marcado de viruelas.

pocket ['pɒkɪt] [po-kit], *s.* 1. Bolsillo, faltriquera. 2. *(Fig.)* Bolsa; interés. 3. Bolsa, cavidad, receptáculo: en una mina, cavidad que contiene el mineral (pepitas de oro). **In pocket,** que tiene ganancia pecuniaria. **Out of pocket,** de su bolsillo, habiendo perdido dinero. **Pocket-book,** (a) portamonedas, bolsa. (b) Librito de memoria, cartera. (c) Dinero, recursos o medios pecuniarios. **Pocket-comb,** peinecito de bolsillo. **Pocket-handkerchief,** pañuelo de bolsillo. **Pocket-knife,** navaja. **Pocket-dictionary,** diccionario manual, de bolsillo. **Pocket-flap,** cartera del bolsillo. **Pocket-hole,** boca de faltriquera. **Pocket-gopher,** *V.* GOPHER. **Pocket-money,** alfileres, dinero para gastos particulares.

pocket, *va.* Embolsar, meter alguna cosa en el bolsillo o faltriquera. **To pocket an affront,** tragarse una injuria, o quedarse con ella en el cuerpo. **To pocket up,** tomar alguna cosa clandestinamente.

pocketed ['pɒkɪtɪd] [po-ki-ted], *a.* Lo que se toma furtivamente.

pocketknife ['pɒkɪtnaɪf] [po-kit-naif], *s.* Cortaplumas, navajita de bolsillo.

pockiness ['pɒkɪnɪs] [po-ki-nes], *s.* Calidad o condición de estar picado de viruelas.

pocky ['pɒkɪ] [po-ki], *a.* 1. Picado de viruelas. 2. Buboso, sifilítico.

pod [pɒd] [pod], *s.* 1. Vaina, legumbre, la corteza en que están encerradas algunas legumbres; cápsula de una planta. 2. Manada, rebaño, colección de animales, especialmente de focas, ballenas, o morsas. 3. La ranura o canal longitudinal que hay en ciertos taladros y barrenas.

pod, *vn.* 1. Llenarse, hincharse (swell up). 2. Criar vainas. 3. Hacer que las focas y vacas marinas se reunan en grupos o rebaños para matarlas.

podder ['pɒdəʳ] [po-daʳ], *s.* El que recoge legumbres.

podge [pɒdʒ] [podch], *s.* *(Prov. Ingl.)* Charco, cenagal, lamedal.

podiatrist ['pɒdɪətrɪst] [po-dia-trist], *s.* Pedicuro, podólogo.

podiatry ['pɒdɪətrɪ] [po-dia-tri], *s.* Podología.

podium ['pɒdɪəm] [po-diom], *s.* *(pl.* PODIA*)* Podio.

poem ['pəʊem] [pouem], *s.* 1. Poema, cualquiera obra en verso. 2. Obra en prosa cuyo estilo muestra imaginación y belleza poéticas.

poet ['pəʊɪt] [poet], *s.* Poeta. **Poet-laureate,** poeta laureado, archipoeta.

poetaster [ˌpəʊɪˈtæstəʳ] [poe-tas-taʳ], *s.* Poetastro, poeta despreciable.

poetess ['pəʊɪtɪs] [poe-tes], **sf.** Poetisa.

poetic, poetical ['pəʊˈetɪk] [poe-tik] [poe-ti-kal], *a.* Poético.

poetically ['pəʊˈetɪkəlɪ] [poe-ti-ka-li], *adv.* Poéticamente.

poetics ['pəʊetɪks] [poe-tiks], *s.* Poética, el tratado que contiene los preceptos del arte de componer obras de poesía.

poetize ['pəʊɪtaɪz] [poe-tais], *vn.* Poetizar, versificar, hacer o componer versos.

poetry ['pəʊɪtrɪ] [poue-tri], *s.* 1. Poética; poesía. 2. Lo que es poético. 3. Versos, poema, obra poética. **Poetry reading,** recital de poesía.

pogrom ['pɒgrəm] [po-grom], *s.* Pogromo.

poh [pɔː] [po], *inter.* ¡Puf! ¡bah! ¡quiá! interjección que expresa aversión o desprecio.

poignancy ['pɔɪnjənsɪ] [poi-ñan-si], *s.* 1. Punta, el sabor que va tirando a agrio. 2. Picante, la acerbidad o acrimonia con que algunas cosas irritan el paladar. 3. Picante, acrimonia, aspereza o mordacidad en el decir.

poignant ['pɔɪnjənt] [poi-ñant], *a.* 1. Picante, acerbo. 2. Punzante. 3. Acre, mordaz, satírico, picante.

poignantly ['pɔɪnjəntlɪ] [poi-ñant-li], *adv.* Picantemente, mordazmente, satíricamente.

poinsettia [pɔɪnˈsetɪə] [poin-se-tia], *s.* Flor de Pascua o de Navidad.

point [pɔɪnt] [point], *s.* 1. Punta, extremo muy agudo. 2. Herramienta o utensilio con un extremo puntiagudo; v. g. punta, especie de buril que usan los abridores y tallistas; en Inglaterra, aguja, carril móvil (railway term); en plural, cambiavía. 3. Agujeta, cordón con herrete. 4. Punto, fin u objeto con que se hace una cosa. 5. Punta, promontorio. 6. Punto, pundonor, puntillo. 7. Agudeza, sal, chiste ingenioso. 8. Punto, la parte más pequeña que se considera indivisible. 9. Punto, instante, momento. 10. Punto, momento crítico, ocasión oportuna. 11. Punto, el estado actual de cualquier especie o negocio. 12. Rumbo, la división del plano en la rosa náutica. 13. Punto, paraje determinado a que se dirige alguna cosa. 14. Puntería. 15. Punta, toda especie de encaje. 16. Punto, parte o cuestión de alguna ciencia. 17. Punto musical. 18. *(Gram.)* Cualquier signo de puntuación, particularmente, entre los impresores, punto final. **Points,** puntos, las vocales en la lengua hebrea. 19. Punto tipográfico, unidad de medida para el tamaño de los tipos. 20. Punto, tanto, unidad de cuenta en los juegos. 21. Rabo, cola de un animal. **To speak to the point,** ir al caso o a lo principal, dejarse de rodeos. **At the point of death,** en artículo de muerte. **At all points,** enteramente. **Point-blank,** (a) directamente, en línea recta. (b) Cara a cara, en facha, en términos formales. **To be at points,** estar de punta de cuernos o contrapuestos. *(Mex.)* Estar quebrados. **I was on the point of coming,** estaba a punto (o a pique) de venir, iba a venir. **In point,** al caso, a propósito. **In point of,** en cuanto, tocante a, con respecto a. **To come to the point,** llegar al caso, al punto; encajar bien. **Knotty point,** punto espinoso, cuestión difícil. **To carry one's point,** salirse con la suya. **He has made five points,** ha hecho cinco tantos.

point, *va.* 1. Apuntar, aguzar, afilar, adelgazar. 2. Apuntar, señalar, indicar. 3. Puntuar. 4. Apuntar, dirigir, asestar el tiro de un arma. **The gun was pointing in my direction,** la pistola apuntaba hacia mí. 5. Apuntar, señalar alguna palabra o frase con puntos en los escritos. 6. *(Albañ.)* Juntar, llenar con argamasa los huecos o intersticios e igualarlos con la llana. *-vn.* 1. Apuntar, señalar con el dedo. 2. Parar, mostrar la caza como hacen los perros de muestra. 3. Señalar, enseñar, dar a conocer. **Point out,** señalar, mostrar (show).

point-blank ['pɔɪntˈblæŋk] [point-blank] *a.* 1. Que tiene una dirección horizontal, a quemarropa. 2. Directo, positivo, formal. *-adv.* Directamente, en línea recta, diametralmente; en facha; positivamente, en términos formales. *-s.* Tiro a quemarropa, tiro asestado.

pointed ['pɔɪntɪd] [poin-ted], *a.* 1. Puntiagudo, puntuado, agudo. 2. Picante, epigramático, satírico (sharp). 3. Dirigido a una persona particular; acentuado. 4. *(Arq.)* Ojival.

pointedly ['pɔɪntɪdlɪ] [poin-ted-li], *adv.* Sutilmente, de un modo picante; con acento y fuerza; explícitamente, en términos formales.

pointedness ['pɔɪntɪdnɪs] [poin-ted-nes], *s.* Picantez; aspereza, acrimonia.

pointer ['pɔɪntər] [poin-tar], *s.* 1. Indicador, índice, lo que indica; en particular, manecilla (watch), apuntador, puntero. 2. Perro de punta y vuelta, ventor, pachón, braco inglés. 3. Pista (clue). 4. *pl.* Las dos estrellas de la Osa mayor, en cuya dirección se halla la estrella polar.

pointing ['pɔɪntɪŋ] [poin-tin], *s.* 1. Acto de afilar o apuntar; afiladura, aguzadura; acto de quitar las puntas. 2. Señalamiento, indicación, el acto de señalar o indicar; particularmente, puntuación: división de las palabras para cantar en la iglesia; acción de juntar o llenar los huecos o grietas con argamasa; puntería (de artillería). 3. Maduración de un absceso. 4. *(Mar.)* Rabo de rata.

pointing-stock ['pɔɪntɪŋˌstɒk] [poin-tin-stok], *s.* Objeto de risa, hazmerreír.

point lace ['pɔɪnleɪs] [point-leis], *s.* V. NEEDLEPOINT.

pointless ['pɔɪntlɪs] [point-les], *a.* 1. Obtuso, sin punto. 2. Vano, inútil.

point of honor ['pɔɪntɒvˌɒnər] [point-ov-o-nar], *s.* Pundonor.

point of view ['pɔɪntɒvˌvjuː] [point-ov-viu], *s.* Punto de vista.

poise [pɔɪz] [pois], *s.* Equilibrio, contrapeso; balanza; reposo.

poise, *va.* 1. Equilibrar, balancear (balance). 2. Igualar en peso, hacer equivaler una cosa a otra. 3. Cargar con algún peso. 4. Pesar, examinar con madurez alguna cosa. 5. Contrapesar, equiparar, cotejar una cosa con otra. 6. Abrumar, oprimir con algún peso grave.

poison ['pɔɪzn] [poi-son], *s.* 1. Veneno. **Poison-nut**, nuez vómica. 2. Veneno, ponzoña, cualquier cosa gravemente nociva a la salud. **Poison-oak, poison-ivy**, especie de zumaque que causa inflamación de la piel. **Poison-sumac, poison-elder,** (a) zumaque, árbol venenoso al tacto. (b) Mata, lo mismo que **poison-oak.**

poison, *va.* 1. Envenenar, atosigar, emponzoñar. 2. Corromper, intoxicar.

poisoner ['pɔɪznər] [poi-so-nar], *s.* Envenenador; corruptor, seductor.

poisoning ['pɔɪznɪŋ] [poi-so-nin], *s.* Envenenamiento, emponzoñamiento; estado mórbido debido a una substancia venenosa.

poisonous ['pɔɪznəs] [pois-nos], *a.* Venenoso, emponzoñado.

poisonousness ['pɔɪznəsnɪs] [pois-nos-nes], *s.* Venenosidad.

poison-pen letter ['pɔɪzn'penˌletər] [poi-son-pen-le-tar], *s.* Anónimo.

poitrel ['pɔɪtrɪl] [poi-trel], *s.* Antepecho, la armadura que en tiempos pasados cubría el pecho del caballo de batalla.

poke [pəʊk] [pouk], *s.* 1. Empuje, empujón, golpe, codazo (push, hit); picadura; la acción de empujar o de picar. **A poke in the ribs,** un codazo en las costillas. 2. Collera con apéndice que sirve para impedir a las bestias que salgan de un cercado. 3. Perezoso, el que se mueve lentamente. 4. Gorra de mujer con ala anterior muy saliente.

poke, *s.* 1. Barjuoleta, bolsa; saquillo. 2. V. POKEWEED.

poke, *va.* 1. Empujar, golpear con alguna cosa puntiaguda, picar. 2. Impeler por medio de un empujón o una picadura. -*vn.* 1. Andar perezosamente. 2. Andar a tientas, buscar alguna cosa a oscuras. **To poke the fire,** hurgar la lumbre, atizar el fuego. **To poke fun at,** burlarse, mofarse de alguno. **To poke the nose everywhere,** meterse en todo.

poker ['pəʊkər] [pou-kar], *s.* 1. Hurgón, atizador, hierro para menear y revolver la lumbre. 2. Juego de naipes. **Poker-faced,** con cara de póker.

pokerish ['pəʊkərɪʃ] [pou-ka-rish], *a.* 1. Alarmante, o que tiende a alarmar. 2. *(Fam.)* Tieso, rígido, inflexible.

pokeweed ['pəʊkwiːd] [pouk-uid], *s. (Bot.)* Hierba carmín, fitolaca.

poky ['pəʊkɪ] [pou-ki], *a.* 1. Flojo, pesado, falto de espíritu; lento. 2. *(G.B.)* Desharrapado, mal vestido. 3. *(G.B.)* Constreñido, apretado. **A poky little house,** una casita diminuta.

polar ['pəʊlər] [pou-lar], *a.* Polar, que pertenece a los polos; que pertenece a los polos magnéticos; que proviene o se halla cerca de los polos. **Polar-stone,** *(Con.)* especie de equino petrificado. **Polar bear,** oso polar, oso blanco.

polariscope ['pəʊlærɪskəʊp] [pou-la-ris-koup], *s.* Polariscopio.

polarity [pəʊ'lærɪtɪ] [pou-la-ri-ti], *s.* 1. Polaridad, facultad de tener o de poder adquirir polos; cualidad de tener polos opuestos. 2. V. POLARIZATION.

polarization [ˌpəʊlərarˈzeɪʃən] [pou-la-rai-sei-shon], *s.* 1. Calidad de tener o adquirir polaridad. 2. Polarización, modificación de la luz de modo que no pueda reflejarse en ciertas direcciones.

polarize, polarise ['pəʊləraɪz] [pou-la-rais], *va.* Polarizar, comunicar polaridad o polarización a una cosa.

pole [pəʊl] [poul], *s.* 1. Polo, cualquiera de los extremos del eje de la esfera. 2. Pértiga, vara larga; cualquier palo largo. 3. Una viga o un palo largo clavado en el suelo. **Pole-mast,** *(Mar.)* palo y mastelero de una sola pieza. **Under bare poles.** *(Mar.)* a palo seco o a la bretona. **Pole of a coach,** lanza de coche. 4. Percha, instrumento de diez pies geométricos de largo; medida de diez y seis pies y medio. 5. Polaco, el natural de Polonia. **The South Pole,** el Polo Sur. **The poles of a magnet,** los polos de un imán.

pole, *va.* 1. Empujar o hacer andar con palos. 2. Llevar, sostener sobre palos. 3. Armar con palos. 4. Agitar con pértiga. -*vn.* Impeler un barco con pértiga.

pole-axe ['pəʊlæks] [poul-aks], *vt.* Desnucar; *(Fig.)* Aturdir, pasmar.

polecat ['pəʊlkæt] [poul-kat], *s.* 1. Veso. Putorius foetidus. 2. Mofeta.

polemic, polemical [pɒ'lemɪk] [po-le-mik] [pɒ'lemɪkəl] [po-le-mi-kal], *a.* Polémico.

polemic, *s.* 1. Polémica (controversy). 2. Controversista, el que escribe o trata sobre puntos dogmáticos.

polemics [pɒ'lemɪks] [po-le-miks], *s.* Polémica.

polestar ['pəʊlstɑːr] [poul-star], *s.* 1. Cinosura, estrella muy resplandeciente en la constelación de la Osa menor; estrella polar. 2. Norte, guía.

pole vault ['pəʊlvɔːlt] [poul-volt], *s.* Salto con pértiga o garrocha.

police [pə'liːs] [po-lis], *s.* Policía. **Police headquarters,** cuartel de policía. **Police officer,** agente de policía.

police, *vt.* 1. Patrullar. 2. Vigilar, supervisar.

policed [pə'liːst] [po-list], *a.* Arreglado, bien administrado.

police dog [pə'liːsdɒg] [po-lis-dog], *s.* Perro policía.

policeman [pə'liːsmən] [po-lis-man], *s.* Policía, gendarme.

policewoman [pə'liːsˌwʊmən] [po-lis-uo-man], *s.* Mujer policía, agente femenino de policía.

policing [pə'liːsɪŋ] [po-li-sin], *s.* Mantenimiento del orden (keeping order).

policy ['pɒlɪsɪ] [po-li-si], *s.* 1. Arte, astucia; prudencia, sagacidad en la dirección y manejo de los asuntos (caution). 2. Curso o plan de acción; particularmente política, dirección de los negocios públicos. 3. Póliza de seguros.

policyholder ['pɒlɪsɪˌhəʊldər] [po-li-si-joul-dar], *s.* Asegurado, poseedor de una póliza de seguros.

polio ['pəʊlɪəʊ] [pou-liou], *s.* Contracción de **Poliomyelitis**, poliomielitis, parálisis infantil.

poliomyelitis ['pəʊlɪəʊmaɪəˈlaɪtɪs] [pou-liou-maia-lai-tis], *s.* Poliomielitis, parálisis infantil.

polish [ˈpɒlɪʃ] [po-lish], s. Betún, pomada, pasta.

polish, va. 1. Pulir, pulimentar, alisar por medio de la frotación, dar lustre, bruñir (smooth). 2. Pulir, limar, civilizar a una persona rústica o tonta; morigerar, hacer cortés, suavizar las costumbre, ilustrar el entendimiento. -vn. Recibir lustre o pulimento. **Polish off,** (Fam.) liquidarse, despacharse. **Polish up,** pulir, perfeccionar.

polisher [ˈpɒlɪʃəʳ] [po-li-shaʳ], s. Pulidor, bruñidor (person or instrument).

polite [pəˈlaɪt] [po-lait], a. Pulido, cortés, urbano, bien criado; que tiene finos modales. **In polite society,** en la buena sociedad.

politely [pəˈlaɪtlɪ] [po-lait-li], adv. Urbanamente, cortésmente, con buenos modales.

politeness [pəˈlaɪtnɪs] [po-lait-nes], s. Cortesía, urbanidad, buena crianza.

politic [ˈpɒlɪtɪk] [po-li-tik], a. 1. Político, sagaz, diestro, astuto. 2. Bien concebido para alcanzar un fin; especioso. 3. Que consta de ciudadanos; adecuado al bien público, político. **Body politic,** cuerpo político, de ciudadanos.

political [pəˈlɪtɪkəl] [po-li-ti-kal], a. 1. Político, que pertenece al gobierno civil o a la administración general de un Estado, que trata de la política o del gobierno. 2. Político, perteneciente a un partido. **Political economy,** economía política. 3. (Des.) Sagaz, astuto.

politically [pəˈlɪtɪkəlɪ] [po-li-ti-ka-li], adv. Políticamente. **Politically aware,** con conciencia política. **Politically correct,** políticamente correcto.

politician [ˌpɒlɪˈtɪʃən] [po-li-ti-shan], s. 1. Político, estadista. 2. hombre astuto y artificioso.

politicize [pəˈlɪtɪsaɪz] [po-li-ti-sais], va. Dar carácter político, politizar.

politics [ˈpɒlɪtɪks] [po-li-tiks], s. pl. 1. Política, la ciencia o arte que trata de la administración y manejo de los negocios públicos. 2. Negocios públicos desde el punto de vista de un partido. 3. Opiniones políticas, preferencia de partido. **To go into politics,** dedicarse a la política.

polka [ˈpɒlkə] [pol-ka], s. Polca, baile originario de Polonia y la música de ese baile.

polka dots [ˈpɒlkədɒt] [pol-ka-dot], s. pl. Diseño de bolitas distribuidas en una tela.

poll [pəʊl] [poul], s. 1. Cabeza de una persona; y de aquí, la persona misma. 2. Matrícula o lista de los que votan en una elección y la votación en una elección. -pl. Paraje donde se vota. 3. Capitación, repartimiento de tributos o contribuciones por cabezas.

poll, va. 1. Descabezar, descopar, desmochar, quitar la cima o copa a los árboles. 2. Descornar, quitar los cuerno a las reses. 3. Encabezar, formar una matrícula con los nombres de las personas que se deben incluir para el objeto con que se forma (lead); preguntar la opinión política de esas personas. 4. Encabezar, registrar o poner en matrícula a uno. 5. Votar en las elecciones. 6. Contar los votos. -vn. Dar voto en las elecciones.

pollack, pollock [ˈpɒlək] [po-lak], s. Pescadilla.

pollard [ˈpɒləd] [po-lad], s. 1. Árbol desmochado o descopado. 2. (Ict.) Coto. V. CHUR. 3. Salvado. 4. Ciervo u otro animal que ha perdido las astas.

pollard, va. (Poco us.) Podar, descopar o desmochar.

pollen [ˈpɒlən] [po-len], s. 1. (Bot.) Polen o polvillo fecundante del órgano masculino de las plantas. **Pollen count,** índice de concentración de polen en el aire. 2. Salvado fino.

poller [ˈpɒləʳ] [po-laʳ], s. 1. Votante, el que tiene voto en una elección. 2. Registrador de votantes. 3. Desmochador, el que desmocha árboles.

pollinate [ˈpɒlɪneɪt] [po-li-neit], vt. Polinizar.

pollination [ˌpɒlɪˈneɪʃən] [po-li-nei-shon], s. (Bot.) Polinización.

polling [ˈpəʊlɪŋ] [pou-lin], s. Votación, acción de votar; escrutinio de los votos. **Polling-booth,** local donde se vota. **Polling-place,** paraje donde se hace el escrutinio de los votos. **Polling-day,** día electoral.

polliwog [ˈpɒlɪwɒg] [po-li-uog], s. (Fam.) Renacuajo. V. TADPOLE.

pollutant [pəˈluːtənt] [po-lu-tant], s. Contaminante.

pollute [pəˈluːt] [po-lut], va. Manchar, ensuciar (dirty, soil). 2. Contaminar, corromper moralmente; viciar (corrupt). 3. Desflorar, violar, deshonrar; profanar. 4. Impurificar, mancillar, quitar la pureza ceremonial (entre los judíos). -a. (Poco us.) Mancillado, deshonrado, contaminado.

polluter [pəˈluːtəʳ] [po-lu-taʳ], s. Corrompedor, corruptor, contaminador; desflorador.

pollution [pəˈluːʃən] [po-lu-shon], s. Polución, contaminación, profanación.

polly [ˈpɒlɪ] [po-li], s. (Fam.) Mariquita, nombre familiar usado en vez de **Mary;** también, una cotorra.

polo [ˈpəʊləʊ] [pou-lou], s. Polo, juego de pelota a caballo. **Polo neck sweater,** suéter de cuello alto o cisne.

polonaise [ˌpɒləˈneɪz] [po-lo-neis], s. 1. Polonesa, prenda de vestir de mujer a modo de gabán corto, ceñido a la cintura. 2. (Mús.) Polaca. 3. Polonesa, polaca, mujer de Polonia.

poltroon [pɒlˈtruːn] [pol-trun], s. 1. Poltrón, collón, cobarde, pusilánime (coward). 2. Poltrón, haragán, holgazán (slack).

poly [ˈpɒlɪ] [po-li], s. Polio (plant).

poly. Prefijo griego que significa muchos o varios.

polyacoustic [ˌpɒlɪəˈkɑstɪk] [po-lia-kas-tik], a. Poliacústico, que multiplica los sonidos.

polyandry [ˈpɒlɪəndrɪ] [po-lian-dri], s. 1. Poliandria, estado de la mujer que tiene más de un marido. 2. Sistema social que incluye la pluralidad de maridos.

polyanthus [ˌpɒlɪˈænθəs] [po-lian-zos], s. (Bot.) Poliantes; prímula.

polychromatic [ˌpɒlɪkrəʊˈmætɪk] [po-li-krou-ma-tik], a. Policromático, que presenta varios colores o cambios de color.

polychrome [ˈpɒlɪkrəʊm] [po-li-kroum], a. Policromo, hecho o impreso en varios o en muchos colores. -s. Cuadro o estatua ejecutado en varios colores.

polyclinic [ˌpɒlɪklaɪnɪk] [po-li-klai-nik], s. 1. Policlínica, institución en que se da instrucción clínica sobre toda clase de enfermedades. 2. Hospital general para el tratamiento de todas las enfermedades.

polyester [ˌpɒlɪˈestəʳ] [po-lies-taʳ], s. Poliéster.

poliethylene [ˌpɒlɪˈeθəliːn] [po-lie-za-lin], s. Polietileno.

polygamist [pɒˈlɪgæmɪst] [po-li-ga-mist], s. Polígamo, polígama, el que practia la poligamia o sostiene sus legalidad.

polygamous [pɒˈlɪgæməs] [po-li-ga-mos], a. 1. Polígamo, que se refiere a la poligamia. 2. (Zool.) Que se une o tiene cópula con más de uno del sexo opuesto. 3. (Bot.) Polígamo, que tiene sobre el mismo pedúnculo flores hembras y hermafroditas.

polygamy [pɒˈlɪgæmɪ] [po-li-ga-mi], s. Poligamia, el estado de un hombre casado con muchas mujeres, o de una mujer casada con muchos maridos a un tiempo.

polyglot [ˈpɒlɪglɒt] [po-li-glot], a. 1. Políglota, escrito en varias lenguas. 2. Políglota, que sabe muchas lenguas.

polygon [ˈpɒlɪgən] [po-li-gon], s. Polígono, figura de varios lados.

polygonal [ˈpɒlɪgənl] [po-li-go-nal], s. Poligonal.

polygraph [ˈpɒlɪgrɑːf] [po-li-graf], sm. Polígrafo.

polygraphy [ˈpɒlɪgrɑːfɪ] [po-li-gra-fi], s. Poligrafía, el arte de escribir usando muchas clases de cifras desconocidas y el arte de descifrarlas.

polyhedral, polyhedrous [ˌpɒlɪˈhiːdrəl] [po-li-hi-dral] [ˌpɒlɪˈhiːdrəs] [po-li-hi-dros], a. Poliedro, que tiene muchas superficies.

polyhedron [ˌpɒlɪˈhiːdrən] [po-li-hi-dron], s. Poliedro, cuerpo sólido de muchas superficies planas.

polymer [ˈpɒlɪməʳ] [po-li-maʳ], s. Polímero.

polymer chemistry [ˈpɒlɪməˌtʃemɪstrɪ] [po-li-ma-che-mistri], s. Química de polímeros.

polymeric ['pɒlɪmərɪk] [po-li-me-rik], *a.* *(Quím.)* Polímero, que contiene los mismo elementos y en la misma cantidad relativa, pero cuyo peso molecular es diferente.

polymerization [,pɒlɪmərar'zeʃən] [po-li-me-rai-sei-shon], *s.* Polimerización.

polymerize ['pɒlɪmərarz] [po-li-me-rais], *va.* Polimerizar.

polymorph ['pɒlɪmɔːf] [po-li-morf], *s.* 1. *(Quím.)* Substancia que posee o presenta el polimorfismo. 2. Ser u organismo polimorfo.

polymorphism [,pɒlɪ'mɔːfɪzəm] [po-li-mor-fi-sem], *s.* Polimorfismo.

polymorphic [,pɒlɪ'mɔːfɪk] [po-li-mor-fik], *a.* Polimorfo.

polynesian [,pɒlɪ'niːzɪən] [po-li-ni-shan], *a.* Polinesiano o polinesio, perteneciétne a la Polinesia.

polynomial [,pɒlɪ'nəʊmɪəl] [po-li-nou-mial], *a.* De varios términos. -*s.* (**Syn.** POLYNOME). 1. Polinomio, cantidad algebraica que contiene varios términos. 2. Vocablo científico que consta de más de tres palabras.

polyp ['pɒlɪp] [po-lip], *s.* *(Zool.)* Pólipo, animalillo gelatinoso, particularmente cuando es compuesto; zóofito.

polypary ['pɒlɪpærɪ] [po-li-pa-ri], *s.* Polípero, formación calcárea o córnea, hecha por varios zoófitos; zoófito compuesto.

polypetalous [,pɒlɪ'petələs] [po-li-pe-ta-los], *a.* Polipétalo, de muchas hojas o pétalos.

polyphonic [,pɒlɪ'fɒnɪk] [po-li-fo-nik], *a.* Polifónico.

polypody ['pɒlɪpɒdɪ] [po-li-po-di], *s.* *(Bot.)* Polipo, planta.

polypus ['pɒlɪpəs] [po-li-pus], *s.* 1. Pólipo, especie de zoófito. V. POLYP. 2. Pólipo, especie de tumor blando.

polystyrene [,pɒlɪ'staɪriːn] [po-li-stai-rin], *s.* Poliestireno.

polysyllabic, [,pɒlɪsɪ'læbɪk] [po-li-si-la-bik], *a.* Polisílabo, polisilábico, que consta de más de tres sílabas.

polysyllable ['pɒlɪsɪlæbl] [po-li-si-la-bol], *s.* Polisílabo, la voz que consta de muchas sílabas, particularmente de más de tres.

polytechnic ['pɒlɪsɪteknɪk] [po-li-tek-nik], *a.* Politécnico, que abraza o practica muchas artes. -*s.* 1. Escuela politécnica, en que se enseñan las artes industriales. 2. Exhibición industrial.

polytheism ['pɒlɪθiːzəm] [po-li-zi-isem], *s.* Politeísmo, la doctrina que enseña que hay más de un Dios.

polytheist ['pɒlɪθiːɪst] [po-li-ziist], *s.* Politeísta, el que admite muchos dioses.

polytheistic, polytheistical [,pɒlɪθiː'ɪstɪk] [po-li-zi-is-tik], *a.* Politeísta, perteneciente o relativo al politeísmo, o que lo profesa.

polyurethane [,pɒlɪ'jʊərɪθeɪn] [po-li-iua-ri-zein], *s.* Poliuretano.

polyvalent [pə'lɪvələnt] [po-li-va-lant], *a.* Polivalente.

polyvinyl ['pɒlɪvaɪnɪl] [po-li-vai-nil], *a.* Polivinílico.

pom ['pɒm] [pom], *s.* Lulú de Pomerania (dog.).

pomace ['pɒmeɪs] [po-meis], *s.* El desecho de manzanas después de sacar la sidra.

pomaceous [pɒ'meɪʃəs] [po-mei-shos], *a.* 1. Pomáceo, relativo a las pomas o manzanas, o hecho de ellas. 2. *(Bot.)* Pomáceo, relativo a un pomo, o fruta de pipa, o a los árboles de las rosáceas que producen pomos.

pomade ['pɒmeɪd] [po-meid], *s.* Pomada, especie de ungüento hecho de varios ingredientes olorosos.

pomander [pəʊ'mændər] [pou-man-da'], *s.* *(Ant.)* Bola o poma olorosa.

pome [pəʊm] [poum], *s.* Pomo, cualquier fruta de pipa; pericarpio carnoso de muchas celdillas en que se hallan las pepitas; como la manzana, el membrillo y la pera.

pomegranate ['pɒməgrænɪt] [po-ma-gra-nit], *s.* 1. *(Bot.)* Granado, el árbol que produce la granada. 2. Granada, la fruta del granado.

pomiferous [pɒ'mɪfərəs] [po-mi-fe-ros], *a.* Pomífero, que produce pomas o manzanas.

pommel ['pʌml] [pa-mel], *s.* 1. Pomo del arzón de una silla; pomo de la empuñadura de una espada, o de la culata de un

cañón. 2. *(Arq.)* Perilla, bolilla, bala redonda. **Pommel of a sword,** pomo de una espada. **Pommel of a saddle,** pomo del arzón de la silla.

pommel, *va.* Cascar, dar a uno golpes hasta hacerle cardenales.

pommy ['pɒmɪ] [po-mi], *s.* *(Pej.)* Inglés (from Australia).

pomp ['pɒmp] [pomp], *s.* Pompa, fausto, vanidad, grandeza, esplendor.

pompeian ['pɒmpeɪɪən] [pom-peian], *a.* Pompeyano, relativo a la ciudad de Pompeya.

pompom ['pɒmpəm] [pom-pom], *s.* Pompón.

pomposity ['pɒmpəsɪtɪ] [pom-po-si-ti], *s.* Fausto, pompa, ostentación; afectación en el lenguaje o los modales.

pompous ['pɒmpəs] [pom-pos], *a.* Pomposo, ostentoso (ostentatious).

pompously ['pɒmpəslɪ] [pom-pos-li], *adv.* Pomposamente, magníficamente.

pompousness ['pɒmpəsnɪs] [pom-pos-nes], *s.* Esplendor artificioso, pompa.

poncho ['pɒntʃəʊ] [pon-chou], *s.* Poncho, prenda de vestir.

pond [pɒnd] [pond], *s.* Estanque de agua, pantano, laguna pequeña (pool). **Horse-pond,** abrevadero. **Fish-pond,** pecina, vivero, nansa. **Mill-pond,** represa de molino. **Pond-snail,** limnea, molusco gasterópodo.

ponder ['pɒndər] [pon-da'], *va.* Ponderar, pesar, examinar con madurez. **To ponder on,** considerar, reflexionar.

ponderable ['pɒndərəbl] [pon-da-ra-bol], *a.* Ponderable, que se puede pesar.

ponderosity [,pɒndə'rɒsɪtɪ] [pon-de-ro-si-ti], *s.* 1. Ponderosidad, peso, gravedad (gravity, weight). 2. Pesadez, languidez, falta de animación, de viveza (lassitude); verbosidad. 3. Cosa de peso o de importancia.

ponderous ['pɒndərəs] [pon-de-ros], *a.* 1. Ponderoso, pesado. 2. Importante, lo que es de importancia. 3. Impulsivo, lo que impele a la ejecución de algo.

ponderously ['pɒndərəslɪ] [pon-de-ros-li], *adv.* Pesadamente.

ponderousness ['pɒndərəsnɪs] [pon-de-ros-nes[, *s.* Ponderosidad, pesadez, peso.

pondweed ['pɒndwiːd] [pond-uid], *s.* *(Bot.)* Potamogeton, planta acuática.

pong ['pɒŋ] [pong], *s.* Hedor, peste, tufo.

pongee ['pɒndʒiː] [pon-yii], *s.* Variedad de tela de seda cruda.

poniard ['pɒnɪəd] [po-niard], *s.* Puñal.

poniard, *va.* Herir con puñal, dar puñaladas.

pontage ['pɒntɪdʒ] [pon-tich], *s.* Pontazgo, pontaje, el derecho que se paga por pasar los puentes y que se destina a repararlos.

pontee ['pɒntʒiː] [pon-tii], *s.* V. PONTIL.

pontiff ['pɒntɪf] [pon-tif], *s.* Pontífice, el Papa.

pontifical [pɒn'tɪfɪkəl] [pon-ti-fi-kal], *a.* 1. Pontifical, perteneciente al sumo pontífice y a los obispos y arzobispos; pontificio, perteneciente al pontífice. 2. Que toca y pertenece a los jefes del sacerdocio de cualquier religión. 3. *(Des.)* El que edifica puentes.

pontifical, *s.* 1. Pontifical, el libro de ceremonias pontificias y de las funciones episcopales. 2. *pl.* Pontificales, el conjunto o agregado de los ornamentos que sirven al obispo para la celebración de los oficios divinos.

pontifically [pɒn'tɪfɪkəlɪ] [pon-ti-fi-ka-li], *adv.* Pontificalmente, según la práctica y estilo de los obispos o pontífices.

pontificate [pɒn'tɪfɪkeɪt] [pon-ti-fi-keit], *s.* Pontificado, papado, la dignidad de pontífice y el tiempo que el pontífice goza de esta dignidad.

pontil ['pɒntɪl] [pon-til], *s.* **ponty** ['pɒntɪ] [pon-ti], *s.* Pontil, varilla de hierro a propósito para fabricar sopletes de vidrio.

pontoon, ponton [pɒn'tuːn] [pon-tun], *s.* 1. Pontón, barco chato y estrecho que sirve para pasar ríos y construir puentes. 2. *(Mar.)* Chata, barco chato provisto de pescantes, etc. V. LIGHTER. 3. Cajón o cilindro impermeable que se emplea para poner a flote una embarcación sumergida.

Pontoon bridge, puente de barcas, pontón flotante. 4. *(Aer.)* Flotador de hidroavión.

pony ['pɒnɪ] [po-ni], *s.* 1. Haca, jaco, caballo que no llega a la marca. 2. Entre colegiales, traducción que se emplea en la preparación de las lecciones. 3. Vaso muy pequeño para licor.

poodly ['puːdlɪ] [pud-li], *s.* Perro de lanas.

pooh ['puː] [pu], **inter.** ¡Bah! ¡ah! (interjección de desdén.

pooh-pooh [puːˈpuː] [pu-pu], *va.* y *vn.* Rechazar, con desprecio; burlar, mofar; hablar con desprecio.

pool [puːl] [pul], *va.* Formar una polla, hucha, un fondo o capital común que ha de dividirse seegún lo convenido. **Pool your issues,** reconciliar las diferencias de opinión, ponerse de acuerdo sobre asuntos controvertidos. *-vn.* Formar un charco.

pool, *s.* 1. Charco. 2. Charca. 3. Hoya (of river). 4. Piscina. 5. Billar, trucos. 6. Yacimiento (of petroleum). **Pool reactor,** reactor nuclear sumergido. **Pool table,** billar, mesa de trucos.

pool, *s.* 1. Polla, nombre que se da en algunos juegos de naipes al dinero que se juega. 2. Combinación para especular en fondos o valores públicos. 3. Combinación de sociedades de compañías de ferrocarriles, etc., para fijar de acuerdo los precios o cotizaciones y para dividirse las ganancias propocionalmente.

poop [puːp] [pup], *s. (Mar.)* Popa o toldilla. **Poop-royal,** *(Mar.)* chopeta.

poop, *va.* Dar o embestir por la popa; se dice del mar o de otra embarcación.

poor [puəʳ] [puaʳ], *a.* 1. Pobre, necesitado, menesteroso, mendigo (miserable). 2. Pobre, escaso, que no es completo o carece de algo. 3. Pobre, humilde, abatido, de poco valor, de poco mérito. 4. Pobre, infeliz, desdichado, desgraciado (unhappy). 5. Tacaño, miserable (mean). 6. Pobre, inútil, lo que para nada sirve. 7. Estéril, seco (dry). 8. Falto de vigor, indispuesto, malo, enfermizo (ill). 9. *(Fam.)* Flaco, seco, enjuto de carnes. 10. Despreciativo, que desprecia; malo. **A poor horse,** un penco, un caballo de poco valor, que para nada sirve. **A poor opinion of one,** mala o despreciativa opinión de alguien. **A poor night,** una mala o incómoda noche. **Poor thing,** pobrecito, pobrecillo. *-s.* Los pobres. **Poor-john,** merluza salada.

poorly ['puəlɪ] [pua-li], *adv.* Pobremente, infelizmente, abatidamente. *-a. (Fam.)* Ligeramente enfermo. **I am poorly,** estoy malo, no me siento bien. **He is very poorly,** está bastante malo.

poorness ['puənɪs] [pua-nes], *s.* 1. Pobreza, necesidad, estrechez, miseria; carestía. 2. Pobreza, escasez o cortedad de ánimo o de otras prendas del alma. 3. Pobreza, esterilidad, falta o escasez de alguna cosa.

poor-spirited ['puəˈspɪrɪtɪd] [pur-aspi-ri-tid], *a.* Abatido, bajo, ruin, cobarde.

pop [pɒp] [pop], *s.* Chasquido, sonido ligero y repentino.

pop, *va.* 1. Meter o empujar de repente; ofrecer inopinadamente. 2. Hacer producir un sonido repentino y explosivo. *-vn.* Entrar o salir de sopetón; llegar, presentarse de repente. **To pop out** o **off,** huir precipitadamente, desaparecer repentinamente, evadir una dificultad. **To pop him off,** dejarle con la palabra en la boca. **To pop the question,** *(Fam.)* hacer una declaración de amor; pedir la mano de una mujer.

popcorn ['pɒpkɔːn] [pop-korn], *s.* 1. Palomitas, rosetas de maíz reventado. 2. Maíz con que se hace lo anterior.

pope ['pəʊp] [poup], *s.* 1. Papa, la cabeza suprema de la Iglesia católica romana. 2. Cualquier sacerdote de la Iglesia griega.

popedom ['pəʊpdɒm] [poup-dom], *s.* Papado, la dignidad de Papa.

popery ['pəʊpərɪ] [pou-pa-ri], *s.* Papismo, nombre que dan los protestantes a la religión católica romana; término despectivo.

pope's-eye ['pəʊpˈaɪ] [poups-ai], *s.* Nombre vulgar de una glándula situada en medio del muslo de un carnero o buey; estimada como buen bocado. **Pope's-head,** *(G.B.)* escobillón para limpiar bóvedas. **Pope's-nose,** obispillo o rabadilla de ave.

popgun ['pɒpgʌn] [pop-gan], *s.* Una escopetilla que arroja una bolita o un tapón de corcho con chasquido; *(Amer.)* cerbatana.

popinjay ['pɒpɪndʒeɪ] [po-pin-yei], *s.* 1. *(Orn.)* Loro, papagayo. 2. *(Orn.)* Pocamaderos. 3. Pisaverde, el mozuelo que presume de galán.

popish ['pəʊpɪʃ] [pou-pish], *a.* Papal, papista, perteneciente al Papa o a la Iglesia católica romana.

popishly ['pəʊpɪʃlɪ] [pou-pish-li], *adv.* A la manera de los papistas o católicos; papalmente, pontificalmente.

poplar ['pɒpləʳ] [pop-laʳ], *s. (Bot.)* Álamo o chopo temblón, cualquier árbol del género Populus, particularmente el álamo blanco, y el de Italia. **White o silver poplar,** álamo blanco. **Lombardy poplar,** álamo de Italia. **Black poplar,** álamo negro, chopo.

poplin ['pɒplɪn] [po-plin], *s.* Popelín, popelina, tela listada.

popper ['pɒpəʳ] [po-paʳ], *s.* 1. Lo que produce chasquido; arma de fuego. 2. Tostador de maíz.

poppet ['pɒpɪt] [po-pit], *s.* 1. V. PUPPET. 2. Válvula de huso. 3. *(Mar.)* Columna de basada, puntal grueso que se apoya contra el fondo del buque que se va a echar al mar.

poppy ['pɒpɪ] [po-pi], *s. (Bot.)* Adormidera, amapola. **California poppy,** amapola de California.

poppycock ['pɒpɪkɒk] [po-pi-kok], *s. (Ger. E.U.)* Tontería presumida, majadería.

poppy-head ['pɒpɪhed] [po-pi-jed], *s.* Cabeza de adormidera.

populace ['pɒpjʊlɪs] [po-piu-lis], *s.* Populacho, la plebe, el cuerpo principal de la plebe, el cuerpo principal del pueblo; a menudo en sentido despectivo, el pueblo bajo, gentuza.

popular ['pɒpjʊləʳ] [po-piu-laʳ], *a.* 1. Popular, perteneciente al pueblo o a la plebe. 2. Popular, amado del pueblo. 3. Popular, lo que es común en el pueblo, o entre el populacho. **Popular applause,** aura popular. **By popular request,** a petición del público.

popularity [ˌpɒpjʊˈlærɪtɪ] [po-piu-la-ri-ti], *s.* Popularidad, la aceptación y aplauso de que uno goza entre el pueblo. **Your TV program is growing in popularity,** tu programa de televisión tiene una popularidad cada vez mayor.

popularize [ˌpɒpjʊləraɪz] [po-piu-la-rais], *va.* Popularizar, propagar entre el pueblo, acreditar a una persona o cosa en el concepto público.

popularly ['pɒpjʊləlɪ] [po-piu-lar-li], *adv.* Popularmente. **Popularly known as,** popularmente conocido como.

populate ['pɒpjʊleɪt] [po-piu-leit], *vn.* Poblar, multiplicar.

population [ˌpɒpjʊˈleɪʃən] [po-piu-lei-shon], *s.* 1. Población, el número total de habitantes de un lugar o una extension dada de territorio. 2. Población, acción de poblar, de proveer de habitantes, de multiplicarlos. **Population explosion,** explosión demográfica.

populism ['pɒpjʊlɪzəm] [po-piu-li-sem], *s.* Populismo.

populist ['pɒpjʊlɪst] [po-piu-list], *a.* Populista.

populous ['pɒpjʊləs] [po-piu-los], *a.* Populoso.

populously ['pɒpjʊ ↓əslɪ] [po-piu-los-li], *adv.* Con mucha gente.

populousness ['pɒpjʊləsnɪs] [po-piu-los-nes], *s.* La abundancia de población; población, el estado de cualquier país en cuanto al número de sus habitantes.

porcate ['pɔːkeɪt] [por-keit], *a.* Surcado; con surcos longitudinales.

porcelain ['pɔːslɪn] [pors-lin], *s.* Porcelana, china, loza fina y translúcida.

porch ['pɔːtʃ] [porch], *s.* Pórtico, vestíbulo, entrada, portal.

porcine ['pɔːsaɪn] [por-sain], *a.* Porcino, propio del puerco.

porcupine ['pɔːkjʊpaɪn] [por-kiu-pain], *s.* Puerco espín, erizo grande, animal roedor.

pore [pɔːʳ] [poʳ], *s.* Poro.

pore, *vn.* Ojear, mirar con atención, tener los ojos fijos en algo.

poriness ['pɔːrɪnɪs] [po-ri-nes], *s.* Porosidad.

pork [pɔːk] [pork], *s.* 1. Carne de puerco. **Fresh pork,** tocino fresco. **Salt pork,** tocino salado. 2. *(Ant.)* Cochino, puerco, cerdo. **Pork-chop,** chuleta, costilla de cerdo. **Corned pork,** carne de puerco salada.

porker ['pɔːkəʳ] [por-ka'], *s.* Puerco, cochino, cerdo, marrano.

pornographic [,pɔːnə'græfɪk] [por-no-gra-fik], *a.* Pornográfico, obsceno.

pornography [pɔː'nɒgrəfɪ] [por-no-gra-fi], *s.* Pornografía, obscenidad.

porosity [pɔː'rɒsɪtɪ] [po-ro-si-ti], **porousness** ['pɔːrəsnɪs] [po-ros-nes], *s.* 1. Porosidad, la propiedad o calidad de poroso. 2. Poro.

porous ['pɔːrəs] [po-ros], *a.* Poroso.

porpoise, porpus ['pɔːpəs] [por-pos], *s.* 1. Puerco marino o marsopa, cetáceo del género Phocæna; tiene unos cinco pies de longitud. 2. Marsuino, cetáceo pequeño, particularmente del género delfín.

porraceous [pɔː'reɪʃəs] [po-rei-shos], *a.* Verdoso.

porridge ['pɔːrɪdʒ] [po-rich], *s.* 1. Gachas, puches, alimento hecho con harina cocida en agua o leche hasta que tome consistencia. 2. Potaje, caldo o guisado de legumbres. **Milk-porriage,** sopa de leche. **Porridge-dish,** sopera.

porridge-pot ['pɔːrɪdʒpɒt] [po-rich-pot], *s.* Marmita, cazuela.

porringer ['pɔːrɪdʒəʳ] [po-rin-ya'], *s.* Escudilla, vasija algo ligera que tiene los lados verticales y algunas veces asas.

port [pɔːt] [port], *s.* 1. Puerto; lugar de entrada y salida para las embarcaciones. **To touch at a port,** hacer escala. **Free port,** puerto franco o libre de derechos. **Bar-port,** puerto con barra. **Close-port,** puerto cerrado. **To leave port,** zarpar. 2. Porta, portañola, ventanilla; abertura en el costado de un buque, sea para una cañón o para dar luz y aire. *V.* PORT-HOLE. **Ballast-ports,** portas de alastrar. **Port-sill,** batiporte, batiente. **Light-ports,** ventanillas. **Port-tackle,** aparejuelo de las portas. 3. Puerta. 4. *(Mec.)* Porta, orificio para el paso de un fluido motor. 5. *(Mar.)* Babor. **Hard a port,** a babor todo. **The ship heels to port,** el buque cae sobre babor. 6. Porte, presencia, continente, aire o garbo de una persona. 7. Vino de Oporto. 8. Porte, la capacidad de la nave para el transporte. **Port-fire,** lanzafuego, botafuego.

port, *va. y vn.* 1. Poner, o andar a babor. 2. *(Mil.)* Llevar un fusil diagonalmente con relación al cuerpo. **Port the helm,** a babor el timón.

portable ['pɔːtəbl] [por-ta-bol], *a.* 1. Manual, portátil. **Portable typewriter,** máquina de escribir portátil. 2. Sufrible, llevadero.

portableness ['pɔːtəblnɪs] [por-ta-bol-nes], *s.* La propiedad de ser manual, portátil o llevadero.

portage ['pɔːtɪdʒ] [por-tich], *s.* 1. Porte, lo que se paga por llevar alguna cosa de un lugar a otro. 2. Conducción, transporte, acarreo, porte de barquichuelos y víveres desde un cuerpo navegable de agua a otro. 3. Carga, cargazón, lo que se transporta o lleva.

portal ['pɔːtl] [por-tal], *s. (Arq.)* 1. Portal, portada, particularmente si es grande e imponente. 2. Construcción arquitectónica que incluye las entradas y portadas de una gran iglesia, etc.

portcullis [pɔːt'kʌlɪs] [port-ka-lis], *s. (Fort.)* Rastrillo formado por una reja fuerte y tupida, que se sube y baja.

portend [pɔː'tend] [por-tend], *va.* Pronosticar, anunciar o indicar un acontecimiento que está para suceder (predict); presagiar (presage).

portent [pɔː'tent] [por-tent], *s.* Portento, señal que indica lo que va a suceder, y particularmente prodigio que trae consigo señales de mal agüero.

portentous [pɔː'tentəs] [por-ten-tos], *a.* 1. Portentoso, ominoso, azaroso, de mal agüero. 2. Prodigioso, portentoso, monstruoso, espantoso; que causa pasmo o terror.

porter ['pɔːtəʳ] [por-ta'], *s.* 1. Portador, porteador, el que lleva o trae de una parte a otra; mozo de cordel, mandadero. 2. Portero. **Porter's lodge,** portería. 3. Portador, cualquier cosa que se usa para llevar. 4. Una especie de cerveza fuerte de color pardo que posee propiedades tónicas.

porterage ['pɔːtərɪdʒ] [por-ta-rich], *s.* 1. Empleo u oficio de un pozo de cordel. 2. Porte, porteo, precio de transporte que se paga a un mozo de cordel.

porterhouse ['pɔːtəhaʊs] [por-ta-jaus], *s.* Mesón.

portfolio [pɔː'fəʊlɪəʊ] [port-fou-liou], *s.* 1. Cartera, bolsa en que se guardan materiales de escribir, dibujos, grabados, etc. 2. *(Fig.)* Cartera, oficio de un ministro de Estado.

port-hole ['pɔːthəʊl] [port-joul], *s.* Ventanilla abierta en el costado de un buque para dar luz y aire; porta, portañola, tronera.

portico ['pɔːtɪkəʊ] [por-ti-kou], *s.* Pórtico, especie de portal cubierto y fundado sobre columnas, que se construye a la entrada de un edificio; soportal, atrio.

porticoed ['pɔːtɪkəʊd] [por-ti-koud], *a.* Provisto de pórtico, o de pórticos.

portion ['pɔːʃən] [por-shon], *s.* 1. Porción, parte (part). 2. Cuota, parte fija y determinada (amount). 3. La parte de herencia que pertenece a cada uno de los hijos en los bienes que quedaron de sus padres. 4. Dote, la hacienda que lleva la mujer cuando se casa.

portion, *va.* 1. Partir, dividir, repartir, distribuir, asignar una parte (divide, share). 2. Dotar. **Portion out,** repartir.

portioner ['pɔːʃənəʳ] [por-sho-na'], *s.* Repartidor.

portionless ['pɔːʃənlɪs] [por-shon-les], *a.* Sin porción, y particularmente, sin dote.

portliness ['pɔːtlɪnɪs] [port-li-nes], *s.* Porte majestuoso, aire de dignidad de una persona.

portly ['pɔːtlɪ] [port-li], *a.* 1. Corpulento, rollizo, gordiflón, algo grueso. 2. Majestuoso, serio, grave.

portman ['pɔːtmən] [port-man], *s.* Habitante de alguno de los cinco puertos del canal de Inglaterra.

portmanteau [pɔːt'mæntəʊ] [port-man-tou], *s.* Portamanteo, maleta ligera.

portrait ['pɔːtreɪt] [por-treit], *s.* Retrato, pintura, efigie o fotografía que representa la imagen de alguna persona; figuradamente, descripción exacta de una persona. **I will paint your portrait,** te retrataré. **Portrait-painter,** retratista.

portraiture ['pɔːtreɪtʃəʳ] [por-trei-cha'], *s.* 1. Retrato, pintura, imagen. 2. Bosquejo. 2. Representación de un objeto.

portray [pɔː'treɪ] [por-trei], *va.* Retratar, formar la imagen de alguna cosa; representar natural y vivamente, ya dibujando, pintando, esculpiendo, o describiendo con palabras; pintar, hacer un retrato.

portrayal [pɔː'treɪəl] [por-treial], *s.* Representación, delineación, retrato. *(Teat.)* Interpretación.

portress [pɔː'trɪs] [por-tris], *sf.* Portera.

portuguese [,pɔːtjʊ'giːz] [por-tiu-guis], *a.* Portugués, de Portugal. *-s.* 1. Portugués, portuguesa, habitante de Portugal. 2. Portugués, idioma de Portugal. **Portuguese man-of-war,** fisalia, acalefo de los mares tropicales.

pose [pəʊz] [pous], *va.* 1. Tomar o hacer tomar una actitud; poner o colocar en cierta actitud o postura, como hace un pintor o escultor. 2. Proponer, afirmar una proposición. *-vn.* Ponerse o colocarse en actitud o postura dadas.

pose, *va.* Parar, confundir, dejar a uno parado sin que sepa qué hacerse; acorralar a uno o dejarle sin salida o respuesta.

pose, *s.* Postura, posición del cuerpo entero, o de una parte de él; particularmente, actitud o postura que ha de reproducirse en un retrato o estatua.

poser ['pəʊzəʳ] [pou-sa'], *s.* 1. Cuestión o problema difícil; argumento perentorio que reduce al silencio. 2. En algunas escuelas inglesas, examinador.

poseur [pəʊ'zɜːʳ] [pou-she'], *s.* **Your friend is a real poseur,** tu amigo es pura pose, es muy afectado.

posh [pɒʃ] [posh], *a. (Fam.)* Elegante, pijo.

posit ['pɒzɪt] [po-sit], *va.* 1. En lógica, afirmar, proponer como principio hecho. 2. Disponer, colocar, poner con relación a otros cuerpos.

position [pə'zɪʃən] [po-si-shon], *s.* 1. Posición, el modo en que está colocada alguna cosa; postura, situación. 2. Postura, actitud, disposición de las partes del cuerpo. 3.

Esfera o radio de influencia, trabajo, o deber; situación elevada. 4. El acto de afirmar un principio o proposición; proposición, aserto. 5. *(Mat.)* Procedimiento para hallar el valor de una cantidad no conocida asumiendo una o más hipótesis; regla de falsa posición. *-vt.* Colocar, poner. **She positioned herself between her sister and her aunt,** se colocó entre su hermana y su tía.

positional [pəˈzɪʃənl] [po-si-sho-nal], *a.* Perteneciente a la posición, postura o situación de una cosa.

positive [ˈpɒzɪtɪv] [po-si-tiv], *a.* 1. Positivo, real, verdadero (true); que existe; opuesto a negativo. 2. Absoluto, que no tiene relación con otra cosa (absolute); inherente; opuesto a relativo. 3. Explícito, preciso, enfático; opuesto a implicado. 4. Prescrito por autoridad competente; imperativo (opuesto a discrecionar); expreso, escrito, dependiente de autoridad, convenido (opuesto a natural). 5. Cierto, seguro, asegurado (sure). **Are you positive?,** ¿está seguro? 6. Terco, porfiado. 7. Primario, principal (opuesto a negativo); que lleva el signo de más ɔ, mayor que cero. 8. Positiva; se dice de la electricidad que tiene una potencia relativamente alta. 9. *(Fotog.)* Positivo, que tiene las luces y las sombras en su relación natural en vez de invertidas. 10. *(Gram.)* Positivo, del grado positivo. *-s.* 1. Afirmación, lo que es cierto. 2. Lo positivo, lo que se puede conocer por los sentidos. 3. Ley absoluta, imperativa. 4. Prueba positiva, cuadro que presenta las luces y sombras como en la naturaleza. 5. *(Gram.)* Grado positivo de comparación. 6. *(Elec.)* Plancha, polo, etc., positivos.

positively [ˈpɒzɪtɪvlɪ] [po-si-tiv-li], *adv.* Positivamente, absolutamente; perentoriamente.

positiveness [ˈpɒzɪtɪvnɪs] [po-si-tiv-nes], **positivity** [ˈpɒzɪtɪvɪtɪ] [po-si-ti-vi-ti], *s.* 1. El estado de lo que es positivo o absoluto. 2. Porfia, terquedad, obstinación, contumacia.

positivism [ˈpɒzɪtɪvɪzəm] [po-si-ti-vi-sem], *s.* 1. Positivismo, calidad de atenerse a lo positivo. 2. Positivismo, sistema de filosofía que sólo admite lo evidente o claramente demostrado. 3. Certeza, o la aserción de la certeza, en el conocimiento.

positivist [ˈpɒzɪtɪvɪst] [po-si-ti-vist], *s.* Positivista, partidario del sistema filosófico del positivismo.

positron [ˈpɒzɪˌtrɒn] [po-si-tron], *s.* *(Elec.)* Positrón.

posse [ˈpɒsɪ] [po-si], *s.* 1. Posibilidad. 2. *V.* POSSE COMITATUS. 3. *(Vulg.)* Gentío.

possess [pəˈzes] [po-ses], *va.* 1. Poseer, gozar, tener en su poder (have). 2. Tomar, apoderarse, hacerse dueño de algo. 3. Señorear, dominar (rule over). 4. Hacer adquirir o poner en posesión a uno de lo que no tiene. 5. Tener a uno poseído o poseso algún espíritu infernal.

possessed [pəˈzest] [po-sest], *pp.* Poseso, poseído. **One possessed,** energúmeno.

possession [pəˈzeʃən] [po-se-shon], *s.* 1. Posesión, el acto de poseer y la misma cosa poseída. **To take possession,** tomar posesión. 2. Propiedad, riquezas, bienes. 3. *(Occult.)* Posesión, el estado del poseso o poseído, del que se halla bajo la influencia d el demonio.

possessive [pəˈzesɪv] [po-se-siv], *a.* Posesivo; poseyente; que denota posesión. **Possessive case,** caso posesivo en la gramática inglesa, que corresponde al caso genitivo. Su signo es el apóstrofo (').

possessor [pəˈzesər] [po-se-sar], *s.* Poseedor, el que tiene la posesión de alguna cosa.

posset [pəˈzet] [po-set], *s.* Leche cortada con vino o con un ácido, azucarada, mezclada con especias y a menudo espesada con pan.

possibility [ˌpɒsəˈbɪlɪtɪ] [po-sa-bi-li-ti], *s.* Posibilidad, lo posible; cosa posible, contingencia.

possible [ˈpɒsəbl] [po-si-bol], *a.* Posible. **It's possible that he loves you,** es posible que él te quiera. **As little as possible,** lo menos posible. *-s.* **The possible,** lo posible (what can be done).

possibly [ˈpɒsəblɪ] [po-si-bli], *adv.* 1. Posiblemente. 2. Quizá, quizás, acaso, por ventura (may be). **This is possibly true,** esto es probablemente verdadero.

possum [ˈpɒsəm] [po-som], *s.* *(Fam.)* *V.* OPOSSUM. **To play possum,** desatenderse, no hacer caso.

post [pəʊst] [poust], *s.* 1. Posta, correo, estafeta, el sistema de transportar la correspondencia ordinaria. 2. Propio, mensajero que se envía con alguna carta de una parte a otra. 3. Puesto, paraje señalado para las operaciones militares. 4. Puesto, empleo, dignidad (employment). 5. Poste, un pilar de piedra o madera. 6. Situación, asiento (sit). 7. Especie, tamaño del papel de escribir. **To travel by post,** correr la posta o ir en posta. **Foot-post,** propio, correo de a pie. **Penny post,** cartero, el que reparte por las casas las cartas del correo. **To be fossed from pillar to post,** andar de Herodes a Pilatos. **I took my post,** tomé mi puesto, fui a mi puesto. **By return of post,** a vuelta de correo. *-a.* Sobornado, ganado para cometer una acción ruin. *(Ant.)* Pronto rápido. **Postboy,** postillón. **Post-chaise, post-coach,** silla o coche de posta. **Post-house,** casa de postas donde se tienen y cuidan los caballos de posta. **Post-card,** *V.* **Postal-card. Post-note.** *V.* **Postal note. Post-road,** camino de posta o correo. **Post-town,** el pueblo donde hay administración de correos.

post, *adv.* Con rapidez, por la posta, de prisa.

post, *vn.* Ir en posta o correr la posta. *-va.* 1. Apostar, situar, colocar en algún puesto o sitio; dar aviso en un lugar público; hacer saber; anunciar. 2. Cartelear, poner carteles infamatorios. 3. Echar al correo o a la estafeta. 4. *(Com.)* Pasar los asientos de un libro al libro mayor; hacer los asientos de las operaciones mercantiles. 5. *(Fam.)* Informar, dar a entender, proveer de informes.

postage [ˈpəʊstɪdʒ] [pous-tich], *s.* Porte de correos, precio fijo para el transporte de correos. **Postage-stamp,** sello de correos, sello de franqueo. *(Amer.)* Estampilla. **Postage meter,** medidor de franqueo.

postal [ˈpəʊstəl] [pous-tal], *a.* Postal, perteneciente al correo o a las cartas. **Postal box,** buzón. **Postal-card,** tarjeta postal. **Postal convention,** convenio postal entre dos países. **Postal note,** billete de correo, pagadero al portador, por una suma menor de cinco pesos. **Postal order,** *(Brit.)* orden postal, billete semejante al anterior, pero cuyo importe está impreso en el mismo documento.

postdate [ˈpəʊstˈdeit] [poust-deit], *va.* Posfechar, poner fecha posterior a la verdadera, diferir.

postdate, *s.* Posfecha, fecha posterior a la verdadera.

poster [ˈpəʊstər] [pous-tar], *s.* 1. Cartel. 2. Colocador o fijador de carteles. 3. Correo; el que viaja en posta o de prisa.

posterior [pɒsˈtɪərɪər] [pos-tia-rio], *a.* Posterior, trasero, que está detrás o viene después. **Posteriors,** nalgas, partes posteriores.

posterity [pɒsˈterɪtɪ] [pos-te-ri-ti], *s.* Posteridad, la raza, prole que proviene del mismo ascendiente; descendientes, hijos; también la descendencia o generación venidera.

postern [ˈpəʊstɜːn] [pous-tern], *s.* 1. Puerta trasera, entrada particular; puerta pequeña, postigo. 2. *(Fort.)* Postigo, poterna.

postgraduate [ˈpəʊstˈgrædjɔɪt] [poust-gra-dueit], *s.* y *a.* Posgraduado.

posthaste [ˈpəʊstˈheist] [poust-jeist], *a.* Hecho a toda prisa, como la del correo. *-s.* Diligencia, presteza en ir y venir, como la del correo. *-adv.* Inmediatamente, con presteza.

posthumous [ˈpɒstjʊməs] [pos-tiu-mos], *a.* 1. Póstumo, nacido después de la muerte del padre; algunas veces extraído del cadáver de la madre. 2. Póstumo, publicado después de la muerte del autor.

posthumously [ˈpɒstjʊməslɪ] [pos-tiu-mos-li], *adv.* Póstumamente.

postil [ˈpɒstɪl] [pos-til], *s.* Postilla, apostilla, la glosa o nota breve puesta al margen de algún impreso o manuscrito, particularmente de la Sagrada Escritura.

postilion ['pɒstɪlɪən] [pos-ti-lion], *s.* 1. Delantero, sota, hablando de cocheros. 2. *(Des.)* Postillón el que guía una silla de posta y el mozo de posta.

posting ['pɒstɪŋ] [pos-tin], *s.* Destino.

postlude ['pɒstluːd] [post-lud], *s.* Postludio, pieza para el órgano que se toca después del oficio divino.

postman ['pəʊstmən] [post-man], *s.* Cartero; correo.

postmark ['pəʊstmaːk] [post-mark], *s.* Matasellos. *-vt.* matasellar.

postmaster ['pəʊstˌmaːstəʳ] [poust-mas-taʳ], *s.* Administrador de correos, director de correos. **Postmaster general,** director general de correos.

post-meridian ['pəʊstməˈriːdɪən] [poust-me-ri-dian], *a.* Postmeridiano, de la tarde; comúnmente se abrevia en P.M.

postmodern ['pəʊstˈmɒdən] [poust-mo-dern], *a.* Postmoderno.

postmortem ['pəʊstˈmɔːtəm] [poust-mor-tem], *adv. (Lat.)* Después de la muerte. **Post-mortem,** *s.* Necropsia, autopsia.

postnatal ['pəʊstˈneɪtl] [poust-nei-tal], *a.* Postnatal, de posparto.

post-nuptial ['pəʊstˈnʌpʃəl] [poust-nap-shal], *a.* Hecho o sucedido después del matrimonio.

post office ['pəʊstˌɒfɪs] [poust-o-fis], *s.* Casa de correos, correo. **Post-office box,** apartado postal o de correos. **Post-office branch,** estafeta, sucursal de correos.

postoperative [ˌpəʊstˈɒpərətɪv] [poust-o-pe-ra-tiv], *a.* Posoperatorio.

postpaid ['pəʊstˈpeɪd] [poust-peid], *a.* Franco, franco de porte; porte pagado.

postpone ['pəʊstˈpəʊn] [poust-poun], *va.* 1. Diferir, suspender. 2. Posponer, colocar alguna cosa en lugar inferior, apreciarla menos que otra, estimar menos que, tener en menos.

postponement ['pəʊstˈpəʊnmənt] [poust-poun-ment], *s.* Aplazamiento, postergación.

postscript ['pəʊsskrɪpt] [pous-skript], *s.* 1. Posdata, la cláusula o capítulo que se añade a la carta ya escrita. 2. (En los papeles públicos) Alcance.

postulant ['pɒstjʊlənt] [pos-tiu-lant], *s.* 1. Postulante, el que hace una petición. 2. Novicio, postulador que quiere hacerse sacerdote o religoso.

postulate ['pɒstjʊleɪt] [pos-tiu-leit], *va.* 1. Postular, pedir para prelado de una iglesia a un sujeto que según derecho no puede ser elegido. 2. Admitir una cosa sin pruebas.

postulate, *s.* 1. Postulado, principio tan claro que no necesita prueba ni demostración. 2. *(Mat.)* Admisión de un primer principio para establecer una demostración.

postulation [ˌpɒstjʊˈleɪʃən] [pos-tiu-lei-shon], *s.* 1. Postulación, el acto de postular. 2. Petición, instancia, súplica (request). 3. Suposición, que no necesita prueba, acción de suponer alguna cosa como verdadera, o un hecho.

posture ['pɒstʃəʳ] [pos-chaʳ], *s.* 1. Postura, modo de tener o poner el cuerpo. 2. Postura, pie, estado, disposición, la situación buena o mala en que uno se halla con respecto a sus negocios o fortuna.

posture, *va.* Colocar, poner alguna cosa en un paraje y postura particular.

postwar ['pəʊstˈwɔːʳ] [poust-uoʳ], *a.* De la posguerra. **The postwar years,** los años de la posguerra.

posy ['pəʊzɪ] [pou-si], *s.* 1. Ramillete de flores. 2. Mote o cifra en un anillo o en otra cosa, particularmente en versos. *(Abrev. de* **poesy.)**

pot [pɒt] [pot], *s.* 1. Marmita; olla (casserole); puchero; vaso más profundo que ancho (vase). **Pots and pans,** cacharros. 2. Pote, taza de metal para beber. 3. La cantidad contenida en una olla. 4. Apuesta, hucha, puesta, lo que se pone al juego (bet). 5. Mucho dinero, una gran suma. **Flower-pot,** tiesto. florero. **Melting-pot,** crisol. **To go to pot,** ir al crisol. estar arruinado, ir hacia la destrucción. **To keep the pot boiling,** (a) mantenerse en actividad; (b) procurar los medios de vivir. **Pot-companion,** compañero de taberna. **Pot-hanger,** llares. **Pot-herb,** hortaliza. **Pot-lid,** cobertera de olla, tapadera de

marmita. **Pot-luck,** comida ordinaria; equivale en castellano a la frase "hacer penitencia"; comer lo que haya en una casa donde no se esperaban convidados. **To take pot-luck,** hacer penitencia. **Pot-valiant,** valeroso a fuerza de beber licores fuerte; se dice del que es valiente sólo cuando está bebido.

pot, *va.* 1. Cocer en una olla o marmita. 2. Poner en tiestos con tierra. 3. Cerrar, preservar o conservar en marmitar para purgar o limpiar. 4. *(Ger.)* Procurar, buscar, como se hace en la caza. *-vn.* 1. Tirar (against). 2. Beber, achisparse (get drunk).

potable ['pəʊtəbl] [pou-ta-bol], *a.* Potable, que se puede beber.

potash ['pɒtæʃ] [po-tash], *s.* 1. Potasa, alcalí que se obtiene de las cenizas de los vegetales. 2. Potasio hidratado (KOH), cuerpo blanco, sólido, licuescente, muy alcalino y de propiedades cáusticas. **Potassium"[]",** *s.* Potasio, metal blanco descubierto por Humphry Davy en la potasa.

potations [pəˈteɪʃənz] [pou-tei-shons], *s.* Libaciones.

potato [pəˈteɪtəʊ] [po-tei-tou], *s.* Patata, papa. **Sweet o Spanish potato,** batata, o patata dulce o de Málaga. (Cuba) Boniato. *(Mex.)* Camote. **Potato-beetle, potato-bug,** dorífero. **Potato-blight, potato-rot,** enfermedad de las patatas.

potbellied ['pɒtˌbelɪd] [pot-be-lid], *a.* Panzudo, ventrudo, barrigudo.

potbelly [ˌpɒtˈbelɪ] [pot-be-li], *s.* Barrigón, barriga grande.

potboiler ['pɒtˌbɔɪləʳ] [pot-boi-laʳ], *s.* Libro, pintura, etc. hecho de prisa únicamente con propósitos pecuniarios.

potency ['pəʊtənsɪ] [pou-tan-si], *s.* Potencia, fuerza; poder, influjo, autoridad.

potent ['pəʊtənt] [pou-tant], *a.* 1. Potente, poderoso, fuerte (strong); que tiene fuerza física, vigor; que tiene fuerza moral, convincente. 2. Poderoso, eficaz, influyente, que ejerce gran autoridad (powerful).

potentate ['pəʊtənteɪt] [pou-tan-teit], *s.* Potentado.

potential [pəˈtenʃəl] [po-ten-shal], *a.* 1. Potencial, posible, existente en potencia, pero no real. 2. Virtual, capaz de existir, pero no existente todavía. 3. *(Fís.)* Potencia, existente por razón de su posición, en contraposición al movimiento; se dice de la energía. 4. *(Gram.)* Potencial, que indica la posibilidad o el poder. 5. Eficaz, potente, poderoso. *-s.* 1. Cosa posible o virtual. 2. *(Gram.)* El modo potencial. 3. Energía potencial, potencia motriz, fuerza capaz de poner en movimiento un cuerpo o una máquina. **Potential mode** (o **mood**), el modo como que se emplean los auxiliares **may, can, must, should, would,** con un infinitivo.

potentiality [pəˌtenʃɪˈælɪtɪ] [po-ten-shia-li-ti], *s.* Potencialidad, la mera capacidad de la potencia independiente del acto.

potentially [pəˈtenʃəlɪ] [po-ten-sha-li], *adv.* Potencialmente, virtualmente.

potently [pəˈtentlɪ] [po-ten-tli], *adv.* Potentemente, poderosamente.

potentness [pəˈtentnɪs] [po-tent-nes], *s.* Potencia, poder.

pother ['pɒðəʳ] [po-zaʳ], *s.* Baraúnda, alboroto, bullicio.

pother, *va. y vn.* Atormentar, fastidiar, molestar; alborotar sin substancia; poner en desorden.

potholder ['pɒthəʊldəʳ] [pot-joul-daʳ], *s.* Portaollas.

pothook ['pɒthuːk] [pot-juk], *s.* 1. Llares, aparato para suspender encima del fuego los calderos y marmitas. 2. Garabato, las letras o escritos mal formados.

potion ['pəʊʃən] [pou-shon], *s.* Poción, brebaje, pócima, bebida medicinal. **Love potion,** filtro de amor.

potpie ['pɒtpaɪ] [pot-pai], *s.* Torta o pastel de carne y verduras.

potpourri [pəʊˈpʊrɪ] [pou-pu-ri], *s.* Menjurjeo, menjunje, popurrí.

potsherd ['pɒtʃɜːd] [pot-sherd], *s.* Tiesto, casco, pedazo de una vasija de barro rota.

pot shot ['pɒtˌʃɒt] [pot-shot], *s.* Tiro o ataque a mansalva o que viola las reglas del deporte.

pottage ['pɒtɪdʒ] [po-tich], *s.* Potaje.

potted ['pɒtɪd] [po-tid], *a.* En maceta o tiesto. *(Fam.)* Borracho, cocido.

potter ['pɒtə'] [po-ta'], *s.* Alfarero. **Potter's clay,** arcilla, barro, tierra de alfareros. **Potter's ware,** alfarería, vasijas de barro.

pottery ['pɒtərɪ] [po-ta-ri], *s.* Alfarería o alfar, fábrica de vasijas de barro. 2. Alfarería, arte de construir vasijas de barro. 3. Efectos de alfarería, vajilla de barro.

pottle ['pɒtl] [po-tel], *s.* 1. Pote, jarro, vaso de beber (glass, jar). 2. Azumbre, medida líquida de cuatro cuartillos. 3. Cesta o cesto pequeño para frutas. **Pottle-bellied,** panzudo, barrigudo, corpulento.

potty ['pɒtɪ] [po-ti], *s. (Fam.)* Orinal para niños. *-a. (Fam.)* Chiflado, chalado.

pouch [paʊtʃ] [pauch], *s.* 1. Saco pequeño, bolsillo, faltriquera (pocket). 2. *(Zool.)* Bolsa, órgano semejante a un saco para contener huevos o hijuelos. 3. *(Bot.)* Silícula; cualquier bolsa o saquillo. **Mail-pouch,** valija del correo. **Tobacco pouch,** petaca.

pouch, *va.* 1. Embolsar, meter en el bolsillo. 2. Tragar o engullir. *-vn.* Hacer pucheritos. *(Amer.)* Jirimionear. *V.* To POUT.

poulp [pʌlp] [polp], *s.* Pulpo, molusco octópodo. *V.* OCTOPUS.

poulterer ['pəʊltərə'] [poul-ta-ra'], *s.* Polero, gallinero.

poultice ['pəʊltɪs] [poul-tis], *s.* Cataplasma, emplasto.

poultice, *va.* Poner una cataplasma.

poultry ['pəʊltrɪ] [poul-tri], *s.* Aves caseras o de corral colectivamente, como gallinas, capones, pollos, pavos, etc. **Poultry-yard.** el corral donde se crían las aves caseras.

pounce [paʊns] [pauns], *s.* 1. Acción de asir con las garras. 2. Garra del ave de rapiña. 3. Grasilla, goma sandáraca reducida a polvo. 4. Cisquero o muñequilla de carbón molido para estarcir algún dibujo; hoy día se llama **stamping-powder.**

pounce, *va.* 1. Horadar, agujerear. 2. Asir con las garras. 3. Polvorear con grasilla. 4. Alisar (un sombrero) frotándolo.

pound [paʊnd] [paund], *s.* 1. Libra, peso que consta diez y seis onzas. 2. Libra esterlina. 3. Corral de concejo; corral en que se encierra el ganado perdido o embargado. 4. Depósito. **Pound-foolish,** gastador, derrochador. **Pound-breach,** traslado ilegal del ganado encerrado en el corral de concejo.

pound, *va.* 1. Golpear pesada y repetidamente (hit, knock); machacar o moler. 2. Encerrar, poner en encierro o depósito (enclose). *V.* IMPOUND. **The waves pound the wall,** las olas golpean el muro.

poundage ['paʊndɪdʒ] [paun-dich], *s.* 1. Tanto por libra; derecho de tanto por libra de peso. 2. Costo de rescatar el ganado acorralado por otros. 3. Acto de acorralar el ganado perdido o embargado.

poundcake ['paʊnˌkeɪk] [paund-keik], *s.* Pastel o torta hechos con una libra de cada ingrediente.

pounder ['paʊndə'] [paun-da'], *s.* 1. Golpeador. 2. Criada, pala de lavar la ropa. 3. Cualquier cosa que toma su denominación del número de libras que tiene. **A thirty-six pounder,** cañón de a treinta y seis. 4. Triturador, bocarte de un molino para minerales. 5. *(G.B)* El que paga un alquiler de cierto número determinado de libras.

pounding ['paʊndɪŋ] [paun-din], *s.* 1. Martilleo; fuertes latidos del corazón (heartbeats). 2. *(Fam.)* Vapuleo, paliza.

pour [pɔː'] [po'], *va.* 1. Echar o vaciar líquidos de una parte a otra. 2. Emitir, arrojar, echar fuera alguna cosa continuamente. 3. Desembolsar pródigamente; dejar caer, desparramar copiosamente (spill). *-vn.* 1. Fluir, correr con rapidez. 2. Caer, descender, precipitarse profusamente (swoop); llover. 3. Salir en masa, venir en muchedumbres, llegar a montones. 4. Esparcirse grandemente. **The northern hordes poured over Italy,** las hordas del norte cayeron sobre Italia. **The ants poured out of the hill,** las hormigas salieron a montones del hormiguero. **To pour out of one vessel into another,** trasegar líquidos; vaciar los líquidos de una parte a otra. **To pour down,** llover a cántaros, diluviar. **He poured out his feelings to her,** le reveló sus sentimientos a ella.

pourer ['pɔːrə'] [po-ra'], *s.* Trasegador, vaciador.

pouring ['pɔːrɪŋ] [po-rin], *a.* **Pouring rain,** lluvia torrencial.

pout [paʊt] [paut], *s.* 1. Mueca que se hace contrayendo los labios, señal de ceño o mal humor. 2. Abadejo; mustela de río.

pout, *vn.* Poner mal gesto, ponerse ceñudo, enfurruñarse, amohinarse. *(Fam.)* Estar de hocico. **Pouting fellow,** hombre ceñudo; cara de vinagre.

pouter ['paʊtə'] [pau-tar], *s.* 1. Hombre ceñudo, que pone mala cara. 2. Guturosa, buchona; paloma de cuello grueso; paloma que tiene la costumbre de dilatar la parte anterior del cuello.

poverty ['pɒvətɪ] [po-ver-ti], *s.* 1. Pobreza, necesidad, estrechez, indigencia, miseria. 2. Falta de substancia, de elementos o de propiedades. 3. Aridez, insuficiencia; tibieza (of sentiment).

poverty-stricken ['pɒvətɪˌstrɪkn] [po-va-ti-stri-ken], *a.* Paupérrimo, necesitado, sumido en la pobreza.

powder ['paʊdə'] [pau-da'], *s.* 1. Polvo, colección de partículas sueltas de una substancia seca. 2. Polvos de tocador. 3. Pólvora. **Powder-box,** polvera. **Powder room,** 1. Salón-tocador de señoras. 2. Pañol de pólvora, Santabárbara.

powder, *va.* 1. Pulverizar, polvificar, moler, desmenuzar y reducir a polvos alguna cosa. 2. Polvorear, esparcir polvo sobre alguna cosa. 3. Salar, rociar con sal.

powdering ['paɪdərɪŋ] [pau-da-rin], *s.* Polvoreamiento, empolvamiento, el acto de pulverizar o el de polvorear; el polvo esparcido.

powdery ['paʊdərɪ] [pau-da-ri], *s.* Polvoriento, lleno o cubierto de polvo; desmenuzable.

power [paʊə'] [paua'], *s.* 1. Facultad, poder, potencia, virtud de hacer alguna cosa (virtue). **That's beyond my power,** eso está fuera de mi alcance, de mis posibilidades. 2. Potencia motriz; fuerza realmente empleada; pujanza. 3. Poder, potestad, dominio, imperio, autoridad, jurisdicción (authority); también, documento legal que confiere tal poder o autoridad. 4. Gran fuerza que produce su efecto. 5. Potencia, el producto que resulta de la multiplicación continua de un número por sí mismo. 6. Poder, las fuerzas militares de un Estado. 7. Potentado, potestad. 8. El estado o cuerpo político de una nación importante e influyente; potencia. 9. Potencia, fuerza mecánica, cualquier forma de energía capaz de hacer trabajo. 10. *(Opt.)* Potencia, facultad de aumentar que tiene un lente. 11. Ente celeste, divinidad. 12. *(Vulg.)* Una gran cantidad, gran número, muchedumbre. **Power-house,** edificio en que están los dínamos, las máquinas de vapor u otros motores primitivos, y de donde se transmite la fuerza mecánica a las varias partes de un ferrocarril eléctrico, o de un sistema de talleres, etc. **As much as lies in his power,** en cuanto está en su poder, en cuanto de él depende. **Heating-power,** potencia (fuerza) calorífica. **Propelling-power,** fuerza motriz, propulsora. **Horse-power,** *V.* HORSE-POWER, en su lugar alfabético. **A power of attorney,** un poder, una procuración. **Civil power,** autoridad civil. **Refractive power, dispersive power,** facultad de refracción, fuerza dispersiva.

powerboat [paʊəˌbəʊt] [paua-bout], *s.* Lancha de motor.

powerbrake ['paʊəˌbreɪk] [paua-breik], *s.* Servofreno.

powercut ['paʊəkʌt] [paua-kat], *s.* Apagón, corte de luz.

powerdive ['paʊədaɪv] [paua-daiv], *s.* Vuelo en picado de un avión a todo motor.

powerful ['paʊəfʊl] [paua-ful], *a.* 1. Poderoso, eficaz, fuerte (strong). 2. Intenso, que tiene gran energía o actividad (intense). 3. Que posee gran autoridad, o que muestra altas cualidades de cuerpo o de ánimo; potente. 4. Que produce gran efecto en el ánimo; convincente.

powerfully ['paʊəfəlɪ] [paua-fu-li], *adv.* Poderosamente, eficazmente, con mucha fuerza.

powerfulness ['paʊəfəlnɪs] [paua-ful-nes], *s.* Poderío, fuerza, energía, eficacia (energy).

powerless ['paʊəlɪs] [paua-les], *a.* Impotente, ineficaz. **I was powerless to stop the fight,** no pude hacer nada para parar la pelea.

powerplant ['paʊəplænt] [paua-plant], *s.* Central eléctrica, central generadora de fuerza motriz.

powwow ['paʊwaʊ] [pau-uau], *vn.* 1. Tratar a los enfermos por medio de conjuros. 2. Reunirse un cuerpo deliberante. 3. *(Fam. E. U.)* Producirse una algarabía en una reunión o conferencia. *-s.* 1. Conjurador indio. 2. Conjuración para curar a los enfermos. 3. Baile, festín que precede a una cacería. 4. Concilio.

pox ['pɒks] [poks], *s.* Una enfermedad cualquiera que produce erupciones pustolosas, particularmente la sífilis y las viruelas. **Small-box,** viruelas. **Pox** o **French pox,** *(Vulg.)* Mal venéreo o gálico. **Chicken-pox,** viruela loca. **Cow-pox,** vacuna.

poxi ['pɒksɪ] [pok-si], *a.* Puñetero.

practicable ['præktɪkəbl] [prak-ti-ka-bol], *a.* Practicable, factible, hacedero; accesible.

practicably ['præktɪkəblɪ] [prak-ti-ka-bli], *adv.* Posiblemente: prácticamente.

practical ['præktɪkəl] [prak-ti-kal], *a.* 1. Práctico, factible. 2. Útil. **Practical joke,** broma pesada. **Practical nurse,** enfermera por la práctica, sin haberse graduado.

practically ['præktɪklɪ] [prak-ti-kli], *adv.* Prácticamente.

practicalness ['præktɪkəlnɪs] [prak-ti-kal-nes], *s.* La propiedad o calidad de práctico.

practice, practise ['præktɪs] [prak-tis], *s.* 1. Práctica, uso, costumbre (habit). 2. Práctica, el ejercicio de alguna cosa en cuanto se distingue de la teoría. **He's out of practice,** le falta práctica. 3. Práctica, método, modo (method). 4. Una regla de aritmética. **Gun practice,** ejercicio de cañón. **To be in good practice,** tener buena parroquia, clientela. **To make it one's practice to,** acostumbrarse a.

practise, practice, *va.* Practicar, ejercer, ejercitar alguna cosa. *-vn.* 1. Practicar, usar continuadamente alguna cosa. 2. Negociar secretamente. 3. Ejercer la medicina; ejercer cualquier oficio. 4. Ensayarse. **To practise at a target,** tirar al blanco. **To practise with the rifle,** ejercitarse en la carabina. **To practise on the fears of,** explotar los temores de.

practiser ['præktɪsə'] [prak-ti-sa'], *s.* 1. Practicante. 2. Práctico; se usa substantivamente esta palabra para designar a los profesores de medicina. 3. El que usa habitualmente estratagemas o malas artes.

practitioner [præk'tɪʃənə'] [prak-ti-sho-nar], *s.* Práctico, el que ejerce su profesión: se aplica más comúnmente al médico.

prae-. Prefijo latino. V. PRE-.

pragmatic [præg'mætɪk] [prag-ma-tik], *a.* 1. práctico, perteneciente a la consumación del deber u oficio; relativo a los asuntos civiles de un Estado soberano. 2. Pragmático, filosófico, ocupado en la evolución científica de las causas y efectos; se dice de la historia, poesía, etc. **Pragmatic sanction,** pragmática sanción, la pragmática; el edicto imperial que servía de ley fundamental.

pragmatical [præg'mætɪkəl] [prag-ma-ti-kal], *a.* 1. Entremetido, impertinente, oficioso; que pretende dictar o gobernar a los demás. 2. Vulgar, trivial.

pragmatically [præg'mætɪklɪ] [prag-ma-ti-kli], *adv.* Impertinentemente; magistralmente.

pragmatism ['prægmætɪzəm] [prag-ma-ti-sem], *s.* Pragmatismo.

prairie ['preərɪ] [prea-ri], *s.* Pradera, pradería (grassland), extensión de terrenos llanos sin árboles y cubiertos de hierba, particularmente en parte del oeste de los Estados Unidos. **Prairie-chicken,** chocha, cerceta de las praderas. **Prairie-dog,** marmota.

praise [preɪz] [preis], *s.* 1. Alabanza, elogio, encomio. 2. Celebridad, fama, renombre, reputación. 3. Loa, alabanza dirigida a Dios; homenaje por gracias o favores recibidos. **Praise be to God,** alabado sea Dios.

praise, *va.* 1. Celebrar, aplaudir (celebrate). 2. Alabar, glorificar, loar, ensalzar (glorify). 3. Bendecir, expresar gratitud por favores recibidos. **The Lord** be praised, alabado sea el Señor.

praiser ['preɪzə'] [prei-sa'], *s.* Loador, admirador, aprobador.

praiseworthiness ['preɪzwɜːðɪnɪs] [preis-uer-zi-nis], *s.* Calidad de loable, de lo que es digno de alabanza; naturaleza loable.

praiseworthly ['preɪzsɜːðlɪ] [preis-uez-li], *adv.* Loablemente, de una manera que merece alabanzas.

praiseworthy ['preɪzsɜːðɪ] [preis-ue-zi], *a.* Digno de alabanza, loable.

pram [præm] [pram], *s.* 1. Barco chato usado en Holanda. 2. Cochecito de niño.

prance [prɑːns] [prans], *vn.* Cabriolar, cabriolear, dar o hacer cabriolas. *-va.* Hacer cabriolas. **Prance about,** brincar.

prancer ['prɑːns] [prans], *s.* Caballo que cabriola.

prancing ['prɑːnsɪŋ] [pran-sin], *s.* 1. Acción de ponerse de manos los caballos. 2. Aire altanero, modo de andar campante y garboso.

prank [præŋk] [prank], *va.* Hermosear, adornar. *-vn.* Vestirse de una manera vistosa, exagerada, con pretensions.

prank, *s.* Travesura, chasco, locura, extravagancia. **Yesterday I played a prank on your brother,** ayer le gasté una broma a tu hermano.

prankish ['præŋkɪʃ] [pran-kish], *a.* Dispuesto o propenso a hacer travesuras.

prate [preɪt] [preit], *vn.* Charlar, hablar mucho sin sustancia.

prate, *s.* Charla, plática o conversación sin substancia.

prater ['preɪtə'] [prei-ta'], *s.* Charlante, charlador, charlatán.

pratfall ['prætfɔːl] [prat-fol], *s.* Revés, batacazo, porrazo.

prating ['preɪtɪŋ] [prei-tin], *s.* Charlatanería, el acto de charlar.

pratingly ['preɪtɪŋlɪ] [prei-tin-li], *adv.* Con charla vana, locuazmente.

prattle ['prætl] [pra-tel], *vn.* Charlar, proferir como los niños.

prattle, *s.* Parlería, habla de los niños; de aquí, charla, charlatanería.

prattler ['prætlə'] [prat-la'], *s.* Charlador.

pravity ['prævɪtɪ] [pra-vi-ti], *s.* Pravedad, iniquidad, perversidad.

prawn [prɔːn] [pron], *s.* Langostino, gamba, camarón.

praxis ['præksɪs] [prak-sis], *s.* 1. Práctica, ejercicio con un fin determinado (practice). 2. Colección de ejemplos, modelos, etc., como los de la gramática.

pray [preɪ] [prei], *vn.* 1. Orar, invocar, rezar a Dios. **Let us pray,** oremos. 2. Rogar, pedir, suplicar (beg). **Pray what is your name?,** sírvase Ud. decirme su nombre, o tenga Ud. la bondad de decirme su nombre. *-va.* Suplicar, rogar, pedir con sumisión y humildad alguna cosa.

prayer ['preə'] [prea'], *s.* 1. Oración, súplica, rezo, deprecación o ruego que se hace a Dios. **The lord's Prayer,** la oración dominical o el Padre nuestro. 2. Súplica, ruego, petición, plegaria. **The Book of Common Prayer,** el ritual de las Iglesias anglicana y americana episcopal. **Prayer-meeting,** reunión para orar y alabar a Dios.

prayer-book ['preəbʊk] [prea-buk], *s.* Libro de devociones, ejercicio cotidiano, devocionario: en especial, ritual que en las Iglesias anglicana y americana episcopal se llama **The Book of Common Prayer.**

prayerful ['preəfʊl] [prea-ful], *a.* Piadoso, que reza mucho; entregado a la oración.

prayerless ['preəlɪs] [prea-les], *a.* Que descuida el rezo; que no reza, que no ora.

prayerlessness ['preəlɪsnɪs] [prea-les-nes], *s.* Omisión, olvido o descuido del rezo, de la oración.

pre-, Prefijo latino que significa ante, delante. **Pre-cooked rice,** arroz precocinado.

preach [priːtʃ] [prich], *va.* 1. Predicar, exponer la palabra divina. 2. Recomendar con instancia. *-vn.* Predicar, reprender públicamente los vicios y exhortar a la virtud.

preacher ['priːtʃə'] [pri-cha'], *s.* Predicador.

preaching ['priːtʃɪŋ] [pri-chin], *s.* Predicación, acción de predicar; la doctrina predicada.

preachment ['priːtʃmənt] [prich-ment], *s.* Prédica, plática o sermón; arenga.

preamble [priːˈæmbl] [priam-bel], *s.* Preámbulo, exordio, prefación. *-va.* Introducir como preliminar, hacer preceder de un preámbulo.

prearrange [priːəˈreɪndʒ] [pria-reinch], *vt.* Concertar, acordar de antemano.

prebend ['prebənd] [pre-bend], *s.* 1. Prebenda, ciertos beneficios eclesiásticos en las catedrales. 2. Prebendado, canónigo.

prebendary ['prebəndərɪ] [pre-ben-da-ri], *s.* 1. Prebendado, canónigo que recibe las rentas de una prebenda. 2. Dignidad u oficio de prebendado.

precarious [prɪˈkɛərɪəs] [pri-kea-rios], *a.* 1. Precario, sujeto a continuo riesgo de pérdida, dependiente de la voluntad de otro, o de la casualidad; incierto (insecure). 2. Peligros, arriesgado, que puede ocasionar daño. 3. Que no está firmemente establecido, que no es fijo; indigno de confianza. **Precarious conclusions,** conclusiones indignas de confianza.

precariously [prɪˈkɛərɪəslɪ] [pri-kea-rios-li], *adv.* Inciertamente, precariamente.

precariousness [prɪˈkɛərɪəsnɪs] [pri-kea-rios-nes], *s.* Condición precaria o peligrosa; incertidumbre, falta de certeza.

precaution [prɪˈkɔːʃən] [pri-ko-shon], *s.* 1. Precaución, reserva, cautela para impedir, obstáculos o daños posibles, o para asegurar o hacerse dueño de alguna propiedad (care). 2. Cuidado que se toma de antemano para precaver algún mal. **To take precautions,** tomar precauciones.

precaution, *va.* Precaver, precautelar, prevenir algún riesgo.

precautionary [prɪˈkɔːʃənərɪ] [pri-ko-sho-na-ri], *a.* Precaucionado, de precaución; destinado a precaver algún mal. **A precautionary signal,** señal de precaución (del Departamento de Señales Meteorológicas).

precautious [prɪˈkɔːʃəs] [pri-ko-shos], *a.* Precavido, cauto (careful).

precede [prɪˈsiːd] [pri-sid], *va.* 1. Anteceder, preceder; de aquí, sobresalir, llevar la preferencia. 2. Colocar, poner alguna cosa delante de otra; proveer de un preludio. *-vn.* 1. Ir delante de otra persona; tener la primacía. 2. Acontecer primeramente.

precedence ['presɪdəns] [pre-si-dans], *s.* Prioridad, anterioridad; precedencia, superioridad.

precedent ['presɪdənt] [pre-si-dant], *a.* Precedente, antecedente.

precedent, *s.* 1. Precedente, ejemplar, lo que se ha hecho en igual caso otras veces, antecedente, cosa que se puede invocar como ejemplo o razón. 2. Decisión judicial que se considera como regla y sirve para guiar decisiones subsiguientes. **This case will set a precedent,** este caso va a sentar un precedente.

precedently ['presɪdəntlɪ] [pre-si-dant-li], *adv.* Antecedentemente, anticipadamente.

preceding [prɪˈsiːdɪŋ] [pri-si-din], *a.* Anterior, que precede.

precentor [prɪˈsentər] [pri-sen-ta], *s.* Chantre, dignidad de alguna iglesia catedral o colegiata.

precept ['priːsept] [pri-sept], *s.* 1. Precepto, mandato u orden que el superior intima. 2. *(For.)* Mandato, hecho por escrito.

preceptive [prɪˈseptɪv] [pri-sep-tiv], *a.* Preceptivo, didáctico, didascálico; que da preceptos para la conducta moral.

preceptor [prɪˈseptər] [pri-sep-ta], *s.* Preceptor, maestro, el que enseña.

precinct ['priːsɪŋkt] [pri-sinkt], *s.* 1. Límite, lindero; lugar cerrado o cercado. 2. Distrito jurisdiccional, división menor territorial, sometida a una autoridad administrativa. 3. Inmediación de un palacio o de una corte. **Voting precinct,** distrito electoral.

precious ['preʃəs] [pre-shos], *a.* 1. Precioso, costoso, de gran valor, muy apreciado, muy estimado (valued). **Precious stones,** piedras preciosas. 2. Caro, amado, que excita el amor. 3. *(Iron.)* Famoso, altivo (famous); sin valor, sin mérito. 4. *(Fam.)* Bastante, considerable. **A precious scoundrel,** un gran belitre. **We lost precious time,** perdimos tiempo precioso.

preciously ['preʃəslɪ] [pre-shos-li], *adv.* Preciosamente, a gran precio.

preciousness ['preʃəsnɪs] [pre-shos-nes], *s.* Preciosidad, valor elevado, la calidad que da a una cosa cualquiera el carácter de preciosa.

precipice ['presɪpɪs] [pre-si-pis], *s.* 1. Precipicio, despeñadero. 2. Situación peligrosa; la ruina temporal o espiritual.

precipitable ['presɪpɪtəbl] [pre-si-pi-ta-bol], *a.* Que puede precipitarse.

precipitance [prɪˈsɪpɪtəns] [pri-si-pi-tans], **precipitancy** [prɪˈsɪpɪtənsɪ] [pri-si-pi-tan-si], *s.* Precipitación, inconsideración; prisa inconsiderada.

precipitant [prɪˈsɪpɪtənt] [pri-si-pi-tant], *a.* 1. Que se precipita, que se lanza hacia adelante con gran velocidad, o que cae de cabeza. 2. Precipitado, arrojado, arrebatado. *-s.* *(Quím.)* Precipitante, cualquiera de los agentes que producen la precipitación.

precipitate [prɪˈsɪpɪtɪt] [pri-si-pi-tit], *va.* 1. Precipitar, despeñar, arrojar. 2. Precipitar, acelerar, apresurar demasiado una cosa 3. Precipitar, exponer a uno a una ruina temporal o espiritual. 4. *(Quím.)* Precipitar, separar el ingrediente disuelto y hacerlo caer en polvo al fondo del disolvente. *-vn.* 1. Precipitarse, caer al fondo. 2. Precipitarse, arrojarse a algún peligro o meterse en él. 3. *(Quím.)* Caer bajo la forma de precipitado.

precipitate, *a.* 1. Precipitado, que se precipita; que cae, corre o se hace lanzar de un lugar elevado. 2. Precipitado, que obra sin debida reflexión, inconsiderado, arrebatado. 3. Urgido o propuesto prematuramente. *-s.* Precipitado, cualquier cosa que se precipita al fondo de una vasija por medio de una operación química.

precipitately [prɪˈsɪpɪtɪtlɪ] [pri-si-pi-tit-li], *adv.* Precipitadamente; apresuradamente.

precipitation [prɪˌsɪpɪˈteɪʃən] [pri-si-pi-tei-shon], *s.* 1. Precipitación, acción o procedimiento de precipitar; la acción química de precipitar; inconsideración, demasiada prisa para o en hacer alguna cosa. 2. Depósito de humedad (lluvia o nieve) desde la atmósfera sobre la superficie de la tierra.

precipitous [prɪˈsɪpɪtəs] [pri-si-pi-tos], *a.* 1. Pendiente, escarpado. 2. Precipitado, arrojado (hasty).

precise [prɪˈsaɪs] [pri-sais], *a.* 1. Preciso, puntual, exacto, no equívoco (exact); estricto, escrupuloso (strict). **At that precise moment,** en ese preciso momento. 2. Formal; afectado. 3. Que no tiene error apreciable; no más que y no menos que. 4. Particular, singular, idéntico. **The precise spot,** el paraje idéntico. **Precise manners,** maneras formales.

precisely [prɪˈsaɪslɪ] [pri-sais-li], *adv.* 1. Precisamente, exactamente. **At three o'clock precisely,** a las tres en punto. 3. Formalmente.

preciseness [prɪˈsaɪsnɪs] [pri-sais-nes], *s.* Precisión, exactitud; afectación o gravedad afectada; formalismo, ceremonia.

precision [prɪˈsɪʒən] [pri-si-shon], *s.* 1. Precisión, limitación exacta, exactitud. **Precision timing,** sincronización. 2. Precisión de estilo, la calidad que expresa exactamente lo que el escritor se propone.

precisive [prɪˈsɪsɪv] [pri-si-siv], *a.* Precisivo, que prescinde; preciso, estricto.

preclude [prɪˈkluːd] [pri-klud], *va.* 1. Prevenir, impedir o estorbar alguna cosa anticipadamente (get ready). 2. Echar fuera, excluir. **The one does not preclude the other,** lo uno no excluye lo otro. **To preclude the possibility of,** hacer imposible.

precocious [prɪˈkoʊʃəs] [pri-kou-shos], *a.* 1. Precoz, que tiene desarrolladas prematuramente las facultades mentales.

2. Precoz, maduro antes del tiempo natural, prematuro, adelantado.

precociousness [prɪˈkəʊʃəsnɪs] [pri-kou-shos-nes], **precocity** [prəˈkɒsɪtɪ] [pri-ko-si-ti], *s.* Precocidad, madurez anticipada, desarrollo prematuro de las facultades mentales.

precogitate [prɪˈkɒdʒɪteɪt] [pri-ko-yi-teit], *va.* Premeditar.

precognition [ˌpriːkɒgˈnɪʃən] [pri-kog-ni-shon], *s.* Precognición, conocimiento anticipado, conocimiento previo.

preconceive [ˈpriːkənˈsiːv] [pri-kon-siv], *va.* Concebir, opinar o imaginar anticipadamente.

preconceived [ˈpriːkənˈsiːvd] [pri-kon-sivd], *a.* Preconcebido.

preconception [ˈpriːkənˈsepʃən] [pri-kon-sep-shon], *s.* 1. Preocupación, concepto anticipado, concepción formada de antemano. 2. Idea preconcebida.

preconcert [ˈpriːkənsɜːt] [pri-kon-sert], *va.* Concertar de antemano.

preconcert, *s.* Acuerdo anticipado, lo convenido con anterioridad.

precondition [ˈpriːkənˈdɪʃən] [pri-kon-di-shon], *s.* Condición previa.

precook [ˌpriːˈkʊk] [pri-kuk], *vt.* Precocinar.

precordial [priːˈkɔːdɪəl] [pri-kor-dial], *a.* Precordial, relativo al diafragma o a las partes anteriores del corazón.

precursive, precursory [prɪˈkɜːsɪv] [pri-ker-siv] [ˈkɜːsərɪ] [pri-ker-so-ri], *a.* Precursor, que va delante; que advierte, informa o predice de antemano.

precursor [prɪˈkɜːsəʳ] [pri-ker-saʳ], *s.* Precursor, el o lo que va delante, que precede a un hombre o a un acontecimiento y anuncia su venida.

predate [ˈpriːˈdeɪt] [pri-deit], *vt.* Antedatar, poner una fecha anterior.

predator [ˈpriːdeɪtəʳ] [pri-dei-taʳ], *s.* Depredador.

predatory [ˈpredətərɪ] [pre-da-to-ri], *a.* Perteneciente a hurto o rapiña; de presa, de botín; rapaz, voraz.

predeceased [ˈpriːdɪˈsiːst] [pri-di-sist], *a.* Muerto antes que otro.

predecessor [ˈpriːdɪsesəʳ] [pri-di-se-saʳ], *s.* Predecesor, antecesor, antepasado, abuelo, persona que ha precedido a alguien en el ejercicio de las mismas funciones.

predestinate [ˈpriːˌdestɪneɪt] [pri-des-ti-neit], *va.* Predestinar, destinar de antemano o desde el principio de las cosas.

predestination [ˈpriːˌdestɪˈneɪʃən] [pri-des-ti-nei-shon], *s.* 1. Predestinación, destinación, anterior de alguna cosa. 2. (*Theol.*) Predestinación, ordenación de la voluntad divina con que **ab aeterno** tiene elegidos a los que por medio de su gracia han de lograr la gloria.

predestine [priːˈdestɪn] [pri-des-tin], *va.* Predestinar; ordenar de antemano. **To be predestined,** estar predestinado.

predeterminate [ˈpriːdɪˌtɜːmɪneɪt] [pri-di-ter-mi-neit], *a.* Predeterminado, determinado de antemano.

predetermination [ˈpriːdɪˌtɜːmɪˈneɪʃən] [pri-di-ter-mi-nei-shon], *s.* Predeterminación.

predetermine [ˈpriːdɪˈtɜːmɪn] [pri-di-ter-min], *va.* Predeterminar, o determinar con anterioridad.

predicable [ˈpredɪkəbl] [pre-di-ka-bol], *a.* Predicable, que se puede afirmar o decir de un sujeto. -*s.* (*Log.*) Predicable, categorema.

predicament [prɪˈdɪkəmənt] [pre-di-ka-ment], *s.* Predicamento, clase, categoría; estado, condición; particularmente, trance apurado, embarazoso, situación difícil o divertida. **Your sister is in a predicament,** tu hermana está en un aprieto.

predicate [ˈpredɪkɪt] [pre-di-kit], *va.* Predicar o más comúnmente predicarse, decir, afirmar o negar en la enunciación una cosa de otra. -*vn.* Afirmarse.

predicate, *s.* 1. (*Gram.*) Predicado, lo que se afirma o niega en una proposición. 2. Calidad inherente a una cosa o que se afirma de ella, atributo.

predication [ˈpredɪkeɪʃən] [pre-di-kei-shon], *s.* Afirmación de alguna cosa.

predicative [prɪˈdɪkətɪv] [pri-di-ka-tiv], *a.* Predicativo.

predict [prɪˈdɪkt] [pri-dikt], *va.* Predecir, decir de antemano lo que ha de acaecer; profetizar, pronosticar. **They predict that he's going to win the tennis match,** predicen que va a ganar el partido de tenis.

predictable [prɪˈdɪktəbl] [pri-dik-ta-bol], *a.* Predecible, previsible. **He's so predictable,** es tan previsible.

predictably [prɪˈdɪktəblɪ] [pri-dik-ta-bli], *adv.* De manera previsible.

prediction [prɪˈdɪkʃən] [pri-dik-shon], *s.* Predicción, profecía (prophecy).

predictive [prɪˈdɪktɪv] [pri-dik-tiv], *a.* Que predice, que anuncia de antemano.

predictor [prɪˈdɪktəʳ] [pri-dik-taʳ], *s.* Adivino, pronosticador.

predigestion [ˌpriːdaɪˈdʒesʃən] [pri-dai-yes-shon], *s.* 1. La digestión artificial o peptonización del alimento, v. g. para las personas achacosas. 2. Masticación, insalivación, funciones preliminares de la digestión.

predilection [priːdɪˈlekʃən] [pri-di-lek-shon], *s.* Predilección, preferencia. **I have predilection for your brother,** tengo predilección por tu hermano.

predisponent [priːˈdɪspənənt] [pri-dis-po-nent], *a.* Predisponente, que predispone, que causa una predisposición.

predispose [ˈpriːdɪsˈpəʊz] [pri-dis-pous], *va.* Predisponer, disponer con anticipación; preparar para recibir alguna impresión.

predisposed [ˈpriːdɪsˈpəʊst] [pri-dis-poust], *a.* Predispuesto.

predisposition [ˈpriːˌdɪspəˈzɪʃən] [pri-dis-po-si-shon], *s.* 1. Predisposición, disposición natural, propensión, predilección (tendency). 2. Predisposición, circunstancia que facilita el desarrollo de una enfermedad. **George has predisposition to fall in love,** Jorge tiene propensión a enamorarse.

predominance [prɪˈdɒmɪnəns] [pri-do-mi-nans], *s.* Predominio, predominación; ascendiente, superioridad en fuerza, infuencia o grado.

predominant [prɪˈdɒmɪnənt] [pri-do-mi-nant], *a.* Predominante.

predominantly [prɪˈdɒmɪnəntlɪ] [pri-do-mi-nant-li], *adv.* Predominantemente.

predominate [prɪˈdɒmɪneɪt] [pri-do-mi-neit], *va.* Predominar, prevalecer, mandar o influir con predominio.

pre-eminence [priːˈemɪnəns] [pri-e-mi-nens], *s.* Preeminencia, excelencia especial, superioridad de posición, calidad o excelencia; supremacía.

pre-eminent [priːˈemɪnənt] [pri-e-mi-nent], *a.* 1. Preeminente, de primer orden o mérito, supremo. 2. Extraordinario, extremo, superlativo.

pre-empt [priːˈempt] [pri-empt], *va.* (*E.U.*) Obtener el derecho de preferencia en la compra de terrenos públicos; establecer un título anterior. -*vn.* Apropiar un terreno público por el privilegio de compra anterior.

pre-emptible [priːˈemptɪbl] [pri-emp-ti-bol], *a.* Sujeto al derecho de compra de una persona determinada.

pre-emption [priːˈempʃən] [pri-emp-shon], *s.* 1. El derecho de comprar antes que otros. 2. (*G.B.*) El privilegio que gozaba antiguamente el rey de comprar las provisiones para la casa real, con preferencia a todos sus súbditos.

pre-emptive [priːˈemptɪv] [pri-emp-tiv], *a.* Preventivo, preferente.

pre-emptor [priːˈemptəʳ] [pri-emp-taʳ], *s.* El que goza el derecho de comprar un terreno con preferencia a todo otro comprador, por ser verdadero colono.

preen [priːn] [priin], *va.* 1. Limpiar, concertar y componer sus plumas las aves. 2. **To preen oneself,** acicalarse una persona (person).

pre-establish [ˈpriːɪsˈtæblɪʃ] [pri-is-ta-blish], *va.* Preestablecer, establecer de antemano o a prevención.

pre-exist [ˈpriːɪgˈzɪst] [pri-ik-sist], *vn.* Preexistir, existir antes.

pre-existence ['pri:ɪɡ'zɪstəns] [pri-ik-sis-tans], *s.* 1. Preexistencia, existencia anterior. 2. Existencia del alma antes de la vida humana.

pre-existent ['pri:ɪɡ'zɪstənt] [pri-ik-sis-tant], *a.* Preexistente.

prefabricate ['pri:'fæbrɪkeɪt] [pri-fa-bri-keit], *vt.* Prefabricar.

prefabricated ['pri:'fæbrɪkeɪtɪd] [pri-fa-bri-kei-tid], *a.* Prefabricado, construido de antemano.

preface ['prefɪs] [pre-fis], *s.* 1. Prefación, prefacio, prólogo; discurso preliminar y corto de un libro; se diferencia de la introducción. 2. Cualquier prólogo, o acción preliminar.

preface, *va.* Hacer o poner un prólogo a un libro; decir alguna cosa en forma de introducción al discurso que se va a hacer. *-vn.* Decir, o hacer, a manera de prólogo.

prefatory ['prefətərɪ] [pre-fa-to-ri], *a.* Preliminar; de la naturaleza de un prólogo, que sirve de prólogo.

prefect ['pri:fekt] [pri-fekt], *s.* 1. Prefecto, una dignidad, un poder tutelar jefe entre los romanos. 2. En Francia y en el Perú, prefecto gobernador de una provincia o departamento.

prefectship ['pri:fektʃɪp] [pri-fekt-ship], *s.* Prefectura, dignidad o territorio de un prefecto.

prefecture ['pri:fektʃəʳ] [pri-fek-chaʳ], *s.* Prefectura; funciones o jurisdicción de un prefecto; también, el edificio oficial para su uso.

prefer [prɪ'fɜːʳ] [pri-feʳ], 1. Preferir, anteponer. 2. Elevar, exaltar (exalt). 3. Proponer en público; ofrecer solemnemente; exhibir o manifestar alguna cosa; presentar. 4. Dar preferencia, como a un acreedor antes de otros. Se usa con la prep. *to,* algunas veces con *above,* y rara vez *before.*

preferable ['prefərəbl] [pre-fe-ra-bol], *a.* Preferible, más deseable, digno de escogimiento.

preferableness ['prefərəblnɪs] [pre-fe-ra-bol-nes], *s.* El estado de lo que es preferible o digno de anteponerse a otra cosa.

preferably ['prefərəblɪ] [pre-fe-ra-bli], *adv.* Preferiblemente, por preferencia, de preferencia.

preference ['prefərəns] [pre-fe-rans], *s.* Preferencia, la acción de preferir, el estado de ser preferido, o la cosa preferida. *(Com.)* **Preference shares,** acciones preferentes.

preferential [ˌprefə'renʃəl] [pre-fe-ren-shal], *a.* Que posee, constituye, implica, o procede de la preferencia.

preferment [prɪ'fɜːmənt] [pri-fer-ment], *s.* 1. Promoción, elevación a alguna dignidad o empleo más eminente que el que uno tenía (promotion). 2. Puesto, empleo u oficio honorífico o lucrativo.

prefiguration [ˌpri:fɪɡə'reɪʃən] [pri-fi-ga-rei-shon], *s.* Prefiguración.

prefigurative ['preɪ'fɪɡərətɪv] [prif-i-gu-ra-tiv], *a.* Que muestra por figuras, por tipos anteriores.

prefigure ['prɪ'fɪɡəʳ] [pri-fi-gaʳ], *va.* Prefigurar, representar anticipadamente la forma o figura de alguna cosa (foresee).

prefix ['pri:fɪks] [pri-fiks], *va.* 1. Prefijar, determinar o señalar anticipadamente. 2. Fijar, establecer.

prefix, *s.* (*Gram.*) Prefijo, afijo, la partícula o sílaba puesta delante de una palabra o término que hace variar su significación.

pregnancy ['preɡnənsɪ] [preg-nan-si], *s.* 1. Preñez, preñado, el estado de la mujer encinta o de la hembra preñada (embarrass). 2. Fertilidad, fecundidad. 2. *(Fig.)* Importancia, gravedad.

pregnant ['preɡnənt] [preg-nant], *a.* 1. Preñada (animals), embarazada, encinta (women). 2. Fértil, abundante, copioso (fertile). 3. Fecundo en consecuencias, grave, que conduce a resultados importantes; seguido comúnmente de *with.* 4. Lleno, repleto; que importa mucho. 5. En retórica y en lógica que implica más de lo que se expresa. 6. Poderoso, convincente.

pregnantly ['preɡnəntlɪ] [preg-nant-li], *adv.* Copiosamente, abundantemente, plenamente, fecundamente.

prehensible [prɪ'hensɪbl] [pri-jen-si-bol], *a.* Capaz de ser aprehendido o asido.

prehensile [prɪ'hensaɪl] [pri-jen-sail], *a.* Prensil.

prehistoric ['pri:hɪs'tɒrɪk] [pri-jis-to-rik], *a.* Prehistórico, perteneciente a la prehistoria, a los tiempos a que no alcanza la historia.

prehistory ['pri:hɪstərɪ] [pri-jis-to-ri], *sf.* Prehistoria.

prejudge ['pri:'dʒʌdʒ] [pri-yach], *va.* Prejuzgar, juzgar o formar juicio de alguna cosa antes del tiempo debido.

prejudgment ['pri:'dʒʌdʒmənt] [pri-yach-ment], *s.* Prejuicio, juicio o condenación sin examen.

prejudice ['predʒʊdɪs] [pre-yu-dis], *s.* 1. Prevención, prejuicio, preocupación del ánimo o de la voluntad; prevención, juicio anticipado, opinión prematura a favor o en contra de una persona. 2. Perjuicio, daño, detrimento. **To the prejudice of,** en o con perjuicio de.

prejudice, *va.* 1. Preocupar, prevenir, impresionar el ánimo o la voluntad de alguno. 2. Perjudicar, hacer daño, causar pérdida a otro.

prejudicial [ˌpredʒʊ'dɪʃəl] [pre-yu-di-shal], *a.* Prejudicial, dañoso, nocivo (harmful).

prejudicially [ˌpredʒʊ'dɪʃəlɪ] [pre-yu-di-sha-li], *adv.* Prejudicialmente, con perjuicio.

prelacy ['preləsɪ] [pre-la-si], *s.* 1. Prelacía, dignidad u oficio de prelado. 2. Episcopado: el cuerpo de obispos.

prelate ['prelɪt] [pre-lit], *s.* Prelado.

prelateship ['prelɪtʃɪp] [pre-lit-ship], *s.* Prelacía, prelatura.

prelature, ['prelɪtʃəʳ] [pre-li-chaʳ], *s.* Prelatura, prelacía.

preliminarily [prɪ'lɪmɪnərɪlɪ] [pri-li-mi-na-ri-li], *adv.* Preliminarmente, por vía de introducción, de una manera preparatoria.

preliminary [prɪ'lɪmɪnərɪ] [pri-li-mi-na-ri], *a.* Preliminar, antecedente, preparativo, introductorio (introductory). *-s.* Preliminar, paso iniciativo, acto preparativo para alguna cosa.

prelude ['preljuːd] [pre-liud], *s.* 1. Preludio, lo que precede y sirve de entrada, prelusión, acción que indica lo que ha de ser la función principal (introduction). 2. *(Mús.)* Preludio, tiento, floreo, arpegio; también, una pieza corta de música que se toca antes de una ceremonia o representación. 3. Presagio, cosa precursora, lo que anuncia un acontecimiento venidero.

prelude, *va. (Mús.)* Florear, hacer floreos. *-vn.* Servir de introducción.

preludial ['preljuːdɪəl] [pre-liu-dial], *a.* Introductorio, de la naturaleza de un preludio; que sirve de prólogo (prologue).

prelusive ['preljuːzɪv] [pre-liu-siv], *a.* Previo, introductorio, que presagia.

premature ['premətʃʊəʳ] [pre-ma-chuaʳ], *a.* Prematuro, intempestivo, precoz, que está maduro o desarrollado antes de tiempo; que se ha hecho, dicho, o concluido antes del tiempo conveniente. **premature fruit, premature judgment,** fruto prematuro, juicio prematuro.

prematurely ['premətʃʊəlɪ] [pre-ma-chua-li], *adv.* Prematuramente; antes del tiempo debido.

prematureness ['premətʃʊənɪs] [pre-ma-chua-nes], *s.* Madurez o sazón antes de tiempo.

premedical ['premedɪkl] [pre-me-di-kal], *a.* Preparatorio para estudiar medicina.

premeditate [prɪ'medɪteɪt] [pri-me-di-teit], *va.* Premeditar, meditar de antemano; proyectar y resolver anticipadamente. *-vn.* Pensar de antemano (reflect).

premeditation [prɪˌmedɪ'teɪʃən] [pri-me-di-tei-shon], *s.* Premeditación, acción de premeditar; designio que ha precedido a la ejecución de un crimen; meditación juiciosa sobre alguna cosa antes de ejecutarla.

premier ['premɪəʳ] [pre-miaʳ], *s.* Primer ministro, el ministro principal del estado. *-a.* Primero, principal.

premiership ['premɪəʃɪp] [pre-mia-ship], *s.* Presidencia del consejo, cargo del primer ministro.

premise ['premɪs] [pre-mis], *va.* 1. Decir o exponer alguna cosa con anterioridad o anticipadamente a otra; sentar o establecer premisas. 2. Postular como una condición precedente.

premise, *s.* 1. Premisa, cada una de las dos primeras proposiciones de un silogismo. 2. Cosa que se da por supuesta; condición existente con anterioridad. 3. *pl.* (*For.*) 1. Asertos, aserciones anteriores, que van delante; hechos afirmados anteriormente. 2. Aquella parte de un instrumento auténtico que da a conocer la fecha, los nombre de los individuos, el terreno o cosa transferida, y la razón o precio. 3. *pl.* Casa, tierra, posesiones. **In the premises,** tocante al asunto de que se trata, en el particular, en esto, acerca de.

premium ['priːmɪəm] [pri-miom], *s.* 1. Premio, galardón, remuneración (guerdon, reward). 2. Prima o premio de un seguro, la cantidad que se paga al asegurador. 3. Prima, la cantidad prometida o dada por premio en ciertas especulaciones mercantiles; interés, beneficio, premio. **Bottomry premium,** premio de un seguro marítimo, por el riesgo de mar. 4. Premio, prima, aumento de valor sobre el nominal o el de par que adquieren ciertas acciones, fondos, o dinero; aumento de valor en la moneda. **At a premium,** con prima, por encima de la par.

premolar [priːˈmoʊləʳ] [pri-mou-laʳ], *s.* Premolar (tooth).

premonish [priːˈmɒnɪʃ] [pri-mo-nish], *va.* (*Ant.*) Prevenir, advertir antes.

premonition [ˌpriːməˈnɪʃən] [pri-mo-ni-shon], *s.* Prevención, advertencia o aviso anticipado (presentiment).

premonitory [priːˈmɒnɪtərɪ] [pri-mo-ni-to-ri], *a.* Preventivo, que previene a otra cosa, que presagia, o amonesta.

premunition [ˌpriːmjʊˈnɪʃən] [pri-miu-ni-shon], *s.* Acción de fortalecer contra el peligro o la objeción; estado de defensa.

prenatal ['priːneɪtl] [pri-nei-tal], *a.* Prenatal, antenatal.

prenominate [priːˈmnɒmɪnɪt] [pri-no-mi-nit], *va.* Nombrar primero o con anterioridad.

prenticeship ['prentɪʃɪp] [pren-ti-ship], *s.* Aprendizaje.

preocupation [priːˌɒkjʊˈpeɪʃən] [prio-kiu-pei-shon], *s.* 1. Preocupación, anticipación en la adquisición de una cosa (worry); el acto o derecho de preocupar; estado de posesión anterior. 2. Preocupación del ánimo (anxiety). 3. (*Des.*) Objeción anticipada.

preoccupied [priːˈɒkjʊpaɪd] [prio-kiu-paid], *pp. y a.* 1. Absorto en las propias ideas o en los negocios (absentminded, inattentive). 2. Que ha sido ocupado anteriormente. 3. Ya en uso, v. g. un nombre científico.

preoccupy [priːˈɒkjʊpaɪ] [prio-kiu-pai], *va.* 1. Preocupar, ocupar antes. 2. Preocupar, prevenir el ánimo; predisponer.

preordain [ˌpriːɔːˈdeɪn] [prior-dein], *va.* (*Teo.*) Preordinar, determinar de antemano.

preordination [priːˌɔːdaɪˈneɪʃən] [prior-dai-nei-shon], *s.* (*Teo.*) Preordinación.

prepaid ['priːˈpeɪd] [pri-peid], *a.* Franco de porte, con porte pagado.

preparation [ˌprepəˈreɪʃən] [pre-pa-rei-shon], *s.* 1. Preparación, acción y efecto de preparar, disposición, adaptación. 2. Preliminar, precaución (care); hecho que sirve para poner por obra algún plan o designio. 3. El hecho o cualidad de estar o ser preparado, dispuesto, listo (readiness). 4. Cosa preparada, como un compuesto medicinal o químico, o una muestra para el estudio científico. 5. Preparación, el procedimiento de componer o de manipular. 6. Estudio preliminar, instrucción, v. g. para un colegio, o para negocios. **Preparations for war,** preparativos de guerra.

preparative [prɪˈpærətɪv] [pri-pa-ra-tiv], *a.* Preparativo, preparatorio, que prepara y dispone. *-s.* Preparativo, la cosa dispuesta y preparada.

preparatively [prɪˈpærətɪvlɪ] [pri-pa-ra-tiv-li], *adv.* Previamente, anticipadamente.

preparatory [prɪˈpærətərɪ] [pri-pa-ra-to-ri], *a.* Preparatorio, previo, antecedente, que sirve de introducción, preliminar.

prepare [prɪˈpɛəʳ] [pri-peaʳ], *va.* 1. Preparar, prevenir, disponer, aparejar, poner en disposición propia para alcanzar el fin que se desea (make ready). 2. Proveer de lo necesario o lo conveniente. 3. Disponer el ánimo hacia un estado conveniente o deseable. *-vn.* Prepararse, disponerse, ponerse en disposición de hacer alguna cosa.

prepared [prɪˈpɛədlɪ] [pri-pead-li], *a.* Listo, preparado. **Prepared food,** producto pre-elaborado.

preparedly [prɪˈpɛədlɪ] [pri-pead-li], *adv.* Con las medidas oportunas tomadas de antemano, con preparación.

preparedness [prɪˈpɛədnɪs] [pri-pead-nes], *s.* Estado de preparación.

preparer [prɪˈpɛərəʳ] [pri-pea-raʳ], *s.* Preparador, el que prepara; preparativo.

prepay ['priːˈpeɪ] [pri-pei], *va.* (pret. y *pp.* PREPAID). Pagar adelantado, pagar anticipadamente; franquear una carta (letter).

prepayment ['priːˈpeɪmənt] [pri-pei-mant], *s.* Pago adelantado; franqueo.

prepense [prɪˈpens] [pri-pens], *a.* Premeditado, concebido o imaginado antes; por lo común en la locución legal **«with malice prepense»,** maliciosa y premeditadamente.

preponderance [prɪˈpɒndərəns] [pri-pon-de-rans], *s.* Superioridad de peso, de influencia, de fuerza, de número; preponderancia.

preponderant [prɪˈpɒndərənt] [pri-pon-de-rant], *a.* preponderante, predominante.

preponderate [prɪˈpɒndəreɪt] [pri-pon-de-reit], *va. y vn.* 1. Preponderar, pesar una cosa más que otra. 2. Preponderar o hacer más fuerza una opinión que otra. 3. Arrastrar, llevarse tras sí. 4. Tener más influencia, crédito o influjo.

preposition [ˌprepəˈzɪʃən] [pre-po-si-shon], *s.* Preposición.

prepositional [ˌprepəˈzɪʃənl] [pre-po-si-sho-nal], *a.* Preposicional, que tiene la fuerza o naturaleza de una preposición.

prepossess [ˌpriːpəˈzes] [pri-po-ses], *va.* 1. Preocupar, llenar de preocupaciones; impresionar, imbuir en favor de. 2. Tomar posesión de algo antes que otro; preocupar. 3. Causar buena impresión, predisponer favorablemente.

prepossessing [ˌpriːpəˈzesɪŋ] [pri-po-se-sin], *a.* Que produce opinión favorable desde luego, atractivo (pleasant, nice); que predispone a favor de algo.

prepossession [ˌpriːpəˈzeʃən] [pri-po-se-shon], *s.* 1. Preocupación, primera impresión que produce una cosa en el ánimo; prevención, opinión preconcebida a favor de alguna persona o cosa (preference). 2. Preocupación, ocupación o posesión anterior.

preposterous [prɪˈpɒstərəs] [pri-pos-te-ros], *a.* 1. Prepóstero, absurdo, contrario a la naturaleza o a la razón; evidentemente impracticable. 2. (*Des.*) Por su origen, trastrocado, hecho al revés o fuera de tiempo. (*Fam.*) Descabellado, sin son ni ton.

preposterously [prɪˈpɒstərəslɪ] [pri-pos-te-ros-li], *adv.* Absurdamente, sin razón, prepósteramente.

preposterousness [prɪˈpɒstərəsnɪs] [pri-pos-te-ros-nes], *s.* Preposteración, trabucación, trastorno o inversión de orden, absurdidad.

prepotency [prɪˈpɒtənsɪ] [pri-po-ten-si], *s.* Prepotencia, predominio.

prepotent ['prɪpɒtənt] [pri-po-tent], *a.* Prepotente, predominante.

prepandial [prɪˈpændɪəl] [pri-pan-dial], *a.* Que ocurre o se hace después de comer.

prepuce ['priːpjuːs] [pri-pius], *s.* Prepucio, piel móvil que cubre el pene.

prerecord ['priːrɪˈkɔːd] [pri-ri-kord], *vt.* Grabar de antemano.

prerequire [prɪˈrekwaɪəʳ] [pri-re-kuaiaʳ], *va.* Requerir antes, demandar de antemano.

prerequisite ['priːˈrekwɪzɪt] [pri-re-kui-sit], *a.* Que se necesita de antemano. *-s.* Requisito necesitado con anticipación para la ejecución de una cosa.

prerogative [prɪˈrɒgətɪv] [pri-ro-ga-tiv], *a.* Prerogativa, privilegio exclusivo o especial. *-a.* Privilegiado.

presage ['presɪdʒ] [pre-sich], **presagement** ['presɪdʒmənt] [pre-sich-ment], *s.* Presagio, pronóstico, presentimiento, anuncio.

presage, *va.* Presagiar, pronosticar, predecir, anunciar.

presageful ['presɪdʒfʊl] [pre-sich-ful], *a.* Que contiene agüero o presagio; ominoso.

presbyter [ˌprez'bɪtəʳ] [pres-bi-taʳ], *s.* Presbítero, sacerdote.

presbyterial [ˌprezbɪ'tɪərɪəl] [pres-bi-tia-rial], *a.* Presbiteral.

presbyterian [ˌprezbɪ'tɪərɪən] [pres-bi-tia-rian], *a.* Presbiteriano. -*s.* Presbiteriano, miembro de la secta protestante.

presbyterianism [ˌprezbɪ'tɪərɪənɪzəm] [pres-bi-tia-ria-ni-sem], *s.* Presbiterianismo.

presbytery ['prezbɪtərɪ] [pres-bi-te-ri], *s.* 1. (Bible) Presbiterio, consejo de ancianos en la Iglesia cristina; cuerpo de ancianos, sean sacerdotes o legos. 2. Presbiterianismo, el sistema de gobierno de una iglesia por presbíteros o ancianos, en oposición a la prelacía y a la independencia. 3. La junta de sacerdotes presbiterianos dentro de un distrito determinado, con un anciano por cada iglesia; tribunal eclesiástico de los presbiterianos. 4. *(Arq.)* Presbiterio, coro. *V.* CHANCEL.

prescience ['presɪəns] [pre-sians], *s.* Presciencia, conocimiento anticipado de las cosas futuras.

prescient ['presɪənt] [pre-siant], *a.* Presciente, que sabe lo futuro, que sabe de antemano; también dotado de vista penetrante.

prescind ['presɪnd] [pre-sind], *va.* y *vn.* 1. Prescindir; separa o apartar una cosa de otra. 2. Prescindir, separar mentalmente una cosa de otra a que está realmente unida. **To prescind from,** hacer abstracción de.

prescribe [prɪs'kraɪb] [pris-kraib], *va.* 1. Prescribir, señalar, ordenar, determinar alguna cosa (order, mark). 2. Recetar a un enfermo, dar instrucciones para el uso de un remedio. -*vn.* 1. Dar leyes o reglas; particularmente, prescribir un remedio que se ha de emplear, el régimen que ha de seguir un enfermo. 2. *(For.)* Prescribir, adquirir un derecho por una larga posesión o por prescripción; perderse, invalidarse por el transcurso del tiempo.

prescript [prɪs'krɪpt] [pris-kript], *s.* 1. Norma, regla. 2. *(For.)* Adquirible por la prescripción.

prescription [prɪs'krɪpʃən] [pris-krip-shon], *s.* 1. Prescripción, acción de prescribir o de dirigir; dirección autoritativa. 2. Precepto, regla (rule). 3. Receta medicinal; también, familiarmente, el medicamento así prescrito. 4. *(For.)* 1. Revindicación o reivindicación, modo de adquirir el dominio de una propiedad por la posesión larga y no interrumpida; también, el número determinado de años después de los cuales se puede reclamar la prescripción. 2. Modo de perder un derecho o título por no haberlo alegado, dentro de un plazo señalado; el número de años después de los cuales no puede alegarse un título o derecho no reclamado; el plazo en que prescribe o se pierde el derecho de incoar un procedimiento criminal.

prescriptive [prɪs'krɪptɪv] [pris-krip-tiv], *a.* 1. Sancionado, autorizado por la costumbre y por el uso prolongado. 2. *(For.)* Adquirido por usufructo o uso inmemorial.

presence ['prezns] [pre-sens], *s.* 1. Presencia, asistencia personal; el estado de una persona que se halla delante de otra, o en el mismo paraje que otra. 2. Presencia, el talle, figura o disposición del cuerpo, proximidad. 3. Presencia, viva memoria de alguna cosa; algo impalpable, pero cercano y perceptible a los sentidos, como una aparición. 4. Asistencia, corte, asamblea de personas, v. g. ante un gran personaje. 5. *(Ant.)* El salón del palacio donde el monarca recibe su corte. 6. Serenidad. **Presence of mind,** presencia de ánimo. **In the presence of,** en presencia de.

present ['preznt] [pre-sent], *a.* 1. Presente, que está delante o en presencia de otro, o concurre con él en el mismo lugar. 2. Presente, actual, hablando de cosas que existen en el tiempo en que uno vive (today). *(Com.)* Actual, corriente. **The present month,** el mes actual o corriente. 3. Presente, que está actualmente fijo en el ánimo. 4. *(Ant.)* Pronto, dispuesto,

aparejado. 5. *(Ant.)* Atento, cuidadoso. **At present,** al presente, ahora. **To be present,** presenciar, asistir, concurrir.

present, *s.* 1. Presente, el don, alhaja o regalo que una persona da a otra. 2. Carta de mandamiento. -*pl.* Las escrituras presentes. **Know all men by these presents,** sepan todos por la presente. **To all to whom these presents shall come, greeting,** a todos los que las presentes vieren, salud. 3. *(Gram.)* Tiempo presente. **Presents remove difficulties,** dádivas quebrantan peñas. 4. *(For.)* Las escrituras o documentos presentes. *a.* 1. Presente: **To be present,** estar presente; **to be present at,** estar presente en. **The present company excepted,** mejorando lo presente. 2. Actual, corriente: **present value, present worth,** valor actual. 3. *(Gram.)* Tiempo presente.

present, *va.* 1. Presentar, introducir, dar a conocer; poner delante de alguien. **To present a person to another,** presentar una persona a otra. 2. Presentar, dar graciosa y voluntariamente algún regalo, ofrecer, regalar. 3. Presentar, manifestar, mostrar. 4. Presentar un beneficio eclesiástico. 5. Representar, exponer. 6. Apuntar, asestar (un arma). 7. *(For.)* Denunciar, citar. **To present arms,** *(Mil.)* Presentar las armas. **To present oneself,** presentarse, ofrecerse. **To present a person with a thing,** regalar una cosa a alguien.

presentability [ˌprezntə'bɪlɪtɪ] [pre-sen-ta-bi-li-ti], *s.* Calidad de presentable.

presentable [prɪ'zentəbl] [pri-sen-ta-bol], *a.* Presentable, que puede presentarse, ofrecerse, mostrarse, exhibirse o representarse.

presentation [ˌprezən'teɪʃən] [pre-san-tei-shon], *s.* 1. Presentación; acción de presentar, de ofrecer; introducción; particularmente, ofrecimiento formal de un regalo. 2. Exhibición, representación, manera de exhibir o de presentar algo a la mente. 3. Presentación, posición del feto al nacer. **On presentation,** *(Com.)* A presentación. 4. Derecho de presentación o de patronato. **The Presentation,** fiesta de la Candelaria. *a.* De regalo y obsequio: **Presentation copy,** ejemplar de regalo con dedicatoria.

presentative ['presntətɪv] [pre-sen-ta-tiv], *a.* 1. Que tiene relación con la presentación mental. 2. Que tiene derecho de presentación.

present-day ['prezntˈdeɪ] [pre-sent-dei], *a.* De la actualidad, de hoy.

presentee [ˌpreznti:] [pre-sen-tii], *s.* Presentado, el sujeto propuesto o nombrado para ocupar un beneficio eclesiástico. 2. El que recibe un regalo.

presenter [prɪ'zentəʳ] [pre-sen-taʳ], *s.* 1. Presentador, el que presenta o propone para un beneficio eclesiástico. 2. El que hace un regalo.

presentiment [prɪ'zentɪmənt] [pri-sen-ti-ment], *s.* Presentimiento, cierto movimiento interior que hace presagiar lo que ha de acontecer, especialmente idea de que amenaza una calamidad o desgracia.

presently ['prezntlɪ] [pre-sent-li], *adv.* 1. Luego, de aquí a poco, dentro de poco. 2. *(Ant.)* Inmediatamente, al punto, sin dilación.

preservable [ˌprezə'vəbl] [pre-ser-va-bol], *a.* Preservable, que se puede preservar.

preservation [ˌprezə'veɪʃən] [pre-sa-vei-shon], *s.* Preservación, conservación (maintenance).

preservative [prɪ'zɜːvətɪv] [pri-ser-va-tiv], *a.* Preservativo, que tiene virtud o eficacia para preservar; conservador. -*s.* 1. Preservativo, lo que sirve para preservar o que tiende a preservar; defensa, salvaguardia (defence); profiláctico. 2. Sustancia añadida a los productos que se conservan para su mantenimiento.

preservatory [prɪ'zɜːvərɪ] [pri-ser-va-to-ri], *a.* Preservativo, que tiene la facultad de preservar o proteger. *s.* 1. Sitio para conservar. 2. Asilo para mujeres pobres o sin trabajo.

preserve [prɪ'zɜːv] [pri-serv], *va.* 1. Asegurar, poner o mantener en seguridad; proteger contra un daño o preservar, sacar de peligro, librar de la destrucción o de la muerte. 2. Preservar, guardar, conservar, mantener en buen estado (maintain). 3. Preservar, poner al abrigo de la corrupción; conservar, hacer almíbar, almibarar. -vn. Hacer conservas de frutas, confitarlas o almibararlas. **To preserve the health,** conservar la salud. **To preserve appearances,** guardar las apariencias.

preserve, s. Conserva, confitura.

preserved [prɪˈzɜːvd] [pri-servd], a. En conserva, confitado, en almíbar. **preserved fruit,** fruta en conserva.

preserver [prɪˈzɜːvəʳ] [pri-ser-vaʳ], s. 1. Preservador, confitero. 2. Antiguamente conservero. 3. Conservador, el que protege o defiende contra la destrucción o el mal.

preside [prɪˈzaɪd] [pri-said], vn. 1. Presidir (lead). 2. Gobernar, dirigir (govern): (se usa con la prep. over). 3. Estar en primer lugar, en lugar distinguido.

presidency [ˈprezɪdənsɪ] [pre-si-dan-si], s. Presidencia; superintendencia; funciones de presidente; tiempo durante el cual ejerce sus funciones un presidente.

president [ˈprezɪdənt] [pre-si-dent], s. 1. Presidente, funcionario elegido o nombrado para presidir una corporación, sociedad o asamblea de personas y dirigir sus deliberaciones, particularmente, el jefe del poder ejecutivo en las repúblicas. 2. Rector de ciertas universidades.

presidentess [ˈprezɪdəntnɪs] [pre-si-dant-nes], s. Presidenta.

presidential [ˌprezɪˈdenʃəl] [pre-si-den-shal], a. Presidencial, perteneciente a una presidencia, o a un presidente; que preside. **Presidential year,** año de elecciones presidenciales.

presidentship [ˈprezɪdəntˈʃɪp] [pre-si-dant-ship], s. Presidencia, cargo.

presider [prɪˈzaɪdəʳ] [pre-sai-daʳ], s. Presidente, el que preside.

presidium [prɪˈsɪdɪəm] [pre-si-diom], s. Presidium (órgano de gobierno soviético).

press [pres] [pres], va. 1. Aprensar, prensar, apretar, estrujar u oprimir en una prensa, laminar (crush, tighten). 2. Aprensar, apretar; afligir, oprimir, angustiar; estrujar a una persona (squeeze). 3. Compeler, obligar (oblige); impeler con violencia. 4. Apresurar, dar prisa (hurry). 5. Apretar, instar con eficacia. 6. Apretar, estrechar, acosar, perseguir de cerca. 7. Recalcar, ajustar o apretar mucho una cosa sobre otra. 8. Hacer levas, enganchar soldados. V. To IMPRESS. 9. Abrazar estrechamente, acariciar. 10. Acosar, incomodar, hostigar, fatigar; abrumar, causar pena. 11. Alisar o dar forma por medio de la presión, satinar. -vn. 1. Obrar por el peso o la fuerza; ejercer presión. 2. Avanzar sobre, adelantarse con ardor o enérgicamente, hacer esfuerzos para progresar, apresurarse. 3. Urgir, instar con vehemencia, apurar. 4. Agolparse la gente alrededor de una persona o cosa, apiñarse. 5. Acercarse demasiado por pura curiosidad; instar importunamente. 6. Hacer fuerza con algún argumento, razón, etc. **To hot-press,** prensar con planchas calientes. **To press a benefit upon one,** hacer a uno algún favor a su pesar. **To press down,** apretar o estrujar a uno hasta hacerle caer o hasta dejarlo imóvil. **He pressed him to his breast,** le estrechó contra su pecho. **Pressed for money,** necesitado; impulsado por la falta de dinero. **To press clothes,** alisar, planchar la ropa. **To press on, to press forward,** impeler hacia adelante, hacer adelantar; apresurarse, adelantarse con ardor. **The feet press the ground,** los pies pisan el suelo. **To press into service,** enganchar soldados.

press, s. 1. Turba, muchedumbre de gente. 2. Acción de esforzarse hacia adelante o de apiñarse. 3. Prisa, urgencia de asuntos; peso (in bussiness). **Press of business,** presión, urgencia de los negocios. 4. Prensa, máquina que sirve para apretar o exprimir, para alisar y dar lustre a los tejidos, para imprimir y otros usos. **Wine-press,** prensa de lagar. **Cloth-press,** prensa de paños. 5. Prensa de impresor, imprenta en general y sus productos; también, el conjunto de los redactores, gacetilleros, repórters, etc., empleados en los diarios o periódicos. 6. Armario, cajón de madera en forma de alacena para poner ropa y otras cosas. 7. Leva, recluta, enganche. V. IMPRESSMENT. **To go to press, to send to**

press, poner en prensa. **To correct for the press,** corregir pruebas de imprenta. **Liberty of the press,** libertad de la prensa, de imprenta. **To have a good** o **bad press,** tener buena o mala prensa. **Press-proof,** 1. La última prueba tomada antes de imprimir. 2. Una prueba tomada con cuidado. **Hot press, cold press,** prensa para satinar, en caliente o en frío. a. 1. De prensa, de imprenta, de enganche. **Press agent,** agente de publicidad; **press galery, press box,** tribuna de prensa; **press conference,** conferencia de prensa. **Press proof** prueba de prensa. (Mil.) **Press gang,** patrulla de enganche; **press money,** prima de enganche.

presser [ˈpresəʳ] [pre-saʳ], s. Aprensador, prensador. 2. Planchador. 3. Prensa (grape). 4. **Presser o presser foot,** prensatelas de una máquina de coser.

pressgang [ˈpresgæŋ] [pres-gang], s. Ronda de matrícula, empleada para enganchar o hacer levas para la marina o el ejército.

pressing [ˈpresɪŋ] [pre-sin], a. 1. Urgente, que insta, importante. 2. Importuno, pesado en sus solicitaciones. -s. V. PRESSURE. **Pressing-boards,** cartones lustrosos para prensar paño. **Pressing-iron,** plancha. **Pressing out,** expresión, acción de extraer el zumo. **Pressing together,** apiñamiento.

pressingly [ˈpresɪŋlɪ] [pre-sin-li], adv. Apretadamente, urgentemente.

pressman [ˈpresmæn] [pres-man], s. 1. Prensador, el que tiene a su cargo una prensa, prensista (Typ.). 2. Obrero que prensa el paño. 3. Reclutador, el que engancha gente para la marina o el ejército. 4. El hombre, soldado o marinero alistado en el servicio público. 5. (Eng.) Periodista.

press-room [ˈpresrʊm] [pres-rum], s. Taller de imprenta, local donde están las prensas de imprimir.

pressure [ˈpreʃəʳ] [pre-shaʳ], s. 1. Presión, la acción de apretar, estrujar o comprimir; prensadura, acción de prensar; el estado de ser apretado, prensado o comprimido. 2. Fuerza mecánica, medida comúnmente en libras; fuerza mecánica de cualquier especie. 3. Fuerza moral determinante, impulso eficaz. 4. Urgencia, prisa, ímpetu, exigencia sobre el tiempo o la energía de alguien (hurry). 5. Ahogo, opresión, aprieto, congoja, vejación, apretura. 6. (Elect.) Tensión. a. De presión, de tensión; **pressure coil,** bobina de tensión. **Pressure gauge,** manómetro, indicador de presión; **Pressure group,** minoría que ejerce influencia sobre los legisladores o la opinión pública.

pressure cooker [ˈpreʃəkʊkəʳ] [pre-sha-ku-kaʳ], s. Olla a presión. (Mex.) Olla express.

pressurize [ˈpreʃəraɪz] [pre-sha-rais], va. (Aer.) Sobrecomprimir. **Pressurized cabin,** cabina a presión.

presswork [ˈpreswɜːk] [pres-uek], s. 1. (Impr.) Manejo y manipulación de la prensa tipográfica, tirada, el trabajo hecho por la prensa. 2. Ebanistería hecha con chapas colocadas al través, encoladas y prensadas mientras están calientes.

prestation [presˈteɪʃən] [pres-tei-shan], s. 1. Pago de dinero, v. g. por peaje, el hacer un servicio o deber; antiguamente, préstamo, cantidad que los clérigos anglicanos pagaban anualmente a los obispos. 2. Prestación de un servicio obligado.

prestidigitation [ˈprestɪˌdɪdʒɪˈteɪʃən] [pres-ti-di-yi-tei-shon], s. Prestidigitación, juegos de manos.

prestige [presˈtiːdʒ] [pres-tich], s. Prestigio, buena reputación, fama, influencia moral o autoridad basada en el poder o los triunfos pasados.

prestigious [presˈtiːdʒɪəs] [pres-ti-yios], a. Prestigioso.

prestimony [ˈprestɪmɒnɪ] [pres-ti-mo-ni], s. Prestimonio, prestamera, prebenda eclesiástia de la Iglesia católica romana.

presto [ˈprestəʊ] [pres-tou], adv. 1. En música, en compás vivo y animado. 2. Presto, luego, al instante (fast).

presumable [prɪˈzjuːməbl] [pri-siu-ma-bol], a. Presumible; razonable.

presumably [prɪˈzjuːməblɪ] [pri-siu-ma-bli], adv. Sin examen, por presunción.

presume [prɪ'zjuːm] [pri-sium], *va.* 1. Presumir, suponer o creer alguna cosa sólo por indicios (assume, suppose); afirmar sin prueba. 2. Presumir, estar muy satisfecho o pagado de sí. 3. Atreverse a hacer una cosa sin derecho o permiso para hacerla (dare). *-vn.* Vanagloriarse, jactarse. **To presume on** o **upon,** suponer; contar con; imaginarse; vanagloriarse de. **To presume upon,** estar muy satisfecho o pagado de, contar con, tener demasiada confianza en algo. **To presume to,** tomarse la libertad de.

presumed [prɪ'zjuːmd] [pri-siumd], *a.* Presunto.

presumer [prɪ'zjuːməʳ] [pri-siu-maʳ], *s.* Un presumido, un hombre arrogante o presuntuoso.

presumption [prɪ'zʌmpʃən] [pri-samp-shon], *s.* 1. Presunción, sospecha, conjetura (suspicion). 2. Presunción, vanidad, confianza en sí mismo. 3. La confianza que se tiene en una cosa presupuesta. 4. Argumento muy fuerte. 5. Temeridad, acción de emprender alguna cosa contra las probabilidades ordinarias. **The presumption is that it will take place,** puede presumirse, pensarse, que eso se realizará.

presumptive [prɪ'zʌmptɪv] [pri-samp-tiv], *a.* 1. Presuntivo, supuesto, presupuesto, que da origen a una presunción, fundado sobre una presunción o un testimonio probable; que puede creerse razonablemente. 2. *(Des.)* Presuntuoso.

presumptively [prɪ'zʌmptɪvlɪ] [pri-samp-tiv-li], *adv.* Según presunción, por vía de conjetura.

presumptuous [prɪ'zʌmptjʊəs] [pri-samp-tiuos], *a.* 1. Presuntuoso, presumido, arrogante, vano, insolente, irreverente. 2. Atrevido, arrojado, que confía excesivamente.

presumptuously [prɪ'zʌmptjʊəslɪ] [pri-samp-tiuos-li], *adv.* Presuntuosamente.

presumptuousness [prɪ'zʌmptjʊəsnɪs] [pri-samp-tiuos-nes], *s.* Presunción, calidad de presuntuoso o arrogante, orgullo, arrogancia, vana confianza, irreverencia.

presuppose [ˌpriːsə'pəʊz] [pri-su-pous], *va.* Presuponer, implicar como antecedente; suponer de antemano.

presupposition [ˌpriːsʌpə'zɪʃən] [pri-sa-pa-si-shon], *s.* Presuposición, presupuesto.

pretence [prɪ'tens] [pri-tens], *s.* Lo mismo que PRETENSE.

pretend [prɪ'tend] [pri-tend], *va.* 1. Aparentar, mostrar o dar a entender lo que no es o lo que no hay, dar por pretexto, fingir (fake, simulate); hacerse el, o que. 2. Pretender, intentar. 3. Pretender, procurar o solicitar alguna cosa. 4. Afirmar falsamente, alegar sin verdad. **To pretend to be,** fingirse, dárselas de. *-vn.* 1. Afectar; presumir o preciarse de; aspirar a lograr alguna cosa o creer tener derecho a ella. **To pretend to,** pretender a 2. Disfrazarse.

pretender [prɪ'tendəʳ] [pri-ten-daʳ], *s.* Pretendiente.

pretendingly [prɪ'tendɪŋlɪ] [pri-ten-din-li], *adv.* Arrogantemente, presuntuosamente.

pretense [prɪ'tens] [pri-tens], *s.* 1. Pretexto, motivo simulado, causa aparente, supuesta razón aparente para ocultar un motivo; ficción, máscara, velo (fiction). 2. Pretensión, afectación, simulación. 3. Pretensión, el derecho bien o mal fundado que alguno juzga tener a una cosa. 4. Intención, designio, proyecto. **Under pretence of,** so pretexto de. **Under false pretences,** con engaño, con dolo.

pretenseless [prɪ'tenslɪs] [pri-tens-les], *a.* Falto de pretensiones.

pretension [prɪ'tenʃən] [pri-ten-shon], *s.* 1. Pretensión, el derecho bien o mal fundado que alguno juzga tener sobre una cosa; pretexto, 2. Ostentación de un carácter particular, sea simulada o mal entendida; afectación. 3. Afirmación atrevida o presuntuosa.

pretentious [prɪ'tenʃəs] [pri-ten-shos], *a.* 1. Con pretensiones, afectado, vanaglorioso, presumido; llamativo. 2. Ambicioso, vasto.

preter-, *s.,* Prefijo latino que significa fuera de, más o más allá.

preterit, preterite ['pretərɪt] [pre-te-rit], *a. (Gram.)* Pasado, pretérito. *-s.* Tiempo pretérito o pasado del verbo. *V.* AORIST.

preterition ['pretərɪʃən] [pre-te-ri-shon], *s.* 1. Preterición. pretermisión. 2. *(Ret.)* Preterición, figura que consiste en

aparentar que se quiere omitir o pasar por alto aquello mismo que se dice expresamente.

preterm [ˌpriː'tɜːm] [pre-term], *a.* Prematuro.

pretermit [ˌpriː'tɜːmɪt] [pre-ter-mit], *v.* 1. Pasar por alto, omitir. 2. Interrumpir.

preternatural [ˌpriːtə'nætʃrəl] [pri-tar-na-chu-ral], *a.* Preternatural, extraordinario, inexplicable, poco común; se diferencia de antinatural.

preternaturally [ˌpriːtə'nætʃrəlɪ] [pri-tar-na-chu-ra-li], *adv.* Preternaturalmente.

pretext ['priːtekst] [pri-tekst], *s.* Pretexto, motivo fingido, razón ficticia; excusa.

pretor ['priːtəʳ] [pri-taʳ], *s.* Pretor, magistrado romano.

pretorian, [priː'tɔːrɪən] [pri-to-rian], *a.* 1. Pretoriano, pretorial, tocante o perteneciente al pretor. 2. Pretoriano, se aplica a los soldados de la guardia de los emperadores romanos.

prettily ['prɪtɪlɪ] [pri-ti-li], *adv.* Lindamente, bonitamente; agradablemente.

prettiness ['prɪtɪnɪs] [pri-ti-nes], *s.* Lindeza; calidad de bonito, cierta belleza, elegancia o gentileza; gracia.

pretty ['prɪtɪ] [pri-ti], *a.* 1. Lindo, bien parecido, bonito, moderadamente bello o hermoso (pretty, nice). 2. Afectado, lindo, hablando irónicamente. 3. Mediano, ni muy pequeño ni muy grande, pasadero; suficiente, bastante. 4. Agradable, dulce, encantador, precioso. **A pretty while,** un buen rato. **A pretty penny,** un dineral, un buen pico. **Pretty-pretty,** chuchería. *-adv.* Algo, algún tanto, un poco. **Pretty well,** medianamente, tal cual, no mal, bastante bien. **Pretty near,** bastante cerca, poco más o menos, a corta distancia.

prevail [prɪ'veɪl] [pri-veil], *vn.* 1. Prevalecer, vencer, ser superior, poder o valer más; sobresalir, predominar (to take root). 2. Influir, tener influjo; obrar con eficacia. 3. Persuadir, inducir, lograr, conseguir, alcanzar de una persona que haga lo que se quiere (persuade). 4. Esparcirse o extenderse grandemente, estar en boga general; ser muy frecuente. **To prevail on, upon, over** o **against,** ser superior, tener más fuerza, dominar, vencer; supeditar. **To prevail on, upon** o **with,** persuadir, inducir, convencer. **He prevailed upon me to come,** me persuadió a que viniese. **Mohammedanism prevails throughout northern Africa,** el mahometismo predomina en todo el norte de África. **It is a fashion which prevails,** es una moda que está en boga.

prevailing [prɪ'veɪlɪŋ] [pri-vei-lin], *a.* 1. Muy esparcido, extendido, general, común. 2. Predominante, poderoso, eficaz.

prevalence ['prevələns] [pre-va-lans], *s.* 1. Predominio, superioridad, fuerza predominante, eficacia, preponderancia. 2. Uso o aceptación general, ocurrencia común, frecuencia.

prevalent ['prevələnt] [pre-va-lant], *a.* 1. Superior, sobresaliente, predominante, poderoso, dominante (leader, major). 2. General, grandemente esparcido, de frecuente ocurrencia, común. 3. Victorioso, eficaz.

prevalently ['prevələntlɪ] [pre-va-lant-li], *adv.* Eficazmente, poderosamente.

prevaricate [prɪ'værɪkeɪt] [pri-va-ri-keit], *vn.* 1. Usar de lenguaje ambiguo o evasivo para engañar, representar falsamente. 2. *(For.)* prevaricato, el crimen del abogado o procurador que hace traición a su parte, favoreciendo a la contraria.

prevarication ['prɪˌværɪ'keɪʃən] [pri-va-ri-kei-shon], *sf.* Evasiva, tergiversación.

prevent [prɪ'vent] [pri-vent], *va.* 1. Prevenir, precaver estorbar, impedir (take care). 2. Prevenir, adelantarse o anticiparse a alguno. 3. *(Ant.)* Preceder, guiar, ir delante guiando y facilitando el camino. *-vn. (Des.)* Venir antes de tiempo.

preventative [prɪ'ventətɪv] [pri-ven-ta-tiv], *a.* y *s.* V. PREVENTIVE.

preventer [prɪ'ventəʳ] [pri-ven-taʳ], *s.* Estorbador, el que o lo que impide o precave; especialmente, *(Mar.)* soga, berlinga, cadena o perno auxiliar. **Preventer-brace,**

contrabraza. **Preventer-tacks,** contraamuras. **Preventer-lifts,** contraamantillos. **Preventer-shrouds,** contraobenques. **Preventer-sheets,** contraescotas. **Preventer-stay,** estay folar. **Preventer-backstays,** contrabrandales.

prevention [prɪˈvenʃən] [pri-ven-shon], *s.* 1. Estorbo, embarazo, la acción de estorbar o impedir, también, lo que impide o sirve de obstáculo. 2. *(Des.)* La acción de ir delante o de tomar la delantera; la acción de preceder. **Prevention is better than cure.** *(Prov.)* Lo mejor es curarse en salud.

preventive [prɪˈventɪv] [pri-ven-tiv], *a.* 1. Impeditivo; que sirve para porteger contra daño; preservativo, lo que tiene virtud de preservar. 2. *(Des.)* Preventivo, que previene o a una cosa. **Preventive service,** resguardo militar. -*s.* Preservativo, profiláctico; medida preventiva o profiláctica.

preventively [prɪˈventɪvlɪ] [pri-ven-tiv-li], *adv.* Prevenidamente, anticipadamente, de antemano.

preview [ˈpriːvjuː] [pri-viu], *s.* Exhibición previa, representación especial (de algún espectáculo) antes de verlo el público. *(Cine)* Avance, preestreno.

previous [ˈpriːvɪəs] [pri-vios], *a.* Previo, anticipado, antecedente, anterior, de antemano. **Previous notice,** aviso dado de antemano. **The previous question,** la cuestión previa. **Previous to,** antecedente; antes de. *V.* PREVIOUSLY.

previously [ˈpriːvɪəslɪ] [pri-vios-li], *adv.* De antemano, anticipadamente, anteriormente. **Previously to July,** antes de julio.

previse [ˈpriːvaɪz] [pri-vais], *va.* 1. Prever; conocer de antemano. 2. Prevenir, avisar o amonestar de antemano.

prevision [ˈpriːvɪʒən] [pri-vi-shon], *s.* Previsión, conocimiento o juicio de lo futuro (pronostic, prediction).

prewar [ˈpriːwɔːr] [pri-uor], *a.* De la preguerra, de antes de la guerra.

prey [preɪ] [prei], *s.* 1. Presa, cualquier animal asido por otro para su alimento; de aqui, botín. pillaje, despojo. 2. Victima. 3. Rapiña, robo. **Beast of prey,** animal de rapiña. animal carnicero. **Bird of prey,** ave de rapiña. **To fall a prey to,** ser presa de.

prey, *vn.* (con *on* o *upon*). 1. Devorar sus presas los animales carniceros. 2. Rapiñar, hurtar, pillar, robar, hacer presa. 3. Irse consumiendo la salud, la vida, etc.; minar, arruinar gradualmente. 4. Pesar, hacer fuerza en el ánimo la razón de alguna cosa; oprimir, agobiar. **To prey upon one's mind,** preocupar, enloquecer.

pribble [ˈprɪbl] [pri-bel], *s.* Disputa o conversaciones tontas.

price [praɪs] [prais], *s.* 1. Precio, el dinero que se paga por alguna cosa. 2. Precio, valor o estimación. 3. Premio, galardón. **Market price,** precio de mercado, precio corriente. **Set price,** precio fijo. **Trade price,** precio con rebaja para los que hacen el mismo comercio. **Full o selling price,** precio de venta al público. **Opening price, closing price,** primer curso, último curso (en la Bolsa). **At any price,** a todo precio; cueste lo que cueste, o lo que costare. **To set a price upon one's head,** poner a precio la cabeza de alguno. **Price-list.** lista de precios, cotización. **Cost price.** precio de coste. **Full price, selling price,** precio de venta al por menor. **Price control,** control de precios. **Price-current,** la lista de los precios corriente por mayor, derechos, etc., de los géneros.

price, *va.* 1. Valuar, estimar, apreciar, fijar el precio de alguna cosa. 2. *(Fam.)* Preguntar o pedir el precio de. **A priced catalogue,** un catálogo con precios.

priceless [ˈpraɪslɪs] [prais-les], *a.* 1. Inapreciable, demasiado precioso para admitir precio; sin precio. 2. *(Des.)* Bajo precio, sin valor ni mérito.

prick [prɪk] [prik], *va.* 1. Punzar, picar, herir de punta (pierce). 2. Fijar por la punta algún instrumento 3. Apuntar, señalar o marcar alguna cosa con la punta de un instrumento (mark); de aquí, escoger; poner en música una canción. 4. Aguzar, avivar, picar, excitar, estimular, pinchar (incite). 5. *(Mar.)* Compasear la carta de marcar. 6. Enderezar o aguzar las orejas; prestar atención. 7. Perseguir una liebre por medio de pistas. -*vn.* 1. Tener o causar la sensación de una punzada o picadura; picarse. 2. Galopar, arrimar las espuelas o dar de

espuelas. 3. Apuntar hacia arriba. 4. *(Prov. Ingl.)* Avinagrarse, ponerse ácido. **To prick on o forward,** aguijonear, pisar, aguzar, avivar, estimular. **To prick up,** enderezar, poner derecha una cosa. **To prick up one's ears,** aguzar las orejas, aguzar los oídos, oír o escuchar atentamente; amusgar. **To prick off o out,** en jardinería, transplantar las plantas tiernas, por vía de preparación para ponerlas en macetas o cuadros. **To prick the sails,** *(Mar.)* Recoser las velas.

prick, *s.* 1. Punzón, aguijón, acicate, cualquier instrumento puntiagudo. 2. Puntura, herida con instrumento punzante; picadura, punzada. 3. Punzada, el sentimiento interior que causa alguna cosa que aflige el ánimo; espina, escrúpulo o remordimiento de conciencia. **Picks of conscience,** remordimientos. 4. Pista, rastro, huella de venado o liebre. 5. Punto, momento; el tiempo fijo en que se hace alguna cosa. 6. El blanco a que tiran los balleteros. **To kick against the pricks.** dar o tirar coces contra el aguijón; obstinarse en resistir a una fuerza superior. *a.* 1. **Pick ear,** oreja agudizada. **Pick punch,** punzón de acero.

prick-eared [ˈprɪkˌɛəd] [prik-ead], *a.* Amusgado; desierto, vivo, impertinente.

pricker [ˈprɪkər] [pri-kar], *s.* 1. Punzón, instrumento puntiagudo; alesna o lesna. 2. El que pica. 3. Jinete, el que espolea o da de espuela al caballo.

pricket [ˈprɪkɪt] [pri-kit], *s.* 1. Punta sobre que se puede asegurar una vela. 2. Siempreviva menor. 3. El gamo de un año cumplido.

pricking [ˈprɪkɪŋ] [pri-kin], *s.* 1. Picadura. 2. Punzada, dolor agudo que se repite de cuando en cuando.

prickle [ˈprɪkl] [pri-kel], *s.* Pincho, púa, espina. **Thorn prickle,** abrojo.

prickliness [ˈprɪklɪnɪs] [pri-kli-nes], *s.* Calidad de espinoso, abundancia de púas, espinas o pinchos.

prickly [ˈprɪklɪ] [pri-kli], *a.* Espinoso, lleno de púas; quisquilloso, poco afable (person).

pride [praɪd] [praid], *s.* 1. Orgullo, presunción, vanidad, engreimiento (vanity). 2. Insolencia, altivez (haughtiness). 3. Ostentación, jactancia o vanagloria. 4. Hermosura notable, belleza, amabilidad, ornamento (beauty); de aquí, majestuosidad, pompa, aparato. 5. Dignidad, elevación, esplendor, ostentación. 6. Amor propio (arrogance). 7. Conocimiento interior de la juventud o del poder; fuego, ardor; de aquí, *(Des.)* propensión al coito que tiene las hembras de algunos animales. **He takes pride in doing good,** se precia o gloria en hacer bien. **Pride of the morning,** niebla o chubasco al amanecer.

pride, *va.* Ensoberbecerse, picarse, preciarse o jactarse de alguna cosa regularmente buena. **To pride oneself,** enorgullecerse, ensoberbecerse.

prideful [ˈpraɪdfʊl] [praid-ful], *a.* Orgulloso, altanero; también vano.

prier [ˈpraɪər] [praiar], *s.* Escudriñador, inquiridor, fisgón, husmeador (curious).

priest [priːst] [prist], *s.* Sacerdote, presbítero, cura, el que preside las ceremonias en un culto religioso.

priestcraft [ˈpriːstkræft] [prist-kraft], *s.* Superchería, artimaña, embuste o fraude de los ministros de la religión.

priestess [ˈpriːstɪs] [pris-tis], *sf.* Sacerdotisa.

priesthood [ˈpriːsthʊd] [prist-jud], *s.* Clero, clerecía, el estado eclesiástico, el sacerdocio.

priestliness [ˈpriːstlɪnɪs] [prist-li-nes], *s.* Las maneras o modales de los sacerdotes.

priestly [ˈpriːstlɪ] [prist-li], *a.* Sacerdotal, perteneciente a un sacerdote o a un cura; que conviene a un cura.

prig [prɪg] [prig], *vn. (Prvov. Ingl.)* Regatear, bajar el precio.

prig, *s.* 1. Mozuelo presumido, pisaverde; pedante. 2. *(Fam.)* ladrón.

priggish [ˈprɪgɪʃ] [pri-guish], *a.* Algo presumido y afectado.

priggishness [ˈprɪgɪʃnɪs] [pri-guish-nes], *s.* Maneras o modales de un pisaverde o un pedante.

prill [prɪl] [pril], *s. V.* BRILL.

prim [prɪm] [prim], *a.* Peripuesto, afectado, relamido, estirado, exageradamente ordenado.

prim, *va.* 1. Cerrar (mouth), apretar, fruncir (lip). 2. Ataviar, poner a uno petimetre o muy majo; hacer carocas o carantoñas.

primacy ['praɪməsɪ] [prai-ma-si], *s.* Primacía, la dignidad y jurisdicción del primado.

primage ['prɪmɪdʒ] [pri-mich], *s. (Mar.)* Capa, quintalada.

primal ['praɪməl] [prai-mal], *a.* Primero, que está al principio; original, principal, lo más importante.

primarily ['praɪmərɪlɪ] [prai-ma-ri-li], *adv.* Primariamente, originalmente; sobre todo, principalmente.

primariness ['praɪmərɪnɪs] [prai-ma-ri-nes], *s.* Primado, primacía, prioridad (supremacy).

primary ['praɪmərɪ] [prai-ma-ri], *a.* 1. Primario, primero, primitivo, original, radical (first, original). 2. Principal, de primer orden, fundamental. 3. Elemental, del primer grado, el más bajo. **Primary education,** enseñanza primaria. -*s.* 1. Primero, lo que ocupa el primer puesto en importancia. 2. *(E. U.)* Reunión de los electores de un partido antes de una elección, para nombrar los candidatos. 3. Pluma grande de las que sirven a las aves para volar; ala delantera (insect). 4. Capital, fundamental, principal. **Primary accent,** acento principal. 5. Elemental. **Primary colors,** colores primarios.

primate ['praɪmɪt] [prai-mit], *s.* 1. Primado, el primero y más preeminente de todos los arzobispos y obispos de un reino. 2. Primates, orden primero de la clase de los mamíferos.

primateship ['praɪmɪtʃɪp] [prai-mit-ship], *s.* Primado, dignidad del primado.

prime [praɪm] [praim], *s.* 1. La primavera de la vida, el estado de mayor vigor o hermosura. 2. El principio de alguna cosa; la madrugada, el alba, el amanecer, el principio del día y a veces se toma por toda la mañana. 3. Ápice, el último grado de perfección. 4. Flor, nata, lo mas escogido o selecto de alguna cosa. 5. Prima, una de las horas canónicas. 6. Señal o signo (') que se pone arriba y hacia la derecha de una letra o guarismo; la pulgada, o el minuto designado por este signo. -*a.* 1. Que está en su mayor verdor o en su estado más floreciente. 2. Primero, original, principal. **At prime cost,** al precio de pie de fábrica, a coste y costas. 3. Primoroso, excelente. 4. Primo, número divisible solamente por sí mismo y por la unidad. 5. Marcado con el signo '. **Prime minister,** primer ministro, el ministro principal del estado.

prime, *va.* 1. Aparejar, preparar. 2. *(Fam.)* Advertir, avisar, noticiar; informar sobre lo que se ha de decir o hacer. 3. Cebar (arm), poner pólvora en la cazoleta de un arma de fuego cargada. 4. Imprimar, cubrir con la primera capa de colores o de argamasa. -*vn.* 1. Servir de cebo; de aquí, poner una persona o cosa en estado de preparación para hacer algo. 2. Llevar agua con el vapor dentro del cilindro; se dice de una caldera de vapor. 3. Acelerarse la marea.

primely ['praɪmlɪ] [praim-li], *adv.* 1. En alto grado, muy bien, excelentemente. 2. *(Des.)* Primeramente, originalmente.

primeness ['praɪmnɪs] [praim-nes], *s.* Primacía, primor, excelencia.

primer ['praɪməʳ] [prai-maʳ], *s.* 1. Cartilla para los niños. 2. Originalmente, el devocionario de Nuestra Señora. 3. Dos grados de letra de imprenta; es decir **long primer,** entredós, filosofía, letra de diez puntos; **y great primer,** texto, letra de dieciocho puntos.

primeval [praɪˈmiːvəl] [prai-mi-val], *a.* Primitivo, primero, original.

priming ['praɪmɪŋ] [prai-min], *s.* 1. El acto de prepararse o alistarse. 2. Cebo, la pólvora que se pone en las cazoletas de las armas de fuego. 3. Lo que es preliminar, o relativamente pequeño, en comparación con otra cosa. 4. Imprimación, la primera capa de colores u óleo que se da a una superficie. 5. En las máquinas de vapor, el primer chorro de mezcla de vapor y agua. **Priming-horn,** polvorín, el frasco para el cebo.

primitive ['prɪmɪtɪv] [pri-mi-tiv], *a.* 1. Primitivo, original; antiguo, que pertenece al principio, al origen, o a los tiempos antiguos, radical, que no es derivado. 2. *(Biol.)* Rudimentario, original, que se halla en estado temprano de su desarrollo. 3. Primitivo, radical, de donde se derivan otras palabras.

primitevely ['prɪmɪtɪvlɪ] [pri-mi-tiv-li], *adv.* Primitivamente.

primitiveness ['prɪmɪtɪvnɪs] [pri-mi-tiv-nes], *s.* Estado o carácter primitivo.

primitivist ['prɪmɪtɪvɪst] [pri-mi-ti-vist], *a.* Primitivista.

primly ['prɪmlɪ] [prim-li], *adv.* De una manera peripuesta, con remilgo, tiesura; puesto de veinticinco alfileres.

primness ['prɪmnɪs] [prim-nes], *s.* Precisión, exactitud, formalidad o gravedad afectada (accuracy, exactness); remilgo en las mujeres.

primogeniture [ˌpraɪməʳˈdʒenɪtʃəʳ] [prai-mou-ye-ni-chaʳ], *s.* 1. Prioridad de nacimiento; derecho de nacimiento. 2. Primogenitura.

primordial [praɪˈmɔːdɪəl] [prai-mor-dial], *a.* Primordial. Original, primitivo. 3. Inicial, rudimentario.

primp [prɪmp] [primp], *v.* Vestir, arreglar.

primrose ['prɪmrəʊz] [prim-rous], *s.* 1. *(Bot.)* Prímula o primavera, una planta y su flor. 2. Color amarillo verdoso claro. -*a.* 1. Perteneciente a la prímula o de su color, amarillo verdoso claro. 2. Florido, gayo. **Primrose path,** sendero florido; vida dada a los placeres de los sentidos.

primus ['prɪməs] [pri-mus], *a.* Primero.

prince [prɪns] [prins], *s.* 1. Príncipe, soberano, monarca. 2. Príncipe, el hijo de un monarca, descendiente varón de una casa real; el que goza de este título de honor. 3. Príncipe, el primero y más excelente en su línea. **Petty prince,** principillo, principote. **Prince Rupert's drops,** *V.* RUPERT'S DROPS. **Prince of the power of the air, prince of this world,** *(Bíblico)* Satanás. **Prince of Wales,** Príncipe de Gales, título del heredero del trono en Inglaterra. **Prince of Darkness,** príncipe de las tinieblas. **Prince of the Church,** príncipe de la Iglesia.

princedom ['prɪnsdəm] [prins-dom], *s.* Principado, soberania.

prince-like ['prɪnslaɪk] [prins-laik], *a.* Correspondiente a un príncipe o semejante a él, principesco.

princely ['prɪnslɪ] [prins-li], *a.* 1. Semejante a un príncipe o característico de él, digno de un príncipe, grande, noble, munífico. 2. Propio de un príncipe; real, magnífico, regio; faustoso, fastuoso, fastoso, augusto. -*adv.* Como un príncipe, digno de un príncipe.

prince's-feather ['prɪnseɪsˈfɛəðəʳ] [prin-ses-fea-daʳ], *s. (Bot.)* 1. Polígono, planta herbácea anual, con espigas de flores color de rosa. 2. Amaranto (de Méjico).

princess [prɪnˈses] [prin-ses], *sf.* Princesa; hija de un monarca, o de una casa real; esposa de un príncipe; reina, o mujer soberana de un Estado. **Princess royal,** hija mayor de un soberano.

principal ['prɪnsɪpəl] [prin-si-pal], *a.* 1. Principal, que tiene el primer lugar y estimación (main). 2. Principal, el que está a la cabeza de algún negocio, y en este sentido se usa como substantivo en ambas lenguas. -*s.* 1. Principal, jefe, presidente, gobernador, director de una escuela u otro establecimiento de educación. 2. *(For.)* Causante, comitente, constituyente. 3. Principal, capital, la cantidad de dinero que se pone a censo, rédito o a ganancias y pérdidas.

principality [ˌprɪnsɪˈpælɪtɪ] [prin-si-pa-li-ti], *s.* 1. Principado, soberanía. 2. *(Ant.)* Superioridad, predomino. -*pl. (Ant.)* En el Nuevo Testamento, potestades celestiales o demoníacas.

principally ['prɪnsɪpəlɪ] [prin-si-pa-li], *adv.* Principalmente, primeramente, en primer lugar.

principalness ['prɪnsɪpəlnɪs] [prin-si-pal-nes], *s.* La calidad de ser principal o jefe, principaldad.

principate ['prɪnsɪpeɪt] [prin-si-peit], *s.* Principado.

principle ['prɪnsəpl] [prin-si-pol], *s.* 1. Principio constitutivo, causa primitiva o primera, fundamento, motivo, causa, origen (bassis, reason). 2. Carácter esencial, esencia. 3. Verdad general, axioma, postulado, proposición admitida como punto de partida. 4. Principio, máxima, regla de conducta. 5. *(Quím.)* Elemento de los cuerpos; constituyente esencial de un compuesto o de una substancia a la cual da su carácter. 6. Dote o facultad natural.

principle, *va.* Imbuir, infundir principios o máximas en el entendimiento; fijar en el ánimo. Se emplea principalmente en el participio pasado. **Men principled against bribery,** hombres de principios opuesto al cohecho. **Men high-principled,** de principios elevados.

prink [prɪŋk] [prink], *vn. y va.* 1. Ataviarse, adornarse; presumir; acicalarse para llamar la atención. 2. Asumir un aire altanero.

print [prɪnt] [print], *va.* 1. Estampar, imprimir, dejar señalada la figura de una cosa en otra. 2. Imprimir, hacer ejemplares de (una cosa) por medio de la prensa. 3. Imprimir, hacer estampar, dar a la prensa o publicar algún libro o escrito. 4. Imprimir, reproducir por medio de la acción de la luz, o de un procedimiento de transferencia. También, en sentido figurado, fijar en el ánimo. 5. Limpiarse las plumas (a bird). -*vn.* 1. Imprimir, ejercer el arte de la tipografía. 2. Sufrir la acción de la luz, cambiar de color, se dice del papel sensibilizado de fotografía. **Printed by,** impreso por; imprenta de. **Printed for,** impreso para.

print, *s.* 1. Impresión, estampa, la calidad y forma de la letra de algún impreso u obra impresa. 2. Impresión; material impreso; caracteres impresos colectivamente. 3. Impreso, el escrito impreso en una o en pocas hojas; papel suelto o volante, diario, etc. 4. Impresión, la marca, señal o huella que una cosa deja en otra, sello. 5. Lámina, plancha, estampa. 6. Indiana, tela impresa. 7. Molde, lo que sirve para dar una forma. 8. Ejemplar positivo sacado de una prueba negativa. **In print,** 1. Impreso, ya en venta, abastecido. 2. *(Des.)* Con exactitud, con formalidad. **Out of print,** agotado, vendido. **Butter print,** molde para mantequilla. **Prints o printed goods,** zarazas. *(Amer.)* Quimones. **Print-shop,** tienda en que se venden estampas o grabados. **Print-works,** taller de estampar telas. **Small print,** tipo menudo.

printed [ˈprɪntɪd] [prin-tid], *a.* Estampado, impreso. **Printed matter,** impresos.

printer [ˈprɪntər] [prin-taˀ], *s.* Impresor, tipógrafo, prensista. 2. *(Fot.)* Aparato para tirar pruebas positivas. **Printer's ink,** tinta de imprenta. **Printer's mark,** pie de imprenta. **Printer's proof,** prueba de imprenta, prueba tipográfica.

printing [ˈprɪntɪŋ] [prin-tin], *s.* 1. Imprenta, tipografía, arte u oficio de imprimir letras, caracters o figuras en papel, telas, etc. 2. Impresión, la acción y efecto de imprimir, lo que está impreso. *V.* PRESSWORK. **Printing-frame,** *(Foto.)* Marco de imprimir. **Printing-machine, printing-press,** prensa, máquina para imprimir o para estampar telas. **Printing-office,** imprenta. **Printig-types,** caracteres de imprenta, letras de molde, tipo.

printless [ˈprɪntlɪs] [print-les], *a.* Lo que no deja señal, impresión ni huella.

prior [ˈpraɪər] [praiaˀ], *a.* Anterior, antecedente, precedente, prior. -*s.* Prior, prelado en algunas órdenes religiosas.

priorate [ˈpraɪəreɪt] [praio-reit], *s.* Priorato, el oficio o dignidad de prior o priora; el tiempo que dura este oficio.

prioress [ˈpraɪərɪs] [praio-ris], *sf.* Priora.

priority [praɪˈɒrɪti] [praio-ri-ti], *s.* Prioridad, anterioridad, antelación. **Priority of debt,** prelación de los acreedores.

priorship [ˈpraɪəʃɪp] [praior-ship], *s.* Priorazgo, priorato.

priory [ˈpraɪəri] [praio-ri], *s.* Priorato, convento en que tiene jurisdicción un prior o una priora.

prism [ˈprɪzəm] [pri-sem], *s.* 1. Prisma. 2. El espectro solar. **Prism binocular,** prismáticos.

prismatic, [prɪzˈmætɪk] [pris-ma-tik], *a.* 1. Prismático, refractado o formado por un prisma; parecido al espectro solar. 2. Prismático, parecido a un prisma, perteneciente a un prisma. 3. Colorido, brillante (bright).

prismatically [prɪzˈmætɪkəlɪ] [pris-ma-ti-ka-li], *adv.* En forma de prisma.

prismoid [ˈprɪzmɔɪd] [pris-moid], *s.* Sólido de forma parecida a la del prisma.

prison [ˈprɪzn] [pri-son], *s.* Prisión, cárcel, edificio público donde se encierra a los presos. **Prison-house,** cárcel, prisión. **Prison-ship,** buque prisión, embarcación destinada a guardar o conducir presos. **Prison-fever, jail-fever,** el tifo, de una forma maligna. **Keeper of a prison,** alcaide, carcelero.

prison, *va.* Encarcelar. *V.* TO IMPRISON.

prisoner [ˈprɪznər] [pri-so-naˀ], *s.* Preso, prisionero. **The prisoner at the bar,** el acusado, el preso que está presente ante el tribunal. **Prisoner's base,** rescate, juego de muchachos.

prisonment [ˈprɪznmənt] [pri-son-ment], *s.* Encierro. *V.* IMPRISONMENT.

pristine [ˈprɪstaɪn] [pris-tain], *a.* Prístino, primitivo, original, que pertenece a los tiempos primitivos.

prittle-prattle [ˈprɪtlˈpætl] [pri-tel-pa-tel], *s. (Fam.)* Charla, habladuría.

privacy [ˈprɪvəsɪ] [pri-va-si], *s.* 1. Retiro, soledad, aislamiento (loneliness). 2. Secreto, asunto que se conserva secreto, o en privado. 3. Retrete; paraje adonde se retira el que quiere estar solo: sitio de retiro.

private [ˈpraɪvɪt] [prai-vit], *a.* 1. Secreto, oculto, solo, solitario, retirado. 2. Privado, que se ejecuta a vista de pocos, familiar y domésticamente; que no es público; propio, particular, peculiar o personal a cada uno, raso, sin graduación. 3. Reticente, poco dispuesto a comunicarse. **In private,** particularmente; en secreto, en particular. **A private man,** un particular. **Private staircase,** escalera secreta o excusada. -*s.* 1. Soldado raso. 2. *pl.* Partes pudendas. **A private hearing,** una audiencia secreta a puertas cerradas. **They wish to be private,** quieren estar solos. **At one's private expense,** a costa propia. **Private theatricals,** comedias caseras.

privateer [ˌpraɪvɪˈtɪər] [prai-va-tiaˀ], *s.* 1. Corsario, navío o embarcación armada en corso, tripulada por simples particulares y a su costa, con licencia de su gobierno para capturar embarcaciones extranjeras en tiempo de guerra. 2. Corsario, el tripulante de un buque corsario.

privateer, *vn.* Armar en corso, cruzrar contra el enemigo a bordo de un buque corsario. **To go privateering,** ir o salir a corso.

privately [ˈpraɪvɪtlɪ] [prai-vit-li], *adv.* Secretamente, ocultamente.

privateness [ˈpraɪvɪtnɪs] [prai-vit-nes], *s.* 1. El estado de la persona que vive como particular, o que vive en la obscuridad. 2. Secreto, silencio. 2. Retiro, recogimiento, apartamiento.

privation [ˈpraɪveɪʃən] [prai-vei-shon], *s.* 1. Privación, carencia, falta de bienestar; cosa dura, penible. 2. *V.* DEPRIVATION. 3. Privación, exoneración, el acto de privar de un empleo u oficio. 4. *(Ecles.)* Suspensión.

privative [ˈprɪvətɪv] [pri-va-tiv], *a.* 1. Privativo, que causa privación. 2. *(Gram.)* Privativo, que significa privación; que muda la significación al negativo. -*s.* 1. Negación, no existencia. 2. *(Gram.)* Prefijo que indica negación, también, adjetivo que indica la ausencia de lo que es ordinariamente inherente, como «ciego» falto de vista.

privatization [ˌpraɪvətaɪˈzeɪʃən] [prai-va-tai-sei-shon], *sf.* Privatización.

privatize [ˈpraɪvətaɪz] [prai-va-tais], *vt.* Privatizar.

privilege [ˈprɪvɪlɪdʒ] [pri-vi-lich], *s.* Privilegio, favor, beneficio, gracia, prerrogativa, inmunidad, exención concedida a ciertas personas solamente, o bajo especiales condiciones. **Writ of privilege,** auto de excarcelación.

privilege, *va.* Privilegiar, exceptuar de un gravamen o carga, conceder una exención, prerrogativa, favor o beneficio.

privileged [ˈprɪvɪlɪdʒd] [pri-vi-lichd], *a.* Privilegiado.

privily [ˈprɪvɪlɪ] [pri-vi-li], *adv.* Privadamente, secretamente.

privity [ˈprɪvɪtɪ] [pri-vi-ti], *s.* 1. Conocimiento particular, conocimiento en común con otro de un asunto privado; en derecho, relación mutua o sucesiva a los mismos derechos de propiedad. 2. Confianza, secreto.

privy [ˈprɪvɪ] [pri-vi], *a.* 1. Consabidor, el que juntamente con otro sabe alguna cosa, confidente, cómplice, instruido, informado, enterado. 2. Privado, escondido, secreto, excusado, clandestino. 3. Particular, propio, destinado a usos particulares, personal. **Privy council,** el consejo privado. **Privy to,** informado de, enterado. -*s.* 1. Parte interesada, partícipe con otro, cómplice. 2. Privada, secreta, letrina, lugar excusado, retrete.

prize [praɪz] [prais], *s.* 1. Premio, recompensa, galardón. **He drew a prize in the lottery,** el se sacó un premio en la lotería. 2. Presa, el botín que se hace al enemigo en conformidad con las leyes de la guerra; buque apresado. **Prize-master,** capitán o cabo de presa. 3. Ganancia, ventaja inesperada (advantage); buena suerte (good luck). **To carry the prize,** llevar, conseguir o ganar el premio. **Prize-court,** tribunal marítimo que juzga las presas. **Prize-fight,** pugilato, lucha en público entre dos combatientes para ganar un premio. **Prize-money,** parte de una presa que toca a cada uno de los oficiales y tripulantes que la han hecho. **Prize-ring,** espacio de dieciséis a veinticuatro pies cuadrados, rodeado de una cuerda y en el cual se verifican los pugilatos. **The prize-ring,** pugilismo como profesión.

prize, *s.* *(Prov. Ingl.)* Alzaprima, punto de apoyo de una palanca.

prize, *va.* 1. Apreciar, estimar, valuar, tasar. 2. Tener en estima. 3. *(Prov. Ingl.)* Alzaprimar, levantar con alzaprima.

prize-fighter ['praɪzfaɪtəʳ] [prais-fai-taʳ], *s.* Púgil, pugilista, el que pelea públicamente por una recompensa.

prize-office ['praɪz'ɒfɪs] [prais-o-fis], *s.* La oficina en que se despachan todos los negocios relativos a las presas hechas en la guerra.

prizer ['praɪzəʳ] [prai-saʳ], *s.* Apreciador, tasador, valorador.

pro [prəʊ] [prou], *s.* En pro, a favor. **Neither pro nor con,** ni en pro ni en contra.

probabilism [ˌprɒbəbɪ'lɪzəm] [pro-ba-bi-li-sem], *s.* Probabilismo, doctrina teológica que sostiene ser lícito seguir la opinión meramente probable, en contraposición a la más probable.

probabilist [ˌprɒbə'bɪlɪst] [pro-ba-bi-list], *s.* Probabilista, el que profesa el probabilismo.

probability [ˌprɒbə'bɪlɪtɪ] [pro-ba-bi-li-ti], *s.* 1. Probabilidad, verisimilitud, calidad de probable. 2. *(E. U.)* Predicción concerniente al tiempo, especialmente los boletines oficiales de la Oficina de Señales Meteorológicas. **In all probability,** según toda probabilidad.

probable ['prɒbəbl] [pro-ba-bol], *a.* Probable, verosímil.

probably ['prɒbəblɪ] [pro-ba-bli], *adv.* Probablemente.

probate ['prəʊbɪt] [prou-bit], *a.* Que se refiere a la comprobación de un testamento. **Probate court,** tribunal encargado de la comprobación de los testamentos, y que tiene jurisdicción en las curadurías. -*s.* Prueba, justificación o verificación de los testamentos en el tribunal privativo y el certificado de esta verificación.

probation [prə'beɪʃən] [pro-bei-shon], *s.* 1. Prueba, evidencia, testimonio (proof). 2. Prueba, la acción y efecto de probar. 3. Prueba, experiencia, examen, ensayo o tentiva que se hace de alguna cosa (exam, test). 4. Probación, noviciado. 5. Libertad condicional o vigilada.

probational [prə'beɪʃənl] [pro-bei-sho-nal], *a.* Probatorio, que sirve de evidencia, de ensayo, o para comprobación.

probationer [prə'beɪʃənəʳ] [pro-bei-sho-naʳ], *s.* 1. Novicio, el religioso que no ha profesado. 2. Novicio, el principiante en cualquier arte o facultad. 3. Delincuente en libertad vigilada.

probative [prə'bətɪv] [pro-ba-tiv], *a.* Probatorio, que sirve de prueba.

probatory [prə'bətərɪ] [pro-ba-to-ri], *a.* Probatorio.

probe [prəʊb] [proub], *s.* 1. *(Cir.)* Tienta. 2. Prueba, ensayo, lo que prueba o ensaya. **Probe-scissors,** tijeras de cirujano, con puntas bulbosas.

probe, *va.* 1. Tentar, reconocer con la tienta alguna herida. 2. Escudriñar, probar, registrar; indagar. 3. Penetrar, atravesar.

probing ['prəʊbɪŋ] [prou-bin], *a.* Penetrante, agudo (question, researchment).

probity ['prɒbɪtɪ] [prou-bi-ti], *s.* Probidad, honradez; veracidad, sinceridad.

problem ['prɒbləm] [pro-blem], *s.* Problema.

problematic, [ˌprɒblɪ'mætɪk] [pro-bli-ma-tik], *a.* Problemático, dudoso, incierto, (enigmatic).

proboscis [prəʊ'bɒsɪs] [prou-bo-sis], *s.* Probóscide, trompa o nariz del elefante, la trompa o trompetilla de los insectos dípteros, u órgano semejante en varios invertebrados. En sentido festivo se aplica a veces a la nariz humana, hocico largo.

procedural [prə'siːdjʊrəl] [pro-si-diu-ral], *a.* Del procedimiento.

procedure [prə'siːdʒəʳ] [pro-si-yaʳ], *s.* 1. Proceder, procedimiento, conducta; un acto, o una serie de actos, manera de obrar. 2. Procedimientos judiciales, actuación, modo de proceder en justicia.

proceed [prə'siːd] [pro-sid], *vn.* 1. Ir adelante, dirigirse al fin propuesto, adelantar, avanzar; andar; proseguir, continuar lo empezado. **Proceed,** prosiga o continúe Ud. **After proceeding some distance,** después de haber avanzado o andado algunos pasos. 2. Proceder, pasar de una cosa a otra. **To proceed to business,** ir a lo que importa; poner manos a la obra. 3. Proceder, provenir (come from), dimanar, seguirse, salir. **Water proceeds from the fountain,** el agua procede de la fuente. 4. Obrar, proceder, portarse, empezar a ejecutar una serie de acciones, especialmente proceder en justicia contra alguno (behavior). 5. Proceder, originarse, venir por generación. 6. Recurrir, acudir, echar mano de, valerse de (profit of). **To proceed to blows,** llegar a las manos, acudir a los golpes. **To proceed to strong measures,** recurrir a, echar mano de medidas rigurosas. 6. Actuar, seguir un proceso o tramitación; proceder; **to proceed against,** proceder contra.

proceeder [prə'siːdəʳ] [pro-si-daʳ], *s.* Adelantador, el que adelanta, el que hace progresos en alguna cosa.

proceeding [prə'siːdɪŋ] [pro-si-din], *s.* 1. Procedimiento, conducta, porte, acto, proceder, transacción (behavior). **The day's proceedings,** las transacciones del día. **A cautions proceeding,** una medida de precaución; conducta cautelosa. 2. Forma u orden judicial, modo de actuar en justicia, procedimiento, proceso, autos. 3. *pl.* Acta de una asamblea o sociedad.

proceeds [prə'siːds] [pro-sids], *s. pl.* Resultados materiales de una acción proceder, productos, réditos.

process ['prəʊses] [prou-ses], *s.* 1. Procedimiento, serie sistemática de operaciones en la producción de alguna cosa (natural o artificial); manipulación, el modo y orden con que se trabaja en la química y en varias artes. 2. Progreso, continuación, adelantamiento, serie, sucesión, transcurso del tiempo. **Process of time,** el lapso o trascurso del tiempo. **In process of time,** con el tiempo. 3. Proceso, el agregado de autos que se forman para alguna causa o pleito civil; forma, expediente, trámite judicial, o modo de actuar en las causas civiles o eclesiásticas. 4. *(Anat. y Zool.)* Eminencia, protuberancia, excrecencia. 5. *(Bot.)* Toda extensión de una superficie o apéndice accesorio.

process, *va.* Someter (alguna materia) a un proceso especial. **Processed cheese,** queso preparado con un método especial.

processal ['prəʊsesəl] [prou-se-sal], *a.* Procesal.

procession [prə'seʃən] [pro-se-shon], *s.* Procesión, cortejo, desfile, cabalgata. **Funeral procession,** acompañamiento fúnebre. **The procession,** el progreso (of idea, of mode).

procession, *vn.* *(Poco us.)* Andar en procesión.

processional [prə'seʃənl] [pro-se-sho-nal], *a.* procesional, que se ordena en forma de procesión o que pertenece a ella. -*s.* 1. Procesionario, libro. 2. Himno que se canta durante una procesión religiosa.

processionary [prə'seʃənərɪ] [pro-se-sho-na-ri], *a.* Procesional, perteneciente a una procesión. **Processionary moth,** lepidóptero nocturno que marcha en filas formando cuña, y cuyas orugas se alimentan de las hojas del roble.

proclaim [prə'kleɪm] [pro-kleim], *va.* 1. Proclamar, promulgar, publicar, propalar. 2. Antiguamente, en Inglaterra, proscribir, poner fuera de la ley. 3. Prohibir por bando; someter (a place) a ciertas restricciones.

proclaimer [prə'kleɪmər] [pro-klei-ma^r], *s.* El que promulga o proclama, proclamador.

proclamation [ˌprɒklə'meɪʃən] [pro-kla-mei-shon], *s.* 1. Proclamación, la publicación de algún decreto, edicto, bando o ley. 2. Decreto, edicto, bando, ley, pragmática (law).

proclitic [prə'klɪtɪk] [pro-kli-tik], *a. (Gram.)* Proclítico; se dice de la voz monosílaba que se une con la siguiente.

proclivity [prə'klɪvɪtɪ] [pro-kli-vi-ti], *s.* Proclividad, propensión, inclinación.

proclivous ['prəklɪvəs] [pro-kli-vos], *a.* Inclinado hacia adelante; se dice de los dientes incisivos.

proconsul [prəʊ'kɒnsəl] [pro-kon-sal], *s.* Procónsul.

proconsular [ˌprəʊ'kɒnsjʊləʳ] [prou-kon-siu-la^r], *a.* Proconsular, que se refiere a un procónsul.

procrastinate [prəʊ'kræstɪneɪt] [prou-kras-ti-neit], *va. y vn.* Procrastinar, diferir, dilatar, dejar de un día para otro, retardar, ser moroso.

procrastination [prəʊkræstɪ'neɪʃən] [prou-kras-ti-nei-shon], *s.* Dilación, demora, tardanza, detención (delay).

procrastinator [prəʊkræstɪ'neɪtəʳ] [prou-kras-ti-nei-ta^r], *s.* El que es moroso, tardo o poco diligente en lo que se debe hacer; vulgarmente, pelmazo.

procreate ['prəʊkrɪeɪt] [prou-krieit], *va.* Procrear engendrar, producir.

procreation [ˌprəʊkrɪ'eɪʃən] [prou-kriei-shon], *s.* Procreación, generación, producción.

procreative ['prəʊkrɪətɪv] [prou-kria-tiv], *a.* Generativo, productivo.

procreator [ˌprəʊkrɪ'eɪtəʳ] [prou-kriei-ta^r], *s.* Procreador; padre.

proctor ['prɒktəʳ] [prok-to^r], *s.* 1. Procurador, el que en virtud de poder o facultad de otro ejecuta en su nombre alguna cosa. 2. Procurador de la curia eclesiástica. 3. Abogado en el tribunal del amirantazgo. 4. Censor de una universidad, funcionario encargado de vigilar a los alumnos y de hacer observar los reglamentos.

proctorship ['prɒktəʃɪp] [prok-to-ship], *s.* Procuración, procuraduría, oficio de procurador.

procurable [prə'kjʊərəbl] [pro-kiua-ra-bol], *a.* Asequible, que puede conseguirse, alcanzarse; proporcionable.

procuracy [prə'kjʊərəsɪ] [pro-kiua-ra-si], *a.* Procuración; gestión, manejo de negocios o intereses ajenos.

procuration ['prɒkjʊreɪʃən] [pro-kiu-rei-shon], *s.* 1. Acción de procurar, de obtener, en especial, alcahuetería. 2. *(For.)* Procuración, poder o comisión que una persona da a otra para que en su nombre haga o ejecute alguna cosa; y el documento en que se da dicho poder. **Procuration-fee,** derecho de comisión sobre un préstamo.

procurator ['prɒkjʊreɪtəʳ] [pro-kiu-rei-ta^r], *s.* Procurador, apoderado.

procure [prə'kjʊəʳ] [pro-kiua^r], *va.* 1. Lograr, obtener, conseguir; procurar, hacer las diligencias para conseguir lo que se desea. 2. Causar, ocasionar. 3. Alcahuetear. -*vn.* Alcahuetear, andar en tercerías.

procurement [prə'kjʊəmənt] [pro-kiua-ment], *s.* 1. Obtención, logro, consecución (attainment). 2. El acto de causar, de poner por obra, de efectuar. **They think it done by her procurement,** creen que se ha hecho por su causa, a solicitud suya o por haberlo ella procurado.

procurer [prə'kjʊərəʳ] [pro-kiua-ra^r], *s.* 1. El que logra, alcanza o consigue alguna cosa. 2. Alcahuete.

procuress [prə'kjʊərɪs] [pro-kiua-ris], *sf.* Alcahueta, tercera.

prod [prɒd] [prod], *va.* Punzar, pungir, empujar o golpear con un instrumento puntiagudo; picar. -*s.* 1. Cualquier instrumento puntiagudo; pincho, aguijón. 2. Picadura, pinchazo, pungimiento, empuje efectuado con un instrumento puntiagudo.

prodigal ['prɒdɪgəl] [pro-di-gal], *a.* 1. Pródigo, manirroto, derrochador. 2. Pródigo, muy generoso o liberal. -*s.* Gastador, disipador.

prodigality [ˌprɒdɪ'gælɪtɪ] [pro-di-ga-li-ti], *s.* Prodigalidad, profusión.

prodigally ['prɒdɪgəlɪ] [pro-di-ga-li], *adv.* Pródigamente.

prodigious [prə'dɪdʒəs] [pro-di-yos], *a.* 1. Enorme, vasto, inmenso, excesivo, extraordinario (huge, vaste). 2. *(Des.)* Prodigioso, portentoso.

prodigiously [prə'dɪdʒəslɪ] [pro-di-yos-li], *adv.* Enormemente, excesivamente, extraordinariamente, prodigiosamente.

prodigiousness [prə'dɪdʒəsnɪs] [pro-di-yos-nes], *s.* Prodigiosidad, enormidad de extensión, estatura, cantidad o grado.

prodigy ['prɒdɪdʒɪ] [pro-di-yi], *s.* 1. Maravilla, persona o cosa extraordinaria; lo que causa admiración. 2. Monstruo, monstruosidad. 3. *(Ant.)* Prodigio, portento.

produce [prə'djuːs] [pro-dius], *va.* 1. Producir, criar, engendrar. 2. Sacar o dar a luz una cosa, exponer a la vista. 3. Causar o ser causa de alguna cosa, efectuar; conducir *a.* 4. Producir, presentar o exhibir alguna cosa en juicio. 5. Manufacturar, fabricar; hacer. 6. *(Geom.)* Prolongar, alargar una línea. 7. *(Teat.)* Presentar al público; poner en escena. -*vn.* Producir, dar producto o resultado conveniente. **Vice produces misery,** el vicio engendra la miseria. **The inhabitants produced their hidden stores,** los habitantes presentaron las provisiones que habían escondido.

produce, *s.* 1. Producto, producción, la cosa producida; particularmente los rendimientos de una hacienda de campo; provisiones. 2. Hijos, descendientes de un animal.

producer [prə'djuːsəʳ] [pro-diu-sa^r], *s.* Productor. **Producer's goods,** elementos de producción, materias primas. 2. Gasógeno, generador de gas pobre. 3. *(Teat.)* Director. 4. *(Cine.)* Productor de una película.

producible [prə'djuːsɪbl] [pro-diu-si-bol], *a.* Producible, lo que se puede producir, exhibir o mostrar.

producing [prə'djuːsɪŋ] [pro-diu-sin], *a.* Productor de.

product ['prɒdʌkt] [pro-dakt], *s.* 1. Producto, producción, la cosa producida; alguna cosa obtenida como resultado de una operación o trabajo. 2. Producción, obra del entendimiento o del arte. 3. Producto, el número que resulta de la multiplicación de otros dos o más números. 4. Producto, provento, renta.

productible [prə'dʌktɪbl] [pro-dak-ti-bol], *a.* Dúctil, susceptible de alargarse sin romperse.

production [prə'dʌkʃən] [pro-dak-shon], *s.* 1. Producción, el acto o procedimiento de producir; en economía política, acto de producir para el consumo. 2. Producto. 3. Producción, composición, obra del ingenio. 4. Alargamiento, producción, extensión.

productive [prə'dʌktɪv] [pro-dak-tiv], *a.* 1. Productivo, que tiene la virtud o la facultad de reproducir. 2. Fecundo, fértil, que da buenas cosechas.

productiveness [prə'dʌktɪvnɪs] [pro-dak-tiv-nes], *s.* Calidad de productivo; fertilidad, fecundidad.

productivity [ˌprɒdʌk'tɪvɪtɪ] [pro-dak-ti-vi-ti], *s.* Productividad.

proem ['prəʊɪm] [prouim], *s.* Proemio, prólogo, prefacio; exordio.

profanation [ˌprɒfə'neɪʃən] [pro-fa-nei-shon], *s.* Profanación, profanamiento, profanidad, impiedad, irreligión; prostitución.

profane [prə'feɪn] [pro-fein], *a.* 1. Profano, irreligioso, impío (ungodly); impuro. 2. Profano, secular, en contraposición a sagrado o religioso.

profane, *va.* 1. Profanar, violar, aplicar alguna cosa sagrada a usos profanos, o tratarla con irreverencia. 2. Profanar, prostituir, hacer uso indecente de una cosa: desperdiciar, hacer mal uso de algo.

profanely [prə'feɪnlɪ] [pro-fein-li], *adv.* Profanamente, impíamente.

profaner [prəˈfeɪnəʳ] [pro-fei-naʳ], s. Profanador, el que profana una cosa sagrada. -a. comp. Más profano.

profanity [prəˈfænɪtɪ] [pro-fa-ni-ti], s. 1. Lenguaje o acto profano; impiedad, blasfemia. 2. La calidad de profano; irreverencia a las cosas sagradas.

profess [prəˈfes] [pro-fes], va. 1. Declarar, manifestar abiertamente su ánimo o intento (declare, say). 2. Profesar, seguir alguna religión u opinión abierta y públicamente. 3. Profesar, ejercer o enseñar en público alguna facultad o arte (teach). 4. Hacer profesión de, fingir (fake, sham). 5. Manifestar, confesar (confess). **To profess oneself a Catholic,** declararse católico. -vn. 1. Profesar, declarar abiertamente. 2. Profesar, ser profesor.

professed, [prəˈfest] [pro-fest], pp. del verbo To PROFESS. 1. Profeso. 2. Declarado, decidido. 3. Ostensible. 4. Alegado, supuesto. **Professed foe,** enemigo declarado. **Professed friend,** amigo decidido. **A professed monk** o **nun,** un religioso profeso; o una religiosa profesa, una monja.

professedly [prəˈfesdlɪ] [pro-fesd-li], adv. 1. Declaradamente, manifiestamente, abiertamente, públicamente. 2. Supuestamente. 3. Confesadamente.

profession [prəˈfeʃən] [pro-fe-shon], s. 1. Profesión, destino, empleo, ejercicio, el modo de vida que requiere una educación liberal o el trabajo mental más bien que el manual. 2. Profesión, protestación, declaración pública de la creencia, opinión, doctrina, etc., de cada uno. 3. Oferta, ofrecimiento, palabra. 4. (Teat.) Arte dramático; los actores.

professional [prəˈfeʃənl] [pro-fe-sho-nal], a. 1. Profesional, que se refiere a una profesión o la práctica; apto para una profesión. 2. Profesional, que tiene relación con una profesión particular, opuesto a *amateur* (aficionado). **Professional duties,** deberes profesionales. -s. 1. El que por profesión y por dinero compite en los juegos y diversiones. 2. Sujeto hábil en su profesión. 3. (Teat.) Actor, actriz. 4. Profesional del deporte.

professionally [prəˈfeʃnəlɪ] [pro-fe-sho-na-li], adv. Por vía de profesión; de profesión; en su profesión.

professionaless [prəˈfeʃnəlɪs] [pro-fe-sho-na-les], a. Sin profesión.

professor [prəˈfesəʳ] [pro-fe-saʳ], s. 1. Profesor, catedrático, el que enseña públicamente alguna facultad, arte, ciencia o doctrina (teacher). 2. Profesor, el que ejerce públicamente alguna facultad o ciencia, catedrático, maestro. 3. Partidario, el que sigue alguna opinión o partido.

professorate [prəˈfesərɪt] [pro-fe-sa-rit], s. Profesorado.

professorial [ˌprofeˈsɔːrɪəl] [pro-fe-so-rial], a. De profesor; profesoral, relativo a un catedrático o profesor.

professorship [prəˈfesəʃɪp] [pro-fe-sa-ship], s. 1. Oficio de profesor, dignidad de catedrático. 2. Cátedra.

proffer [ˈprofəʳ] [pro-faʳ], va. Proponer, ofrecer algo para su aceptación, brindar.

proffer, s. Oferta, propuesta, ofrecimiento; la cosa ofrecida.

proficiency [prəˈfɪʃəns] [pro-fe-shan-shi], s. Estado o calidad de adepto o proficiente, maña, habilidad, perfeccionamiento en un arte, pericia (ability).

proficient [prəˈfɪʃənt] [pro-fe-shant], a. proficiente, adelantado, versado, instruido en una ciencia, un arte; hábil.

profile [ˈprəʊfaɪl] [prou-fail], s. 1. Contorno, recorte; diseño en perfil o como en una sección vertical. 2. Perfil, el rostro humano representado de lado; el contorno del cuerpo visto de lado. **In profile,** de perfil.

profile, va. Retratar o pintar de perfil; perfilar.

profit [ˈprofɪt] [pro-fit], s. 1. Provecho, beneficio, ventaja, utilidad, producto (advantage). 2. Ganancia, utilidad o interés pecuniario (gain); exceso de los ingresos o cantidades recibidas sobre los desembolsos o gastos. **Gross profit,** ganancia total. **Net profit,** ganancia neta, beneficio neto. **Profit and loss,** ganancias y pérdidas. **To make profit of a thing,** sacar ventaja de una cosa, hacer su agosto. **To yield profit,** dar ganancia o provecho. 3. Interés, renta.

profit, va. Aprovechar a, servir, ser útil, ventajoso para; hacer bien, ayudar. -vn. 1. Sacar utilidad o provecho de alguna cosa, utilizarse; lucrar, ganar. 2. Mejorarse, servir, ser útil, traer beneficio. **To profit by experience,** ganar, mejorarse, por la experiencia. **To be profited by,** ganar en.

profitability [ˌprofɪtəˈbɪlɪtɪ] [pro-fi-ta-bi-li-ti], s. 1. Rentabilidad. 2. Provecho, utilidad. 3. Ventaja.

profitable [ˈprofɪtəbl] [pro-fi-ta-bol], a. 1. Rentable. 2. Útil, provechoso, ventajoso.

profitableness [ˈprofɪtəblnɪs] [pro-fi-ta-bol-nes], s. Ganancia, lucro; ventaja, provecho.

profitably [ˈprofɪtəblɪ] [pro-fi-ta-bli], adv. Provechosamente, útilmente, ventajosamente.

profiteer [ˌprofɪˈtɪəʳ] [pro-fi-tiaʳ], s. Explotador, que se aprovecha de las circunstancias para ganar demasiado dinero, usurero, acaparador. -vn. Obtener ganancias elevadas aprovechándose de alguna circunstancia, p. ej. la guerra.

profitless [ˈprofɪtlɪs] [pro-fit-les], a. Sin ventaja, sin provecho; inútil.

profitlessly [ˈprofɪtlɪslɪ] [pro-fit-les-li], adv. Infructuosamente.

profit sharing [ˈprofɪtˌʃeərɪŋ] [pro-fit-shea-rin], s. Distribución de ganancias entre los trabajadores.

profligacy [ˈprofligəsɪ] [pro-fli-ga-si], s. Estragamiento, libertinaje, desenfreno, disolución, abandono, corrupción desvergonzada.

profligate [ˈprofligeɪt] [pro-fli-gueit], a. Abandonado, entregado a los vicios; libertino, libre, licencioso, desmandado, perdido. -s. Un hombre libertino, disipado, relajado, perdido, calavera, vicioso o de vida airada.

pro form [ˈprəʊfɔːm] [prou-form], Locución latina que se usa para significar o que una cosa se hace meramente por cumplir con alguna fórmula o que es fingida. **Pro forma accounts,** cuentas simuladas. **Pro forma bills,** letras simuladas o supuestas.

profound [prəˈfaʊnd] [pro-faund], a. 1. Profundo, hondo (deep). 2. Profundo, recóndito, abstruso. 3. Profundo, grande, extremo en su clase. 4. Profundo, intenso o denso en su especie (intense). 5. Profundo, humilde en sumo grado (humble). -s. 1. Profundo, abismo. 2. Profundo, mar, océano.

profoundly [prəˈfaʊndlɪ] [pro-faund-li], adv. Profundamente.

profoundness [prəˈfaʊndnɪs] [pro-faund-nes], s. Profundidad, penetración.

profundity [prəˈfʌndɪtɪ] [pro-fan-di-ti], s. 1. Profundidad, hondura. 2. Profundidad, sublimidad o grandeza de ciencia o ingenio.

profuse [prəˈfjuːs] [pro-fius], a. 1. Profuso; pródigo. 2. Exuberante.

profusely [prəˈfjuːslɪ] [pro-fius-li], adv. 1. Profusamente; pródigamente. 2. Exuberantemente.

profuseness [prəˈfjuːsnɪs] [pro-fius-nes], **profusion.** Profusión, prodigalidad; abundancia, copia, superabundancia; gastos extravagantes.

progenitive [prəʊˈdʒenɪtɪv] [prou-ye-ni-tiv], a. Generativo.

progenitor [prəʊˈdʒenɪtəʳ] prou-ye-ni-taʳ], s. Progenitor; ascendiente en línea directa.

progeniture [prəʊˈdʒenɪtʃʊəʳ] [prou-ye-ni-chuaʳ], s. Progenitura.

progeny [ˈprodʒɪnɪ] [pro-yi-ni], s. 1. Progenie, progenitura, casta, descendientes, linaje. 2. Producto, resultado.

prognosis [proɡˈnəʊsɪs] [prog-nou-sis], s. (Med.) 1. Conclusión o predicción respecto a la marcha futura y terminación de una enfermedad; también, el arte de pronosticar lo que debe suceder en las enfermedades por los síntomas que presentan. 2. Cualquier pronóstico o predicción; presciencia.

prognosticable [proɡˈnostɪkəbl] [prog-nos-ti-ka-bol], a. Pronosticable.

prognostic [proɡˈnostɪk] [prog-nos-tik], s. Pronóstico, juicio conjetural que se hace de lo que ha de suceder; (Med.) síntoma indicativo de la terminación de una enfermedad. -a. Pronóstico, que sirve para indicar lo que ha de suceder.

prognosticate [proɡˈnostɪkeɪt] [prog-nos-ti-keit], va. Pronosticar, indicar de antemano.

prognostication [prɒɡ.nɒstɪˈkeɪʃən] [prog-nos-ti-kei-shon], *s*. Pronosticación, acción de pronosticar; lo que pronostica, presagio, pronóstico.

prognosticator [prɒɡˌnɒstɪˈkeɪtəʳ] [prog-nos-ti-kei-taʳ], *s*. Pronosticador.

program, programme [ˈprəʊɡræm] [prou-gram], *s*. 1. Anuncio o cartel en que se indican por su orden las partes que forman una función pública. 2. Curso de procedimientos dispuesto de antemano; cartel, enumeración o lista de las tareas y deberes ordinarios o cotidianos; prospecto. 3. Programa; prólogo, introducción.

program, *va*. Programar.

programmer [ˈprəʊɡræməʳ] [prou-gra-maʳ], *s*. Programador.

programming [ˈprəʊɡræmɪŋ] [prou-gra-min], *s*. Programación.

progress [ˈprəʊɡres] [prou-gres], *s*. 1. Progreso, aprovechamiento, adelantamiento; desarrollo, mejoramiento, adelanto (development, evolution). 2. Viaje, jornada, curso (travel); carrera, p. ej. la del séquito de un monarca; corriente; paso, pasaje. **To make slow progress,** adelantar lentamente. **Dinner was in progress,** estaban comiendo. **To make little progress,** progresar o adelantar poco.

progress, *vn*. Progresar, hacer progresos o adelantamientos en alguna cosa. 2. Marchar, avanzar. 3. *(Mús.)* Pasar de una nota o tono siguiente. 4. Hacer progresar.

progression [prəˈɡreʃən] [pro-gre-shon], *s*. 1. Progresión, adelantamiento, la acción de ir o dirigirse hacia adelante. 2. *(Mat.)* Progresión, serie de números o cantidades en proporción continua.

progressional [prəˈɡreʃənl] [pro-gre-sho-nal], *a*. Progresivo.

progressive [prəˈɡresɪv] [pro-gre-siv], *a*. Progresivo, que va hacia adelante; que aspira al progreso o lo favorece; que va mejorando, perfeccionándose.

progressive, *s*. Progresista.

progressively [prəˈɡresɪvlɪ] [pro-gre-siv-li], *adv*. Progresivamente.

progressiveness [prəˈɡresɪvnɪs] [pro-gre-siv-nes], *s*. Calidad de progresivo, estado de progreso; marcha progresiva, adelanto.

prohibit [prəˈhɪbɪt] [pro-ji-bit], *va*. 1. Prohibir, vedar (forbid). 2. Impedir, embarazar (stop). **Prohibited goods,** contrabando o géneros prohibidos.

prohibiter [prəˈhɪbɪtəʳ] [pro-ji-bi-taʳ], *s*. El que prohibe alguna cosa; impedidor.

prohibition [prəʊɪˈbɪʃən] [proui-bi-shan], *s*. 1. Prohibición; auto prohibitorio. 2. *(E. U.)* Prohibición legal de la manufactura y venta de licores alcohólicos como bebida. 3. Auto inhibitorio. *a. (EE.UU.)* Antialcohólico; prohibicionista: **prohibition law,** ley seca. **Prohibition party,** partido prohibicionista.

prohibitionism [ˌprəʊɪˈbɪʃənɪʒəm] [proui-bi-sha-ni-sem], *s*. Prohibicionismo.

prohibitionist [ˌprəʊɪˈbɪʃənɪst] [proui-bi-sha-nist], *s*. Partidario de la prohibición; en especial *(E. U.)* partidario de prohibir por ley la fabricación y venta de licores alcohólicos para el consumo público como bebida.

prohibitive [prəˈhɪbɪtɪv] [pro-hi-bi-tiv], **prohibitory** [prəˈhɪbɪtərɪ] [pro-hi-bi-to-ri], *a*. Prohibitivo, prohibitorio; que implica prohibición.

project [ˈprɒdʒekt] [pro-yekt], *va*. 1. Echar, arrojar, despedir. 2. Delinear, trazar. 3. Proyectar (shadows), idear, trazar. 4. Hacer salir o sobresalir. *-vn*. Volar, salir fuera de la línea perpendicular, hacer o formar proyectura o vuelo; proyectar.

project, *s*. Proyecto, idea, pensamiento; dibujo, diseño, plan (plain).

projector [ˈprɒdʒektəʳ] [pro-yek-taʳ], *s*. 1. Proyectista. 2. Proyector, aparato de proyección de películas cinematográficas.

projectile [prəˈdʒektaɪl] [pro-yek-tail], *a*. 1. Impelido o puesto en movimiento por alguna fuerza o potencia. 2. Arrojador, que arroja o lanza. 3. Arrojadizo, que se puede arrojar o se destina a ser arrojado. *-s*. Proyectil, cuerpo arrojadizo que se lanza para herir o matar.

projection [prəˈdʒekʃən] [pro-yek-shon], *s*. 1. Lanzamiento, el acto de lanzar o arrojar. 2. Proyección, el acto de comunicar movimiento a algún cuerpo arrojadizo. 3. Plan, minuta o borrón de un proyecto, de un pensamiento, etc. 4. Delineación. 5. El punto crítico de una preparación culinaria o de otra clase. *a*. De proyección: **projection machine,** proyector cinematográfico.

projectionist [prəˈdʒekʃnɪst] [pro-yek-sho-nist], *s*. Proyectista.

projector [prəˈdʒektəʳ] [pro-yek-taʳ], *s*. 1. Proyectista, arbitrista. 2. Aparato para proyecciones.

projecture [prəˈdʒektʃəʳ] [pro-yek-chaʳ], *s. (Arq.)* Proyectura, vuelo.

prolapse [ˈprəʊlæps] [prou-laps], *s. (Med.)* Prolapso, procidencia, caída o descenso de una víscera u órgano movible.

prolate [prəˈleɪt] [pro-leit], *a*. Alargado, en dirección a los polos.

prolepsis [prəˈlepsɪs] [pro-lep-sis], *s*. 1. Prolepsis, anticipación; figura retórica por la cual se anticipa una objeción, refutándola de antemano.

proleptic, [prəˈleptɪk] [pro-lep-tik], *a*. Previo, antecedente.

proles [prəʊlz] [prouls], *s*. Prole, hijos (children); en derecho, descendencia, hijos legítimos.

proletarian [ˌprəʊləˈtɛərɪən] [prou-le-ta-rian], *a*. Proletario; bajo, vulgar, despreciable. *-s*. 1. Proletario, persona de la clase última o más pobre. 2. Gañán, jornalero, peón.

proletariat [ˌprəʊləˈtɛərɪət] [prou-le-ta-riat], *s*. Proletariado, la clase de los proletarios; en su empleo primitivo, populacho, gentuza; en el uso moderno y socialista, la clase obrera, como creadora de la riqueza; operarios, trabajadores.

proliferate [prəˈlɪfəreɪt] [pro-li-fe-reit], *va*. Producir, dar. *-vn*. Reproducirse, particularmente con rapidez, como las celdillas en la formación de los tejidos (cell). 2. Multiplicarse abundantemente.

proliferous [prəˈlɪfərəs] [pro-li-fe-ros], *a*. 1. Prolífero, que produce prole o descendientes. 2. *(Bot.)* Que tiene un desarrollo excesivo de partes u órganos.

prolific, prolifical [prəˈlɪfɪk] [pro-li-fik], *a*. 1. Prolífico, fértil, fecundo, muy productivo. 2. *V.* PROLIFEROUS.

prolifically [prəˈlɪfɪkəlɪ] [pro-li-fi-ka-li], *adv*. Fecundamente, abundantemente.

prolix [ˈprəʊlɪks] [prou-liks], *a*. 1. Prolijo, demasiado largo, dilatado, difuso. 2. Fastidioso, enfadoso, latoso (annoying).

prolixity [prəʊˈlɪksɪtɪ] [prou-lik-si-ti], *s*. Prolijidad, estado o calidad de polijo; verbosidad.

prolixly [ˈprəʊlɪkslɪ] [prou-liks-li], *adv*. Prolijamente.

prologue [ˈprəʊlɒɡ] [prou-log], *s*. Prólogo, exordio, prefacio.

prolong [prəˈlɒŋ] [pro-long], *va*. 1. prolongar, alargar, dilatar, extender. 2. *(Des.)* Diferir, retardar.

prolongation [ˌprəʊlɒŋˈɡeɪʃən] [prou-lon-guei-shon], *s*. Prolongación, dilatación, extensión.

prolusion [prəˈluːʒən] [pro-lu-shon], *s*. Prolusión, prelusión, preludio, introducción.

promenade [ˌprɒmɪˈnɑːd] [pro-mi-nad], *vn*. Pasearse. *-s*. 1. Paseo, acción de pasearse (walk); paseo ceremonioso. 2. Paseo, sitio o lugar público destinado a pasear. *a*. De paseo: **promenade concert,** concierto durante el cual la gente baila. *(Mar.)* **Promenade deck,** cubierta de paseo.

prominence [ˈprɒmɪnəns] [pro-mi-nens], *s*. 1. Estado de lo que es prominente o eminente; eminencia, altura; distinción, importancia. 2. Prominencia, protuberancia; lo que hace salidizo; *(Arq.)* salidizo, resalto.

prominent [ˈprɒmɪnənt] [pro-mi-nent], *a*. 1. Prominente, saliente, proyectante, que se eleva sobre lo que está a su inmediación, en relieve (protuberant, high). 2. Conspicuo por su posición, carácter o importancia; eminente, sobresaliente, distinguido. **Prominent eyes,** ojos saltones. **Prominent figures,** figuras de alto relieve.

promiscuity [ˌprɒmɪsˈkjuːɪtɪ] [pro-mis-kiui-ti], *sf.* Promiscuidad, inmoralidad.

promiscuous [prəˈmɪskjʊəs] [pro-mis-kiuos], *a.* 1. Promiscuo, mezclado confusamente, compuesto de individuos o partes mezclados confusamente. 2. Ejercido o repartido, sin distinción; común, no restringido, sin restricción.

promiscuously [prəˈmɪskjʊəslɪ] [pro-mis-kiuos-li], *adv.* promiscuamente, sin orden; en común.

promiscuousness [prəˈmɪskjʊəsnɪs] [pro-mis-kiuos-nes], *s.* Mezcla, confusión.

promise [ˈprɒmɪs] [pro-mis], *s.* 1. Promesa, palabra dada, prometido. 2. Espectativa, esperanza. *(Bibl. y ant.)* Promisión. 3. Prometido, alguna cosa prometida. **To break one's promise,** faltar a su palabra, o promesa. **Land of promise,** tierra de promisión. **Promise of marriage,** promesa de matrimonio.

promise, *va.* 1. Prometer, ofrecer hacer o no hacer (una cosa); hacer promesa de dar alguna cosa. 2. Hacer concebir una esperanza. 3. *(Ant. o fam.)* Prometer, asegurar o aseverar. - *vn.* 1. Prometer, hacer promesas; empeñarse a hacer o no hacer alguna cosa. 2. Dar buenas esperanzas; anunciarse, hacer concebir esperanzas; pormeterse, tener gran esperanza o confianza en que se logrará alguna cosa.

promised [ˈprɒmɪst] [pro-mist], *a.* Prometido.

promisee [ˈprɒmɪsiː] [pro-mi-sii], *s. (For.)* El o la que ha recibido una promesa.

promiser [ˈprɒmɪsəʳ] [pro-mi-saʳ], *s.* Prometedor.

promising [ˈprɒmɪsɪŋ] [pro-mi-sin], *a.* Prometedor, que promete mucho, que es de gran esperanza.

promisor [ˈprɒmɪsəʳ] [pro-mi-saʳ], *s.* Autor de una promesa; prometedor.

promissorily [ˈprɒmɪsərɪlɪ] [pro-mi-so-ri-li], *adv.* Por vía de promesa.

promissory [ˈprɒmɪsərɪ] [pro-mi-so-ri], *a.* Promisorio, que encierra en sí promesa. **Promissory note,** pagaré, vale, escrito por el cual se compromete el firmante a pagar una cantidad.

promontory [ˈprɒmɒntrɪ] [pro-mon-tri], *s.* Promontorio, cabo o punta de tierra que entra en el mar.

promote [prəˈməʊt] [pro-mout], *va.* 1. Promover, fomentar, hacer adelantar, favorecer, desarrollar, extender, establecer, aumentar; alentar, hacer florecer. 2. Promover, ascender, elevar a uno a otro empleo más preminente que el que tenía. **To promote the arts and sciences,** hacer florecer las artes y las ciencias. 3. Fundar, organizar una empresa, buscar capitales para ella.

promoter [prəˈməʊtəʳ] [pro-moutaʳ], *s.* 1. Promotor, promovedor, el que da el impulso principal. 2. Promovedor, el que ayuda (obteniendo un capital o de otra manera) a promover o estabecer una empresa rentística o de comercio.

promotion [prəˈməʊʃən] [pro-mou-shon], *s.* Promoción, acción de promover o estado de ser promovido; elevación, ascenso de alguno a una dignidad, grado o empleo superior al que tenía.

promotive [prəˈməʊtɪv] [pro-mou-tiv], *a.* Promovedor, que tiende a fomentar, promover, adelantar, alentar o favorecer.

prompt [prɒmpt] [prompt], *a.* 1. Pronto, dispuesto, aparejado para la ejecución de alguna cosa (ready); puntual, exacto en hacer las cosas a su tiempo sin dilatarlas (exact). 2. Hecho o ejecutado de todo corazón o de buena voluntad; que sucede al tiempo debido o señalado. **Prompt payment,** pago puntual en la fecha señalada. **prompt cash,** pago al contado, inmediato.

prompt, *va.* 1. Impulsar, excitar, hurgar, incitar, conmover (incite, spur on). 2. Sugerir, insinuar, advertir o hacer a uno acordarse de alguna cosa (suggest). 3. Apuntar; dar ocasión, mover.

prompter [ˈprɒmptəʳ] [promp-taʳ], *s.* 1. Admonitor, el que amonesta; la persona que incita a obrar. 2. Apuntador, el que apunta; apuntador de teatro.

promptitude [ˈprɒmptɪtjuːd] [promp-ti-tiud] **promptness** [ˈprɒmpt] [prompt], *s.* Prontitud, presteza, rapidez de decisión y de acción; facilidad, buena voluntad.

promptly [ˈprɒmptlɪ] [prompt-li], *adv.* Prontamente, a su tiempo, al momento.

promulgate [ˈprɒməlgeɪt] [pro-mul-gueit], *va.* Promulgar, publicar alguna cosa solemnemente, proclamar.

promulgation [ˌprɒməlˈgeɪʃən] [pro-mal-guei-shan], *s.* Promulgación.

pronate [ˈprəʊneɪt] [prou-neit], *va.* Poner o echar boca abajo.

pronation [ˌprəʊˈneɪtəʳ] [prou-nei-taʳ], *s.* Pronación, un movimiento por el cual el antebrazo y la palma de la mano se vuelven hacia abajo.

pronator [ˈprəʊneɪtəʳ] [prou-nei-taʳ], *s.* Pronador, músculo del antebrazo que sirve para volver la palma de la mano hacia tierra.

prone [prəʊn] [proun], *a.* 1. Inclinado hacia abajo. 2. Echado boca abajo. 3. Precipitoso, pendiente. 4. Prono, inclinado, dispuesto, propenso.

proneness [ˈprəʊnnɪs] [proun-nes], *s.* 1. Inclinación hacia abajo; pendiente, cuesta (pent). 2. Inclinación, propensión o disposición a alguna cosa mala.

prong [prɒŋ] [prong], *s.* Cualquier instrumento puntiagudo; parte saliente como la púa, diente o punta de un tenedor o de una horca de labrador.

pronged [prɒŋd] [prongd], *a.* Dentellado, dentado, provisto de púas. **A four-pronged fork,** un tenedor de cuatro dientes.

pronominal [prəʊˈnɒmɪnl] [prou-no-mi-nal], *a.* Pronominal, de la naturaleza del pronombre; concerniente al pronombre.

pronoun [ˈprəʊnən] [pro-nan], *s.* Pronombre, parte de la oración.

pronounce [prəˈnaʊns] [pro-nauns], *va.* 1. Pronunciar, proferir, articular (words, sounds); articular correctamente. 2. Pronunciar, decir, recitar una arenga, un discurso, etc (speech). 3. Pronunciar, fallar, dar sentencia. 4. Declarar. **To pronounce one a brave man,** declarar que uno es un valiente. *-vn.* Hablar magistralmente.

pronounceable [prəˈnaʊnəbl] [pro-naun-sa-bol], *a.* Pronunicable, que se puede pronunciar o articular.

pronounced [prəˈnaʊnst] [pro-naunst], *a.* Pronunciado, marcado, fuerte, decidido. **Pronounced opinions,** opiniones decididas.

pronouncer [prəˈnaʊnsəʳ] [pro-naun-saʳ], *s.* Pronunciador.

pronouncing [prəˈnaʊnsɪŋ] [pro-naun-sin], *pa.* del verbo PRONOUNCE. *-a.* De pronunciación, que enseña la pronunciación. **A pronouncing dictionary,** un diccionario de pronunciación.

pronunciation [prəˌnʌnsɪˈeɪʃən] [pro-nan-siei-shon]; *s.* Pronunciación, el acto o la manera de pronunciar palabras; articulación; articulación solemne, v. g. para bendecir.

proof [pruːf] [pruf], *s.* 1. Prueba, la razón, argumento, etc., con que se prueba algo; lo que demuestra la verdad o falsedad de alguna cosa (evidence). 2. Prueba, el ensayo o experiencia que se hace de alguna cosa (essay). 3. Prueba, la consistencia y firmeza de alguna cosa; impenetrabilidad; también, armadura, impenetrable. 4. Prueba, la primera plana que se tira para corregir las erratas de imprenta. 5. Grado regulador, que sirve de tipo para los licores alcohólicos. 6. Prueba, la primera impresión de un negativo. 7. *(Mat.)* Operación por la cual se comprueba la exactitud de un cálculo. **Proof-sheet,** pliego de prueba, prueba. **To put to the proof,** poner a prueba. *-a.* 1. Empleado en probar, cotejar o corregir. 2. Impenetrable, que está hecho a prueba o que no es de prueba. **Proof brandy,** aguardiente de prueba. **Bomb-proof,** a prueba de bomba. **Water-proof,** a prueba de agua, impermeable. **To be proof against,** ser o estar a prueba de. **Proof against all temptations,** a prueba de toda tentación. **Proof spirit,** licor que contiene alcohol por la mitad de su volumen. **The proof of the pudding is in the eating,** al freír será el reír. **Waterproof,** a prueba de agua, impermeable.

proof, *v.* 1. Probar, sacar prueba de. 2. Hacer resistente: impermeabilizar.

proofless ['pruːflɪs] [pruf-les], *a.* Falto de prueba, no probado; sin fundamento.

proofread ['pruːfriːd] [pruf-rid], *va.* Corregir pruebas de imprenta.

prop [prɒp] [prop], *va.* 1. Sostener, apoyar, impedir que caiga una cosa; apuntalar; poner un rodrigón, etc. 2. *(Fig.)* Sostener, apoyar, mantener firme, sustentar. 3. *(Min.)* Entibar.

prop, *s.* 1. Apoyo, puntal. 2. Apoyo, amparo, columna, báculo (column, help). 3. Sostén, cualquier cosa que sirve para sostener a otra; apeo, sustentáculo (bassis); *(Min.)* entibo, ademe; *(Agr.)* rodrigón, tentemozo; machón, contrafuerte. **Props of the cut-water,** *(Mar.)* Escoras del tajamar.

propagable ['prɒpəgəbl] [pro-pa-ga-bol], *a.* Que puede propagarse, que es capaz de propagación.

propaganda [ˌprɒpəˈgændə] [pro-pa-gan-da], *s.* Propaganda.

propagandist [ˌprɒpəˈgændəndɪst] [pro-pa-gan-dist], *s. & a.* Propagandista, propagador. **Propagandist doctrine,** doctrina propagandista.

propagandize [ˌprɒpəˈgændəndaɪz] [pro-pa-gan-dais], *v.* Hacer propaganda.

propagate ['prɒpəgeɪt] [pro-pa-gueit], *va.* 1. Propagar, multiplicar la especie, engendrar. 2. Propagar, dilatar, extender, aumentar. 3. Engendrar, causar, ocasionar, formar. 4. Propagarse.

propagation [ˌprɒpəˈgeɪʃən] [pro-pa-guei-shon], *s.* 1. Propagación, la multiplicación de la especie. 2. Propagación, la dilatación o extensión de alguna cosa.

propagator [ˌprɒpəˈgeɪtər] [pro-pa-guei-taʳ], *s.* Propagador.

propel [prəˈpel] [pro-pel], *va.* Impeler, mover alguna cosa hacia adelante; servir como con un medio de propulsión o impulsión; lanzar (un proyectil).

propellent [prəˈpelənt] [pro-pe-lent], *a.* Motor, propulsor, que hace mover, o empuja hacia adelante.

propeller [prəˈpeləʳ] [pro-pe-laʳ], *s.* 1. Impulsor, el o lo que impele. 2. Hélice, parte del mecanismo propulsor de un buque de vapor; propulsor en general. 3. Buque de hélice. **Screw propeller,** propulsor de hélice. 4. *(Auto)* **Propeller shaft,** eje de propulsión, eje cardán.

propense [prəˈpens] [pro-pens], *a.* *(Ant.)* Propenso, inclinado, dispuesto.

propension [prəˈpenʃən] [pro-pe-shon], *s.* Propensión, tendencia.

proper ['prɒpəʳ] [pro-paʳ], *a.* 1. Propio, conveniente, idóneo, a propósito, apto para algún fin (own). 2. Propio, conforme al uso, conveniente, correspondiente, justo, correcto (correspondant). 3. Propio, peculiar, particular. 4. Propio, natural, en contraposición a lo postizo o accidental. 5. Justo, exacto, literal, plano (exact). 6. *(Ant. o Prov.)* Esbelto, bien dispuesto, de buena presencia, bien parecido; aseado. 7. *(Ant.)* Propio, mismo. **Proper sense,** sentido propio, justo o literal. **Proper surroundings,** alrededores, medio, atmósfera, circunstancias propias, convenientes. **Proper name,** nombre propio, de pila.

properly ['prɒpəlɪ] [pro-per-li], *adv.* 1. Propiamente, justamente, convenientemente; correctamente; oportunamente, con mucha razón, a propósito. 2. Correctamente. 3. Decorosamente. **Properly speaking,** hablando claro; hablando en términos precisos, etc. **More properly,** mejor dicho.

properness ['prɒpənɪs] [pro-pa-nes], *s.* 1. Propiedad, la calidad particular que conviene privativamente a alguna cosa. 2. Corrección. 3. Decoro.

propertied ['prɒpətɪd] [pro-pa-tid], *a.* Propietario, que posee bienes.

property ['prɒpətɪ] [pro-pa-ti], *s.* 1. Propiedad (attribute), calidad particular o privativa. 2. Propiedad, derecho de posesión, dominio; derecho o interés legal de valor; el derecho de ejercer una ocupación o empleo particular. 3. Propiedad, lo que puede ser poseído legalmente; hacienda, los bienes poseídos. **Personal property,** bienes muebles, los

que pueden acompañar a la persona del dueño. **Real property,** bienes inmuebles, bienes raíces. **A man of large property,** un gran hacendado, un rico propietario. 4. **Properties,** *s. pl.* Trajes, vestidos, armas, etc., propias y usadas en el tiempo y lugar en que se supone la acción de un drama. 5. *(Teat.)* Guardarropía, accesorios.

prophecy ['prɒfəsɪ] [pro-fe-si], *s.* 1. Profecía hecha por inspiración divina; predicción de las cosas futuras. 2. Plática o discurso hecho bajo inspiración divina.

prophesier ['prɒfɪsɪəʳ] [pro-fi-siaʳ], *s.* Profeta, el que predice.

prophesy ['prɒfɪsɪ] [pro-fi-si], *va.* 1. Profetizar, predecir, especialmente bajo la inspiración divina; prefigurar. 2. Hablar o porferir en nombre de Dios; interpretar, declarar. -*vn.* 1. Hablar con influencia divina; comunicar entre Dios y el hombre. 2. Profetizar; predecir. 3. Explicar las Escrituras.

prophet ['prɒfɪt] [pro-fit], *s.* 1. Profeta, el que transmite mensajes divinos o que interpreta la voluntad divina. 2. Profeta, el que predice lo venidero; especialmente el profeta inspirado. 3. Guía, superior religioso.

prophetess ['prɒfɪtɪs] [pro-fi-tis], *sf.* Profetisa.

prophetic [prəˈfetɪk] [pro-fe-tik], *a.* Profético: que predice.

prophetically [prəˈfetɪkəlɪ] [pro-fe-ti-ka-li], *adv.* Proféticamente.

prophylactic [ˌprɒfɪˈlæktɪk] [pro-fi-lak-tik], *a.* Profiláctico, preservativo, preventivo.

prophylaxis [ˌprɒfɪˈlæksɪs] [pro-fi-lak-sis], *s.* Profilaxis, higiene, tratamiento médico, preventivo.

propinquity [prəˈpɪŋkwɪtɪ] [pro-pin-kui-ti], *s.* 1. Propincuidad, cercanía (place). 2. Proximidad (time). 3. Propincuidad, parentesco.

propitiable [prəˈpɪʃɪəbl] [pro-pi-shia-bol], *a.* Que se puede propiciar o volver propicio, favorable.

propitiate [prəˈpɪʃɪeɪt] [pro-pi-shieit], *vn.* Propiciar, ablandar, aplacar, conciliar.

propitiation [prəˌpɪʃɪˈeɪʃən] [pro-pi-shiei-shon], *s.* 1. Propiciación, acción de volver propicio. 2. Propiciación, lo que hace propicio; sacrificio que se ofrece a Dios para aplacarle.

propitiator [prəˌpɪʃɪˈeɪtəⁿ] [pro-pi-shiei-taʳ], *s.* Propiciador.

propitiatory [prəˈpɪʃɪətərɪ] [pro-pi-shia-to-ri], *s.* Propiciatorio, que tiene virtud de mover y hacer propicio. -*s.* 1. Propiciación. 2. Propiciatorio, placa de oro que en la ley antigua se colocaba sobre el arca de la Alianza.

propitious [prəˈpɪʃəs] [pro-pi-shos], *a.* 1. Propicio, benéfico, benigno, inclinado a hacer bien. 2. De buen agüero, feliz, favorable.

propitiously [prəˈpɪʃəslɪ] [pro-pi-shos-li], *adv.* Propiciamente, favorablemente.

propitiousness [prəˈpɪʃəsnɪs] [pro-pi-shos-nes], *s.* Calidad de propicio; beneficencia, naturaleza favorable, favor, benignidad.

propolis ['prɒpəlɪs] [pro-po-lis], *s.* Propóleos, tanca, betún de las abejas. Se llama también cera aleda. *V.* BEE-GLUE.

proponent [prəˈpəʊnənt] [pro-pou-nent], *s.* Proponente, proponedor.

proportion [prəˈpɔːʃən] [pro-por-shon], *s.* 1. Proporción, relación de las partes entre sí o con el todo; extensión, número o grado relativo. 2. Proporción debida, ajuste conveniente, simetría, forma, tamaño (shape, size). 3. *(Mat.)* Proporción, la semejanza o igualdad de dos razones; regla de tres. 4. Parte que corresponde: porción, cuota. **In proportion,** en proporción, en correspondencia, a medida que. **Out of proportion,** desproporcionado.

proportion, *va.* Proporcionar, disponer y ordenar una cosa en la debida proporción; formar con simetría.

proportionable [prəˈpɔːʃənəbl] [pro-por-sho-na-bol], *a.* Proporcionable, proporcionado.

proportionably [prəˈpɔːʃənəblɪ] [pro-por-sho-na-bli], *adv.* Proporcionablemente, proporcionadamente.

proportional [prəˈpɔːʃənl] [pro-por-sho-nal], *a.* Proporcional, perteneciente a la proporción o que la incluye. **Proportional representation,** representación proporcional. -*s.* *(Mat.)* Proporcional, número o cantidad proporcional.

proportionality [ˌprəpɔːʃəˈnælɪtɪ] [pro-por-sho-na-li-ti], *s.* Proporcionalidad.

proportionally [prəˈpɔːʃnəlɪ] [pro-por-sho-na-li], *adv.* Proporcionalmente, en proporción.

proportionate [prəˈpɔːʃnɪt] [pro-por-sho-nit], *a.* Proporcionado, en debida proporción con algo; competente.

proportionate, *va.* Proporcionar, ajustar en proporción.

proportionately [prəˈpɔːʃnɪtlɪ] [pro-por-sho-nit-li], *adv.* Proporcionadamente.

proportionateness [prəˈpɔːʃnɪtnɪs] [pro-por-sho-nit-nes], *s.* Proporcionalidad, proporción.

proportionment [prəˈpɔːʃənmənt] [pro-por-shon-ment], *s.* 1. Acción y efecto de proporcionar; ajustar. 2. Proporción (state, condition).

proposal [prəˈpəʊzl] [pro-pou-shal], *s.* 1. Propuesta, proposición, ofrecimiento, oferta que ha de ser considerada o aceptada. 2. Declaración: proposición de matrimonio. 3. Plan o línea de conducta propuestos por uno.

propose [prəˈpəʊz] [pro-pous], *va.* 1. Proponer, ofrecer algo para su consideración o aceptación; ofrecer, presentar. 2. Proponer, pensar, tener intención de, formar un designio. **To propose a toast,** proponer un brindis. *-vn.* 1. Proponerse, hacer propósito, hacer resolución de. 2. Ofrecer, en especial hacer una oferta de matrimonio.

proposer [prəˈpəʊzəʳ] [pro-pou-saʳ], *s.* Proponente, proponedor.

proposition [ˌprɒpəˈzɪʃən] [pro-po-si-shon], *s.* 1. Proposición, una oración breve en que se afirma o niega alguna cosa. 2. Proposición, la acción de proponer; propuesta. 3. Expresión de un juicio por medio de palabras. 4. Lo que se propone como asunto del discurso; exposición de un tema; propósito. 5. *(Mat.)* Proposición, cualquier principio que se establece y ha de ser demostrado. 6. *(Mús.)* Enunciado de un tema. 7. *(Fam.)* Negocio, ocupación, proyecto, asunto, problema; oficio; artículo de comercio; sujeto, tipo, individuo.

propositional [ˌprɒpəˈzɪʃənl] [pro-po-si-sho-nal], *a.* Considerado como una proposición.

propound [prəˈpaʊnd] [pro-paund], *va.* 1. Proponer, plantear. 2. Sentar o sostener una proposición. 3. Hacer preguntas a uno.

propounder [prəˈpaʊndəʳ] [pro-paun-daʳ], *s.* Proponente, proponedor.

proprietary [prəˈpraɪətərɪ] [pro-prai-ta-ri], *a.* 1. Propietario, que tiene derecho exclusivo a una cosa. 2. *(Com.)* Patentado, registrado. *-s.* 1. Propietario, dueño. 2. Conjunto de propietarios. 3. Derecho exclusivo a la posesión: justa pretensión a la propiedad de una cosa.

proprietor [prəˈpraɪətəʳ] [pro-praia-taʳ], *s.* Propietario, la persona que tiene derecho a una cosa, o al título legal de la misma; amo; dueño.

proprietress [prəˈpraɪətrɪs] [pro-praia-tris], *sf.* Propietaria.

propriety [prəˈpraɪətɪ] [pro-praia-ti], *s.* 1. Concordancia con el uso establecido, conveniencia, conducta o acción conveniente, decencia en los modales. 2. Exactitud y uniformidad gramatical y retórica; propiedad, perfecta conveniencia de la palabra o estilo con el asunto que se expresa; sentido propio (of words). 3. Reglas de conducta, la educación, el trato social. **To offend against propriety,** faltar a las reglas de la buena crianza.

props [prɒps] [props], *s. (Teat.)* Guardarropía, accesorios. 2. Encargado de la guardarropía.

propt, *pp. irr.* de TO PROP.

propulsion [prəˈpʌlʃən] [pro-pal-shon], *s.* Propulsión, propulsa; impulso, impulsión.

propulsive [prəˈpʌlsɪv] [pro-pal-siv], **propulsory** [prəˈpʌlsərɪ] [pro-pal-so-ri], *a.* Propulsor, que hace adelantar.

pro rata [ˌprəʊˈrɑːtə] [pro-ra-ta], *a. (Com.)* Prorrata, a proporción.

prorate [ˈprəʊreɪt] [prou-reit], *va.* Prorratear.

prorogation [ˌprəʊrəˈgeɪʃən] [prou-ro-guei-shon], *s.* Prorrogación, ampliación, prolongación, extensión, continuación o dilatación del tiempo señalado para una cosa.

The prorogation of the session of Parliament, suspensión de las sesiones del Parlamento hasta cierto día señalado.

prorogue [prəˈrəʊg] [pro-roug], *va.* 1. Prorrogar, ampliar, extender, dilatar o continuar el tiempo señalado (adjourn, extend). 2. Diferir. **To prorogue Parliament,** suspender las sesiones del Parlamento hasta un día señalado.

prosaic [prəˈdʒeɪɪk] [prou-seik], *a.* 1. Prosaico, tocante o parecido a la prosa; que está en prosa. 2. No imaginativo, falto de interés, común, trivial.

prosaically [prəˈdʒeɪɪkəlɪ] [prou-sei-ka-li], *adv.* Prosaicamente, de un modo prosaico.

prosaicism, prosaism [prəˈdʒeɪɪsɪzəm] [prou-sei-si-sem], *s.* Estilo, carácter prosaico; frase, locución prosaica; prosaísmo.

proscenium [prəˈsiːnɪəm] [prou-si-niom], *s. (Teat.)* Proscenio, el lugar entre la escena y la orquesta.

proscribe [prəʊsˈkraɪb] [prous-kraib], *va.* 1. Proscribir, declarar a uno reo de muerte; poner a uno fuera de la protección de las leyes; expulsar de la sociedad. 2. Condenar, reprobar, hablando de doctrinas, máximas, etc.; prohibir, vedar.

proscriber [prəʊsˈkraɪbəʳ] [prous-krai-baʳ], *s.* El que proscribe, prohibe o veda.

proscription [prəʊsˈkrɪpʃən] [prous-krip-shon], *s.* 1. Proscripción, acción de proscribir, de poner fuera de la ley, o de la sociedad. 2. Interdicción, restricción.

proscriptive [prəʊsˈkrɪptɪv] [prous-krip-tiv], *a.* Proscriptivo, que proscribe o condena; perteneciente a, o de la naturaleza de la proscripción.

prose [prəʊz] [prous], *s.* 1. Prosa, la forma corriente y suelta del lenguaje. 2. Habla común, trivial y tediosa. 3. Discurso pesado, lata. 3. Charla, plática. *-a.* Prosaico, de prosa, en prosa; insulso, fastidioso. **Prose writer,** prosista.

prosecute [ˈprɒsɪkjuːt] [pro-si-kiut], *va.* 1. Proseguir, seguir, continuar, llevar adelante. 2. Anhelar, buscar o seguir con empeño; pretender, solicitar. 3. Procesar, hacer causa a uno, enjuiciar, demandar. 4. Ejercer (a profession, activity). *-vn.* Querellarse ante el juez; seguir un pleito; sostener una acusación criminal.

prosecution [ˌprɒsɪˈkjuːʃən] [pro-si-kiu-shon], *s.* 1. Prosecución, la acción de proseguir una cosa. 2. Seguimiento de una causa criminal; demanda, acusación, proceso. 3. Parte actora. 4. Ministerio fiscal.

prosecutor [ˈprɒsɪkjuːtəʳ] [pro-si-kiu-taʳ], *s.* El que prosigue o continúa alguna cosa, el actor o acusador en una causa criminal; demandante, acusador privado. **Prosecutor public,** fiscal.

prosecutrix [ˈprɒsɪkjuːtrɪks] [pro-si-kiu-triks], *sf.* Acusadora, demandante en una causa criminal.

proselyte [ˈprɒsɪlaɪt] [pro-si-lait], *s.* Prosélito, persona convertida a una religión, a una secta, a un partido, o a alguna opinión.

proselyte, proselytize [ˈprɒsɪlaɪz] [pro-si-li-tais], *va.* Convertir, hacer prosélitos.

proselytism [ˈprɒsɪlɪtɪzəm] [pro-si-li-ti-sem], *s.* Proselitismo, el acto de hacer prosélitos; estado de conversión.

proser [ˈprəʊzəʳ] [prou-saʳ], *s.* Prosista, hablador sin sustancia, escritor enojoso, insulso, pesado, latoso.

prosily [ˈprɒsɪlɪ] [pro-si-li], *adv.* 1. Prosaicamente, de un modo prosaico. 2. Pesadamente, fastidiosamente.

prosiness [ˈprɒsɪnɪs] [pro-si-nes], *s.* Calidad de prosaico; insulsez.

prosody [ˈprɒsədɪ] [pro-so-di], *s.* 1. Prosodia, la parte de la gramática que enseña la pronunciación y cantidad de las sílabas. 2. Métrica.

prospect [ˈprɒspekt] [pros-pekt], *va. y vn.* 1. Catear, *(Amer.)* buscar oro, petróleo; descubrir minerales o minas. 2. Dar buenas esperanzas, prometer. **To prospect for,** andar en busca de, buscar un yacimiento.

prospect, *s.* 1. Perspectiva, vista o aspecto de diversos objetos mirados de lejos; paisaje, panorama (landscape). 2. Perspectiva, lo que se prevé o espera; indicación que justifica una expectativa o esperanza; aspecto, futura probabilidad fundada en las indicaciones presentes. 3. Situación con respecto a los puntos cardinales, la dirección en que se halla el frente de una cosa. 4. Indicación de la presencia de un mineral 5. *(Des.)* Vistillas, lugar alto desde donde se ve y descubre mucho terreno. 6. Expectativa, esperanza, probabilidad, perspectiva. 7. Cliente, comprador probable. 8. *(Min)* Indicio de veta o venero. 9. *(Min)* Oro, etc., obtenido de una muestra de un mineral. 10. Mina parcialmente explotada. **In prospect,** en prespectiva, probable. **These houses afford a fine prospect,** estas casas tiene hermosas vistas. **There is no prospect of his coming,** no hay esperanzas de que venga; no tiene trazas de venir. **The house has a western prospect,** la casa da al poniente. **A prospect of gold,** indicación (pepita o polvo) de oro. **Man of goods prospect,** hombre de provenir.

prospecting ['prɒspektɪŋ] [pros-pek-tin], *s. (Min)* 1. Exploración en busca de yacimientos. 2. Cateo.

prospective ['prɒspektɪv] [pros-pek-tiv], *a.* 1. Anticipado, venidero, que está por venir, o en expectativa. 2. Previsor, prevenido, que mira hacia adelante o toma en cuenta lo futuro. *-s.* Vista, perspectiva.

prospectus ['prɒspektəs] [pros-pek-tus], *s.* Prospecto, el anuncio que se hace de algún plan o proyecto, o de alguna obra antes de darse a luz.

prosper ['prɒspəʳ] [pros-paʳ], *va.* Prosperar, acrecentar en bienes. *-vn.* 1. Prosperar, gozar de fortuna o prosperidad. 2. Medrar, mejorar de fortuna.

prosperity [prɒs'perɪtɪ] [pros-pe-ri-ti], *s.* Prosperidad, felicidad, fortuna.

prosperous ['prɒspeərəs] [pros-pe-ros], *a.* 1. Próspero, feliz, dichoso, afortunado, favorable (happy, lucky). 2. Floreciente, propicio (propicious). **Prosperous gales,** vientos propicios.

prosperously ['prɒspərəslɪ] [pros-pe-ros-li], *adv.* Prósperamente.

prosperousness ['prɒspərəsnɪs] [pros-pe-ros-nes], *s.* Prosperidad.

prostate ['prɒsteɪt] [pros-teit], *s. (Anat.)* Próstata, glándula situada al principio de la uretra en el hombre y los mamíferos machos.

prostatic [prɒs'tætɪk] [pros-ta-tik], *a.* Prostático, perteneciente o relativo a la próstata.

prosthesis [prɒs'θɪsɪs] [pros-zi-sis], *s.* 1. Prótesis, adición de una o más letras a una palabra, especialmente al principio. 2. *(Cir.)* La operación de hacer partes artificiales y ajustarlas al cuerpo, como los dientes postizos, piernas de corcho, etc.

prostitute ['prɒstɪtjuːt] [pros-ti-tiut], *va.* Prostituir, exponer a todo género de torpeza y sensualidad.

prostitue, *s.* 1. Mercenario. 2. Prostituta, ramera. *-a.* 1. Prostituto, prostituido, venal. 2. Vil, entregado a los vicios, deshonrado. envilecido, corrompido.

prostitution [ˌprɒstɪ'tjuːʃən] [pros-ti-tiu-shon], *s.* Prostitución.

prostrate ['prɒstreɪt] [pros-treit], *a.* 1. Postrado, humillado, prosternado. 2. Postrado, abatido; humillado. 2. Echado a la larga. 3. *(Biol.)* Procumbente, echado, tendido.

prostrate, *va.* 1. Echar a tierra o por el suelo; tender a la larga. 2. Postrar, demoler, derribar; arruinar. 3. Prostrarse, hincarse de rodillas. 4. *(Med.)* Postrar, enflaquecer, quitar el vigor a alguno. **To prostrate oneself,** postrarse, prosternarse.

prostration [prɒs'treɪʃən] [pros-trei-shon], *s.* 1. Prostación. 2. Abatimiento, depresión.

prosy ['prəʊzɪt] [prou-si], *a.* 1. Prosaico. 2. Latoso, insulso.

protagonist [prəʊ'tægənɪst] [prou-ta-go-nist], *s.* 1. Protagonista, personaje principal del drama griego; jefe. 2. Portavoz, campeón, defensor de una causa.

protect [prə'tekt] [pro-tekt], *va.* Proteger, amparar, defender, patrocinar, favorecer.

protection [prə'tekʃən] [pro-tek-shon], *s.* 1. Protección, amparo, patrocinio (defence, patronage). 2. Protección, proteccionismo, sistema económico que, para proteger la industria y el comercio de un país, dificulta la importación de productos extranjeros, recargando los derechos de aduana. 3. Salvoconducto, pasaporte.

protectionism [prə'tekʃənɪzəm] [pro-tek-sho-ni-sem], *s.* Proteccionismo, sistema económico de los proteccionistas. V. PROTECTION, 2ª acep.

protective [prə'tektɪv] [pro-tek-tiv], *a.* 1. Protector, que sirve de abrigo. 2. Protector, que protege. **Protective coloring,** coloración protectora, mimetismo. **Protective tariff,** tarifa (o arancel) proteccionista.

protective, *a.* protector, protectorio, que protege, que sirve de abrigo. *-s.* 1. Alguna cosa que protege; amparo, abrigo. 2. Cubierta aséptica para una herida.

protector [prə'tektəʳ] [pro-tek-taʳ], *s.* 1. Protector, patrono, patrocinador. 2. Cosa que protege; **chest protector,** peto de lana; **point protector,** guardapuntas.

protectorate [prə'tektərɪt] [pro-tek-to-rit], *s.* Protectorado, protectoría, el oficio, dignidad o jurisdicción de protector.

protegé ['prɒtezeɪ] [pro-te-yei], *s.* Protegido, favorito, ahijado, paniaguado.

protegée ['prɒtezeɪ] [pro-te-yei], *s.* Protegida, favorita, ahijada, paniaguada.

proteic ['prɒteɪk] [pro-teik], *a. (Quim.)* Proteico.

protein ['prɒteɪn] [pro-tein], *s.* Proteína.

protest ['prəʊtest] [prou-test], *vn.* 1. Protestar, declarar solemnemente su dictamen o parecer, afirmar (avow). 2. Protestar de o contra; recusar (reject). *-va.* Protestar una letra de cambio, hacer o sacar protesto contra el que no la quiere aceptar o pagar después de haberla aceptado. **To protest for non-acceptance,** protestar por falta de aceptación. **To protest for non-payment,** protestar por falta de pago.

protest, *s.* Protesta, protesto. **Under protest,** haciendo constar su protesta, protestando, con reservas; de mala gana. **To accept a bill under protest,** aceptar una letra bajo o so protesto. **Protest of a bill,** protesto de una letra de cambio o libranza.

protestant ['prɒtestənt] [pro-tes-tant], *a.* 1. Protestante, el que protesta. 2. Protestante, nombre que se da a las religiones anglicana, luterana y calvinista y a las sectas que se derivan de ellas.

protestant, *s.* Protestante, nombre que se da a los que profesan cualquiera de las sectas protestantes.

protestantism ['prɒtɪstəntɪzəm] [pro-tis-tan-ti-sem], *s.* Protestantismo, la creenica de los protestantes.

prostestation [ˌprɒtes'teɪʃən] [pro-tes-tei-shon], *s.* protestación; protesta, declaración solemne de una opinión, etc.

protester ['prɒtestəʳ] [pro-tes-taʳ], *s.* El que protesta, protestante.

proto-, Prefijo derviado del griego que significa primero; en química significa el más bajo.

protocol ['prəʊtəkɒl] [prou-to-kol], *s.* 1. Trazo, esbozo, v. g. de un tratado; declaración o memoria informal de un acuerdo entre dos países; acta de una conferencia. 2. Protocolo, registro. 3. Convenio entre patronos y obreros en que se establecen las bases para resolver los conflictos.

protocol, *v.* 1. Protocolizar, protocolar. 2. Inscribir en un convenio o protocolo.

proton ['prəʊtɒn] [prou-ton], *s. (Fís. y Quím.)* Protón.

protoplasm ['prəʊplæzəm] [prou-to-pla-sem], *s. (Biol.)* Protoplasma.

prototype ['prəʊtətaɪp] [prou-tou-taip], *s.* Prototipo, el original de alguna copia.

protoxid ['prəʊtɒksɪd] [prou-tok-sid], *s.* protóxido, el óxido que contiene un solo átomo de oxígeno.

protozoa ['prəʊtəzuː] [prou-to-su], *s. pl.* Protozoarios, protozoos.

protract [prə'trækt] [pro-trakt], *va.* 1. Alargar, prolongar, dilatar, diferir en tiempo. 2. Levantar un plano; trazar un mapa por medio del pitipié y del semicírculo (transferidor). 3. *(Anat.)* Extender, empujar o impulsar hacia adelante.

protracter [prə'træktəʳ] [pro-trak-taʳ], *s.* 1. Alargador. 2. V. PROTRACTOR.

protractile [prə'træktaɪl] [pro-trak-tail], *a.* Capaz de ser impulsado o extendido hacia adelante.

protraction [prə'trækʃən] [pro-trak-shon], *s.* 1. Prolongación, dilatación, extensión. 2. Demora. 3. Trazado de un plano por medio del transportador.

protractive [prə'træktɪv] [pro-trak-tiv], *a.* Dilatorio; el que alarga o prolonga.

protractor [prə'træktəʳ] [pro-trak-taʳ], *s.* 1. Transferidor, instrumento para medir o trazar ángulos. 2. *(Anat.)* Músculo que mueve un miembro hacia adelante. 3. Regla o molde. 4. V. PROTRACTER, 1ª acep.

protrude [prə'truːd] [pro-trud], *va.* Empujar, impeler, llevar hacia adelante; hacer salir o sobresalir. **To protrude one's tongue,** sacar la lengua. *-vn.* 1. Empujarse o moverse hacia adelante, salir al aire. 2. Salir fuera, sobresalir.

protrusible, protrusile [prə'truːzɪbl] [pro-tru-si-bol], *a.* Que puede ser extendido o impulsado hacia adelante.

protrusion [prə'truːʒən] [pro-tru-shon], *s.* El acto de empujar o llevar una cosa hacia adelante; rempujón, empujón.

protrusive [prə'truːzɪv] [pro-tru-siv], *a.* Que impulsa hacia adelante, que hace salir o proyectar.

protuberance, [prə'tjuːbərəns] [pro-tiu-be-rans], *s.* 1. Protuberancia, prominencia de los huesos o de otras partes del cuerpo. 2. Prominencia, la elevación de una de las partes de cualquier cuerpo sobre las que están alrededor.

protuberant [prə'tjuːbərənt] [pro-tiu-be-rant], *a.* Prominente, saliente.

protuberate [peə'tjuːbərɪt] [pro-tiu-be-rit], *vn.* Sobresalir, formar prominencia.

proud [praʊd] [praud], *a.* 1. Soberbio, orgulloso, altivo, atrevido, envanecido, presumido, presuntuoso, fiero, ufano. 2. Alto, quisquilloso, engreído; grande, noble. 3. Arrogante, insolente, impaciente. 4. Soberbio, magnífico, pomposo, ostentoso, espléndido, grande. 5. *(Med.)* Fungoso. 6. *(Des.)* Salida: se dice de las hembras de los animales. 7. Fogoso (horse). 8. Hinchado, embravecido (sea). 9. Bello, espléndido, noble. **He is very proud of his birth,** está muy pagado de su nacimiento. **A proud day for Athens,** un gran día para Atenas. **Proud-stomached,** altivo, arrogante. **Proud titles,** títulos pomposos.

proudly ['praʊdlɪ] [praud-li], *adv.* Soberbiamente, orgullosamente; pomposamente.

prove [pruːv] [pruv], *va. (pret.* PROVED, *pp.* PROVED o PROVEN). 1. Probar, justificar, manifestar, hacer patente, mostrar. 2. Probar, examinar, experimentar. 3. Abrir y hacer público un testamento con las fórmulas prescritas por las leyes. 4. *(Arit.)* Hacer la prueba de. 5. Sacar una prueba de. *-vn.* 1. Resultar, venir a parar, salir bien o mal, según la prueba, hallarse. 2. *(Ant.)* Hacer prueba o experiencia de una cosa. **It will prove otherwise,** saldrá de otro modo. **Prove all things,** probadlo todo. **To prove incorrect,** resultar inexacto. **To prove useful,** ser o resultar útil. **If what you say proves true,** si lo que Ud. dice resulta verdadero. **To prove oneself,** mostrarse, hacer prueba de, mostrar que uno es. **To prove the patience of,** poner a prueba la paciencia de.

proven ['pruːvən] [pru-van], *pp. irr.* de PROVE (limitado a los tribunales o a documentos judiciales). Probado, demostrado. **Not proven,** veredicto admisible en el derecho escocés, que declara la acusación como no probada, aunque tampoco refutada.

provenance [ˌprɒvɑːˈnsɑːl] [pro-van-sal], *s.* Origen, procedencia.

provender ['prɒvɪndəʳ] [pro-vin-daʳ], *s.* 1. Provisión de heno y grano para el ganado. 2. Provisión, víveres.

provenience [ˌprɒviːˈnɪəns] [pro-vi-niens], *s.* Origen, procedencia.

prover ['pruːvəʳ] [pru-vaʳ], *s.* Persona que prueba o saca pruebas.

proverb ['prɒvɜːb] [pro-verb], *s.* 1. Proverbio, adagio o refrán; apotegma. 2. Sentencia enigmática. 3. Alguna cosa proverbial; ejemplo típico o notorio.

proverbial [prəˈvɜːbɪəl] [pro-ver-bial], *a.* 1. Proverbial. 2. Conocido, notorio.

proverbialist [prəˈvɜːbɪəlɪst] [pro-ver-bia-list], *s.* Proverbiador; proverbista.

proverbially [prəˈvɜːbɪəlɪ] [pro-ver-bia-li], *adv.* Proverbialmente.

provide [prəˈvaɪd] [pro-vaid], *va.* 1. Proveer, prevenir, proporcionar, tener prontas las cosas necesarias para algún fin (furnish). 2. Proveer, abastecer, surtir (supply); dar, suministrar (give). 3. Atesorar. 4. Estipular, contratar mutuamente. *-vn.* 1. Proveer, proporcionar medios para el uso futuro; abastecer de víveres. 2. Precaverse, tener cuidado, encargarse de; tomar precauciones, prepararse. 3. Hacer una estipulación previa. **To provide against,** precaver, prevenir anticipadamente algún riesgo, daño o peligro. **to provide for,** proveer, cuidar de antemano, dar a uno lo que necesita, estar preparado para algún acontecimiento, negocio, etc.; tomar precauciones. **Provided that,** con tal que; siempre que; como, bajo condición; bien entendido. **The Lord will provide,** Dios proveerá.

provided [prəˈvaɪdɪd] [pro-vai-did], *a.* Provisto, equipado, dotado: **provided school,** escuela municipal. 2. Proporcionado, dado, heredado. *-conj.* **Provided that,** con tal que, siempre que, a condición de o que.

providence ['prɒvɪdəns] [pro-vi-dans], *s.* 1. Providencia, previsión, prevención o disposición anticipada. 2. Providencia divina, o simplemente Providencia, la mira y cuidado que tiene Dios acerca de sus criaturas. 3. Prudencia, frugalidad, economía.

provident ['prɒvɪdənt] [pro-vi-dant], *a.* 1. Próvido, providente, prevenido; cuidadoso, cauto, circunspecto, prudente, avisado. 2. Frugal, económico.

providential [ˌprɒvɪˈdenʃəl] [pro-vi-den-shal], *a.* Providencial, que resulta de o que evidencia la acción de la providencia divina.

providentially [ˌprɒvɪˈdenʃəlɪ] [pro-vi-den-sha-li], *adv.* Providencialmente, por la sabia disposición de la Providencia.

providently ['prɒvɪdəntlɪ] [pro-vi-dent-li], *adv.* Próvidamente, prudentemente.

provider [prəˈvaɪdəʳ] [pro-vai-daʳ], *s.* Proveedor, provisor, abastecedor, suministrador.

province ['prɒvɪns] [pro-vins], *s.* 1. Provincia, una de las partes en que generalmente se dividen los reinos o estados, distrito. 2. El oficio, empleo, obligación o incumbencia particular de cada uno; competencia; departamento. 3. Esfera, campo de actividad. **That is not my province,** eso no me toca, no me pertence o no es encargo mío, o eso no es de mi cargo. **It is the province of,** pertenece o está al cargo de.

provincial ['prɒvɪnʃəl] [pro-vin-shal], *a.* 1. Provincial, perteneciente a una provincia de un mismo estado. 2. Provincial, rudo, campesino, grosero.

provincial, *s.* 1. Provincial, el natural o habitante de una provincia; que no es de la capital. 2. Provincial, el religioso que tiene el gobierno y superioridad sobre todas las casas y conventos de una provincia.

provincialism [prəˈvɪnʃəlɪzəm] [pro-vin-sha-li-sem], *s.* Provincialismo, modo particular de hablar de los habitantes de una provincia.

provincialist ['prɒvɪnʃəlɪst] [pro-vin-sha-list], *s.* Provincial, el que usa de provincialismos; habitante de una provincia.

proving ['pruːvɪŋ] [pru-vin], *s.* Prueba, acción y efecto de probar. **Proving-ground,** lugar para probar los cañones y otras armas de fuego y las municiones para las mismas.

provision [prəˈvɪʒən] [pro-vi-shon], *s.* 1. Provisión, prevención de comestibles o de otras cosas necesarias (supply); víveres, bastimentos. 2. Provisión, los comestibles u otras cosas recogidas (stores). 3. La acción de proveerse, prevenirse o disponerse, precaución o medidas de precaución. 4. Señalamiento, asignación de alimentos, asistencias, etc. 5 Ajuste, convenio, estipulación. 6. Requisito. 7. Medida, disposición, providencia. **Till further provision be made,** hasta más proveer. **To make provision for,** proveer a; asegurar el porvenir de. 8. Cláusula, estipulación, condición. 9. Provisiones, vituallas, bastimentos.

provision, v. Aprovisionar, abastecer.

provisional [prə'vɪʒənl] [pro-vi-sho-nal], a. provisional; establecido, dispuesto, o mandado interinamente.

provisionally [prə'vɪʒnəlɪ] [pro-vi-sho-na-li], adv. Provisionalmente, interinamente.

proviso [prə'vaɪzəo] [pro-vai-sou], s. 1. Caución, estipulación, condición provisional, requisito. 2. Cláusula o artículo que lo establece.

provisory [prə'vɪʒərɪ] [pro-vi-so-ri], a. Provisorio, provisional, condicional, temporero.

provocation [ˌprɒvə'keɪʃən] [pro-vo-kei-shon], s. 1. Provocación, lo que provoca, causa ira o resentimiento. 2. Estímulo para ejecutar una cosa. 3. Cosa que irrita o exaspera.

provocative [prə'vɒkətɪv] [pro-vo-ka-tiv], a. 1. Provocativo, estimulante. 2. Irritante, exasperador (irritating). -s. Llamativo, lo que puede estimualr o producir apetito.

provoke [prə'vəok] [pro-vouk], va. 1. Provocar, irritar o estimular a uno para que se enoje. 2. Provocar, excitar, incitar, inducir. 3. Provocar, facilitar, ayudar, causar, promover. 4. (Des.) Desafiar. -vn. Causar enojo, excitar la cólera de alguno.

provoker [prə'vəokər] [pro-vou-kar], s. Provocador, persona o cosa que provoca.

provoking [prə'vəokɪŋ] [pro-vou-kin], a. 1. Provocativo, provocante. 2. Irritante, exasperador.

provokingly [prə'vəokɪŋlɪ] [pro-vou-kin-li], adv. Insolentemente, de un modo provocativo.

prow [praʊ] [prau], s. Proa, la parte delantera de una embarcación; tajamar. -a. (Des.) Valeroso.

prowess ['praʊɪs] [prauis], s. Proeza, hazaña, valentía.

prowl ['praʊl] [praul], va. 1. Recorrer. 2. Rapiñar, hurtar; estafar (swindle). -vn. Andar o vagar de una parte a otra en busca de presa o pillaje.

prowler ['praʊlər] [prau-lar], s. Vagamundo, andorrero; el que anda vagando; ladrón, estafador.

proximal ['prɒksɪməl] [prok-si-mal], a. (Biol.) Próximo, relativamente más cercano al centro del cuerpo, lo opuesto a distal.

proximity [prɒk'sɪmɪtɪ] [prok-si-mi-ti], s. proximidad, cercanía, inmediación.

proxy ['prɒksɪ] [prok-si], s. 1. Procuración, comisión, poder. **To marry by proxy,** casarse por poder. 2. Apoderado, poderhabiente, el que tiene poder de otro para ejecutar algo en su nombre, sustituto, delegado. (Contracción de Procuracy).

prude [pru:d] [prud], sf. Mojigata, remilgada, gazmoña que afecta honestidad, modestia o santidad.

prudence ['pru:dəns] [pru-dans], s. Prudencia, cordura, discreción.

prudent ['pru:dənt] [pru-dant], a. Prudente, cuerdo, discreto, circunspecto (careful).

prudential [pru:'denʃəl] [pru-den-shal], a. Prudencial, que toca a la prudencia; dictado por la prudencia.

prudentially [pru:'denʃəlɪ] [pru-den-sha-li], s. adv. Prudencialmente.

prudentials [pru:'denʃəlz] [pru-den-shals], s. Máximas de prudencia.

prudently [pru:'dəntlɪ] [pru-dant-li], adv. Prudentemente.

prudery ['pru:dərɪ] [pru-da-ri], s. Melindre, remilgo, la afectada y demasiada delicadeza en las acciones o en el modo de ejecutarlas; gazmoñería, mojigatez, la afectación de modestia, honestidad o prudencia.

prudish ['pru:dɪʃ] [pru-dish], a. Gazmoño, mojigato, el que afecta modestia, honestidad o prudencia; serio o grave con afectación.

prune [pru:n] [prun], va. y vn. 1. Podar, cortar o quitar las ramas superfluas de los árboles y plantas. 2. Escamondar los árboles. 3. Limpiar alguna cosa quitando lo superfluo. **To prune up,** vestir, adornar. 4. Limpiar y componer sus plumas las aves. V. PREEN.

prune, s. 1. Ciruela pasa; ciruela. 2. (Fam) Bendito, simple.

prunelle ['pru:nel] [pru-nel], s. Pasa amarilla.

pruner ['pru:nər] [pru-nar], s. Podador.

pruning ['pru:nɪŋ] [pru-nin], s. Acción de podar o mondar; poda, monda, remonda, limpia de los árboles. **Pruning-hook,** podón, márcola, corvillo. **Pruning-knife,** cuchilla para podar. **Pruning-shears,** podaderas, tijeras para podar.

prurience ['proərɪəns] [prua-rians], s. 1. Comezón, prurito; particularmente, curiosidad liviana, sensualidad. 2. Deseo inmoderado.

prurient ['proərɪənt] [prua-riant], a. 1. Dispuesto a la lascivia o liviandad. 2. Que padece prurito o comezón; anheloso.

prussian ['prʌʃən] [pra-shan], a. y s. Prusiano, natural de Prusia o lo perteneciente a este reino. **Prusian blue,** azul de Prusia.

prussic ['prʌsɪk] [pra-sik], a. (Quím.) Prúsico. **Prussic acid,** V. Hydrocyanic acid.

pry [praɪ] [prai], va. y vn. 1. Espiar, acechar, atisbar, observar, reconocer (spy, exam). Se usa particularmente con out. **To pry out a secret,** arrancar un secreto. **To pry into other people's concerns,** meterse en asuntos ajenos, meterse uno en lo que no le importa; curiosear, entremeterse, sonsacar. 2. Alzaprimar, mover o levantar con una placa. **To pry apart,** separar. **To pry off,** despegar. **To pry open,** abrir, forzar.

pry, s. 1. Mirada escrudiñadora y atenta; inspección, atisbo, fisgoneo, observación curiosa e impertinente. 2. Curioso, indiscreto, entrometido. 3. (Fam.) Palanca, barra o palo para levantar un peso.

prying ['praɪɪŋ] [praiin], a. Fisgón, curioso, entrometido.

psalm [sɑːm] [salm], s. Salmo; cántico sagrado que contiene alabanzas; himno.

psalmbook ['sɑːmbok] [salm-buk], s. Salterio, libro de salmos.

psalmist ['sɑːmɪst] [sal-mist], s. Salmista; por antonomasia, David.

psalmody ['sælmədɪ] [sal-mo-di], s. Salmodia.

psalter ['sɔːltər] [sol-tar], s. Saterio o libro de salmos; en especial las versiones de las Iglesias católica y anglicana.

psaltery ['sɔːltərɪ] [sol-ta-ri], s. 1. Salterio, instrumento músico de los antiguos hebreos. 2. Salterio, instrumento músico de la edad media, con trece cuerdas y una tabla harmónica.

pseudo ['sjuːdəo] [siu-dou], a. Pseudo, seudo o falso, adjetivo griego que se pone delante de algunas voces. **Pseudo philosopher,** pseudo filósofo.

pseudomorph ['sjuːdəomɔːf] [siu-dou-morf], s. 1. Seudomorfo, mineral que tiene la forma exterior cristalina de otro mineral. 2. Forma irregular o falsa.

pseudonym ['sjuːdənɪm] [siu-do-nim], s. 1. Seudónimo, nombre ficticio empleado por un autor par que se ignore el suyo propio. 2. (Biol.) El nombre vernáculo.

pseudonymous [sjuː'dənɪməs] [siu-do-ni-mos], a. Seudónimo, de nombre supuesto.

pseudopod ['sjuːdəopɒd] [siu-dou-pod], s. (Biol.) Seudópodo, una prolongación temporal del protoplasma de una célula o de un animal unicelular, que le sirve para tomar su alimento, para moverse, etc.

pshaw [pʃɔː] [psho], inter. ¡Vaya! ¡fuera! ¡quita! ¡malhaya! ¡puf!

psoriasis [sə'raɪəsɪs] [so-raiasis], s. Soriasis, enfermedad crónica de la piel que presenta gurpos de escamas.

psyche [saɪk] [saik], s. 1. Psique, Psiquis. 2. El alma.

psychedelic [saɪkə'delɪk] [sai-ka-de-lik], a. Psicodélico o sicodélico.

psychiatrist [saɪ'kaɪətrɪst] [sai-kaia-trist], s. (Med.) Psiquiatría o siquiatría.

psychic, psychical ['saɪkɪk] [sai-kik] ['saɪkɪkəl] [sai-ki-kal], a. 1. Psíquico, referente a las facultades del alma, desde el punto de vista intelectual y moral. 2. Natural, como opuesto a espiritual. 3. Sensible a las fuerzas psíquicas.

psychoanalysis [ˌsaɪkəoə'nælɪsɪs] [sai-koua-na-li-sis], s. (Med.) Psicoanálisis o sicoanálisis.

psychoanalyst [ˌsaɪkəʊ'ænəlɪst] [sai-koua-na-list], *s.* Psicoanalista o sicoanalista.

psychoanalytic [ˌsaɪkəʊˌænə'lɪtɪk] [sai-koua-na-li-tik], *a.* Psicoanalítico o sicoanalítico.

psychoanalyze [ˌsaɪkəʊə'nælaɪz] [sai-koua-na-laos], *va.* Psicoanalizar, o sicoanalizar, hacer psicoanálisis o sicoanálisis.

psychological, psychologic [ˌsaɪkə'lɒdʒɪkəl] [sai-ko-lo-yi-kal], *a.* Psicológico. **Psychological testing,** psicotecnia.

psychologist [saɪ'kɒlədʒɪst] [sai-ko-lo-yist], *s.* Psicólogo, el que estudia o está versado en la psicología.

psychology [saɪ'kɒlədʒɪ] [sai-ko-lo-yi], *s.* Psicología, la ciencia que trata del alma humana, sus facultades y funciones; también, tratado sobre el alma.

psychomancy [saɪ'kɒmænsɪ] [sai-ko-man--si], *s.* Sicomancia, arte supersticiosa de evocar o llamar a las almas de los muertos.

psychopathic [ˌsaɪkəʊ'pæθɪk] [sai-kou-pa-zik], *a. (Med.)* Psicopático o sicopático.

psychosis [saɪ'kəʊsɪs] [sai-kou-sis], *s. (Med.)* Psicosis o sicosis.

psychosomatic ['saɪkəʊsəʊ'mætɪk] [sai-kou-sou-ma-tik], *a.* Psicosomático.

psychotherapy [ˌsaɪkəʊ'θerəpɪ] [sai-kou-ze-ra-pi], *s. (Med.)* Psicoterapia o sicoterapia.

ptarmigan ['tɑːmɪɡən] [tar-mi-gan], *s. (Ornit.)* Perdiz blanca.

pteridophyte ['terɪdəʊfaɪt] [te-ri-dou-fait], *s. (Bot.)* Pteridofita.

pterodactyl [ˌterəʊ'dæktɪl] [te-rou-dak-til], *s. (Paleont.)* Pterodáctilo.

ptolemaic ['tɒləmaɪk] [to-lo-maik], *a.* Tolemaico, lo que pertence al sistema astronómico de Tolomeo.

Ptolemy ['tɒləmɪ] [to-lo-mi], *n.pr.* Tolomeo.

ptomain, ptomaine ['təʊmeɪn] [tou-mein], *s.* Ptomaína.

pub [pʌb] [pab], *s. (Engl.)* Cervecería, taberna.

puberty ['pjuːbətɪ] [piu-ber-ti], *s.* 1. Pubertad, la edad en que adquieren las personas de ambos sexos aptitud para reproducirse. 2. *(Bot.)* El período en que una planta empieza a echar flores.

pubes ['pjuːz] [piubs] *s.* Pubis, pubes, parte inferior del vientre.

pubescence [pjuː'besəns] [piu-be-sans], *s.* 1. Pubescencia, pubertad. 2. *(Bot.)* Pelusa, vello.

pubescent [pjuː'besənt] [piu-be-sant], *a.* 1. Pubescente, cubierto de pelos, particularmente de pelos delgados, cortos y suaves, como las hojas de ciertas plantas; que tiene pelusa, velloso. 2. Púber: se dice de la persona que ha llegado a la edad de la pubertad.

pubic ['pjuːbɪk] [piu-bik], *a.* Pubiano, púbico: que se refiere al pubis o a la región púbica.

pubis ['pjuːbɪs] [piu-bis], *s. (Anat.)* Pubis, parte del hueso coxal.

public ['pʌblɪk] [pa-blik], *a.* 1. Público, común, que pertenece a todo el pueblo (common). 2. Público, notorio, patente, manifiesto (evident, obvious). 3. General, universal. 4. Público: se aplica a la potestad, autoridad, espíritu, etc. cuando se tienen o poseen para el bien de todo el pueblo o cuando se emplean en él. **Public enemy,** enemigo público. **Public health,** higiene pública, sanidad. **Public lands,** tierras nacionales o de dominio público. **Public opinion,** opinión pública. **Public school,** escuela pública, en Ingl. también se llaman así a ciertas instituciones que preparan a los jóvenes para el acceso a la Universidad (Eton, Harrow, Winchester.) **Public-house,** 1. posada, taberna, hostería, fonda. 2. *(Ingl.)* Cervecería, establecimiento autorizado para vender bebidas alcohólicas. **To make public,** publicar o hacer pública alguna cosa. *-s.* Público, el pueblo. **In public,** en público, públicamente, a la vista de todos. **Public-hearted,** animado del bien público, ansioso por el bien del pueblo. **Public-spirited,** patriótico, el que prefiere el bien común o del público a su interés particular. **Public utility,** empresa de servicios públicos. **Into public,** en la vida pública o de sociedad. **Public works,** obras públicas.

publican ['pʌblɪkən] [pa-bli-kan], *s.* 1. Publicano, arrendador o cobrador de derechos públicos entre los romanos. 2. *(Vulg.)* Mesonero, posadero, tabernero.

publication [ˌpʌblɪ'keɪʃən] [pa-bli-kei-shon], *s.* 1. Publicación, el acto de publicar. 2. La acción de poner en venta alguna obra impresa, y la misma obra publicada, promulgación. 3. Notificación pública, edicto.

publicist ['pʌblɪsɪst] [pa-bli-sist], *s.* 1. Publicista, el autor que escribe sobre el derecho público, o de los estados o naciones. 2. Escritor sobre asuntos de interés público. 3. Agente de publicidad.

publicity [pʌb'lɪsɪtɪ] [pa-bli-si-ti], *s.* Publicidad, notoriedad. *a.* De publicidad, publicitario. **Publicity bureau,** agencia de publicidad.

publicize ['pʌblɪsaɪz] [pa-bli-sais], *va.* Publicar, divulgar.

publicly ['pʌblɪklɪ] [pa-bli-kli], *adv.* Públicamente, a la vista de todos.

publish ['pʌblɪʃ] [pa-blish], *va.* 1. Publicar, hacer manifiesta al público alguna cosa. 2. Publicar un libro, anunciar que está de venta. 3. **To publish the banns,** correr las amonestaciones.

publisher ['pʌblɪʃər] [pa-bli-shar], *s.* Publicador, editor, el que publica un libro o escrito y lo pone en venta.

publishing ['pʌblɪʃɪŋ] [pa-bli-shin], Publicación (books, etc.) **Publishing house,** editorial, casa editora.

puccoon ['pʌkuːn] [pa-kun], *s.* Orcaneta.

puce [pjuːs] [pius], *s.* Color castaño rojizo.

puck [pʌk] [pak], *s.* 1. Coco, fantasma, duende legendario de los ingleses, como el del «Sueño de una noche de verano», de Shakespeare. 2. *(Ornit.)* Chotacabras. 3. Disco de caucho usado en hokey sobre hielo.

pucker ['pʌkər] [pa-kar], *va.* Arrugar, hacer pliegues. *-s.* 1. Pliegue, arruga, (gather). 2. *(Fam.)* Agitación, perplejidad, embrollo.

puckish ['pʌkɪʃ] [pa-kish], *a.* Travieso.

pudding ['pʌdɪŋ] [pa-din], *s.* 1. Pudín. 2. Manjar farináceo, que se come con carne, o como plato principal de una comida. 3. Salchicha, morcilla. **Black-pudding,** morcilla. *(Amer.)* Morcón. **Pudding dish, pudding pan,** tartera. **Pudding face,** cara gorda e inexpresiva. 4. *(Geol.)* **Pudding stone,** pudinga.

puddle ['pʌdl] [pa-del], *s.* 1. Lodazal, cenagal. 2. *V.* PUDDLING. 3. Charco, poza (pool). 4. Mezcla impermeable de arcilla y arena. 5. Lío, confusión.

puddle, *va.* 1. Afinar, convertir en hierro batido, agitando sin cesar el hierro derretido y eliminando el carbono. 2. Cimentar, cubrir el fondo de un canal para que no filtre. 3. Enlodar; enturbiar el agua con lodo. 4. Ensuciar, enturbiar. 5. Impermeabilizar con una mezcla de arcilla y arena. 6. Lavar un mineral arcilloso.

puddler ['pʌdlər] [pad-lar], *s.* 1. El que enloda o cimenta con lodo; refinador de hierro. 2. Utensilio para agitar el metal derretido. 3. Horno de afinar.

puddling ['pʌdlɪŋ] [pad-lin], *s.* 1. Acto y efecto de cimentar o enlodar o de batir el hierro, agitándolo en el horno de afinación. 2. Amasijo, masa de arcilla y tierra gredosa para cimentar.

puddly ['pʌdlɪ] [pad-li], *a.* 1. Lodoso, cenagoso. 2. Lleno de charcos, encharcado.

pudency ['pʌdənsɪ] [pa-den-si], *s.* Modestia, pudor, recato.

pudgy ['pʌdʒɪ] [pad-chi], *a. (Fam.)* Corto y grueso, v. g. las manos; regordete, gordiflón.

pudicity ['pʌdɪsɪtɪ] [pa-di-si-ti], *s.* Pudicicia, pudor, modestia, recato.

puerile ['pjʊəraɪl] [piue-rail], *a.* Pueril, que es propio de muchachos.

puerility [pjʊə'rɪlɪtɪ] [piue-ri-li-ti], *s.* Puerilidad, muchachada.

puerilism ['pjʊərɪlɪzəm] [piue-ri-li-sem], *s.* Infantilismo.

puerperal [pjʊ'ɜːpərəl] [piu-er-pe-ral], *a. (Med.)* Puerperal, perteneciente o que se refiere al parto, que resulta del parto.

puerperous [pjʊ'ɜːpərəs] [piu-er-pe-ros], *a.* Parturiente, de parto, que pare.

Puerto Rican [ˈpwɜːtəʊˈriːkən] [puer-tou-ri-kan], *a.* Portorriqueño.

puff [pʌf] [paf], *s.* 1. Resoplido, bufido, soplo, bocanada de humo. 2. Borla para empolvar o echar polvos en el pelo. 3. Bollos. 4. Tocados, etc., de los vestidos de mujer 4. La exageración en alabar y recomendar alguna cosa para llamar la atención sobre ella. 5. Colcha, edredón. Bulto; mesa hinchada, abultada. 6. Chupada (of a cigar). 7. Borla para empolvarse. 7. *V.* PUFFBALL. **Puff of wind,** ventarrón, ventolera. **Puff-paste,** hojaldre, hojuela de pasta. **Spanish puff,** buñuelo. **Puff-adder,** víbora muy venenosa de África, con cuyo veneno emponzoñan los indígenas sus saetas. 8. *Interj.* ¡Puf!, ¡bah!

puff, *va.* 1. Hinchar, inflar o llenar alguna cosa de aire. 2. Soplar, apartar algo de donde estaba por medio del viento (blow). 3. Ensoberbecer, engreír, envanecer (make vain). 4. Alabar o ensalzar desmedidamente una persona o cosa con el objeto de llamar la atención hacia ella y de hacerla parecer mejor y más excelente de lo que en sí es. *(Fam.)* Cacarear. -*vn.* 1. Inflarse, hincharse con aire alguna cosa. 2. Inflarse, hinchar, engreírse, envanecerse. 3. Bufar, manifestar enojo o desprecio. 4. Resoplar, fumar, resollar con fuerza, jadear, hipar. 5. Mover alguna cosa muy agitadamente.

puff at, bufar haciendo desprecio de alguna cosa; despreciar.

puff away, disipar a soplos, disiparse una cosa por la acción del viento; arrojar a una persona o cosa de donde estaba, dando resoplidos o con enojo o desprecio.

puff form, arrancar de repente alguna cosa del sitio que ocupaba por miedo de una ráfaga de viento, una bocanada de aire o un soplo. **To puff with pride,** llenar o henchir de viento o vanidad, ponerse inflado, soplado, hinchado o hueco de vanidad.

puffer [ˈpʌfəʳ] [pa-faʳ], *s.* 1. El que resopla o sopla; el que es jactancioso, vanaglorioso o muy inflado de vanidad; el que pondera desmedidamente alguna cosa. 2. Bombeador. 3. Postor simulado en una subasta. 4. Tren en el lenguaje infantil.

puffin [ˈpʌfɪn] [pa-fin], *s.* 1. *(Orn.)* Alca de pico muy deprimido. Fratercula. 2. *(Bot.)* Bejín.

puffiness [ˈpʌfɪnɪs] [pa-fi-nes], *s.* 1. Hinchazón, regularmente de estilo. 2. *(Med.)* Hinchazón, tumescencia que cede a la presión.

puffing [ˈpʌfɪŋ] [pa-fing], *s.* 1. Hinchazón, el efecto de hincharse, envanecerse o engreírse. 2. La acción de soplar, inflar, hinchar o de apartar algo de su lugar por medio del viento. 3. Ponderación desmesurada del mérito o valor de algo. 4. Una especie de bollo. -*a.* Abofellado, fofo, hueco (clothes, laces).

puffingly [ˈpʌfɪŋlɪ] [pa-fin-li], *adv.* Hinchadamente; con afán.

puffy [ˈpʌfɪ] [pa-fi], *a.* 1. Flatulento, hinchado, inflado, entumecido. 2. Que sopla a intervalos; 3. Hinchado, inflado, fofo (fluffy, fat). 3. Acampanado (style). **A swelling, puffy style,** un estilo pomposo o acampanado.

pug [pʌg] [pag], *s.* 1. *V. Pug-dog.* 2. Nariz roma, chata. 3. Nombre cariñoso que se da regularmente a los monos, a los perros pequeños y a veces a las personas. 4. Barro amasado. **Pug-dog,** faldero, perrillo de pelo corto y nariz roma. **Pug-nose,** nariz roma, respingada, cuya punta mira hacia arriba. **Pug-nosed,** romo.

pug, *va.* 1. Cimentar, embarrar, el fondo de un canal, enlodar con arcilla. 2. Llenar con argamasa para apagar el sonido. 3. Amasar.

pugging [ˈpʌgɪŋ] [pa-guin], *s.* 1. Amasijo, mezcla grosera de arcilla y aserrín que se pone entre los pisos para amortiguar el ruido. 2. Acción de forrar, de cimentar.

pugh [pʌf] [paf], *inter.* ¡Fuera! ¡puf! voz que indica desprecio, y particularmente que una cosa huele muy mal.

pugilism [ˈpjuːdʒɪlɪzəm] [piu-yi-li-sem], *s.* Pugilismo o pugilato, la lid a puñadas, boxeo.

pugilist [ˈpjuːdʒɪlɪst] [piu-yi-list], *s.* Púgil, pugilista, boxeador.

pugilistic [ˈpjuːdʒɪlɪstɪk] [piu-yi-lis-tik], *a.* De pugilato, perteneciente al pugilato, pugilístico.

pug-mill [ˈpʌgmɪl] [pag-mil], *a.* Artesa de ladrillería; amasadera, máquina en que se muele y mezcla la arcilla.

pugnacious [pʌgˈneɪʃəs] [pag-nei-shos], *a.* Pugnaz, belicoso.

pugnacity [pʌgˈnæsɪtɪ] [pag-na-si-ti], *s.* Pugnacidad.

pug-nosed [ˈpʌgnəʊzd] [pag-nousd], *a.* 1. De nariz respingona. 2. Chato (dog).

puissance [ˈpɔɪsəns] [pui-sans], *s.* Pujanza, fuerza, poder, potencia (power).

puissant [ˈpɔɪsənt] [pui-sant], *a.* Pujante, poderoso, fuerte.

puke [pjuːk] [piuk], *s.* *(Vulg.)* 1. Vómito, nausea. 2. Vomitivo. 3. Cosa o persona repugnante. **To have a puke,** vomitar.

puke, *va.* y *vn.* *(Vulg.)* Vomitar.

pulchritude [ˈpʌlkrɪtjuːd] [pal-kri-tiud], *s.* Pulcritud, esmero en el adorno y aseo de la persona; hermosura, aseo, donaire; belleza.

puling [ˈpjuːlɪŋ] [pa-lin], *s.* 1. Pío, voz del pollo. 2. Gritería de niños; gemido.

pull [pɔl] [pul], *va.* 1. Tirar, atraer o traer hacia sí con violencia, estirar. **To pull ahead,** *(Mar.)* Tirar avante. 2. Coger, recoger (flowers, fruits); obtener tirando. 3. Sacar, extraer, arrancar. 4. Rasgar, desgarrar, hacer tiras. 5. Bogar, remar, conducir remando. 6. Sacar una prueba con la prensa de mano. 7. Pelar, desplumar (birds). 8. Torcer, distender (a muscle, tendon). 9. Beber, dar un tiento. 10. Sacar una prueba de imprenta. 11. Sorprender (low gambling house). 12. Refrenar un caballo para que no gane una carrera. 13. Dar un golpe oblicuo a la pelota. 14. Prender (a person). **To pull a face,** hacer una mueca. **To pull a long face,** poner cara larga. **To pull oneself together,** recobrarse, serenarse. **To pull the trigger,** apretar el gatillo. **To pull the wool over one's eyes,** engañar con falsas apariencias. **To pull up stakes,** liar los bártulos, mudarse. -*vn.* Tirar con esfuerzo, tirar de una cuerda. **To pull asunder o away,** arrancar, separar con violencia o quitar por fuerza una cosa de donde estaba. **To pull back,** tirar, apartar o retirar hacia atrás, hacer recular o cejar. **To pull down,** derribar, subvertir, demoler, degradar, privar, deponer; bajar, humillar, abatir. **To pull in,** tirar, atraer hacia adentro, cerrar. **To pull in pieces,** hacer pedazos, hacer trizas. **To pull off,** tirar, quitar, sacar alguna cosa a viva fuerza, arrancar; deshacer o desbaratar, levantar, quitar una cosa que estaba encima de otra o la cubría, como un sello, un parche, una máscara, etc. **To pull out,** tirar, quitar, sacar, arrancar. **To pull up,** extirpar, arrancar de cuajo o de raíz, desarraigar; alzar, levantar. **To pull the wool over one's eyes,** engañar a uno como un chino, jugársela a uno de codillo.

pull, *s.* 1. Tirón, estirón, sacudimiento, sacudida. 2. Contienda, combate. 3. Cuesta, subida, ascensión difícil. 4. Atracción. 5. Trato, tiento. 6. Chupada, calada (a cigar). 7. Ventaja, superioridad. 8. Influencia, aldabas. 9. Acto de refrenar un caballo para que no gane una carrera. 10. Golpe oblicuo a la pelota.

pullback [ˈpɔlbæk] [pul-bak], *s.* Estorbo, lo que tira hacia atrás o impide adelantar.

puller [ˈpɔləʳ] [pu-laʳ], *s.* El que tira o arranca.

pullet [ˈpɔlɪt] [pu-lit], *s.* Polla, la gallina medianamente crecida.

pulley [ˈpɔli:] [pu-li], *s.* Polea, garrucha. **Pulley-piece,** *(Mar.)* Armadura de barca.

pullulate [ˈpʌljʊleɪt] [pa-liu-leit], *vn.* 1. Pulular, germinar, ahijar o multiplicar mucho las plantas. 2. Pulular, se dice de los errores que se multiplican o crecen.

pullman [ˈpɔlmən] [pul-man], *s.* Coche dormitorio o salón.

pulmonary [ˈpʌlmənərɪ] [pal-ma-na-ri], *a.* Pulmonar, pulmoníaco, que pertenece o se refiere a los pulmones. **Pulmonary artery,** arteria pulmonar.

pulp [pʌlp] [palp], *s.* 1. Pulpa, la parte más carnosa del cuerpo animal. 2. Pulpa, la carne o parte mollar de las frutas. 3. Pulpa, masa blanda y húmeda; pasta para hacer papel. 4. (*Bot.*) Arila, tegumento propio de ciertas semillas, como la del café.

pulpiness [ˈpʌlpɪnɪs] [pal-pi-nes], s. Estado pulposo, calidad de pulposo.

pulpit [ˈpʌlpɪt] [pal-pit], s. 1. Púlpito. 2. Clero. 3. Tribuna, tarima. **Pulpit-cloth**, paño de púlpito.

pulpiteer [ˈpʌlpɪtɪəʳ] [pal-pi-tiaʳ], s. Predicador.

pulpous [ˈpʌlpəs] [pal-pos], **pulpy** [ˈpʌlpɪ] [pal-pi], a. Pulposo, mollar.

pulpousness [ˈpʌlpəsnɪs] [pal-pos-nes], s. La calidad de pulposo.

pulque [ˈpʌlk] [palk], s. Pulque, bebida fermentada del maguey.

pulsate [pʌlˈseɪt] [pal-seit], vn. Pulsar, latir una arteria, el corazón, etc.; latir con impulso rítmico.

pulsatile [ˈpʌlsətɪl] [pal-sa-til], a. 1. Pulsativo, de latido; se dice de la cosa que pulsa. 2. (*Mús.*) De percusión.

pulsation [pʌlˈseɪʃən] [pal-sei-shon], s. Pulsación, latido.

pulsative [ˈpʌlsətɪv] [pal-sa-tiv], a. Pulsativo, pulsador, que pulsa.

pulsator [pʌlˈseɪtəʳ] [pal-sei-taʳ], s. 1. Golpeador, apaleador. 2. Pulsómetro. 3. Máquina en que se agitan los diamantes para despojarlos de la tierra que llevan adherida.

pulsatory [ˈpʌlsətərɪ] [pal-sa-to-ri], a. Pulsador, que pulsa, que late, que produce pulsaciones, se dice del movimiento más bien que de la cosa.

pulse [pʌls] [pals], s. 1. Pulso, el latido de las arterias que es perceptible al tacto. 2. Pulsación, vibración. 3. Legumbres (chickpeas, lentils). **To feel one's pulse**, tomar el pulso, tantear o sondear con arte la voluntad de una persona.

pulse, s. Legumbres colectivamente (de las leguminosas), v. g. garbanzos, habas lentejas, etc.

pulse, vn. 1. Pulsar, latir las arterias o el corazón. 2. Vibrar.

pulsion [ˈpʌlʃən] [pal-shon], s. Impulso, virtud impulsa.

pulsometer [ˈpʌlsəmiːtəʳ] [pal-so-mi-taʳ], s. Pulsómetro, aparato de bomba que funciona por medio del vapor.

pulverization [ˌpʌlvəraɪˈzeɪʃən] [pal-va-rai-sei-shon], s. Pulverización.

pulverize [ˈpʌlvəraɪz] [pal-ve-rais], va. Pulverizar, reducir a polvo.

puma [ˈpjuːmə] [piu-ma], s. (*Zool.*) Puma, tigre americano.

pumice [ˈpʌmɪs] [pa-mis], va. Apomazar, allanar o pulir con piedra pómez. **Pumice-stone**, piedra pómez.

pump [pʌmp] [pamp], s. 1. Bomba, máquina para sacar agua o hacer circular un fluido, o para comprimirlo, llevándolo o impeliéndolo por aberturas o cañerías. **Suction-pump**, bomba aspirante. **Lifting-pump**, bomba elevadora. **Force-pump**, bomba impelente. **Air-pump**, máquina neumática; bomba de aire, en las máquinas de vapor. **Feed-pump**, donkey-pump, bomba alimenticia. **Chain-pump**, bomba de cadena. **Pump-dale**, (*Mar.*) Dala. **Pump-hook**, (*Mar.*) sacanabo. **To fetch the pump**, (*Mar.*) cargar la bomba. **To man the pump**, (*Mar.*) Armar la bomba. **To work a pump**, hacer funcionar una bomba. 2. Zapato de hombre, fino y de suela delgada.

pump, va. y vn. 1. Dar a la bomba, sacar agua de la bomba, bombear. 2. Sondear, tantear. 3. Sonsacar, examinar con astucia. 4. Bañar a chorro. **Pumping-shaft**, pozo en que se hallan las bombas de una mina.

pumper [ˈpʌmpəʳ] [pam-paʳ], s. 1. Bombero, el que saca agua con una bomba. 2. Sonsacador, el que tantea, sondea o sonsaca.

pumping [ˈpʌmpɪŋ] [pam-pin], a. De accionar la bomba, de sacar con bomba. *Pumping engine*, bomba mecánica, bomba de vapor.

pumpkin [ˈpʌmpkɪn] [pamp-kin], s. Calabaza.

pun [pʌn] [pan], s. Equívoco, chiste, juego de vocablos.

pun, vn. 1. Jugar del vocablo, decir equívocos. 2. Burlarse de alguno con equívocos o retruécanos.

punch [pʌntʃ] [panch], va. 1. Punzar, horadar con punzón (pick). 2. (*Fam.*) Dar puñetazos; empujar con el codo o con la mano; dar golpes con la mano.

punch, s. 1. Punzón, instrumento de hierro que remata en la punta y sirve para horadar; sacabocado o sacabocados. 2. Ponche, bebida compuesta de licores espirituosos, agua, limón y azúcar. 3. (*Fam.*) Golpe. 4. Arlequín o bufón de los volatines. -a. Fuerte, gordo. **Conductor's punch**, sacabocados de conductor (en los ferrocarriles).

punch-bowl [ˈpʌntʃbɔːl] [panch-bol], s. Ponchera, la taza para hacer ponche.

puncheon, punchin [ˈpʌntʃɪən] [pan-chion], s. 1. Medida de líquidos que contiene veinte arrobas. 2. Punzón; cuño.

puncheon, s. (*Carp.*) Pie derecho, poste grueso de madera que se pone en pie debajo del caballete de un edificio.

puncher [ˈpʌntʃəʳ] [pan-chaʳ], s. 1. Punzador, el que punza u horada. 2. Vaquero.

punctate, punctated [ˈpʌnkteɪt] [pank-teit], a. 1. (*Bot. y Zool.*) Puntuado, sembrado de puntos o de glándulas internas translúcidas. 2. Formado en punta, puntiagudo.

punctilio [pʌŋˈktɪlɪəʊ] [pank-ti-liou], s. Puntillo, punto de honra, delicadeza o pundonor.

punctilious [pʌŋˈktɪlɪəs] [pank-ti-lios], a. Puntilloso, nimiamente escrupuloso; muy puntilloso, demasiado delicado en puntos de honor y trato, demasiado exacto o preciso.

punctiliousness [pʌŋˈktɪlɪəsnɪs] [pank-ti-lios-nes], s. Pundonor o escrupulosidad nimia (preciseness); exactitud, atención minuciosa a los pormenores (exactness).

puncto [ˈpʌŋktəʊ] [pank-tou], s. Punto de toque en la esgrima.

punctual [ˈpʌŋktjʊəl] [pank-tiual], a. 1. Puntual, diligente y exacto. 2. Puntual, indudable, cierto. 3. Preciso, fijo, cierto, determinado.

punctuality [ˌpʌŋktjʊˈælɪtɪ] [pank-tiu-a-li-ti], **punctualness** [ˈpʌŋktjʊəl] [pank-tiual] s. Puntualidad, exactitud.

punctually [ˈpʌŋktjʊəlɪ] [pank-tiua-li], adv. Puntualmente, exactamente.

punctuate [ˈpʌŋktjʊeɪt] [pank-tiueit], va. Puntuar, señalar con puntos; colocar las notas o signos ortográficos. -vn. usar signos de puntuación.

punctuation [ˌpʌŋktjʊˈeɪʃən] [pank-tu-ei-shon], s. Puntuación, el arte de puntuar, y el conjunto de puntos o signos ortográficos de un escrito.

puncture [ˈpʌŋktʃəʳ] [pank-chaʳ], va. Punzar, agujerear con un instrumento puntiagudo, picar. -s. 1. Puntura, agujero hecho con algún instrumento puntiagudo, punzadura, punzada, picadura, picada. 2. (*Zool.*) Concavidad menuda, hoyo.

pundit [ˈpʌndɪt] [pan-dit], s. Bracmán sabio, particularmente el versado en el conocimiento del idioma sanscrito, así como en las ciencias, leyes y religión de la India.

pungency [ˈpʌndʒənsɪ] [pan-yan-si], s. 1. Picante, naturaleza picante, poder de picar o punzar, la acerbidad o acrimonia que tiene algunas cosas que exacerban el sentido del gusto. 2. Punta, sabor, picante. 3. Picante, la acrimonia o mordacidad en el decir. 4. Agudeza, viveza.

pungent [ˈpʌndʒənt] [pan-yent], a. 1. Picante, que afecta los órganos de los sentidos, especialmente del gusto y el olfato, con una sensación picante (spicy, sharp). 2. Acre, mordaz, acerbo, áspero. 3. (*Zool.*) Propio para picar. 4. (*Bot.*) Que termina en una punta dura.

punic [ˈpʌnɪk] [pa-nik], a. Púnico, perteneciente a los cartagineses; entre los romanos, falso, pérfido. -s. Lengua púnica, idoma de los cartagineses.

puniceous [ˈpʌnɪʃəs] [pa-ni-shos], a. Purpúreo, morado, claro.

puniness [ˈpʌnɪnɪs] [pa-ni-nes], s. Pequeñez; delicadeza de salud.

punish [ˈpʌnɪʃ] [pa-nish], va. 1. Castigar, mortificar, afligir con una restricción o pérdida, como pena, o con el propósito de corregir o reformar; penar. 2. Castigar, pegar, imponer una pena en expiación de una falta o un crimen.

punishable [ˈpʌnɪʃəbl] [pa-ni-sha-bol], a. Punible, digno de castigo, sujeto a castigo por la ley.

punisher ['pʌnɪʃəʳ] [pa-ni-shaʳ], s. Castigador.

punishing ['pʌnɪʃɪŋ] [pa-ni-shin], s. Castigo. -a. Agotador, duro.

punishment ['pʌnɪʃmənt] [pa-nish-ment], s. Castigo. (Fam.) Vapuleo, serie de golpes, p. ej. en un pugilato.

punitive ['pʌnɪtɪv] [pa-ni-tiv], a. Penal, punitivo.

punk [pʌŋk] [pank], s. Yesca. -a. (Fam.) 1. Muy malo, de ínfima calidad. 2. (Fam.) Malo en cuanto a salud.

punning ['pʌnɪŋ] [pa-nin], s. Costumbre de hacer retruécanos o juegos de vocablos.

punster ['pʌnstəʳ] [pans-taʳ], s. Truhán; el que hace retruécanos; jugador de vocablos.

punt [pʌnt] [pant], va. 1. Impeler un barco, empujando con una vara contra el fondo. 2. Llevar, conducir, en un barquichuelo. 3. En el juego de la pelota de viento, impeler la pelota golpeándola con el pie; de aquí, dar, impeler. -vn. 1. Ir cazando o pescando en una lancha o barquichuelo; también, impeler un bote, empujándolo. 2. Impeler una pelota golpeándola con los pies.

punt, vn. Apuntar, parar: se usa en ciertos juegos para indicar el acto de apuntar o poner dinero a las cartas.

punt, s. 1. Barquichuelo que tiene el fondo plano: se usa en aguas poco profundas y se impulsa con una pértiga. 2. (Mar.) Plancha de agua. 3. Puntapié de volea.

punter ['pʌntəʳ] [pan-taʳ], s. 1. El que impele la pelota de viento golpeándola con el pie. 2. El que apunta o apuesta a las cartas en ciertos juegos.

puny ['pʌnɪ] [pa-ni], a. Débil, enfermizo; tierno; chico, pequeño; inferior.

pup [pʌp] [pap], vn. Parir la perra.

pup, s. Cachorro, cachorrito.

pupa ['pjuːpə] [piu-pa], s. Ninfa, crisálida.

pupal ['pjuːpəl] [piu-pal], a. De crisálida.

pupate ['pjuːpeɪt] [piu-peit], v. Transformarse en crisálida.

pupil ['pjuːpɪl] [piu-pil], s. 1. Pupila, la niña del ojo. 2. Discípulo, alumno, alumna. 3. Pupilo, el menor que está bajo la dirección de un tutor.

pupilage ['pjuːpɪlɪdʒ] [piu-pi-lich], s. Pupilaje, el estado del que se halla bajo la dirección de un tutor.

pupilary, ['pjuːpɪlərɪ] [piu-pi-la-ri], a. Pupilar, perteneciente a un pupilo o a la niña del ojo. **Pupilary margin**, borde la pupila del ojo.

puppet ['pʌpɪt] [pa-pit], s. 1. Títere, muñeco, figurilla que se mueve artificiosamente. 2. Títere, voz de desprecio empleada respecto a una persona que obra bajo la autoridad de otra. 3. Monuelo, voz de desprecio. 4. (Mec.) Válvula de uso, se llama también, **puppet-valve. Puppet-man**, titiritero. **Puppet-show**, representación de títeres, comedia de muñecos.

puppy ['pʌpɪ] [pa-pi], s. 1. Cachorro, perrillo. 2. Trasto, monicaco, nombre de desprecio que se da al enfadoso impertinente, pisaverde, monigote.

puppy, va. y vn. V. TO PUP.

puppyish ['pʌpɪʃ] [pa-pish], a. Parecido a un cachorro, a la manera de un pisaverde.

purblind ['pɜːblaɪnd] [per-blaind], a. Cegato, corto de vista, que sufre ofuscamiento de la vista.

purchasable [pɜːˈtʃæsəbl] [per-cha-sa-bol], a. Comprable, que puede adquirirse por dinero.

purchase [pɜːˈtʃɪs] [per-chis], va. 1. Comprar, adquirir por dinero el dominio de una cosa (buy). 2. Ganar, obtener, adquirir por medio de esfuerzo, o con peligro (gain, obtain). **He purchased it dearly**, le costó caro. **I have purchased it by great labor**, buen trabajo me ha costado ganarlo. 3. (Des.) Expiar una falta pagando un multa. 4. Renta o producto.

purchase, s. 1. Compra; adquisición, el acto de comprar; adquisición por medio de dinero u otro equivalente de cambio, o por esfuerzo o peligro. 2. Compra, adquisición, lo que se ha comprado. 3. Ventaja mecánica. V. LEVERAGE. 4. (Mec.) Fuerza; potencia; aparato. **His life is not worth a day's purchase**, no le doy un día de vida.

purchaser [pɜːˈtʃɪsəʳ] [per-chi-saʳ], s. Comprador, adquiridor.

pure [pjʊəʳ] [piuaʳ], a. 1. Puro, libre, sin mezcla, exento de toda substancia extraña, limpio, claro (light, pure). 2. Puro, limpio, sin mancha ni mancilla, exento de imperfecciones, de toda mancha moral; inocente, también que no está echado a perder, alterado ni corrompido; pulido, clásico (de dicción). 3. Puro, casto, inmaculado; santo, virtuoso. 4. Puro, simple, mero, sencillo.

purebred [pjʊəˈbred] [piua-bred], a. De pura raza.

purée ['pjʊəreɪ] [piua-rei], s. Puré (potatoes, apple, etc.)

purely ['pjʊəlɪ] [piua-li], adv. Puramente, meramente, simplemente, de una manera pura; sin mezcla, sin corrupción ni delito; inocentemente, castamente. **Purely accidental**, meramente accidental, fortuito.

pureness ['pjʊənɪs] [piua-nes], s. 1. Pureza, limpieza, claridad. 2. Pureza, inocencia, integridad (simplicity); castidad. 3. Pureza en las voces, frases y expresiones.

purgation [pɜːˈgeɪʃən] [per-guei-shon], s. 1. Purgación, purificación, la acción de purgar o purificar; en particular, de exonerar el vientre por medio de un purgante. 2. (For.) Purgación, el acto de purgar.

purgative ['pɜːgətɪv] [per-ga-tiv], a. Purgativo, purgante. -s. Purgante, medicamento cuyo uso interno produce evacuaciones alvinas.

purgatory ['pɜːgətərɪ] [per-ga-to-ri], s. Purgatorio.

purge [pɜːdʒ] [perch], va. 1. Purgar, purificar, limpiar, separando todo lo que es impuro, extraño o superfluo, acrisolar (cleanse, purify). 2. Purgar, desvanecer las sospechas, indicios que existen contra alguno; justificar. 3. Purgar con purga medicinal. 4. Clarificar. 5. Lavar los pecados. -vn. Purificarse.

purge, s. 1. Purga, purgante, 2. Purgación, acción u operación de purgar.

purger ['pɜːdʒəʳ] [per-chaʳ], s. Purificador, purgador; purga, purgante.

purging ['pɜːdʒɪŋ] [per-chin], a. Purgativo. -s. 1. Purgación, purificación, la acción y efecto de purgar. 2. Diarrea. 3. Purificación, expiación.

purification [ˌpjʊərɪfɪˈkeɪʃən] [piua-ri-fi-kei-shon], s. Purificación, en los mismos sentidos que en castellano.

purificator [ˌpjʊərɪfɪˈkeɪtəʳ] [piua-ri-fi-kei-taʳ], s. Purificador.

purifier ['pjʊərɪfaɪəʳ] [piua-ri-faiaʳ], s. Depurador, purificador.

purify ['pjʊərɪfaɪ] [piua-ri-fai], va. 1. Purificar, hacer puro o claro, quitar o extraer de cualquier cosa todo aquello que le es extraño; limpiar, refinar, clarificar. 2. Librar del pecado o de su corrupción. 3. Purificar, limpiar según las ceremonias de una religión; librar de manchas. 4. Purificar o refinar un idoma dejándolo castizo y libre de impropiedades. -vn. Purificarse.

purifying ['pjʊərɪfaɪɪŋ] [piua-ri-fain], s. Purificación, la acción u operación de purificar.

purism ['pjʊərɪzəm] [piu-ri-sem], s. Purismo, calidad de purista; pureza afectada, particularmente en el empleo de las palabras.

purist ['pjʊərɪst] [piu-rist], s. Purista, el que afecta pureza en el lenguaje o la observa con nimia escrupulosidad.

puritan ['pjʊərɪtən] [piu-ri-tan], s. 1. Puritano. 2. Colono de la Nueva Inglaterra.

puritanic, ['pjʊərɪtənɪk] [piu-ri-ta-nik], a. Puritano, que pertenece a los puritanos, riguroso, severo, rígido.

puritanism ['pjʊərɪtənɪzəm] [piu-ri-ta-ni-sem], s. Puritanismo, la doctrina de los puritanos.

purity ['pjʊərɪtɪ] [piua-ri-ti], s. Pureza, integridad, castidad (integrity); limpieza, inocencia, exactitud en las voces, frases y expresiones; la calidad o el estado de lo puro en cualquier sentido.

purl [pɜːl] [perl], vn. 1. Murmurar o susurrar los arroyos. 2. Ondear o hacer ondas el agua; hacer ondas la luz; undular. -s. 1. Suave murmullo.

purl, va. Perfilar, guarnecer con un bordado o fleco, orlar. -s. 1. Perfil, orla, guarnición de bordado; espiral de hilo de oro o plata. 2. Pliegue de vestido. 3. Variedad de punto o encaje del siglo XVI. 4. Suave murmullo. 5. Onda, rizo. 6. Cerveza o vino de ajenjos; cerveza aromatizada. **Purl-man,** el que vende dicha bebida.

purlieu ['pɜːljuː] [per-liu], *s.* Las tierras que confinan con algún monte o vedado; lindes, mojoneras de un campo o de una heredad; límites, confines, lindero.

purlieus ['pɜːliəs] [per-lios], *s.* Alrededores, cercanías.

purling ['pɜːlɪŋ] [per-lin], *s.* Murmullo suave de una pequeña corriente de agua. *-a.* y *pa.* Que susurra o murmura.

purlingly ['pɜːlɪŋlɪ] [per-lin-li], *adv.* A la manera de un suave murmullo, suavemente.

purloin ['pɜːlɔːn] [per-loin], *va.* 1. Hurtar, robar, ratear. 2. Inutilizar.

purloiner ['pɜːlɔɪnəʳ] [per-loi-naʳ], *s.* Ladrón, ratero.

purparty ['pɜːpɑːtɪ] [per-par-ti], *s. (For.)* Parte, división.

purple ['pɜːpl] [per-pel], *a.* 1. Purpúreo, se dice del color que resulta de la mezcla del rojo y azul y que tira a violado; de aquí, imperial, regio. 2. *(Poét.)* Purpurino, purpúreo; teñido de sangre, sangriento. *-s.* 1. Púrpura, color purpúreo. 2. Vestido de color de púrpura propio de los reyes; de aquí, dignidad de los reyes y de los cardenales. **Purples,** pintas, tabardillo pintado.

purple, *va.* purpurar, teñir de púrpura.

purplish ['pɜːplɪʃ] [per-plish], *a.* Purpurino, algo purpúreo.

purport ['pɜːpɔːt] [per-port], *s.* 1. Significado, sentido, tenor de algún escrito; intento, la cosa intentada. 2. Contenido, la substancia de algún escrito o instrumento, no expresada con las palabras exactas que deberían emplearse.

purport, *va.* y *vn.* Significar, querer decir, implicar; dar a entender.

purpose ['pɜːpəs] [per-pos], *s.* 1. Mira, intención, designio, proyecto, efecto (intention, project). 2. Ventaja práctica, efecto o resultado práctico, utilidad, resulta, consecuencia; uso, caso (utility). 3. Resolución fija, determinación, constancia. 4. Intento; tener, significación. 5. Propósito; proposición; cuestión, materia de discusión. **To the purpose,** a o al propósito. **To no purpose,** inútilmente. **To small purpose,** para bien poco. **To very little purpose,** casi para nada. **On purpose,** expresamente, de propósito, de intento, adrede. **To the purpose,** *(Fam.)* De perilla; como anillo al dedo. **To my purpose,** según lo que deseo, según mi intención, según las miras que tengo. **As for the purpose,** en cuanto al objeto, a propósito. **To speak to the purpose,** hablar (como hace) al caso, como se debe. **What they say is not to the purpose,** lo que dicen no viene al caso, está fuera del caso. **For what purpose?** ¿Con qué fin, para qué? **Common purposes,** usos ordinarios. **Public purposes,** utilidades públicas, usos públicos. **To come to the purpose,** ir al grano, o al caso. **What purpose would that answer?,** ¿para qué serviría eso?

purpose, *va.* y *vn.* Proponer, determinar o hacer algún propósito; tener la intención de; proponer o proponerse, tener designio de, formar una resolución; contar con algo.

purposely ['pɜːpəslɪ] [per-pos-li], *adv.* Adrede, de intento, de propósito, expresamente.

purposive ['pɜːpəsɪv] [per-po-siv], *a.* 1. Dirigido a un fin o propósito. 2. Intencional.

purpurin ['pɜːpərɪn] [per-pa-rin], *s.* Purpurina.

purr ['pɜːʳ] [peʳ], *s.* 1. El susurro que hace el gato cuando está satisfecho. 2. Marisco bivalvo comestible. 3. Ronroneo, zumbido de motor.

purr, *vn.* 1. Susurrar. 2. Ronronear los gatos cuando están contentos; producir un sonido bajo, continuo y zumbante como el de un carrete. 3. Zumbar el motor. *-va.* Mostrar los gatos su contento por medio del ronroneo.

purse ['pɜːs] [pers], *s.* 1. Bolsa, bolso o bolsillo; portamonedas. 2. Recursos, posibles, efectivo. 3. Suma de dinero ofrecida como premio o regalo; dinero recogido en una colecta.

purse, *va.* 1. Embolsar, echar, meter o guardar el dinero en la bolsa. 2. Cerrar una cosa formando pliegues como los de una bolsa. 3. Contraer, fruncir, arrugar.

purseful ['pɜːsfʊl] [pers-ful], *a.* Rico. *-s.* La cantidad que contiene una bolsa.

purser ['pɜːsəʳ] [per-saʳ], *s. (Mar.)* Mayordomo, sobrecargo, contador de navío.

pursiness ['pɜːsɪnɪs] [per-si-nes], *s.* Dificultad en la respiración; de aquí, gordura.

purslane, purslain ['pɜːsleɪn] [pers-lein], *s. (Bot.)* Verdolaga, planta rastrera.

pursuable ['pɜːsjʊəbl] [per-siua-bol], *a.* Proseguible.

pursuance ['pɜːsjʊəns] [per-siuans], *s.* 1. Prosecución, continuación. 2. Persecución, seguimiento. 3. Cumplimiento, ejecución.

pursuant ['pɜːsjʊənt] [per-siuant], *a.* Hecho en consecuencia o en conformidad con alguna cosa.

pursue ['pɜːsjuː] [per-siu], *va.* y *vn.* 1. Perseguir, hacer padecer o sufrir a alguno. 2. Perseguir, seguir, acosar, ir tras del que huye o en su seguimiento. 3. Proseguir, continuar; seguir, adoptar. 4. Proceder contra alguno, procesarle. 5. Procurar, solicitar.

pursuer ['pɜːsjʊəʳ] [per-siuaʳ], *s.* 1. Perseguidor. 2. La persona que procura con empeño el logro de algún objeto. 3. *(Scot.)* Demandante.

pursuit [pəˈsjuːt] [per-sut], *s.* 1. Perseguimiento, acosamiento, seguimiento, la acción de ir tras uno o de acosarle (harassment). 2. Persecución, el acto de perseguir. 3. Conato, empeño, esfuerzo en la ejecución de alguna cosa (effort). 4. Prosecución, continuación o seguimiento de alguna cosa; busca, solicitud. 5. Ocupación, pretensión. **Pursuits,** *s. pl.* Ocupaciones, estudios, investigaciones, tareas.

pursy ['pɜːsɪ] [per-si], *a.* 1. Corto de aliento, asmático; que resuella con fatiga; de aquí, obeso. 2. Engreído por el dinero.

purulent ['pjʊərʊlənt] [piua-ru-lant], *a.* Purulento.

purvey ['pɜːvɪ] [per-vi], *va.* y *vn.* 1. Proveer, surtir, procurar, suministrar. 2. Proveer, abastecer de lo necesario para hacer una cosa.

purveyance [pɜːˈveɪəns] [per-vians], *s.* Abastecimiento, abasto, provisión de los bastimentos necesarios (supply).

purveyor [pɜːˈveɪəʳ] [per-veiaʳ], *s.* Abastecedor, surtidor, suministrador, provedor.

purview ['pɜːvjuː] [per-viu], *s.* 1. Extensión, esfera, alcance de una cosa, p. ej. de la autoridad oficial, o de una historia. 2. Cuerpo o substancia de un estatuto; límite o alcance de una disposición legal.

pus [pʌs] [pas], *s.* Pus, humor que se segrega en los tejidos inflamados, como en las úlceras, o en las heridas no cicatrizadas.

push [pʌʃ] [pash], *va.* 1. Empujar, impeler con fuerza hacia adelante (shove). 2. Llevar adelante con energía, proseguir con empelo, promover. 3. Obligar, estrechar, apretar (press). 4. Importunar, molestar (bather). 5. *(Ant.)* Herir de punta; embestir. *-vn.* 1. Ejercer presión regular al mover alguna cosa; dar impulso; lo opuesto a *draw,* tirar hacia sí. 2. Adelantarse, apresurarse, darse prisa; hacer todos los esfuerzos para lograr alguna cosa. 3. Acometer; dar una topetada los animales cornudos.

push away, empujar a distancia, alejar, rechazar; apartar con la mano.

push back, rechazar, hacer retroceder.

push down, abatir, derribar, echar por tierra; forzar, empujar hacia abajo.

push forward, adelantarse dando empujones. **To push oneself forward,** entrar uno donde no se le llama; abrirse camino en el mundo.

push further, seguir adelante.

push in, hacer entrar, introducir empujando, entremeterse, meterse uno donde no le llaman.

push off, apartar con la mano; alejarse del muelle, de la ribera u orilla: hacerse mar adentro. *(Mar.)* Desatracar.

push on, echar adelante, incitar, aguijonear; empujar, hacer adelantarse, apresurar. **Push on!,** ¡Adelante!

push out, empujar hacia fuera, hacer salir; echar, expulsar; alejarse de la ribera, desatracar, hacerse mar adentro.

push, *s.* 1. Impulso, impulsión, empujón, empuje, empujo. 2. Asalto, ataque. 3. Conato, esfuerzo; *(Fam.)* energía, actividad resuelta. 4. Momento crítico, emergencia, apuro, aprieto, prueba. **He has been put to a push,** se ha visto en un apuro. 5. *(Mec.)* Lo que se empuja para inducir acción, v. g. un botón de presión. 4. Avance (venciendo obstáculos). 6. Cornada, estocada. **Push-button,** botón o perilla que, bajo presión, establece o corta una corriente eléctrica; botón de presión. **Push-pin,** 1. juego de alfileres. 2. Pasador de la caja del reloj.

pushball ['pʊʃbɔːl] [pash-bol], *s.* 1. Pelota gigantesca para un juego especial. 2. Juego en que se emplea dicha pelota.

pusher ['pʊʃəʳ] [pa-shaʳ], *s.* 1. Empujador. 2. Persona emprendedora. 3. *(Avia.)* Avión de propulsión.

pushing ['pʊʃɪŋ] [pa-shin], *a.* Activo, diligente, eficaz; emprendedor; vigoroso, robusto, fuerte.

pushover ['pʊʃˌoʊvəʳ] [push-ou-vaʳ], *s.* 1. Adversario débil. *(Méx.)* Pichón. 2. Problema de fácil solución.

pushpin ['pʊʃpɪn] [pash-pin], *s.* 1. Juego de los alfileres, crucillo. 2. Chinche, clavito.

pusillanimous [ˌpjuːsɪˈlænɪməs] [piu-si-la-ni-mos], *a.* Pusilánime, cobarde, falto de ánimo.

puss [pʊs] [pus], *s.* 1. Miz, minino, voz de que ordinariamente se usa para llamar a los gatos, por extensión, una muchacha o joven. **A sly puss,** una muchacha taimada. 2. Liebre. 3. *V.* PUSS-MOTH. 3. *(Fam.)* Cara, boca, gesto. **Puss-in-the-corner,** el juego de muchachos llamado «de las cuatro esquinas». **Puss in Boots,** el gato con botas.

pussy ['pʊsɪ] [pu-si], *s.* Gatita (forma diminutiva). **Pussy-cat,** 1. Gata, gato. 2. *(Bot.)* El amento del sauce llamado *pussy-willow.* **Pussy-willow,** sauce pequeño americano.

pustule ['pʌstjuːl] [pas-tiul], *s.* Pústula, postilla pequeña. *(Vulg.)* Grano, nacido.

put [pʊt] [put], *va. (pa.* PUTTING, *pret.* y *pp.* PUT). 1. Poner, colocar (place). 2. Poner, disponer o prevenir alguna cosa. 3. Poner, confiar, cometer, entregar (give). 4. Poner, dedicar a alguno o inclinarle a que tome algún empleo u oficio. 5. Poner, reducir o estrechar a una persona a que haga algo contra su voluntad. 6. Poner, exponer, proponer, presentar para ser para ser discutido, hacer o dirigir (a question). 7. Expresar en palabras, declarar, intepretar. 8. Arrojar, lanzar con un movimiento del brazo hacia arriba y adelante. 9. *(Ant.)* Poner, imponer, obligar a alguna cosa. - *vn.* 1. Dirigir su rumbo o curso, dirigirse. 2. *(Ant.)* Ir, moverse. 3. Brotar, germinar, arrojar el árbol sus hojas, flores, botones o renuevos.

put about, 1. *(Mar.)* Cambiar de rumbo. 2. Molestar, turbar, desconcertar.

put asunder, apartar.

put away, apartar, quitar, poner a un lado; echar fuera, despedir, desterrar; repudiar.

put back, apartar, retirar hacia atrás; retroceder, volver atrás; perder el terreno, atrasar, retardar. *(Mar.)* Arriba, volver de arribada. **To put back the clock,** atrasar el reloj.

put by, arrimar, arrinconar, desviar, apartar, poner a un lado, despachar, despedir, echar fuera, disuadir o desviar de un propósito, eludir, evitar, estorbar, distraer, rehusar; despreciar, no hacer caso; refutar.

put down, deprimir, abatir, humillar, dar un tapaboca o un remoquete; hacer callar a uno, suprimir, abolir, hacer caer en desuso alguna cosa, impugnar, confutar, poner debajo. **To put down in writing,** asentar, notar, poner por escrito.

put forth, extender, alargar la mano u otra cosa, publicar, dar a luz, producir, brotar, germinar o arrojar las plantas; proponer; emplear el poder, la fuerza, etc., para el logro de una cosa. *(Mar.)* Dejar un puerto.

put forward, llevar adelante; apresurarse, adelantarse. **To put oneself forward,** presentarse; hacerse o darse a conocer.

put in, insertar, ingerir, introducir una cosa entre otras; indicar para un empleo u oficio, volver a poner en su lugar, v. g. un miembro dislocado; hacer esfuerzos, hacer algo con vigor, entrar en un lugar para procurarse abrigo, provisiones o asistencia. *(Mar.)* Entrar en un puerto. **To put in at,** arribar a un sitio de abrigo. **To put in fear,** amedrentar, intimidar. **To put in for,** pretender, solicitar; hacer oposición a algún

destino; salir a la palestra o ponerse entre los pretendientes a alguna dignidad, oficio, etc. **To put in mind,** recordar. **To put in practice,** poner en uso, usar, ejercitar. **To put in print,** imprimir. **To put in writing,** poner por escrito.

put into, unir; meter dentro de, guardar en; hacer declarar, expresarse. **To put into port,** *(Mar.)* Arribar, entrar de arribada en un puerto.

put off, diferir, dilatar, dejar para otro tiempo; dejar o desistir de una obra, etc.; quitarse algo de encima del cuerpo, despojarse de alguna cosa que se llevaba puesta; poner a un lado, apartar; poner en voga, acreditar, recomendar; dar al público, entretener, desentenderse; embocar, encajar. Salir a la mar; echar el bote al agua. **Put off your clothes,** desnúdese Ud.

put on, ponerse alguna cosa; atribuir, hacer algún cargo, imputar, acusar; incitar, promover, imponer una pena; hacerse o engañarse; empezar un nuevo género de vida; hacerse pasar uno por lo que no es. **Put on your hat,** cúbrase Ud., póngase Ud. el sombrero. **To put on shore,** echar a tierra, desembarcar.

put out, brotar, arrojar o germinar las plantas, echar, sacar, expeler o arrojar a una persona o cosa del lugar que ocupaba; despedir, despachar, echar fuera; apagar o matar la lumbre, la luz o el fuego; cegar, dejar ciego, borrar lo escrito o impreso, poner dinero a interés, dar a logro, sacar o dar a luz; publicar, divulgar; olvidar las máximas o resoluciones que uno se había propuesto seguir; distraer. **To put out of all hope,** quitar o hacer perder completamente la esperanza; hacer caer en la desesperación. **To put out of doors,** poner en la calle. **To put out of heart,** desalentar. **To put out of joint,** dislocar o desencajar los huesos. **To put out of order,** desordenar, descomponer, sacar las cosas de su quicio o de su puesto; desconcertar, echar a perder alguna cosa. **To put out the flag,** enarbolar una bandera. **To put one out,** aturdir, confundir; perturbar, cortar, sonrojar, avergonzar, dejar parado, confuso, chafado o despatarrado a alguno, turbar o desordenar.

put over, enviar, remitir o dirigir a uno a otra persona para tomar informes; remitirse, referirse; diferir, dilatar, posponer. Conducir al otro lado; navegar por travesía, atravesar.

put to, dejar, abandonar; exponer; sujetar a; unir, como se hace con las caballerías; añadir, aumentar, ayudar; echar, juntar los animales machos con las hembras para la generación. **To put to bed,** acostar, desvestir y poner en cama, como se hace con los niños; disponer a una mujer para el parto. **To put to flight,** hacer huir. **To put to his oath,** hacer prestar juramento en justicia. **To put to death,** quitar la vida, hacer morir, matar. **To put to it,** añadir, aumentar; perturbar, atormentar, incomodar; apretar, estrechar, acosar, perseguir de cerca, obligar, precisar, poner las peras a cuarto. **To be put to it,** hallarse en un aprieto, verse entre la espada y la pared. **To put to rights,** poner en orden, arreglar debidamente. **To put to sea,** hacerse a la vela. **To put to the sword,** pasar a cuchillo. **To put to the vote,** recoger los votos; poner a votación. **To put to the venture,** arriesgar, aventurar, poner en peligro.

put together, acumular, juntar, acopiar, amontonar, hacinar, reunir.

put up, poner a un lado o en su propio lugar; preservar, encajonar (fruits); hacer conservas; guardar, esconder, ocultar, adelantarse o ir hacia alguno, pretender, solicitar, salir a la palestra, ponerse entre los pretendientes a algún empleo, oficio, etc.; dejar impune un delito, exponer al público, salir de repente, acumular, amontonar, hacer brotar o germinar una planta. **To put up a thing for sale,** poner una cosa en venta. **To put up a prayer,** rogar, pedir, suplicar; hacer una oración o deprecación. **To put up at,** apearse en, alojarse en. **To put up to,** incitar, urgir, instigar a alguno para que ejecute lo que se desea; empeñar en algún asunto; enseñar, dar instrucciones sobre algo. **To put up with,** sufrir sin quejarse; aguantar, tolerar, sufrir, perdonar o disimular una falta; tener paciencia; conformarse con.

put upon, poner a colocar sobre; imponer como obligación o deber; exponer a algún riesgo, hacer padecer; engañar. **To put a trick upon one,** hacer una mala partida o pegar un petardo a alguno. **To put upon trial,** poner a prueba o someter a juicio. **To put a stop,** impedir, hacer alto, poner fin a. **To put an end,** acabar. **To put one's hand to the plough,** poner manos a la obra. **Put the case,** suponga Ud., dé Ud. por sentado.

put, *pret.* y *pp.* de To PUT.

put, s. 1. Acción del verbo *put,* en cualquiera de sus acepciones, particularmente golpe, tiro, lanzamiento. 2. Especie de juego de naipes. 3. *(E. U.)* Contrato por el cual una persona adquiere, mediante pago, el privilegio de vender o remitir a otra determinado artículo por un precio estipulado; lo opuesto a *call.* 4. **To stay put,** estar quieto, en su lugar.

put, s. *(Prov. Ingl.)* Patán, palurdo.

putative ['pju:tətɪv] [piu-ta-tiv], *a.* Putativo, reputado, supuesto.

put-off ['pʊtɒv] [put-of], *a.* 1. Deshechado. 2. Aplazado. 3. Retraso, dilatorias, aplazamiento. 4. Evasiva, excusa.

put-out ['pʊtaʊt] [put-aut], *a.* Enojado, contrariado.

putredinous ['pʊtrɪ'di:nəs] [pu-tri-di-nos], *a.* Podrido, corrompido, pútrido, que tiene su origen en la putrefacción, de olor fétido (bad, putrid).

putrefaction [ˌpjuːtrɪ'fækʃən] [pu-tri-fak-shon], *s.* Putrefacción, corrupción, acto o procedimiento de pudrirse, corromperse; calidad de podrido.

putrefactive [ˌpjuːtrɪ'fæktɪv] [pu-tri-fak-tiv], *a.* Putrefactivo, corruptivo, perteneciente a la putrefacción; expuesto a pudrirse; que puede causar putrefacción.

putrefy ['pjuːtrɪfaɪ] [pu-tri-fai], *va.* 1. Pudrir o podrir, corromper, podrecer, hacer descomponer con olor fétido, resolver en podre alguna cosa. 2. Hacer gangrenoso o carioso. *-vn.* Pudrirse, corromperse, podrecer, echarse a perder, hacerse fétido por la pudrición.

putrescence [pjuː'tresəns] [pu-tre-sens], *s.* Pudrición, pudrimiento, putrefacción, corrupción.

putrescent [pjuː'tresənt] [pu-tre-sent], *a.* Podrido, pútrido, que se halla en estado de putrefacción.

putrid ['pjuːtrɪd] [pu-trid], *a.* Podrido, pútrido, corrompido (rotten).

putt [pʌt] [pat], *s.* Tirada en el juego de golf enfocada hacia el agujero.

puttee ['pʌtiː] [pa-ti], *s.* Polaina, banda arrollada a la pierna.

putter ['pʌtəʳ] [pa-taʳ], *s.* 1. En el juego de golf, *putter,* bastón empleado para hacer caer la pelota en el agujero. 2. Ponedor, colocador. 3. **Putter of questions,** el que hace las preguntas.

putter, *vn. (Fam.)* Inquietarse por bagatelas, entretenerse en cosas que no valen la pena. V. POTTER.

putty ['pʌtɪ] [pa-ti], *s.* 1. Masilla (o potea), pasta de greda levigada, mezclada con aceite de linaza que usan los vidrieros. 2. V. Putty-powder. **Putty-powder, jewelers' putty,** óxido de estaño, a veces mezclado con óxido de plomo; polvos para pulir el vidrio, los metales, la joyería, etc.

putty, *va.* Cubrir o llenar con masilla.

puzzle ['pʌzl] [pa-sel], *s.* 1. Embarazo, embrollo; pena, inquietud, perplejidad. 2. Acertijo, adivinanza, enigma. **Crossword puzzle,** crucigrama.

puzzle, *va.* 1. Embrolar, enredar, confundir, aturrullar; poner dificultades u obstáculos; inquietar, molestar. 2. **To puzzle out,** resolver, desenredar, descifrar. *-vn.* Enredarse, embrollarse, confundirse. **To puzzle over,** tratar de descifrar o resolver, devanarse los sesos.

puzzler ['pʌzləʳ] [pas-laʳ] *s.* 1. Embrollador, enredador, inquietador, molestador, zumbón. 2. Resolvedor de enigmas, rompecabezas.

pygmean ['pɪgmɪən] [pig-mian], o **pygmy** ['pɪgmɪ] [pig-mi], *a.* Pigmeo.

pyorrhea [ˌpaɪə'rɪə] [paia-ria], *s. (Med.)* Piorrea.

pyramid ['pɪrəmɪd] [pi-ra-mid], *s.* Pirámide. 1. Monumento grande en forma de pirámide cuadrilateral. 2. *(Mat.)* Sólido que tiene por base un polígono cualquiera y cuyas caras son triángulos que se unen en un vértice. 3. En Bolsa aumentar

uno la extensión de sus operaciones al alza o a la baja, empleando el beneficio obtenido en cada una de ellas.

pyramidal ['pɪrəmɪdl] [pi-ra-mi-dal], **pyramidical**a. Piramidal.

Pyrenean [ˌpɪrə'niːən] [pi-ra-nian], *a.* Pirenaico, perteneciente o relativo a los montes Pirineos.

pyretic [paɪ'retɪk] [pai-re-tik], *a.* 1. Pirético, febril, con fiebre, que proviene de la fiebre. 2. Febrífugo, que quita la fiebre. *-s.* Medicamento febrífugo.

pyrex [paɪ'reks] [pai-reks], *s.* Loza refractaria, resistente a la lumbre.

pyrexia [paɪ'reksɪə] [pai-rek-sia], *s.* Pirexia, fiebre, condición febril, también, paroxismo de fiebre.

pyritic, [paɪ'rɪtɪk] [pai-ri-tik], *a.* Piritoso, perteneciente o parecido a la pirita; que tiene las propiedades de ésta.

pyro-, pyr-, Prefijo griego que significa fuego.

pyro [paɪə'rəʊ] [pai-rou], *s. (Fam.)* Abreviatura de ácido pirogálico.

pyrogenous [paɪ'rədʒɪnəs] [pai-ro-yi-nos], *a.* 1. Pirógeno, producido por la fusión, ígneo. 2. Febril, que excita la fiebre.

pyrography [paɪ'rəgrəfɪs] [pai-ro-gra-fi], *s.* Pirografía, el arte o procedimiento de producir un diseño sobre madera por medio de una punta hecha ascua o de una llama fina; también, el de estampar madera con planchas o cilindros calientes.

pyrology [paɪ'rɒlədʒɪ] [pai-ro-lo-yi], *s.* Pirología, análisis por medio del soplete.

pyromancy [ˌpaɪrə'mænsɪ] [pai-ro-man-si], *s.* Piromancia, adivinación por el fuego.

pyrotechnic, pyrotechnical [ˌpaɪrəʊ'teknɪk] [paia-rou-tek-nik], *a.* Pirotécnico, que pertenece a los fuegos artificiales o al arte de hacerlos.

pyrotechnics [ˌpaɪrəʊ'teknɪks] [paia-rou-tek-niks], *s.* Pirotécnica.

pyrotechny [ˌpaɪrəʊ'teknɪ] [paia-rou-tek-ni], *s.* Pirotecnia.

pyrrhic ['pɪrɪk] [pi-rik], *s.* Pirriquio, pie dompuesto de dos sílabas breves. *-a.* Pírrico, perteneciente a un pirriquio, o a una antigua danza guerrera. **Pyrrhic victory,** victoria pírrica.

pythagorean [paɪˌθægə'rɪən] [pai-za-go-rian], *a.* Pitagórico, perteneciente a la doctrina de Pitágoras.

pythian ['pɪθɪən] [pi-zian], *a.* Pitio, pertenciente a los juegos de Apolo en Delfos.

python ['paɪθən] [pai-zon], *s.* 1. Pitón.

pythoness ['paɪθənɪs] [pai-zo-nes], *sf.* Pitonisa, especie de adivina o maga.

pyx [pɪks] [piks], *s.* 1. Copón, píxide, la cajita en que se guarda la hostia. 2. Caja de brújula.

Q

q [kjuː] [kiu], Se pronuncia en inglés como en castellano la *c* fuerte. *Que, qui,* en principio o en medio de dicción, se pronuncian *cue, cui;* y en las voces derivadas del francés como *c.* Ejemplos; banquet, *báncuet;* quiver, *cuiver.* En las voces derivadas del francés, cuando estas sílabas están al fin de dicción, en unas se pronuncia como *c,* y en otras como en castellano, v. g. antique, *antic;* etiquette, *étiquet.*

Qatar [kæ'tɑːʳ] [ka-taʳ], *s.* Qatar.

quack [kwæk] [kuak], *vn.* 1. Graznar como un pato. 2. Charlatanear, charlar, chacharear, echar bocandas o balodranadas; jactarse. *-s.* Graznido, grito del pato.

quack, *s.* y *a.* 1. Charlatán, el que charla mucho jactándose y ponderando sus conocimientos en las ciencias o artes. 2. Curandero, matasanos, el que hace de médico sin serlo. 3. Empírico, matasanos, mal médico, medicastro.

quackery ['kwækərɪ] [kua-ke-ri], *s.* Charlatanería, habladuría, baldronada.

quad [kwɒd] [kuod], *s.* 1. *(Fam.)* Cuatrillizo (quadruplet). 2. *(Impr.)* Cuadrado, cuadratín. V. QUADRAT. 3. *(Teleg.)* V. QUADRUPLEX. 4. V. QUADRUPLET. 5. Cuadrángulo o patio, como el de un colegio o de una cárcel; de aquí, cárcel.

quadra [ˈkwɒdrə] [kuo-dra], *s. (Arq.)* 1. Bastidor, marco. 2. Plinto, el miembro más bajo de un podio.

quadragesima [ˌkwɒdrəˈdʒesɪmə] [kuo-dra-ye-si-ma], *s.* Cuadragésima, cuaresma.

quadragesimal [ˌkwɒdrəˈdʒesɪməl] [kuo-dra-ye-si-mal], *a.* Cuadragesimal, que pertenece a la cuaresma.

quadrangle [ˈkwɒdræŋgl] [kuo-dran-guel], *s.* 1. Cuadrángulo, figura que se compone de cuatro ángulos. 2. *(Arq.)* Patio cuadrado u oblongo, como el que suele haber dentro de un colegio u otro edificio grande.

quadrangular [ˈkwɒdræŋgjələʳ] [kuo-dran-guiu-laʳ], *a.* Cuadrangular, que tiene o forma cuatro ángulos.

quadrant [ˈkwɒdrənt] [kuo-drant], *s.* 1. Cuadrante, la cuarta parte del círculo. 2. Cuadrante de altura, instrumento matemático, instrumento astronómico reemplazado hoy por el sextante u octante. 3. *(Elect.)* V. HENRY.

quadrantal [ˈkwɒdrəntəl] [kuo-dran-tal], *a. (Mat.)* Cuadrantal.

quadrat [ˈkwɒdræt] [kuo-drat], *s.* Cuadrado, cuadratín.

quadrate [ˈkwɒdreɪt] [kuo-dreit], *a.* 1. Cuadro, cuadrado; se dice de todo lo que tiene cuatro lados iguales. 2. *(Des.)* Lo que contiene números cuadrados. -*s.* 1. *(Anat.)* Hueso o músculo cuadrado. 2. *(Astr.)* Aspecto de los astros en que distan de sí 90°; cuadrado. 3. *(Mús.)* Becuadro (#).

quadrate, *vn.* 1. Cuadrar, adaptarse, conformarse, ajustarse o venir bien una cosa con otra. 2. Equilibrar un cañón en la cureña.

quadratic [kwɒˈdrætɪk] [kuo-dra-tik], *a.* Cuadrático, perteneciente al cuadro o cuadrado. **Quadratic equation,** ecuación cuadrática, cuadrática. -*s.* Cuadrática, ecuación que encierra el cuadrado de la raíz que se busca.

quadrature [ˈkwɒdrətʃəʳ] [kuo-dra-chaʳ], *s.* 1. Cuadratura, reducción de una figura curvilínea a un cuadrado 2. Cuadratura, el aspecto cuadrado de la luna con el sol; posición relativa de dos cuerpos celestes que se hallan a una distancia de 90° uno del otro, al ser visto desde el centro de un tercer cuerpo.

quadrennial [kwɒˈdrenɪəl] [kuo-dre-nial], *a.* 1. Cuadrienal, que comprende o dura cuatro años. 2. Que sucede una vez cada cuatro años.

quadribasic [ˈkwɒdrɪˌbæsɪk] [kuo-dri-ba-sik], *a. (Quím.)* Cuadribásico.

quadrifarious [ˈkwɒdrɪˌfɛərɪəs] [kuo-dri-fa-rios], *a. (Biol.)* Dispuesto en cuatro filas o hileras.

quadrifid [ˈkwɒdrɪfɪd] [kuo-fri-fid], *a.* Hendido en cuatro partes.

quadriga [ˈkwɒdrɪgə] [kuo-dri-ga], *s.* Cuadriga, carro antiguo tirado por cuatro caballos de frente.

quadrilateral [ˌkwɒdrɪˈlætərəl] [kuo-dri-la-te-ral], *a.* Cuadrilátero, que tiene cuatro lados. -*s.* Figura que tiene cuatro lados.

quadrilateralness [ˌkwɒdrɪˈlætərəlnɪs] [kuo-dri-la-te-ral-nes], *s.* Calidad de cuadrilátero.

quadrille [kwəˈdrɪlɪ] [kua-dril], *s.* 1. Cuadrilla (dance). 2. La música de este baile. 3. Cuatrillo, cascarela, un juego de naipes entre cuatro. -*vn.* Bailar el baile así llamado o tocar la música del mismo.

quadrillion [kwəˈdrɪlɪən] [kua-dri-lion], *s.* Cuadrillón, número cardinal; según el sistema americano y francés, la quinta potencia de mil, o la unidad seguida de quince ceros; por el sistema inglés, la cuarta potencia de un millón, la unidad seguida de veinticuatro ceros.

quadrilocular [ˌkwɒdrɪˈlɒkjələʳ] [kua-dri-lo-kiu-laʳ], *a. (Bot.)* Cuadrilocular, que está dividido en cuatro compartimientos.

quadrinomial [ˌkwɒdrɪˈnɒmɪəl] [kua-dri-no-mial], *a.* Cuadrínomo, compuesto de cuatro términos. -*s.* Cuadrinomio, cantidad algebraica que consta de cuatro términos.

quadripartite [ˈkwɒdrɪˌpɑːtaɪt] [kua-dri-par-tait] *a.* Cuádruple, que se compone de cuatro partes.

quadripartitely [ˈkwɒdrɪˌpɑːtaɪtlɪ] [kua-dri-par-tait-li], *adv.* De un modo cuádruple.

quadriphyllous [ˈkwɒdrɪˈfaɪləs] [kua-dri-fai-los], *a.* Cuadrifolio, que tiene cuatro hojas.

quadrireme [ˈkwɒdrɪˌriːm] [kua-dri-rim], *s.* Galera con cuatro bancos de remos.

quadrisyllable [ˌkwɒdrɪˈsaɪləbl] [kua-dri-sai-la-bol], *s.* Cuadrisílabo.

quadrivium [ˈkwɒdrɪvɪəm] [kua-dri-viom], *s.* Cuadrivio, el lugar donde concurren cuatro sendas o caminos.

quadroon [kwɒˈdruːn] [kua-drun], *s.* Cuarteron, hijo de blanco y mulata o de mulato y mujer blanca.

quadrumana [kwɒˈdruːmænə] [kua-dru-ma-na], *s. pl.* Cuadrumanos, orden de mamíferos que en las cuatro extremidades tienen el dedo pulgar separado de modo que puede tocar a los otros dedos.

quadrumanous [ˌkwɒdruˈmænəs] [kua-dru-ma-nous], *a.* Cuadrumano, que tiene cuatro manos.

quadruped [ˈkwɒdrʊped] [kuo-dru-ped], *s.* Cuadrúpedo, el animal de cuatro pies.

quadrupedal [ˈkwɒdrʊpedl] [kuo-dru-pe-dal], *a.* Cuadrupedal, de cuatro pies, o perteneciente a ellos.

quadruple [ˈkwɒdrʊpl] [kuo-dru-pol], *a.* Cuádruple. -*s.* Pieza de ocho o de cuatro doblones.

quadruplet [kwɒˈdruːplɪt] [kuo-dru-plit], *s.* 1. Juego de cuatro cosas que funcionan como una sola; v. g. una bicicleta de cuatro asientos. 2. Cuatrillizo.

quadruplex [kwɒˈdruːplɪks] [kuo-dru-pleks], *a.* Cuádruple, cuádruplo; sistema telegráfico en que se pueden enviar a la misma vez cuatro mensajes, dos en cada dirección. -*s.* Instrumento telegráfico cuádruple.

quadruplicate [kwɒˈdruːplɪkeɪt] [kuo-dru-pli-keit], *va.* Cuadruplicar, multiplicar por cuatro.

quadruplication [ˌkwɒdruplɪˈkeɪʃən] [kuo-dru-pli-kei-shon], *s.* Cuadruplicación.

quadruply [kwɒˈdruːplaɪ] [kuo-dru-plai], *adv.* Al cuádruplo, cuatro veces tanto o cuatro tantos más.

quaff [kwɒf] [kuof], *va.* Beber a grandes tragos; beber con gusto. -*vn.* Beber demasiado.

quaffer [ˈkwɒfəʳ] [kuo-faʳ], *s.* Bebedor desmedido; borracho.

quag [ˈkwæg] [kuag], **quagmire** [ˈkwægmaɪəʳ] [kuag-maiaʳ], *s.* Tremedal, el sitio o paraje cenagoso que con poco movimiento retiembla.

quagga [ˈkwægə] [kua-ga], *s. (Zool.)* Cuaga, mamífero del África Meridional, parecido a la cebra.

quaggy [ˈkwægɪ] [kua-gui], *a.* Pantanoso; blando.

quail [kweɪl] [kueil], *s.* 1. *(Orn.)* Codorniz, ave gallinácea. 2. Colín, ave gallinácea de la América del Norte; ave semejante del género Callipepla. 3. Turnice, gallinácea.

quail, *va.* 1. *(Ant.)* Intimidar. 2. Temblar. **I quail at the idea,** la idea me da pavor (it terrifies me). 3. *(Ant.)* V. To QUELL. -*vn.* Desanimarse, descorazonarse, perder el valor.

quail-pipe [ˈkweɪlˌpaɪp] [kueil-paip], *s.* Reclamo de codornices.

quaint [kweɪnt] [kueint], *a.* 1. De apariencia anticuada y extraña, pero no desagradable; raro, a la vez que gracioso, gentil, o lindo. 2. Original, singular, fantástico, pintoresco (picturesque). 3. *(Ant.)* Primorosamente labrado; que sirve de adorno. **She is so quaint,** ella tiene un ingenio tan original.

quaintly [ˈkweɪntlɪ] [kueint-li], *adv.* Graciosamente, con gracia; lindamente, fantásticamente, de una manera singular, original, extraña.

quaintness [ˈkweɪntnɪs] [kueint-nes], *s.* Primor, singularidad, apariencia anticuada.

quake [kweɪk] [kueik], *vn.* Temblar, temblequear o tembletear, temblar con frecuencia; estar agitado por sacudimientos cortos y frecuentes, estremecerse, oscilar, ser movedizo. **The earth will quake sooner or later,** la tierra temblará tarde o temprano.

quake, *s.* Temblor, movimiento trémulo; tiritona. Terremoto (earthquake).

Quaker [ˈkweɪkəʳ] [kuei-kaʳ], *s.* Cuáquero, cuákero.

quakerism [ˈkweɪkərɪzəm] [kuei-ka-ri-sem], *s.* La doctrina y maneras de los cuáqueros.

quaking ['kweɪkɪŋ] [kuei-kin], *pa.* de QUAKE. Que tiembla; movedizo. **Quaking-grass,** 1. Plantas gramíneas del género Briza. 2. La planta gramínea que se llama comúnmente *rattlesmake-grass.*

qualifiable ['kwɒlɪfaɪəbl] [kuo-li-faia-bol], *a.* Calificable, que puede calificarse; susceptible de modificaciones.

qualification [ˌkwɒlɪfɪˈkeɪʃən] [kuo-li-fi-kei-shon], *s.* 1. Calificación, la acción y efecto de calificar a una persona o cosa. **She has a very good qualification,** tiene una muy buena calificación. 2. Requisito, la circunstancia o condición que se requiere para alguna cosa; calidad, cualidad natural o adquirida que hace a una persona o cosa propia para un puesto, objeto o destino, en especial, capacidad o poder legal; adaptación, negación parcial, atenuación, mitigación.

qualificator [ˌkwɒlɪfɪˈkeɪtər] [kuo-li-fi-kei-taʳ], *s.* Calificador del santo oficio.

qualified ['kwɒlɪfaɪd] [kuo-li-faid], *pp.* y *a.* 1. Titulado, apto, competente, que posee las cualidades necesarias. **A highly qualified candidate,** un candidato muy cualificado, muy preparado. 2. Limitado, con reservas, restringido. **Qualified success,** éxito relativo, cierto éxito.

qualifier ['kwɒlɪfaɪəʳ] [kuo-li-faiaʳ], *s.* 1. (Sport) Clasificado. 2. Calificador.

qualify ['kwɒlɪfaɪ] [kuo-li-fai], *va.* 1. Hacer apto o idóneo para alguna colocación, empleo u ocupación. 2. Dotar, adornar la naturaleza de dotes y prerrogativas. 3. Habilitar, hacer hábil y capaz a alguno. 4. Calificar, dar por buena o mala una cosa según sus cualidades y circunstancias. 5. Modificar, limitar, restringir. 6. Templar, suavizar. **A person qualified to exercise an employment,** una persona capaz de ejercer un empleo o con los requisitos necesarios para desempeñarlo. **A man well qualified,** un hombre dotado de bellas prendas. -*vn.* 1. Prepararse, hacer lo necesario para poder desempeñar un cargo, o gozar determinadas ventajas. 2. Titularse, sacarse el título de algo. 3. (Sport) Clasificarse. 4. (E. U.) Prestar juramento, antes de entrar en funciones. **A qualified voter,** elector habilitado, que ha cumplido con la ley. **To qualify the sense of words,** modificar el sentido de las palabras. **An adjective qualifies a noun,** el adjetivo califica al nombre. **To qualify liquors,** saborear o diluir los licores.

qualifying ['kwɒlɪfaɪɪŋ] [kuo-li-fain], *a.* Eliminatorio, ronda eliminatoria.

qualitative ['kwɒlɪtətɪv] [kuo-li-ta-tiv], *a.* Cualitativo, que denota cualidad; que se refiere únicamente a la cualidad. **Qualitative analysis,** análisis cualitativo.

qualitatively ['kwɒlɪtətɪvlɪ] [kuo-li-ta-tiv-li], *adv.* Cualitativamente.

quality ['kwɒlɪtɪ] [kua-li-ti], *s.* 1. Calidad o cualidad, la propiedad natural de cada cosa, lo que hace que una cosa sea lo que es; elemento característico (characteristic). 2. Condición; grado; grado de excelencia; prenda, excelencia relativa. **Excellent quality,** primera calidad. 3. Natural, genio, índole. 4. Propiedad, poder o virtud de producir efectos determinados. 5. Papel, parte especial, función. 6. (Prov. o des.) Posición social, el conjunto o cuerpo de los nobles o las personas de distinción. **Man of quality,** hombre de buena cuna, de distinción.

quality control ['kwɒlɪtɪˌkɒntrəl] [kuo-li-ti-kon-trol], *s.* Control de calidad.

qualm [kwɑːm] [kualm], *s.* 1. Acceso de náusea. 2. Delicadeza de conciencia; escrúpulo moral, remordimiento. **She has no qualms about leaving you,** no tiene ningún reparo o escrúpulo en dejarte. 3. Recelo, duda (misgiving).

qualmish ['kwɑːmɪʃ] [kual-mish], *a.* 1. Con náuseas. 2. Escrupuloso.

qualmishness ['kwɑːmɪʃnɪs] [kual-mish-nes], *s.* El estado de la persona que tiene predisposición a náuseas.

quandary ['kwɒndərɪ] [kuon-da-ri], *s.* Incertidumbre, dilema, duda, suspensión; laberinto. **Your sister is in a quandary,** tu hermana está en un dilema.

quantifiable ['kwɒntɪfaɪəbl] [kuon-ti-faia-bol], *a.* Cuantificable.

quantifier ['kwɒntɪfaɪəʳ] [kuon-ti-faiaʳ], *s.* Cuantificador.

quantify ['kwɒntɪfaɪ] [kuon-ti-fai], *vt.* Cuantificar.

quantitative ['kwɒntɪtətɪv] [kuon-ti-ta-tiv], *a.* Cuantitativo, que se refiere a la cantidad. **Quantitative analysis,** análisis cuantitativo, el que se emplea para determinar la cantidad de cada elemento o ingrediente.

quantitatively ['kwɒntɪtətɪvlɪ] [kuon-ti-ta-tiv-li], *adv.* Cuantitativamente.

quantity ['kwɒntɪtɪ] [kuon-ti-ti], *s.* 1. Cantidad, propiedad de alguna cosa que se puede aumentar o disminuir o que está sujeta a número, peso o medida. 2. Medida o peso indeterminado. 3. Cantidad (amount), porción grande o pequeña de alguna cosa. **In quantity,** en grandes cantidades. 4. Cantidad, el tiempo que se emplea en pronunciar una sílaba; duración relativa de las notas musicales. 5. (Elec.) La fuerza de una corriente, en contraposición a la potencia o intensidad.

quantum ['kwɒntəm] [kuon-tom], *s.* 1. Tanto, la cantidad a que llega alguna cosa, cuantía (amount). 2. (Fís.) Cuanto, quántum. (Mec.) Cuántico.

quarantine ['kwɒrəntiːn] [kuo-ran-tin], *s.* 1. Cuarentena, el espacio de tiempo que están en el lazareto o privados de comunicación los que se presume vienen de países inficionados o contagiados. 2. Lazareto, lugar destinado para hacer la cuarentena. 3. Cuarenta días. 4. (For.) El derecho que la ley de Inglaterra concedía a las viudas de continuar en posesión de la casa de su marido por cuarenta días después del fallecimiento de éste. -*vt.* Poner en cuarentena.

quarrel ['kwɒrəl] [kuo-rel], *s.* 1. Pendencia, riña, contienda. **To pick a quarrel,** armar pendencia. 2. Alteración, porfía, disputa. 3. Desavenencia, rompimiento de amistades. 4. Motivo o causa de disputa 5. El diamante con que se corta el cristal. 6. Una especie de flecha usada antiguamente con extremidad cuadrada. 7. V. QUARY, 5ª acep.

quarrel, *vn.* 1. Reñir, pelear, disputar, contender. 2. Desamistarse, discordar, desavenirse mutuamente. 3. Tachar, poner en alguna cosa faltas o tachas. **To quarrel with one's bread and butter,** quitarse el pan de la boca, perjudicarse a sí mismo.

quarreler ['kwɒrələʳ] [kuo-re-laʳ], *s.* Quimerista.

quarrelsome ['kwɒrəlsəm] [kuo-rel-som], *a.* Pendenciero, quimerista, irascible.

quarrelsomely ['kwɒrəlsəmlɪ] [kuo-rel-som-li], *adv.* Alborotadamente, con ganas de reñir.

quarrier ['kwɒrɪəʳ] [kuo-riaʳ], *s.* Cantero, picapedrero, obrero que trabaja en las canteras.

quarry ['kwɒrɪ] [kuo-ri], *s.* 1. Cantera, el sitio de donde se saca piedra para labrar; mina. 2. El ave en que hace presa el halcón; presa. 3. (Des.) Un montón de caza muerta; cuir, piel. 4. Cuadrado, cuadro, rombo. 5. Cuadrado o rombo pequeño de vidrio, teja, etc. 6. V. QUAREL, 6ª acep.

quarry, *va.* 1. Sacar piedra o trabajar en una cantera. 2. (Des.) Devorar, hacer presa.

quarryman ['kwɒrɪmən] [kuo-ri-man], *s.* Cavador de cantera, dueño de una cantera; cantero, picapedrero, obrero en una cantera.

quart [kwɔːt] [kuort], *s.* 1. Cuarto de galón. 2. Una vasija que sirve para medir líquidos. 3. (Mús.) Cuarta, intervalo de cuatro tonos.

quart, *s.* 1. (Esgr.) V. CARTE. 2. Cuarta en el juego de los cientos.

quartan ['kwɔːtən] [kuor-tan], *a.* Perteneciente a la cuarta en una serie; particularmente que sucede cada cuarto día. -*s.* Cuartana, calentura intermitente que se repite cada cuarto día.

quarter ['kwɔːtəʳ] [kuor-taʳ], *s.* 1. Cuarto, cuarterón o cuarta parte de cualquiera cosa, cuarto de quintal. **A quart of a year,** un cuarto de año. 2. Cuarta, la división de los medios vientos. 3. Cuartel, barrio, paraje o sitio particular de alguna población. 4. Barrio (district of town), barriada, vecindad, parte de alguna comarca; distrito, región. **From all quarters,** de todas partes. 5. (Mil.) Cuartel, el sitio o paraje en que está alojado o acuartelado un cuerpo de soldados. **Winter quarters,** cuarteles de invierno. 6. Estación, sitio, puesto señalado, como el de los oficiales y de la tripulación en un buque de guerra; ordinariamente en plural. 7. Morada, residencia temporal; cuartos alquilados; generalmente en plural. 8. Región que comprende la cuarta parte, poco más o menos, de un espacio; cada una de cuatro partes correlativas, como las de un zapato, del casco de una caballería, etc. 9. Cuarterón, entrepaño. 10. (Mar.) Cuadra de popa. **Wind on the quarter o quartering wind,** (Mar.) Viento a la cuadra. **Quarter-cask,** cuarterola. **Quarter-cloths,** (Mar.) viento o la cuadra. **Quarter-day,** El día en que principia cada una de las cuatro estaciones del año; día en que se paga el alquiler. **Quarter-deck,** (Mar.) alcázar. **Quarter-deck ladder,** escalera de costado, o escalera real. **Quarter-gunners,** (Mar.) Artilleros de brigada de marina. **Quarter-netting,** (Mar.) Redes de combate. **Quarter-pieces,** (Mar.) Artilleros de brigada de marina. **Quarter-netting,** (Mar.) Redes de combate. **Quarter-pieces,** (Mar.) Montantes. **Quarter-plates,** tamaño de una placa fotográfica de 3 1/4 y 4 1/4 pulgadas; placa o cuadro de este tamaño. **Quarter-point,** (Mar.) Cuarto viento o rumbo de la brújula **Quarter-rails,** (Mar.) Batayolas. **Quarter-section,** en los Estados Unidos y el Canadá, el cuarto de una milla cuadrada; pieza de terreno de media milla cuadrada o 160 acres. **Quarter-sessions,** tribunal formado por tres magistrados inferiores o jueces de paz, que se reunen una vez cada trimestre en todos los condados de Inglaterra, para juzgar a los acusados de ciertos delitos leves. **Quarter wind,** (Mar.) viento por anca. **All hands to quarters,** todos a su puesto. **In quarters,** en cuartos; en cuarteles o en campamento, en cuartos alquilados. **They took up their quarters at,** se alojaron en o en casa de. **From another quarter,** de otra parte. **The moon is then in its third quarter,** la luna está entonces en su tercer cuarto. -a. Cuarto, que tiene la cuarta parte de una cosa.

quarter, s. Cuartel, gracia, acto de hacer gracia de la vida a un enemigo que no puede defenderse y rendido a discreción, de aquí, clemencia, indulgencia. **To ask for, to cry quarter,** pedir gracia. **To give no quarter,** no dar cuartel.

quarter, va. 1. Cuartear, partir o dividir en cuartas partes; descuartizar, hacer cuartos. 2. Partir, romper a la fuerza. 3. Dividir en cuarteles una población. 4. Acuartelar, repartir la tropa en cuarteles. 5. Dar de comer o mantener a uno con comida sea por dinero o sin él. 6. Alojar, hospedar. 7. (Her.) Cuartelar los escudos de armas.

quarterage [ˈkwɔːtərɪdʒ] [kuor-ta-rich], s. Sueldo o salario que se paga cada trimestre.

quarterback [ˈkwɔːtəbæk] [kuor-ta-bak], s. En el fútbol americano, uno de los cuatro jugadores colocados detrás de la línea.

quartered [ˈkwɔːtərɪd] [kuor-ta-rid], a. 1. Partido o separado en cuatro partes. 2. Hecho de madera dividida o aserrada a lo largo en cuartos, para mostrar la veta. 3. Alojado, acuartelado. **Quartered oak,** madera de roble aserrado a lo largo en cuartos para mostrar la veta.

quarterly [ˈkwɔːtəlɪ] [kuor-ta-li], a. Que contiene la cuarta parte; que se hace cada tres meses, trimestral. **Quarterly wages,** salario de un trimestre. **The quarterly review,** la revista trimestral, un periódico que se publica cada tres meses. -s. Periódico que sale a la luz cada tres meses.

quarterly, adv. 1. Una vez cada trimestre. 2. En cuartos, por cuartos.

quarterman [ˈkwɔːtəmən] [kuor-ta-man], s. (Mar.) Sotomaestro.

quarter-master [ˈkwɔːtəˌmɑːstəʳ] [kuor-ta-mas-taʳ], s. (Mil.) Cuartelmaestre, comisario ordenador; (Mar.) cabo de brigadas, oficial inferior que ayuda al piloto y tiene a su cargo las brújulas, los aparatos de señales, etc. **Quarter-master-general,** intendente de ejército.

quartern [ˈkwɔːtən] [kuor-tern], s. (Ingl.) 1. La cuarta parte de ciertas medidas y pesos, como de un cuartillo. 2. **Quartern loaf,** pan de cuatro libras.

quarter note [ˈkwɔːtənəʊt] [kuor-ta-nout], s. (E. U.) Negra.

quartet, quartette [kwɔːˈtet] [kuor-tet], s. 1. Cuarteto, composición vocal o instrumental para cuatro voces. 2. Las cuatro personas que tocan o cantan esta composición. 3. (Poet.) Cuarteto, estrofa de cuatro versos. 4. Cuatro cosas de una misma clase.

quartile [ˈkwɔːtaɪl] [kuor-tail], s. Cuadrado o aspecto cuadrado en la astrología.

quarto [ˈkwɔːtəʊ] [kuor-tou], a. En cuarto: se dice del libro cuyo pliego doblado forma cuatro hojas u ocho páginas. -s. Un libro en cuarto.

quartz [kwɔːts] [kuorts], s. (Min.) Cuarzo, cristal de roca.

quartzose, quartzous, quartzy [ˈkwɔːtsəs] [kuor-tsous], a. Cuarzoso, que contiene cuarzo, o compuesto de cuarzo.

quasar [ˈkweɪzɑːʳ] [kuei-saʳ], s. Cuasar.

quash [kwɒʃ] [kuosh], va. 1. Someter, oprimir, suprimir por fuerza, domar. **To quash a rebellion,** suprimir o sofocar una revolución. 2. (For.) Anular, invalidar, abrogar, derogar. -vn. Estremecerse al oír algún ruido.

quasi- [ˈkweɪzaɪ] [kuei-sai], [ˈkwɑːzɪ] [kua-si] pref. Prefijo latino que significa casi o «como si».

quasi-contract [ˈkwɑːzɪˌkɒntrækt] [kua-si-kon-trakt], s. Cuasicontrato.

quassia o quassia wood [ˈkweɪzɪə] [kuei-sia], s. (Bot.) Leño o palo de cuasia (quaisa) o simarruba; es muy amarga y tiene propiedades tónicas.

quassin [ˈkwɒsɪn] [kuo-sin], s. El principio amargo de la cuasia, un compuesto blanco cristalizable.

quater-cousin [ˌkwɒtəˈkʌzɪn] [kuo-ta-ka-sin], s. Primo en cuarto grado; amigo.

quaternary [kwəˈtɜːnərɪ] [kuo-ter-na-ri], a. 1. Cuaternario, compuesto de cuatro cosas; dispuesto de cuatro en cuatro. 2. Cuarto en orden. 3. Cuadrángulo. 4. De la época cuaternaria. -s. Época la más reciente de la historia geológica.

quaternion [kwəˈtɜːnɪən] [kuo-ter-nion], s. 1. Cuaternidad. 2. Una fila de cuatro soldados; juego o sistema de cuatro.

quatrain [ˈkwɒtreɪn] [kuo-trein], s. Cuarteto, combinación métrica de cuatro versos.

quaver [ˈkweɪvəʳ] [kuei-vaʳ], vn. 1. Gorgoritear, gorjear, trinar, hacer quiebros con la voz en la garganta. 2. Temblar, moverse alguna cosa con un movimiento trémulo.

quaver, s. 1. Gorjeo, trino; pasaje en la música; trino en los instrumentos. 2. (Mús.) Corchea, un signo de la música. **Quaver rest,** aspiración de corchea.

quavering [ˈkweɪvərɪŋ] [kuei-va-rin], s. Gorgorito, trinado, trino.

quay [kiː] [ki], s. Muelle, malecón; desembarcadero artificial donde pueden cargar y descargar las embarcaciones.

quayside [ˈkiːsaɪd] [ki-said], s. Muelle.

queachy, queenchy [ˈkwiːtʃɪ] [kui-chi], a. Movedizo, que tiembla bajo los pies, como el terreno húmedo o pantanoso.

quean [kiːn] [kin], s. 1. Mujercilla, la mujer de mala vida. 2. Una joven o muchacha.

queasiness [ˈkwiːzɪnɪs] [kui-si-nes], s. Debilidad, fiaqueza de estómago, hastío, desgana, inapetencia, sensación de mareo.

queasy [ˈkwiːzɪ] [kui-si], a. 1. Nauseabundo: se dice del que es propenso al vómito. **My stomach is a bit queasy,** tengo el estómago un poco revuelto. 2. Nauseabundo, nauseoso, nauseativo, que provoca al vómito o produce náuseas. 3. Fastidioso, que causa hastío. 4. Asqueroso, que da asco. 5. Delicado, nimio, escrupuloso. 6. Delicado, expuesto a contingencias; difícil de manejar o tratar. 7. Intranquilo (uneasy).

queen [kwiːn] [kuin], sf. 1. Reina, la esposa del rey. 2. Mujer soberana en un reino. 3. Mujer que brilla más que las otras en una fiesta o solemnidad. **queen dowager,** reina viuda. 4. El caballo en los naipes. 5. La dama en el juego de damas y la reina en el ajedrez. 6. Reina (de las abejas); la sola hembra completamente desarrollada en un enjambre de abejas u hormigas. **Queen consort,** esposa del rey, que no tiene parte en el gobierno. **Queen mother,** reina madre. **Queen regent,**

reina regente. **Queen regnant,** reina reinante, la que ejerce el domino por derecho propio. **Queen-of-the-mead-ows,** espirea, ulmaria, «reina de los prados», género de plantas de la familia de las rosáceas.

queen bee [ˈkwiːnˌbiː] [kuin-bi], *s.* Reina de las abejas.

queenhood [ˈkwiːnhʊd] [kuin-jud], *s.* Realeza, estado o condición de una reina.

queenly [ˈkwiːnlɪ] [kuin-li], *a.* Parecido a una reina; que tiene el carácter o el porte de una reina; de reina, regio; propio de una reina.

queenship [ˈkwiːnʃɪp] [kuin-ship], *s.* Dignidad, domino o poder de una reina.

queer [ˈkwɪəʳ] [kuiaʳ], *a.* 1. Raro (odd), extraño, orginal, singular. 2. Cuestionable, defavorable, no propicio, misterioso. 3. Estrafalario, estrambótico. -*s.* *(Ger.)* 1. Moneda falsa. 2. Maricón, marica.

queerly [ˈkwɪəlɪ] [kuia-li], *adv.* Particularmente, singularmente, raramente, misteriosamente.

queerness [ˈkwɪənɪs] [kuia-nes], *s.* Rareza, particularidad, ridiculez.

quell [kwel] [kuel], *va.* 1. Hacer cesar, hacer ceder, subyugar, sojuzgar. **To quell tumults,** apaciguar o sosegar tumultos. 2. Apaciguar, calmar, aquietar, mitigar (v. g. un dolor). -*vn.* Minorarse, ir a menos, apaciguarse, calmarse.

quench [kwentʃ] [kuench], *va.* 1. Apagar, matar la lumbre, la luz, el fuego y también se dice de la sed, saciar; ahogar, extinguir. 2. Apagar, sosegar, extiguir alguna pasión de ánimo. 3. Extinguir, acabar, borrar la memoria de alguna cosa. 4. Destruir.

quenchable [ˈkwentʃəbl] [kuen-cha-bol], *a.* Extinguible, apagable, destruible.

quencher [ˈkwentʃəʳ] [kuen-chaʳ], *s.* Apagador.

quenchless [ˈkwentʃlɪs] [kuench-les], *a.* Inextinguible, que no se puede apagar; implacable, que no se puede calmar.

quercine [ˈkwɜːsɪn] [kuer-sin], *a.* De encinas o robles, perteneciente a estos árboles.

quercitron [ˈkwɜːsɪtrən] [kuer-si-tron], *s.* 1. Corteza del roble negro americano con que se tiñe de amarillo. 2. El roble negro americano.

quercus [ˈkwɜːkəs] [kuer-kus], *s.* Género típico de las quercíneas, que comprende los robles y las encinas.

querent [ˈkwerənt] [kue-rent], *s.* Querellante, el que se querella.

querist [ˈkwerɪst] [kue-rist], *s.* Inquiridor, preguntador; la persona curiosa o preguntona.

querl, quirl [ˈkwɜːl] [kuerl], *va.* Dar vueltas, doblar en redondo. -*s.* Sinuosidad, doblez redondeada, enroscadura.

quern [ˈkwɜːn] [kuern], *s.* Molino de mano antiguo (para granos).

querulous [ˈkwerʊləs] [kue-ru-los], *a.* Querelloso, quejoso, dispuesto a quejarse; de índole inclinada a la murmuración.

querulously [ˈkwerʊləslɪ] [kue-ru-los-li], *adv.* Querellosamente, quejosamente, con sentimiento.

querulousness [ˈkwerʊləsnɪs] [kue-ru-los-nes], *s.* La disposición a quejarse continuamente.

query [ˈkwerɪ] [kue-ri], *s.* 1. Cuestión, pregunta a que se debe responder; de aquí, una duda. 2. Signo de duda o interrogación; nota que se pone para que se investigue la exactitud de alguna cosa; se indica a menudo con el signo interrogativo (?).

query, *va.* 1. Expresar una duda respecto a; marcar con un signo de interrogación. 2. Preguntar, inquirir, pesquisar. -*vn.* 1. Dudar de. 2. Preguntar, proponer cuestiones o hacer preguntas. **I'd like to query this bill,** me parece que hay un error en esta cuenta.

quest [kwest] [kuest], *s.* 1. Pesquisa, inquisición, averiguación. 2. Busca, buscada. 3. *(Des.)* El conjunto de los que van en busca de alguna cosa.

question [ˈkwestʃən] [kues-tion], *s.* 1. Cuestión, pregunta (inquiry), interrogación. 2. Cuestión, proposición de que se trata, asunto; materia u objeto de discusión o de deliberación; problema. 3. Cuestión, disputa, debate, controversia. 4.

Proposición que ha de resolverse o discutirse en una asamblea deliberante. 5. Objeción interpuesta o admitida; duda. 6. Cuestión de tormento. 7. Examinación jurídica. **The question is,** el caso es. **Leading question,** pregunta hecha de modo que indica la respuesta que se ha de dar. **Out of the question,** fuera de la cuestión, que no es digno de consideración, que no se debe pensar en ello. **Past question,** fuera de duda, indudablemente, ciertamente. **To ask one a question,** hacer a uno una pregunta. **To beg the question,** suponer lo que está bajo discusión. **To call in question,** poner en cuestión, en duda. **To be beside the question,** salirse de la cuestión. **to put a question,** hacer una pregunta, dirigir una interpelación. **The previous question was put and carried,** pidieron y votaron la cuestión previa. **Not a fair question,** pregunta no permitida, pregunta indiscreta. **What is the question?,** ¿De qué se trata? **That is the question,** he ahí la cuestión, lo que se ha de examinar, decidir; he ahí de lo que se trata. **There can be no question about it,** no cabe duda acerca de ello.

question, *vn.* 1. Inquirir, preguntar, escudriñar. 2. Cuestionar, poner en cuestión o en duda; dudar que; también poner objeción a, tachar, recusar, controvertir. -*va.* 1. Preguntar, examinar a uno por preguntas. 2. Dudar, dificultar. 3. Desconfiar, no tener confianza. **He questions my prudence,** desconfía de mi prudencia.

questionable [ˈkwestʃənəbl] [kues-tio-na-bol], *a.* Cuestionable, que puede ponerse en cuestión; expuesto a sospecha o cuestión; dudoso, sospechoso. **A remark in questionable taste,** un comentario de dudoso buen gusto.

questionableness [ˌkwestʃənəblnɪs] [kues-tio-na-bol-nes], *s.* Calidad o estado de lo cuestionable, naturaleza sospechosa, dudosa, controvertible.

questioner [ˈkwestʃənəʳ] [kues-tio-naʳ], *s.* Inquisidor, preguntador, preguntón.

questioning [ˈkwestʃənɪŋ] [kues-tio-nin], *a.* Inquisitivo. -*s.* Interrogatorio (interrogation), cuestionamiento.

questioningly [ˈkwestʃənɪŋlɪ] [kues-tio-nin-li], *adv.* De manera inquisidora o inquisitiva.

questionist [ˈkwestʃənɪst] [kues-tio-nist], *s.* 1. En la Universidad de Cambridge, aspirante a un grado. 2. *(Des.)* Escudriñador, inquiridor.

questionless [ˈkwestʃənlɪs] [kues-tio-lis], *a.* Que no hace preguntas. -*adv.* *(Des.)* Ciertamente, interrogatorio.

question mark [ˈkwestʃənˌmɑːk] [kues-tion-mark], *s.* Signo de interrogación.

questionnaire [ˌkwestʃənɛəʳ] [kues-tio-neaʳ], *s.* Cuestionario.

questor [ˈkwestəʳ] [kues-taʳ], *s.* Cuestor, magistrado romano.

questus [ˈkwestəs] [kues-tas], *s.* *(For.)* Bienes adquirido y no heredados.

quetzal [ˈkwetsəl] [kue-chal], *s.* 1. Quetzal, ave de Guatemala. 2. Quetzal, moneda guatemalteca.

queue [ˈkjuː] [kiu], *s.* 1. Cola, trenza de cabellos en forma de cuerda. 2. Fila, hilera de personas que esperan en el orden de su llegada. **Join the queue,** póngase en la cola. 3. Cola, como la de un violín. -*vi.* Hacer cola.

queue jumping [ˈkjuːˌdʒʌmpɪŋ] [kiu-yam-pin], *s.* Saltarse la cola, colarse. **She accused me of queue jumping,** me acusó de saltarme la cola, de colarme.

quibble [ˈkwɪbl] [kui-bel], *vn.* 1. Sutilizar, buscar escapatorias; evadir el punto en cuestión o la verdad llana y lisa, por medio de argucias. 2. *(Des.)* Jugar del vocablo, decir equívocos. -*s.* Subterfugio, escaparatorio, evasión de un punto o cuestión; argucia, sutileza.

quibbler [ˈkwɪbləʳ] [kui-blaʳ], *s.* Tramoyista.

quibblingly [ˈkwɪblɪŋlɪ] [kui-blin-li], *adv.* De una manera evasiva, con argucias y sutilezas.

quiche [ˈkwɪʃ] [kuish], *s.* Quiche.

quick [kwɪk] [kuik], *a.* 1. Veloz, acelerado, ligero, pronto, hecho con celeridad, rápido, presto; que llega en poco tiempo. **Be quick,** despáchese Ud., dése Ud. prisa. 2. Vivo, diligente, ágil, activo. 3. Ardiente, penetrante. 4. Vivo, viviente. **Quick work,** *(Mar.)* Obra viva. 5. Vivo de genio, despierto de inteligencia; que responde fácilmente a las impresiones. 6. Irritable, petulante. 7. Preñada, embarazada, encinta; se dice más comúnmente, **quick with child.** 8. Que produce interés o provecho; disponible, efectivo. **A quick motion,** un movimiento rápido, veloz. **A quick ear,** un oído vivo, fino. **A quick wit,** una inteligencia viva. **A quick fire,** un fuego ardiente. **A quick pulse,** pulso irritable; se distingue del pulso frecuente. **The quick and the dead,** los vivos y los muertos. **To be quick about** o **at anything,** hacer de prisa una cosa, ejecutarla prontamente. *-adv.* Con presteza, vivamente, velozmente, rápidamente. **Quick-eyed,** de ojos vivos, con vista penetrante. **Quick-grass.** *V.* COUCH-GRASS. **Quick-scented.** que tiene el olfato fino. **Quick-sighted,** que tiene vista aguda, penetrante. **Quick-sightedness,** agudeza de vista, penetración. **Quick-tempered,** fácil de encolerizarse, irascible, colérico. **Quick-witted,** de inteligencia viva, agudo, perspicaz. **Quick-hedge,** seto vivo. **Quick-match,** mecha de estopilla, cuerdamecha.

quick, *s.* 1. Lo que tiene vida, particularmente la carne viva, lo vivo; *(Fig.)* la sensibilidad. **To cut** o **sting to the quick,** herir a uno en lo vivo. 2. *(Bot.)* Planta de seto. *V.* QUICKSET.

quickbeam [ˈkwɪkbiːm] [kuik-bim], *s.* *(Bot.)* Fresno silvestre.

quicken [ˈkwɪkən] [kui-ken], *va.* 1. Vivificar, dar vida, resucitar, devolver la vida. 2. Acelerar, urgir, avivar; apresurar. 3. Avivar, excitar, aguzar, animar. *-vn.* 1. Avivarse, vivificarse, recibir vida. 2. Moverse de prisa. 3. Sentir moverse la criatura; se dice de una madre. **His pulse is quickened,** su pulso se ha acelerado.

quickening [ˈkwɪkənɪŋ] [kui-ke-nin], *s.* 1. Acción y efecto de vivificar, o de hallarse vivo. 2. En la jurisprudencia médica, la primera vez que la mujer embarazada siente moverse el feto dentro de la matriz.

quickie [ˈkwɪkɪ] [kui-ki], *s.* *(Fam.)* Uno rápido. **A quickie drink,** una copa rápida.

quickfreeze [ˈkwɪkˈfriːz] [kuik-fris], *va.* Congelar rápidamente.

quicklime [ˈkwɪklaɪm] [kuik-laim], *s.* Cal viva.

quickly [ˈkwɪklɪ] [kui-kli], *adv.* Prontamente, con presteza. **Do it as quickly as you can,** hazlo tan pronto como puedas.

quickness [ˈkwɪknɪs] [kuik-nes], *s.* Presteza, vivacidad, prontitud, celeridad, actividad; sagacidad, viveza, penetración.

quicksand [ˈkwɪksænd] [kuik-sand], *s.* Arenas movedizas.

quickset [ˈkwɪkset] [kuik-set], *s.* 1. Arbusto o árbol con que se hace un seto, particularmente el espino blanco. 2. Seto vivo. **Quickset hedge,** seto vivo.

quickset, *va.* Cercar con un seto vivo; plantar con el espino majuelo.

quicksilver [ˈkwɪksɪlvəʳ] [kuik-sil-vaʳ], *s.* Azogue, mercurio.

quicksilvered [ˈkwɪksɪlvəd] [kuik-sil-vard], *a.* Azogado, dado de azogue o mercurio.

quickstep [ˈkwɪkstep] [kuik-step], *s.* 1. *(Mús.)* Marcha escrita en compás acelerado; pasacalle. 2. Paso acelerado.

quid [kwɪd] [kuid], *s.* 1. Un pedacito de cualquier cosa que se está mascando, (tobacco). 2. *(GB)* Libra esterlina.

quid pro quo [ˈkwɪd] [kuid], *s.* Retribución.

quiddity [ˈkwɪdɪtɪ] [kui-di-ti], *s.* 1. Esencia. 2. Cavilación, argucia, distinción u objeción fútil, ligera.

quiddle [ˈkwɪdl] [kui-del], *vn.* Gastar el tiempo en pequeñeces, divertirse en bagatelas.

quidnunc [ˈkwɪdnʌnk] [kuid-nank], *s.* Curioso insaciable, persona que quiere saber todo lo que pasa; novelero, amigo de cuentos.

quiesce [ˈkwaɪes] [kuaies], *vn.* 1. Aquietarse, callarse. 2. Convertirse en muda una letra.

quiescence [kwaɪˈesns] [kuai-esens], **quiescency** [ˈkwaɪesnsɪ] [kuai-esen-si], *s.* Quietud, reposo, descanso.

quiescent [kwaɪˈesnt] [kuai-esent], *a.* 1. Quieto, descansado, flato de movimiento, en reposo. 2. No

agitado, tranquilo, libre de ansiedad o emoción. 3. Mudo, que no se pronuncia.

quiet [ˈkwaɪət] [kuaiat], *a.* 1. Quedo, quieto, falto de movimiento. 2. Pacífico, apacible, dulce de genio, sosegado, tranquilo. 3. Silencioso. **Be quiet!,** ¡cállate! *-s.* 1. Silencio (silence). 2. Quietud, sosiego, reposo, descanso, tranquilidad, calma.

quiet, *va.* Aquietar, apaciguar, sosegar, tranquilizar. **Quiet down,** calmar, acallar.

quieter [ˈkwaɪətəʳ] [kuaia-taʳ], *s.* Apaciguador.

quietism [ˈkwaɪətɪzəm] [kuaia-ti-sem], *s.* 1. Tranquilidad de ánimo. 2. Quietismo, molinismo.

quietist [ˈkwaɪətɪst] [kuaia-tist], *s.* Quietista, molinista.

quietly [ˈkwaɪətlɪ] [kuaiat-li], *adv.* Quietamente, pacíficamente, con sosiego. En voz baja.

quietness [ˈkwaɪətnɪs] [kuaiat-nes], **quietude** [ˈkwaɪətjuːd] [kuaia-tiud], *s.* Quietud, sosiego, tranquilidad, paz, reposo.

quietus [ˈkwaɪətəs] [kuaia-tus], *s.* Carta de pago, finiquito, descanso; muerte.

quiff [kwɪf] [kuif], *s.* Copete, tupé.

quill [kwɪl] [kuil], *s.* 1. Pluma grande de las alas o de la cola de las aves; cañón de pluma. 2. Cañón o pluma para escribir; también, un escritor y con el artículo significa la profesión literaria. 3. La púa del puerco espín. 4. Parte cilíndrica, parecida al cañón de una pluma, canilla, cañita de tejedor. **Quill-men,** gente de pluma.

quilling [ˈkwɪlɪŋ] [kui-lin], *s.* Faralá, vuelo de un material plegado, cada uno de los pliegues de ese material.

quilt [ˈkwɪlt] [kuilt], *s.* Colcha o cobertura acolchada para la cama; sobrecama acolchada. **Continental quilt,** edredón nórdico.

quilt, *va.* Colchar, acolchar.

quilted [ˈkwɪltɪd] [kuil-ted], *a.* Acolchado, guateado.

quilter [ˈkwɪltəʳ] [kuil-taʳ], *s.* Colchonero.

quilting [ˈkwɪltɪŋ] [kuil-tin], *s.* 1. *(Mar.)* Cajera. 2. El acto de acolchar. 3. **Quiltings,** cojines colchados.

quinary [ˈkwɪnərɪ] [kui-na-ri], *a.* Quinario, que consta de cinco partes.

quince [kwɪns] [kuins], *s.* 1. *(Bot.)* membrillo, fruto amarillento que produce el árbol del mismo nombre. 2. Membrillo o membrillero, árbol que produce los membrillos. **Japan** o **Japanese quince,** membrillo japonés, arbusto de adorno, estimado por sus flores encarnadas o carmesíes.

quincuncial [ˈkwɪnkənʃəl] [kuin-kan-shal], *a.* Que tiene la figura de quincunce o tresbolillo.

quincunx [ˈkwɪnkʌnks] [kuin-kanks], *s.* 1. Quincunce, tresbolillo, plantío de árboles en cuadro, uno en cada esquina y otro en medio. 2. Quincunce. 3. *(Astr.)* el aspecto de un astro distante de otro cinco signos.

quindecagon [ˈkwɪndɪˈkægən] [kuin-di-ka-gon], *s.* Quindecágono, figura de quince lados y otros tantos ángulos.

quinia, quinin, quinine [kwɪˈniːn] [kui-nin], *s.* Quinina, alcaloide activo, febrífugo, que se extrae de la quina.

quinidin, quinidine [ˈkwɪnɪdiːn] [kui-ni-din], *s.* Quinidina, compuesto blanco cristalizable, isómero de la quinina, contenido en la quina.

quinquagesima [ˌkwɪŋkəˈdʒesɪmə] [kuin-kua-ye-si-ma], *s.* Período de cincuenta días. **Quinquagesima Sunday,** domingo de quincuagésima, el que precede al primero de cuaresma.

quinquangular [kwɪŋˈkæŋɡjʊləʳ] [kuin-kuan-guiu-laʳ], *a.* Que tiene cinco ángulos.

quinquefoliate [ˈkwɪŋkwɪfəlɪeɪθ] [kuin-kui-fo-lieit], *a.* Quinquefoliado, quinquedigitado, de cinco hojas.

quinquelobate [ˈkwɪŋkwələbeɪt] [kuin-kue-lo-beit], *a.* Que tiene cinco lóbulos.

quinquennial [ˌkwɪŋˈkwenɪəl] [kuin-kue-nial], *a.* Quinquenal, que dura un quinquenio o sucede una vez en cinco años.

quinquina [ˈkwɪŋkɪnə] [kuin-ki-na], *s.* Quinaquina.

quinsy [ˈkwɪnzɪ] [kuin-si], *s.* Angina, esquinancia, inflamación de las amígdalas, especialmente cuando es supurativa.

quint [kwɪnt] [kuint], *s.* 1. Registro de órgano que suena una quinta más alta que los teclados que se tocan. 2. El conjunto de cinco. 3. La cuerda E del violín. 4. Quinta, cinco cartas de un palo seguidas en orden en algunos juegos.

quintain [ˈkwɪnteɪn] [kuin-tein], o **quintins**, poste o pilar que se ponía antiguamente en los picaderos.

quintal [ˈkwɪntəl] [kuin-tal], *s.* Quintal, el peso de cien libras o cuatro arrobas.

quintessence [kwɪnˈtesns] [kuin-te-sens], *s.* Quintaesencia, lo más puro y acrisolado de cualquiera cosa.

quintessential [ˌkwɪntɪˈsenʃəl] [kuin-ti-sen-shal], *a.* Perteneciente a la quinta esencia. Por excelencia.

quintessentially [ˌkwɪntɪˈsenʃəlɪ] [kuin-ti-sen-sha-li], *adv.* Intrínsecamente, esencialmente.

quintet, quintette [kwɪnˈtet] [kuin-tet], *s.* Quinteto, trozo de música compuesto para cinco voces o cinco instrumentos; también las cinco personas que lo ejecutan.

quintillion [kwɪnˈtɪljən] [kuin-ti-lion], *s.* Número cardinal, entre los franceses y los americanos, la sexta potencia de mil; el guarismo uno seguido de dieciocho ceros; en el sistema inglés, la quinta potencia de un millón.

quintuple [ˈkwɪntjʊpl] [kuin-tiu-pel], *a.* Quíntuplo.

quintuplet [ˈkwɪntjuːplɪt] [kuin-tiu-plit], *s.* Quintillizo.

quip [kwɪp] [kuip], *s.* Pulla, chufleta, dicho picante; chanza pesada, sarcasmo. Ocurrencia, salida. *-vt.* Decir bromeando o haciendo un chiste.

quire [ˈkwaɪəʳ] [kuaiaʳ], *s.* 1. Mano de papel, cuaderno compuesto de 24 o 25 hojas. **Book in quires,** libro en papel o sin coser. 2. Juego de todas las hojas necesarias para hacer un libro; de aquí, libro. 3. *(Ant.)* Coro. V. CHOIR.

quire, *va.* Plegar el papel en manos.

quire, *vn. (Poco us.)* Cantar en concierto, cantar a coro.

quirk [kwɜːk] [kuerk], *s.* 1. Desvío repentino, vuelta corta, recodo. 2. Arranque de la imaginación, capricho, pulla, expresión aguda y picante. 3. Sutileza, delicadeza, distinción artificiosa; argucia, refugio, rodeo. 4. Aire de música muy corto. 5. Copada, caveto, muesca pequeña entre las molduras. 6. Singularidad, peculiaridad. **By a quirk of fate,** por uno de esos caprichos del destino.

quirk, *va.* Acanalar, estriar; hacer copadas o cavetos. **Quirking plane,** cepillo de cavetos.

quirky [ˈkwɜːkɪ] [kuer-ki], *a.* 1. Lleno de argucias, artificioso, que emplea escapatorias. 2. Que consta de vueltas o recodos. 3. Extravagante, estrafalario.

quirt [ˈkwɜːt] [kuert], *s.* Látigo con mango corto de madera o cuero rígido y correa de cuero crudo retorcido.

quisling [ˈkwɪzlɪŋ] [kuis-lin], *s.* Quisling, traidor de su patria.

quit [kwɪt] [kuit], *va. (pret. y pp.* QUIT o QUITTED). 1. Dejar, abandonar, parar, cesar de, desistir; renunciar, ceder, resignar; por extensión, salir, alejarse de. **Quit talking and listen!,** ¡deja de hablar y escucha! 2. *(Ant.)* Pagar; hacer pago de, o para. 3. *(Fam. o des.)* Absolver, dar por libre, descargar; de aquí, desembarazar, justificar. V. ACQUIT. *-vn.* Desistir de, o cesar de hacer una cosa. **To quit an employment,** dejar, abandonar un empleo. **To give notice to quit,** dar aviso o notificar para que se deje una casa, habitación, etc. **To quit work,** cesar de trabajar. **Quit your nonsense,** basta de tonterías. **He quit the place for good,** salió del lugar para siempre. **To quit cost,** pagar los gastos, reembolsar. **To quit scores,** ajustar, arreglar cuentas con alguno, desquitarse con alguien.

quit, *pp.* de To QUIT. Libertado, libre, descargado, absuelto.

quitchgrass [ˈkwɪtʃɡrɑːs] [kuich-gras], *s. (Bot.)* Grama.

quitclaim [ˈkwɪtkleɪm] [kuit-kleim], *va.* Renunciar o ceder un título o reclamación. *-s. (For.)* Renuncia, cesión definitva sin reserva alguna que hace una persona a favor de otra, ya se trate de una demanda, reclamación, litigio judicial, o derecho de acción. **Quitclaim deed,** documento que contiene la renuncia a la propiedad de un terreno.

quite [kwaɪt] [kuait], *adv.* 1. Completamente (completely), perfectamente, totalmente, enteramente, absolutamente. **I quite agree with you,** estoy completamente de acuerdo contigo. **She's not quite ten,** todavía no ha cumplido los diez. 2. En grado considerable, bastante, muy. **It's quite warm today,** hoy hace bastante calor. **Quite a lot of money,** bastante dinero.

quitrent [ˈkwɪtrənt] [kui-trent], *s.* Censo feudal que pagaba antiguamente el dueño de una propiedad y por medio del cual se libraba del servicio feudal.

quits [kwɪts] [kuits], *inter.* En paz: expresión que se usa cuando se paga enteramente un alcance o deuda. **To be quits,** *(Fam.)* Estar o quedar en paz.

quittance [ˈkwɪtəns] [kui-tans], *s.* 1. Finiquito, descargo, desempeño, pago, satisfacción. 2. Recompensa, remuneración.

quitter [ˈkwɪtəʳ] [kui-taʳ], *s.* El que abandona o renuncia una cosa, poco perseverante..

quiver [ˈkwɪvəʳ] [kui-vaʳ], *s.* Carcaj, aljaba.

quiver, *vn.* Temblar, estremecerse.

quivered [ˈkwɪvəd] [kui-vard], *s.* Armado con aljaba; metido como flecha en aljaba.

quivering [ˈkwɪvərɪŋ] [kui-va-rin], *s.* Tremor, temblor.

quixotic [ˈkwɪksɒtɪk] [kuik-so-tik], *a.* Quijotesco, relativo o parecido a Don Quijote; de aquí, romancesco o caballeresco hasta la extravagancia.

quixotism [ˈkwɪksətɪzəm] [kuik-so-ti-sem], *s.* Quijotismo, porte o modo de proceder ridículo.

quiz [kwɪz] [kuis], *s.* 1. Cuestión o sugestión disparatada o poco seria; chanza, chulada, burla: acertijo, enigma. 2. Burlón, zumbón, chancero, candongo, chuleador. 3. *(Fam.)* El acto de preguntar a un díscipulo o a una clase oralmente o por escrito. 4. Concurso (competition), prueba (test). **Quiz show,** programa concurso.

quiz, *va.* 1. Candonguear, chulear, chancear. 2. Mirar con un lente, con un monóculo. 3. Examinar a un díscipulo o clase haciéndoles preguntas. **Quizzing-glass,** monóculo, lente para un ojo.

quizmaster [ˈkwɪzmɑːtəʳ] [kuis-mas-taʳ], *s.* Presentador de un concurso.

quizzical [ˈkwɪzɪkəl] [kui-si-kal], *a.* 1. Burlón, dado a chulear o chasquear. 2. Raro, singular, extraño.

quizzically [ˈkwɪzɪkəlɪ] [kui-si-ka-li], *adv.* Socarronamente, burlonamente.

quodliblet [ˈkwɒdlɪblɪt] [kuod-li-blet], *s.* 1. *(Mús.)* Fantasía, miscelánea, a veces poco armoniosa. 2. Sutileza, punto delicado y disputable.

quodlibetic, quodlibetical [ˌkwɒdlɪˈblɪtɪk] [kuod-li-be-tik], *a.* 1. No restringido a un asunto particular; discutido a voluntad por gusto o curiosidad. 2. Dado a sutilezas y argucias como ejercicio intelectual.

quoif [kɔɪf] [koif], *s.* Cofia, escofieta. V. COIF.

quoin [kɔɪn] [koin], *s.* 1. *(Arq.)* Adarja, piedra saliente, diente, ángulo de una pared: esquina, ángulo exterior de un edificio; clave, piedra cuneiforme con que se cierra el arco o bóveda. *(Mec.)* Cuña o pieza cuneiforme de que se usa para algún fin; cuña de imprenta, para apretar la forma. **Stowing-quoins** *(Mar.)* cuñas de abarrotar, abarrotes. *-va.* Acuñar, meter cuñas.

quoit [kɔɪt] [koit], *s.* Tejo, disco de hierro con un agujero redondo en el centro, de que se usa en un juego parecido al de los tejos. *-pl.* Especie de juego de tejos.

quoit, *vn.* Jugar al tejo. *-va.* Tirar el tejo a la raya.

quondam [ˈkwɒndæm] [kon-dam], *a.* De tiempos anteriores, de otro tiempo, que fue. **My quondam king,** mi antiguo rey o el que fue mi rey en otro tiempo.

quorum [ˈkwɔːrəm] [kuo-rum], *s.* 1. Junta o número suficiente de personas pertenecientes a un cuerpo deliberante o a una corporación para resolver o determinar algún asunto. 2. *(Ingl.)* Comisión especial de jueces de paz.

quota [ˈkwəʊtə] [kuou-ta], *s.* Cuota, parte o porción determinada que toca a cada uno; prorrata, contingente.

Quota of troops, contingente de tropas. **quota system;** sistema de cuotas.

quotable ['kwəʊtəbl] [kuou-ta-bol], *a.* Citable, que puede citarse o es digno de ser citado.

quotation [kwəʊ'teɪʃən] [kuo-tei-shon], *s.* 1. Citación, el acto de citar. 2. Cita, las palabras citadas; párrafo de un libro, citado por vía de aclaración o prueba en apoyo. 3. *(Com.)* Cotización, indicación del precio de las mercancías. 4. **Quotation mark,** virgulilla, signo tipográfico que se pone al principio y al fin de un pasaje citado («...»). En inglés se emplean como invertidas al principio y apóstrofos al fin.

quote ['kwəʊt] [kuout], *va.* 1. Citar, notar, repetir, reproducir un párrafo de un escrito o discurso, como aclaración, autoridad o prueba en apoyo. 2. *(Com.)* Cotizar, indicar el precio de un artículo. -*s.* 1. Cita (passage). 2. Presupuesto (estimate). **Between quotes,** entre comillas.

quoter ['kwəʊtə'] [kuou-ta'], *s.* Citador, el que cita.

quoth [kwəʊθ] [kuouz], *v. imp.* **Quoth I,** dije yo, digo yo. **Quoth he,** él dijo.

quotha ['kwəʊθə] [kuou-za], *inter.* ¡De veras! ¡vaya! Expresa ordinariamente algún desprecio.

quotidian [,kwəʊ'tɪdɪən] [kuou-ti-dian], *a.* Cotidiano, diario, que sucede cada día. -*s.* Calentura cotidiana.

quotient ['kwəʊʃənt] [kuou-shent], *s.* *(Mat.)* Cociente. **Intelligence Quotient, I. Q.,** cociente intelectual.

quoting ['kwəʊtɪŋ] [kuou-tin], *s.* Citación, el acto de citar.

quran ['kuːrən] [ku-ran], *s.* Alcorán. *V.* KORAN.

R

r[ɑːˈ] [aʳ], Se pronuncia en general como en castellano. La *r* sola se pronuncia muchas veces como *rr,* y las dos *rr* como una *r* sola. Cuando es final, se le da al sílaba *er,* cuando es final, se le da el sonido de *ar* o *or,* como si estuviera sola y separada de la dicción; v. g. desire *(desaiar);* digger *(digguer).* Como abreviatura, *R* quiere decir *rey* o *real,* o en las recetas de los médicos, *recipe,* esto es, *toma.*

rabbet ['ræbɪt] [ra-bit], *va. (Carp.)* Acepillar un pedazo de madera para que ajuste con otro; hacer con el inglete una ranura en la madera; rebajar con el guillante.

rabbet, *s.* 1. Ranura, rebajo o ensambladura de dos pedazos de madera, para que encajen uno en otro. **Rabbet-plane,** guillame, cepillo angosto y largo. 2. *(Mar.)* Alefriz.

rabbi ['ræbɪ] [ra-bi], **rabbin** ['ræbɪn] [ra-bin], *s.* Rabí, rabino, el doctor de la ley judaica.

rabbinic, ['ræbɪnɪk] [ra-bi-nik], *a.* Rabínico.

rabbinist ['ræbɪnɪst] [ra-bi-nist], *s.* Rabinista.

rabbit ['ræbɪt] [ra-bit], *s.* 1. Conejo, pequeño animal roedor del género Lepus. **Doe-rabbit,** coneja. **Young rabbit,** gazapillo, gazapo. **Rabbit nest o hole,** conejera. **Welsh rabbit,** *(Fam.)* quesadilla, tostada con queso, queso tostado, sazonado, y que se *s (Arq.)* ralemente con tostada. 2. *(Mar.)* Alefriz.

rabbit-hutch ['ræbɪthʌtʃ] [ra-bit-jach], *sf.* Conejera.

rabbit-warren ['ræbɪt,wɒrən] [ra-bit-uo-ren], *s.* Conejera, conejar; madriguera.

rabble ['ræbl] [ra-bel], *s.* 1. La gentuza, gentualla, canalluza, canalla, chusma, la ínfima plebe (pey). 2. Gentío, muchedumbre (mob). **Rabble-rouser,** agitador. **A rabble arch,** una arenga, una soflama (harangue).

rabble, *s.* Hurgón o botador de punta curva, como el que se usa en las fundiciones.

rabid ['ræbɪd] [ra-bid], *a.* 1. Rabioso, que padece el mal de rabia. 2. Que proviene de la rabia o pertenece a ella. 3. Rabioso, fanático, violento, furioso, feroz (fierce).

rabidly ['ræbɪdlɪ] [ra-bid-li], *adv.* **He's rabidly anti-French,** es un anti-francés rabioso, furibundo.

rabies ['reɪbɪːz] [rei-bis], *s.* Rabia, hidrofobia, enfermedad a menudo mortal que se desarrolla en los perros y se transmite al hombre por la mordedura del animal atacado.

raccoon [rəˈkuːn] [ra-kun], *s.* Mapache, cuadrúpedo carnívoro nocturno de América, de la familia de los úrsidos.

race [reɪs] [reis], *s.* 1. Raza, casta; serie continua de los descendientes que provienen de la misma estirpe; casta, especies de los animales domésticos; descendencia, prole, generación; famlia, tribu, pueblo. 2. Linaje, generación, genealogía. 3. Clase, especie de seres o animales con caracteres que los unen o los separan de otros. 4. *(Ant.)* Sabor o gusto particular, como el del vino. *(Fr.)* **The human race,** el género humano. **Race riot,** disturbio racial.

race, *s.* 1. Carrera, apuesta, lucha de velocidad, ya sea a pie o a caballo; en botes o yates, en trineos o coches, nadando o patinando; carreras para ganar un premio. **Boat race,** regata. **To run in a race,** tomar parte en una carrera. 2. De aquí, una competencia cualquiera. 3. Progresión, y particularmente carrera, movimiento acelerado. 4. Duración de la vida; curso, carrera. 5. Corriente de agua violenta o rápida o el canal para ella; canal estrecho, caz, saetín. 6. Paso, carrera de la lanzadera. **To run a race,** luchar a la carrera, a correr. **The Derby races,** las carreras de Derby. **Race-course,** 1. Lugar o campo para carreras. 2. Canal de molino, saetín. **Race-cup,** premio de carrera. **Race-ground,** campo de carreras; terreno dispuesto para las carreras de caballos. **Race-horse,** caballo criado para las carreras.

race, *va.* 1. Obligar a correr de prisa (como para ganar un premio). 2. Correr, disputar el premio de una carrera. -*vn.* 1. Correr con mucha ligereza, de prisa. 2. Moverse la maquinaria a un paso acelerado.

racecard ['reɪskɑːd] [reis-kard], *sm.* Programa de carreras.

racer ['reɪsə'] [rei-sa'], *s.* 1. Corredor, el que disputa el premio de la carrera o corre por apuesta. 2. Caballo de carrera.

race track ['reɪstræk] [reis-trak], *s.* Hipódromo.

raceway ['reɪsweɪ] [reis-uei], *s.* Canal de agua artificial, canal de molino.

rachitic [rəˈkaɪtɪk] [ra-ki-tik], *a.* 1. Raquítico, que padece raquitis. 2. Perteneciente a una raquis.

racial ['reɪʃəl] [rei-shal], *a.* Racial. **Racial integration,** integración racial. **Racial segregation,** separación racial. **Racial pride,** orgullo de raza.

racialism ['reɪʃəlɪzəm] [rei-sha-li-sem], *s. (G.B.)* Racismo.

racialist ['reɪʃəlɪst] [rei-sha-list], *a. (G.B.)* Racista.

racially ['reɪʃəlɪ] [rei-sha-li], *adv.* Racialmente, desde un punto de vista racial.

racing ['reɪsɪŋ] [rei-sin], *s.* **Horse racing,** carreras de caballos. -*a.* De carreras. **Racing car,** coche de carreras.

racism ['reɪsɪzəm] [rei-si-sem], *s.* Racismo, creencia en la superiordiad racial de un grupo.

racist ['reɪsɪst] [rei-sist], *s.* Racista. -*a.* Racista.

rack [ræk] [rak], *s.* 1. Estante (shelf). **Clothes rack,** perchero. **Drying rack,** tendedero. 2. Instrumento para extender alguna cosa: tormento; potro o cuestión de tormento. **To put to the rack,** dar tormento. 3. Dolor, pena, angustia. 4. Rueca, palo a que se afirma el lino para hilarlo. 5. Cremallera, barra dentada que se mueve por medio de una rueda dentada también. **Rack and pinion,** engranaje de cremallera y piñón. 6. Morillos de asador. 7. Enrejado de madera dentro del cual se pone el heno para el ganado. 8. Nubarrón. 9. Astillero o percha en que se ponen astas, picas o lanzas. **Racks of a cart,** adrales, laderas de carro. 10. Destrucción. **To go to rack and ruin,** caer en ruinas y destrucción.

rack, *va.* 1. Dar tormento. 2. Atormentar, afligir, molestar, sacudir (shake). **I was racked with pain,** sufría dolores atroces. **She was racked with guilt,** estaba atormentada por el remordimiento. 3. Apretar, oprimir con exacciones violentas. 4. Vagar o moverse apresuradamente de una parte a otra. 5. Trasegar, mudar el licor de una vasija a otra. **To rack wine,** trasegar el vino. 6. Alargar, extender. **Rack up,** acumular.

racket ['rækɪt] [ra-kit], *s.* 1. Baraúnda, confusión (noise). 2. Jerga, habla confusa. 3. *(Dep.)* Raqueta, paleta para jugar al volante. 4. *(Fam.)* Tinglado, asunto turbio.

racketeer ['rækɪtɪəʳ] [ra-ki-tiaʳ], s. Mafioso.

racking ['rækɪŋ] [ra-kin], s. 1. Tortura. 2. Remordimiento de conciencia; tortura de ánimo. 3. Trasiego de vino u otros licores.

rack-rent ['rækrent] [rak-rent], s. Arriendo o arrendamiento exorbitante.

raconteur [ˌrækɒn'tɜːʳ] [ra-kon-teʳ], a. 1. Picante, lleno de interés, vigoroso (estilo o lenguaje), brioso, animado (lively). 2. De aroma o sabor peculiar, agradable y característico. 3. Perteneciente a la raza, al tipo o al origen.

radar ['reɪdɑːʳ] [rei-daʳ], s. (Radio) Radar.

radial ['reɪdɪəl] [rei-dial], a. 1. Que pertenece al radio, o al rayo; que parte del centro, que tiene radios. **Radial tire,** neumático radial. 2. (Zool.) Radial, perteneciente al hueso radio, o a una parte divergente del centro. 3. (Bot.) Perteneciente a la ligulada de la flor compuesta.

radiance ['reɪdɪəns] [rei-dians], s. Brillo, resplandor, esplendor, brillantez, lucimiento.

radiant ['reɪdɪənt] [rei-diant], a. Radiante, radioso, resplandeciente, brillante (bright). -s. 1. (Geom.) Línea recta que procede de un punto dado, alrededor del cual se supone que gira. 2. Punto luminoso de donde emana la luz. 3. Lo que despide rayos.

radiantly ['reɪdɪəntlɪ] [rei-diant-li], adv. Con brillo, con esplendor, con alegría.

radiate ['reɪdɪeɪt] [rei-dieit], vn. Radiar, despedir o arrojar rayos de luz, salir como los rayos de luz; echar rayos, centellear, relumbrar. -va. Dar luz, llenar de luz, iluminar, irradiar. **Heat radiates from the sun,** el sol irradia calor.

radiated ['reɪdɪeɪtɪd] [rei-dieitid], a. 1. Radiado, dispuesto en forma de radio, que parte de un centro común. 2. Partido o separado en rayos, o marcado en rayos. 3. (Zool.) Radiado, que tiene simetría de radios; perteneciente a la división de los animales radiados. 4. (Bot.) Que tiene florecillas liguladas.

radiation [ˌreɪdɪ'eɪʃən] [rei-diei-shon], s. (Fís.) Radiación, irradiación. **Radiation sickness,** enfermedad, provocada por la radiación.

radiator ['reɪdɪeɪtəʳ] [rei-diei-taʳ], s. Radiador.

radical ['rædɪkəl] [ra-di-kal], a. 1. Radical. 2. Extremo. 3. Extremista. -s. Radical.

radicalism ['rædɪkəlɪzəm] [ra-di-ka-li-sem], s. Radicalismo.

radicalize ['rædɪkəlaɪz] [ra-di-ka-lais], vt. Radicalizar.

radically ['rædɪkəlɪ] [ra-di-ka-li], adv. Radicalmente.

radicand ['rædɪkænd] [ra-di-kand], s. Radicando.

radicate ['rædɪkeɪt] [ra-di-keit], va. Arraigar.

radio ['reɪdɪəʊ] [rei-diou], s. 1. Radio (receiver), radio (broadcasting, medium). 2. Radiocomunicación. **Radio amateur,** radioaficionado. **Radio announcer,** locutor de radio. **Radio astronomy,** radioastronomía. **Radio beacon,** radiobaliza, radiofaro. **Radio broadcasting,** radiodifusión. **Radio communication,** radiocomunicación, radiotelecomunicación. **Radio compass, Radio direction finder.** radiocompás. **Radio frequency,** radiofrecuencia. **Radio listener,** radioescucha, radioyente. **Radio message,** radiograma. **Radio navigation,** 1. Radionavegación. 2. (Aer.) Radioaviación. **Radio navigator,** radionavegante. **Radio operator,** radiotelegrafista. **Radio station,** radiodifusora, estación. **Radio telescope,** radiotelescopio. **Radio tube,** lámpara de radio, válvula. **Radio wave meter,** ondímetro.

radio, vi. Llamar por radio, transmitir por radio un mensaje. **To radio for help,** pedir ayuda por radio.

radioactive ['reɪdɪəʊ'æktɪv] [rei-diou-ak-tiv], a. Radiactivo, radioactivo.

radioactivity ['reɪdɪəʊæk'tɪvɪtɪ] [rei-diou-ak-ti-vi-ti], s. Radiactividad, radioactividad.

radiobiology [ˌreɪdɪəʊbaɪ'ɒlədʒɪ] [rei-diou-baio-lo-yi], s. Radiobiología.

radiocarbon [ˌreɪdɪəʊ'kɑːbən] [rei-diou-kar-bon], s. Radiocarbono. **Radiocarbon dating,** determinación de antigüedad con radiocarbono.

radiogram ['reɪdɪəʊgræm] [rei-diou-gram], s. Radiograma.

radiograph ['reɪdɪəʊgrɑːf] [rei-diou-graf], s. Radiografía. -va. Radiografiar.

radiographer [ˌreɪdɪ'ɒgrəfəʳ] [rei-dio-gra-faʳ], s. Radiógrafo.

radiography [ˌreɪdɪ'ɒgrəfɪ] [rei-dio-gra-fi], s. Radiografía.

radioisotope ['reɪdɪəʊ'aɪsətəʊp] [rei-diou-ai-so-toup], s. Radioisótopo.

radiolocation [ˌreɪdɪəʊlə'keɪʃən] [rei-diou-lo-kei-shon], s. Radiolocalización.

radiologist [ˌreɪdɪ'ɒlədʒɪst] [rei-dio-lo-yist], s. Radiólogo.

radiology [ˌreɪdɪ'ɒlədʒɪ] [rei-dio-lo-yi], s. Radiología.

radiometer [ˌreɪdɪəʊ'miːtəʳ] [rei-diou-mi-taʳ], s. Radiómetro.

radiophone ['reɪdɪəʊfəʊn] [rei-diou-foun], s. 1. Radioteléfono. 2. (Fís.) Radiófono.

radiophoto ['reɪdɪəfətəʊ] [rei-dio-fo-tou], s. Radiofotografía.

radioscopy [ˌreɪdɪ'ɒskəpɪ] [rei-dios-ko-pi], s. Radioscopia.

radio set ['reɪdɪəʊset] [rei-diou-set], s. Aparato de radio.

radiotelephone ['reɪdɪəʊ'telɪfəʊn] [rei-diou-te-li-foun], s. 1. Radiotelefonía. 2. Radioteléfono.

radiotherapy ['reɪdɪəʊ'θerəpɪ] [rei-diou-ze-ra-pi], s. Radioterapia.

radish ['rædɪʃ] [ra-dish], s. Rábano.

radium ['reɪdɪəm] [rei-diom], s. Radio

radius ['reɪdɪəs] [rei-dios], s. Radio.

radon ['reɪdɒn] [rei-don], s. Radón.

raffia ['ræfɪə] [ra-fia], s. Rafia.

raffish ['ræfɪʃ] [ra-fish], a. 1. Chillón, vulgar (coarse). 2. Extravagante, adefesio.

raffle ['ræfl] [ra-fel], va. y vn. Rifar, sortear. **To raffle off,** rifar. -s. Rifa, sorteo, tómbola. **Charity raffle,** tómbola (de beneficiencia).

raft [rɑːft] [raft], s. 1. (Naut.) Balsa, almadía; jangada. 2. (E.U.) Amontonamiento de troncos de árboles en un río. 3. (Ger.) Gran número, montón (large amount).

raft, va. Llevar sobre una balsa o jangada.

rafter ['rɑːftəʳ] [raf-taʳ], s. Cabrio, viga.

raftport ['rɑːftpɔːt] [raft-port], s. (Mar.) Porta de cañón, tronera.

rag [ræg] [rag], s. 1. Trapo, andrajo, harapo, jirón (piece of cloth). **Rag doll,** muñeca de trapo. 2. pl. Vestidos usados, rasgados. 3. Canto agudo o saliente de un trozo de metal o de una roca; risco. 4. (Coloq.) Periodicucho.

ragamuffin ['rægəmʌfɪn] [ra-ga-ma-fin], s. 1. Andrajoso, hombre vil y despreciable; mendigo, pordiosero; trapiento, pelagatos, chispero. 2. Pilluelo, golfillo.

rage [reɪdʒ] [reich], s. 1. Rabia, ira, enojo, furor, arrebato de cólera. **I'm in a rage,** estoy furioso. 2. Furor, furia (violent anger), violencia, vehemencia, intensidad extrema (things). 3. Ardor, anhelo. 4. (Fam.) Antojo, cosa que todos o muchos desean con vehemencia; boga, moda (fashion).

rage, vn. 1. Rabiar, enojarse, enfurecerse, encolerizarse. **I raged against this TV program,** protesté furiosamente contra ese programa de televisión. 2. Rugir, bramar, arder furiosamente. **The fire raged for five days,** el furioso incendio se prolongó durante cinco días.

ragged ['rægɪd] [ra-guid], a. 1. Roto, andrajoso, harapiento. 2. Desigual, escabroso, áspero.

raging ['reɪdʒɪŋ] [rei-yin], a. Furioso, violento, rabioso.

ragingly ['reɪdʒɪŋlɪ] [rei-yin-li], adv. Furiosamente, airadamente.

raglan ['ræglən] [ra-glan], s. Raglán, gabán holgado de hombre. **Raglan sleeves,** mangas raglán (muy holgadas, típicas de dicho gabán).

ragman ['rægmən] [rag-man], s. Trapero.

ragout [ræ'guː] [ra-gu], s. Guisado, estofado.

ragstone ['rægstəʊn] [rag-stoun], s. Especie de piedra de amolar.

ragtime ['rægtaɪm] [rag-taim], s. Música popular sincopada.

ragweed ['rægwiːd] [rag-uid], s. (Bot.) Ambrosía.

raid [reɪd] [reid], va. o vn. 1. (Mil.) Invadir, súbitamente, como para hacer la guerra o pillar. **The police raided the building,** la policía hizo una redada en el edificio. 2. (Fam.) Entrar o apoderarse por fuerza legal. -vn. Merodear, hacer una invasión, pillar. -*s.* Correría, irrupción, incursión hostil; invasión repentina, prendimiento. **Air raid,** ataque aéreo.

raider ['reɪdəʳ] [rei-daʳ], *s.* Asaltante (attacker, robber), atracador.

rail [reɪl] [reil], *s.* 1. Barra, baranda, barandilla, antepecho, barrera. 2. Riel, carril, raíl. 3. *(Mar.)* Batayola, cairel, galón. **Head-rails.** *(Mar.)* Perchas. **Rough-tree-rails,** *(Mar.)* Barandas. **Waist-rails,** *(Mar.)* Varengas. 4. Carril, considerado como medio de transporte. **By rail,** por ferrocarril. **To run off the rails,** descarrilar. **Rail card,** tarjeta de descuento para viajes en tren.

rail, *s.* Ave zancuda, género típico de la familia de los rálidos; tiene las alas y la cola cortas, las patas, los dedos y el pico largos.

rail, *va.* 1. Cercar con balaustradas, barandillas o barreras. 2. Poner rieles o carriles. -*vn.* Injuriar de palabra, emplear un lenguaje insolente y ultrajante; decir mal; se emplea con *at* o *against.*

railer ['reɪləʳ] [rei-laʳ], *s.* Maledicente, murmurador (gossip).

railing ['reɪlɪŋ] [rei-lin], *s.* 1. Serie de barras; barandilla, balaustrada, cerca, estacada, verja, enverjado. 2. Carriles, material para una vía férrea. 3. Lenguaje injurioso.

raillery ['reɪləri] [rei-la-ri], *s.* Chocarrería, bufonada satírica, burla.

railroad ['reɪlrəʊd] [reil-roud], *va. (E. U.)* 1. Apresurar, hacer algo rápidamente, como con la rapidez de un tren. **She was railroaded into accepting the offer,** la apremiaron para que aceptara la oferta. 2. Condenar injustamente (convict unfairly).

railway ['reɪlweɪ] [reil-uei], *s.* (En la Gran Breataña se usa más la palabra *railway;* en los Estados Unidos, *railroad).* 1. Ferrocarril, vía férrea, camino de hierro sobre el que van los coches o material rodante. 2. Sistema de carriles, estaciones, material rodante, etc., empleado en el transporte por ferrocarril 3. Corporación o personas que poseen o explotan una línea férrea. **Railroad car,** carro, coche de ferrocarril. **Railroad crossing,** encrucijada, crucero; cruce de vía; también, lugar en que el camino ordinario corta la vía férrea. **Railroad gauge,** entrevía, anchura entre los carriles de una vía férrea. **Railroad siding,** desviadero, vía suplementaria; en Cuba, chucho. **Street railroad o railway,** ferrocarril urbano, tranvía, sea eléctrico o de sangre. **Narrow-gauge railway,** ferrocarril de vía estrecha o angosta.

raiment ['reɪmənt] [rei-ment], *s.* Ropa, traje, prendas de vestir.

rain [reɪn] [rein], *vn.* Llover. **It rains,** llueve. **To rain pitchforks,** llover a cántaros. **Rain or shine,** que llueva o no, con buen o mal tiempo, pase lo que pase (whatever the situation). -*va.* Hacer llover, hacer caer alguna cosa en mucha abundancia. **Rain down,** llover. **Insults rained down on you,** le llovieron insultos. **Rain out, rain off,** suspenderse, cancelarse.

rain, *s.* 1. Lluvia. 2. Caída de lluvia; caída de alguna cosa a manera de lluvia. **Heavy rain,** aguacero. **The rains,** la estación de las lluvias. **Rain cloud,** nube de lluvia.

rainbow ['reɪnbəʊ] [rein-bou], *s.* Arco iris. **Rainbow trout,** trucha arco iris.

raincoat ['reɪnkəʊt] [rein-kout], *s.* Impermeable, abrigo impermeable.

rainfall ['reɪnfɔːl] [rein-fol], *s.* 1. Aguacero, caída de lluvia. 2. Cantidad de lluvia y de nieve derretida y medida como lluvia, que cae en un período de tiempo determinado.

rain forest ['reɪnˌfɒrɪst] [rein-fo-rist], *s.* Bosque húmedo, bosque tropical, bosque de zona de gran precipitación pluvial.

rain-ga(u)ge ['reɪngeɪdʒ] [rein-gueich], *s.* Pluviómetro, udómetro, pluvímetro, instrumento para medir la lluvia que cae en lugar y tiempo dados.

rainproof ['reɪnpruːf] [rein-pruf], *a.* Impermeable, a prueba de lluvia.

rain storm ['reɪnstɔːm] [rein-storm], *s.* Temporal de lluvias.

rain water ['reɪnwɔːtəʳ] [rein-uo-taʳ], *s.* Agua llovediza, agua de lluvia.

rainy ['reɪnɪ] [rei-ni], *a.* Lluvioso. **Rainy season,** estación de las lluvias.

raise [reɪz] [reis], *va.* 1. Levantar, alzar, poner en pie, poner derecho. 2. Levantar, construir, fabricar, edificar (build). 3. Levantar, aumentar, subir, dar mayor incremento, mayor valor o un precio más alto a alguna cosa. 4. Levantar, engrandecer, enhiestar, elevar, ensalzar, exaltar, promover. 5. Animar, excitar, incitar, poner en movimiento. 6. Causar, ocasionar, producir, hacer nacer, hacer crecer, criar; cultivar (cultivate) hacer concebir, inspirar, dar lugar a, hacer surgir, hacer brotar. **We raise cattle,** nos dedicamos a la cría de ganado. 7. Resucitar, vivificar, dar vida, revivir, poner en estado de actividad o vigor. **Lazarus was raised from the dead,** Lázaro resucitó de entre los muertos. 8. Levantar, reclutar, alistar. 9. Sacar contribuciones, recaudar (collect); recoger o juntar dinero sacándoselo a otros por cualquier medio. 10. Levantar, quitar o oven impuesto, poner fin a. **To raise a siege,** levantar un sitio. **To raise an outery,** exclamar; armar un alboroto. **To raise the country,** sublevar, alborotar, revolucionar un país. **To raise the nap of the cloth,** perchar los paños, sacarles el pelo con el palmar. **To raise the dust,** hacer o levantar polvo. **To raise the curtain** (en el teatro), correr o levantar el telón.

raise, *s.* Aumento, subida de sueldo.

raiser ['reɪzəʳ] [rei-saʳ], *s.* 1. Levantador, el que alza o levanta; el que engrandece, exalta o ensalza. 2. Causador, productor, autor. 3. Fundador (founder). 4. El que saca contribuciones; el que levanta ejércitos.

raisin ['reɪzən] [rei-san], *s.* Pasa, la uva seca. **Bloom raisins,** pasas gorronas.

raising ['reɪzɪŋ] [rei-sing], *s.* 1. Crianza. 2. Levantamiento. 3. Izamiento (de una bandera, etc.).

raja, rajah ['rɑːdʒə] [ra-cha], *s.* Rajá, soberano de la India.

rake [reɪk] [reik], *s.* 1. Rastro, mielga, rastrillo (garden tool), instrumento de los labradores y hortelanos. 2. *(Mar.)* Lanzamiento, la caída para afuera de la roda o codaste. 3. Calavera, tunante, libertino o perdido (contracción de *Rakehell)* **Coal rake or oven rake,** hurgón.

rake, *va.* 1. Recoger con rastrillo, rastrillar; raer. 2. Rebuscar, escudriñar, buscar, mirar o examinar con atención. 3. Pasar por encima con el movimiento de un rastrillo; raspar ligeramente. 4. Cubrir, arrastrando tierra u otra cosa. 5. *(Mil.)* Enfilar, tiarar a lo largo de; *(Mar.)* barrer de popa a proa. -*vn.* 1. Usar del rastro o de la mielga. 2. Buscar a tientas, buscar minuciosamente, escudriñar; ahorrar, acumular con cuidado. 3. Pasar con rapidez o violencia. 4. Tunar, vaguear, andar vagando, vivir, como un libertino. *(Fam.)* **They are raking it in,** están haciendo mucho dinero, se están forrando. **Rake over,** rastrillar, volver sobre. **Rake up,** rastrillar, conseguir.

rake, *vn.* Inclinarse, estar fuera de la perpendicular.

rake-off ['reɪkɒf] [reik-of], *s. (Coloq.)* Tajada, pellizco.

raker ['reɪkəʳ] [rei-kaʳ], *s.* 1. Raedera, raspadera. 2. Rastrillador, raedor; el que recoge alguna cosa con rastro o rastrillo.

rakish ['reɪkɪʃ] [rei-kish], *a.* 1. Libertino, licencioso, perdido, disoluto (dissolute). 2. Desenfadado (casual, jaunty). **They wear their hats at a rakish angle,** llevan el sombrero ladeado con gracia o desenfado. 3. *(Mar.)* Que tiene los mástiles inclinados hacia atrás de una manera insólita.

rally ['rælɪ] [ra-li], *va.* 1. *(Mil.)* Reunir y reanimar, rehacer, replegar, volver a juntar las tropas fugitvas o dispersas y ponerlas de nuevo en orden. 2. Ridiculizar; dar chanza o zumba. -*vn.* 1. Recuperarse, reponerse (recover). *(Fin.)* Repuntar, recuperarse. 2. *(Mil.)* Reunirse (gather), reanimarse; recobrar las fuerzas, el vigor. 3. Burlarse de alguno, chancearse, zumbarse. **A rallying-word,** grito o voz de batalla o de guerra: voz para animar las tropas o la gente. **They all rallied round him,** todos acudieron a ofrecerle apoyo.

rally, *s.* 1. Unión o reunión pronta para un fin común, v. gr. de tropas dispersas. Concentración (mass meeting). **Political rally,** mitin. 2. Recuperación, acto de recobrar la condición normal después de un período de agotamiento o depresión;

acción rápida y vigorosa de cualquier especie. 3. *(Dep.)* Peloteo. 4. *(Fin.)* Repunte. 5. *(Med.)* Mejoría.

ram [ræm] [ram], *s.* 1. *(Zool.)* Morueco, carnero padre. 2. Instrumento para dar o aplastar con golpes fuertes, pisón. 3. Espolón, remate de la proa de los buques acorazados; también, ariete, buque blindado con espolón. 4. Ariete, máquina militar para batir las murallas. 5. Aries, signo del zodíaco.

ram, *va.* 1. Apisonar, dar, golpear, con un pisón, espolón o ariete. 2. Impeler con violencia, hacer entrar por fuerza; apretar; atacar un arma. 3. Atestar, henchir, atracar. **To ram down a paving,** apisonar o pisonar el empedrado. *-vi.* Estrellarse, chocar contra algo o alguien. **Ram home,** hacer entender a la fuerza.

Ramadan [ˈræməˈdæn] [ra-ma-dan], *s.* Ramadán, la cuaresma de los mahometanos, noveno mes del año musulmán.

ramble [ˈræmbl̩] [ram-bel], *vn.* 1. Vagar, corretear, ir a la ventura, andar vagando sin dirección fija, pasear (walk). 2. Hacer algo o hablar sin objeto determinado. 3. Dar vueltas, serpentear. 4. Mostrar falta o carencia de plan o sistema: se dice de las cosas. 5. Divagar, irse por las ramas (digress). **Ramble on,** divagar sobre algo.

ramble, *s.* 1. Correría, acción de ir de una parte a otra sin dirección, sin objeto fijo, paseo, caminata (long walk). 2. Sendero que serpentea, que tiene muchas vueltas y revueltas. **I will go for a ramble,** iréa dar un paseo.

rambler [ˈræmblər] [ram-blar], *s.* 1. Vagabundo, vagamundo, tunante, callejero. 2. Excursionista (walker). 3. Rosa trepadora.

rambling [ˈræmblɪŋ] [ram-bling], *a.* 1. Que se va por las ramas, que divaga. 2. Laberíntico, intrincado. 3. Trepador. *- s. (Dep.)* Excursionismo.

ramification [ˌræmɪfɪˈkeɪʃən] [ra-mi-fi-kei-shon], *s.* Ramificación, repercusión.

ramify [ˈræmɪfaɪ] [ra-mi-fai], *vn.* Ramificarse, dividirse en ramas. *-va.* Dividir una cosa en ramificaciones.

ramjet [ˈræmdʒet] [ram-yet], *s. (Aer.)* **Ramjet engine,** motor de retropropulsión a base de aire comprimido y combustible.

rammer [ˈræmər] [ra-mar], *s.* 1. Maza. **Paving rammer,** pisón, empedrador. 2. Atacador. 3. La baqueta de fusil o escopeta.

rammish [ˈræmɪʃ] [ra-mish], *a.* Que huele a chotuno: también libidinoso.

ramose [ˈræməʊz] [ra-mous], *a.* Ramoso.

ramp [ræmp] [ramp], *s.* 1. Rampa (slope), declive, desnivel. 2. *(Des.)* Salto, brinco, pernada, zancada.

ramp, *vn.* 1. Saltar, brincar, bailar, enredar o divertirse dando saltos o brincos. 2. Trepar como planta. *-va.* Sesgar.

rampage [ˈræmpeɪdʒ] [ram-peich], *s. (Fam.)* Alboroto, agitación turbulenta; brinco dado con cólera o violencia. *-vi.* Pasar arrasando.

rampancy [ˈræmpənsɪ] [ram-pan-si], *s.* Exuberancia (lushness), superabundancia, extravagancia en acciones o sentimientos.

rampant [ˈræmpənt] [ram-pant], *a.* 1. Exuberante, excesivo, desenfrenado (unbridled), no restringido: lozano, que crece con abundancia. 2. Endémico. **Disease was rampant,** proliferaban las enfermedades. 2. *(Her.)* Rampante, en ademán de agarrar o asir. 3. *(Arq.)* Que tiene un estribo o contrafuerte más alto que otro.

rampart [ˈræmpɑːt] [ram-part], *s.* 1. Plataforma, terraplén (bank); muralla (wall), el terraplén con su parapeto. 2. Baluarte, amparo, defensa.

rampion [ˈræmpɪən] [ram-pion], *s. (Bot.)* Rapónchigo.

ramrod [ˈræmrɒd] [ram-rod], *s.* Baqueta de fusil (rod); atacador de cañón.

ramshackle [ˈræmˌʃækl̩] [ram-sha-kel], *a.* Próximo a caerse en pedazos; viejo y descuidado, poco sólido, destartalado.

ran [ræn] [ran], *pret.* de TO RUN.

ranch [rɑːntʃ] [ranch], *s. (E. U. del Oeste)* 1. Rancho, granja donde se cría ganado en grande escala. 2. Granja.

rancher [ˈrɑːntʃər] [ran-cha'], *s.* Hacendado, dueño de un rancho, ranchera.

ranch house [ˈrɑːntʃˌhɑʊs] [ranch-jaus], *s.* Casa, chalet de una sola planta, bungalow.

ranching [ˈrɑːntʃɪŋ] [ran-chin], *sf. (E.U.)* Ganadería.

rancid [ˈrænsɪd] [ran-sid], *a.* Rancio, de olor o gusto fuerte, el de substancias oleosas que empiezan a echarse a perder; acedo; rancioso. **To go rancid,** ponerse rancio.

rancidness [ˈrænsɪdnes] [ran-sid-nes], **rancidity** [rænˈsɪdɪtɪ] [ran-si-di-ti], *s.* Rancidez, ranciadura, lo rancio; olor rancioso, como el del aceite añejo.

rancor [ˈræŋkər] [ran-ko'], *s.* Rencor (spite), enemistad antigua, encono, inquina, malicia (malice), odio profundo.

rancorous [ˈræŋkərəs] [ran-ko-ros], *a.* Rencoroso: vengativo, malévolo.

rancour, *s. V.* RANCOR.

rand [rænd] [rand], *s.* Calzo del zapato.

random [ˈrændəm] [ran-dom], *s.* 1. Falta de propósito o intención definidos; ventura, acaso; se emplea hoy sólo en la locución. **At random,** a la aventura, por acaso; a diestro y siniestro, al tuntún, a trochemoche. 2. Desatino, desacierto; cosa hecha o escogida sin método. *-a.* Fortuito, impensado, casual; desatinado, al azar. **Random shot,** *(Art.)* Tiro por elevación. **Random access,** acceso aleatorio o directo. **Random-access memory,** memoria de acceso aleatorio o directo.

randomly [ˈrændɒmlɪ] [ran-dom-li], *adv.* Al azar.

randy, randie [ˈrændɪ] [ran-di], *a.* 1. *(Esco.)* Desordenado, tumultuoso, alborotado. 2. *(Coloq.)* Caliente, cachondo (horny).

rang [ræŋ] [rang], *pret.* de TO RING.

range [reɪndʒ] [reindch], *va.* 1. Recorrer, pasar, repasar, particularmente buscando alguna cosa; andar vagando; navegar, pasar cerca de la costa. 2. Colocar (place), ordenar, poner en hileras, en filas; arreglar. 3. Arreglar, clasificar, disponer en clases, divisiones sistemáticas o partidos, colocar en orden. *-vn.* 1. Vagar. 2. Colocarse; proseguir un rumbo. 3. Extenderse, estar situado en la misma dirección o en una línea paralela a otra; de aquí, tomar el mismo partido. 4. Variar, pasar de un punto a otro. **The thermometer may range forty degrees in one day,** el termómetro puede variar cuarenta grados *(Fah.)* en un día. 5. Tener lugar igual o correspondiente. 6. Ir, caminar,. se dice de los proyectiles con referencia a su alcance y dirección.

range, *s.* 1. Extensión o espacio en que cabe alguna cosa o al través del cual se mueve, período de tiempo que separa las reapariciones periódicas de una cosa; duración. 2. Vasta extensión de terrenos de pasto. 3. Alcance, v. g. el de un arma de fuego; extensión en que se hace sentir una influencia; duración. **It was out of range,** estaba fuera de alcance. 4. *(Mús.)* Registro. 5. Fila, hilera, ringlera, línea. 6. Gama (variety). 7. Línea de un tiro de artillería; sitio para tirar al blanco. **Range of a cable,** *(Mar.)* Cornamusas, piezas para amarrar varios cabos de labor. **Range of mountains,** cordillera de montañas, cadena de montañas (chain).

rangefinder [ˈreɪndʒˌfaɪndər] [reindch-fain-da'], *s. (Mil.)* Telémetro.

ranger [ˈreɪndʒər] [reind-cha'], *s.* 1. Guardamayor de bosque. 2. Tunante, tuno, bribón, ladrón. 3. Perro ventor. 4. Soldado de las tropas de asalto en EE.UU.

Rangoon [ræŋˈɡuːn] [ran-gun], *s.* Rangún.

rangy [ˈreɪndʒɪ] [rein-yi], *a.* Largo y delgado, larguirucho.

rank [ræŋk] [rank], *a.* 1. Lozano, exuberante, fértil; espeso, cerrado 2. Rancio, que tiene olor fuerte y desabrido, repugnante (revolting), fétido. 3. Insigne, acabado, rematado. 4. Grosero, áspero, basto. 5. Flagrante (glaring). *-s.* 1. Fila (line), la serie de hombres puestos en línea; hilera, ringlera. **To break lines,** romper filas. 2. Clase, orden, grado de dignidad, categoría (status). 3. Calidad, dignidad o empleo honorífico. **A man of rank,** hombre de condición o de distinción.

rank, *va.* Poner en fila, colocar, ordenar (arrange), disponer, estar clasificado. **She's ranked first,** está clasificado primero. -*vn.* Colocarse, alinearse.

ranking ['ræŋkɪŋ] [ran-kin], *s.* Clasificación, ranking. -*a.* De grado superior o más alto.

rankish ['ræŋkɪʃ] [ran-kish], *s.* Algo rancio.

rankle ['ræŋkl] [ran-kel], *vn.* Enconarse, inflamarse, irritarse. -*vi.* Doler. **What still rankles with me,** lo que todavía me duele, lo que no le puedo perdonar.

rankly ['ræŋklɪ] [ran-kli], *adv.* 1. Toscamente, groseramente. 2. Pomposamente. 3. Ranciamente.

rankness ['ræŋknɪs] [rank-nes], *s.* 1. Exuberancia, fertilidad, fecundidad, abundancia (abundance). 2. Olor muy fuerte. 3. Carácter excesivo.

ransack ['rænsæk] [ran-sak], *va.* 1. Escudriñar, rebuscar, explorar o registrar todas las partes de (search). 2. *(Des.)* Saquear, pillar, robar (pillage).

ransacking ['rænsækɪŋ] [ran-sa-kin], *s.* Rebusco.

ransom ['rænsəm] [ran-som], *s.* 1. Rescate, la cantidad que se paga para obtener la libertad de un preso o de un esclavo, o de mercancías capturadas o retenidas; también, en otros tiempos, multa considerable. 2. Rescate, obtención de la libertad mediante el pago de una suma. **Ransom demand,** nota exigiendo un rescate.

ransom, *va.* Rescatar, redimir, librar el cautiverio, de presidio, etc., pagando un rescate o una indemnización.

ransomless ['rænsəmlɪs] [ran-som-les], *a.* Irrescatable, irredimible, que no se puede rescatar o redimir.

rant [rænt] [rant], *vn.* Declamar con extravagancia, delirar, disparatar; vocear.

rant, *s.* Lenguaje altisonante, campanudo, retumbante.

ranter ['rɒntər] [ran-tar], *s.* Declamador, orador que emplea vehemencia inútil, energúmeno.

ranunculus [rə'nʌŋkjələs] [ra-na-kiu-los], *s.* *(Bot.)* Ranúnculo, botón de oro; género de plantas y su flor, típico de las ranunculáceas.

rap [ræp] [rap], *va.* y *vn.* 1. Golpear o dar un golpe vivo y repentino (knock). **To rap at the door,** tocar o llamar a la puerta. 2. Proferir de una manera seca y violenta, amonestar, reprender (rebuke). 3. *(Coloq.)* Cotorrear (chat).

rap, *va.* *(pret.* y *pp.* RAPT o RAPPED). 1. Arrebatar; generalmente en el participio pasado *rapt.* 2. Quitar, tomar alguna cosa con violencia; tomar ávidamente para llevárselo.

rap, *s.* 1. Golpe (blow), ligero y vivo o el sonido de él; sopapo. **A rap on the knuckles,** golpecito dado sobre los artejos. 2. Medio penique falso o contrahecho; de aquí fruslería, cosa sin valor. **I don't care a rap,** no se me da (importa) un bledo. 3. Madeja. **Rap on the nose,** papirote. 4. *(Coloq.)* Charla, cháchara (chat). **Rap sheet,** antecedentes penales.

rapacious [rə'peɪʃəs] [ra-pei-shos], *a.* 1. Rapaz, que tiene inclinación o está dado al hurto, robo o rapiña. 2. Voraz, acostumbrado a tomar por fuerza el alimento. 3. Codicioso (greedy), avaricioso.

rapaciously [rə'peɪʃəslɪ] [ra-pei-shos-li], *adv.* Con rapacidad.

rapacity [rə'pæsɪtɪ] [ra-pa-si-ti], *s.* Rapacidad.

rape [reɪp] [reip], *s.* 1. Rapto, fuerza, la violencia que se hace a una mujer para gozarla; estupro. **To commit a rape,** forzar a una mujer; cometer un rapto. 2. Rapiña, robo; acción de coger y llevarse algo. 3. Escobajo, el racimo separado de las uvas. 4. *(Bot.)* nabo silvestre; colza, planta de cuya semilla se saca aceite. **Rape-seed,** nabina o simiente de colza o nabo silvestre. 5. Filtro para hacer vinagre.

rape, *vt.* 1. Violar. 2. Expoliar (plunder).

rapeseed ['reɪpsiːd] [reip-sid], *s.* Semilla de colza. **Rapeseed oil,** aceite de colza.

rapid ['ræpɪd] [ra-pid], *a.* Rápido (quick), veloz; raudo, que se mueve con celeridad; que está hecho o acabado en poco tiempo; que va prontamente al término. -*s.* Racial, raudal, corriente impetuosa de los ríos; caída desde menor altura que la de una catarata; se usa generalemnte en plural.

rapidity [rə'pɪdɪtɪ] [ra-pi-di-ti], **rapidness** ['ræpɪdnɪs] [ra-pid-nes], *s.* Rapidez, velocidad, celeridad.

rapidly ['ræpɪdlɪ] [ra-pid-li], *adv.* Rápidamente, velozmente.

rapids ['ræpɪdz] [ra-pids], *s.pl.* Rápidos.

rapier ['reɪpɪər] [rei-piar], *s.* Espadín; florete, espetón, estoque, arma blanca con la que sólo se puede herir de punta.

rapine ['ræpaɪn] [ra-pain], *s.* Rapiña, robo, violencia, fuerza.

rapist ['ræpɪst] [ra-pist], *s.* Violador.

rappee ['ræpiː] [ra-pi], *s.* Rapé o tabaco rapé.

rappel ['ræpəl] [ra-pal], *vi.* Descender en rappel.

rapper ['ræpər] [ra-par], *s.* 1. Golpeador, medio espiritista. 2. Llamador o aldabón de puerta. 3. *(Vulg.)* Un juramento.

rapping ['ræpɪŋ] [ra-ping], *s.* Llamada, golpeteo (knocking).

rapport [ræ'pɔːr] [ra-por], *s.* Armonía, concordancia de relación, relación simpática. *(Fr.)* **Close rapport,** relación estrecha.

rapprochement [ræ'prɒʃmənt] [ra-prosh-mant], *s.* Acercamiento.

rapscallion [ræp'skælɪən] [raps-ka-lion], *s.* Vagabundo, canalla.

rapt [ræpt] [rapt], *a.* Transportado, encantado, en éxtasis, embelesado (spellbound). **He was listening with rapt attention,** estaba escuchando embelesado.

raptor ['ræptər] [rap-tar], *s.* Ave raptora, rapaz.

rapture ['ræptʃər] [rap-cha], *s.* 1. Rapto, enajenamiento, pasmo, éxtasis, arrebatamiento, arrobamiento, embeleso transporte. 2. Acto o expresión de arrobamiento, del mayor placer.

raptured ['ræptʃəd] [rap-chad], *a.* (Poco us.) Absorto (absorbed), arrobado, arrebatado, transportado, fuera de sí.

rapturous ['ræptʃərəs] [rap-cha-ros], *a.* Maravilloso, pasmoso, hechicero.

rapturously ['ræptʃərəslɪ] [rap-cha-ros-li], *adv.* Con éxtasis, con transportes, con el mayor placer, efusivamente.

rare [reər] [rea], *a.* 1. Raro, que sucede pocas veces, que no se halla frecuentemente, poco común (uncommon). 2. Muy apreciado por causa de rareza, de gran valor, sobresaliente, excelente; preciso. 3. *(Culin.)* Asado imperfectamente, que conserva el color de la carne cruda y sus jugos, medio crudo: se dice de la carne. *V.* UNDER-DONE. 4. Raro, ralo (de la atmósfera), enrarecido (rarefied). 5. Muy esparcido en el espacio; lejanos entre sí.

rarebit ['reəbɪt] [rea-bit], *s.* Tostada con queso. *V.* RABBIT.

rarefaction [ˌreərɪ'fækʃən] [rea-ri-fak-shon], *s.* Rarefacción.

rarefiable ['reərɪfɑɪəbl] [rea-ri-faia-bol], *a.* Capaz de rarefacción.

rarefied ['reərɪfɑɪd] [rea-ri-faid], *a.* Enrarecido.

rarefy ['reərɪfɑɪ] [rea-ri-fai], *va.* Rarificar, rarefacer, enrarecer; dilatar un cuerpo por la dispersión de sus partículas en un espacio mayor. -*vn.* Rarefacerse, extenderse, dilatarse.

rarely ['reəlɪ] [rea-li], *adv.* Raramente, por maravilla, rara vez.

rareness ['reənɪs] [rea-nes], *s.* 1. Rareza, calidad de lo poco común; singularidad; superioridad, excelencia. 2. Tenuidad. *V.* RARITY, 3ª acep.

rareripe ['reərɪpɑɪp] [rea-ri-paip], *a.* Precoz, que madura temprano. -*s.* Fruta precoz.

rarity ['reərɪtɪ] [rea-ri-ti], *s.* 1. Raridad, rareza. 2. Cosa a que se atribuye gran precio a causa de su rareza. 3. Raridad, tenuidad, calidad de raro o ralo, lo opuesto a densidad.

rascal ['rɑːskəl] [ras-kal], *s.* Pícaro (crafty), bribón, bellaco, pillo, un hombre bajo, vil, ruin o indigno; belitre.

rascality [rɑːs'kælɪtɪ] [ras-ka-li-ti], *s.* Bellaquería, ruindad, carácter pícaro; acción vil o ruin; pillada.

rascally ['rɑːskəlɪ] [ras-ka-li], *a.* Vil (vile), bajo, ruin, indigno, infame.

rase [reɪz] [reis], *va.* 1. Arrasar, destruir, echar por tierra. 2. *(Ant.)* Rasar, pasar rozando. 3. *(Des.)* V. ERASE.

rash ['rɑːskəl] [ras-kal], *a.* Temerario, inconsiderado, atolondrado, irreflexivo, precipitado. -*s.* Roncha; sarpullido, erupción del cutis.

rasher ['ræʃər] [ra-shar], *s.* Lonja, torrezno.

rashly [ˈræʃlɪ] [rash-li], *adv.* Temerariamente, imprudentemente, con precipitación.

rashness [ˈræʃnɪs] [rash-nes], *s.* 1. Temeridad, audacia, arrojo, irreflexión, precipitación. 2. Acción temeraria o inconsiderada.

rasp [rɑːsp] [rasp], *s.* 1. Escofina, raspa, raspador, rascador. 2. La acción o el sonido de escofinar.

rasp, *va.* Raspar, escofinar. *-vi.* Hacer un ruido áspero.

raspberry [ˈrɑːzbərɪ] [ras-be-ri], *s.* 1. (*Bot.*) Frambuesa. 2. Frambueso, planta que produce las frambuesas. 3. (*Coloq.*) Pedorreta. **Raspberry-bush,** (*Bot.*) Frambueso.

rasping [ˈrɑːspɪŋ] [ras-pin], *a.* Raedor, raspante; ronco (hoarse), áspero; de aquí, irritante, que irrita o veja, atormentador. *-s.* Raspadura, raedura.

Rasta [ˈræstə] [ras-ta], *s.* (*Coloq.*) Rasta.

Rastafarian [ˌræstəˈfɛərɪən] [ras-ta-fea-rian], *s.* Rastafari.

rasure [ˈræʃʊəʳ] [ra-shuaʳ], *s.* Raspadura, raedura, borradura, testadura.

rat [ræt] [rat], *s.* (*Zool.*) 1. Rata, pequeño cuadrúpedo roedor que infesta las casas, los graneros, las embarcaciones, etc. 2. (*E.U.*) Postizo para el pelo. **To smell a rat,** oler el poste. **Rattrap,** ratonera. **Rat-catcher,** cazador de ratas o ratones. **Rat poison,** cualquier veneno para matar ratas. **Rat-tail file,** lima de cola de rata.

rat, *va.* y *vn.* 1. (*Fam.*) Reemplazar los operarios que pertenecen a un gremio por otros no agremiados. 2. (*Fam.*) Trabajar por menor jornal que el fijado por los gremios de oficio; no tomar parte en una huelga. 3. Cazar ratas.

ratable [ˈrætəbl] [ra-ta-bol], *a.* 1. sometida a contribucioón por ley. 2. Valuado, tasado, proporcionalmente. 3. Valuable, que puede valuarse.

ratably [ˈrætəblɪ] [ra-ta-bli], *adv.* A prorrata o según prorrata.

ratafia [ˈrætəfɪə] [ra-ta-fia], *s.* Ratafía, especie de rosoli hecho con aguardiente y almendras de albaricoque.

ratan [ˈrætən] [ra-tan], *s.* Rota, caña de Indias; roten, junco o bastón hecho del tallo de la rota. *V.* RATTAN.

ratany, ratanhy [ˈrætənɪ] [ra-ta-ni], *s.* Ratania.

rat-a-tat [ˌrætəˈtæt] [ra-ta-tat], *s.* Golpeteo.

ratbag [ˈrætbæg] [rat-bag], *s.* (*Coloq.*) Cascarrabias.

ratch [rætʃ] [rach], *s.* Una rueda de reloj que tiene doce dientes.

ratchet [ˈrætʃɪt] [ra-chit], *s.* 1. Rueda, dentada con fiador, fiador, (*Amer.*) trinquete. 2. Diente del caracol en la relojería.

rate [reɪt] [reit], *s.* 1. Tasa, razón, proporción, medida de alguna cosa; cantidad o grado relativo o comparativo. **At the rate of,** a razón de. 2. Precio o valor fijo; (*Com.*) curso, tasa, tipo. 3. Clase, grado, orden, clase de un navío o de una embarcación (buque mercante). 4. Variación diaria del reloj. 5. Modo, manera. **At any rate,** de todos modos, de cualquier modo; sea como fuere. **An extravagant rate,** precio exorbitante. 6. Velocidad (speed), ritmo (rythm). 7. (*Gran Bret.*) Derecho parroquial; contribución impuesta para usos locales en contraposición a las del gobierno general. **Book of rates,** arancel de los derechos de aduana. **First-rate,** de primera clase, lo mejor. **Market rate,** tipo del mercado. **A first-rate author,** un escritor de primer orden. **A first-rate singer,** un cantante de primera fuerza. **Poor-rate,** tasa o contribución para socorrer a los pobres. **A second-rate ship,** un buque de segunda clase. **At that rate,** de ese modo; si es así. **At the rate you are going on,** al paso que va Ud. **At a furious rate,** a todo correr.

rate, *va.* 1. Tasar, evaluar, apreciar, arreglar y fijar el valor relativo de alguna cosa. 2. Imponer, repartir una tasa o derecho (sobre). 3. Tomar la medida de; calcular la variación diaria de un reloj o cronómetro, comparándolo con un regulador de hora exacta. *-vn.* Ser estimado o valuado; tener valor. **Italy doesn't rate with me,** para mí Italia no vale gran cosa.

rate, *va.* y *vn.* Regañar, reñir a uno; poner a alguno como nuevo. *V.* BERATE.

rateen, *s. V.* RATTEEN.

ratepayer [ˈreɪtpɛəʳ] [reit-peaʳ], *s.* Contribuyente.

rather [ˈrɑːðəʳ] [ra-daʳ], *adv.* 1. De mejor gana; más bien, antes; puede ser; tal vez, quizá; algo, un poco. **He looks**

rather like Tony, se parece un poco a Tony. 2. Antes, con preferencia a otra cosa. 3. Antes bien, más presto. 4. Por mejor decir; al contrario. 5. (*Fam.*) Muy; en sentido irónico. **I would rather go than stay,** más quisiera irme que quedarme. **I had rather,** (o mejor) **I would rather,** me gustaría más, preferiría. **This work is rather expensive,** no deja de ser cara esta obra. **He was rather noisy,** era bastante ruidoso. **I would rather not,** preferiría que no, más bien no. **Men loved darkness rather than light,** los hombres preferían las tinieblas a la luz. **The rather as, the rather for,** tanto más que; tanto mejor que. **She is rather pretty,** es bastante bonita. **The yellow, or rather the buff, tint,** el matiz amarillo, por mejor decir, el de ante.

ratification [ˌrætɪfɪˈkeɪʃən] [ra-ti-fi-kei-shan], *s.* Ratificación, confirmación, aprobación.

ratifier [ˈrætɪfaɪəʳ] [ra-ti-faiaʳ], *s.* Ratificador.

ratify [ˈrætɪfaɪ] [ra-ti-fai], *va.* Ratificar, aprobar o confirmar.

rating [ˈreɪtɪŋ] [rei-tin], *s.* 1. Determinación de una tasa, precio o grado. 2. (*Tech.*) Categoría, clase. **Ratings,** índice de audiencia.

ratio [ˈreɪʃɪəʊ] [rei-shiou], *s.* 1. Razón, relación de grado, número, etc.; cantidad relativa, proporción. 2. (*Mat.*) Razón, relación entre dos números o dos cantidades de la misma naturaleza. 3. (*Ant.*) Razón, causa, argumento. **In the inverse ratio,** en razón inversa.

ratiocinate [ˌrætɪˈɒsɪneɪt] [ra-tio-si-neit], *vn.* Raciocinar.

ration [ˈræʃən] [ra-shon], *s.* (*Mil.*) Ración, la porción de pan, carne, forraje, etc., que se da para cada día en el ejército o en la marina. **Ration book,** cartilla de racionamiento.

ration, *va.* Racionar, distribuir artículos de primera importancia cuando hay escasez. **Ration out,** distribuir en forma racionada.

rational [ˈræʃənl] [ra-sho-nal], *a.* 1. Racional; fundado en la razón. 2. Razonable (sensible), según razón, motivado. 3. Juicioso (sane), de juicio. 4. Racional, que sólo se concibe por la razón.

rational, *s.* Un ser racional.

rationale [ˌræʃəˈnɑːl] [ra-sho-nal], *s.* Razón fundamental; base. **What's the rationale behind your decision?** ¿en qué se basa su decisión?

rationalism [ˈræʃənəlɪzm] [ra-sho-na-li-sem], *s.* 1. Racionalismo, lo opuesto a *supernaturalism.* 2. La doctrina de que la razón proporciona ciertos elementos que son base de la experiencia y sin los cuales la experiencia es imposible: lo contrario de *empiricism,* racionalismo.

rationalist [ˈræʃənəlɪst] [ra-sho-na-list], *s.* El que procede, obra o explica alguna cosa solamente por las reglas de la razón.

rationalist, *a.* Racionalista, perteneciente al racionalismo; conforme con los principios del racionalismo.

rationality [ˌræʃəˈnælɪtɪ] [ra-sho-na-li-ti], *s.* Racionalidad, la conveniencia o conformidad de las cosas con la razón.

rationalization [ˌræʃənəlaɪˈzeɪʃən] [ra-sho-na-lai-sei-shon], *s.* (*Psic., Mat.*) Racionalización. (*Neg.*) Racionalización, reconversión.

rationalize [ˈræʃənəlaɪz] [ra-sho-na-lais], *va.* 1. Explicar racionalmente. 2. Reorganizar racionalmente.

rationally [ˈræʃənəlɪ] [ra-sho-na-li], *adv.* Racionalmente, con sensatez.

rationing [ˈræʃənɪŋ] [ra-sho-nin], *s.* Racionamiento, distribución de artículos de primera importancia en época de escasez.

ratoon [rəˈtuːn] [ra-tun], *s.* 1. Vástago, renuevo que brota de la raíz de una planta desbrozada, como de la caña de azúcar. 2. Una de las hojas de en medio en la planta del tabaco.

rattan [rəˈtæn] [ra-tan], *s.* 1. Roten, rota (rotino); (*Amer.*) bejuco. 2. Bastón o varilla de roten.

ratteen [rəˈtiːn] [ra-tiin], *s.* Ratina, tela de lana que tiene granillo.

ratter [ˈrætəʳ] [ra-taʳ], *s.* Cazarratones.

rattle [ˈrætl] [ra-tel], *vn.* 1. Zumbar, zurrir, hacer un ruido bronco y confuso; rechinar. 2. Hablar rápida y tontamente, parlotear. 3. Moverse o funcionar con ruido desapacible. *-va.* 1. Sonar o tocar alguna cosa de modo que haga ruido;

hacer producir una serie de sonidos breves y agudos en rápida sucesión; sacudir con ruido, vibrar (vibrate). 2. Atolondrar o aturdir con ruido. 3. Proferir, articular, o producir de una manera ruidosa. 4. *(Coloq.)* Poner nervioso. 5. *(Mar.)* Atar los rebenques *a*. **The wind rattled the shutters,** el viento sacudió los postigos de la ventana. **To rattle away,** parlotear; rodar a distancia, haciendo ruido. **To rattle in the throat,** tener un moribundo el hipo o sarrillo, familiarmente, hervirle el pecho. *(Mex.)* Tener el estertor. **Rattle off,** recitar, decir de un tirón. **Rattle on,** parlotear sin parar. **Rattle through,** decir rápidamente, apurar.

rattle, *s.* 1. Sonido o ruido repetido vivamente; rechino, zumbido, zurrido. 2. Sonajero o sonajillas de niños, matraca; también la serie de anillos sueltos y córneos en la cola de la culebra de cascabel. 3. Parla, charla, habla rápida y ruidosa. **The rattles,** 1. Estertor del moribundo. 2. *V.* CROUP.

rattleheaded ['rætl'hedɪd] [ra-tel-je-did], *a.* Ligero de cascos, asquivano.

rattlepate ['rætlpeɪt] [ra-tel-peit], **rattleskull** ['ætlskʊl] [ra-tel-skul], *s.* Hablantín, parlanchín.

rattlesnake ['rætlsneɪk] [ra-tel-sneik], *s.* Culebra de cascabel, crótalo. **Rattlesnake-root,** lechera, hierba perenne del género Prenanthes, con raíz gruesa y amarga.

rattling ['rætlɪŋ] [ra-tlin], *s.* El hipo o sarrillo de los moribundos; estertor, ruido; rechino, zollipo o sollozo con hipo. *-a. (Ger.)* vivo, sorprendente, alegre.

ratty ['rætɪ] [ra-ti], *a.* 1. *(Coloq.)* Raído (shabby), hecho pedazos. 2. Malhumorado (bad-tempered).

raucous ['rɔːkəs] [ro-kos], *a.* Ronco, de sonido áspero, bronco, escandaloso, estentóreo (loud), estridente (shrill)

raucously ['rɔːkəslɪ] [ro-kos-li], *adv.* A voz en cuello (loudly), escandalosamente, estridentemente (shrilly).

raucousness ['rɔːkəsnɪs] [ro-kos-nes], *sf.* Estridencia.

raunchy ['rɔːntʃɪ] [ron-chi], *a.* 1. *(Coloq.)* Picante, escabroso, aguardentoso. 2. Raído (shabby).

ravage ['rævɪdʒ] [ra-vich], *va.* Saquear (plunder), pillar; asolar, talar, destruir. **Spain was ravaged by the Civil War,** España fue asolada por la Guerra Civil.

ravage, *s.* Asolamiento, ruina, destrozo, destrucción; saqueo.

ravager ['rævɪdʒəʳ] [ra-vi-chaʳ], *s.* Pillador, saqueador; asolador.

ravages ['rævɪdʒɪz] [ra-vi-chis], *s.pl.* Estragos. **Ravages of time,** los estragos del tiempo.

rave [reɪv] [reiv], *vn.* 1. Delirar (talk deliriously), desvariar, disparatar, decir extravagancias, encolerizarse, enfurecerse, ponerse fuera de sí o salirse de sus casillas. 2. Obrar, moverse o arrojarse de una manera tumultuosa y ruidosa; correr con ímpetu como un torrente. También se usa este verbo en sentido activo. **To rave after,** querer a toda costa, despepitarse por algo. **He raved about his painting,** disparataba con motivo de su cuadro.

ravel ['rævəl] [ra-val], *va.* 1. Deshilar, deshilachar, destejer, deshacer un tejido, desenlazar, a menudo con *out.* 2. *(Ant.)* Enredar, enmarañar (acepción original). *-vn.* 1. Deshilarse, destorcerse, dehacerse, se usa a menudo con *out.* 2. *(Ant.)* Enredarse, confundirse. **To ravel out,** deshilarse un tejido.

ravelin ['rævəlɪn] [ra-ve-lin], *s. (Fort.)* Rebellín, obra exterior separada de la fortificación.

raveling, ravelling ['rævəlɪn] [ra-ve-lin], *s.* 1. Hilacha. 2. Acto de deshilachar o deshilacharse.

raven ['reɪvn] [rei-ven], *s. (Orn.)* Cuervo. *-a.* Negro y luciente como el plumaje del cuervo.

raven, *va.* y *vn.* 1. Apresar, proporcionarse algo con violencia; prender por fuerza. 2. Devorar (devour), tragar con voracidad; echarse sobre la presa, hacer presa de. *-s.* Presa, botín, alimento obtenido a viva fuerza; despojo, rapiña (pillage).

ravening ['rævnɪŋ] [rav-nin], *s.* Rapiña, voracidad. *-pa.* de TO RAVEN.

ravenous ['rævənəs] [ra-ve-nos], *a.* Voraz (voracious), hambriento, tragón, golosazo; rapaz.

ravenously ['rævənəslɪ] [ra-ve-nos-li], *adv.* Vorazmente.

raver ['reɪvəʳ] [rei-vaʳ], *s.* Juerguista.

ravin ['rævɪn] [ra-vin], *s.* Presa, rapiña.

ravine [rə'viːn] [ra-vin], *s.* Barranca, quebrada, hondonada.

raving ['reɪvɪŋ] [rei-vin], *s.* Desvarío, delirio. *-pa.* de TO RAVE.

ravingly ['reɪvɪŋlɪ] [rei-vin-li], *adv.* Disparatadamente, locamente.

ravioli [ˌrævɪ'əʊlɪ] [ra-vio-li], *s.* Raviolis.

ravish ['rævɪʃ] [ra-vish], *va.* 1. Arrebatar, llevar tras sí, atraer, encantar. 2. Estuprar, forzar a una mujer, violar (rape). 3. *(Ant.)* Arrebatar, quitar, tomar por fuerza.

ravisher ['rævɪʃəʳ] [ra-vi-shaʳ], *s.* Estuprador, forzador, arrebatador.

ravishing ['rævɪʃɪŋ] [ra-vi-shin], *pa.* Encantador, pasmoso, embriagador.

ravishingly ['rævɪʃɪŋlɪ] [ra-vi-shin-li], *adv.* De una manera encantadora.

ravishment ['rævɪʃmənt] [ra-vish-ment], *s.* 1. Rapto, transporte, éxtasis, arrobamiento 2. Fuerza, estupro, violación de una mujer.

raw [rɔː] [ro], *a.* 1. Crudo, que no está cocido, asado o frito, no aderezado ni guisado (uncooked). 2. Raído, desollado vivo, que no está cubierto con pellejo o piel, o que está lastimado: se dice también de los huesos que no tiene carne encima. 3. Crudo, frío y húmedo, cortante. 4. Sin preparar, crudo, en estado natural; verde; no suavizado o sin tono, v. g. los colores; bruto, sin refinar, sin purificar. 5. Nuevo, nuevamente hecho o fabricado. 6. Novato, falto de experiencia, poco versado, ignorante, indisciplinado. **Raw weather,** tiempo crudo o frío y húmedo. **Raw silk,** seda cruda o en rama. **Raw spirits,** licores puros o sin mezcla. **A raw apple,** una manzana cruda. **Cucumbers are generally eaten raw,** los pepinos se comen generalmente crudos. **Raw flesh,** carne desollada, viva. **Raw soldiers, troops,** soldados bisoños, tropas bisoñas, mal aguerridas. **Raw hand,** tirón, novato, novicio. **Raw material,** materia bruta, materia prima. **Raw sugar,** azúcar bruto, sin refinar.

rawboned ['rɔː'bəʊnd] [ro-bound], *a.* Huesudo, membrudo; magro, enjuto.

raw deal ['rɔːdiːl] [ro-dil], *s.* Mala pasada.

rawhead ['rɔːhed] [ro-jed], *s.* Espectro, fantasma, espantajo. **Rawhead and bloody bones,** coco, espantajo de niños.

rawhide ['rɔːhaɪd] [ro-jaid], *a.* Hecho de cuero crudo. *-s.* 1. Cuero crudo, sin curtir (leather). 2. Látigo hecho de este cuero.

rawish ['rɔːɪʃ] [rouish], *a.* algo crudo; un poco frío o húmedo.

rawness ['rɔːnɪs] [ro-nes], *s.* Crudeza, falta de experiencia.

ray [reɪ] [rei], *s.* 1. La línea a lo largo de la cual se propaga una forma cualquiera de energía radiante; rayo de luz. 2. Rayo, una de las varias líneas que salen de un objeto. 3. Rayo, línea recta por donde se considera que va o se dirige una cosa. 4. Línea, raya; fila derecha. 5. *(Zool.)* Parte o prominencia parecida a un rayo; como la espina de la aleta de los peces, el brazo de una estrella de mar, etc. 6. *(Bot.)* Lígula, florecilla ligulada de las sinantéreas. 7. *(Zool.)* Raya, pez cartilaginoso, que tiene el cuerpo muy ancho y aplanado por delante. 8. *(Mús.)* Re.

ray, *va.* 1. Rayar, hacer rayas; proveer de rayas. 2. Emitir.

ray-cloth ['reɪklɒθ] [rei-kloz], *s.* Paño que no está teñido.

ray-grass ['reɪgrɑːs] [rei-gras], *s. (Bot.)* Joyo, cominillo.

rayon ['reɪɒn] [reion], *s.* Rayón, fibra de celulosa modificada.

raze [reɪz] [reis], *va.* 1. Arrasar, demoler (demolish), echar por tierra, destruir enteramente. 2. *V.* RAZEL. 3. *(Ant.)* Extirpar; tachar, borrar.

razor ['reɪzəʳ] [rei-saʳ], *s.* Navaja de barbero o de afeitar, verdugillo. **To set a razor,** amolar una navaja de afeitar; vaciarla. **Razor-grinder,** vaciador de navajas de afeitar. **Razor-strop,** suavizador, asentador de navajas. **Razor-sheath o razor-shell,** navaja, una especie de marisco. **Razor-bill,** *(Orn.)* alca, ave palmeada.

razor blade ['reɪzəbleɪd] [rei-sa-bleid], *s.* Hoja de afeitar.

razor-sharp ['reɪzəʃɑːp] [rei-sa-sharp], *a.* Muy afilado, muy agudo.

razz ['ræz] [ras], *vt. (Coloq.)* Tomarle el pelo, vacilar.

razzmatazz [ˌræzməˈtæz] [ras-ma-tas], *s. (Coloq.)* Bulla, alboroto.

re [riː] [ri], *pref.* Partícula inseparable que denota repetición o acción retrógrada.

re [reɪ] [rei], *s. (Mús.)* Re, segunda nota de la escala musical.

reabsorb [ˈriːəbˈzɔːb] [riab-sorb], *va.* Reabsorber; absorber o embeber de nuevo lo que se había derramado, extravasado.

reabsorption [ˈriːəbˈzɔːpʃən] [riab-sorp-shon], *s.* Reabsorción, acción de absorber de nuevo.

reach [riːtʃ] [riich], *va.* 1. Alargar, extender, tender. 2. Alcanzar. 3. Llegar o alcanzar a alguna cosa distante; conseguir; penetrar. 4. alcanzar o llegar hasta algún término. 5. Coger o tomar alguna cosa de un paraje distante y darla. **Reach me my hat,** alcánceme Ud. el sombrero: entréguEme Ud. mi sombrero. 6. Lograr, obtener, conseguir (con esfuerzo) -*vn.* 1. Extenderse, llegar. 2. Alcanzar, penetrar; esforzarse. 3. Coger alguna cosa con la mano. 4. *(Mar.)* Ceñir el viento, navegar de bolina. **He reached out his plate,** alargó su plato. **To reach home,** llegar a casa. **The letter reached me,** la carta llegó a mis manos. **To reach the heart,** llegar al corazón, tocar al corazón. **As far as the eye could reach,** tan lejos como alcanzaba la vista. **To reach into,** penetrar en. **To reach after,** procurar, hacer esfuerzos para alcanzar u obtener. **To reach back,** remontar, alcanzar. **To reach down,** bajar, descender. **In an overcoat which reached below his knees,** en un sobretodo que le llegaba más abajo de las rodillas.

reach, *s.* 1. Alcance, extensión. **Reach of thought,** capacidad. 2. Alcance, poder, facultad; capacidad. **It is not within my reach,** no puedo alcanzarlo; no está a mi alcance, o no puedo entenderlo bien; capacidad de llegar, de tocar con la mano o con algo que se tiene en la mano, de aquí, alcance, extensión de la inteligencia, de la influencia mental. 3. Punto, posición, o resultado ganados o asequibles. 4. Extensión no interrumpida de una corriente de agua; vista. 5. Lanza o barra que une el eje posterior de un vehículo con la parte delantera. 6. *(Mar.)* El acto de navegar, o la distancia navegada en una sola bordada. **Out of reach,** fuera de alcance. **One boundless reach of sky,** una extensión ilimitada de cielo.

reachable [ˈriːtʃəbl] [ri-cha-bol], *a.* Accesible, alcanzable.

react [riːˈækt] [ri-akt], *va.* 1. Reaccionar, producir una acción como en respuesta o resistencia a otra. 2. Rechazar, resistir a la acción de un cuerpo por una fuerza contraria. 3. Obrar recíprocamente dos o más agentes químicos o físicos.

reactance [riːˈæktəns] [ri-ak-tans], *s.* Reactancia, reacción de autoinducción.

reaction [riːˈækʃən] [ri-ak-shon], *s.* 1. Reacción, acción opuesta o contraria; la tendencia hacia un estado precedente u opuesto; la fuerza que opone el cuerpo impelido a la del impulsor. 2. Acción mútua o recíproca de agentes químicos. 3. Cualquier acción debida a un estímulo. **How was his reaction?,** ¿cómo fue su reacción?

reactionary [riːˈækʃənrɪ] [ri-ak-sho-na-ri], *a.* Reaccionario, -*s.* y *a.* Derechista, reaccionario (en sus tendencias políticas).

reactionist [riːˈækʃənɪst] [ri-ak-sho-nist], *s.* Reaccionario, partidario conservador, contrario a la revolución.

reactivate [riːˈæktɪveɪt] [ri-ak-ti-veit], *vt.* Reactivar.

reactive [riːˈæktɪv] [ri-ak-tiv], *a.* Reactivo, que causa, produce u opera reacción; que tiende a operar una reacción, o que tiene la fuerza de obrar en sentido contrario.

reactor [riːˈæktəʳ] [ri-ak-taʳ], *s. (Elec.)* Reactor.

read [riːd] [rid], *va. (pret.* y *pp.* READ [red] [red]). 1. Leer; pasar la vista por lo escrito. **She reads herself to sleep,** ella lee hasta quedarse dormida. 2. Leer alto, proferir los sonidos que de ordinario se dan a las palabras. 3. Comprender, leer, ver, percibir, reconocer, descubrir o comprender por caracteres, signos o rasgos. 4. Interpretar, explicar; imputar, v. g. una significación oculta. 5. Leer, observar o anunciar las indicacioes de un instrumento. 6. Saber por medio de libros. 7. Estudiar, aprender (learn). 8.

(Mús.) Leer, seguir de un modo inteligente, tocar o cantar las notas de una composición. 9. Producir un resultado cualquiera por medio de la lectura. **To read one to sleep,** adormecer (a uno) leyendo. 10. Enseñar, como con un libro; amonestar, aconsejar, avisar. -*vn.* 1. Leer, notar o comprender los caracteres o el contenido de un libro o manuscrito. 2. Leer, saber; se usa a menudo con *of o about.* 3. Leer en alta voz el contenido de un libro o manuscrito. 4. Aprender leyendo, estudiar; entregarse al estudio, practicar mucho la lectura. Se usa a menudo con *up.* 5. Leerse, aparecer en la lectura. 6. Comprender o expresar la música escrita. 7. Dar una conferencia pública o una serie de ellas. **The deed having been read,** dada lectura del instrumento auténtico. **To read off hand,** leer de corrida. **To read between the lines,** leer entre líneas, es decir, inferir lo que no está expresado claramente. **To read by sound,** recibir un despacho telegráfico, oyendo los sonidos del instrumento receptor. **The passage reads thus,** el pasaje dice así o lee así: (presenta esta variante). **To read aloud,** leer en alta voz. **To read law,** leer, estudiar derecho. **To read about,** leer acerca de algo, hacer un curso de, aprender leyendo. **To read again, to read over again,** volver a leer, leer otra vez.

read on, proseguir o continuar leyendo.

read out, expulsar a un miembro de una asociación.

read over, leerlo todo, recorrer un escrito.

read [red] [red], *pp.* del verbo TO READ. Leído, que se instruye leyendo; instruído; erudito. **Well-read man,** hombre leído o erudito.

readability, [ˌriːdəˈbɪlɪtɪ] [ri-da-bi-li-ti], *s.* Calidad de legible: de aquello cuya lectura causa placer.

readable [ˈriːdəbl] [ri-da-bol], *a.* Leíble, legible, que se puede leer, de lectura fácil y agradable.

reader [ˈriːdəʳ] [ri-daʳ], *s.* 1. Lector, el que lee. 2. Libro de lectura. Lay-**reader,** lego autorizado para leer las oraciones en una iglesia. **A great reader,** un gran lector.

readership [ˈriːdəʃɪp] [ri-da-ship], *s.* Lectores. **The Washington Post has a readership of over 10 million,** el Washington Post tiene una tirada de 10 millones.

readily [ˈredɪlɪ] [re-di-li], *adv.* 1. Prontamente, luego; con placer, de buena gana (gladly). 2. Fácilmente (easily), inmediatamente. **These books are readily available,** estos libros se pueden conseguir fácilmente.

readiness [ˈredɪnɪs] [re-di-nes], *s.* 1. Calidad de dispuesto, preparado o listo para, en condición conveniente. 2. Prontitud, facilidad, aptitud, desembarazo. **Readiness of wit,** viveza o vivacidad de talento o de ingenio. 3. Voluntad, gana, buena voluntad (willingness), disposición favorable. **Readiness of speech,** facilidad de palabra. **Readiness in doing anything,** prontitud para hacer alguna cosa. **We had got all in readiness,** todo lo habíamos preparado.

reading [ˈriːdɪŋ] [ri-din], *s.* 1. Lección, lectura, acción de leer, en cualquiera de las acepciones de este verbo; relación pública; lectura de un proyecto de ley. 2. Estudio de los libros; investigación literaria, educación literaria. 3. Lectura, lo que se lee, o que se señala para su lectura. 4. La indicación de un instrumento graduado. 5. Lección, variante, texto; la forma en que aparece algún pasaje, palabra o cosa en un manuscrito o libro determinado. 6. Glosa, interpretación, de una adivinanza, etc.; delineación. -*a.* Que lee mucho; que le gusta mucho leer. **Reading-room,** gabinete de lectura; sala donde hay libros, o diarios y publicaciones periódicas para leer. **Reading matter,** material de lectura; la parte literaria o de noticias en algún periódico, en oposición a los anuncios.

readjust [ˈriːəˈdʒʌst] [riad-yast], *va.* 1. Ajustar de nuevo, poner en su primer estado. 2. Ajustar de una manera diferente; poner en relación diferente.

readjustment [ˈriːəˈdʒʌstmənt] [riad-yast-ment], *s.* Reajuste, readaptación.

readmission [ˈriːədˈmɪʃən] [riad-mi-shon], *s.* Readmisión.

readmit [ˈriːədˈmɪt] [riad-mit], *va.* Readmitir, volver a admitir, admitir de nuevo.

ready ['redɪ] [re-di], *a.* 1. Preparado, dispuesto (willing), aparejado para alguna cosa, aprestado; provisto de todo lo que es necesario; en condición para usar u obrar. **Ready to burst**, a punto de reventar. **To make ready**, preparar. 2. Inclinado, propenso, dispuesto. 3. Que está para; no lejos de, en el momento de. 4. Listo, pronto (quick); contante, de contado; que no se difiere. **Ready money**, dinero contante. **Ready payment**, paga pronta. 5. Fácil, lo que no cuesta trabajo. 6. A la mano, al alcance; socorrido, útil, disponible sin dilación. 7. Pronto, ligero. **All things are ready**, todo está listo, todo se halla dispuesto. **Ready for departure**, preparado para salir o irse, listo para la marcha. **A ready retort**, una réplica pronta. **Ready to find fault**, inclinado a poner faltas. **A ready method**, un método fácil. **He was ready to die**, estaba para morir, en vísperas de morir. **Ready-made**, ya hecho; confeccionado. **Ready-witted**, de ingenio vivo, pronto. -*adv.* Prontamente, presto.

ready-cooked ['redɪ'kukt] [re-di-kukt], *a.* Listo para comer.

ready-to-serve [ˌredɪtə'sɜːv] [re-di-to-serv], *a.* Preparado.

reaffirm ['riːə'fɜːm] [ria-ferm], *s.* Reiterar (restate), reafirmar.

reaffirmance ['riːə'fɜːməns] [ria-fer-mans], *s.* Segunda confirmación.

reagent [riːˈeɪdʒənt] [ri-ei-chant], *s.* (*Quím.*) Reactivo.

real [rɪəl] [rial], *a.* 1. Real, verdadero (true), que existe de hecho; no imaginario ni teórico. 2. Efectivo, genuino (genuine); no artificial, no falso ni contrahecho; sincero. 3. (*For.*) Perteneciente o referente a las tierras o bienes raíces; que se refiere a las cosas en contraposición a las personas. **Real sherry wine**, vino de Jerez legítimo. **Real property**, propiedad inmueble, bienes raíces. **Real estate**, bienes raíces. -*s.* Real, una antigua moneda de España. **A real vellon**, un real de vellón. -*adv.* Muy, mucho. **I'm real tired**, estoy muy cansada.

realign [riːə'laɪn] [ria-lain], *vt.* Realinear.

realism [rɪəlɪzəm] [ria-li-sem], *s.* 1. Realismo, la negación del ideal; copia de la naturaleza sin ninguna idealidad, en la literatura y en las artes. 2. Doctrina filosófica de los realistas.

realist ['rɪəlɪst] [ria-list], *s.* Realista.

realistic [rɪə'lɪstɪk] [ria-lis-tik], *a.* 1. Realista, conforme a los principios y métodos del realismo. 2. Que parece estar vivo.

realistically [rɪə'lɪstɪkəlɪ] [ria-lis-ti-ka-li], *adv.* De manera realista. **Looking at it realistically**, siendo realistas.

reality [riːˈælɪtɪ] [ria-li-ti], *s.* 1. Realidad, entidad. 2. Carácter o cosa real. 3. (*Raro. For.*) V. REALTY. **In reality**, en realidad, en verdad.

realizable ['rɪəlaɪzəbl] [ria-lai-sa-bol], *a.* Realizable, que se puede realizar.

realization [ˌrɪəlaɪ'zeɪʃən] [ria-lai-sei-shon], *s.* 1. Realización. 2. Comprensión (understanding).

realize ['rɪəlaɪz] [ria-lais], *va.* 1. Percibir como realidad; comprender la verdadera naturaleza de algo, sentir, apreciar completa y vivamente; considerar, admitir como real. 2. Realizar (achieve), hacer real; poner en existencia verdadera. 3. Hacer parecer como verdadero; presentar al ánimo como existente. 4. Ganar, obtener como ganancia o provecho (obtain). 5. (*Com.*) Realizar, vender géneros, convertir su propiedad en dinero. **His hopes could never be realized**, sus esperanzas no pudieron realizarse jamás. **To realize much profit from**, obtener grandes ganacias de algo.

real-life [ˌrɪəl'laɪf] [rial-laif], *a.* De la vida real. **Real-life situation**, situación real.

really ['rɪəlɪ] [ria-li], *adv.* Realmente, efectivamente, verdaderamente. **I really don't care**, la verdad es que no me importa.

realm [relm] [relm], *s.* 1. Reino (kingdom). **The peers of the realm**, los pares o grandes del reino; los próceres. 2. Dominio, jurisdicción o alcance de un poder o influencia cualquiera. 3. División del globo con respecto a su fauna.

realtor ['rɪəltɔːr] [rial-tar], *s.* Agente inmobiliario.

realty ['rɪəltɪ] [rial-ti], *s.* (*For.*) Bienes raíces; fincas, bienes heredados, patrimonio en tierras.

ream [riːm] [rim], *s.* Resma, el mazo de veinte manos de papel.

ream, *va.* Ensanchar o aumentar gradualmente un agujero.

reamer ['riːmər] [ri-mar], *s.* Escariador, exprimidor.

reanimate ['riːˈænɪmeɪt] [ria-ni-meit], *va.* Reanimar, hacer revivir, dar nuevas fuerzas o vigor, resucitar.

reap [riːp] [rip], *va.* 1. Segar, cortar y recoger las mieses; cosechar los frutos de un campo (harvest). 2. Obtener o sacar fruto de alguna cosa. **What benefit shall you reap by it?** ¿Qué provecho sacará Ud. de ello? -*vn.* 1. Hacer el agosto, hacer la siega, hacer la cosecha por medio de una segadora o de otro modo. 2. Recibir como recompensa, o como fruto de su trabajo.

reaper ['riːpər] [ri-par], *s.* 1. Segador, el que siega. 2. Segadora, máquina para segar las mieses. Contiene a menudo una agavilladora o mecanismo para atar los haces. V. HARVESTER.

reaping ['riːpɪŋ] [ri-pin], *s.* Siega, cosecha, acción de segar, de hacer el agosto. **Reaping-hook**, hoz, segadera, instrumento para segar las mieses. **Reaping-machine**, segadora; máquina con que se cortan y agavillan las mieses. **Reaping-time**, siega, el tiempo de segar las mieses.

reappear ['riːə'pɪər] [ria-piar], *vn.* Reaparecer.

reappearance ['riːə'pɪərəns] [ria-pia-rans], *s.* 1. Reaparición, nueva aparición. 2. Segunda entrada en escena de un actor.

reappoint ['riːə'pɔɪnt] [ria-point], *v.* Designar o fijar de nuevo, dar una nueva cita, y particularmente nombrar de nuevo para un empleo.

reapportion ['riːə'pɔːʃən] [ria-por-shon], *va.* Proporcionar otra vez, repartir de nuevo.

reappraisal ['riːə'preɪzəl] [ria-prei-sal], *s.* Revaluación.

rear [rɪər] [riar], *a.* Postrero, trasero, que está, se queda o viene detrás; último, posterior. **Rear wall**, pared trasera o posterior. -*s.* 1. Fondo, la parte posterior 2. Lugar o posición a espaldas o detrás de alguna persona o cosa. 2. (*Mil.*) Retaguardia; la última clase. **Rear-guard**, retaguardia. **Rear rank**, última fila. **To be in the rear**, estar a la cola. **To bring up the rear**, cerrar la marcha, hacer o formar la cola.

rear, *va.* 1. Levantar, alzar, ensalzar, elevar. 2. Erigir, construir (build). 3. Criar (raise), cuidar de alguna persona desde su niñez hasta la edad madura; educar, instruir. 4. Levantar desde una condición caída; reanimar, ensalzar, exaltar. -*vn.* Encabritarse (horse). **To rear a family**, criar una familia. **To rear a building**, erigir, construir un edificio. **The horse reared**, el caballo se encabritó.

rear-admiral ['rɪər'ædmərəl] [riar-ad-mi-ral], *s.* Contraalmirante.

rearm ['riːˈɑːm] [ri-arm], *va.* Rearmar.

rearmament ['riːˈɑːməmənt] [ri-ar-ma-ment], *s.* Rearme.

rearrange ['riːə'reɪndʒ] [ria-reindch], *va.* Volver a arreglar. **I will rearrange the furniture**, volveré a cambiar los muebles de lugar.

rear-view ['rɪəˌvjuː] [ria-viu], *s.* **Rear-view mirror**, espejo de retrovisión, retrovisor.

rearward ['rɪəwəd] [ria-uod], *a.* Postrero, que viene último o a la cola. -*adv.* Detrás, hacia o en la parte posterior. -*s.* (*Ant*) Retaguardia; la última base.

reason ['riːzn] [ri-son], *s.* 1. Razón, la facultad de discurrir (faculty); la potencia intelectual; racionalidad. 2. Fundamento, motivo, causa (cause). 3. Razón, justicia, derecho. 4. Razón, argumento, prueba. 5. (*Lóg.*) Principio o motivo lógico para pensar, antecedente, premisa, particularmente la premisa menor. 6. Intuición, conocimiento infuso. 7. Moderación. **To yield to reason**, ceder a la razón. **In reason**, le daremos lo que sea justo. **By reason of**, a causa de. **It stands to reason**, así lo quiere, lo pide la razón. **There is reason to suspect that fellow**, hay motivos para tener sospechas de ese individuo.

reason, *vn.* Razonar, raciocinar; debatir, disputar, pensar (think). -*va.* Investigar, escudriñar, examinar; discutir. **Reason out**, entender razonando.

reasonable ['riːznəbl] [ri-so-na-bol], *a.* 1. Racional, razonable, conforme o según la razón; dirigido por la razón, que piensa u obra según los consejos de la razón; justo, equitativo. **Reasonable doubt,** duda razonable. 2. Arreglado, mediano, mediocre.

reasonableness ['riːznəblnɪs] [ri-so-na-bol-nes], *s.* Racionalidad; naturaleza razonable, conformidad con la razón; moderación; justicia (fairness), equidad (equity).

reasonably ['riːznəblɪ] [ri-so-na-bli], *adv.* Razonablemente. **Reasonably priced goods,** artículos a precios razonables.

reasoned ['riːznd] [ri-sond], *a.* Razonado.

reasoner ['riːznəʳ] [ri-so-naʳ], *s.* Razonador, el que razona o discute.

reasoning ['riːznɪŋ] [ri-so-nin], *s.* Razonamiento, lógica.

reasonless ['riːznlɪs] [ri-son-les], *a.* Sin razón, desrazonable.

reassemble ['riːəsembl] [ria-sem-bel], *va.* Juntar de nuevo, reunir, recoger.

reassert ['riːəsɜːt] [ria-sert], *va.* Asegurar, afirmar de nuevo.

reassess ['riːəses] [ria-ses], *vt.* Volver a estudiar, reexaminar.

reassing ['riːəsɪŋ] [ria-sin], *va.* Asignar, destinar o repartir de nuevo, retroceder.

reassurance ['riːəʊərəns] [ria-shua-rans], *s.* 1. Confianza establecida; afirmación repetida, certeza restablecida. 2. *(Com.)* Segundo seguro, el acto de volver a asegurar las mercancías o géneros por haber quebrado, o temerse que quiebren los primeros aseguradores.

reassure ['riːəʊəʳ] [ria-shuaʳ], *va.* Alentar, volver a asegurar. **I will try to reassure them that everything is alright,** trataré de tranquilizarles asegurándoles que todo está bien.

reassuring ['riːəʊərɪŋ] [ria-shua-rin], *a.* Tranquilizador. **It's reassuring to know that you are here with us,** es tranquilizador saber que estás aquí con nosotros.

reassuringly ['riːəʊərɪŋlɪ] [ria-shua-rin-li], *adv.* De modo tranquilizador.

reattachment ['riːətætʃmənt] [ria-tach-ment], *s. (For.)* El reembargo de alguna cosa.

reawaken ['riːəweɪkən] [ria-uei-ken], *vt.* Volver a despertar, renacer (rebirth). *-vi.* Volver a despertarse.

reawakening ['riːəweɪknɪŋ] [ria-ueik-nin], *s.* Renacer, despertar.

rebate ['riːbeɪt] [ri-beit], *va.* y *vn.* 1. Rebajar, deducir, disminuir de una cuenta, de una factura; hacer una rebaja. 2. Embotar.

rebatement ['riːbeɪtmənt] [ri-beit-ment], *s.* Rebaja, descuento (discount), deducción, diminución. **Tax rebate,** devolución de impuestos.

rebecca [rɪˈbekə] [ri-be-ka], *s.* Rabel, la forma primitiva del violín, con una, dos, o tres cuerdas.

rebel ['rebl] [re-bel], *vn.* Rebelarse, levantarse, sublevarse, alzarse. *-s.* Rebelde.

rebellion [rɪˈbeljən] [ri-be-lion], *s.* Rebelión, levantamiento, revuelta (revolt), sublevación.

rebellious [rɪˈbeljəs] [ri-be-lios], *a.* Rebelde, amotinado (insurgent), sedicioso, sublevado.

rebelliously [rɪˈbeljəslɪ] [ri-be-lios-li], *adv.* Con rebeldía.

rebelliousness [rɪˈbeljəsnɪs] [ri-be-lios-nes], *s.* Rebeldía, falta de obediencia o subordinación.

rebirth ['riːbɜːθ] [ri-berz], *s.* Renacimiento.

reblossom [rɪˈblɒsəm] [ri-blo-som], *vn.* Volver a florecer, florecer de nuevo.

rebound ['riːbaʊnd] [ri-baund], *vn.* 1. Repercutir; botar, saltar la pelota, rebotar (ricochet). 2. Volverse contra. 3. *(Des.)* Resonar. **The jest rebounded on him,** la burla se volvió contra él; la espada se le volvió garabato. *-va.* Rechazar.

rebound, *s.* Resalto, repercusión, rebote.

rebounding ['riːbaʊndɪŋ] [ri-baun-din], *s.* Rebote.

rebroadcast ['riːbrɔːdkɑːst] [ri-brod-kast], *s.* Retransmisión radiodifusora.

rebuff [rɪˈbʌf] [ri-baf], *s.* 1. Desaire, mala acogida. 2. Repulsa, denegación (refusal). 3. Resistencia, repentina y viva; jaque, vencimiento.

rebuff, *va.* 1. Rechazar, rebatir con violencia. 2. Desairar, denegar, acoger mal.

rebuild [rɪˈbɪld] [ri-bild], *va.* (*pret.* y *pp.* REBUILT). Reedificar, construir de nuevo.

rebuke [rɪˈbjuːk] [ri-biuk], *va.* 1. Reprender, consurar; dar una reprimenda; regañar, reñir (scold). 2. *(Ant.)* Hacer callar, refrenar por medio de un mandato o una orden.

rebuke, *s.* 1. Reprensión, reprimenda, amonestación, censura. 2. Bofetada.

rebuker [rɪˈbjuːkəʳ] [ri-biu-kaʳ], *s.* Represor, censor.

rebus ['riːbəs] [ri-bas], *s.* Un jeroglífico acertijo; quisicosa, manera peculiar de expresar palabras o frases por la representación de objetos cuyos nombres tiene semejanza a las palabras o las sílabas de que se componen.

rebut [rɪˈbʌt] [ri-bat], *va. (For.)* Refutar (refute), contradecir, por prueba en contrario. *-vn.* Replicar, responder a la dúplica del demandante.

rebuttal [rɪˈbʌtl] [ri-ba-tal], *s.* Refutación, acción de refutar; la presentación de pruebas para refutar una deposición ya hecha.

rebutter [rɪˈbʌtəʳ] [ri-ba-taʳ], *s. (For.)* 1. Respuesta a una contraréplica. 2. El que refuta, o que presenta testimonio en contrario.

recalcitrance [rɪˈkælsɪtrəns] [ri-kal-si-trans], *sf.* Terquedad, obstinación.

recalcitrant [rɪˈkælsɪtrənt] [ri-kal-si-trant], *a.* Recalcitrante, rehacio, obstinado en la resistencia, contumaz (obstinate).

recalcitrate [rɪˈkælsɪtreɪt] [ri-kal-si-treit], *vn.* Recalcitrar, resistir con tenacidad a quien se debe obedecer.

recall [rɪˈkɔːl] [ri-kol], *va.* 1. Revocar, anular, hacer volver, mandar volver. 2. Traer a la memoria, recordar (remember). 3. Quitar el cargo o empleo. **To recall an ambassador,** retirar a un embajador de su misión, mandarle volver a su país. **I cannot recall the circumstances,** no puedo recordar las circunstancias.

recall, *s.* 1. Revocación. 2. El acto de volver a llamar. 3. Memoria (memory). **To have total recall,** tener una memoria excelente.

recant [rɪˈkænt] [ri-kant], *va.* y *vn.* 1. Retractarse, desdecirse. **He was obliged to recant,** le obligaron a cantar la palinodia. 2. *(Relig.)* Abjurar (abjure).

recantation [ˌriːkænˈteɪʃən] [ri-kan-tei-shon], *s.* Retractación, recantación, palinodia.

recanter [rɪˈkæntəʳ] [ri-kan-taʳ], *s.* El que se desdice.

recap ['riːkæp] [ri-kap], *s.* 1. Capa de caucho que se superpone a neumáticos gastados. 2. Resumen (summary). *-va.* 1. Recubrir neumáticos gastados. 2. Recapitular, resumir (summarize).

recapacitate [ˌriːkæˈpæsɪteɪt] [ri-ka-pa-si-teit], *va.* Recapacitar.

recapitulate [ˌriːkæˈpɪtjʊleɪt] [ri-ka-pi-tiu-leit], *va.* Recapitular, resumir.

recapitulation ['riːkəpɪtjʊˈleɪʃən] [ri-ka-pi-tiu-lei-shon], *s.* Recapitulación, resumen; resunción.

recaption ['riːkæptʃən] [ri-kap-chon], *s. (For.)* Nuevo embargo, secuestro o prisión.

recapture ['riːkæptʃəʳ] [ri-kap-chaʳ], *va.* Volver a tomar; represar.

recapture, *s.* Represa de una embarcación; acción de prender o capturar de nuevo.

recast ['riːkɑːst] [ri-kast], *va.* (*pret.* y *pp.* RECAST). 1. Fundir otra vez, volver a fundir. 2. Formar, amoldar, de nuevo, cambiando la forma, disposición, etc., v. g. de un discurso u obra dramática. 3. Calcular de nuevo. 4. Arrojar otra vez.

recede [rɪˈsiːd] [ri-sid], *vn.* 1. Cejar, retroceder, recular (withdraw), retirarse, alejarse. 2. Desistir, volverse atrás; desdecirse. 3. Inclinarse o tenderse a distancia, formar declive, apartarse. **He receded from his demand,** desistió de su demanda.

receipt [rɪˈsiːt] [ri-sit], *s.* 1. Recibimiento, cobranza. 2. Lo que se recibe; ingresos, sumas o cantidades recibidas. 3. Recibo, el escrito en que se declara haber recibido dinero u otra cosa. 4. Receta, memoria de aquello de que se debe componer alguna cosa. *V.* RECIPE. 5. *(Ant.)* Receptoria. **Receipt and outgo,** entrada y salida. **On receipt of,** al recibo de. **Receipt-book,** registro de recetas; *(Com.)* libro de ingresos o recibos. **Receipt in fall (of all demands),** recibo por saldo de cuentas. *(Fin.)* **Receipts,** ingresos, entradas.

receipt, *va.* Dar recibo de algo, extender el recibo de un pago.

receipted, *pp.* Que lleva un recibo.

receivable [rɪˈsiːvəbl] [ri-si-va-bol], *a.* Recibidero, admissible. **Bills receivable,** valores a recibir, o por cobrar.

receive [rɪˈsiːv] [ri-siv], *va.* 1. Recibir, tomar lo que se da o presenta. 2. Recibir, aceptar, aprobar, admitir. 3. Recibir, admitir (admit), hospedar, acoger. 4. Recibir, percibir, cobrar. 5. Concebir. 6. Recibir, comulgar. **To receive rents,** cobrar rentas. **To receive one graciously,** hacer buena acogida a alguno.

receiver [rɪˈsiːvəʳ] [ri-si-vaʳ], *s.* 1. Recibidor, depositario. 2. Encubridor de hurtos. 3. *(Elec.)* Receptor. **Telephone receiver,** audífono.

receivership [rɪˈsiːvəʃɪp] [ri-si-va-ship], *s.* Sindicatura.

receiving set [rɪˈsiːvɪŋset] [ri-si-vin-set], *s.* Radiorreceptor.

recension [rɪˈsenʃən] [ri-sen-shon], *s.* 1. Revisión crítica de un texto, y el mismo texto revisado. 2. Crítica, examen crítico.

recent [ˈriːsnt] [ri-sent], *a.* Reciente, moderno, nuevo, fresco, flamante, acaecido no hace mucho tiempo. **In recent years,** en los últimos años.

recently [ˈriːsntlɪ] [ri-sent-li], *adv.* Recientemente, nuevamente, hace poco. **Until quite recently,** hasta hace bien poco.

recentness [ˈriːsntnɪs] [ri-sent-nes], *s.* Novedad, fecha, origen reciente.

receptacle [rɪˈseptəkl] [ri-sep-ta-kol], *s.* 1. Receptáculo, cualquier cosa que sirve para contener otras. 2. *(Bot.)* Receptáculo, extremo del pedúnculo, casi siempre grueso y carnoso, donde se asientan las hojas o vertícilos de la flor.

reception [rɪˈsepʃən] [ri-sep-shon], *s.* 1. Recepción, el acto de recibir, y el estado de ser recibido; acogimiento, acogida (welcome). **What sort of reception did you get?,** ¿qué tal te han recibido? 2. Admisión (admission). 3. Recepción de una oficina, de un hotel. 4. Recepción en un acto social (social event). 5. Recepción de radio o televisión. **Reception room,** salón donde se puede recibir.

receptionist [rɪˈsepʃənɪst] [ri-sep-sho-nist], *s.* Recepcionsita, recibidor.

receptive [rɪˈseptɪv] [ri-sep-tiv], *a.* Capaz de recibir; que tiene la facultad de recibir, dispuesto a recibir. **I'm receptive to any suggestion,** estoy abierto a cualquier sugerencia.

recess [rɪˈses] [ri-ses], *s.* 1. Nicho, alcoba; la parte entrante en la pared de un cuarto. 2. Suspensión de cualquiera empresa, acción o trabajo; vacaciones, interrupción de trabajos; prórroga. 3. Retiro, el lugar apartado y distante del concurso y bullicio de la gente; soledad, escondrijo (secluded place). **The most secret recess of the human heart,** lo más escondido o lo más oculto del corazón humano.

recession [rɪˈseʃən] [ri-se-shon], *s.* 1. Retirada, retiro, la acción de retirarse. 2. Restitución, desistimiento; concesión. 3. *(Com.)* Recesión.

recessional [rɪˈseʃənl] [ri-se-sho-nal], *s.* Himno que se canta cuando el sacerdote o el coro dejan el presbiterio después del servicio divino.

rechange [riˈtʃeɪndʒ] [ri-cheinch], *va.* Recambiar.

recharge [riːˈtʃɑːdʒ] [ri-charch], *va.* 1. Acusarse mutuamente, acusar al acusador. 2. Recargar, cargar o acometer de nuevo.

recharge, *s.* Recarga.

rechargeable [ˈriːˈtʃɑːdʒəbl] [ri-char-ya-bol], *a.* Recargable.

recidivism [rɪˈsɪdɪvɪzəm] [ri-si-di-vi-sem], *s.* Reincidencia, la recaída en alguna culpa o pecado.

recidivist [rɪˈsɪdɪvɪst] [ri-si-di-vist], *s.* Reincidente.

recipe [ˈresɪpɪ] [re-si-pi], *s.* 1. Receta, instrucciones para hacer un guiso o preparar un plato. **Recipe book,** libro de recetas.

recipience [rɪˈsɪpɪəns] [ri-si-pians], *s.* Acción de recibir; facultad de recibir.

recipient [rɪˈsɪpɪənt] [ri-si-piant], *s.* Recipiente, el que o lo que recibe; destinatario de una carta por ejemplo. *-a.* Recipiente.

reciprocal [rɪˈsɪprəkəl] [ri-si-pro-kal], *a.* Recíproco, mutuo (mutual), alternativo, que obra por movimiento de vaivén. *-s.* 1. El cociente obtenido dividiendo la unidad por un número. 2. Una cosa que alterna con otra.

reciprocally [rɪˈsɪprəkəlɪ] [ri-si-pro-ka-li], *adv.* Recíprocamente, mutuamente.

reciprocalness [rɪˈsɪprəkəlnɪs] [ri-si-pro-kal-nes], *s.* Reciprocidad, mutua correspondencia.

reciprocate [rɪˈsɪprəkeɪt] [ri-si-pro-keit], *va.* Producir un movimiento de vaivén; hacer pasar adelante y atrás; dar y recibir mutuamente, *-vn.* Reciprocar, obrar recíprocamente. **Reciprocating motion,** movimiento alternativo o de vaivén. **Your love isn't reciprocated,** tu amor no es correspondido.

reciprocation [rɪˌsɪprəˈkeɪʃən] [ri-si-pro-kei-shon], *s.* Reciprocación, reciprocidad; acto de dar y recibir mutuamente; alternación, alternativa; movimiento alternativo.

reciprocity [ˌresɪˈprɒsɪtɪ] [re-si-pro-si-ti], *s.* Reciprocidad, calidad de recíproco; derecho u obligación recíproca; particularmente, derechos o ventajas iguales y mutuos entre los ciudadanos de dos países respecto a los privilegios comerciales que han de gozar ambos.

recital [rɪˈsaɪtl] [ri-sai-tal], *s.* 1. Relación, narración; repetición. 2. Recitación en público de algo que se ha confiado a la memoria. 3. *(Mús.)* El acto de tocar una composición una sola persona. 4. Explicación, repetición. 5. Recital (performance).

recitation [ˌresɪˈteɪʃən] [re-si-tei-shon], *s.* Recitación, recitado.

recitative [ˌresɪtəˈtiːv] [re-si-ta-tiv], *s.* Recitativo o recitado, estilo músico en que se canta recitando. *-a.* Recitativo.

recite [rɪˈsaɪt] [ri-sait], *va.* 1. Recitar (declaim), referir, narrar, relatar, contar hechos o detalles; entrar en los pormenores. 2. Decir o pronunciar de memoria; recitar, recitar una lección. 3. Citar.

reciter [rɪˈsaɪtəʳ] [ri-sai-taʳ], *s.* Recitador.

reck [rek] [rek], *va.* y *vn.* *(Poet. o ant.)* Tener cuidado o inquietarse de. **He recked not of danger,** no le inquietó el peligro.

reckless [ˈreklɪs] [re-kles], *a.* Descuidado, atrevido (daring), temerario, precipitado; indiferente sin miramiento, con desvergüenza; atolondrado respecto al peligro.

recklessly [ˈreklɪslɪ] [re-kles-li], *adv.* Imprudentemente, de modo temerario. **You are driving recklessly,** conduces imprudentemente.

recklessness [ˈreklɪsnɪs] [re-kles-nes], *s.* 1. Descuido, atrevimiento, falta de atención, abandono a los vicios; ociosidad, indiferencia, inconsideración, imprudencia (imprudence). 2. Indiferencia, apatía.

reckon [ˈrekən] [re-kon], *va.* 1. Contar, numerar. 2. Estimar, considerar (consider). **I shall reckon it a favor,** lo miraré como un favor. 3. Poner en el número de, en el grado de. *-vn.* 1. Contar, computar, calcular (calculate); formalizar una cuenta. 2. Pagar una multa. 3. Contar, fiar, tener confianza; con *on* o *upon* contar con. **I reckon on your friendship,** cuento con la amistad de Ud. 4. *(Prov. o ant.)* Suponer, creer (think). **What do you reckon?,** ¿qué opinas? **Reckon up,** sumar, calcular. **Reckon with,** vérselas con (face); tener en cuenta (take into account). **Reckon without,** no tener en cuenta.

reckoner [ˈrekənəʳ] [re-ko-naʳ], *s.* 1. Contador, calculador. 2. Libro u otro expediente para facilitar una computación. **Ready-reckoner,** libro de cuentas ya hechas.

reckoning [ˈrekənɪŋ] [rek-nin], *s.* 1. Cuenta; cuenta de cargo y data; cuenta de huésped. 2. Cuenta, suposición; cálculos (calculation). **By my reckoning,** según mis cálculos. 3. Ajuste de demandas o cuentas. 4. Escote. 5. Juicio (judgement). **The day of reckoning;** el día del Juicio Final. 6. *(Mar.)* Estima. **Dead reckoning,** *(Mar.)* rumbo estimado, estima, cálculo aproximado de la distancia recorrida por un buque, según la guíndola. **To be out in one's reckoning,**

estar lejos de la cuneta, engañarse en el cálculo. **Reckoning-book,** libro en que se sienta lo que se recibe y gasta o de cuenta y razón. **Everyone must pay his reckoning,** cada uno debe pagar su escote.

reclaim [rɪˈkleɪm] [ri-kleim], *va.* 1. Reformar, corregir; amansar, domesticar. 2. Reducir alguna cosa al estado que se requiere; volver al estado de cultivo las tierras incultas, desiertas o inundadas. 3. Reclamar, oponerse; pedir en contra. 4. Recuperar (recover).

reclaimable [rɪˈkleɪməbl] [ri-klei-ma-bol], *a.* Reclamable, que puede ser reclamado, corregido o cultivado.

reclaimant [rɪˈkleɪmənt] [ri-klei-mant], *s.* (Poco us.) Disidente, el que se opone a alguna determinación o reclama contra ella.

reclamation [ˌrekləˈmeɪʃən] [re-kla-mei-shon], *s.* Reclamación, restauración.

recline [rɪˈklaɪn] [ri-klain], *va.* Reclinar, inclinar. -*vn.* Recostarse (lean back), descansar, reposar.

recline, *a.* (Poco us.) Reclinado, inclinado.

recliner [rɪˈklaɪnəʳ] [ri-klai-naʳ], *s.* Asiento reclinable o abatible.

reclose [rɪˈkləʊz] [ri-klous], *va.* Volver a cerrar.

reclothe [rɪˈkləʊð] [ri-kloz], *va.* Volver a vestir, vestir de nuevo.

recluse [rɪˈkluːs] [ri-klus], *a.* Recluso, encerrado, retirado del mundo o de la vista pública. -*s.* Una persona retirada del mundo, persona que vive en el retiro, en el aislamiento, ermitaño (hermit).

reclusely [rɪˈkluːslɪ] [ri-klus-li], *adv.* Retiradamente.

recluseness [rɪˈkluːsnɪs] [ri-klus-nis], *s.* Retiro (retreat), recogimiento, estado de la persona que vive encerrada; soledad, aislamiento.

reclusion [rɪˈkluːʒən] [ri-klu-shon], *s.* Reclusión, retirada del mundo.

reclusive [rɪˈkluːsɪv] [ri-klu-siv], *a.* Que proporciona retiro, que vive en el aislamiento o el retiro.

recognition [ˌrekəgˈniːʃən] [re-kog-ni-shon], *s.* 1. Reconocimiento (identification), el acto de reconocer. 2. Reconocimiento (acknowledgment, acceptance) 3. Recuerdo, memoria. 4. Agradecimiento; saludo amistoso.

recognizable [ˈrekəgnaɪzəbl] [re-kog-nai-sa-bol], *a.* Que puede ser reconocido.

recognizably [ˈrekəgnaɪzəblɪ] [re-kog-nai-sa-bli], *adv.* Evidentemente.

recognizance [ˈrekəgnaɪzəns] [re-kog-nai-sans], *s.* Reconocimiento; obligación, sumisión con condición de hacer un acto determinado, v. gr. comparecer ante un tribunal.

recognize [ˈrekəgnaɪz] [re-kog-nais], *va.* 1. Reconocer (identify). 2. Declarar que se tiene conocimiento de una cosa; reconocer, admitir formalmente. 3. Confesar, admitir (accept), conceder. -*vn.* Subscribir una obligación auténtica.

recognize, *va.* Volver a conocer, a percibir.

recognized [ˈrekəgnaɪzd] [re-kog-naisd], *a.* Reconocido.

recognizor [ˈrekəgnaɪzəʳ] [re-kog-nai-saʳ], *s.* (For.) El que da algún vale a favor de otro.

recoil [rɪˈkɔɪl] [ri-koil], *s.* 1. Reculada; coz, retroceso, rebufo de un arma de fuego. 2. Repugnancia, temor. **Recoil-spring,** resorte para disminuir el rebufo.

recoil, *vn.* 1. Recular de horror o repugnancia, quedarse helado; retirarse. 2. Cejar, retroceder. 3. Volver atrás. 4. Rebufar (un arma de fuego). **The blood recoils with horror at the sight,** la sangre se hiela en las venas ante tal cuadro.

recoilless [rɪˈkɔɪlɪs] [ri-koi-les], *a.* Sin retroceso (gun).

recoin [rɪˈkɔɪn] [ri-koin], *va.* Acuñar de nuevo.

recollect [ˌrekəˈlekt] [re-ko-lekt], *va.* 1. Acordarse, traer a la memoria, recordar (remember). 2. Recobrarse, volver en sí.

recollect, *va.* Recoger, juntar de nuevo; reunir.

recollect, recollet, *s.* Recoleto, miembro de una orden reformada de franciscanos.

recollection [ˌrekəˈlekʃən] [re-ko-lek-shon], *s.* 1. Memoria (memory), recuerdo, recordación, reminiscencia. 2. Recuerdo, memoria, la cosa traída a la memoria. **I have no**

recollection of having seen you before, no recuerdo haberte visto antes.

recommence [ˌriːkəˈmens] [ri-ko-mens], *va.* Empezar de nuevo, reanudar. -*vi.* Reanudarse.

recommencement [ˈriːkəmensmənt] [ri-ko-mens-ment], *s.* La acción de comenzar de nuevo alguna cosa.

recommend [ˌrekəˈmend] [re-ko-mend], *va.* 1. Recomendar, alabar (praise), empeñarse por alguno elogiándole; encomendar, poner al cuidado de uno. 2. Aconsejar (advise), avisar por lo que toca a un curso de acción.

recommendable [ˌrekəˈmendəbl] [re-ko-men-da-bol], *a.* Recomendable; digno de alabanza.

recommendation [ˌrekəmenˈdeɪʃən] [re-ko-men-dei-shon], *s.* 1. Recomendación. 2. Recomendación, la alabanza o elogio que se hace de alguno con el fin de recomendarle a otro.

recommendatory [ˌrekəˈmendətərɪ] [re-ko-men-da-to-ri], *a.* Recomendatorio.

recommender [ˌrekəˈmendəʳ] [re-ko-men-daʳ], *s.* El que recomienda.

recompact [ˈrekɒmpækt] [re-kom-pakt], *va.* Reunir, volver a unir, volver a pegar.

recompense [ˈrekəmpens] [re-kom-pens], *va.* 1. Recompensar, compensar, satisfacer, dar el equivalente; reintegrar. 2. Indemnizar; resarcir de un daño.

recompense, *s.* Recompensa, equivalente devuelto; compensación, indemnización.

recompilement [ˌrekəmˈpaɪlmənt] [re-kom-pail-ment], *s.* Nueva compilación.

recompose [ˈrekəmpəʊz] [re-kom-pous], *va.* 1. Volver a componer; tranquilizar de nuevo. 2. Recomponer, rehacer; componer de nuevo (la luz blanca); lo contrario de *descompose,* descomponer.

recomposition [ˌrekɒmpəˈsɪʃən] [re-kom-po-si-shon], *s.* 1. Nueva composición. 2. *(Quím.)* Recomposición.

reconcilable [ˈrekənsaɪləbl] [re-kon-sai-la-bol], *a.* Reconciliable, componible; conciliable, que puede concordar con algo; compatible.

reconcilably [ˈrekənsaɪləblɪ] [re-kon-sai-la-bli], *adv.* De una manera compatible.

reconcile [ˈrekənsaɪl] [re-kon-sail], *va.* 1. Reconciliar, componer o ajustar diferencias; restablecer la amistad entre personas enojadas. 2. Conciliar, componer, concordar, arreglar (una querella), poner de acuerdo; adaptar. 3. Restablecer. **I cannot reconcile myself to his way of thinking,** no puedo adaptarme a su modo de pensar. **To reconcile oneself to,** resolverse o determinarse a. **If you can reconcile it to your conscience,** si Ud. puede conciliarlo con su conciencia.

reconcilement [ˈrekənsaɪlmənt] [re-kon-sail-ment], *s.* Reconciliación, la acción de reconciliar, o el estado de hallarse reconciliado.

reconciler [ˈrekənsaɪləʳ] [re-kon-sai-laʳ], *s.* Reconciliador; conciliador, pacificador.

reconciliation [ˌrekənsɪlɪˈeɪʃən] [re-kon-si-liei-shon], *s.* Reconciliación; conciliación, ajuste, acomodamiento; renovación de la amistad; acuerdo entre cosas que parecen opuestas, diferentes o incompatibles.

reconciliatory [ˈrekənsɪlɪətərɪ] [re-kon-si-lia-to-ri], *a.* Reconciliador, que reconcilia o tiende a reconciliar.

recondense [ˈrekəndəns] [re-kon-dens], *va.* Volver a condensar.

recondite [rɪˈkɒndaɪt] [ri-kon-dait], *a.* 1. Recóndito, secreto, oculto (hidden), impenetrable. 2. Profundo; que trata, que se ocupa en asuntos abstrusos.

recondition [ˌriːkənˈdɪʃən] [re-kon-di-shon], *va.* Reacondicionar, reparar, restaurar.

reconduct [ˈrekəndʌkt] [re-kon-dakt], *va.* Conducir de nuevo, volver a conducir.

reconnaisance [rɪˈkɒnɪsəns] [ri-ko-nai-sans], *s.* Reconocimiento; examen de una región, v. g. para operaciones militares.

reconnoitre [ˌrekəˈnɔːtəʳ] [re-ko-no-taʳ], *va.* Reconocer, examinar el estado de las cosas para dar parte de él;

examinar con la vista; inspeccionar, v. g. los militares, ingenieros o geólogos.

reconquer ['riːˈkɒŋkəʳ] [ri-kon-kaʳ], *va.* Reconquistar.

reconquest ['riːˈkɒŋkwest] [re-kon-kuest], *s.* Reconquista.

reconsider ['riːkənˈsɪdəʳ] [ri-kon-si-daʳ], *va.* Considerar de nuevo, volver a considerar; someter a nuevo examen una cuestión ya debatida.

reconsideration ['riːkənˌsɪdəˈreɪʃən] [ri-kon-si-de-ra-shon], *s.* El acto de considerar de nuevo; el acto de someter a nueva discusión una propuesta rechazada anteriormente.

reconstitute ['riːˈkɒnstɪtjuːt] [ri-kons-ti-tiut], *vt.* Reconstituir.

reconstitution ['riːˈkɒnstɪˈtjuːʃən] [ri-kons-ti-tiu-shon], *sf.* Reconstitución.

reconstruct ['riːkənˈstrʌkt] [ri-kon-strakt], *va.* Reedificar, construir de nuevo; en los Estados Unidos, reorganizar y reintegrar en la Unión un Estado separado de ella.

reconstruction ['riːkənˈstrʌkʃən] [ri-kon-strak-shon], *s.* 1. Reconstrucción (rebuilding). 2. Reconstitución (re-creation).

reconvene ['riːkənˈviːn] [ri-kon-vin], *va.* Convocar, juntar o reunir de nuevo-

reconversion ['riːkənˈvɜːʃən] [ri-kon-ver-shon], *s.* Reconversión.

reconvert ['riːkənˈvɜːt] [ri-kon-vert], *vt.* Reorganizar, reconvertir.

reconvey ['riːkənveɪ] [ri-kon-vei], *va.* 1. Volver a llevar o enviar; volver a poner una cosa en su antiguo sitio. 2. Retroceder; transferir a anterior poseedor.

record ['rekɔːd] [ri-kord], *va.* 1. Registrar, anotar (write down) o poner alguna cosa en los libros de registro; inscribir una relación auténtica u oficial de algo; protocolar; archivar. **Historians record how the Spanish Empire fell,** los historiadores narran la caída del Imperio Español. 2. Celebrar la memoria de alguna cosa, fijar en el ánimo, imprimir en la memoria. 3. Indicar, registrar, grabar. 4. *(Ant.)* Referir, relatar. **Where the barometer recorded but 28.5 inches,** donde el barómetro indicó no más que 28.5 pulgadas (726 milímetros).

record, *s.* 1. Registro, copia auténtica de un documento; protocolo, historia; record. 2. Relación de sucesos consignados en un libro para conservarlos. 3. Disco que reproduce sonidos musicales o de otra clase en un gramófono. **Record company,** compañía discográfica. 4. Registro de actos, en especial de los atletas; también el más notable de esos actos. **To hold the world record,** ostentar el récord mundial. 5. Atestación, testimonio. **Records,** archivo (file), papeles archivados; fastos; memorias. **Old records,** archivos. **Keeper of the records,** archivero. **On o upon record,** registrado; *(Fig.)* inscrito en los anales de la historia. **There is no record of it in history,** no hay nota de ello, no se hace mención de ello en la historia. **To make a record,** tomar razón, registrar, archivar; también, igualar o superar al más notable ejercicio atlético que se recuerda. *-a.* Sin precedentes.

recorded ['rekɔːdɪd] [ri-kor-did], *a.* 1. Grabado. 2. Escrito (written), documentado.

recorder ['rekɔːdəʳ] [ri-kor-daʳ], *s.* 1. Registrador, archivero. 2. Juez recopilador, magistrado o ministro superior que recopila y examina la evidencia o resultado de las deposiciones de los testigos para que el jurado *(jury)* decida; y que dicta la sentencia *(verdict)* según la decisión del jurado. 3. Indicador, contador, aparato para indicar. 4. *(Mús.)* Flauta.

recordership ['rekɔːdəʃɪp] [ri-kor-da-ship], *s.* Cargo o función de reegistrador o archivero, y el tiempo de su duración.

recording ['rekɔːdɪŋ] [ri-kor-din], *s.* Grabación.

recount ['rekaʊnt] [ri-kaunt], *va.* Recontar; referir, relatar; recitar, detallar, mencionar con pormenores.

re-count, *va.* Contar de nuevo.

re-count, *s.* Repetición de una cuenta; cuenta hecha de nuevo, recuento.

recoup ['rekɑʊp] [ri-kaup], *va.* 1. Retener (alguna cosa debida) para indemnizarse. 2. Obtener compensación por una pérdida. 3. Reparar (una pérdida), indemnizar, resarcir.

recourse ['rekɔːs] [ri-kors], *s.* 1. Recurso, remedio (option), auxilio, refugio. 2. *(For.)* Recurso, derecho de acción contra una persona o una propiedad para obtener garantías. 3. Acceso, entrada al trato o comunicación.

recover [rɪˈkʌvəʳ] [ri-ka-vaʳ], *va.* 1. Recobrar (regain), volver a cobrar lo que antes se tenía. 2. Reparar, remediar, resarcir. **To recover a loss,** resarcir un daño. 3. *(For.)* Obtener fallo judicial contra alguien. 4. *(Ant.)* Rescatar, restablecer, reparar a alguno de la enfermedad, ir recobrando la salud perdida; volver a un estado o condición anterior. 5. *(For.)* Ganar un pleito. **To recover one's health,** restablecerse, recobrar la salud. **To recover oneself,** volver en sí; tomar valor.

recover, *va.* Volver a cubrir o tapar.

recoverable [rɪˈkʌvərəbl] [ri-ka-ve-ra-bol], *a.* Curable; recuperable; exigible, que se puede lograr por medio de un pleito. **The debt was recoverable,** era exigible la deuda. **No damages are recoverable,** no se deben daños y perjuicios.

recoverableness [rɪˈkʌvərəblnɪs] [ri-ka-ve-ra-bol-nes], *s.* El estado o la calidad de recuperable.

recovery [rɪˈkʌvərɪ] [ri-ka-ve-ri], *s.* 1. Recobro, recuperación; acto de recobrar, de volver a entrar en posesión; de una propiedad, de volver a ganar. 2. Mejoría, convalecencia, restablecimiento de la salud. 3. El acto de hacer libres los bienes vinculados. 4. Recuperación de cosas robadas o perdidas, rescate (retrieval). 5. Fallo, decisión judicial en favor de alguien. 6. Remedio. **It is a thing past recovery,** no tiene remedio. **Past recovery,** desahuciado, sin remedio; en estado crítico.

recreancy ['rekrɪənsɪ] [re-krian-si], *s.* Deslealtad, apostasía; pusilanimidad.

recreant ['rekrɪənt] [re-kriant], *a.* 1. Falso, desleal; apóstata. 2. Cobarde, apocado, pusilánime.

re-create ['rekrɪeɪt] [re-krieit], *va.* Recrear, deleitar, divertir (amuse); aliviar.

recreation [ˌrekrɪˈeɪʃən] [re-kriei-shon], *s.* Recreación, recreo, entretenimiento, diversión, pasatiempo, esparcimiento (leisure); descanso.

re-creation [ˌrekrɪˈeɪʃən] [re-kriei-shon], *s.* Nueva creación, formación de nuevo.

recreational [ˌrekrɪˈeɪʃənl] [re-kriei-sho-nal], *a.* Recreativo.

recreative ['rekrɪeɪtɪv] [re-kriei-tiv], *a.* Recreativo, agradable (enjoyable); entretenido.

recreativeness ['rekrɪeɪtɪvnɪs] [re-kriei-tiv-nes], *s.* La calidad de lo que divierte o agrada.

recriminate [rɪˈkrɪmɪneɪt] [re-kri-mi-neit], *va.* y *vn.* Recriminar, acusar al acusador, acusarse mutuamente.

recrimination [rɪˌkrɪmɪˈneɪʃən] [ri-kri-mi-nei-shon], *s.* Recriminación, acto de recriminar, reproche.

recriminator [rɪˌkrɪmɪˈneɪtəʳ] [ri-kri-mi-ni-taʳ], *s.* *(For.)* Recriminador.

recross ['rekrɒs] [ri-kros], *va.* Volver a pasar.

recrudesce [ˌriːkruːˈdes] [ri-kru-des], *vn.* Recrudecer, recrudecersse, tomar nuevo incremento un mal físico o moral; encrudecerse.

recrudescence [ˌriːkruːˈdesəns] [ri-kru-de-sens], *s.* Encrudecimiento, recrudescencia, acción y efecto de recrudecer; aumento o actividad mayor de los fenómenos morbosos después de una mejoría sensible.

recrudescent [ˌriːkruːˈdesənt] [ri-kru-de-sent], *a.* Recrudescente, que recrudece.

recruit [rɪˈkruːt] [ri-krut], *va.* 1. Abastecerse, proveerse uno de lo que necesita; de aquí, restablecer (re-establish), reparar, rehacer; reemplazar. 2. Reclutar tropas. **To recruit oneself,** reparar las fuerzas, restablecerse. *-vn.* Restablecerse, reponerse, rehacerse; reanimarse, recobrar la salud o la fuerza.

recruit, *s.* 1. *(Mil.)* Recluta, soldado bisoño; marinero novicio. 2. El reemplazo de cualquier cosa que hace falta.

recruiting [rɪˈkruːtɪŋ] [ri-kru-tin], *s.* Recluta, el acto de reclutar o reemplazar.

recruitment [rɪˈkruːtmənt] [ri-krut-ment], *s.* Reclutamiento.

rectal [ˈrektəl] [rek-tal], *a.* Relativo o perteneciente al recto.

rectangle [ˈrektˌæŋgl] [rek-tan-guel], *s.* Rectángulo, paralelogramo de ángulos rectos.

rectangled [ˈrektˌæŋgld] [rek-tan-gueld], **rectangular** [ˈrektˌæŋgjolaʳ] [rek-tan-guiu-laʳ], *a.* Rectangular, que tiene ángulos rectos.

rectifiable [ˈrektɪfaɪəbl] [rek-ti-faia-bol], *a.* Rectificable; que puede rectificar, capaz de ser corregido.

rectification [ˌrektɪfɪˈkeɪʃən] [rek-ti-fi-kei-shon], *s.* Rectificación, acción de rectificar: (a) enmendación; (b) el procedimiento de refinar o purificar (un líquido) por destilaciones repetidas; (c) (*Mat.*) determinación de una línea recta cuya longitud es igual al arco de una curva.

rectifier [ˈrektɪfaɪəʳ] [rek-ti-faiaʳ], *s.* Rectificador, el que o lo que rectifica; particularmente un refinador de licores espirituosos.

rectify [ˈrektɪfaɪ] [rek-ti-fai], *va.* (*pret.* y *pp.* RECTIFIED). 1. Rectificar, corregir, enmendar, reformar. 2. Rectificar los licores y darles mayor perfección o purificar por cristalizaciones repetidas.

rectilineal [ˌrektɪˈlɪnɪəl] [rek-ti-li-nial], **rectilinear** [ˌrektɪˈlɪnɪəʳ] [rek-ti-li-niaʳ], *a.* Rectilíneo, que se compone de líneas rectas.

rectitude [ˈrektɪtjuːd] [rek-ti-tiud], *s.* 1. Rectitud, derechura. 2. Rectitud en las acciones, equidad (equity).

rector [ˈrektəʳ] [rek-taʳ], *s.* (*Relig.*) 1. Rector, párroco, cura propio. 2. Jefe, superior, principal de ciertos colegios u otros establecimiento de educación.

rectoral [ˈrektərəl] [rek-to-ral], *a.* Rectoral, relativo o perteneciente a un rector.

rectorate [ˈrektəreɪt] [rek-to-reit], *s.* Rectorado, el oficio y cargo de rector y el tiempo que dura; rectoría.

rectorship [ˈrektəʃɪp] [rek-to-ship], *s.* V. RECTORATE.

rectory [ˈrektərɪ] [rek-to-ri], *s.* 1. Habitación de un rector, casa de un cura, particularmente cuando forma parte de la propiedad de una iglesia. 2. (*Ingl.*) Rectoría, feligresía de un cura con sus edificios, tierras y rentas.

rectum [ˈrektəm] [rek-tam], *s.* (*Anat.*) Recto, la tercera y última porción del intestino grueso.

recumbence [rɪˈkʌmbəns] [ri-kam-bans], *s.* 1. Estado o postura del que está reclinado. 2. (*Des.*) La acción de esperar con confianza.

recumbent [rɪˈkʌmbənt] [ri-kam-bant], *a.* Recostado, reclinado.

recuperate [rɪˈkuːpəreɪt] [ri-ku-pe-reit], *va.* 1. Recuperar, recobrar, volver a ganar. 2. V. RECOUP. *-vn.* (*E.U.*) Restablecerse, recobrar la salud o las fuerzas.

recuperation [rɪˌkuːpəˈreɪʃən] [ri-ku-pe-rei-shon], *s.* Recuperación (recovery), restablecimiento.

recuperative [rɪˈkuːpərətɪv] [ri-ku-pe-ra-tiv], *a.* Recuperativo, que tiende a la recuperación.

recur [rɪˈkɜːʳ] [ri-keʳ], *vn.* 1. Acaecer, suceder, otra vez o repetidas veces, particularmente a intervalos regulares; volver, presentarse de nuevo. **A recurring paroxysm,** un paroxismo que se repite. 2. Ofrecerse a la imaginación o a la memoria. 3. (*Des.*) Recurrir, acudir.

recurrence [rɪˈkʌrəns] [ri-ka-rans], *s.* 1. Repetición, reaparición. 2. Recurso.

recurrent [rɪˈkʌrənt] [ri-ka-rant], *a.* 1. Que vuelve de vez en cuando; periódico. **A recurrent nightmare,** una pesadilla recurrente. 2. (*Anat.*) Recurrente, que corre hacia atrás, como una arteria, o un nervio.

recurve [rɪˈkɜːv] [ri-kerv], *va.* Encorvar, torcer hacia atrás o abajo.

recurved [rɪˈkɜːvd] [ri-kervd], **recurvous** [rɪˈkɜːvəs] [ri-ker-vos], *a.* Encorvado.

recusancy [ˈrekjozənsɪ] [re-kiu-san-si], *s.* La acción de recusar y la calidad de recusante.

recusant [ˈrekjozənt] [re-kiu-sant], *s.* y *a.* Recusante, no conformista.

recusation [ˌrekjoˈseɪʃən] [re-kiu-sei-shon], *s.* (*For.*) Recusación, acto de recusar a un juez por motivo de parentesco, predisposición contra una de las partes, etc.

recycle [ˌriːˈsaɪkl] [ri-sai-kel], *va.* 1. Recircular. 2. Reciclar.

recycling [ˌriːˈsaɪklɪŋ] [ri-sai-klin], *s.* Reciclaje, reciclado.

red [red] [red], *a.* 1. Colorado, rojo, encarnado; rubio. 2. Revolucionario, anárquico. *-s.* 1. Rojez, el color rojo, el encarnado, el color encarnado; color parecido al de la sangre. 2. Uno de muchos colores rojos. 3. Republicano rojo; ultraradical en sus opiniones. **Adrianople o Turkey red,** carmesí. **The Red Sea,** el Mar Rojo. **Cherry red,** rojo cereza. **A deep red,** un rojo subido. **Light red,** rojo claro. **To turn red,** ponerse colorado, sonrojarse. **Red ant,** (a) hormiga leonada, la hormiga común de las casa. (b) Hormiga que esclaviza a otras. **Red cedar,** cedro colorado; junípero. **Red chalk,** creta roja, creta colorada con el peróxido de hiero. **Red deer,** ciervo común; ciervo de Virginia. **Red-haired,** de pelo rojo o de un rubio ardiente. **Red herring,** arenque seco y ahumado. **Red man,** indio de América. **Red liquor, red mordant,** disolución de acetato de alúmina empleado como mordiente en el tinte. **Red snow,** nieve colorada por un alga. **Red silver,** plata roja, mineral de plata rojizo; piragirita. **Red spider,** ácaro rojo. **Red thrush,** tordo rojo. **Red ocher,** ocre rojo. **Red-tapist,** formalista, covachuelista, empleado del Gobierno. **Red tape,** (a) balduque, cinta estrecha (rojiza) para atar legajos; (b) (*Fig.*) formalismo, apego a la rutina, exclusivismo de escuela.

redact [rɪˈdækt] [ri-dakt], *vt.* Redactar.

redaction [rɪˈdækʃən] [ri-dak-shon], *sf.* Redacción.

red-baiting [ˈredbeɪtɪŋ] [red-bei-tin], *s.* Acosamiento de los comunistas.

redbird [ˈredbɜːd] [red-berd], *s.* (*Orn.*) 1. Cardenal. 2. Tánagra, (*Fam.*) tángara escarlata. 3. Pinzón real.

red-blooded [ˈredˈblʌdɪd] [red-bla-did], *a.* 1. Valiente, intrépido. 2. Viril.

red-book [ˈredbok] [red-buk], *s.* El registro de las personas que tienen tierras, pensiones o empleos por el rey; guía de la corte.

redbreast [ˈredbrest] [red-brest], *s.* (*Orn.*) Pitirrojo, petirrojo, pechicolorado.

redcap [ˈredkæp] [red-kap], *s.* 1. Cardelina, jilguero europeo. 2. Cargador (en las estaciones de ferrocarril).

redcoat [ˈredkɔːt] [red-kout], *s.* Casaca colorada; voz con que designan en Inglaterra a los soldados.

red-coral [ˈredkɔːrəl] [red-ko-ral], *s.* Coral rojo, especie de zoófito.

red cross [ˈredkrɒs] [red-kros], *s.* 1. Cruz de San Jorge, emblema de los ingleses. 2. Cruz griega, roja sobre fondo blanco. **Red Cross Society,** sociedad de la Cruz Roja, formada para socorrer a los enfermos y heridos en la guerra. **Red-cross knight,** templario; caballero de la orden de San Jorge.

redden [ˈredn] [re-den], *va.* Teñir de color rojo o encarnado. *-vn.* Ponerse colorado; ruborizarse (blush).

reddish [ˈredɪʃ] [re-dish], *a.* Bermejizo, rojizo; que tira a rojo.

reddishness [ˈredɪʃnɪs] [re-dish-nes], *s.* Bermejura, el color bermejo.

redditive [ˈredɪtɪv] [re-di-tiv], *a.* (Poco us.) Se dice en gramática de la partícula que responde a una pregunta.

reddle [ˈredl] [re-del], *s.* Almazarrón, almagre.

redecorate [ˈriːˈdekəreɪt] [ri-dei-ko-reit], *vt.* Pintar.

redecoration [riːˌdekəˈreɪʃən] [ri-de-ko-rei-shon], *sf.* Renovación.

redeem [rɪˈdiːm] [ri-dim], *va.* 1. Recomprar, adquirir de nuevo; volver a tomar posesión de una cosa enajenada, reembolsando su valor al que la posee. 2. Redimir, rescatar, libertar; sacar del cautiverio. 3. Redimir del pecado y sus consecuencias: se dice de Jesucristo. 4. Cumplir una promesa, una palabra dada. 5. Resarcir, recompensar, reintegrar, reparar. **To redeem out of pawn,** desempeñar.

redeemable [rɪˈdiːməbl] [ri-di-ma-bol], *a.* Redimible, rescatable.

redeemer [rɪˈdiːməʳ] [ri-di-maʳ], *s.* Redentor, el Salvador del mundo.

redeeming [rɪˈdiːmɪŋ] [ri-di-min], *a.* Que rescata, redime o libra; que recompensa, que reembolsa. *-s.* Redención, rescate; recompensa (reward), reintegro.

redemption [rɪ'dempʃən] [ri-dem-shon], s. 1. Redención, salvación (saving), rescate; la acción de rescatar o redimir, o la calidad de rescatado. (a) Liberación de una propiedad gravada con hipoteca, desempeño de bienes muebles. (b) Pago de una deuda u obligación. 2. Redención del pecado por la expiación de Jesucristo. **You are beyond redemption,** no tienes remedio.

redemptional [rɪ'dempʃənl] [ri-dem-sho-nal], **redemptory,** a. Perteneciente a la redención o rescate.

redemptive [rɪ'demptɪv] [ri-dem-tiv], a. De rescate, que sirve para rescatar o redimir; relacionado con la redención.

redeploy ['riːdɪ'plɔɪ] [ri-di-ploi], vt. Reorientar, dar nuevo destino.

redeployment ['riːdɪ'plɔɪmənt] [ri-di-ploi-ment], s. Reorientación, reorganización, reubicación.

redevelop [ˌriːdɪ'veləp] [ri-di-ve-lop], vt. Reurbanizar.

redevelopment [ˌriːdɪ'veləpmənt] [ri-di-ve-lop-ment], s. Reurbanización.

red-handed ['red'hændɪd] [red-jan-did], a. Que tiene las manos ensangrentadas, como las de un asesino; en flagrante, en el acto.

redhead ['red'hed] [red-jed], s. y a. Pelirrojo.

red-hot ['red'hɒt] [red-jot], a. 1. Candente, ardiente, enrojecido al fuego. 2. (Fig.) Demasiado entusiasta; extremo. **A red-hot partizan,** un partidario extremo. **Red hot player,** as. **Red-hot poker,** (Bot.) trítomo.

redial [riː'daɪəl] [ri-daial], vi. Volver a marcar el teléfono. -s. Rellamada.

redid [ˌriː'dɪd] [ri-did] pret. of **redo.**

rediscover ['riːdɪs'kʌvər] [ri-dis-ka-va], vt. Redescubrir.

rediscovery ['riːdɪs'kʌvərɪ] [ri-dis-ka-va-ri], s. Redescubrimiento.

redistribute ['riːdɪs'trɪbjuːt] [ri-dis-tri-biut], vt. Redistribuir.

redistribution ['riːdɪs'trɪbjuːʃən] [ri-dis-tri-biu-shon], s. Redistribución.

red-lead ['red'liːd] [red-lid], s. Minio, bermellón, azarcón, rúbrica sinópica.

red-letter ['red'letər] [red-le-ta], a. Indicado por una o más letras rojas. **Red-letter day,** día de fiesta o feriado; de aquí, día favorable, propicio.

redly ['redlɪ] [red-li], adv. Con color rojo, rojizamente.

redness ['rednɪs] [red-nes], s. Encarnado, rojo; rojez, rojura, bermejura.

redolence ['redəʊləns] [re-dou-lens], s. Fragancia, perfume.

redolent ['redəʊlənt] [re-dou-lent], a. Fragante, fragante, oloroso (scented). **His style is redolent of the Impressionists,** su estilo recuerda el de los impresionistas.

redouble [riː'dʌbl] [ri-da-bel], va. Reduplicar, redoblar, aumentar; repetir frecuentemente. -vn. Redoblarse, aumentarse dos veces tanto.

redoubt [rɪ'daʊt] [ri-daut], s. (Fort.) V. REDOUT.

redoubtable [rɪ'daʊtəbl] [ri-dau-ta-bol], a. Formidable, terrible, imponente (imposing).

redound [rɪ'daʊnd] [ri-daund], vn. 1. Operar por su turno; de aquí, contribuir, redundar, venir a parar una cosa en perjuicio o daño de otro, provenir, resultar. 2. (Des.) Recudir, resaltar, recaer. **Undertakings which will redound to the honor of their country,** empresas que contribuirán a la gloria de su país.

redout [rɪ'daʊt] [ri-daut], s. Reducto, fuerte de varios lados, sin baluarte; fortificación de tierra para uso provisional.

redraft ['riː'drɑːft] [ri-draft], s. 1. Nuevo dibujo, copia, o borrón. 2. Resaca, letra de cambio contra el endosante de otra protestada, para reembolsarse.

redraw [riː'drɔː] [ri-dro], va. Hacer un segundo dibujo o borrón, una segunda copia. -vn. (Com.) Resacar, girar una letra de resaca.

redress [rɪ'dres] [ri-dres], va. 1. Enderezar; corregir, enmendar, reformar, rectificar; hacer justicia. 2. Aliviar o aligerar el peso, carga, etc. 3. Aliviar, consolar. **To redress grievances,** deshacer agravios.

redress, s. Reforma, corrección, enmienda, enderezamiento; desagravio; alivio, consuelo. **To seek redress,** buscar justicia, buscar la reparación de algún agravio.

redresser [rɪ'dresər] [ri-dre-sa], s. Reformador.

redressible [rɪ'dresɪbl] [ri-dre-si-bol], a. Reformable, corregible; capaz de ser aliviado.

redressive [rɪ'dresɪv] [ri-dre-siv], a. (Poco us.) Consolatorio; correctivo, reformatorio.

redshank ['redʃæŋk] [red-shank], s. (Orn.) Especie de maubecha del género Totanus.

redskin ['redskɪn] [red-skin], s. Piel roja, indio de América.

redstreak ['redstriːk] [red-streik], s. Manzana de rosa.

red tape ['redteɪp] [red-teip], s. 1. Cinta roja. 2. Papeleo, expedienteo.

reduce [rɪ'djuːs] [ri-dius], va. 1. Reducir, dar una forma o condición determinadas. 2. Reducir, convertir, reformar, enmendar. 3. Reducir, disminuir, minorar. 4. Reducir, sujetar, someter, sojuzgar; poner en orden. 5. Degradar, envilecer. 6. (Arit. y Alg.) Cambiar la denominación de los números, simplificar (simplify). 7. (Cir.) Reducir, volver a su lugar partes dislocadas; volver alguna cosa al lugar donde antes estaba o al estado que antes tenía. 8. (Quím.) Desoxidar un mineral; separar de una tierra, de un óxido, el metal que contienen. **To reduce to the ranks,** volver a las filas; convertir a un oficial en simple soldado. **Reducing-scale,** escala de reducción; escala de partes iguales para reducir las dimensiones de un plano.

reduced [rɪ'djuːst] [ri-diust], a. 1. Reducido (lower). 2. Reducido, empobrecido (impoverished).

reducer [rɪ'djuːsər] [ri-diu-sa], s. Reductor, reducidor; (Art. y Of.) Empate en disminución.

reducible [rɪ'djuːsəbl] [ri-diu-si-bol], a. Reducible, que se puede reducir.

reduction [rɪ'dʌkʃən] [ri-dak-shon], s. Reducción, reducimiento, acción y efecto de reducir o disminuir; disminución; conquista; desoxidación. **Reduction-works,** establecimiento metalúrgico para la extracción del metal de los minerales; fundición.

reductive [rɪ'dʌktɪv] [ri-dak-tiv], a. Reductivo, perteneciente a la reducción.

reductively [rɪ'dʌktɪvlɪ] [ri-dak-tiv-li], adv. Por consecuencia.

redundance [rɪ'dʌndəns] [ri-dan-dans], **redundancy** [rɪ'dʌndənsɪ] [ri-dan-dan-si], s. Redundancia, exceso, superabundancia. **Redundance of words,** pleonasmo.

redundant [rɪ'dʌndənt] [ri-dan-dant], a. 1. Redundante, superabundante, superfluo (superfluous), excesivo. 2. Redundante, recargado en el estilo, verboso, tautológico.

redundantly [rɪ'dʌndəntlɪ] [ri-dan-dant-li], adv. Superfluamente.

reduplicate [rɪ'djuːplɪkeɪt] [ri-diu-pli-keit], va. Reduplicar, redoblar, reiterar, multiplicar.

reduplicate, s. Reduplicado, duplicado, reiterado.

reduplication [rɪˌdjuːplɪ'keɪʃən] [ri-diu-pli-kei-shon], s. Reduplicación.

reduplicative [rɪ'djuːplɪkətɪv] [ri-diu-pli-ka-tiv], a. Reduplicativo, reduplicado.

redwing ['redwɪŋ] [red-uin], s. 1. Tordo, rojo del antiguo continente. 2. Mirlo americano con manchas rojas sobre las alas.

redwood ['redwʊd] [red-vud], s. 1. Árbol inmenso de California de las coníferas, o su madera; la Sequoia sempervirens. 2. Algún otro árbol de madera rojiza, como el sándalo rojo, el sibucao, etc.

re-echo ['riː'ekəʊ] [ri-ekou], vn. Responder o resonar el eco.

reed [riːd] [rid], s. 1. (Bot.) Caña, planta hueca y nudosa que se cría en lugares húmedos. También el tallo de esta planta. **Reed-cane,** caña. 2. (Mús.) Caña, lengüeta; laminilla delgada, elástica, de caña, madera, o metal, que casi tapa una abertura, produciendo los tonos musicales de los órganos, etc. 3. Churumbela, un instrumento semejante a la chirimía; de aquí, poesía pastoral. 4. Tubo que contiene pólvora, y la conduce al agujero de explosión en una mina. 5. (Arq.) Baqueta, junquillo, moldura semicilíndrica. 6. Peine (cárcel), una parte de los telares donde se juntan los hilos. 7.

(Poet.) Flecha, saeta. 8. Abomaso, el cuarto o verdadero estómago de los rumiantes. **Reed-bird,** *V.* BOBOLINK (Dolichonyx). **Reed-bunting,** emberizo, verderol; verderón de los cañaverales. Emberiza sehosniclus. **Reed-mace,** enea, planta del género Typha. **Reed-organ,** armonio, órgano pequeño   provisto de lengüetas (de latón) y de teclado. **Reed-work,** lengüetería del órgano.

reeducate ['riːˈedjʊkeɪt] [rie-diu-keit], *vt.* Reeducar, rehabilitar.

reedy ['riːdɪ] [ri-di], *a.* 1. Lleno de cañas, cañado, cañoso. 2. Parecido a una caña o a una lengüeta. 3. De tono delgado y agudo, como el producido por una lengüeta.

reef [riːf] [rif], *s.* 1. Arrecife, escollo o banco de políperos situado casi a flor de agua. 2. Bajío, banco de arena en el mar. 3. Filón, vena metálica. 4. *(Mar.)* Rizo. **To take in a reef,** tomar un rizo. **To let out a reef,** largar un rizo. **Reef-band,** faja de rizos. **Reef-cringle,** anillo de vela. **Reef knot,** nudo de rizos. **Reef-line,** cabo de tomar rizos. **Reef-tackles,** aparejuelos o palanquines de rizos.

reef, *va. (Mar.)* Tomar rizos a las velas, acortarlas cuando hay mucho viento; disminuir la extensión de las velas plegando una parte y amarrándola a la verga. **To be close-reefed,** *(Mar.)* estar con todos los rizos tomados.

reefer ['riːfəʳ] [ri-faʳ], *sf.* Chaquetón.

reek [riːk] [rik], *s. (Esco.)* 1. Humo, vaho, vapor. 2. Aventura, hazaña (en sentido burlesco), calaverada. 3. Hedor (stench).

reek, *va.* y *vn.* Ahumar, exponer al humo; humear, vahear, vahar. Hoy implica un olor desagradable. **To reek with sweat,** humear de sudor. **To reek with filth,** estar excesivamente sucio.

reeky ['riːkɪ] [ri-ki], *a.* Ahumado, ennegrecido. *V.* AULD REEKIE.

reel [riːl] [ril], *s.* 1. Aspa, devanadera, argadijo, carrete; utensilio giratorio que sirve para aspar o devanar madejas, etc. 2. Un baile como una contradanza, vivo y animado, y la música del mismo. **Reel of a log,** *(Mar.)* carretel. **Fishing-reel,** carrete, para cuerda de pescar. **Hose-reel,** carrete para manguera. **Reel-click,** retén, fiador, para regularizar el movimiento de la cuerda de pescar.

reel, *va.* Aspar, recoger el hilo en el aspa haciéndolo madeja. *-vn.* Hacer eses, dar vueltas y giros como un borracho; vacilar al andar; bambolear (move unsteadily). **He reeled out of the room,** salió de la habitación tambaleándose. **Reel in,** enrollar, recoger. **Reel off,** recitar de un tirón.

reelect ['riːˈlekt] [rii-lekt], *va.* Reelegir, elegir de nuevo.

reelection ['riːˈlekʃən] [rii-lek-shon], *s.* Reelección, elección repetida.

reembark [ˌriːmˈbɑːk] [riim-bark], *va.* y *vn.* Reembarcar; reembarcarse, embarcarse otra vez.

reembarkation ['riːembɑːˈkeɪʃən] [riim-ba-kei-shon], *s.* Reembarco, reembarcación, embarcación.

reemerge ['riːˈmɜːdʒ] [rii-merch], *vi.* Volver a salir, reaparecer (reappear), resurgir.

reemergence ['riːˈmɜːdʒəns] [rii-mer-yens], *s.* Reaparición; nueva aparición.

reenact ['riːˈnækt] [rii-nakt], *va.* Recrear (recreate), reconstruir una escena.

reenactment ['riːˈnæktmənt] [rii-nakt-ment], *s.* Restablecimiento, revalidación (law).

reenforce ['riːnfɔːs] [riin-fors], *va.* Reforzar, añadir nuevas fuerzas a, fortalecer; proveer de tropas adicionales. *-s.* Lo que da más fuerza o fortalece; refuerzo.

reenforcement [ˌriːnˈfɔːsmənt] [riin-fors-ment], *s.* Refuerzo, nuevo socorro; tropas o embarcaciones adicionales en auxilio de otras.

reengage ['riːnˈgeɪdʒ] [riin-gueich], *va.* Empeñar, alquilar, apalabrar, comprometer, obligar de nuevo; volver a acometer de nuevo.

reengagement ['riːnˈgeɪdʒmənt] [riin-gueich-ment], *s.* Empeño o combate renovado; nuevo empeño o ataque; acción de estipular o apalabrar segunda vez.,

reenlist ['riːnlɪst] [riin-list], *va.* y *vn.* Alistar o alistarse de nuevo; enganchar o engancharse de nuevo.

reenter ['riːˈentəʳ] [rien-taʳ], *va.* 1. Volver a entrar; entrar de nuevo. 2. Repasar con el buril.

reentering ['riːˈentərɪŋ] [rien-ta-rin], *a. V.* REENTRANT.

reentrance ['riːˈentrəns] [rien-trans], o **re-entry** ['riːˈentrɪ] [rien-tri], *s.* 1. Segunda entrada, entrada repetida. 2. **Reentry,** *(For.)* la acción de volver a entrar en posesión de tierras, habitaciones, rentas, etc.

reentrant ['riːˈentrənt] [rien-trant], *a.* Reentrante, se dice de un ángulo.

reestablish ['riːɪsˈtæblɪʃ] [riis-ta-blish], *va.* Restablecer.

reestablishment ['riːɪsˈtæblɪʃmənt] [riis-ta-blish-ment], *s.* Restablecimiento, restauración.

reeve ['riːv] [riiv], *va. (Mar.)* Pasar, guarnir, introducir un cabo en el motón.

reeve, *s.* Mayordomo.

reexamination ['riːɪgzæmɪˈneɪʃən] [riik-sa-mi-nei-shon], *s.* Reexaminación.

reexamine ['riːɪgˈzæmɪn] [riik-sa-min], *va.* Reexaminar.

reexport ['riːˈekspɔːt] [rieks-port], *va.* Reexportar, volver a exportar; exportar lo que había sido importado.

ref [ref] [ref], *s. (Coloq.)* Árbitro.

reface ['riːˈfeɪs] [ri-feis], *vt.* Forrar de nuevo, revestir de nuevo.

refashion ['riːˈfæʃən] [ri-fa-shon], *va.* Rehacer, modelar, de nuevo.

refasten ['riːˈfæsn] [ri-fa-sen], *va.* Atar (tie), amarrar, asegurar, unir de nuevo; volver a atar.

refection ['riːˈfekʃən] [ri-fek-shon], *s.* Refección, refacción, refocilación, alimento moderado.

refective ['riːˈfektɪv] [ri-fek-tiv], *a.* Refocilador, que refocila o repara. *-s.* Restaurador.

refectory [rɪˈfektərɪ] [ri-fek-to-ri], *s.* Refectorio; el comedor, la sala destinada para comer (dining hall).

refer [rɪˈfɜːʳ] [ri-ferʳ], *va.* 1. Referir, remitir, enviar; dirigir, encaminar u ordenar alguna cosa para algún fin, dirigir para informes. 2. Someter al examen o consideración (de otra persona); someter a la decisión de un árbitro. 3. Asignar, atribuir. *-vn.* 1. Referirse, hacer relación una cosa a otra, aludir. 2. Referir a otra persona, a un banco, etc., para que dé recomendaciones o informes. 3. Dirigirse a, recurrir a, acudir. 4. Apuntar, dar a conocer por medio de una cruz, asterisco u otro signo de imprenta. **He refers to the Bank of T.,** refiere (para informes) al Banco de T.

referee [ˌrefəˈriː] [re-ra-rii], *s.* Árbitro, arbitrador, el sujeto a cuya decisión queda alguna cosa.

reference ['refərəns] [re-frans], *s.* 1. Referencia, remisión; alusión, mención. 2. Nota, señal u otra indicación en un libro o escrito que refiere al lector a otro pasaje o libro. 3. La persona a quien se puede acudir (para informes o recomendación); fiador; la misma recomendación; referencia, aviso del crédito de que puede gozar una persona, casa de comercio, etc. 4. Arbitramento o arbitramiento. **On reference to,** dirigiéndose a. **With reference to,** con referencia, con relación a; en cuanto a, respecto.

referendum [ˌrefəˈrendəm] [re-ra-ren-dom], *s.* 1. Acción de someter algo un diplomático a su gobierno, v. gr. una proposición no contenida en sus instrucciones. 2. Referendum, especie de plebiscito sobre ciertas cuestiones políticas o económicas.

referential [ˌrefəˈrenʃəl] [re-fe-ren-shal], *a.* Que contiene un informe; que se refiere a algo.

refill ['riːfɪl] [ri-fil], *s.* Repuesto (de un envase comercial). *-va.* Volver a llenar.

refine [rɪˈfaɪn] [ri-fain], *va.* Refinar, purificar, pulir, perfeccionar alguna cosa; hacer o hacerse cortés y cultivado, elegante. *-vn.* 1. Sutilizar, discurrir con demasiada sutileza, astucia, malicia, etc. 2. Purificarse o hacerse algo más puro. 3. Pulirse, hacerse demasiado delicado o afectado. **To be refined,** ser muy prendado, distinguirse por su cortesía, urbanidad o cultura.

refined [rɪˈfaɪnd] [ri-faind], *a.* Refinado (thing); culto, elegante, fino (elegant).

refinedly [rɪˈfaɪndlɪ] [ri-faind-li], *adv.* Afectadamente.

refinedness [rɪ'faɪndnɪs] [ri-faind-nes], *s. V.* REFINEMENT.

refinement [rɪ'faɪnmənt] [ri-fain-ment], *s.* 1. Refinación, la acción de refinar. 2. Refinadura, la acción de refinar metales o licores. 3. La demasiada delicadeza, sutileza o esmero en lo que se discurre, inventa o hace. 4. Adelantamiento, en elegancia o pureza. 5. Astucia refinada. 6. Afectación de elegancia o elegancia afectada. 7. Prendas, dotes, elegancia, gracias, adorno.

refiner [rɪ'faɪnəʳ] [ri-fai-naʳ], *s.* Refinador, persona o cosa que refina.

refinery [rɪ'faɪnərɪ] [ri-fai-na-ri], *s.* Refinería, lugar donde se purifica alguna materia cruda, v. gr. el azúcar o el petróleo.

refining [rɪ'faɪnɪŋ] [ri-fai-nin], *s.* Refinadura de metales o licores, etc.

refit [rɪ'fɪt] [ri-fit], *va.* 1. Reparar, componer, aderezar, rehabilitar. 2. (*Mar.*) Embonar o reparar el casco de una embarcación.

reflect [rɪ'flekt] [ri-flekt], *va. y vn.* 1. Reflejar, reflectar, reverberar, devolver, hablando de la luz, el calor, el sonido o algún cuerpo elástico. 2. Reflejar, rechazar, repercutir. 3. Reflejar, devolver una imagen. 4. Repensar, volver a pensar con atención. 6. Improperar, dar en rostro a alguno con una mala acción, echar en cara, reprobar, hacer observaciones injuriosas. 7. Desdorar, deslustrar, deslucir, manchar. 8. Relustrar o refluir en; ser responsable de. **Errors of wives reflect on husbands,** los maridos pagan las faltas de las mujeres.

reflecter [rɪ'flektəʳ] [ri-flek-taʳ], *s.* Reverbero, el cuerpo que refleja.

reflection [rɪ'flekʃən] [ri-flek-shon], *s.* 1. Reflexión de los rayos de la luz, etc., reverberación; imagen producida por reflexión. 2. Reflexión, consideración, meditación. 3. Censura, nota, tacha, baldón. 4. (*Anat.*) Doblez, el efecto de doblar una cosa sobre sí misma. **On, upon, reflection,** pensando en ello. **They will not bear any reflections upon their nephew,** no sufren que se diga mal de su sobrino.

reflective [rɪ'flektɪv] [ri-flek-tiv], *a.* 1. Reflexivo, que refleja o reflecta. 2. Reflexivo, que reflexiona; meditativo, meditabundo.

reflector [rɪ'flektəʳ] [ri-flek-taʳ], *s.* 1. (*Opt.*) Reflector, lo que refleja, como un espejo de metal pulimentado; telescopio de reflexión. 2. (*Des.*) El que reflexiona, medita o cosidera atentamente.

reflex [rɪ'fleks] [ri-fleks], *a.* 1. Reflejo, dirigido hacia atrás. 2. (*Fix.*) Perteneciente a una acción reflexiva o producido por ella. **Reflex action (motion o movement),** acción refleja, la producida por la transmisión de un impulso a un centro nervioso; v. g. el pestañeo involuntario cuando se amenaza al ojo. *-s.* 1. Imagen producida por la reflexión; una simple copia. 2. Reflejo, reverberación, resalto de la luz o del color de un cuerpo en otro.

reflex, *va.* Reflejar, dirigir, inclinar o volver hacia atrás.

reflexion [rɪ'flekʃən] [ri-flek-shon], *s.* (*Ant.*) Reflexión: se usa siempre en sentido físico y no moral. *V.* REFLECTION.

reflexive [rɪ'fleksɪv] [ri-flek-siv], *a.* (*Gram.*) Reflexivo, aquello cuya acción recae sobre el mismo que la ejecuta. **Reflexive pronoun, reflexive verb,** pronombre, verbo reflexivo.

reflexively [rɪ'fleksɪvlɪ] [ri-flek-siv-li], *adv.* Reflexivamente.

reflourish [rɪ'flɔːrɪʃ] [ri-flo-rish], *vn.* Reflorecer.

reflow [rɪ'flaʊ] [ri-flau], *vn.* Reefluir, volver hacia atrás o hacer retroceso un líquido.

refluence, refluency [rɪ'fluəns] [ri-fluans], *s.* Reflujo, el estado o calidad de refluente; acción de refluir.

refluent [rɪ'fluənt] [ri-fluant], *a.* Refluente, que refluye, que vuelve hacia atrás.

reflux ['riːflʌks] [ri-flaks], *s.* Reflujo, movimiento hacia atrás, o en dirección opuesta; menguante, decadencia.

reforest ['riːfɒrɪst] [ri-fo-rist], *va.* Restablecer bosques.

reforestation ['riːfɒrɪsteɪʃən] [ri-fo-ris-tei-shon], *s.* Reforestación, restablecimiento de bosques.

reform ['riːfɔːm] [ri-form], *va.* 1. Volver a formar. 2. Reformar, restituir una cosa a su antigua forma. 3. Reformar, corregir, enmendar, cambiar de malo a mejor, o persuadir a otros a que se enmienden; hacer mejor moralmente, librar de malas costumbres. 4. (*Mil.*) Reformar, licenciar parte de las tropas de un ejército, cuerpo, etc. *-vn.* Reformarse, corregirse, enmendarse.

reform, *s.* Reforma, arreglo, cambio favorable y progresivo, especialmente en la administración. **Civil-service reform,** (*E.U.*) reforma en el servicio civil, nacional, o de un Estado particular.

reformation [ˌrefə'meɪʃən] [re-for-mei-shon], *s.* 1. Reforma, el acto de reformar o enmendar, y la calidad de reformado; enmienda en el método de vida o en las maneras. 2. Reforma, la gran revolución religiosa del siglo XVI., que terminó con el establecimiento del protestantismo. 3. Nueva formación, acción y efecto de formar de nuevo.

reformative [rɪ'fɔːmətɪv] [ri-for-ma-tiv], *a.* Reformador, que forma de nuevo.

reformatory [rɪ'fɔːmətərɪ] [ri-for-ma-to-ri], *a.* Reformatorio, que tiene autoridad o tendencia para producir reforma o enmienda. *-s.* Casa de corrección, establecimiento destinado a corregir individuos culpables de delitos; cuando es para jóvenes se llama **reform school.**

reformer ['riːfɔːməʳ] [ri-for-maʳ], *s.* 1. Reformador, reformista. 2. Uno de los que emprendieron la Reforma protestante.

reformist [rɪ'fɔːmɪst] [ri-for-mist], *s.* Religioso reformado.

refract [rɪ'frækt] [ri-frakt], *va.* Refringir, refractar.

refracted [rɪ'fræktɪd] [ri-frak-tid], *a.* Refracto.

refraction [rɪ'frækʃən] [ri-frak-shon], *s.* Refracción, la desviación del rayo de luz que pasa de un medio a otro de diferente densidad.

refractive [rɪ'fræktɪv] [ri-frak-tiv], *a.* Refringente, que refringe; refractor, que causa refracción.

refractor [rɪ'fræktəʳ] [ri-frak-taʳ], *s.* Telescopio de refracción; refractor.

refractorily [rɪ'fræktərɪlɪ] [ri-frak-to-ri-li], *adv.* Tercamente, obstinadamente, de un modo incorregible.

refractoriness [rɪ'fræktərɪnɪs] [ri-frak-to-ri-nes], *s.* Contumacia, obstinación, terquedad, porfía.

refractory [rɪ'fræktərɪ] [ri-frak-to-ri], *a.* 1. Refractario, contumaz, terco, díscolo, obstinado, indócil, rebelde, incorregible. 2. (*Quím.*) Infundible, que resiste a los medios ordinarios de reducción.

refragable [rɪ'frægəbl] [ri-fra-ga-bol], *a.* Capaz de impugnación, lo que se puede refutar.

refrain [rɪ'freɪn] [ri-frein], *va.* Refrenar, contener, reprimir, moderar, detener. *-vn.* Refrenarse, abstenerse de obrar o intervenir, dejar de hacer, contenerse, guardarse de hacer una cosa.

refrain, *s.* Estrambote, estribillo, verso o copla que se repite a intervalos en una canción o estancia.

refrangible [rɪ'frændʒɪbl] [ri-fran-yi-bol], *a.* Capaz de refracción.

refresh [rɪ'freʃ] [ri-fresh], *va.* 1. Refrescar, poner fresco, renovar, volver a dar vigor, vivificar. 2. Refrescar, templar el calor, enfriar. 3. Refrigerar, aliviar, descansar, tomar algún descanso, alivio o recreo. *-vn.* Refrescarse, recobrar nuevas fuerzas, rehacerse.

refresher [rɪ'freʃəʳ] [ri-fre-shaʳ], *s.* Refrescador, refrigerador, el o lo que refresca.

refreshing [rɪ'freʃɪŋ] [ri-fre-shin], *a.* Refrescante, refrigerante; que alivia; a menudo en sentido sarcástico, como **refreshing impudence,** descaro, frescura. *-s.* Refrescadura.

refreshment [rɪ'freʃmənt] [ri-fresh-ment], *s.* 1. Refresco, refrigerio, alivio, lo que da nueva fuerza o vigor. 2. Refresco, alimento moderado que se toma para reparar las fuerzas; agasajo de refrescos, dulces, etc., que se hace en las visitas o reuniones. En este sentido se usa en plural, por regla general.

refrigerant [rɪ'frɪdʒərənt] [ri-fri-ya-rant], *a.* Refrigerante, refrigerativo, que disminuye el calor, que enfría. *-s.* Refrigerante, medicamento o remedio que disminuye el calor.

refrigerate [rɪ'frɪdʒəreɪt] [ri-fri-ya-reit], *va.* Refrigerar, refrescar, hacer que se ponga fría alguna cosa, enfriar.

refrigerating [rɪˈfrɪdʒəreɪtɪŋ] [ri-fri-ya-rei-tin], *s.* Refrigeración.

refrigeration [rɪˌfrɪdʒəˈreɪʃən] [ri-fri-ya-reishon], *s.* Refrigeración, enfriamiento, acción y efecto de enfriar.

refrigerative [rɪˈfrɪdʒərətɪv] [ri-fri-ya-ra-tiv], *a.* Refrigerante. -*s.* Refrigerante.

refrigerator [rɪˈfrɪdʒəreɪtəʳ] [ri-fri-ya-rei-taʳ], *s.* 1. Lo que enfría; refrigerador, caja o cuarto para conservar algo frío por medio de hielo; garapiñera. 2. Refrigerante, vaso que rodea el capitel de un alambique para enfriar pronto. **Refrigerator car,** (*F.C.*) carro de refrigeración; furgón provisto de una cámara de hielo para el transporte de artículos maleantes.

refuel [ˈriːfjʊəl] [ri-fiual], *vn.* Repostar combustible.

refuge [ˈrefjuːdʒ] [re-fiuch], *s.* 1. Refugio, acogida, amparo, protección contra un peligro o una calamidad. 2. Abrigo, asilo, lo que abriga o protege; plaza fuerte, guarida. 3. Recurso, expediente, subterfugio.

refugee [ˌrefjʊˈdʒiː] [re-fiu-yii], *s.* Refugiado.

refulgence [rɪˈfʌldʒəns] [ri-fal-yans], *s.* Refulgencia, resplandor, claridad, esplendor, brillantez.

refulgent [rɪˈfʌldʒənt] [ri-fal-yant], *a.* Refulgente, brillante, resplandeciente.

refund [ˈriːfʌnd] [ri-fand], *va.* 1. Restituir; volver a pagar, reembolsar. 2. Consolidar una deuda; reemplazar por un empréstito recién consolidado.

refundable [rɪˈfʌndəbl] [ri-fan-da-bol], *a.* Que se puede restituir o volver a pagar.

refusable [rɪˈfjuːzəbl] [ri-fiu-sa-bol], *a.* Recusable, que se puede recusar.

refusal [rɪˈfjuːzəl] [ri-fiu-sal], *s.* 1. Negativa, repulsa, denegación; desaire. 2. Elección, opción, el privilegio de aceptar o recusar, o rehusar; la preferencia para hacer una cosa.

refuse [rɪˈfjuːz] [ri-fius], *va. y vn.* 1. Recusar, negar, no conceder lo que se pide, no consentir, no permitir, no convenir. 2. Rehusar, desechar, no aceptar, repulsar, denegar. 3. Desairar.

refuse [ˈrefjuːz] [re-fius], *s.* Desecho, zupia, desperdicio; sobra, residuo. -*a.* Rechazado, desechado, sin valor.

refuser [rɪˈfjuːzəʳ] [ri-fiu-saʳ], *s.* El que recusa o rehusa.

refutable [rɪˈfjuːtəbl] [ri-fiu-ta-bol], *a.* Refutable, que puede ser refutado.

refutation [ˌrefjʊˈteɪʃən] [re-fiu-tei-shon], *s.* Refutación.

refute [ˈrefjuːt] [re-fiut], *va.* Refutar, contradecir.

regain [rɪˈgeɪn] [ri-guein], *va.* Recobrar, recuperar; volver a ganar lo perdido; ganar de nuevo; conseguir, acercarse otra vez.

regal [ˈriːgəl] [ri-gal], *a.* Real, regio, perteneciente a un rey; propio de un rey. -*s.* Organillo portátil y muy pequeño del siglo XVI.

regale [rɪˈgeɪl] [ri-gueil], *va.* Regalar, agasajar, festejar; recrear, deleitar.

regale, *s.* (*sing.* de REGALIA). 1. Patronato regio, prerrogativa real. 2. (*Ant.*) Banquete, festín suntuoso, jolgorio; regalo; complacencia.

regalement [rɪˈgeɪlmənt] [ri-gueil-ment], *s.* Regalo, presente, dádiva.

regalia [rɪˈgeɪlɪə] [ri-guei-lia], *s. pl.* 1. Insignias reales. 2. Insignias, distintivos, adornos propios de algunos cuerpos.

regality [rɪˈgælɪtɪ] [ri-ga-li-ti], *s.* Realeza, soberanía, poder soberano.

regally [ˈriːgəlɪ] [ri-ga-li], *adv.* Soberanamente, como rey, de un modo regio.

regard [rɪˈgɑːd] [ri-gard], *va.* 1. Observar o mirar de cerca, reparar, atender, poner atención. 2. Considerar desde cierto punto de vista, reputar, juzgar, estimar. 3. Estimar, hacer aprecio y estimación de alguno, hacer caso de alguna cosa, apreciar; hacer alto; respetar, venerar. 4. Tocar, pertenecer, tener relación a, concernir, mirar a. **As regards,** tocante a, en cuanto a, por lo que toca a. **As regards that I cannot agree with you,** en cuanto a eso, no puede convenir con usted

regard, *s.* 1. Miramiento, atención, circunspección, consideración. 2. Respeto, veneración, acatamiento. I

profess a great regard for him, lo estimo mucho. **With regard to what you say,** en cuanto a lo que usted dice. 3. Reputación, fama común. 4. Respecto, relación; con *with* o *in,* y seguido de *to* u *of.* **With regard to, in regard of** o **to,** con relación a, en cuanto a, relativamente a. 5. Consideración, afectos, amistades; fórmula de urbanidad. 6. Mirada. **With the kindest regards,** con la mayor consideración. **My kindest regards,** mil afectos de mi parte. **To have a great regard for,** tener mucha consideración por, hacer gran caso de. **Without any regard to,** sin miramientos. **Regard being had (to),** atendido que, en vista de.

regardant [rɪˈgɑːdənt] [ri-gar-dant], *a.* (*Her.*) Mirante.

regarder [rɪˈgɑːdəʳ] [ri-gar-daʳ], *s.* Espectador, mirón.

regardful [rɪˈgɑːdfʊl] [ri-gard-ful], *a.* Atento, circunspecto; cuidadoso.

regardfully [rɪˈgɑːdfʊlɪ] [ri-gard-fu-li], *adv.* Atentamente, respetuosamente.

regarding [rɪˈgɑːdɪŋ] [ri-gar-din], *prep.* Con relación a, relativamente a, en cuanto a. **Anxious regarding his plans,** ansioso en cuanto a sus planes.

regardless [rɪˈgɑːdlɪs] [ri-gard-les], *a.* Descuidado, negligente; desacatado, indiferente.

regardlessly [rɪˈgɑːdlɪslɪ] [ri-gard-les-li], *adv.* Descuidadamente, desatentamente.

regardlessness [rɪˈgɑːdlɪsnɪs] [ri-gard-les-nes], *s.* Descuido, negligencia; desacatamiento. *s.* Regata, contienda entre botes u otras embarcaciones menores, para ganar una apuesta.

regatta [rɪˈgætə] [ri-ga-ta], *sf.* Regata.

regency [ˈriːdʒənsɪ] [ri-yan-si], *s.* 1. Regencia, el gobierno de un reino cuando el príncipe no puede gobernar por cualquiera causa. 2. Regencia, el gobierno de un regente; también el conjunto de regentes.

regeneracy [rɪˈdʒənərəsɪ] [ri-ye-ne-ra-si], *s.* Regeneración, acción y efecto de regenerar.

regenerate [rɪˈdʒenərɪt] [ri-ye-na-reit], *va.* 1. Regenerar, reproducir. 2. Reengendrar. 3. (*Teol.*) Renovar espiritualmente; infundir buenos principios.

regenerate, *a.* Regenerado, reengendrado; nacido a una nueva vida, renovado espiritualmente.

regenerateness [rɪˈdʒenərɪtnɪs] [ri-ye-na-rit-nes], **regeneration** [rɪˌdʒenəˈreɪʃən] [ri-ye-na-rei-shon], *s.* regeneración; renacimiento.

regenerative [rɪˈdʒenərətɪv] [ri-ye-ne-ra-tiv], *a.* Regenerador, que regenera.

regeneratory [rɪˈdʒenərətərɪ] [ri-ye-na-ra-to-ri], *a.* Regeneratorio, que tiene la propiedad de regenerar o renovar.

regent [ˈriːdʒənt] [ri-yent], *a.* 1. Regente, que ejerce autoridad en lugar de otro. 2. Regente, reinante; que rige o gobierna. -*s.* 1. Regente, regenta, el o la que rige un reino en nombre y lugar del rey. 2. Gobernador, gobernante. 3. Regente, miembro de una universidad encargado de ciertas funciones especiales de administración.

regentship [ˈriːdʒəntʃɪp] [ri-yent-ship], *s.* Regencia, empleo de regente.

reggae [ˈregeɪ] [re-guei], *sm.* Reggae.

regicidal [ˈredʒɪsaɪdl] [re-yi-sai-dal], *a.* Regicida, que mata a un rey o reina; perteneciente al regicidio.

regicide [ˈredʒɪsaɪd] [re-yi-said], *s.* 1. Regicidio, asesinato de un rey o reina. 2. Regicida, el que mata a un rey o soberano.

régime [reɪˈʒiːm] [rei-yim], *s.* Régimen, manera o sistema de gobernar; administración particular; sistema social.

regimen [ˈredʒɪmən] [re-yi-man], *s.* 1. Régimen, dieta, observancia metódica de las prescripciones higiénicas en cuanto a los alimentos, vestidos, ejercicio, etc. 2. Goberno metódico, sujeción, freno. 3. (*Gram.*) Régimen, dependencia mutua que tienen las partes de la oración, expresada con o sin preposiciones, según los casos.

regiment [ˈredʒɪmənt] [re-yi-mant], *s.* 1. Regimiento, cierto número de compañías de soldados de que es jefe un coronel. 2. (*Des.*) Regimiento, gobierno.

regimental [ˌredʒɪˈmentl] [re-yi-men-tal], *a.* Regimental, perteneciente a un regimiento. **Regimentals,** uniforme militar.

region [ˈriːdʒən] [ri-yon], *s.* 1. Región, extensión indefinida aunque considerable (country); área; se dice hablando de la tierra, del aire o del cuerpo humano. 2. Región, país, distrito, comarca; lugar, espacio. 3. *(Anat. y Zool.)* Región, porción del cuerpo.

regional [ˈriːdʒənl] [ri-yo-nal], *a.* Regional, perteneciente a una región; local, topográfico.

regionalism [ˈriːdʒənəlɪzəm] [ri-yo-na-li-sem], *s.* Regionalismo.

regionalist [ˈriːdʒəlɪst] [ri-yo-na-list], *a.* Regionalista.

register [ˈredʒɪstəʳ] [re-yis-taʳ], *s.* 1. Registro, asiento o apuntamiento de alguna cosa; relación formal u oficial, y el libro que la contiene; rol, lista, archivo, protocolo (list); libro de parroquia. 2. Registrador; escribano de hipotecas. *V.* REGISTRAR. **Register of a ship,** matrícula de navío. **Register-ships,** *(Mar.)* navíos de registro, los que tenían permiso del rey de España para traficar en los puertos de América. 3. Lo que registra; aparato mecánico para registrar ciertos hechos, como la velocidad, la presión, etc.; o para contar el valor de los billetes de pasaje, el dinero cobrado en las tiendas, etc. 4. *(Quím.)* Registro, celosía, placa o plancha de los hornos que sirve para abrirlos o cerrarlos y regular el calor. 5. *(Mús.)* (a) Compás de la voz o de un instrumento; (b) registro, listón de madera que puesto o retirado cambia las voces del órgano. 6. *(Com.)* Certificado de nacionalidad; documento de aduana que contiene la descripción de un buque, su nombre, cabida, nacionalidad, dueños, etc. 7. *(Impr.)* Registro, la correspondencia igual de las dos páginas de una misma hoja. **To sign in the register,** firmar en el registro, registrarse (in hotel). **To call the register,** pasar lista. **Register of votes,** registro electoral.

register, *va.* 1. Registrar, inscribir en un registro o en una lista. 2. Notar según una escala. *-vn.* 1. Inscribir unos un nombre en un registro. 2. *(Impr.)* Estar en un registro. **To register a letter,** certificar una carta.

registered [ˈredʒɪstəd] [re-yis-tad], *a.* Certificado, registrado (baggage, mail, trademark).

registrar [ˌredʒɪsˈtrɑːʳ] [re-yis-traʳ], *s.* Registrador, el empleado a cuyo cargo está algún registro.

registration [ˌredʒɪsˈtreɪʃən] [re-yis-trei-shon], *s.* Asiento, registro; empadronamiento, encabezamiento.

registry [ˈredʒɪstrɪ] [re-yis-tri], *s.* 1. Asiento. 2. Archivo, el lugar en que se guardan papeles o instrumentos. 3. Protocolo, registro.

reglet [ˈreglɪt] [re-glit], *s.* 1. *(Arq.)* Filete, moldura pequeña. 2. *(Impr.)* corondel, regleta.

regraft [rɪˈgræft] [ri-graft], *va.* Ingerir o ingertar de nuevo.

regrant [rɪˈgrænt] [ri-grant], *va.* Volver a conceder.

regrate [rɪˈgreɪt] [ri-greit], *va.* 1. Antiguamente, monopolizar, hacer monopolio, revender provisiones en el mismo lugar de su primera venta a un precio mayor. 2. Raspar, quitar la superficie exterior de una piedra para darle mejor apariencia.

regress [ˈriːgres] [ri-gres], *vn.* 1. Regresar, volver, retornar (come back, turn back). 2. *(Astr.)* Retrogradar, moverse en dirección opuesta a la del movimiento general de los astros.

regression [rɪˈgreʃən] [ri-gre-shon], *s.* Regresión, retroceso o el acto de volver atrás.

regressive [rɪˈgresɪv] [ri-gre-siv], *a.* Retrógrado, que vuelve o retorna; retroactivo.

regret [rɪˈgret] [ri-gret], *s.* 1. Pesadumbre, cuidado, sentimiento; dolor al recordar algún acontecimiento pasado; pesar. 2. Compunción, dolor de conciencia, tristeza llena de remordimientos. 3. *pl. (Fam.)* Pésame, recusación; excusa cortés que se da como respuesta a una invitación. **To my great regret,** muy a pesar mío. **I have no regrets,** no me arrepiento.

regret, *vn.* Sentir, tener pena, dolor o pesadumbre; echar de menos (miss).

regrettable [rɪˈgretəbl] [ri-gre-ta-bol], *a.* Que ha de ser sentido; propio para causar pesadumbre.

regular [ˈregjələʳ] [re-guiu-laʳ], *a.* 1. Regular, regulado, que es o está ajustado, y conforme a una regla, que está en regla. 2. Arreglado, que guarda regla y orden, gobernado por una regla o reglas, metódico; que vuelve o se repite sin omisión. 3. Regular, conforme a ley o costumbre; autorizado debidamente, permanente. 4. *(Mil.)* Regular, perteneciente a un ejército permanente. **A regular doctor,** un médico titulado; el médico llamado por otros alópata. *-s.* 1. Soldado que pertenece a un ejército permanente. 2. El que está empleado regularmente. 3. Regular, el que vive, bajo una regla en un instituto religioso. **Regular customer,** cliente habitual. **As regular as clockwork,** tan bien ordenado como un reloj. **He is a regular attendant at church on Sundays,** asiste regularmente a la iglesia los domingos. **A person of regular habits,** persona ordenada en sus costumbres. **A regular feast,** un verdadero banquete.

regularity [ˌregjəˈlærɪtɪ] [re-guiu-la-ri-ti], *s.* Regularidad, conformidad, simetría, método, buen orden.

regularize [ˈregjələraɪz] [re-guiu-la-rais], *vt.* Formalizar, normalizar, regularizar.

regularly [ˈregjələlɪ] [re-guiu-la-li], *adv.* Regularmente.

regulate [ˈregjəleɪt] [re-guiu-leit], *va.* 1. Regular, regularizar, arreglar, ordenar, poner y mantener en orden (arrange, settle). 2. Medir, ajustar, dirigir, disciplinar, ajustar según regla y método (direct, run).

regulation [ˌregjəˈleɪʃən] [re-guiu-lei-shon], *s.* Regulación, arreglo, método; reglamento, orden, regla de conducta o de gobierno; mandato. **Regulation size, length,** tamaño, longitud de reglamento.

regulative [ˈregjələtɪv] [re-guiu-la-tiv], *a.* Reglamentario, regulador, que tiende o sirve para regular.

regulator [ˈregjəleɪtəʳ] [re-guiu-lei-taʳ], *s.* 1. Regulador; el que regula, arregla u ordena alguna cosa. 2. Regulador, reloj que sirve de norma para el arreglo de los demás relojes. 3. Regulador, mecanismo que en las máquinas sirve para regular el movimiento; índice que acelera o atrasa la marcha de un reloj.

regulus [ˈregjələs] [re-guiu-los], *s.* 1. *(Quím.)* Régulo, la parte más pura de los minerales, que en estado de fusión cae al fondo del crisol. 2. *(Astr.)* Régulo, estrella blanca de primera magnitud en la constelación León.

regurgitate [rɪˈgɜːdʒɪteɪt] [ri-guer-yi-teit], *va.* Volver a echar, echar otra vez, volver a verter o a trasegar. *-vn. (Med.)* Regurgitar, salirse algún líquido o humor de la parte que le contiene por la mucha abundancia.

regurgitation [rɪˈgɜːdʒɪˈteɪʃən] [ri-guer-yi-tei-shon], *sf.* Regurgitación.

rehabilitate [ˌriːəˈbɪlɪteɪt] [ria-bi-li-teit], *va.* Rehabilitar, restablecer, reintegrar en su primer estado o capacidad, en sus anteriores derechos, títulos o privilegios.

rehabilitation [ˈriːəˌbɪlɪˈteɪʃən] [ria-bi-li-tei-shon], *s.* Rehabilitación.

rehash [ˈriːˈhæʃ] [ri-jash], *va.* Volver a picar, esto es, dar nueva forma a una cosa (se emplea despreciativamente. *-s.* Algo rehecho con materiales usados antes; fárrago.

rehearsal [rɪˈhɜːsəl] [ri-jer-sal], *s.* 1. Repetición, la acción de repetir; recitación, relación. 2. Ensayo, la prueba de una pieza de teatro o de música, por lo común en privado.

rehearse [rɪˈhɜːs] [ri-jers], *va.* 1. Repetir, recitar, referir. 2. Repasar; ensayar una pieza de teatro o de música, para poder corregirla antes de la representación pública.

reign [reɪn] [rein], *vn.* 1. Reinar, poseer y ejercer el poder soberano. 2. Reinar, dominar, predominar (dominate). 3. Reinar, prevalecer, estar en boga.

reign, *s.* 1. Soberanía, reino, poder soberano. 2. Predominio, dominio, influencia predominante. 3. Reinado, espacio de tiempo en que gobierna un rey o reina. **In/under the reing of,** bajo el reinado de.

reigning [ˈreɪnɪŋ] [rei-nin], *a.* Reinante, predominante, prevaleciente.

reimburse [ˌriːɪmˈhɜːs] [rim-bers], *va.* 1. Reembolsar, devolver el dinero desembolsado. 2. Indemnizar.

reimburser [ˌriːmˈbɜːsəʳ] [rim-ber-saʳ], *s.* El que reembolsa o indemniza.

reimbursement [ˌriːmˈbɜːsmənt] [rim-bers-ment], *s.* Reembolso.

reimpression [ˌriːmˈpreʃən] [riim-pre-shon], *s.* Reimpresión, impresión repetida; nueva edición. V. REPRINT.

rein [reɪn] [rein], *s.* Rienda, tanto en el sentido físico como en el moral; correa de las bridas; *(Fig.)* gobierno, dirección. **To give rein to,** aflojar las riendas, dar licencia para obrar como se quiera. **To take the reins,** tomar las riendas, tomar la dirección del gobierno.

rein, *va.* 1. Gobernar; dirigir por medio de riendas. 2. Refrenar, tener en freno, contener. **Rein back/in,** refrenar.

reincarnate [ˌriːnˈkɑːneɪt] [riin-kar-neit], *vt.* Reencarnar.

reincarnation [ˈriːnkɑːˈneɪʃən] [riin-kar-nei-shon], *s.* Reencarnación.

reincorporate [ˌriːnˈkɔːpəreɪt] [riin-kor-po-reit], *va.* Reincorporar, volver a incorporar.

reincorporation [ˌriːnkɔːpəˈreɪʃən] [riin-kor-po-rei-shon], *s.* Reincorporación.

reindeer [ˈreɪndɪəʳ] [rein-diaʳ], *s.* Reno.

reinfect [ˈreɪnfekt] [rein-fekt], *va.* Infectar o inficionar de nuevo, volver a inficionar.

reinforce [ˌriːnˈfɔːs] [riin-fors], *va.* V. REENFORCE.

reinforcement [ˌriːnˈfɔːsmənt] [rein-fors], *s.* V. REENFORCEMENT.

reinsert [ˌriːnˈsɜːt] [riin-sert], *va.* Insertar o ingerir de nuevo una cosa en otra.

reinstate [ˈriːnˈsteɪt] [riin-steit], *va.* 1. Reinstalar, reintegrar, volver a poner en el estado precedente, restablecer; volver a revestir de autoridad. 2. En los seguros contra incendios, reparar o reponer, en lugar de pagar el valor de la propiedad dañada.

reinsurance [ˈriːnˈʃʊərəns] [riin-shua-rans], *s.* Seguro de una propiedad ya asegurada; reparto de un seguro cuantioso entre varias compañías.

reinsure [ˈriːnˈʃʊəʳ] [riin-shuaʳ], *va.* Asegurar por segunda vez, volver a asegurar.

reinvest [ˈriːnˈvest] [riin-vest], *va.* Dar nueva autoridad o renovar la que se dio.

reinvigorate [ˈriːnˈvɪɡəreɪt] [riin-vi-go-reit], *va.* Vigorizar o fortificar de nuevo.

reinvigoration [ˈriːnvɪɡəˈreɪʃən] [riin-vi-go-rei-shon], *s.* El acto de reforzar o vigorizar de nuevo.

reissue [ˈriːˈɪʃjuː] [ri-ishiu], *va.* 1. Reimprimir (a book, magazine, etc.). 2. Emitir por segunda vez (a film). *-s.* Reimpresión, reaparición.

reiterate [ˈriːˈɪtəreɪt] [ri-i-te-reit], *va.* Reiterar, repetir, decir o ejecutar algo repetidas veces (repeat).

reiteratedly [ˈriːˌɪtəˈreɪtɪdlɪ] [ri-i-te-rei-tid-li], *adv.* Reiteradamente, repetidas veces.

reiteration [riːˌɪtəˈreɪʃən] [rii-te-rei-shon], *s.* Reiteración, repetición.

reiterativ [ˈriːˈɪtərətɪv] [ri-i-te-ra-tiv], *a.* Reiterativo.

reject [ˈriːdʒekt] [ri-yekt], *va.* 1. Rechazar, rebatir, repulsar (repel, push away). 2. Desechar, no admitir, rehusar, repugnar (decline, refuse); despreciar, desestimar.

rejectable [ˈriːdʒektəbl] [ri-yek-ta-bol], *a.* Recusable, inadmisible.

rejecter, rejector [ˈriːdʒektəʳ] [ri-yek-taʳ], *s.* El que rechaza, rebate o repugna.

rejection [ˈriːdʒekʃən] [ri-yek-shon], *s.* Rechazamiento, desecho, la acción de desechar, rechazar, etc.

rejective [ˈriːdʒektɪv] [ri-yek-tiv], *a.* Rechazador, que tiende a rechazar o rehusar.

rejectment [ˈriːdʒekt] [ri-yekt], *s.* Desecho, cosa que no sirve; también, rechazamiento.

rejig [riːˈdʒɪɡ] [ri-yig], *vt.* Reajustar, recomponer (readjust).

rejoice [rɪˈdʒɔɪs] [ri-yois], *vn.* Regocijarse, recrearse, sentir júbilo, alegría (enjoy), *-va.* Regocijar, alegrar, dar o causar alegría.

rejoicing [rɪˈdʒɔɪsɪŋ] [ri-yoi-sin], *s.* Alegría, fiesta, regocijo, júbilo. *-a.* Gustoso, agradable, divertido, alegre (happy).

rejoin [riːˈdʒɔɪn] [ri-yoin], *va.* Reunirse, volver a juntarse, volver a la compañía de; reunirse después de una separación. *-vn.* 1. Replicar, responder a una respuesta. 2. *(For.)* Contrarreplicar, contestar contradiciendo la réplica del demandador.

rejoinder [rɪˈdʒɔɪndəʳ] [ri-yoin-daʳ], *s.* Respuesta, réplica; contrarréplica. **As a rejoinder to,** como contestación a.

rejoint [riːˈdʒɔɪnt] [ri-yoint], *va.* 1. *(Alb.)* Llenar las degolladuras con mortero. 2. Reponer, reunir las junturas o articulaciones de algo.

rejudge [rɪˈdʒʌdʒ] [ri-yach], *va.* Rever, volver a ver, revistar, examinar o juzgar de nuevo.

rejuvenate [rɪˈdʒuːvɪneɪt] [ri-yu-vi-neit], *va.* Rejuvenecer, remozar.

rejuvenation [rɪˌdʒuːvɪˈneɪʃən] [ri-yu-vi-nei-shon], *s.* Remozamiento, el acto de remozar, de renovar.

rekindle [ˈriːˈkɪndl] [ri-kin-del], *va.* Volver a encender; inflamar, despertar o excitar de nuevo.

relapse [rɪˈlæps] [ri-laps], *vn.* 1. Recaer, volver alguno a adolecer de la enfermedad de que padeció; sufrir una recaída. 2. Recaer, volver a caer en algún error, delito, etc.; reincidir; renegar, pasarse de un culto a otro. **To have a relapse,** tener una recaída *(Med.).*

relapse, *s.* Recaída; reincidencia, repetición de una falta; recidiva de una enfermedad.

relate [rɪˈleɪt] [ri-leit], *va.* 1. Relatar, referir, contar, narrar (tell). 2. Emparentar, contraer parentesco. *-vn.* Estar en relación o asociación de pensamiento o de hecho (be in relation with); tocar, pertenecer, ser concerniente a, referirse.

related [rɪˈleɪtɪd] [ri-lei-tid], *pp.* y *a.* Conexo, que está en relación o enlace (with); emparentado, consanguíneo; del mismo género, de la misma familia.

relater [rɪˈleɪtəʳ] [ri-lei-taʳ], *s.* Relator, el que narra o relata.

relation [rɪˈleɪʃən] [ri-lei-shon], *s.* 1. Relación, respecto, consonancia, conexión, concernencia, interdependencia (relationship, connection). 2. Referencia, alusión. 3. Relación, comunicación o correspondencia de una persona o cosa con otra. 4. Parentesco (family). 5. Pariente, parienta. **All his relations,** toda su parentela. **Near relation,** pariente cercano. 6. Relación, narración. **In relation to,** con relación a, respecto a. **Good relations,** buenas relaciones. **To bear no relation to,** no tener nada que ver con. **Close relation,** pariente cercano.

relational [rɪˈleɪʃənl] [ri-lei-sho-nal], *a.* Relacional.

relationship [rɪˈleɪʃən] [ri-lei-shon], *s.* Parentesco, conexión por consanguinidad o afinidad; estado o calidad de ser emparentado. **Relationship by blood,** consanguinidad.

relative [ˈrelətɪv] [re-la-tiv], *a.* 1. Relativo, que tiene relación con, que se refiere a; pertinente. 2. Relativo, inteligible sólo en relación con otra cosa, que no existe por sí mismo. 3. Relativo, que representa un antecedente. **Relative greatness,** grandeza relativa. *-s.* 1. Pariente, deudo. 2. Pronombre relativo. 3. Cualquier cosa que tiene relación con otra. **With relative ease,** con relativa facilidad.

relatively [ˈrelətɪvlɪ] [re-la-tiv-li], *adv.* Relativamente, por comparación.

relativeness [ˈrelətɪvnɪs] [re-la-tiv-nes], *s.* El estado de lo que tiene relación con otra cosa.

relativism [ˈrelətɪvɪzəm] [re-la-ti-vi-sem], *s.* Relativismo.

relativist [ˈrelətɪvɪst] [re-la-ti-vist], *s.* Relativista.

relativistic [ˌrelətɪˈvɪstɪk] [re-la-ti-vis-tik], *s.* Relativista.

relativity [ˌreləˈtɪvɪtɪ] [re-la-ti-vi-ti], *s.* Relatividad. **Theory of relativity,** teoría de la relatividad.

relaunch [ˈriːlɔːntʃ] [ri-lonch], *va.* Relanzar.

relax [rɪˈlæks] [ri-laks], *va.* 1. Relajar, aflojar, laxar; ablandar. 2. Aflojar, soltar lo que estaba tirante. 3. Relajar, anular o relevar de alguna obligación. 4. Relajar, esparcirse o divertir el ánimo, solazar. 5. Relajar, disminuir la pena o castigo. 6. Abrir; desatar. 7. Aliviar el estreñimiento. 8. Hacer lánguido, languidecer. *-vn.* Aflojar, ceder o perder algo de su rigor o serveridad. **To relax one's muscles,** relajar o aflojar los músculos. **Relax!,** ¡cálmate!, ¡tranquilo!

relaxant [rɪˈlæksənt] [ri-lak-sant], *a.* Relajante.

relaxation [ˌriːlækˈseɪʃən] [ri-lak-sei-shon], *s.* 1. Aflojamiento, flojedad de lo que estaba tirante. 2. Relajación, descanso o intermisión en algún trabajo o tarea; descanso, reposo, recreo, distracción, mitigación, lenidad. 3. Relajamiento de nervios, músculos, etc. **To take some relaxation,** relajarse, esparcirse.

relay [ˈriːleɪ] [ri-lei], *s.* 1. Relevo. 2. Remuda. 3. Carrera de relevos. 4. Tramo (in a race). 5. Posta. 6. (*Elec.*) Relevador, relé. *-va.* Reexpedir. **Relay race,** carrera de relevos.

release [rɪˈliːs] [ri-lis], *va.* 1. Soltar, dar libertad a un preso (free). 2. Libertar, poner en libertad. 3. Libertar, eximir de alguna obligación; ceder, condonar, remitir; relajar, aflojar, relevar, apartarse, renunciar; eximir, exonerar. 4. Aliviar los dolores, los pesares. **To release someone on bail,** poner en libertad bajo fianza.

release, *s.* 1. Libertad, soltura (freedom). 2. Remisión de una pena; alivio en los sufrimientos, en los pesares; aligeramiento final de algo opresivo. 3. Descargo, exoneración de una obligación; el recibo de una deuda firmado por el acreedor; finiquito. 4. Un modo de traspasar la posesión de cualquier heredad. 5. Cesión (of a right); abandono de una pretensión. 6. Disparo, lanzamiento (shot). **Deed of release,** acta de cesión. **A release of gaz,** un escape de gas. **To be on general release,** exhibirse en todos los cines (film).

relegate [ˈrelɪgeɪt] [re-li-gueit], *va.* Desterrar, relegar; colocar en posición inferior u obscura; apartar.

relegation [ˌrelɪˈgeɪʃən] [re-li-guei-shon], *s.* Relegación como a obscuridad, destierro.

relent [rɪˈlent] [ri-lent], *vn.* 1. Apiadarse, compadecerse, enternecerse (pity, be sorry on), ceder, aplacarse, desenojarse. 2. (*Des.*) Relentecer, ponerse tierna y blanda alguna cosa, ablandarse, templarse. **His heart relents,** su corazón se enternece.

relenting [rɪˈlentɪŋ] [ri-len-tin], *a.* Enternecido, dispuesto a enternecerse o a ceder. *-s.* Enternecimiento, desenojo; sentimiento de compasión.

relentless [rɪˈlentlɪs] [ri-lent-les], *a.* Despiadado, empedernido, implacable, inexorable.

relentlessly [rɪˈlentlɪslɪ] [ri-lent-les-li], *adv.* Inexorablemente, de manera implacable.

relessee, relessor [rɪˈlɪsiː] [ri-li-si] [rɪˈlesəʳ] [ri-le-saʳ], *s.* V. RELEASEE, RELEASOR. (Formas irregulares.)

relet [rɪˈlet] [ri-let], *vt.* Realquilar.

relevance [ˈreləvəns] [re-le-vans], *s.* Cualidad de pertinente o aplicable; aplicabilidad.

relevant [ˈreləvənt] [re-le-vant], *a.* 1. Pertinente, a propósito, aplicable, apropiado. 2. Que alivia o auxilia.

reliability, [rɪˌlaɪəˈbɪlɪtɪ] [re-laia-bi-li-ti], *s.* Calidad del que o de lo que es digno de confianza.

reliable [rɪˈlaɪəbl] [ri-laia-bol], *a.* Seguro, digno de confianza, confiable; discreto, prudente, de sano juicio.

reliance [rɪˈlaɪəns] [ri-laians], *s.* Confianza, seguridad.

reliant [rɪˈlaɪənt] [ri-laiant], *a.* Confiado, particularmente el que tiene confianza en sí mismo.

relic [ˈrelɪk] [re-lik], *s.* 1. Reliquia, residuo o resto de lo que ha desaparecido o está destruido. 2. Reliquia, cosa apreciada en memoria de alguien fallecido, como un santo o mártir.

relict [ˈrelɪkt] [re-likt], *s.* Viuda (widow).

relief [rɪˈliːf] [ri-lif], *s.* 1. Alivio, alejamiento completo o parcial de un mal que aflige el cuerpo o el ánimo; aligeramiento (alleviation). 2. Consuelo, socorro, ayuda caritativa (help); lo que alivia el pesar; refuerzo. 3. (*Mil.*) Relevo, mudanza de centinela. 4. Desagravio, satisfacción o compensación de la injuria u ofensa recibida; reparación. 5. Relieve, realce, en obras de escultura o arquitectura; labor o figura que resalta en una superficie plana. 6. Parte que aparentemente se destaca en una pintura. 7. Elevación de una persona; hecho u objeto que descuella. **High relief, low relief,** alto relieve, bajo relieve. **To stand in bold relief,** resaltar vigorosamente. **Indoor relief,** socorro dado a los indigentes en una casa de caridad. **Outdoor relief,** socorro a domicilio. **By way of light relief,** a modo de diversión. **That's a relief!,** ¡menos mal!

relievable [rɪˈliːvəbl] [ri-li-va-bol], *a.* Consolable, capaz de alivio.

relieve [rɪˈliːv] [ri-liv], *va.* 1. Relevar, remediar, socorrer (help, repair), librar completa o parcialmente de algo doloroso u opresivo, o de sus efectos. 2. Aliviar, consolar. 3. (*Mil.*) Relevar (sentry). 4. Desagraviar, hacer justicia. 5. Mitigar, suavizar, vivificar el estilo o lenguaje. 6. Poner en relieve, hacer resaltar una labor o figura. **To feel relieved,** sentirse aliviado. **To relieve one's feelings,** desahogarse.

reliever [rɪˈliːvəʳ] [ri-li-vaʳ], *s.* El que socorre o releva.

relight [rɪˈlaɪt] [ri-lait], *va.* Volver a encender o encender de nuevo. *-vn.* Volver a desmontarse de un caballo; volver a bajarse de un carruaje.

religion [rɪˈlɪdʒən] [ri-li-yon], *s.* Religión, culto que se tributa a Dios y el conjunto de creencias religiosas de un individuo o de un país.

religionary [rɪˈlɪdʒənərɪ] [ri-li-yo-na-ri], *a.* Religioso, perteneciente a la religión.

religious [rɪˈlɪdʒəs] [ri-li-yos], *a.* 1. Religioso, pío, devoto. 2. Perteneciente o que se refiere a una religión. 3. Verdadereamnete fiel, concienzudo. 4. Religioso, perteneciente a una orden monástica.

religiously [rɪˈlɪdʒəslɪ] [ri-li-yos-li], *adv.* Religiosamente; exactamente, puntualmente.

religiousness [rɪˈlɪdʒəsnɪs] [ri-li-yos-nes], *s.* Religiosidad, piedad, moralidad religiosa.

relinquish [rɪˈlɪŋkwɪʃ] [ri-lin-kuish], *va.* 1. Abandonar, dejar, ceder. 2. Dejar de demandar o pretender; resignar, renunciar (a).

relinquishment [rɪˈlɪŋkwɪʃmənt] [ri-lin-kuish-ment], *s.* Abandono, dejación, cesión.

reliquary [ˈrelɪkwərɪ] [re-li-kua-ri], *s.* 1. Relicario, la caja o lugar en que se guardan las reliquias de los santos. 2. (*For.*) El que después de haber presentado sus cuentas resulta deudor de cierta suma; el que paga poco a poco.

relish [ˈrelɪʃ] [re-lish], *s.* 1. Gusto, apetencia, sabor (taste). 2. Gusto agradable de los alimentos o bebidas; (*Fig.*) cualidad que hace a una cosa agradable; afición, entusiasmo (liking). 3. Sabor (flavor). 4. Cata, la porción pequeña de alguna cosa que se da para catar o probar. **A relish for good literature,** un gusto por la buena literatura. **He has no relish for studying,** no le agrada estudiar. **To do something with relish,** hacer algo de buena gana.

relish, *va.* 1. Saborear, dar sabor, gusto o sainete a las cosas. 2. Gustar de, tener afición a alguna cosa. *-vn.* 1. Saber bien, tener buen gusto; ser sabroso. 2. Gustar, agradar. **I don't relish the plan,** no me gusta el plan. **Do you relish some dancing?,** ¿te apetece ir a bailar?

relishable [ˈrelɪʃəbl] [re-li-sha-bol], *a.* Gustoso, sabroso, apetitoso.

relive [ˈriːˈlɪv] [ri-liv], *vn.* **Revivir,** vivir de nuevo.

relocate [ˈriːləʊˈkeɪt] [ri-lou-keit], *va.* Establecer de nuevo, colocar en un nuevo lugar.

relocation [riːləʊˈkeɪʃən] [ri-lou-kei-shon], *s.* Nueva colocación.

reluctance [rɪˈlʌktəns] [ri-lak-tans], *s.* Repugnancia, desgana, disgusto, mala gana. **With reluctance,** de mala gana.

reluctant [rɪˈlʌktənt] [ri-lak-tant], *a.* Repugnante, que no quiere, que no tiene ganas; no dispuesto a ceder; que obra con repugnancia.

rely [rɪˈlaɪ] [ri-lai], *vn.* Confiar en, tener confianza en, contar con (trust on); asegurarse de, fiarse en o de; se usa con *on* o *upon*. **Do not rely upon them,** no se fíe usted de ellos, no cuente usted con ellos. **We are relaying on you,** contamos con usted.

remain [rɪˈmeɪn] [ri-mein], *vn.* 1. Quedar, restar, faltar; quedarse atrás después del alejamiento o de la destrucción de otras personas o cosas; quedarse solo. 2. Remanecer, permanecer, persistir, continuar en un estado determinado. **Few remain,** quedan pocos. **They remained a fortnight in Caracas,** se quedaron quince días en Caracas. **She still remains a maiden,** aún permanece soltera o aún no se ha casado. **To remain still,** quedarse de pie. **It only remains to**

tell you,sólo resta decirle a usted o sólo tengo ya que decir a usted

remainder [rɪ'meɪndəʳ] [ri-mein-daʳ], s. Resto, residuo, resta, alcance. -a. Restante, que queda de una cantidad, de una cuenta, etc.

remains [rɪ'meɪnz] [ri-meins], s. pl. 1. Cadáver, el cuerpo muerto del hombre. 2. Sobras, restos, reliquias. 3. Las obras póstumas de un autor. 4. Esqueletos humanos; ruinas.

remake [rɪ'meɪk] [ri-meik], va. Rehacer, volver a hacer, hacer de nuevo.

remand [rɪ'mɑːnd] [ri-mand], va. 1. Volver a llamar; traer o enviar a alguno al paraje donde había estado antes. 2. (For.) Volver a enviar a la prisión; enviar a otro tribunal.

remand, remandment [rɪ'mɑːndmənt] [ri-mand-ment], s. Nuevo envío a la prisión; mandato judicial para el traslado a otro tribunal.

remark [rɪ'mɑːk] [ri-mark], s. Observación, advertencia, nota, reparo.

remark, va. 1. Expresar con palabras o por escrito; hacer observaciones; señalar, distinguir (mark) 2. Notar, observar; reparar (notice).

remarkable [rɪ'mɑːkəbl] [ri-mar-ka-bol], a. Reparable, notable, interesante, considerable o digno de consideración o atención; extraordinario, poco común, que puede excitar admiración.

remarkableness [rɪ,mɑː'kəblnɪs] [ri-mar-ka-bol-nes], s. Singularidad: la calidad que hace a una cosa notable o digna de atención particular.

remarkably [rɪ'mɑːkəblɪ] [ri-mar-ka-bli], adv. Notablemente, extraordinariamente.

remarker [rɪ'mɑːkəʳ] [ri-mar-kaʳ], s. Observador; anotador.

remarriage ['riː'mærɪdʒ] [ri-ma-rich], s. Segundas nupcias.

remarry ['riː'mærɪ] [ri-ma-ri], va. y vn. Casar o casarse de nuevo; volver a casar o casarse.

remediable ['rɪ'miːdɪəbl] [ri-mi-dia-bol], a. Remediable; curable.

remedial ['rɪ'miːdɪəl] [ri-mi-dial], a. Reparador; de la naturaleza de un remedio.

remediless ['rɪ'miːdɪlɪs] [ri-mi-di-les], a. Irremediable, sin recurso; incurable; irreparable.

remedy ['remədɪ] [re-me-di], s. 1. Remedio, medicamento. **It is past remedy,** no tiene remedio; es incurable. 2. Remedio, el medio que se toma para reparar algún daño; recurso. **To have no remedy at law,** no tener recurso legal.

remedy, va. Curar, sanar, remediar, reparar. **That's soon remedied,** eso es fácil de remediar.

remember [rɪ'membəʳ] [ri-mem-baʳ], s. va. 1. Acordarse, tener presente o retener en la memoria, rememorar. 2. Acordarse, hacer memoria. 3. Mentar, hacer mención de alguna cosa; recordar, traer a la memoria. -vn. Acordarse. **Remember me to her,** déle usted recuerdos de mi parte. **To remember someone in one's will,** mencionar a alguien en su testamento. **I don't remember hearing it,** no recuerdo haberlo oído.

rememberer [rɪ'membərəʳ] [ri-mem-ba-raʳ], s. Recordante.

remembrance [rɪ'membrəns] [ri-mem-brans], s. 1. Memoria, retentiva. **To call to remembrance,** traer a la memoria; acordarse de alguna cosa. 2. Relación o apuntamiento de. 3. Recuerdo, aviso. 4. Memoria, recuerdo, señal.

remind [rɪ'maɪnd] [ri-maind], va. Acordar, recordar, avisar, excitar y mover a otro a que tenga presente alguna cosa; poner en la memoria; reavivar la memoria.

reminder [rɪ'maɪndəʳ] [ri-main-daʳ], s. Recuerdo, lo que trae algo a la memoria; advertencia.

remindful [rɪ'maɪndf ʊl] [ri-maind-ful], a. 1. Rememorativo, que sirve para hacer recordar; que sirve de aviso. 2. Atento, cuidadoso, vigilante.

reminisce [,remɪ'nɪs] [re-mi-nis], vn. Tener reminiscencias, narrar recuerdos.

reminiscence [,remɪ'nɪsəns] [re-mi-ni-sens], s. Reminiscencia.

reminiscent [,remɪ'nɪsənt] [re-mi-ni-sent], a. Que recuerda lo pasado.

reminiscential [,remɪnɪ'senʃəl] [re-mi-ni-sen-shal], a. Perteneciente a la reminiscencia.

remiss [rɪ'mɪs] [ri-mis], a. Remiso, flojo, lento, perezoso, negligente; falto de energía. **Remiss in duty,** lento, negligente en cumplir con su deber. **To grow remiss,** entibiarse, aflojar.

remissibility [rɪ,mɪsɪ'bɪlɪtɪ] [ri-mi-si-bi-li-ti], s. Calidad de remisible o perdonable.

remissible [rɪ'mɪsɪbl] [ri-mi-si-bol], a. Remisible, perdonable.

remission [rɪ'mɪʃən] [ri-mi-shon], s. 1. Remisión, la acción de remitir; particularmente, remisión, perdón, absolución de culpa o delito. 2. Remisión, disminución o mengua de actividad o fuerza. 3. (Med.) Remisión, disminución temporal del rigor de una enfermedad. 4. Rebaja, minoración, v.g. de una multa. 5. Descanso en el trabajo o estudio. 6. Remesa. V. REMITTANCE. **Remission of sins,** remisión de los pecados.

remissly [rɪ'mɪslɪ] [ri-mis-li], adv. Flojamente, negligentemente.

remissness [rɪ'mɪsnɪs] [ri-mis-nes], s. Remisión, flojedad, negligencia y poca solicitud en la ejecución de alguna cosa.

remissory [rɪ'mɪsərɪ] [ri-mi-so-ri], a. Remisorio, que tiene virtud o facultad para remitir o perdonar.

remit [rɪ'mɪt] [ri-mit], va. 1. Remitir, enviar dinero de una parte a otra; transmitir. 2. Remitir, perdonar culpas, hacer gracia. 3. Exonerar, eximir de una multa u otra pena; dejar de exigir. 4. Relajar, aflojar. 5. Referir, someter a la consideración de otro. -vn. 1. Enviar dinero; hacer remesas. 2. Disminuir; debilitarse, hacerse más llevadera alguna cosa; bajar, templarse, suavizarse. **The fever begins to remit,** la calentura empieza a bajar.

remitment [rɪ'mɪtmənt] [ri-mit-ment], s. Remisión, acción y efecto de remitir; gracia, perdón, exoneración; remesa.

remittal [rɪ'mɪtl] [ri-mi-tal], s. 1. Cesión, renuncia, abandono (renunciation). 2. Remesa. V. REMITTANCE.

remittance [rɪ'mɪtəns] [ri-mi-tans], s. Remesa, la remisión de dinero o valores que se hace de una parte a otra; letra de cambio; también los valores enviados.

remittent [rɪ'mɪtənt] [ri-mi-tant], a. Remitente, que tiene aumentos y disminuciones alternativas sin cesación completa, v. g. una fiebre. -s. Fiebre o calentura remitente.

remitter [rɪ'mɪtəʳ] [ri-mi-taʳ], s. 1. Remitente, el que hace una remesa; el que compra una libranza postal. 2. (For.) Restitución, v. g. a un derecho o título anterior.

remix [,riː'mɪks] [ri-miks], sm. (Mús.) Remix.

remnant ['remnənt] [rem-nant], s. Remanente, resto, residuo; retal, retazo de alguna tela.

remodel ['riː'mɒdl] [ri-mo-del], va. Modelar de nuevo; reconstruir.

remonstrance [rɪ'mɒnstrəns] [ri-mons-trans], s. 1. Representación, súplica motivada, el acto de hacer reconvenciones. 2. Represión, amonestación, reconvención. 3. La custodia o viril en que se pone la hostia en las iglesias católicas. V. MONSTRANCE.

remonstrant [rɪ'mɒnstrənt] [ri-mons-trant], a. Motivado, que contiene motivos o razones eficaces. -s. El que representa a lo vivo; protestante.

remonstrate [rɪ'mɒnstreɪt] [ri-mons-treit], vn. Representar a lo vivo; objetar, reconvenir, oponer, presentar razones contra.

remora [rɪ'mɒrə] [ri-mo-ra], s. 1. Rémora (fish). 2. Un instrumento de cirugía usado antiguamente.

remorse [rɪ'mɔːs] [ri-mors], s. 1. Remordimiento, compunción (regret), dolor que se siente por haber cometido una mala acción. 2. (For.) Compasión, piedad (pity). **To feel remorse,** arrepentirse, compadecerse.

remorseful [rɪ'mɔːsf ʊl] [ri-mors-ful], a. Lleno de remordimientos; tierno, compasivo.

remorseless [rɪ'mɔːslɪs] [ri-mors-les], a. Cruel, insensible a los remordimientos.

remorselessly [rɪ'mɔːslɪslɪ] [ri-mors-lis-li], adv. Sin remordimiento, sin piedad.

remorselessness [rɪˈmɔːslɪsnɪs] [ri-mors-les-nes], *s.* Crueldad, apatía ante la desgracia.

remote [rɪˈməʊt] [ri-mout], *a.* 1. Remoto. 2. Lejano. 3. Ajeno. 4. Leve, mínimo. 5. Inabordable. **Remote control,** telemando, teledirección. **To operate by remote control,** teledirigir, teleguiar. **Remote viewing,** clarividencia. **In some remote future,** en un futuro lejano.

remote-control [rɪˈməʊtlənˈtrəʊl] [ri-mout-kon-troul], *a.* Teledirigido, teleguiado.

remotely [rɪˈməʊtlɪ] [ri-mout-li], *adv.* Remotamente, lejos, a lo lejos.

remoteness [rɪˈməʊtnɪs] [ri-mout-nes], *s.* Alejamiento, distancia.

remount [ˈriːˈmaʊnt] [ri-maunt], *va.* 1. Remontar, volver a montar, subir de nuevo. 2. *(Mil.)* Remontar, hacer la remonta, dar nuevos caballos a los soldados. -*vn.* Volver a subir.

removability [rɪˌmuːvəˈbɪlɪtɪ] [ri-mu-va-bi-li-ti], *s.* 1. Movilidad, facultad de moverse. 2. Amovilidad, calidad de amovible.

removable [rɪˈmuːvəbl] [ri-mu-va-bol], *a.* 1. Removible, que se puede remover o alejar; transportable. 2. Amovible (persons).

removal [rɪˈmuːvəl] [ri-mu-val], *s.* 1. Remoción, acto y efecto de remover; removimiento; alejamiento, apartamiento; traslado de un lugar a otro. 2. Cambio de lugar; cambio de morada. 3. Deposición. 4. Alivio, curación, quite. 5. Acto de poner fin o término a alguna cosa. **From our removal from Havana,** desde nuestra salida de la Habana. **A removal to a new post,** un traslado a un nuevo puesto. **Removal allowance,** subvención de mudanza.

remove [rɪˈmuːv] [ri-muv], *va.* 1. Remover, alejar, mudar una cosa de un lugar a otro; alzar o levantar la casa. 2. Remover, deponer del empleo o destino. 3. Alejar, apartar; quitar (threat, waste). 4. Destruir, poner fin, hacer desaparecer (do away with). -*vn.* Mudarse, trasladarse de un paraje a otro, alejarse, apartarse, cambiar de sitio, cambiar de habitación. **Remove that chair,** quite usted esa silla. **We must remove him from his post,** es menester destituirle de su puesto. **They will remove on the first of May,** cambiarán de casa el primero de mayo. **Cousin once removed,** hijo o hija de un primo carnal, sobrino segundo.

remove, *s.* 1. Cambio de puesto o paraje, mudanza, mudada. 2. Partida, el acto de partir de un lugar para ir a otro. 3. Escalón, el grado que se sube en dignidad. 4. Grado de parentesco; grado, paso, intervalo. 5. Plato o entrada de una comida.

remover [rɪˈmuːvəʳ] [ri-mu-vaʳ], *s.* El que remueve.

remunerable [rɪˈmjuːnərəbl] [ri-miu-na-rei-bol], *a.* Remunerable, capaz o digno de recompensa.

remunerate [rɪˈmjuːnəreɪt] [ri-miu-na-reit], *va.* Remunerar, recompensar, premiar.

remuneration [rɪˌmjuːnəˈreɪʃən] [ri-miu-na-rei-shon], *s.* Remuneración, recompensa, retribución.

remunerative [rɪˈmjuːnərətɪv] [ri-miu-na-ra-tiv], *a.* Remuneratorio; gananciono, provechoso, lucrativo.

remunerator [rɪˈmjuːnəreɪtəʳ] [ri-miu-na-rei-taʳ], *s.* Remunerador.

renaissance [rəˈnɛsɑːns] [re-ne-sans], *s.* 1. Renacimiento, vuelta a la vida. 2. Renacimiento (arts, literature).

renal [ˈriːnl] [ri-nal], *a.* Renal, que pertenece a los riñones.

renascence, renascency [rɪˈnæsəns] [ri-ne-sans], *s.* 1. Renacimiento. 2. *V.* RENAISSANCE, 2ª acep.

renascent [rɪˈnæsənt] [ri-ne-sant], *a.* Renaciente.

rencounter [rɪnˈkaʊntəʳ] [rin-kan-taʳ], *s.* 1. Reencuentro, choque, combate, refriega. 2. Quimera, pendencia, riña casual, colisión hostil repentina.

rencounter, *va. y vn.* 1. Encontrar, hallar impensadamente. 2. Encontrarse al enemigo de repente, embestirse, acomterse, atacarse.

rend [ˈrend] [rend], *va. y vn.* 1. Lacerar, hacer pedazos, desgarrar, rasgar, hender. 2. Separar, desunir. 3. Remover a viva fuerza; arrancar.

rend, *s. (Mar.)* Costura de los tablones.

render [ˈrendəʳ] [ren-daʳ], *s.* 1. Desgarrador. 2. Pago de un arriendo o alquiler.

render, *va.* 1. Hacer, cambiar dando un carácter determinado. 2. Dar, suministrar, prestar, rendir (give, supply). 3. Interpretar, v. g. una composicón musical. 4. Traducir (translate). 5. Volver, devolver, restituir (give back). 6. Derretir y clarificar. 7. Aplicar algo a una pared, v. g. la primera capa de yeso. **To render thanks to God,** dar gracias a Dios. **To render an account,** pasar factura. **To render assistance to,** prestar auxilio a. **To render justice,** hacer justicia. **To render smooth,** alisar. **To render into Spanish,** traducir al castellano. **This rends it impossible,** esto lo hace imposible. **To render down,** derretir. **To render up,** entregar, dejar, ceder.

rendering [ˈrendərɪŋ] [ren-da-rin], *s.* 1. Acción de dar, devolver o asignar. 2. Traducción, versión. 3. Interpretación artística. 4. Acto de derretir y clarificar. **Rendering-pan,** caldera para extraer la manteca.

rendezvous [ˈrɒndɪvuː] [ran-di-vu], *s.* 1. Cita para concurrir en un día u hora convenida a un lugar o sitio previamente señalado. 2. Lugar señalado para juntarse o reunirse.

rendezvous, *vn.* Acudir, juntarse, reunirse en paraje y hora señalados.

rendible [ˈrendɪbl] [ren-di-bol], *a.* Que puede ser desgarrado o lacerado.

rending [ˈrendɪŋ] [ren-din], *s.* Quebranto, dolor o pesar agudo.

rendition [renˈdɪʃən] [ren-di-shon], *s.* 1. Versión, traducción. 2. Interpretación artística. 3. Rendición, acción de rendirse. 4. La cantidad producida, rédito.

renegade [ˈrenɪgeɪd] [re-ni-gueid], *s.* 1. Renegado, apóstata de su fe religiosa. 2. Desertor. 3. Vagabundo, perdido.

renege, renig [rɪˈniːg] [ri-nig], *vn.* En los naipes, renuncia.

renew [rɪˈnjuː] [ri-niu], *va. y vn.* 1. Renovar, renovarse, hacer o hacerse nuevo. 2. Hacer, comenzar de nuevo; hacer revivir. 3. *(Teol.)* Regenerar espiritualmente. **To renew one's strength,** renovar fuerzas.

renewable [rɪˈnjuːəbl] [ri-niua-bol], *a.* Renovable.

renewal [rɪˈnjuːəl] [ri-niual], *s.* Renovación.

reniform [ˈrenɪfɔːm] [re-ni-form], *a.* Reniforme, que se parece a un riñón o tiene su figura.

rennet [ˈrenɪt] [re-nit], *s.* 1. Cuajo. 2. Cuajaleche, cardo lechero. 3. Quimosina.

renominate [rɪˈnɒmɪneɪt] [ri-no-mi-neit], *va.* Nombrar de nuevo, particularmente, para un segundo período del mismo cargo o empleo.

renounce [rɪˈnaʊns] [ri-nauns], *va.* 1. Renunciar. 2. Rechazar, negar, renegar, abandonar, abjurar (abandon, beat off). 3. En los naipes, no jugar carta de un palo, teniéndola.

renouncement [rɪˈnaʊnsmənt] [ri-nauns-ment], *s.* Renuncia.

renovate [ˈrenəʊveɪt] [re-nou-veit], *va.* 1. Renovar. 2. Limpiar enteramente, purificar.

renovation [ˌrenəʊˈveɪʃən] [re-nou-vei-shon], *s.* Renovación, acción y efecto de renovar; limpiadura; en teología, regeneración.

renovator [ˈrenəʊveɪtəʳ] [re-nou-vei-taʳ], *s.* Renovador, el o lo que renueva.

renown [rɪˈnaʊn] [ri-naun], *s.* Renombre, fama, gloria, reputación, celebridad. **A man of renown,** un hombre célebre.

rent [rent] [rent], *s.* 1. Renta; arrendamiento; alquiler, arriendo; también, el derecho de recibir esa compensación. 2. Desgarrón, rasgón, desgarro; rotura, rompimiento; cisma. **Rent-free,** *adv.* Sin pagar alquiler. **Rent-day,** día de pagar el alquiler o arrendamiento. **Rent rebate,** devolución de alquiler. **To rent a house,** alquilar una casa a alguien.

rent, *va.* 1. Arrendar, tomar en arrendamiento alguna renta o posesión. 2. Arrendar, dar en arriendo, alquilar.

rentable [ˈrentəbl] [ren-ta-bol], *a.* Arrendable.

rental [ˈrentl] [ren-tal], **rent-roll** [ˈrentrəʊl] [rent-roul], *s.* 1. Renta, arriendo, producto total de una propiedad alquilada. 2. Lista de rentas.

renter [ˈrentəʳ] [ren-taʳ], *s.* Rentero, arrendador, alquilador.

renunciation [rɪˌnʌnsɪ'eɪʃən] [ri-nan-siei-shon], *s.* Renuncia, renunciación.

reopen ['riː'əʊpən] [ri-ou-pen], *va.* Volver a abrir.

reorder ['riː'ɔːdəʳ] [ri-or-daʳ], *va.* 1. Volver a pedir o encargar. 2. Arreglar, ordenar.

reorganization ['riːˌɔːgənaɪ'zeɪʃən] [rior-ga-na-isei-shon], *s.* Reorganización.

reorganize ['riː'ɔːgənaɪz] [rior-ga-nais], *va.* Reorganizar.

rep [rep] [rep], *s.* Cierto tejido de superficie cordelada.

repack ['riː'pæk] [ri-pak], *vt.* Reembalar, reenvasar; volver a hacer (suitcase).

repair [rɪ'pɛəʳ] [ri-peaʳ], *va.* 1. Reparar, componer, aderezar, recorrer. **To repair a house,** reparar, recorrer una casa. 2. Resarcir, recompensar. 3. Suplir, cumplir lo que falta; acudir, aplicar, embonar, restaurar, renovar; *(Mar.)* carenar.

repair, *vn.* 1. Ir a alguna parte, encaminarse a, irse; retirarse, refugiarse. 2. Volver; dirigirse a, recurrir a.

repair, *s.* 1. Reparo, reparación, restauración, compostura. 2. Recorrida, embonada o reparo del casco de una embarcación. 3. *(Ant.)* Morada, asilo, guarida. **Out of repair,** descompuesto. **Repair-shop,** taller de reparaciones, particularmente de las máquinas.

repairable [rɪ'pɛərəbl] [ri-pea-ra-bol], *a.* Reparable.

repairer [rɪ'pɛərəʳ] [ri-pea-raʳ], *s.* Reparador.

reparation [ˌrepə'reɪʃən] [re-pa-rei-shon], *s.* 1. Reparación, renovación. 2. Recompensa; satisfacción, compensación.

reparative [rɪ'pɛərətɪv] [ri-pea-ra-tiv], *a.* Reparativo, restaurativo, que tiene virtud de reparar o restaurar.

repartee [ˌrepɑː'tiː] [re-par-tii], *s.* Respuesta o réplica aguda o picante; agudeza, chiste, donaire; gracia.

repartition [ˌrepə'tɪʃən] [re-pa-ti-shon], *s.* Repartimiento, repartición.

repass ['riː'pɑːs] [ri-pas], *va.* Repasar, volver a pasar; pasar en dirección opuesta.

repassage ['riː'pɑːsɪdʒ] [ri-pa-sich], *s.* Libertad o permiso de pasar.

repast ['riː'pɑːst] [ri-past], *s.* Refrigerio, comida, alimento. **Light repast,** colación. **To make a light repast,** tomar un refrigerio; hacer colación, tomar un pisto.

repatriate ['riː'pætrɪət] [ri-pa-trieit], *va.* Repatriar, enviar o conducir a su patria al que está fuera de ella.

repay [riː'peɪ] [ri-pei], *va.* Volver a pagar, recompensar, retornar, restituir; reconocer un beneficio recibido, dar un equivalente; pagar en la misma moneda. -*vn.* Hacer un pago, dar satisfacción o desquite. **It repays visit,** merece la pena visitarlo. **To repay someone in full,** pagar a alguien todo lo que se le debe, liquidar las cuentas con alguien.

repayable [riː'peɪəbl] [ri-peia-bol], *a.* Reintegrable, reembolsable. **Repayable on demand,** reembolsable a petición. **Repayable in 12 instalments,** a pagar en 12 cuotas.

repayment [riː'peɪmənt] [ri-pei-ment], *s.* Pago, devolución de lo comprado o gastado.

repeal [rɪ'piːl] [ri-pil], *va.* Abrogar, anular, revocar, abolir, como una ley (annul, cancel).

repeal, *s.* Revocación, abrogación, anulación.

repealable [rɪ'piːləbl] [ri-pi-la-bol], *a.* Revocable, anulable, abrogable, capaz de ser abrogado.

repealer [rɪ'piːləʳ] [ri-pi-laʳ], *s.* Revocador, anulador.

repeat [rɪ'piːt] [ri-pit], *s.* *(Mús.)* Repetición, línea de puntos que se pone en la pauta para indicar que un trozo de música debe ejecutarse dos veces. **Repeat broadcast,** retransmisión.

repeat, *va.* 1. Repetir, volver a hacer o decir; reiterar. 2. Recitar de memoria, repasar, ensayar. **Don't repeat it to anybody,** no se lo cuentes a nadie. **Can you repeat the design of this car?,** ¿puede hacer un coche igual que éste?

repeatedly [rɪ'piːtɪdlɪ] [ri-pi-tid-li], *adv.* Repetidamente, repetidas veces.

repeater [rɪ'piːtəʳ] [ri-pi-taʳ], *s.* 1. Repetidor. 2. Reloj de repetición. 3. Arma (gun) de repetición. 4. Repetidor, instrumento para transmitir de nuevo señales telegráficas. 5. *(E.U.)* El que vota o procura votar más de una vez en la misma elección.

repeating [rɪ'piːtɪŋ] [ri-pi-tin], *a.* Periódico *(Mat.)*.

repel [rɪ'pel] [ri-pel], *va.* 1. Repeler, rechazar, hacer retroceder por fuerza; refutar. 2. Repeler, alejar; lo contrario de atraer. 3. *(Med.)* Repercutir los humores. -*vn.* Rechazar, resistir; tener una cualidad o tendencia repulsiva.

repellent [rɪ'pelənt] [ri-pe-lent], *a.* 1. Repelente, que repele o rechaza. 2. A prueba de agua, impermeable. -*s.* 1. Impermeable, tela. 2. *(Med.)* Remedio repercusivo. **Repellent to insects,** que ahuyenta a los insectos.

repent [rɪ'pent] [ri-pent], *a.* *(Zool.)* Rastrero, que se arrastra; *(Bot.)* que echa raíces desde un tallo horizontal.

repent, *va.* y *vn.* Arrepentirse (de), tener pesar de haber hecho alguna cosa ofensiva o de haber pecado. **You will repent it,** le pesará a usted.

repentance [rɪ'pentəns] [ri-pen-tans], *s.* Arrepentimiento, penitencia, contrición.

repentant [rɪ'pentənt] [ri-pen-tant], *a.* Arrepentido, que se arrepiente, contrito.

repenting [rɪ'pentəntɪŋ] [ri-pen-tin], *s.* Arrepentimiento.

repentingly [rɪ'pentɪŋlɪ] [ri-pen-tin-li], *adv.* Con pesar o arrepentimiento.

repeople ['riː'piːp] [ri-pi-pol], *va.* Repoblar, volver a poblar.

repercuss [rɪpəkəs] [ri-per-kos], *va.* Repercutir, reverberar, rechazar.

repercussion [ˌriːpə'kʌʃən] [ri-per-ka-shon], *s.* Repercusión, reverberación (vibration), rechazo; frecuente reiteración del mismo tono, nota o acorde.

repercussive [rɪ'pəkəsɪv] [ri-per-ka-siv], *a.* Repercusivo

repertoire ['repətwɑːʳ] [re-par-tuaʳ], *s.* V. REPERTORY, 2ª acep.

repertory [repətərɪ] [re-per-to-ri], *s.* 1. Depósito, lugar donde se recogen las cosas; colección. 2. Repertorio, reportorio, lista de obras dramáticas o musicales que están por representar. 3. Tabla en que las cosas están dispuestas de tal modo que se pueden hallar fácilmente; lista, índice.

repetition [ˌrepɪ'tɪʃən] [re-pi-ti-shon], *s.* Repetición, reiteración; repaso; acción de repetir y lo que se repite.

rephrase [rɪ'freɪs] [ri-freis], *vt.* Decir de otra forma, expresar con otras palabras.

repine [rɪ'paɪn] [ri-pain], *vn.* Afligirse, apurarse, quejarse, murmurar, ser muy dado a hallar o poner faltas.

repiner [rɪ'paɪnəʳ] [ri-pai-naʳ], *s.* Murmurador, sentidor, triste, melancólico.

repining [rɪ'paɪnɪŋ] [ri-pai-nin], *s.* Pesar; murmuración, queja, descontento, quejoso.

replace [rɪ'pleɪs] [ri-pleis], *va.* 1. Reemplazar (take the place of). 2. Reponer, colocar (put). 3. Poner un substituto en lugar de otra persona. 4. Devolver, reembolsar (give back); restituir. 5. Colocar en otro lugar. **Please, replace the receiver,** cuelgue, por favor (phone). **She had to be replaced,** tuvo que ser destituida.

replaceable [rɪ'pleɪsəbl] [ri-plei-sa-bol], *a.* Reemplazable, que se puede reemplazar o reponer.

replacement [rɪ'pleɪsmənt] [ri-pleis-ment], *s.* 1. Remplazo, reposición, reintegración. 2. Colocación en su lugar. 3. Pieza de repuesto. 4. Substitución. **Replacement engine,** motor de repuesto.

replait [rɪ'pleɪt] [ri-pleit], *va.* Plegar repetidas veces.

replant [rɪ'plɑːnt] [ri-plant], *va.* Replantar, plantar de nuevo.

replay [rɪ'pleɪ] [ri-plei], *nf.* Repetición (on TV); desempate, partido para desempatar (Sports).

replenish [rɪ'plenɪʃ] [ri-ple-nish], *va.* Rellenar, llenar, surtir generosamente (refill); proveer con abundancia.

replenishment [rɪ'plenɪʃmənt] [ri-ple-nish-ment], *s.* Acción y efecto dellenar, proveer, o surtir.

replete [rɪ'pliːt] [ri-plit], *a.* Relleno, repleto, lleno (full). **Replete with,** lleno de.

repletion [rɪ'pliːʃən] [ri-pli-shon], **repleteness** [rɪ'pliːtnɪs] [ri-plit-nes], *s.* Repleción, plenitud.

replica ['replɪkə] [re-pli-ka], *s.* 1. (Fine Arts) Duplicado ejecutado por el artista mismo y que se considera como original. 2. *(Mús.)* Pasaje que se ha de ejecutar segunda vez.

replicant ['replɪkənt] [re-pli-kant], *s.* Replicador, replicante, el que responde.

replicate ['repli̩keɪt] [re-pli-keit], *a.* Replegado, plegado hacia atrás.

replication ['repli̩keɪʃən] [re-pli-kei-shon], *s.* 1. Réplica, respuesta (answer). 2. (*For.*) Réplica del actor contradiciendo la respuesta del demandado. 3. Una repetición o copia. 4. Pliegue sistemático de una superficie.

reply [rɪ'plaɪ] [ri-plai], *s.* Réplica, respuesta, contestación.

reply, *va.* 1. Contestar, responder a lo que se habla o escribe. 2. Replicar, instar, argüir con otro.

repoint [rɪ'pɔɪnt] [ri-point], *vt.* Rejuntar.

repopulate ['riːpɒpjʊleɪt] [ri-po-piu-leit], *vt.* Repoblar.

report [rɪ'pɔːt] [ri-port], *va.* 1. Esparcir, divulgar (circulate, spread); referir, contar (tell); informar, hacer relación, dar parte, noticia, o hacer exposición; manifestar (say). 2. Relatar, dar cuenta por razón de observación o indagación personal. 3. Certificar, formal u oficalmente (un resultado, una condición). -*vn.* 1. Hacer relación, dar parte. 2. Servir como reporter o noticiero. 3. (*E.U.*) Comparecer en un paraje señalado, o ante alguien y anunciarse. **It is reported,** corre la voz, se dice. **To be reported o reported of,** ser objeto de informes favorables o desfavorables. **To report progress,** exponer el estado de la cuestión.

report, *s.* 1. Relación, parte, noticia, manifiesto, anuncio, informe (announcement, statement). 2. Voz, rumor, opinión (rumour). **Flying report,** noticia volandera, suelta. **There was a report of his arrival,** corrió la voz de su llegada. **By report,** según se dice. 3. Fama, reputación pública. 4. Relación de pleitos o causas. 5. **Report of fire-arms,** estallido, tiro, trueno. **Report of a gun,** un cañonazo. **Report of a musket,** un escopetazo. **Report of a pistol,** un pistoletazo, un trabucazo. 6. Declaración de efectos hecha en la aduana. **Reported speech,** discurso indirecto. **There is a report that,** corre la voz de que, se rumorea que. **To know something by report,** saber algo de oídas. **He reports for the X newspaper,** es reportero del periódico X. **To report back to someone,** rendir cuentas a alguien, informar. **A comittee was set up to report on the matter,** se creó una comisión para investigar el asunto. **Report back inmediately!,** ¡preséntese inmediatamente!

reportage [ˌrepɔːˈtɑːʒ] [re-por-tash], *sm.* Reportaje.

reporter [ˌrɪpɔːtəʳ] [ri-por-taʳ], *s.* 1. Taquígrafo, repórter, el que busca y recoge noticias para los periódicos. 2. Relator, redactor de las causas o pleitos importantes en los tribunales. **Reporter's gallery,** tribuna de los taquígrafos o de los periodistas (en una asamblea legislativa).

repose [rɪ'pəʊz] [ri-pous], *va.* 1. Extender en una postura de descanso; reponer por medio del descanso. 2. Fijar, fiar, confiar, poner su confianza o esperanza en. -*vn.* 1. Reposar, dormir, descansar. 2. Estar seguro, tener seguridad; fiarse de. 3. Tenderse a la larga, reclinarse, recostarse.

repose, *s.* 1. Reposo, descanso, tranquilidad, sueño (rest, sleep). 2. Calma, quietud; moderación en los modales.

reposite [rɪ'pɒzɪt] [ri-po-sit], *va.* Depositar, reponer.

reposition [ˌrɪpɒ'zɪʃən] [ri-po-si-shon], *s.* Reposición, restablecimiento.

repository [rɪ'pɒzɪtərɪ] [ri-po-si-to-ri], *s.* Repositorio, depósito, despensa, lugar en que se pueden guardar géneros; también, lugar de exhibición y venta, almacén, tienda.

repossess ['riːpə'zes] [ri-po-ses], *va.* Recobrar, recuperar (recover). **To repossess oneself of,** volver a tomar posesión de algo.

repossession ['riːpə'zeʃən] [ri-po-se-shon], *s.* reposesión, recuperación de una posesión.

reprehend [ˌreprɪ'hend] [re-pri-jend], *va.* Reprender, reñir, censurar, tachar.

reprehender [ˌreprɪ'hendəʳ] [re-pri-jen-daʳ], *s.* Reprensor.

reprehensible [ˌreprɪ'hensɪbl] [re-pri-jen-si-bol], *a.* Reprensible, censurable.

reprehensibly [ˌreprɪ'hensɪblɪ] [re-pri-jen-si-bli], *adv.* Censurablemente.

reprehension [ˌreprɪ'henʃən] [re-pri-jen-shon], *s.* Reprensión, amonestación, censura.

reprehensive [ˌreprɪ'hensɪv] [re-pri-jen-siv], *a.* Reprensor, que indica o contiene una reprensión, propenso a reprender, a reconvenir.

represent [ˌreprɪ'zent] [re-pri-sent], *va.* 1. Representar, manifestar, describir, por medio de palabras, cuadros o personificaciones (describe); hacer el papel de; recitar en público. 2. Presentar de nuevo a la mente. 3. Estar en lugar de otro, hacer las veces de, ser apoderado de alguien.

represent, *va.* Presentar de nuevo, en particular de un modo diferente.

representable [ˌreprɪ'zentəbl] [re-pri-sen-ta-bol], *a.* Representable, que se puede representar; digno de representación.

representation [ˌreprɪzen'teɪʃən] [re-pri-sen-tei-shon], *s.* 1. Representación, acción y efecto de representar (show). 2. Lo que representa o exhibe algo por medio de semejanza, como un modelo, una figura, un cuadro, una descripción o ejecución de una obra dramática. 3. Derecho de hacer las veces de otro; también el derecho de ser representado en una asamblea legislativa. 4. Asamblea de representación. 5. Representación, manifestación, aserto, afirmación (revealing, show). **To make representation,** quejarse, presentar una petición o una queja.

representative [ˌreprɪ'zentətɪv] [re-pri-sen-ta-tiv], *a.* 1. Representativo, apto o autorizado para representar; que sirve para representar; típico. 2. Representante, que hace las veces de otro, que hace el papel de delegado o agente. -*s.* 1. Representante, el que representa a una persona ausente; delegado nombrado por elección para un cuerpo legislativo; en los Estados Unidos, miembro de la cámara popular del Congreso o de la Legislatura de un estado. 2. Símbolo, tipo, ejemplo típico (example). **A person not fully representative,** una persona no adecuada para representar a algo.

representatively [ˌreprɪ'zentətɪvlɪ] [re-pri-sen-ta-tiv-li], *adv.* Por delegación o poder, como representante.

representer [ˌreprɪ'zentəʳ] [re-pri-sen-taʳ], *s.* Representante.

repress [rɪ'pres] [ri-pres], *va.* Sojuzgar, sujetar, reprimir, domar.

repression [rɪ'preʃən] [ri-pre-shon], *s.* Represión, la acción y efecto de represar o de reprimir.

repressive [rɪ'presɪv] [ri-pre-siv], *a.* Represivo, que sirve para reprimir o refrenar.

reprieve [rɪ'priːv] [ri-priv], *va.* 1. Suspender la ejecución de una sentencia de muerte. 2. Aliviar, o libertar temporalmente de peligro, pena o dolor.

reprieve, *s.* 1. La dilación o la suspensión temporal en la imposición de un castigo. 2. Suspensión temporal del dolor.

reprimand ['reprɪmɑːnd] [re-pri-mand], *va.* Reprender, corregir (correct, repress); reñir, y especialmente censurar; reconvenir en público.

reprint ['riːprɪnt] [ri-print], *va.* Reimprimir, imprimir de nuevo.

reprint, *s.* Reimpresión, nueva edición de una obra; copia hecha en otro país.

reprisal [rɪ'praɪzəl] [ri-prai-sal], *s.* Represalia.

reprise [rɪ'priːz] [ri-pris], *s.* 1. Represalia. 2. Estribillo de copla.

reproach [rɪ'prəʊtʃ] [ri-prouch], *va.* Reprochar, vituperar, increpar, reconvenir (censure, upbraid), echar en cara; vituperar, afear, censurar. **They were reproached as devoid of courage,** se les increpó por su falta de valor. **What have they to reproach him with?,** ¿qué tienen que echarle en cara?

reproach, *s.* Reproche, oprobio; tacha, nota, infamia, causa de reproche o culpa; vituperación, reconvención, increpación. **Free from reproach,** exento de tacha o faltas. **This is a reproach to us,** esto es deshonroso para nosotros. **Beyond reproach,** intachable.

reproachable [rɪ'prəʊtʃəbl] [ri-prou-cha-bol], *a.* Censurable, reprensible, digno de reproche o increpación.

reproachful [rɪ'prəʊtʃfʊl] [ri-prouch-ful], *a.* Que contiene o expresa reproche, improperio, tacha o reconvención; increpador, injurioso; ceñudo; infame. **A reproachful look,**

una mirada reprochadora, ceñuda. **Reproachful words,** palabras injuriosas. **Reproachful life,** vida infame o licenciosa.

reproachfully [rɪˈprəʊtʃfəlɪ] [ri-prouch-fu-li], *adv.* De una manera increpadora, por vía de improperio u oprobio; con ceño, con reproche.

reproachfulness [rɪˈprəʊtʃfənɪs] [ri-prouch-ful-nes], *s.* Calidad de lo que es digno de reproche; reconvención; ceño; oprobio, disposición a improperar o vituperar.

reprobate [ˈreprəʊbeɪt] [re-prou-beit], *a.* 1. Malvado, vicioso, abandonado a los vicios; privado de todo sentimiento del deber, rérobo. 2. *(Ant.)* Falso, de mala ley; bajo, inferior.

reprobate, *va.* Reprobar, condenar; desaprobar, no aprobar.

reprobation [ˌreprəʊˈbeɪʃən] [re-prou-bei-shon], *s.* Reprobación, desaprobación, condenación.

reprobative, [ˈreprəʊbətɪv] [re-prou-ba-tiv], *a.* Reprobador, reprobatorio, que reprueba.

reproduce [ˌriːprəˈdjuːs] [ri-pro-dius], *va.* Reproducir, volver a producir o producir de nuevo.

reproduction [ˌriːprəˈdʌkʃən] [ri-pro-dak-shon], *s.* 1. Reproducción, el acto o poder de reproducir: (a) en biología, reproducción, generación de animales o plantas; (b) reminiscencia, el procedimiento de la memoria que presenta de nuevo al conocimiento interior objetos conocidos anteriormente. 2. Reproducción, la cosa reproducida; renacimiento del drama; copia, traslado del original, en las bellas artes. **Reproduction furniture,** mobiliario de estilo.

reproductive, reproductory [ˌriːprəˈdʌktɪv] [ri-pro-dak-tiv], *a.* Reproductivo, reproductor, perteneciente a la reproducción; empleado en la reproducción física o mental.

reprographic [ˌriːprəˈgræfɪk] [ri-pro-gra-fik], *sf.* Reprografía.

reproof [ˌriːˈpruːf] [ri-pruf], *s.* Improperio, reprensión, censura, tacha echada en cara a uno, peluca. **To administer a reproof,** reñir, reprender.

reprovable [ˌriːˈpruːvəbl] [ri-pru-va-bol], *a.* Censurable, tachable, reprensible.

reproval [rɪˈpruːvəl] [ri-pru-val], *sf.* Reprobación.

reprove [rɪˈpruːv] [ri-pruv], *va.* 1. Culpar, censurar autoritativa, directa y abiertamente (blame). 2. Acusar, expresar desaprobación (de un acto o hecho); reprender, condenar. 3. *(Ant.)* Convencer.

reprover [rɪˈpruːvəʳ] [ri-pru-vaʳ], *s.* Represor, censor.

reptant [ˈreptənt] [rep-tant], *a.* Rastrero, que se arrastra.

reptile [ˈreptaɪl] [rep-tail], *a.* 1. Reptil, que camina rozando la tiera con el vientre. 2. Bajo, taimado, vil; venenoso. -*s.* 1. Reptil. 2. Persona vil y baja.

reptilian [repˈtɪlɪən] [rep-ti-lian], *a.* De reptil, perteneciente a los reptiles.

reptilious [repˈtɪlɪəs] [rep-ti-lios], *a.* Semejante a un reptil.

republic [rɪˈpʌblɪk] [ri-pa-blik], *s.* 1. República. 2. Comunidad de personas.

republican [rɪˈpʌblɪkən] [ri-pa-bli-kan], *a. y s.* Republicano.

republicanism [rɪˈpʌblɪkənɪzəm] [ri-pa-bli-ka-ni-sem], *s.* 1. Republicanismo, sistema republicano de gobierno. 2. Predilección por los principios republicanos. 3. Política del partido republicano de los Estados Unidos.

republication [riːˌpʌblɪˈkeɪʃən] [ri-pa-bli-kei-shon], *s.* 1. Segunda o nueva publicación; copia hecha en otro país. 2. Renovación de un testamento.

republish [rɪˈpʌblɪʃ] [ri-pa-blish], *va.* Publicar de nuevo.

repudiable [rɪˈpjuːdɪəbl] [ri-piu-dia-bol], *a.* Repudiable.

repudiate [rɪˈpjuːdɪeɪt] [ri-piu-dieit], *va.* 1. Repudiar (hate); renunciar, echar o lanzar de sí. 2. Repeler a la mujer propia.

repudiation [rɪˌpjuːdɪˈeɪʃən] [ri-piu-diei-shon], *s.* Repudiación, repudio.

repugnance [rɪˈpʌgnəns] [ri-pag-nans], **repugnancy** [rɪˈʌgnənsɪ] [ri-pag-nan-si], *s.* Repugnancia, desgana, aversión (reluctance).

repugnant [rɪˈpʌgnənt] [ri-pag-nant], *a.* Repugnante, contrario, incompatible, opuesto; inconsistente.

repugnantly [rɪˈpʌgnəntlɪ] [ri-pag-nant-li], *adv.* Con repugnancia, de muy mala gana.

repulse [rɪˈpʌls] [ri-pals], *s.* Repulsa, rechazo, rehuso; sofión.

repulse, *va.* Repulsar, desechar, repeler.

repulsion [rɪˈpʌlʃən] [ri-pal-shon], *s.* 1. *(Fís.)* Repulsión. 2. Estado de ser repulsado; aversión, repugnancia, mala acogida.

repulsive [rɪˈpʌlsɪv] [ri-pal-siv], *a.* Repulsivo, repugnante, chocante, que rechaza, que causa aversión.

repulsiveness [rɪˈpʌlsɪvnɪs] [ri-pal-siv-nes], *s.* Carácter repugnante, chocante; lo que rechaza toda familiaridad.

reputable [rɪˈpjɒtəbl] [ri-piu-ta-bol], *a.* 1. Honroso, decoroso, honorífico, estimable (decent, proper), digno de estimación. 2. Lícito, exento de tacha. **Reputable conduct,** conducta decorosa, exenta de tacha.

reputably [rɪˈpjɒtəblɪ] [ri-piu-ta-bli], *adv.* Honrosamente, con decoro.

reputation [ˌrepjʊˈteɪʃən] [re-piu-tei-shon], *s.* Reputación buena o mala; estimación, fama, crédito, nombre, renombre, nombradía. **To ruin anybody's reputation,** dar mala reputación a alguien. **Of no reputation,** sin reputación. **A firm of reputation,** una empresa acreditada. **By reputation,** según se dice.

repute [rɪˈpjuːt] [ri-piut], *va.* Reputar, estimar, juzgar, tener por. **To be reputed,** pasar por, tener fama de, ser juzgado como. **Reputed father,** padre putativo.

repute, *s.* Fama, crédito, reputación, estimación; opinión común. **In good repute,** de buena reputación. **In evil repute,** de mala fama.

reputedly [rɪˈpjuːtɪdlɪ] [ri-piu-tid-li], *adv.* Según la opinión común.

request [rɪˈkwest] [ri-kuest], *s.* 1. Petición, ruego, súplica, encargo, instancia, solicitud (petition, plea). 2. Crédito, estimación, boga. **At the request of,** a petición, a solicitud de. **In request,** en boga, en crédito; en lenguaje comercial, pedido, buscado. **At the request of,** a instancia de, a petición de. **To play a song by request,** tocar una canción a petición del público.

request, *va.* Rogar, pedir, suplicar, encargar, solicitar. **To request an answer,** pedir una contestación, una respuesta.

requicken [rɪˈkwɪkn] [ri-kui-ken], *va.* Reanimar, hacer revivir.

requiem [ˈrekwɪem] [re-kuiem], *s.* 1. Misa de requiem o de difuntos. 2. Descanso, paz, quietud.

requirable [rɪˈkwaɪəbl] [ri-kuaia-bol], *a.* Que se puede requerir o solicitar.

require [rɪˈkwaɪəʳ] [ri-kuaiaʳ], *va.* 1. Requerir, demandar, solicitar, pedir alguna cosa como de derecho. 2. Requerir, necesitar, exigir; haber menester o hallar indispensable. **To require one to report,** requerir de alguno que dé informes sobre algo. **The work will require money and men,** la obra exigirá dinero y hombres. **This plants requires watering frequently,** esta planta hay que regarla con frecuencia. **If required,** en caso de necesidad.

requirement [rɪˈkwaɪəmənt] [ri-kuaia-ment], *s.* Demanda, requerimiento, el acto de pedir con autoridad; requisito, lo que se requiere para alguna cosa, necesidad. **The requirements of health,** los cuidados que exige la salud. **Our requirements are few,** con poco nos arreglamos, tenemos pocas necesidades.

requirer [rɪˈkwaɪərəʳ] [ri-kuaia-raʳ], *s.* Requeridor, solicitador.

requisite [ˈrekwɪzɪt] [re-kui-sit], *a.* Necesario, preciso, indispensable. -*s.* Requisito.

requisiteness [ˈrekwɪzɪtnɪs] [re-kui-sit-nes], *s.* Necesidad, precisión.

requisition [ˌrekwɪˈzɪʃən] [re-kui-si-shon], *s.* 1. Pedimento, petición, demanda formal, requisición (plea). 2. Necesidad, requisito, menester (need). 3. Cualidad de ser solicitado, boga. **In requisition,** en boga; pedido, buscado. 4. *(For.)* Requisitoria, requerimiento, pedido.

requisitory [ˈrekwɪzɪtərɪ] [re-kui-si-to-ri], *a.* 1. Que implica una petición, demanda o súplica. 2. (Poco us.) Demandado, pedido, solicitado.

requital [rɪˈkwaɪtl] [ri-kuai-tal], *s.* 1. Retorno, paga, satisfacción, compensación por lo bueno o lo malo; desquite, pena del talión. **In requital of,** en pago, en compensación de. 2. Premio, galardón, recompensa.

requite [rɪˈkwaɪt] [ri-kuait], *va.* 1. Retornar, pagar en la misma moneda, volver satisfaciendo o recompensando; desquitar, vengar una injuria. 2. Reconocer, pagar, recompensar. **He requited me evil for good,** me ha devuelto mal por bien.

reredos [ˈrɪədɒs] [ria-dos], *s.* 1. Retable, adorno arquitectónico, que se coloca detrás de un altar. 2. Placa de hierro que se pone en el fondo de un hogar o chimenea.

reroute [riˈruːt] [ri-rut], *va.* Reenrumbar, reencaminar.

rerun [riˈrʌn] [ri-ran], *s.* Repetición, por ejemplo de una película.

resale [ˈriːseɪl] [ri-seil], *sf.* Reventa.

rescind [rɪˈsɪnd] [ri-sind], *va.* Rescindir, anular, abrogar.

rescission [rɪˈsɪʒən] [ri-si-shon], *s.* Rescisión, anulación, abrogación.

rescissory [rɪˈsɪsərɪ] [ri-si-so-ri], *a. (For.)* Rescisorio, que tiene el poder de rescindir.

rescribe [rɪˈskraɪb] [ris-kraib], *va. (Des.)* 1. Rescribir, contestar. 2. Volver a escribir la misma cosa.

rescript [ˈrɪskrɪpt] [ris-kript], *s.* Rescripto, edicto.

rescuable [ˈreskjuəbl] [res-kiua-bol], *a.* Que puede ser rescatado o librado de algún peligro o riesgo.

rescue [ˈreskjuː] [res-kiu], *va.* Librar, libertar (free); recobrar, rescatar (ransom); preservar, sacar de algún peligro o riesgo. *(Fam.)* Quitar o sacar de las manos. **To come to the rescue of,** acudir al rescate de. **Rescue dig,** excavación de urgencia. **Rescue vessel,** buque de salvamento. **Rescue team,** equipo de salvamento.

rescue, *s.* Libramiento, recobro; la acción de libertar con violencia a un preso; socorro, preservación de un peligro o de un enemigo.

rescuer [ˈreskjuːəʳ] [res-kiuaʳ], *s.* Librador, libertador, salvador.

research [rɪˈsɜːtʃ] [ri-serch], *s.* Escudriñamiento, averiguación o examen diligente de una cosa; investigación sistemática y científica. **Research and development,** investigación y desarrollo. **A piece of research,** una investigación. **Research team,** equipo de investigación.

research, *va.* y *vn.* Buscar, investigar. **A well researched study,** un estudio bien preparado.

researcher [rɪˈsɜːtʃəʳ] [ri-ser-chaʳ], *s.* Científico investigador, rebuscador.

reseat [riˈsiːt] [ri-sit], *va.* 1. Sentar o asentar de nuevo. 2. Poner un fondo o asiento nuevo. **To reseat a chair,** poner asiento nuevo a una silla.

resect [rɪˈsekt] [ri-sekt], *va.* Acortar, cercenar, cortar una porción de (un hueso o nervio).

resection [riˈsekʃən] [ri-sek-shon], *s.* Acortamiento, resección, operación de cortar una porción de un hueso o nervio.

resemblance [rɪˈzembləns] [ri-sem-blans], *s.* Semejanza, similitud, conformidad (likeness, similarity); lo que se asemeja, imagen exterior; retrato fiel. **To bear no resemblance to somebody,** no parecerse en absoluto.

resemble [rɪˈzembl] [ri-sem-bel], *va.* 1. Asemejarse, parecerse. **He resembles his father,** se parece a su padre. 2. *(Des.)* Asemejar; comparar, poner en paralelo. **She doesn't resemble her sister,** no se parece a su hermana.

resent [rɪˈzent] [ri-sent], *va.* Resentirse, dar muestras de sentimiento o pesar; encolerizarse, tomar una cosa como injuria o afrenta, indignarse. **I don't resent your saying it,** no me ofende que lo digas. **I resent that!,** ¡protesto contra eso!

resenter [rɪˈzentəʳ] [ri-sen-taʳ], *s.* El que se resiente de un agravio.

resentful [rɪˈzentfʊl] [ri-sent-ful], *a.* Enfadadizo, vidrioso, el que se enfada con facilidad; resentido.

resentment [rɪˈzentmənt] [ri-sent-ment], *s.* Resentimiento, enojo y mala voluntad en vista del mal verdadero o supuesto hecho contra sí mismo o los amigos de uno; disgusto profundo y persistente, desazón, pesar.

reservation [ˌrezəˈveɪʃən] [re-sa-vei-shon], *s.* 1. Reservación, acción y efecto de reservar, y la cosa reservada (booking). 2. Restricción mental, segunda intención, pensamiento secreto, lo que sobreentiende cautelosamente el que habla. 3. Reserva, reservación; término forense. 4. Separación o destino de una porción designada de territorio, bajo las leyes territoriales de los Estados Unidos, para un uso particular, v. g. para residencia de una tribu de indios; también, el territorio así reservado. **I had reservations about it,** tenía algunas dudas sobre ello. **To make a reservation,** hacer una reserva, reservar (hotel, restaurant,...).

reserve [rɪˈzɜːv] [ri-serv], *va.* 1. Reservar (book), guardar para adelante, guardar alguna cosa para otra ocasión. 2. Tener por suyo, retener, conservar. 3. Exceptuar, excluir de alguna cosa concedida o estipulada. **He reserves the right to,** se reserva el derecho de.

reserve, *s.* 1. Reserva, reservación, guarda o custodia de una cosa para otro tiempo o uso; reservación de tierras. 2. Reserva, circunspección, cautela, silencio en lo que a uno se refiere (restriction); reticencia; recato, modestia. 3. Reservación, excepción. 4. *(Mil.)* Reserva, retén. **Reserve fund,** fondo de reserva. **Without reserve,** sin reserva, sin excepción, enteramente. **To play in the reserves,** jugar de suplente (Sports).

reserved [rɪˈzɜːvd] [ri-servd], *a.* 1. Reservado, modesto, cauteloso, circunspecto, discreto, distante. 2. Retenido, guardado, preservado.

reservedly [rɪˈzɜːvdlɪ] [ri-servd-li], *adv.* Reservadamente, bajo sigilo; con reserva, con cautela.

reservedness [rɪˈzɜːvdnɪs] [ri-servd-nes], *s.* Reserva, cautela, circunspección, recato.

reserver [rɪˈzɜːvəʳ] [ri-ser-vaʳ], *s.* El que reserva.

reservist [rɪˈzɜːvɪst] [ri-ser-vist], *a.* Soldado de reserva.

reservoir [rɪˈzɜːvɔəʳ] [ri-ser-vuaʳ], *s.* Depósito, regularmente de agua, que puede ser charca, estanque, arca o algibe; por extensión se da también este nombre al depósito de cualquier otra cosa.

reset [ˈriːset] [ri-set], *va.* Poner, colocar o fijar de nuevo. *-s.* Acción de poner o fijar otra vez; o lo que está fijado o puesto de nuevo.

reset, *va. (Der. esco.)* Recibir objetos hurtados.

resettle [ˈriːsetl] [ri-se-tel], *va.* Restablecer, repoblar, poblar de nuevo. *-vn.* Restablecerse, poblarse, fijarse de nuevo. **To resettle in the same parish,** fijarse de nuevo en la misma parroquia.

resettlement [ˈriːsetlmənt] [ri-se-tel-ment], *s.* Restablecimiento, repoblación.

reshape [ˈriːʃeɪp] [ri-sheip], *vt.* Reformar, rehacer.

reside [rɪˈzaɪd] [ri-said], *vn.* 1. Residir, morar en algún lugar. 2. Residir, estar o formar parte de, ser inherente.

residence [ˈrezɪdəns] [re-si-dans], *s.* 1. Residencia, morada, domicilio (living, stay), habitación o lugar donde se vive. 2. El acto de residir, o la calidad de residente; vecindad. **Certificate of residence,** carta de vecindad; certificación de residencia. **A doctor in residence,** un médico interno. **To take up one's residence,** establecerse, fijar su residencia.

residency [ˈrezɪdənsɪ] [re-si-dan-si], *s. V.* RESIDENCE.

resident [ˈrezɪdənt] [re-si-dent], *a.* 1. Residente, que reside o mora en un lugar. 2. Permanente, no migratorio; se dice de las aves. 3. Inherente. *-s.* 1. El que o la que reside, en cualquier sentido; particularmente, vecino, el que tiene casa y hogar en un pueblo, habitante. 2. Residente: se llama así el ministro que reside en alguna corte extranjera, sin el carácter de embajador. **To be resident in a village,** residir en un pueblo. **Residents association,** asociación de vecinos.

residential [ˌrezɪˈdenʃəl] [re-si-den-shal], *a.* Residencial.

resider [rɪˈsaɪdəʳ] [ri-sai-daʳ], *s.* Residente, morador, habitante.

residual [rɪˈzɪdjʊəl] [ri-si-diual], **residuary** [rɪˈzɪdjʊərɪ] [ri-si-diua-ri], *a.* 1. Restante, perteneciente a un residuo, de la naturaleza de un residuo; lo que queda cuando han desaparecido todas las cosas de un mismo género, o todas las causas conocidas. **Residual magnetism,** magnetismo restante, el que queda después de suprimida la fuerza imanante. 2. **Residuary,** *(For.)* que está en relación con el resto de una herencia o que se refiere a él. **Residuary legatee,** legatario universal.

residue [ˈrezɪdjuː] [re-si-diu], *s.* Residuo, resto, resta, sobrante.

residuum [rɪˈzɪdjʊəm] [ri-si-diuam], *s.* Residuo, lo que queda de una substancia con la que se ha hecho alguna operación; resta, lo que queda después de cualquier procedimiento de sustracción.

resign [rɪˈzaɪn] [ri-sain], *va.* 1. Dimitir, resignar, renunciar, ceder, hacer dejación. 2. Resignarse, rendirse, entregarse o humillarse a la voluntad de otro.

resign, *va.* Firmar de nuevo, firmar otra vez.

resignation [ˌrezɪɡˈneɪʃən] [re-sig-nei-shon], **resignment** [rɪˈzaɪnmənt] [ri-sain-ment] *s.* Resignación, conformidad con la voluntad de Dios.

resigner [rɪˈzaɪnəʳ] [ri-sai-naʳ], *s.* Resignante, el que resigna un beneficio.

resilience [rɪˈzɪlɪəns] [ri-si-lians], *s.* Resalto, elasticidad, el poder, acto o efecto, de volver a una posición anterior.

resilient [rɪˈzɪlɪənt] [ri-si-liant], *a.* Resaltante, elástico.

resin [ˈrezɪn] [re-sin], *s.* Resina.

resinaceous [ˌrezɪˈneɪʃəs] [re-si-ni-shos], *a.* V. RESINOUS, 1ª acep.

resinoid [ˈrezɪnɔɪd] [re-si-noid], *a.* Parecido a una resina. -*s.* Sustancia que se parece a una resina.

resinous [ˈrezɪnəs] [re-si-nos], *a.* 1. Resinoso, de la naturaleza de las resinas, o que contiene resina. 2. Obtenido de la resina, como la electricidad.

resinousness [ˈrezɪnəsnɪs] [re-si-nos-nes], *s.* La calidad de lo que es resinoso.

resist [rɪˈzɪst] [ri-sist], *va. y vn.* Resistir, rechazar, repeler (stand up to); oponerse (opposit); impedir, detener por la inercia (stop); esforzarse en poner obstáculos, en contrariar, en hacer frustrar un proyecto, etc; negarse *a.* **To resist the evidence of one's senses,** negarse a admitir el testimonio de los sentidos. **I couldn't resist taking it,** no pude resistirme a cogerlo.

resistance, resistence [rɪˈzɪstəns] [ri-sis-tans], *s.* 1. Resistencia, oposición, defensa. 2. Fuerza que impide un movimiento; impedimento, obstáculo. 3. *(Elec.)* Resistencia, la cualidad de un cuerpo que limita la fuerza de una corriente eléctrica. **Resistance-box,** caja del carrete de resistencia. *V.* RHEOSTAT. **Resistance-coil,** rosca, carrete, de alambre aislado de resistencia eléctrica conocida, del que se usa para medir las resistencias no conocidas. **To offer resistance,** oponer resistencia.

resistant, resistent [rɪˈzɪstənt] [ri-sis-tant], *a.* Resistente, que resiste.

resister [rɪˈzɪstəʳ] [ri-sis-taʳ], *s.* Insumiso.

resistible [rɪˈzɪstɪbl] [ri-sis-ti-bol], *a.* Resistible.

resistless [rɪˈzɪstlɪs] [ri-sist-les], *a.* 1. Irresistible, que o a quien no se puede resistir. 2. Que no ofrece resistencia, indefenso.

resistor [rɪˈzɪstəʳ] [ri-sis-taʳ], *s.* Resistencia.

resoluble [ˈrezəljəbl] [re-so-lu-bol], *a.* 1. Soluble, que se puede disolver, desatar, o desleír. 2. Resoluble.

resolute [ˈrezəluːt] [re-so-lut], *a.* Resuelto, determinado; firme, constante.

resolutely [ˈrezəluːtlɪ] [re-so-lut-li], *adv.* Resueltamente.

resoluteness [ˈrezəluːtnɪs] [re-so-lut-nes], *s.* Resolución, determinación, firmeza, ánimo, constancia (spirit, firmness).

resolution [ˌrezəˈluːʃən] [re-so-lu-shon], *s.* 1. Resolución, determinación, ánimo, valor, arresto (courage); firmeza, constancia (steadiness). 2. Resolución, determinación de algún asunto; el propósito, línea de conducta o acuerdo tomado. 3. Resolución, solución de alguna duda o dificultad, de un problema o de una ecuación. 4. Análisis, la solución de las partes de algún compuesto; resolución, disolución de un todo; análisis químico, mecánico o mental; descomposición. 5. Resolución, la propuesta formal que se ofrece a la aceptación, o que se acepta por un cuerpo legislativo o deliberante. 6. Resolución de un tumor, de una inflamación, etc. **Man of resolution,** hombre de tesón; hombre determinado o decidido. **To put a resolution to a meeting,** someter a votación una moción. **Good resolutions,** buenas intenciones.

resolutive [rɪˈzezəljuːtɪv] [re-so-liu-tiv], *a.* Resolutivo.

resolvable [rɪˈzɒlvəbl] [ri-sol-va-bol], *a.* Resoluble, lo que se puede resolver, analizar, o aclarar.

resolve [rɪˈzɒlv] [ri-solv], *va. y vn.* 1. Resolver o resolverse, determinar, decidir, decidirse, declarar, declararse (declare, decide); tratar de, estar dispuesto a (be ready to). 2. Expresar o declarar como opinión o intención (express); tomar un acuerdo; aprobar por medio de votos. 3. Resolver, analizar (exam). 4. Resolver, convertir, reducir un todo a partes menudas deshaciéndolo; descomponer en sus partes constituyentes. 5. Enterar, explicar alguna cosa. 6. Resolver, desatar, dar solución a una dificultad o a una duda. 7. Resolver, disipar, desvanecer humores, tumores, etc. 8. *(Fig.)* Transformarse en o reducirse una cosa a otra mejor. 9. Fijarse en una opinión. 10. *(Ant.)* Derretir, desleír. -*vr.* Resolverse, cambiar un cuerpo deliberante de una forma de organización o proceder de otra. -*vn.* Resolverse, tomar una resolución; decidirse a, determinarse a. **I have resolved upon it,** me he decidido, he determinado. **The House resolved to take up the bill,** la Cámara resolvió aprobar el proyecto de ley. **This will resolve her doubts,** esto resolverá sus dudas. **It was resolved that,** se acordó que.

resolve, *s.* Resolución, determinación, propósito.

resolvedly [rɪˈzɒlvɪdlɪ] [ri-sol-vid-li], *adv.* Resueltamente, valerosamente.

resolvedness [rɪˈzɒlvɪdnɪs] [ri-sol-vid-nes], *s.* Resolución determinada.

resolvent [rɪˈzɒlvənt] [ri-sol-vent], *a.* Resolvente, que tiene la facultad de resolver o descomponer una cosa en sus elementos o partes constituyentes. -*s.* Solutivo, el medicamento que tiene la virtud de disipar los humores o tumores; todo lo que tiene el poder de resolver, en cualquier sentido.

resolver [rɪˈzɒlvəʳ] [ri-sol-vaʳ], *s.* El que resuelve, determina o disuelve.

resonance [ˈrezənəns] [re-so-nans], *s.* Resonancia, retumbo, la calidad de sonoro; resonación.

resonant [ˈrezənənt] [re-so-nant], *a.* 1. Resonante, retumbante, reverberante, repercusivo, hablando de un paraje que refleja bien o demasiado el sonido. 2. Sonoro, sonoroso (voices, instruments).

resonator [ˈrezəneɪtəʳ] [re-so-nei-taʳ], *s.* Resonador, lo que resuena; la faringe con las fosas nasales, y el nombre de ciertos aparatos.

resorption [rɪˈzɔːpʃən] [ri-sorp-shon], *s.* Reabsorción, resorción.

resorptive [rɪˈzɔːptɪv] [ri-sorp-tiv], *a.* Reabsorbedor, relativo a la reabsorción, o causado por ella.

resort [rɪˈzɔːt] [ri-sort], *vn.* 1. Acudir, recurrir, frecuentar, concurrir (frequent, meet). 2. Ir o ponerse en camino para alguna parte; venir, llegar o concurrir en abundancia personas o cosas a algún lugar. 3. *(For.)* Faltar a lo prometido o pactado.

resort, *s.* 1. Concurso, concurrencia; visita, el acto de visitar o frecuentar un lugar; también, el lugar o sitio frecuentado, punto de reunión. 2. Recurso, acción de recurrir a alguno; el medio que se emplea en un caso urgente; refugio. 3. *(Ant.)* Concurso de gente junta en un mismo lugar.

resorter [rɪˈzɔːtəʳ] [ri-sor-taʳ], *s.* El que concurre a algún sitio o le frecuenta o visita.

resound

resound [rɪˈzaʊnd] [ri-saund], *va.* 1. Publicar, repetir, repercutir el sonido. 2. Cantar, celebrar. **The echo resounded his lamentations,** el eco repitió sus lamentos. - *vn.* 1. Resonar, retumbar, hacer gran ruido o estruendo. 2. Devolver o reforzar un sonido; formar eco; llenarse de sonido. 3. Mostrar resonancia. 4. Tener fama, ser célebre o celebrado.

resound, *va.* Volver a sonar, sonar repetidas veces.

resource [rɪˈsɔːs] [ri-sors], *s.* 1. Recurso, arbitrio, medio, expediente (recourse, mean). 2. Facultad de hallar, procurar o aplicar los medios convenientes, el poder de ejecución *(sing. o pl.)* 3. *pl.* Recursos, posibles, medios pecuniarios; ventajas naturales de un país. **Finantial resources,** medios financieros. **Natural resources,** recursos naturales.

resourceful [rɪˈsɔːsfʊl] [ri-sors-ful], *a.* Fértil en recursos o expedientes; lleno de medios o ventajas.

resourceless [rɪˈsɔːslɪs] [ri-sors-les], *a.* Desprovisto de recursos, o de ventajas naturales.

resow [ˌriːˈsəʊ] [ri-sou], *va.* Resembrar.

respect [rɪsˈpekt] [ris-pekt], *va.* 1. Respetar, venerar, tener respeto a una persona, acatar, estimar; tener como sagrado o inviolable. 2. Mirar, apreciar, hacer caso de alguna cosa. 3. Tocar, tener, relación una cosa a otra, concernir, referir. **It respects you directly,** le toca a usted directamente. **To respect persons,** dejarse influir demasiado por el estado social; ceder a las circunstancias exteriores de la persona con perjuicio del derecho y la equidad.

respect, *s.* 1. Respecto, la razón, relación o proporción de una cosa con otra. 2. Miramiento, respeto, veneración, acatamiento, atención, consideración a las personas beneméritas o a lo que es justo. **To show respect,** tener respeto a alguno. 3. Carácter respetable. 4. Consideración, motivo. **With respect to what you say,** tocante a lo que usted dice. **To make oneself respected,** hacerse respetar. **In some respect,** de algún modo. **In other respects,** por otra parte. 5. Porte que indica deferencia; en plural, **respects,** memorias, expresiones, recuerdos, cumplimientos que se hacen o envía por cortesía unas personas a otras. **Out of respect for you,** por consideración a usted, por usted **In respect to.** Con respecto a; en comparación de. 6. Acepción, tendencia, disposición indebida, en detrimento de la justicia.

respectability, respectableness [rɪsˌpektəˈblɪlɪtɪ] [ris-pek-ta-bi-li-ti], *s.* Respetabilidad, calidad de respetable; crédito, carácter o posición honoríficos. **Of no respectability,** sin consideración, en situación dudosa u obscura.

respectable [rɪsˈpektəbl] [ris-pek-ta-bol], *a.* 1. Respetable, estimable, honroso, de buen nombre, en buena reputación. 2. Pasable, tal cual, bastante bueno, considerable; mediano. **A respectable man,** hombre de mucho respeto, de crédito sentado; hombre formal. **Respectable talents,** talentos bastante notables, de consideración. **In respectable society,** entre personas educadas. **At a respectable distance,** a una distancia respetable.

respectably [rɪsˈpektəblɪ] [ris-pek-ta-bli], *adv.* 1. Respetablemente, con respeto. 2. Pasablemente, bastante bien, medianamente.

respected [rɪsˈpektɪd] [ris-pek-tid], *a.* Considerado, respetado, estimado.

respecter [rɪsˈpektər] [ris-pek-tar], *s.* El que respeta. **To be a respecter of persons,** hacer acepción de personas.

respectful [rɪsˈpektfʊl] [ris-pekt-ful], *a.* Respetuoso, lleno de respeto.

respectfully [rɪsˈpektfəlɪ] [ris-pekt-fu-li], *adv.* Respetuosamente.

respectfulness [rɪsˈpektfʊlnɪs] [ris-pekt-ful-nes], *s.* Conducta respetuosa.

respecting [rɪsˈpektɪŋ] [ris-pek-tin], *prep.* Con respecto a, en cuanto a, relativamente a, por lo que toca a.

respective [rɪsˈpektɪv] [ris-pek-tiv], *a.* Respectivo, relativo o referente a una cosa particular; cada uno, particular; sendos.

respectively [rɪsˈpektɪvlɪ] [ris-pek-tiv-li], *adv.* Respectivamente, relativamente.

respirable [rɪsˈpaɪərəbl] [ris-pai-ra-bol], *a.* Respirable, que se puede respirar, propio de la respiración.

respiration [ˌrespɪˈreɪʃən] [res-pi-rei-shon], *s.* 1. Respiración, acción de aspirar y de respirar el aire. 2. *(Bot.)* Respiración, acción de tomar las plantas el oxígeno, y después de su oxigenación expeler los productos de ésta. 3. El sonido que se oye en la auscultación.

respirator [ˌrespɪˈreɪtər] [res-pi-rei-tar], *s.* Respirador, aparato de alambre fino, o de gasa, que se pone sobre la boca o la nariz como protección contra el frío, el polvo, el humo, etc.

respiratory [rɪsˈpaɪərətərɪ] [ris-pai-ra-to-ri], *a.* Respiratorio, que sirve para la respiración o que pertenece a ella; causado por la respiración. **Respiratory track,** vías respiratorias.

respire [rɪsˈpaɪər] [ris-paia], *vn.* 1. Resollar, respirar; tener vida, vivir (live). 2. Descansar, aliviarse del trabajo, tomar aliento (rest). -*va.* 1. Respirar, inspirar y arrojar el aire o gas. 2. Exhalar, echar vaho.

respite [ˈrespaɪt] [res-pait], *s.* 1. Suspensión de la ejecución de la pena capital. 2. Pausa; plazo, respiro, tregua. **To get no respite,** no poder descansar. **Without respite,** sin tregua, sin respiro.

respite, *va.* Dar treguas, suspender o diferir una cosa; conceder plazo o espera.

resplendence [rɪsˈplendəns] [ris-plen-dens], *s.* Resplandor, brillo, lustre.

resplendent [rɪsˈplendənt] [ris-plen-dent], *a.* Resplandeciente, brillante.

resplendently [rɪsˈplendəntlɪ] [ris-plen-dant-li], *adv.* Lustrosamente, brillantemente.

respond [rɪsˈpɒnd] [ris-pond], *vn.* 1. Responder, contestar a lo que se habla o escribe. 2. Responder; corresponder; venir bien, ajustarse una cosa a otra.

respondent [rɪsˈpɒndənt] [ris-pon-dent], *s.* Respondedor; demandante.

responsal [rɪsˈpɒnsl] [ris-pon-sal], *s.* Respuesta litúrgica.

response [rɪsˈpɒns] [ris-pons], *s.* 1. Respuesta, contestación a una pregunta o carta (answer). 2. En el oficio divino la respuesta que da la congregación a lo que dice el oficiante. 3. Replica a una objeción en los argumentos.

responsibility [rɪsˌpɒnsəˈbɪlɪtɪ] [ris-pon-sa-bi-li-ti], *s.* 1. Responsabilidad. 2. Deber, obligación, fideicomiso o depósito; aquello de que es uno responsable. 3. Solvencia; también la capacidad de ejecutar un contrato. **Joint responsibility,** responsabilidad solidaria. **To accept responsibility for,** hacerse responsable.

responsible [rɪsˈpɒnsɪbl] [ris-pon-si-bol], *a.* 1. Responsable, obligado a satisfacer algún cargo, deber, deuda u otro servicio. 2. Que tiene capacidad, mental y moral, para distinguir entre lo bueno y lo malo, y para ser legalmente resonable por su conducta; perteneciente a dicha capacidad o condición. 3. Solvente. 4. Abonado; que envuelve o implica responsabilidad u obligación. **A responsible post,** un puesto de responsabilidad. **A fully responsible man,** un hombre muy responsable, de toda formalidad. **To act in a responsible fashion,** actuar con seriedad, con formalidad. **Those responsible will be punished,** se castigará a los responsables.

responsibleness [rɪsˈpɒnsɪblnɪs] [ris-pon-si-bolnes], *s.* Responsabilidad.

responsibly [rɪsˈpɒnsɪblɪ] [ris-pon-si-bli], *adv.* **To act responsibly,** actuar formalmente, con seriedad.

responsive [rɪsˈpɒnsɪv] [ris-pon-siv], *a.* 1. Respondiente; correspondiente, que concuerda con, idóneo, conforme. 2. Respondedor, que responde, que constituye una respuesta. 3. *(For.)* Que contiene respuesta pertinente.

responsiveness [rɪsˈpɒnsɪvnɪs] [ris-pon-siv-nes], *s.* Calidad de lo que corresponde a otra cosa o concuerda con ella; simpatía, conformidad.

responsory [rɪsˈpɒnsərɪ] [ris-pon-so-ri], *a.* Que responde, que contiene respuesta. -*s.* Responsorio, ciertas preces y versículos que se dicen en el rezo divino.

rest [rest] [rest], *s.* 1. Descanso, tregua, interrupción o cesación de la ocupación, trabajo, o de una acción o movimiento cualquiera (relief, repose); sueño, reposo. 2. Reposo de los muertos, el descanso final o último. 3.

Quietud, paz, tranquildad (peace). 4. Sustentáculo, apoyo, arrimo, estribo; esperanza final (hope). 5. Resto, residuo, sobra. 6. Los demás, los otros. 7. Descansadero, el lugar donde se descansa. 8. Cuja, ristre. 9. Pausa en la música y el signo que la indica. 10. Censura en la poesía. **To disturb a person's rest,** turbar el reposo de alguien. **To have a good night's rest,** pasar una buena noche, dormir bien. **Give me the rest,** déme usted lo restante, lo demás. **Minim rest,** *(Mús.)* media pausa. **Give it a rest!,** ¡déjalo! **Rest area,** apartadero, área de descanso *(E. U.).* **Rest day,** día de descanso. **To come to rest,** detenerse, pararse. **To take a rest,** tomar un descanso, descansar.

rest, *vn.* 1. Descansar, dormir, reposar; apoyar, afianzar. 2. Morir, tener descanso en el sepulcro. 3. Parar, estar quedo o sin movimiento. 4. Estar en paz, tener el ánimo sosegado. 5. Estar sostenido por; estar tendido, establecido o fundado sobre; apoyarse en, reposar, yacer. 6. Fiarse en, atenerse a, poner su cofianza en; contar con alguien. 7. *(For.)* Dar una parte por terminada la vista de un pleito. 8. Allanarse a algún convenio. 9. Quedar, permanecer. **Rest assured,** esté usted seguro. 10. Restar, quedar. -*va.* Poner a descansar, hacer cesar un trabajo o esfuerzo; *(vr.)* ponerse a descansar; poner, apoyar o asentar una cosa sobre otra para que esté cómoda o quieta. **Rest from your task,** descanse usted de su tarea. **To rest against/on a tree,** apoyarse en o contra un árbol. **To rest on one's word,** fiar en la palabra de alguno. **To retire to rest,** retirarse a descansar, acostarse a dormir. **To rest one's case** *(Jur.)*, terminar un alegato. **She never rests,** nunca descansa. **May he rest in peace,** descanse en paz. **His arm rested on my shoulder,** su brazo estaba apoyado en mi hombro.

restart [ˈriːsˈtɑːt] [ris-tart]. *vt.* Volver a empezar, volver a arrancar (engine).

restaurant [ˈrestərɒŋ] [res-to-ran], *s.* Restaurante, fonda, lugar donde se sirve de comer.

restful [ˈrestˌʊl] [rest-ful], *a.* 1. Lleno de reposo, que da descanso. 2. Quieto, sosegado, tranquilo. **A restful scene,** una escena tranquila, reposada.

restfully [ˈrestfəlɪ] [rest-fu-li], *adv.* Tranquilamente, reposadamente.

restiff [ˈrestɪf] [res-tif], *a. (Ant.) V.* RESTIVE.

resting [ˈrestɪŋ] [res-tin], *s.* Reposo, descanso. **Resting-place,** (a) lugar de descanso; *(Fig.)* el sepulcro. (b) Meseta de escalera.

restitution [ˌrestɪˈtjuːʃən] [res-ti-tiu-shon], *s.* 1. Restitución, restablecimiento, recobro. 2. Reparación, acción de dar un equivalente, como por un daño o por una pérdida; indemnización. 3. Recuperación de una posición o condición anterior. 4. *(Fís.)* Propiedad de elasticidad.

restive [ˈrestɪv] [res-tiv], *a.* Repropio: se dice de los caballos y mulos tercos y reacios y también de las personas; pertinaz, obstinado.

restiveness [ˈrestɪvnɪs] [res-tiv-nes], *s.* Terquedad, obstinación, rebeldía.

restless [ˈrestlɪs] [rest-les], *a.* 1. Inconstante, mudable. 2. Inquieto, impaciente. 3. Insomne, desvelado.

restlessness [ˈrestlɪsnɪs] [rest-les-nes], *s.* Insomnio, vigilia, desvelo; desasosiego; agitación continua; inquietud, impaciencia.

restock [restɒk] [res-tok], *va.* Renovar, surtir nuevamente.

restorable [ˈrestərəbl] [res-to-ra-bol], *a.* Restituible.

restoration [ˌrestəˈreɪʃən] [res-to-rei-shon], *s.* 1. Restauración, el acto de restaurar, reparar, o reponer alguna cosa en el estado o estimación que tenía; rehabilitación, restablecimiento, renovación. 2. La cosa restablecida o restaurada a su estado original, v. gr. una obra de arte. 3. Restauración, el restablecimiento de los Estuardos en Inglaterra, de los Judíos en Palestina después de la cautividad babilónica, etc. 4. *(Teol.)* Redención final del pecado, salvación universal.

restorative [rɪsˈtɔːrətɪv] [ris-to-ra-tiv], *a. y s.* Restaurativo, restaurante, que tiene el poder de restaurar; medicamento que restaura las fuerzas.

restore [rɪsˈtɔːr] [ris-to^r], *va.* 1. Restituir, restablecer una cosa en el estado que antes tenía (re-establish); reparar, reconstruir (mend, repair). 2. Reproducir, reedificar, representar como antes existía, con la ayuda de materiales o restos existentes. 3. Recuperar, recobrar, restaurar, restablecer después de una interrupción; devolver la salud. 4. Restituir, devolver lo que ha sido perdido, tomado o quitado; compensar, resarcir, dar un equivalente. 5. Reponer, reintegrar, colocar a uno en el empleo o estado de que fue privado. **To restore one to liberty,** darle a uno su libertad, ponerle en libertad. **To restore something to its place,** devolver algo a su sitio. **Order was restored,** se restableció el orden.

restore, *va.* Depositar o almacenar de nuevo.

restorer [rɪsˈtɔːrər] [ris-to-ra^r], *s.* Restaurador.

restoring [rɪsˈtɔːrɪŋ] [ris-to-rin], *s.* Restauración; restitución.

restrain [rɪsˈtreɪn] [ris-trein], *va.* 1. Restringir, restriñir, detener, apretar; reprimir, contener, refrenar (hold, stop). 2. Impedir. 3. Restriñir, constreñir, limitar, coartar (limit). 4. *(For.)* Prohibir, vedar la comisión de un acto ilegal.

restrainable [rɪsˈtreɪnəbl] [ris-trei-na-bol], *a.* Restringible.

restrained [rɪsˈtreɪnd] [ris-treind], *a.* Comedido, moderado.

restrainedly [rɪsˈtreɪnɪdlɪ] [ris-trei-nid-li], *adv.* Con restricción.

restrainer [rɪsˈtreɪnər] [ris-trei-na^r], *s.* Restringente, lo que restringe; especialmente en fotografía, un agente químico que retarda la acción del revelador.

restraint [rɪsˈtreɪnt] [ris-treint], *s.* Sujeción, limitación, refrenamiento, freno, constreñimiento; oposición; prohibición.

restrict [rɪsˈtrɪkt] [ris-trikt], *va.* Restringir, limitar, ceñir o coartar.

restricted [rɪsˈtrɪktɪd] [ris-trik-tid], *a.* Restringido, reducido (area), prohibido (prohibited).

restriction [rɪsˈtrɪkʃən] [ris-trik-shon], *s.* Restricción, limitación o modificación.

restrictive [rɪsˈtrɪktɪv] [ris-trik-tiv], *a.* Restrictivo, que restringe, ciñe o limita; que sirve para limitar o restringir.

restrictively [rɪsˈtrɪktɪvlɪ] [ris-trik-tiv-li], *adv.* Limitadamente.

rest room [ˈrestrɒm] [rest-rum], *s.* 1. Sala de descanso. 2. Retrete, excusado.

restructure [ˌriːsˈtrʌktʃər] [ris-trak-cha^r], *vt.* Restructurar.

restructuring [ˌriːsˈtrʌtʃərɪŋ] [ris-trak-cha-rin], *sf.* Reestructuración.

result [rɪˈzʌlt] [ri-salt], *vn.* 1. Seguirse, inferirse, como consecuencia o resultado; ser efecto físico o lógico. 2. Resultar, venir a parar, acabar, terminar en; tener un resultado: (seguido de *in*). **This will result in good (or evil),** esto acabará en bien o en mal). **To result from,** resultar de. **To result in,** provocar, causar. **It resulted in accident,** causó un accidente.

result, *s.* 1. Resulta, resultado; ilación, consecuencia; efecto, conclusión. 2. Resulta, lo que últimamente se resuelve en alguna conferencia o deliberación; decisión aprobada por una asamblea deliberante. **As a result of,** a consecuencia de. **In the result,** finalmente.

resultance [rɪˈzʌltəns] [ri-sal-tans], *s.* Resultado, resultancia.

resultant [rɪˈzʌltənt] [ri-sal-tant], *a.* Resultante. -*s.* 1. Resultante, fuerza o velocidad que resulta de la concurrencia de otras en un mismo punto, o la que produce el mismo efecto que las demás juntas. 2. Lo que se sigue como consecuencia, resultado.

resulting [rɪˈzʌltɪŋ] [ri-sal-tin], *pa.* 1. Resultante, que dimana como consecuencia, efecto o conclusión. 2. *(For.)* Que vuelve a ser o recaer. **Resulting use,** usufructo que vuelve a recaer en quien lo ha instituido.

resumable [rɪˈzjuːməbl] [ri-siu-ma-bol], *a.* Que se puede reasumir.

resume [rɪˈzjuːm] [ri-sium], *va.* 1. Empezar de nuevo, continuar después de una interrupción. 2. Reasumir; recobrar la posesión de algo, reocupar, recuperar lo perdido o tomado; volver a tomar. *-vn.* Tomar el hilo, reanudar. **To resume a journey,** volver a ponerse en viaje, en camino. **To resume a business,** reanudar un negocio. **To resume a discourse,** tomar el hilo de un discurso.

resumption [rɪˈzʌmpʃən] [ri-samp-shon], *s.* Reasunción; recobro.

resumptive [rɪˈzʌmptɪv] [ri-samp-tiv], *a.* Que vuelve a tomar o a resumir.

resurface [riːˈsəːfɪs] [ri-ser-fis], *va.* Revestir, poner nueva superficie.

resurrect [ˌrezəˈrekt] [re-sa-rekt], *va.* (*Fam.*) 1. Volver a la vida, o al uso y aceptación. 2. Desenterrar, exhumar. **To resurrect a doctrine,** volver a poner una doctrina en aceptación corriente.

resurrection [ˌrezəˈrekʃən] [re-sa-rek-shon], *s.* 1. Resurrección. 2. Renovación, restablecimiento.

resurvey [rɪˈzəːveɪ] [ri-ser-vei], *va.* 1. Apear, deslindar, medir de nuevo un terreno. 2. Rever, volver a ver. *-s.* Nuevo apeo, deslinde, o medición de terreno.

resuscitate [rɪˈsʌsɪteɪt] [ri-sa-si-teit], *va.* Resucitar, hacer revivir; renovar. *-vn.* Resucitar, volver a la vida.

resuscitation [rɪˌsʌsɪˈteɪʃən] [ri-sa-si-tei-shon], *s.* Resurrección, renacimiento, renovación.

ret [ret] [ret], *va.* Enriar, embalsar el cáñamo o el lino.

retail [ˈriːteɪl] [ri-teil], *va.* 1. Vender por menor, revender. 2. Decir o relatar una cosa detalladamente.

retail, *s.* Venta por menor; reventa. **To sell by retail,** vender al por menor o al menudeo.

retailer [ˈriːteɪləʳ] [ri-tei-laʳ], *s.* Lonjista, tendero, comerciante por menor, revendedor.

retain [ˈriːteɪn] [ri-tein], *va.* 1. Retener, guardar, conservar. 2. Tomar a sueldo o ajustar a un mozo, sirviente, etc.; especialmente a un abogado, pagarle honorarios anticipados. *-vn.* Pertenecer, ser dependiente o criado. (*Arq.*) Servir de sostén. **To retain youthful vigor,** conservar el vigor de la juventud. **Retaining-fee,** *V.* RETAINER, 4ª acep. **Retaining-wall,** pared maestra, muro de apoyo.

retainable [ˈriːteɪnəbl] [ri-tei-na-bol], *a.* Que se puede retener.

retainer [rɪˈteɪnəʳ] [ri-tei-naʳ], *s.* 1. Adherente, partidario. 2. Dependiente, criado, acompañante de otro en un campamento. 3. Retenedor. 4. El honorario o estipendio que se paga anticipadamente a un abogado para que defienda una causa o pleito.

retake [ˈriːteɪk] [ri-teik], *va.* Volver a tomar.

retaliate [rɪˈtælɪeɪt] [ri-ta-lieit], *va.* Talionar, castigar con la pena del talión; pagar en la misma moneda; desquitarse, vengarse.

retaliation [rɪˌtælɪˈeɪʃən] [ri-ta-liei-shon], *s.* Desquite, despique; desagravio, satisfacción; pago, retorno, defensa. **By way of retaliation,** por vía de represalias. **Law of retaliation,** Ley del talión.

retaliative [rɪˈtælɪətɪv] [ri-ta-lia-tiv], *a.* Vengativo; que se desquita.

retaliatory [rɪˈtælɪətərɪ] [ri-ta-lia-to-ri], *a.* Que usa de represalias, se desquita o paga en la misma moneda.

retard [rɪˈtɑːd] [ri-tard], *va.* 1. Disminuir la velocidad, retardar, atrasar. 2. Retardar, detener, diferir, dilatar. *-vn.* (*Des.*) Atrasarse.

retardation [ˌrɪtɑːˈdeɪʃən] [ri-tar-dei-shon], *s.* Retardación, retardo, atraso; acción de retardar el movimiento, dilación.

retarder [rɪˈtɑːdəʳ] [ri-tar-daʳ], *s.* El o lo que retarda o impide.

retardment [rɪˈtɑːdmənt] [ri-tard-ment], *s.* (Poco us.) Retardo.

retch [retʃ] [rech], *vn.* Esforzarse para vomitar, arquear.

retent [ˈretənt] [re-tent], *s.* Lo retenido, guardado, o conservado.

retention [rɪˈtenʃən] [ri-ten-shon], *s.* 1. Retención, la acción y efecto de retener; acto de guardar una cosa en poder o posesión de uno; conservación de una costumbre u opinión. 2. La facultad de retener o conservar. 3. Retentiva, memoria.

retentive [rɪˈtentɪv] [ri-ten-tiv], *a.* 1. Retentivo, que tiene virtud de retener. 2. (*Med.*) Retentriz, potencia o poder de retener.

retentiveness [rɪˈtentɪvnɪs] [ri-ten-tiv-nes], *s.* Retentiva, facultad, poder de retener; tenacidad (de la memoria).

reticence [ˈretɪsəns] [re-ti-sans], *s.* 1. Reticencia, la calidad, la costumbre o el acto de guardar silencio, o de ser reservado, sobre lo que debiera decirse. 2. (*Ret.*) Reticencia.

reticent [ˈretɪsənt] [re-ti-sant], *a.* Reticente.

reticently [ˈretɪsəntlɪ] [re-ti-sant-li], *adv.* Reservadamente, con reserva.

reticle [ˈretɪkl] [re-ti-kol], *s.* (*Astr.*) Retículo, redecilla de alambres, que sirve de micrómetro y para otros usos en los telescopios, etc.

reticular [rɪˈtɪkjələʳ] [ri-ti-kiu-laʳ], *a.* Reticular, en forma de red; perteneciente a un retículo.

reticulate [rɪˈtɪkjəleɪt] [ri-ti-kiu-leit], *va.* Formar un tejido en forma de red.

reticulation [rɪˌtɪkjəˈleɪʃən] [ri-ti-kiu-lei-shon], *s.* Disposición en forma de red.

reticule [ˈretɪkjuːl] [re-ti-kiul], *s.* 1. Ridículo, bolsa de señora para llevar el pañuelo, el bordado de aguja, artículos pequeños, etc. 2. *V.* RETICLE.

reticulum [rɪˈtɪkjuːləm] [re-ti-kiu-lom], *s.* 1. Retículo, tejido en forma de red. 2. Redecilla, segunda de las cuatro cavidades en que se divide el estómago de los rumiantes.

retiform [ˈretɪfɔːm] [re-ti-form], *a.* Con líneas que se cruzan a manera de red.

retina [ˈretɪnə] [re-ti-na], *s.* Retina, membrana del fondo del ojo que contiene el aparato nervioso esencial para la visión.

retinitis [ˌretɪˈnaɪtɪs] [re-ti-nai-tis], *s.* Retinitis, inflamación de la retina.

retinoid [ˈretɪnɔɪd] [re-ti-noid], *a.* Resiniforme, parecido a una resina.

retinue [ˈretɪnjuː] [re-ti-niu], *s.* 1. Tren, comitiva, acompañamiento de criados. 2. Serie de resultados.

retire [rɪˈtaɪəʳ] [ri-taiaʳ], *vn.* 1. Retirarse; retroceder, volver atrás. 2. Retirarse, refugiarse, ponerse a salvo. 3. Dejar algún empleo público. 4. Recogerse, apartarse, separarse. **A retired life,** vida privada. **To retire from business,** retirarse de los negocios. *-va.* 1. Pagar completamente y retirar de la circulación comercial. **To retire the bonds of a city,** retirar los bonos de una ciudad. 2. Jubilar, retirar, un oficial del ejército o de la marina. 3. (*Ant.*) Remover, apartar, separar. **To retire from a post,** dimitir de un cargo. **To retire on a pension,** jubilarse.

retired [rɪˈtaɪəd] [ri-taiad], *pa.* 1. Retirado; secreto, apartado, aislado, solitario. 2. Retirado, jubilado. **To live a retired life,** llevar una vida retirada, solitaria; vivir lejos del mundo. **Retired officer,** oficial retirado. **To put on the retired list,** poner en retiro, conceder la jubilación.

retiredly [rɪˈtaɪədlɪ] [ri-taiad-li], *adv.* Solitariamente, privadamente.

retiredness [rɪˈtaɪədnɪs] [ri-taiad-nes], *s.* Retiro, recogimiento, soledad.

retiree [rɪˈtaɪəriː] [ri-taia-ri], *s.* Jubilado.

retirement [rɪˈtaɪəmənt] [ri-taia-ment], *s.* 1. Retiro, retiramiento. 2. Retiro, lugar apartado; la morada o asilo a donde uno se retira a pasar una vida sosegada. 3. Retiro, el estado del que se ha separado del mundo, de los negocios, etc.; jubilación.

retiring [rɪˈtaɪərɪŋ] [ri-taia-rin], *pa.* 1. Recatado; modesto, discreto. 2. Perteneciente a un empleado jubilado o militar en situación de retiro.

retort [rɪˈtɔːt] [ri-tort], *va.* 1. Redargüir; pagar una palabra descortés o picante con otra igual o más fuerte. (*Fam.*) Retrucar. 2. Encorvar, doblar, torcer. 3. Replicar. 4. (*Des.*) Rechazar, repeler.

retort, *s.* 1. Redargución; réplica aguda, picante, o mordaz (answer); acción de redargüir. 2. Retorta, vasija.

retorter [rɪˈtɔːtəʳ] [ri-tor-taʳ], *s.* El que replica o redarguye.

retortion [rɪˈtɔːʃən] [ri-tor-shon], *s.* Retorcimiento; retorsión.

retouch [ˈriːˈtʌtʃ] [ri-tach], *va.* Retocar, volver a tocar, modificar, dar la última mano. **To retouch an essay, a**

painting, retocar un ensayo, un cuadro. -*s.* Retoque, última mano.

retoucher [ri:'tʌtʃəʳ] [ri-ta-chaʳ], *s.* El que retoca, particularmente las impresiones fotográficas para perfeccionarlas.

retrace [ri:'treis] [ri-treis], *va.* 1. Volver a seguir las huellas o pisadas de alguno; traer o representar a la memoria o a la imaginación la idea de una cosa pasada. 2. Repasar, narrar, recitar. 3. Retrazar, volver a trazar.

retract [rɪ'trækt] [ri-trakt], *va.* 1. Retractar, desdecir una declaración, palabras, etc.; denegar, retirar. 2. Retraer, encoger, como con las uñas de un gato. -*vn.* 1. Retractarse, desdecirse (be drawn in), cantar la palinodia. 2. Encogerse, retirarse, retraerse.

retractable, retractible [rɪ'træktəbl] [ri-trak-ta-bol], *a.* Retractable, que se puede retractar, o encoger.

retractation [ˌrɪtræk'teɪʃən] [ri-trak-tei-shon], *s.* Retracción.

retractile [rɪ'træktaɪl] [ri-trak-tail], *a.* Retráctil, se dice de las uñas de los animales que se hallan ocultas en el estado de reposo.

retraction [rɪ'trækʃən] [ri-trak-shon], *s.* Retracción; contracción; retractación; renuncia.

retractive [rɪ'træktɪv] [ri-trak-tiv], *a.* Que retira o retracta.

retractor [rɪ'træktəʳ] [ri-trak-taʳ], *s.* El o lo que retrae; en particular, un músculo retractor; también, un instrumento o aparato destinado a levantar las carnes después de cortadas, en una amputación.

retread [rɪ'triːd] [ri-trid], *va.* 1. Volver a andar, volver a pisar. 2. Recubrir. **To retread a tire,** recubrir una llanta o neumático.

retreat [rɪ'triːt] [ri-trit], *s.* 1. Retiro, soledad. 2. Retirada, en lugar que sirve de acogida segura; refugio, asilo. 3. *(Mil.)* Retirada. **To sound the retreat,** tocar retirada. 4. *(Arq.)* Releje. 5. Receso. **To beat the retreat,** dar el toque de retreta *(Mil.).* **To be in full retreat,** retirarse en masa.

retreat, *vn.* Retirarse, refugiarse. **The waters are retreating,** las aguas están bajando.

retrench [rɪ'trentʃ] [ri-trench], *va.* 1. Cercenar, cortar, acortar, disminuir. 2. *(Mil.)* Atrincherar. -*vn.* Reducirse o ceñirse a sus medios, vivir con economía, cercenar los gastos.

retrenchment [rɪ'trentʃmənt] [ri-trench-ment], *s.* 1. Cercenadura, cercenamiento, rebaja, disminución. 2. Atrincheramiento, trinchera.

retribution [ˌretrɪ'bjuːʃən] [re-tri-biu-shon], *s.* Retribución, recompensa; especialmente, imposición de una pena.

retributive [rɪ'trɪbjʊtɪv] [ri-tri-biu-tiv], *a.* 1. Retribuyente, que retribuye, que tiende a remunerar o a castigar. 2. Distributivo. **Retributive justice,** justicia distributiva.

retrievable [rɪ'triːvəbl] [ri-tri-va-bol], *a.* Recuperable; reparable.

retrievableness [rɪ'triːvəblnɪs] [ri-tri-va-bol-nes], *s.* El estado o la condición de lo que puede repararse.

retrieval [rɪ'triːvəl] [ri-tri-val], *s.* El acto o procedimiento de recuperar, restaurar, etc.; reintegración de una pérdida o quiebra.

retrieve [rɪ'triːv] [ri-triv], *va.* 1. Recuperar, mejorar de condición o estado (improve), recobrar, restablecer, restaurar (re-establish). 2. Reparar, componer, remediar las malas consecuencias de algo, expiar (repair). 3. Buscar y traer a la mano; se dice de los perros. -*vn.* Hallar y traer algo los perros como la caza muerta o herida. **To retrieve something from the sea,** rescatar algo del mar.

retriever [rɪ'triːvəʳ] [ri-tri-vaʳ], *s.* 1. El o lo que recobra o restaura. 2. Perro adiestrado para buscar y traer la caza, sabueso.

retro- ['retrəʊ] [re-trou]. Prefijo que significa atrás o hacia atrás, y que a veces implica oposición.

retroact ['retrəʊækt] [re-trou-akt], *va.* Obrar en oposición o hacia atrás; tener fuerza retroactiva.

retroaction ['retrəʊækʃən] [re-trouak-shon], *s. (For.)* Retroacción, ficción legal que supone a una cosa anterior al tiempo en que sucedió.

retroactive [ˌretrəʊ'æktɪv] [re-trouak-tiv], *a.* Retroactivo, que obra o tiene fuerza sobre el tiempo anterior.

retrocede ['retrəsiːd] [re-tro-sid], *va.* Retroceder, ceder a uno el derecho o cosa que él había cedido antes. -*vn.* Retroceder, volver hacia atrás.

retrocession [ˌretrəʊ'seʃən] [re-trou-se-shon], *s.* Retrocesión, retroceso; movimiento retrógrado; inclinación hacia atrás.

retroflex ['retrəʊfleks] [re-trou-fleks], *a.* Que muda bruscamente de dirección doblándose hacia atrás.

retroflexion [ˌretrəʊ'flekʃən] [re-trou-flek-shon], *s.* Retroflexión, inflexión hacia atrás; se dice particularmente del fondo del útero.

retrograde ['retrəʊgreɪd] [re-trou-greid], *a.* Retrógrado; contrario, opuesto.

retrograde, *vn.* Retrogradar, retroceder.

retrogression ['retrəʊgreʃən] [re-trou-gre-shon], *s.* Retrogradación.

retrogressive ['retrəʊgresɪv] [re-trou-gre-siv], *a.* Retrógrado, que va o vuelve hacia atrás; que se inclina hacia abajo.

retrorocket ['retrəʊrɒkɪt] [re-trou-ro-kit], *s. (Aer.)* Retrocohete.

retrospect ['retrəʊspekt] [re-trous-pekt], *s.* Reflexión o consideración de las cosas pasadas.

retrospection [ˌretrəʊ'spekʃən] [re-trous-pek-shon], *s.* El acto y la facultad de considerar las cosas pasadas.

retrospective ['retrəʊspektɪv] [re-trous-pek-tiv], *a.* Retrospectivo, que se refiere al tiempo pasado.

retroversion ['retrəʊvɜːʃən] [re-trou-ver-shon], *s.* Retroversión, inclinación hacia un lado o hacia atrás; se dice particularmente de la matriz.

retry ['riː'traɪ] [ri-trai], *vt.* Volver a procesar.

return [rɪ'tɜːn] [ri-tern], *vn.* 1. Volver, ir otra vez al paraje donde uno ha estado ya; regresar (al lugar de donde se salió); retornar (come back). 2. Volverse, irse de nuevo, aparecer o presentarse de nuevo. 3. Volver, repetir, reiterar o empezar de nuevo lo mismo que se había hecho antes. 4. Restituirse o volver al estado anterior (restore, give back). 5. Responder, reponer, replicar (answer). 6. Volver a la posesión de alguien. -*va.* 1. Devolver, transmitir, remitir; volver a enviar. 2. Volver, corresponder, pagar, retribuir. 3. Volver, restituir lo que se ha recibido o tomado. 4. Dar cuenta o hacer relación, especialmente de una manera oficial a los superiores de uno, o a determinada autoridad. 5. Dar en cambio, recompensar, agradecer o reconocer (un favor, etc.); corresponder. 6. Dar como aumento, interés o provecho; ser origen o manantial de; redituar, producir. 7. Elegir, anunciar como elegido para un cuerpo legislativo. **To return to the same kind of life,** volver a las andadas. **To return a kindness,** corresponder a un beneficio. **To return good for evil,** devolver bien por mal. **To return thanks,** dar las gracias. **To return a verdict,** dar pronunciar un jurado su fallo. **To return home,** regresar a casa. **They were about to return,** estaban a punto de volver. **She has not yet returned,** ella no está de vuelta todavía. **To return blow for blow,** devolver golpe por golpe. **To return like for like,** pagar con la misma moneda.

return, *s.* 1. Retorno, regreso. 2. Ganancia, utilidad, provecho, rédito. 3. Retorno, reconocimiento de un beneficio, pago, paga, satisfacción, recompensa, retribución. 4. Retorno, cambio o trueque de unas mercaderías por otras. 5. Vicisitud, revolución. 6. Vuelta, repetición de alguna cosa. 7. Remesa, remisión de alguna cosa de una parte a otra. 8. Relación, cuenta que se da de alguna cosa. 9. Restitución, la acción de restituir. 10. Recaída. 11. *(Arq.)* Continuación de las molduras hasta alguna esquina. 12. Relación, parte oficial; *(pl.)* lista, nómina, padrón o censo; *(Mil.)* lista de muertos y heridos. 13. Respuesta, réplica, redargüición. 14. Reaparición, retorno. 15. *(Ingl.)* Elección, nombramiento para el Parlamento. **To make a return,** (a) hacer una relación oficial; (b) redituar, producir utilidad o ganancia; (c) devolver, corresponder, hacer restitución; (d) pagar en la misma moneda, desquitarse, no quedar a deber nada; responder, sacudirse. **Goods of a quick return,** mercancías de pronto despacho. **On my return from,** a mi regreso de. **In return,** en cambio, en recíproca correspondencia.

Return-ticket, billete de ida y vuelta. **Return-request,** *(E. U.)* solicitud impresa o escrita en un sobre para que se devuelva la carta a ciertas señas, si no se entrega en un plazo determinado. **Election returns,** colección de datos e informes sobre el resultado de una elección. **By return of post,** a vuelta de correo. **In return,** en cambio. **Return of income,** declaración de renta. **Return on sales,** rendimiento de las ventas. **Return address,** señas del remitente.

returnable [rɪ'tɜːnəbl] [ri-ter-na-bol], *a.* 1. Que se puede retornar o volver. 2. *(For.)* Devolutorio, debido y exigido en tiempo y lugar determinados; v. gr. una citación judicial.

returnee [rɪtɜ'niː] [ri-ter-nii], *s.* Persona que vuelve.

returner [rɪ'tɜːnəʳ] [ri-ter-naʳ], *s.* Persona que devuelve, restituye, o vuelve a enviar; el que remite dinero.

retuse [rɪ'tjuːz] [ri-tius], *a.* Muy obtuso, terminado en una extremidad redondeada con el centro deprimido; se dice de hojas y conchas.

reunify ['riːjunɪfaɪ] [ri-iu-ni-fai], *vt.* Reunificar.

reunion [riːˈjunjən] [ri-iu-nion], *s.* 1. Reunión; reconciliación; nueva unión, cohesión o concordia. 2. Reunión, conjunto de personas reunidas.

reunite ['riːjuˈnaɪt] [ri-iu-nait], *va.* Reunir, juntar; reconciliar. *-vn.* Reunirse, volver a unirse, reconciliarse. **He was reunited with his wife,** volvió con su mujer, se reconcilió con su mujer.

revaluation [riːˌvælˈjoʊeɪʃən] [ri-va-liuei-shon], *s.* Revaluación.

revamp ['riːˈvæmp] [ri-vamp], *va.* Poner nueva suela a un zapato; de aquí, remendar, rehacer.

reveal [rɪ'viːl] [ri-vil], *va.* 1. Revelar, manifestar o descubrir algún secreto. 2. Revelar, manifestar Dios lo futuro o lo que está oculto.

revealer [rɪ'viːləʳ] [ri-vi-laʳ], *s.* Revelador, el que revela.

reveille [rɪ'væli] [ri-va-li], *s. (Mil.)* Diana, el toque militar al romper el día.

revel ['revl] [re-vel], *vn.* Jaranear, andar en borracheras; divertirse con gran ruido o algazara.

revel, *s.* Algazara, regocijos ruidosos; jarana, borrachera, banquete con gran algazara.

revelation [ˌrevəˈleɪʃən] [re-ve-lei-shon], *s.* 1. Revelación, acción y efecto de revelar, y también la cosa revelada, especialmente la revelación divina. 2. *(Fil.)* Conocimiento inmediato de lo verdadero. 3. Apocalipsis, el último de los libros del Nuevo Testamento. **It was a revelation to me,** fue una revelación para mí.

revelatory ['revələtərɪ] [re-va-la-to-ri], *a.* Revelador.

reveler ['revləʳ] [rev-laʳ], *s.* Jaranero, la persona que gusta de andar en fiestas estrepitosas; hombre disoluto; juerguista.

revelry ['revəlrɪ] [re-val-ri], *s.* Jarana, borrachera, banquete estrepitoso, regocijos ruidosos.

revenge [rɪ'vendʒ] [ri-vench], *va.* Vengar, tomar satisfacción del agravio o injuria recibida; vengarse de; aplicar una pena en cambio de otro mal sufrido. **To revenge an affront,** vengarse de una afrenta. **To be revenged on someone,** vengarse de alguien.

revenge, *s.* 1. Desquite, despique, desagravio, ley del talión. 2. Venganza. **To take revenge on,** vengarse de.

revengeful [rɪ'vendʒful] [ri-vench-ful], *a.* 1. Vengativo. 2. Vengador.

revengefully [rɪ'vendʒfəlɪ] [ri-vench-fu-li], *adv.* Con venganza.

revengefulness [rɪ'vendʒfulnɪs] [ri-vench-ful-nes], *s.* Venganza, ansia de vengarse.

revenue ['revənjuː] [re-ve-niu], *s.* 1. Rentas públicas, ingresos del Estado, el producto total de las contribuciones, tasas, impuestos, derechos de aduanas, etc. 2. Renta, rédito, entrada (de los bienes de un particular). **Revenue officer,** empleado de aduana. **Revenue stamp,** timbre **del** impuesto.

reverberant [rɪ'vɜːvərənt] [ri-ver-be-rant], *a.* Repercusivo; retumbante, resonante.

reverberate [rɪ'vɜːvəreɪt] [ri-ver-be-reit], *va.* y *vn.* 1. Resonar, retumbar, repetir el sonido; hacer eco. 2. Reverberar, reflejar la luz; rechazar.

reverberation [rɪˌvɜːvəˈreɪʃən] [ri-ver-ba-rei-shon], *s.* Retumbo, eco o repercusión del sonido; rechazo; reverberación o reflexión de la luz y el calor.

reverberator [rɪ'vɜːvəreɪtəʳ] [ri-ver-be-rei-taʳ], *s.* Reverberador, lo que reverbera o refleja el sonido, la luz, el calor; reverbero.

reverberatory [rɪ'vɜːvərətərɪ] [ri-ver-be-ra-to-ri], *s.* Horno de reverbero. *-a.* De reverbero, que reverbera o refleja, destinado a producir reverberación. **Reverberatory furnace,** horno de reverbero.

revere [rɪ'veəʳ] [ri-veaʳ], *va.* Reverenciar, respetar, venerar, honrar.

reverence ['revərəns] [re-ve-rans], *s.* 1. Reverencia, respeto, veneración. 2. Reverencia, inclinación del cuerpo o de parte de él en señal de respeto. 3. Reverencia, el título honorífico que se da a las personas religiosas. **To pay reverence,** rendir homenaje; inclinarse, hacer reverencia. **Your Reverence,** Reverencia.

reverence, *va.* Reverenciar, respetar, venerar.

reverend ['revərənd] [re-ve-rend], *a.* 1. Reverendo, venerable, el tratamiento que se da a las dignidades eclesiásticas. **Right reverend** (tratamiento que se da a un obispo), muy reverendo, o **Most reverend** (a un arzobispo), reverendísimo.

reverent ['revərənt] [re-ve-rant], *a.* Reverente; sumiso, humilde, lleno de respeto.

reverential [ˌrevəˈrenʃəl] [re-ve-ren-shal], *a.* Reverencial, respetuoso.

reverentially [ˌrevəˈrenʃəlɪ] [re-ve-ren-sha-li], **reverently** [ˌrevəˈrentlɪ] [re-ve-rent-li], *adv.* Reverencialmente, respetuosamente.

reverie, revery ['revərɪ] [re-ve-ri], *s.* Estado *del* ánimo preocupado por ideas vagas; ensueño; arrebato, rapto, arrobamiento, distracción.

reversal [rɪ'vɜːsəl] [ri-ver-shal], *s.* 1. Inversión (order); *(For.)* revocación de un fallo o una sentencia. 2. En el espectro solar, el cambio de una línea obscura en una brillante y viceversa.

reverse [rɪ'vɜːs] [ri-vers], *va.* 1. Invertir (order), volver al revés, volver lo de arriba abajo, volver patas arriba; invertir, poner lo de dentro afuera. 2. Volcar, voltear, trastornar. 3. *(For.)* Revocar, anular, abolir. 4. Poner o mudar una cosa en lugar de otra. 5. *(Mec.)* Comunicar un movimiento o efecto opuesto; dar contravapor. **He quickly reversed the engine,** a toda prisa dio contravapor a la locomotora. *-vn.* Cambiarse en lo contrario o volver a un estado anterior. **Reversing lever, gear,** palanca de retroceso o inversión, aparato que invierte el movimiento de una máquina de vapor.

reverse, *s.* 1. Lo contrario, lo opuesto. **Quite the reverse,** todo lo contrario. 2. Respaldo, el lado extremo o superficie de atrás, inferior o secundario; en especial, reverso o revés de una moneda o medalla. 3. Cambio a una posición, dirección o estado opuestos. 4. Vicisitud, mudanza, contratiempo, descalabro.

reversedly [rɪ'vɜːsɪdlɪ] [ri-ver-sid-li], *adv.* Con lo de arriba abajo; al revés.

reverseless [rɪ'vɜːslɪs] [ri-vers-les], *a.* Que no se puede invertir o mudar de arriba abajo.

reversible [rɪ'vɜːsɪbl] [ri-ver-si-bol], *a.* 1. Capaz de ser volteado o invertido; que admite posición o dirección opuesta; de dos caras. 2. Revocable por la ley, anulable.

reversion [rɪ'vɜːʃən] [ri-ver-shon], *s.* 1. Futura, la sucesión de empleo o renta a que uno tiene derecho después de la muerte de otro. 2. Reversión, vuelta de una heredad a su precedente poseedor o sus herederos; derecho de reversión.

reversionary [rɪ'vɜːʃnərɪ] [ri-ver-sho-na-ri], *a.* Que toca a uno por derecho de reversión.

reversioner [rɪ'vɜːʃnəʳ] [ri-ver-sho-naʳ], *s.* El que tiene derecho de reversión o sucesión.

revert [rɪ'vɜːt] [ri-vert], *va. (Ant.)* Invertir, volver al revés; volver atrás. *-vn.* 1. Retroceder, volverse atrás, mirar atrás, volver a una posición, condición o estado anteriores. 2. Tomar el hilo, referirse a alguna cosa anteriormente conocida o mencionada. 3. *(Biol.)* Volver hacia una forma hereditaria, anterior o primitiva, o mostrar algunos de sus rasgos característicos. 4. Volver o tocar a uno por derecho de reversión. **To revert to a subject,** volver a un tema.

revert, s. *(Mús.)* Vuelta.

revertible [rɪ'vɜːtɪbl] [ri-ver-ti-bol], a. Reversible, que ha de volver al poseedor precedente.

revery, s. V. REVERIE.

revest [rɪ'vest] [ri-vest], va. 1. Volver a vestir. 2. Restablecer en la posición de algún empleo.

revestiary [rɪ'vestʃərɪ] [ri-ves-cha-ri], s. Guardarropa. **Revestiary of a church,** sacristía.

revet [rɪ'vet] [ri-vet], va. Revestir la pared con cal, piedra u otros materiales.

revetment [rɪ'vetmənt] [ri-vet-ment], s. *(Fort.)* Revestimiento de una muralla o pared; pared fuerte destinada a sostener las tierras.

revictual ['riːˈvɪtl] [ri-vik-chual], va. Volver a proveer de víveres.

review [rɪ'vjuː] [ri-viu], va. 1. Rever, ver de nuevo; examinar, considerar, repasar. 2. Volver a ver, ver otra vez. 3. *(Mil.)* Revistar, pasar revista a la tropa. 4. Criticar, dar cuenta de; analizar una obra. -vn. Escribir o hacer una revista.

review, s. 1. Revista, la segunda vista o examen de una cosa hecha con cuidado y diligencia; repaso *(examination)*. 2. Revista, nombre dado a algunas obras periódicas en que se analizan y examinan críticamente las producciones literarias. 3. *(Mil.)* Revista o reseña de la tropa. 4. Escrutinio *(scrutiny, inspection.)* **Quearterly review,** revista trimestral. **Annual review,** análisis anual. **The case came up for review,** el asunto se sometió a revisión. **Salaries are under review,** los sueldos están sujetos a revisión.

reviewer [rɪ'vjuːəʳ] [ri-viuaʳ], s. 1. El que escribe en los periódicos llamados revistas: crítico, el que da cuenta de las publicaciones nuevas en una revista; revistero. 2. Revisor, el que revé o pasa revista; examinador, inspector.

revile [rɪ'vaɪl] [ri-vail], va. Ultrajar, despreciar, injuriar, difamar.

revilement [rɪ'vaɪlmənt] [ri-vail-ment], s. Contumelia, oprobio, injuria, ultraje.

reviler [rɪ'vaɪləʳ] [ri-vai-laʳ], s. Injuriador.

reviling [rɪ'vaɪlɪŋ] [ri-vai-lin], s. Oprobio, injuria, ultraje.

revilingly [rɪ'vaɪlɪŋlɪ] [ri-vai-lin-li], adv. Injuriosamente, afrentosamente, con oprobio.

revise [rɪ'vaɪz] [ri-vais], va. 1. Rever, volver a examinar detenidamente alguna cosa. 2. Revisar, modificar, corregir por una autoridad; mejorar, reformar *(change, improve).* **Revised,** pp. revisado, examinado de nuevo, corregido. **To revise for exams,** repasar para los exámenes. **Revised Version,** la traducción corregida de la Biblia en inglés. **Authorized Version,** versión autorizada.

revise, s. 1. Revista. 2. *(Impr.)* La segunda prueba de un pliego. **Second revise,** la tercera prueba del pliego que se está imprimiendo.

reviser, revisor [rɪ'vaɪzəʳ] [ri-vai-saʳ], s. Revisor, censor, el que corrige, particularmente pruebas de imprenta.

revision [rɪ'vɪʒən] [ri-vi-shon], s. 1. Revisión, el acto de rever. 2. Versión o edición revisada o corregida.

revisit ['riːˈvɪzɪt] [ri-vi-sit], va. Volver a visitar, visitar de nuevo.

revisory [rɪ'vɪzərɪ] [ri-vi-so-ri], a. Revisor, que revisa. **A revisory comission,** una comisión revisora.

revival [rɪ'vaɪvəl] [ri-vai-val], s. 1. Restauración, restablecimiento. 2. Renovación de interés por la religión; despertamiento religioso. **The Revival of Learning,** el Renacimiento.

revivalism [rɪ'vaɪvəˌlɪzəm] [ri-vai-va-li-sem], s. Evangelismo.

revivalist [rɪ'vaɪvəlɪst] [ri-vai-va-list], s. El que contribuye al despertamiento del sentimiento religioso.

revive [rɪ'vaɪv] [ri-vaiv], vn. 1. Revivir, volver a vivir, tener nueva vida. 2. Revivir, restablecerse, renovarse o reanimarse después de un estado de decaimiento; cobrar nuevo vigor; volver en sí, recobrar los sentidos. 3. Renacer, florecer de nuevo. -va. 1. Resucitar, dar nueva vida a un muerto. 2.

Restablecer, renovar, restaurar. 3. Avigorar, dar nuevo vigor; despertar, avivar; animar, excitar. 4. Restablecer, volver a poner en vigor (una ley, costumbre, etc.). 5. Hacer recordar, despertar la memoria. **Trade begins to revive,** el comercio empieza a revivir. **To revive the memory of great men,** hacer revivir la memoria de los grandes hombres. **This will revive him,** esto lo reanimará. **To revive someone's courage,** infundir ánimo a alguien.

reviver [rɪ'vaɪvəʳ] [ri-vai-vaʳ], s. Vivificador.

revivify [rɪ'vɪvɪfaɪ] [ri-vi-vi-fai], va. y vn. Revivificar, hacer revivir; dar nueva vida, nuevo vigor; restablecerse, revivir.

rrevocable ['revəkeɪbl] [re-vo-kei-bol], a. Revocable, que se puede revocar.

revocableness [ˌrevə'keɪblnɪs] [re-vo-kei-bol-nes], s. Calidad de revocable.

revocation [ˌrevə'keɪʃən] [re-vo-kei-shon], s. 1. Revocación, acción y efecto de revocar. 2. *(For.)* Anulación de un instrumento, acto o promesa por parte de quien los hizo.

revoke [rɪ'vəʊk] [ri-vouk], va. Revocar, anular, invalidar, declarar nulo lo que se ha hecho (law, will). -vn. Renunciar, no jugar la carta del palo que se pide.

revolt [rɪ'vəʊlt] [ri-voult], vn. 1. Rebelarse, levantarse, sublevarse, amotinarse. 2. Desertar, cambiar de casaca. -va. 1. Rebelar, revolucionar, sublevar. 2. Chocar excesivamente, indignar, irritar, dar asco. **The room revolted me,** la habitación me dio asco.

revolt, s. 1. Revuelta, sublevación, levantamiento, 2. Rebelión, rebeldía. 3. Deserción. **To rise in revolt,** sublevarse, rebelarse.

revolter [rɪ'vəʊltəʳ] [ri-voul-taʳ], s. Rebelde, sublevado, amotinado.

revolting [rɪ'vəʊltɪŋ] [ri-voul-tin], a. Que causa horror o repugnancia.

revoltingly [rɪ'vəʊltɪŋlɪ] [ri-voul-tin-li], adv. De un modo repugnante en alto grado.

revolute [rɪ'vəljuːt] [ri-vo-liut], a. *(Bot.)* Enrollado hacia atrás, doblados los márgenes sobre la superficie inferior.

revolution [ˌrevə'luːʃən] [re-vo-lu-shon], s. 1. Revolución, rotación, vuelta al mismo punto; se dice de los planetas, del tiempo, de las estaciones y de los siglos; cada uno de los giros completos de un astro en su órbita. 2. Revolución, cualquier giro, vuelta, o sinuosidad sobre un eje, v. g. una espiral. 3. Repetición de cambios o acontecimientos sucesivos; ciclo; espacio de tiempo que transcurre entre esas repeticiones. 4. Revolución, mudanza violenta en los negocios de un Estado o en la forma de su gobierno.

revolutionary [ˌrevə'luːʃənərɪ] [re-vo-lu-sho-na-ri], a. Revolucionario, perteneciente a una revolución en el Estado; que tiende a producir una revolución. -s. Revolucionario, partidario de una revolución política.

revolutionist [ˌrevə'luːʃənɪst] [re-vo-lu-sho-nist], s. Revolucionario, el partidario de una revolución política.

revolutionize [ˌrevə'luːʃənaɪz] [re-va-lu-sho-nais], va. Revolucionar, conmover, sublevar, trastornar.

revolvable [rɪ'vɒləbl] [ri-vol-va-bol], a. Que puede girar, capaz de dar vueltas.

revolve [rɪ'vɒlv] [ri-volv], vn. 1. Revolverse, moverse en línea curva de modo que vuelva periódicamente al punto de partida. 2. Girar, moverse alrededor o circularmente, rodar. 3. Moverse en ciclos, suceder periódicamente. 4. Ser considerado bajo todos los aspectos. -va. 1. Arrollar, revolver, hacer girar o mover en una órbita o círculo. 2. Hacer rodar, dar vueltas sobre un eje. 3. Revolver, discurrir, meditar, contemplar. **Everything revolves round him,** todo depende de él

revolver [rɪ'vɒlvəʳ] [ri-vol-vaʳ], s. 1. Lo que gira o rueda. 2. Revólver, pistola que contiene varias recámaras en un cilindro giratorio.

revolving [rɪ'vɒlvɪŋ] [ri-vol-vin], **Revolving credit,** crédito rotativo. **Revolving door,** puerta giratoria.

revue [rɪ'vjuː] [ri-viu], s. Revista teatral.

revulsion [rɪ'vʌlʃən] [ri-val-shon], s. 1. Cambio repentino, v. g. en las ideas; reacción fuerte de cualquier especie. *(Med.)*

Revulsión, reacción. 2. Apartamiento, retroceso; separación violenta, reculada.

revulsive [rɪˈvʌsɪv] [ri-val-siv], *a.* *(Med.)* Revulsivo, revulsorio, que causa una fuerte reacción.

reward [rɪˈwɔːd] [ri-uord], *va.* Premiar, remunerar, recompensar, gratificar. **She rewarded me with a kiss,** me premió con un beso.

reward, *s.* 1. Premio, recompensa, remuneración (prize); gratificación, hallazo, salario (earnings). 2. Merecido, el castigo o pena. **As a reward for,** en recompensa de.

rewardable [rɪˈwɔːdəbl] [ri-uor-da-bol], *a.* Digno o capaz de premio.

rewarder [rɪˈwɔːdər] [ri-uor-daᵣ], *s.* Premiador, remunerador.

rewind [rɪˈwaɪnd] [ri-uain], *vt.* Dar cuerda (watch), devanar; rebobinar (Elec., Cinema).

reword [rɪˈwɔːd] [ri-uord], *va.* 1. Repetir en otras palabras, expresar de otra manera. 2. Repetir las mismas palabras.

rework [rɪˈwɜːk] [ri-uek], *vt.* Refundir, rehacer.

rhapsodist [ˈræpsədɪst] [rap-so-dist], *s.* 1. Rapsodista, el que hace o compone rapsodias. 2. El que se expresa con exagerado sentimiento.

rhapsodize [ˈræpsədaɪz] [rap-so-dais], *va. y vn.* Cantar o recitar centones o rapsodias.

rhapsody [ˈræpsədɪ] [rap-so-di], *s.* Rapsodia, centón, obra compuesta de diferentes trozos debidos a varios autores.

rhea [ˈriːə] [ria], *s.* 1. Rea, hija de Urano y madre de los dioses. 2. Ave parecida al avestruz que habita en las llanuras de la América del Sur.

Rhenish [ˈrenɪʃ] [re-nish], *a.* Perteneciente o relativo al río Rin o a sus riberas. -*s.* Vino del Rin.

rheostat [ˈriːəstæt] [rious-tat], *s.* Reóstato, aparato que sirve para medir la resistencia eléctrica de los conductores.

rhesus [ˈriːsəs] [ri-sos], *s.* **Rhesus positive,** factor Rhesus positivo. **Rhesus factor,** factor Rhesus, factor Rh.

rhetoric [ˈretərɪk] [re-to-rik], *s.* 1. Retórica, el arte de hablar con propiedad y elegancia. 2. Libro de texto sobre el discurso o la retórica. 3. Retóricas, sofesterías o razones que no son del caso.

rhetorical [rɪˈtɒrɪkəl] [ri-to-ri-kal], *a.* Retórico, que pertenece a la retórica.

rhetorically [rɪˈtɒrɪkəlɪ] [ri-to-ri-ka-li], *adv.* Retóricamente.

rhetorician [rɪˈtɒrɪʃən] [ri-to-ri-shan], *s.* Retórico, persona versada en los principios y reglas de la retórica, o que la enseña.

rheum [ruːm] [rum], *s.* Reuma, destilación, fluxión, romadizo.

rheumatic [ruːˈmætɪk] [ru-ma-tik], *a.* Reumático, perteneciente al reumatismo o que lo padece.

rheumatism [ˈruːmətɪzəm] [ru-ma-ti-sem], *s.* Reumatismo, enfermedad que se manifiesta por dolores mudables más o menos vivos en los músculos o las articulaciones.

rheumy [ˈruːmɪ] [ru-mi], *a.* Lleno de humedad, o de humor acre.

rhinoceros [raɪˈnɒsərəs] [rai-nou-se-ros], *s.* Rinoceronte, un animal cuadrúpedo paquidermo, con uno o dos cuernos cortos y encorvados osbre la nariz, y con el labio superior movedizo y prensil.

rhizome, [ˈraɪzəʊm] [rai-soum], *s. (Bot.)* Rizoma, tallo horizontal y subterráneo; se llama también **rootstock.**

rhomb [rɒm] [rom], **rhombus** [ˈrɒmbəs] [rom-bos], *s.* Rombo, paralelogramo que consta de cuatro lados iguales y tiene dos ángulos mayores que los otros dos.

rhombic [ˈrɒmbɪk] [rom-bik], *a.* Que tiene figura de rombo.

rhomboid [ˈrɒmbɔɪd] [rom-boid], *s. (Geom.)* Romboide, paralelogramo cuyos lados contiguos son desiguales y dos de sus ángulos mayores que los otros dos.

rhombus, *s. V.* RHOMB.

rhumb [ruːmb] [rumb], *s.* 1. *(Mar.)* Rumbo. 2. **Rhumb o rhumb-line,** línea loxodrómica.

rhubarb [ˈruːbɑːb] [ru-barb], *s.* 1. Ruibarbo, raíz medicinal purgante. 2. Ruipónticoa, rapóntigo (plant).

rhyme, [raɪm] [raim], *s.* Rima, consonancia; poesía o poema. **Without rhyme or reason,** sin ton ni son.

rhyme, rime, *vn.* Versificar, hacer versos; rimar. *V.* RIME.

rhimer, rimer [ˈraɪmər] [rai-maᵣ], *s.* Versista, el que hace versos.

rhythm [ˈrɪðəm] [ri-dem], *s.* 1. Ritmo, proporción entre el tiempo de un movimiento y el de otro diferente; combinación métrica. 2. Cadencia, medida, armonía. 3. *(Med.)* Periodicidad, ocurrencia en paroxismos.

rhythmic, rhythmical [ˈrɪðmɪk] [riz-mik] [ˈrɪðmɪkəl] [riz-mi-kal], *a.* Rítmico; armónico.

rib [rɪb] [rib], *va.* Marcar con rayas, listones o filetes; hacer una tela con listones salientes; proveer de costillas; encerrar como dentro de un costillar,

rib, *s.* 1. Costilla, el hueso largo y encorvado que nace del espinazo y viene hacia el pecho. 2. Cualquier pedazo de madera u otro material que fortalece el costado de alguna cosa; faja, listón largo y estrecho parecido a una costilla, como una moldura saliente de un tejado; cabrio, viga de tejado; cuaderna; varilla o ballena (de paraguas); tirante, varenga de hierro; vivo (en las telas o medias). 3. *(Bot.)* Costilla, nervadura gruesa de las hojas. 4. Costilla, la mujer propia; en alusión a la frase del Génesis. **Ribs of a ship,** ligazones de navío. **Ribs of a parrel,** *(Mar.)* liebres de racamento. **Rib cage,** tórax.

ribald [ˈrɪbəld] [ri-bald], *s.* Hombre bajo e impúdico. -*a.* Obsceno, lascivo, groseramente abusivo, toscamente chistoso, insultante.

ribaldry [ˈrɪbəldrɪ] [ri-bal-dri], *s.* Escabrosidad, obscenidad.

riband [ˈrɪbənd] [ri-band], *s. (Ant.) V.* RIBBON.

ribbed [ˈrɪbd] [rid], *a.* Provisto de costillas. **Ribbed sweater,** jersey de cordoncillo.

ribbon [ˈrɪbən] [ri-ban], *s.* 1. Colonia, cinta o listón de seda. 2. Cinta, listón, faja; parecido a una cinta, como el muelle de un reloj o una lista pintada sobre el costado de una embarcación. 3. *pl. (Fam.)* Riendas. **Satin ribbons,** cintas o listones de raso. **Velvet ribbons,** cintas de terciopelo. **Silk plush ribbon,** cinta rizada de felpa. **Hat-band ribbon,** cinta para sombreros. **Hat-bindery ribbon,** rivecillo para sombreros. **Waist ribbon,** cinta para cinturones. **Ribbon-grass,** alpiste. **To tear to ribbons,** hacer trizas.

ribbon, *va.* Encintar, adornar o engalanar con cintas.

ribbon, *a.* Hecho de cinta, o semejante a una cinta. **Ribbon-weaver,** cintero, tejedor de cintas.

riboflavin [ˌraɪbəʊˈfleɪvɪn] [rai-bou-flei-vin], *s.* Riboflavina.

ribwort [ˈrɪbwɔːt] [rib-uort], *s. (Bot.)* Llantén lanceolado.

rice [raɪs] [rais], *s. (Bot.)* Arroz, planta gramínea y su fruto. Oryza sativa. **Rice-field,** arrozal, campo sembrado de arroz. **Rice-bird,** *V.* BOBOLINK. Se llama así en los Estados Unidos del Sur, porque se alimenta de arroz en el otoño. **Rice-paper,** (a) papel de paja de arroz. (b) Papel de China; papel vegetal muy delicado que emplean los chinos para pintar flores, insectos, etc., de varios colores y para hacer flores artificiales.

rich [rɪtʃ] [rich], *a.* 1. Rico, opulento, acaudalado, hacendado (wealthy). 2. Precioso, costoso, de precio, compuesto de materiales raros o preciosos (expensive); de valor, suntuoso. 3. Abundante, copioso, generoso (abundant); fértil, pingüe. **Rich soil,** tierra pingüe. **Rich wine,** vino generoso. 4. Rico, sabroso, muy grato al paladar; dulzarrón; a menudo implica exceso perjudicial de manteca o grasas; muy sazonado. 5. Rico, excelente muy bueno en su clase; abundante en cualidades recomendables. 6. *(Fam.)* Muy jocoso; divertido o ridículo. **A rich soil,** un suelo rico, fértil, fecundo. **Rich jewels,** joyas costosas, de mucho valor. **Rich gravy,** pringue, salsa demasiado grasa. **A rich joke,** un chiste muy divertido. **That's rich!,** ¡qué gracioso! **The rich,** los ricos.

riches [ˈrɪtʃɪz] [ri-chis], *s. pl.* 1. Riqueza, opulencia, abundancia de bienes y cosas preciosas. 2. Esplendor, pompa, magnificencia.

richly [ˈrɪtʃlɪ] [rich-li], *adv.* 1. Ricamente, opulentamente, magníficamente. 2. Copiosamente, abundantemente.

richness [ˈrɪtʃnɪs] [rich-nes], *s.* 1. Riqueza, opulencia; primor, suntuosidad, magnificencia. 2. Fertilidad. 3. Abundancia, copia. 4. Pinguosidad, crasitud; calidad de lo rico en general o de lo que da buenas ganancias.

rick [rɪk] [rik], *s.* Niara, rima o rimero de haces de grano o heno.

rickets ['rɪkɪts] [ri-kits], *s.* Raquitis, raquitismo, enfermedad de la temprana niñez, caracterizada por el reblandecimiento de los huesos y consecuente deformidad.

rickety ['rɪkɪtɪ] [ri-ki-ti], *a.* 1. Desvencijado, cayéndose, que está para caerse por falta de solidez. 2. Raquítico, que padece de raquitis.

rickshaw ['rɪkʃɔː] [rik-sho], *s.* Vehículo japonés tirado por un hombre.

ricochet ['rɪkəʃeɪ] [ri-ko-shei], *va.* Hacer fuego de rebote. -*vn.* Rebotar sobre una superficie una o varias veces, como hace una bala de cañón cuando se dispara casi horizontalmente. -*s.* (*Art.*) Fuego de rebote.

rid [rɪd] [rid], *va.* 1. Desembarazar, desocupar. 2. (*Ant.*) Librar, libertar, redimir. 3. (*Ant.*) Desechar, expeler. **To rid oneself of a troublesome business,** zafarse de algún asunto escabroso, de una carga o de la que ofende; librar. **To rid oneself of,** desembarazarse de. **To be o to get rid of,** estar exento; desembarazarse o librarse de; deshacerse de. **To rid a room of insects,** eliminar los insectos de una habitación.

rid, 1. *pret.* y *pp.* de to RID. 2. (*Ant.*) *pret.* de to RIDE.

riddance ['rɪdəns] [ri-dans], *s.* 1. Libramiento o preservación de un mal o peligro. 2. Zafada, la acción de zafarse de alguna cosa que molesta. **To make a clear riddance,** desembarazar alguna parte de las personas o cosas que estorban.

ridden ['rɪdn] [ri-den], *pp.* de to RIDE.

riddle ['rɪdl] [ri-del], *s.* 1. Enigma, adivinanza, pregunta intrincada (conundrum). 2. Cualquier cosa difícil de atinar o comprender. -*va.* Resolver enigmas. -*vn.* Hablar enigmáticamente.

riddle, *va.* y *vn.* 1. Acribillar, agujerear en muchas partes con balas. 2. Cribar, acribar, pasar a través de una criba. -*s.* Criba, cribo, cedazo grueso, especialmente el empleado en una fundición o para lavar el oro.

ride [raɪd] [raid], *vn.* (*pret.* RODE, *pp.* RIDDEN). 1. Cabalgar, andar, ir o pasear a caballo; manejar, enseñar o adiestrar un caballo. 2. Ruar, andar en coche o carruaje. 3. Moverse o caminar una cosa puesta encima de otra. 4. Flotar, sostenerse en un fluido; estar fondeado; andar por el mar o estar en él. **To ride at anchor,** surgir, estar fondeado. -*va.* 1. Sentarse, y ser llevado sobre algo; correr. 2. Flotar sobre las olas, henderlas, dominarlas. 3. Montar, guiar un caballo; atravesar a caballo; andar por, o viajar, cualquiera que sea el medio empleado. **Can you ride?,** ¿sabe usted montar a caballo?

ride away, marcharse, irse.

ride behind, cabalgar a la grupa.

ride down, echar a tierra y pisar paseando a caballo; de aquí, pisotear, tratar insolente y arrogantemente.

ride on, seguir adelante.

ride out, (*Mar.*) luchar felizmente contra una tempestad. **To ride shank's mare,** (*Fam.*) andar a pie.

ride up, acercarse, subir. **To ride easy,** (*Mar.*) mantenerse bien al ancla.

ride, *s.* 1. Paseo a caballo o en coche. 2. El espacio de terreno destinado para paseo. **To give somebody a rough ride,** hacer pasar un mal rato a alguien. **To go for a ride,** pasear a caballo.

rider ['raɪdəʳ] [rai-daʳ], *s.* 1. Caballero, cabalgador; jinete; picador; ciclista. 2. Ruante, el que va en coche o carruaje. 3. El cochero u otra persona que maneja los caballos de un carruaje, y también los que corren caballos. 4. Cosa que va a horcajadas sobre otra; nombre que se da algunas veces a una hoja añadida a un instrumento ya concluido, y a las cláusulas añadidas a las leyes aprobadas en el Parlamento.

riders ['raɪdəz] [rai-dars], *s. pl.* (*Mar.*) Sobreplanes, especie de cuadernas o costillas interiores. **Floor-riders,** sobreplanes del fondo. **Lower futtock-riders,** genoles de sobreplanes. **Second futtock-riders,** ligazones de sobreplanes.

ridge [rɪdʒ] [ridch], *va.* Alomar, formar lomos o camellones; cubrir con listones salientes o arrugas. -*vn.* Estar marcado con arrugas o listones salientes.

ridge, *s.* 1. Cualquier protuberancia que se levanta desigualmente y que es larga en proporción a su anchura y altura; listón saliente, arruga, elevación prolongada, serie de colinas, serranía, serrijón; cerro. 2. Cumbre, cima o pico de montaña. 3. Escollo, arrecife, banco de piedra que sale del mar. 4. Caballón, el lomo que se levanta en el campo arado entre surco y surco; camellón. 5. Caballete, el lomo que se levanta en medio del tejado. **A ridge of hills,** una cadena de colinas, cerro. **Ridge-ropes of the head-nettings,** (*Mar.*) nervios de las redes de proa. **Ridges of horse's mouth,** las arrugas que tienen los caballos en el paladar. **Ridge-pole, ridge-plate,** cima, madero que termina la armazón del alero.

ridgy ['rɪdʒɪ] [rid-chi], *a.* Desigual, que se levanta con desigualdad, cerril; que tiene listones salientes.

ridicule ['rɪdɪkjuːl] [ri-di-kiul], *s.* 1. Ridiculez, extravagancia. 2. Ridículo, el dicho que ridiculiza a alguno.

ridicule, *va.* Ridiculizar, escarnecer, tornar en ridículo, hacer mofa de alguien.

ridiculous [rɪ'dɪkjʊləs] [ri-di-kiu-los], *a.* 1. Ridículo, risible. 2. Ridículo, extravagante, nimio.

ridiculously [rɪ'dɪkjʊləslɪ] [ri-di-kiu-los-li], *adv.* Ridículamente.

ridiculousness [rɪ'dɪkjʊləsnɪs] [ri-di-kiu-los-nes], *s.* Calidad de ridículo.

riding ['raɪdɪŋ] [rai-din], *s.* 1. La acción de andar a caballo o en coche; paseo a caballo o en coche; excursión, cabalgata. 2. Distrito o porción en que se dividen algunos condados en Inglaterra. -*a.* Lo que se emplea para caminar a caballo o en coche. (*Mar.*) Fondeado. **Riding easy,** (*Mar.*) descansado al ancla. **Riding hard,** (*Mar.*) tormentoso al ancla. **Riding-cloak, riding-coat,** redingote. **Ridign-habit,** traje de montar. **Riding-hood,** capirote, gabán, capilla, capucho. **Riding-school,** picadero, escuela de equitación. **Riding-whip, riding-rod,** látigo de montar.

rife [raɪf] [raif], *a.* 1. Abundante en número o cantidad; muy esparcido, corriente, común. 2. Lleno, seguido de *with.* **Rumors of war were rife,** los rumores de guerra eran cosa corriente. **The small-pox has been very rife this year,** este año ha habido epidemia de viruelas o han sido muy comunes las viruelas.

rifely ['raɪflɪ] [raif-li], *adv.* Abundantemente, comúnmente.

rifeness ['raɪfnɪs] [raif-nes], *s.* Abundancia, frecuencia.

riffraff ['rɪfræf] [rif-raf], *s.* Gentuza, canalla, desperdicio: se dice de la gente más baja.

rifle ['raɪfl] [rai-fel], *va.* 1. Robar, pillar. 2. Rayar un arma de fuego. -*vn.* Proveer a un arma de fuego de raya o muesca espiral. **To rifle a case,** desvalijar una maleta. **To be rifle with,** abundar en, estar lleno de.

rifle, *s.* Carabina, escopeta con cañón estriado por dentro, rifle. **Rifle range,** 1. Alcance de un tiro del rifle. 2. Lugar en que se puede tirar al blanco.

rifleman ['raɪflmən] [rai-fel-man], *s.* Escopetero, carabinero, riflero, el hombre armado con rifle o que es hábil en su manejo.

rifler ['raɪfləʳ] [rai-flaʳ], *s.* Pillador, robador.

rift [rɪft] [rift], *s.* 1. Hendedura, rendija, grieta, reventón; cuarteadura. 2. Desemboque, vado, sitio poco profundo en un arroyo. 3. Espuma que forman las olas al romperse en la playa.

rift, *va.* Hender, dividir. -*vn.* Reventar; regoldar.

rig [rɪg] [rig], *va.* 1. Ataviar, asear, adornar; con *out.* 2. Aparejar, equipar; con *out o up.* **To rig out a boom,** (*Mar.*) botar afuera.

rig, *s.* 1. Aparejo, disposición especial de los mástiles, jarcias, velas, etc., en el casco de un buque. 2. (*Fam.*) Modo de vestir, traje; tren de carruaje y caballos para pasear en coche; apresto, aparejo, equipo; aparato de pesca. 3. (*Prov.*) Burla, mala partida.

rigadoon [ˌrɪgə'duːn] [ri-ga-dun], *s.* Rigodón, baile, especie de contradanza provenzal.

rigger ['rɪgəʳ] [ri-gaʳ], *s.* (*Mar.*) Aparejador.

rigging ['rɪgɪŋ] [ri-guin], *s.* 1. *(Mar.)* Aparejo, el conjunto de velas, jarcia y motonería de un buque. 2. *(Ger.)* Vestido.

right [raɪt] [rait], *a.* 1. Recto, justo, equitativo (fair, just), sincero, razonable, honesto (decent, proper). 2. Derecho, recto, justo, conforme a la ley moral o a la voluntad de Dios. 3. Idóneo, propio, conveniente (fit, suitable); fundado. 4. Verdadero, cierto, real, que ni es falso ni erróneo (truth); legal, legítimo. 5. Derecho, igual, no torcido ni inclinado a uno u otro lado, directo, que está en línea recta. 6. Bien arreglado, convenientemente dispuesto, ajustado, en buen orden. 7. Derecho (lo contrario de izquierdo). 8. Sano, en buen estado de cuerpo o de ánimo. 9. Derecho; se dice del lado mejor acabado en las telas. **The right way,** el camino recto o directo. **Right angle,** ángulo recto. **The right side,** el lado derecho (de una tela). **To be right,** tener razón. **Right sailing,** *(Mar.)* navegación recta o por alguno de los cuatro puntos cardinales. **Right-angled,** de ángulos rectos, rectangular. **Right-minded,** recto, honrado. *-inter.* ¡Bien! ¡bueno! *-adv.* 1. Rectamente, justamente, exactamente, perfectamente, precisamente. 2. Derechamente, en derechura. 3. Muy. 4. Inmediatamente, al instante. 5. Ahora mismo. **It is right,** está bien; está justo. **You are right o you are in the right,** tiene usted razón. **Right or wrong,** a tuertas o a derechas, con razón o sin ella. **You say right,** dice usted bien, tiene usted razón. **Right reverend,** reverendísimo. **Right honorable,** muy honorable, o respetable. *-s.* 1. Derecho, la ley moral; justicia, equidad, rectitud. 2. Razón, lo que está conforme con los hechos o con la verdad, que no contiene maldad ni error. 3. Derecho; título justo y equitativo; propiedad, dominio. 4. Poder, autoridad. 5. Privilegio, prerrogativa. 6. La derecha, lo opuesto a la izquierda. **To rights,** derechamente, derecho, sin torcer. **To the right,** a la derecha. **On his right,** a su derecha. **To be right,** tener razón. **To maintain one's right,** sostener su derecho. **To set to rights,** poner en orden; componer; reconciliar. **Right of way,** derecho de vía. **That soon put rights,** eso se corrige fácilmente. **To put a clock right,** poner un reloj en hora. **To put a mistake right,** corregir un error. **To be in one's right mind,** estar en sus cabales. **He's a right idiot,** es un puro idiota. **I'll be right over,** voy ahora mismo, voy enseguida.

right, *va.* 1. Hacer justicia, proceder con justicia. **To right oneself,** tomarse justicia por su mano. 2. *(Mar.)* Adrizar o levantar una embarcación que estaba ladeada. **To right a wrong,** deshacer un agravio, acabar con un problema.

rightabout ['raɪtəbaʊt] [rait-abaut], *s.* 1. Media vuelta. 2. Vuelta hacia la derecha.

right away ['raɪtəweɪ] [rait-auei], *adv.* Inmediatamente, en seguida.

righteous ['raɪtʃəs] [rai-chos], *a.* Justo, recto, equitativo; honrado.

righteously ['raɪtʃəslɪ] [rai-chos-li], *adv.* Justamente, rectamente, honradamente.

righteousness ['raɪtʃəsnɪs] [rai-chos-nes], *s.* Rectitud, justicia, equidad; honradez.

righter ['raɪtəʳ] [rai-taʳ], *s.* El que hace justicia; enderezador de entuertos o agravios.

rightful ['raɪtfʊl] [rait-ful], *a.* Legítimo, justo, recto.

rightfully ['raɪtfəlɪ] [rait-fu-li], *adv.* Legalmente, rectamente, justamente.

rightfulness ['raɪtfəlnɪs] [rait-ful-nes], *s.* Derechura; justicia, rectitud, equidad.

right-hand ['raɪthænd] [rait-jand], *a.* 1. Situado o perteneciente a mano derecha. 2. Se dice de la persona con quien más se cuenta o en quien se confía principalmente. **Right-hand man,** *(Fam.)* el brazo derecho, el colaborador principal; el auxiliar en quien se confía sobre todo.

right-handed ['raɪthændɪd] [rait-jan-ded], *a.* 1. Que se sirve ordinariamente de la mano derecha; de aquí, mañoso, hábil. 2. Que rueda o gira de izquierda a derecha, como las manecillas de un reloj. 3. Hecho con la mano derecha. **Right-handed screw,** tornillo (de rosca) a la derecha.

rightist ['raɪtɪst] [rai-tist], *s.* Derechista, conservador.

rightly ['raɪtlɪ] [rait-li], *adv.* Rectamente, justamente, bien, como se debe; exactamente; directamente.

rightness ['raɪtnɪs] [rait-nes], *s.* Rectitud, justicia; derechura.

right off ['raɪtɒf] [rait-of], *adv.* En seguida.

rigid ['rɪdʒɪd] [ri-yid], *a.* Tieso; rígido, inflexible; austero, severo; rigoroso; estricto, exacto, como el razonamiento.

rigidity [rɪ'dʒɪdɪtɪ] [ri-yi-di-ti], *s.* 1. Rigidez, rigor, austeridad; tesura. 2. Tosquedad, falta de garbo, gracia o aire; terquedad.

rigidly ['rɪdʒɪdlɪ] [ri-yid-li], *adv.* Tiesamente; inflexiblemente; con rigidez.

rigidness ['rɪdʒɪdnɪs] [ri-yid-nes], *s.* Rigidez, inflexibilidad.

riglet ['rɪglɪt] [ri-glit], *s. V.* REGLET.

rigmarole ['rɪgmərəʊl] [rig-ma-raul], *s.* Jerigonza, galimatías, desatino; un conjunto de palabras vacías de sentido.

rigor, rigour ['rɪgəʳ] [ri-goʳ], *s.* 1. Rigor, la tesura de los nervios que los hace inflexibles. 2. Rigor de calentura. 3. Rigor, severidad, dureza, austeridad; tesón, terquedad. 4. Rigor, exactitud en lo que es justo y recto. 5. Tesura, dureza, inflexiblidad de las cosas.

rigorous ['rɪgərəs] [ri-go-ros], *a.* Rigoroso, severo, cruel.

rigorously ['rɪgərəslɪ] [ri-go-ros-li], *adv.* Rigorosamente.

rigorousness ['rɪgərəsnɪs] [ri-go-ros-nes], *s.* Severidad, rigor.

rigour (es la manera usual de escribir esta palabra en Inglaterra). *V.* RIGOR.

rile [raɪl] [rail], *va. (Prov o fam.)* Sulfurar, encolerizar. *V.* ROIL.

rill [rɪl] [ril], *s.* Riachuelo, arroyuelo.

rillet ['rɪlɪt] [ri-lit], *s.* Arroyuelo. *V.* RIVULET.

rim [rɪm] [rim], *s.* 1. Canto, borde, margen, orilla. 2. Cerco, arco. **The rim of the belly,** el peritoneo.

rime [raɪm] [raim], *s.* 1. Escarcha. 2. Resquicio, hendedura, rendija, agujero, abertura.

rime, *va.* y *vn.* (Rhyme es forma etimológicamente incorrecta, aunque muy usada). 1. Rimar, versificar; componer en rima. 2. Rimar, ser una voz consonante de otra; corresponder, convenir, armonizarse (things).

rimer, rhymer ['raɪməʳ] [rai-maʳ], *s.* Rimador, versista; también, poetastro.

rimmed [rɪmd] [rimd], *a.* Bordeado, con borde.

rimy ['rɪmɪ] [ri-mi], *a.* Escarchado, blanco con escarcha; frío.

rind [raɪnd] [raind], *s.* Corteza, hollejo.

rind, *va.* Descortezar, quitar el hollejo.

ring [rɪŋ] [ring], *s.* 1. Círculo, cerco, cualquier objeto circular que tiene una abertura casi igual a su diámetro; anillo, aro, arillo, cintillo (hoop, rim); virola, argolla. 2. Sortija, anillo; aro de oro u otro metal que se lleva, principalmente para adorno, en los dedos de la mano. **Staple-ring,** argolla con espiga. 3. Circo, arena, como para una carrera, lucha o espectáculo. 4. Corro o corrillo de gente. 5. Combinación de varias o muchas personas, frecuentemente para fines ilícitos o censurables, v. g. en los negocios o en la política. 6. Ojera, círculo amoratado alrededor de los ojos. **A wedding ring,** un anillo de boda. **A seal ring,** una sortija que sirve de sello. **Ear-ring,** zarcillo. **Ring-bolt,** *(Mar.)* cáncamo, argolla. **Ring-bone,** *(Vet.)* sobrehueso de caballo. **Ring-dial,** reloj de sol en un anillo. **Ring-ropes,** *(Mar.)* bozas rabizadas. **Ring-streaked,** rayado en círculo. **Ring-shaped,** anular. **A sarcastic ring in the voice,** un tono sarcástico en la voz. **I'll give you a ring,** te llamaré.

ring, *s.* 1. Campano o repique de campanas; el juego de campanas de una torre. 2. *(Mar.)* Arganeo, virola con chaveta. 3. Sonido, ruido, rumor, susurro; estruendo.

ring, *va.* 1. Rodear, formar corro alrededor de; circundar. 2. Poner un anillo; anillar, ensortijar; adornar con anillos, sortijas o argollas. 3. *(Hort.)* Quitar una tira circular de corteza. -vn. 1. Moverse en círculo o en espiral. 2. Formar círculo.

ring, va. (pret. RANG, a veces RUNG; pp. RUNG). 1. Sonar, tocar, tañer. 2. Repicar, o tañer campanas. 3. Anunciar, proclamar, celebrar, v. g. con un repique de campanas. 4. Repetir a menudo o con énfasis; reiterar. 5. Llamar, convocar, por medio de una campana. -vn. 1. Sonar, dar de sí un sonido sonoro como una campana. 2. Sonar mucho, clara o fuertemente; retiñir, retumbar, resonar. 3. Zumbar los oídos. 4. Estar lleno del ruido, fama o nombre de una cosa.

ring back, volver a llamar.

ring down, bajar (curtain).

ring in, anunciar.

ring off, colgar (phone).

ring round/up, llamar (phone).

ring-dove [ˈrɪŋdʌv] [ring-dav], s. Paloma torcaz, zurita o zorita.

ringer [ˈrɪŋəʳ] [rin-gaʳ], s. Campanero, tocador de campanas.

ringing [ˈrɪŋɪŋ] [rin-guin], pa. Resonante, retumbante; que replica, que toca las campanas. **A ringing cheer,** viva resonante. -s. 1. Acción de sonar o hacer tocar las campanas; campaneo, repique de campana; retintín (del sonido de una campana). 2. (Hort.) Acción de quitar una tira circular de la corteza.

ringleader [ˈrɪŋliːdəʳ] [ring-li-daʳ], s. Cabeza de partido o bando; cabecilla, abanderizador.

ringlet [ˈrɪŋlɪt] [rin-glit], s. 1. Anillejo, círculo. 2. Sortija, bucle en el cabello, rizo. (Cuba) Crespo.

ringside [ˈrɪŋsaɪd] [ring-said], s. **Ringside seat,** butaca de primera fila.

ringtail [ˈrɪŋteɪl] [ring-teil], s. (Orn.) Especie de milano.

ringworm [ˈrɪŋwɜːm] [ring-uerm], s. Tiña, enfermedad del cutis; aparece en manchas circulares y la causa un parásito fungoso.

rinse [rɪns] [rins], va. 1. Lavar, limpiar, inundando o sumergiendo en un líquido. 2. Enjuagar, aclarar.

rinser [ˈrɪnsəʳ] [rin-saʳ], s. Lavandero, el que limpia.

rinsing [ˈrɪnsɪŋ] [rin-sin], s. Enjuagadura, acción de enjuagar, y el líquido con que se enjuaga; lo que se quita enjuagando.

riot [ˈraɪət] [raiot], s. 1. Tumulto, sedición, alboroto, motín, asonada. 2. Desenfreno, desorden, exceso; borrachera.

riot, vn. 1. Andar en borracheras, vivir desenfrenadamente, entregarse a los vicios. 2. Causar alborotos, sediciones, tumultos o motines.

rioter [ˈraɪətəʳ] [raio-taʳ], s. Hombre disoluto, bullicioso o sedicioso; alborotador, amotinador, abanderizador. (Fam.) Bullanguero, jaranero, libertino.

riotous [ˈraɪətəs] [raio-tos], a. 1. Sedicioso, faccioso, amotinado. 2. Desenfrenado, desarreglado, libertino, disoluto.

riotously [ˈraɪətəslɪ] [raio-tos-li], adv. Desenfrenadamente, disolutamente; bulliciosamente.

riotousness [ˈraɪətəsnɪs] [raio-tos-nes], s. Disolución, desenfreno, desorden; el estado de la persona o personas que están alborotadas o fuera de orden.

rip [rɪp] [rip], va. 1. Rasgar, lacerar, romper (slash, tear), dividir (a cloth) a lo largo de una línea de resistencia mínima; comúnmente con up, u off; hender. 2. Descoser, soltar. **To rip up,** rajar. **To rip off a plank,** (Mar.) descoser un tablón. 3. Penetrar al fondo de, sondear; poner a descubierto; descubrir un secreto; se usa con up. 4. Aserrar la madera en la dirección general de la veta; (carp.) hilar, linear. -vn. henderse, romperse. **To rip along,** ir a buen tren, correr rápidamente. **To rip off,** rajar, abrir de golpe, quitar, arrancar. **To rip out,** soltar, dejar escapar, hablar con vehemencia. **To rip out an oath,** jurar con violencia, jurar a la ligera, blasfemar. **Rip-saw,** sierra de hender o máquina para aserrar tablas. **To rip a box open,** abrir una caja rompiéndola.

rip, s. 1. Laceración, rasgadura, rasgón, paraje rasgado o roto. 2. Sierra de hender. V. **Rip-saw.**

riparian [raɪˈpeərɪən] [rai-pea-rian], a. Ribereño, que pertenece a la ribera de un río. **Riparious.** (Bot. y Zool.) Ribereño, que vive o se cría a lo largo de las riberas de un río.

ripe [raɪp] [raip], a. 1. Maduro, sazonado, en sazón. 2. Acabado, consumado, qeu se acerca a la perfección. 3. Pronto, preparado, a propósito. 4. Rosado, colorado; parecido a la madurez del fruto.

ripen [ˈraɪpən] [rai-pen], vn. Madurar, llegar a madurez. -va. Madurar, poner alguna cosa en estado de madurar.

ripely [ˈraɪplɪ] [raip-li], adv. Maduramente; a propósito.

ripeness [ˈraɪpnɪs] [raip-nes], s. Madurez.

ripper [ˈrɪpəʳ] [ri-paʳ], s. El que rasga o descose.

ripping [ˈrɪpɪŋ] [ri-pin], s. 1. Rompimiento, la acción de romper. 2. Laceración, la acción de lacerar. 3. Descubrimiento.

ripple [ˈrɪpl] [ri-pel], va. Formar pequeñas ondas, rizar la superficie del agua. -vn. 1. Agitarse, rizarse la superficie del agua. 2. Sonar como el agua que corre sobre un lecho áspero o pedregoso; murmurar.

ripple, va. Desgargolar, sacudir el cáñamo para que despida el cañamón.

ripple, s. 1. Oleadita, escarceo del agua, pequeña onda producida por una brisa suave, o al correr del agua sobre un lecho pedregoso. 2. Cualquier sonido semejante al murmullo de las aguas. 3. Ondulación, rizo, algo parecido a una oleadita.

ripple, s. Un peine que sirve para desgargolar.

rippling [ˈrɪplɪŋ] [ri-plin], s. 1. La acción de desgargolar el cáñamo. 2. El escarceo del agua cuando lo produce una brisa suave o el lecho pedregoso de un arroyo.

riprap [ˈrɪpræp] [rip-rap], va. Reforzar por medio de piedras partidas o deshechas. -s. 1. Piedras trituradas para hacer cimientos o muros, particularmente para formar una base o cimiento en agua profunda. 2. Cimiento hecho de piedras echadas en montón.

rise [raɪz] [rais], vn. (pret. ROSE, pp. RISEN). 1. Ascender, subir una cosa hacia arriba (lift); elevarse, levantarse (get up). 2. Levantarse, ponerse en pie (después de arrodillarse, sentarse o acostarse); de aquí, suspender sus tareas una asamblea deliberante, cerrar una sesión. 3. Levantarse, salir de la cama. 4. Nacer, asomar por el horizonte; salir el sol. 5. Nacer, salir; se dice de las plantas cuando empiezan a despuntar. 6. Saltar, salir, brotar alguna cosa de la tierra. **To rise from table,** levantarse de la mesa (after lunch). **That stream rises from a spring,** aquel arroyo nace de un manantial. 7. Levantarse, sublevarse, rebelarse. 8. Levantarse, suscitarse una disputa, una competencia, etc. 9. Ascender, subir o adelantar en empleo o dignidad; aumentar en fortuna, hacerse más rico. 10. Hincharse hacia arriba. **A river rises after rain,** un río sube, se hincha o aumenta después de la lluvia. 11. Encarecerse, subir o aumentarse el precio de una cosa. 12. Elevarse en el estilo; elevarse o ensalzarse en honores, fama o fortuna. 13. Resucitar. **The Lord is risen indeed,** el Señor ha resucitado en verdad. **To rise up against anyone,** acomete a alguno. 14. provenir, motivar, nacer, originarse. **To rise to one's feet,** ponerse en pie, levantarse. **That rises (o arises) from your negligence,** eso proviene de la negligencia de usted Sinónimo. ARISE.

rise, s. 1. Levantamiento, erección, la acción y efecto de levantar o levantarse. 2. Elevación, altura, eminencia. 3. Subida, la acción y efecto de subir; ascensión. 4. Subida, el sitio o lugar en declive, que va subiendo. 5. Subida, la mejoría o elevación de las cosas con respecto a su estado o precio. 6. Crecida, creciente (de un río, etc.); alza en los fondos públicos. **Rise and fall in the public stocks,** alza y baja en los fondos públicos. 7. Salida del sol. 8. Fuente, principio, origen, manantial, causa. 9. Elevación, ascenso en grado, honores, riquezas, reputación, etc.; elevación de la voz. **A rise of ground,** una elevación del terreno. **The rise of a hill,** la pendiente de una colina. **The rise of mercury in the thermometer,** la subida del mercurio en el termómetro. **To take a rise of someone,** burlarse de alguien.

risen, pp. de to RISE.

riser [ˈraɪzəʳ] [rai-saʳ], s. 1. El que se levanta. **An early riser,** madrugador, el que madruga. **Late riser,** persona que se levanta tarde. 2. Contrahuella, la cara vertical de un peldaño de escalera.

risibility [ˌrɪzɪˈbɪlɪtɪ] [ri-si-bi-li-ti], *s.* Risibilidad, la facultad de reír.

risible [ˈrɪzɪbl] [ri-si-bol], *a.* 1. Risible, lo que causa risa. 2. Risible, ridículo, digno de risa o burla.

rising [ˈraɪzɪŋ] [rai-sin] *a.* Naciente, nuevo, saliente. -*s.* 1. Levantamiento, renacimiento, vuelta a la vida; sublevación, insurrección, motín; acto de asomar en el horizonte; término de una sesión. 2. *(Prov. Ingl. y E.U.)* Levadura, fermento; también la cantidad de masa que se prepara de una vez. 3. Prominencia, protuberancia; en especial, lobanillo, lupia. **With rising alarm,** con creciente alarma. **She's rising 20,** pronto cumplirá 20 años.

risk [rɪsk] [risk], *s.* Riesgo, contingencia, peligro (danger, peril). **To run a risk,** correr peligro. **At the risk of one's life,** arriesgando la vida. **At one's own risk,** bajo su propia responsabilidad.

risk, *va.* Arriesgar, poner en riesgo, aventurar, exponer.

risker [ˈrɪskəʳ] [ris-kaʳ], *s.* El que arriesga.

risky [ˈrɪskɪ] [ris-ki], *a.* 1. Peligroso, arriesgado, expuesto a riesgos. 2. Imprudente, arriesgado, temerario.

risotto [rɪˈzɒtəʊ] [ri-so-tou], *s.* Arroz (rice).

rite [raɪt] [rait], *s.* Rito, la ceremonia solemne o religiosa; acto u observancia ceremonial. **Funeral rites,** ritos fúnebres o exequias.

ritual [ˈrɪtjʊəl] [ri-chual], *a.* Ritual, ceremonial, -*s.* 1. Formalidad o método prescrito para una ceremonia religiosa o ceremonial; sistema o conjunto de ritos. 2. Ritual, libro que enseña el orden de las sagradas ceremonias.

ritualism [ˈrɪtjʊəlɪzəm] [ri-chua-li-sem], *s.* Ritualismo, el estudio de los ritos o el exagerado apego a ellos; ritualidad, observancia de las formalidades prescritas para hacer una cosa.

ritualist [ˈrɪtjʊəlɪst] [ri-chua-list], *s.* Ritualista, rubriquista.

ritualistic [ˌrɪtjʊəˈlɪstɪk] [ri-chua-lis-tik], *a.* Ritualista, apegado al ritualismo, que aprecia mucho los ritos, particularmente los de la Iglesia antes de la Reforma.

ritually [ˈrɪtjʊəlɪ] [ri-chua-li], *adv.* Según el ritual o los ritos; conforme a los ritos.

rival [ˈraɪvəl] [rai-val], *a.* Émulo, contrario, opuesto (opposite, enemy). -*s.* Rival, competidor. **A rival firm,** una empresa de la competencia.

rival, *va.* 1. Competir, emular, entrar en competencia con alguno; rivalizar con (compete); ser el igual de otro. 2. *(Ant.)* Ser rival o competidor de alguien; esforzarse en alcanzar el mismo fin a que otro aspira. -*vn.* Rivalizar.

rivalry [ˈraɪvəlrɪ] [rai-val-ri], *s.* Rivalidad, competición, emulación; lucha o esfuerzo para obtener un fin que otro se propone alcanzar al mismo tiempo; esfuerzo para igualar o exceder a otro en mérito o perfección.

rive [raɪv] [raiv], *va.* (*pret.* RIVED, *pp.* RIVED o RIVEN). Rajar, ender. -*vn.* Henderse.

river [ˈrɪvəʳ] [ri-vaʳ], *s.* 1. Río. 2. *(Fig.)* Río, copia, flujo copioso, torrente. **River-basin,** cuenca de río, el área que desagua. **River-bed,** lecho, álveo, madre de un río. **Up (the) river,** río arriba. **Down (the) river,** río abajo. **River-dragon,** cocodrilo, caimán. **River-god,** Dios tutelar de río. **River-horse,** hipopótamo. **River fishing,** pesca fluvial.

rivermouth [ˈrɪvəmaʊθ] [ri-va-mauz], *s.* Estuario.

riverside [ˈrɪvəsaɪd] [ri-var-said], *s. y a.* Orilla de un río; ribera, el espacio a lo largo de un río.

rivet [ˈrɪvɪt] [ri-vit], *s.* Remache, la vuelta de la punta de un clavo remachado; roblón.

rivet, *va.* 1. Remachar, asegurar un clavo después de introducido doblándole la punta. 2. Roblar, doblar o remachar una pieza de hierro para asegurarla. 3. Remachar, asegurar o afianzar fuertemente alguna cosa.

rivulet [ˈrɪvjʊlɪt] [ri-viu-lit], *s.* Riachuelo, río pequeño.

RNA, ribonucleic acid, *s.* Ácido ribonucleico.

roach [rəʊtʃ] [rouch], *s.* 1. Escarcho. 2. Cucaracha.

road [rəʊd] [roud], *s.* 1. Carretera, camino; vía abierta al paso del público, particularmente desde una población a otra; vía, carretera (way). 2. Camino, el viaje que se hace de una parte a otra. **The high road,** el camino real. 3. *(Mar.)* Rada, bahía o ensenada en la que pueden anclar los buques. **By-road,** atajo, trocha, camino privado o poco frecuentado. **Cross-road,** encrucijada; camino de atajo. **Turnpike road,** camino con portazgo, calzada; y familiarmente, camino real. **Road-bed,** fundación de un camino; construcción sobre la que se asientan los rieles de un ferrocarril. **Road-roller,** pisón, rodillo para allanar caminos. **Road-runner,** pájaro, cuchillo de tierra, de cola larga, de los Estados Unidos del Sudoeste; habita en las llanuras y corre con gran velocidad. **"Road narrows",** estrechamiento de la calzada. **Road accident,** accidente de tráfico. **To take the road,** ponerse en camino. **She's on the road of recovery,** se está reponiendo. **Across the road,** enfrente, al otro lado de la calle. **My car is off the road,** mi coche está en el garaje.

roadbed [ˈrəʊdbed] [roud-bed], *s.* 1. Infraestructura. 2. Calzada (of the road).

roadblock [ˈrəʊdblɒk] [roud-blok], *s.* 1. *(Mil.)* Barricada. 2. Obstáculo colocado en caminos, particularmente por representantes de la autoridad.

roadhouse [ˈrəʊdhaʊs] [roud-jaus], *s.* Posada o restaurante cerca de una carretera.

roadie [ˈrəʊdɪ] [rou-di], *s. (Mus)* El que se encarga del transporte del equipo.

roadster [ˈrəʊdstəʳ] [rouds-taʳ], *s.* 1. Caballo que anda bien; también, bicicleta para los caminos ordinarios. 2. *(Mar.)* Un buque al ancla.

roadway [ˈrəʊdweɪ] [roud-uei], *s.* Carretera, calzada, parte del camino reservada para los carruajes.

roam [rəʊm] [roum], *vn.* Vagar, vaguear, andar vagando sin dirección fija, correr acá y acullá. -*va.* Correr, corretear.

roamer [ˈrəʊməʳ] [rou-maʳ], *s.* Vagabundo, andariego (tramp).

roaming [ˈrəʊmɪŋ] [rou-min], *a.* Paseos, vagabundeo.

roan [rəʊn] [roun], *a.* Roano, ruano (horse). -*s.* 1. Caballo ruano; color ruano. 2. Badana curtida de color ruano, o que imita al marroquín.

roar [rɔːʳ] [roʳ], *vn.* 1. Rugir, bramar como el león u otra bestia feroz. 2. Aullar, dar aullidos. 3. Bramar; se dice del mar y de los vientos. 4. Mugir el toro.

roar, *s.* 1. Rugido, el bramido del león. 2. Grito, gritería, vocerío. 3. Bramido, estruendo, ruido grande. 4. Mugido, el bramido del toro.

roaring [ˈrɔːrɪŋ] [rou-rin], *s.* Rugiente, que ruge.

roast [rəʊst] [roust], *va.* 1. Asar; cocer la carne o un manjar en el asador o en el horno. 2. Tostar o calentar mucho, calentar hasta un grado extremo, calcinar. 3. *(Fam.)* Burlarse, mofarse; chiflar, rechiflar (ironically).

roast, *a.* Asado, tostado (abrev. de **roasted**). **Roast meat,** asado o carne asada. **Roast beef,** carne de vaca asada, rosbif. -*s.* Carne asada, o una pieza a propósito o que está para asar; asado. **To rule the roast,** *(Vulg.)* mandar, tener vara alta, gobernar.

roaster [ˈrəʊstəʳ] [rous-taʳ], *s.* Cocinero que asa; asador, tostador, persona que asa o tuesta; tostador, aparato para tostar o calcinar; animal u objeto a propósito para ser asado.

roasting [ˈrəʊstɪŋ] [rous-tin], *ger.* de TO ROAST. -*s.* 1. Acción de asar, de tostar; tostadura. 2. En metalurgia es el acto de quemar el mineral para disipar su materia volátil; torrefacción, calcinación, beneficio por medio del fuego. 3. Burla pesada, rechifla; zurra.

rob [rɒb] [rob], *va.* Robar, coger y llevarse una propiedad con violencia y sin derecho; pillar; saquear, quitar, hurtar; privar. **To rob on the high-way,** saltear. **To rob a stage-coach,** robar una diligencia. **To rob Peter to pay Paul,** robar a Pedro para pagar a Pablo. **I've been robbed,** me han robado.

robber [ˈrɒbəʳ] [ro-baʳ] *s.* Ladrón, salteador de caminos, saqueador, despojador del bien ajeno.

robbery [ˈrɒbərɪ] [ro-be-ri], *s.* Robo, la acción de robar; robo a mano armada; asalto, pillaje, saqueo.

robe [rəʊb] [roub], *s.* 1. Manto, toga, traje talar o ropa larga que se lleva por encima de otros vestidos, particularmente como señal de oficio o dignidad (cloth); traje de ceremonia (dress). 2. Túnico; alguna cosa que cubre, como un manto. 3.

Manta de coche, de pieles u otro material. **A counsellor's robe,** garnacha. **Robe of state,** traje de gala. **Master of the robes,** jefe del guardarropa.

robe, *va.* Vestir de gala o de ceremonia; vestir, ataviar. *-vn.* Vestirse, ponerse trajes; cubrirse. **Fields robed with green,** campos cubiertos de verdura. **Robing-room,** guardarropa, sitio para ponerse y quitarse los trajes de ceremonia; vestuario de las iglesias. **To robe in black,** vestirse de negro.

robin ['rɒbɪn] [ro-bin], *s.* 1. *(Orn.)* Pechicolorado, petirrojo. 2. Petirrojo, tordo norteamericano.

robot ['rəʊbɒt] [rou-bot], *s.* 1. Robot, autómata mecánico. 2. Piloto automático de aviones.

robotic ['rəʊbɒtɪk] [rou-bo-tik], *a.* Robótico, robotizado.

robust ['rəʊbʌst] [rou-bast], *a.* Fuerte, robusto, vigoroso. **A robust defence,** una gran defensa, una defensa enérgica.

robustness [rəʊbʌstnɪs] [rou-bast-nes], *s.* Robustez, fuerza, vigor.

rock [rɒk] [rok], *s.* 1. Roca, peñasco (stone); escollo. 2. Fundamento sólido o inmutable; solidez, defensa, protección, amparo (protection). 3. Arrecife, algo sobre lo cual se puede naufragar; causa de ruina o daño. 4. *(Prov. o des.)* Rueca. **Chalk-rock,** roca cretácea. **Trap rock,** roca dolerita. *V.* TRAP. **Rock alum (roche alum),** alumbre de roca, alumbre en estado nativo. **Rock-bound,** rodeado de peñascos. **Rock-candy,** azúcar candi. **Rock-crusher,** máquina para triturar rocas o minerales. **To run on the rocks,** estar en peligro.

rock, *va.* 1. Mecer. 2. Arrullar; calmar, sosegar. *-vn.* Bambolear; oscilar. **The town was rocked by strikes,** la ciudad fue sacudida por huelgas.

rock bottom ['rɒk'bɒtəm] [rok-bo-tom], *s.* Lo más profundo, el fondo.

rock-crystal ['rɒk‚krɪstl] [rok-kris-tal], *s. (Min.)* Cristal de roca, cuarzo.

rocker ['rɒkəʳ] [ro-kaʳ], *s.* 1. Columpio de una cuna; una de las piezas curvas sobre que se mece una cuna o silla mecedora; *(E.U.)* silla mecedora. 2. Cunera. 3. Balancín. 4. Rockero *(Mús.).* **She's off his rocker,** está loca, le falta un tornillo.

rocket ['rɒkɪt] [ro-kit], *s.* 1. Cohete, volador. 2. Jaramago de los jardines. **Base rocket,** reseda. **Sky-rocket,** cohete. **To give a rocket,** reñir, echar un rapapolvo. *-vi.* **To rocket to fame,** hacerse famoso. **To rocket upwards,** subir como un cohete.

rocket launcher ['rɒkɪt‚lɔːntʃəʳ] [ro-kit-lon-chaʳ], *s.* Lanzacohetes.

rocket missile ['rɒkɪt‚mɪsɪl] [ro-kit-mi-sil], *s.* Proyectil-cohete.

rocket plane ['rɒkɪtpleɪn] [ro-kit-plein], *s.* Avión cohete.

rocketry ['rɒkɪtrɪ] [ro-ki-tri], *s.* Cohetería.

rocket ship ['rɒkɪtʃɪp] [ro-kit-ship], *s.* Navecohete, barco para lanzar proyectiles; cohete.

rock garden ['rɒk‚gɑːdn] [rok-gar-den], *s.* Jardín rocoso.

rockiness ['rɒkɪnɪs] [ro-ki-nes], *s.* 1. Gran número de rocas. 2. El estado de lo que se halla lleno de peñascos; naturaleza roqueña.

rocking ['rɒkɪŋ] [ro-kin], *pa.* Mecedor; vacilante, oscilatorio. **Rocking-chair,** mecedora, (Cuba) columpio. **Rocking-horse,** caballo mecedor, caballito de madera, cuyos pies descansan sobre dos arcos que permiten al jinete mecerse en él.

rocking, *s.* Balanceo.

rock-oil ['rɒk‚ɔɪl] [rok-oil], *s.* Petróleo.

rock-ribbed ['rɒk‚rɪbd] [rok-ribd], *a.* Inflexible, fuerte, firme.

rockrose ['rɒkrəʊz] [rok-rous], *sf.* Jara, heliantero.

rock-salt ['rɒksɔːlt] [rok-solt], *s.* Sal de piedra, sal gema.

rock-solid [‚rɒk'sɒlɪd] [rok-so-lid], *a.* Sólido como una piedra.

rock-water ['rɒk'wɔːtəʳ] [rok-uo-taʳ], *s.* Agua cristalina de las rocas.

rockwork ['rɒkwɜːk] [rok-uek], *s.* Grutesco, roca artificial, conjunto de piedras aseguradas con argamasa y dispuestas de modo que imitan una roca natural.

rocky ['rɒkɪ] [ro-ki], *a.* Peñascoso, roqueño, roquero, formado de rocas, lleno de rocas; duro, endurecido. **The Rocky Mountains,** las Montañas Rocosas.

rococo [rəʊˈkəʊkəʊ] [rou-kou-kou], *a. y s.* Churrigueresco; estilo arquitectónico en que abundan los adornos con profusión excesiva y de mal gusto.

rod [rɒd] [rod], *s.* 1. Varilla, vara, caña, rama pequeña de una planta leñosa; bastón (stick);·de aquí, disciplina, corrección; dominación, poder. **Angling-rod,** caña de pescar. **Curtain-rod,** varilla de cortina. 2. Vara de medir; pértica, medida de dieciseis pies y medio o poco más de cinco metros; vara de alguacil o de otro cargo análogo. 3. *(Mec.)* Vástago, barra, varilla, vara que forma parte de una máquina. 4. Varillas. 5. Uno de los cuerpos microscópicos parecidos a varillas que se hallan en la retina. 6. Línea particular de alcurnia o linaje; raza, tribu. **Black-rod,** nombre que se da al ujier de la cámara de los pares de Inglaterra. **Connecting rod,** biela. **Spare the rod and spoil the child,** quien bien te quiere te hará llorar. **To have a rod in pickle for someone,** guardársela a alguien. **To rule with a rod of iron,** gobernar con el palo, con mano de hierro. **To give the rod,** dar azotes, azotar.

rode [rəʊd] [roud], *pret.* de TO RIDE.

rodent ['rəʊdənt] [rou-dent], *a.* Roedor, que roe; perteneciente al orden zoológico de los roedores. *-s.* Roedor, animal del orden de los roedores.

rodeo ['rəʊdɪəʊ] [rou-diou], *s.* Rodeo, jaripeo.

rodomontade [‚rɒdəmɒnˈteɪd] [ro-do-mon-teid], *s.* Fanfarronada.

roe [rəʊ] [rou], *s.* 1. Corzo. 2. Hueva, huevecillos de los pescados.

roebuck ['rəʊbʌk] [rou-bak], **roe-deer** [rou-diaʳ], *s.* Corzo.

rogation [rəʊˈgeɪʃən] [rou-guei-shon], *s.* 1. Rogaciones, letanías en las procesiones de las cuatro témporas. 2. Proyecto de la ley presentado al pueblo romano. 3. Ruego, súplica. **Rogation-week,** semana de rogaciones.

rogue [rəʊg] [roug], *s.* 1. Bribón, pícaro, villano, ruin, vagabundo (knavish). 2. Perillán; voz familiar y cariñosa; tunante, astuto, travieso. **A cunning rogue, un** pícaro taimado. **To be a great rogue,** *(Fam.)* ser caña. **A thorough rogue,** pícaro de cuatro suelas. **Rogues' yarn,** *(Mar.)* hilo de ladrones. 3. *(Der. inglés)* Pordiosero, mendigo holgazán y robusto; vagabundo. 4. Elefante feroz y peligroso, separado del resto de la manada. **You rogue!,** ¡canalla!, ¡sinvergüenza!

roguery ['rəʊgərɪ] [rou-gue-ri], *s.* Picardía, travesura, retozo.

roguish ['rəʊgɪʃ] [rou-guish], *a.* 1. Pícaro, ruin, travieso, picaresco (mischievous). 2. Juguetón, chistoso. **Roguish eyes,** ojos picarescos, burlones, ojitos traviesos.

roguishly ['rəʊgɪʃlɪ] [rou-guish-li], *adv.* Pícaramente.

roguishness ['rəʊgɪʃnɪs] [rou-guish-nes], *s.* Picardía; ladronera, tunantada, bribonada; mala partida, partida de tuno. **The roguishness of his look,** lo picaresco, lo travieso d   e su mirada.

roil [rɔɪl] [roil], *va.* 1. Enturbiar, o espesar algo agitándolo; enlodar. 2. Vejar, irritar.

roister ['rɔɪstəʳ] [rois-taʳ], *vn.* Bravear, fanfarronear, echar bravatas. *-s.* Fanfarrón, baladrón.

role [rəʊl] [roul], *s.* Papel de un actor; funciones o carácter asumidos.

roll [rəʊl] [roul], *vn.* 1. Rodar, hacer rodar (drag along). 2. Volver, girar, voltear, dar vuelta o vueltas a alguna cosa (spin, turn). 3. Arrollar, fajar. 4. Rollar.. arrollar papel, cinta, tela, etc. 5. Laminar, pasar por el laminador; cilindrar, extender en rodillos. 6. Alisar, allanar por medio de un rodillo (de pastelero) o de un alisador. 7. Envolver (wrap). 8. Empujar o llevar hacia adelante sobre rodillos. 9. Dar de sí los sonidos musicales de una manera llena y creciente. -

vn. 1. Rodar, dar vueltas sobre el suelo o cualquier plano. 2. Volver, girar, rodar, andar o moverse alrededor o en torno, correr o moverse sobre ruedas; girar sobre un eje. 3. Revolver, revolverse; agitarse las olas. 4. Menear los ojos o moverlos de uno a otro lado. 5. Voltear o caer dando vueltas. 6. Ondear, ondular, moverse como las olas; moverse tumultuosamente, fluctuar, flotar sobre un mar agitado. 7. Retumbar, producir un sonido profundo y resonante, como el trueno. 8. Bambolearse, moverse de un lado a otro. 9. Arrollarse en forma de cilindro u ovillo; ser allanado, alisado o extendido con un rodillo. 10. Vivir con lujo; manar, tener abundancia de algo. 11. Dar un redoble de tambores. **To roll about/along,** rodar, divagar, andar de acá para allá. **To roll away,** quitar, separar, apartar. **To roll by,** pasar (procession). **To roll down,** bajar rodando una cuesta, una escalera, etc. **To roll in money,** nadar en dinero. **To roll off,** caer rodando. **To roll out,** sacar algo rodando (barrel). **To roll up,** rollar, arrollar; hacer un ovillo. **To roll a walk with a roller,** allanar la tierra con un rodillo.

roll, *s.* 1. Rodadura, la acción de rodar. 2. Rodador, lo que rueda o cae rodando. 3. Rollo de papel de cinta, de tabaco, etc., rodillo, cilindro de madera o metal; tela rollada en forma de cilindro. V. ROLLER. 4. Rollo o volumen; se dice de los libros de los antiguos por la figura que les daban. 5. Rol, lista, nómina, catálogo, matrícula (catalog, list). 6. Documentos públicos que han sido archivados, y a veces también se toma por los archivos donde se guardan. 7. Redoble (drums); retumbo del trueno (thunder). 8. Bamboleo. 9. Superficie ondeante, ondulante, como la del mar. 10 (*Arq.*) Roleo, voluta. 11. Bollo, mollete. **Master of the rolls,** la segunda dignidad judicial en Inglaterra. **French roll,** pan francés, panecillo. **Silver-smith's roll,** cilindro de escarchar. **To call the roll,** pasar lista. **To walk with a roll,** andar bamboleándose, dando tumbos. **To give a roll,** bambolearse, balancearse.

rollaway ['rəʊləweɪ] *sf.* (*E.U.*) **Rollaway-bed,** cama abatible.

roll call ['rəʊlkɔːl] [roul-kol], *s.* Lista, pase de lista.

roller ['rəʊləʳ] [rou-laʳ], *s.* 1. Rodillo, cilindro que rueda para disminuir la fricción; cilindro muy pesado para allanar la tierra. 2. Venda, faja. 3. Rodillo, alisador, palo redondo que usan algunos menestrales para alisar, pulir, estirar. 4. (*Mar.*) Polines, roletes, liana. 5. Ola larga y creciente.

roller bearing ['rəʊlə'beərɪŋ] [rou-la-bea-rin], *s.* Cojinete de rodillos.

roller coaster ['rəʊlə'kəʊstəʳ] [rou-la-kous-taʳ], *s.* Montaña rusa.

roller skate ['rəʊləˈskeɪt] [rou-la-skeit], *s.* Patín de ruedas.

roller towel ['rəʊlə'taʊəl] [rou-la-taual], *s.* Toalla sin fin.

rollick ['rɒlɪk] [ro-lik], *vn.* Travesear, moverse con aire retozón; portarse indolente y jovialmente.

rollicking ['rɒlɪkɪŋ] [ro-li-kin], *ger.* y *a.* Que se mueve de una manera negligente o fanfarrona; jovial; juguetón, travieso.

rolling ['rəʊlɪŋ] [rou-lin], *a.* y *ger.* de TO ROLL. 1. Rodadero, rodadizo; que rueda, que da vueltas. 2. Undulado, entrecortado por colinas y valles. 3. Vuelto hacia atrás o hacia abajo como lo que está bajo un rodillo. -*s.* Rodadura, movimiento de lo que rueda; acto de rodar o de la persona que emplea una herramienta de laminar. **Rolling prairies,** praderadas entrecortadas, ondulantes. **Rolling-mill,** (a) establecimiento para hacer láminas, barras, rieles o varillas de metal, trabajándolo entre pares de cilindros. (b) Laminador, máquina para laminar los metales. **Rolling-plant,** (a) V. **Rolling-stock. Rolling-pin,** rodillo de pastelero. **Rolling-stock,** material rodante, el conjunto de locomotoras, coches, vagones, carros, etc., de un ferrocarril. **Rolling stone,** rodillo de piedra para allanar la tierra, canto rodante. **Rolling-tackle,** (*Mar.*) Aparejo de rolín.

roll-top desk ['rəʊltɒp‚desk] [roul-top-desk], *s.* Escritorio con tapa corrediza.

roly-poly ['rəʊlɪ'pəʊlɪ] [rou-li-pou-li], *a.* Rechoncho, gordiflón. -*s.* 1. Pudín en forma de rollo, cocido o sometido a la acción del vapor. 2. (*Fam.*) Persona gordinflona.

ROM *Abreviatura de* **Read-Only-Memory,** memoria de sola lectura (*Inform.*).

romaic [rəʊ'meɪk] [rou-meik], *a.* Romaico, perteneciente al idioma o al pueblo griego moderno, o característico de ellos.

romaine [rəʊ'meɪn] [rou-mein], *s.* (*E.U.*) Romana. **Romaine lettuce,** lechuga romana.

roman ['rəʊmən] [rou-man], *a.* 1. Romano, relativo a Roma o a los romanos. 2. Semejante a un romano por su carácter; noble, valeroso; también, austero, severo. 3. Católico romano, papal. **Roman letter, Roman type,** letra romana, tipo romano, forma ordinaria de caracteres de imprenta. **Roman candle,** candela romana, pieza de fuegos artificiales.

romance [rəʊ'mæns] [rou-mans], *a.* Romance; se aplica a cada una de las lenguas modernas derivadas del latín popular, entre las cuales se distinguen el español, el italiano y el francés.

romance, *s.* Romance; ficción, cuento, fábula (tale); romanza (*Mús.*). **The romance of history,** lo atractivo de la historia. **The romance of the sea,** el encanto del mar.

romance, *vn.* Mentir; fingir fábulas.

romancer [rəʊ'mænsəʳ] [rou-man-saʳ], *s.* 1. Romancero, el que compone romances. 2. Mentiroso, chismeador, chismoso.

romancist [rəʊ'mænsɪst] [rou-man-sist], *s.* Romancero, escritor de romances.

romanesque [‚rɒmə'nesk] [rou-ma-nesk], *a.* 1. Romanesco, románico; se dice de cierto estilo de arquitectura caracterizado por el arco redondo y por su general solidez. 2. Romance; se dice en particular del provenzal.

romanist [rəʊ'mænɪst] [rou-ma-nist], *s.* y *a.* Un católico romano.

romantic [rəʊ'mæntɪk] [rou-man-tik], *a.* 1. Quijotesco: se dice del modo, porte ridículo o empeños extravagantes de alguno. 2. Romántico, novelesco, que pertenece a los romances y novelas; extravagante, improbable, ridículo. 3. Encantado: se dice de los sitios amenos y deliciosos. 4. Fabuloso, fingido, de novela, de cuento.

romantically [rəʊ'mæntɪkəlɪ] [rou-man-ti-ka-li], *adv.* Estravagantemente, ridículamente.

romanticism [rəʊ'mæntɪsɪzəm] [rou-man-ti-si-sem], *s.* Romanticismo.

romanticist [rəʊ'mæntɪsɪst] [rou-man-ti-sist], *a.* Romántico.

romanticize [rəʊ'mæntɪsaɪz] [rou-man-ti-sais], *vt.* Romantizar, hacer romántico.

romish ['rəʊmɪʃ] [rou-mish], *a.* 1. Romano, que pertenece a los romanos. 2. Romano, que pertenece al Papa o a la Iglesia católica.

romp [rɒmp] [romp], *s.* 1. La muchacha retozona que es amiga de juguetear con descompostura. 2. El retozo descompuesto y poco modesto.

romp, *vn.* Retozar, brincar o juguetear descompuestamente.

rompers ['rɒmpəz] [rom-pars], *s. pl.* Mameluco, trajecito de niño de una sola pieza en forma de pantalón.

rompish ['rɒmpɪʃ] [rom-pish], *a.* Inclinado a retozos o juegos poco modestos.

rondeau ['rɒndəʊ] [ron-dou], *s.* 1. Redondilla. 2. (*Mús.*) Rondó.

rondo ['rɒndəʊ] [ron-dou], *s.* 1. (*Mús.*) Rondó, cierta composición musical. 2. Redondilla.

rood [ruːd] [rud], *s.* 1. La santa cruz o el crucifijo. 2. Un cuarto de acre cuadrado. 3. Pértica. V. ROD. **Rood-screen,** gloria, mampara del presbiterio. **Roodloft,** crucero.

roof [ruːf] [ruf], *s.* 1. Tejado, techado, techo de bóveda; (*Poet.*) bóveda, cielo (sky). 2. Paladar, la parte interior y superior de la boca. 3. Imperial de un coche o diligencia. 4.

Casa, hogar, habitación (room). **Rooftree,** cumbrera, maderamen de techo; el techo mismo. **Flat roof,** azotea; techo casi horizontal. **Gambrel roof,** techo a la holandesa. **Mansard roof,** techo aboardillado, a la francesa. **Slate roof,** techo de pizarras. **Tile roof,** tejado, techo cubierto de tejas. **To live under the same roof,** vivir bajo el mismo techo. **To raise the roof,** poner el grito en el cielo (as a protest).

roof, *va.* 1. Techar, cubrir con techo. 2. Encerrar en una casa; abrigar, alojar. **The house is roofed in wood,** la casa tiene techo de madera.

roof garden [ˈruːfˌɡɑːdn] [ruf-gar-den], *s.* Azotea con jardín.

rooftile [ˈruːftaɪl] [ruf-tail], *s.* Teja, cobija.

roofed [ˈruːft] [ruft], **roofy** [ˈruːfɪ] [ru-fi], *a.* Techado.

roofing [ˈruːfɪŋ] [ru-fin], *sf.* Techumbre.

roofless [ˈruːflɪs] [ruf-les], *a.* Sin techo.

rook [rʊk] [ruk], *s. (Orn.)* 1. Corneja de pico blanco. 2. Roque, torre, pieza del juego de ajedrez. 3. *(Des.)* Trampista, tramposo, fullero.

rookery [ˈrʊkərɪ] [ru-ke-ri], *s.* 1. Los árboles donde hacen sus nidos muchas cornejas. 2. Nido de las aves marinas; lugar donde anualmente se reúnen las focas para procrear. 3. Alojamiento viejo y en mal estado; también, vecindario bajo, vil.

rooky [ˈrʊkɪ] [ru-ki], *a.* Habitado por cornejas.

room [rʊm] [rum], *vn. (Fam.)* Habitar ciertas piezas, alojarse. *-s.* 1. Lugar, paraje, sitio (place). 2. Lugar, el espacio que ocupa cualquier cuerpo; puesto. 3. Lugar, causa, motivo, razón para hacer o no hacer una cosa (reason). 4. Lugar, tiempo, ocasión, oportunidad (chance, opportunity). 5. Cuarto, aposento, cámara, pieza de una casa. **The next room,** la pieza inmediata. **A front room,** aposento o cuarto a la calle. **A back room,** cuarto o pieza interior. **State-room,** *(Mar.)* camarotes principales; pañol. **There is no room for your horse,** no hay cabida para el caballo en este sitio. **There is no room for doubt,** no deja lugar a dudas *(Fig.).* **There is room for one,** hay sitio para una persona. **To give room,** hacer lugar, retirarse, dar puesto. **To make room,** abrir paso, hacer lugar, despejar la vía. **There is no room for doubt,** no hay duda posible. **Dining-room,** comedor. **Drawing-room,** salón. **Room temperature,** temperatura ambiente. **Room-mate,** compañero de cuarto; la persona que habita un cuarto con otra u otras. **Room clerk,** recepcionista (in a hotel).

roomer [ˈrʊmər] [ru-ma'], *s.* Inquilino en un cuarto.

rooming house [ˈrʊmɪŋˌhaʊs] [ru-min-jaus], *s.* Casa de huéspedes.

roomy [ˈrʊmɪ] [ru-mi], *a.* Espacioso, dilatado, capaz.

roost [ruːst] [rust], *s.* 1. Pértiga de gallinero; de aquí, cualquier lugar provisional de descanso. **Henroost,** gallinero. 2. Sueño, descanso, reposo, hablando de las aves domésticas. 3. *(E. U.)* Perchada, reunión de aves perchadas en un mismo sitio. **To rule the roost,** dominar, mandar, como el gallo de pelea sobre los otros.

roost, *vn.* 1. Dormir o descansar las aves en una pértiga. 2. *(Fest.)* Estar alojado en alguna parte. **To come home to roost,** no hay deuda que no se pague.

rooster [ˈruːstər] [rus-ta'], *s.* Gallo, el macho de las aves domésticas o de corral.

root [ruːt] [rut], *s.* 1. Raíz de los árboles y plantas. 2. Raíz, la parte inferior o el pie de cualquiera cosa. 3. Raíz, origen, principio de donde procede una cosa; estirpe, tronco, el fundador de una familia. 4. *(Gram.)* Raíz, voz primitiva o lo que queda de ella, después de quitarle los prefijos y subfijos. 5. Raíz: metafísicamente hablando se dice de las pasiones o afectos que están profundamente fijos en el alma. 6. *(Arit.)* Raíz, número que multiplicado por sí mismo produce la potencia. **Roots,** raíces: se da este nombre genérico más particularmente a las plantas de las cuales se come la parte que está bajo tierra. 7. *(Mús.)* Base, nota fundamental. 8. Raigón (de diente). **Root-stock,** rizoma. **Cube root,** raíz cúbica. **To take root o strike root,** echar raíces, arraigarse. **The root of all evil,** la raíz, el origen de

todos los males. **Root cause,** causa primordial. **Root sign,** raíz *(Mat.).*

root, *vn.* y *va.* 1. Arraigar, echar o criar raíces. 2. Hozar, levantar la tierra con el hocico. 3. Arraigarse o afianzarse alguna planta en la tierra. 4. Arraigarse, inveterarse los males, vicios, etc. 5. Arraigarse, echar raíces en el alma o hacer en ella una impresión profunda alguna pasión o afecto; imprimir, grabar profundamente. 6. Estar establecido, fijo en alguna parte. **To root about/around,** hocicar (animal), investigar (person). **To root for,** gritar por, apoyar a. **To root through,** explorar, examinar *(Fig.).* **To root up o out,** arrancar de raíz, desarraigar; extinguir, extirpar; desterrar.

root beer [ˈruːtˌbɪər] [rut-bia'], *s.* Cerveza de baja graduación alcohólica hecha de raíces.

rooted [ˈruːtɪd] [ru-tid], *a.* Radical; arraigado.

rootedly [ˈruːtɪdlɪ] [ru-tid-li], *adv.* Radicalmente; fijamente.

rootlet [ˈruːtlɪt] [rut-let], *s. dim.* Raicilla, radícula.

rooter [ˈruːtər] [ru-ta'], *s.* 1. El o lo que desarraiga, y hoza como un puerco o jabalí; el que arranca de raíz. 2. *(Ger.)* El que anima por medio de aplausos; aplaudidor.

rooty [ˈruːtɪ] [ru-ti], *a.* 1. Lleno de raíces. 2. Parecido a raíces.

rope [rəʊp] [roup], *s.* 1. Soga, cuerda, cordel, maroma. 2. Sarta, ristra, trenza; hilera, fila. **Rope of onions,** ristra de cebollas. **Ropes of a ship,** *(Mar.)* jarcia, cordaje. **Rope's end,** chicote de cabo. **Entering-rope,** guardamancebo del portalón. **Bolt-rope,** relinga. **Buoy-rope,** orinque. **Guest-rope,** guía de falsa amarra. **Rope-yard,** cordelería. **To be at the end of one's rope,** quedarse en la calle, estar sin recursos. **Rope-bands,** *pl. (Mar.)* envergues. **Rope-dancer,** volatín, bailarín de cuerda. **Rope-ladder,** escala de cuerdas. **Rope-maker,** cordelero, soguero. **Rope's-end,** castigar, golpeando con un cabo de cuerda. **Rope-work,** obra, trabajo hecho de cuerdas. **To know the ropes,** saber cuántas son cinco; entender bien un asunto.

rope, *va.* 1. Atar, amarrar o unir por medio de una cuerda. 2. Rodear con soga (como un circo o arena). 3. *(E. U.)* Coger con un lazo. *-vn.* Hacer hebras o madeja. **To rope in,** *(Ger. E. U.)* atraer a una empresa, engañar con arte y maña. **To rope off,** acordonar. **To rope up,** cordar.

ropemaker [ˈrəʊpˌmeɪkər] [roup-meika'], *s.* Cordelero.

rope-trick [ˈrəʊptrɪk] [roup-trik], *s.* Cualquier juego de manos que se ejecuta con cuerdas. 2. *(Des.)* Picardía o villanía que merece la horca.

ropewalk [ˈrəʊpwɔːk] [roup-uok], *s.* Cordelería, soguería. **Rope-walker,** volatinero, persona que con habilidad y arte anda y voltea por el aire sobre una maroma.

ropeyarn [ˈrəʊpjɑːn] [roup-yarn], *s. (Mar.)* Filástica.

ropiness [ˈrəʊpɪnɪs] [rou-pi-nes], *s.* Viscosidad; tenacidad.

ropish [ˈrəʊpɪʃ] [rou-pish], **ropy** [ˈrəʊpɪ] [rou-pi], *a.* Viscoso, pegajoso, glutinoso.

rosary [ˈrəʊzərɪ] [rou-sa-ri], *s.* 1. Rosario. 2. Rosario, rezo de este nombre. 3. Guirnalda o corona de rosas; de aquí, colección de piezas literarias escogidas. 4. Cuadro de rosas; jardín de rosales.

rose [rəʊz] [rous], *pret.* de TO RISE.

rose, *s.* 1. Rosal, planta que produce las rosas; género, tipo de las rosáceas. 2. Rosa, flor del rosal. 3. Color de rosa. 4. Lo que tiene alguna semejanza a una rosa; rosa, roseta, lazo de cintas para adorno; *(Arq.)* rosetón; el remate circular y lleno de orificios del caño de una regadera. **Honey of roses,** miel rosada. **Rose-bush,** *(Bot.)* rosal. **Every rose has its thorn,** *(Prov.)* a cada gusto su susto; o no hay rosa sin espinas. **Dog-rose,** agavanzo, escaramujo, rosal silvestre. Se llama también **wild brier. Bengal o monthly rose,** rosa de China; rosa de todo el año. **Tea-rose, tea-scented rose,** cualquiera de las numerosas variedades de rosas con fragancia semejante a la de la rosa de té. **Wild rose,** rosal silvestre. **Under the rose,** bajo cuerda, secretamente. **Rose-beetle, rose-bug, rose-chafer,** varios escarabajos o insectos coleópteros dañinos a los rosales. **Rose-window,** ventana con florón o rosetón.

roseate ['rəʊzɪɪt] [rou-siit], a. Rosado, róseo.

rosebud ['rəʊzbʌd] [rous-bad], s. 1. Capullo de rosa. 2. Una joven en la flor de su juventud.

rosemary ['rəʊzmərɪ] [rous-ma-ri], s. *(Bot.)* Romero, rosmarino, arbusto aromático de la famlia de las labiadas, con flores azules.

roset ['rəʊzet] [rou-set], s. Rosicler, el color encendido parecido al de la rosa encarnada.

rosette ['rəʊzɪɪt] [rou-sit], s. 1. Rosa, roseta, lazo de cintas que sirve de adorno o de distintivo; rosetón, adorno de arquitectura. 2. Cosa semejante a una rosa.

rosewater ['rəʊzˌwɔːtəʳ] [rous-uo-taʳ], s. Agua rosada, agua de rosas.

rosewood ['rəʊzwʊd] [rous-vud], s. palo de rosa: árbol del género Dalbergia.

rosin ['rɒzɪn] [ro-sin], s. 1. Trementina, resina que despide el pino. 2. *V.* RESIN.

rosin, va. Dar con resina.

roster ['rɒstəʳ] [ros-taʳ], s. 1. Escalafón, registro de personal. 2. Lista, nómina, matrícula. 3. *(Mil.)* Lista de deberes, orden de prestar servicio.

rostral ['rɒstrəl] [ros-tral], a. Rostral, perteneciente a un pico o rostro de ave, o a un espolón; *(Zool.)* que tiene rostro.

rostrate ['rɒstreɪt] [ros-treit], a. Adornado con espolones de galeras u otros buques.

rostrum ['rɒstrəm] [ros-trom], s. 1. Tribuna, plataforma desde donde habla un orador, o el que preside; los oradores colectivamente. 2. La tribuna en que arengaban los oradores romanos. 3. Rostro, el pico del ave; hocico; parte sobresaliente. 4. *(Mar.)* Rostro, la punta de la proa o del espolón que sobresale. 5. Cañón del alambique.

rosy ['rəʊzɪ] [rou-si], a. 1. Róseo, rosado, de rosa; sonrojado, que se sonroja. 2. *(Fig.)* Glorioso, agradable, lisonjero, optimista. 3. Rosado, que está compuesto de rosas. **Rosy cheeks,** mejillas sonrosadas. **Rosy-fingered,** con dedos de rosa; epíteto homérico de la aurora. **Rosy-hued,** rosado, color de rosa, con tez rosada.

rot [rɒt] [rot], vn. 1. Pudrirse o podrirse; corromperse, echarse a perder, malearse. 2. Padecer de morriña las ovejas. 3. Corromperse moralmente. 4. Irse consumiendo poco a poco; estar estancado; ir a menos. -va. 1. Pudrir, resolver en poder. 2. Enriar. *V.* RET. **To rot away,** corromperse, descomponerse.

rot, s. 1. Putrefacción, podre, podredumbre. 2. Enfermedad que agota, como las de los pulmones; morriña, una enfermedad que da a las ovejas. 3. *(Bot.)* Enfermedad de las plantas, causado por los hongos y las bacterias. 4. *(Ger.)* Borricada, dicho tonto, opinión necia. **It has rot,** está podrido. **Don't talk rot!,** ¡no digas burradas!

rota ['rəʊtə] [rou-ta], s. 1. Rol, nómina, lista de nombres que indica el orden y clase de sus deberes. *V.* ROSTER. 2. Orden de los deberes u obligaciones de uno, rutina.

Rotary ['rəʊtərɪ] [rou-ta-ri], a. Giratorio, rotante, que rueda o da vueltas como una rueda. **Rotary club,** club rotario. **Rotary press,** máquina rotativa.

rotate ['rəʊteɪt] [rou-teit], va. y vn. 1. Girar, dar vueltas, o hacer rodar sobre un eje (to gyrate, revolve, rotate). 2. Alternar, cambiar, como las cosechas, los funcionarios, etc.; desamelgar un terreno. -a. 1. *(Bot.)* Rotante en forma de rueda, como la corola de ciertas flores; de venas, en posición radial. 2. *(Ento.)* Que forma círculo alrededor de una parte.

rotating ['rəʊteɪtɪŋ] [rou-tei-tin], a. Rotativo, giratorio.

rotation [rəʊ'teɪʃən] [rou-tei-shon], s. Rotación, turno, alternativa, vicisitud. **In rotation o by rotation,** por turno, alternativamente. **Rotation of crops,** desamelgamiento, rotación de las cosechas.

rotative ['rəʊtətɪv] [rou-ta-tiv], **rotatory** ['rəʊtətərɪ] [rou-ta-to-ri], a. 1. Rotante, rotatorio, que está en rotación o que la causa. 2. *(Rotatory)* Alternativo, sucesivo.

rotator [rəʊ'teɪtəʳ] [rou-tei-taʳ], s. 1. Lo que causa rotación; músculo rotador. 2. Hélice.

rote [rəʊt] [rout], s. Las palabras aprendidas sólo por rutina, por repetición rutinaria. **To learn by rote,** aprender de memoria, como el papagayo.

rotiform ['rəʊtɪfɔːm] [rou-ti-form], a. Rotifome, en forma de rueda.

rotor ['rəʊtəʳ] [rou-taʳ], s. Rotor, indicador giratorio. **Rotor, hub,** cubo de rotor.

rotten ['rɒtn] [ro-ten], a. 1. Podrido, corrompido; endeble. 2. Cariado. 3. Fétido, hediondo. 4. Malo, abdominable, desagradable, ofensivo. **Rotten egg,** huevo empollado. **Rotten trick,** acción de pícaro.

rottenness ['rɒtnnɪs] [ro-ten-nes], s. 1. Podredumbre, putrefacción, corrupción. 2. Mala calidad o estado.

rotten-stone ['rɒtnˌstəʊn] [ro-ten-stoun], s. Trípol o trípoli (tierra podrida), substancia usada para pulir.

rotter ['rɒtəʳ] [ro-taʳ], s. Persona indeseable, sinvergüenza, gandul (idling, loafing).

rotund [rəʊ'tʌnd] [rou-tand], a. 1. Rotundo (language). 2. Redondo, circular, esférico, orbicular.

rotunda [rəʊ'tʌndə] [rou-tan-da], s. *(Arq.)* Rotonda, rotunda, salon o edificio circular que generalmente tiene cúpula.

rotundity [rəʊ'tʌndɪtɪ] [rou-tan-di-ti], s. 1. Rotundidad. 2. Redondez, esfericidad. 3. Objeto o protuberancia redondos.

rouble ['ruːbl] [ru-bel], s. *V.* RUBLE.

rouge [ruːʒ] [rush], s. 1. El encarnado, el color encarnado. 2. Arrebol, colorete, aceite que se ponen en el rostro las mujeres. 3. Azafrán de Marte, rojo de joyero para pulir. *V.* CROCUS. -a. Colorado, encarnado.

rouge, va. y vn. Arrebolarse, afeitarse, darse la cara con arrebol o colorete, o tenerla compuesta con este aceite; pulir con azafrán de Marte.

rough [rʌf] [raf], a. 1. Áspero, tosco, escabroso (harsh, sour): se dice de lo que no está llano, liso o igual en la superficie; erizado; peludo, encrespado; desgreñado, mal peinado. 2. Tosco o áspero al tacto. 3. Áspero, acerbo o agrio al gusto. 4. Bronco, ingrato al oído. 5. Áspero, escabroso (roads, paths). 6. Duro, cruel, severo, áspero de genio, desapacible, rígido. 7. Bruto, tosco, inculto, grosero, brusco, insolente, arrogante. 8. Tempestuoso, borrascoso, agitado, alborotado (sea). 9. Formado o ejecutado deprisa, no acabado; aproximativo, general. **Rough diamond,** diamante en bruto. **Rough wine,** vino áspero. **Rough sea,** mar alborotado. **Rough wind,** viento borrascoso. **Rough words,** palabras duras y chocantes. **A rough sketch,** boceto, bosquejo. **A rough guess,** una valuación aproximada. **Rough with prickles,** erizado de púas. **A dog with rough hair,** un perro de pelo encrespado. **At a rough guess,** a ojo de buen cubero. -s. 1. Estado tosco, en bruto, no pulido o mal acabado. 2. Vista general, aproximada. 3. Pillo, alborotador. 3. Matón, bravucón. *V.* RUFFIAN. **Rough-draft, draught,,** bosquejo, boceto.

rough, va. 1. Hacer, poner áspero, tosco, escabroso. 2. Labrar imperfectamente. **To rough-draw,** bosquejar, trazar rudamente. **To rough-hew,** formar el modelo tosco de alguna cosa; desbastar, cortar toscamente sin allanar. **To rough it,** pasar trabajos, vivir en duras condiciones. **To rough-dry,** secar, enjugar (de prisa y corriendo) sin planchar. **Rough-rider,** 1. Jinete que cabalga de una manera descuidada. 2. Escudero instructor, el que adiestra los caballos. **Rough-shod,** herrado con herraduras para el hielo (es decir, con clavos); se halla a menudo en la locución, **To ride rough-shod,** ir en derechura al grano, conducirse de una manera imperiosa.

roughage ['rʌfɪdʒ] [ra-fich], s. 1. Forraje o alimento áspero de difícil digestión. 2. Material tosco o grosero.

rough-and-ready ['rʌfən'redɪ] [raf-an-re-di], a. 1. Tosco de maneras pero de eficaz acción. 2. Decidido, activo pero poco fino.

rough-and-tumble ['rʌfən'tʌmbl] [raf-an-tam-bel], a. 1. Rudo y desordenado pero resistente. 2. Accidentado, borrascoso. 3. Pelea violenta sin sujeción a reglas.

roughcast ['rʌfkɑːst] [raf-kast], va. Hacer alguna cosa toscamente, bosquejar una figura o cuadro.

roughcast, s. 1. Modelo en bruto. 2. Revoque tosco; mezcla o mortero grueso.

roughen ['rʌfn] [ra-fen], va. Poner áspero. -vn. Volverse rudo.

rough-hewn ['rʌf'hju:n] [raf-jiun], *a.* Desbastado, mal acabado; a menudo en sentido figurado; rudo, tosco, de modales groseros.

roughly ['rʌflɪ] [raf-li], *adv.* Ásperamente, rudamente, tempestuosamente, desapaciblemente, desagradablemente.

roughness ['rʌfnɪs] [raf-nes], *s.* 1. Aspereza, rudeza, tosquedad, desigualdad (de la superficie). 2. Severidad, dureza (en la disciplina). 3. Grosería de modales o de conducta; rudeza de genio, calidad de brusco. 4. Calidad de lo que está mal acabado o no trabajado. 5. Tempestad, tormenta.

roughride ['rʌfraɪd] [raf-raid], *v.* 1. Domar caballos. 2. Dominar, imponerse.

roughrider ['rʌfraɪdəʳ] [raf-rai-daʳ], *s.* 1. Domador de caballos.

roulette [ru:'let] [ru-let], *s.* 1. Ruleta, cierto juego de azar. 2. Roleta, disco de acero templado de que usan los grabadores.

round ['raʊnd] [raund], *a.* 1. Redondo, circular, cilíndrico, esférico (spherical). 2. Que tiene superficie curva; no angular ni plano; convexo o cóncavo. 3. Lleno, hablando de los períodos; fácil, cuando se trata del estilo. 4. Redondo, cabal, sin picos ni quebrados, hablando de cuentas o de números. 5. Grande, cuantioso; liberal, amplio. 6. Franco, claro, sincero, liso, llano, ingenuo. 7. Cómodo en el andar, vivo, veloz, acelerado. 8. De cadencia llena, de tono sonoro. 9. Franco, justo, honrado. 10. Semicircular, o caracterizado por el arco semicircular. **A round assertion**, una afirmación rotunda, clara y positiva. **To make round**, redondear, dar figura redonda. **A round fee**, gajes u honorarios amplios, generosos. **To bring up with a round turn**, oligar a hacer una parada repentina. -*s.* 1. Círculo, orbe, esfera, redondez. 2. Vuelta, giro, rotación, revolución. 3. Paso, escalón, peldaño, uno de los palos atravesados en una escalera portátil. 4. (*Mil.*) Ronda. 5. Andanada de cañones; salva, descarga de muchas armas de fuego a un tiempo, tiro, descarga, una sola carga de municiones de guerra. 6. Ruta, camino, circuito. 7. Rutina, serie de movimientos repetidos. 8. Un baile. 9. Redondilla, canción corta, compuesta de modo que produce un efecto armónico al cantarla varias voces que empiezan a intervalos sucesivos. 10. Tajada redonda de carne de buey. **In the whole round of our life**, en todo el curso de nuestra vida. **To go the rounds**, ir de ronda. **Everyone fired five rounds**, cada uno hizo cinco disparos. -*adv.* Circularmente, redondamente, en circunferencia; por todas partes, por todos lados. -*prep.* Alrededor de; en contorno. **Round the world**, por todo el mundo. **My head turns round**, se me va la cabeza. **To take a round**, dar una vuelta. **To go round**, andar alrededor. **All the year round**, todo el año.

round, *va.* 1. Cercar, rodear, ceñir, abrazar todo alrededor, dar vuelta una cosa alrededor de otra. 2. Redondear. 3. Moverse alrededor. 4. Relevar, fabricar alguna cosa en relieve o resalte. **To round in**, (*Mar.*) Halar en redondo. **To round up the beams**, volver para arriba los baos. -*vn.* 1. Redondearse, hacerse redondo. 2. Susurrar, hablar al oído, hablar quedo. 3. Rondar.

roundabout ['raʊndəbaʊt] [raund-abaut], *a.* Indirecto, vago, que hace rodeos; desviado. -*s.* 1. Chaqueta, chaleco. 2. Tío vivo. *V. Merry-go-round.* 3. Danza a la redonda.

roundelay ['raʊndɪleɪ] [raun-di-lei], *s.* 1. Una melodía sencilla. 2. Redondilla. 3. Baile en círculo, corro. 4. Bandeja o mesita redonda. 5. (*Arq.*) Ventaja, nicho o panel circular. **Roundel**, la figura redonda.

round-hand ['raʊndhænd] [raund-jand], *s.* Carácter de letra que suprime los ángulos, haciendo todos los trazos redondeados.

roundhead ['raʊndhed] [raund-jed], *s.* Cabeza redonda; apodo que se daba antiguamente a los puritanos en Inglaterra.

round-house ['raʊndhaʊs] [raund-jaus], *s.* 1. (*Mar.*) Toldilla, la cubierta superior de un navío en la parte de popa o la que cubre la cámara alta. 2. (*E. U.*) Rotunda, casa de máquinas, edificio semicircular para las locomotoras con una plataforma giratoria en su centro.

roundish ['raʊndɪʃ] [raun-dish], *a.* Algo o casi redondo.

roundly ['raʊndlɪ] [raund-li], *adv.* Redondamente; claramente, sin cumplimientos, abiertamente; francamente; absolutamente; ligeramente.

roundness ['raʊndnɪs] [raund-nes], *s.* Redondez; claridad, sinceridad, buena fe.

round-shouldered ['raʊnd'ʃəʊldəd] [raund-shoul-ded], *a.* Algo jorobado, cargado de espaldas.

round steak ['raʊndsti:k] [raund-steik], *s.* Bistec de mediana calidad.

round-up ['raʊndʌp] [raund-ap], *va.* Rodear, recoger los hatos en un rodeo. -*s.* Rodeo de hatos para marcarlos con hierro candente o para reunirlos.

rouse [raʊz] [raus], *va.* 1. Despertar, cortar el sueño, al que está durmiendo (wake up). 2. Despertar, hacer que uno vuelva sobre sí o recapacite; excitar, animar, poner en acción. 3. Levantar la caza, hacerla salir de su nido o cama. 4. (*Mar.*) Halar o arronzar un calabrote o cable. -*vn.* 1. Despertar, dejar de dormir. 2. Despertar, hacerse más advertido o avisado.

rouse, *s.* Tragazo, trago demasiado grande de licor.

rouser ['raʊzəʳ] [rau-saʳ], *s.* 1. Despertador, excitador. 2. (*Fam.*) bola, mentira, embuste. 3. Cosa sorprendente, admirable, estupenda.

roust [raʊst] [raust], *va.* (*Fam.*) Despertar y hacer huir (animals). -*vn.* Ser activo, moverse con energía.

roustabout ['raʊstəbaʊt] [raust-abaut], *s.* (*E.U. y Aus.*) Peón, trabajador de cubierta en los vapores de río; también, gañán.

rout [raʊt] [raut], *s.* 1. Rota, derrota de un ejército, huida en confusión. 2. Jabardo, jabardillo, garulla, chusma, junta o reunión de gente baja. 3. (*Ant.*) Tertulia, reunión de gente decente. 4. Clamor, griterío. 5. Séquito.

rout, *va.* 1. Derrotar, vencer y poner en confusión, hacer huir, destruir. 2. Arrojar, sacar o hacer salir con violencia, como de un retiro; con *out,* por lo común. **To rout out**, poner al descubierto; hacer salir a la fuerza: **to rout one out of the bed**, arrancar a uno de la cama.

route [ru:t] [rut], *s.* 1. Ruta, itinerario, derrota. 2. Camino, carretera. 3. Rumbo. 4. Trazado. -*va.* 1. Enrumbar, encaminar. 2. Predisponer.

routine ['ru:ti:n] [ru-tin], *a.* 1. Rutinario. 2. Rutinero. 3. Soso, insulso. 4. Mediano, regular.

routine, *s.* Rutina, serie de actos prescritos o habituales; costumbre, estilo o hábito adquirido por mera práctica.

rove [rəʊv] [rouv], *va.* Corretear (to walk around, ramble). -*vn.* 1. Vagar, vaguear, errar, correr acá y acullá. 2. Disparar una especie de flecha que los ingleses llaman *rover.* **To rove about the seas**, piratear.

rove, *va.* (*Art. y Of.*) 1. Unir y alargar las madejas, torcer el hilo antes de encanillarlo, pasándolo entre pares de cilindros arrolladores. 2. Enhebrar, pasar por un ojo o agujero; pasar una cuerda por una polea.

rove, *s.* 1. Madeja de lana tirada. 2. Anillo de metal que se usa como remache de clavo en la construcción de barcos. 3. Correría, acto de correr acá y acullá.

rover ['rəʊvəʳ] [rou-vaʳ], *s.* 1. Errante, andorrero, tunante, vago, vagabundo. 2. Veleta, la persona inconstante y mudable. 3. Ladrón, pirata. 4. Una especie de flecha.

roving ['rəʊvɪŋ] [rou-vin], *s.* Primera torsión que se da a un hilo de algodón, lana, etc. -*a.* Errante, vagabundo. 2. **Roving frame**, mechera en fino.

row [raʊ] [rau], *s.* 1. Hilera, fila, línea. 2. Paseo en lancha o bote. 3. Riña, pelotera, alboroto.

row, *vn.* (*Mar.*) Remar, trabajar con el remo. -*va.* Bogar, conducir remando: pasear por agua. **Rowboat**, bote, lancha, barca de remos. **Row-lock**, chumacera, escalamera.

row, *vn.* Pelearse, armar un zipizape, tomar parte en un *s.* Camorra, zipizape; zambra, quimera, alboroto.

rowdy ['raʊdɪ] [rau-di], *s. y a.* Pillo, pelafustán, quimerista, alborotador. (*Méx.*) Lepero, pelagatos, canalla.

rowdyism ['raʊdrɪzəm] [rau-dii-sem], *s.* Pillería, pelagatería; alboroto.

rowen [ˈraʊɪn] [rauin], *s.* 1. Segunda cosecha en el mismo campo. 2. *(Prov.) pl.* Campo que queda en rastrojo para dar pastos en el otoño.

rower [ˈraʊəʳ] [rauaʳ], *s.* Remero, bogador.

royal [ˈrɔɪəl] [roial], *a.* 1. Real, que pertenece a un rey o monarca (regal, kingly). 2. Regio, majestuoso, magnífico, noble, magnánimo, ilustre. 3. De calidad o tamaño superior. 4. Eminentemente agradable o primoroso. **We had a royal time**, nos divertimos en grande. *-s.* 1. Un tamaño de papel; es de 19 por 24 pulgadas para escribir y de 20 por 25 para imprenta. 2. *(Mar.)* Juanete, la vela más alta. 3. Mogote de ciervo.

royalism [ˈrɔɪəlɪzəm] [roia-li-sem], *s.* Realismo, monarquismo.

royalist [ˈrɔɪəlɪst] [roia-list], *s.* Realista, partidario de los reyes.

royally [ˈrɔɪəlɪ] [roia-li], *adv.* Regiamente, a lo regio, a manera de rey; magníficamente, noblemente.

royalty [ˈrɔɪəltɪ] [roial-ti], *s.* 1. Realeza, soberanía, dignidad real; majestad real. 2. Los emblemas de la soberanía, que se expresan metafóricamente por las palabras corona y cetro. 3. Regalía, parte de las utilidades que paga el editor, fabricante, etc., al autor, inventor o propietario que se han reservado ciertos privilegios. 4. Derechos, regalías, prerrogativas reales.

rub [rʌb] [rab], *va.* 1. Estregar, fregar, limpiar, frotar, rascando o estregando una cosa con otra (to scrub, scour). 2. Rozar, tocar ligeramente dos cosas entre sí. 3. Rascar, frotar con las uñas u otra cosa la piel. 4. Raspar, raer un papel, una lámina, etc. 5. Inquietar, incomodar, fastidiar. *-vn.* 1. Estregarse o frotarse dos cosas entre sí. 2. Desenredarse, salir o librarse de algún peligro o enredo, adelantarse con dificultad. 3. Producir un efecto mental, particularmente un efecto duro o penoso; hastiar, molestar.

rub away, continuar frotando o estregando; quitar frotando.

rub along/on, ir viviendo con trabajo: salir de apuros.

rub down a horse, limpiar un caballo.

rub in, hacer penetrar en los poros frotando o refregando; *(Fam.)* reiterar, insitir demasiado.

rub off, quitar; limpiar una cosa estregándola con otra.

rub out, borrar. **To rub the wrong way**, frotar a contrapelo; de aquí causar irritación, contradecir, incomodar.

rub up, aguijonear, excitar, animar; retocar, repasar, pulir, pulimentar.

rub, *s.* 1. Frotamiento, ludimiento, colisión de dos cuerpos uno con otro. 2. Estregamiento, estregadura. 3. Tropiezo, embarazo, obstáculo, dificultad. 4. Sarcasmo, denuesto; algo que ofende el amor propio.

rubbish [ˈrʌbɪʃ] [ra-bish], *s.* Escombro, ripio, rudera, broza, ruinas; morralla, desecho, zupia, desperdicio; andrajos.

rubber [ˈrʌbəʳ] [ra-baʳ], *a.* Hecho de caucho o goma elástica. **Rubber cloth**, tela revestida de caucho. **Rubber dam**, hoja de caucho de que se sirven los dentistas para mantener seca la cavidad de un diente. *-s.* 1. Caucho, hule, goma elástica (en Perú, jebe); se llama también, **Indian-rubber. Hard rubber**, vulcanita, caucho químicamente compuesto con azufre y expuesto a la acción del calor; substancia que tiene muchas aplicaciones. 2. El que estrega alguna cosa. 3. Rodilla, estropajo, aljofifa para estregar o limpiar; estregadera; escofina; cualquiera cosa con que se estrega, limpia, frota o raspa. 4. Partida en el juego llamado *whist.* **Rubber band**, bandita de goma elástica o de caucho. **Rubber heel**, tacón de goma o de caucho.

rubberize [ˈrʌbəraɪz] [ra-ba-rais], *va.* Engomar, encauchar, impregnar con goma o caucho, p. ej. la seda.

rubbers [ˈrʌbəz] [ra-bars], *s. pl.* Zapatos de goma o de caucho.

rubber stamp [ˌrʌbəˈstæmp] [ra-ba-stamp], *s.* Sello de goma. *-va.* 1. Sellar con sello de goma. 2. *(Vul.)* Aprobar rutinariamente.

rubble [ˈrʌbl] [ra-bel], *s.* 1. Ripios, cascote, morrillo, piedras, de forma irregular; se llama también *rubble-stone.* 2. Enripiado, mampostería; por otro nombre, *rubble-work.*

rub down [ˈrʌbdaʊn] [rab-daun], *s.* Fricción, mensaje. *-va.* Friccionar, dar masaje.

rubicund [ˈruːbɪkənd] [ru-bi-kand], *a.* Rubicundo.

rubied [ˈrʌbiːd] [ra-bid], *a.* Encendillo como rubí o de color de rubí.

rubiform [ˈrʌbɪfɔːm] [ra-bi-form], *a.* Rojo, rubio.

rubify [ˈrʌbɪfaɪ] [ra-bi-fai], *va.* Rubificar, poner colorada alguna cosa.

ruble [ˈruːbl] [ru-bel], *s.* Rublo.

rubric [ˈruːbrɪk] [ru-brik], *a.* Rubro, rojo, rojizo. *-s.* 1. Rúbrica, regla que enseña la práctica de las ceremonias y ritos de la Iglesia (porque solían estamparse con letras encarnadas). 2. Rúbrica, rasgo o señal que ponen algunos después de su firma.

rubricate [ˈruːbrɪkeɪt] [ru-bri-keit], *v.* Marcar, iluminar o imprimir con color rojo. 2. Poner rúbrica o epígrafe.

ruby [ˈruːbɪ] [ru-bi], *s.* 1. Rubí, piedra preciosa de color rojo o de carmín transparente. 2. Carmín, color encarnado vivo. 3. Piedra preciosa en la máquina de un reloj. *-a.* Rubicundo, de rojo vivo; semejante a un rubí. *-va.* Rubificar, enrojecer; hacer parecer a un rubí. **Ruby-throat**, colibrí norteamericano.

ruched [ruːʃt] [rusht], *s.* Rizado de muselina o cinta para los vestidos (o mangas) de mujer.

ruck [rʌk] [rak], *s.* 1. Arruga, fruncido. 2. Los que quedan rezagados en una cadena. 3. La masa, el vulgo; lo común.

ruck, *v.* Arrugar, ajar.

ruckle [ˈrʌkl] [ra-kel], *v.* Arrugar, fruncir (to frown).

rucksack [ˈrʌksæk] [rak-sak], *s.* Mochila, morral.

ruction [ˈrʌkʃən] [rak-shon], *s. (Fam.)* Alboroto, tumulto.

rudder [ˈrʌdəʳ] [ra-daʳ], *s.* Timón, la pieza de madera que sirve para gobernar el buque; gobernalle. **Ruder-pintles**, *(Mar.)* Machos del timón.

ruddiness [ˈrʌdɪnɪs] [ra-di-nes], *s.* 1. Color de rubí; rubicundez. 2. Hermosura y encendimiento del color del rostro; tez lustrosa y encendida.

ruddy [ˈrʌdɪ] [ra-di], *a.* 1. Colorado, rojizo, encendido, rubio. 2. Ardiente, vívido. 3. *(Fam.)* Maldito, condenado. **A ruddy face**, el rostro con colores muy vivos, cara de tomate.

rude [ruːd] [rud], *a.* 1. Rudo, brutal, rústico, grosero, impolítico, descortés. **Rude language**, lenguaje brutal. 2. Violento, turbulento; severo, inflexible. 3. Tosco, basto, ignorante, sin crianza, sin educación. 4. Informe, imperfecto, mal hecho. 5. Desigual, escabroso. 6. Chapucero, imperfecto. 7. Rústico, inculto. **To be rude**, ser descortés o grosero, portarse con poca modestia o con poca crianza.

rudely [ˈruːdlɪ] [rud-li], *adv.* Rudamente, ásperamente, groseramente, brutalmente; con poca delicadeza.

rudeness [ˈruːdnɪs] [rud-nes], *s.* Grosería, descortesía; rudeza, dureza, aspereza; brutalidad, insolencia; ignorancia.

rudiment [ˈruːdɪmənt] [ru-di-ment], *s.* 1. Rudimiento, cualquiera de los primeros principios de un arte, ciencia o profesión; principio. 2. Lo que es rudimentario; parte, órgano, estructura rudimentarios, germen.

rudimental [ˌruːdɪˈmentl] [ru-di-men-tal], *a.* Rudimental, perteneciente o relativo a los rudimentos.

rudimentary [ˌruːdɪˈmentərɪ] [ru-di-men-ta-ri], *a.* 1. Rudimental, rudimentario, de la naturaleza de un rudimento; en estado de rudimento; germinal, elemental. 2. Que queda imperfectamente desarrollado; abortivo.

rue [ruː] [ru], *va.* Llorar, lamentar, sentir, ponderar un infortunio *-vn.* Compadecerse, sentir, arrepentirse, estar pesaroso. **You will rue the day of your birth**, lamentará Ud. el día en que nació. **You shall rue it**, te ha de pesar.

rue, *s.* 1. *(Bot.)* Ruda, planta, tipo de las rutáceas. 2. Infusión o decocción hecha de esta planta; trago amargo o ácido. 3. Amargura, pesar, arrepentimiento. 4. Decepción.

rueful [ˈruːfʊl] [ru-ful], *a.* Lamentable, lastimoso, triste, deplorable; terrible.

ruefully [ˈruːfəlɪ] [ru-fu-li], *adv.* Tristemente.

ruff [rʌf] [raf], *s.* 1. Lechuguilla, el cuello o cabezón que se usaba antiguamente. 2. Aspereza, la calidad de áspero que tienen las cosas. 3. Apéndice natural, como un collar de plumas salientes o de pelo alrededor del cuello de un ave o de un mamífero. 4. Paloma moñuda. 5. Pavo marino. 6. Fallo, fallada (cards).

ruff, v. 1. Alechugar. 2. Fallar (cards).

ruffed ['rʌft] [raft], a. 1. Que lleva gorguera. 2. Que tiene collar de pelo o pluma. **Ruffed grouse**, especie de perdiz norteamericana.

ruffian ['rʌfɪən] [ra-fian], s. Malhechor, ladrón, bandolero. -a. Brutal, inhumano, semejante a un bandolero o merodeador. **Ruffianish**, a. Propio de un malvado; tunantón.

ruffianly ['rʌfɪənlɪ] [ra-fian-li], a. Forajido, no sujeto a ley; parecido a un bandido.

ruffle ['rʌfl] [ra-fel], va. 1. Desordenar, confundir; desazonar, enfadar. 2. Rizar, hacer dobleces en la ropa y otras cosas; adornar con puños o manguitos 3. Incomodar, irritar; vejar. -vn. 1. Rizarse, tomar en dobleces; de aquí, moverse alguna cosa tremolando en el aire. 2. Fastidiarse, incomodarse, aburrirse. 3. (Ant.) Alborotarse, exasperarse. **To ruffle it**, fanfarronear.

ruffle, va. Tocar marcha (los tambores).

ruffle, s. 1. Vuelta o puño de camisola. 2. Vuelo de las mangas de mujer. 3. Enojo, irritación, conmoción temporal; también, escarceo del agua. 4. Un toque de tambor en la milicia. **Laced ruffles**, vueltas de encaje.

rug [rʌg] [rag], s. 1. Paño burdo. 2. Frazada, manta peluda muy basta. 3. Perro de lanas o de aguas. 4. Ruedo, tapete; felpudo. 5. Manta (of a horse).

rugate ['rʌgeɪt] [ra-gueit], a. V. RUGOSE.

rugby ['rʌgbɪ] [rag-bi], s. Rugby.

rugged ['rʌgɪd] [ra-guid], a. 1. Áspero, desigual, tosco, escabroso. 2. Basto, inculto, desapacible. 3. Descomedido, desvergonzado, severo; arrugado, ceñudo, regañón. **That rugged teacher, adversity**, aquel maestro severo, la adversidad. 4. Peludo. 5. Bronco, ingrato al oído. 6. (Fam. E. U.) Robusto, vigoroso. 7. Tempestuoso, borrascoso. **A rugged beard**, unas barbas incultas.

ruggedly ['rʌgɪdlɪ] [ra-guid-li], adv. Rudamente, ásperamente.

ruggedness ['rʌgɪdnɪs] [ra-guid-nes], s. Rudeza, aspereza.

ruin ['ruːɪn] [ruin], s. 1. Ruina, caída, decadencia; bancarrota, pérdida de reputación u honra, corrupción, vicio. 2. Estado de ruina, desolación o degradación; perdición. 3. Ruina, causa de destrucción. **To bring one to ruin**, perder a uno. **To go to ruin**, arruinarse, perderse, venir a menos. **Ruins**, escombros, ruinas o despojos de fábricas o edificios arruinados; residuos.

ruin, va. Arruinar, derribar, demoler, destruir, empobrecer; seducir. -vn. 1. Caer en ruinas, arruinarse; decaer. 2. Producir o causar ruina.

ruination [ˌruːɪˈneɪʃən] [rui-nei-shon], s. Arruinamiento, ruina, perdición.

ruinous ['ruːɪnəs] [rui-nos], a. Ruinoso; pernicioso, fatal, funesto.

ruinously ['ruːɪnəslɪ] [rui-nos-li], adv. Perniciosamente, ruinosamente.

rulable ['ruːləbl] [ru-la-bol], a. Que se puede gobernar, mandar o dirigir; sujeto a reglas. 2. Permisible según regla; lícito, permitido.

rule [ruːl] [rul], s. 1. Mando, poder, autoridad, señorío. 2. Regla, modelo o ejemplo que debe servir de medida para ajustar las acciones y pensamientos; método o principio de acción. 3. Regla, el listón que sirve para trazar las líneas derechas, cartabón. 4. Regularidad, buen orden. 5. Auto, fallo de un tribunal; también, regla, estatuto. 6. Raya, filete, regla de imprenta. 7. Raya, línea rayada o reglada. 8. Reglamento. **To be the rule**, ser de regla o de reglamento. **To bear rule**, mandar. **To make it a rule to**, hacerse una regla, una ley, de. **Two-foot rule**, regla de dos pies de largo. **Rule of proportion**, regla de tres o de proporción. **Standing rules**, reglamento, estatuto (of a society, corporation).

rule, va. 1. Gobernar, mandar, reprimir, subyugar, contener, moderar (to govern, direct, run). 2. Establecer una regla, un reglamento; dirigir, disciplinar, decidir según reglas. 3. Arreglar, conducir. 4. Rayar, marcar con rayas o líneas, marcar o trazar con una regla, reglar. **To ruel paper**, reglar papel. **To rule out**, (For.) No admitir, no recibir, desechar. **To rule the roast**, mandar, terminar. **To rule with a rod of iron**, gobernar con mano de hierro. -vn. 1. Señorear, dominar, tener mando o autoridad; regir. 2. Poner, sentar, establecer, una regla que debe observarse; formular una decisión. 3. Tener influencia predominante, prevalecer. 4. (Com.) Quedar, permanecer en determinado nivel o estado. 5. Mantenerse a un tipo; estar los precios altos, bajos. **To rule over**, regir, gobernar, dominar. **He is ruled by his wife**, su mujer le manda.

ruler ['ruːləʳ] [ru-laʳ], s. 1. Gobernador, el que tiene el supremo mando. 2. Regla para trazar las líneas derechas. 3. Rayador de papel. **Paralled ruler**, regla para trazar paralelas.

ruling ['ruːlɪŋ] [ru-lin], s. 1. Decisión, fallo u orden de un tribunal, un juez o una persona que preside. 2. Rayadura, acción de rayar o trazar líneas. **Ruling-machine**, máquina para rayar. **Ruling-pen**, tiralíneas. a. 1. Regidor, gobernante. 2. Predominante, imperante. 3. Que sirve para rayar.

rullion ['ruːlɪən] [ru-lion], s. Zapato de cuero sin adobar.

rum [rʌm] [ram], s. 1. Ron, aguardiente de caña dulce. (Méx.) Chinguirito. 2. (Fam.) Cualquier licor embriagante. -a. (Fam. Ingl.) 1. Extraño, raro. 2. Que da placer. **Rum customer**, persona o animal con quien no se puede jugar.

rumble ['rʌmbl] [ram-bel], va. y vn. 1. Producir un sonido sordo y continuo o de redoble, como el trueno; retumbar, rugir (gut). 2. Moverse, avanzar haciendo ese sonido. 3. Alborotar, hacer tumulto, estar en tumulto o alboroto.

rumble, s. 1. Ruido, rumor, sonido sordo y prolongado; estruendo producido por un carruaje o tren. 2. Asiento elevado detrás de un coche. **Rumble seat**, asiento elevado detrás de un automóvil.

rumen ['ruːmən] [ra-men], s. Omaso, panza o primer estómago de los rumiantes.

ruminant ['ruːmɪnənt] [ru-mi-nant], a. y s. 1. Rumiador, rumiante. 2. Meditativo.

ruminate ['ruːmɪneɪt] [ru-mi-neit], va. 1. Rumiar, masticar segunda vez lo que han comido los animales rumiantes. 2. Rumiar, considerar despacio y pensar con reflexión y madurez alguna cosa.

rumination [ˌruːmɪˈneɪʃən] [ru-mi-nei-shon], s. Rumia, rumiadura, mediatación, consideración.

rummage ['rʌmɪdʒ] [ra-midch], va. y vn. 1. Resolver, explorar, de una manera desordenada, escudriñar, andar revolviendo todo lo que se encuentra 2. Agitar bien (un líquido o el contenido de un barril, etc.) 3. (Con out o up) Hallar, algo que se ha buscado sin orden ni método. -vn. Ir buscando y rebuscando por todas partes, trastornándolo todo. -s. Revuelta, trastorno, desorden, acto de rebuscar desordenadamente, de prisa y revolviendo.

rummager ['rʌmɪdʒəʳ] [ra-mid-chaʳ], s. Saqueador, explorador.

rummy ['rʌmɪ] [ra-mi], s. Variedad de juego de naipes.

rumor, rumour ['ruːməʳ] [ru-moʳ], s. Rumor, voz no confirmada que corre entre el público.

rumor, va. Esparcir o divulgar alguna noticia; hacer correr un rumor. **It is rumored**, se dice.

rumorer ['ruːmərəʳ] [ru-mo-raʳ], s. El que esparce rumores.

rump [rʌmp] [ramp], s. Rabadilla u obispillo de ave; anea, nalga de animal y a veces también de hombre en desprecio; solomillo de vaca. **Rump Parliament**, nombre que se da en la historia inglesa a ciertos períodos del parlamento en el tiempo de Cromwell.

rumple ['rʌmpl] [ram-pel], va. Arrugar, hacer pliegues o protuberancias irregulares.

rumple, s. Arruga, doblez o pliegue irregulares.

run [rʌn] [ran], *va.* (*pret.* RAN, *pp.* RUN, *ger.* RUNNING) 1. Hacer correr, (en cualquiera de sus acepciones intransitivas), recorrer. 2. Introducir con precipitación una cosa en otra, hacer entrar, herir de punta; picar. 3. Arrojar con violencia. 4. Efectuar corriendo, ejecutar, hacer. 5. Cazar (running). 6. Descargar, verter, echar de sí. 7. Hacer derretirse o liquidarse. 8. Coser en una línea continua. 9. Aventurar, arriesgar. 10. Derretir, fundir. 11. Manejar, dirigir (una máquina, institución, empresa). 12. Conducir, llevar o dirigir el juicio o la imaginación. *-vn.* 1. Correr, ir corriendo, seguir corriendo, pasar o caminar con velocidad; pasar como un meteoro; volar, hender el aire; moverse rápidamente de un punto a otro; viajar; apresurarse, huir. 2. Correr el tiempo; correr peligro. 3. Cambiarse o pasar rápidamente de un estado a otro; resbalarse, deslizarse. 4. Correr, ir tras uno, seguir o buscar a alguno. 5. Competir, lidiar, ser competidor. **To run for Congress**, ser competidor de otros para un puesto en el Congreso. 6. Correr, estar admitido o recibido; estar en fuerza una costumbre, opinión, etc., estilarse, acostumbrarse; estar en actividad; hallarse en operación, como una máquina. 7. Correr, decirse o saberse públicamente una cosa. 8. Desarrollarse por medio de acrecimiento o transición; frecuentemente con *in, into, to* o *up*. **To run to seed**, Granar. 9. Ocupar el entendimiento o imaginación en la contemplación de un asunto; con *on* o *upon*. 10. Proceder, continuar o proseguir en la ejecución de una cosa con orden fijo y determinado; repetirse en sucesión. 11. Correr, fluir, gotear un líquido; derretirse o liquidarse un cuerpo. 12. Correr, perseguir, acosar; acometer o arremeter impetuosamente. 13. Correr, pasar, tener curso; extenderse a lo largo, ya sea distancia o dirección. 14. Correr a porfía. 15. Ser el estilo de un escrito fácil y fluido. 16. Ocurrir o suceder algo; ser, existir con las naturales variaciones de tamaño, calidad, etc. 17. Tender, ir hacia, inclinarse, tener predisposición hacia algo. 18. En música, tocar una serie de notas en sucesión rápida. 19. Presentarse gran número de personas a retirar dinero de un banco. 20. Rezumarse, derramarse. 21. Hacer contrabando.

run about, andar de una parte a otra o correr de aca para allá sin objeto determinado.

run across, atravesar corriendo; hallar (casualmente), encontrar; extenderse en. **A friend whom I ran across in London**, un amigo con quien me encontré en Londres.

run after, Anhelar por, aspirar a; buscar con ansia alguna cosa.

run against, chocar, topar, encontrarse, darse encontrones; oponerse; ser una cosa contraria u opuesta a otra.

run aground, zozobrar, encallar.

run ahead, correr delante; llevar ventaja.

run along, correr un fluido o líquido, la voz, un sonido, etc., por todo un espacio.

run away, huir, escapar, tomar soleta, zafarse. **To run away with**, arrebatar, precipitar.

run back, retroceder, volver atrás; volver el pensamiento o la imaginación a la contemplación de una cosa pasada.

run behind, correr detrás, quedarse atrás; no hacer frente a sus gastos.

run by, Ser conocido por; pasar por, por vía de.

run down, agobiar, oprimir, envilecer; cansar o perseguir a una persona o a un animal haciéndole correr demasiado; fluir, destilar, gotear, chorrear.

run in, coincidir; convenir; ocupar enteramente. **To run into**, ocuparse, emplearse; pasar. **To run in the blood o in the family**, seguir o extenderse por generaciones sucesivas; estar en la sangre. **To run in**, rodar (car). **Running in**, estar en rodaje.

run into the ground, (*Fam. E. U.*) 1. llevar al exceso; 2. tener mal éxito, manejar mal y fracasar.

run off, pasar rápidamente de una cosa a otra; imprimir; decir sin estudio, ensartar, repetir.

run on, mencionar de paso; continuar.

run out, salir, o salirse corriendo; esparcirse, escurrirse, correrse o fluir una cosa; atrasarse o gastar más de lo que se tiene de renta; acabarse o concluirse; extenderse o dilatarse; consumir.

run over, rebosar, derramarse, salirse un liquido del vaso u otra cosa que lo contiene; decir, contar o referir una cosa con todos sus pormenores; repasar, volver a pasar o contar; recorrer, registrar o mirar con cuidado.

run through, atravesar, pasar de parte a parte; traspasar, atravesar, pasar de una parte a otra.

run to, acudir, correr o ir con diligencia al socorro de alguno.

run under, navegar a la altura de algún lugar.

run up, recorrer con la imaginación alguna cosa anterior a otra; levantar, dar más altura; coser de una manera provisional; contar o sumar rápidamente; incurrir, contraer por medio de repetidas ediciones; crecerse, aumentarse; construir de prisa; alzar, levantar en alto (bandera, etc.); estrecharse, encogerse un tejido mojado; (*E.U. del Oeste*) ahorcar.

run up and down, correr de una parte a otra.

run upon, acometer, encontrarse, chocarse. **To run counter**, oponerse; correr en una dirección opuesta. **To run foul of**, (*Mar.*) chocar, abordar. **To run races**, efectuar carreras; apostar carreras, apostar a correr. **To run the hazard o the danger**, correr peligro. **To run to seed**, granar, desarrollar las simientes con exceso. **To run the gantlet**, pasar por baquetas. **The title runs thus**, el título dice así. **To run aground**, varar. **To run out a warp**, (*Mar.*) tender una espía. **To run close-hauled**, (*Mar.*) correr a bolina balada. **To run in for the land**, andar con la proa a tierra. **The sled runs over the snow**, el trineo se desliza sobre la nieve. **The watch has run down**, el reloj se ha parado. **To run the leaves**, desarrollar las hojas con exceso. **A sore which runs**, una úlcera que supura. **The note has yet twenty days to run**, el pagaré vence dentro de veinte días. **The memory of man runs not to the contrary**, no hay memoria de un ejemplo en contrario.

run, *s.* 1. Corrida, carrera, curso. 2. Vuelta, viajecito, excursión (walk); también, adelantamiento regular o continuo. 3. Curso o período de operación; también, lo que se produce o ejecuta en ese período. (v. g. en una fábrica.). 4. Curso, movimiento de un liquido, lo que fluye: especialmente un arroyuelo. 5. Curso, serie, continuación (acts). 6. Voluntad, gusto, libre uso, libertad de ir y venir a voluntad. 7. Aceptación, aprobación. 8. Carrera, hilera. 9. La acción de acudir muchas personas a sacar sus depósitos de un banco. 10. Sitio frecuentado, especialmente por los animales; terreno de pasto. 11. Migración, v. g. de los peces al lugar del desove, ribazón. 12. Caída, dirección relativa. 13. (*Mús.*) Sucesión rápida de notas. 14. Aptitud para correr. 15. (*Teat.*) Rampa. 16. Duración, vida (of things). **Good** o **ill run at play**, buena o mala suerte en el juego. **A run for one's money**, compensación por el esfuerzo hecho o por el dinero gastado. **A day's run**, (*Mar.*) Singladura, el camino que hace una embarcación en 24 horas. **In the long run**, al fin, al cabo; a la corta o a la larga; tarde o temprano. **On the run**, huyendo, corriendo; en movimiento.

runabout ['rʌnəbaʊt] [ran-abaut], *s.* 1. Persona callejera, vagabundo. 2. Automóvil pequeño. 3. Lancha pequeña de motor.

runagate ['rʌnəgeɪt] [rana-gueit], *a.* 1. Renegado, apóstata; vagabundo. 2. Fugitivo.

runaway ['rʌnəweɪ] [ran-auei], *a.* y *s.* 1. Fugitivo, desertor; que huye. 2. Efectuado o causado por medio de la fuga. **Runaway match**, casamiento que sigue a un rapto o una fuga. 3. Caballo desbocado.

rune [ruːn] [run], *s.* 1. Runa, cada uno de los caracteres que empleaban en la escritura los antiguos escandinavos. 2. Cualquier verso, poema, sentencia o dicho obscuro; misterio. 3. Misterio, magia.

rung, *pret.* y *part.* de TO RING.

rung [rʌŋ] [rang], *s.* 1. Paso, escalón, cualquiera de los peldaños de una escalera de mano. 2. *(Mar.)* Varengas, planes. 3. Listón, barrote.

runic [ˈrʌnɪk] [ra-nik], *a.* Rúnico, runo; perteneciente o relativo a las runas o al idioma de los godos y dinamarqueses. -*s.* Una forma de caracteres modernos de imprenta, v. g. runic.

runlet [ˈrʌnlɪt] [ran-lit], *s.* Arroyuelo. *V.* RIVULET.

runner [ˈrʌnəʳ] [ra-naʳ], *s.* 1. Corredor; correo, mensajero. 2. Vástago, renuevo; *(Prov. Ingl.)* tallo delgado, echado a la larga, que se arraiga por nudos y extremos. 3. La parte sobre la que un objeto corre o se desliza; corredera. 4. Corredera, la muela superior del molino. 5. Anillo movible. pasador corredizo. 6. Operador de una máquina o locomotora. **Runner of a tackle,** *(Mar.)* Amante de aparejo. **runner of a crowfoot,** *(Mat.)* Perigallo de araña.

runner-up [ˈrʌnərʌp] [ra-nar-ap], *s.* Concursante que queda en segundo lugar.

runnet [ˈrʌnɪt] [ra-nit], *s. V.* RENNET.

running [ˈrʌnɪŋ] [ra-nin], *s.* Carrera, corrida, curso. 2. Acto de forzar un bloqueo. 3. Habilidad para correr. 4. *(Fam.)* Excursión, recorrido. 5. Marcha, funcionamiento. **To be in, o out of, the running,** tener o no tener esperanzas o posibilidades de ganar. **To make the running,** llevar la delantera. -*a.* 1. Corredor. 2. Que fluye, que contiene pus. 3. Corriente, que corre. **Running expenses,** gastos corrientes. 4. Corredizo. **Running knot,** nudo corredizo. **Running board,** estribo de un automóvil. **Running gear,** tren de rodaje, ejes y ruedas de un vehículo. **Running horse,** caballo corredor. **Running sore,** una herida con pus. **Running water,** agua corriente.

runnion [ˈrʌnɪən] [ra-nion], *s.* Pelafustán, pandorgo, persona despreciable.

run-off [ˈrʌnɒf] [ran-of], *s.* 1. Agua de desagüe. 2. Carrera o competencia final para determinar el vencedor.

runt [rʌnt] [rant], *s.* 1. Redrojo, el animal más pequeño y débil de una lechigada o hata; animal detenido en su crecimiento. 2. Enano.

runway [ˈrʌnweɪ] [ran-uei], *s.* 1. vía o sendero por el que corre algo. 2. Lecho de un arroyo. 3. Senda por la que pasan animales. 4. Pista de aterrizaje para aviones.

rupee [ruːˈpiː] [ru-pi], *s.* Rupia.

rupture [ˈrʌptʃəʳ] [rap-chaʳ], *s.* 1. Rompimiento, rotura. 2. Rompimiento, riña, desavenencia, hostilidad. 3. Potra, hernia, quebradura.

rupture, *va.* Reventar, romper o hacer pedazos una cosa, quebrar, separar con violencia. -*vn.* Abrirse, henderse, sin extrema violencia.

rural [ˈrʊərəl] [ru-ral], *a.* Rural, campesino, campestre, rústico.

ruse [ruːs] [rus], *s.* Astucia, engaño, estafa, acción con que se pretende engañar.

rush [rʌʃ] [rash], *s.* 1. Junco, junquillo, enea. 2. Friolera, bagatela, cosa de poco valor. *V.* RUSH-LIGHT. **It is not worth a rush,** no vale un bledo o un ardite. **Rush-bottomed,** con fondo de junco. **Rushlight,** una especie de vela o lamparilla de noche con pábilo de junco. **Rush-mat,** estera de junco.

rush, *s.* 1. Ímpetu, movimiento furioso, método o procedimiento enérgico (impulse, momentum). 2. Prisa grande, presión, demanda extraordinaria; gran cantidad de algo que causa ímpetu o prisa. 3. Concurso, gentío, agolpamiento de gente, apretura. 4. *(E. U.)* Lucha, contienda violenta entre dos grupos de personas, cada uno de los cuales procura rechazar al otro. 5. Carrera precipitada.

rush, *vn.* Arrojarse, abalanzarse, tirarse, dispararse: se dice de una persona o de un animal que da una embestida o salto impetuoso. -*va.* Empujar o arrojar con violencia, ejecutar con precipitación. **To rush forward,** abalanzarse, arrojarse con ímpetu. **To rush in,** entrar de rondón. **To rush in upon,** sorprender. **To rush out,** salir precipitadamente. **To rush**

through, ejecutar con precipitación o de prisa, exponerse atrevidamente:

rusher [ˈrʌʃəʳ] [ra-shaʳ], *s.* 1. Embestidor. 2. Persona enérgica. 3. El que lleva el balón en el fútbol americano.

rushy [ˈrʌʃɪ] [ra-shi], *a.* 1. Juncoso, lleno de juncos. 2. De anea o espadaña.

rusk [rʌsk] [rask], *s.* 1. Galleta, rosca. 2. Pan tostado al horno.

russet [ˈrʌsɪt] [ra-sit], *a.* 1. Bermejizo; color mezlca de anaranjado y purpúreo; vulgarmente, moreno rojizo o amarillento. 2. Burdo, tosco, grosero 3. Acabado, pero no teñido de negro, se aplica al calzado. 4. Curtido y sin colorear (hide). -*s.* 1. Color producido por la mezcla de anaranjado y purpúreo. 2. Vestido de labrador o de un hombre del campo. 3. Variedad de manzana de color verdusco con manchas pardas.

Russia [ˈrʌʃə] [ra-sha], *s.* 1. Rusia. *V.* APENDICE. 2. Piel de Rusia; vaqueta de Moscovia.

russian [ˈrʌʃən] [ra-shan], *a.* Ruso, de Rusia. -*s.* Ruso, natural o habitante de Rusia.

rust [rʌst] [rast], *s.* 1. Orín, herrumbre, robín, el moho u óxido que cría el hierro o cualquier otro metal; el óxido rojizo de hierro. 2. *(Bot.)* Añublo, tizón, enfermedad que ataca los trigos y se debe a un honguillo parásito; el hongo que produce esa enfermedad. 3. Orín, mancha, defecto. **Rust of corn,** tizón. **To gather rust,** enmohecerse, criar moho u orín.

rust, *vn.* 1. Enmohecerse, ponerse mohoso, cubrirse de moho o de orín. 2. Enmohecerse, embotarse: se dice del entendimiento o valor cuando se entorpecen por la falta de ejercicio. -*va.* 1. Enmohecer, poner mohoso, cubrir de orín una cosa de metal. 2. Entorpecer el entendimiento, el valor o el ingenio por no ponerlo en ejercicio.

rustic [ˈrʌstɪk] [ras-tik], *a.* 1. Rústico, agreste, villano, campesino, sencillo, sin artificio, inculto, grosero. 2. Que nota o pertenece a algún estilo irregular de trabajo o adorno propio del campo. -*s.* Patán, villano, rústico, hombre del campo.

rustical [ˈrʌstɪkəl] [ras-ti-kal], *a. (Ant.)* Rústico, áspero.

rusticity [rʌsˈtɪsɪtɪ] [ras-ti-si-ti], *s.* Rusticidad, simplicidad, grosería, rudeza.

rustily [ˈrʌstɪlɪ] [ras-ti-li], *adv.* Con herrumbre, enmohecimiento o falta de uso.

rustiness [ˈrʌstɪnɪs] [ras-ti-nes], *s.* El estado de lo que se halla cubierto de orín o moho; falta de uso.

rustle [ˈrʌsl] [ra-sel], *va. y vn.* 1. Susurrar, hacer, o hacer producir una serie de sonidos rápidos y suaves (como los de las hojas, de las sedas, etc.); producir un sonido de rozamiento. 2. Conducirse con energía y actividad. 3. Robar ganado. -*s.* Rozamiento, ruido que hacen las hojas, las sedas, cuando se las frota o agita; susurro.

rustler [ˈrʌsləʳ] [ras-laʳ], *s.* 1. El o lo que susurra o produce ruido parecido al roce. 2. *(Ger. E. U.)* Hombre activo o emprendedor. 3. *(E.U)* Actividad febril, esfuerzo, lucha.

rustless [ˈrʌslɪs] [ras-les], *a.* Inoxidable.

rustproof [ˈrʌstpruːf] [rast-pruf], *a.* Inoxidable.

rusty [ˈrʌstɪ] [ras-ti], *a.* 1. Oxidado, mohoso, herrumbroso, tomado de herrumbre o producido por ella. 2. Parecido a orín o herrumbre en el color; rojizo o amarillento. 3. Entorpecido, debilitado por falta de uso; que ha perdido su habilidad por falta de práctica. 4. Ronco, rudo, bronco (de tonos o sonidos). 5. Rojizo. **Rusty bacon,** tocino rancio.

rut [rʌt] [rt], *va.* Hacer carriles, rodadas o surcos en el camino o suelo, *(Fig.)* arrugar. -*s.* 1. Carril, rodada, la impresión o señal que deja la rueda en la tierra por donde pasa. 2. Costumbre, hábito arraigados; sendero trillado, pisado.

rut, *vn.* Bramar los venados, ciervos y otros animales cuando están en celo; estar en celo. -*s.* 1. Brama, unión del macho con la hembra, celo, excitación sexual en varios animales, v. g. los venados. 2. Mugido, bramido, ruido, batahola, alboroto. **Rutting-time,** tiempo de brama, estación del celo.

rutabaga [ˌruːtəˈbeɪɡə] [ru-ta-bei-ga], *s.* Rutabaga, nabo sueco, variedad de nabo.

ruth [ruːθ] [ruz], *s. (Ant.)* Compasión, conmiseración; desgracia, miseria.

ruthless [ˈruːθlɪs] [ruz-les], *a.* Cruel, endurecido, insensible, falto de piedad.

ruthlessly [ˈruːθlɪslɪ] [ruz-lis-li], *adv.* Cruelmente, inhumanamente.

ruthlessness [ˈruːθlɪsnɪs] [ruz-lis-nes], *s.* Crueldad, falta de piedad, de compasión, apatía por las desgracias ajenas.

rutting [ˈrʌtɪŋ] [ra-tin], *a. (Bio.)* En celo.

ruttish [ˈrʌtɪʃ] [ra-tish], *a.* 1. Que tiende a hacer o correr en las rodadas. 2. Lascivo, libidinoso; salido.

rutty [ˈrʌtɪ] [ra-ti], *a.* Lleno de carriles.

rye [raɪ] [rai], *s.* 1. *(Bot.)* Centeno, especie de grano, planta gramínea y sus simientes. 2. *(Fam. E. U.)* Whisky destilado de centeno. **Rye-worm**, gusano larva de una mosca europea, nociva a los tallos del centeno. **Spurred rye**, centeno atizonado, cornezuelo. V. ERGOT.

rye bread [ˈraɪbred] [rai-bred], *s.* Pan de centeno.

rye-grass [ˈraɪɡrɑːs] [rai-gras], *s. (Bot.)* Grama de centeno.

S

s [es] [es] El sonido de la *s* varía en la lengua inglesa: en muchas voces tiene un sonido agudo, como en *soon, yes, muffs*; y en otras suave, como en *praise, ribs, churches*. Cuando precede a la *h*, tiene un sonido especial que conserva también en la mayor parte de las voces en que está seguida de *u* o *ion*, como en *pleasure, evasion*. En algunas voces es muda, como en *island, viscount*; *s* es signo del posesivo o genitivo; también, contracción de *is*, es. **it's good**, es bueno. -Como abreviatura significa la *S, sociedad, sud o sur*; como F. R. *s.*, Miembro de la Sociedad Real. *s.* E. Sudeste; *s.* S.E., sudsudeste, etc.

sabal [ˈsæbl] [sa-bal], *s.* Sabal, género de palmeras de los trópicos, que tiene hojas grandes en forma de abanico.

sabbatarian [ˌsæbəˈtɛərɪən] [sa-ba-tea-rian], *a.* y *s.* Nombre de unos sectarios que guardaban con el mayor rígor la fiesta del domingo; y por extensión se llama así a los que observan muy estrictamente la abstinencia de todo trabajo en este día.

sabbath [ˈsæbəθ] [sa-baz], *s.* Sábado, el día séptimo de la semana destinado entre los judíos al descanso. **The Christian Sabbath**, domingo, el primer día de la semana. **Sabbath-breaker**, infractor o quebrantador del domingo. **Sabbath-day**, el día dedicado a obras de piedad y al reposo.

sabbatical [səˈbætɪkəl] [sa-ba-ti-kal], *a.* Sabático, perteneciente al sábado entre los judíos.

sabbatism [ˈsæbətɪzəm] [sa-ba-ti-sem], *s.* La observancia supersticiosa y rígida del sábado.

saber, sabre [ˈseɪbæʳ] [sei-baʳ], *s.* Sable, arma blanca, espada de un solo filo. -*va.* Acuchillar, herir a sablazos.

sabian [ˈsæbɪən] [sa-bian], *a.* Sabeo, perteneciente a los sabeos o a su culto. -*s.* Sabeo, adorador del sol, entre los persas y caldeos, secta que reconoció la unidad de Dios.

sabianism [ˌsæbɪəˈnɪzəm] [sa-bia-ni-sem], *s.* Sabeísmo.

sabine [ˈsæbaɪn] [sa-bain], *s. (Bot.)* Sabina. V. SAVIN.

sable [ˈseɪbl] [sei-bol], *s.* Cabellina, especie de comadreja o marta y también la piel de dicho animal. -*a.* 1. *(Her.)* Sable negro. 2. Ropas de luto.

sabot [ˈsæbəʊ] [sa-bou], *s.* 1. Zueco, almadreña. 2. Disco adherido a un proyectil para hacerle mantener determinada posición dentro del cañón de un arma de fuego. 3. Pieza de empalme para acortar una cuerda del arpa.

sabotage [ˈsæbətɑːʒ] [sa-bo-tash], *s.* Sabotaje. -*va.* Sabotear.

saboteur [ˌsæbəˈtɜːʳ] [sa-bo-teʳ], *s.* Saboteador.

sabre [ˈseɪbəʳ] [sei-baʳ], *s.* V. SABER.

sabretache [ˌsæbəˈtæʃ] [sei-ba-tash], *s.* Portapliegos o escarcela del uniforme de caballería.

sabulous [ˈsæbələs] [sa-bo-los], *a.* Sabuloso, arenoso.

sac [sæk] [sak], *s. (Biol.)* Saco, bolsa membranosa; cavidad o receptáculo.

saccade [ˈsækeɪd] [sa-keid], *s.* 1. Sofrenada. 2. *(Mús.)* Golpe de arco que hace sonar varias cuerdas a la vez de un violín.

saccate [ˈsækeɪt] [sa-keit], *a.* En forma de bolsa o saco.

saccharin [ˈsækərɪn] [sa-ka-rin], *s.* 1. Sacarina, compuesto azucarado que se obtiene del alquitrán de hulla. 2. Otro compuesto de un sabor amargo.

saccharine [ˈsækəriːn] [sa-ka-rin], *a.* Sacarino, azucarado.

saccharose [ˈsækərəʊs] [sa-ka-rous], *s.* Azúcar (de caña, de remolacha).

sacerdotal [ˌsæsəˈdæʊtl] [sa-sa-dou-tal], *a.* Sacerdotal.

sacerdotalism [ˌsæsədəʊtəˈlɪzm] [sa-sa-dou-ta-li-sem], *s.* Carácter y métodos sacerdotales; celo por las cosas sacerdotales, también, artimaña de un ministro de la religión.

sachem [ˈsætʃɪm] [sa-kim], *s.* Jefe hereditario de una tribu de indios norteamericanos, cacique.

sachet [ˈsæʃeɪ] [sa-shei], *s.* Saquito para polvos perfumados.

sack [sæk] [sak], *s.* 1. Saco, saca, costal, talega (bag). 2. Medida de tres fanegas. 3. Sacó, el saqueo de una plaza. 4. Chaqueta, casaca suelta con mangas que usaron las personas de uno y otro sexo en los siglos XVII y XVIII; bata de mujer. 5. *(Des.)* Vino dulce de Canarias. 6. Botín. **To give sack**, dar calabazas, ser despedido. **To hold the sack**, quedarse con las manos vacías. *a.* De sacos o sacos. **sack race**, carrera de sacos.

sack, *va.* 1. Meter en sacos. 2. Saquear. 3. Despedir, dar calabazas. **To sack up**, ensacar.

sackbut [ˈsækbʌt] [sak-bat], *s.* 1. Sacabuche, un instrumento músico primitivo parecido al trombón. 2. En la Biblia, un instrumento de cuerda.

sackcloth [ˈsækklɒθ] [sak-kloz], *s.* 1. Arpillera, brea. 2. Cilicio.

sack coat [ˈsækkəʊt] [sak-kout], *s.* Saco holgado de hombre.

sacker [ˈsækəʳ] [sa-kaʳ], *s.* Saqueador, el que saquea.

sackful [ˈsækfʊl] [sak-ful], *s.* Costal o saco lleno, lo bastante para llenar un saco.

sacking [ˈsækɪŋ] [sa-kin], *s.* Tela para sacos, harpillera.

sacral [ˈseɪkrəl] [sei-kral], *s.* Sacro sagrado.

sacrament [ˈsækrəmənt] [sa-kra-ment], *s.* 1. El juramento o ceremonia solemne que impone una obligación. 2. Sacrmento. 3. El sacramento de la eucaristía. 4. Juramento, compromiso solemne. **To receive the sacrament**, comulgar. **The Blessed** o **Holy Sacrament**, el Santísimo Sacramento.

sacramental [ˌsəkrəˈmentl] [sa-kra-men-tal], *s.* Sacramental.

sacramentarian [ˌsækrəˈmentɛərɪən] [sa-kra-men-tea-rian], *a.* Sacramental, perteneciente a los sacramenteos o a los sacramentarios. -*s.* Sacramentario, el que rechaza la doctrina luterana de la eucaristía.

sacramentary [ˌsækrəˈmentərɪ] [sa-kra-men-ta-ri], *a.* Sacramental, concerniente a los sacramentos. -*s.* Sacramentario, antiguo libro que contenía todas las ceremonias y oraciones usadas en la celebración de los sacramentos.

sacred [ˈseɪkrɪd] [sei-krid], *a.* Sagrado, sacro, consagrado; santo, concerniente a la religión, en relación con seres divinos o sobrenaturales; digno de reverencia; inviolable. **His sacred majesty**, la persona sagrada del rey.

sacredly [ˈseɪkrɪdlɪ] [sei-krid-li], *adv.* Sagradamente, inviolablemente, religiosamente, santamente.

sacredness [ˈseɪkrɪdnɪs] [sei-krid-nes], *s.* Santidad, carácter sagrado; consagración a Dios o a su culto, inviolabilidad.

sacrifice [ˈsækrɪfaɪs] [sa-kri-fais], *va.* 1. Sacrificar, inmolar. 2. Sacrificar, abandonar, renunciar o perder una cosa por conservar otra. 3. Destruir, matar. -*vn.* Sacrificar, ofrecer sacrificios.

sacrifice, *s.* 1. Sacrificio, el acto de sacrificar u ofrecer a la deidad alguna cosa y la misma cosa sacrificada u ofrecida, víctima. 2. Sacrificio, renuncia de alguna cosa apreciable hecha con repugnancia por amor, respeto o reconocimiento. 3. Pérdida sufrida sin compensación, destrucción, v. g. de una o más vidas. 4. *(Com.)* Sacrificio, rebaja en los precios que anula la ganancia o implica pérdida. **To sell at a sacrifice**, vender sin beneficio.

sacrificer ['sækrɪfaɪsə^r] [sa-kri-fai-sa^r], s. Sacrificador.

sacrificial [ˌsækrɪ'fɪʃəl] [sa-kri-fi-shal], a. Sacrificador, que pertenece a los sacrificios, empleado en los sacrificios, de la naturaleza de un sacrificio. ofrecido como expiación del pecado.

sacrilege ['sækrɪlɪdʒ] [sa-kri-lich], s. Sacrilegio, lesión o violación de alguna cosa sagrada.

sacrilegious [ˌsækrɪ'lɪdʒəs] [sa-kri-li-yos], a. Sacrílego.

sacrilegiously [ˌsækrɪ'lɪdʒəslɪ] [sa-kri-li-yos-li], adv. Sacrílegamente.

sacrist ['sækrɪst] [sa-krist], s. 1. V. SACRISTAN. 2. Copista de música y encargado de los libros de coro de una iglesia.

sacristan ['sækrɪstən] [sa-kris-tan], s. Sacristán, el empleado que cuida de los ornamentos y del aseo de la iglesia y sacristía.

sacristy ['sækrɪstɪ] [sa-kris-ti], s. Sacristía (de una iglesia).

sacrum ['sækrəm] [sa-krom], s. Sacro, hueso del espinazo, formado por cinco vértebras entre la región lumbar y el cóccix.

sad [sæd] [sad], a. 1. Triste, lúgubre, pensativo, melancólico (sorrowful, mournful). 2. Infausto, lastimoso, calamitoso. 3. Malo, perverso, cruel, funesto. 4. (Ant.) Obscuro, sombrío o triste en el color. 5. (Fam.) Travieso, malicioso, dispuesto a hacer diabluras. 6. (Prov.) Pesado, indigesto; se dice del pan. 7. Malo, pobre, de inferior calidad. **Sad news**, noticias infaustas o funestas. **To grow sad**, entristecerse. **To make sad**, entristecerse, afligir. **A sad fellow**, diablillo, hombre malicioso; un pícaro.

sadden ['sædn] [sa-den], va. y vn. 1. Entristecer, constristar, causar o dar tristeza, poner triste. 2. Hacer más obscuro un color. 3. Entristecerse, melancolizarse, ponerse triste. 4. Ensombrecer.

saddle ['sædl] [sa-del], s. 1. Silla de montar (horse, bicycle). (S. Amer.) Galápago, silla de caballo. 2. Cojinete relleno de material blando (pelote, etc.) para el lomo de un caballo. 3. Entre carniceros, cuarto trasero de una res. 4. Lo que tiene la forma o posición de una silla. **Saddleback**, cuesta o montaña con dos cumbres separadas por una ligera depresión. **Saddle of mutton**, lomos de carnero. **Saddle-bow**, arzón. **Saddle-cloth**, mantilla de silla. **Saddle-tree**, fuste de silla. **Pack-saddle**, basto, albarda. **Saddle-backed**, ancho de espaldas; encorvado. **Saddle-bag**, alforja. (Mex.) Cojinillo. **Saddle-horse**, caballo de silla. **Saddle-maker**, V. SADDLER. **Saddle-shaped**, en forma de silla de montar; (Geol.) en arco, encorvado y sin fractura en la cima.

saddle, va. 1. Ensillar, poner o echar la silla al caballo u otro animal cuadrúpedo. 2. Cargar, poner a cuestas. 3. **To saddle with**, cargar o hacer cargar con algo molesto.

saddle-galled ['sædlgɔːld] [sa-del-gould], a. Lastimado por la silla. (Mex.) Desollado, en el sentido de despellejado.

saddler ['sædlæ^r] [sad-la^r], s. Sillero, el que hace sillas de montar.

saddlerock ['sædlrɒk] [sa-del-rok], s. (E. U.) Ostra grande de primera calidad oriunda de Long. Island, Estado de Nueva York.

saddlery ['sædlərɪ] [sad-le-ri], s. Herraje de talabartero o sillero.

sadism ['seɪdɪzəm] [sei-di-sem], s. Sadismo.

sadist ['seɪdɪst] [sei-dist], s. Sadista.

sadly ['sædlɪ] [sad-li], adv. Tristemente, miserablemente, mal. **Sadly hurt**, herido de peligro. **To be sadly off**, tener uno sus asuntos en mal estado.

sadness ['sædnɪs] [sad-nes], s. Tristeza, pesadumbre, melancolía, abatimiento; aspecto tétrico, serio.

safari [sæ'fɑːrɪ] [sa-fa-ri], sm. Safari.

safe [seɪf] [seif], a. 1. Seguro, salvo, ileso, libre y exento de todo peligro, daño o riesgo (harmless, sound, unhurt, unscathed). 2. Intacto, sin lesión. 3. Seguro, que ofrece toda clase de seguridades; hablando de personas; leal, digno de confianza. 4. Cierto, exento de error. 5. Incapacitado para dañar u ofender, p. ej. por estar encarcelado, o haber muerto. **It is not safe for us to stay here**, no estamos

seguros aquí. **Safe conscience,**, conciencia pura o tranquila. **I wish you safe home**, deseo que llegue Ud. con felicidad. **Safe and sound**, sano y salvo. **Safe load**, carga máxima.

safe, s. 1. Lugar seguro para guardar objetos; en especial, caja de seguridad, arca o cofre fuerte a prueba de fuego o de ladrones. 2. Alacena para conservar carnes o manjares, despensa. **Safe-keeping**, depósito, guardia o custodia segura; acto y efecto de poner una cosa en seguridad.

safe-conduct ['seɪf'kɒndəkt] [seif-kon-dakt], s. Convoy, salvoconducto.

safe-deposit ['seɪfdɪˌpɒzɪt] [seif-di-po-sit], s. Cámara de seguridad, acorazada (box, vault).

safeguard ['seɪfgɑːd] [seif-gard], s. 1. Salvaguardia, defensa, carta de seguridad. 2. Escolta. 3. Defensa, abrigo.

safeguard, va. Guardar, proteger.

safely ['seɪflɪ] [seif-li], adv. Seguramente, sin peligro, a salvo, felizmente.

safeness ['seɪfnɪs] [seif-nes], s. Estado o condición de hallarse en seguridad.

safety ['seɪftɪ] [seif-ti], s. 1. Seguridad, resguardo, salvamento; exención de todo mal, daño o perjuicio. 2. Seguro de un arma. **Safety-belt**, cinto de seguridad, salvavidas. **Safety-lamp**, lámpara de seguridad o de Davy, para los mineros: lámpara envuelta en tela metálica. **Safety-match**, fósforo que se enciende solamente sobre una superficie especialmente preparada. **Safety-pin**, imperdible, alfiler de seguridad. **Safety-valve**, válvula de seguridad (en las máquinas de vapor). **In safety**, con seguridad, sin peligro.

saffian ['sæfɪən] [sa-fian], s. Cuero de cabra o cordero curtido con zumaque y teñido con colores vivos.

saffron ['sæfrən] [sa-fron], s. (Bot.) Azafrán (planta, las hebras o los estigamas de las flores, y el color). -a. Azafranado, de color de azafrán. **Saffron thistle**, alazor, cártamo.

sag [sæg] [sag], va. Hacer ceder o doblegar por el medio. -vn. 1. Ceder a su propio peso, doblegarse, hundirse, particularmente en el medio; doblegarse, colgar toscamente. 2. Aflojar, flaquear, como bajo un infortunio. 3. (Mar.) Irse a la ronza. 4. Tardar, ser lento de movimiento. -s. 1. Hundimiento, depresión, bolsa, comba, combaduría. 2. Flecha de un cable. 3. (Com.) Baja de precios.

saga ['sɑːɡə] [sa-ga], s. Saga, leyenda de los escandinavos.

sagacious [sə'ɡeɪʃəs] [sa-guei-shos], a. Sagaz, vivo, sutil, penetrante.

sagaciously [sə'ɡeɪʃəslɪ] [sa-guei-shos-li], adv. Sagazmente.

sagacity [sə'ɡæsɪtɪ] [sa-ga-si-ti], s. Sagacidad, astucia; sutileza.

sage [seɪdʒ] [seich], s. 1. (Bot.) Salvia, planta de la familia de las labiadas. **Sage-brush**, artemisia, una especie parecida, arbusto. **Sage-cheese**, queso aromatizado con hojas de salvia. 2. Sabio, filósofo. **The seven sages**, los siete sabios de Grecia. -a. Sabio; prudente; grave, sagaz; cuerdo.

sagely ['seɪdʒlɪ] [seich-li], adv. Sabiamente; cuerdamente, prudentemente.

sageness ['seɪdʒnɪs] [seich-nis], s. Sabiduría; gravedad; prudencia, cordura.

sagittal ['sædʒɪtəl] [sa-yi-tal], a. Sagital.

sagittarius [ˌsædʒɪ'teɪrɪəs] [sa-yi-te-rios], s. (Astr.) Sagitario.

sago ['seɪɡəʊ] [sei-gou], s. (Bot.) Sagú, meollo de varias especies de palma de la India oriental, muy alimenticio.

sahib ['sɑːhɪb] [sa-ib], s. Señor; tratamiento empleado en Persia y en el Indostán.

said [seɪd] [seid], pp. de SAY. (For.) Citado, antedicho, ya nombrado.

sail [seɪl] [seil], s. (Mar.) 1. Vela, el paño de lona extendido sobre un palo y verga a fin de recibir el viento e impeler la nave. **Main-sail**, vela mayor. **Main-top-sail**, gavia. **Main-top-gallant-sail**, juanete mayor. **Main-top-gallant-royal**, sobrejuanete mayor. **Fore-sail**, trinquete. **Fore-top-sail**, velacho. **Fore-top-gallant-sail**, juanete de proa. **Mizzen-**

sail, mesana. **Mizzen-top-sail**, sobremesana. **Mizzen-top-gallant-sail**, juanete de mesana. **Stay-sail**, vela de estay. **Fore-stay-sail**, trinquetilla. **Studding-sail**, rastrera, ala. **Sprit-sail**, cabadera. **To set sail**, hacerse a la vela. **To strike sail**, arriar una vela. 2. Vela, la misma embarcación. (En este sentido el plural no lleva *s*, y tiene la misma forma que el singular). 3. Velas, número de embarcaciones. **Fleet of seventeen sail of the line**, escuadra de diez y siete navíos de línea. 4. Excursión, paseo en barco de vela. **Sail-boat**, barco de vela, barca, yate. **Sail-cloth**, lona, lienzo para velas y toldos. **Sail-loft**, tinglado, almacén de velas o lona, taller donde se hacen velas. **Sail-maker**, fabricante de velas. **Under full sail**, a todo trapo. 5. Aspa, brazo de molino.

sail, *vn.* 1. Darse a la vela, hacerse a la vela, dar las velas al viento, navegar. 2. Viajar por mar, río o lago; ir en una embarcación. 3. Volar sin aletear; flotar, ir por el aire (una nube). 4. *(Fam.)* Pasar sobre, moverse majestuosamente. -*va.* 1. Navegar, manejar o guiar una embarcación. 2. Navegar por, viajar en, cruzar en una embarcación. **To sail back**, navegar hacia atrás, entrar a descansar en algún puerto. **To sail along the coast**, costear. **To sail before the wind**, *(Mar.)* Navegar a dos puños. **To sail with the wind on the beam**, *(Mar.)* Navegar con el viento a través. **To sail with a scant wind**, *(Mar.)* Navegar de bolina. **To sail close-hauled**, *(Mar.)* Navegar ciñendo el viento.

sailable ['seɪləbl] [sei-la-bol], *a.* Navegable (a la vela).

sailer ['seɪləʳ] [sei-laʳ], *s.* Navío, buque, embarcación que sirve para navegar. **Good o fine sailer**, navío velero.

sailfish ['seɪlfɪʃ] [seil-fish], *s.* Variedad de pez espada.

sailing ['seɪlɪŋ] [sei-lin], *s.* 1. Acto de darse a la vela. 2. Navegación, arte de navegar. **Plain sailing**, 1. Avance, adelantamiento sin dificultades, literal o figuradamente; coser y cantar. 2. *V. Plane sailing.* **Plane sailing**, acción de navegar sobre la carta de marcar. **Great-circle sailing**, navegación circular. **Sailing orders** o **instructions**, orden de salida o marcha dada a un buque de guerra.

sailor ['seɪləʳ] [sei-loʳ], *s.* Marinero, hombre de mar, marino (seaman). **Sailor's wages**, mesadas, soldadas, sueldo de los marineros o de la tripulación. **Sailor** o **sailor hat**, sombrero de paja.

sailvard ['seɪlvɑːd] [seil-vard], *s.* Verga.

saint [seɪnt] [seint], *s.* 1. Santo, la persona de virtud y piedad eminentes; (en el Nuevo Testamento, cualquier cristiano fiel); en especial, santo, santa, persona canonizada por la Iglesia (holy). 2. Un ángel. -*a.* como título se escribe con mayúscula, y por lo común en abreviatura, St. **St. Andrew's cross**, cruz de San Andrés. 3. Nombre de una planta de la familia de las hipericíneas. **St. John's wort**, hierba de San Juan, hipérico. **St. Vitu's dance**, baile de San Vito, enfermedad caracterizada por movimientos convulsivos. **St. Bernard**, perro grande y sagaz, oriundo del hospicio de San Bernardo en los Alpes. **St. John's bread**, algarrobo, árbol. *V.* CAROB.

saint, *va.* Canonizar. -*vn.* 1. Obrar como un santo. 2. **To saint it**, hacer el santo.

sainted ['seɪntɪd] [sein-tid], *a.* Santo; piadoso, virtuoso, sagrado.

sainthood ['seɪnthʊd] [seint-jud], *s.* Santidad.

saint-like ['seɪntlaɪk] [seint-laik], *a.* Propio de un santo o de los santos.

saintliness ['seɪntlɪnɪs] [seint-li-nes], *s.* Santidad, santificación.

saintly ['seɪntlɪ] [seint-li], *adv.* Santamente; piadosamente, virtuosamente.

saintship ['seɪntʃɪp] [seint-ship], *s.* Santidad, carácter de santo.

sake [seɪk] [seik], *s.* Causa, motivo, fin, objeto, razón, amor, respecto, consideración (cause, reason). **For God's sake**, por amor de Dios. **For brevity's sake**, en obsequio de la brevedad. **Do it for my sake**, hágalo Ud. por mí. **For your sake**, por Ud., por respeto a o de Ud., en obsequio o gracia de Ud. *(Vulg.)* Por amor de Ud. **For politeness' sake**, por política.

sal [sæl] [sal], *s.* Sal; término de química o farmacia. **Sal ammoniac**, sal amoniaco, cloruro de amoníaco. **Sal soda**, sosa, carbonato de sodio para lavar. **Sal volatile**, carbonato armónico.

salaam, salam [sə'lɑːm] [sa-lam], *va.* y *vn.* Saludar a la oriental. -*s.* Reverencia oriental profunda, que se hace con la palma de la mano derecha sobre la frente.

salable ['seɪləbl] [sei-la-bol], *a.* Vendible, que puede ser vendido, de fácil venta (marketable).

salableness ['seɪləblnɪs] [sei-la-bol-nes], *s.* La calidad que constituye a una cosa vendible o de despacho.

salacious [sə'leɪʃəs] [sa-lei-shos], *a.* Salaz, lascivo, lujurioso.

salaciousness [sə'leɪʃəsnɪs] [sa-lei-shos-nes], **salacity** [sə'læsɪtɪ] [sa-la-si-ti], *s.* Salacidad, lascivia, lujuría.

salad ['sæləd] [sa-lad], *s.* Ensalada. **Salad-bowl**, ensaladera. **Salad dish**, plato para ensalada. **Salad dressing**, salsa para la ensalada. **Salad greens**, verduras para ensalada (tales como lechuga, espinaca, etc.) **Salad oil**, aceite para ensalada (generalmente de oliva).

salal ['sæləl] [sa-lal], *s.* Arbusto americano de bayas comestibles.

salamander ['sæləˌmændəʳ] [sa-la-man-daʳ], *s.* Salamandra, salamanquesa.

salami [sə'lɑːmɪ] [sa-la-mi], *sm.* Salami.

salary ['sæləɾɪ] [sa-la-ri], *va.* Asalariar, dar jornal, salario o sueldo. -*s.* Salario, sueldo, paga, jornal (wages). **Salaried**, *pp.* Asalariado, que recibe un salario.

sale [seɪl] [seil], *s.* 1. Venta, acción y efecto de vender (selling). 2. Almoneda, venta a pública subasta. 3. Oportunidad de vender, demanda por parte de los compradores; voga, mercado. 4. Salida, despacho, demanda. **Sale by auction**, almoneda, subasta. **For sale** o **on sale**, de venta, ofrecido o pronto para la venta. **On sale or return**, contrato o pacto de retroventa. *a.* 1. De ventas, para la venta, sobre la venta. 2. Hecho, corriente, de confección, de serie. **Sales agent**, agente de ventas. **Sales tax**, impuesto sobre las ventas.

saleable, saleableness ['seɪləbl] [sei-la-bol], *V.* SALABLE, SALABLENESS.

sales agent ['seɪlzˌeɪdʒənt] [seils-ei-yant], *s.* Agente vendedor.

salesclerk ['seɪlzklɜːk] [seils-klerk], *s.* Dependiente, vendedor (in a shop).

salesgirl ['seɪlzgɜːl] [seils-guerl], *s.* Dependienta, vendedora (in a shop).

salesman ['seɪlzmən] [seils-man], *vn.* Vendedor, el que vende géneros en una tienda.

salesmanship ['seɪlzmənʃɪp] [seils-man-ship], *s.* Arte de vender.

salesperson ['seɪlzˌpɜːsn] [seils-per-son], *s.* Dependiente, vendedor (en una tienda).

salesroom ['seɪlzrʊm] [seils-rum], *s.* Sala de ventas, sala de exhibición de mercancías.

sales tax ['seɪlztæks] [seils-taks], *s.* Impuesto sobre las ventas.

saleswoman ['seɪlzwʊmən] [seils-uo-man], *sf.* Vendedora, la que vende géneros en una tienda; vulgarmente, **saleslady.**

salient ['seɪlɪənt] [sei-lient], *a.* Saltante, saliente, salido.

saliferous [sə'lɪfəɾəs] [sa-li-fe-ros], *a. (Geol.)* Salífero, que contiene sal.

salify ['sælɪfaɪ] [sa-li-fai], *va. (Quím.)* Salificar, formar una sal.

saline ['seɪlaɪn] [sei-lain], *a.* Salino, que tiene propiedades de sal. -*s.* Una sal de magnesio o de uno de los álcalis.

salineness ['sælɪnnɪs] [sa-lin-nes], *s.* La calidad o propiedad de salino.

salinity [sə'lɪnɪtɪ] [sa-li-ni-ti], *sf.* Salinidad.

saliva [sə'laɪvə] [sa-lai-va], *s.* Saliva.

salivary ['sælɪvəɾɪ] [sa-li-va-ri], *a.* Salival; salivoso.

salivate ['sælɪveɪt] [sa-li-veit], *va. (Med.)* Excitar la secreción excesiva y continua de saliva.

salivation ['sælɪveɪʃən] [sa-li-vei-shon], *s.* Babeo, salivación, la excreción abundante de saliva, producida ordinariamente por algún remedio.

sallow ['sæləʊ] [sa-lou], *a.* Cetrino, descolorido, amarillo, pálido, lívido; se dice principalmente de la piel humana. -*s.* (*Bot.*) Sarga, una especie de sauce.

sally ['sælɪ] [sa-li], *s.* 1. (*Mill.*) Salida, surtida. 2. Paseo, excursión. 3. Impetu, arranque, pronto de alguna pasión o del genio; arrancada. 4. Despropósito, desahogo, un pronto, un arrebato, un repente o una viveza nacida de irreflexión; humorada, extravagancia. 5. (*Arq.*) Salidizo, saliente, vuelo. **Sallies of wit**, agudezas, rasgos, dichos prontos y vivos; courrencias graciosas o saladas. **To make sallies into the country**, recorrer un terreno, dar frecuentes paseos por el campo.

sally, *vn.* Salir, hacer una salida repentinamente; salir, avanzar con ánimo resuelto.

sallyport ['sælɪpɔːt] [sa-li-port], *s.* (*Fort.*) Surtida, la puerta por donde los sitiados hacen sus salidas.

salmon ['sæmən] [sa-mon], *s.* 1. Salmón, pez de mar de carne rosada. 2. Color de la carne de salmón, anaranjado rosado. **Salmon louse**, lombriz que se halla en las agallas del salmón. **Salmon-trout**, trucha salmonada.

saloon [səˈluːn] [sa-lun], *s.* 1. (*E. U.*) Una cantina o taberna donde se venden licores. 2. Sala de asamblea. 3. Sala grande de un vapor. 4. **Saloon carriage**, vagón-salón en un ferrocarril.

salt [sɔːlt] [solt], *s.* 1. Sal, cloruro de sodio, substancia cristalina de sabor propio bien señalado y muy soluble en el agua. 2. (*Quím.*) Sal, cuerpo compuesto de un ácido y una base. 3. *pl.* Sales medicinales, cuando no se especifican, sal de higuera, sulfato de magnesia. 3. Sabor, gusto. 5. Sal, agudeza, gracia o viveza en lo que se dice. -*a.* 1. Salado, impregnado de sales; salobre, que tiene sabor de sal, salino. 2. Curado o conservado con sal. 3. Que contiene agua salada o que crece en ella. **Salt-box**, caja para guardar la sal en la cocina, salero de cocina. **Saltcellar**, salero de mesa. **Salt-bush**, cualquiera de ciertas hierbas de Australia, principalmente del género Atriplex. **Salt-junk**, carne de buey dura, seca y salada para rancho de marinero. **Salt-lick**, lamedero, lugar adonde acuden los animales para lamer la sal de depósitos superficiales. **Glauber's salt**, sal de Glauber, sulfato de sodio. **Rochelle salt**, tartrato de potasio y sodio. **Rock salt**, sal gema. **Not (to be) worth one's salt**, no valer uno el pan que come. **To be sent o to go up Salt River**, (*Ger. E. U.*) Ser vencido, se dice de candidatos políticos, y es alusión a un pequeño río del Kentucky. **Salt-mines**, minas de sal, salinas. **Salt-maker**, salinero, el que trabaja en las minas de sal o en las salinas. **Salt meat**, *s.* Carne salada; cocina. **Salt-pan**, 1. Caldera o vasija en que se hace la sal evaporando el agua salada, 2. Saladar, *V. Salt-pit.* **Salt-pit**, salina, lagunajo, el sitio donde se cría u obtiene la sal por evaporación natural, salina. **Salt-spring**, fuente de agua salada. **Salt-tub**, saladero. **Salt-works**, salina, lugar donde se hace o cuaja la sal.

salt, *va.* 1. Salar, sazonar con sal, curar con sal, salpimenar. 2. (*Fig.*) sazonar, purificar. 3. (*Ger.*) Depositar fraudulentamente mineral rico en una mina sin valor. 4. Amañar (a thing). 5. Cargar precios exagerados en una factura. **To salt one's money away**, ahorrar, guardar o colocar uno bien su dinero.

saltant ['sɔːltənt] [sol-tant], *a.* Saltante.

saltation [sɔːlˈteɪʃən] [sol-tei-shon], *s.* 1. Saltación, palpitación. 2. Progreso o modificación por saltos.

salter ['sɔːltər] [sol-tar], *s.* 1. Salador, el que sala. 2. Salinero, el que vende sal. 3. Preparador de sales o drogas; droguista.

saltern ['sɔːltən] [sol-tern], *s.* Salina, el lugar donde se beneficia la sal.

saltigrade ['sɔːltɪgreɪd] [sol-ti-greid], *a.* Saltígrado, que anda a saltos, se aplicaen particular a una clase de arañas.

saltiness ['sɔːltɪnɪs] [sol-ti-nes], *sf.* Salinidad, salobridad.

salting ['sɔːltɪŋ] [sol-tin], *s.* 1. Salazón, acción de salar. 2. Tierra que inunda regularmente la marea. **Salting-tub**, saladero.

saltish ['sɔːltɪʃ] [sol-tish], *s.* Sabroso, algo salado.

saltless ['sɔːltlɪs] [solt-les], *a.* Soso, desabrido, insulso, insípido.

saltmarsh ['sɔːltmɑːʃ] [solt-marsh], *s.* Saladar o marisma.

saltness ['sɔːltnɪs] [solt-nes], *s.* Sabor de sal, saladura.

saltpeter, saltpetre ['sɔːltpiːtər] [solt-pi-tar], *s.* Nitro, salitre. **Saltpetre-house**, salitrería. **Saltpetre-makers**, alitrero.

saltwort ['sɔːltwɔːt] [solt-uort], *s.* Barrilla, sosa, nombre de diferentes plantas de los géneros Salsola y Salicornía.

saltworks ['sɔːltwɜːks] [solt-ueks], *s.* Salinas.

salty ['sɔːltɪ] [sol-ti], *a.* Salado, salobre, salobreño.

salubrious [səˈluːbrɪəs] [sa-lu-brios], *a.* Salubre, saludable.

salubrity [səˈluːbrɪtɪ] [sa-lu-bri-ti], **salubriousness** [səˈluːbrɪəsnɪs] [sa-lu-brios-nes] *s.* Salubridad.

salutary ['sæljʊtərɪ] [sa-liu-ta-ri], *a.* Saludable, salubre, sano, salutífero.

salutation [ˌsæljʊˈteɪʃən] [sa-liu-tei-shon], *s.* Salutación, saludo, bienvenida, enhorabuena, parabién.

salutatory ['sæljʊtətərɪ] [sa-liu-ta-to-ri], *a.* Saludador. -*s.* La oración con que principian los ejercios el día de recepción de grados en los colegios y universidades americanos; discurso de bienvenida.

salute [səˈljuːt] [sa-liut], *va.* 1. Saludar, mostrar benevolencia, respeto o deferencia. 2. Honrar con una salva de artillería o fusilería, o porte de armas, enarbolar el pabellón, etc., saludar. 3. (*Ant.*) Bear. -*vn.* Ofrecer un saludo.

salute, *s.* 1. Salutación; saludo, acción o actitud de saludar. 2. Salva, descarga de armas en honor de alguien, saludo hecho portando el arma; honras militares, navales, u otras de carácter oficial. 3. Beso, abrazo.

salvage ['sælvɪdʒ] [sal-vich], *s.* 1. Salvamento. 2. Derecho de salvamento que se cobra de las cosas salvadas en un naufragio. 3. Lo recuperado en un incendio o un naufragio. -*va.* Salvar (en un naufragio, incendio, etc.).

salvation [sælˈveɪʃən] [sal-vei-shon], *s.* Salvación, estado del que se halla libre de peligro; salvación, consecución de la bienaventuranaza eterna. **Salvation Army**, ejército de salvación, una organización religiosa.

salvationist [sælˈveɪʃənɪst] [sal-vei-sho-nist], *s.* Miembro del Ejército de Salvación.

salve [sælv] [salv], *s.* 1. Emplasto, ungüento; auxilio, socorro, remedio. 2. Remedio, alivio, consuelo. 3. (*Fam.*) Adulación. **Lip-salve**, pomada para los labios.

salve, *va.* 1. Curar una herida o úlcera aplicando ungüentos o emplastos (to cure). 2. Salvar, socorrer, remediar, auxiliar. 3. Salvar, evitar algún inconveniente, impedimento, dificultad o riesgo.

salver ['sælvər] [sal-var], *s.* Salvilla, bandeja.

salvia ['sælvɪə] [sal-via], *s.* (*Bot.*) Salvia.

salvo ['sælvəʊ] [sal-vou], *s.* 1. Reservación, excusa, escapatoria, subterfugio, restricción mental; excepción. 2. Salva de artillería, saludo militar o naval.

samaritan [səˈmærɪtən] [sa-ma-ri-tan], *a.* Samaritano, samarita, de Samaría. -*s.* 1. Samarita, samaritano. 2. Persona benévola; en alusión a la parábola de San Lucas.

samba ['sæmbə] [sam-ba], *s.* Samba, baile y canto populares del Brasil.

sambo ['sæmbəʊ] [sam-bou], *s.* 1. Mestizo, negro, apodo peyorativo. 2. Zambo.

same [seɪm] [seim], *a.* Mismo, idéntico; igual. **The same**, lo mismo, la misma cosa, otro tanto, todo uno. **It is all the same to me**, para mí es todo uno; no me importa; lo mismo me da. **Much the same as**, casi como. **If it is the same to you**, si le es a Ud. lo mismo, o igual. **All the same**, a pesar de todo.

sameness ['seɪmnɪs] [seim-nes], *s.* 1. Identidad. 2. Semejanza fiel.

samlet ['seɪmlɪt] [seim-let], *s.* Salmón pequeño, salmonete. (En vez de *Salmonet*).

samp [sæmp] [samp], *s.* (*E. U.*) Maíz descortezado sin moler o gachas hechas con él.

samphire ['sæmfaɪər] [samp-jaia'], *s.* (*Bot.*) Hinojo marino.

sample ['sɑːmpl] [sam-pel], *s.* 1. Muestra, prueba. 2. Ejemplo, dechado, patrón. **Sample copy**, ejemplar de muestra; **sample case**, muestrario.

sample, *va.* Sacar una muestra de algo, probar o examinar por medio de una porción o muestra. **Sample book**, muestrario, libro de muestras.

sampler ['sɑːmpləʳ] [sam-plaʳ], *s.* 1. El que prueba o examina por medio de muestras, el que prepara o exhibe muestras de artículos de comercio. 2. Dechado, labor de las niñas.

sanative ['sænətɪv] [sa-na-tiv], *a.* Curativo, sanativo, que sana (curative).

sanatorium [ˌsænə'tɔːrɪəm] [sa-na-to-riom], *s.* 1. Lugar adonde acuden las gentes para conservar la salud, v. g. una estación balnearia o un punto de veraneo en los climas tropicales. 2. Casa de salud, sanatorio.

sanctification [ˌsæŋktɪfɪ'keɪʃən] [sank-ti-fi-kei-shon], *s.* Santificación; consagración.

sanctifier ['sæŋktɪfaɪəʳ] [sank-ti-faiaʳ], *s.* Santificador.

sanctify ['sæŋktɪfaɪ] [sank-ti-fai], *va.* Santificar.

sanctimonious [ˌsæŋktɪ'məʊnɪəs] [sank-ti-mou-nios], *a.* Beato, mojigato, parecido o semejante a santo.

sanctimoniusness [ˌsæŋktɪ'məʊnɪəsnɪs] [sank-ti-mou-nios-nes], *s.* Apariencia de santidad, aire falso de santidad, mojigatería.

sanctimony ['sæŋktɪ'məʊnɪ] [sank-ti-fi-mou-ni], *s.* 1. Santimonia, santidad. 2. Apariencia de santidad; beatería.

sanction ['sæŋkʃən] [sank-shon], *s.* 1. Sanción, el acto solemne por el que se ratifica, autoriza o confirma una ley o estatuto. 2. Sanción, establecimiento o ley: mandato, decreto. 3. Ratificación, confirmación, justificación. *-va.* Sancionar, dar fuerza de ley; autorizar, ratificar, validar; venir en apoyo de, confirmar.

sanctitude ['sæŋktɪtjuːd] [sank-ti-tiud], *s.* (*Ant.*) Carácter sagrado, santidad.

sanctity ['sæŋktɪtɪ] [sank-ti-ti], *s.* 1. Santidad, el estado o la naturaleza de sagrado o santo, pureza espiritual. 2. Calidad de sagrado, solemnemente obligatorio, o inviolable; inviolabilidad.

sanctuary ['sæŋktjʊərɪ] [sank-chua-ri], *s.* 1. Santuario, lugar santo o sagrado; templo, altar de santo. Entre los israelitas, la parte más retirada del tabernáculo o templo. 2. Asilo, refugio sagrado. **To take sanctuary**, acogerse a sagrado.

sanctum ['sæŋktəm] [sank-tom], *s.* Paraje sagrado; familiarmente, una pieza reservada, una oficina particular. **Sanctum sanctorum**, Sancta sanctórum.

sanctus ['sæŋktəs] [sank-tos], *s.* Sanctus, parte de la misa antes del canon, en que se repite esta palabra tres veces. **Sanctus bell**, campanilla que sirve para anunciar la elevación de la sagrada hostia en la misa.

sand [sænd] [sand], *s.* 1. Arena, partículas o granos pequeños de piedra sueltos o separados (grit). 2. Arenal, tierra estéril cubierta de arena. 3. *pl.* 1. Arenales, playa de arena; regiones donde no se halla más que arena. 2. Partículas o granos arenosos semejantes a los del reloj de arena; de aquí, momentos de tiempo o de vida. 4. (*Ger. E. U.*) 1. Fuerza de carácter, sufrimiento, valor. 2. Dinero contante, caudales. **Sand-bank**, banco de arena. **Small sand**, arenilla. (*Mex.*) Marmajita o margajita. **Sand-bag**, saco de arena, saco para arena; se emplea para construir fortificaciones, para lastre, etc., y también como arma ofensiva. **Sand-bar**, barra, banco de arena en la embocadura de un río, o a lo largo de la playa, etc. **Sand-blast**, aparato para impeler un chorro de arena a fin de desgastar o grabar modelos en el vidrio, mármol, etc. **Sand-fly**, mosca de los arenales, insecto pequeño muy incómodo del género Simulium. **Sand-glass**, reloj de arena. **Sand-wasp**, avispa de arena, toda avispa que cava en la tierra. **Sand-bath**, (*Quím.*) Baño de arena. **Sand-blind**, corto de vista. **Sand-box**, 1. Salvadera (para echar arenilla sobre lo que se escribe). 2. Depósito de arena que se pone en una locomotora y sirve para echar arena delante de las ruedas e impedir que resbalen.

sand, *va.* Enarenar, cubrir o mezclar con arena.

sandal ['sændl] [san-dal], *s.* Sandalia.

sandalwood ['sændlwʊd] [san-dal-vud], *s.* Sándalo, árbol de la India, y su madera olorosa. **Red sandalwood o sanderswood**, madera de sándalo rojo.

sandbag ['sændbæg] [sand-bag], *s.* 1. Saco de arena. 2. Porra de arena.

sandbag, *v.* 1. Tapar u obstruir con sacos de arena. 2. Golpear con una porra de arena.

sandblast ['sændblɑːst] [sand-blast], *s.* Chorro de arena. *-va.* Limpiar paredes, etc.) mediante un chorro de arena.

sandbox-tree ['sændbɒksˌtriː] [sand-boks-tri], *s.* (*Bot.*) Hura, especie de nogal de América.

sand dune ['sændˌdjuːn] [sand-diun], *s.* Duna.

sanded ['sændɪd] [san-did], *a.* 1. Arenoso, arenisco, lleno o cubierto de arena. 2. Color de arena; marcado con puntos menudos, pecoso.

sanders ['sændəz] [san-dars], *s.* (*Bot.*) sándalo. V. SANDALWOOD.

sandiness ['sændɪnɪs] [san-di-nes], *s.* 1. Naturaleza arenosa. 2. Rubio ardiente de la tez o cabellera.

sandiver ['sændɪvəʳ] [san-di-vaʳ], *s.* Anatrón, la sal y espuma del vidrio que se saca en las fábricas.

sandpaper ['sændˌpeɪpəʳ] [sand-pei-paʳ], *s.* Papel de lija.

sandpiper ['sændˌpaɪpəʳ] [sand-pai-paʳ], *s.* Actitis o tringa, ave zancuda semejante a la agachadiza, que por lo común frecuenta las orillas del mar en las bandadas.

sandpit ['sændpɪt] [sand-pit], *s.* Arenal.

sandstone ['sændstəʊn] [sand-stoun], *s.* Piedra arenisca, roca que consta de granos de cuarzo.

sandstorm ['sændstɔːm] [sand-storm], *s.* Tormenta de arena.

sandwich ['sændwɪdʒ] [sand-uich], *s.* 1. Sandwich, emparedado. 2. Combinación de dos cosas iguales con una distinta en el medio. **Sandwich man**, individuo metido entre dos carteles anunciadores que ambula por las calles. *-va.* Colocar entre dos capas, intercalar.

sandy ['sændɪ] [san-di], *a.* 1. Arenoso, arenisco, abundante en arena, que consta o está cubierto de arena, o de arena, o que la contiene. 2. Rufo, del color de la arena, rubio ardiente.

sane [seɪn] [sein], *a.* Sano de mente, que está en posesión de todas sus facultades mentales; que proviene de una mente sana.

saneness ['seɪnnɪs] [sein-nes], *s.* Sanidad del ánimo.

sang [sæŋ] [sang], *pret.* de TO SING.

sang, *s.* Instrumento chino de viento que contiene trece tubos.

sangaree [ˌsæŋɡəriː] [san-ga-ri], *s.* Sangría, bebida que se compone de vino tinto, agua, azúcar, una raja de limón, etc.

sanguiferous [sæŋ'ɡɪfərəs] [san-gui-fe-ros], *a.* Sanguífero, sanguificativo.

sanguifier ['sæŋɡɪfaɪəʳ] [san-gui-faiaʳ], *s.* La cosa que se puede convertir en sangre por medio de la digestión y sanguificación.

sanguify ['sæŋɡɪfaɪ] [san-gui-fai], *vn.* Sanguificar, criar sangre.

sanguinariness [ˌsæŋɡɪ'neərɪnɪs] [san-gui-nea-ri-nes], *s.* Calidad de sanguinario.

sanguinary ['sæŋɡɪnərɪ] [san-gui-na-ri], *a.* 1. Sanguinario, cruel, bárbaro, inhumano. 2. Sangriento.

sanguine ['sæŋɡwɪn] [san-güin], *a.* 1. Sanguíneo, sanguino, de color de sangre. 2. Sanguíneo: se dice de uno de los temperamentos o complexiones. 3. Ardiente, violento, vehemente; atrevido, temerario, impetuoso; confiado, lleno de esperanza. *-s.* Color de sangre.

sanguinely ['sæŋɡwɪnlɪ] [san-güin-li], *adv.* Ardientemente; confiadamente, con esperanzas de buen éxito.

sanguineness ['sæŋɡwɪnnɪs] [san-güin-nes], *s.* 1. Estado o calidad del que está lleno de esperanza, confianza, ardor o arrojo; originalmente, temperamento sanguíneo. 2. Plenitud de sangre, plétora, color de sangre en la piel.

sanguineous [sæŋ'ɡwɪnɪəs] [san-güi-nios], *a.* 1. Sanguino, que abunda en sangre o la aumenta y cría. 2. Sanguíneo, sanguino, que pertenece a la sangre, que constituye la sangre. 3. Encarnado, de color de sangre.

sanify ['sænɪfaɪ] [sa-ni-fai], *v.* Sanear, dar condiciones de salubridad.

sanious ['sænɪəs] [sa-nios], *a.* Purulento, sanioso, icoroso.

sanitarian [ˌsænɪˈtɛərɪən] [sa-ni-tea-rian], *a.* Sanitario, perteneciente a la salud pública o a las reglas de la higiene. -*s.* promovedor de una reforma sanitaria.

sanitarium [sænˈtɛərɪəm] [sa-ni-tea-riom], *s.* *V.* SANATORIUM (2ª acep.)

sanitary [ˈsænɪtərɪ] [sa-ni-ta-ri], *a.* Sanitario, higiénico, relativo a la salud. **Sanitary napkin**, servilleta sanitaria, almohadilla higiénica.

sanitate [ˈsænɪteɪt] [sa-ni-teit], *v.* Higienizar, sanear.

sanitation [sænɪˈteɪʃən] [sa-ni-tei-shon], *s.* Saneamiento, higiene.

sanity [ˈsænɪtɪ] [sa-ni-ti], *s.* Juicio sano, sentido común; sanidad, estado sano de la inteligencia, del espíritu y de la voluntad.

sanskrit, sanscrit [ˈsænskrɪt] [sans-krit], *s.* y *a.* Sánscrito, lengua sagrada del Indostán, que tiene gran afinidad con las principales de Europa.

Santa Claus [ˈsæntəˈklɔːz] [san-ta-klos], *s.* Papá Noel, San Nicolás.

santon [ˈsæntən] [san-ton], *s.* Santón, monje o fraile turco. (*Esp.*)

sap [sæp] [sap], *s.* 1. Savia, el jugo o suco nutricio de los árboles y plantas. 2. (*Mil.*) Zapa, una especie de mina. 3. Vigor, vitalidad. 4. (*Fam.*) Dinero. 5. Tonto, bobo. *V. Sap-wood.* **Sap-green**, verde del jugo del ramno. **Sap-wood**, albura, alburno, la madera nueva próxima a la corteza de un árbol.

sap, *va.* 1. Zapar, minar una muralla o fortificación. 2. Minar, abrir camino por debajo de tierra. 3. Minar, procurar cautelosamente la ruina o destrucción de una cosa. -*vn.* Caminar por mina o debajo de tierra, obrar ocultamente o por bajo mano, introducirse furtiva y cautelosamente en alguna parte.

saphenous [ˈsæfɪnəs] [sa-fi-nos], *a.* (*Anat.*) Superficial, manifiesto, se dice de ciertas venas y nervios de la pierna.

sapid [ˈsæpɪd] [sa-pid], *a.* Sabroso, gustoso, deleitable al paladar.

sapidity, sapidness [səˈpɪdɪtɪ] [sa-pi-di-ti], *s.* Sabor, gusto, de los alimentos.

sapling [ˈsæplɪŋ] [sa-plin], *s.* Renuevo, árbol joven, de aquí, un joven, y en particular, cachorro de lebrel.

sapper [ˈsæpəʳ] [sa-paʳ], *s.* (*Mil.*) Zapador, el que zapa.

sapphic [ˈsæfɪk] [sa-fik], *a.* Sáfico, que se refiere a la poetisa griega Safo. -*s.* Sáfico, especie de verso.

sapphire [ˈsæfaɪəʳ] [sa-faiaʳ], *s.* 1. Zafir o zafiro, piedra preciosa de color cerúleo, variedad dura y transparente del vorindón. 2. Color azul obscuro, cerúleo.

sappiness [ˈsæpɪnɪs] [sa-pi-nes], *s.* 1. El estado o la calidad de lo que abunda en savia, jugosidad. 2. Mentecatería, conducta pueril.

sappy [ˈsæpɪ] [sa-pi], *a.* 1. Que abunda en savia. 2. Jugoso, que abunda en jugos. 3. Inmaturo, mentecato, débilmente, sentimental, propenso a puerilidades.

saracen [ˈsærəsən] [sa-ra-san], *s.* Sarraceno.

saracenic [ˌsærəˈsiːnɪk] [sa-ra-si-nik], *a.* Sarracénico, perteneciente a los sarracenos, moro.

sarcasm [ˈsɑːkæzəm] [sar-ka-sem], *s.* Sarcasmo, ironía acerba, burla o sátira picante (irony).

sarcastic [sɑːˈkæstɪk] [sar-kas-tik], *a.* Sarcástico, mordaz, picante, irónico.

sarcastically [sɑːˈkæstɪkəlɪ] [sar-kas-ti-ka-li], *adv.* Mordazmente, sarcásticamente.

sarcel [ˈsɑːsl] [sar-sel], *s.* Una de las plumas del alón de cualquier ave, y particularmente del halcón.

sarcenet [ˈsɑːsnɪt] [sars-nit], *s.* *V.* SARSENET.

sarcologic [ˌsɑːkəˈlɒdʒɪk] [sar-ko-lo-yik], *a.* Sarcológico, referente a la sarcología.

sarcology [ˈsɑːkələdʒɪ] [sar-ko-lo-yi], *s.* Sarcología, la parte de la anatomía que trata de las partes blandas.

sarcoma [sɑːˈkəʊmə] [sar-kou-ma], *s.* Sarcoma, tumor o excrecencia que se cría en alguna parte del cuerpo sin cambio de color; frecuentemente es maligno.

sarcophagous [sɑːˈkəfəgəs] [sar-ko-fa-gos], *a.* Carnívoro: se dice del animal que se mantine de carne.

sardine [sɑːˈdiːn] [sar-din], *s.* Sardio, especie de cornerina, se considera y emplea como piedra preciosa.

sardinian [sɑːˈdiːnɪən] [sar-di-nian], *a.* Sardo, de Cerdeña.

sardonic [sɑːˈdɒnɪk] [sar-do-nik], *s.* 1. Sardónico, insincero y burlón; burlador. 2. Antiguamente, forzado, no natural (risa). **Sardonic laughter**, risa sardónica.

sardonyx [sɑːˈdɒnɪks] [sar-do-niks], *s.* Sardónice, piedra preciosa, sardonio, sardónique o sardónix, variedad de ónice que consta de capas de calcedonia de colores claros, alternadas con capas rojizas de cornerina.

sarrasin [ˈsɑːrəsiːn] [sa-ra-sin], *s.* Rastrillo de defensa. *V.* PORTCULLIS.

sarsaparilla [ˌsɑːsəpəˈrɪlə] [sar-sa-pa-ri-la], *s.* (*Bot.*) Zarzaparrilla.

sarsenet, sarsnet [ˈsɑːsnɪt] [sars-nit], *s.* Tafetán de Florencia, especie de tela delgada de seda que se emplea para forros.

sartorial [sɑːˈtɔːrɪəl] [sar-to-rial], *a.* Sartorio, de sastre; perteneciente a un sastre.

sash [sæʃ] [sash], *va.* Poner una banda o ceñidor a una persona.

sash, *s.* 1. Banda o faja de seda que usan los oficiales militares, ya terciada, ya ceñida; cíngulo, cinturón, ceñidor, cinto. 2. Bastidor o marco de ventana, o vidriera; vidriera corrediza, la que se sube y baja con poleas y cuerdas. 3. Chal largo y muy angosto.

sassafras [ˈsæsəfræs] [sa-sa-fras], *s.* (*Bot.*) Sasafrás, árbol americano de las lauráceas.

sat [ˈsæt] [sat], *pret.* y *pp.* del verbo TO SIT.

satan [ˈseɪtn] [sei-tan], *s.* Satanás, el diablo, el feje de los ángeles caídos.

satanic [səˈtænɪk] [sa-ta-nik], *a.* Satáncio, diabólico, infernal.

satanically [səˈtænɪkəlɪ] [sa-ta-ni-ka-li], *adv.* Diabólicamente, satánicamente.

satchel [ˈsætʃəl] [sa-chal], *s.* Burjaca o bursaca; mochila, bolsa, maletilla, saco de mano.

sate [seɪt] [seit], *va.* hartar, saciar a uno de comida. *V.* SATIATE.

sateen [sæˈtiːn] [sa-tin], *s.* Rasete, cierta tela lustrosa de algodón y a veces de estambre.

satellite [ˈsætəlaɪt] [sa-te-lait], *s.* 1. (*Astr.*) Satélite. **Man-made satellite**, satélite artificial. 2. Satélite, subalterno obsequioso, persona que asiste o acompaña a otra que se halla en el poder.

satiable [ˈseɪʃəbl] [sei-sha-bol], *a.* Saciable, que puede saciarse.

satiate [ˈseɪʃɪeɪt] [sei-shieit], *va.* 1. Saciar, hartar, llenar, satisfacer completamente los deseos y pasiones. 2. Saturar, colmar, sobrecargar, sobrellenar. -*vn.* Hartarse, saciarse.

satiate, *a.* Harto, saciado, satisfecho, saturado (satisfied).

satiation [ˌseɪʃɪˈeɪʃən] [sa-shiei-shon], *s.* Hartazgo, el acto y efecto de hartarse o saciarse; saciedad.

satiety [ˈseɪʃɪətɪ] [sei-shia-ti], *s.* Saciedad, hartura, plenitud que sobrepasa los deseos, repleción.

satin [ˈsætɪn] [sa-tin], *s.* 1. Raso, tela de seda lustrosa, tupida y suave. **Satin-bird**, pájaro muy vistoso de Australia. **Satin-damask**, raso con rico dibujo de flores o arabescos, lisos o en relieve. **Satin-flower**, lunaria, planta y su flor.

satinet [ˈsætɪnɪt] [sa-ti-nit], *s.* 1. Satinete, especie de tela fuerte de lana y algodón. 2. Rasete, especie de raso delgado.

satinwood [ˈsætɪnwʊd] [sa-tin-wud], *s.* Palo águila, madera dura y lustrosa, una de varias maderas de las Indias orientales y occidentales que se emplean en la ebanisteria.

satiny [ˈsætɪnɪ] [sa-ti-ni], *a.* Arrasado, parecido al raso o propio de él.

satire [ˈsætaɪəʳ] [sa-taiaʳ], *s.* 1. Sátira, obra en que se motejan las costumbres, vicios, etc. 2. Sátira, cualquier dicho agudo, picante y mordaz.

satiric [sə'tɪrɪk] [sa-ti-rik], *a.* Satírico, que contiene una sátira; de la naturaleza de la sátira.

satirically [sə'tɪrɪkəlɪ] [sa-ti-ri-ka-li], *adv.* Satíricamente.

satirist ['sætərɪst] [sa-ti-rist], *s.* Escritor de sátiras, autor satírico.

satirize ['sætɪraɪz] [sa-ti-rais], *va.* Satirizar, motejar con sátiras, escribir sátiras.

satisfaction [ˌsætɪs'fækʃən] [sa-tis-fak-shon], *s.* 1. Satisfacción, contento, cumplimiento del deseo o gusto. 2. Satisfacción, recompensa o reparación por algún delito, agravio o injuria. 3. Lo que satisface o recompensa, razón compensación; pago (de una deuda o cuenta). **In full satisfaction of a debt, of a demand**, en pago final de una deuda, en saldo de una cuenta.

satisfactorily [ˌsætɪs'fæktərɪlɪ] [sa-tis-fak-to-ri-li], *adv.* Satisfactoriamente, suficientemente; de una manera satisfactoria o convincente.

satisfactoriness [ˌsætɪs'fæktərɪnɪs] [sa-tis-fak-to-ri-nes], *s.* Calidad de satisfactorio.

satisfactory [ˌsætɪs'fæktərɪ] [sa-tis-fak-to-ri], *a.* 1. Satisfactorio, que da o produce satisfacción o contento, expiatorio; suficiente. 2. Expiatorio.

satisfy ['sætɪsfaɪ] [sa-tis-fai], *va.* 1. Satisfacer, saciar un gusto o una pasión, contentar. 2. Satisfacer, sosegar las pasiones de ánimo. 3. Satisfacer, recompensar, resarcir, pagar. 4. Satisfacer, dar solución a alguna duda o dificultad. -*vn.* Satisfacer, dar satisfacción a.

saturable ['sætʃəreɪbl] [sa-cha-rei-bol], *a.* Saturable, capaz de saturación.

saturate ['sætʃəreɪt] [sa-cha-reit], *va.* 1. (*Quím.*) Saturar, echar en un líquido toda la cantidad de un sólido que puede disolverse en él. 2. Empapar, mojar; imbuir, inculcar completamente; llenar al extremo.

saturation [ˌsætʃə'reɪʃən] [sa-cha-rei-shon], *s.* Saturación.

Saturday ['sætədɪ] [sa-te-di], *s.* Sábado.

Saturn ['sætən] [sa-tarn], *s.* 1. Saturno (planet). 2. Saturno, una de las divinidades latinas.

saturnalia [ˌsætə'neɪlɪə] [sa-tar-nei-lia], *s.* 1. Saturnales, fiestas en honor del dios Saturno. 2. Epoca o escenas de licenciar y desorden.

saturnian ['sætənɪən] [sa-tar-nian], *a.* 1. Saturnal, feliz, dichoso, perteneciente a la edad dorada. 2. Saturnal, perteneciente al planeta Saturno.

saturnine ['sætənaɪn] [sa-tar-nain], *a.* 1. Saturnino, bajo la influencia del planeta Saturno, melancólico, triste, silencioso, poco sociable. 2. (*Ant. Quím.*) Plomizo, perteneciente al plomo. **Saturnine poisoning**, envenenamiento por el plomo.

satyr ['sætər] [sa-tar], *s.* 1. Sátiro, divinidad mitológica de los bosques, con orejas semejantes a las de la cabra. 2. Persona muy lasciva.

sauce [sɔːs] [sos], *s.* 1. Salsa, mezcla de varias cosas desleídas para condimentar los guisados. 2. Plato hecho con pulpa de frutas cocida ligeramente con azúcar. 3. (*Fam.*) lenguaje impertinente o impudente. **Sauce-boat, sauce-dish**, salsera.

sauce, *va.* 1. Condimentar, sazonar. 2. (*Fam.*) Ser impertinente; decir desvergüenzas, insolencias.

saucebox ['sɔːsbɒks] [sos-boks], *s.* El muchacho o persona desvergonzada y atrevida.

saucepan ['sɔːspən] [sos-pan], *s.* Cacerola, cazo pequeño con un mango largo para hacer salsas y otros guisos.

saucer ['sɔːsər] [so-sar], *s.* 1. Platillo. 2. Platillo usado para servir las confituras, frutas, etc.; salsera. 3. (*Mar.*) Parte que recibe el espigón del cabrestante.

saucily ['sɔːsɪlɪ] [so-si-li], *adv.* Descaradamente, desvergonzadamente, con impudencia o insolencia.

sauciness ['sɔːsɪnɪs] [so-si-nes], *s.* Descaro, insolencia, impudencia, desvergüenza.

saucisse ['sɔːsɪs] [so-sis], *s.* (*Art.*) Salchicha, saco embetunado y lleno de pólvora para dar fuego a una mina (*Fr.*).

saucy ['sɔːsɪ] [so-si], *a.* Descarado, atrevido, desvergonzado, insolente, impudente (insolent).

sauerkraut ['saʊəkraʊt] [saua-kraut], *s.* Col ácida, preparación alemana de col desmenuzada, sazonada con sal y fermentada bajo presión.

sauna ['sɔːnə] [so-na], *sf.* Sauna.

saunders ['sɔːndəz] [son-ders], *s.* Plato de carne picada y puré de patatas.

saunter ['sɔːntər] [son-ta], *vn.* Vagar, andar ocioso, despacio y sin objeto; de aquí, haraganear.

sauntering ['sɔːntərɪŋ] [son-te-rin], *s.* Vagancia, acción de vagar ocioso.

saurian ['sɔːrɪən] [so-rian], *a.* Saurio, parecido a un lagarto. - *s. pl.* Saurios, los reptiles conocidos con el nombre de lagartos.

sausage ['sɒsɪdʒ] [so-sich], *s.* 1. Salchicha, chorizo, longaniza. 2. Cierto globo cautivo de observación. 3. Alemán. **Large sausage**, salchichón. (*Prov.*) Butifarra.

sauté ['saʊteɪ] [sou-tei], *a.* Salteado.

savable, saveable ['sævəbl] [sa-va-bol], *a.* Conservable, salvable, que se puede salvar o conservar.

savage ['sævɪdʒ] [sa-vich], *a.* 1. Salvaje, que no está domesticado, silvestre, feroz, bárbaro, inculto. 2. Salvaje, no civilizado, que vive de una manera ruda o primitiva. 3. Feroz, cruel, enfurecido. 4. (Poco us.) Inculto, inhabitado, alejado de las habitaciones humanas. -*s.* Salvaje, el hombre bárbaro o inculto.

savagely ['sævɪdʒlɪ] [sa-vich-li], *adv.* Bárbaramente, cruelmente, inhumanamente.

savageness ['sævɪdʒnɪs] [sa-vich-nes], *s.* Salvajez; barbarie, ferocidad, crueldad.

savanna [sə'vænə] [sa-va-na], *s.* Sabana, campo grande cubierto de hierbas, y por extensión cualquier pradera muy extensa sin árboles.

savant ['sævənt] [sa-vant], *s.* Sabio, persona erudita.

save [seɪv] [seiv], *va.* 1. Salvar, librar de algún riesgo o peligro, poner en seguro; guardar, conservar (to keep). 2. Ahorrar, excusar algo del gasto; economizar, conservar las cosas no gastándolas con profusión. 3. Salvar, dar la bienaventuranza eterna. 4. Salvar, evitar algún inconveniente, obstáculo o riesgo. 5. Aprovecharse, tomar o emplear a propósito, en tiempo oportuno. 6. Ahorrar, evitar, excusar penas, trabajos, molestias, etc. 7. Reservar, proteger, eximir. 8. **To save up**, ahorrar dinero. **To save quarrels**, impedir o prevenir las contiendas. **To save harmless**, sanear, indemnizar. **God save the king!** ¡Dios salve al rey! ¡Viva el rey! **To save oneself the trouble**, ahorrarse la molestia o el trabajo. **To save appearances**, guardar las apariencias.

save, *prep.* Salvo, excepto, menos, a excepción de. -*conj.* Sino, a menos que, si no es más que.

saveable ['seɪvəbl] [sei-va-bol], *a.* 1. Salvable. 2. Guardable, conservable.

saver ['seɪvər] [sei-va], *s.* Libertador; el que guarda, ahorra o economiza. **Saver life**, salvavidas.

saving ['seɪvɪŋ] [sei-vin], *a.* 1. Ahorrativo, frugal, económico; que no hace gastos inútiles, que no es pródigo (thrifty). 2. Salvador, que salva. 3. Sin pérdida, ni ganacia. 4. Calificativo, que hace excepción o reserva. **A saving clause**, cláusula que contiene una salvedad o reserva. -*s.* 1. Economía, ahorro, el acto de ahorrar o lo que se ahorra. 2. Excepción en favor de una cosa. 3. *pl.* Ahorros. **Savings account**, cuenta de ahorros. **Savings bank**, banco de ahorros, caja de ahorros. -*prep.* Con excepción de fuera de, excepto. **Saving your reverence**, con perdón de usted.

savingly ['seɪvɪŋlɪ] [sei-vin-li], *adv.* Económicamente, parcamente.

savingness ['seɪvɪŋnɪs] [sei-vin-nes], *s.* Ahorro, economía, frugalidad.

savior, saviour ['seɪvjər] [sei-via], *s.* Salvador, el Redentor del género humano.

savoir-faire ['sævwɑː'fɛər] [sa-vua-fe], *s.* Don de gentes.

savor, savour ['seɪvər] [sei-va], *s.* 1. Sabor, gusto, olor, perfume u olor y sabor combinados. 2. Sabor, calidad aproximada o carácter determinado.

savor, savour, *va.* 1. Saborear, dar sabor gusto. 2. (*Ant.*) Tener gusto a. -*vn.* 1. Saber, tener sabor perceptible al gusto. 2. Oler, exhalar algún olor. 3. Tener sabor u olor a alguna cosa (con *of*); manifestar una calidad determinada. En este último sentido se usa casi siempre moralmente hablando. **Words savoring of pride**, palabras de orgulloso dejo.

savorily ['seɪvərɪlɪ] [sei-va-ri-li], *adv.* Con gusto, sabrosamente.

savoriness ['seɪvərɪnɪs] [sei-va-ri-nes], *s.* Paladar, fragancia.

savory ['seɪvərɪ] [sei-va-ri], *s.* (*Bot.*) Ajedrea.

savory, savoury, *a.* Sabroso, fragante, aperitivo, agradable.

savoy [sə'vɔɪ] [sa-voi], *s.* (*Bot.*) Variedad de col o berza con hojas arrugadas.

saw [sɔː] [so], *s.* 1. Sierra, serrucho, instrumento para aserrar. **Hand-saw**, sierra o serrucho de mano. **Pil-saw o whip-saw**, serrucho, sierra grande con dos asideros. **Tenon-saw**, sierra de ingletes. 2. Refrán, proverbio, sentencia. **Band saw**, sierra continua (de hoja sin fin). **Cross-cut saw**, sierra de trozar. **Fret saw**, sierra de calar. **Compass o keyhole saw**, sierra de rodear, de punta, para abrir bocallaves. **Jig saw**, sierra de vaivén. **Sawbuck**, (*E. U.*) Caballete de aserrador con extremos en forma de X. **Saw-blade**, hoja de sierra. **Saw-fly**, mosca de sierra, tentredo, insecto himenóptero, cuya hembra con su largo ovipositor penetra las plantas y la madera blanda y deposita sus huevos en la incisión. **Saw-set**, trabador, triscador, instrumento para triscar los dientes de una sierra.

saw, pret. del verbo *TO SEE*.

saw, *va.* (*pp.* SAWED y SAWN). Serrar, aserrar. -*vn.* 1. Ser cortado o capaz de ser cortado con una sierra. 2. Usar una sierra, ejecutar movimientos como los del que maneja una sierra. 3. (*Fam.*) Tocar el violín.

sawbones ['sɔːbəʊnz] [so-bouns], *s.* (*Fam.*) Cirujano.

sawdust ['sɔːdʌst] [so-dast], *s.* Aserraduras, serrín.

sawfish ['sɔːfɪʃ] [so-fish], *s.* Priste, pez marino del orden de los selacios.

sawmill ['sɔːmɪl] [so-mil], *s.* Molino de aserrar.

sawn ['sɔːn] [son], *pp. irr.* de SAW. Aserrado.

sawpit ['sɔːpɪt] [so-pit], *s.* Aserradero.

saw-wort ['sɔːwɔːt] [so-uort], *s.* (*Bot.*) Serrátula.

saw-wrest ['sɔːwrest] [so-rest], *s.* Triscador. V. **Saw-set**, en SAW.

sawyer ['sɔːjəʳ] [so-yaʳ], *s.* 1. Aserrador, serrador o más bien chiquichaque, el aserrador de piezas grandes. 2. (*E. U.*) Árbol que ha caído en un río. V. SNAG. **Sawhorse o trestle,**, caballete de aserrador.

sax [sæks] [saks], *s.* Hachuela de pizarrero.

saxhorn ['sækshɔːn] [saks-jorn], *s.* (*Mús.*) Bombardino.

saxifrage ['sæksɪfrɪdʒ] [sak-si-frich], *s.* (*Bot.*) Saxigraga, género de plantas.

saxon ['sæksn] [sak-son], *a.* Sajón, de Sajonia, perteneciente a los sajones o a su lengua. -*s.* 1. Sajón, sajona, habitante de Sajonia. 2. Lengua sajona. 3. Anglosajón, aquel cuya lengua, materna es el inglés.

saxophone ['sæksəfəʊn] [sak-so-foun], *s.* Saxofono, instrumento con embocadura semejante a la del clarinete y unas 20 llaves.

say [seɪ] [sei], *s.* 1. Habla, la locución o palabras que se hablan, discurso, afirmación: lo que uno ha dicho o tiene que decir. 2. Derecho o turno de hablar o elegir. 3. **The say**, la última palabra, la autoridad decisiva. **To have a say in the affair**, tener voz en el asunto.

say, *va.* (*pret. y pp.* SAID). 1. Decir, hablar, pronunciar alguna cosa; recitar, repetir (talk, tell, speak). 2. Decir, alegar, afirmar. 3. Suponer, presumir como probable o verdadero o como hipótesis provisional. **To say over again**, volver a decir, repetir o decir segunda vez. **That is to say**, esto es decir o quiere decir. **I have something to say to you**, tengo que hablar con Ud. **No sooner said than done**, dicho y hecho. **To say a lesson**, recitar una lección. **My watch says quarter past twelve**, mi reloj señala las doce y cuarto. **It is said, they say**, se dice, dicen. -*vn.* Decir, hacer una aserción. **To say on**, continuar hablando. **I say!** ¡Hola! ¡escucha, oye! **All he could say for himself**, todo lo que pude decir o alegar en su favor.

saying ['seɪɪŋ] [seiin], *s.* Dicho, lo que se dice; aserto, relato, adagio, sentencia, proverbio (proverb, sentence,

expression). **An old saying**, refrán antiguo. **As the saying is**, como se dice, como dijo el otro.

scab [skæb] [skab], *s.* 1. Costra de una herida o úlcera. 2. Roña, especie de sarna que padecen las bestias. 3. Sarnoso, roñoso; apodo que se da al hombre ruin; de aquí (recent). 2. Despreciativamente, obrero que no pertenece a un gremio, o que no quiere hacer causa común con él, esquirol.

scab, *vn.* Criar costra sobre una llaga o herida.

scabbard ['skæbəd] [ska-bard], *s.* 1. Vaina de espada. 2. Funda de botón; toda cobertura.

scabbed ['skæbd] [skabd], **scabby** ['skæbɪ] [ska-bi], *a.* 1. Cubierto de costras, costroso. 2. Sarnoso, roñoso. 3. Vil, despreciable, ruin.

scabbiness ['skæbɪnɪs] [ska-bi-nes], *s.* La calidad de ser costroso, roñoso o sarnoso y el estado del que padece costras o roña.

scabies ['skeɪbiːz] [skei-bis], *s.* Sarna. V. ITCH.

scabious ['skæbɪəs] [ska-bios], *a.* Sarnoso. -*s.* (*Bot.*) Escabiosa, planta del género Scabiosa, de la familia de las dipsáceas.

scabrous ['skæbrəs] [ska-bros], *a.* Escabroso, desigual, áspero.

scabrousness ['skæbrəsnɪs] [ska-bros-nes], *s.* 1. Escabrosidad. 2. Aspereza, rugosidad. 3. Dificultad.

scabwort ['skæbwɔːt] [skab-uort], *s.* (*Bot.*) Enula campana. V. ELECAMPANE.

scad ['skæd] [skad], *s.* 1. Escombro, pez. V. HORSEMACKEREL. 2. Alosa, sábalo.

scaffold ['skæfəld] [ska-fold], *s.* 1. Andamio para sostener a los obreros o los materiales, v. g. en la construcción de un edificio. 2. Cadalso para ejecutar a un reo; patíbulo. 3. Tablado, andamio para un espectáculo o fiesta.

scaffold, *va.* 1. Construir tablados, instalar o poner andamios. 2. Entablar, tener los cadáveres sobre una especie de andamio, como hacen ciertas tribus indias.

scaffolding ['skæfəldɪŋ] [ska-fol-din], *s.* 1. Construcción temporal de tablados o andamios: material para andamios. 2. Armazón, bastidor de apoyo, sostén, particularmente en embriología.

scaglia ['skæɡlɪə] [ska-glia], *s.* Piedra caliza italiana que corresponde a la greda de Inglaterra.

scalable ['skæləbl] [ska-la-bol], *a.* Que se puede escalar.

scalar ['skæləʳ] [ska-laʳ], *a.* Escalar.

scalawag ['skæləwæɡ] [ska-la-uag], *s.* 1. (*Ger. E. U.*) Tuno, bribón. 2. Animal inferior o sin valor, res raquítica. 3. (*E. U.*) Republicano del sur, después de la guerra de Secesión.

scald [skɔːld] [skold], *va.* 1. Escaldar, quemar con algún líquido, hirviendo o caliente. 2. Coger ligeramente en un líquido, muy caliente. 3. Limpiar con agua muy caliente.

scald, *s.* 1. Quemadura, escaldadura, lesión de la piel y de la carne causada por un líquido hirviente. 2. Quema, acción de escaldar.

scald, *s.* V. SCALL.

scald, *a.* Tiñoso; vil, ruin, miserable.

scaldhead ['skɔːldhed] [skold-jed], *s.* Tiña, especie de lepra.

scale [skeɪl] [skeil], *s.* 1. Platillo de balanza y también la balanza misma. 2. Libra, un signo del zodíco. 3. Escama (de peces y de reptiles). 4. Escama, constrita de la piel; formación parecida a una escama, p. ej. en las alas de las mariposas. 5. Costra, costrita. 6. (*Bot.*) Escama, hoja abortada o rudimentaria cuyo color varía mucho. 7. Incrustación en las calderas; chispa, revestimiento de óxido que se forma sobre el hierro calentado. 8. Lámina pequeña de algún metal; laminita o plancha, hoja u capa muy pequeña de alguna cosa. 9. Escala, escalera portátil; escalón. 10. Escalada. 11. (*Mat.*) Escala o pitipié, línea dividida en partes iguales; escala, instrumento o medida matemática; escala de un mapa. 12. (*Mús.*) Gama. 13. Graduación regular, división de una cosa en grados. **Pair of scales**, peso de cruz. **Money-scales**, pesilla para pesar el oro y la plata. **Scale-beam**, astil o brazo de balanza. **Scales of iron**, las chispas que salen del hierro blando, cuando se le martilla. **Scale-insect**, cualquiera de los insectos cocidos, o pulgón de la corteza. **Scale-pan**, platillo de balanza. **On a large scale**, en gran escala, en grande. **On a small scale**, en pequeña escala, en pequeño.

scale, *va.* 1. Escamar, quitar las escamas; descortezar. 2. Quitar el cardenillo a los metales. 3. Cercenar, escatimar. 4. Cubrir con escamas. 5. Incrustar. *-vn.* Descostrarse; separarse en hojas o láminas delgadas; incrustarse.

scale, *va.* 1. Escalar, subir, encaramarse. 2. Medir por escala, hacer un dibujo por escala. 3. Reducir (wages, salary) según una escala. 4. Balancear, averiguar el peso por medio de balanzas; comparar, pesar, igualar. *-vn.* Servir como escalera.

scaled ['skeɪlɪd] [skei-lid], *pa.* 1. Escamado, que tiene quitadas las escamas. 2. Escamoso, que tiene escamas. 3. Subido, escalado.

scaling ['skeɪlɪŋ] [skei-lin], *s.* 1. Escamadura, la acción de escamar. 2. Escalada, la acción de escalar una fortaleza. 3. Medición por escala. 4. Disposición en escamas, imbricación. **Scaling-ladders**, escalas de sitio. *-pa.* de TO SCALE.

scall ['skɔːl] [skol], *s.* Tiña, erupción cutánea pustolosa, a menudo epidémica entre los niños; erupción costrosa o escamosa.

scalled ['skɔːld] [skold], *a.* Tiñoso, que padece tiña; costroso.

scallion ['skæljən] [ska-lion], *s. (Bot.)* Ascalonia, cebolleta.

scallop ['skɒləp] [sko-lop], *s.* 1. Peine, molusco bivalvo, pechina. 2. Venera, concha que llevaban como señal los romeros. 3. Recortadura, festón semicircular, recorte, onda.

scallop, *va.* 1. Festonear, hacer cortaduras en forma de dientes o festones. 2. Asar ostras, cocerlas en su concha.

scalp ['skɔːlp] [skolp], *s.* Cuero cabelludo.

scalp, *va.* 1. Levantar los tegumentos que cubren el cráneo. 2. *(Fam.)* Comprar y vender a precios reducidos (v. g. billetes de ferrocarril). 3. *(E.U.)* Privar a alguien de su cargo político.

scalpel ['skɔːlpəl] [skol-pel], *s.* Escalpelo; bisturí, instrumento de hoja fina y aguda empleado en cirugía y en las disecciones.

scalping ['skɔːlpɪŋ] [skol-pin], *s.* Acción de arrancar la piel del cráneo, como hacen los salvajes con los enemigos vencidos. **Scalping-knife**, cuchillo que se usa para levantar los tegumentos del cráneo dejándoles pendientes los cabellos.

scaly ['skɔːlɪ] [sko-li], *a.* 1. Escamoso, escamudo; que está cubierto de escamas; de la naturaleza de una escama. 2. Incrustado (caldera). 3. *(Fam.)* Vil, ruin, deshonrado.

scamp [skæmp] [skamp], *s.* Bribón, tuno, pícaro; originalmente, vagabundo, fugitivo.

scamper ['skæmpəʳ] [skam-paʳ], *vn.* Escaparse de prisa, huir, poner pies en polvorosa. *-s.* 1. Fuga, huída precipitada. 2. Chapucero, frangollón.

scan [skæn] [skan], *va.* 1. Escudriñar, examinar cuidadosamente. 2. Escandir, medir las sílabas o los pies que tiene un verso; leer versos marcando los pies que tienen.

scandal ['skændl] [skan-dal], *s.* 1. Escándalo (disturbance); difamación, maledicencia. 2. Oprobio, ignominia, mancha, infamia, causada por conducta deshonorosa o vergonzosa; baldón, caída. **Scandal-bearer, scandal-monger**, murmurador, detractor, el que va de una a otra parte diciendo mal de los demás.

scandalize ['skændəlaɪz] [skan-da-lais], *va.* 1. Difamar; acusar falsamente. 2. Escandalizar, causar escándalo.

scandalous ['skændələs] [skan-da-los], *a.* Escandaloso; vergonzoso, infame; chocante, ofensivo, calumnioso, difamatorio.

scandalously ['skændələslɪ] [skan-da-los-li], *adv.* Ignominiosamente; escandalosamente; de una manera difamante.

scandalousness ['skændələsnɪs] [skan-da-los-nes], *s.* Calidad de escandaloso u ofensivo, carácter escandaloso.

scandent ['skændənt] [skan-dent], *a.* Trepador; que trepa, o que sirve para trepar.

Scandinavian [ˌskændɪˈneɪvɪən] [skan-di-nei-vian], *a.* y *s.* Escandinavo, lo perteneciente a la Escandinavia; el natural de este país, o su lengua.

scanner ['skænəʳ] [ska-naʳ], *s.* Escáner *(Inform., Med)*; Antena giratoria (Radar).

scanning ['skænɪŋ] [ska-nin], *s.* Acción de escandir versos.

scansion ['skænʃən] [skan-shon], *s.* La medida de los versos por sus pies, escansión.

scansorial [ˌskænˈʃɔːrɪəl] [skan-sho-rial], *a.* Trepador, que trepa; apto para trepar, que tiene la costumbre de trepar.

scant ['skænt] [skant], *va.* Escasear, cercenar, limitar la provisión de algo; de aquí, dar de mala gana o insuficientemente, estrechar, dar escasa ración, acortar los gajes o los alimentos. *-vn. (Mar.)* Bajar en fuerza, caer, disminuirse; también, cambiar a una dirección menos favorable.

scant, *a.* Escaso, parco, apenas suficiente; corto, limitado; angosto, estrecho; insuficientemente provisto de alguna cosa. **Scant of**, corto de, insuficientemente provisto de.

scantily ['skæntɪlɪ] [skan-ti-li], *adv.* Escasamente, parcamente, estrechamente, a duras penas; insuficientemente.

scantiness ['skæntɪnɪs] [skan-ti-nes], *s.* Estrechez, angostura y corta capacidad; escasez, rareza de una cosa; falta de espacio, de extensión; proporciones estrechas, restringidas, exigüidad, insuficiencia.

scantly, *adv. (Ant.)* V. SCANTILY.

scantness ['skæntnɪs] [skant-nes], *s.* V. SCANTINESS.

scanty ['skæntɪ] [skan-ti], *a.* 1. Corto, estrecho, pequeño, falto de extensión. 2. Limitado en número o cantidad, escaso. 3. Económico, que ahorra. 3. Mezquino, cicatero.

scape ['skeɪp] [skeip], *s.* 1. *(Bot.)* Bohordo, tallo herbáceo radical que no tiene hojas. 2. *(Ento.)* Parte semejante a un tallo cerca de la base, p. ej. de una antena. 3. *(Orn.)* Cañón entero de una pluma. 4. Fuste de una columna. 5. El grito de una agachadiza asustada.

scape-goat ['skeɪpgəʊt] [skeip-gout], *s.* 1. El chivo que los judíos acostumbraban a poner en liberted en la fiesta de la expiación. 2. Persona obligada a sufrir por las culpas de otras.

scapegrace ['skeɪpgreɪs] [skeip-greis], *s.* Persona incorregible; pícaro, travieso, bribón.

scapement ['skeɪpmənt] [skeip-ment], *s.* En relojería, escape. V. ESCAPEMENT.

scapula ['skæpjʊlə] [ska-piu-laʳ], *s.* Escápula, omoplato, hueso de la espaldilla.

scapular ['skæpjʊləʳ] [ska-piu-laʳ], *a.* Escapular, que pertenece a la escápula. *-s.* 1. Escapulario. 2. *(Cir.)* Vendaje para el omoplato.

scar [skɑːʳ] [skaʳ], *s.* 1. Cicatriz, chirlo, señal que queda después de curada una herida o llaga. 2. Toda marca o señal que resulta de una lesión. 3. *(Ict.)* Escaro. 4. Roca pelada, peñasco. 5. Parte desnuda de una ladera.

scar, *va.* Hacer alguna herida o cicatriz en el cuerpo.

scarab ['skærəb] [ska-rab], **scarabee**, *s.* Escarabajo sagrado, ateuco, insecto coleóptero al que daban culto los antiguos egipcios. (Ateuchus sacer.)

scarabæid ['skærəb] [ska-rab], *a.* y *s.* Escarabídeo, perteneciente o parecido al escarabajo.

scaramouch ['skærəmuːʃ] [ska-ra-mush], *s.* Botarga, bufón, fanfarrón (bragging, swaggering).

scarce ['skɑːrs] [skars], *a.* 1. Raro, que no es abundante. 2. Escaso, que se encuentra o halla pocas veces; que no sucede a menudo; que escasea con relación a la demanda. **Money is scarce**, el dinero anda escaso. **To make oneself scarce**, no dejarse ver mucho.

scarcely ['skɑːrslɪ] [skars-li], *adv.* Apenas, con dificultad, no bien, luego que.

scarceness ['skɑːrsnɪs] [skars-nes], **scarcity** ['skɑːrsɪtɪ] [skar-si-ti], *s.* Carestía, penuria, escasez; rareza, raridad.

scare ['skeəʳ] [skeaʳ], *va.* Espantar, causar miedo o espanto; amedrentar, intimidar. **To scare away**, espantar o ahuyentar la caza, los pájaros, etc.

scarecrow ['skeəkrəʊ] [skea-krau], *s.* 1. Espantajo, maniquí para espantar los cuervos y otras aves. 2. Lo que da miedo. 3. Espantajo, esperpento, persona estrafalaria o desgalichada.

scaremonger ['skɛəmɒŋgəʳ] [skea-mon-gaʳ], *s.* Propagador de noticias alarmantes.

scarf [skɑːf] [skarf], *s.* 1. Banda, cuando pasa del hombro al costado; faja, cuando ciñe la cintura. 2. Corbata, corbata ya preparada y colgante. 3. **Scarf o scarf-joint**, *(Carp.)* ensamblaje, ensambladura, de dos piezas de madera; uno de los maderos cortados para ensamblarlo.

scarf, *va.* 1. Ensamblar, unir varias piezas de madera entre sí para formar una obra. 2. Adornar con una banda; terciar, poner en banda. 3. Envolver, cubrir, adornar.

scarface ['skɑːfeɪs] [skar-feis], *s.* Caracortada.

scarfing ['skɑːfɪŋ] [skar-fin], *s.* Acción de ensamblar; ensambladura, encabezadura, empalme.

scarfskin ['skɑːfskɪn] [skarf-skin], *s.* Cutícula, epidermis.

scarification [ˌskɛərɪfɪˈkeɪʃən] [skea-ri-fi-kei-shon], *s.* Escarificación, sajadura, el acto de escarificar y las ligeras incisiones que produce esa operación.

scarificator [ˌskɛərɪfɪˈkeɪtəʳ] [skea-ri-fi-kei-taʳ], *s.* Escarificador, instrumento con varias puntas aceradas o lancetas, que se usa para escarificar.

scarifier ['skɛərɪfaɪəʳ] [skea-ri-faiaʳ], *s.* 1. Sajador, escarificador, el que escarifica. 2. *V.* SCARIFICATOR. 3. Especie de cultivadora.

scarify ['skɛərɪfaɪ] [skea-ri-fai], *va.* 1. Escarificar, hacer incisiones en la piel, sirviéndose del escarificador, de una lanceta o de un bisturí; sajar. 2. Revolver la superficie del terreno. 3. *(Fig.)* Criticar severamente; satirizar de una manera mordaz. 4. Hacer cortes en la corteza de un árbol.

scarious, scariose ['skɛərɪəs] [skea-rios], *a. (Bot.)* Escarioso; seco, delgado, membranáceo y no verde.

scarlatina [ˌskɑːləˈtiːnə] [ska-la-ti-na], *s.* Escarlatina.

scarless ['skɑːlɪs] [skar-les], *a.* Sin cicatrices; ileso.

scarlet ['skɑːlɪt] [skar-lit], *s.* Escarlata, grana, color fino encarnado vivo que tiende a anaranjado, y el paño teñido del mismo color. **Scarlet-oak**, *(Bot.)* coscoja. *-a.* 1. Bermejo, de color escarlata. 2. Vestido de color escarlata. **Scarlet-fever**, escarlatina, escarlata, fiebre contagiosa, caracterizada por un sarpullido escarlata sobre la piel y en la garganta, y al que sigue la exfoliación de la epidermis.

scarp ['skɑːp] [skarp], *va.* Hacer escarpa, cortar en declive, *- s. (For.)* Escarpa; declive, pendiente.

scarry ['skɑːrɪ] [skea-ri], *a.* Que tiene cicatrices.

scart ['skɑːt] [skart], *s.* 1. Rasguño, señal (scratch). 2. Tacaño. 3. Soplo de aire.

scart, *v.* 1. Rasguñar, rascar. 2. Grabar.

scary ['skɛərɪ] [skea-ri], *a. (Fam.)* Medroso, asustadizo.

scat [skæt] [skat], *inter.* ¡Zape! voz que se usa para espantar al gato y otros animales pequeños.

scathe, scath ['skeɪθ] [skeiz], *va.* 1. Desbaratar, dañar severamente, hacer gran daño. 2. Quemar, abrasar. 3. Fustigar, criticar.

scathe, *s.* Desbarate, desbarato, el acto y efecto de desbaratar o dañar.

scatheless ['skeɪθlɪs] [skeiz-les], *a.* Libre de daño o perjuicio; sano y salvo.

scathing ['skeɪðɪŋ] [skei-zin], *a.* Duro, mordaz (attack).

scatter ['skætəʳ] [ska-taʳ], *va.* 1. Esparcir, disipar, alejar cosas una de otra; malgastar, disipar. 2. Dispersar, hacer huir, vencer. *-vn.* Dispersarse, esparcirse; disiparse, partir en muchas direcciones diferentes. **Scatter-brain**, persona atolondrada, casquivana. **Scatter-brained**, atolondrado, voluble, inconstante.

scattered ['skætəd] [ska-ted], *a. part.* 1. Disperso, disipado; esparcido. 2. *(Bot.)* Apartado, irregular, sin apariencia alguna de orden regular. **Scattered flock**, rebaño disperso.

scattering ['skætərɪŋ] [ska-te-rin], *a.* 1. Que se dispersa. 2. Disperso. 3. Dividido, repartido. *s.* 1. Dispersión, esparcimiento, desperdigamiento. 2. Cosa desparramada.

scatteringly ['skætərɪŋlɪ] [ska-te-rin-li], *adv.* Esparcidamente.

scavenge ['skævɪndʒ] [ska-vinch], *va.* 1. Limpiar o retirar la basura, particularmente de las calles. 2. Expulsar gases quemados.

scavenger ['skævɪndʒəʳ] [ska-vin-chaʳ], *s.* 1. Basurero, el que se lleva o saca la basura de las calles y letrinas. 2. Animal que se alimenta de carroña. **Scavenger-beetle**, escarabajo que se alimenta de carroña, especialmente un clavicornio.

scenario [sɪˈnɑːrɪəʊ] [si-na-riou], *s.* Guión (film, play).

scenarist ['siːnərɪst] [si-na-rist], *s. (Cine)* Guionista.

scend ['send] [send], *vn.* Arfar, cabecear el buque levantando alternativamente la popa y la proa.

scene [siːn] [sin], *s.* 1. Escena, perspectiva, vista, paisaje; una localidad y todo lo que con ella se relaciona. 2. Escena, sitio o tablado del teatro en que se representa una obra dramática u otro espectáculo; teatro, lugar donde sucede un acontecimiento, real o fingido (stage). 3. Escena, división de un acto; la acción o asunto de la pieza que se representa. 4. Escena, escenario, las decoraciones del teatro. 5. Acción notable, extraordinario, sea o no intencional; especialmente un arrebato, un impulso apasionado, un escándalo. **To bring on the scene**, poner en escena. **The scene of war**, el teatro de la guerra. **The scene is at Granada**, la escena pasa en Granada. **Scene-painter**, pintor escénico, o de decoraciones.

sceneful ['siːnfʊl] [sin-ful], *a.* Abundante en escenas o imágenes.

scenery ['siːnərɪ] [si-na-ri], *s.* 1. Perspectiva, vista, paisaje. 2. Decoraciones teatrales; escenario.

scenic ['siːnɪk] [si-nik], *a.* Escénico, tocante o perteneciente a la escena; artístico; pintoresco.

scenographical [siːˈnɒgrəfɪkəl] [si-no-gra-fi-kal], *a.* Escenográfico.

scenography [siːˈnɒgrəfɪ] [si-no-gra-fi], *s.* Escenografía, la perfecta delineación y representación de un objeto en perspectiva.

scent [sent] [sent], *s.* 1. Olfato, el sentido con que se percibe el olor (smell, nose). 2. Olor, perfume, la fragancia o el mal olor que exhala alguna cosa. 3. Rastro, la senda o camino que lleva la caza y se descubre por el olor; pista. 4. Indicio, presentimiento. 4. Perfume, esencia.

scent, *va.* 1. Oler, percibir con el olfato. 2. Perfumar. 3. Concebir una sospecha de algo. *-vn.* Seguir la pista, rastrear.

scentless ['sentlɪs] [sent-les], *a.* 1. Desprovisto del sentido del olfato; que no halla la pista. 2. Inodoro, sin olor; que no tiene olor.

sceptic ['skeptɪk] [skep-tik], *a.* Escéptico. *V.* SKEPTIC.

scepticism ['skeptɪsɪzəm] [skep-ti-si-sem], *s.* Escepticismo. *V.* SKEPTICISM.

scepter, sceptre ['skeptəʳ] [skep-taʳ], *s.* Cetro, insignia de los emperadores y reyes.

sceptred ['skeptrɪd] [skep-trid], *a.* 1. Que lleva o tiene cetro. 2. Real, regio.

schedule ['ʃedjuːl] [she-diul], *va.* Incluir en una lista, catálogo o inventario; inventariar, hacer una lista de. *-s.* 1. *(For.)* Añadidura, aditamento. 2. Lista, catálogo. 3. Plan, programa. 4. Horario (de los trenes). 5. Temario.

schematic [skɪˈmætɪk] [ski-ma-tik], *a.* Esquemático; de la naturaleza de un plan, diseño o representación generales; de una constitución general, típico.

scheme [skiːm] [skim], *s.* 1. Plan, proyecto, designio. 2. Planta, esquema, modelo; diseño, bosquejo en perfil, diagrama, construcción gráfica. 3. Sistema, arreglo, disposición. 4. Treta, artificio sutil.

scheme, *va.* y *vn.* Formar un plan, proyectar; trazarse un plan; formar proyectos.

schemer ['skiːməʳ] ['skiːməʳ] [ski-maʳ], *s.* Proyectista, invencionero.

schemy ['skiːmɪ] [ski-mi], *a. (Fam.)* Astuto, intrigante.

schism ['skɪzəm] [ski-sem], *s.* 1. Cisma, escisión o separación en una Iglesia. 2. Cisma, cuerpo eclesiástico separado de un cuerpo mayor o más antiguo. 3. División, desavenencia.

schismatic ['skɪzmætɪk] [skis-ma-tik], *s.* Cismático, el fundador o partidario de un cisma.

schismatically [ˌskɪzˈmætɪkəlɪ] [skis-ma-ti-ka-li], *adv.* Cismáticamente.

schismatize ['skɪzmætaɪz] [skis-ma-tais], *vn.* Tomar parte en un cisma.

schist ['skɪst] [skist], *s.* Esquisto, toda roca que fácilmente se divide en hojas.

schizophrenia [ˌskɪtsəʊˈfriːnɪə] [ski-sou-fri-nia], *s.* Esquizofrenia.

schizophrenic [ˌskɪtsəʊˈfrɪnɪk] [ski-sou-fri-nik], *a.* Esquizofrénico.

scholar ['skɒləʳ] [sko-laʳ], *s.* 1. Escolar, estudiante; discípulo (pupil, alumnus). 2. Hombre erudito, docto o literato; letrado, sabio o sabia. 3. El que adquiere conocimientos de cualquier especie. 4. El estudiante que en las universidades de Inglaterra goza una beca pensionada en algún colegio. **Day scholar**, externo, discípulo externo. **Felllow-scholar**, condiscípulo, camarada de colegio o escuela de estudios. **A classical scholar**, humanista, helenista, latinista. **To be no scholar**, haber recibido poca instrucción; no saber leer ni escribir.

scholarly, scholar-like ['skɒləlɪ] [sko-lar-li], *a.* De estudiante, de escolar, que conviene a un estudiante. *-adv.* Como sabio, como hombre letrado.

scholarship ['skɒləʃɪp] [sko-lar-ship], *s.* 1. Saber, el conocimiento de las ciencias o de las letras; erudición, ciencia. 2. Educación literaria. 3. Beca, plaza o prebenda en algún colegio, fundada para la manutención de un estudiante.

scholastic [skəˈlæstɪk] [sko-las-tik], *a.* 1. Escolástico; estudiante, estudiantil; perteneciente a las escuelas o a la educación. 2. Escolástico, que se refiere a la teología de la edad media; pedantesco.

scholastical [skəˈlæstɪkəl] [sko-las-ti-kal], *a.* Escolástico, escolar, estudiantino, estudiantil.

scholastically [skəˈlæstɪkəlɪ] [sko-las-ti-ka-li], *adv.* Escolásticamente.

scholasticism [skəˈlæstɪsɪzəm] [sko-las-ti-si-sem], *s.* Escolasticismo; el método o las sutilezas de las escuelas.

school [skuːl] [skul], *s.* 1. Escuela, la casa o paraje donde se enseña; una institución para la enseñanza (academy, college). 2. El cuerpo de alumnos de una escuela. 3. Cualquier clase o ejercicio de una escuela. 4. Todos los discípulos de un maestro (filósofo o doctor célebre, artista, etc.) o sistema; el sistema mismo. 5. Esfera o medios de enseñanza o de disciplina. 6. Método de vida. **Common school**, escuela libre y pública de los Estados Unidos. **Boarding-school**, pupilaje, la casa donde se admiten pupilos para vivir en ella y recibir educación. **Fencing-school**, sala o escuela de esgrima. **Dancing-school**, sala o escuela de baile. **Charity-school**, escuela gratuita. **Law school**, escuela de derecho. **In school**, en clase. **To go to school**, entrar en clase. **School book**, un libro usado en las escuelas. **Schoolboy**, muchacho de escuela. **Schoolfellow**, condiscípulo. **Schoolgirl**, niña que va a la escuela. **Schoolhouse**, la escuela, casa de escuela. **Private school**, escuela particular, a diferencia de la pública. **Public school**, escuela pública, la establecida y mantenida por la autoridad civil. **School-teacher**, maestro o maestra de escuela.

school, *va.* 1. Instruir, enseñar. 2. Amaestrar, adiestrar. 3. Reprender enseñando sus obligación al que faltó a ella, disciplinar.

school, *vn.* Ir o moverse juntos, como los peces; moverse en masa. *-s.* Ribazón, manjúa, majal, la multitud de peces que nadan juntos, como en tropa.

school board ['skuːlbɔːd] [skul-bord], *s.* Junta de educación.

schooling ['skuːlɪŋ] [sku-lin], *s.* 1. Instrucción dada o adquirida en una escuela; enseñanza preparatoria. 2. Precio de la escuela, remuneración pagada a un maestro de escuela. 3. Reprimenda.

schoolman ['skuːlmən] [skul-man], *s.* 1. Un erudito muy versado en las disputas y controversias de las escuelas. 2. Escritor sobre teología escolástica.

schoolmaster ['skuːlˌmɑːstəʳ] [skul-mas-taʳ], *s.* Maestro de escuela; maestro, el o lo que forma, instruye y guía.

schoolmate ['skuːlmeɪt] [skul-meit], *s.* Compañero de colegio, de escuela, de clase.

schoolmistress ['skuːlˌmɪstrɪs] [skul-mis-tris], *sf.* Maestra de niños o niñas.

schooner ['skuːnəʳ] [sku-naʳ], *s.* (*Mar.*) 1. Goleta, embarcación con dos palos (hoy con tres y aun cuatro) y velas cangrejas. 2. (*E.U.*) Furgón con toldo que usan los emigrantes en las llanuras del Oeste de los Estados Unidos. 3. (*Fam. E.U.*) Vaso alto y grande para cerveza.

schwah [ʃwɑː] [shua], *sf.* Vocal neutra.

sciatic [saɪˈætɪk] [skai-atik], *a.* Ciático, esquiático, que se refiere a la cadera. **The sciatic nerve**, el nervio ciático.

sciatica [saɪˈætɪkə] [saia-ti-ka], *s.* Ciática, neuralgia de la cadera y del muslo, es decir, del nervio ciático.

science ['saɪəns] [saians], *s.* 1. Ciencia, conocimiento, sabiduria. 2. Certidumbre, destreza, habilidad de ejecución que resulta del conocimiento que se tiene de algo. 3. Conjunto, sistema de conocimientos sobre un asunto. **Science fiction**, ciencia-ficción.

sciential ['saɪənʃəl] [saian-shal], *a.* Que produce el saber o que conduce a la ciencia; inteligente, hábil, instruído.

scientific [ˌsaɪənˈtɪfɪk] [saian-ti-fik], *a.* 1. Científico. 2. De acuerdo con las reglas, principios o procedimientos de la ciencia; sistemático, exacto. 3. Versado en la ciencia o en una ciencia; sabio, muy hábil.

scientifically [ˌsaɪənˈtɪfɪkəlɪ] [saian-ti-fi-ka-li], *adv.* Científicamente.

scientist ['saɪəntɪst] [saian-tist], *s.* Científico, sabio.

scimeter, scimitar ['sɪmɪtəʳ] [si-mi-taʳ], *s.* Cimitarra. *V.* SIMITAR.

scintilla ['sɪntɪlə] [sin-ti-la], *s.* Centella, chispa; de aquí, partícula, traza, tilde, jota.

scintillant ['sɪntɪlənt] [sin-ti-lant], *a.* Centelleante, que echa chispas.

scintillate ['sɪntɪleɪt] [sin-ti-leit], *vn.* Chispear, centellear.

scintillation [ˌsɪntɪˈleɪʃən] [sin-ti-lei-shon], *s.* Chispazo, centelleo, chispeo (sparkling).

scion ['saɪən] [saion], *s.* 1. Verduguillo, rama destinada a ser injertada o plantada; esqueje. 2. Vástago, renuevo, tallo tierno de un árbol o planta. 3. Hijo, hija o descendiente.

scission ['sɪʃən] [si-shon], *s.* 1. Escisión, fisión. 2. Corte, separación.

scissors ['sɪzəz] [si-sors], *s. pl.* Tijeras.

scissure ['sɪʃəʳ] [si-shaʳ], *s.* Cisura, hendedura, cortadura longitudinal.

sclerosis [sklɪˈrəʊsɪs] [skli-rou-sis], *s.* Esclerosis, toda especie de endurecimiento morboso de los tejidos.

sclerotic [sklɪˈrəʊtɪk] [skli-rou-tik], *a.* 1. Escleroso, denso, endurecido, se dice particularmente de la esclerótica o córnea opaca del ojo. 2. Que padece esclerosis.

scoff [skɒf] [skof], *vn.* Mofarse, burlarse o hacer burla (se usa con at).

scoff, *s.* 1. Mofa, escarnio, burla. 2. Hazmerreír.

scoffer ['skɒfəʳ] [sko-faʳ], *s.* Mofador, despreciador.

scoffingly ['skɒfɪŋlɪ] [sko-fin-li], *adv.* Con mofa y escarnio.

scold [skəʊld] [skould], *va.* y *vn.* Regañar, reñir, rezongar, reefunfuñar. **A scolding-match**, (*Fam.*) una pelotera.

scollop ['skɒləp] [sko-lop], *s.* y *v. V.* SCALLOP.

scomber ['skɒmbəʳ] [skom-baʳ], *s.* Escombro, caballa, género típico de los escombéridos.

sconce [skɒns] [skons], *s.* 1. Baluarte, defensa, abrigo, defensa. 2. (*Fam.*) Cabeza; el contenido del cráneo; seso, juicio, sentido. 3. Yelmo. 4. Anaquel fijo. 5. Multa.

sconce, *s.* Candelabro de pared; linterna provista de una pantalla exterior. (*Mex.*) Pantalla.

sconce, *va.* 1. Fortificar con un baluarte o defensa. 2. Multar, imponer una pena pecuniaria (to fine)..

scoop [skuːp] [skup], *s.* 1. Cuchara o cucharón; paleta, pala cóncava (de mano); utensilio que sirve para traspalar la hulla, para rastrear las ostras, para tomar porciones de harina, azúcar, etc. 2. Acto de cavar o ahuecar. 3. Paletada, la cantidad cavada o sacada de una vez. 4. Cavidad en forma de taza; hueco 5. (*Mar.*) Vertedor, achicador. 6. Arte de dar una noticia en la prensa antes que los demás.

scoop, *va.* 1. Sacar con cucharón o achicador, vaciar. 2. Cavar, socavar.

scooper [ˈskuːpəʳ] [sku-paʳ], *s.* El que achica o socava; cavador.

scoot [skuːt] [skut], *vn.* 1. *(Fam. E.U.)* Irse de prisa; tomar las de Villadiego. 2. Pasar, volar, ligeramente por encima de una cosa, como un ave.

scooter [ˈskuːtəʳ] [sku-taʳ], *s.* 1. Patineta, patinete. *(Mex.)* Patín del diablo. 2. Velero de fondo plano para el agua o hielo.

scope [skəʊp] [skoup], *s.* 1. Alcance de vista o acción; punto de mira; lugar, espacio en que ejercer las facultades. 2. Objeto, fin, intento, designio, intención. **To have free scope**, tener carta blanca para hacer lo que se quiera, no tener freno ni sujeción, obrar libremente. **To give full scope to the imagination**, dar rienda suelta a la imaginación.

scope. Sufijo que significa indicador; se emplea principalmente en los nombres de los instrumentos de observación; v. g. **telescope**, telescopio.

scorbutic, scorbutical [skɔːˈbjuːtɪk] [skor-biu-tik], *a.* Escorbútico.

scorch [skɔːtʃ] [skorch], *va.* 1. Chamuscar, quemar por encima o por afuera; tostar (to singe). 2. Agostar, abrasar (el sol) con calor extremo. -*vn.* 1. Quemarse, secarse. 2. Agostarse, abrasarse (las plantas). 3. *(Ger.)* Moverse o ser impelido a gran velocidad.

scorcher [ˈskɔːtʃəʳ] [skor-chaʳ], *s.* 1. Lo que chamusca o abrasa. 2. Persona o cosa que se mueve o puede moverse a gran velocidad, como un caballo, un ciclista, etc. 3. Día muy caluroso.

scorching [ˈskɔːtʃɪŋ] [skor-chin], *a.* Ardiente, abrasador, caliente.

scordium [ˈskɔːdɪəm] [skor-diom], *s.* *(Bot.)* Escordio, germandria acuática.

score [skɔːʳ] [skoʳ], *s.* 1. Muesca, canalita, incisión, entalladura; señal, marca, línea, raya. 2. Cuenta, escote; deuda. 3. De aquí, mala voluntad, diferencia, controversia; también, razón, motivo, cuenta, consideración. 4. Talla, el número de tantos en los juegos y deportes. 5. *(Mús.)* Partitura, conjunto de las partes de una composición musical; los pliegos o el libro que las contienen. 6. Veintena, veinte. **To pay one's score**, pagar sus deudas, su escote. **Put that to my score**, póngame Ud. eso en cuenta. **On the score of**, en consideración a, con motivo de. **Upon what score?**, ¿con qué motivo? ¿por qué razón? **An opera in score**, una ópera puesta en partitura. **Three-score**, sesenta. **Fourscore**, ochenta. **Sixcore**, ciento veinte.

score, *va.* 1. Rayar, marcar con líneas, muescas o cortaduras; escoplear. 2. Marcar con latigazos, azotar; de aquí, censurar severamente. 3. Borrar, tachar, testar. 4. Apuntar, sentar, poner en cuenta; llevar a una cuenta. 5. Ganar tantos en un juego. 6. *(Mús.)* Escribir la parte correspondiente a un instrumento de orquesta. 7. Calificar, valorar una prueba o examen (to examine). 8. Alcanzar, obtener, ganar. -*vn.* 1. Marcar la tarja, sentarse en cuenta; marcar los tantos en un juego. 2. Ganar tantos en un juego; obtener una ventaja. 3. Hacer muescar, rayas o señales.

scorer [ˈskɔːrəʳ] [sko-raʳ], *s.* 1. Marcador, el que marca; el que lleva cuenta de las jugadas o de los tantos ganados por los que toman parte en un juego cualquiera. 2. Martillo, instrumento que emplean los leñadores para marcar los árboles.

scoring [ˈskɔːrɪŋ] [sko-rin], *s.* Marcador, tanteo *(Dep.).*

scorn [ˈskɔːn] [skorn], *va.* y *vn.* 1. Despreciar, desdeñar; rechazar desdeñosamente, profesar desprecio por. 2. Mofar, escarnecer, hacer escarnio. 3. Burlarse de uno, ponerle en ridículo. **My friends would scorn me if**, mis amigos me despreciarían si.

scorn, *s.* 1. Desdén, desprecio (contempt); sentimiento o tratamiento desdeñoso debido a la mala opinión que se tiene de una persona o de un objeto. 2. Irrisión, escarnio, expresión de desdén, mofa. 3. Objeto de desdén, de desprecio. **He is the scorn of all the town**, es objeto del desprecio de toda la ciudad.

scorner [ˈskɔːnəʳ] [skor-naʳ], *s.* Desdeñador, escarnecedor.

scornful [ˈskɔːnfʊl] [skorn-ful], *a.* Desdeñoso, insolente, lleno de desprecio.

scornfully [ˈskɔːnfəlɪ] [skorn-fu-li], *adv.* Desdeñosamente, despreciablemente, con desdén.

scornfulness [ˈskɔːnfəlnɪs] [skorn-ful-nes], *s.* Calidad de desdeñoso. **The scornfulness of his look**, lo desdeñoso de su mirada.

scorpio [ˈskɔːpɪəʊ] [skor-piou], *s.* *(Astr.)* Escorpión, una constelación del Zodíaco, y su signo.

scorpion [ˈskɔːpɪən] [skor-pion], *s.* 1. Escorpión, alacrán. 2. Escorpión, constelación del zodíaco. 3. Especie de látigo o azote. **Scorpion-fly**, escorpión mosca, insecto neuróptero cuya cola se parece a la del escorpión. **Scorpion-grass**, una especie cualquiera de miosotis, v. g. la «Nomeolvides». **Scorpion-wort**, hierba del alacrán.

scot [skɒt] [skot], *s.* *(Ant.)* Escote; tasa, contribución. **Scot and lot**, derechos parroquiales. **Scot-free**, libre de escote; impune.

scotch [skɒtʃ] [skoch], *va.* 1. Escoplear, hacer muescar, hacer cortes o cortaduras pequeñas en alguna cosa. 2. Herir ligeramente. 3. Allanar la piedra con un pico. 4. Poner una galga o amarra a un vehículo. 5. Estorbar, frustrar. **We have scotched the snake, not killed it**, hemos herido pero no matado esta serpiente.

scotch, *s.* 1. Cortadura, corte, incisión. 2. Línea trazada en el suelo, p. ej. para jugar al infernáculo. *V.* HOP-SCOTCH. 3. Calzo, cuña, galga, amarra de un carruaje. 4. Obstáculo, impedimento.

Scotch, Scottish [ˈskɒtɪʃ] [sko-tish], *a.* Escocés, lo perteneciente a Escocia. **Scotch thistle**, cardo borriquero; cardo, emblema nacional de Escocia. **Scotch-collops**, *s. pl.* ternera cortada en tajadas o picada. **Scotch-fiddle**, *(Vulg.)* sarna.

scotcher [ˈskɒtʃəʳ] [sko-chaʳ], *s.* Travesaño.

scot-free [ˈskɒtfriː] [skot-fri], *a.* Impune.

scotism [ˈskɒtɪzəm] [sko-ti-sem], *s.* Escotismo, doctrina escolástica de Escoto.

Scotsman [ˈskɒtsmən] [skoch-man], *s.* Escocés, el natural de Escocia.

scoundrel [ˈskaʊndrəl] [skaun-drel], *s.* Belitre, bergante, un pícaro, un bribón, un hombre vil y ruin.

scoundrelism [ˈskaʊndrəlɪzm] [skaun-dre-li-sem], *s.* Picardía, bajeza.

scoundrelly [ˈskaʊndrəlɪ] [skaun-dre-li], *adv.* De pícaro, de bribón, bajo, vilmente.

scour [ˈskaʊəʳ] [skauaʳ], *va.* 1. Fregar, estregar (to rub). 2. Limpiar, ahuyentar de una parte a los que son perjudiciales en ella. 3. Limpiar, quitar la suciedad de una cosa estregándola; lavar, recorrer, componer; blanquear. **To scour cloth**, escurar el paño o sacarle el aceite con greda y jabón. 4. Purgar con violencia. 5. Formar, v. gr. el cauce de un arroyo, disminuyendo por el roce. 6. Pasar atravesando con cuidado, recorrer, explorar. 7. Correr, pasar rápidamente cerca de algo. 8. Ahuyentar, expeler. 9. Barrer, expulsar. 10. Batir un monte. -*vn.* 1. Limpiar, estregar, los utensilios de una casa. 2. Corretear, correr de una parte a otra. 3. Soltársele a uno el vientre. **To scour about**, vagar, ser un vagabundo. **To scour away**, huir.

scour, *s.* 1. Acción limpiadora de una corriente rápida. 2. Sustancia usada para desgrasar tejidos. 3. Diarrea del ganado.

scourer [ˈskaʊərəʳ] [skauraʳ], *s.* 1. Limpiador, sacamanchas. 2. Purga. 3. Vagabundo. 4. Ladrón nocturno.

scourge [ˈskɜːdʒ] [skerch], *s.* Azote (birch), correa, látigo, instrumento de corrección; lo que agota o mata; castigo severo; calamidad. **The Scourge of God**, el azote de Dios.

scourge, *va.* 1. Azotar, dar con un látigo, flagelar, dar golpes con unas disciplinas. 2. Castigar (por delitos o faltas con intención de corregir); mortificar, hostigar, acosar.

scourger [ˈskɜːdʒəʳ] [sker-chaʳ], *s.* Azotador, castigador, mortificador.

scouring [ˈskaʊrɪŋ] [skau-rin], *s.* 1. Fregado, fregadura, estregadura, acción de fregar o estregar; acción de escurar o desengrasar. 2. Diarrea, hez, deshecho.

scout [skaʊt] [skaut], *s. (Mil.)* 1. Descubridor, explorador, batidor del campo; centinela avanzada; espía. 2. Buque de observación. 3. Avión de reconocimiento. 4. Muchacho explorador. **A good scout**, buena persona, buen muchacho.

scout, *vn. (Mil.)* Reconocer secretamente los movimientos del enemigo, ir como explorador.

scout, *va.* 1. Rechazar con desdén. 2. *(Con at.)* Burlarse, reírse de algo o de alguien.

scoutmaster ['skaʊtˌmɒːstəʳ] [skaut-mas-taʳ], *s.* Jefe de niños exploradores.

scow [skaʊ] [skau], *s.* 1. Chalana, barcaza. 2. *(Fam.)* Yate de regatas.

scowl [skaʊl] [skaul], *vn.* 1. Mirar con ceño, poner mala cara, ponerse ceñudo, poner mal gesto, enfurruñarse. 2. Tener aspecto amenazador. *-va.* Rechazar, repeler.

scowl, *s.* Ceño (frown), sobrecejo, semblante ceñudo, enfadado, disgustado o emperrado.

scowling ['skaʊlɪŋ] [skau-lin], *s.* El acto de mirar de sobrecejo, mal gesto o ceño.

scowlingly ['skaʊlɪŋlɪ] [skau-lin-li], *adv.* Con ceño.

scrabble ['skræbl] [skra-bel], *va.* 1. Escarabajear, garabatear. 2. Recoger, amontonar de prisa. *-vn.* 1. Emborronar, trazar caracteres irregulares o informes. 2. *(Fam.)* V. SCRAMBLE. *-s.* Acción de escarabajear, de emborronar.

scrabble, *s.* Garabato, borrón, escrito o dibujo hecho de cualquier modo.

scrag [skræg] [skrag], *s.* 1. Cualquier cosa flaca o macilenta y basta o áspera; pedazo de carne magra, particularmente del cuello; el cuello. 2. V. REMNANT.

scrag, *v. (Fam.)* Ahorcar, dar garrote, torcer el pescuezo a.

scragged ['skrægɪd] [skra-guid], *a.* 1. Áspero, desigual, escabroso. 2. Flaco, descarnado.

scragginess ['skrægɪnɪs] [skra-gui-nes], *s.* Flaqueza, extenuación; aspereza, desigualdad.

scraggy ['skrægɪ] [skra-gui], *a.* Áspero, desigual; flaco, macilento, descarnado.

scramble ['skræmbl] [skram-bel], *va.* 1. Preparar, arreglar, deprisa o confusamente. 2. Preparar huevos revolviéndolos mientras se fríen. *-vn.* 1. Trepar, andar con ayuda de pies y manos, o subir gateando a una altura; trepar, las plantas. 2. Hacer esfuerzos para alcanzar; contender y disputar ansiosamente acerca de quien ha de coger una cosa. **To scramble for**, esforzarse por coger o alcanzar. **To scramble over**, pasar gateando. **To scrable up**, trepar, subir. **Scrambled eggs**, huevos revueltos.

scramble, *s.* 1. Trepa, la acción de trepar o subir gateando a una altura. 2. Lucha, esfuerzo para obtener algo, contienda o pelea entre dos o más personas por agarrar o posesionarse de una cosa; arrebatiña, hecho desordenado. 3. *(Aer.)* Despegue de emergencia.

scrambler ['skræmbləʳ] [skram-blaʳ], *s.* 1. El que disputa con otro u otros por agarrar algo. 2. Trepador, el que trepa o sube gateando a una altura.

scrap [skræp] [skrap], *s.* 1. Migaja, mendrugo, sobras. 2. Pedacito, fragmentos. 3. Desperdicios, desechos, retales, chatarra. **Scrap book**, libro de recortes. **Scrap heap**, montón de desechos o desperdicios. **Scrap iron, scrap metal**, hierro viejo, despojos de metal o de hierro. **Scrap of paper**, pedazo de papel.

scrap, *v.* Desechar, descartar, echar a la basura. 2. Derogar. 3. Desguazar un buque. 4. *(Fam.)* Reñir, pelear.

scrape [skreɪp] [skreip], *va. y vn.* 1. Raer, raspar la superficie de alguna cosa para quitar o borrar algo de ella (to rasp). 2. Arañar, recoger con afán de varias partes y en pequeñas porciones lo necesario para algún fin; amontonar poco a poco. 3. Hacer un ruido desagradable tocando en la superficie de una cosa; rascar o tocar mal un instrumento. 4. Hacer cortesías o reverencias con muy poca gracia. **To scrape out**, borrar o quitar algo de la superficie de una cosa raspándola. **To scrape off**, quitar raspando. **To scrape together**, amontonar a fuerza de industria y ahorro. **To scrape acquaintance with**, insinuarse, entrar en las buenas gracias de alguien.

scrape, *s.* 1. Raspadura, acción y efecto de raspar; ruido de raspar, roce de los pies en el suelo. 2. Enredo, maraña; embarazo, dificultad, berenjenal, empeño, lance apretado. 3. Cortesía tosca o con poca gracia 4. Riña. 5. Lío, aprieto, apuro. **I am out of the scrape**, zafé el cuerpo, salí de enredos.

scrapepenny ['skreɪpˌpenɪ] [skreip-pe-ni], *s.* Avaro, tacaño.

scraper ['skreɪpəʳ] [skrei-paʳ], *s.* 1. Rascador, raspador, instrumento para raspar o rascar. 2. Arañador de dinero. 3. Aprendiz o persona que toca mal el violín. 4. *(Mar.)* Rasquetas. 5. Estregadera, raedera; garatura (del pelambrero).

scraping ['skreɪpɪŋ] [skrei-pin], *s.* 1. Raedura, raspadura, acción de raspar, de raer. 2. Raspaduras, lo que se saca raspando. 3. *pl.* Ahorros, cosas amontonadas.

scrappy ['skræpɪ] [skrei-pi], *a.* Escaso, pobre (meal); inconexo (speech).

scratch ['skrætʃ] [skrach], *va. y vn.* 1. Rascar, raspar; raer, arañar; garrapatear. 2. Rasguñar o hacer un rasguño o araño. 3. Rayar (el vidrio). 4. Escribir mal, garrapatear. 5. Cavar, excavar raspando. 6. Cancelar, borrar, testar. **To scratch out one's eyes**, sacar a uno los ojos con las uñas.

scratch, *s.* 1. Rasguño, araño, arañazo, rascadura; marca o incisión hecha en una superficie; raya ligera, arañazo. 2. La línea desde la cual parten los que se disputan el premio en una carrera. 3. *pl.* Galápago, espundia, enfermedad en el casco del caballo. 4. Peluca para una parte de la cabeza. 5. *(E.U.)* En el juego de billar, bambarria, chiripa, acierto o logro casual. **Scratches**, grietas en los pies de los caballos. V. la 3ª acep.

scratcher ['skrætʃəʳ] [skra-chaʳ], *s.* Arañador, el que araña o rasguña.

scratchpad ['skrætʃpæd] [skrach-pad], *s.* Cuaderno de apuntes, cuaderno para borrador.

scratchwork ['skrætʃwɜːk] [skrach-uek], *s.* Pintura al fresco.

scrawl [skrɔːl] [skrol], *va.* Garrapatear, garabatear, escribir mal, hacer garabatos.

scrawl, *s.* Escrito desigual o cosa escrita de prisa y mal; lo que está escrito o dibujado sin habilidad; garabatos, garrapatos.

scrawler ['skrɔːləʳ] [skro-laʳ], *s.* Garabateador, el que escribe garabatos.

scrawniness ['skrɔːnɪnɪs] [skro-ni-nes], *s.* Flaqueza, flacura, falta de carnes.

scrawny ['skrɔːnɪ] [skro-ni], *a.* Flaco, enjuto y huesudo, falto de carnes.

screak [skriːk] [skrik], *s.* 1. Chillido. 2. Crujido, chirrido.

screak, *v.* 1. Chillar. 2. Rechinar, crujir.

scream [skriːm] [skrim], *va.* Gritar, proferir en voz alta y penetrante; dar alaridos; vociferar, vocear. *-vn.* Chillar, gritar, dar gritos agudos o penetrantes.

scream, *s.* Grito, alarido que comúnmente denota miedo o dolor; grito agudo o penetrante, chillido.

screamer ['skriːməʳ] [skri-maʳ], *s.* El que o lo que grita o vocea.

screaming ['skriːmɪŋ] [skri-min], *s.* Gritería, acción de dar un grito; vocería, alarida.

scree ['skriː] [skri], *s. (Eng.)* Piedra, canto; montón de cantos.

screech ['skriːtʃ] [skrich], *vn.* Dar alaridos o chillidos.

screechowl ['skriːtʃhaʊl] [skrich-jaul], *s. (Orn.)* Zumaya o zumacaya, alucón; toda lechuza que da chillidos en vez de graznar.

screechy ['skriːtʃɪ] [skri-chi], *a.* Chillante, que se asemeja a un chillido; agudo, penetrante y discorde.

screed [skriːd] [skrid], *s.* 1. Tirada crítica; invectiva, arenga. 2. Plantilla, gálibo; listón, tira de madera o capa de mortero que se pone a intervalos en una pared para igualar la superficie. 3. Jirón, tira larga, retazo.

screen [skriːn] [skrin], *s.* 1. Biombo, mampara, algo que separa o intercepta; cancel, pantalla, antipara, persiana; tabique, reja; albitana, cerca para resguardar las plantas de la acción del viento; de aquí, abrigo, defensa. 2. Pantalla de chimenea. 3. Criba, harnero, zaranda.

screen, va. 1. Abrigar, ocultar, esconder; proteger, defender; sustraer (a un castigo). 2. Cribar, cerner. **Screenings**, s. pl. desperdicios, restos de alguna cosa pasada por una criba o harnero.

screenplay ['skriːnpleɪ] [skrin-plei], s. Argumento de película cinematográfica.

screw [skruː] [skru], s. 1. Tornillo, cilindro de metal, madera, etc., ahuecado en espiral por su superficie exterior; también, tuerca, rosca, cilindro hueco rayado en espiral en su superficie interior (nail). 2. Tornillo, clavo cilíndrico con filete en espiral; lo que se parece a un tornillo; hélico; vapor de hélice; concha de hélice. 3. Vuelta de tornillo. 4. (Ger.) Cicatero, tacaño, también, presión, fuerza. **Set-screw, thumb-screw, binding-screw**, tornillo montado o de presión. **Right-handed screw**, tornillo de filete a la derecha. **Left-handed screw**, tornillo zurdo o reverso. **Round-head screw**, tornillo de cabeza redonda (de gota de sebo). **Screw steamer**, vapor de hélice. **Screw eyes**, armellas. **Screw nails**, clavos de rosca. **Female-screw**, tuerca. **Screw-tap**, matriz o molde para hacer tornillos. **Cork-screw**, tirabuzón, sacacorchos. **Screw-plate**, taraja. **Screw-taps for the screw-plate**, mochuelos de taraja. **Screw-driver**, destornillador.

screw, va. 1. Atornillar, torcer o afianzar con tornillo. 2. Retorcer, afear alguna cosa retorciéndola. 3. Forzar, apretar, comprimir, oprimir, estrechar. 4. Torcer, deformar; hacer gestos con la boca o cara. -vn. 1. Retorcerse o dar vueltas una cosa en forma de rosca o espiral. 2. Ejercer extorsión u opresión. **To screw down**, atornillar, cerrar, fijar con tornillo. **To screw in**, hacer entrar una cosa en otra dándole vueltas o revolviéndola como se hace a un tornillo; insinuar, introducir alguna palabra o discurso con maña en una conversación. **To screw out**, hacer salir a viva fuerza alguna cosa de donde estaba metida; echar a perder algo al sacarlo de donde estaba. **To screw out of one**, sonsacar con astucia y maña. **To screw one's wits**, calentarse los sesos. **To screw one's face into**, contraer las facciones. **To screw up one's courage**, darse ánimo, cobrar ánimo.

scribble ['skrɪbl] [skri-bel], va. 1. Escribir de prisa y sin cuidado (letra o estilo). 2. Escarabajear, borrajear, garrapatear.

scribble, s. 1. Escrito de poco mérito o mal formado. 2. Garabato, garrapato.

scribbler ['skrɪblər] [skri-blar], s. Escritor o autor de poca nota.

scribe ['skraɪb] [skraib], s. 1. Escritor; escribiente. 2. Notario público. 3. Escriba, doctor de la ley entre los hebreos. 4. Amanuense, copista. **I am no great scribe**, yo no escribo muy bien.

scribe, va. 1. Marcar, rayar, con un instrumento puntiagudo. 2. Ensamblar, ajustar.

scrimmage ['skrɪmɪdʒ] [skri-mich], s. Contienda, lucha cuerpo a cuerpo, escaramuza.

scrimp ['skrɪmp] [skrimp], va. y vn. Estrechar, reducir, acortar; ser pasimonioso, portarse con tacañería o sordidez. - a. Estrecho, reducido, corto. -s. Mísero, un avaro.

scrimpingly ['skrɪmpɪŋlɪ] [skrim-pin-li], adv. De una manera mezquina, parsimoniosa o sórdida.

scrimpy ['skrɪmpɪ] [skrim-pi], a. 1. (Fam.) Demasiado estrecho, escaso, desmasiado corto; reducido, muy pequeño. 2. Tacaño, cicatero.

scrip [skrɪp] [skrip], s. 1. Cédula, esquela. 2. Certificado o certificación de un banco o compañía atestando que el accionista tiene interés en uno u otra. 3. Bolsa, morral, zurrón, taleguilla. (En vez de **Script**). **Scrip-holder**, tenedor de vales o certificados provisionales.

script [skrɪpt] [skript], s. 1. Escritura, mano, carácter ordinario de letra. 2. (Impr.) Plumilla inglesa, tipo que imita la forma de la letra escrita. 3. (For.) Escritura, v. g. un testamento o codicilo.

scriptural ['skrɪptʃərəl] [skrip-cha-ral], a. Bíblico, contenido en la Sagrada Escritura, o autorizado por ella.

scripture ['skrɪptʃər] [skrip-char], s. Escritura, la Escritura Sagrada de cualquier pueblo; en especial, la Biblia.

scrofula ['skrɒfjʊlə] [skro-fiu-la], s. Lamparón, escrófula.

scrofulous ['skrɒfjʊləs] [skro-fiu-los], a. Escrofuloso, que tiene lamparones, que padece de escrófula.

scroll [skrəʊl] [skroul], s. 1. El rollo de papel o pergamino que contiene un escrito o se destina a escribir en él. 2. Rasgo, traza o diseño en lugar de un sello. 3. Adorno en espiral; encaracolado, voluto, roleo. **Scroll-saw**, sierra de contornear.

scrotal ['skrəʊtl] [skrou-tal], a. Escrotal, relativo al escroto.

scrotum ['skrəʊtəm] [skrou-tom], s. Escroto, bolsa que contiene los testículos.

scrub [skrʌb] [skrab], va. Fregar, estregar; limpiar fregando o rascando; restregar (con la mano o con un estropajo).

scrub, a. 1. Achaparrado, desmirriado; inferior, mezquino. 2. En que participan luchadores novicios o poco hábiles. (Se dice de carreras, etc.). -s. 1. Belitre, un hombre vil. 2. Estropajo; escoba vieja; una cosa inútil y despreciable.

scrubby ['skrʌbɪ] [skra-bi], a. Estropajoso; vil, despreciable, bajo; achaparrado.

scruff ['skrʌf] [skraf], s. Nuca, parte alta de la cerviz, unión de la cabeza y el espinazo.

scruffy ['skrʌf] [skraf], a. Dejado, sucio, desaliñado.

scrum [skrʌm] [skram], nf. Melé.

scrumpy ['skrʌmpɪ] [skram-pi] a. Muy rico, de rechupete.

scrunch ['skrʌntʃ] [skranch], vt. Ronzar.

scruple ['skrʌpl] [skra-pel], s. 1. Escrúpulo, duda. 2. Escrúpulo, la tercera parte de una dracma. 3. Cualquiera cantidad muy pequeña.

scruple, vn. Escrupulizar, tener duda; vacilar por razones de conciencia.

scrupulous ['skruːpjʊləs] [skru-piu-los], a. 1. Escrupuloso, delicado, riguroso, concienzudo; dudoso, temeroso; cuidadoso, cauto. 2. Exacto, preciso, estricto, exigente.

scrupulously ['skruːpjʊləslɪ] [skru-piu-los-li], adv. Escrupulosamente.

scrupulousness ['skruːpjʊləsnɪs] [skru-piu-los-nes], s. Escrupulosidad, delicadeza de conciencia; calidad de escrupuloso o concienzudo; exactitud, nimiedad en el examen y averiguación de las cosas.

scrutable ['skruːtəbl] [skru-ta-bol], a. Escudriñable.

scrutineer ['skruːtɪnɪər] [skru-ti-niar], s. Escudriñador.

scrutinize ['skruːtɪnaɪz] [skru-ti-nais], va. Escudriñar, examinar en sus detalles o a fondo, averiguar, inquirir, sondear.

scrutinous ['skruːtɪnəs] [skru-ti-nos], a. Curioso.

scuba ['skuːbə] [sku-ba], s. Escafandra autónoma. **Scuba gear**, equipo para buceo, escafandra autónoma.

scud [skʌd] [skad], vn. Correr, volar o moverse rápidamente; atravesar de prisa; correr como una embarcación en una borrasca, con pocas velas puestas, o sin ellas. **To scud before the wind**, correr viento en popa. **To scud before the sea**, (Mar.) correr a dos puños. -s. 1. Carrera precipitada, el acto de correr o moverse rápidamente. 2. Nubes ligeras, impulsadas por el viento; la variedad de nubes próximas a la tierra; también, espuma del mar.

scuddle ['skʌdl] [ska-del], vn. (Des.) Huir, apretar a correr.

scuff [skʌf] [skaf], va. y vn. (Fam.) 1. Ponerse áspera una superficie con el uso o desgaste. 2. Arrastrar los pies al andar.

scuffle ['skʌfl] [ska-fel], s. Quimera a puñetazos, pendencia, contienda, riña, altercación, reyerta a fuerza de agarrar, de tirar o de empujar. (Fam.) Retozo, jugueteo.

scuffle, vn. Reñir, pelear, altercar. (Fam.) Retozar, juguetear.

scull [skʌl] [skal], s. 1. Remo de espadilla, remo largo colocado a popa de una barquilla y que puede bogarlo un hombre solo. 2. Remo ligero y corto de espadilla. 3. Botecito, barquilla para remar con espadilla.

scull, va. y vn. Cinglar, impeler un bote con un solo remo colocado a popa, y moviéndolo alternativamente a uno y otro lado.

scullboat ['skʌlbəʊt] [skal-bout], s. Barquillo, botecito; (Mar.) sereni.

sculler ['skʌlə^r] [ska-la^r], *s.* Bote de un remero; remero de bote; cinglador, el que cingla.

scullery ['skʌlərɪ] [ska-la-ri], *s.* Espetera; fregadero.

scullion ['skʌlɪən] [ska-lion], *s.* 1. Marmitón, pinche, galopín de cocina. **Scullion wench**, fregona. 2. Sollastre, ente vil, despreciable.

sculper ['skʌlpə^r] [skal-pa^r], *s.* Buril, cincel. Se escribe también SCORPER.

sculpt ['skʌlpt] [skalpt], *vt.* Esculpir.

sculptor ['skʌlptə^r] [skalp-ta^r], *s.* Escultor, el que modela efigies en barro o las esculpe en piedra, bronce, etc.; cincelador (en metales).

sculptress ['skʌlptrɪs] [skalp-tris], *f.* Escultora, la mujer que esculpe o entalla.

sculptural ['skʌlptʃərəl] [skalp-cha-ral], *a.* Escultural, relativo a la escultura, como arte, o propio de ella.

sculpture ['skʌlptʃə^r] [skalp-cha^r], *s.* Escultura, el arte de esculpir y entallar.

sculpture, *va.* 1. Esculpir, labrar o formar una efigie o imagen en madera, mármol o piedra. 2. Entallar, cincelar.

scum [skʌm] [skam], *s.* 1. Nata, espuma, la materia impura o inútil que sobrenada en algunos líquidos cuando están en ebullición o fermentación; conjunto de plantas diminutas sobre el agua estancada; espuma, burbujas. 2. Hez, escoria; *(Fig.)* desecho. **Scum of metals**, la escoria o deshecho de los metales. **Scum of the people**, la hez del pueblo, la canalla.

scum, *va.* Espumar, quitar la espuma, la nata o la escoria que arrojan de sí los líquidos o su superficie.

scumble ['skʌmbl] [skam-bel], *va.* Templar los colores de una pintura o dibujo frotándolos con un color relativamente seco, dar glacis. **Scumbling**, glaica, unión de colores.

scummer ['skʌmə^r] [ska-ma^r], *s.* Espumadera.

scummy ['skʌmɪ] [ska-mi], *a.* Espumoso, cubierto de escoria, o de la naturaleza de ésta.

scupper ['skʌpə^r] [ska-pa^r], *s.* Imbornal o embornal, uno de los agujeros que hay sobre la cubierta para vaciar el agua. **Scupper-nails**, estoperoles.

scurf [skɜːf] [skerf], *s.* 1. Caspa (dandruff), desescamación harinosa de la cutícula, epidermis, exfoliada en escamas; tiña de los árboles. 2. Cualquier partícula de cosa sucia o substancia escamosa adherida a una superficie. 3. Hez, escoria, chusma.

scurfiness ['skɜːfɪnɪs] [sker-fi-nis], *s.* El estado de lo que tiene caspa o epidermis exfoliada en escamas.

scurfy ['skɜːfɪ] [sker-fi], *a.* Casposo, costroso.

scurrility [skʌ'rɪlɪtɪ] [ska-ri-li-ti], *s.* Baldón, improperio; lenguaje grosero; broma baja, soez; bufonería, bufonada.

scurrilous ['skʌrɪləs] [ska-ri-los], *a.* Vil, grosero, bajo; chocante; injurioso; difamatorio, oprobioso.

scurrilously ['skʌrɪləslɪ] [ska-ri-los-li], *adv.* De manera grosera, procazmente.

scurry ['skʌrɪ] [ska-ri], *va.* y *vn.* Moverse o hacer mover precipitadamente; escaparse de prisa; apretar a correr. *-s.* 1. Movimiento precipitado. 2. Prisa, vuelta, remolino.

scurvied ['skɜːvd] [skervd], *a.* Escorbútico, atacado de escorbuto.

scurvily ['skɜːvɪlɪ] [sker-vi-li], *adv.* Vilmente; groseramente, mezquinamente, ignominiosamente.

scurviness ['skɜːvɪnɪs] [sker-vi-nes], *s.* Ruindad; malignidad, indignidad; torpeza, vileza.

scurvy ['skɜːvɪ] [sker-vi], *s.* Escorbuto, enfermedad caracterizada por manchas lívidas bajo la piel, inflamación y sanguinolencia de las encías y agotamiento general; la causa el uso prolongado a borde de carnes saladas sin legumbres frescas. *-a.* 1. Vil, ruin, despreciable, bajo. 2. *(Des.)* Escorbútico. 3. Grosero.

scut [skʌt] [skat], *s. (Prov. Ingl.)* Colita, rabito, rabo o cola pequeña.

scutch [skʌtʃ] [skach], *va.* Agramar, espadillar, macerar a golpes el lino, cáñamo, etc.

scutcheon ['skʌtʃɪən] [ska-chion], *s.* 1. Escudo de armas. 2. Escudete de metal; plancha con el nombre de una persona.

scutcher ['skʌtʃə^r] [ska-cha^r], *s.* Agramadera, útil para agramar.

scuttle ['skʌtl] [ska-tel], *s.* 1. Escotillón, puerta o tapa cerradiza en el suelo de la embarcación. **Cabin-scuttles**, *(Mar.)* luces o lumbreras de camarote. **Scuttles of the mast**, *(Mar.)* fogonaduras. 2. Cualquier agujero. 3. Cubo metálico para carbón; se llama también **coal-scuttle o coal-hod.** 4. Carrera corta; paso acelerado.

scuttle, *va.* Hacer aberturas en el fondo, en los lados o en la cubierta de un buque; echar a pique. *-vn.* Apretar a correr. *V.* SCURRY. **To scuttle a vessel**, barrenar un barco, para echarlo a pique.

scuzzy ['skʌzɪ] [ska-si], *a.* Cutre.

scythe [saɪð] [skais], *s.* Guadaña, dalle (para segar o cortar la hierba).

sea [siː] [sii], *s.* 1. Mar, toda el agua salada que rodea la tierra; océano (ocean). 2. Mar, considerable extensión del océano rodeada en parte de tierra; menos frecuentemente, lago ancho. 3. Olaje, oleada, oleaje; ola grande, el curso de las ondas. 4. Mar, la abundancia excesiva o vasta extensión de una cosa. 5. Cualquier cosa muy tempestuosa. **At sea**, (a) en el mar. (b) No saber qué hacer, estar perplejo. **Beyond sea**, allende el mar, ultramarino. **The main sea**, alma mar, mar ancha. **Narrow sea**, estrecho de mar. **Heavy sea**, oleada, ola fuerte. **High-swelling sea**, mar de leva. **The sea runs very high**, la mar está muy crecida. **To put to sea**, salir a la mar, hacer a la vela. **Half-seas-over**, medio borracho. **A high sea**, una mar gruesa. **Sea-bank**, (a) muralla de mar, especie de dique opuesto a las aguas del mar. (b) Orilla del mar. **Sea-beat, sea-beaten**, batido o golpeado por las olas de la mar. **Sea-biscuit**, galleta de marinero. **Sea-boat**, embarcación marinera. **A good sea-boat**, embarcación velera. **Sea-born**, nacido en la mar, marino. **Sea-breach**, irrupción de mar que rompe un dique. **Sea-bream**, besugo, pez de los espáridos. **Sea-breeze**, brisa, viento de mar, que sopla del mar hacia tierra. **Sea-brief**, *(Mar.)* carta de mar o marítima. **Sea-built**, construido para la mar o para navegar. **Sea-cabbage, sea-colewort, sea-kale**, *(Bot.)* berza marina. **Sea-calf**, foca o becerro marino. **Sea-cap**, gorra de marinero. **Sea-captain**, capitán de navío o de otra embarcación. **Sea-card**, *(Mar.)* rosa náutica. **Sea-chart**, *(Mar.)* carta de marear. **Sea-cucumber**, cohombro de mar, holoturia que recibe este nombre a causa de su figura. **Sea-dragon**, araña o dragón marino, un pez. **Sea-eagle**, halieto, águila pescadora, ave marítima rapaz, de plumaje leonado y cola blanca. **Sea-ear**, oreja de mar, aulone, molusco gasterópodo. **Sea-egg**, *V.* **Sea-urchin. Sea-fennel**, *(Bot.)* hinojo marino. **Sea-fight**, batalla o combate naval. **Sea-fish**, pez o pescado de mar. **Sea-fowl**, ave marítima o ave de mar; conjunto de aves marinas. **Sea-gate**, (a) oleada larga. (b) Punto de salida al mar. (c) Compuerta de marea. **Sea-girt**, rodeado o cercado por el mar. **Sea-green**, (a.) verdemar. (s.) Color verde azulado oscuro, como el del mar. **Sea-gull**, gaviota, ave de los láridos. **Sea-hedgehog**, equino. **Sea-hog**, marsopa, marsopla o cachalote. **Sea-holly**, *(Bot.)* cardo corredor. **Sea-holm**, isleta no habitada. **Sea-horse**, caballo marino, hipocampo; hipopótamo. **Sea-king**, rey de piratas de los pueblos del norte. **Sea-legs**, pie marino, facultad de andar por la cubierta de un buque sin caerse ni dar tumbos. **Sea-letter**, patente de mar, documento que lleva un buque neutral y que indica su nacionalidad, matrícula, clase de cargamento, etc. **Sea-lettuce**, lechuga de mar, alga marina verde que se usa a menudo como alimento. **Sea-level**, nivel del mar. **Sea-lion**, león marino, foca de largas orejas. **Sea-lungs**, pólipo coelentorado (etenophora). **Sea-mark**, baliza, boya, señal que se pone con palo, mástil, tonel o cualquier otra cosa en los parajes donde la navegación es peligrosa. **Sea-mew**, gaviota, particularmente la europea. **Sea-monster**, monstruo marino. **Sea-moss**, (a) carolina, ova, alga marina comestible, especialmente la rosada. (b) Polípero marino parecido al musgo. **Sea-nettle**, ortiga de mar, acalefo que causa picazón en la piel. **Sea-nymph**, ninfa marina. **Sea-onion**, cebolla albarrana, escila marítima. **Sea-ooze**, cieno de mar. **Sea-otter**, nutria marina. **Sea-pen**, pluma de mar, pólipo en forma de pluma rizada. **Sea-piece**, pintura marítima o naval, pintura que representa cualquier cosa perteneciente al mar o a la navegación. **Sea-pool**, marisma; lago o laguna de agua salada. **Sea-porcupine**, cierto pez espinoso de mar. **Sea-raven**, (a) V. SCULPIN. (b) Cormorán, ave afín al pelícano. **Sea-risk**, riesgo o peligro de mar. **Sea-rocket**, (Bot.) alga marina. **Sea-room**, alta mar, espacio suficiente para maniobrar una embarcación. **Sea-rover**, pirata; corsario. **Sea-serpent**, serpiente acuática o de mar; animal marino enorme, parecido a la serpiente que algunos pretenden haber visto. **Sea-service**, el servicio de marina o de mar. **Sea-shark**, tiburón. **Sea-shell**, concha marina. **Sea-star**, V. STARFISH. **Sea-term**, término naval, voz náutica. **Sea-tossed**, batido por el mar. **Sea-unicorn**, unicornio de mar, nombre vulgar del narval. **Sea-urchin**, equino, erizo de mar; equinodermo. Echinus. **Sea-voyage**, viaje por mar. **Sea-wall**, muralla de mar, especie de dique para romper el ímpetu de las olas; banco de arena, piedras, etc., arrojadas por el mar. **Sea-walled**, rodeado o protegido por el mar, como por una pared. **Sea-water**, agua del mar, agua salada. **Sea-wave**, ola. **Sea-wolf**, lobo marino.

sea-anemone ['siː.ə'nemənɪ] [sia-ne-mo-ni], s. Anémone de mar, especie de actinia, pólipo que se parece a la flor del mismo nombre.

sea-bass ['siː.bæs] [si-bas], s. Serrano, pez de mar muy estimado, abundante desde la Florida hasta el Cabo Cod, en Massachusetts; se llama también **bluefish** y **black-fish** o **rock-bass**.

seaboard ['siː.bɔːd] [si-bord], a. Vecino al mar o cerca de él. -s. Orilla, borde del mar.

sea-coast ['siː.kəʊst] [si-koust], s. Costa marítima, orilla, borde del mar.

sea-cow ['siː.kaʊ] [si-kau], s. Manato, manatí, vaca marina.

sea-dog ['siː.dɒg] [si-dog], s. 1. Foca común. 2. León marino, foca grande de California. 3. Tiburón espinoso, perro de mar. 4. Marinero viejo o persona aficionada al mar; (Fam.) lobo marino.

seafarer ['siːˌfɛərərˈ] [si-fea-raʳ], s. Marinero, navegante (navigating).

seafaring ['siːˌfɛərɪŋ] [si-fea-rin], a. Marino, marinero, navegante.

seafood ['siː.fuːd] [si-fud], s. Mariscos.

seagoing ['siːˌgəʊɪŋ] [si-gouin], a. 1. Propio para la navegación de altura. 2. Navegante, experto en la navegación por alta mar.

seal [siːl] [sil], s. 1. Sello para cerrar las cartas y la impresión que hace en la oblea o lacre. 2. Selladura, la acción de sellar. 3. El lacre que tiene la señal formada por el sello; señal o marca característica. 4. El acto de sellar, concluir o poner fin a una cosa. 5. Sello; firma; autenticación, fianza; sacramento. 5. Timbre. 6. Lo que impide la entrada o salida de un gas o el aire en un tubo o recipiente. **Great seal**, gran sello. **Prity seal**, sello privaco (o pequeño). **To affix one's seal**, poner uno su sello. **Under the hand and seal of**, firmado y sellado por. **Keeper of the selas**, guardasellos.

seal, va. 1. Sellar, poner el sello sobre una cosa. 2. Sellar, estampar una cosa en otra. 3. Sellar, concluir, poner fin. 4. Sellar, afirmar, afianzar, confirmar. 5. Cerrar una carta, un paquete, con lacre u otra sustancia. 6. Santiguar; bautizar, confirmar. 7. Guardar secreto. 8. Confirmar, ratificar, decidir irrevocablemente. **To seal up**, cerrar. 9. Poner una chapeleta para impedir el retroceso de gas o aire. **To seal with sealing wax**, lacrar.

seal, vn. Cazar focas. -s. Foca, becerro marino, mamífero acuático o carnívoro que vive principalmente en las latitudes árticas. (A.S.seol).

sealed ['siːld] [sild], a. Sellado, cerrado, secreto: sealed book, libro cerrado. **Sealed orders**, intrucciones secretas que se dan en un pliego cerrado.

sealer ['siːləˈ] [si-laʳ], s. 1. Sellador. 2. Cazador de focas.

sealing ['siːlɪŋ] [si-lin], s. 1. Selladura, sello, cerramiento (straping, banding). 2. Precintado. 3. Caza de focas. **Sealing tape**, cinta engomada para precintar.

sealing-wax ['siːlɪŋwæks] [si-lin-uaks], s. Lacre.

seal-ring ['siːlrɪŋ] [sil-rin], s. Sortija con sello.

sealskin ['siːlskɪn] [sil-skin], s. Piel de foca o una prenda de vestir hecha de ella.

seam [siːm] [sim], s. 1. Costura, línea visible de unión entre dos partes o piezas. 2. Grieta, hendedura, rendija, raja. 3. Listón saliente o reborde que se forma al juntar dos cosas, o que queda en una pieza de fundición al salir del molde. 4. Costrón, cicatriz; arruga. 5. (Geol.) Filón, vena, capa delgada, yacimiento de mineral o roca. 6. **Sutura.** (Mar.) Costura de los tablones. **To pay the seams**, (Mar.) embrear las costuras.

seam, va. 1. Hacer costuras, coser. 2. Señalar con cicatrices.

seamaid ['siːmeɪd] [si-meid], sf. Sirena.

seaman ['siːmən] [si-man], s. 1. Marinero, hombre de mar; marino experimentado. 2. Tritón, el macho de la sirena. **Seaman's wages**, sueldos o mesadas de los marineros.

seamanship ['siːmənʃɪp] [si-man-ship], s. La habilidad o pericia en la navegación o en el arte de hacer maniobrar una embarcación.

seamless ['siːmlɪs] [sim-les], a. Sin costura. **Seamless hose**, medias sin costura.

seamster ['siːmstəˈ] [sims-taʳ], sm. (Ant.) Costurero.

seamstress ['semstrɪs] [sems-tris], sf. Costurera, la mujer que tiene por oficio coser ropa blanca. Se escribe también **sempstress**.

seamy ['siːmɪ] [si-mi], a. Que tiene o muestra costuras; (Fig.) lo peor. **The seamy side**, el lado peor, el aspecto menos favorable.

seance ['seɪɑːns] [seians], s. Sesión; en especial, reunión de espiritistas.

seaplane ['siːpleɪn] [si-plein], s. Hidroavión.

seaport ['siːpɔːt] [si-port], s. Puerto de mar.

sear [sɪəˈ] [siaʳ], a. 1. Seco, marchito, ajado; se dice ordinariamente de las plantas que se han secado. 2. Gastado, cascado. 3. Chamusco, quemadura.

sear, va. 1. Disecar, marchitar, tostar, chamuscar. 2. Cauterizar, quemar la superficie de una cosa. 3. Hacer calloso o insensible. 4. Marcar con hierro. 5. Endurecer, empedernir.

sear, s. Linguete o fiador en la llave de un arma de fuego que mantiene el gatillo en seguro o montado. **Sear-spring**, muelle real.

search [sɜːtʃ] [serch], va. y vn. 1. Explorar, escudriñar, buscar, registrar, hallar buscando (to explore, to scan). **To search a house**, registrar una casa. 2. Inquirir, indagar. 3. Tentar, reconocer la cavidad de una herida; probar, poner a prueba. 4. Investigar, indagar, hacer pesquisas o averiguaciones, informarse de. 5. Exploración con un instrumento. **To search after**, preguntar por alguno; indagar, inquirir. **To search into**, examinar, investigar. **To search for**, buscar, tratar de descubrir; inquirir o procurar; hallar alguna cosa. **To search out**, hallar o encontrar alguna cosa buscándola. **To search for arms**, cacheo. **Right of search**, derecho de visitas.

search, s. 1. Registro, el acto de registrar. **The right of search**, el derecho de registrar o visitar un barco. 2. Pesquisa, averiguación. 3. Busca, buscada, el acto de buscar. 4. Examen, pesquisa, indagación, investigación. 5. Penetración del entendimiento. **Search-light**, holofote, luz eléctrica con reflector que proyecta un rayo luminoso de gran intensidad; se usa mucho en la navegación por la costa y en los buques de guerra.

searchable ['sɜːtʃəbl] [ser-cha-bol], a. Que puede buscarse, escudriñarse, explorarse.

searcher ['sɜːtʃəˈ] [ser-chaʳ], s. 1. Buscador, escudriñador, pesquisidor, indagador, inquiridor; vista, inspector, empleado de aduana encargado de registrar el equipaje de los viajeros. 2. Todo instrumento o aparato empleado para examinar o investigar; gato, instrumento con garfios que sirve para escudriñar el interior de un cañón; sonda para las piedras de la vejiga; buscador, ocular de microscopio.

searching ['sɜːtʃɪŋ] [ser-chin], *a.* Penetrante, escrutador; completo, cabal. **Searching party**, grupo de personas enviadas en busca de otra y otras.

search-warrant ['sɜːtʃˌwɒrənt] [serch-uo-rant], *s.* Mandato judicial disponiendo el registro de una casa, lugar u objeto.

seashore ['siːʃɔːʳ] [si-sho'], **seaside** ['siːsaɪd] [si-said], *s.* 1. Ribera, costa u orilla del mar (strand). 2. Litoral, costa; playa.

seasick ['siːsɪk] [si-sik], *a.* Mareado, que se marea en el mar.

seasickness ['siːsɪknɪs] [si-sik-nes], *s.* Mareo, náuseas causadas por el balanceo de un buque; indisposición muy molesta.

season ['siːzn] [si-son], *s.* 1. Estación, una de las cuatro partes en que se divide el año. 2. Sazón, tiempo determinado, tiempo oportuno o conveniente; temporada; período de tiempo. 3. Época, momento; tiempo fijo. **Dull season**, *(Com.)* estación muerta. **In season, in due season**, en tiempo oportuno. **To be in season**, ser de la estación, del tiempo. **In season**, en sazón, a su tiempo. **Close season**, veda.

season, *va.* 1. Sazonar, dar sazón al manjar; condimentar. 2. Imbuir, persuadir, infundir. 3. Sazonar, poner las cosas en el punto y madurez que deben tener. 4. Templar, moderar, hacer más agradable o menos riguroso y severo. 5. Aclimatar, acostumbrar, habituar. -*vn.* 1. Secarse, endurecerse, v. g. el maderaje. 2. Sazonarse, madurarse, hacerse propio para el uso; aclimatarse (person).

seasonable ['siːznəbl] [si-so-na-bol], *a.* Oportuno, conveniente, favorable, a propósito, de estación.

seasonably ['siːznəblɪ] [si-so-na-bli], *adv.* En sazón, oportunamente.

seasoned ['siːznd] [si-sond], *a.* 1. Sazonado. 2. Picante, curado. 3. Aclimatado, habituado. **Seasoned traveler**, viajero consumado.

seasoner ['siːznəʳ] [si-so-na'], *s.* Sazonador.

seasoning ['siːznɪŋ] [si-so-nin], *s.* 1. Sazón, condimento que se da a los manjares. 2. Salsa, o sal de un cuento o de un escrito; sainete de un dicho, etc.; lo que se añade para aumentar el placer del goce. 3. El procedimiento de secarse y endurecerse (la madera). 4. Aclimatación.

seat [siːt] [sit], *s.* 1. Asiento, cualquier cosa que sirve para sentarse, silla, banco (bottom). 2. Asiento, fondo, parte de la silla en que uno se coloca. 3. Fondillos de los calzones; nalga. 4. Sitio, posición, paraje o lugar en que se halla situada alguna cosa. 5. Residencia, morada, domicilio. **Country-seat**, sitio, casa de campo. 6. Privilegio, derecho o manera de sentarse.

seat, *va.* 1. Sentar, asentar, colocar en asientos. 2. Tener asientos para (persons). 3. Colocar o acomodar a alguno en un empleo elevado. 4. Asentar, poner alguna cosa de manera que esté firme. 5. Poner un asiento a una silla; echar fondillos (trousers). **The hall will seat eight hundred**, la sala tiene asientos para ochocientas personas.

seating ['siːtɪŋ] [si-tin], *s.* 1. Acción de sentar o de sentarse. 2. Material para entapizar las sillas o sofás. 3. *(Mec.)* Lecho, base. **Seating capacity**, cubo, cabida.

seaward ['siːwɔːd] [si-uord], *adv.* Hacia el mar. -*a.* Dirigido hacia el mar.

seaway ['siːweɪ] [si-uei], *s.* 1. Ruta oceánica. 2. Vía fluvial que permite la navegación de embarcaciones marítimas. 3. Mar gruesa o alborotada.

seaweed ['siːwiːd] [si-uid], *s.* 1. Alga marina (y aun la que vive en el agua dulce); ova. 2. Toda planta que crece en el mar.

seaworthy ['siːˌwɜːðɪ] [si-uer-zi], *a.* Se dice de la embarcación que es a propósito para navegar.

sebaceous [sɪ'beɪʃəs] [si-bei-shos], *a.* Sebáceo, seboso, perteneciente o parecido al sebo, que contiene materia pingüe.

sec [sek] [sek], *a.* 1. Segundo. 2. Seco (wine).

secant ['siːkənt] [si-kant], *a.* Cortante, que divide en dos partes. -*s.* Secante, línea que corta un cuerpo; secante, el radio prolongado hasta encontrarse con la tangente.

secede [sɪ'siːd] [si-sid], *vn.* Apartarse, separarse de un cuerpo político o religioso.

seceder [sɪ'siːdəʳ] [si-si-da'], *s.* Separatista, el que se aparta.

secession [sɪ'seʃən] [si-se-shon], *s.* Apartamiento, separación, antiguamente secesión.

secessionist [sɪ'seʃnɪst] [si-se-sho-nist], *s.* Partidario de la separación; secesionista, el que en la guerra civil de los Estados Unidos mantenía el derecho de los Estados del Sur a la separación política.

seclude [sɪ'kluːd] [si-klud], *va.* Apartar, excluir, alejar a alguien de una compañía o sociedad; alejarse de otros; encerrar, confinar en estado de aislamiento. **Secluded**, *pp.* alejado, apartado, desviado; retirado en el aislamiento, en la soledad.

seclusion [sɪ'kluːʒən] [si-klu-shon], *s.* 1. Separación; exclusión, aislamiento, soledad. 2. Lugar apartado, retiro. 3. Reclusión, encierro.

second ['sekənd] [se-kond], *a.* 1. Segundo, lo que sigue inmediatamente al primero. **Second son**, segundón. 2. Secundario, subordinado; inferior. 3. Segundo, otro, idéntico a otro. **Second-class**, de segunda clase, de grado inferior. **Second-hand**, de segunda mano, de lance, que ha sido poseído o usado por otro; por intermedio de otro. **Second-rute**, de segunda clase o categoría. **The twenty-second**, el vigésimo segundo. **To be second to none**, no ser inferior a nadie. -*s.* 1. Segundo, brazo derecho; el que ayuda a otro en una empresa, en un negocio; apoyo, auxilio; defensor, sostenedor. 2. Padrino, el que apadrina a otro en un desafío. 3. Segundo, una de las sesenta partes en que se divide el minuto de hora o de grado. 4. Segundo, intervalo músico entre dos sonidos sucesivos. 5. Dos, días dos en las fechas. **The second best**, el mejor después del primero. En los certámenes, el accésit. **To come off second best**, llevar lo peor, o la peor parte en una contienda.

second, *va.* 1. Apoyar, sostener, apadrinar, ayudar, auxiliar, favorecer; apoyar un proyecto de ley en los cuerpos deliberantes, como preliminar a su discusión o aceptación. 2. Segundar, asegundar, ser segundo o seguirse al primero.

secondarily [ˌsekən'dærɪlɪ] [se-kon-da-ri-li], *adv.* Secundariamente, en segundo lugar.

secondary ['sekəndərɪ] [se-kon-da-ri], *a.* 1. Secundar, de segunda clase, influencia o grado; subordinado, subalterno; subsecuente; resultante; accesorio; que depende de otro; que gira alrededor de un planeta principal. 2. De, o perteneciente a una corriente eléctrica inducida o a su circuito. -*s.* 1. Lugarteniente, delegado, diputado. 2. Algo de tamaño o importancia secundarios. 3. *(Astr.)* Círculo secundario; planeta secundario, satélite. 4. Una de las plumas grandes que crecen en la segunda articulación del ala de un ave. 5. Ala posterior de las mariposas y otros insectos.

seconder ['sekəndəʳ] [se-kon-da'], *s.* El que apoya, secunda o sostiene la proposición que ha hecho algún otro.

second-hand ['sekənd'hænd] [se-kond-jand], *s.* 1. Segunda mano, la posesión que se recibe del primer poseedor. 2. Manecilla de reloj que indica los segundos. **At second-hand**, por imitación; secundariamente; de segunda mano, de lance.

secondly ['sekəndlɪ] [se-kond-li], *adv.* En segundo lugar.

second-sight ['sekəndsaɪt] [se-kond-sait], *s.* Conocimiento de lo futuro.

secrecy ['siːkrəsɪ] [si-kre-si], *s.* 1. Secreto, silencio cuidadoso, sigilo. 2. Soledad, retiro. 2. Fidelidad en guardar sigilo o secreto.

secret ['siːkrɪt] [si-kret], *a.* 1. Secreto, oculto (concealed, hidden). 2. Secreto, retirado, escondido. 3. Secreto, callado, reservado, que no se sabe generalmente. 4. Callado, reservado, silencioso, que guarda un secreto. 5. Obsceno, vergonzoso, que no debe salir a luz. **Secret service**, servicio secreto, policía secreta. -*s.* 1. Secreto, el silencio cuidadoso de no revelar lo que se quiere tener oculto, y la misma cosa que se quiere guardar callada. 2. Secreto, una cosa no conocida o sabida sólo por una o muy pocas personas. 3. Razón oculta; lo que cuando es conocido, explica; llave. 4. *pl.* Partes pudendas o genitales. **In secret**, secretamente, en secreto. Secreto; cuidado o disimulación silenciosa; la cosa que se oculta o no se descubre. **Open secret**, secreto a voces.

secretary ['sekrətrɪ] [se-kre-ta-ri], *s.* 1. Secretario, el que cuida de la correspondencia de otros y escribe sus cartas, despachos y documentos públicos o privados. 2. Secretario, ministro, funcionario cuyo empleo es presidir y dirigir un ministerio. 3. Escritorio, papelera, mueble. **Secretary of War**, ministro de guerra. **Secretary-bird**, secretario (Serpentarius), ave de rapiña de África.

secretaryship ['sekrətrɪʃɪp] [se-kra-tri-ship], *s.* Secretaría, el cargo o empleo de secretario.

secrete [sɪ'kriːt] [si-krit], *va.* 1. Desviar, escender, tener secreto, ocultar, encubrir. 2. *(Med.)* Secretar, separar, elaborar algo de la sangre o de la savia por el procedimiento de la secreción.

secretion [sɪ'kriːʃən] [si-kri-shon] *s.* 1. Secreción, el procedimiento por el cual se separan de la sangre o de la savia ciertos elementos para convertirse en nuevas sustancias. 2. Secreción, la substancia secretada. 3. Ocultación, escondimiento, el acto de esconder.

secretive ['siːkrətɪv] [si-kra-tiv], *a.* 1. Secreto, callado, silencioso, reservado, dispuesto a ocultar. 2. Secretivo, secretorio, que promueve la secreción.

secretiveness ['siːkrətɪvnɪs] [si-kra-tiv-nes], *s.* Inclinación a ocultar o esconder.

secretly ['siːkrɪtlɪ] [si-krit-li], *adv.* Secretamete, ocultamente.

secretness ['siːkrɪtnɪs] [si-krit-nes], *s.* 1. Secreto, sigilo. 2. La calidad que constituye a uno propio para guardar un secreto.

sect [sekt] [sekt], *s.* 1. Secta, la comunidad de hombres que siguen la doctrina y opinión particular de algún maestro célebre, especialmente en materias religiosas; denominación, una comunión que no está de acuerdo con una iglesia establecida. 2. Partido, pandilla, orden.

sectarian [sek'teəriən] [sek-tea-rian], *a.* y *s.* Sectario, que profesa o sigue alguna secta con tesón; fanático. -*s.* Sectario, miembro (fanático) de una secta.

sectarianism [sek'teəriənɪzəm] [sek-tea-ria-ni-sem], *s.* Carácter o tendencia de secta; adhesión excesiva a una secta.

sectile ['sektaɪl] [sek-tail], *a.* Sectil, que se puede cortar, dividir o separar en secciones.

section ['sekʃən] [sek-shon], *s.* 1. Sección, cortadura, división; parte, porción distinta, subdivisión de un capítulo o de una ley; en los Estados Unidos, área de terreno público, una milla en cuadro que contiene 640 acres y constituye la trigésimasexta parte de una municipalidad o **township**. 2. Sección, corte, representación de un edificio, de una máquina, de una formación geológica, etc., de manera que muestre el interior. 3. Corte muy delgado de alguna cosa, especialmente para su examen con el microscopio. 4. *(Impr.)* El signo que indica una subdivisión. 5. Barrio, distrito. 6. Comarca, región. 7. Compartimento. 8. Tramo. **Section-cutter**, instrumento para cortar secciones muy delgadas para el examen microscópico.

sectional ['sekʃənl] [sek-sho-nal], *a.* 1. Seccionario, perteneciente a una parte; local. 2. Hecho de secciones, como un vapor. 3. Parcial, incompleto.

sectionalism ['sekʃənəlɪzəm] [sek-sho-na-li-sem], *s.* Regionalismo, prejuicios regionales.

sector ['sektər] [sek-ta^r], *s.* 1. *(Geom.)* Sector, parte del círculo comprendida entre dos radios y el arco comprendido entre ellos. 2. Un instrumento matemático o astronómico en forma de sector geométrico; compás de proporción.

sectoral ['sektərə] [sek-to-ral], *a. (Econ.)* Sectorial.

secular ['sekjʊlər] [se-kiu-la^r], *a.* 1. Secular, seglar, mundano, temporal. 2. Secular; se dice del clero no sujeto a las reglas monásticas. 3. Secular, lo que sucede una vez en un siglo. 4. Efectuado en el curso de un siglo o siglos. -*s.* Seglar, lego, por oposición a eclesiástico, sea secular o regular.

secularism ['sekjʊlərɪzəm] [se-kiu-la-ri-sem], *sm.* Laicismo.

secularization ['sekjʊləraɪ'zeɪʃən] [se-kiu-la-rai-sei-shon], *s.* Secularización, acción y efecto de secularizar.

secularize ['sekjʊləraɪz] [se-kiu-la-rais], *va.* Secularizar, hacer secular o mundano; transferir la jurisdicción civil de un distrito o de un país de manos de eclesiásticos a las de seglares.

secularly ['sekjʊlərlɪ] [se-kiu-la-li], *adv.* A lo seglar o como seglar; como un hombre apegado al mundo.

secure [sɪ'kjʊər] [se-kiua^r], *a.* 1. Seguro, tranquilo, sin temor o inquietud. 2. Descuidado, negligente, que no hace caso, lleno de confianza. 3. Seguro, libre y exento de peligro, daño o riesgo. 4. Seguro, cierto, indudable. 5. Confiado en sí mismo.

secure, *va.* 1. Asegurar, resguardar, poner en seguridad o al abrigo; salvar, proteger, poner en salvo. 2. Asegurar, dar firmeza y seguridad a una cosa, afianzar; dar garantías. 3. Encerrar, aprisionar, poner bajo llave, impedir que algo se escape o pierda. 4. Lograr, obtener, adquirir, hacerse dueño de. **To secure one**, asegurar o poner en lugar seguro a una persona; prender. **I have secured my place**, he obtenido ya un asiento.

securely [sɪ'kjʊəlɪ] [se-kiua-li], *adv.* Seguramente, con seguridad, sin riesgo; tranquilamente.

secureness [sɪ'kjʊənɪs] [si-kiua-nes], *s.* Seguridad, calidad de seguro; falta de cuidado.

security [sɪ'kjʊərɪtɪ] [si-kiu-ri-ti], *s.* 1. Seguridad, el estado de las cosas que las hace firmes, seguras y libres de todo riesgo y peligro; protección, defensa. 2. Seguridad, tranquilidad, confianza; también exceso de confianza, falta de cautela, descuido. 3. Seguridad, fianza, obligación de indemnidad a favor de alguno. -*pl.* Vales, valores, garantías de pago. **To stand security**, salir fiador por otro. **Security risk**, persona de dudosas antecedentes y peligrosa para la seguridad nacional.

sedan [sɪ'dæn] [si-dan], *s.* 1. Sedán, automóvil sedán. 2. Silla de manos.

sedate [sɪ'deɪt] [si-deit], *a.* Sereno, apacible, sosegado, formal, serio, juicioso.

sedately [sɪ'deɪtlɪ] [si-deit-li], *adv.* Tranquilamente, formalmente.

sedateness [sɪ'deɪtnɪs] [si-deit-nes], *s.* Serenidad, tranquilidad, calma, quietud.

sedation [sɪ'deɪʃən] [si-dei-shon] *sf.* Tratamiento mediante calmantes, sedación.

sedative ['sedətɪv] [se-da-tiv], *a.* Sedativo, calmante. -*s.* Sedativo, medicamento calmante.

sedentary ['sedntrɪ] [se-dan-tri], *a.* 1. Sedentario; se aplicaa la vida o ejercicio de poca acción y movimiento. 2. Poltrón, flojo, perezoso. 3. *(Zool.)* Sedentario, que queda fijado o unido a un objeto.

sedge [sedʒ] [sedch], *s. (Bot.)* Juncia, cárice, esparganio, cualquier planta de la familia de las ciperáceas; vulgarmente, junco, enea. **Sedge-warbler, sedge-bird**, curruca, pajarillo cantor de Europa. **Sedge root**, chufa (tubérculo).

sedgy ['sedʒɪ] [sed-chi] *a.* Cubierto de juncias o cárices.

sediment ['sedɪmənt] [se-di-ment], *s.* 1. Sedimento, hez, poso, zurrapas. 2. *(Geol.)* Detritus transportado o depositado por el agua.

sedimental ['sedɪməntl] [se-di-men-tal], *a.* Sedimental, perteneciente a los sedimentos.

sedimentary ['sedɪ'mentərɪ] [se-di-men-ta-ri], *a.* Sedimentario, sedimentoso, que participa de la naturaleza del sedimento o está formado por él. **Sedimentary rocks**, rocas sedimentarias.

sedimentation ['sedɪmen'teɪʃən] [se-di-men-tei-shon], *s.* Sedimentación.

sedition [sə'dɪʃən] [se-di-shon], *s.* Sedición, tumulto, levantamiento popular contra la autoridad; motín, revuelta, sublevación.

seditious [sə'dɪʃəs] [se-di-shos], *a.* 1. Sedicioso. 2. Culpable de sedición, tumultuoso; amotinado.

seditiously [sə'dɪʃəslɪ] [se-di-shos-li], *adv.* Sediciosamente.

seditiousness [sə'dɪʃəsnɪs] [se-di-shos-nes], *s.* Calidad de sedicioso; excitación a la sedición.

seduce [sɪ'djuːs] [si-dius], *va.* 1. Seducir, desviar del deber, de la rectitud o de la verdad, instigar a alguna cosa mala. 2. En especial, seducir a una mujer. 3. Invitar, tentar. 3. Arrastrar, llevar a algo malo.

seducement [sɪ'djuːsmənt] [si-dius-ment], *s.* Seducción, acción de seducir o los medios empleados para ello.

seducer [sɪ'djuːsəʳ] [si-diu-saʳ], *s.* Seductor, seductora; el o la que seduce.

seducible, seduceable [sɪ'djuːsəbl] [si-diu-sa-bol], *a.* Capaz de ser seducido o de dejarse seducir.

seduction [sɪ'dʌkʃən] [si-dak-shon], *s.* 1. Seducción. 2. Atractivo.

seductive [sɪ'dʌktɪv] [si-dak-tris], *a.* Seductivo, atractivo, halagüeño; persuasivo.

seductress [sɪ'dʌktrɪs] [si-dak-tris], *sf.* Seductora, la que seduce o corrompe.

sedulous ['sedjʊləs] [se-diu-los], *a.* Diligente, aplicado, cuidadoso, asiduo.

sedulousness ['sedjʊləsnɪs] [se-diu-los-nes], *s.* Ahinco, cuidado, celoso, diligencia, asiduidad, aplicación.

see [siː] [sii], *s.* Silla pontifical o episcopal; sede, diócesis o episcopado.

see, *va. (pret.* SAW, *pp.* SEEN, *ger.* SEEING). 1. Ver, percibir con los ojos; mirar, observar (to look at, observe, regard, view, watch). 2. Ver, percibir con la mente; concebir, comprender, conocer. 3. Ver, distinguir, descubrir, reparar; notar, inquirir, indagar, informarse; también conocer, sufrir. **See whether I am right**, averigüe Ud. si tengo razón. **I have seen better days**, he conocido mejores tiempos. 4. Ver, visitar a un sujeto o estar con él con un objeto cualquiera, tener relaciones con alguien; hacer o recibir visitas. 5. Acompañar, escoltar. 6. Tener como cargo o cuidado (seguido de cláusula que empiece con **that**). **See that the work is done**, cuide Ud. de que se haga el trabajo. 7. Considerar, juzgar, tener por. -*vn.* 1. Ver, percibir con la vista. 2. Discernir, penetrar, comprender. 3. Preguntar;. informarse, considerar, advertir; reflexionar; pensar en algo. **To see afar off**, ver de lejos, ver a lo lejos. **To see for**, buscar, inquirir. **To see into**, ver y examinar una cosa a fondo, ver el interior de una cosa o penetrar en ella. **To see one another**, visitarse, verse. **I'll see about it**, yo lo veré, yo lo pensaré. **Let me see**, déjeme Ud. ver, pensar o examinar (la cosa de que se trata). **To see a person home**, acompañar a una persona a su casa. **Let's see, let us see**, veamos; a ver. **I see**, ya veo, ya comprendo. **To see out**, ver u oír hasta el fin; ver partir; eclipsar, dejar deslucido a otro. **To see through**, comprender, reconocer; llevar a cabo; ayudar a uno en la ejecución de algo. **To see to**, tener cuidado, pensar, poner atención en algo. **See to it**, tenga Ud. cuidado de ello, piense Ud. en ello.

see, *inter.* ¡Mira!

seed [siːd] [siid], *s.* 1. Semilla, simiente; grano de los vegetales. **Seed of a fruit**, pepita, cuesco. **Animal seed**, esperma, semen. 2. Origen, causa primitiva, principio productivo. 3. Progenie, casta, generación. 4. Excesiva madurez, decadencia. **Seed-basket**, sembradera, cesto para grano. **Seed-bud**, botón, el germen o rudimento del fruto. **Seed-corn**, trigo o maíz para sembrar. **Seed-drill**, sembradora, máquina de sembrar. **Seed-lac**, laca seca en granos. **Seed-vessel**, pericarpio, la parte de una planta en que están contenidas las semillas. **To run to seed**, producir semillas, convertirse todo en semillas; agotarse. **Seed-cake**, bollo o torta hecha con semillas aromáticas (anisado). **Seedlip, seedlop**, sementero. **Seed-plot**, semillero, plantel.

seed, *va.* 1. Sembrar, esparcir las semillas. 2. Adornar con figuras parecidas a semillas. 3. Despepitar. -*vn.* 1. Sembrar semillas. 2. Granar, desgargolar, llegar a la madurez, y producir la semilla.

seeder ['siːdəʳ] [sii-daʳ], *s.* Sembradora, máquina de sembrar.

seediness ['siːdɪnɪs] [si-di-nes], *s.* La condición o calidad de lo que está lleno de simiente.

seed-pearl ['siːdpɜːl] [siid-perl], *s.* Aljófar, rostrillo, granillos de perlas.

seed-time ['siːdtaɪm] [siid-taim], *s.* Sementera, siembra.

seedling ['siːdlɪŋ] [siid-lin], *s.* 1. Planta de semillero. 2. Semilla, germen.

seedsman ['siːdzmən] [siids-man], *s.* 1. Sembrador, el que siembra granos. 2. Tratante en semillas o simientes.

seedy ['siːdɪ] [sii-di], *a.* 1. Granado, lleno de granos, abundante en semillas. 2. Desharapado, pobre y andrajoso, descamisado.

seeing ['siːɪŋ] [siin], *s.* Vista, visión, el acto de ver. *a.* Vidente. -*conj.* **Seeing o seeing that**, visto que, siendo así que, puesto que.

seek [siːk] [siik], *va. (pret.* y *pp.* SOUGHT). 1. Buscar, ir en busca de, procurar hallar alguna cosa. 2. Inquirir; solicitar, pretender. 3. Intentar, procurar. 4. Preguntar, interrogar, suplicar. 5. Acudir, dirigirse, recurrir. 6. Explorar, registrar. -*vn.* Buscar, hacer preguntas o diligencias para hallar. **To seek after**, buscar, inquirir; solicitar, pretender; perseguir; pesquisar. **To seek for**, andar buscando, inquiriendo o preguntando por una cosa; procurar conseguir un objeto. **To seek of**, solicitar. **To seek out**, buscar por todos lados; pesquisar, hacer pesquisas o investigaciones; solicitar, hacer esfuerzos por conseguir un fin; seguir los perros la caza por el olfato. **To seek to**, acudir. **To seek one's life**, querer matar o asesinar a uno.

seeker ['siːkəʳ] [sii-kaʳ], *s.* Buscador, inquiridor, investigador.

seel ['siːl] [siil], *va.* 1. Tapar o coser los ojos a los halcones. 2. Cerrar los ojos; cegar. 3. Engañar. *vn.* Tumbarse sobre una banda. *V.* TO HEEL.

seem ['siːm] [siim], *vn.* 1. Parecer, tener apariencia o señales de, darse un aire a alguno. 2. Parecerle a uno alguna cosa. **It seems**, parece, según parece.

seemer ['siːməʳ] [sii-maʳ], *s.* El que parece.

seeming ['siːmɪŋ] [sii-min], *s.* Apariencia, parecer, exterior; particularmente, apariencia falsa. -*a.* Aparente, especioso, parecido; que tiene apariencia de algo.

seemingly ['siːmɪŋlɪ] [sii-min-li], *adv.* Al parecer, aparentemente.

seemingness ['siːmɪŋnɪs] [sii-min-nes], *s.* Exterioridad, apariencia; plausibilidad.

seemliness ['siːmlɪnɪs] [siim-li-nes], *s.* Gracia, gallardía; decoro, decencia, bien parecer; propiedad, la conformidad y correspondencia que deben guardar las cosas y personas entre sí.

seemly ['siːmlɪ] [siim-li], *a.* Decente, propio, correspondiente, decoroso, que conviene. **It is not seemly to**, no conviene que. -*adv.* Decentemente, de una manera conveniente.

seen [siːn] [siin], *pp.* de TO SEE.

seep [siːp] [siip], *va.* y *vn. (E.U. y Esco.)* 1. Colar, pasar. 2. Colarse, rezumarse, pasar a través de los poros. 3. Perder un líquido por haberse derramado o rezumado. 4. Escurrirse una cosa mojada.

seepage ['siːpɪdʒ] [sii-pich], *s.* Coladura de un líquido; cantidad de un fluido que pasa por los poros de algo y se pierde.

seer [sɪəʳ] [siaʳ], *s.* 1. Profeta, adivinador, el que prevé los acontecimientos futuros. 2. Veedor, el que ve o mira.

seeress ['sɪəz] [sias], *s.* Profetisa, vidente, adivina.

seerhand ['sɪəhænd] [sia-jand], *s.* Turbante indio.

seersucker ['sɪəsʌkəʳ] [sia-sa-kaʳ], *s. (Com.)* Sirsaca, carranclán fino y rayado de la India.

seesaw ['siːsɔː] [si-so], *s.* 1. Vaivén, movimiento alternativo. 2. Juego de muchachos, y la tabla de que se sirven para este juego. -*a.* De vaivén, que vacila.

seesaw, *vn.* Balancear, dar o hacer balances.

seethe [siːð] [siiz], *va. (pp.* SEETHED, y antiguamente SODDEN o SOD). Hacer cocer, hacer hervir. -*vn.* Hervir, bullir, ponerse en movimiento algún licor por la acción del calor. **To seethe over**, derramarse el líquido o salirse de su cotinente por estar hirviendo.

seether [ˈsiːðəʳ] [sii-zaʳ], s. Caldera, marmita.

seething [ˈsiːðɪŋ] [si-zin], a. Hirviente, efervescente.

segment [ˈsegmənt] [seg-ment], s. 1. Segmento, parte cortada o dividida; sección. 2. Segmento de un círculo.

segmentation [ˌsegmənˈteɪʃən] [seg-men-tei-shon], s. Acción y efecto de dividir en segmentos.

segregate [ˈsegrɪgeɪt] [se-gri-gueit], va. y vn. Segregar, separar o apartar una cosa de otra; segregarse. -a. Segregado, apartado, separado; selecto.

segregation [ˈsegrɪˈgeɪʃən] [se-gri-guei-shon], s. Segregación, separación, apartamiento.

seine [seɪn] [sin], va. y vn. Pescar con buitrago o red barredera. -s. Buitrago, red barredera.

seismic [ˈsaɪzmɪk] [sais-mik], a. Seísmico, perteneciente a los terremotos o producido por ellos.

seismograph [ˈsaɪzməgrɑːf] [sais-mo-graf], s. Seismógrafo, seismómetro, instrumento que señala automáticamente los fenómenos de un terremoto, mide su dirección, su intensidad, etc.

seismology [saɪzˈmɒlədʒɪ] [sais-mo-lo-yi], s. Seismología, ciencia que trata de los terremotos.

seizable [ˈsiːzəbl] [si-sa-bol], a. Capaz de o expuesto a ser asido o embargado.

seize [siːz] [siis], va. y vn. 1. Asir, agarrar, coger (to seize, take). 2. Embargar, secuestrar o efectos. 3. Apoderarse una pasión de ánimo de alguna persona. 4. *(For)* Tomar bajo la custodia de la ley. 5. *(Mar.)* Amarrar, dar una ligadura. 6. Fascinar, impresionar. 7. Aprovechar una oportunidad. 8. Comprender bien. **To seize on**, apoderarse, agarrar con firmeza una cosa. **To seize upon**, coger, agarrar o asir una cosa echándose sobre ella; embargar. **To seize again**, volver a agarrar o asir lo que se había soltado; volver a embargar lo que se había desembargado. **To be seized with fear**, sobrecogerse de miedo. **To be seized (o seised) of**, *(For)* estar en posesión de, poseer.

seizer [ˈsiːzəʳ] [si-saʳ], s. Agarrador, secuestrador; el que ase, embarga o se apodera de algo. Como término forense se escribe también SEIZOR y SEISOR.

seizing [ˈsiːzɪŋ] [si-sin], s. 1. El acto de asir o tomar posesión de una cosa y la misma cosa de que se toma posesión. 2. La cuerda con que se amarra; acción de atar las racias con una cuerda.

seizure [ˈsiːʒəʳ] [si-shaʳ], s. 1. El acto de asir. 2. La cosa asida o agarrada. 3. Captura, la acción de apoderarse de alguna cosa por fuerza; embargo, secuestro. 4. *(Med.)* Ataque, acceso de una enfermedad. 5. *(Mec.)* Atasco, trabamiento.

seldom [ˈseldəm] [sel-dom]. adv. Raramente, rara vez.

select [sɪˈlekt] [si-lekt], va. Escoger, entresacar; tomar con preferencia a otro o entre muchos; elegir.

select, a. 1. Selecto, escogido, tomado con preferenca a otros. 2. *(Fam.)* Exclusivo, **Select society**, sociedad selecta, escogida.

selected [sɪˈlektɪd] [si-lek-tid], a. Escogido, seleccionado.

selection [sɪˈlekʃən] [si-lek-shon], s. 1. Selección, elección, escogimiento. 2. Elegido o escogido; colección hecha con cuidado.

selective [sɪˈlektɪv] [si-lek-tiv], a. Perteneciente o relativo a la selección; que escoge.

selectness [sɪˈlektnɪs] [si-lekt-nes], s. La calidad o propiedad de ser selecto.

selector [sɪˈlektəʳ] [si-lek-taʳ], s. El que elige o escoge.

selenium [sɪˈliːnɪəm] [si-li-niom], s. *(Quím.)* Seleni, metaloide que se reduce con facilidad a polvo; notable por las variaciones de su resistencia eléctrica bajo la influencia de la luz y del calor.

self [self] [self], a. (pl. SELVES). 1. Mismo, idéntico, propio; desusado excepto en el compuesto **selfsame**. 2. Puro, no mezclado (colores). -s. 1. Persona, personalidad, individuo. 2. Se, sí mismo; yo mismo. **Self** se une a los pronombres personales, a algunos adjetivos posesivos y al pronombre **one** para formar pronombres reflexivos o para dar más

fuerza a la expresión. **The selfsame thing**, la misma cosa. **Myself**, yo mismo, me. **Himself, herself, itself**, se. **Ourselves, yourselves, themselves**, nos, os, se. **Oneself**, sí mismo, se. **The gracious self**, tu graciosa persona. **My other self**, mi otro yo. **To lay a thing by itself**, poner una cosa aparte. **To live like oneself**, vivir según su calidad. Esta palabra se usa muy frecuentemente en composición. La mayor parte de estas voces tienen el sentido que claramente les da su segundo componente; algunas que requieren explicación se hallarán aquí. **Self-abased**, humillado por la conciencia de su propia vergüenza. **Self-binder**, máquina de segar con atador automático. **Self-centered**, concentrado en sí mismo. **Self-command**, dominio sobre sí mismo. **Self-complacency**, complacencia en sí mismo. **Self-conceit**, egotismo, vanidad, arrogancia. **Self-conceited**, presumido, arrogante, presuntuoso. **Self-confidence**, confianza en sí mismo. **Self-concious**, (a) consciente de sí mismo con exageración. (b) Esciente, conocedor de la propia existencia. **Self-contradiction**, contradicción consigo mismo. **Self-control**, imperio sobre sí mismo. **Self-convicted**, convicto por confesión propia; que se condena a sí mismo. **Self-deception**, la acción de engañarse a sí mismo o de formarse ilusiones vanas. **Self-defense**, la acción de engañarse a sí mismo o de formarse ilusiones vanas. **Self-delusion**, V. **Self-defection**. **Self-denial**, abnegación de sí mismo. **Self-denying**, que hace abnegación de sí mismo. **Self-devotion**, dedicación de una persona, de sus deseos e intereses al servicio de una causa o de otra persona. **Self-esteem**, estimación, buena opinión de sí mismo; a veces, demasiado buen concepto de sí mismo. **Self-evident**, patente, evidente por sí mismo; que lleva la convicción al ánimo con sólo enunciarlo. **Self-examination**, examen de sí mismo, examen de conciencia. **Self-existence**, existencia por sí mismo, independiente de todo otro ser; uno de los atributos de Dios. **Self-existent, self-existing**, existente por sí mismo, en virtud de su propia esencia o naturaleza. **Self-government**, (a) dominio, imperio, sobre sí mismo; (b) gobierno de un pueblo por sí mismo. **Self-help**, ayuda propia. **Selfhood**, personalidad, individualidad, egoísmo. **Self-importance**, altivez; concepto extravagante de la importancia propia. **Self-instructor**, el maestro de sí mismo. **Self-interest**, el propio interés. **Selfish**, interesado, egoísta. **Self-love**, amor propio, amor de sí mismo. **Self-luminous**, luminoso por su propia naturaleza, que emite luz. **Self-moving**, automotor, que se mueve por sí mismo. **Self-murder**, suicidio. **Self-murderer**, suicida. **Self-possession**, sangre fría, tranquilidad de ánimo. **Self-preservation**, preservación de sí mismo. **Self-regulating**, regulador automático. **Self-reliance**, confianza en sí mismo, en el propio juicio, en los propios recursos. **Self-reliant**, confiado en sí mismo. **Self-righteous**, que es justo en tu propia estimación. **Self-sacrifice**, sacrificio o subordinación de sí mismo o de los propios deseos al deber o al bien de otros. **Self-sufficience, self-sufficiency**, presunción, confianza desmedida en sí mismo. **Self-sufficient**, (a) que tiene entera confianza en sí mismo, en su fuerza; de aquí, orgulloso, arrogante. (b) Que se basta a sí mismo. **Self-will**, obstinación, terquedad, porfía. **Self-willed**, obstinado, terco. **Self-winding**, de cuerda automática (reloj). **Self-worship**, egolatría.

self-address [ˈselfəˈdres] [self-a-dres], va. Rotular.

self-assurance [ˈselfəˈʊərəns] [self-a-shua-rans], s. Confianza en sí mismo.

self-contained [ˈselfkənˈteɪnd] [self-kon-teind], a. Reservado, independiente.

self-controlled [ˈselfkənˈtrəʊld] [self-kon-troul], a. Dueño de sí mismo.

self-expression [ˈselfɪksˈpreʃən] [self-iks-pre-shon], s. Expresión de la personalidad.

selfial [ˈselfɪəl] [sel-fial], a. Relativo o perteneciente a sí mismo; personal, particular.

self-improvement [ˈselfaɪmˈpruːvmənt] [self-im-pruv-ment], s. Mejoramiento de sí mismo.

self-induction ['selfɪn'dʌkʃən] [self-in-dak-shon], *s. (Elec.)* Autoinducción.

self-indulgence ['selfɪn'dʌldʒəns] [self-in-dal-yans], *s.* Satisfacción de los propios deseos.

selfish ['selfɪʃ] [sel-fish], *a.* 1. Interesado, ensimismado, egoísta. 2. Que cree o enseña que el amor propio es causa principal de los acto humanos.

selfishly ['selfɪʃlɪ] [sel-fish-li], *adv.* Interesadamente; con mucho amor propio, por egoísmo.

selfishness ['selfɪʃnɪs] [sel-fish-nes], *s.* Egoísmo, amor propio, egotismo.

selfless ['selflɪs] [self-les], *a.* Desinteresado, generoso.

self-made ['selfmeɪd] [self-meid], *a.* Formado por esfuerzo propio. **Self-man**, hombre que se ha hecho una posición por su propio esfuerzo.

self-preservation ['self‚prezə'veɪʃən] [self-pre-sa-vei-shon], *s.* 1. Propia conservación. 2. Instinto de conservación.

self-propulsion ['selfprə'pʌlʃən] [self-pro-pal-shon], *s.* Autopropulsión.

self-reliance ['selfrɪ'laɪəns] [self-ri-laians], *s.* Confianza en sí mismo.

self-respect ['selfrɪs'pekt] [self-ris-pekt], *s.* Respeto de sí mismo, propia estimación, dignidad, decoro.

self-sacrifice ['self'sækrɪfaɪs] [self-sa-kri-fais], *s.* Sacrificio personal, abnegación.

self-same ['selfseɪm] [self-seim], *a.* Idéntico, mismísimo.

self-satisfied ['self'sætɪsfaɪd] [self-sa-tis-faid], *a.* Ensimismado.

self-seeker ['self'siːkəʳ] [self-sii-ka], *s.* Egoísta.

self-service ['self'sɜːvɪs] [self-ser-vis], *s.* Autoservicio.

self-starter ['self'stɑːtəʳ] [self-star-ta], *s.* Arranque automático.

self-sufficiency ['selfsə'fɪʃənsɪ] [self-sa-fi-shan-si], *s.* 1. Autosuficiencia, capacidad de bastarse a sí mismo 2. Confianza desmedida en sí mismo, presunción.

self-winding ['self'wɪndɪŋ] [self-uin-din], *a.* De cuerda automática.

sell [sel] [sel], *s. (Fam.)* Engaño, estafa.

sell, *va.* (*pret. y pp.* SOLD). 1. Vender, traspasar a otro la propiedad de la cosa que uno posee, por un precio convenido. 2. Vender; se dice respecto de las cosas inmateriales cuando se las sacrifica al interés. 3. Vender, entregar por dinero; hacer traición. -*vn.* 1. Vender, hacer el comercio, traficar. 2. Venderse, ser vendido, hallar compradores; tener buen despacho una cosa o venderse bien. **To sell for ready money**, vender al contado. **To sell on credit**, vender al fiado o a plazos. **To sell underhand**, vender bajo mano. **To sell off**, vender el todo de muchas cosas juntas. **To sell by auction**, almonedear. **To sell at retail, wholesale**, vender al por menor, al por mayor. **To sell one's soul**, vender su alma al diablo. **To sell short**, vender para una fecha futura lo que aún no se tiene.

seller ['seləʳ] [se-la], *s.* Vendedor.

sellout ['selaʊt] [sel-aut], *s.* 1. Liquidación realización. 2. *(Fam.)* Traición. 3. *(Teat.)* Función para la que están vendidas todas las localidades.

selter, seltzer ['seltəʳ] [sel-ta], *s.* Agua de Seltz, agua mineral que contiene mucho ácido carbónico.

selvage ['selvɪdʒ] [sel-vich], *s.* 1. Orilla de paño. 2. Borde, orilla, particularmente cuando es diferente del resto. 3. Chapa lateral de la cerradura por donde sale el pestillo. **Selwages**, *(Mar.)* estrobos para los obenques y brandales.

semantics [sɪ'mæntɪks] [si-man-tiks], *s. pl.* Semántica.

semaphore ['seməfɔːʳ] [se-ma-fo], *s.* Semáforo, aparato para hacer señales, especialmente con brazos, discos, pabellones o linternas móviles; telégrafo de señales (en los ferrocarriles).

semblance ['sembləns] [sem-blans], *s.* Semejanza, exterior, apariencia; además, máscara, velo, ficción; imagen; forma visible o imaginaria,

semen ['siːmən] [si-men], *s.* 1. Semen, substancia que para la generación tienen los animales del sexo masculino. 2. *(Bot.)* Simiente, semilla.

semester [sɪ'mestəʳ] [si-mes-ta], *s.* Semestre.

semi- ['semɪ] [se-mi], Semi: prefijo que usado en composición significa medio, la mitad de cualquier cosa. **Semiannual**, semianual, semestral; que se verifica cada seis meses.

semiannual ['semɪ'ænjʊəl] [se-mia-nual], *a.* Semestral.

semiautomatic [‚semɪˌɔːtə'mætɪk] [se-mio-to-ma-tik], *a.* Semiautomático.

semibreve ['semɪbriːv] [se-mi-briv], *s. (Mús.)* Semibreve, redonda, la figura o nota fundamental de la música que vale un compás menor. **Semibreve rest**, aspiración de semibreve.

semicircle ['semɪˌsɜːkl] [se-mi-ser-kel], *s.* Semicírculo, medio círculo.

semicircular ['semɪˌsɜːkjʊləʳ] [se-mi-ser-kiu-la], *a.* Semicircular.

semicolon ['semɪ'kəʊlən] [se-mi-kou-lon], *s.* Punto y coma (;), signo ortográfico.

semidouble ['semɪˌdʌbl] [se-mi-da-bel], *a. (Bot.)* Semidoble, que tiene los estambres exteriores convertidos en pétalos y los interiores perfectos. -*s.* Semidoble, el oficio o fiesta de la Iglesia romana que se celebra con menor solemnidad que los oficios y fiestas dobles.

semifinals ['semɪ'faɪnlz] [se-mi-fi-nals], *s. pl* Semifinales.

semifinished ['semɪ'fɪnɪʃt] [se-mi-fi-nisht], *a.* Semiacabado.

seminal ['semɪnl] [se-mi-nal], *a.* 1. Seminal, lo perteneciente al semen o lo que lo contiene. 2. *(Bot.)* Seminal, lo que pertenece a las semillas de las plantas. 3. Embrionario.

seminar ['semɪnɑːʳ] [se-mi-na], *s.* Seminario, reunión del profesor con estudiantes para realizar trabajos de investigación.

seminary ['semɪnərɪ] [se-mi-na-ri], *s.* 1. Seminario, la casa o lugar destinado para educación de niños y jóvenes. 2. Seminario, el principio o raíz de que nacen o se propagan algunas cosas. 3. Semillero, sitio en que se crían las plantas hasta la época en que han de transplantarse: (sentido original). **Theological seminary**, seminario eclesiástico. -*a.* 1. Seminal. 2. Perteneciente a un seminario.

semination [‚semɪ'neɪʃən] [se-mi-nei-shon], *s. (Ant.)* 1. Sembradura, la acción de sembrar; diseminación. 2. *(Bot.)* El esparcimiento natural de las semillas.

semiotic [semɪ'ɒtɪk] [se-mio-tik], *a.* Semiótico.

semiquadrate [semɪ'kwɒdreɪt] [se-mi-kua-dreit], *s. (Astr.)* Semicuadrado, el aspecto de dos planetas cuando distan entre sí cuarenta y cinco grados.

semiquaver ['semɪˌkweɪvəʳ] [se-mi-kuei-va], *s. (Mús.)* Semicorchea.

semiskilled ['semɪ'skɪld] [se-mi-skild], *a.* Semicualificado, semiexperto.

Semite ['siːmaɪt] [si-mait], *a.* Semítico, concerniente a Sem, o a los pueblos clasificados entre sus descendientes. -*s.* Conjunto de las lenguas semíticas.

semitone ['semɪtəʊn] [se-mi-toun], *s. (Mús.)* Semitono, intervalo equivalente a la mitad de un tono.

semitonic ['semɪˌtəʊnɪk] [se-mi-tou-nik], *a.* Relativo a un semitono; de medio tono.

semitrailer ['semɪ'treɪləʳ] [se-mi-trei-la], *s. (E.U.)* Trailer.

semivowel ['semɪ'vaʊəl] [se-mi-vauel], *s.* Semivocal.

semiweekly ['semɪˌwiːklɪ] [se-mi-ui-kli], *a.* Bisemanal. -*adv.* Bisemanalmente. -*s.* Publicación bisemanal.

sempiternal [sempɪ'tɜːnl] [sem-pi-ter-nal], *a.* Sempiterno, que tiene principio pero no tiene fin.

senary ['senərɪ] [se-na-ri], *a.* Senario, compuesto de seis unidades, que contiene seis.

senate ['senɪt] [se-neit], *s.* 1. Senado, junta de los senadores (assembly of elders); el más alto de los dos cuerpos legislativos de los países constitucionales (v. g. los Estados Unidos, España, Francia e Italia). 2. La junta directiva de ciertas universidades. 3. Consejo, un cuerpo legislativo. 4. Cualquier junta o concurrencia de personas graves, respetables y circunspectas. **Senate-house**, senado, el lugar donde se juntan los senadores.

senator ['senɪtəʳ] [se-ni-ta], *s.* Senador, miembro de un senado; consejero.

senatorial ['senɪtɔːrɪəl] [se-ni-to-rial], *a.* 1. Senatorio, perteneciente o relativo al senado o al senador. 2. *(E.U.)* Que tiene derecho de elegir un senador, v. g. un distrito senatorio.

senatorship ['senɪtəʃɪp] [se-ni-ta-ship], *s.* El empleo o dignidad de senador.

send [send] [send], *va. (pret. y pp.* SENT). 1. Enviar, despachar, mandar una persona a alguna parte (to dispatch, ship). 2. Enviar, remitir cosas de una parte a otra. 3. Emitir, arrojar, lanzar, despedir, producir. 4. Difundir, extender, propagar. 5. Enviar, conceder, dar; hacer venir, sobrevenir o acontecer; infligir. 6. Hacer mirar hacia algo o alguien. *-vn.* Enviar, despachar, un agente, mensaje o mensajero.

send away, despedir a un criado; enviar a escardar o despedir a alguno ásperamente.

send back, mandar volver, enviar de vuelta, enviar otra vez, hacer volver.

send down, enviar abajo, hacer bajar.

send for, enviar a buscar, enviar a llamar; enviar por uno o a decirle que venga; enviar o despachar a una persona para que traiga consigo a otra o alguna cosa.

send in, hacer entrar, mandar entrar, venir o servir; anunciar, decir su nombre; introducir. **To send in one's papers**, dimitir renunciar.

send forth, enviar adelante, hacer marchar; producir, dar a luz; publicar, promulgar; empujar; emitir, exhalar.

send forward, enviar hacia adelante.

send off, expedir, hacer partir.

send up, (a) enviar arriba, mandar subir. (b) *(Fam. E.U.)* Enviar a la cárcel. **To send about one's business**, mandar a paseo. **To send word**, mandar o pasar aviso, participar una noticia por escrito o por un propio, enviar un mensaje o recado por medio de una persona.

send, *vn.* 1. *(Mar.)* Cabecear la embarcación de proa a popa. 2. Enviar recado o mensajero. 3. **To send for**, mandar por, enviar a buscar, hacer venir. V. SCEND.

sender ['sendə'] [sen-da'], *s.* 1. El que envía. 2. *(Com.)* Expedicionario. 3. Transmisor.

sending ['sendɪŋ] [sen-din], *s.* 1. Envío, remesa. 2. Transmisión. **Sending key**, manipulador.

send-off ['sendɒf] [send-of], *s.* 1. Envío. 2. Despedida afectuosa.

Seneca ['senɪkə] [se-ni-ka], *s.* Séneca.

senescence ['senɪsəns] [se-ni-sens], *s.* Senectud, vejez.

senescent ['senɪsənt] [se-ni-sent], *a.* Que envejece; característico de la vejez.

senile ['siːnaɪl] [si-nail], *a.* Senil, que pertenece a los viejos y a la vejez.

senior ['siːnɪə'] [si-nio'], *a.* 1. Mayor, de mayor edad. 2. Más antiguo o anciano por su cargo o título; superior en grado o dignidad. 3. Perteneciente al último año del curso de estudio en un colegio americano. *-s.* 1. Antiguo, anciano. 2. *(Eng.)* Individuo de la Junta de Gobierno de un colegio. *(Eng.)* Estudiante encargado de la disciplina de los demás. **Senior of a college**, antiguo de colegio, que en algunas partes se llama también senior. **Senior high school**, los dos últimos años de una escuela secundaria.

seniority [siːnɪˈɒrɪtɪ] [si-nio-ri-ti], *s.* 1. Antigüedad. 2. Precedencia. **Seniority scale**, escalafón.

senna ['senə] [se-na], *s. (Bot.)* Sen o sena.

senocular ['senəkjələ'] [se-no-kiu-la'], *a.* Que tiene seis ojos (like some spiders).

sensation [sen'seɪʃən] [sen-sei-shon], *s.* 1. Sensación, la impresión de los objetos en los órganos de los sentidos percibida por el cerebro. 2. Lo que produce sentimientos de interés o excitación; estado de excitación.

sensational [sen'seɪʃənl] [sen-sei-sho-nal], *a.* 1. De sensación; que produce excitación o que se destina a producirla. 2. Que se refiere a la sensación, a la percepción por los sentidos.

sense [sens] [sens], *s.* 1. Sentido, la potencia o facultad que tienen los seres animados de percibir las impresiones de los objetos externos (felt, experienced). 2. Sentido, entendimiento, razón, seso (a menudo en plural). **A man of sense**, hombre de juicio. 3. Sentido, el modo particular de entender una cosa o el juicio que se forma de ella; el juicio del mayor número. 4. Sensación, percepción por los sentidos; sentimiento, percepción moral. 5. Sentido, significado, interpretación, significación. 6. Percepción sensitiva, sensibilidad. **To gratify one's senses**, satisfacer los sentidos. **Common sense**, sentido común. **To be out of one's senses**, estar fuera de sí, estar loco. **To come to one's senses**, volver en sí: recobrar el buen sentido. **Sense organs**, órganos de los sentidos. **Sense perception**, percepción sensitiva.

sense, *v.* 1. Sentir, percibir por los sentidos. 2. Sentir, percibir intuitivamente, darse cuenta de, comprender.

senseless ['senslɪs] [sens-les], *a.* 1. Insensible, falto de sentimiento; privado de sentido, que no puede sentir, que no tiene conciencia de sí mismo. 2. Insensato, necio, absurdo, falto de razón. 3. Sin sentido, absurdo. **Senseless of**, insensible a.

senselessly ['senslɪslɪ] [sens-les-li], *adv.* Insensatamente, de un modo insensato.

senselessness ['senslɪsnɪs] [sens-les-nes], *s.* Tontería, insensatez, necedad, absurdo.

sensibility [ˌsensɪˈbɪlɪtɪ] [sen-si-bi-li-ti], *s.* 1. Sensibilidad, la facultad de percibir las impresiones que recibimos de los objetos externos. 2. Sensibilidad, la predisposición o propensión de los sentidos a recibir de una manera viva o fuerte las impresiones exteriores. 3. Precisión, hablando de instrumentos.

sensible ['sensəbl] [sen-si-bol], *a.* 1. Sensible, capaz de sentir; capaz de producir impresiones en los sentidos; perceptible, por los sentidos; sensitivo, perceptible por los sentidos; sensitivo, perceptible o percibido por la inteligencia. 2. Sensato, sensitivo, capaz de emociones. 3. Convencido, persuadido. 4. Cuerdo, razonable, juicioso, sensato. 5. (Poco us.) Sensitivo, afectado por los cambios más ligeros. **To be sensible**, tener tacto, buen juicio; conocer, esetar persuadido; ver, concebir. **To be sensible of**, hacerse cargo de. **I am sensible (that) I have done amiss**, estoy persuadido de que he hecho mal.

sensibleness ['sensəblnɪs] [sen-si-bol-nes], *s.* 1. La posibilidad de que una impresión sea percibida por los sentidos. 2. Sensación, sensibilidad. 3. Impresión, sentimiento producido en el ánimo por alguna cosa que lo aflige. 4. Cordura, sensatez.

sensibly ['sensəblɪ] [sen-si-bli], *adv.* 1. Perceptiblemente, sensiblemente. 2. Exteriormente. 3. Juiciosamente, con prudencia y cordura.

sensitive ['sensɪtɪv] [sen-si-tiv], *a.* 1. Sensitivo, sensible, impresionable, de viva sensibilidad; que afecta a los sentidos; en fotografía, sensibilizado, hecho sensible a la acción de la luz. 2. Sensitivo, perteneciente a los sentidos. **Sensitive-plant**, sensitiva, planta que al tocarla se contrae como si tuviera sensación: (mimosa pudica) planta de la familia de las leguminosas.

sensitively ['sensɪtɪvlɪ] [sen-si-tiv-li], *adv.* Sensiblemente, con pesar, con sentimiento.

sensitiveness ['sensɪtɪvnɪs] [sen-si-tiv-nes], *s.* 1. Sensibilidad, calidad de sensitivo o sensible, tanto física como mentalmente. 2. Delicadeza, precisión.

sensitize ['sensɪtaɪz] [sen-si-tais], *va.* Sensibilizar, hacer sensible, particularmente a la acción de la luz (v. g. la placa fotográfica). **Sensitized paper**, papel sensibilizado (para fotografía).

sensorial [sen'sɔːrɪəl] [sen-so-rial], *a.* Sensorio, perteneciente al sensorio o a la sensación.

sensory ['sensɔːrɪ] [sen-so-ri], *s.* Sensorio, cualquiera de los órganos de los sentidos.

sensory, *a.* Sensorio, perteneciente a la facultad de sentir; que produce la sensación.

sensual ['sensjʊəl] [sen-siual], *a.* 1. Sensual, que pertenece a los sentidos o al apetito carnal; carnal, lo contrario de espiritual. 2. Sensual, lascivo, lujurioso, voluptuoso.

sensualist ['sensjʊəlɪst] [sen-siua-list], *s.* Persona sensual o dada a la sensualidad, a la satisfacción de los sentidos. 2. *(Filos.)* Sensualista, partidario del sensualismo.

sensuality [ˌsensjʊˈælɪtɪ] [sen-siua-li-ti], *s.* Sensualidad, lascivia, voluptuosidad: el estado o calidad de sensual; entregado a los placeres sensuales.

sensualize ['sensjʊəlaɪz] [sen-siua-lais], *va.* Hacer sensual, voluptuoso o lascivo.

sensually ['sensjʊəlɪ] [sen-siua-li], *adv.* Sensualmente, con sensualidad, voluptuosamente.

sensuous ['sensjʊəs] [sen-siuos], *a.* Afectivo, patético; que afecta los sentidos, que se deriva de los sentidos o se refiere a ellos; tierno, apasionado. Se diferencia de **sensual.**

sensuousness ['sensjʊəsnɪs] [sen-siuos-nes], *s.* Afición a lo bello y a los objetos o adornos de lujo; calidad de los sentidos, de ser susceptibles a las influencias externas.

sent ['sent] [sent], pret. y *pp.* de TO SEND.

sentence ['sentəns] [sen-tens], *s.* 1. Sentencia, dictamen, juicio o parecer que da uno acerca de la cosa sobre la que se le consulta (judgement, decision). 2. Sentencia, declaración de juicio o resolución de un juez, vistos los méritos de una causa. 3. Sentencia, dicho grave y sucinto. 4. *(Gram.)* Sentencia, período, frase, párrafo breve que contiene sentido completo. 5. *(Mús.)* frase. **To serve a sentence**, cumplir una condena.

sentence, *va.* 1. Sentenciar, condenar. 2. Dictaminar.

sentential [sentənˈʃəl] [sen-ten-shal], *a.* *(Gram.)* De frase, perteneciente a un período completo.

sententious [senˈtenʃəs] [sen-ten-shos], *a.* 1. Sentencioso, abundante en sentencias, en máximas. 2. Lacónico, breve; enérgico, expresivo en su lenguaje.

sententiously [senˈtenʃəslɪ] [sen-ten-shos-li], *adv.* 1. Sentenciosamente. 2. Concisamente.

sententiousness [senˈtenʃəsnɪs] [sen-ten-shos-nes], *s.* Laconismo, brevedad con energía.

sentience ['senʃəns] [sen-shans], *s.* Conciencia, sensibilidad, percepción.

sentient ['senʃənt] [sen-shant], *a.* 1. Sensible, que siente o tiene sensación, dotado de la facultad de percibir por los sentidos; lo contrario de inanimado y vegetal. 2. Sensitivo. **Sentient of**, consciente de. -*s.* Senciente, el que siente.

sentiment ['sentɪmənt] [sen-ti-mant], *s.* 1. Sentimiento, afecto, impresión que se siente en el ánimo, sea de alegría, de tristeza, etc. (feeling, sense). sentimiento noble, tierno o artístico y su expresión; también la cualidad de afectar o de ser afectado por una emoción delicada, intelectual o afectuosa. 2. Sentimiento de simpatía o afecto personal hacia una persona del sexo opuesto, a diferencia del amor o la pasión. 3. Sentimiento, dictamen, opinión o juicio interior que se forma de las cosas. 4. Sentido, pensamiento (in words); brindis. 5. Afecto. 6. Concepto, frase, pensamiento. **A man of honorable sentiments**, hombre de nobles sentimientos.

sentimental [ˌsentɪˈmentl] [sen-ti-men-tal], *a.* Sentimental, que pertenece a los sentimientos o afectos; propenso a sentimientos tiernos; que los excita; muy sensible.

sentimentalist [ˌsentɪˈmentəlɪst] [sen-ti-men-ta-list], *s.* Persona sentimental, propensa la sentimiento más bien que a la razón, o que afecta gran sensibilidad.

sentimentality [ˌsentɪmenˈtælɪtɪ] [sen-ti-men-ta-li-ti], *s.* Afectación de exquisita sensibilidad, o de afectos muy tiernos.

sentimentalize [ˌsentɪˈmentəlaɪz] [sen-ti-men-ta-lais], *va.* y *vn.* Afectar gran sensibilidad.

sentinel ['sentɪnl] [sen-ti-nel], **sentry** [sen-tri], *s.* 1. Centinela, el soldado que está de guardia; el acto de hacer guardia. **To stand sentry**, estar de centinela. 2. Lo que sirve de guarda o protección. **Sentry-box**, garita de centinela.

sepal ['sepəl] [se-pal], *s.* *(Bot.)* Sépalo, cada una de las hojuelas de cáliz.

separable ['sepərəbl] [se-pa-ra-bol], *a.* Separable, capaz de separarse.

separably ['sepərəblɪ] [se-pa-ra-bli], *adv.* De manera que se puede separar.

separate ['seprɪt] [se-pa-reit], *va.* 1. Separar, dividir, desunir, apartar cosas que están juntas o unidas; desviar. 2. Ocupar una posición entre dos cosas; poner aparte. 3. Considerar

separadamente; estimar como cosas diferentes. 4. Desnatar la leche. -*vn.* Apartarse, desunirse, separarse.

separate, *a.* Separado, desunido, segregado, sin lazo, distinto, diferente; separado del cuerpo.

separately ['seprɪtlɪ] [se-pa-ra-tli], *adv.* Separadamente, a parte, sin conexión, distintamente; uno a uno.

separateness ['seprɪtnɪs] [se-pa-reit-nes], *s.* Estado de separación.

separation [ˌsepəˈreɪʃən] [se-pa-rei-shon], *s.* 1. Separación, desunión; acción de separar; estado de separación (dissociation, abstraction). 2. Análisis químico, descomposición de un mixto en sus elementos constitutivos. 3. Separación, divorcio.

separatist ['sepərətɪst] [se-pa-ra-tist], *s.* Cismático, el que se ha separado de la religión dominante en su país.

separative ['sepərətɪv] [se-pa-ra-tiv], *a.* Separativo, que separa o tiende a la separación; distintivo.

separator ['sepəreɪtəʳ] [se-pa-rei-taʳ], *s.* 1. Separador, cualquier útil o aparato para separar las cosas, como en el zurrón del grano. 2. Separador, el o lo que separa.

sepia ['siːpɪə] [si-pia], *s.* 1. Sepia, materia colorante que se saca de la jibia, tratándola con álcalis; color de sepia; dibujo hecho con sepia. 2. Sepia, jibia. V. CUTTLEFISH. 3. Jibión, hueso de la jibia. -*a.* Perteneciente a la sepia, hecho en sepia.

sepoy ['siːpɔɪ] [si-poi], *s.* Cipayo.

sepsis ['sepsɪs] [sep-sis], *s.* 1. Sepsis, putrefacción venenosa. 2. Infección procedente de un virus pútrido, que contiene organismos microscópicos.

sept [sept] [sept], *s.* Raza, casta, generación, linaje.

septal ['septl] [sep-tal], *a.* 1. De septo, perteneciente a un septo o que lo forma. 2. Perteneciente a un linaje.

september [sepˈtembəʳ] [sep-tem-baʳ], *s.* Septiembre, el noveno mes del año.

septenary ['septənərɪ] [sep-te-na-ri], *a.* Septenario, lo que se compone de siete. -*s.* El número siete.

septennial [sepˈtenɪəl] [sep-te-nial], *a.* Sieteñal, que dura un septenio, que sucede una vez en siete años.

septet [sepˈtet] [sep-tet], *s.* Grupo de siete personas, cosas o partes; compañía de siete cantores o tañedores; composición musical en siete partes, septeto.

septic ['septɪk] [sep-tik], *a.* Séptico, putrefactivo, que causa putrefacción, pútrido. **Septic tank**, fosa séptica.

septicæmia, septicemia [ˌseptɪˈsiːmɪə] [sep-ti-si-mia], *s.* Septicemia, envenenamiento de la sangre. V. SEPTEMIA.

septuagenary [ˌseptjʊəˈdʒɪˈnɛərɪ] [sep-tua-ye-na-ri], *a.* Septuagenario, que consiste o se compone de setenta.

septuagesima [ˌseptjʊəˈdʒəsɪmə] [sep-tua-ye-si-ma], *s.* Septuagésima, el tercer domingo anterior a la primera semana de cuaresma.

septuagesimal [ˌseptjʊəˈdʒesɪməl] [sep-tua-ye-si-mal], *a.* Septuagésimo.

septum ['septəm] [sep-tom], *s.* *(Anat.)* Septo, la cosa que se divide o separa a otras entre sí.

septuple ['septjʊpl] [sep-tiu-pol], *a.* Séptuplo.

sepulchral [sɪˈpʌlkrəl] [si-pal-kral], *a.* Sepulcral, fúnebre.

sepulcher, sepulchre [sɪˈpʌlkəʳ] [si-pal-kaʳ], *s.* Sepulcro, sepultura.

sepulcher, sepulchre, *va.* Sepultar, enterrar, poner en un sepulcro.

sepulture [sɪˈpʌltʃəʳ] [si-pal-chaʳ], *s.* Sepultura, entierro.

sequel ['siːkwəl] [si-kual], *s.* 1. Secuela, lo que sigue como porción final; párrafo o capítulo final. 2. Resultado, consecuencia, éxito de una cosa. **In the sequel**, en seguida, después.

sequence ['siːkwəns] [si-kuans], *s.* 1. Serie, continuación ordenada y sucesiva de cosas (standardized). 2. Orden de sucesión; arreglo. 3. Efecto, consecuencia. 4. *(Mús.)* Sucesión regular de frases melodiosas y semejantes en diferentes diapasones. 5. Enlace lógico, ilación. 6. *(Cinem.)* Secuencia. **Sequence of a suit of cards**, runfla de un palo, en los naipes.

sequent ['siːkwənt] [si-kuant], *a.* Siguiente, en orden de tiempo; consiguiente.

sequester [sɪˈkwestəʳ] [si-kues-taʳ], *va.* 1. Separar, apartar, retirar. 2. Secuestrar, poner en secuestro. 3. Privar a uno de lo que poseía hasta que se decida una controversia o se satisfaga una demanda. 4. Secuestrar, embargar. 5. Confiscar. *-vn.* Renunciar; v. g. la renuncia que hace una viuda a toda intervención en la liquidación de la herencia de su marido.

sequestrable [sɪˈkwestrəbl] [si-kues-tra-bol], *a.* Que se puede secuestrar y separar; capaz de división.

sequestrate [sɪˈkwestreɪt] [si-kues-treit], *va.* 1. Secuestrar, apropiar o confiscar para uso del gobierno; tomar posesión provisional de algo a consecuencia de un acuerdo equitativo entre acreedores. 2. *(Ant.)* Retirar, apartar, separar.

sequestration [ˌsiːkwesˈtreɪʃən] [si-kues-trei-shon], *s.* 1. Secuestración de bienes. 2. Separación, retiro. 3. Privación del uso y de las utilidades de alguna cosa.

sequestrator [ˌsiːkwesˈtreɪtəʳ] [si-kues-trei-taʳ], *s.* Secuestrador, el que secuestra.

sequoia [sɪˈkwɔɪə] [si-kuoia], *s.* Secoya (**redwood**), palo rojo, y Sequoia gigantea (**big tree**), árbol grande.

seraglio [seˈrɑːɡlɪəʊ] [se-ra-gliou], *s.* 1. Serrallo, el antiguo palacio de los sultanes en Constantinopla. 2. Harem; de aquí, burdel, lupanar.

serape [ˈserəp] [se-rap], *s.* Sarape, manta mejicana.

seraph [ˈserəf] [se-raf], *s.* Serafín, ángel o espíritu del primer coro celestial.

seraphic [səˈræfɪk] [se-ra-fik], *a.* Seráfico.

sere [sɜːʳ] [seʳ], *a.* Seco, marchito.

serenade [ˌserəˈneɪd] [se-re-neid], *s.* Serenata, música que se toca durante la noche para festejar a alguien.

serenade, *va.* Dar una serenata.

serene [seˈriːn] [se-rin], *a.* 1. Sereno, claro, despejado de nubes y nieblas (calm, unruffled). 2. Sereno, apacible, sosegado, tranquilo. 3. De exaltada posición; se aplica a ciertos príncipes y personajes elevados en Alemania y Francia. **Most serene**, serenísimo.

serenely [səˈriːnlɪ] [se-rin-li], *adv.* 1. Serenamente, con serenidad y despejo. 2. Con sosiego y apacibilidad de ánimo.

sereneness [səˈriːnnɪs] [se-rin-nes], *s.* Serenidad de ánimo, tranquilidad, calma.

serenity [səˈriːnɪtɪ] [se-ri-ni-ti], *s.* 1. Serenidad, claridad, despejo de nubes en el cielo. 2. Serenidad, sosiego, apacibilidad. 3. Tranquilidad, calma, paz, quietud. 4. Serenidad, título de honor que se da a algunos príncipes.

serf [sɜːf] [serf], *s.* Siervo, criado o esclavo ocupado en la labranza.

serfdom [ˈsɜːfdəm] [serf-dom], *s.* Servidumbre, estado o condición de los siervos o esclavos.

serge [sɜːdʒ] [serch], *s.* Sarga, tela fuerte de seda o más comúnmente de estambre que forma cordoncillo. **Sil serge**, sarga de seda. **Woollen serge**, anascote. **Serge-maker**, fabricante de sarga.

sergeancy [ˈsɜːdʒənsɪ] [ser-yan-si], *s.* V. SERGEANTSHIP.

sergeant [ˈsɑːdʒənt] [sar-yant], *s.* 1. Sargento, oficial subalterno en la milicia inmediatamente superior al cabo. 2. Alguacil, ministro inferior de justicia. 3. *(Ingl.)* Abogado de primera clase. 4. Escudero. **Sergeant at arms**, macero del rey; oficial de las asambleas legislativas que ejecuta los mandatos del presidente y mantiene el orden.

sergeantship [ˈsɑːdʒəntʃɪp] [sar-yant-ship], *s.* Sargentía, el empleo y oficio de sargento; grado de sargento.

serial [ˈsɪərɪəl] [sia-rial], *a.* 1. Consecutivo, perteneciente a una serie; a manera de serie. 2. Publicado por series, por entregas, y a intervalos regulares. 3. Sucesivo, dispuesto en hileras o filas. *-s.* Obra que se publica por entregas, por series. **Interface serial**, interface en serie. **Serial number**, número de serie.

serialize [ˈsɪərɪəlaɪz] [se-ria-lais], *vt.* Publicar en serie, en entregas, serializar.

serially [ˈsɪərɪəlɪ] [se-ria-li], *adv.* En serie; por serie.

sericate [ˈserɪkeɪt] [se-ri-keit], *a.* Sedoso; velludo.

sericulture [ˌserɪˈkʌltʃəʳ] [se-ri-kal-chaʳ], *s.* Sericultura, industria de la seda.

series [ˈsɪərɪz] [sia-ris], *s.* Serie, continuación ordenada y sucesiva de las cosas; enlace, encadenamiento, unión (enchainment, union).

serious [ˈsɪərɪəs] [sia-rios], *a.* 1. Serio, sensato, reflexivo, grave, severo (honest, solemn). 2. Serio, formal; verdadero, sincero. 3. Serio, grave, importante, de consecuencia. 4. Solemne, articularmente en lo relativo a la religión. **Are you serious?** ¿habla usted de veras? ¿habla usted formalmente? **A serious business**, asunto de gravedad. **Serious wounded**, gravemente herido.

seriously [ˈsɪərɪəslɪ] [sia-rios-li], *adv.* Seriamente, de veras, fuera de chanza, formalmente, con formalidad. **I can't take him seriously**, no puedo tomarle en serio. **Do you say so seriously?**, ¿me lo dices en serio?

seriousness [ˈsɪərɪəsnɪs] [se-rios-nes], *s.* Seriedad, gravedad.

sermocination [ˌsɜːməsɪˈneɪʃən] [ser-mo-si-nei-shon], *s.* *(Ret.)* Una forma de prosopopeya en que uno responde a la pregunta que él mismo ha hecho.

sermon [ˈsɜːmən] [ser-mon], *s.* 1. Sermón, discurso cristiano hecho para el púlpito, oración evangélica. 2. Cualquier discurso de carácter grave y formal; exhortación, amonestación, reprensión particular. **Funeral sermon**, oración fúnebre. **Collection of sermons**, sermonario.

sermonize [ˈsɜːmənaɪz] [ser-mo-nais], *va.* 1. Predicar la palabra de Dios. 2. Predicar, sermonear, reprender o echar sermones.

seron, seroon [ˈsɜːruːn] [se-run], *s.* Serón, zurrón, sera grande en que se llevan higos, dátiles, pasas, etc. **A serron of indigo**, un zurrón de añil. **A seroon of cinnamon**, churla de canela. **A serron of cocoa**, sobornal de cacao.

serosity [səˈrɒsɪtɪ] [se-ro-si-ti], *s.* Serosidad, la parte más acuosa de un humor animal.

serotine [ˈsɜːrətɪn] [se-ro-tin], *s.* Especie de murciélago.

serous [ˈsɪərəs] [se-ros], *a.* Seroso, que produce serosidad o suero, o es semejante a estos líquidos.

serpent [ˈsɜːpənt] [ser-pent], *s.* 1. Serpiente, sierpe, animal que se arrastra por la tierra (snake). 2. Buscapiés, una especie de cohete sin varilla que corre muy arrimado a la tierra. 3. Serpentón, instrumento músico de viento, especie de bajón. 4. Persona traidora, llena de malicia (devil). 5. Satanás.

serpentine [ˈsɜːpəntaɪn] [ser-pen-tain], *a.* 1. Serpentino, que se asemeja o pertenece a la serpiente o sierpe. 2. Serpentino, caracoleado, que se mueve caracoleando como la serpiente. **Serpentine marble**, serpentina, especie de mármol manchado como piel de serpiente. *-s.* 1. Serpentina, piedra de color verde, rojizo o amarillo, a veces transparente y otras opaca; un silicato de magnesio. 2. *(Des.)* Serpentín, variedad de alambique.

serpentize [ˈsɜːpəntaɪz] [ser-pan-tais], *vn.* Serpentear, andar haciendo vueltas o tornos, como la serpiente.

serpigo [ˈsɜːpɪɡəʊ] [ser-pi-gou], *s.* Serpigo, erupción cutánea a modo de tiña seca.

serrated [seˈreɪtɪd] [se-rei-tid], *a.* Dentellado; *(Bot.)* serrado, cuyos dientes se dirigen hacia adelante.

serration [seˈreɪʃən] [se-rei-shon], *s.* Endentadura, recortadura semejante a la de los dientes de una sierra.

serrature [ˈserətʃəʳ] [se-ra-chaʳ], *s.* *(Biol.)* Estructura serrada, endentadura.

serried [ˈserɪd] [se-rid], *a.* Apretado, compacto en filas o hileras, como los soldados.

serum [ˈsɪərəm] [si-ram], *s.* Suero, la parte más acuosa de la sangre o de la leche.

servable [ˈsɜːvəbl] [ser-va-bol], *a.* Servible, que puede ser servido.

servant [ˈsɜːvənt] [ser-vant], *s.* 1. Criado, sirviente, persona que sirve a otra por un salario (domestic). **Woman-servant, servant-girl, servant-maid**, criada. **Servant-man**, criado. 2. Siervo, esclavo (slave). 3. Servidor, el que por cortesía se pone a la disposición de otro. **Your humble servant**, un servidor. **Your obedient servant**, suyo afectísimo (formal letters).

serve [sɜːv] [serv], *va.* 1. Servir, estar al servicio de otro, trabajar para otro. 2. Servir, estar sujeto a otro o estar a sus órdenes. 3. Servir, aprovechar, valer alguna cosa o ser de alguna utilidad; ayudar, ser útil. 4. Servir de tal o cual cosa, hacer las veces de otro, auxiliar a otro; prestar servicios. 5. Servir, asistir a la mesa llevando a ella los manjares. 6. Servir, ejercer algún empleo o cargo en propiedad o como substituto de otro. 7. Maniobrar, mantener en acción, hacer funcionar (v.g. un cañón). 8. Servir, tener las cosas el efecto o uso para que se destinan o ser a propósito para el objeto que se intenta conseguir con ellas; bastar, ser suficiente, satisfacer, contentar. 9. Servir, obsequiar, divertir. 10. Abastecer, surtir, v. g. con aprovisionamiento regular o hecho en períodos fijos. 11. (For.) Entregar una citación o requerimiento. 12. Servir, prestar culto o adoración a Dios. 13. (Mar.) Aforrar. 14. Portarse para con alguien, recompensar, tratar. 15. En la crianza de ganado, cubrir el macho a la hembra. -vn. 1. Servir, ser criado, estar al servicio de otro, emplearse en interés de otro. 2. Estar en sujeción. 3. Cumplir los deberes de un empleo, servir a su país, como en el ejército o en la marina. 4. Bastar, ser suficiente y eficaz; de aquí, ser favorable, conveniente o apto para algún propósito. 5. Sacar o dar saque, tirar, arrojar la pelota en el juego de este nombre. **To serve for**, servir de. **To serve himself o**, servirse de o hacer uso de. **To serve an office**, servir un empleo, desempeñar algún puesto público. **To serve one a trick**, jugar a uno una mala partida, pegarle un chasco. **To serve one's ends.** servir o ser útil para que otro consiga lo que intenta. **To serve one's turn**, bastar, ser suficiente. **To serve out one's time**, acabar el tiempo de servicio. **To serve the time**, andar con el tiempo, contemporizar. **I'll serve him in his kind**, le pagaré en la misma moneda. **When occasion shall serve**, cuando la ocasión sea favorable. **To serve a warrant**, intimar o ejecutar un auto de prisión.

server ['sɜːvəʳ] [ser-vaʳ], s. 1. Servidor, el que sirve. 2. Lo que se emplea para servir, como una bandeja o una vajilla. (Tennis) Saque. (USA) Camarero (waiter).

service ['sɜːvɪs] [ser-vis], s. 1. Servicio, el acto y tiempo de servir como criado, dependiente, empleado, soldado o marinero; la condición o el trabajo de un criado. 2. Servidumbre, el acto de servir en la casa real y en las de los grandes. 3. Servicio, el uso útil que se hace de una cosa; utilidad, ventaja. 4. Culto divino, los divinos oficios; la celebración de los oficios. 5. Servicio, favor, asistencia, ayuda, servicio que se hace en beneficio de un igual o de un amigo (help). 6. Servicio; tomado absolutamente es el militar o el naval. 7. Servicio, cubierto, entrada, el número de platos que se ponen y mudan juntos en la mesa. 8. Acomodo, conveniencia de una persona para servir en una casa. 9. (For.) (a) Deber, obligación que tiene un criado o un arrendatario. (b) Entrega legal de una citación a la persona designada. 10. (Mar.) Forro de cable. 11. (Bot.) V. SERVICE-TREE. **I am at your service**, estoy a su disposición. **It is of no service**, no vale nada, de nada sirve. **Out of service**, desacomodado, sin acomodo, sin conveniencia. **To see service**, servir, prestar servicio. **To be of service to**, ser útil a, servir. **To do good service**, ser de utilidad, servir bien. **Service elevator**, montacargas. **Service agreement**, contrato de mantenimiento. **To press into service**, obligar a trabajar, utilizar, servirse de.

serviceable ['sɜːvɪsəbl] [ser-vi-sa-bol], a. 1. Servible, que puede servir. 2. Capaz de prestar largo servicio; duradero. 3. (Ant.) Servicial, diligente en servir; oficioso.

serviceably ['sɜːvɪsəblɪ] [ser-vi-sa-bli], adv. Útilmente, duraderamente.

serviceman ['sɜːvɪsmən] [ser-vis-man], s. Militar, soldado.

service station [sɜːvɪ'steɪʃən] [ser-vis-stei-shon], s. Taller de reparaciones de automóviles.

service-tree ['sɜːvɪstriː] [ser-vis-tri], s. Serbal.

servicewoman ['sɜːvɪsˌwʊmən] [ser-vis-uo-man], s. Mujer soldado, mujer militar.

servient ['sɜːvɪənt] [ser-vient], a. (For.) Subordinado; contrapuesto a **dominant**.

servile ['sɜːvaɪl] [ser-vail], a. 1. Servil, bajo, abyecto; abatido, humilde. 2. Perteneciente a esclavos o propio de ellos; digno de un esclavo. 3. Adulador, lisonjero. 4. (Gram.) Servil, que no pertenece a la raíz de la palabra. -s. 1. Esclavo, o individuo de espíritu servil. 2. Letra o sílaba servil, que no es de la forma de su radical.

servilely ['sɜːvaɪlɪ] [ser-vai-li], adv. Servilmente, de una manera servil; con bajeza.

servility [sɜː'vɪlɪtɪ] [ser-vi-li-ti], s. 1. Servidumbre, esclavitud, estado de siervo. 2. Servidumbre, la sujeción de las pasiones o afectos que dominan la voluntad. 3. Bajeza, vileza de ánimo.

servility, s. Servilismo.

serving ['sɜːvɪŋ] [ser-vin], a. Sirviente, que sirve, que está al servicio de otro. -s. Acción de servir. **Serving-maid**, criada sirvienta. **Serving-mallet**, (Mar.) maceta de forrar. **Serving-man**, sirviente, criado.

servitor ['sɜːvɪtəʳ] [ser-vi-taʳ], s. 1. Partidario; compañero en una expedición o conquista con respecto al jefe que la manda. 2. Servidor, el que se ofrece a la disposición de otro. 3. Un fámulo de colegio en la universidad de Oxford.

servitorship ['sɜːvɪtəʃɪp] [ser-vi-ta-ship], s. Famulato, el empleo de fámulo de un colegio.

servitude ['sɜːvɪtjuːd] [ser-vi-tiud], s. 1. Servidumbre, esclavitud; estado de sujeción; domesticidad, condición de criado o sirviente; dependencia de otro. 2. (Angloindio) Servicio militar o naval. 3. (For.) Bienestar, alivio. V. EASEMENT.

servo ['sɜːvəʊ] [ser-vou], s. Servo.

sesame ['sesəmɪ] [se-sa-mi], s. Ajonjolí, sésamo, planta herbácea anual de la India, de cuyo fruto se extrae aceite. **Open sesame!**, ¡ábrete sésamo!

sesamoid ['sesəmɔɪd] [se-sa-moid], a. Sesamoide, que se parece al sésamo. -s. Término aplicado a los huesecillos o cartílagos que se desarrollan en el espesor de las articulaciones.

sesqui-. Prefijo que significa uno y medio.

sessile ['sesaɪl] [se-sail], a. (Biol.) Sésil, fijado inmediatamente en la base; que carece de sostén o tallo particular.

session ['seʃən] [se-shon], s. 1. Sesión, junta de una corporación organizada, de una compañía, de magistrados o senadores; reunión, asamblea de los miembros de una corporación (reunion, meeting). 2. Todo el tiempo que duran las sesiones de una junta, un congreso, etc. 3. El tribunal inferior y el cuerpo gobernante de la Iglesia presbiteriana.

sessional ['seʃənl] [se-sho-nal], a. Relativo a una sesión.

set [set] [set], va. (pret. y pp. SET). 1. Asentar, sentar, poner derecho o en pie (seat, make firm). 2. Poner, colocar, fijar, disponer una cosa en el sitio, grado u orden que debe tener (fix); montar; plantar (en la tierra). 3. Poner, fijar, poner fijo, inmóvil; de aquí, embarazar, detener, impedir; desarrollar en forma rudimentaria, como el fruto o simiente. 4. Establecer, determinar, ordenar, señalar, destinar. 5. Arreglar, poner en orden para el uso (get ready); preparar, alistar, poner o parar en el juego; reducir a regla. 6. Estimar, considerar, reputar (con **at**); valuar, fijar un precio (con **by u on**). 7. Engastar, encajar y embutir una cosa en otrar. 8. Trabar, triscar los dientes de la sierra alternando a uno y otro lado. 9. Poner en movimiento en una dirección dada. 10. Embarazar, inquietar, perturbar la mente. 11. (Impr.) Parar tipo, componer; a menudo con **up**. 12. Poner algunos versos en música; también, dar, fijar el tono (de un himno, etc.). 13. (Cir.) Reducir una dislocación. 14. Hacer empollar (las gallinas). 15. Tender, poner lazos; (Mar.) tender, desplegar. -vn. 1. Ponerse el sol o los astros u ocultarse bajo el horizonte. 2. Cuajarse un líquido o convertirse en sólido. 3. Pararse, quedarse parada o fija alguna persona o cosa; fijarse, detenerse. 4. Componer, poner alguna letra en música. 5. (Fam.) Empollar (hen). 6. Moverse o fluir (running) en una dirección dada; tender, inclinarse. 7. Aplicarse a alguna cosa o dedicarse a ella con esmero. 8. Empezar a desarrollarse un fruto rudimentario; transformarse las flores en semillas o frutos. 9. (Fam.) Sentar, caer bien una prenda de vestir. **To set at liberty**, poner en libertad. **To set to work**, poner a la obra. **To set a house on fire**, pegar fuego a una casa. **To set**

a bone, poner un hueso en su lugar. **To set fast**, sujetar, consolidar; Adelantar un reloj. **To set thinking**, hacer pensar. **To set a task**, imponer una tarea.

set about, emprender una cosa o ponerse a hacerla, dedicarse a algún empleo, ocupación o destino.

set abroad, divulgar, publicar o hacer pública alguna cosa.

set again, reponer, volver a poner, colocar otra vez. **To set against**, indisponer o poner mal a uno con otro, incitar o irritar a alguno en contra de otro; oponer u oponerse.

set agoing, hacer ir; poenr en juego o movimiento; dar impulso.

set aground, arrendar un terreno.

set apart, poner aparte, dejar para otra vez; arrinconar o abandonar por algún tiempo.

set aside, dejar alguna cosa o suspender su ejecución para hacerla después, poner a un lado o aparte; despreciar, no hacer caso; rechazar; abrogar, anular. *(Fam.)* Arrinconar. **To set at defiance**, provocar, desafiar, apostárselas con otro. **To set at naught**, despreciar, tener en nada. **Set at rest**, poner en reposo; dejar una cosa.

set away, quitar, separar, echar a un lado.

set back, recular, hacerse atrás; llevar hacia atrás.

set before, presentar, poner a la vista; dar a escoger una cosa poniéndola a la vista.

set by, estimar, hacer aprecio, hacer caso, considerar, reputar; abandonar por un poco de tiempo la ejecución de una cosa.

set down, poner en tierra o por tierra; desembarcar (un viajero); depositar; poner por escrito, hacer algún apunte; resolver una cosa definitivamente; considerar como verdad establecida; atribuir, acusar, imputar; censurar o humillar; poner más bajo.

set forth, manifestar, exponer, representar; promulgar; exponer, dar a conocer, enunciar; hacer valer (razones); ensalzar, alabar; avanzar, adelantarse, irse, marcharse, ponerse en camino; levantar, poner más alta alguna cosa; arreglar o poner en orden; enviar una expedición.

set forward, adelantar, ganar la delantera; promover; empujar, impeler, llevar hacia adelante; acercar; animar, dar aliento; ponerse en camino, irse.

set from, salir de una parte, emprender la marcha.

set in, subir, fluir con constancia hacia tierra; se dice de la marea, y por extensión de cualquier influencia general; comenzar, ponerse a; encajar, embutir; y *(Des.)* poner a una persona en estado de que comience a hacer algo.

set off, poner aparte; reservar, separar del resto por medio de una línea o linde; comparar, contraponer; poner en relieve, realzar, adornar, hermosear, embellecer, poner bonito o hermoso, componer, adornar, hermosear, embellecer, poner bonito o hermoso, componer o adornar un gabinete, casa, etc.; salir de alguna parte, partir; salir los caballos de las barreras para principiar la corrida en las carreras de caballos.

set on, determinar, resolver; fijar la atención en alguna cosa; acometer, arremeter, atacar, asaltar; emplear a alguno para que haga una cosa determinada, animar, incitar, azuzar; echar a andar, marcharse; emprender un asunto, negocio u ocupación. **He set on the mob**, incitó al populacho. **To set one's mind on**, aplicarse a. **To set on edge**, dar dentera. **To set on shore**, desembarcar. **To set one's hand to**, poner su firma, firmar (un convenio); *(Fig.)* aceptar, admitir. **To set one's house in order**, arreglar sus negocios y particularmente prepararse para la muerte.

set out, echar a andar, irse, marcharse, ponerse en camino, partir, emprender un viaje; mostrar, hacer ver, dar a conocer; proveer de equipos o pertrechos; publicar, manifestar, hacer patente; dar a luz; dar principio a alguna cosa, principiar a ejercer algún oficio, empleo u ocupación; asignar, señalar; adornar, hermosear; trazar los contornos de una figura; fluir hacia afuera, como la marea o una corriente; plantar (tree, plants, etc.).

set to, aplicarse con vigor; ponerse a trabajar. **To set to rights**, rectificar; poner una cosa en orden. **Set one to work**, poner a alguno a trabajar, darle trabajo o hacer que

trabaje. **To set pen to paper**, escribir, poner la pluma sobre el papel.

set together, poner en orden; juntar, poner junto.

set up, ensalzar, exaltar, elevar; erigir, fundar, instituir o levantar; enderezar o poner derecha o empinada una cosa; adelantarse o ponerse delante; hacer una proposición; establecer y establecerse; empezar alguno a traficar por sí o por su cuenta; principiar un sistema nuevo de vida; hacer profesión pública de una opinión, de una virtud, etc., preciarse de; poner a la vista; *(Impr.)* componer; dar un grito; hacer ruido; meter bulla. **To set up a coach**, echar coche. **To set up a shop**, poner tienda. **To set up a tent**, levantar una tienda. **To set up for**, darse uno por lo que no es; darse por lo que es; erigirse en medianero, dictador, etc.; preciarse de; concurrir. **To set up for oneself**, obrar por sí; trabajar por su cuenta. **To set up to sale**, poner en venta.

set upon, echar a andar; echarse sobre uno, acometer, asaltar; fijar la atención; determinar resueltamente. **To be set upon by footpads**, ser atacado por salteadores. **To set a price**, fijar un precio. **To set a stone**, engastar una piedra preciosa. **To set a time**, señalar un tiempo o plazo dterminado. **To set free**, libertar, poner en libertad. **To set nets**, poner lazos. **To set one over a thing**, dar a uno el encargo de hacer o de inspeccionar la ejecución de una cosa. **To set one's hand to**, firmar. **To set one's mind against**, concebir odio o tirria contra alguno. **To set sail**, hacerse a la vela.

set, *a.* 1. De opinión fija; obstinado, terco, resuelto. 2. Señalado, establecido por autoridad; prescrito. 3. Regular, arreglado, ajustado, formal, estudiado; reflexionado. 4. Puesto, sentado, colocado; fijo, inmóvil. 5. Hecho, construido, fabricado, fijo, montado, engastado.

set, *s.* 1. Juego, un determinado número de cosas que tienen cierta proporción y conexión entre sí; colección, serie, grupo, clase; compañía, cuadrilla, banda, hablando de personas. **A set of books**, una colección de libros. **Set of buckles**, juego de hebillas. **Set of diamonds**, aderezo de diamantes. **Set of horses**, tiro de caballos para arrastrar un coche o carruaje; yunta de caballos para arar. **Set of bed-curtains**, colgadura de cama. **A set of oars, of chairs**, un juego de remos, de sillas. 2. Conjunto o agregado de muchas cosas. **Set of china**, vajilla de porcelana. **Set of teeth**, dentadura. **Set form**, formulario. 3. Juego, la disposición con que están unidas ciertas cosas, siempre más de dos, de suerte que sin separarse puedan ejecutar algún movimiento. 4. Acción y efecto de dar dirección, posición o forma fija; curso, movimiento, tendencia; encorvadura; porte; triscamiento de los dientes de ciertas sierras. 5. Ocaso o puesta del sol. 6. Planta o pie de árbol, plantel, tallo listo para plantarlo. 7. Un fruto en su estado rudimentario.

set, *s.* Ajuste, caída de una prenda de vestir. *V.* FIT.

setback ['setbæk] [set-bak], *s.* 1. Obstáculo, impedimento al paso, embarazo; vuelta forzosa a un punto por donde se pasó antes. 2. Contracorriente.

set-bolt ['setbɒlt] [set-bolt], *s.* *(Mar.)* Botador, perno de trabante.

set-down ['setdaʊn] [set-daun], *s.* Reprimenda; *(Fam.)* peluca.

set-off ['setɒf] [set-of], *s.* *(For.)* 1. Compensación; cualquier contrapeso, tanto en el sentido recto como en el figurado. 2. Adorno; brillo, relieve, lo que realza. 3. Parte saliente de una pared. *V.* OFFSET. 4. La acción de reconocer un deudor la justicia de la petición de su acreedor, presentando al propio tiempo alguna demanda contra él que iguala la deuda o parte de ella.

seton ['setən] [se-ton], *s.* *(Cir. and Vet.)* Sedal.

setose, setous ['setəʊz] [se-tous], *a.* Cerdoso.

setscrew ['setskruː] [set-skru], *s.* Tornillo de sujeción o de presión.

sett [set] [set], *sf.* Madriguera.

settee [se'tiː] [se-ti], *s.* 1. Canapé. 2. *(Mar.)* Bajel de dos palos que se emplea en el mar Mediterráneo.

setter ['setər] [se-taʳ] *s.* 1. El o lo que pone, coloca o fija. 2. Perro de ajeo; perro adiestrado para indicar la caza por medio de una postura fija. 3. Espión, espía (spy). 4. Corchete, alguacil. 5. El que compone música para adaptarla a versos o letra.

setting ['setɪŋ] [se-tin], *s.* 1. Ocultación aparente del sol y de los astros debajo del horizonte (sunset). 2. Acción y efecto de colocar, fijar, engastar, embutir (fixing), etc. 3. Alguna cosa engastada, embutida, etc., la cosa insertada. 4. Engaste, engastadura, montadura, el marco en que está puesta una cosa; de aquí, cercado, alrededor. 5. (*Fam.*) Nidada, un número de huevos juntos para ser empollados. **Setting of the wind or current**, (*Mar.*) dirección del viento o la corriente. 6. (*Music*) Arreglo, versión.

setting, *a.* Poniente. **Setting sun**, sol poniente.

settle ['setl] [se-tel], *s.* Escaño.

settle, *va.* 1. Colocar, dar colocación a una persona. 2. Fijar, asegurar, afirmar, arreglar (fix, place). 3. Establecer, promulgar leyes, reglamentos, etc.; poner en el comercio, dar una profesión, estado; casar. 4. Hacer a una cosa más unida o compacta. 5. Colonizar, poblar, establecer en un país (colony). 6. Clarificar, quitar la hez. 7. Sosegar, calmar, serenar (calm). 8. Aclarar un pasaje, quitarle toda ambigüedad; determinar el sentido de un texto; resolver, decidir. 9. Decidir, determinar, poner fin a, fijar la opinión; acabar. 10. Arreglar, poner en orden (arrange). 11. Liquidar una cuenta, pagar una deuda (liquidate). 12. Hacer firme y transitable un camino. *-vn.* 1. Reposarse, asentarse, hacer sedimento, caer al fondo de algun líquido una parte de lo que está disuelto o suspenso en él. 2. Establecerse o fijar su residencia en algún paraje. 3. Disponer un método de vida; tomar estado; casarse; instalarse. 4. Fijarse una cosa o permanecer quieta por mucho tiempo en un paraje. 5. Sosegarse, calmar, serenarse. 6. Contraerse. 7. Dar en dote, señalar o asignar una cantidad de dinero como arras a la esposa. 8. Decidirse, determinarse, elegir (choose); ponerse resueltamente a hacer alguna cosa (undertake, start on). 9. Hacer arreglos con acreedores; saldar una cuenta. 10. Posarse; reposar. 11. Dejarse caer gradualmente, ir al fondo. **To settle to the bottom**, ir al fondo. **To be settled**, estar domiciliado. **The Puritans settled New England**, los puritanos colonizaron la Nueva Inglaterra. **This last blow settled him**, este último golpe acabó con él. **To settle the succession to the throne**, regularizar la sucesión al trono. **To settle down**, ponerse a; fijarse, detenerse. **Let the wine settle**, deje usted reposar el vino. **To settle an estate upon one**, instituir o nombrar a uno irrevocablemente heredero de alguna propiedad. **To be settling down at**, estar acostumbrado a. **To settle up**, ajustar cuentas. **To settle upon**, constituir la dote o señalar la propiedad que tiene la mujer al tiempo de su casamiento, para que no pueda entrar en la posesión del marido; decidirse a. **I have settled upon him a good annuity**, le he constituido una buena renta vitalicia. **To settle disputes**, componer las disputas o pendencias; zanjar las dificultades; convenirse, arreglar, hacer las paces entre los que están reñidos. **To settle accounts**, ajustar cuentas. **I'll settle him**, me lo cargaré.

settled ['setld] [se-teld], *a.* Permanente, fijo (fix).

settledness ['setldnɪs] [se-teld-nes], *s.* Estabilidad, permanencia; el estado fijo de alguna cosa.

settlement ['setlmənt] [se-tel-ment], *s.* 1. La acción de establecer (establishment). 2. Establecimiento, la colocación o suerte estable de alguna persona; instalación de un cura párroco, etc. 3. Colonia, el sitio o lugar donde se establecen colonos (colony); núcleo rural (village). 4. (*Ingl.*) Asiento, domicilio. 5. El acto de posesionar legalmente. 6. Dote que se da en arras a una mujer, y la acción de constituir o señalar la dote que una mujer lleva al matrimonio. 7. Acomodo, empleo, destino. 8. Ajuste, finiquito, convenio (agreement); (*Com.*) liquidación. **To reach a settlement**, acordar, llegar a un acuerdo.

settler ['setlər] [se-tlar], *s.* 1. El que compone, arregla y fija alguna cosa. **Settler of averages**, el medidor de averías o el que fija el importe de las averías. 2. El colono que se establece por primera vez en una colonia. 3. Poblador, establecedor, fundador (colonist, founder).

settling ['setlɪŋ] [se-tlin], *s.* 1. Establecimiento, colonización, arreglo (agreement, establishment); la acción del verbo **settle** en todas sus acepciones. 2. *pl.* Heces, zurrapas; sedimento, poso.

set-to ['settu:] [set-tu], *s.* Lucha, combate, disputa, debate.

setup ['setʌp] [set-ap], *s.* Arreglo, disposición, organización.

setwall ['setwɔ:l] [set-uol], *s.* Valeriana común de Europa.

seven ['sevn] [se-ven], *a.* y *s.* Siete, número cardinal y su signo. **The seven wonders of the world**, las siete maravillas del mundo.

sevenfold ['sevnfəʊld] [se-ven-fould], *a.* Séptuplo, siete veces una cantidad. *-adv.* Siete veces.

sevenscore ['sevnskɔːʳ] [se-ven-skoʳ], *a.* Ciento cuarenta, siete veces veinte.

seventeen ['sevntiːn] [se-ven-tin], *a.* y *s.* Diez y siete.

seventeenth ['sevntiːnθ] [se-ven-tinz], *a.* Décimo séptimo, el ordinal de diez y siete.

seventh ['sevnθ] [se-venz], *s.* y *a.* Séptimo. **Seventh heaven**, séptimo cielo, éxtasis. *-s.* (*Mús.*) Séptima.

seventieth ['sevntɪθ] [se-ven-tiez], *a.* Septuagésimo, número ordinal de setenta.

seventy ['sevntɪ] [se-ven-ti], *a.* y *s.* Setenta, siete veces diez.

sever ['sevəʳ] [se-vaʳ], *va.* 1. Separar, apartar, cortar, desunir, hacer una división o separación entre dos cosas que están unidas o que deben estarlo (divide, cut). 2. Arrancar, sacar, quitar o separar con violencia alguna cosa. 3. Partir, romper, deshacer (break). *-vn.* Separarse, desunirse, entreabrirse; partirse.

several ['sevrəl] [se-ve-ral], *a.* 1. Diversos, varios, algunos (some); más de uno o de dos, sin ser numerosos. 2. Diverso, distinto, solo, considerado como individuo, separado. 3. Particular, singular. 4. (*For.*) Distinto, relacionado individual y separadamente; respectivo. *-s.* Cada persona o cosa tomada por sí: varios, cada uno en particular. **Our several claims**, nuestras reclamaciones respectivas.

severally ['sevrəlɪ] [se-ve-ra-li], *adv.* Separadamente, distintamente, individualmente (one by one); a parte, cada uno de por sí. **Jointly and severally**, solidariamente.

severalty ['sevrəltɪ] [se-ve-ral-ti], *s.* (*For.*) Posesión privativa de un terreno.

severance ['sevərəns] [se-ve-rans], *s.* Separación, partición. **Severance pay**, salario al que se despide de un empleo.

severe [sɪ'vɪəʳ] [si-viaʳ], *a.* 1. Severo, doloroso, acre, riguroso (hard, rude). 2. Severo, riguroso, áspero, duro, cruel, inexorable. 3. Severo, exacto, rígido, conforme a reglas rígidas, que rechaza todo ornato de estilo; austero. 4. Severo, grave, serio, mesurado. **A severe test**, una prueba dura, severa. **A severe blow**, un rudo golpe. **A severe climate**, un clima riguroso. **A severe cold**, un fuerte resfriado.

severely [sɪ'vɪəlɪ] [si-via-li], *adv.* Severamente, cruelmente; con rigor, con severidad; estrictamente, rigurosamente.

severity [sɪ'verɪtɪ] [si-ve-ri-ti], *s.* 1. Severidad, rigor aspereza, crueldad. 2. Severidad, observancia rígida, exactitud, puridad y austeridad de estilo; austeridad. 3. Severidad, seriedad, gravedad (gravity, seriousness). **Severity of life**, austeridad de vida. **The severity of a test**, el rigor de una prueba.

sew [səʊ] [sou], *va.* Coser, juntar con aguja e hilo. *-vn.* Coser, ocuparse cosiendo. **To sew again**, recoser. **To sew up**, encerrar, coser en. **The deal is sewn up**, el negocio está concluido definitivamente.

sew, *va.* (*Prov. Ingl.*) Desaguar un estanque, vaciar.

sewage ['sjuːɪdʒ] [siuich], *s.* Drenaje. **Sewage disposal**, depuración de aguas residuales. *V.* SEWERAGE.

sewer ['sjʊəʳ] [siuaʳ], *s.* Cosedor, el que cose.

sewer, *s.* 1. Albañal, el canal o conducto para expeler las inmundicias; alcantarilla, desaguadero (drain). 2. (*Des.*) Maestresala.

sewerage ['sjʊərɪdʒ] [siua-rich], *s.* 1. Desagüe sistemático por medio de albañales o cloacas; la conducción de las inmundicias desde los edificios. 2. Sistema de albañales o alcantarillas. **Sewerage system**, alcantarillado.

sewing ['səʊɪŋ] [souin], *s.* Costura, el acto de coser; lo que se ha cosido a la aguja. **Sewing-machine**, máquina de coser.

Sewing-needle, aguja de coser. **Sewing-thread**, hilo de coser o para coser; hilo de número.

sex [seks] [seks], s. 1. Sexo, condición orgánica que distingue al macho de la hembra en los animales y en las plantas. 2. Sexo. **Sex act**, coito, acto carnal. **Sex maniac**, maníaco sexual. **Sex of-fender**, delincuente sexual. **Sex-shop**, sex-shop, sexería.

sexagenarian [ˌseksədʒɪˈnɛərɪən] [sek-sa-yi-nea-rian], s. Sexagenario, persona de edad entre los sesenta y los setenta años.

sexagesima [ˌseksəˈdʒəsɪmə] [sek-sa-ye-si-ma], s. Sexagésima.

sexagesimal [ˌseksəˈdʒesɪməl] [sek-sa-ye-si-mal], a. Sexagesimal, basado en el número sesenta, que procede por potencias de sesenta.

sexed [sekst] [sekst], a. (Bio.) Sexuado. **Highly sexed**, obseso sexual.

sexennial [sekˈsɪnɪəl] [sek-si-nial], a. Que dura seis años, acontece cada seis años o pertenece al sexenio.

sexiness [ˈseksɪnɪs] [sek-si-nes], s. Carácter sexual; sexy.

sexism [ˈseksɪzəm] [sek-si-sem], s. Sexismo.

sexist [ˈseksɪst] [sek-sist], a. Sexista.

sexless [ˈsekslɪs] [seks-les], a. Neutro, que no tiene sexo.

sexologist [sekˈsɒlədʒɪst] [sek-so-lo-yist], a. Sexólogo.

sexology [sekˈsɒlədʒɪ] [sek-so-lo-yi], s. Sexología.

sekshop [ˈsekʃɒp] [sek-shop], sf. Sex-shop, sexería.

sextain [ˈseksteɪn] [seks-tein], s. Sextilla, composición métrica que consta de seis versos.

sextant [ˈsekstənt] [seks-tant], s. 1. La sexta parte de un círculo. 2. Sextante, un instrumento astronómico, usado principalmente por los marinos para determinar la latitud de un lugar. 3. Constelación pequeña.

sextet [seksˈtet] [seks-tet], a. Sexteto.

sextile [seksˈtɪl] [seks-til], s. (Astr.) Sextil, el aspecto de dos astros que distan entre sí sesenta grados.

sextillion [seksˈtɪlɪən] [seks-ti-lion], a. Sextillón, un número cardinal; según la numeración americana y francesa la séptima potencia de mil; según la numeración inglesa, la sexta potencia de un millón.

sexton [ˈsekstən] [seks-ton], s. Sacristán de una iglesia que cuida del edificio, de los entierros, etc.; en lo antiguo, sepulturero, el que por oficio abría las sepulturas.

sextuple [ˈsekstjʊpl] [seks-tiu-pel], a. Séxtuplo.

sexual [ˈseksjʊə] [seks-siual], a. Sexual, que concierne al sexo; que tiene sexo o se caracteriza por él; generativo, genital.

sexuality [ˌseksjʊˈælɪtɪ] [sek-siua-li-ti], s. Sexualidad, condición de lo que tiene sexo o está caracterizado por él.

sexually [ˈseksjʊəlɪ] [sek-siua-li], adv. De una manera sexual; respecto al sexo.

sexy [ˈseksɪ] [sek-si], a. Atractivo, sexy, provocativo.

Seychelles [seɪˈʃelz] [sei-shels], s.pl. Seychelles.

sh [ʃ] [sh], interj. ¡chist!, ¡chitón!

shabbily [ˈʃæbɪlɪ] [sha-bi-li], adv. Vilmente, ruinmente, mezquinamente; con vestidos usados, rapados.

shabbiness [ˈʃæbɪnɪs] [sha-bi-nes], s. Vileza, bajeza, miseria, roñería (meanness); estado andrajoso, desharrapado.

shabby [ˈʃæbɪ] [sha-bi], a. 1. Usado, rapado, andrajoso, en mal estado (ragged), ensuciado por el largo uso. 2. Desharrapado, descamisado; mísero, ruin, tacaño (low, mean). 3. Vil, bajo, despreciable, indigno de un hombre honrado.

shack [ʃæk] [shak], s. 1. (E.U. y Canadá) Choza, cabaña tosca o de troncos. 2. (E.U. y prov. Ingl.) Pasto de bellotas; pasto para el invierno. **To shack up**, amontonarse.

shackle [ˈʃækl] [sha-kel], va. 1. Encadenar, atar, ligar con cadenas (enchain); poner obstáculos o trabas, estorbar (difficult). 2. (Elec.) Poner un aislador entre los extremos (cortados) de algo, v. g. de un alambre.

shackle, s. 1. Anillo o argolla de metal (para atar a un preso); grillo, esposa. 2. Grillo, traba, impedimento. 3. Cadena, grillete; eslabón o gancho para unir los coches de ferrocarril. **Shackle-bolt**, cáncamo de grillete; perno de horquilla.

shad [ʃæd] [shad], s. Alosa, sábalo, saboga; pez del género Alosa.

shaddock [ˈʃædɒk] [sha-fok], s. Pamplemusa, árbol de las Antillas.

shade [ʃeɪd] [sheid], s. 1. Sombra, la oscuridad causada por la interceptación de los rayos de la luz. 2. Sombra, el color oscuro y bajo que se pone entre los demás colores que sobresalen en una pintura. 3. Matiz, graduación de un color (hue). 4. Matiz, diferencia ligera (nuance); poco, cantidad pequeña (little) **To put something in the shade**, eclipsar, dejar algo pequeño, dejar insignificante. **I'm a shade better**, estoy algo mejor. 5. Cortina para minorar la luz; pantalla, lo que sirve para interceptar la luz o proteger contra los rayos de luz, el polvo, etc. (curtains); pantalla, sombrerillo de lámpara; visera de gorra; toldo (awning, marquee). 6. Sombra, espectro, fantasma (ghost). 7. Sombra, la representación o semejanza imperfecta de alguna cosa. 8. Un sitio oscuro o cubierto de sombras; sombra, lo que hacen los árboles, que también se llama umbría. 9. Exterior, ligera apariencia; ficción, máscara, imagen. **Window-shades**, cortinas de encerado para ventanas. **Glass shade**, guarda brisa, brisero. **Shades**, gafas de sol.

shade, va. 1. Oscurecer, privar de la luz y claridad (darken). 2. Asombrar, cubrir con la sombra; ocultar una cosa de modo que no le dé la luz. 3. Entoldar, cubrir algún sitio con toldos para resguardarse del sol o del calor (shelter). 4. Abrigar, esconder, amparar, proteger, poner al abrigo de o dar abrigo. 5. Sombrear, poner sombras en la pintura o dibujo; matizar, juntar, casar acertadamente diversos colores. 6. Rasguear las letras, hacer ciertos trazos más gruesos que otros al escribir. **Shade off**, degradar (color).

shader [ˈʃeɪdər] [shei-daʳ], s. El que oscurece.

shadeless [ˈʃeɪdlɪs] [sheid-les], a. Privado de sombra.

shadily [ˈʃeɪdɪlɪ] [shei-di-li], adv. Con sombra, en la sombra; de una manera sospechosa.

shadiness [ˈʃeɪdɪnɪs] [shei-di-nes], s. La calidad y estado de lo que se halla cubierto de sombra o bajo la sombra.

shading [ˈʃeɪdɪŋ] [shei-din], a. Sombreado; gradual; degradación.

shadow [ˈʃædəʊ] [sha-dou], s. 1. Sombra, oscuridad que produce en un cuerpo otro que se interpone entre él y la luz; sombrajo, sombraje. 2. (Lit.) Sombras, oscuridad, tinieblas (darkness, gloom). 3. Sombra, el fondo oscuro o partes sombreadas de una pintura. 4. Cualquier sitio oscuro o cubierto de sombras (dark). 5. Sombra, espectro, fantasma (spectre). 6. Compañero inseparable o lo que sigue a otra cosa como si fuese su sombra (mate). 7. Tipo, representación mística de alguna cosa. 8. Traza o apariencia ligera; el más leve grado, poco. 9. Sombra, refugio, amparo, protección (protection). **Without a shadow of doubt**, sin la más mínima duda, sin lugar a dudas. **To cast a shadow**, proyectar una sombra. **To be in the shadow of**, estar amenazado por.

shadow, va. 1. Anublar, oscurecer, dar sombra, poner a la sombra. 2. Representar imperfectamente o de un modo misterioso; representar por medio de un símbolo, simbolizar. 3. Seguir, acompañar de cerca como una sombra; espiar, cazar, como hace un perro **To be shadowed**, ser perseguido. 4. Matizar. -vn. 1. Anublarse, oscurecerse. 2. Casarse o confundirse los colores. **To shadow forth**, simbolizar, anunciar.

shadowboxing [ˈʃædəʊbɒksɪŋ] [sha-dou-bok-sin], s. Boxeo con un contendiente imaginario a manera de entrenamiento.

shadowy [ˈʃædəʊɪ] [sha-doui], a. 1. Umbroso, umbrío; obscuro, sombreado, tenebroso, misterioso. 2. Oscuro, sin realidad, vago; indefinido; que tiene relación con un espectro. 3. Típico, simbólico.

shady [ˈʃeɪdɪ] [shei-di], a. 1. Opaco, oscuro, sombrío, lleno de sombra; que hace sombra. **It's shady here**, aquí hay sombra. 2. Al abrigo de los rayos y del calor del sol; refrescado por la sombra. 3. Impropio de la luz o que la evita; moralmente sospechoso.

shaft [ʃɑːft] [shaft], s. 1. Flecha, dardo, saeta, arma arrojadiza (arrow); también mango de un arma. 2. Chapitel de una torre; caña o fuste de columna: *(Mec.)* eje, árbol, mástil (axle, spinder); barra larga y cilíndrica, particularmente si gira; limón o limonera de carro; lanza de coche; varas de las sillas de manos. 3. Cañón o tubo de pluma. **Shaft of a carriage**, varas y juego de un coche.

shaft, *s.* 1. Socavón, tiro o pozo de mina, para la ventilación o para extraer materiales. 2. Túnel de un horno de fundición.

shag [ʃæg] [shag], *s.* 1. Pelo áspero y lanudo. 2. Felpa, tejido que tiene pelo, por el haz; *(Amer.)* tripe; jergón. 3. Cormorán, cuervo marino. **Shag-bag**, guitón, pícaro; pordiosero.

shag, *va.* y *vn. (pret.* y *pp.* SHAGGED). Hacer peludo, velludo; hacer escabroso, desigual; colgar o yacer en forma de mechón pesado.

shagbark [ʃæbɑːk] [shag-bark], *s.* Caria (blanca). V. HICKORY.

shagged [ʃægɪd] [sha-guid], *a.* Velludo; achaparrado.

shagginess [ʃægɪnɪs] [sha-gui-nes], *s.* Calidad de peloso o afelpado.

shaggy [ʃægɪ] [sha-gui], *a.* 1. Peludo, velludo, hirsuto; afelpado, lanudo; de aquí, escabroso, áspero, desigual. 2. Cubierto de pelo, lana, etc., desigual y enredado (hairy, furry).

shagreen [ʃæˈɡriːn] [sha-grin], *s.* 1. Piel de zapa, lija que se emplea para alisar maderas, etc. 2. Especie de cuero granilloso, teñido de verde por regla general y que proviene del Oriente.

shah [ʃɑː] [sha], *s.* 1. Chah, soberano de Persia. 2. Título de honor común en los países mahometanos, como adición al nombre.

shake [ʃeɪk] [sheik], *va. (pret.* SHOOK (SHAKED), *pp.* SHAKEN). 1. Sacudir, menear con fuerza, agitar o mover rápida o violentamente alguna cosa, hacer bambolear o bambonear (beat, flap, move up and down). 2. Arrojar, lanzar, despedir con ímpetu (cast, throw). 3. Debilitar; poner a una cosa en riego o peligro (risk); *(Fig.)* desalentar, amilanar (discourage). 4. Despertar repentinamente, excitar, agitar; estorbar o dañar a causa de un choque: (a veces con **up**). 5. Estrechar la mano. 6. *(Mús.)* V. TRILL. 7. *(Fam. E.U.)* Desembarazarse, librarse de algo, echar de sí, despedir. *-vn.* 1. Bambonear o bambolear; vacilar, titubear. 2. Temblar, moverse con movimiento inquieto y perturbado. 3. Temblar, tener mucho miedo (fear). **To shake one's head**, mover la cabeza. **The wind shakes the house**, el viento hace temblar la casa. **To shake hands**, darse un apretón de manos. **To shake hands with**, darse la mano, despedirse; dar la mano a otro, ponerse de acuerdo. **To shake for fear**, temblar de miedo. **To shake from**, echar de sí, poner a un lado. **To shake in**, introducir una cosa sacudiéndola o meneándola violentamente. **To shake off**, sacudir una cosa para que se mueva; hacer caer una cosa a fuerza de sacudirla; zafarse de, echar de sí, libertarse de algo que incomoda. **To shake to pieces**, sacudir o menear violentamente alguna cosa hasta que caiga en pedazos. **To shake out**, sacudir, hacer salir, hacer caer. **To shake out of**, arrancar. **To shake up**, sacudir, remover; agitar, poner en debida forma sacudiendo. **To shake with laughter**, morirse de risa, o perecer de risa.

shake, *s.* 1. Concusión, sacudimiento, sacudida, impulso dado a una cosa. 2. Vibración; movimiento de undulación causado por un impulso dado al cuerpo que se mueve (vibration). 3. La acción de darse o apretarse las manos. 4. Tabla de ripia desigual y no raspada que se usa para cubrir chozas, etc. 5. *pl.* Escalofrío de la fiebre intermitente. 6. *(Ger.)* Periquete; instante. 7. *(Mús.)* Trino. V. TRILL. 8. Duela. V. SHOOK. 9. Grieta, hendedura en un tronco. **Milk shake**, batido.

shakedown [ʃeɪkdaʊn] [sheik-daun], *s.* 1. Cama improvisada. 2. *(Fam.)* Variedad de baile ruidoso y rápido. 3. *(Fam.)* Extorsión, exigencia de dinero por compulsión o persuasión.

shaken [ʃeɪkn] [shei-ken], *pp.* del verbo SHAKE. Sacudido; agitado; rajado, hendido (madero).

shaker [ʃeɪkəʳ] [shei-kaʳ], *s.* Coctelera.

shake-up [ʃeɪkʌp] [sheik-ap], *s.* 1. Sacudimiento. 2. Reorganización con cambio de personal.

shaking [ʃeɪkɪŋ] [shei-kin], *s.* Sacudimiento; temblor.

Shakesperarian [ʃeɪksˈpɪərɪən] [sheiks-pia-rian], *a.* Perteneciente o relativo a Shakespeare, o en el estilo de este autor.

shakiness [ʃeɪkɪnɪs] [shei-ki-nes], *s.* Debilidad, inestabilidad (unstability).

shako, shacko [ʃækəʊ] [sha-kou], *s.* Chacó, morrión militar.

shaky [ʃeɪkɪ] [shei-ki], *a.* 1. Habitualmente trémulo; vacilante, débil; poco firme. 2. *(Com.)* Falta de crédito o solvencia; indigno de confianza. 3. Agrietado, hendido.

shale [ʃeɪl] [sheil], *s.* Arcilla esquistosa que se hiende fácilmente en láminas frágiles y desiguales.

shall [ʃæl] [shal], *v. defec. (pret.* SHOULD, V. la SINOPSIS). Se usa como auxiliar para denotar el tiempo futuro del verbo en el modo indicativo. En las oraciones afirmativas *shall* se usa en la primera persona para anunciar simplemente un acontecimiento venidero, y en las segundas y terceras para expresar mandato, amenaza o promesa. **I shall do it**, lo haré o tengo intención de hacerlo. **You shall do it**, lo hará usted, yo mando que usted lo haga o yo aseguro que le obligaré a usted a hacerlo; usted ha de hacerlo. **He shall go**, él irá, yo le haré ir, yo haré que vaya o yo prometo hacerle ir. En las oraciones interrogativas *shall* sirve en la primera persona para expresar simplemente la interrogación, en la segunda para averiguar la intención de la persona a quien se pregunta, y en la tercera para indagar la voluntad de la persona con quien hablamos, respecto al supuesto de la oración. **Shall I go to town?**, ¿voy a la ciudad? ¿debo ir a la ciudad? ¿iré a la ciudad? ¿quiere usted que vaya a la ciudad? **Thou shalt not kill**, no matarás. **You shall pay for this!**, ¡me las pagarás! **Shall you go to town?**, ¿irá usted a la ciudad? **How shall we spend the evening?** ¿cómo pasaremos la velada? Después de otro verbo *shall* en la segunda y tercera persona sirve simplemente para anunciar. **He says that he shall set out tomorrow**, dice que partirá mañana.

shallop [ʃæləp] [sha-lop], *s.* Chalupa, barco prolongado mayor que el esquife o bote; bote abierto, de cualquier tamaño.

shallot [ʃəˈlɒt] [sha-lot], *s.* Chalote ascalonia, planta afín al ajo.

shallow [ʃæləʊ] [sha-lou], *a.* 1. Somero, inmediato a la superficie, que tiene poco fondo, poco profundo. 2. Superficial, trivial, insípido; necio, bobo. **A shallow stream**, una corriente poco profunda. *-s. (Mar.)* Bajío, banco de arena. **Shallow-brained, shallow-pated**, aturdido, ligero de cascos, necio.

shallowness [ʃæləʊnɪs] [sha-lou-nes], *s.* 1. Falta de hondura; poca profundidad. 2. Ligereza, necedad, falta de reflexión, bobada.

shaly [ʃælɪ] [sha-li], *a.* De, o perteneciente a la arcilla esquistosa.

sham [ʃæm] [sham], *va.* y *vn.* Engañar, chasquear, hacer una burla, dar un chasco; fingir, hacer creer una cosa falsa; usar de ficción. **To sham illness**, fingirse enfermo. **She's just shamming**, está fingiendo.

sham, *s.* Socolor, pretexto, apariencia falsa; fingimiento, ilusión, impostura, fraude. *-a.* Fingido, disimulado, no genuino, supuesto; postizo. **Sham-fight**, batalla figurada, combate fingido. **A sham quarrel**, una contienda simulada.

shamble [ʃæmbl] [sham-bol], *vn.* Andar bamboleándose o con paso poco seguro. *-s.* Modo de andar bamboleándose; paso poco seguro.

shambles [ʃæmblz] [sham-belz], *s. pl.* 1. Matadero, el lugar o sitio donde se matan las reses; lugar donde ha ocurrido una matanza. 2. Carnicería, el sitio donde se vende la carne para el abasto público.

shambling [ʃæmblɪŋ] [sham-blin], *a.* Que se mueve inseguramente, renqueando. *-pa.* de SHAMBLE.

shame [ʃeɪm] [sheim], *s.* 1. Vergüenza, rubor, bochorno, empacho (embarrassment, flush). 2. Pundonor. 3. Vergüenza, ignominia, oprobio, deshonra, afrenta (humiliation). **For shame! shame on you!** ¡qué vergüenza! ¡qué asco! ¡bah! **Have you no shame?**, ¿no te da vergüenza? 4. Lástima, pena. **It's a shame that**, es una lástima que.

shame, *va.* 1. Avergonzar, causar vergüenza; afrentar, deshonrar. 2. impeler, incitar, por un sentimiento de vergüenza: con *into* o *out of*. **To shame one out of his negligence**, echar en cara a uno su negligencia, hacerle sonrojar por su descuido.

shamefaced [ˈʃeɪmfeɪst] [sheim-feist], *a.* Tímido, vergonzoso, modesto, pudoroso.

shamefacedly [ˈʃeɪmfeɪsɪdlɪ] [sheim-fei-sid-li], *adv.* Vergonzosamente, con rubor o modestia.

shamefacedness [ˈʃeɪmfeɪsɪdnɪs] [sheim-fei-sid-nes], *s.* Timidez, modestia, pudor, vergüenza, rubor, empacho (timidity).

shameful [ˈʃeɪmfʊl] [sheim-ful], *a.* 1. Vergonzoso, ignominioso, bochornoso, oprobioso, deshonroso, afrentoso. 2. Deshonesto, indecente.

shamefully [ˈʃeɪmfəlɪ] [sheim-fu-li], *adv.* Vergonzosamente, ignominiosamente; indignamente, indecentemente.

shameless [ˈʃeɪmlɪs] [sheim-les], *a.* 1. Desvergozado, sin vergüenza, descarado, desollado. 2. Hecho sin la menor vergüenza; falto de decoro, de pudor.

shamelessly [ˈʃeɪmlɪslɪ] [sheim-les-li], *adv.* Desvergonzadamente, atrevidamente, descaradamente, sin empacho, desahogadamente.

shamelessness [ˈʃeɪmlɪsnɪs] [sheim-les-nes], *s.* Desvergüenza, descaro, desuello, avilantez, impudencia.

shaming [ˈʃeɪmlɪŋ] [shei-min], *a.* Vergonzoso, humillante. **This is too shaming!**, ¡qué vergüenza!

shammy [ˈʃæmɪ] [sha-mi], *s.* Gamuza, especie de cabra montés. **Shamois-leather**, gamuza: escríbese a veces **Shammy-leather**. *V.* CHAMOIS.

shampoo [ʃæmˈpuː] [sham-pu], *va.* 1. Lavar y limpiar la cabeza, frotándola con espuma de jabón y agua. 2. Frotar con fuerza el cuerpo de una persona que sale de un baño caliente. *-s.* El acto de frotar el cuerpo, o de limpiar la cabeza; champú. (hairdresser's) **A shampoo and set**, lavado y marcado. **To give oneself a shampoo**, lavarse la cabeza.

shamrock [ˈʃæmrɒk] [sham-rok], *s.* (*Bot.*) Trébol, como emblema nacional de Irlanda; también, una de otras varias plantas trifolioladas, p. ej. la acedera.

Shangai [ˌʃæŋˈhaɪ] [shan-jai], *sm.* Shangai.

shank [ʃæŋk] [shank], *s.* 1. Pierna, la parte del cuerpo del animal que está entre la rodilla y el pie. 2. Zanca, pierna larga de las aves. 3. Asta o ástil, el mango o parte más larga de algún instrumento; tallo, soporte comparado a una pierna; cuerpo del tip; fuste de una columna; enfranque de un zapato; rabo o cola de botón. 4. (*Bot.*) *V.* PEDICELO o FOOTSTALK. 5. (*Ger. E.U.*) Resto o última parte. **The shank of the evening**, la última parte de la anochecida. **Shank of an anchor**, asta de ancla. **Spindle shank**, pierna de un huso. **Shank-painter**, (*Mar.*) boza de la uña del ancla.

shanked [ˈʃæŋkt] [shankt], *a.* Enastado, que tiene asta o mango; de piernas, de tallo. **Long-shanked**, zancudo, con zancas largas.

shan't [ʃɑːnt] [shant], (*Fam.*) Abreviación de *shall not*.

shanty [ˈʃæntɪ] [shan-ti], *s.* (*pl.* SHANTIES). Cabaña, choza; abrigo desvencijado o provisional.

shape [ʃeɪp] [sheip], *va. y vn.* (*pp.* SHAPED, rara vez SHAPEN; y antiguamente SHOPEN). 1. Formar, dar figura o forma, modelar, tallar (form, carve, work). 2. Proporcionar, ajustar a un fin particular, modificar; disponer, ordenar un rumbo o marcha determinados (determine, settle). 3. Imaginar, concebir, figurarse alguna cosa (image). **To shape a course**, (*Mar.*) ponerse en rumbo. **To shape well**, desarrollarse en buenas condiciones, prometer, esperanzar. **Shape up**, rendir más, trabajar mejor.

shape, *s.* 1. Hechura, forma, figura; contorno de los objetos. 2. Talle, la disposición o proporción del cuerpo humano. 3. Expresión desarrollada o fórmula definida de algo; aplicación. **To put an idea into shape**, hacer aplicación de una idea. 4. Exterior, apariencia, aspecto (look). 5. Modelo, ejemplar, norma. 6. (*Fam.*) Manera, modo de hacer. **To take shape**, formarse, tomar forma. **To be in good shape**, estar en buenas condiciones, estar en forma (fit).

shapeless [ˈʃeɪplɪs] [sheip-les], *a.* Informe, disforme, desproporcionado, imperfecto.

shapelessness [ˈʃeɪplɪsnɪs] [sheip-les-nes], *s.* Irregularidad o deformidad en la forma o figura de una cosa.

shapeliness [ˈʃeɪplɪnɪs] [sheip-li-nes], *s.* Simetría, belleza, proporción.

shapely [ˈʃeɪplɪ] [sheip-li], *a.* Simétrico, que tiene simetría; que está bien hecho o bien proporcionado.

shaper [ˈʃeɪpəʳ] [shei-paʳ], *s.* Persona o instrumento que da forma; máquina de tallar o estampar.

shard [ʃɑːd] [shard], *s.* 1. Tiesto, casco, el pedazo quebrado de alguna vasija de barro. 2. Elitro (v.g. de un coleóptero).

share [ʃɛəʳ] [sheaʳ], *va.* 1. Distribuir, repartir entre muchos (divide up, distribute); con *between* o *among*. 2. Participar, recibir de otro alguna cosa como parte que toca a uno; tener parte en algo; gozar o soportar con otros. 3. Dividir, compartir, partir (divide up); con *with*. 4. Cortar, separar. *-vn.* Participar, tener parte en alguna cosa o tocar algo de ella. **To share alike**, repartir igualmente, tener una parte igual. **I don't share that idea**, no comparto esa idea.

share, *s.* 1. Parte, porción de una cosa dividida o repartida entre varios. 2. Cuota, parte que toca a cada persona que participa en un negocio; (*y Com.*) acción, parte o porción del fondo de una compañía de comercio, y el papel o vale que representa cada parte. 3. Interés, participación, porción asignada. **To hold a share**, tener interés en alguna cosa, tener o poseer una acción de alguna compañía. 4. Reja del arado. **To each his share**, a cada uno su parte. **Share and share alike**, por igual, por partes iguales. **On shares**, con condición de tener una parte. **Railway share**, acción de ferrocarril. **To fall to the share of**, tocar, caer en parte. **Share in the profits**, participación en beneficios. **It fell to my share**, me correspondió a mí. **To do one's share**, hacer uno lo que le corresponde. (*Fin.*) **Share index**, índice de cotización en bolsa. **Share issue**, emisión de acciones.

sharebone [ˈʃɛəbəʊn] [shea-boun], *s.* Hueso del empeine, del pubis.

sharecropper [ˈʃɛəˌkrɒpəʳ] [shea-kro-paʳ], *s.* Mediero, inquilino.

shares [ʃɛəz] [shears], *s.* Repartidor; partícipe.

shareholder [ˈʃɛəhəʊldəʳ] [shea-joul-daʳ], *s.* (*Com.*) Accionista, el dueño de una o más acciones.

sharer [ˈʃɛərəʳ] [shea-raʳ], *s.* Repartidor; partícipe.

shark [ʃɑːk] [shark], *s.* 1. Tiburón. 2. Estafador (swindler). 3. Experto.

sharker [ˈʃɑːkəʳ] [shar-kaʳ], *s.* Petardista. *V.* SHARPER.

sharp [ʃɑːp] [sharp], *a.* 1. Agudo, lo que tiene punta, filo o corte delgado y sutil, puntiagudo, aguzado, cortante (cutting). 2. Que forma un ángulo agudo, abrupto, angular. 3. Agudo, perspicaz, de vivo ingenio, astuto, mañoso (clever, shrewd, discerning). 4. De aguda vista, de buen oído (keen). 5. Agudo, penetrante. 6. Acre, mordaz, picante, agrio; sarcástico. 7. Severo, rígido; vivo, violento. 8. Ansioso, ardiente; vehemente, penetrante, áspero (v. g. la arena); pronto; impetuoso, fogoso, vivo (combate, debate); vigilante, atento; mordaz, excesivamente frío (viento, escarcha); listo, avisado. 9. Distinto, claramente delineado o definido. 10. (*Mús.*) Elevado más alto que su propio tono; precedido de un sostenido. *-s.* 1. (*Mús.*) Sostenido, (#) signo musical que indica elevación de un semitono, el mismo tono así indicado. 2. Aguja de coser de la forma más larga y más delgada. 3. Estafador. 4. (*Fest. E.U.*) De aquí, maestro en un arte, sujeto hábil, experto. *-adv.* 1. De una manera severa, sarcástica. 2. (*Fam.*) Al instante, exactamente, puntualmente. **We shall go at four o'clock sharp**, iremos a las cuatro en punto. **Look sharp**, está o estad alerta. **To pull up sharp**, frenar de repente, frenar en seco. **A sharp knife**, un cuchillo cortante. **A sharp needle, roof**, una aguja puntiaguda, un techo puntiagudo, o en punta. **Sharp sight**, vista penetrante. **Sharp features**, facciones enjutas. **Sharp criticism**, una crítica acerba. **Sharp-edged**, afilado, agudo, aguzado. **Sharp-eyed**, de vista penetrante. **Sharp-pointed**, puntiagudo, de punta aguda, acerada.

sharp, *va.* 1. Afilar, aguzar. 2. Elevar medio tono; marcar con un sostenido. -*vn.* 1. *(Mús.)* Cantar o tocar más alto que el tono debido. 2. Ratear; engañar, trampear, petardear.

sharp bend [ˈʃɑːpbend] [sharp-bend], *s.* Curva cerrada (en una carretera).

sharpen [ˈʃɑːpən] [shar-pen], *va.* 1. Afilar, aguzar, adelgazar; amolar. 2. Aguzar o sutilizar el ingenio. 3. Hacer más severo, intenso, acre, fogoso o ansioso. -*vn.* Aguzarse, hacerse más agudo, más vivo o picante; afilarse.

sharpener [ˈʃɑːpnəʳ] [sharp-naʳ], *s.* Amolador, afilador. **Pencil-sharpener**, cortalápiz, sacapuntas.

sharper [ˈʃɑːpəʳ] [shar-paʳ], *s.* 1. Fullero. 2. Caballero de industria.

sharpie [ˈʃɑːpiː] [shar-pi], *s.* *(Fam.)* Púa.

sharply [ˈʃɑːplɪ] [sharp-li], *adv.* 1. Con filo, corte o punta. 2. Severamente, rigorosamente. 3. Agudamente, vivamente. 4. Agudamente, sutilmente, ingeniosamente.

sharpness [ˈʃɑːpnɪs] [sharp-nes], *s.* 1. Agudeza, sutileza o delicadeza de los filos, cortes o puntas (keenness). 2. Agudeza, sutileza, perspicacia, viveza de ingenio (shrewdness). 3. Acrimonia, aspereza, mordacidad (pungency). 4. Acritud, agrura, acrimonia. 5. Violencia, rigor (rudeness). 6. Destemple, inclemencia del tiempo.

sharpshooter [ˈʃɑːpˌʃuːtəʳ] [sharp-shu-taʳ], *s.* Tirador experto.

sharp-sighted [ˈʃɑːpˈsaɪtɪd] [sharp-sai-tid], *a.* Perspicaz, el que tiene vista de lince o muy penetrante.

sharp-visaged [ˈʃɑːpˈvɪsaːdʒt] [sharp-vi-sacht], *a.* Cariaguileño.

sharp-witted [ˈʃɑːpˈwɪtɪd] [sharp-ui-tid], *a.* Agudo de ingenio.

shatter [ˈʃætəʳ] [sha-taʳ], *va.* 1. Destrozar, hacer pedazos o astillas, hacer añicos alguna cosa (smash, break into pieces); estrellar, romper alguna cosa de un golpe haciéndola pedazos. 2. Arruinar la salud, distraer, perturbar. **He was shattered to hear it**, al enterarse se quedó atónito. -*vn.* 1. Hacerse pedazos, quebrarse, romperse. 2. Tener un sonido como el de las cosas al romperse; dar un estallido. **The window shattered**, la ventana se hizo añicos.

shattered [ˈʃætəd] [sha-terd], *a.* Abrumado, destrozado; *(Fam.)* hecho polvo.

shattering [ˈʃætərɪŋ] [sha-te-rin], *a.* Contundente, demoledor.

shattery [ˈʃætərɪ] [sha-te-ri], *a.* Desmenuzable, quebradizo, que se puede reducir fácilmente a pedazos.

shave [ʃeɪv] [sheiv], *va.* 1. Rasurar, quitar o cortar la barba o el cabello, rapar. 2. Afeitar, hacer o cortar la barba. 3. Raspar, raer alguna cosa quitando una parte de su superficie. 4. Rozar, tocar o tropezar ligeramente. 5. Cortar alguna cosa reduciéndola a partes muy menudas. -*vn.* 1. Afeitarse, hacerse la barba. 2. Llevarse la mejor parte en un trato o negocio.

shave, *s.* Afeitado, rasurado. **That was a close shave**, eso fue un milagro. **To have a shave**, afeitarse.

shaveling [ˈʃeɪvlɪŋ] [sheiv-lin], *s.* Hombre rapado; monje o fraile.

shaven [ˈʃeɪvn] [shei-ven], *pp. of* **shave.**

shaver [ˈʃeɪvəʳ] [shei-vaʳ], *s.* 1. Barbero, el que afeita. 2. Desollador, el que hace su negocio, el que no mira más que su interés. 3. Robador, ladrón. 4. *(Fam.)* Muchacho, jovencito. **He is a keen shaver**, es trujamán experto.

shaving [ˈʃeɪvɪŋ] [shei-vin], *s.* 1. Raedura, la parte menuda que se rae de alguna cosa. 2. Raspadura, rasura, lo que se quita de la superficie raspando. 3. Rasurado, afeitado. **Shaving-brush**, brocha de afeitar. **Shaving-dish**, bacía. **Shaving-knife**, navaja de afeitar. **Cloth-shaving**, paño de afeitar. **Shaving-soap**, jabón para afeitarse. **Shaving (of wood)**, acepilladuras, virutas, alisaduras. **Shavings**, virutas.

shaw [ʃɔː] [sho], *s.* *(Prov. brit.)* Bosquecillo, bosque pequeño, soto.

shawl [ʃɔːl] [shol], *s.* Chal, pañolón, pañuelo grande o manteleta. *(Amer.)* Manta, pañuelos para rebozo.

shawn [ʃɔːn] [shon], *s.* *(Ant.)* Oboe, instrumento músico.

she [ʃiː] [shi], *pron. fem.* 1. Ella, aquella; (delante de un pronombre relativo) la que, aquella que. **She who speaks**, la que habla. 2. La hembra. **She-ass**, borrica, burra. **She-goat**, cabra.

sheaf [ʃiːf] [shif], *s.* (en *pl.* SHEAVES). 1. Gavilla, haz, garba, un manojo de cañas de trigo, centeno o cebada atadas. 2. Paquete, lío. 3. *V.* SHEAVE. **Sheaf of arrows**, haz de flechas.

sheaf, *va.* Agavillar.

shear [ʃɪəʳ] [shiaʳ], *va. (pret.* SHEARED o SHORE, *pp.* Sheared o SHORN). 1. Atusar, recortar o igualar el pelo con tijera; trasquilar; (cut down). 2. Tundir, cortar el pelo de los paños e igualarlo con tijera; trasquilar. 3. Esquilar, quitar con la tijera el pelo, vellón o lana de los ganados. 4. Cortar cualquier cosa mediante el roce o presión de otras dos, como cortar hierba con los dientes, etc. **Shearing-time**, esquileo, el tiempo en que se esquila. **Shearing-machine**, esquiladora mecánica.

shearer [ˈʃɪərəʳ] [shia-raʳ], *s.* Esquilador, trasquilador, el que esquila.

shears [ˈʃɪəz] [shiars], *s. pl.* 1. Tijeras grandes; cizallas, tijeras para cortar los metales. 2. Las corroderas de un torno o de una máquina para taladrar. 3. Cualquier cosa que tiene la figura de tijeras. 4. *V.* SHEERS.

shearman [ˈʃɪəmən] [shia-man], *s.* Esquilador; tundidor.

shearwater [ˈʃɪəwɔːtəʳ] [shia-uo-taʳ], *s.* Pico-tijera, ave marina del género Puffinus.

sheath [ʃiːθ] [shiz], *s.* 1. Vaina, caja, funda, estuche (box, cover). 2. Cubierta, lo que cubre una parte o un órgano, v. g. la parte inferior de las hojas en las plantas gramíneas.

sheathe [ʃiːð] [shid], *va.* 1. Envainar, meter en la vaina. 2. Poner vaina a una espada o puñal (sword). 3. Defender alguna cosa poniéndole un forro o cubierta, forrar (cover). 4. Embotar la acritud o acrimonia de las partículas acres de los cuerpos. **To sheathe a ship's bottom**, *(Mar.)* aforrar el fondo de un navío.

sheathing [ˈʃiːðɪŋ] [shi-din], *s.* 1. Forro exterior, revestimiento, lo que forma una funda o cubierta. 2. El acto de envainar o forrar. 3. Forro exterior de navío. **Copper-sheathing**, *(Mar.)* forro de cobre. **Pump-sheathing**, *(Mar.)* forro de bomba de agua. **Sheathing-nails**, clavos de entablar.

sheathless [ˈʃiːðlɪs] [shid-les], *a.* Sin vaina, sin estuche; desenvainado.

sheath-winged [ˈʃiːðwɪŋd] [shid-uingd], *a.* Armado de estuches para cubrir las alas.

sheave [ʃiːv] [shiv], *s.* 1. Roldana, rueda de una polea, garrucha. 2. Rueda excéntrica o su disco. **Lignumvitæ sheaves**, *(Mar.)* roldanas de palo santo. **Sheave-holes of the sheets**, *(Mar.)* escorteras.

sheaves [ʃiːvz] [shivs], *pl.* de SHEAF.

shebang [ʃəˈbæŋ] [she-bang], *s.* *(E.U.)* **The whole shebang**, todo ello.

shed [ʃed] [shed], *va. (pret.* y *pp.* SHED). 1. Arrojar, quitarse, desprenderse de algo, como una culebra de su piel o un ave de sus plumas, mudar (remove, take away). 2. Verter, derramar, hacer correr (pour away). 3. Esparcir, dejar caer. 4. Exhalar, emitir (exhale). **To shed feathers**, pelechar. -*vn.* Caer, desunirse, separarse; mudar los cuernos algunos animales. **To shed 10 kg in two months**, perder (adelgazar) 10 kg en dos meses.

shed, *s.* 1. Vertiente, superficie inclinada que vierte el agua. 2. En composición significa efusión o derramamiento. 3. Separación, reparto. 4. El declive o la bajada de una colina.

shed, *s.* 1. Sotechado, soportal, cobertizo, tinglado. 2. Tejadillo o colgadizo que sale de una pared para servir de cobertizo a algún puesto de vender. 3. Cabaña, barraca.

shedder [ˈʃedəʳ] [she-daʳ], *s.* Derramador, el que vierte o derrama.

sheen [ʃiːn] [shiin], *s.* Resplandor, brillantez; particularmente un lustre o brillo débil, como el de la luz reflejada.

sheeny [ˈʃiːnɪ] [shii-ni], *a.* Lustroso, luciente, brillante (bright, shining).

sheep [ʃiːp] [shiip], *s. (sing.* y *pl.).* 1. Oveja, carnero, rumiante del género Ovis. 2. *pl.* Ovejas; llámase así en sentido místico a los feligreses o fieles con respecto a sus obispos o párrocos. 3. Papanatas, hombre simple. 4. Badana, piel de carnero preparada para la encuadernación. **Sheep-bot**, mosca del carnero, o su larva, que infesta la nariz de los carneros. **Sheepcote, sheepfold**, redil, el cercado o corral para encerrar el ganado. **Sheep-dog**, perro de pastor. **Sheep-dip**, (a) decocción insecticida, v. g. de tabaco, en la cual se introduce a los carneros para librarlos de parásitos. (b) Limpiadura de la lana antes de esquilar. **Sheep-dung**, sirle, sirria. **Sheep-hook**, cayado. **Sheep-master**, ganadero, el dueño de ganado lanar. **Sheep-shearer**, esquilador de carneros. **Sheep-shank**, (a) la pierna de un carnero. (b) (Mar.) Margarita en un cabo. **Sheepwalk**, (G.B.) dehesa, tierra destinada solamente para pasto del ganado lanar.

sheepish [ˈʃiːpɪʃ] [shii-pish], a. Vergonzoso, corto de genio; tímido, pusilánime.

sheepishly [ˈʃiːpɪʃlɪ] [shii-pish-li], adv. Tímidamente, con pusilanimidad o falta de ánimo.

sheepishness [ˈʃiːpɪʃnɪs] [shii-pish-nes], s. Empacho, timidez, cortedad de genio; pusilanimidad.

sheep's-eye [ˈʃiːpzaɪ] [shiips-ai], s. Mirada al soslayo; ojeada modesta y amorosa.

sheep-shearing [ˈʃiːpˌʃeərɪŋ] [ship-shea-rin], s. Esquileo, acción de esquilar y la época en que se esquila el ganado lanar.

sheepskin [ˈʃiːpskɪn] [ship-skin], s. Piel de carnero, badana.

sheer [ʃɪəʳ] [shiaʳ], a. 1. Puro, claro, sin mezcla, absoluto, consumado, cabal (absolute, pure). 2. Muy fino y delgado, ligero (light) (v. g. un tejido). 3. Escarpado, casi vertical, a pico. -adv. De un golpe, de una vez. -s. (Mar.) Arrufo, arrufadura, la corvadura que hacen las cubiertas y costados de los barcos. **A ship with a great sheer**, (Mar.) bajel muy arrufado. **In sheer desperation**, en último caso, en último extremo. **Sheer curtain**, visillos.

sheer, vn. (Mar.) Alargarse, desviarse del rumbo o derrota. **To sheer off**, huir, largarse, escaparse.

sheet [ʃiːt] [shiit], s. 1. Pedazo ancho y muy delgado de cualquier objeto o substancia: v. g. sábana, pieza de lienzo para cubrir la cama. 2. Pliego, hoja de papel, pedazo de papel de cierto tamaño (paper); un diario; hoja, lámina delgada de metal, vidrio, madera, etc. 3. Cualquier cosa grande extendida; superficie grande y ancha, p. ej. la de una extensión de agua. 4. En plural, hojas, en la significación de un libro o escrito. 5. (Mar.) Escota, cuerda o maroma con que se templa la vela de la nave alargándola o acortándola. 6. Vela; uso literario. **A sheet of ice**, una capa de hielo. **Winding-sheet**, mortaja, la sábana en que se envuelven los cadáveres. **Top-sail sheets**, (Mar.) Escotines. **To haul aft the sheets**, (Mar.) cazar las escotas. **To haul home the top-sail sheets**, (Mar.) cazar el escotín a besar. **To ease off the sheets**, (Mar.) dar un salto a las escotas. **To let fly the sheets**, (Mar.) arriar las escotas en banda. **To sail with flowing sheets**, (Mar.) navegar a escota larga. **Sheet-anchor**, esperanza, el ancla mayor de un buque; (Fig.) áncora de salvación, apoyo seguro, último recurso. **Sheet-cable**, cable mayor, cable de proa esperanza. **Sheet-lightning**, relámpago a manera de un resplandor muy extenso, y que es debido al reflejo de un relámpago lejano.

sheet, va. 1. Ensabanar, cubrir o envolver en sábanas. 2. Proveer de o suministrar sábanas. 3. Envolver en alguna cosa grande; extender en láminas u hojas. **To sheet a bed**, poner sábanas en una cama.

sheeting [ˈʃiːtɪŋ] [shii-tin], s. Tela para hacer sábanas. **Russia sheeting**, Brin de Rusia.

sheet metal [ˈʃiːtmetl] [shiit-me-tal], s. Hoja metálica, metal laminado.

sheik [ʃeɪk] [sheik], s. Jeque, anciano o superior entre los árabes; jefe de familia o de tribu en los países mahometanos.

shekel [ˈʃekl] [she-kel], s. 1. Siclo, moneda usada entre los hebreos. 2. Peso usado entre los asirios y los babilonios. 3. pl. (Ger.) Dinero, pasta.

sheldrake [ˈʃeldreɪk] [shel-dreik], s. 1. Tadorna, ave acuática de Europa muy parecida al ánade. 2. Mergánsar. 3. V. CANVASBACK. Se escribe también *shelduck* y *skeldrake*.

shelf [ʃelf] [shelf], s. (pl. SHELVES). 1. Anaquel o estante de armario, de alacena o de vasares; entrepaño; tabla fija a la pared para sostener objetos. 2. Bajío, banco de arena. **To leave on the shelves**, (Fig.) arrinconar, dar carpetazo.

she'll [ʃiːl] [shil], **She will, she shall.**

shell [ʃel] [shel], s. 1. Casco, la parte exterior de cualquiera cosa cuando es dura y consistente. 2. Cáscara de nuez, de huevo, de avellana, etc. 3. Vaina, vainilla, la corteza de algunas legumbres. 4. Silicua, la corteza de las semillas de las plantas silicuosas. 5. Concha, la cubierta exterior de una animales testáceos o crustáceos. 6. La parte exterior de una cosa. 7. Corteza, la exterioridad de alguna cosa inmaterial (bark, skin). 8. (Art.) Bomba, proyectil hueco metálico, lleno de una substancia explosiva (bomb); también, cásula metálica para un arma de retrocarga. 9. (Poét.) La lira en su forma primitiva, una concha de tortuga con cuerdas. 10. (Mar.) Casco o caja de motón. **Shell-gold**, oro de concha u oro molido para dorar. **Shell-proof**, a prueba de bomba. **Shell-silver**, plata de concha. **Shell-work**, obra de concha.

shell, va. 1. Descascarar, descortezar, quitar las cáscaras, cortezas o vainas (nuts, fruits). 2. Encerrar en una cáscara, vaina o casco. 3. Bombardear, lanzar bombas. 4. (E. U.) Separar los granos de maíz de la mazorca. -vn. Descascararse; lavantarse la cubierta de una cosa en costras. **Shell out**, desembolsar, aflojar (money).

shellac [ʃəˈlæk] [sha-lak], s. Goma laca en hojuelas.

shellbark [ˈʃelbɑːk] [shel-bark], s. Caria; cada una de las dos especies, Carya alba o sulcata, o sus frutos.

sheller [ˈʃeləʳ] [she-laʳ], s. Descascarador.

shellfire [ˈʃelfaɪəʳ] [shel-faiaʳ], s. Cañoneo, fuego de metralla, bombardeo.

shell-fish [ˈʃelfɪʃ] [shel-fish], s. Marisco, animal acuático provisto de concha, v. g. un molusco o un crustáceo.

shelling [ˈʃelɪŋ] [she-lin], s. Bombardeo.

shell shock [ˈʃelʃɒk] [shel-shok], s. Condición psiconeurótica que sufren soldados expuestos a los peligros de la guerra moderna.

shelly [ˈʃelɪ] [she-li], a. Conchudo, cubierto de conchas.

shelter [ˈʃeltəʳ] [shel-taʳ], s. 1. Guarida, amparo, abrigo, abrigaño (asylum, refuge); todo lo que protege contra un peligro o contra la intemperie; casa, vivienda, hogar (house). 2. Protector, defensor (guardian). 3. Protección, asilo, refugio. **Under shelter**, al abrigo, al refugio.

shelter, va. 1. Guarecer, abrigar, poner al abrigo o a cubierto, dar casa o habitación. 2. Refugiar, acoger, amparar, proteger, defender (protect, harbor). 3. Encubrir, ocultar, tapar (hide, cover). -vn. Refugiarse, guarecerse, acogerse. **To seek shelter for the night**, buscar donde resguardarse durante la noche, buscar refugio para la noche.

shelterless [ˈʃeltəlɪs] [shel-ta-les], a. Desamparado, sin asilo, sin refugio; desabrigado.

shelve [ʃelv] [shelv], va. 1. Poner sobre un anaquel; (Fig.) poner a un lado, diferir indefinidamente, retirar. 2. Proveer de estantes o anaqueles.

shelve, vn. Inclinarse gradualmente, estar en pendiente.

shelves [ʃelvz] [shelvs], pl. de SHELF.

shelving [ˈʃelvɪŋ] [shel-vin], a. Inclinado, lo que está en declive o pendiente (pent). -s. 1. Conjunto de estantes o anaqueles; material para construir anaqueles. 2. Lugar inclinado, en declive; tonga, tongada.

shenanigans [ʃəˈnænɪɡənz] [sha-na-ni-gans], spl. Artimañas, bromas, trampas.

shepherd [ˈʃepəd] [she-pard], s. 1. Pastor, el que guarda y guía ovejas y carneros. 2. Zagal. 3. Pastor, párroco, cura, el que tiene cura de almas. **Shepherd-dog**, perro de pastor. V. COLLIE. **Shepherd's crook**, cayado de pastor. **Shepherd's**

purse o pouch, *(Bot.)* bolsa de pastor. **Shepherd's watch,** hierba pajarera, anagálida.

shepherdess ['ʃepədɪs] [she-par-des], *sf.* Pastora, zagala, doncella aldeana.

sherbet ['ʃɜːbɪt] [sher-bit], *s.* Sorbete, refresco hecho del zumo de alguna fruta, con azúcar, agua, esencia, etc., y al que se da cierto grado de congelación.

sherd ['ʃɜːd] [sherd], *s.* Tiesto, casco, pedazo quebrado de alguna vasija de barro.

sherif ['ʃerɪf] [she-rif], *s.* 1. Jerife, descendiente de Mahoma por su hija Fátima. 2. Magistrado principal de la Meca.

sheriff ['ʃerɪf] [she-rif], *s.* Jerife, el magistrado a quien está encargada la ejecución de las leyes en cada condado de Inglaterra o de los Estados Unidos.

sherry ['ʃerɪ] [she-ri], *s.* Vino de Jerez.

shield [ʃiːld] [shild], *s.* 1. Escudo, broquel, arma defensiva. 2. Escudo, amparo, patrocinio. 3. Protector, defensor. 4. *(Her.)* Escudo de armas, el espacio en que se representan los blasones de una familia. 5. Una parte que protege; todo lo que sirve para cubrir o proteger alguna cosa. **Shield-bearer,** escudero, el que lleva el escudo; también, falena (del género Aspidisca) cuya larva es nociva a los árboles frutales. **Shield-fern,** cualquier helecho del género Aspidium; aspidia.

shield, *va.* Escudar, amparar, resguardar, defender (protect, shelter).

shift [ʃɪft] [shift], *va.* 1. Cambiar, hacer mudar de lugar, sitio o puesto a una cosa (change); transportar, conducir, llevar un paraje a otro (transport, carry); trasladar de un paraje o de un tiempo a otro. 2. Cambiar por otra u otras cosas de la misma clase; vestirse o quitarse algo del cuerpo. -*vn.* 1. Cambiarse, mudarse de un paraje a otro. 2. Ingeniarse, darse maña, buscar arbitrios, discurrir trazas y modos para conseguir o ejecutar una cosa. 3. Tergiversar, usar de frases equívocas. 4. *(Des.)* Mudarse el vestido, la camisa, etc., ponerse otra ropa blanca. **To shift about,** cambiar completamente de dirección. **To shift for oneself,** mirar por sí mismo; ingeniarse o buscar recursos para salir por sí mismo de algún mal paso. **To shift off,** eludir la dificultad, salir o librarse de algún aprieto por medio de artificios; cuando se toma en buen sentido corresponde también a tomar un sesgo, un medio, un temperamento o un arbitrio en cualquier asunto, pero más generalmente es andar u obrar con ardides, con doblez o con segundas. **To shift a tackle,** *(Mar.)* enmendar un aparejo. **To get someone to shift,** hacer que alguien cambie de actitud. **To shift the helm,** cambiar el timón, poner el timón a la contra. **To shift a berth,** mudar fondo. **To shift the blame on,** echar la culpa a. **To shift the cargo,** volver a la estiva. **The ballast shifts,** el lastre se corre. **To shift about/around,** cambiar de trabajo o de sitio a menudo.

shift, *s.* 1. Cambio, el acto de cambiar de lugar, dirección o forma, o una cosa por otra (change). 2. Sustitución, la cosa sustituida por otra (replacement); recurso, expediente (expedients, means), el medio extraordinario para el logro de algún fin, y de aquí, artimaña, artificio, maña, astucia, subterfugio, fraude, evasión, excusa frívola y sólo por salir del paso. 3. Camisa de mujer. 4. Tanda de obreros; tarea, el tiempo que trabaja cada tanda de operarios (work). **To work in shifts,** trabajar por turnos. **To make shift to,** ingeniárselas, arreglarse para. **To make shift without,** pasarse sin. **To make a shift,** largarse, cambiar de sitio.

shiftable ['ʃɪftəbl] [shif-ta-bol], *a.* Mudable.

shifter ['ʃɪftər] [shif-tar], *s.* 1. El que traslada o cambia algo, v. g. la escena de un teatro. 2. Tramoyista, el que usa de ficciones y engaños; invencionero.

shifting ['ʃɪftɪŋ] [shif-tin], *a.* Movedizo.

shift-key ['ʃɪftkiː] [shift-ki], *a.* *(Inform.)* Tecla de mayúsculas.

shiftless ['ʃɪftlɪs] [shift-les], *a.* Falto de recursos, perezoso, ineficiente.

shifty ['ʃɪftɪ] [shif-ti], *a.* Engañoso, tramposo, sospechoso.

shilling ['ʃɪlɪŋ] [shi-lin], *s.* 1. Chelín, antigua moneda británica.

shilly-shally ['ʃɪlɪˌʃælɪ] [shi-li-sha-li], *vn., adv.* y *a.* Estar irresoluto, no saber qué hacer. Repetición de **shall I?** que se usa para expresar familiarmente duda o indecisión. *(Fam.)* Con que sí, y con que no.

shimmer ['ʃɪmər] [shi-mar], *vn.* Despedir luz o claridad trémula, lucir con intermitencias. -*s.* Luz incierta o trémula; débil resplandor.

shimmy ['ʃɪmɪ] [shi-mi], *s.* 1. Baile en que se mueven mucho las caderas y los hombros. 2. Vibración anormal, como la de las ruedas delanteras de un automóvil.

shin ['ʃɪn] [shin], *s.* Espinilla, la parte anterior de la canilla de la pierna. -*vi* **Shin up,** trepar.

shindy ['ʃɪndɪ] [shin-di], *s.* Alboroto, pendencia ruidos en la que se dan y reciben golpes.

shine [ʃaɪn] [shain], *vn.* 1. Lucir, relucir, brillar, resplandecer, relumbrar (lighten). 2. Relucir, sobresalir, resaltar alguna virtud (stand out, glitter). **The sun is shining,** hay sol. **To shine a light on,** proyectar una luz sobre. 3. Lucir, sobresalir, distinguirse una persona por sus prendas, ingenio, etc., sobresalir, exceder (excel). 4. Favorecer, ser propicio. -*va.* Pulir, bruñir, dar lustre (shoes).

shine, *s.* 1. Resplandor, lustre, brillo (light). 2. Buen tiempo, claridad (clearness). **Sunshine,** claridad del sol. 3. *(Ger. E. U.)* Inclinación, afecto, gusto.

shiner ['ʃaɪnər] [shai-na], *s.* 1. El que o lo que brilla o hace relucir. 2. *(Fam.)* Moneda lustrosa o de oro. 3. Pez plateado.

shingle ['ʃɪŋl] [shin-guel], *va.* 1. Cubrir con ripias o tajamaniles. 2. Cortar los cabellos por igual y muy cortos en toda la cabeza. 3. Batir el hierro, expeler las impurezas por medio de golpes o presión fuertes.

shingle, *s.* 1. Ripia, tablita delgada para cubrir las casas. *(Cuba)* Tejamaní. *(Mex.)* Tajamanil. 2. *(Fest. E. U.)* Muestra pequeña con el nombre de una persona, como para oficina, bujete, etc.

shingle, *s.* Cascajo, piedra redondeada y gastada por el agua, y mayor que el cascajo ordinario.

shingles ['ʃɪŋlz] [shin-guels], *s.* Herpes, enfermedad cutánea, sintomática de un desorden nervioso, que se presenta en forma de erupción vesicular o pustulosa.

shingly ['ʃɪŋlɪ] [shin-gli], *a.* Guijarroso, riscoso.

shininess ['ʃaɪnɪnɪs] [shai-ni-nes], *s.* Brillo (brightness).

shining ['ʃaɪnɪŋ] [shai-nin], *a.* Brillante, resplandeciente; luciente. -*s.* Lucimiento, esplendor, lustre; resplandor, brillo.

shinto, shintoism ['ʃɪntəʊ] [shin-tou] ['ʃɪntəʊɪzəm] [shin-tou-isem], *s.* Culto de los primitivos japoneses, especie de culto de los antepasados.

shiny ['ʃaɪnɪ] [shai-ni], *a.* Lustroso, brillante, resplandeciente, luciente.

ship [ʃɪp] [ship], *s.* Nave, bajel, navío, buque, embarcación de cubierta y con velas. **Ship of the line,** *(Mar.)* navío de alto bordo o de línea. **Ship of war,** navío, buque de guerra. **Merchant ship,** buque mercante. **Store-ship,** *(Mar.)* navío almacén. **To ballast a ship,** *(Mar.)* lastrar un buque. **Burden of a ship,** *(Mar.)* porte, capacidad de carga de un buque. **Ship-biscuit,** galleta. V. HARDTACK. **Ship-boy,** (a) paje de escoba. (b) Grumete. **Ship-builder,** constructor de buques, ingeniero naval. **Ship-chandler,** proveedor de buques (lona, jarcia, etc.). **Ship-chandlery,** caballería, tienda de artículos de marina; jarcia, etc. **Ship-fever,** tifus; así llamado porque era en otro tiempo común a bordo. **Ship-load,** cargamento, cargazón. **Ship-money,** antiguo derecho sobre buques.

ship, *va.* 1. Embarcar, poner a bordo. 2. Transportar por mar; y en el comercio, trasportar por ferrocarril o de cualquier otro modo. 3. Contratar y recibir a bordo la tripulación. 4. Recibir a bordo de cualquier embarcación, p. ej. una ola. 5. Armar, montar los mástiles, el timón, los remos. -*vn.* 1. Ir a bordo, embarcarse. 2. Alistarse como marinero. **To ship the oars,** armar los remos. **To ship off,** expedir. **To ship out,**

mandar, enviar.

shipboard [ˈʃɪpbɔːd] [ship-bord], *s. (Mar.)* Bordo; se usa solamente en las frases adverbiales **a-shipboard** u **on shipboard**, a bordo.

shipbreaker [ˈʃɪpˌbreɪkəʳ] [ship-brei-kaʳ], *s.* Desguazador.

shipmaster [ˈʃɪpˌmɑːstəʳ] [ship-mas-taʳ], *s. (Mar.)* Capitán de embarcación.

shipmate [ˈʃɪpmeɪt] [ship-meit], *s.* Camarada de a bordo.

shipment [ˈʃɪpmənt] [ship-ment], *s.* Embarque, envío, remesa, cargo, cargamento.

shipper [ˈʃɪpəʳ] [shi-paʳ], *s.* 1. Cargador, el que entrega a una compañía de transportes los objetos que desea expedir. 2. *(Com.)* Lo que se puede trasportar sin deterioro en la calidad, aroma o sabor.

shipping [ˈʃɪpɪŋ] [shi-pin], *s.* 1. Navíos o bajeles colectivamente. 2. Embarques, expedición de mercancías. - *a.* Naval, marítimo, relativo a embarques, relativo a expedición de mercancías. **Shipping clerk**, dependiente encargado de remisiones. **Shipping company**, compañía naviera. **Shipping documents**, documentos de embarque o de expedición. **Shipping lane**, ruta de navegación. **Shipping room**, departamento de embarque o de expedición de mercancías.

shipshape [ˈʃɪpʃeɪp] [ship-sheip], *a.* Bien orientado, en buen orden, bien arreglado, bien instalado, como a bordo de un buque.

shipworm [ˈʃɪpwɜːm] [ship-uem], *s.* Broma, especie de carcoma que se introduce en la madera de los buques y la destruye. Teredo.

shipwreck [ˈʃɪprek] [ship-rek], *s.* 1. Naufragio, pérdida o ruina de la embarcación en el mar. 2. Los restos de un naufragio. 3. Desastre, desgracia.

shipwreck, *va.* Causar naufragio; echar a pique alguna embarcación. **To be shipwrecked**, naufragar. **Shipwrecked**, naufragado, que se ha ido a pique.

shipwright [ˈʃɪpraɪt] [ship-rait], *s.* Carpintero de ribera; constructor de buques.

shipyard [ˈʃɪpjɑːd] [ship-yard], *s.* Astillero (de construcción naval).

shirk [ʃɜːk] [sherk], *s.* El que falta a su obligación o trabajo, que se emperaza.

shirk, *va. y vn.* 1. Evitar, esquivar, eludir la ejecución de algo, faltar, desatender la obligación o trabajo (avoid, evade). 2. *(Des.)* Trampear, defraudar.

shirker [ˈʃɜːkəʳ] [sher-kaʳ], *a.* Vago, gandul, holgazán.

shirr [ʃɜːʳ] [sheʳ], *va.* 1. Acordonar, fruncir en líneas paralelas. 2. Pasar huevos por crema o nata en vez de agua. -*s.* 1. Acordonamiento, pliegues que se hacen por medio de hilos de fruncir. 2. Hilo de caucho o goma, tejido en una tela para hacerla elástica.

shirred [ʃɜːd] [sherd], *pp. y a.* 1. Acordonado. 2. Provisto de hilos de goma elástica. 3. pasado por crema (eggs).

shirt [ʃɜːt] [shert], *s.* 1. Camisa, camiseta. 2. Revestimiento o forro interior de un horno de fundición. **Shirt-bosom, shirt-front**, pechera de camisa. **Shirt-sleeve**, manga de camisa. **In one' shirt-sleeves**, en mangas de camisa. **Shirt-waist**, corpiño de camisa, prenda de vestir que llega sólo a la cintura, llevada por las mujeres y los niños. **Keep your shirt on!**, ¡calma!, ¡con calma!

shirting [ˈʃɜːtɪŋ] [sher-tin], *s.* Tela para hacer camisas.

shirttail [ˈʃɜːteɪl] [sher-teil], *s.* Faldón.

shirtwaist [ˈʃɜːtweɪst] [shert-ueist], *s. (E.U.)* Blusa.

shit [ʃɪt] [shit], *s.* Caca, excremento. **Oh shit!, Shit!**, ¡mierda! **To beat the shit**, dar una paliza a alguien. **I don't give a shit!**, ¡me importa un comino, me importa un rábano!

shiver [ˈʃɪvəʳ] [shi-vaʳ], *s.* 1. Temblor, escalofrío (chill). 2. Cacho o pedazo pequeño de una cosa (piece). **To give a shiver**, estremecerse, sentir escalofríos. 3. Cachivache; trozo, pedazo, fragmento, casco; la parte o porción de cualquiera cosa que se rompe, revienta o salta en pedazos. 4. *(Mar.)* Roldana. V. SHEAVE.

shiver, *vn.* 1. Tiritar de frío, temblar de miedo. 2. Cascarse, hacerse pedazos, quebrantarse. -*va.* 1. Estrellar, romper alguna cosa de un golpe haciéndola pedazos, hacer astillas, añicos (break into pieces); vibrar, sacudir (shake). 2. Disponer una vela de modo que bata al viento en lugar de recibirlo de lleno.

shivering [ˈʃɪvərɪŋ] [shi-ve-rin], *s.* 1. Horripilación, escalofrío, temblor, estremecimiento. 2. Quebranto, desmembramiento.

shivery [ˈʃɪvərɪ] [shi-ve-ri], *a.* 1. Trémulo, parecido a un escalofrío. 2. Predispuesto a calofriarse. 3. Friolento, friolero. 4. Quebradizo.

shoal [ʃəʊl] [shoul], *s.* 1. Sitio en que el agua es poco profunda. 2. Bajío, banco de arena. **By shoals**, a cientos. 3. Concurrencia, multitud, muchedumbre; cardume, manjúa. V. SCHOOL. **Shoal of herrings**, cardume de arenques. -*a.* Poco profundo, bajo. **Shoal water**, agua poco profunda.

shoal, *va. y vn.* 1. Disminuir en profundidad. 2. Atroparse, juntarse en tropas; reunirse una gran muchedumbre.

shoalines [ˈʃəʊlɪnɪs] [shou-li-nes], *s.* Falta de profundidad, calidad de somero.

shock [ʃɒk] [shok], *s.* 1. Choque, encuentro violento, colisión, concusión, sacudimiento (impact, jolt); reencuentro, combate. 2. Agitación súbita del ánimo; emoción pasmosa. **To be in shock**, estar conmocionado. 3. *(Med.)* Agotamiento de las funciones corporales, v. g. a consecuencia de una lesión repentina. 4. Conmoción, sacudimiento del cuerpo producido por la electricidad. 5. Ofensa (offence); desazón. **A shock result**, resultado sorprendente. **Shock therapy**, terapia de choque. **To give someone a shock**, sobresaltar, asustar, conmocionar.

shock, *s.* 1. Hacina, el montón donde se juntan y ordenan los haces de trigo u otro grano. 2. Mechón de cabellos toscos y enredados. 3. Perro lanudo. **Shock-dog**, perro de lanas. -*a.* Afelpado, lanudo.

shock, *va. y vn.* 1. Sacudir, mover violentamente (shake). 2. Ofender, disgustar (offend). 3. Chocar, encontrarse con violencia una cosa con otra. 4. Chocar, provocar, enojar a otros. 5. Chocar, disgustar, enfadar; horrorizar, herir. 6. Hacinar, hacer hacinas de grano. **Shock absorber**, amortiguador.

shocking [ˈʃɒkɪŋ] [sho-kin], *a.* Espantoso, horrible, chocante, que disgusta, choca o hiere; ofensivo.

shockproof [ˈʃɒkpruːf] [shok-pruf], *a.* A prueba de choques.

shock troops [ˈʃɒktruːps] [shok-trups], *s. pl.* Tropas especialmente escogidas para la ofensiva en la guerra.

shock wave [ˈʃɒkweɪv] [shok-ueiv], *s.* Onda de choques.

shoddy [ˈʃɒdɪ] [sho-di], *a.* 1. Hecho de lana artificial o que la contiene. 2. Falso, no legítimo. -*s.* 1. Lana artificial, imitada. 2. Tela que contiene imitación de lana. 3. *(Fam.)* Ostentación vulgar, impostura.

shoe [ʃuː] [shu], *s.* 1. Zapato, el calzado del pie. 2. Algo que se asemeja a un zapato por su posición o su uso; p. ej. la herradura de las caballerías; suela de trineo, zapata de ancla; galga de carruaje; *(Mar.)* calzo, soler; contera de bastón o de la vaina de un arma blanca; canal para conducir el trigo o el mineral a la tolva, etc. **Shoe-black**, limpiabotas. **Horse-shoe**, herradura de caballo. **Shoe of a wheel**, llanta. **Wooden shoes**, zuecos, chanclos. **Shoe-blacking**, betún para zapatos. **Shoestring, shoe-lace, shoe-tie**, cordón o lazo de zapato. **To put on one's shoes**, calzarse. **To cast a shoe**, desherrarse un animal. **I would not stand in his shoes**, *(Coll.)* no quisiera halarme en su pellejo, o no le arriendo la ganancia.

shoe, *va. (pret.* SHOD, *pp.* SHOD o SHODDEN). Calzar; guarnecer la parte inferior de alguna cosa con otra más fuerte. **To shoe a horse**, herrar un caballo.

shoeblack [ˈʃuːblæk] [shu-blak], *s.* Limpiabotas.

shoebrush [ˈʃuːbrʌʃ] [shu-brash], *s.* Cepillo para zapatos.

shoehorn [ˈʃuːhɔːn] [shu-jorn], *s.* Calzador, utensilio para calzarse bien los zapatos.

shoeing [ˈʃuːɪŋ] [shuin], *s.* El acto de herrar.

shoemaker [ˈʃuːˌmeɪkəʳ] [shu-mei-kaʳ], *s.* Zapatero.

shoemaking [ˈʃuːˌmeɪkɪŋ] [shu-mei-kin], *s.* Zapatería, fabricación o comercio de calzado.

shoe polish [ˈʃuːˌpɒlɪʃ] [shu-po-lish], *s.* Betún o grasa para calzado.

shoer [ˈʃuːəʳ] [shuaʳ], *s.* Persona que calza; y particularmente herrador, el que hierra las caballerías.

shoe store [ˈʃuːstɔːʳ] [shu-stoʳ], *s.* Zapatería, tienda de calzado.

shoe tree [ˈʃuːtriː] [shu-tri], *s.* Horma para zapato.

shole [ˈʃəʊl] [shoul], *s. (Mar.)* Solera, trozo de tablón sobre el que se apoyan las escoras cuando el terreno es flojo.

shone [ʃɒn] [shon], *pret.* de TO SHINE.

shoo [ʃuː] [shu], *va. y vn.* Ahuyentar (las aves domésticas) gritando «shoo»; vocear o gritar «shoo.» *-inter.* ¡Fuera! se usa para ahuyentar las gallinas.

shook [ʃuː] [shu], *pret.* de TO SHAKE.

shoot [ʃuːt] [shut], *va. (pret. y pp.* SHOT). 1. Tirar, dar, herir o matar con arma de fuego; fusilar, pasar por las armas. 2. Arrojar, lanzar, disparar, despedir alguna cosa con impulso y violencia, tirar, como una saeta o dardo. 3. Tirar, descargar un arma de fuego. 4. Descargar, vaciar el contenido de algo. *(E.U.)* **Shoot no rubbish**, prohibido echar basura. 5. Empujar, hacer salir (push). 6. Traspasar, atravesar rápidamente, pasar por encima o por debajo de. 7. Volar, hacer saltar con pólvora. 8. Ajustar (line) cepillando. *-vn.* 1. Tirar, disparar las armas. 2. Lanzarse, correr rápidamente, v. g. un proyectil; caer una estrella. 3. Brotar, espigar, germinar; crecer (grow). 4. Latir, punzar, sentir algún dolor agudo y repentino (pain). 5. Sobresalir (stand out). **To shoot an arrow**, lanzar un flecha. **To shoot a bear**, matar un oso. **To shoot a deserter**, fusilar a un desertor. **To shoot a bolt**, echar, correr un cerrojo. **To shoot away**, salir disparado, como una bala. **To shoot by/past**, pasar como un rayo. **To shoot down**, abatir, derribar. **To shoot rapids**, pasar, salvar el recial de un río (rapid). **To shoot forth**, lanzarse o abalanzarse. **To shoot off**, tirar, descargar (gun); llevarse. **To shoot through**, atravesar, pasar de parte a parte.

shoot, *s.* 1. Vástago, pimpollo, el renuevo o ramo tierno del árbol o planta (sprout). 2. Recial, lugar angosto de un río, por el cual se precipita las aguas impetuosamente. 3. Artesa inclinada. *V.* CHUTE. 4. Tiroso, punzada.

shooting [ˈʃuːtɪŋ] [shu-tin], *s.* 1. *pl.* Disparos, tiros; tiroteo. 2. *sm.* Asesinato, crimen (murder). 3. Caza (hunting). **To go shooting**, ir de caza. **Within shooting range**, a tiro. **Shooting-gallery**, galería de tiro al blanco (game). **Shooting-party**, partida de caza.

shop [ʃɒp] [shop], *s.* 1. Tienda, paraje donde se venden géneros al por menor; en los Estados Unidos se llama comúnmente **store**, almacén. **Baker's shop**, panadería. 2. Taller u oficina donde se trabaja alguna manufactura. **Silversmith's shop**, platería. **Jeweller's shop**, joyería, platería. **Watch-maker's shop**, relojería. **To keep a shop**, poner un negocio. **To shut up shop**, cerrar la tienda, el almacén; desistir de una empresa. **To smell of the shop**, oler a tienda, sugerir demasiado la propia ocupación. **To talk shop**, hablar con exceso, sin necesidad o fuera de tiempo de la propia ocupación, oficio o negocios. **Shop-bill**, *(Ingl.)* lista de mercancías que se pone en el escaparate de una tienda. **Shop-boy, shop-girl**, mancebo, muchacha de almacén. **Shop steward**, enlace sindical. **Shop-walker, floor-walker**, vigilante (para impedir raterías en tienda o almacén).

shop, *vn. (Fam.)* Andar de tienda en tienda comprando. **To shop around**, comparar precios de unas tiendas con otras.

shopkeeper [ˈʃɒpˌkiːpəʳ] [shop-ki-paʳ], *s.* Tendero.

shoplifter [ˈʃɒpˌlɪftəʳ] [shop-lif-taʳ], *s.* El ladrón que ratea algo en una tienda.

shoplifting [ˈʃɒpˌlɪftɪŋ] [shop-lif-tin], *s.* Ratería hecha en una tienda durante las horas de venta.

shopping [ˈʃɒpɪŋ] [sho-pin], *s.* Compra. **Shopping center**, centro comercial. **To go shopping**, 1. Ir de compras. 2. Ir de tiendas.

shop window [ˈʃɒpˌwɪndəʊ] [shop-uin-dou], *s.* Vitrina, escaparate o vidriera de tienda.

shore [ʃɔːʳ] [shoʳ], *s.* 1. Costa, ribera, grao, playa (coast, beach); borde, orilla de un río o lago (bank). **To go on shore**, *(Mar.)* ir a tierra. 2. Puntal, costón; *(Mar.)* escora, botante; *(Min.)* entibo, ademe. **Shore of a pair of shears**, *(Mar.)* puntal diagonal de cabria. **A bold shore**, una costa escarpada. **Close inshore**, arrimado a la tierra.

shore, *va.* 1. Apuntalar, poner puntales. 2. *(Mar.)* Escorar. 3. Llevar a tierra, a la orilla. 4. Circundar, como lo hace una orilla o ribera.

shoreline [ˈʃɔːˌlaɪn] [shor-lain], *s.* 1. Costa o ribera. 2. Contorno de la playa.

shorn [ʃɔːn] [shorn], *pp.* de TO SHEAR.

short [ʃɔːt] [short], *a.* 1. Corto, de poca extensión; de escasa estatura; corto, de poca duración (brief). 2. Limitado, circunscrito (limited); breve, sucinto, conciso, compendiado (concise). 3. Brusco, seco, malhumorado, de áspero trato (rude). 4. Que no alcanza, inadecuado, deficiente (inadequated). 5. Próximo, cercano, que debe llegar u ocurrir en tiempo no lejano (next). 6. Corto de alcances (stupid). 7. Quebradizo, que se desmiga fácilmente (como una pasta). 8. *(Com.)* Algo que el vendedor no tiene en su posesión al vendérselo, pero que se obliga a entregarlo en época determinada. 9. Breve, que se pronuncia rápidamente; que no lleva acento. **To fall short of one's expectations**, no salir con lo que se esperaba. **Within a short time**, dentro de poco tiempo. **Short of money**, escaso de dinero. **The translation falls short of the original**, la traducción no llega o es inferior al original. **In short**, en suma, en resumen. **A very short while**, un ratito. **Short of this**, fuera de esto, además de esto, amén de esto. **In a short time**, luego, pronto. **To be short, to cut short o in short**, para abreviar. **To be short of**, estar lejos de; no responder a. **To be short of money**, andar escaso de dinero. **To come short of**, faltar, no alcanzar, no corresponder, estar lejos de. **To cut short**, cortar la palabra, interrumpir bruscamente; destruir, hacer cesar; abreviar. **To fall short**, estar corto; escasear, faltar. **To grow short**, hacerse corto, comenzar a ser corto. **To run short**, faltar. **To take short**, tomar o coger de improviso. **Short-handed**, que carece de un número suficiente de operarios, marineros, etc. **Short-bodied**, que tiene el cuerpo pequeño. **Short-breathed**, que respira con dificultad. **Short-nosed**, romo, chato, de nariz aplastada. **Short ribs**, costillas falsas. **Short-winded**, asmático, corto de respiración. **Short-waisted**, corto de talle.

short, *s.* 1. Sumario, resumen, compendio. 2. Sílaba o vocal breve. 3. *pl.* Salvado mezclado con harina gruesa. 4. *-pl.* En la fabricación de cuerdas, el cáñamo de calidad inferior. 5. *pl.* Calzón corto. **The short and the long of it**, en resumidas cuentas. *-adv.* Brevemente, breve.

shortage [ˈʃɔːtɪdʒ] [shor-tich], *s.* 1. Escasez, falta. 2. Desfalco, déficit.

shortcake [ˈʃɔːtkeɪk] [short-keik], *s.* Torta de frutas.

short-change [ˈʃɔːtˈtʃeɪndʒ] [short-cheinch], *va.* Defraudar al dar los cambios, engañar.

short circuit [ˈʃɔːtˈsɜːdɪt] [short-ser-kit], *s.* Corto circuito. *-va.* Causar un corto circuito.

shortcoming [ˈʃɔːtˈkʌmɪŋ] [short-ka-min], *s.* 1. Defecto, falta de completa ejecución (fault); negligencia del deber, omisión (negligence). 2. Falta de los productos usuales, de las cosechas acostumbradas.

shorten [ˈʃɔːtn] [shortn], *va.* 1. Acortar, recortar, hacer más corto. 2. Abreviar, compendiar, resumir. 3. Recortar, cercenar lo que sobra en alguna cosa. 4. Impedir, limitar, restringir. 5. Hacer quebradiza la pastelería. *-vn.* Acortarse, abreviarse, disminuirse.

shortening [ˈʃɔːtnɪŋ] [short-nin], *s.* 1. Acción de acortar, de abreviar. 2. Lo que hace quebradiza una cosa, v. gr. la manteca o mantequilla usada para hacer quebradizas las pastas, los hojaldres, etc.

shorthand [ˈʃɔːthænd] [short-jand], *s.* Taquigrafía, estenografía. **To take shorthand**, escribir en taquigrafía, taquigrafiar. **Shorthand typist**, taquimecanógrafa.

short-handed [ˈʃɔːthændɪd] [short-jan-did], *a.* Escaso de mano de obra, falto de trabajadores.

shorthorn [ˈʃɔːthɔːn] [short-jorn], *s.* Ganado vacuno de cuernos cortos.

short-lived [ˈʃɔːtlɪvd] [short-livd], *a.* Corto de vida; pasajero, que dura poco (brief).

shortly [ˈʃɔːtlɪ] [short-li], *adv.* 1. Presto, luego, al instante. 2. Brevemente, en pocas palabras.

short-necked [ˈʃɔːtˈnekɪd] [short-ne-kid], *a.* Cuellicorto, el que tiene el cuello o pescuezo corto.

shortness [ˈʃɔːtnɪs] [short-nes], *s.* 1. Cortedad; pequeñez. 2. Brevedad de palabras. 3. Flaqueza de memoria. 4. Defecto, imperfección. **Shortness of breath**, respiración dificultosa, asma.

shorts [ˈʃɔːtz] [shorts], *s. pl.* 1. Calzoncillos. 2. Calzones cortos de hombre o de mujer. **Bathing shorts**, calzones de baño.

short-sighted [ˈʃɔːtˈsaɪtɪd] [short-sai-tid], *a.* Cegato, el que es miope o corto de vista, y el que es rudo o de cortos alcances. **Short-sightedness**, (a) miopía, cortedad de vista. (b) Cortedad de alcances.

short-tempered [ˈʃɔːtˈtempəd] [short-tem-pard], *a.* De mal carácter.

short-term [ˈʃɔːttɜːm] [short-term], *a.* De período breve.

short wave [ˈʃɔːtweɪv] [short-ueiv], *s.* (*Radio*) Onda corta.

shorty [ˈʃɔːtɪ] [shor-ti], *s.* Persona baja, enano, tapón.

shot [ʃɒt] [shot], *s.* 1. Munición, postas o municiones (munitions); perdigones, la munición menuda que sirve para cargar las escopetas (pellets). 2. Bala, proyectil sólido (bullet). **Grape-shot**, metralla. **Shot between wind and water**, balazo a flor del agua. 3. Tiro, la acción de tirar o disparar; el acto de lanzar un arma arrojadiza, y particularmente el de descargar un arma de fuego. 4. Tiro, alcance, la distancia a que llega lo que se arroja o dispara. **Within pistol-shot**, a tiro de pistola. 5. Tirador, el que se ejercita en tirar. 6. Tirada, jugada, v. g. en el billar. 7. *V.* BLAST. 8. Escote, la parte a prorrata cabe a cada uno de los que se han divertido o comido en compañía. *V.* SCOT. **Bird shot, fowling shot**, munición menuda. **Buck shot, deer shot**, munición de balines, postas. **Cannon shot**, cañonazo. **A good shot**, un buen tirador. **Shot-tower**, torre para hacer municiones. **She was off like a shot**, se fue rápidamente, como una bala. **To be a poor shot**, ser mal tirador. **Not by a long shot**, (*Ger.*) ni por asomo, ni con mucho. *pret. and pp. of* SHOOT.

shotgun [ˈʃɒtgʌn] [shot-gan], *s.* Escopeta, arma de fuego ligera para cazar.

shot-put [ˈʃɒtpʊt] [shot-put], *s.* Lanzamiento de peso, en el deporte.

shotten [ˈʃɒtn] [sho-ten], *a.* (*Prov. o des.*) 1. Dislocado. 2. Desovado: se dice de los peces cuando han soltado sus huevos o huevas. 3. Cuajada (custard).

should [ʃʊd] [shud], *pret.* de SHALL. Indica un tiempo condicional y en general se usa en los mismos casos en que se emplea *shall* en el futuro de indicativo, aunque el uso de *should* no es tan fijo como el de *shall. Should*, se usa muy frecuentemente como verbo defectivo con la significación de deber o haber de. **I should go**, yo iría o yo debería ir. **If I should go**, si yo fuese. **You should go**, usted debería ir. **You should tell him**, deberías decírselo. **I should be very sorry**, yo lo sentiría mucho. **Why should I?**, ¿por qué yo?, ¿por qué lo voy a hacer? **Should I do that?**, ¿debería yo hacer eso? **Should** se encuentra también solo en la oración para evitar la repetición del verbo que se ha usado inmediatamente antes. **Should be**, expresión muy común que se usa casi siempre irónicamente para expresar que una persona o cosa no es lo que debería ser. **For fear he shoud fall**, por temor de que él se cayese. **I should have seen you earlier**, yo debería haberle visto a usted más temprano. **She**

should be there by now, ella debería haber llegado ya. **Should he not come in a day or two**, si no viniese dentro de uno o dos días.

shoulder [ˈʃəʊldə(r)] [shoul-da(r)], *s.* 1. (*Anat.*) Hombro, la parte alta de la espalda del ser humano de donde nacen los brazos. 2. Brazuelo; cuarto delantero, la parte más alta de las patas delanteras de los cuadrúpedos. 3. (*Fig.*) Lo que sostiene o apoya; sostén, soporte, parte saliente; contera de bastón, virola de cuchillo, rodete mecánico; (*Mec.*) espaldón de espiga; regatón de lanza, etc. **Shoulder bone o blade**, espaldilla, omoplato, escápula. **Shoulder of pork**, pernil. **To give one the cold shoulder**, recibir a uno con indiferencia o fríamente; no hacerle caso. **Shoulder-of-mutton sail**, vela triangular, guaira. **Shoulder to shoulder**, hombro a hombro, cooperando y apoyándose mutuamente, como una fila de soldados. **Shoulder-belt**, tahalí. **Shoulder-knot**, charretera mocha, capona. **Shoulder-strap**, (a) correón (de los silleteros, aguadores, etc.). (b) Charretera, divisa militar de oro, plata o seda que se asegura al hombro; dragona.

shoulder, *va.* 1. Empujar con insolencia. 2. Echar, cargar al hombro. **Shoulder arms**, (*Mil.*) armas al hombro. **Broad-shouldered**, ancho de espaldas.

shouldn't [ˈʃʊdnt] [shu-dent], **should not.**

shout [ʃaʊt] [shaut], *va.* 1. Vocear, exclamar. 2. Afectar voceando; repeler, animar con gritos. *-vn.* Exclamar, dar gritos y voces en señal de triunfo o para incitar o mover los ánimos; vitorear, dar vivas, aclamar. **There were shouts of applause**, hubo gran ovación, grandes aplausos. **To shout a protest**, protestar en voz alta. **To shout at**, silbar a alguno; reprobar con voces, gritos o silbidos lo que alguno hace o dice. **Shout down**, abuchear, hundir a gritos. **Shout out**, gritar, hablar en tono muy alto.

shout, *s.* Exclamación, aclamación, gritería. **Shout of applause**, viva.

shouter [ˈʃaʊtə(r)] [shau-ta(r)], *s.* Gritador, el que grita y exclama.

shouting [ˈʃaʊtɪŋ] [shau-tin], *s.* Vocerío, griterío; aclamación. *-a.* Que vocea, o mueve los ánimos dando gritos.

shove [ʃʌv] [shav], *va. y vn.* 1. Empujar, hacer fueza para mover o separar alguna cosa (push); impeler, llevar adelante. 2. Llevar un barco con sogas por encima del agua. 3. Moverse hacia adelante con velocidad. **To shove along o forward**, empujar o llevar hacia adelante; hacer avanzar o adelantarse. **To shove away**, rechazar, alejar. **To shove back**, hacer retroceder. **To shove off**, alejarse de, dejar. **To shove from**, empujar, rechazar a empujones. **To shove on**, poner, ponerse (disk, coat). **To shove out**, empujar hacia afuera, hacer salir.

shove, *s.* Empellón, empujón.

shovel [ˈʃʌvl] [sha-vel], *s.* Pala. **A shovel hat**, sombrero de canal. **Fire shovel**, badila.

shovel, *va.* Traspalar, mover o pasar con la pala alguna cosa de un lado a otro.

shovel-board [ˈʃʌvlbɔːd] [sha-vel-bord], *s.* Tabla para jugar al tejo; y el mismo tejo (juego).

shoveler [ˈʃʌvlə(r)] [sha-ve-la(r)], *s.* (*Orn.*) Espátula, pato cuchareta.

shovelful [ˈʃʌvlfʊl] [sha-vel-ful], *s.* Palada.

show [ʃəʊ] [shou], *va.* (*pret.* SHOWED, *pp.* SHOWN ó SHOWED). 1. Mostrar, exponer a la vista o en público, enseñar (reveal, teach); hacer ver. 2. Señalar, mostrar, descubrir, manifestar (say, point out). 3. Probar, demostrar (demonstrate). 4. Publicar, dar a conocer una cosa. 5. Enseñar, explicar (explain). 6. Conducir. *-vn.* Parecer, tener apariencia o señales de; dar señal. **To show forth**, exponer, mostrar; publicar, manifestar. **To be first shown**, estrenarse (film). **To show in o into**, introducir o meter a alguno en alguna parte. **Show her in**, hágale usted entrar. **To show off**, hacer ver, descubrir, hacer gala de; dejar ver. **To show (oneself) off**, darse importancia. **To show out**, acompañar a la puerta. **To show round**, mostrar, guiar. **To show up**, hacer subir; exponer, descubrir un fraude, descorrer un velo; presentarse a la hora o en el día señalados.

show, s. 1. Espectáculo público; exhibición o la cosa exhibida (exhibition); muestra, lo que está expuesto a la vista; títeres. 2. Ostentación, boato, prosopopeya, pompa. 3. Manifestación, lo que manifiesta; seña, indicación, promesa. 4. Apariencia con o sin realidad; pretexto, máscara, velo. 5. *(Fam. E.U.)* Oportunidad, lance, suerte. **To make show of anger,** aparentar enfado. **In open show,** públicamente. **To make a fine show,** hacer gran papel. **To make a show of riches,** hacer gala de sus riquezas. **Show-bill,** cartel, cartelón. Muestrario de tienda, caja de muestras. **Show biz, show bussiness,** el mundo del espectáculo. *(E.U.)* **Showboat,** barco-teatro. **Show-window,** ventana o escaparate de tienda. **Cattle-show,** exposición de ganado. **A vote by show of hands,** votación que se efectúa alzando las manos. **With a show of friendship,** con apariencia de amistad; bajo pretexto de amistad.

showcase [ˈʃəʊkeɪs] [shou-keis], s. Muestrario, vitrina, mostrador, escaparate.

shower [ˈʃaʊəʳ] [shauaʳ], s. 1. Lluvia, nubada de corta duración, aguacero. **A heavy shower,** chaparrón, turbión. 2. Lluvia, abundancia. 3. Ducha. **Shower-bath,** baño de ducha, chorro de agua que se aplica al cuerpo humano.

shower, s. Mostrador, el que muestra.

shower, va. 1. Mojar o anegar con lluvia. 2. Derramar (pour). 3. Distribuir con liberalidad. -vn. 1. Llover, caer agua de las nubes (rain). 2. Llover, venir o caer sobre uno alguna cosa con abundancia.

showeriness [ˈʃaʊərɪnɪs] [shaua-ri-nes], s. Tiempo lluvioso.

showerless [ˈʃaʊəlɪs] [shaua-les], a. Sin lluvia, que no tiene nubadas.

showery [ˈʃaʊərɪ] [shaua-ri], a. Lluvioso, abundante en aguaceros.

showily [ˈʃəʊɪlɪ] [shoui-li], adv. Vistosamente, ostentosamente, magníficamente.

showiness [ˈʃəʊɪnɪs] [shoui-nes], s. Ostentación, vista, esplendor, magnificencia.

showman [ˈʃəʊmən] [shou-man], s. 1. Hábil empresario de espectáculos. 2. Dueño o director de algún circo u otro espectáculo.

showmanship [ˈʃəʊmənʃɪp] [shou-man-ship], s. Habilidad para la presentación de espectáculos teatrales.

shown, pp. de TO SHOW.

showroom [ˈʃəʊrʊm] [shou-rum], s. Sala de exhibiciones.

showy [ˈʃəʊɪ] [shoui], a. Ostentoso, magnífico, suntuoso, vistoso (lively, attractive).

shrank [ʃræŋk] [shrank], pret. de TO SHRINK.

shrapnel [ˈʃræpnl] [shrap-nel], s. Granada de metralla, bomba llena de balas y con carga de pólvora.

shred [ʃred] [shred], va. Picar, hacer pedazos muy pequeños alguna cosa, desmenuzar.

shred, s. 1. Cacho, tira, pedazo, pequeño (bit, piece); retazo, harapo. 2. Fragmento, partícula (fragment); punto, átomo, nada, jota, tilde. **There isn't a shred of truth in it,** eso no tiene nada de verdad. **In shreds,** hecho jirones, destrozado.

shredder [ˈʃredəʳ] [shre-daʳ], s. Picadora, trituradora.

shrew [ʃruː] [shru], s. 1. Sierpe, víbora, mujer de mal genio, maligna y turbulenta. 2. *(Zool.)* Musgaño, musaraña, mamífero carnicero muy pequeño.

shrewd [ʃruːd] [shrud], a. 1. Astuto, perspicaz, de vivo ingenio, sagaz, sutil (clever, sagacious). 2. *(Ant.)* Artificioso, solapado. 3. *(Ant.)* Agudo, cortante. 4. *(Des.)* Enfadoso, enojoso; maligno. **A man of shrewd discernment,** un hombre de sutil dicernimiento. **This is a shrewd thing to do,** hacer eso es lo más prudente. **A shrewd question,** una pregunta astuta.

shrewdly [ˈʃruːdlɪ] [shrud-li], adv. 1. Astutamente, con astucia, sagazmente, sutilmente. 2. *(Ant.)* Con artificio, con cautela, solapadamente.

shrewdness [ˈʃruːdnɪs] [shrud-nes], s. 1. Sagacidad, travesura, astucia, sutileza de genio. 2. *(Ant.)* Malignidad, maldad; agudeza, mordacidad.

shrewish [ˈʃruːɪʃ] [shruish], a. Regañón, regañador, quimerista, pendenciero; diabólico.

shrewishness [ˈʃruːɪʃnɪs] [shruish-nes], s. Pervesidad, maldad; travesura; mal genio.

shrewmouse [ˈʃruːmaʊs] [shru-maus], s. Musgaño, musaraña.

shriek [ʃriːk] [shrik], vn. Chillar, dar chillidos (squeak); gritar, dar gritos. **To shriek abuse at someone,** insultar, lanzar improperios a alguien. **This color shrieks at one,** es un color chillón.

shriek, s. Chillido; grito de espanto o dolor. **To utter a shriek,** dar un chillido.

shrieking [ˈʃriːkɪŋ] [shri-kin], a. 1. Chillón, gritón (color, person). 2. Chillidos, gritos.

shrill [ʃrɪl] [shril], a. Agudo, penetrante, sutil: se aplica al sonido.

shrill, va. y vn. Chillar, producir un sonido agudo, sutil y penetrante.

shrillness [ˈʃrɪlnɪs] [shril-nes], s. La aspereza del sonido y de la voz.

shrilly [ˈʃrɪlɪ] [shri-li], adv. Ásperamente, agudamente, con un ruido penetrante.

shrimp [ʃrɪmp] [shrimp], s. 1. Camarón, crustáceo marino comestible. 2. Enano, hombre pequeño, de muy poca estatura. **To go shrimping,** pescar camarones.

shrine [ʃraɪn] [shrain], s. 1. Relicario, caja o urna para guardar reliquias. 2. Altar, o sepulcro de santo; capilla; paraje o cosa consagrados por razones históricas, religiosas, u otras. -va. V. ENSHRINE.

shrink [ʃrɪŋk] [shrink], va. *(pret.* SHRANK, *pp.* SHRUNK, SHRUNKEN, y antiguamente SHRINKED). 1. Encogerse, contraerse alguna cosa ocupando menos lugar, estrecharse (contract), angostarse, acortarse (shorten); disminuir. 2. Evitar un peligro o huir y apartarse de él; retroceder; temblar, estremecerse (shake, tremble); retirarse. 3. Encogerse, apocarse el ánimo (sadden). -va. Encoger, contraer. **To shrink from danger,** retirarse del peligro. **To shrink for fear,** temblar de miedo. **To shrink in the wash,** encogerse al lavar (clothes). **To shrink back,** retirarse a la vista de algún peligro o de alguna cosa desagradable; detenerse en la ejecución de alguna cosa por temor a las consecuencias. **To shrink away,** acortarse, angostarse, desaparecer por grados; sustraerse, huir. **To shrink up,** estrechar, estrecharse; encogerse, arrugarse por efecto de la sequedad; temblar, estremecerse. **To shrink on,** asegurar firmemente en su lugar, v. g. la llanta de una rueda. **Shrink-wrap,** envasar al vacío.

shrink, s. 1. Encogimiento, acortamiento, contracción de nervios causada por miedo u horror. 2. *(E.U.)* Psiquiatra.

shrinkage [ˈʃrɪŋkɪdʒ] [shrin-kich], s. Merma, disminución de volumen de los metales, de la madera u otras materias (contraction); el peso o volumen perdidos a consecuencia de esa disminución.

shrinkingly [ˈʃrɪŋkɪŋlɪ] [shrin-kin-li], adv. Encogiéndose, retrocediendo, con vacilación.

shrivel [ˈʃrɪvl] [shri-vel], vn. Arrugarse, encogerse; acorcharse las frutas; encarrujarse, ensortijarse (hilo, pelo, hojas, etc.); a menudo con la prep. *up.* -va. 1. Arrugar, doblar, encoger (wrinkle). 2. Estrechar; disminuir el alcance, vigor o actividad de algo (narrow).

shriven [ˈʃrɪvn] [shri-ven], pp. de TO SHRIVE.

shroud [ʃraʊd] [shraud], s. 1. Mortaja, la vestidura que ponen, o la sábana en que envuelven al cadáver para sepultarlo. 2. Cubierta, carpeta, vestidura.

shroud, va. 1. Amortajar, poner la mortaja a un difunto. 2. Cubrir, ocultar, guarecer, abrigar. -vn. Guarecerse, refugiarse, encogerse.

shrouds [ʃraʊdz] [shauds], s. pl. *(Mar.)* Obenques, cabos gruesos. **Bowsprit-shrouds,** mostachos del bauprés. **Main-shrouds,** obenques mayores. **Preventer-shrouds,** obenques volantes. **Main-top-gallant-shrouds,** obenquitos del juanete mayor. **Bumkin-shrouds,** pie de serviola. **Futtock-shrouds,** arraigadas.

shrove [ʃrəʊv] [shrouv], s. V. SHRIFT; se usa solamente en voces compuestas. v. g.

shrovetide [ˈʃrəʊvtaɪd] [shrouv-taid], **shrove Tuesday** [ˈʃrəʊvˈtjuːsdeɪ] [shouv-tius-dei], s. Martes de carestolendas o de carnaval, el día que precede al miércoles de ceniza.

shrub [ʃrʌp] [shrab], s. 1. (Bot.) Arbusto; mata. 2. Especie de bebida que se hace de aguardiente de caña, limón y azúcar.

shrubbery [ˈʃrʌbərɪ] [shra-be-ri], s. Plantío de arbustos o arbolitos; repajo, matorral, maleza.

shrubby [ˈʃrʌb] [shra-bi], a. Parecido a un arbusto; lleno de arbustos. **Shrubby place**, maleza, matorral.

shrug [ʃrʌg] [shrag], vn. Encogerse (shoulders). -va. Encoger, contraer.

shrug, s. Encogimiento de hombros.

shrunk [ʃrʌŋk] [shrank], pret. y pp. de TO SHRINK.

shrunken [ʃrʌŋkən] [shran-ken], pp. de TO SHRINK.

shuck [ʃʌk] [shak], va. Descascarar, descortezar (peal); en los Estados Unidos, quitar el hollejo al maíz, o la concha a una ostra. -s. (Prov.) 1. Cáscara, vaina, hollejo. 2. (E.U.) Concha de ostra o almeja.

shudder [ˈʃʌdəʳ] [sha-daʳ], vn. Estremecerse, temblar de miedo o de horror.

shuddering [ˈʃʌdərɪŋ] [sha-de-rin], s. Temblor, estremecimiento producido por horror o miedo (chill, fright).

shuffle [ˈʃʌfl] [sha-fel], va. y vn. 1. Barajar, mezclar y revolver unas personas o cosas con otras; empujar, hacer pasar de un lado a otro. 2. Barajar los naipes o mezclarlos entre sí antes de repartirlos. 3. Poner en confusión, desordenar. 4. Reunir o echar muchas cosas juntas, con fraude o prisa; poner a un lado descuidadamente; se usa con las preposiciones up, out, off, in, etc. 5. Eludir o evitar una dificultad saliendo de ella con algún artificio. 6. Trampear, entrampar, usar de algún artificio o fraude. 7. Tergiversar, ir buscando efugios con rodeos o trampas (distort). 8. Hacer esfuerzos, proceder con dificultad (effort). 9. Arrastrar los pies, andar de un modo irregular; taconear al bailar.

shuffle aside, apartar, relegar a alguien de su puesto.

shuffle along, arrastrar los pies; hacer esfuerzos para salir de un mal paso.

shuffle into, introducir a alguien con artificio o cautela.

shuffle off, evadirse, huir de una dificultad; hacer esfuerzos por salir de un mal paso; echar fuera, despedir.

shuffle up, formar algo tumultuosa o fraudulentamente. Hacer las cosas a la carrera.

shuffle, s. 1. Barajadura, el acto de barajar o confundir el orden de las cosas (mixture). 2. Treta, fraude, artificio, evasión, efugio fraudulento para salir de una dificultad (fraudulence). 3. Mezcla, confusión, desorden; movimiento desordenado. **To walk in a shuffle**, caminar arrastrando los pies. **Shuffleboard**, V. SHOVEL-BOARD.

shuffler [ˈʃʌfləʳ] [sha-flaʳ], s. Tramoyista, el que usa de ficciones y engaños; petardista, enredador, embrollón, chismoso, maula.

shuffling [ˈʃʌflɪŋ] [sha-flin], s. 1. Confusión, desorden. 2. Tramoya, enredo, chisme, embrollo. 3. Tropezón, tropiezo.

shun [ʃʌn] [shan], va. y vn. Huir, evitar, rehuir, rechazar; escaparse, recatarse de (evade).

shunt [ʃʌnt] [shant], va. 1. Desviar (train): apartar un tren, hacerlo pasar a otra vía. V. SWITCH. 2. Establecer una vía adicional para la corriente eléctrica; distribuir por medio de conductores. 3. Evadir, eludir; echar el cascabel a uno. **To shunt someone to and fro**, zarandear, mandar a alguien de aquí para allá. **They shunted him from one window to another**, le mandaban de una ventanilla a otra. -vn. Desviarse, usar de una cambiavía (railway); de aquí, mudar de curso o de opinión.

shush [ʃʌʃ] [shash], vt. Hacer callar, acallar. **Shush!**, ¡silencio!, ¡chitón!

shut [ʃʌt] [shat], va. (pret. y pp. SHUT). 1. Cerrar, encerrar (enclose). 2. Cerrar, prohibir, impedir (prohibit); se usa con las preposiciones against o to. 3. Cerrar, negar a uno la entrada. 4. Concluir o acabar alguna cosa (finish). 5. Encoger (shrink). 6. Cerrar, ajustar. -vn. Cerrarse, apretarse, estrecharse o apiñarse. **They shut at 7h**, cierran a las 7. **To shut against**, cerrar a. **To shut from**, excluir de, ocultar a. **To shut off**, impedir la entrada (al vapor, etc.), impedir la

entrada (al vapor, etc.), impedir que algo fluya, interceptar. **To shut out**, impedir que uno entre cerrándole la puerta; evitar que el ánimo se ocupe en una cosa. **To shut out rain**, impedir que entre la lluvia. **To shut close**, cerrarse bien. **To shut down on**. (Fam.) hacer cesar, suprimir, reprimir. **To shut up**, cerrar completamente; callarse, dejar de hablar; concluir, acabar, terminar; tapar; condenar (una puerta, ventana, etc.); aprisionar. **To shut up shop**, V. SHOP.

shut, s. Cerradura; postigo (lock). -a. 1. Cerrado. 2. Sordo, cerrado; se dice de ciertas consonantes como t, p, k, b. 4. (Prov.) Libre, exento. **Are you shut of him?**, ¿se descartó Ud. de él?

shut-down [ˈʃʌtdaʊn] [shat-daun], s. Cesación de trabajo (factory, enterprise, etc.)

shut-in [ˈʃʌtɪn] [shat-in], s. Inválido recluído en un hospital o en su casa.

shut-out [ˈʃʌtaʊt] [shat-aut], s. 1. Encerramiento para impedir la entrada. 2. En los deportes, triunfo en que el lado contrario no logra ningún punto.

shutter [ˈʃʌtəʳ] [sha-taʳ], s. 1. Cerrador, el que cierra. 2. Cerradura, todo lo que cierra; obturador de una cámara fotográfica. 3. Contraventana, postigo de ventana.

shuttle [ˈʃʌtl] [sha-tel], s. Lanzadera, un instrumento de los tejedores.

shuttlecock [ˈʃʌtlkɒk] [sha-tel-kok], s. Volante, rehilete.

shy [ʃaɪ] [shai], a. 1. Tímido, miedoso, fácil de asustar (bashful, timid). 2. Reservado, cauteloso, esquivo, vergonzoso, contenido (shameful). 3. Prudente, circunspecto, precavido (prudent, wise). 4. Evasivo, que huye o escapa. 5. Huraño, intratable (elusive). (E.U.) **She's 25 dollars shy**, ha perdido 25 dólares, le faltan 25 dólares.

shy, va. 1. Hacer desviar; se usa con off o away. 2. Echar con un movimiento lateral. -vn. Desviarse repentinamente, como con espanto; se dice de un caballo. -s. V. FLING. **To shy away**, alejarse asustado, escapar de miedo.

shyly [ˈʃaɪlɪ] [shai-li], adv. Con esquivez, reserva o cautela; tímidamente, con sospecha; con circunspección.

shyness [ˈʃaɪnɪs] [shai-nes], s. Reserva, timidez, vergüenza (shame).

shyster [ˈʃaɪstəʳ] [shais-taʳ], s. (Fam. E.U.) Abogado de mala reputación, trapisondista.

si [sɪ] [si], s. Si, séptima nota de la escala música.

Siam [saɪˈæm] [saiam], sm. Siam.

Siamese [saɪəˈmiːz] [saia-mis], a. Siamés, perteneciente o relativo al reino de Siam. -s. Siamés, el natural o habitante de Siam.

Siberian [saɪˈbɪərɪən] [sai-be-rian], a. Siberiano, de Siberia.

sibilant [ˈsɪbɪlənt] [si-bi-lant], a. Sibilante.

sibilation [sɪbɪˈleɪʃən] [si-bi-lei-shon], s. Silbido.

siby [ˈsɪbɪ] [si-bi], s. Sibila, profetisa, adivina.

Sicilian [sɪˈsɪlɪən] [si-si-lian], a. y s. Siciliano, de Sicilia.

Sicily [ˈsɪsɪlɪ] [si-si-li], s. Sicilia.

sic [sɪk] [sik], adv. **She said sic**, cito palabras textuales.

sick [sɪk] [sik], a. 1. Malo, enfermo, doliente (ill). 2. Ahitado, ahito con náusea. 3. Disgustado, fatidiado. 4. Corrompido. **I am sick of him**, estoy harto de él o me tiene muy disgustado o cansado. **The sick**, los enfermos. **Sick to death**, enfermo de peligro, de muerte. **To be sick at the stomach**, tener náuseas. **To be sick at heart**, llevar la muerte en el alma. **Sick-bed**, lecho de enfermo. **He gets sick in trains**, se marea en los trenes. **To be sick at heart**, estar muy deprimido.

sick, va. Buscar; en imperativo para incitar un perro a morder o atacar; de aquí, animar, excitar al ataque. **Sick up**, arrojar, devolver.

sicken [ˈsɪkn] [si-ken], va. 1. Enfermar, causar enfermedad, poner enfermo; dar asco, dar ganas de vomitar. 2. Debilitar, extenuar (weaken). -vn. 1. Enfermar, caer enfermo (to fall ill). 2. Hartarse, fastidiarse, cansarse (to get weary). 3. Tener hastío o asco de alguna cosa. **To sicken at**, sentir náuseas de. 4. Debilitarse, extenuarse. **Our heart sickens at the sight of him**, nuestro corazón se despedaza o desgarra a su vista.

sickening [ˈsɪknɪŋ] [sik-nin], a. Nauseabundo, asqueroso, repugnante.

sickish ['sɪkɪʃ] [si-kish], *a.* 1. Enfermizo, algo malo. 2. Nauseabundo, que da asco.

sickishly ['sɪkɪʃlɪ] [si-kish-li], *adv.* De un modo nuaseabundo, asquerosamente.

sickle ['sɪkl] [si-kel], *s.* Hoz, segadera, instrumento para segar las mieses y hierbas. **Sickle cell**, célula falciforme.

sickliness ['sɪklɪnɪs] [si-kli-nes], *s.* Achaque, indisposición habitual; estado enfermizo; insalubridad.

sickly ['sɪklɪ] [si-kli], *a.* 1. Enfermizo, achacoso, malsano, valetudinario. 2. Lánguido, endeble, débil (weak).

sickness ['sɪknɪs] [sik-nes], *s.* 1. Enfermedad, indisposición, mal, falta de salud (illness, pain). 2. Basca, náusea. **Falling sickness**, epilepsia. **Sickness rate**, morbilidad.

side [saɪd] [said], *s.* 1. (*Anat.*) Lado, costado, cada una de las partes del cuerpo del animal desde el nacimiento del brazo hasta el hueso de la cadera. 2. Lado, lo que está a la derecha o a la izquierda de un todo. 3. Orilla, margen; falda, ladera. 4. Lado, facción, partido, bando, parte. 5. Lado, cara, una de dos o más superficies o partes contrapuestas. 6. Lazo de parentesco. 7. (*Mar.*) Bordo, costado, banda. **Starboard side**, (*Mar.*) banda de estribor. **Side of the waist**, (*Mar.*) amurada del combés. **Lee-side**, (*Mar.*) costado de sotavento. **Weather-side**, (*Mar.*) costado de barlovento. **Right o wrong side of a stuff**, la cara o revés de una tela. **He is of my side**, está por mí, es de mi partido o sigue mi opinión. **This and the other side**, por acá y por allá. **The right or left side**, el lado derecho o izquierdo. **By the side of**, al lado de, por el lado de. **On this side**, a, de, o por este lado. **On that side**, de o por aquel lado. **On the other side**, del o al otro lado; más allá; a la otra parte. **To be on the safe side**, por precaución, para mayor seguridad. **On all sides**, por todas partes. **Relations by the mother's side**, parientes por parte de madre. **Side-arms**, armas blancas. *-a.* Lateral, de lado; oblicuo. **Side-wheel**, *a.* Que tiene ruedas a los costados (vapor). *-s.* Rueda lateral; una de las dos ruedas de paleta de un vapor.

side, *va. y vn.* 1. Tomar parte por alguno o declararse por él. 2. Declararse por un partido, facción o bando. 3. Unirse con alguno. 4. Igualar. **To side with one**, ser del mismo partido u opinión. **To side against**, ir en contra, tomar el partido contrario.

sideboard ['saɪdbɔːd] [said-bord], *s.* 1. Aparador. 2. Adral (truck).

sideburns ['saɪdbɜːns] [said-berns], *s. pl.* Patillas.

side dish ['saɪd] [said], *s.* Entremés, platillo.

sideface ['saɪdfeɪs] [said-feis], *s.* Cabeza de perfil.

sidekick ['saɪdkɪk] [said-kik], *s.* Compinche, compañero (work).

side light ['saɪdlaɪt] [said-lait], *s.* 1. Luz lateral. 2. Información que se obtiene incidentalmente.

side line ['saɪdlaɪn] [said-lain], *s.* Negocio u ocupación accesorios.

sidelong ['saɪdlɒŋ] [said-lon], *a.* Lateral, de lado. *-adv.* Lateralmente, de lado.

sideral, *a.* V. SIDEREAL.

sidereal [saɪ'dɪːrɪəl] [sai-di-rial], *a.* Sidéreo, perteneciente a las estrellas.

sidesaddle ['saɪdˌsædl] [said-sadl], *s.* La silla que usaban las mujeres para montar a caballo.

sideshow ['saɪdʃəʊ] [said-shou], *s.* 1. Diversión secundaria (en un circo, etc.). 2. Carreta, feria.

sidestep ['saɪdstep] [said-step], *va.* 1. Hacerse a un lado. 2. Evadir (situation, problem)

sidestreet ['saɪdstriːt] [said-strit], *sf.* Calle secundaria.

sideswipe ['saɪdzwaɪp] [saids-uaip], *va.* (*Fam.*) Rozar oblicuamente a manera de golpe.

side-taking ['saɪdˈteɪkɪŋ] [said-tei-kin], *s.* El empeño que se toma por una facción o partido.

side-track ['saɪdtræk] [said-trak], *va.* (*E.U.*) Desviar, apartar un carro o vagón de ferrocarril, para desembarazar la vía principal; (*Fig.*) desviar, alejar de la dirección o del asunto principal; reducir a la inacción. *-vn.* Ir sobre un apartadero. *-a.* Apartadero, desviadero. V. SIDING, 1ª acep.

sidewalk ['saɪdˌwɔːk] [said-uok], *s.* Acera. (*Mex.*) Banqueta.

sideways ['saɪdˌweɪz] [said-ueis], **sidewise** ['saɪdwaɪz] [said-uais], *adv.* De lado, oblicuamente, al través.

siding ['saɪdɪŋ] [sai-din], *s.* 1. Apartadero, desviadero (railway), ramal inmediato a la vía principal, por el que se desvían los coches de un tren. 2. Costaneras, el entablado de los costados. 3. La acción de empeñarse en un partido o facción.

sidle ['saɪdl] [sai-del], *va.* 1. Ir de lado por algún paso estrecho. 2. Estar echado de lado. **To sidle up**, acercarse sigilosamente.

siege [siːdʒ] [sidch], *s.* Sitio, asedio, cerco. **To lay siege to a fortress**, poner sitio a una fortaleza.

sierra [sɪ'erə] [sie-ra], *s.* Sierra, cadena de montañas.

siesta [sɪ'estə] [sies-ta], *sf.* **To have a siesta**, dormir la siesta.

sieve [sɪv] [siv], *s.* 1. Cedazo, tamiz; zaranda, criba, cribo. 2. Persona gárrula que repite cuanto se le dice. 3. Canasto que contiene dos tercios de fanega. **Sievemaker**, cedacero, fabricante de tamices.

sift [sɪft] [sift], *va.* 1. Cerner, separar con el cedazo la harina del salvado; pasar o cerner por tamiz; cribar, zarandear, pasar por la criba o la zaranda. 2. Examinar, escudriñar (scan). 3. Dividir, separar una cosa de otra (divide). *-vn.* Caer o pasar al través de un tamiz o cedazo. **To sift out**, inquirir, investigar. **To sift a question to the bottom**, examinar una cuestión a fondo.

sifter ['sɪftər] [sif-tar], *s.* Cernedor, persona o cosa que cierne; escudriñador; cedazo, zaranda, criba.

sigh [saɪ] [sai], *vn.* 1. Suspirar, dar suspiros; lamentar, llorar. 2. Suspirar, desear ardientemente, anhelar; a menudo con la prep. *for.* *-va.* (*Poét.*) Decir suspirando; lamentar; algunas veces con la prep. *out.* **To sigh away**, consumir (el tiempo) en suspiros.

sigh, *s.* Suspiro, susurro.

sighing ['saɪɪŋ] [saiin], *a.* Susurro, suspiros.

sighingly ['saɪɪŋlɪ] [sain-li], *adv.* Suspirando, con suspiros.

sight [saɪt] [sait], *s.* 1. Vista, la facultad o potencia de ver (faculty of seeing). 2. Vista, el objeto de la visión. 3. Vista, los ojos o cada uno de ellos separadamente (eyes). 4. Vista, la acción y efecto de ver, y el modo con que se mira; alcance de la visión, y de lo que con ella se descubre. 5. Conocimiento claro de alguna cosa (knowing); oportunidad para investigar o estudiar; opinión, parecer (opinion). 6. Espectáculo, objeto que causa admiración u horror. 7. Visera de morrión. 8. Mira o punto del cañón de escopeta (gun). 9. Puntería, acto de apuntar con un arma de fuego (aiming); observación hecha con un instrumento. 10. Agujero, abertura para mirar. **At sight**, a primera vista, a libro abierto. **At first sight**, a primera vista. (*Com.*) A la vista. **To come in sight**, asomarse, empezar a aparecer. **To pay at sight**, pagar a la vista. **Ten days after sight**, a diez días vista. **To translate at sight**, traducir oralmente. **To know someone by sight**, conocer a alguien de vista. (*E.U.*) **Out of sight**, fantástico, maravilloso, fabuloso. **To get a sight of**, lograr ver. **Sights**, monumentos, curiosidades, cosas de interés.

sight, *va.* 1. Avistar, alcanzar con la vista (see); ver con un instrumento. 2. Poner miras a un arma. 3. Apuntar a un blanco (aim).

sighted ['saɪtɪd] [sai-tid], *a.* Que tiene vista; se emplea en composición. V. **Far-sighted, short-sighted, sharp-sighted.**

sighting ['saɪtɪŋ] [sai-tin], *sf.* Observación.

sightless ['saɪtlɪs] [sait-les], *a.* 1. Ciego, falto de vista (blind). 2. Que está fuera de vista.

sightly ['saɪtlɪ] [sait-li], *a.* Vistoso, hermoso, deleitable o agradable a la vista.

sightseeing ['saɪtˌsiːɪŋ] [sait-siin], *s.* Acto de visitar objetos o puntos de interés.

sightseer ['saɪtˌsɪər] [sait-siar], *s.* Persona que visita puntos u objetos de interés, turista.

sign [saɪn] [sain], *s.* 1. Signo, señal, nota, indicio (note, mark). 2. Portento, milagro. 3. Tablilla, muestra o señal que se pone encima de alguna puerta para dar a entender un lugar de negocio o de recreo. 4. Signo, constelación del zodíaco. 5. Firma, rúbrica. **Signed and sealed**, firmado y sellado. 6. Seña, la señal con que se da a entender una cosa sin hablar.

7. Señal, huella, vestigio (trace, signal). **To make the sign of the cross**, hacer la señal de la cruz. **Sign manual**, firma o rúbrica de una persona. **Signboard**, muestra de establecimiento. **To show signs**, dar muestras de.

sign, va. 1. Señalar, poner señal en alguna cosa. 2. Firmar, rubricar. 3. Representar, significar. 4. Hacer señas. **To sign away**, ceder, firmar una cesión. **Sign in**, registrarse, firmar en el registro. **Sign off**, terminar, finalizar una emisión (Rad., TV). **Sign on**, contratar, firmar un contrato o inscripción. **Sign up, = sign on.**

signal ['sɪgnl] [sig-nal], a. Insigne, señalado, notable, memorable (notable, distinguished). -s. 1. Señal, aviso. 2. Signo, indicio (trace). **A signal exploit**, una hazaña señalada, memorable. **A signal failure**, fracaso completo. **Sailing-signals**, señales de hacerse a la vela. **Signal book**, código de señales. **Signal-code**, código o sistema de señales, especialmente en el mar. **Signal flag**, bandera de señales, **Signal-light**, fanal. **Signalman**, guardavía, el que hace señales. -vt. **To signal one's approval**, aprobar, hacer seña de aprobación.

signalize ['sɪgnəlaɪz] [sig-na-lais], va. Señalar, distinguir; singularizar, particularizar; hacer notable.

signally ['sɪgnəlɪ] [sig-na-li], adv. Insignemente, grandemente; señaladamente.

signatory ['sɪgnətərɪ] [sig-na-to-ri], s. y a. Signatario, firmante.

signature ['sɪgnətʃəʳ] [sig-na-chaʳ], s. 1. Subscripción, la firma en una carta o en cualquier otra cosa. 2. Signatura, señal de imprenta en los pliegos para su coordinación. 3. (Mús.) Signatura, signo o signos que se ponen a la derecha de la llave en el pentagrama, para indicar la entonación de las notas (signos de bemol o sostenido). 4. (Ant.) Señal, marca.

signer ['saɪnəʳ] [sai-naʳ], s. Firmante, el que firma o ha firmado.

signet ['sɪgnɪt] [sig-nit], s. 1. Sello; el sello privado del rey. 2. Signáculo, la impresión de un sello sobre el papel.

significance [sɪgˈnɪfɪkəns] [sig-ni-fi-kans], s. 1. Significación, calidad de expresivo o significante. 2. Energía, eficacia, énfasis. 3. Importancia, momento, consecuencia, peso.

significant [sɪgˈnɪfɪkənt] [sig-ni-fi-kant], a. 1. Significante, expresivo, significativo; enfático, enérgico. 2. Importante, que es de algún momento o consecuencia. 3. Que figura, que tiene un significado o culto o encubierto.

significantly [sɪgˈnɪfɪkəntlɪ] [sig-ni-fi-kant-li], adv. Expresivamente, con energía y fuerza.

significantness [sɪgˈnɪfɪkəntnɪs] [sig-ni-fi-kant-nes], s. La calidad que constituye a una cosa significativa o importante.

signification [ˌsɪgnɪfɪˈleɪʃən] [sig-ni-fi-kei-shon], s. Significación, significado, sentido de alguna frase o palabra; la acción de significar o demostrar.

significative [sɪgˈnɪfɪkətɪv] [sig-ni-fi-ka-tiv], a. Significativo, expresivo, enérgico; que tiene una significación, particularmente una signifiación oculta.

significatory [sɪgˈnɪfɪkətərɪ] [sig-ni-fi-ka-to-ri], a. Significativo. -s. (Des.) Señal, indicio.

signify ['sɪgnɪfaɪ] [sig-ni-fai], va. 1. Significar, notificar, declarar, manifestar, hacer saber (tell, declare); dar a entender. 2. Significar, representar una cosa a otra distinta de sí misma; ser signo o indicio de algo, denotar. 3. Importar, ser de alguna consecuencia. -vn. Tener sentido; importar, ser de alguna consecuencia. **What does it signify?** ¿Qué importa? ¿qué significa eso? **It doesn't signify**, no importa, da igual.

signing ['saɪnɪŋ] [sai-nin], sm. Fichage (sport).

silage ['saɪlɪdʒ] [sai-lich], s. Ensilaje.

silence ['saɪləns] [sai-lens], s. 1. Silencio, taciturnidad; privación voluntaria de hablar, quietud. 2. Silencio, secreto. **Death-like silence**, silencio sepulcral. **Silence gives consent**, quien calla otorga. -inter. ¡Silencio! ¡punto en boca! voz con la cual se manda callar.

silence, va. 1. Imponer silencio, mandar o hacer callar. 2. Parar, detener el movimiento de algo, aquietar.

silencer ['saɪlənsər] [sai-lan-saʳ], s. Silenciador, apagador.

silent ['saɪlənt] [sai-lent], a. 1. Silencioso, mudo, que no produce sonido; taciturno, callado. 2. Que no hace mención o alusión. 3. Quieto, tranquilo, sosegado, calmoso. 4. (Com.) Comanditario, perteneciente a la comandita. **Silent partner**, socio comanditario. **To remain silent**, callar, guardar silencio, no chistar. **Be silent**, calle usted. **Silent film**, película muda.

silently ['saɪləntlɪ] [sai-lent-li], adv. Silenciosamente, sin ruido; sin hacer mención de una cosa o pasándola por alto.

silentness ['saɪləntnɪs] [sai-lent-nes], s. Silencio.

silhouette [ˌsɪluːˈet] [si-luet], va. Hacer aparecer en silueta. -s. Silueta, imagen de perfil, tomada por el contorno de la sombra.

silica ['sɪlɪkə] [si-li-ka], s. Sílice, binóxido de silicio, ácido silícico.

silicate ['sɪlɪkeɪt] [si-li-keit], s. Silicato, sal compuesta de ácido silícico y una base.

silicic ['sɪlɪsɪk] [si-li-sik], a. Silícico, perteneciente a la sílice. **Silicic acid**, ácido silícico, sílice.

silicious [sɪˈlɪʃəs] [si-li-shos], a. Silícico, silícico, silíceo, que consta de sílice o cuarzo. **Silicious earth**, tierra primitiva o sencilla de sílice o pedernal.

silicon ['sɪlɪkən] [si-li-kan], s. (Quím.) Silicio, elemento no metálico, el más abundante después del oxígeno.

silicone ['sɪlɪkəʊn] [si-li-koun], sf. Silicona.

silicosis [ˌsɪlɪˈkəʊsɪs] [si-li-kou-sis], sf. Silicosis.

silk [sɪlk] [silk], a. Hecho de seda, sedoso, sedeño. **A silk dress**, un vestido de seda. -s. 1. Seda. 2. Tejido de seda. **Raw silk**, seda cruda o en rama. **Sewing-silk**, seda para coser. **Black corded silk**, paño de seda. **Figured silk**, seda labrada. **Floss silk**, seda floja; escarzo, atanquía, filadiz. **Shot silk**, seda tornasolada. **Twilled silk**, tela cruzada de seda. **Watered silk**, seda ondeada, muaré. **Silk-cotton**, seda vegetal, borrilla de las simientes del bómbice, que se emplea para rellenar los mohadones, etc. **Silk-cotton-tree**, bómbice, ceiba. **Silk goods**, géneros de seda. **Silk-throwing**, torcedura de la seda. **Waste silk**, borra de seda. **Silk-dyer**, tintorero de sedas. **Silk-thrower, silk-throwster**, devanador o torcedor de seda. **Silk-weaver**, tejedor de seda.

silken ['sɪlkən] [sil-ken], a. 1. Sedoso, hecho de seda; sedeño; blando, suave. 2. Vestido de seda.

silkiness ['sɪlkɪnɪs] [sil-ki-nes], s. Blandura, molicie, suavidad; lisonja; sonsaca.

silk-raising ['sɪlkˌreɪzɪŋ] [silk-rei-shin], sf. Sericultura.

silkweed ['sɪlkwiːd] [silk-uid], s. 1. Asclepias.

silk-worm ['sɪlkwɜːm] [silk-uerm], s. Gusano de seda, larva de una mariposa nocturna de los bombácidos.

silky ['sɪlkɪ] [sil-ki], a. 1. Hecho de seda. 2. Sedoso, sedeño, que tiene las propiedades de la seda; suave como la seda; lustroso.

sill [sɪl] [sil], s. Umbral de puerta; (carp.) solera, viga de carrera, antepecho de ventana, alféizar, repisa; nabo; madero horizontal para sostener otras piezas. **Cap-sill**, (Min.) cabezal, cumbrera. **Ground-sill**, solera, viga de carrera. **Window-sill**, antepecho de ventana.

sillily ['sɪlɪlɪ] [si-li-li], adv. Simplemente, tontamente, neciamente.

silliness ['sɪlɪnɪs] [si-li-nes], s. Simpleza, bobería, tontería, necedad.

silly ['sɪlɪ] [si-li], a. 1. Necio, tonto, mentecato, imbécil (stupid); inocente, cándido, fácil de engañar (simple). 2. Sencillo, ingenuo, sin artificio. 3. (Fam.) Bobo, baboso, babieca, papamoscas. **Silly of me!**, ¡qué tonto soy! **To make somebody look silly**, dejar en ridículo a alguien. **Don't be silly**, no seas tonto. **That was a silly thing to do**, eso fue una estupidez.

silo ['saɪləʊ] [sai-lou], s. 1. Silo. 2. (Mil.) Plataforma subterránea de lanzamiento.

silt [sɪlt] [silt], s. Cieno, fango, aluvión; sedimento térreo arrastrado por las aguas. -va. y vn. Obstruir o obstruirse con aluvión; también, colar, pasar al través.

silver ['sɪlvəʳ] [sil-vaʳ], s. 1. Plata, metal precioso. -a. De plata, hecho de plata; plateado. **A silver voice**, voz argentina o sonora como la plata. **Silver leaf**, hoja de plata. **Curde mass of silver**, plata bruta, o en bruto. *(Prov.)* Plata virgen. 2. Monedas de plata consideradas como dinero. 3. Vajilla o servicio de mesa de plata. **Silver alloy**, aleación de plata. *(E.U.)* **Silver beet**, acelga. **Silver foil**, hoja de plata. **Silver plate**, artículos plateados, mercadería plateada. **Silver-plated**, plateado. **Silver thimble**, dedal de plata. **Silver-beater**, batihoja, batidor de plata. **Silver-fir**, *(Bot.)* abeto. **Silver-luce**, encaje o galón de plata. **Silver-medal**, medalla de plata. **Silver-mine**, mina de plata. **Silver-ore**, mineral de plata. **Silver-thistle**, *(Bot.)* acanto o branca ursina. **Silver-weed**, *(Bot.)* agrimonia. **Silver fox**, zorro plateado.

silver, va. 1. Platear, dar la blancura o el brillo de la plata.

silvering ['sɪlvərɪŋ] [sil-ve-rin], s. 1. Capa de plata aplicada sobre alguna cosa. 2. Plateadura, arte o procedimiento de platear; azogamiento. 3. *(Foto.)* Acto de sensibilizar el papel con una sal de plata.

silver-plate ['sɪlvə'pleɪt] [sil-va-pleit], va. Enchapar, platear.

silver-plated [ˌsɪlvə'pleɪtɪd] [sil-va-plei-tid], a. Enchapado, plateado.

silver screen ['sɪlvəskriːn] [sil-va-skrin], s. Pantalla cinematográfica.

silversmith ['sɪlvəsmɪθ] [sil-va-smiz], s. Platero, el artífice que labra la plata; fabricante de efectos de plata.

silverware ['sɪlvəweəʳ] [sil-va-uea'], s. Plata labrada; vajilla de plata; artículos de plata.

silver wedding ['sɪlvə'wedɪŋ] [sil-va-ue-din], s. Bodas de plata.

silvery ['sɪlvərɪ] [sil-va-ri], a. 1. Plateado, dado de plata. 2. Argentino que se asemeja a la plata en lustre, color o sonido.

simian ['sɪmɪən] [si-mian], s. Simio o mono. *-a.* Perteneciente o parecido a un mono.

similar ['sɪmɪləʳ] [si-mi-la'], a. 1. Similar, homogéneo. 2. Semejante, similitudinario, que se parece o tiene semejanza con otra cosa.

similarity [ˌsɪmɪ'lærɪtɪ] [si-mi-la-ri-ti], s. Semejanza, conformidad, homogeneidad.

similarly ['sɪmɪləlɪ] [si-mi-lar-li], adv. Semejantemente.

simile ['sɪmɪlɪ] [si-mi-li], s. Símil, ejemplo, parábola; similitud, comparación.

similitude [sɪ'mɪlɪtjuːd] [si-mi-li-tiud], s. 1. Similitud, semejanza. 2. Ejemplo, comparación.

simitar ['sɪmɪtəʳ] [si-mi-ta'] s. Cimitarra.

simlin ['sɪmlɪn] [sim-lin], s. *(E.U. del Sur y del Oeste)* Variedad de calabaza.

simmer ['sɪməʳ] [si-ma'], vn. *(Culin.)* Hervir a fuego lento.

simous ['sɪməs] [si-mos], a. Que tiene nariz chata y vuelta hacia arriba.

simper ['sɪmpəʳ] [sim-pa'], vn. Sonreír, comúnmente sonreír bobamente, o con afectación.

simper, s. Sonrisa, por lo común sonrisa tonta o afectada.

simple ['sɪmpl] [sim-pel], a. 1. Simple, manso, apacible, sencillo, llano, ingenuo (candid, simple). 2. Simple, puro, sencillo, que no tiene mezcla ni composición (pure); mero, no complicado (uncomplicated). **Simple substance**, substancia sencilla o elemento de alguna cosa. 3. Simple, fácil de engañar; mentecato, necio, bobo (foolish). 4. Poco importante, insignificante, ordinario. *-s.* Simple, planta, hierba o mineral que sirve por sí sola para medicina. **Simple manners**, modales sencillos. **She's a bit simple**, es un poco tonta, está algo tocada. **Simple-hearted**, sencillo, franco, sincero. **Simple-minded**, sencillo, cándido, ingenuo. **Simple-mindedness**, sencillez, candor.

simpleton ['sɪmpltən] [sim-pel-ton], s. Simplón, simplonazo.

simplicity [sɪm'plɪsɪtɪ] [sim-pli-si-ti], s. 1. Sencillez, ingenuidad, llaneza, candor (pureness). 2. Simplicidad, el estado de lo que no es compuesto. 3. Simpleza, bobería, necedad, imbecilidad (silliness).

simplification [ˌsɪmplɪfɪ'keɪʃən] [sim-pli-fi-kei-shon], s. Simplificación, acción o procedimiento de simplificar.

simplify ['sɪmplɪfaɪ] [sim-pli-fai], va. Simplificar, hacer una cosa más sencilla o menos complicada.

simplistic ['sɪmplɪstɪk] [sim-plis-tik], a. Simplista.

simply ['sɪmplɪ] [sim-pli], adv. 1. Sencillamente, sin arte. 2. Simplemente, sin añadidura ni composición (purely). 3. Meramente, solamente (merely). 4. Simplemente, tontamente.

simulant ['sɪmjʊlənt] [si-miu-lant], a. Que simula, imita o finge; que tiene la forma o apariencia (thing); se emplea especialmente en biología.

simulate ['sɪmjʊleɪt] [si-miu-leit], va. Simular, fingir.

simulation [ˌsɪmjʊ'leɪʃən] [si-miu-lei-shon], s Simulación, doblez de ánimo, hipocresía.

simulator ['sɪmjʊleɪtəʳ] [si-miu-lei-ta'], sm. Simulador.

simultaneity [ˌsɪməltə'nɪɪtɪ] [si-mal-ta-nia-ti], s. Simultaneidad, calidad de simultáneo.

simultaneous [ˌsɪməl'teɪnɪəs] [si-mal-tei-nios], a. Simultáneo, que existe, se hace o sucede a un mismo tiempo.

simultaneously [ˌsɪməl'teɪnɪəslɪ] [si-mal-tei-nios-li], adv. Simultáneamente, a un tiempo, de conformidad.

sin [sɪn] [sin], s. 1. Pecado, trangresión de la ley de Dios o de sus preceptos; maldad. 2. Transgresión, falta, ofensa (offence). **Like sin**, con vehemencia. **To fall into sin**, caer en el pecado.

sin, vn. Pecar, faltar a la ley de Dios o a sus preceptos.

since [sɪns] [sins], adv. 1. Desde que, desde, desde entonces. **Ever since**, desde entonces. 2. Antes de ahora. **Some months since**, hace algunos meses. **Long since**, hace mucho tiempo. **Not long since**, hace poco, no hace poco acá. **It is half an hour since the train left**, hace media hora que partió el tren. *-conj.* Ya que, puesto que, en vista de (because); pues, puesto que. **Since it's so**, siendo esto así o puesto que es así. **Since he's the Minister**, como es el ministro. *-prep.* Desde, después. **Since she arrived**, desde que llegó.

sincere [sɪn'sɪəʳ] [sin-sia'], a. 1. Sincero, real, verdadero, genuino. 2. Sincero, sin doblez, franco, abierto.

sincerely [sɪn'sɪəlɪ] [sin-sia-li], adv. Sinceramente, verdaderamente; francamente, con franqueza y buena fe.

sincerity [sɪn'serɪtɪ] [sin-se-ri-ti], s. Sinceridad, integridad, franqueza.

sine [saɪn] [sain], s. *(Mat.)* Seno, perpendicular tirada desde el extremo de un arco de círculo al radio que pasa por el otro extremo. **Coversed sine**, cosenoverso. **Versed sine**, senoverso.

sine, prep. *(Lat.)* Sin. **Sine die**, indefinidamente, sindía señalado para reunirse de nuevo; hasta nueva orden. **Sine qua non**, cosa o condición esencial.

sinecure ['saɪnɪkjʊəʳ] [sai-ni-kiua'], s. Renta o sueldo sin empleo, beneficio simple. *(Vul.)* Una olla boba.

sinew ['sɪnjuː] [si-niu], va. Fortalecer o juntar como con tendones; proveer de tendones, dar fuerza. *-s.* 1. Tendón, cuerda fibrosa. 2. Nervio, fortaleza, la parte más firme y poderosa de alguna cosa.

sinewed ['sɪnjuːd] [si-niud], a. Nervoso, nervioso; fuerte, robusto.

sinewy ['sɪnjuːɪ] [si-niui], a. Nervudo, vigoroso.

sinful ['sɪnfʊl] [sin-ful], a. Pecaminoso, malvado, mal inclinado, corrompido, perverso, perdido. **A sinful man**, pecador. **A sinful woman**, pecadora.

sinfully ['sɪnfʊlɪ] [sin-fu-li], adv. Malvadamente, con maldad, de un modo criminal.

sinfulness ['sɪnfʊlnɪs] [sin-ful-nes], s. Maldad, corrupción, perversidad, mala conducta.

sing [sɪŋ] [sing], vn. y va. *(pret.* SANG o SUNG, *pp.* SUNG). 1. Cantar, hacer con la voz modulaciones armoniosas y agradables. 2. Murmurar el arroyuelo. 3. Gorjear los pájaros. 4. Gorjearse o hacer gorgoritos los niños cuando principian a hablar. 5. Rechinar; zumbar (ears) 6. *(Poét.)* Cantar, celebrar (celebrate). 7. **To sing out**, gritar, dar voces; avisar. **To sing out of tune (o false)**, cantar falso. **To sing a child to sleep**, dormir a un niño cantando. **To sing along**, acompañar cantando, cantar a coro. **To sing up**, cantar más fuerte.

Singapore [ˌsɪŋɡəˈpɔːʳ] [sin-ga-poʳ], *sm.* Singapur.

singe [sɪnʤ] [sindch], *va.* 1. Chamuscar, quemar alguna cosa ligeramente por la parte exterior (scorch); socarrar, sollamar, aperdigar un ave, purificar algo pasándolo por las llamas. 2. Dañar, perjudicar (damage, hurt). **Her reputation was singed**, su reputación quedó perjudicada.

singer [ˈsɪŋɡəʳ] [sin-gaʳ], *s.* Cantor, cantora, cantante.

singing [ˈsɪŋɪŋ] [sin-guin], *s.* Canto, música, vocal, concierto, armonía (song, harmony). **Singing bird**, pájaro cantor. **Singing book**, cuaderno de solfa, de canto. **Singing-master**, maestro de canto, el que enseña a cantar.

single [ˈsɪŋɡl] [sin-guel], *a.* 1. Único, simple, solo, no doble (only). **Single block**, (*Mar.*) motón sencillo. **Not a single word**, ni una sola palabra. 2. Particular, individual. 3. Solo, sin compañía (lonely). 4. Soltero, soltera. 5. Puro, incorrupto (pure). **To live single**, vivir en el estado de celibato. **A single sole**, una suela sencilla. **A single man or woman**, un soltero, una soltera. **Single-handed**, (a) solo, sin ayuda; (b) manco, que tiene una sola mano; (c) que se puede usar con una sola mano. **Single-loader**, arma de fuego de retrocarga que recibe un solo cartucho de una vez. **Single-minded**, ingenuo, sincero, sin doble. **Single mother**, madre soltera. **Single combat**, combate singular. **Simple-hearted**, sencillo de corazón, cándido, ingenuo. **Single life**, celibato. **Single people**, solteros, personas no casadas.

single, *va.* 1. Singularizar, particularizar. 2. Separar, retirar (separate, remove). 3. Tomar por sí solo.

single-breasted [ˈsɪŋɡlˈbrestɪd] [sin-guel-bres-tid], *a.* De una sola hilera de botones.

single file [ˈsɪŋɡlfaɪl] [sin-guel-fail], *adv.* En hilera, uno tras otro.

singleness [ˈsɪŋɡlnɪs] [sin-guel-nes], *s.* Sencillez, llaneza, sinceridad, ingenuidad.

single-track [ˈsɪŋɡltræk] [sin-guel-trak], *a.* De una sola vía. **Single-track mind**, mente estrecha, de interés muy limitado.

singly [ˈsɪŋɡlɪ] [sin-gli], *adv.* Individualmente, sencillamente, de uno en uno, uno a uno, separadamente; francamente, abiertamente.

singsong [ˈsɪŋsɒŋ] [sing-song], *s.* 1. Cadencia uniforme. 2. Sonsonete, verso malo; gorigori. *V.* DOGGEREL.

singular [ˈsɪŋɡjʊləʳ] [sin-guiu-laʳ], *a.* 1. Sencillo, singular; aislado, que está aparte, peculiar. 2. Singular, extraño, extraordinario, raro, excelente. 3. (*Ant.*) Único, sin ejemplo. **Singular conduct**, conducta singular, extraña. **The singular number**, el número singular.

singularity [ˌsɪŋɡjʊˈlærɪtɪ] [sin-guiu-la-ri-ti], *s.* 1. Particularidad, distinción. 2. Singularidad, cosa extraordinaria. rara o excelente.

singularize [ˈsɪŋɡjʊləraɪz] [sin-guiu-la-rais], *va.* Singularizar. particularizar.

singularly [ˈsɪŋɡjʊləlɪ] [sin-guiu-lar-li], *adv.* Singularmente, separadamente, particularmente.

sinic [ˈsɪnɪk] [si-nik], *s.* Chinesco, chino.

sinical [ˈsɪnɪkl] [si-ni-kal], *a.* Relativo al seno de un arco.

sinister [ˈsɪnɪstəʳ] [si-nis-taʳ], *a.* 1. Siniestro, izquierdo (left). 2. Siniestro, viciado, avieso, mal intencionado. 3. Siniestro, infeliz, funesto, aciago.

sinistrad [ˈsɪnɪstrəd] [si-nis-trad], *adv.* Hacia el lado izquierdo del cuerpo.

sinistral [ˈsɪnɪstrəl] [si-nis-tral], *a.* Siniestro, izquierdo, vuelto hacia la izquierda.

sinistrous [ˈsɪnɪstrəs] [si-nis-tros], *a.* Siniestro, malvado, depravado.

sinistrously [ˈsɪnɪstrəslɪ] [si-nis-tros-li], *adv.* 1. Siniestramente, depravadamente. 2. Hacia la izquierda.

sink [sɪŋk] [sink], *vn.* (*pret.* SANK o SUNK, *pp.* SUNK o SUNKEN). 1. Hundirse, sumirse, irse abajo. 2. Hundirse, sumergirse, irse a pique una nave (submerge). 3. Hundirse, bajarse, sentarse o apretarse una obra, un monte, etc. 4. Pasar o penetrar una cosa por medio o hasta el interior de otra; dejarse penetrar, calar; imprimirse o fijarse una cosa, v. g. en la memoria. 5. Bajarse, descender, desaparecer (disappear). 6. Bajar, disminuir, menguar; debilitarse, sucumbir, perecer (weaken, die). 7. Dejarse caer, ceder a su propio peso. 8. Abatirse, acoquinarse, amilanarse (depress). 9. (*Ant.*) Arruinarse, decaer, declinar, empeorar, ir a menos. -*va.* 1. Hundir, sumergir, echar al fondo. **To sink a ship**, (*Mar.*) echar a pique un buque. 2. Cavar, penetrar. 3. Deprimir, abatir, humillar (humiliate). **To sink into powerty**, caer en la miseria. 4. Destruir, exterminar, extinguir (extinguish). 5. Disminuir, bajar, rebajar. 6. Abatir, derribar, hacer caer. 7. Disipar (wealths, rights). 8. Suprimir, ocultar, hacer desaparecer. 9. Decorar por medio de líneas o calados; inscribir o hacer una incisión en algo, p. ej. en un cuño. **To sink away**, pasar la vida indolentemente o sin utilidad alguna. **To sink down**, caer por grados; penetrar profundamente. **To sink under**, atribularse en o con, anonadarse. **Sinking-fund**, fondo de amortización. **Sinking spirit**, abatimiento de ánimo. **The water sinks**, el agua baja, disminuye. **He was left to sunk or swim**, le abandonaron a su suerte (*Fig.*). **The moon was sinking**, la luna iba desapareciendo. **The stone sank into his forehead**, la piedra penetró en su frente. **Now we're sunk!**, ¡estamos perdidos! **To sink on one's knees**, caer de rodillas.

sink, *s.* 1. Alcantarilla, albañal. 2. Sentina, cualquier lugar lleno de inmundicia.

sinker [ˈsɪŋkəʳ] [sin-kaʳ], *s.* Hundidor, el que o lo que hunde; plomo para la cuerda de pescar. **Die-sinker o punch-sinker**, tallador, abridor o grabador en hueco.

sink-unit [ˈsɪŋkˈjuːnɪt] [sink-iu-nit], *s.* Fregadero, lavadero.

sinless [ˈsɪnlɪs] [sin-les], *a.* Impecable, exento de pecado, puro.

sinlessness [ˈsɪnlɪsnɪs] [sin-les-nes], *s.* Impecabilidad.

sinner [ˈsɪnəʳ] [si-naʳ], *s.* Pecador, pecadora.

Sinology [saɪˈnɒlədʒɪ] [sai-no-lo-yi], *sf.* Sinología.

sinuate [ˈsɪnjʊeɪt] [si-niueit], *va.* Formar obliciudades, sinuosidades o senos. -*a.* Sinuoso, ondulado.

sinuation [ˌsɪnjʊˈeɪʃən] [si-niu-ei-shon], *s.* Tortuosidad, corvadura.

sinuosity [ˌsɪnjʊˈɒsɪtɪ] [si-niuo-si-ti], *s.* Sinuosidad.

sinuous [ˈsɪnjʊəs] [si-niuos], *a.* Sinuoso.

sinus [ˈsaɪnəs] [si-nos], *s.* 1. Seno, ensenada, bahía, la parte del mar que se interna entre dos puntas de tierra. 2. Seno, cavidad, abertura, hueco, concavidad.

sip [sɪp] [sip], *va.* Sorber, echar sorbitos, traguitos o copitas; absorber lentamente; chupar, extraer.

sip, *s.* Sorbo, trago pequeño. **A little sip**, sorbito.

siphon [ˈsaɪfən] [sai-fon], *s.* 1. Sifón, cañón o tubo corvo que sirve para sacar licores y para otros varios usos. 2. *vt.* Sacar con sifón. **Siphon off**, reducir de manera gradual, quitar poco a poco (Funds), malversar.

sipper [ˈsɪpəʳ] [si-paʳ], *s.* Sorbedor, el que sorbe.

sippet [ˈsɪpɪt] [si-pit], *s.* Sopita, sopilla, sopa, pedazo de pan empapado en algún licor.

sir [sɜːʳ] [seʳ], *s.* 1. Señor, término de cortesía. 2. Título que se da en Inglaterra, puesto siempre delante del nombre de pila, a los barones y a los caballeros de las órdenes militares. **Dear Sir**, muy señor mío (letters).

sire [saɪəʳ] [saiaʳ], *s.* 1. Padre. 2. Se usa hablando de los animales irracionales; v. g. **This horse had a good sire**, este caballo tuvo buen padre. 3. Algunas veces se usa en composición, como **grand-sire**, abuelo; **great grand-sire**, bisabuelo. 4. Señor, tratamiento del soberano.

sire, *va.* Engendrar, producir, hablando de animales y particularmente de caballos.

siren [ˈsaɪərən] [saia-ran], *s.* 1. Sirena, ninfa legendaria del mar, mitad mujer y mitad pez, que por la dulzura de su canto arrastraba a los navegantes hacia los escollos; de aquí una mujer peligrosa y hechicera. 2. Cantadora melodiosa. **Siren song**, canto de sirena. 3. Aparato para producir un silbido fuerte por medio del vapor. *V.* FOGHORN. -*a.* Encantador.

sirius [ˈsɪrɪəs] [si-rios], *s.* (*Astr.*) Sirio, canícula, la estrella más brillante del firmamento.

sirloin [ˈsɜːlɔɪn] [ser-loin], *s.* Lomo de buey o vaca; la parte que queda encima del riñón.

sirocco [sɪˈrɒkəʊ] [si-ro-kou], *s.* Siroco o jaloque, el viento que viene de la parte intermedia entre levante y mediodía. *V.* SIMOOM.

siskin [ˈsɪskɪn] [sis-kin], *s.* Verderón, pájaro del género Spinus.

sissy [ˈsɪsɪ] [si-si], *s.* 1. Marica, maricón. 2. Bragazas.

sister [ˈsɪstəʳ] [sis-taʳ], *sf.* 1. Hermana, la que tiene los mismos padres que otra persona o el padre o madre solamente. 2. Hermana, la mujer de la misma creencia, del mismo ser o naturaleza, de la misma especie o de la misma profesión que otra. **The sister kingdom**, denominación con que los ingleses designan a Irlanda y los irlandeses a Inglaterra. **Foster sister**, hermana de leche. **The Three o Fatal Sisters**, Las Parcas. *(E.U.)* **Sister city**, ciudad gemela.

sister-blocks [ˈsɪstəblɒks] [sis-ta-bloks], *s. (Mar.)* Motones herrados.

sisterhood [ˈsɪstəhʊd] [sis-ta-jud], *s.* 1. Hermandad, el oficio u obligación de hermana. 2. Conjunto de hermanas. 3. Hermandad, congregación de mujeres bajo ciertas reglas o votos.

sister-in-law [ˈsɪstərɪnlɔː] [sis-ta-in-lo], *sf.* Cuñada, hermana política.

sisterly [ˈsɪstəlɪ] [sis-ta-li], *a.* Con hermandad, como correponde a hermanas; perteneciente a las hermanas.

sit [sɪt] [sit], *vn. (pret.* SAT, *pp.* SAT.) 1. Sentarse, asentarse, estar sentado. 2. Sentarse, poner el cuerpo en alguna disposición o de algún modo particular; posarse, permanecer inmóvil y en pie (birds). 3. Estar situada o colocada una cosa (place). 4. Fijarse algo profundamente en el ánimo, en el corazón, etc. 5. Sentar, venir o ajustar bien o mal un vestido, un adorno, etc. 6. Sentar bien o mal una cosa, agradar o ser conforme y conveniente al gusto (please). 7. Hallarse reunida alguna junta, consejo, asamblea, etc. 8. Estar en sesión los individuos de una junta, tribunal, etc. 9. Sostenerse en el puesto que se ocupa estando sentado; mantenerse a caballo. 10. Descansar, apoyarse sobre alguna cosa. 11. Empollar. 12. Servir de modelo a un pintor o fotógrafo; tomar una posición determinada para un fin especial. *-va.* Asentar, sentar, poner a uno en un asiento. **To sit by**, sentarse junto a uno o arrimado a una persona. **To sit close**, juntarse, acercarse. **Sit by me**, siéntese usted a mi lado. **He sits a horse well**, se tiene o se mantiene bien a caballo, monta bien. **To sit at table**, sentarse a la mesa. **To sit down**, sentarse, estar sentado; residir, morar; quedar satisfecho. **To sit down before a fortress**, bloquear una fortaleza o principiar a ponerle sitio. **To sit a horse well**, montar bien a caballo. **To sit for one's picture**, sentarse delante de un retratista para que haga el retrato. **To sit out**, estar desocupado o sin puesto ni empleo, estar holgando; perseverar. **To sit up**, sentarse el que estaba echado, poner erguido; velar. **To sit upon**, juzgar, cuando se habla de jueces; estar reunidos en sesión los individuos de una junta, asamblea, etc. **To make someone sit up**, dar qué pensar a alguien. **Sit still**, esté usted quieto, no se levante usted. **To sit well**, venir bien una cosa con otra. **Do sit down!**, ¡siéntese, por favor! **To sit a lecture out**, aguantar hasta el final de una conferencia. **Sit-up**, ejercicio de abdominales (Gymnastics).

sitar [ˈsɪtəʳ] [si-taʳ], *s.* Guitarra oriental que tiene dos cuerdas de alambre del mismo tono, y una de acero, un cuarto de tono más alta que aquellas.

sit-down strike [ˈsɪtdaʊnˌstraɪk] [sit-daun-straik], *s.* Huega de brazos caídos.

site [saɪt] [sait], *s.* Sitio, situació, solar.

sited [ˈsaɪtɪd] [sai-tid], *a.* Puesto, colocado, situado.

sith [sɪθ] [siz], *adv., prep. y conj. (Des. o poét.) V.* SINCE.

siting [ˈsɪtɪŋ] [si-tin], *sf.* Emplazamiento, situación.

sitter [ˈsɪtəʳ] [si-taʳ], *s.* 1. El que se sienta o está sentado; en particular, la persona que se hace retratar o fotografiar. 2. El ave que está empollando huevos.

sitting [ˈsɪtɪŋ] [si-tin], *s.* 1. La acción de sentarse y la postura que uno tiene cuando está sentado. 2. El tiempo que está uno delante del pintor para que le retrate. 3. Sesión, junta. 4. Sentada, asentada. 5. Empolladura, la acción de empollar huevos; también, nidada o cría de pajarillos. *-a.* 1. Sentado,

de persona sentada; ave que empolla. 2. *(Bot.)* Sesil, sin pedimento. *V.* SESSILE. **Sitting member**, miembro en funciones. **At one sitting**, en una sesión, de un tirón.

sitting room [ˈsɪtɪŋrʊm] [si-tin-rum], *s.* Sala de recibo.

situate [ˈsɪtjʊeɪt] [si-tiu-eit], *a.* Situado, colocado. *vt.* Situar, colocar.

situation [ˌsɪtjʊˈeɪʃən] [si-tiu-ei-shon], *s.* 1. Situación, estado, vecindad, cercanía, localidad (location). 2. Acomodo, plaza, empleo, ocupación (place, job). 3. Combinación de circunstancias, complicación; situación, punto en el desarrollo de una obra literaria que excita vivamente el interés. **In a situation**, con empleo, empleado. **Out of a situation**, sin empleo, cesante.

situational [ˌsɪtjʊˈeɪʃənl] [si-tiu-ei-sho-nal], *a.* Situacional.

six [sɪks] [siks], *a. y s.* Seis. **Six and seven**, confusión, desorden. **At sixes and sevens**, a la buena ventura, en estado de descuido, desorden, confusión o contrariedad.

sixpence [ˈsɪkspəns] [siks-pens], *s.* Seis peniques.

sixpenny [ˈsɪkspenɪ] [siks-pe-ni], *a.* Que vale o se vende por seis peniques.

sixshooter [ˈsɪksˈʃuːtəʳ] [siks-shu-taʳ], *s.* Revólver con cilindro de seis cartuchos.

sixteen [ˈsɪkstiːn] [siks-tiin], *a. y s.* Dieciséis.

sixteenth [ˈsɪkstiːnθ] [siks-tiinz], *a.* Décimosexto. **The sixteenth century**, el siglo décimosexto o diez y seis.

sixth [ˈsɪksθ] [siksz], *a. y s.* Sexto. **Sixth sense**, sexto sentido, profunda intuición.

sixth, *s.* 1. La sexta parte de cualquier cosa. 2. *(Mús.)* Sexta, una de las concordancias originales. **The sixth of June**, el seis de junio. **Edward the Sixth**, Eduardo Sexto.

sixthly [ˈsɪksθlɪ] [siksz-li], *adv.* En sexto lugar.

sixtieth [ˈsɪkstɪɪz] [siks-tiiz], *a.* Sexagésimo. *-s.* Una de las sesenta partes iguales de una cosa.

sixty [ˈsɪkstɪ] [siks-ti], *a. y s.* Sesenta.

sizable, sizeable [ˈsaɪzəbl] [sai-sa-bol], *a.* Que tiene tamaño proporcionado; algo grande.

size [saɪz] [sais], *s.* Tamaño, talla; calibre, dimensión, corpulencia, estatura, grandor (measurement, extension). **A room of immense size**, una habitación de grandes dimensiones. **Great size operation**, operación de gran envergadura. 2. Marco de zapatero. 3. Tipo de medida, cantidad especificada. **What size shoe do you take?**, ¿qué número calza usted? **Size of ropes**, *(Mar.)* Mena, el grueso de cabos y cuerdas.

size, *s.* 1. Sustancia viscosa y pegajosa; engrudo; disolución de materia gelatinosa, como la cola, el almidón o la resina, que se emplea para encolar el papel. 2. Cola de retazo, sisa empleada para dorar.

size, *va.* 1. Ajustar, arreglar, igualar, hacer venir una cosa a la medida de otra (equalize). 2. Fijar, arreglar: se dice comúnmente de los pesos y medidas; distribuir o clasificar según tamaño. 3. Evaluar, apreciar, tasar (fix, rate).

size, *va.* Engrudar, encolar, pegar una cosa a otra con cualquier materia glutinosa. 2. Lavar una pared para blanquearla.

sizeable [ˈsaɪzəbl] [sai-sa-bol], *a.* Considerable, bastante grande.

sizeably [ˈsaɪzəblɪ] [sai-sa-bli], *adv.* Considerablemente.

sized [ˈsaɪzt] [saist], *a.* Que pertenece al tamaño, magnitud o grandor de las cosas. **Large-sized ropes**, *(Mar.)* Cabos de mena mayor.

sizer [ˈsaɪzəʳ] [sai-saʳ], *s.* 1. Instrumento par medir el tamaño de las perlas. 2. *V.* SIZAR.

siziness [ˈsaɪzɪnɪs] [sai-si-nes], *s.* Viscosidad.

sizing [ˈsaɪzɪŋ] [sai-sin], *s.* 1. Encoladura, acción de encolar. 2. Cola; capa de cola.

sizy [ˈsaɪzɪ] [sai-si], *a.* Viscoso, pegajoso.

sizz [ˈsɪz] [sis], *vn.* Chisporrotear, silbar.

sizzle [ˈsɪzl] [si-sel], *va. y vn. (Prov.)* Quemar, chamuscar, quemarse o chamuscarse produciendo un silbido, como sucede bajo la acción violenta del calor. *-s. (Fam.)* Sonido como el silbido; chisporroteo, temperatura excesivamente alta.

skate [skeɪt] [skeit], *va.* Patinar, deslizarse sobre el hielo u otra superficie lisa, sirviéndose al efecto de patines. **Skate over/round**, esquivar, eludir, evitar. -*s.* 1. Patín, especie de calzado armado de hierro para correr sobre el hielo. 2. Lija. **Roller-skate**, patín de ruedas. **Get your skates on!**, ¡date prisa!

skater ['skeɪtəʳ] [skei-taʳ], *s.* Patinador.

skating ['skeɪtɪŋ] [skei-tin], *s.* Patinaje.

skean ['skiːn] [skiin], *s.* Daga, puñal irlandés antiguo.

skedaddle [skɪ'dædl] [ski-da-del], *vn. (Ger.)* Tomar las de Villadiego, poner pies en polvorosa.

skee [skiː] [skii], *s.* Especie de patín noruego para deslizarse sobre el hielo y la nieve, consiste en una plancha de madera larga y estrecha, a la cual se asegura la parte anterior del pie.

skeet ['skiːt] [skiit], *s. (Mar.)* Bañadera, especie de cucharones para bañar las velas, cubiertas o costados de la embarcación.

skein [skeɪn] [skein], *s.* Madeja, mazo, cadejo. **To wind off a skein**, devanar una madeja.

skeletal ['skelɪtl] [ske-li-tal], *a.* De esqueleto, perteneciente al esqueleto, que forma esqueleto.

skeleton ['skelɪtn] [ske-li-ton], *a.* Que consiste meramente en un esqueleto o armazón, extenuado. -*s.* 1. Esqueleto, armazón descarnada y completa del cuerpo animal. 2. Armazón o armadura; esbozo o plan de una cosa, particularmente de una obra literaria. **Skeleton key**, llave maestra. **The skeleton at the feast**, el aguafiestas. **A skeleton in the closet**, un secreto vergonzoso.

skep ['skep] [skep], *s.* Especie de cesto para llevar trigo, colmena, casa de abejas.

skeptic, sceptic ['skeptɪk] [skep-tik], *s.* Escéptico, el que duda de todo y particularmente de la religión cristiana.

skeptical ['skeptɪkl] [skep-ti-kal], *a.* Escéptico.

skeptically ['skeptɪklɪ] [skep-ti-kli], *adv.* Escépticamente.

sketch [sketʃ] [skech], *s.* 1. Diseño, esbozo, bosquejo, la primera mano que se da a una pintura u otra obra material (rough copy). 2. Esquicio, boceto, traza, rasguño, borrón, el primer diseño de una obra de pintura o escultura (drawing). 3. Bosquejo, borrón, el plan de cualquier obra intelectual.

sketch, *va.* 1. Esquiciar, trazar, delinear, rasguñar una figura, un cuadro, etc. 2. Bosquejar una pintura o cualquier obra material. 3. Bosquejar, presentar o hacer el bosquejo o borrón de una obra intelectual.

sketchily ['sketʃɪlɪ] [ske-chi-li], *adv.* A manera de esbozo, bosquejo o boceto.

sketchiness ['sketʃɪnɪs] [ske-chi-nes], *s.* Calidad o condición de esbozo, bosquejo o borrón.

sketching ['sketʃɪŋ] [ske-chin], *s.* Dibujo, arte de dibujar.

sketchy ['sketʃɪ] [ske-chi], *a.* Bosquejado, esquiciado; no acabado, incompleto.

skew [skjuː] [skiu], *a.* Oblicuo, torcido, atravesado, al sesgo, de través. -*s.* 1. Movimiento, curso o posición oblicuos. 2. Mirada al sesgo, oblicua. **To be on skew**, estar mal puesto, estar torcido.

skew, *va.* Poner al sesgo; dar forma o poner oblicua o torcidamente; echar de través. -*vn.* 1. Andar o moverse oblicuamente. 2. Mirar al sesgo.

skewed ['skjuːd] [skiud], *a.* Torcido, desviado.

skewer ['skjuːəʳ] [skiuaʳ], *s.* Aguja de hardear; espetón.

ski [skiː] [ski], *s.* Esquí. -*vn.* Esquiar. **Ski lift**, telesquí, teleférico. **Ski jumping**, saltos de esquí.

skid [skɪd] [skid], *va.* Proveer de baraderos, poner, arrastrar o tirar sobre baraderos o carenotes. -*s.* 1. Carenote, baradero. 2. Calzo, rastra (de rueda).

skiddoo [skɪ'duː] [ski-du], *vi. (E. U.)* Irse, largarse.

skid row ['skɪdrəʊ] [skid-rou], *s.* Hampa, barrio de holgazanes y degenerados.

skier ['skɪəʳ] [skiaʳ], *a.* Esquiador, esquiadora.

skiff [skɪf] [skif], *s.* Esquife, bote o barco pequeño.

skilful ['skɪlfʊl] [skil-ful], *a.* Práctico, experimentado, diestro, hábil, experto.

skilfully ['skɪlfʊlɪ] [skil-fu-li], *adv.* Diestramente, sagazmente, mañosamente.

skilfulness ['skɪlfʊlnɪs] [skil-ful-nes], *s.* Habilidad, destreza, capacidad o arte para hacer una cosa.

skill [skɪl] [skil], *s.* Conocimiento práctico; habilidad, destreza, saber; maña o gracia en hacer o para hacer una cosa; arte, artificio.

skilled ['skɪld] [skild], *a.* Práctico, instruido; diestro, hábil.

skilless ['skɪlɪs] [ski-les], *a.* Inexperto, falto de conocimiento o destreza.

skillful ['skɪlfʊl] [skil-ful], *a.* Diestro, hábil.

skillfully ['skɪlfʊlɪ] [skil-fu-li], *adv.* Hábilmente.

skim [skɪm] [skim], *va.* 1. Desnatar, quitar la nata a la leche u otros líquidos. 2. Espumar, quitar la espuma. 3. Pasar ligeramente por encima de una cosa tocando su superficie. 4. Tratar superficialmente acerca de alguna cosa. -*vn.* Deslizarse o moverse una cosa con rapidez por encima de otra, tocando suavemente su superficie. **To skim the ocean**, *(Mar.)* Peinar las olas.

To skim along, rozar, resbalar.

To skim over, resbalar, rozar, recorrer un libro, tocar ligeramente una cuestión.

skim, *s.* Acción de desnatar o espumar; espuma, desecho.

skimmer ['skɪməʳ] [ski-maʳ], *s.* Espumadera.

skimp ['skɪmp] [skimp], 1. *V.* STINT. 2. Ejecutar con descuido. -*vn.* 1. Ser mezquino o tacaño. 2. Hacer un trabajo con poco cuidado.

skimpy ['skɪmpɪ] [skim-pi], *a.* 1. Corto, escaso. 2. Tacaño, que escatima.

skin [skɪn] [skin], *s.* 1. Cutis, pellejo sutil que cubre exteriormente el cuerpo humano; piel de un animal, tegumento. **He is nothing but skin and bone**, está en los huesos. **I would not be in his skin**, no quisiera hallarme en su pellejo. 2. Cuero, piel del animal que sirve para hacer pergamino, cordobán, suela y otras cosas. 3. Odre, pellejo o cuero que sirve para contener líquidos. 4. Pellejo, tegumento o capa exterior que cubre ciertos frutos. **Sheep-skin dressed with wool**, zalea. **Fore-skin**, prepucio. **Scarf skin**, epidermis, cutícula. **Skin deep**, superficie, no más profundo que el cutis. **Calf skin**, piel de becerro. **Sheep skin**, badana, zalea. **Skin-deep**, superficial, epidérmico. **Dressed skin**, piel adobada o curtida.

skin, *va.* 1. Desollar, quitar el pellejo o la piel. 2. Cubrir con la piel o pellejo. 3. Cubrir superficialmente. -*vn.* Cubrirse de pellejo o tegumento; cicatrizarse. **To skin over**, curarse o cicatrizarse una llaga o herida; cuajarse superficialmente; hacerse costras.

skin diving ['skɪnˌdaɪvɪŋ] [skin-dai-vin], *s.* Buceo sin escafandra pero con un dispositivo que permite la respiración en el agua.

skinflint ['skɪnflɪnt] [skin-flint], *s.* Avaro, cicatero, miserable.

skin graft ['skɪngræft] [skin-graft], *s.* Piel para injertos.

skinhead ['skɪnhed] [skin-jed], *s.* Cabeza rapada.

skinless ['skɪnlɪs] [skin-les], *a.* Desprovisto de pellejo, sin piel o que tiene una película muy delgada, como ciertas frutas y granos.

skinner ['skɪnəʳ] [ski-naʳ], *s.* 1. Pellejero, el que tiene por oficio vender y adobar los pellejos. 2. Peletero, el que trabaja o vende pieles finas.

skinned [skɪnd] [skind], *a.* Que tiene pellejo, hecho de cuero, correoso.

skinniness ['skɪnɪnɪs] [ski-ni-nes], *s.* Flaqueza, falta de carnes, extenuación.

skinny ['skɪnɪ] [ski-ni], *a.* Flaco, falto de carnes.

skin-tight ['skɪntaɪt] [skin-tait], *a.* Ceñido al cuerpo.

skip [skɪp] [skip], *va.* 1. Pasar por alto, omitir (miss out, omit). 2. Saltar ligeramente por encima de algo. 3. Hacer saltar sucesivamente, como salta una piedra plana sobre el agua. -*vn.* 1. Saltar ligeramente, brincar, cabriolar, triscar, dar o hacer cabriolas. 2. Dar saltos o pernadas, brincar hacia alguna cosa o desde ella. 3. Pasar por alto sin hacer caso de.

skip, *s.* 1. Cabriola, salto, brinco. 2. Omisión, acción de pasar por alto sin hacer caso.

skipper ['skɪpəʳ] [ski-paʳ], *s.* 1. Persona o cosa que brinca o salta. 2. Un bailarín o bailarina. 3. Escombresocio, pez. 4. Especie de mariposa; debe su nombre a la manera como vuela. 5. Gusanillo de queso.

skipper, *s.* Maestro o patrón de una pequeña embarcación; paje de escoba. **Skipper's daughter**, cabrilla de mar.

skipping ['skɪpɪŋ] [ski-pin], *s.* Acción de saltar. **Skipping-rope**, comba, cuerda para el juego de niños llamado también comba.

skippingly ['skɪpɪŋlɪ] [ski-pin-li], *adv.* A saltos, a brincos.

skirmish ['skɜːmɪʃ] [sker-mish], *s.* Escaramuza, pelea ligera; contienda, pendencia.

skirmish, *vn.* Escaramuzar.

skirmisher ['skɜːmɪʃəʳ] [sker-mi-shaʳ], *s.* Escaramuzador.

skirret ['skɜːrɪt] [ske-rit], *s.* (*Bot.*) Chirivía, planta de las umbelíferas.

skirt [skɜːt] [skert], *s.* 1. Falda, saya, faldilla, la parte del vestido desde la cintura abajo, también, enagua. 2. Faldón, falda suelta al aire o la parte inferior de una colgadura, etc., orla, filete. 3. Orilla, margen, borde.

skirt, *va.* 1. Orillar, guarnecer la orilla de una tela o ropa. 2. Poblar, adornar o formar la orilla o el margen de un río, monte, país, etc.

skit [skɪt] [skit], *s.* 1. Pasquín, sátira breve. 2. Burla, capricho.

skittish ['skɪtɪʃ] [ski-tish], *a.* 1. Espantadizo, que fácilmente se asusta, tímido. 2. Retozón, inclinado a retozar. 3. Repropio, terco, reacio. 4. Caprichoso, quisquilloso, suspicaz. 5. Voluble, inconstante.

skittishly ['skɪtɪʃlɪ] [ski-tish-li], *adv.* Caprichosamente.

skittishness ['skɪtɪʃnɪs] [ski-tish-nes], *s.* Desenvoltura, volubilidad, inconstancia.

skittle ['skɪtl] [ski-tel], *s.* Bolo, juego de bolos; por lo común en plural.

skive [skaɪv] [skaiv], *va.* 1. Raspar, adelgazar, p. ej. el cuero. 2. Moler y pulir, v. g. la superficie de una joya. -*s.* Disco de joyero para pulir el diamante.

skiver ['skaɪvəʳ] [skai-vaʳ], *s.* 1. Cuero hendido con cuchillo, cuero para pastas. 2. Cuchillo o máquina para raspar o adelgazar.

skulk [skʌlk] [skalk], *vn.* Andar a sombra de tejado; ocultarse, substraerse a la vista.

skull [skʌl] [skal], *s.* 1. Cráneo; calavera, casco de la cabeza de un animal vertebrado. 2. Remo para cinglar. V. SCULL.

skullcap ['skʌlkæp] [skal-kap], *s.* 1. Casquete, gorra muy ajustada a la cabeza. 2. Sincipucio. V. SINCIUT. 3. Escutelaria, planta de la familia de las labiadas.

skunk [skʌŋk] [skank], *s.* 1. Zorrillo. 2. Canalla.

sky [skaɪ] [skai], *s.* 1. Región etérea, cielo, firmamento, el orbe diáfano que rodea la tierra. **Cloudy sky**, cielo encapotado. 2. Atmósfera. 3. Tiempo, la constitución o temperamento del aire. 4. Una nube. 5. Una sombra. **Sky-blue**, azul celeste. **Sky-born**, nacido en el cielo. **Sky-clad**, (*Fam.*) Desnudo, **sky-high**, tan alto como el cielo.

sky-color [skaɪˈkʌləʳ] [skai-ka-laʳ], *s.* Color azul o celeste.

sky-colored [skaɪˈkʌləd] [skai-ka-lad], **sky-dyed** [skaɪˈdaɪd] [skai-daid], *a.* Azul celeste.

skylark ['skaɪlɑːk] [skai-lark], *s.* (*Orn.*) Alondra, calandria. -*vn.* (*Fam.*) Chacotear, estar de chacota, triscar, jaranear. **Skylarking**, chacota, jarana.

skylight ['skaɪlaɪt] [skai-lait], *s.* Claraboya, lumbrera, montera; ventanilla que mira al cielo.

skyline ['skaɪlaɪn] [skai-lain], *s.* 1. Línea del horizonte. 2. Perspectiva de una ciudad con rascacielos.

skyrocket ['skaɪˌrɒkɪt] [skai-ro-kit], *s.* Cohete.

skysail ['skaɪseɪl] [skai-seil], *s.* (*Mar.*) Sosobre, vela ligera colocada encima del sobrejuanete.

skyscraper ['skaɪˌskræpəʳ] [skai-skra-paʳ], *s.* Racacielos.

skyward, skywards ['skaɪwəd] [skai-uod], *adv.* Hacia el cielo.

slab [slæb] [slab], *s.* 1. Costero, el madero que se saca de la parte más exterior del árbol; bloque. 2. Losa, piedra alisada; plancha o pedazo plano y grueso de metal, piedra u otro material.

slabber ['slæbəʳ] [sla-baʳ], *vn.* Babear, expeler o echar de sí la baba o saliva; dejar caer el alimento líquido al comer; ensuciar, hacer un lodazal.

slabberer ['slæbərəʳ] [sla-ba-raʳ], *s.* 1. Baboso, la persona que echa babas. 2. Ensuciador, el que ensucia.

slabbering ['slæbərɪŋ] [sla-be-rin], *s.* 1. Babeo, el acto de babear. 2. El acto de derramar, ensuciar o mojar.

slabby ['slæbɪ] [sla-bi], *a.* 1. Espeso, viscoso. 2. Mojado, lleno de humedad.

slack [slæk] [slak], *a.* 1. Flojo, poco apretado o poco tirante. 2. Flojo, perezoso, negligente, descuidado, tardo (negligent). 3. Lento, tardo, sosegado, espacioso (sluggish). 4. Que fluye lentamente. **Slack water**, estado del mar entre flujo y reflujo. **Trade is slack**, el comercio no marcha bien, decae. **Slack ropes**, (*Mar.*) Cabos sueltos en banda. -*s.* 1. Cabo de cuerda colgante; parte de una cuerda que no está bastante tirante. 2. Cisco, carbón menudo.

slacken ['slækn] [sla-ken], *va.* y *vn.* 1. Aflojar, poner floja una cosa que estaba tirante. 2. Ablandar, poner blanda una cosa que estaba endurecida. 3. Apagar, v. g. la cal. 4. Aflojar, amainar, amortiguar. 5. Remitir; diferir, tardar, descuidar. 6. Despegar o despegarse. 7. Aflojar, entibiarse, perder el vigor, aplicación, etc. 8. Decaer, desfallecer. 9. Relajar, laxar o ablandar. 10. Relajar, aliviar. **The fever slackens**, cede la calentura. **The wind slackens**, el viento amaina. **To slacken off**, dejar de trabajar, trabajar menos, aflojar el ritmo. **To slack up**, retardar, detener la rapidez de algo: alojar, amainar.

slacker ['slækəʳ] [sla-kaʳ], *s.* Cobarde, el que elude pelear en la guerra.

slackly ['slæklɪ] [slak-li], *adv.* Flojamente, lentamente.

slackness ['slæknɪs] [slak-nes], *s.* 1. Flojedad, remisión, descaido. 2. Debilidad (weakness).

slacks ['slæks] [slaks], *s.* 1. Pantalones holgados (man or woman).

slag [slæg] [slag], *s.* 1. Escoria, la hez de los metales. 2. Escoria volcánica.

slain [sleɪn] [slein], *pp.* del verbo *TO SLAY*.

slake [sleɪk] [sleik], *va.* 1. Apagar, extinguir (extinguish). 2. Remojar; desleír. 3. Moderar (control, moderate). 4. Aflojar, ceder, bajar o disminuirse la fuerza o vigor de una cosa. -*vn.* 1. Apagar, extinguir. 2. Remojar; desleír. 3. Moderar. 4. Aflojar, ceder, bajar o disminuirse la fuerza o vigor de una cosa. -*vn.* Apagarse, llegar a ser hidratado; se dice de la cal. **To slake lime**, apagar la cal. **To slake one's thirst**, apagar uno la sed.

slalom ['slɑːləm] [sla-lom], *vn.* Esquiar zigzagueando, eslálom.

slam [slæm] [slam], *va.* 1. Arrojar, tirar o empujar con violencia y estrépito. **To slam the door**, cerrar de golpe, o dar un golpe a la puerta. 2. Dar capote, hacer uno de los jugadores en alguna mano todas las bazas. -*vn.* Cerrarse o dar de golpe y con estrépito.

slam, *s.* 1. Empuje o cierre con estrépito y violencia; golpe. 2. Capote en el juego.

slander ['slændəʳ] [slan-daʳ], *va.* Calumniar, denigrar, infamar, hablar mal.

slander, *s.* 1. Calumnia, acusación falsa, denigración, mancha o borrón en la fama de alguno, impostura (lie). 2. Infamia, descrédito, deshonra (dishonesty).

slanderer ['slɑːndərəʳ] [slan-da-raʳ], *s.* Calumniador, impostor, maldiciente.

slandering ['slɑːndərɪŋ] [slan-de-rin], *s.* Murmuración, maledicencia. -*a.* Maldiciente, calumnioso.

slanderous ['slɑːndərəs] [slan-de-ros], *a.* Infamatorio, calumnioso.

slanderously ['slɑːndərəslɪ] [slan-de-ros-li], *adv.* Calumniosamente.

slang [slæŋ] [slang], *s.* 1. Jerga, jerigonza, lenguaje popular inelegante y no autorizado; o empleo de expresiones correctas, pero dándoles un sentido impropio o grotesco. 2. Jacrandina, caló, lenguaje propio de gitanos. **To talk slang**, hablar en argot.

slangy ['slæŋgɪ] [slan-gui], *a.* 1. De la naturaleza de la jerga, que le pertenece o la contiene. 2. Dado al uso de la jerga.

slank ['slæŋk] [slank], *pret.* del verbo SLINK.

slant [slɑːnt] [slant], *va.* y *vn.* Dar una dirección oblicua; inclinarse, sesgarse.

slanting ['slɑːntɪŋ] [slan-tin], *a.* Sesgado, oblicuo, inclinado, en declive. *-s.* 1. Dirección oblicua; plano inclinado, declive. **The conversation is taking on a new slant,** la conversación está tomando un nuevo giro. 2. Pulla, chufleta, dicho sarcástico.

slantingly ['slɑːntɪŋlɪ] [slan-tin-li], *adv.* Sesgadamente, de través o al través.

slap [slæp] [slap], *va.* Golpear, dar un golpe (strike): regularmente se usa para denotar un golpe con la mano abierta o una manotada. **To slap one over the face,** dar una bofetada o bofetón, dar un sopapo. **To slap down,** derribar de una bofetada. **Slap in the face,** cachete, torta. *interj.* ¡zas!

slap, *s.* Manotada, el golpe dado con la mano, y por extensión cualquier golpe dado con una cosa ancha. **Slap on the face,** bofetada, bofetón. *-adv.* De golpe y porrazo, de sopetón.

slapdash ['slæpdæʃ] [slap-dash], *a. y adv. (Fam.)* De una vez, de un golpe.

slapper ['slæpəʳ] [sla-paʳ], *sf.* Furcia.

slapstick ['slæpstɪk] [slap-stik], *s.* Comedia grotesca en que abundan los porrazos.

slash [slæʃ] [slash], *va.* Acuchillar, dar cuchilladas. *-vn.* Tirar tajos y reveses con una espada, a trochemoche.

slash, *s.* Cuchillada, corte en carne viva; chirlo, jabeque; latigazo, azote; en especial, corte, cortadura en una tela.

slat [slæt] [slat], *va. y vn.* Arrojar con violencia o con un empellón; lanzar con descuido; sacudirse, hacer ruido.

slat, *s.* Tablilla, pedazo delgado y estrecho de madera y algunas veces de metal o piedra. **Blind-slat,** tablilla de persiana.

slatch [slætʃ] [slach], *s. (Mar.)* 1. El medio de un cabo suelto. 2. Intervalo de buen tiempo.

slate [sleɪt] [sleit], *s.* 1. Pizarra, especie de piedra que se divide en hojas delgadas para cubrir los tejados. 2. Pizarra para escribir. 3. *(E. U.)* Lista de candidatos preparada de antemano: programa redactado con anticipación. **Slate-colored,** de color de pizarra. **Slate-pencil,** pizarrín, pizarrete. **Slate-quarry,** pizarral, cantera de pizarra. **To start with a clean slate,** hacer borrón y cuenta nueva.

slate, *va.* Empizarrar, cubrir con pizarra.

slater ['sleɪtəʳ] [slei-taʳ], *s.* Pizarrero, el que cubre los tejados con pizarra; herramienta con canto de pizarra para quitar el pelo de las pieles.

slattern ['slætən] [sla-tern], *a.* Puerco, desaliñado. *-s.* Mujer desaliñada.

slatternly ['slætənlɪ] [sla-tern-li], *adv.* Desaliñadamente. *-a.* Puerco, desaliñado.

slaty ['sleɪtɪ] [slei-ti], *a* Pizarreño, pizarroso, que participa de la naturaleza de la pizarra; que consiste de pizarra o se parece a ella.

slaughter ['slɔːtəʳ] [slo-taʳ], *s.* Carnicería, matanza, mortandad de gente, estrago que se hace en la guerra.

slaughter, *va.* 1. Matar atrozmente, hacer una carnicería; hacer pedazos. 2. Matar animales en la carnicería.

slaughter-house ['slɔːtəhɑʊs] [slo-ta-jaus], *s.* Matadero.

slaughterman ['slɔːtəmən] [slo-ta-man], *s.* Matador, asesino.

slaughterous ['slɔːtərəs] [slo-ta-ros], *a.* Mortífero, destructivo.

Slav [slɑːv] [slav], *a.* Eslavo. *V.* SLAVONIC. *-s.* Persona de la raza eslava.

slave [sleɪv] [sleiv], *s.* 1. Esclavo, esclavo, persona sin libertad, bajo el dominio de otra. 2. Esclavo, el que se somete a sus pasiones. **Slave-driver,** capataz de esclavos. **Slave-born,** nacido en la esclavitud. **Slave labor,** trabajo de esclavos. **Slave-holding,** poseedor de esclavos. **To slave away,** trabajar como un negro.

slave, *vn.* Trabajar como esclavo. *-va. (Poét. o ant.)* Esclavizar.

slaver ['sleɪvəʳ] [slei-vaʳ], *s.* Negrero, persona o buque que hacía el tráfico de negros para venderlos como esclavos.

slaver, *s.* Baba.

slaver, *vn.* Babosear.

slavery ['sleɪvərɪ] [slei-va-ri], *s.* 1. Esclavitud, servidumbre, el estado de esclavo. 2. Esclavitud, servidumbre, yugo, el estado de sujeción injusta y forzada en que un superior tiene a su inferior o el fuerte al débil.

slavey ['sleɪvɪ] [slei-vi], *sf.* Fregona.

Slavic ['slævɪk] [sla-vik], *a. V.* SLAVONIC.

slavish ['sleɪvɪʃ] [slei-vish], *a.* Servil, bajo, humilde.

slavishly ['sleɪvɪʃlɪ] [slei-vish-li], *aadv.* Servilmente.

slavishness ['sleɪvɪʃnɪs] [slei-vish-nes], *s.* 1. Bajeza, vileza. 2. Servidumbre, esclavitud.

slavonic [sləˈvɒnɪk] [sla-vo-nik], *a.* 1. Eslavo, esclavón, relativo a los pueblos o a las lenguas de origen eslavo. *V.* SLAV. 2. *V.* SALVONIAN.

slaw [slɔː] [slo], *s.* Col cortada en rebanadas y servida cruda o cocida como ensalada.

slay [sleɪ] [slei], *va. pret.* SLEW, *pp.* SLAIN) matar, dar muerte violenta, quitar la vida.

slayer ['sleɪəʳ] [sleiaʳ], *s.* Matador, asesino. **Man-slayer,** homicida.

sleave ['sliːv] [sliiv], *s.* Seda o hilo destorcido.

sleaze, sleaziness ['sliːz] [sliis] ['sliːzɪnɪs] [slii-si-nes], *sm.* Desaliño, desaseo; mala fama, sordidez,

sleazy ['sliːzɪ] [slii-si], *a.* Falto de firmeza en su textura, flojo, ligero. **Sleazy cloth** paño de soplillo.

sled ['sled] [sled], *va. y vn.* 1. Llevar o pasearse sobre un trineo; usar una narria. *-s.* Narria, rastra, trineo. 2. Macho, el mazo grande que tienen en las herrerías para forjar el hierro.

sleek ['sliːk] [sliik], *a.* 1. Liso, bruñido, alisado (smooth, even). 2. Suave, blando, zalamero, insinuante, de palabras melífluas: en los Estados Unidos, generalmente, *slick. V.* SLICK.

sleek, *va.* 1. Peinar o componer el pelo o la lana. 2. Alisar, pulir, poner lisa o lustrosa alguna cosa. 3. Hacer menos desagradable u ofensivo; aquietar, pacificar.

sleekly ['sliːklɪ] [slii-kli], *adv.* Con lisura, igualdad o lustre.

sleekness ['sliːknɪs] [sliik-nes], *s.* Lisura, igualdad y lustre de una superficie.

sleeky ['sliːkɪ] [slii-ki], *a.* 1. *V.* SLEEK. 2. *(Esco.)* Zalamero, socarrón, taimado.

sleep [sliːp] [sliip], *va. y vn. (pret. y pp.* SLEPT). 1. Dormir, descansar o reposar en el sueño. 2. Dormir o dormirse, descuidarse u obrar en algún negocio con poca actividad o solicitud. 3. Reposar, descansar; también, yacer muerto. 4. Dormir una cosa o no hablarse de ella. 5. Entumecerse un miembro por hallarse interumpida la circulación de la sangre. 6. Girar sin movimiento perceptible: se dice de un trompo o peonza.

sleep around, acostarse con cualquiera.

sleep away, disipar o malgastar el tiempo durmiendo.

sleep in, dormir hasta tarde.

sleep out, dormir fuera; dormir al aire libre.

sleep over, consultar con la almohada, posponer una decisión hasta pasada la noche, considerar maduramente; vivir locamente, pasar el tiempo sin provecho.

sleep upon, no hacer caso de una cosa; descuidarse en el cumplimiento de su obligación. **To sleep in Jesus,** estar muerto, dormir en el Señor, estar gozando de Dios. **To sleep like a top,** dormir como un lirón. **To sleep on,** seguir durmiendo. **To sleep one's liquor away,** disipar o malgastar el tiempo durmiendo. **To sleep soundly,** dormir a pierna suelta; dormir profundamente, con sueño profundo.

sleep, *s.* 1. Sueño, el acto de dormir; descanso, reposo. 2. Estado de inacción, de inercia o reposo; muerte, el reposo del sepulcro. 3. *(Bot.)* Posición que toman durante la noche las hojas de las plantas. **To go to sleep,** dormirse. **To put to sleep,** adormecer. **Sleep-walker,** sonámbulo. **Sleep-walking,** sonambulismo. **To have a sleep,** echar una cabezada. **To sleep the sleep of the just,** dormir con la conciencia tranquila.

sleeper ['sliːpəʳ] [slii-paʳ], *s.* 1. El que duerme. 2. *(E. U.)* Coche dormitorio. *V. Sleeping-car.* 3. Animal adormecido durante el invierno.

sleeper, *s.* Durmiente, carrera, travesaño, vigueta; *(mar.)* curva de yugo que se sitúa por la parte interior, aplicando sus brazos contra los yugos inferiores o contra el forro.

sleepily [ˈsliːpɪlɪ] [slii-pi-li], *adv.* Con somnolencia, pesadez o torpeza.

sleepiness [ˈsliːpɪnɪs] [slii-pi-nes], *s.* Somnolencia, adormecimiento; letargo.

sleeping [ˈsliːpɪŋ] [slii-pin], *s.* Sueño, reposo, descanso. -*pa.* Durmiente; calmante, adormecedor. **Sleeping-car,** coche dormitorio de ferrocarril. En Inglaterra se llama más comúnmente **sleeping-carriage o coach. Sleeping-draft o potion,** bebida calmante, narcótico. **Sleeping-partner,** comanditario.

sleepless [ˈsliːplɪs] [sliip-les], *a.* Desvelado, falto de sueño. **Sleepless night,** noche que se pasa en vela.

sleeplessness [ˈsliːplɪsnɪs] [sliip-les-nes], *s.* Insomnio, desvelo.

sleepy [ˈsliːpɪ] [slii-pi], *a.* 1. Soñoliento, adormecido. 2. Soporífero, soporoso; letárgico. **To be sleepy,** tener sueño.

sleepyhead [ˈsliːpɪhed] [slii-pi-jed], *s.* Dormilón.

sleet [sliːt] [sliit], *s.* Aguanieve, nieve o granizo mezclado con lluvia.

sleet, *vn.* Caer agua nieve, nevar y llover al mismo tiempo; caer granizo menudo.

sleety [ˈsliːtɪ] [slii-ti], *a.* Lo que contiene agua nieve.

sleeve [sliːv] [sliiv], *s.* 1. Manga, la parte de la vestidura que cubre los brazos hasta la muñeca. 2. *(Mec.)* Dedal largo, tubo o cilindro hueco que rodea un árbol o vara. 3. Junta de manguito o manguito de tuerca. **To laugh in the sleeve at,** reírse con disimulo de alguna persona o cosa. **To say in one's sleeve,** decir para su capote o para su sayo. **To hang on one's sleeve,** estar una persona sujeta o dependiente de la voluntad de otra. **To wear one's heart on one's sleeve,** llevar el corazón en la mano. **Hanging sleeves,** mangas perdidas. **Sleeve-band,** cinta con que se aprieta la manga. **Sleeve-button,** botón de manga. **Sleeve-coupling,** junta de manguito. **Sleeve-links,** gemelos de mangas. **Sleeve-nut,** manguito de tuerca; tuerca larga con filete a la derecha en un extremo y filete a la izquierda al otro, para juntar y acercar dos barras o tubos.

sleeved [ˈsliːvd] [sliivd], *a.* Que tiene mangas, antiguamente, mangado. **A sleeved waistcoat,** chupa con mangas.

sleeveless [ˈsliːvlɪs] [sliiv-les], *a.* 1. Sin mangas, que no tiene mangas. 2. *(Ant.)* Falto de razón o fundamento, fuera de camino. **Sleeveless tale,** fábula absurda o ridícula.

sleigh [sleɪ] [slei], *s.* Trinco, vehículo ligero y sin ruedas para caminar sobre la nieve y el hielo.

sleighing [ˈsleɪŋ] [sleiin], *s.* 1. Acción de ir en trineo. 2. La condición de los caminos que permite el uso de un trineo.

sleight [slaɪt] [slait], *s.* Ardid, artificio, estratagema, astucia, maña. **Sleight of hand,** juego de manos.

slender [ˈslendər] [slen-dar], *a.* 1. Delgado, sutil, tenue, de poco diámetro o circunferencia en proporción a su largo o altura (thin, slim). 2. Flaco, débil, enclenque, falto de vigor, delicado (delicate, dainty). 3. Escaso, de poca base o fundamento. 4. Pequeño, corto, insuficiente (short); mediano. 5. Delgado en sonido o calidad; falto de volumen. **Slender estate,** hacienda corta, pocos haberes. **Slender income,** renta corta. **A slender pittance,** una escasa pitanza. **Slender income,** renta corta. **A slender pittance,** una escasa pitanza. **Slender waist,** cintura o talle delgado. **Slender wit,** entendimiento limitado; ingenio o saber superficial, corto mérito. **Slender dinner,** comida escasa.

slenderness [ˈslendənɪs] [slen-da-nes], *s.* 1. Delgadez, sutileza, delicadeza. 2. Tenuidad, debilidad. 3. Escasez, falta de abundancia. 4. Pequeñez. 5. Debilidad, falta de vigor, falta de solidez.

slept [slept] [slept], *pp.* y *pret.* del verbo TO SLEEP.

sleuth [sluːθ] [sluz], *s.* 1. Pista, rastro de un hombre o animal. 2. *(Fam.)* Detective. **Sleuth-hound,** sabueso ventor. -*va.* Hacer el papel de detective.

slew [sluː] [slu], *pret.* del verbo TO SLAY.

sley [sleɪ] [slei], *va.* Dividir o torcer en hilos; poner la urdimbre en el telar. *V.* SLAY.

slice [slaɪs] [slais], *va.* 1. Rebanar, hacer rebanadas; cortar haciendo tiras o tajadas; a menudo con *up.* 2. Tajar, cortar, partir, dividir; se usa frecuentemente con *off.* **Slice through,** pasarse por encima, cortar.

slice, *s.* 1. Rebanada, tajada, lonja. 2. Una de las varias herramientas que se emplean para rebanar o partir; pala; espátula. 3. Golpe con efecto a la derecha (golf).

sliced [slaɪst] [slaist], *a.* Cortado en rebandas (bread).

slicer [ˈslaɪsər] [slai-saʳ], *s.* 1. Rebanador, el o lo que rebana. 2. Sierra circular o aparato de hender de los joyeros.

slick [slɪk] [slik], *va.* Alisar, hacer lindo, lustroso. -*a.* 1. Liso, resbaladizo, de tersura grasienta. 2. De palabras melifluas, adulador, rendido. 3. *(Fam.)* Diestro; mañosamente hecho. -*s.* Punto liso sobre la superficie del agua o en el pelo de un animal.

slicker [ˈslɪkər] [sli-kaʳ], *s.* 1. Impermeable. 2. *(Vul.)* Pillo, trampista.

slid [slɪd] [slid], *pret.* y *pp.* del verbo TO SLIDE.

slidden [slɪdn] [sli-den], *pp.* del verbo TO SLIDE.

slide [slaɪd] [slaid], *vn.* 1. Resbalar, deslizarse, irse los pies por encima de una superficie lisa (slip up, slith). 2. Escabullirse, escurrirse o deslizarse una cosa. 3. Correr o resbalar por encima del hielo. 4. Salirse, huir o escurrirse de entre las manos. 5. Correr, pasar, deslizarse o irse una cosa fácilmente. 6. Irse introduciendo, ir entrando, penetrar una cosa en otra poco a poco, y también se dice de las opiniones, modas, etc. 7. Errar, pecar. 8. No hacer caso de; con *let.* **Let the matter slide,** no haga usted caso del asunto. -*va.* Hacer colar, introducir o hacer recibir por medio del algún artificio una opinión, argumento, etc. **To slide away,** colarse, pasar sin ser observado; deslizarse o escurrirse una cosa de entre las manos. **To slide in,** introducirse en una parte sin ser sentido; introducir una cosa con maña y artificio. **To slide into,** pasar imperceptiblemente de un estado a otro, y regularmente se usa para expresar el pase de lo bueno a lo malo. **To slide over,** pasar ligeramente; recorrer ligera o superficialmente una cosa.

slide, *s.* 1. Tapa corrediza; tapa o pantalla fotográfica; portaobjetos para el microscopio o para la linterna óptica, cajón que se abre deslizándose. 2. Rebalón, acción de resbalar. 3. Sitio donde resbalan las personas o cosas; resbaladero, para deslizarse sobre la nieve; plano inclinado: paso llano y fácil; muesca, encaje (de un bastidor). 4. Falla, dislocación de una veta; desmoronamiento, caída de una masa de tierra. 5. Diapositiva, transparencia. 6. *(Mús.)* Ligado. **Slide-bolt,** pestillo corredizo, cerrojo de seguridad. **Microscope slide,** platina, porta-objetos. **To let things slide,** dejar las cosas de lado, no ocuparse de las cosas. **Slide-rest,** *(Mec.)* Soporte de corredera, carrillo portaherramientas. **Slide-valve,** válvula de corredera.

slider [ˈslaɪdər] [slai-daʳ], *s.* El que resbala.

slide rule [ˈslaɪdruːl] [slaid-rul], *s.* Regla de cálculo.

sliding [ˈslaɪdɪŋ] [slai-din], *s.* Deslizamiento, la acción y efecto de deslizar. **Sliding knot,** nudo escurridizo.

slight [slaɪt] [slait], *a.* 1. Ligero, leve, de poca importancia, de poco momento (light, brief). 2. Pequeño, corto, breve, limitado (short, brief). 3. Negligente, descuidado (negligent). 4. Necio, imprudente. 5. Fútil, débil, sin fuerza (weak). 6. Flojo, delgado (thing, weak). -*s.* Desaire, descuido, indiferencia, una acción u omisión que implica falta de cortesía, o desprecio; menosprecio. **The wound is only slight,** la herida es leve. **To make slight of,** despreciar, menospreciar, hacer poco caso de alguien o algo.

slight, *va.* 1. Menospreciar, despreciar, desdeñar, desestimar, no hacer caso, desairar, ver mal, sonrojar. 2. Hacer o ejecutar algo con poco cuidado. *V.* SHIRK. **To slight,** hacer una cosa con descuido o poco cuidado; tratar a una persona con poco aprecio o menospreciarla. **Not in the slightest,** ni en los más mínimo, en absoluto.

slighter [ˈslaɪtər] [slai-taʳ], *s.* menospreciador, desairador, indiferente; el que descuida.

slighting [ˈslaɪtɪŋ] [slai-tin], *a.* Despectivo, menospreciativo.

slightingly [ˈslaɪtɪŋlɪ] [slai-tin-li], *adv.* Con desprecio.

slightly [ˈslaɪtlɪ] [slait-li], *adv.* 1. Sin fuerza, ligeramente. **Slightly wounded,** ligeramente herido. 2. Negligentemente, descuidadamente.

slightness [ˈslaɪtnɪs] [slait-nes], *s.* 1. Debilidad, falta de vigor. 2. Descuido, negligencia.

slim [slɪm] [slim], *a.* 1. Delgado, sutil, tenue. 2. Poco lógico, débil. 3. Insubstancial, construido ligeramente, poco sólido. 4. Falto de vigor, enclenque. 5. Insuficiente, escaso, magro, flaco. *-vi.* **Slim down,** adelgazar, perder peso. **Slimmed down,** saneado, reconvertido.

slime [slaɪm] [slaim], *s.* 1. Cualquier sustancia viscosa o mucilaginosa, particularmente la sucia y adhesiva; lama, légamo, barro pegajoso, fango; exudación mucosa de ciertos animales y plantas. 2. Lodo mineral. 3. Cualquier cualidad o cosa repugnante. *-va. y vn.* 1. Ensuciar, cubrir o cubrirse de lama légamo o exudación mucosa. 2. Deslamar, quitar el légamo o sustancia viscosa.

slimy [ˈslaɪmɪ] [slai-mi], *a.* Viscoso, pegajoso, legamoso; mucoso.

sling [slɪŋ] [sling], *s.* 1. Honda, instrumento hecho de cuero o cuerda para arrojar piedras con violencia. 2. Hondazo. 3. El vendaje en que descansa un brazo roto, dislocado o herido; barbiquejo, cabestrillo. 4. *(Mar.)* Eslinga. **Slings of the yard,** cruz de la verga; estribos de las vergas. **Slings of the buoy,** guarnición de la boya.

sling, *s. (E. U.)* Bebida compuesta de aguardiente, whisky o ginebra con azúcar nuez moscada.

sling, *va.* 1. Tirar con honda; tirar, arrojar. 2. Colgar, suspender como en un cabestrillo; izar, columpiar o subir en alto, eslingar con una cuerda o polea. *-vn.* 1. Oscilar repentinamente; ir girando. 2. Moverse con paso suelto y fácil. **Sling away,** tirar. **Sling out,** brotar, expulsar.

slingshot [ˈslɪŋʃɒt] [slin-shot], *s.* Tirador.

slink [slɪŋk] [slink], *vn. (pret. y pp.* SLUNK o SLANK). Escabullirse, escaparse, escurrirse furtivamente.

slink, *va. y vn. (Reg.)* Abortar, malparir; se dice de las bestias.

slip [slɪp] [slip], *va. (pret. y pp.* SLIPPED o SLIPT). 1. Tirar, echar a un lado o arrojar una cosa que oprime o sujeta; hacer mover suave y fácilmente. 2. Meter o introducir secretamente. 3. Soltar, desatar, separar o arrancar una cosa de otra. 4. Dejar. 5. Perder alguna cosa por descuido o negligencia. 6. *(Mar.)* Largar (soltar), un cable o cabo. 7. Malparir (animal). 8. Dislocarse un hueso. 9. *(Ant.)* Recorrer, mirar o considerar alguna cosa superficialmente. *-vn.* 1. Resbalar, deslizarse, irse los pies. 2. Salirse alguna cosa de su lugar. 3. Rebalar, caer en alguna falta o error. 4. Escapar, huir, dejar un lugar o sitio repentinamente (escape from). 5. Pasar rápidamente sin ser visto ni sentido. 6. Deslizarse, decir o hacer una cosa con descuido o inadvertencia. 7. Borrarse algo de la memoria u olvidarlo.

slip away, desaparecer, marcharse o huir precipitadamente.

slip down dejarse caer.

slip into, introducirse alguno donde no le llaman; insinuarse en el ánimo de una persona con maña.

slip off, quitarse alguna cosa de encima del cuerpo.

slip out, salir de alguna parte sin ser observado o con disimulo; dislocarse un hueso. **To slip out a word,** escaparse alguna palabra. **To slip one's clothes on,** vestirse de prisa. **To slip the cable,** *(Jar.)* Alargar el cable por el ojo o por el chicote.

slip, *s.* 1. Resbalón, el acto de resbalar. 2. Desliz, falta, tropiezo. 3. Esqueje, estaca, vástago desgajado. 4. Escapada, huida. 5. Tira, pedazo largo y angosto. 6. Pasaje o espacio largo en proporción a su anchura: en los Estados Unidos, espacio entre dos muelles, dique, embarcadero, como un *ferry-slip.* 7. Equivocación, error, engaño. 8. Falta, ligera dislocación de los estratos. 9. *(Impr.)* Galerada, molde que aún no está en páginas. 10. Lo que se pone o quita fácilmente, como una funda de almohada o una prenda de vestir holgada; guardapiés, zagalejo; traílla, la cuerda o correa con que se lleva al perro atado. **Slip of paper,** tira de papel. **Slip of the tongue,** lapsus linguae, yerro de lengua. **Glass slip,** portaobjetos para el microscopio; con el objeto montado en su lugar se llama *slide.*

slipboard [ˈslɪpbɔːd] [slip-bord], *s.* Corredera.

slipknot [ˈslɪpnɒd] [slip-not], *s.* Lazo corredizo.

slip-on [ˈslɪpɒn] [slip-on], *s.* Prenda de vestir que entra por la cabeza. **Slip-on sweater,** suéter o chaqueta tejida que no tiene botonadura.

slipped [ˈslɪpt] [slipt], *a.* **Slipped disk,** hernia discal.

slipper [ˈslɪpəʳ] [sli-paʳ], *s.* Chinela, pantuflo, zapato ligero y bajo, zapatilla.

slipperiness [ˈslɪpərɪnɪs] [sli-pa-ri-nes], *s.* 1. La calidad que constituye a una cosa resbaladiza. 2. La facilidad en deslizarse o resbalarse. 3. El estado de lo que es muy movedizo o poco firme.

slippery [ˈslɪpərɪ] [sli-pe-ri], *a.* 1. Resbaladizo, escurridizo, deslizadizo. 2. Movedizo, poco firme, poco sólido: se dice regularmente del terreno. 3. Que se escapa de entre las manos; engañador, indigno de confianza. **A slippery witness,** un testigo engañador, indigno de confianza.

slippy [ˈslɪpɪ] [sli-pi], *a.* **To be slippy,** darse prisa (hurry up).

slipshod [ˈslɪpʃɒd] [slip-shod], *a.* En chancletas. **To go slipshod,** *(Fam.)* Andar o ir en chancleta, o chancletas.

slit [slɪt] [slit], *va. (pret. y pp.* SLIT o SLITTED). 1. Hacer una larga incisión (en algo). 2. Tajar, cortar a lo largo en tiras o jirones.

slit, *s.* Raja, hendedura; corte relativamente largo; abertura larga y estrecha.

slither [ˈslɪðəʳ] [sli-zaʳ], *vi.* Deslizarse, ir rodando, resbalar.

slitting [ˈslɪtɪŋ] [sli-tin], *s. y pa.* de SLIT. Acción de dar un corte largo o de cortar largas tiras. **Slitting-mill,** 1. Taller donde se cortan planchas de metal en tiras para hacer clavos. 2. Sierra de disco empleada por los joyeros para labrar las piedras preciosas. 3. Sierra múltiple para aserrar tablillas, etc.

sliver [ˈslɪvəʳ] [sli-vaʳ], *va. y vn.* 1. Cortar, romper o romperse en trozos largos, a lo largo. 2. Desgajar, desgajarse, romperse.

sliver, *s.* Brizna, astilla. V. SPLINGER. 2. Torzal, mecha de fibras textiles.

sloats [ˈsləʊts] [slouts], *s. pl.* Teleras de carro.

slobber [ˈslɒbəʳ] [slo-baʳ], *s.* Baba. V. SLAVER.

slobber, *va.* Babosear.

slobbery [ˈslɒbrɪ] [slo-ba-ri], *a.* Baboso, mojado.

sloe [sləʊ] [slou], *s.* Endrina, la fruta del endrino; también, el mismo endrino.

slog [slɒg] [slog], *s.* **It was a slog,** me costó trabajo. *-vt.* Golpear. *-vi.* Trabajar arduamente, sudar tinta.

slog along, Caminar con dificultad, costosamente.

slog away. To slog away at something, afanarse por realizar algo.

slog on = slog along.

slog out. To slog it out, luchar hasta el final (fighting).

slogan [ˈsləʊgən] [slou-gan], *s.* Eslogan, pintada (graffiti).

slogger [ˈslɒgəʳ] [slo-gaʳ], *s.* Trabajador.

sloop [ˈsluːp] [slup], *s. (Mar.)* Balandra, embarcación pequeña. **Sloop-of-war,** *(Mar.)* Corbeta, embarcación de guerra.

slop [slɒp] [slop], *va.* 1. Verter, derramar. 2. Verter agua u otro líquido sobre algo; mojar, ensuciar, enlodar. *-vn.* Verterse, derramarse.

slop, *s.* 1. La mancha que se hace dejando caer algún líquido; lugar mojado. 2. *pl.* Agua sucia; desechos líquidos. 3. *pl.* Atole, u otro alimento líquido (por desprecio): zupia, purrela, aguachirle. **Slop-basin, slop-bowl,** barreño o receptáculo, para aguas sucias. **Slop-jar,** jarro o tinaja para aguas sucias, particularmente pieza de un juego de tocador. **Slop-pail, slop-bucket,** cubo o tina para agua sucia. **Slop-shop,** bazar *(E.U.).*

slope [sləʊp] [sloup], *s.* 1. Sesgo, la oblicuidad o torcimiento de alguna cosa hacia un lado; escotadura. 2. Declive, descenso, bajada, loma. 3. Escarpa. *-a.* Sesgo, torcido, inclinado, en pendiente. *-adv.* Al sesgo, oblicuamente.

sloping [ˈsləʊpɪŋ] [slou-pin], *a.* Inclinado, en declive.

slopingly ['sləʊpɪŋlɪ] [slou-pin-li], *adv.* Sesgadamente, al sesgo.

sloppily ['slɒpɪlɪ] [slou-pi-li], *adv.* De modo descuidado (carelessly).

sloppiness ['slɒpɪnɪs] [slou-pi-nes], *s.* Calidad de mojado y sucio; estado cenagoso.

sloppy ['slɒpɪ] [slo-pi], *a.* 1. Mojado y sucio: lodoso, cenagoso, lleno de lodo o cieno. 2. Hecho de una manera descuidada.

slosh [slɒʃ] [slosh], *va.* y *vn.* V. SPLASH. -*s.* V. SLUSH.

slot [slɒt] [slot], *s.* 1. *(Mec.)* Muesca, ranura, canal o hendedura larga y estrecha. 2. Pista, huella de venado.

slot, *va.* 1. Ajustar en una ranura. 2. Acanalar, cortar una ranura o muesca.

sloth [sləʊθ] [slouz], *s.* 1. Pereza, negligencia, dejadez, flojedad. 2. Perezoso, un animal arbóreo de la América tropical.

slothful ['sləʊθfʊl] [slouz-ful], *a.* Perezoso, tardo, lento; dejado, negligente.

slothfully ['sləʊθfʊlɪ] [slouz-fu-li], *adv.* Perezosamente, flojamente, con dejadez.

slothfulness ['sləʊθfʊlnɪs] [slouz-ful-nes], *s.* Pereza, tardanza, pesadez, haraganería.

slot-machine ['slɒtməʃiːn] [slot-ma-shin], *s.* Máquina con ranuras para monedas en que se juega dinero.

slouch [slaʊtʃ] [slauch], *s.* 1. Mirada cabizbaja; inclinación del cuerpo. 2. Patán, rústico, villano.

slouch, *va.* y *vn.* 1. Estar o andar cabizbajo. 2. Poner una cosa más baja o caída y suelta de lo que estaba. **Slouch-hat,** sombrero gacho o con las alas caídas. **Slouch about/around,** andar cabizbajo, sin saber qué hacer; gandulear.

slough [slaʊ] [slau], *s.* Lodaza, el sitio pantanoso y lleno de lodo, *(Fig.)* abismo de la desesperación. **The slough of despond,** el abismo de la desesperación.

slough, *s. (E.U.)* 1. Pantano; canal de agua, abra llena de cañas. 2. Lodazal.

slough, *va.* y *vn.* Echar o ser echado, como el tejido muerto: echar de sí una costra. -*s.* 1. El pellejo suelto o fuera del cuerpo de ciertos animales que lo mudan: en la culebra y en la serpiente se llama camisa y en algunos insectos tela; por extensión se dice también a veces del pellejo humano. 2. Escara de una herida o úlcera; el tejido muerto separado y desechado de las partes vivas.

sloughy ['slaʊɪ] [slaui], *a.* Lodos, pantanoso.

sloughy, *a.* Que tiene tejidos muertos y desechados, o que es propio de ellos.

Slovak ['sləʊvæk] [slou-vak], *a.* Eslovaco.

sloven ['slʌvn] [sla-ven], *s.* Persona desaliñada y desaseada.

slovenliness ['slʌvnlɪnɪs] [sla-ven-li-nes], *s.* 1. Desaliño, desaseo en el vestir. 2. Asquerosidad, porquería. 3. Negligencia, descuido, dejadez.

slovenly ['slʌvnlɪ] [sla-ven-li], *a.* 1. Desaliñado, desaseado, puerco, sucio. 2. Dejado, descuidado. -*adv.* Desliñadamente, con desaseo, con dejadez.

slow [sləʊ] [slou], *va.* y *vn.* Retardar, aflojar el paso, diferir, ir más despacio, a menudo con las preposiciones *up* o *down.* -*s.* 1. Tardío, lento, pausado, detenido, tardo en obrar, en moverse o en cualquier otra cosa. 2. Tardío, tardo, que sucede después de tiempo oportuno. 3. Tardo, lento, torpe, pesado. 4. Tardo, torpe, poco expedito en comprender las cosas o en explicarse. **Slow coach,** indolente, perezoso, negligente, dejado. **Slow-ared,** pesado en el andar. **Slow-witted,** torpe, estúpido. **Life here is slow,** aquí se vive a ritmo lento. **To be slow pay,** ser moroso. **My watch goes too slow,** mi reloj atrasa. **The match is very slow,** el partido es muy aburrido.

slowdown ['sləʊdaʊn] [slou-daun], *sf. (E.U.)* Huelga de manos caídas.

slowly ['sləʊlɪ] [slou-li], *adv.* Lentamente, pausadamente, con lentitud.

slow motion ['sləʊ'məʊʃən] [slou-mo-shon], *s.* Movimiento lento, tardío. **Slow motion camera,** cámara lenta.

slowness ['sləʊnɪs] [slou-nes], *s.* 1. Lentitud, tardanza, detención. 2. Pesadez o torpeza de entendimiento, negadez. 3. Dilación, retardación, retardo. 4. Deliberación.

slowworm ['sləʊwɜːm] [slou-uerm], *s.* Cecilia, serpiente pequeña.

slub [slʌb] [slab], *va.* Torcer un poco (torzales de lana) antes de encanillar; ovillar. -*s.* Hilo my poco retorcido, mechón.

slubber ['slʌbəʳ] [sla-baʳ], *va.* 1. Hacer alguna cosa de mala gana o con prisa intempestiva, chafallar. 2. Manchar, ensuciar. -*vn.* Estar muy de prisa, hacer algo muy de prisa y aturdidamente.

slubber, *s.* Canillero, el que hace canillas o mechones de hilo; ovillador de lana.

sludge ['slʌdʒ] [sladch], *s.* Lodo, cieno.

slue [sluː] [slu], *va.* (pa. SLUING, *pp.* SLUED). 1. Revirar, mover a un lado como sobre un eje. 2. Volver, girar. -*s.* Giro, vuelta.

slug [slʌg] [slag], *s.* 1. Haragán, holgazán, zángano. 2. Babosa, caracol que se cría sin concha, también la larva de un tentredo (mosca de sierra) u otro insecto parecido a la babosa. 3. El pedazo de metal que se mete en algún arma de fuego en lugar de bala. 4. *(Impr.)* Lingote, tira de metal más gruesa que un renglón.

slug, *va.* Cargar (firearm) con trozos de metal en lugar de balas.

slug, *va.* y *vn. (Ger.)* Dar fuertes puñadas.

sluggard ['slʌgəd] [sla-gard], *s.* Haragán, holgazán.

sluggish ['slʌgɪʃ] [sla-guish], *a.* Perezoso, flojo, dejado, descuidado, indolente.

sluggishly ['slʌgɪʃlɪ] [sla-guish-li], *adv.* Perezosamente, lentamente, con flojedad.

sluggishness ['slʌgɪʃnɪs] [sla-guish-nes], *s.* Pereza, flojedad, negligencia, dejadez.

sluice [sluːs] [slus], *s.* 1. Canal, acequia, acueducto, azud; compuerta, especie de puerta pequeña en los canales o en las presas de ríos. 2. *(Fig.)* Salida, la cosa a través de la cual sale o fluye algo.

sluice, *va.* 1. Mojar, regar, por medio de acequias; lavar la tierra que contiene el mineral en una acequia. 2. Soltar la presa o quitar la compuerta de un canal, acquia, etc.

sluicy ['sluːsɪ] [slui-si], *a.* Que fluye en torrente, como el agua luego que se suelta una presa.

slum [slʌm] [slam], *s.* Barrio bajo y sucio de una población; garito. -*vn.* Visitar los barrios bajos, particularmente cuando se hace por mera curiosidad. **To live in a slum,** vivir en los barrios bajos, vivir en una casucha. **Slum area,** barrio bajo.

slumber ['slʌmbəʳ] [slam-baʳ], *vn.* 1. Dormitar, estar medio dormido (sleep); *(poét.)* dormir. 2. Dormirse o descuidarse uno en las obligaciones de su empleo u oficio o en lo que tiene que hacer.

slumber, *s.* Sueño ligero y tranquilo.

slumberous ['slʌmbərəs] [slam-be-ros], *a.* Soñoliento, soporífero.

slummy ['slʌmɪ] [sla-mi], *a.* Sórdido, muy pobre.

slump [slʌmp] [slamp], *vn.* Romper una costra y hundirse en una materia blanda cualquiera, como la nieve, *(Fam.)* salir mal, faltar, hacer bancarrota. -*s.* Rompimiento y hundimiento; desplome; mal éxito, quiebra.

slung [slʌŋ] [slang], *pret.* y *pp.* del verbo *TO* SLING. **Slung-shot,** rompecabezas, arma ofensiva.

slunk [slʌŋk] [slank], *pret.* y *pp.* del verbo *TO* SLINK.

slur [slɜːʳ] [sleʳ], *va.* 1. Menospreciar, rebajar, desdorar a alguno. 2. Pasar ligeramente, ocultar. 3. Hacer algo o hablar de una manera confusa; juntar palabras o sílabas. 4. *(Mús.)* Ligar las notas. 5. Manchar, ensuciar.

slur, *s.* 1. Estigma, observación en desdoro; estigma; borrón o mancha ligera en la reputación. 2. *(Mús.)* Ligadura que indica que las notas han de encadenarse. 3. *(Impr.)* Porción manchada de una impresión.

slurp [slɜːp] [slerp], *vt.* Sorber.

slurred [slɜːd] [slerd], *a.* Poco correcto (speech).

slurry ['slʌrɪ] [sla-ri], *s.* Lodo, compuesto acuoso.

slush [slʌʃ] [slash], *va.* 1. Ensebar, engrasar con una sustancia lubricante. 2. *(Alb.)* Llenar de argamasa; generalmente con la preposición *up.* 3. Lavar, echando agua sobre un puente o cubierta. -*s.* 1. Materia blanda y mojada, como la nieve que se derrite, o el fango: cieno, lodo blando. 2. Grasa lubricante; pintura para evitar el enmohecimiento.

slushy ['slʌʃɪ] [sla-shi], *a.* Cubierto de nieve a medio derretir o de cieno; parecido a estas substancias.

slut [slʌt] [slat], *sf.* 1. Perra, la hembra del perro. 2. Una mujer sucia o asquerosa; en otro tiempo se aplicaba también a los hombres.

sluttish ['slʌtɪʃ] [sla-tish], *a.* Asqueroso, puerco, sucio, desaliñado, despreciable.

sluttishly ['slʌtɪʃlɪ] [sla-tish-li], *adv.* Asquerosamente.

sluttishness ['slʌtɪʃnɪs] [sla-tish-nes], *s.* Asquerosidad, porquería, suciedad.

sly [slaɪ] [slai], *a.* Astuto, taimado, pícaro, socarrón, disimulado, artificioso, falso, martagón, marrajo. **Sly blade,** encallecido en astucias, camastrón, gran perillán.

slyboots ['slaɪˌbuːts] [slai-buts], *s. (Fam.)* Mañuelas, martagón, mátalas-callando, sueco, socarrón; la persona astuta y cauta que sabe manejar diestramente sus negocios.

slyly ['slaɪlɪ] [slai-li], *adv.* Astutamente, disimuladamente, con artificio, con maña, con segundas; a hurtadillas, callandito, bonitamente.

slyness ['slaɪnɪs] [slai-nes], *s.* Mañuela, socarronería, la maña con astucia y bellaquería; disimulo; con segunda o con segunda intención.

smack [smæk] [smak], *vn.* 1. Saber, tener algún sabor particular (taste). 2. Oler o tener sabor u olor (smell): se dice de las opiniones, doctrinas, etc. **His language smacks of atheism,** su lenguaje huele a ateísmo o tiene sabor u olor de ateísmo. 3. Saborearse, hacer ruido, desuniendo los labios, como después de catar o probar alguna cosa. 4. Besarse mutuamente estrechando los labios. -*va.* Besar, dar un beso. **To smack one's lips,** relamerse.

smack, *s.* 1. Sabor, gusto. 2. Tintura, conocimiento ligero o superficial. 3. Gusto, semejanza, resabio, tintura; el residuo que queda de alguna cosa que ha estado unida a otra, después de separarse. 4. Un poco o una cantidad corta de cualquier cosa. 5. La acción de separar los labios haciendo ruido con ellos. 6. Beso fuerte y ruidoso, o que se oye. 7. Manotada. 8. Chasquido, golpe. 9. *(Mar.)* Esmaque, embarcación pequeña. **I'll have a smack at it,** lo intentaré, lo voy a probar.

smacker ['smækəʳ] [sma-kaʳ], *s.* Beso o golpe con ruido.

small [smɔːl] [smol], *a.* 1. Pequeño, menudo, chico; corto (short, little). **When we were small,** cuando éramos pequeños. 2. Poco; de poco momento, peso o importancia. 3. Falto de amplitud moral o mental; corto, despreciable, mezquino (mean, stingy). 4. Que funciona o que comercia de una manera limitada. 5. Débil, flojo. 6. Tierno, blando; fino, delgado, de poco bulto o volumen. 7. Oscuro, bajo, vulgar, plebeyo. **To cut small,** hacer pedazos menudos alguna cosa. **Small change,** calderilla. **Small print,** carácter de letra muy menuda. **To make small,** achicar. -*s.* 1. La parte estrecha de cualquier cosa y en particular del lomo o filo. 2. Cosa o cantidad pequeña. -*adv.* En tono bajo o suave. **Small arms,** armas blancas. **Small beer,** cerveza débil o floja. **Small-clothes,** calzones cortos. **Small coal,** carbón menudo, cisco. **Small fry,** los peces pequeños en general; de aquí, gente menuda o cosas pequeñas. **Small talk,** conversación sin importancia, vulgaridades. **The small hours,** las primeras horas de la mañana, la una, las dos, etc. **Small craft,** conjunto de embarcaciones menores; *(Fig.)* cosas o personas pequeñas en general. **Small pica,** V. PICA. **A small voice,** una vocecita, una voz delgada (o suave). **Small wares,** mercería.

smallage ['smɔːlɪdʒ] [smo-lich], *s.* Apio particularmente en estado silvestre.

smallish ['smɔːlɪʃ] [smo-lish], *a.* Algo pequeño, corto, menudo.

smallness ['smɔːlnɪs] [smol-nes], *s.* Pequeñez; debilidad.

smallpox ['smɔːlpɒks] [smol-poks], *s.* Viruelas.

smalt ['smɔːlt] [smolt], *s.* Esmalte, un vidrio azul oscuro, teñido por el óxido de cobalto; esmaltín que sirve para pintar.

smart [smaːt] [smart], *s.* 1. Escozor, dolor vivo y punzante (pain). 2. Dolor, aflicción. 3. *(Vulg.)* Bullebulle, el que afecta viveza y actividad; muchacho muy despierto. -*a.* 1. Punzante, agudo, acerbo, agrio, picante. 2. Vivo, eficaz, activo, vivaracho; *(E. U.)* inteligente, despierto, hábil, de talento, avisado, despejado, ingenioso, despabilado (clever). 3. Agudo, ingenioso, sutil. 4. Mordiente, mordaz, picante. 5. *(Ingl.)* Elegante, petimetre, a la moda; estimable, gallardo.

smart, *va.* 1. Escocer, percibir una sensación muy desagradable parecida a la de una quemadura. 2. Escocer, sentir en el ánimo una impresión desagradable, dolerse. **I will make you smart for it,** le haré a usted arrepentirse. **My eyes are smarting,** me duelen los ojos. **To smart under,** resentirse.

smarten ['smaːtn] [smar-ten], *va.* Hermosear, embellecer; hacer a uno gallardo, donoso.

smartly ['smaːtlɪ] [smart-li], *adv.* 1. Agudamente, vivamente, sensiblemente. 2. Agudamente, con agudeza de ingenio, con finura, con delicadeza, elegantemente.

smartness ['smaːtnɪs] [smart-nes], *s.* 1. Agudeza, vigor. 2. Viveza, vivacidad, perspicacia de ingenio, agudeza, sutileza.

smarty ['smaːtɪ] [smar-ti], *a.* Sabelotodo, listillo.

smash [smæʃ] [smash], *va. y vn.* 1. Hacer pedazos o añicos (break into pieces); hacer astillas, romper o romperse de golpe; *(Fam.)* hacer bancarrota. 2. Machacar, allanar, aplastar (squash, crush). -*s.* 1. Machacamiento, acto de machacar o romper; se usa a menudo con la prep. *up;* ruina, quiebra. 2. Bebida de licores espirituosos. **To go to smash,** arruinarse, quebrar. **Smash down,** romper. **Smash up,** destrozar, hacer pedazos.

smashup ['smæʃʌp] [smash-ap], *s.* 1. Choque o colisión desastroso. 2. Quiebra total.

smatter ['smætəʳ] [sma-taʳ], *vn.* 1. Saber una cosa superficialmente y muy por encima. 2. Hablar superficialmente y sin conocimiento.

smatterer ['smætərəʳ] [sma-ta-raʳ], *s.* El que sabe una cosa superficialmente o a medias.

smattering ['smætərɪŋ] [sma-te-rin], *s.* Tintura, conocimiento superficial de una cosa o de varias.

smear [smɪəʳ] [smiaʳ], *va.* 1. Salpicar, untar, cubrir de una substancia viscosa, emporcar, ensuciar. 2. Calumniar, difamar. -*s.* 1. Mancha, embarradura. 2. Calumnia, difamación.

smeary ['smɪərɪ] [smia-ri], *a.* Graso; pegajoso.

smell [smel] [smel], *va. (pret. y pp.* SMELLED o SMELT). 1. Oler, percibir, descubrir, conocer; olfatear, oliscar. **To smell a rat,** oler el poste. **I will smell him out,** yo le descubriré. -*vn.* 1. Oler, despedir o echar de sí fragancia o hedor. **It smells good,** huele bien. 2. Oler, parecerse o tener señas y visos de alguna cosa ordinariamente mala. **To smell of,** oler a. **To smell strong,** despedir un olor fuerte.

smell, *s.* 1. Olfato, sentido del olfato. 2. Olor (odour); perfume (scent). 3. Fragancia o hediondez. 4. Olor, traza, vestigio. **To be offensive to the smell,** herir, ofender el olfato. **To have a keen sense of smell,** tener buen olfato. **It smells good,** huele bien. **Smell out,** husmear, olfatear.

smeller ['smeləʳ] [sme-laʳ], *s.* Oledor, el que huele.

smellfeast ['smelfiːst] [smel-fist], *s.* Parásito, gorrista, mogollón.

smelliness ['smelɪnɪs] [sme-li-nes], *sf.* Hediondez.

smelling ['smelɪŋ] [sme-lin], *s.* El acto de oler. **Smelling-bottle,** vasito o redomilla para olores. **Smelling salts,** sales aromáticas. **Sweet-smelling,** *a.* Hediondo, que huele mal.

smelly ['smelɪ] [sme-li], *a.* Maloliente, que huele mal, apestoso.

smelt ['smelt] [smelt], *pret. y pp.* del verbo *TO* SMELL.

smelt, *s.* Esperlán.

smelt, *va.* Fundir, derretir minerales para extraer el metal.

smelter ['smeltə^r] [smel-ta^r], s. Fundidor.

smile [smɑɪl] [smail], vn. 1. Sonreírse, reírse un poco o levemente. 2. Manifestar alegría o lozanía. **The meadows smile,** ríen los prados. 3. Favorecer, ser propicio. **Fortune smiles on him,** la fortuna le favorece. 4. Despreciar o no hacer caso de alguna cosa sonriéndose. -va. Expresar o efectuar por medio de una sonrisa. **To smile one's thanks,** dar las gracias con una sonrisa. **To smile at, on o upon,** sonreír a uno. **To give somebody a smile,** sonreír a alguien. **To smile assent,** consentir con una sonrisa.

smile, s. 1. Sonrisa. 2. Aspecto agradable o risueño. 3. Disposición favorable o propicia; favor, bendición.

smiley ['smɑɪlɪ] [smai-li], a. Risueño, sonriente (eyes, face).

smiling ['smɑɪlɪŋ] [smai-lin], a. Risueño, sonriente.

smilingly ['smɑɪlɪŋlɪ] [smai-lin-li], adv. Con cara risueña, con sonrisa, sonriendo.

smirch [smɜːtʃ] [smerch], va. 1. Ensuciar, tiznar, mancillar, deslucir. 2. (Fig.) Desdorar, denigrar, difamar, deshonrar.

smirk [smɜːk] [smerk], vn. Sonreírse con desenvoltura; sonreírse agradablemente, tener cara de risa. **To smirk upon,** Mirar risueño. **Smirking look,** cara risueña.

smirker ['smɜːkə^r] [smer-ka^r], s. El que muestra risa en el semblante.

smit [smɪt] [smit], pp. o pret. del verbo TO SMITE.

smitch ['smɪtʃ] [smich], s. (Fam.) Pedacito, partícula.

smite [smɑɪt] [smait], va. (pret. SMOTE o SMIT, pp. SMITTEN o SMIT). 1. Herir, golpear. 2. Afligir, castigar. 3. Herir o tocar al alma, mover o excitar algún afecto, ganar el corazón. **She has mitten you,** te ha encantado o te ha robado el corazón o el alma. **An idea smote me,** se me ocurrió una idea. **It smites my heart,** me llega al alma. 4. Quemar o abochornar el calor las tierras o frutos. 5. Arruinar, destruir, asolar. 6. Cortar, partir o romper por medio de un golpe. 7. (Ant.) Matar, quitar la vida. -vn. Venir con fuerza repentina; chocar.

smiter ['smɑɪtə^r] [smi-ta^r], s. El que hiere o aflige; golpeador.

smith [smɪθ] [smiz], s. Forjador de metales. **Blacksmith,** herrero. **Smith and farrier,** herrador, albéitar. **Locksmith,** cerrajero. **Goldsmith,** orífice. **Silversmith,** platero.

smithereens ['smɪθərənz] [smi-ze-rens], s. pl. (Fam.) Añicos, fragmentos producidos por golpes.

smithery ['smɪθərɪ] [smi-ze-ri], s. 1. Herrería, el arte u oficio del herrero. 2. Herrería, taller en que se funde el hierro o en que se hacen obras de hierro en grueso.

smithy ['smɪθɪ] [smi-zi], s. Forja, hornaza de herrero o cerrajero.

smitten ['smɪtn] [smi-ten], pp. de TO SMITE.

smock [smɒk] [smok], s. Camisa de mujer. **Smock-frock,** blusa de obrero o labriego. **Smock-faced,** de cara afeminada. -a. (Des.) Afeminado, parecido a una mujer.

smocking ['smɒkɪŋ] [smo-kin], sm. Adorno con frunces.

smog [smɒg] [smog], s. Mezcla de niebla y humo propia de algunas grandes ciudades.

smoke [smɔʊk] [smok], s. Humo, vapor espeso que exhala lo que se está quemando. **To end in smoke,** volverse humo. **Smoke-consumer,** aparato o útil fumívoro que sirve para consumir más completamente los gases de la combustión. **Smoke-consuming,** Fumívoro. **Smoke-house,** cuarto cerrado para ahumar o acecinar carnes, pieles, etc. **Smoke-jack,** torno de asador que se mueve por medio del humo. **Smoke-stack,** chimenea, cañón por donde pasa el humo (de un vapor, locomotora, etc.). **Smoke-tree,** arbusto o árbol de adorno con largos tallos parecidos a plumas: zumaque veneciano.

smoke, s. 1. Humear, echar de sí humo. 2. Arder, estar encendido. **To go up in smoke,** quedar destruido en un incendio. 3. Moverse con velocidad levantando polvo. 4. Oler, descubrir. 5. Fumar, consumir tabaco en cigarro o pipa. -va. 1. Ahumar, poner al humo alguna cosa para que se cure; sahumar. 2. Fumar, quemar tabaco en hoja; aspirar el humo del tabaco. **To have a smoke,** echar un pitillo. 3. Ahumar, ahogar con humo; echar, hacer salir por medio del

humo; se usa frecuentemente con la prep. out. 4. (Ant.) Oler, descubrir, indagar. **To smoke out,** expeler a uno con intención de que no vuelva.

smoked [smɔʊkt] [smoukt], a. Ahumado.

smoke-dry ['smɔʊkdraɪ] [smouk-drai], va. Ahumar, secar al humo.

smokeless ['smɔʊklɪs] [smouk-les], a. Desahumado; sin humo, que no da humo. **Smokeless powder,** pólvora sin humo.

smoker ['smɔʊkə^r] [smou-ka^r], s. 1. Sahumador; fumador. 2. Caja o aparato con que se echa humo sobre las abejas para aquietarlas. 3. (E. U.) Coche de fumar. 4. (Fam.) Tertulia en que se permite fumar.

smoke screen ['smɔʊkskriːn] [smouk-skrin], s. Cortina de humo.

smoking ['smɔʊkɪŋ] [smou-kin], s. Acción de ahumar o de fumar. **Smoking-car (smoking-carriage** en Inglaterra), coche de fumar. **No smoking (allowed),** se prohibe fumar.

smoky ['smɔʊkɪ] [smou-ki], a. Humeante; humoso.

smolder, smouler ['smɔʊldə^r] [smoul-da^r], vn. 1. Arder sin llama y humear. 2. Existir en estado latente.

smooch ['smuːtʃ] [smuch], vi. Acariciarse, besuquearse.

smooth [smuːð] [smuz], a. 1. Liso, pulido, bruñido, alisado (polish, neat). 2. Llano, igual; uniforme, sin variación (flat); fácil, libre de impedimentos u obstáculos. 3. Suave, mansa, hablando de la corriente; suave, dulce, delicado, tierno (delicate, sweet). 4. Lisonjero, halagüeño, adulador, carantoñero. 5. Cortés, afable. 6. (Gram. **griega**) No aspirado; contrapuesto a rough. 7. Que no tiene un sabor acídulo ni astringente; se dice de los licores. **A smooth surface,** una superficie lisa, igual. **Smooth water,** agua mansa. **Smoothbore,** ánima lisa. **Smooth-faced,** 1. barbilampiño, sin barba; 2. alisado; 3. de semblante apacible y sereno. **Smooth-grained,** que tiene vetas lisas. **Smooth-sliding,** que se desliza con suavidad e igualdad. **Smooth-paced,** lo que anda con paso igual. **Smooth-shaven,** que está rasurado por igual. **Smooth-spoken, smooth-tongued,** de palabras meliflúas, lisonjeras.

smooth, va. 1. Allanar, poner llana o igual la superficie de alguna cosa. 2. Alisar, poner lisa alguna cosa. 3. Allanar, facilitar. 4. Pacificar, aquietar; calmar, ablandar, lisonjear. **Smoothing-iron,** hierro para alisar. **Smoothing-plane,** cepillo corto. **Smooth back,** alisarse, peinarse hacia atrás. **Smooth out,** arreglar. **To smooth over difficulties,** allanar dificultades.

smoothly ['smuːðlɪ] [smuz-li], adv. 1. Igualmente, con igualdad, sin desigualdad. 2. Lisamente, llanamente. 3. Fácilmente, libremente. 4. Blandamente, inocentemente. 5. Halgüeñamente, con halagos, afablemente.

smoothness ['smuːðnɪs] [smuz-nes], s. 1. Lisura, igualdad y lustre de la superficie, llanura. 2. Bruñido, tersura. 3. Suavidad, dulzura o dulzor de las cosas al gusto. 4. Blandura, suavidad o dulzura en el estilo, en el discurso, etc.

smote [smɔʊt] [smout], pret. de TO SMITE.

smother ['smʌðə^r] [sma-da^r], va. 1. Ahogar, sofocar, impedir la respiración; también, hacer morir por falta de aire. 2. Ahogar, apagar (fuego, llama). 3. Suprimir, ocultar, disfrazar. 4. Embadurnar, embarrar. 5. Hablando de cocina, encerrar y cocer algo dentro de una masa apretada. -vn. 1. Ahogarse, asfixiarse, carecer de respiración. 2. Estar oculto por falta de aire, v. g. un fuego. 3. (Fig.) Hallarse oculto, suprimido.

smother, s. 1. Supresión, el efecto de suprimir; ahogo, sofocación. 2. Humareda, polvareda.

smoulder ['smɔʊldə^r] [smoul-da^r], v. V. SMOLDER.

smouldering ['smɔʊldərɪŋ] [smoul-de-rin], a. Lleno de humo sin salida, sofocante.

smudge [smʌdʒ] [smadch], va. 1. Tiznar, manchar con tizne u hollín; ensuciar. 2. (E. U.) Fumigar, ahumar, v. g. para ahuyentar los mosquitos o evitar la escarcha. -s. 1. Tizne, hollín; ensuciamiento con una materia seca u hollín. 2.

Fuego humoso para ahuyentar los insectos, impedir la escarcha o acecinar la carne. 3. Raspas de pintura y barniz.

smudgy ['smʌdʒɪ] [smad-chi], *a.* 1. Tiznado, holliniento, ensuciado. 2. Humeante, v. g. un fumigador, llamado *smudge,* 2ª acep.

smug [smʌg] [smag], *a.* Atildado, pulido con afectación, nimiamente compuesto y satisfecho de sí mismo.

smuggle ['smʌgl] [sma-guel], *va.* 1. Hacer o ejercer el contrabando, matutear, entrar o sacar géneros por alto. 2. Pasar o introducir algo clandestinamente, a escondidas. *-vn.* Hacer contrabando.

smuggler ['smʌglər] [sma-glaʳ], *s.* Contrabandista, metedor, matutero.

smuggling ['smʌglɪŋ] [sma-glin], *s.* Comercio de contrabando, meteduría.

smugly ['smʌglɪ] [sma-gli], *adv.* Pulidamente, afectadamente.

smugness ['smʌgnɪs] [smag-nes], *s.* Afectación y nimiedad en el vestir.

smut [smʌt] [smat], *s.* 1. Tiznón, la mancha que se hace en alguna cosa untándola con tizne; suciedad. 2. Tizón, tizoncillo, enfermedad de las plantas producida por un hongo parásito. 3. Obscenidad, impureza, palabras sucias u obscenas.

smut, *va.* 1. Tiznar, manchar o señalar con tizne; ensuciar. 2. Atizonar, añublar. 3. Destizonar, quitar el tizón de los granos. 4. *(Fig.)* Mancillar la reputación, echar un baldón, infamar. *-vn.* Añublarse, atizonarse los trigos.

smutch ['smʌtʃ] [smach], *va.* Tiznar, manchar con tizne, hollín u otro unto semejante.

smuttily ['smʌtɪlɪ] [sma-ti-li], *adv.* 1. Con humo o tizne, suciamente. 2. Impúdicamente, deshonestamente, obscenamente.

smuttiness ['smʌtɪnɪs] [sma-ti-nes], *s.* 1. Tizne, el humo que se pega a las cosas; tiznón, la mancha que deja el tizne. 2. Obscenidad, impureza.

smutty ['smʌtɪ] [sma-ti], *a.* 1. Tiznado, manchado con tizne, hollín o carbón. 2. Humoso: se dice del lugar que contiene humo o donde se esparce. 3. Añublado, atizonado: se dice de los granos que tienen la enfermedad llamada tizón o añublo. 4. Obsceno, impuro.

snack [snæk] [snak], *s.* 1. Parte, porción. **To go snacks,** ir a medias, compartir. 2. Tentempie, refrigerio, una comida ligera. **Snackbar,** bar, cafetería.

snaffle ['snæfl] [sna-fel], *s.* Brida con muserola; bridón, bocado de freno sin camas; se llama también *snaffle-bit.*

snaffle, *va.* 1. Refrenar, sujetar y reducir al caballo con el freno. 2. Refrenar, contener, reprimir. 3. Ganguear, hablar por la nariz.

snag [snæg] [snag], *s.* 1. Nudo en la madera, ramo desgajado, protuberancia. 2. Sobrediente, diente que sale sobre otro. 3. Pitón, punta de las astas del ciervo. 4. *(E.U.)* En los ríos del Oeste, tronco de un árbol fijo al fondo por un extremo y casi a flor de agua por el otro; de aquí, cualquier obstáculo oculto e ignorado. **To strike a snag,** chocar contra un tronco sumergido; encontrar un obstáculo no sospechado. **Snag-boat,** buque de vapor para arrancar árboles fijos en el fondo de un río.

snagged ['snægd] [snagd], *a.* Lleno de sobredientes; nudoso.

snaggy ['snægɪ] [sna-gui], *a.* 1. Lleno de troncos de árbol, v. g. un río. 2. Nudoso, lleno de nudos o tocones (tree). 3. Parecido a una rama desgajada, a un nudo o un pitón.

snail [sneɪl] [sneil], *s.* 1. Caracol, molusco gasterópodo. 2. Babosa, caracol gasterópodo sin concha (principalmente en los E. U.) 3. Posma, persona roncera, lerda y pesada. **Snail-clover,** alfalfa, mielga. **Snail-pace,** paso de tortuga, de caracol.

snake [sneɪk] [sneik], *s.* 1. Culebra, serpiente; también en sentido figurado. 2. Lagarto, lagartija u otro animal anfibio de forma semejante. **Snake-bit,** mordedura de serpiente. **Snake-killer,** 1. secretario, un ave. 2. *V. Road-runner.* **Snake-skin,** piel de serpiente.

snake, *va.* 1. *(Fam. E. U.)* Tirar de algo por un extremo arrastrándolo por el suelo. 2. Efectuar algo por medio de

movimientos parecidos a los de las culebras. *-vn.* Culebrear; embutir, entrañar.

snakeroot ['sneɪkruːt] [sneik-rut], *s. (Bot.)* Serpentaria. **Virginian snakeroot,** serpentaria de Virginia, díctamo de Virginia. **Indian snakeroot,** raíz de serpiente.

snaky ['sneɪkɪ] [snei-ki], *a.* 1. Que pertenece o se asemeja a la culebra; culebrino, serpentino, serpenteando, culebreando, tortuoso, formando eses. 2. Astuto, solapado; insinuante, traidor. 3. *(E.U.)* Lleno de culebras.

snap [snæp] [snap], *va.* 1. Hacer estallar una cosa; dar, apretar, cerrar con golpe o estadillo. 2. Romper, destrozar, hacer pedazos o astillas una cosa con ruido y violencia. 3. Agarrar a alguno, echar la mano o la garra, asir de repente y con pecipitación; a menudo con la prep. *up.* 4. Interrumpir a uno con petulancia, cortarle la palabra. 5. *(Fam.)* Fotografiar instantáneamente, a menudo fotografiar a uno sin que él lo sepa. 6. *(E.U.)* Lanzar por el aire. *-vn.* 1. Chasquear, dar un chasquido. 2. Estallar una cosa, romperse o quebrarse dando un estallido. 3. Lanzarse rápidamente, como cuando la tensión cesa de repente. 4. Coger de golpe, procurar coger; tirar a morder; por lo común con la prep. *at.* 5. Emitir, o parecer emitir luz; se dice de los ojos. 6. Hablar severa y abruptamente. 7. Fallar, no salir un tiro. **To snap in two,** quebrar, romper en dos pedazos. **To snap at,** tirar una mordiscada, tirar a morder o procurar morder. **To snap one's fingers,** castañetear; burlarse de. **Snap back,** contestar. **Snap off,** romper, separar, morder (dog). **Snap up,** lanzarse, apresurarse.

snap, *s.* 1. Chasquido, sonido rápido y agudo; castañeteo (with fingers). 2. Estallido, el sonido que hace una cosa al henderse o abrirse de golpe. 3. Corchete, cerrajita, garra que se cierra con chasquido. 4. Mordiscón, mordedura; cierre repentino, como el de las garras de una trampa. 5. Galletica. *V. Ginger-snap.* 6. *(Fam.)* Vigor de carácter o de estilo; energía. 7. Período corto (of cold). *-a.* Hecho o ejecutado repentinamente sin consideración o sin demora. **Snap-shot,** 1. Disparo hecho rápidamente, sin apuntar. 2. Fotografía tomada instantáneamente, sin preparación.

snapdragon ['snæpˌdrægən] [snap-dra-gon], *s.* 1. Hierba becerra. 2. Tenazas de cidriero. 3. Juego que consiste en coger con los dedos pasas, etc., que se ponen en aguardiente ardiendo.

snapper ['snæpər] [sna-paʳ], *s.* 1. Mordedor. 2. Pez comestible de gran tamaño del género Lutjanus (u otro afin) que se halla en el Golfo de México. 3. *V.* Snapping turtle, **Snappers,** castañuelas, castañetas.

snapping ['snæpɪŋ] [sna-pin], *s.* Acción del verbo *snap,* en cualquiera de sus acepciones. **Snapping turtle,** gran tortuga voraz, particularmente la Chelydra serpentina, común en la América del Norte.

snappish ['snæpɪʃ] [sna-pish], *a.* 1. Mordaz; regañón, agrio, mohino, pendenciero. 2. Arisco; pronto o dispuesto a morder, como un perro.

snappishly ['snæpɪʃlɪ] [sna-pish-li], *adv.* Mordazmente; agriamente, con aspereza.

snappishness ['snæpɪʃnɪs] [sna-pish-nes], *s.* Aspereza, sequedad o despego en el trato (rudeness).

snare [snɛəʳ] [sneaʳ], *s.* 1. Cepo, lazo, buitrón, trampa para coger la caza y los animales monteses. 2. Lazo, garlito, celada, asechanza para ofuscar y engañar a una persona. 3. Trampa, petardo, la apariencia engañosa con que se deslumbra o se burla a alguno. 4. Tirante para templar un tambor. **Sharedrum,** tambor con tirantes de cuerda.

snare, *va.* Enmarañar, enredar, tender trampas o lazos. *-vn.* Usar de trampas o cepos.

snarl [snɑːl] [snarl], *vn.* Regañar, dar muestras de enfado, gruñir entre dientes. *-s.* Regaño, gruñido entre dientes; *(Fam.)* contienda, riña. **Snarl-up,** embotellamiento, congestión de tráfico.

snarl, *va.* y *vn.* 1. Enredar, enmarañar; enredarse, enmarañarse; confundir (blur, confuse). 2. Embutir, estampar (artículos huecos de metal). *-s.* 1. Nudo, hilo enredado; cabellos desgreñados; complicación, enredo. 2. *(Fam.),* Riña, escaramuza. 3. Nudo en la madera.

snarler ['snɑːləʳ] [snar-laʳ], *s.* Regañón, el que tiene costumbre de regañar.

snarly ['snɑːlɪ] [snar-li], *a.* Enredoso, insidioso.

snatch [snætʃ] [snach], *va.* 1. Arrebatar, coger o tomar alguna cosa con precipitación. 2. Agarrer, echar la mano o la garra, asir de repente. 3. Arrebatar, quitar o tomar con violencia. 4. Transportar o llevar de una parte a otra con precipitación. - *vn.* 1. Procurar agarrar o arrebatar. 2. Tirar a morder, tirar un mordisco.

snatch, *s.* 1. El acto de echar la garra o agarrar. 2. Arrebatamiento, la acción de arrebatar. 3. Arrebatiña, el acto de arrojarse muchos en confusión a coger algo. 4. Una pequeña porción de cualquier cosa; un bocado, hablando de comida; un pequeño espacio o intervalo, hablando de tiempo. 5. Respuesta evasiva.

snatcher ['snætʃəʳ] [sna-chaʳ], *s.* Arrebatador.

snatchingly ['snætʃɪŋlɪ] [sna-chin-li], *adv.* Arrebatadamente, precipitadamente.

sneak [sniːk] [snik], *vn.* 1. Venir o irse a la sordina, a cencerros tapados o secretamente. 2. Arrastrar o andar arrastrando por la tierra. 3. Obrar con bajeza o ruindad. 4. Ratear. **To sneak along,** andar cabizbajo. *s.*

sneaker ['sniːkəʳ] [sni-kaʳ], *s.* 1. El que obra con bajeza. 2. *(Prov. Ingl.)* Tacita de ponche u otra bebida.

sneaking ['sniːkɪŋ] [sni-kin], *a.* 1. Furtivo, a hurtadillas, ratero; servil, bajo, vil. 2. Mantenido o concebido secretamente. **A sneaking fondness,** afición que se guarda secreta.

sneakingly ['sniːkɪŋlɪ] [sni-kin-li], *adv.* Servilmente, con bajeza; rateramente.

sneakingness ['sniːkɪŋnɪs] [sni-kin-nes], *s.* Bajeza, lisonja baja; vileza, ruindad.

sneak thief ['sniːkθiːf] [snik-zif], *s.* Ratero, ladrón de poca monta.

sneer [snɪəʳ] [sniaʳ], *vn.* 1. Mirar o hablar con desprecio. 2. Fisgarse o burlarse sonriéndose.

sneer, *s.* 1. Mirada de desprecio. 2. Fisga, risa falsa o burlona, mofa, escarnio.

sneerer, *s.* Mofador, fisgón, escarnecedor.

sneering ['snɪərɪŋ] [snia-rin], *a.* Burlón, mofador, escarnecedor. -*s.* Escarnio, rechifla.

sneeringly ['snɪərɪŋlɪ] [snia-rin-li], *adv.* Con desprecio; escarneciendo; con aire desdeñoso.

sneeze [sniːz] [snis], *vn.* Estornudar, dar un estornudo.

sneeze, *s.* Estornudo.

sneezing ['sniːzɪŋ] [sni-sin], *s.* Estornudo, acción de estornudar. **Sneezing-powder,** cebadilla.

snick [snɪk] [snik], *va. (Esco.)* Cortar (como con tijeras). -*s. (Prov. Ingl.)* Corte pequeño, tijeretada. **Snick and snee, snick or snee,** *(Ant.)* Riña a navajazos o cuchilladas; también, jocosamente, un cuchillo.

snicker ['snɪkəʳ] [sni-kaʳ], *vn.* Reírse tontamente o con desprecio; dar risotadas.

snide [snaɪd] [snaid], *a. (Ger.)* Fraudulento, engañoso, socarrón, bellaco.

sniff [snɪf] [snif], *va.* 1. Atraer alguna cosa con el aliento por medio de inhalaciones rápidas y cortas. 2. Dar un respingo, como expresión de desprecio o desdén. -*vn.* Resollar con fuerza hacia adentro; oler; sorberse los mocos, algunas veces como expresión de sospecha, desprecio o resentimiento. -*s.* 1. Acción de respirar o aspirar prontamente; olfateo rápido. 2. Lo que se aspira oliendo o respirando prontamente. **To go out for a sniff of air,** salir a tomar el aire.

sniffer ['snɪfəʳ] [sni-faʳ], *a.* **Sniffer dog,** perro antidroga.

sniffle ['snɪfl] [sni-fel], *s.* Lloriqueo, moqueo. -*vn.* Lloriquear, moquear.

sniffy ['snɪfɪ] [sni-fi], *a.* Desdeñoso, estirado.

snifter ['snɪftəʳ] [snif-taʳ], *s.* Copita, trago.

snigger ['snɪgəʳ] [sni-gaʳ], *s.* Risa disimulada. *vi.* Reírse disimuladamente.

sniggering ['snɪgərɪŋ] [sni-ga-rin], *s.* Cachondeo, risitas.

sniggle ['snɪgl] [sni-guel], *vn. (Ingl.)* Pescar anguilas en presa; entrampar, enmarañar.

snip [snɪp] [snip], *va.* Tijeretear, dar tijeretadas; cortar con tijeras. **To snip off,** cortar de un golpe con tijeras.

snip, *s.* 1. Tijeretada (cut). 2. Pedazo pequeño; cosa o persona pequeña. **A snip of a girl,** una muchachita. 3. Parte, porción. 4. Zote, zopenco.

snipe [snaɪp] [snif], *sf. (Orn.)* Beacina, agachadiza, ave zancuda del género Gallinago; gallina de agua. -*vi.* Tirar desde. **To snipe at somebody,** tirar a alguien desde un escondite.

sniper ['snaɪpəʳ] [sni-paʳ], *s.* Tirador o cazador emboscado.

snippet ['snɪpɪt] [sni-pit], *s.* 1. Parte o porción pequeña; pitanza. 2. Gallineta pequeña.

snitch [snɪtʃ] [snich], *s.* Napias, narices (nose).

snivel ['snɪvl] [sni-vel], *s.* Moquita, el moco líquido que destila de la nariz.

snivel, *vn.* 1. Moquear, echar mocos. 2. Llorar como una criatura. 3. Jeremiquear, hacer pucheros. *(Mex.),* Jirimiquar.

sniveller ['snɪvləʳ] [sniv-laʳ], *s.* 1. Lloraduelos, el que es muy llorón. 2. El que es mocoso o echa muchos mocos.

snivelling ['snɪvlɪŋ] [sniv-lin], *a.* Llorón, que hace pucheros.

snob [snɒb] [snob], *s.* Esnob o snob, persona ignorante y jactanciosa.

snobbery ['snɒbərɪ] [sno-ba-ri], *s.* Esnobismo.

snobbish ['snɒbɪʃ] [sno-bish], *a.* Esnob, ignorante y jactancioso.

snobbishness ['snɒbɪʃnɪs] [sno-bish-nes], *s.* Esnobismo, ignorancia jactanciosa.

snood ['snuːd] [snud], *s.* 1. *(Esco.)* Cintillo, cinta para la cabellera de que usaron las jóvenes solteras escocesas; (emblema de la virginidad). 2. *(Dial.)* Sedal *(Prov. sotileza),* trozo de crin o hilo de tripa para asegurar un anzuelo. V. SNELL.

snoop ['snuːp] [snup], *s.* Curioso, fisgón.

snooty ['snuːtɪ] [snu-ti], *a.* Presumido.

snooze [snuːz] [snus], *vn. (Fam.)* Dormitar, dormir la siesta; estar amodorrado, soñoliento. -*s. (Fam.)* Sueño ligero.

snore [snɔːʳ] [snoʳ], *va.* Pasar (el tiempo) roncando. -*vn.* Roncar, hacer ruido con el resuello cuando se duerme.

snore, *s.* Ronquido.

snorer ['snɔːrəʳ] [sno-raʳ], *s.* Roncador, el que ronca.

snoring ['snɔːrɪŋ] [sno-rin], *s.* Ronquido.

snorkel ['snɔːkl] [snor-kel], *s.* Doble tubo de respiración para submarinos. **Snarked pen,** pluma fuente que se llena de tinta mediante un tubo aspirante.

snort ['snɔːt] [snort], *va.* y *vn.* Resoplar, bufar como un caballo fogoso.

snot [snɒt] [snot], *s. (mucus)* Moco que sale de la nariz.

snotty ['snɒtɪ] [sno-ti], *a. (Bajo)* Mocoso, lleno de mocos; sucio.

snout [snaʊt] [snaut], *va.* Proveer de hocico, boquerel o embocadura. -*s.* 1. Hocico, el morro de los animales. 2. Jeta u hocico de puerco. 3. Trompa de elefante. 4. Cañón de un fuelle, tobera; boquerel de manguera, embocadura de un cañón. **Snout-beetle,** gorgojo. **Snout-ring,** narigón para puercos.

snow [snəʊ] [snou], *s.* 1. Nieve, vapor condensado por el frío y resuelto en copos blancos. 2. Algo que se parece a la nieve. 3. Nieves, nevada, nevasca. **Snowbird,** 1. pinzón de las nieves, pájaro americano que vuela en bandadas durante el invierno. Junco hyemalis. 2. V. *Snow-bunting.* **Snow-blind,** cegado por la reverberación de la luz sobre la nieve. **Snow-blindness,** ceguera causada por la reverberación de la luz sobre la nieve. **Snow-broth,** agua de nieve o de cualquier líquido muy frío. **Snow-bunting,** verderón de las nieves, pájaro de los fringílidos; el macho en la estación de la cría es blanco de nieve con manchas negras. **Snow-capped** *capt.),* coronado de nieve con la cima cubierta de nieve. **Snow-drift,** montón, masa de nieve acumulada por el viento. **Snow-plough,** limpianieves (railway). **Snow-shed,** guardaaludes, estructura de maderos construida sobre la vía férrea para protegerla contra los derrumbamientos de masas de nieve desde las alturas vecinas. **Snow-shoe,** zueco, calzado para andar sobre la nieve. V. SKEE. **Snowslide,**

snowslip, alud, avalancha de nieve. **Snow-storm,** nevasca, nevada, nevisca; borrasca de nieve.

snow, *vn.* Nevar, caer nieve. -*va.* 1. Cubrir, obstruir, detener o aprisionar con nieve; se usa con *in, over, under o up.* 2. Dejar caer como nieve; nevar.

snowball ['snəʊbɔːl] [snou-bol], *va.* Lanzar bolas de nieve. -*s.* Pella o pelota de nieve.

snowbound ['snəʊbaʊnd] [snou-baund], *a.* Bloqueado o incomunicado por la nieve.

snowdrop ['snəʊdrɒp] [snou-drop], *s.* (*Bot.*) Campanilla blanca; flor de la leche, planta de las amarilídeas. **Snowdrop-tree,** árbol pequeño del género Halesia.

snowfall ['snəʊfɔːl] [snou-fol], *s.* Nevada.

snowflake ['snəʊfleɪk] [snou-fleik], *s.* 1. Copo de nieve. 2. Verderol de las nieves. 3. (*Bot.*) Campanilla.

snowshoe ['snəʊʃuː] [snou-shu], *s.* Raqueta de nieve.

snowsuit ['snəʊsuːt] [snou-sut], *s.* Traje-pantalón (generalmente infantil) que protege contra la nieve y el frío.

snow-white ['snəʊwaɪt] [snou-uait], *a.* Nevado, blanco como la nieve.

snowy ['snəʊɪ] [snoui], *a.* 1. Nevoso, que frecuentemente tiene nieve. 2. De nieves, cargado de nieve, dispuesto a nevar. 3. Nevado, blanco como la nieve. 4. Puro, sin mancha.

snub [snʌp] [snab], *va.* 1. Desairar, acoger mal, tratar con aspereza. 2. Reprender, reñir, regañar. 3. Parar de repente.

snub, *s.* 1. Reprensión, repulsa, desaire. 2. Nariz chata. -*a.* Chato; corto y ancho; se dice de la nariz. **Snub-nosed,** el que tiene la nariz roma y ancha.

snuff [snʌf] [snaf] *s.* 1. Moco o pavesa de candela y la misma candela cuando está casi toda concluída. 2. El olor que despide de sí una cosa. 3. Tabaco en polvo, polvo, polvillo; rapé. 4. (*Vulg.*) Refunfuñadura.

snuff, *va.* Atraer o introducir una cosa en la nariz con el aliento. **To snuff up,** tomar por la nariz. 2. Oler, percibir, el olor de alguna cosa. 3. Despabilar, limpiar o quitar la pavesa o pábilo a la vela. -*vn.* Resoplar hacia adentro, (*vulg.*), sorberse los mocos. V. *TO* SNIFF.

snuffbox ['snʌfbɒks] [snaf-boks], *s.* Caja de tabaco en polvo o de rapé; tabaquera.

snuffer ['snʌfəʳ] [sna-faʳ], *s.* 1. Despabilador, el que despabila. 2. *pl.* Despabiladeras, las tijeras con que se despabila o quita el pábilo a la luz.

snuffiness ['snʌfɪnɪs] [sna-fi-nes], *s.* Condición de lo que está cubierto de tabaco o rapé.

snuffle ['snʌfl] [sna-fel], *vn.* Ganguear, hablar gangoso, hablar por las narices. -*s.* 1. Gangueo, acción de ganguear. 2. *pl.* Romadizo, catarro nasal.

snuffy ['snʌfɪ] [sna-fi], *a.* Cubierto de tabaco; que huele a rapé.

snug [snʌg] [snag], *a.* 1. Abrigado estrecha y cómodamente; bien puesto, lindo, bonito. 2. Estrecho o compacto; ajustado, con lugar suficiente pero no demasiado; conveniente, cómodo, acomodado. -*s.* (*Mec.*) Tope, reborde.

snuggery ['snʌgərɪ] [sna-gue-ri], *s.* (*Fam.*) Pieza o habitación cómoda y bien arreglada; en las fondas inglesas, pieza inmediata al mostrador de licores.

snuggle ['snʌgl] [sna-guel], *vn.* Dormir abrigado.

so [səʊ] [sou], *adv.* 1. Así, del mismo modo que, así como, por lo mismo; por tanto, por consiguiente; a causa de, así pues; lo mismo que. 2. Tal, tan o tanto, tan…como, tanto como; correlativo de *as.* 3. De modo o de manera que. 4. Por tanto, por lo cual, por cuya razón. 5. Con tal que, con esta condición o bajo la condición de. 6. A este punto, a este tiempo; entonces; a tal punto, de modo que, tan bien como. 7. Casi, poco más o menos. 8. Lo, ello, eso; (se emplea para evitar la repetición de una voz o de una frase). 9. Sea, así sea; bien, bueno. 10. (*Fam.*) ¿Verdad, de veras? (por elipsis en vez de *is it so?*). -*conj.* Bien, supuesto que. **So as to,** de manera que. **So much,** tanto. **So much as,** siquiera, a lo menos. **So, then,** con que, de modo que. **So that,** de suerte que, de modo que, de tal manera que. **So be it,** amen, así sea, quiéralo Dios. **And so forth,** y así de lo demás, y todo

lo demás. **If it be so that,** si fuese así, si fuese verdad que. **So much as,** por mucho que. **So so,** así, así, tal cual, medianamente; bien bien o bueno bueno, como exclamación para expresar que se ha concluído una cosa o que se sabe algo. **Do you so?** ¿Hace usted eso? **They are not so,** no lo son, no son así. **If so,** si así es, o de ese modo. **I hope so; I think so,** así lo espero; lo creo. **How so?,** ¿cómo es eso? **Why so?** ¿Por qué así? **So-called,** llamado así; seudo (delante de un nombre), supuesto. **So much for,** he aquí lo que es; he ahí. **So far,** hasta aquí, hasta ahí; tan lejos. **(Mr.) So and so,** Señor Fulano, fulano de tal. **Be he never so powerful,** por poderoso que sea. **If ever so little,** por poco que. -*inter.* ¡So! (para que se paren las caballerías o vacas).

soak [səʊk] [souk], *va.* 1. Empapar, remojar, poner en remojo alguna cosa para que se empape. 2. Empapar, mojar, humedecer del todo, regar. 3. Chupar o embeber en sí por los poros; absorber. 4. Beber con exceso. -*vn.* 1. Remojarse, estar puesto en remojo. 2. Calarse, introducirse algún líquido en un cuerpo poroso; con *in, into o through.* 3. Beborrotear, empinar el codo.

soak, *s.* 1. Procedimiento o acto de empapar, remojo. 2. El líquido en que se empapa alguna cosa. 3. (*Fam.*) Bebedor, borrachón, zampacurtillos; orgía en que se bebe mucho.

soakage ['səʊkɪdʒ] [sou-kich], *s.* Remojo, acción de remojar o remojarse; merma, cantidad de líquido que se rezuma y se pierde.

soaker ['səʊkəʳ] [sou-kaʳ], *s.* 1. El o lo que empapa o remoja. 2. (*Fam.*) Borrachón de vicio.

so-and-so ['səʊənsəʊ] [souan-sou], *s.* **Mr so-and-so,** don Fulano de Tal.

soap [səʊp] [soup], *s.* Jabón, pasta o masa que sirve para lavar y blanquear la ropa y otras cosas; un compuesto cualquiera de un ácido grasiento y una base. **Soap-ashes,** las cenizas que quedan después de hacer jabón. **Soap-ball,** jaboncillo, bola de jabón. **Soap-boiler,** jabonero; caldera para jabón. **Soap-bubble,** ampolla de jabón. **Soap-earth,** V. STEATITE. **Soap-house,** jabonería. **Soap-maker,** jabonero. **Soap-suds,** jabonaduras.

soap, *va.* Jabonar, o enjabonar, lavar con jabón.

soap opera ['səʊp,ɒpərə] [soup-o-pe-ra], *s.* Comedia sentimental, culebrón.

soapstone ['səʊpstəʊn] [soup-stoun], *s.* Esteatita, galaxia; jaboncillo, jabón de sastre.

soapwort ['səʊpwɔːt] [soup-uort], *s.* (*Bot.*) Saponaria.

soapy ['səʊpɪ] [sou-pi], *a.* Jabonoso, saponáceo, que tiene las cualidades del jabón.

soar [sɔːʳ] [soʳ], *vn.* 1. Remontarse, elevarse en el aire. 2. Remontarse, encumbrarse, elevarse, sublimarse (rise); aspirar, anhelar. **Soaring style,** estilo muy elevado o sublime. **Her spirits soared,** se reanimó de golpe. -*s.* Vuelo o remonte de las aves hacia lo alto.

sob [sɒb] [sob], *s.* Sollozo, suspiro.

sob, *vn.* Sollozar, suspirar.

sober ['sɒbəʳ] [so-baʳ], *a.* 1. Cuerdo, sano en su juicio, sensato (sensible); sereno, con el ánimo tranquilo; de sangre fría. 2. Grave, serio, sabio, modesto (serious, grave). 3. Sobrio, templado, moderado, arreglado, especialmente en el beber (moderate). 4. Sobrio, no embriagado. 5. Oscuro, sombrío, de color apagado. **To get o grow sober,** recobrar la sobriedad; volverse sensato y formal, no beber más. **To be stone-cold sober,** estar totalmente sobrio. **In sober earnest,** de veras, con seriedad, formalmente. **The sober plumage of a wren,** el plumaje sombrío de un troglodita.

sober, *va.* Desemborrachar, sacar a uno del estado de borracho; de aquí, poner grave, serio o pensativo. -*vn.* Volverse sobrio, cuerdo, moderado, sensato. **To sober down,** serenar o serenarse; hacer volver o volverse cuerdo; sosegar, sosegarse.

soberly ['sɒbəlɪ] [so-ber-li], *adv.* Sobriamente, con moderación o templanza; juiciosamente.

soberness ['sɒbənɪs] [so-ber-nes], **sobriety** [sə'braɪətɪ] [sou-braia-ti], *s.* 1. Sobriedad, templanza; moderación, cordura. 2. Seriedad, gravedad. 3. Calma, sangre fría.

sobriquet ['səʊbrɪkeɪ] [sou-bri-kei], *sf.* Mote, apodo.

so-called ['səʊ'kɔːld] [sou-kold], *a.* Denominado, llamado; supuesto.

soccer ['sɒkəʳ] [so-kaʳ], *s.* Fútbol, balompié.

sociable ['səʊʃəbl] [sou-sha-bol], *a.* Sociable, amigable, familiar, comunicativo.

sociability [ˌsəʊʃə'bɪlɪtɪ] [sou-sha-bi-li-ti], *s.* Sociabilidad, franqueza.

sociably ['səʊʃəblɪ] [sou-sha-bli], *adv.* Sociablemente, francamente, amigablemente.

social ['səʊʃəl] [sou-shal], *a.* 1. Social, sociable, afable, franco. 2. Social, perteneciente a la sociedad. 3. Organizado para vivir en sociedad, como una raza o pueblo. 4. *(Zool.)* Social, que vive en comunidad; p. ej. las abejas, hormigas o avispas: agregado, compuesto, colonial. **Social administration,** administración social. **Social life,** vida social. **Social worker,** asistente social. **Social scientist,** sociólogo.

socialism ['səʊʃəlɪzəm] [sou-sha-li-sem], *s.* Socialismo.

socialist ['səʊʃəlɪst] [sou-sha-list], *a. y s.* Socialista, partidario del socialismo.

socilistic [ˌsəʊʃə'lɪstɪk] [sou-sha-lis-tik], *a.* Socialista, perteneciente al socialismo.

socialization [ˌsəʊʃəlaɪ'zeɪʃən] [sou-sha-lai-sei-shon], *s.* Socialización.

socialize ['səʊʃəlaɪz] [sou-sha-lais], *s.* Socializar.

society [sə'saɪətɪ] [so-saia-ti], *s.* 1. Sociedad, la unión de los hombres entre sí formada por la naturaleza o por las leyes. 2. Sociedad, academia, junta o reunión para cultivar o promover las ciencias o las artes. 3. Compañía, sea para objetos de comercio o para otra cosa. 4. Compañía, trato amistoso o civil, visita o tertulia en las casas. **Fashionable society,** la buena, la alta sociedad. **A danger to society,** un peligro para la sociedad.

sociocultural [ˌsəʊsɪəʊ'kʌltʃərəl] [sou-siou-kal-cha-ral], *a.* Sociocultural.

socioeconomic ['səʊsɪəʊˌiːkə'nɒmɪk] [sou-sioui-ko-no-mik], *a.* Socioeconómico.

sociological [ˌsəʊsɪəʊ'lɒdʒɪkəl] [sou-siou-lo-yi-kal], *a.* Sociológico.

sociologist [ˌsəʊsɪ'ɒlədʒɪst] [sou-sio-lo-yist], *s.* Sociólogo.

sociology [ˌsəʊsɪ'ɒlədʒɪ] [sou-sio-lo-yi], *s.* Sociología, ciencia que estudia las leyes de la evolución y organización de la sociedad.

sock [sɒk] [sok], *s.* 1. Calcetín, escarpín, media calceta. 2. Zueco, especie de calzado que usaban los cómicos antiguos. 3. Reja de arado, particularmente de quita y pon.

socket ['sɒkɪt] [so-kit], *s.* Cualquier hueco en que encaja alguna cosa; cuenca, encaje, contera, el cañón de candelero donde se mete la vela, y la arandela o cazoleta del mismo cañón. **Socket of the eye,** cuenca del ojo. **Socket of a tooth,** alvéolo de un diente. **Socket of the capstan,** *(Mar.)* Concha de cabrestante.

socko ['sɒkəʊ] [so-kou], *a.* *(E.U.)* Estupendo, fantástico.

Socratic, Socratical [sɒ'krætɪk] [so-kra-tik], *a.* Socrático, lo perteneciente o relativo a Sócrates.

sod [sɒd] [sod], *va.* *(pret.* SODDED, *ger.* SODDING*).* Cubrir de césped un terreno. *-s.* Césped, turba, terrón.

soda ['səʊdə] [sou-da], *s.* Sosa, soda; carbonato u óxido de sodio; sal soda. **Soda-fountain,** fuente de agua de soda. **Soda-water,** agua de soda. **Soda cracker,** galleta de soda.

sodality [sə'dælɪtɪ] [sou-da-li-ti], *s.* Cofradía, hermandad.

sodden ['sɒdn] [so-den], *va.* Major, empapar con agua, saturar. *-vn.* Empaparse, mojarse; ponerse blanda o corrompida una cosa.

sodden, *pp.* del verbo to SEETHE. 1. Mojado, empapado en agua. 2. que parece cocido o medio cocido.

sodium ['səʊdɪəm] [sou-diom], *s.* Sodio, elemento metálico color de plata y alcalino.

sodomy ['sɒdəmɪ] [so-do-mi], *s.* Sodomía, delito contrario a las leyes de la naturaleza.

soever ['səʊ'evəʳ] [sou-e-vaʳ], *adv.* Que sea; quiera, por o por más. Esta voz hace siempre relación a un pronombre o adverbio que está en la misma frase. **What great thing soever,** cualquier acción señalada que. **Whosoever,** quienquiera. **Wheresoever,** donde quiera. **Howsoever,** como quiera, de cualquier modo que sea. **Which way soever,** por donde quiera, de cualquier modo que sea.

sofa ['səʊfə] [sou-fa], *s.* Sofá, canapé ancho y cómodo.

soft [sɒft] [soft], *a.* 1. Blando, suave al tacto, mole, suavecito; dúctil, maleable, flexible, que cede fácilmente (flobby). 2. Liso, dulce y suave al tacto (smooth). 3. Melodioso, de sonido débil y grato al oído: no fuerte ni áspero. 4. Benigno, tierno, blando; delicado, sensible a la impresión del aire. 5. Pastoso, jugoso, cuando se habla de la suavidad y blandura de una cosa. 6. Atento, cortés, obsequioso; apacible; fácil, dócil. 7. De matices delicados, templado; no reluciente ni demasiado vivo. 8. Afeminado. 9. Dulce, sin sales minerales, que puede disolver el jabón, se aplica al agua. 10. Silbante; sonante, vocal o fuerte. 11. Bituminoso; se dice de la hulla en contraposición al carbón de piedra. **A soft skin,** un cutis suave. **Soft iron,** hierro dulce o maleable. **Soft to the touch,** blando al tacto. **Soft toy,** muñeco de peluche. **A soft voice,** una voz dulce, suave, baja. **A soft answer turneth away wrath,** una respuesta blanda disipa la ira. **Soft water,** agua dulce. *-inter.* ¡Poco a poco!, ¡quedo, quedito!, ¡despacio! *-adv.* *(Des.)* Blandamente, suavemente, flexiblemente.

soft-boiled ['sɒftˌbɔɪld] [soft-boild], *a.* Pasado por agua. **Soft-boiled eggs,** huevos tibios, huevos pasados por agua.

soft coal ['sɒftkəʊl] [soft-koul], *s.* Carbón bituminoso.

soften ['sɒfn] [so-fen], *va.* 1. Ablandar, reblandecer, poner blanda o suave una cosa dura o tiesa. 2. Mitigar, templar, amansar, suavizar. 3. Enternecer o mover a compasión; aplacar al que está enojado. 4. Enervar, afeminar. *-vn.* 1. Ablandarse, reblandecerse. 2. Templarse, amansarse, enternecerse.

softener ['sɒfnəʳ] [sof-naʳ], *s.* 1. El o lo que ablanda. 2. El que templa, amansa o aplaca a uno. 3. Brocha ancha para casar o amortiguar los colores.

softening ['sɒfnɪŋ] [sof-nin], *pa.* del verbo SOFTEN. *-s.* Reblandecimiento; blandura; enternecimiento; suavidad.

softish ['sɒftɪʃ] [sof-tish], *a.* Blandito, blandujo.

softly ['sɒftlɪ] [soft-li], *adv.* Blandamente, callandito, bonitamente, suavemente, tranquilamente, sin ruido; lentamente, con lentitud, paso a paso. **Speak softly,** hable usted bajo.

softness ['sɒftnɪs] [soft-nes], *s.* 1. Blandura, la calidad de las cosas blandas. 2. Blandura, dulzura, afabilidad en el trato. 3. Complacencia, deferencia, atención para con los deseos de los demás. 4. Afeminación, pusilanimidad.

soft-pedal ['sɒft'pedl] [soft-pe-dal], *va.* *(Vul.)* Reprimir, suavizar.

soft-soap [sɒft'səʊp] [soft-soup], *va.* *(Vul.)* Dar coba, halagar con fines mezquinos.

softwood ['sɒftwʊd] [soft-vud], *s.* 1. Madera blanda. 2. Madera de árbol conífero.

soggy ['sɒgɪ] [so-gui], *a.* Empapado en agua: húmedo y pesado; mojado.

soil [sɔɪl] [soil], *va.* 1. Ensuciar, emporcar, manchar (dirty). 2. Abonar, estercolar, engrasar las tierras.

soil, *va.* Alimentar con verde en un corral o cercado; purgar con alimento verde.

soil, *s.* 1. Terreno, la tierra considerada respecto de sus cualidades vegetativas. 2. Región. **Native soil,** el país natal. **Soil good for wheat,** terreno a propósito para trigo. 3. Suciedad, mancha, porquería. 4. Mancha, borrón en la fama de alguno. 5. Abono, estiércol.

soiled [sɔɪld] [soild], *a.* Sucio, manchado (dirty).

soiling ['sɔɪlɪŋ] [soi-lin], *s.* 1. Ensuciamiento. 2. Alimento verde, alcacer para las bestias.

soirée ['swɑːreɪ] [sua-rei], *s.* Tertulia.

sojourn ['sɒdʒɜːn] [so-yern], *vn.* Residir o morar en un paraje o lugar por algún tiempo.

sojourn, *s.* Morada o residencia casual o por algún tiempo.

sojouner ['sɒdʒɜːnəʳ] [so-yer-naʳ], *s.* Morador, residente temporal, transeunte.

sol [sɒl] [sol], *s.* 1. Sueldo, moneda de cobre de Francia; sol, moneda de plata del Perú. 2. Sol, nota de música. 3. El sol, dios del sol.

solace ['sɒlɪs] [so-lis], *va.* Solazar, divertir; consolar; recrear, alegrar. -*vr.* **To solace oneself,** consolarse, solazarse, recrearse, divertirse.

solace, *s.* Consuelo, alivio, recreo, complacencia.

solar ['sɔʊləʳ] [sou-laʳ], *a.* Solar, relativo al sol. **Solar cell,** célula solar. **Solar heating,** calefacción solar. **Solar system,** sistema solar. **Solar year,** año solar. **Solar battery,** batería solar.

solarium [sɒʊˈlɛərɪəm] [sou-lei-riom], *s.* Solana, pieza para tomar el sol.

sold [sɒʊld] [sould], *pret.* y *pp.* del verbo *TO* SELL. **Sold out,** agotado, vendido en su totalidad.

solder ['sɒʊldəʳ] [soul-daʳ], *va.* Soldar, pegar y unir con metal.

solder, *s.* Soldadura, el metal a propósito para soldar.

solderer ['sɒʊldərəʳ] [soul-da-raʳ], *s.* Soldador, el que tiene el oficio de soldar.

soldering ['sɒʊldərɪŋ] [soul-da-rin], *s.* Soldadura, acción de soldar. **Soldering-iron,** soldador, el instrumento con que se suelda.

soldier ['sɒʊldʒəʳ] [soul-diaʳ], *s.* 1. Soldado, soldado raso. 2. Militar, el que profesa la milicia, también guerrero experto, valiente, o esforzado. **A foot-soldier,** soldado de a pie o de infantería.

soldierly ['sɒʊldʒəlɪ] [soul-diar-li], *a.* Soldadesco, militar, perteneciente a los soldados.

soldiery ['sɒʊldʒərɪ] [soul-dia-ri], *s.* Soldadesca, el conjunto de los soldados.

sole [sɒʊl] [soul], *va.* Solar, echar suelas a los zapatos. **To half-sole,** poner o echar medias suelas.

sole, *s.* 1. Planta del pie; suela del zapato. 2. Lenguado. 3. Suelo, la superficie inferior de cualquier cosa que toca la tierra. **Sole of a gun-carriage,** solera de cureña. **Sole of the rudder,** zapata del timón. -*a.* 1. Único, solo. 2. (*For.*) Soltero, soltera. **A sole proprietor,** único propietario. **The sole support of a numerous family,** el único sostén de una numerosa familia.

solecism ['sɒləsɪzəm] [so-la-si-sem], *s.* 1. (*Gram.*) Solecismo, error en la construcción o sintaxis. 2. Una falta cualquiera, incongruencia.

solecistic ['sɒləsɪstɪk] [so-la-sis-tik], *a.* Incongruo, incongruente, que falta a las reglas de la sintaxis.

solecize ['sɒləsaɪz] [so-la-sais], *vn.* Cometer solecismos.

solely ['sɒʊlɪlɪ] [sou-li-li], *adv.* Únicamente, solamente.

solemn ['sɒləm] [so-lem], *a.* 1. Solemne, grave. 2. Augusto, majestusoso, gave, serio, circunspecto.

solemnness ['sɒləmnɪs] [so-lem-nes], *s.* Seriedad, gravedad, carácter o tono solemne.

solemnity [sɒˈlemnɪtɪ] [so-lem-ni-ti], *s.* 1. Solemnidad, pompa. 2. Solemnidad, rito, ceremonia, fiesta. 3. Gravedad, seriedad.

solemnization ['sɒləmnaɪˈzeɪʃən] [so-lem-nai-sei-shon], *s.* Solemnización, celebración, celebridad.

solemnize ['sɒləmnaɪz] [so-lem-nais], *va.* Solemnizar, celebrar solemnemente. **To solemnize a marriage,** celebrar un matrimonio.

solemnly ['sɒləmnlɪ] [so-lemn-li], *adv.* Solemnemente, majestuosamente; con todas las formalidades.

soleness ['sɒʊlnɪs] [soul-nes], *s.* (Poco us.) Independencia, el estado de hallarse solo y sin dependencia de otro.

solenoid ['sɒʊlənɔɪd] [sou-le-noid], *s.* Solenoide, hilo eléctrico, la forma más sencilla de un imán.

solfa ['sɒlˈfɑː] [sol-fa], *va.* y *vn.* Solfear, cantar marcando el compás y pronunciando los nombres de las notas.

solicit [səˈlɪsɪt] [so-li-sit], *va.* 1. Solicitar, pretender o buscar alguna cosa con diligencia y cuidado, pedir con instancia; importunar, rogar. 2. Pedir, implorar. 3. Solcitar, inducir, incitar a hacer alguna cosa; excitar el deseo, en especial incitar a cometer una acción ilícita. -*vn.* Pedir, hacer una petición o solicitud.

solicitation [səˌlɪsɪˈteɪʃən] [so-li-si-tei-shon], *s.* Solicitación.

solicitor [səˈlɪsɪtəʳ] [so-li-si-taʳ], *s.* 1. Procurador, agente, solicitador o diligenciero, el que solicita en nombre de otro. 2. Solicitador, persona que pide o ruega. **Solicitor in Chancery,** procurador o abogado en el tribunal de la chancillería.

solicitous [səˈlɪsɪtəs] [so-li-si-tos], *a.* Solícito, deseoso (con *about o for*); que siente solicitud o se interesa por algo, atento a o por; inquieto, cuidadoso, ansioso por algo.

solicitously [səˈlɪsɪtəslɪ] [so-li-si-tos-li], *adv.* Solícitamente, diligentemente, ansiosamente.

solicitude [səˈlɪsɪtjuːd] [so-li-si-tiud], *s.* Solicitud, cuidado, afán, instancia cuidadosa.

solid ['sɒlɪd] [so-lid], *a.* 1. Sólido, consistente. 2. Sólido, compacto, macizo (compact). 3. Sólido, firme, fuerte, denso, sano (strong). 4. Sólido, verdadero. 5. Sólido, real, efectivo, duradero; grave, sesudo. -*s.* 1. Sólido, la parte del cuerpo animal que contiene los fluidos. 2. (*Geom.*) Sólido, cuerpo que tiene extensión, anchura y altura o profundidad. **To be frozen solid,** estar completamente helado. **Solid geometry,** geometría del espacio.

solidarity [sɒlɪˈdærɪtɪ] [so-li-da-ri-ti], *s.* 1. Solidaridad. 2. Mancomunidad.

solidification [səˌlɪdɪfɪˈkeɪʃən] [so-li-di-fi-kei-shon], *s.* Solidificación, consolidación.

solidify [səˈlɪdɪfaɪ] [so-li-di-fai], *va.* Solidificar, hacer sólido, volver sólido un cuerpo líquido o gaseoso. -*vn.* Volverse sólido.

solidity [səˈlɪdɪtɪ] [so-li-di-ti], *s.* 1. Solidez, firmeza, dureza, densidad. 2. Solidez, verdad, certeza, integridad.

solidly ['sɒlɪdlɪ] [so-lid-li], *adv.* Sólidamente, firmemente.

solid-state ['sɒlɪdˈsteɪt] [so-lid-steit], *attr.* Estado sólido. **Solid-state physics,** física del estado sólido.

solidus ['sɒlɪdəs] [so-li-dus], *s.* (*Tip.*) Barra.

soliloquize, soliloquise [səˈlɪləkwaɪz] [so-li-lo-kuais], *vn.* Hacer un soliloquio, un monólogo; soliloquiar, hablar a solas.

soliloquy [səˈlɪləkwɪ] [so-li-lo-kui], *s.* Soliloquio, habla o discurso de una persona a solas, o consigo misma.

soliped ['sɒlɪpt] [so-lipt], *s.* Solípedo, el animal cuyos pies no están hendidos, como los del caballo.

solitaire [sɒlɪˈtɛəʳ] [so-li-teaʳ], *s.* 1. Solitario, diamante u otra joya que se engasta separadamente. 2. Solitario, uno de los varios juegos en que toma parte una sola persona.

solitarily [sɒlɪˈtɛərɪlɪ] [so-li-tea-ri-li], *adv.* Solitariamente, en soledad, sin compañía.

solitariness [sɒlɪˈtɛərɪnɪs] [so-li-tea-ri-nes], *s.* Soledad, retiro.

solitary [sɒlɪˈtɛərɪ] [so-li-ta-ri], *a.* 1. Solitario, que vive en la soledad (alone). 2. Solitario, retirado, poco frecuentado, desierto, desamparado, hablando de sitios o parajes. 3. Solo, único; hecho, ejecutado o sucedido aisladamente. 4. (*Zool.*) Solitario, que vive solo o en parejas; simple, no compuesto. 5. Incomunicado, se dice de una clase de prisión. -*s.* Solitario, ermitaño.

solitude ['sɒlɪtjuːd] [so-li-tiud], *s.* 1. Soledad, vida solitaria, la falta de compañía (loneliness). 2. Soledad, desierto, paraje solitario.

sollar ['sɒləʳ] [so-laʳ], *s.* 1. Descanso, plataforma en una mina. 2. Cámara elevada en una iglesia.

solo ['sɒʊlɒʊ] [sou-lou], *s.* (*Mús.*) Solo, la composición que uno canta solo o que se toca con un solo instrumento.

soloist ['sɒʊlɒʊɪst] [sou-louist], *s.* Solista.

Solomon ['sɒləmən] [so-lo-mon], *s.* Salomón.

solstice ['sɒlstɪs] [sols-tis], *s.* (*Astr.*) Solsticio, época en que el sol está más distante del ecuador. **Summer solstice,** solsticio de verano o estival. **Winter solstice,** solsticio de invierno.

solstitial [sɒlsˈtɪʃəl] [sols-ti-shal], *a.* Solsticial, relativo a los solsticios.

solubility [sɒljʊˈbɪlɪtɪ] [so-liu-bi-li-ti], *s.* Solubilidad.

soluble ['sɒljʊbl] [so-liu-bol], *a.* Soluble.

solute ['sɒljʊt] [so-liut], *a.* (*Bot.*) Completamente separado, libre.

solution [sə'lu:ʃən] [so-lu-shon], *s.* 1. Solución, desleimiento de una cosa sólida y el compuesto que resulta de este desleimiento. 2. Solución, desenlace de una dificultad o de un argumento. 3. Resolución de una duda, de un problema o ecuación. 4. Separación, desunión.

solutive ['sɒlutɪv] [so-lu-tiv], *a.* Solutivo; laxativo, laxante.

solvability [sɒlvə'bɪlɪtɪ] [sol-va-bi-li-ti], *s.* Solubilidad, calidad de soluble.

solvable ['sɒlvəbl] [sol-va-bol], *a.* Disoluble, soluble, que se puede resolver o disolver; se dice de un argumento o de un problema.

solve [sɒlv] [solv], *va.* 1. Desenredar, desenlazar, librar de perplejidades, aclarar. 2. Resolver, solver, disolver, explicar.

solvency ['sɒlvənsɪ] [sol-ven-si], *s.* Solvencia, posibilidad de pagar uno sus deudas.

solvent ['sɒlvənt] [sol-vent], *a.* 1. Solvente o resolvente, que puede desleir o desatar. 2. Solvente, abonado, que puede pagar sus deudas. -*s.* 1. Disolvente, líquido que puede disolver una substancia. 2. *(Med.)* Medicamento que se emplea para disolver las concreciones u obstrucciones mórbidas de un órgano.

solvible ['sɒlvɪbl] [sol-vi-bol], *a.* Soluble. V. SOLVABLE.

somatic [sɒʊ'mætɪk] [sou-ma-tik], *a.* 1. Corporal, corpóreo, físico. 2. Perteneciente a la cavidad del cuerpo o a sus paredes.

somber, sombre ['sɒmbəʳ] [som-baʳ], *a.* 1. Sombrío, obscuro, nebuloso (dark). 2. Triste, tétrico, severo, lúgubre, melancólico (sad).

sombrous ['sɒmbrəs] [som-bros], *a. (Poét.)* V. SOMBER.

some [sʌm] [sam], *a.* 1. Algo de, un poco, expresando una cantidad indeterminada. 2. Algún, alguno, alguna, unos pocos, ciertos, expresando un número indeterminado. 3. Algunos, algunas personas, ciertas personas. 4. Uno, alguno, cualquier o cualquiera. 5. Unos, unas, poco más o menos; cerca de. **Give me some bread,** déme usted pan o un poco de pan. **Some day,** algún día. **Some other time,** otro día. **Some time since,** hace algún tiempo. **Some two thousand,** unos dos mil. **Some persons say,** algunos, o ciertas personas dicen. **Some 30 people,** unas 30 personas. **Some shoes,** zapatos, unos zapatos. **Some difficulty,** cierta dificultad. -*pron.* Algunos, algunas, unos y otros, parte, una parte, una porción. **Some are rich and some poor,** unos son ricos y otros pobres. **Are there any matches? There are some,** ¿hay fósforos? Sí, los hay. **Give me some,** déme usted unos cuantos.

-some, sufijo: desinencia, que se emplea en la formación de ciertos adjetivos que indican una cantiad regular o suficiente de la cualidad expresada; v. gr. Blithe*some,* alegre, lleno de alegría; quarrel*some,* pendenciero, irascible.

somebody ['sʌmbədɪ] [sam-ba-di], *s.* 1. Alguien, alguna persona; persona no conocida o no especificada. 2. Una persona de suposición, un personaje. **Somebody else,** algún otro.

someday ['sʌmdeɪ] [sam-dei], *adv.* Algún día.

somehow ['sʌmhaʊ] [sam-jau], *adv.* De algún modo o manera.

somersault ['sʌməsɔːlt] [sa-ma-solt], *s.* Salto mortal, el que dan los volatines en el aire.

something ['sʌmθɪŋ] [sam-sin], *s.* 1. Alguna cosa, algo; una cosa no especificada. 2. Cosa que tiene existencia real. 3. Cosa de importancia y suposición. **Something strange,** algo extraño. **Something else,** otra cosa. **I have something to do,** tengo que hacer. -*adv.* Algo, algún tanto. **This is something like,** esto sí que me gusta. **Did you say something?,** ¿has dicho algo? **I need something to drink,** necesito beber. **It's something chronic,** es horrible.

sometime ['sʌmtaɪm] [sam-taim], *adv.* En algún tiempo, en otro tiempo, antiguamente.

sometimes ['sʌmtaɪmz] [sam-taims], *adv.* Algunas veces, a veces, de cuando en cuando.

somewhat ['sʌmwɒt] [sam-uot], *s.* 1. Alguna cosa, algo; un poquito, poco más o menos, por poco que sea. 2. Sujeto o cosa de consecuencia. -*adv.* Algo, algún tanto, un poco. **Somewhat busy,** algo ocupado.

somewhere ['sʌmwɛəʳ] [sam-uea], *adv.* En alguna parte. **Somewhere else,** en alguna otra parte. **I left it somewhere or other,** lo dejé por ahí. **Somewhere in Spain,** en alguna parte de España.

somnambulism [sɒm'næmbjʊlɪzəm] [som-nam-biu-li-sem], *s.* Sonambulismo, estado del sonámbulo.

somnambulist [sɒm'næmbjʊlɪst] [som-nam-biu-list], *s.* Sonámbulo, el que estando dormido se levanta de la cama y anda como si estuviera despierto.

somniferous [sɒm'nɪfərəs] [som-ni-fe-ros], *a.* Somnífero, soporífero.

somnific [sɒm'nɪfɪk] [som-ni-fik], *a.* Narcótico, soporífero.

somnolence ['sɒmnələns] [som-no-lens], *s.* Somnolencia, inclinados a dormir, ganas de dormir.

somnolent ['sɒmnələnt] [som-no-lent], *a.* 1. Soñoliento, poseído de sueño, o muy inclinado a él. 2. Soñoliento, adormecedor que tiende a causar sueño.

son [sʌn] [son], *s.* 1. Hijo, se dice del hijo varón con relación al padre o a la madre. 2. Hijo, descendiente; como **The sons of Adam,** los hijos de Adán. 3. Hijo de confesión, hijo espiritual. 4. Hijo, expresión de cariño. 5. Hijo o natural de un país o pueblo. 6. Hijo: se usa para expresar una cosa producida por otra con respecto a la cosa que la produjo. 7. Hijo, la segunda persona de la Santísima trinidad. **Godson,** ahijado. **Grandson,** nieto.

sonant ['sɒʊnənt] [sou-nant], *a.* 1. Sonante; se dice de las vocales, y de ciertas consonantes, como la *n, g, th, b,* en contraposición a *surd, voiceless,* mudas. 2. Sonante, sonoro, que resuena.

sonar ['sɒʊnɑːʳ] [sou-naʳ], *s.* Contracción de la expresión inglesa *Sonic Navigation Ranging,* dispositivo para conocer la presencia o situación de submarions y otros objetos sumergidos.

sonata [sə'nɑːtə] [so-na-ta], *s. (Mús.)* Sonata, composición instrumental para piano en tres o cuatro movimientos; contrapuesto a *cantata.*

song [sɒŋ] [song], *s.* 1. Canción, cantar, cantinela, copla, canto; balada, poema lírico. 2. Poesía, verso (poetry). 3. Bagatela, nimiedad, poca cosa. **To sell for a mere song,** vender por un pedazo de pan. **To sing the same song,** cantar la misma cantinela, repetir la misma cosa. **An old song,** bagatela. **To sing a song,** cantar una canción. **Drinking song,** canción báquica. **Love song,** canción de amor. **The Song of Songs, the Song of Solomon,** el Cantar de los Cantares. **Song-book,** cancionero, libro de canciones. **There's no need to make a song and dance,** no es para tanto, no hay que exagerar.

songbird ['sɒŋbɜːd] [song-berd], *s.* Pájaro cantor.

songful ['sɒŋfʊl] [song-ful], *a.* Melodioso, lleno de canto.

songless ['sɒŋlɪs] [song-les], *a.* Que no canta; sin canto.

songster ['sɒŋstəʳ] [songs-taʳ], *s.* Cantor, el que sabe cantar; pájaro cantor.

songstress ['sɒŋtrɪs] [songs-tres], *sf.* Cantora, cantarina, cantatriz.

song writer ['sɒŋraɪtəʳ] [song-rai-taʳ], *s.* Compositor de canciones.

sonic ['sɒnɪk] [so-nik], *a.* Sónico. **Sonic barrier,** barrera sónica.

soniferous [sɒ'nɪfərəs] [so-ni-fe-ros], *a.* Sonante, sonoro.

son-in-law ['sʌnɪnlɔː] [san-in-lo], *s.* Yerno.

sonnet ['sɒnɪt] [so-nit], *va.* y *vn.* Celebrar con sonetos, componer sonetos. -*s.* Soneto, composición métrica de catorce versos.

sonny ['sɒnɪ] [so-ni], *s.* Hijo, hijito.

sonometer [sɒ'nɒmɪtəʳ] [so-no-mi-taʳ], *s.* Sonómetro.

sonorous ['sɒnərəs] [so-no-ros], *a.* Sonoro, de buen sonido, sonoroso, retumbante, resonante.

sonorously ['sɒnərəslɪ] [so-no-ros-li], *adv.* Sonoramente, armónicamente.

sonship ['sɒnʃɪp] [son-ship], *s.* Filiación, calidad de hijo, relación del hijo para con sus padres.

soon ['su:n] [sun], *adv.* Presto, pronto, prontamente; temprano; de buena gana. **As soon as,** luego que, tan pronto como. **As soon as I saw him,** luego que le ví. **Too soon,** demasiado temprano o demasiado pronto. **How soon shall you be back?,** ¿cuánto tardará usted en volver? **Come back soon,** vuelve pronto. **Soon after,** poco después, inmediatamente después. **Sooner,** antes. **I would sooner die,** antes la muerte; preferiría morir. **Soon after sunrise,** poco después de salir el sol. **Sooner or later,** tarde o temprano.

soonest ['su:nɪst] [su-nest], *adv.* Superlativo de SOON. Lo más pronto posible. **At the soonest,** cuanto antes.

soot [su:t] [suut], *va.* Cubrir de hollín o ensuciar con él. -*s.* Hollín.

sooted ['su:tɪd] [su-tid], *a.* Holliniento.

sooth [su:θ] [suuz], *a. (Esco. o ant.)* Agradable, delicioso, verdadero, real. -*s. (Des.)* Verdad, realidad. **In sooth,** en realidad.

soothe [su:ð] [suuz], *a.* 1. Calmar, ablandar, apaciguar, suavizar. 2. Agradar, complacer, lisonjear. 3. Paliar, excusar.

soother ['su:ðəʳ] [suu-zaʳ], *s.* 1. Apaciguador, el que clama, ablanda o suaviza. 2. *(Des.)* Lisonjero, adulador.

soothing ['su:ðɪŋ] [suu-zin], *a.* Calmante, dulcificante, consolador; tierno, dulce. -*s.* Acción de calmar, apaciguar, suavizar o paliar.

soothingly ['su:ðɪŋlɪ] [su-zin-li], *adv.* Con dulzura, con tono acariciador (speak); tiernamente.

soothsay ['su:θseɪ] [suz-sei], *vn.* Adivinar, decir lo que está por venir; decir la buena ventura.

soothsayer ['su:θseɪəʳ] [suz-seiaʳ], *s.* 1. Adivino. 2. *V.* MANTIS.

sootiness ['su:tɪnɪs] [su-ti-nes], *s.* La calidad de estar una cosa llena de hollín, fuliginosidad.

sooty ['su:tɪ] [su-ti], *a.* 1. Holliniento, que tiene hollín. 2. Fuliginoso, denegrido, obscurecido, tiznado.

sop [sɒp] [sop], *s.* 1. Sopa, pedazo de pan o de otra cosa empapado en cualquier líquido para comerlo. 2. Dádiva, regalo, lo que se da para apaciguar o aplacar a alguien. 3. Cualquier masa húmeda o empapada.

Sophia [səʊˈfɪə] [sou-fia], *sf.* Sofía.

sophism ['sɒfɪzəm] [so-fi-sem], *s.* 1. Sofisma, argumento falaz. 2. Doctrina de los antiguos sofistas.

sophist ['sɒfɪst] [so-fist], *s.* 1. Sofista, nombre antiguo de los profesores de filosofía y retórica. 2. Sofista, el que se vale de sofismas para engañar.

sophistic ['sɒfɪstɪk] [so-fis-tik], *a.* Sofístico, fingido, de la naturaleza del sofisma.

sophistically ['sɒfɪstɪkəlɪ] [so-fis-ti-ka-li], *adv.* Sofísticamente.

sophisticalness ['sɒfɪstɪkəlnɪs] [so-fis-ti-kal-nes], *s.* Sofistería, aparente y fingida sutileza de los argumentos y razones.

sophisticate ['sɒfɪstɪkeɪt] [so-fis-ti-keit], *va.* 1. Sofisticar, hacer sofismas. 2. Sofisticar, falsificar, alterar o adulterar alguna cosa.

sophisticated [səˈfɪstɪkeɪtɪd] [so-fis-ti-kei-tid], *a.* 1. Complejo, sofisticado, complicado. 2. Refinado, astuto.

sophistication [səˌfɪstɪˈkeɪʃən] [so-fis-ti-kei-shon], *s.* 1. Complejidad. 2. Refinamiento, esmero.

sophistry ['sɒfɪstrɪ] [so-fis-tri], *s.* Sofistería, argumento falaz.

sophomore ['sɒfəmɔːʳ] [so-fo-moʳ], *s.* En los colegios, estudiante de segundo año (en un curso completo de cuatro años).

soporific [ˌsɒpəˈrɪfɪk] [so-po-ri-fik], *a.* Soporífero, soporoso, que causa, motiva o inclina al sueño. -*s.* Medicamento soporífero, que hace dormir.

sopping ['sɒpɪŋ] [so-pin], *a.* Mojado. **Sopping wet,** empapado.

soppy ['sɒfɪstɪkəlɪ] [so-fis-ti-ka-li], *a.* Mojado, saturado de humedad; blando y muy húmedo.

soprano [səˈprɑːnəʊ] [so-pra-nou], *a.* De tiple o soprano. -*s.* 1. Tiple, soprano, la más aguda de las voces humanas. 2. Las notas o la música propias de esa voz. 3. Tiple, persona que tiene este tono de voz.

sorb [sɔːb] [sorb], *s.* Sorba o serba, el fruto del serbo o serbal y el mismo serbal o serbo.

sorcerer ['sɔːsərəʳ] [sor-se-reʳ], *s.* Hechicero.

sorceress ['sɔːsəres] [sor-se-res], *sf.* Hechicera.

sorcery ['sɔːsərɪ] [sor-se-ri], *s.* Hechizo, encantación, encanto, hechicería.

sordes ['sɔːdz] [sords], *s. pl.* Sarro, substancia feculenta que se adhiere a los dientes; el pus o materia de las llagas.

sordet ['sɔːdɪt] [sor-dit], *s. V.* SORDINE.

sordid ['sɔːdɪd] [sor-did], *a.* 1. Avariento, tacaño, codicioso. 2. Sórdido, impuro, indecente, escandaloso; vil, bajo. 3. *(ant.)* Sórdido, sucio.

sordidly ['sɔːdɪdlɪ] [sor-did-li], *adv.* Codiciosamente, con codicia y bajeza.

sordidness ['sɔːdɪdnɪs] [sor-did-nes], *s.* 1. Sordidez, mezquindad, miseria. 2. Bajeza, vileza. 3. Sordidez, suciedad, porquería o fealdad de alguna cosa.

sordine ['sɔːdiːn] [sor-din], *s.* Sordina, lo que se pone a un instrumento músico para apagar su tono.

sore [sɔːʳ] [soʳ], *s.* 1. La parte del cuerpo que está dolorida, una parte escoriada, una llaga o úlcera; lastimadura, matadura (cattle). 2. Mal, dolor, pena, memoria dolorosa, controversia. -*a.* 1. Delicado, tierno, dolorido, malo. 2. Escrupuloso, resentido. **To be sore with someone,** estar enfadado, estar resentido con alguien. 3. Doloroso, penoso, violento, vehemente. **Sore ears,** mal de oídos. **Sore eyes,** mal de ojos, ojos enfermos. **A sore point,** un punto delicado. **The sore place,** la parte enferma. **A sore sight,** un espectáculo doloroso. -*adv. (ant.)* Muy penosamente.

sorel ['sɒrəl] [so-rel], *a. y s. V.* SORREL. **She has been sorely tried,** ha sufrido lo impensable.

sorely ['sɔːlɪ] [sor-li], *adv.* Penosamente.

soreness ['sɔːnɪs] [sor-nes], *s.* 1. Dolencia, mal. 2. El estado de una llaga o úlcera muy dolorida. 3. Amargura o intensidad de una pena.

sorghum ['sɔːgəm] [sor-gom], *s.* 1. Sorgo, zahina, planta gramínea que se cultiva por su jugo sacarino. 2. *(E. U.)* Melaza que se hace con el jugo del sorgo.

sorority [səˈrɒrɪtɪ] [so-ro-ri-ti], *s.* Hermandad de mujeres con fines sociales.

sorrel ['sɒrəl] [so-rel], *a.* Alazán rojo: se aplica al caballo que es de color alazán. -*s.* 1. Color alazán o rojizo. 2. Caballo u otro animal alazán. 3. Gamo en su tercer año. 4. *(Bot.)* Acedera, hierba del género Rumex. **Field o sheep-sorrel,** acedera pequeña. **Wood-sorrel,** acederilla.

sorrily ['sɒrɪlɪ] [so-ri-li], *adv.* Mal, malamente, pésimamente, lastimosamente.

sorriness ['sɒrɪnɪs] [so-ri-nes], *s.* Ruindad, vileza, bajeza; mediocridad.

sorrow ['sɒrəʊ] [so-rou], *s.* 1. Pesar, dolor, sentimiento (pain). **Full of sorrow,** lleno de pesar. 2. Tristeza, pesadumbre, pena, sinsabor, desabrimiento (sadness). **To my sorrow,** con gran sentimiento mío. **Sorrow-stricken,** agobiado de dolor.

sorrow, *vn.* Entristecerse, ponerse triste y melancólico.

sorrowful ['sɒrəʊfʊl] [so-rou-ful], *a.* Pesaroso, afligido, angustiado, lleno de sentimiento o pena; triste, melancólico, que expresa pesar; doloroso, lastimoso.

sorrowfully ['sɒrəfəlɪ] [so-ro-fu-li], *adv.* Con angustia, con pena, con aflicción, con sentimiento.

sorrowing ['sɒrəʊɪŋ] [so-rouin], *s.* Aflicción, tristeza, lamentación.

sorrowless ['sɒrəʊlɪs] [so-rou-les], *a.* Sin pena, sin dolor, sin aflicción.

sorry ['sɒrɪ] [so-ri], *a.* 1. Apesadumbrado, pesaroso, triste, afligido, desconsolado (sad). 2. Triste, melancólico, funesto. 3. Despreciable, ruin, vil, pícaro, malvado (depicable, mean). 4. Pobre, escaso, miserable, pobrete (miserable). **I am sorry for it,** lo siento. **I am sorry for you,** lo siento por usted. **A sorry sight,** un triste espectáculo. **Very sorry!,** ¡lo siento!, ¡perdone! **There's no need to be sorry for her,** no hay que compadecerle.

sort [sɔːt] [sort], *s.* 1. Suerte, género, especie, clase, calaña (class, kind). **Three sorts of wine,** tres clases de vino o vino de tres clases. 2. Suerte, calidad, condición (quality). 3.

Clase u orden de personas, conjunto de personas. 4. Manera, modo, forma (way). **In like sort,** de la misma suerte. **I know his sort,** a esos ya me los conozco, conozco su calaña. **All sorts of people,** toda clase de gentes. **Perfect of its sort,** perfecto en su línea. **I have a sort of idea that,** tengo cierta/alguna idea de que. **Out of sorts,** 1. Indispuesto; 2. Malhumorado, triste, apesadumbrado; 3. *(Impr.)* falto de una clase o fundición especial de letra o guarismos.

sort, *va.* 1. Separar o dividir en distintas clases, se usa a menudo con *over.* 2. Colocar, ordenar, arreglar, a menudo con *out.* 3. Proporcionar, conformar, adaptar. *-vn.* 1. Hermanarse, unirse con otros de la misma especie. 2. Ajustarse, acomodarse una cosa con otra. 3. Salir o suceder alguna cosa bien o mal.

sortable [ˈsɔːtəbl] [sor-ta-bol], *a.* Acomodado, conveniente, apto, oportuno.

sortie [ˈsɔːtiː] [sor-ti], *s.* Salida que hace un número de tropas de la plaza sitiada.

sortilege [ˈsɔːtɪlɪdʒ] [sor-ti-lech], *s.* 1. Sortilegio. 2. Sorteo, la acción de sortear.

so-so [ˈsəʊsəʊ] [sou-sou], *a.* Pasadero, pasable. *-adv.* Así, así, en forma regular.

sot [sɒt] [sot], *s.* 1. Zaque, el hombre borracho. 2. Zote, hombre ignorante y torpe.

sot, *va.* Atontar, aturdir, atolondrar. *-vn.* Beborretear hasta embriagarse.

sottish [ˈsɒtɪʃ] [so-tish], *a.* 1. Torpe, rudo, tardo. 2. Embotado, entorpecido por los excesos.

sou [səʊ] [sou], *s.* Sueldo, moneda.

soubriquet [ˈsəʊbrɪkeɪ] [sou-bri-kei], *s.* Sobriquet.

soufflé [ˈsuːfleɪ] [su-flei], *s.* Suflé.

sough [saʊ] [sau], *va.* y *vn.* Producir un sonido como de suspiro, v. g. el del viento entre las ramas de los pinos, susurrar, murmurar. *-s.* 1. Susurro, suspiro profundo, murmullo (sigh). 2. *(Prov. Ingl.)* Desaguadero subterráneo.

sought [sɔːt] [saut], *pret.* y *pp.* del verbo TO SEEK.

soul [səʊl] [soul], *s.* 1. Alma, el espíritu inmortal del hombre. 2. Alma, lo que es principio de la vida en todos los seres vivientes. 3. Alma, esencia, virtud principal. 4. Alma, individuo, persona, criatura racional. **There was not a soul in the house,** no había nadie en casa. 5. Alma, viveza, espíritu, gallardía. 6. Fuerza o fervor individual, cordialidad, corazón: ardor, móvil; nobleza, generosidad. 7. Espíritu separado del cuerpo. **With all muy soul,** con el mayor gusto, con toda mi alma, con mis cinco sentidos. **Upon my soul,** en mi ánima o en mi conciencia.

souled [səʊld] [sould], *a.* Animado, el que tiene alma racional, se usa en composición.

soulful [ˈsəʊlfʊl] [soul-ful], *a.* Lleno de lo que apela al alma o a los sentimientos y los satisface; conmovedor, espiritual. A este adjetivo corresponden el adverbio *soulfully* y el sustantivo *soulfulness.*

soulfully [ˈsəʊlfʊlɪ] [soul-fu-li], *adv.* Sentimentalmente.

soulless [ˈsəʊlɪs] [soul-les], *a.* Desalmado, vil, bajo, ruin, despreciable, sin conciencia.

sound [saʊnd] [saund], *a.* 1. Sano, sin lesión o enfermedad alguna. 2. Sano, perfecto, entero. 3. Puro, seguro, ortodoxo: cuando se habla de doctrinas. 4. Seguro, cierto, indudable (certain). 5. Recto, justo, firme (right). 6. Profundo; completo, cabal. 7. Solvente, que puede cumplir sus obligaciones. **Sound sleep,** sueño profundo. *-adv.* Sanamente, vigorosamente. *-s.* 1. Mar poco profundo. 2. Sonda, cualquier paraje en la mar donde la sonda alcanza al fondo. 3. *(Geol.)* Estrecho, brazo de mar. 4. Tienta, sonda, instrumento de cirugía. 5. Son, sonido; vibración de un cuerpo sonante. 6. Alcance del oído. 7. Ruido (noise); apariencia grande en las cosas. 8. Vejiga natatoria (fish). **Sound-post,** el alma del violín. **Sound reasoning,** raciocinio sólido, seguro. **Sound system,** sistema fonológico. **Sound-board,** V. *Sounding-board.* **Within sound of,** al alcance de. **Of sound and disposing mind and**

memory, *(For.)* De mente y memoria sanas; capaz de hacer testamento.

sound, *va.* 1. Sonar, tocar, tañer, hacer que alguna cosa emita un sonido. **To sound alarm,** tocar alarma. 2. Celebrar, publicar (publish). 3. Dar aviso, mandar, prescribir u ordenar por medio de un sonido. 4. Probar por el sonido; auscultar o percutir; examinar por medio de los sonidos. *-vn.* 1. Sonar, hacer o causar ruido. 2. Sonar, hacer una cosa alusión a otra. 3. Ser llevado por el sonido; esparcirse, divulgarse. 4. Dar una señal por medio de un toque o sonido. **That sounds very odd,** eso suena raro, eso parece raro.

sound, *va.* 1. *(Mar.)* Sondar o sondear, echar la plomada para cerciorarse de la profundidad del agua. 2. Sondar o sondear, inquirir o rastrear cautelosamente alguna cosa; sondar o tantear. 3. *(Med.)* Sondar, tentar, reconocer con la tienta.

sounder [ˈsaʊndəʳ] [saun-daʳ], *s.* 1. Resonador, el o lo que da un sonido; resonador telegráfico que transmite un mensaje por medio del sonido. 2. Sondeador, aparato para sondear, p. ej. en el mar. 3. Tienta.

sounding [ˈsaʊndɪŋ] [saun-din], *a.* Sonante, sonoro; retumbante. **High-sounding,** sonoro, retumbante, campanudo. **Sounding-board,** tabla de armonía (de un piano); secreto, cajón de los órganos; tornavoz, sombrero de púlpito. *-s.* 1. Acción de sonar, resonar, sondar o tentar. 2. *(Mar.)* Braceaje, medida por brazas; sonda. 3. *pl.* Sondas, cantidad de brazas. 4. Muestras, v. g. de conchas sacadas del agua por el sondeador. **Sounding-lead,** *(Mar.)* escandallo. **Lead-sounding,** sonda de escandallo. **Sounding-line,** sondaleza. **Off o out of soundings,** fuera de sondas.

soundless [ˈsaʊndlɪs] [saund-les], *a.* 1. Mudo, sin sonido. 2. Insondable.

soundly [ˈsaʊndlɪ] [saund-li], *adv.* Sanamente, con salud, vigorosamente, firmemente; verdaderamente, seguramente, con rectitud y justicia. **To sleep soundly,** dormir profundamente.

soundness [ˈsaʊndnɪs] [saund-nes], *s.* 1. Sanidad, salud; vigor, firmeza. 2. Verdad, rectitud, pureza. 3. Fuerza, solidez. 4. Rectitud, justicia. 5. Pureza de la fe, ortodoxia.

soundproof [ˈsaʊndpruːf] [saund-pruf], *a.* Insonoro, a prueba de ruidos.

sound track [ˈsaʊndtræk] [saund-trak], *s.* Banda o huella de sonido de una película cinematográfica.

sound wave [ˈsaʊndweɪv] [saund-ueiv], *s.* Onda sonora.

soup [suːp] [sup], *s.* Sopa, caldo de carne o legumbres; se diferencia de *broth,* que es caldo solo, colado. **Peas-soup,** sopa de guisantes. **Milk-soup,** sopa de leche. **Soup-ladle,** cucharón. **Soup-plate,** plato hondo o sopero. **Soup-tureen,** sopera. **Mock turtle soup,** imitación de la sopa de tortuga. **In the soup,** *(Fest. E. U.)* en apuros, en aprieto.

soupy [ˈsuːpɪ] [su-pi], *a.* Espeso.

sour [ˈsaʊəʳ] [sauaʳ], *s.* Agrio, zumo ácido o substancia agria. *-a.* 1. Agrio, ácido, acerbo al gusto. 2. Agrio, acre, áspero, desabrido. 3. Penoso, doloroso. **Sour apple,** manzana agria o verde. **Sour dock,** acedera. **Sour-krout, sourcrout,** berza ácida. V. SAUERKRAUT. **to taste sour,** tener gusto agrio. **To turn sour,** volverse agrio. **A sour countenance,** un aspecto avinagrado. **Sour-goard,** pan de mico, árbol de la familia de las malváceas. Adansonia. **Sour grass,** acedera pequeña.

sour, *va.* 1. Agriar, acedar, poner agria o ácida alguna cosa. 2. Agriar, desabrir, exasperar, irritar, indisponer los ánimos o las voluntades. 3. Descontentar, desagradar. 4. Macerar; hacer fermentar (la cal). *-vn.* 1. Agriarse, ponerse agria alguna cosa; revenirse, fermentar. 2. Irritarse, enojarse. 3. Corromperse, echarse a perder. 4. Volverse áspera, viscosa y perjudicial a las mieses (soil).

source [sɔːs] [sors], *s.* 1. Creador, originador; origen. 2. Lugar donde se halla algo, o donde se saca; principio. 3. Manantial, el origen del agua u otra cosa (spring). **To have from a good source,** saber de buena tinta.

sourish [ˈsaʊərɪʃ] [saua-rish], *a.* Agrillo, algo agrio. **This wine has a sourish taste,** este vino tiene punta de agrio.

sourness ['saʊənɪs] [saua-nes], s. 1. Acedía, el sabor ácido y agrio; agrio, agrura. 2. Acrimonia, la aspereza o desabrimiento en el genio o en las palabras.

souse [saʊs] [saus], s. 1. Salmuera, adobo; escabeche, la cabeza, patas u orejas de cerdo adobadas (pickle). 2. (E. U. y Prov. Ingl.) Zambullida (water). 3. Ataque repentino, lanzamiento de un halcón sobre su presa. -adv. Zas, con violencia.

souse, va. 1. Zambullir, chapuzar, meter en el agua (plunge). 2. Arrojar, derramar, verter un líquido. 3. Escabechar, poner en escabeche; adobar. 4. Arrojarse, dar un golpe con violencia, como hace el ave de rapiña a la presa. -vn. Lanzarse, arrojarse como el ave de rapiña se arroja sobre la presa.

south [saʊθ] [sauz], s. 1. Mediodía, sud o sur, la parte meridional de la esfera, punto cardinal opuesto al norte. 2. Comarca o región situada en dirección al sur. 3. (E. U.) Los estados que se separaron de la Unión en 1861. 4. (Des.) Viento del sur. -a. Meridional, austral, del sur, del mediodía. **South wind,** viento del sur. **The South Pole,** El Polo Sur. **To be south,** dar a mediodía. **South Sea,** mar Pacífico o del sur. -adv. 1. Hacia el mediodía, por la parte del sur. 2. Desde el sur.

South Africa [saʊθ'æfrɪkə] [sauz-a-fri-ka], s. Sudáfrica, África del Sur.

South African [saʊθ'æfrɪkən] [sauz-a-fri-kan], a. Sudafricano.

South America [ˌsaʊθə'merɪkə] [sauz-a-me-ri-ka], s. Sudamérica, América del Sur.

South American [ˌsaʊθə'merɪkən] [sauz-a-me-ri-kan], a. Sudamericano.

southeast [saʊθ'iːst] [sauz-ist], s. Sudeste, el punto que media entre el este y el sur. -a. Sudeste, del sudeste, al sudeste.

southeaster [saʊθ'iːstəʳ] [sauz-is-taʳ], s. Temporal o viento de sudeste.

southeasterly [saʊθ'iːstəlɪ] [sauz-is-ta-li], a. y adv. Hacia el sudeste, al sudeste; que sopla del sudeste.

Southeastern [saʊθ'iːstən] [sauz-is-tarn] a. del sudeste, perteneciente o situado al sudeste.

souther ['saʊðəʳ] [sau-zaʳ], s. Viento o borrasca del sur.

southerly ['saʊθəlɪ] [sau-za-li], a. Casi meridional, hacia el sur o mediodía; del sur, que proviene del sur.

southern ['sʌðən] [sau-zarn], a. Meridional, austral, del sur; situado al sur. **The Soouthern Cross,** La Cruz del Sur; constelación del hemisferio austral. **Southernmost,** lo más al sur, lo más al mediodía.

southerner ['sʌðənəʳ] [sau-zar-naʳ], s. Persona nativa del sur de E.U.A.

southernwood ['sʌðən'wʊd] [sau-zarn-wud], s. (Bot.) Abrótano, lombriguera.

southing ['sʌθɪŋ] [sau-zin], a. Que camina hacia el sur. -s. 1. Diferencia de latitud medida hacia el sur. 2. Posición extrema de un astro hacia el sur en su movimiento diurno.

southmost ['sʌθməʊst] [sauz-moust], a. El más cercano al mediodía.

southpaw ['saʊθpɔː] [sauz-po], s. (esp. E. U.) Zurdo.

south-south-east [ˌsaʊtsaʊθ'iːst] [sauz-sauz-ist], s. Sudsudeste.

south-south-west [ˌsaʊzsaʊz'west] [sauz-sauz-uest], s. Sudsudoeste.

southward ['saʊθwəd] [sauz-uod], s. Las regiones del sur o mediodía.

southwardly ['saʊθwədlɪ] [sauz-uod-li], adv. Hacia el mediodía. **Southward of the line,** al sur de la línea (ecuador).

southwest ['saʊθ'west] [sauz-uest], s. Sudoeste, punto entre el sur y el oeste. -a. Sudoeste, del sudoeste, al sudoeste.

southwester ['saʊθ'westəʳ] [sauz-ues-taʳ], s. 1. Viento, borrasca o tempestad del sudoeste. 2. Chapona, sueste, sombrero de lona encerada, con el ala estrecha por delante y muy ancha por detrás. **Southwesterly,** a. y adv. del sudoeste, hacia el sudoeste; que sopla del sudoeste. **Southwestern,** del sudoeste, perteneciente o situado al sudoeste. **Southwestward,** hacia el sudoeste.

souvenir [ˌsuːvə'nɪəʳ] [su-ve-niaʳ], s. Memoria, prenda de recuerdo, lo que sirve para traer lo pasado a la memoria.

sovereing ['sɒvrɪŋ] [so-ve-rein], s. 1. Soberano, monarca, el que tiene la autoridad suprema. 2. Antigua moneda inglesa de oro. -a. 1. Soberano, supremo, independiente, superior a todo en su género o clase. 2. Soberano, singular, preeminente, de eficacia segura; lo más influyente o poderoso.

sovereignly ['sɒvrənlɪ] [so-ve-rein-li], adv. Soberanamente, perfectamente, excelentemente.

sovereignty ['sɒvrəntɪ] [so-ve-rein-ti], s. Soberanía.

soviet ['səʊvɪət] [sou-viet], s. y a. Soviet, soviético.

sow [saʊ] [sou], s. 1. Puerca, marrana, la hembra del puerco. V. PIG. 2. Un pedazo de plomo según sale de la fundición. 3. Goa, el pedazo de hierro según sale de la hornada donde se funde la mina. 4. **Sow** o **sowbug,** cochinilla de tierra, insecto isópodo que se cría en parajes húmedos. **Sow-pig,** lechona. **Wild-sow,** jabalina o puerca montés, la hembra del jabalí. **Sow-thistle,** cerraja, cardo ajonjero, planta semejante a la achicoria.

sow, va. y vn. (pret. SOED, pp. SOWN o SOWED). 1. Sembrar, arrojar y esparcir, como las semillas por la tierra; empanar, sembrar grano. 2. Sembrar, desparramar, esparcir, propagar. -vn. Sembrar, hacer la sementera; literal y figuradamente. **To sow one's wild oats,** (Fig. Fam.) Correr sus mocedades, hacer travesuras juveniles.

sowbread ['saʊbred] [sou-bred], s. (Bot.) Pamporcino o pan porcino, una planta.

sowens, sowans ['saʊəns] [souans], s. sing. y pl. (Esco.) Puches o gachas preparadas con los desechos de la harina de avena.

sower ['saʊəʳ] [souaʳ], s. 1. Sembrador, el que siembra; desparramador, el que desparrama, sembradera, máquina para sembrar. 2. Propagador, el que propaga.

sowing ['saʊɪŋ] [souin], s. Sementera, siembra, acción de sembrar los granos, sembradura. **Sowing-machine,** sembradera, instrumento o máquina para sembrar. **Sowing-time,** sementera, tiempo a propósito para sembrar.

sown ['saʊn] [soun], pp. del verbo TO SOW.

soy [sɔɪ] [soi], s. (E.U.) Soja. **Soy bean,** soya.

spa [spɑː] [spa], s. 1. Estación termal, balneario. 2. Manantial de aguas minerales.

space [speɪs] [speis], va. Espaciar; (Impr.) poner espacios entre las palabras o las líneas. -s. 1. Espacio; extensión (limitada o ilimitada), trecho; distancia; área. 2. Espacio, el intervalo de tiempo, de aquí, un poco de tiempo. 3. Tiempo, sazón, oportunidad. 4. Intersticio. 5. (Impr.) Espacio, pieza de metal más baja que la letra y más delgada que un cuadratín de ene, para dividir una dicción de otra. 6. (Mús.) Espacio, intervalo que hay entre raya y raya del pentagrama. **Space between,** el espacio intermedio. **To stare into space,** mirar al vacío, distraídamente. **A space,** algún tiempo, un poco de tiempo, durante algún tiempo, por algún tiempo.

space capsule ['speɪsˌkæpsjuːl] [speis-kap-siul], s. Cápsula espacial.

space centre ['speɪsˌsentəʳ] [speis-sen-taʳ], s. Centro espacial.

spacecraft ['speɪskrɑːft] [speis-kraft], s. Nave espacial.

space fiction ['speɪsˌfɪkʃən] [speis-fik-shon], s. Ficción científica, novelas de aventuras interplanetarias.

space flight ['speɪsflaɪt] [speis-flait], s. Vuelo espacial.

spaceman ['speɪsmæn] [speis-man], s. Astronauta, piloto espacial, cosmonauta.

spacemanship ['speɪsmænʃɪp] [speis-man-ship], s. Destreza o maestría aeronáutica o de los aeronautas.

space platform ['speɪsˌplætfɔːm] [speis-plat-form], s. Plataforma espacial.

space rocket ['speɪsrɒkɪt] [speis-ro-kit], s. Proyectil-cohete.

spaceship ['speɪsʃɪp] [speis-ship], s. Astronave.

space station [ˈspeɪsˌsteɪʃən] [speis-stei-shon], *s.* Estación astral.

space suit [ˈspeɪssuːt] [speis-sut], *s.* Traje espacial.

space travel [ˈspeɪstrævl] [speis-tra-vel], *s.* Astronáutica, viajes astronáuticos o interestelares.

spacey [ˈspeɪsɪ] [spei-si], *a.* Psicodélico, ausente.

spacious [ˈspeɪʃəs] [spei-shos], *a.* Espacioso, vasto, amplio, extenso, de mucho espacio, capaz, ancho.

spaciously [ˈspeɪʃəslɪ] [spei-shos-li], *adv.* Espaciosamente, con gran extensión.

spaciousness [ˈspeɪʃəsnɪs] [spei-shos-nes], *s.* Espaciosidad, capacidad, extensión, amplitud.

spade [ˈspeɪd] [speid], *s.* 1. Azadón, legón, con que se labra la tierra (tool). 2. Un ciervo o gamo de tres años. 3. Espadas, uno de los cuatro palos de que se compone la baraja de naipes (cards). 4. Animal castrado.

spade, *va.* Azadonar, cavar con azadón.

spadeful [ˈspeɪdfʊl] [speid-ful], *s.* Azadonada, cantidad que puede contener o remover un azadón.

spadix [ˈspædɪks] [spa-diks], *s.* (Bot.) Espádice, (m.) receptáculo común de varias flores, encerrado en la espata.

spaghetti [spəˈɡetɪ] [spa-gue-ti], *s.* Macarrón a la italiana.

Spain [speɪn] [spein], *s.* España.

span [spæn] [span], *s.* 1. Palmo, la distancia que hay desde la punta del dedo pulgar de la mano abierta y extendida hasta el extremo del dedo meñique, y que se estima en nueve pulgadas. 2. Instante, momento, rato breve, espacio pequeño de tiempo. 3. (Arq.) Tramo, luz de puente; ojo, apertura de arco o bóveda. 4. Tronco, pareja; (E.U. pareja de caballos; África del sur,, de bueyes). 5. Lo que mide o limita; traba; (Mar.) eslinga, amante. **Span-rope,** (Mar.) Nervio. **Span-shackle,** (Mar.) Abrazadera o cepo del pescante del ancla. **Span-new,** (ant. o dial.) Flamante, enteramente nuevo. **Spanworm,** oruga o larva de los geometrinos. **The whole span of something,** algo en toda su extensión. **A brief span,** una breve temporada.

span, *va.* 1. Medir a palmos; medir con la mano. 2. Alcanzar, llegar de un lado a otro; echar sobre, extenderse sobre. 3. Amarrar, ligar, atar. *-vn.* Proceder por etapas a jornadas regulares.

span, *pret. ant.* del verbo To SPIN.

spandrel (o **spandril**)[ˈspændrəl] [span-drel], *s.* (Arq.) Enjuta, embecadura; tímpano, espacio triangular entre dos arcos.

spangle [ˈspæŋɡl] [span-guel], *s.* 1. Lentejuela, planchita de metal plana y reluciente. 2. Cualquier cuerpo luminoso o cualquier cosa que relumbra.

spangle, *va.* Adornar alguna cosa con lentejuelas. **Spangled skies,** el cielo estrellado.

Spanglish [ˈspæŋɡlɪʃ] [span-glish], *s.* Espinglés, hispinglés (Hum.), mezcla de español e inglés.

Spaniard [ˈspænjəd] [spa-niad], *s.* 1. Español; natural o habitante de España. 2. Arbusto espinoso de la Nueva Zelandia.

spaniel [ˈspænjəl] [spa-niel], *s.* Perro de aguas, de tamaño pequeño con orejas grandes y colgantes y pelo largo y sedoso.

Spanish [ˈspænɪʃ] [spa-nish], *a.* Español, de España; que se refiere o pertenece a aquel país. *-s.* Español, el lenguaje castellano. **Spanish bayonet,** cualquier especie de yuca, particularmente **Spanish broom,** retama de España, atocha. **Spanish chalk,** esteatita, jaboncillo. **Spanish-black,** negro de España; corcho quemado. **Spanish-flies,** *s. pl.* Cantáridas. **Spanish-leather,** cordobán, cuero de Córdoba. **Spanish mackere,** escombro de ambas costas del Atlántico. **Spanish main,** la parte del Mar de las Antillas inmediata a la América del Sur, con inclusión del camino que solían seguir los buques mercantes españoles en sus viajes entre Europa y América. **Spanish moss,** musgo negro o de Florida.

Spanish America [ˈspænɪʃəˈmerɪkə] [spa-nish-a-me-ri-ka], *s.* América Hispana, Hispanoamérica.

Spanish-American [ˈspænɪʃəˈmerɪkən] [spa-nish-a-me-ri-kan], *a. y s.* Hispanoamericano.

spanishness [ˈspænɪʃnɪs] [spa-nish-nes], *sf.* Cualidad de español, españolismo.

spank [spæŋk] [spank], *va.* Golpear con la mano abierta o con un objeto sobre las nalgas; dar nalgadas. *vn.* Correr, ir de prisa. **To spank along,** ir corriendo, ir volando.

spanker [ˈspæŋkəʳ] [span-kaʳ], *s.* 1. El o lo que da nalgadas. 2. Maricangalla, vela del palo de mesana. 3. (Fam.) Alguna cosa extraordinariamente grande y hermosa. 4. (Fam.) El o lo que va rápidamente, a grandes pasos.

spanking [ˈspæŋkɪŋ] [span-kin], *a.* 1. Que se mueve rápidamente, pronto, veloz. 2. (Fam.) Extraordinariamente grande o hermoso. 3. Zurra, paliza. **To give a spanking,** zurrar, dar una zurra.

spanner [ˈspænəʳ] [spa-naʳ], *s.* 1. El o lo que mide o alcanza; en especial una entre varias clases de herramientas; llave de pasador. 2. V. *Spanworm,* al fin del título SPAN.

spar [spaːʳ] [spaʳ], *s.* 1. Espato, especie de fósil reluciente. 2. Un palo delgado y corto. 3. (Mar.) Berlinga, percha, bordón, mástil. 4. Asna, cabrio, cabrial, madero redondo que forma parte de una grúa o cabria de enarbolar. 5. Lucha a puñadas. **Iceland spar,** espato de Islandia. **Spar-deck,** cubierta de guindaste.

spar, *vn.* Fingir un combate a puñadas, como hacen los púgiles para ejercitarse. *va.* 1. Proveer de berlingas o mástiles; mover o alzar por medio de mástiles y poleas. 2. (Des.) Atracar o cerrar, cerrar con una tranca.

spare [speəʳ] [speaʳ], *va.* 1. Ahorrar, economizar, excusar gastos o moderarlos (save); economizar o conservar las cosas para que no se gasten o consuman, guardar o reservar una cosa; pasar o pasarse sin alguna cosa. 2. Perdonar, dejar libre a alguno de la pena que merecía (forgive); ahorrar, abstenerse de injuriar o molestar, hacer gracia de; permitir vivir. 3. Dispensar de, dar, conceder, conferir, disponer de (give). *-vn.* 1. Hacer gracia, usar de clemencia; de aquí, abstenerse, detenerse, refrenarse, desistir. 2. Ser frugal, ahorrativo, vivir con frugalidad y economía. **Not to spare oneself,** no economizar su trabajo, sus esfuerzos. **To spare the life of a prisoner,** perdonar la vida a un prisionero, permitirle vivir. **To have to spare,** tener de sobra. **Can you spare this book?,** ¿puede usted privarse de este libro?

spare, *a.* 1. Disponible a voluntad. 2. Sobrante, de sobra, que está de repuesto para un caso de necesidad o reserva; suplementario, adicional. 3. Descarnado, delicado, débil. 4. Escaso, sobrio, no abundante; apenas suficiente. **Spare time,** tiempo desocupado, ocio, tiempo libre. (Fam.) Ratos perdidos, horas de descanso. **Spare tyre,** rueda de repuesto. **Spare hours,** horas de recreo o perdidas para el trabajo. **Spare money,** dinero de reserva, dinero ahorrado para una necesidad. **Spare of speech,** escaso de palabras, que habla poco. **Spare bed,** cama de repuesto o de sobra. **To spare at the spigot and let out at the bunghole,** (Prov.) Economizar una gota y desperdiciar una bota. **Spare stores,** (Mar.) Pertrechos de respeto. **Spare rigging,** (Mar.) Crujía, postizas.

spareness [ˈspeənɪs] [spea-nes], *s.* Magrura, escasez; ahorro; frugalidad.

sparer [ˈspeərəʳ] [spea-raʳ], *s.* Ahorrador, la persona que ahorra.

sparetime [ˈspeətaɪm] [spea-taim], *atr.* Tiempo libre.

sparing [ˈspeərɪŋ] [spea-rin], *a.* 1. Escaso, corto, limitado, poco; de abastecimient limitado. 2. Frugal, económico, ahorrativo, sobrio. **Sparing in commendations,** sobrio de elogios. **Sparing efforts,** esfuerzos limitados.

sparingly [ˈspeərɪŋlɪ] [spea-rin-li], *adv.* 1. Escasamente, parcamente, frugalmente, económicamente. 2. Rara vez, con poca frecuencia. 3. Cautamente, con precaución, con prudencia. **To live sparingly,** vivir parcamente.

sparingness [ˈspeərɪŋnɪs] [spea-rin-nes], *s.* 1. Ahorro, escasez, ahorramiento. 2. Precaución, cautela.

spark [spaːk] [spark], *s.* 1. Chispa, partícula encendida de fuego. 2. (Poét.) Centella, la chispa que se desprende del pedernal herido. 3. Resplandor pasajero, emanación brillante, chispa eléctrica, centella, punto reluciente. 4. Vislumbre. 5. Chispa, diamante muy pequeño. 6. Petímetre, pisaverde, el joven que cuida demasiadamente de su compostura. 7. Amante, galán. **A spark of reason,** una chispa de razón, un destello de buen sentido. **A spark of life,** un átomo de vida. **To make the sparks fly,** provocar riña. **Spark-arrester, spark-catcher,** chispero, sombrerete (locomotive).

spark, vn. 1. Chispear, echar chispas, centellear. 2. Formar chispas eléctricas o pequeños arcos, v.g. en el conmutador: se dice de los dinamos. -va. (Fam.) Galantear, pretender en matrimonio.

sparkish ['spɑːkɪʃ] [spar-kish], a. Alegre, vivo, galán, vestido de gala.

sparkic ['spɑːkɪk] [spar-kik], s. Centella, chispa.

sparkle ['spɑːkl] [spar-kel], vn. 1. Chispear, despedir chispas o resplandores; centellear (glitter). 2. Chispear, relucir, o brillar mucho (glint). 3. Chispear, producir burbujas, como ciertos vinos.

sparkler ['spɑːklə'] [spar-kla'], s. La persona que tiene los ojos muy vivos o como suele decirse, que echan chispas.

sparkling ['spɑːklɪŋ] [spar-klin], pa. Centelleante, brillante, chispeante, espumoso (shining). **Sparkling eyes,** ojos brillantes, chispeantes. **Sparkling wine,** vino que chispea.

sparklingly ['spɑːklɪŋlɪ] [spar-klin-li], adv. Con brillantez o brillo, con esplendor.

sparklingness ['spɑːklɪŋnɪs] [spar-klin-nes], s. Brillantez, brillo, lustre, esplendor.

spark plug ['spɑːkplʌg] [spark-plag], s. Bujía.

sparrow ['spærəʊ] [spa-rou], s. 1. Gorrión, pardal, pájaro de color oscuro, particularmente del género Passer. 2. Otro pájaro cantor parecido al gorrión.

sparrowgrass ['spærəʊˌgrɑːs] [spa-rou-gras], s. (Fam.) Espárrago. (Corrupción de asparagus).

sparrowhawk ['spærəʊhɔːk] [spa-rou-jok], s. Gavilán, ave de rapiña.

sparse [spɑːs] [spars], a. Esparcido, desparramado, difundido en pequeño número, no denso.

sparsely ['spɑːslɪ] [spars-li], adv. Aquí y allá, a grandes trechos, no densamente.

sparsity ['spɑːsɪtɪ] [spar-si-ti], s. Calidad de disperso o esparcido.

Spartan ['spɑːtən] [spar-tan], a. Espartano, de Esparta. -s. Espartano, habitante o natural de Esparta.

spasm ['spæzəm] [spa-sem], s. Espasmo, contracción violenta e involutaria de los músculos.

spasmodic ['pæz'mɒdɪk] [spas-mo-dik], a. Espasmódico, convulsivo.

spasmodically [spæz'mɒdɪkəlɪ] [spas-mo-di-ka-li], adv. Espasmódicamente, por saltos, a ratos.

spastic ['spæstɪk] [spas-tik], a. Espástico. V. SPASMODIC.

spat [spæt] [spat], va. y vn. Desovar los mariscos o moluscos. -s. Huevas de los mariscos o moluscos, particularmente de la ostra; ostras pequeñas hasta que se fijan en un lugar. (spat. pret. de spit).

spat, va. y vn. (E. U.) 1. Dar un golpe ligero con la mano, dar palmadas; también, reñir ligeramente. 2. Azotar (la lluvia). V. PATTER. -s. 1. Manotada, manotón con la mano abierta; sopapo, bofetada. 2. Gota grande de lluvia, salpicadura, salpicón. 3. (E. U.) Riña, disputa (fight). V. PAT.

spathe ['spæθ] [spaz], s. (Bot.) Espata, bolsa membranácea que envuelve muchas flores; en especial, espádice.

spathic ['spæθɪk] [spa-zik], a. (Min.) Espático, parecido al espato.

spatial, spacial ['speɪʃəl] [spei-shal], a. Del espacio, perteneciente a él, o de su naturaleza.

spats [spæts] [spats], s. pl. Polainas.

spatter ['spætə'] [spa-ta'], va. y vn. 1. Salpicar, manchar con agua sucia. 2. Rociar, esparcir en gotas. 3. Difamar, quitar la fama o la reputación.

spatter, s. 1. Salpicadura; rociamiento, rociada; acción y efecto de salpicar, de rociar. 2. Salpicadura, la substancia con que se salpica o rocía. 3. Ruido como de la lluvia que cae. **Spatterdashes,** polainas.

spattle ['spætl] [spa-tel], va. (Cerám.) Motear la vajilla de loza. **Spatting-machine,** máquina para motear los objetos de cerámica.

spatula ['spætjʊlə] [spa-tiu-la], s. Espátula, paleta de acero de que usan los boticarios, los esmaltadores, los escultores, etc.

spatulate ['spætjʊleɪt] [spa-tiu-leit], a. Espatulado, en forma de espátula; estrecho en la base y redondeado por el extremo, forma de muchas hojas.

spavin ['spævɪn] [spa-vin], s. Esparaván, enfermedad que padecen las caballerías en la articulación del corvejón.

spawn [spɔːn] [spon], s. 1. Freza, huevas de los peces, anfibios, moluscos o crustáceos. 2. Producto o fruto de una cosa (despectively). 3. Ostras pequeñas antes de fijarse; también pececillos. V. SPAT. 4. (Bot.) Micelio de un honguillo (como el de la seta).

spawn, va. y vn. 1. Desovar, poner sus huevos o huevas los peces, anfibios o moluscos. 2. Producir o soltar de sí alguna cosa, como desovan los peces. 3. Engendrar, procrear; proceder, dimanar. En este último sentido es voz de desprecio. **Spawn of the devil,** (Vulg.) hijo del diablo o demonio.

spawner ['spɔːnə'] [spo-na'], sf. Pez hembra.

spawning ['spɔːnɪŋ] [spo-nin], s. Freza, desove, el acto de desovar los peces. **Spawning-time,** desove, el tiempo en que desovan los peces.

spay [speɪ] [spei], va. Castrar las hembras de los animales.

speak [spiːk] [spik], va. y vn. (pret. SPOKE; pp. SPOKEN). 1. Hablar, articular, pronunciar, proferir palabras o voces (talk); expresarse en un idioma; decir. 2. Perorar, arengar, hacer alguna arenga o razonamiento. 3. Razonar, conversar, disputar. 4. Hablar, rogar, abogar o interceder por una persona. 5. Hablar, revelar, hacer mención, dar aviso; explicarse. 6. Sonar. 7. Proclamar, celebrar. 8. Hablar a otro, dirigirse a uno, llamar un buque a otro con bocina.

speak about, hablar de, tratar de. **To speak fair,** hablar bien de algo o de alguien.

speak for, (a) hablar a favor o en nombre de otro; (b) ser prueba, evidencia de algo. **To speak for itself,** hablar por sí mismo, ser manifiesto. **To speak one's mind,** decir lo que se piensa, hablar en plata.

speak out, hablar claro, o en romance, hablar atrevidamente.

speak to, hablar a, (Fam.) poner de oro y azul, reprender.

speak up, hablar en voz alta, elevar la voz; osar hablar; decir claridades. **To speak thick,** hablar con media lengua, hablar tartajoso. **To speak through the nose,** ganguear, hablar gangoso. **Speaking personally,** en cuanto a mí, en lo que a mí se refiere. **So to speak,** por decirlo así. **Not to be on speaking terms,** 1. No conocer a uno sino de vista; no tener trato con alguien. 2. No hallarse en buenos términos con otra persona.

speakable ['spiːkəbl] [spi-ka-bol], a. 1. Decible, capaz de decirse o hablarse. 2. Capaz de hablar.

speaker ['spiːkə'] [spi-ka'], s. 1. El que habla, vocero. 2. Orador, el que arenga o habla en público. 3. Presidente de un cuerpo legislativo. **The Speaker of the House,** el presidente de la cámara de los diputados. **An easy o ready speaker,** un orador de fácil palabra.

speakership ['spiːkəʃɪp] [spi-ka-ship], s. Oficio o cargo del presidente de una asamblea legislativa.

speaking ['spiːkɪŋ] [spi-kin], a. Parlante, que habla. **A speaking likeness,** un retrato viviente, que está hablando. -s. Habla, discurso, declamación. **Speaking-tube,** tubo acústico (para hablar entre dos piezas algo distantes una de otra) o desde la calle a uno de los pisos. **Speaking-trumpet,** bocina, especie de trompeta que sirve para hablar de lejos; portavoz. **French-speaking,** de habla francesa, francófono.

spear [spɪə'] [spia'], s. 1. Lanza, azagaya, venablo. 2. Arpón de pesca. 3. (Poét.) Lancero. 4. Brizna, tallo delgado de hierba. **Pump-spear,** (Mar.) Asta de bomba. **Spear-box,** (Mar.) Guarnición de bomba. **Spear-grass,** hierba de los prados. **Spear-head,** punta de lanza. **Spear-wort,** un ranúnculo, francesilla llama.

spear, va. Alancear, atravesar o prender con lanza o con arpón. -vn. Brotar.

spearmint ['spɪəmɪnt] [spia-mint], *s. (Bot.)* Hierbabuena puntiaguda, menta verde.

special ['speʃəl] [spe-shal], *a.* 1. Especial, extraordinario, singular, que se diferencia de lo común, ordinario o general. 2. Especial, particular, privativo, peculiar. 3. Específico, que caracteriza y distingue una especie de otra, de especie, diferencial. **Special delivery,** entrega inmediata (post). **Special-delivery stamp,** timbre de entrega inmediata.

specialist ['speʃəlɪst] [spe-sha-list], *s.* Especialista, persona que se dedica a una ciencia o arte, o que descuella en ellas.

specialization [ˌspeʃələɪˈzeɪʃən] [spe-sha-lai-sei-shon], *s.* Especialización.

specially ['speʃəlɪ] [spe-sha-li], *adv.* Especialmente, singularmente, particularmente, sobre todo.

speciality [ˌspeʃɪˈælɪtɪ] [spe-shia-li-ti], *s.* Especialidad, calidad de especial.

specialize ['speʃəlaɪz] [spe-sha-lais], *vn.* Especializar, especializarse.

specialized ['speʃəlaɪzd] [spe-sha-laisd], *a.* Especializado.

specially ['speʃəlɪ] [spe-sha-li], *adv.* Especialmente, sobretodo, particularmente.

specialty ['speʃəltɪ] [spe-shal-ti], *s.* 1. Especialidad, empleo o estudio limitado a una clase determinada de trabajo, las tareas de un especialista. 2. Artículo fabricado para uso especial, artículo que se vende principal o exclusivamente. 3. *(For.)* Cualquier obligación hecha y firmada formalmente.

specie ['spiːʃiː] [spi-shi], *s.* Dinero contante en oro o plata, numerario.

species ['spiːʃiːz] [spi-shis], *s. (sing. and pl.)* 1. *(Biol.)* Especie, grupo de animales o plantas subordinado al género (genus) y capaz de multiplicarse entre sí ilimitadamente. 2. Especie, razón general o concepto que comprende a muchos individuos de la misma naturaleza. 3. De aquí, en el lenguaje popular, clase, género, suerte, variedad; forma. 4. *(ant.)* Especie, imagen o idea de algún objeto que se representa en el alma. 5. *(Farm.)* Polvos compuestos.

specific [spəˈsɪfɪk] [spe-si-fik], *a.* 1. Específico, que caracteriza y distingue una cosa de otra. 2. Específico: se dice del medicamento que se supone capaz de curar una enfermedad determinada. 3. Expreso, formal, preciso; especificado, determinado, distinto. 4. Peculiar. **Specific name,** nombre específico, el de la especie; sigue siempre al del género y principia generalmente con letra minúscula.

specific, *s.* Específico o medicamento específico. **Specific gravity,** peso específico.

specifically [spəˈsɪfɪkəlɪ] [spe-si-fi-ka-li], *adv.* 1. Específicamente, de un modo específico. 2. En cuanto a su naturaleza o diferencia específica. 3. En un sentido o caso particular.

specification [ˌspesɪfɪˈkeɪʃən] [spe-si-fi-kei-shon], *s.* Especificación; la mención individual o particular de una cosa.

specify ['spesɪfaɪ] [spe-si-fai], *va.* Especificar, declarar con individualidad, mencionar específicamente.

specimen ['spesɪmɪn] [spe-si-men], *s.* Muestra, ejemplar.

specious ['spiːʃəs] [spi-shos], *a.* 1. Especioso, plausible, recto y verdadero en apariencia, por lo común sólo en apariencia. 2. *(ant.)* Especioso, hermoso, vistoso.

speciousness ['spiːʃəsnɪs] [spi-shos-nes], *s.* Calidad de especioso.

speck [spek] [spek], **speckle** ['spekl] [spe-kel], *s.* 1. Manchita, mácula, punto descolorido en alguna cosa; nube en un ojo; lunar, señal. 2. Punto, cosa muy pequeña, partícula, átomo.

speck, speckle, *va.* Abigarrar, manchar, señalar con manchitas, espolvorear, motear.

spectacle ['spektəkl] [spek-ta-kol], *s.* 1. Espectáculo, lo que se expone a la vista pública, ostentación. 2. Espectáculo, suceso lastimoso, exhibición deplorable. 3. *pl.* Anteojos, lunetas de vidrio o cristal que sirven para corregir algún defecto de la visión o para proteger los ojos de la luz demasiado viva, gafas. 4. *pl. (Zool.)* Marcas o señales a manera de gafas.

spectacled ['spektəkld] [spek-ta-kold], *a.* El que lleva o usa ante-ojos.

spectacular [spekˈtækjɔləʳ] [spek-ta-kiu-laʳ], *a.* Espectacular, caracterizado por fausto y magnificencia. *-s.* Programa espectacular de televisión, de carácter extraordinario.

spectator ['spekteɪtəʳ] [spek-tei-taʳ], *s.* Espectador, el que mira con atención.

spectatress ['spektəkl] [spek-ta-tres], *sf.* Espectadora.

specter, spectre ['spektəʳ] [spek-taʳ], *s.* Espectro, visión, fantasma.

spectral ['spektrəl] [spek-tral], *a.* 1. Espectral, perteneciente a un espectro o fantasma. 2. *(Opt.)* Espectral, relativo a los espectros solares o causado por ellos.

spectrometer [spekˈtrɒmɪtəʳ] [spek-tro-mi-taʳ], *s.* Espectrómetro, aparato para el análisis espectral.

spectroscope ['spektrəskəʊp] [spek-tros-koup], *s.* Espectroscopio, instrumento óptico que sirve para estudiar el espectro luminoso.

spectroscopic [spektrəˈskɒpɪk] [spek-tros-ko-pik], *a.* Espectroscópico, que se refiere al espectroscopio o se ve con él.

spectroscopy [spekˈtrɒskəpɪ] [spek-tros-ko-pi], *s.* Espectroscopia.

spectrum ['spektrəm] [spek-trom], *s.* 1. Espectro, imagen con los colores del arco iris, producida por la descomposición de la luz. 2. Imagen de un objeto reluciente que se ve después de apartar de él la vista. **A wide espectrum of possibilities,** un amplio abanico de posibilidades. **Solar spectrum,** espectro solar.

specula ['spekjɔlə] [spe-kiu-la], *s. pl.* Espejos. V. SPECULUM.

specular ['spekjɔləʳ] [spe-kiu-laʳ], *a.* 1. Especular, terso, limpio, que tiene las cualidades de un espejo. 2. *(Des.)* Auxiliar de la vista.

speculate ['spekjɔleɪt] [spe-kiu-leit], *va. y vn.* 1. Especular, meditar, contemplar, considerar, reflexionar. 2. Especular, hacer una compra o inversión que puede ofrecer pérdida, pero con la esperanza de obtener una ganancia.

speculation [ˌspekjɔˈleɪʃən] [spe-kiu-lei-shon], *s.* 1. Especulación, la acción y efecto de especular. 2. Un proyecto o pensamiento que se ha discurrido o meditado, pero que no se ha puesto en práctica. 3. Especulativa, teórica; en oposición a la práctica en las artes y ciencias. 4. Meditación, contemplación o consideración detenida de alguna cosa. 5. *(Com.)* Especulación, acción de comprar, vender, etc., para obtener una ganancia. **To buy on speculation,** comprar como especulación.

speculative ['spekjɔlətɪv] [spe-kiu-la-tiv], *a.* 1. Especulativo, contemplativo, muy pensativo, dado a la especulación o contemplación. 2. Especulativo, teórico, que determina sólo en la especulación de las cosas. 3. Especulador (en sentido comercial).

speculatively ['spekjɔlətɪvlɪ] [spe-kiu-la-tiv-li], *adv.* Especulativamente, teóricamente; por vía de especulación (intelecutual o comercial).

speculativeness ['spekjɔlətɪvnɪs] [spe-kiu-la-tiv-nes], *s.* Carácter especulativo.

speculator ['spekjɔleɪtəʳ] [spe-kiu-lei-taʳ], *s.* 1. Especulador, la persona que especula comercialmente. 2. *(Des.)* Un observador, un contemplador.

speculum ['spekjɔləm] [spe-kiu-lom], *s.* 1. Espejo. 2. *(Cir.)* Espéculum: nombre dado a varios instrumentos de cirugía que sirven para tener dilatadas las cavidades mientras se las examina.

sped [sped] [sped], *pret. y pp.* de *TO* SPEED.

speech [spiːtʃ] [spich], *s.* 1. Habla, lenguaje, palabra o facultad de hablar. 2. Habla, conversación; el acto de hablar; dicho, expresión hecha por palabras. **To lose one's speech,** perder el habla. 3. Discurso; oración, arenga. 4. Idioma o lengua particular, dialecto (language). *(Fig.)* Cualquier modo de expresar el pensamiento por sonidos o señales. **Make a speech,** dar un discurso. **Without further speech,** sin decir más.

speechless ['spiːtʃlɪs] [spich-les], *a.* 1. Mudo, privado de la facultad de hablar. 2. Cortado, sobrecogido, callado, turbado, desconcertado, sin habla.

speechlessness ['spiːtʃlɪsnɪs] [spich-les-nes], *s.* Mudez, la falta de habla.

speechmaker ['spiːtʃmeɪkərˈ] [spich-mei-kaʳ], *s.* El que hace arengas.

speed [spiːd] [spid], *va.* (*pret.* y *pp.* SPED o SPEEDED). 1. Ayudar, dar ayuda o auxilio; favorecer; hacer salir bien o que tenga buen éxito alguna cosa. 2. Despachar, expedir, resolver y determinar algún negocio; acelerar el paso o movimiento. 3. Enviar a uno de prisa; apresurar, dar prisa, acelerar. **May Heaven speed this undertaking!** ¡El cielo favorezca esta empresa!, -*vn.* Ir, moverse o hacer alguna cosa con presteza y prontitud, despacharse, darse prisa. 2. Salir bien, tener buen éxito, tener acierto en lo que se emprende. 3. Hallarse en cualquier situación buena o mala. **Speed along,** ir a gran velocidad. **Speed up,** activar, acelerar.

speed, *s.* 1. Rapidez; el acto y estado de progresar rápidamente; presteza, velocidad, prisa, apresuramiento, diligencia. 2. Carrera, medida o razón del movimiento (race); velocidad relativa; (*Mec.*) andar. 3. Éxito, suceso, salida, fin, despacho bueno o malo de una cosa. **High speed,** galope o carrera tendida. **With all speed,** a toda prisa, con toda la celeridad posible. **At full speed,** a toda velocidad; (hablando de personas) a carrera tendida, velozmente; (hablando de caballos) a escape, a rienda suelta, a escape tendido; (de carruajes) a la carrera, a todo correr. **To make speed,** hacer diligencias, acelerarse, apresurarse. **What speed are you doing?,** ¿a qué velocidad vas? **Good speed!,** ¡buen viaje!

speedboat ['spiːdbəʊt] [spid-bout], *s.* Lancha rápida.

speeder ['spiːdərˈ] [spi-daʳ], *s.* Corredor, el que corre a velocidades excesivas.

speedily ['spiːdɪlɪ] [spi-di-li], *adv.* Rápidamente, velozmente; de prisa, pronto, con toda diligencia, con apresuramiento.

speediness ['spiːdɪnɪs] [spi-di-nes], *s.* Celeridad, velocidad, rapidez; prontitud, diligencia, prisa.

speed limit ['spiːdˌlɪmɪt] [spid-li-mit], *s.* Límite de velocidad.

speedometer [spɪˈdɒmɪtərˈ] [spi-do-mi-taʳ], *s.* Velocímetro, celerímetro.

speed-up ['spiːdʌp] [spid-ap], *s.* Aceleramiento.

speedway ['spiːdweɪ] [spid-uei], *s.* Autopista, supercarretera; pista (track).

speedwell ['spiːdwel] [spid-uel], *s.* (*Bot.*) Verónica, planta de las escrofulariáceas.

speedy ['spiːdɪ] [spi-di], *a.* 1. Ligero, veloz, rápido, que se mueve con velocidad. 2. Pronto, diligente, acelerado, vivo, que emplea poco tiempo en hacer una cosa. **A speedy answer,** una contestación pronta.

spell [spel] [spel], *s.* 1. Hechizo, encanto (fake). 2. Turno, orden y alternativa entre varios sujetos para el trabajo; tanda. 3. Tanda, tarea que se señala para un tiempo determinado. 4. (*Fam.*) Poco tiempo. **By spells,** por turnos, a su vez. **A spell of eight hours,** tanda (o tiempo) de ocho horas. **Spellbound,** encantado, bajo el poder del encanto. **To be under spell,** estar hechizado, encantado. **To cast a spell over someone,** hechizar a alguien.

spell, *va.* (*pret.* y *pp.* SPELLED o SPELT). 1. Deletrear, pronunciar o escribir cada letra, separada y de por sí. 2. Descifrar, p. ej. una inscripción; aprender calentándose los sesos, estudiar; se usa a veces con *over* o *out.* 3. Hechizar, encantar. -*vn.* 1. Formar palabras con las letras; particularmente, escribir correctamente o con buena ortografía. 2. (*Poét.* y *poco us.*) Contemplar, meditar.

spell, *va.* (*Fam.* o *Prov.*) Relevar, reemplazar, tomar el puesto de otro en alguna ocupación. **To spell the pump,** rendir los marineros a la bomba. **To spell the watch,** llamar a la guardia. -*vt.* Spell out, deletrear (read letter by letter).

spellbinder ['spelˌbaɪndərˈ] [spel-bain-daʳ], *s.* Orador fascinante.

speller ['spelərˈ] [spe-laʳ], *s.* El que deletrea.

spelling ['spelɪŋ] [spe-lin], *s.* 1. Deletreo, acción de deletrear; arte de deletrear correctamente; ortografía. 2. Manera como se deletrea una palabra y la misma palabra deletreada. **Spelling checker,** corrector ortográfico. **Spelling error,** error ortográfico.

spelt ['spelt] [spelt], *s.* (*Bot.*) Espelta.

spelt, *pret.* y *pp.* del verbo SPELL.

spencer ['spensərˈ] [spen-saʳ], *s.* Especie de sobretodo, que se llevaba al principio del siglo XIX.

spend [spend] [spend], *va.* (*pret.* y *pp.* SPENT). 1. Gastar, expender, emplear el dinero en alguna cosa (lay out). 2. Malgastar, disipar. 3. Gastar, consumir, destruir, extinguir (destroy). 4. Gastar, echar a perder. 5. Gastar, ocupar, emplear. **I shall spend the winter with my sister,** pasaré el invierno, con mi hermana. 6. Cansar, fatigar. -*vn.* 1. Hacer gastos. 2. Gastarse, perderse, consumirse. **To spend a mast,** (*Mar.*) Perder un palo. **To spend the holidays,** pasar las vacaciones. **To spend freely,** gastar demasiado, despilfarrar.

spender ['spendərˈ] [spen-daʳ], *s.* 1. El que gasta. 2. Gastador, el que gasta mucho, pródigo, manirroto. **To be a big spender,** ser una persona generosa.

spending ['spendɪŋ] [spen-din], *s.* Gasto.

spendthrift ['spendθrɪft] [spend-zrift], *s.* Pródigo, gastador, manirroto, derrochador, malgastador.

spent ['spent] [spent], *pret.* y *pp.* del verbo TO SPEND.

sperm [spɜːm] [sperm], *s.* Esperma. **Sperm bank,** banco de esperma. **Sperm whale,** cachalote.

spermaceti [spɜːməˈsetɪ] [sper-ma-se-ti], *s.* Espermaceti o esperma de ballena, substancia grasienta que se saca del aceite contenido en la cabeza de los cachalotes. **Sperm-oil, spermaceti-oil,** aceite de esperma, de cachalote.

spermatozoon [spɜːmətəˈʒəʊɒn] [sper-ma-to-souon], *s.* Espermatozoide, espermátulo o espermatozoario; cuerpo filamentoso y viviente que se halla en el semen de los animales y que da a éste su facultad fecundante.

spew [spjuː] [spiu], *va.* y *vn.* Vomitar, echar algo del estómago; arrojar, echar con aborrecimiento.

spewing ['spjuːɪŋ] [spiuin], *s.* Vómito.

sphenoid ['sfenɔɪd] [sfe-noid], *a.* Esfenoidal, encajado a modo de cuña. -*s.* Esfenoides, hueso impar, en medio de los de la base del cráneo.

spheral ['sfɪərəl] [sfia-ral], *a.* 1. Esférico, redondeado, simétrico. 2. Referente a las esferas celestes; armonioso.

sphere [sfɪə] [sfia], *s.* 1. Esfera, cuerpo esférico. 2. Globo, sea celeste o terrestre. 3. Esfera, el círculo o extensión de los conocimientos científicos, y la clase, estado o condición de las personas; círculo de acción, extensión de poder o influencia.

sphere, *va.* Colocar en una esfera; redondear, poner redonda alguna cosa.

spheric ['sferɪk] [sfe-rik], *a.* 1. Clestial, perteneciente a un astro, o a las esferas en que los antiguos suponían colocados a los astros; exaltado. 2. *V.* SPHERICAL.

spherical ['sferɪkəl] [sfe-ri-kal], *a.* 1. Esférico, de forma de esfera o globo. 2. Planetario, perteneciente a los planetas.

spherically ['sferɪkəlɪ] [sfe-ri-ka-li], *adv.* En forma esférica.

spheroid ['sferɔɪd] [sfe-roid], *s.* Esferoide, cuerpo cuya figura se aproxima a la de la esfera.

spheroidal ['sferɔɪdəl] [sfe-roi-dal], *a.* Esferoidal, que tiene forma o figura de esferoide.

spherule ['sferjʊl] [sfe-riul], *s.* Esfera menuda, glóbulo, esférula.

sphincter ['sfɪŋktərˈ] [sfink-taʳ], *s.* (*Anat.*) Esfínter, un músculo que rodea una abertura o tubo y sirve para cerrarlo.

sphinx ['sfɪŋks] [sfinks], *s.* 1. Esfinge (*f.*); monstruo fabuloso, con cabeza de mujer y cuerpo de león, que proponía enigmas y devoraba a los que no podían explicarlos. La esfinge egipcia no tenía alas, la griega sí. 2. Persona misteriosa o enigmática. 3. Esfinge (*m.*), género de insectos lepidópteros. *V.* HAWK-MOTH.

spice [spaɪs] [spais], *s.* 1. Especia, cualquier sustancia para dar sabor a la comida (*Culin.*); (*Mex.*) Olor. 2. Saborete, lo que da sabor, gusto o interés; grano, dosis. 3. (*Poét.*) Olor aromático, perfume agradable. **Spice-bush,** benjuí, arbusto americano aromático de las lauráceas. **Spices,** especiería, especias. **the espice,** (*Fig.*) la nata, la flor de.

spice, *va.* Especiar, echar especias, sazonar o condimentar con especias; *(Fig.)* dar gusto o picante a una cosa, dicho o escrito.

spicer ['spaɪsəʳ] [spai-saʳ], *s.* 1. El que sazona con especias. 2. *(Des.)* Especiero, el que vende especias o trata en ellas.

spicery ['spaɪsəɪ] [spai-se-ri], *s.* 1. Especiería, droguería. 2. Dispensa o lugar donde se guardan las especias. 3. Propiedad o carácter aromático.

spicily ['spaɪsɪlɪ] [spai-si-li], *adv.* De una manera picante.

Spick ['spɪk] [spik], *s.* (E. U.) Hispano.

spick-and-span ['spɪkən'spæn] [spik-an-span], *a.* Nuevo, flamante, fresco.

spicknel ['spɪknɪl] [spik-nel], *s. (Bot.)* Pinillo oloroso, hierba perenne de Europa.

spicula ['spɪkjələ] [spi-kiu-la], *s.* 1. *(Bot.)* Espiguita, espiga menuda. 2. V. SPICULE.

spicule ['spɪkjəl] [spi-kiul], *s.* Cuerpo pequeño y puntiagudo, púa. 1. *(Zool.)* púa que se halla en los invertebrados, como la esponja. 2. *(Bot.)* Espiguita, espiguilla. 3. *pl.* Agujas de la escarcha o hielo, la única forma en que puede existir la humedad a grandes alturas de la atmósfera.

spicy ['spaɪsɪ] [spai-si], *a.* 1. Que produce especias o abunda en ellas. 2. Aromático, que tiene fragancia, especiado. 3. *(Fig.)* Sabroso, picante.

spider ['spaɪdəʳ] [spai-daʳ], *s.* 1. Araña, insecto arácnido. 2. Arácnido, lo que es semejante a la araña. 3. **Spider o spider-crab,** araña de mar, cangrejo de patas largas y delgadas, centollo. 4. Sartén con mango largo; originalmente cazo con pies. **Spider-like,** parecido a una araña. **Spider-flower,** una especie cualquiera del género Cleome. **Spider-line,** hilo de tela de araña para micrómetros. **Spider's web,** telaraña.

spiderman ['spaɪdəmən] [spai-dar-man], *s.* Hombre araña, obrero empleado en la construcción de edificios altos.

spiffing ['spɪfɪŋ] [spi-fin], *a.* Estupendo, fenomenal.

spigot ['spɪgət] [spi-got], *s.* Llave de fuente, tapón para cerrar la espita.

spike [spaɪk] [spaik], *s.* 1. Espiga de grano, inflorescencia con flores sesiles dispuestas juntamente a lo largo de un eje común. 2. Espigón, clavo largo, perno. 3. Punta o punta larga. 4. *(Bot.)* Alhucema, espliego. **Oil of spike,** aceite de espliego. **Spike heel,** tacón de aguja. **Spikes,** zapatillas con clavos *(Sport).*

spike, *va.* 1. Afianzar, sujetar o clavar con espigones. 2. Aguzar, adelgazar por la punta. 3. Clavar, tapar o inutilizar el oído de un cañón. **To spike a cannon,** *(Mil.)* Clavar un cañón.

spikenard ['spaɪknɑːd] [spaik-nard], *s.* 1. Nardo, confección aromática hecha de las hojas del nardo y sus espigas. 2. *(Bot.)* Espicanardo, espique o nardo. 3. Hierba americana que se parece a la zarzaparrilla silvestre. 4. Uno de los varios aceites vegetales.

spiky ['spaɪkɪ] [spai-ki], *a.* Parecido a un clavo, puntiagudo, armado de púas.

spile [spaɪl] [spail], *va.* 1. Horadar un barril y ponerle espita, tapón o espiche. 2. Clavar estacas o pilotes. *-s.* 1. Pilote (estaca). V. PILE. 2. Clavija de madera que sirve de tapón, espiche, agujero en un barril o tonel que permite la entrada del aire o la salida de los gases de fermentación. 3. *(E. U.)* Llave de sangrar el arce azucarero.

spiling ['spaɪlɪŋ] [spai-lin], *s.* Pilotaje, conjunto u obra de pilotes.

spill [spɪl] [spil], *s. (Prov.)* 1. Astilla de madera. 2. Clavillo: fósforo de cartón. 3. Caída, vuelco, vertido.

spill, *va.* (pret. y *pp.* SPILLED o SPILT). 1. Derramar, verter, dejar caer, perder (pour): se dice de las substancias líquidas y polvorientas o de objectos pequeños y sueltos. 2. Arrojar, volcar (tip over). 3. Destruir, desperdiciar, malbaratar, disipar (destroy). 4. *(Mar.)* Apagar, descargar el viento del seno de una vela para aferrarla. *-vn.* Derramarse, verterse, volcarse; rebosar; perderse o destruirse. *-vi.* **Spill over,** desbordarse.

spillage ['spɪlɪdʒ] [spi-lich], *s.* Vertido.

spiller ['spɪləʳ] [spi-laʳ], *s.* Sedal de caña de pescar.

spillway ['spɪlweɪ] [spil-uei], *s.* Canal de desagüe.

spilt ['spɪlt] [spilt], *pret.* and *pp. of* spill.

spin [spɪn] [spin], *va.* (pret. SPUN, ant. SPAN, pp. SPUN). 1. Hilar, reducir el algodón, lino, cáñamo, lana, seda, a hilo, etc. 2. Alargar, prolongar, decir, contar, parlotear, a menudo con *out.* **To spin out long discourses,** hacer largos discursos. 3. Hacer girar (como gira una peonza). 4. Hacer durar, procurar que pase el tiempo. *-vn.* 1. Hilar, ejercer el arte de hilar. 2. Correr hilo a hilo; hilar, echar filamentos viscosos las arañas o los gusanos de seda y formar con ellos telarañas o capullos. 3. Girar; moverse en derredor como un huso. 4. V. SPURT. **Spin around,** girar, dar vueltas. *-s.* Revolución, vuelta; paseo. **To go for a spin,** dar un paseo, ir a dar una vuelta. **To put a spin on the ball,** dar efecto a la pelota *(Sport).*

spinach ['spɪnɪdʒ] [spi-nich], *s. (Bot.)* Espinaca.

spinal ['spaɪnl] [spai-nal], *a.* Espinal. **Spinal column,** espina dorsal, espinazo.

spindle ['spɪndl] [spin-del], *s.* 1. Huso, instrumento de madera con que se hila; instrumento de hierro que se introduce en un cañón para devanar seda; broca. 2. Gorrón, eje, carretel, árbol sobre el cual gira una cosa. 3. Cosa muy delgada que se supone parecida a un huso. **Spindle of the vane,** *(Mar.)* huso, eje o fierro de la grímpola. **Spindle of the capstan,** *(Mar.)* Pínola del cabrestante. **Spindle of the steering-wheel,** *(Mar.)* Maza de la rueda del timón. **Spindle-leegged, -shanked,** zanquivano, el que tiene las piernas largas y delgadas. **Spindle-shaped,** fusiforme, en figura de huso.

spindle, *vn.* Crecer los tallos de las plantas muy altos y delgados.

spindle-tree ['spɪndl̩triː] [spin-del-tri], *s. (Bot.)* Bonetero, arbusto de Europa.

spine ['spaɪn] [spain], *s.* 1. Espinazo o espina, columna vertebral. 2. Espina, púa delgada o puntiaguda.

spinel ['spaɪnl] [spai-nel], *s.* Espinel, especie de rubí.

spinet [spɪ'net] [spi-net], *s.* Espineta, clavicordio pequeño.

spinnaker ['spɪnəkəʳ] [spi-na-kaʳ], *s.* Una vela grande en forma de foque para regatas, y que se pone al lado opuesto de la vela mayor.

spinner ['spɪnəʳ] [spi-naʳ], *s.* 1. Hilador, hilandera, hilandero. 2. Araña de jardín. 3. V. SPINNERET.

spinneret [spɪnə'ret] [spi-na-ret], *s.* Fileras, órgano propio de la araña o del gusano de seda, que les sirve para tejer la telaraña o la seda.

spinning ['spɪnɪŋ] [spi-nin], *s.* 1. Hila, acción o arte de hilar, filatura (of thread). **Spinning-jenny,** telar o aparato para hilar más de un hilo a la vez. **Spinning-mill,** hilandería. **Spinning-mule,** telar para hilar algodón. V. MULE. **Spinning-wheel,** torno de hilar. 2. Rotación (motion).

spinose ['spɪnəʊs] [spi-nous], *a.* Espinoso, lleno de espinas.

spinous ['spɪnəʊs] [spi-nous], *a.* Espinoso.

spiny ['spaɪnɪ] [spai-ni], *a.* 1. Espinoso, provisto de espinas. 2. Penoso, difícil, inquietante.

spiracle ['spɪrəkl] [spi-ra-kol], *s.* 1. Respiradero, abertura u orificio para dar paso al aire o al agua al respirar; estigma, orificio de las tráqueas de los insectos; estoma, poro microscópico que se halla en la epidermis de las plantas; respiradero de los cetáceos. 2. Cono muy pequeño formado en la lava líquida por los gases que de ella se escapan.

spiral ['spaɪərəl] [spai-ral], *a.* Espiral; dispuesto en espiral o en hélice. *-s.* 1. Espira, curva espiral que partiendo de un punto y aumentando progresivamente su radio, da vueltas en torno de sí misma a manera de caracol. 2. Hélice. *-vi.* **Spiral down/up,** bajar/subir en espiral (plane).

spirally ['spaɪərəlɪ] [spai-ra-li], *adv.* Espiralmente, en figura o a modo de espiral.

spire ['spaɪəʳ] [spaiaʳ], *s.* 1. Espira, línea curva que sin cerrar el círculo va dando vueltas en forma de caracol. 2. Obelisco, pirámide; torre. 3. La aguja o chapitel de un campanario o torre. 4. Tallo delgado, brizna de hierba. 5. Cúspide, cima, de alguna cosa.

spire, *va.* Edificar con chapitel. *-vn.* 1. Rematar en punta. 2. Germinar, como la cebada al hacer cerveza.

spirit [ˈspɪrɪt] [spi-rit], *s.* 1. Espíritu, substancia incorpórea o inmaterial. 2. Espíritu, alma racional (soul). 3. Espíritu, ánimo, valor, energía, brío, esfuerzo, denuedo. 4. Viveza, agudeza, fuego, ardor, fogosidad (passion). 5. Espectro, fantasma, visión (ghost). 6. Hombre de corazón, espíritu emprendedor. 7. Elación, fortaleza, grandeza de alma. 8. Espíritu, genio o inclinación para una cosa. 9. Ingenio, talento. 10. Genio, condición, carácter especial; motivo, principio de acción (cause). 11. Espíritu, el verdadero sentido o intento; opuesto a letra. 12. Espíritu, el vigor o la energía natural que alienta y fortifica el cuerpo (courage). 13. Extracto o quinta esencia de una cosa. 14. El licor espirituoso que ha sido sacado por destilación, particularmente, el alcohol. **Spirits**, *s. pl.* (a) Espíritus, los vapores sutilísimos que se exhalan de un licor o cuerpo cualquiera. (b) Espíritus, las partes más sutiles y puras de los cuerpos. (c) Humor o buen humor, la buena disposición en que uno se halla para ejecutar una cosa (mood); alegría, vivacidad, viveza. **To be in good** o **high spirits,** estar alegre, de buen humor o contento. **To have a high spirit,** tener el alma grande; ser altivo. **To cast out spirits,** exorcizar espíritus. **Spirits** o **spirit of wine,** espíritu de vino, alcohol común. **Spirits of turpentine,** aceite de trementina, aguarrás. **Low spirits,** abatimiento. **High spirits,** alegría, buen humor, optimismo. **To keep up one's spirits,** mantener el valor. **Spirit-stirring,** animador, que estimula el valor. **To show spirit,** mostrar buen ánimo. **Pyroxylic spirit, wood spirit,** éter piroleñoso, alcohol metílico. **Ardent spirits,** licores espirituosos. **Spirit-lamp,** lámpara de alcohol. **Spirit-level,** nivel de aire (en el éter y el alcohol). **The Spirit,** el Espíritu Santo.

spirit, *va.* 1. Llevar, conducir secreta y misteriosamente como por medio de un espíritu; arrebatar, llevarse; se usa con **away** u otro adverbio. 2. *(Ant.)* Incitar, animar, dar espíritu.

spirited [ˈspɪrɪtɪd] [spi-ri-tid], *a.* Vivo, fogoso, brioso; lleno de vida, de fuerza, de vigor; arrebatado. **A spirited horse,** un caballo fogoso, impetuoso. **High-spirited,** que posee grandeza de alma. **Low-spirited,** que es cobarde o se amilana con facilidad. **Mean-spirited,** de ánimo mezquino, estrecho; miserable.

spiritedly [ˈspɪrɪtɪdlɪ] [spi-ri-tid-li], *adv.* Animosamente, con espíritu, vigor o energía.

spiritedness [ˈspɪrɪtɪdnɪs] [spi-ri-tid-nes], *s.* Arrebato de calor, energía; ardor; corazón, valor, vigor, ánimo, fuerza.

spiritism [ˈspɪrɪtɪzəm] [spi-ri-ti-sem], *s.* Espiritismo; voz de uso no bien determinado. *V.* SPIRITUALISM.

spiritless [ˈspɪrɪtlɪs] [spi-rit-les], *a.* 1. Abatido, amilanado, sin espíritu o vigor; sin carácter, gastado; sin imaginación. 2. Sin espíritu, sin alma, muerto.

spiritlessly [ˈspɪrɪtlɪslɪ] [spi-rit-les-li], *adv.* Sin vigor, sin espíritu, sin energía (sad, depressive).

spiritlessness [ˈspɪrɪtlɪsnɪs] [spi-rit-les-nes], *s.* Abatimiento, amilanamiento, falta de vigor o energía (depression).

spiritous [ˈspɪrɪtəs] [spi-ri-tuos], *a.* 1. Espiritoso o espirituoso, refino o refinado. **Spiritous liquors,** licores espirituosos. 2. Vivo, activo.

spiritual [ˈspɪrɪtjʊəl] [spi-ri-tiual], *a.* 1. Espiritual, incorpóreo, que consta de espíritu; mental, intelectual, inmaterial. 2. Espiritual, que pertenece al espíritu; santo, puro; que no es carnal, sensual ni corporal; que proviene del Espíritu Santo. 3. Espiritual, eclesiástico, en oposición a temporal o civil; piadoso, religioso. 4. *V.* SPIRITUALISTIC.

spiritualism [ˈspɪrɪtjʊəlɪzəm] [spi-ri-tiua-li-sem], *s.* 1. Espiritismo, doctrina de los que creen en la comunicación con los espíritus mediante una persona que se llama *médium.* 2. Espiritualismo, sistema filosófico opuesto al materialismo, que acepta la existencia de seres espirituales y en particular la inmortalidad del alma. 3. Espiritualidad.

spiritualist [ˈspɪrɪtjʊəlɪst] [spi-ri-tiua-list], *s.* 1. Espiritista, partidario del espiritismo. 2. Espiritualista, partidario del espiritualismo.

spirituality [ˌspɪrɪtjʊˈælɪtɪ] [spi-ri-tiua-li-ti], *s.* 1. Espiritualidad, inmaterialidad, calidad de espiritual, de santo y puro; carácter o naturaleza espiritual; vida interior. 2. Los bienes espirituales o eclesiásticos.

spiritualize [ˈspɪrɪtjʊəlaɪz] [spi-ri-tiua-lais], *va.* 1. Espiritualizar, dar carácter espiritual; tratar, considerar como si tuviese sentido espiritual. 2. Animar, vivificar.

spiritually [ˈspɪrɪtjʊəlɪ] [spi-ri-tiua-li], *adv.* Espiritualmente; con el carácter de espíritu, en espíritu.

spirituous [ˈspɪrɪtjʊəs] [spi-ri-tiuos], *a.* 1. Espiritoso o espirituoso, destilado, que contiene alcohol; embriagante, ardiente. 2. *(Des.)* Espiritoso, vivo, animoso, que tiene mucho espíritu. **Spirituous liquors,** licores espirituosos o ardientes.

spirituousness [ˈspɪrɪtjʊəsnɪs] [spi-ri-tiuos-nes], *s.* La calidad de ser un licor espirituoso.

spirt [spɜːt] [spert], *va.* y *s. V.* SPURT.

spiry [ˈspaɪrɪ] [spai-ri], *a. (Poét. o des.)* Piramidal, espiral; con numerosos campanarios.

spit [spɪt] [spit], *s.* 1. Asador, varilla puntiaguda de hierro que se introduce en la carne para asarla. 2. Lengua de tierra o banco de arena largo y estrecho que se extiende mar adentro desde la orilla. 3. *(Prov. Ingl.)* Azadonada. **Turn-spit,** asador, máquina para asar.

spit, *s.* 1. Escupidura, escupitajo, esputo, escupido, saliva. 2. Escupidura, el acto de escupir. 3. Espuma o huevos de varios insectos. **Spitbox,** escupidera. **To be the very spit of someone,** ser la viva imagen de alguien.

spit, *va. (pret. y pp.* SPIT, SPAT). 1. Escupir. 2. Arrojar, impulsar o echar en ráfagas o gotas. *-vn.* 1. Escupir, salivar, echar saliva o esputos, gargajear. 2. Producir sonido semejante al que se hace escupiendo. 3. Caer en gotas o copos dispersos. **Spit it out!,** ¡desembucha!, ¡dilo!

spit, *va. (pret. y pp.* SPITTED). 1. Espetar, clavar en el asador; atravesar de parte a parte. 2. Ensartar en una varilla.

spitchcook [ˈspɪtʃkʊk] [spich-kuk], *va.* Dividir un ave o pescado a lo largo y asarlos.

spitchcook, Anguila tajada y asada.

spite [spaɪt] [spait], *s.* 1. Rencor, despecho, malevolencia, odio, mala voluntad (rancor, hate). 2. Acción de malquerencia; lo que se hace por rencor; vejación. **Spite of** o **in spite of,** a pesar de, a despecho, contra la voluntad o gusto de alguno. **In spite of all my endeavors,** a pesar de todos mis esfuerzos.

spite, *va.* Dar pesar, causar indignación; picar, impacientar; mostrar resentimiento, vejar maliciosamente.

spitfire [ˈspɪtfaɪəʳ] [spit-faiaʳ], *s.* Persona colérica, dada a decir palabras duras o maliciosas.

spiteful [ˈspaɪtfʊl] [spait-ful], *a.* Rencoroso, enconoso; malicioso, maligno, malévolo.

spitefully [ˈspaɪtfəlɪ] [spait-fu-li], *adv.* Malignamente, con rencor, con tirria; por despecho; con el deseo de hacer daño.

spitefulness [ˈspaɪtfəlnɪs] [spait-fal-nes], *s.* Malignidad, malevolencia, malicia, rencor, encono; deseo de perjudicar que proviene de irritación y mala voluntad.

spitter [ˈspɪtəʳ] [spi-taʳ], *s.* 1. El que espeta. 2. Escupidero. 3. Gamezno, el gamo pequeño y nuevo.

spittle [ˈspɪtl] [spi-tel], *s.* Saliva, humor acuoso que se forma en la boca; escupido, esputo, gargajo.

spitz [ˈspɪts] [spits], *s.* Perro pequeño de hocico puntiagudo y pelo largo y tupido, perro de Pomerania.

splash [splæʃ] [splash], *va.* 1. Chapotear, hacer saltar, golpear el agua. 2. Salpicar, humedecer con un líquido (como agua sucia); enlodar. *-vn.* Chapotear, golpear el agua con los pies o las manos. *-s.* 1. Salpicadura, acto de salpicar, o chapotear; ruido, choque del agua. 2. Salpicadura, mancha de agua sucia que ha salpicado. **Splash about,** desparramar, derrochar. **Splash down,** amerizar. **Splash up,** salpicar.

splashback, splashboard [ˈsplæʃbæk] [splash-bak] [ˈsplæʃbɔːd] [splash-bord], *s.* Guardafango, salpicadero (car).

splashy ['splæʃɪ] [spla-shi], *a.* Cenagoso, lodoso, sucio; húmedo.

splatter ['splætəʳ] [spla-taʳ], *va.* y *vn.* Hacer un ruido ligero como de chapoteo; también, hablar entre dientes, hablar en vascuence.

splay [spleɪ] [splei], *va.* 1. Achaflanar, hacer en chaflán. 2. Exponer a la vista, mostrar; cortar un ave, un pez, etc. 3. Despaldar o despaldillar a un caballo. -*a.* Extendido, desplegado, ancho; pesado. -*s.* Alféizar, derrame que hace la pared en el corte de una ventana o puerta.

spleen [spli:n] [splin], *s.* 1. Bazo, órgano esponjoso que está en el hipocondrio izquierdo; antiguamente se consideraba como el asiento de varios afectos. (De aquí los sentidos figurados.). 2. Ira, rencor, odio, animosidad, mal humor. 3. Hipocondría, vapores hipocondríacos. 4. Esplín, melancolía. **To vent one's spleen,** descargar uno la bilis o el rencor.

spleened ['spli:nd] [splind], *a.* Privado del bazo.

spleenful ['spli:nfʊl] [splin-ful], *a.* Bilioso, colérico, enfadoso, regañón, triste, melancólico (sad, irritated).

spleenish ['spli:nɪʃ] [spli-nish], *a.* (Poco us.) Algo caprichudo o regañón; algo bilioso o melancólico.

spleenless ['spli:nlɪs] [splin-les], *a.* Blando, suave, apacible.

spleenwort ['spli:nwɔːt] [splin-uort], *s.* (*Bot.*) Escolopendra.

spleeny ['spli:nɪ] [spli-ni], *a.* Triste, melancólico, bilioso; irritable, enfadadizo.

splendent ['splendənt] [splen-dent], *a.* Esplendente; resplandeciente.

splendid ['splendɪd] [splen-did], *a.* 1. Esplendente, brillante, resplandeciente. 2. Espléndido, magnífico. 3. Ilustre, glorioso, heroico.

splendidly ['splendɪdlɪ] [splen-did-li], *adv.* Espléndidamente.

splendiferous [splendɪˈfərəs] [splen-di-fe-ros], *a.* Espléndido.

splendor, splendour ['splendəʳ] [splen-doʳ], *s.* Esplendor, pompa, magnificencia; brillantez, gran resplandor.

splenetic [splɪˈnetɪk] [spli-ne-tik], *a.* Atrabiliario, atrabilioso, bilioso, melancólico; caprichudo, regañón, de mal humor.

splenic ['splenɪk] [sple-nik], *a.* Esplénico, perteneciente o relativo al bazo. **Splenic artery,** arteria esplénica.

splice [splaɪs] [splais], *va.* 1. Ayustar, entrelazar las puntas de dos cabos; empalmar. 2. Unir, juntar, empalmar maderos. 3. (*Fest.*) Unir en matrimonio. **To splice the main brace,** (*Ger.*) tomar un trago de licor espirituoso.

splice, *s.* (*Mar.*) Ayuste, empalme, de cabo. **To bend with a splice,** (*Mar.*) ajustar con costura. **Eye-splice,** (*Mar.*)costura de ojo. **Long-splice,** (*Mar.*) costura larga o española, ayuste largo. **Short-splice,** (*Mar.*) costura corta o flamenca: empalmadura. **To get spliced,** contraer matrimonio, casarse.

splicer ['splaɪsəʳ] [splai-saʳ], *s.* Máquina de montaje.

splicing ['splaɪsɪŋ] [splai-sin], *s.* Ayuste, empalme. **Splicing-fid,** (*Mar.*) pasador, para abrir los cabos y ayustar.

splint [splɪnt] [splint], *va.* Entablillar, asegurar con tablillas un miembro fracturado. -*s.* 1. Tira plana y delgada, particularmente la que sirve para hacer cuévanos, asientos de sillas, etc.; astilla. 2. Tablilla para entablillar los miembros rotos o descoyuntados. 3. *V.* **Splint-bone. Splint-bone,** sobrehueso, uno de los pequeños huesos rudimentarios laterales, en las partes del caballo y otros animales afines.

splinter ['splɪntəʳ] [splin-taʳ], *va.* 1. Astillar, hacer astillas, hender en fragmentos. 2. Entablillar o entabletar un miembro fracturado. -*vn.* Hacerse pedazos, romperse en astillas.

splinter, *s.* 1. Astilla, esquirla, brizna, de un cuerpo sólido; por lo general, es agudo y angular más bien que plano. 2. Rancajo, punta o astilla de madera clavada en la carne. 3. Astillazo que salta de una piedra cuando se está labrando.

splinterprooft ['splɪntəpruːf] [splin-ta-pruf], *a.* Inastillable.

split [splɪt] [split], *va.* (*pret.* y *pp.* SPLIT o SPLITTED). 1. Hender, dividir, partir, rajar (cleave); estrellar. **Let's split the difference,** partamos la diferencia. 2. Dividir, hender o separar a lo largo. *V.* RIVE. 3. Dividir en dos o más capas, como se hace con el cuero. 4. Dividir, desunir los ánimos introduciendo discordias. -*vn.* 1. Henderse, estrellarse, rajarse, romperse; estallar. 2. Dividirse en dos o más partidos

opuestos. 3. Henderse, rajarse a lo largo. **To split upon a rock,** estrellarse contra una roca. **The votes are split 7-5,** los votos están repartidos 7 a 5. **My head is splitting,** me duele mucho la cabeza. **To split with laughing,** reventar de risa. -*s.* 1. Hendedura, hendidura, grieta, abertura longitudinal. 2. División, cisma, rompimiento. 3. Raja, pedazo separado. -*a.* 1. Hendido. 2. Limpiado y acecinado (fish). **Split off,** separar. **Split up,** dividir, parcelar (estate).

split-level ['splɪtˌlevl] [split-le-vel], *a.* De piso escalonado.

splitter ['splɪtəʳ] [spli-taʳ], *s.* Hendedor, el que hiend o raja.

split-up ['splɪtʌp] [split-ap], *sf.* Separación, división, ruptura.

splotch [splɒtʃ] [sploch], *va.* Manchar o ensuciar con manchitas de diferente color. -*s.* Manchita de color distinto de las que la rodean; borrón.

splurge [splɜːdʒ] [splerch], *vn.* Hacer gran papel; hacer alarde vanidoso (show). -*s.* Ostentación vana de sí mismo.

splutter ['splʌtəʳ] [spla-taʳ], *va.* y *vn.* Farfullar, hablar indistinta y atropelladamente (speech). -*s.* Chisporroteo; sonido como el que se produce al farfullar. Baraúnda, batahola, confusión. (Variación de **Sputter**).

spoil [spɔɪl] [spoil], *va.* 1. Inutilizar, echar a perder; deteriorar, destruir la utilidad o belleza de una cosa; estropear (damage, worsen). 2. Corromper, pervertir, arruinar (corrupt, pervert). 3. Pillar, robar; despojar, saquear, robar (steal). 4. Mimar demasiado (pamper). -*vn.* 1. Inutilizarse, corromperse, dañarse, echarse a perder alguna cosa. 2. Hacer pillaje o robo. **Spoiled child,** niño mimado, gachón, consentido.

spoil, *s.* 1. Despojo, botín; lo que se coge al enemigo. 2. *pl.* (*E. U.*) Los gajes o beneficios de un cargo público; recompensa por servicios políticos. 3. Pillaje, robo. 4. Camisa o despojo de serpiente o culebra, la piel de que se desnuda.

spoiler ['spɔɪləʳ] [spoi-laʳ], *s.* 1. Despojador, desposeedor; robador, ladrón. 2. Corruptor, pervertidor, el que echa a perder a otro corrompiéndole a contemplándole.

spoilsman ['spɔɪlsmən] [spoils-man], *s.* (*E. U.*) El que trabaja por un partido político por los gajes del oficio; partidario del reparto de los despojos entre los que mandan.

spoke [spəʊk] [spouk], *s.* 1. Radio de rueda, rayo de rueda. 2. Barra que se introduce en la rueda para impedir que gire. 3. Escalón de escalera. 4. (*Mar.*) Cabilla del timón. -*va.* Poner rayos a una rueda. **Spoke-shave,** rebajador de rayos.

spoke, *pret.* del verbo TO SPEAK.

spoken ['spəʊkn] [spou-ken], *pp.* del verbo TO SPEAK. Hablado.

spokesman ['spəʊksmən] [spouks-man], *s.* Interlocutor, el que habla en nombre de otro o lleva la voz o la palabra en nombre de otros.

spoliation [spəʊlɪˈeɪʃən] [spou-li-ei-shon], *s.* 1. Despojo. 2. (*For.*) Espoliación de bienes.

spondee ['spɒndiː] [spon-di], *s.* (*Poét.*) Espondeo, pie que consta de dos sílabas largas.

sponge [spʌndʒ] [spandch], *s.* 1. Esponja, animal fijo y marino por regla general, sin tentáculos y con poros en la pared del cuerpo. 2. Esponja, producción marina, masa flexible y porosa habitada por pólipos, que con mucha facilidad absorbe cualquier líquido y lo suelta comprimiéndola. 3. Todo utensilio parecido a una esponja que sirve como absorbente; lanada o escobillón; masa para hacer pan; masa de metales finamente divididos. 4. Mogollón, gorrista, parásito humano. **Sponge-cake,** bizcocho, bizcochuelo, bollo ligero y esponjoso.

sponge, *va.* 1. Borrar o limpiar alguna cosa con esponja. 2. Atraer y chupar la sustancia o bienes de otros. 3. Comer de gorra; chasquear. 4. Escobillonar. -*vn.* 1. Embeberse como una esponja. 2. Pescar o recoger esponjas. 2. Vivir de gorra, comer de gorra. **Sponge up,** absorber.

spongecake ['spʌndʒkeɪk] [spandch-keik], *sm.* Bizcocho.

spongelet ['spʌndʒlɪt] [spandch-let], *s.* 1. (*Bot.*) *V.* SPONGIOLE. 2. Esponjita, esponja pequeña.

sponger ['spʌndʒəʳ] [spand-chaʳ], *s.* Esponja, pegote, mogollón, gorrista, gorrón.

sponginess ['spʌndʒɪnɪs] [spand-chi-nes], *s.* La calidad que constituye a una cosa esponjosa.

sponging ['spʌnʤɪŋ] [spand-chin], *s.* 1. Socaliña, estafa, pillería. 2. Limpiamiento o limpiadura.

spongy ['spʌnʤɪ] [spand-chi], *a.* 1. Esponjoso, esponjado, lleno de poros, que es de la calidad de la esponja. 2. Embebido, empapado, lleno como una esponja.

sponsor ['spɒnsəʳ] [spon-saʳ], *s.* 1. Fiador, fianza, el que abona a otro. 2. Padrino o madrina de bautismo.

sponsor, *va.* Auspiciar, fomentar, apadrinar.

sponsorship ['spɒnsəʃɪp] [spon-sa-ship], *m.* Patrocinio. **Under the sponsorship of,** bajo el patrocinio de, patrocinado por.

spontaneity [spɒntə'neɪɪtɪ] [spon-ta-nei-ti], *s.* Espontaneidad, voluntariedad, cualidad de espontáneo.

spontaneous [spɒn'teɪnɪəs] [spon-tei-nios], *a.* 1. Espontáneo, que tiene su principio en sí mismo; que se hace o se produce por sí mismo y no por una causa exterior. 2. Que se produce o se cría sin trabajo humano; indígena, silvestre, esporádico. **Spontaneous generation,** generación espontánea. *V.* ABIOGENESIS.

spontaneously [spɒn'teɪnɪəslɪ] [spon-tei-nios-li], *adv.* Espontáneamente, voluntariamente.

spook [spuːk] [spuk], *s.* (*Fam. y fest.*) Fantasma, espectro, aparición, coco (spectrum).

spool [spuːl] [spul], *s.* 1. Canilla en que los tejedores devanan el hilo o la seda; carrete pequeño. 2. La cantidad de hilo que contiene la canilla.

spool, *va.* Encañar, encanillar, devanar en canilla o en carrete. **Spooling-wheel,** el torno para devanar la seda.

spoom [spuːm] [spum], *vn.* (*Ant.*) Pasar con velocidad; (*Mar.*) navegar, viento en popa.

spoon [spuːn] [spun], *s.* Cuchara. **Table spoon,** cuchara (para sopa). **Dessert spoon,** cucharilla de postre. **Teaspoon,** cucharilla de café. **Knife, fork, and spoon,** cubierto. **To be born with a silver spoon in one's mouth,** nacer en buena cuna.

spoon, *va.* y *vn.* Usar una cuchara; alzar con cuchara; pescar con garfio de cuchara. **Spoon off,** quitar con una cuchara (cream). **Spoon up,** recoger con cuchara.

spoonbill ['spuːnbɪl] [spun-bil], *s.* (*Orn.*) 1. Ave de cuchara, espátula, ave zancuda. 2. Pez notable por el achatamiento y prolongación de las mandíbulas.

spoondrift ['spuːndrɪft] [spun-drift], *s.* (*Mar.*) Rocío del mar.

spoon-feed ['spuːnfiːd] [spun-fid], *vt.* 1. Dar de comer con cuchara (baby). 2. (*Fig.*) Tratar como a un niño.

spoon-fed ['spuːnfed] [spun-fed], *a.* Demasiado mimado.

spoonful ['spuːnfʊl] [spun-ful], *s.* Cucharada.

spoonmeat ['spuːnmiːt] [spun-mit], *s.* El manjar que se come con cuchara.

spoonwort ['spuːnwɔːt] [spun-uort], *s.* (*Bot.*) Coclearia.

sporadic [spə'rædɪk] [spo-ra-dik], *a.* (*Med.*) Esporádico; solo, aislado; caso de una enfermedad que no es epidémica ni endémica, sino aislada.

spore [spɔːʳ] [spoʳ], *s.* 1. (*Bot.*) Espora (o esporo), corpúsculo reproductor de las plantas criptógamas, análogo a las semillas. 2. (*Biol.*) Espora (o esporo), cuerpo redondo u ovoide, menudo, orgánico, que se desarrolla en un nuevo individuo, como en los protozoarios y las bacterias. 3. Organismo diminuto, germen.

sport [spɔːt] [sport], *s.* 1. Juego, retozo; burla, chanza. 2. Juguete, diversión, divertimiento, entretenimiento, recreo, pasatiempo. 3. Juguete, objeto de risa y broma. 4. Cacería a caballo o a pie, partida de pesca, natación. 5. (*Biol.*) Animal o planta que exhibe variación espontánea del tipo normal. **Sports complex,** complejo deportivo. **Sports ground,** campo de deportes. **Field-sports,** diversiones del campo, como la caza, etc. **To make sport of,** burlarse de. **In sport,** en broma.

sport, *va.* 1. Divertirse, alegrarse, regocijarse (enjoy). 2. Ostentarse, vanagloriarse (to be arrogant). -*vn.* 1. Chancear, juguetear, estar de burla, de juego o de chunga; andarse con chanzas y con burlas; estrenar, lucir. 2. (*Biol.*) Variar de repente o espontáneamente del tipo normal.

sportful ['spɔːtfʊl] [sport-ful], *a.* Festivo, alegre, chistoso, placentero, agradable.

sportiness ['spɔːtɪnɪs] [spor-ti-nes], *sf.* Deportividad. (*Fig.*) Cursilería.

sporting ['spɔːtɪŋ] [spor-tin], *a.* Deportivo.

sportive ['spɔːtɪv] [spor-tiv], *a.* Festivo, alegre, juguetón, retozón; aficionado a bromear.

sportively ['spɔːtɪvlɪ] [spor-tiv-li], *adv.* De un modo retozón o festivo.

sportiveness ['spɔːtɪvnɪs] [spor-tiv-nes], *s.* Alegría, juego, festividad, holganza, chanza, retozo.

sportless ['spɔːtlɪs] [sport-les], *a.* Triste, sin gana de juego, sin diversión.

sportsman ['spɔːtsmən] [sports-man], *s.* Cazador, el que caza por diversión; pescador; aficionado a las diversiones campestres.

sportsman-like ['spɔːtsmənlaɪk] [sports-man-laik], *a.* Aficionado a los ejercicios atléticos, a la caza, pesca, natación, etc.; conforme a las reglas de estas diversiones.

sportsmanship ['spɔːtsmənʃɪp] [sports-man-ship], *s.* Espíritu deportivo. **Good sportsmanship,** caballerosidad deportiva, honradez deportiva.

sportswoman ['spɔːtswʊmən] [sports-uo-man], *f.* Mujer aficionada a los ejercicios de destreza y fuerza y a las diversiones al aire libre.

spot [spɒt] [spot], *s.* 1. Sitio, lugar o paraje particular (place). **Upon the spot,** en el sitio mismo, en el acto, al punto, inmediatamente; también, alerta, despierto. **He was on the spot,** estaba alerta, en el sitio mismo. **He died upon the spot,** murió en el acto. **In spots,** (*Fam.*) en algunos respectos; aquí y allí. 2. Un espacio pequeño de terreno, trozo de tierra. 3. Mancha, la impresión que hace en algún cuerpo la cosa que cayendo sobre él muda su color; borrón. 4. Mancha, la deshonra que se hereda o se contrae; mácula, borrón, deshonra, ignominia, desgracia. 5. Lunar, mancha natural en cualquier parte del cuerpo. 6. Espacio, cuña (Radio, TV). **To do something on the spot,** hacer algo en el acto. **To put someone on the spot,** poner a alguien en un aprieto. **To break out in spots,** salir granos en la piel.

spot, *va.* 1. Abigarrar, motear, poner a una cosa varios colores sin orden ni unión. 2. Manchar, ensuciar haciendo perder el color. 3. Manchar, deslustrar la fama o la reputación. 4. Corromper, alterar o mudar. 5. Tachonar, sembrar de.

spotless ['spɒtlɪs] [spot-les], *a.* Limpio, inmaculado, sin mancha, nítido.

spotlessness ['spɒtlɪsnɪs] [spot-les-nes], *s.* Inocencia, el estado del que no tiene tacha, mancha.

spotlight ['spɒtlaɪt] [spot-lait], *s.* (*Teat.*) 1. Reflector. 2. Farol de luz concentrada. **To be on the spotlight,** hacerse conspicuo.

spotlit ['spɒtlɪt] [spot-lit], *a.* Iluminado.

spotted ['spɒtɪd] [spo-tid], *a.* y *pp.* 1. Manchado, ensuciado con manchas. 2. Moteado, con manchas (dress); apulgarado, v. g. la ropa blanca; esquizado, como el mármol. **Spotted fever,** tabardillo pintado, la fiebre del tabardillo.

spotter ['spɒtəʳ] [spo-taʳ], *s.* La persona que mancha o ensucia; el que mancha o deshonra.

spottiness ['spɒtɪnɪs] [spo-ti-nes], *s.* Estado o calidad de lo que tiene manchas.

spotting ['spɒtɪŋ] [spo-tin], *sm.* Moteamiento, punteo.

spotty ['spɒtɪ] [spo-ti], *a.* Lleno de manchas, puerco, sucio (dirty).

spouse [spaʊs] [spaus], *s.* Esposo, esposa.

spouseless ['spaʊslɪs] [spaus-les], *a.* Soltero o viudo; sin esposo, sin esposa.

spout [spaʊt] [spaut], *s.* 1. Caño o cañón por donde sale el agua a chorro; tubo de desagüe; canilla de tonel, espita; gárgola o figurón que arroja el agua por la boca en las canales de los tejados. 2. Cuello de vasija; pico de cafetera, de tetera. **Water-spout,** surtidor de agua que salta, tromba o manga marina, remolino; chaparrón, turbión. **Rain-spout,** lluvia muy abundante.

spout, *va.* y *vn.* 1. Arrojar o echar agua u otro líquido con mucho ímpetu. 2. Salir, saltar o hacer salir o saltar cualquier líquido con mucho ímpetu. 3. Borbotar, salir a borbotones o con mucha fuerza el agua u otro líquido. 4. Chorrear, correr a chorro. 5. *(Fam.)* Decir de una manera declamatoria; recitar, declamar. **To spout down,** llover a chaparrones. **To spout up,** resaltar, salir o saltar el agua hacia arriba.

sprain [spreɪn] [sprein], *va.* Torcer violentamente los ligamentos que rodean alguna articulación sin dislocar el hueso. **He has sprained his ankle,** se ha torcido el tobillo.

sprain, *s.* Torcedura o tensión violenta de los tendones o ligamentos sin dislocación.

sprang ['spræŋ] [spran], *pret.* del verbo TO SPRING.

sprawl [sprɔːl] [sprol], *s.* Postura informal, desgarbada; extensión. **Urban sprawl,** urbanización caótica.

sprawl, *va.* y *vn.* 1. Tenderse a la larga; tender o mover, tenderse o moverse con los miembros en posición poco graciosa. 2. Tener una posición extendida y falta de gracia (p. ej. las viñas). -*s.* El acto de tenderse sin gracia, o esa posición misma.

spray [spreɪ] [sprei], *va.* 1. Rociar, pulverizar un líquido, esparcirlo en partículas menudas (liquid). 2. Rociar, aplicar el líquido pulverizado, como se hace con el rociador. -*vn.* Rociar, esparcir un líquido en menudas gotas. -*s.* 1. Rociada, rocío, agua u otro líquido que se esparce en gotas menudas, espuma del mar. 2. Rociador. *V.* ATOMIZER. **Spray out,** salir a chorro.

spray, *s.* 1. Ramita de árbol o planta que lleva otras ramitas o flores; ramaje menudo. 2. Dibujo o adorno parecido a una colección de ramillas o flores.

spraygun ['spreɪgʌn] [sprei-gan], *sf.* Pistola para rociar, pulverizador.

spraying ['spreɪɪŋ] [spreiin], *s.* 1. Rociadura. 2. Pulverización.

spread [spred] [spred], *va. (pret. y pp.* SPREAD). 1. Tender, extender, alargar, desplegar, engrandecer la superficie de algo; desenvolver. 2. Esparcir, divulgar, difundir o extender noticias, doctrinas, etc.; publicar, diseminar, propagar. 3. Esparcir o difundir luz, olor, etc. 4. Envolver, cubrir de una capa delgada. 5. Desplegar a la vista, exhibir. 6. Pertrechar, equipar a propósito con cosas arregladas en orden. 7. Tender, alejar, forzar más a parte, a mayor distancia una cosa de otra. -*vn.* 1. Extenderse, alargarse, desplegarse. 2. Esparcirse, difundirse. 3. Desarrollarse, propagarse, exhalarse. 4. Alejarse por fuerza. **To spread abroad,** esparcir, divulgar, hacer una cosa pública, y también susurrarse, correr o saberse una cosa que estaba secreta. **To spread over,** cubrir una cosa con otra extendiéndola por toda su superficie. **To spread the cloth,** poner la mesa. **The fire spread rapidly,** el fuego se expandió rápidamente.

spread, *s.* 1. Extensión, dilatación, amplitud. 2. Expansión, dilatación. 3. Ambito. 4. Desarrollo; propagación. 5. Colcha de cama; tapete de mesa, mantel. 6. *(Fam.)* Festío, banquete.

spreader ['spredə'] [spre-da'], *s.* Divulgador; él o lo que esparce.

spreading ['spredɪŋ] [spre-din], *a.* 1. Extenso, ancho; que se extiende; *(Bot.)* divergente; frondoso. 2. Que se esparce, que se propaga. **Under a spreading chestnut-tree,** debajo de un castaño frondoso. -*s.* Acción y efecto del verbo **spread;** extensión, propagación, etc.

spree [spriː] [sprii], *vn.* Beber mucho, emborracharse. -*s.* Borrachera, jarana, juerga. *V.* CAROUSAL.

sprig [sprɪg] [sprig], *s.* 1. Ramita, rama pequeña, renuevo, pimpollo. 2. Tachuela sin cabeza.

sprig, *va.* Adornar con ramitas; bordar ramos o flores.

spriggy ['sprɪgɪ] [spri-gui], *a.* Ramoso.

sprightliness ['spraɪtlɪnɪs] [sprait-li-nes], *s.* Viveza, despejo, alegría, vivacidad.

sprightly ['spraɪtlɪ] [sprait-li], *a.* Alegre, despejado, despierto, vivo, vivaracho.

spring [sprɪŋ] [spring], *va. (pret.* SPRANG o SPRUNG, *pp.* SPRUNG). 1. Soltar el resorte o muelle (de una trampa, una cerradura, etc.). 2. Presentar a la vista, producir o ejecutar de repente o inesperadamente. 3. Hacer volar o saltar una mina. 4. Combar, encorvar por fuerza una cosa, esforzar demasiado, rendir un palo o verga. 5. *(Arq.)* Arrancar o vaciar un arco o bóveda; principiarlos de un punto dado. 6. Insertar una cosa en un lugar donde cabe muy apretadamente, encorvándola o forzándola. 7. Saltar por encima; pasar por arriba de algo saltando. 8. Ojear la caza, espantarla o ahuyentarla con voces para que se levante. -*vn.* 1. Saltar, brincar (jump). 2. Saltar o saltar un líquido. 3. Salir con mucha fuerza; aparecerse de repente. 4. Moverse súbitamente, como con una fuerza elástica o por medio de un resorte. 5. Alabearse, combarse, desviarse de un plano o línea normal. 6. Brotar, arrojar, apuntar los árboles y plantas (sprout); echar o arrojar hierba o cualquier otra cosa la tierra. 7. Nacer, proceder, provenir, tomar su origen, derivar de, venir, dimanar, originarse, traer su origen (derive, come). 8. Levantarse, elevarse más arriba que los objetos circunvecinos. 9. Comenzar, nacer, empezar a levantarse un arco o bóveda.

spring again, renacer, brotar de nuevo, volver a saltar.

spring away, saltar a un lado, lanzarse de un salto. **To spring back,** saltar hacia atrás; retroceder, recular.

spring forth, brotar, crecer, salir; lanzarse, precipitarse.

spring forward, abalanzarse, arrojarse, tirarse, dispararse.

spring from, surgir, proceder de.

spring up, nacer, brotar, crecer, desarrollarse; salir a luz, presentarse a la vista; subir, engrandecerse.

spring upon, abalanzarse *a.* **To spring a leak,** *(Mar.)* descubrir una vía de agua, hacer agua el buque. **The chamois sprang from rock to rock,** la gamuza saltaba de roca en roca. **To spring a charge of perjury,** hacer inesperadamente una acusación de perjurio.

spring, *s.* 1. Resorte, elasticidad, fuerza elástica; muelle, resorte; cualquier cuerpo elástico que vuelve a su forma normal cuando cesa de estar comprimido. **Spring-lock,** cerradura de golpe. 2. Salto, brinco, corcovo; reculada, movimiento súbito con fuerza. 3. Energía o potencia, causa de acción. 4. Primavera, estación del año en la cual comienzan las plantas a brotar y crecer. 5. Manantial, el nacimiento del agua o fuente; surtidor. **Spring-water,** agua de fuente. 6. Manantial, origen, principio. 7. Entrada de agua; tangidera; barloa. 8. Combadura, o la cosa combada. (esta voz forma muchos compuestos, en su mayor parte de significación evidente). **Spring-back,** lomo plegado (book). **Spring-board,** trampolín. **Spring mattress,** colchón de muelles. **In one spring,** de un salto.

spring beauty ['sprɪŋˌbjuːtɪ] [spring-biu-ti], *s. (Bot.)* Claitonia.

springbok ['sprɪŋbɒk] [spring-bok], *s.* Gacela del Sur de África.

spring-cleaning ['sprɪŋˈkliːnɪŋ] [spring-kli-nin], *sf.* Limpieza general.

springer ['sprɪŋə'] [sprin-ga'], *s.* 1. Saltador, brincador. 2. *(Arq.)* imposta; sotabanco, cojinete, sillar de arranque. 3. Perro de España, hábil en ojear la caza.

spring-halt ['sprɪŋhɔːlt] [spring-jolt], *s.* Cojera de caballo.

springiness ['sprɪŋɪnɪs] [sprin-gui-nes], *s.* Elasticidad, resorte, fuerza elástica.

springlike ['sprɪŋlaɪk] [spring-laik], *a.* Primaveral.

springtide ['sprɪŋtaɪd] [spring-taid], *s.* Estación de primavera. **Spring-tide,** marea fuerte en las épocas del novilunio y plenilunio.

springy ['sprɪŋɪ] [sprin-gui], *a.* 1. Elástico. 2. Lleno de fuentes o manantiales.

sprinkle ['sprɪŋkl] [sprin-kel], *va.* 1. Asperjar, rociar, esparcir (spread); regar o desparramar en gotas. 2. Polvorear, empolvar (sugar, salt). 3. Distribuir aquí y allá, sembrar; arrojar o esparcir cosas de modo que caigan separadas. 4. Bautizar rociando. -*vn.* 1. *(Impers.)* Lloviznar, llover un poco, como al principio de un aguacero (rain). **It sprinkles,** está lloviznando. 2. Caer en gotas o en partículas.

sprinkle, *s.* La cantidad pequeña de cualquier cosa que se esparce o derrama rociando algo; caída en gotas o partículas o lo que cae de esta manera, de aquí, pequeña cantidad, una pizca, un poco. **A sprinkle of salt,** una pizca de sal. **A sprinkle of oil,** unas gotas de aceite.

sprinkler ['sprɪŋklə'] [sprin-kla'], *s.* El o lo que asperja o derrama; (a) regadera; (b) aspersorio, instrumento con que se rocía; hisopo para esparcir agua bendita.

sprinkling ['sprɪŋklɪŋ] [sprin-klin], *s.* 1. Lo que se esparce; pequeña cantidad, una pizca, un poco. 2. Aspersión, rociadura, esparcimiento de gotas de un líquido. 3. Diversidad de colores. **A sprinkling of rain,** una lluvia fina, una llovizna. **A springkling of knowledge,** una pizca de conocimiento.

sprint [sprɪnt] [sprint], *vn.* Esprintar. *-s.* Corrida, carrera corta y rápida (race).

sprinter ['sprɪntəʳ] [sprin-taʳ], *s.* Velocista.

sprit [sprɪt] [sprit], *s.* (*Mar.*) Botavara, verga de abanico.

sprite ['spraɪt] [sprait], *s.* 1. Espíritu aéreo, duende, trasgo; hada. 2. (*Ant.*) Fantasma, espectro.

spritsail ['sprɪtseɪl] [sprit-seil], *s.* (*Mar.*) Cebadera. **Spritsail braces,** brazos de cebadera. **Spritsail-top-sail,** (*Mar.*) sobrecebadera.

sprocket ['sprɒkɪt] [spro-kit], *s.* 1. Diente de rueda, cabilla para el engranaje de rueda y cadena. 2. Erizo, rueda de cabillas; rueda para engranarse en una cadena; se llama también **sprocket-wheel. Sprocket-gear,** engranaje de rueda y cadena (como en una bicicleta).

sprog ['sprɒg] [sprog], *s.* Bebé.

sprout [spraʊt] [spraut], *va.* 1. Hacer germinar o brotar. 2. Quitar los botones o vástagos. *-vn.* 1. Germinar, brotar el germen; arrojar hojas, flores o renuevos; echar botones. 2. Crecer. 3. Extenderse en ramificaciones. **To sprout new leaves,** echar nuevas hojas.

sprout, *s.* Vástago, renuevo, retoño. **Sprouts,** *s. pl.* Bretones, coles de Bruselas (*Culin.*)

spruce [spru:s] [sprus], *a.* Lindo, pulido, gentil. *-s.* (*Bot.*) Pruche, pinabete, especie de abeto del género Picea. **Essence of spruce,** esencia o jugo de pruche. **Norway spruce,** pinabete, pícea de Noruega. Picea excelsa. **Hemlock spruce,** abeto del Canadá- **Douglas spruce,** V. PINE. **Black spruce,** abeto negro.

spruce, *vn.* Vestirse con esmero. **Spruce up,** arreglar.

sprucely ['spru:slɪ] [sprus-li], *adv.* Lindamente, bellamente, vivamente.

spruceness ['spru:snɪs] [sprus-nes], *s.* Lindeza, hermosura, belleza, gentileza.

sprue ['spru:] [spru], *s.* 1. Bebedero de molde; escoria del orificio de colada. 2. (Local, E.U.) Aftas. *V.* THRUSH.

sprung [sprʌŋ] [sprang], *pret.* y *pp.* del verbo TO SPRING. **A sprung mast,** (*Mar.*) palo rendido.

spry [spraɪ] [sprai], *a.* Vivo, listo, ágil, activo en sus movimientos.

spryness ['spraɪnəs] [sprai-nes], *s.* Agilidad, presteza, calidad de listo.

spud [spʌd] [spad], *s.* 1. Uno de los diversos utensilios parecidos a un azadón o un escopio; escarda; limpiaojos (de cirujano); navaja corta. 2. (*Prov.*) (a) Mano de criatura; (b) patata.

spume [spju:m] [spium], *s.* Espuma o nata que sobrenada en los líquidos en estado de ebullición o fermentación.

spume, *vn.* Espumar, echar o hacer espuma.

spumescent ['spju:məsənt] [spiu-me-sent], *a.* Lo que arroja de sí mucha espuma cuando se pone a hervir.

spun [spʌn] [span], *pret.* y *pp.* del verbo TO SPIN. **Spun glass,** vidrio hilado.

spunge [spʌndʒ] [spandch], *s.* 1. Esponja. 2. (*Art.*) Lanada. *-s. y v. V.* SPONGE. (Forma antigua, pero recomendada recientemente por la Sociedad Filológica).

spungy ['spʌndʒɪ] [spand-chi], *a.* 1. Esponjoso. 2. Húmedo.

spunk [spʌŋk] [spank], *s.* 1. Yesca. 2. (*Fam.*) Corazón, genio (violento) coraje, valor; también, enojo.

spunky ['spʌŋkɪ] [span-ki], *a.* (*Fam.*) Vivo, valeroso, valiente; también, enfadadizo, enojadizo.

spur [spɜːʳ] [speʳ], *s.* 1. Espuela para picar a un jinete a la caballería en que va montado. 2. Espuela, aguijón, estímulo; excitación. 3. Espolón del gallo; uña puntiaguda; pincho; acicate. **Artificial cock-spurs,** navajas de gallo. 4. Estribación, estribo, risco, saliente brusco de una colina o montaña. 5. (*Bot.*) Prolongación en forma de cucurucho detrás de ciertas flores. **On the spur of the moment,** de prisa, bajo el impulso del momento. **Spur-gear,** rueda

dentada. **Spur-gearing,** engranaje de ruedas dentadas. **Spur-wheel,** rueda de engranaje recto. **To win one's spurs,** ganar la dignidad de cabalero; ejecutar una hazaña o acción notable que da fama y renombre. **Spurs of the beams,** (*Mar.*) penadas de los baos. **Spurs of the bitts,** (*Mar.*) curvas de las bitas.

spur, *va.* y *vn.* 1. Espolear, picar con la espuela. 2. Espolear, poner espuelas, avivar, incitar, estimular. 3. Hacer andar o mover a viva fuerza. 4. Calzar o ponerse las espuelas en el pie, en una bota, etc. 5. Andar muy deprisa, apretar el paso. 6. Viajar con toda diligencia. **To spur on,** espolear, aguijar, avivar o estimular mucho; adelantarse o avanzar con osadía e intrepidez.

spurgall ['spɜːgəl] [sper-gal], *va.* Espolear, herir o picar haciendo herida con la espuela.

spurgall, *s.* Espoleadura, la picadura o llaga que hace la espuela.

spurious ['spjʊərɪəs] [spiua-rios], *a.* 1. Espurio, adulterado, contrahecho, degenerado, no genuino. 2. Espurio, bastardo. 3. (*Biol.*) Falso. 4. (*Bot.*) Aparente, pero no real y verdadero.

spuriously ['spjʊərɪəslɪ] [spiua-rios-li], *adv.* Falsamente, de un modo espurio.

spuriousness ['spjʊərɪəsnɪs] [spiua-rios-nes], *s.* 1. Falsedad, falsificación. 2. La calidad o estado de ser espuria, adulterada o contrahecha alguna cosa. 3. Bastardía, la calidad del que es bastardo o hijo espurio.

spurn [spɜːn] [spern], *va.* 1. Desdeñar, despreciar, menospreciar; tratar o mirar con desprecio, rechazar con desdén. 2. Rechazar a puntapiés; cocear o acocear. *-vn.* Oponerse con insolencia o desprecio; desechar con desdén, rechazar desdeñosamente. **To spurn away,** echar fuera a puntapiés.

spurn, *s.* Coz; maltrato, ajamiento.

spurning ['spɜːnɪŋ] [sper-nin], *s.* Desdén, menosprecio; tratamiento insolente y lleno de desprecio.

spurred ['spɜːd] [sperd], *a.* 1. Con espuelas; con espolones. 2. (*Biol.*) Que tiene espuela o espolón; atizonado (como ciertos granos). **Spurred rye,** centeno atizonado. *V.* ERGOT.

spurt [spɜːt] [spert], *va.* y *vn.* Arrojar (liquid) en chorro o a chorros; hacer salir o salir en chorro; brotar, salir impetuosamente. *-s.* 1. Chorro, derrame repentino de un líquido. 2. Explosión de ira.

spurt, *vn.* Hacer un esfuerzo repentino y extremo; esforzarse por breve tiempo con toda energía o rapidez. *-s.* 1. Aumento de energía o rapidez por poco tiempo; esfuerzo extraordinario de poca duración. **Final spurt,** esfuerzo final (race). 2. Período breve.

sputter ['spʌtəʳ] [spa-taʳ], *s.* 1. Chisporroteo, el acto de chisporrotear; acción de farfullar. 2. Saliva que se arroja farfullando; saliva.

sputterer ['spʌtərəʳ] [spa-ta-raʳ], *s.* 1. Escupidor, gargajiento, gargajoso, el que escupe mucho. 2. Faramallero, faramallón.

sputum ['spjuːtəm] [spiu-tom], *s.* Esputo, lo que se arroja en cada expectoración; expectoración característica de tal o cual enfermedad.

spy [spaɪ] [spai], *s.* Espía, persona enviada al campo enemigo para informarse de sus planes; emisario secreto; el que vigila las acciones de otro. **Spy ring,** red de espionaje. **Spy story,** novela de espías.

spy, *vn.* 1. Columbrar, ver desde lejos. 2. Espiar, observar con aplicación intensa. 3. Explorar, reconocer un país; examinar o descubrir por medio de procedimientos ocultos; con *out.* **To spy out,** atisbar, divisar, columbrar. **Spyboat,** barca exploradora. **Spyglass,** anteojo de larga vista, catalejo. **Spy out,** reconocer, hacer un reconocimiento, supervisar.

spy-in-the-sky [ˌspaɪɪnðəˈskaɪ] [spai-in-de-skai], *sm.* Satélite espía.

spy-plein ['spaɪpleɪn] [spai-plein], *s.* Avión espía.

sq. (*Mat.*) *Abreviatura de* **square,** cuadrado.

squab [skwɒb] [skuob], *a.* 1. Acabado de salir de la cáscara; implume. 2. Rechoncho, cachigordo, regordete; se dice del que es gordo y muy pequeño. *-s.* 1. Pichón, pichoncillo. 2. Persona rechoncha, regordeta. 3. Cojín muy relleno; canapé lleno de crin o pluma. *-adv.* Zas, voz con que se expresa el sonido de un golpe repentino o el mismo golpe.

squabbe [skwɒb] [skuob], *vn.* Reñir, andar en pendencias o en contestaciones, armar querellas o disputas, disputar.

squabbe, *s.* Pendencia, riña, querella, disputa, contienda, sarracina o tremolina.

squabbler ['skwɒblə'] [skuo-bla'], *s.* Pendenciero, amigo de armar riñas o pendencias.

squad [skwɒd] [skuod], *s. (Mil.)* Escuadra de soldados o de la policía; pelotón; pequeño grupo de personas. **Squad drill,** ejercicio de pelotón.

squad-car ['skwɒdkɑ:'] [skuod-ka'], *sm.* Coche-patrulla.

squadron ['skwɒdrən] [skuo-dron], *s.* 1. *(Mar.)* Escuadra de naves de guerra; división de una armada. 2. Escuadrón, una de las prociones en que se divide un regimiento de caballería; consta de dos *troops* o pelotones. 3. Cuadro, la formación de un cuerpo de tropas en figura cuadrada; un conjunto o número de soldados en formación.

squalid ['skwɒlɪd] [skuo-lid], *a.* De apariencia mezquina y pobre, desaliñado, sucio (dirty).

squalidness ['skwɒlɪdnɪs] [skuo-lid-nes], *s.* Mezquindad, pobreza, suciedad.

squall [skwɔ:l] [skuol], *va.* y *vn.* chillar, dar chillidos; vocear como un niño encolerizado. *-v. impers.* Estar borrascoso; soplar en ráfagas.

squall, *s.* 1. Chillido, sonido de la voz agudo y desapacible. 2. *(Mar.)* Racha, golpe repentino de viento, pero que dura poco; chubasco. **Southerly squall,** *(Mar.)* racha, solana. **Violent squall,** *(Mar.)* ráfaga, movimiento violento del aire. **Squall of wind and rain,** *(Mar.)* chubasco.

squaller ['skwɔ:lə'] [skuo-la'], *s.* Chillador, chillón, el que chilla mucho.

squalling ['skwɔ:lɪŋ] [skuo-lin], *a.* Berreador, chillón.

squally ['skwɔ:lɪ] [skuo-li], *a.* Chubascoso, borrascoso.

squalor ['skwɔ:lə'] [skuo-la'], *s.* Suciedad, inmundicia, mugre.

squander ['skwɒndə'] [skuon-da'], *va.* 1. Malgastar, gastar pródigamente, disipar, desperdiciar, malbaratar. 2. *(Ant.)* Dispersar.

squanderer ['skwɒdərə'] [skuon-da-ra'], *s.* Malbaratador, gastador, disipador, pródigo.

square [skwɛə'] [skuea'], *a.* 1. Cuadrangular, cuadrado, cuadrángulo. **Twelve inches square,** doce pulgadas en cuadro. 2. Paralelo, exactamente correspondiente; en ángulos rectos, rectangular. 3. Cuadrado, perfecto, exacto, justo, cabal, sin defecto ni imperfección; honrado, equitativo, justo. 4. Ancho, con líneas comparativamente rectas. 5. *(Fam.)* Abundante, que satisface; p. ej. **Square kilometre,** kilómetro cuadrado. **A square meal,** una comida completa. 6. Horizontal, y en ángulos rectos con la quilla; se dice de las vergas. 7. *(Mat.)* Elevado a la segunda potencia. **A square man,** un hombre bien formado o bien proporcionado. **Square dealing,** buena fe, honradez en los tratos. **To be square,** *(Fam.)* estar a mano, o corriente, o pagados. **Square measure,** medida cuadrada o de superficie. **The account is square,** la cuenta está justa. **Square root,** *(Mat.)* raíz cuadrada. **Square-rigged,** *(Mar.)* aparejo de cruzamen. **Square-sail,** *(Mar.)* vela redonda. **Square-yard,** *(Mar.)* verga redonda. **Square-timbers,** *(Mar.)* maderos escuadrados. *-s.* 1. *(Geom.)* Cuadro, cuadrado, figura de cuatro lados iguales y cuatro ángulos rectos. 2. Cuadrado, el producto de un número multiplicado por sí mismo; la segunda potencia. 3. Objeto cuadrado o casi cuadrado; v. gr. cristal de ventana; casilla de tablero de damas. 4. Plaza, lugar ancho y cuadrado cercado de casas. 5. *(Amer.)* Manzana de casas en una población. 6. Escuadra, instrumento compuesto comúnmente de dos reglas que forman un ángulo recto; cartabón. 7. Nivel, la proporción debida, orden; exactitud, proceder honrado, equidad. 8. Cuadro formado por las tropas. **Out of square,** que no está en ángulo recto o escuadra. **To be square with someone,** estar en paz.

square, *va.* 1. Cuadrar, formar en cuadro. 2. Escuadrar, formar en ángulos rectos. 3. *(Mat.)* Cuadrar, reducir a un cuadrado o a su valor; multiplicar un número por sí mismo.

4. Medir, reducir a una misma medida. 5. *(Carp.)* Cuadrar, trabajar los maderos en cuadro. 6. Ajustar, arreglar, acomodar; hacer el balance de una cuenta. 7. Conformar o ajustar; *(Mar.)* bracear en cuadro; colocar las vergas paralelas a la cubierta y en ángulos rectos con la quilla. *-vn.* 1. Cuadrar, estar en ángulos rectos, conformarse o ajustarse una cosa con otra. 2. Convenir, concordarse, estar en exacta conformidad; corresponder a una asedio. 3. Tomar una actiutd pugilística; se usa con *off,* por regla general. **To square the circle,** cuadrar el círculo, construir geométricamente un cuadrado equivalente al área de un círculo dado. **To square the yards,** *(Mar.)* poner las vergas en cruz.

squared ['skwɛəd] [skuead], *a.* Cuadriculado (paper).

square dance ['skwɛə,dɑːns] [skuea-dans], *s.* Contradanza, especie de lanceros.

squarely ['skwɛəlɪ] [skuea-li], *adv.* En cuadro, cuadradamente; convenientemente, justamente, honradamente.

squareness ['skwɛənɪs] [skuea-nes], *s.* Cuadratura, la calidad o condición de cuadrado.

squash [skwɒʃ] [skuosh], *s.* 1. Zumo, jugo. **Orange squash,** zumo de naranja. 2. Aplastamiento; masa u objeto aplastado o magullado. 3. La colisión de los cuerpos blandos entre sí; caída de un cuerpo blando y pesado. 4. Squash (game).

squash, *s.* Cidracayote (calabaza), fruto mollar y comestible de varias hierbas anuales rastreras y americanas, de las cucurbitáceas; también la planta misma. **Summer squash,** cidracayote de verano; se come verde cocida y sin quitarle las semillas. **Squash-vine,** cucúrbita, cidracayote, planta. **Squash-beetle,** coleóptero crisomélido, con rayas amarillas y negras, que se alimenta del cidracayote, del meló, y plantas semejantes.

squash, *va.* Aplastar, deshacer, la figura que tenía alguna cosa haciéndola una pasta; magullar. **Squash in,** apiñar, apretar. **Can you squash my shoes in?,** ¿puedes calzarte mis zapatos? **Squash up,** hacer sitio, apretarse, hacerse a un lado.

squat ['skwɒt] [skuot], *vn.* 1. Agacharse, agazaparse, acurrucarse, ponerse en cuclillas. 2. Establecerse en u ocupar un terreno público o ajeno sin justo título.

squat, *a.* 1. Agachado, puesto en cuclillas. 2. Rechoncho, grueso y corto (fatty). *-s.* Porrazo, caída repentina.

squatter ['skwɒtə'] [skuo-ta'], *s.* Advenedizo, entremetido, injusto ocupante, colono usurpador. *(Mex. Fam.)* paracaidista.

squaw [skwɔː] [skuo], *s.* Mujer o muchacha india (de la América del Norte).

squawk ['skwɔːk] [skuok], *vn.* 1. Graznar. 2. *(Fig.)* Delatar, denunciar.

squeak [skwiːk] [skuik], *vn.* 1. Chillar, dar un chillido; producir un sonido agudo y discordante (wheel). 2. Romper el silencio por miedo de algún daño.

squeak, *s.* Grito, quejido lastimoso. **To have a narrow squeak,** escaparse por los pelos **He couldn't get a squeak out of her,** no pudo sacarle ni palabra.

squeaky ['skwiːkɪ] [skui-ki], *a.* Chirriador, chillón, que cruje.

squeal ['skwiːl] [skuil], *vn.* 1. Gritar, dar alaridos; lanzar gritos agudos de mayor duración que los del **squeak.** 2. *(Ger.)* Hacer delaciones. *-s.* Grito penetrante como el de un cerdo.

squeamish ['skwiːmɪʃ] [skui-mish], *a.* 1. Fastidioso, enfadoso (annoying); nimio, demasiado delicado o escrupuloso. 2. Fastidiado, disgustado; con náuseas. **Squeamish stomach,** estómago delicado. **I'm not squeamish,** me da igual, me trae sin cuidado.

squeamishly ['skwiːmɪʃlɪ] [skui-mish-li], *adv.* Fastidiosamente, enfadosamente; con náuseas.

squeamishness ['skwiːmɪʃnɪs] [skui-mish-nes], *s.* Fastidio, disgusto, delicadeza excesiva.

squeegee ['skwiːdʒiː] [skui-yi], *va.* Alisar, allanar una estampa fotográfica con un cilindro alisador. *-s.* Alisador de goma que se usa en la fotografía.

squeeze [skwiːz] [skuis], *va.* 1. Apretar, comprimir; estrechar, estrujar, exprimir el jugo. 2. Exprimir, estrujar (press); tupir. 3. Poner en cierta posición o lugar por medio de fuerza o presión; apretar fuertemente. 4. Arrancar el tributo, las contribuciones, etc.; acosar, agobiar (pursue); disminuir los jornales hasta el más bajo tipo. 5. Hacer un molde o impresión en papel húmedo por medio de la presión.

squeeze in, hacer entrar apretando.

squeeze out, hacer salir, exprimir. **To squeeze money out of someone,** sacar dinero a alguien.

squeeze past, deslizarse, pasar.

squeeze through, pasar o hacer pasar al través. **To squeeze to death,** *(Fam.)* matar a apachurrones. *-vn.* Escaparse o salirse alguna cosa que estaba oprimida.

squeeze up, hacer sitio, correrse a un lado.

squeeze, *s.* 1. Apretadura, presión compresión, apretón. 2. Facsímile de una moneda o inscripción, que se obtiene oprimiendo sobre ella una substancia blanda.

squeezer ['skwiːzəʳ] [skui-saʳ], *s.* Exprimidor (de frutas, etc.)

squelch [skwelʧ] [skelch], *s.* Caída fuerte, porrazo.

squelch, *va.* 1. Hacer callar a uno, dar un tapaboca, humillándole; desconcertar. 2. Poner fin; derrotar, vencer, sojuzgar; se usa a menudo con *out.* *-vn.* Ser vencido, desconcertado.

squib [skwib] [skuib], *s.* 1. Cohete, cañuto de papel lleno de pólvora u otra materia combustible; buscapié. 2. Sátira, chiste, chanza.

squib, *va.* y *vn.* Usar de sátiras o pullas; atacar con ellas.

squid [skwid] [skuid], *s.* 1. Calamar, molusco con diez tentáculos. 2. Cebo artificial, que tiene a menudo la forma de un pez.

squint [skwint] [skuint], *a.* 1. Ojizaino, que mira atravesado y con malos ojos. 2. Bizo, bisojo; persona que por vicio o defecto de los ojos tuerce la vista.

squint, *s.* 1. Estrabismo, enfermedad o vicio de los ojos bizcos. 2. Mirada bizca; mirada furtiva; también, vista parcial. 3. Tendencia indirecta. **To have a squint,** bizquear, mirar bisojo. **To give a squint at,** mirar de soslayo.

squint, *va.* y *vn.* 1. Bizquear, mirar bizco o atravesado. 2. Ladear o torcer la vista o los ojos.

squint-eyed ['skwintˈaid] [skuint-aid], *a.* 1. Ojizaino. bizco, bisojo. 2. Atravesado, torcido y de mala intención; ambiguo, oscuro.

squinting ['skwintiŋ] [skuin-tin], *s. (Med.)* Estrabismo, estrambosidad, la enfermedad o vicio de los bizcos o bisojos.

squintingly ['skwintiŋli] [skuin-tin-li], *adv.* Con un modo de mirar atravesado, como un bizco.

squire ['skwaiəʳ] [skuaiaʳ], *s.* 1. Escudero, el paje o sirviente que llevaba el escudo al caballero en la antigua caballería. 2. Escudero, título de hidalguía en Inglaterra; propietario de antigua heredad; *(local, E. U.)* alcalde, juez de paz. **Squire Brown,** señor Brown. *V.* ESQUIRE.

squire, *va.* Acompañar a una persona por cortesía y como caballero.

squirm [skwɜːm] [skuerm], *vn.* 1. Torcerse, encorvar el cuerpo como a consecuencia de un dolor o sufrimiento. 2. Mostrar señales de dolor o pena. 3. (Con out) Escaparse con trabajo, con poca destreza. *-s.* Torcimiento; movimiento causado por el dolor.

squirrel ['skwirəl] [skui-ral], *s.* Ardilla. *-vt.* **Squirrel away,** almacenar.

squirt [skwɜːt] [skuert], *va.* y *vn.* Arrojar algún líquido con fuerza y violencia; hacer salir o salir a chorros; jeringas. **Squirting cucumber,** cohombro de asno. *V.* ELATERIUM.

squirt, *s.* 1. Chorro, golpe de alguna cosa líquida que sale con fuerza. 2. Jeringazo, el acto de jeringar. 3. Jeringa, instrumento con el cual se arroja con violencia alguna cosa líquida.

squirter ['skwɜːtəʳ] [skuer-taʳ], *s.* El que jeringa o arroja un líquido con una jeringa.

squishy ['skwiʃi] [skui-shi], *a.* Blando.

St., *s.* Abreviatura de **Saint,** San o Santo.

stab [stæb] [stab], *va.* y *vn.* 1. Herir o matar a puñaladas, dar de puñaladas; atravesar con un arma puntiaguda. 2. Atravesar el corazón, dar una puñalada.

stab, *s.* 1. Puñalada, la herida que se da con el puñal; estocada. 2. Golpe mortal; herida (wound). 3. Pinchazo, dolor agudo (pain). **To have a stab at something,** intentar, probar algo.

stabber ['stæbəʳ] [sta-baʳ], *s.* Asesino, el que mata alevosamente.

stabbing ['stæbiŋ] [sta-bin], *sf.* Puñalada.

stability [stəˈbiliti] [sta-bi-li-ti], *s.* 1. Estabilidad, calidad de estable; permanencia, duración, solidez, consistencia (consistence). 2. Constancia, firmeza, fijeza en las resoluciones.

stabilization [ˌsteibələˈzeiʃən] [stei-ba-lai-sei-shon], *s.* Estabilización.

stabilize ['steibilaiz] [stei-bi-lais], *va.* Estabilizar, fijar.

stabilizer ['steibəlaizəʳ] [stei-bi-lai-saʳ], *s.* Estabilizante (cooking).

stable ['steibl] [stei-bol], *a.* Estable, establecido firmemente; durable, permanente (permanent); firme, fijo, constante, decidido, de principios o conducta fijos y sin cambio (fix); sólido. *-s.* 1. Establo, caballeriza; cuadra para albergar las caballerías o el ganado vacuno. 2. Conjunto de caballos de carrera.

stable, *va.* Meter los caballos en la cuadra o el ganado en el establo. *-vn.* Vivir en establo como las bestias. **To close the door after the horse has gone,** a buenas horas mangas verdes.

stable-boy ['steiblboi] [stei-bol-boi], **stable-man** ['steiblmən] [stei-bol-man], *s.* Establero, mozo de caballos.

stableness ['steiblnis] [stei-bol-nes], *s.* Estabilidad. *V.* STABILITY.

stabling ['steibliŋ] [stei-blin], *s.* 1. Acción de meter los caballos en la cuadra o el ganado en el establo. 2. Lugar en una cuadra o establo.

staccato [stəˈkɑːtəʊ] [sta-ka-tou], *a. (Mús.)* Staccato, voz italiana que significa destacado.

stack [stæk] [stak], *s.* 1. Niara, rima o rimero (de haces de grano o heno). 2. Pila o hacina de leña o de heno, cónica por lo común, montón; pabellón de fusiles. 3. Ringlera o fila de fogones o cañones de chimenea. 4. *(Fam.)* Copia, abundancia.

stack, *va.* Hacinar, el heno o leña; apilar, amontonar; poner las armas en pabellones.

stacker ['stækəʳ] [sta-kaʳ], *s.* Apiladora.

stadium ['steidiəm] [stei-diom], *s.* 1. Estadio, lugar público en la Grecia antigua para las carreras a pie. 2. Estado, medida griega de longitud de 185 metros o 600 pies ingleses. 3. Grado de progreso o adelantamiento.

staff [stɑːf] [staf], *s.* *(pl.* STAVES o STAFFS). 1. Báculo, palo, cayado (stick). 2. Apoyo, sostén, alivio, arrimo (help). 3. Palo o bastón que se usa como arma ofensiva y defensiva; garrote. 4. Vara, insignia de jurisdicción y empleo. 5. Vara de agrimensor; jalón de mira; alidade. 6. *(Mil.)* Estado mayor de un ejército; plana mayor de un regimiento. 7. Conjunto de personas asociadas para llevar a cabo alguna empresa particular; p. ej. **The editorial staff,** el conjunto de redactores, la redacción. 8. *(Mús.)* Pentagrama, las cinco paralelas que se usan para notar las notas de la música. 8. Asta (de lanza, pica, bandera, etc.). 10. Sonda acanalada que sirve de guía al litótomo. **Ensign-staff,** *(Mar.)* asta de bandera de popa. **Jack-staff,** *(Mar.)* asta de bandera de proa. **Flag-staff,** asta de bandera. **Staff-officer,** oficial de estado mayor. **Medical staff,** cuerpo de sanidad militar. **Staff nurse,** enfermera cualificada. **Staff training,** formación del personal.

staff, *s.* Compuesto plástico, que consta principalmente de yeso, mezclado con un poco de cemento, glicerina y dextrina en agua; se usa para edificar provisionalmente o para adorno de edificios.

staffwood ['stɑːfwʊd] [staf-vud], *s.* Duelas, botada, la madera para toneles.

stag [stæg] [stag], *s.* 1. Ciervo, mamífero rumiante, particularmente cuando tiene cinco o más años de edad y puntas terminales en las astas. 2. El macho de otros venados o a animales cervales. 3. *(Fam.)* Varón, en contraposición a la mujer. **To go stag to a party,** ir solo a una fiesta.

stag-beetle ['stægˌbiːtl] [stag-bi-tel], *s.* Ciervo volante, escarabajo cornudo de los lucánidos.

stage [steɪdʒ] [steidch], *s.* 1. Tablado, andamio que se levanta para algún espectáculo o fiesta. 2. Escenario, tablas, escena, parte del teatro o de la sala concierto, en que se verifica la representación; teatro. 3. De aquí, la profesión de actor. 4. Teatro, escena de acción *(Teat.).* 5. Parada, descansadero; etapa, jornada, distancia recorrida sin detención (journey); distancia que separa dos puntos en que descansan los viajeros. 6. Grado, estado; progreso, período de una enfermedad. 7. Disco, portaobjetos (microscope). 8. *(E. U.)* Diligencia. V. **Stage-coach.** 9. *(Arq.)* Escalón, paso de escalera. **Hanging-stage,** plancha de viento; andamio para los pintores. **To bring upon the stage,** poner en escena. **To come o to go upon the stage,** entrar en escena. **To go off, to quit the stage,** abandonar la escena; retirarse del teatro. **By short stages,** a pequeñas etapas, a cortas jornadas. **Stage of growth,** grado de crecimiento. **Stage-micrometer,** micrómetro del portaobjetos. **Mechanical stage,** disco de microscopio que puede moverse en dos direcciones en ángulos rectos. **Stage-coach,** diligencia o coche de diligencia, coche público para los viajeros. **Stage-driver,** mayoral, cochero de diligencia. **Stage-horse,** caballo de parada; caballo de diligencia.

stage, *va.* Representar, exhibir en público; arreglar para el escenario. *-vn.* Viajar en diligencia.

stagecraft ['steɪdʒkrɑːft] [steidch-kraft], *s.* Habilidad para las producciones teatrales.

stagefright ['steɪdʒfraɪt] [steidch-frait], *s.* Terror que inspira el público.

stage lights ['steɪdʒlaɪts] [steidch-laits], *s. pl.* Candilejas, luces en el proscenio de un teatro.

stagey ['steɪdʒɪ] [steid-chi], *a.* Dramático, teatral.

staggard ['stægəd] [sta-gard], *s.* Ciervo de cuatro años.

stagger ['stægəʳ] [sta-gaʳ], *vn.* 1. Hacer eses, dar vueltas o giros como un borracho (roll, sway); bambolear. 2. Desmayarse, perder el sentido (faint). 3. Vacilar, titubear, dudar, estar incierto, no estar resuelto (doubt). *-va.* 1. Causar vértigos o vahídos. 2. Asustar, dar o causar susto. 3. Hacer vacilar, dudar o titubear. 4. Hacer bambolear, temblar o tambalear. **You stagge me!,** ¡me asombras!

staggers ['stægəz] [sta-gars], *s.* 1. Vértigo, especie de apoplejía que padecen los caballos, y el ganado lanar. 2. Vértigo, vahído.

staghound ['stæghaʊnd] [stag-jaund], *s.* Sabueso o perro para cazar ciervos.

staging ['steɪdʒɪŋ] [steid-chin], *s.* Andamiaje, plataforma provisional.

stagnant ['stægnənt] [stag-nant], *a.* Estancado, detenido, encharcado, estantí; que cesa de circular.

stagnate ['stægneɪt] [stag-neit], *vn.* 1. Estancarse, detenerse; estar estancado, llegar a ponerse cenagoso, encharcándose. 2. Estar embotado, embotarse; volverse inactivo o inerte.

stagnation [stæg'neɪʃən] [stag-nei-shon], *s.* Estagnación, estancación, estancamiento, sea en sentido literal o figurado; paralización de los negocios.

staid [steɪd] [steid], *a.* Grave, serio, sosegado.

staid, *pret.* y *pp.* de TO STAY.

staidness ['steɪdnɪs] [steid-nes], *s.* Gravedad, sosiego, carácter serio.

stain [steɪn] [stein], *va.* 1. Manchar, ensuciar (dirt); chafarrinar. 2. Manchar, ajar, desdorar, empañar la fama, la reputación, etc. 3. Colorar, teñir, como el cidrio o la madera; pintar cristales (paint). 4. Teñir, impregnar de color un tejido para hacer más visible su estructura microscópica. *-vn.* Recibir o comunicar un tinte o color, teñirse. **A bacillus which stains readily with anilin colors,** un bacilo que se tiñe fácilmente con los colores de anilina. **Stained glass,** vidrio de color.

stain, *s.* 1. Mancha, mácula, borrón. 2. Tinte, color con que se tiñe. 3. Deslustre, deshonra, desdoro. **Without a stain on his character,** sin una mancha en su reputación.

stainer ['steɪnəʳ] [stei-naʳ], *s.* El que mancha o ensucia; el que tiñe; el que desdora o deslustra. **Glass-stainer,** colorador de vidrios, fabricante de vidrios de color.

stainless ['steɪnlɪs] [stein-les], *a.* Limpio, libre de manchas, inmaculado. **Stainless steel,** acero inoxidable.

stair [steəʳ] [steaʳ], *s.* 1. Escalón, peldaño. 2. *pl.* Escalera, una serie de escalones. **One pair of stairs,** el primer alto o el primer piso. **Spiral o corkscrew stairs,** escalera de caracol. **Flight of stairs,** tramo de escalera, **Stair-carpet,** alfombra de escalera. **Stair-rod,** varilla para sujetar la alfombra de escalera, en el piso superior. **Downstairs,** abajo, en el piso inferior. **To go o come upstairs,** subir la escalera. **To go o come downstairs,** bajar la escalera.

staircase ['steəkeɪs] [stea-keis], *s.* Escalera: caja de escalera.

stairway ['steəweɪ] [stea-uei], *s.* Escalera. V. STAIRCASE.

stake [steɪk] [steik], *s.* 1. Estaca, poste (post); jalón, estaquilla; rodrigón, palo que se pone para apoyar las vides y árboles tiernos. 2. Pira, poste al que se ata a una persona para quemarla viva. 3. Tas, yunque pequeño. **Stake-boat,** bote anclado para marcar la dirección y distancias en las regatas. **The issue at stake,** el punto en cuestión. **To be at stake,** estar en peligro, estar en contienda.

stake, *s.* 1. Apuesta; posta en los juegos de envite; tosta o polla. 2. Riesgo, peligro, contingencia. 3. Premio (de contienda). 4. Interés en una empresa; ganancia o pérdida contingente.

stake, *va.* 1. Estacar (fix); fijar o poner palos, estacas, etc., para que sostengan o apoyen algo. 2. Poner, apostar (bet). 3. Poner en el juego. 4. Arriesgar, exponer (risk). **To stake all,** envidar el resto, echar el resto, aventurarlo todo.

stalactite ['stæləktaɪt] [sta-lak-tait], *s.* Estalactita, una especie de concreción pétrea que se forma en las bóvedas de las cavernas.

stalagmite ['stæləgmaɪt] [sta-lag-mait], *s.* Estalagmita, concreción pétrea en el piso de una caverna; parte opuesta a la estalactita, y que a menudo se une con ésta.

stale [steɪl] [steil], *a.* Añejo, viejo, rancio, añejado (old); alterado, deteriorado. **To grow stale,** añejarse, enranciarse. *-s.* 1. Cerveza que ha empezado a volverse agria. 2. Mate en el juego de ajedrez; tablas. 3. Orines.

stale, *va.* Añejar, hacer viejo. *-vn.* Mear, orinar (animals).

stalely ['steɪlɪ] [stei-li], *adv.* De mucho tiempo.

stalemate ['steɪlmeɪt] [steil-meit], *s.* Tablas, empate, en el juego de ajedrez. *-va.* Hacer tablas en el juego de ajedrez.

staleness ['steɪlnɪs] [steil-nes], *s.* Vejez, antigüedad; rancidez.

stalk [stɔːk] [stok], *va.* 1. Cazar a la espera; acercarse a hurtadillas para matar (game). 2. Pasar, sobre algo con porte majestuoso. *-vn.* 1. Andar con paso majestuoso afectando señorío. 2. Andar a hurtadillas, avanzar a paso de lobo.

stalk, *s.* 1. Paso levantado y orgulloso. 2. Tallo, pie, tronco; eje de las plantas, particularmente las herbáceas. 3. Pedúnculo, rabo de flor, de fruta; pecíolo, rabo de hoja; troncho de ciertas hortalizas, raspa de las uvas. **Partial flower-stalk,** pedunculillo o pedúnculo parcial. 4. *(Zool.)* Tallo, parte que sostiene. 5. Cualquier pie o sostén, como el de una copa.

stalking-horse ['stɔːkɪŋˌhɔːs] [sto-kin-jors], *s.* 1. El caballo verdadero o figurado que sirve a los cazadores para ocultarse y cazar. 2. Máscara, disfraz.

stalky ['stɔːkɪ] [sto-ki], *a.* Duro como el tallo.

stall [stɔːl] [stol], *s.* 1. Pesebre, compartimiento de una cuadra o establo donde se encierra y se da de comer a un caballo o una vaca. 2. Puesto, tienda portátil, puestecillo de cosas para vender; tabla de carnicería. 3. Silla o asiento de un prebendado en el coro. 4. Asiento de luneta o butaca de teatro. 5. Compartimiento de explotación en una mina de carbón. **Butcher's stall,** tabla de carnicero. **Cobbler's stall,** zapatería de viejo.

stall, *va.* 1. Encerrar, meter o tener encerrada o atada al pesebre una res en el establo, especialmente para cebarla. 2. Instalar, investir, poner en posesión de una cosa (install). 3.

Atascar, atollar, meter en el barro; parar o detener con obstáculos (hamper, hold up). -*vn.* Estar atascado, atollado; hundirse en el cieno, en la nieve, etc. **The train was stalled in a snow-storm,** el tren quedó detenido por una nevada. **To stall someone off,** tener a alguien a raya. **Stop stalling!,** ¡déjese de evasivas! **The talks are stalled,** las conversaciones están en un callejón sin salida.

stall-fed ['stɔːlfed] [stol-fed], *a.* Cebado a estaca, mantenido en establo.

stallion ['stælɪən] [sta-lion], *s.* Caballo padre, garañón, el destinado para la cría.

stalwart ['stɔːlwət] [stol-uot], *a.* (*Ant.*) 1. Fuerte, duro, firme, bravo. 2. Digno de guardarse o mantenerse. 3. (*E.U.*) Constante; fiel a su partido político.

stamen ['steɪmen] [stei-men], *s.* (*pl.* STAMENS, rara vez STAMINA). Estambre, órgano masculino de la flor, que contiene el polen.

stamina ['stæmɪnə] [sta-mi-na], *s.* 1. Fuerza vital, vigor. 2. Sostén, la parte firme de un cuerpo, la que sirve de apoyo.

staminal ['stæmɪnl] [sta-mi-nal], *a.* 1. Estaminal, concerniente a los estambres. 2. Relativo a la fuerza vital, esencial.

staminate ['stæmɪneɪt] [sta-mi-neit], *a.* 1. Estaminífero, provisto de estambres, pero sin pistilos. 2. Estamíneo, que tiene estambres.

stammer ['stæməʳ] [sta-maʳ], *va.* y *vn.* Tartamudear; balbucear o balbucir. -*s.* Tartamudeo; balbucencia o balbuceo.

stammerer ['stæmərər] [sta-ma-raʳ], *s.* Tartamudo.

stammering ['stæmərɪŋ] [sta-me-rin], *a.* Tartamudo. -*s.* Tartamudeo.

stamp [stæmp] [stamp], *vn.* Patear, patalear, dar patadas o golpes con los pies en el suelo. -*va.* 1. Estampar, señalar o imprimir una cosa en otra. 2. Sellar; timbrar (letters); fijar el sello de correo; estampillar, marcar con una estampilla. 3. Acuñar. 4. Machacar, moler, majar (crush, mash). 5. Patear, golpear con los pies. 6. Atribuir, una cualidad distintiva; marcar, infamar, estigmatizar. 7. Marcar, imprimir, fijar en la mente (print, impress). **To stamp on one's memory,** grabar en la memoria, memorizar. **To stamp down,** apisonar, comprimir con los pies. **Stamp out,** apagar (extinguish), extirpar, desarraigar.

stamp, *s.* 1. Impresión, marca o señal que deja una cosa que se estampa en otra y la misma cosa que hace la señal. 2. Imagen grabada en madera o metal. 3. Cuño, troquel para sellar la moneda; cuño, sello, la señal o marca que queda impresa en la moneda. 4. Estampador, mano de mortero; instrumento o útil para estampar. 5. Sello o marca, la señal que se pone en las cosas que pagan derechos; timbre, sello legal; sello de correos, estampilla. 6. (*Min.*) Bocarte, máquina para quebrantar y machacar el mineral antes de fundirlo. **Stamps,** papel sellado. **Stamp-duties,** derechos de papel sellado o de sello. 7. Temple, calidad de la índole, humor o genio; suerte, clase; laya, calaña. **Stamp act,** ley del timbre. **Stamp album,** álbum para sellos. **Stamp collecting,** filatelia. **Stamp-office,** oficina del timbre. **Postage stamp,** sello de correos o de franqueo. **Trading stamp,** cupón, bono, vale. **To bear the stamp of,** llevar el timbre, la estampilla de; llevar la señal, marca o sello de algo. **Men of the same stamp,** hombres de la misma calaña.

stampede ['stæmpiːd] [stam-pid], *va.* y *vn.* 1. Ahuyentar, con estampido; hacer huir con terror pánico. 2. Obrar por común impulso, tomar de repente un acuerdo, v. gr. en una reunión política. -*s.* 1. Estampida, huida con pánico. 2. Movimiento repentino e impulsivo de un gran número de personas o animales.

stamper ['stæmpəʳ] [stam-paʳ], *s.* 1. Estampador; impresor. 2. Herramienta o máquina para estampar o machacar; pilón, punzón de forja, bocarte; triturador que se emplea en la fabricación de la pólvora.

stamping ['stæmpɪŋ] [stam-pin], *s.* 1. Timbrado, timbre, acción de estampar, de estampillar, de timbrar, pataleo, pateo. 2. Machaqueo, trituración. **Stamping-machine,**

estampador mecánico; máquina de perforar. **Stamping-mill,** bocarte, molino triturador de minerales.

stanch [stɑːntʃ] [stanch], *va.* 1. Restañar la sangre. 2. Estancar o detener el curso de alguna cosa líquida. -*vn.* Estancarse, detenerse.

stanch, *a.* 1. Firme, seguro, celoso, verdadero, constante, fiel, adicto. 2. Sano, bien acondicionado, en buen estado; que no está roto. **A stanch friend,** una amigo fiel, adicto. **A stanch ship,** un buque fuerte, sólido. **A stanch hound,** un sabueso seguro, que no pierde la pista.

stanchion ['stɑːnʃən] [stan-shon], *s.* Puntal, el madero que se pone hincado en la tierra firme para sostener las paredes o otras cosas. **Stanchions of a ship,** (*Mar.*) puntales. **Quarter stanchions,** (*Mar.*) candeleros o grampones. **Awning-stanchions,** (*Mar.*) candeleros del toldo.

stanchless ['stɑːntʃlɪs] [stanch-les], *a.* Lo que no se puede restañar o detener.

stanchness ['stɑːntʃnɪs] [stanch-nes], *s.* Firmeza, resolución, determinación, celo.

stand [stænd] [stand], *vn.* (*pret.* y *pp.* STOOD). 1. Estar en pie o derecho, estar de pie o levantado, estar en posición vertical; mantenerse derecho (straight). 2. Sostenerse, tenerse tieso o firme, resistir (resist). 3. Permanecer, quedarse o subsistir en algún paraje. 4. Pararse, detenerse, hacer alto, hacer mansión en algún sitio (stop, house). 5. Cesar, pararse, quedar suspenso, parado o sin movimiento, suspenderse. 6. Mantenerse firme, resistir; durar. 7. Subsistir en un estado fijo. 8. Tenerse, ponerse, estar en cierta postura. 9. Enderezarse o ponerse de punta. 10. Poseer rectitud moral. 11. Estar situado, estar colocado, hallarse. 12. Tener un puesto determinado con respecto a la clase o al orden. 13. Persistir, perseverar. 14. Ser consistente, acordar, convenir; Quedar de acuerdo, quedar corrientes. 15. Estar, hallarse, tener, ser. 16. Estar mal satisfecho, poner tachas u objeciones; ser exigente o difícil. **One must not stand upon trifles,** no hay que pararse en fruslerías. 17. Valer, tener fuerza o valor. 18. Consistir, estribar una cosa en otra; depender lógicamente; se usa con *on, upon, o by.* 19. Presentarse como candidato u opositor. 20. Erizarse el pelo. 21. Tomar una dirección, hacer correr, dirigirse. **To stand on the same tack,** correr la misma bordada, correr bajo de las mismas amuras. -*va.* 1. Poner derecho, colocar, tener derecho. 2. Aguantar, sufrir, tolerar, llevar con paciencia. 3. Someterse, soportar. 4. Importar, ser útil, ser de provecho. 5. (*Fam.*) Pagar el coste de algo. **To stand treat,** pagar una comida, una convidada. 6. Sostener, defender, resistir.

stand about, rodear, cercar.

stand against, oponerse, resistir; mantenerse firme contra alguno.

stand alone, estar, mantenerse solo; ser el único de su especie.

stand aloof, (from), mantenerse separado de algo, lejos; no participar en algo.

stand aside, apartarse, mantenerse alejado.

stand back, retroceder, mantenerse detrás.

stand by, sostener, favorecer, ayudar, auxiliar; atenerse a una cosa, contar con; hallarse presente sin tomar parte en lo que se hace; estar cerca, quedarse allí; sostenerse o apoyarse. (*Mar.*) Velar, estar listo, mantenerse listo. **To stand by an award,** sujetarse al juicio de árbitros. **To stand by itself,** estar solo o apartado. **To stand by the halliards,** (*Mar.*) velar la driza. **I stood by at the operation,** yo asistí a la operación; me hallaba presente. **Stand by me,** esté usted a mi lado; ayúdeme usted.

stand far off, mantenerse o estar lejos.

stand for, estar por, estar en lugar de, representar; significar, querer decir; solicitar, pretender, presentarse como candidato u opositor; sostener, defender, ser del partido, opinión, etc., de otro, mantener o sostener una opinión; dirigirse a o hacia, llevar rumbo hacia. **A mark which stood for the highest grade,** una señal que indicaba el grado más alto. **Who stood for the child?,** ¿quiénes sacaron de pila al niño? **To stand fire,** aguantar el fuego (enemy).

stand forth, adelantarse, ponerse omantenerse delante; avanzar; presentarse.

stand from under, alejarse de alguna cosa que está por caer. *(Imper.)* ¡Agua va!

stand in , costar, montar, importar tanto; hablando de cantidades. **To stand in awe of,** sentir temor de alguien o algo. **To stand in hand,** importar, ser ventajoso o importante. **To stand in good stead,** servir, ser útil. **To stand inshore,** *(Mar.)* correr hacia la tierra. **To stand in the way,** cerrar el paso, hallarse en el camino, impedir, ser un obstáculo.

stand off, mantenerse a cierta distancia, estar separado; negar, no conceder lo que se desea; no convenir en una cosa; no ser amigos, tener las voluntades desunidas; evitar el encontrarse o el verse, hacerse o volverse atrás; salir hacia fuera. **Stand off,** hágase usted allá, sepárase usted, no se acerque o no se arrime usted **To stand off and on,** *(Mar.)* bordear, barloventear, vuelta al mar, vuelta a la tierra.

stand on end o to stand upon an end, erizarse, mantenerse derecho, quedar vertical. **To stand on tiptoe,** ponerse de puntillas.

stand out, mantenerse firme sostenerse con resolución y firmeza, resistir, hacer frente, oponerse abiertamente; separarse, apartarse; no convenir, negar o no conceder una cosa; salir mucho una cosa de la superficie, resaltar, destacarse, estar en relieve, formar eminencias o protuberancias. **To stand out to sea,** llevar la proa al mar. **Stand out of the way!,** ¡quítese usted de en medio! ¡fuera! **It stands to reason,** es conforme a razón, es razonable.

stand together, mantenerse juntos, concertarse y adherirse. **To stand to it,** mantenerse firme en una contienda.

stand towards, acercarse.

stand under, sufrir, sostener; estar bajo, estar colocado debajo de.

stand up, levantarse, alzarse, ponerse en pie; hacer o formar un partido o reunión para defender algo. **To stand up for,** (a) defender, mantener, sostener, apoyar. (b) Personarse por, sacar la cara por.

stand upon, estar colocado sobre, estar en; adherirse a; interesar, concernir, tocar, pertenecer; estimar, valuar, hacer mucho caso de una cosa; picarse de, tener su orgullo en; insistir. **Do not stand upon ceremony,** sin cumplimientos.

stand with, acordarse, convenirse; estar conforme con; disputar, andar en contestaciones. **To stand still,** estarse quieto; estancarse el agua. **Stand still!** ¡Esté usted quieto! ¡no se mueva usted! **To stand sentry,** estar de centinela. **As the case stands,** en el estado en que se hallan las cosas.

stand, *s.* 1. El puesto o sitio donde está uno esperando. 2. Posición, situación, estación, el punto o paraje señalado para que alguno se ponga en él; lugar en que uno se dedica ordinariamente a sus asuntos o negocios. 3. Construcción sobre la cual pueden ponerse personas o cosas; plataforma, tribuna; mostrador (de comerciante); puesto en un mercado, velador para poner la luz, consola; salvilla para servir la bebida; estante, vasar; mesita; atril (de música); estante, pie, sostén, soporte. 4. Parada, pausa o alto, la acción de pararse o detenerse. 5. Parada, el término de la acción de una cosa; estado de lo inactivo. 6. Oposición, resistencia. 7. El estado fijo de una cosa que ni puede adelantar ni retroceder. 8. Armamento, equipo completo de armas y munición para un solo soldado. 9. Vegetación sobre el campo, v. g. de las hierbas. **Cruet-stand,** taller, angarillas, pie de las ampolletas de aceite y vinagre que se usan en las mesas. **To keep a stand,** qudarse siempre en el mismo estado. **Flower-stand,** estante para flores, jardinera. **Music-stand,** pupitre para papeles de música, estrado para orquesta.

standard ['stændəd] [stan-dard], *s.* 1. Marco o patrón para servir de norma; ley, medida de extensión, de cantidad, de valor o de precio que se establece por la ley o de común asenso. 2. Patrón, modelo, dechado, norma, regla fija. 3. Ley; grados de fino del oro o la plata.

standard, *s.* 1. Árbol o palo que se queda en pie derecho. 2. *(Mar.)* Curva capuchina. 3. Mueble fijo o pesado. 4. Estandarte, insignia de la milicia; estandarse, pétalo superior (o posterior) de la corola papilionácea, -*a.* Regulador; que sirve de tipo de modelo o de marco, de ley; clásica (una obra). **Standard authors,** autores clásicos. **Standard gauge,** (a) medida o marco que sirve de norma. (b) Entrevía común de ferrocarril, la de 56 pulgadas. **Standard work,** obra maestra o clásica.

standardization [ˌstændədaɪˈzeɪʃən] [stan-da-dai-sei-shon], *s.* Estandarización.

standby ['stændbaɪ] [stand-bai], *s.* Adherente fiel; persona o cosa digna de confianza.

stander ['stændəʳ] [stan-daʳ], *s.* El que está en pie.

standing ['stændɪŋ] [stan-din], *a.* 1. Derecho o en pie, levantado, de pie; erecto, con pedestal, con pie (erect). 2. Permanente, fijado, establecido (fixed); fijo o establecido permanentemente. 3. Duradero, estable, constante. 4. Estancado, encharcado, sin vertiente o sin salida. 4. Estancado, encharcado, sin vertiente o sin salida. 5. Fijo, que no puede moverse con facilidad. **Standing army,** ejército permanente. **Standing-place, standing-room,** sitio en que se está de pie, o en que se puede estar de pie. **Standing-room only,** espacio sólo para estar en pie (donde las asientos están todos tomados). **Standing water,** agua muerta, remansada, encharcada o estancada, el agua que no corre. **Standing trees,** los árboles que quedan en pie en los montes después de una corta. 6. *(Mar.)* Muerto, arraigado. **Standing rigging,** *(Mar.)* jarcia, muerta, aparejo fijo.

standing, *s.* 1. Posición, carácter o calidad de las personas o familias en la estimación de otras; posición relativa. 2. Posición, puesto, sitio o paraje destinado para colocarse, sitio o paraje que tiene bastante firmeza y solidez para poder mantenerse de pie en él. 3. La duración de alguna cosa; fecha. 4. Antigüedad, la calidad de ser antiguo. 5. Parada; acción de quedarse en pie. **Of four years' standing,** que tiene cuatro años de fecha; establecido desde hace cuatro años. **Friends of old standing,** amigos antiguos, amigos de mucho tiempo. **We are of the same standing,** somos contemporáneos, o somos iguales. **A person of high standing,** persona o sujeto de consecuencia, posición o carácter. *(Fam.)* Sujeto de alto copete.

standish ['stændɪʃ] [stan-dish], *s.* Escribanía de mesa.

stand-pipe ['stændpaɪp] [stand-paip], *s.* Columna, tubo de alimentación de agua, en un depósito.

standpoint ['stændpɔɪnt] [stand-point], *s.* Puesto, posición con relación a la que se consideran las cosas; punto de vista.

standstill ['stændstɪl] [stand-stil], *s.* Parada, alto; pausa completa; descanso. **To be at a standstill,** quedar parado, no andar.

stand-offish [ˌstændˈɒfɪʃ] [stand-o-fish], *sf.* Reservado, frío, poco amable.

stand-offishly [ˌstændˈɒfɪʃlɪ] [stand-o-fish-li], *adv.* Fríamente, con poca amabilidad.

standpoint ['stændpɔɪnt] [stand-point], *sm.* Punto de vista.

stank [stæŋk] [stank], pret. de TO STINK.

stannic ['stænɪk] [sta-nik], *a.* Estánico, perteneciente al estaño, particularmente en sus compuestos más altos.

stanza ['stænzə] [stan-sa], *s. (Poét.)* Estancia, estrofa, grupo de cuatro o más líneas en rima; cada uno de esos grupos o divisiones de un poema.

stapes ['steɪpz] [steips], *s. (Anat.)* Estribo, el huesecillo más interior del oído. *(Lat.)*

staple ['steɪpl] [stei-pel], *s.* 1. Género, producción principal de un país (production). 2. Elemento o material principal (element). 3. Hebra o filamento de algodón o de lana. 4. Materia prima, materia bruta. 5. Emporio de comercio, mercado. -*a.* 1. Principal, producido y vendido regular y constantemente. 2. Ajustado o establecido según las leyes del comercio, conforme a los usos o leyes del comercio. **Staple commodities,** las principales manufacturas o géneros de algún emporio o escala de comercio.

staple, *s.* Cerradero, la chapa de hierro en que entra y se asegura el pestillo o cerrojo; picolete, grapa o chapa en forma de U con extremos puntiagudos.

staple, *va.* Clasificar las hebras (de lana), según su longitud. **Short-stapled, long-stapled,** de hebra corta, de hebra larga.

stapler ['steɪplə'] [stei-pla'], *s.* 1. Engrapador. 2. Comerciante en productos de consumo principal.

star [stɑː'] [sta'], *s.* 1. *(Astron.)* Estrella, uno de los cuerpos luminosos que aparecen en el cielo de noche. **Shooting stars,** estrellas errantes o voladoras. 2. Estrella, hado, suerte, destino (destiny). 3. Cruz, placa, la insignia honorífica que llevan los caballeros de varias órdenes. 4. Asterisco, marca de referencia o cita en los libros. 5. Actor, actriz que hace el papel principal; el que sobresale en su profesión. **Binary** o **double star,** estrella doble, par de estrellas que giran alrededor de su centro común de gravedad. **North star, pole-star,** estrella polar. **Star of Bethlehem.** *(Bot.)* leche de gallina. **star-paved,** sembrado o lleno de estrellas, estrellado. **Star-proof,** que no puede ser atravesado por la luz de las estrellas. **Star-shaped,** esteliforme, en forma de estrella. **Star sign,** signo del Zodíaco. **Star-spangled,** sembrado de estrellas; se dice en especial del pabellón de los Estados Unidos. **Star-stone,** piedra de estrella, especie de fósil. **To be born under a lucky star,** nacer con buena estrella.

starboard ['stɑːbɔːd] [star-bord], *s. (Mar.)* Estribor, el costado derecho de una embarcación.

starch [stɑːtʃ] [starch], *s.* 1. Almidón, fécula, substancia blanca, pulverulenta, insípida e inodora (CHO), insoluble en el agua fría y en el alcohol, que se extrae de todos los vegetales excepto los hongos. 2. Engrudo de almidón. 3. *(Fig.)* Modales rígidos; coraje, brío.

starch, *va.* Almidonar, atiesar, la ropa blanca con almidón.

star-chamber ['stɑːtʃeɪmbə'] [star-cheim-ba'], *a.* Secreto y arbitrario.

starched ['stɑːtʃt] [starcht], *a.* 1. Almidonado. 2. Tieso, nimiamente grave y circunspecto.

starcher ['stɑːtʃə'] [star-cha'], *s.* Almidonador o almidonadora.

starchly ['stɑːtʃlɪ] [starch-li], *adv.* Tiesamente, fuertemente; con afectación.

starchmaker ['stɑːtʃmeɪkə'] [starch-mei-ka'], *s.* Almidonero, el que hace almidón.

starchy ['stɑːtʃɪ] [star-chi], *a.* 1. Almidonado, engrudado; *(Fig.)* tieso, de modales rígidos. 2. De almidón, combinado con almidón: *(med.)* feculoso.

stardust ['stɑːdʌst] [star-dast], *sm* Encanto.

stare [steə'] [stea'], *va.* Clavar o fijar la vista, encararse con alguno; hacer que uno haga o deje de hacer algo por medio de miradas fijas y penetrantes; mirar de fijo. -*vn.* 1. Abrir grandes ojos; mirar con asombro, con insolencia. 2. Saltar a la vista; salir una cosa en la superficie de otra. 3. Enderezarse, levantarse los cabellos. **To stare in the face,** dar en cara o en los ojos, saltar a los ojos, venirse a los ojos, ser tan claro como la luz del día, ser una cosa tan clara que no se puede negar. **To stare into the distance,** estar mirando a las nubes.

stare, *s.* Mirada fija, mirada con los ojos dilatados; mirada atontada o de asombro.

starer ['steərə'] [stea-ra'], *s.* El que clava la vista en algún objeto.

starfish ['stɑːfɪʃ] [star-fish], *s.* Estrella de mar, asteria, animal marino equinodermo de brazos radiados.

star-gazer ['stɑːgeɪzə'] [star-guei-sa'], *s.* Astrónomo, astrólogo.

star-gazing ['stɑːgeɪzɪŋ] [star-guei-sin], *s.* El acto de mirar a las estrellas.

staring ['steərɪŋ] [stea-rin], *pa.* 1. Abierto, grande, fijo; que mira fijamente. 2. Que salta a la vista; llamativo. **Staring colors,** colores llamativos, muy vivos.

stark [stɑːk] [stark], *a.* 1. Tieso, rígido (stiff), como en la muerte, de aquí, muerto. 2. *(Fig.)* Tieso, inflexible, severo (harsh). 3. Completo, cabal; puro. 4. *(Ant.)* Fuerte, vigoroso, poderoso (strong). **Stark madness,** locura completa. **Stark nonsense,** pura tontería. **stark and stiff,** rígido, muerto. -*adv.* Completamente, enteramente. **He is stark mad,** está

rematadamente loco o es un loco rematado. **Stark naked,** completamente desnudo, en cueros.

starkly ['stɑːklɪ] [stark-li], *adv.* Tiesamente, totalmente, del todo.

starless ['stɑːlɪs] [star-les], *a.* Sin estrellas; sin la luz de las estrellas.

starlight ['stɑːlaɪt] [star-lait], *s.* Luz de las estrellas. -*a.* Estrellado. **Starlight night,** noche estrellada o muy clara.

starlike ['stɑːlaɪk] [star-laik], *a.* Estrellado, lustroso, brillante, radiante como una estrella o como las estrellas.

starling ['stɑːlɪŋ] [star-lin], *s.* 1. *(Orn.)* Estornino; pájaro del antiguo continente (Sturnus); también, pájaro americano del género Sturnella. 2. El ángulo o esquina del estribo de un puente.

starred ['stɑːd] [stard], *a.* Estrellado, lleno de estrellas; adornado con estrellas; afortunado.

starry ['stɑːrɪ] [sta-ri], *a.* 1. Estrellado, sembrado de estrellas o de puntos brillantes. 2. Alumbrado por las estrellas. 3. Centelleante, radiante como las estrellas. 4. Esteliforme, que tiene la forma de una estrella. 5. Estelar, perteneciente o relativo a las estrellas.

starwort ['stɑːwɔːt] [star-uort], *s. (Bot.)* Estrellada.

start [stɑːt] [start], *va.* 1. Suscitar, mover por primera vez; (a) sobrecoger, asustar; ojear o espantar la caza; hacer levantar (un animal o ave); desemboscar, hacer salir un animal montés de su guarida; (b) poner en movimiento, hacer funcionar o marchar (una cosa inanimada); dar la señal de partida; (c) aflojar, dislocar. 2. Principiar, dar nueva dirección; originar, empezar. 3. Proponer de una manera inesperada, poner sobre el tapete; suscitar objeciones. 4. Trasegar, sacar el contenido; desfondar; alabear, despegar. 5. *(Ant.)* Descubrir, inventar. -*vn.* 1. Sobrecogerse, sobresaltarse, asustarse, estremecerse, conmoverse súbitamente por alguna pasión. 2. Saltar, dar un salto, levantarse de repente. 3. Partir, ponerse en camino; principiar la carrera; emprender cualquier negocio; coger o tomar la delantera; estrenarse, comenzar. 4. Salir, proceder, ir adelante; proceder, derivar. 5. Aflojarse de su lugar; descoyuntarse; alabearse, combarse (wood). 6. *(Ant.)* Desviarse, apartarse.

start aside, echarse a un lado, ladearse.

start after, salir, empezar a perseguir o buscar; partir después (de otra cosa).

start back, saltar hacia atrás; partir a la vuelta.

start for, partir, ponerse en camino hacia; presentarse como candidato.

start from, salir, partir de un lugar; tomar su origen; comenzar.

start off, salir; partir, ponerse en camino; principiar a moverse.

start on, meterse con.

start out, principiar a hacer una cosa, irse, marcharse. **To start out of one's sleep,** despertarse sobresaltado.

start up, levantarse precipitadamente, ponerse derecho; elevarse; salir a luz alguna cosa de repente; ponerse en movimiento, empezar a funcionar (a machine). **To start a car,** dar la señal para que un coche del tranvía se ponga en camino. **To start a subject,** poner un asunto sobre el tapete. **To start wine,** trasegar el vino. **To start a fire,** provocar un incendio. **To have a start,** tener ventaja, llevar ventaja sobre alguien. **Start moving!,** ¡muévase!, ¡menéarse!

start, *s.* 1. Estremecimiento, agitación repentina; sobresalto, susto repentino o de una impresión imprevista. 2. Partida; primer paso, primer movimiento, comienzo, principio (beginning). 3. Salto, bote, la acción de apartarse de pronto para evitar un encuentro imprevisto. 4. Ímpetu, arranque, pronto de alguna pasión o del genio (impulse); estampida. 5. Arranque, la acción de partir de carrera para proseguir corriendo. 6. Delantera, distancia en que uno se adelanta a otro; ventaja (advantage). 7. Grieta, raja, aflojamiento. **To get the start,** coger la delantera. **By starts,** a saltos, por botes. **By fits and starts,** a saltos y corcovos. **To give a start,** asustar, dar un susto. **Upon the start,** al primer paso, al principio, en el momento de partir. **To make a fresh start,** empezar de nuevo, hacer vida nueva.

starter ['stɑːtəʳ] [star-taʳ], s. 1. El que da la señal de partida (de un automóvil o en una carrera). 2. Palanca de marcha en las máquinas. 3. El perro que levanta la caza. 4. Arranque o marcha de un automóvil. **Self-starter,** marcha automática. **Elevator starter,** jefe de ascensoristas.

starting ['stɑːtɪŋ] [star-tin], s. 1. Sobresalto, estremecimiento, susto (fright). 2. Partida. 3. Impulso, movimiento repentino (impulse). 4. (Mec.) Salida, arrancada, acto de poner en movimiento. 5. Comienzo. **Starting-point,** punto de partida. **Starting-place o starting-post,** la barrera de donde se arranca a correr.

startle ['stɑːtl] [star-tel], va. Espantar, asustar, dar miedo; sobrecoger, alarmar, hacer estremecer. -vn. (Ant.) Sobresaltarse, sobrecogerse, temblar de miedo.

starvation [stɑːˈveɪʃən] [star-vei-shon], a. Que causa o que tiende a causar inanición o indigencia. -s. inanición, debilidad grande por falta de alimento; el acto de morir de hambre o el estado de padecer hambre; la muerte procedente de la falta de alimento; por extensión, indigencia, carencia de cualquier cosa esencial a la vida.

starve [stɑːv] [starv], vn. 1. Morir de hambre, morirse de hambre. 2. Perecer, morir por falta de alimento. 3. Sufrir mentalmente, o hallarse sumido en la miseria. 4. (Ingl.) Morir de frío. -va. 1. Matar de hambre, hacer morir por falta de alimento. 2. Hambrear, sujetar a una persona por hambre; reducir a un estado de extrema hambre. 3. (Ingl.) Hacer morir de frío; helar. 4. Amilanar, privar de fuerza o vigor. **To starve oneself,** dejarse morir de hambre. **To starve someone of something,** privar a alguien de algo.

starveling ['stɑːvlɪŋ] [starv-lin], s. El animal extenuado por falta de alimento o muerto de hambre. -a. Hambriento, muerto de hambre, famélico, hambrón.

starving ['stɑːv] [starv], a. Famélico, hambriento.

stasis ['steɪsɪs] [stei-sis], s. (Med.) Estancación de la sangre, particularmente en los vasos capilares.

state [steɪt] [steit], s. 1. Estado, modo de existencia, relación a las circunstancias, condición, ser actual o disposición en que se halla o considera una persona o cosa. 2. Estado, el cuerpo político de una nación; en especial, uno de los Estados Unidos de América. 3. Estado, el país o dominio de algún príncipe. 4. Fausto, pompa, aparato, gran ceremonia; dignidad, grandeza. 5. Trono, el asiento real usado en los actos de ceremonia majestuosa. 6. El gobierno civil, en contraposición al eclesiástico. **State-affairs,** negocios públicos, negocios o asuntos de estado. **In a state of** o **to,** en estado de. **Married state,** matrimonio. **Single state,** celibato. **In state,** con gran pompa, de gran ceremonia. **To lie in state,** estar expuesto en cama de respeto. **Secretary of State,** ministro de Estado, de Relaciones Exteriores. **As stated above,** como se ha indicado arriba.

state, a. 1. De estado; político, público. 2. De lujo; usado en grandes ceremonias; propio para ocasiones de pompa. 3. De un estado de los Estados Unidos. **State fair,** feria estatal. **State paper,** documento del Estado; pliego, documento o tratado político. **State-house,** (E.U.) edificio del Estado, en que se reune la legislatura de un estado. **State's evidence,** (a) testimonio aducido en una causa criminal; (b) el cómplice que por librarse del castigo declara sobre un delito en perjuicio de otros. **State prison,** V. PENITENTIARY.

state, va. 1. Exponer, enunciar, declarar formal o particularmente hablando o por escrito; relatar, decir, contar. 2. (For.) Declarar como cosa positiva. 3. (Alg.) Proponer, plantear (un problema).

statecraft ['steɪtkrɑːft] [steit-kraft], s. Política, diplomacia, el arte de gobernar, de dirigir los asuntos públicos.

stated ['steɪtɪd] [stei-tid], a. part. Establecido, que sucede en épocas señaladas o fijas; regular, fijo, perteneciente a los cuerpos en equilibrio; opuesto a dinámico.

statehood ['steɪthʊd] [steit-jud], sf. Categoría de estado.

stateless ['steɪtlɪs] [steit-les], a. Apátrida.

stateliness ['steɪtlɪnɪs] [steit-li-nes], s. 1. Grandeza, majestad, aparato majestuoso, dignidad. 2. Fausto o pompa afectada; altivez.

stately ['steɪtlɪ] [steit-li], a. Augusto, sublime, majestuoso, imponente, soberbio; con apariencia de grandeza y magnificencia; lleno de dignidad, grande, excelso, noble, elevado. **A stately edifice,** un soberbio edificio. **Stately manners,** modales nobles, llenos de dignidad. -adv. Majestuosamente, suntuosamente.

statement ['steɪtmənt] [steit-ment], s. 1. Declaración, exposición, acción de declarar o exponer; resumen, narración, relación, cuenta. 2. Relato, informe. 3. Cuenta y razón.

stateroom ['steɪtrʊm] [steit-rum], s. 1. Camarote, cuarto particular para dormir, como en un vapor o coche dormitorio; contiene generalmente dos camas. 2. Gran salón, o pieza principal de un palacio.

statesman ['steɪtsmən] [steits-man], s. Estadista, político; hombre de Estado notable por su talento.

statesmanlike ['steɪtsmənlaɪk] [steits-man-laik], a. De una manera propia de un hombre de Estado, o estadista.

statesmanship ['steɪtsmənʃɪp] [steits-man-ship], s. Calidad de estadista. V. STATECRAFT.

stateswoman ['steɪtswʊmən] [steits-uo-man], sf. La mujer que se mezcla en los asuntos de estado.

static ['stætɪk] [sta-tik], a. Estático.

static, s. Parásitos. **Statis suppressor,** antiparásito, antiparasitario.

statics ['stætɪks] [sta-tiks], s. Estática, la ciencia que trata del equilibrio de los cuerpos.

station ['steɪʃən] [stei-shon], s. 1. El puesto donde se coloca alguno; lugar señalado (place). 2. Paradero, estación de ferrocarril o de la policía. 3. Condición o posición social (social condition). 4. En agrimensura, punto desde el cual o alrededor del cual se hacen las medidas de ángulos o distancias; también, la distancia que sirve de medida normal. 5. Puesto militar, parada, descansadero. **Station-house,** edificio donde están de guardia los ministros de la policía; estación de ferrocarril para viajeros, habitación de los individuos de una estación de salvamento. **Humble station,** baja posición social. **To get ideas above one's station,** darse aires de superioridad.

station, va. Apostar, disponer, colocar.

stationary ['steɪʃənərɪ] [stei-sho-na-ri], a. 1. Estacionario, estacional. 2. Fijo, sin movimiento. 3. Que continúa en el mismo estado, sin hacer progreso alguno. **Stationary engine,** máquina fija.

stationer ['steɪʃənəʳ] [stei-sho-naʳ], s. Papelero, el que vende papel, tinta, lacre y demás efectos necesarios para escribir.

stationery ['steɪʃənərɪ] [stei-sho-na-ri], s. Papel y avíos necesarios para escribir. **Stationery store,** papelería.

stationmaster ['steɪʃənˌmɑːstəʳ] [stei-shon-mas-taʳ], s. Jefe de estación.

station wagon ['steɪʃənˌwægən] [stei-shon-va-gon], s. Camioneta, furgoneta.

statist ['steɪtɪst] [stei-tist], s. Estadístico, el versado en la estadística.

statistic [stəˈtɪstɪk] [sta-tis-tik], a. Estadístico, perteneciente a la estadística; que contiene tablas estadísticas, que trata de la estadística, o dado a ella.

statistically [stəˈtɪstɪkəlɪ] [sta-tis-ti-ka-li], adv. Estadísticamente, por medios estadísticos.

statistician [stəˈtɪstɪʃən] [sta-tis-ti-shan], s. Estadístico, persona versada en trabajos estadísticos.

statistics [stəˈtɪstɪks] [sta-tis-tiks], s. 1. Estadística, conjunto de datos relativos al estado social. 2. Estadística, ciencia.

statuary ['stætjʊərɪ] [sta-tiua-ri], s. 1. Estatuas consideradas colectivamente. 2. Estatuaria; estatuario, escultor.

statue ['stætjuː] [sta-tiu], s. Estatua.

statuesque [stætjʊˈesk] [sta-tiuesk], a. Parecida a una estatua.

statuette [ˌstætjʊˈet] [sta-tiuet], *s.* Estatua pequeña, figurilla.

stature [ˈstætʃəʳ] [sta-chaʳ], *s.* Estatura, altura, talla, tamaño.

status [ˈsteɪtəs] [stei-tos], *s.* 1. Manera de ser; condición o relación legal, posición. 2. Posición relativa. **Social status,** posición social. **To have sufficient status,** tener bastante categoría.

status quo [ˈsteɪtəsˈkwəʊ] [stei-tos-kuou], *sm.* Statu quo.

statute [ˈstætjuːt] [sta-tiut], *s.* Estatuto, ley, pragmática. decreto, reglamento.

statutory [ˈstætjʊtərɪ] [sta-tiu-to-ri], *a.* Perteneciente o relativo a un estatuto, establecido por la ley.

staunch [stɔːntʃ] [stonch], *a.* Sano de quilla y costados. V. STANCH.

staunchly [ˈstɔːntʃlɪ] [stonch-li], *adv.* Firmemente, lealmente.

stave [steɪv] [steiv], *va. (pret.* STAVED o STOVE). 1. Romper las duelas; quebrar una cosa, abriendo un agujero; quebrantar, destrozar. 2. Agujerear una cosa destrozándola. o rompiéndola, desfondar. 3. Cubrir de duelas, poner duelas. 4. Rechazar, desviar como con un bastón; retardar, diferir; se usa con **off,** por lo general. 5. Descabezar algún barril o tonel para desocuparlo. **To stave and tail,** separar a los perros cuando riñen, dándoles de palos y tirándoles de la cola. **Stave in,** romper, partir a golpes. **Stave off,** rechazar, mantener a distancia; aplazar (delay).

stave, *s.* 1. Duela de barril, tabla de tonel. **Staves and heading,** duelas y fondos. 2. Tabla recta que forma parte del brocal de un pozo. 3. *(Mús.)* Pentagrama. 4. Estrofa, estancia.

staves [ˈsteɪvz] [steivs], *s.* 1. *pl. regular de* STAVE. 2. *pl.* irregular de STAFF.

stay [steɪ] [stei], *s.* 1. Morada, mansión, el acto o tiempo de quedarse en un paraje (lodge); parada, detención, estancia (visit). 2. *(For.)* Cesación temporal de un procedimiento judicial. 3. Embarazo, impedimento, obstáculo. 4. Lo que reprime o apoya; puntal; apoyo, sostén (support); sustentáculo, atesador, fiador; *(Arq.)* arbotante, apeo, estribo; tentemozo. 5. Varilla de ballena en un corsé; en plural, una forma antigua de corsé. 6. Estabilidad, fijeza, perseverancia, persistencia (perseverance). **Make no stay,** no se detenga usted. **I shall make some stay in London,** me detendré algo en Londres. **Stay of proceedings,** sobreseimiento.

stay, *s. (Mar.)* Estay, cabo grueso que sirve para sostener un palo o mastelero por la parte delantera. **Main-stay,** estay mayor. **The ship missed stays,** el buque falló la virada. **Stay-sails,** velas de estay. **Fore-stay,** estay de trinquete. **Foretop-stay,** estay del velacho.

stay, *vn. (pret. y pp.* STAYED). 1. Quedarse, permanecer, estarse, continuar en el mismo sitio, en el mismo estado o en la misma situación (remain). 2. Parar o pararse, cesar en el movimiento o en la acción, no pasar adelante (stop). 3. Tardar, detenerse. 4. *(Des.)* Aguardarse, esperarse. *-va.* 1. Parar, detener o impedir el movimiento o acción de otro. 2. Contener, poner freno, reprimir (repress). 3. Sostener, apoyar.

stay away, quedar alejado, ausentarse, no parecer.

stay behind, no salir, quedarse.

stay for, aguardar o esperar a uno.

stay from, impedir la acción o efecto de una cosa; separar; torcer o hacer torcer el camino.

stay in, quedarse en su casa, no salir.

stay off, no ir a trabajar o al colegio.

stay on, quedar sobre, descansar sobre; permanecer, cotinuar en el mismo estado.

stay out, quedarse fuera, no entrar.

stay over, pernoctar, pasar la noche.

stay up, velar, no acostarse. **Stay-at-home,** casero, persona que rara vez sale de su casa. **Stay-a-while,** mata espinosa que se adhiere a cuantos la rozan. **To stay the stomach,** tomar un ligero refrigerio, tomar las once.

stay-at-home [ˈsteɪəthəʊm] [stei-at-joum], *a.* Hogareño, casero, que le gusta estar en casa.

stayer [ˈsteɪəʳ] [steiaʳ], *s.* El que permanece, se queda o está quieto en una parte; el que para o retiene; el que apoya o favorece.

stead [sted] [sted], *s.* 1. Lugar, sitio; las veces de; (precedido de **in**). 2. Auxilio, ayuda. 3. *(Des.)* Armazón de cama. V. BEDSTEAD. **In his stead,** en su sitio, en su lugar; en vez de él. **In stead of,** en lugar de, en vez de, V. INSTEAD. **To stand in stead,** ser útil, servir una cosa para lo que se quiere destinarla. **In my stead,** en mi lugar.

steadfast, stedfast [ˈstedfæst] [sted-fast], *a.* 1. Fijo, firme, estable, permanente. 2. Constante, inmutable. 3. Resuelto, determinado.

steadfastly [ˈstedfæstlɪ] [sted-fast-li], *adv.* Firmemente, con constancia, con resolución. **He fixed his eyes stead fastly on her,** él estuvo con los ojos clavados en ella.

steadfastness [ˈstedfæstnɪs] [sted-fast-nes], *s.* 1. Inmutabilidad, estabilidad. 2. Firmeza, constancia, resolución, persistencia.

steadily [ˈstedɪlɪ] [ste-di-li], *adv.* Firmemente; invariablemente.

steadiness [ˈstedɪnɪs] [ste-di-nes], *s.* 1. Firmeza, la seguridad en que se halla una cosa que no falsea ni se mueve; estabilidad. 2. Firmeza, entereza, constancia. 3. Regularidad, conducta arreglada.

steady [ˈstedɪ] [ste-di], *a.* 1. Firme, fijo, seguro, asegurado. 2. Juicioso, formal, asentado, prudente. 3. Firme, constante, no variable; que se mueve o funciona con regularidad. 4. Libre de excesos; de vida arreglada.

steady, *va.* Hacer firme, sostener, fijar alguna cosa.

steak [steɪk] [steik], *s.* Tajada de carne para asar. **Beef-steak,** tajada de vaca, bistec.

steal [stiːl] [stil], *va. y vn. (pret.* STOLE, *pp.* STOLEN). 1. Robar, hurtar, pillar, estafar con tretas y engaños (swindle). 2. Pretender o arrogarse algo sin derecho, v.g. la calidad de autor; cometer plagio. 3. Introducir clandestinamente o sin ser observado; pasar furtivamente, a hurtadillas. 4. Colarse, escabullirse, escapar sin visto (escape). 5. Robar o atraer con eficacia y como violentamente el afecto o ánimo.

steal along, pasar en silencio, deslizarse sin ruido, avanzar a paso de lobo.

steal away, steal off, marcharse a hurtadillas; escabullirse.

steal away from, quitar del medio, hacer desaparecer, ocultar, esconder. **Thou shalt not steal,** no hurtarás.

steal down, descender furtivamente.

steal forth, salir clandestinamente.

steal in, into, penetrar furtivamente, introducirse a hurtadillas.

steal over, ganar insensiblemente, apoderarse suavemente de algo; deslizarse a escondidas.

steal up, subir a ocultas, clandestinamente. **To steal up on someone,** acercarse a alguien sigilosamente.

steal upon, aproximarse sin ruido, sorprender; apoderarse de algo; deslizarse, penetrar calladamente. *-s. (Fam.)* Hurto, el acto de hurtar; robo.

stealer [ˈstiːləʳ] [sti-laʳ], *s.* Ladrón, el que roba o hurta.

stealing [ˈstiːlɪŋ] [sti-lin], *s.* Hurto, robo; la acción de hurtar, y la cosa robada.

stealth [stelθ] [stelz], *s.* La calidad o costumbre de obrar a hurtadillas o en secreto. **By stealth,** a hurtadillas, a escondidas, de oculto, a escondite, en secreto.

stealthy [ˈstelθɪ] [stel-zi], *a.* Furtivo, hecho de oculto o a escondidas.

steam [stiːm] [stim], *s.* 1. Agua en el estado gaseoso; vapor, o vaho que exhala todo cuerpo húmedo que se calienta (vapor); en especial el fluido elástico producido por la ebullición del agua. 2. Niebla, vaho visible. **Steam-engine,** máquina de vapor. **To cut off, to expand to shut off steam,** cortar, disminuir, interrumpir, el vapor. **To get up** o **generate steam,** producir o generar vapor. **With all steam on,** a todo vapor. **Steam is on,** hay presión. **Super-heated, surcharged steam,** exceso de vapor. **High-pressure steam,** vapor a alta presión. **Steam bath,** baño de vapor. **Steam-chest,** caja o cámara de vapor. **Steam-gauge,** manómetro de vapor.

Steam-hammer, martinete de vapor. **Steam-pipe,** cañería o conducto de vapor.

steam, *va.* 1. Saturar con vapor; someter a la acción del vapor. 2. Secar, quitar la humedad a una cosa, v.g. los adobes. *-vn.* 1. Vahear, emitir o echar de sí vaho o vapor. 2. Moverse por medio del vapor. 3. Evaporarse o reducirse a vapor. **To steam ahead,** avanzar. **To steam up,** empañar (window).

steamboat [ˈstiːmbəʊt] [stim-bout], *s.* Barco de vapor, vapor de río.

steamer [ˈstiːməʳ] [sti-maʳ], *s.* 1. Barco, vapor. 2. Vaporizador. **Steamer rug,** manta de viaje. **Steamer trunk,** baúl de camarote.

steamfitter [ˈstiːmfɪtəʳ] [stim-fi-taʳ], *s.* Montador de calderas de vapor.

steamheat [ˈstiːmhiːt] [stim-jit], *s.* Calefacción mediante vapor.

steamroller [ˈstiːmˌrəʊləʳ] [stim-rou-laʳ], *s.* 1. Apisonadora. 2. *(Fig.)* Actividad arrolladora, fuerza abrumadora. *-va.* Abrumar.

steamship [ˈstiːmʃɪp] [stim-ship], *s.* Vapor, buque de vapor. **Steamship line,** línea marítima, línea de vapores.

steam shovel [ˈstiːmˌʃʌvl] [stim-sha-vel], *s.* Pala mecánica.

steamy [ˈstiːmɪ] [sti-mi] *a.* Vaporoso, empañado (window).

steed [stiːd] [stid], *s.* Caballo, corcel.

steel [stiːl] [stil], *s.* 1. Acero. 2. Arma o instrumento hecho de acero, p. ej. espada, cuchillo, etc. 3. *(Fig.)* Dureza, firmeza. **Alloy steel,** aleación de acero. **Ball-bearing steel,** acero para cojinetes. **Steel helmet,** casco de acero. **Bessemer steel,** aero Bessemer. **Chrome steel,** acero cromado o al cromo. **Damask steel,** aero damasquinado. **Stainless steel,** acero inoxidable. **Steel wool,** lana de acero (for cleaning).

steel, *va.* 1. Acerar, poner acero, cubrir o armar de acero. 2. Fortalecer, endurecer, hacer más firme, acorazar. 3. Dar apariencia de acero a una cosa. *-a.* Hecho o compuesto de acero o parecido a él; de aquí, endurecido, inflexible, duro, sin piedad. **Steel-blue,** azulado, como ciertos aceros. **Steel-clad,** cubierto o armado de acero. **Steel-engraving,** grabado en acero. **Steel-pen,** pluma de acero. **Tincture of steel,** *(Ingl.)* tintura de cloruro de hierro. **Steel-works,** talleres en que se fabrica el acero. **Tool-steel,** acero de superior calidad y de gran temple que se usa para hacer herramientas cortantes. **To steel oneself,** fortalecerse. **To steel somebody,** infundir valor a alguien.

steel-grey [ˈstiːlɡrəɪ] [stil-grei], *a.* Gris metálico.

steeliness [ˈstiːlɪnɪs] [sti-li-nes], *s.* Dureza, insensibilidad.

steel-plated [ˌstiːlˈpleɪtɪd] [stil-plei-tid], *a.* Chapado en acero.

steelworker [ˈstiːlˌwɜːkəʳ] [stil-ue-keʳ], *s.* Obrero en una fundición de acero.

steely [ˈstiːlɪ] [sti-li], *a.* 1. Acerado, con acero o de acero. 2. *(Poét.)* Acerino, de acero o perteneciente a este metal. 3. Fuerte, inflexible, firme, duro.

steep [stiːp] [stip], *a.* Escarpado, derecho, pino, rápido. *-s.* Precipicio, despeñadero, altura o cuesta my difícil de subir.

steep, *va.* 1. Empapar, penetrar con algún líquido, macerar (soak, macerate). 2. Mojar completamente, impregnar, remojar; poner en infusión. 3. Embalsar. *-vn.* Mezclarse gradualmente en una infusión. **Steeped in,** empapado de, saturado de. **To steep tea,** poner el té en infusión. **Steeping-tub,** *(Mar.)* tina de desalar. **Steeping-trough,** el sitio donde los cerveceros echan la cebada para entallecer. *-adj. (Fam.)* Excesivo, exorbitante. **A steep climb,** una cuesta muy empinada.

steeping [ˈstiːpɪŋ] [sti-pin], *s.* Mojadura, maceración, acción de empapar, de remojar.

steeple [ˈstiːpl] [sti-pel], *s.* 1. Campanario, torre elevada de una iglesia. 2. Iglesia (el edificio); nombre dado por los primeros cuáqueros.

steeplechase [ˈstiːplˌtʃeɪs] [sti-pel-cheis], *s.* Corrida a caballo por el campo, con tapias zanjas u otros obstáculos.

steepled [ˈstiːpld] [sti-peld], *a.* Con torre o campanario.

steeplejack [ˈstiːpldʒæk] [sti-pel-yak], *s.* Reparador de chimeneas, torres, etc.

steeply [ˈstiːplɪ] [sti-pli], *a.* Empinado. **The road climbs steeply,** la carretera es muy empinada. **To rise prices steeply,** subir mucho los precios.

steepness [ˈstiːpnɪs] [stip-nes], *s.* Calidad de escarpado o pendiente.

steer [ˈstɪəʳ] [stiaʳ], *s.* 1. Novillo, novillejo, utrero. 2. *(E.U.)* Buey de cualquier edad que sea.

steer, *va.* 1. Gobernar, guiar o dirigir el rumbo o la embarcación (guide). 2. Guiar o manejar la rueda o el volante de un vehículo (guide, drive). *-vn.* 1. Navegar, andar bien o mal una nave. 2. Gobernarse, conducirse. 3. Estar sujeto a la acción del timón o de cualquier dirección. **To steer clear of,** evitar chocar con algo, mantenerse alejado de.

steerage [ˈstɪərɪdʒ] [stia-rich], *s.* 1. Antecámara de un bajel, proa, rancho de la gente, que ocupan principalmente los inmigrantes. 2. Alojamiento de los marineros, oficiales más jóvenes, sirvientes, etc. (en un buque de guerra). 3. Gobierno, dirección; la acción de gobernar o dirigir. **To have steerage-way,** *(Mar.)* tener salida para gobernar. **Steerage passenger,** pasajero de proa, de bodega, o de combés. **Steerage-way,** estela, surco del buque; movimiento de una embarcación suficiente para poder gobernarla por el timón.

steering wheel [ˈstɪərɪŋwiːl] [stia-rin-uil], *s.* 1. Volante (de un automóvil). 2. *(Mar.)* Rueda del timón.

steerman [ˈstɪəmən] [stiar-man], *s. (Mar.)* Piloto, timonel, timonero.

stellar [ˈsteləʳ] [ste-laʳ], *a.* Astral, estrellar, relativo o perteneciente a las estrellas.

stellate [ˈsteleɪt] [ste-leit], *a.* Estrellado, de forma estrellada, parecido a las estrellas.

stelliform [ˈstelɪfɔːm] [ste-li-form], *a.* Esteliforme, en forma de estrella.

stellular [ˈsteljʊləʳ] [ste-liu-lar], *a.* Estrellado, sembrado de pequeñas estrellas.

stellionate [ˈstelɪəneɪt] [ste-lio-neit], *s. (For.)* Estelionato, el delito que comete el que vende una finca como libre no siéndolo.

stem [stem] [stem], *s.* 1. Tallo, tronco, cuerpo principal de un árbol, arbusto o planta, el eje que sube. 2. Vástago, pedúnculo de una flor, fruta u hoja, pecíolo. 3. Una parte delgada cualquiera que se asemeja más o menos al tallo del árbol, al pedúnculo de la flor, etc.; pie (de copa); cañón de pluma; barra, rasgo perpendicular que se añade al cuerpo de una nota. 4. *(Mar.)* Roda, roa, tajamar, un trozo derecho de madera en el cual se unen los costados del bajel por la parte delantera. **A woody stem,** un tallo leñoso. **Herbaceous stems,** tallos herbáceos. **From stem to stern,** de proa a popa. **Stem-winder,** reloj de bolsillo.

stem, *va.* 1. Navegar contra la corriente, ir contra viento o marea. 2. Oponerse a la corriente o a las opiniones más aceptadas, resistir. 3. Hacer impermeable una unión o encaje, tapándola o cubriéndola. 4. Quitar los pedúnculos; desgranar (p. ej. las uvas, las pasas). 5. Poner patas o pies a una cosa. **To stem from,** proceder de. **To stem the torrent,** detener el torrente. **To stem the tide,** rendir la marea.

stemless [ˈstemlɪs] [stem-les], *a.* Sin pie o sostén, sin pedúnculo; en botánica, sin tallo.

stempel, stemple [ˈstempl] [stem-pel], *s.* 1. Estemple, montante, asnado, madero grueso con que se aseguran de trecho en trecho los costados de la mina. 2. Travesaño de madera.

stemson [ˈstemsən] [stem-son], *s. (Mar.)* Contrarroda, sobrerroda, trabazón de palos fuertes que aseguran la roda del navío.

stench [stentʃ] [stench], *s.* Hedor, hediondez (stink), también en sentido figurado.

stencil [ˈstensl] [sten-sil], *va.* 1. Estarcir, hacer letras o dibujos calados con un patrón (in typing). 2. Pintar con un modelo calado. *-s.* 1. Patrón, modelo calado para estarcir. 2. Adorno, hecho con planchas de estarcir.

stenciler [ˈstensɪləʳ] [sten-si-laʳ], *s.* El que estarce letras o dibujos, particularmente para adornar los techos de las habitaciones.

stenograph [ˈstensl] [stensl], *s.* 1. Carácter o escritura en la estenografía. 2. Máquina parecida a la de escribir, para hacer caracteres fonéticos.

stenographer [steˈnɒɡrəfəʳ] [ste-no-gra-faʳ], *s.* Estenógrafo, taquígrafo, persona que ejerce la estenografía.

stenographic [ˌstenəˈɡræfɪk] [ste-no-gra-fik], *a.* Estenográfico, perteneciente a la estenografía.

stenography [ste'nɒgrəfɪ] [ste-no-gra-fi], _s._ Taquigrafía o estenografía. _V._ SHORTHAND.

stenotyping [ˌstenɒ'taɪpɪŋ] [ste-no-tai-pin], _s._ Estenomecanografía.

stentorian [sten'tɔːrɪən] [sten-to-rian], _a._ Estentóreo, muy fuerte y grueso; se dice de la voz.

step [step] [step], _va. (pret. y pp._ STEPPED o STEPT). 1. Colocar, poner o mover el pie, como al andar. 2. Ejecutar, llevar a cabo dando los pasos necesarios; atravesar o medir dando pasos; se usa a menudo con _off._ 3. Plantar un mástil. - _vn._ 1. Dar un paso, mover el pie o los pies como al andar, correr o bailar; avanzar, retroceder o mudar de posición con un movimiento del pie. 2. Andar una corta distancia, pasear, dar una vuelta. 3. Andar paso a paso, gravemente o con dignidad y resolución.

step after, seguir o ir detrás.

step aside, desviarse, apartarse, ponerse a un lado.

step back, retroceder, volver atrás; volver a tornar el pensamiento hacia lo pasado.

step down, bajar, descender.

step forth, presentarse resueltamente, ir andando con pasos mesurados o muy poco a poco.

step forward, dar un paso hacia adelante.

step in, entrar en un carruaje o subir a él; entrar, venir de repente, ocurrirse a la imaginación. **Step inside!,** ¡pasa!, ¡adelante!

step on, poner el pie sobre algo, pisar, andar sobre.

step out, salir, dar un paso fuera; bajar, v. g. de un carruaje. **To step over,** atravesar, pasar de una parte a otra.

step short, _(Mil.)_ Dar pasos de quince pulgadas cada uno, acortando el paso.

step up, subir.

step, _s._ 1. Paso, la acción de andar el espacio o distancia que naturalmente se adelanta de un pie a otro, y el mismo espacio (pace). 2. Paso, este mismo espacio tomado como medida 3. Paso o escalón, el peldaño de escalera (stair); umbral de puerta. 4. Paso, un espacio muy corto. 5. Escalón, el grado a que se asciende en la consecución de una cosa o el paso y modo con que alguno adelanta en lo que desea. 6. Paso, el adelantamiento que se hace en cualquiera cosa. 7. Pisada, paso, la huella que queda impresa al andar. 8. Paso, el modo de andar. 9. Paso, el modo de vida de alguno o su conducta. 10. _(Mús.)_ Intervalo equivalente a un grado de la escala o del pentagrama. 11. Pedestal de máquina, quicio de eje vertical; _(Mar.)_ carlinga, madero fijo sobre la quilla en el que entra la mecha del palo. **Steps,** _pl._ pasos, diligencias para la prosecución de algún negocio. **Step of a mast,** carlinga. **By such steps,** por tales medios. **to retrace one's steps,** volver sobre sus pasos. **To take a step,** dar un paso; tomar alguna medida. **In step,** de acorde, en unión (como en la marcha).

step-, prefijo que en composición tiene la significación de parentesco de afinidad, como **Step-father,** padrastro. **Step-mother,** madrastra. **Step-son,** hijastro. **Step-daughter,** hijastra. **Step-brother,** hermanastro. **Step-sister,** hermanastra.

stepladder ['stepˌlædəʳ] [step-la-daʳ], _s._ Escalera de mano.

steppe [step] [step], _s._ Estepa.

stepping-stone ['stepɪŋstəʊn] [ste-pin-stoun], _s._ 1. Pasadera, estriberón 2. _(Fig.)_ Escalón. 3. _(Fig.)_ Trampolín.

stereo ['sterɪəʊ] [ste-riou], _Abreviatura de_ **stereophonic.**

stereographic ['sterɪəʊˌgræfɪk] [ste-riou-gra-fik], _a._ Estereográfico, perteneciente al estereografía.

stereophonic [ˌsterɪəʊ'fɒnɪk] [ste-riou-fo-nik], _a._ Estereofónico.

stereophony [ˌsterɪəʊ'fɒnɪ] [ste-riou-fo-ni], _sf._ Estereofonía.

stereoscope ['sterɪəskəʊp] [ste-rios-koup], _s._ Estereoscopio, instrumento óptico con dos lentes prismáticos, en que se ven como de relieve las figuras de un dibujo o fotografía doble.

stereoscopic [ˌstrɪəs'kɒpɪk] [ste-rios-ko-pik], _a._ Estereoscópico, perteneciente al estereoscopio o propio para usarlo en él. **Stereoscopic pictures,** cuadros estereoscópicos. **Stereoscopic camera,** cámara estereoscópica.

stereotype ['sterɪətaɪp] [ste-rio-taip], _va._ 1. Estereotipar, clisar; convertir las formas de caracteres movibles en planchas permanentes. 2. Estereotipar, imprimir con planchas firmes y estable en lugar de las comunes hechas con letras sueltas; imprimir de una manera indeleble. -_s._ Estereotipo, clisé; plancha de metal de estereotipar, que se saca de una matriz; letra o viñeta clisada. **Stereotype plate,** plancha estereotípica, clisé.

stereotyped ['sterɪətaɪpd] [ste-rio-taipd], _a._ 1. Estereotipado. 2. Sin originalidad.

sterile ['steraɪl] [ste-rail], _a._ 1. Estéril, infructífero, que no engendra; que no contiene polen o no produce un pistilo. 2. Que no produce, sin ventaja, sin resultado.

sterility [ste'rɪlɪtɪ] [ste-ri-li-ti], _s._ Esterilidad, condición o calidad de estéril.

sterilization [ˌsterɪlaɪˌzeɪʃən] [ste-ri-lai-sei-shon], _s._ Esterilización.

sterilize ['sterɪlaɪz] [ste-ri-lais], _va._ 1. Esterilizar, hacer infecundo. 2. Destruir las bacterias u otros organismos microscópicos. **To sterilize milk,** hervir la leche para destruir las bacterias.

sterilizer ['sterɪlaɪzeʳ] [ste-ri-lai-saʳ], _s._ Esterilizador; aparato para destruir las bacterias.

sterling ['stɜːlɪŋ] [ster-lin], _a._ 1. Esterlina. 2. Genuino, hecho a ley, puro, verdadero. **A person of sterling worth,** una persona de grandes méritos. **A pound sterling,** una libra esterlina. **Sterling silver,** plata de ley.

stern [stɜːn] [stern], _a._ 1. Austero, duro, rígido; severo, inflexible, cruel (severe). 2. Áspero, agrio de genio (rude); que infunde miedo, que repele. -_s._ 1. _(Mar.)_ Popa, el remate posterior de un bajel. **Stern-fast,** codera. **Square-stern,** popa llana. **Pink-stern,** popa de pinque. **Stern-frame,** cuaderna de popa o del cuerpo popés. **Stern-port,** _(Mar.)_ 1. Porta de guardatimón. 2. La parte o extremidad posterior de cualquiera cosa, cola. **Stern-chase,** en que la nave que persigue va siguiendo en la estela de la otra. **Stern-chaser,** pieza de retirada. **Stern-post,** codaste, estambor, guardatimón, pieza fijada en la quilla y que sostiene el timón. **Stern-sheets,** el espacio que queda a popa de los bancos de un bote. **A stern warning,** un aviso terminante. **Sternway,** reculada, movimiento de retroceso. **Stern-wheeler,** _(E.U.)_ Bote de vapor, de poco calado, que tiene a popa una sola rueda grande paleta.

sternly ['stɜːnlɪ] [stern-li], _adv._ Austeramente, severamente, rigurosamente.

sternness ['stɜːnnɪs] [stern-nes], _s._ Austeridad, severidad, rigor, dureza, aspereza de genio.

sternum ['stɜːnnəm] [stern-nom], _s._ _(Anat.)_ Esternón, hueso situado en la parte anterior y media del tórax.

steroid ['stɪərɔɪd] [ste-roid], _s._ Esteroide.

stertor ['stɜːtəʳ] [ster-taʳ], _s._ Estertor, respiración ronca y anhelosa.

stertorous ['stɜːtərəs] [ster-to-ros], _a._ Estertoroso, caracterizado por el estertor.

stet [stet] [stet], _(Impr.)_ Reténgase.

stethoscope ['steθəskəʊp] [ste-zos-koup], _s._ Estetoscopio, instrumento acústico para explorar el estado del pecho.

stethoscopic [ˌsteθəs'kɒpɪk] [ste-zos-kou-pik], _a._ Estetoscópico, relativo al estetoscopio.

stevedore ['stiːvɪdɔːʳ] [sti-vi-doʳ], _s._ Estibador, descargador.

stew [stjuː] [stiu], _va. y vn._ Estofar, cocer a fuego lento. -_s._ 1. Estofado, guisado; carne o pescado estofados _(Culin.)_ 2. _(Fam.)_ Estado de excitación nerviosa y ansiedad; agitación mental. 3. _(Ant.)_ Estufa, aposento recogido y abrigado al que se da calor artificialmente. 4. _pl. (Ant.)_ Burdel, lupanar. **Stew-pan,** la cazuela o cacerola donde se estofa la carne.

steward ['stjuːəd] [stiuad], _s._ 1. Administrador; el que administra o maneja una propiedad o los asuntos de otro. 2. Mayordomo de mesa o de colegio; a bordo, despensero, el que tiene a su cargo la despensa y los camarotes de los viajeros; senescal. **Steward of a farm,** _(Cuba)_ Mayoral.

Steward of a dinner, etc., comisionado, encargado de un convite, función, etc. **Steward's room,** despensa.

stewardess ['stjuːədɪs] [stiua-des], *sf.* 1. *(Mar.)* Camarera de a bordo. 2. *(Aer.)* Azafata, aeromoza.

stewardship ['stjuːədʒɪp] [stiuad-ship], *s.* Mayordomía, gobierno, administración.

sthenic ['sθɪnɪk] [szi-nik], *a.* 1. Que manifiesta energía o actividad, como una parte o un órgano. 2. Que tiene el poder de inspirar o animar.

stich [stɪtʃ] [stich], *s.* 1. Un versículo de la Biblia. 2. Verso, línea de poesía; se usa frecuentemente en composición; v. gr. *hemistich,* hemistiquio. 3. Hilera de árboles.

stick [stɪk] [stik], *s.* 1. Palo, palillo, pedazo de madera largo y delgado; vara, raja de leña. 2. Pieza de madera de construcción. 3. Bastón, vara que se lleva en la mano. 4. Ristra, serie de cosas dispuestas en sarta. 5. Estique, instrumento de madera que usan los escultores para modelar en barro. 6. Arco (para instrumento de cuerda). **Sticks,** *pl.* támaras o rozo, leña menuda de palitos, astillas, etc., para quemar; chabasca, ramitas delgadas. **Broomstick,** palo de escoba. **Round stick,** taco en el juego de billar. **Shooting-stick,** *(Impr.)* Atacador de imprenta. **Stick of furniture,** mueble. **Stick of sealing-wax,** barra de lacre. **Drum-sticks,** palillos de tambor o bolillos. **Chop-sticks,** palillos para comer. **Fan-sticks,** varillas de abanico. **To pick up sticks,** recoger la leña menuda o támaras. **Blow with a stick,** bastonazo, garrotazo. **To be in a clef stick,** estar en un aprieto, estar entre la espada y la pared. **A funny old stick,** un tipo raro, un tipo divertido.

stick, *s.* Herida o golpe penetrante con arma o instrumento punzante; estocada.

stick, *s.* 1. Estado de hallarse pegadas unas cosas a otras. 2. Acción de parar, parada; demora, dilación; vacilación, escrúpulo.

stick, *va. (pret.* y *pp.* STUCK), 1. Hacer penetrar, hacer entrar un instrumento de punta; hundir, pasar o atravesar con puñal u otros instrumento puntiagudo. 2. Hincar, introducir o clavar una cosa en otra; fijar alguna cosa con un instrumento puntiagudo; sujetar, fijar con alfileres, tachuelas, etc. 3. Matar o herir de una puñalada o cuchillada. 4. Picar, punzar; llenar de puntas; cubrir de algo que penetra. **A paper stuck with pins,** un papel cubierto o bien provisto de alfileres. 5. Pegar, juntar, unir con una substancia adhesiva. 6. *(Ger.)* Engañar. 7. Componer tipo. 8. *(Agr.)* Plantar jalones. -*vn.* 1. Cogerse, ser mantenido o apoyado para no hundirse. 2. Hacer comba hacia fuera, hacer barriga, sobresalir; se usa con *out, through* y *from.* 3. Pegarse, adherirse o unirse una cosa con otra tenazmente. 4. Pegarse, estar siempre con uno a su pesar o introducirse en una parte sin ser llamado. 5. Pegarse, insinuarse alguna cosa en el ánimo. 6. Pararse, detenerse; dudar, tener escrúpulo, fluctuar, vacilar. 7. Perseverar, ser constante en alguna cosa. 8. Atollarse, meterse en algún empeño o embarazo del que no se puede salir fácilmente. **To stick at it,** *(Fam.)* Persistir.

stick around, quedarse por ahí, esperar.

stick at, detenerse, sentir escrúpulo de; acusar la conciencia o tener cargo de conciencia. **He sticks at everything,** *(Fam.)* se ahoga en poca agua. **He sticks at nothing,** *(Fam.)* Nada le detiene o contiene, de nada tiene escrúpulo.

stick by, sostener, apoyar; pegarse a alguno. **To stick close,** mantenerse juntos; unirse fuertemente. **To stick fast,** pegarse, adherirse fuertemente. **To stick in the mire,** hundirse en el cieno.

stick down, pegar, colar.

stick in, clavar, picar, punzar, encajar; hundirse.

stick out, salir, sobresalir, hacer barriga; mantenerse firme, no ceder, resistir. **His bones stick out,** se le ven los huesos, está descarnado.

stick to, pegarse o adherirse tenazmente, aferrarse a una idea, opinión; atenerse a.

sticker ['stɪkər] [stik-ar], *s.* Etiqueta engomada.

stickiness ['stɪkɪnɪs] [sti-ki-nes], *s.* 1. Tenacidad, la dificultad en desasirse o despegarse una cosa de otra. 2. Viscosidad, glutinosidad (viscosity).

sticking-plaster ['stɪkɪŋˌplɑːstər] [sti-kin-plas-tar], *s.* Emplasto adhesivo, tafetán inglés o de Inglaterra.

stickle ['stɪkl] [sti-kel], *vn.* Altercar, disputar o porfiar acerca de menudencias; insistir o vacilar por razones de poca importancia.

stickleback ['stɪklbæk] [sti-kel-bak], *s.* Esino, pez pequeño de aguas dulces o saladas.

stickler ['stɪklər] [sti-klar], *s.* Un disputador porfiado o cansado; el que es partidario ardiente o defiende con ardor a su partido.

stickpin ['stɪkpɪn] [stik-pin], *s.* Alfiler de corbata. *(Méx.),* Fistol.

sticky ['stɪkɪ] [sti-ki], *a.* Pegajoso, viscoso, tenaz.

stiff [stɪf] [stif], *a.* 1. Tieso; duro, firme y sólido, que con dificultad se dobla o rompe (rigid). 2. Envarado, entorpecido, torpe, embotado, que funciona con dificultad o fricción. 3. Rígido, duro, inflexible; tenso, tendido (taut). 4. Espeso, viscoso, consistente (viscous). 5. Obstinado, terco (stubborn). 6. Afectado, poco natural, que carece de gracia. 7. Duro; hablando del estilo. 8. Fuerte, que tiene movimiento fuerte y regular. 9. Difícil, severo (difficult). 10. *(Com.)* Firme en los precios. 11. *(Mar.)* Que aguanta bien el viento; que se inclina poco cuando lleva mucho velamen. **To grow stiff,** estirarse, endurecerse. **Stiff breeze,** brisa fuerte. **A stiff paste,** una pasta espesa. **Stiff gale,** viento fuerte. **Stiff news,** noticias fundadas o dignas de creerse. **Stiff neck,** (a) afección reumática de los músculos del cuello; (b) tortícolis. *V. Wry neck.* **To be stiff in the legs,** tener las piernas entumecidas.

stiffen ['stɪfn] [sti-fen], *va.* 1. Atiesar, poner tieso o tirante; endurecer, dar firmeza; espesar. 2. Envarar o entorpecer los miembros. 3. Arreciar de frío. -*vn.* 1. Atiesarse o ponerse tiesa una cosa, endurecerse; enderezarse; espesarse. 2. Envarar o entorpecerse los miembros. 3. Obstinarse. *adv.* **To be worried stiff,** estar muy preocupado.

stiffen, *vt.* Endurecer, hacer más rígido; agarrotar, entumecer.

stiffener ['stɪfənər] [sti-fa-nar], *s.* Abultador, colchoncillo, cojinillo; atiesador; contrafuerte de zapato.

stiff-hearted ['stɪfˈhɑːtɪd] [stif-jar-tid], *a.* Obstinado, terco.

stiffly ['stɪflɪ] [sti-fli], *adv.* Tiesamente, obstinadamente, inflexiblemente.

stiff-necked ['stɪfˈnekt] [stif-nekt], *a.* Obstinado, terco, pertinaz, testarudo, cabezudo.

stiffness ['stɪfnɪs] [stif-nes], *s.* 1. Tesura, inflexibilidad; rigidez de lo que no se puede doblar; imposibilidad de moverse. 2. *(Med.)* Rigor, tensión que impide el movimiento. 3. Inflexibilidad, terquedad, obstinación; modales severos, altaneros. 4. Dureza de estilo. 5. Espesura, consistencia de una masa. **Stiffness of limbs,** envaramiento o entorpecimiento de los miembros.

stifle ['stɪfl] [sti-fel], *va.* 1. Sofocar, ahogar. 2. Apagar, extinguir, acabar, terminar, poner fin. 3. Suprimir, calar, ocultar. -*vn.* Ahogarse, morir por falta de respiración.

stigma ['stɪgmə] [stig-ma], *s.* 1. Borrón, mancha, nota de infamia; antiguamente, marca, señal que se hacía con un hierro candente. 2. Estigma, extremo superior del pistilo destinado a recibir el polen. 3. *(Anat. y Zool.)* Marco o poro; orificio de la tráquea en los insectos. 4. Estigma, llaga milagrosa (correspondiente a las cinco heridas de Jesucristo).

stigmatic [stɪgˈmætɪk] [stig-ma-tik], *a.* 1. Señalado con una marca; *(Ant. de infamia);* ignominioso; de aquí, deformado, desfigurado. 2. *(Bot.)* Estigmático, referente al estigma de una flor.

stigmatize ['stɪgmətaɪz] [stig-ma-tais], *va.* 1. Estimagtizar, señalar con una nota de infamia. 2. Marcar con estigmas, como los puntos que presenta la piel en el sarampión.

stile [staɪl] [stail], *s.* 1. Un portillo con escalones para pasar de un cercado a otro. 2. Gnomon, el estilo de hierro con que señalan las horas en los relojes de sol. 3. Estilo. *V.* STYLE. **Turn-stile,** un torno en forma de cruz que se pone en algunos sitios o cercados para pasar fácilmente.

stiletto [stɪˈletəʊ] [sti-le-tou], *s.* Verduguillo, un puñal o estoque pequeño con tres cortes. 2. Punzón, instrumento puntiagudo para agujerear.

still [stɪl] [stil], *va.* 1. Acallar, aplacar o sosegar el llanto; hacer callar, hacer cesar un ruido cualquiera. 2. Acallar, aquietar, aplacar, apaciguar. 3. Parar o detener el movimiento de alguna cosa. 4. *(Des.)* Destilar, alambicar.

still, *a.* 1. Inmóvil, que no puede moverse: fijo, que está sin movimiento (fixed); tranquilo, quedo (calm). 2. Silencioso, quieto, que guarda silencio, que no hace ruido: de aquí, suavizado, de sonido débil; apacible, sosegado (quiet). 3. Sin efervescencia; se dice de los vinos. 4. Muerto, inanimado. **Still water,** agua encharcada o tranquila. **Still wine,** vino no espumoso. **Still as the grave,** silencioso como la tumba. **The aire is still,** la atmósfera está tranquila. **To stand still,** detenerse, permanecer quedo, no moverse. **Still life,** naturaleza muerta (en una pintura). **Still-born,** aborto, que ha nacido muerto. *-s.* 1. Silencio, calma, tranquilidad, quietud, sosiego. 2. Alambique, vaso que sirve para destilar. *-adv.* 1. Todavía, aún, sin cesar, siempre, hasta ahora. 2. No obstante, sin embargo, a pesar de eso. 3. Más, además. **Still more,** todavía más, aún más. **Still better,** mejor aún. **I can still recall it,** todavía lo recuerdo.

still-burn [ˈstɪlbɜːn] [stil-bern], *va.* Quemar por destilación.

stiller [ˈstɪləʳ] [sti-laʳ], *s.* 1. Persona que apacigua, que calma. 2. *(Prov. Ingl.)* Disco que se coloca sobre un cubo lleno para impedir que el líquido salpique.

stilling [ˈstɪlɪŋ] [sti-lin], *s.* Poino, el codal que sustenta y sirve de apoyo a las cubas en la bodega.

stilly [ˈstɪlɪ] [sti-li], *a. (Poét.)* Tranquilo, silencioso; suave, de sonido débil. *-adv.* Silenciosamente, quietamente.

stillness [ˈstɪlnɪs] [stil-nes], *s.* Silencio, sosiego, calma quietud, tranquilidad.

stilt [stɪlt] [stilt], *s.* 1. Zanco, palo con horquilla o estribo en que se afirma el pie para andar. 2. Prisma o trípode de barro para sostener un artículo de alfarería en el horno. 3. *(Esco.)* Esteva del arado. 4. Zanco de manto, ave del orden de las zancudas, género Himantopus.

stilted [ˈstɪltɪs] [stil-tid], *a.* Subido en zancos, hinchado, pomposo, engreído.

stimulant [ˈstɪmjʊlənt] [sti-miu-lant], *a.* Estimulante, que estimula, que excita o es propio para excitar. *-s.* 1. Estimulante, lo que excita, lo que aguijonea. 2. Remedio estimulante, substancia que excita la acción orgánica del sistema humano; en plural, licores embriagantes.

stimulate [ˈstɪmjʊlaɪt] [sti-miu-leit], *va.* 1. Estimular, aguijonear, punzar, avivar. 2. *(Med.)* Estimular, avivar o acelerar la acción orgánica de las partes del cuerpo. *-vn.* 1. Servir como estímulo o aguijón. 2. Tomar estimulantes o licores embriagantes.

stimulating [ˈstɪmjʊleɪtɪŋ] [sti-miu-lei-tin], *a.* Estimulante; *(Med.)* Estimulador.

stimulation [ˌstɪmjʊˈleɪʃən] [sti-miu-lei-shon], *s.* 1. Estímulo, aguijón, incitamiento para obrar. 2. Estimulación, la acción y efecto de estimular.

stimulative [ˈstɪmjʊlətɪv] [sti-miu-la-tiv], *a.* Estimulante. *-s.* Estímulo; excitación.

stimulus [ˈstɪmjʊləs] [sti-miu-los], *s.* 1. Estímulo, aguijón; motivo, incentivo. 2. Estimulante, lo que determina una excitación en un nervio o músculo. 3. *(Bot.)* Dardo, aguijón.

sting [stɪŋ] [sting], *va. y vn. (pret. y pp.* STUNG) 1. Picar, pinchar, hacer una picadura, usar de un aguijón. 2. Causar o producir tormento la memoria de una cosa. 3. Atormentar, carcomer, remorder la conciencia. **To sting someone to do something,** incitar a uno a hacer algo, provocar. **My conscience stung me,** me remordió la conciencia.

sting, *s.* 1. Aguijón, la púa o punta aguda con que pican algunos insectos. 2. Punzada, picadura, picada. 3. Cualquier cosa que produce un dolor vivo o una punza; *(Bot.)* púa, filamento hueco y tieso que secreta un fluido picante, como el de las ortigas. 4. Remordimiento de conciencia. 5.

Aguijón, estímulo. **A sting of remorse,** una punzada de remordimiento. 6. *(E. U.)* Timo, tongo.

stingily [ˈstɪndʒɪlɪ] [stin-yi-li], *adv.* Avaramente, miserablemente, tacañamente.

stinginess [ˈstɪndʒɪnɪs] [stin-yi-nes], *s.* Tacañería, avaricia, miseria, ruindad.

stinging [ˈstɪŋɪŋ] [stin-guin], *s.* Picadura, punzada, punzadura.

stingless [ˈstɪŋlɪs] [stin-les], *s.* Que no tiene aguijón; sin púa.

stingy [ˈstɪndʒɪ] [stin-yi], *a.* 1. Mezquino, tacaño, ruin, avaro, miserable (mean). 2. Escaso, poco, limitado (few).

stink [stɪŋk] [stink], *van. (pret.* STANK o STUNK, *pp.* STUNK). Heder, oler mal, apestar.

stink, *s.* Hedor, hediondez.

stinkard [ˈstɪŋkəd] [stin-kard], *s.* La persona hedionda o muy puerca.

stinker [ˈstɪŋkəʳ] [stin-kaʳ], *s.* Cualquier cosa hedionda o que arroja de sí muy mal olor.

stinking [ˈstɪŋkɪŋ] [stin-kin], *a.* Hediondo.

stinkingly [ˈstɪŋkɪŋlɪ] [stin-kin-li], *adv.* Hediondamente, con hediondez; vilmente, cobardemente.

stinkingness [ˈstɪŋkɪŋnɪs] [stin-kin-nes], *s.* Hediondez.

stinkpot [ˈstɪŋkpɒt] [stink-pot], *s.* Olla llena de materiales hediondos; bomba asfixiante.

stinky [ˈstɪŋkɪ] [stin-ki], *a.* Apestoso, hediente, maloliente.

stint [stɪnt] [stint], *va.* 1. Limitar, restringir dentro de límites fijos; roporcionar o servir escasamente. 2. Señalar, repartir una tarea determinada. *-vn.* Ceñirse, ser económico o parsimonioso.

stin, *s.* 1. Cuota, porción fija o determinada, v. g. tarea de trabajo. 2. Límite, restricción. 3. Maubecha pequeña, tríngido, ave de las escolopácidas. Tringa.

stipe [staɪp] [staip], *s. (Bot.)* 1. Estipo, el tallo de las palmas y de las plantas que lleva fronde. 2. Estipo, el sustentáculo de cualquier órgano de las plantas y particularmente del sombrerete en los hongos.

stipend [ˈstaɪpend] [stai-pend], *s.* Estipendio, sueldo o salario pagado en épocas fijas como compensación de servicios prestados; en Escocia, sueldo de un clérigo.

stipendiary [staɪˈpendɪərɪ] [stint], *a.* Estipendiario. *-s.* Estipendiario, el que hace algún servicio por estipendio señalado.

stipitate [ˈstɪpɪteɪt] [sti-pi-teit], *a. (Bot.)* Estiposo, que tiene estipo, que está mantenido por un sustentáculo.

stipple [ˈstɪpl] [sti-pel], *va.* Picar, puntear, hacer puntitos, dibujando, pintando o grabando. *-s.* Picado, punteado.

stippling [ˈstɪplɪŋ] [sti-plin], *s.* Picado, acto o procedimiento de dibujar, de graban picando.

stipulate [ˈstɪpjʊleɪt] [sti-piu-leit], *va.* 1. Estipular, especificar las cláusulas o palabras de un convenio. 2. Mencionar expresmente; especificar, particularizar. *-vn.* Estipular, contratar mutuamente.

stipulate, *a.* Estipulífero, provisto de estípulas.

stipulation [ˌstɪpjʊˈleɪʃən] [sti-piu-lei-shon], *s.* 1. Estipulación, acción de estipular, calidad de estipualdo. 2. Estipulación, cláusula, condición, convenio enunciado en un contrato; convenio, contrato mutuo; pacto.

stipule [ˈstɪpjʊl] [sti-piul], *s.* 1. *(Bot.)* Estípula, apéndice foliáceo en la base del pecíolo de ciertas hojas. 2. *(Orn.)* Pluma reciente.

stir [stɜːʳ] [steʳ], *va.* 1. Cambiar de lugar las partes componentes de un todo, mover o menear una cosa, particularmente con un movimiento circularmente, como con una cuchara (move, change place). 2. Agitar, alterar, revolver, enturbiar, inquietar, irritar (shake). 3. Suscitar, animar, incitar; conmover, excitar los afectos y sentimientos. 4. Agitar, ventilar o controvertir una cuestión o materia de negocios o de ciencias. **To stir the fire,** atizar o avivar la lumbre. *-vn.* 1. Moverse o menearse, ponerse en movimiento. 2. Mudar de posición, moverse, cambiar de lugar. 3. Levantarse temprano. 4. *(Ant.)* Agitarse, bullir o no estarse quieto. **To stir up,** conmover, excitar, animar, aguijonear; poner en movimiento; despertar.

stir, *s.* 1. Movimiento, conmoción, actividad en alguna cosa. 2. Interés, público o general, excitación, conmoción. 3. Estruendo, alboroto.

stirrer ['stɜːrəʳ] [ste-reʳ], *s.* 1. Promovedor, movedor, promotor, motor; instigador, incitador. 2. Madrugador, el que madruga.

stirring ['stɜːrɪŋ] [ste-rin], *s.* 1. Movimiento. 2. El acto de levantarse por la mañana. *-a.* 1. Activo, acostumbrado a una vida activa. 2. Alentador, animador.

stirrup ['stɪrəp] [sti-rap], *s.* 1. Estribo, piezas en que apoya el pie el jinete. 2. *(Mar.)* Estribo. **Stirrups of the yards or of the horses,** *(Mar.)* estribos de guardamancebos de las vergas. **Stirrups of the yard-arms,** *(Mar.)* estribos de los pelones de las vergas. **Stirrups of the chain-plates,** *(Mar.)* estribos de las cadenas. **Stirrup-bearer,** tirante de estribo. **Stirrup-leather,** la correa de que cuelga el estribo.

stitch [stɪtʃ] [stich], *va.* 1. Coser, unir con aguja, seda, hilo, etc., dos pedazos de cualquier cosa. 2. Coser, unir, juntar. *-vn.* Coser o hacer bordados; coser, tener el oficio de sastre o costurera. **To stitch up,** remendar; recoser lo que estaba descosido. **To stitch down,** ribetear.

stitch, *s.* 1. Puntada, punto, el paso de la aguja por la tela que se va cosiendo. 2. Punto, cada una de las lazadas o nuditos de las medias, calcetas, etc. 3. Punzada, dolor punzante. 4. Caballón o surco que traza el arado. 5. Distancia, jornada, división o porción de un viaje. **Back-stitch,** punto atrás, pespunte. **Cross-stitch,** punto cruzado, punto de escarpí. **Chain-stitch,** punto de cadena. **Lock-stitch,** punto de cadeneta. **Lock-stitch o chain-stitch sewing-machines,** máquinas de coser punto de cadeneta o de cadena.

stitcher ['stɪtʃəʳ] [sti-chaʳ], *s.* 1. Cosedor, cosedora, ribeteadora, persona que cose. 2. En la encuadernación, máquina para coser los libros.

stitching ['stɪtʃɪŋ] [sti-chin], *s.* 1. Pespunte, hilera de puntos en una tela. 2. Punto atrás.

stithy ['stɪθɪ] [sti-zi], *s.* 1. Fragua. *V.* SMITHY. 2. Yunque o ayunque, bigornia.

stoat [stəʊt] [stout], *s.* Armiño.

stock [stɒk] [stok], *s.* 1. Tronco, la parte de los árboles y plantas desde el suelo hasta donde se divide en ramas. 2. Tronco, estirpe o cepa de una familia o linaje; estirpe, familia, linaje. 3. *(For.)* Línea directa de una familia. 4. Ganado en general; se llama comúnmente *live stock.* 5. *(Com.)* Capital comercial; valores, acciones, en plural, surtido de mercancías, mercancías almacenadas. 6. Acopio, provisión cuantiosa; fondo; abundancia, cantidad de primeras materias; enseres; muebles; efectos existentes. 7. Mango, manija; berbiquí de barrena; caja de fusil; aquella parte de un mecanismo que sirve para apoyar o mantener las piezas vivas. **Stock of a gun,** caja de escopeta. 8. *(Mar.)* Grada de construcción, astillero. **To be on the stocks,** estar en vías de construcción. **A ship on the stocks,** *(Mar.)* Navío en las gradas o en el astillero. **Stock-blocks,** *(Mar.)* polines de la grada. **Stock of an anchor,** *(Mar.)* Cepo de ancla. 9. Corbatín, especie de corbata. 10. Baceta o monte, los naipes que quedan después de haber dado. 11. Alelí. *V.* GILLYFLOWER. 12. Leño, el trozo del árbol después de cortado; de aquí, tronco, zoquete, estólido, un hombre tonto o insensible. 13. Stocks, cepo prisión, antiguo instrumento de castigo en el cual se sujetaban los pies o brazos del delincuente. 14. Colonia de abejas, abejar. **To lay in a stock,** hacer provisión, surtir sus almacenes; proveerse. **Stock in trade,** mercancías disponibles en almacén. **To take (account of) stock,** hacer inventario. **Live stock,** ganados. **Stock farmer,** ganadero. **Joint-stock company,** sociedad por acciones, sociedad anónima. **Railroad stocks,** acciones de ferrocarril. **Stock-yard,** corral para ganados, corral grande en que se encierra el ganado destinado al matadero o al transporte. **Stock-broker,** corredor de valores públicos. **Stock-dove,** *(Orn.)* paloma torcaz. **Stock-fish,** bacalao seco. **Stock-gilly flower,** *(Bot.)* Alelí doble. **Stock-jobber,** agiotista, el que negocia en los efectos o valores públicos a menudo de un modo irregular. **Stock-jobbing,** agiotaje de valores públicos.

stock, *va.* 1. Proveer, abastecer, surtir, llenar. 2. Acumular, juntar, acopiar. 3. Encepar, poner en un cepo.

stockade ['stɒkeɪd] [sto-keid], *va.* Empalizar, rodear de empalizadas. *-s.* 1. Empalizada, estacada, fila de estacas clavadas en tierra. 2. Construcción de pilotaje para proteger un muelle.

stockbroker ['stɒkˌbrəʊkəʳ] [stok-brou-kaʳ], *s.* Agente de bolsa.

stockbroking ['stɒkˌbrəʊkɪŋ] [stok-brou-kin], *s.* Correduría de bolsa.

stock company ['stɒkˌkʌmpənɪ] [stok-kam-pa-ni], *s.* *(Com.)* 1. Sociedad anónima. 2. *(Teat.)* Compañía teatral de repertorio.

stockholder ['stɒkˌhəʊldəʳ] [stok-joul-daʳ], *s.* Accionista.

stockiness ['stɒkɪnɪs] [sto-ki-nes], *sf.* Robustez.

stockinet ['stɒkɪnɪt] [sto-ki-nit], *s.* Elástica, tejido elástico propio para ropa interior.

stocking ['stɒkɪŋ] [sto-kin], *va.* Proveer de medias, poner las medias a uno. *-s.* Media, la vestidura de la pierna y del pie. **Silk stockings,** medias de seda. **Worsted stockings,** medias de lana o de estambre. **Thread stockings,** medias de hilo. **Knit stockings,** medias de punto. **Wove stokings,** medias de telar.

stocking-frame ['stɒkɪŋˈfreɪm] [sto-kin-freim], *s.* Telar de medias.

stocking-weaver ['stɒkɪŋˈwiːvəʳ] [sto-kin-uea-vaʳ], *s.* Tejedor de medias.

stokish ['stɒkɪʃ] [sto-kish], *a.* Estúpido, insensible, como un tronco, duro.

stock market ['stɒkˌmɑːkɪt] [stok-mar-kit], *s.* Bolsa de valores.

stockpile ['stɒkpaɪl] [stok-pail], *s.* Acumulación de materias primas y otros productos para hacer frente a escaseces.

stockpile, *va.* Acumular materias primas para hacer frente a escaseces.

stockroom ['stɒkrʊm] [stok-rum], *s.* Depósito de mercancías (en un almacén, oficina, etc.)

stocks ['stɒks] [stoks], *s. pl.* 1. Cepo, especie de prisión. 2. Valores públicos, acciones. 3. Gradas de construir buques. *V.* STOCK.

stock-still ['stɒkˈstɪl] [stok-stil], *a.* Inmóvil (como un poste).

stocky ['stɒkɪ] [sto-ki], *a.* Rechoncho.

stockyard ['stɒkjɑːd] [stok-yard], *s.* Corral de ganado.

stodgy ['stɒdʒɪ] [stod-yi], *a.* Regordete.

stoic ['stəʊɪk] [stoik], *s.* Estoico, el filósofo que seguía la escuela de Zenón, de aquí, persona indiferente al placer o al dolor; también, ascético severo.

stoical ['stəʊɪkəl] [stoi-kal], *a.* 1. Estoico, perteneciente a la secta o filosofía estoica. 2. Estoico, severo, firme, inflexible e imperturbable como un estoico.

stoically ['stəʊɪklɪ] [stoi-kli], *adv.* Estoicamente, de un modo inflexible e imperturbable.

stoicism ['stəʊɪsɪzəm] [stoui-si-sem], *s.* Estoicismo, la doctrina o secta de los estoicos.

stoke [stəʊk] [stouk], *va. y vn.* Atizar, mantener vivo el fuego en las máquinas de vapor.

stoker ['stəʊkəʳ] [stou-kaʳ], *s.* Fogonero, el que cuida del fuego.

stole ['stəʊl] [stoul], *s.* 1. Estola, vestidura para la celebración de oficios sagrados. 2. Estola, chal. **Fur stole,** estola de piel.

stole, stolen ['stəʊlən] [stou-len], *pret.* y *pp.* del verbo TO STEAL.

stolid ['stɒlɪd] [sto-lid], *a.* Estólido, impasible, estúpido.

stolidity [stɒ'lɪdɪtɪ] [sto-li-di-ti], *sf.* Impasibilidad; flema, terquedad.

stomach ['stʌmək] [sto-mak], *s.* 1. Estómago, la parte del cuerpo en que se hace la primera digestión de los alimentos. 2. Barriga, abdomen; uso común, pero inexacto. 3. Apetito, gana de comer; afición, inclinación.

stomach, *va.* Aceptar sin oposición; sufrir, aguantar.

stomachal ['stʌməkəl] [sta-ma-kal], *a.* Estomacal, perteneciente al estómago o que aprovecha al estómago; cordial.

stomacher ['stʌməkəᵊʳ] [sta-ma-kaʳ], *s.* Peto, prenda de vestir que se pone en el pecho.

stomaching ['stʌməkɪŋ] [sta-ma-kin], *s.* Resentimiento.

stomachless ['stʌməklɪs] [sta-mak-les], *a.* Sin estómago, desganado, sin gana o sin apetito.

stomatitis ['stʌmətaɪtɪs] [sta-ma-tai-tis], *s.* Estomatitis, inflamación de la boca.

stone [stəʊn] [stoun], *s.* 1. Piedra, un cuerpo natural, sólido y duro. 2. Roca, como material. 3. Trozo de piedra con forma propia para un uso especial; v. gr. piedra de molino, de amolar; piedra sepulcral. 4. Piedra preciosa. 5. Pida, cálculo, la materia dura que se engendra en el cuerpo humano, particularmente en los riñones y en la vejiga. 6. Hueso, cuesco, pepita de las frutas. 7. *(Ingl.)* Un peso de catorce libras. 8. *(Bajo)* Testículo. **Mill-stone,** muela o piedra de molino. **Flint-stone,** piedra de la escopeta, de lumbre o de pedernal. **Imposing-stone,** *(Impr.)* Piedra de imponer. **To leave no stone unturned,** no dejar piedra por mover, no economizar ningún esfuerzo, hacer todo lo posible. **Stone-breaker,** V. *Stone-crusher.* **Stone-coal,** carbón de piedra; carbón muy duro o antracita. **Stone-cold,** frío como la piedra, como el mármol. **Stone-color,** color de la piedra expuesta al aire; gris azulado. **Stone-crusher,** triturador o bocarte de piedra. **Stone-cutting,** labra de las piedras. **Stone-dead,** muerto como una piedra. **Stone-mason,** albañil. **Stone-parsley,** perejil perenne. **Stone-pine,** pino dulce del Mediterráneo. **Stone's cast, stone's throw,** tiro de piedra, distancia a que alcanza una piedra lanzada con la mano. **Stone Age,** Edad de Piedra. **Stone-blind,** enteramente ciego, física o mentalmente. **Stone-cutter,** picapedrero, cantero, el que labra las piedras. **Stone-fruit,** fruta de hueso. **Stone-hawk,** *(Orn.)* Halcón apedreado. **Stone-pit, stone-quarry,** cantera. *-a.* De piedra, hecho de piedra. **Stone me!,** ¡caramba!, ¡caray!

stone, *va.* 1. Apedrear; asaltar o matar a pedradas. 2. Quitar los cuescos o huesos a las frutas. 3. Revestir de piedras, trabajar en albañilería.

stonebreak ['stəʊnˈbreɪk] [stoun-breik], *s. (Bot.)* Quebrantapiedras, saxífraga.

stone-deaf ['stəʊnˈdef] [stoun-def], *a.* Sordo como una tapia.

stoner ['stəʊnəʳ] [stou-naʳ], *s.* Apedreador; despepitador de frutas.

stoneware ['stəʊnwɛəʳ] [stoun-ueaʳ], *s.* Cacharro de barro.

stonewashed ['stəʊnˌwɒʃt] [stoun-uosht], *a.* Lavado a piedra (jeans).

stonework ['stəʊnwɜːk] [stoun-uek], *s.* Obra hecha de piedra o cantería.

stonily ['stəʊnɪlɪ] [stou-ni-li], *adv.* Fríamente, glacialmente.

stony ['stəʊnɪ] [stou-ni], *a.* 1. Pedregoso, lleno de piedras. 2. *(Ant. o poét.)* De piedra, hecho de piedra; pétreo. 3. Duro, inflexible, inexorable. 4. Petrificante, que transforma en piedra.

stood [stʊd] [stud], *pret. y pp.* del verbo STAND.

stooge [stuːdʒ] [studch], *s.* 1. *(Teat.)* El que ayuda subrepticiamente a un actor. *(Mex.)* Palero. 2. El que ejecuta tareas serviles para otra persona. *-vi.* **Stooge about/around,** vagabundear, estar sin hacer nada.

stool [stuːl] [stul], *s.* 1. Banquillo sin respaldo; taburete, escabel. 2. Tarimilla, banqueta. V. FOOTSTOOL. 3. Sillico, silleta: y de aquí, cámara, excremento, evacuación de vientre: (comúnmente en plural). 4. Planta madre; vástago acodado. 5. Señuelo o añagaza (para atraer las aves). **Stool-pigeon,** 1. cimbel, cimillo. 2. persona empleada para embaucar a otras. **Close-stool, night-stool,** sillico para excrementos. **To go to stool,** hacer del cuerpo, ir a la secreta. **Foot-stool,** escabel, tarimilla para poner los pies.

stoop [stuːp] [stup], *vn.* 1. Encorvarse, combarse, inclinarse hacia adelante (bend). 2. Encorvarse o bajarse hasta el suelo. 3. Bajarse, someterse, sujetarse (submit). 4. Bajarse, humillarse, abatirse (humiliate); emplearse en cosas menos honoríficas que las pertenecientes a alguno por su clase o estado. 5. Ceder, rendirse (surrender, yield). 6. Condescender, acomodarse al gusto y voluntad de otro. 7. Lanzarse, arrojarse como el halcón se arroja sobre la presa. *-va.* Someter o sujetar; hacer bajar; bajar la cabeza. **To stoop to,** rebajarse a.

stoop 1, *s.* 1. Inclinación hacia adelante y abajo; también, inclinación habitual de los hombros hacia adelante. 2. Descenso, caída de alguna dignidad o estado a otro inferior. 3. Caimiento, declinación, abatimiento. 4. Caída del halcón sobre la presa.

stoop 2, *s.* *(E.U.)* Gradería, pórtico exterior, meseta descubierta a la entrada de una casa.

stoope 3, *s.* 1. Copa o frasco para beber. 2. Pila de agua bendita.

stoopingly ['stuːpɪŋ] [stu-pin-li], *adv.* Hacia abajo, con inclinación hacia abajo.

stop [stɒp] [stop], *va.* 1. Detener, parar, impedir que una cosa siga el movimiento que lleva; cortar, interceptar (cut off). 2. Detener, suspender, diferir, dilatar la ejecución de una cosa; reprimir, refrenar de antemano. 3. Tapar, cerrar o cubrir algún agujero o abertura (close). 4. Retener, v. g. los salarios o jornales. **To stop a leak,** tapar, cegar una vía de agua. **To stop the progress of vice,** detener los progresos del vicio. **To stop the way,** obstruir el camino, cerrar el paso. *-vn.* 1. Parar o pararse, cesar el movimiento o la acción, detenerse, hacer alto. 2. Llegar al fin, cesar (end). 3. *(Fam.)* Quedarse algún tiempo, alojarse o morar en algún paraje o casa. 4. *(Mús.)* Cambiar el tono o diapasón por medio de un agujero o un traste. **To stop up,** tapar, cerrar (a hole, a road). **To stop one's career,** cortarle a uno los pasos. **To stop one's mouth,** tapar la boca, no dejar hablar. **Stop a moment,** deténgase usted un instante. **My watch has stopped,** mi reloj se ha parado. **To stop short,** quedarse cortado. **To stop payment,** *(Com.)* suspender los pagos; dar punto a los negocios. **Stop it!,** ¡ya vale!, ¡basta ya! **Not to stop at,** no pararse en, no contentarse con, no mirar en. **To stop away,** ausentarse. **To stop by,** pararse, detenerse por un corto espacio de tiempo. **To stop in,** quedarse en casa. **To stop over,** pasar la noche, pernoctar. **To stop up,** tapar, cegar, cerrar. **To stop oneself,** abstenerse.

stop, *s.* 1. Parada, la acción de parar o detenerse; pausa, alto (pause). 2. Interrupción; suspensión, detención. 3. Dilación, retardación, retardo. 4. Oposición, obstáculo, impedimento, embarazo (impediment). 5. Cesación; represión. 6. *(Mús.)* Palanca, tecla o mango para cambiar el diapasón de un instrumento de música; traste de guitarra; registro de órgano. 7. Punto, signo de puntuación. **Full stop,** punto final. 8. *(Mec.)* Retén, fiador, seguro. **To put a stop to,** suspender, poner término a, hacer cesar. **To make a stop,** hacer alto, detenerse; hacer una pausa. **To come to a dead stop,** cortarse, pararse repentinamente. **A 15 min. stop,** un descanso de 15 min. **Stop-gap,** lo que cierra un agujero; *(Mar.)* abarrote. Se usa también como adjetivo. **To make a stop in Madrid,** hacer escala en Madrid. **To bet a stop,** quedar paralizado. **A stop of a few weeks,** una estancia de unas pocas semanas. **To pull out all the stops,** desplegar todos los recursos *(Fig.)*

stopcock ['stɒpkɒk] [stop-kok], *s.* 1. Llave de fuente. 2. Canilla de tonel: espita.

stop light ['stɒplaɪt] [stop-lait], *s.* Señal luminosa de parada.

stopover ['stɒpəʊvəʳ] [stop-ou-vaʳ], *s.* Escala, parada intermediaria en el camino.

stoppage ['stɒpɪdʒ] [sto-pich], *s.* 1. Obstrucción, cesación de movimiento, detención, embarazo, impedimento. 2. Retención (sobre los sueldos). **Stoppage in transit,** *(For.)* embargo hecho por el vendedor de las mercancías durante su transporte a manos del comprador, en caso de insolvencia de éste.

stopper ['stɒpəʳ] [sto-paʳ], *va.* Entaponar, tapar con un tapón; *(Mar.)* bozar, amarrar con bozas. *-s.* 1. Persona o cosa que tapa, que cierra; tarugo, tapón; *(Mar.)* bozas, pedazos cortos de cabo grueso que sirven para suspender cualquier cuerpo pesado o para tener un cable. 2. Persona o cosa que detiene.

Anchor-stopper, *(Mar.)* capón. **Stopper-bolts,** *(Mar.)* argollas de boza.

stopping ['stɒpɪŋ] [sto-pin], *s.* Parada; empaste (tooth).

stopple ['stɒpl] [sto-pel], *va.* Entaponar, atarugar, o cerrar con tapón. -*s.* Tapón.

stop watch ['stɒpwɒtʃ] [stop-uoch], *s.* Cronómetro, reloj cuya marcha se inicia y detiene a voluntad. Se utiliza en deportes.

storage ['stɔːrɪdʒ] [sto-rich], *s.* 1. Almacenaje, acción y efecto de almacenar, de guardar en almacén. 2. Espacio para almacenar las mercancías. 3. Almacenaje, lo que se paga por guardar en un almacén. **Storage battery,** acumulador, batería de acumuladores.

store [stɔːʳ] [stoʳ], *s.* 1. Copia, abundancia, gran cantidad, acopio, provisión (provision, supply). 2. *pl.* Pertrechos, equipos; víveres, provisiones; municiones, bastimentos. 3. Almacén, depósito. 4. En los Estados Unidos y en algunas colonias inglesas, tienda, almacén. V. SHOP. **Store of victuals,** provisiones de boca. **Stores for an army,** municiones, pertrechos o provisiones de guerra. -*a.* Almacenado, guardado en almacén. **What is in store for someone,** lo que le espera a uno. **To lay in a store of,** hacer acopio de.

store, *va.* 1. Surtir, proveer, abastecer; municionar, pertrechar. **To store a ship,** *(Mar.)* Abastecer un buque. 2. Atesorar, guardar, acumular, acopiar; tener en reserva. 3. Almacenar, poner o guardar en almacén. **To store away,** poner en reserva. **To store up,** acumular.

storer ['stɔːrəʳ] [sto-raʳ], *s.* El que atesora, acumula, acopia o guarda.

storehouse ['stɔːhaʊs] [stor-jaus], *s.* Almacén.

storekeeper ['stɔːˌkiːpəʳ] [stor-ki-paʳ], *s.* 1. Guardaalmacén; jefe de depósito; tendero, comerciante. 2. *(Mar.)* Pañolero.

storeroom ['stɔːrʊm] [stor-rum], *s. (Mar.)* Despensa; pañol. **Boatswain's store-room,** *(Mar.)* pañol de proa.

storied ['stɔːrɪd] [sto-rid], *a.* 1. Historiado, que tiene una historia notable. 2. Historiado, adornado con cuadros históricos. 3. Referido por la historia. 4. Que tiene pisos.

stork [stɔːrk] [stork], *s. (Orn.)* Cigüeña.

storm [stɔːm] [storm], *s.* 1. Tempestad, tormenta, borrasca; vendaval; conmoción de la atmósfera, por lo regular con lluvia, etc. **A thunder-storm,** tronada. **A rain and wind storm,** turbonada. **Snow-storm,** tormenta de nieve, nevasca. 2. Tormenta, adversidad, calamidad, desgracia o infelicidad en el estado de una persona. 3. Asalto, el ataque para apoderarse a viva fuerza de una plaza o puesto. 4. Conmoción, tumulto, alboroto. 5. Acometimiento tumultuoso, lluvia (particularmente de proyectiles). **To raise, to stir up a storm,** levantar una tempestad, promover desórdenes. **To take by storm,** tomar por asalto. **Storm-beaten, storm-beat, storm-tossed,** azotado, combatido por la tempestad. **Storm-petrel o stormy petrels.** V. PETREL. **Storm-sail,** tallavientos, vela pequeña de trinquete que se usa en las borrascas.

storm, *va.* Asaltar, tomar por asalto, atacar a viva fuerza. -*vn.* 1. *(Impersonal)* Tempestar, haber tempestad, haber tormenta. **It stormed yesterday,** ayer hubo tempestad. 2. Levantarse una borrasca o tempestad. 3. Reventar o estallar de cólera, prorrumpir en injurias, denuestos o insultos.

stormbird ['stɔːmbɜːd] [storm-berd], *s.* Procelaria, ave que anuncia borrasca en el mar.

storm door ['stɔːmdɔːʳ] [storm-doʳ], *s.* Contrapuerta, doble puerta (para proteger contra el viento y el frío).

storminess ['stɔːmɪnɪs] [stor-mi-nes], *s.* Estado borrascoso, tempestuoso.

stormwater ['stɔːmwɔːtəʳ] [storm-uo-taʳ], *s.* Agua de lluvia.

storm window ['stɔːmˌwɪndəʊ] [storm-uin-dou], *s.* Contraventana, doble ventana (protection).

stormy ['stɔːmɪ] [stor-mi], *a.* 1. Tempestuoso, borrascoso. 2. Violento, turbulento.

story ['stɔːrɪ] [sto-ri], *s.* 1. Historia, relación de las cosas pasadas. 2. Cuento, fábula, conseja (tale); historieta, noveleta. *(Fam.)* Cuento de viejas, hablilla. 3. Enredo, trama de una obra literaria o dramática. 4. *(Fam.)* Mentira, fábula

(lie); eufemismo usado generalmente por los niños o para con los niños. 5. Anécdota. 6. Alto, cada uno de los pisos o suelos de una casa (floor). **A house three stories high,** casa de tres altos o de tres pisos. **As the story goes,** según se dice, según cuenta la historia. **A true story,** una historia o anécdota verdadera. **Fairy story,** cuento de hadas.

story, *va.* 1. Historiar, narrar (tell). 2. Colocar las cosas poniéndolas ordenadamente unas debajo de otras.

story-teller ['stɔːrɪˌtelaʳ] [sto-ri-te-laʳ], *s.* Cuentista, chismeador, chismoso; embustero, el que dice con frecuencia mentiras.

stout [staʊt] [staut], *a.* 1. Fornido, robusto, corpulento; fuerte, vigoroso, firme. 2. Resuelto, intrépido, animoso. 3. Terco, inflexible. -*s.* Cerveza fuerte.

stoutly ['staʊtlɪ] [staut-li], *adv.* Vigorosamente, valientemente; con resolución.

stoutness ['staʊtnɪs] [staut-nes], *s.* 1. Valor, ánimo, fuerza. 2. Intrepidez, arrojo. 3. Terquedad, obstinación; aspereza.

stove [stəʊv] [stouv], *s.* 1. Estufa (heating); estufa de cocina (cooking); hornillo para poner fuego. 2. Estufa para plantas. 4. Horno cerámico. **Foot-stove,** rejuela.

stove, *pret.* y *pp.* de TO STAVE.

stow [stəʊ] [stou], *va.* 1. Ordenar, colocar con orden (order); llenar de una manera compacta o metódica; hacinar. 2. *(Mar.)* Ocultar (hide); también, alojarse. **To stow in bulk,** *(Mar.)* Arrumar a bulto. **Stow away,** esconder.

stowage ['stəʊɪdʒ] [stouich], *s.* 1. Arreglo, colocación en su sitio; el estado de la cosa que se halla almacenada o guardada. 2. Sitio, espacio donde se guardan o almacenan cosas (store). 3. El dinero que se paga por el almacenaje. 4. *(Mar.)* Estiba; arrumaje. **To shift the stowage,** *(Mar.)* Mudar la estiba.

stowaway ['stəʊəweɪ] [stoua-uei], *s.* Polizón, el que se oculta en un buque o tren de ferrocarril para obtener pasaje gratis.

stower ['stəʊəʳ] [stouaʳ], *s.* Estibador.

strabismus [strəˈbɪzməs] [stra-bis-mos], *s. (Med.)* Estrabismo, defecto visual de los bizcos.

straddle ['strædl] [stra-del], *vn.* Estar en pie o andar esparrancado o muy abierto de piernas; ponerse a horcajadas. -*s.* 1. Acción de ponerse a horcajadas. 2. El espacio que separa las piernas del que se pone a horcajadas.

straggle ['strægl] [stra-guel], *vn.* 1. Extraviarse, descaminarse o andar descaminado del cuerpo principal o de sus compañeros. 2. Rodar, andorrear, corretear, ir de una parte a otra. 3. Extenderse más de lo ordinario las ramas de algún árbol o arbusto. 4. Estar disperso, hallarse a intervalos irregulares. **The village straggles on for kilometres,** el pueblo se extiende varios kilómetros. **Straggling soldier,** soldado rezagado. **Straggling branches,** ramas dispersas, apartadas. **Straggle away/off,** dispersarse.

straggler ['stræglaʳ] [stra-glaʳ], *s.* 1. Rezagado, el que se queda atrás. 2. Vagamundo, tunante. 3. La rama que sale más que las otras. 4. Objeto aislado o desviado.

straight [streɪt] [streit], *a.* 1. Derecho, recto; que no es rizado ni pasudo; sin inclinación ni torcedura. **As straight as a die,** derecho como una vela. 2. Justo, equitativo; correcto, exacto. 3. Directo, recto, sin rodeos, libre de estorbos. **Straight timbers,** palos derechos. -*adv.* 1. Directamente, en derechura, en línea recta. 2. Luego, al punto, inmediatamente. **She's straight,** es de fiar. **To make straight,** enderezar o poner derecha una cosa. **To make straight again,** volver a enderezar lo que se había torcido. **Straight line,** línea recta. **Straight razor,** navaja de barbero *(E.U.).* **The child went straight to his room,** el niño fue derecho a su habitación. **Straight ahead/on,** todo recto, todo seguido. **Let's get this straight,** pongamos las cosas claras. **Straight away,** inmediatamente, en el acto, en seguida. **Straight (poker),** escalera (poker).

straightaway ['streɪtəˈweɪ] [streit-a-uei], *adv.* Adelante, en línea recta. -*s.* Curso directo.

straightedge ['streɪtedʒ] [streit-edch], *s.* Regla o barra de metal o madera para trazar líneas rectas.

straighten ['streɪtn] [strei-ten], *va.* 1. Enderezar, poner derecho. 2. Sacar del desorden, arreglar; se usa a menudo con *up.*

straightener ['streɪtnər] [streit-naʳ], *s.* El que pone una cosa en el estado que debe tener.

straightforward [ˌstreɪtˈfɔːwəd] [streit-for-uard], *a.* Que no desvía, que anda derecho; de aquí, honrado, de corazón recto, sincero. *-adv.* Directamente adelante. Se escribe también *straightforwards.*

straightly ['streɪtlɪ] [streit-li], *adv.* 1. En línea recta, directamente. 2. Con mucha tensión.

straightness ['streɪtnɪs] [streit-nes], *s.* Rectitud, derechura; tensión.

strain [streɪn] [strein], *va.* 1. Extender con esfuerzo; estirar, ensanchar o alargar una cosa con violencia o más de lo que es debido (stretch strongly). 2. Llevar al extremo o más allá de lo que es debido y razonable. 3. *(Mec.)* Forzar, deformar permanentemente; obligar demasiado; torcer, retorcer. 4. Constreñir, incomodar, molestar, inquietar. 5. Apretar a uno contra sí abrazándole. 6. Colar, pasar por manga, cedazo, etc., algún líquido; se usa frecuentemente con *out. -vn.* 1. Esforzarse, hacer grandes esfuerzos. 2. Filtrarse, colarse. **To strain the voice,** forzar la voz o levantarla más de lo que se debe. **To strain close,** comprimir. **Do not strain yourself,** no se canse usted, no se violente usted **To strain a point,** hacer un esfuerzo. **To strain milk,** colar la leche. **The ship is strained.** *(Mar.)* Se han levantado o largado las costuras.

strain, *s.* 1. Tensión, estiramiento, estirón; esfuerzo (effort). 2. Lesión o daño que se sufre a consecuencia de un esfuerzo excesivo; contorsión, retorcimiento, torcedura, esguince. V. SPRAIN. 3. Estilo, tono, modo de hablar o de pensar. 4. *(Mús.)* Aire, melodía (melody); acorde, acentos. 5. Parte distintiva de un poema, canto; composición en verso. 6. Estirpe, descendencia, raza, linaje (race); clase. 7. Genio o disposición heredada. **Strain of madness,** vena de locura. **Melodious strains,** acordes melodiosos. **The strains of a waltz,** los compases de un vals. **Too high a strain,** un tono demasiado alto. **A strain of buff-coloured pansies,** una clase de pensamientos color de ante. **The strain on a rope,** la tensión de una cuerda. **To put a great strain on someone,** someter a alguien a un gran esfuerzo.

strainer ['streɪnər] [strei-naʳ], *s.* Colador, coladera, coladero, pasador.

strait [streɪt] [streit], *a.* 1. Estrecho, angosto (narrow). 2. Estrecho e íntimo, hablando de la amistad o del parentesco. 3. Estrecho, rígido, austero, exacto (exact). 4. Estrecho, escaso, miserable. 5. *(Des.)* Recto, derecho. *-s.* 1. Estrecho, el brazo angosto de mar. 2. Garganta de una montaña; desfiladero, angostura o paso estrecho. 3. Estrecho, aprieto, peñigro, riesgo. **Strait-jacket, strait-waistcoat,** camisa de fuerza.

straiten ['streɪtn] [strei-ten], *va.* 1. Acortar, ceñir, limitar; angostar, cercenar. 2. Estrechar, reducir a menos espacio; disminuir. 3. Estrechar, apretar, reducir a estrechez o aprieto; incomodar.

strait-jacket ['streɪtˌdʒækɪt] [streit-ya-kit], *s.* Camisa de fuerza.

strait-laced ['streɪnˈleɪst] [streit-leist], *a.* 1. Metido en pensa, apretado, muy comprimido. 2. Estricto, estrecho, demasiado riguroso. 3. Santurrón.

straitly ['streɪtlɪ] [streit-li], *adv.* 1. Estrechamente; estrictamente, rigurosamente. 2. Íntimamente, con intimidad.

straitness ['streɪtnɪs] [streit-nes], *s.* 1. Estrechez, angostura, corta extensión de lugar o tiempo. 2. Estrechez, aprieto, lance apretado. 3. Estrechez, escasez notable, penuria, falta de lo necesario. 4. Rigor, severidad, austeridad.

strake [streɪk] [streik], *s. (Mar.)* Traca o hilada, costura de tablas de popa a proa. **To heel a strake,** *(Mar.)* Tumbarse de una traca; hablando de la embarcación.

strand [strænd] [strand], *va. y vn.* Encallar; echarse sobre la costa; en sentido figurado, quedarse desamparado. *-s.* Costa, marina, playa del mar; rara vez, ribera de un río; arenal a la orilla de un río.

strand, *va.* 1. Romper uno de los cabos de una cuerda. 2. Torcer, retorcer los cabos de un cordel. *-s.* 1. Cabo, uno de los hilos de que se compone una cuerda. 2. Hebra, fibra, filamento. **Heart-strand,** corazón de un cabo.

strange [streɪndʒ] [streinch], *a.* 1. Extraño, singular, raro, sorprendente, extraordinario, singularmente bueno o malo. 2. Extraño, que no es de la misma casa o familia, que pertenece a otra parte; de una clase o carácter diferente; desconocido. 3. Forastero, el que no es del lugar donde está. 4. Extranjero, el que es o viene de país extraño. 5. De modales hurraños, reservado, poco tratable. **A strange face,** cara desconocida. *-inter.* ¡Cosa rara! ¡Cáspita! **How strange!,** ¡qué raro! **To make strange, to make oneself strange,** (a) mostrar o afectar asombro, sorpresa o ignorancia; con *of.* (b) pretender ser extranjero. **I felt strange at first,** me sentí incómodo al principio. **Strange woman,** en la Biblia, ramera.

strangely ['streɪndʒlɪ] [streinch-li], *adv.* 1. Extrañamente, singularmente, extraordinariamente. 2. Como los extranjeros; con relación a extranjeros.

strangeness ['streɪndʒnɪs] [streinch-nes], *s.* 1. Extranjería, la condición o calidad de ser uno extranjero o de otro dominio o país. 2. Extrañeza, reserva, alejamiento, esquivez. 3. Maravilla. 4. Extravagancia o desarreglo en el porte o conducta.

stranger ['streɪndʒər] [strein-chaʳ], *s.* 1. Extranjero, el extraño o el que no pertenece a la casa, familia, corporación, etc., de que se trata, desconocido. 2. Extranjero, el que es de otra nación. 3. El que no conoce o no sabe alguna cosa especificada; con *to.* **A child, who is still a stranger to the world,** un hijo que todavía no conoce el mundo. **He is a stranger to me,** me es desconocido. **You are a great stranger here,** se vende usted muy caro, no se le ve a usted. **You're quite a stranger!,** ¡apenas te dejas ver!

strangle ['stræŋgl] [stran-guel], *va.* 1. Estrangular. 2. Ahogar, sofocar. 3. Reprimir, suprimir. *-vn.* Padecer, estrangulación, morir estrangulado, estrangularse.

stranglehold ['stræŋglhəʊld] [stran-guel-jould], *s.* 1. (Fighting) Llave con que se semiasfixia al adversario. 2. Lo que priva de libertad de movimiento o expresión.

strangler ['stræŋglər] [stran-glaʳ], *s.* 1. El que ahoga o da garrote. 2. El que extingue o sofoca alguna cosa.

strangulate ['stræŋgjʊleɪt] [stran-guiu-leit], *va.* Estrangular.

strangulated ['stræŋgjʊleɪtɪd] [stran-guiu-lei-tid], *a. part.* 1. *(Med.)* Estrangulado, estrechado de tal manera que se halla suspendida la circulación. 2. *(Bot. y Zool.)* Estrechado a intervalos, como por medio de vendas o cuerdas.

strangulation [ˌstræŋgjʊˈleɪʃən] [stran-guiu-lei-shon], *s.* 1. Estrangulación, acción y efecto de estrangular; ahogamiento, la acción y efecto de ahogar o de dar garrote. 2. *(Med.)* Estrangulación, toda constricción ejercida sobre una parte de manera que suspenda la circulación.

strap [stræp] [strap], *s.* 1. Correa, tira de cuero larga, estrecha y flexible; una tira de paño. 2. Cuero, asentador de navajas. V. STROP. 3. Capona, charretera mocha; tirante o trabilla de pantalón. 4. *(Mar.)* Gaza, cabo con que se guarnecen los motones por la parte exterior de su circunferencia. 5. Oreja de zapato; tirante de bota. 6. Correones; precinta, trabilla.

strapping ['stræpɪŋ] [stra-pin], *a. (Fam.)* Abultado. **Strapping woman,** mujerona.

strata ['strætə] [stra-ta], *s. pl.* de STRATUM.

stratagem ['strætɪdʒəm] [stra-ti-yem], *s.* 1. Estratagema, ardid de guerra. 2. Estratagema, astucia, fingimiento o engaño artificioso.

strategic ['strətɪdʒɪk] [stra-ti-yik], *a.* Estratégico.

strategist ['strətɪdʒɪst] [stra-ti-yist], *s.* Estratégico, persona versada en el arte de la estrategia.

strategy ['strætɪdʒɪ] [stra-ti-yi], *s.* 1. Estrategia, el arte de dirigir las operaciones militares para conseguir la victoria. 2. El empleo de astucia y estratagemas (business, politics).

stratify ['strætɪfaɪ] [stra-ti-fai], *va.* Estratificar, colocar por capas o lechos.

stratosphere ['strætəʊsfɪər] [stra-tous-fiaʳ], *s.* Estratosfera.

stratum ['strɑ:təm] [stra-tom], *s.* Estrato, lecho o capa de cualquier cosa que está tendida naturalmente sobre otra. 1. Estrato, capa de roca; 2. *(Anat. y Zool.)* Capa de tejido.

stratus ['streɪtəs] [strei-tos], *s.* Nube que se presenta en forma de faja, a poca altura sobre el horizonte.

straw [strɔ:] [stro], *s.* 1. Paja. 2. Un comino, un bledo, una monada o fruslería. **I don't care a straw,** no me importa un pito. **Stack of straw,** pajar. **To break a straw,** reñir. *-a.* 1. Hecho o relleno de paja. 2. De ningún valor, falso, ficticio. **Straw bail,** caución o fianza simuladas. **Straw bond,** bono o caución ficticios. **Straw color,** color de paja, amarillo claro. **Straw-bed,** jergón de paja. **Straw-built,** pajizo, hecho de paja. **Straw-colored,** pajizo claro, de color de paja; pajado. **Straw-hat,** sombrero de paja. **Straw-worm,** gorgojo.

strawberry ['strɔ:bərɪ] [stro-be-ri], *s.* 1. *(Bot.)* Fresa, la mata que produce la fresa. 2. Fresa, la fruta producida por la planta de este nombre.

strawberry-tree ['strɔ:bərɪtri:] [stro-be-ri-tri], *s. (Bot.)* Madroño, árbol de las ericáceas.

stray [streɪ] [strei], *vn.* 1. Descarriarse, extraviarse, andar descarriado (to lose one's way); perder el camino, andar vagando sin saber el camino. 2. Errar, faltar a la justicia y equidad; desviarse del deber. **They had strayed 5 km from the road,** se habían desviado 5 km. del camino.

stray, *s.* 1. Descarriamiento, descarrío, la acción de descarriar o descarriarse. 2. Una persona o animal descarriado o perdido. **In a few stray cases,** en casos aislados.

streak [stri:k] [strik], *s.* 1. Raya, lista, línea de color distinto del que tiene el fondo de una cosa; reguero; rayo de luz. 2. Vena, rasgo de ingenio: traza, pizca; también antojo, capricho. 3. Raspadura, color del polvo fino de un mineral cuando está limitado. 4. *(Mar.)* Costura de tablas, traca, hilada. V. STRAKE.

streak, *va.* Rayar, hacer líneas de varios colores; barajar o entreverar colores.

streaky ['stri:kɪ] [stri-ki], *a.* Rayado, alistado, veteado, abigarrado; bordado.

stream [stri:m] [strim], *s.* 1. Corriente, flujo o curso del agua u otro líquido que corre. 2. Arroyo, río, torrente (river). 3. Flujo, movimiento de lo que sale o entra sin intermisión, v. g. de la gente; chorro (of liquid, gas, light). 4. Corriente, el curso que llevan algunas cosas. *(Fig.)* Fuente. **Stream of words,** flujo de palabras. **Stream-anchor,** anclote, ancla de espía. **An unbroken stream of cars,** una riada de coches, una gran fila de coches. **A small stream,** arroyuelo. **In the stream,** en franquicia. **In one continuous stream,** ininterrumpidamente. **Down stream, up stream,** agua abajo, agua arriba. **Against the stream,** contra la corriente. **Stream tin,** estaño de aluvión, en grano.

stream, *va. y vn.* 1. Correr, manar o fluir los líquidos. 2. Manar, brotar; salir en abundancia y a modo de un torrente. 3. Arrojar o derramar alguna cosa con abundancia y sin interrupción. 4. Lavar, v. g. los minerales, en agua corriente. 5. Hacer ondear; flotar, extenderse ondeando, como una bandera. 6. Moverse llevando tras sí un rastro de luz, como un meteoro. **To stream the buoy,** *(Mar.)* Echar la boya al agua.

streamer ['stri:mər] [stri-maʳ], *s.* Flámula, gallardete, banderola; faja de luz en una aurora boreal; bandera o cinta pendiente.

streamlet ['stri:mlet] [strim-let], *s.* Arroyuelo, arroyo pequeño; hilo de agua.

streamline ['stri:mlaɪn] [strim-lain], *va.* Dar líneas aerodinámicas, dar formas que permitan flujo continuo.

streamlined ['stri:mlaɪnd] [strim-laind], *a.* 1. Aerodinámico, modernizado. 2. Adelgazado.

streamy ['stri:mɪ] [stri-mi], *a.* 1. Que abunda en agua corriente, surcado de arroyos; que mana a chorros. 2. Parecido a rayos de luz o que los echa.

street [stri:t] [strit], *s.* Calle, camino público en una población, y el espacio que queda entre las dos aceras formadas por las casas. **By-street,** calle apartada, callejuela. **Cross street,** calle traviesa. **Main street,** calle mayor,

principal. **Street car,** carro urbano, coche de tranvía. **Street railway,** tranvía, ferrocarril urbano. **Street-walker,** mujer pública o prostituta.

strength [streŋθ] [strenz], *s.* 1. Fuerza, vigor, robustez (force). 2. Fuerza, virtud, eficacia (effectiveness); potencia motriz; potencia intelectual o moral, poder en general, facultad de obrar o sufrir (power, faculty); validez, fuerza legal; fuerza, vigor, nervio del estilo o de las palabras; fuerza o fuerzas, la gente de guerra y demás aprestos militares. 3. Fortaleza, consistencia, firmeza, tenacidad, solidez de una cosa material. 4. Fortaleza o vigor de ánimo. 5. Grado de intensidad, de vehemencia; grado de potencia o de concentración; seguridad, confianza. 6. *(Ant.)* Fuerza, una plaza murada y guarnecida para defenderse. **By strength of,** a fuerza de. **The strength of public opinion,** la fuerza de la opinión pública. **Strength of will,** resolución. **Her strength failed her,** le abandonaron las fuerzas, se sintió desfallecer.

strengthen ['streŋθən] [stren-zen], *va.* 1. Fortalecer, fortificar, dar fuerza y vigor. 2. Confirmar, corroborar, reforzar. 3. Animar, alentar, infundir brío. *-vn.* Fortalecerse, coger o cobrar fuerzas; hacerse fuerte o más fuerte, reforzarse.

strengthener ['streŋθənər] [strenz-naʳ], *s.* Corroborante.

strenuous ['strenjʊəs] [stre-niuos], *a.* 1. Estrenuo, fuerte, persistente, enérgico; acérrimo, tenaz. 2. Que necesita gran esfuerzo. **To be strenuous,** tener entereza, no doblegarse o no condescender con facilidad; ser activo en sumo grado.

strenuously ['strenjʊəslɪ] [stre-niuos-li], *adv.* Acérrimamente, con mucha fuerza y vigor; vigorosamente, enérgicamente.

strenuousness ['strenjʊəsnɪs] [stre-niuos-nes], *s.* Ánimo, esfuerzo, vigor, fortaleza, ardor, celo.

streptococcus [ˌstreptəˈkɒkəs] [strep-to-ko-kos], *s.* Estreptococo.

streptomycin [ˌstreptəˈmaɪsɪn] [strep-to-mai-sin], *s. (Med.)* Estreptomicina.

stress [stres] [stres], *s.* 1. Fuerza, peso, importancia, entidad, consideración, valor (worth, value); punto, esencial (essential). 2. Violencia, tensión, fuerza que se hace o se padece. 3. Influencia ejercida por la fuerza, compulsión, coacción. 4. Acento tónico, fuerza, énfasis. **By stress of weather,** *(Mar.)* a causa de un temporal. **Stress of the war,** lo recio de la guerra. **Stress of the voice,** el esfuerzo que se hace con la voz en las sílabas en que está el acento. **To lay great stress upon,** dar mucha importancia a; insistir, apoyar fuertemente sobre, algo, hacer hincapié. **Under stress of,** impulsado por. **Stress mark,** tilde. **To lay great stress on,** insistir mucho, recalcar.

stress, *va.* Sujetar a tensión o peso, como se hace con un madero; dar importancia o énfasis a; meter en dificultades, acongojar.

stressed ['strest] [strest], *a.* Acentuado.

stretch [stretʃ] [strech], *va. y vn.* 1. Extender, alargar, tender; poner muy tensa o estirada alguna cosa. 2. Estirar, extender o alargar alguna cosa más de lo que se debe; dilatar. 3. Violentar o dar una interpretación o sentido siniestro a un texto, ley, etc. 4. Hacer un gran esfuerzo, forzar; hacer violencia; exagerar, llevar al extremo. 5. *(Mar.)* Hacer toda fuerza de vela. **To stretch out to sea,** *(Mar.)* Tirar a la mar. 6. Alargarse, extenderse, dar de sí, dilatarse; estirarse; ocupar cierto espacio; *(Fig.)* esforzarse, exagerar. 7. Desplegarse. **To stretch as far as,** extenderse, llegar hasta. **To stretch the wings,** extender las alas. **To stretch forth,** alargar, extender. **To stretch out,** extender, estirar, alargar; extenderse, desplegarse, yacer desplegado, prolongar o prolongarse. **To stretch up,** alargar, extender. **Stretched in bed,** tendido en la cama o tendido a la larga. **To stretch oneself,** estirarse o desperazarse.

stretch, *s.* 1. Extensión, dilatación. 2. Estirón, esfuerzo. 3. Violencia o interpretación forzada del sentido de un texto, ley, etc. 4. *(Fam.)* El punto a donde puede llegar la acción o esfuerzo de una cosa. 5. *(Mar.)* Bordada, el camino que hace una embarcación entre dos viradas. **The stretch of its wings was three feet,** la extensión de sus alas era de tres pies. **The**

utmost stretch of imagination, el mayor esfuerzo de la imaginación.

stretcher [ˈstretʃəʳ] [stre-chaʳ], *s.* 1. El o lo que alarga o estira. 2. Camilla, cama portátil para conducir los heridos; andas, féretro con varas. 3. En albañilería, un ladrillo o piedra que yace a lo largo de la hilera. 4. Viga, madero largo, tirante que se emplea en la construcción; *(Mar.)* codaste, codal. 5. Pedestal, el madero contra el cual pone los pies el remero para bogar. **Carpet-stretcher,** atizador para alfombras. **Glove-stretcher,** ensanchador de guantes. **Wire-stretcher,** estirador de alambre.

stretching [ˈstretʃɪŋ] [stre-chin], *s.* La acción y el efecto del verbo *stretch,* en cualquiera de sus acepciones; tendedura, alargamiento, estiramiento; dilatación; esperezo (after sleep).

strew [struː] [stru], *va.* (*pp.* STREWED y STREWN). Esparcir, derramar, desparramar; sembrar, salpicar. **To strew with flour** o **with sugar,** espolvorear o polvorear con harina o con azúcar. **To strew with salt,** polvorear con sal.

stria [ˈstraɪə] [straia], *s. (Arq.)* 1. Estría, la media caña que tienen a lo largo las columnas y pilastras. 2. Las rayas o surcos de ciertas conchas.

striate [ˈstraɪt] [strait], *va.* Estriar, marcar con estrías.

striated [straɪˈeɪtɪd] [strai-ei-tid], *a.* Estriado, formado con estrías.

stricken [ˈstrɪkn] [stri-ken], *pp.* del verbo TO STRIKE. 1. Herido (particularmente por un proyectil). 2. Afligido. 3. Entrado en años.

strickle [ˈstrɪkl] [stri-kel], *s. (Prov. Ingl.)* Rasero, instrumento que sirve para rasar o igualar las medidas de áridos.

strict [strɪkt] [strikt], *a.* 1. Estricto, rígido, estrecho, ajustado, puro (precise). 2. Exacto, riguroso, escrupuloso (exact). 3. Severo, áspero (rude). 4. *(Zool.)* Limitado, ceñido, estrecho. 5. Ajustado, apretado. 6. Estirado, tirante.

strictly [ˈstrɪktlɪ] [strikt-li], *adv.* Exactamente, rigurosamente, con rigor, con severidad, estrictamente; puntualmente. **To remain strictly neutral,** guardar la más rigurosa neutralidad. **Strictly confidential,** estrictamente confidencial. **Strictly private,** propiedad privada, prohibido el paso.

strictness [ˈstrɪktnɪs] [strikt-nes], *s.* 1. Exactitud, puntualidad, regularidad. 2. Severidad, rigor, austeridad; escrupulosidad. 3. Tirantez.

stricture [ˈstrɪktʃəʳ] [strik-chaʳ], *s.* 1. Sello, marca o impresión hecha en una cosa. 2. Observación o reflexión ligera hecha sobre un discurso, un escrito, estricto, etc. 3. Contracción o estrechez de un canal o conducto en un cuerpo; constricción.

stride [straɪd] [straid], *s.* Tranco, trancada o zancada, un paso largo.

stride, *va.* (*pret.* STRODE, *pp.* STRIDDEN, antiguamente STRID; *pa.* STRIDING). 1. Pasar a zancadas, cruzar a grandes trancos. 2. Cabalgar, montar a horcajadas. *-vn.* Atrancar, dar trancos, zancadas o pasos largos. **Stride away/off,** alejarse dando grandes zancadas. **To stride up and down,** andar de aquí para allá.

stridency [ˈstraɪdənsɪ] [strai-den-si], *s.* Estridencia.

strident [ˈstraɪdənt] [strai-dant], *a.* Estridente; se aplica al sonido agudo, desapacible y chirriante.

stridor [ˈstraɪdəʳ] [strai-daʳ], *s.* Estridor, sonido agudo, desapacible y chirriante. *(Lat.)*

strife [straɪf] [straif, *s.* Contienda, disputa, refriega, pleito, debate (fight); antipatía. **Domestic strife,** riñas domésticas.

strike [straɪk] [straik], *va.* (*pret.* STRUK, *pp.* STRUCK o STRICKEN). 1. Golpear, sacudir o dar golpes (hit, knock); pegar; atravesar de un golpe, herir (hurt); hacer impresión sobre algo; sacar fuego por medio de un golpe; cortar, separar, quitar; (en este sentido se usa con *off*). 2. Arrojar con violencia una cosa contra otra. 3. Acuñar o sellar moneda. 4. Contratar; convenir, concertar (convene); hacer un balance. 5. Imprimir o fijar fuertemente en la memoria, en el ánimo, etc. 6. Herir o tocar haciendo impresión, como

en la vista, en la imaginación, etc. 7. Mover o conmover repentinamente el ánimo. 8. Chocar, encontrar y ver repentinamente; de aquí, descubrir, divisar. 9. Borrar, tachar, rayar; se usa con *out, off, from,* o alguna cláusula adverbial. 10. Arriar, calar; bajar una vela; levantar el campo. **To strike the colors or the flag,** arriar la bandera. **To strike on a rock,** *(Mar.)* Escollar. **To strike soundings,** *(Mar.)* Sondear, tocar el fondo (sondeando). 11. Tocar, tañer o dar el martillo en la campana del reloj; dar la hora; batir un tambor; hacer resonar. **The clock strikes twelve,** el reloj da las doce. 12. Hacer huelga, dejar de trabajar para obtener por ese medio una concesión. 13. Dar golpe, hacer eco, hacer impresión o llamar la atención alguna cosa; sorprender, sorprenderse, causar admiración, amedrentar. *-vn.* 1. Golpear, dar golpes; tropezar, dar; aporrear, batir. 2. Sonar, dar o hacer sonido. 3. *(Mar.)* Varar, encallar la embarcación; amainar las velas. 4. Suceder casualmente; encontrarse, tropezar con; se usa con *upon.* 5. Entrar atrevida o repentinamente en un sendero o camino: ir adelante, avanzar; estallar, manifestar. 6. Declararse en huelga, para obtener aumento de jornales, disminución de horas de trabajo o corrección de abusos. 7. Arriar el pabellón, rendirse. 8. Echar raíces; fijarse en las conchas, como lo hacen las ostras pequeñas. 9. Tomar cierta dirección, como los estratos geológicos. 10. Esparcirse, acabarse poco a poco, o cambiarse, p. ej. los colores de una tela. 11. Penetrar; saturarse de sal, como el pescado salado.

strike against o **upon,** chocar o encontrarse un cuerpo con otro; estrellarse. **To strike a lead,** encontrar una veta o vena de mineral; de aquí *(Fam.),* hallar el medio de obtener una ganancia o conseguir buen éxito.

strike at, atacar, acometer, atacarse; alcanzar el tiro de una arma arrojadiza o de una de fuego.

strike back, dar golpe por golpe.

strike down, echar abajo de uno o muchos golpes; derribar, hacer caer; aterrar, echar por tierra.

strike for, *(Fam.)* Dirigirse hacia; acometer, atacar en favor o defensa de. **To strike home,** alcanzar el punto deseado, dar en el clavo.

strike in, meterse, desaparecer de la superficie; juntarse, unirse a otros después que éstos han empezado; interrumpir; conformarse con, adaptarse a; entrar repentinamente.

strike into, comenzar repentinamente; entrar, penetrar, hundirse en.

strike in with, conformarse, convenir, condescender.

strike off, borrar, cancelar, rayar; cortar o separar alguna parte de un todo, quitar; *(Fam.)* imprimir, hacer una tirada. **To strike off one's head,** cortar la cabeza a uno.

strike on, dar contra, tropezar, encontrar, descubrir.

strike out, borrar, cancelar; producir algún efecto por medio de la colisión de dos cuerpos; formar o producir algún designio, resolución, plan, etc., o por un esfuerzo repentino del ánimo: arrojarse, lanzarse, hacer un esfuerzo nadando o patinando.

strike through, mostrarse repentinamente una cosa por medio de otra diversa; traspasar, atravesar, pasar de parte a parte; calar.

strike up, producir un sonido cualquiera por medio de golpes; tocar, tañer.

strike with admiration, llenar de admiración o chocar. **To strike fire,** sacar fuego del pedernal con el eslabón. **To strike work,** hallar trabajo, y (rara vez) declararse en huelga. **A thought strikes me,** se me ocurre un pensamiento, tengo una idea. **As it strikes me,** según me parece, a mi juicio, en mi opinión. **To strike blind,** cegar o poner ciego de repente.

strike, *s.* 1. Golpe, acción de dar, pegar o golpear. 2. Huelga, cesación del trabajo por cierto número de trabajadores. 3. *(Fam.)* Descubrimiento de un filón o del mineral que se buscaba; buen éxito completo o inesperado. 4. Rasero, medida. V. STRICKLE.

strikeblock [ˈstraɪkblɒk] [straik-blok], *s. (Carp.)* Cepillo bocel.

strikebreaker [ˈstraɪkˌbreɪkəʳ] [straik-brei-kaʳ], s. Esquirol, rompehuelgas.

striker [ˈstraɪkəʳ] [strai-kaʳ], s. 1. Golpeador, el que golpea. 2. Huelguista, trabajador que deja el trabajo y se declara en huelga.

striking [ˈstraɪkɪŋ] [strai-kin], a. 1. Que sorprende y admira; fuerte, obvio, parecido, semejante; de bulto, patente, evidente, seguro (evident). **Striking news,** noticias extraordinarias o muy inesperadas. 2. Que hace huelga. **A striking woman,** una mujer imponente. **It's striking that,** es chocante que.

string [strɪŋ] [strin], s. 1. Cordón, cuerdecita por lo común redonda de hilo, etc., para colgar o atar algo; bramante. 2. Cualquier hilo en que se ha ensartado alguna cosa y las cosas ensartadas; ristra. 3. Cinta, presilla, cordel (cord). 4. La cuerda de un arco. 5. Hilera, un número de cosas colocadas en orden sucesivo. 6. Cuerda de cualquier instrumento músico. 7. Fibra, nervio, tendón (nerve). 8. Cadena, encadenamiento (chain). 9. Cuelga, ristra. **A string of onions,** ristra de cebollas. **A string of carriages, of lies,** una hilera de carruajes, una sarta de mentiras. 10. (Mar.) Durmiente del alcázar y castillo. **A whole string of errors,** una serie de errores. **To pull strings,** mover palancas, tocar resortes.

string, va. 1. Encordar, poner cuerdas a los instrumentos de música o a otra cosa cualquiera. 2. Templar algún instrumento músico de cuerdas. 3. Ensartar, enhilar; encordelar, enhebrar; atar con bramante. 4. Estirar, poner tensa o estirada una cosa. 5. Quitar las fibras, las briznas **To string along,** embaucar. **To string up,** (Fam.) Ahorcar. **To string out,** extenderse en línea larga e irregular. 2. Presentar la apariencia de hebras o briznas.

string bean [ˈstrɪŋbiːn] [strin-bin], s. Habichuela verde, judía. (Mex.) Ejote.

stringed [ˈstrɪŋd] [stringd], a. Encordado, encordelado; ensartado. **Stringed instrument,** instrumento de cuerda. **6 stringed,** de 6 cuerdas.

stringency [ˈstrɪndʒənsɪ] [strin-yan-si], s. Calidad de riguroso, estricto o severo; severidad, estrechez.

stringent [ˈstrɪndʒənt] [strin-yent], a. 1. Estricto, riguroso, severo (harsh). 2. Impedido por obstáculos. 3. Que aprieta, que comprime; (Com.) estancado.

stringer [ˈstrɪŋəʳ] [strin-gaʳ], s. 1. Durmiente, madero pesado que sirve de apoyo. 2. El que encuerda, enhiebra, ensarta, etc.

stringless [ˈstrɪŋlɪs] [string-les], a. Que no tiene cuerdas.

stringy [ˈstrɪŋɪ] [strin-gui], a. Fibroso, filamentoso; tenaz, duro, correoso.

strip [strɪp] [strip], va. (pret. y pp. STRIPPED o STRIPT). 1. Desnudar, despojar, quitar a uno el vestido o lo que tiene encima. 2. Despojar o privar a uno de lo que goza o tiene. 3. Robar. 4. Descortezar, quitar la corteza. 5. Ordeñar hasta agotar. 6. Desgarrar o cortar en tiras o jirones. 6. Desnudar, quitar lo que cubre o se halla encima, como se hace en varias operaciones mecánicas. **To strip a mast,** (Mar.) Desaparejar un palo. **To strip off,** desnudar, quitar, arrancar.

strip, s. Tira, faja, pedazo angosto y comparativamente largo (de madera, de tela); jirón. V. STRIPE. **Narrow strip,** tirita, tirilla. **Weather-strip,** gualdrín.

stripe [straɪp] [straip], va. Rayar, hacer rayas. **Striped and plaid,** rayado y listado.

stripe, s. 1. Raya, lista, banda o línea de color diferente de la superficie contigua. 2. Banda, trozo largo de tela. 3. Cardenal, la señal amoratada que queda en el cuerpo de resultas de un golpe. 4. Carácter distintivo; calaña, clase; género.

striped [straɪpt] [straipt], a. Listado, rayado, con franjas.

stripling [ˈstrɪplɪŋ] [stri-plin], s. Mozalbete, mozuelo.

striptease [ˈstrɪptiːz] [strip-tis], s. (Teat.) Espectáculo en que una actriz se desnuda poco a poco.

stripy [ˈstraɪpɪ] [strai-pi], a. Rallado, listado.

strive [straɪv] [straiv], vn. (pret. STROVE, pp. STRIVEN). 1. Esforzarse, procurar, hacer lo posible para conseguir alguna cosa. 2. Empeñarse en adquirir o conseguir algo, familiarmente pernear o trabajar mucho en la consecución de una cosa. 3. Debatir, disputar, contender; oponerse, estar en oposición una cosa con otra. 4. Competir una cosa con otra. **To strive for mastery,** disputarse la supremacía.

striver [ˈstraɪvəʳ] [strai-vaʳ], s. Competidor.

striving [ˈstraɪvɪŋ] [strai-vin], s. Esfuerzos.

strode [strəʊd] [stroud], pret. de TO STRIDE.

stroke [strəʊk] [strouk], s. 1. Golpe, el choque de un cuerpo contra otro, acción de golpear; golpe o tiro que alcanza o hiere a alguno. 2. Cada uno de los movimientos repetidos de una serie, como los de un émbolo o remo; remada, curso o carrera del émbolo o pistón; dirección o extensión de dicho movimiento. 3. Toque en la pintura; pincelada, plumada. 4. Fractura, cardenal o herida causada por un golpe; cualquier daño causado como por un golpe; golpe, infortunio o desgracia repentina; ataque, apoplejía (Med.). 5. Golpe en las obras de ingenio, la parte que tiene más gracia y oportunidad en ellas. **I know his stroke,** conozco su modo de obrar. 6. Jugada, golpe (Golf, Cricket). 6. Campanada de reloj. **It is on the stroke of eight,** están al dar las ocho. 7. Acción eficaz, hazaña; suceso, éxito. 8. Ligero movimiento acariciador. 9. (Med.) Ataque. **Stroke of a pen o pencil,** plumada, pincelada. **Stroke of wit,** chiste, gracia, humorada, dicho gracioso, especie salada. **Good stroke!,** ¡muy bien! **To arrive on the stroke,** llegar a tiempo, llegar a la hora justa. **To give a stroke,** acariciar, hacer una caricia.

stroke, va. 1. Pasar la mano por la espalda, halagar, acariciar (caress). 2. Frotar suavemente. 3. Ranurar la piedra con cincel. 4. Alisar los pliegues con la aguja.

stroll [strəʊl] [stroul], vn. Tunar, vagar, vaguear, andar vagando; callejear, pasearse. -s. Paseo voluntario; vagancia, callejeo. **To take, to go for a stroll,** dar un paseo, pasearse.

stroller [ˈstrəʊləʳ] [strou-laʳ], s. 1. El que se pasea o anda lentamente o sin objeto fijo; tunante, vagamundo o vagabundo. 2. Cómico ambulante, de la legua.

strolling [ˈstrəʊlɪŋ] [strou-lin], a. part. Vagabundo, que vaga; que se pasea ociosamente; ambulante.

strong [strɒŋ] [strong], a. 1. Fuerte, forzudo, vigoroso, robusto, muscular, que tiene grandes fuerzas. 2. Fuerte, que tiene mucha resistencia; que produce impresión notable sobre los sentidos que posee una cualidad en alto grado; sólido, firme, concentrado; espirituoso de cuerpo, que contiene mucho alcohol. 3. Capaz, hábil. 4. Violento, impetuoso; de aquí, vivo, brillante, picante. 5. Fuerte, sano. 6. Ardiente, activo, eficaz, enérgico; celoso, caluroso. 7. Resuelto, determinado. 8. (Com.) Que manifiesta tendencia al alza, como el mercado o los precios. **Strong meat,** carne difícil de digerir. **His army is ten thousand strong,** tiene un ejército de diez mil hombres. **A strong partizan,** un celoso partidario. **A strong argument,** un argumento poderoso. **Strong box,** cofre, fuerte, caja de hierro para guardar valores. **Strong-minded,** de carácter, de inteligencia vigorosa; despreocupado, descreído. **Strong-backed,** ancho de caderas, robusto. **Strong-bodied,** corpulento, robusto. **Strong-bodied wine,** vino de mucho cuerpo. **Strong-fisted, strong-handed,** fuerte de manos y puños. **Strong-hand,** fuerza, violencia.

strongly [ˈstrɒŋlɪ] [strong-li], adv. Fuertemente, rigorosamente, vehementemente; con violencia.

stronghold [ˈstrɒŋhəʊld] [strong-jould], s. Plaza fuerte; lugar hecho fácilmente defendible por la naturaleza o por el arte.

strongroom [ˈstrɒŋrʊm] [strong-rum], s. Cuarto acondicionado para guardar cosas de valor.

strontium [ˈstrɒntɪəm] [stron-tiom], s. (Quím.) Estroncio, elemento amarillento; se emplean sus sales en la pirotecnia para producir llamas rojas.

strop [strɒp] [strop], va. Asentar navajas, suavizar la navaja con el cuero. -s. 1. Suavizador o asentador de navajas; tira de cuero o lona que sirve para afilar las navajas de afeitar. 2. *(Mar.)* Estrovo, cordaje de las poleas.

strophe ['strəʊfɪ] [strou-fi], *s.* Estrofa; estancia, cualquiera de las partes simétricamente iguales de que consta una oda, canción, etc.

strove [strəʊv] [strouv], *pret.* del verbo TO STRIVE.

struck [strʌk] [strak], *pret. y pp.* del verbo TO STRIKE.

structural ['strʌktʃərəl] [strak-cha-ral], *a.* Perteneciente a la estructura, caracterizado por la estructura o que la tiene.

structuralize ['strʌktʃərəlaɪz] [strak-cha-ra-lais], *va.* Estructurar, disponer.

structure ['strʌktʃəʳ] [strak-chaʳ], *s.* 1. Construcción, el efecto de construir; lo que se construye; combinación de partes relacionadas, p. ej. una máquina, un edificio, etc. 2. Estructura, hechura, distribución y unión orgánica de las partes u órganos en un cuerpo u objeto. 3. *(Ant.)* Edificación. **The microscopic structure of malachite,** la estructura microscópica de la malaquita.

struggle ['strʌgl] [strak-guel], *vn.* 1. Bregar, forcejar, resistirse para desasirse, soltarse o librarse de algo. 2. Esforzarse o hacer esfuerzos para conseguir algo. 3. Luchar, contender, agitarse.

struggle, *s.* Esfuerzo, contienda, lucha, disputa; resistencia.

strum ['strʌm] [stram], *va. y vn.* Arañar, tañer un instrumento de cuerda de una manera descuidada, ruidosa y sin expresión.

strumpet ['strʌmpɪt] [stram-pet], *s.* Ramera, puta, mujer abandonada.

strung [strʌŋ] [strang], *pret. y pp.* del verbo STRING.

strut [strʌt] [strat], *vn.* 1. Contonearse, pavonearse. 2. Inflarse, ensoberbecerse.

strut, *s.* 1. Riostra, jabalcón, tornapunta de caballete. 2. Instrumento de hueso o madera que se usa ajustando los pliegues de una lechuguilla.

strutting ['strʌtɪŋ] [stra-tin], *s.* Contoneo, la acción de contonearse; paso arrogante, altanero.

strychnine ['strɪkniːn] [strik-nin], *s.* Estricnina, alcaloide sumamente venenoso.

stub [stʌb] [stab], *s.* 1. Tocón, cepa, de un árbol pequeño, arbusto o mate; lo que queda de un tronco o tallo después de cortada la parte principal. 2. Zoquete; parte o pieza corta que sobresale de una superficie; fragmento, resto. 3. *(E. U.)* En un libro de cheques, talón, matriz. 4. Colilla (cigarette). **Stub-book,** libro talonario. **Stub-iron,** hierro hecho de clavos viejos de herradura. **Stub pen,** pluma de escribir con punta muy roma. **Stub-twist,** hierro de varios colores hecho con clavos de herradura usados; sirve para hacer cañones de fusil.

stub, *va.* 1. *(E. U.)* Dar o tropezar contra una cosa situada casi al nivel del suelo. 2. Extirpar, arrancar sacando las raíces. 3. Quitar los tocones o cepas. 4. Reducir a un tocón; hacer cachigordete. **Stub out,** apagar (cigarette). **Stub up,** quitar, desarraigar.

stubbed ['stʌbd] [stabd], *a.* 1. Cortado o extirpado por el tronco. 2. Grueso y corto. 3. Fuerte, vigoroso, como un tronco. 4. Grosero, áspero de trato o modales.

stubbiness ['stʌbɪnɪs] [sta-bi-nes], *s.* El estado de lo que es corto y grueso.

stubble ['stʌbl] [sta-bel], *s.* Rastrojo, el residuo de la mies después de segada.

stubborn ['stʌbən] [sta-bon], *a.* 1. Cabezudo, obstinado, contumaz, terco, testarudo, porfiado, tenaz. 2. Inflexible, inquebrantable, intratable. **Stubborn facts,** hechos innegables.

stubbornly ['stʌbənlɪ] [sta-bon-li], *adv.* Obstinadamente, inflexiblemente, tercamente.

stubbornness ['stʌbənnɪs] [sta-bon-nes], *s.* Obstinación, aferramiento, terquedad, pertinacia; porfía.

stubby ['stʌbɪ] [sta-bi], *a.* Cachigordete; gordo, corto y tieso.

stub-nail ['stʌbneɪl] [stab-neil], *s.* Puntilla, hita.

stucco ['stʌkəʊ] [sta-kou], *va. y vn.* Revestir, cubrir de estuco; formar adornos de estuco. -*s.* 1. Estuco, yeso fino para encostrar las paredes. 2. Trabajo de estuco; cualquier cemento o argamasa para el exterior de los edificios.

stuck [stʌk] [stak], *pret. y pp.* del verbo STICK.

stud 1 [stʌd] [stad], *s.* 1. Poste de tabique, pie derecho, poste intermedio y corto. 2. Tachón, tachuela grande, clavo de adorno; botón de camisa. 3. Refuerzo de eslabón.

stud 2, *s.* Yeguada, caballada, manada de yeguas y caballos padres. **Stud-book,** registro genealógico de caballos. **Stud-horse,** caballo padre.

stud, *va.* Tachonar, adornar con tachones.

studding-sails ['stʌdɪŋseɪlz] [sta-din-seils], *s. pl. (Mar.)* Velas ligeras que se extienden más afuera que las mayores en los peñoles de las vergas. **Lower studding-sails,** rastreras. **Upper studding-sails,** alas.

student ['stjuːdənt] [stiu-dent], *s.* 1. Estudiante, discípulo, persona que estudia. 2. Sabio, letrado. **Law or medical student,** pasante de abogado o médico.

studentship ['stjuːdəntʃɪp] [stiu-dent-ship], *s.* Beca.

studied ['stʌdɪd] [sta-did], *a.* 1. Estudiado, hecho con cuidado, premeditado. 2. *(Des.)* Docto, versado o instruido.

studier ['stʌdɪəʳ] [sta-diaʳ], *s.* El que ha cultivado o cultiva con esmero alguna ciencia.

studio ['stjuːdɪəʊ] [stiu-diou], *s.* Estudio, taller de un artista. **Studio couch,** sofá cama.

studious ['stjuːdɪəs] [stiu-dios], *a.* 1. Estudioso, aplicado al estudio. 2. Cuidadoso, solícito, diligente. 3. Estudiado, hecho con deliberación.

studiously ['stjuːdɪəslɪ] [stiu-dios-li], *adv.* Estudiosamente, diligentemente, con aplicación.

studiousness ['stjuːdɪəsnɪs] [stiu-dios-nes], *s.* Estudiosidad, aplicación al estudio.

study ['stʌdɪ] [sta-di], *s.* 1. Estudio, la aplicación a saber y comprender alguna ciencia o arte. 2. Estudio, aplicación, cuidado o diligencia para hacer alguna cosa. 3. Meditación profunda. 4. Embarazo, perplejidad. 5. Estudio, instrucción, conocimientos adquiridos. 6. Estudio, la pieza donde una persona tiene su bilbioteca y estudia. **To be in a brown study,** estar absorto en una idea; estar pensando en las avutardas; mirar las telarañas. **To make a study of,** investigar, hacer un estudio sobre algo.

study, *va.* 1. Estudiar, aplicarse a aprender alguna facultad o ciencia. 2. Estudiar, observar o examinar con cuidado. 3. Aprender a fuerza de aplicación. 4. Considerar, meditar; idear, proyectar, discurrir medios, aplicarse a; se usa a menudo con *out o up,* **To study up a scheme,** estudiar un plan o proyecto. -*vn.* 1. Estudiar, estar pensando o discurriendo de intento en alguna cosa. 2. Procurar, hacer las diligencias para conseguir lo que se desea.

stuff [stʌf] [staf], *s.* 1. Material, la materia que se requiere para hacer alguna cosa; materia prima. 2. Esencia, parte, elemental, elemento fundamental, sea material o espiritual. 3. Bienes en general; mobiliario, mueblaje, los muebles de una casa. 4. Cosa de poco o ningún valor y estimación; droga; desechos, desperdicios; ideas o sentimientos sin valor; fruslería; se usa muchas veces con interjección. 5. Tejido o tela de cualquier especie; particularmente, todo tejido de lana que es más delgado y ligero que el paño; estofa. **Silk and cotton stuff,** filosofía. 6. Jarope, cualquier droga o medicamento. 7. Betún, compuesto de sebo, trementina, etc., para preservar el maderamen de una embarcación. 8. Tablas, tablillas. **It's poor stuff,** no sirve para nada. **Is this your stuff?,** ¿es tuyo esto? **Thick stuff,** *(Mar.)* Tablones. -*inter.* ¡bagatela! ¡niñería! ¡fruslería! **Hot stuff,** persona estupenda, cosa maravillosa. **He's hot stuf at golf,** es un hacha al golf, juega muy bien al golf. **Get stuffed!,** ¡vete a la porra! **To do one's stuff,** actuar, hacer uno su trabajo.

stuff, *va.* 1. Henchir, llenar; colmar, rellenar. 2. Rehenchir, llenar de borra, lana o crina; en taxidermia, rehenchir, rellenar la piel de un animal. 3. Atetar; apretar. 4. Mechar; introducir especias o hierbas aromáticas en la carne. **To stuff a turkey,** rellenar un pavo. 5. Tapar, atascar (las narices o boca). -*vn.* Atracarse, engullir, llenarse de comida; tragar. **To stuff away,** devorar, zampar (food). **To stuff up,** obstruirse. **To get stuffed up,** quedarse atascado, quedarse obstruido.

stuffing [ˈstʌfɪŋ] [sta-fin], *s.* 1. El material con que atesta o rellena una cosa; atestadura *(Mec.)* empaquetado; relleno culinario; borra, pelote de telas de lana. 2. Relleno, la acción y efecto de rellenar. **Stuffing-box,** *(Mex.)* Caja de empaquetado, prensa-estopas.

stuffy [ˈstʌfɪ] [sta-fi], *a.* 1. Mal ventilado; que causa sensación de malestar. 2. Que impide la respiración.

stultify [ˈstʌltɪfaɪ] [stal-ti-fai], *va.* 1. Embrutecer, atontar, hacer parecer absurdo, inconsistente o contradictorio; se emplea frecuentemente como verbo reflexivo. 2. *(For.)* Alegar locura o estupidez.

stum [stʌm] [stam], *s.* Mosto, el zumo exprimido de la uva antes de fermentar y hacerse vino; vino fermentado en parte. *V.* MUST.

stum, *va.* Hacer cesar la fermentación (del mosto), añadiendo mostaza u otros ingredientes.

stumble [ˈstʌmbl] [stam-bel], *vn.* 1. Tropezar, dar con los pies en un estorbo; dar un traspié, un paso en falso; moverse de una manera incierta o desatinada. 2. Hallar casualmente alguna persona o cosa o dar por casualidad con ella; *con on* o *upon.* -*va.* 1. Hacer tropezar a uno; hacer a uno dar un traspié o deslizarse. 2. Ofender. **To stumble through a speech,** dar un discurso de cualquier manera. **To stumble across/upon,** encontrar por casualidad, tropezar.

stumble, *s.* Traspié, tropiezo, resbalón; desliz, paso en falso (en sentido recto y figurado); desatino.

stumbler [ˈstʌmblər] [stam-blar], *s.* Tropezador, el que tropieza.

stumbling-block [ˈstʌmblɪŋblɒk] [stam-blin-blok], *s.* Tropezadero, tropiezo; piedra de escándalo.

stump [stʌmp] [stamp], *s.* 1. Tocón, cepa, el resto del tronco de un árbol que sobresale de la tierra después de cortado. 2. En general, la parte de un cuerpo sólido que queda después de haber separado o cortado una porción considerable de su substancia. **Stump of a finger,** tocón o zoquete de un dedo. **Stump of a leg,** muñón de una pierna. **Stump of a tooth,** raigón de un diente. **Cabbage-stump,** troncho de berza. **Up a stump,** *(Fam. E. U.)* Estar en un brete, verse perplejo. 3. *pl.* Las piernas; generalmente en la locución **to stir one's stumps,** *(Fam. E. U.)* mover las piernas, es decir, ponerse en movimiento, zarandearse. 4. Tribuna o estrado desde donde se pronuncia un discurso político; de aquí, arenga política en tiempo de elecciones. 5. *(Fam.)* Desafío, invitación a una controversia. 6. Esfumino, rollito de piel suave o de papel cortado en punta para esfumar. -*a.* 1. Parecido a un tocón. 2. Perteneciente a una arenga política. **Stump-speaker,** orador político. **To be on the stump,** hacer una campaña *(E.U.).*

stump, *va.* 1. Pronunciar un discurso electoral. 2. *(Fam.)* Desafiar, provocar; hacer parar por razón de obstáculos verdaderos o imaginarios; tropezar, dar contra un obstáculo, v. g. con el pie. -*vn.* 1. Andar renqueando, renquear; andar sobre los muñones de piernas amputadas. 2. *(Fam.)* Pronunciar discursos políticos. **To stump about/along,** andar cojeando, andar pisando muy fuerte. **To stump up,** desembolsar, apoquinar.

stumpy [ˈstʌmpɪ] [stam-pi], *a.* 1. Lleno de tocones o trozos. 2. Parecido a un tocón, cachigordete, rechoncho.

stun [stʌn] [stan], *va.* 1. Aturdir con un golpe; privar del sentido por medio de una conmoción cerebral. 2. Atolondrar, ensordecer, por algún tiempo, v. g. por medio de un ruido explosivo. 3. Aturrullar, dejar pasmado. -*s.* Choque, golpe o sacudimiento que aturde o deja estupefacto; atudimiento, el efecto de aturdir.

stung [stʌŋ] [stan], *pret.* y *pp.* del verbo STING.

stunned [stʌnd] [stand], *a.* Atontado, aturdido.

stunner [ˈstʌnər] [sta-naʳ], *s.* 1. El o lo que aturde, atolondra o aturrulla. 2. *(Ger.)* Cosa extraordinaria, de apariencia o efecto sorprendente.

stunt 1 [stʌnt] [stant], *va.* Impedir crecer o no dejar medrar; detener en el crecimiento; hacer achaparrado. **To grow stunted,** achapararrse o no crecer los árboles. -*s.* 1. Detenimiento, en el progreso o desarrollo; cesación del crecimiento. 2. Animal o cosa achaparrados.

stunt 2, *(Fam. E. U.) va.* Hacer ejercicios corporales de fuerza y destreza. -*s.* Suerte o ejercicio corporal que requiere pericia y destreza.

stupe [stjuːp] [stiup], *s. (Med.)* Fomentación, compresa; el paño empapado en un cocimiento para fomentar alguna llaga.

stupe, *va.* Fomentar, aplicar paños empapados en un cocimiento a una parte enferma.

stupefacient [ˌstjuːpɪˈfeɪʃənt] [stiu-pi-fei-shant], *a.* Estupefaciente, que causa estupor, falta de sensación o pasmo. -*s.* Un medicamento narcótico.

stupefaction [ˌstjuːpɪˈfækʃən] [stiu-pi-fak-shon], *s.* Estupefacción, pasmo o estupor; atolondramiento, aturdimiento, asombro.

stupefier [ˈstjuːpɪfaɪər] [stiu-pi-faiaʳ], *s.* Lo que causa estupidez o insensibilidad.

stupefy [ˈstjuːpɪfaɪ] [stiu-pi-fai], *va.* 1. Embrutecer, entorpecer los sentidos o las facultades; dejar estupefacto. 2. Atontar, atolondrar; asombrar, causar gran sorpresa, dejar turulato.

stupefying [ˈstjuːpɪfaɪɪŋ] [stiu-pi-fain], *a.* Pasmoso.

stupendous [stjuːˈpendəs] [stiu-pen-dos], *a.* Estupendo; inmenso, vasto; de tamaño, volumen o grado maravilloso.

stupendously [stjuːˈpendəslɪ] [stiu-pen-dos-li], *adv.* Estupendamente, de un modo asombroso.

stupid [ˈstjuːpɪd] [stiu-pid], *a.* 1. Estúpido, insensato, notablemente torpe en comprender o en raciocinar. 2. Tosco, grosero. **A stupid thing,** una patochada, tontada o brutalidad.

stupidity [stjuːˈpɪdɪtɪ] [stiu-pi-di-ti], **stupidness** [ˈstjuːpɪdnɪs] [stiu-pid-nes], *s.* Estupidez, tontería, embrutecimiento.

stupidly [ˈstjuːpɪdlɪ] [stiu-pid-li], *adv.* Torpemente, estúpidamente, con insensatez.

stupor [ˈstjuːpər] [stiu-poʳ], *s.* 1. Estupor, entorpecimiento de los sentidos o de las facultades intelectuales. 2. Atontamiento, torpeza notable para comprender, estupidez densa.

sturdily [ˈstɜːdɪlɪ] [ster-di-li], *adv.* Robustamente, resueltamente; firmemente, porfiadamente, vigorosamente.

sturdiness [ˈstɜːdɪnɪs] [ster-di-nes], *s.* 1. Fuerza, fortaleza. 2. Terquedad, obstinación.

sturdy [ˈstɜːdɪ] [ster-di], *a.* 1. Fuerte, robusto, de buena y cabal salud; endurecido, vigoroso. 2. Bronco, terco, firme e inflexible, resuelto. **Sturdy beggars,** mendigos robustos o que pueden trabajar. **Sturdy independence,** fuerte espíritu de independencia.

sturgeon [ˈstɜːdʒən] [ster-yon], *s.* Esturión.

stutter [ˈstʌtər] [sta-tar] *vn.* Tartamudear, hablar con dificultad, entrecortadamente y repitiendo las sílabas; tartalear en la pronunciación. -*s.* Tartamudeo, la acción o el vicio de tartamudear o tartalear.

stutterer [ˈstʌtərər] [sta-ta-raʳ], *s.* Tartamudo, el que tartamudea; farfulla, el que habla balbuciente y de prisa.

stuttering [ˈstʌtərɪŋ] [sta-ta-rin], *a.* Tartamudo.

sty [staɪ] [stai], *s. (pl.* STIES) 1. Zahurda, pocilga o cochiquera. 2. Zaquizamí, habitación sucia; lupanar, burdel. 3. Orzuelo del ojo, tumor inflamatorio del borde libre de un párpado.

style 1 [staɪl] [stail], *s.* 1. Estilo, el modo y forma de escribir o hablar particular a cada uno; manera de expresar el pensamiento; dicción distintiva y característica. 2. Estilo, el uso y moda que hay y se guarda comúnmente: manera de obrar; manera, moda, tono, género. **Style of address,** tratamiento; encabezamiento. **Style of living,** estilo de vida. **Old style,** año conforme al cómputo de Julio César. **New style,** cómputo del año conforme a la corrección de Gregorio XIII en 1582. El primero es 13 días más tarde que el segundo. 3. Estilo o modo peculiar de pintar o de componer en la música; carácter de la composición y ejecución; carácter general de las obras de un artista. 4. Estilo, un punzón de hierro con el cual escribían los antiguos sobre tablillas preparadas con una capa de cera. 5. Util para grabar; estilete de cirugía. 6. *(Zool.)* Punzón, prolongación o parte puntiaguda. 7. Título, apellido, renombre o epíteto. **To be in style,** estar de moda. **To live in style,** vivir con lujo.

style 2, *s.* 1. Estilo o gnomon del reloj de sol. 2. *(Bot.)* Estilo, la parte del pistilo que está entre el estigma y el embrión.

style, *va.* Intitular, nombrar, dar o poner un nombre, título o renombre.

stylet ['staɪlɪt] [stai-lit], *s.* 1. Estilete, cualquier instrumento delgado y puntiagudo; punzón pequeño. 2. *(Zool.)* Prolongación puntiaguda.

styling ['staɪlɪŋ] [stai-lin], *s.* Estilización.

stylish ['staɪlɪʃ] [stai-lish], *a.* Elegante, a la moda, de buena forma y estilo.

stylist ['staɪlɪst] [stai-list], *s.* Estilista. Consultor respecto a estilos de ropa, peinados, etc.

stylistic [staɪˈlɪstɪk] [stai-lis-tik], *a.* Estilístico.

stylized ['staɪlaɪzd] [stai-laisd], *a.* Estilizado.

styloid ['staɪlɔɪd] [stai-loid], *a.* Estilóideo, parecido a un estilo o punzón.

stylus ['staɪləs] [stai-los], *s.* 1. Estilo, punzón. 2. Aguja de fonógrafo.

styptic ['stɪptɪk] [stip-tik], *a.* y *s. (Med.)* Estíptico, que tiene virtud de astringir y de contener la hemorragia.

stypticity [stɪpˈtɪsɪtɪ] [stip-ti-si-ti], *s.* Estipticidad.

styx ['stɪks] [stiks], *s.* Estigia, laguna del infierno mitológico.

suasion ['sweɪzn] [suei-son], *s.* Persuasión; anticuado, excepto en la locución, *moral suasion.*

suave ['swaːv] [suav], *a.* Suave, tratable, de modales corteses, afable.

suavity ['swɑːvɪtɪ] [sua-vi-ti], *s.* Suavidad, dulzura, blandura, delicia.

sub- [sʌb] [sab], prefijo que unido con otras voces significa el grado inferior de alguna cosa.

subalpine ['sʌbælpaɪn] [sab-al-pain], *a.* Subalpino.

subaltern ['sʌbltən] [sab-al-tern], *a.* Subalterno, inferior, subordinado, dependiente. -*s.* 1. Oficial subalterno; alférez, teniente, oficial inferior al capitán. 2. *(Lógica)* Clase o naturaleza especificada como comprendida en otra general.

subcommittee ['sʌbkəmɪtɪ] [sab-ko-mi-ti], *s.* Una comisión parcial nombrada de entre los individuos de otra para un objeto particular.

subconscious ['sʌbˈkɒnʃəs] [sab-kon-shos], *a.* Subconsciente.

subcontract ['sʌbˈkɒntrækt] [sab-kon-trakt], *s.* Subcontrato, contrato que hace a su vez el contratista de una obra o trabajo.

subdivide ['sʌbˈdɪvaɪd] [sab-di-vaid], *va.* Subdividir.

subdivision ['sʌbdɪˌvɪʒən] [sab-di-vi-shon], *s.* Subdivisión, en botánica y zoología, división o grupo subordinado.

subdue [səbˈdjuː] [sab-diu], *va.* 1. Sojuzgar, subyugar, sujetar, dominar, mandar con violencia. 2. Domar; enternecer, suavizar. 3. Sojuzgar, conquistar, vencer con habilidad o industria; mejorar las tierras; extirpar las malas hierbas. **In a subdued tone,** en tono sumiso; bajando la voz. **To subdue one's flesh,** mortificar el cuerpo o reprimir los impulsos y apetitos de la carne.

subduer ['sʌbˈdjuːəʳ] [sab-diuaʳ], *s.* Sojuzgador, conquistador.

sub-entry ['sʌbˈentrɪ] [sab-en-tri], *s.* Subasiento.

subgroup ['sʌbgruːp] [sab-grup], *s.* Subgrupo.

subhuman ['sʌbˈhjuːmən] [sab-jiu-man], *a.* Infrahumano.

subjacent ['sʌbˈdʒæsənt] [sab-ya-sent], *a.* Subyacente, situado debajo de otra cosa o más bajo que ella.

subject ['sʌbdʒɪkt] [sab-yikt], *va.* 1. Sujetar, someter, sojuzgar, dejar sujeto a. 2. Exponer, arriesgar. 3. Presentar, colocar una cosa delante para que se la considere y juzgue y se disponga de ella. 4. Sujetar, poner en estado de dependencia, subordinar. 5. *(Ant.)* Someter, poner debajo. **To subject someone to a test,** poner a alguien a prueba.

subject, *a.* 1. Sujeto, expuesto o propenso a alguna tendencia o agencia. 2. Sujeto, sometido a otro, avasallado, que está bajo la dependencia de otro. 3. Situado debajo a los pies de otra cosa. -*s.* 1. Súbdito, súbdita; vasallo. 2. Sujeto, materia, aquello de que se trata actualmente, asunto, argumento,

tema: *(Gram.)* sujeto, término de una proposición de la cual se afirma o niega alguna cosa, y particularmente el caso nominativo. 3. Sujeto, lo mismo que persona cuando se trata de sus buenas o malas cualidades. 4. La materia u objeto de alguna ciencia o arte; idea o plan general de una obra artística; asunto. 5. Cadáver destinado a la disección para explicar o enseñar la anatomía; persona expuesta a una enfermedad o que la padece. **Subject-matter,** asunto, materia de que se trata. **To be subject to,** ser propenso a, estar sujeto a. **Subject to the approval to,** sujeto a la aprobación de.

subjection ['sʌbˈdʒekʃən] [sab-yek-shon], *s.* 1. Sujeción, yugo, dependencia, servidumbre. 2. Sujeción, el acto de sujetar o sujetarse.

subjective ['sʌbˈdʒektɪv] [sab-yek-tiv], *a.* 1. Subjetivo, que se refiere al sujeto pensante; en contraposición a objetivo. 2. Subjetivo, que tiene relación con el sujeto de que se trata.

subjectively ['sʌbˈdʒektɪvlɪ] [sab-yek-tiv-li], *adv.* Subjetivamente, de una manera subjetiva.

subjectiveness ['sʌbˈdʒektɪvnɪs] [sab-yek-tiv-nes], *s.* Subjetividad, calidad de subjetivo.

subjectivisim ['sʌbˈdʒektɪvɪzəm] [sab-yek-ti-vi-sem], *sm.* Subjetivismo.

subjectivity [ˌsʌbdʒekˈtɪvɪtɪ] [sab-yek-ti-vi-ti], *sf.* Subjetividad.

subjoin ['sʌbˈdʒɔɪn] [sab-yoin], *va.* Añadir al fin, sobreañadir, juntar a.

subjugate ['sʌbˈdʒʊgeɪt] [sab-yu-gueit], *va.* Subyugar, conquistar, someter, sujetar.

subjugation ['sʌbdʒʊˈgeɪʃən] [sab-yu-guei-shon], *s.* Sujeción, servidumbre, yugo.

subjunctive ['sʌbˈdʒʌŋktɪv] [sab-yank-tiv], *a.* Subjuntivo del modo subjuntivo, perteneciente al modo del verbo que denota la suposición, la duda, la condición o dependencia. - *s. (Gram.)* Subjuntivo, modo subjuntivo.

sublease ['sʌbˈliːs] [sab-lis], *va.* Subarrendar. V. SUBLET.

sublimate ['sʌblɪmɪt] [sa-bli-meit], *s. (Quím.)* Sublimado, la parte más sutil y volátil de los mixtos, extraída de las partes crasas por medio del fuego. **Corrosive sublimate,** solimán, sublimado corrosivo, cloruro sobreoxigenado de mercurio.

sublimate, *va.* 1. *(Quím.)* Sublimar, elevar por medio del fuego las partes volátiles de los cuerpos, y volver a solidificarse. 2. Sublimar, separar de la escoria; *(Fig.)* refinar, purificar.

sublimation [ˌsʌblɪˈmeɪʃən] [sa-bli-mei-shon], *s.* 1. Sublimación. 2. Refinamiento, perfección, quinta esencia.

sublime [səˈblaɪm] [sa-blaim], *a.* 1. Sublime, excelso, elevado, exaltado. 2. Majestuoso, imponente, solemne. 3. Del grado más alto, supremo, extremo, el más grande. 4. *(Poét.)* Altivo, orgulloso, arrebatado, transportado. -*s.* El estilo sublime o elevado.

sublime, *va.* y *vn.* 1. Sublimar, exaltar, engrandecer, ensalzar o poner a gran altura. 2. *(Quím.)* Sublimar o sublimarse.

sublimely [səˈblaɪmlɪ] [sa-blaim-li], *adv.* Sublimemente, elevadamente, de un modo sublime.

submarine [ˌsʌbməˈriːn] [sab-ma-rin], *a.* Submarino, que está debajo de la superficie del mar.

submerge [səbˈmɜːdʒ] [sab-merch], *va.* 1. Sumergir, zambullir, meter alguna cosa debajo del agua; de aquí, ahogar. 2. Sumergir, anegar, inundar. -*vn.* Zambullirse, sumergirse, yacer debajo del agua; estar escondido o enterrado, oculto a la vista.

submergence [səbˈmɜːdʒəns] [sab-mer-yans], *s.* Sumersión, acción y efecto de sumergir.

submission [səbˈmɪʃən] [sab-mi-shon], *s.* 1. Sumisión, sometimiento, la acción y efecto de someterse; obediencia. 2. Sumisión, rendimiento, deferencia, obsequio, respeto; resignación. 3. *(Ant.)* El reconocimiento de una falta, la confesión de un error. 4. *(For.)* Acción de referir o someter, o el acuerdo de someter el punto controvertido al arbitraje.

submissive [səbˈmɪsɪv] [sab-mi-siv], *a.* Sumiso, obediente, rendido, sometido, obsequioso.

submissively [səb'mɪsɪvlɪ] [sab-mi-siv-li], *adv.* Humildemente, respetuosamente, con sumisión, rendimiento o respeto.

submissiveness [səb'mɪsɪvnɪs] [sab-mi-siv-nes], *s.* Obsequio, sumisión, rendimiento.

submit [səb'mɪt] [sab-mit], *va.* 1. Someter, sujetar (en este sentido es generalmente verbo reflexivo). 2. Someter, referir o dejar una resolución o determinación al juicio, fallo, discreción o arbitrio de otro. 3. Presentar como el propio parecer o versión. -*vn.* 1. Someterse, sujetarse, rendirse, conformarse, consentir en una cosa, ceder. 2. Estar sometido. **We must all submit,** no hay más remedio que someternos, o tenemos que consentir o conformarnos.

subnormal ['sʌb'nɔːməl] [sab-nor-mal], *a.* Anormal, inferior al grado normal. **Subnormal temperature,** temperatura bajo la normal. -*s. (Mat.)* Subnormal, parte del eje de una curva comprendida entre la ordenada y la normal.

suborbital ['sʌb'ɔːbɪtəl] [sab-or-bi-tal], *a.* Suborbital, situado debajo de la órbita del ojo.

suborder ['sʌb'ɔːdəʳ] [sab-or-daʳ], *s.* 1. *(Bot. y Zool.)* Suborden, división primaria de un orden. 2. *(Arq.)* Orden subordinado, empleado principalmente para adorno.

subordinate ['sʌb'ɔːdɪneɪt] [sab-or-di-neit], *a.* Subordinado, inferior, dependiente o bajo las órdenes de otro.

subordinate, *va.* 1. Subordinar, poner o colocar en un orden o categoría inferior; de aquí, tener o considerar como de menor importancia. 2. Someter, sujetar.

subordinately ['sʌb'ɔːdɪneɪtlɪ] [sab-or-di-neit-li], *adv.* Subordinadamente, como dependiente, como inferior a otro.

subordination ['sʌb,ɔːdɪ'neɪʃən] [sab-or-di-nei-shon], *s.* Subordinación.

suborn ['sʌ'bɔːn] [sa-born], *va.* Sobornar, corromper, cohechar.

suborner ['sʌ'bɔːnəʳ] [sa-bor-naʳ], *s.* Sobornador, cohechador, el que soborna.

subpoena [səb'poiːnə] [sab-poi-na], *s.* Comparendo, la citación que un superior o un juez hace a una persona, mandándola comparecer bajo alguna pena. -*va.* Notificar por medio de una citación de comparendo; emplazar.

subrogate ['sʌbrəgɪt] [sab-ro-guit], *a.* Sustituido, subrogado.

subrogation [,sʌbrə'geɪʃən] [sab-ro-guei-shon], *s.* Subrogación.

subscribe [səb'skraɪb] [sabs-kraib], *va. y vn.* 1. Subscribir, suscribir, dar el consentimiento firmando al pie o al fin de algún escrito. 2. Certificar uno con su firma; firmar, rubricar. 3. Subscribir, convenir con el dictamen de otro, aprobar, consentir, dar el consentimiento. 4. Subscribirse a una obra. 5. Subscribirse para la ejecución de cualquier empresa, articipando una suma determinada para tener derecho a las ganacias.

subscriber [səb'skraɪbəʳ] [sabs-krai-baʳ], *s.* 1. Subscriptor, suscriptor, el que subscribe o firma. 2. Subscriptor, el que subscribe o contribuye a alguna obra o a cualquiera otra empresa u objeto.

subscript ['sʌbskrɪpt] [sabs-kript], *a. y s.* Cualquier cosa escrita debajo de otra.

subscription [səb'skrɪpʃən] [sabs-krip-shon], *s.* 1. Subscripción. la acción y efecto de subscribir. 2. Subscripción, la firma de una carta o documento. 3. Subscripción, la acción de contribuir a cualquier empresa. 4. La suma o número individual o total que se subscribe para cualquier objeto. 5. Pacto, convenio en cuanto está demostrado por la firma del que lo hace.

subsection ['sʌb,sekʃən] [sab-sek-shon], *s.* Subdivisión, clase menor.

subsecutive [səb'sɪkwɪtɪv] [sab-si-kui-tiv], *a.* Subsiguiente, subsecuente.

subsequence ['sʌbsɪkwəns] [sab-si-kuens], *s.* Subsecuencia.

subsequent ['sʌbsɪkwənt] [sab-si-kuent], *a.* Subsiguiente.

subsequently ['sʌbsɪkwəntlɪ] [sab-si-kuent-li], *adv.* Posteriormente, subsiguientemente.

subserve [səb'sɜːv] [sab-serv], *va.* Servir, estar subordinado, servir como instrumento o de instrumento, favorecer. -*vn.* Servir como subordinado.

subservience [səb'sɜːvɪəns] [sab-ser-vians], *s.* Servicio, utilidad, socorro; la acción de servir de instrumento en la ejecución de una cosa y la aptitud para ello.

subservient [səb'sɜːvɪənt] [sab-ser-viant], *a.* Subalterno, subordinado, inferior; obsequioso; útil, apto o a propósito para servir de instrumento.

subserviently [səb'sɜːvɪəntlɪ] [sab-ser-viant-li], *adv.* Subordinadamente, de un modo secundario pero útil; útilmente.

subside [səb'saɪd] [sab-said], *vn.* 1. Apaciguarse, calmarse, cesar una tempestad, agitación, o pasión turbulenta; minorar, cesar. 2. Bajar, rebajar, ir a un nivel más bajo (un fluido); desplomarse, dejarse caer. 3. Sumergirse, irse a fondo.

subsidence [səb'saɪdəns] [sab-sai-dans], *s.* 1. Apaciguamiento, calma. 2. Desplome, desmoronamiento. 3. Sumersión, acción de sumergir o de irse a fondo.

subsidiary [səb'sɪdɪərɪ] [sab-si-dia-ri], *a.* 1. Subsidiario. 2. Auxiliar, que ayuda.

subsidize ['sʌbsɪdaɪz] [sab-si-dais], *va.* Subvencionar, dar un subsidio; suministrar fondos a una empresa.

subsidy ['sʌbsɪdɪ] [sab-si-di], *s.* Subsidio, ayuda, socorro en dinero que da el Estado a una empresa individual o comercial considerada como de interés público; subvención. 2. Subsidio, dinero que da un Estado a una potencia aliada.

subsign ['sʌbsaɪn] [sab-sain], *va.* Subscribir, firmar.

subsist [səb'sɪst] [sab-sist], *vn.* 1. Subsistir, permanecer, durar alguna cosa o conservarse (endure). 2. Subsistir, existir, vivir, estar por sí en su propia naturaleza y ser (survive). 3. Sustentarse, tener con que vivir y mantenerse de un modo correspondiente a su estado o calidad. -*vn.* Alimentar o mantener a uno.

subsistence [səb'sɪstəns] [sab-sis-tans], *s.* 1. Existencia. 2. Subsistencia, sustento. 3. Calidad de subsistente; también, una cualidad inherente. **Subsistence money,** la cantidad de dinero que se necesita o se emplea en mantenerse o en el sustento diario.

subsistent [səb'sɪstənt] [sab-sis-tant], *a.* 1. Subsistente, que subsiste. 2. Inherente.

subsoil ['sʌbsɔɪl] [sab-soil], *va.* Arar, voltear la tierra con un arado de subsuelo. -*s.* Subsuelo, capa de tierra situada inmediatamente debajo del terreno superficial.

substance ['sʌbstəns] [sabs-tans], *s.* 1. Substancia, la entidad o esencia que subsiste o existe por sí. 2. Substancia, ser, esencia, naturaleza de las cosas. 3. Substancia, la parte más esencial de una cosa. 4. Realidad, la existencia física y real de una cosa. 5. Substancia, lo mismo que cuerpo o materia. 6. Substancia, la hacienda, caudal o bienes.

substantial [səb'stænʃəl] [sabs-tan-shal], *a.* 1. Substancial, que pertenece a la substancia, es propio de ella o la incluye. 2. Real, existente, verdadero. 3. Corpóreo, material. 4. Substancial, substancioso. 5. Fuerte, vigoroso, sólido. 6. Acomodado, el que tiene medios de subsistir o es moderadamente rico. -*s.* Lo que tiene substancia; realidad, cosa real. **Substantials,** las partes esenciales o más importantes. **Substantial damages,** daños generales.

substantialize [səb'stænʃəlaɪz] [sabs-tan-sha-lais], *va.* Hacer real y efectiva alguna cosa.

substantially [səb'stænʃəlɪ] [sabs-tan-sha-li], *adv.* Substancialmente; realmente; sólidamente.

substantialness [səb'stænʃəlnɪs] [sabs-tan-shal-nes], *s.* Firmeza, fuerza, duración.

substantiate [səb'stænʃɪeɪt] [sabs-tan-shieit], *va.* 1. Verificar, establecer, comprobar, justificar. 2. *(Ant.)* Dar cuerpo. *V.* EMBODY.

substantival [,sʌbstən'taɪvəl] [sabs-tan-tai-val], *a.* 1. *(Gram.)* Substantivo, perteneciente a un nombre o substantivo. 2. Existente por sí mismo.

substantive ['sʌbstəntɪv] [sabs-tan-tiv], *a.* 1. *(Gram.)* Substantivo, que puede usarse como nombre substantivo; que denota existencia. 2. Que tiene substancia o realidad; de aquí, duradero. 3. Esencial. 4. Expresado explícitamente. 5. Que tiene individualidad distinta; que posee medios o recursos independientes, v. g. un país. -*s.* 1. Nombre, substantivo; cualquier cosa que se emplea como substantivo,

p. ej. una forma del verbo, una locución o cláusula. 2. El o lo que es independiente.

substantively ['sʌbstəntɪvlɪ] [sabs-tan-tiv-li], *adv.* 1. Substancialmente, en substancia, esencialmente. 2. Substantivamente, como substantivo.

substation ['sʌbˌsteɪʃən] [sabs-tei-shon], *sf. (Elec.)* Subestación.

substitute ['sʌbstɪtjuːt] [sabs-ti-tiut], *va.* Substituir, poner una persona o cosa en lugar de otra. -*s.* Sustituto, suplente. **This is a poor substitute for the real thing,** esto no sustituye plenamente lo auténtico. -*a.* Sucedáneo, de repuesto.

substitution [ˌsʌbstɪ'tjuːʃən] [sabs-ti-tiu-shon], *s.* Substitución; reemplazo; acción y efecto de substituir.

substratum ['sʌbˌstrɑːtəm] [sabs-tra-tom], *s.* Lecho, capa o cama debajo de otras.

substructure ['sʌbˌstrʌktʃəᵣ] [sabs-trak-cha^r], *s. (Arq.)* Infraestructura, soporte, las partes de un edificio que están debajo de todas las otras. Se contrapone a *superstructure,* superestructura.

subsume [sʌb'sjuːm] [sab-sium], *vt.* Subsumir.

subsystem ['sʌbˌsɪstəm] [sab-sis-tem], *sm.* Subsistema.

subtense ['sʌbtəns] [sab-tens], *s. (Geom.)* Subtensa, cuerda.

subter ['sʌbtəᵣ] [sab-ta^r], Prefijo que en composición significa debajo; opuesto a *super,* sobre.

subterfuge ['sʌbtəfjuːdʒ] [sabs-ta-fiuch], *s.* Subterfugio, efugio, evasión, salida, excusa falsa.

subterranean [ˌsʌbtə'reɪnɪən] [sab-ta-rei-nian], *a.* Subterráneo, que está debajo de tierra.

subtext ['sʌbtekst] [sab-tekst], *sm.* Subtexto.

subtile ['sʌbtaɪl] [sab-tail], *a.* 1. Sútil, delicado, tenue, etéreo (delicate); refinado (refined); penetrante (sharp). **A subtile spider's web,** una telaraña sutil. **A subtile perfume,** un perfume penetrante. 2. Sutil, perspicaz, ingenioso, penetrante, agudo. 3. Artero, artificioso, astuto. *V.* SUBTLE. (La tendencia actual es a emplear *subtile* como atributo de las cosas y *subtle,* como característico del ánimo.)

subtilize ['sʌtɪlaɪz] [sa-ti-lais], *va.* y *vn.* 1. Sutilizar. adelgazar una cosa. 2. Sutilizar, limar o pulir una cosa. -*vn.* Sutilizar, discurrir ingeniosamente; por lo regular se toma en mala parte.

subtility ['sʌtɪlɪtɪ] [sa-ti-li-ti], *s.* 1. Sutileza, sutilidad, delgadeza o tenuidad. 2. La demasiada sutileza, delicadeza o esmero. 3. Astucia, artificio, artería.

subtitle ['sʌbˌtaɪtl] [sab-tai-tel], *sm.* Subtítulo.

subtle ['sʌtl] [sa-tel], *a.* 1. Sutil, astuto, artificioso, mañoso, artero. 2. Perspicaz, penetrante, agudo; demasiado refinado. 3. Apto, hábil, mañoso. 4. Ejecutado con arte primoroso, ingeniosamente ideado. 5. *V.* SUBTILE, en cualquiera de sus acepciones.

subtleness ['sʌtlnɪs] [sa-tel-nes], **subtlety** ['sʌtltɪ] [sa-tel-ti], *s.* Sutileza, astucia, artificio.

subtly ['sʌtl] [sa-tel], *adv.* Sutilmente, delicadamente, artificiosamente.

subtract [səb'trækt] [sab-trakt], *va.* 1. Substraer, apartar, separar. 2 *(Arit.)* Restar, substraer un número menor de otro mayor.

subtraction [səb'trækʃən] [sab-trak-shon], *s.* 1. Substracción, la acción y efecto de substraer. 2. *(Arit.)* Resta o substracción.

subtropical ['sʌbˈtrɒpɪkəl] [sab-tro-pi-kal], *a.* 1. Subtropical, de cualidades intermedias entre las de las zonas templadas y las tropicales. 2. Perteneciente a la región cercana a los círculos tropicales.

suburb ['sʌbɜːb] [sa-berb], *s.* Suburbio, arrabal o aldea cerca de la ciudad.

suburban [sə'bɜːbən] [sa-ber-ban], *a.* Suburbano. -*s.* Residente en un suburbio.

suburbanite [sə'bɜːbənaɪt] [sa-ber-ba-nait], *s.* El que vive en un suburbio.

suburbia [sə'bɜːbɪə] [sa-ber-bia], *s.* 1. Suburbios, alrededores, extramuros barrios residenciales o ciudades que rodean una metrópolis. 2. Tipo de vida que los caracteriza.

subvention [səb'venʃən] [sab-ven-shon], *s.* Subvención, la acción y efecto de subvenir o amparar; ayuda. *V.* SUBSIDY.

subversion [səb'vɜːʃən] [sab-ver-shon], *s.* Subversión, ruina, estrago, trastorno o destrucción.

subversive [səb'vɜːsɪv] [sab-ver-siv], *s.* Subversión, ruina, estrago, trastorno o destrucción.

subversive, *a.* Subversivo.

subvert [sʌb'vɜːt] [sab-vert], *va.* Subvertir, destruir, trastornar, arruinar.

subverter [səb'vɜːtəᵣ] [sab-ver-ta^r], *s.* Subversor, destructor.

subvertible [səb'vɜːtɪbl] [sab-ver-ti-bol], *a.* Subvertible, que se puede subvertir; trastornable, destruible.

subway ['sʌbweɪ] [sab-uei], *s.* Subterráneo, ferrocarril subterráneo, metro, metropolitano.

succeed [sək'siːd] [sak-sid], *vn.* y *va.* 1. Suceder, entrar en lugar de otro o seguirse a él. 2. Suceder, llenar una persona o cosa el hueco de otra u ocupar su lugar. 2. Salir bien de alguna empresa o empeño; conseguir, lograr, acertar. 4. Hacer salir bien una empresa o empeño; hacer prosperar. **To succeed in doing a thing,** acertar, lograr hacer una cosa. **Nothing succeeds with them,** nada les sale bien. **Maria Theresa succeeded to the throne,** María Teresa sucedió en el trono. **To succeed each other** o **one another,** sucederse (los unos a los otros).

succeeder [sək'siːdəᵣ] [sak-si-da^r], *s.* Sucesor, el que sucede a otro o entra en su lugar.

succeeding [sək'siːdɪŋ] [sak-si-din], *a.* Subsiguiente, que sigue inmediatamente a otra cosa; futuro.

success [sək'ses] [sak-ses], *s.* 1. Suceso, salida, resultado o fin bueno, buen éxito, fortuna, ventaja o triunfo. 2. *(Ant. o Fam.)* Mal resultado. 3. Persona o asunto afortunados.

successful [sək'sesfʊl] [sak-ses-ful], *a.* Próspero, dichoso, afortunado, exitoso, feliz, que ha salido bien.

successfully [sək'sesfəlɪ] [sak-ses-fu-li], *adv.* Felizmente, prósperamente, con felicidad o buen éxito.

successfulness [sək'sesfəlnɪs] [sak-ses-ful-nes], *s.* Feliz éxito, buen suceso, dicha.

succession [sək'seʃən] [sak-se-shon], *s.* 1. Sucesión, la acción de suceder. 2. Linaje, descendencia. 3. Sucesión o herencia; derecho de sucesión; advenimiento al trono.

successive [sək'sesɪv] [sak-se-siv], *a.* Sucesivo, que sigue o va después de otra cosa.

successively [sək'sesɪvlɪ] [sak-se-siv-li], *adv.* Sucesivamente, consiguientemente.

successiveness [sək'sesɪvnɪs] [sak-se-siv-nes], *s.* (Poco us.) Sucesión.

successless [sək'seslɪs] [sak-ses-les], *a.* Desafortunado, desgraciado, infeliz.

successor [sək'sesəᵣ] [sak-se-sa^r], *s.* 1. Sucesor, el que sucede a otro. 2. Heredero.

succinct [sək'sɪŋkt] [sak-sinkt], *a.* 1. Sucinto, breve, compendioso. 2. *(Ento.)* Enfaldado, sostenido por un hilo de seda, como la ninfa de una mariposa.

succinctly [sək'sɪŋktlɪ] [sak-sinkt-li], *adv.* Sucintamente, compendiosamente, con brevedad, con precisión, en pocas palabras.

succinctness [sək'sɪŋktnɪs] [sak-sinkt-nes], *s.* Brevedad, concisión. *va.* Socorrer, ayudar, auxiliar dar socorro.

succor, succour ['sʌkəᵣ] [sa-ka^r], *s.* Socorro, ayuda, auxilio, favor, asistencia. **To fly, to run for succor,** volar, correr en busca de socorro.

succorer ['sʌkərəᵣ] [sa-ka-ra^r], *s.* Socorredor, el que socorre, auxiliador.

succorless ['sʌkələs] [sa-ka-les], *a.* Desamparado, sin protección, sin ayuda.

succulence ['sʌkjʊləns] [sa-kiu-lans], *s.* Jugosidad.

succulent ['sʌkjʊlənt] [sa-kiu-lant], *a.* Suculento, jugoso.

succumb [sə'kʌmb] [sa-kamb], *vn.* 1. No poder llevar o aguantar un trabajo o una carga; quedar rendido o vencido debajo de otro. 2. Morir. **He succumbed to his wounds,** murió de sus heridas.

succussion [sə'kʌʃən] [sa-ka-shon], *s.* Sacudimiento, la acción de sacudir.

such [sʌtʃ] [sach], *a*. 1. Tal, igual, semejante; cierto. 2. Enfáticamente, cosa extremada, intolerable. **We are come to such a pass,** hemos llegado a situación tan extrema. **Such a place,** cierto lugar. *-pron.* Tal, un tal; el que, la que, los que, las que; aquel, aquella, aquello. **There is no such thing,** no hay tal cosa. **At such a time,** en tal tiempo. **Mr. such a one,** don fulano, o el señor fulano de tal. **Such as,** el que, los que, lo que, cualquiera que. **In such case,** en tal caso. **No such thing!,** ¡ni hablar! *-adv.* Tan. **Such good people,** una gente tan buena. **It's such a long time ago,** hace tanto tiempo.

suchlike [ˈsʌtʃlaɪk] [sach-laik], *a*. Semejante, tal.

suck [sʌk] [sak], *va. y. vn.* 1. Chupar, sacar o atraer con los labios un jugo o substancia. 2. Mamar, atraer y sacar la leche de los pechos. 3. Extraer o sacar alguna cosa formando un vacío o casi vacío por medio de la rarefacción o extracción del aire, como el agua que se extrae con las bombas. 4. Chupar o ir sustrayendo la hacienda de otro con pretextos y engaños. **To suck down,** tragar. **To suck in,** sorber. **To such out/up,** extraer o sacar algo chupando o por medio de una bomba; dar a la bomba; vaciar una cosa sacando lo que contenía a fuerza de chupar; sacar una cosa de otra.

suck, *s.* 1. *(Med.)* Succión, la acción de chupar o de extraer algo chupando. 2. La acción de mamar. 3. Leche, lo que dan las madres a sus criaturas. **To give suck,** amamantar, dar de mamar.

sucker [ˈsʌkər] [sa-kaᵣ], *s.* 1. Chupador, el que chupa. 2. Chupadero, lo que chupa. 3. Chupón. 4. Émbolo y el sopapo de bomba. 5. Tubo aspirador. 6. Caramelo, paleta de dulce. 7. *(Vul.)* Bobo, persona cándida y crédula.

sucket [ˈsʌkɪt] [sa-kit], *s.* Dulce que se chupa, como el caramelo.

sucking [ˈsʌkɪŋ] [sa-kin], *s.* Chupadura, la acción de chupar; la acción de mamar. **Sucking-fish,** rémora. **Sucking pig,** lechoncillo.

suckle [ˈsʌkl] [sa-kel], *va.* 1. Amamantar, dar la teta, dar de mamar. 2. Criar, nutrir a un niño con la leche de los pechos.

suckling [ˈsʌklɪŋ] [sa-klin], *s.* Mamantón, la cría o la criatura que está aún mamando.

sucrose [ˈsuːkrəʊz] [su-krous], *s.* Sacarosa.

suction [ˈsʌkʃən] [sak-shon], *s.* Succión, el acto de chupar; la producción de un vacío parcial. **Suction-hose,** manguera de alimentación. **Suction-pump,** bomba aspirante.

Sudanese [suːdəˈniːz] [su-da-nis], *a.* Sudanés, del Sudán o perteneciente a él. *-s.* Sudanés.

sudden [ˈsʌdn] [sa-den], *a.* 1. Repentino, pronto, no prevenido, imprevisto, súbito. 1. Apresurado, ideado, usado o hecho deprisa; precipitado. *-s. (Des.)* Repentón, suceso o lance que sobreviene sin pensar. **On a sudden,** de repente, sin esperanza, súbitamente.

suddenly [ˈsʌdnlɪ] [sa-den-li], *adv.* Repentinamente, de repente, súbitamente.

suddenness [ˈsʌdnnɪs] [sa-den-nes], *s.* Precipitación, calidad de repentino.

suds [sʌdz] [sads], *s. pl.* 1. Jabonaduras, el agua que queda mezclada con el jabón y su espuma. 2. Espuma. **To be in the suds,** *(Vulg.)* Verse apurado.

sue [suː] [su], *va. y vn.* 1. Poner por justicia; perseguir o demandar a alguno en justicia. 2. Seguir un pleito; procesar o hacer causa a alguno. 3. Ganar un pleito o una demanda. 4. Ejecutar u obligar a uno por justicia a pagar lo que debe. 5. Rogar, pedir, suplicar. *-vn.* Pretender en matrimonio, galantear. **To sue for,** pedir o demandar judicialmente. **To sue for damages,** demandar por daños y perjuicios. **To sue out,** conseguir u obtener una cosa a fuerza de ruegos.

suede [ˈsweɪd] [sueid], *s.* Piel de ante. **Suede cloth,** tela parecida a la piel de ante.

suet [sʊɪt] [suit], *s.* Sebo, grasa dura y sólida de la región de los riñones (oxen, lambs).

suety [ˈsʊɪtɪ] [sui-ti], *a.* Seboso.

suffer [ˈsʌfər] [sa-faᵣ], *va. y vn.* 1. Sufrir, padecer algún dolor, pesar, etc. 2. Sufrir, tolerar, aguantar, llevar algún mal con paciencia, sufrimiento y tolerancia (bear, tolerate). 3. Sufrir, permitir; admitir (admit). 4. Sufrir alguna pena o castigo. 5. Causar daño o detrimento. **To suffer for,** sufrir, padecer por, llevar la pena de algo. **To be suffered,** tolerable, soportable. **Not to be suffered,** intolerable, insoportable. **I can't suffer it,** no puedo aguantarlo. **To suffer for divorce,** solicitar el divorcio, presentar demanda de divorcio. **To be suffered,** ser demandado.

sufferable [ˈsʌfərəbl] [sa-fa-ra-bol], *a.* Sufrible, sufridero, soportable, tolerable.

sufferableness [ˈsʌfərəblnɪs] [sa-fa-ra-bol-nes], *s.* El estado de lo que puede tolerarse.

sufferably [ˈsʌfərəblɪ] [sa-fe-ra-bli], *adv.* De un modo soportable.

sufferance [ˈsʌfərəns] [sa-fa-rans], *s.* 1. Tolerancia, permisión, consentimiento, tácito. 2. *(Ant.)* Sufrimiento, paciencia, conformidad, resignación, tolerancia, aguante. 3. *(Ant.)* Pena, dolor, trabajo, tormento. 4. En las aduanas, permiso para expedir ciertas clases de efectos.

sufferer [ˈsʌfərəᵣ] [sa-fe-raᵣ], *s.* 1. Sufridor, el que sufre dolor físico o moral; doliente. 2. Perdidoso. 3. El que tolera tácitamente. **Fellow-sufferer,** compañero de infortunio. **A sufferer in o by,** víctima de.

suffering [ˈsʌfərɪŋ] [sa-fe-rin], *s.* Pena, dolor (físico o moral), el padecimiento o la pérdida sufrida, tormento. *-pa.* Paciente, doliente.

suffice [səˈfaɪs] [sa-fais], *vn.* Bastar, ser suficiente. *-va.* Satisfacer, ser bastante o suficiente. **Suffice it to say,** baste decir.

sufficiency [səˈfɪʃənsɪ] [sa-fi-shan-si], *s.* 1. Suficiencia, capacidad o idoneidad para algún fin u objeto. 2. Lo suficiente, lo bastante o lo que basta, lo que es menester. 3. Cualidad, eficacia. 4. Presunción, exagerada confianza en sí mismo, alto concepto del propio valor. **Self-sufficiency,** presunción en las fuerzas propias. **To have a sufficiency,** estar acomodado.

sufficient [səˈfɪʃənt] [sa-fi-shent], *a.* 1. Suficiente, bastante, lo que es menester (enough). 2. Suficiente, bastante o capaz para alguna cosa; apto, idóneo. **Sufficient witness,** testigo sin tacha. **To be sufficient,** bastar, ser suficiente.

sufficiently [səˈfɪʃəntlɪ] [sa-fi-shant-li], *adv.* Suficientemente, bastantemente, bastante; bastante bien.

suffix [ˈsʌfɪks] [sa-fiks], *va.* Añadir, anexar, como sufijo a afijo.

suffix, *s.* 1. Sufijo, afijo, sílaba o letra que se añade al final de una palabra para modificar la significación de ésta. 2. Cualquier título o designación añadidos.

suffocate [ˈsʌfəkeɪt] [sa-fo-keit], *va.* 1. Sofocar, sufocar, ahogar, impedir el aliento o la respiración. 2. Matar sofocado. 3. Apagar, extinguir, ahogar, v. g. un fuego. *-vn.* Sofocarse, ahogarse, perder la respiración.

suffocating [ˈsʌfəkeɪtɪŋ] [sa-fo-kei-tin], *a.* Sofocante, sofocador, que ahoga.

suffocation [sʌfəˈkeɪʃən] [sa-fo-kei-shon], *s.* Sofocación, ahogo, impedimiento de la respiración.

suffocative [ˈsʌfəkətɪv] [sa-fo-ka-tiv], *a.* Sofocante, sofocador.

suffragan [ˈsʌfrəgən] [sa-fra-gan], *a.* Auxiliar. *-s.* 1. Sufragáneo: se dice de un obispo con respecto a su metropolitano. 2. Obispo auxiliar.

suffrage [ˈsʌfrɪdʒ] [sa-frich], *s.* 1. Sufragio, voto en favor de alguna medida u opinión: de aquí, aprobación, consentimiento. 2. El derecho o privilegio de votar.

suffragette [sʌfrəˈdʒet] [sa-fra-yet], *s.* Sufragista, partidaria del voto femenino.

suffragist [ˈsʌfrəgɪst] [sa-fra-guist], *s.* Sufragista, partidario del sufragio femenino.

suffuse [səˈfjuːz] [sa-fius], *va.* Difundir, extender; derramar, verter, cubrir con un color o tinte. **Cheeks suffused with blushes,** mejillas cubiertas de rubor. **Eyes suffused by tears,** ojos bañados de lágrimas.

suffusion [səˈfjuːʃən] [sa-fiu-shon], *s.* 1. *(Med.)* Sufusión o efusión de humores debajo del cutis. 2. Sufusión, congestión ligera difundida. 3. Mezcla de colores en el plumaje.

sugar [ˈʃʊgəʳ] [shu-gaʳ], *s.* 1. Azúcar, compuesto dulce cristalizable. (C12H22O11) que se saca principalmente del jugo de la caña dulce y de la remolacha. 2. Cualuier cosa muy dulce. **Beet-sugar,** azúcar de remolacha. **Grape-sugar,** azúcar de uvas, glucosa. **Maple-sugar,** azúcar de arce. **Sugar-beet,** remolacha. **Sugar-bowl,** azucarero. **Sugar-cane,** caña dulce o de azúcar. **Loaf-sugar,** azúcar de pilón. **Brow o clayed sugar,** azúcar moreno o terciado, cogucho; *(Amer.)* chancaca, panoche, panela. **White o refined sugar,** azúcar refinado. **Sugar-coated,** garapiñado, cubierto de azúcar. **Sugar cube/lump,** terrón de azúcar. **Sugar-plum.** confite, dulce. **Sugar of lead,** azúcar de plomo o sal de Saturno. **Sugar-house,** ingenio o trapiche donde se fabrica el azúcar; refino u oficina donde se refina (sugar-refinery). **To sweeten with sugar,** azucarar, confitar. **Oh, sugar!,** ¡caramba!, ¡caracoles!

sugar, *va.* 1. Azucarar, endulzar o suavizar el mal sabor de una cosa con azúcar; también en sentido figurado. 2. *(E. U. y Canadá)* Hacer el azúcar de arce.

sugar mill [ˈʃʊgəmɪl] [shu-ga-mil], *s.* Trapiche, molino de azúcar.

sugary [ˈʃʊgərɪ] [shu-ga-ri], *a.* 1. Azucarado, sacarino, compuesto de azúcar, dulce. 2. Goloso, aficionado al azúcar y a los dulces. 3. *(Fig.)* Melosa, seductivo, halagüeño.

suggest [səˈdʒest] [sa-yest], *va.* 1. Sugerir, echar una indirecta, insinuar, informar indirecta y discretamente. 2. Sugerir, advertir o acordar alguna especie. 3. Sugerir, instigar una acción, influir para que se ejecute. **This suggests that,** esto hace pensar que, esto sugiere que. **Prudence suggests a retreat,** la prudencia nos aconseja retirarnos. **What are you suggesting?,** ¿qué insinúa usted?

suggestible [səˈdʒestɪbl] [sa-yes-ti-bol], *a.* Sugestionable.

suggestion [səˈdʒestʃən] [sa-yes-chon], *s.* Sugestión, sugerencia, la acción de sugerir y la cosa sugerida; instigación. **My suggestion is that,** yo propongo que. **There is no suggestion of danger,** no hay indicio de peligro. *(Culin.)* **A suggestion of salt,** una pizca de sal.

suggestive [səˈdʒestɪv] [sa-yes-tiv], *a.* Sugerente. que sugiere; que inspira el ánimo o estimula la reflexión.

suggestively [səˈdʒestɪvlɪ] [sa-yes-tiv-li], *adv.* Indecentemente.

suicidal [sʊɪˈsaɪdl] [sui-sai-dal], *a.* 1. Que pertenece o que tiende al suicidio. 2. Destructor de sí mismo, ruinoso a sus propios intereses.

suicide [ˈsʊɪsaɪd] [sui-said], *s.* 1. Suicidio, el acto de quitarse la vida. 2. Suicida. 3. *(Fig.)* Ruina política, social, o comercial que uno mismo se atrae o causa. *-vn. (Vulg.)* Suicidarse.

suing [ˈsʊɪŋ] [suin], *s.* 1. Solicitación o diligencia para conseguir alguna cosa. 2. Galanteo, pretensión en matrimonio. 2. *V.* SUIT, 2ª acep.

suit [suːt] [sut], *s.* 1. Petición, súplica, solicitación. 2. Galanteo, obsequio o cortejo hecho a una mujer. 3. Pleito o litigio judicial. 4. Juego, un número determinado de cosas que tienen cierta conexión o correspondencia entre sí; colección completa de cosas semejantes, reunión, surtido. 5. Vestido, el conjunto de prendas que componen el abrigo del cuerpo. **I have bought four suits of clothes,** he comprado cuatro vestidos completos. 6. Palo en la baraja. 7. *V.* SUITE, 2ª acep. **Suit of hangings,** colgaduras. **A suit of armor,** una armadura completa. **Suit in chancery,** procedimiento ante la cancillería. **To bring (a) suit,** entablar un pleito, incoar una demanda judicial. **To follow suit,** (a) jugar el mismo palo; (b) seguir el ejemplo, imitar lo que otro hace.

suit, *va. y vn.* 1. Adecuar, proporcionar, acomodar, ajustar o casar dos o más cosas para que digan bien entre sí o para que hagan buen juego. 2. Adaptar, acomodar o hacer venir bien una cosa con otra. 3. Venir, ajustarse, acomodarse o conformarse una cosa a otra o una cosa con otra. 4. Convenir, concordar. 5. Sentar, caer o venir bien un vestido o adorno; ser aparente o bueno. **This coat does not suit me,** no me sienta esta levita. **That suits you very well,** eso le conviene a usted perfectamente; eso le va o cae a usted muy bien.

He is well suited with his place, está muy contento con su empleo.

suitable [ˈsuːtəbl] [su-ta-bol], *a.* Conforme, proporcionado, conveniente.

suitableness [ˈsuːtəblnɪs] [su-ta-bol-nes], *s.* Conformidad, conveniente, conforme.

suitcase [ˈsuːtkeɪs] [sut-keis], *s.* Maleta.

suite [swiːt] [suit], *s.* 1. Serie, continuación ordenada y sucesiva de cosas. 2. Séquito de un alto personaje; tren, acompañamiento, comitiva. **Suite of apartments,** vivienda o habitación con varias piezas o aposentos; vivienda.

suitor [ˈsuːtəʳ] [su-taʳ], *s.* 1. Prentendiente suplicante, el que pretende o suplica; aspirante; postulante. 2. Amante, pretendiente, cortejo, el que galantea o hace la corte a una mujer. 3. Pleitante, el que pleitea.

sulfate [ˈsʌlfeɪt] [sal-feit], etc. *V.* SULPHATE, SULPHUR, etc.

sulk [sʌlk] [salk], *vn.* Estar malcontento o de mal humor; ser terco u obstinado. *-s.* **Sulks,** murria mohína, mal humor.

sulkily [ˈsʌlkɪlɪ] [sal-ki-li], *adv.* De mal humor, con mala gana.

sulkiness [ˈsʌlkɪnɪs] [sal-ki-nes], *s.* Mal humor, ceño; estado de la persona que refunfuña.

sulky [ˈsʌlkɪ] [sal-ki], *a.* 1. Malcontento, caprichoso, regañón, áspero de genio, vinagre. 2. Obstinado, terco.

sulky, *s. (pl.* SULKIES). Calesín de un solo asiento, solitario.

sullen [ˈsʌlən] [sa-len], *a.* 1. Malcontento; malhumorado. 2. Intratable, duro de genio, berrinchudo (rude). 3. Remolón, taciturno, cazurro.

sullenly [ˈsʌlənlɪ] [sa-len-li], *adv.* Ásperamente, con ceño, de mal humor; tercamente.

sullenness [ˈsʌlənnɪs] [sa-len-nes], *s.* 1. Ceño, enojo, berrín o berrinche, demostración de enfado; mal humor o mal genio, tristeza sombría. 2. Obstinación, terquedad, pertinacia.

sully [ˈsʌlɪ] [sa-li], *va.* Manchar, ensuciar, tachar, mancillar, ennegrecer. *-s.* Mancha.

sulpha drugs [ˈsʌlfədrʌg] [sul-fa-drag], *s. pl.* Sulfonamidas.

sulphate [ˈsʌlfeɪt] [sal-feit], *s. (Quím.)* Sulfato, sal de ácido sulfúrico con una base.

sulphid, sulphide [ˈsʌlfaɪd] [sal-faid], *s.* Sulfuro, compuesto de azufre con un elemento o radical.

sulphite [ˈsʌlfeɪt] [sal-feit], *s.* Sal de ácido sulfuroso.

sulphur [ˈsʌlfəʳ] [sal-faʳ], *s.* Azufre, elemento amarillo claro, no metálico, que se halla en muchas partes en estado nativo.

sulphureous, sulphurous [sʌlˈfjʊərɪəs] [sal-fiua-rios], *a.* Sulfúreo, azufroso, azufrado, que tiene azufre.

sulphuric [sʌlˈfjʊərɪk] [sal-fiu-rik], *a.* Sulfúrico, perteneciente al azufre, o procedente de él. **Sulphuric acid,** ácido sulfúrico, líquido muy corrosivo (H2SO4) que se usa en las artes; aceite de vitriolo.

sultan [ˈsʌltən] [sl-tab], *s.* Sultán, nombre que dan los turcos a su emperador.

sultana [sʌlˈtɑːnə] [sal-ta-na], *sf.* Sultana, la primera de las mujeres del sultán.

sultriness [ˈsʌltrɪnɪs] [sal-tri-nes], *s.* Bochorno.

sultry [ˈsʌltrɪ] [sal-tri], *a.* Abochornado, caluroso, bochonorso, sin ventilación, sofocante.

sum [sʌm] [sam], *s.* 1. Suma, el agregado de muchas cosas; particularmente se toma por el de dinero, y en este caso corresponde muy frecuentemente a cantidad 2. Suma, sumario, resumen, compendio, o recopilación de alguna cosa (resume). 3. Suma, la conclusión o sustancia de alguna cosa y también su resultado. 4. Cima, lo sumo, lo último. **For a certain sum agreed upon,** por cierta cantidad alzada. **To do sums in one's head,** hacer un cálculo mental.

sum, *va.* 1. Sumar, juntar dos o más números o cantidades. 2. Sumar, recopilar, compendiar, abreviar alguna materia difusa o extensa. **To sum up,** recapitular, resumir.

sumac, sumach [ˈsuːmæk] [su-mak], *s.* 1. *(Bot.)* Zumaque, cualquier arbusto o árbol del género Rhus. 2. Polvos de las hojas secas de ciertas especies de zumaque, que se emplean para curtir y teñir.

summarily [ˈsʌmərɪlɪ] [sa-ma-ri-li], *adv.* Sumariamente, en compendio, en pocas palabras.

summarize [ˈsʌmaraɪz] [sa-ma-rais], *va.* Epitomar, resumir, reducir.

summary [ˈsʌmərɪ] [sa-ma-ri], *a.* Sumario, breve, compendioso, sucinto, corto. -*s.* Sumario, resumen, compendio o suma.

summer [ˈsʌməʳ] [sa-maʳ], *a.* Estival o estivo, de verano. -*s.* 1. Verano, estío. **Indian summer,** el veranillo de San Martín, de 15 de octubre al 15 de noviembre. **Summer-house,** cenador, glorieta de jardín. **Summer solstice,** solsticio de verano. **Summer-time, -tide,** estío, estación de verano. **Summer-boarder,** veraneante. **To spend the summer,** veranear. **Summer-fallow,** *va.* Arar en el verano y dejar en barbecho. 2. (*Poét.*) Año de vida, particularmente de vida alegre; período próspero.

summer, *s.* 1. Viga solera, viga maestra. 2. Sotabanco, piedra grande sobre una columna para sostener una o más bóvedas. **Summer-tree,** los traveseros en que descansan las vigas maestras.

summer, *vn.* Veranear, pasar el verano. -*va.* Calentar; preservar del frío.

summersault [ˈsʌmasɔːlt] [sa-ma-solt], **summerset** [ˈsʌmaset] [sa-ma-set], *s.* Salto mortal.

summit [ˈsʌmɪt] [sa-mit], *s.* Ápice, el extremo superior de una cosa, cima, punta; cima, cumbre, de un edificio, montaña, etc. **Summit conference,** reunión en la cima.

summon [ˈsʌmən] [sa-mon], *va.* 1. Citar, ordenar a alguno que se presente en fecha y lugar señalados. 2. Citar, notificar, requerir por auto de juez; requerir o pedir la inmediata presencia de alguien o algo, dar o servir como señal para presentarse; convocar; mandar. 3. Excitar, animar. 4. Intimar la rendición. **To summon away,** llamar aparte, mandar alejarse. **To summon back,** llamar, volver a llamar. **To summon up,** armarse de; evocar.

summoner [ˈsʌmənəʳ] [sa-mo-naʳ], *s.* El que cita o notifica.

summons [ˈsʌmənz] [sa-mons], *s.* Citación, notificación, requerimiento; intimación; aviso o amonestación hecha con autoridad.

sump [sʌmp] [samp], *s.* 1. Sumidero, pozo perdido, pozanco, estanque en una salina. 2. Hoyo de albañilería cubierto de arcilla para recibir los metales fundidos. 3. (*Aut.*) Colector de aceite.

sumpter [ˈsʌmptəʳ] [samp-taʳ], *s.* Caballo o mulo de carga, acémila.

sumption [ˈsʌmpʃən] [samp-shon], *s.* Premisa mayor de un silogismo.

sumptuary [ˈsʌmptjʊərɪ] [samp-chua-ri], *a.* 1. Suntuario, que pertenece al arreglo, suspensión o moderación de los gastos o del lujo en las comidas y vestidos. 2. (Poco us.) Que hace las veces de una acémila.

sumptuous [ˈsʌmptʃʊəs] [samp-chuos], *adv.* Suntuosamente, con esplendor, con pompa.

sumptuousness [ˈsʌmptʃʊəsnɪs] [samp-chuos-nes], *s.* Suntuosidad, magnificencia, pompa.

sun [sʌn] [san], *s.* 1. Sol. 2. Sol, cualquier astro que es centro de un sistema planetario. 3. Sol, cualquier cosa sumamente espléndida o que da luz física o moral. 4. Solana, el sitio donde el sol da de lleno. **Under the sun,** debajo del sol, en este mundo. **The sun rises, sets,** el sol sale, se pone. **The sun is up, is down,** el sol ha salido ya, se ha puesto. **Sun-bath,** exposición del cuerpo a los rayos directos del sol; algunas veces con un fin terapéutico. **Sun-bed,** tumbona. **Sun-proof,** aprueba de sol. **Sun-spot,** mácula, mancha oscura, irregular, en la cara del sol, dentro de los 35° de su ecuador. **To have a place in the sun,** tener buena posición. **Put it where the sun doesn't shine!,** ¡métetelo donde te quepa! (*Vulg.*) (*E. U.*)

sun, *va.* Asolear, poner al sol, secar al sol. **To sun oneself,** tomar el sol. -*vr.* **To sun oneself,** tomar el sol, broncearse.

sunbeam [ˈsʌnbiːm] [san-bim], *s.* Rayo de sol.

sunbeat [ˈsʌnbiːt] [san-bit], *a.* Asoleado, calentado por el sol; iluminado por el sol.

sunbird [ˈsʌnbɜːd] [san-berd], *s.* Suimanga, ave de las Indias orientales.

sunbonnet [ˈsʌnbɒnɪt] [san-bo-nit], *s.* Gorra o cofia de mujer para andar al sol, especie de papalina.

sunbright [ˈsʌnbraɪt] [san-brait], *s.* Quemadura del sol.

sunburnt [ˈsʌnbɜːnt] [san-bernt], *a.* Tostado por el sol, asoleado; atezado.

sunclad [ˈsʌnklæd] [san-klad], *a.* Brillante, lustroso.

Sunday [ˈsʌndɪ] [san-di], *s.* Domingo, el primer día de la semana, el día del Señor. **Sunday-letter,** letra dominical.

Sunday-school, escuela dominical; conjunto de los discípulos y maestros de dicha escuela.

sunder [ˈsʌndəʳ] [san-daʳ], *s.* Dos, dos partes.

sunder, *va.* y *vn.* Separar, apartar, dividir; romper o romperse; separarse.

sundew [ˈsʌndjuː] [san-diu], *s.* (*Bot.*) Rocío del sol, cualquier planta del género Drosera; notables por ser insectívoras.

sundial [ˈsʌndɪəl] [san-dail], *s.* Reloj de sol, cuadrante.

sundown [ˈsʌndaʊn] [san-daun], *s.* 1. Puesta del sol. V. SUNSET. 2. (*E. U.*) Sombrero de ala ancha para las mujeres.

sundries [ˈsʌndriːz] [san-dris], *s. pl.* (*Com.*) Géneros diversos.

sundry [ˈsʌndrɪ] [san-dri], *a.* Varios, muchos, diversos.

sunfast [ˈsʌnfɑːst] [san-fast], *a.* De color firme, a prueba de sol.

sunfish [ˈsʌnfɪʃ] [san-fish], *s.* 1. Ojón, pez de mar del género Mola, de cuerpo muy corto y forma redondeada. 2. Pez norteamericano de agua dulce, semejante a la perca: pertenece al género Lepomis.

sunflower [ˈsʌnflaʊəʳ] [san-flauaʳ], *s.* (*Bot.*) Girasol, helianto.

sung [sʌŋ] [sang], *pret. y pp.* del verbo TO SING.

sunglasses [ˈsʌnɡlɑːsɪz] [san-gla-ses], *s. pl.* Anteojos para el sol.

sunhemp [ˈsʌnhempl] [san-jemp], *s.* (*Bot.*) Cáñamo de sol: especie de cáñamo de las Indias orientales.

sunk [sʌŋk] [sank], *pret. y pp.* del verbo TO SINK.

sunlamp [ˈsʌnlæmp] [san-lamp], *s.* Lámpara de rayos ultravioletas.

sunless [ˈsʌnlɪs] [san-les], *a.* Sin calor o sin sol; sombrío; sin luz, obscuro.

sunlight [ˈsʌnlaɪt] [san-lait], *s.* La luz del sol.

sunlike [ˈsʌnlaɪk] [san-laik], *a.* Semejante o parecido al sol; resplandeciente.

sunny [ˈsʌnɪ] [sa-ni], *a.* 1. Resplandeciente, semejante al sol. 2. Soleado, expuesto al sol; tostado por el sol, atezado. 3. Brillante como el sol. **Sunny day,** día claro. 4. (*Fig.*) Alegre, risueño. **A sunny smile,** una sonrisa alegre. **It is sunny,** hace sol. **To be on the sunny side of 50,** tener menos de 50 años.

sunrise [ˈsʌnraɪz] [san-rais], **sunrising** [ˈsʌnraɪzɪŋ] [san-rai-sin], *s.* 1. Salida o nacimiento del sol. **Before sunrise,** antes de salir el sol o antes de amanecer. 2. Oriente.

sunset [ˈsʌnset] [san-set], *s.* La puesta o el ocaso del sol. **Until sunset,** hasta que el sol se ponga.

sunshade [ˈsʌnʃeɪd] [san-sheid], *s.* Quitasol o sombrero de anchas alas.

sunshine [ˈsʌnʃaɪn] [san-shain], *s.* 1. Solana, el sitio o paraje donde el sol da de lleno. 2. El influjo del sol; la claridad del sol. **In the sunshine,** al sol.

sunshiny [ˈsʌnʃaɪnɪ] [san-shai-ni], *a.* Claro o resplandeciente como el sol.

sunstroke [ˈsʌnstrəʊk] [san-strouk], *s.* Insolación, congestión repentina del cerebro, a menudo con síntomas semejantes a los de la apoplejía, y causada por el calor excesivo.

sunward [ˈsʌnwəd] [san-uard], *adv.* Hacia el sol.

sunwise [ˈsʌnwaɪz] [san-uais], *adv.* Con el sol (en su movimiento diurno).

sup [sʌp] [sap], *va.* Sorber, beber a sorbos. -*vn.* Cenar.

sup, *s.* Sorbo, bocanada de cualquiera cosa líquida.

super- [ˈsʌpəʳ] [sa-paʳ], Prefijo que en composición significa *sobre.*

superable [ˈsʌpərəbl] [sa-pa-ra-bol], *a.* Superable, que se puede vencer.

superabound [ˌsuːpərəˈbaʊnd] [su-pa-ra-baund], *vn.* Superabundar, abundar con exceso.

superabundance [ˌsuːpərəˈbʌndəns] [sa-pa-ra-ban-dans], *s.* Superabundancia, lo superfluo.

superabundantly [ˌsuːpərəˈbʌndəntlɪ] [su-pa-ra-ban-dant-li], *adv.* Superabundantemente.

superannuate [ˌsuːpəˈrænjʊeɪt] [su-per-a-niueit], *va.* Inhabilitar o declarar a uno inhábil para ejercer u obtener algún cargo a causa de su mucha edad; jubilar, dar retiro a una persona de mucha edad por estar imposibilitada de ejercer su cargo. **Superannuated,** *pp.* Imposibilitado, viejo, fuera de servicio; anticuado, añejo; jubilado.

superb [suːˈpɜːb] [su-perb], *a.* Soberbio, grande, magnífico, espléndido.

superbly [suːˈpɜːblɪ] [su-perb-li], *adv.* Soberbiamente.

supercargo [ˈsuːpəˌkɑːgəʊ] [su-pa-kar-gou], *s.* Sobrecargo, encomender: se dice del que se embarca en un buque de comercio como comisionado para la venta del cargamento o parte de él, por cuenta del dueño.

supercharge [ˈsuːpətʃɑːdʒ] [su-par-charch], *va.* Sobrecargar, sobrealimentar.

supercharger [ˈsuːpətʃɑːdʒəʳ] [su-par-char-yaʳ], *s.* Compresor, sobrecargador, sobrealimentador.

superciliary [ˌsuːpəˈsɪlɪərɪ] [su-pa-si-lia-ri], *a.* Perteneciente a la ceja: situado en la sobreceja.

superciliousness [ˌsuːpəˈsɪlɪəsnɪs] [su-pa-si-lios-nes], *s.* Arrogancia, altanería, altivez, orgullo, presunción.

superficial [ˌsuːpəˈfɪʃəl] [su-per-fi-shal], *a.* 1. Superficial, que toca o pertenece a la superficie, está o se queda en ella. 2. Superficial, aparente, sin solidez ni substancia, insubstancial.

superficialness [ˌsuːpəˈfɪʃəlnɪs] [su-per-fi-shal-nes], *s.* Superficialidad, calidad de superficial.

superficially [ˌsuːpəˈfɪʃəlɪ] [su-per-fi-sha-li], *adv.* Superficialmente, ligeramente, por encima.

superfine [ˈsuːpəfaɪn] [su-pa-fain], *a.* Superfino. -*s.* El paño superfino o más fino.

superfineness [ˈsuːpəfaɪnnɪs] [su-pa-fain-nes], *s.* La calidad de superfino.

superfluous [suːˈpɜːfluəs] [su-per-fluos], *a.* Superfluo, que está demás, sobrante.

superfluousness [suːˈpɜːfluəsnɪs] [su-per-fluos-nes], **superfluity** [suːˈpɜːfluɪtɪ] [su-per-flui-ti], *s.* 1. Superfluidad, demasía. 2. Superfluidad, lo superfluo o lo que está demás.

superheat [ˌsuːpəˈhiːt] [su-pa-jit], *va.* Sobrecalentar.

superhighway [ˈsuːpəˌhaɪweɪ] [su-pa-jai-uei], *s.* Autopista.

superhuman [ˈsuːpəˈhjuːmən] [su-par-jiu-man], *a.* Sobrehumano.

superimpose [ˌsuːpərɪmˈpəʊz] [su-par-im-pous], *va.* Sobreponer, poner encima de otra cosa.

superinduce [ˈsuːpərɪnˈdjuːs] [su-par-in-dius], *va.* Sobreañadir, añadir con exceso o sobre lo que se había añadido antes; producir o ser causa de algo como adición a otra cosa que existía anteriormente.

superintend [ˌsuːpərɪnˈtend] [su-par-in-tend], *va.* Vigilar, celar, cuidar solícitamente; dirigir.

superintendence [ˌsuːpərɪnˈtendəns] [su-par-in-ten-dans], *s.* Superintendencia.

superintendent [ˌsuːpərɪnˈtendənt] [su-par-in-ten-dant], *s.* Superintendente, la persona a cuyo cargo está la dirección y cuidado de alguna cosa.

superior [suːˈpɪərɪəʳ] [su-pia-riaʳ], *a.* 1. Superior, que está más alto o en lugar más prominente con respecto a otra cosa. 2. Superior, que es más excelente o digno que otra cosa. 3. Superior, que excede a otra cosa en vigor, virtud, etc. -*s.* Superior, la persona que manda, gobierna o dirige a otras.

superiority [suːˌpɪərɪˈɒrɪtɪ] [su-pe-ri-o-ri-ti], *s.* 1. Superioridad, preeminencia, excelencia (excelence). 2. Superioridad, autoridad, dominio (authority).

superlative [suːˈpɜːlətɪv] [su-per-la-tiv], *a.* Superlativo, lo más grande o excelente en su clase.

superlatively [suːˈpɜːlətɪvlɪ] [su-per-la-tiv-li], *adv.* Superlativamente, en grado superlativo, extremadamente, en sumo grado.

superman [ˈsuːpəmən] [su-per-man], *s.* Superhombre.

supermarket [ˈsuːpəmɑːkɪt] [su-per-mar-kit], *s.* Supermercado.

supernatural [ˈsuːpəˌnætʃərəl] [su-per-na-cha-ral], *a.* Sobrenatural, que excede o pasa los términos de la naturaleza.

supernova [suːpəˈnəʊvə] [su-per-nou-va], *s.* Supernova.

supernumerary [ˌsuːpəˈnjuːmərərɪ] [su-per-niu-me-ra-ri], *a.* Supernumerario, que está sobre el número señalado; suplementario, superfino. -*s.* Supernumerario; figurante, comparsa (de teatro); cosa suplementaria.

superpose [ˈsuːpəpəʊz] [su-per-pous], *va.* Sobreponer, superponer, colocar sobre otra cosa; en geometría, suponer que una figura está sobrepuesta a otra.

superposition [ˈsuːpəpəzɪʃən] [su-per-po-si-shon], *s.* Superposición, acción de sobreponer; calidad de sobrepuesto.

superpower [ˈsuːpəpaʊəʳ] [su-per-pauaʳ], *s.* Superpotencia.

superscribe [ˈsuːpəskraɪb] [su-per-skraib], *va.* Sobreescribir, escribir o poner un letrero en alguna cosa; poner sobreescrito a una carta.

superscript [ˈsuːpəskrɪpt] [su-per-skript], *s.* Carácter sobrescrito.

superscription [ˈsuːpəskrɪpʃən] [su-per-skrip-shon], *s.* 1. La acción de sobreescribir. 2. Sobreescrito.

supersede [ˌsuːpəˈsiːd] [su-per-sid], *va.* Sobreseer, hacer diferir o suspender; invalidar, hacer inútil o vana alguna cosa; impedir.

supersession [ˈsuːpəseʃən] [su-per-se-shon], *s.* Sobreseimiento; anulación.

supersonic [ˈsuːpəsɒnɪk] [su-per-so-nik], *a.* Supersónico.

superstition [ˌsuːpəˈstɪʃən] [su-pers-ti-shon], *s.* 1. Superstición, modo excesivo, indiscreto o vano en las prácticas de piedad o del culto religioso. 2. Superstición, culto que se da a quien no se debe o que se da de un modo indebido. 3. Superstición, nimia exactitud o esmero vano en el cumplimiento y observancia de algunas cosas, sobre todo en la moral.

superstitious [ˌsuːpəˈstɪʃəs] [su-pers-ti-shos], *a.* Supersticioso; nimiamente escrupuloso.

superstitiously [ˌsuːpəˈstɪʃəslɪ] [su-pers-ti-shos-li], *adv.* Supersticiosamente.

superstitiousness [ˌsuːpəˈstɪʃəsnɪs] [su-pers-ti-shos-nes], *s.* Superstición, calidad de supersticioso.

superstructure [ˈsuːpəstrʌktʃəʳ] [su-per-strak-chaʳ], *s.* Superestructura.

supervene [ˌsuːpəˈviːn] [su-per-vin], *vn.* Sobrevenir, acaecer o suceder; seguir inmediatamente a otra cosa.

supervenient [ˌsuːpəˈviːnɪənt] [su-per-vi-niant], *a.* Superveniente, añadido, adicional.

supervise [ˈsuːpəvaɪz] [su-per-vais], *va.* Inspeccionar, revistar, vigilar o celar por incumbencia u oficio la ejecución de una cosa.

supervision [ˌsuːpəˈviːʃən] [su-per-vi-shon], *s.* Superintendencia.

supervisor [ˈsuːpəvaɪzəʳ] [su-per-vai-soʳ], *s.* 1. Sobrestante, superintendente, inspector. 2. (*E. U.*) Funcionario de una municipalidad que tiene parte en la gestión administrativa de la misma. **Board of Supervisors,** la junta administrativa de una ciudad o de un condado.

supervisory [ˈsuːpəvaɪzərɪ] [su-per-vai-so-ri], *a.* De supervisión. **A supervisory post,** cargo de supervisor.

supine [ˈsuːpaɪn] [su-pain], *a.* 1. Supino, que está echado boca arriba. 2. Supina; se aplica la ignorancia que procede negligencia o descuido en aprender lo que se puede y debe saber. 3. Negligente, indolente, descuidado.

supinely [ˈsuːpaɪnlɪ] [su-pain-li], *adv.* Boca arriba; descuidadamente, con negligencia.

supineness ['suːpaɪnɪs] [su-pain-nes], **supinity** ['suːpaɪnɪtɪ] [su-pai-ni-ti], *s.* 1. La situación o postura del que está echado boca arriba. 2. Descuido, negligencia, dejadez.

supper ['sʌpəʳ] [sa-paʳ], *s.* Cena, el alimento que se toma por la noche; también, banquete. **The Lord's Supper,** la última cena o la institución de la Eucaristía.

supperless ['sʌpəlɪs] [sa-pa-les], *a.* Sin cenar.

suppertime ['sʌpətaɪm] [sa-pa-taim], *sf.* Hora de cenar.

supping ['sʌpɪŋ] [sa-pin], *s.* El acto de sorber; el acto de cenar.

supplant [səˈplɑːnt] [sa-plant], *va.* 1. Suplantar, derribar a uno de su empleo, fortuna, favor o valimiento para ponerse en su lugar y alzarse con lo que el otro goza o para instalar a otro en su lugar. 2. Desbancar a uno de un puesto. 3. Dar una zancadilla.

supplanter [səˈplɑːntəʳ] [sa-plan-taʳ], *s.* Suplantador, el que suplanta a otro.

supplanting [səˈplɑːntɪŋ] [sa-plan-tin], *s.* Suplantación, la acción y efecto de suplantar.

supple ['sʌpl] [sa-pel], *a.* 1. Flexible, manejable, que se deja doblar fácilmente. 2. Flexible, blando, dócil, obediente, deferente. 3. Adulatorio, lisonjero.

supple, *va.* y *vn.* 1. Hacer flexible y manejable alguna cosa. 2. Hacer dócil u obediente a una persona. 3. Ablandarse, hacerse flexible.

supplement ['sʌplɪmənt] [sa-pli-ment], *s.* 1. Suplemento. **Supplement of a newspaper,** alcance, suplemento. 2. El ángulo que se añade a otro para formar dos ángulos rectos.

supplemental [ˌsʌplɪˈmentl] [sa-pli-men-tal], *a.* 1. Suplementario, suplemental; que suple o puede suplir a otra cosa: adicional. 2. Suplementario, se dice del ángulo que sumado con otro completa 180 grados.

suppleness ['sʌplnɪs] [sa-pel-nes], *s.* Flexibilidad, blandura; docilidad, condescendencia.

suppliant ['sʌplɪənt] [sa-pliant], *a.* Deprecatorio; humilde, rendido, postrado. -*s.* Suplicante, el que suplica.

supplicant ['sʌplɪkənt] [sa-pli-kant], *s.* Suplicante.

supplicate ['sʌplɪkeɪt] [sa-pli-keit], *va.* Suplicar, rogar, pedir.

supplication [ˌsʌplɪˈkeɪʃən] [sa-pli-kei-shon], *s.* Súplica, suplicación, petición, ruego.

supplier [səˈplaɪəʳ] [sa-plaiaʳ], *s.* Proveedor, suministrador.

supply [səˈplaɪ] [sa-plai], *va.* 1. Suplir, completar, integrar o llenar lo que falta en alguna cosa (complete). 2. Surtir, abastecer, proveer (provide); suministrar, proporcionar, dar. 3. Suplir, poner o ponerse una persona o una cosa en el lugar que otra ocupaba o había de ocupar. **The tradesmen who supply us,** nuestros proveedores.

supply, *s.* 1. Provisión, abastecimiento, surtido (provision); conjunto de cosas necesarias para un objeto. 2. Cantidad suficiente para un uso dado; acopio de provisiones. 3. Substituto, beneficiado temporal. 4. *pl.* Pertrechos, materiales, víveres, enseres. **To be in want of supplies,** carecer de provisiones. **Demand and supply,** oferta y demanda. **Supplies,** provisiones, víveres.

support [səˈpɔːt] [sa-port], *va.* 1. Sostener, mantener, impedir la caída de algo, servir de apoyo; apoyar (el peso de). 2. Proveer, suministrar fondos. 3. Sostener, v. g. un trato o diálogo. 4. Soportar, sufrir, tolerar. 4. Soportar, sufrir, tolerar. 5. Asistir, amparar, ayudar. 6. Defender, atestiguar, probar, demostrar. 7. *(Teatro)* Hacer un papel subordinado a otro; hacer un papel. **To support a family,** mantener a una familia. **To support oneself,** mantenerse, ganarse la vida.

support, *s.* 1. Sostén, el acto de sostener y aquello con que se sostiene. 2. Apoyo, protección. 3. Sustento, lo necesario para vivir. **In support of,** en favor de, en apoyo de; para sostener, apoyar, etc. **Point of support,** punto de apoyo. **Support buying,** compra proteccionista. **Support price,** precio de apoyo. **Moral support,** apoyo moral.

supportable [səˈpɔːtəbl] [sa-por-ta-bol], *a.* Soportable, tolerable, llevadero; sostenible.

supportably [səˈpɔːtəblɪ] [sa-por-ta-bli], *adv.* De una manera tolerable, soportable.

supporter [səˈpɔːtəʳ] [sa-por-taʳ], *s.* 1. Sostenimiento, sustentáculo. 2. Apoyo, amparo, columna. 3. Sosteniente, sostenedor. 4. Defensor, protector. 5. *(Her.)* Soporte, cada una de las figuras de animales que sostienen el escudo de armas; se usa casi siempre en plural. 6. *(Arq.)* Atalante o telamón. **Supporter's club,** peña deportiva (sport).

supposable [səˈpəʊzəbl] [sa-pou-sa-bol], *a.* Que se puede suponer o que es de suponer; no inconcebible.

supposal [səˈpəʊzəl] [su-pou-sal], *s.* Suposición.

supposableness [səˈpəʊzəblnɪs] [sa-pou-sa-bol-nes], *s.* La capacidad de poderse suponer una cosa; probabilidad.

suppose [səˈpəʊz] [sa-pous], *va.* 1. Suponer, dar por sentada alguna cosa sin prueba ni autoridad. 2. Suponer, fingir o presuponer alguna cosa. 3. Imaginar algo; creer sin examen. **It is to be supposed,** es de creer o se puede suponer. **Supposing it to be true,** suponiendo que sea esto verdad. **Supposing that,** dado caso que. **Let's suppose that,** pongamos que, supongamos. **Suppose we go on holidays?,** ¿qué te parece si nos vamos de vacaciones?

supposed [səˈpəʊzd] [sa-pousd], *a.* Pretendido, supuesto.

supposer [səˈpəʊzəʳ] [sa-pou-saʳ], *s.* Suponedor.

supposition [ˌsʌpəˈzɪʃən] [sa-po-si-shon], *s.* Suposición, hipótesis.

suppositional [ˌsʌpəˈzɪʃənl] [sa-po-si-sho-nal], *a.* Hipotético, supositivo que se funda en suposición o hipótesis.

supposititious [ˌsʌpəˈzɪʃəs] [sa-po-si-shous], *a.* 1. Supuesto, falso, ilegítimo, fingido (false). 2. Supuesto, imaginado.

supposititiousness [ˌsʌpəˈzɪʃəsnɪs] [sa-po-si-shos-nes], *s.* Suposición, falsedad; substitución de una cosa por otra.

suppositive [ˌsʌpəˈzɪtɪv] [sa-po-si-tiv], *a.* Supuesto.

suppositively [ˌsʌpəˈzɪtɪvlɪ] [sa-po-si-tiv-li], *adv.* En suposición.

suppository [səˈpɒzɪtərɪ] [sa-po-si-to-ri], *s.* Supositorio, cala.

suppress [səˈpres] [sa-pres], *va.* 1. Suprimir, detener, estorbar o impedir el curso de alguna cosa. 2. Suprimir, ocultar, no explicar lo que se debe o algunamateria, omitir o callar de propósito (hide). 3. Destruir (destroy).

suppressant [səˈpresənt] [sa-pre-sant], *a.* Inhibidor *(Med.).*

suppression [səˈpreʃən] [sa-pre-shon], *s.* 1. Supresión; represión, acción de reprimir. 2. *(Med.)* Suspensión de una secreción; falta de secreción, a diferencia de retención.

suppressive [səˈpresɪv] [sa-pre-siv], *a.* Represivo, que tiende a reprimir o que puede reprimir; que suprime o ahoga.

suppressor [səˈpresəʳ] [sa-pre-saʳ], *s.* Supresor, el que suprime.

suppurate ['sʌpjʊəreɪt] [sa-pu-reit], *va.* Supurar, criar pus o materia alguna herida o llaga. -*vn.* Supurar, echar pus o materia.

suppuration [ˌsʌpjʊəˈreɪʃən] [sa-pua-rei-shon], *s.* Supuración, la acción y efecto de supurar.

supramundane ['suːprəˈmʌndeɪn] [su-pra-man-dein], *a.* Sobrenatural, superior a las cosas terrenales.

supranational ['suːprəˈnæʃənl] [su-pra-na-sho-nal], *a.* Supranacional.

suprarenal ['suːprəˈriːnə] [su-pra-ri-nal], *a.* Suprarenal, que está colocado encima de los riñones.

supremacy [sʊˈpreməsɪ] [su-pre-ma-si], *s.* Supremacía, autoridad suprema, estado de supremo.

supreme [sʊˈpriːm] [su-prim], *a.* Supremo, lo más elevado, lo más grande.

supremely [sʊˈpriːmlɪ] [su-prim-li], *adv.* Supremamente, en el más alto grado.

surbase [sɜːˈbeɪs] [ser-beis], *s.* 1. Cornisa, moldura sobre un pedestal. 2. Moldura o borde por encima de una base.

surcease [ˈsɜːsiːz] [ser-sis], *vn.* Cesar, supenderse; acabarse enteramente.

surcease, *s. (Ant.)* Cesación.

surcharge [ˈsɜːtʃɑːdʒ] [ser-charch], *s.* 1. Sobrecarga, sobrepeso, más carga. 2. Sobrecarga, recargo, nuevo g r a v a m e n .

surcharge, *va.* Sobrecargar, recargar, cargar con exceso.

surd [sɜːd] [serd], *a.* y *s.* 1. Sordo, no vocal ni sonante; producido por los órganos vocales sin voz ni tono; por ejemplo las consonantes p, t, s, o k, opuesto a sonante. 2. *(Mat.)* Irracional, que no puede ser expresado en números racionales; v. g. la raíz cuadrada de dos.

sure [ʃʊəʳ] [shua], *a.* 1. Seguro, cierto, indudable, hablando de noticias o hechos (true). 2. Seguro, infalible, efectivo (effective), hablando de medios, recursos, remedios, etc. 3. Seguro, firme, sentado, hablando del paso, de la mano, del pulso, etc. 4. Seguro, firme, constante, estable (secure, steady), que no está en peligro de faltar o de caerse. **As sure as fate,** con toda seguridad. *(E.U.)* **Sure!,** ¡claro!, ¡seguro! **Sure thing!,** ¡por supuesto! **To be sure,** seguramente, sin duda; ya se ve. **To be sure of foot,** tener el pie o paso seguro. **To be sure of oneself,** estar seguro de uno mismo. **To be sure to,** no faltar, no carecer. **To make sure,** asegurar, cerciorar. **To make sure of,** asegurarse de, verificar, apoderarse de; contar con o sobre alguien. *-adv. (Fam. o des.)* Ciertamente, indudablemente, sin duda alguna. **Sure enough,** a buen seguro, con certeza.

sure-fire [ˈʃʊəfaɪəʳ] [shua-faia], *a.* Seguro, de éxito seguro.

sure-footed [ˈʃʊəfʊtɪd] [shua-fu-tid], *a.* Se dice del animal que no tropieza y de los afectos de ánimo que obran sin interrupción.

surely [ˈʃʊəlɪ] [shua-li], *adv.* Ciertamente, seguramente, sin duda. Se usa generalmente de un modo expletivo para afirmar más. **Surely not?,** ¿será posible?

sureness [ˈʃʊənɪs] [shua-nes], *s.* Certeza, seguridad. V. SURETY.

surety [ˈʃʊətɪ] [shua-ti], *s.* 1. Seguridad, exención de riesgo o el estado de las cosas que las hace firmes, seguras y libres de todo riesgo o peligro. 2. Seguridad, certeza que se tiene de que una cosa no faltará o no engañará. 3. Seguridad, fianza, responsabilidad de daños u obligacón a favor de alguno, regularmente en materia de intereses. 4. Seguridad o caución que se da o se toma. 5. Fiador, obligado, el que se obliga por otro. **Of a surety,** de seguro, como cosa cierta. **To be surety for,** ser fiador, salir garante; responder de alguien o algo. **To stand surety for someone,** ser fiador de alguien.

suretyship [ˈʃʊətɪʃɪp] [shua-ti-ship], *s.* Seguridad, fianza u obligación de indemnidad en favor de alguno.

surf [sɜːf] [serf], *s.* 1. Marejada; oleaje, embate del mar al romper sobre la playa (sea). (Variación de **sough**). 2. Espuma (foam).

surface [ˈsɜːfɪs] [ser-fis], *va.* Poner o hacer una superficie sobre algo; allanar, alisar, igualar. *-s.* Superficie, sobrefaz, la parte externa o exterior de alguna cosa. **To skin the surface of,** rozar la superficie; correr de prisa y superficialmente. **Surface tension,** tensión superficial. **By surface mail (land),** por vía terrestre.

surfboard [ˈsɜːbɔːd] [serf-bord], *s.* Tabla para flotar sobre la rompiente.

surfboarder [ˈsɜːbɔːdəʳ] [serf-bor-da], *s.* Surfista.

surfeit [ˈsɜːfɪt] [ser-fit], *va.* y *vn.* 1. Ahitar, hartar, saciar, atracar, sobrecargar de alimentos. 2. Saciar o satisfacer el ánimo. 3. Ahitarse, saciarse, hartarse de comida o bebida.

surfeit, *s.* Ahito, empacho, exceso en comer y beber; indigestión, embarazo gástrico o del estómago.

surfeiter [ˈsɜːfɪtəʳ] [ser-fi-ta], *s.* Glotón, el que come o bebe con exceso.

surge [sɜːdʒ] [serch], *s.* Olaje, oleada *(Naut.);* prolongadas ondulaciones del mar; el acto de levantarse y moverse las olas. **A surge of people,** una oleada de gente.

surge, *vn.* Agitarse o embravecerse el mar; levantarse e hincharse, y moverse hacia adelante las olas. *-va.* Hacer mover hacia adelante con movimiento de expansión, v. g. las olas, las ondas sonoras, etc. **To surge the capstan,** lascar el cabretante.

surgeon [ˈsɜːdʒən] [ser-yon], *s.* 1. Cirujano. 2. Médico, oficial médico. **Surgeon-dentist,** cirujano dentista. **Surgeon-general,** en los E.U. médico mayor, jefe de sanidad militar o naval, con grado equivalente al de general de ejército.

surgery [ˈsɜːdʒərɪ] [ser-ye-ri], *s.* Cirugía (operation). **Surgery hours,** horas de consulta.

surgical [ˈsɜːdʒɪkəl] [ser-yi-kal], *a.* Quirúrgico, que pertenece a la cirugía.

surgically [ˈsɜːdʒɪkəlɪ] [ser-yi-ka-li], *adv.* Quirúrgicamente.

surgy [ˈsɜːdʒɪ] [ser-yi], *a.* Agitado o embravecido como el mar.

surlines [ˈsɜːlaɪnz] [ser-lains], *s.* Grosería, mal genio, mal humor; entono.

surly [ˈsɜːlɪ] [ser-li], *a.* 1. Arisco, insolente; áspero de genio; impertinente. 2. Grosero, tosco, rudo, v. g. una respuesta. 3. Furioso, tempestuoso, p. ej. el tiempo. **A surly dog,** un perro arisco. **To give a surly answer,** contestar de mala manera.

surmise [sɜːmaɪz] [ser-mais], *va.* Conjeturar, suponer, imaginar alguna cosa sin fundamento o razón suficiente.

surmise, *s.* 1. Conjetura, imaginación; aprensión falsa, juicio o discurso sin fundamento; noción imperfecta. 2. Indirectas, rumores. **I surmised as much,** ya lo suponía.

surmount [sɜːˈmaʊnt] [ser-maunt], *va.* 1. Vencer, superar, a fuerza de voluntad. 2. Sobrepujar, pasar por encima de una cosa; levantarse o elevarse sobre ella. 3. Pasar, sobrepujar.

surmountable [sɜːˈmaʊntəbl] [ser-maun-ta-bol], *a.* Vencible, superable.

surname [ˈsɜːneɪm] [ser-neim], *s.* 1. Apellido, el nombre o sobrenombre de la familia. 2. Renombre o epíteto que se añade al nombre de una persona.

surname, *va.* Apellidar, nombrar, denominar, llamar con algún renombre o título a una persona.

surpass [sɜːˈpɑːs] [ser-pas], *va.* Sobresalir, sobrepujar, superar, exceder (exceed).

surpassing [sɜːˈpɑːsɪŋ] [ser-pa-sin], *a.* Sobresaliente, superior, que sobrepuja a los demás; excelente.

surplice [ˈsɜːpləs] [ser-plis], *s.* Sobrepelliz, vestidura de lienzo que usa el clero en las funciones de su ministerio.

surpliced [ˈsɜːpləst] [ser-plist], *a.* Con sobrepelliz, que lleva sobrepelliz-

surplus [ˈsɜːpləs] [ser-plas], *s.* Sobrante, demasía, sobras, lo que sobra de alguna cosa. **Surplus value,** plusvalía.

surprise [səˈpraɪz] [ser-prais], *s.* 1. Sorpresa, la acción por la cual se sorprende. 2. Estado de sorpresa; admiración, asombro, emoción producida por algo que sucede súbitamente; ataque repentino. **To be surprised,** quedar atónito, quedar asombrado. **Much to my surprise, to my great surprise,** para gran sorpresa mía. **Surprise attack,** ataque por sorpresa.

surprise, *va.* 1. Sorprender, sobrecoger, coger descuidado o de improviso. 2. Sorprender, dejar admirado o maravillado. **You surprise me!,** ¡me asombras!

surprising [səˈpraɪzɪŋ] [ser-prai-sin], *a.* Maravilloso, asombroso, admirable, que causa sorpresa.

surprisingly [səˈpraɪzɪŋlɪ] [ser-prai-sin-li], *adv.* Pasmosamente, maravillosamente, de un modo admirable.

surreal [səˈrɪəl] [sa-rial], *a.* Surrealista.

surrealism [səˈrɪəlɪzəm] [sa-ria-li-sem], *s.* Surrealismo.

surrender [səˈrendəʳ] [sa-ren-da], *va.* 1. Rendir, entregar a otro, y particularmente poner en manos del enemigo. 2. Ceder, traspasar, renunciar a, abandonar, entregar. 3. Renunciar a favor de otro. *-vn.* Ceder, rendirse, entregarse. **I surrender!,** ¡me rindo!

surrender, *s.* 1. Rendición, entrega. 2. Renuncia o dejación voluntaria; abandono, sumisión. 3. *(For.)* Cesión de bienes. **The surrender of a right,** la renuncia de un derecho. **Surrender of property,** cesión de bienes.

surreptitious [sʌrəpˈtɪʃəs] [sa-rap-ti-shos], *a.* Subrepticio, hecho oculta o fraudulentamente.

surreptitiously [ˌsʌrəpˈtɪʃəslɪ] [sa-rap-ti-shos-li], *adv.* Subrepticiamente, fraudulentamente.

surrogacy [ˈsʌrəgəsɪ] [sa-ro-ga-si], *sf.* Subrogación.

surrogate [ˈsʌrəgeɪt] [sa-ro-gueit], *va.* Subrogar, substituir o poner una persona o cosa en lugar de otra.

surrogate, *s.* 1. Subrogado, delegado de un juez eclesiástico. 2. *(Local E.U.) (For.)* Juez de testamentarías, o de bienes de difuntos o intestados.

surround [səˈraʊnd] [sa-raund], *va.* 1. Circundar, cercar, rodear. 2. Rodear, circundar, constituir una cerca o borde alrededor de algo; ceñir. 3. Asediar, v. g. una plaza o fortaleza.

surrounding [səˈraʊndɪŋ] [sa-raun-din], *s.* 1. *pl.* Alrededores, contornos o cualquier parte de ellos. 2. El acto del que rodea o ciñe. *a.* Circundante, de alrededor.

surtax [ˈsɜːtæks] [ser-taks], *s.* Impuesto adicional, sobretasa.

surveil [səˈveɪl] [ser-veil], *vt. (E.U.)* Vigilar.

surveillance [sɜːˈveɪləns] [ser-vei-lans], *s.* Vigilancia, acción de vigilar; Estado del que se halla vigilado.

survey [ˈsɜːveɪ] [ser-vei], *va.* 1. Apear, acotar, medir o deslindar las tierras y heredades. 2. Mirar, inspeccionar o reconocer desde lo alto (look at). 3. Inspeccionar, examinar (inspect), vigilar o celar por incumbencia u oficio los edificios, etc., y tasarlos. 4. Mirar una cosa examinándola. **To survey a coast,** *(Mar.)* reconocer una costa y levantar el plano de ella.

survey, *s.* 1. Apeo o delinde de tierras o heredades; también, un departamento o cuerpo para practicar la agrimensura; medición. 2. Perspectiva, vista o aspecto de muchos objetos juntos mirados de lejos. 3. Reconocimiento, inspección, examen, vista.

surveying [ˈsɜːveɪɪŋ] [ser-vein], *s.* Agrimensura, arte de medir terrenos y levantar planos.

surveyor [səˈveɪər] [ser-veio], *s.* 1. Agrimensor, apeador, medidor de tierras. 2. Sobrestante, superintendente. 3. Perito. **Surveyor of the navy,** *(Mar.)* perito. **Surveyor of the custom-house,** vista de la aduana.

survival [səˈvaɪvəl] [ser-vai-val], *s.* 1. Supervivencia, la acción de sobrevivir. 2. Persona o cosa que sobrevive; costumbre que ha durado mucho más tiempo que las condiciones que la originaron. **Survival of the fittest,** *(Biol.)* la supervivencia de los más idóneos; la conservación y propagación de ciertas formas favorecidas en la lucha por la existencia (teoría de la evolución). **Survival kit,** equipo de emergencia.

survive [səˈvaɪv] [ser-vaiv], *vn.* 1. Sobrevivir, vivir después de muerto otro. 2. Vivir o durar una cosa más que otra (remain).

surviving [səˈvaɪvɪŋ] [ser-vai-vin], *a.* Sobreviviente.

survivor o surviver [səˈvaɪvər] [ser-vai-va], *s.* El que sobrevive a otro o vive después de su muerte.

susceptibility [səˌseptəˈbɪlɪtɪ] [sa-sep-ta-bi-li-ti], *s.* Susceptibilidad, la disposición a recibir las impresiones.

susceptible [səˈseptəbl] [sa-sep-ti-bol], *a.* 1. Susceptible, capaz de recibir o dispuesto a admitir en sí. 2. Sensible, que recibe fácilmente las impresiones morales; que se conmueve fácilmente, impresionable. **He is very susceptible,** *(Fam.)* es muy enamorado.

susceptibly [səˈseptəblɪ] [sa-sep-ta-bli], *adv.* De una manera susceptible.

susceptive [səˈseptɪv] [sa-sep-tiv], *a.* Susceptivo, susceptible.

suspect [ˈsʌspekt] [sas-pekt], *va. y vn.* 1. Imaginar la existencia de algo; conjeturar, suponer, tener una opinión sin certidumbre. 2. Recelar; desconfiar de; inferir la culpa posible de una persona sin pruebas, sin razón suficiente. 3. Sospechar, formar o tener sospecha; tener por sospechoso. **He suspects nothing,** no sospecha de nada.

suspect, *s.* Persona sospechosa de un delito; persona vigilada como sospechosa. **To be suspected,** estar bajo sospecha, ser sospechoso.

suspectedly [ˈsʌspektɪdlɪ] [sas-pek-tid-li], *adv.* De una manera sospechosa; de manera que excita las sospechas.

suspend [səsˈpend] [sas-pend], *va.* 1. Suspender, colgar, poner pendiente una cosa en el aire. 2. Suspender,

interrumpir, cesar, aplazar, detener o parar por algún tiempo la ejecución de una cosa. 3. Suspender, privar temporalmente a uno del ejercicio de su empleo o ministerio. 4. Hacer depender. *-vn. (Com.)* Suspender pagos.

suspender [səsˈpendər] [sas-pen-da], *s.* El o lo que suspende; cada uno de los tirantes del pantalón; liga. **Suspenders,** ligas.

suspense [səsˈpens] [sas-pens], *s.* 1. Suspensión, duda o detención en algún movimiento del ánimo, incertidumbre. 2. Suspensión, detención, parada o interrupción. *-s.* (Poco us.) 1. Suspenso, parado, detenido. 2. Suspenso, irresuelto, irresoluto. **The suspense is killing me!,** ¡no puedo aguantar tanta emoción! **In suspense,** en suspenso, pendiente.

suspension [səsˈpenʃən] [sas-pen-shon], *s.* Suspensión, acción de suspender; estado de lo que se halla suspendido; *(Quím.)* estado de una substancia que permanece en un líquido sin precipitarse; detención; cesación temporal; duda. **Suspension bridge,** puente colgante o de suspensión. **Suspension of hostilities,** suspensión de hostilidades, armisticio.

suspensory [səsˈpensərɪ] [sas-pen-so-ri], *a.* Suspensorio, que sirve para suspender. *-s.* Suspensorio, vendaje para sostener el escroto.

suspicion [səsˈpɪʃən] [sas-pi-shon], *s.* 1. Sospecha, recelo, desconfianza; conjetura. 2. *(Fam.)* Pizca, grano, brizna.

suspicious [səsˈpɪʃəs] [sas-pi-shos], *a.* Suspicaz, desconfiado, receloso (distrustful); sospechoso.

suspiciously [səsˈpɪʃəslɪ] [sas-pi-shos-li], *adv.* Sospechosamente, con sospecha, de un modo sospechoso.

suspiciousness [səsˈpɪʃəsnɪs] [sas-pi-shos-nes], *s.* Recelo, suspicacia, desconfianza, inclinación a sospechar.

sustain [səsˈteɪn] [sas-tein], *va.* 1. Sostener, sustentar o mantener alguna cosa, llevar, soportar (bear); *(Mús.)* prolongar con la misma fuerza. 2. Sostener, apoyar, afianzar. 3. Sostener, mantener o defender; establecer, probar (establish). 4. Sostener, sustentar o dar lo necesario para mantenerse. 5. Sostener, ayudar, patrocinar (sponsor). 6. Sostener, sufrir, tolerar, aguantar. **To sustain a loss,** perder algo, sufrir una pérdida.

sustainable [səsˈteɪnəbl] [sas-tei-na-bol], *a.* Sostenible, que se puede sostener; defendible, que se puede defender.

sustainer [səsˈteɪnər] [sas-tei-na], *s.* 1. Sostenedor, defensor, protector. 2. El que sufre.

sustenance [ˈsʌstɪnəns] [sas-ti-nans], *s.* Sostenimiento, sustento, mantenimiento; alimentos, víveres, manutención; subsistencia.

suttle [ˈsʌtl] [sa-tel], *a. y s.* Neto; peso limpio.

sutural [ˈsuːtʃərəl] [su-cha-ral], *a.* Sutural, perteneciente a una sutura o colocado en ella.

suture [ˈsuːtʃər] [su-cha], *s.* 1. Sutura, costura; unión de los huesos del cráneo; *(Bot.)* línea poco saliente, rafe. 2. Sutura.

suzerain [ˈsuːzəreɪn] [su-sa-rein], *s.* Persona revestida de suprema autoridad.

svelte [svelt] [svelt], *a.* 1. Esbelto. 2. Airoso, elegante. 3. Aliñado.

swab [swɒb] [suob], *s.* Instrumento que consta de una sustancia blanda y absorbente al extremo de un mango; se emplea para limpiar la boca de un paciente, el alma de un cañón, etc. *(Mar.)* Lampazo, estropajo grande hecho de filáciga.

swab, *va.* Fregar, limpiar; *(Mar.)* lampacear, limpiar con lampazo.

swabber [ˈswɒbər] [suo-ba], *s.* Paje de escoba, galopín.

swaddle [ˈswɒdl] [suo-del], *va.* Fajar, rodear, ceñir o envolver con fajas; generalmente significa envolver o fajar una criatura en pañales.

swaddle, *s.* Faja.

swaddling-cloth [ˈswɒdlɪŋklɒʊð] [suo-dlin-klouz], *s.* Mantilla, pañal, envoltura de niños.

swag [swæg] [suag], *vn.* 1. Colgar, inclinarse alguna cosa hacia abajo por su propio peso. 2. Fachendear, echar plantas, echarla de bravo, de majo, de grande de ingenio.

swage [sweɪdʒ] [sueich], *va.* Estampar, dar figura al metal con una matriz. -*s.* Herramienta para hacer molduras en las fajas de hierro. **Swage-block,** dicha herramienta; variedad de yunque.

swagger [ˈswægəʳ] [sua-gaʳ], *vn.* Baladronear, hacer o decir baladronadas; echarlas de valiente. **To swagger about,** contonearse, pavonearse. -*s.* Contoneo, pavoneo.

swaggerer [ˈswægərəʳ] [sua-ga-raʳ], *s.* Jaquetón, jaque, valentón, fanfarrón, baladrón.

swaggy [ˈswægɪ] [sua-gui], *a.* Colgante, pendiente, que cuelga o está suspenso.

Swahili [swɑˈhiːlɪ] [sua-ji-li], *s.* Suajili, swahili.

swain [sweɪn] [suein], *s.* Zagal, joven aldeano, pastorcillo, amante, enamorado.

swallow [ˈswɒləʊ] [suo-lou], *s.* 1. Trago. 2. *(Orn.)* Golodrino, golondrina, pájaro de la familia de los hirundínidos. 3. Vencejo, avión. **At one swallow,** de un trago. **Swallow-tail,** algo que por su forma se parece a la cola de la golondrina; cola de milano, especie de espiga de ensambladura. **Swallow-tailed coat,** frac.

swallow, *va.* 1. Tragar, deglutir, engullir, hacer pasar alguna cosa por el tragadero. 2. Recibir o hacer desaparecer; tragar; se usa comúnmente con up. 3. Tragar, recibir o creer alguna cosa de ligero y sin examinarla. 4. Soportar con paciencia y sumisión. 5. Retractar, retirar, desdecir. **To swallow up,** tragar; absorber; sumir, precipitar como en un abismo; apropiar o hacer propia alguna cosa. **The mist swallowed us up,** la niebla nos envolvió. **To swallow an insult,** tolerar un ultraje. -*s.* 1. Bocado, trago, lo que se traga de una vez. 2. El acto de tragar, deglución. 3. Tragadero esófago. 4. Abismo, sima; agujero de un sumidero.

swam [swæm] [suam], *pret.* del verbo TO SWIM.

swamp [swɒmp] [suomp], *s.* Pantano, terreno encharcado; sitio bajo y húmedo. **Swamp fever,** paludismo.

swamp, *va.* 1. Sumergir, cubrir de agua (submerge); echar a pique un barco (sink); hacer zozobrar. 2. Meter en terreno pantanoso; encharcar (flood); de aquí, sumergir en dificultades, confundir en un tropel; arruinar, hundir. -*vn.* Caer en grandes dificultades, empantanarse, irse a pique; zozobrar. **They have swamped us with applications,** nos han abrumado con solicitudes.

swampland [ˈswɒmplænd] [suomp-land], *sf.* Pantano, marisma.

swampy [ˈswɒmpɪ] [suom-pi], *a.* Pantanoso. **To become swampy,** empantanarse.

swan [swɒn] [suon], *s.* Cisne, ave palmípeda de cuello largo y flexible y plumaje blanco. **Swan-like,** semejante al cisne. **Swandown, swan's down,** (a) plumón de cisne. (b) Moletón, una tela muy suave. *V.* **Canton flannel,** (c) paño de vicuña, tela de lana muy suave y gruesa. **Swan-skin,** (a) piel de cisne; (b) lanilla, bayeta superfina. -*vi.* **To swan around,** vagabundear, gandulear. **To swan off,** irse tranquilamente. **Swan song,** canto del cisne.

swank [swæŋk] [suank], *sf.* Ostentación, alarde. *vi.* Darse humos, fanfarronear. **To swank about,** pavonearse.

swap [swɒp] [suop], *adv. (Prov. Ingl.)* De prisa, con presteza; vivamente.

swap, *va.* Cambiar, cambalachear. -*vn.* Hacer cambalaches o trueques. -*s. (Fam.)* Cambalache, trueque, cambio. **To swap stories,** contarse chistes. **It's a fair swap,** es un cambio equitativo.

sward [swɔːd] [suord], *va.* Sembrar, cubrir de césped. -*vn.* Volverse verde, herboso, cubrirse de hierbas. -*s.* La haz o superficie de la tierra cubierta de hierbas, césped.

swarm [swɔːm] [suorm], *s.* 1. Enjambre, copia grande de abejas o de seres vivientes y pequeños de cualquiera clase. 2. Enjambre, gentío, multitud de gente reunida. 3. Hormiguero. **A swarm of mosquitoes,** un enjambre de mosquitos.

swarm, *va.* Ocupar en enjambres, producir en enjambres. -*vn.* Enjambrar, jabardear, hacer mucha cría las abejas, y también criar en enjambres de la colmena. 2. Enjambrar, multiplicar o producir en abundancia. 3. Hervir, bullir, hormiguear de gente, de soldados, etc., para ponderar la muchedumbre. 4. Abundar o haber grande abundancia de alguna cosa; manar en abundancia. **To swarm up a tree,** trepar a un árbol.

swarm, *va.* y *vn. (Fam.)* Trepar, subir, ayudándose con pies y manos.

swart [swɔːt] [suort], *a.* 1. Prieto, moreno, atezado, negro. 2. Triste; contrario.

swarthiness [ˈswɔːðɪnɪs] [suor-zi-nes], *s.* Color moreno, atezamiento, tez morena.

swarthy [ˈswɔːðɪ] [suor-zi], *a.* Atezado, tezado, tostado por el sol; moreno, negruzco, curtido.

swash [swɒʃ] [suosh], *s.* 1. El impulso del agua cuando surte o fluye con violencia. 2. Canal angosto por el cual fluyen las mareas. **Swash-buckler,** matasiete, espaadachín, fanfarrón.

swash, *va.* Verter, derramar o salpicar agua en bastante cantidad. -*vn.* 1. Hacer ruido como salpicando con agua. 2. Salpicar, hacer saltar el agua. 3. Balandronear; meter bulla o hacer mucho ruido.

swasher [ˈswɒʃəʳ] [suo-shaʳ], *s.* Jaquetón, baladrón, fanfarrón.

swashing [ˈswɒʃɪŋ] [suo-shin], *pa.* 1. El acto de fanfarronear, de echarlas de valiente. 2. Violento, abrumador. **A swashing blow,** un golpe violento.

swashy [ˈswɒʃɪ] [suo-shi], *a.* Batiente, a la manera del mar.

swastika [ˈswɒstɪkə] [svas-ti-ka], *s.* Svástica.

swatch [swɒtʃ] [suoch], *s.* Muestra pequeña de alguna tela o tejido.

swath [swɔːθ] [suoz], *s.* 1. Faja de hierba que el guadañero deja tras sí; ringlera de heno o mies acabada de segar. 2. Guadañada, el espacio cortado de una vez por una máquina o útil; se emplea en sentido figurado en ambos casos.

swathe [sweɪð] [sueiz], *va.* Fajar, liar, rodear; envolver.

swathe, *s.* Faja, venda, atadura; pañal de niño.

sway [sweɪ] [suei], *va.* 1. Hacer que se incline o ladee alguna persona; de aquí, preocupar el ánimo o la voluntad de alguno. 2. Blandir o vibrar alguna cosa en el aire; mover con la mano, v. g. un cetro. 3. Mandar, dominar, gobernar; dirigir, ejercer influencia o autoridad sobre alguno; regir. 4. *(Mar.)* Izar, guindar. -*vn.* 1. Ladearse, inclinarse o torcerse una cosa por su propio peso hacia un lado. 2. Inclinarse o ladearse el ánimo hacia una cosa o persona. 3. Tener influjo, mando o dominio. **To sway up,** guindar.

sway, *s.* 1. Poder, imperio, dominación, mando, influjo (influence). **To bear sway,** llevar el cetro. **To hold sway,** gobernar, regir, estar en el poder. 2. Vibración, la acción de vibrar o blandir un arma. 3. Sacudimiento, estremecimiento, bamboleo. **Sway-backed,** *(Fam.)* pando.

sweal [swɪəl] [suial], *va.* 1. Derretirse, y correrse como el sebo de una vela. 2. Consumirse, quemarse despacio.

swear [sweəʳ] [sueaʳ], *va.* y *vn. (pret.* SWORE.; *pp.* SWORN). 1. Jurar, afirmar o negar una cosa bajo juramento. 2. Jurar, declarar, ratificar, confirmar o prometer alguna cosa con juramento. 3. Jurar, echar votos o juramentos, blasfemar. 4. Jurar, resolverse u ofrecerse con juramento a hacer una cosa; prestar juramento. 5. Hacer jurar o prometer a uno bajo juramento. 6. Juramentar, tomar juramento a alguno. **To swear by,** *(Fam.)* poner confianza implícita en. **To swear in,** hacer prestar juramento. **To swear off,** renunciar. **To swear off smoking,** renunciar a fumar. *a.* **The witness has been sworn,** el testigo ha prestado juramento.

swearer [ˈsweərəʳ] [suea-raʳ], *s.* Jurador, votador, el que tiene el vicio de jurar.

swearing [ˈsweərɪŋ] [suea-rin], *s.* Jura, juramento.

sweat [swet] [suet], *s.* 1. Sudor, la serosidad que sale del cuerpo del animal por los poros en forma de gotas; secreción cutánea, transpiración. 2. Sudor, trabajo, fatiga. 3. Evaporación de humedad. **To be in a sweat,** estar sudando, estar nadando en sudor. **By the sweat of his brow,** con el sudor de su frente. **Sweat-shop,** taller donde se trabaja un número excesivo de horas por jornal insuficiente.

sweat, *va.* y *vn. (pret.* y *pp.* SWEAT o SWEATED). 1. Sudar, exhalar o expeler el sudor. 2. Sudar, trabajar con fatiga y desvelo, física o moralmente. 3. Exhalar o echar de sí humedad en forma de vapor; dejar salir por los poros; p. ej. una planta o un jarro; resudar. 4. Hacer sudar. 5. Echar de sí alguna cosa a modo de sudor. **To sweat off,** quitarse peso sudando. **To sweat out a distemper,** curarse de una enfermedad por medio del sudor. **To sweat it out,** armarse de paciencia, aguantar, soportar. 6. Sujetar las pieles a un procedimiento de fermentación para despojarlas del pelo. 7. Recortar o cercenar las monedas, especialmente de una manera ilegal. 8. Tomarse mucho trabajo, extenuarse, fatigarse.

sweater ['swetəʳ] [sue-taʳ], *s.* Chaqueta o blusa tejida. *(Amer.)* Suéter.

sweatiness ['swetɪnɪs] [sue-ti-nes], *s.* El estado de lo que se halla lleno de sudor; calor; humedad.

sweating ['swetɪŋ] [sue-tin], *s.* Transpiración, acción de sudar. **Sweeating-room,** sudadero, lugar del baño destinado para sudar.

sweaty ['swetɪ] [sue-ti], *s.* Sudado, sudoso, en transpiración; trabajoso, laborioso, lo que hace sudar.

Swede ['swiːd] [suid], *s.* 1. Natural o habitante de Suecia. 2. Nabo sueco. *V.* RUTABAGA.

Swedish ['swiːdɪʒ] [sui-dish], *a.* Sueco, perteneciente a Suecia. *-s.* Idioma sueco.

sweep [swiːp] [suip], *va.* y *vn.* *(pret.* y *pp.* SWEPT). 1. Barrer, limpiar con la escoba. 2. Barrer, no dejar nada de lo que había en alguna parte. 3. Arrebatar, llevar con celeridad y violencia; arrastrar por; mover o hacer moverse una cosa a la fuerza y como barriéndola, en sentido literal o figurado; abrazar con la mirada. 4. Marchar pomposamente, llevar una cosa con pompa u orgullo. 5. Pasar o moverse con celeridad llevándose tras sí cuanto se encuentra. 6. Deshollinar o limpiar chimeneas.

sweep along, arrastrar con fuerza o majestuosamente; ostentar, desplegar; rozar.

sweep away, robar o llevarse cuanto se halla; arrebatar, arrastrar, eliminar, suprimir. **To sweep the bottom,** *(Mar.)* rastrear.

sweep down, descender (barriendo); precipitarse en; descender.

sweep up, barrer en montón; limpiar, recoger.

sweep, *s.* 1. Barredura, barrido, el acto de barrer. 2. Destrucción violenta y general. 3. La figura o línea que describe en su movimiento una cosa agitada violentamente; vuelta, giro. 4. Alcance, extensión o área alcanzada; alcance de la vista; dirección o extensión de un movimeinto no hecho en línea recta; curva, encorvadura. 5. El o lo que barre; deshollinador; pieza de una máquina o lo largo de la cual se efectúa un rozamiento; remo largo y pesado; aspa de molino. 6. Calzada o camino en forma curva delante de un edificio. 7. *pl.* Barreduras. **They made a sweep for drugs,** hicieron una redada buscando droga. **To make a clean sweep,** ganar todos los puntos (sport, cards).

sweeper ['swiːpəʳ] [sui-paʳ], *s.* Barrendero, el que barre. **Carpet-sweeper,** escoba mecánica para barrer alfombras. **Chimney-sweeper,** deshollinador, limpiachimeneas.

sweepings ['swiːpɪŋz] [sui-pins], *s. pl.* Barreduras, la inmundicia que se junta con la escoba cuando se barre.

sweep-net ['swiːpnet] [suip-net], *s.* Esparavel, red redonda de pescar.

sweepstakes ['swiːpsteɪks] [suips-teiks], *s.* y *pl.* 1. El que gana todo cuanto se apuesta o se juega. 2. Palio, el premio que se señalaba en la carrera al que llegaba primero.

sweet [swiːt] [suit], *a.* 1. Dulce, grato, gustoso, agradable a los sentidos (nice); dulce al gusto o al paladar; que no es ni ácido ni amargo, azucarado; que no está salado; suave, b l a n d o o grato al tacto; oloroso, fragante al olfato, melodioso, dulce y agradable al oído. 2. Hermoso, lindo, agradable o bello a la vista. 3. Benigno, suave, dulce, apacible, amable, cuando se habla del genio, del trato, etc.; encantador, agradable, que impesiona agradablemente el ánimo, la imaginación. 4. Fresco, que no está corrompido o no es añejo. *-s.* 1. Dulzura, deleite. 2. Cosa dulce; más usado en plural, dulces,

golosinas. 3. Dulzura, placer, satisfacción. 4. Persona querida; querido, querida; es voz de cariño. **Sweet music,** música suave, melodiosa. **A sweet face,** una cara linda. **Sweet pinks,** claveles olorosos, fragantes. **A sweet girl,** una muchacha encantadora. **To smell sweet,** oler bien, tener buen olor. **Sweet-apple, sweet-sop,** anona, chirimoya. **Sweet cicely,** perifollo. *V.* CICELY. **Sweet corn,** variedad de maíz, preferida como comestible. **Sweet-fern,** planta de la familia de las miricáceas. **Sweet-gum,** liquidámbar de américa y la goma que de él se obtiene. **Sweet herbs,** hierbas olorosas que se usan como condimento. **Sweet-oil,** aceite de oliva. **Sweet-pea,** guisante de olor. **Sweet-tempered,** de carácter dulce, complaciente. **Sweet-tongued,** melifluo, pico de oro. **Sweet-scented,** perfumado. **Sweet-smelling,** odorífero, fragante. **Sweet-spoken,** melifluo. **Sweet-toothed,** goloso. **Sweet-William,** *(Bot.)* dianto, clavel barbado. **Sweet-willow, sweet-gale,** mirto holandés, pimienta de Brabante, arbusto de las miricáceas.

sweetbread ['swiːtbred] [suit-bred], *s.* Páncreas, glándula abdominal; o timo, glándula del cuello, cuando se emplean como alimento; lechecillas o mollejas de ternera.

sweetbrier ['swiːtraɪəʳ] [suit-braiaʳ], *s.* *(Bot.)* Escaramujo oloroso, agavanzo.

sweeten ['swiːtn] [sui-ten], *va.* 1. Dulzurar, dulcificar, endulzar, poner dulce lo que no lo era; azucarar, edulcorar. 2. Suavizar, mitigar, moderar, aplacar; aumentar el placer de; dar encanto a. 3. Embalsamar; purificar, quitar los malos olores; hacer salubre. *-vn.* Endulzarse.

sweetener ['swiːtnəʳ] [suit-naʳ], *s.* 1. Dulcificante, lo que dulcifica. 2. El que mitiga, calma o suaviza; el que palia.

sweetflag ['swiːtflæg] [suit-flag], *s.* *(Bot.)* Cálamo aromático.

sweetheart ['swiːthɑːt] [suit-jart], *s.* Enamorada, dulce amiga; querida, amante; la mujer a quien se corteja o galantea; se usa también a veces para significar galán, galanteador, cortejo, el amante de una mujer.

sweeting ['swiːtɪŋ] [sui-tin], *s.* 1. Camuesa, especie de manzana; variedad particular de manzana dulce. 2. *(Ant.)* querido; voz de cariño.

sweetish ['swiːtɪʃ] [sui-tish], *a.* Algo dulce.

sweetly ['swiːtlɪ] [suit-li], *adv.* Dulcemente, con dulzura, suavemente.

sweetmeat ['swiːtmiːt] [suit-mit], *s.* Dulce, cualquiera especie de confitura en seco; dulces secos.

sweetness ['swiːtnɪs] [suit-nes], *s.* Dulzura, calidad de dulce, melodioso, oloroso, o benigno; suavidad, blandura, apacibilidad, bondad.

sweetrush ['swiːtrʌʃ] [suit-rash], *s.* *(Bot.)* cálamo armático. *V.* SWEETFIAG.

swell, [swel] [suel], *vn.* *(pp.* SWELLED o SWOLLEN). 1. Hincharse, engrosarse, llenarse y entumecerse alguna cosa por cualquier causa que sea. 2. Hincharse, elevarse alguna parte del cuerpo; abotagarse. 3. Hincharse, envanecerse, engreírse, ensoberbecerse. 4. Escribir o hablar usando un estilo hinchado. 5. *(Mar.)* Embravecerse o agitarse el mar, hervir las olas. *-va.* 1. Hinchar, engrosar, inflar, entumecer; abultar. 2. Aumentar, agravar. 3. Hinchar, engreír, envanecer. 4. Cantar o tocar usando el crescendo y disminuendo combinados. **To swell to a great amount,** elevarse a una gruesa suma. **Rains swell the rivers,** las lluvias engrosan los ríos. **The sails swelled,** se hincharon las velas. **Swollen with pride,** inflado, hinchado de orgullo. **To swell out,** arrojar el árbol sus hojas; espetarse, ampollarse, bufar.

swell, *a.* 1. *(Ger.)* De petimetres, de mal gusto o de moda extremada. 2. Perteneciente a una hinchazón o torcedura. *-s.* 1. Entumecencia, hinchazón, bulto; cualquier aumento de volumen. 2. Oleada, ola larga y continua, oleaje, marejada; de aquí, ondulación del terreno. 3. Prominencia, protuberancia. 4. *(Mús.)* (a) La unión de crescendo y diminuendo, y los signos (<>) que la indican. (b) Aparato por el cual se puede aumentar o disminuir la fuerza del sonido. 5. *(Ger.)* Persona que sigue las modas con exageración. **Swell-organ,** parte del órgano cuyos cañones están encerrados en una caja; órgano de expresión. **Swell-pedal,** pedal de expresión. **We had a swell time,** lo pasamos muy bien.

swelling ['swelɪŋ] [sue-lin], *s.* 1. Hinchazón, el efecto de hincharse. 2. Tumor, abotagamiento de las carnes, bulto. 3. Cualquier prominencia, salida, chichón, bollo. 4. Acceso, transporte. *-pa.* de SWELL. Que se hincha, que se infla. **Swelling sails,** velas que se hinchan. **Swelling sea,** mar agitada, de oleaje. **Swelling breast,** seno agitado; pecho que se desarrolla.

swelter ['sweltəʳ] [suel-ta*r*], *va.* y *vn.* 1. Abrumar de calor. 2. Ahogarse o estar abrumado de calor.

sweltering ['sweltərɪŋ] [suel-te-rin], *a.* Sofocante, caluroso. **It's sweltering here,** hace demasiado calor aquí.

swept [swept] [suept], *pret.* y *pp.* del verbo SWEEP.

swerve [swɜːv] [suerv], *va.* Desviar, apartar de una dirección; dar efecto (to a ball). *-vn.* Desviarse, apartarse, separarse, extraviarse. *s.* Desvío, viraje brusco; esguince; regate (Sport).

swift [swɪft] [suift], *va. (Mar.)* Tortorar, dar tortores. **To swift a boat,** *(Mar.)* dar tortores a un bote.

swift, *a.* 1. Veloz, acelerado, pronto, ligero, rápido (fast). 2. Capaz de moverse con velocidad. 3. Pronto, repentino (sudden); que viene o sucede sin previo aviso. 4. Pronto, que obra sin tardar; vivo, diligente, activo (live). *-s.* 1. *(Orn.)* Vencejo, avión, pájaro semejante a la golondrina, notable por la rapidez de su vuelo. 2. Un ejemplar de varias clases de lagartos pequeños. 3. Carrete, devanadera con eje de quita y pon. 4. Corriente o curso rápido de un río; torrente o avenida impetuosa. **A swift stream,** una corriente rápida. **Swift-footed, swift of foot,** de paso rápido, ligero para correr. **Swift destruction,** ruina repentina.

swifter ['swɪftəʳ] [suif-ta*r*], *s. (Mar.)* Tortor, andarible; falso obenque.

swiftly ['swɪftlɪ] [suift-li], *adv.* Velozmente, rápidamente, ligeramente.

swiftness ['swɪftnɪs] [suift-nes], *s.* Velocidad, ligereza, rapidez, celeridad, prontitud en el movimeinto.

swig [swɪg] [suig], *va.* y *vn.* Beber a grandes tragos.

swig, *va. (Mar.)* Aballestar, estirar una cuerda fija por un extremo y atada por el otro a un objeto movible. *-s.* Acción de halar un cable o cabo que está amarrado por ambos extremos.

swill [swɪl] [suil], *va.* 1. Beber con exceso. 2. Emborrachar, embriagar. 3. Lavar, enjuagar.

swill, *s.* 1. Bazofia, alimento líquido para los puercos hecho con los restos de la cocina. 2. Tragantada, trago grande a algún licor.

swiller ['swɪləʳ] [sui-la*r*], *s.* Bebedor insaciable.

swim [swɪm] [suim], *vn. (pret.* SWAM o SWUM, *pp.* SWUM). 1. Nadar. mantenerse el hombre u otro animal sobre el agua o ir sobre ella. 2. Nadar, ir una cosa por encima del agua sin hundirse. 3. Nadar, abundar en alguna cosa. 4. Llevarse o ir con la corriente; conformar uno su conducta a la moda o la opinión general. 5. Padecer vaguidos o vahídos. **His head swims,** se le va la cabeza. 6. Pasar alguna cosa por delante de la vista con un movimiento trémulo. *-va.* 1. Pasar a nado. 2. Hacer flotar. 3. Empapar, calar, mojar en el agua para que floten las partes más ligeras. **He can't swim a stroke,** no sabe nadar en absoluto. **To swim away,** salvarse a nado. **To swim over a river,** atravesar un río a nado. **To swim with the tide,** seguir la corriente o ir con la corriente.

swim, *s.* 1. La acción o diversión de nadar. 2. Movimiento de deslizarse o bambolearse. **Swim bladder,** vejiga natatoria. **Swim fin,** aleta. **Swim trunks,** taparrabo. **To be in the swim,** estar en auge. 2. Estar al corriente. **I like a swim,** me gusta la natación. **To go for a swim,** ir a nadar.

swimmable ['swɪməbl] [sui-ma-bol], *a.* Que se puede atravesar a nado.

swimmer ['swɪməʳ] [sui-ma*r*], *s.* Nadador.

swimming ['swɪmɪŋ] [sui-min], *s.* 1. Natación. 2. Mareo, vahído, vértigo. *-a.* 1. Natatorio. 2. Nadador, natátil. 3. Lloroso. **Swimming-cap,** gorro de baño. **Swimming hole,** nadadero. **Swimming pool,** piscina, alberca. **Swimming stroke,** brazada. **To be fond of swimming,** ser aficionado a nadar.

swimmingly ['swɪmɪŋlɪ] [sui-min-li], *adv.* A las mil maravillas, sin tropiezo.

swindle ['swɪndl] [suin-del], *va.* Petardear, estafar, sonsacar, trampear, sacar dinero u otra cosa con pretextos falsos, pillar alguna cosa con tretas y engaños. *-s.* Estafa, trampa.

swindler ['swɪndləʳ] [suin-dla*r*], *s.* Estafador, petardista, tramposo.

swine [swaɪn] [suain], *a.* Marrano, puerco, cerdo, cochino. **Wild swine,** jabalí. **Sea-swine,** marsopa, marsopla o cachalote, un cetáceo. **Swine-plague,** peste de los puercos, enfermedad infecciosa causada por un microbio, que ataca los pulmones y el aparato digestivo de los cerdos. **Swine-pox,** variedad de viruelas locas. **Swine-thistle, V.** Sowthistle. What a swine he is!, ¡es un canalla!

swine-bread ['swaɪnbred] [suain-bred], *s.* 1. *(Bot.)* Trufa, criadilla de tierra. 2. Pande, puerco, planta. V. CYCLAMEN.

swine-herd ['swaɪnhɜːd] [suain-jerd], *s.* Porquero, porquerizo, el que guarda los puercos.

swing [swɪŋ] [suing], *va. (pret.* SWUNG o SWANG, *pp.* SWUNG). 1. Vibrar, hacer oscilar; balancear, bambolear, dar un movimiento trémulo a alguna cosa. 2. Mover, voltear o hacer dar vueltas en el aire; blandir (gun). 3. Hacer girar sobre un punto o eje. 4. Hacer subir, engoznar, colocar sobre goznes. *-vn.* 1. Vibrar, oscilar, moverse libremente a uno y otro lado un cuerpo, suspenso en el aire. 2. Columpiarse, moverse en el columpio. 3. Balancearse, dar o hacer balances. 4. Volverse, dar vueltas en alguna dirección fija, como sobre un eje. 5. *(Mar.)* Bornear, hacer cabeza, dar vuelta sobre las anclas. **To swing about,** rodear o dar vueltas alrededor de alguna cosa. **Swingbar, V.** SWINGLETREE. **Swing-plough,** arado de reja reversible. **To swing around the circle,** pasar por la serie completa. **To swing clear,** evitar un choque. **To swing round,** girar (turn).

swing, *s.* 1. Vibración, oscilación (movement), el movimiento libre e igual a un lado y a otro de un cuerpo suspenso en el aire. 2. Balanceo, bamboleo, balance. 3. Columpio, soga fija por sus extremos para columpiarse. 4. Inclinación o propensión irresistible. 5. Ímpetu de algún cuerpo puesto en movimiento; alcance. 6. Libre carrera o libertad desenfrenada. 7. Respaldo de articulación (camera). **Swingtree of a gun carriage,** *(Art.)* balancín de cureña. **In full swing,** en plena operación. **To give a swing,** balancear. **It has a swing of 5 metres,** tiene un recorrido de 5 metros. **To take a swing at somebody,** asestar un golpe a alguien. **What you lose on the swings your gain on the roundabouts,** lo que no va en lágrimas va en suspiros. **To walk with a swing,** andar a ritmo. **To be in full swing,** estar en plena actividad.

swing, *s.* Música de jazz, variedad de música popular de E.U.

swinge [swɪndʒ] [suindch], *va.* (SWINGED, *pa.* SWINGEING). Azotar, castigar, dar una felpa o una zurribanda.

swinger ['swɪŋəʳ] [suin-ga*r*], *s.* El que se columpia, voltea o da vueltas en el aire. **He's a swinger,** es muy moderno.

swinging ['swɪŋɪŋ] [suin-guin], *s.* 1. Oscilación, vibración. 2. Balanceo. 3. Borneo. *-pa.* del verbo SWING.

swingle ['swɪŋl] [suin-guel], *va.* Espadillar, sacudir el lino o cáñamo con la espadilla. *-s.* 1. Espadilla, instrumento para espadillar lino o cáñamo. Se llama también **swinglestaff y swing-knife.** 2. La barra corta del mayal con que se golpea el trigo al trillarlo. 3. V. SWINGLETREE.

swingletree ['swɪŋltriː] [suin-guel-tri], *s.* Bolea, balancín de tiro, afianzado en la punta de la lanza de un coche o arado. Se escribe también **singletree.**

swinish ['swaɪnɪʃ] [sui-nish], *a.* Porcuno, que es propio del puerco o perteneciente a él; cochino, grosero, sucio.

swipe [swaɪp] [suaip], *va.* 1. *(Fam.)* Dar un golpe fuerte. 2. *(Ger.)* Hurtar. *-s.* 1. *(Fam.)* fuerte. 2. Cigueñal o cigoñal, una pértiga que se usa para sacar agua.

swirl [swɜːl] [suerl], *va. y vn.* Hacer girar o girar, como en un torbellino; girar en remolino la nieve, el viento, el polvo o el agua. *-s.* 1. Remolino, torbellino; movimiento de lanzarse, como el de un pez. 2. Torcedura, forma espiral.

swish [swɪʃ] [suish], *va. y vn.* Mover o moverse con movimiento como de barrer y produciendo un sonido silbante. *-s.* Sonido silbante, como el de un látigo al cortar el aire; el movimiento que produce dicho sonido. *-s.* Elegante (smart).

Swiss [swɪs] [suis]. *a.* Suizo, de suiza. *-s.* Suizo, suiza; habitante de Suiza.

switch [swɪtʃ] [suich], *s.* 1. Varilla, vara pequeña (stick); *(Amer.)* cuje. 2. Moño de cabello natural o postizo en el peinado de las mujeres. 3. Aguja, *(Amer.)* cambiavía, carril movible o artificio para pasar un tren de uno a otro lado. 4. *(Elec.)* Conmutador, pieza de los aparatos eléctricos que sirve para cambiar de conductor una corriente. 5. Acción u operación de desviar un tren por medio de una aguja.

switch, *va.* 1. Varear, dar golpes o sacudir con una vara; sacudir a uno el polvo, medirle las costillas. 2. Precintar, asegurar con cujes o flejes. 3. Desviar, hacer pasar a otra vía un coche o un tren de ferrocarril. 4. *(Elec.)* Mudar de un circuito a otro. **To switch off,** desconectar, desenchufar. **To switch on,** encender, enchufar. **To switch round,** invertir, cambiar.

switchback [ˈswɪtʃbæk] [suich-bak], *s.* Vía de ferrocarril en zigzag.

switchblade [ˈswɪtʃbleɪd] [suich-bleid], *s.* Puñal, cuchillo o navaja de hoja automática.

switchboard [ˈswɪtʃbɔːd] [suich-bord], *s.* Conmutador telefónico.

switch box [ˈswɪtʃbɒks] [suich-boks], *s.* *(Elec.)* Caja de interruptores.

switchman [ˈswɪtʃmən] [suich-man], *s.* Guarda-agujas, empleado encargado de manejar las agujas de ferrocarril.

switchyard [ˈswɪtʃjɑːd] [suich-yard], *s.* *(F.C.)* Patio de maniobras.

Switzerland [ˈswɪtsələnd] [sui-cha-land], *s.* Suiza.

swivel [ˈswɪvl] [sui-vel], *va. y vn.* Girar sobre un eje. *-s.* 1. Alacrán, eslabón giratorio. 2. Pedrero, colisa, cañoncito que gira sobre un eje. 3. La lanadera de un telar de cintas. **Swivel chair,** silla giratoria. **Swivel-gun,** pedrero.

swollen [ˈswəʊlən] [suo-len], *pp.* del verbo TO SWELL. *a.* Hinchado.

swoon [swuːn] [suun], *vn.* Desmayarse, desfallecer, perder el sentido.

swoon, *s.* Desmayo, desfallecimiento, pasmo, síncope.

swoop [swuːp] [suup], *va.* 1. Descender y agarrar la presa al vuelo o hallándose en movimiento; se usa a menudo con up. 2. Coger, agarrar. *-vn.* Caer, precipitarse sobre algo, como el ave sobre su presa.

swoop, *s.* El acto de echarse un ave de rapiña sobre su presa.

sword [sɔːd] [suord], *s.* 1. Espada, arma blanca; sable. 2. *(Fig.)* Poder de la espada; dominio; derecho de vida y muerte; el poder militar en contraposición al civil. **Broadsword,** espada ancha, sable. **Cut and thrust sword,** espada-sable. **To put to the sword,** pasar a filo de espada, pasar a cuchillo. **To fire and sword,** a fuego y sangre. **Sword-arm,** brazo derecho. **Sword-belt.** cinturón. **Sword-cane,** bastón de estoque. **Sword dance,** danza de espadas. **Sword-guard, sword-hilt,** empuñadura, puño, guarda de la espada. **Sword-play,** asalto y defensa con la espada. **Sword-shaped,** ensiforme, que tiene la forma de una espada. **Sword-law,** la ley del más fuerte. **Sword-player,** esgrimidor. **To cross swords with someone,** reñir con alguien.

swordfish [ˈsɔːdfɪʃ] [suord-fish], *s.* Pez espada, pez

de alta mar.

swordsman [ˈsɔːdsmən] [suords-an], *s.* (*pl.* SWORDSMEN). 1. Tirador, hombre hábil en el manejo de la espada, espadachín. 2. Soldado, hombre de espada.

swore [swɔːr] [suoʳ], *pret.* del verbo TO SWEAR.

sworn [swɔːn] [suorn], *pp.* del verbo TO SWEAR.

swum [swʌm] [suam], *pret. y pp.* del verbo TO SWIM.

swung [swʌŋ] [suang], *pret. y pp.* del verbo TO SWING.

sybarite [ˈsɪbəraɪt] [si-ba-rait], *s.* Sibarita, habitante de la antigua ciudad griega de Sibaris, famosa por su lujo.

sybaritic [ˌsɪbəˈrɪtɪk] [si-ba-ri-tik], *a.* Sibarítico: se dice del que es dado a la molicie y a los deleites; y de las fiestas, diversiones, etc., muy extravagantes y continuadas.

sycamore [ˈsɪkəmɔːr] [si-ka-moʳ], *s.* 1. *(Bot.)* Sicomoro, higuera sicomoro, árbol de Siria y Egipto. 2. *(E.U.)* Plátano de América, falso plátano, árbol afín al arace. *V.* BUTTONWOOD.

sycophancy [ˈsɪkəfənsɪ] [si-ko-fan-si], *s.* 1. La calidad, carácter o práctica de sicofante. 2. Adulación.

sycophant [ˈsɪkəfənt] [si-ko-fant], *s.* Adulador, parásito, sicofante; gorrista, mogollón.

syllabic [sɪˈlæbɪk] [si-la-bik], *a.* Silábico.

syllabically [sɪˈlæbɪkəlɪ] [si-la-bi-ka-li], *adv.* Por sílabas.

syllabication [sɪˌlæbɪˈkeɪʃən] [si-la-bi-kei-shon], *s.* Silabeo, el acto de formar sílabas.

syllable [ˈsɪləbl] [si-la-bol], *s.* 1. Sílaba. 2. Cualquiera cosa concisa o breve.

syllabus [ˈsɪləbəs] [si-la-bos], *s.* Extracto, compendio, resumen de los principales puntos de un discurso.

syllogism [ˈsɪlədʒɪzəm] [si-lo-yi-sem], *s.* 1. Silogismo, argumento que consta de tres proposiciones, la última de las cuales se deduce de las otras dos. 2. Razonamiento deductivo contraposición al inductivo.

syllogistic [ˌsɪləˈdʒɪstɪk] [si-lo-yis-tik], *a.* Silogístico.

syllogize [ˈsɪlədʒaɪz] [si-lo-yais], *vn.* Silogizar, hacer silogismos o argüir en forma silogística.

sylph [sɪlf] [silf], *s.* 1. Silfo, sílfide. *(F.),* nombre que los cabalistas daban a los duendes; una joven delgada y primorosa. 2. Colibrí sudamericano del género Cyanolesbia, con cola larga horcada y de colores brillantes.

sylva [ˈsɪlvə] [sil-va], *s.* Conjunto de los árboles de las selvas.

sylvan [ˈsɪlvən] [sil-van], *a.* Selvático, silvático, silvestre; de aquí, rústico, rural. *-s.* Silvando, dios de las selvas.

symbiosis [ˌsɪmbɪˈəʊsɪs] [sim-biou-sis], *s.* Simbiosis.

symbol [ˈsɪmbəl] [sim-bol], *s.* 1. Símbolo, figura emblemática o nota significativa, emblema, signo, tipo. 2. Signo, carácter, marca o abreviatura que representa algo, como una operación o cantidad en las matemáticas, una substancia en química, un planeta en astronomía, etc. 3. Símbolo, el credo o sumario de los artículos de la fe. **The symbol of sulphuric acid is H2SO4,** el símbolo del ácido sulfúrico es H2SO4.

symbolic [sɪmˈbɒlɪk] [sim-bo-lik], *a.* Simbólico. **Symbolic logic,** lógica simbólica.

symbolically [sɪmˈbɒlɪkəlɪ] [sim-bo-li-ka-li], *adv.* Simbólicamente.

symbolism [ˈsɪmbəlɪzəm] [sim-bo-li-sem], *s.* Simbolismo, representación por medio de símbolos; sistema de símbolos.

symbolize [ˈsɪmbəlaɪz] [sim-bo-lais], *va. y vn.* Simbolizar, parecerse una cosa a otra o representarla con semejanza; guardar mucha semejanza una cosa con otra.

symmetrical [sɪˈmetrɪkəl] [si-me-tri-kal], *a.* Simétrico, proporcionado, que tiene simetría.

symmetry [ˈsɪmɪtrɪ] [si-mi-tri], *s.* Simetría, la proporción y correspondencia de unas partes con otras y de éstas con el todo.

sympathetic [ˌsɪmpəˈθetɪk] [sim-pa-ze-tik], *a.* 1. Simpático; que causa o experimenta simpatía; que obra por simpatía, que depende de ella; de acuerdo. 2. Compasivo, amable, benévolo. **They were sympathetic but could not help,** se compadecieron de nosotros pero no podían ayudarnos.

sympathetically [ˌsɪmpəˈθetɪkəlɪ] [sim-pa-ze-ti-ka-li], *adv.* Simpáticamente, con simpatía.

sympathize [ˈsɪmpəθaɪz] [sim-pa-zais], *vn.* 1. Compadecerse, simpatizar, acompañar a otro en el sentimiento o dolor; aliviar las penas de alguno mostrando sentimiento por ellas. 2. Padecer una parte u órgano en simpatía con otra. 3. Convenir, armonizarse, ajustarse. **I really do sympathize,** lo siento de verdad. **They called to sympathize,** vinieron a dar el pésame.

sympathy [ˈsɪmpəθɪ] [sim-pa-zi], *s.* 1. Simpatía, la correspondencia natural o imaginada que tienen ciertos cuerpos entre sí. 2. Simpatía, solidaridad, la comformidad de genios e inclinaciones entre dos personas. 3. *(Med.)* Simpatía, la relación o correspondencia que existe entre la acción de dos órganos separados uno de otro. **She has my sympathy,** la compadezco. **To express one's sympathy,** dar el pésame. **Sympathy vote,** voto de consolación.

symphonic [sɪmˈfɒnɪk] [sim-fo-nik], *a.* 1. Sinfónico, perteneciente o relativo a la sinfonía. 2. Homónimo; se dice de los vocablos del mismo sonido.

symphonious [sɪmˈfɒnɪəs] [sim-fo-nios], *a.* Armonioso.

symphonist [sɪmˈfɒnɪst] [sim-fo-nist], *s.* Sinfonista, el que compone sinfonías.

symphony [ˈsɪmfɒnɪ] [sim-fo-ni], *s.* Sinfonía, concierto de diferentes voces o instrumentos de música.

symposium [sɪmˈpəʊzɪəm] [sim-pou-siom], *s.* 1. Festín o banquete amenizado con la conversación de los comensales. 2. De aquí, una colección de comentarios, opiniones o sueltos cortos que se pubican juntos, v. g. en un periódico.

symptom [ˈsɪmptəm] [simp-tom], *s.* 1. *(Med.)* Síntoma, cualquier fenómeno morboso o mudanza sensible en la apariencia o en el modo de funcionar los órganos. 2. Síntoma o señal que indica la existencia de alguna otra cosa.

symptomatic [ˌsɪmptəˈmætɪk] [sim-to-ma-tik], *a.* Sintomático, perteneciente al síntoma, de la naturaleza de un síntoma o indicio; según los síntomas.

synagogue [ˈsɪnəgɒg] [si-na-gog], *s.* 1. Sinagoga, el lugar o edificio en que se reúnen los judíos a orar y a oír la doctrina de su religión. 2. Sinagoga, congregación o junta religiosa de los judíos.

synapse [ˈsaɪnæps] [sai-naps], *s.* Sinapsis.

synchronic [sɪŋˈkrɒnɪk] [sin-kro-nik], *a.* Sincrónico, lo que sucede al mismo tiempo que otra cosa.

synchronism [ˈsɪŋkrənɪzəm] [sin-kro-ni-sem], *s.* Sincronismo, contemporaneidad, concurrencia de sucesos o eventos acaecidos a un mismo tiempo.

synchronization [ˌsɪŋkrənaɪˈzeɪʃən] [sin-kro-nai-sei-shon], *s.* Sincronización.

synchronize [ˈsɪŋkrənaɪz] [sin-kro-nais], *va.* Sincronizar.

synchronous [ˈsɪŋkrənəs] [sin-kro-nos], *a.* Sincrónico, coetáneo, concurrente, simultáneo, que se hace al mismo tiempo.

synchrotron [ˈsɪŋkrəˌtrɒn] [sin-kro-tron], *s.* Sincrotón.

syncopate [ˈsɪŋkəpeɪt] [sin-ko-peit], *va.* 1. Sincopar. 2. *(Mús.)* Hacer una sincopa.

syncopation [ˌsɪŋkəˈpeɪʃən] [sin-ko-pei-shon], *s.* 1. Síncopa, supresión de una letra o sílaba en medio de una palabra. 2. Síncopa musical.

syncope [ˈsɪŋkəpɪ] [sin-ko-pi], *s.* 1. Síncope, la pérdida completa y repentina del sentido y movimiento. 2. *(Gram.)* Síncopa, la supresión de una letra o sílaba en medio de la dicción. 3. *(Mús.)* Síncopa, nota que se toca al fin de un tiempo y al principio de otro.

syncretic [sɪnˈkrɛtɪk] [sin-kre-tik], *a.* Sincrético.

syncretism [ˈsɪŋkrətɪzəm] [sin-kre-ti-sem], *s.* Sincretismo.

syndic [ˈsɪdɪk] [sin-dik], *s.* Síndico.

syndicalism [ˈsɪdɪkəlɪzəm] [sin-di-ka-li-sem], *s.* Sindicalismo.

syndicate [ˈsɪdɪkɪt] [sin-di-kit], *va.* y *vn.* Combinar en una asociación comercial o manejar por medio de ella. -*s.* 1. Asociación de personas para la prosecución de una

empresa que exige grandes caudales. 2. Sindicado, junta de síndicos.

syndrome [ˈsɪdrəʊm] [sin-droum], *sm.* Síndrome.

synecdoche [sɪˈnɛkdəkɪ] [si-nek-do-ki], *s.* Sinécdoque, figura retórica.

synod [ˈsɪnəd] [si-nod], *s.* Sínodo, el concilio que celebra el obispo con los eclesiásticos de su diócesis.

synodal [ˈsɪnədl] [si-no-dal], *a.* Sinódico.

synonym [ˈsɪnənɪm] [si-no-nim], *s.* 1. Sinónimo, voz o palabra que tiene el mismo o casi el mismo sentido que otra: opuesto a *antonym.* 2. Equivalente de un vocablo en otra lengua.

synonymous [sɪˈnɒnɪməs] [si-no-ni-mos], *a.* Sinónimo, que expresa la misma cosa con diferentes voces: se dice de una cosa respecto de otra con la cual tiene estrecha relación.

synonymy [sɪˈnɒnəmɪ] [si-no-na-mi], *s.* Sinonimia, la calidad de expresar la misma cosa con diferentes voces.

synopsis [sɪˈnɒpsɪs] [si-nop-sis], *s.* Sinopsis, suma, sumario.

synoptic [sɪˈnɒptɪk] [si-nop-tik], *a.* Sinóptico; perceptible o comprensible a primera vista.

synovial [saɪˈnəʊvɪəl] [sai-nou-vial], *a.* Sinvoial, perteneciente a la sinovia o que la produce.

syntactic [sɪnˈtæktɪk] [sin-tak-tik], *a.* Sintáctico, perteneciente o relativo a la sintaxis.

syntax [ˈsɪntæks] [sin-taks], *s.* Sintaxis, la parte de la gramática que enseña el uso de las partes de la oración.

synthesis [ˈsɪnθəsɪs] [sin-ze-sis], *s.* 1. Síntesis, composición, lo contrario de *análisis;* reunión de substancias separadas, o de partes subordinadas en una nueva forma. 2. Combinación de los elementos radicales de una palabra en la formación de un idioma. 3. *(Log.)* Razonamiento que procede de todo a una parte o de lo general a lo particular. 4. *(Cir.)* Reunión de partes divididas.

synthesize [ˈsɪnθəsaɪz] [sin-za-sais], *va.* Sintetizar.

synthetic [ˈsɪnˈθetɪk] [sin-ze-tik], *a.* 1. Sintético, relativo a la síntesis, lo contrario de analítico. 2. Sintético, fabricado químicamente. **Synthetic rubber,** caucho sintético, caucho artificial.

syphilis [ˈsɪfɪlɪs] [si-fi-lis], *s.* Sífilis, mal gálico, enfermedad específica, venérea e infecciosa.

syphilitic [ˌsɪfɪˈlɪtɪk] [si-fi-li-tik], *a.* Sifilítico, perteneciente a la sífilis, o que la padece.

syphon [ˈsaɪfən] [sai-fon], *s.* Sifón. V. SIPHON.

Syrian [ˈsɪrɪən] [si-rian], *a.* y *s.* Sirio, de la Siria; habitante de la Siria moderna o antigua.

syringe [sɪˈrɪndʒ] [si-rindch], *s.* Jeringa, un instrumento para echar ayudas y hacer inyecciones.

syringe, *va.* Jeringar, echar ayudas con una jeringa; lavar haciendo inyecciones.

syrup [ˈsɪrəp] [si-rop], *s.* Jarabe. V. SIRUP.

system [ˈsɪstəm] [sis-tem], *s.* 1. Sistema, el orden y situación natural de muchas cosas que obran simultáneamente. 2. Sistema, el conjunto y enlace de principios o verdades relativas a una materia; clasificación metódica. 3. Un todo compuesto de partes constituyentes; p. ej. un sistema de ferrocarril. 4. *(Biol.)* Conjunto de estructuras orgánicas que obran en combinación; el sistema nervioso, digestivo, etc. **System analyst,** analista de sistemas. **System disk,** disco de sistema *(Inform.)* **Systems software,** software del sistema.

systematic [ˌsɪstəˈmætɪk] [sis-te-ma-tik], *s.* y *a.* Sistemático.

systematical [ˌsɪstəˈmætɪkəl] [sis-te-ma-ti-kal], *a.* Sistemático, metódico, puesto con orden.

systematically [ˌsɪstəˈmætɪkəlɪ] [sis-te-ma-ti-ka-li], *adv.* Sistemáticamente.

systematize [ˈsɪstəmətaɪz] [sis-te-ma-tais], *va.* Reducir a sistema.

systemic [sɪsˈtemɪk] [sis-te-mik], *a.* 1. Sistemático. 2. Perteneciente al cuerpo como un todo.

systole [ˈsɪstəlɪ] [sis-to-li], *s.* Sístole, el movimiento del corazón y de las arterias cuando se contraen; opuesto al llamado *diástole.*

systolic [ˈsɪstəlɪk] [sis-to-lik], *a.* Sistólico, relativo a la sístole.

T

t [ti:] [ti], Esta letra tiene en general el mismo sonido que en español, aunque un poco más fuerte. Cuando precede a una *i* seguida de vocal, se pronuncia como *sh;* v. g. en las palabras *nation y patient;* en muchas voces acabadas en *une, ure, ure,* etc., tiene el sonido de *ch,* como en *nature, virtue,* etc.: también en algunas veces muda, p. ej. en *to listen, often, to soften,* etc. -La *th* tiene tres sonidos; uno suave, entre la *d* y la *z* castellana, como en *thus, that,* etc.; otro agudo, parecido al de la *z* española como en *thin, thought,* etc.; y el último como el de la *t* simple, v. g. en *Thames, Thomas,* etc.

tab [tæb] [tab], *s.* 1. Jirón, lengüeta, proyección, apéndice o parte saliente de una cosa. 2. Cuenta. **To keep tab,** *(Fam.)* Llevar cuenta, poner en cuenta. **To pick up the tap,** pagar la cuenta, asumir responsabilidades *(Fig.).* 3. Tabulación.

tabard ['tæbəd] [ta-bard], *s.* Tabardo, prenda de abrigo ancha y larga con las mangas bobas, que se usó en tiempos pasados.

tabarder ['tæbədəʳ] [ta-bar-daʳ], *s.* El que llevaba tabardo.

tabasco [təˈbæskəo] [ta-bas-kou], *s.* Salsa de pimienta de Tabasco.

tabby ['tæbɪ] [ta-bi], *s.* 1. Tabí, especie de tela de seda ondeada y prensada. 2. Gato moteado; y particularmente una gata. *-a.* 1. Ondeado, que tiene la apariencia de hacer ondas (clothes). 2. Abigarrado, salpicado de varios colores.

tabby, *va.* Ondear y prensar las telas de seda formando en ellas aguas u ondas.

tabernacle ['tæbənækl] [ta-ba-na-kol], *s.* 1. Tabernáculo, tienda: entre los judíos el lugar donde estaba el arca del testamento. 2. Tabernáculo, templo, santuario; cualquier habitación o vivienda en el lenguaje de la Sagrada Escritura.

tab key ['tæbki:] [tab-ki], *s.* Tecla de tabulación *(Tip., Inform.).*

tablature ['tæblətʃəʳ] [ta-bla-chaʳ], *s.* 1. *(Anat.)* Una de las láminas de tejido óseo que forman las paredes del cráneo. 2. Pintura mural.

table ['teɪbl] [tei-bol], *s.* 1. Mesa, un mueble para el servicio doméstico o para adorno. 2. Mesa, tomado absolutamente es la mesa para comer, y también la comida o manjares que se ponen o sirven en ella. **To keep a good table,** tener buena mesa. 3. El conjunto de personas que están comiendo a un tiempo en la mesa. 4. Tabla, el índice de los libros o cualquier lista o catálogo dispuesto en orden sucesivo: clasificación o serie de números o signos dispuestos para facilitar su examen. 5. Tabla, pintura hecha en tabla o piedra. 6. Tabla, plancha, superficie plana o lisa de cualquier metal o piedra para grabar, esculpir o pintar en ella. 7. Palma de la mano. **Tables,** tablas o tablas reales, un juego muy semejante al del chaquete. **To burn the tables,** volverse la tortilla; hacer cambiar la suerte. **To turn the tables upon one,** devolver la pelota a alguno. **Side-table,** bufete, aparador. **Table-cloth,** mantel; tela para manteles; alemanisco. **Table-covers,** sobremesa: *(Amer.)* Cubremesas. **Table-land,** mesa, meseta, terreno elevado y llano. **Table-linen,** adamascado. **Table-set** o **service,** vajilla, juego de artículos necesarios para poner completamente una mesa. **Table-boarder,** pupilo, pensionista, el que come a la mesa, pero se aloja en otra parte. **Table salt,** sal de mesa. **Table-talk,** propósitos de sobremesa; conversación familiar. **Table-beer,** cerveza, floja, cerveza de pasto. **Table-book,** libro vistoso que se tiene por lo regular sobre una mesa: y *(Des.)* una especie de librito de memoria para escribir con lápiz. **To put a proposal on the table,** hacer una propuesta; *(E.U.)* aplazar la discusión de una propuesta. **To rise from the table,** levantarse de la mesa.

table, *va.* y *vn.* 1. Dar carpetazo a un proyecto de ley; posponer la discusión o consideración de un acuerdo. 2. Poner sobre la mesa, v. g. un naipe. 3. Hacer el índice de algún escrito; hacer un catálogo en orden sucesivo. 4. *(Carp.)* Ensamblar, acoplar.

table d'hôte ['tɑːblˈdəot] [ta-bol-dout], *s.* Menú.

tablemat ['teɪblmæt] [tei-bol-mat], *s.* Salvamanteles.

table-spoon ['teɪblspuːn] [tei-bol-spun], *s.* Cuchara de mesa o de sopa.

table-sponful ['teɪblˌspuːnfʊl] [tei-bol-spun-ful], *s.* Cucharada.

tablet ['tæblɪt] [ta-blit], *s.* 1. Tableta, tablilla; hoja de marfil, etc., sobre la cual se puede escribir; juego o conjunto de hojas de papel unidas, o una sola de esas hojas. V. PAD. 2. Mesa pequeña o cualquier superficie plana pequeña: particularmente, plancha para una inscripción. 3. Tableta, medicamento en forma de pastilla cuadrada. **Votive tablet,** tablilla, plancha grabada conmemorativa de un voto.

tableware ['teɪblwɛəʳ] [tei-bol-ueaʳ], *s.* Servicio de mesa.

tabloid ['tæblɔɪd] [ta-bloid], *s.* Pequeño periódico con noticias condensadas y muchas ilustraciones. *-a.* Comprimido o condensado, como una crítica, un drama, etc.

taboo, tabu [təˈbuː] [ta-bu], *va.* Declarar tabú; *(Fig.)* prohibir, excluir, desterrar. *-s.* Tabú, especie de prohibición religiosa de los habitantes de la Polinesia, por la que se consideran como sagrados ciertos objetos, lugares, días, personas, etc.; de aquí, preocupación, ostracismo.

tabor, tabour ['tæbəʳ] [ta-boʳ], *s.* Tamboril, tambor pequeño; pandero.

tabouret ['tæbərɪt] [ta-bo-rit], *s.* 1. Tambor, pequeño o tamboril. 2. Taburete. 3. Bastidor de bordar.

tabourine ['tæbɔriːn] [ta-bu-rin], *s.* Tamboril.

tabular ['tæbjolə'] [ta-biu-laʳ], *a.* 1. Perteneciente a una tabla; dispuesto en forma de lista o catálogo. 2. Tabular, en forma de placa o plancha: llano; laminado. 4. Computado con una tabla matemática.

tabulate ['tæbjoleɪt] [ta-biu-leit], *va.* 1. Disponer en forma de tabla o lista; disponer en cuadros sinópticos. 2. Formar con una superficie plana.

tabulate, *va.* 1. Disponer en forma de tabla o lista: disponer en cuadros sinópitocs. 2. Formar con una superficie plana.

tabulated ['tæbjoleɪtɪd] [ta-biu-lei-tid], *a.* Liso, plano, igual.

tabulation [ˌtæbjoˈleɪʃən] [ta-biu-lei-shon], *s.* Colocación, distribución en cuadros o listas.

tachograph ['tækəɡrɑːf] [ta-ko-graf], *s.* Tacógrafo.

tachometer [tæˈkɒmɪtəʳ] [ta-ko-mi-taʳ], *s.* Tacómetro.

tachygraphy [təˈkɪɡrɑːfɪ] [ta-ki-gra-fi], *s.* Taquigrafía, el arte de escribir con celeridad por medio de signos. V. STENOGRAPHY.

tacit ['tæsɪt] [ta-sit], *a.* Tácito, que sin expresarse se supone o infiere.

tacitly ['tæsɪtlɪ] [ta-sit-li], *adv.* Tácitamente, de un modo tácito.

taciturn ['tæsɪtɜːn] [ta-si-tern], *a.* Taciturno, callado, que por costumbre gasta pocas palabras.

tack [tæk] [tak], *va.* 1. Atar, afianzar como con tachuelas; clavar, ligeramente. 2. Pegar, coser o unir una cosa a otra; añadir como suplementario, anexar. V. APPEND. *-vn.* Virar, dar vuelta la nave para tomar otro rumbo; virar por avante, cambiar de bordada. **To tack something on to a letter,** añadir algo a una carta.

tack, *s.* 1. Tachuela, clavito con cabeza; puntilla. 2. Lo que asegura; hilván. 3. *(Mar.)* 1. Amura, jarcia para fijar el ángulo de ciertas velas; 2. Bordada, virada, el giro que hacen las embarcaciones a un lado y a otro alternativamente para ganar el viento. 4. De aquí, un cambio de política; nuevo plan de acción. **On the port tack,** amurado a babor. **On the starboard tack,** amurado a estribor. **To stand on the other tack,** cambiar de amura. **To be on wrong tack,** estar equivocado.

tackle ['tækl] [ta-kel], *va.* 1. Agarrar, asir, forcejear. 2. En el juego de *football,* salir al encuentro de un adversario y procurar impedir que corra. *-s.* 1. Aparejo, artificio para levantar o mover algo, combinación de cuerdas, poleas, ganchos, etc.; jarcia. 2. Todo género de instrumentos, aparejos, aperos, o avíos. **Fishing-tackle,** enseres, avíos de pescar. 3. Acción de agarrar, o de impedir que otro corra. **Main-tackle,** aparejo real. **Fore-tackle,** aparejo del trinquete. **Stay-tackle,** aparejo de amurar. **Tackle-fall,** tira de aparejo. **Tackle-hooks,** ganchos de aparejos.

tackling ['tæklɪŋ] [ta-klin], s. 1. Aparejo, palanquín. 2. Instrumentos, aperos, herramientas.

tacky ['tækɪ] [ta-ki], a. Malo, raído (shabby); vulgar, de pacotilla (shaddy).

tact [tækt] [takt], s. 1. Tacto, discernimiento, buen sentido; finura, tino. 2. Tacto, sentido del tacto.

tactic ['tæktɪk] [tak-tik], a. Táctico, perteneciente o relativo a la táctica.

tactician [tæk'tɪʃən] [tak-ti-shan], s. Táctico, el instruido en la táctica militar o naval.

tactics ['tæktɪks] [tak-tiks], s. pl. 1. Táctica, el arte de los movimientos, formaciones o evoluciones militares o navales. 2. Manejo hábil; ardides.

tactile ['tæktaɪl] [tak-tail], a. Tangible, referente al tacto; tocable, que se puede tocar.

tactless ['tæktlɪs] [takt-les], a. Falto de tacto, finura o tino; desatinado.

tactual ['tæktʃʊəl] [tak-chual], a. Táctil.

tadpole ['tædpəʊl] [tad-poul], s. Renacuajo, cría acuática de un animal anfibio.

taffeta ['tæfɪtə] [ta-fi-ta], s. Tafetán sencillo o liso.

taffy ['tæfɪ] [ta-fi], s. 1. Melcocha, arropía. 2. (Ger. E. U.) Zalamería.

tag [tæg] [tag], s. 1. Herrete; marbete, rótulo, cédula atada por un extremo; lo que está atado o cuelga. 2. Pingajo, arrapiezo.

tag, va. 1. Herretear, echar herretes a alguna cosa; marcar con un marbete o rótulo. 2. Atar, afianzar. **Tagged lace,** agujeta. 3. Seguir de cerca, marchar sobre los talones de alguno.

tag, va. Alcanzar y tocar.

tail [teɪl] [teil], s. 1. Cola, la extremidad que en la parte posterior tienen los animales, aves y peces. 2. Cola, la punta prolongada de algunas ropas talares. 3. Cola, la parte posterior o inferior de alguna cosa; la parte opuesta a la cabeza: apéndice terminal; rastro luminoso de un cometa; rasgo que se pone a una nota música y que la hace subir o bajar. 4. Acompañamiento, escolta. **To turn tail,** volver la espalda, mostrar los talones, fugarse. **Bob tail,** cola cortada. 5. (For.) Limitación de propiedad.

tail, va. Tirar de la cola. **To tail away,** ir disminuyendo.

tailblock ['teɪlblɒk] [teil-blok], s. (Mar.) Motón de rabiza.

tailcoat ['teɪlkəʊt] [teil-kout], s. Frac.

tailed ['teɪld] [teild], a. Rabudo, que tiene cola o rabo.

tailing ['teɪlɪŋ] [tei-lin], s. 1. pl. Restos, partes inferiores, particularmente de los minerales. 2. Extremo interior de un ladrillo o piedra dentro de una pared.

tail light ['teɪllaɪt] [teil-lait], s. Luz o farol de cola.

tailor ['teɪləʳ] [tei-laʳ], s. Sastre, el que tiene por oficio hacer vestidos. **Tailor-bird,** pájaro oriental que cose o ensarta hojas con algodón para formar su nido. **Tailor's dummy,** maniquí.

tailoress ['teɪlərɪs] [tei-la-res], f. Sastra, mujer que tiene por oficio hacer vestidos.

tailoring ['teɪlərɪŋ] [tei-la-rin], s. Sastrería.

tailor-made ['teɪləmeɪd] [tei-la-meid], a. Hecho a la medida.

tail-piece ['teɪlpiːs] [teil-pis], s. Florón o cualquier otro adorno grabado al fin de un libro o de un capítulo; (Tip.) culo de lámpara; cola de violín o guitarra.

tail spin ['teɪlspɪn] [teil-spin], s. (Aer.) Barrena.

tailtackle ['teɪltækl] [teil-ta-kel], s. (Mar.) Aparejo o palanquín de rabiza.

tail wheel ['teɪlwiːl] [teil-uil], s. (Aer.) Rueda de cola.

tail wind ['teɪlwɪnd] [teil-uind], s. Viento de cola o trasero, viento de popa.

taint [teɪnt] [teint], va. 1. Manchar, ensuciar, infeccionar. 2. Corromper, viciar, echar a perder; envenenar.

taint, s. Mácula, mancha, tanto en el sentido físico como en el moral: tacha, lunar; infección, corrupción.

taintless ['teɪntlɪs] [teint-les], a. Incorrupto, no contaminado, puro, sin mancha.

take [teɪk] [teik], va. (pret. TOOK, pp. TAKEN). 1. Tomar, coger, asir o agarrar una cosa con la mano (hand). 2. Tomar, recibir o aceptar de cualquier modo que sea (accept). 3. Tomar, ocupar o adquirir por medio de la fuerza o por medio de la fuerza o por medio de artificios; apoderarse de. 4. Tomar, percibir o cobrar (earn, receive). 5. Tomar, quitar; hurtar o pillar; arrebatar, llevar; restar, deducir, substraer (deduct). 6. Tomar o hacer a uno prisionero; prender. 7. Escoger; de aquí, usar, emplear, adoptar. 8. Tomar, entender o interpretar alguna cosa en un sentido determinado (understand). 9. Cautivar, embargar las potencias del alma; deleitar, causar deleite, gusto o placer. 10. Tomar, aprender o concebir alguna cosa. 11. Ejecutar cualquier acción expresada generalmente por el sustantivo que va unido con el verbo. 12. Contraer una enfermedad; resfriarse (con cold). 13. Informarse midiendo, pesando o computando. 14. Pasar por encima, cruzar. **A horse takes a hedge,** el caballo salta por encima del seto. 15. Copiar, sacar una copia. 16. Tomar, tragar alguna cosa como medicina. 17. Suponer o dar por sentada alguna cosa. 18. Dar en alguna parte determinada. 19. Incluir en un curso, visitar. -vn. 1. Tomar, lograr; salir bien, tener buen éxito; acusar gusto o agrado. 2. Quitar; abstraer o deducir alguna cosa; detraer, detractar, derogar. 3. Efectuarse una cosa, seguir el curso, orden o efecto natural. 4. Agarrarse, arraigarse, prender las plantas. 5. Encaminarse, dirigirse, ir o moverse hacia. 6. Prender el fuego. 7. Aplicarse, tener afición a, inclinarse naturalmente; se usa por lo común con to. 8. Hacer un cuadro, imagen o fotografía. **That takes a great deal of time,** eso toma mucho tiempo. **Take my word for it,** créame usted bajo mi palabra.

take after, imitar, tomar por ejemplo; parecerse.

take again, volver a tomar o tomar segunda vez.

take asunder, separar, desunir, despegar. **To take away,** quitar, sacar; llevarse; alzar o levantar la mesa; apartar o separar alguna cosa.

take back, (Fam.) Retractar, desdecirse.

take down, bajar o poner más baja una cosa; bajar o conducir de alto abajo; abatir, humillar; tragar. **To take for granted,** dar por sentado. **To take form,** despojar, privar de, minorar, substraer.

take in, cercar, rodear o ceñir; contener, comprender o incluir en sí; entender, comprender; admitir, recibir, tomar; acoger, recoger, dar asilo; contraer, disminuir el volumen de algo; encoger; ganar por conquista; (Fam.) estafar, engañar. **To take in hand,** emprender, tomar por su cuenta, tomar en mano. **To take into one's head,** ponérsele a uno en la cabeza, metérsele en la mollera.

take off, despegar (plane); separar, quitar de delante o del medio, arrebatar; levantar o apartar, v. g. una máscara; destruir; invalidar o hacer nula y de ningún valor una cosa; tragar de un golpe; comprar; remedar, ridiculizar; copiar; sacar un retrato; despegar o separar dos cosas que estaban unidas entre sí. **To take off an arm,** cortar, amputar un brazo. **To take off the edge of a knife,** embotar un cuchillo: quitar el filo. **To take off form,** debilitar, disminuir; apartar de, desviar de.

take on, quejarse, lamentarse, melancolizarse, estar triste.

take out, llevar o sacar afuera; hacer salir o echar a alguno de un paraje; sacar, quitar, arrebatar; arrancar, extraer. **To take the creases out of cloth,** quitar los dobleces del paño o alisarlo. **To take out a patent,** obtener un privilegio de invención. **To take out of,** extraer.

take over, 1. (Engl.) apoderarse, adquirir, tomar posesión de algo; 2. derivar.

take to, aplicarse al estudio; tomar afición a alguna cosa; recurrir. **To take to heart,** tomar a pecho. **To take to pieces,** hacer pedazos; desarmar una cosa que tiene varias piezas; de aquí, confutar un argumento punto por punto.

take up, tomar al fiado, tomar prestado; atacar; comenzar o dar principio a alguna cosa; ocupar la atención; recurrir en último resultado; prender, arrestar; ligar un vaso en las operaciones quirúrgicas; admitir una cosa sin examen; reprender, amonestar; principiar una cosa en el punto donde otro la dejó; alzar o levantar alguna cosa del suelo; ocupar o llenar un sitio cualquiera; comprender o incluir en sí; adoptar una opinión, doctrina, etc.; saldar, pagar (una letra de cambio, un pagaré, etc.); cobrar o recoger, hablando de contribuciones; aprovechar en el estudio o en cualquier otra materia; detenerse o contenerse; reformar uno su vida o sus costumbres. **To take up a quarrel,** entremeterse en alguna disputa o pendencia. **To take up a space,** ocupar o llenar completamente un sitio o espacio. **To take one up sharply,** reprender a alguno agriamente. **To take up short,** quedarse cortado. **To take up with,** contentarse; vivir o habitar con; ocupar.

take upon, tomar sobre sí algún cargo, obligación, responsabilidad, etc.; entremeterse, mezclarse o meterse en una cosa; afectar señorío, hacerse el personaje, el caballero; arrogarse, atribuirse. **To take upon trust,** tomar a crédito; saber algo por haberlo oído decir; creer alguna cosa bajo la fe o crédito de otro. **To take upon oneself,** tomar a su cargo o encargarse de la ejecución de una cosa.

take with, agradar, satisfacer, contentar, gustar. **To take a journey,** hacer un viaje. **To take a leap,** dar un salto o brinco. **To take a linking to,** aficionarse a. **To take a turn o a walk,** dar una vuelta, un paseo. **To take a thing kindly,** tomar una cosa en buen sentido, no tomarlo por donde quema; y también quedar contento de alguna cosa que otro ha hecho. **To take advice,** aconsejarse o tomar consejo. **To take an oath,** jurar o hacer juramento. **To take breath,** tomar aliento, reposarse después de algún esfuerzo. **To take home,** llevar, traer a casa. **To take care,** cuidar, tener cuidado; ser cuidadoso, tener solicitud por algo. **To take the chair,** tomar, ocupar el sillón presidencial, presidir. **To take the field,** entrar en campaña, comenzar las hostilidades. **To take fire,** encenderse; atufarse, tomar fuego. **To take fright at,** atemorizarse de o por, sobresaltarse. **To take heed,** estar alerta, tener cuidado. **To take hold,** coger, apoderarse. **To take landscapes,** fotografiar o pintar paisajes. **To take leave of,** despedirse de. **To take no trouble to gain an end,** no dar pie ni patada. **To take offence at,** agraviarse de, picarse. **To take pains,** esmerarse, darse la pena. **To take pity on,** apiadarse o compadecerse de. **To take place,** suceder, efectuarse, verificarse, tener efecto alguna cosa. **To take notice,** poner atención. **Not to take notice,** no hacer caso, no poner cuidado. **Take notice,** (For.) aviso, aviso o noticia al público; advertencia. **To take refuge,** acogerse a. **To take sanctuary,** acogerse a lugar sagrado. **To take shelter,** guarecerse. **To take ship,** embarcarse. **To take the law,** poner pleito. **To be taken ill,** enfermar. **The enemy took to flight,** el enemigo huyó. **To take to business,** ser aficionado a los negocios o consagrarse a ellos. **A book which will not take,** un libro que no tendrá buen éxito, que no se venderá. **The daughter takes after her father,** la hija se parece o sale a su padre.

take, s. 1. Toma, tomadura, acción de tomar, y la porción que se toma de una vez. 2. (Impr.) tomada, la porción que toma el cajista de una vez. **Take-off,** (a) imitación burlesca, caricatura; (b) el punto donde los pies dejan el suelo al saltar. **Take-up,** atesador, pieza que estira el hilo en las máquinas de coser al levantarla la aguja.

take-home pay ['teɪkhɔ͡ʊmˌpeɪ] [teik-joum-pei], s. Salario neto (después de haberse descontado los impuestos y otras sumas por diversos conceptos).

taken ['teɪkən] [tei-ken], pp. de TO TAKE.

take-off ['teɪkɒf] [teik-of], s. 1. Despegue (plane). 2. Partida o salida (in travel). 3. (Fam.) Imitación en son de caricatura. -vn. 1. Despegar. 2. Salir, partir.

taker ['teɪkə͡ʳ] [tei-ka͡ʳ], s. Tomador.

taking ['teɪkɪŋ] [tei-kin], a. 1. Encantador, seductor, atractivo; halagüeño (charm). 2. (Fam.) Contagioso. -s. 1. Acción del que toma o embarga; secuestro, embargo. 2. Afición a alguna

cosa: inclinación, afecto; se usa con for. 3. pl. Recibos. 4. (Fam.) Captura; de aquí, situación difícil, trance apurado.

talc [tælk] [talk], s. (Min.) Talco.

talcum powder ['tælkəmˌpaʊdə͡ʳ] [tal-kom-pau-da͡ʳ], s. Talco, polvo de talco.

tale [teɪl] [teil], s. 1. Cuento, cuentecillo o narración de alguna aventura, incidente, etc (story). 2. Relación, relato. 3. Fábula, conseja. 4. Cuenta, operación aritmética (Mat.)

tale-bearer ['teɪlˌbɛərə͡ʳ] [teil-bea-ra͡ʳ], s. Soplón, chismoso, cuentero.

tale-bearing ['teɪlˌbɛərɪŋ] [teil-bea-rin], s. Soplo, cuento o chisme.

talent ['tælənt] [ta-lent], s. 1. Talento, dotes de la naturaleza. 2. Talento, aptitud notable, capacidad, habilidad natural, ingenio. 3. Talento, moneda o suma de monedas que usaron los antiguos.

talented ['tæləntɪd] [ta-len-tid], a. Talentoso, que tiene talento.

talent scout ['tæləntˌskaʊt] [ta-lent-skaut], s. Persona encargada de descubrir posibles futuros actores, cantantes, etc.

tale-teller ['teɪlˌtelə͡ʳ] [teil-te-la͡ʳ], s. Chismeador, chismoso.

talisman ['tælɪzmən] [ta-lis-man], s. Talismán; carácter, figura o imagen adivinatoria y supersticiosa.

talk [tɔːk] [tok], va. 1. Decir, hablar de; conversar sobre algo. 2. Hablar (language). -vn. 1. Hablar, conversar. 2. Charlar, hablar mucho y fuera de propósito. 3. Contar, referir (tell). 4. Razonar, conferenciar (speech).

talk away, to talk on, continuar hablando, hablar siempre; pasar el tiempo hablando, conversando.

talk back, contestar, replicar.

talk into, convencer a fuerza de hablar, persuadir, hacer ejecutar.

talk out of, disuadir; sonsacar.

talk over, discutir, persuadir, convencer. **To talk to the purpose,** hablar al alma.

talk up, pronunciarse, explicarse claramente; (Fam.) discutir con intención de promover; alabar, engrandecer.

talk, s. 1. Plática, conversación de una persona con otra. 2. Habla, la locución o palabras que se hablan. 3. Charla, cháchara, parloteo. 4. Voz común, fama, rumor. 5. El asunto de una conversación. **Small talk,** palique, charla. (Vulg.) Dichitos. **It's just talk,** son sólo rumores. **To have a talk with,** mantener una conversación con alguien, hablar con alguien.

talkative ['tɔːkətɪv] [to-ka-tiv], a. Locuaz, charlante, amigo de charlar.

talkativeness ['tɔːkətɪvnɪs] [to-ka-tiv-nes], s. Localidad, charlatanería, garrulidad, flujo de palabras.

talker ['tɔːkə͡ʳ] [to-ka͡ʳ], s. 1. El que habla o conversa con otro. 2. Hablador, el que habla mucho, parlador, charlador. 3. Fanfarrón, el que echa fanfarronadas.

talkie ['tɔːkɪ] [to-ki], s. Película sonora.

talking machine ['tɔːkɪŋməˌʃiːn] [to-kin-ma-shin], s. Fonógrafo, tocadiscos.

talking picture ['tɔːkɪŋˌpɪktʃə͡ʳ] [to-kin-pik-cha͡ʳ], s. Película sonora, película hablada.

talking-to ['tɔːkɪŋtuː] [to-kin-tu], s. **To give someone a talking-to,** echar la bronca, echar un rapapolvos a alguien.

tall [tɔːl] [tol], a. 1. Alto, de alta talla o estatura. 2. Alto, elevado. 3. (Ant.) Excelente, admirable, renombrado.

tallage ['tɔːlɪdʒ] [to-lich], s. Alcabala; impuesto.

tallow ['tæləʊ] [ta-lou], va. Ensebar, untar con sebo. -s. Sebo. **Raw tallow,** sebo puro o en rama. **Melted tallow,** sebo colado. **Tallow-chandler,** velero, el que hace velas de sebo. **Tallow-chandler's shop,** velería. **Tallow-tree,** (Bot.) árbol del sebo. **Tallow dip,** vela de sebo.

tallowy ['tæləʊɪ] [ta-loui], a. Seboso, grasoso; del color o de la apariencia de sebo.

tally ['tælɪ] [ta-li], s. 1. Tarja, palo partido por el medio para ir marcando lo que se saca o compra fiado o de adelantado, haciendo muescas en él. 2. Cualquier cosa hecha de modo que ajuste con otra.

tally, *va.* 1. Ajustar, acomodar, hacer alguna cosa a medida de otra o de modo que venga bien con ella. 2. Tarjar, llevar la cuenta de alguna cosa señalando las partidas por rayas o muescas en una tarja o caña. **To tally the sheets,** *(Mar.)* Cazar y atracar las escotas. *-vn.* Cuadrar, conformarse o ajustarse una cosa con otra.

tallyho ['tælɪ'həʊ] [ta-li-jou], *inter.* Grito del cazador a los sabuesos. *-s.* Coche de cuatro caballos.

talon ['tælən] [ta-lon], *s.* 1. Garra, el pie del ave de rapiña. 2. Talón de hoja de espada.

talus ['tæləs] [ta-los], *s.* 1. *(Anat.)* Astrágalo, hueso del tobillo; tobillo. 2. *(Arq.)* Pendiente, inclinación, talud. 3. *(Geol.)* Masa pendiente de fragmentos debajo de un peñasco. *(Lat.)*

tamable ['teɪməbl] [tei-ma-bol], *a.* Domable, domesticable, capaz de ser amansado, domado o domesticado

tamarind ['tæmərɪnd] [ta-ma-rind], *s.* Tamarindo, árbol tropical oriundo de la India, y su fruto.

tamarisk ['tæmərɪsk] [ta-ma-risk], *s.* *(Bot.)* Tamarisco, tamariz.

tambour ['tæmbʊər] [tam-bua^r], *s.* 1. Tambor. 2. Tambor, para bordar y la obra hecha a tambor. 3. Tamboril. 4. Cancel de una iglesia; *(Arq.)* tambor, el casco de una cúpula que estriba en los arcos torales.

tambour, *va.* Bordar a tambor.

tambourine [ˌtæmbə'riːn] [tam-ba-rin], *s.* Pandereta con cascabeles o con rodajas metálicas.

tame [teɪm] [teim], *a.* 1. Amansado, domado, domesticado, manso (pet). 2. Dócil, sometido, tratable (gentle, mild). 3. Abatido, humilde, sumiso (obedient). 4. Pálido, falto de animación o efecto, sin color (sad). **A tame narrative,** un relato pálido, sin color.

tame, *va.* 1. Domar, domesticar, amansar, hablando de fieras o animales. 2. Avasallar, abatir; suavizar, domeñar, poner dócil o tratable.

tamely ['teɪmlɪ] [teim-li], *adv.* Humildemente, abatidamente, bajamente.

tameness ['teɪmnɪs] [teim-nes], *s.* 1. Calidad de amansado o domesticado; domesticidad de los animales; mansedumbre. 2. Sumisión, timidez, cobardía, genio o carácter apocado.

tamer ['teɪmər] [tei-ma^r], *s.* 1. Domador, vencedor. 3. El que domestica animales.

tamis ['tæmɪz] [ta-mis], *s.* Tamiz, cedazo hecho de tela.

tamkin ['tæmkɪn] [tam-kin], *s. (Art.)* Tapaboca.

tamp [tæmp] [tamp], *va.* Cebar el barreno de una cantera para volar la roca.

tamper ['tæmpər] [tam-pa^r], *vn.* Procurar alterar oficiosamente; entremeterse, meterse en camisa de once varas; se usa generalmente con *with.*

tampon ['tæmpən] [tam-pon], *s. (Med.)* Tapón.

tan [tæn] [tan], *va.* 1. Curtir, zurrar, adobar o aderezar pieles. 2. Curtir, tostar, quemar, poner marchito o moreno, hablando del sol o del aire.

tan, *s.* 1. Casca, la corteza del roble molida para curtir las pieles. 2. Moreno amarillento que tira a rojo. 3. Tez morena como requemada por el sol y el aire. **Tan-bark,** casca para curtir. **Tan-it o vat,** el tanque o pozo donde se adoban las pieles en las tenerías. **Tan-yard, tenería.**

tandem ['tændəm] [tan-dam], *a.* Que tiene los caballos colocados en fila, uno tras otro. *-s.* 1. Dos o más caballos enganchados y guiados uno tras otro; el vehículo con los caballos así enganchados. 2. Bicicleta o biciclo de doble silla, para dos ciclistas. *-adv.* Uno delante de otro.

tang [tæŋ] [tang], *s.* 1. Resabio, el sabor que deja alguna cosa en la boca. 2. *(Vulg.)* Sainete, sabor, gusto. 3. Sonido, tañido, tono. 4. Cola, espiga, rabera de una herramienta; parte saliente.

tang, *vn.* Retumbar, hacer ruido.

tangent ['tændʒənt] [tan-yent], *a. y s. (Geom.)* Tangente.

tangential ['tændʒən ʃəl] [tan-yen-shal], *a.* De una línea tangente; que se mueve en tangente.

tangerine [ˌtændʒə'riːn] [tan-ya-rin], *a. y s.* 1. Tangerino, tangerina, natural de Tánger o perteneciente a esta ciudad.

2. Naranja tangerina, variedad pequeña y aromática de corteza roja.

tangibility [ˌtændʒə'bɪlɪtɪ] [tan-yi-bi-li-ti], *s.* La calidad que hace a una cosa capaz de ser percibida por el tacto.

tangible ['tændʒəbl] [tan-yi-bol], *a.* Tangible.

tangle ['tæŋgl] [tan-guel], *va.* 1. Enredar, enmarañar, embrollar, embarazar. 3. Confundir. *-vn.* Enmarañarse, enredarse; confundirse.

tangle, *s.* 1. Enredo o enlace desordenado de una cosa con otra; trenza de pelo. 2. Estado de confusión.

tangle, *s.* Cada una de las dos especies de laminaria, alga marina.

tangly ['tæŋglɪ] [tan-gli], *a.* 1. Enredado o desordenado. 2. Abundante en hierbas marinas.

tango ['tæŋgəʊ] [tan-gou], *s.* Tango.

tangy ['tæŋɪ] [tan-gui], *a.* Picante, fuerte.

tank [tæŋk] [tank], *s.* Cisterna de madera o metal, aljibe, arca de aguas; *(Amer.)* tanque, **Tank-car,** carro tanque, vagón de ferrocarril que lleva un tanque de hierro, por lo común de forma cilíndrica; sirve para transportar petróleo, etc. **Tank-engine,** locomotora con tanque de agua encima de la caldera, pero sin ténder. *-vi.* **To tank along,** ir como un rayo, a toda pastilla. **To get tanked up,** emborracharse.

tankage ['tæŋkɪdʒ] [tan-kich], *s.* 1. Acto de poner en tanques. 2. Precio que se paga por guardar algo en tanques. 3. Cabida o capacidad de un tanque o tanques. 4. Residuo de las grasas.

tankard ['tæŋkɑːd] [tan-kar], *s.* Cántaro o jarro grande, a veces con tapa.

tanker ['tæŋkər] [tan-ka^r], *s.* Barco petrolero.

tanner ['tænər] [ta-na^r], *s.* Curtidor, zurrador, el que curte o adoba pieles.

tannery ['tænərɪ] [ta-na-ri], *s.* Tenería o cortiduría.

tannic ['tænɪk] [ta-nik], *a. (Quím.)* Tánico, perteneciente a la casca, o que se saca de ella. **Tannic acid,** ácido tánico o tanino, compuesto astringente (C14H10O9) que forma escamas brillantes cuando se saca de las nueces de agalla. Sirve para curtir y para hacer tinta.

tannin ['tænɪn] [ta-nin], *s.* Tanino, principio curtiente. V. *Tannic acid.*

tanning ['tænɪŋ] [ta-nin], *s.* Curtimiento, zurra, procedimiento para adobar o aderezar las pieles.

tansy ['tænzɪ] [tan-si], *s. (Bit.)* Tanaceto. **Wild tansy,** Argentina.

tantalize ['tæntəlaɪz] [tan-ta-lais], *va.* Atormentar a alguno mostrándole objetos o placeres que no puede alcanzar.

tantalum ['tæntələm] [tan-ta-lom], *s. (Min.)* Tántalo, cuerpo simple metálico.

tantamount ['tæntəməʊnt] [tan-ta-maunt], *a.* Equivalente, que equivale.

tantivy ['tæntɪvɪ] [tan-ti-vi], *adv.* De prisa, a rienda suelta.

tantrum ['tæntrəm] [tan-trom], *s.* Acceso de cólera o petulancia.

tap [tæp] [tap], *va.* 1. Sacar un líquido; decentar un barril; horadar para poner la canilla a un tonel. 2. Extraer el jugo de un árbol por incisión. *-s.* 1. Canilla, espita, tubo o caño que se pone en la cuba para sacar el vino. 2. *(Mec.)* Taladro, herramienta en forma de tornilla para hacer el filete o rosca interior. 3. Licor especial o calidad particular de licor. 4. *(Fam.)* Mostrador de taberna. **On tap,** contenido en un barril, que se saca de un barril, cubo o tonel.

tap, *va. y vn.* 1. Golpear o tocar ligeramente. 2. Remontar (el calzado). 3. Dar golpecitos. *-s.* 1. Palmada suave, golpecito con una cosa pequeña. 2. Remiendo echado al talón de un zapato. 3. *pl.* Toque militar de corneta o tambor para apagar las luces. **To tap at the door,** llamar dando golpecitos a la puerta. **To tap for some information,** intentar obtener información, tratar de sacar información a alguien. **To tap out,** enviar (message).

tap dance ['tæpdɑːns] [tap-dans], *s.* Baile zapateado de los E. U.

tape [teɪp] [teip], *s.* Cinta (cassette), cintilla, tejido de hilo o algodón; tira de metal delgado; *(Amér.)* melindre. **Tape line,**

tape measure, cinta para medir. **Tape recorder,** grabadora. **Linen tape,** cinta de hiladillo. **They have got it all taped,** lo tienen todo organizado, en perfecto funcionamiento. **Red tape,** (a) balduque, cinta estrecha para atar legajos. (b) expediente, formalismo, método rutinario (en el despacho de los asuntos públicos).

tape deck ['teɪpdek] [teip-dek], *f.* Unidad de cinta (cassette).

taper ['teɪpəʳ] [tei-paʳ], *s.* 1. Bujía, cerilla, vela pequeña; cirio (de iglesia); hacha, blandón. 2. Disminución gradual de tamaño en un objeto de forma prolongada.

taper, *vn.* Ahusarse. *-va.* Ahusar, adelgazar.

tape recorder ['teɪprɪˌkɔːdəʳ] [teip-ri-kor-daʳ], *s.* Magnetófono, grabadora de cinta.

tape-recording ['teɪprɪˌkɔːdɪŋ] [teip-ri-kor-din], *a.* Magnetofónico.

taproom ['teɪprʊm] [teip-rum], *s.* Cantina, taberna.

tapestry ['tæpɪstrɪ] [ta-pis-tri], *va.* Entapizar, adornar con colgaduras o tapices. *-s.* Tapiz; tapicería, colgadura.

tapeworm ['teɪpwɜːm] [teip-uem], *s.* Tenia, lombriz solitaria.

tapioca [ˌtæpɪˈəʊkə] [ta-pio-ka], *s.* Tapioca, fécula de la yuca brava o mandioca.

tapir ['teɪpəʳ] [tei-paʳ], *s.* Tapir, mamífero paquidermo de los países intertropicales.

taproot ['tæprʊt] [tap-rut], *s.* Tallo de la raíz; raíz principal.

taps ['tæpz] [taps], *s. pl. (Mil.)* Toque de queda.

taps, *s. pl. (Mil.)* Toque de queda

tapster ['tæpstəʳ] [taps-taʳ], *s.* Mozo de cervecería.

tar [tɑːʳ] [taʳ], *s.* 1. Alquitrán, brea. 2. En estilo vulgar, significa marinero u hombre de mar, como apodo. (Abrev. de TARPAULIN, 3ª acep.) **Coal-tar,** alquitrán de hulla. **Mineral tar,** betún, alquitrán mineral. **Tar-box,** caja que contiene ungüento de brea para los carneros. **Tar-water,** agua de alquitrán.

tar, *va.* 1. Alquitranar, embrear. 2. Brear, dar brega a alguno, molestarle o chasquearle. **To tar and feather,** embrear y emplumar.

tarantula [təˈræntjʊlə] [ta-ran-tiu-la], *s.* Tarántula, una espcie de araña de gran tamaño.

tardily ['tɑːdɪlɪ] [tar-di-li], *adv.* 1. Lentamente (slowly). 2. Tardíamente; pasado el tiempo oportuno; fuera de tiempo (out of time).

tardiness ['tɑːdɪnɪs] [tar-di-nes], *s.* Lentitud, tardanza.

tardy ['tɑːdɪ] [tar-di], *a.* 1. Tardío, que sucede después del tiempo oportuno. 2. Tardo, lento; negligente, que obra de mala gana.

tare [tɛəʳ] [teaʳ], *s.* 1. *(Bot.)* Cizaña. 2. *(Bot.)* Lenteja; algarroba común, o una de otras varias especies de plantas. 3. *(Com.)* Tara, la parte del peso que se rebaja en los géneros o mercancías por razón de la caja, saca u otro envase en que vienen incluidos: merma.

tare, *va.* Destarar, restar la tara al pesar una cosa.

target ['tɑːgɪt] [tar-guit], *s.* 1. Blanco a que se tira. 2. Tarja, especie de escudo o rodela. 3. *(Fig.)* Objeto de ataque, centro de observación. **Target-practise,** tiro al blanco.

tariff ['tærɪf] [ta-rif], *s.* Tarifa, arancel, tabla o catálogo de los derechos que deben pagar los géneros.

tarn [tɑːn] [tarn], *s. (Ingl. y Esco.)* Lago pequeño entre las montañas.

tarnish ['tɑːnɪʃ] [tar-nish], *va.* 1. Deslustrar, empañar, deslucir, quitar el lustre. 2. Mancillar, deshonrar; disminuir la pureza de. *-vn.* Deslustrarse, deslucirse, perder el lustre; enmohecerse, tomarse de orín (metals). *-s.* 1. Falta de lustre, deslustre; de aquí, mancha. 2. La película delgada y de color que se forma en la superficie del mineral expuesta al aire.

tarot ['tærəʊ] [ta-rou], *s.* Tarot.

tarpaulin [tɑːˈpɔːlɪn] [tar-po-lin], *s.* 1. El cáñamo embreado, alquitranado o lienzo de alquitrán; alquitranado o lienzo de alquitrán; encerado. **Tarpawlingnails,** *(Mar.)* Estoperoles. 2. Sombrero de cuero encerado. 3. *(Fam.)* Marinero, en son de burla.

tarpon ['tɑːpɒn] [tar-pon], *s.* Sábalo (pez).

tarragon ['tærəgən] [ta-ra-gon], *s. (Bot.)* Estragón.

tarrier ['tærɪəʳ] [ta-riaʳ], *s.* 1. Tardador, el que tarda o se tarda. 2. *(Dial.)* V. TERRIER.

tarring ['tɑːrɪŋ] [ta-rin], *a.* Asfaltado.

tarry ['tɑːrɪ] [ta-ri], *vn.* 1. Tardar, detenerse, pararse, quedarse atrás; aplazar la partida o la llegada. 2. Morar, habitar o estar de asiento en algún lugar.

tarry, *s.* Cubierto de brea o de alquitrán; semejante al alquitrán o a la brea.

tarsus ['tɑːsəs] [tar-sos], *s.* 1. *(Anat.)* Tarso, empeine del pie. 2. Lámina de tejido conexivo en el párpado. 3. Tarso, la tercera articulación del pie de las aves. 4. *(Zool.)* Segmento terminal de las patas de los artrópodos.

tart [tɑːt] [tart], *a.* 1. Acedo, agridulce, que tiene punta de agrio. 2. Acre, desapacible, picante, mordaz.

tart, *s.* Tarta, pastelillo de fruta. *-vt.* **To tart up,** remodelar, renovar.

tartan ['tɑːtən] [tar-tan], *s.* 1. Tartán, tela de lana con cuadros o listas cruzadas de diferentes colores. 2. El cuadro o dibujo de dicha tela. 3. Vestido de tartán. 4. *(Mar.)* Tartana, especie de embarcación con un solo mástil y una vela latina.

tartar ['tɑːtəʳ] [tar-taʳ], *s.* 1. Tártaro, sal que se forma dentro de las cubas de vino. V. ARGOL. 2. Sarro, incrustación que se forma sobre los dientes, principalmente el fosfato de cal. **Cream of tartar,** crémor tártaro. **Tartar emetic,** tártaro emético.

Tartar, *s.* Tártaro, habitante de la Tartaria. **To catch a Tartar,** hallar uno la horma de su zapato.

tartaric [tɑːˈtærɪk] [tar-ta-rik], *a.* Tártrico, perteneciente al tártaro, o que se deriva de él; ácido tártrico.

tartarize ['tɑːtəraɪz] [tar-ta-rais], *va.* Tartarizar, impregnar o tratar con tártaro.

tartarous ['tɑːtərəs] [tar-ta-ros], *a.* Tartáreo, hecho de tártaro, compuesto de tártaro o que tiene las propiedades de tártaro.

tartly ['tɑːtlɪ] [tar-tli], *adv.* Agriamente, austeramente.

tartness ['tɑːtnɪs] [tart-nes], *s.* 1. Agrura, acedía, sabor ácido o agrio. 2. Acrimonia, aspereza o desabrimiento en el genio o en las expresiones.

tartrate ['tɑːtreɪt] [tar-treit], *s.* Tartrato, sal del ácido tártrico.

task [tɑːsk] [task], *s.* 1. Tarea, la obra o trabajo que se debe concluir en tiempo determinado (work); deber, tarea, lección que hay que aprender. 2. Trabajo molesto, labor, faena. 2. Trabajo molesto, labor, faena. **To take to task,** reprender, regañar, censurar.

tasker ['tɑːskəʳ] [tas-kaʳ], *s.* El que da, pone o señala tareas.

tassel ['tæsəl] [ta-sel], *s.* 1. Borla o borlita de seda, oro o plata en figura de bellota, con muchos hilos. 2. Borla, especie de botón de seda, oro o plata del que salen muchos hilos, en figura de campanillas. 3. Inflorescencia de ciertas flores, v. g. las del maíz o del sauce.

tasselled ['tæsəld] [ta-seld], *a.* Adornado con borlas o campanillas.

taste [teɪst] [teist], *va. y vn.* 1. Gustar, sentir, percibir y distinguir con el paladar el gusto o sabor de las cosas. 2. Gustar, probar, catar, gustar de tomar algo. 3. Gustar, experimentar, ensayar. 4. Gustar, querer alguna cosa, tener complacencia en ella; agradar, parecer bien. 5. Saber o tener un sabor que puede percibir el sentido del gusto. **To taste of,** saber a, tener sabor a.

taste, *s.* 1. Gusto, sensación de los sabores (flavor); sabor, gustadura; paladeo, saboreo. 2. Gusto, sentido por el cual se distinguen los sabores. 3. Cata, sorbo, trago, la porción pequeña de alguna cosa que se da para catar o probarla; *(Fig.)* ligera cantidad, un poco, muy poco; muestra, ejemplar; ensayo, prueba, experimento. 4. Gusto, discernimiento; la facultad estética; facultad de sentir y discernir lo bello o la excelencia artística. 5. Inclinación y aptitud especiales para una ocupación (liking). 6. Manera con que se hace una obra o labor, en lo referente al buen gusto, a la gracia y elegancia de la misma. **A man of taste,** hombre de gusto. **To have a taste for,** gustarle a uno una cosa, o tener gusto para hacerla. **Sweet to the taste,** de sabor dulce. **People of taste,** gente de buen gusto.

tastebud ['teɪstbʌd] [teist-bad], *s.* Papila del gusto.

tasted ['teɪstɪd] [teis-tid], *a.* Que tiene sabor o gusto particular.

tasteful ['teɪstfʊl] [teist-ful], *a.* Conforme al buen gusto, que tiene buen gusto, hecho con gusto. 2. *(Ant.)* Sabroso.

tastefully ['teɪstfəlɪ] [teist-fu-li], *adv.* Según el buen gusto, con gusto.

tastefulness ['teɪstfəlnɪs] [teist-ful-nes], *s.* Gusto, discernimiento, gracia, elegancia.

tasteless ['teɪstlɪs] [teist-les], *a.* 1. Insípido, desabrido, soso o que no tiene sabor ni sazón. 2. Falto o privado del sentido del gusto. 3. Insípido, que no tiene espíritu o que no tiene gracia ni sal.

tastelessly ['teɪstlɪslɪ] [teist-les-li], *adv.* Insípidamente, sin gusto o falta de viveza o gracia.

tastelessness ['teɪstlɪsnɪs] [teist-les-nes], *s.* Insipidez, falta de gusto o falta de viveza o gracia.

taster ['teɪstəʳ] [teis-taʳ], *s.* 1. Catador, el que cata o prueba la vianda o bebida. 2. Copita para catar o probar licores.

tasty ['teɪstɪ] [teis-ti], *a.* 1. Sabroso. 2. *(Fam.)* Hecho o expresado con gusto, con gracia o con sal; forma poco castiza. **Tasty food,** alimentos sabrosos.

tat [tæt] [tat], *va.* y *vn.* Hacer encaje de hilo a mano con lanzadera y por medio de lazos y nudos.

tatter ['tætəʳ] [ta-taʳ], *va.* Hacer andrajos, jirones o harapos; se usa casi exclusivamente en el participio pasado. **Tattered,** harapiento.

tatter ['tætəʳ] [ta-taʳ], *s.* Andrajo, pingajo, arrapiezo, harapo. **To be all in tatters,** estar hecho un andrajo o estar hecho jirones.

tatting ['tætɪŋ] [ta-tin], *s.* Encaje o guarnición de hilo, hecho a mano con lanzadera; y el procedimiento empleado para hacerlo. V. TAT.

tattle ['tætl] [ta-tel], *va.* Charlar, parlar, chacharear. V. BLAB. *-vn.* Chismear, traer y llevar chismes.

tattle, *s.* Charla, cháchara, charlatanería; chisme; parlería, como la de los niños.

tattler ['tætləʳ] [ta-tlaʳ], *s.* 1. Charlador, parlador, hablador, chacharero. 2. *(Orn.)* Agachadiza del género Totamus, de pico recio y agudo.

tattoo [tə'tuː] [ta-tuu], *s.* 1. *(Mil.)* Retreta, el toque del tambor que avisa a los soldados que se retiren al cuartel. 2. Figura dibujada en el cutis con tinta indeleble, tatuaje.

tattoo, *va.* Pintar o pintarse el cutis con figuras, o rayarlo con colores.

tattooing [tə'tuːɪŋ] [ta-tuin], *s.* La acción y efecto de pintarse figuras en el cutis; la figura así dibujada.

tattooist [tə'tuːɪst] [ta-tuist], *s.* Tatuador.

taught [tɔːt] [tot], *pret.* y *pp.* del verbo TEACH. *-a. (Des.)* V. TAUT.

taunt [tɔːnt] [tont], *va.* Mofar, hacer burla o zumba de alguna persona, dar chanza; echar en cara, vituperar.

taunt, *s.* Mofa, burla, escarnio, chanza, zumba.

taunter ['tɔːntəʳ] [ton-taʳ], *s.* Mofador, burlón, zumbón.

tauntingly ['tɔːntɪŋlɪ] [ton-tin-ku], *adv.* Con mofa, con vituperio; en tono de sarcasmo; en tono insultante.

taupe [tɔːp] [top], *s.* Gris pardo.

taurine ['tɔːriːn] [to-rin], *a.* 1. Taurino, de toro, semejante o relativo al toro. 2. *(Astr.)* Relativo al signo Tauro del zodíaco.

taut [tɔːt] [tot], *a.* 1. *(Mar.)* Tieso, tendido. 2. Listo, preparado, en forma debida.

tautly ['tɔːtlɪ] [tot-li], *adv.* Con tersura; con voz tensa.

tautology [tɔː'tɒlədʒɪ] [to-to-lo-yi], *s.* Tautología, repetición de una misma idea en otros términos.

tavern ['tævən] [ta-varn], *s.* Taberna; fonda, posada, establecimiento público donde por dinero se hospeda la gente; figón. **Tavern-haunter,** el que frecuenta figones o tabernas. **Tavern-keeper,** tabernero; posadero.

taw [tɔː] [to], *va.* Curtir pieles blancas con alumbre, a diferencia de curtir corambres con zumaque.

taw, *s.* Bolita de mármol con que juegan los niños; línea desde la cual los jugadores lanzan las bolas.

tawdrily ['tɔːdrɪlɪ] [to-dri-li], *adv.* De una manera chillona; vistosamente y sin elegancia.

tawdriness ['tɔːdrɪnɪs] [to-dri-nes], *s.* Oropel, apariencia, brillo falso de oropel; calidad de chillón (colors); algo cursi.

tawdry ['tɔːdrɪ] [to-dri], *a.* Vistoso sin elegancia; adornado con exceso; de colores chillones; se dice sólo de lo que relumbra mucho y vale poco.

tawny ['tɔːnɪ] [to-ni], *a.* Curtido, moreno; leonado, que tira a pardo y amarillo.

tax [tæks] [taks], *s.* 1. Impuesto, tributo, contribución, gabela que se paga al Estado; estos nombres se usan comúnmente en plural. 2. Gabela, carga, servidumbre pesada. **Tax-collector, tax-gatherer,** recaudador de contribuciones. **Tax-payer,** contribuyente. **Tax-list,** célula, lista de bienes raíces sobre los cuales se han pagado las contribuciones.

tax, *va.* 1. Imponer tributos o contribuciones. 2. *(For.)* Tasar costas, tasar las costas. 3. Cargar, abrumar; exigir demasiado. 4. *(Biblia)* Registrar para la imposición de tributos. 5. *(Fam.)* Pedir como precio. 6. Acusar, hacer cargos; se usa con *of* o *with.* **To tax with insincerity,** tachar, acusar a alguien de doblez.

taxable ['tæksəbl] [tak-sa-bol], *a.* 1. Lo que se puede cargar o está sujeto a impuestos. 2. Pechero.

taxation [tæk'seɪʃən] [tak-sei-shon], *s.* 1. La imposición o repartimiento de derechos, contribuciones o impuestos. 2. *(Des.)* Imputación, la atribución de alguna culpa, falta o delito.

taxer ['tæksəʳ] [tak-saʳ], *s.* 1. El que impone tributos. 2. Acusador, el que acusa.

tax exempt ['tæksɪg'zempt] [taks-ik-sempt], *a.* Exento de impuestos.

taxi ['tæksɪ] [tak-si], *va.* 1. Ir en un taxi. 2. *(Aer.)* Deslizarse un avión sobre la superficie al despegar o al aterrizar.

taxicab ['tæksɪkæb] [tak-si-kab], *s.* Taxi, automóvil de plaza.

taxidermic ['tæksɪdɜːmɪk] [tak-si-der-mik], *a.* Taxidérmico, relativo a la taxidermia.

taxidermist ['tæksɪdɜːmɪst] [tak-si-der-mist], *s.* Taxidermista, el que practica la taxidermia.

taxidermy ['tæksɪdɜːmɪ] [tak-si-der-mi], *s.* Taxidermia, arte de disecar los animales muertos para conservarlos con apariencia de vivos.

taxonomy [tæk'sɒnəmɪ] [tak-so-no-mi], *s.* Taxonomía, la ciencia de clasificar, como parte de la biología.

tea [tiː] [tii], *s.* 1. Té: se da este nombre a un arbusto, a las hojas de este arbusto y a la infusión que se hace con ellas. 2. Cualquier infusión o decocción que sirve como bebida o medicamento. 3. Refección ligera de la tarde; también, reunión en la cual se sirve té. **Tea-board,** batea, bandeja o azafate para servir el té. **Tea-canister,** caja para té. **Tea-pot,** tetera, vasija en que se hierve y se sirve el té. **Tea-kettle,** marmita en que se tiene hirviendo el agua para hacer el té. **Not for all the tea in China,** ni por todo el oro del mundo.

tea bag ['tiːbæg] [ti-bag], *s.* Bolsita para hacer té.

teacart ['tiːkɑːt] [ti-kart], *s.* Mesita de ruedas para servir el té.

teach [tiːtʃ] [tich], *va.* 1. Enseñar, dar lecciones. 2. Enseñar, doctrinar, dar documentos. 3. Instruir, informar, hacer saber. *-vn.* Tener por oficio la enseñanza pública o particular.

teachability [ˌtiːtʃə'bɪlɪtɪ] [ti-cha-bi-li-ti], *f.* Educabilidad.

teachable ['tiːtʃəbl] [ti-cha-bol], *a.* Dócil; susceptible de enseñanza.

teacher ['tiːtʃəʳ] [ti-chaʳ], *s.* 1. Maestro, preceptor, enseñador. 2. Predicador. **Assistant teacher,** pasante, segundo maestro, profesor auxiliar.

teaching ['tiːtʃɪŋ] [ti-chin], *s.* 1. Enseñanza, acción, arte u ocupación de enseñar. 2. Instrucción, doctrina, la cosa enseñada.

teacup ['tiːkʌp] [ti-kap], *s.* Taza para té; cabida de dicha taza. **Teacupful,** cabida de una taza para té; unos 125 gramos.

teak [tiːk] [tik], *s.* Teca.

teal [tiːl] [til], *s. (Orn.)* Cerceta, zarceta, especie de ánade silvestre.

team [tiːm] [tim], *s.* 1. Equipo, bando. 2. Yunta (oxen, etc.). **Team championship,** campeonato por equipos. **Team mate,** compañero de equipo. **Team spirit,** compañerismo.

team, *va.* 1. Conducir con un tronco o una yunta. 2. Uncir, enganchar, poner el tiro a un vehículo. -*vn.* Guiar un tiro de caballos.

teamster ['tiːmstər] [tim-sta^r], *s.* Conductor de tiro de caballos o bueyes.

teamwork ['tiːmwɜːk] [tim-uek], *s.* Trabajo de cooperación, espíritu de solidaridad de un equipo.

teapoy ['tiːpɔɪ] [ti-poi], *s.* Mesita de adorno para servicio de té.

tear [tɛər] [tea^r], *s.* 1. Lágrima de los ojos; lloro, llanto. 2. Gota, porción parecida a una gota.

tear, *va.* (*pret.* TORE, *ant.* TARE, *pp.* TORN). 1. Desgarrar, romper, despedazar, rasgar, hacer pedazos, lacerar (rip up). 2. Rasguñar, arañar. 3. Arrancar, separar una persona o cosa de otra con violencia. 4. Atormentar (torment). *vn.* 1. Separarse, dividirse algo cuando se tira de ello (divide). 2. Menearse, moverse o correr con velocidad, precipitadamente (run). **To tear to tatters,** hacer jirones. **To tear one's hair,** arrancarse los cabellos. **To tear asunder,** separar con violencia. **To tear away,** arrancar, arrebatar; desmembrar, separar. **To tear oneself away,** (*Fam.*) arrancarse de un lugar, partir uno contra su voluntad. **To tear down,** despedazar, destruir, echar por tierra. **To tear off,** arrancar o separar con violencia; arrojarse, ir precipitadamente. **To tear up,** arrancar las plantas. **To tear along,** correr a rienda suelta. **To tear into a room,** entrar a una habitación de manera precipitada. **To tear past,** pasar como un rayo. **This dress tears easily,** este vestido se rasga fácilmente.

tearful ['tɪəfʊl] [tia-ful], *a.* Lloroso, lagrimoso, lleno de lágrimas.

tear gas ['tɪəgæs] [tia-gas], *s.* Gas lacrimógeno.

tea room ['tiːruːm] [ti-rum], *s.* Salón o sala de té.

tease [tiːz] [tis], *va.* 1. Jorobar, molestar, atormentar, importunar, hacer rabiar (annoy). 2. Cardar, rastrillar, lana o lino. 3. Sacar el pelo al paño con la capota del cardón. 4. Despedazar, separar por medio de instrumentos, como los tejidos al examinarlos (separate). -*s.* (a) lo que atormenta. (b) acción o efecto de molestar o atormentar.

teasel ['tiːzl] [ti-sel], *s. V.* TEAZEL.

teaser ['tiːzər] [ti-sa^r], *s.* La persona o cosa importuna, molesta o enfados.

teaspoon ['tiːspuːn] [ti-spun], *s.* Cucharita. **Teaspoonful,** cucharadita.

teat [tiːt] [tit], *s.* 1. Pezón del pecho, tetilla. 2. Ubre, la teta del animal.

teazel ['tiːzl] [ti-sel], *s.* 1. Cardencia, cualquier planta de las dipsáceas; también, capota, la cabeza de la cardencha para levantar pelo en el paño. 2. Aparato mecánico que usan los pelaires.

technical ['teknɪkəl] [tek-ni-kal], *a.* 1. Técnico. 2. Legalista. **Technical term,** tecnicismo, voz técnica.

technicality [ˌteknɪ'kælɪtɪ] [tek-ni-ka-li-ti], *s.* 1. Tecnicidad. 2. Tecnicismo. 3. Argucia.

technically ['teknɪkəlɪ] [tek-ni-ka-li], *adv.* Técnicamente.

technician [tek'nɪʃən] [tek-ni-shan], *s.* Técnico.

technicolor ['teknɪˌkʌlər] [tek-ni-ka-la^r], *s.* Tecnicolor. Marca registrada.

technics ['teknɪks] [tek-niks], *s.* 1. Conjunto de principios de las artes en general. 2. Tecnisimo, conjunto de reglas, términos y métodos técnicos.

technique [tek'niːk] [tek-nik], *s.* Técnica, manera de ejecutar algo artísticamente, y en particular de tocar un instrumento de música según las relgas del arte.

technocracy [tek'nɒkrəsɪ] [tek-no-kra-si], *s.* Tecnocracia.

technocrat ['teknəʊkræt] [tek-nou-krat], *s.* Tecnócrata.

technological [ˌteknə'lɒdʒɪkəl] [tek-no-lo-yi-kal], *a.* Tecnológico, pertencience o relativo a la tecnología.

technology [tek'nɒlədʒɪ] [tek-no-lo-yi], *s.* 1. Tecnología, conjunto de los conocimientos propios de los oficios mecánicos y de las artes industriales. 2. Aplicación de la ciencia a las artes.

ted [ted] [ted], *va.* Extender o esparcir el heno o hierba recién segada para que se seque.

tedder ['tedər] [te-da^r], *s.* 1. Traba o trabas; impedimiento, restricción. 2. El o lo que esparce el heno o la hierba para que se seque.

tedious ['tiːdɪəs] [ti-dios], *a.* Tedioso, fastidioso, enfadoso, molesto, pesado.

tediously ['tiːdɪəslɪ] [ti-dios-li], *adv.* Fastidiosamente.

tediousness ['tiːdɪəsnɪs] [ti-dios-nes], *s.* 1. Tedio, fastidio, aburrimiento. 2. Pesadez.

teem [tiːm] [tiim], *va.* (*Ant.*) Parir, dar a luz la hembra; producir o causar una cosa a otra. -*vn.* 1. Estar llena alguna cosa, estar rebosando de, abundar en; hervir; hervir en o de. **A lake which teems with fishes,** un lago lleno de peces, abundante en peces. 2. Parir, salir a luz o al público una cosa que no se sabía. 3. Verter el acero derretido.

teemer ['tiːmər] [ti-ma^r], *s.* La hembra que pare.

teeming ['tiːmɪŋ] [tii-min], *a. part.* 1. Prolífico, fecundo. 2. Lleno; que rebosa; producido en gran cantidad.

teen-age ['tiːneɪdʒ] [tin-eich], *a.* Adolescente, de trece a diez y nueve años.

teen-ager ['tiːnˌeɪdʒər] [tin-ei-cha^r], *s.* Adolescente, joven de trece a diez y nueve años.

teens ['tiːnz] [tins], *s. pl.* Los números cuyos nombres terminan en -*teen;* en especial de edad de trece a diez y nueve años. **She is not yet out of her teems,** aun no llega a los veinte.

teeter ['tiːtər] [tin-ta^r], *vn.* Balancearse, columpiarse. -*s.* Movimiento oscilante; vaivén.

teeth [tiːθ] [tiz], *s. pl.* de TOOTH. **Wisdom-teeth,** muelas del juicio.

teeth, teethe ['tiːð] [tiz], *vn.* Endentecer, echar los dientes.

teething ['tiːðɪŋ] [ti-zin], *s.* Dentición, formación y salida de los dientes; época o tiempo de la dentición.

teetotal ['tiːˈtəʊtl] [ti-tou-tal], *a.* 1. Entero, completo total. 2. Relativo a la abstinencia completa de bebidas alcohólicas.

teetotaler ['tiːˈtəʊtlər] [ti-tou-ta-la^r], *s.* El que se abstiene absolutamente del uso de bebidas alcohólicas.

teetotalism ['tiːˈtəʊtəlɪzəm] [ti-tou-ta-li-sem], *s.* Abstinencia completa de bebidas alcohólicas.

tegument ['tegjəmənt] [te-guiu-ment], *s.* Tegumento, cubierta exterior.

te-hee ['tiːˈhiː] [ti-jii], *vn.* Reír entre dientes. -*s.* Risa ahogada.

telecommunication ['telɪkəˌmjuːnɪˈkeɪʃən] [te-li-ko-miu-ni-kei-shon], *s.* Telecomunicación.

telecommute ['telɪkəmˌjuːt] [te-li-ko-miut], *vi.* Trabajar a distancia.

telecommuter ['telɪkəmˌjuːtər] [te-li-ko-miu-ta^r], *s.* Trabajador a distancia.

telecopy ['telɪˌkɒpɪ] [te-li-ko-pi], *s.* Telecopia.

telefax ['telɪfæks] [te-li-faks], *m.* Telefax.

telefilm ['telɪfɪlm] [te-le-film], *m.* Telefilm

telegram ['telɪgræm] [te-li-gram], *s.* Telegrama, despacho telegráfico, mensaje enviado por el telégrafo.

telegraph ['telɪgrɑːf] [te-li-graf], *s.* Telégrafo, aparato para transmitir noticias con brevedad y a largas distancias.

telegraph, *va.* y *vn.* Telegrafiar, enviar por el telégrafo; dictar despachos o entregarlos para su transmisión.

telegraphic [ˌtelɪˈgræfɪk] [te-li-gra-fik], *a.* Telegráfico, perteneciente o relativo al telégrafo.

telegraphist [tɪˈlegrəfɪst] [ti-le-gra-fist], *s.* Telegrafista, empleado de una oficina telegráfica o persona versada en telegrafía.

telegraphy [tɪˈlegrəfɪ] [ti-le-gra-fi], *s.* Telegrafía, el arte de construir y manejar los telégrafos.

telemetric [ˌtelɪˈmetrɪk] [te-li-me-trik], *a.* Telemétrico.

telemetry [tɪˈlemɪtrɪ] [ti-le-mi-tri], *s.* Telemetría.

teleological [ˌtelɪəˈlɒdʒɪkl] [te-lio-lo-yi-kal], *a.* Teleológico, perteneciente a la teleología.

teleology [ˌtelɪˈɒlədʒɪ] [te-lio-lo-yi], *s.* Teleología, doctrina de las causas finales.

telepathic [ˌtelɪˈpæθɪk] [te-li-pa-zik], *a.* Telepático.

telepathy [tɪˈlepəθɪ] [ti-le-pa-zi], *s.* Telepatía, comunicación del pensamiento de una persona o otra por medios no generalmente reconocidos.

telephone [ˈtelɪfəʊn] [te-li-foun], *s.* Teléfono. -*va.* y *vn.* Telefonear. **Telephone book,** guía telefónica. **Telephone booth,** cabina telefónica. **Telephone office,** central telefónica. **Telephone operator,** telefonista.

telephonic [ˌtelɪˈfɒnɪk] [te-li-fo-nik], *a.* Telefónico.

telephony [tɪˈlefənɪ] [ti-le-fo-ni], *s.* Telefonía.

telephoto [ˈtelɪˈfəʊtəʊ] [te-li-fou-tou], *s.* *(Trademark)* Telefoto. -*a.* Telefotografico. **Telephoto lens,** teleobjetivo.

telephotography [ˌtelɪfəˈtɒgrəfɪ] [te-li-fo-to-gra-fi], *s.* Telefotografía.

teleplay [ˈtelɪpleɪ] [te-li-plei], *s.* Teleteatro.

teleprompter [ˈtelɪˌprɒmptər] [te-li-promp-tar], *s.* *(Trademark)* Apuntador electrónico.

telescope [ˈtelɪskəʊp] [te-lis-koup], *s.* Telescopio.

telescope, *va.* y *vn.* Impeler o moverse dos cosas en dirección contraria y chocar de modo que una encaje en la otra, como las secciones de un telescopio o anteojo de larga vista.

telescopic [ˌtelɪsˈkɒpɪk] [te-lis-ko-pik], *a.* 1. Telescópico, perteneciente al telescopio; hecho con auxilio del telescopio. 2. Telescópico, que no se puede ver sino con el telescopio. 3. Que ve de lejos. 4. *(Mec.)* Con secciones que encajan una dentro de otra.

teleshopping [ˈtelɪˌʃɒpɪŋ] [te-li-sho-pin], *s.* *pl.* *(E. U.)* Compras por teléfono, telecompra.

teletype [ˈtelɪˌtaɪp] [te-li-taip], *s.* Teletipo.

televiewer [ˈtelɪˌvjuːər] [te-li-viua'], *s.* Televidente, telespectador.

televise [ˈtelɪvaɪz] [te-li-vais], *va.* Televisar.

television [ˈtelɪˌvɪʒən] [te-li-vi-shon], *s.* Televisión. **Television camera,** tomavista. **Television set,** televisor, telerreceptor. **Television studio,** telestudio.

tell [tel] [tel], *va.* y *vn.* (*pret.* y *pp.* TOLD). 1. Decir, principalmente cuando significa contar, mandar o adivinar (say). **Before I tell my story,** antes que yo diga o cuente mi historia. **Nobody can tell what will happen tomorrow,** nadie puede decir o adivinar lo que sucederá mañana. **He told me to call again,** me dijo o me mandó que volviera o que volviese. 2. Decir, informar, hacer saber. 3. Descubrir, revelar o decir algún secreto. **It will tell in his favor or against him,** eso irá o será a su favor en su contra. 4. Dar una orden o mandato a otro; disponer, ordenar. 5. Contar, numerar. 6. *vn.* Producir efecto. **He was told to do it,** se le mandó hacerlo. **Every blow told,** cada golpe produjo efecto. **Tell me another!,** ¡vaya! **To tell a lie,** mentir. **Tell that to the marines!,** ¡cuéntaselo a otro! **I tell you that!,** ¡se me ocurre una idea!

teller [ˈtelər] [te-la'], *s.* 1. Relator de noticias o cuentos. 2. Computista. *Teller,* en la tesorería pública, o en los bancos, empleado, bajo las denominaciones de *Receiving teller,* recibidor. **Paying teller,** pagador. **Entering teller,** contador. 3. Escrutador, el que recibe y cuenta los votos.

telling [ˈtelɪŋ] [te-lin], *pa.* Que hace o produce efecto. **A telling speech,** un discurso eficaz.

telltale [ˈteltel] [tel-teil], *s.* 1. Soplón, chismoso, chismeador, correvedile. 2. Indicador, aparato, generalmente automático, que da informes o noticias; axiómetro, instrumento que indica los movimientos del timón.

telluric [ˈteluərɪk] [te-liu-rik], *a.* Telúrico, de o perteneciente a la tierra o al telurio.

tellurium [teˈluərɪəm] [te-liu-riom], *s.* *(Min.)* Telurio, un elemento no metálico y raro, de color entre plata y estaño.

temerarious [ˌteməˈrærɪəs] [te-me-ra-rios], *a.* Temerario, imprudente.

temerity [tɪˈmerɪtɪ] [ti-me-ri-ti], *s.* Temeridad, arrojo u osadía imprudente.

temper [ˈtempər] [tem-pa'], *va.* 1. Templar, moderar, entibiar o suavizar la fuerza de alguna cosa; atemperar. 2. Mezclar varios ingredientes entre sí para componer o formar un compuesto. 3. Atemperar, acomodar; temperar, ablandar. 4.

Templar, dar a los metales aquel punto de dureza que requieren para su perfección.

temper, *s.* 1. Condición, carácter, genio, disposición del ánimo (character). 2. Temple, la calidad o el estado del genio y natural apacible o áspero; disposición, carácter. 3. Irritación, cólera, ira (anger, rage). 4. Moderación, calma, sangre fría (cold blood). 5. Temple, el punto de dureza que se da a los metales. 6. Grado de densidad debida a una mezcla, v. g. en la argamasa. 7. Cal de defecación (for sugar). 8. *(Ant.)* Temperamento, la complexión, constitución o disposición del cuerpo.

tempera [ˈtempərə] [tem-pe-ra], *s.* Témpera, pintura al temple.

temperament [ˈtempərəmənt] [tem-pe-ra-ment], *s.* 1. Temperamento (character), la constitución o complexión propia de cada individuo. 2. *(Mús.)* Sistema de templar los instrumentos que practica una ligera alteración en los espacios muy breves, para evitar la disonancia o confusión de los sonidos. 3. Disposición mental. 4. Mal genio (moodiness).

temperamental [ˌtempərəˈmentl] [tem-pe-ra-men-tal], *a.* 1. Propio y peculiar del temperamento físico o del temple moral de cada uno. 2. Innato (innate).

temperance [ˈtempərəns] [tem-pe-rans], *s.* 1. Templanza, temperancia, moderación, sobriedad. 2. Paciencia, calma. 3. En especial el principio y la práctica de la abstinencia total de bebidas alcohólicas (abstinence from alcohol).

temperate [ˈtempərɪt] [tem-pe-rit], *a.* 1. Templado, moderado, contenido, sobrio. 2. Abstemio, que no bebe vino ni licores alcohólicos. 3. Templado, ni frío ni caliente.

temperately [ˈtempərɪtlɪ] [tem-pe-rit-li], *adv.* Moderadamente, templadamente.

temperateness [ˈtempərɪtnɪs] [tem-pe-rit-nes], *s.* Templanza, moderación; serenidad de ánimo.

temperature [ˈtemprɪtʃər] [tem-pri-cha'], *s.* 1. *(Fís.)* Temperatura. 2. *(Med.)* Temperatura, fiebre.

tempered [ˈtempəd] [tem-pard], *a.* 1. Templado, acondicionado. 2. Dispuesto, inclinado. **Ill-tempered,** áspero, agrio de genio, mal condicionado. *(Fam.)* De la cáscara amarga. **Even-tempered,** de humor igual. **Good-tempered,** de buen temple o carácter.

tempest [ˈtempɪst] [tem-pist], *s.* 1. Tempestad, tormenta, temporal. 2. Conmoción o perturbación de ánimo: tempestad o violencia de genio o natural. **Tempest-beaten,** batido por la tempestad. **Tempest-tossed,** sacudido por la tormenta. **A tempest in a teapot,** una tormenta en un vaso de agua.

tempestuous [temˈpestjʊəst] [tem-pes-tiuos], *a.* Tempestuoso; borrascoso; impetuoso, turbulento.

templar [ˈtemplɑ'] [tem-pla'], *s.* Templario.

template [ˈtemplɪt] [tem-plit], *s.* V. TEMPLET.

temple [ˈtempl] [tem-pel], *s.* 1. Templo, edificio dedicado al culto de Dios o de una divinidad; por excelencia, el templo de Jerusalén que se destinaba al culto de Jehová; en Francia, templo protestante, en contraposición a iglesia católica romana. 2. Cada uno de los dos colegios de legistas que hay en Londres y en París, y que en otro tiempo estuvieron habitados por los templarios. 3. *(Anat.)* Sien, la parte de la cabeza que está al extremo de las cejas. 4. Vara o regla en los telares con púas en sus extremidades para mantener igual y extendida la tela: se usa por lo común en plural.

templet [ˈtemplɪt] [tem-plit], *s.* 1. Patrón, modelo, gálibo, pieza plana de madera o metal que sirve para dar forma a alguna cosa. 2. Solera, cuña, piedra o madero corto y grueso para igualar el peso o empuje.

tempo [ˈtempəʊ] [tem-pou], *s.* *(Mús.)* Ritmo, compás, grado relativo de movimiento; también; cadencia, modo o estilo particular del compás. *(Ital.)* **A tempo,** en debido compás. **Tempo rubato,** en compás irregular («compás robado»).

temporal [ˈtempərəl] [tem-po-ral], *a.* 1. Temporal, transitorio, pasajero (not eternal). 2. Temporal, secular, en oposición a eclesiástico. 3. Temporal, perteneciente a las sienes.

temporality ['tempərəlıtı] [tem-po-ra-li-ti], *s.* Temporalidades, bienes seculares.

temporally ['tempərəlı] [tem-po-ra-li], *adv.* Temporalmente, transitoriamente; con respecto a la vida presente. **I live here temporally,** vivo aquí temporalmente.

temporary ['tempərərı] [tem-po-ra-ri], *a.* Temporario, temporal, provisional, que dura por limitado tiempo. **As a temporary measure,** como medida provisional.

temporize ['tempəraız] [tem-po-rais], *vn.* 1. Temporizar, diferir, ganar tiempo. 2. Temporizar, contemporizar; atenerse, someterse a las circunstancias.

temporizer ['tempəraızər] [tem-po-rai-sar], *s.* Temporizador, entretenedor, el que gana tiempo dilatándolo.

tempt [tempt] [temptt], *va.* 1. Tentar, poner a prueba, solicitar al mal, al pecado; instigar, inducir, estimular. 2. Poner a prueba la paciencia de uno, provocar, excitar. **To tempt fate,** tentar a la suerte.

temptable ['temptəbl] [temp-ta-bol], *a.* El que es capaz de dejarse tentar, instigar o seducir a la comisión de una acción mala.

temptation [temp'teıʃən] [temp-tei-shon], *s.* 1. Tentación, la acción de tentar. 2. Tentación, movimiento interior que induce a lo malo. 3. Tentación, movimiento interior que provoca el deseo hacia alguna cosa. **To resist the temptation,** resistir la tentación.

tempter ['temptər] [temp-ta'], *s.* 1. Tentador, el que tienta o induce al mal. 2. Tentador, el demonio o espíritu maligno.

tempting ['temptıŋ] [temp-tin], *a.* Tentador, atractivo, apetecible (desirable).

temptingly ['temptıŋlı] [temp-tin-li], *adv.* Con tentación.

temptress ['temptrıs] [temp-tres], *s.* Tentadora, mujer que fascina y atrae.

ten [ten] [ten], *a.* y *s.* Diez.

tenable ['tenəbl] [te-na-bol], *a.* Defendible, capaz de ser defendido o sostenido.

tenacious [tı'neıʃəs] [ti-nei-shos], *a.* 1. Tenaz, que es difícil de despegarse, de partes muy unidas unas a otras; tieso, no flexible. 2. Tenaz, pegajoso, adhesivo. 3. Tenaz, que retiene fuertemente; terco, porfiado (fighter), firme en su intento o propósito.

tenaciously [tı'neıʃəslı] [ti-nei-shos-li], *adv.* Tenazmente, con tenacidad, con obstinación.

tenacity [tı'næsıtı] [ti-na-si-ti], *s.* 1. Tenacidad, calidad de adhesivo o pegajoso. 2. Tenacidad, terquedad (stubbornness), porfía.

tenancy ['tenənsı] [te-nan-si], *s.* Tenencia (holding), posesión temporal de lo que pertenece a otro; estado o período de inquilinato o arrendamiento; título legal.

tenant ['tenənt] [te-nant], *s.* 1. Arrendatario, arrendador, inquilino, rentero, el que tiene posesión temporal de alguna cosa que arrienda de otro. 2. Residente, morador, el que reside o mora en algún lugar. **Tenant for life,** residente, usufructuario o inquilino vitalicio.

tenant, *vn.* Arrendar, tener en arriendo o en posesión temporal alguna cosa que pertenece a otro.

tenantless ['tenəntlıs] [te-nant-les], *a.* Desarrendado, sin inquilinos; deshabitado (unoccupied).

tenantry ['tenəntrı] [te-nan-tri], *s.* 1. Arriendo. 2. El conjunto de los arrendatarios de un hacendado o propietario.

tench [tentʃ] [tench], *s.* Tenca, pez europeo de agua dulce de los ciprínidos. (*Tinca*).

tend [tend] [tend], *vn.* 1. Propender, tener tendencia (have tendency), tender; tener por resultado, ejercer influencia en cierta dirección; contribuir. 2. Ir hacia, moverse, encaminarse o dirigirse en cierta dirección. **Education tends to refinement,** la educación tiende al refinamiento. **His path tended upward,** su sendero se dirigía hacia arriba.

tend, *va.* 1. Guardar, vigilar, velar, cuidar o tener cuidado de alguna cosa. 2. Atender, estar con cuidado y atención a lo que se hace. 3. (*Des.*) Asistir, acompañar. 4. (*Mar.*) Vigilar en un buque al ancla, para evitar que cuando cambie la marea se enreden el ancla y las cadenas. -*vn.* 1. Asistir, servir como

criado o dependiente; con *on* o *upon.* 2. Estar atento a (take care of), ocuparse en; pensar en. (Abrev. de ATTEND.) **To tend a child,** tener cuidado de un niño. **To tend a flock of sheep,** vigilar un rebaño de carneros. **To tend upon a master,** servir a un amo.

tendance ['tendəns] [ten-dans], *s.* 1. (*Ant.*) Cuidado, atención. 2. (*Des.*) Corte: tren. *V.* ATTENDANCE.

tendency ['tendənsı] [ten-dan-si], *s.* 1. Tendencia (inclination), propensión; dirección o inclinación hacia algún designio, fin o resultado. 2. Lo que tiende a causar un efecto.

tendentious [ten'denʃəs] [ten-den-shos], *a.* Tendencioso.

tender ['tendər] [ten-da'], *a.* 1. Tierno, blando, delicado, flexible; que cede a cualquier impresión extraña. 2. Tierno, delicado, compasivo, sensible, que se afecta fácilmente (affectionate). 3. Capaz de afectos o sentimientos tiernos. 4. Delicado, afeminado. 5. Tierno, amoroso, afectuoso, cariñoso. 6. Indulgente, benigno. 7. Delicado, arduo, arriesgado. 8. Delicado, escrupuloso. 9. Tierno, se aplica al tiempo o a la edad de la niñez. **Tender of all over,** cuidadoso de, solícito de los sentimientos de otros. **Tender-hearted,** tierno de corazón, compasivo.

tender, *s.* 1. Oferta (offer), ofrecimiento, propuesta que se hace sobre cualquier asunto. 2. (*For.*) Oferta formal de pago; moneda que se ofrece en pago; también sumisión, oferta formal de hacer cierto trabajo por una suma especificada.

tender, *s.* 1. Escampavía, patache, bajel pequeño que ordinariamente sigue a otro mayor. 2. Ténder, (*Amer.*) alijo, carro que lleva el combustible y el agua para la locomotora. 3. Guarda, pesona que cuida a alguno: servidor.

tender, *va.* 1. Ofrecer, presentar, proponer. 2. (*For.*) Ofrecer en pago sin condiciones. -*vn.* Hacer una oferta o propuesta, licitación.

tender, *va.* 1. Enternecer, ablandar, poner tierno. 2. (*Ant.*) Estimar a uno, hacer caso de algo, querer.

tenderfoot ['tendərfʊt] [ten-da-fut], *s.* (*Ger. E. U. y Australia*) El recién llegado que no está acostumbrado todavía a la vida en los bosques o en los campos de mineros, etc.; cualquier persona inexperta, novato (inexperienced).

tenderize ['tendəraız] [ten-da-rais], *vt.* Ablandar.

tenderizer ['tendəraızər] [ten-da-rai-sa'], *s.* Maza para ablandar la carne por ejemplo.

tenderling ['tendəlıŋ] [ten-der-lin], *s.* 1. Uno de los pitones de venado o ciervo. 2. (*Poco us.*) Favorito, persona mimada.

tenderloin ['tendəlɔın] [ten-der-loin], *s.* Filete, la parte más jugosa y tierna del solomillo.

tenderly ['tendəlı] [ten-der-li], *adv.* Tiernamente, con ternura y cariño.

tenderness ['tendənıs] [ten-der-nes], *s.* 1. Terneza, ternura, delicadeza, suavidad; calidad de tierno. 2. Facilidad de enternecerse, dulzura, benevolencia. 3. Delicadeza, miramiento, escrupulosidad, nimiedad. 4. Afecto, cariño.

tendinous ['tendınəs] [ten-di-nos], *a.* Tendinoso, que tiene tendones o se compone de ellos.

tendon ['tendən] [ten-don], *s.* 1. Tendón, cuerda o cordón que une los extremos de los músculos a los huesos y sirve para el movimiento. 2. La ternilla del casco del caballo.

tendril ['tendrıl] [ten-dril], *s.* Zarcillo: en algunas plantas un cordoncillo o hilo que está enroscado a ellas y que en las vides se llama también tijeretas.

tendriled ['tendrıld] [ten-drild], *a.* Provisto de zarcillos; se usa para formar palabras compuestas.

tenement ['tenımənt] [te-ni-mant], *s.* 1. Habitación, vivienda, alojamiento, parte de una casa en que se aloja una familia; por lo común en una clase inferior de habitaciones. 2. (*For.*) Cualquier cosa, de carácter permanente que puede poseerse en propiedad, como tierras, rentas, franquicias, etc. 3. Fábrica, edificio y particularmente casa habitación.

tenet ['tenıt] [te-nit], *s.* Dogma; aserción, aserto, proposición que se sienta como verdadera, principio (principle).

tenfold ['tendfəʊld] [ten-fould], *a.* Décuplo, que contiene un número diez veces exactamente. -*adv.* De manera décupla.

tennis ['tenɪs] [te-nis], *s.* Tenis. **Tennis ball,** pelota de tenis. **Tennis court,** cancha de tenis. **Tennis match,** partido de tenis. **Tennis tournament,** torneo de tenis.

tenon ['tenən] [te-non], *va.* 1. Espigar, formar espiga en un madero. 2. Juntar a espiga y mortaja. -*s.* 1. *(Carp.)* Espiga, almilla, la punta de algún madero o palo que entra en una mortaja. 2. Pieza que se pone a una estatua para reforzarla. **Tenon-saw,** sierra de ingletes.

tenor ['tenəʳ] [te-noʳ], *s.* 1. Tenor, curso, constitución u orden firme y estable de alguna cosa. 2. Tenor, contenido, substancia y efecto de un escrito o instrumento; contenido literal de un escrito. 3. Carácter y tendencia generales. 4. *(Mús.)* Tenor, voz media entre la de contralto y barítono; persona que tiene esta voz. 5. Viola u otro instrumento de sonido intermedio entre el alto y el bajo. -*a.* De tenor, perteneciente a la voz o instrumento de tenor. **The even tenor of one's way,** su método regular de vida.

tenpenny ['tenpenɪ] [te-pe-ni], *a.* De diez peniques, que vale diez peniques; también, clavo de cierto tamaño.

tenpins ['tenpɪnz] [ten-pins], *s.* *(E. U.)* Juego con diez bolos de madera.

tense [tens] [tens], *a.* 1. Tieso, estirado, tenso, tirante, nervioso (nervous). 2. Tenso (strained). **It was a very tense finish,** fue una final muy emocionante. -*s.* *(Gram.)* Tiempo del verbo.

tense, *va.* Poner tenso, tensar. *(Coloq.)* **Tense up,** ponerse tenso.

tensely ['tenslɪ] [tens-li], *adv.* Con tensión, tensamente.

tenseness ['tensnɪs] [tens-nes], *s.* Contracción, tensión, tirantez, el estado de lo que se halla tirante.

tensibility [ˌtensɪ'bɪlɪtɪ] [ten-si-bi-li-ti], *s.* El estado y la disposición de lo que se puede estirar o poner tenso.

tensible ['tensɪbl] [ten-si-bol], *a.* Capaz de tensión, que puede estirarse.

tensile ['tensaɪl] [ten-sail], *a.* Tensor. **Tensile strength,** resistencia a la tensión.

tension ['tenʃən] [ten-shon], *s.* 1. Tensión, extensión o dilatación de alguna cosa, tirantez. 2. Gran aplicación del espíritu. 3. *(Mec.)* Tensión, regulador del hilo en una máquina de coser. 4. Estado de tirantez en las relaciones entre dos gobiernos. 5. *(Elec.)* Tensión. **High tension,** alta tensión.

tensive ['tensɪv] [ten-siv], *a.* Tirante, estirado; causado por tensión o que la causa.

tensor ['tensəʳ] [ten-saʳ], *s.* Tensor, músculo extensor.

ten-strike ['tenstraɪk] [ten-straik], *s.* Jugada en que se derriban los diez bolos con una sola bocha; de aquí. **To make a ten-strike,** poner una pica en Flandes.

tent [tent] [tent], *s.* 1. *(Mil.)* Tienda de campaña; pabellón. 2. Cualquier habitación provisional. 3. Lechino, porción de bilas que unidas en figura de clavo se emplean en cirugía para varios usos. 4. *(Zool.)* Tela sedosa que cubre a ciertas orugas. 5. Tintillo, especie de vino de color rojo vivo. **Tent-bed,** catre de tijera. **Tent-cloth,** terliz. **To pitch tents,** armar las tiendas de campaña; acamparse. **To strike the tents,** plegar tiendas, levantar el campo. **Tent-pole,** mástil, montante de tienda. **Tent-wine,** vino de Alicante. **Dark-tent,** tienda portátil con cámara oscura para usarla al aire libre. **Tent-caterpillar,** oruga norteamericana gregaria que hila una tela grande y sedosa y es muy nociva.

tent, *vn.* Alojarse en tienda o pabellón. -*va.* Tentar, reconocer con la tienta la cavidad de una herida.

tentacle ['tentəkl] [ten-ta-kol], *s.* 1. *(Zool.)* Tentáculo, apéndice móvil y blando (conmúnmente de la cabeza) que tienen muchos moluscos y zoófitos y que les sirve para tocar y hacer presa. 2. *(Bot.)* Tentáculo, filamento glandular sensible.

tentative ['tentətɪv] [ten-ta-tiv], *a.* 1. Que toca o pertenece a la tentativa, prueba o ensayo. 2. Provisional, provisorio. 3. Indeciso (hesitant). -*s.* Tentativa, ensayo.

tentatively ['tentətɪvlɪ] [ten-ta-tiv-li], *adv.* 1. Provisionalmente (provisionally), provisoriamente. 2. Indecisamente (hesitantly), cautelosamente. **They started very tentatively,** empezaron muy cautelosamente.

tenter ['tentəʳ] [ten-taʳ], *s.* Rama, especie de bastidor que se usa en las fábricas de paño para estirarlo en todas direcciones. **Tenterhooks,** clavijas de rama, escarpias o alcayatas. **To be on the tenters,** hallarse entre la espada y la pared.

tenter, *va.* Estirar con ganchos. -*vn.* Estirarse, alargarse, dilatarse.

tenth [tenθ] [tenz], *a.* Décimo, deceno, el ordinal de diez. **Alphonso Tenth,** Alfonso Décimo. **The tenth of October,** el diez de octubre. -*s.* La décima parte. 3. El diezmo.

tenthly ['tenθlɪ] [tenz-li], *adv.* En décimo lugar.

tentwort ['tentwɔːt] [tent-uort], *s.* *(Bot.)* Culantrillo.

tenuity [te'njʊɪtɪ] [te-niui-ti], *s.* Tenuidad, raridad, sutileza (subtlety), delgadez; rarefacción del aire o de un fluido.

tenuous ['tenjʊəs] [te-niuos], *a.* Tenue, delgado, delicado, endeble (weak).

tenure ['tenjʊəʳ] [te-niuaʳ], *s.* 1. Tenencia, ocupación, dependencia. 2. Ejercicio, ocupación. 3. Puesto permanente, titularidad (job security).

tepee ['tiːpiː] [ti-pi], *s.* Cabaña de los indios de E.U., tipi.

tepefy ['tiːpiːfaɪ] [ti-pi-fai], *va.* y *vn.* Entibiar, hacer tibio; ponerse tibio.

tepid ['tepɪd] [te-pid], *a.* Tibio, templado, entre caliente y frío.

tepidity [te'pɪdɪtɪ] [te-pi-di-ti], *s.* Tibieza.

tepor ['tepəʳ] [te-paʳ], *s.* Calor moderado.

tequila [tɪ'kiːlə] [ti-ki-la], *s.* Tequila.

terce [tɜːs] [ters], *s.* Tercerola, una especie de tonel que contiene la tercera parte de una pipa. V. TIERCE.

tercentenary [ˌtɜːsen'tiːnərɪ] [ter-sen-ti-na-ri], *a.* De tres siglos, de trescientos años. -*s.* Aniversario tricentésimo.

term [tɜːm] [term], *s.* 1. Término (word), dicción, vocablo, la voz o palabra con la cual se explica alguna cosa; particularmente, una voz técnica. 2. *pl.* Palabras significativas, discurso, oración. 3. *(Lóg.)* Palabras que pueden ser sujeto o atributo de la proposición; uno de los tres elementos de un silogismo. 4. Término, espacio de tiempo, período (period), plazo de tiempo determinado y prescrito: en este sentido llaman los ingleses término al tiempo en que los tribunales superiores de justicia están abiertos. **The President's first term in office,** el primer mandato del presidente. 5. *pl.* Condiciones, estipulaciones propuestas, sean o no aceptadas: de aquí, relato, pie, base de acuerdo, relaciones mutuas. **Upon what terms?,** ¿en qué términos? 6. Término, límite, confín, hablando de la extensión de lugar. 7. *(Mat.)* Lo que limita una línea, superficie o volumen, parte de una expresión algebraica unida a otra por el signo de adición o substracción. **The term of four years,** el plazo de cuatro años. **In set terms,** en términos escogidos. **To be on good terms with,** estar sobre buen pie con, estar bien con. **Not on any terms,** por ningún concepto, a ningún precio, de ninguna manera. **To bring to terms,** traer a un arreglo, imponer condiciones. **To come to terms,** decidirse a un arreglo, ceder, someterse. **To make terms,** efectuar un acuerdo o arreglo, estar acordes. **Michaelmas term,** época (de tribunal) de la festividad de San Miguel, del 24 de octubre al 21 de diciembre. **Hilary term,** sesiones de los tribunales desde el 11 de enero al miércoles anterior a la Pascua de Resurrección.

term, *va.* Nombrar, llamar, calificar de (describe).

termagancy ['tɜːməgənsɪ] [ter-ma-gan-si], *s.* Carácter pendenciero.

termagant ['tɜːməgənt] [ter-ma-gant], *a.* Turbulento; pendenciero. -*s.* Sierpe, fiera, áspid: se aplica a la mujer de mal genio y que siempre está gruñendo o armando pendencias.

termer ['tɜːməʳ] [ter-maʳ], *s.* El abogado, procurador, agente, etc., que en Inglaterra sigue a los jueces a los diferentes puntos donde establece su tribunal.

terminable ['tɜːmɪnəbl] [ter-mi-na-bol], *a.* Limitable.

terminal ['tɜːmɪnl] [ter-mi-nal], *a.* 1. Terminal, último y que pone término a una cosa. *(Bot.)* que crece en la punta de una rama o tallo. -*s.* 1. Punto o parte que termina; estación o figura terminal. 2. *(Inform.)* Terminal.

terminate ['tɜ:mɪneɪt] [ter-mi-neit], *va.* y *vn.* 1. Terminar, acabar, ser fin o término, poner término, límite o fin. **This train terminates here,** éste es el final del recorrido de este tren. 3. Terminar, componer una desavenencia o disputa.

termination [ˌtɜ:mɪˈneɪʃən] [ter-mi-nei-shon], *s.* 1. Terminación, la acción y efecto de acabarse, terminarse o resolverse una cosa; fin, conclusión. 2. Limitación, la acción de limitar. 3. Límite, lindero (boundary), cabo, extremidad; en especial, el cabo de un conductor eléctrico. 4. Terminación, desinencia, la última sílaba de una voz según la variedad de sus significados. 5. *(Med.)* Interrupción. **Termination of pregnancy,** interrupción del embarazo.

terminative ['tɜ:mɪnətɪv] [ter-mi-na-tiv], *a.* Terminativo.

terminology [ˌtɜ:mɪˈnɒlədʒɪ] [ter-mi-no-lo-yi], *s.* 1. Terminología, el arte o ciencia del uso debido de los términos. 2. Conjunto de los términos técnicos o nomenclatura de una persona, clase o ciencia particulares.

terminus ['tɜ:mɪnəs] [ter-mi-nos], *s.* 1. Término final, fin; particularmente la estación terminal de un ferrocarril y la ciudad en que está situada dicha estación. 2. Término, límite, mojón. 3. Término arquitectónico.

termite ['tɜ:maɪt] [ter-mait], *s.* Termita, comején, homiga blanca.

terminer ['tɜ:mɪnəʳ] [ter-mi-naʳ], *s. (For.)* La comisión que se da a los jueces ingleses para que oigan y determinen las causas en sus respectivos distritos.

termless ['tɜ:mlɪs] [term-les], *a.* Ilimitado, que no tiene límites ni términos.

termly ['tɜ:mlɪ] [term-li], *adv. (Poco us.) (For.)* En cada término.

tern ['tɜ:n] [tern], *s.* Golondrina de mar, ave palmípeda semejante a la gaviota, pero menor. Sterna. -*a. V.* TERNATE.

ternary ['tɜ:nərɪ] [ter-na-ri], *a.* Ternario, compuesto de tres. -*s.* Terna; ternario.

ternate ['tɜ:neɪt] [ter-neit], *a.* Clasificado o arreglado de tres en tres.

terra ['terə] [te-ra], *s.* Tierra *(Lat.)* **Terra alba** tierra de pipa. **Terra-cotta,** tierra cocida (terracota). **Terra firma,** tierra firme. **Terra incognita,** tierra desconocida.

terrace ['terəs] [te-ras], *va.* Terraplenar, hacer un terraplén o formar en terraplenes sucesivos. -*s.* 1. Terraplén, terrapleno, bancal, espacio elevado y llano que tiene uno o más lados inclinados. 2. Terraplén que sostiene una hilera de casas o las mismas casas asi colocadas. 3. Terrado, azotea. 4. Balcón (balcony), galería abierta. **Terraces,** gradas, tribunas.

terraced ['terəst] [te-rast], *a.* 1. *(Agr., Geog.)* En terrazas o bancales. 2. Adosado.

terracota ['teraˈkɒtə] [te-ra-ko-ta], *f.* Terracota.

terrane, terrain [teˈreɪn] [te-rein], *s. (Geol.)* Cualquier roca o serie de rocas relacionadas sin intermisión.

terrapin ['terəpɪn] [te-ra-pin], *s.* Emido, tortuga de carne deliciosa, de la costa atlántica de los Estados Unidos.

terrestrial [tɪˈrestrɪəl] [ti-res-trial], *a.* Terrestre, terreno.

terrestrialness [tɪˈrestrɪəlnɪs] [ti-res-trial-nes], *s.* La naturaleza y calidad de la tierra.

terrible ['terəbl] [te-ra-bol], *a.* 1. Terrible, pavoroso, espantoso, horroroso (horrific). **I feel terrible,** me encuentro muy mal. 2. Tremendo, grande, desmedido, desmesurado. **What a terrible shame!,** ¡qué lástima más grande!

terribly ['terəblɪ] [te-ra-bli], *adv.* Terriblemente, espantosamente, horriblemente.

terrier ['terɪəʳ] [te-rieʳ], *s.* 1. Zorrero, perro zorrero o raposero, notable por su valor en la persecución de los animales nocivos. 2. Nutria macho solitaria. 3. *(For ant. Ingl.)* Descripción o catálogo de posesiones, heredades o bienes raíces.

terrific [təˈrɪfɪk] [te-ri-fik], *a.* 1. Espantoso, terrífico, que amedrenta, que causa terror. 2. *(Fam.)* Extraordinario, maravilloso. **I had a terrific time,** lo pasé fenomenalmente.

terrified ['terɪfaɪd] [te-ri-faid], *a.* Aterrorizado, aterrado.

terrify ['terɪfaɪ] [te-ri-fai], *vt.* Aterrorizar. **Planes terrify me,** los aviones me aterrorizan.

terrifying ['terɪfaɪɪŋ] [te-ri-fain], *a.* Aterrador, espantoso, espeluznante (appalling).

territorial ['terɪˈtɔːrɪəl] [te-ri-to-re-al], *a.* Territorial; en especial, perteneciente a uno o a todos los Territorios de los Estados Unidos.

territory ['terɪtərɪ] [te-ri-to-ri], *s.* 1. Territorio, extensión de tierra sobre la cual ejerce su jurisdicción un estado soberano. 2. Extensión de tierra, región, distrito. 3. Comarca de los Estados Unidos no elevada todavía a la categoría de Estado y sometida a un régimen provisional.

terror ['terəʳ] [te-roʳ], *s.* 1. Espanto, terror (fear), pavor, gran miedo; objeto de miedo, de espanto. 2. *(Fam.)* Persona fastidiosa.

terrorism ['terərɪzəm] [te-ro-ri-sem], *s.* Terrorismo.

terrorist ['terərɪst] [te-ro-rist], *s.* Terrorista.

terrorize ['terəraɪz] [te-ro-rais], *vt.* Aterrorizar, tener atemorizado.

terror-stricken ['terəˌstrɪkən] [te-ro-stri-ken], *a.* Horrorizado, aterrado.

terse [tɜ:s] [ters], *a.* 1. Sucinto; breve y comprensivo, conciso, lacónico (laconic), compendioso; limado y elegante sin afectación. 2. *(Des.)* Terso (smooth), liso, pulido.

tersely ['tɜ:slɪ] [ters-li], *adv.* Concisa y elegantemente, lacónicamente.

terseness ['tɜ:snɪs] [ters-nes], *s.* Calidad de conciso y sucinto (en el estilo).

tertian ['tɜ:ʃən] [ter-shan], *a.* Terciano, que vuelve u ocurre cada tercer día. -*s.* Terciana, calentura intermitente que repite cada tercer día.

tertiary ['tɜ:ʃərɪ] [ter-sha-ri], *a.* 1. Terciario, tercero en orden o grado. 2. *(Geol.)* Terciario, de la época terciaria. -*s.* 1. Época geológica posterior a la cretácea. 2. *(Orn.)* Pluma terciaria de un ave.

test [test] [test], *s.* 1. Prueba, toque, examen que se hace de una persona o cosa, test (multiple-choice type). 2. Juicio o distinción que se hace entre dos cosas. 3. Piedra de toque, criterio, norma de juicio. 4. Juramento u otra prueba testimonial de los principios de la fe. 5. Reacción química, por medio de la cual se puede establecer la identidad de un compuesto o de uno de sus constituyentes; reactivo. **Blood test,** análisis de sangre. **To put to the test,** experimentar, probar, poner a prueba. **To stand the test,** ser de prueba, soportar la prueba. **Test-tube,** probeta que se usa en los laboratorios. **Test-paper,** papel reactivo.

test, *s.* 1. Cubierta exterior rígida; concha. 2. *(Bot.)* Tegumento exterior de una semilla.

test, *va.* 1. Experimentar ensayar, hacer la prueba, el ensayo de algo. **These cosmetics have been tested on animals,** se han utilizado animales en las pruebas de laboratorio de estos cosméticos. 2. Sujetar a condiciones que demuestren el verdadero carácter de una cosa. 3. Examinar, evaluar, analizar (analyze), comprobar.

testable ['testəbl] [tes-ta-bol], *a.* Capaz de ser testigo o de servir de testigo.

testacean ['testeɪʃən] [tes-tei-shan], *a.* y *s.* Testáceo, que tiene concha; invertebrado provisto de concha.

testaceous ['testeɪʃəs] [tes-tei-shos], *a.* Testáceo: que tiene concha dura.

testament ['testəmənt] [tes-ta-ment], *s.* 1. Testamento (will), declaración de la última voluntad que hace una persona disponiendo de sus bienes y hacienda. 2. El Viejo y Nuevo Testamento, los libros de la Sagrada Escritura.

testamentary [ˌtestəˈmentərɪ] [tes-ta-men-ta-ri], *a.* Testamentario.

testate ['testeɪt] [tes-teit], *a.* Que ha hecho testamento, que ha testado.

testator ['testeɪtəʳ] [tes-tei-taʳ], *s.* Testador, el que hace testamento.

testatrix ['testərɪks] [tes-ta-triks], *f.* Testadora, la mujer que hace testamento.

tested ['testɪd] [tes-tid], *a.* Ensayado, probado, experimentado; examinado.

tester ['testəʳ] [tes-taʳ], *s.* 1. Probador, el que prueba o hace examen. 2. Cielo de cama. 3. Frasco de muestra (sample).

testicle ['testɪkl] [tes-ti-kol], *a.* Testículo, cada una de las glándulas seminales.

testification [ˌtestɪfɪ'keɪʃən] [tes-ti-fi-kei-shon], *s.* Testificación, el acto de testificar.

testifier ['testɪfaɪəʳ] [tes-ti-faiaʳ], *s.* Testigo, testificante.

testify ['testɪfaɪ] [tes-ti-fai], *va.* 1. Testificar, atestiguar, afirmar. 2. Atestar, declarar bajo juramento o ante el juez. 3. Servir de prueba. -*vn.* 1. Dar testimonio, servir de testigo. 2. Servir de evidencia o indicación. 3. Aseverar.

testily ['testɪlɪ] [tes-ti-li], *adv.* Impertinentemente, con petulancia; con morosidad.

testimonial [ˌtestɪ'məʊnɪəl] [tes-ti-mou-nial], *a.* Testimonial, que da testimonio, que hace fe. -*s.* 1. Prenda o prueba formal de amistad, recuerdo que se da a menudo en público, homenaje (tribute). 2. Certificación o certificado en que se asegura la verdad de algún hecho, recomendación (reference, recommendation).

testimony ['testɪmənɪ] [tes-ti-mo-ni], *s.* 1. Testimonio, atestación, testificación, declaración. 2. Testimonio, prueba, justificación o comprobación de la certeza y verdad de alguna cosa. 3. *(Bibl.)* Tablas de la Ley, el Antiguo Testamento. **I must bear testimony,** debo hacer la justicia. **In testimony whereof,** en testimonio de lo cual.

testiness ['testɪnɪs] [tes-ti-nes], *s.* Enfado (anger), enojo, mal humor, aspereza de genio.

testing ['testɪŋ] [tes-tin], *s.* Pruebas. -*a.* Duro, arduo (arduous).

testing ground ['testɪŋgraʊnd] [tes-tin-graund], *s.* Terreno de pruebas.

testosterone [te'stɒstərəʊn] [tes-tos-te-roun], *s.* Testosterona.

test-tube ['testʰtjuːb] [test-tiub], *s.* Probeta.

testy ['testɪ] [tes-ti], *a.* Enojadizo, descontentadizo, irritable (touchy), de mal genio.

tetanic ['tetənɪk] [te-ta-nik], *a.* Tetánico, relativo al tétanos o que lo produce.

tetanoid ['tetənɔɪd] [te-ta-noid], *a.* Parecido al tétano o que produce síntomas del tétanos.

tetanus ['tetənəs] [te-ta-nos], *s.* Tétanos, tétano, enfermedad nerviosa caracterizada por rigidez y tensión de los músculos sometidos al imperio de la voluntad.

tetchy ['tetʃɪ] [te-chi], *a.* Irritable.

tête-a-tête ['teɪtɑː'teɪt] [teit-a-teit], *s.* Cara a cara, silla a silla, a solas.

tether ['teðəʳ] [te-daʳ], *va.* Trabar, atar, restriñir. -*s.* Soga (rope), cadena (chain).

tetra ['tetrə] [te-tra], *pref.* Prefijo griego que significa cuatro.

tetrachord ['tetrəkɔːd] [te-tra-kord], *s. (Mús.)* Tetracordio, media octava.

tetragon ['tetrəgən] [te-tra-gon], *s. (Geom.)* Tetrágono, cuadrilátero.

tetragonal ['tetrəgənl] [te-tra-go-nal], *a.* Tetrágono, cuadrangular, que tiene cuatro ángulos.

tetrahedral ['tetrə'hiːdrəl] [te-tra-ji-dral], *a.* Tetraedral, tetraédico, relativo al tetraedro.

tetrahedron ['tetrə'hiːdrən] [te-tra-ji-dron], *s.* Tetraedro, sólido terminado por cuatro planos o caras.

tetrameter [te'træmɪtəʳ] [te-tra-mi-taʳ], *s.* Tetrámetro, verso de cuatro bases o medidas.

tetter ['tetəʳ] [te-taʳ], *s.* Sarpullido, empeine, enfermedad vesicular del cutis.

teuton ['tjuːtən] [tiu-ton], *s.* 1. Teutón, teutona, individuo de la raza germánica. 2. Los arios del noroeste de Europa con inclusión de los alemanes y los escandinavos.

teutonic [tjʊ'tɒnɪk] [tiu-to-nik], *a.* Teutónico, germánico. -*s.* Tudesco, idioma o idiomas de los teutones.

tew [tjuː] [tiu], *va. (Prov. o Com.)* Cascar, trabajar; agramar. **To tew hemp,** espadar o espadillar cáñamo.

Texan ['teksən] [tek-dan], *s.* y *a.* Tejano.

text [tekst] [tekst], *s.* 1. Texto, las palabras propias de un autor a distinción de las notas o comentarios que se hacen de ellas. 2. Verso o pasaje breve de la Sagrada Escritura. 3. De aquí, tema, tesis o asunto de un discurso. 4. Grado de ietra o tipo; p. ej. German text, tipo alemán. **Textbook,** libro de texto; manual, libro de escuela; libro con espacios en blanco para notas o comentarios; libreto de ópera.

text-hand ['teksthænd] [tekst-jand], *s.* Escritura o carácter de letra muy grueso.

textile ['tekstaɪl] [teks-tail], *a.* Textil, hilable, capaz de hilarse o de reducirse a hilos y ser tejido.

textual ['tekstʃʊəl] [tekst-chual], *a.* Textual, que conviene con el texto y es propio de él; versado en el texto.

textualist ['tekstʃʊəlɪst] [tekst-chua-list], *s.* Textualista, el que usa con frecuencia del texto de una obra, y también el que es dado a citar textos.

texture ['tekstʃəʳ] [tekst-chaʳ], *s.* 1. Textura, tejido, disposición y orden en los hilos de una tela, y por extensión se dice también de la disposición y orden de las fibras que componen las partes del cuerpo del animal. 2. Tela, tejido, obra tejida. 3. Textura, la colocación y orden de una cosa que se sigue o ata con otra.

textured ['tekstʃəd] [tekst-chad], *a.* Con textura, con relieve.

Thai [taɪ] [tai], *a.* Tailandés. -*s.* Tailandés, persona natural de Tailandia, lengua tailandesa.

Thailand ['taɪlænd] [tai-land], *s.* Tailandia.

thallium ['θælɪəm] [za-liom], *s.* Talio.

Thames [temz] [tems], *s.* **The Thames,** el Támesis.

than [ðæn] [dan], *conj.* 1. Que: partícula comparativa. **Your house is larger than mine,** la casa de Ud. es mayor que la mía. **He has more money than I,** tiene más dinero que yo. 2. De: se usa en lugar de que cuando va delante de los números, en sentido afirmativo. **Fewer than twenty,** menos de veinte. **More than a thousand,** más de mil. **More than once,** más de una vez.

thank [θæŋk] [zank], *va.* Agradecer, expresar gratitud a uno, dar gracias a. **I shall thank you for that favor,** le agradeceré a Ud. o le estimaré a Ud. que me haga ese favor. **Thank you,** gracias. **Thank God,** a Dios gracias. -*s. pl.* Gracias, agradecimiento, acción de agradecer, expresión de gratitud. **Thanks to you,** gracias a usted. **To return thanks,** hacer presentes sus agradecimientos.

thankful ['θæŋkfʊl] [zank-ful], *a.* Grato, agradecido. **I am very thankful to him,** le estoy muy agradecido.

thankfully ['θæŋkfəlɪ] [zank-fu-li], *adv.* Con gratitud o reconocimiento (gratefully). **He smiled up at me,** me sonrió agradecido.

thankfulness ['θæŋkfəlnɪs] [zank-ful-nes], *s.* Agradecimiento, gratitud, reconocimiento.

thankless ['θæŋklɪs] [zank-les], *a.* 1. Desagradecido (ungrateful), ingrato el que no reconoce los favores recibidos. 2. Lo que no merece gracias.

thanklessness ['θæŋklɪsnɪs] [zank-les-nes], *s.* Desagradecimiento, ingratitud.

thanks [θæŋks] [zanks], *s.pl.* Agradecimiento (gratitude). **Speech of thanks,** discurso de agradecimiento. -*interj.* ¡Gracias!

thanksgiving ['θæŋksgɪvɪŋ] [zanks-gui-vin], *s.* 1. Acción de gracias; particularmente, reconocimiento por las mercedes recibidas de Dios. 2. Celebración pública en reconocimiento del favor de Dios; día señalado para esa celebración. Thanksgiving Day, día de acción de gracias en reconocimiento de la protección y merced divinas; en los Estados Unidos es el último jueves de noviembre.

thankworthy ['θæŋkwɜːθɪ] [zank-uer-zi], *a.* Digno de reconocimiento; meritorio (commendable).

that [ðæt] [dat], *a.* Ese, esa, eso; el, la, aquello especialmente designado. **That boy,** ese muchacho. **That book is better than this,** ese (aquel) libro es mejor que éste. -*pron.* 1. Aquél, aquello, aquélla, como pronombre demostrativo. 2. Que, quien, el cual, la cual, lo cual, como pronombre relativo, y puede hacer relación a personas o cosas. **That of,** el de, la de.

That which, el que, la que, lo que. **What of that,** ¿qué importa eso? ¿qué quiere Ud. decir con eso? ¿qué resulta de eso? *That* se usa frecuentemente para evitar la repetición de una palabra. **That way,** por aquel camino, por allí. **That is,** es decir o eso es. **That may be,** eso puede ser, es posible. **See that,** vea Ud. eso. **What street is that,** ¿qué calle es ésa? **Upon that,** sobre esto, en cuanto a eso; luego. **All that is just,** todo lo que es justo. **And all that,** y todo eso; y otras hierbas. **To put this and that together,** deducir conclusiones. **It was I, not he, that wrote it,** fui yo, y no él, quien lo escribió. *-conj.* 1. Porque. 2. Para que. 3. Que, de modo que. **So that, insomuch that,** por cuanto; de modo que, de suerte que. **Not but that,** no es decir que. **Save that,** salvo que. **Supposing that,** supuesto que, dado que. *-adv.* Tan. **I'm not that interested, really,** la verdad es que no estoy tan interesado.

thatch [θætʃ] [zach], *s.* Cubierta de cañas, bálago, paja u hojas de palmera, que sirve de techado.

thatch, *va.* Techar con bálago o cañas, o poner un techo de paja.

thatched [θætʃt] [zacht], *a.* De paja, con el tejado de paja.

thatcher [ˈθætʃəʳ] [za-chaʳ], *s.* Trastejador de cañas o bálago.

thaw [θɔː] [zo], *vn.* 1. Deshelarse, derretirse (melt), hacerse líquido lo que está helado. 2. Deshacerse los hielos. *-va.* Deshelar, liquidar lo que está helado. **It thaws,** deshiela, se derrite la nieve o el hielo. **Thaw out,** descongelar.

thaw, *s.* 1. Deshielo, blandura del tiempo que deshace las nieves o el hielo. 2. El derretimiento o disolución de lo que está helado.

the [ðə] [da], *art.* 1. El, la; lo: *the* se usa delante de un substantivo tomado en sentido determinado (véase la Sinopsis de la Gramática inglesa). Delante de un comparativo no se traduce en español. **All the region,** toda la región. **The poor,** los pobres. 2. Por. **Three dollars the yard,** tres dólares la yarda, por yarda. 3. Cuanto. **The more you have the more you want,** cuanto más tienes más quieres.

theater, theatre [ˈθɪətəʳ] [zia-taʳ], *s.* 1. Teatro, el edificio (building) o paraje en que se junta el público a ver algún espectáculo o función. **Movie theater,** cine. **Operating theater,** quirófano. 2. Teatro (drama), literatura y representaciones dramáticas, en general, en conjunto. 3. Anfiteatro, lugar provisto de gradas. 4. Cualquier paraje o región que es escena de los acontecimientos.

theatrical [θɪˈætrɪkəl], *a.* 1. Teatral, que pertenece o toca al teatro. 2. Fingido, como por un actor; hecho para producir efecto, teatral, histriónico (exaggerated).

theatrically [θɪˈætrɪkəlɪ] [zia-tri-ka-li], *adv.* De un modo teatral.

thee [ðiː] [di], *pron.* Te, a ti: el caso objetivo de la segunda persona del singular del pronombre personal; se emplea en la oración, en poesía y en prosa elevada.

theft [θeft] [zeft], *s.* Hurto (robbery), la acción de hurtar y la misma cosa hurtada.

their [ðeəʳ] [deaʳ], *pron. pos.* Su, suyo, suya, de ellos, de ellas. **Theirs,** el suyo, la suya, los suyos, las suyas, de ellos o de ellas. **A friend of theirs,** un amigo suyo o de ellos.

theism [ˈθiːɪzəm] [zii-sem], *s.* Teísmo; deísmo.

theist [ˈθiːɪst] [ziist], *s.* Teísta, deísta.

theistic [ˈθiːɪstɪk] [zi-is-tik], *a.* Teísta, del teísmo, de los teístas.

them [ðem] [dem], *pron.* El caso objetivo de *They.* Los, las, les, ellos, ellas, a aquellos, a aquellas. **I love them,** los o las amo.

theme [θiːm] [ziim], *s.* 1. Tema (subject), el asunto o materia de un discurso. **Theme park,** parque temático. 2. Tesis, disertación, particularmente en las escuelas y colegios. 3. *(Mús.)* Tema, motivo, sobre el cual se hacen variaciones.

themselves [ðəmˈselvz] [dem-selvs], *pron. pl.* Ellos mismos, ellas mismas; sí mismos: caso oblicuo del pronombre personal recíproco y a veces también se usa como nominativo. **They only think of themselves,** sólo piensan en sí mismos.

then [ðen] [den], *adv.* 1. Entonces, en aquel tiempo (at that time), a la sazón. 2. Luego, después, en seguida. 3. En otro tiempo. *-conj.* 1. En tal caso, por consiguiente, pues. 2. Luego, por esta razón. **now and then,** de cuando en cuando; de vez en cuando. **Now...then...,** ya...ya... **Now then,** ahora pues, pues, por consiguiente. **And then,** con esto; y además de esto; y entonces; y en seguida. **And what then?** ¿y qué más? ¿y qué se seguirá de eso? *-a.* De entonces, de aquel tiempo; (uso cuestionable). **The then leader,** el entonces líder.

thenar [ˈθenəʳ] [de-naʳ], *a.* De la palma de la mano, o del juanete del pie.

thence [ðens] [dens], *adv.* 1. Desde allí (from there), de allí, hablando de lugar. 2. Desde entonces, desde ese tiempo, después de aquel tiempo. 3. De ahí, por eso, por esa razón, por ese motivo.

thenceforth [ˈðensˈfɔːθ] [dens-forz], *adv.* Desde entonces, de allí en adelante.

thenceforward [ðensˈfɔːwəd] [dens-for-uord], *adv.* Desde entonces; en adelante.

theocracy [θɪˈɒkrəsɪ] [zio-kra-si], *s.* Teocracia, el gobierno cuyos jefes son mirados como ministros o delegados de Dios.

theocratic [θɪˈɒkrætɪk] [zio-kra-tik], *a.* Teocrático.

theodolite [θɪˈɒdəlaɪt] [zio-do-lait], *s.* Teodolito, instrumento geodésico, que se usa para medir ángulos, distancias y alturas.

theologian [θɪəˈləʊdʒɪən] [zio-lou-yian], *s.* Teólogo, persona versada en la teología: profesor de teología.

theological [θɪəˈlɒdʒɪkəl] [zio-lo-yi-kal], *a.* Teologal, teológico.

theologically [θɪəˈlɒdʒɪkəlɪ] [zio-lo-yi-ka-li], *adv.* Teológicamente.

theology [θɪˈɒlədʒɪ] [zio-lou-yi], *s.* Teología, ciencia que trata de Dios y sus atributos.

theorem [ˈθɪərəm] [zio-rem], *s.* 1. Teorema, proposición que se puede demostrar. 2. *(Geom.)* Proposición en que se va a averiguar la verdad de una cosa.

theoretic [θɪəˈretɪk] [zio-re-tik], *a.* Teórico, especulativo, que pertenece a la teoría; que comprende y entiende especulativamente la esencia de las cosas sin prueba práctica.

theoretically [θɪəˈretɪkəlɪ] [zio-re-ti-ka-li], *adv.* Teóricamente, especulativamente.

theoric [ˈθɪərɪk] [zio-rik], *s.* Teórica, especulativa. *-a.* Teórico.

theorist [ˈθɪərɪst] [zio-rist], *s.* Teórico, el que no conoce más que la teoría de un arte o ciencia.

theorize [ˈθɪəraɪz] [zio-rais], *vn.* Exponer o formar teorías, especular.

theory [ˈθɪərɪ] [zio-ri], *s.* 1. Teoría, teórica, especulativa, conocimiento teórico. 2. Teoría, serie de leyes que sirven para relacionar determinado orden de fenómenos. 3. La ciencia en contraposición al arte. 4. Explicación filosófica de los fenómenos. **In theory,** en teoría.

theosophical [θɪəˈsɒfɪkəl] [zio-so-fi-kal], *a.* Teosófico, perteneciente a la teosofía.

theosophy [θɪˈɒsəfɪ] [zio-so-fi], *s.* Teosofía, doctrina de varias sectas que pretenden admitir la verdad esencial existente como base de toda religión, filosofía y ciencia; la religión universal.

therapeutic [ˌθerəˈpjuːtɪk] [ze-ra-piu-tik], *a.* Terapéutico, curativo.

therapeutics [θerəˈpjuːtɪks] [ze-ra-piu-tiks], *s.* Terapéutica, la parte de la medicina que trata del modo de obrar los medicamentos y de su aplicación.

therapist [ˈθerəpɪst] [ze-ra-pist], *s.* Persona versada en la terapéutica.

therapy [ˈθerəpɪ] [ze-ra-pi], *s.* Terapia.

there [ðeəʳ] [deaʳ], *adv.* 1. Allí, allá, ahí. 2. Allá, hacia aquel lugar, en aquella dirección. **There she is,** héla ahí. **There is,** allí está, helo ahí o allí, éste o ése es, míralo allí. *There,* forma con el verbo *to be* el impersonal *there be* que corresponde al verbo castellano *haber* usado como impersonal, con la diferencia que en inglés el verbo está en el mismo número que el nombre a que se refiere. **There can not be,** no puede haber. **There is a place,** hay un lugar, o un sitio. **There are many things,** hay muchas cosas. **There was a king,** hubo un rey. **There were many soliders,** había muchos soldados. *There* precede también a otros verbos para dar énfasis a la oración. **There came a man,** vino un hombre. **Here and there,** de aquí para allí, acá y acullá. - *interj. (Fam.)* **There!** ¡toma! y bien; ¡vaya!

thereabouts [ðɛərəbaʊts] [dear-a-bauts], *adv.* 1. Por ahí, por allá, por allí, cerca (near), en los contornos; acerca de; hablando de algún lugar o paraje o del número, cantidad o estado de alguna cosa. 2. Tocante a eso.

thereafter [ðɛərˈɑːftər] [dear-af-ta^r], *adv.* 1. Después de eso, en seguida. 2. Según, conforme, en conformidad.

thereat [ðɛərˈæt] [dear-at], *adv.* 1. Por eso; de eso. 2. Allá, en aquel paraje o lugar. 3. A aquel.

thereby [ˈðɛərˈbaɪ] [dear-bai], *adv.* Con eso, por medio de eso; con ello, con aquello; de este modo.

therefore [ˈðɛərfɔːr] [dear-fo^r], *adv. y conj.* 1. Por esto, por eso, por aquello, por esta razón, por tanto o por lo tanto, por consiguiente, de consiguiente o a consecuencia de eso. 2. En recompensa de esto o de aquello.

therefrom [ðɛərˈfrɒm] [dear-from], *adv.* De allí, de allá; de eso, de aquello.

therein [ðɛərˈɪn] [dear-in], *adv.* En esto, en aquello, en eso.

thereinto [ðɛərˈɪntɒ] [dear-in-tu], *adv.* En aquello, en eso; dentro de aquello o de esto.

thereof [ðɛərˈɒv] [dear-ov], *adv.* De esto, de aquello, de ello.

thereon [ðɛərˈɒn] [dear-on], *adv.* En eso, sobre eso.

thereout [ðɛərˈaʊt] [dear-aut], *adv.* De allí; fuera de allí; fuera de eso o de aquello.

thereto [ðɛərˈtuː] [dear-tu], *adv.* A eso, a ello.

thereunder [ðɛərˈʌndər] [dear-an-da^r], *adv.* Debajo de eso.

there upon [ˈðɛərəˈpɒn] [dear-a-pon], *adv.* En consecuencia de eso; sobre eso; al instante.

therewith [ðɛəˈwɪθ] [dea-uiz], *adv.* Con eso o con aquello, luego, inmediatamente.

therewithal [ðɛəˈwɪθəl] [dea-ui-zal], *adv.* A más, además; al mismo tiempo.

therm [θɜːm] [zerm], *s.* Termia.

thermal [ˈθɜːməl] [zer-mal], *a.* Termal, perteneciente al calor, caliente. **Thermal alarm,** alarma automática que suena cuando la temperatura alcanza cierto grado. **Thermal waters,** aguas termales.

thermic [ˈθɜːmɪk] [zer-mik], *a.* Termal, perteneciente o debido al calor.

thermodynamics [ˈθɜːməʊdaɪˈnæmɪks] [zer-mou-dai-na-miks], *s.* Termodinámica, parte de la física que trata de la fuerza mecánica del calor.

thermoelectric [ˈθɜːməʊɪˈlektrɪk] [zer-moi-lek-trik], *a.* Termoeléctrico, relativo a la termoelectricidad.

thermometer [θəˈmɒmɪtər] [zer-mo-mi-ta^r], *s.* Termómetro, instrumento que sirve para medir los grados del calor y del frío.

thermonuclear [ˈθɜːməʊˈnjuːklɪər] [zer-mou-niu-klia^r], *a.* Termonuclear.

thermos [ˈθɜːməs] [zer-mos], *s.* Termo (marca registrada).

thermostat [ˈθɜːməstæt] [zer-mos-tat], *s.* Termostato, aparato para regular automáticamente la temperatura por medio de la expansión diferencial de ciertas substancias.

thesaurus [θɪˈsɔːrəs] [zi-so-ros], *s.* 1. Antiguo almacén griego. 2. Almacén de palabras o de conocimientos, léxico o enciclopedia, diccionario ideológico o de ideas afines.

these [ðiːz] [dis], *pron. pl.* de THIS. Estos, estas.

thesis [ˈθiːsɪs] [zi-sis], *s.* 1. Tesis (dissertation), conclusión, la proposición que se sienta y que se intenta defender. 2. Cuestión, proposición. 3. Tesis, parte no acentuada del pie de verso, disminución del tono de la voz al pronunciar la tesis. *V.* ARSIS.

thespian [ˈθespɪən] [zes-pian], *a.* Trágico, dramático; relativo a Tespis, considerado como el padre de la tragedia griega. - *s.* Actor, actriz.

they [ðeɪ] [dei], *pron. pl.* de HE, SHE o IT. Ellos, ellas. **They didn't come,** ellos no vinieron. **They say he's a millionaire,** dicen o se dice que es millonario.

thick [θɪk] [zik], *a.* 1. Espeso, denso (dense), condensado. 2. Cenagoso, turbio, feculento. 3. Grueso, corpulento, macizo. 4. Continuado, repetido, frecuente. 5. Espeso, que está muy junto y apretado; abundante en. 6. Basto, grosero, tosco. 7. Sobrecargado de vapor, nebuloso, brumoso, sombrío. 8. Embotado, obtuso de inteligencia (stupid), torpe. 9. *(Fam.)* Íntimo, excesivamente familiar. **Thick-lipped,** bezudo. **To speak thick,** hablar con media lengua. **Thick of hearing,** duro de oído, que oye con dificultad. -*s.* 1. Grueso, espesor. 2. Lo más denso, nutrido, tupido o recio. **The thick of the fight,** lo más fuerte del combate. **To go through thick and thin,** atropellar por todo. -*adv.* Frecuentemente, continuadamente; de una manera fuerte. **Thick-headed,** espeso, pesado, que tiene la cabeza dura; torpe de inteligencia. **Thick-set,** (a) rechoncho, grueso, abultado de carnes; (b) plantado muy espeso o dejando poco espacio entre las plantas o árboles. **Thick-skinned,** (a) de pellejo espeso, (b) paquidermo. **Thick stuff,** *(Mar.)* tablones, palmejares. **Scarf thick stuff,** palmejares de los escarpes.

thicken [ˈθɪkən] [zi-ken], *va. y vn.* 1. Espesar, condensar lo líquido o lo fluido. 2. Espesar. 3. Dar fuerza, dar más valor, confirmar. 4. Engrosar, aumentar. 5. Crecer. 6. Condensarse, enturbiarse, cerrarse. **It thickens,** *(Fam. Fig.)* ¡ya escampa!

thicket [ˈθɪkɪt] [zi-kit], *s.* Bosquecito o monte espeso o muy frondoso, soto, espesura o frondosidad; matorral.

thickish [ˈθɪkɪʃ] [zi-kish], *a.* Algo espeso o denso, un poco turbio.

thickly [ˈθɪklɪ] [zi-kli], *adv.* 1. Profundamente. 2. Con frecuencia, continuadamente. **Thickly settled,** muy poblado.

thickness [ˈθɪknɪs] [zik-nes], *s.* 1. Espesor, espesura, densidad (denseness). 2. Espesor, la tercera dimensión de un cuerpo, en oposición al largo y al ancho. 3. Consistencia, el estado de las cosas líquidas cuando se coagulan y toman cuerpo. 4. Grosor de un montón de papel, de las capas de alguna substancia, etc. **It comes in two thickness,** viene en dos grosores. **Thickness of hearing,** dureza de oído.

thick-skulled [ˈθɪkskʌld] [zik-skuld], *a.* Tardo, torpe (clumsy), rudo, de cabeza dura.

thief [θiːf] [zif], *s.* 1. Ladrón, el que roba, estafador. 2. El o lo que causa una pérdida, v. g. de tiempo, de la reputación, etc. 3. *(Prov.)* Seta, pavesa o moco de una luz.

thieve [θiːv] [ziv], *vn.* Hurtar, robar (steal).

thievery [ˈθiːvərɪ] [zi-va-ri], *s.* 1. Latrocinio, hurto, robo (robbery), la acción y costumbre de hurtar o robar. 2. Hurto, robo, la cosa hurtada o robada.

thieving [ˈθiːvɪŋ] [zi-vin], *a. (Coloq.)* Ladrón.

thievish [ˈθiːvɪʃ] [zi-vish], *a.* Inclinado a hurtar, dado al vicio del hurto.

thievishness [ˈθiːvɪʃnɪs] [zi-vish-nes], *s.* Latrocinio.

thigh [θaɪ] [zai], *s.* Muslo, la parte del cuerpo del animal desde la juntura de la cadera hasta la rodilla.

thimble [ˈθɪmbl] [zim-bel], *s.* 1. Dedal. 2. *(Mar.)* Guardacabo. **Thimbleberry,** la frambuesa negra; y también, el frambueso de flor blanca; ambos del Canadá y los Estados Unidos.

thin [θɪn] [zin], *a.* Delgado, delicado, sutil, débil. 2. Flaco (slim), falto de carnes. 3. Ralo, claro que no tiene densidad o solidez. 4. Poco, corto, ligero, escaso, delgado, tenue, pequeño. 5. Claro, poco trabado, que no está turbio o espeso. 6. Raro, diseminado, no espeso ni abundante, poco numeroso. 7. Escaso, pequeño, falto de ingredientes o cualidades características. **A thin plate of metal,** una placa delgada de metal. **A thin crop,** una cosecha escasa. **A thin disguise,** un disfraz ligero. **Thin blood,** sangre clara. **Thin air,** aire enrarecido. **A thin suspicion,** una sospecha sin fundamento. **To make thin,** descarnar; hacer enflaquecer. **To grow thin,** enflaquecer. **To make thinner,** adelgazar.

thin, *va.* 1. Enrarecer, atenuar, poner ralo. 2. Adelgazar. 3. Aclarar, clarificar los licores. 4. Aclarar, entresacar un bosque, una arboleda, etc. 5. Dejar claro, disminuir el número. 6. Diluir, rebajar, aclarar. **Thin down,** (a) adelgazar (become slimmer); (b) diluir, aclarar. **Thin out,** (a) disminuir, hacerse menos denso; (b) entresacar.

thine [ðaɪn] [dain], *pron.* tuyo. *-a.* Tu, tus: se emplea en vez de *thy* delante de una vocal. **Thine eyes,** tus ojos. **The glory is thine,** la gloria es tuya.

thing [θɪŋ] [zing], *s.* 1. Cosa, en contraposición a persona, objeto (object), substancia. 2. Asunto (matter, affari), objeto o existencia no conocida o no caracterizada por un nombre definido; asunto, hecho. **I'm fed up with the whole thing,** estoy harto del asunto. 3. Evento (event), circunstancia, acontecimiento. **Above all things,** sobre todas las cosas o sobre todo. 4. *pl.* Cosas, efectos personales, pertenencias (belongings); hábitos, vestidos. 5. Se usa algunas veces por desprecio o como diminutivo hablando de personas. **I pity the poor little thing,** tengo lástima del pobrecito o de la pobrecita. **Anything,** algo, cualquier cosa que sea. **Anything but,** otra cosa que, nada menos que. **No such thing,** no hay tal cosa; nada. **The thing,** lo conveniente, lo que está de moda, lo necesario o lo que se desea. **To make a good thing of,** *(Fam.)* Sacar gran provecho de una cosa. **As things stand,** en el punto en que están las cosas.

thingumabob [ˈθɪŋəmɪbɒb] [zin-ga-mi-bob], *s. (Coloq.)* Cosa, chisme.

think [θɪŋk] [zink], *va. y vn.* 1. Pensar, imaginar, meditar, discurrir, considerar, idear. 2. Pensar, reflexionar, examinar con cuidado. 3. Pensar, intentar hacer una cosa o hacer ánimo de ejecutarla. 4. Pensar, creer (believe), juzgar, formar concepto. 5. Proponerse (plan), formar designio, tener intención de. 6. *(vn.)* Traer a la memoria, pensar en, se usa con *on* o *upon.* **To think of,** o **to think upon,** pensar en, reflexionar acerca de, meditar, considerar; tener la mira en. **To think well o ill of one,** pensar bien o mal de uno, tener buena o mala opinión de él. **As you think fit,** como Ud. guste, como Ud. quiera. **To think scorn,** desdeñarse. **Methinks, methought,** me parece a mí, creía yo. **You have to think ahead,** tienes que ser previsor. **Think back,** recordar. **A well thought-out proposal,** una propuesta bien elaborada. **Think over things,** primero piénsatelo bien. **Think through,** planear detenidamente. **Think up,** inventar, crear, idear. *-s.* **I'll have to have a think about it,** tendré que pensarlo.

thinker [ˈθɪŋkəʳ] [zin-kaʳ], *s.* Pensador.

thinking [ˈθɪŋkɪŋ] [zin-kin], *s.* 1. Pensamiento, ideas, la acción y efecto de pensar, meditación, reflexión. 2. Juicio, parecer, opinión. **Way of thinking,** modo de pensar, opinión, parecer. **To my thinking,** a mi parecer, en mi opinión. *-a.* Pensante, inteligente.

think tank [ˈθɪŋktæŋk] [zink-tank], *s.* Gabinete estratégico, comité asesor.

thinly [ˈθɪnlɪ] [zin-li], *adv.* 1. Delgadamente, delicamente. 2. Poco en corto número, apenas (scarcely). **Thinly sown,** claro: se dice del sembrado.

thinner [ˈθɪnəʳ] [zi-naʳ], *s.* Disolvente (solvent), diluyente.

thinness [ˈθɪnnɪs] [zin-nes], *s.* 1. Tenuidad, delgadez, sutileza. 2. Escasez. 3. Raleza, lo contrario de espesura. 4. Fineza (slimness), ligereza. 5. Falta de vistosidad, poca consistencia.

thin-skinned [ˈθɪnˈskɪnd] [zin-skind], *a.* Susceptible.

third [θɜːd] [zerd], *a.* Tercer, tercero, ordinal de *three,* tres. **Third rate,** de tercer orden, de tercera clase. **George the Third,** Jorge Tercero. *-s.* 1. Tercio, la tercera parte. 2. *(Mús.)* Tercera. **Two-thirds,** dos terceras partes. *-adv.* En tercer lugar. **Third class,** de tercera clase.

thirdly [ˈθɜːdlɪ] [zerd-li], *adv.* En tercer lugar.

thirst [θɜːst] [zerst], *s.* 1. Sed, deseo o apetito de beber. **To quench the thirst,** apagar la sed. 2. Sed, deseo vehemente o anhelo y gana ardiente de alguna cosa. **Thirst of riches,** ansia o sed de riquezas. **Thirst for vengeance,** sed de venganza.

thirst, *va. y vn.* 1. Tener o padecer sed. 2. Desear con anhelo y ansia. 3. Desear beber. **To thirst after** o **for,** ansiar, anhelar (yearn), desear con ansia o vehemencia.

thirstiness [ˈθɜːstɪnɪs] [zers-ti-nes], *s.* 1. Sed, deseo de beber. 2. Sed, el deseo ansia ardiente por alguna cosa.

thirsty [ˈθɜːstɪ] [zers-ti], *a.* 1. Sediento, que padece o tiene sed. 2. Sediento, que desea con ansia alguna cosa. **Blood thirsty,** sanguinario.

thirteen [ˈθɜːˈtiːn] [zer-tiin], *a. y s.* Trece. **She is thirteen,** ella tiene trece años.

thirteenth [ˈθɜːˈtiːnθ] [zer-tiinz], *a.* Décimo tercio, ordinal de trece. **On the thirteenth of January,** el trece de enero.

thirtieth [ˈθɜːtɪɪθ] [zer-tiez], *a.* Trigésimo, ordinal de treinta.

thirty [ˈθɜːtɪ] [zer-ti], *a. y s.* Treinta.

this [ðɪs] [dis], *a.* Este, esta, esto, que está presente; se refiere a lo que está presente o más cerca que otra cosa. *-pron.* Éste, ésta, esto. **This plant,** esta planta. **This or that,** esto o aquello, el uno o el otro. **These three years I come seeking fruit,** hace tres años que vengo a buscar fruta. **By this time,** ahora, al presente, a este tiempo. **This is the way,** este es el camino.

thistle [ˈθɪsl] [di-sel], *s. (Bot.)* Cardo; una de varias plantas espinosas de la familia de las compuestas. **Canada thistle, cursed thistle,** cardo silvestre. **Carline thistle,** ajonjera, carlina común. **Fuller's thistle,** cardón, cardencha, cardo de batanero. **Milk thistle, Our Ladyps thistle,** cardo lechoso, cardo de Nuestra Señora. **Thistle down,** vello, borrilla de cardo. **Scotch thistle,** cardo que se considera como emblema nacional de Escocia. **Thistle-finch, thistle-bird,** jilguero. *V.* GOLDFINCH.

thistly [ˈθɪslɪ] [dis-li], *adv.* Lleno de cardos.

thither [ˈθɪðəʳ] [di-daʳ], *adv.* 1. Allá, hacia aquel lugar, en aquella direccion. 2. A ese fin, punto o resultado. **Hither and thither,** acá y allá.

tho' [ðəʊ] [dou], *conj.* Contracción de THOUGH.

thole [θəʊl] [zoul], *s.* 1. Tolete, escálamo, gavilán donde se apoya el remo al tiempo de remar. Thole-pin, tolete. 2. Uno de los dos asideros por donde se coge el mango de la guadaña.

thong [θɒŋ] [zon], *s.* Correa o correhuela, tira larga de cuero.

Thor [θɔːʳ] [zoʳ], *s.* El dios escandinavo de la guerra y de la agricultura, bienhechor de la humanidad.

thoracic [θɔːˈræsɪk] [zo-ra-sik], *a.* Torácico, que pertenece al tórax.

thorax [ˈθɔːræks] [zo-raks], *s.* 1. Tórax, cavidad del pecho de los animales vertebrados. 2. Región media del cuerpo de un insecto entre la cabeza y el abdomen.

thorium [ˈθɔːrɪəm] [zo-riom], *s. (Quím.)* Torio.

thorn [θɔːn] [zorn], *va.* 1. Penetrar o traspasar con una espina o púa. 2. Asegurar con una espina. 3. proveer de espinas para cualquier objeto. *-s.* 1. *(Bot.)* Espina (spine), púa que nace del tejido leñoso o vascular de ciertas plantas. 2. Espino, arbusto del género Crataegus; majuelo. *V.* HAWTHORN. 3. Espina, pesadumbre, zozobra (anxiety), cualquier cosa que molesta. **To be upon thorns,** estar en ascuas. **Thorn-apple,** *(Bot.)* Estramonio.

thornback [ˈθɔːnbæk] [zorn-bak], *s. (Ict.)* Raya espinosa.

thornless [ˈθɔːnlɪs] [zorn-les], *a.* Falto de espinas o púas.

thorny [ˈθɔːnɪ] [zor-ni], *a.* 1. Espinoso, lleno de espinas. 2. Espinoso, arduo, penoso. **Thorny-woodcock,** especie de limazo con cáscara.

thorough [ˈθʌrə] [za-ro], *a.* Entero, cabal, completo, perfecto, acabado; consumado, pefecto, meticuloso (meticulous); (en mala parte) loco rematado, pícaro consumado. *-prep. (Des.)* V. THROUGH.

thoroughbred [ˈθʌrəbred] [za-ro-bred], *a.* De sangre pura; osado, valeroso; de forma elegante. **Thoroughbred horse,** caballo de pura sangre.

thoroughfare [ˈθʌrəfɛəʳ] [za-ro-feaʳ], *s.* Paso, tránsito o camino libre por donde se puede pasar. **No thoroughfare,** no se pasa; calle cerrada; el público no entra.

thorough-going [ˈθʌrəgəʊɪŋ] [za-ro-gouing], *a.* Completo, muy eficaz, entero; que va hasta el fin.

thoroughly [ˈθʌrəlɪ] [za-ro-li], *adv.* Enteramente, cabalmente, a fondo, rigurosamente (strictly).

thoroughness [ˈθʌrənɪs] [za-ro-nes], *s.* Meticulosidad, esmero (care).

thorough-paced [ˈθʌrəpeɪst] [za-ro-peist], *a.* Cabal, completo, perfecto.

thorough-wax [ˈθʌrəwæks] [za-ro-uaks], *s.* Oreja de liebre. *V.* HARE'S-EAR.

thorp [θɔːp] [zorp], *s.* Lugar, aldea.

those [ðəʊz] [dous], *a. pl.* de THAT. Aquellos, aquellas; esos, esas. *pron. pl.* Aquéllos, aquéllas, ésos, ésas. **Those who o those which,** los que o las que. **Those of,** los de o las de.

thou [ðaʊ] [dau], *pron.* Tú, segunda persona del pronombre personal. *Thou* no se usa en inglés en el lenguaje familiar, a no ser por los cuáqueros; pero se usa frecuentemente en la poesía y en el estilo sublime. **Thou and thee,** trato demasiado familiar.

thou, *va.* Tutear; hablar o tratar con demasiada familiaridad; hablar a uno en tono de desprecio. **To thee and thou,** tutear.

though [ðəʊ] [dau], *conj.* Aunque, bien que, no obstante, sin embargo, aun cuando. **What though,** aun que, qué, importa que. **Though he were dead, yet shall he live,** aun cuando él muera, vivirí. **As though,** como si; como que; con todo. *-adv.* Sin embargo. **It's easy, though, to understand their feelings,** sin embargo, es fácil comprender sus sentimientos.

thought [θɔːt] [zot], *pret.* y *pp.* del verbo THINK. *-s.* 1. Pensamiento, el acto y efecto de pensar; la especie concebida o formada; meditación seria, reflexión. 2. Pensamiento, juicio, dictamen, opinión. 3. Designio, proyecto, intención. 4. Memoria, recordación. 5. Cuidado, solicitud, atención. 6. *(Fam.)* Poquito, una migaja. **To entertain ill thoughts of one.** tener mala opinión de alguna persona. **The thought strikes me,** me ocurre la idea. **To take thought,** sentir inquietud. **To have some thoughts of,** tener el proyecto o la idea de; pensar en.

thoughtful [ˈθɔːtfʊl] [zot-ful], *a.* 1. Pensativo (pensive), meditabundo. 2. Atento (kind), cuidadoso, considerado. **How thoughtful of you!,** ¡qué considerado por tu parte!

thoughtfully [ˈθɔːtfəlɪ] [zot-fu-li], *adv.* Cuidadosamente, solícitamente, consideradamente (considerately); de un modo muy pensativo o meditabundo; con reflexión, con inquietud.

thoughtfulness [ˈθɔːtfəlnɪs] [zot-ful-nes], *s.* Meditación profunda, reflexión; cuidado, afán, inquietud; previsión.

thoughtless [ˈθɔːtlɪs] [zot-les], *a.* 1. Atolondrado, descuidado, irreflexivo (unthinking). 2. Desconsiderado (inconsiderate), incauto; insensato, disipado, impróvido.

thoughtlessly [ˈθɔːtlɪslɪ] [zot-les-li], *adv.* Descuidadamente, negligentemente, sin consideración, sin reflexión (without thinking), sin cuidado.

thoughtlessness [ˈθɔːtlɪsnɪs] [zot-les-nes], *s.* 1. Descuido, omisión, inadvertencia, desconsideración. 2. Ligereza, indiscreción, atolondramiento.

thought-provoking [ˈθɔːtprəˌvəʊkɪŋ] [zot-pro-vou-kin], *a.* Que hace pensar o reflexionar.

thousand [ˈθaʊzənd] [zau-sand], *a.* 1. Mil, diez veces ciento. 2. También se usa indefinidamente para denotar un número o cantidad muy grande. **He will find a thousand occasions for doing it,** hallará mil ocasiones de hacerlo. *-s.* 1. Mil. 2. Millar; guarismo que significa mil. **By thousands,** por millares, a millares.

thousandth [ˈθaʊzəndθ] [zau-sandz], *a.* Milésimo, el ordinal de mil. *-s.* Milésima parte de un todo.

thrall [θrɔːl] [zrol], *va.* *(Poet. o des.)* Esclavizar, avasallar.

thraldom [ˈθrɔːldəm] [zrol-dom], *s.* Esclavitud (slavery), servidumbre.

thrash [θræʃ] [zrash], *va.* 1. Trillar o apalear grano; desgranar; batir; sacudir; apalear; azotar. 2. Golpear (beat) o dar de palos a alguno, zurrar. *(Vulg.)* Sobar. *-vn.* 1. Trillar el grano. 2. Arrojarse, agitarse, moverse violentamente. 3. Trabajar, ocuparse en cosas serviles. **Thrash out,** discutir, tratar de resolver.

thrasher [ˈθræʃəʳ] [zra-shaʳ], *s.* 1. Trillador, apaleador de granos. 2. Máquina para trillar. 3. Malviz, especie de tordo americano. 4. *V.* THRESHER.

thrashing [ˈθræʃɪŋ] [zra-shin], *s.* Paliza (beating), zurra.

thread [θred] [zred], *s.* 1. Hilo, torzal delgado. 2. Filete (de tornillo, de rosca). 3. Filamento (filament), hilito. 4. Hilo, continuación de alguna cosa que se está haciendo. Skein of

thread, madeja de hilo. **Thread-like,** semejante a hilo, como hilo, filiforme. **Thread and thrum,** hilo o hilaza, mezcla de bueno y malo. **Thread of a conversation,** hilo de una conversación.

thread, *va.* 1. Enhebrar. 2. Ensartar (skewer), colar, atravesar a lo largo, pasar por. **He threaded his way through the crowd,** se abrió paso entre la multitud. 3. Coser.

threadbare [ˈθredbɛəʳ] [zred-beaʳ], *a.* Raído (worn-out), muy usado, gastado hasta verse los hilos.

threadworm [ˈθredwɜːm] [zred-uem], *s.* Lombricilla filiforme, ascáride; se llama también *pinworm.*

threat [θret] [zret], *s.* Amenaza. **To obtain money with threats,** obtener dinero con amenazas.

threaten [ˈθretn] [zre-ten], *va.* 1. Amenazar (menace), hacer amenazas a, aterrar. 2. Amenazar o amargar; hablando de cosas, es pronosticar algún mal.

threatener [ˈθretnəʳ] [zret-naʳ], *s.* Amenazador.

threatening [ˈθretnɪŋ] [zret-nin], *s.* Amenaza, acción de amenazar. *-a.* Amenazador, terrible, amenazante.

threateningly [ˈθretnɪŋlɪ] [zret-nin-li], *adv.* Con amenazas.

threatful [ˈθretfʊl] [zret-ful], *a.* Lleno de amenazas.

three [θriː] [zri], *a.* Tres, número cardinal. *-s.* Tres, la suma de tres unidades; el guarismo que representa este número. **Three-celled,** trilocular, que tiene tres células. **Three-cleft,** *(Bot.)* Trífido, que está dividido en tres. **Three-cornered,** triangular, de tres cuernos, de tres esquinas o ángulos. **Three-decker,** navío de tres puentes. **Three deep,** en tres hileras o filas. **Three-leaved,** trifoliado, de tres hojas. **Three-parted,** *(Bot.)* Tripartido. **Three-ply,** triple, de tres pliegues. **Three-lobed,** trilobulado, dividido en tres lóbulos. **Three-quarter,** de las tres cuartas partes. **Three-stringed,** de tres cuerdas. **Three-valved,** de tres válvulas, de tres conchas.

threefold [ˈθriːfəʊld] [zri-fould], *a.* Tríplice, triplo.

treepence [ˈθrepəns] [zre-pens], *s.* Tres peniques, moneda pequeña de plata que tenía este valor.

threepenny [ˈθrepənɪ] [zre-pe-ni], *a.* Vil (vile).

threepile [ˈθriːpaɪl] [zri-pail], *s.* Terciopelo.

threescore [ˈθriːskɔːʳ] [zri-skoʳ], *a.* y *s.* Sesenta; tres veces una veintena. **Threescore years and ten,** setenta años.

thresh [ˈθreʃ] [zresh], *va.* *V.* TO THRASH.

thresher [ˈθreʃəʳ] [zre-shaʳ], *s.* 1. Zorra marina, especie de tiburón. 2. Para otras acepciones, véase THRASHER.

threshold [ˈθreʃhəʊld] [zresh-jould], *s.* 1. Umbral (doorway), quicio, piedra o madero colocado al pie de la abertura de una puerta; entrada. 2. Punto de partida de entrada.

threw [θruː] [zru], *pret.* del verbo TO THROW.

thrice [θraɪs] [zrais], *adv.* Tres veces; de una manera o grado triple; de aquí, completamente.

thrid [θrɪd] [zrid], *vn.* Colar, pasar por un paraje estrecho.

thrift [θrɪft] [zrift], *s.* 1. Economía, frugalidad (frugality), cuidado y prudencia en el manejo de sus negocios. 2. Ganancia, utilidad, ahorro. 3. Crecimiento rápido, desarrollo, como el de una planta. 4. *(Bot.)* Planta llamada también *sea-pink,* una de las varias especies del género Armeria.

thriftily [ˈθrɪftɪlɪ] [zrif-ti-li], *adv.* Frugalmente, económicamente.

thriftiness [ˈθrɪftɪnɪs] [zrif-ti-nes], *s.* Frugalidad, parsimonía, economía.

thriftless [ˈθrɪftlɪs] [zrift-les], *a.* Manirroto, pródigo; extravagante.

thrifty [ˈθrɪftɪ] [zrif-ti], *a.* 1. Frugal, económico; de gastos moderados. 2. Próspero, feliz en los negocios. 3. Floreciente, que crece o se desarrolla con rapidez.

thrill [θrɪl] [zril], *va.* 1. Penetrar, hacer experimentar una emoción viva, emocionar. 2. Hacer estremecerse. *-vn.* 1. Estremecerse o conmoverse por alguna pasión violenta; experimentar una emoción viva. 2. Penetrar, herir el oído con sonidos o gritos violentos y agudos. 3. Temblar, moverse temblando. **To thrill with pleasure,** temblar de gusto. **To thrill the blood,** hervir la sangre. *-s.* Temblor (tremor), estremecimiento, emoción (excitement). **Meeting him was a real thrill,** fue verdaderamente emocionante conocerle.

thriller [ˈθrɪləʳ] [zri-laʳ], *f.* Novela, película de suspense o misterio.

thrilling [ˈθrɪlɪŋ] [zri-lin], *a.* Que pasma, que conmueve; vivo.

thrive [θraɪv] [zraiv], *vn.* 1. Medrar, prosperar, adelantar, tener éxito, enriquecerse. 2. Crecer con vigor, desarrollarse (grow).

thriver [ˈθraɪvəʳ] [zrai-vaʳ], *s.* El que medra o prospera.

thriving [ˈθraɪvɪŋ] [zrai-vin], *a.* Próspero. **A thriving black market,** un floreciente mercado negro.

thrivingly [ˈθraɪvɪŋlɪ] [zrai-vin-li], *adv.* Prósperamente.

thro' [θraʊ] [zru], *adv.* y *prep.* abrev. de THROUGH.

throat [θrəʊt] [zrout], *s.* 1. Garganta, la parte interior del cuello, también gaznate. **I have a sore throat,** me duele la garganta. **To cut the throat,** degollar. 2. El camino principal de alguna parte. 3. Pasaje u orificio; *(Bot.)* entrada del tubo de la corola; garganta, parte estrecha. 4. *(Mar.)* Cangreja. **Throat-halliard,** *(Mar.)* Driza de cangreja. **Throat-pipe,** traquiarteria. **Throat-seizing,** garganteadura.

throaty [ˈθrəʊtɪ] [zrou-ti], *a.* Ronco; de garganta, gutural.

throb [θrɒb] [zrob], *vn.* 1. Latir (beat), palpitar. 2. Vibrar, de cualquier modo que sea. *V.* THRILL.

throb, *s.* Latido, pulsación, palpitación.

throbbing [ˈθrɒbɪŋ] [zro-bin], *a.* Vibrante, palpitante.

throes [θrəʊz] [zrous], *s.pl.* Angustia, gran dolor, dolor de parto, agonía de la muerte.

thrombosis [θrɒmˈbəʊsɪs] [zrom-bou-sis], *s.* *(Med.)* Trombosis.

throne [θrəʊn] [zroun], *s.* 1. Trono, asiento regio, la sede de un obispo en una catedral. **To ascend the throne,** ascender al trono. 2. Poder soberano; el que tiene el poder soberano. **Thrones,** *pl.* Tronos, hablando de los espíritus angélicos.

throng [θrɒŋ] [zron], *s.* Tropel de gente, multitud amontonada, muchedumbre (crowd).

throng, *va.* 1. Apretar, rellenar cierto espacio. 2. Apretar o estrujar a uno la concurrencia muy numerosa y apiñada de gente. *-vn.* Venir en tropel, amontonarse la gente, acudir en gran número. **The audience thronged the hall,** el auditorio llenó la sala de bote en bote.

throttle [ˈθrɒtl] [zro-tel], *s.* 1. Gaznate, garguero, traquiarteria. 2. *(Mec.)* Válvula de cuello o de paso en las máquinas de vapor; también se llama *throttle-valve*. **At full throttle,** a toda máquina. 3. Acelerador (accelerator).

throttle, *va.* Ahogar (strangle), sofocar. *-vn.* Sofocarse, ahogarse, respirar con dificultad.

through [θruː] [zru], *a.* Que va desde el principio hasta el fin con pocas paradas o sin ninguna. **A through train,** tren terminal. *-adv.* 1. De un lado a otro. **I am wet through,** estoy calado hasta los huesos, enteramente. 2. Desde el principio hasta el fin, todo el camino. 3. Hasta el fin, de parte a parte. 4. *(Fam.)* A buen fin. *-prep.* 1. Al través de, de un extremo a otro par, de parte a parte, de medio a medio. 2. Por medio de, por entre, de o al través, enteramente, del todo. **Through your influence,** mediante el influjo de Ud.; por mediación de Ud. 3. En, en medio de; por. 4. Con motivo de, por efecto de, por causa de. **Fish swim through the water,** los peces nadan por o en medio del agua. **Through all Spain,** por toda España. **To carry through,** llevar a buen fin. **To fall through,** salir mal, fracasar. **This train runs through,** este tren va hasta el término.

throughout [θruːˈaʊt] [zru-aut], *prep.* Por todo, en todo, a lo largo de; durante todo (all over). **Throughout Europe,** en toda Europa. *-adv.* En todas partes.

throughway [ˈθruːweɪ] [zru-uei], *s.* Autopista.

throve [θrəʊv] [zrouv], *pret.* del verbo TO THRIVE.

throw [θrəʊ] [zrou], *va.* y *vn.* (*pret.* THREW, *pp.* THROWN). 1. Echar, arrojar, tirar, disparar (fire), lanzar. 2. Echar, tirar, tender, derribar al suelo (pull down). 3. Echarse, arrojarse. 4. Tirar los dados. 5. Impeler, empujar con violencia; estrellar. 6. Desmontar (unseat), desarzonar, echar al suelo. 7. Echar, tirar algo apresurada o negligentemente. 8. Despojarse de; desechar o mudar, v. g. como lo hace una serpiente con su piel. 9. Torcer la seda, convertir los filamentos en hilo. 10. Parir (animals). 11. Perder con premeditación (race, game). 12. Dar forma a los objetos de alfarería.

throw about, echar alrededor de; arrojar por uno y otro lado.

throw aside, arrojar, poner de lado.

throw away, arrojar, rechazar, desperdiciar, malgastar; desechar, echar a un lado, arrinconar.

throw back, rechazar hacia atrás; volver.

throw down, derribar, destruir, echar por tierra; subvertir, trastornar.

throw in, echar dentro, arrojar en; intercalar, insertar; añadir, dar de más., dar además de lo convenido.

throw off, echar o arrojar de sí o de alguna parte; expeler, hacer salir, dejar o renunciar una cosa.

throw on, ponerse, echarse encima. **To throw open,** abrir de par en par.

throw out, proferir, hacer creer; echar afuera, expeler, excluir, esparcir, exhalar, emitir, v. g. una opinión; hacer observaciones, insinuar. **To throw out of,** arrojar por. **To throw overboard,** *(Mar.)* Echar en la mar o tirar a la mar. **To throw silk,** torcer seda. **To throw together,** improvisar.

throw up, arrojar por alto o en alto; echar al aire; elevar, levantar; renunciar a, abandonar, deshacerse de un cargo, vomitar.

throw, *s.* 1. Tiro, el movimiento de una cosa arrojada o lanzada con violencia, y también el espacio que recorre la cosa así arrojada. 2. Un rato, un corto espacio de tiempo. 3. Golpe, esfuerzo. 4. **Within a stone's throw,** a tiro de piedra. 5. Cubrecama (bedspred). 6. Echarpe, chal (shawl).

throwback [ˈθruːbæk] [zru-bak], *s.* Atavismo, retroceso.

thrum [θrʌm] [zram], *s.* Cadillos, hilo basto; hilo destorcido.

thrum, *va.* Rascar las cuerdas de un instrumento, tocarlas mal: golpear ligeramente con los dedos, tamborilear. *-s.* Sonido que se hace golpeando ligeramente.

thrush [θrʌʃ] [zrash], *s.* 1. *(Orn.)* Tordo, ave de los géneros Turdus o Mrula; zorzal, malvís. 2. *(Med.)* Afta, úlcera que se forma en la superficie interior de la boca. 3. *(Vet.)* Higo, enfermedad que ataca el talón del caballo.

thrust [θrʌst] [zrast], *va.* y *vn.* (*pret.* y *pp.* THRUST). 1. Introducir con violencia. 2. Empujar (push), impeler. 3. Apretar, estrechar, cerrar. 4. Entremeterse, meterse, mezclarse en lo que a uno no le toca. 5. Introducirse en alguna parte sin ser llamado. 6. Acometer con ímpetu y violencia, embestir con uno. 7. Obligar a hacer algo por fuerza.

thrust aside, rechazar, empujar a un lado.

thrust away, rechazar, apartar, arrojar, alejar.

thrust back, rechazar.

thrust down, echar abajo, introducir, hacer entrar.

thrust forward, empujar hacia adelante, echar adelante.

thrust in, meter o introducir por fuerza o con violencia.

thrust out, echar o arrojar afuera.

thrust together, apretar o estrujar unas cosas con otras.

thrust through, dar de puñaladas, atravesar de parte a parte con algún instrumento punzante.

thrust upon, imponer a, hacer aceptar a, hacer creer cosas falsas a otro.

thrust, *s.* 1. Empuje repentino, empuje a lo largo; empujón (push), estocada; lanzada; cualquier bote o golpe que se tira con un arma o instrumento punzante. 2. Arremetida, ataque (attack), ofensiva (advance). 3. *(Mec.)* Empuje mutuo entre dos cuerpos en contacto, presión horizontal hacia el exterior; tracción, impulso del tornillo, empuje de la hélice. 4. *(Fís.)* Empuje, potencia o capacidad de empuje.

thrusting [ˈθrʌstɪŋ] [zras-tin], *s.* Ambicioso.

thud [θʌd] [zad], *vn.* Hacer un ruido sordo. *-s.* Sonido sordo y pesado, como el de un cuerpo duro que da contra otro comparativamente blando, el golpe que produce dicho sonido.

thug [θʌg] [zag], *s.* 1. Miembro de una secta de asesinos fanáticos de la India. 2. De aquí, asesino, matón (bully).

thumb [θʌm] [zam], *s.* Pulgar, el dedo primero y más grueso de los de la mano. **Thumb-nut,** tuerca con orejetas. **Thumb-screw,** tuerca con orejetas, tornillo de presión, antiguo instrumento de tortura.

thumb, *va.* Manosear con poca destreza (grope); emporcar alguna cosa con los dedos al manosearla. **Thumb through,** hojear.

thumbnail [ˈθʌmneɪl] [zam-neil], *s.* Uña del pulgar. **Thumbnail sketch,** esbozo en miniatura.

thumbnotch ['θʌmnɒtʃ] [zam-noch], *s.* Recorte en diccionarios, índices, etc. para facilitar su consulta.

thumbtack ['θʌmtæk] [zam-tak], *s.* Chinche, tachuela.

thump [θʌmp] [zamp], *s.* Porrazo, golpe que causa un sonido sordo (blow); puñada.

thump, *va.* y *vn.* 1. Aporrear, cascar, apuñear, acachetear. **He thumped the table with his fist,** pegó un puñetazo en la mesa. 2. Dar un porrazo o un golpe, golpear pesadamente.

thumping ['θʌmpɪŋ] [zam-pin], *a. (Coloq.)* Aplastante.

thunder ['θʌndəʳ] [zan-daʳ], *s.* 1. Trueno, el ruido que acompaña al rayo. 2. Cualquier estruendo o ruido violento. **The thunder of the traffic,** el estruendo del tráfico. 3. *(Fig.)* Rayo: denunciación fulminante, excomunión. **Thunder-storm,** tormenta acompañada de truenos.

thunder, *va.* y *vn.* 1. Tronar, oírse el ruido del trueno. 2. Tronar, dar estampidos o estallidos como los de las armas de fuego. 3. Tempestar, atronar, aturdir a voces o a gritos, gritar (shout). 4. Fulminar o arrojar rayos. 5. Fulminar penas, excomuniones, etc. **It thunders,** truena.

thunderbolt ['θʌndəbəʊlt] [zan-da-boult], *s.* 1. Rayo o centella despedida de las nubes. 2. Fulminación, censura, excomunión eclesiástica.

thunderclap ['θʌndəklæp] [zan-da-klap], *s.* Trueno, rayo, tronada o tempestad con truenos.

thundercloud ['θʌndəklaʊd] [zan-da-klaud], *s.* Nubarrón.

thunderer ['θʌndərəʳ] [zan-da-raʳ], *s.* Tonante o tronador.

thunderous ['θʌndərəs] [zan-da-ros], *a.* Atronador, que produce truenos.

thunderstrike ['θʌndəstraɪk] [zan-da-straik], *va.* Fulminar, herir con rayo o centella; aturdir o espantar con alguna cosa muy extraordinaria y sorprendente. Este verbo se usa poco a no ser en el participio pasado, **thunderstruck,** anonadado, estupefacto, turulato. **To be thunderstruck,** *(Fam.)* Quedarse helado o de una pieza.

thundery ['θʌndərɪ] [zan-da-ri], *a.* Tormentoso.

thurible ['θjʊərɪbl] [ziua-ri-bol], *s.* Turíbulo, incensario, braserillo que sirve para incensar.

Thursday ['θɜːzdɪ] [zres-di], *s.* Jueves, el quinto día de la semana.

thus [ðʌs] [das], *adv.* 1. Así, de este modo (in this way), de esta suerte, en estos términos. 2. Sí, tanto; a ese grado. 3. Siendo así, en estas condiciones. 4. Por lo tanto, por consiguiente (consequently). (*Thus* se limita hoy al estilo literario y formal, y lo reemplaza *so* en el uso ordinario). **Thus it is,** así es que, así es como. **Thus far,** hasta aquí. **Thus much,** basta no más, baste esto. **Thus it comes to pass,** así es como viene a ser, a acontecer.

thus, *s.* Incienso, resina aromática.

thwack [dwæk] [duak], *va.* Aporrear, pegar, zurrar, golpear con alguna cosa plana o redondeada. V. WHACK. -*s.* Zurra, tunda, golpe dado con alguna cosa plana (blow). (Var. de WHACK).

thwart [dwɔːt] [duort], *a.* Travesero, transversal, travieso. -*vt.* 1. *(Ant.)* Mover obstáculos, contrarrestar, frustrar. **The police managed to thwart the robbers,** la policía logró burlar a los ladrones. 2. *(Poco us.)* Ir en contra; estar en oposición con o a.

thy [ðaɪ] [dai], Adjetivo posesivo correspondiente a *Thou,* tu, tus.

thyme [ðaɪm] [daim], *s. (Bot.)* Tomillo, cualquier hierba olorosa del género Thymus.

thymus ['θaɪməs] [dai-mos], *s.* Timo, glándula sin conducto que se halla en el cuello de muchos vertebrados.

thyroid ['θaɪrɔɪd] [zai-roid], *a.* Tiroideo. -*s.* Tiroides (glándula).

thyself [ðaɪ'self] [daiself], *pron. recip.* Tú mismo, ti mismo. **Love thy neighbor as thyself,** ama a tu prójimo como a ti mismo.

ti [tiː] [ti], *s. (Mús.)* Si.

tiara [tɪ'ɑːrə] [tia-ra], *s.* Tiara, ornamento de la cabeza; diadema.

Tibet [tɪ'bet] [ti-bet], *s.* El Tíbet.

Tibetan [tɪ'betən] [ti-be-tan], *s.* 1. Tibetano. 2. Lengua tibetana. -*a.* Tibetano.

tibia ['tɪbɪə] [ti-bia], *s.* 1. Tibia, el hueso más grueso (interior) de la pierna; un hueso semejante del ave. 2. Cuarta articulación de la pata de un insecto. 3. Flauta primitiva.

tibial ['tɪbɪəl] [ti-bial], *a.* Tibial que pertenece al hueso tibia.

tic [tɪk] [tik], *s.* Tic.

tick [tɪk] [tik], *s.* 1. El golpe del reloj o cosa semejante; tic tac, ruido ligero producido por un movimiento acompasado. 2. Marca indicadora que se usa al confrontar una cosa. 3. *(Zool.)* Garrapata, rezno, un insecto que se agarra fuertemente a los animales. 4. Funda de almohada. 5. *(Fam.)* Crédito, préstamo de dinero o géneros sin más seguridad que la confianza que se tiene en el que lo recibe. **To buy upon tick,** comprar al fiado. **Bed-tick,** cotí o terliz con que se hacen almohadas y colchones.

tick, *va.* 1. Sonar produciendo tic tac; indicar la hora con ruido ligero; se usa a menudo con *off.* 2. Confrontar, haciendo una marca indicadora. -*vn.* Hacer sonido de tic, tac, batir. **Tick over,** estar en marcha, marchar al ralentí. **The business is just ticking over,** el negocio va tirando.

ticker ['tɪkəʳ] [ti-kaʳ], *s.* El o lo que produce un sonido de tic tac; es especial, 1. *(Fam. E. U.)* instrumento telegráfico receptor, particularmente un indicador de valores; 2. *(Ger.)* reloj de bolsillo. 3. *(Coloq.)* Corazón (heart).

ticker tape ['tɪkəteɪp] [ti-ka-teip], *s.* Cinta de teletipo. **A ticker-tape parade,** un desfile triunfal.

ticken ['tɪkn] [ti-ken], *ticking* ['tɪkɪŋ] [ti-kin], *s.* Terliz, cotí o cotín para colchones.

ticket ['tɪkɪt] [ti-ket], *s.* 1. Billete, boleta, *(Mex.)* boleto; tarjeta de entrada; billete, cédula de transporte por ferrocarril. 2. Rótulo, marbete; marca que se pone a alguna cosa para reconocerla, etiqueta (label). 3. *(E. U.)* Balota; de aquí, lista de candidatos en una elección (list of candidates). **Excursion ticket, roundtrip ticket,** billete de ida y vuelta *(F. C.)* **Play-house ticket,** boletín o boleta de teatro. **Lottery-ticket,** cédula o billete de lotería.

ticket, *va.* Fijar, pegar un rótulo o marbete a; rotular (label), marcar.

ticketholder ['tɪkɪthəʊldəʳ] [ti-kit-joul-daʳ], *s.* Persona en posesión de una entrada, boleto, billete.

ticking-off ['tɪkɪŋɒf] [ti-kin-of], *s. (Coloq.)* Regaño, rapapolvo.

tickle ['tɪkl] [ti-kel], *vt.* 1. Hacerle cosquillas a, hacerle gracia a (amuse). -*vi.* Picar. -*s.* Cosquilleo.

tickler ['tɪkləʳ] [ti-klaʳ], *s.* 1. El que hace cosquillas. 2. Recordatorio, ayuda, memoria.

tickling ['tɪklɪŋ] [ti-klin], *s.* Cosquillas.

ticklish ['tɪklɪʃ] [ti-klish], *a.* 1. Cosquilloso, que siente mucho las cosquillas. 2. Instable, incierto. 3. Arduo, delicado, difícil, peliagudo (tricky, thorny).

ticklishness ['tɪklɪʃnɪs] [ti-klish-nes], *s.* La propiedad de ser cosquilloso.

tickseed ['tɪksiːd] [tik-sid], *s.* Cualquier planta del género Cercopsis cuyas semillas parecen garrapatas.

tick-tack ['tɪktæk] [tik-tak], *s.* 1. Tic, tac, sonido recurrente o reiterado como el producido por un reloj. 2. Chaquete, una especie de juego muy conocido.

tic-tac-toe [ˌtɪktæk'təʊ] [tik-tak-tou], *s.* Tres en raya.

tid [tɪd] [tid], *a. (Des.)* Delicado, gustoso. **Tid-bit,** golosina.

tidal ['taɪdl] [tai-dal], *a.* 1. De marea, determinado por las mareas; que crece y mengua periódicamente. 2. Periódico; regularizado o medido en cuanto al tiempo por el flujo y reflujo de la marea. **Tidal basin,** dique de marea, en el cual la marea mengua y crece. **Tidal harbor,** puerto en que se notan las mareas. **Tidal wave,** (a) marejada, oleada de vasta extensión pero de pocos pies de altura, que sigue al sol y a la luna de este a oeste y causa las mareas; (b) impropiamente, avenida o desbordamiento de la marea.

tiddler ['tɪdləʳ] [tai-dlaʳ], *s. (Coloq.)* Pececito.

tiddlywinks ['tɪdlɪwɪŋkz] [ti-dli-uinks], *s.* Juego en que se emplean pequeños discos de colores en una taza.

tide [taɪd] [taid], *s.* 1. Marea, el flujo y reflujo de las aguas del mar. 2. Corriente (current); curso, marcha; flujo. 3. Tiempo, estación. **Time and tide,** el tiempo y la hora. **Springtide,** estación de primavera. 4. Período de tiempo de seis horas y doce minutos, el intervalo que media entre pleamar y bajamar en el océano. **Whitsuntide,** pentecostés. **The tide ebbs,** la marea mengua. **The tide flows,** la marea crece. **Flood tide,** creciente, flujo, marea alta. **High o full tide,** plenamar, pleamar. **Ebb tide, low tide,** bajamar. **Tide-way,** canal de marea. **Neap-tides,** aguas chifles o muertas. **Spring-tide,** agua viva, marea, mayor. **To go with the tide,** seguir la corriente. **This should tide us over until next year,** nos arreglaremos con esto hasta el próximo año.

tide, *va.* 1. Llevar (la marea) hacia algún paraje. 2. Superar una dificultad; aguardar tiempo u ocasión más favorable; se usa con *over.* **To tide it up,** *(Mar.)* Montar con la marea.

tideless ['taɪdlɪs] [taid-les], *a.* Que no tiene marea; sin marea.

tidesman ['taɪdzməns] [taids-man], *s.* 1. *V.* TIDEWAITER. 2. Empleado cuyo oficio depende del estado de la marea.

tidewater ['taɪd,wɔ:təʳ] [taid-uo-taʳ], *s.* Marejada. *-a.* Costanero.

tidily ['taɪdɪlɪ] [tai-di-li], *adv.* Aseadamente (neatly); mañosamente, en buen orden.

tidiness ['taɪdɪnɪs] [taid-di-nes], *s.* Aseo (neat), buen arreglo, maña.

tidings ['taɪdɪŋz] [tai-dins], *s. pl.* Nuevas, relato, noticias.

tidy ['taɪdɪ] [tai-di], *a.* 1. Airoso, bien dispuesto, limpio (clean), aseado. 2. De disposición o hábitos metódicos. 3. *(Des. o Fam.)* Considerable, bastante. *-s.* Funda para muebles.

tidy, *va.* y *vn.* *(Fam.)* Asear, componer; poner en orden.

tie [taɪ] [tai], *va. (pret. y pp.* TIED, *pa.* TYING). 1. Anudar, atar, ligar o enlazar dos o más cosas haciendo nudos; juntar con un lazo. 2. Unir o enlazar íntimamente; atar, encadenar. 3. Restringir dentro de límites, limitar, confinar. 4. Sentar el mismo número en la cuenta; traer a igualdad en la suma. 5. Unir las notas con un rasgo. **To tie up,** arremangar, recoger; levantar (tie); impedir, obstruir; poner fuera del gobierno o poder de alguien; envolver algo (en una cubierta). **Tie down,** atar, amarrar. **Tie in,** concordar, cuadrar (coincide).

tie, *s.* 1. Lazo, atadura, ligadura, lo que sirve para atar o ligar. 2. Lazo (bond), vínculo del matrimonio, de la amistad, etc.; apego, adhesión, unión. 3. Una trenza de pelo. 4. Par, igualdad cabal de número en pro y en contra, empate (equal score). 5. Lo que sirve para atar; maroma, cordaje. 6. *(Mús.)* Ligadura, línea curva que junta dos notas en el mismo grado del pentagrama. 7. Tirante, ligazón. 8. Traviesa de ferrocarril. 9. *(E. U.) pl.* Zapatos bajos atados con cordones. **Tie-beam,** tirante; solera de puente.

tied [taɪd] [taid], *a.* Empatado.

tier [tɪəʳ] [tiaʳ], *s.* Atador, lo que ata; lo que se ata; en especial, delantal de niño.

tier, *s.* 1. Fila (row), ringlera. 2. Escalón, nivel. **Tier of guns,** *(Mar.)* Andanada de cañones. **Cable-tier,** pozo de cable. **Tier of a cable,** andana.

tierce ['tɪəs] [tiers], *s.* 1. Tercerola, el tonel que contiene la tercera parte de una pipa. 2. *(Mús.)* Tercera, la consonancia que comprende el intervalo de dos tonos y medio. 3. Tercera, término del juego de los cientos. 4. Tercia, hora canónica. 5. En la esgrima, posición del puño vuelto hacia dentro.

tiered ['tɪəd] [tiard], *a.* En gradas. **A three-tiered cake,** un pastel de tres pisos.

tie-up ['taɪʌp] [taiap], *s.* 1. Interrupción de trabajo por huelga, descompostura de maquinaria, etc. 2. Paralización momentánea del tráfico (stoppage).

tiff [tɪf] [tif], *s.* 1. Pique, disgusto; arranque, palabra picante, pelea (brawl), riña. 2. Bebida, cualquier licor simple o compuesto.

tiff, *va.* Merendar. (Angloindio). *-vn.* Picarse, atufarse, reñir.

tiffany ['tɪfənɪ] [ti-fa-ni], *s.* Tafetán sencillo.

tiger ['taɪgəʳ] [tai-gaʳ], *s.* 1. Tigre, mamífero carnicero y feroz de la raza felina. 2. Jaguar. 3. Volante (criado). **Tiger-beetle,** cicindela, insecto coleóptero. **Tiger-lily,** lirio de tigre. (Lilium tigrinum).

tigerish ['taɪgərɪʃ] [tai-ga-rish], *a.* De tigre, parecido al tigre.

tight [taɪt] [tait], *a.* 1. Bien cerrado, construido sólida y fuertemente; impermeable, impenetrable a los fluidos; *(Mar.)* estanco. 2. Tirante, fuertemente apretado, tieso, tenso. 3. Premioso, estrecho, muy ajustado. **A tight shoe,** un zapato demasiado estrecho. 4. *(Com.)* Escaso, difícil de obtener; se dice del dinero. 5. *(Fam.)* Compacto, acomodado. 6. *(Fam. E. U.)* Mezquino, miserable. 7. Difícil de pasar o de salir de (problematic). 8. *(Fam.)* Embriagado, borracho. **Tight-fitting,** muy ajustado. **Water-tight,** estanco, impermeable. **Tight lacing,** trabas; corsé demasiado ajustado. **To tie tight,** apretar. **A tight ship,** *(Mar.)* Navío estanco.

tighten ['taɪtn] [tai-ten], *va.* y *vn.* Estirar, atiesar; apretar (press); atiesar, ponerse más tenso.

tight-lipped ['taɪtlɪpt] [tait-lipt], *a.* Reservado, callado (quiet), poco comunicativo.

tightly ['taɪtlɪ] [tait-li], *adv.* Con firmeza, bien apretado; de una manera apretada, estirada, tiesa; con estrechez. **He was holding her hand tightly,** la tenía agarrada fuerte de la mano.

tightness ['taɪtnɪs] [tait-nes], *s.* 1. Tensión, tirantez. 2. Estrechez. 3. Condición de lo que se halla bien cerrado; impermeabilidad. 4. Parsimonia, tacañería. 5. Opresión.

tightrope ['taɪtrəʊp] [tait-roup], *s.* Cuerda tirante de volatinero.

tights ['taɪts] [taits], *s. pl.* Calzón ajustado para facilitar los movimientos y mostrar las formas.

tight squeeze ['taɪtskwi:z] [tait-skuis], *s.* Aprieto (predicament), apuro, conflicto.

tightwad ['taɪtwɒd] [tait-uod], *s. (Coloq.)* Apretado.

tigress ['taɪgrɪs] [tai-gres], *f.* La hembra del tigre.

tike [taɪk] [taik], *s. (Prov.)* 1. Patán, rústico. 2. Perro degenerado.

tile [taɪl] [tail], *s.* 1. Teja, baldosa, pieza de barro cocido de varias figuras para cubrir los techos, suelos, etc. 2. Placa de porcelana, mármol u otro material que se usa para adornar las paredes. **Ridge-tile,** teja acanalada. **Dutch tiles,** azulejos. **Tile-maker,** tejero. **Tile-kiln,** tejar, el lugar donde se fabrican las tejas.

tile, *va.* 1. Tejar, cubrir de tejas. 2. Desaguar por medio de tejas. 3. Asegurar contra una intrusión.

tiling ['taɪlɪŋ] [tai-lin], *s.* 1. El acto o procedimiento de cubrir con tejas. 2. Tejas en general; tejado, el techo cubierto de tejas.

till [tɪl] [til], *s.* Cajón (drawer) o gaveta para guardar dinero. -*prep.* Hasta, hasta dónde. *-conj.* Hasta que.

till, *va.* Cultivar, labrar, dar a la tierra las labores necesarias.

tillable ['tɪləbl] [ti-la-bol], *a.* Labrantío, capaz de cultivo. **Tillable land,** tierra cultivable, labrantía o de pan llevar.

tillage ['tɪlɪdʒ] [ti-lich], *s.* Labranza, el trabajo de cultivar la tierra, cultivo de la tierra, la agricultura.

tiller ['tɪləʳ] [ti-laʳ], *s.* 1. Agricultor, labrador. 2. Mango, palanca; en especial, barra o caña del timón; de aquí, medio de guiar. **At the tiller,** al timón. 3. Retoño, renuevo, resalvo de un árbol. **Tiller-rope,** *(Mar.)* guardín de la caña. **Tiller-hole,** *(Mar.)* Limera. **Tiller-transom,** *(Mar.)* Descanso de la caña del timón. **To ship the tiller,** *(Mar.)* montar la caña del timón.

tiller, *vn.* Echar retoños de la raíz.

tilling ['tɪlɪŋ] [ti-lin], *s.* Labranza.

tilt [tɪlt] [tilt], *s.* 1. Inclinación desde la vertical o la horizontal; declive (slope). 2. Justa o torneo, un ejercicio y fiesta militar de los antiguos caballeros. 3. Lanzada. 4. Tienda, cubierta, todo, tendal. **Tilt-boat,** *(Mar.)* Carroza. **Tilt-hammer,** martinete de báscula.

tilt, *va.* 1. Empinar, inclinar (slope), levantar en alto alguna cosa de modo que se salga lo que hay en ella. 2. Martilla, forjar con el martinete. 3. Apuntar la lanza. 4. Entoldar, cubrir con toldos. -vn. 1. Inclinarse hacia un lado, ladearse. 2. Justar, combatir en una justa.

tilth [tɪlθ] [tilz], s. 1. Labranza, cultivo. 2. Profundidad a que alcanza el cultivo de un terreno.

timbal, tymbal ['tɪmbəl] [tim-bal], s. Timbal, atabal.

timber ['tɪmbəʳ] [tim-baʳ], s. 1. Madera de construcción; maderamen, maderaje. 2. Árboles de monte, los árboles no cortados. 3. Viga maestra (beam), el madero principal de una fábrica. 4. Cuaderna, miembro; pieza de construcción que se levanta de dos lados de la quilla. **Filling-timbers,** (Mar.) Cuadernas de henchimiento. **Floor-timbers,** varengas. **Stern-timbers,** gambotas de popa. **Head-timbers,** gambotas de proa. **Cant-timbers,** cuadernas que no están perpendicularmente sobre la quilla. **Ship-timber,** madera para construcciones navales. **Top-timbers,** reveses. **Round timber,** madera en troncos, tronco entero. **Squared timber,** madera escuadrada. **Old timber,** madera de demolición. **Standing timber,** árboles en pie. **Timber-merchant,** maderero, el que trata en madera. **Timber-sow,** carcoma, gusano que roe la madera. **Timber trade,** la industria maderera. **Timber-work,** maderaje, maderamen, el conjunto de maderas para edificios, etc. **Timber-yard,** astillero.

timber, va. Enmaderar, proveer de madera de construcción.

timbered ['tɪmbəd] [tim-bad], adj. part. 1. Cubierto de árboles crecientes o de monte alto. 2. Edificado, construido, provisto de madera.

timberland ['tɪmbəlænd] [tim-ba-land], s. Terreno maderero.

timber line ['tɪmbəlaɪn] [tim-ba-lain], s. Límite de la vegetación arbórea.

timber wolf ['tɪmbəwɒlf] [tim-ba-vulf], s. Lobo gris.

timbre ['tɛmbr] [tembʳ], s. 1. Timbre, calidad de una voz, de un instrumento músico. 2. (Her.) Timbre, la insignia que se coloca sobre el escudo de armas para distinguir los grados de nobleza.

time [taɪm] [taim], s. 1. Tiempo, la medida de la duración de las cosas. 2. Tiempo, un término limitado; plazo. 3. Tiempo, sazón, oportunidad, la ocasión y coyuntura de hacer algo. 4. Tiempo, tomado por un largo espacio de él; edad, época, como **To take time,** tomarse tiempo o dejar la ejecución de una cosa por un largo espacio de tiempo. **In Tudor times,** en la época de los Tudor, en tiempos de los Tudor. 5. (Mús.) Compás, medida de los sonidos con respecto a su duración: grado del movimiento. V. TEMPO. 6. Vez (indicando la repetición). **At a time,** a la vez. **At times,** a veces. **Every time,** cada vez, todas las veces. **Many times** muchas veces, a menudo. **Many and many a time,** muchísimas veces. 7. Intervalo, el espacio de un tiempo a otro; hora, división del día indicada por el reloj. **What time is it?** ¿Qué hora es? **Tell me the time,** dígame Ud. la hora. 8. El término de la preñez. 9. La hora del parto o de la muerte. 10. Relación temporal o inflexión que toma el verbo. **In time,** a tiempo, con el tiempo. **In our times,** en nuestros días. **From time to time,** de cuando en cuando. **The time to come,** lo futuro, lo venidero. **Time out of mind,** tiempo inmemorial. **In old times, in times of yore,** antiguamente, en otros tiempos, en tiempos antiguos. **From this time forth,** desde ahora, desde hoy en adelante, en lo venidero. **At any time,** cuando Ud. guste o cuando Ud. quiera. **At no time,** jamás. **At this time,** al presente, ahora. **At that time,** en aquella ocasión, en aquel tiempo, entonces. **This time a twelvemonth,** de aquí a un año. **At all times,** en todos los tiempos, en todas las edades. **In a day's time** en el espacio de un día. **In an hour's time,** en una hora. **In the day-time,** de día o por el día. **In the night-time,** de noche o por la noche. **To pass the time away,** pasar el tiempo; recrearse, divertirse, darse una pavonada. **By that time,** para entonces o entonces. **A woman near her time,** una mujer en días de parir. **To take time by the forelock,** (Prov.) tomar o asir la ocasión por los cabellos. **From time to time,** de vez en cuando, de cuando en cuando. **A long time since,** hace largo tiempo. **In no time,** en un instante, al momento. **Time enough,** hay tiempo; es

bastante pronto. **Behind time,** atrasado, retardado. **There is no time to spare,** no hay tiempo que perder. **To lose time,** perder el tiempo, retrasar (el reloj). **At some time or other,** un día u otro. **To keep time,** guardar compás. **To beat time,** marcar el compás. **To be on time,** (E. U.) Ser puntual. **Out of time,** fuera de compás. **For the time being,** por ahora, por o para entonces; de ahora, actual, en este tiempo. **Time-pleaser, time-server,** el que contemporiza o se acomoda con demasiada facilidad al gusto ajeno. **Time-serving,** complaciente, contemplativo, lisonjero, que adora el sol que nace. **Timetable,** cartel, cédula o lista de las horas en que suceden o se hacen ciertas cosas; p.ej. las horas de llegada y salida de trenes, barcos, etc. **Time warp,** salto en el tiempo. **Time worn,** usado, gastado por el tiempo.

time, va. 1. Adaptar al tiempo, hacer alguna cosa a tiempo oportuno. 2. Concertar, arreglar el tiempo. 3. (Mús.) Llevar el compás. 4. (Sport) Cronometrar.

time card ['taɪmˌkɑːd] [taim-kard], s. Tarjeta en que se marca la hora de entrada y salida de empleados o trabajadores.

time clock ['taɪmˈklɒk] [taim-klok], s. Reloj para marcar la hora de entrada y salida de empleados o trabajadores.

time exposure ['taɪmɪkˌspəʊʒəʳ] [taim-iks-pou-saʳ], s. Exposición de tiempo (en fotografía).

time keeper ['taɪmkiːpəʳ] [taim-ki-paʳ], s. 1. Reloj, reloj astronómico. 2. Marcador de tiempo.

timeless ['taɪmlɪs] [taim-les], a. 1. Independiente o superior a todas las limitaciones del tiempo, que no tiene fin, eterno (eternal). 2. Intempestivo, que se hace fuera de tiempo o de ocasión oportuna.

time limit ['taɪmlɪmɪt] [taim-li-mit], s. Plazo.

timeliness ['taɪmlɪnɪs] [taim-li-nes], s. Tiempo conveniente, oportunidad; calidad de oportuno.

timely ['taɪmlɪ] [taim-li], adv. Temprano, con tiempo; bien pronto, a tiempo oportuno, a propósito. -a. Oportuno (opportune), en tiempo.

time out [ˌtaɪmˈaʊt] [taim-aut], s. Tiempo muerto.

timepiece ['taɪmˌpiːs] [taim-pis], s. Cualquier reloj o instrumento que marca las horas.

timer ['taɪməʳ] [tai-maʳ], s. 1. Marcador de tiempo (person or instrument). 2. El que sirve o trabaja por determinado lapso.

timesheet ['taɪmʃiːt] [taim-shiit], f. Hoja de asistencia.

timetable ['taɪmˌteɪbl] [taim-tei-bol], m. Horario, programa.

timewasting ['taɪmweɪstɪŋ] [taim-ueis-tin], a. Lo que hace perder tiempo.

timid ['tɪmɪd] [ti-mid], a. Tímido (shy), temeroso, que evita la publicidad, pusilánime (faint-hearted), medroso, huraño.

timidity [tɪˈmɪdɪtɪ] [ti-mi-di-ti], **timidness** ['tɪmɪdnɪs] [ti-mid-nes], s. Timidez, temor, miedo, pusilanimidad.

timidly ['tɪmɪdlɪ] [ti-mid-li], adv. Tímidamente, con timidez.

timing ['taɪmɪŋ] [tai-min], s. 1. (Mus., Sport) Ritmo. 2. (Auto) **Check the timing,** revise el encendido. **The timing of the election,** la fecha escogida para las elecciones.

timorous ['tɪmərəs] [ti-mo-ros], a. Temeroso (spineless), medroso, asombradizo, espantadizo, timorato (prudish).

timpani ['tɪmpənɪ] [tim-pa-ni], s.pl. Timbales.

timpanist ['tɪmpənɪst] [tim-pa-nist], s. Timbalero.

tin [tɪn] [tin], s. 1. Estaño, metal maleable y blanco. 2. Hoja de lata, hojalata, lámina cubierta de estaño. 3. Objeto de hojalatería. 4. (Ger.) Dinero, moneda. **Tinfoil,** hoja de estaño, alinde. **Tin-man,** hojalatero, alinde. **Tin-man,** hojalatero, estañero. **Tin-plate,** hoja de lata. **Tin-pot,** jarro o vasija de hoja de lata. **Tintype,** (E. U.) Fotografía hecha sobre una plancha de hojalata. V. FERROTYPE. **Tin-ware,** hojalatería, efectos de hojalata.

tin, va. 1. Estañar, cubrir o bañar con estaño. 2. Cubrir, v. g. un tejado, con hoja de lata. 3. Meter en una caja o bote de hojalata. **To tin over,** estañar completamente una cosa o cubrirla toda con estaño.

tin can ['tɪnkæn] [tin-kan], s. Lata, bote.

tincture [ˈtɪŋktʃər] [tink-cha^r], *s.* 1. Tintura, tinte, el color que queda en la cosa teñida. 2. Tintura, en farmacia es la solución de una substancia simple o compuesta en alcohol o espíritu de vino. 3. tintura. el conocimiento superficial de alguna ciencia o arte; gusto, gustillo.

tincture, *va.* 1. Teñir, colorar, tinturar. 2. Dar un sabor o un gusto particular a las cosas. 3. Tinturar, instruir o informar a grandes rasgos de alguna cosa.

tinder [ˈtɪndər] [tin-da^r], *s.* Yesca, toda materia muy seca y dispuesta de suerte que cualquier chispa de fuego prenda en ella; mecha.

tinderbox [ˈtɪndəbɒks] [tin-da-boks], *s.* Yesquero.

tine [taɪn] [tain], *s.* 1. Púa de rastrillo; diente de tenedor. 2. Angustia, aflicción de ánimo.

ting [tɪŋ] [ting], *va. y vn.* Dar o producir un solo sonido metálico y agudo. -*s.* Un sonido metálico solo y agudo, como el de una campana; retintín. (*Imitativo*)

tinge [tɪndʒ] [tindch], *va.* 1. Colorar, teñir (dye), dar un tinte ligero, colorear. 2. Dar ligero gusto a una cosa; modificar mezclando con algo. -*s.* 1. Tinte, color ligero, matiz. 2. Gusto, gustillo, cualidad comunicada por una substancia extraña.

tingle [ˈtɪŋgl] [tin-guel], *vn.* 1. Picar, punzar, hormiguear, experimentar una picazón, como la que se siente en la piel cuando se expone al frío. 2. Producir picazón u hormigueo. **My ears tingle,** me hormiguean las orejas. -*s.* 1. Picazón, hormigueo, comezón. 2. Retintín. *V.* JINGLE.

tingling [ˈtɪŋglɪŋ] [tin-glin], *s.* Punzada de dolor, picazón, comezón.

tingly [ˈtɪŋglɪ] [tin-gli], *a.* **My leg feels tingly,** siento un hormigueo en la pierna. **Tingly feeling,** sensación de hormigueo.

tinhorn [ˈtɪnhɔːn] [tin-jorn], *s.* (*Coloq.*) Fanfarrón. -*a.* Fanfarrón (show-off).

tinker [ˈtɪŋkər] [tin-ka^r], *va.* Remendar como lo hace un calderero, a veces, chafallar, remendar chapuceramente. -*vn.* 1. Trabajar como calderero o latonero. 2. Chafallar, remendar de un modo chapucero. -*s.* Latonero, calderero remendón; desabollador.

tinkle [ˈtɪŋkl] [tin-kel], *va. y vn.* 1. Cencerrear, retiñir, hacer retintines, sonar o dejar oír ligeros sonidos metálicos repetidos. 2. Zumbar los oídos. -*s.* Tintineo, tilín.

tinkling [ˈtɪŋklɪŋ] [tin-klin], *s.* Retintín, retín, sucesión de sonidos agudos, ligeros y sonoros.

tinned [tɪnd] [tind], *a.* Enlatado, de lata.

tinner [ˈtɪnər] [ti-na^r], *s.* 1. Minero de estaño. 2. Estañero, hojalatero.

tinny [ˈtɪnɪ] [ti-ni], *a.* De estaño, perteniente o parecido al estaño.

tinpot [ˈtɪnpɒt] [tin-pot], *a.* De poco valor, de pacotilla.

tinsel [ˈtɪnsəl] [tin-sel], *s.* 1. Oropel, laminitas de latón reluciente, lentejuelas; (*Fig.*) falso brillo. 2. Brocadillo, restaño, tejido al que se pegan o cosen lentejuelas u oropel. -*a.* De oropel, que tiene brillo falso. -*va.* Adornar con oropel.

tint [tɪnt] [tint], *va.* Teñir, colorar (color), dar un color, matizar. -*s.* 1. Tinte, color con que se tiñe, matiz, grado de fuerza que se da a los colores. 2. Matiz, efecto de luz, sombra, etc., producido en el grabado o cruzando las líneas, etc. **Neutral tint,** matiz neutro.

tinted [ˈtɪntɪd] [tin-tid], *a.* Coloreado, teñido.

tinwork [ˈtɪnwɜːk] [tin-uerk], *s.* Fábrica o mina de estaño.

tiny [ˈtaɪnɪ] [tai-ni], *a.* Muy pequeño, menudo, minúsculo, diminuto (minute).

tip [tɪp] [tip], *s.* 1. Punta, extremidad (extremity), cabo. **He was standing on the tips of his toes,** estaba de puntillas. 2. Casquillo, regatón; virola que se pone al extremo de una cosa.

tip, *s.* 1. Propina. 2. Aviso amistoso y útil, fundado en informes confidenciales, consejo (advice). 3. Toque ligero, golpecito. 4. Vertedero, basurero.

tip, *va.* 1. Guarnecer o cubrir la extremidad o punta de una cosa con un metal cualquiera. 2. Golpear ligeramente o dar golpecitos suaves. 3. Ladear, inclinar (tilt), levantar un extremo o lado de. 4. (*Fam.*) Dar una propina. 5. (*Ger.*) Dar informes secretos respecto de algún suceso, particularmente

cuando median apuestas, pronosticar (forecast). -*vn.* 1. Ladearse, inclinarse a un lado. 2. Hacer un regalo en dinero, dar propina. **To tip the wink,** guiñar, dar guiñadas. **To tip at nine-pins,** birlar, en el juego de bolos. **Tipped with silver,** montado en plata. **Tip off,** avisar, dar el chivatazo. **Tip over,** volcar. **Tip up,** voltear, darle la vuelta.

tip-off [ˈtɪpɒf] [tip-of], *s.* Dato, soplo, chivatazo.

tipped [ˈtɪpd] [tipd], *a.* Con filtro.

tippet [ˈtɪpt] [tipt], *s.* Palatina, adorno que usan las mujeres al cuello.

tipple [ˈtɪpl] [ti-pel], *va. y vn.* 1. Beber con exceso, beborrotear, pero no hasta el extremo de embriagarse. 2. Achisparse, empinar el codo.

tippler [ˈtɪplər] [ti-pla^r], *s.* Bebedor, el que bebe mucho o es aficionado a los licores. (*Fam.*) Tomista.

tipsily [ˈtɪpsɪlɪ] [tip-si-li], *adv.* Como borracho.

tipstaff [ˈtɪpstɑːf] [tip-staf], *s.* 1. Alguacil de vara. 2. Vara de justicia.

tipster [ˈtɪpstər] [tips-ta^r], *s.* Pronosticador.

tipsy [ˈtɪpsɪ] [tip-si], *a.* 1. Borracho, embriagado, achispado (merry). 2. Oscilante.

tiptoe [ˈtɪptəʊ] [tip-tou], *s.* Punta del pie. **To walk on tiptoe** o **on one's tiptoes,** andar de puntillas. **To be on tiptoe, to stand a tiptoe,** tenerse, ponerse de puntillas, estar aguardando, alerta.

tiptop [ˈtɪptɒp] [tip-top], *a.* (*Fam.*) Lo mejor en su clase. -*s.* Cumbre, cima, el más alto punto. **In tiptop condition,** en excelente estado, como nuevo.

tirade [taˈreɪd] [tai-reid], *s.* Tirada crítica: invectiva (diatribe).

tire [ˈtaɪər] [taia^r], *s.* Llanta, neumático. **Tire blowout,** reventón de llanta o neumático. **Tire cover,** cubrellantas. **Tire gauge,** medidor de presión de las llantas o neumáticos.

tire, *va.* Cansar, fatigar, aburrir, fastidiar, enfadar. -*vn.* 1. Cansarse, padecer cansancio o fatiga, aburrirse, fastidiarse. 2. Hacer presa en. **To tire out,** cansar mucho, reventar de cansancio o fatiga.

tired [ˈtaɪəd] [taiad], *a.* 1. Cansado (weary), fatigado, fastidiado. **I'm tired,** estoy cansado. 2. Mustio (faded), gastado.

tiredness [ˈtaɪədnɪs] [taiad-nes], *s.* Cansancio, lasitud, demasiada fatiga.

tireless [ˈtaɪəlɪs] [taia-les], *a.* 1. Infatigable, incansable. 2. Falto de llanta (wheel).

tiresome [ˈtaɪəsəm] [taia-som], *a.* Tedioso, fastidioso, molesto (irritating), pesado, enfadoso.

tiresomeness [ˈtaɪəsəmnɪs] [taia-som-nes], *s.* Tedio, fastidio (annoyance), aburrimiento, displicencia.

tiring [ˈtaɪərɪŋ] [taia-rin], *a.* Cansador, cansado.

'ti [tɪs] [tis] Abreviatura poética de IT IS. **'Tis ill done,** es o está mal hecho.

tisane [tɪˈzæn] [ti-san], *s.* Tisana, bebida medicinal. *V.* PTISAN.

tisic [ˈtɪsɪk] [ti-sik], *s.* Tisis, tísica. *V.* PHTHISIC.

tissue [ˈtɪʃuː] [ti-shu], *s.* 1. (*Biol.*) Tejido, cada una de las agregaciones de elementos anatómicos, entrelazados o simplemente adheridos entre sí, que forman las partes sólidas de los cuerpos orgánicos. 2. Tejido ligero parecido a la gasa; originalmente, tisú, tela de oro o plata. 3. Serie conexa, encadenamiento; ficción. 4. Papel de seda. 5. Pañuelo de papel (paper handkerchief). 6. Trama (web). **Woody tissue,** tejido leñoso. **The whole story is a tissue of fabrications,** todo ello no es más que un tejido de mentiras. **Tissue-paper,** papel de seda.

tissue, *va.* Entretejer, mezclar en el tejido diferentes materias.

tit [tɪt] [tit], *s.* 1. Paro. *V.* TOMTIT y TITLARK. 2. Haca, caballo pequeño. 3. Teta (breast). 4. Golpecito; en la locución **Tit for tat,** taz a taz o taz por taz; tal para cual; esto por eso. **To give tit for tat,** no quedar a deber nada; estar a mano. (*Vulg.*) Estar pata, o patas.

titanic [taɪˈtænɪk] [tai-ta-nik], *a.* 1. Titánico, titanio, perteneciente o parecido a los Titanes; de aquí, vasto, gigantesco. 2. Titánico, perteneciente al titanio, particularmente en su más alto grado de combinación.

titanium [taɪ'tænɪəm] [tai-ta-niom], s. (Min.) Titanio, metal gris.

titbit ['tɪtbɪt] [tit-bit], s. 1. Bocado regalado, trozo escogido, exquisitez. 2. Chisme (gossip).

titchy ['tɪtʃɪ] [ti-chi], a. (Coloq.) Enano.

tithable ['tɪðʃəbl] [ti-cha-bol], a. Diezmable, sujeto a pagar diezmo.

tithe [taɪð] [taiz], s. 1. Diezmo. 2. La décima parte de una cosa, de aquí, una porción pequeña. **Collector of tithes,** diezmero. **Tithe-free,** libre o exento de diezmo.

tithe, vn. Diezmar, pagar el diezmo; percibir y cobrar el diezmo, -va. Imponer tributo.

tither ['taɪðəʳ] [tai-zaʳ], s. Dezmero o diezmero, el que recauda el diezmo.

tithing ['taɪðɪŋ] [tai-zin], s. 1. Diezmo, acción de levantar el diezmo. 2. Decena, el agregado de diez familias que se unían antiguamente para formar una subdivisión política en algunas provincias de Inglaterra.

titillate ['tɪtɪleɪt] [ti-ti-leit], va. 1. Titilar, cansar titilación o una especie de cosquilleo agradable. 2. Excitar. 3. Despertar (stimulate).

titillating ['tɪtɪleɪtɪŋ] [ti-ti-lei-tin], a. Excitante, estimulante (stimulating).

titillation [ˌtɪtɪ'leɪʃən] [ti-ti-lei-shon], s. Titilación, picazón o una especie de cosquilleo agradable.

title ['taɪtl] [tai-tel], s. 1. Título, de un libro, de un capítulo, etc.; inscripción, rótulo o rotulata. 2. Título, nombre de dignidad o de una calidad honorífica. 3. Título, renombre o distintivo con que se conoce a alguna persona. 4. Título, la demostración auténtica del derecho que se tiene a alguna cosa, acta, título, documento que establece el derecho a una propiedad. 5. La portada o frontispicio de un libro. (Cin. T. V.) **Titles,** títulos de crédito.

title, va. 1. Titular; intitular; conferir un título; dar el nombre de. 2. Titular, estampar el nombre en la cubierta o el lomo de un libro.

titled ['taɪtld] [tai-teld], a. Con título.

title holder ['taɪtlˌhəʊldəʳ] [tai-tel-joul-daʳ], s. Campeón (champion).

title page ['taɪtlpeɪdʒ] [tai-tel-peich], s. La portada o frontispico de un libro; (Amer.) carátula.

titling ['taɪtlɪŋ] [tai-tlin], s. Farlusa o gorrión silvestre. V. TITLARK.

titmouse ['tɪtmaʊz] [tit-maus], s. (Orn.) Paro, pájaro pequeño que tiene el pico corto y cubierto de plumas.

titter ['tɪtəʳ] [ti-taʳ], vn. Sonreírse, reír entre dientes, reír con disimulo.

titterer ['tɪtərəʳ] [ti-ta-raʳ], s. El o la que ríe entre dientes o sofocando la risa.

tittering ['tɪtərɪŋ] [ti-te-rin], s. Risa entre dientes, sonrisa.

tittle ['tɪtl] [ti-tel], s. 1. Tilde, vírgula, vigulilla. 2. Tilde, ápice, cosa mínima.

tittle-tattle ['tɪtlˌtætl] [ti-tel-ta-tel], s. 1. Charla (chat), plática sin substancia. 2. (Coloq.) Chismes. 3. Soplón (informer).

tittle-tattle, vn. Charlar (chat); susurrar.

titular ['tɪtjʊləʳ] [ti-tiu-laʳ], a. 1. Titular, nominal, que tiene solamente el nombre o título. 2. Titular, perteneciente a un título, revestido de un título. -s. Titular, el que tiene el título de un cargo.

titularly ['tɪtjʊlərlɪ] [ti-tiu-lar-li], adv. Con sólo el título.

tiz [tɪz] [tis], s. **To get into a tiz,** inquietarse, ponerse nervioso.

TNT, s. (Quím.) Abreviatura de trinitrotoluene, TNT, potente explosivo.

to [tuː] [tu], adv. y prep. Hasta, hacia; a, en dirección hacia; también es el signo del infinitivo en inglés. 1. Es a o al, cuando es signo del objeto indirecto o dativo, si éste no es un pronombre personal, y en general siempre que precede al nombre después de los verbos que significan movimiento, dirección, unión, pertenencia, preferencia o atención; como, **Give it to him,** dáselo a él. **I'll go to London,** iré a Londres. **I spoke to you,** hablé a Ud. **I am going to speak to him,** voy a hablarle. **It belongs to Peter,** pertenece a Pedro. **I prefer this book to mine,** prefiero este libro al mío. **I have no enmity to him,** no le tengo mala voluntad. **That is nothing to me,** nada me importa eso. 2. Cuando denota la intención u objeto con que se ejecuta alguna cosa, corresponde a para, por o a en castellano. **She went there only to see me,** fue allá sólo por verme, a verme, para verme o con sólo el objeto o la intención de verme. **I come to speak to him,** vengo a hablarle, para hablarle o con el objeto de hablarle. 3. Después de un participio pasivo o de un adjetivo denotando su objeto, equivale a para. **Born to die,** nacido para morir. **Ready to go out,** dispuesto a salir. **That is lost to me,** eso se perdió para mí. 4. Es también que en castellano, particularmente cuando expresa una acción futura o venidera. **We are still to see,** tenemos todavía que ver. **To have to, to be obliged to,** tener que, deber. **Why are we to go?,** ¿por qué tenemos que ir nosotros? 5. Hasta; tan lejos como. **To this day,** hasta hoy o hasta el día de hoy. **To the number of,** hasta el número de. **Even to,** hasta. **I see to the bottom,** veo hasta el fondo. 6. Hacia, a. **To the east was an open country,** hacia el este se extendía un terreno llano. 7. En, cuando indica una relación de movimiento hacia algo. **From door to door,** de puerta en puerta. 8. Menos (marcando la hora). **It is ten minutes to nine,** son las nueve menos diez minutos. 9. De o del. **He is a friend to the poor,** es amigo de los pobres. **Philip the Second was son to Charles the Fifth,** o **was successor to Charles the Fifth,** Felipe Segundo fue hijo de Carlos Quinto o fue sucesor de Carlos Quinto. **Surgeon to the king,** cirujano del rey. **The road to Madrid,** el camino de Madrid. **Woe to the man,** ¡ay del hombre, o infeliz del hombre! 10. En la mayor parte de los casos to no se traduce, cuando es signo de infinitivo. **He loves to travel,** le gusta viajar. En otros casos se traduce por a, de, para, a fin de, según el sentido. **She has the desire to learn,** ella tiene deseo de aprender. **Bound to succeed,** resuelto a triunfar. **To arrive at the truth,** a fin de averiguar la verdad. To como signo del infinitivo se omite: (a) después de los verbos auxiliares do, can, may, must, shall, will; (b) después de dare, osar, atreverse, help, ayudar, need, necesitar, please, servirse, go, ir; (c) después del objeto de los verbos bid, mandar, feel, sentir, have, haber, hear, oír, let, dejar, make, hacer, y a veces, find, hallar y know, saber; (d) después de ciertas locuciones. **According to,** según. **As to,** en cuanto a, por lo que toca a. **So as to,** de manera que, a fin de. **To and fro,** de acá para acullá; de aquí para allí. **To and fro motion,** vaivén. **Twenty to one,** veinte a uno. **Sharp to the taste,** punzante al paladar. **Not to muy knowledge,** no que yo sepa. **To my knowledge,** me consta que. **To drink to excess,** beber con esceso. **As to that,** por lo que toca a eso, en cuanto a eso, respecto a eso. **For the time to come,** en lo venidero. **To the end that,** a fin que. **I am glad to see you,** me alegro de ver a Ud. **To speak to the purpose,** hablar al caso. **To go to and again,** ir y volver. **To and again,** de un lado y otro. **Face to face,** cara a cara.

toad [təʊd] [toud], s. (Zool.) 1. Sapo, escurzo, anfibio terrestre sin cola. 2. Cualquier persona como objeto de desprecio. **Toad-eater,** pegote, parásito, sicofante. **You lying toad!,** ¡mentiroso de porquería!

toadfish ['təʊdfɪʃ] [toud-fish], s. Sapo marino.

toadflax ['təʊdflæks] [toud-flaks], s. (Bot.) Linaria, lino bastardo; planta de las escrofulariáceas; se llama también **butter-and-eggs,** mantequilla y huevos.

toadstone ['təʊdstəʊn] [toud-stoun], s. (Min.) Piedra del sapo, batraquita, nombre vulgar de una especie de piedra llena de agujeritos.

toadstool ['təʊdstuːl] [toud-stul], s. (Bot.) Hongo bejín, hongo bastardo, cualquier seta venenosa.

toady ['təʊdɪ] [tou-di], va. y vn. Adular servilmente; hacer zalamerías, ser zalamero. -a. Adulador (flatterer), zalamero, pelota (creep).

toast [təʊst] [toust], *va.* 1. Tostar, hacer asar, secar o calentar a la lumbre. 2. *(Fam.)* Calentar o calentarse al fuego. **I'm just toasting myself in front of the fire,** me estoy calentando junto al fuego. 3. Brindar, echar un brindis a, beber a la salud de alguno.

toast, *s.* 1. Tostada, rebanada de pan tostado. **Toast rack,** portatostadas. 2. Brindis (tribute), la acción de brindar a la salud de una persona. **I'd like to propose a toast,** me gustaría proponer un brindis.

toaster [ˈtəʊstəʳ] [tous-taʳ], *s.* 1. El que brinda. 2. El o lo que tuesta, tostador; parrillas.

tobacco [təˈbækəʊ] [to-ba-kou], *s.* 1. Tabaco, las hojas curadas y preparadas del tabaco que se fuman, mastican o se toman por la nariz reducidas a polvo. 2. Tabaco, planta solanácea, originaria de la América tropical. Nicotiana tabacum. **Tobacco-heart,** estado morboso del corazón debido al uso excesivo del tabaco. **Tobacco-pipe,** pipa de tabaco. **Tobacco-pipe clay,** tierra de pipa. **Tobacco-box,** tabaquera. **Tobacco-pouch,** bolsa para tabaco. **Tobacco-worm,** oruga muy perjudicial al tabaco en los E.U.

tobacconist [təˈbækənɪst] [to-ba-ko-nist], *s.* 1. Fabricante de tabaco. 2. Tabaquero, vendedor de tabaco, que en España se llama comúnmente estanquero.

toboggan [təˈbɒɡən] [to-bo-gan], *s.* Tobogán. *-vn.* Deslizarse en un tobogán. *(Fig.)* Disminuir repentinamente en valor.

tocsin [ˈtɒksɪn] [tok-sin], *s.* Campana y campanada de alarma; toque, señal dada con una campana.

tod [tɒd] [tod], *s. (Ingl.)* Zorro.

today [təˈdeɪ] [to-dei], *s.* El día presente; también la época o siglo presente. **Today's papers,** los periódicos de hoy. *-adv.* Hoy. **Today of all days,** precisamente hoy.

toddle [ˈtɒdl] [to-del, *vn.* Bambolear, marchar con paso incierto, como el de un niño. **They toddled into the room,** entraron en la habitación con paso incierto.

toddler [ˈtɒdləʳ] [tod-laʳ], *s.* Niño chiquito de dos a tres años de edad. **Toddler clothes,** ropa de niño de esa edad.

toddy [ˈtɒdɪ] [to-di], *s.* 1. Ponche, bebida de licor espirituoso, agua caliente y azúcar; licor alcohólico en general. 2. Vino de palmera, jugo que exuda por las incisiones hechas en varias palmas.

to-do [təˈduː] [to-du], *s. (Fam.)* Confusión, trapisonda, lío (mess).

tody [ˈtɒdɪ] [to-di], *s.* Todi, pájaro verde de Jamaica, de la familia de los alciónidos.

toe [təʊ] [tou], *s.* 1. Dedo del pie. 2. Uña, pezuña, parte delantera del casco del caballo y otros animales. 3. Extremo (de media, del calzado); el extremo inferior o pie de alguna cosa. **The great toe,** el dedo gordo del pie. **From top to toe,** de pies a cabeza.

toe, *va.* 1. Tocar con los dedos del pie. 2. Asegurar con clavos un puntal. **Three-toed,** con tres dedos.

toenails [ˈtəʊneɪlz] [tou-neils], *s. pl.* Uñas de los dedos del pie,

toff [tɒf] [tof], *s. (Coloq.)* Encopetado.

toffee [ˈtɒfɪ] [to-fi], *s.* Toffee, caramelo.

tofu [ˈtəʊfuː] [tou-fu], *s.* Tofu, queso de soja.

toga [ˈtəʊɡə] [tou-ga], *s.* Toga, vestidura exterior de un ciudadano romano.

together [təˈɡeðəʳ] [to-gue-daʳ], *adv.* 1. Juntamente, en compañía de otro. **Let us go together,** vamos juntos. 2. A un tiempo o al mismo tiempo. 3. De seguida, sin interrupción. **Together with,** a una con, juntos. **Six weeks together,** seis semanas seguidas. **Together,** *(Mar.)* a una. *-a. (Coloq.)* Centrado, equilibrado.

togetherness [təˈɡeðənɪs] [to-gue-da-nes], *s.* Unión.

toggle [ˈtɒɡl] [to-guel], *s.* 1. Cazonete de aparejo. 2. Palanca acodillada. **Toggle-joint,** junta de codillo.

toggle switch [ˈtɒɡlˌswɪtʃ] [to-guel-suich], *s.* Interruptor de palanca acodillada, interruptor de presión.

togs [tɒɡz] [togs], *s. pl. (Coloq.)* Ropa.

toil [tɔɪl] [toil], *vn.* 1. Trabajar, aplicarse con desvelo a la ejecución de alguna cosa: fatigarse, molestarse, trabajar mucho.

2. Adelantarse a paso lento. **To toil through,** abrirse penosamente camino de parte a parte. **To toil up,** subir con pena.

toil, *s.* 1. Faena, trabajo, pena, fatiga, afán. 2. Red para pescar, cazar o para cualquier otra cosa; generalmente en sentido figurado. **Toil of a spider,** telaraña o red de araña.

toilet [ˈtɔɪlɪt] [toi-lit], *s.* 1. Acto de vestirse. 2. Modo de vestir de una persona, arreglo personal. 3. Tocador. 4. Retrete, excusado, lavatorio. **Toiled articles,** artículos de tocador. **Toilet bag,** neceser. **Toilet paper,** papel de excusado. **Toilet soap,** jabón de tocador. **Toilet water,** agua de tocador.

toiletries [ˈtɔɪlɪtriːz] [toi-li-tris], *s. pl.* Artículos de tocador o de perfumería.

toilet-train [ˈtɔɪlɪtˌtreɪn] [toi-lit-trein], *vt.* Enseñar a pedir para ir al baño (to a child).

toilful [ˈtɔɪlfʊl] [toil-ful], *a.* Trabajoso, repleto de trabajos.

toilsome [ˈtɔɪlsəm] [toil-sam], *a.* Laborioso, trabajoso; penoso, fatigoso (tiring).

toilsomely [ˈtɔɪlsəmlɪ] [toil-sam-li], *adv.* Laboriosamente; fatigosamente.

toilsomeness [ˈtɔɪlsəmnɪs] [toil-sam-nes], *s.* Trabajo, afán; fatiga, penalidad que causa el trabajo prolijo o muy continuado.

token [ˈtəʊkən] [tou-ken], *s.* 1. Señal, muestra, marca, seña, nota. 2. Prenda, recuerdo, prueba de amistad. 3. Medalla, tanto, ficha de metal semejante a una moneda, que a veces ponen en circulación los comerciantes, dándoles un valor monetario determinado. **As a token of,** en señal de. *-a.* Simbólico, por puro formulismo.

token, *va.* Mostrar, denotar.

tokenism [ˈtəʊkənɪzəm] [tou-ke-ni-sem], *s.* Formulismo.

Tokyo [ˈtəʊkjəʊ] [tou-kiou], *s.* Tokio.

told [təʊld] [tould], *pret.* y *pp.* del verbo TO TELL.

tolerable [ˈtɒlərəbl] [to-le-ra-bol], *a.* 1. Tolerable (endurable). sufrible, pasadero, llevadero. 2. Pasadero, medianamente bueno, mediocre.

tolerableness [ˈtɒlərəblnɪs] [to-le-ra-bol-nes], *s.* La calidad de lo que es tolerable, pasadero o medianamente bueno.

tolerably [ˈtɒlərəblɪ] [to-le-ra-bli], *adv.* Tolerablemente, medianamente, así así. **He sings tolerably well,** canta razonablemente, pasablemente.

tolerance [ˈtɒlərəns] [to-le-rans], *s.* 1. Tolerancia (forbearance), indulgencia. 2. Paciencia.

tolerant [ˈtɒlərənt] [to-le-rant], *a.* Tolerante.

tolerantly [ˈtɒlərəntlɪ] [to-le-rant-li], *adv.* Con tolerancia.

tolerate [ˈtɒləreɪt] [to-le-reit], *va.* 1. Tolerar, permitir, disimular, llevar con paciencia. 2. Soportar, aguantar (endure).

toleration [ˌtɒləˈreɪʃən] [to-le-rei-shon], *s.* Tolerancia, tolerancia civil.

toll [təʊl] [toul], *s.* 1. Peaje, portazgo o pontazgo, el derecho o impuesto pagado por los que viajan, derecho de molienda. **To pay toll,** estar sujeto a peaje, pagar portazgo. **To take toll.** cobrar una tasa, un peaje. **Toll-bridge,** puente de peaje. **Toll-gate** barrera de peaje. **Toll-house,** oficina de portazgos, domicilio del portazguero junto a la barrera. **Toll-man,** peajero, portazguero. 2. El sonido de las campanas. **miller's toll,** maquila de molinero.

toll, *va.* y *vn.* 1. Pagar o cobrar el derecho de portazgo. 2. Repicar; tañer (peal), o tocar una campana, lentamente, con toques aislados repetidos a intervalos iguales. 3. Tocar a muerto (una campana). 4. Llamar o convocar con campana. **To toll the hour,** dar la hora.

tollbooth [ˈtəʊlbuːð] [toul-buz], *va.* Encarcelar, poner preso.

toll call [ˈtəʊlkɔːl] [toul-kol], *s.* Llamada telefónica de larga distancia.

toller [ˈtəʊləʳ] [tou-laʳ], *s.* El que toca las campanas.

toll-free [ˈtəʊlfriː] [toul-fri], *a.* Exento de peaje.

tom [tɒm] [tom], *s.* Gato macho.

tomahawk [ˈtɒməhɔːk] [to-ma-jok], *va.* Golpear o matar con el hacha india llamada *tomahawk. -s.* Hacha de armas de los indios americanos.

tomato [təˈmeɪtəʊ] [to-mei-tou], *s. (Bot.)* Tomate. **Tomato sauce,** salsa de tomate.

tomb [tuːm] [tum], *s.* Tumba, sepulcro.

tombola [tɒmˈbəʊlə] [tom-bou-la], *s.* Tómbola.

tomboy [ˈtɒmbɔɪ] [tom-boi], *s.* Marimacho, doncella pizpireta y respingona.

tombstone [ˈtuːmstəʊn] [tum-stoun], *s.* Lápida o piedra sepulcral.

tomcat [ˈtɒmkæt] [tom-kat], *s.* Gato no castrado.

tome [təʊm] [toum], *s.* Tomo, libro grueso.

tomfool [ˈtɒmˈfuːl] [tom-ful], *s.* Tonto, necio; también, persona divertida, chancera.

tomfoolery [tɒmˈfuːlərɪ] [tom-fu-la-ri], *s.* Proceder o conducta necia, payasadas.

tomorrow [təˈmɒrəʊ] [to-mo-rou], *s.* El día de mañana, el día inmediato, que sigue al presente. **I wonder what tomorrow will bring,** me pregunto qué nos deparará el futuro, *-adv.* Mañana. **Tomorrow morning,** mañana por la mañana.

tom-tit [ˈtɒmtɪt] [tom-tit], *s. (Orn.)* Paro. V. TIT.

tom-tom [ˈtɒmtɒm] [tom-tom], *s.* 1. Tam-tam, especie de tambor indio. 2. Gongo. *V.* GONG.

ton [tʌn] [tan], *s.* 1. Tonelada, medida de capacidad y el peso de dos mil libras o veinte quintales; este peso se llama *short ton,* en contraposición al *long ton* de 2,240 libras. 2. *(Des.)* Medida de dos toneles. *V.* TUN.

tonal [ˈtəʊnl] [tou-nal], *a. (Mús.)* Tonal, relativo a los tonos o a la tonalidad.

tonality [təˈnælɪtɪ] [tou-na-li-ti], *s.* 1. Tonalidad, sistema de sonidos que sirve de fundamento a una composición musical. 2. Conjunto de tonos que tiene un cuadro.

tone [təʊn] [toun], *s.* 1. Tono de la voz o del habla, y a veces también se toma por la misma voz o habla. **Don't speak to me in that tone of voice!,** ¡no me hables en ese tono! 2. Tono o timbre en la música, intervalo de un segundo mayor. 3. Tonillo, modo particular de hablar o de leer. 4. Tono en medicina es el estado de tensión, elasticidad o firmeza propio y peculiar de cada órgano para ejercer su función respectiva. 5. Estilo o tendencia característica; tono. 6. Tono, efecto general de un cuadro, su armonía con relación el colorido y claroscuro; matiz de color. 7. Nivel (level). **To raise the tone,** levantar el nivel.

tone, *va.* 1. Dar el tono; modificar el tono; entonar (cuadros, fotografías). 2. Templar. *V.* TUNE. 3. *V.* INTONE. *-vn.* 1. Corresponder en tono o matiz. 2. Tomarse un matiz dado. **To tone down,** (a) *(Pint.)* suavizar el tono, pintar con colores menos vivos; (b) moderar la calidad y volumen del sonido; (c) modificar en cuanto a la expresión o al efecto. **To tone up,** (a) aumentar la calidad o fuerza; (b) elevar el tono músico; (c) dar o adquirir mayor fuerza o vigor corporal, tonificar (revitalize).

toneless [ˈtəʊnlɪs] [toun-les], *a.* Que está fuera de tono, sin estilo característico.

toner [ˈtəʊnəʳ] [tou-naʳ], *s.* Tónico, loción tonificante.

tongs [tɒŋz] [tongs], *s. pl.* Tenazas, instrumento para prender, asir o agarrar alguna cosa; alicates. **Coal-tongs,** tenazas de chimenea, para coger las brasas. **Oyster-tongs,** gafas para pescar ostras. **Sugar-tongs,** tenacillas para azúcar. **Hammer and tongs,** *(Fam.)* con violencia, con todas sus fuerzas.

tongue [tʌŋ] [tang], *s.* 1. Lengua, el órgano del gusto y de la palabra. 2. Lengua (language), idioma o modo de hablar de una nación. 3. Lengua, habla, lenguaje, lo que se habla. 4. Lengüeta, lo que tiene forma de una pequeña lengua; espiga, saliente pequeño de una tabla; clavo de nebilla; lengua de tierra; badajo de campana. **Foul tongue,** lengua maldiciente; *(Med.)* lengua cargada. **To hold the tongue,** callar. **Tongue-tie,** *va.* Atar la lengua a uno, hacer callar. *-s.* Frenillo, defecto físico que impide a los niños mamar y hablar con facilidad. **Tongue-tied,** con frenillo; con la lengua atada, mudo. **Tongue twister,** trabalenguas.

tongue, *va.* 1. Modificar el sonido de (la flauta, corneta, etc.) por medio de la lengua. 2. Poner lengüetas para machihembrar. *-vn.* Usar de la lengua hablando o tocando un instrumento de viento; picotear.

tongued [tʌŋd] [tangd], *a.* El o lo que tiene lengua. **A fine-tongued fellow,** un zalamero, uno que usa palabras muy melosas.

tongueless [ˈtʌŋlɪs] [tang-les], *a.* 1. Mudo (dumb), sin habla. 2. Deslenguado, sin lengua. 3. Confuso, turbado. 4. Aquello de que nadie habla.

tonic [ˈtɒnɪk] [to-nik], *a.* 1. Tónico (pick-me-up), nombre dado a todo medicamento que excita la acción vital. 2. Tónico, perteneciente al tono o a los tonos; en música, perteneciente a la nota tónica o dominante. 3. Tenso, perteneciente a la tensión, *(Med.)* rígido, tieso. *-s.* 1. Tónico, medicamento fortificante. 2. *(Mús.)* Tónica (dominante) primera nota de la escala del tono en que está escrita una pieza de música.

tonicity [tɒˈnɪsɪtɪ] [to-ni-si-ti], *s.* Tonicidad, calidad de tónico; salud y vigor en general.

tonight [təˈnaɪt] [to-nait], *s.* La noche inmediata, la que sigue al día de hoy; esta noche. *-adv.* Esta noche.

toning [ˈtəʊnɪŋ] [to-nin], *s.* Entonación, el acto o procedimiento de entonar; en fotografía, el arte o acto de tratar una impresión plateada con una disolución de cloruro de oro para cambiarle el color y aumentar su permanencia.

tonnage [ˈtʌnɪdʒ] [ta-nich], *s.* 1. Tonelaje o porte de un buque manifestado en toneladas; arqueo; también arqueo o cabida del conjunto de los buques de un país. 2. Alcabala o derecho de aduana que se cobra a tanto por tonelada.

tonsil [ˈtɒnsl] [ton-sil], *s.* Tonsila, amígdala, cuerpo glanduloso situado a uno y otro lado de la faringe. **She had her tonsils out,** le operaron de las amígdalas.

tonsilitis, tonsillitis [ˌtɒnsɪˈlaɪtɪs] [ton-si-lai-tis], *s.* Amigdalitis, inflamación de las tonsilas.

tonsillectomy [ˌtɒnsɪˈlektəmɪ] [ton-si-lek-ta-mi], *s. (Med.)* Amigdalotomía, extirpación de las amígdalas.

tonsorial [tɒnˈsɔːrɪəl] [ton-so-rial], *a.* Barberil, perteneciente a los barberos.

tonsure [ˈtɒnʃəʳ] [ton-shaʳ], *s.* 1. Tonsura, la acción de cortar el pelo. 2. Tonsura, grado preparatorio para recibir las órdenes menores, que confiere el prelado con la ceremonia de cortar al aspirante un poco de cabello. 3. Lugar de la cabeza en que se cortan esos cabellos.

tony [ˈtəʊnɪ] [tou-ni], *a. (Coloq.)* Fino, elegante.

too [tuː] [tu], *adv.* 1. Demasiadamente, demasido (excessively). 2. Además, igualmente, también (as well), así mismo, aun. 3. Muy (very). **I'm not too very sure,** no estoy muy seguro.

took [tʊk] [tuk], *pret.* del verbo TAKE.

tool [tuːl] [tul], *va. y vn.* Marcar o adornar con una herramienta. *-s.* 1. Herramienta (instrument), apero, utensilio, trebejo, el instrumento que sirve para cualquier trabajo manual. **Garden tools,** herramientas de jardinería. 2. Por extensión, máquina como torno que se emplea para hacer máquinas. 3. La persona que sirve de instrumento a otra para hacer alguna cosa mala. **Edge-tool,** instrumento cortante.

toot [tuːt] [tut], *va. y vn.* Tocar el cuerno de caza, una bocina o un silbato. *-s.* Bocinazo.

tooth [tuːθ] [tuz], *s. (pl.* TEETH). 1. Diente, hueso pequeño engastado en la quijada que sirve para mascar los manjares. **Back-tooth,** muela. **Eye-tooth,** colmillo. **Tooth-brushes,** cepillos para dientes. 2. Diente de sierra, de rueda o de otro cualquier instrumento. 3. *(Bot. y Zool.)* Diente, dentecillo. 4. Gusto, paladar. 5. *pl. (Fig.)* Fuerza que hace oposición. **In the teeth of the wind,** contra la fuerza del viento. **To have a sweet tooth,** tener el paladar delicado, gustar de dulces y golosinas. **To show one's teeth,** enseñar los dientes, amenazar. **To cast in the teeth,** echar en cara, mostrar los dientes. **Tooth and nail,** con todo tesón, con todo empeño, con todas sus fuerzas. **In spite of one's teeth,** a despecho, a pesar de uno.

tooth, *va.* 1. Dentar, proveer de dientes. 2. Encajar unos dientes en otros. 3. *(Mar.)* Endentar.

toothache [ˈtuːθeɪk] [tuz-eik], *s.* Dolor de muelas.

toothbrush [ˈtuːθbrʌʃ] [tuz-brash], *s.* Cepillo de dientes.

toothed [tuːθt] [tuzt], *a.* Dentado, que tiene dientes. **Toothed wheel,** rueda dentada.

toothfairy [ˈtuːθfɛərɪ] [tuz-fea-ri], *s.* Ratoncito Pérez.

toothless [ˈtuːθlɪs] [tuz-les], *a.* Desdentado, que no tiene o ha perdido los dientes.

toothpaste [ˈtuːθpeɪst] [tuz-peist], *s.* Dentífrico, pasta de dientes, pasta dentífrica.

toothpick [ˈtuːθpɪk] [tuz-pik], *s.* Mondadientes, palillo, escarbadientes. **Tooth-pick case,** palillero.

toothshell [ˈtuːθʃel] [tuz-shel], *s.* Dental, una especie de concha parecida a un diente.

toothsome [ˈtuːθsəm] [tuz-sam], *a.* Sabroso, gustoso, grato al paladar o al gusto.

toothwort [ˈtuːθwɔːt] [tuz-uort], *s. (Bot.)* Dentaria.

toothy [ˈtuːθɪ] [tu-zi], *a.* Dentudo.

tooting [ˈtuːtɪŋ] [tu-tin], *s.* El acto de tocar la trompa o la corneta; sonido de trompa.

top [tɒp] [top], *s.* 1. Cima, cumbre (height), cabeza, remate, coronilla, coronamiento (de pared), copa, punta, cielo, el extremo, lo más alto y elevado de cualquier cosa; y según esta sea se le aplican dichas voces. 2. Cumbre o ápice del favor, de la fortuna, de la gloria, etc. 3. Superficie. 4. El último grado; el puesto más elevado (highest rank); la persona superior en alguna calidad moral a todas las demás. **She worked her way to the top,** se abrió camino hasta la cima de su profesión. 5. Corona de la cabeza. 6. Tupé, el pelo que se trae en la parte anterior de la cabeza. 7. La cabeza o punta de una planta. **Tops of boots,** campanas, vueltas de o para las botas. 8. Trompo, peón, con que juegan los muchachos haciéndole dar vueltas. **Whipping-top,** peonza. **From top to bottom,** de arriba abajo. **From top to toe,** de pies a cabeza, de arriba a bajo. 9. *(Mar.)* Cofa, tablero colocado horizontalmente en el cuello de un palo para afirmar la obencadura. **Main-top,** cofa mayor. **Fore-top,** cofa de trinquete. **Mizzen-top,** cofa de mesana. **Top-mast,** mastelero. **Top-block,** motón de virador. **Top-lantern,** farol de la cofa. **Top-rails,** batayolas de las cofas. **Top-rope,** amante del virador. **Top-sails,** gavias. **Top-sail-sheets,** escotines. **Top-tackle,** aparejo, del virador. **Top-armor, or armings,** empavesadas de las cofas. *-a.* Lo más elevado en lugar, grado o posición; primero, principal. **The service is top class,** el servicio es de primera.

top, *va. y vn.* 1. Elevarse o levantarse por encima de otra cosa. 2. Sobrepujar. 3. Aventajar, exceder, superar (surpass). 4. Predominar, exceder mucho en altura una cosa respecto de otra. 5. Predominar, prevalecer o tener más fuerza. 6. Cubrir el mango, el cabo, la punta o la extremidad de cualquier cosa con otra diversa. 7. Esforzarse, esmerarse. 8. Descabezar o desmochar los árboles. 9. Encumbrarse, llegar a la cumbre de alguna cosa. 10. *(Fam.)* Ejecutar alguna cosa a la perfección. **To top a yard,** *(Mar.)* Amantillar o embicar las vergas. **Topping lifts,** *(Mar.)* Amantillos. 11. Suicidarse (commit suicide).

toparch [ˈtɒpɑːk] [top-ark], *s.* Toparca, *(m.)* persona principal en un lugar o en un territorio reducido.

topaz [ˈtəʊpæz] [tou-pas], *s.* 1. Topacio, piedra preciosa amarilla compuesta de sílice, alúmina y fluor. 2. Topaza, colibrí del género Topaza, de vivos colores y de tamaño relativamente grande.

topcoat [ˈtɒpkəʊt] [top-kout], *s.* Abrigo o sobretodo liviano, gabán (overcoat).

tope [ˈtəʊp] [toup], *vn.* Soplar, beber mucho.

tope, *s.* Altar, bóveda o torre budista, construída para guardar reliquias.

toper [ˈtəʊpəʳ] [tou-paʳ], *s.* Borrachón, bebedor. *(Fam.)* Tomista.

topful [ˈtɒpfʊl] [top-ful], *a.* Lleno hasta arriba.

top-gallant [ˈtɒpgælənt] [top-ga-lant], *s.* 1. *(Mar.)* Juanete, la vela que va encima de la gavia. 2. Cumbre, cima; cualquier cosa muy elevada.

topiary [ˈtɒpɪərɪ] [to-pia-ri], *a.* Que pertenece al arte de entretejer ramos.

topic [ˈtɒpɪk] [to-pik], *s.* 1. Asunto (matter), objeto de un discurso; tema. 2. *pl. (Ret.)* Lugares comunes, tópicos. 3. El remedio tópico o que se aplica directamente a la parte enferma.

topical [ˈtɒpɪkəl] [to-pi-kal], *a.* 1. Tópico, perteneciente a algún principio o punto general o a algún lugar determinado. 2. Local, limitado; que se emplea exteriormente.

top-knot [ˈtɒpkɒt] [top-not], *s.* Fontanche, un moño alto sobre la frente adornado con cintas.

topless [ˈtɒplɪs] [top-les], *a.* 1. Que no tiene cima o ápice. 2. Sin la parte de arriba.

topman [ˈtɒpmən] [top-man], *s.* Aserrador de arriba (garments).

topmost [ˈtɒpməʊst] [top-moust], *a.* Lo más alto.

topnotch [ˈtɒpnɒtʃ] [top-noch], *a. (Fam.)* De primera, excelente, insuperable.

topographer [təˈpɒgrəfəʳ] [to-po-gra-faʳ], *s.* Topógrafo, el que describe o delinea algún terreno.

topographic [ˌtɒpəˈgræfɪk] [to-po-gra-fik], *a.* Topográfico.

topographist [təˈpɒgrəfɪst] [to-po-gra-fist], *s.* V. TOPOGRAPHER.

topography [təˈpɒgrəfɪ] [to-po-gra-fi], *s.* 1. Topografía, descripción detallada o delineación de un terreno o región. 2. Conjunto de caracteres físicos de una región.

topping [ˈtɒpɪŋ] [to-pin], *a.* 1. Eminente, distinguido (distinguished). 2. De grandes pretensiones, empenachado, arrogante. *-s.* Cubierta, mango, punta, la extremidad o cabo que se pone a una cosa.

toppingy [ˈtɒpɪŋɪ] [to-pin-gui], *adv.* Aventajadamente, con todo primor.

topple [ˈtɒpl] [to-pel], *va.* Hacer caer, volcar. *-vn.* Volcarse o caer hacia adelante una cosa. **She toppled over,** perdió el equilibrio y se cayó.

top-sail [ˈtɒpseɪl] [top-seil], *s. (Mar.)* Gavia, vela de gavia. **To have the top-sails set,** *(Mar.)* Tener las gavias largas. **To back the top-sails,** *(Mar.)* Poner las gavias en facha.

top-secret [ˈtɒpˈsiːkrɪt] [top-si-krit], *a.* Estrictamente confidencial, absolutamente secreto.

topsy-turvy [ˈtɒpsɪˈtɜːvɪ] [top-si-ter-vi], *adv.* Al revés, con lo de abajo arriba, desordenado (messy). **A topsy-turvy world,** un mundo patas arriba, loco.

toque [təʊk] [touk], *s.* 1. Cofia, toca, especie de gorra de mujer. 2. Toca, la alta cofia cónica de los antiguos Dux de Venecia.

tor [tɔːʳ] [toʳ], *s.* 1. Peñasco, altura. 2. Torre, torrecilla.

Torah [ˈtɔːrə] [to-ra], *s.* **The Torah,** la Torá.

torch [ˈtɔːtʃ] [torch], *s.* 1. Antorcha (flame), hacha. 2. Linterna. 3. Incendiario (arsonist).

torch-bearer [ˈtɔːtʃˌbeərəʳ] [torch-bea-raʳ], *s.* Hachero, el que alumbra con hacha.

torchlight [ˈtɔːtʃlaɪt] [torch-lait], *s.* Luz de antorcha, en contraposición a la luz del sol.

torch-thistle [ˈtɔːtʃˌðɪzl] [torch-zi-sel], *s. (Bot.)* Céreo, cirio.

tore [tɔːʳ] [toʳ], *pret.* del verbo TO TEAR. *-s.* 1. *(Arq.)* Tondino; toro; bocel. 2. *(Prov. Ingl.)* La hierba inútil que queda en los campos en invierno.

torment [ˈtɔːmənt] [tor-ment], *va.* Atormentar, martirizar (tease), afligir, causar molestia o enfado.

torment, *s.* Tormento, pena, dolor violento, angustia, tortura (torture).

tormenter, tormentor [ˈtɔːməntəʳ] [tor-men-taʳ], *s.* Atormentador.

torn [tɔːrn] [tôrn], *pp.* del verbo TO TEAR.

tornado [tɔːˈneɪdəʊ] [tor-nei-dou], *s.* Tornado, huracán que ocurre por lo general en el borde o límite sudeste de un ciclón.

torpedo [tɔːˈpiːdəʊ] [tor-pi-dou], *s. (pl.* TORPEDOES). 1. Torpedo, aparato o máquina de guerra que sirve para volar barcos. 2. Torpedo, tremielga, tembladera, pez eléctrico o raya eléctrica. **Torpedo boat,** torpedero, buque veloz para lanzar torpedos.

torpid [ˈtɔːpɪd] [tor-pid], *a.* Adormecido, entorpecido, privado de movimiento.

torpidness ['tɔːpɪdnɪs] [tor-pid-nes], *s.* 1. Entorpecimiento, pasmo o adormecimiento de algún miembro. 2. Letargo, sopor (drowsiness), apatía, estupor o embotamiento de los sentidos o del ánimo.

torque [tɔːk] [tork], *s.* 1. Collar. 2. *(Mec.)* Esfuerzo de torsión.

torrent ['tɒrənt] [to-rent], *s.* 1. Torrente, corriente o avenida impetuosa de aguas. 2. Torrente, abundancia o muchedumbre de cosas que vienen a un mismo tiempo.

torrential [tɒˈrenʃəl] [to-ren-shal], *a.* Torrencial, que todo lo arrastra tras de sí en su carrera como un torrente.

torrid ['tɒrɪd] [to-rid], *a.* Tórrido, muy ardiente (burning); tostado. **The torrid zone,** zona tórrida, la que está entre los trópicos.

torridness ['tɒrɪdnɪs] [to-rid-nes], *s.* El estado o la calidad de lo que es muy ardiente.

torsion ['tɔːʃən] [tor-shon], *s.* Torcedura, torsión, acción y efecto de torcer. **Torsion,** acción y efecto de torcer. **Torsion balance,** balanza de torsión.

torso ['tɔːsəʊ] [tor-sou], *s.* Torso, tronco de una estatua sin cabeza y sin miembros.

tort [tɔːt] [tort], *s. (For.)* Tuerto, agravio, sinrazón.

tortile ['tɔːtɪl] [tor-til], *a.* Torcido, doblado.

tortoise ['tɔːtəs] [tor-tos], *s.* Tortuga. **Tortoiseshell o turtleshell,** carey, concha de tortuga. **Sea tortoise o turtle,** tortuga de mar. **Land tortoise,** tortuga de tierra, galápago.

tortuous ['tɔːtjʊəs] [tor-tuos], *a.* Tortuoso (winding), torcido, sinuoso.

tortuosity [ˌtɔːtjʊˈɒsɪtɪ] [tor-tuo-si-ti], *s.* 1. Tortuosidad. 2. Estragamiento de costumbres.

tortuosness ['tɔːtjʊəsnɪs] [tor-tuos-nes], *s.* Tortuosidad.

torture ['tɔːtʃəʳ] [tor-chaʳ], *s.* 1. Tortura, tormento, dolor. **Under torture he gave their names,** dio sus nombres porque lo torturaron.

torture, *va.* 1. Atormentar, someter al tormento, hacer sufrir la tortura. 2. Atomentar o afligir la memoria de una cosa. 3. Torcer en una forma anormal; alterar el sentido, p. ej. de un texto.

tortured ['tɔːtʃed] [tor-chad], *a.* Atormentado. **Tortured to death,** muerto en el tormento.

torturer ['tɔːtʃərəʳ] [tor-cha-raʳ], *s.* Atormentador, torturador.

toss [tɒs] [tos], *va.* 1. Tirar (throw), arrojar o echar alguna cosa con la mano. 2. Tirar, lanzar, arrojar o disparar con violencia; lanzar al aire. **Let's toss a coin,** echémoslo a cara o cruz. 3. Agitar (shake), mover bruscamente, en especial hacia arriba, v. gr. la cabeza; sacudir. **To toss in a blanket,** mantear. 4. Agitar, discutir, repetir lo dicho. *-vn.* 1. Estar en continua agitación, no estarse quieto. 2. Corcovear, dar corcovos en el aire. **To toss one about o to and fro,** traer a alguno al retortero o al peloteo, traerle engañado con falsas promesas. **To toss aside,** arrojar a un lado; dejar de usar, no hacer caso de alguien o algo. **To toss off,** tragar de golpe, beber sin tomar aliento; también, echar a un lado, disponer de. **To toss up,** tirar o lanzar en alto; levantar o alzar algo; jugar a cara o cruz.

toss, *s.* 1. Sacudimiento, sacudida, lanzamiento (throw). 2. Un modo de mover la cabeza con afectación hacia arriba. **With a toss of his head,** con un movimiento brusco de la cabeza.

tosser ['tɒsəʳ] [to-saʳ], *s.* 1. Sacudidor, manteador. 2. Cualquiera persona o cosa que agita a otra.

tossing ['tɒsɪŋ] [to-sin], *s.* 1. Sacudimiento, sacudida. 2. Agitación (agitation). 3. Manteamiento.

tossingly ['tɒsɪŋlɪ] [to-sin-li], *adv.* Con sacudidas o sacudimientos.

tosspot ['tɒspɒt] [tos-pot], *s. (Ant.)* Borrachón; glotón.

tot [tɒt] [tot], *s.* 1. Niño, niña que marcha con paso incierto, pequeño (young child). 2. Copita (alcohol). *(Coloq.)* **Tot up,** sumar.

total ['təʊtl] [tou-tal], *a.* Total, completo, entero (whole), todo. **A complete stranger,** una persona totalmente desconocida. *-s.* Total, el todo.

total, *vt.* 1. Ascender, elevarse a, un total de, sumar (add up), totalizar. 2. **The car was totaled,** el coche quedó totalmente destrozado.

totalitarian [ˌtəʊtælɪˈteərɪən] [tou-ta-li-tea-rian], *a.* Totalitario, dictatorial.

totality [təʊˈtælɪtɪ] [tou-ta-li-ti], *s.* Totalidad.

totalizator ['təʊtəlaɪzeɪtəʳ] [tou-ta-lai-sei-taʳ], *s.* Máquina para registrar apuestas en las carreras de caballos.

totally ['təʊtəlɪ] [tou-ta-li], *adv.* Totalmente.

tote [təʊt] [tout], *va. (Fam. E. U. del Sud).* 1. Llevar carga sobre los hombros. 2. Entre los cortadores de árboles, acarrear provisiones y pertrechos desde el depósito o almacén a los bosques donde trabajan.

tote bag ['təʊtbæg] [tout-bag], *s.* Bolso grande, bolsón.

totem ['təʊtəm] [tou-tem], *s.* Totem, poste totémico.

totter ['tɒtəʳ] [to-taʳ], *vn.* 1. Bambolear, tambalear, temblar, estar para caer o estar cayéndose, desmoronarse, amenazar ruina, bambolearse. 2. Vacilar, titubear. **The regime is tottering,** el régimen está a punto de caer, está tambaleándose.

tottering ['tɒtərɪŋ] [to-ta-rin], *a.* Vacilante; que bambonea o bambolea, que amenaza ruina, inseguro (unsteady). *-s.* 1. Bamboleo o bamboneo. 2. Vacilación.

totteringly ['tɒtərɪŋlɪ] [to-ta-rin-li], *adv.* De un modo vacilante.

tottery ['tɒtərɪ] [to-ta-ri], *a.* Vacilante, inestable.

toucan ['tuːkən] [tu-kan], *s. (Orn.)* Tucán, ave trepadora de América del género Rhamphastos, notable por su enorme pico.

touch [tʌtʃ] [tach], *va.* 1. Tocar, ponerse en contacto, particularmente con una parte del cuerpo; rozar ligeramente (brush). 2. Tocar, poner la mano en una cosa sin cogerla; palpar. 3. Tocar, llegar, juntar una cosa a otra sin que quede espacio en medio. 4. Llegar a alguna parte. 5. Tocar o examinar los metales en la piedra de toque para saber su calidad y quilates. 6. Hacer relación a una persona o cosa. 7. Tocar o comunicar a uno un contagio físico o moral. 8. Mover, enternecer, imprimir en el corazón afectos de amor, piedad, etc., conmover; irritar, excitar la ira, aguijonear, herir, afligir, afectar (affect, concern). **He was touched by her kindness,** su amabilidad lo enterneció. 9. Tocar, tratar de una cosa ligeramente. 10. Esquiciar, trazar. 11. Tocar, hacer sonar en algún instrumento hiriendo sus cuerdas. 12. Influir, tocar a; concernir, importar. *-vn.* 1. Tocar, estar cercano o contiguo, estar en contacto; tocarse. 2. Imponer las manos sobre una persona para curarla de una enfermedad, v. gr. los lamparones. **To touch at,** llegar a algún paraje sin detenerse. **To touch at a port,** hacer escala en algún puerto. **Touch down,** *(Aerosp.)* aterrizar. **To touch off,** descargar (un cañón); hacer o acabar de prisa, bosquejar. **Touch on,** tocar, mencionar. **To touch up,** retocar, corregir. **To touch upon a thing,** tocar, hablar de una cosa por incidencia. **To touch one,** tocar a uno, concernirle. **That touches him to the quick,** le toca a lo vivo. **To touch and go,** *(Mar.)* tocar y aparejar; tratar de una asunto ligeramente.

touch, *s.* 1. Toque, el acto de tocar una cosa tentándola o palpándola o llegándose inmediatamente a ella; tocamiento, palpamiento, la acción y efecto de tocar. 2. Contacto, el acto de tocarse dos cuerpos. 3. Tacto, uno de los sentidos corporales, y el acto de tocar. 4. Toque, golpe; manera o método característico; ejecución, la última mano. 5. Toque en la pintura y escultura, pincelada, rasgo. 6. Cantidad pequeña de alguna cosa mezclada con otra; dolorcito, latido, dolor corto; un poco, una sospecha. 7. Indirecta. 8. Tiento, ensayo ligero. 9. La acción y la manera de tañer algún instrumento de música; también, la resistencia que opone el teclado a los dedos del que toca; tañimiento. 10. Buena inteligencia, armonía, simpatía, correspondencia. 11. Toque en el oro o plata con la piedra de toque. 12. Habilidad (skill). 13. Toque, la prueba, examen o experiencia que se hace de algún sujeto. 14. Movimiento interior del alma. **I will have a touch at it,** le daré un tiento. **Touch-and-go:** (a) dispuesto a dispararse al más leve toque; (b) *(Mar.)* que roza el fondo sin perder velocidad; que escapa a duras penas; (c) ligero y alegre. U. t. c. s. **Touch-back,** s. (Término del juego de pelota llamado *foot-ball*) El acto de tocar el suelo con la pelota detrás de la meta del propio jugador, después de haberla lanzado con el pie uno de los jugadores del bando opuesto. **Touch-down,** (Término de *foot-ball*) el acto o la jugada consistente en tocar el suelo con la pelota detrás de la meta del campo enemigo.

touchable ['tʌtʃəbl] [ta-cha-bol], *a.* Tangible (concrete), que se puede tocar.

touch-and-go ['tʌtʃən'gəʊ] [tach-an-gou], *s.* Situación sumamente incierta o precaria. *-a.* Incierto, casual, inestable.

touché [tu:'ʃeɪ] [tu-shei], *interj.* Apúntate un tanto.

touched ['tʌtʃt] [tacht], *a. (Fam.)* Tocado.

touch-hole ['tʌtʃhəʊl] [tach-joul], *s.* Fogón, oído del cañón.

touching ['tʌtʃɪŋ] [ta-chin], *prep.* Tocante, en orden a lo cual, por lo que toca a, concerniente a, en cuanto a, en orden a, acerca de. *-a.* Patético, lastimero, tierno, enternecedor (moving), afectuoso. *-s.* Toque, acto de tocar; contacto.

touchingly ['tʌtʃɪŋlɪ] [ta-chin-li], *adv.* Patéticamente, tiernamente, de un modo afectuoso.

touchstone ['tʌtʃstəʊn] [tach-stoun], *s.* Piedra de toque; examen, prueba; criterio.

touchy ['tʌtʃɪ] [ta-chi], *a.* Vidrioso, enojadizo, susceptible (sensitive), quisquilloso, cosquilloso. **Touchy subject,** tecla.

tough [tʌf] [taf], *a.* 1. Correoso (leathery), tenaz, flexible, que se extiende y se doblega fácilmente sin romperse. 2. Tieso, que no puede doblarse con facilidad. 3. Fuerte (strong), duro, que no puede romperse sin esfuerzo; vigoroso, de gran fortaleza para el sufrimiento. 4. Viscoso, glutinoso. 5. *(Fam.)* Difícil, penoso. *-adv. (Coloq.)* **Stop acting tough,** no te hagas el gallito. *-s. (Coloq.)* Matón.

toughen ['tʌfn] [ta-fen], *va. y vn.* Hacer o hacerse correoso; endurecer, hacer duro, llegar a ser duro.

toughie ['tʌfɪ] [ta-fi], *s. (Coloq.)* 1. **The exam was a real toughie,** el examen fue dificilísimo. 2. Matoncito.

toughly ['tʌflɪ] [taf-li], *adv.* Fuertemente.

toughness ['tʌfnɪs] [taf-nes], *s.* 1. Flexibilidad. 2. Tenacidad; viscosidad. 3. Tesura, rigidez de lo que no se puede doblar. 4. Actitud agresiva (aggressiveness).

toupee ['tu:peɪ] [tu-pei], *s.* Tupé, mechón de cabello.

tour ['tʊər] [tua'], *s.* 1. Viaje, peregrinación. **To take** o **make a tour,** viajar. 2. Vuelta, paseo o viaje corto, excursión; circuito. 3. Vuelta, giro, revolución de los planetas. 4. Jornada, servicio; término militar de otros tiempos. 5. *(Mús., Teat.)* Gira, tournée. **Tour guide,** guía de turismo. **Tour operator,** operador turístico. *(Mil.)* **Tour of duty,** período de servicio.

tour, *vt.* 1. Recorrer, viajar por. 2. *(Mús., Teat.)* Ir de gira, hacer una gira por.

tour de force ['tʊədə'fɔːs] [tua-de-fors], *s.* Hazaña, tour de force.

touring ['tʊərɪŋ] [tu-rin], *a.* Ambulante, que está de gira.

tourism ['tʊərɪzəm] [tu-ri-sem], *s.* Turismo.

tourist ['tʊərɪst] [tu-rist], *s.* Turista, viajero, excursionista. **Tourist court,** campo de turistas, especie de hotel para turistas. **The tourist season,** la temporada turística.

touristy ['tʊərɪstɪ] [tu-ris-ti], *a. (Coloq.)* Demasiado turístico.

tournament ['tʊənəmənt] [tur-na-ment], *s.* Torneo, justa.

tourney ['tʊənɪ] [tur-ni], *vn.* Tornear, combatir o pelear en el torneo.

tourniquet ['tʊənɪkeɪ] [tur-ni-kei], *s.* Torniquete, instrumento quirúrgico para impedir la hemorragia en operaciones y heridas de las extremidades.

touse [taʊz] [taus], *vt.* Pegar, dar una tunda a alguien.

tousle ['taʊzl] [tau-sel], *va.* Desordenar, alborotar (el cabello); comúnmente en el participio pasado.

tousled ['taʊzld] [tau-seld], *a.* Desgreñado (unkempt), despeinado (el cabello).

tout [taʊt] [taut], *vi.* **To tout for customers,** andar a la caza de clientes. *-vt.* Ofrecer (offer); promocionar (promote).

tow [taʊl] [tau], *s.* Estopa, la borra del lino y del cáñamo. **Tow-head,** persona que tiene los cabellos de color rubio subido o alborotados. **Tow-headed,** que tiene los cabellos muy rubios.

tow, *s.* 1. Lo que va o está remolcado o espiado; bajeles, barcos, etc. 2. Atoaje o espía, la maniobra de espiar un barco. **Tow-boat,** barco remolcador. **Tow-line, tow-rope,** cabo de remolque, sirga, remolque. **Tow-path,** camino de sirga.

tow, *va.* Remolcar, atoar, espiar, halar, tirar o llevar a remolque por medio de un cabo que se tiende por la proa, amarrado a un anclote o al muelle. **To take in tow,** *(Mar.)* tomar a remolque. **They towed the car away,** se llevaron el coche a remolque.

towage ['tʊɪdʒ] [touich], *s.* 1. Derechos de sirga. 2. Atoaje o espía, la maniobra de atoar o espiar un barco.

toward, towards [tə'wɔːdz] [to-uords], *prep.* Hacia, con dirección a; con, para con; cerca, cerca de, cosa de, alrededor de, con respecto a, tocante a. **Toward o towards evening,** hacia o cerca del anochecer. **Toward God,** para con Dios.

towardly [tə'wɔːdlɪ] [to-uard-li], *a.* Dócil (meek), complaciente, deferente.

towel ['taʊəl] [taual], *s.* Toalla, paño de manos, tela de lino o lienzo para enjugar una cosa frotándola. **Roller towel,** toalla continua, giratoria. *-vt.* Secar con toalla.

toweling ['taʊəlɪŋ] [taua-lin], *s.* Toalla, felpa.

tower ['taʊər] [taua'], *s.* 1. Torre de iglesia, campanario, etc. 2. Torre, torreón: ciudadela, fortaleza. 3. Vuelo alto, elevación. 4. Un peinado muy elevado que se usaba antiguamente. **The Tower of London,** la Torre de Londres.

tower, *vn.* 1. Elevarse una cosa a una altura desmesurada. 2. Remontarse o tomar viento libre las aves cuando vuelan muy alto. **Tower above,** destacar sobre.

towered ['taʊəd] [tauad], *a.* Torreado, guarnecido de torres.

towering ['taʊərɪŋ] [taua-rin], *a.* Destacado, sobresaliente.

town [taʊn] [taun], *s.* 1. Ciudad, villa, pueblo grande. 2. *(E. U.)* Municipalidad, subdivisión de un condado. 3. *(Ingl.)* Plaza, cualquier porción o número de casas rodeadas de muros. **A fortified town,** plaza de armas. **A trading town,** ciudad mercantil. **Seaport town,** ciudad marítima, puerto de mar. **In town,** en la ciudad: en la metrópoli. **On the town,** *(E. U.)* 1. Indigente, que no tiene para vivir más que los socorros de la ciudad. 2. Que vive de la prostitución. **Man about town,** hombre acaudalado que vive en la ociosidad y cómodamente, y frecuenta los clubs y lugares públicos. **Women of the town,** damas cortesanas, rameras. **Town clerk,** secretario de ayuntamiento. **Town crier,** pregonero. **Town hall,** casa de ayuntamiento o casa consistorial. **Town house,** (a) casa consistorial, casa de ayuntamiento o ayuntamiento, casa de consejo, y en algunas partes de España consistorio; (b) la casa que uno tiene en la ciudad cuando se habla de una persona que tiene otra fuera de ella: los ingleses regularmente entienden por *town house* la casa que se tiene en Londres. **Town planning,** urbanismo.

township ['taʊnʃɪp] [taun-ship], *s.* 1. *(E. U.)* Territorio de una ciudad; cuerpo municipal; subdivisión de un condado. 2. Extensión de terrenos públicos de los Estados Unidos, de seis millas cuadradas. 3. *(Ingl.)* Límites o territorio de una ciudad.

townsman ['taʊnzmən] [tauns-man], *s.* 1. Vecino de alguna villa o pueblo. 2. Conciudadano, paisano, el que es de la misma ciudad o pueblo que otro.

townspeople ['taʊnzpiːpl] [tauns-pi-pol], *s.* Vecinos del lugar, gente de la ciudad.

towntalk ['taʊntɔːk] [taun-tok], *s.* La cosa o suceso que es tema de conversación en un pueblo.

toxemia [tɒk'siːmɪə] [tok-si-mia], *s.* Toxemia, envenenamiento de la sangre.

toxic ['tɒksɪk] [tok-sik], *a.* 1. Venenoso, ponzoñoso, tóxico. 2. Causado por ponzoña o veneno.

toxicity [,tɒk'sɪsɪtɪ] [tok-si-si-ti], *f.*

toxicological [,tɒksɪ'kɒlədʒɪkəl] [tok-si-ko-lo-yi-kal], *a.* Toxicológico, perteneciente o relativo a al toxicología.

toxicology [,tɒksɪ'kɒlədʒɪ] [tok-si-ko-lo-yi], *s.* Toxicología, parte de la medicina que trata de los venenos.

toxin ['tɒksɪn] [tok-sin], *s.* Toxina.

toy [tɔɪ] [toi], *s.* 1. Juguete. 2. Objeto menudo que imita a otro mayor y que sirve de entretenimiento y diversión. 3. Retozo, retozadura. 4. *(Ant.)* Humorada, capricho, cuento. - *a.* 1. De juguete. **Toy soldier,** soldadito de juguete. 2. Enano (miniature).

toy, *va.* y *vn.* 1. Jugar, enredar, retozar, divertirse. 2. Juguetear. 3. Regodearse o deleitarse haciendo caricias y halagos.

toyish ['tɔɪʃ] [toiish], *a.* Juguetón, caprichoso, semejante a un miriñaque.

toyshop ['tɔɪʃɒp] [toi-shop], *s.* La tienda donde se venden juguetes, juguetería.

trace [treɪs] [treis], *s.* 1. Rastro, huella, pisada. 2. Vestigio, rastro, señal (indication) o apariencia de lo que fue. **They can't find any trace of my letter,** no encuentran mi carta por ninguna parte. 3. Pizca; cantidad o calidad apenas perceptible. 4. Tirante o tiradera que se pone a las mulas o caballos.

trace, *va.* 1. Trazar (chart), delinear, hacer las líneas de un dibujo. 2. Calcar, copiar en una placa transparente. 3. Rastrear, seguir la huella o la pista. 4. Trazar, señalar el camino, la conducta, etc., que se debe seguir. 5. Formar idea de una cosa por algún vestigio o resto de ella o de otra. 6. Imitar o seguir el ejemplo, el estilo, etc. 7. Investigar, descubrir, escudriñar; rastrear. **Tracing-line,** *(Mar.)* Perigallo. 8. Recorrer, seguir su camino por, o a lo largo de.

traceable ['treɪsəbl] [trei-sa-bol], *a.* Que se puede trazar o rastrear, aquello cuyo rastro se puede seguir.

trace element ['treɪsˌelɪmənt] [treis-e-li-ment], *s.* Oligoelemento.

tracer ['treɪsəʳ] [trei-saʳ], *s.* 1. Trazador, investigador, escudriñador, imitador. 2. Tiralíneas, instrumento de dibujante. 3. Cédula o fórmula de investigación, que se envía de un punto a otro para averiguar el paradero de cartas extraviadas en el correo.

tracery ['treɪsərɪ] [trei-sa-ri], *s.* 1. *(Arq.)* Recortaduras, adornos góticos en piedra. 2. Randa. 3. Arte de trazar o de hacer recortaduras.

trachea [trəˈkɪə] [tra-kia], *s.* 1. Tráquea, traquearteria, conducto cartilaginoso por el cual pasa el aire desde la laringe a los bronquios y pulmones. 2. Tráquea, conducto del aire en ciertos artrópodos, como los insectos. 3. *(Bot.)* Ducto, vasos en espiral.

tracheal [trəˈkɪəl] [tra-kial], *a.* Traqueal, perteneciente o relativo a la tráquea.

tracheotomy [ˌtrækɪˈɒtəmɪ] [tra-kio-to-mi], *s.* Traqueotomía, operación quirúrgica, incisión en la tráquea para extraer un cuerpo extraño para impedir la sofocación del paciente en ciertas enfermedades.

tracing ['treɪsɪŋ] [trei-sin], *s.* 1. Acción de trazar. 2. Calco, copia hecha en papel transparente.

tracing paper ['treɪsɪŋˌpeɪpəʳ] [trei-sin-pei-paʳ], *s.* Papel de calco.

track [træk] [trak], *s.* 1. Vestigio, rastro, huella, pisada. 2. Rodada, carril, el surco que dejan en los caminos las ruedas de los carros o carruajes. 3. *(Mar.)* Estela, la señal que el navío deja en el agua cuando va navegando. 4. Rumbo, ruta; curso. 5. Camino (road), senda o vereda muy pasajera. 6. Vía (way), los carriles de una vía férrea; carril sobre el que puede moverse alguna cosa. 7. Campo de carreras. **Double track** *(F.C.)* vía doble. **Side-track,** desviadero. V. SIDE. **Track-walker,** guardavía, empleado que tiene a su cargo la vigilancia constante de un trozo de la vía férrea. 8. Tema, pieza (song). 9. Riel.

track, *va.* 1. Rastrear, seguir el rastro, buscar alguna cosa por él o seguir a alguno por las pisadas. **Track down,** localizar, encontrar. 2. *(Mar.)* sirgar. **Tracking-path,** sirguería. **Tracking-rope,** sirga.

trackage ['trækɪdʒ] [tra-kich], *s.* 1. Tirada, remolque. 2. Carril, el conjunto de rieles de un ferrocarril. **A trackage of eight hundred miles,** extensión de rieles de ochocientas millas.

track and field [ˌtrækənˈfiːld] [trak-an-fild], *s.* Atletismo.

tracker ['trækəʳ] [tra-kaʳ], *s.* 1. *(Mar.)* Sirguero. 2. Rastreador. **Tracker dog,** perro rastreador.

trackless ['træklɪs] [trak-les], *a.* Que no presenta rastro o vestigio de que hayan andado por encima.

track meet ['trækmiːt] [trak-mit], *s.* Competencia de pista y campo.

tract [trækt] [trakt], *s.* 1. Trecho, espacio o extensión de lugar. 2. Región, comarca, un espacio grande de territorio. 3. Curso, serie, continuación. 4. Folleto, discurso, especialmente sobre un tema de religión o de moral; opúsculo. **A tract of land,** un terreno erial o sin cultivo.

tractable ['træktəbl] [trak-ta-bol], *a.* 1. Tratable, manejable, complaciente (indulgent), dócil. 2. Fácil de manejar o trabajar.

tractably ['træktəblɪ] [trak-ta-bli], *adv.* Afablemente, dócilmente, con dulzura en el trato.

tractate ['trækteɪt] [trak-teit], *s.* Tratado, breve, opúsculo, folleto.

tractile ['træktɪl] [trak-til], *a.* Dúctil (malleable).

traction ['trækʃən] [trak-shon], *s.* 1. Tracción, acción y efecto de traer, particularmente de arrastrar los coches o carros sobre una vía o superficie, v. g. del ferrocarril. 2. Contracción, tensión de un músculo. 3. Tracción o fricción de las ruedas sobre una vía. 4. Agarre (grip), adherencia. **Traction engine,** tractor, máquina de tracción.

tractive ['træktɪv] [trak-tiv], *a.* Traedor, que trae.

tractor ['træktəʳ] [trak-taʳ], *s.* Tractor. **Tractor-trailer,** camión con remolque.

trade [treɪd] [treid], *s.* 1. Comercio, tráfico; negocio, trato. 2. Ocupación, oficio, ejercicio: generalmente se entiende del comercio o artes mecánicas en contraposición a la profesión de las ciencias o artes liberales. 3. Conjunto de artesanos del mismo oficio. 4. Volumen del tráfico y cambio (de dinero) hecho en cualquier lugar determinado. 5. *(E.U.)* En la política, convenio de mala ley. **Trade-mark,** marca de fábrica. **Trade-union o trades- union,** gremio de oficios, sociedad de obreros formada para favorecer sus intereses comunes. **What trade does he follow?** ¿Qué oficio tiene?

trade, *va.* y *vn.* 1. Negociar, comerciar, tratar (deal). 2. Traficar, vender, cambiar. **Trade in,** entregar como parte del pago. **Trade on,** explotar, capitalizar.

traded ['treɪdɪd] [trei-did], *a.* Versado, práctico.

trade-in ['treɪdɪn] [treid-in], *s.* Trueque (transaction), objeto dado como pago parcial para la compra de otro similar. Se usa también como verbo activo.

trader ['treɪdəʳ] [trei-daʳ], *s.* 1. Negociante, comerciante (merchant), traficante, negociador. 2. Factor.

trade school ['treɪdskʊl] [treid-skul], *s.* Escuela vocacional, escuela de artes y oficios.

trades-people ['treɪdzˌpiːpl] [treids-pi-pol], *s.* La gente menestral o artesana.

tradesman ['treɪdzmən] [treids-man], *s.* 1. Tendero, mercader, el que tiene tienda. 2. Artesano, menestral.

trade-winds ['treɪdwɪndz] [treid-uinds], *s. pl.* Vientos, alisios, vientos generales, monzones en el Océano Indico.

trading ['treɪdɪŋ] [trei-din], *s.* Comercio, trato. -*a.* Mercantil, comercial. **Trading post,** factoría. **Trading stamps,** sellos de premio.

tradition [trəˈdɪʃən] [tra-di-shon], *s.* 1. Tradición, noticia de alguna cosa antigua que viene de padres a hijos y se comunica por relación sucesiva de unos a otros. 2. Costumbre antigua que casi tiene fuerza de ley. **By tradition,** por tradición.

traditional [trəˈdɪʃənl] [tra-di-sho-nal], *a.* Tradicional, comunicado por tradición.

traditionally [trəˈdɪʃnəlɪ] [tra-di-sho-na-li], *adv.* Por tradición, tradicionalmente (customarily).

traduce [trəˈdjuːs] [tra-dius], *va.* Detractar, difamar (libel), decir mal de uno, murmurar de él, vituperar o afear su conducta; calumniar, denigrar.

traducer [trəˈdjuːsəʳ] [tra-diu-saʳ], *s.* Calumniador, detractor, difamador, murmurador.

traducible [trəˈdjuːsəbl] [tra-diu-sa-bol], *a.* Que puede ser difamado o calumniado.

traduction [trəˈdʌkʃən] [tra-dak-shon], *s. (Poco us.)* 1. Calumnia (defamation), denigración. 2. *(Des.)* Propagación; derivación.

traffic [ˈtræfɪk] [tra-fik], *s.* 1. Tráfico, comercio. 2. Tránsito, transporte. 3. Mercadería, géneros. **Traffic jam,** atasco. **Traffic lane,** vía para el tránsito. **Traffic light,** semáforo, farol o luz de tránsito. **Traffic sign,** señal de tránsito.

traffic, *va.* Negociar, trocar efectos, vender. -*vn.* 1. Traficar, comerciar o negociar en géneros o mercaderías. 2. Hacer alguna cosa vil o infame por interés.

trafficker [ˈtræfɪkəʳ] [tra-fi-kaʳ], *s.* Traficante, comerciante (dealer).

tragedian [trəˈdʒiːdɪən] [tra-yi-dian], *s.* 1. El escritor de tragedias. 2. El actor que representa tragedias.

tragedy [ˈtrædʒɪdɪ] [tra-yi-di], *s.* 1. Tragedia, obra dramática en que se representan sucesos de gran trascendencia o muy conmovedores, por personajes ilustres y con desenlace generalmente funesto. 2. Tragedia, cualquier suceso fatal, funesto, desgraciado o infausto.

tragic [ˈtrædʒɪk] [tra-yik], *a.* 1. Trágico, que pertenece a la tragedia. 2. Trágico, fatal, funesto (terrible), desgraciado.

tragically [ˈtrædʒɪkəlɪ] [tra-yi-ka-li], *adv.* Trágicamente, fatalmente, infaustamente.

tragicalness [ˈtrædʒɪkəlnɪs] [tra-yi-kal-nes], *s.* Tristeza, horror, calamidad, infortunio.

tragicomedy [ˈtrædʒɪˈkɒmɪdɪ] [tra-yi-ko-mi-di], *s.* Tragicomedia, uno de los géneros en que se han dividido las piezas dramáticas.

tragicomic [ˈtrædʒɪˈkɒmɪk] [tra-yi-ko-mik], *a.* Tragicómico, jocoserio, cosa entre lastimosa y risible.

trail [treɪl] [treil], *va.* y *vn.* 1. Rastrear, seguir a algún animal por el rastro; cazar siguiendo la pista. 2. Arrastrar (drag) o llevar arrastrando una cosa por el suelo. 3. Llevar colgando alguna cosa larga. 4. Arrastrar o llevar tras sí. **Trailing arbutus,** *V.* ARBUTUS y MAYFLOWER.

trail, *s.* 1. Rastro (trace), pisada, huella, pista. **The storms left a trail of destruction,** las tormentas destruyeron todo a su paso. 2. Cola, la punta prolongada del vestido o de otra cosa que se lleva arrastrando; cola (de meteoro). 3. Sendero, vereda. v. g. la senda que cruza un yermo. 4. Circunstancia o circunstancias que sugieren y guían las pesquisas en dirección o sentido determinados. **Trail of light,** rastro luminoso. **A false trail,** una pista falsa. **Trail-board,** *(Mar.)* Moldura entre las curvas bandas.

trailer [ˈtreɪləʳ] [trei-laʳ], *s.* 1. Carro de remolque. 2. Remolque-habitación. **Trailer court,** estacionamiento para dichas habitaciones. 3. *(Cin., T.V.)* Avance, trailer.

train [treɪn] [trein], *va.* 1. Disciplinar, ejercitar o hacer que uno aprenda alguna cosa mediante el ejercicio y práctica de ella. 2. Amaestrar, enseñar, criar, adiestrar: en esta significación va casi siempre con la partícula *up.* 3. Preparar, poner en cierta condición física prescrita, por medio de la dieta y el ejercicio. 4. Poner en espaldera, hacer trepar o dirigir en una dirección particular (una planta). 5. Apuntar un cañón. -*vn.* 1. Criar, dar enseñanza, someter a un régimen. 2. Seguir un curso metódico de ejercicios gimnásticos, o de otra clase. **To train a horse,** amaestrar o adiestrar un caballo. **To train soldiers,** disciplinar tropa.

train, *s.* 1. Procesión; fila de vehículos; tren de ferrocarril. 2. Reguero de pólvora. 3. Séquito, tren, comitiva; recua. 4. Serie, continuación ordenada. 5. La cola de las aves; cola de vestido. 6. *(Mec.)* Tren, serie de piezas que obran juntas para transmitir el movimiento. 7. Lazo, celada (trap); trampa. **Down train,** tren descendente, tren de ida. **Up train,** tres ascendente, tren de regreso. **Excursion train,** tren de ida y vuelta de recreo. **Freight train,** *(E.U.)* **goods train,** *(GB)* tren de mercancías, tren de carga. **Through train,** tren directo o terminal.

trainbands [ˈtreɪnbændz] [trein-bands], *s. pl.* Milicias, cuerpos militares formados por los vecinos de algún país o ciudad.

trained [treɪnd] [treind], *a.* 1. Calificado, cualificado. 2. Amaestrado, entrenado. **A highly trained army,** un ejército muy bien adiestrado. 3. Educado.

trainee [treɪˈniː] [trei-nii], *s.* Aprendiz, recluta. **A trainee hairdresser,** un aprendiz de peluquero.

trainer [ˈtreɪnəʳ] [trei-naʳ], *s.* 1. Maestro, director, el que enseña o dirige. 2. Zapatilla de deporte.

training [ˈtreɪnɪŋ] [trei-nin], *s.* La acción de enseñar alguna cosa por medio de la práctica; educación, instrucción (instruction). **Training-school,** *(E.U.)* escuela de instrucción práctica y ejercicio (v. gr. para preparar e instruir a las enfermeras).

trainload [ˈtreɪnləʊd] [trein-loud], *s.* Carga completa de un tren.

trait [treɪt] [treit], *s.* Golpe, toque; rasgo (characteristic), acción; forma, figura, facción.

traitor [ˈtreɪtəʳ] [trei-taʳ], *s.* Traidor.

traitorous [ˈtreɪtərəs] [trei-to-ros], *a.* Pérfido (perfidious), aleve, alevoso, traidor.

traitorously [ˈtreɪtərəslɪ] [trei-to-ros-li], *adv.* Traidoramente, alevosamente, con perfidia.

traitress [ˈtreɪtrɪs] [trei-tris], *f.* Traidora.

traject [ˈtrædʒekt] [tra-yekt], *va.* Tirar, arrojar; traspasar. *V.* TO THROW.

trajectory [trəˈdʒektərɪ] [tra-yek-to-ri], *s.* Trayectoria, curva que describe el proyectil de un arma de fuego.

tram [træm] [tram], *s.* 1. *(GB)* Tranvía; coche de tranvía. 2. Riel plano; carril de tranvía. 3. Carreta de carbón. **Tram-car,** *(GB)* coche de tranvía. **Tramway, tramroad,** 1. tranvía, ferrocarril urbano; 2. camino provisto de rieles planos, para vehículos de ruedas.

trammel [ˈtræməl] [tra-mel], *s.* 1. Impedimento, obstáculo (obstacle); estorbo. 2. Trabas que ponen a los caballos para que sienten el paso. 3. Llares, garabato pendiente de una chimenea. 4. Compás de vara.

trammel, *va.* Trabar, poner trabas (hamper); estorbar, embarazar con limitaciones, impedir.

tramp [træmp] [tramp], *va.* 1. Andar con paso pesado; pisar con fuerza. **The prisoners tramped along in the rain,** los prisioneros marchaban pesadamente bajo la lluvia. 2. Andar o viajar a pie. -*vn.* 1. Pisar pesadamente; ir, andar, marchar a pie. 2. Corretear, vagabundear.

tramp, *s.* 1. Marcha pesada y continua, como de una muchedumbre. 2. Ruido producido por una marcha pesada y continua. 3. Viaje o paseo largo a pie. 4. *(E.U.)* Vago, peón, el que camina o viaja a pie; en especial, vagabundo (vagrant), correntón. 5. Vapor que va de puerto en puerto, tomando carga donde la haya. 6. Mujerzuela, golfa.

trample [ˈtræmpl] [tram-pel], *va.* 1. Hollar, pisotear (crush) o pisar repetidamente alguna cosa. **He was trampled to death,** murieron aplastados. 2. Pisar, poner bajo los pies; hollar, menospreciar, ajar o tratar con desprecio: por lo común con *on.* -*vn.* Marchar pesadamente, torpemente (en sentido literal y figurado); pisar muy fuerte.

trampler [ˈtræmpləʳ] [tram-plaʳ], *s.* Pisador, el que pisa.

trampoline [ˈtræmpəlɪn] [tram-po-lin], *s.* Trampolín, cama elástica.

trance [trɑːns] [trans], *s.* 1. Rapto, éxtasis (ecstasy), arrobamiento del ánimo, enajenamiento. 2. Estado de insensibilidad: (a) síncope prolongado; (b) catalepsia, condición hipnótica.

tranced [trɑːnst] [transt], *a.* Arrobado, elevado, arrebatado, enajenado.

tranquil [ˈtræŋkwɪl] [tran-kuil], *a.* Tranquilo, sosegado (quiet), pacífico, apacible.

tranquility [træŋˈkwɪlɪtɪ] [tran-kui-li-ti], *s.* Tranquilidad, calma (calm), serenidad (serenity).

tranquillize [ˈtræŋkwɪlaɪz] [tran-kui-lais], *va.* Tranquilizar, sosegar, calmar, aquietar.

tranquilizer [ˈtræŋkwɪlaɪzəʳ] [tran-kui-lai-saʳ], *s.* Tranquilizante, calmante.

tranquilly [ˈtræŋkwɪlɪ] [tran-kui-li], *adv.* Tranquilamente, con quietud, con sosiego.

trans-, [trænz] [trans], Prefijo que significa al través de, más allá, por entre.

transact [trænˈzækt] [tran-sakt], *va.* Llevar a cabo, hacer, ejecutar, conducir, despachar o dar curso a un negocio.

transaction [træn'zækʃən] [tran-sak-shon], *s.* 1. Manejo, conducta de cualquier asunto; transacción (deal). 2. Negociación, negocio, asunto, lo que está hecho. 3. *pl.* Trabajos de una sociedad docta; memorias. **Let me know all the transactions,** dígame Ud. todo lo que pasa a todo lo que pase. **During these transactions,** mientras pasaba o sucedía esto.

trasactor [træn'zæktə^r] [tran-sak-ta^r], *s.* Negociador, el que negocia.

transalpine [trænz'ælpaɪn] [tran-sal-pain], *a.* Transalpino, situado al otro lado de los Alpes, particularmente al norte, es decir, el lado más lejano de Roma.

transatlantic ['trænzət'læntɪk] [tran-sakt-lan-tik], *a.* Trasalático. **Transatlantic air-ship,** aeronave trasatlántica. **Transatlantic liner,** barco trasatlántico, trasatlántico.

transcend [træn'send] [tran-send], *va.* 1. Sobrepujar, elevarse sobre alguien o algo en excelencia o grado; sobresalir. 2. Exceder, propasar, pasar de los límites. *-vn.* Ser trascendente, transcendental o sobresaliente.

transcendence [træn'sendəns] [tran-sen-dans], *s.* 1. Trascendencia, excelencia, superioridad marcada. 2. *(Teol.)* Existencia superior y más allá de la de otros seres; existencia de Dios, aparte del universo y no limitada por el tiempo ni el espacio.

transcendent [træn'senənt] [tran-sen-dant], *a.* 1. Sobresaliente, excelente en sumo grado. 2. Trascendente, superior al universo material; espiritual.

transcendental [ˌtrænsen'dentl] [tran-sen-den-tal], *a.* 1. Trascendental, no comprendido en las categorías; que traspasa los límites de la ciencia experimental. **Trascendental meditation,** meditación trascendental. 2. Eminente o excelente en sumo grado, sobresaliente. 3. Superior o fuera del sentido común o contrario a él.

transcendently [træn'sendəntlɪ] [tran-sen-dent-li], *adv.* Excelentemente, primorosamente.

transcontinental [ˌtrænzˌkɒntɪ'nentl] [trans-kon-ti-nen-tal], *a.* Transcontinental.

transcribe [træn'skraɪb] [trans-kraib], *va.* Transcribir, copiar (copy), trasladar un escrito o impreso.

transcriber [træn'skraɪbə^r] [trans-krai-ba^r], *s.* Copiante, amanuense. *(Amer.)* Escribiente.

transcript [træn'skrɪpt] [trans-kript], *s.* Trasunto, copia o traslado de un original.

transcription [træn'skrɪpʃən] [trans-krip-shon], *s.* 1. Transcripción. 2. Trasunto, traslado, copia. 3. Radiodifusión a base de discos fonográficos. 4. Disco empleado con este fin.

transcriptive [træn'skrɪptɪv] [trans-krip-tiv], *a.* Perteneciente a la copia o el traslado.

transept ['trænsept] [tran-sept], *s.* El crucero de una iglesia; el espacio entre el altar y el coro.

transfer ['trænsfə^r] [trans-fa^r], *va.* 1. Transferir, transportar, pasar o llevar una cosa desde un lugar a otro. 2. Transferir, ceder o renunciar a otro el derecho o la posesión de una cosa; en este sentido va acompañado por lo común de *to* y algunas veces de *upon.* **Harry transferred to another department,** Harry se trasladó a otro departamento.

transfer, *s.* 1. Traspaso, acción y efecto de traspasar; transferencia, acción y efecto de transferir; traslación, transporte. 2. La cosa transferida o traspasada. 3. Lugar, método o medio de transferir. 4. Traspaso, acta de cesión de una propiedad. 5. Calcomanía (decal).

transferable [træn'sfɜːrəbl] [trans-fe-ra-bol], *a.* Transferible, que puede ser transferido o traspasado, que se puede trasladar. **Not transferable,** intransferible.

transference ['trænsfərəns] [trans-fe-rans], *s.* Transferencia, acción y efecto de transferir. **Thought transference,** transmisión del pensamiento.

transfiguration [ˌtrænsfɪgə'reɪʃən] [trans-fi-ga-rei-shon], *s.* Transfiguración (transformation), mudanza de una figura en otra. *(Relig.)* **The Transfiguration,** la Transfiguración.

transfigure [træns'fɪgə^r] [trans-fi-ga^r], *va.* Transformar, transmutar, mudar de figura.

transfix [træns'fɪks] [trans-fiks], *va.* 1. Traspasar o atravesar con una cosa puntiaguda. 2. Paralizar. **We were transfixed with terror,** nos quedamos paralizados de terror.

transfixion [træns'fɪkʃən] [trans-fik-shon], *s.* Transfixión, la acción de herir pasando de una parte a otra.

transform [træns'fɔːm] [trans-form], *va.* 1. Transformar, cambiar la forma de algo, metamorfosear, transmutar. 2. Convertir, cambiar el carácter o la naturaleza de. 3. *(Mat.)* Cambiar una expresión en otra equivalente. *-vn.* Transfigurarse, transformarse.

transformable [træns'fɔːməbl] [trans-for-ma-bol], *a.* Transformable, convertible, que se puede transformar.

transformation [ˌtrænsfə'meɪʃən] [trans-for-mei-shon], *s.* Transformación, la mudanza de una forma o figura en otra; cambio, conversión; metamorfosis; en la alquimia, transmutación.

transformative [træns'fɔːmətɪv] [trans-for-ma-tiv], *a.* Transformativa, que tiene virtud de transformar.

transformer [træns'fɔːmə^r] [trans-for-ma^r], *s.* Transformador, el o lo que transforma; en especial, aparato eléctrico para convertir una corriente en otra de cantidad y potencia diferentes (más bajas o más altas).

transfuse [træns'fjuːz] [trans-fius], *va.* 1. Transfundir, trasvasar (decant), echar un licor poco a poco de un vaso en otro. 2. Transfundir, hacer pasar cierta cantidad de sangre de las venas de una persona o un animal a las de otro. 3. Restablecer (las fuerzas).

transfusion [træns'fjuːʒən] [trans-fiu-shon], *s.* Transfusión, la acción de transfundir. **Blood transfusion,** transfusión de sangre.

transgress [træns'gres] [trans-gres], *va.* 1. Traspasar, transgredir, violar o quebrantar alguna ley, estatuo o precepto, infringir (infringe). 2. Propasar, exceder, ir más allá de los límites. *-vn.* 1. Transgredir una ley; pecar (sin). 2. En geología, tapar.

transgression [træns'greʃən] [trans-gre-shon], *s.* 1. Transgresión, quebrantamiento de alguna ley. 2. *(Relig.)* Pecado (sin), falta.

transgressor [træns'gresə^r] [trans-gre-sa^r], *s.* Transgresor.

tranship ['trænʃɪp] [tran-ship], *vt.* Transbordar.

transient ['trænzɪənt] [tran-sient], *a.* Pasajero, transitorio, transeúnte.

transiently ['trænzɪəntlɪ] [tran-sient-li], *adv.* Ligeramente, de paso, de un modo transitorio.

transistor [træn'zɪstə^r] [tran-sis-ta^r], *s.* Transistor, aparato eléctrico que reemplaza al tubo al vacío.

transit ['trænzɪt] [tran-sit], *s.* 1. Tránsito, paso o acto de pasar. **Passengers in transit,** pasajeros en tránsito. 2. Pasaje (passage) o vía determinada, particular. 3. *(Astr.)* Tránsito, el paso de un astro sobre el disco de otro; paso de un astro por el meridiano de un lugar dado.

transition [træn'zɪʃən] [tran-si-shon], *s.* 1. Transición (change), tránsito, el paso o la acción de pasar de un lugar, condición o estado a otro; mudanza. 2. Transición, artificio oratorio con que se pasa de un discurso a otro. 3. *(Mús.)* Transición. V. MODULATION.

transitional [træn'zɪʃənəl] [tran-si-sho-nal], *a.* Perteneciente a la transición o al tránsito.

transitive ['trænzɪtɪv] [tran-si-tiv], *a.* Transitivo; se aplica al verbo cuya acción recae directamente sobre el complemento.

transitively ['trænzɪtɪvlɪ] [tran-si-tiv-li], *adv.* De un modo transitivo.

transitorily [ˌtrænzɪ'tɔːrɪlɪ] [tran-si-to-ri-li], *adv.* Transitoriamente.

transitory ['trænzɪtərɪ] [tran-si-to-ri], *a.* Transitorio, caduco, perecedero, pasajero (temporary) de corta duración.

translatable [trænz'leɪtəbl] [trans-lei-ta-bol], *a.* Traducible, que se puede traducir.

translate [trænz'leɪt] [trans-leit], *va.* 1. Traducir, verter de un idioma a otro; explicar, interpretar. 2. Trasladar a un obispo de una silla episcopal a otra. 3. Transformar, cambiar. 4. Dar a conocer, explicar, aclarar. 5. *(Ant.)* Arrebatar al cielo. **To translate into English,** traducir al inglés.

translation [trænz'leɪʃən] [trans-lei-shon], *s.* 1. Translación, la acción de transportar, transferir, trasladar o mudar de un paraje a otro; traslación de un obispo, la acción de mudarle de un obispado a otro. 2. Traducción, versión, traslación, la acción de traducir de un idioma a otro. **I've only read it in translation,** sólo lo he leído traducido. 3. *(Ret.)* Traslación.

translator [trænz'leɪtə^r] [trans-lei-ta^r], *s.* 1. Traductor, el que traduce de una lengua a otra. 2. Repetidor telegráfico.

transliterate [trænz'lɪtəreɪt] [trans-li-ta-reit], *va.* Representar las letras de una lengua, o su sonido, por las letras de otra.

translucence [trænz'luːsns] [trans-lu-sens], *s.* Translucidez, calidad de translúcido.

translucent [trænz'luːsnt] [trans-lu-sent], **translucid** [translu-sid], *a.* 1. Translúcido, que deja pasar la luz sin permitir distinguir los objetos; semitransparente. 2. Transparente (inexactamente).

transmigrate ['trænzmaɪ'greɪt] [trans-mai-greit], *vn.* Transmigrar, mudar de habitación de un país a otro.

transmigration [ˌtrænzmaɪ'greɪʃən] [trans-mai-grei-shon], *s.* 1. Transmigración, la mudanza de habitación de un país a otro hecha por una familia o una nación entera. 2. La transmigración de las almas o la transmigración pitagórica.

transmigratory [trænz'mɪgrətərɪ] [trans-mi-gra-to-ri], *a.* Que pasa de una condición o estado a otro.

transmissible [trænz'mɪsəbl] [trans-mi-sa-bol], *a.* Transmisible, susceptible de transmisión.

transmission [trænz'mɪʃən] [trans-mi-shon], *s.* 1. Transmisión (conveyance). 2. Emisión (broadcasting). 3. *(Mec.)* Caja de cambios.

transmissive [trænz'mɪsɪv] [trans-mi-siv], *a.* Transmisible; que se debe a la transmisión, transmitido.

transmit [trænz'mɪt] [trans-mit], *va.* 1. Transmitir *(convey),* ceder o traspasar lo que se posee al dominio de otro. 2. Conducir, transferir, trasladar. 3. *(T.V.)* Transmitir, emitir (broadcast).

transmittable [trænz'mɪtəbl] [trans-mi-ta-bol], *a.* Transmisible, que se puede transmitir o conducir.

transmitter [trænz'mɪtə^r] [trans-mi-ta^r], *s.* 1. Transmisor, lo que transmite. 2. Transmisor (telegráfico o telefónico).

transmutable [trænz'mjuːtəbl] [trans-miu-ta-bol], *a.* Transmutable.

transmutably [trænz'mjuːtəblɪ] [trans-miu-ta-bli], *adv.* De un modo transmutable.

transmutation [ˌtrænzmjuː'teɪʃən] [trans-miu-tei-shon], *s.* 1. Transmutación, conversión *(conversion),* mudanza. 2. Cambio de estado, mudanza sucesiva, alternación, cambio de un metal vil en precioso.

transmute [trænz'mjuːt] [trans-miut], *va.* Transmutar, convertir o mudar una cosa en otra; cambiar la naturaleza, sustancia o forma.

transmuter [trænz'mjuːtə^r] [trans-miu-ta^r], *s.* El o lo que transmuta.

transnational [trænz'næʃənəl] [trans-na-sho-nal], *s.* El acto de nadar de un lado a otro.

transom ['trænsəm] [tran-som], *s.* 1. Travesaño, el madero que atraviesa una abertura; de aquí, ventana pequeña encima de una puerta, que sirve para dar ventilación. 2. *(Art.)* Telera, una de las piezas de madera que juntan las gualderas de las cureñas. 3. *(Mar.)* Yugo o peto de popa. **Wing transoms,** yugos principales o de la curz o popa. **Deck-transoms,** yugos de la cubierta. **Helm-port-transoms,** contra-yugos. **Hilling-transoms,** yugos de henchimiento.

transparency [træns'pærənsɪ] [trans-pa-ren-si], *s.* 1. Transparencia, diafanidad, calidad de transparente. 2. Transparente, letrero o cuadro sobre tela, vidrio o substancia transparente, detrás del cual se ponen una o más luces. 3. Diapositiva, transparencia (slide).

transparent [træns'pærənt] [trans-pa-rent], *a.* 1. Transparente, diáfano (clear). 2. *(Fig.)* Fácil de entender o discernir; también, franco, sincero.

transpiration [ˌtrænspɪ'reɪʃən] [trans-pi-rei-shon], *s.* Transpiración (sweat), expulsión insensible de algún humor o líquido por los poros.

transpire [træns'paɪə^r] [trans-paia^r], *va.* Transpirar (sweat), echar de sí por medio de la transpiración. -*vn.* 1. Transpirar, evaporarse insensiblemente; rezumarse. 2. Translucirse, empezarse a saber lo que estaba oculto. **It finally transpired that,** finalmente resultó que. 3. *(Neol. y erróneo)* Acontecer, suceder.

transplant ['trænsplɑːnt] [trans-plant], *va.* 1. Transplantar, mudar las plantas de un paraje a otro para que prevalezcan. 2. *(Med.)* Transplantar.

transplantation [ˌtrænsplɑːn'teɪʃən] [trans-plan-tei-shon], *s.* Transplantación, trasplante.

transport ['trænspɔːt] [trans-port], *va.* 1. Transportar, llevar de un paraje a otro; particularmente, deportar, desterrar, extrañar, enviar de un estado a otro país; llevar a presidio. 2. Arrebatar, llevar tras sí conmover, transportar.

transport, *s.* 1. Transportamiento, arrobamiento, rapto, efecto de una viva pasión; acceso. 2. Transporte, el acto de transportar. 3. Transporte, la embarcación para llevar o conducir soldados, las municiones de guerra, etc.; se dice también. **Transport ship o Transport vessel.** 4. El criminal que ha sido condenado a la pena de extrañamiento o deportación. 5. Remesa (shipment).

transportable [træns'pɔːtəbl] [trans-por-ta-bol], *a.* Capaz de ser transportado.

transportation [ˌtrænspɔː'teɪʃən] [trans-por-tei-shon], *s.* 1. Transportación. 2. Extrañamiento, deportación, o destierro a otro país. 3. *(E.U.)* Vehículos que se usan para el transporte; también, el coste del transporte.

transporter [træns'pɔːtə^r] [trans-por-ta^r], *s.* El que transporta.

transposal [træns'pəʊzl] [trans-pou-sal], *s.* Transposición.

transpose [træns'pəʊz] [trans-pous], *va.* 1. Transponer, mudar de un lugar a otro alguna cosa. 2. Quitar o mudar de su lugar o puesto. 3. *(Mús.)* Escribir o tocar en un tono lo que está escrito en otro.

transposition [ˌtrænspə'zɪʃən] [trans-po-si-shon], *s.* Transposición, la acción del transponer.

transship [træns'ʃɪp] [trans-ship], *va.* Transbordar.

transshipment [træns'ʃɪpmənt] [trans-ship-ment], *s.* Transbordo (transfer), el traslado de la carga de un buque o carro a otro, para que continúe sin interrupción el transporte de dicha carga.

transsexual [trænz'seksjʊəl] [trans-seks-siual], *s.* Transexual.

transubstantiate [trænsəb'stænʃɪeɪt] [trans-sabs-tan-shieit], *va.* Transubstanciar, convertir totalmente de una substancia en otra.

transubstantiation ['trænsəbˌstænʃɪ'eɪʃən] [trans-sabs-tan-shiei-shon], *s.* Transubstanciación, conversión total de una substancia en otra; en especial, del pan y el vino en el cuerpo y sangre de Nuestro Señor Jesucristo, en la Eucaristía.

transversal [trænz'vɜːsl] [trans-ver-sal], *a.* Transversal, que atraviesa de un lado a otro. -*s.* Transversal, línea transversal.

transversally [trænz'vɜːsəlɪ] [trans-ver-sa-li], *adv. (Poco us.)* Transversalmente.

transverse [trænz'vɜːs] [trans-vers], *a.* Transversal, transverso, que está al través.

transversely [trænz'vɜːslɪ] [trans-vers-li], *adv.* Transversalmente, oblicuamente.

trap [træp] [trap], *s.* 1. Trampa (snare), cepo, armadijo para coger ladrones o animales dañinos. **Mouse-trap,** ratonera. 2. Garlito, red, lazo. **To be caught in the trap,** caer en el garlito, o en la trampa. *(Mex.)* Caer en la ratonera. 3. Entre tiradores, aparato que en un momento dado deja salir un animal u objeto destinado a servir de blanco, v. gr. un pichón vivo a una bola de vidrio. 4. Válvula de sumidero, construcción que sirve para retener en un punto fijo una cantidad de líquido que sólo permite el paso a las inmundicias. 5. *V.* TRAP-DOOB. 6. *(Fam.)* Un carruaje. 7. *pl.* Efectos personales. 8. Juego del palo corvo.

trap, *va.* 1. Hacer caer en el lazo, en la trampa o en el garlito; atrapar (catch, snare), armar lazos o asechanzas. 2. Enjaezar, adornar.

trapdoor [ˈtræpdɔːʳ] [trap-doʳ], *s.* Una especie de puerta disimulada que se abre por medio de algunos resortes ocultos, trampilla. **Trap-door spider,** araña de gran tamaño que habita en hoyos cilíndricos hechos en la tierra y protegidos por una puertecilla con gozne, de una sustancia sedosa.

trape [treip] [treip], *va.* *(Fam. o des.) V.* TRAPES.

trapes, traipse [treips] [treips], *vn.* Mangonear; andar vagando o tunando.

trapes, *s.* *(Vulg.)* Mujer ociosa y desaliñada.

trapeze [trəˈpiːz] [tra-pis]. *s.* Trapecio, palo corto suspendido por sus extremos con cuerdas y que sirve para hacer ejercicios gimnásticos. **Trapeze artist,** trapecista.

trapezium [trəˈpiːzɪəm] [tra-pi-siom], *s.* 1. *(Geom.)* Trapezoide, cuadrilátero irregular que no tiene ningún lado paralelo a otro. 2. *(Anat.)* Trapecio, hueso radial del carpo.

trapezoid [ˈtræpɪzɔɪd] [tra-pi-soid], *s.* *(Geom.)* Trapecio, cuadrilátero irregular que tiene paralelos solamente dos de sus lados.

trapezoidal [ˈtræpɪzɔɪdl] [tra-pi-soi-dal], *a.* Trapezoidal, de figura de trapecio.

trapper [ˈtræpəʳ] [tra-paʳ], *s.* El que pone trampas o lazos para coger animales de piel vendible, trampero, cazador (hunter).

trappings [ˈtræpɪŋz] [tra-pins], *s. pl.* Jaeces; adornos, galas, parafernalia (paraphernalia).

Trappist [ˈtræpɪst] [tra-pist], *a.* Trapense, de la Trapa.

trash [træʃ] [trash], *s.* 1. Heces, porquería, desecho, zupia o cualquier otra cosa de ninguna entidad ni valor, basura (garbage). 2. Una persona vil o indigna, escoria (worthless people). 3. Tierra, greda.

trash, *va.* 1. Podar: deshojar, quitar las hojas. 2. Tirar a la basura. 3. Criticar. poner verde. 4. Destrozar.

trashman [ˈtræʃmən] [trash-man], *s.* Basurero, persona que recoge la basura.

trashy [ˈtræʃɪ] [tra-shi], *a.* Vil, despreciable, inútil, de ningún valor, malo (bad). **Trash novel,** novelucha.

trauma [ˈtrɔːmə] [tro-ma], *s.* 1. Cualquier lesión del cuerpo causada por violencia, herida. 2. *(Psych.)* Trauma (shock).

traumatic [trɔːˈmætɪk] [tro-ma-tik], *a.* Traumático, relativo a las heridas o el traumatismo.

traumatize [ˈtrɔːmətaɪz] [tro-ma-tais], *vt.* Traumatizar.

travail [ˈtræveɪl] [tra-veil], *va.* 1. Trabajar, afanarse, hacer esfuerzos. 2. Estar de parto, padecer los dolores de parto. -*va.* *(Des.)* Cansar, fatigar (tire), atormentar, mortificar, aquejar.

travail, *s.* 1. Afán, fatiga, trabajo. 2. Dolores de parto.

travel [ˈtrævl] [tra-vel], *va. y vn.* 1. Viajar, hacer viajes, andar viajando; caminar; particularmente, visitar países extranjeros. 2. Volar o pasar con celeridad el tiempo, las noticias, etc. 3. Trabajar, afanarse.

travel, *s.* Viaje (trip), la jornada o camino que se hace de una parte a otra. 2. Afán, fatiga. 3. *(Mec.)* Movimiento de un mecanismo; carrera del émbolo o pistón. 4. *pl.* **Travels,** viajes, relación de las cosas que algún viajero ha observado en sus viajes. **Travel agency,** agencia de viajes. **Travel agent,** agente de viajes. **Travel-stained, travel-soiled,** manchado por el polvo del camino. **Travel-worn,** fatigado por el viaje.

traveled [ˈtrævld] [tra-veld], *a.* Que ha viajado mucho.

traveler [ˈtrævləʳ] [tra-ve-laʳ], *s.* 1. Viajante, viajero. 2. *(Mar.)* Arraca de las vergas de juanete. **Traveler's check,** cheque de viajeros o de viaje.

traveling [ˈtrævlɪŋ] [tra-ve-lin], *a.* Viajero, ambulante, itinerante (itinerant). **Traveling companion,** compañero de viaje. **Traveling salesman,** representante.

travelogue [ˈtrævəlɒg] [tra-ve-log], *s.* Conferencia sobre un viaje, generalmente con ilustraciones.

traversable [ˈtrævɜːsəbl] [tra-ver-sa-bol], *a.* Atravesable, que se puede atravesar; negable, contestable.

traverse [ˈtrævəs] [tra-vers], *a.* Travieso, que está atravesado o puesto al través. **Traverse-course,** *(Mar.)* rumbo compuesto. **Traverse-board,** tabla que lleva dibujada la rosa marina de los vientos; de uso antiguo. **Traverse-table,** libro del diario; tabla de las diferencias de latitud, etc. -*s.* 1. Cualquier cosa que está colocada de modo que cruza a otra; travesaño: travesero; cerco travesero. 2. *(Fort.)* Través, trinchera con parapeto pequeño. 3. *(Geom.)* Línea transversal. 4. El acto de recorrer o viajar; viaje, pasaje. 5. Negación, acto de negar; objeción legal. 6. *(Mar.)* Bordada en dirección oblicua. 7. En agrimensura, línea corta que parte de una línea principal y sirve para determinar la posición de un punto lateral. **Traverse of fortune,** reveses de fortuna. **Traverse-jury,** *V. Petit-jury.*

traverse, *va.* 1. Atravesar, cruzar (cross). 2. Recorrer o atravesar todo un espacio determinado. 3. Examinar o escudriñar con cuidado. 4. *(For.)* Negar, oponerse o hacer oposición a alguna sentencia o resolución judicial por los medios legales. 5. Estorbar, impedir, contrariar, poner obstáculos o impedimentos. -*vn.* 1. Atravesarse, hacer vaivén, moverse de un lado a otro. 2. Dar vueltas, girar como sobre un pie.

travesty [ˈtrævɪstɪ] [tra-vis-ti], *va.* Disfrazar; trovar, imitar burlescamente, presentar o tomar las cosas bajo una forma ridícula. -*s.* Imitación grotesca o burlesca; el acto de disfrazar; tratamiento burlesco de un tema elevado o noble.

trawl [trɔːl] [trol], *va.* Arrastrar el albareque. *V.* TROLL. -*vn.* Pescar con albareque, pescar con red de arrastre. -*s. V. Trawl-line y Trawl-net.* **Trawl-line,** cuerda gruesa y muy larga, provista de boyas y de la cual cuelgan a cortos trechos sedales con anzuelos cebados: se usa en la pesca del bacalao. **Trawl-net,** red de gran tamaño en forma de saco, remolcada por un bote.

trawler [ˈtrɔːləʳ] [tro-laʳ], *s.* Barca pesquera de arrastre.

tray [treɪ] [trei], *s.* 1. Bandeja, salvilla: *(Amer.)* azafate (de plata, metal o charol). 2. Encaje, cajoncito: caja ligera, poco profunda y sin tapa, que se usa en los baúles, en las colecciones científicas. **Tea-tray,** bandeja, batea. **Chopping-tray,** artesilla de cocina.

treacherous [ˈtretʃərəs] [tre-cha-ras], *a.* 1. Traidor, pérfido, falso, engañador; indigno de confianza. **A treacherous act,** una traición. **Treacherous memory,** memoria infiel o que olvida fácilmente las cosas. **A treacherous smile,** risa falsa o risa de traidor. 2. Peligroso (dangerous), traicionero (unpredictable). **Treacherous weather,** condiciones climáticas adversas.

treacherously [ˈtretʃərəslɪ] [tre-cha-ras-li], *adv.* Traidoramente (disloyally), a traición, pérfidamente.

treacherousness [ˈtretʃərəsnɪs] [tre-cha-ras-nes], *s.* La calidad de traidor, pérfido o falso.

treachery [ˈtretʃərɪ] [tre-cha-ri], *s.* Perfidia, deslealtad, traición, falsedad. **An act of treachery,** una traición.

treacle [ˈtriːkl] [tri-kel], *s.* 1. Melote, miel de cañas, miel de prima, jarabe de azúcar, melaza. 2. Triaca, composición de varios medicamentos simples.

treacly [ˈtriːklɪ] [tri-kli], *a.* Meloso, empalagoso.

tread [tred] [tred], *va. y vn.* (*pret.* TROD, *pp.* TRODDEN). 1. Pisar, hollar, poner el pie sobre alguna cosa. 2. Andar por encima de alguna cosa; sentir algo bajo los pies; apretar con el pie. 3. Pisotear. 4. Patalear (stamp), dar patadas en el suelo violentamente. 5. Hollar, ajar, abatir, pisar o despreciar. 6. Caminar con majestad o dándose importancia. 7. Pisar, (en las aves); gallear, cubrir el gallo a las gallinas. **To tread inward** o **outward,** andar metiendo los pies hacia dentro o volviéndolos hacia fuera. **To tread back,** desandar, volver atrás. **To tread in the foot-steps of one,** seguir las pisadas de alguno o imitarle. **Someone trod on my foot,** alguien me pisó. **Trodden path,** camino trillado.

tread, *s.* 1. Paso (step), la acción de pisar. **She was walking with a heavy tread,** andar con paso cansino. 2. Pisada, la huella o señal que deja estampada el pie en la tierra. 3. Pisada o pisadura, la parte sobre la cual se apoya algo al moverse o que sirve para pisar; escalón de escalera; cara de rueda, de corredera o de riel; centro del torno. 4. Galladura. 5. Escalón, peldaño.

treader ['tredə'] [tre-da'], *s.* Pisador.

treadle ['tredl] [tre-dl], *s.* 1. Cárcola, el listón de madera o metal en que ponen el pie los torneros y tejedores 2. Galladura (del huevo), chalaza. 3. Pedal.

treadmill [tredmɪl] [tred-mil], *s.* 1. Molino de rueda de escalones, mecanismo que servía antiguamente como medio de castigo. 2. *(Fig.)* Uniformidad fatigosa del trabajo o esfuerzo, rutina (routine).

treason ['tri:zn] [tri-son], *s.* 1. Traición, falta de lealtad debida al Estado. 2. Perfidia, falsedad. **High treason,** alta traición o delito de lesa majestad. **Petit treason,** llamábase en Inglaterra traición pequeña o baja al delito de asesinato cuando un criado mataba a su amo, una mujer a su marido o un fiel a su prelado.

treasonable ['tri:zənəbl] [tri-so-na-bol], *a.* Pérfido, desleal, traidor, de traición.

treasonableness ['tri:zənəblnɪs] [tri-so-na-bol-nes], *s.* El estado o la calidad que constituye a uno traidor; traición.

treasure ['treʒə'] [tre-sha'], *s.* Tesoro, abundancia de caudal y dinero guardado y conservado; riquezas acumuladas; lo que es precioso o muy estimado. **Treasure-house,** tesorería. **Treasure-trove,** tesoro hallado, tesoro de oro, plata, etc., que alguien halla y no tiene dueño conocido.

treasure, *va.* Atesorar, recoger tesoros y riquezas; guardar con cuidado.

treasurer ['treʒərə'] [tre-sha-ra'], *s.* Tesorero. **Treasurer of the navy,** tesorero general de marina.

treasury ['treʒərɪ] [tre-sha-ri], *s.* 1. Tesorería, la oficina o despacho del tesorero. **King's treasury,** el real erario, la tesorería general. 2. Antología (anthology).

treat [tri:t] [trit], *va.* 1. Tratar, portarse (de cierta manera) para con alguno. 2. Tratar, manejar una cosa materialmente, aplicar un procedimiento particular a una cosa. 3. Tratar, escribir, discurrir o disputar sobre alguna materia; expresar por medio del arte. 4. Agasajar, regalar, pagar el coste de alguna comida o más particularmente de alguna bebida; pagar una convidada. -*vn.* 1. Tratar de, trata; negociar (deal), ajustar, conferir y hablar sobre algún negocio para conformar y avenir a los interesados en él. 2. Negociar, arreglar un tratado. 3. *(Fam.)* Regalar, pagar el coste de la comida o bebida de otro.

treat, *s.* 1. Trato, convite, banquete (banquet), festín. 2. Complacencia, regalo, gran placer. **A high treat,** un gusto grande, un gran placer. **To stand treat,** *(Fam.)* convidar a alguno, esto es, hacer o pagar el gasto; obsequiar.

treatment ['tri:tmənt] [trit-ment], *s.* 1. Trato, modo de tratar o tratarse. 2. Tratamiento, modo de tratar una persona o cosa; método que se emplea para la curación de una enfermedad; procedimiento metalúrgico. 3. *(Med.)* Tratamiento. **She's having treatment for her back,** está recibiendo tratamiento por mi problema de espalda.

treaty ['tri:tɪ] [tri-ti], *s.* 1. Tratado, ajuste, convenio concluido entre dos o más gobiernos. 2. Negociación para llegar a un acuerdo.

treble ['trebl] [tre-bel], *a.* 1. Tríplice, triplo, triple. 2. *(Mús.)* Atiplado, tiplisonante. **A treble block,** *(Mar.)* cuadernal de tres ojos.

treble, *va.* Triplicar, multiplicar por tres. -*vn.* Triplicarse, multiplicarse tres veces.

treble, *s. (Mús.)* Tiple, la voz más alta en la consonancia musical. **Treble voice,** voz de tiple o soprano. **Treble clef,** clave de sol.

trebly ['treblɪ] [tre-bli], *adv.* Triplicadamente, tres veces tanto.

tree [tri:] [tri], *s.* 1. Árbol, el mayor de los vegetales; vegetal leñoso cuya altura no baja de 20 pies. 2. Dibujo, cuadro en forma de árbol. 3. Madero, trozo pesado de madera. 4. Horca; cruz. **Tree of life o lignum vitae,** árbol de la vida, guayaco, palo santo. **Fruit-tree,** árbol frutal. **Genealogical tree,** árbol genealógico. **Tree-fern,** helecho arborescente, helecho de árbol. **Tree-frog, tree-toad,** rana arbórea del género. Hyla o de otro afín. **Tree-mallow,** lavatera de árbol, planta malvácea. **Tree of heaven,** árbol del cielo, ailanto, árbol originario de las Molucas. **Tree trunk,** tronco. **Tyburn tree,** la horca. **Up a tree,** *(Fam.)* 1. puesto entre la espada y la pared; 2. desinteresado, neutral.

treeless ['tri:lɪs] [tri-les], *a.* Sin árboles.

treenail ['tri:neɪl] [tri-neil], *s. (Mar.)* Cabilla, clavija de palo larga y redonda que se usa en la construcción de los buques.

trefoil ['trefɔɪl] [tre-foil], *s.* 1. Trébol. V. CLOVER. 2. Adorno en forma de hoja de trébol. **Marsh trefoil,** trébol palustre. **Shrub trefoil,** citiso, ervellada, corona de rey.

trek [trek] [trek], *vn. (pret.* y *pp.* TREKKED) (África del sur). 1. Viajar de un lugar a otro en carromatos. 2. Emigrar. 3. Tirar de una carga. -*s.* Caminata (hike). **It's quite a trek to the shops,** hay un buen paseo hasta llegar a las tiendas.

trekking ['trekɪŋ] [tre-kin], *s.* Senderismo, trekking.

trellis ['trelɪs] [tre-lis], *s.* Enrejado; espaldera o espaldar de los jardines.

tremble ['trembl] [trem-bel], *vn.* 1. Temblar, temblequear o templetear. 2. Temblar, tener mucho miedo, estremecerse. 3. Tiritar de frío (shiver). 4. Temblar, amenazar ruina. 5. Trinar, hacer trino con la voz o con un instrumento. -*s.* Temblor.

trembling ['tremblɪŋ] [trem-blin], *s.* Temblor, -*a.* Que tiembla, temblante, trembloso, trémulo. **Trembling poplar, trembling-tree,** temblón, álamo temblón, particularmente el americano.

tremblingly ['tremblɪŋlɪ] [trem-blin-li], *adv.* Trémulamente, con temblor o temblando.

tremendous [tre'mendəs] [tre-men-dos], *a.* 1. Tremendo, enorme (great, huge), digno de ser temido; que causa pasmo por su magnitud, fuerza o consecuencias. 2. Formidable (very good). **We had a tremendous time,** lo pasamos estupendamente.

tremendously [tre'mendəslɪ] [tre-men-dos-li], *adv.* De un modo tremendo.

tremendousness [tre'mendəsnɪs] [tre-men-dos-nes], *s.* Terribilidad; susto; espanto (fright), miedo.

tremor ['tremə'] [tre-ma'], *s.* Tremor, temblor (quiver); vibración. **He was speaking with a tremor in his voice,** hablaba con voz temblorosa.

tremulous ['tremjʊləs] [tre-miu-los], *a.* Trémulo, tremulento, que tiembla.

tremulously ['tremjʊləslɪ] [tre-miu-los-li], *adv.* Trémulamente.

tremulousness ['tremjʊləsnɪs] [tre-miu-los-nes], *s.* Temblor, calidad de trémulo.

trench [trentʃ] [trench], *va.* y *vn.* 1. Surcar, hacer surcos; hacer zanjas, fososo o cauces. 2. Atrinchear, cerrar o ceñir con trincheras: en este sentido lleva tras sí por lo común la preposición *about*. 3. Usurpar o apropiarse de lo ajeno. V. ENCROACH. **To trench upon the liberty of the citizens,** atacar la liberad de los ciudadanos. **To trench the ballast,** *(Mar.)* Separar el lastre con mamparos.

trench, *s.* 1. Foso, zanja (ditch), caz, cauce. 2. *(Mil.)* Trinchera. **Trench warfare,** guerra de trincheras.

trenchant ['trentʃənt] [tren-chant], *a.* 1. Afilado, cortante. 2. Desabrido, mordaz (scathing), cáustico (caustic), picante como la sátira.

trench coat ['trentʃkəʊt] [trench-kout], *s.* Trinchera, abrigo impermeable, gabardina (raincoat).

trencher ['trentʃə'] [tren-cha'], *s.* 1. Trinchero, un plato de madera para trinchar; bandeja. 2. Las viandas, la comida; los placeres de la mesa; de aquí, la mesa. **Trencher-friend, trencher-fly,** parásito gorrón, gorrista, pegote. **Trencherman,** comedor; compañero de mesa. **Trenchermate,** compañero de mesa.

trend [trend] [trend], *vn.* Tomar rumbo o dirección, dirigirse, tender, inclinarse. -*s.* 1. Dirección o rumbo en general; inclinación hacia un punto particular, tendencia (tendency). 2. Tendencia, moda (fashion).

trendie ['trendiː] [tren-di], *s. (Prov. o des.) V.* TRUNDLE.

trendsetter ['trenˌsetəʳ] [trend-se-taʳ], *s.* Persona que inicia una moda.

trental ['trenɪl] [tren-tal], *s.* Treintenario de misas.

trepan [trɪ'pæn] [tri-pan], *va.* 1. *(Cir.)* Trepanar, hacer la operación del trepano. 2. *(Esco.)* Coger en el garlito.

trepanner [trɪ'pænəʳ] [tri-pa-naʳ], *s.* 1. El cirujano que hace la operación del trépano. 2. Engañador.

trephine [tre'fiːn] [tre-fin], *va.* Trepanar. *-s.* Trefino, especie de trépano pequeño.

trepid ['trepɪd] [tre-pid], *a.* Trépido, trémulo; opuesto a *intrepid.*

trepidation [ˌtrepɪ'deɪʃən] [tre-pi-dei-shon], *s.* Trepidación, miedo (fear), terror, inquietud (worry).

trespass ['trespəs] [tres-pas], *va.* 1. Quebrantar, traspasar o violar alguna ley, precepto o estatuto, antiguamente transgredir; pecar, faltar. 2. Infringir (infringe), violar, ofender; se usa con *against.* **To trespass on one's patience,** abusar de la paciencia de alguno. 3. Ocupar ilegítimamente la propiedad de otro.

trespass. *s.* 1. Transgresión (transgression), traspaso, el quebrantamiento o violación de alguna ley, precepto, etc.; ofensa, culpa, pecado. 2. Ocupación ilegítima o injusta de la propiedad ajena.

trespasser ['trespəsəʳ] [tres-pa-saʳ], *s.* Transgresor, violador de una ley; pecador, intruso (intruder).

tress [tres] [tres], *s.* Trenza; rizo de cabellos; en plural, cabellos abundantes.

tressed ['trest] [trest], *a.* Trenzado.

trestle ['tresl] [tre-sel], *s.* 1. Caballete, madero que descansa sobre cuatro pies divergentes; caballete de aserrador. 2. Obra de celosía y caballete para sostener los durmientes de un puente de ferrocarril, etc. **Trestle-trees,** pl. *(Mar.)* Baos de los palos. **Cross and trestle-trees,** *(Mar.)* Baos y crucetas. **Trestle-work,** obra (puente) de caballete.

trey [treɪ] [trei], *s.* Naipe o dado señalado con tres puntos; el tres.

tri- [traɪ] [trai], *pref.* Prefijo que significa tres, tres veces.

triable ['traɪəbl] [traia-bol], *a.* 1. Que se puede experimentar. 2. Averiguable en juicio.

triad ['traɪəd] [traiad], *s.* Triada, reunión de tres personas o cosas. *-a. (Quím.)* Que vale tres en combinación.

trial ['traɪəl] [traial], *s.* 1. Esfuerzo, ensayo, probadura, tentativa. 2. Conocimiento adquirido por experiencia; prueba. 3. Padecimiento (trouble), desgracia, aflicción. 4. *(Dep.)* Prueba de selección. 5. Ensayo, muestra o experiencia. 6. Juicio (judgement). *(For.)* El día de la vista de una causa o proceso; el examen para pronunciar sentencia. **To bring a prisoner to trial,** poner en juicio o en tela de juicio a una persona acusada de algún delito. **Trial by jury,** juicio por jurado. **The trial lasted six weeks,** el pleito (o el proceso) duró seis semanas. **On trial,** a prueba. **Trial trip,** viaje de prueba. *-a.* De prueba. **I will employ you on a trial basis,** te voy a contratar a prueba. **Trial order,** pedido de prueba. **Trial run,** representación teatral por cierto tiempo a manera de prueba.

triangle ['traɪæŋgl] [traian-guel], *s.* 1. Triángulo. 2. *(Mús.)* Triángulo, instrumento de percusión que consiste en una varilla de metal plegada en forma de triángulo, la cual se hace sonar golpeándola con otra varilla metálica. **Isosceles triangle,** triángulo isósceles. **Spherical triangle,** triángulo esférico.

triangular [traɪ'æŋgjʊləʳ] [traian-guiu-laʳ], *a.* Triangular.

triangulate [traɪ'æŋgjʊleɪt] [traian-guiu-leit], *va.* Dividir o disponer en triángulos; en particular, ligar por medio de triángulos los puntos notables de una comarca para levantar su plano.

triathlon [traɪ'æθlən] [traiaz-lon], *s.* Triatlon.

tribal ['traɪbəl] [trai-bal], *a.* De una tribu, perteneciente a una tribu, tribal.

tribe [traɪb] [traib], *s.* 1. Tribu, una de las partes en que se dividía el pueblo entre los antiguos. 2. Raza (race), casta. 3. *(Biol.)* Grupo de plantas o de animales de un orden o grado no determinado.

tribesman ['traɪbzmən] [traibs-man], *s.* Miembro de una tribu.

triblet ['traɪlɪt] [trai-blit], *s.* Un instrumento que usan los plateros para hacer anillos.

tribulation [ˌtrɪbjʊ'leɪʃən] [tri-biu-lei-shon], *s.* Tribulación, congoja (sorrow), pena, aflicción.

tribunal [traɪ'bjuːnl] [trai-biu-nal], *s.* Tribunal (court), el lugar destinado para la administración de justicia; juzgado.

tribune ['trɪbjuːn] [tri-biun], *s.* 1. Tribuno, magistrado civil y también un jefe militar entre los romanos; cualquier campeón de la plebe. 2. Tribuna, lugar elevado desde donde se dirige la palabra a una asamblea.

tribuneship ['trɪbjuːnʃɪp] [tri-biun-ship], *s.* Tribunado, la dignidad del tribuno civil.

tributary ['trɪbjʊtərɪ] [tri-biu-ta-ri], *a.* 1. Tributario, que está obligado a pagar tributo en reconocimiento de dominio u obsequio. 2. Sujeto, subordinado. *-s.* Tributario.

tribute ['trɪbjuːt] [tri-biut], *s.* 1. Tributo, homenaje (acknowledgment). 2. Tributo (payment). **To pay the tribute of nature,** morir, pagar tributo a la muerte.

trice [traɪs] [trais], *s.* Momento, instante, tris; se usa sólo en la locución *in a trice,* en un abrir y cerrar de ojos.

trice, *va. (Mar.)* Izar, hacer subir por medio de una jarcia; también, amarrar, ligar.

tricentenary [ˌtraɪsen'tiːnərɪ] [trai-sen-ti-na-ri], *a.* Tricentenario.

triceps ['traɪseps] [trai-seps], *s.* Tríceps, músculo que tiene tres cabezas.

trick [trɪk] [trik], *s.* 1. Treta fraudulenta, artimaña (ruse), engaño, fraude, superchería, embuste, artería, astucia, socaliña. **A knavish trick,** acción ruin. **He played me a trick,** me gastó una mala pasada. *(Fam.)* Hacer travesuras. 2. Chasco, burla, broma (joke); travesura, parchazo. 3. Costumbre, hábito adquirido, maña. 4. Baza, en el juego de naipes. *-a.* De juguete, de mentira.

trick, *va.* 1. Engañar, defraudar, jugar una pieza, pegar un pachazo. 2. Ataviar, componer, asear; por lo común, con *out.* *-vn.* Trampear, vivir de trampas.

trickery ['trɪkərɪ] [tri-ka-ri], *s.* Artimañas.

tricking ['trɪkɪŋ] [tri-kin], *s.* Atavío, adorno.

trickish ['trɪkɪʃ] [tri-kish], *a.* Astuto, artificioso, aleve, mañoso, embustero (liar), trapacero.

trickle ['trɪkl] [tri-kel], *vn.* Gotear, correr a gotas, caer gota a gota; escurrir. **He trickled water over the leaves,** dejó caer un hilito de agua sobre las hojas. *-s.* Hilo.

trick or treat [ˌtrɪkə'triːt] [tri-ka-trit], *s.* Frase con la cual en la noche de Halloween los niños amenazan con una jugarreta si no reciben un regalo.

trickster ['trɪkstəʳ] [tris-taʳ], *s.* Engañador, embaucador; maula, gato.

tricksy ['trɪksɪ] [trik-si], *a.* 1. Juguetón, retozón, travieso. 2. Artificioso, aleve, embustero.

tricky ['trɪkɪ] [tri-ki], *a.* 1. Falso, artificioso, trapacero. 2. Vicioso (el animal). 3. Taimado, astuto (devious).

tricolor ['trɪkələʳ] [tri-ka-laʳ], *a.* Tricolor, de tres colores. *-s.* Bandera nacional de los franceses.

tricycle ['traɪsɪkl] [trai-si-kol], *s.* Triciclo, velocípede de tres ruedas.

tride [traɪd] [traid], *a.* Trido, menudo y vivo: se dice del paso del caballo.

trident ['traɪdənt] [trai-dent], *s.* Tridente, el cetro de tres puntas de Neptuno.

tried ['traɪd] [traid], *a.* Probado.

triennial [traɪ'enɪəl] [trai-e-nial], *a.* Trienal, que dura tres años o sucede cada tercer año.

trier ['traɪəʳ] [traiaʳ], *s.* 1. Experimentador, ensayador. 2. Juez, censor, examinador. 3. Toque, ensayo, prueba.

trifle ['traɪfl] [trai-fel], *s.* 1. Bagatela, paparrucha, fruslería, friolera, cualquier cosa de poca substancia y valor; ando, poca cosa. 2. Crema aromatizada, confección ligera. **To stop at trifles,** reparar en pelillos.

trifle, *va.* Emplear en bagatelas, malgastar (el tiempo). *-vn.* 1. Obrar ligeramente, no hacer caso de una cosa; ser ligero, hablar con ligereza. 2. Chancear, juguetear, emplear o gastar el tiempo en cosas vanas e inútiles; se usa por lo general con *with.* 3. Manosear, palpar, juguetear, jugar con algo ligeramente y sin objeto, v. gr. un abanico; se usa con *with.* V. DALLY y TOY. **To trifle with one,** burlarse de uno; entretener a alguno, jugar con él. **To trifle away time,** malgastar el tiempo o emplearlo en bagatelas.

trifle, *s.* 1. Nimiedad (trivial thing). 2. Insignificancia. **It's a trifle too salty,** está un pelín salado.

trifler ['traɪfləʳ] [trai-flaʳ], *s.* Persona frívola, casquivana.

trifling ['traɪflɪŋ] [trai-flin], *a.* Frívolo, vano, inútil (useless); inconsiderable, de ninguna consecuencia. **Trifling story,** un cuento insípido o que hace dormir.

triflingly ['traɪflɪŋlɪ] [trai-flin-li], *adv.* Frívolamente, inútilmente, sin consecuencia.

triflingness ['traɪflɪŋnɪs] [trai-flin-nes], *s.* Frivolidad, ligereza (triviality); insignificancia, poca importancia.

triform ['traɪfɔːm] [trai-form], *a.* Triforme.

trig [trɪg] [trig], *va.* Atar o trabar las ruedas de un carruaje, impedir que una rueda dé vueltas. *-s.* Calzo de rueda o de barril; galga.

trig, *a.* 1. Bien puesto, bien acicalado. 2. Sano, en buen estado, firme.

trigger ['trɪgəʳ] [tri-gaʳ], *s.* 1. Gatillo, disparador (gun). **To pull the trigger,** apretar el gatillo. 2. Disparador de una máquina. 3. Pararruedas, calzo que detiene una rueda al bajar por algún terreno pendiente.

trigger-happy ['trɪgəˌhæpɪ] [tri-ga-ja-pi], *a. (Coloq.)* Que dispara a la menor provocación.

triglyph ['trɪglɪf] [tri-glif], *s. (Arch.)* Triglifo, un miembro del friso dórico.

trigon ['trɪgɒn] [tri-gon], *s.* 1. Triángulo, trígono. 2. Trígono. V. TRINE.

trigonometric ['trɪgɒnəˈmetrɪk] [tri-go-no-me-trik], *a.* Trigonométrico.

trigonometry [ˌtrɪgəˈnɒmɪtrɪ] [tri-go-no-mi-tri], *s.* Trigonometría, el arte que enseña la resolución analítica de los triángulos, tanto planos como esféricos.

trike [traɪk] [traik], *m.* Triciclo.

trilateral ['traɪˈlætərəl] [trai-la-te-ral], *a.* Trilátero, trilateral.

trilateralness ['traɪˈlætərəlnɪs] [trai-la-te-ral-nes], *s.* La calidad de lo que es trilátero.

trilby ['trɪlbɪ] [tril-bi], *s.* Sombrero de fieltro.

trilingual ['traɪˈlɪŋgwəl] [trai-lin-gual], *a.* Trilingüe, que está en tres lenguas, o que las emplea.

trill [trɪl] [tril], *s.* Trino, trinado, gorjeo (warbling), quiebro de la voz.

trill, *va.* Trinar, hacer trinos, quiebros o trinados. *-vn.* Gotear, correr gota a gota.

trillion ['trɪlɪən] [tri-lion], *s.* Trillón un millón de millones según la numeración frances y americana; según la inglesa, la tercer potencia de un millón.

trillium ['trɪlɪəm] [tri-liom], *s. (Bot.)* Trilio.

trilogy ['trɪlədʒɪ] [tri-lo-yi], *s.* Trilogía, conjunto de tres obras dramáticas que continúan el mismo tema general.

trim [trɪm] [trim], *a.* 1. Bien puesto, en buen estado, ajustado con precisión; bien cuidado, ataviado, acicalado. 2. Esbelto (slim), estilizado. 3. Elegante, de buen corte (neat).

trim, *va.* 1. Dar forma a, restablecer la figura, ajustar, adaptar; en carpintería, alisar, desbastar. 2. Desbastar, poner en orden o quitando cantos y esquinas; podar, mondar (plants); cortar (hair, beard). 3. Despabilar una lámpara o vela; por extensión, quitar los carbonos de una lámpara eléctrica de arco y reemplazarlos con otros nuevos. 4. Componer, adornar (decorate); guarnecer (dress), franjear, orillar. 5. Balancear, igualar o equilibrar los pesos de dos cosas. *-vn.* 1. Vacilar, titubear entre dos partidos; nadar entre dos aguas. 2. Estar o mantenerse en equilibrio (ship). **To trim off,** afeitar, recortar e igualar los bojes, espalderas u otras plantas. **To trim up,** adornar, hermosear, componer. **To trim a**

discourse, pulir un discurso. **To trim a lamp o a light,** despabilar una lámpara o vela. **To trim a ship,** *(Mar.)* Orientar un buque. **To trim the sails,** orientar las velas. **To trim the hold,** abarrotar.

trim, *s.* 1. Atavío, adorno, aderezo. **She was in her nicest trim,** estaba muy compuesta. 2. Traje, vestido; estilo (adorno o aspecto). 3. Recorte (cut). **Just a trim, please,** córteme sólo las puntas, por favor. 4. La disposición en que se arreglan las diversas partes de un buque para que navegue bien; también, el grado comparativo de inmersión de la proa y popa. **Trim of the hold,** disposición de la estiva. **Trim of the sails,** disposición de las velas. **Out of sailing trim,** mal dispuesto para navegar, pesado.

trimester [trɪˈmestəʳ] [tri-mes-tar], *s.* Trimestre.

trimly ['trɪmlɪ] [trim-li], *adv.* Primorosamente, con buen arreglo, bien.

trimmed ['trɪmd] [trimd], *a.* Ataviado, adornado. **Sharp trimmed,** *(Mar.)* A la trinca.

trimmer ['trɪməʳ] [tri-maʳ], *s.* 1. El que ajusta, desbasta, poda, etc. 2. Veleta, hombre de todos partidos. 3. Herramienta o máquina para igualar y desbastar.

trimming ['trɪmɪŋ] [tri-min], *s.* 1. Guarnición de vestido, franja, orla. 2. Desbaste; ajuste; arreglo; poda. 3. *pl.* Accesorios (accompaniments), pertenencias, como los enmaderamientos de adorno o la ferretería de una casa. **He will give him a good trimming,** *(Fam.)* El le ajustará la golilla, él le dará una buena felpa.

trine [train] [train], *s. (Astr.)* El aspecto trino de los planetas, cuando distan entre sí ciento veinte grados.

Trinidad ['trɪnɪdæd] [tri-ni-dad], *s.* Trinidad. **Trinidad and Tobago,** Trinidad y Tobago.

trinitrotoluene [traɪˈnaɪtrəʊˈtɒljuːiːn] [trai-ni-trou-to-liuin], *s. (Quím.)* Trinitrotolueno, explosivo muy potente. Se usa más en la forma abreviada de TNT.

Trinity ['trɪnɪtɪ] [tri-ni-ti], *s.* 1. Trinidad, la unión de tres personas en un solo Dios. **The Holy Trinity,** la Santísima Trinidad. 2. V. TRIAD y TRIO. **Trinity House,** la casa del gremio de marineros y pilotos en Inglaterra.

trinket ['trɪŋkɪt] [trin-kit], *s.* Joya, dije, adorno pequeño, bujería, chuchería (knickknack), cosa de poco valor para componerse.

trinomial [traɪˈnəʊmɪəl] [trai-nou-mial], *a.* 1. *(Biol.)* Que tiene tres nombres o terminos, el genérico, el específico y el subestpecífico. 2. *(Alg.)* Que consta de tres términos. *-s.* Trinomio, cantidad, algebraica compuesta de tres términos.

trio [trɪəʊ] [triou], *s.* 1. Triada, reunión de tres. 2. *(Mús.)* Trío, composición para tres voces o para tres instrumentos.

trip [trɪp] [trip], *va.* 1. Hacer caer a uno echándole la zancadilla. 2. Armar un lazo o zancadilla, usar de alguna treta o artificio. 3. Coger a uno en falta o cogerle en renuncio. 4. Bailar, ligera o ágilmente; mover los pies ligeramente y con ritmo. 5. *(Mec.)* Soltar, disparar; desatar. 6. Zarpar, levar anclas. *-vn.* 1. Tropezar (stumble), trompicar, resbalar, deslizarse los pies. 2. Deslizarse, decir o hacer una cosa con descuido e indeliberadamente, equivocarse, engañarse, tener un desliz o un descuido. 3. *(Mar.)* Zarpar. 4. Correr, andar con pasos ligeros, andar muy aprisa. 5. Dar una vuelta; hacer un viaje corto. **To trip the anchor,** *(Mar.)* Hacer que el ancla largue el fondo, levar el ancla. **Trip-hammer,** martinete de fragua. V. *Tilt-hammer.* **Trip over,** tropezar y caerse. **Trip up,** equivocarse, meter la pata.

trip, *s.* 1. Vuelta, un viaje corto (journey), excursión (excursion). **A trip to the zoo,** una visita al zoo. 2. Tropezón (stumble), resbalón, el acto de resbalar: caída, desliz, paso falso. 3. Paso o movimiento ágil. 4. *(Mar.)* Bordada de una embarcación que barlovenea. 5. Zancadilla, la acción de atravesar o echar el luchador el pie por detrás del de su contrario para derribarlo.

tripartite ['traɪpɑːtaɪt] [trai-par-tait], *a.* Tripartido, tripartito.

tripe [traɪp] [traip], *s.* 1. Tripas, cuajar, estómago de un animal rumiante preparado como alimento. **Tripe-woman,**

tripicallera, la mujer que vende tripas y callos. 2. *(Coloq.)* Paparruchas, chorradas (nonsense).

tripedal ['trɪpedəl] [trai-pe-dal], *a.* Lo que tiene tres pies.

triphase ['traɪfeɪz] [trai-feis], *a.* Trifásico.

triple ['trɪpl] [tri-pel], *a.* Tríplice, triple, triplo. *-va.* Triplicar. **Triple-expansion,** de triple expansión, con tres cilindros de tamaños graduados en los que el vapor se dilata sucesivamente, v. gr. en una máquina de vapor para buques. **Triple jump,** triple salto de longitud.

triplet ['trɪplɪt] [tri-plit], *s.* 1. Terno, número de tres de una misma especie. 2. Cada uno de tres hermanos nacidos de un parto, trillizo. 3. Tercerilla, una composición poética.

triplex ['trɪplɪks] [tri-pliks], *a.* Tríplice, de tres partes.

triplicate ['trɪplɪkɪt] [tri-pli-kit], *a.* Triplicado, triplo, tres tanto, tres veces más. *-s:* Triplicado, tercera copia de algo.

triply ['trɪplɪ] [tri-pli], *adv.* Triplemente, de una manera triple, por triplicado.

tripod ['traɪpɒd] [trai-pod], *s.* Trípode: aparato de tres pies para sostener instrumentos geodésicos, fotográficos, etc.

tripoli ['trɪpəlɪ] [tri-po-li], *s.* Trípoli, un género de greda silícea con que se pule y da lustre a los cristales, metales, etc. V. *Rotten-stone.*

tripper ['trɪpəʳ] [tri-paʳ], *s.* Andarín ágil, el que se mueve con ligereza; el que da una zancadilla, el o lo que suelta, disparador.

tripping ['trɪpɪŋ] [tri-pin], *a.* Veloz, ligero, ágil (agile). *-s.* 1. Baile ligero y a saltos. 2. Tropiezo, tropezón (stumble), traspié, paso falso.

trippingly ['trɪpɪŋlɪ] [tri-pin-li], *adv.* Velozmente, con agilidad y ligereza.

trippy ['trɪpɪ] [tri-pi], *a. (Fam.)* Flipante.

triptych ['trɪptɪk] [trip-tik], *s.* Tríptico.

trireme ['traɪriːm] [trai-rim], *s. (Ant.)* Trirreme, galera de tres órdenes de bancos de remeros por banda.

trisect ['trɪsekt] [tri-sekt], *va.* Trisecar, tripartir, dividir en tres partes.

trisection ['trɪsekʃən] [tri-sek-shon], *s.* Trisección, la acción de trisecar o dividir una cosa en tres partes.

tristful ['trɪstfʊl] [trist-ful], *a. (Ant.)* Triste (sad), melancólico.

trisyllabic ['traɪsɪ'læbɪk] [trai-si-la-bik], *a.* Trisílabo: se dice de la dicción o palabra de tres sílabas.

trite ['traɪt] [trait], *a.* Usado, repetido, envejecido, trillado (hackeneyed); trivial, vulgar.

tritely ['traɪtlɪ] [trait-li], *adv.* Vulgarmente.

triteness ['traɪtnɪs] [trait-nes], *s.* Vulgaridad (coarseness), trivialidad, cosa muy usada o muy común.

Triton ['traɪtn] [trai-ton], *s.* 1. Tritón, deidad, marina. 2. Gasterópodo del género Tritón. 3. Salamandra pequeña, batracio acuático.

tritone ['traɪtəʊn] [trai-toun], *s. (Mús.)* Trítono, intervalo de tres tonos.

triturable ['trɪtʃərəbl] [tri-tiu-ra-bol], *a.* Triturable, que se puede triturar.

triturate ['trɪtʃəreɪt] [tri-tiu-reit], *va.* Triturar, reducir a polvo.

trituration [,trɪtʃə'reɪʃən] [tri-tiu-rei-shon], *s.* Trituración, la acción de triturar.

triumph ['traɪʌmf] [traiomf], *s.* 1. Triunfo, vencimiento, victoria (victory). 2. Triunfo, la solemnidad y aplauso con que se celebra una victoria; la entrada solemne y pomposa en Roma con que se honraba en la antigüedad a los generales vencedores. 3. Alegría grande; brillo semejante a una pompa triunfal.

triumph, *vn.* 1. Triunfar, entrar en triunfo. 2. Triunfar (win), vencer en la guerra o en una disputa. 3. Gloriarse de haber vencido, hacer alarde de alguna ventaja o vencimiento.

triumphal [traɪ'ʌmfəl] [traiom-fal], *a.* Triunfal. *-s.* Triunfo.

triumphant [traɪ'ʌmfənt] [traiom-fant], *s.* 1. Triunfante, victorioso. 2. Triunfante, glorioso, exaltado.

triumphantly [traɪ'ʌmfəntlɪ] [traiom-fant-li], *adv.* Triunfantemente, en triunfo, victoriosamente; con alegría insolente.

triumpher [traɪ'ʌmfəʳ] [traiom-faʳ], *s.* Triunfador (winner).

triumvir [traɪ'ʌmvɪʳ] [traiam-viʳ], *s.* Triunviro, uno de los tres magistrados romanos que formaban el triunvirato.

triumvirate [traɪ'ʌmvɪrɪt] [traiom-vi-rit], *s.* Triunvirato.

trivet ['trɪvɪt] [tri-vit], *s.* Trébedes (de cocina), trípode.

trivia ['trɪvɪə] [tri-via], *s. pl.* Trivialidades, banalidades (banalities), nimiedades.

trivial ['trɪvɪəl] [tri-vial], *a.* Trivial, vulgar, ordinario, bajo; frívolo (frivolous).

triviality [,trɪvɪ'ælɪtɪ] [tri-via-li-ti], *s.* Trivialidad, banalidad, nimiedad. **We exchanged trivialities,** hablamos de cosas intrascendentes.

trivialize ['trɪvɪəlaɪz] [tri-via-lais], *vt.* Trivializar, quitarle importancia.

trivially ['trɪvɪəlɪ] [tri-via-li], *adv.* Trivialmente; comúnmente; frívolamente.

trivialness ['trɪvɪəlnɪs] [tri-vial-nes], *s.* Trivialidad; vulgaridad; frivolidad, poca importancia.

triweekly ['traɪwiːklɪ] [tri-ui-kli], *a.* 1. Que sucede o se hace tres veces por semana. 2. Que se hace o sucede cada tercera semana.

troat ['trəʊt] [trout], *vn.* Bramar, hacer oír su voz el venado cuando está en celo.

trochaic [trɒ'keɪk] [tro-keik], *a.* Trocaico, lo que consta de troqueos.

troche ['trəʊtʃ] [trouch], *s.* Tablilla, trocisco, que contiene un medicamento pulverizado mezclado con azúcar y goma.

trochee ['trɒkiː] [tro-ki], *s. (Poet.)* Troqueo, pie que consta de una sílaba larga y otra breve.

trod, trodden [trɒd] [trod], [trɒdn] [tro-den], *pret.* y *pp.* del verbo TO TREAD.

trode ['trəʊd] [troud], *pret.* del verbo TREAD.

troglodyte ['trɒglədaɪt] [tro-glo-dait], *s.* 1. Troglodita, habitante de las cavernas; se aplica a una raza prehistórica. 2. *(Fig.)* Ermitaño, solitario. 3. Mono semejante al hombre. 4. Reyezuelo, troglodita. V. WREN.

troika ['trɔɪkə] [troi-ka], *f.* Troica.

Trojan ['trəʊdʒən] [trou-yan], *a.* y *s.* Troyano, de Troya. **The trojan horse,** el caballo de Troya. **To work like a Trojan,** trabajar como un burro.

troll [trəʊl] [troul], *va.* 1. Cantar en sucesión (parts of a song), cantar de una manera alegre. 2. Pescar con caña por la popa de un bote o barco. 3. Voltear, dar vueltas a alguna cosa. *-vn.* 1. Cantar alegremente. 2. Pescar con caña. 3. Girar (spin), moverse circularmente. 4. Rodar, andorrear, corretear.

troll, *s.* 1. Cantar que se entona en partes sucesivas. 2. Rodadura, movimiento de rodar o girar. 3. Carrete de la caña de pescar. 4. *(Mit.)* Gnomo, enano.

trolley ['trɒlɪ] [tro-li], *s.* 1. Trole, rueda pequeña con muesca para que gire en contacto con un conductor eléctrico y comunique la corriente al coche de tranvía. **Trolley bus,** trolebús. 2. Carrito, mesa rodante, vagoneta.

trolling ['trɒlɪŋ] [tro-lin], *s.* El procedimiento o acto de pescar tirando el anzuelo y cordel por la popa de una embarcación y casi a flor de agua.

trollop ['trɒləp] [tro-lap], *s.* Gorrona, mujer desliñada y poco recatada, mujerzuela (slut).

trombone [trɒm'bəʊn] [trom-boun], *s.* Trombón, sacabuche, instrumento músico de metal.

tromp ['trɒmp] [tromp], *vi.* Pisotear, pisar.

troop [truːp] [trup], *s.* 1. Tropa, junta de mucha gente unida y acuadrillada entre sí para algún fin; cuadrilla, turba. 2. Tropa (unit), el cuerpo de soldados o gente de guerra. 3. Tropa, conjunto de gente de guerra a caballo. **Troops,** tropas, ejército.

troop, *vn.* 1. Atroparse, juntarse la gente en cuadrillas. 2. Juntarse, tumultuarse, agavillarse la gente. 3. Marchar en cuerpo o en orden militar, desfilar (parade). 4. Marchar en compañía de otros muchos. **To troop away** o **off,** retirarse en cuerpo o en cuadrillas.

troop carrier ['tru:p͵kærɪəʳ] [trup-ka-riaʳ], *s.* Transporte de tropas.

trooper ['tru:pəʳ] [tru-paʳ], *s.* Soldado de a caballo (cavalryman).

trope ['trəʊp] [troup], *s.* Tropo, uso de una expresión en sentido figurado; lenguaje figurado.

trophic ['trəʊfɪk] [trou-fik], *a.* Trófico, perteneciente a la nutrición y a sus procedimientos.

trophied ['trəʊfaɪd] [trou-faid], *a.* Adornado de trofeos.

trophy ['trəʊfɪ] [trou-fi], *s.* 1. Trofeo, despojo del enemigo vencido. 2. Trofeo, monumento público en memoria del vencimiento. 3. *(Poet.)* Trofeo, triunfo.

tropic ['trɒpɪk] [tro-pik], *s.* Trópico. **The Tropic of Cancer,** el trópico de Cáncer. **The Tropics,** el Trópico.

tropical ['trɒpɪkəl] [tro-pi-kal], *a.* 1. *(Astr.)* Tropical, que pertenece al trópico o círculo menor de la esfera. 2. *(Reto.)* Trópico: se dice del estilo en que se usan mucho los tropos.

troposphere ['trɒpəsfʊəʳ] [tro-pos-fiaʳ], *s.* Troposfera.

trot [trɒt] [trot], *va.* 1. Hacer trotar. 2. Pasar al trote, por encima de algo. *-vn.* 1. Trotar, ir o caminar al trote. 2. Trotar, andar de prisa o con celeridad.

trot, *s.* 1. Trote, modo de andar del caballo más levantado y vivo que el paso regular. 2. Andar o movimiento constante. 3. Niño, niña. *V.* TOT.

troth [trəʊθ] [trouz], *s.* 1. Verdad, fe, fidelidad. **In troth,** en verdad. 2. Esponsales.

trotter ['trɒtəʳ] [tro-taʳ], *s.* Caballo trotón. **Trotters** o **sheep's trotters,** manos o pies de carnero.

trotting ['trɒtɪŋ] [tro-tin], *m. (Sport)* Trote.

troubadour ['tru:bədɔːʳ] [tru-ba-doʳ], *s.* Trovador, poeta provenzal de la Edad Media.

trouble ['trʌbl] [tra-bel], *va.* 1. Disturbar, perturbar, causar disturbio. 2. Desazonar, afligir, inquietar, preocupar (worry). 3. Molestar (bother), enfadar, aguar el gusto a uno; atribular. 4. Incomodar, dar que hacer; importunar. **Do not trouble youself,** no se moleste Ud. 5. Revolver, enturbiar, poner turbio. 6. Pedir, rogar, suplicar (fórmula de cortesía). **May I trouble you to hand me the book?** ¿tiene Ud. la bondad de darme el libro? **What need you trouble yourself?** ¿por   qué se incomoda o se apura Ud.? **Do not trouble my head with it,** no me quiebre Ud. la cabeza con eso.

trouble, *s.* 1. Problema (problem), turbación, confusión, disturbio (strife), desorden. 2. Molestia, inquietud, incomodidad. 3. Aflicción, calamidad, pena, congoja. **Can you do it without trouble?** ¿puede Ud. hacerlo sin molestarse? 4. Enfado, impertinencia, engorro. **To be in trouble,** estar inquieto, estar agitado, estar afligido; hallarse en un apuro, sufrir alguna calamidad. **To be at the trouble, to put to trouble,** dar que hacer. **It is not worth the trouble,** no vale la pena.

troubled ['trʌbld] [tra-beld], *a. pp.* del verbo. TO TROUBLE. **I am troubled with the gout,** padezco mal de gota. **To fish in troubled water,** pescar en agua turbia o en río revuelto. Preocupado (disturbed).

troubler ['trʌbləʳ] [tra-blaʳ], *s.* Alborotador, perturbador, inquietador.

trouble shooter ['trʌbl͵ʃuːtəʳ] [tra-bel-shu-taʳ], *s. (Fam.)* El encargado de descubrir y allanar o corregir fallas, conciliador (mediator).

troublesome ['trʌblsəm] [tra-bel-som], *a.* 1. Penoso, molesto, oneroso, fatigoso, pesado, gravoso. 2. Importuno, molesto, enfadoso, impertinente, incómodo, fastidioso.

troubling ['trʌblɪŋ] [tra-blin], *a.* Alarmante, inquietante.

troublous ['trʌbləs] [tra-blos], *a.* 1. Turbulento, confuso, tumultoso. 2. Inquieto, impaciente.

trough [trɒf] [trof], *s.* 1. Artesa, gamella, gamellón; dornajo, cubeta. *(Am.)* Batea. **Stone trough,** pilón. 2. Depresión larga y estrecha, como entre dos colinas o el intermedio o espacio entre dos olas.

trounce [traʊns] [trauns], *va. (Fam.)* Zurrar, dar palos, castigar severamente.

troupe [truːp] [trup], *s.* Compañía de cómicos, acróbatas, etc.

trouper ['tru:pəʳ] [tru-paʳ], *s.* Comediante, actor que viaja. **A good trouper,** persona que sabe viajar sin importarle incomodidades. **She's a real trouper,** siempre está dispuesta a echar una mano.

trouser ['traʊzəʳ] [trau-saʳ], *a.* Del pantalón.

trousers ['traʊzəz] [trau-sars], *s. pl.* Pantalones; calzones largos o de marinero.

trousseau ['tru:səʊ] [tru-sou], *s.* Ajuar de novia.

trout [traʊt] [traut], *s.* Trucha, pez delicado que se coge en los ríos y arroyos. **Trout flies,** moscas artificiales para la pesca de truchas.

trout-hook ['traʊthʊk] [traut-juk], *s.* Anzuelo de trucha.

trover ['trəʊvəʳ] [trou-vaʳ], *s. (For.)* El derecho de repetir contra quien ha hallado o posee por cualquier título los bienes ajenos y no los quiere entregar a su dueño.

trowel ['traʊəl] [traual], *s.* Trulla, llana, paleta, palustre, instrumento que usan los albañiles.

troy ['trɔɪ] [troi], **troy-weight** [troi-ueit], *s.* Peso de troy, peso para el oro, la plata y las drogas medicinales, que es de doce onzas cada libra.

truancy ['truːənsɪ] [truan-si], *s.* Novillos, ausencia de la escuela sin permiso; haraganería.

truant ['truːənt] [truant], *s. y a.* Holgazán (lazy), haragán, ocioso, tunante. **To play the truant,** hacer novillos, ausentarse de la escuela sin licencia.

truce [truːs] [trus], *s.* 1. Tregua, cesación temporal de hostilidades, suspensión de armas. **To call a truce,** suspender las hostilidades. 2. Descanso, interrupción, intermisión, intervalo.

truck [trʌk] [trak], *va. y vn.* Trocar, permutar, cambiar, hacer un cambio o trueque; traficar, vender. *-s.* 1. Efectos para vender o trocar, particularmente los de fácil manejo. 2. *(E.U.)* Hortalizas para el mercado. 3. *(Fam.)* Artículos sin valor; desechos, desperdicios, zupias. 4. *(Fam.)* Cambio (change), permuta, trueque.

truck, *va. y vn.* Acarrear, transportar por medio de camiones. *-s.* 1. Camión, carretón fuerte para transportar mercancías pesadas. 2. Carretilla de mano para barriles, cajas, baúles, etc. **Truck frame,** bastidor para camión. **Dumping truck,** volquete.

truckage ['trʌkɪdʒ] [tra-kich], *s.* Carreteo, y el precio que se paga por llevar efectos en carretones.

trucker ['trʌkəʳ] [tra-kaʳ], *s.* Camionero, transportista.

trucking ['trʌkɪŋ] [tra-kin], *s.* Transporte por carretera.

truckle ['trʌkl] [tra-kel], *vn.* Someterse, ceder, sujetarse, besar la correa; estar en un estado de sujeción e inferioridad.

truckle-bed ['trʌklbed] [tra-kel-bed], *s.* Carriola, cama con ruedas que puede rodarse debajo de otra cama más alta.

truckman ['trʌkmən] [trak-man], *s.* 1. Carretero. 2. Trocador, el que hace trueques.

truculence ['trʌkjʊləns] [tra-kiu-lans], *s.* Fiereza, crueldad.

truculent ['trʌkjʊlənt] [tra-kiu-lant], *a.* Truculento (gruesome), cruel.

trudge [trʌdʒ] [tradch], *vn.* Andar o ir a pie; caminar con afán, fatiga y trabajo.

true [truː] [tru], *a.* 1. Verdadero (real), cierto, seguro, efectivo. 2. Verdadero, real, sin engaño, doblez o tergiversación, ingenuo, sincero; verídico. 3. Genuino (genuine), puro, propio y natural. 4. Fiel (faithful), constante, leal; exacto. **A true translation,** traducción que concuerda con su original. **True-blue,** leal, fiel. **True-born,** legítimo, verdadero; de nacimiento legítimo. **True-bred,** de casta legítima. **True-hearted,** leal, sincero, fiel, franco, de buena fe. **True-heartedness,** fidelidad, sinceridad, franqueza, buena fe.

true bill ['tru:'bɪl] [tru-bil], *s.* Acusación de parte de un gran jurado.

true-blue ['tru:'blu:] [tru-blu], *a.* Rancio. *s.* Partidario.

true-love [ˈtruːlʌv] [tru-lav], *a. (Bot.)* Pariseta de cuatro hojas, hierba París o uva de oso. **True-lover's knot,** lazo de amor.

trueness [ˈtruːnɪs] [tru-nes], *s.* Fidelidad (faithfulness), sinceridad, candidez, franqueza.

truepenny [ˈtruːpeni] [tru-pe-ni], *s. (Fam.)* Hombre de bien, mozo honrado.

truffle [ˈtrʌfl] [tra-fel], *s. (Bot.)* Criadilla de tierra, trufa, hongo subterráneo.

truism [ˈtruːɪzəm] [trui-sem], *s.* 1. Verdad indudable y que no puede negarse. 2. *(Fam.)* Verdad evidente, pero no importante; perogrullada (platitude).

truly [ˈtruːlɪ] [tru-li], *adv.* Verdaderamente, en verdad; realmente, en realidad; exactamente (accurately), con precisión; sinceramente (sincerely), de buena fe. **Yours truly, yours very truly,** su seguro servidor.

trump [trʌmp] [tramp], *s.* 1. *(Poét. o ant.)* Trompeta, clarín. 2. Triunfo, en el juego de naipes. **Diamonds are trumps,** oros son triunfos. **To put to one's trumps,** apretarle en un discurso o argumento. 3. *(Fam.)* Persona muy agradable; un real mozo. 4. *(Esco.)* Birimbao.

trump, *va.* 1. Jugar triunfo, matar con un triunfo. 2. Engañar. **To trump up,** forjar; idear, suponer o inventar; tomado siempre en mala parte.

trumpery [ˈtrʌmpərɪ] [tram-pe-ri], *s.* 1. Hojarasca, oropel, cualquier cosa de poco valor o utilidad; bujería, baratija. 2. Palabras vanas, inútiles o de poca substancia, piropo, relumbrón. 3. Engaño, fraude, falsedad (falseness).

trumpet [ˈtrʌmpɪt] [tram-pit], *s.* Trompeta, clarín; trompa, instrumento músico militar. **Speaking-trumpet,** bocina. **Hearing-trumpet, ear-trumpet,** trompetilla acústica. **Trumpet-creeper, trumpet-vine,** jazmín trompeta, planta trepadora con flores escarlata en forma de trompeta. **Trumpet-honey-suckle,** madreselva. **Trumpet-tongued,** vocinglero, con lengua de trompeta. **Trumpet-shell,** trompa o bocina marina.

trumpet, *va.* 1. Pregonar a son de trompeta, trompetear. 2. Modelar en forma de boca de trompeta. - Dar de sí un sonido como de trompeta.

trumpeter [ˈtrʌmpɪtəʳ] [tram-pi-taʳ], *s.* 1. Trompetero, trompeta, trompetista. 2. Pregonero, el que publica y hace patente alguna cosa. 3. Agamí, ave sudamericana de las zancudas. 4. Trompa marina, pez cetáceo.

truncate [trʌŋˈkeit] [tran-keit], *va.* Truncar o troncar, cortar la cima o la extremidad de algo.

truncated [trʌŋˈkeit] [tran-keit], *a.* Truncado, cortado; terminado bruscamente en su extremidad.

truncating [trʌŋˈkeitɪŋ] [tran-kei-tin], *s. (Inform.)* Truncamiento.

truncheon [ˈtrʌntʃən] [tran-chon], *s.* Porra, cachiporra.

trundle [ˈtrʌndl] [tran-del], *s.* 1. Rodaja, rueda pequeña. 2. *V. Trundle-bed.* 3. Rodadura, la acción de rodar. 4. Rueda baja: carreta de ruedas bajas. **Trundle-bed,** carriola, cama baja o tarima con ruedas. **Trundle-shot,** *(Mar.)* Palanquetas. **Trudle-tail,** cola redonda.

trundle, *va. y vn.* Rodar, moverse por la tierra dando vueltas.

trunk [trʌŋk] [trank], *a.* De, o perteneciente a un cuerpo principal. **Trunk line,** línea principal de un sistema de transportes, p. ej. un ferrocarril o un canal. -*s.* 1. Tronco, la parte inferior de los árboles desde el suelo hasta donde se divide en ramas. 2. Tronco, el cuerpo humano o de algún otro animal sin la cabeza, piernas o brazos. 3. Tronco, la parte principal de una cosa dividida en ramales, como las arterias, venas, etc. 4. Fuste de columna. 5. Baúl (box) o cofre. **Nests of trunks,** juegos de cuatro cofres o baúles. 6. Trompa, la nariz del elefante. 7. Cañón o conducto cuadrangular de madera, v. g. en un órgano. **Trunk-hose,** calzones largos de los siglos XVI y XVII. **Trunk-maker,** cofrero. **Trunk road,** carretera principal.

trunks [trʌŋkz] [tranks], *s. pl.* Calzones cortos de hombre.

trunnion [ˈtrʌnɪən] [tra-nion], *s.* 1. *(Art.)* Muñón, cada una de las dos piezas cilíndricas que sostienen a un cañón sobre la cureña. **Trunnion plates,** chapos de testera, contramuñoneras. 2. Tuerca de cilindro oscilante.

truss [trʌs] [tras], *s.* 1. Braguero para las quebraduras, suspensión. 2. Armadura, armazón, conjunto de piezas principales de un puente u otra construcción. 2. Mazorca, conjunto de flores terminales. 4. Haz, atado, lío, paquete, brazado. En Inglaterra, 36 libras de paja y 60 de heno hacen un *truss*. **Truss-maker,** el que hace bragueros o suspensorios.

truss, *va.* 1. Atirantar, apuntalar, sostener con un armazón. 2. Espetar; añanzar el ave antes de guisarla. 3. *(Ant.)* Empaquetar, enfardelar, hacer un lío o fardo. **To truss up,** empaquetar, liar; ahorcar como criminal.

trust [trʌst] [trast], *s.* 1. Confianza (confidence, faith), seguridad o esperanza firme en otra persona, confidencia. 2. *(For.)* Fideicomiso, cargo, depósito, cualquier cosa confiada a la honradez o fidelidad de otra persona. 3. Crédito por el cual se presta a uno alguna cosa sin más seguridad que la confianza que en él se tiene. 4. Crédito por el cual se admite y cree algo; crédito en sentido comercial. 5. El estado de la persona en quien se ha hecho confianza. 6. Esperanza, expectación, creencia. 7. *(Com.)* Combinación, asociación de compañías industriales para fijar la producción, precio, etc., de una mercadería, o para asumir la dirección y las ganacias de un negocio. **A place of great trust,** un puesto de mucha importancia. **To give upon trust,** dar fiado. **In trust,** en confianza, en depósito. **Trust deed of sale,** *(For.)* Escritura de venta condicionada.

trust, *va. y vn.* 1. Confiar, tener confianza en o hacer confianza de, contar con. 2. Confiar, esperar con firmeza y seguridad. 3. Confiar, encargar y fiar. 4. Confiarse, fiarse, poner en confianza. 5. Creer, dar crédito. 6. Vender al fiado. 7. Creer en, dar fe, aceptar como verdadero. 8. Esperar con confianza (hope); estimar algo como verdadero, deseando a la vez que lo sea. **I hope you enjoyed yourself,** espero que te hayas divertido.

trusted [ˈtrʌstɪd] [tras-tid], *a.* Leal, de confianza.

trustee [trʌsˈtiː] [tras-tii], *s.* Tenedor de bienes; encomendero, el que tiene a su cargo la propiedad de otro, depositario; fidei-comisario.

truster [ˈtrʌstəʳ] [tras-taʳ], *s.* Fiador, el que fía.

trusteeship [ˈtrʌstɪʃɪp] [tras-ti-ship], *s.* Oficio o funciones de administrador o depositario.

trust fund [ˈtrʌstfənd] [tras-fand], *s.* Fondo fiduciario.

trustily [ˈtrʌstɪlɪ] [tras-ti-li], *adv.* Fielmente; lealmente, honradamente.

trustiness [ˈtrʌstɪnɪs] [tras-ti-nes], *s.* Fidelidad, probidad, integridad y honradez en las acciones.

trusting [ˈtrʌstɪŋ] [tras-tin], *a.* Confiado.

trustless [ˈtrʌstlɪs] [trast-les], *a.* Pérfido, inconstante, sin fe, sin que merezca confianza o crédito.

trusthworthiness [ˈtrʌstˌwɜːðɪnɪs] [trast-uer-zi-nes], *s.* Integridad, honradez (honesty).

trustworthy [ˈtrʌstˌwɜːðɪ] [trast-uer-zi], *a.* Digno de confianza, seguro.

trusty [ˈtrʌstɪ] [tras-ti], *a.* 1. Fiel, leal (loyal), constante, íntegro, que merece confianza o crédito. 2. Fuerte, seguro, que no cede fácilmente.

truth [truːθ] [truz], *s.* 1. Verdad, la total correspondencia de lo que se dice o expresa con lo que interiormente se juzga. **Tell me the truth,** dime la verdad. 2. Verdad, axioma. 3. Fidelidad, constancia. 4. Realidad. 5. Exactitud. 6. Honradez. **Of a truth** o **in truth,** a la verdad o en verdad; en realidad, seriamente.

truthful [ˈtruːθfʊl] [truz-ful], *a.* Verídico; verdadero, conforme a la verdad.

truthfully [ˈtruːθfəlɪ] [truz-fu-li], *adv.* Sinceramente.

truthless [ˈtruːθlɪs] [truz-les], *a.* 1. Falso (false), contrario a la verdad. 2. Sin fe, desleal.

try [trai] [trai], *va. (pret. y pp.* TRIED) 1. Examinar, ensayar, probar, hacer prueba, intentar (attempt). 2. Experimentar, probar y examinar prácticamente las virtudes o propiedades de una cosa. 3. Tentar, probar, tantear. 4. Tentar, intentar, poner los medios para lograr algo. 5. Procesar; juzgar o examinar algún pleito o causa criminal; formar causa a uno. 6. Procurar, emprender, intentar (try). 7. Decidir o terminar una diferencia. 8. Purificar, refinar por medio de la calefacción. 9. Imponer una carga a, fatigar (v. g. la vista). -vn. 1. Esforzarse, ensayar, procurar, hacer lo posible. 2. # *(Mar.)* Capear. **We shall try it out,** veremos en qué para. **Try for,** tratar de conseguir. **Try on,** probarse, medirse. -s. Prueba, ensayo, intento (attempt), esfuerzo. **It's worth a try,** vale la pena intentarlo.

trying ['traɪɪŋ] [traiin], *a. part.* Penoso, difícil de soportar; fatigoso; contrariador.

tryout ['traɪaut] [trai-aut], *s.* Prueba, examen, ensayo.

try-sail ['traɪseɪl] [trai-seil], *s. (Mar.)* La vela mayor de un paquete. **Try-sail-mast,** pie de amigo de la mayor.

tryst [trɪst] [trist], *s.* Cita (appointment) o lugar de cita. **To bide tryst,** acudir a una cita, ser exacto a la cita.

tsar [zɑːr] [saʳ], *s.* Zar.

tsetse fly ['tsetsɪflaɪ] [tse-tsi-flai], *s.* Tsetsé, mosca chupadora de sangre del interior del continente africano. Su picadura no causa daño al hombre, pero es mortal para el ganado mayor y los caballos.

t-shirt ['tiːʃɜːt] [ti-shert], *s.* Camiseta de mangas muy cortas que suele usarse exteriormente.

tub [tʌb] [tab], *va.* 1. Encubar, poner en una cuba. 2. Bañar (a uno) en bañera. -vn. Bañarse en bañera. -s. 1. Cuba, recipiente de madera redondo de formado de varias duelas; tina de madera. 2. Cantidad que puede contener una cuba. 3. Lo que se parece a una cuba; bote pesado. 4. Cubeta, tonel pequeño. 5. Baño tomado en una bañera. **Bath-tub,** bañera, baño. **Mash-tub,** cuba de tracear la cerveza. **Wash-tub,** cuba, tina de lavar.

tuba ['tjuːbə] [tiu-ba], *s.* Tuba (instrumento musical).

tubby ['tʌbɪ] [ta-bi], *a. (Coloq.)* Rechoncho, regordete.

tube [tjuːb] [tiub], *va.* Proveer de un tubo o tubos. -s. 1. Tubo (pipe), cañón, cañuto, fístola o cualquier otro conducto largo y muy delgado; sifón. 2. *(Anat.)* Conducto, órgano tubular, particularmente el que conduce aire. 3. *(Coloq.)* **The tube,** la tele. 4. *(G.B., Coloq.)* **The tube,** el metro.

tuber ['tjuːbəʳ] [tiu-baʳ], *s.* 1. *(Bot.)* Tubérculo, porción corta y engrosada de un tallo subterráneo, como la patata. 2. *(Anat.)* Hinchazón, prominencia.

tubercle ['tjuːbəkl] [tiu-bar-kel], *s.* 1. Eminencia natural, poco notable, particularmente de un hueso. 2. *(Med.)* Tubérculo, tumorcillo granular, producto morboso dentro de un órgano; en los pulmones causa la consunción pulmonar. 3. *(Bot.)* Excrecencia pequeña.

tubercular [tjəˈbɜːkjələʳ] [tiu-ber-kiu-laʳ], *a.* 1. Tuberculoso; en forma de nudo o excrecencia. 2. *(Med.)* Tuberculoso, relativo o perteneciente al tubérculo; de la naturaleza de los tubérculos.

tuberculin [tjəˈbɜːkjəlɪn] [tiu-ber-kiu-lin], *s.* Tuberculina, preparación para el diagnóstico de la tuberculosis.

tuberculosis [tjəˌbɜːkjəˈləʊsɪs] [tiu-ber-kiu-lou-sis], *s.* Tuberculosis, tuberculización, enfermedad diatésica que consiste en el desarrollo de tubérculos en uno o varios órganos, especialmente en los pulmones.

tuberculous, tuberculose [tjəˈbɜːkjələs] [tiu-ber-kiu-los], *a.* Tuberculoso, tuberculífero, que padece tuberculosis, que tiene tubérculos.

tubing ['tjuːbɪŋ] [tiu-bin], *s.* Tubería, tubo en secciones; sistema de tubos.

tubular ['tjuːbjələʳ] [tiu-biu-laʳ], *a.* Tubular, largo y hueco como tubo o cañón.

tubule ['tjuːbjuːl] [tiu-biul], *s.* Tubo pequeño.

tuck [tʌk] [tak], *s.* 1. Alforza o pliegue para disminuir el largo de una bata, vestido, falda, etc. 2. Cartera, prolongación de una de las cubiertas de un libro, cuya extremidad se inserta en un corte o en una presilla de la otra cubierta. 3. *(Mar.)* Falda, arca de popa. 4. *(Des.)* Estoque, espada, angosta y larga.

tuck, *va.* 1. Arremangar, recoger o encoger lo que cuelga. 2. Meter entre la ropa; arropar, tapar y cubrir bien a uno con ropa. **To tuck up one's clothes,** arremangarse.

tucker ['tʌkəʳ] [ta-kaʳ], *s.* 1. El o lo que hace alforzas; alforzador de máquinas de coser. 2. Escote, especie de adorno que cubre el pecho de las mujeres.

tucker, *va. (Fam. E.U.)* Cansar, fatigar; por lo común con *out.* **To be tuckered out,** estar muy cansado.

Tuesday ['tjuːzdɪ] [tius-di], *s.* Martes, el tercer día de la semana. **Shrove Tuesday,** martes de carnestolendas.

tuff [tʌf] [taf], *s.* Tufo, piedra esponjosa volcánica compuesta de fragmentos.

tuft [tʌft] [taft], *s.* 1. Copete, conjunto de cosas pequeñas y flexibles que están atadas por la base; v. gr. borla, lazo, penacho; mazorca de hierbas, de flores, etc.; ramillete; mechón de cabellos en lo alto de la frente; melena de crines, de lana. 2. Reunión de pequeños vasos sanguíneos en un punto, a manera de nudo. **Tuft of hair,** moño. **Tuft-hunter,** zalamero, adulador de los poderosos.

tuft, *va.* 1. Adornar con borlas, lazos o penachos. 2. Separar en grupos, en mazorcas o en ramilletes. 3. En tapicería, fijar a intervalos regulares con copetes o botones.

tufty ['tʌftɪ] [taf-ti], *a.* 1. Afelpado, felpudo, velludo. 2. Encopetado. 3. Lleno de lazos, borlas, etc.

tug [tʌg] [tag], *va.* Tirar con fuerza, hacer fuerza hacia sí, arrastrar con esfuerzo, halar, remolcar. -vn. Luchar, esforzarse.

tug, *s.* 1. Tirada con esfuerzo o la acción de tirar de una cosa con toda violencia. 2. Esfuerzo grande hecho para arrancar o tirar de alguna cosa. 3. Remolcador de vapor. **Tug-boat,** remolcador. *V.* 3ª acep.

tugger ['tʌgəʳ] [ta-gaʳ], *s.* El que tira o arranca con mucha fuerza.

tug-of-war ['tʌgəvˈwɔːr] [tag-ov-uoʳ], *s.* 1. Competencia en que dos grupos tiran de una cuerda. 2. Lucha por la supremacía.

tuition [tjʊˈɪʃən] [tiui-shon], *s.* 1. Tutoría, instrucción; enseñanza. 2. Precio de la enseñanza o instrucción.

tulip ['tjuːlɪp] [tiu-lip], *s. (Bot.)* Tulipán, planta y flor.

tulip-tree ['tjuːlɪptriː] [tiu-lip-tri], *s. (Bot.)* Tulipero, árbol grande de la familia de las magnoliáceas, con flores parecidas a las del tulipán.

tulle [tjuːl] [tiul], *s.* Tul.

tumble ['tʌmbl] [tam-bel], *vn.* 1. Caer, dar en tierra. 2. Hundirse, desplomarse, venir abajo o al suelo, venir a tierra. 3. Rodar abajo, bajar rodando. 4. Voltear, dar alguna cosa vueltas por sí misma o dar vueltas o saltos como los volteadores; saltar, dar saltos o brincos; revolcarse. 5. *(Ger.)* Comprender, entender. -va. 1. Arrojar con descuido y con bastante fuerza. 2. Desordenar, desarreglar, trastornar, derribar, volcar. 3. Ajar o arrugar los vestidos. **To tumble down,** hundirse, caer. **To tumble into bed,** echarse en la cama. **To tumble out,** echar fuera de, arrojar con violencia. **To tumble over,** trastornar, volcar, poner lo de arriba abajo. **Tumble-down,** que amenaza ruina, destrozado.

tumble, *s.* Caída, vuelco, voltereta.

tumblebug ['tʌmblbʌg] [tam-bel-bag], *s.* Escarabajo pelotero, que hace una bola de estiércol para depositar en ella sus huevos.

tumbler ['tʌmbləʳ] [tam-blaʳ], *s.* 1. Volteador, el que da vueltas, saltabanco, titiritero. 2. Vaso sin pie para beber, a diferencia de la copa. 3. Pichón volteador. **The tumbler of a lock,** rodete fiador, de cerradura.

tumbrel ['tʌmbrəl] [tam-bral], *s.* 1. *(Art.)* Carro de artillería. 2. Chirrión, carro de basura.

tumefaction [ˌtjuːmɪˈfækʃən] [tiu-mi-fak-shon], *s. (Med.)* Tumefacción, la hinchazón o elevación de alguna parte del cuerpo.

tumefy ['tjuːmɪfaɪ] [tiu-mi-fai], *va.* Hacer entumecerse o hincharse.

tumescence [tjuːˈmesns] [tiu-me-sens], *s.* Tumescencia, principio de un tumor.

tumescent [tjuːˈmesnt] [tiu-me-sent], *a.* Tumefacto, tumescente.

tumid [ˈtjuːmɪd] [tiu-mid], *a.* 1. Túmido, hinchado, prominente. 2. Túmido, inflado, hablando del estilo.

tumor, tumour [ˈtjuːməʳ] [tiu-maʳ], *s.* Tumor, hinchazón, y bulto que se forma en alguna parte del cuerpo.

tumular [ˈtjuːmjɒləʳ] [tiu-ma-laʳ], *a.* Tumulario, en forma de montecillo.

tumult [ˈtjuːmʌlt] [tiu-malt], *s.* 1. Tumulto, alboroto, motín, desorden, concurso grande de gente que causa desorden. 2. Agitación de ánimo.

tumultuous [ˈtjuːmʌltjʊəs] [tiu-mal-tios], *a.* 1. Tumultuario, tumultuoso, que causa o levanta tumultos o que está sin orden ni concierto. 2. Turbulento, confuso, alborotado y desordenado.

tumultuously [ˈtjuːmʌltjʊəslɪ] [tiu-mal-tios-li], *adv.* Tumultuariamente, en tumulto; sin orden ni concierto.

tumultuousness [ˈtjuːmʌltjʊəsnɪs] [tiu-mal-tios-nes], *s.* Turbulencia, tumulto.

tumulus [ˈtjuːmjɒləs] [tiu-miu-los], *s.* Túmulo, montón de tierra, que por lo general cubría una sepultura.

tun [tʌn] [tan], *s.* 1. Tonel, cubeta o barril grande. 2. Cuba o tanque de cervecero para la fermentación; contiene a menudo unos 3.000 litros o más. 3. Cantidad de cerveza fermentada de una vez. 4. Tonelada, medida indeterminada y bastante grande; v. g. de dos pipas de vino (252 galones). *V.* TON.

tun, *va.* Entonelar, envasar, embarrilar vino u otros licores.

tuna (o **tunny**) **fish** [ˈtjuːnə] [tiu-na], *s.* Atún.

tunable [ˈtjuːnəbl] [tiu-na-bol], *a.* 1. Que se puede templar. 2. *(Des.)* Armonioso, musical.

tundra [ˈtʌndrə] [tan-dra], *s.* Tundra, llanura undulada de Rusia y Siberia, cubierta de musgo y a veces húmeda o pantanosa.

tune [tjuːn] [tiun], *s.* 1. Tono, la canción métrica para la música compuesta de varias coplas; tonada. 2. Tono, el sonido que hace la voz cuando se habla o canta y el que hace un instrumento cuando se toca. 3. Concordancia o armonía, tanto, hablando de la música como hablando metafóricamente de costumbres, actos morales, etc. 4. Tono, el estado particular del ánimo y a veces también del cuerpo para ejecutar, aprender, etc. **The fiddle is in tune or out of tune,** el violín está afinado o desafinado.

tune, *va.* 1. Templar un instrumento músico. 2. Cantar armoniosamente. 3. Poner acordes dos o más cosas o ajustarlas perfectamente entre sí. *-vn.* 1. Modular, cantar con armonía y variedad de la voz. 2. Ajustarse o concertar dos o más voces o instrumentos.

tuneful [ˈtjuːnfʊl] [tiun-ful], *a.* Armonioso, acorde, melodioso.

tuneless [ˈtjuːnlɪs] [tiun-les], *a.* Desentonado, disonante, discordante, fuera de tono.

tuner [ˈtjuːnəʳ] [tiu-naʳ], *s.* Afinador de instrumentos musicales.

tungsten [ˈtʌŋstən] [tangs-ten], *s.* *(Quím.)* Tungsteno, metal polvoriento, de color plomizo, duro y pesado.

tunic [ˈtjuːnɪk] [tiu-nik], *s.* 1. Túnica, vestidura interior, con o sin mangas, que usaban los antiguos. 2. Vestidura exterior moderna fruncida al talle, o ceñida con un cinturón, v. g. una blusa o un ropaje exterior. 3. Túnica, telilla o película que cubre algunos órganos de las plantas. 4. *(Anat.)* Túnica, membrana sutil que cubre algunas partes del cuerpo.

tunicle [ˈtjuːnɪkl] [tiu-ni-kol], *s.* 1. Túnica, tegumento o envoltura. 2. Túnica fina, ligera o delicada. 3. Tunicela, vestidura eclesiástica.

tuning [ˈtjuːnɪŋ] [tiu-nin], *s.* Temple, acción y efecto de templar. **Tuning-fork,** diapasón. **Tuning-hammer, tuning-key,** templador, llave de afinador.

tunnage [ˈtjuːnɪdʒ] [tiu-nich], *s.* El derecho de tonelada que se cobraba en las aduanas. *V.* TONNAGE.

tunnel [ˈtʌnl] [ta-nel], *s.* 1. Túnel, socavón, o paso subterráneo, abierto artificialmente para el paso de trenes, para conducir aguas, o establecer otra comunicación. 3. Cañón de chimenea, de ladrillera, etc. **Tunnel-net,** red profunda ancha por la boca y de forma cónica.

tunnel, *va.* 1. Hacer, construir un socavón o túnel a través de una colina o por debajo de un río. 2. Disponer en forma de túnel o socavón.

tunny (o **tuna**) **fish** [ˈtʌnɪfɪʃ] [ta-ni-fish], *s.* Atún.

tup [tʌp] [tap], *s.* Morucco, carnero padre.

turban [ˈtɜːbən] [ter-ban], *s.* 1. Turbante, tocado con que los orientales se cubren la cabeza. 2. Tocado de mujer. 3. Sombrero moderno para mujeres y niños, con ala muy estrecha o sin ella. 4. Espira de molusco univalvo.

turbaned [ˈtɜːbənd] [ter-band], *a.* Que tiene o lleva turbante.

turbary [ˈtɜːbərɪ] [ter-ba-ri], *s.* El derecho de cavar turbas o céspedes de tierra, y el sitio donde se cavan.

turbid [ˈtɜːbɪd] [ter-bid], *a.* 1. Turbio, túrbido, espeso; cenagoso. 2. Turbulento, confuso, turulato, en estado de confusión.

turbine [ˈtɜːbaɪn] [ter-bain], *s.* Turbina, rueda hidráulica que gira sobre un eje vertical y que aprovecha la mayor parte posible de la fuerza motriz.

turbojet [ˈtɜːbəʊdʒet] [ter-bou-yet], *s.* Turborreator, avión de turborreacción.

turboprop [ˈtɜːbəʊprɒp] [ter-bo-prop], *s.* Avión de turbohélice.

turbot [ˈtɜːbət] [ter-bot], *s.* Rodaballo, rombo.

turbulence [ˈtɜːbjʊləns] [ter-biu-lans], *s.* Turbulencia, alboroto, tumulto, confusión.

turbulent [ˈtɜːbjʊlənt] [ter-biu-lant], *a.* 1. Turbulento, agitado, tumultuoso, violento. 2. Predispuesto a la sublevación o insubordinación. 3. Que tiende a disturbar o poner en confusión. **A turbulent sea,** *(Mar.)* Mar bravo. **Turbulent weather,** *(Mar.)* Tiempo tormentoso. **Turbulent temper,** genio turbulento o inquieto.

turbulently [ˈtɜːbjʊləntlɪ] [ter-biu-lant-li], *adv.* Turbulentamente, agitadamente, con confusión.

turdoid [ˈtɜːdɔɪd] [ter-doid], *a.* Parecido o perteneciente a los tordos o túrdidos.

tureen [təˈriːn] [ta-rin], *s.* Sopera, vasija honda en que se sirve la sopa.

turf [tɜːf] [terf], *s.* 1. Césped, trozo de tierra cubierto de hierba menuda. 2. Turba. *V.* PEAT. 3. Alfombra de hierba. 4. Circo, terreno donde se efectúan las carreras de caballos; ocupación de hacer correr caballos; en la locución *the turf.*

turf, *va.* Encespedar, cubrir con céspedes.

turfiness [ˈtɜːfɪnɪs] [ter-fi-nes], *s.* La abundancia de césped o de turba.

turfy [ˈtɜːfɪ] [ter-fi], *a.* 1. Cubierto de céspedes, parecido al césped. 2. Perteneciente a las carreras de caballos. **Turfy ground,** cespedera.

turgid [ˈtɜːdʒɪd] [ter-yid], *a.* 1. Túnido, inflado, hinchado. 2. *(Fig.)* Ampuloso, engreído, pomposo; se dice del estilo.

turgidity [tɜːˈdʒɪdɪtɪ] [ter-yi-di-ti], *s.* El estado de turgencia o hinchazón.

turk [tɜːk] [terk], *s.* *(Orn.)* Pavo, pava: *(Mex.)* Guajalote: *(Cuba)* Guamajo.

Turkey [ˈtɜːkɪ] [ter-ki], *f.* Turquía.

Turkey corn, *(Bot.)* Maíz. **Turkey millet,** *(Bot.)* Alcandía. **Turkey-gobbler,** pavo o guanajo. **Turkey-buzzard,** aura. *(Mex.)* zopilote, buitre americano.

turkish [ˈtɜːkɪʃ] [ter-kish], *a.* Turco. **Turkish bath,** baño turco. **Turkish towel,** toalla gruesa y afelpada propia para el baño. *-s.* Idioma turco.

turmeric [ˈtɜːkmərɪk] [terk-ma-rik], *s.* Cúrcuma, planta de la India parecida al jengibre; y su raíz, de que se saca color amarillo.

turmoil [ˈtɜːmɔɪl] [ter-moil], *s.* Disturbio, inquietud, baraúnda, alboroto.

turmoil, *vn.* Inquietarse, estar en agitación.

turn [tɜːn] [tern], *va.* 1. Volver, dar vuelta o vueltas a alguna cosa. 2. Volver, mudar, cambiar, de un estado a otro. 3. Volver, poner a alguna persona o cosa en el estado que antes tenía. 4. Volver, torcer o inclinar una cosa de un lado a otro; volver o tornar lo de arriba abajo. 5. Volver, cambiar, convertir o transformar una cosa en otra. 6. Volver, hacer mudar a fuerza de persuasión o razones la opinión que se tenía; convertir; pervertir. 7. Volver, verter, traducir o trasladar de una lengua a otra. 8. Volver, dirigir, encaminar o enderezar una cosa a otra material o inmaterialmente. 9. Volver, rechazar. 10. Alterar, variar, cambiar. 11. Tornear, trabajar al torno. 12. Aplicar o destinar una cosa a un uso diferente del que antes tenía. 13. Adaptar una cosa a otra. 14. Discurrir, reflexionar. 15. Embotar. 16. Hacer circular dinero, géneros, etc. 17. Transferir. 18. Hacer vertiginoso, dar asco o náuseas. *-vn.* 1. Volver, girar, rodar, andar o moverse alrededor o en torno. 2. Voltear, dar alguna cosa vueltas por sí misma. 3. Dar vueltas, andar rodando, andar de acá para allá. 4. Volver, torcer o dejar el camino o línea recta. 5. Volverse a, inclinar el cuerpo o el rostro hacia alguna persona o cosa determinada. 6. Mudarse, transformarse, mudar de posición, de situación, de estado, de opinión, etc. 7. Hacerse o llegar uno a ser lo que antes no era 8. Mudarse, desdecirse, cambiar de casaca. 8. Volverse o avinagrarse el vino, acedarse la leche. 10. Estribar, fundarse; depender de. 11. Trastornársele o irsele a uno la cabeza.

turn about, volverse hacia otra parte; rodar o andar dando vueltas alrededor.

turn against, hacer frente; defenderse.

turn aside, descaminar, alejar; alejarse, ponerse a un lado.

turn away, despedir o despachar, hacer que se vuelvan las personas o cosas que ya no se necesitan; despedir o echar a una persona; desviar o desviarse, volver o volverse al otro lado; apartar o separar; echar, sacar o arrojar con violencia; deshacerse de.

turn back, volver atrás o volver otra vez, volverse; volver o devolver una cosa a la persona de quien se recibió, restituir; retroceder, desandar lo andado.

turn down, (a) plegar, doblar; (b) rechazar, reclinar, rehusar. (c) voltear hacia abajo. **To turn down the bedspread,** doblar hacia abajo la sobrecama. **To turn down one's coat collar,** doblar hacia abajo el cuello del abrigo.

turn from, desviar de; apartarse de.

turn in, replegar, plegar muchas veces, hacer pliegues; doblar hacia dentro. **To turn in and out,** serpear o serpentear.

turn into, mudar, cambiar, transformar, convertir, transformarse, mudar de forma o de figura. **She is turned of forty,** ella tiene cuarenta años cumplidos.

turn off, cerrar una llave o canilla, despachar, arrojar o echar a una persona con desprecio, echar a cajas destempladas, despedir o echar enhoramala; renunciar, hacer dejación de alguna cosa, apartar, separar o divertir el pensamiento, la atención, etc.; mudar de camino o tomar otro camino; llevar a cabo, ejecutar. **To turn off a day's work,** llevar a cabo el trabajo del día.

turn out, (a) echar fuera, expeler, arrojar, lanzar, echar con violencia, volver lo de dentro afuera, llegar a ser, resultar; (b) *(Mar.)* levantarse; (c) echar al campo los animales. **So it turned out,** así resultó, sucedió que.

turn over, transferir, pasar a otro; diferir, dilatar; enviar; volver la hoja de un libro. **To turn over a new leaf,** enmendarse, empezar vida nueva.

turn to, recurrir o acudir a uno; transformar o transformarse; volverse hacia una persona o cosa; dirigirse hacia. **To turn to advantage o to account,** sacar ventaja o utilidad de una cosa; hacer que redunde en beneficio. **To turn to good account,** sacar provecho de una cosa. **To turn to and fro,** volver de un lado a otro. **To turn to windward,** *(Mar.)* barloventear, abarloar.

turn up, arregazar, arremangar; volver el triunfo en los juegos de naipes; acontecer, suceder; venir a mano,

reaparecer. **To turn up the ground,** cavar la tierra, disponer la tierra para el cultivo.

turn upon, estribar, fundarse, apoyarse; producir un suceso, desgracia, etc., cualquier efecto en alguna persona o lugar; recaer sobre; revolver sobre. **To turn upside down,** trastornar, volver lo de arriba abajo; zozobrar un navío. **To turn home,** retirarse, volverse o irse a casa. **To turn one home,** enviar a alguno a casa. **To turn physician,** hacerse médico o recibirse de médico. **To turn short,** dar media vuelta; volverse bruscamente. **To turn tail,** andar u obrar con doblez o con segunda; buscar rodeos. **To turn the brain,** volver loco. **To turn the head,** trastornar la cabeza o el juicio; volverse loco. **To turn the scale,** hacer inclinarse la balanza; volver la tortilla. **To turn the stomach,** causar asco o hastío; causar náuseas. **My head turns,** se me va la cabeza, me da vueltas la cabeza. **Turn over o please turn over,** *(p. t. o.)* a la vuelta.

turn, *s.* 1. Vuelta, giro, movimiento circular. 2. Rodeo, revuelta. 3. Vuelta, paseo corto, viaje a sitio poco distante. 4. Turno, vez, tanda; alternación, orden sucesivo o alternado de las cosas. 5. Ocasión, oportunidad. 6. Mudanza, cambio; fase, faz. 7. Proceder, procedimiento, modo de obrar, portarse o comportarse las personas. 8. Genio, inclinación, propensión. 9. Acción, pasada buena o mala que se hace a alguno; chasco, pieza; servicio, favor, asistencia. 10. Provecho, utilidad. 11. Forma, figura, hechura. 12. Modo de decir las cosas; colocación de las voces de una sentencia. **To take a turn,** dar una vuelta, un paseo. **To take another turn,** cambiar de faz. **Things have taken a different turn,** las cosas han tomado otro aspecto. **By turns,** por turno, alternativamente. **He has a turn for agriculture,** es aficionado a la agricultura o tiene inclinación a la agricultura. **It is your turn,** a Ud. le toca. **At every turn,** a cada instante, a cada momento. **A friendly turn,** un favor. **An ill-natured turn,** un chasco pesado, una pieza.

turncoat ['tɜːnkəʊt] [tern-kout], *s.* El que muda de partido o de opiniones, el que cambiar de casaca; desertor, renegado apóstata.

turner ['tɜːnəʳ] [ter-naʳ], *s.* 1. Torneador, tornero. **Turner's lathe,** torno. 2. Gimnasta, miembro de un club atlético.

turning ['tɜːnɪŋ] [tern-nin], *s.* 1. Vuelta, rodeo; las vueltas y revueltas que hace una cosa tortuosa. 2. Recodo, ángulo, rodeo (street, river). 3. *pl.* Virutas que se hacen torneando. **Turning-point,** (a) punto decisivo, crisis; (b) punto donde se trueca la dirección de un movimiento.

turnip ['tɜːnɪp] [ter-nip], *s.* Nabo, planta hortense y su raíz comestible.

turnkey ['tɜːnkiː] [tern-ki], *s.* Bastonero o ayudante del alcaide de una cárcel; demandadero de una cárcel.

turnout ['tɜːnaʊt] [tern-aut], *s.* 1. Tren, séquito, conjunto de personas que concurren a una reunión o diversión pública. 2. Vía doble o lateral en un camino angosto; desviadero corto en un ferrocarril. 3. Equipaje, carruaje de lujo. 4. Producto de una fábrica en un tiempo dado. 5. Salida de personas; en especial huelga de obreros.

turnover ['tɜːnˌəʊvəʳ] [tern-ou-vaʳ], *a.* Doblado hacia abajo, p. ej. un cuello de camisa. *-s.* 1. Vuelco; vuelta. 2. Variedad de pastelillo. 3. Utensilio para dar vuelta a los guisos. 4. Cambio de partido, opinión, etc. 5. Ciclo en el movimiento de mercancías. 6. Proporción en el cambio de personal de una empresa.

turnpike ['tɜːnpaɪk] [tern-paik], *s.* 1. Camino en que hay barreras de portazgo; camino público. 2. Barrera, los maderos que se ponen en algún camino público para el cobro del portazgo o de los derechos que se pagan para componer los caminos; portazgo. 3. *V.* TURNSTILE.

turnstone ['tɜːnstəʊn] [tern-stoun], *s.* *(Orn.)* Revuelvepiedras.

turntable ['tɜːnteɪbl] [tern-tei-bol], *s.* 1. *(F.C.)* Plataforma giratoria, placa giratoria. 2. Plato tocadiscos. 3. Giratoria.

turpentine ['tɜːpəntaɪn] [ter-pan-tain], *s.* Trementina, la goma que destilan el pino, abeto, enebro y otros árboles de la misma especie. **Turpentine-tree,** terebinto, especie de alfóncigo.

turpeth ['tɜːnpəθ] [tern-pez], *s.* 1. Turbit, raíz del albohol turbit, planta parecida a la jalapa. 2. **Turpeth mineral,** turbit mineral, sulfato mercurial de propiedades eméticas.

turpitude ['tɜːpɪtjuːd] [ter-pi-tiud], *s.* Torpeza, vileza, infamia; deshonestidad.

turquoise ['tɜːkwɔɪz] [ter-kuois], *s.* Turquesa, piedra preciosa azul.

turret ['tʌrɪt] [ta-rit], *s.* Torrecilla, torre pequeño.

turreted ['tʌrɪtɪd] [ta-ri-tid], *a.* Hecho en figura de torre o que se eleva como una torre.

turtle ['tɜːtl] [ter-tel], *s.* 1. Tortuga de mar. 2. *(Impr.)* Bastidor grueso en forma de segmento de cilindro, que se usa para sostener el tipo en una prensa giratoria. 3. *V.* **Turtle-dove. Turtle-dove,** tórtola. **Small land turtle,** *(Amer.)* tortuga de tierra, galápago, jicotea. **Turtle-shell,** carey. **To turn turtle,** zozobrar, volverse hacia arriba el casco de una embarcación.

tush [tʌʃ] [tash], *inter. (Ant.)* ¡Tarara! ¡bah! interjección para expresar impaciencia o desprecio.

tusk [tʌsk] [task], *s.* 1. Colmillo, diente agudo de algunas fieras. 2. Punta parecida a un diente.

tusked ['tʌskt] [taskt], *a.* Colmilludo.

tussle ['tʌsl] [ta-sel], *va. y vn. (Fam.)* Luchar con; tener una agarrada, una sarracina. -*s.* Sarracina, refriega con desorden, pendencia.

tussock ['tʌsək] [ta-sok], *s.* 1. Montecillo de hierbas crecientes o de cárices. 2. Penacho de pelo o de plumas. 2. Penacho de pelo o de plumas. **Tussock-moth,** mariposa nocturna del género Orygia, cuya oruga tiene penachos peludos.

tut [tʌt] [tat], *inter.* ¡Tate! ¡Basta! ¡Quita allá! Se usa para expresar ligera reprensión o impaciencia.

tutelage ['tjuːtɪlɪdʒ] [tiu-ti-lich], *s.* Tutela, tutoría, el cargo de tutor.

tutelary ['tjuːtɪlərɪ] [tiu-ti-la-ri], *a.* Tutelar. **A tutelar angel,** ángel de la guardia. **A tutelar saint,** santo tutelar o patrón.

tutor ['tjuːtəʳ] [tiu-taʳ], *s.* Tutor, ayo, preceptor.

tutor, *va.* 1. Enseñar, instruir. 2. Señorear, mandar imperiosamente.

tutoress ['tjuːtərɪs] [tiu-ta-res], tutriz, aya.

tutorial [tjuːˈtɔːrɪəl] [tiu-to-rial], *a.* Tutorial; *(Jur.)* Tutelar.

tutty ['tjuːtɪ] [tiu-ti], *s.* Tutía, atutía, óxido de cinc impuro que se obtiene en los hornos de fundición y sirve como polvo para pulir.

tuwhit-tuwhoo [tʊˈwɪtəˈwuː] [tu-uita-vuu], *vn.* Gritar el buho. -*s.* Grito del buho.

tuxedo [tʌkˈsɪdəʊ] [tak-si-dou], *s.* Smoking.

twaddle ['twɒdl] [tuo-del], *va. y vn.* Charlar, parlotear, chacharar con aire de persona docta. -*s.* Habladuría, charla; palique; tonterias, disparates.

twain [tweɪn] [tuein], *a. (Ant.)* Dos.

twang [twæŋ] [tuang], *va. y vn.* 1. Producir un sonido agudo y penetrante. 2. Restallar, chasquear o estallar alguna cosa como la honda o el látigo. 3. Tañer, hiriendo las cuerdas de un instrumento músico.

twang, *s.* 1. Retintín, el modo y tonillo afectado de hablar; acento muy fuerte al pronunciar. 2. Cualquier sonido agudo y penetrante, como el de una cuerda música de la cual se tira.

twangling ['twæŋlɪŋ] [tuan-glin], *s.* Ruido desapacible.

'twas [twɒz] [tuos], contracción de IT WAS. Fue.

tweak [twiːk] [tuik], *va.* Pellizcar y torcer, apretar entre los dedos. -*s.* Pellizco, sacudida.

tweed [twiːd] [tuid], *a.* Hecho del paño cruzado escocés de lana, por lo general o de dos colores.

tweedle ['twiːdl] [tui-del], *va.* Manosear, tentar y tocar ligeramente con las manos.

'tween [twiːn] [tuin], *prep.* Entre; contracción de BETWEEN.

tweeter ['twiːtəʳ] [tui-taʳ], *s.* Altavoz para sonidos agudos.

tweezers ['twiːzəz] [tui-sars], *s. pl.* Tenacillas, pinzas pequeñas para objetos diminutos.

twelfth [twelf] [tuelf], *a.* Duodécimo, número ordinal de doce. -*s.* 1. Una de doce partes iguales. 2. *(Mús.)*

Duodécima, intervalo de una octava más una quinta. **Twelfth Night,** víspera del día de Reyes, de la Epifanía.

twelfth-tide ['twelftaɪd] [tuelf-taid], *s.* El día de los Reyes o la Epifanía.

twelve [twelv] [tuelv], *a. y s.* Doce. **Twelve-month,** un año o doce meses. **Twelve-penny,** de a doce peniques. **Twelve-score,** doce veces veinte, doscientos cuarenta.

twentieth ['twentɪθ] [tuen-tiez], *a.* Vigésimo, ordinal de veinte.

twenty ['twentɪ] [tuen-ti], *a. y s.* Veinte. **Twenty-one,** veintiuno. **Twenty-wine,** veintinueve.

twibil ['twɪbɪl] [tui-bil], *s.* Una especie de hacha de dos filos.

twice [twaɪs] [tuais], *adv.* 1. Dos veces. 2. Al doble, duplicadamente. **Twice-born,** renacido.

twiddle ['twɪdl] [tui-del], *va. (Fam. o dial.)* Tocar ligeramente; hacer dar vueltas.

twig [twɪg] [tuig], *s.* 1. Ramita, rama pequeña (de árbol). 2. Rama pequeña de una arteria u otro vaso.

twilight ['twaɪlaɪt] [tuai-lait], *s.* 1. Crepúsculo. 2. Cualquier luz débil. 3. Aprehensión o percepción indistinta. **By twilight,** entre dos luces. -*a.* Obscuro, sombrío, crepuscular. **Twilight sleep,** anestesia parcial para partos.

twill [twɪl] [tuil], *va.* Tejer con líneas diagonales; cruzar un tejido. -*s.* Tela cruzada; cruzado.

twin [twɪn] [tuin], *s.* 1. Gemelo, mellizo; *(Mex.)* Cuate; *(Cuba)* Jimagua; *(Amer.)* Morocho. 2. *(Astr.)* Géminis, signo boreal, el tercero de los del zodíaco. -*a.* 1. Gemelo, gemela. 2. Doble; gemíneo, en parejas.

twin, *vn.* 1. Nacer mellizo. 2. Parir dos o más hijos de un parto. 3. Hermanearse, parearse.

twine [twaɪn] [tuain], *va.* 1. Torcer, formar de muchos hilos una cuerda; enroscar, enredar o liar alrededor o dando vueltas. 2. Unir o combinar una cosa con otra de modo que formen un cuerpo entre sí. -*vn.* 1. Enroscarse, ensortijarse. 2. Caracolear, hacer tornos, dar vueltas. **To twine about,** abrazar.

twine, *s.* 1. Hilo de acarreto o bramante. *(Amer.)* Hilo mestizo, guita. *(Mex.)* Mecate. **Fine twine,** mecatito. **Sail-twine,** *(Mar.)* Hilo de vela. 2. Enroscadura, el efecto de eroscarse. 3. Abrazo.

twinge [twɪndʒ] [tuinch], *va. y vn.* Causar un dolor agudo o una pena a otro, hacer mal a alguien, atormentar; padecer un dolor local agudo y repentino.

twinge, *s.* Dolor agudo o punzante, y el tormento que causa; tirón de orejas; dolor de costado; pena del ánimo, remordimiento.

twinkle ['twɪŋkl] [tuin-kel], *vn.* 1. Centellear, chispear, despedir rayos de luz de una manera trémula. 2. Parpadear, mover los párpados; abrir y cerrar los ojos; pestañear guiñando.

twinkling ['twɪŋklɪŋ] [tuin-klin], *s.* 1. Vislumbre, resplandor tenue de la luz. 2. La acción de parpadear; pestañeo, guiñada. 3. Momento, instante. **In the twinkling of on eye,** en un abrir y cerrar de ojos. 4. Vibración trémula.

twin-screw ['twɪnskruː] [tuin-skru], *a.* En arquitectura marítima, de doble hélice.

twirl [twɜːl] [tuerl], *va.* Voltear, dar vueltas a una cosa, como con los dedos. -*vn.* Volver, dar vueltas.

twirl, *s.* Rotación, movimiento rápido, alrededor de algo, vuelta dada en círculo, giro.

twirler ['twɜːləʳ] [tuer-laʳ], *s.* El o lo que da vueltas a una cosa; *(Fam. E.U.)* tormenta giratoria, ciclón.

twist [twɪst] [tuist], *va.* 1. Torcer, dar vueltas a alguna cosa, alrededor apretándola; retorcer, torcer mucho. 2. Entrelazar o entretejer una cosa con otra. 3. Tejer. 4. Trenzar o hacer trenzas. 5. Ceñir, rodear. -*vn.* 1. Insinuarse o introducirse una cosa en otra muy íntimamente; enroscarse, envolverse. 2. Torcerse; hacerse una rosca. 3. Retortijarse, ensortijarse. **Twisted bread,** rosca pan retorcido.

twist, *s.* 1. Trenza, cualquiera cosa hecha de varias otras torcidas, tejidas, entretejidas o entrelazadas entre sí; cordoncillo, hilo de seda. 2. Torcedura, la acción y efecto de torcer. 3. Torzal, la unión de varias cosas que hacen como hebras torcidas y dobladas unas con otras. 4. Cada hilo o hebra de un cordón o cuerda y el mismo cordón. 5. Rollo de tabaco. **To give one's arm a twist,** torcerse el brazo.

twister ['twɪstəʳ] [tuis-taʳ], *s.* 1. Torceador; cordelero, soguero, cabestrero. 2. Torcedor, instrumento que sirve para torcer o retorcer. 3. Entre marinos, torbellino, viento giratorio; en los Estados Unidos del Oeste, ciclón, gran tormenta. *V.* TORNADO. 4. Pelota arrojada con cierta torcedura peculiar o que lleva un movimiento giratorio sobre su eje.

twit [twɪt] [tuit], *va.* Molestar, recordando algo desagradable; reprender, dar en rostro con, echar algo en cara.

twitch [twɪtʃ] [tuich], *va.* Tirar bruscamente. *-vn.* Moverse con una contracción espasmódica, encogerse.

twitch, *s.* 1. Tensión o tirantes dolorosa de las fibras: retortijón. 2. Acción de tirar bruscamente; tirón repentino. 3. Acial.

twitter ['twɪtəʳ] [tui-taʳ], *vn.* Gorjear los pájaros.

twitter, *s.* 1. Gorjeo (de los pájaros). 2. *(Fam.)* Estado de agitación del ánimo.

'twixt [twɪkst] [tuikst], contracción de BETWIXT.

two [tuː] [tu], *a. y s.* Dos. **Two and two,** dos a dos. **To kill two birds with one stone,** matar dos pájaros de un tiro. **Two-legged animal,** animal bípedo o de dos pies. **Two-cleft** bífido, hendido en dos. **Two-faced,** de dos caras; doble, no sincero, disimulado. **Two-horse,** de dos caballos, tirado por dos caballos; de la fuerza de dos caballos. **Two-edged,** que tiene dos filos o cortes.

two-fisted [ˌtuːˈfɪstɪd] [tu-fis-tid], *a. (Fam.)* Viril, vigoroso.

twofold ['tuːfəʊld] [tu-fould], *a.* Doble, duplicado. *-adv.* Duplicadamente, al doble.

two-handed ['tuːhændɪd] [tu-jan-did], *a.* 1. De dos manos, que exige el uso de ambas manos a la vez. 2. Construido para usarlo dos personas. 3. Ambidextro. **Two-handed sword,** espadón.

twopenny ['tuːpenɪ] [tu-pe-ni], *a.* De dos peniques, del valor de dos peniques; de aquí, vil, de ningún valor.

two-ply ['tuːplaɪ] [tu-plai], *a.* De dos capas, de dos tramas.

two-seater ['tuːsiːðəʳ] [tu-si-taʳ], *s.* Velhículo de dos asientos.

two-tongued ['tuːtɒŋd] [tu-tongd], *a.* Falso, doble.

two-way ['tuːweɪ] [tu-wei], *a.* De dos direcciones; de tránsito en ambas direcciones.

tycoon [taɪˈkuːn] [tai-kun], *s.* Magnate industrial o político.

tymbal ['tɪmbəl] [tim-bal], *s.* Tímbal, atabal.

tympani ['tɪmpənɪ] [tim-pa-ni], *s.* 1. *(Impr.)* Tímpano, una hoja o más comúnmente varias hojas de papel colocadas en una prensa para mejorar la calidad de la tirada. 2. Tímpano, membrana u hoja delgada que se pone tensa. *V.* TYMPANUM, 3ª acep.

tympanum ['tɪmpənəm] [tim-pa-nom], *s.* 1. *(Anat.)* Tímpano, membrana extendida y tensa como la de un tambor, que separa el conducto auditivo externo del oído medio; el oído medio. 2. *(Bot.)* Timpanillo, membrana que tapa el orificio de la cápsula de ciertos musgos. 3. *(Arq.)* Tímpano, vacío que hay entre el cerramiento del rontis y su cornisa; timpanillo o tímpano, adorno en el arranque de un arco.

tympany ['tɪmpənɪ] [tim-pa-ni], *s.* *(Anat.)* Timpanitis. *V.* TYMPANITES.

type [taɪp] [taip], *s.* 1. Tipo, símbolo, signo, figura. 2. Emblema, figura simbólica. 3. Tipo, ejemplar distintivo de un grupo o de una clase. 4. Tipo, letra de imprenta, y cada una de sus clases o variedades. 5. *(Biol.)* Plan, tipo, modelo de estructura; representación ideal de una especie. **Type-bar,** línea de tipos que se funde en una sola pieza. **Type-founder,** fundidor de letras de imprenta. **Type-foundry,** fundición de tipos. **Type-setter,** cajista mecánico; máquina para componer tipos. **Type-setting,** que compone tipos; composición de letras de imprenta. **Type-wheel,** rueda tipográfica.

typewrite ['taɪpraɪt] [taip-rait], *va. y vn. (pp.* TYPEWRITTEN). Escribir a máquina, poner algo por escrito con una máquina de escribir. **A type-written letter,** una carta escrita a máquina. *(Neol.)*

typewriter ['taɪpraɪtəʳ] [taip-rai-taʳ], *s.* Máquina de escribir.

typewritting ['taɪpˌraɪtɪŋ] [taip-rai-tin], *s.* 1. El acto, arte u operación de usar una máquina de escribir. 2. Trabajo hecho con dicha máquina.

typhoid ['taɪfɔɪd] [tai-foid], *a.* Tifoideo, parecido al tifus o a la fiebre tifoidea. *-s.* Fiebre tifoidea, caracterizada por gran postración e irritación de los intestinos, con diarrea.

typhoon [taɪˈfuːn] [tai-fun], *s.* Tifón, huracán del mar de la China.

typhous ['taɪfəs] [tai-fos], *s.* Tífico, perteneciente o relativo al tifo.

typhus ['taɪfəs] [tai-fos], *s. (Med.)* tifo, tifus, fiebre aguda, continua, caracterizada por perturbación profunda del sistema nervioso y sanguíneo y por irritación del cerebro, a la que sigue el estupor. **Typhus abdominalis,** fiebre tifoidea.

typical ['tɪpɪkəl] [ti-pi-kal], *a.* Típico, figurativo, lo que sirve para representar otra cosa; simbólico, alegórico.

typically ['tɪpɪkəlɪ] [ti-pi-ka-li], *adv.* Figurativamente.

typify ['tɪpɪfaɪ] [ti-pi-fai], *va.* Representar, simbolizar.

typing ['taɪpɪŋ] [tai-pin], *s.* Mecanografía, dactilografía, escritura en máquina.

typist ['taɪpɪst] [tai-pist], *s.* Mecanógrafo.

typographer [taɪˈpɒɡrəfəʳ] [tai-pó-gra-faʳ], *s.* Tipógrafo, impresor.

typographic [ˌtaɪpəˈɡræfɪk] [tai-po-gra-fik], *a.* 1. Tipográfico, lo que pertenece al arte de imprimir o a la imprenta. 2. Emblemático.

typography [taɪˈpɒɡrəfɪ] [tai-po-gra-fi], *s.* 1. Representación emblemática o figurativa. 2. Tipografía, imprenta, el arte de imprimir.

tyrannic [tɪˈrænɪk] [ti-ra-nik], *a.* Tiránico, cruel, despótico.

tyrannically [tɪˈrænɪkəlɪ] [ti-ra-ni-ka-li], *adv.* Tiránicamente.

tyrannicalness [tɪˈrænɪkəlnɪs] [ti-ra-ni-kal-nes], *s.* Calidad de tirano.

tyrannicide [tɪˈrænɪsaɪd] [ti-ra-ni-said], *s.* Tiranicidio, la acción de quitar la vida a un tirano.

tyrannize ['tɪrənaɪz] [ti-ra-nais], *va. y vn.* 1. Tiranizar. 2. Obrar o proceder con tiranía, severidad, rigor o inclemencia.

tyranny ['tɪrənɪ] [ti-ra-ni], *s.* 1. Tiranía; gobierno absoluto; gobierno despótico. 2. Opresión, rigor, crueldad, severidad.

tyrant ['taɪrənt] [tai-rant], *s.* Tirano, déspota, señor absoluto y severo.

tyre ['taɪəʳ] [taiaʳ], *s. (Anglindio)* Leche cuajada.

tyre, *s. (Aut.)* Llanta, neumático *(GB);* cámara de aire (inner tube). **Tyre-burst,** reventón, pinchazo.

tyro ['taɪərəʊ] [taia-rau], *s.* Tirón, bisoño, principiante, novicio, nuevo en algún arte o disciplina.

tzar, tzarina [zɑːʳ] [saʳ], [sa-ri-na], *s. V.* CZAR, CZARINA.

U

u [juː] [iu], vigésima primera letra del alfabeto inglés, tiene tres diferentes sonidos; el uno es semejante al del diptongo castellano *iu*, como en *muse, tube, cure* (mius, tiub, quiuaʳ); se pronuncia también como en español en las voces *full, truth,* etc; y por último tiene un sonido entre la *a* y la *o* españolas en *but, cut, tub,* etc. Véase la Introducción.

ubiquitous [juːˈbɪkwɪtəs] [iu-bi-kui-tos], *a.* ubicuo, omnipresente, que está o se halla en todas partes. *-s.* Ubiquitario. *V.* UBIQUITARIAN.

ubiquity [juːˈbɪkwɪtɪ] [iu-bi-kui-ti], *s.* 1. Ubicuidad, existencia en todas partes al mismo tiempo; omnipresencia. 2. Existencia perenne, sin principio ni fin.

udder ['ʌdəʳ] [a-daʳ], ubre, teta de las hembras de los cuadrúpedos.

UEFA *Abreviatura de* **Union of European Football Associations.**

ufologist [juːˈfɒlədʒɪst] [iu-fo-lo-yist], *s.* Ufólogo.

ufology [juːˈfɒlədʒɪ] [iu-fo-lo-yi], *s.* Ufología.

ugh [əːh] [ef], *inter.* ¡Puf! ¡uf! Denota repugnancia o disgusto.

uglify ['ʌɡlɪfaɪ] [a-gli-fai], *vt.* Afear.

uglily ['ʌɡlɪlɪ] [a-gli-li], *adv.* Feamente, deformemente, vilmente.

ugliness [ˈʌɡlɪnes] [a-gli-nes], *s.* 1. Fealdad, deformidad, disformidad. 2. Fealdad, torpeza, corrupción de costumbres.

ugly [ˈʌɡlɪ] [a-gli], *a.* 1. Feo, disforme, deforme, malparecido; asqueroso. 2. Repugnante, contrario a la moral; que causa aversión. 3. Malo por su carácter o sus consecuencias. 4. *(FAm. E.U.)* Obstinado.

UHF *Abreviatura de* **Ultra High Frequency,** frecuencia ultraelevada.

Ukrainian [juːˈkreɪnɪən] [iu-krei-nian], *a.* Ucranio.

ulcer [ˈʌlsəʳ] [al-saʳ], *s.* Úlcera.

ulcerate [ˈʌlsəreɪt] [al-sa-reit], *va.* Ulcerar.

ulceration [ˌʌlsəˈreɪʃən] [al-sa-rei-shon], *s.* Ulceración.

ulcerous [ˈʌlsərəs] [al-sa-ros], *a.* Ulceroso.

ullage [ˈʌlɪdʒ] [a-lich], *s.* El hueco o vacío de un tonel, la parte que está sin llenar.

ulnar [ˈʌlnəʳ] [al-naʳ], *a.* Cubital, relativo al cúbito.

Ulster [ˈʌlstəʳ] [als-taʳ], *sm.* Ulster.

ulterior [ʌlˈtɪərɪəʳ] [al-tia-riaʳ], *a.* Ulterior, que está de la parte de allá; oculto, no revelado; que viene después, posterior; secundario.

ultima [ˈʌltɪmə] [al-ti-ma], *s.* Sílaba última o final de una palabra.

ultimate [ˈʌltɪmɪt] [al-ti-mit], *a.* 1. Último, final. 2. Fundamental, esencial; primario.

ultimately [ˈʌltɪmɪtlɪ] [al-ti-mit-li], *adv.* Últimamente; esencialmente.

ultimatum [ˌʌltɪˈmeɪtəm] [al-ti-mei-tom], *s.* 1. Ultimátum, en lenguaje diplomático, resolución terminante y definitiva, comunicada por escrito. 2. Cualquier cosa última o fundamental.

ultra.- [ˈʌltrə] [al-tra], Prefijo latino que significa más allá o además. *-a.* Exagerado, extremo.

ultramarine [ˌʌltrəməˈriːn] [al-tra-ma-rin], *s.* Ultramar, ultramarino, el color azul formado del lapislázuli. *-a.* Ultramarino, que está o se considera de la otra parte del mar.

ultramodern [ˌʌltrəˈmɒdən] [al-tra-mo-dern], *a.* Ultramoderno.

ultramontane [ˌʌltrəˈmaʊntɪn] [al-tra-maun-tin], *a.* 1. Ultramontano, que está más allá o de la otra parte de los montes; al sur de los Alpes. 2. Ultramontano, ultracatólico, que se refiere al ultramontanismo.

ultra-red [ˌʌltrəˈred] [al-tra-red], *a.* Infrarrojo, ultrarrojo.

ultrasonic [ˈʌltrəˈsɒnɪk] [al-tra-so-nik], *a.* Ultrasónico. **Ultrasonic wave,** ultrasonido. *-s.* Ultrasonido.

ultrasound [ˈʌltrəsaʊnd] [al-tra-saund], *s.* Ultrasonido.

ultraviolet [ˈʌltrəˈvaɪəlɪt] [al-tra-vaio-lit], *a.* Ultravioleta. **Ultraviolet ray,** rayo ultravioleta.

ululate [ˈjuːljʊleɪt] [iu-liu-leit], *vn.* Ulular, gritar como un buho.

ululation [ˌjuːljʊˈleɪʃən] [iu-liu-lei-shon], *s.* Ululato, clamor, grito como el del buho.

umbel [ˈʌmbəl] [am-bal], *s. (Bot.)* Umbela, inflorescencia cuyos pedúnculos nacen en el mismo punto y se elevan a igual o casi igual altura, a modo de quitasol.

umber [ˈʌmbəʳ] [am-baʳ], *s.* 1. Tierra de sombra usada por los pintores; tierra parda que consta de un óxido hidratado de hierro mezclado con óxido manganésico y arcilla. 2. *(Ict.)* Umbla, umbra.

umber, *va.* Sombrear, hacer oscuro, como con tierra de sombra.

umbilical [ʌmbɪˈlaɪkəl] [am-bi-lai-kal], *a.* Umbilical, que pertenece o se refiere al ombligo; central.

umilicus [ʌmbɪˈlaɪkəs] [am-bi-lai-kos], *s.* 1. Ombligo. 2. Depresión o concavidad semejante a un ombligo, v. g. en una planta o concha.

umbrage [ˈʌmbrɪdʒ] [am-brich], *s.* 1. Pique, resentimiento; sentimiento que causa el verse aventajado u oscurecido por otro; sentimiento producido por una injuria. 2. Sombra, la que hacen los árboles; umbría; sombrajo.

umbrageous [ʌmˈbrɪdʒəs] [am-bri-yos], *a.* Sombrío, umbroso.

umbrella [ʌmˈbrelə] [am-bre-la], *s.* Paraguas; quitasol, sombrilla.

umpirage [ˈʌmpɪrɪdʒ] [am-pi-rich], *s.* Arbitramento.

umpire [ˈʌmpaɪəʳ] [am-paiaʳ], *s.* 1. Árbitro, arbitrador, el componedor amigable de alguna disputa o contienda. 2. Árbitro dirimente, el que decide en caso de desavenencia o empate entre los árbitros. *-va.* y *vn.* Arbitrar, decidir o juzgar como árbitro.

un- [ʌn] [an], Prefijo que significa no; se usa para expresar negación o estado incompleto y corresponde muchas veces a des- o in-.

unabashed [ˈʌnəˈbæʃt] [a-na-basht], *a.* Descocado, falto de rubor o de vergüenza.

unabated [ˈʌnəˈbeɪtɪd] [a-na-bei-tid], *a.* No disminuido; completo, cabal.

unabbreviated [ˈʌnəˈbriːvɪeɪtd] [a-na-bri-viei-tid], *a.* No abreviado, que no está compendiado; no reducido.

unable [ʌnˈeɪbl] [an-ei-bol], *a.* Inhábil, incapaz, impotente; imposibilitado.

unaccented [ˈʌnækˈsentɪd] [an-ak-sen-tid], *a.* No acentuado, falto de acento.

unacceptable [ˈʌnəkˈseptəbl] [an-ak-sep-ta-bol], *a.* Inaceptable; poco conveniente, desagradable.

unaccessible [ˈʌnəkˈsesəbl] [an-ak-se-si-bol], *a.* Inaccesible.

unaccommodated [ˈʌnəˈkɒmədeɪtɪd] [an-a-ko-mo-dei-tid], *a.* Desacomodado, falto de los medios convenientes para mantener su estado.

unaccompanied [ˈʌnəˈkʌmpənɪd] [an-a-kam-pa-nid], *a.* Desacompañado, solo, sin compañía; sin acompañamiento.

unaccomplished [ˈʌnəˈkʌmplɪʃt] [an-a-kam-plisht], *a.* 1. Incompleto, imperfecto, no acabado. 2. Falto de prendas o gracias.

unaccountable [ˈʌnəˈkaʊntəbl] [an-a-kaun-ta-bol], *a.* Inexplicable, extraño, extraordinario, que no puede explicar; que no se puede concebir.

unaccountably [ˈʌnəˈkaʊntəblɪ] [an-a-kaun-ta-bli], *adv.* Extrañamente, de un modo extraordinario, raro, de un modo que no puede explicarse.

unaccustomed [ˈʌnəˈkʌstəmd] [an-a-kas-tamd], *a.* Desacostumbrado, fuera del uso y costumbre común; insólito, no habitual.

unacknowledged [ˈʌnəkˈnɒlɪdʒ] [an-ak-no-lich], *a.* No reconocido; negado; inconfeso, no declarado; por contestar, v. gr. una carta de la cual no se ha acusado recibo.

unacquainted [ˈʌnəˈkweɪntɪd] [an-a-kuein-tid], *a.* Desconocido, ignorado, que no conoce, que no sabe. **I am entirely unacquainted with it,** me es del todo desconocido. **To be unacquainted,** no conocer; ignorar.

unadjusted [ʌnəˈdʒʌstɪd] [an-ad-yas-tid], *a.* No ajustado, no arreglado.

unadmired [ˈʌnədˈmaɪəd] [an-ad-maiad], *a.* Despreciado, no apreciado, olvidado.

unadorned [ˈʌnədˈdɔːnd] [an-a-dornd], *a.* Desadornado, sin adorno.

unadulterated [ˈʌnədˈʌltəreɪtɪd] [an-a-dal-te-rei-tid], *a.* Genuino, puro, natural, sin mezcla, no falsificado.

unadventurous [ˈʌnədˈventʃərəs] [an-ad-ven-cha-ras], *a.* Prudente, circunspecto, no atrevido, que no se arriesga.

unadvisable [ˈʌnədˈvaɪzəbl] [an-ad-vai-sa-bol], *a.* Poco cuerdo, que no es prudente o conveniente.

unadvised [ˈʌnədˈvaɪst] [an-ad-vaist], *a.* Imprudente, indiscreto, inconsiderado, hecho sin reflexión.

unadvisedly [ˈʌnədˈvaɪzɪdlɪ] [an-ad-vai-sid-li], *adv.* Imprudentemente, temerariamente.

unaffected [ˈʌnəˈfektɪd] [an-a-fek-tid], *a.* 1. Real, verdadero, ingenuo, natural, sincero, sin artificio. 2. Natural, sencillo, franco, sin afectación. 3. Que no se conmueve, que se mantiene impasible o inalterable.

unaffectedly [ˈʌnəˈfektɪdlɪ] [an-a-fek-tid-li], *adv.* Sencillamente, naturalmente, sin afectación.

unaffectedness [ˈʌnəˈfektɪdnɪs] [an-a-fek-tid-nes], *s.* Sencillez, lisura, ingenuidad, naturalidad.

unaffecting [ˈʌnəˈfektɪŋ] [an-a-fek-tin], *a.* Que no mueve los afectos del ánimo, frío, insípido.

unaided [ʌnˈeɪdɪd] [an-ei-did], *a.* Sin ayuda, sin socorro.

unalienable [ʌnəˈlɪənəbl] [an-a-li-na-bol], *a.* Inajenable, inalienable.

unalienably [ʌnəˈlɪənəblɪ] [an-a-li-na-bli], *adv.* De un modo inalienable.

unallowable [ʌnəˈlaʊəbl] [an-a-laua-bol], *a.* Inadmisible.

unallowed [ʌnəˈləʊd] [an-a-loud], *a.* Ilícito, no permitido.

unalterable [ʌnˈɒltərəbl] [an-al-te-ra-bol], *a.* Inalterable, invariable, inmutable.

unalterableness [ʌnˈɒltərəblnɪs] [an-al-te-ra-bol-nes], *s.* Inalterabilidad.

unalterably [ʌnˈɒltərəblɪ] [an-al-te-ra-bli], *adv.* Inalterablemente.

unambiguous [ˈʌnæmˈbɪgjʊəs] [an-a-bi-guiuos], *a.* Claro, indudable, que no admite duda.

unambitious [ˈʌnæmˈbɪʃəs] [an-a-bi-shos], *a.* No ambicioso, sin ambición.

un-American [ˈʌnəˈmerɪkən] [an-a-me-ri-kan], *a.* No americano; que carece de los rasgos característicos de los Estados Unidos, ya se trate de sus habitantes, constumbres, política, etc.

unamiable [ˈʌnˈeɪmɪəbl] [an-ei-mia-bol], *a.* Que no es amable; nada amable.

unamiableness [ˈʌnˈeɪmɪəblnɪs] [an-ei-mia-bol-nes], *s.* Falta de amabilidad.

unanimity [juːnəˈnɪmɪtɪ] [iu-na-ni-mi-ti], *s.* Unanimidad, conformidad de sentimientos, unión de voluntades.

unanimous [juːˈnænɪməs] [iu-na-ni-mos], *a.* Unánime, que está de común acuerdo.

unanimously [juːˈnænɪməslɪ] [iu-na-ni-mos-li], *adv.* Unánimemente, de común acuerdo.

unanimousness [juːˈnænɪməsnɪs] [iu-na-ni-mos-nes], *s.* Unanimidad.

unanswerable [ʌnˈɑːnsərəbl] [an-an-se-ra-bol], *a.* Incontrovertible, incontestable, indisputable, que no admite duda o disputa, tan convincente que no admite respuesta.

unanswerableness [ʌnˈɑːnsərəblnɪs] [an-an-se-ra-bol-nes], *s.* Calidad de incontrovertible, o indisputable.

unanswerably [ʌnˈɑːnsərəblɪ] [an-an-se-ra-bli], *adv.* Indisputablemente.

unanswered [ʌnˈɑːnsəd] [an-an-sard], *a.* 1. Por contestar, no contestado. 2. No respondido, no impugnado. 3. Que no es recompensado como se debe, no reconocido.

unappalled [ˈʌnəˈpɔːld] [an-a-pold], *a.* Intrépido, arrojado.

unapparelled [ˈʌnəˈpɔːld] [an-a-porld], *a.* Desnudo, sin vestido.

unappealable [ˈʌnəˈpiːləbl] [an-a-pi-la-bol], *a.* Que no admite apelación a un tribunal superior; de última instancia, conclusivo, final.

unappeasable [ˈʌnəˈpiːsəbl] [an-a-pi-sa-bol], *a.* Implacable.

unapplied [ˈʌnəˈplaɪd] [an-a-plaid], *a.* Que no se aplica o destina a una cosa determinada.

unapportioned [ˈʌnəˈpɔːʃənd] [an-a-por-shond], *a.* Que no es proporcionado.

unapproachable [ˈʌnəˈprəʊtʃəbl] [an-a-prou-cha-bol], *a.* Inaccesible.

unappropriated [ˌʌnəˈprəʊpɪeɪtɪd] [an-a-prou-priei-tid], *a.* No concedido, destinado ni reservado para un uso especial; impropio, no adecuado a una persona o conjunto de personas en particular.

unapt [ˈʌnæpt] [an-apt], *a.* 1. Poco inclinado, poco propenso, inverosímil. 2. Inepto, incapaz; nada a propósito; inhábil; lerdo.

unaptly [ˈʌnæptlɪ] [an-apt-li], *adv.* Ineptamente, mal, sin maña, sin habilidad.

unaptness [ˈʌnæptnɪs] [an-apt-nes], *s.* Ineptitud, inaptitud, falta de inclinación, torpeza de ingenio.

unarmed [ʌnˈɑːmd] [an-armd], *a.* 1. Desarmado, sin armas, sin defensa. 2. *(Zool. y Bot.)* Inerme, desprovisto de púas, espinas, placas, etc.

unashamed [ˈʌnəˈʃeɪmd] [an-a-sheimd], *a.* Que no tiene vergüenza.

unasked [ʌnˈɑːskt] [an-askt], *a.* No solicitado, no llamado, no convidado.

unassailable [ˌʌnəˈseɪləbl] [an-a-sei-la-bol], *a.* Incapaz de ser asaltado, atacado o combatido.

unassailed [ˌʌnəˈseɪld] [an-a-seild], *a.* No acometido.

unassayed [ˌʌnəˈseɪd] [an-a-seid], *a.* No ensayado; no intentado.

unassisted [ˈʌnəˈsɪstɪd] [an-a-sis-tid], *a.* Sin socorro, sin auxilio, sin ayuda.

unassuming [ˈʌnəˈsjuːmɪŋ] [an-a-siu-min], *a.* Modesto, nada atrevido, nada presuntuoso.

unassured [ˈʌnəˈʃʊəd] [an-a-shuad], *a.* 1. Que no está asegurado; poco seguro. 2. Que no merece confianza.

unattached [ˈʌnəˈtætʃt] [an-a-tacht], *a.* 1. Suelto, que no está pegado o unido a otra cosa. 2. En especial, (a) no embargado por motivo de una deuda; (b) *(Mil.)* de reemplazo, no destinado a un cuerpo o regimiento.

unattackable [ˈʌnəˈtækəbl] [an-a-ta-ka-bol], *a.* Inatacable, que no se puede atacar.

unattainable [ˈʌnəˈteɪnəbl] [an-a-tei-na-bol], *a.* Insequible, que no se puede alcanzar o lograr.

unattainted [ˈʌnəˈteɪntɪd] [an-a-tein-ted], *a.* Incorrupto.

unattempted [ˈʌnəˈtemptɪd] [an-a-temp-tid], *a.* No experimentado, no ensayado, no intentado.

unattended [ˈʌnəˈtendɪd] [an-a-ten-did], *a.* Solo, sin comitiva, sin séquito, sin acompañamiento. **Unattended to,** descuidado, negligente.

unattested [ˈʌnəˈtestɪd] [an-a-tes-tid], *a.* No atestiguado, falto de atestación.

unattired [ˈʌnəˈtaɪəd] [an-a-taiad], *a.* No ataviado o adornado.

unattractive [ˈʌnəˈtræktɪv] [an-a-trak-tiv], *a.* Falto de atracción, poco atractivo.

unatributed [ˌʌnəˈtrɪbjʊtɪd] [an-a-tri-biu-tid], *a.* Que no se atribuye.

unau [ˈʌnəʊ] [an-au], *a.* El perezoso común del Brasil, mamífero desdentado, con dos dedos en cada pie.

unauthorized, unauthorised [ˈʌnəˈɔːθəraɪzd] [an-o-zo-raisd], *a.* Desautorizado, sin autorización.

unavailable [ˈʌnəˈveɪləbl] [an-a-vei-la-bol], *a.* Infructuoso, inútil; no disponible, no utilizable, no aprovechable.

unavailableness [ˈʌnəˈveɪləblnɪs] [an-a-vei-la-bol-nes], *s.* Ineficacia, inutilidad, condición de no disponible.

unavailing [ˈʌnəˈveɪlɪŋ] [an-a-vei-lin], *a.* Inútil, vano, infructuoso, ineficaz.

unavoidable [ˈʌnəˈvɔɪdəbl] [an-a-voi-da-bol], *a.* Inevitable.

unavoidableness [ˌʌnəˈvɔɪdəblnɪs] [an-a-voi-da-bol-nes], *s.* La calidad de lo que no se puede evitar.

unavoidably [ˌʌnəˈvɔɪdəblɪ] [an-a-voi-da-bli], *adv.* Inevitablemente.

unawarded [ˌʌnəˈwɔːdɪd] [an-a-uor-did], *a.* No determinado o juzgado.

unaware [ˌʌnəˈwɛəʳ] [an-a-ueaʳ], *a.* 1. Que ignora una cosa determinada, que no presta atención a. 2. *(Ant.)* Descuidado, negligente. **To be not unaware,** no ignorar, estar impuesto de.

unawares [ˌʌnəˈwɛəz] [an-a-ueas], *(Poét.)*, *adv.* Inopinadamente, repentinamente, de improviso; sin pensar, inadvertidamente; sin premeditación.

unbacked [ˈʌnˈbækt] [an-bakt], *a.* 1. Sin ayuda, sin apoyo (rentístico). 2. Que carece de respaldo, como un taburete.

unbailable [ʌnˈbeɪləbl] [an-bei-la-bol], *a.* Que no admite fianza.

unbalance [ˈʌnˈbæləns] [an-ba-lans], *s.* Desequilibrio.

unbalanced [ˈʌnˈbælənst] [an-ba-lanst], *a.* 1. Que no está en equilibrio, no balanceado. 2. *(Com.)* No ajustado para su balance, dícese de las cuentas. 3. Falto de equilibrio mental, lunático, destornillado.

unbaptized [ˈʌnbæpˈtaɪzd] [an-bap-taisd], *a.* No bautizado, de aquí, no cristiano, impío, profano.

unbar [ˈʌnbɑːʳ] [an-baʳ], *va.* Desatrancar, quitar la tranca o los barrotes.

unbarrel [ˈʌnˈbærəl] [an-ba-rel], *va.* Sacar de un tonel o barril lo que contiene.

unbearable [ʌnˈbɛərəbl] [an-bea-ra-bol], *a.* Intolerable, insufrible, que no se puede sufrir o llevar con paciencia.

unbearably [ʌnˈbɛərəblɪ] [an-bea-ra-bli], *adv.* Insoportablemente.

unbearded [ˈʌnˈbɜːbd] [an-ber-bed], *a.* 1. Imberbe. 2. Falto de aristas, no barbado.

unbeaten [ˈʌnˈbiːtn] [an-bi-ten], *a.* 1. No pisado, no frecuentado. 2. batido; no apaleado, no golpeado. 3. Invicto, no derrotado.

unbecoming [ˈʌnbɪˈkʌmɪŋ] [an-bi-ka-min], *a.* Indecente, indecoroso, impropio, mal parecido, que sienta o cae mal, que no conviene al lugar, a las circunstancias; que no sienta bien al que lo lleva (vestido o adorno).

unbecomingly [ˈʌnbɪˈkʌmɪŋlɪ] [an-bi-ka-min-li], *adv.* Indecorosamente, de una manera impropia, inconveniente.

unbecomingness [ˈʌnbɪˈkʌmɪŋnɪs] [an-bi-ka-min-nes], *s.* Indecencia, falta de decencia o de decoro.

unbefitting [ˈʌnbɪˈfɪtɪŋ] [an-bi-fi-tin], *a.* Inconveniente, que no conviene.

unbegotten [ˈʌnbɪˈgɒtn] [an-bi-go-ten], *a.* 1. Ingénito, no engendrado. 2. Increado, que existe por sí mismo.

unbeknown [ˈʌnbɪˈnəʊn] [an-bi-noun], *a.* (*Prov.*) Desconocido, que ejecuta una acción desconocida, sin conocimiento de otro.

unbelief [ˈʌnbɪˈliːf] [an-bi-lif], *s.* 1. Incredulidad, dificultad o repugnancia, en creer. 2. Incredulidad, irreligión, falta de fe.

unbeliever [ˈʌbɪˈliːvəʳ] [an-bi-li-vaʳ], *s.* Incrédulo, falto de fe religiosa, infiel.

unbelieving [ˈʌnbɪˈliːvɪŋ] [an-bi-li-vin], *a.* Incrédulo, infiel.

unbeloved [ˈʌnbɪˈlʌvd] [an-bi-lavd], *a.* Que no es amado.

unbend [ˈʌnˈbend] [an-bend], *va.* (*pret. y pp.* UNBENT o UNBENDED). 1. Enderezar lo que estaba doblado o torcido, aflojar, soltar lo que estaba tirante. 2. Dar descanso o aliviar de la fatiga; esparcir, distraer el ánimo, solazarse. 3. (*Mar.*) Desenvergar, desentalingar. **To unbend the sails,** desenvergar las velas. **To unbend the anchor,** desentalingar el ancla. **To unbend a cable,** desentalingar un cable.

unbending [ˈʌnˈbendɪŋ] [an-ben-din], *a.* Inflexible, que no se encorva; que no se dobla, que no cede; resuelto o determinado firmemente.

unbending, *a.* Laxante, destinado a diversión, de descanso. - *s.* Laxación, descanso.

unbenign [ˈʌnˈbenɪn] [an-be-nin], *a.* Maligno, malévolo; duro, nada cariñoso.

unbent [ˈʌnˈbent] [an-bent], *a.* Aflojado, flojo, suelto; destorcido.

unbiased, unbiassed [ˈʌnˈbaɪəst] [an-baiast], *a.* Exento de prevención, de preocupación; imparcial.

unbidden [ˈʌnˈbɪdn] [an-bi-den], *a.* 1. Que no ha sido invitado. 2. Espontáneo de propio movimiento; producido naturalmente.

unbind [ˈʌnˈbaɪnd] [an-baind], *va.* (*pret. y pp.* UNBOUND). Destar; desvendar.

unblamed [ˈʌnˈbleɪmd] [an-bleimd], *a.* Que no tiene tacha; inocente.

unbleached [ˈʌnˈbliːtʃt] [an-blicht], *a.* Crudo, no blanqueado (cloths).

unblemished [ʌnˈblemɪʃt] [an-ble-mist], *a.* Irreprensible; sin mancha, sin tacha.

unblest [ˈʌnˈblest] [an-blest], *a.* Maldito; desdichado, infeliz, desgraciado.

unblinking [ˈʌnˈblɪŋkɪŋ] [an-blin-kin], *a.* Desvergonzado.

unblown [ˈʌnˈbləʊn] [an-blaun], *a.* 1. Que aún no se ha abierto; que aún está por florecer. 2. Mudo, que no se hace sonar (trompeta). 3. Que no está hinchado ni movido por el viento; no inflado.

unblunted [ˈʌnˈblʌntɪd] [an-blan-tid], *a.* Que no está embotado, desembotado.

unblushing [ˈʌnˈblʌʃɪŋ] [an-bla-shin], *a.* Que no se avergüenza, desvergonzado.

unblushingly [ˈʌnˈblʌʃɪŋlɪ] [an-bla-shin-li], *adv.* Sin avergonzarse, descaradamente.

unbolt [ˈʌnˈbəʊlt] [an-boult], *va.* Desatrancar, tirar el cerrojo de.

unbolted [ˈʌnˈbəʊltɪd] [an-boul-tid], *a.* 1. Que no está cernido, no pasado por tamiz. 2. No asegurado con cerrojos, que se le ha quitado o corrido el cerrojo.

unbooted [ˈʌnˈbuːtɪd] [an-bu-tid], *a.* Descalzo, sin botas.

unborn [ˈʌnˈbɔːn] [an-born], *a.* Innato, que no ha nacido aún.

unbosom [ʌnˈbʊzəm] [an-bu-som], *va.* Abrir su pecho a uno; revelar un secreto, confiar o decir en confianza un secreto.

unbought [ˈʌnˈbɔːt] [an-bout], *a.* 1. Que no ha sido comprado, que se ha adquirido de balde. 2. Que no se ha vendido, hablando de mercancías.

unbound [ˈʌnˈbaʊnd] [an-bound], *a.* 1. No encuadernado. 2. Suelto, desatado. 3. *pret. y pp.* de TO UNBIND.

unbounded [ˈʌnˈbaʊndɪd] [an-boun-did], *a.* Infinito, que no tiene fin, límite o término; ilimitado; libre, no empeñado.

unbrace [ˈʌnˈbreɪs] [an-breis], *va.* Aflojar, soltar, desabrochar; destapar.

unbraid [ˈʌnˈbreɪd] [an-breid], *va.* Destejer, destrenzar; desenredar.

unbreakable [ˈʌnˈbreɪkəbl] [an-brei-ka-bol], *a.* Irrompible.

unbreathed [ˈʌnˈbiːθd] [an-brizd], *a.* 1. No respirado, no comunicado a otro. 2. (*Des.*) No ejercitado.

unbreathing [ˈʌnˈbiːθɪŋ] [an-bri-zin], *a.* Inanimado, inánime, que no respira.

unbred [ˈʌnˈbred] [an-bred], *a.* Descortés, malcriado, inánime, que no respira.

unbreeched [ˈʌnˈbriːtʃt] [an-bricht], *a.* Desbragado, sin bragas.

unbribed [ˈʌnˈbraɪbɪd] [an-brai-bid], *a.* Desinteresado; incorrupto, íntegro.

unbridle [ˈʌnˈbraɪdl] [an-bri-del], *va.* Desenfrenadr, desembridar.

unbridled [ʌnˈbraɪdld] [an-bri-deld], *a.* Desenfrenado, licencioso, que no tiene freno o sujeción en sus acciones.

unbroached [ˈʌnˈbrəʊtʃt] [an-broucht], *a.* Que no ha sido barrenado o decentado.

unbroken [ˈʌnˈbrəʊkən] [an-brou-ken], *a.* 1. Intacto, que no está roto, entero. 2. Inviolado. 3. No interrumpido, regular; llano. 4. No debilitado, firme, fuerte. 5. No adiestrado (caballería).

unbuckle [ˈʌnˈbʌkl] [an-ba-kel], *va.* Deshebillar, soltar las hebillas.

unburden [ʌnˈbɜːdn] [an-ber-den], *va.* Descargar, quitar o aliviar la carga.

unburied [ˈʌnˈberɪd] [an-be-rid], *a.* Insepulto, no enterrado.

unburned, unburnt [ʌnˈbɜːnt] [an-bernt], *a.* No quemado.

unburnished [ʌnˈbɜːnɪʃt] [an-ber-nisht], *a.* No bruñido.

unburning [ʌnˈbɜːnɪŋ] [an-ber-nin], *a.* Que no quema ni consume con su calor.

unburthen [ʌnˈbɜːðn] [an-ber-den], *va. V.* UNBURDEN.

unbusinesslike [ʌnˈbɪznɪslaɪk] [an-bis-nis-laik], *a.* Poco hábil, o que no conviene, para los negocios; poco práctico, poco serio.

unbutton [ˈʌnˈbʌtn] [an-ba-ton], *va.* Desabotonar.

uncage [ʌnˈkeɪdʒ] [an-keich], *va.* Sacar o hacer salir de una jaula, libertar.

uncalled [ʌnˈkɔːld] [an-kold], *a.* No llamado, no citado, no pedido. **Uncalled for,** no merecido por las circunstancias; poco necesario, gratuito.

uncanny [ʌnˈkænɪ] [an-ka-ni], *a.* (*Esco.*) 1. Misterioso, pavoroso. 2. Inhábil, incauto. 3. Poco seguro, peligroso. 4. Severo.

uncap [ʌnˈkæp] [an-kap], *va.* 1. Destapar, quitar la tapa o cubierta (como de una lente); quitar el casquillo de un fusil. 2. Quitar la superficie del panal (de miel). -*vn.* Saludar, quitándose la gorra o casquete.

uncared [ʌnˈkɛəd] [an-kead], *a.* Desamparado, descuidado, abandonado (seguido de *for*).

uncase [ʌnˈkeɪs] [an-keis], *va.* 1. Desenvainar, sacar de la caja o vaina; (*Mil.*) desplegar (la bandera); de aquí, revelar. 2. Desnudar.

uncaught [ʌnˈkɔːt] [an-kot], *a.* Aún no cogido.

uncaused [ʌnˈkɔːst] [an-kost], *a.* Sin motivo, sin causa, lo que se hace sin razón.

uncautious [ʌnˈkɔːʃəs] [an-ko-shos], *a*. Incauto, impróvido. *V*. INCAUTIOUS.

unceasing [ʌnˈsiːsɪŋ] [an-si-sin], *a*. Incesante, que no cesa; continuo.

unceasingly [ʌnˈsiːsɪŋlɪ] [an-si-sin-li], *adv*. Sin cesar, incesantemente, continuamente.

uncensored [ʌnˈsensəd] [an-sen-sord], *a*. No censurado.

unceremonious [ˈʌnˌserɪˈməʊnɪəs] [an-se-si-mou-nois], *a*. Brusco, poco cortés.

uncertain [ʌnˈsɜːtn] [an-ser-ten], *a*. 1. Incierto, dudoso. 2. Incierto, inconstante; precario. 3. Irresoluto, indeciso; que no sabe, que no está seguro de. 4. Variable, poco seguro; no fijado, no determinado. 5. Sin significación exacta.

uncertainly [ʌnˈsɜːtnlɪ] [an-ser-tan-li], *adv*. Inciertamente.

uncertainty [ʌnˈsɜːtntɪ] [an-ser-tan-ti], *s*. Incertidumbre, duda, ambigüedad, irresolución; instabilidad, contingencia.

unchain [ʌnˈtʃeɪn] [an-chein], *va*. Desencadenar, quitar las cadenas.

unchangeable [ʌnˈtʃeɪndʒəbl] [an-chein-ya-bol], *a*. Impermutable, inmutable.

unchangeableness [ʌnˈtʃeɪndʒəblnɪs] [an-chein-ya-bol-nes], *s*. Inmutabilidad, estabilidad; constancia, firmeza de propósito.

unchangeably [ʌnˈtʃeɪndʒəblɪ] [an-chein-ya-bli], *adv*. Inmutablemente.

unchanged [ʌnˈtʃeɪndʒt] [an-cheincht], *a*. Invariado, no alterado.

unchanging [ʌnˈtʃeɪndʒɪŋ] [an-chein-yin], *a*. Inalterable, inmutable.

uncharitable [ʌnˈtʃærɪtəbl] [an-cha-ri-ta-bol], *a*. Nada caritativo, duro.

uncharitableness [ʌnˈtʃærɪtəblnɪs] [an-cha-ri-ta-bol-nes], *s*. Falta de caridad, dureza.

uncharitably [ʌnˈtʃærɪtəblɪ] [an-cha-ri-ta-bli], *adv*. Sin caridad.

unchaste [ʌnˈtʃeɪst] [an-cheist], *a*. Impúdico, deshonesto, lascivo, incontinente.

unchastity [ʌnˈtʃeɪstɪtɪ] [an-cheis-ti-ti], *s*. Incontinencia, lascivia, impureza, impudencia.

unchecked [ʌnˈtʃekt] [an-chekt], *a*. 1. Desenfrenado, que no es reprimido, detenido, contenido. 2. Que no está confrontado, verificado.

unchristian [ʌnˈkrɪstɪən] [an-kris-tian], *a*. Anticristiano, opuesto o contrario a las leyes o máximas cristianas; indigno de un cristiano.

unchurch [ʌnˈtʃɜːtʃ] [an-cherch], *va*. 1. Excomulgar, expulsar de la iglesia. 2. Negar la validez de los sacramentos y órdenes de una iglesia; dícese p. ej. de una secta.

uncial [ˈʌnsɪəl] [an-sial], *a*. Uncial: dícese de una clase de letra muy abultada que se halla en algunos manuscritos antiguos, entre los siglos IV y VIII.

uncircumcised [ˈʌnˈɜːkəmsaɪzd] [an-ser-kam-saisd], *a*. Incircunciso.

uncivil [ʌnˈsɪvɪl] [an-si-vil], *a*. Incivil, descortés, desatento, impolítico.

uncivilly [ʌnˈsɪvɪlɪ] [an-si-vi-li], *adv*. Groseramente.

uncivilized [ˈʌnˈsɪvɪlaɪst] [an-si-vi-laist], *a*. Bárbaro, tosco, salvaje, que no está civilizado.

unclad [ʌnˈklæd] [an-klad], *pret*. y *pp*. del verbo UNCLOTHE. No vestido.

unclarified [ˈʌnˈklærɪfaɪd] [an-kla-ri-faid], *a*. Que no está purificado o clarificado.

unclasp [ʌnˈklɑːsp] [an-klasp], *va*. 1. Desabrochar; abrir el broche de un libro. 2. Librar de un abrazo.

uncle [ˈʌŋkl] [an-kel], *s*. 1. Tío, el hermano del padre o de la madre; el marido de la tía. 2. Hombre viejo; particularmente, negro viejo en los Estados Unidos del Sur. 3. (*Ger*.) *V*. PAWNBROKER. **Uncle Sam**, el gobierno o un representante típico de los Estados Unidos; explicación festiva de las iniciales U.S.

unclean [ʌnˈkliːn] [an-klin], *a*. Inmundo, puerco, sucio, impuro; obsceno.

uncleanliness [ʌnˈkliːnlɪnɪs] [an-klin-li-nes], *s*. Suciedad, inmundicia, falta de limpieza.

uncleanly [ˈʌnˈkliːnlɪ] [an-klin-li], *a*. Inmundo, puerco, impuro; indecente.

uncleanness [ˈʌnˈkliːnnɪs] [an-klin-nes], *s*. Suciedad, asquerosidad; impureza, obscenidad.

unclog [ʌnˈklɒg] [an-klog], *va*. Desembarazar, exonerar, descargar.

uncloister [ˈʌnˈkɔɪstəʳ] [an-klois-taʳ], *va*. Exclaustrar; poner en libertad; sacar a una persona o cosa de donde estaba encerrada.

unclose [ʌnˈkləʊz] [an-klous], *va*. Abrir; descubrir, revelar.

unclosed [ˈʌnˈkləʊzt] [an-kloust], *a*. Abierto; descercado.

unclothe [ʌnˈkləʊð] [an-kloud], *va*. (*pret*. y *pp*. regular y también UNCLAD). Desnudar, quitar la ropa, poner desnudo.

unclouded [ˈʌnˈkləʊdɪd] [an-kloudid], *a*. Claro, despejado, libre de nubes, sereno.

uncoil [ʌnˈkɔɪ] [an-koil], *va*. Desarrollar, desenrollar, extender lo que estaba arrollado.

uncoined [ˈʌnˈkɔɪnd] [an-koind], *a*. No acuñado.

uncollectable [ˌʌnkəˈlektəbl] [an-ko-lek-ta-bol], *a*. Que no se puede cobrar o recaudar; irrecuperable.

uncollected [ˌʌnkəˈlektɪd] [an-ko-lek-tid], *a*. Disperso, no recogido.

uncolored, uncoloured [ˈʌnˈkʌləd] [an-ka-led], *a*. Descolorado, que no está teñido; incolor, que carece de color; exento de preocupación.

uncombed [ˈʌnˈkəʊmd] [an-koumd], *a*. Despeinado, no peinado; desgreñado.

uncomeliness [ˈʌnˈkʌmlɪnɪs] [an-koum-li-nes], *s*. Fealdad; indecencia; falta de hermosura en las cosas; falta de gracia en las personas.

uncomely [ˈʌnˈkʌmlɪ] [an-koum-li], *a*. Indecente; feo; desagradable; grosero,

uncomfortable [ʌnˈkʌmfətəbl] [an-kam-for-ta-bol], *a*. Desconsolado, triste; que no se encuentra bien; penoso, desagradable, molesto, enfadoso, pesado, incómodo, que no es confortante.

uncomfortably [ʌnˈkʌmfətəblɪ] [an-kam-for-ta-bli], *adv*. Desconsoladamente; penosamente, trabajosamente, incómodamente; tristemente.

uncommon [ʌnˈkɒmən] [an-ko-mon], *a*. Poco frecuente, raro, extraño, extraordinario, nada común; de aquí, digno de observación.

uncommonly [ʌnˈkɒmənlɪ] [an-ko-mon-li], *adv*. Extraordinariamente; raramente, infrecuentemente, con poca frecuencia.

uncommonness [ʌnˈkɒmənnɪs] [an-ko-mon-nes], *s*. Rareza, singularidad, extrañeza.

uncommunicated [ˈʌnkəˈmjuːnɪkeɪtɪd] [an-ko-miu-ni-kei-tid], *a*. No comunicado.

uncommunicative [ˈʌnkəˈmjuːnɪkətɪv] [an-ko-miu-ni-ka-tiv], *a*. Poco comunicativo, reservado.

uncompleted [ˈʌnkəmˈpliːtɪd] [an-kom-pli-tid], *a*. Inacabado, no completado, imperfecto.

uncompressed [ˈʌnkəmˈprest] [an-kom-prest], *a*. Que no está comprimido.

uncompromising [ˈʌnkəmˈprəmaɪsɪŋ] [an-kom-pro-mai-sin], *a*. Que no admite compromisos; inflexible, intratable, firme.

unconceived [ˈʌnkənˈsiːvd] [an-kon-sivd], *a*. Impensado; no concebido.

unconcern [ˈʌnkənˈsɜːn] [an-kon-sern], *s*. Indiferencia, descuido.

unconcerned [ˈʌnkənˈsɜːnd] [an-kon-sernd], *a*. Indiferente, descuidado, negligente.

unconcernedly [ˈʌnkənˈsɜːndlɪ] [an-kon-sernd-li], *adv*. Indiferentemente, sin tomar interés.

uncondemned [ˈʌnkənˈdemnd] [an-kon-demnd], *a*. Que no está condenado; tolerado, admitido; que no está prohibido, que no se desaprueba.

unconditional [ˈʌnkənˈdɪʃənl] [an-kon-di-sho-nal], *a*. Absoluto, sin condiciones, incondicional.

unconditioned [ˈʌnkənˈdɪʃənd] [an-kon-di-shond], *a.* 1. Exento de condiciones, no limitado ni restringido. 2. *(Fil.)* Incondicional, no limitado por condiciones de tiempo o espacio; exento de relaciones, absoluto.

unconfined [ˈʌnkənˈfaɪnd] [an-kon-faind], *a.* Libre, ilimitado, sin trabas, sin obstáculos.

unconfirmed [ˈʌnkənˈfɜːmd] [an-kon-fermd], *a.* Que no está confirmado, apoyado, establecido; que no ha recibido el rito de la confirmación.

unconformable [ˈʌnkənˈfɔːməbl] [an-kon-for-ma-bol], *a.* Contrario, incompatible, que no puede concordar con otra cosa, falto de conformidad; que presenta desacuerdo geológico.

unconformity [ˈʌnkənˈfɔːmɪtɪ] [an-kon-for-mi-ti], *s.* Desconformidad, desemejanza, falta de conformidad, desacuerdo; falta de paralelismo entre los estratos contiguos.

uncongenial [ˈʌnkənˈdʒiːnɪəl] [an-kon-yi-nial], *a.* 1. Poco simpático, antipático, sin afinidad. 2. Que no conviene a la naturaleza o al carácter de; desagradable.

unconnected [ˈʌnkəˈnektɪd] [an-ko-nek-tid], *a.* Inconexo, que no tiene conexión o relación con otra cosa.

unconnectedly [ˈʌnkəˈnektɪdlɪ] [an-ko-nek-tid-li], *adv.* De un modo inconexo.

unconquerable [ʌnˈkɒŋkərəbl] [an-kon-ke-ra-bol], *a.* Invencible, insuperable.

unconscionable [ʌnˈkɒnʃnəbl] [an-kon-sho-na-bol], *a.* 1. Desrazonable, injusto, excesivo. 2. No sensato, falto de razón. 3. Falto de conciencia, que obra contra los dictados de ésta. **An unconscionable liar,** un embustero de tomo y lomo.

unconscionably [ʌnˈkɒnʃnəblɪ] [an-kon-sho-na-bli], *adv.* Sin razón, sin conciencia.

unconscious [ʌnˈkɒnʃəs] [an-kon-shos], *a.* 1. Inconsciente, privado temporalmente de la conciencia de sí mismo. 2. No sabedor, que no sabe, que ignora. 3. De existencia ignorada o no conocida.

unconsciously [ʌnˈkɒnʃəslɪ] [an-kon-shos-li], *adv.* Sin tener, conciencia de ello; sin saberlo, involuntariamente.

unconsciousness [ʌnˈkɒnʃəsnɪs] [an-kon-shos-nes], *s.* 1. Inconsciencia. 2. Insensiblidad.

unconsecrated [ʌnˈkɒnsɪkreɪtɪd] [an-kon-si-krei-tid], *a.* No consagrado.

unconsidered [ˈʌnkənˈsɪdəd] [an-kon-si-derd], *a.* Inconscientemente.

unconstitutional [ˈʌnˌkɒnstɪˈtjuːʃənl] [an-kons-ti-tiu-sho-nal], *a.* Inconstitucional, no conforme a la constitución del estado.

unconstitutionally [ˈʌnˌkɒnstɪˈtjuːʃənlɪ] [an-kons-ti-tiu-sho-na-li], *adv.* Inconstitucionalmente.

unconstrainable [ˈʌnkɒnsˈtreɪnəbl] [an-kons-trei-na-bol], *a.* Incapaz de ser constreñido; libre.

unconstrained [ˈʌnkɒnsˈtreɪnd] [an-kons-treind], *a.* Libre, voluntario, espontáneo, hecho libremente.

uncontrollable [ˈʌnkənˈtrəʊləbl] [an-kon-trou-la-bol], *a.* Ingobernable; incontrastable, irresistible.

uncontrollably [ˈʌnkənˈtrəʊləblɪ] [an-kon-trou-la-bli], *adv.* Irresistiblemente, de un modo incontrastable.

uncontrolled [ˈʌnkənˈtrəʊld] [an-kon-trould], *a.* Sin freno, libre.

unconventional [ˈʌnkənˈvenʃənl] [an-kon-ven-sho-nal], *a.* Que no se ajusta a las reglas convenidas; informal, libre.

unconverted [ˈʌnkənˈvɜːtɪd] [an-kon-ver-tid], *a.* Infiel, no convertido.

uncooked [ˈʌnˈkʊkt] [an-kukt], *a.* Crudo, sin hacer.

uncool [ˈʌnˈkuːl] [an-kul], *a.* Nada sofisticado; anticuado (unfashioned); emocionado, nervioso (excitable).

uncord [ˈʌnˈkɔːd] [an-kord], *va.* Desatar, deshacer la cuerda.

uncork [ˈʌnˈkɔːk] [an-kork], *va.* Sacar el corcho o tapón de destapar.

uncorrected [ˈʌnkəˈrektɪd] [an-ko-rek-tid], *a.* Incorrecto, no corregido.

uncorrupt [ˈʌnkərʌpt] [an-ko-rapt], *a.* Incorrupto, no pervertido; honrado, íntegro. *V.* INCORRUPT.

uncorrupted [ˈʌnkəˈrʌptɪd] [an-ko-rap-tid], *a.* Incorrupto, no viciado o pervertido.

uncostly [ˈʌnkəʊstlɪ] [an-koust-li], *a.* Que no es costoso, no dispendioso.

uncountable [ˈʌnˈkaʊntəbl] [an-kaun-ta-bol], *a.* Innumerable, que no puede contarse.

uncouple [ˈʌnˈkʌpl] [an-ka-pel], *va.* Desatrabillar, quitar la trabilla; soltar; separar. **Uncoupled,** soltado, suelto; de aquí, soltero, no casado.

uncortliness [ˈʌnˈkɔːtlɪnɪs] [an-kort-li-nes], *s.* Falta de elegancia, grosería, maneras bruscas.

uncourtly [ˈʌnˈkɔːtlɪ] [an-kort-li], *a.* Inelegante, que no tiene maneras cortesanas; incivil.

uncouth [ʌnˈkuːθ] [an-kuz], *a.* 1. Tosco, grosero, sin gracia, imbécil; rústico. 2. Extraño, singular, extraordinario.

uncouthly [ʌnˈkuːθlɪ] [an-kuz-li], *adv.* Groseramente, toscamente, singularmente.

uncouthness [ʌnˈkuːθnɪs] [an-kuz-nes], *s.* Extrañeza, rareza, singularidad.

uncover [ʌnˈkʌvəʳ] [an-ka-vaʳ], *va.* 1. Destapar, descubrir, quitar lo que cubre. 2. Revelar, poner al descubierto, hacer saber abiertamente. -*vn.* Descubrirse, quitarse el sombrero o gorra.

uncowl [ʌnˈkaʊk] [an-kaul], *va.* Quitar la capucha de.

uncritical [ʌnˈkrɪtɪkəl] [an-kri-ti-kal], *a.* Que no tiene sentido crítico.

uncross [ʌnˈkrɒs] [an-kros], *a.* Descruzar (legs).

uncrossed [ʌnˈkrɒst] [an-krost], *a.* No anulado; no frustrado.

uncrowded [ˈʌnˈkraʊdɪd] [an-krau-did], *a.* Holgado, desahogado.

uncrown [ʌnˈkraʊn] [an-kraun], *va.* Destronar, privar de la corona.

unction [ˈʌŋkʃən] [ank-shon], *s.* 1. Unción, la acción de ungir. 2. Unción, untura, untadura; también, ungüento. 3. La extremaunción. 4. Unción: dícese de lo que enternece y de lo que mueve el corazón a la piedad y amor de Dios.

unctuosity [ˈʌŋtjʊˈɒsɪtɪ] [ank-tiuo-si-ti], *s.* Untuosidad.

unctuous [ˈʌŋtjʊəs] [ank-tiuos], *a.* Untuoso, craso.

uncultivable [ʌnˈkʌltɪvəbl] [an-kal-ti-va-bol], *a.* Incultivable, que no se puede cultivar.

uncultivated [ʌnˈkʌltɪveɪtɪd] [an-kal-ti-vei-tid], *a.* 1. Inculto; que no tiene cultivo ni labor. 2. Inculto, rústico, grosero, que no tiene cultura.

uncumbered [ˈʌnˈkʌmbəd] [an-kam-berd], *a.* Desembarazado, libre.

uncurl [ˈʌnˈkɜːl] [an-kerl], *va.* y *vn.* 1. Desenrizar el pelo, deshacer o descomponer los rizos. 2. Extender una cosa que estaba doblada, haciendo vuelta o circunvoluciones.

uncurrent [ʌnˈkʌrənt] [an-ka-rent], *a.* Que no tiene curso; que no es legal; no admitido.

uncurtain [ʌnˈkɜːtɪn] [an-ker-tin], *va.* Quitar las cortinas de.

uncut [ʌnˈkʌt] [an-kat], *a.* Que no está cortado, que está entero o completo.

undamaged [ʌnˈdæmɪdʒ] [an-da-mich], *a.* Ileso, libre de daño.

undate [ʌnˈdeɪt] [an-deit], *a.* Ondeado, que presenta undulaciones.

undated [ʌnˈdeɪtɪd] [an-dei-tid], *a.* 1. Sin fecha. 2. *V.* UNDATE.

undaunted [ʌnˈdɔːntɪd] [an-don-tid], *a.* Impávido, denodado; arrojado, ardiente, impertérrito, intrépido.

undauntedly [ʌnˈdɔːntɪdlɪ] [an-don-tid-li], *adv.* Intrépidamente, con osadía, con arrojo.

undauntedness [ʌnˈdɔːntɪdnɪs] [an-don-tid-nes], *s.* Intrepidez, arrojo, impavidez.

undecayed [ʌnˈdɪkeɪd] [an-di-keid], *a.* Inmarchitable, incapaz de marchitarse; inalterable, duradero.

undeceive [ʌndɪˈsiːv] [an-di-siv], *va.* Desengañar, hacer conocer el engaño, advertir el error, hablar sin rebozo.

undeceived [ˈʌndɪˈsiːvd] [an-di-sivd], *a.* Desengañado.

undecided [ʌndɪˈsaɪdɪd] [an-di-sai-did], *a.* Indeciso, indeterminado, que no se ha decidido o determinado.

undecipherable [ˌʌndɪˈsaɪfərəbl] [an-di-sai-fa-ra-bol], *a.* Indescifrable.

undeclinable [ˌʌndɪˈklaɪnəbl] [an-di-klai-na-bol], *a.* Indeclinable.

undeclined [ˌʌndɪˈklaɪnd] [an-di-klaind], *a.* Recto, derecho.

undefaced [ˌʌndɪˈfeɪst] [an-di-feist], *a.* Entero, sano, no desfigurado.

undefiled [ˌʌndɪˈfaɪld] [an-di-faild], *a.* Impoluto, puro, limpio, libre de mancha.

undefinable [ˌʌndɪˈfaɪnəbl] [an-di-fai-na-bol], *a.* Indefinible.

undefined [ˌʌndɪˈfaɪnd] [an-di-faind], *a.* Indefinido.

undemonstrable [ˌʌndɪˈmɒnstrəbl] [an-di-mons-tra-bol], *a.* Indemostrable, que no se puede demostrar.

undeniable [ˌʌndɪˈnaɪəbl] [an-di-naia-bol], *a.* Innegable, incontestable, irrefragable.

undeniably [ˌʌndɪˈnaɪəblɪ] [an-di-naia-bli], *adv.* Irrefragablemente, de un modo incontestable o innegable.

under [ˈʌndəʳ] [an-daʳ], *a.* 1. Inferior, situado más abajo. 2. Subalterno, subordinado. 3. Bajo (de tono). -prep. y *adv.* 1. Debajo, denota dependencia o subordinación. 2. Debajo, más abajo, denota que una cosa está cubierta con otra. 3. Debajo, en un puesto inferior respecto al superior. 4. Bajo de, inferior *a.* 5. So: en español úsase sólo delante de las palabras *capa, color y pena.* 7. Menos, menos que, por menos, en menos. 8. En; por; mediante, por el medio de; con relación a; que es asunto u objeto de. **Under discussion,** en discusión. 9. En tiempo de, en la época de. 10. En virtud de; autorizado o atestiguado por. **Under my hand and seal,** sellado y firmado por mí. 11. Conforme a, según. **Under contract,** conforme al contrato. 12. Plantado o sembrado con. **A hectare under corn,** una hectárea sembrada de maíz. **To be under restraint,** estar sujeto. **To be under age,** ser menor o no haber salido de la minoridad. **Under the care of,** al cuidado de. **I am under an obligation to him,** le debo favores. **Under sail, under canvas,** (*Mar.*) a la vela. **Under pain of death,** so pena de muerte. (*Under armas,* bajo las armas. **Under cover,** al abrigo, a cubierto; dentro de un sobre. **To be under a cloud,** hallarse en apuros, sufrir en su reputación. **To bring under,** someter, sujetar. **To keep under,** reprimir, subyugar, dominar. **Under an assumed name,** bajo un nombre supuesto. **The son is under tutors,** el hijo está sometido a sus tutores. **Under consideration,** en consideración. *Under* se usa muy frecuentemente en la formación de palabras compuestas.

underage [ˈʌndərɪdʒ] [an-da-rich], *a.* Menor de edad.

underarmed [ˈʌndərˈɑːmd] [an-da-armd], *a.* Sin suficientes armas.

underbid [ˈʌndəˈbɪd] [an-da-bid], *va.* Ofrecer menos que otro, particularmente por trabajo o materiales.

underbind [ˈʌndəˈbaɪnd] [an-da-bind], *va.* Atar por debajo.

underbrush [ˈʌndəbrʌʃ] [an-da-brash], *s.* Maleza, los arbustos y arbolillos que crecen debajo de los grandes árboles.

undercarriage [ˈʌndəˌkærɪdz] [an-da-ka-rich], *s.* 1. Bastidor de automóvil. 2. (*Aer.*) Tren de aterrizaje.

undercharge [ˈʌndəˈtʃɑːdʒ] [an-da-charch], *va.* 1. Cobrar menos que lo acostumbrado. 2. Cobrarle (a alguien) muy poco. 3. Cargar un arma con muy poco explosivo.

underclerk [ˈʌndəˈklɜːk] [an-da-klerk], *s.* Subsecretario o segundo secretario; escribiente.

underclothes [ˈʌndəkləʊðz] [an-da-klouzs], **underclothing** [ˈʌndəˈkləʊðɪŋ] [an-da-klou-zin], *s.* Prendas de vestir interiores, ropa interior.

under cover [ˈʌndəˈkʌvəʳ] [an-da-ka-vaʳ], *adv.* En secreto, subrepticiamente.

undercurrent [ˈʌndəˌkʌrənt] [an-da-ka-rent], *s.* Corriente inferior, debajo de la superficie; (*Fig.*) tendencia oscura u oculta.

undercut [ˈʌndəkʌt] [an-da-kat], *va.* 1. Socavar, cavar debajo de (v. g. una masa de hulla) para facilitar su extracción. 2. En tenis, cortar la pelota con golpe por debajo. 3. Vender a precios más bajos (que el competidor). 4. Trabajar por menos salario (que otros). -*s.* 1. Socava. 2. En tenis, golpe que se da por debajo a la pelota.

underdeveloped [ˈʌndədɪˈveləpt] [an-da-di-ve-lopt], *a.* Subdesarrollado.

underdevelopment [ˈʌndədɪˈveləpmənt] [an-da-di-ve-lop-ment], *s.* Subdesarrollo.

underdog [ˈʌndədɒg] [an-da-dog], *s.* 1. Perdidoso. 2. Víctima. 3. El de abajo.

underestimate [ˈʌndərˈestɪmɪt] [an-dar-es-ti-mit], *va.* Subestimar.

underexposure [ˈʌndərˈɪksˈpəʊʒəʳ] [an-dar-iks-pou-shaʳ], *s.* Poca exposición (en una fotografía).

underfeed [ˈʌndəˈfiːd] [an-da-fid], *va.* 1. Desnutrir, alimentar muy poco. 2. Alimentar (una caldera) por debajo.

underfilling [ˈʌndəˈfiːlɪŋ] [an-da-fi-lin], *s.* Cimiento de un edificio.

underfoot [ˈʌndəˈfʊt] [an-da-fut], *a.* Debajo de los pies.

underframe [ˈʌndəˈfreɪm] [an-da-freim], *s.* Infraestructura.

underfurnish [ˈʌndəˈfɜːnɪʃ] [an-da-fer-nish], *va.* Escasear; proveer con menos de lo que se necesita.

undergird [ˈʌndəˈgɜːd] [an-da-guerd], *va.* Ceñir por debajo.

undergo [ˈʌndəˈgəʊ] [an-da-gou], *va.* (*pret.* UNDERWENT, *pp.* UNDERGONE). 1. Sufrir, padecer, aguantar, sostener, experimentar. 2. Pasar por; arrostrar, exponerse a, correr peligro o riesgo. 3. Estar sometido a, existir bajo.

undergraduate [ˈʌndəˈgrædjʊeɪt] [an-da-gra-diueit], *s.* Alumno no graduado.

underground [ˈʌndəgraʊnd] [an-da-graund], *s.* 1. Subterráneo. 2. Metro, metropolitano. 3. Resistencia. -*a.* Subterráneo. **Underground garage,** aparcamiento subterráneo.

undergrown [ˈʌndəgrəʊn] [an-da-graun], *a.* Achaparrado, de talla menor que la mediana.

undergrowth [ˈʌndəgrəʊθ] [an-da-grauz], *s.* 1. Maleza, chamarasca, lo que nace debajo de los árboles grandes en los bosques y florestas. 2. Calidad de achaparrado o pequeño.

underhand [ˈʌndəhænd] [an-da-jand], *adv.* Bajo mano, por bajo cuerda, clandestinamente. -*a.* Secreto, clandestino, socarrón, disimulado.

underhanded [ˌʌndəˈhændɪd] [an-da-jan-did], *a.* Disimulado clandestinamente, con segunda intención.

underlay [ˈʌndəleɪ] [an-da-lei], *va.* Reforzar o fortalecer con alguna cosa puesta por debajo. -*vn.* Inclinarse un filón fuera de la perpendicular. -*s.* 1. (*Impr.*) Pedazo de papel, etc., que se pone debajo de ciertas partes de una forma para alzarlas al debido nivel. 2. (*Min.*) Inclinación de un filón.

underlie [ˌʌndəˈlaɪ] [an-da-lai], *vn.* (*pret.* UNDERLAY, *pp.* UNDERLAIN). 1. Estar debajo. 2. *va.* Ser la razón fundamental o sostén de. **The principle that underlay his plan,** el principio que sirvió de fundamento a su plan. 3. Estar sujeto a.

underline [ˈʌndəlaɪn] [an-da-lain], *va.* Subrayar, notar las palabras con rayas puestas debajo de ellas.

underling [ˈʌndəlɪŋ] [an-da-lin], *s.* 1. Un agente inferior. 2. Un hombre vil y despreciable; mequetrefe.

underlying [ˌʌndəˈlaɪɪŋ] [an-da-laiin], *a.* Subyacente; fundamental.

undermine [ˌʌndəˈmaɪn] [an-da-main], *va.* 1. Minar, cavar o abrir camino por debajo de la tierra. 2. Zapar, minar, abrir minas. 3. Minar los cimientos o los fundamentos de una cosa. 3. Dañar o injuriar por medios ocultos.

undermost [ˌʌndəˈməʊst] [an-da-moust], *a.* Ínfimo, el más bajo. -*adv.* Debajo de todo.

underneath [ˈʌndəˈniːθ] [an-da-niz], *adv.* Debajo, en la parte inferior o en un paraje inferior.

undernourished [ˈʌndəˈnʌrɪʃt] [an-da-na-risht], *a.* Desnutrido, mal alimentado.

underpaid [ˈʌndəˈpeɪd] [an-da-peid], *pp.* y *a.* Mal pagado, insuficientemente, retribuido.

underpart [ˈʌndəpɑːt] [an-da-part], *s.* Parte inferior o no esencial.

underpass [ˈʌndəpɑːs] [an-da-pas], *s.* Paso bajo, paso inferior (en un camino, calle, etc.).

underpay [ˈʌndəˈpeɪ] [an-da-pei], *va.* Pagar insuficientemente. -*s.* Retribución insuficiente.

underpin [ˌʌndəˈpɪn] [an-da-pin], *va.* Apuntalar, sostener desde abajo, cuando se quita un puntal anterior.

underpinning [ˌʌndəˈpɪnɪŋ] [an-da-pi-nin], *s.* 1. Apuntalamiento (de un edificio). 2. *(Fam.)* Las piernas de una persona.

underpraise [ʌndəˈpreɪs] [an-da-preis], *va.* Alabar una cosa menos de lo que merece.

underprivileged [ˈʌndəˈprɪvɪlɪdʒd] [an-da-pri-vi-li-chid], *s.* y *a.* Necesitado, desamparado, desvalido.

underprize [ˈʌndəˈpraɪz] [an-da-prais], *va.* Despreciar, desestimar, rebajar la estimación o valor de una cosa.

underproduction [ˈʌndəprəˈdʌkʃən] [an-da-pra-dak-shan], *s.* Producción insuficiente.

underprop [ˈʌndəprɒp] [an-da-prop], *va.* Apuntalar.

underrate [ʌndəˈreɪt] [an-da-reit], *va.* Despreciar, no dar a una cosa todo el valor o la estimación que se merece.

underrun [ʌndəˈrʌn] [an-da-ran], *va.* 1. Correr por debajo 2. *(Mar.)* Recorrer; poner un cable debajo de un barco y tirar de él. **To underrun the cables,** *(Mar.)* Recorrer los cables.

underscore [ʌndəˈskɔːʳ] [an-da-skoʳ], *va.* Subrayar, poner una línea bajo una letra o palabra.

under-secretary [ˈʌndəˈsekrətərɪ] [an-da-se-kri-ta-ri], *s.* Subsecretario.

undersell [ˈʌndəˈsel] [an-da-sel], *va.* Vender por menos o más barato que otro.

underset [ʌndəˈset] [an-da-set], *va.* Poner debajo.

undershirt [ʌndəˈʃɜːt] [an-da-shert], *s.* Elástica, camiseta.

undershot [ʌndəˈʃʌt] [an-da-shat], *a.* Impelido por agua que corre debajo; se dice de una rueda hidráulica.

undersign [ʌndəˈsaɪn] [an-da-sain], *va.* Subscribir, firmar al pie de un escrito; se usa principalmente en el participio pasado, *undersigned,* el abajo firmante.

undersized [ˈʌndəˈsaɪzd] [an-da-saisd], *a.* De talla menor que mediana.

underskirt [ˈʌndəskɜːt] [an-da-skert], *s.* 1. Fondo, refajo, enagua. 2. Falda principal de un vestido adornado con sobrefalda.

underslung [ˈʌndəslʌŋ] [an-da-slang], *a.* Colgante, suspendido debajo del bastidor o del eje (de un vehículo).

understand [ʌndəˈstænd] [an-da-stand], *va.* y *vn.* (*pret.* y *pp.* UNDERSTOOD). 1. Entender, percibir, alcanzar, comprender. 2. Entender, saber, ser sabedor, tener claro conocimiento de. 3. Entender, conocer, penetrar. **I understand that,** tengo entendido que. 4. Sobrentender, entender una cosa no expresa, pero que debe suponerse en vista de lo que antecede. **The preposition is understood,** la preposición está sobreentendida. **I gave him to understand,** le di a entender, le hice comprender. **That is understood,** está entendido; por supuesto. **It being understood,** bien entendido. **Be it understood,** entiéndase.

understanding [ʌndəˈstændɪŋ] [an-da-stan-din], *s.* 1. Entendimiento, una de las tres potencias que se atribuyen al alma; comprensión. 2. Inteligencia, capacidad, conocimiento. 3. El espíritu en tanto que concibe. 4. Inteligencia, correspondencia, armonía, amistad, recíproca. **A secret understanding,** inteligencia, concierto o acuerdo secreto. **A good understanding,** buena armonía. **To come to an understanding,** convenirse; quedar o ponerse de acuerdo. -*a.* Inteligencia, perito.

understandingly [ʌndəˈstændɪŋlɪ] [an-da-stan-din-li], *adv.* De una manera inteligente.

understate [ˈʌndəˈsteɪt] [an-da-steit], *va.* 1. Declarar con menos fuerza que la verdad merece. 2. Declarar como menos que lo verdadero.

understatement [ˈʌndəˈsteɪtmənt] [an-da-steit-ment], *s.* Expresión exageradamente moderada.

understood [ʌndəˈstʊd] [an-da-stud], *pret.* y *pp.* del verbo TO UNDERSTAND.

understrapper [ˈʌndəˈstræpəʳ] [an-da-stra-paʳ], *s.* Substituto, agente inferior; el hombre que sirve de instrumento o apoyo de maldades.

understudy [ˈʌndəˈstʌdɪ] [an-da-sta-di], *s.* Actor listo para remplazar a otro en determinado momento.

undertake [ʌndəˈteɪk] [an-da-teik], *va.* y *vn.* 1. Emprender, comenzar alguna cosa que se supone difícil o peligrosa. 2. Emprender, tomar a su cargo, tomar por su cuenta, entrar en una empresa. 3. Emprender, determinarse a hacer o tratar alguna cosa. 4. Oponerse. 5. Responder, salir fiador. 6. Aventurar, arriesgar.

undertaker [ʌndəˈteɪkəʳ] [an-da-tei-kaʳ], *s.* 1. Emprendedor; empresario; particularmente, el que prepara y dirige los entierros; *(Amer.)* zacateca. 2. El que toma a su cargo una empresa o le da comienzo; contratista.

undertaking [ʌndəˈteɪkɪŋ] [an-da-tei-kin], *s.* 1. Empresa, empeño; lo que se ha emprendido. 2. Oficio de preparar y dirigir entierros. 2. *(For.)* Empeño o garantía.

undertone [ʌndəˈtəʊn] [an-da-toun], *s.* 1. Tono bajo la voz. 2. Matiz suavizado de un color. 3. Sentido o indicación que se implica pero no se expresa.

undertook [ʌndəˈtʊk] [an-da-tuk], *pret.* del verbo TO UNDERTAKE.

undertow [ˈʌndətəʊ] [an-da-tau], *s.* Resaca, el movimiento de la ola al retirarse de la playa; también, contracorriente hacia el fondo del mar.

undervaluation [ˈʌndəˌvæljʊˈeɪʃən] [an-da-va-liu-ei-shon], *s.* Estimación muy baja, apreciación de algo en menos de lo que vale.

undervalue [ʌndəˈvæluː] [an-da-va-liu], *va.* Despreciar, dar menos valor a alguna cosa de lo que se debe; apreciar en menos.

undervalue, *s.* Menosprecio, poco valor, escasa estimación.

underwear [ˈʌndəwɛəʳ] [an-da-ueaʳ], *s.* Ropa interior.

underwent [ˈʌndəwent] [an-da-uent], *pret.* del verbo TO UNDERGO.

underwood [ˈʌndəwʊd] [an-da-vud], *s.* Monte bajo, los arbustos o árboles enanos que nacen entre los grandes. *V.* UNDERBRUSH.

underwork [ˈʌndəwɜːk] [an-da-uerk], *va.* Competir con, trabajando por menos jornal. -*vn.* Trabajar menos de lo que se debe; dejar imperfecta alguna cosa por falta de trabajo. -*s.* Trabajo subordinado o de rutina.

underworkman [ˈʌndəˈwɜːkmən] [an-da-uerk-man], *s.* El oficial u obrero que hace un trabajo manual bajo la dirección del maestro o de otro oficial superior a él.

underworld [ˈʌndəwɜːld] [an-da-uerld], *s.* 1. Infierno. 2. Hampa, mundo de vicio, bajos fondos sociales.

underwrite [ˈʌndəraɪt] [an-da-rait], *va.* 1. Subscribir, firmar al pie de un escrito. 2. Asegurar, particularmente contra los riesgos del mar. 3. Obligarse o comprometerse a comprar todas las acciones de una nueva empresa o compañía, a las cuales no se subscribe el público.

underwritten [ˈʌndəˌrɪtn] [an-da-ri-ten], *pp.* de TO UNDERWRITE.

underwriter [ˈʌndəˌraɪtəʳ] [an-da-rai-taʳ], *s.* Asegurador, corporación o persona que asegura mercancías u otras cosas.

underwrote [ˈʌndərəʊt] [an-da-rout], *pret.* del verbo TO UNDERWRITE.

underwrought [ˈʌndəˌrɔːt] [an-da-raut], *pret.* y *pp.* ant. del verbo TO UNDERWORK.

undeserved [ˈʌndɪˈzɜːvd] [an-di-servd], *a.* No merecido, inmerecido.

undeservedly [ˈʌndɪˈzɜːvdlɪ] [an-di-servd-li], *adv.* Sin mérito, sin merecerlo o sin haberlo merecido; injustamente.

undeserving [ˈʌndɪˈzɜːvɪŋ] [an-di-ser-vin], *a.* Indigno de gozar o conseguir una cosa; no benemérito.

undesigned [ˈʌndɪˈsaɪnd] [an-di-saind], *a.* Involuntario, indeliberado, hecho sin intención.

undesigning [ˈʌndɪˈsaɪnɪŋ] [an-di-sai-nin], *a.* Sincero, sencillo; el que obra sin malicia; el que hace una cosa sin objeto o designio determinado.

undesirable [ˈʌndɪˈzaɪrəbl] [an-di-sai-ra-bol], *a.* Que no es deseable, poco deseable.

undesired [ˈʌndɪˈzaɪəd] [an-di-saiad], *a.* No deseado, no solicitado.

undesiring [ˈʌndɪˈzaɪərɪŋ] [an-di-saia-rin], *a.* Negligente, tibio; no deseoso, indiferente.

undesirous [ˈʌndɪˈzaɪrəs] [an-di-sai-ros], *a.* Que no desea, no deseoso.

undestroyed [ˈʌndɪstrɔɪd] [an-dis-troid], *a.* No destruído.

undetected [ˈʌndɪˈtektɪd] [an-di-tek-tid], *a.* Sin ser descubierto.

undetermined [ˈʌndɪˈtɜːmɪnd] [an-di-ter-mind], *a.* Indeterminado, sin fijar, sin decidir; indeciso, incierto.

undeterred [ˈʌndɪˈtɜːd] [an-di-terd], *a.* Que no está asustado; no impedido, no estorbado.

undeviating [ʌnˈdiːvɪeɪtɪŋ] [an-di-viei-tin], *a.* Regular, directo; que sigue su curso natural; sin rodeo, siempre el mismo.

undevoted [ˈʌndɪvaʊtɪd] [an-di-vau-tid], *a.* Opuesto; no dedicado a.

undevout [ˈʌndɪvaʊt] [an-di-vaut], *a.* Indevoto, irreligioso, incrédulo.

undid [ˈʌndɪd] [an-did], *pret.* de TO UNDO.

undigested [ˈʌndaɪˈdʒestɪd] [an-dai-yes-tid], *a.* Indigesto, no digerido; mal ordenado.

undiminished [ˈʌndɪˈmɪnɪʃt] [an-di-mi-nisht], *a.* Entero, no disminuido.

undine [ˈʌndiːn] [an-din], *s. (Mit.)* Ondina, ninfa de las aguas.

undirected [ˈʌndaɪˈrektɪd] [an-dai-rek-tid], *a.* Que no está dirigido o no lleva dirección alguna; que no tiene gobierno; entregado a sí mismo; (carta) sin señas.

undiscerned [ˈʌndɪˈsɜːnd] [an-di-sernd], *a.* No descubierto.

undiscernedly [ˈʌndɪˈsɜːndlɪ] [an-di-sernd-li], *adv.* Ocultamente.

undiscernible [ˈʌndɪˈsɜːnəbl] [an-di-ser-na-bol], *a.* Invisible, imperceptible.

undisciplined [ʌnˈdɪsɪplɪnd] [an-di-si-plind], *a.* Indisciplinado, falto de enseñanza; falto de corrección.

undiscoverable [ˈʌndɪsˈkʌvərəbl] [an-dis-ka-ve-ra-bol], *a.* Que no se puede descubrir; imposible de encontrar.

undiscovered [ˈʌndɪsˈkʌvəd] [an-dis-ka-verd], *a.* No descubierto o visto, escondido.

undisguised [ˈʌndɪsˈgaɪzd] [an-dis-gaisd], *a.* Sin disfraz, cándido, franco, abierto, sencillo.

undismayed [ˈʌndɪsˈmeɪd] [an-dis-meid], *a.* Que no ha perdido el ánimo o valor; que está o se mantiene firme.

undisposed [ˈʌndɪsˈpəʊzd] [an-dis-pousd], *a.* No dispuesto. **Undisposed of,** disponible, no vendido, no decidido de otra manera.

undisputed [ˈʌndɪsˈpjuːtɪd] [an-dis-piu-tid], *a.* Evidente, incontestable, incontrovertible.

undissembled [ˈʌndɪˈsembld] [an-di-sem-blid], *a.* No disimulado, no disfrazado; franco, abierto, ingenuo.

undissolving [ʌnˈdɪzɒlvɪŋ] [an-di-sol-vin], *a.* Que no se derrite.

undistempered [ˈʌndɪsˈtempəd] [an-dis-tem-perd], *a.* 1. Sano, bueno, que no padece enfermedad. 2. Tranquilo, sosegado, que nada tiene que lo inquiete.

undistinguished [ˈʌndɪsˈtɪŋgwɪʃt] [an-dis-tin-güisht], *a.* 1. Indistinto, que no se distingue o no se diferencia. 2. Indistinto, que no percibe clara y distintamente.

undistinguishing [ˈʌndɪsˈtɪŋgwɪʃɪŋ] [an-dis-tin-güi-shin], *a.* Que no distingue o no hace diferencia alguna entre las cosas; que carece de discernimiento.

undisturbed [ˈʌndɪsˈtɜːbd] [an-dis-terbd], *a.* Que no está turbado, inquietado; sin alteración ni desarreglo; quieto, tranquilo, no agitado; impasible, que por nada se turba.

undivided [ˈʌndɪˈvaɪdɪd] [an-di-vai-did], *a.* Indiviso, entero. **An undivided estate,** una propiedad indivisa.

undivulged [ˈʌndɪˈvʌldʒɪd] [an-di-val-yid], *a.* Secreto.

undo [ʌnˈduː] [an-du], *va. (pret.* UNDID, *pp.* UNDONE). 1. Deshacer, anular, el efecto de; reponer en el estado anterior. 2. Arruinar, perder; causar pesadumbre a. 3. Desatar, desliar; desarmar, desmontar. 4. No hacer, dejar sin hacer. **He intends to undo me,** me quiere perder. **To come undone,** deshacerse, desatarse. **To leave undone,** no hacer, dejar de hacer. **To remain undone,** quedar por hacer. **I am undone,** estoy perdido, estoy arruinado.

undock [ˈʌnˈdɒk] [an-dok], *va.* Sacar un buque del dique.

undoing [ˈʌnˈduːɪŋ] [an-duin], *s.* 1. Acción de deshacer. 2. Ruina, pérdida.

undone [ˈʌnˈdʌn] [an-dan], *pp.* del verbo UNDO.

undoubted [ʌnˈdaʊtɪd] [an-dau-tid], *a.* No dudado, evidente, fuera de duda, cierto.

undoubtedly [ʌnˈdaʊtɪdlɪ] [an-dau-tid-li], *adv.* Indudablemente.

undrawn [ʌnˈdrɔːn] [an-dron], *pp.* No sacado; no atraído, no arrastrado; que no ha sido sorteado (billete de lotería, etc.).

undreamed [ʌnˈdriːmd] [an-drimd], *a.* Impensado, inesperado. **Undreamed of,** inopinado.

undress [ʌnˈdres] [an-dres], *va.* 1. Desnudar, quitar la ropa. 2. Desvendar, quitar el vendaje de (una herida, etc.). *-vn.* Desnudarse.

undress, *s.* Paños menores, ropa de levantarse; ropa de casa. **To be in an undress,** *(Fam.)* estar de trapillo. **Undress,** *(Mil.)* uniforme diario, traje de cuartel. *-a.* Perteneciente al traje diario; de aquí, informal.

undried [ʌnˈdraɪd] [an-draid], *a.* Que aún no está seco o no secado; verde (frutos, etc.).

undriven [ʌnˈdrɪvn] [an-dri-ven], *a.* Quieto, fijo; no impelido hacia ningún lado.

undue [ʌnˈdjuː] [an-diu], *a.* 1. Indebido, más que suficiente, excesivo, desmedido. 2. Irregular; ilícito, injusto, contra razón, ley o costumbre. 3. Que no es debido, no vencido.

undulate [ˈʌndjʊleɪt] [an-diu-leit], *vn.* Undular, ondear o hacer ondas, presentar la apariencia de una undulación. *-va.* Hacer ondear.

undulation [ˌʌndjʊˈleɪʃən] [an-diu-lei-shon], *s.* Undulación, movimiento a modo de las onds.

undulatory [ˈʌndjʊlətərɪ] [an-diu-la-to-ri], *a.* Undulatorio; se dice del movimiento semejante al de las ondas.

unduly [ˈʌnˈdjuːlɪ] [an-diu-li], *adv.* Indebidamente; ilícitamente.

undutiful [ˈʌnˈdjʊtɪfəl] [an-diu-ti-ful], *a.* Inobediente, desobediente, que falta a sus deberes. **An undutiful son,** un mal hijo, un hijo desobediente.

undutifully [ˈʌnˈdjʊtɪfəlɪ] [an-diu-ti-fu-li], *adv.* Inobedientemente, con inobediencia; sin respeto, contra su obligación.

undying [ʌnˈdaɪɪŋ] [an-daiin], *a.* Imperecedero, que no muere; inmortal.

unearth [ʌnˈɜːθ] [an-erz], *va.* Sacar de la tierra, desarragiar; revelar, descubrir.

unearthly [ʌnˈɜːθlɪ] [an-erz-li], *a.* Que no xes terrenal, sobrenatural, aterrador, que infunde miedo, espantoso.

uneasily [ʌnˈiːzɪlɪ] [an-i-si-li], *adv.* Inquietamente, incómodamente, con mucho trabajo; penosamente.

uneasiness [ʌnˈiːzɪnɪs] [an-i-si-nes], *s.* Inquietud, desasosiego, incomodidad, disgusto, malestar; pena, pesadumbre.

uneasy [ʌnˈiːzɪ] [an-i-si], *a.* 1. Inquieto, cuidadoso, ansioso, desasosegado. 2. Impertienente, molesto, enfadoso, incómodo. 3. Embarazado, incomodado, que carece de gracia, desazonado. 4. Difícil de efectuar, dificultoso.

uneaten [ʌnˈiːtn] [an-i-ten], *a.* No comido, no devorado.

unedifying [ˈʌnˈedɪfaɪɪŋ] [an-e-di-faiin], *a.* Que no edifica con su ejemplo.

uneducated [ˈʌnˈedjʊkeɪtɪd] [an-e-diu-kei-tid], *a.* Falto de educación, sin instrucción; ignorante.

uneffaced [ˈʌnˈfeɪst] [an-i-feist], *a.* Que no está borrado o cancelado.

unemployed [ˈʌnˈɪmplɔɪd] [an-im-ploid], *a.* 1. Desocupado, sin ocupación, sin empleo; ocioso. 2. No empleado, no invertido, que no produce.

unencumbered [ˈʌnɪnˈkʌmbəd] [an-in-kam-berd], *a.* Sin trabas; exento de cargas de cualquier clase.

unending [ʌnˈendɪŋ] [an-en-din], *a.* Sin fin, perpetuo, eterno.

unendowed [ˈʌnɪnˈdəʊd] [an-in-doud], *a.* Indotado.

unenduring [ˈʌnɪnˈdjʊərɪŋ] [an-in-diua-rin], *a.* Poco duradero, de corta duración.

unengaged [ˈʌnɪnˈgeɪdʒd] [an-in-gueich], *a.* Desocupado, libre, no comprometido.

unenjoyed [ˈʌnɪnˈjɔɪd] [an-in-yoid], *a.* Que no se goza o no se ha gozado.

unenjoying [ˈʌnɪnˈjɔɪɪŋ] [an-in-yoiin], *a.* Que no goza.

unenligtened [ˈʌnɪnˈlaɪtnd] [an-in-lai-tend], *a.* No iluminado.

unenterprising [ˈʌnˈentəpraɪzɪŋ] [an-en-ta-prai-sin], *a.* Que no es emprendedor.

unenviable [ˈʌnˈenvɪəbl] [an-en-via-bol], *a.* Poco envidiable.

unenvied [ˈʌnˈenvɪəd] [an-en-vid], *a.* No envidiado, que no causa envidia.

unequable [ˈʌnˈiːkwəbl] [an-i-kua-bol], *a.* Desigual, variable, irregular.

unequal [ˈʌnˈiːkwəl] [an-i-kual], *a.* 1. Desigual, que no es igual en extensión, duración o propiedades. 2. Ineficaz, insuficiente, inferior. 3. Desporporcionado: de aquí, no equitativo, injusto, parcial. 4. Falto de uniformidad. 5. *(Bot.)* Poco simétrico.

unequalled [ˈʌnˈiːkwəld] [an-i-kuald], *a.* Sin igual, sin semejante, sinpar, incomparable.

unequally [ˈʌnˈiːkwəlɪ] [an-i-kua-li], *adv.* Desigualmente; fuera de proporción, insuficientemente.

unequivocal [ˈʌnɪˈkwɪvəkəl] [an-i-kui-vo-kal, *a.* Inequívoco, que no admite duda o equivocación.

unerring [ˈʌnˈɜːrɪŋ] [an-e-rin], *a.* Infalible, sumamente cierto y seguro, inerrable.

uneringly [ˈʌnˈɜːrɪŋlɪ] [an-e-rin-li], *adv.* Infaliblemente, con toda seguridad y certidumbre.

unessayed [ˈʌnˈseɪd] [an-i-seid], *a.* No ensayado; no intentado.

unesteemed [ˈʌnɪsˈtiːmd] [an-is-timd], *a.* No estimado o apreciado.

uneven [ˈʌnˈiːvən] [an-i-ven], *a.* 1. Desigual, que no es llano, escabroso, barrancoso, quebrado. 2. Desigual, que no corresponde o conviene con otra cosa: que no es regular o uniforme. 3. Impar, no divisible por dos.

unevenly [ˈʌnˈiːvənlɪ] [an-i-ven-li], *adv.* Desigualmente.

unevenness [ˈʌnˈiːvənnɪs] [an-i-ven-nes], *s.* 1. Desigualdad, escabrosidad o aspereza ocasionada por no estar llana una cosa; falta de regularidad. 2. Desigualdad, inconstancia, poca firmeza o estabilidad.

uneventful [ˈʌnɪˈventfʊl] [an-i-vent-ful], *a.* Exento de acontecimientos notables; tranquilo.

uneventfully [ˈʌnɪˈventfʊlɪ] [an-i-vent-fu-li], *adv.* Tranquilamente, sin suceso notable, monótonamente.

unexacted [ˈʌnɪgˈsæktɪd] [an-ik-sak-tid], *a.* Que no es exigido; que ha sido producido naturalmente y sin auxilio del arte.

unexamined [ˈʌnɪgˈsəmaɪnd] [an-ik-sa-maind], *a.* No examinado.

unexampled [ˈʌnɪgˈzɑːmpld] [an-ik-sam-peld], *a.* Que no tiene igual, sin ejemplo, único en su línea.

unexceptionable [ˌʌnɪgˈsepʃnəbl] [an-ik-sep-sho-na-bol], *a.* Libre de toda objeción o reparo; irreprensible, irrecusable.

unexceptional [ˈʌnɪgˈsepʃnəl] [an-ik-sep-sho-nal], *a.* Que no hace excepción; ordinario, usual o corriente.

unexcised [ˈʌnɪgˈsaɪst] [an-ik-saist], *a.* 1. No cortado. 2. Que no está sujeto al derecho de sisa.

unexempt [ˈʌnɪgˈsempt] [an-ik-sempt], *a.* No exento, sujeto.

unexpanded [ˈʌnɪkˈspændɪd] [an-ik-pan-did], *a.* Encogido, no extendido.

unexpected [ˈʌnɪksˈpektɪd] [an-iks-pek-tid], *a.* Inesperado, impensado, no prevenido, inopinado, repentino, que no se esperaba.

unexpectedly [ˈʌnɪksˈpektɪdlɪ] [an-iks-pek-tid-li], *adv.* De repente, impensadamente, inesperadamente, inopinadamente, sin pensarlo; de improviso.

unexpectedness [ˈʌnɪksˈpektɪdnɪs] [an-iks-pek-tid-nes], *s.* Repentino, lance inesperado o imprevisto.

unexpired [ˈʌnɪksˈpaɪəd] [an-iks-paiad], *a.* No acabado, no concluido.

unexplored [ˈʌnɪksˈplɔːd] [an-iks-plord], *a.* Inexplorado, no conocido, no descubierto.

unexported [ˈʌnɪksˈplɔːtɪd] [an-iks-por-tid], *a.* No extraído o llevado fuera del país.

unexposed [ˈʌnɪksˈpəʊzd] [an-iks-poust], *a.* No expuesto (a la luz, etc.)

unfaded [ʌnˈfeɪdɪd] [an-fei-did], *a.* No marchito, no ajado; que conserva sus colores o su frescura.

unfading [ʌnˈfeɪdɪŋ] [an-fei-din], *a.* Inmarcesible, que no pasa; imperecedero, imperdible.

unfailing [ʌnˈfeɪlɪŋ] [an-fei-lin], *a.* 1. Inagotable, que produce siempre. 2. Seguro, cierto, que no puede faltar, infalible.

unfair [ˈʌnˈfɛəʳ] [an-feaʳ], *a.* Doble, falso; injusto; que no es hornado en sus tratos, que obra de mala fe.

unfairly [ʌnˈfɛəlɪ] [an-fea-li], *adv.* De mala fe; injustamente, con doblez.

unfairness [ʌnˈfɛənɪs] [an-fea-nes], *s.* Falta de equidad; deslealtad, mala fe.

unfaithful [ʌnˈfeɪθfʊl] [an-feiz-ful], *a.* Infiel, falto de fe; pérfido, desleal, traidor. **The unfaithful,** los incrédulos, los infieles.

unfaithfully [ʌnˈfeɪθfʊlɪ] [an-feiz-fu-li], *adv.* Infielmente, deslealmente, pérfidamente.

unfaithfulness [ʌnˈfeɪθfʊlnɪs] [an-feiz-ful-nes], *s.* Infidelidad, perfidida, alevosía, deslealtad.

unfallen [ʌnˈfɔːln] [an-fo-len], *a.* Que no ha caído, que está en pie.

unfalteringly [ʌnˈfɔːltərɪŋlɪ] [an-fol-te-rin-li], *adv.* Sin vacilar.

unfamiliar [ʌnfəˈmɪlɪəʳ] [an-fa-mi-liaʳ], *a.* Poco familiar, poco común; no conocido familiarmente.

unfashionable [ʌnˈfæʃnəbl] [an-fa-sho-na-bol], *a.* Que no es de moda, que no sigue la moda; opuesto a la moda, raro, singular.

unfashionableness [ʌnˈfæʃnəblnɪs] [an-fa-sho-na-bol-nes], *s.* La condición de no seguir los caprichos de la moda, llaneza en el vestir; el vestir a la antigua.

unfashionably [ʌnˈfæʃnəblɪ] [an-fa-sho-na-bli], *adv.* Contra la moda.

unfashioned [ʌnˈfæʃnənd] [an-fa-shond], *a.* Informe, tosco, basto, que está sin limar o sin pulir.

unfasten [ʌnˈfɑːsn] [an-fa-sen], *va.* Desatar, soltar, aflojar.

unfathered [ʌnˈfɑːðəd] [an-fa-derd], *a* Huérfano de padre; que carece de autor.

unfathomable [ʌnˈfæðəməbl] [an-fa-do-ma-bol], *a.* Insondable, impenetrable, que no tiene fondo.

unfathomably [ʌnˈfæðəməblɪ] [an-fa-do-ma-bli], *adv.* De un modo insondable.

unfavorable [ʌnˈfeɪvərəbl] [an-fei-va-ra-bol], *a.* Contrario, adverso, no favorable, no propicio.

unfavorably [ˈʌnˈfeɪvərəblɪ] [an-fei-va-ra-bli], *adv.* Contrariamente, de una manera poco favorable.

unfearing [ˈʌnˈfɛərɪŋ] [an-fea-rin], *a.* Intrépido, animoso, sin temor.

unfeasible [ʌnˈfiːzɪbl] [an-fi-si-bol], *a.* No hacedero, no factible, impracticable.

unfed [ʌnˈfed] [an-fed], *a.* Falto de alimento, no nutrido.

unfeeling [ʌnˈfiːlɪŋ] [an-fi-lin], *a.* Insensible, apático; duro de corazón, cruel.

unfeelingly [ʌnˈfiːlɪŋlɪ] [an-fi-lin-li], *adv.* Cruelmente; insensiblemente.

unfeigned [ʌnˈfeɪnd] [an-feind], *a.* Que no es fingido, real, verdadero, genuino; ingenuo.

unfeignedly [ʌnˈfeɪnədlɪ] [an-fei-nid-li], *adv.* Ingenuamente, sinceramente; verdaderamente.

unfelt [ʌnˈfelt] [an-felt], *a.* No percibido, no sentido.

unfenced [ʌnˈfenst] [an-fenst], *a.* Abierto, no cercado, que no tiene defensa.

unfermented [ˈʌnfəˈmentɪd] [an-fa-men-tid], *a.* No fermentado.

unfertile [ʌnˈfɜːtaɪl] [an-fer-tail], a. Infecundo, estéril.

unfetter [ʌnˈfetəʳ] [an-fe-taʳ], va. Desencadenar, quitar los grillos a, poner en libertad.

unfigured [ʌnˈfɪgəd] [an-fi-gad], a. Lo que no representa forma o figura animal.

unfilled [ʌnˈfɪld] [an-fild], a. Vacío, no lleno; vacante.

unfinished [ʌnˈfɪnɪʃt] [an-fi-nisht], a. Incompleto, imperfecto, no acabado, no concluido.

unfit [ʌnˈfɪt] [an-fit], a. Desconveniente, nada apto, poco propio para; poco hecho para; inepto, incapaz. (Se usa a menudo con *for* o *to*).

unfit, va. Inhabilitar, hacer incapaz o inhábil para alguna cosa.

unfitly [ʌnˈfɪtlɪ] [an-fit-li], adv. Impropiamente, incongruentemente; sin aptitud.

unfitness [ʌnˈfɪtnɪs] [an-fit-nes], s. Ineptitud, insuficiencia, falta de aptitud o de disposición, impropiedad.

unfitting [ʌnˈfɪtɪŋ] [an-fi-tin], a. Impropio, poco o nada a propósito, desconvenible.

unfix [ʌnˈfɪks] [an-fiks], va. 1. Soltar, aflojar. 2. Liquidar, deshelar.

unfixed [ʌnˈfɪkst] [an-fikst], a. Errante, vacilante; irresoluto, voluble.

unflagging [ʌnˈflægɪŋ] [an-fla-guin], a. Persistente, que no se cansa.

unfledged [ˈʌnfledʒ] [an-fledch], a. Implume, que no tiene todavía plumas; inmaturo, inexperimentado.

unfleshed [ʌnˈfleʃt] [an-flesht], a. No encarnizado; incruento, que no ha probado aún la sangre.

unflinching [ʌnˈflɪntʃɪŋ] [an-flin-chin], a. Que no retrocede; resuelto, no vencido.

unfold [ʌnˈfəʊld] [an-fould], va. 1. Desplegar, desdoblar, descoger, desarrollar, abrir una cosa plegada. 2. Revelar, descubrir, poner en claro, manifestar lo que está oculto, secreto o escondido; desencerrar. -vn. Abrirse, descubrirse, desarrollarse.

unforbearing [ʌnfɔːˈbeərɪŋ] [an-for-bea-rin], a. Intolerante, poco indulgente, impaciente.

unforbid [ʌnfɔːˈbɪd] [an-for-bid], **unforbidden** [ʌnfɔːˈbɪdn] [an-for-bi-den], a. Permitido, no prohibido.

unforced [ʌnˈfɔːst] [an-forst], a. Sin estar obligado, libre, espontáneo, voluntario, natural, no fingido.

unforeseen [ˈʌnfɔːˈsiːn] [an-for-sin], a. Imprevisto, inopinado, no previsto.

unforgetful [ʌnfɔːˈgetfʊl] [an-for-get-ful], a. No olvidadizo; que no olvida.

unforgettable [ˈʌnfəˈgetəbl] [an-for-ge-ta-bol], a. Inolvidable, imperecedero.

unforgiving [ˈʌnfəˈgɪvɪŋ] [an-for-gui-vin], a. Duro, inexorable, implacable.

unforgotten [ʌnfɔːˈgɒtn] [an-for-go-ten], a. No olvidado, presente, fijo en la memoria.

unformed [ˈʌnˈfɔːmd] [an-formd], a. 1. Informe, sin forma regular, falto de estructura. 2. Crudo, de un carácter no completamente desarrollado. 3. *(Biol.)* No organizado, sin estructura. **Unformed stars,** estrellas que se hallan fuera de una constelación.

unfortified [ʌnˈfɔːtɪfaɪd] [an-for-ti-faid], a. 1. No fortificado, que no tiene murallas o fortificaciones. 2. Débil, endeble.

unfortunate [ʌnˈfɔːtʃnɪt] [an-forch-nit], a. Desafortunado, infortunado, desgraciado, infeliz.

unfortunately [ʌnˈfɔːtʃnɪtlɪ] [an-forch-nit-li], adv. Por desgracia, infelizmente.

unfortunateness [ʌnˈfɔːtʃnɪtnɪs] [an-forch-nit-nes], s. Infortunio, desgracia, desventura.

unfought [ʌnˈfaʊt] [an-faut], a. Sin pelear o sin haber peleado. **Unfought for,** no disputado, sin lucha.

unfound [ʌnˈfaʊnd] [an-faund], a. No hallado, imposible de hallarse.

unfounded [ʌnˈfaʊndɪd] [an-faun-did], a. Infundado, sin fundamento. 2. No fundado ni establecido.

unframed [ʌnˈfreɪmd] [an-freimd], a. Sin forma o figura.

unfraught [ʌnˈfrɔːt] [an-frot], a. No cargado, exento de carga.

unfreezable [ʌnˈfriːzəbl] [an-fri-sa-bol], a. Incogelable.

unfrequent [ʌnˈfrɪkwent] [an-fri-kuent], Poco o nada frecuente. V. INFREQUENT.

unfrequented [ˈʌnfrɪˈkwentɪd] [an-fri-kuen-tid], a. Solitario, poco o nada frecuentado.

unfrequently [ʌnˈfrɪkwentlɪ] [an-fri-kuent-li], adv. Rara vez, raramente, por maravilla.

unfriended [ʌnˈfrrendɪd] [an-fren-did], a. Desamparado, sin protección, sin amigos.

unfriendliness [ʌnˈfredlɪnɪs] [an-frend-li-nes], s. Falta de amistad, falta de benevolencia.

unfriendly [ʌnˈfrendlɪ] [an-frend-li], a. 1. Áspero, poco amistoso, poco atento, seco, nada afable, enemigo. 2. Poco favorable, poco propicio, perjudicial.

unfrock [ˈʌnˈfrɒk] [an-frok], va. Exclaustrar, privar del carácter eclesiástico.

unfruitful [ˈʌnˈfruːtfʊl] [an-frut-ful], a. 1. Estéril, infructífero, que no da o no produce fruto. 2. Lo que no produce el fruto que se esperaba de ello; infructuoso.

unfruitfulness [ˈʌnˈfruːtfʊlnɪs] [an-frut-ful-nes], s. Esterilidad, infecundidad; infructuosidad.

unfulfilled [ˈʌnfʊlˈfɪld] [an-ful-fild], a. No cumplido, no observado.

unfunded [ˈʌnˈfaʊndɪd] [an-fand-did], a. No consoliddo, sin fondos para el pago de los intereses.

unfurl [ʌnˈfɜːl] [an-ferl], va. Desplegar, desdoblar, extender. **To unfurl the sails,** *(Mar.)* Desaferrar las velas.

unfurnish [ʌnˈfɜːnɪʃ] [an-fer-nish], va. 1. Desamueblar, quitar los muebles; desprovisto.

ungainliness [ʌnˈgeɪnlɪnɪs] [an-guein-li-nes], s. Falta de gracia, torpeza.

ungainly [ʌnˈgeɪnlɪ] [an-guein-li], a. Desmañado, falto de gracia, torpe, poco diestro, pesado.

ungear [ʌnˈgɪəʳ], [an-guiaʳ], va. Desengranar, desconectar, desembragar.

ungenerous [ʌnˈdʒenərəs] [an-ye-ne-ros], a. Falto de generosidad, indigno, innoble, bajo.

ungenerously [ʌnˈdʒenərəslɪ] [an-ye-ne-ros-li], adv. Sin generosidad; indignamente, bajamente.

ungenial [ʌnˈdʒiːnɪəl] [an-yi-nial], a. Malsano, hablando de lo que hace daño a la salud; muy riguroso, hablando del clima; poco favorable a la naturaleza, a la constitución, a los hábitos adquiridos, etc.; áspero, rudo, brusco.

ungenialness [ʌnˈdʒiːnɪəlnɪs] [an-yi-nial-nes], s. La falta de conformidad en las cosas con la salud, constitución, hábitos adquiridos, etc.

ungenteel [ʌndʒenˈtiːl] [an-yen-til], a. Rudo, descortés, bajo, tosco, grosero, de mal tono, de mal gusto.

ungentle [ʌnˈdʒentl] [an-yen-tel], a. Áspero, riguroso, severo, intratable, duro de genio.

ungentlemanlike [ʌnˈdʒentlmənlaɪk] [an-yen-tel-man-laik], a. Indigno de un hombre bien criado; que no conviene a un caballero.

ungentleness [ʌnˈdʒentlnɪs] [an-yen-tel-nes], s. Dureza de genio, rudeza, aspereza, severidad, falta de amabilidad en el trato.

ungently [ʌnˈdʒentlɪ] [an-yen-tli], adv. Ásperamente, rudamente, con severidad.

ungifted [ʌnˈgɪftɪd] [an-guif-tid], a. Que no está dotado de talento.

ungird [ʌnˈgɜːd] [an-guerd], va. Desceñir, decinchar.

ungirt [ʌnˈgɜːt] [an-guert], a. Desceñido, suelto o sin atar.

ungiving [ʌnˈgɪvɪŋ] [an-gui-vin], a. Que no da nada.

unglazed [ʌnˈgleɪzd] [an-gleisd], a. 1. Que no tiene vidrieras o sin vidrieras: se dice de las ventanas. 2. No encharolado; no barnizado; no satinado (papel); que está sin vidriar: se dice de las vasijas de barro.

ungodliness [ʌnˈgɒdlɪnɪs] [an-god-li-nes], s. Impiedad, irreligión, falta de piedad y religión.

ungodly [ʌnˈgɒdlɪ] [an-god-li], a. Impío, malvado, irreligioso, profano.

ungorged [ʌnˈgɜːdʒd] [an-gorchd], a. Insaciable; no saciado.

ungovernable [ʌnˈɡʌvənəbl] [an-ga-ver-na-bol], *a.* Indomable, ingobernable, indisciplinable, incapaz de gobierno, de dirección o de disciplina.

ungovernableness [ʌnˈɡʌvənəblnɪs] [an-ga-va-na-bol-nes], *s.* Indocilidad.

ungoverned [ʌnˈɡʌvənd] [an-ga-vernd], *a.* Desgoberando, desarreglado, desenfrenado, descomedido, desaforado; que no guarda regla ni orden.

ungraceful [ʌnˈɡreɪsfʊl] [an-greis-ful], *a.* Tosco, desairado, desgraciado, falto de gracia o de gentileza.

ungracefulness [ʌnˈɡreɪsfʊlnɪs] [an-greis-ful-nes], *s.* Tosquedad, falta de gracia o de gentileza.

ungracious [ʌnˈɡreɪʃəs] [an-grei-shos], *a.* Desagradable, repugnante, ofensivo, chocante; falto de cortesía.

ungraciously [ʌnˈɡreɪʃəslɪ] [an-grei-shos-li], *adv.* Malvadamente, groseramente, sin gracia.

ungraciousness [ʌnˈɡreɪʃəsnɪs] [an-grei-shos-nes], *s.* Descortesía, bellaquería, grosería.

ungrammatical [ˌʌnɡrəˈmætɪkəl] [an-gra-ma-ti-kal], *a.* Incorrecto, contrario a las reglas de la gramática.

ungranted [ʌnˈɡræntɪd] [an-gran-tid], *a.* No concedido, no dado, no otorgado.

ungrateful [ʌnˈɡreɪtfʊl] [an-greit-ful], *a.* 1. Desagradecido, ingrato, que olvida o desprecia los beneficios recibidos. 2. Desagradable, no agradable. 3. Ingrato; dícese del terreno poco fecundo.

ungratefully [ʌnˈɡreɪtfəlɪ] [an-greit-fu-li], *adv.* 1. Ingratamente, desagradecidamente. 2. Desagradablemente, de mala gana, sin gusto.

ungratefulness [ʌnˈɡreɪtfəlnɪs] [an-greit-ful-nes], *s.* Ingratitud, desagradecimiento; desagrado.

ungratified [ʌnˈɡrætɪfaɪd] [an-gra-ti-faid], *a.* No satisfecho, no contentado.

ungrounded [ʌnˈɡraʊndɪd] [an-graun-did], *a.* Infundado, que no tiene razón ni fundamento.

ungrudgingly [ʌnˈɡrʌdʒɪŋlɪ] [an-grad-chin-li], *adv.* De buena gana, con gusto, voluntariamente.

unguarded [ʌnˈɡɑːdɪd] [an-gar-did], *a.* 1. Desguarnecido, sin guarda o sin defensa. 2. Descuidado, negligente; incauto, indiscreto.

unguent [ˈʌŋɡwənt] [an-güent], *s.* Ungüento.

unguicular [ʌnˈɡjʊɪkjʊləʳ] [an-güi-kiu-laʳ], *a.* Unguiculado, que tiene los dedos terminados por uñas.

unguided [ʌnˈɡaɪdɪd] [an-gai-did], *a.* No dirigido, no gobernado, sin guía.

ungulate [ʌnˈɡjʊleɪt] [an-giu-leit], *a.* y *s.* Ungulado (animal) que tiene casco o pesuña.

unhair [ʌnˈhɛəʳ] [an-jeaʳ], *a.* Profano, impío; profanado.

unhammered [ʌnˈhæməd] [an-ja-merd], *a.* No martillado.

unhand [ʌnˈhænd] [an-jand], *va.* Soltar las manos.

unhandily [ʌnˈhændɪlɪ] [an-jan-di-li], *adv.* Poco diestramente, desmañadamente.

unhandsome [ʌnˈhænsəm] [an-jan-som], *a.* 1. Feo, desaliñado, falto de gracia o hermosura. 2. Innoble, bajo; doble, falso.

unhandsomely [ʌnˈhænsəmlɪ] [an-jan-som-li], *adv.* 1. Groseramente, sin gracia; feamente, con fealdad, mal. 2. Con doblez; groseramente.

unhandsomeness [ʌnˈhænsəmnɪs] [an-jan-som-nes], *s.* 1. Fealdad, falta de belleza. 2. Tosquedad, falta de gentileza. 3. Doblez; grosería.

unhandy [ʌnˈhændɪ] [an-jan-di], *a.* Desmañado, torpe, poco hábil, poco diestro.

unhang [ʌnˈhæŋ] [an-jang], *va.* Descolgar, quitar las colgaduras; desprender (tapicerías). **To unhang the tiller,** desmontar la caña del timón.

unhappily [ʌnˈhæpɪlɪ] [an-ja-pi-li], *adv.* Infelizmente, miserablemente, mal, por desgracia.

unhappiness [ʌnˈhæpɪnɪs] [an-ja-pi-nes], *s.* Infelicidad, desgracia, infortunio, mala ventura; miseria, desdicha, calamidad.

unhappy [ʌnˈhæpɪ] [an-ja-pi], *a.* 1. Infeliz, desgraciado, desdichado (persons, things). 2. Desafortunado, desventurado (persons).

unharmed [ʌnˈhɑːmd] [an-jarmd], *a.* Ileso, sano y salvo, que no ha recibido ningún daño.

unharmful [ʌnˈhɑːmfʊl] [an-jarm-ful], *a.* Inocente, que no es nocivo o no hace daño.

unharness [ʌnˈhɑːnɪs] [an-jar-nes], *va.* 1. Desenjaezar, quitar los jaeces a los caballos. 2. Quitar las guarniciones a las bestias de carga. 3. Desarmar, quitar la armadura.

unhasp [ʌnˈhæsp] [an-jasp], *va.* Soltar el pestillo.

unhatched [ʌnˈhætʃɪd] [an-ja-chid], *a.* 1. No salido del cascarón. 2. No traslúcido, no descubierto, que no ha salido a la luz.

unhealed [ʌnˈhiːld] [an-jild], *a.* No curado.

unhealthful [ʌnˈhelθfʊl] [an-jelz-ful], *a.* Malsano, insalubre, que no es provechoso para la salud o es perjudicial a ella.

unhealthiness [ʌnˈhelθɪnɪs] [an-jel-zi-nes], *s.* Insalubridad, calidad de malsano o contrario a la salud; la falta de salud.

unhealthy [ʌnˈhelθɪ] [an-jel-zi], *a.* 1. Enfermizo, achacoso, valetudinario, falto de salud. 2. Insalubre, malsano. *V.* UNEHALTHFUL.

unheard [ʌnˈhɜːd] [an-jerd], *a.* 1. Que no se oye o no se ha oído. 2. Desconocido, oscuro, sin fama. **Unheard of,** inaudito, extraño, singular, nunca oído; sin ejemplo.

unheated [ʌnˈhiːtɪd] [an-ji-tid], *a.* No calentado, frío.

unheeded [ʌnˈhiːdɪd] [an-ji-did], *a.* No atendido, despreciado: aplícase a aquello de que se hace poco caso.

unheeding [ʌnˈhiːdɪŋ] [an-ji-din], *a.* Negligente, descuidado, distraído.

unhelped [ʌnˈhelpt] [an-jelpt], *a.* Desamparado, no ayudado, no socorrido, sin auxilio.

unhesitating [ʌnˈhezɪteɪtɪŋ] [an-je-si-tei-tin], *a.* Que no vacila; pronto, listo.

unhesitatingly [ʌnˈhezɪteɪtɪŋlɪ] [an-je-si-tei-tin-li], *adv.* Sin vacilar; prontamente.

unhewn [ʌnˈhjuːn] [an-jiun], *a.* Tosco, basto, bruto o en bruto; no pulido.

unhindered [ʌnˈhɪndəd] [an-jin-dad], *a.* Libre, sin trabas; no opuesto, no impedido.

unhinge [ʌnˈhɪndʒ] [an-jinch], *va.* Desgoznar, desgonzar, desquiciar, sacar de quicio; desordenar, poner en confusión.

unhitch [ʌnˈhɪtʃ] [an-jich], *va.* Descolgar, desatar, desenganchar.

unholiness [ʌnˈhəʊlɪnɪs] [an-jou-li-nes], *s.* Impiedad, profanidad; maldad, perversidad.

unholy [ʌnˈhəʊlɪ] [an-jou-li], *adv.* Profano, impío, malvado, perverso.

unhood [ʌnˈhuːd] [an-jud], *va.* Desganchar, desenganchar, desaferrar; descolgar.

unhoop [ʌnˈhuːp] [an-jup], *va.* Quitar los aros, arcos o cercos de los barriles o toneles.

unhoped [ʌnˈhuːpt] [an-jupt], *a.* Inesperado.

unhopeful [ʌnˈhuːpfʊl] [an-joup-ful], *a.* Que no ofrece buenas esperanzas; falto de grandes esperanzas.

unhorse [ʌnˈhɔːs] [an-jors], *va.* Botar o sacar de la silla al jinete, hacerle perder los estribos.

unhouse [ʌnˈhaʊs] [an-jaus], *va.* Desalojar, echar a uno de la casa o alojamiento.

unhuman [ʌnˈhjuːmən] [an-jiu-man], *a.* Inhumano. *V.* INHUMAN.

unhumbled [ʌnˈhʌmbld] [an-jam-beld], *a.* No humillado; altanero, sin pudor, sin vergüenza.

unhurt [ʌnˈhɜːt] [an-jert], *a.* Ileso, sano y salvo, que no ha recibido ningún daño.

unhurtful [ʌnˈhɜːtfʊl] [an-jert-ful], *a.* Inocente.

unhurtfully [ʌnˈhɜːtfəlɪ] [an-jert-fa-li], *adv.* Inocentemente.

unhygienic [ˈʌnhaɪˈdʒiːnɪk] [an-jai-yi-nik], *a.* Antihigiénico.

unicameral [ˈjuːnɪˈkæmərəl] [iuni-ka-me-ral], *a.* Que consiste de una sola cámara; v. g. un cuerpo legislativo.

unicorn ['juːnɪˈkɔːn] [iuni-korn], *s.* Unicornio, animal fabuloso de un solo cuerno.

unification [ˌjuːnɪfɪˈkeɪʃən] [iuni-fi-kei-shon], *s.* Unificación.

unify ['juːnɪfaɪ] [iuni-fai], *va.* Unificar, unir.

uniform ['juːnɪfɔːm] [iuni-form], *a.* 1. Uniforme, que tiene la misma forma, invariable; semejante. 2. Acorde, armonioso, que conviene con otra cosa; consistente, constante. Uniforme, traje reglamentario que usan los militares y otros empleados. **In full uniform,** de gran uniforme, de gala.

uniformity [juːnɪˈfɔːmɪtɪ] [iuni-for-mi-ti], *s.* Uniformidad, conformidad o igualdad, semejanza de una cosa consigo misma o con otras.

uniformly ['juːnɪfɔːmlɪ] [iuni-form-li], *adv.* Uniformemente, correspondientemente, igual o concordemente, sin variación alguna.

unilateral ['juːnɪˈlætərəl] [iuni-la-te-ral], *a.* Unilateral.

unilateralism ['juːnɪˈlætərəlɪzəm] [iuni-la-te-ra-li-sem], *s.* Opinión unilateral.

unilingual ['juːnɪˈlɪŋgwəl] [iuni-lin-gual], *a.* Monolingüe.

unimaginable [ˌʌnɪˈmædʒməbl] [a-ni-ma-yi-na-bol], *a.* Inimaginable, lo que no se puede imaginar.

unimaginably [ˌʌnɪˈmædʒməblɪ] [a-ni-ma-yi-na-bli], *adv.* De un modo no imaginable.

unimpaired ['ʌnɪmˈpɛəd] [a-nim-pead], *a.* 1. Intacto, ileso, inalterado. 2. No disminuido, no gastado, no usado.

unimpeachable [ˌʌnɪmˈpiːtʃəbl] [a-nim-pi-cha-bol], *a.* Incensurable, intachable; irreprensible; digno de confianza.

unimportant ['ʌnɪmˈpɔːtənt] [a-nim-por-tant], *a.* 1. Nada importante, que nada significa, insignificante. 2. Natural, sin afectación.

unimpressionable ['ʌnɪmˈprezənəbl] [a-nim-pre-sho-na-bol], *a.* Poco impresionable, poco conmovido, que no cede fácilmente a una impresión física o moral.

unimpressive ['ʌnɪmˈpresɪv] [a-nim-pre-siv], *a.* Que no impresiona, mueve o afecta.

unimprovable [ˌʌnɪmˈpruːvəbl] [a-nim-pru-va-bol], *a.* Incapaz de mejora, adelantamiento o reforma.

unimprovableness [ˌʌnɪmˈpruːvəblnɪs] [a-nim-pru-va-bol-nes], *s.* Incapacidad de mejora o reforma.

unimproved [ˌʌnɪmˈpruːvd] [a-nim-pruvd], *a.* No adelantado, no mejorado; inculto.

unindustrious [ˌʌnɪnˈdʌstrɪəs] [an-in-das-trios], *a.* Desidioso, descuidado, dejado.

uninflammable [ˌʌnɪnˈflæmɪbl] [an-in-fla-ma-bol], *a.* Incombustible.

uninfluenced [ˌʌnɪnˈfluənst] [an-in-fluanst], *a.* 1. No influido, libre de toda influencia. 2. Exento de preocupaciones.

uninformed [ˌʌnɪnˈfɔːmd] [an-in-formd], *a.* 1. Inculto, sin cultura, ignorante. 2. Inanimado.

uninhabitable [ˌʌnɪnˈhæbɪtəbl] [an-in-ja-bi-ta-bol], *a.* Inhabitable, que no se puede habitar.

uninhabitableness [ˌʌnɪnˈhæbɪtəblnɪs] [an-in-ja-bi-ta-bol-nes], *s.* El estado de lo que no se puede habitar.

uninhabited [ˌʌnɪnˈhæbɪtɪd] [an-in-ja-bi-tid], *a.* Inhabitado, desierto.

uninjured [ˌʌnɪnˈdʒuəd] [an-in-yuad], *a.* Ileso, no dañado, que no ha recibido ningún daño; no perjudicado, intacto.

uninscribed [ˌʌnɪnsˈkraɪbd] [an-ins-kraibd], *a.* Falto de inscripción.

uninspired [ˌʌnɪnsˈpaɪəd] [an-ins-paiad], *a.* Que no ha recibido ninguna inspiración sobrenatural.

uninstructed [ˌʌnɪnsnˈtrʌktɪd] [an-ins-trak-tid], *a.* Rudo, ignorante, sin educación, sin instrucción.

uninstructive [ˌʌnɪnsˈtrʌktɪv] [an-ins-trak-tiv], *a.* No instructivo.

uninsured ['ʌnɪnˈʃuəd] [an-in-shuad], *a.* Que no está asegurado.

unintelligent [ˌʌnɪnˈtelɪdʒənt] [an-in-te-li-yent], *a.* Falto de inteligencia, ignorante, estúpido.

unintelligibility [ˌʌnɪnˌtelɪdʒəˈbɪlɪtɪ] [an-in-te-li-ya-bi-li-ti], *s.* La incapacidad de ser entendido; oscuridad impenetrable; calidad de ininteligible.

unintelligible [ˌʌnɪnˈtelɪdʒəbl] [an-in-te-li-ya-bol], *a.* Ininteligible.

unintelligibly [ˌʌnɪnˈtelɪdʒəblɪ] [an-in-te-li-ya-bli], *adv.* De un modo o manera ininteligible.

unintentional ['ʌnɪnˈtenʃən] [an-in-ten-sho-nal], *a.* Hecho sin intención, objeto, plan o designio.

unintentionally ['ʌnɪnˈtenʃənlɪ] [an-in-ten-sho-na-li], *adv.* Sin intención, sin quererlo, involuntariamente.

uninterested [ʌnˈɪntrɪstɪd] [an-in-tris-tid], *a.* Desinteresado.

uninterrupted ['ʌnˌɪntəˈrʌptɪd] [an-in-te-rap-tid], *a.* Continuo, no interrumpido, sin interrupción.

uninterruptedly ['ʌnˌɪntəˈrʌptɪdlɪ] [an-in-te-rap-tid-li], *adv.* Sin interrupción, continuamente.

unintroduced [ʌnˈɪntrədjuːst] [an-in-tro-diust], *a.* Entrometido, intruso, no presentado de un modo regular.

uninvited ['ʌnɪnˈvaɪtɪd] [an-in-vai-tid], *a.* No convidado, no rogado.

union ['juːnjən] [iu-nion], *s.* 1. Unión, el acto de unir una cosa con otra; junta, reunión. 2. Unión, conformidad, concordia de los ánimos o dictámenes; confederación, liga o asociación; gremio de oficios. 3. Estado matrimonial. 4. Proporción, simetría, armonía. 5. Emblema de unión representado en un pabellón. 6. Unión, conexión para cañones o varillas. **Union Jack,** pabellón de la Gran Bretaña e Irlanda reunidas.

unionism ['juːnjənɪzm] [iu-nio-ni-sem], *s.* 1. Unionismo. 2. Sindicalismo.

unionist ['juːnjənɪst] [iu-nio-nist], *a.* Unionista.

unipersonal ['juːnɪˈpɜːsnəl] [iu-ni-per-so-nal], *a.* 1. Que existe en una sola persona. 2. *(Gram.) V.* IMPERSONAL.

unique [juːˈniːk] [iu-nik], *a.* Solo, sin igual, único en su género o especie; de aquí, singular, raro.

unisex ['juːnɪseks] [iu-ni-seks], *a.* Unisexo, que sirve para ambos sexos.

unisexual [ˌjuːnɪˈseksjʊəl] [iu-ni-sek-siual], *a.* 1. *(Bot.)* Unisexual, de un solo sexo. 2. *(Ento.)* Que consta de hembras solamente.

unison ['juːnɪzn] [iu-ni-son], *s.* 1. Unisonancia, la concurrencia de dos o más voces, cuerdas o instrumentos en un mismo tono de música. 2. Unísón, concierto músico por un mismo tono. *-a.* Unísono.

unit ['juːnɪt] [iu-nit], *s.* 1. Unidad, una sola persona o cosa; lo que forma un todo. 2. Unidad, lo que constituye el número uno como indivisible y absoluto.

unitarian [ˌjuːnɪˈtɛərɪən] [iu-ni-tea-rian], *s.* Unitario, sectario que niega la doctrina de la Trinidad, que no reconoce en Dios más que una sola persona.

unitarianism [ˌjuːnɪˈtɛərənɪzəm] [iu-ni-tea-ria-ni-sem], *s.* Unitarismo, doctrina de los unitarios.

unite ['juːnɪt] [iu-nit], *va.* 1. Unir, juntar dos o más cosas haciendo de ellas un todo. 2. Unir, concordar o conformar las voluntades, ánimos o pareceres. *-vn.* Unirse, juntarse, convenirse, concertarse.

united ['juːnaɪtɪd] [iu-nai-tid], *a.* Unido, juntado.

United Arab Emirates [juːˈnaɪtɪdˈærəbeˈmɪərɪts] [iu-nai-tid-a-rab-e-mi-reits], *spl.* Emiratos Árabes Unidos.

United Kingdom [juːˈnaɪtɪdˈkɪŋdəm] [iu-nai-tid-kin-dom], *s.* Reino Unido.

United Nations [juːˈnaɪtɪdˈneɪʃənz] [iu-nai-tid-nei-shons] *spl.* Naciones Unidas.

United States (of America) [juːˈnaɪtɪdˈsteɪtsˌəvəˈmerɪkə] [iu-nai-tid-steits-ov-a-me-ri-ka], *spl.* Estados Unidos (de América).

unitedly ['juːnaɪtɪdlɪ] [iu-nai-tid-li], *adv.* Unidamente, juntamente, con unión; de acuerdo; de una vez.

uniter ['juːnɪtəʳ] [iu-nai-taʳ], *s.* La persona o cosa que une.

unity ['juːnɪtɪ] [iu-ni-ti], *s.* 1. Unidad, el estado de lo que es uno. 2. Unión, concordia, conformdidad, armonía. 3. *(Mat.)* El número uno; la razón de dos cantidades iguales. 4. En literatura y en las artes, combinación en un conjunto homogéneo y artístico.

univalve [ˈjuːnɪvælv] [iu-ni-valv], *a.* Univalvo: se dice de los mariscos y conchas de una pieza. -*s.* Molusco, univalvo, gasterópodo; concha de una pieza.

universal [ˌjuːnɪˈvɜːsəl] [iu-ni-ver-sal], *a.* 1. Universal, común, general, total, que se extiende a todo o lo comprende todo. 2. Que existe o que se considera como un todo. 3. *(Art. y Of.)* Universal, propio para una gran variedad de usos o aplicaciones.

universalism [ˌjuːnɪˈvɜːsəlɪzm] [iu-ni-ver-sa-li-sem], *s.* Universalismo, doctrina de la salvación final de todas las almas y de que lo bueno triunfará al fin universalmente.

universalist [ˌjuːnɪˈvɜːsəlɪst] [iu-ni-ver-sa-list], *s.* Universalista, partidario del universalismo.

universality [ˌjuːnɪˈvɜːsælɪtɪ] [iu-ni-ver-sa-li-ti], *a.* Universalidad, generalidad, estado o calidad de lo universal.

universal joint [ˌjuːnɪˈvɜːsældʒɔɪnt] [iu-ni-ver-sal-yoint], *s.* *(Mec.)* Unión, junta o articulación universal o de Cardán.

universally [ˌjuːnɪˈvɜːsælɪ] [iu-ni-ver-sa-li], *adv.* Universalmente, generalmente.

universe [ˈjuːnɪvɜːs] [iu-ni-vers], *s.* Universo, el conjunto de todas las cosas creadas; mundo.

university [juːnɪvɜˈsɪtɪ] [iu-ni-ver-si-ti], *s.* 1. Universidad, establecimiento de instrucción superior donde se enseñan las ciencias y artes liberales. 2. Todos los estudiantes de ese establecimiento.

univocal [juːnɪvəʊkl] [iu-ni-vou-kal], *a.* 1. Unívoco, que tiene un solo sentido; no equívoco. 2. Cierto, regular.

unjoin [ʌnˈdʒɔɪn] [an-yoin], *va.* Separar, dividir, desunir.

unjoint [ʌnˈdʒɔɪnt] [an-yoint], *va.* Dislocar, desencajar, descoyuntar.

unjointed [ʌnˈdʒɔɪntɪd] [an-yoin-tid], *a.* Desunido; falto de articulaciones.

unjoyful [ʌnˈdʒɔɪfʊl] [an-yoi-ful], *a.* Triste, melancólico, lúgubre, de mal humor.

unjudged [ʌnˈdʒʌdʒ] [an-yadch], *a.* No juzgado, no decidido; pendiente, en litigio.

unjust [ʌnˈdʒʌst] [an-yast], *a.* Injusto, inicuo, desrazonable, contrario a la justicia.

unjustifiable [ʌnˈdʒʌstɪfaɪəbl] [an-yas-ti-faia-bol], *a.* Injustificable, inexcusable, sin disculpa, sin excusa.

unjustifiably [ʌnˈdʒʌstɪfaɪəblɪ] [an-yas-ti-faia-bli], *adv.* Inexcusablemente, de una manera injustificable.

unjustly [ʌnˈdʒʌstlɪ] [an-yas-tli], *adv.* Injustamente, inicuamente.

unkempt [ʌnˈkempt] [an-kempt], *a.* 1. Despeinado, desgreñado, desmelenado. 2. *(Fig.)* Sin pulimento, sin arte, inculto, tosco.

unkennel [ʌnˈkenl] [an-ke-nel], *va.* 1. Desalojar o echar a un animal de su cama, madriguera, huronera, etc. 2. Poner al descubierto una cosa que estaba secreta.

unkept [ʌnˈkept] [an-kept], *a.* No retenido, no guardado.

unkind [ʌnˈkaɪnd] [an-kaind], *a.* Adusto, no benévolo, duro, poco amable; áspero, seco.

unkindliness [ʌnˈkaɪndlɪnɪs] [an-kaind-li-nes], *a.* Aspereza, sureza, severidad, rigor.

unkindly [ʌnˈkaɪndlɪ] [an-kaind-li], *adv.* Duramente, ásperamente, con rigor o severidad, con desafecto, con poco cariño. **To treat one unkindly,** maltratar a uno, no mostrarle afabilidad.

unkindness [ʌnˈkaɪndnɪs] [an-kaind-nes], *s.* 1. Desafecto, desamor, falta de cariño o de afabilidad. 2. Malignidad, propensión o gusto en hacer o decir mal.

unkink [ʌnˈkɪŋk] [an-kink], *va.* Quitar las torceduras o los nudos.

unknowable [ʌnˈnəʊəbl] [an-noua-bol], *a.* Incognoscible.

unknowing [ʌnˈnəʊəɪŋ] [an-nouin], *a.* Ignorante.

unknowingly [ʌnˈnəʊɪŋlɪ] [an-nouin-li], *adv.* Ignorantemente, sin saberlo.

unknown [ʌnˈnəʊn] [an-noun], *a.* 1. Oculto, desconocido, ignorado, no conocido antes, ignoto. 2. Mayor de lo que se cree o se imagina; superior a todo cómputo. 3. Incógnito, sin que se sepa, sin noticia de. **Unknown to me,** sin mi noticia de, sin saberlo yo, sin mi concurrencia o participación.

unlace [ʌnˈleɪs] [an-leis], *va.* Desabrochar; desenlazar.

unlade [ʌnˈleɪd] [an-leid], *va.* 1. Descargar, quitar o aliviar la carga. 2. Desembarcar, sacar y poner en tierra lo que estaba embarcado.

unladylike [ʌnˈleɪdɪlaɪk] [an-lei-di-laik], *a.* Impropio de una señora o dama; poco afeminado.

unlaid [ʌnˈleɪd] [an-leid], *a. y pp.* TO UNLAY. 1. Que no está colocado ni puesto; en especial que no tiene líneas paralelas filigrana (papel). 2. No apaciguado ni aquietado. 3. Destorcido (como los cabos de una cuerda).

unlamented [ˈʌnləˈmentɪd] [an-la-men-tid], *a.* No lamentado, no llorado.

unlatch [ʌnˈlætʃ] [an-lach], *va.* Abrir levantado el picaporte.

unlawful [ˈʌnˈlɔːfʊl] [an-lo-ful], *a.* Ilegal, ilícito, contrario u opuesto a las leyes; ilegítimo. **Unlawful interest,** usura.

unlawfully [ˈʌnˈlɔːfʊlɪ] [an-lo-fu-li], *adv.* Ilegalmente, ilegítimamente, ilícitamente, contra las leyes o en violación de las leyes. **Unlawfully born,** ilegítimo, bastardo.

unlawfulness [ˈʌnˈlɔːfʊlnɪs] [an-lo-ful-nes], *s.* 1. Ilegalidad, calidad de ilegal. 2. Ilegitimidad.

unlearn [ˈʌnˈlɜːn] [an-lern], *va.* Desaprender, olvidar lo que se ha aprendido.

unlearned [ˈʌnˈlɜːnɪd] [an-ler-nid], *pp. y a.* Indocto, ignorante; ignorado, no aprendido; mal hecho.

unleavened [ˈʌnˈlevnd] [an-le-vend], *a.* Ácimo, que no tiene levadura o fermento.

unless [ənˈles] [an-les], *conj.* 1. A menos que, no sea que (seguido de verbo en subjuntivo): a menos de que, a menos de (seguido de verbo en infinitivo). 2. Excepto, si no, si no es (delante de un pronombre, etc.).

unlettered [ˈʌnˈletəd] [an-le-tard], *a.* Indocto, iliterato.

unlicensed [ˈʌnˈlɪsənst] [an-li-senst], *a.* No autorizado, sin privilegio, sin patente; sin permiso o licencia.

unlicked [ˈʌnˈlɪkt] [an-likt], *a.* Mal formado, irregular.

unlighted [ˈʌnˈlaɪtɪd] [an-lai-tid], *a.* No iluminado, oscuro; no encendido.

unlike [ˈʌnˈlaɪk] [an-laik], *a.* 1. Desemejante, diferente, disímil, distinto, nada parecido. 2. Inverosímil, improbable. **Not unlike,** parecido, semejante.

unlikelihood [ʌnˈlaɪklɪhʊd] [an-laik-li-jud], **unlikeliness** [ˈʌnˈlaɪklɪnɪs] [an-laik-li-nes], *s.* Improbabilidad, inverisimilitud.

unlikeness [ˈʌnˈlaɪknɪs] [an-laik-nes], *s.* Disimilitud, desemejanza.

unlimited [ˈʌnˈlɪmɪtɪd] [an-li-mi-ted], *a.* 1. Ilimitado, sin límites ni término; indefinido. 2. Franco, absoluto.

unlimitedly [ˈʌnˈlɪmɪtɪdlɪ] [an-li-mi-ted-li], *adv.* Ilimitadamente, sin límites, sin medida.

unlink [ˈʌnˈlɪŋk] [an-link], *va.* Deseslabonar, desenlabonar, soltar los eslabones; separar, deshacer.

unload [ˈʌnˈləʊd] [an-loud], *va.* 1. Descargar, quitar o aliviar la carga; desahogar, aligerar. 2. *(Fam. E.U.)* Vender, particularmente en grandes cantidades; se dice de las mercancías averiables o difíciles de conservar en buen estado. -*va.* Descargar la carga.

unlock [ˈʌnˈlɒk] [an-lok], *va.* 1. Abrir una cerradura (cerrada con llave). 2. *(Impr.)* Desapretar (forms). 3. Dar libre acceso; hacer disponible. 4. Revelar (secreto).

unlooked-for [ˈʌnˈluːktfɔːr] [an-lukt-foʳ], *a.* Inesperado, inopinado.

unloose [ˈʌnˈluːz] [an-lus], *va.* Desatar. -*vn.* Hacerse pedazos.

unloved [ˈʌnˈlʌvd] [an-lavd], *a.* Desamado, no amado.

unloveliness [ˈʌnˈlʌvlɪnɪs] [an-lav-li-nes], *s.* Aspereza de genio, falta de amabilidad.

unlovely ['ʌn'lʌvlɪ] [an-lav-li], *a.* Desamable, desagradable, fastidioso.

unloving ['ʌn'lʌvɪŋ] [an-la-vin], *a.* Poco amante, poco afectuoso, que no ama.

unluckily ['ʌn'lʌkɪlɪ] [an-la-ki-li], *adv.* Desgraciadamente, desafortunadamente, por desgracia.

unluckiness ['ʌn'lʌkɪnɪs] [an-la-ki-nes], *s.* Desastre, desgracia, infortunio, mala suerte.

unlucky ['ʌn'lʌkɪ] [an-la-ki], *a.* 1. Desgraciado, desafortunado, desdichado. 2. Funesto, infausto, azaroso, aciago, siniestro, de mal agüero.

unmade ['ʌn'meɪd] [an-meid], *a.* Increado; deshecho; que no se ha hecho aún o que se ha olvidado hacerlo.

unmaidenly ['ʌn'meɪdnlɪ] [an-mei-den-li], *a.* Impropio de una doncella.

unmake ['ʌn'meɪk] [an-meik], *va.* 1. Deshacer, destruir, aniquilar. 2. Deponer (autoridad).

unman ['ʌn'mæn] [an-man], *va.* 1. Privar de fuerza viril o de firmeza; afeminar, acobardar, desanimar. 2. Desguarnecer, quitar la guarnición (square, fortress). 3. Castrar, capar. 4. Privar del juicio o de la razón.

unmanageable ['ʌn'mænədʒəbl] [an-ma-ne-ya-bol], *a.* Inmanejable, indómito, intratable.

unmanaged ['ʌn'mænɪdʒ] [an-ma-nicht], *a.* No manejado, no domado; indisciplinado.

unmanlike ['ʌn'mænlaɪk] [an-man-laik], *a.* 1. Indigno de un hombre o contrario a los sentimientos que deben dirigir la conducta de los hombres. 2. Afeminado, enervado, muelle.

unmanned ['ʌn'mænd] [an-mand], *a.* Que no está dirigido o gobernado por hombres.

unmannered ['ʌn'mænəd] [an-ma-nerd], *a.* Rudo, brutal, grosero; mal criado, soez.

unmannerly ['ʌn'mænəlɪ] [an-ma-na-li], *a.* Impolítico, malcriado, mal educado, falto de crianza, descortés, grosero. *-adv.* Descortésmente, groseramente, sin política, sin crianza.

unmarked ['ʌn'maːkt] [an-markt], *a.* No mirado, no observado, no señalado.

unmarketable ['ʌn'maːktəbl] [an-mark-ta-bol], *a.* Invendible, que no se halla en buen estado para el mercado; echado a perder, no pedido.

unmarriageable ['ʌn'mærɪdʒəbl] [an-ma-ri-cha-bol], *a.* Incasable, no casadero; que no está en edad o condición de casarse.

unmarried ['ʌn'mærɪd] [an-ma-rid], *a.* Célibe, no casado; soltero, soltera.

unmask ['ʌn'maːsk] [an-mask], *va.* Desenmascarar, quitar la máscara a una persona; descubrir, descorrer o quitar el velo.

unmasked ['ʌn'maːskt] [an-maskt], *a.* Patente, manifiesto.

unmastered ['ʌn'maːstəd] [an-mas-tard], *a.* No domado, no vencido; que no está todavía aprendido o adquirido.

unmatchable ['ʌn'mætʃəbl] [an-ma-cha-bol], *a.* Que no tiene por; único, incomparable.

unmatched ['ʌn'mætʃt] [an-macht], *a.* Único, sin igual, sin par, sin nada que se le asemeje.

unmeaning ['ʌn'miːnɪŋ] [an-mi-nin], *a.* Sin significación, vacío de sentido, que no significa nada. **Unmeaning words,** palabras vanas o vacías de sentido; vulgarmente, greguería o jerga.

unmelted ['ʌn'meltɪd] [an-mel-tid], *a.* No derretido.

unmentionable [ʌn'menʃnəbl] [an-men-sho-na-bol], *a.* Impropio, que no debe mencionarse. *-pl. (Fest.)* Calzones, pantalones.

unmerciful [ʌn'mɜːsɪfʊl] [an-mer-si-ful], *a.* 1. Inclemente, riguroso, cruel, desapiadado. 2. *(Fam.)* Excesivo, exorbitante, fuera de razón.

unmercifully [ʌn'mɜːsɪfəlɪ] [an-mer-si-fu-li], *adv.* Cruelmente, rigurosamente, desapiadadamente, inhumanamente, sin misericordia.

unmercifulness [ʌn'mɜːsɪfʊlnɪs] [an-mer-si-ful-nes], *s.* Inclemencia, crueldad, inhumanidad.

unmerited [ʌn'merɪtɪd] [an-me-ri-tid], *a.* Desmerecido, inmerecido.

unmethodical ['ʌnmɪ'θɒdɪkəl] [an-mi-zo-di-kal], *a.* Que no es metódico; desarreglado, irregular, falto de método.

unmindful [ʌn'maɪndfʊl] [an-maind-ful], *a.* Olvidadizo, que con facilidad se olvida de las cosas; descuidado, dejado, negligente, que no hace caso, que no presta atención.

unmindfulness [ʌn'maɪndfʊlnɪs] [an-maind-ful-nes], *s.* Descuido, dejadez, negligencia, falta de atención.

unmistak(e)able ['ʌnmɪs'teɪkəbl] [an-mis-tei-ka-bol], *a.* Inequívoco, que no puede tomarse por otra cosa; evidente.

unmitigated [ʌn'mɪtɪgeɪtɪd] [an-mi-ti-guei-tid], *a.* Duro, no mitigado, no suavizado; desmesurado; de aquí, tan malo como es posible serlo. *V.* UNCONSCIONABLE.

unmixed, unmixt [ʌn'mɪkst] [an-mikst], *a.* Puro, sin composición, sin mezcla; simple, sencillo.

unmolested ['ʌnmə'lestɪd] [an-mo-les-tid], *a.* Quieto, tranquilo, no molestado.

unmourned [ʌn'mɔːnd] [an-mornd], *a.* No llorado, no lamentado.

unmoved [ʌn'muːvd] [an-muvd], *a.* 1. Inmoto, que no se mueve. 2. Inmoble, inmovible, constante, firme e invariable. 3. Inalterable, impasible, no conmovido, no enternecido.

unmoving [ʌn'muːvɪŋ] [an-mu-vin], *a.* 1. Falto de movimiento. 2. Seco, árido, que no mueve los afectos del ánimo.

unmusical [ʌn'mjuːzɪkəl] [an-miu-si-kal], *a.* Disonante, discordante, discorde, poco musical.

unmuzzle [ʌn'mʌzl] [an-ma-sel], *va.* Quitar el bozal a, desbozalar.

unnamed [ʌn'neɪmd] [an-neimd], *a.* Innominado, no nombrado, anónimo, sin nombre.

unnatural [ʌn'nætʃrəl] [an-na-chu-ral], *a.* 1. Innatural, no natural, contrario a las leyes o a los sentimientos de la naturaleza; cruel, monstruoso, inhumano. 2. Desnaturalizado, falto de los afectos o sentimientos naturales. 3. Forzado, artificial, fuera de lo natural. **An unnatural parent,** un padre desnaturalizado.

unnaturally [ʌn'nætʃrəlɪ] [an-na-chu-ra-li], *adv.* Contra la naturaleza o contra las leyes de la naturaleza.

unnaturalness [ʌn'nætʃrəlnɪs] [an-na-chu-ral-nes], *s.* La calidad que constituye a una cosa contraria a lo que es natural o común.

unnavigable ['ʌn'nævɪgəbl] [an-na-vi-ga-bol], *a.* Innavegable. *V.* INNAVIGABLE.

unnecessarily [ʌn'nesɪsərɪlɪ] [an-ne-si-sa-ri-li], *adv.* Sin necesidad; inútilmente; fuera de propósito.

unnecessariness [ʌn'nesɪsərɪnes] [an-ne-si-sa-ri-nes], *s.* Superfluidad; inutilidad; falta de necesidad.

unnecessary [ʌn'nesɪsərɪ] [an-ne-si-sa-ri], *a.* Innecesario, excusado, superfluo, inútil.

unneedful [ʌn'niːdfʊl] [an-nid-ful], *a.* Inútil, innecesario.

unneighborly [ʌn'neɪbəlɪ] [an-nei-bo-li], *a.* Áspero, adusto; nada cortés, poco atento con sus vecinos.

unnerve ['ʌn'nɜːv] [an-nerv], *va.* Enervar, quitar las fuerzas, enflaquecer.

unnerved ['ʌn'nɜːvd] [an-nerved], *a.* y *pp.* Enervado, debilitado, sin fuerzas.

unnoted ['ʌn'nəʊtɪd] [an-nou-tid], *a.* Desaparcibido, sin ser notado; oscuro, sin reputación, poco conocido.

unnoticed [ʌn'nəʊtɪst] [an-nou-tist], *a.* No observado, pasado por alto, dejado aparte.

unnumbered [ʌn'nʌmbəd] [an-nam-berd], *a.* Innumerable, sin número.

unobjected ['ʌnəb'dʒektɪd] [an-ob-yek-tid], *a.* No imputado; no objetado.

unobjectionable ['ʌnəb'dʒekʃnəbl] [an-ob-yek-sho-na-bol], *a.* Irreprensible, irrecusable; exento de objeciones.

unobservable ['ʌnəb'zɜːvəbl] [an-ob-ser-va-bol], *a.* Imperceptible, inapreciable, que no se puede observar.

unobservant [ˌʌnəbˈzɜːvənt] [an-ob-ser-vant], *a.* Inobservante, que no observa; que no presta atención, que no hace caso.

unobserved [ˌʌnəbˈzɜːvd] [an-ob-servd], *a.* Desapercibido, no notado, que pasa o sucede sin observarse, sin llamar la atención o sin que se haga caso de ello.

unobstructed [ˌʌnəbsˈtrʌktɪd] [an-obs-trak-tid], *a.* Libre, no obstruido, no impedido.

unobstructive [ˌʌnəbsˈtrʌktɪv] [an-obs-trak-tiv], *a.* Que no impide o embaraza.

unoccupied [ˈʌnˈɒkjʊpaɪd] [an-o-kiu-paid], *a.* Desocupado, vacante, libre; sin ocupación. **Unoccupied land,** baldío, erial.

unofficial [ˈʌnəˈfɪʃəl] [an-o-fi-shal], *a.* Extraoficial, no oficial.

unopened [ˈʌnˈəʊpənd] [an-ou-pend], *a.* Cerrado, que aún no se ha abierto.

unopposed [ˌʌnəˈpəʊzd] [an-o-pousd], *a.* Sin oposición o que no encuentra oposición.

unorganized [ˈʌnˈɔːɡənaɪzd] [an-or-ga-naist], *a.* Inorganizado, no organizado; inorgánico, falto de estructura.

unoriginal [ˌʌnəˈrɪdʒɪnəl] [an-o-ri-yi-nal], *a.* No original.

unorthodox [ˈʌnˈɔːθədɒks] [an-or-zo-doks], *a.* Heterodoxo.

unostentatious [ˈʌnˌɒstenˈteɪʃəs] [an-os-ten-tei-shos], *a.* Libre de ostentación, de fausto; no presumido, modesto, simple.

unpack [ˈʌnˈpak] [an-pak], *va.* Desempaquetar, desempapelar, desenvolver, desembalar, desenfardar.

unpaid [ˈʌnˈpeɪd] [an-peid], *a.* No pagado, que no se ha pagado; el que no recibe lo que se le debe; el que trabaja sin recibir pago alguno.

unpained [ˈʌnˈpeɪnd] [an-peind], *a.* Sin dolor, lo que no duele.

unpainful [ˈʌnˈpeɪnfʊl] [an-pein-ful], *a.* Que no causa o produce dolor.

unpainted [ˈʌnˈpeɪntɪd] [an-pein-tid], *a.* Que no está pintado; sin afeites.

unpaired [ˈʌnˈpɛəd] [an-peard], *a.* Desapareado, no apareado; no reunido.

unpalatable [ʌnˈpælɪtəbl] [an-pa-li-ta-bol], *a.* Desabrido, desagradable al paladar.

unparalleled [ʌnˈpærəleɪd] [an-pa-ra-leld], *a.* Único, sin igual, sin par; sin paralelo.

unpardonable [ʌnˈpɑːdnəbl] [an-par-do-na-bol], *a.* Irremisible, que no merece perdón.

unpardonably [ʌnˈpɑːdnəblɪ] [an-par-do-na-bli], *adv.* Irremisiblemente, sin remisión, sin perdón.

unparliamentary [ˈʌnˌpɑːləˈmentərɪ] [an-par-la-men-ta-ri], *a.* Contrario a las reglas del parlamento o a las que gobiernan a un cuerpo deliberante.

unparted [ʌnˈpɑːtɪd] [an-par-tid], *a.* Indiviso.

unpatented [ˈʌnˌpeɪtɪntɪd] [an-pei-tin-tid], *a.* No privilegiado, sin patente.

unpaved [ʌnˈpeɪvd] [an-peivd], *a.* No empedrado.

unpawned [ʌnˈpɔːnd] [an-pond], *a.* Desempeñado, libre de empeño.

unpeople [ʌnˈpiːpl] [an-pi-pol], *va.* Despoblar.

unperceivable [ˌʌnpəˈsiːvəbl] [an-par-si-va-bol], *a.* Imperceptible; ininteligible.

unperceived [ˌʌnpəˈsiːvd] [an-par-sivd], *a.* No percibido, no descubierto.

unpick [ˈʌnˈpɪk] [an-pik], *vt.* Descoser (seam).

unpiloted [ˌʌnprˈləʊtɪd] [an-pi-lou-tid], *a.* Que no es conducido por un piloto; sin guía, sin conductor.

unpin [ˈʌnˈpɪn] [an-pin], *va.* Desprender lo que está prendido con alfileres.

unplaced [ˈʌnˈpleɪst] [an-pleist], *a.* Desacomodado, no colocado.

unplagued [ˈʌˈplægd] [an-plagd], *a.* Libre de alguna cosa que cause dolor; no atormentado.

unplanted [ˈʌnˈplæntɪd] [an-plan-tid], *a.* Espontáneo, que no ha sido plantado; que crece espontáneamente.

unpleasant [ʌnˈpleznt] [an-ple-sant], *a.* Desagradable, enfadoso, molesto, displicente.

unpleasantly [ʌnˈplezntlɪ] [an-ple-sant-li], *adv.* Desagradablemente, enfadosamente, desabridamente.

unpleasantness [ʌnˈplezntnɪs] [an-ple-sant-nes], *s.* Desagrado, disgusto, desazón, enfado.

unpleased [ʌnˈpliːst] [an-plist], *a.* Descontento, disgustado, enfadado, enojado.

unpleasing [ʌnˈpliːzɪŋ] [an-pli-sin], *a.* Desagradable, ofensivo, enfadoso, molesto.

unpleasingly [ʌnˈpliːzɪŋlɪ] [an-pli-sin-li], *a.* Desagradablemente; ofensivamente.

unplug [ˈʌnˈplʌg] [an-plag], *vt.* Desconectar, desenchufar.

unplugged [ˌʌnˈplʌgd] [an-plagd], *a.* (*Mús.*) Sin elementos electrónicos, unplugged.

unpoetic, unpoetical [ˈʌnpəʊˈetɪk] [an-pou-etik] [ˈʌnpəʊˈetɪkəl] [an-pou-eti-kal], *a.* Que no es poético, que no está conforme con las reglas de la poesía.

unpolished [ˈʌnˈpɒlɪʃt] [an-po-lisht], *a.* 1. Áspero, tosco, que no está liso, que no está pulido. 2. Basto, rudo, grosero, impolítico. **An unpolished diamond,** diamante en bruto. **Unpolished ore,** mineral sin bruñir.

unpolite [ˈʌnˈpɒlaɪt] [an-po-lait], *a.* Grosero, descortés, impolítico. *V.* IMPOLITE.

unpolluted [ˌʌnəˈluːtɪd] [an-po-lu-tid], *a.* Impoluto, inmaculado, limpio, sin mancha.

unpopular [ˈʌnˈpɒpjʊləʳ] [an-po-piu-laʳ], *a.* Impopular, que es contrario a las opiniones dominantes, que no agrada al pueblo.

unpossessing [ˈʌnpəˈsesɪŋ] [an-po-se-sin], *a.* El que no posee o el que no tiene derecho a la posesión de alguna cosa.

unpracticable [ʌnˈpræktɪkəbl] [an-prak-ti-ka-bol], *a.* *V.* IMPRACTICABLE.

unpractised [ʌnˈpræktɪst] [an-prak-tist], *a.* Inexperto, no versado, no enseñado.

unprecedented [ˈʌnˈpresɪdəntɪd] [an-pre-si-dan-tid], *a.* Inaudito, sin precedente o sin ejemplar.

unpredictable [ˈʌnprɪˈdɪktəbl] [an-pri-dik-ta-bol], *a.* Que no se puede pronosticar.

unprejudiced [ˈʌnˈpredʒʊdɪst] [an-pre-yu-dist], *a.* No preocupado, libre o exento de preocupaciones; imparcial.

unpremeditated [ˈʌnprɪˈmedɪteɪtɪd] [an-pri-me-di-tei-tid], *a.* Inopinado; no premeditado, no pensado con anterioridad.

unprepared [ˈʌprɪˈpɛəd] [an-pri-pead], *a.* Desprevenido, desproveído, desprovisto, no preparado.

unpreparedness [ˈʌnprɪˈpɛədnɪs] [an-pri-pead-nes], *s.* Desprevención, falta de prevención.

unprepossessing [ˈʌnˌpriːpəˈzesɪŋ] [an-pri-po-se-sin], *a.* Poco atractivo, poco insinuante, que no inspira opinión favorable al principio o a primera vista.

unpressed [ˈʌnprest] [an-prest], *a.* No prensado; no obligado, no forzado.

unpretending [ˈʌnprɪˈtendɪŋ] [an-pri-ten-din], *a.* Modesto, moderado, falto de pretensión.

unprevailing [ˈʌnprɪˈveɪlɪŋ] [an-pri-vei-lin], *a.* Nulo; no corriente; ineficaz.

unprincipled [ʌnˈprɪnsɪpld] [an-prin-si-pold], *a.* El que no tiene principios u opiniones fijas en la moral o en la religión; malvado.

unprinted [ˈʌnprɪntɪd] [an-prin-tid], *a.* 1. Manuscrito, no impreso. 2. Liso (cloths).

unprisoned [ˈʌnprɪˈprɪzənd] [an-pri-sond], *a.* Suelto, que no está preso.

unprized [ˈʌnpraɪzd] [an-praist], *a.* No apreciado.

unproductive [ˈʌnprəˈdʌktɪv] [an-pro-dak-tiv], *a.* Improductivo, que no produce; estéril.

unprofessional [ˈʌnprəˈfeʃənl] [an-pro-fe-sho-nal], *a.* Que no pertenece a una profesión (liberal); extraño a una profesión; no profesional, contrario a las reglas de una profesión.

unprofitable [ʌnˈprɒfɪtəbl] [an-pro-fi-ta-bol], *a.* Poco ventajoso, no lucrativo, que no produce nada; inútil, vano, que para nada sirve.

unprofitableness [ʌnˈprɒfɪtəblnɪs] [an-pro-fi-ta-bol-nes], *a.* Inutilidad.

unprofitably [ʌnˈprɒfɪtəblɪ] [an-pro-fi-ta-bli], *adv.* Inútilmente, sin provecho, sin beneficio.

unprohibited [ˌʌnprəˈhɪbɪtɪd] [an-pro-ji-bi-tid], *a.* No prohibido, permitido.

unpromising [ˈʌnˈprɒmɪsɪŋ] [an-pro-mi-sin], *a.* De poca apariencia, que no promete mucho, que no da grandes esperanzas.

unpronounceable [ˈʌnprəˈnaʊnsəbl̩] [an-pro-naun-sa-bol], *a.* Que no se puede pronunciar.

unpronounced [ʌnˈprənaʊnst] [an-pro-naunst], *a.* Inarticulado, no pronunciado.

unpropitious [ˈʌnprəˈpɪʃəs] [an-pro-pi-shos], *a.* Infausto, no favorable, poco propicio.

unprosperous [ʌnˈprɒspərəs] [an-pros-pe-ros], *a.* Desafortunado, desgraciado, infeliz.

unprotected [ˈʌnprəˈtektɪd] [an-pro-tek-tid], *a.* Desvalido, sin protección; falto de impuestos protectores.

unproved [ʌnˈpruːvd] [an-pruvd], *a.* No probado, no demostrado.

z Desproveído, desprovisto, falto, cogido desprevenido. **Unprovided for,** no preparado a, no previsto. **Unprovided with,** desprovisto de, que carece de.

unprovoked [ˈʌnprəˈvəʊkt] [an-pro-voukt], *a.* No provocado; sin motivo, sin provocación.

unpublished [ˈʌnˈpʌblɪʃt] [an-pa-blisht], *a.* Secreto, oculto, no publicado; inédito.

unpunctual [ˈʌnˈpʌŋktjʊəl] [an-pank-tiual], *a.* Inexacto, que no es puntual.

unpunishable [ˈʌnˈpʌnɪʃəbl̩] [an-pa-ni-sha-bol], *a.* Que no es punible, que no admite castigo.

unpunished [ˈʌnˈpʌnɪʃt] [an-pa-nisht], *a.* Impune, no castigado.

unpursued [ˈʌnˈpɜːsjuːd] [an-per-siud], *a.* Quieto, no perseguido.

unqualified [ˈʌnˈkwɒlɪfaɪd] [an-kuo-li-faid], *a.* 1. Inhábil, inepto, incapaz, que no tiene las cualidades necesarias o no es a propósito para alguna cosa. 2. Que no tiene la autorización necesaria o legal. 3. Dado o hecho sin restricción; completo, entero. **They have his unqualified approbation,** ellos tienen la entera aprobación de él.

unqualify [ˈʌnˈkwɒlɪfaɪ] [an-kuo-li-fai], *va.* Inhabilitar. *V.* DISQUALIFY.

unquenchable [ʌnˈkwentʃəbl̩] [an-kuen-cha-bol], *a.* Inextinguible, insaciable.

unquenched [ʌnˈkwentʃt] [an-kuencht], *a.* No extinguido, no apagado.

unquestionable [ʌnˈkwestʃənəbl̩] [an-kues-cho-na-bol], *a.* Indudable, indiscutible, que no admite disputa.

unquestionably [ʌnˈkwestʃənəblɪ] [an-kues-cho-na-bli], *adv.* Indudablemente, sin duda, sin disputa.

unquestioned [ʌnˈkwestʃənd] [an-kues-chond], *a.* 1. Incontestable, indisputable. 2. Tenido por cierto, no dudado. 3. No examinado, no preguntado.

unquickened [ʌnˈkwɪknd] [an-kui-kend], *a.* Inanimado.

unquiet [ʌnˈkwaɪət] [an-kuaiet], *a.* Inquieto, desosegado; agitado, turbado.

unquietly [ʌnˈkwaɪətlɪ] [an-kuaiet-li], *adv.* Inquietamente, con desasosiego o inquietud.

unquietness [ʌnˈkwaɪətnɪs] [an-kuaiet-nes], *s.* Inquietud, desasosiego.

unracked [ʌnˈrækt] [an-rakt], *a.* No trasegado, no clarificado. **Unracked wine,** vino por trasegar.

unravel [ʌnˈrævəl] [an-ra-vel], *va.* 1. Desenredar, deshacer el enredo; deshilar, sacar los hilos de un tejido. 2. Desembrollar, aclarar, explciar. 3. Desatar o desenredar, dar salida a un lance, enredo o trama en las piezas dramáticas. - *vn.* Desenredarse; desenlazarse.

unravelment [ʌnˈrævəlmənt] [an-ra-vel-ment], *s.* Desenlace (de una pieza).

unreached [ʌnˈriːtʃt] [an-richt], *a.* No alcanzado, no conseguido.

unread [ʌnˈred] [an-red], *a.* No leído, sin leer; iliterato, indocto, ignorante.

unreadiness [ˈʌnˈredɪnɪs] [an-re-di-nes], *s.* Pesadez; desprevención, falta de prevención o de preparación; lentitud; carencia de facilidad.

unready [ʌnˈredɪ] [an-re-di], *a.* 1. Lento; que no es pronto en ver o apreciar. 2. Desprevenido, que no está prevenido o preparado; que no está pronto o dispuesto.

unreal [ˈʌnˈrɪəl] [an-rial], *a.* 1. No real, imaginario, vano, sin realidad. 2. Inmaterial, incorporal. 3. Insincero, falto de sinceridad.

unreason [ˈʌnˈriːzn] [an-ri-son], *s.* Sinrazón, necedad, disparate.

unreasonable [ʌnˈriːznəbl̩] [an-ri-so-na-bol], *a.* Inmoderado, excesivo, exorbitante, desrazonable.

unreasonableness [ʌnˈriːznəblnɪs] [an-ri-so-na-bol-nes], *s.* 1. Sinrazón, despropósito, falta de razón. 2. Exorbitancia.

unreasonably [ʌnˈriːznəblɪ] [an-ri-so-na-bli], *adv.* Irracionalmente, exorbitantemente, excesivamente.

unreclaimed [ˈʌnrɪˈkleɪmd] [an-ri-kleimd], *a.* Incorregible, incapaz de corrección.

unrecognizable [ˈʌnˈrekəgnaɪzəbl̩] [an-re-kog-nai-sa-bol], *a.* Irreconocible.

unrecorded [ˌʌnrɪˈkɔːdɪd] [an-ri-kor-did], *a.* Sepultado en el olvido, no recordado en monumentos públicos; no archivado.

unreduced [ˌʌnrɪˈdjuːst] [an-ri-diust], *a.* No reducido, no sujetado.

unreeve [ʌnˈriːv] [an-riv], *va.* *(Mar.)* Despasar, desguarnir.

unrefined [ˈʌnrɪˈfaɪnd] [an-ri-faind], *a.* 1. No refinado, no purificado, en bruto. 2. Inculto, rudo, de estilo o modales poco cultos o refinados.

unreformed [ˈʌnrɪˈfɔːmd] [an-ri-formd], *a.* 1. No reformado, no corregido. 2. Impenitente, obstinado en la culpa.

unrefracted [ˈʌnrɪˈfræktɪd] [an-ri-frak-tid], *a.* No refracto.

unregarded [ˈʌnrɪˈɡɑːdɪd] [an-ri-gar-did], *a.* Desatendido, descuidado, desdeñado, despreciado.

unregenerate [ˈʌnrɪˈdʒenərɪt] [an-ri-ye-ne-rit], *a.* No regenerado.

unregistered [ˈʌnˈredʒɪstəd] [an-re-yis-ted], *a.* No archivado; no registrado, inscrito o apuntado.

unrelated [ˈʌnrɪˈleɪtɪd] [an-ri-lei-tid], *a.* 1. Que no tiene parentesco con otra persona. 2. Que no tiene relación o conexión con otra cosa, no afín.

unrelenting [ˈʌnrɪˈlentɪŋ] [an-ri-len-tin], *a.* Incompasivo, duro de corazón, inflexible.

unreliable [ˈʌnrɪˈlaɪəbl̩] [an-ri-laia-bol], *a.* Indigno de confianza; que no merece creencia o fe (person or thing).

unrelieved [ˈʌnrɪˈliːvd] [an-ri-livd], *a.* No socorrido, no aliviado.

unremitted [ˈʌnrɪˈmɪtɪd] [an-ri-mi-tid], *a.* Continuo; no perdonado.

unremitting [ˈʌnrɪˈmɪtɪŋ] [an-ri-mi-tin], *a.* Perseverante, constante, incansable.

unremoved [ˈʌnrɪˈmuːvd] [an-ri-muvd], *a.* No remóvido; inmoble, incapaz de ser removido; no alejado, no desviado.

unremunerative [ˈʌnrɪˈmjuːnərətɪv] [an-ri-miu-ne-ra-tiv], *a.* Que no es remunerador.

unrepealed [ˈʌnrɪˈpiːld] [an-ri-pild], *a.* No abrogado.

unrepentant [ˈʌnrɪˈpentənt] [an-ri-pen-tant], *a.* Impenitente, obstinado en la culpa.

unreplenished [ˈʌnrɪˈplɪnɪʃt] [an-ri-pli-nisht], *a.* No lleno, no surtido o provisto.

unrepresented [ˈʌnˌreprɪˈzentɪd] [an-re-pri-sen-tid], *a.* No representado, que no tiene representante.

unrequested [ˈʌnrɪˈkwestɪd] [an-ri-kues-tid], *a.* Espontáneo, que no se ha pedido, rogado o demandado.

unreserve [ˈʌnrɪˈzɜːv] [an-ri-serv], *a.* Franqueza, ingenuidad, candor.

unreserved [ˈʌnrɪˈzɜːvd] [an-ri-servd], *a.* 1. Que no es reservado, retenido; ilimitado, sin restricción. 2. Franco, abierto; libre.

unreservedly [ˈʌnrɪˈzɜːvdlɪ] [an-ri-servd-li], *adv.* Sin reserva; sin reticencia, francamente, abiertamente.

unreservedness [ˌʌnrɪ'zɜːvdnɪs] [an-ri-servd-nes], *s.* Candor, franqueza, ingenuidad.

unresisted [ˌʌnrɪ'zɪstɪd] [an-ri-sis-tid], *a.* Sin resistencia; irresistible.

unresisting [ˌʌnrɪ'zɪstɪŋ] [an-ri-sis-tin], *a.* Que no resiste, que no ofrece resistencia, sin resistencia.

unresolvable [ˌʌnrɪ'zɒlvəbl] [an-ri-sol-va-bol], *a.* Indisoluble, insoluble.

unresolved [ˌʌnrɪ'zɒlvd] [an-ri-solvd], *a.* 1. Irresoluto, indeterminado, indeciso. 2. No desatado, no aclarado, que no está resuelto.

unrest [ʌn'rest] [an-rest], *s.* Inquietud, desasosiego.

unresting [ʌn'restɪŋ] [an-res-tin], *a.* Que no descansa jamás; que no toma reposo.

unrestrained [ˌʌnrɪ'streɪnd] [an-ri-streind], *a.* 1. Desenfrenado, libre, licencioso, insubordinado; suelto. 2. Ilimitado, sin límites.

unretracted [ˌʌnrɪ'træktɪd] [an-ri-trak-tid], *a.* Que no se ha retractado, que no se ha desdicho; no encogido ni retraído.

unrevealed [ˌʌnrɪ'viːld] [an-ri-vild], *a.* Oculto, no revelado, que se guarda secreto.

unrewarded [ˌʌnrɪ'wɔːdɪd] [an-ri-uor-did], *a.* No premiado, no recompensado.

unriddle [ʌn'rɪdl] [an-ri-del], *va.* 1. Desatar o adivinar un enigma, explicar un problema. 2. Desenmarañar.

unrig [ʌn'rɪg] [an-rig], *va. (Mar.)* Desaparejar.

unrighteous [ʌn'raɪtʃəs] [an-rai-chos], *a.* Inicuo, malo, perverso; injusto.

unrighteously [ʌn'raɪtʃəslɪ] [an-rai-chos-li], *adv.* Inicuamente, perversamente.

unrightful [ʌn'raɪtfʊl] [an-rait-ful], *a.* Injusto, contrario a derecho; no legítimo.

unripe [ʌn'raɪp] [an-raip], *a.* Verde, inmaturo, que no ha llegado a la madurez, que no está maduro.

unripeness [ʌn'raɪpnɪs] [an-raip-nes], *s.* Falta de madurez.

unrisen [ʌn'rɪzn] [an-ri-sen], *a.* Que no se ha levantado; que no ha salido todavía (astro).

unrivalled [ʌn'raɪvəld] [an-rai-vald], *a.* Sin rival, sin igual o paralelo.

unroll [ʌn'rəʊl] [an-roul], *va.* 1. Desarrollar, extender lo que estaba arrollado. 2. Desplegar a la vista. *-vn.* Abrirse desarrollándose; desarrollarse.

unroof [ʌn'ruːf] [an-ruf], *va.* Destechar, quitar el techo.

unroost [ʌn'ruːst] [an-rust], *va.* Arrojar o echar de la percha de un gallinero; y por extensión, echar a una persona de su puesto, empleo, etc.

unroot [ʌn'ruːt] [an-rut], *va.* Desarraigar, extirpar, arrancar de raíz.

unrope [ʌn'rəʊp] [an-roup], *vt.* Desatar.

unruffled [ʌn'rʌfld] [an-ra-feld], *a.* Calmado, tranquilo, sereno.

unruled [ʌn'ruːld] [an-ruld], *a.* 1. No rayado, no reglado (papel). 2. Absoluto, independiente; lo que no tiene quien lo dirija o gobierne.

unruly [ʌn'ruːlɪ] [an-ru-li], *a.* Indómito, desenfrenado, indomable, indomeñable; revoltoso, levantisco; terco, intratable; desarreglado.

unsaddle [ʌn'sædl] [an-sa-del], *va.* Desensillar, quitar la silla a las caballerías.

unsafe [ʌn'seɪf] [an-seif], *a.* peligroso, no seguro, que tiene riesgo o peligro.

unsafely [ʌn'seɪflɪ] [an-seif-li], *adv.* Peligrosamente.

unsaid [ʌn'seɪd] [an-seid], *a.* No proferido, no mencionado, que no se ha dicho.

unsalable [ʌn'seɪləbl] [an-sei-la-bol], *a.* Invendible, que no se puede vender, lo que no tiene salida.

unsalted [ˌʌn'sɒltɪd] [an-sol-tid], *a.* Desalado; no salado.

unsatisfactory [ˈʌnˌsætɪs'fæktərɪ] [an-sa-tis-fak-to-ri], *a.* Poco satisfactorio, que no satisface o no convence.

unsatisfied [ʌn'sætɪsfaɪd] [an-sa-tis-faid], *a.* No satisfecho, descontento; no harto; no convencido, no persuadido; no saldado.

unsatisfying [ʌn'sætɪsfaɪɪŋ] [an-sa-tis-faiin], *a.* Que no satisface, que no sacia.

unsaturated [ʌn'sætʃəreɪtɪd] [an-sa-cha-rei-tid], *a. (Quím.)* No saturado; no combinado en el máximo grado.

unsavory, unsavoury [ʌn'seɪvərɪ] [an-sei-va-ri], *a.* 1. Insípido, soso, desabrido; empalagoso. 2. Hediondo, fétido. 3. Desagradable, displicente; de mala conducta o relacionado con alguna cosa moralmente mala. **To make unsavory,** desazonar o desabrir una cosa, ponerla sosa, insulsa o insípida.

unsay [ʌn'seɪ] [an-sei], *va.* Retractar lo que se ha dicho o desdecirse de ello.

unscholarly [ʌn'skɒlərlɪ] [an-sko-la-li], *a.* Impropio o indigno de una persona instruida; iliterato, no erudito.

unschooled [ʌn'skuːld] [an-skuld], *a.* Indocto, ignorante, falto de enseñanza.

unscientific [ˈʌnˌsaɪən'tɪfɪk] [an-saian-ti-fik], *a.* No científico, poco científico.

unscorched [ʌn'skɔːtʃt] [an-skorcht], *a.* No chamuscado, no tostado, no quemado.

unscrew [ʌn'skruː] [an-skru], *va.* Desatornillar, destornillar; *(Fig.)* desenganchar, apartar, separar.

unscrupulous [ʌn'skruːpjʊləs] [an-sku-piu-los], *a.* Poco escrupuloso, inmoral, falto de principios morales.

unscrupulously [ʌn'skruːpjʊləslɪ] [an-sku-piu-los-li], *adv.* Sin moralidad, sin conciencia.

unseal [ʌn'siːl] [an-sil], *va.* Desellar, romper o quitar el sello, abrir lo que está sellado.

unsealed [ʌn'siːld] [an-sild], *a.* Desellado, sin sello, abierto, no sellado.

unseasonable [ʌn'siːzbəbl] [an-si-so-na-bol], *a.* Intempestivo, fuera de sazón, fuera de propósito, inoportuno; indebido, poco conveniente. **At unseasonable hours,** a deshora o a deshoras.

unseasonably [ʌn'siːzbəblɪ] [an-si-so-na-bli], *adv.* Intempestivamente, fuera de propósito, fuera de tiempo o sazón, en mala ocasión.

unseasoned [ʌn'siːzənd] [an-si-sond], *a.* 1. No sazonado, soso; no aclimatado. 2. No acostumbrado, no habituado; no aguerrido, no endurecido. 3. Verde, no seca (madera).

unseat [ʌn'siːt] [an-sit], *va.* Quitar de un asiento o posición fija: 1. Desarzonar, echar al suelo (from a horse); 2. Privar del derecho de tomar asiento como legislador; echar abajo (ministery).

unsectarian [ˌʌnsek'tɛərɪən] [an-sek-ta-rian], *a.* No sectario, no propio de una secta; abierta a todos.

unsecure [ˌʌnsɪ'kjʊər] [an-si-kiuar], *a.* Inseguro, en peligro. *V.* INSECURE.

unseeing [ʌn'siːɪŋ] [an-siin], *a.* Ciego, falto de vista.

unseemiliness [ʌn'siːmlɪnɪs] [an-sim-li-nes], *s.* Indecencia, indecoro.

unseemly [ʌn'siːmlɪ] [an-sim-li], *a.* Indecente; indecoroso; malparecido, impropio.

unseen [ʌn'siːn] [an-sin], *a.* 1. Invisible, que no se ve; no evidente. 2. Inapercibido, que no se ha visto; que no se ha visto más de una vez.

unselfish [ʌn'selfɪʃ] [an-sel-fish], *a.* Desinteresado, no egoísta.

unselfishly [ʌn'selfɪʃlɪ] [an-sel-fish-li], *adv.* Desinteresadamente, sin egoísmo.

unsent [ʌn'sent] [an-sent], *a.* No enviado. **Unsent-for,** no llamado, no enviado a llamar, no convidado.

unserviceable [ʌn'sɜːvɪsəbl] [an-ser-vi-sa-bol], *a.* Inútil, sin utilidad ni ventaja, que no es bueno para nada.

unset [ʌn'set] [an-set], *a.* No plantado; no puesto.

unsettle [ʌn'setl] [an-se-tel], *va.* 1. Inquietar, alterar, perturbar. 2. Hacer incierta o poco segura alguna cosa, poner en desorden; desarreglar; trastornar (el espíritu, la razón). 3. Dislocar, remover, trastornar; conmover.

unsettled [ʌn'setld] [an-se-teld], *a.* 1. Inestable, poco estable, no fijado. 2. Que no tiene domicilio o residencia fija; vago. 3. Inconstante, irresuelto, indeterminado, incierto. 4.

Pendiente, no acabado. 5. Desarreglado, descompuesto, turbado; turbio, que no ha hecho poso. 6. *(Com.)* No arreglado, no liquidado. 7. No habitado, no poblado, sin habitantes.

unsex ['ʌn'seks] [an-seks], *va.* Quitar las propiedades, hábitos, etc., que corresponden a su sexo; particularmente, hacer o hacer parecer poco femenino (a una mujer).

unsexual ['ʌn'seksjʊəl], *a.* Asexual, no característico o peculiar de uno de los sexos.

unshackle ['ʌn'ʃækl] [an-sha-kel], *va.* Destrabar, desencadenar, quitar las trabas a; libertar.

unshaded ['ʌn'ʃeɪdɪd] [an-shei-did], *a.* Que no está sombreado; que no tiene sombra.

unshadowed ['ʌn'ʃædəʊɪd] [an-sha-douid], *a.* Claro, sereno, exento de sombra.

unshakable ['ʌn'ʃeɪkəbl] [an-shei-ka-bol], *a.* Inmutable, impasible.

unshaken ['ʌn'ʃeɪkən] [an-shei-ken], *a.* Firme, estable, seguro, inmoble, inmovible.

unshared ['ʌn'ʃɛəd] [an-shead], *a.* Que no ha sido dividido; que no ha cabido a alguno en partición.

unshaven ['ʌn'ʃeɪvn] [an-shei-ven], *a.* No afeitado, sin estar afeitado.

unsheathe ['ʌn'ʃiːð] [an-shidz], *va.* Desenvainar, sacar de la vaina.

unshed ['ʌn'ʃed] [an-shed], *a.* No derramado, no esparcido.

unsheltered ['ʌn'ʃeltəd] [an-shel-terd], *a.* Desvalido, falto de abrigo o protección.

unship ['ʌn'ʃɪp] [an-ship], *va.* Desembarcar, sacar a tierra lo que está embarcado. **To unship the rudder,** *(Mar.)* Desmontar el timón. **To unship the oars,** *(Mar.)* Desarmar los remos.

unshocked ['ʌn'ʃɒkt] [an-shokt], *a.* No ofendido, no disgustado.

unshod ['ʌn'ʃɒd] [an-shod], *a.* y *pp.* Descalzo; desherrado.

unshoe ['ʌn'ʃuː] [an-shu], *va. (pret. y pp.* UNSHOD). Desherrar.

unshorn ['ʌn'ʃɔːn] [an-shorn], *a.* Que no ha sido esquilado. **Unshorn sheep,** ovejas por esquilar.

unshot ['ʌn'ʃɒt] [an-shot], *a.* 1. Que no se ha descargado, no disparado. 2. No herido.

unshut ['ʌn'ʃʌt] [an-shat], *a.* Abierto, no cerrado.

unsightly ['ʌn'saɪtlɪ] [an-sait-li], *a.* Feo, disforme, desagradable a la vista.

unsinful ['ʌn'sɪnfʊl] [an-sin-ful], *a.* Impecable, que no peca; exento de pecado.

unsized ['ʌn'saɪzd] [an-saisd], *a.* No encolado, sin cola (papel).

unskilled ['ʌn'skɪld] [an-skild], *a.* No diestro, desmañado, inhábil, inexperimentado; ignorante.

unsleeping ['ʌn'sliːpɪŋ] [an-sli-pin], *a.* En vela, siempre despierto.

unsmiling ['ʌn'smaɪlɪŋ] [an-smai-lin], *a.* Sin sonrisa.

unsmoked ['ʌn'sməʊkt] [an-smoukt], *a.* No ahumado; no fumado; (pipa nueva) en la cual no se ha fumado.

unsociable ['ʌn'səʊʃəbl] [an-sou-sha-bol], *a.* Insociable, intratable, huraño.

unsociableness ['ʌn'səʊʃəblnɪs] [an-sou-sha-bol-nes], *s.* Insociabilidad.

unsociably ['ʌn'səʊʃəblɪ] [an-sou-sha-bli], *adv.* Insociablemente.

unsocial ['ʌn'səʊʃəl] [an-sou-shal], *a.* Insocial, intratable, huraño.

unsoiled ['ʌn'sɔɪld] [an-soild], *a.* Impoluto, libre de mancha.

unsold ['ʌn'səʊld] [an-sould], *a.* No vendido, no despachado; que no ha tenido salida.

unsolder ['ʌn'səʊldə'] [an-soul-da'], *va.* Quitar la soldadura.

unsoldierly ['ʌn'səʊldʒəlɪ] [an-soul-dia-li], *a.* Indigno de un soldado, contrario u opuesto a la disciplina militar.

unsolicited ['ʌnsəˈlɪsɪtɪd] [an-so-li-si-tid], *a.* No solicitado, no buscado.

unsolicitous ['ʌnsəˈlɪsɪtəs] [an-so-li-si-tos], *a.* Poco solícito, deseoso, o celoso de; poco cuidadoso de.

unsolved ['ʌn'sɒlvd] [an-solvd], *a.* Sin resolver, sin explicar, sin desatar; oscuro, confuso.

unsophisticated ['ʌnsəˈfɪstɪkeɪtɪd] [an-so-fis-ti-kei-tid], *a.* Puro, que no ha sido falsificado o adulterado; sencillo, no artificial; inexperimentado, falto de experiencia.

unsorted ['ʌn'sɔːtɪd] [an-sor-tid], *a.* 1. No apartado, no separado. 2. Fuera de tiempo o de propósito.

unsought ['ʌn'sɔːt] [an-sot], *a.* Hallado o encontrado sin buscarlo.

unsound ['ʌn'saʊnd] [an-saund], *a.* 1. Enfermizo, de poca salud; achacoso. 2. Defectuoso, que no es sano; falto de vigor, de fuerza, de solidez; poco firme; falto de salud, enfermo. 3. Sentido, hendido: dícese de la vasija que no está sana. 4. Erróneo, falso; heterodoxo, no ortodoxo. 5. Demasiado fofo o blando. 6. Podrido, corrompido.

unsounded ['ʌn'saʊndɪd] [an-saun-did], *a.* Que no ha sido sondeado o examinado con la sonda; que no se ha sondeado o sabido a fondo.

unsoundness ['ʌn'saʊndnɪs] [an-saund-nes], *s.* 1. Heterodoxia, oposición a las doctrinas ortodoxas. 2. Falta de solidez o de fuerza. 3. Corrupción.

unspared ['ʌn'spɛəd] [an-spead], *a.* No ahorrado.

unsparing ['ʌn'spɛərɪŋ] [an-spea-rin], *a.* 1. Liberal, generoso, pródigo, no económico. 2. Inhumano, falto de piedad, cruel.

unsparingly ['ʌn'spɛərɪŋlɪ] [an-spea-rin-li], *adv.* 1. Liberalmente, pródigamente, con profusión. 2. Sin piedad, inhumanamente.

unspeakable [ʌn'spiːkəbl] [an-spi-ka-bol], *a.* 1. Inefable, indecible, inexplicable. 2. *(Fam.)* Extremadamente malo; execrable. **The unspeakable,** el execrable turco.

unspeakably ʌn'spiːkəblɪ] [an-spi-ka-bli], *adv.* Inefablemente, indeciblemente.

unsped ['ʌn'sped] [an-sped], *a.* No despachado o expedido.

unspent ['ʌn'spent] [an-spent], *a.* Que no está agotado; no gastado, no debilitado.

unsphere ['ʌn'sfɪə'] [an-sfia'], *va.* Sacar de su esfera o lugar.

unspoiled ['ʌn'spɔɪld] [an-spoild], *a.* No saqueado; ileso, libre de daño; intacto.

unspotted [n'spɒlɪd] [an-spou-tid], *a.* Inmaculado, limpio, sin mancha.

unstable ['ʌn'steɪbl] [an-stei-bol], *a.* Instable, poco estable; inconstante, variable, mudable, vacilante; irresoluto, indeciso.

unstaid ['ʌn'steɪd] [an-steid], *a.* Voluble, mudable, ligero, atolondrado, inconstante.

unstaidness ['ʌn'steɪdnɪs] [an-steid-nes], *s.* Indiscreción, imprudencia; inconstancia.

unstained ['ʌn'steɪnd] [an-steind], *a.* Inmaculado, libre de mancha; no teñido; sin color (vidrio).

unsteadfast ['ʌn'stedfɑːst] [an-sted-fast], *a.* Instable, inconstante, no fijo, irresoluto.

unsteadily ['ʌn'stedɪlɪ] [an-ste-di-li], *adv.* Ligeramente, inconstantemente, de un modo inconsecuente; indiscretamente.

unsteadiness ['ʌn'stednɪs] [an-ste-di-nes], *s.* Inestabilidad, inconstancia.

unsteady ['ʌn'stedɪ] [an-ste-di], *a.* Voluble, inconstante, veleidoso, inconsiguiente o inconsecuente, que no tiene firmeza o resolución; poco asegurado, poco fijo; poco firme, inseguro.

unstep ['ʌn'step] [an-step], *va. (Mar.)* Desmontar, quitar un mástil de su hueco o encaje.

unstinted ['ʌn'stɪntɪd] [an-stin-tid], *a.* No limitado; liberal.

unstop ['ʌn'stɒp] [an-stop], *va.* Abrir camino, dar paso libre; destapar.

unstopped ['ʌn'stɒpt] [an-stopt], *a.* Que no encuentra resistencia o que no halla nada que se le oponga.

unstrained ['ʌn'streɪnd] [an-streind], *a.* Natural, no violento.

unstring ['ʌn'strɪŋ] [an-strin], *va.* 1. Desencordar, quitar las cuerdas a un instrumento de música. 2. Desliar, desatar, aflojar.

unstruck ['ʌn'strʌk] [an-strak], *a.* No conmovido, no asustado, impávido.

unstrung ['ʌn'strʌŋ] [an-strang], *pret.* y *pp.* del verbo TO UNSTRING.

unstudied ['ʌn'stʌdɪd] [an-sta-did], *a.* 1. Que no ha sido estudiado; que no ha sido premeditado, no preparado, natural. 2. No dado al estudio.

unstuffed [ˈʌnˈstʌft] [an-staft], *a.* No llenado, no rellenado, no atiborrado.

unsubdued [ˈʌnsəbˈdjuːd] [an-sab-diud], *a.* Indomado, no sujetado, no subyugado; indómito, invicto.

unsubmissive [ˈʌnsəbˈmɪsɪv] [an-sab-mi-siv], *a.* Insumiso, no sometido, rebelde.

unsubstantial [ˈʌnsəbˈstænʃəl] [an-sab-stan-shal], *a.* Insubstancial, de poca o ninguna substancia; poco sólido; de poco valor; no real, imaginario; no duradero; inmaterial, no esencial.

unsuccessful [ˈʌnsəkˈsesfʊl] [an-sak-ses-ful], *a.* Que no ha conseguido lo que esperaba, que ha salido mal; infructuoso, sin éxito, desgraciado, desafortunado, adverso.

unsuccessfully [ˈʌnsəkˈsesfəlɪ] [an-sak-ses-fa-li], *adv.* Infelizmente, desafortunadamente.

unsuccessfulness [ˈʌnsəkˈsesfəlnɪs] [an-sak-ses-fal-nes], *s.* Infortunio, desgracia, desdicha.

unsuitable [ˈʌnˈsuːtəbl] [an-su-ta-bol], *a.* No adaptado, no apropiado; que no conviene, poco adecuado; desproporcionado, desigual, incongruente.

unsuitableness [ˈʌnˈsuːtəblnɪs] [an-su-ta-bol-nes], *s.* Incongruencia, desconveniencia; incompatibilidad.

unsuited [ˈʌnˈsuːtɪd] [an-su-tid], *a.* No a propósito, incongruo, impropio, incongruente.

unsullied [ˈʌnˈsʌlɪd] [an-sa-lid], *a.* Inmaculado, no ensuciado, puro, libre de mancha.

unsung [ˈʌnˈsʌŋ] [an-sang], *a.* No cantado, no celebrado en verso.

unsupported [ˈʌnsəˈpɔːtɪd] [an-sa-por-tid], *a.* Que no tiene apoyo o sostén; que no tiene quien lo defienda o apoye; no hay quien lo defienda o apoye; no favorecido; no sostenido; no provisto.

unsure [ˈʌnˈʃʊəʳ] [an-shua'], *a.* Incierto, no seguro.

unsurmountable [ˈʌnsəˈmaʊntəbl] [an-sa-maun-ta-bol], *a.* Insuperable. *V.* INSURMOUNTABLE.

unsurpassable [ˈʌnsəˈpɑːsəbl] [an-sa-pa-sa-bol], *a.* 1. Impasable. 2. Insuperable.

unsuspected [ˈʌnsəsˈpektɪd] [an-sas-pek-tid], *a.* No sospechado.

unsuspicious [ˈʌnsəsˈpɪʃəs] [an-sas-pi-shos], *a.* Sencillo, que no es suspicaz; confiado, no inclinado a sospechar, no sospechoso, no receloso.

unswear [ˈʌnˈsweəʳ] [an-suea'], *va.* y *vn.* (*pret.* UNSWORE, *pp.* UNSWORN). Abjurar; retractarse de un juramento.

unsweetened [ˈʌnˈswiːtnd] [an-sui-tend], *a.* No dulcificado, sin endulzar.

unswerving [ˈʌnˈswɜːvɪŋ] [an-suer-vin], *a.* Inmutable, firme. **Unswerving faith,** fe inquebrantable.

unsympathetic [ˈʌnˌsɪmpəˈθetɪk] [an-sim-pa-ze-tik], *a.* Falto de simpatía, poco simpático, poco benévolo, que no simpatiza.

unsystematic [ˈʌnˌsɪstɪˈmætɪk] [an-sis-ti-ma-tik], *a.* Que no es sistemático, falto de sistema.

untainted [ˈʌnˈteɪntɪd] [an-tein-tid], *a.* Inmaculado; que no está corrompido, no echado a perder; que no está viciado, infestado o apestado.

untaken [ˈʌnˈteɪkn] [an-tei-ken], *a.* No tomado, no cogido. **Untaken up,** no ocupado, no llenado.

untamable [ˈʌnˈteɪməbl] [an-tei-ma-bol], *a.* Indomable; indomesticable.

untamed [ˈʌnˈteɪmd] [an-teimd], *a.* Indómito, indomado, no domado, no suavizado, no domesticado; feroz; insumiso, rebelde.

untangible [ˈʌnˈtændʒəbl] [an-tan-yi-bol], *a.* (*Ant.*) *V.* INTANGIBLE.

untangle [ˈʌnˈtæŋl] [an-tan-guel], *va.* Desenredar, desenmarañar, desembarazar.

untarnished [ˈʌnˈtɑːnɪʃt] [an-tar-nisht], *a.* No mancillado, no deslucido, no deslustrado (en sentido literal y figurado); sin mancha.

untasted [ˈʌnˈteɪstɪd] [an-teis-tid], *a.* Que no se ha gustado, probado o catado.

untaught [ˈʌnˈtɔːt] [an-tot], *a.* 1. Rudo, ignorante, mal criado. 2. Inexperto, novato, falto de experiencia.

untaxed [ˈʌnˈtækst] [an-takst], *a.* Exento de tasa, de contribución; no acusado.

unteach [ˈʌnˈtiːtʃ] [an-tich], *va.* (*Ant.*) (*pret.* y *pp.* UNTAUGHT). Desenseñar, hacer olvidar lo que antes se había enseñado.

unteachable [ˈʌnˈtiːtʃəbl] [an-ti-cha-bol], *a.* Incapaz de ser enseñado. **Unteachable man,** hombre indócil.

untempered [ˈʌnˈtempəd] [an-tem-pard], *a.* No templado, sin temple; no atemperado, no suavizado.

untempted [ˈʌnˈtemptɪd] [an-temp-tid], *a.* No tentado, libre o exento de tentaciones.

untenable [ˈʌnˈtenəbl] [an-te-na-bol], *a.* 1. Lo que no se puede poseer. 2. Incapaz de defensa, insostenible.

untenanted [ˈʌnˈtenəntɪd] [an-te-nan-tid], *a.* Desarrendado, sin arrendatario; vacío, desocupado.

untended [ˈʌnˈtendɪd] [an-ten-did], *a.* *V.* UNATTENDED.

untender [ˈʌnˈtendəʳ] [an-ten-da'], *a.* Duro, áspero, falto de ternura, intensible.

untendered [ˈʌnˈtendəd] [an-ten-dard], *a.* No ofrecido.

untented [ˈʌnˈtentɪd] [an-ten-tid], *a.* Que no tiene tiendas de campaña.

unthinking [ˈʌnˈθɪŋkɪŋ] [an-zin-kin], *a.* Descuidado, desatento, indiscreto; irreflexivo.

unthought-of [ˈʌnˈθɔːtɒv] [an-zot-ov], *a.* Impensado, descuidado; dado al olvido o echado en el olvido.

unthread [ˈʌnˈθred] [an-zred], *va.* Desenhebrar, deshilachar, sacar los hilos de algún tejido.

unthrift [ˈʌnˈθrɪft] [an-zrift], *s.* 1. Carencia de ahorro, de economía; prodigalidad. 2. (*Des.*) Gastador, pródigo, el que gasta mucho.

unthrifty [ˈʌnˈθrɪftɪ] [an-zrift-ti], *a.* Pródigo, manirroto.

untidily [ˈʌnˈtaɪdɪlɪ] [an-tai-di-li], *adv.* Sin aseo, sin orden, sin arreglo ni limpieza.

untidiness [ˈʌnˈtaɪdɪnɪs] [an-tai-di-nes], *s.* Descompostura, desaliño, falta de aseo y orden.

untidy [ˈʌnˈtaɪdɪ] [an-tai-di], *a.* Desaliñado, descompuesto, falto de orden y aseo, desaseado; sucio.

untie [ˈʌnˈtaɪ] [an-tai], *va.* 1. Desatar, desprender, desenlazar o soltar lo atado, deshacer (un nudo). 2. Aflojar o soltar lo apretado. 3. (*Des.*) Aclarar, explicar, resolver una dificultad.

until [ənˈtɪl] [an-til], *prep.* Hasta. -*conj.* Hasta el punto en que; hasta el lugar o grado que, hasta que. **Until the hour comes,** hasta que venga o llegue la hora.

untile [ˈʌnˈtaɪl] [an-tail], *va.* Destejar, quitar las tejas de los tejados.

untilled [ˈʌnˈtɪld] [an-tild], *a.* Inculto, no cultivado.

untimely [ˈʌnˈtaɪmlɪ] [an-taim-li], *a.* Intempestivo, precoz, prematuro, adelantado, que no está en sazón, que es antes de tiempo. -*adv.* Intempestivamente, antes de tiempo, sin sazón, abortivamente.

untiring [ˈʌnˈtaɪrɪŋ] [an-tai-rin], *a.* Incansable, infatigable.

untitled [ˈʌnˈtaɪtld] [an-tai-teld], *a.* Que no tiene título, sin título.

unto [ˈʌnˈtʊ] [an-tu], *prep.* A, en, dentro; hacia. Forma poética o arcaica equivalente a *to,* excepto como signo del infinito.

untold [ˈʌnˈtəʊld] [an-tould], *a.* 1. Que no se ha referido, que no se ha dicho, no narrado. 2. No computable; desmedido, sumamente grande. **To leave untold,** no decir, no relatar, dejar en el tintero.

untouched [ˈʌnˈtʌtʃt] [an-tacht], *a.* 1. Intacto, que no ha sido tocado; ileso. 2. Insensible, no conmovido, no afectado, que no se conmueve por nada.

untoward [ˌʌntəˈwɔːd] [an-to-uord], *a.* 1. Displicente, enfadoso, incómodo, vejador; desfavorable, siniestro, adverso. 2. Indócil, que no cede fácilmente, testarudo, refractario.

untowardly [ˌʌntəˈwɔːdlɪ] [an-to-uord-li], *adv.* Tercamente, indócilmente, perversamente; adversamente, infelizmente, siniestramente.

untowardness [ˌʌntəˈwɔːdnɪs] [an-to-uord-nes], *s.* Perversidad, terquedad.

untraced ['ʌn'treɪst] [an-treist], *a.* No hollado, no pisado, sin senda, sin huella; (dibujo) no calcado.

untrained ['ʌn'treɪnd] [an-treind], *a.* Indisciplinado, indócil, no ejercitado, inexperimentado; que no está adiestrado.

untrammelled ['ʌn'træməld] [an-tra-meld], *a.* Sin trabas; no limitado, libre.

untransferable ['ʌntræns'fɜːrəbl] [an-trans-fa-ra-bol], *a.* No enajenable, que no se puede transferir o enajenar.

untranslatable ['ʌntræns'leɪtəbl] [an-trans-tei-ta-bol], *a.* Intraducible, que no se puede traducir de un idioma a otro.

untravelled ['ʌn'trævld] [an-tra-veld], *a.* No frecuentado por viajeros o pasajeros; se dice también del que no ha viajado por países extranjeros.

untried ['ʌn'traɪd] [an-traid], *a.* Que no se ha experimentado, ensayado o probado; que no ha sido juzgado.

untrimmed ['ʌn'trɪmd] [an-trimd], *a.* No guarnecido; no ajustado; largo, no cortado, no afeitado, descuidado (hair, beard).

untrodden ['ʌn'trɒdn] [an-tro-den], *a.* Que no ha sido pisado ni hollado o señalado con los pies; de aquí, no frecuentado.

untroubled ['ʌn'trʌbld] [an-tra-beld], *a.* 1. Quieto, tranquilo, sosegado, apacible. 2. Claro, transparente.

untrue ['ʌn'truː] [an-tru], *a.* 1. Falso, que no es verdadero; incierto, contrario a la verdad, falto de realidad. 2. Falso, engañoso, pérfido.

untruly ['ʌn'truːlɪ] [an-tru-li] *adv.* Falsamente.

untruss ['ʌn'trʌs] [an-tras], *va.* Desatar.

untrustworthy ['ʌn'trʌst,wɜːðɪ] [an-trast-uer-zi], *a.* Indigno de confianza.

untrusty ['ʌn'trʌstɪ] [an-tras-ti], *a.* Infiel, pérfido, que no merece confianza.

untruth ['ʌn'truːθ] [an-truz], *s.* 1. Falsedad, mentira. 2. Infidelidad, traición.

untuck ['ʌn'tʌk] [an-tak], *va.* Deshacer un pliegue a; desguarnecer una cama.

untunable ['ʌn'tjuːnəbl] [an-tiu-na-bol], *a.* Desentonado, discorde, disonante.

untune ['ʌn'tjuːn] [an-tiun], *va.* 1. Hacer desentonar o salir de tono; desacordar o destemplar un instrumento. 2. Trastornar, sacar las cosas de su quicio.

unturned ['ʌn'tɜːnd] [an-ternd], *a.* No torneado; no movido. **To leave no stone unturned,** no dejar piedra por mover.

untutored ['ʌn'tjuːtəd] [an-tiu-tord], *a.* Mal educado, que no ha sido instruido, enseñado o disciplinado.

untwine ['ʌn'twaɪnl] [an-tuain], *va.* 1. Desenrollar, desarrollar, desencoger lo que está arrollado. 2. Separar una cosa que está enroscada con otra.

untwist ['ʌn'twɪst] [an-tuist], *va.* Destorcer, deshacer lo torcido.

untypical ['ʌn'tɪpɪkəl] [an-ti-pi-kal], *a.* Atípico.

unused ['ʌn'juːzd] [an-iusd], *a.* Inusitado, no usado, insólito.

unuseful [ʌn'juːzfʊl] [an-ius-ful], *a.* Inútil.

unusual [ʌn'juːʒʊəl] [an-iu-shual], *a.* Raro, extraordinario, extraño; inusitado; desacostumbrado.

unusually [ʌn'juːʒʊəlɪ] [an-iu-shua-li], *adv.* Inusitadamente, raramente, rara vez.

unusualness [ʌn'juːʒʊəlnɪs] [an-iu-shual-nes], *s.* Rareza, raridad.

unutterable [ʌn'ʌtərəbl] [an-a-te-ra-bol], *a.* Inefable, inenarrable, inexplicable, indecible.

unvalued [ʌn'væljuːd] [an-va-liud], *a.* Desestimado, menospreciado. 2. Inestimable, que no tiene valor fijo.

unvaried [ʌn'veərɪd] [an-va-rid], *a.* Invariado, no mudado, no cambiado; uniforme, que es siempre lo mismo.

unvarnished [ʌn'vɑːnɪʃt] [an-var-nisht], *a.* No barnizado, falto de barniz; sin adorno.

unvarying [ʌn'veərɪɪŋ] [an-va-rin], *a.* Que no varía, constante, uniforme.

unveil [ʌn'veɪld] [an-veild], *va.* Quitar el velo, descubrir lo que está cubierto, mostrar a la vista.

unventilated [ʌn'ventɪleɪtɪd] [an-ven-ti-lei-tid], *a.* No ventilado.

unverifiable [ʌn'verɪfaɪəbl] [an-ve-ri-faia-bol], *a.* Sin aire, sin ventilar.

unversed [ʌn'vɜːst] [an-verst], *a.* No conocedor, poco ducho.

unvirtuous [ʌn'vɜːtjʊəs] [an-ver-tiuos], *a.* Vicioso, falto de virtud (vicious).

unvisited ['ʌn'vɪzɪtɪd] [an-vi-si-tid], *a.* No visitado.

unvoiced [ʌn'vɔɪst] [an-voist], *a.* No expresado. **His opinions remain unvoiced,** sus opiniones continúan no expresadas.

unwakened [ʌn'weɪkənd] [an-uei-kend], *a.* No despierto.

unwanted [ʌn'wɒntɪd] [an-uon-tid], *a.* No deseado (child); superfluo.

unwarily [ʌn'weərɪlɪ] [an-uea-ri-li], *adv.* Incautamente, inadvertidamente, imprudentemente, sin previsión, sin precaución (rash).

unwariness [ʌn'weərɪnɪs] [an-uea-ri-nes], *s.* Imprevisión, falta de precaución, falta de cuidado, de cautela.

unwarlike [ʌn'wɔːlaɪk] [an-uor-laik], *a.* Que no es belicoso, pacífico (orderly, peaceable).

unwarned [ʌn'wɔːnd] [an-uornd], *a.* No avisado, no prevenido, no advertido.

unwarrantable [ʌn'wɒrəntəbl] [an-uo-ran-ta-bol], *a.* 1. Inexcusable, indisculpable, sin excusa ni disculpa. 2. Insostenible, que no se puede defender.

unwarrantably [ʌn'wɒrəntəblɪ] [an-uo-ran-ta-bli], *adv.* Injustamente, de un modo inexcusable; de un modo que no puede admitir ninguna defensa.

unwarranted [ʌn'wɒrəntɪd] [an-uo-ran-tid], *a.* Incierto, que no es seguro ni fijo.

unwary [ʌn'weərɪ] [an-uea-ri], *a.* 1. Incauto, imprudente, inconsiderado, irreflexivo, que no pone cuidado en el peligro (incautious). 2. *(Des.)* Inopinado. **If you are unwary he will cheat you,** si eres incauto, él te estafará.

unwashed ['ʌn'wɒʃt] [an-uosht], *a.* Puerco, sucio, que no se ha lavado. **The great unwashed,** *(Fest.)* El populacho, la canalla.

unwasted [ʌn'weɪstɪd] [an-ueis-tid], *a.* Entero, ileso, no consumido (clear, whole, full)..

unwasting [ʌn'weɪstɪŋ] [an-ueis-tin], *a.* Que no se disminuye o se consume, inagotable.

unwavering [ʌn'weɪvərɪŋ] [an-uei-va-rin], *a.* Que no vacila; determinado, resuelto, constante.

unweakened [ʌn'wiːkənd] [an-ui-kend], *a.* No debilitado.

unwearable [ʌn'weərəbl] [an-uea-ra-bol], *a.* Poco propio para ser llevado, que ya no puede usarse o llevarse.

unwearying [ʌn'weərɪɪŋ] [an-uea-riin], *a.* 1. No cansado, no fatigado. 2. Infatigable, incansable.

unwed [ʌn'wed] [an-ued], *a.* Soltero, no casado (bachelor).

unweighed [ʌn'weɪgd] [an-ueigd], *a.* No pesado, sin ser pesado; que no ha sido escudriñado, examinado.

unwelcome [ʌn'welkəm] [an-uel-kam], *a.* Que no es bienvenido, que no se ve con placer; mal recibido, mal acogido; desagradable, incómodo, inoportuno, que viene fuera de tiempo. **His news are unwelcome in this moment,** sus noticias son inoportunas en este momento.

unwell [ʌn'wel] [an-uel], *a.* 1. Indispuesto, que no está bien; enfermizo, mal. 2. Menstruante, la que está con el menstruo. **He felt unwell this morning,** se sintió indispuesto esta mañana.

unwept [ʌn'wept] [an-uept], *a.* No llorado, no lamentado; no vertido (lágrimas).

unwet [ʌn'wet] [an-uet], *a.* Enjuto, que no está mojado; seco, sin humedad.

unwholesome [ʌn'həʊlsəm] [an-joul-som], *a.* Malsano, insalubre, perjudicial a la salud; nocivo, malo.

unwieldily [ʌn'wiːldɪlɪ] [an-uil-di-li], *adv.* Pesadamente, de un modo dificultoso de manejar.

unwieldiness [ʌn'wiːldɪnɪs] [an-uil-di-nes]; *s.* Pesadez, dificultad de manejarse o moverse.

unwieldy [ʌn'wiːldɪ] [an-uil-di], *a.* Pesado, ponderoso, abultado, que se mueve con dificultad.

unwilling [ʌn'wɪlɪŋ] [an-ui-lin], *a.* Desinclinado, que no quiere o que no tiene deseo o gana de hacer alguna cosa; mal dispuesto, de mala voluntad. **To be unwilling,** tener repugnancia. **Willing or unwilling,** que quiera que no quiera, a buenas o a malas.

unwillingly [ʌn'wɪlɪŋlɪ] [an-ui-lin-li], *adv.* De mala gana, con repugnancia, por fuerza, a duras penas.

unwillingness [ʌnˈwɪlɪŋnɪs] [an-ui-lin-nes], *s.* Mala gana, repugnancia.

unwind [ˈʌnˈwaɪnd] [an-uaind], *va. (pret.* y *pp.* UNWOUND). Devanar (hilo); desenredar, desenmarañar. - *vn.* Devanarse, desarrollarse.

unwise [ˈʌnˈwaɪz] [an-uais], *a.* Imprudente, indiscreto; ignorante, tonto (foolish).

unwisely [ˈʌnˈwaɪzlɪ] [an-uais-li], *adv.* Neciamente; imprudentemente, indiscretamente.

unwished [ˈʌnˈwɪʃt] [an-uisht], *a.* No buscado, no deseado.

unwittlily [ˈʌnˈwɪtlɪlɪ] [an-uit-li-li], *adv.* Sin gracia, tontamente, fastidiosamente.

unwitting [ʌnˈwɪtɪŋ] [an-ui-tin], *a.* Que no tiene saber ni conocimiento de lo que se trata; que no sabe.

unwittingly [ʌnˈwɪtɪŋlɪ] [an-ui-tin-li], *adv.* Sin saberlo, inconscientemente (unintentionally). **He was unwittingly cruel to her,** era cruel con ella inconscientemente.

unwomanly [ʌnˈwʊmənlɪ] [an-uo-man-li], *a.* Indigno de una mujer; que no conviene a una mujer.

unwonted [ʌnˈwəʊntɪd] [an-uon-tid], *a.* 1. No acostumbrado, poco común, poco habitual, extraordinario (unusual). 2. *(Des.)* Insólito, desacostumbrado (se decía de personas).

unwontedness [ʌnˈwəʊntɪdnɪs] [an-uon-tid-nes], *s.* Rareza, raridad, la calidad de ser rara alguna cosa.

unwooded [ʌnˈwuːdɪd] [an-wu-did], *a.* No poblado de árboles, sin bosque.

unworking [ʌnˈwɜːkɪŋ] [an-uer-kin], *a.* Perezoso, holgazán, que no trabaja.

unworthily [ʌnˈwɜːðɪlɪ] [an-uer-zi-li], *adv.* Indignamente.

unworthiness [ʌnˈwɜːðɪnɪs] [an-uer-zi-nés], *s.* Indignidad, falta de mérito; bajeza.

unworthy [ʌnˈwɜːðɪ] [an-uer-zi], *a.* Indigno, falto de mérito, que no merece; vil, bajo (shameful, disgraceful)..

unwound [ʌnˈwaʊnd] [an-uaund], *a.* Sin cuerda (un reloj, etc.).

unwounded [ˈʌnˈwaʊndɪd] [an-wun-ded], *a.* No herido, ileso, libre de daño.

unwrap [ˈʌnˈræp] [an-rap], *va.* Desenvolver. **He unwrapped the gift,** desenvolvió el obsequio.

unwreathe [ˈʌnˈreθ] [an-rez], *va.* Desenvolver, quitar la guirnalda; destrenzar, deshacer lo entretejido.

unwritten [ˈʌnˈrɪtn] [an-ri-ten], *a.* Verbal, no escrito, tradicional, comunicado por tradición.

unwrought [ˈʌnˈraʊt] [an-raut], *a.* No trabajado, no fabricado; en bruto; crudo; grosero. **Unwrought wax,** cera virgen.

unyielded [ʌnˈjiːldɪd] [an-yil-did], *a.* No cedido.

unyelding [ʌnˈjiːldɪŋ] [an-yil-din], *a.* Inflexible, reacio, terco, que no cede.

unyoke [ˈʌnˈjəʊk] [an-youk], *va.* Desuncir, quitar el yugo; de aquí, separar, desunir. -*vn.* Ser libertado de un yugo; suspender el trabajo, cesar.

unzip [ˈʌnˈzɪp] [an-zip], *v.* Bajar la cremallera de. **Will you unzip this dress please?,** me baja la cremallera del vestido por favor?

up [ʌp] [ap], *a.* Que se mueve o se inclina hacia arriba; levantado, sobre el horizonte; ascendiendo. **Up train,** tren ascendente. **Up grade,** terraplén, cuesta ascendente. -*s.* Lo alto, lo elevado, tierra elevada; estado de prosperidad: se usa principalmente en la locución **ups and downs,** altibajos. -*adv.* 1. Arriba, en lo alto, hacia arriba; lo contrario de *down,* abajo. 2. En pie o derecho; de pie o levantado. 3. Hasta, de manera que esté al mismo grado, nivel, etc. **Up to date,** hasta la fecha, moderno, al día. 4. *(Fam.)* Informado en, en estado igual a, formando una partida igual. **Up to his tricks,** tan pillo como él. **Up in geology,** impuesto en geología. 5. Excitado, animado; en pie, sublevado, insurrecto; en progreso o ejecución. **To be up in arms,** sublevarse, tomar las armas, insurreccionarse. **What's up?** ¿qué pasa? ¡qué se trama? 6. En prominencia, bajo consideración. 7. Guardado en un lugar. **To lay up money,** acumular dinero. **To put up preserves,** preparar conservas de frutas. 8. Al término, llegado, acabado. **The hour is up,** ha llegado la hora. **It is all up now,** todo se

acabó. 9. Completamente, en todo. **Twenty houses were burned up,** veinte casas se quemaron completamente. **To go up,** subir. **Hard up,** *(Fam.)* en apuros, a la cuarta pregunta. **Up hill,** cuesta arriba. **Up-stairs,** arriba, en lo alto de la escalera. *-prep.* Hacia arriba a lo largo, subiendo; en lo alto de; en el interior de. **Up to,** hasta; a la altura de; al corriente de; dispuesto *a. -inter.* ¡Arriba! **The sun is up,** el sol ha salido. **To be up,** estar levantado, haberse levantado o salido de la cama; haberse levantado, amotinado o revolucionado; estar en una posición o situación elevada. **Now up, now down,** tan pronto arriba, como abajo. **Up there!** ¡alto ahí! **Up up!** ¡arriba levántese Ud.! **Drink it up,** bébalo Ud. todo. **Up and down,** acá y allá, por todas partes; arriba y abajo; por detrás y por delante, por todos lados; de un lado a otro.

upbear [ˈʌpˈbeəʳ] [ap-beaʳ], *va. (pret.* UPBORE. *pp.* UPBORNE). Sostener en alto; levantar en alto.

upbraid [ˈʌpˈbreɪd] [ap-breid], *va.* Echar en cara, vituperar, afear; reconvenir (to reproach, rebuke, scold).

upbraiding [ˈʌpˈbreɪdɪŋ] [ap-brei-din], *s.* Reconvención.

upbringing [ˈʌpˈbrɪŋɪŋ] [ap-brin-guin], *s.* Educación, crianza. **He had a stern upbringing,** tuvo una severa educación.

upcast [ˈʌpkɑːst] [ap-kast], *a.* Tirado o arrojado a lo alto. -*s.* 1. Tiro por alto en el juego de bolos. 2. Pozo de ventilación ascendente en una mina.

update [ˈʌpdeɪt] [ap-deit], *v.* Actualizar. **She has to update her ideas,** ella tiene que actualizar sus ideas.

updating [ˈʌpˈdeɪtɪŋ] [ap-dei-tin], *sf.* Actualización, puesta al día.

upgrade [ˈʌpɡreɪd] [ap-greid], *s.* Cuesta, pendiente (slope).

upheaval [ˈʌpˈhiːvəl] [ap-ji-val], *s.* 1. Solevación, solevantamiento. 2. *(Geol.)* Levantamiento de la corteza terrestre. 3. Trastorno del orden establecido (disturbance).

upheave [ˈʌpˈhiːv] [ap-jiv], *va.* Solevantar, levantar con esfuerzo. -*vn.* Levantarse, alzarse.

upheld [ʌpˈheld] [ap-jeld], *pret.* y *pp.* de TO UPHOLD.

up-hill [ˈʌphɪl] [ap-jil], *a.* Difícil, penoso, fatigoso. *(Fam.)* Cuesta arriba. -*adv.* Bajo dificultades, con obstáculos.

uphold [ʌpˈhəʊld] [ap-jould], *vn.* 1. Levantar en alto. 2. Sostener, apoyar, proteger, mantener (to support, confirm, maintain)..

upholster [ʌpˈhəʊlstəʳ] [ap-jouls-taʳ], *va.* 1. Guarnecer almohadones, sillas, sofás, etc.; proveerlos de relleno, resortes, cubiertas, etc. 2. Entapizar, adornar con tapices, colgaduras, etc. 3. Proveer de una cubierta de cualquier clase. **He upholstered the chair,** tapizó la silla.

upholsterer [ʌpˈhəʊlstərəʳ] [ap-jouls-ta-raʳ], *s.* Tapicero, guarnecedor de sofás, etc.: el que tiene por oficio poner alfombras, cortinas, etc. **Upholsterer-bee,** *V.* LEAF-CUTTER.

upholstery [ʌpˈhəʊlstərɪ] [ap-jouls-te-ri], *s.* 1. Géneros de que se usa para guarnecer sillas, almohadones, etc. 2. Tapicería, conjunto de tapices de una pieza o un edificio. 3. Tapicería, arte y oficio de tapicero.

upkeep [ˈʌpkiːp] [ap-kip], *s.* 1. Sostenimiento, mantenimiento. 2. Costo de reparación.

upland [ˈʌplænd] [ap-land], *s.* Terreno elevado, país montañoso. -*a.* Alto, elevado. **Upland cotton, uplands,** algodón superfino.

uplift [ˈʌplɪʃt] [ap-lift], *va.* Levantar en alto o en vilo.

upon [əˈpɒn] [a-pon], *prep.* 1. Sobre, encima, en, con, cerca de, a, por. Corresponde a *on,* por lo general. *V.* ON. 2. De. **Cattle live upon grass,** los ganados se alimentan de hierba. **To depend upon one,** depender de alguien. 3. *a.* **Upon the right hand,** a mano derecha. **Upon the first opportunity,** a la primera ocasión. 4. **Upon,** seguido de un nombre de día o de una fecha, no se traduce y lo mismo sucede con el gerundio. **Upon the fifth of May,** el cinco de mayo. **Upon seeing this,** viendo esto. **Upon one's guard,** prevenido. **Upon his coming,** cuando venga. **To be upon duty,** estar de guardia. **I was upon a journey,** yo estaba viajando. **Upon the whole matter,** por lo demás, fuera de esto. **Upon my honor,** a fe mía. **Upon your arrival,** a la llegada de Ud. **He has nothing to live upon,** no tiene con qué vivir. **Upon Sunday,** El domingo. **Upon pain of death,** so pena de muerte, bajo pena de muerte.

Upon corresponde en castellano a preposiciones muy diversas, tanto con respecto al lugar, como al tiempo y al modo; también se usa muy a menudo unida a los verbos para variar o modificar su significado.

upper [ˈʌpəʳ] [a-paʳ], *a.* (comparativo de UP). 1. Superior, más alto o en lugar preeminente a otra cosa. 2. Superior, más elevado, más excelente o más eminente. **The upper regions,** las altas regiones, las regiones superiores. **The upper House,** la cámara alta. **Upper-hand,** superioridad, ventaja. **Upperdeck,** *(Mar.)* cubierta alta. **Upper-works,** *(Mar.)* obras muertas. **Upper-leather,** pala de zapato. -*s.* 1. Pala del zapato. 2. Borceguíes que se llevan sobre el calzado.

upper berth [ˈʌpəˈbɜːθ] [a-pa-berz], *s.* Cama o litera alta (en un tren, etc.).

upper class [ˈʌpəˈklɑːs] [a-pa-klas], *s.* Clase aristócrata. -*a.* 1. De la aristocracia. 2. De las clases superiores (de un colegio).

upper-crust [ˈʌpəˈkrʌst] [a-pa-krast], *a.* De categoría.

uppercut [ˈʌpəkʌt] [a-pa-kat], *s.* En el boxeo, golpe en corto de abajo arriba.

uppermost [ˈʌpəməʊst] [a-pa-moust], *a.* Lo más alto, supremo, lo más elevado, lo más preeminente, excelente o eminente. **To be uppermost,** predominar; estar encima.

uppish [ˈʌpɪʃ] [a-pish], *a.* *(Fam.)* Engreído, altivo, soberbio (proud, haughty).

uppishness [ˈʌpɪʃnɪs] [a-pish-nes], *s.* Altivez.

upraise [ˈʌpˈreɪz] [a-preis], *va.* Exaltar; alzar, elevar.

upright [ˈʌpraɪt] [ap-rait], *a.* 1. Derecho, vertical, a plomo, recto; puesto en pie (erect, vertical). 2. Recto, justo, equitativo (just, honest). **Bolt upright,** derecho como un huso, tieso como una barra de hierro. **To sit upright,** estar derecho; incorporarse (en la cama). -*s.* *(Arq.)* el plan de un frontispicio; el alzado o diseño que muestra la obra en su frente; montante, pieza vertical.

uprightly [ˈʌpˌraɪtlɪ] [ap-rait-li], *adv.* 1. Perpendicularmente, sin torcerse. 2. Derechamente, rectamente, con rectitud, sinceramente.

uprightness [ˈʌpˌraɪtnɪs] [ap-rait-nes], *s.* 1. Elevación perpendicular. 2. Rectitud, probidad, integridad.

uprise [ˈʌpraɪz] [ap-rais], *vn.* Levantarse, elevarse.

uprising [ˈʌpraɪzɪŋ] [ap-rai-sin], *s.* 1. La acción de levantarse de la cama; acción de salir por el horizonte o desde cualquier lugar más bajo. 2. Salida del sol. 3. Agitación grande entre mucha gente. 4. Motín, insurrección, sublevación (rebellion, revolt). 5. Subida, cuesta.

uproar [ˈʌprɔːʳ] [ap-roʳ], *s.* Tumulto, batalla, alboroto, conmoción (noise, shouting).

uproarious [ʌpˈrɔːrɪəs] [ap-ro-rios], *a.* Ruidoso, tumultuoso, particularmente con fiesta y algazara.

uproot [ʌpˈruːt] [ap-rut], *va.* Desarraigar, arrancar de raíz.

upset [ˈʌpset] [ap-set], *va.* 1. Trastornar, poner lo de arriba abajo; volcar, hacer volcar (un carruaje) (to overturn). 2. De aquí, turbar mucho. 3. Desordenar, desarreglar. *(Mar.)* Zozobrar. **He upset a glass of wine over the table,** volcó un vaso de vino sobre la mesa. **Upset price,** precio inicial.

upshot [ˈʌpʃɒt] [ap-shot], *s.* Remate, fin, conclusión; suma total (result, end).

upside [ˈʌpsaɪd] [ap-said], *s.* La parte superior, lo de arriba. **Upside down,** lo de arriba abajo, al revés; *(Fam.)* patas arriba; en confusión.

upstage [ˈʌpsteɪdʒ] [ap-steich], *adv.* Hacia el fondo. *a.* Arrogante (snobbish, haughty)

upstage, *v.* Eclipsar.

upstairs [ˈʌpsteəz] [ap-stears], *adv.* Arriba, en el piso de arriba.

upstanding [ˈʌpstændɪŋ] [ap-stan-din], *a.* Sano, franco, honesto (strong, healthy, frank, honest).

upstart [ˈʌpstɑːt] [ap-start], *s.* Hombre de fortuna, el villano o el hombre humilde que de repente se eleva a los honores, riquezas o poder.

upstay [ˈʌpsteɪ] [ap-stei], *va.* Sostener, apoyar.

upstream [ˈʌpˈstriːm] [ap-strim], *adv.* Aguas arriba.

uptake [ˈʌpteɪk] [ap-teik], *va.* Tomar o coger una cosa en las manos. *a.* Ser listo, ser duro de mollera.

up-town [ˈʌpˈtaʊn] [ap-taun], *a.* *(Fam. E.U.)* Perteneciente a la parte superior de una ciudad o residente en ella. -*adv.* En o hacia lo alto de la ciudad.

upturn [ˈʌpˈtɜːn] [ap-tern], *va.* Volver hacia arriba; volver patas arriba; de aquí, poner en confusión.

upward [ˈʌpwəd] [ap-uord], *a.* Lo que mira o se dirige hacia arriba.

upward, upwards, *adv.* 1. Hacia arriba. 2. Más **Ten pounds and upwards,** diez libras o más. **Upwards and downwards,** por arriba y por abajo.

uranic [jʊəˈrænɪk] [iua-ra-nik], *a.* 1. Uranio, relativo al espacio celeste; celeste, astronómico. 2. Uránico, relativo al segundo óxido de uranio.

uranium [jʊəˈreɪnɪəm] [iua-ra-niom], *s.* *(Min.)* Uranio. **Oxidulated uranium,** uranio oxidulado.

Uranus [jʊəˈreɪnəs] [iua-rei-nos], *s.* Urano, planeta más distante del sol que Saturno.

urban [ˈɜːbən] [er-ban], *a.* Urbano, situado en una ciudad o habitante de ella; parecido a una ciudad. **He dislikes urban life,** le disgusta la vida urbana.

urbane [ɜːˈbeɪn] [er-bein], *a.* Cortesano, urbano, de buenas maneras (courteous, gentleman).

urbanity [ɜːˈbænɪtɪ] [er-ba-ni-ti], *s.* Urbanidad, cortesanía, buen modo o buenos modales.

urbanize [ˈɜːbənaɪz] [er-ba-nais], *vt.* Urbanizar.

urchin [ˈɜːtʃɪn] [er-chin], *s.* 1. Niño travieso o malo; corresponde en general a bribonzuelo (mischievous). 2. Erizo, animal rodeado de púas como espinas. 3. Erizo de mar.

urea [ˈjʊərɪə] [iu-ria], *s.* Urea, principio inmediato de la orina (COH4N2), incoloro, soluble y cristalizable.

uremia [jʊˈriːmɪə] [iu-ri-mia], *s.* Uremia, estado morboso ocasionado por la acumulación de urea en la sangre.

uremic [juˈriːmɪk] [iu-ri-mik], *a.* Urémico, relativo a la uremia.

ureter [jʊˈriːtəʳ] [iu-ri-taʳ], *s.* Uréter, el canal por donde desciende la orina de los riñones a la vejiga.

urethra [jʊˈriːtrə] [iu-ri-tra], *s.* Uretra, el canal excretor de la orina.

urethral [jʊˈriːtrəl] [iu-ri-tral], *a.* Urético, uretral.

urge [ɜːdʒ] [erch], *va.* 1. Impeler, empujar, apretar con fuerza en una dirección cualquiera, esforzar. 2. Incitar, excitar, estimular, hurgar. 3. Apresurar, acelerar. 4. Apretar, acosar, seguir de cerca. 5. Solicitar, importunar. 6. Urgir, instar, aguijonear, precisar. **He urged her to drive carefully,** le instó a conducir cuidadosamente. -*vn.* 1. Presentar, avanzar, sostener argumentos o pretensiones. 2. Estimular, animar, insistir sobre.

urgency [ˈɜːdʒənsɪ] [er-chen-si], *s.* Urgencia, aprieto o necesidad urgente.

urgent [ˈɜːdʒənt] [er-chent], *a.* Urgente, importuno; insistente, imperativo. **There is a urgent message for you,** hay un mensaje urgente para ti.

urgently [ˈɜːdʒəntlɪ] [er-chent-li], *adv.* Instantemente, con instancia.

urger [ˈɜːdʒəʳ] [er-chaʳ], *s.* El que compele, obliga o insta; solicitador, abrumador.

uric [ˈjʊrɪk] [iu-rik], *a.* Úrico, perteneciente a la orina o derivado de ella. **Uric acid,** ácido úrico.

urinal [jʊˈraɪnl] [iu-rai-nal], *s.* 1. Orinal, el vaso en que se recoge la orina. 2. Urinario, meadero cómodo y decente.

urinalysis [jʊrəˈnælɪsɪs] [iu-ra-na-li-sis], *s.* Urinálisis, análisis de orina.

urinary [ˈjʊrɪnərɪ] [iu-ri-na-ri], *a.* Urinario.

urinate [ˈjʊrɪneɪt] [iu-ri-neit], *vn.* Orinar, mear. **He always urinates in the street,** él siempre orina en la calle.

urine [ˈjʊrɪn] [iu-rin], *s.* Orina, orín.

urinous [ˈjʊrɪnəs] [iu-ri-nos], *a.* Urinario, perteneciente a la orina o que participa de sus calidades. **A urinous odor,** un olor como de orina.

urn [ɜːn] [ern], *s.* 1. Urna. 2. Recipiente metálico grande provisto de un grifo para té o café.

urogenital [ˌjʊərəʊˈdʒenɪtl] [iu-rou-ye-ni-tal], *a.* Urogenital.

urologist [jʊəˈrɒlədʒɪst] [iu-ro-lo-yist], *s.* Urólogo.

urology [jʊəˈrɒlədʒɪ] [iu-ro-lo-yi], *sf.* Urología.

Ursa Major ['ɜːsə'meɪdʒəʳ] [er-sa-mei-yaʳ], *sf.* Osa Mayor.

Ursa Minor ['ɜːsə'maɪnəʳ] [er-sa-mai-noʳ], *sf.* Osa Menor.

urticaria [ˌɜːtɪ'keərɪə] [er-ti-kea-ria], *s.* (*Med.*) Urticaria.

urtication [ˌɜːtɪ'keɪʃən] [er-ti-kei-shon], *s.* Acción de picar con ortigas, particularmente flagelación practicada con ortigas frescas como tratamiento contra la parálisis.

Uruguayan [ˌjʊərə'gwaɪən] [iua-ra-güaian], *a.* y *s.* Uruguayo.

us [ʌs] [as], *pron.* Nos o nosotros, el caso objetivo o dativo de WE. **Give us this day our daily bread,** el pan nuestro de cada día dánosle hoy.

usable, useable ['juːzəbl] [iu-sa-bol], *a.* Que se puede usar, a propósito para el uso.

usage ['juːzɪdʒ] [iu-sich], *s.* 1. Trato, tratamiento, el modo de tratar a una persona o cosa (treatment). 2. Uso, costumbre, hábito, práctica corriente (custom, habit). 3. Empleo de formas o palabras, sancionado o no.

usance ['juːzəns] [iu-sans], *s.* 1. (*Com.*) Usanza, cierto término a que se libran las letras de cambio, el cual varía según los países. 2. (*Ant.*) Uso, aprovechamiento, empleo de alguna cosa. **To draw a bill at usance,** librar una letra a uso o a estilo.

USA *Abreviatura de* **United States of America,** Estados Unidos de América.

USD *Abreviatura de* **US Dollars,** dolars americanos.

use [juːs] [ius], *s.* 1. Uso, la acción y efecto de usar alguna cosa. 2. Uso, el servicio y aprovechamiento actual de una cosa; utilidad, provecho, ventaja; goce, manejo. 3. Necesidad, ocasión de emplear. 4. Uso, costumbre, hábito, práctica. **Uses of the sea,** (*Mar.*) usos de la mar. 5. (*For.*) Uso, goce, derecho de usar de una cosa ajena con ciertas limitaciones. **Of use,** útil, que sirve, que es a propósito para algún fin. **Of no use,** inútil, que de nada sirve; que no viene al caso. **Out of use,** sin uso, inusitado, olvidado, que no es de moda. **To be in use,** estar en uso, servir, ser usado. **To be of no use,** no servir para nada, no ser de ninguna utilidad, ser inútil. **For the use of,** para el uso de. **I have no further use for it,** no lo necesito ya; no me sirvo más de ello. **To make use of,** hacer uso de, servirse de, usar de; utilizar. **To put to use,** poner en uso.

use, *va.* 1. Usar, emplear, gastar, hacer uso de, servirse o valerse de; usar de (to employ, consume). 2. Practicar, poner en práctica; hacer práctica de. 3. Tratar, dar a alguno buen o mal trato, portarse bien o mal con él. 4. Acostumbrar, habituar. -*vn.* Tener costumbre, hacer uno por costumbre; soler, acostumbrar; enseñarse o hacerse a sufrir trabajos, dolores, etc.; hoy siempre en imperfecto. **I used to go there,** solía ir allá. **To use ill,** maltratar o tratar mal. **They use the computer,** ellos se sirven del ordenador. **To use oneself,** acostumbrarse, habituarse. **To use up,** usar completamente, gastar, consumir; agotar, fatigar con exceso.

used [juːzd] [iusd], *a.* 1. Usado, gastado (employed). **Used car,** automóvil de segunda mano. 2. Acostumbrado, habituado (accustomed). **He is used to that,** está acostumbrado a eso.

useful ['juːsfʊl] [ius-ful], *a.* Útil; provechoso, beneficioso (helpful). **Here are the things that might be useful to you,** aquí estan las cosas que pueden serte útiles.

usefully ['juːsfəlɪ] [ius-fu-li], *adv.* Útilmente; con provecho.

usefulness ['juːsfəlnɪs] [ius-ful-nes], *s.* Utilidad.

useless ['juːslɪs] [ius-les], *a.* Inútil. **It's useless to say it,** es inútil decirlo.

uselessly ['juːslɪslɪ] [ius-les-li], *a.* Inútilmente.

uselessness ['juːslɪsnɪs] [ius-les-nes], *s.* Inutilidad.

user ['juːzəʳ] [iu-saʳ], *s.* El que usa, se sirve o se vale de alguna cosa.

usher ['ʌʃəʳ] [a-shaʳ], *s.* 1. Ujier, portero de cámara, conserje, aposentador, acomodador: persona cuyo oficio es conducir a los asientos en un cine o teatro. 2. (*Ingl.*) Sotamaestro. **He was one of the ushers of the cinema,** es uno de los acomodadores del cine.

usher, *va.* 1. Introducir; acompañar o ir delante, aposentador (to conduct). 2. Anunciar, dar la primera noticia.

USP *Abreviatura de* **Unique Sales Proposition.**

USSR *Abreviatura de* **Union of Soviet Socialist Republics,** Unión de Repúblicas Socialistas Soviéticas (URSS).

usual ['juːʒʊəl] [iu-shual], *a.* Usual, acostumbrado, ordinario, común, usado, habitual (customary). **As usual, he was late,** llegó tarde, como siempre.

usually ['juːʒʊəlɪ] [iu-shua-li], *adv.* Usualmente, comúnmente, ordinariamente, frecuentemente, regularmente, normalmente, por lo regular, por lo común. **Usually we finish work at 5 o'clock,** normalmente terminamos de trabajar a las 5 en punto.

usualness ['juːʒʊəlnɪs] [iu-shual-nes], *s.* Costumbre, práctica muy usada y corriente; frecuencia.

usufruct ['juːzjʊfrʌkt] [iu-su-frakt], *s.* Usufructo, el goce o disfrute de los frutos o rentas de una cosa sin tener la propiedad.

usurer ['juːʒərəʳ] [iu-sa-raʳ], *s.* Usurero, el que presta dinero con usura o a un interés exorbitante.

usurious [juː'zjʊərɪəs] [iu-siua-rios], *a.* Usurario; que presta dinero a usura; en que hay usura.

usuriousness [juː'zjʊərɪəsnɪs] [iu-siua-rios-nes], *s.* Usura.

usurp [juː'zɜːp] [iu-serp], *va.* 1. Usurpar, tomar por fuerza y tener en posesión de uno sin derecho ni autoridad legal. 2. Usurpar, arrogarse como si se tuviera derecho a ello.

usurpation [juːzɜː'peɪʃən] [iu-sar-pei-shon], *s.* Usurpación.

usurper [juː'zɜːpəʳ] [iu-sar-paʳ], *s.* Usurpador.

usury ['juːʒʊrɪ] [iu-su-ri], *s.* Usura, el interés exorbitante que se paga por el dinero prestado; originalmente, el préstamo de dinero a interés.

utensil [juː'tensl] [iu-ten-sil], *s.* Utensilio, lo que sirve para el uso y comodidad de la vida; herramienta o útil para el uso doméstico agrícola. **Kitchen utensils,** utensilios de cocina. **Farming utensils,** aperos de labranza.

uterine ['juːtəraɪn] [iu-ta-rain], *a.* 1. Uterino, que pertenece al útero. 2. Uterino, se aplica a los hermanos de madre solamente. *s.* Útero, madre, matriz (the womb).

utilitarian [ˌjuːtɪlɪ'teərɪən] [iu-ti-li-tea-rian], *a.* Utilitario, relativo a la utilidad; que sólo pretende conseguir lo útil; que antepone a todo la utilidad. -*s.* Utilitario, el que antepone a todo la utilidad.

utilitarianism [juːtɪlɪ'teərɪənɪzəm] [iu-ti-li-ta-ria-ni-sem], *s.* 1. Utilitarismo, sistema de los utilitarios, doctrina que hace la utilidad el fin y criterio de acción y la base de la moralidad. 2. Devoción a los intereses meramente materiales.

utility [juː'tɪlɪtɪ] [iu-ti-li-ti], *s.* Utilidad, ventaja (usefulness).

utilize, utilise ['juːtɪlaɪz] [iu-ti-lais], *va.* Utilizar, emplear útilmente, aprovecharse de, hacer útil. **You must utilize all available resources,** debes utilizar todos los recursos disponibles.

utmost ['ʌtməʊst] [at-moust], *a.* Extremo, sumo; mayor, más grande; más posible; más distante; último, postrero. -*s.* Lo sumo, lo mayor, lo más sobresaliente, preeminente. **Do your utmost,** haga Ud. cuanto pueda o todo lo que pueda.

utopia [juː'təʊpɪə] [iu-tou-pia], *s.* 1. Utopía, isla imaginaria que tenía un perfecto sistema social y político. 2. Lugar, reino o condición idealmente perfectos.

utopian [juː'təʊpɪən] [iu-tou-pian], *a.* Imaginario, utópico, ideal.

utter ['ʌtəʳ] [a-taʳ], *a.* 1. Total, todo, entero, cabal (complete, total). 2. Extremo, excesivo, sumo. 3. Perentorio, terminante. 4. (*Ant.*) Exterior, de fuera, que está situado a la parte de afuera.

utter, *va.* 1. Proferir, pronunciar o articular las palabras. 2. Expresar, manifestar o representar con palabras lo que se siente. 3. Descubrir, publicar, revelar. 4. Dar circulación, emitir.

utterable ['ʌtərəbl] [a-ta-ra-bol], *a.* Que se puede proferir o pronunciar.

utterance ['ʌtərəns] [a-te-rans], *s.* 1. Prolación, el acto de proferir o pronunciar; habla, lenguaje, expresión, estilo o modo de hablar. 2. La cosa proferida o expresada. 3. (*Des.*) Extremidad o extremo, el último punto.

utterer [ˈʌtərərəʳ] [a-te-raʳ], *s.* El que pronuncia o profiere; divulgador.

utterly [ˈʌtəlɪ] [a-ter-li], *adv.* Totalmente, enteramente, del todo; de lleno.

uttermost [ˈʌtəməʊst] [a-ta-moust], *a.* Extremo, sumo. *-s.* Lo sumo. *V.* UTMOST.

UV *a. Abreviatura de* **Ultraviolet**, ultravioleta.

uvula [ˈjuːvjələ] [iu-via-la], *s.* Úvula, campanilla, gallillo.

uxorious [ʌkˈsɔːrɪəs] [ak-so-rios], *a.* Gurrumino: se dice del marido que acapara con exceso a su mujer.

uxoriously [ʌkˈsɔːrɪəslɪ] [ak-so-rios-li], *adv.* Con gurrumina.

uxoriousness [ʌkˈsɔːrɪəsnɪs] [ak-so-rios-nes], *s.* Gurrumina, condescendencia y contemplación excesiva con la mujer propia.

V

v [viː] [vi], consonante se pronuncia en inglés como en español. En general los españoles confunden algo el sonido de esta letra con el de la *b*, aunque deben pronunciarse de muy diverso modo: para la *b* se han de juntar los labios por la parte exterior de la boca, y para la *v* los dientes superiores con el labio inferior.

v, *s.* 1. Pieza o dos piezas en forma de V; v. g. en maderas de construcción. 2. Guarismo romano que representa cinco.

vacancy [ˈvækənsɪ] [va-kan-si], *s.* 1. Vacuidad, calidad de vacío (emptiness). 2. Vacío, espacio vacío, hueco; laguna, interrupción del pensamiento. 3. Vacante, puesto, destino o lugar que está por proveer, sin beneficiado. 4. Vacante, el tiempo de huelga o descanso. **We have a vacancy for a secretary,** tenemos una vacante de secretaria.

vacant [ˈvækənt] [va-kant], *a.* 1. Vacío, desocupado, hueco; descargado (empty, unoccupied). 2. Libre, desembarazado. 3. Vacante, lo que vaca. 4. Ocioso; lerdo, bobo, negligente, fútil. **He looks rather vacant,** tiene la mirada perdida.

vacantly [ˈvækəntlɪ] [va-kant-li], *adv.* Distraídamente (forgetful, idle).

vacate [ˈvækeɪt] [va-keit], *va.* 1. Vaciar, dejar vacío; dejar vacante; dejar o renunciar la posesión de un empleo, dignidad, etc. 2. Anular, invalidar. **To vacate the sale,** rescindir la venta. *-vn.* Dejar, salir, irse, marcharse; vacar.

vacation [ˈvækeɪʃən] [va-kei-shon], *s.* 1. Vacación, días feriados, suspensión de los tribunales de justicia (vacation, a day off). 2. Vacación, suspensión de estudios, negocios o trabajo por algún tiempo, y el lugar o espacio de tiempo libre o desocupado. 3. Vacación, acción de vacar; anulación. **On vacation,** de vacaciones.

vaccinate [ˈvæksɪneɪt] [vak-si-neit], *va.* Vacunar, inocular el fluido vacuno (u otro virus) como preservativo de la misma enfermedad que lo origina.

vaccination [ˌvæksɪˈneɪʃən] [vak-si-nei-shon], *s.* Vacunación, operación de vacunar.

vaccine [ˈvæksiːn] [vak-sin], *a.* 1. Vacuno, perteneciente o relativo a las vacas. 2. Perteneciente a la vacuna. *-s.* Vacuna, virus de ciertos granos preparado para la vacunación o introducción por ella.

vaccinia [væksˈnɪə] [vak-si-nia], *s.* Vacuna, grano o viruela que sale a las vacas en las ubres y particularmente la vacuna inoculada.

vacillate [ˈvæksɪleɪt] [vak-si-leit], *vn.* Vacilar; titubear, estar incierto, irresoluto; no estar firme (to falter, flicker, hesitate). **He vacillated between accepting and not accepting,** vacilaba entre aceptar y no aceptar.

vacillation [ˌvæksɪˈleɪʃən] [vak-si-lei-shon], *s.* 1. Vacilación.

vacuity [væˈkjuːɪtɪ] [va-kui-ti], *s.* 1. Vacuidad, estado de lo vacío, vacuo. 2. Espacio vacío, vacío. 3. Ociosidad, exención de esfuerzo mental. 4. Falta de inteligencia, estupidez. 5. Inanidad falta de realidad, nada.

vacuous [ˈvækjʊəs] [va-kiuos], *a.* Vacío, vacuo (stupid). **His face had a vacuous expression,** su cara tenía una expresión vacía.

vacuum [ˈvækjəm] [va-kium], *s.* Vacío. **Vacuum bottle,** termos. **Vacuum cleaner,** aspiradora eléctrica o al vacío. **Vacuum pump,** bomba al vacío. **Vacuum tube,** tubo o válvula de vacío.

vade-mecum [ˈvɑːdɪˈmeɪkəm] [va-di-mei-kum], *s.* Vademécum o vade.

vagabond [ˈvægəbɒnd] [va-ga-bond], *a.* 1. Vagabundo, vagamundo, sin domicilio fijo. 2. Errante, que vaga acá y allá. 3. Fluctuante, al acaso. *-s.* Un vagamundo, un hombre sin casa ni hogar. **To play the vagabond,** vagamundear.

vagary [ˈveɪgərɪ] [vei-ga-ri], *s.* Capricho, extravagancia, humorada, antojo (caprice, fad, quirk). **The vagaries of the nature,** los caprichos de la naturaleza.

vagina [ˈvædʒaɪnə] [va-yai-na], *s.* 1. Vaina o cubierta parecida a una vaina. 2. Vagina, conducto sexual, que se extiende desde la vulva hasta la matriz. 3. *(Bot.)* Parte tubular que envuelve a otra.

vaginal [ˈvædʒaɪnəl] [va-yai-nal], *a.* Vaginal, perteneciente a una vaina o a la vagina.

vaginate [ˈvædʒɪneɪt] [va-yi-neit], *a.* 1. Envainado, contenido en una vaina, que tiene vaina. 2. Vaginado, tubular.

vagrancy [ˈveɪgrənsɪ] [vei-gran-si], *s.* Tuna, la vida holgazana, libre y vagamunda. **Vagrancy is a crime in some countries,** el vagabundeo es un delito en algunos países.

vagrant [ˈveɪgrənt] [vei-grant], *a.* 1. Vagabundo, vagamundo, errante. 2. Que tiene curso o movimiento errante. *-s.* Un vago, un vagabundo.

vague [veɪg] [vei], *a.* 1. Vago, indeterminado, que carece de precisión; indistino (not clear, distinct). 2. Despistado, impreciso (imprecise, impractical, forgetful). 3. *(Ant.)* Vago, vagante, que anda ocioso sin oficio del beneficio.

vaguely [ˈveɪglɪ] [veig-li], *adv.* Vagamente, ligeramente. **I remember him vaguely,** le recuerdo vagamente.

vain [veɪn] [vein], *a.* 1. Vano, inútil, sin efecto, sin realidad, substancia o entidad (unsuccessful). 2. Vano, vanidoso, presuntuoso, desvanecido. 3. Ostentoso, suntuoso, llamativo; se dice de las cosas. 4. Vano, insubsistente, poco durable o estable. 5. Vano, sin fundamento, razón o prueba, vacío (empty, meaningless). **In vain,** en vano, inútilmente. **To labor in vain,** trabajar en balde.

vainglorious [veɪnˈglɔːrɪəs] [vein-glo-rios], *a.* Vanaglorioso, vano, jactancioso, ufano.

vaingloriously [veɪnˈglɔːrɪəslɪ] [vein-glo-rios-li], *adv.* Vanagloriosamente, con jactancia.

vaingloriousness [veɪnˈglɔːrɪəsnɪs] [vein-glo-rios-nes], *s.* Vanagloria.

vainglory [veɪnˈglɔːrɪ] [vein-glo-ri], *s.* Vanagloria, jactancia.

vainly [ˈveɪnlɪ] [vein-li], *adv.* Vanamente, arrogantemente; inútilmente (unsuccessfully). **Vainly he tried to find someone to marry him,** vanamente intentó encontrar a alguien para que se casara con él.

vainness [ˈveɪnnɪs] [vein-nes], *s.* Vanidad, satisfacción de sí mismo, envanecimiento.

vair [veəʳ] [veaʳ], *s.* 1. *(Her.)* Vero, piel de ardilla blanca y azul. 2. Especie de forro de pieles, blanco y azul, usado en los trajes de la nobleza (siglo XIV).

valance [ˈvæləns] [va-lans], *s.* 1. Cenefa, doselera de cama colgada; gotera del dosel de una cama o de cortinas de ventana, orladura. 2. Damasco de seda, o de seda y lana, que sirve de cubierta a los muebles. Este tejido se llama también *valencia.*

vale [veɪl] [veil], *s.* 1. *(Poét.)* Valle, una llanura situada entre montañas o alturas (a valley). 2. Canal pequeño; reguera.

vale, *inter.* ¡Agur! ¡adiós!.

valediction [ˌvælɪˈdɪkʃən] [va-li-dik-shon], *s.* Vale, despedida (farewell); último vale.

valedictory [ˌvælɪˈdɪktərɪ] [va-li-dik-to-ri], *a.* De despedida o que pertenece a la despedida. *-s.* Discurso de despedida en los colegios, a fin de curso.

valence [ˈvæləns] [va-lans], *s. (Quím.)* Valencia, la propiedad poseída por los elementos o radicales de combinarse con otros elementos o de remplazarlos en una proporción definida y constante.

valentine ['vælǝntaɪn] [va-len-tain], *s.* 1. La postal de los enamorados el día de San Valentín. 2. El amante o cortejo que se elige el día de San Valentín (el 14 de febrero).

valerian [vǝ'lɪǝrɪǝn] [va-le-rian], *s.* 1. *(Bot.)* Valeriana, hierba benedicta. 2. Medicamento preparado con la raíz de esta planta, se usa como antiespasmódico.

valet ['væleɪ] [va-lei], *s.* 1. Criado. **Valet-de-chambre,** ayuda de cámara. 2. Palo herrado y puntiagudo de que se usa para adiestrar los caballos.

valetudinarian ['vælɪˌtjuːdɪ'nɛǝrɪǝn] [va-li-tiu-di-nea-rian], *a.* Valetudinario, enfermizo, delicado de salud. -*s.* La persona valetudinaria, enfermiza o delicada.

valiant ['vælɪǝnt] [va-liant], *a.* Valiente, esforzado, animoso, valeroso (brave, courageous, heroic). **He was valiant in battle,** era valiente en la batalla.

valiantly ['vælɪǝntlɪ] [va-liant-li], *adv.* Valientemente, con brío, con ánimo, esforzadamente.

valiantness ['vælɪǝntnɪs] [va-liant-nes], *s.* Valentía, valor, esfuerzo, aliento, ánimo.

valid ['vælɪd] [va-lid], *a.* 1. Válido, apreciado o estimado generalmente, basado o sostenido en los hechos, justo; valedero (reasonable, acceptable). 2. *(Ant.)* Válido, fuerte, esforzado. **That is not a valid excuse,** esta no es una excusa válida.

validate ['vælɪdeɪt] [va-li-deit], *vt.* Convalidar.

validation [ˌvælɪ'deɪʃǝn] [va-li-dei-shon], *sf.* Convalidación.

validity [vǝ'lɪdɪtɪ] [va-li-di-ti], *s.* Validez, calidad de válido.

valise [vǝ'liːz] [va-lis], *s.* Maleta, saco de viaje o de mano; valija (case, suitcase).

valley ['vælɪ] [va-li], *s.* 1. Valle, llanura de tierra entre dos alturas (vale, dale). 2. *(Arq.)* Gotera formada por el encuentro de dos declives de un techado. **He lives in a beautiful green valley between the mountains,** él vive en un bonito valle verde entre montañas.

valor ['vælǝʳ] [va-laʳ], *s.* Valor, brío, fortaleza, intrepidez en presencia del peligro (courage, bravery).

valorous ['vælǝrǝs] [va-lo-ros], *a.* Valeroso, valiente, animoso, intrépido (plucky, brave, courageous).

valorously ['vælǝrǝslɪ] [va-lo-ros-li], *adv.* Valerosamente, con intrepidez, con arrojo.

valuable ['væljʊǝbl] [va-liua-bol], *a.* 1. Precioso, estimable, apreciable. 2. Digno de atención o consideración, importante, que vale mucho.

valuation [ˌvæljʊ'eɪʃǝn] [va-liu-ei-shon], *s.* Tasa, valuación; avalúo.

valuator ['væljʊˌeɪtǝʳ] [va-liu-ei-taʳ], *s.* Tasador, evaluador.

value ['væljʊː] [va-liu], *s.* 1. Valor, utilidad o deseabilidad de una cosa; valor intrínseco. 2. Valor, precio del mercado. 3. Valor, aprecio, estimación. 4. Valor, significación exacta, sentido; importancia. 5. *(Mús.)* Valor, duración relativa de una nota. 6. *(Biol.)* Grado o lugar en una clasificación. **To set a great value on a thing,** hacer mucho aprecio de una cosa.

value, *va.* 1. Valuar, valorar, señalar el valor o la estimación de; tasar. 2. Estimar, apreciar, hacer mucho aprecio o estimación de una cosa 3. Llevar cuenta de; hacer caso de; considerar, tomar en consideración.

valueless ['væljuːlɪs] [va-liu-les], *a.* Indigno, despreciable, que no vale nada.

valuer ['væljʊǝʳ] [va-liuaʳ], *s.* Tasador, apreciador, estimador.

valve [vælv] [valv], *s.* 1. Válvula, cualquier artefacto que abre y cierra una abertura o pasaje a voluntad, para dejar escapar o retener un fluido, gas, etc. 2. *(Anat.)* Válvula, pliegue membranoso de los vasos del cuerpo, que abriéndose y cerrándose da o impide el paso a los humores. **Air valve,** válvula atmosférica o de aire. **Ball valve,** válvula esférica. **Cut-off valve,** válvula de corredera, de cajón. **Throttle valve,** válvula de cuello o reguladora.

valvular ['vælvjʊlǝʳ] [val-viu-laʳ], *a.* Valvular, perteneciente a la válvula, de la naturaleza de una válvula. **Valvular heart-disease,** enfermedad orgánica de las válvulas del corazón.

valvule ['vælvjuːl] [val-viul], *s.* Valvulilla, válvula pequeña.

vamp [væmp] [vamp], *s.* 1. Pala de zapato, empeine, capellada, la parte superior del calzado. 2. Algo que se añade a una cosa vieja para darle apariencia nueva. 3. *(Fam.)* Acompañamiento músico improvisado. 3. Vampiresa.

vamp, *va.* 1. Echar capellado o empeine *a.* 2. Remendar una cosa vieja con otra nueva. 3. *(Fam.)* Improvisar un acompañamiento musical *a.* **To wamp a pair of shoes,** echar capelladas a un par de zapatos.

vampire ['væmpaɪǝʳ] [vam-paiaʳ], *s.* 1. Vampiro, ente fabuloso o espectro que por las noches chupa la sangre de los vivos mientras duermen. 2. *(Fig.)* Vampiro, persona que se enriquece a expensas del pueblo; insaciable. 3. Vampiro, murciélago muy grande de la América tropical que chupa la sangre de los animales y del hombre, cuando los halla dormidos.

van [væn] [van], *s.* 1. Vanguardia, la parte más avanzada de un ejército o armada. 2. Los jefes de una empresa. 3. *(Ant.)* Aventador; bieldo. *(Abrev. de Vanguard.)* 3. Camioneta, furgoneta, furgón. **He drives a van,** conduce una camioneta.

vanadium [vǝ'neɪdɪǝm] [va-nei-diom], *s.* *(Quím.)* Vanadio, metal blanco que se halla muy rara vez.

vandal ['vændǝl] [van-dal], *a.* Bárbaro, vándalo. -*s.* Vándalo, hombre de una raza teutónica que en el siglo quinto saqueó a Roma; de aquí, el que con intención destruye o desfigura lo que es bello o artístico.

vandalism ['vændǝlɪzǝm] [van-da-li-sem], *s.* Vandalismo, los hechos o el espíritu de los vándalos; espíritu de destrucción.

vandalize ['vændǝlaɪz] [van-da-lais], *v.* Destrozar. **His car has been vandalized,** su coche ha sido destrozado.

vane [veɪn] [vein], *s.* 1. Veleta, banderilla de metal que se coloca en un sitio elevado para que señale la dirección en que viene el viento. 2. *(Mar.)* Grímpola. 3. Aspa de molino, paleta (de hélice). 4. Barba de pluma. 5. Pínula de instrumentos matemáticos. **Dog-vane,** cataviento. **Vane-stock,** armazón de la grímpola. **Vane-spindle,** huso o hierro de la grímpola.

vang [væŋ] [vang], *s.* *(Mar.)* Burra de mesana.

vanguard ['væŋgɑːd] [van-gard], *s.* Vanguardia.

vanilla [vǝ'nɪlǝ] [va-ni-la], *s.* 1. Vainilla, género de plantas orquídeas trepadoras y americanas, de flores olorosas. 2. Su fruto, que se suele mezclar con el chocolate. **Her son likes vanilla ice-cream,** a su hijo le gusta el helado de vainilla.

vanish ['vænɪʃ] [va-nish], *vn.* Desvanecerse, desaparecer, ocultarse o quitarse de la vista con presteza. **The ship vanished over the horizon,** el barco desapareció por el horizonte.

vanishing point ['vænɪʃɪŋˌpɔɪnt] [va-ni-shin-point], *s.* Punto de fuga (en la perspectiva).

vanity ['vænɪtɪ] [va-ni-ti], *s.* 1. Vanidad, falta de substancia, entidad o realidad; inutilidad. 2. Vanidad, fausto, ostentación, pompa vana, presunción. 3. Lo que es vano.

vanity case ['vænɪtɪˌkeɪs] [va-ni-ti-keis], *s.* Polvera.

vanquish ['væŋkwɪʃ] [van-kuish], *va.* 1. Vencer, conquistar, rendir, sujetar al enemigo o figuradamente (to defeat, conquer). 2. Confutar o impugnar a uno. **You must vanquish yours fears,** debes vencer tus miedos.

vanquishable ['væŋkwɪʃǝbl] [van-kui-sha-bol], *a.* Vencible, que puede vencerse.

vanquisher ['væŋkwɪʃǝʳ] [van-kui-shaʳ], *s.* Vencedor.

vantage ['væntɪdʒ] [van-tich], *s.* Ventaja, superioridad sobre un competidor. **Vantage-ground,** la situación del que en una disputa o contienda posee alguna ventaja que no tiene su contrario.

vapid ['væpɪd] [va-pid], *a.* 1. Exhalado, evaporado; insípido (bebidas). 2. Pesado, falto de animación, de viveza, insulso (dull, uninteresting).

vapidity [væ'pɪdɪtɪ] [va-pi-di-ti], *s.* Insipidez; el estado de lo que no tiene espíritu o fuerza por haberse evaporado.

vapor, vapour ['veɪpǝʳ] [vei-paʳ], *s.* 1. Vapor, vaho, exhalación; nube ligera, fluido visible en la atmósfera. 2. Vapor, fluido aeriforme, la forma gaseosa de una sustancia que por lo general es sólida o líquida. 3. Lo transitorio e insubstancial. 4. Vanidad, presunción, soberbia, arrogancia.

5. *pl. (Ant.)* Vapores, melancolía, mal hipocondríaco o del bazo. **Vapor-bath,** baño de vapor.

vapor, *vn.* 1. Evaporarse, exhalarse. 2. Baladronear, hacer o decir baladronadas. **-va.** *(Ant.)* Evaporar, reducir una cosa a vapor; exhalar.

vaporish ['væpɔːriʃ] [va-po-rish], *a.* 1. Vaporoso, que echa de sí vapor. 2. Caprichoso.

vaporizable ['veɪpəraɪzəbl] [vei-pa-rai-sa-bol], *a.* Que puede ser vaporizado.

vaporization [ˌveɪpəraɪˈzeɪʃən] [vei-pa-rai-sei-shon], *s.* Vaporización.

vaporize, vaporise ['veɪpəraɪz] [vei-pa-rais], *va.* Vaporizar, convertir en vapor; evaporar. *-vn.* Vaporizarse, disiparse en vapor.

vaporizer ['veɪpəraɪzəʳ] [vei-pa-rai-saʳ], *s.* Vaporizador.

vaporous ['veɪpərəs] [vei-pa-ras], *a.* 1. Vaporoso, que tiene la naturaleza o carácter del vapor; nebuloso. 2. Cargado de vapores. 3. Hipocondríaco. 4. Vano, quimérico, caprichudo.

variable ['veəriəbl] [vea-ria-bol], *a.* 1. Variable, alterable, mudable (changeable, mobile, moody). 2. Inconstante, veleidoso. 3. *(Mat.)* Variable, que no tiene valor determinado. *-s.* 1. Lo que varía o está sujeto a mudanza. 2. *(Mat.)* Cantidad variable.

variableness ['veəriəblnɪs] [va-ria-bol-nes], *s.* Instabilidad, inconstancia, ligereza.

variably ['veəriəblɪ] [va-ria-bli], *adv.* Variablemente.

variance ['veəriəns] [va-rians], *s.* 1. Variación, acción de variar, mudanza. 2. Discordia, desavenencia, oposición. **They are always at variance,** siempre están riñendo, disputando, de cuernos, o de punta. *(Mex.)* Estar contrapunteados.

variant ['veəriənt] [va-riant], *a.* 1. Variante, que presenta variación, diverso. 2. Variable, inconstante, que tiende a variar; veleidoso. 3. Mudable, poco estable, indeciso. *-s.* Cosa que se diferencia de otra en la forma solamente; sinónimo estricto.

variation [ˌveəriˈeɪʃən] [va-riei-shon], *s.* 1. Variación, mudanza. 2. Grado en que varía una cosa. 3. *(Gram.)* Inflexión de nombres y verbos. 4. *(Mús.)* Floreos, variaciones de un tema musical. 5. *(Astr.)* Desigualdad del movimiento lunar, cambio en los elementos de una órbita. 6. *(Biol.)* Variación, desviación de la forma típica en estructura o funciones, como a consecuencia de las condiciones y circunstancias que rodean a la planta o animal descritos.

varicolored ['værɪˈkʌləd] [va-ri-ka-lad], *a.* Abigarrado, de varios colores.

varicose ['værɪkəʊs] [va-ri-kous], *a.* Varicoso, que tiene o padece varices. **She has had varicose veins for three years.** tiene varices desde hace tres años.

varied ['veərɪd] [va-rid], *pp.* de VARY. Cambiado, variado, mezclado.

variegate ['veərɪɡeɪt] [va-ri-gueit], *va.* Jaspear, vetear, varetear, formar listas de diversos colores.

variegation [ˌveərɪˈɡeɪʃən] [va-ri-guei-shon], *s.* Jaspeadura; veteado, jaspeado.

variety [vəˈraɪɪtɪ] [va-rai-ti], *s.* 1. Variedad, diversidad o diferencia de algunas cosas entre sí. 2. Colección de cosas diversas en un grupo. 3. Posesión de diferentes propiedades características por un solo individuo. 4. *(Biol.)* Variedad, subdivisión de una especie. 5. Clase limitada de cosas que se diferencian por ciertas propiedades comunes de una clase más extensa, a la cual pertenecen.

variola [vəˈraɪələ] [va-raio-la], *s.* Viruela. *(Lat.)*

variolous [vəˈraɪələs] [va-raio-las], *a.* Varioloso, que pertenece a las viruelas.

various ['veərɪəs] [va-rios], *a.* 1. Vario, diverso, diferente (different, varied). 2. Vario, inconstante, mudable. 3. Vario, que tiene variedad, siendo más de uno y fácil de distinguir; varios. 4. Desemejante, que tiene diversidad de aspecto o apariencia; veteado, abigarrado. **Various people have come to the party,** gente variada ha venido a la fiesta.

variously ['veərɪəslɪ] [vea-rios-li], *adv.* Variamente.

varix ['vərɪks] [va-riks], *s.* Várice o variz, vena dialtada e hinchada.

varnish ['vɑːnɪʃ] [var-nish], *s.* 1. Barniz, disolución de una o más substancias resinosas en alcohol, etc., y usada para dar lustre a los metales, maderas y otras cosas. 2. Barniz, la paliación, capa o color con que se disimula o encubre algo.

varnish, *va.* 1. Barnizar, dar con barniz. 2. Paliar, disimular o encubrir los defectos de una cosa. 3. Cubrir una cosa con barniz o con cualquier otra substancia para adornarla.

varnisher ['vɑːnɪʃəʳ] [var-ni-shaʳ], *s.* 1. Embarnizador, barnizador, charolista. 2. El que encubre o palia.

varsity ['vɑːsɪtɪ] [var-si-ti], *s.* y *a. (Fam.)* Universidad. (Corrupción de *university*).

varvel ['vɑːvl] [var-vel], *s.* Uno de los anillos de metal que en tiempos pasados se fijaban a las patas del halcón y sobre el cual se grababa el nombre de su dueño.

vary ['veərɪ] [vea-ri], *va.* y *vn.* 1. Variar, diversificar. 2. Variar, cambiar, tener mudanzas o mutaciones. 3. Variar, mudar, hacer cambiar algo; mudarse, cambiarse, alterarse. 4. Discrepar, discordar, llegar a ser diferente; diferir en opiniones o sentimientos, estar en desacuerdo. 5. Desviarse a un lado; alejarse del norte o acercarse al norte la aguja imantada.

vascular ['væskjʊləʳ] [vas-kiu-laʳ], *a.* Vasculoso, vascular, perteneciente a los vasos de los seres orgánicos; que tiene vasos circulatorios y particularmente numerosos vasos sanguíneos.

vascularity [ˌvæskjʊˈlærɪtɪ] [vas-kiu-la-ri-ti], *s.* Vascularidad, calidad de vascular, presencia de vasos circulatorios.

vasculose ['væskjʊləʊz] [vas-kiu-lous], *a. (Bot.)* Vasculoso, vascular.

vase [vɑːz] [vas], *s.* Florero, jarrón. **She has a beatifull vase of flowers,** tiene un bonito jarrón de flores.

vasectomy [væˈsektəmɪ] [va-sek-to-mi], *sf.* Vasectomía.

vaseline ['væsɪliːn] [va-si-lin] *s.* Vaselina, sustancia crasa que se saca de la brea del petróleo; variedad del *petrolatum* de la farmacopea americana. *V.* PETROLATUM.

vassal ['vɑːnɪʃ] [var-nish], *s.* 1. Vasallo, súbdito. 2. Esclavo, siervo.

vast [vɑːst] [vast], *a.* Vasto, extenso, extendido, dilatado; inmenso, muy numeroso, grande o crecido, enorme (great). *-s. (Poét.)* Inmensidad, espacio vasto.

vastly ['vɑːstlɪ] [vast-li], *adv.* En sumo grado, muy, mucho, excesivamente, inmensamente. **He is vastly superior to me,** es inmensamente superior a mí.

vat [væt] [vat], *s.* Tina, cuba grande (large vessel, tank). **A tanner's vat,** noque, estanquillo o pozuelo en que ponen a curtir las pieles.

Vatican ['vætɪkən] [va-ti-kan], *s.* 1. Vaticano, palacio pontificio en Roma. 2. Gobierno del Papa.

vaticinate [væˈtɪsɪneɪt] [va-ti-si-neit], *vn.* Vaticinar, adivinar.

vaudeville ['vəʊdəvɪl] [vo-da-vil], *s.* 1. Zarzuela. 2. Jácara, romance, cantar del pueblo.

vault [vɔːlt] [volt], *s.* 1. Bóveda, todo techo arqueado o artesonado. 2. Cueva, bodega, subterráneo como el en que se guarda el vino. 3. Cielo, firmamento. 4. Bóveda, lugar subterráneo en las iglesias para enterrar a los difuntos. 5. Privada, letrina. 6. Volteta, voltereta, salto.

vault, *va.* Abovedar, hacer bóveda. *-vn.* Voltear, dar vueltas en el aire; saltar por encima, particularmente con ayuda de una percha o garrocha, o apoyando las manos sobre algo.

vaulted ['vɔːltɪd] [vol-tid], *a.* Abovedado, arqueado, artesonado. **Vaulted sky,** la bóveda estrellada.

vaulter ['vɔːltəʳ] [vol-taʳ], *s.* Volteador, saltador, volatín.

vaunt [vɔːnt] [vont], *va.* y *vn.* 1. Ostentar o manifestar orgullo o jactancia; hacer ostentación, gala o alarde de alguna calidad, acción, etc. 2. Jactarse, vanagloriarse, alabarse.

vaunt, *s.* Jactancia, ostentación vana; gala, alarde.

vaunter ['vɔːntəʳ] [von-taʳ], *s.* Baladrón, fanfarrón, blasonador.

vauntingly ['vɔːntɪŋlɪ] [von-tin-li], *adv.* Con jactancia.

VCR *Abreviatura de* **Video-Cassette Recorder.**

veal [viːl] [vil], *s.* Ternera, la carne de ternero o ternera y también se llama así a veces al mismo ternero vivo. **Veal-cutlet,** tajada de ternera, chuleta. **Veal-pie,** pastel de ternera. **There is a good veal in this restaurant,** hay una buena ternera en ese restaurante.

vectis ['vektɪs] [vek-tis], *s.* Instrumento obstétrico de una sola hoja para facilitar el parto.

vector ['vektəʳ] [vek-taʳ], *va.* Vectorizar, trazar vectores.

vector, *s.* (*Aer.*) Vector.

Veda ['veɪdə] [vei-da], *s.* Veda (literalmente ciencia); la ciencia divina de Brama, existente por sí misma; en plural, los cuatro libros sagrados de la India.

veer [vɪəʳ] [viaʳ], *vn.* (*Mar.*) Virar, cambiar de dirección, como el viento; (*Fig.*) ser variable o veleidoso. -va. 1. Virar, dirigir el buque a otro rumbo. 2. Dejar arriar, aflojar, alargar. **To veer and haul,** lascar y halar; largar y escasear. **The wind veers and hauls,** el viento se alarga y escasea. **To veer away the cable,** arriar el cable.

veery ['vɪərɪ] [via-ri], *s.* Tordo leonado y melodioso común en todo el Este de la América del Norte.

vegan ['viːgən] [vi-gan], *s.* Vegetariano estricto.

veganism ['viːgənɪzəm] [vi-ga-ni-sem], *sm.* Vegetarianismo puro, estricto.

vegetable ['vedʒɪtəbl] [ve-yi-ta-bol], *s.* 1. Vegetal, vegetable, hortaliza, legumbre, verdura, la parte o el todo de una planta comestible. 2. En sentido científico, planta de cualquiera clase, vegetal. -a. 1. Vegetable, vegetal, lo que vegeta. 2. Perteneciente a las legumbres u hortalizas. **The lettuce is a good vegetable,** la lechuga es una buena verdura.

vegetal ['vedʒɪtəl] [ve-yi-tal], *a.* 1. Vegetal, perteneciente o relativo a las plantas. 2. Que vegeta, común a las plantas y a los animales; p. ej. la nutrición, el crecimiento, etc.

vegetarian [ˌvedʒɪˈtɛərɪən] [ve-yi-tea-rian], *a.* y *s.* Fitófago, el que sólo se alimenta de vegetales. **He is on a vegetarian diet,** sigue una dieta vegetariana.

vegetarianism [ˌvedʒɪˈtɛərɪənɪzəm] [ve-yi-tea-ria-ni-sem], *s.* Abstinencia de todo alimento animal; la teoría de que el alimento de hombre debería ser exclusivamente vegetal.

vegetate ['vedʒɪteɪt] [ve-yi-teit], *vn.* 1. Vegetar, crecer. 2. Vegetar, vivir maquinalmente, con vida puramente orgánica.

vegetation [ˌvedʒɪˈteɪʃən] [ve-yi-tei-shon], *s.* 1. Vegetación. 2. Vegetación, conjunto de las plantas en general.

vegetative ['vedʒɪtətɪv] [ve-yi-ta-tiv], *a.* 1. Vegetativo, vegetante, dotado de la calidad de vegetar; que hace vegetar; que concurre a las funciones de nutrición y reproducción. 2. Que tiene existencia meramente física.

vegetativeness ['vedʒɪtətɪvnɪs] [ve-yi-ta-tiv-nes], *s.* Potencia vegetativa.

veggie ['vedʒɪ] [ve-yi], *a.* Vegetariano.

vehemence ['viːməns] [vi-mans], *s.* Vehemencia, impetuosidad, violencia.

vehement ['viːmənt] [vi-mant], *a.* Vehemente, impetuoso, violento; ansioso (violent, passionate).

vehemently ['viːməntlɪ] [vi-mant-li], *adv.* Vehementemente, patéticamente.

vehicle ['viːkl] [vei-kol], *s.* 1. Vehículo, cualquier carruaje u otro medio de transporte. 2. (*Phys. & Med.*) Vehículo, lo que sirve para hacer pasar una cosa más fácilmente, y con el mismo sentido se usa también en lo figurado. 3. (*Fig.*) Vehículo, lo que sirve para transmitir, medio. 4. Excipiente. **TV and radio are important vehicles of news,** la televisión y la radio son importantes vehículos de noticias.

vehicular [vɪˈhɪkjʊləʳ] [ve-ji-kiu-laʳ], *a.* Perteneciente o relativo al vehículo.

veil [veɪl] [veil], *va.* 1. Velar, cubrir con velo. 2. Encubrir, ocultar, disimular, disfrazar, tapar.

veil, *s.* 1. Velo, prenda del traje femenino de calle, hecha de tul u otra tela ligera, con la cual suelen cubrirse las mujeres la cabeza o el rostro. 2. Velo, cortina o tela que cubre un objeto. 3. Velo, cubierta, disfraz, máscara, pretexto.

vein [veɪn] [vein], *s.* 1. Vena, vaso sanguíneo que lleva la sangre al corazón. 2. Nervio del ala de un insecto. 3. (*Bot.*) Vena, nervio, hacecillo de hebras en las hojas de las plantas.

4. Vena, veta de metales en las minas; lo que llena una hendedura en la roca, particularmente cuando es depositado por soluciones acuosas; filón de mineral. 5. Vena; se da este nombre a las listas de varios colores que se hallan en algunas piedras y maderas. 6. Humor, genio. 7. La disposición favorable para hacer alguna cosa. 8. La inclinación del ingenio o talento. **A poetical vein,** vena, numen poético.

veined [veɪnd] [veind], *a.* Venoso; veteado.

veinous ['veɪnəs] [vei-nos], *a.* Venoso. **The blood passes through the veins,** la sangre pasa a través de las venas.

veld [veld] [veld], *sf.* Sábana.

vellum ['veləm] [ve-lom], *s.* Vitela, piel de vaca o ternera adobada y muy pulida; cualquier pergamino.

velocipede [vəˈlɒsɪpiːd] [ve-lo-si-pid], *s.* Velocípedo, forma primitiva de la bicicleta; también, velocípedo de tres ruedas para niños.

velocity [vɪˈlɒsɪtɪ] [vi-lo-si-ti], *s.* Velocidad, rapidez (speed).

velodrome ['viːləˌdrəʊm] [vi-lo-droum], *s.* Velódromo.

velvet ['velvɪt] [vel-vit], *s.* 1. Terciopelo, tela de seda velluda. 2. (*Zool.*) Vello, piel que cubre y nutre el cuerno de algunos animales cuando empieza a salir. -a. 1. Hecho de terciopelo. 2. Suave como el terciopelo, aterciopelado.

velveteen [ˌvelvɪˈtiːn] [vel-vi-tin], *s.* Pana, terciopelo de algodón. **She likes a velveteen dress,** a ella le gusta el vestido de terciopelo.

velvety ['velvɪtɪ] [vel-vi-ti], *a.* Aterciopelado, semejante al terciopelo, suave como él.

venal ['viːnl] [vi-nal], *a.* 1. Venal, mercenario. 2. (*Ant.*) Venal, perteneciente a las venas. *V.* VENOUR.

vend [vend] [vend], *va.* Vender; particularmente, llevar en un carretón y ofrecer a la venta.

vendee [venˈdiː] [ven-di], *s.* Comprador.

vender ['vendəʳ] [ven-daʳ], *s.* Vendedor, vendedora; vendedor ambulante, buhonero (hawker, pedlar).

vendetta [venˈdetə] [ven-de-ta], *s.* Vindicta, venganza personal, feudo de sangre entre dos personas o familias (fierce dispute).

vendible ['vendɪbl] [ven-di-bol], *a.* Vendible, venal, que está expuesto para venderse. -s. Cualquier cosa vendible; géneros de venta.

vending ['vendɪŋ] [ven-din], *sf.* Distribución, venta.

vending-machine ['vendɪŋməˈʃiːn] [ven-din-ma-shin], *s.* Máquina expendedora.

vendor ['vendəʳ] [ven-daʳ], *s.* Vendedor; forma más usada en documentos legales.

veneer [vəˈnɪəʳ] [ve-niaʳ], *va.* 1. Chapear, enchapar, cubrir (surface) con hojas delgadas, especialmente de maderas vistosas. 2. Revestir con chapas delgadas de otras substancias que la madera. 3. Tapar, ocultar lo desagradable, disfrazar.

veneer, *s.* 1. Hoja para chapear, chapa de material para producir un efecto rico en una superficie. 2. Capa exterior y delgada que se da a una cosa para adorno. 3. Apariencia o elegancia meramente exterior. **His veneer is very good,** su apariencia es muy buena.

veneering [vəˈnɪərɪŋ] [ve-nia-rin], *s.* 1. Chapeadura, el arte de chapear. 2. Material que sirve para hacer hojas de chapear.

venerable ['venərəbl] [ve-ne-ra-bol], *a.* 1. Venerable, digno de veneración; hoy implica generalmente vejez. 2. Venerable, que infunde reverencia, sagrado, consagrado.

venerablenes ['venərəblnɪs] [ve-ne-ra-bol-nes], *s.* La calidad que constituye a una persona venerable o digna de veneración y respeto.

venerably ['venərəblɪ] [ve-ne-ra-bli], *adv.* Venerablemente.

venerate ['venəreɪt] [ve-na-reit], *va.* Venerar, reverenciar, respetar, honrar lo noble, lo viejo o lo sagrado (to honor greatly, respect).

veneration [ˌvenəˈreɪʃən] [ve-na-rei-shon], *s.* Veneración, respeto.

venerator [ˌvenəˈreɪtəʳ] [ve-na-rei-taʳ], *s.* Venerador.

venereal [vɪˈnɪərɪəl] [vi-nia-rial], *a.* 1. Venéreo, que pertenece a la Venus o que procede del acto sexual. 2. Venéreo, transmitido por el coito con una persona que tiene el mal venéreo; perteneciente a las enfermedades así comunicadas. 3. Que excita el deseo sexual. 4. *(Des.)* De cobre.

Venetian [vɪ'niːʃən] [vi-ni-shan], *a.* Veneciano, de Venecia. - *s.* Veneciano, natural de Venecia. **Venetian blinds,** persianas, celosías. **Venetian chalk,** talco gráfico. **Venetian window,** ventana de tres aberturas o huecos separados.

Venezuelan [ˌveneˈzweɪlən] [ve-ni-suei-lan], *a.* y *s.* Venezolano.

vengeance ['vendʒəns] [ven-yans], *s.* 1. Venganza, castigo retributivo, imposición de una pena merecida (revenge). 2. Despique, desquite, venganza rencorosa. **With a vengeance,** con violencia, con fuerza, con toda su alma; extremamente. **He soon had his opportunity for vengeance,** pronto tuvo su oportunidad de venganza. **Seek vengeance,** buscar venganza.

vengeful ['vendʒful] [vench-ful], *a.* Vengativo.

venial ['viːnɪəl] [vi-nial], *a.* 1. Venial, remisible. 2. Permitido, lícito (pardonable, not serious).

venially ['viːnɪəlɪ] [vi-nia-li], *adv.* Venialmente, levemente, ligeramente.

veniality [ˌviːnɪˈælɪtɪ] [vi-nia-li-ti], *s.* Venialidad, calidad de venial.

venison ['venɪzn] [ve-ni-son], *s.* Venado, carne de venado.

venom ['venəm] [ve-nom], *s.* 1. Veneno, licor ponzoñoso que secretan ciertos animales, como las serpientes y los alacranes (poison). 2. Ponzoña, lo que produce efecto ponzoñoso; maldad; rencor (great ill-feeling, anger).

venomous ['venəməs] [ve-no-mos], *a.* 1. Venenoso, ponzoñoso. 2. Que comunica veneno; *(Fig.)* dañoso, perjudicial. 3. Malo, rencoroso, maligno, propenso a obrar mal.

venomously ['venəməslɪ] [ve-no-mos-li], *adv.* Venenosamente.

venomousness ['venəməsnɪs] [ve-no-mos-nes], *s.* Venenosidad; natural venenoso.

venous ['viːnəs] [vi-nos], *a.* 1. Venoso, perteneciente a las venas o contenido en ellas. 2. Veteado, marcado con venas o nervios; v. gr. el ala de un insecto. **Venous blood,** sangre venosa; se diferencia de la arterial por su color más obscuro y por contener más ácido carbónico.

vent [vent] [vent], *s.* 1. Respiradero, tronera, lumbrera, cualquier abertura por donde puede salir el aire y ventilarse una cueva, bodega, etc; salida de cualquiera clase; ventosa, oído, fogón de un arma de fuego. 2. Ano. 3. Articulación, expresión, acción de pronunciar; se usa hoy por lo general en la locución **to give vent to,** dar expresión a, dar salida a. 4. Desahogo. **To give one's passion vent,** desfogar o desahogar la cólera. **His jacket has a vent in the back,** su chaqueta tiene una abertura en la espalda.

vent, *va.* 1. Dar salida o abrir un respiradero, tronera, etc. 2. Descubrir o divulgar un proyecto, un secreto, etc.; expresar públicamente; articular. 3. Dejar escapar. 4. Dar libre carrera a; aliviar, dando salida a algo. 5. Descargar. **He was angry with himself and vented his rage on his son,** estaba enfadado consigo mismo y descargó su rabia con su hijo.

vental ['ventl] [ven-tal], *a.* Del viento, perteneciente al viento.

venter ['ventər] [ven-tar], *s.* 1. Cualquiera de las tres cavidades principales del cuerpo. 2. Vientre; de aquí, en derecho, madre.

ventilate ['ventɪleɪt] [ven-ti-leit], *va.* 1. Ventilar, producir circulación del aire en; renovar el aire de una habitación. 2. Ventilar, controvertir, disputar, discutir; examinar. 3. *(Ant.)* Aventar.

ventilation [ˌventɪˈleɪʃən] [ven-ti-lei-shon], *s.* 1. Ventilación, el movimiento del aire que pasa, corre o se transpira. 2. Ventilación, el acto de controvertir, disputar o contender sobre alguna cosa para examinarla.

ventilator ['ventɪleɪtər] [ven-ti-lei-tar], *s.* Ventilador, aparato o abertura para renovar el aire.

ventose ['ventoz] [ven-tous], *a.* Ventoso, flatulento; de aquí, hablador.

ventral ['ventrəl] [ven-tral], *a.* 1. Ventral, perteneciente al vientre. 2. *(Bot.)* Perteneciente a la superficie anterior de un órgano. **Ventral fins,** aletas abdominales.

ventricle ['ventrɪkl] [ven-tri-kol], *s. (Anat.)* Ventrículo: se da este nombre a dos cavidades del corazón y a cuatro del cerebro.

ventricular ['ventrɪkjʊlər] [ven-tri-kiu-lar], *a.* Ventricular, relativo al ventrículo.

ventriloquism [ven'trɪləkwɪzəm] [ven-tri-lo-kui-sem], *s.* Ventriloquía, arte del ventrílocuo.

ventriloquist [ven'trɪləkwɪst] [ven-tri-lo-kuist], *s.* Ventrílocuo.

venture ['ventʃər] [ven-char], *s.* 1. Riesgo, peligro. 2. Caso o empresa arriesgada, especulación en los negocios. 3. La cosa aventurada o arriesgada. **At a venture,** a ventura o a la ventura.

venture, *vn.* 1. Osar, atreverse. 2. Aventurarse, arriesgarse. **To venture at, on o upon,** probar ventura, pretender o emprender alguna cosa que se considera difícil de conseguir. *-va.* Aventurar, arriesgar (to hazard, risk). **To venture abroad, to venture out,** atreverse a descender. **To venture up,** atreverse a subir; emprender la subida.

venturer ['ventʃərər] [ven-cha-rar], *s.* Aventurero.

venturesome ['ventʃəsəm] [ven-cha-som], *a.* 1. Atrevido, emprendedor, osado (daring). 2. Aventurado, que envuelve riesgo o azar; dudoso.

venturous ['ventʃrəs] [ven-chu-ras], *a.* Osado, atrevido (daring, presumptuous).

venturously ['ventʃrəslɪ] [ven-chu-ras-li], *adv.* Osadamente.

venturousness ['ventʃrəsnɪs] [ven-chu-ras-nes], *s.* Arrojo, temeridad.

venue ['venjuː] [ve-niu], *s. (For.)* Vecindad o paraje donde radica la causa del pleito. **A change of venue,** cambio de tribunal en un pleito.

Venus ['viːnəs] [vi-nos], *s.* 1. Venus, diosa romana del amor; originariamente la diosa latina de la primavera y de las vides. 2. *(Astr.)* Venus, el planeta más cercano a la tierra, y el astro más brillante en el firmamento después del sol y de la luna. **Venus's comb,** *(Bot.)* Peine de pastor. **Venus's looking-glass,** *(Bot.)* Campanilla, planta del género Specularia. **Venus's navelwort,** *(Bot.)* Ombligo de Venus, planta de las borrajíneas. **Venus's fan,** especie de zoófito. **Venus's fly-trap,** atrapa-moscas, planta sensitiva con hojas que se cierran y aprisionan los insectos posados en ellas.

veracious [vəˈreɪʃəs] [ve-rei-shos], *a.* 1. Veraz, verídico. 2. Verdadero.

veracity [vəˈræsɪtɪ] [ve-ra-si-ti], *s.* Veracidad, la propiedad o hábito de decir siempre la verdad.

veranda [vəˈrændə] [ve-ran-da], *s.* Pórtico abierto o galería que se extiende a lo largo de uno o más lados de una casa.

verb [vɜːb] [verb], *s. (Gram.)* Verbo, una de las partes de la oración.

verbal ['vɜːbəl] [ver-bal], *a.* 1. Verbal, que se refiere a las palabras; que tiene relación con las palabras (más bien que con las ideas). 2. Verbal, de viva voz; proferido, no escrito. 3. Literal, palabra por palabra. 4. Verbal, derivado del verbo o que participa de su naturaleza. **A verbal contract,** contrato verbal o de palabra.

verbalism ['vɜːbəlɪzəm] [ver-ba-li-sem], *s.* Observación hecha de viva voz.

verbally ['vɜːbəlɪ] [ver-ba-li], *adv.* Verbalmente; palabra por palabra.

verbatim [vɜːˈbeɪtɪm] [ver-bei-tim], *adv.* Al pie de la letra, palabra por palabra.

verbena [vɜːˈbiːnə] [ver-bi-na], *s.* Verbena, planta herbácea anual que se cultiva en los jardines.

verbiage ['vɜːbɪɪdʒ] [ver-biich], *s.* Verbosidad, el uso de palabras inútiles; superabundancia de palabras.

verbose [vɜːˈbəʊs] [ver-bous], *a.* Verboso, abundante en palabras inútiles, difuso, prolijo.

verbosity [vɜːˈbɒsɪtɪ] [ver-bo-si-ti], *s.* Verbosidad.

verdancy ['vɜːdənsɪ] [ver-dan-si], *s.* Verdor, calidad de lo verde.

verdant ['vɜːdənt] [ver-dant], *a.* 1. Verde, que verdea; fresco. 2. Falto de experiencia, sencillo.

verdict ['vɜːdɪkt] [ver-dikt], *s.* 1. Veredicto, el fallo del jurado; declaración o decisión sobre un hecho dictada por el jurado. **General verdict,** la decisión absoluta y sin reserva del jurado, tanto con respecto al hecho como a la ley. **Special verdict,** la decisión del jurado especificando simplemente el hecho y dejando al juez la aplicación de la ley. 2. Dictamen, parecer, voto.

verdigris ['vɜːdɪɡrɪs] [ver-di-gris], *s.* 1. Verdete, acetato de cobre. 2. Cardenillo, verdín, la herrumbre u orín del cobre.

verdin ['vɜːdɪn] [ver-din], *s.* Paro de Méjico, de cabeza amarilla.

verditer ['vɜːdɪtəʳ] [ver-di-taʳ], *s.* Verdete, color azul o verde claro, hecho con el carbonato o acetato de cobre y que se emplea en pintura y tintorería.

verdure ['vɜːdjʊəʳ] [ver-diuaʳ], *s.* Verde, verdura, verdor; vegetación.

verdurous ['vɜːdjʊərəs] [ver-diua-ros], *a.* Verde; adornado de verde.

verge [vɜːdʒ] [verdch], *s.* 1. Canto extremo, borde, margen, vera, veril. 2. Línea que deslinda o limita; círculo, anillo; de aquí, alcance, esfera, oportunidad. 3. Vara, insignia de jurisdicción y autoridad eclesiástica u otra. 4. Árbol de volante (en los escapes verticales de relojería). 5. *(Arch.)* Fuste de columna. 6. *(Zool.)* Verga, órgano de la generación en ciertos moluscos y crustáceos. **On** o **upon the verge of,** al borde de; en vísperas de, a dos dedos de; a la extremidad de.

verge, *vn.* Acercarse a, aproximarse a; tender.

verger ['vɜːdʒəʳ] [ver-chaʳ], *s.* 1. Alguacil de vara; macero de una universidad inglesa. 2. Aposentador, pertiguero de una catedral, sacristán. *V.* USHER.

Vergil ['vɜːdʒɪl] [ver-yil], *sm.* Virgilio.

verifiable ['verɪfaɪəbl] [ve-ri-faia-bol], *a.* Verificable, que se puede demostrar o comprobar.

verification [ˌverɪfɪ'keɪʃən] [ve-ri-fi-kei-shon], *s.* Verificación, comprobación, confirmación por argumento o evidencia.

verify ['verɪfaɪ] [ve-ri-fai], *va.* 1. Verificar, justificar, probar, comprobar, demostrar la exactitud de. 2. Cumplir, ejecutar (una promesa). 3. *(For.)* Afirmar bajo juramento.

verily ['verɪlɪ] [ve-ri-li], *adv.* Verdaderamente, ciertamente, en verdad; sinceramente, en realidad (truly).

verisimilar [ˌverɪ'sɪmɪləʳ] [ve-ri-si-mi-laʳ], *a.* (Poco us.) Verosímil o verisímil, que tiene apariencia de verdadero.

verisimilitude [ˌverɪsɪ'mɪlɪtjuːd] [ve-ri-si-mi-li-tiud], *s.* Verisimilitud, apariencia de verdad.

veritable ['verɪtəbl] [ve-ri-ta-bol], *a.* Verdadero, cierto, real, genuino (genuine, real).

verity ['verɪtɪ] [ve-ri-ti], *s.* Verdad, calidad de correcto, realidad; cosa realmente existente, hecho; máxima, axioma, principio (truth, axiom).

verjuice ['vɜːdʒuːs] [ver-yus], *s.* 1. Agraz, zumo de la uva sin madurar. 2. Aspereza de modales o lenguaje; mordacidad.

vermeil ['vɜːmeɪl] [ver-meil], *s.* 1. Plata o bronce sobredorados. 2. Barniz transparente de agua. 3. Granate rojo anaranjado. 4. *(Poét. o des.)* Color bermellón.

vermicelli [ˌvɜːmɪ'selɪ] [ver-mi-se-li], *s.* Fideos, especie de pasta o masa delgada, vermiforme.

vermicide ['vɜːmɪsaɪd] [ver-mi-said], *s.* Vermífugo, medicamento que mata las lombrices intestinales.

vermicule ['vɜːmɪkjuːl] [ver-mi-kiul], *s.* Gusanillo, gusano pequeño, lombricilla.

vermiform ['vɜːmɪfɔːm] [ver-mi-form], *a.* Vermiforme, que tiene la forma o figura de lombriz o gusano; lombriza. **Vermiform appendix,** apéndice vermiforme del intestino ciego.

vermifuge ['vɜːmɪfjuːdʒ] [ver-mi-fiuch], *s.* Vermífugo, antihelmíntico, medicina contra las lombrices.

vermilion [və'mɪlɪən] [ver-mi-lion], *s.* 1. Bermellón, cinabrio, sea natural o artificial. 2. Cualquier color sumamente rojo.

vermilion, *va.* Enrojar, teñir de rojo.

vermin ['vɜːmɪn] [ver-min], *s.* 1. Bicho, sabandija, cualquier animal dañino o nocivo, nombre colectivo para denotar los insectos parásitos, los ratones, gusanos, piojos, etc. 2. *(Fig.)* Gente despreciable y asquerosa.

verminous ['vɜːmɪnəs] [ver-mi-nos], *a.* *(Med.)* Verminoso, lleno de lombrices o con disposición a criarlas.

vermouth ['vɜːməθ] [ver-moz], *s.* Vermut, vermú.

vernacular [və'nækjʊləʳ] [ver-na-kiu-laʳ], *a.* 1. Indígena, vernáculo, del país natal. 2. Local, característico de una localidd o país determinados. **Vernacular tongue,** la lengua nativa o el idioma vernáculo.

vernal ['vɜːnl] [ver-nal], *a.* Vernal, que pertenece a la primavera, que sucede en la primavera; joven, de la juventud.

vernier ['vɜːnɪəʳ] [ver-niaʳ], *s.* Nonio, vernier, escala movible.

veronica [və'rɒnɪkə] [ve-ro-ni-ka], *s.* 1. Lienzo en que aparecen estampadas las facciones de Nuestro Señor Jesucristo. 2. *(Bot.)* Verónica, género de plantas de las escrofuláriáceas.

verruca [və'ruːkə] [ve-ru-ka], *s.* Verruga (wart).

versatile ['vɜːsətaɪl] [ver-sa-tail], *a.* 1. Versátil, que tiene aptitud para tareas u ocupaciones nuevas y variadas. 2. Versátil, de genio o carácter inconstante o voluble. 3. Versátil, que se puede volver fácilmente (como sobre un quicio o eje).

versatility [ˌvɜːsə'tɪlɪtɪ] [ver-sa-ti-li-ti], *s.* 1. Aptitud para muchas ocupaciones, posesión de variados talentos. 2. Veleidad, la calidad de lo que es versátil o de genio o carácter voluble e inconstante; mutabilidad, inconstancia.

verse [vɜːs] [vers], *s.* 1. Verso, número determinado de sílabas que forman consonancia y cadencia. 2. Metro, copla, composición en verso. 3. Versículo, subdivisión pequeña de algún capítulo. **To make verses,** versificar, hacer versos. **This song has three verses,** esa canción tiene tres versos.

versed [vɜːst] [verst], *a.* Versado, práctico o diestro en una materia o cosa. **Versed sine,** seno verso, función trigonométrica.

verseman ['vɜːsmən] [vers-man], *s.* Poeta, versista, el que hace versos.

versicle ['vɜːsɪkl] [ver-si-kol], *s.* Versículo; versículo, párrafo breve de un libro litúrgico.

versification [ˌvɜːsɪfɪ'keɪʃən] [ver-si-fi-kei-shon], *s.* Versificación, acción, arte o práctica de hacer versos.

versify ['vɜːsɪfaɪ] [ver-si-fai], *vn.* Versificar, hacer versos. - *va.* Recitar, decir o representar alguna composición en verso.

version ['vɜːʃən] [ver-shon], *s.* 1. Versión, traducción de una lengua a otra (traslation). 2. Versión, el modo que tiene cada uno de referir un mismo suceso. 3. Versión, operación obstétrica para cambiar la posición del feto cuando éste se presenta mal para el parto. **Authorized** o **King James's Version, Revised Version,** dos versiones inglesas de la Biblia. *V.* AUTHORIZE y REVISE.

versus ['vɜːsəs] [ver-sos], *prep.* En contra (against). Se abrevia **vs.** y se emplea en demandas y litigios, como por ej.: **The State versus John Doe,** El Estado en contra de Fulano de Tal.

vert [vɜːt] [vert], *s.* 1. *(Der. inglés)* Todo árbol, arbusto o cualquier otra planta que crece dentro de un bosque y puede ocultar a un ciervo. 2. *(Her.)* Sinople o sínoble.

vertebra ['vɜːtɪbrə] [ver-ti-bra], *s.* Vértebra, cada uno de los huesos enlazados entre sí que forman el espinazo.

vertebral ['vɜːtɪbrəl] [ver-ti-bral], *a.* 1. Vertebral, perteneciente a las vértebras. 2. Vertebrado, provisto de vértebras.

vertebrate ['vɜːtɪbreɪt] [ver-ti-breit], *a.* Vertebrado, que tiene una columna vertebral. -*s.* Animal vertebrado.

vertex ['vɜːteks] [ver-teks], *s.* Vértice; cima, cumbre; extremidad superior de una pirámide, de un cono, etc.: cenit.

vertical ['vɜːtɪkəl] [ver-ti-kal], *a.* Vertical, perpendicular al horizonte; que está directa y perpendicularmente sobre nuestro vértice o cabeza.

verticality [ˌvɜːtɪ'kælɪtɪ] [ver-ti-ka-li-ti], *s.* La situación o carácter vertical.

vertically ['vɜːtɪkəlɪ] [ver-ti-ka-li], *adv.* Verticalmente.

vertiginous [vɜː'tɪdʒɪnəs] [ver-ti-yi-nos], *a.* 1. Vertiginoso, que padece vértigos. 2. Que tiende a causar vértigo. 3. Giratorio, que da vueltas.

vertigo ['vɜːtɪɡəʊ] [ver-ti-gou], *s.* Vértigo, vahido de cabeza. **She suffers from vertigo,** ella sufre de vértigo.

vervain ['vɜːveɪn] [ver-vein], *s. (Bot.)* Planta no cultivada del género Verbena.

verve [vɜːv] [verv], *s.* 1. Energía, entusiasmo, fervor. 2. Inspiración artística.

very ['verɪ] [ve-ri], *a.* 1. Verdadero, real. 2. Grande, lo que tiene calidades comúnmente malas en grado eminente. **He is a very thief,** es un ladrón consumado. 3. Idéntico, mismo. **At that very hour,** a aquella misma hora o precisamente a aquella hora. 4. Completo. 5. Justo, preciso (exactly, precisely) -*adv.* Muy, mucho, sumamente. **Very much,** mucho o muchísimo; muy (antes de un participio). **Very** se usa también de un modo expletivo para aumentar el énfasis de la oración. **She has a car of her very own,** tiene su propio coche.

vesicle ['vesɪkl] [ve-si-kol], *s.* Vesícula, vejigüela, vejiguilla; ampolla o quiste pequeño; protuberancia llena de aire que tienen ciertas plantas acuáticas.

vesicular [vəˈsɪkjʊləʳ] [ve-si-kiu-laʳ], *a.* Vesicular, en forma de vesícula; vesiculoso.

vesper ['vespəʳ] [ves-paʳ], *s.* 1. Véspero o héspero, la estrella vespertina. 2. Tarde, el anochecer. 3. Campana que llama a vísperas. 4. *pl.* Vísperas, una de las horas del oficio divino que se dice por la tarde. -*a.* Vespertino, perteneciente a la tarde o a las vísperas.

vespertine ['vespətiːn] [ves-per-tin], *a.* Vespertino.

vessel [vesl] [ve-sel], *s.* 1. Vasija, el vaso para echar o guardar licores u otras cosas. 2. Vaso, nombre dado por los anatómicos a los canales que contienen la sangre y la linfa en el cuerpo humano. 3. Buque, bajel, embarcación. 4. *(Bot.)* V. DUCT.

vest [vest] [vest], *s.* 1. Chaleco (a waistcoat). V. WAISTCOAT. 2. Chaqueta antigua de mujer; guarnición del vestido de mujer por el frente. 3. Elástica, camiseta interior. 4. Vestido, vestidura.

vest, *va.* 1. Revestir (authority), investir. 2. Investir, dar la investidura de alguna cosa; poner en posesión, dar a cargo. 3. Vestir, cubrir o adornar el cuerpo con el vestido. **To vest with,** vestir de, revestir de. **To vest in,** revestir de, investir de, poner en posesión de.

vestal ['vestl] [ves-tal], *s.* Vestal, entre los romanos la virgen consagrada a la diosa Vesta. -*a.* Virgíneo, virginal.

vestibule ['vestɪbjuːl] [ves-ti-biul], *s.* Vestíbulo, atrio, pórtico, portal, zaguán (a entrance hall). **I'll meet you in the vestibule of the theater,** me encontraré contigo en el vestíbulo del teatro.

vestige ['vestɪdʒ] [ves-tich], *s.* 1. Vestigio, señal que queda de una cosa (a trace). 2. *(Biol.)* Parte u órgano, pequeño o atrofiado, aunque normalmente desarrollado en los antepasados.

vestigial ['vestɪdʒɪəl] [ves-ti-yial], *a. (Biol.)* Que se ha atrofiado o degenerado.

vesting ['vestɪŋ] [ves-tin], *s.* Material para hacer chalecos.

vestment ['vestmənt] [vest-ment], *s.* Prenda de vestir, vestido; vestidura de dignidad, de pompa; vestimenta que usan los sacerdotes; también, sabanilla (de altar).

vest-pocket [vestˈpɒkɪt] [vest-po-kit], *a.* Para el bolsillo del chaleco. **Vest-pocket Dictionary,** Diccionario de bolsillo.

vestry ['vestrɪ] [ves-tri], *s.* 1. Vestuario, habitación donde se guardan vestidos y se revisten los eclesiásticos y a veces los coristas. 2. Sacristía, una pieza contigua a la iglesia, donde se guardan las vestiduras, los ornamentos y otras cosas pertenecientes al culto divino. 3. En la Iglesia episcopal protestante, reunión de hombres que tienen a su cargo la administración de los asuntos de la parroquia. 4. En las iglesias no litúrgicas, capilla o cuarto para la escuela dominical contiguo a la iglesia. **Vestryman,** miembro de la junta parroquial *(vestry).*

vesture ['vestʃəʳ] [ves-chaʳ], *s.* 1. Vestido, lo que viste o cubre, capa; traje, hábito. 2. En el antiguo derecho inglés, todo lo que cubre el terreno excepto los árboles.

vet [vet] [vet], *v.* Someter a investigación, examinar, repasar.

vetch [vetʃ] [vech], *s. (Bot.)* Algarroba, arverjona; cualquier planta del género Vicia.

vetchy ['vetʃɪ] [ve-chi], *a.* Abundante en algarrobas.

veteran ['vetərən] [ve-te-ran], *s.* y *a.* 1. Veterano, militar viejo. 2. Veterano, hombre antiguo, práctico y experto en cualquier profesión o ejercicio.

verterinarian [ˌvetərɪˈnɛərɪən] [ve-te-ri-nea-rian], *s.* Albéitar, veterinario.

veterinary ['vetərɪnərɪ] [ve-te-ri-na-ri], *a.* Veterinario, perteneciente a la veterinaria o a las enfermedades y lesiones de los animales domésticos y a su tratamiento. **Veterinary science,** veterinaria.

veto ['viːtəʊ] [vi-tou], *va.* 1. Poner el veto a (v.g. a un proyecto de ley). 2. Vedar o prohibir con autoridad; rehusar la aprobación de. -*s.* 1. Veto, derecho que tiene el poder ejecutivo de negar la sanción de una ley votada por los cuerpos legislativos. 2. Acción de vetar, de poner el veto a; comunicación oficial en que se niega la sanción a un proyecto de ley. 3. Cualquier prohibición hecha con autoridad.

vetting ['vetɪŋ] [ve-tin], *s.* Exament, investigación (check).

vex [veks] [veks], *va.* 1. Vejar, molestar; apesadumbrar, desazonar, hacer padecer a uno (to annoy, distress). 2. Enojar, irritar, enfadar, provocar, hacer salir a uno de sus casillas. *(Vulg.)* Moler, jorobar. 3. Turbar, perturbar. **To be vexed,** incomodarse, enojarse, picarse.

vexation [vekˈseɪʃən] [vek-sei-shon], *s.* Vejación, molestia, maltrato; provocación, enojo, enfado.

vexatious [vekˈseɪʃəs] [vek-sei-shos], *a.* Penoso, molesto, enfadoso; provocativo.

vexatiousness [vekˈseɪʃəsnɪs] [vek-sei-shos-nes], *s.* Molestia, vejación, inquietud.

vexer ['veksəʳ] [vek-saʳ], *s.* El que inquieta, enfada, molesta o provoca.

VHF *Abreviatura de* **Very High Frequency,** frecuencia muy alta.

via ['vaɪə] [vaia], *prep.* Por la vía de, por. **Via Nicaragua,** por Nicaragua.

viability [ˌvaɪəˈbɪlɪtɪ] [vaia-bi-li-ti], *s.* Viabilidad, calidad de viable.

viable ['vaɪəbl] [vaia-bol], *a.* Viable, capaz de vivir; que sale a luz con fuerza bastante para seguir viviendo.

viaduct ['vaɪədʌkt] [vaia-dakt], *s.* Viaducto, obra a manera de puente, para el paso de un camino sobre una hondonada.

vial ['vaɪəl] [vaial], *s.* Redoma, ampolleta; botella, vaso.

viand ['vaɪənd] [vaiand], *s.* Vianda, la carne o comida que se sirve a la mesa.

viatic ['vaɪətɪk] [vaia-tik], *a.* De viaje, de viático.

viaticum [vaɪˈætɪkəm] [vaia-ti-kom], *s.* 1. Viático, prevención o provisión para algún viaje. 2. Viático, la comunión que se administra a los enfermos en peligro de muerte.

vibrant ['vaɪbrənt] [vai-brant], *a.* Vibrante, que vibra.

vibrate ['vaɪbreɪt] [vai-breit], *va.* 1. Vibrar, blandir, dar un movimiento trémulo a alguna cosa larga y delgada (to jar, rattle, vibrate). 2. Vibrar, arrojar con ímpetu y violencia una cosa, especialmente hablando de las que en su movimiento hacen vibraciones. -*vn.* 1. Vibrar, moverse alguna cosa suspensa en el aire de un lado a otro, con movimiento igual. 2. Vibrar o moverse una cosa haciendo vibraciones.

vibratile ['vaɪbrətɪl] [vai-bra-til], *a.* Vibrátil, a propósito para el movimiento vibratorio.

vibration [vaɪˈbreɪʃən] [vai-brei-shon], *s.* Vibración: se dice del vaivén de un cuerpo libre suspenso en el aire, y del movimiento trémulo de las cuerdas tirantes, de los rayos de luz, etc.

vibratory ['vaɪbrətərɪ] [vai-bra-to-ri], *a.* Vibratorio, oscilatorio.

vicar ['vɪkəʳ] [vi-kaʳ], *s.* 1. Vicario, el que hace las veces de un superior en ciertas funciones, particularmente las eclesiásticas. 2. Teniente de cura de una parroquia; cura beneficiado.

vicarage ['vɪkərɪdʒ] [vi-ka-rich], *s.* 1. Vicaría, vicariato, beneficio curado. 2. Vicaría, casa del vicario.

vicarial [vɪˈkeərɪəl] [vi-ka-rial], *a.* Vicarial, lo perteneciente al vicario y a su oficio.

vicarious [vɪˈkeərɪəs] [vi-ka-rios], *a.* 1. Vicario, hecho o ejecutado por vía de sustitución; sufrido en vez de otro. 2. Diputado, delegado, substituto, que obra en virtud de poderes de otra persona o la substituye. 3. Vicarial, perteneciente al vicario.

vicarship ['vɪkəʃɪp] [vi-kar-ship], *s.* Vicariato.

vice [vaɪs] [vais], *s.* 1. Vicio, maldad, habitual disposición al mal, malignidad; lo opuesto a virtud (defect, failing, fault). 2. Vicio, defecto o imperfección del cuerpo o del alma; falta, culpa, desliz. 3. El bufón de los volátiles. 4. Vicio, resabio o mala costumbre del caballo. 5. *V.* VISE. **Continual lying is a vice**, mentir continuamente es un vicio.

vice, Prefijo que sólo se usa en composición para significar que la persona de quien se habla tiene las veces o autoridad de aquella que denota la voz con que se forma la composición. **Vice-admiral**, (a) vicealmirante, el jefe principal de una escuadra después del almirante; (b) vicealmirante, uno de los grados de los oficiales generales de marina en Inglaterra. **Vice-admiralty**, vicealmirantazgo. **Vice-agent**, agente, la persona que hace algo en lugar de otro. **Vice-chancellor**, vicecanciller, vicecancelario. **Vice-consul**, vicecónsul, el que hace las veces de cónsul. **Vice-presidency**, vicepresidencia, dignidad de vicepresidente y el tiempo que dura. **Vice-president**, vicepresidente; en especial el Vicepresidente de los Estados Unidos de América.

viceroy ['vaɪsrɔɪ] [vais-roi], *s.* Virrey, el que con este título gobierna en nombre y con autoridad del rey.

viceroyalty ['vaɪsˈrɔɪəltɪ] [vais-roial-ti], *s.* Virreinato.

vice versa ['vaɪsˈvɜːsə] [vais-ver-sa], *adv.* Viceversa. **Kevin dislikes Mary and vice versa**, a Kevin no le gusta Mary y viceversa.

vicinage ['vɪsɪnɪdʒ] [vi-si-nich], *s.* 1. Vecindad, cercanía o proximidad de unos parajes a otros. 2. Calidad de próximo o vecino.

vicinity [vɪˈsɪnɪtɪ] [vi-si-ni-ti], *s.* Vecindad, cercanía, proximidad.

vicious ['vɪʃəs] [vi-shos], *a.* 1. Vicioso, endepravado, entregado al mal (evil, cruel). 2. Vicioso, defectuoso, imperfecto; (horse) asombradizo. 3. *(Fam.)* Maligno, rencoroso, enconado. **Vicious circle**, círculo vicioso.

viciously ['vɪʃəslɪ] [vi-shos-li], *adv.* De manera perversa, viciosamente.

viciousnes ['vɪʃəsnɪs] [vi-shos-nes], *sf.* Crueldad, viciosidad.

vicissitude [vɪˈsɪsɪtjuːd] [vi-si-si-tiud], *s.* Vicisitud, orden o acontecimiento sucesivo o alternativo; alternativa, vuelta o retorno; mudanza; instabilidad.

victim ['vɪktɪm] [vik-tim], *s.* 1. Víctima, criatura viva ofrecida en sacrificio a una divinidad (dupe, martyr, prey). 2. Persona sacrificada con un objeto cualquiera. 3. El que padece una condición enferma o un sentimiento mórbido. 4. El que ha sido embaucado, estafado. **The murderer's victims were all women**, las víctimas de los crímenes son todas mujeres.

victimize ['vɪktɪmaɪz] [vik-ti-mais], *va. (Fam.)* Hacer víctima, estafar, embaucar.

victor ['vɪktəʳ] [vik-taʳ], *s.* Vencedor, el que consigue una victoria.

victoria [vɪkˈtɔːrɪə] [vik-to-ria], *s.* 1. *(Bot.)* Victoria, ninfea gigantea del Amazonas. 2. Carruaje bajo y ligero de cuatro ruedas, con cielo de quita y pon.

victorious [vɪkˈtɔːrɪəs] [vik-to-rios], *a.* Victorioso (successful, winning).

victoriously [vɪkˈtɔːrɪəslɪ] [vik-to-rios-li], *adv.* Victoriosamente.

victoriousness [vɪkˈtɔːrɪəsnɪs] [vik-to-rios-nes], *s.* Triunfo, victoria.

victory ['vɪktərɪ] [vik-to-ri], *s.* Victoria, conquista; triunfo, vencimiento, vencida.

victress ['vɪktrɪs] [vik-tres], *sf.* Vencedora.

victual ['vɪktʃəl] [vik-chal], *s.* Vitualla, el conjunto de cosas necesarias para la comida, víveres.

victual, *va.* Abastecer, proveer de bastimentos. **Victualling department**, *(Ingl.)* Administración naval, servicio de las subsistencias de la marina. **Victualling ship**, buque que lleva los víveres para otro o para la flota.

victualler ['vɪktʃələʳ] [vik-cha-laʳ], *s.* 1. Abastecedor, porveedor, el que provee de bastimentos o vituallas. 2. Hostalero, bodegonero, el que tiene fonda, bodegón, etc., donde se da de comer. 3. El buque donde se llevan los bastimentos para una flota.

vicugna, vicuña [vɪˈkjuːnə] [vi-kiu-na], *s.* Vicuña, cuadrúpedo parecido a la llama y originario del Perú, cuya lana es muy estimada.

videlicet [vɪˈdiːlɪset] [vi-di-li-set], *adv.* A saber: comúnmente se escribe *viz. V.* VIZ.

video ['vɪdɪəʊ] [vi-diou], *s.* Vídeo.

vie [vaɪ] [vai], *va.* y *vn.* 1. Competir, contender dos o más personas entre sí, aspirar con empeño unos y otros a una misma cosa. 2. Disputar sobre una cosa; obrar o ejecutar algo en competencia; hacer una cosa por emulación.

Viennese [ˌvɪəˈniːz] [via-nis], *a.* Vienés, vienesa, de Viena en Austria. *-s. (sing.* y *pl).* Vienés, natural o habitante de Viena.

Vietnamese [ˌvjetnəˈmiːz] [viet-na-mis], *a.* y *s.* Vietnamita.

view [vjuː] [viu], *va.* 1. Mirar; ver, percibir o examinar con la vista, mirar con atención, examinar, inspeccionar, reconocer (to look at, regard, inspect). 2. Mirar mentalmente, considerar. **I viewed his opinion as unnecesary**, considero su opinion como innecesaria.

view, *s.* 1. Vista, la acción y efecto de ver (outlook, picture). 2. Vista, el hecho mismo de ver y el modo con que se mira; vista intelectual; opinión, noción, parecer (opinion). 3. Vista, visión, la facultad o potencia de ver; el alcance a donde llega la vista. 4. Perspectiva, vista o aspecto de diversos objetos juntos mirados de lejos; cuadro, dibujo, lámina, particularmente lo que representa un paisaje, lo que se presenta a las miradas. 5. Vista, intento o propósito. 6. Examen, inspección o escrutinio de una cosa. 7. Apariencia. 8. *(For.)* Inspección hecha, v. g. por el jurado, de una propiedad o de un local o paraje. **With this view**, con esta mira, con este intento. **At first view**, de una ojeada, de una mirada. **Field of view**, *(Opt.)* campo de la visión. **To take a nearer view of**, ver, examinar de más cerca. **In view of**, en vista de, dado. **On view**, expuesto. **Point of view**, punto de vista. **This house has a beautiful view of the bay**, esta casa tiene una hermosa vista de la bahía. **Tell me your view**, dime tu opinión.

viewer ['vjuːəʳ] [viuaʳ], *s.* Veedor, el que ve, mira o registra con curiosidad; mirador, el que mira.

viewfinder ['vjuːˌfaɪndəʳ] [viu-fain-daʳ], *s.* En fotografía, visor o buscador.

viewless ['vjuːlɪs] [viu-les], *a.* Invisible.

viewpoint ['vjuːpɔɪnt] [viu-point], *s.* Punto de vista.

vigil ['vɪdʒɪl] [vi-yil], *s.* 1. Vela, la acción de velar o la vigilia y el tiempo que se vela. 2. Vela, el ejercicio de devoción en las horas acostumbradas de descanso. 3. Vigilia, la víspera de alguna festividad en que se ayuna. **Keep vigil**, velar.

vigilance ['vɪdʒɪləns] [vi-yi-lans], *s.* 1. Desvelo, el estado del que no puede dormir. 2. Vigilancia, cuidado (watchfulness). **Vigilance committee**, junta de vigilancia, para la administración de pronta justicia.

vigilant ['vɪdʒɪlənt] [vi-yi-lant], *a.* Vigilante, cuidadoso, atento.

vigilante [ˈvɪdʒɪˈlæntɪ] [vi-yi-lan-ti], *s.* Vigilante. En E.U. miembro de un cuerpo espcial de vigilancia privada.

vigilantly ['vɪdʒɪləntlɪ] [vi-yi-lant-li], *adv.* Con vigilancia y cuidado.

vignette [vɪˈnjet] [vi-niet], *va.* 1. Hacer una fotografía con fondo o borde cuya sombra va disipándose gradualmente. *-s.* 1. Viñeta, un dibujo o estampita apaisada que se pone por adorno al principio o al fin de los libros o capítulos de una obra impresa. 2. Grabado, dibujo, fotografía, etc., la sombra de cuyo fondo va disipándose gradualmente hasta desaparecer.

vigor, vigour ['vɪgə^r] [vi-ga^r], *s.* 1. Vigor, fuerza, actividad. 2. Energía, eficacia.

vigorous ['vɪgərəs] [vi-go-ros], *a.* Vigoroso.

vigorously ['vɪgərəslɪ] [vi-go-ros-li], *adv.* Vigorosamente, con energía, con fuerza.

vigorousness ['vɪgərəsnɪs] [vi-go-ros-nes], *s.* Vigorosidad, robustez; actividad.

vigour ['vɪgə^r] [vi-ga^r], *s.* V. VIGOR; forma usual en G.B. (strength, energy). **He began his new job with vigour and enthusiasm**, empezó su trabajo con vigor y entusiasmo.

Viking ['vaɪkɪn] [vai-kin], *s.* Uno de los piratas del norte que infestaron las costas de Europa desde el siglo octavo hasta el undécimo.

vile [vaɪl] [vail], *a.* Vil, bajo, indigno, despreciable, malvado, perverso (horrible, wicked, disgusting).

vilely ['vaɪllɪ] [vail-li], *adv.* Vilmente, bajamente, servilmente.

vileness ['vaɪlnɪs] [vail-nes], *s.* Vileza, bajeza, infamia, abyección; acción o modo de pensar bajo y traidor.

vilification [ˌvɪlɪfɪ'keɪʃən] [vi-li-fi-kei-shon], *s.* Envilecimiento, acción de envilecer o vilipendiar: difamación.

vilifier ['vɪlɪfaɪə^r] [vi-li-faia^r], *s.* Difamador, el que vilipendia.

vilify ['vɪlɪfaɪ] [vi-li-fai], *va.* 1. Envilecer, hacer despreciable una cosa. 2. Ajar, desacreditar, difamar, vilipendiar, calumniar.

villa ['vɪlə] [vi-la], *s.* Quinta, casa de campo.

village ['vɪlɪdʒ] [vi-lech], *s.* Lugar, aldea, población pequeña y abierta. **They live in a little village**, ellos viven en una aldea pequeña.

villager ['vɪlɪdʒə^r] [vi-li-cha^r], *s.* Lugareño, aldeano; villano.

villain ['vɪlən] [vi-lan], *s.* 1. Villano, bellaco, malvado (knave). 2. Pechero, patán feudal.

villainous ['vɪlənəs] [vi-la-nos], *a.* 1. Bellaco, vil, ruin: villano. 2. Malvado, capaz de grandes crímenes. 3. *(Fam.)* Muy malo, asqueroso, repugnante.

villainously ['vɪlənəslɪ] [vi-la-nos-li], *adv.* Vilmente.

villainousness ['vɪlənəsnɪs] [vi-la-nos-nes], *s.* Maldad, perversidad, villanía.

villainy ['vɪlənlɪ] [vi-lan-li], *s.* V. VILLANY.

villanage ['vɪlənɪdʒ] [vi-la-nich], *s.* V. VILLENAGE.

villanize ['vɪlənaɪz] [vi-la-nais], *va.* Avillanar, envilecer, hacer vil o despreciable.

villanous ['vɪlənəs] [vi-la-nos], *a.* V. VILLAINOUS.

villany ['vɪlənlɪ] [vi-la-ni], *s.* Villanía, vileza, bastardía, infamia.

villein ['vɪlɪn] [vi-lin], *s.* Villano.

vim [vɪm] [vim], *s. (Fam.)* Fuerza o vigor; energía, espíritu (energy, vigor).

viminal ['vɪmɪnl] [vi-mi-nal], *a.* Mimbroso, hecho de mimbres.

VIN *Abreviatura de* **Vehicle Identification Number**.

vinaigrette [ˌvɪner'gret] [vinei-gret], *s.* 1. Vasito o redomilla para contener una sal o esencia. 2. (Poco us.) Salpicón, salsa fría con vinagre.

vincible ['vɪnsɪbl] [vin-si-bol], *a.* Vencible, que puede ser vencido.

vinculum ['vɪnkələm] [vin-ko-lom], *s.* Vínculo.

vindicable ['vɪndɪkəbl] [vin-di-ka-bol], *a.* Sostenible, justificable, vindicable.

vindicate ['vɪndɪkeɪt] [vin-di-keit], *va.* 1. Vindicar, defender, justificar. 2. *(For.)* Vindicar, recobrar justamente alguna persona aquello de que ha sido desposeída. 3. Vengar.

vindication [ˌvɪndɪ'keɪʃən] [vin-di-kei-shon], *s.* Vindicación, justificación, defensa.

vindicative ['vɪndɪkətɪv] [vin-di-ka-tiv], *a.* Vindicativo, justificativo, vindicador. **She was cruel and vindicative**, era cruel y vindicativa.

vindicator ['vɪndɪkeɪtə^r] [vin-di-kei-ta^r], *s.* Defensor, protector, vindicador.

vindicatory ['vɪndɪkətərɪ] [vin-di-ka-to-ri], *a.* Vindicativo, vindicatorio, justificativo; que contribuye a la vindicación.

vindictive [vɪn'dɪktɪv] [vin-dik-tiv], *a.* Vengativo, inclinado a tomar venganza de cualquier agravio.

vindictively [vɪn'dɪktɪvlɪ] [vin-dik-tiv-li], *adv.* Vengativamente, por venganza.

vindictiveness [vɪn'dɪktɪvnɪs] [vin-dik-tiv-nes], *s.* Ansia de venganza, carácter vengativo.

vine [vaɪn] [vain], *s.* 1. Parra, toda planta que tiene el tallo débil y rastrero o trepador, enredadera. 2. Vid, planta que produce las uvas; parra, una planta cualquiera del género Vitis. **Vine-clad**, cubierto de enredaderas, de vides; por extensión, cubierto de viñas. **Vine-dresser**, a. viñador, deslechugador; (b) oruga de una mariposa norteamericana que corta las hojas de la vid. **A vine-branch**, un sarmiento. **Vine-knife**, podadera. **Vine-fretter, vine-grub**, pulgón de la vid. **Vine-leaf**, hoja de vid o de sarmiento. **vine-pest**, filoxera; enfermedad de la vid. **Wild wine**, vid silvestre. **Vine-stock**, cepa, el tronco de la vid.

vinegar ['vɪnɪgə^r] [vi-ni-ga^r], *s.* 1. Vinagre, líquido ácido obtenido por la fermentación del vino, de la sidra, etc. 2. Vinagre, lo que es agrio metafóricamente; v. gr. una cara. **Vinegar aspect**, cara de vinagre, cara áspera y desapacible. **Vinegar-cruet**, vinagrera.

vinery ['vaɪnərɪ] [vai-ne-ri], *s.* 1. Invernadero para las uvas. 2. Las vides en general.

vineyard ['vɪnjəd] [vin-yard], *s.* 1. Viña, viñedo, el terreno plantado de muchas vides. 2. *(Fig.)* Viña, lugar para cultura espiritual; la iglesia.

vinous ['vaɪnəs] [vai-nos], *a.* 1. Vinoso, que tiene las calidades o propiedades del vino. 2. *(Zool.)* De color de vino.

vintage ['vɪntɪdʒ] [vin-tich], *s.* Vendimia; cosecha de uvas, época. **Vintage car**, coche de época.

vintager ['vɪntədʒə^r] [vin-ta-ya^r], *s.* Vendimiador.

vintner ['vɪntnə^r] [vint-na^r], *s.* Vinatero, tabernero, tratante en vinos.

viny ['vaɪnɪ] [vai-ni], *a.* Perteneciente a las vides o las enredaderas: que produce vides o enredaderas.

vinyl ['vaɪnl] [vai-nil], *s. (Quím.)* Vinilo. -*a.* Vinílico.

viol ['vaɪəl] [vaiol], *s.* 1. Viola, instrumento músico de la edad media que tenía generalmente seis cuerdas; predecesor del violín. 2. Instrumento de cuerda parecido al violín. 3. *(Mar.)* Virador, calabrote afianzado con mojeles al cable y traído al cabrestante volante para mejor levar el ancla, cuando el cabrestante principal no basta.

viola [vɪ'əʊlə] [vi-ou-la], *s.* 1. Viola, instrumento de la misma figura que el violín, aunque algo mayor; alto. 2. *V. VIOL.*, 2ª acep. **She plays the viola in the new school**, ella toca la viola en el colegio nuevo.

violaceous ['vaɪələʃəs] [vaio-lei-shos], *a.* Violáceo, de color de violeta; perteneciente a la violeta o a esta familia de plantas.

violate ['vaɪəleɪt] [vaio-leit], *va.* 1. Violar, quebrantar o traspasar la ley, preceptos, derechos, etc (to break). 2. Violar, profanar las cosas sagradas (to treat). 3. Violar, forzar a una mujer, y si es doncella, se llama estuprar (to rape).

violation [ˌvaɪə'leɪʃən] [vaio-lei-shon], *s.* 1. Violación, la acción y efecto de violar o profanar. 2. Violación, la acción de forzar a una mujer. 3. Estupro, violación de una doncella.

violator ['vaɪəleɪtə^r] [vaio-lei-ta^r], *s.* 1. Violador. 2. Estuprador.

violence ['vaɪələns] [vaio-lens], *s.* 1. Violencia, fuerza o ímpetu en las acciones. 2. Violencia, vehemencia, impetuosidad. 3. Violencia, la fuerza con que se obliga a alguno a que haga lo que no quiere. 4. Violencia, la fuerza que se hace para sacar a una cosa de su estado u orden natural.

violent ['vaɪələnt] [vaio-lent], *a.* 1. Violento, impetuoso, que obra con fuerza. 2. Violento, vehemente, arrebatado. 3. Fuerte, extremo. 4. Severo, duro, violento, que obra con fuerza indebida. 5. Que resulta de la fuerza externa o del daño. **He has a violent temperament**, tiene un temperamento violento.

violently ['vaɪələntlɪ] [vaio-lent-li], *adv.* Violentamente, con vehemencia, con impetuosidad.

violet ['vaɪəlɪt] [vaio-lit], *s*. 1. Violeta, una flor; toda planta del género Viola. 2. Color violado, el séptimo del espectro solar. -*a*. Violado, del color de la violeta. **Violet ray**, rayo violeta.

violin [ˌvaɪə'lɪn] [vaio-lin], *s*. 1. Violín, instrumento músico de cuatro cuerdas, que se toca con arco. 2. Violín, el que lo toca. *V*. VIOLINIST. **He plays violin very bad**, toca el violín muy mal.

violinist [ˌvaɪə'lɪnɪst] [vaio-li-nist], *s*. Violín, violinista, el que toca el violín (violin player).

violoncellist [ˌvaɪələn'tʃelɪst] [vaio-lon-che-list], *s*. Violoncelista, el que toca el violoncelo.

violoncello [ˌvaɪə'lɪn] [vaio-lin], *s*. 1. Violoncelo, violonchelo, una especie de violón pequeño. 2. Violoncelo, registro pedal del órgano.

viper ,['vaɪpəʳ] [vai-paʳ], *s*. 1. Víbora, una especie de culebra venenosa. 2. Cualquiera persona o cosa dañina o dañosa.

viperine ['vaɪpərɪn] [vai-pe-rin], *a*. Viperino, venenoso, nocivo; maléfico, pérfido.

virago [vɪ'rɑːgəʊ] [vi-ra-gou], *s*. 1. Marimacho, Mari-Ramos, mujer regañona, colérica. 2. *(Ant.)* Marimacho, guerrera, amazona.

virgilian [vɜː'dʒɪlɪən] [ver-yi-lian], *a*. Virgiliano, propio y característico del poeta Virgilio.

virgin ['vɜːdʒɪn] [ver-yin], *s*. 1. Virgen, doncella, la mujer que no ha conocido varón. 2. Religiosa que ha hecho voto de virginidad. 3. Virgo, un signo del zodíaco. 4. *(Zool.)* Que produce huevos sin ser impregnada. -*a*. 1. Virginal, perteneciente a una virgen, modesto, casto. 2. Puro, incólume, inmaculado. 3. Virgen; se aplica a la tierra que no ha sido arada ni cultivada, a las cosas que están en su primera entereza, y a las producciones naturales que están en su ser primitivo, sin que las haya alterado el arte o el uso.

virginal ['vɜːdʒɪnl] [ver-yi-nal], *a*. Virginal, que pertence a las vírgenes o es propio de ellas.

virginity [vɜː'dʒɪnɪtɪ] [ver-yi-ni-ti], *s*. Virginidad, el estado de la mujer que no ha conocido varón.

virile ['vɪraɪl] [vi-rail], *a*. 1. Viril, lo que es propio del varón. 2. Varonil, que tiene el vigor del varón, masculino (sexually potent). **He is young and virile**, es joven y viril.

virility [vɪ'rɪlɪtɪ] [vi-ri-li-ti], *s*. Virilidad, carácter de lo viril, edad viril.

virology [ˌvaɪə'rɒlədʒɪ] [vaia-ro-lo-yi], *s*. Virología.

virtu ['vɜːtʊ] [ver-tu], *s*. 1. Calidad poco común, curiosa o hermosa; por lo común, en la locución *objects o articles of virtu*. 2. Gusto para objetos curiosos o raros. *(Ital.)*

virtual ['vɜːtjʊəl] [ver-tiua-li], *a*. Virtual.

virtually ['vɜːtjʊəlɪ] [ver-tiua-li], *adv*. Virtualmente.

virtue ['vɜːtjuː] [ver-tiu], *s*. 1. Virtud: tiene las mismas acepciones en las dos lenguas, tanto en lo físico como en lo moral. 2. Castidad, particularmente de la mujer. 3. Virtud, moralidad, castidad (chastity, virginity). **Virtues**, virtudes, el quinto coro de los espíritus celestiales.

virtuoso [ˌvɜːtjʊ'əʊzəʊ] [ver-tiu-ou-sou], *s*. Persona aficionada a estudiar las antigüedades, las curiosidades de la naturaleza, las nobles artes o la música; particularmente, músico muy hábil. Es voz italiana.

virtuous ['vɜːtjʊəs] [ver-tiuos], *a*. 1. Virtuoso, moralmente puro y bueno; digno de aprobación: se dice de las personas y de sus acciones, y cuando se habla de mujeres regularmente se entiende casta. 2. *(Ant.)* Virtuoso, se aplicaba a las cosas que tienen la actividad y virtud natural que les corresponde; eficaz.

virtuously ['vɜːtjʊəslɪ] [ver-tiuos-li], *adv*. Virtuosamente

virtuousness ['vɜːtjʊəsnɪs] [ver-tiuos-nes], *s*. Virtuosidad, la calidad o propiedad que constituye a una persona o cosa virtuosa.

virulence ['vɪrʊləns] [vi-ru-lens], *s*. 1. Virulencia, calidad de virulento; naturaleza sumamente ponzoñosa. 2. Malignidad, mordacidad.

virulent ['vɪrʊlənt] [vi-ru-lent], *a*. Virulento, venenoso, ponzoñoso; que tiene la naturaleza del virus; mordaz, maligno, cáustico (dangerous). **In his speech he made a virulent attack**, en su discurso el hizo un virulento ataque.

virulently ['vɪrʊləntlɪ] [vi-ru-lant-li], *adv*. Malignamente.

virus ['vaɪərəs] [vaia-ras], *s*. Virus, el humor maligno de cualquier mal; principaio morbífico que es el agente para la transmisión de varias enfermedades infecciosas; en sentido figurado, malignidad, infección moral, amargura mental, mordacidad.

visage ['vɪzɪdʒ] [vi-sidch], *s*. Rostro, cara, semblante, aspecto distintivo (face)..

viscera ['vɪsərə] [vi-sa-ra], *s. pl.* de VISCUS.

visceral ['vɪsərəl] [vi-sa-ral], *a*. 1. Visceral, perteneciente o relativo a las vísceras. 2. Ventral, abdominal.

viscid ['vɪsɪd] [vi-sid], *a*. 1. Viscoso, pegajoso, glutinoso. 2. *(Fís.)* Imperfectamente, fluido; se aplica a una substancia, como el alquitrán, que cambia de forma bajo la influencia de una fuerza.

viscose ['vɪskəʊs] [vis-kous], *a*. Viscoso.

viscosity [vɪs'ɒsɪtɪ] [vis-ko-si-ti], *s*. Viscosidad, calidad de viscoso.

viscount ['vaɪkaʊnt] [vai-kaunt], *s*. Vizconde, título de nobleza inmediato al de conde.

viscountesse ['vaɪkaʊntɪs] [vai-kaun-tis], *sf*. Vizcondesa.

viscous ['vɪskəs] [vis-kos], *a*. Viscoso, glutinaoso, pegajoso.

viscus ['vɪskəs] [vis-kos], *s*. (*pl*. VISCERA). Víscera, uno de los órganos contenidos en las grandes cavidades del cuerpo, el abdomen, el tórax y el cráneo, más, común en plural, vísceras, entrañas.

vise [vaɪs] [vais], *s*. Tornillo de banco, útil que sirve para asir y asegurar aquello en que se trabaja; torno.

visibility [ˌvɪzɪ'bɪlɪtɪ] [vi-si-bi-li-ti], *s*. Visibilidad, calidad de visible.

visible ['vɪzəbl] [vi-sa-bol], *a*. 1. Visible, que se puede ver, perceptible a la vista. 2. Visible, evidente, claro, manifiesto. -*s*. *(Des.)* La cosa visible.

visibly ['vɪzəblɪ] [vi-sa-bli], *adv*. Visiblemente; evidentemente, manifiestamente.

Visigoth ['vɪzɪgɒθ] [vi-si-goz], *s*. Visigodo, visigoda; godo del oeste.

vision ['vɪʒən] [vi-shon], *s*. 1. Visión, vista, la facultad o el sentido de la vista; la acción de ver o el acto de la potencia visiva. 2. Visión, objeto de la vista. 3. Visión, fantasma, sueño; revelación inspirada y profética.

visionary ['vɪʒənərɪ] [vi-sho-na-ri], *a*. 1. Imaginario, que carece de realidad; impracticable, infactible, que no se puede hacer. 2. Visionario, el que cree o se figura visiones o fantasmas. -*s*. Visionario, el hombre que se figura y cree con faclidad cosas quiméricas; hombre poco práctico.

visit ['vɪzɪt] [vi-sit], *va*. 1. Visitar, ir a ver a alguno. 2. Visitar: se dice del reconocimiento o examen que hace una autoridad eclesiástica o civil de las personas o de los negocios que tienen relación con sus atribuciones. 3. *(Teol.)* Visitar, enviar Dios a los hombres algún consuelo, visitarse, irse a ver recíprocamente, hacer visitas, ir de visita. 4. Inflingir (to inflict). 5. Castigar (to punish, torment). **They visited the ruins of Pompeii**, visitaron las ruinas de Pompeya.

visit, *s*. 1. Visita, visitación, acto de cortesía. 2. Visita personal, de inspección y examen; v. gr. la ida del médico a la casa del enfermo; la visita de un obispo, etc.

visitable ['vɪzɪtəbl] [vi-si-ta-bol], *a*. Visitable, lo que se puede visitar; lo que está sujeto a ser visitado o reconocido por alguna autoridad.

visitant ['vɪzɪtənt] [vi-si-tant], *s*. Visitador.

visitation [ˌvɪzɪ'teɪʃən] [vi-si-tei-shon], *s*. 1. Visitación, visita. 2. Inspección y examen oficiales, como de un establecimiento, colegio, etc.; visita de un obispo. 3. Disposición divina de gracia o de retribución; castigo del cielo. **Death by visitation of God**, muerte natural.

visitatorial [ˌvɪzɪ'tətɔːrɪəl] [vi-si-ta-to-rial], *a*. Lo que pertenece a un visitador o a la autoridad que visita.

visiting ['vɪzɪtɪŋ] [vi-si-tin], *a*. De visita. **Visiting card**, tarjeta de visita.

visitor ['vɪzɪtəʳ] [vi-si-taʳ], *s*. Visitador.

visor ['vaɪzəʳ] [vai-soʳ], *s*. *V*. VIZOR. Visera.

vista [ˈvɪstə] [vis-ta], *s.* Vista, perspectiva; perspectiva mental que comprende una serie de acontecimientos.

visual [ˈvɪzjʊəl] [vi-shual], *a.* Visual.

visualize [ˈvɪzjʊəl] [vi-shual], *vt.* 1. Visualizar; imaginarse, representarse (in mind). 2. Prever (foresee).

visually [ˈvɪzjʊəlɪ] [vi-shua-li], *adv.* Visualmente.

vital [ˈvaɪtl] [vai-tal], *a.* 1. Vital, perteneciente a la vida; que contribuye a la vida o le es necesario. 2. Esencial, indispensable; vital, de suma importancia (essential, necessary, lively, energetic). 3. Que afecta a la vida; fatal, mortal. **It's vital that you get to the hospital soon**, el esencial que ilegues al hopital pronto.

vitality [vaɪˈtælɪtɪ] [vai-ta-li-ti], *s.* Vitalidad, principio o fuerza vitales (liveliness, energy).

vitalize [ˈvaɪtəlaɪz] [vai-ta-lais], *va.* Vivificar, hacer vital, dar vida; animar, reanimar.

vitally [ˈvaɪtəlɪ] [vai-ta-li], *adv.* Vitalmente, de una manera vital; esencialmente.

vitals [ˈvaɪtlz] [vai-tals], *s. pl.* Las partes vitales de un ser viviente; *(Fig.)* lo esencial, la vida, órganos vitales.

vitamin [ˈvɪtəmɪn] [vi-ta-min], *s.* Vitamina.

vitiate [ˈvɪʃɪeɪt] [vi-shieit], *va.* 1. Viciar, dañar, corromper, echar a perder (to spoil, to make impure). 2. Viciar, hacer nulo, invalidar.

vitiation [ˌvɪʃɪˈeɪʃən] [vi-shiei-shon], *s.* Depravación, corrupción; estado de lo corrompido; invalidacón (de un acto o contrato).

viticulture [ˈvɪtɪkʌltʃəʳ] [vi-ti-kal-chaʳ], *s.* Viticultura, cultivo de la vid; arte de cultivar las vides.

vitreous [ˈvɪtrɪəs] [vi-trios], *a.* 1. Vítreo, hecho de vidrio o que tiene sus propiedades. 2. Vítreo, parecido al vidrio en alguna propiedad; vidrioso. **Vitreous body** o **humor**, humor vítreo del ojo.

vitreousness [ˈvɪtrɪəsnɪs] [vi-trios-nes], *s.* Vidriosidad, la semejanza con el vidrio.

vitrescent [ˈvɪtrəsənt] [vi-tre-sent], *a.* Capaz de vitrificarse.

vitrifaction [ˌvɪtrɪˈfækʃən] [vi-tri-fak-shon], *s.* Vitrificación, acción o procedimiento de vitrificar; estado o calidad de lo vitrificado.

vitriform [ˈvɪtrɪfɔːm] [vi-tri-form], *a.* Vítreo, que tiene la apariencia del vidrio.

vitrify [ˈvɪtrɪfaɪ] [vi-tri-fai], *va.* Vitrificar. -*vn.* Vitrificarse, reducirse a vidrio.

vitriol [ˈvɪtrɪəl] [vi-triol], *s.* 1. Aceite de vitriolo, ácido sulfúrico. 2. Sulfato, vitriolo. **Blue** o **Roman vitriol**, vitriolo azul, sulfato de cobre. **Green vitriol** o **copperas**, vitriolo verde o marcial, caparrosa, sulfato de hierro. **White vitriol**, vitriolo blanco, sulfato de cinc.

vitriolic [ˌvɪtrɪˈblɪk] [vi-trio-lik], *a.* 1. Vitriólico. 2. Cáustico, mordaz (extremely bitter, violent). **His speech was cruel and vitriolic**, su discurso fue cruel y mordaz.

vituperable [vɪˈtjuːpərəbl] [vi-tiu-pa-rei-bol], *a.* Vituperable (very abusive, insulting).

vituperate [vɪˈtjuːpəreɪt] [vi-tiu-pa-reit], *va.* Vituperar, censurar, decir mal.

vituperation [vɪˌtjuːpəˈreɪʃən] [vi-tiu-pa-rei-shon], *s.* Vituperación, el acto de vituperar o censurar.

vivacious [vɪˈveɪʃəs] [vi-vei-shos], *a.* 1. Vivo, animado, alegre, despejado (lively, bright). 2. De larga vida. 3. *(Bot.)* Vivaz, perenne. **He is vivacious and attactive**, él es animado y atractivo.

vivaciousness [vɪˈveɪʃəsnɪs] [vi-vei-shos-nes], *s.* 1. Vivacidad, viveza de genio, animación. 2. *(Des.)* Ancianidad, vida larga.

vivarium [vɪˈvæːrɪəm] [vi-va-riom], *s.* Vivar, vivero.

vivid [ˈvɪvɪd] [vi-vid], *a.* 1. Vivo, despejado, lleno de vida, intenso; brillante (color) (brilliant, bright). 2. Vivo, de apariencia viviente, animado, enérgico (clear, striking, active, lively). 3. Activo, que obra con vivo interés. **His imagination is more vivid than most people's**, su imaginación es más viva que la de la mayoría de la gente.

vividly [ˈvɪvɪdlɪ] [vi-vid-li], *adv.* Vivamente, con vivacidad, con vigor.

vividness [ˈvɪvɪdnɪs] [vi-vid-nes], *s.* Vivacidad, calidad de brillante, intensidad; fuerza, brillo.

vivification [ˌvɪvɪfɪˈkeɪʃən] [vi-vi-fi-kei-shon], *s.* Vivificación.

vivify [ˈvɪvɪfaɪ] [vi-vi-fai], *va.* Vivificar, dar vida a; dar vigor, reanimar.

viviparous [vɪˈvɪpərəs] [vi-vi-pa-ros], *a.* 1. *(Zool.)* Vivíparo: se dice del animal que pare los hijos vivos, a distinción de los que ponen huevos. 2. *(Bot.)* Que produce bulbos o simientes que germinan mientras están aún unidas a la planta.

vivisect [ˈvɪvɪsekt] [vi-vi-sekt], *va.* Disecar un animal vivo para hacer estudios fisiológicos. -*vn.* Practicar la vivisección.

vivisection [ˌvɪvɪˈsekʃən] [vi-vi-sek-shon], *s.* Vivisección, disección de los animales para fines científicos.

vixen [ˈvɪksn] [vik-sen], *s.* 1. Zorra o raposa, la hembra del zorro o raposo (a female fox). 2. Mujer regañona, colérica, displicente, quimerista.

vizar [ˈvɪzəʳ] [vi-saʳ], *s. (Ant.)* visera, máscara, carátula.

vizier, vizir [ˈvɪzɪəʳ] [vi-shiaʳ] *s.* Visir, o el gran visir, el primer ministro del imperio otomano.

vizor [ˈvaɪzəʳ] [vai-soʳ] *s.* 1. Visera, ala pequeña que tienen en la parte anterior las gorras, etc., para resguardar la vista. 2. Visera, del yelmo.

VLF *Abreviatura de* **Very Low Frequency**.

vocable [ˈvəʊkəbl] [vou-ka-bol], *s.* Vocablo, palabra, sonido vocal.

vocabulary [vəʊˈkæbjʊlərɪ] [vou-ka-biu-la-ri], *s.* 1. Vocabulario, lista de palabras, diccionario. 2. Nomenclatura, conjunto de palabras usadas por una persona o contenidas en una obra. **These words are found in the criminal vocabulary**, esas palabras se encuentran en el diccionario criminal.

vocal [ˈvəʊkəl] [vou-kal], *a.* Vocal, oral. **Vocal cords**, cuerdas vocales.

vocalist [ˈvəʊkəlɪst] [vou-ka-list], *s.* Cantor, cantora, particularmente los de voz cultivada, lo contrario de *instrumentalist*.

vocalization [ˌvəʊkəlaɪˈzeɪʃən] [vou-ka-lai-sei-shon], *s.* Vocalización, acción y efecto de vocalizar.

vocalize [ˈvəʊkəlaɪz] [vou-ka-lais], *va.* 1. Proferir o formar la voz, vocalizar. 2. Poner los puntos vocales, v. g. en fonografía, o en un idioma semítico. -*vn.* Vocalizar, solfear sin nombrar las notas.

vocally [ˈvəʊkəlɪ] [vou-ka-li], *adv.* 1. Vocalmente, con la voz. 2. Verbalmente.

vocation [vəʊˈkeɪʃən] [vou-kei-shon], *s.* 1. Vocación, oficio, carrera, profesión. 2. Llamamiento espiritual o que Dios hace al hombre para el servicio religioso.

vocational [vəʊˈkeɪʃənl] [vou-kei-sho-nal], *a.* 1. Vocacional. 2. Profesional, práctico, relativo a un oficio o profesión. **Vocational guidance**, orientación profesional. **Vocational school**, escuela de artes y oficios, escuela profesional. **Vocational training**, preparación o instrucción técnica y práctica. **Vocational tests**, pruebas vocacionales de aptitud.

vocative [ˈvɒkətɪv] [vo-ka-tiv], *s.* Vocativo.

vociferate [vəʊˈsɪfəreɪt] [vou-si-fa-reit], *vn.* Vociferar; clamorear.

vociferation [vəʊsɪfəˈreɪʃən] [vou-si-fa-rei-shon], *s.* Vocería, gritos, confusión de voces.

vociferous [vəʊˈsɪfərəs] [vou-si-fe-ros], *a.* Vocinglero, clamoroso, vociferante (loud, noisy).

vogue [vəʊg] [voug], *s.* Crédito, estimación; moda (fashion). **To be in vogue**, estar en boga, usarse mucho, ser de moda.

voice [vɔɪs] [vois], *s.* 1. Voz, el sonido proferido con la boca por el ser humano y algunos animales; calidad o carácter de ese sonido. 2. Facultad de hablar. 3. Opinión o elección expresados; sufragio, voz, voto. 4. Enseñanza, admonición, instrucción. 5. El que habla, particularmente en pro de otra persona. 6. *(Gram.)* Voz, del verbo. **He has a very deep voice**, tiene una voz muy profunda.

voice, *va.* 1. Poner en habla, expresar, proclamar, decir su parecer (to express). 2. Dar el tono; acordar o templar un instrumento. 3. *(Mús.)* Escribir la parte vocal.

voiced [ˈvɔɪst] [voist], *a.* 1. *(Gram.)* Sonoro. 2. Expreso, expresado, formulado

voiceless [ˈvɔɪslɪs] [vois-les], *a.* 1. Mudo. 2. *(Gram.)* Sordo.

void [vɔɪd] [void], *a.* 1. Vacío, desocupado, hueco; vacante. 2. *(For.)* Nulo, sin ningún efecto, sin valor ni fuerza (not valid, binding). 3. Falto, privado, desprovisto. 4. Vano, falto de realidad. -*s.* Vacuo, vacío, el espacio enteramente desocupado. **Her marriage was declared void**, su matrimonio fue declarado nulo.

void, *va.* 1. Vaciar, desocupar, evacuar. 2. Dejar un lugar, desocuparlo o separarse de él. 3. Anular, invalidar, hacer nula alguna cosa. **To void out**, echar fuera, arrojar.

voidable [ˈvɔɪdəbl] [voi-da-bol], *a.* 1. Anulable. 2. Que sepuede evacuar o expeler.œ

voidance [ˈvɔɪdəns] [voi-dans], *s.* Vaciamiento, la acción y efecto de vaciar.

voile [vɔɪl] [voil], *sf.* Gasa.

volatile [ˈvɒlətaɪl] [vo-la-tail], *a.* 1. Volátil, que tiene la propiedad de volatilizarse o exhalarse fácilmente a la temperatura ordinaria. 2. Voluble, ligero, inconstante (changeable, unstable). 3. Pasajero, transitorio. **Her son has a volatile personality**, su hijo tiene una personalidad volátil.

volatileness [ˈvɒlətaɪlnɪs] [vo-la-tail-nes], *s.* 1. Volatilidad, calidad de volátil, de transformarse en gas. 2. Volatilidad, volubilidad, instabilidad, ligereza.

volatilize [vɒˈlætəlaɪz] [vo-la-ti-lais], *va.* Volatilizar, sutilizar los cuerpos reduciéndolos a partes volátiles. -*vn.* Volatilizarse, transformarse en vapor o gas.

volcanic [vɒlˈkænɪk] [vol-ka-nik], *a.* Volcánico, perteneciente o relativo al volcán.

volcano [vɒlˈkeɪnəʊ] [vol-kei-nou], *s.* Volcán, abertura en la tierra y más comúnmente en una montaña, por donde salen de tiempo en tiempo humo, llamas y materias encendidas o derretidas. **The village was destroyed when the volcano erupted**, el pueblo fue destruido cuando el volcán erupcionó.

volition [vəˈlɪʃən] [vo-li-shon], *s.* Voluntad, facultad de querer; volición, el acto en que la voluntad se determina por alguna cosa (willingly).

volitional [vəˈlɪʃənl] [vo-li-sho-nal], *a.* Volitivo, de la voluntad.

volley [ˈvɒlɪ] [vo-li], *s.* 1. Descarga de armas de fuego; andanada; salva. 2. Rociada de palabras picantes, de insultos, etc. 3. Voleo.

volley, *va.* y *vn.* Lanzar una descarga de; ser descargado o sonar al mismo tiempo; estallar.

volleyball [ˈvɒlɪbɔːl] [vo-li-bol], *s.* Balonvolea, vólibol.

volleyed [ˈvɒlɪəd] [vo-liad], *a.* Tirado, descargado.

volt [vəʊlt] [voult], *s.* Voltio, unidad práctica de la fuerza electromotriz; la fuerza que se aplica a un conductor de la resistencia de un ohmio produce una corriente de un amperio. **Volt-ammeter, volt-meter**, voltímetro, aparato que se emplea para medir potenciales eléctricas. **Volt-ampere**, V. WATT. **Volt-coulomb**, V. JOULE.

volt, *s.* La vuelta que se hace dar al caballo en el picadero.

voltage [ˈvəʊltɪdʒ] [voul-tich], *s.* Voltaje, fuerza electromotriz expresada en voltios; conjunto de voltios que actúan en un sistema eléctrico.

voltaic [vɒlˈteɪk] [voul-teik], *a.* *(Fís.)* Voltaico, perteneciente a la electricidad que se desarrolla por medio de la acción química o del contacto; galvánico.

volubility [ˌvɒljʊˈbɪlɪtɪ] [vo-liu-bi-li-ti], *s.* 1. Volubilidad, facilidad de expresión, verbosidad. 2. *(Des.)* Volubilidad, la facilidad de moverse alrededor de alguna cosa.

voluble [ˈvɒljʊbl] [vo-liu-bol], *a.* 1. De fácil palabra, locuaz (very talkative). 2. Voluble, que gira fácilmente, dispuesto para dar vueltas. 3. *(Bot.)* Voluble, que sube en espiral.

volume [ˈvɒljuːm] [vo-lium], *s.* 1. Volumen, un libro encuadernado (a book). **A folio volume**, un tomo en folio, 2. Un rollo formado por cualquier cosa arrollada; rollo de vitela sobre el cual escribían los antiguos. 3. Volumen, bulto, caudal de río. 4. Importe, suma, gran cantidad. 5. *(Mat.)* Volumen, espacio ocupado por un cuerpo. 6. Volumen, plenitud del sonido o del tono.

volumetric [ˌvɒljuːˈmetrɪk] [vo-liu-me-trik], *a.* *(Fís.)* Volumétrico, perteneciente a la medida de los compuestos comparando los volúmenes.

voluminous [vəˈljuːmɪnəs] [vo-liu-mi-nos], *a.* 1. Voluminoso, abultado, extenso. 2. Copioso, difuso. 3. Se dice del escritor que ha publicado muchas obras o de la obra que está escrita en muchos volúmenes.

voluminously [vəˈljuːmɪnəs] [vo-liu-mi-nos], *adv.* En muchos tomos o volúmenes; copiosamente, abultadamente.

voluminousness [vəˈljuːmɪnəs] [vo-liu-mi-nos], *s.* El estado de lo que se halla contenido en muchos volúmenes o es voluminoso.

voluntarily [ˌvɒlənˈtærɪlɪ] [vo-lon-ta-ri-li], *adv.* Voluntariamente, espontáneamente, de libre voluntad.

voluntary [ˈvɒləntərɪ] [vo-lon-ta-ri], *a.* Voluntario, espontáneo, que nace de la voluntad libremente o que se hace de libre voluntad. **Their actions was completely voluntary**, sus acciones fueron completamente voluntarias. -*s.* 1. Voluntario, el que se compromete a hacer o emprender una cosa voluntariamente. 2. Solo para órgano que se toca antes o después del oficio divino.

volunteer [ˈvɒləntɪəʳ] [vo-lon-tiaʳ], *s.* Voluntario, el que se ofrece para cualquier servicio por su propia voluntad; especialmente, el soldado que sirve sin haber sido reclutado.

volunteer, *va.* y *vn.* Ofrecer o contribuir voluntariamente; servir como coluntario, sentar plaza, ofrecerse. **She volunteered for a dangerous mission**, ella se ofreció voluntaria para una peligrosa misión.

voluptuary [vəˈlʌptjʊərɪ] [vo-lap-tua-ri], *s.* Hombre voluptuoso o entregado a los placeres.

voluptuous [vəˈlʌptjʊəs] [vo-lap-tuos], *a.* 1. Voluptuoso, que proporciona o produce placer a los sentidos. 2. Voluptuoso, dado a los placeres del lujo o a los deleites sensuales. 3. De formas voluptuosas (mujer).

voluptuously [vəˈlʌptjʊəslɪ] [vo-lap-tuos-li], *adv.* Voluptuosamente, lujuriosamente; con lujo.

voluptuousness [vəˈlʌptjʊəsnɪs] [vo-lap-tuos-nes], *s.* Sensualidad, deleite o placer sensual; voluptuosidad.

vomer [ˈvəmərˡ] [vo-maʳ], *s.* Vómer, huesecillo impar de las fosas nasales.

vomit [ˈvɒmɪt] [vo-mit], *va.* y *vn.* 1. Vomitar, arrojar violentamente lo que estaba en el estómago (to throw out, disgorge, puke, spew). 2. Vomitar, arrojar afuera con violencia; salir con violencia.

vomit, *s.* 1. Vómito, lo que se vomita; acción de vomitar (sick). 2. Vomitivo, el medicamento que hace vomitar.

vomiting [ˈvɒmɪtɪŋ] [vo-mi-tin], *s.* 1. Vómito, acción de vomitar. 2. Vómito, lo que se vomita.

voodoo [ˈvuːduː] [vu-du], *s.* Conjunto de supersticiones aún existentes en las Antillas y los Estados Unidos del Sur, acerca de los hechizos, la magia, vudú, etc. **These tribes used to practise voodoo**, esas tribus suelen practicar vudú.

voracious [vəˈreɪʃəs] [vo-rei-shos], *a.* Voraz, muy comedor, que devora; (apetito) devorador; rapaz (ravenous).

voraciously [vəˈreɪʃəslɪ] [vo-rei-shos-li], *adv.* Vorazmente, con voracidad.

voracity [vəˈræsɪtɪ] [vo-ra-si-ti], *s.* Voracidad, calidad de voraz.

vortex [ˈvɔːteks] [vor-teks], *s.* Remolino, torbellino, vórtice.

votary [ˈvəʊtərɪ] [vou-ta-ri], *s.* El que se dedica o consagra a algún género particular de vida, el que está muy apasionado por alguna persona o cosa. **A votary of love**, un amante, un enamorado. **A votary of learning**, uno que se entrega al estudio.

vote [vəʊt] [vout], *s.* 1. Voto, sufragio, parecer, dictamen; opinión expresada en una decisión o elección. 2. Medio por el cual se expresa un voto; por ejemplo, una palabra, una papeleta o el acto de elevar la mano. 3. Votación, decisión. **To put to the vote**, poner a votación, proceder a votar. **A casting vote**, voto decisivo.

vote, *va.* Votar, elegir o determinar por votos. *-vn.* Votar, dar uno su voto.

voter [ˈvəʊtəʳ] [vou-taʳ], *s.* Votante, voto, elector, la persona que vota o tiene derecho a votar.

voting [ˈvəʊtɪŋ] [vou-tin], *a.* Votante. **Voting machine**, máquina electoral.

votive [ˈvəʊtɪv] [vou-tiv], *a.* Votivo, dado u ofrecido por voto.

vouch [vaʊtʃ] [vauch], *va.* 1. Poner o tomar a alguno por testigo. 2. Atestiguar, certificar, afirmar, atestar, testificar, 3. Apelar al testimonio de alguno. **I can vouch for his honesty**, puedo garantizar su honestidad. *-vn.* Dar testimonio de, salir fiador de; certificar.

voucher [ˈvaʊtʃəʳ] [vau-chaʳ], *s.* 1. Documento justificativo, particularmente el o lo que acusa recibo de dinero u objetos de valor. 2. Testigo, el que atestigua alguna cosa; fiador, responsable, garante.

vouchsafe [ˈvaʊtʃseɪf] [vauch-seif], *va.* Conceder, permitir, otorgar. *-vn.* Condescender, dignarse.

vow [vaʊ] [vau]. *s.* 1. Voto, promesa hecha de un modo solemne, particularmente a Dios, a la virgen o a un santo. 2. Voto, cualquier promesa solemne de las que constituyen el estado religioso.

vow, *va. y vn.* 1. Dedicar o consagrar a Dios, a la Virgen o a un santo. 2. Voto, cualquier promesa solemne de las que constituyen el estado religioso.

vowel [vaʊəl] [vauel], *s.* Vocal, la letra que por sí forma sílaba; el sonido producido por la vibración de las cuerdas vocales. *-a.* Vocal. *-va.* Proveer de vocales, p. ej. un escrito árabe o hebreo.

vox [vɒks] [voks], *s.* Voz (en la música). **Vox humana**, registro de lengüeta para producir en el órgan tonos parecidos a la voz humana.

voyage [ˈvɔɪdʒ] [vo-yich], *s.* Viaje por mar, río o lago; navegación. **Voyage out and home**, viaje redondo. **Twenty day's voyage**, veinte días de viaje o de travesía.

voyage, *vn.* Navegar, viajar por mar, río o lago, hacer un viaje por mar. *-va.* Transitar, pasar por.

voyager [ˈvɔɪdʒəʳ] [vo-yi-chaʳ], *s.* Viajero por mar; navegador.

VR *Abreviatura de* **Virtual Reality**, Realidad Virtual.

vs *Abreviatura de* **versus**, contra.

Vulcan [ˈvʌlkən] [val-kan], *s.* 1. Vulcano, dios del fuego en la antigua Roma. 2. Planeta que se suponía existir entre el sol y Mercurio.

vulcanite [ˈvʌlkənaɪt] [val-ka-nait], *s.* Vulcanita. variedad negruzca de caucho azufrado o vulcanizado.

vulcanization [ˌvʌlkənarˈzeɪʃen] [val-ka-nai-sei-shon], *s.* Vulcanización, el procedimiento de tratar el caucho con azufre a una temperatura elevada.

vulcanize [ˈvʌlkənaɪz] [val-ka-nais], *va.* Vulcanizar, combinar el caucho con azufre a una temperatura más o menos elevada; sujetar a la vulcanización.

vulgar [ˈvʌlgəʳ] [val-gaʳ], *a.* 1. Vulgar, lo que pertenece al vulgo. 2. Vulgar, común, ordinario (bourgeois, common, ordinary). 3. Vulgar, vernáculo: se dice de las lenguas que se hablan, en contraposición a las lenguas muertas. 4. Público, generalmente sabido. 5. Vil, bajo, contrario al buen gusto. *-s.* Vulgo, plebe, populacho. **She uses vulgar expresions**, ella usa expresiones vulgares. **Vulgar fraction**, fracción común.

vulgarism [ˈvʌlgərɪzəm] [val-ga-ri-sem], *s.* Vulgaridad, expresión ofensiva al buen gusto; el modo de vivir correspondiente al vulgo.

vulgarity [vʌlˈgærɪtɪ] [val-ga-ri-ti], *s.* 1. Vulgaridad, la calidad o propiedad perteneciente al vugo (coarseness). 2. Vulgaridad, bajeza, dicho o hecho bajo, mal tono, modales vulgares.

vulgarize, vulgarise [ˈvʌlgəraɪz] [val-ga-rais], *va.* Vulgarizar, hacer vulgar. *-vn.* Conducirse de un modo vulgar, bajo.

vulgarly [ˈvʌlgəlɪ] [val-ga-li], *adv.* Vulgarmente, comúnmente; bajamente, como del vulgo.

vulnerability [ˌvʌlnərəˈbɪlɪtɪ] [val-na-ra-bi-li-ti], *s.* V. VULNERABLENNESS.

vulnerable [ˈvʌlnərəbl] [val-ne-ra-bol], *a.* Vulnerable, que puede ser herido. **The enemy's position is vulnerable**, la posición del enemigo es vulnerable.

vulnerableness [ˈvʌlnərəblnɪs] [val-ne-ra-bol-nes], *s.* La calidad de vulnerable.

vulnerary [ˈvʌlnərərɪ] [val-ne-ra-ri], *a.* Vulneraio, eficaz para curar llagas o heridas. *-s.* Medicamento vulnerario.

vulpine [ˈvʌlpaɪn] [val-pain], *a.* 1. Zorruno, vulpino. 2. Astuto, ladino.

vulture [ˈvʌltʃəʳ] [val-chaʳ], *s. (Orn.)* Buitre, ave de rapiña.

vulturous [ˈvʌltʃərəs] [val-cha-ras], *a.* Buitrero, perteneciente al buitre o que le es propio.

vulva [ˈvʌlvə] [val-va], *s.* Vulva, abertura exterior de la vagina.

vulvar [ˈvʌlvəʳ] [val-vaʳ], *a.* De la vulva; perteneciente o relativo a la vulva.

vying [ˈvaɪɪŋ] [vaiin], *Ger.* **Vie.**

vyingly [ˈvaɪɪŋlɪ] [vaiin-li], *adv.* De manera que emule o rivalice.

W

w [ˈdʌbljʊ] [da-bel-iu], es una letra ambigua en la lengua inglesa, siendo consonante al principio de dicción y vocal cuando forma diptongo en medio o al final de las palabras. Se pronuncia de un modo muy semejante a la *u* vocal castellana; es muda, cuando precede a la *r*, como en *wright, wrong*; cuando está delante de la *h* y *o*, como en *whole, who*; y en algunas otras voces, como *sword, answer*, etc.

wabble [ˈwɒbl] [uo-bel], *vn.* 1. *(Fam.)* Balancearse vacilando, como una peonza que gira lentamente. 2. Vacilar. *-s.* Movimiento irregular de cuerpos que están desigualmente equilibrados y en rotación.

wabbly [ˈwɒblɪ] [uo-bli], *a.* Que hace eses o se balancea vacilando.

wacke [ˈwæk] [uak], *s.* Roca parda terrosa o arcillosa.

wacky [ˈwækɪ] [ua-ki], *a.* 1. Chiflado, chalado. 2. Estrambótico, extravagante, descabellado.

wad [wɒd] [uod], *s.* 1. Manojo o atado de paja. 2. Borra o pelote para rehenchir cojines, sillas, etc. 3. *(art.)* Taco, el bodoquillo que se pone sobre la carga en las pieas de artillería. 4. Mineral de manganeso y cobalto. 6. Lío, bolita. 7. Fajo.

wad, *va.* 1. Acolchar, emborrar, atacar. 2. Empaquetar con entreforro o algodón en rama para protección (v. gr. las mercancías preciosas); forrar con entretela.

wad-hook [ˈwɒdhʊk] [uod-juk], *s. (Art.)* Sacatrapos.

wadding [ˈwɒdɪŋ] [uo-din], *s.* Entretela, entreforro, lo que sirve para forrar, particularmente algodón en rama; conjunto de pelotes; taco.

waddle [ˈwɒdl] [uo-del], *vn.* Anadear, andar moviendo las caderas de un lado a otro, andar como el pato.

wade [weɪd] [ueid], *va.* Atravesar a vado. *-vn.* 1. Vadear, pasar algún río sin echarse a nado; andar en el agua, en el barro, por entre las hierbas altas, en toda sustancia que cede al pie. 2. Pasar o penetrar con dificultad. **He waded the river**, el vadeaba el río.

wader [ˈweɪdəʳ] [uei-daʳ], *s.* 1. El o lo que vadea. 2. **Wader o wading bird**, zancudas, orden de aves.

wadi [ˈwɒdɪ] [uo-di], *s.* Valle que contiene el lecho de un torrente que generalmente se agota en la estación seca. *(Arabe)*.

wafer [ˈweɪfəʳ] [uei-faʳ], *va.* Poner una oblea; pegar o cerrar con oblea. *-s.* Oblea; hostia; barquillo. **Wafer-iron**, barquillero, molde de hierro para hacer barquillos. **Wafer-man**, oblero, el que hace obleas; barquillero, el que hace y vende barquillos.

waffle ['wæfl] [ua-fel], *s.* Barquillo o suplicación, fruta de sartén.

waffle, *v.* Hablar mucho y decir poco. **If you ask him a question, he'll only waffle,** si tu le preguntas él sólo hablará mucho y dirá poco.

waft ['wɑːft] [uaft], *va.* 1. Llevar por el aire o por encima del agua (to buoy, drift, hang, float). 2. Hacer flotar, sobrenaðar.

waft, *s.* 1. Cuerpo flotant. 2. El movimiento de una bandera u otra cosa que se tremola para hacer alguna señal.

waftage ['wɑːftɪdʒ] [uaf-tich], *s.* La conducción por el aire o por el agua.

wafter ['wɑːftəʳ] [uaf-taʳ], *s.* Embarcación ligera; fragata, convoy, conserva.

wag [wæg] [uag], *va.* 1. Mover o menear ligeramente (to move, gossip). **To wog the tail,** colear. 2. Hacer gestos y movimientos ridículos, -*va.* 1. Oscilar, inclinarse alternativamente en direcciones opuestas. 2. Proceder regularmente (vida). 3. Irse.

wag, *s.* 1. Voleado, coleadura; movimiento alternativo de la cabeza. 2. Un chocarrero, retozón o juguetón, burlón; bufón; un taratira. **To play the wag,** andarse en chanzas o con burlas, estar de chunga, gastar chanzas pesadas.

wage [weɪdʒ] [ueich], *s.* 1. Paga por algún servicio, comúnmente en plural. 2. Prenda. *V.* WAGES. **Wage-earner, wage-worker,** trabajador, jornalero, el que trabaja por un jornal. 3. Salario, sueldo.

wage, *va.* 1. Hacer emprender con vigor, sostener (to carry on, engage). **To wage war,** hacer guerra. 2. Preparar la alfarería, amasándola o trabajándola. **To wage one's law,** se llama así en la jurisprudencia inglesa el derecho que tiene cualquier persona ejecutada por deudas, de presentarse al tribunal para probar que no debe el todo o parte de lo que se le pide.

wager ['weɪdʒəʳ] [uei-chaʳ], *s.* 1. Apuesta, la acción de apostar, y también lo que se apuesta (a bet). 2. Prenda, cosa depositada. **To lay a wager,** apostar, hacer una apuesta. **Wager of law,** la acción de ofrecer ante un tribunal la justificación o prueba de un hecho, etc.

wager, *va.* Apostar, **I'll wager ten dollars that I can do it,** apuesto diez dólares a que puedo hacerlo.

wagerer ['weɪdʒərəʳ] [uei-cha-raʳ], *s.* Apostador, el que apuesta.

wages ['weɪdʒɪz] [uei-ches], *s. pl.* de WAGE. Salario, jornal, soldada, paga o recompensa por algún servicio. **Monthly wages,** salario mensual; mesada.

waggery ['weɪdʒərɪ] [uei-che-ri], *s.* Chocarrería, bufonada; travesura, bellaquería.

waggish ['wægɪʃ] [ua-guish], *a.* Bromista, gracioso.

waggishness ['wægɪʃnɪs] [ua-guish-nes], *s.* Retozo, juguete, chocarrería: la propensión a gastar chanzas pesadas.

waggle ['wægl] [uaguel], *va.* Mover ligeramente de un lado a otro. -*vn.* Anadear; menearse; bullir. -*s.* Movimiento alternativo rápido, oscilación.

Wagnerian [vɑːgˈnɪərɪən] [vag-nia-rian], *a.* Relativo a Ricardo Wagner, el compositor alemán de música, o a sus obras.

wagon, waggon ['wægən] [ua-gon], *s.* 1. Galera, carro grande o carretón de cuatro ruedas para llevar géneros o equipajes; en general, cualquier vehículo de cuatro ruedas, coche. 2. *(G.B.)* Vagón, furgón de ferrocarril para el transporte de géneros. **Wagon-load,** galerada, carretada, la carga que cabe en una galera o carretón; unidad de medida. **Wagon-maker, waggon-maker, wagon-wright,** carretero, el que hace carros.

wagonage, waggonage ['wægənɪdʒ] [ua-go-nich], *s.* Porte, carretaje.

wagontrain ['wægən,treɪn] [ua-gon-trein], *s. (Mil.)* Tren de provisiones.

wagtail ['wægteɪl] [uag-teil], *s. (Orn.)* Aguzanieve, nevatilla, motacila.

waif [weɪf] [ueif], *s.* 1. Audorrero, (niño) errante, descuidado, sin hogar, abandonado, 2. Algo llevado de aquí para allá, como por el viento o el agua; artículo desemparejado, perdido. 3. *(For.)* Cosa robada que el ladrón perseguido abandona en el camino; bienes mostrencos, los que no tienen dueño conocido.

wail [weɪl] [ueil], *va. y un.* 1. Deplorar o llorar los males, desdichas, etc. 2. Lamentar o lamentarse. 3. Gemir, dar gemidos y sollozos (to utter sorrowful, complaining cries).

wailing ['weɪlɪŋ] [uei-lin], *s.* Lamento, gemido, sollozo, clamor.

wain [weɪn] [uein], *s.* Carruaje. **Charles's Wain,** *(Fam.)* Osa Mayor.

wainscot ['weɪnskət] [uein-skot], *s.* Enmaderamiento de ensambladura, el friso con que se cubren y adornan las paredes de una sala o gabinete.

wainscot, *va.* Cubrir y adornar las paredes de una sala con piezas de ensambladura; entablar, guarnecer; poner friso de madera.

wainscoting ['weɪnskətɪŋ] [uein-sko-tin], *s.* Entablamento, entabladura; capa de mezcla que cubre la pared.

waist [weɪst] [ueist], *s.* 1. Cintura, la parte inferior del talle. 2. (Hablando del vestido de las mujeres), justillo, corpiño, jubón, monillo, talle; ajustador. 3. *(Mar.)* Combés de una nave. **Waistboards,** *(Mar.)* Falcas, las tablas que se ponen en los cantos de las bordas para impedir la entrada de las olas. **Waistcloths,** *(Mar.)* Empavesadas. **She has a very small waist,** ella tiene una cintura muy pequeña.

waistband ['weɪstbænd] [ueist-band], *s.* Cintura de pantalón, de enagua.

waistcoat ['weɪstkəʊt] [ueist-kout], *s.* Chaleco, prenda de vestir sin mangas que llega hasta la cintura y que se lleva debajo de la levita o chaqueta. **Waistcoat button,** botón de chaleco o chupa, botón pequeño.

waistline ['weɪstlaɪn] [ueist-lain], *s.* Cintura.

wait [weɪt] [ueit], *va.* Esperar, aguardar; dilatar, diferir (la partida o un acto) (to remain, stay). -*vn.* 1. Estar aguardando o esperando, estar en expectativa (to expect). 2. Quedar dispuesto, listo *a.* 3. Servir; hacer servicios personales; ser criado, sirviente o mozo (de fonda). **To wait at table,** servir a la mesa. **To wait for,** esperar a; acechar. **To wait on o upon,** ir a ver a alguno, visitar o hacer una visita; presentar sus respetos a; servir, seguir, servir a la mesa o como criado; seguirse, inferirse, ser una cosa consecuencia de otra; acompañar o ir acompañando, especialmente a los recién casados; poner cuidado en, velar sobre; volver a conducir a una persona al paraje de donde se salió con ella. **I shall have the honor to wait on you tomorrow,** mañana tendré el gusto de ponerme a las órdenes de Ud.

wait, *s.* 1. Espera, aguadamiento, acto de esperar; tardanza, detención, demora, el tiempo ocupado en aguardar. 2. *(Des.)* Asechanza, celada. **To lie in wait,** asechar, poner asechanzas. **To lay wait,** formar emboscadas, preparar un paraje para un ataque. **To wait up,** esperar levantada.

waiter ['weɪtəʳ] [uei-taʳ], *s.* 1. Camarero, criado de fondo, mozo de café o taberna, sirviente, criado. 2. Azafate o bandeja para servir el café, el té, las bebidas, etc. **Dumb-waiter,** ascensor doméstico (para elevar objetos de la cocina a los pisos altos); *(G.B.)* aparador giratorio. **He is a very good waiter,** él es un buen camarero.

waiting ['weɪtɪŋ] [uei-tin], *s.* El acto de aguardar o esperar; servicio, el acto de servir. **Gentleman in waiting,** gentilhmbre de servicio. **Waiting-maid, waiting-woman, waiting-gentlewoman,** doncella, camarera. **Waiting-room,** sala de espera. **Waiting list,** lista de espera.

waitress ['weɪtrɪs] [uei-tres], *s.* Camarera.

waive ['weɪv] [ueiv], *va.* 1. Dejar pasar; renunciar temporalmente; ceder, resignar (to abandon). 2. *(Der. ant. Ingl.)* Proscribir a una mujer. **He waived his profession,** él renunció a la profesión.

waiver ['weɪvəʳ] [uei-vaʳ], *s. (For.)* Renuncia voluntaria de un derecho, privilegio, o ventaja.

waiving ['weɪvɪŋ] [uei-vin], *s. (For. ant.)* El acto de proscribir a una mujer: recusación de la protección de las leyes a una mujer.

wake [weɪk] [ueik], *vn.* 1. Velar, estar sin dormir; velar, pasar la noche. 2. Despertar, despertarse, dejar el sueño, dejar de dormir. 3. Hacerse más vivo y advertido. -va. 1. Despertar, cortar o quitar el sueño. 2. Despertar, excitar, remover (to revival, arouse, excite). 3. Resucitar. 4. Velar a los difuntos. **Your son woke up early to go to the beach**, tu hijo se despertó temprano para ir a la playa.

wake, s. 1. Vela o vigilia de un muerto durante toda la noche; costumbre común entre los irlandeses. *(Cuba y Mex.)* Velorio. 2. *(Gram Bret.)* Vela, romería o fiesta de la dedicación de una iglesia, que antiguamente se guardaba velando toda la noche. 3. *(Des.)* Vela, vigilia, la acción de estar despierto. 4. *(Mar.)* Estela, la señal que la embarcación deja en el agua a su paso. **A ship in the wake of another**, *(Mar.)* Un bajel en la estela o las aguas de otro.

wakeful ['weɪkfʊl] [ueik-fol], a. Vigilante, que vela o está despierto, que no tiene sueño o que no duerme.

wakefully ['weɪkfʊlɪ] [ueik-fu-li], adv. Vigilantemente.

wakefulness ['weɪkfʊlnɪs] [ueik-ful-nes], s. Vigilia, desvelo, falta de sueño, insomnio; estado de una persona que no puede dormir.

waken ['weɪkən] [uei-ken], vn. Despertar, despertarse, dejar de dormir. -va. Despertar, avivar, hacer que uno vuelva en sí.

wake-robin ['weɪkˌrɒbɪn] [ueik-ro-bin], s. *(Bot.)* 1. Aro o yaro, planta británica con hojas verdes obscuras y sagitadas. 2. *(E. U.)* Una especie cualquiera del género. Trillium, hierba perenne de las liliáceas. Se llama también *birthroot.*

waking ['weɪkɪŋ] [uei-kin], s. Vela, el tiempo que uno está en vela o despierto estado de vigilia. -a. 1. Que despierta. 2. Despierto, que no duerme. 3. De vela o vigilia; en que no se duerme. **Waking hours**, horas de vela.

wale [weɪl] [ueil], va. Hacer rayas sobre el cuerpo, azotar, -s. 1. Raya, señal hecha sobre la piel azotando. 2. Relieve, especie de labor o figura que se forma en el damasco y otras telas. 3. *(Mar.)* Cinta. **Main-wale**, cinta de la segunda cubierta.

walk [wɔːk] [uok], vn. 1. Andar, o ir al paso (to sail, stump). 2. Pasear, pasearse; ir a pie; andar por gusto o por ejercicio. 3. Andar o caminar a paso corto, hablando de caballerías. 4. Obrar, conducirse, portarse; vivir. 5. Aparecer, hablando de fantasmas, espectros o duendes. 6. *(Fam.)* Irse obligado a ello, liar al petate, ser despedido. -va. 1. Pasear, sacar a pasar o hacer pasear; recorrer, andar en 2. Atravesar, pasar de una parte a otra. 3. Conducir, dirigir; hacer ir al paso (un caballo).

walk after, seguir a uno o ir tras él.

walk away, irse, marcharse.

walk back, volver, regresar.

walk down, bajar, andar bajando.

walk forth, salir.

walk in, entrar, pasar adelante; pasearse en; *(Bibl.)* vivir en.

walk out, salir, irse afuera. **To walk the hospitals**, estudiar la clínica médica o quirúrgica en los hospitales. **To walk the streets**, andar por las calles o pasear las calles.

walk up, subir, andar subiendo; (con *to*) acercarse a. **To walk up and down**, pasearse de arriba a abajo.

walk, s. 1. Paseo el acto de pasear o pasearse. 2. El modo de andar. 3. Paso, el movimiento seguido del caballo cuando no trota ni galopa. 4. Paseo, el lugar o sitio destinado para pasarse; senda; alameda, camino cuyas orillas tienen árboles. **The street walk**, la calzada de la calle, el enlosado o entarimado. 5. Carrera, estado, empleo, vocación. 6. Método de vida, conducta, porte. **To go for a walk**, ir a pasearse, ir a paseo. **The humble walks of life**, las humildes sendas de la vida.

walker ['wɔːkər] [uo-kar], s. Paseador, andador; peatón, peón, el que anda a pie. **Night-walker**, cantonera. **Street-walker**, prostituta.

walkie-talkie ['wɔːkɪ'tɔːkɪ] [uo-ki-to-ki], s. Radioteléfono portátil.

walking ['wɔːkɪŋ] [uo-kin], s. Paseo, la acción de pasear o pasearse. **Walking-beam**, balancín (de máquina vertical de vapor). **Walking-cane**, bastón ligero. **Walking-staff**, bordón, bastón. **Walking-stick**. (a) bastón; (b) insecto fasmídeo de cuerpo prolongado y parecido a las ramillas

entre las cuales vive. **Walking-spirit**, ánima en pena, duende, fantasma. **To give one his walking-ticket**, despedirle, enviarle a pasear; darle calabazas.

walkout ['wɔːkaʊt] [uok-aut], s. *(Fam. E.U.)* Huelga de obreros, salida en señal de protesta.

walkover ['wɔːkˌəʊvər] [uok-ou-va'], s. Triunfo fácil, o sin oposición apreciable.

wall [wɔːl] [uol], s. 1. Pared. 2. Muralla, muro, obra de albañilería para cercar, separar (rampart) etc. 3. Muralla de un recinto fortificado; a menudo en plural. 4. Banco de roca natural; tapia. 5. Lado de cualquier cavidad, costado de vasija o receptáuclo. **Partition-wall**, tabique. **To take the wall**, tomarse la acera, tomarse el mejor puesto sin querer cederlo a otro. **Main wall**, pared maestra. **To be driven to the wall**, verse entre la espada y la pared. **To go to the wall**, verse obligado a rendirse, verse en apuros. **Wall-creeper**, *(Orn.)* pico murario. **Wall-fruit**, fruta de espalera o espaldera. **Wall-louse**, chince. **Wall-pepper**, *(Bot.)* siempreviva, hierba puntera. **Wall-piece**, pieza o pedreo, cañón de muralla. **Wall-rue**, *(Bot.)* ruda muraria. **Wall-tree**, espaldera. **One wall of the room is yellow**, una pared de la habitación es amarilla.

wall, va. 1. Emparedar, tapiar. 2. Murar, cercar o guarnecer con muros o murallas; fortificar, murar, cerrar, tapiar.

wallaby ['wɒləbɪ] [uo-la-bi], s. Especie menor de cangarú.

wallet ['wɒlɪt] [uo-lit], s. 1. Cartera de bolsillo. 2. Alforjas, mochila. **He lost all his money because his wallet had been stolen**, perdió todo su dinero porque su cartera había sido robada.

wall-eyed ['wɔːl'aɪd] [uol-aid], a. 1. *(Med.)* Que tiene los ojos divergentes o muy abiertos; lo opuesto a bizco. 2. *(Ant.)* Zarco, el que tiene los ojos de un color azul muy claro.

wall-flower ['wɔːl'flaʊər] [uol-flaua'], s. 1. *(Bot.)* Alelí doble, planta crucífera. 2. Mujer a la que nadie saca a bailar, que se queda sin pareja en un baile.

wallop ['wɒləp] [uo-lop], vn. Bullir, hervir. -va. *(Ger.)* Zurrar, tundir, castigar a golpes (to strike, whack), -s. Linternazo, porrazo.

wallow ['wɒləʊ] [uo-lou], vn. 1. Moverse con pesadez o poca gracia. 2. Encenagarse, meterse o revolcarse en el cieno o porquería. 3. Sumergirse o estar encenagado en algún vicio. **To wallow in riches**, manar en riquezas. **To wallow in pleasures**, vivir en medio de los placeres.

wallow, s. Revuelco, el acto de revolcarse.

wallower ['wɒləʊər] [uo-loua'], s. El o lo que se revolca en el fango o lodo.

wallowing-place ['wɒləʊɪŋˌpleɪs] [uo-louin-pleis], s. Cenagal; revolcaldero.

walnut ['wɔːlnʌt] [uol-nat], s. *(Bot.)* 1. Nuez, el fruto del nogal o la madera de este árbol. 2. Nogal, árbol alto de la familia de las juglándeas y cuyo fruto es la nuez. **The table is made of nogal**, la mesa está hecha de madera de nogal.

walrus ['wɔːlrəs] [uol-ras], s. Morsa, mamífero de gran tamaño parecido a la foca. Vive en los mares áricos.

waltz [wɔːlts] [uolts], vn. Valsar, bailar el vals. -s. Vals.

waltzer ['wɔːltsər] [uol-tsa'], s. El o la que valsa: valsador, valsadora.

wamble ['wæmbl] [uam-bel], vn. *(Prov. o des.)* Nausear, padecer náuseas o ganas de vomitar.

wampum ['wæmpəm] [uam-pom], s. Cuentas formadas de las partes interiores de conchas y enhebradas, que servían como dinero y como adorno a los indios americanos.

wan [wɒn] [uon], s. Pálido, descolorido. **To grow wan**, palidecer, ponerse palido.

wand [wɒnd] [uond], s. 1. Vara, ramo delgado. 2. Vara, insignia de autoridad o jurisdicción. 3. Varita de virtudes, vara de adivinar. **Mercury's wand**, caduceo.

wander ['wɒndər] [uon-da'], va. y vn. 1. Errar, andar vagando, vagar, vaguear (to move, go, walk from place to place). 2. Rodar, andorrear, corretear, andar de una parte a otra sin objeto fijo. 3. Discurrir, andar o caminar por diversas partes y lugares. 4. Delirar. 5. Extraviarse; desviarse del asunto, p. ej. durante una discusión. **Groups of nomads**

wander across the desert, grupos de nómadas vaguean a través del desierto.

wanderer [ˈwɒndərəʳ] [uon-da-raʳ], s. Tunante, vagamundo, andorrero. vago; errante, extraviado (drifter, hobo, roam). **Wanderer from**, persona que se aleja o desvía de; transgresor.

wandering [ˈwɒndərɪŋ] [uon-da-rin], s. 1. Viajes o paseos de unas partes a otras sin objeto determinado. 2. Extravío, pérdida del camino. 3. Habla errante e incoherente, como la del que delira. -a. 1. Errante, que anda errante. 2. Descaminado, descarriado; delirante. 3. Vagamundo.

wane [wɒn] [uon], vn. Menguar, disminuir; decaer, ir en decadencia. **The daylight is waning**, la luz del día está disminuyendo

waning [ˈweɪnɪŋ] [uei-nin], ·s. Decadencia, decremento, declinación, caimiento. **Wane of the moon**, menguante de la luna.

wangle [wæŋgl] [uan-guel], vn. (Fam.) Sacudirse, extricarse (de alguna dificultad, etc.). -va. 1. Engatusar, persuadir con artificios o engaños. 2. Agenciarse, arreglar, procurar, conseguir (to obtain, achieve) **To wangle an invitation**, obtener una invitación con artimañas.

wannabe [ˈwɒnəbiː] [uo-na-bi], s. Amateur, imitador barato.

wanness [wɒnnɪs] [uon-nes], s. Palidez; descaecimiento, languidez, falta de fuerzas.

want [wɒnt] [uont], va. 1. Necesitar, haber menester, tener necesidad de alguna cosa; estar desprovisto de (to need). 2. Hacer falta, sentir la necesidad de. 3. Querer, desear, tener o sentir deseo (to desire). **What do you want?** ¿qué quiere Vd.? 4. Dispensarse de, pasarse sin. -vn. 1. Estar necesitado, indigente (to lack). 2. Carecer, tener falta de algo. 3. Faltar, no existir alguna prenda, calidad o circunstancia. **Who wants to enter into difficulties?**, ¿quién quiere meterse en dificultades? **I shall want your asssistance**, necesitaré su ayuda de Vd. **You are wanted**, tienen necesidad de Ud., por Ud. preguntan. **Wanted** (término de anuncios), se encesita. **I want you to do it**, quiero que Vd. lo haga.

want, s. 1. Necesidad, la falta de las cosas necesarias para la conservación de la vida; pobreza, indigencia, miseria (poverty). 2. Falta, privación o carencia de una cosa necesaria o útil (a lack). **To be in want**, estar pobre o necesitado. 3. La cosa que se necesita; falta de una cosa que se quiere tener. **For want of**, por falta de. **To die of want**, morir de miseria.

wantage [ˈwɒntɪdʒ] [uon-tich], s. Lo que falta; déficit.

wanting [ˈwɒntɪŋ] [uon-tin], a. Falto, defectuoso, necesitado, escaso. **To be wanting**, faltar.

wanton [ˈwɒntən] [uon-ton], a. 1. Juguetón, retozón, de buen humor travieso. 2. Extravagante. 3. No atado, suelto (flotante). 4. Lascivo, inclinado a la lascivia; libre, licencioso, atrevido, disoluto (immoral). 5. Falto de razón inexcusable, imperdonable; sin provocación (motiveless, without reason). -s. 1. Hombre o mujer lasciva. 2. Persona frívola.

wanton, vn. 1. Retozar, juguetear, entretenerse jugueteando y retozando. 2. Hacer picardías, por maldad. 3. Pasar el tiempo en liviandades.

wantonly [ˈwɒntənlɪ] [uon-ton-li], adv. 1. Alegremente, con retozos; de picardía; de pura maldad; por hacer mal; sólo por juguete. 2. Lascivamente, inmodestamente.

wantonness [ˈwɒntənnɪs] [uon-ton-nes], s. 1. Lascivia, impudicicia, deshonestidad. 2. Licencia, libertad, inmoderado, descompostura, desgarro. 3. Juguete, entretenimiento, chanza, chacota.

wantwit [ˈwɒntwɪt] [uont-uit], s. Idiota, tonto (rude, silly).

war [wɔːʳ] [uoʳ], s. 1. Guerra, hostilidad armada entre naciones o partidos opuestos. 2. El arte militar, la profesión de las armas. 3. Las armas que se usan para hacer la guerra. 4. (Poét. o des.) Ejércitos. 5. Oposición, contrariedad. **Wardance**, danza de los salvajes antes de ir a la guerra o en celebración de uan victoria. **War to the knife**, guerra a muerte. **Articles of war**, código militar o naval. **Man-of-war**, navío, buque de guerra. **War Department**, ministerio de la guerra. **War-cry**, grito de guerra (de nación o partido).

War-whoop, grito de guerra (de los indios americanos). **War-worn**, usado o gastado por la guerra; abrumado por la guerra; se aplica particularmente a un veterano.

war, vn. Guerrear, estar en guerra.

warble [ˈwɔːbl] [uor-bel], va. Cantar con quiebros y trinos, como un pájaro; trinar, gorjear. **To warble her praises**, cantar sus alabanzas (de una mujer). -vn. 1. Trinar, hacer quiebros y trinos con la voz; trinar, gorjear (los pájaros). 2. Murmurar (un arroyo). -s. Canto, gorjeo. **The warble of a bird in summer**, el canto de un pájaro en verano.

warbler [ˈwɔːbləʳ] [uor-blaʳ], s. 1. Cantor o músico que hace trinos. 2. Curruca, silvia, pájaro; nombre dado a varios pájaros de escaso canto.

warbling [ˈwɔːblɪŋ] [uor-blin], a. Melodioso; (arroyo) de suave murmullo. -s. Canto armonioso de una persona; canto, gorjeo de las aves.

ward [wɔːd] [uord], va. 1. Guardar, defender, proteger, preservar (to cover, protect, featherbed). 2. Parar o detener un golpe. **To ward off**, evitar, desviar el golpe. -vn. Vigilar, velar.

ward, s. 1. Pupilo o menor en tutela. 2. Barrio, cuartel o distrito de alguna ciudad. 3. Sala, división de hospital, de cárcel, etc. 4. Pupilaje, tutela, tutoría. 5. Guarda, el acto de guardar o custodiar. 6. Guardas de llave o cerradura. 7. Defensa, el arma con que uno se defiende; posición, defensiva, en la que está uno a cubierto de la espada del adversario. 8. Guarda, guardián, conserje. **He has send his ward to his house**, ha enviado a su pupilo a su casa.

warden [ˈwɔːdn] [uor-den], s. 1. Custodio, guardián, el que guarda o custodia alguna cosa. 2. Alcaide de una cárcel o carcelero. 3. Conserje, que tiene a su cuidado ciertos establecimientos; en Inglaterra, director de ciertos colegios. 4. En la Iglesia anglicana, cada uno de los dos mayordomos que cuidan de los asuntos de una parroquia. V. CHURCH-WARDENS Y VESTRY. **The wardens and vestry**, los mayordomos y la junta parroquial. 5. Una especie de pera. **Warden of the Cinque Ports**, el gobernador de los Cinco Puertos, un empleo muy honorífico en Inglaterra. **The warden of a port**, capitán de un puerto. **Wardens**, maestros o jurados en algún oficio.

wardenship [ˈwɔːdnʃɪp] [uor-den-ship], s. El oficio de guarda o custodio; conserjería; bedelía; alcaidía.

warder [ˈwɔːdəʳ] [uor-daʳ], s. Guarda, guardia.

wardmote [ˈwɔːdməʊt] [uord-mout], s. Junta de barrio o cuartel para la dirección y gobierno de sus asuntos.

wardrobe [ˈwɔːdrəʊb] [uor-droub], s. 1. Guardarropa. 2. Conjunto de ropa que posee una persona, vestuario. **She bought a complete new wardrobe in Paris**, ella compró el nuevo vestuario en Paris.

wardroom [ˈwɔːdrʊm] [uord-rum], s. Cuartel de oficiales.

wards [ˈwɔːdz] [uords], prep. Hacia (in a direction).

wardship [ˈwɔːdʃɪp] [uord-ship], s. Tutela, tutoría, pupilaje.

ware [wɛəʳ] [ueaʳ], s. 1. Mercadería, mercancía, artículos de la misma clase; se emplea por lo común en palabras compuestas; v. gr. **tableware**, vajilla de mesa; **earthenware**, loza, vajilla de barro. 2. pl. Géneros que se venden, mercancías, artículos de comercio. **Hardware**, quinquillería. **China ware**, porcelana, loza fina. **Hollow ware**, ollas, marmitas, y otros artículos de hierro para cocinar. **Small wares**, artículos menudos; mercería, pasamanería. -a. (Ant.) WARY y AWARE.

warehouse [ˈwɛəhaʊs] [uea-jaus], s. Almacén, el edificio donde se guardan los géneros; 1. Lugar para guardar los efectos que todavía no están listos para el mercado; 2. Almacén donde se cuidan géneros mediante pago. **Bonded warehouse**, depósito, sitio donde se depositan las mercancías que aún no han pagado los derechos de aduana. **Warehouse-keeper**, **warehouseman**, guardaalmacén; almacenero. **Warehouse-rent**, almacenaje.

warehouse, va. Almacenar, poner en almacén.

wareroom [ˈwɛərʊm] [uea-rum], s. Pieza para el almacenaje o para la venta de géneros o mercancías.

warfare [ˈweəfɛəʳ] [uea-feaʳ], s. 1. Guerra, el arte y profesión militar. 2. La vida del soldado, servicio militar. 3. Lucha, combate.

warhead [ˈweəhed] [uea-jed], s. Punta de combate.

warhorse [ˈweəhɔːs] [uea-jors], s. 1. Caballo de guerra o a propósito para la guerra. 2. (Fam.) El que ha tenido large experiencia, especialmente en la guerra o en la política; veterano.

warily [ˈweərɪlɪ] [uea-ri-li], adv. Cautamente, cautelosamente, astutamente, con astucia.

wariness [ˈweərɪnɪs] [uea-ri-nes], s. Cautela, precaución, previsión prudente.

warlike [ˈwɔːlaɪk] [uor-laik], a. Guerrero, belicoso, militar.

warlock [ˈwɔːlɒk] [uor-lok], s. (Ant.) Brujo; también, duende (elf, goblin).

warm [wɔːm] [uorm], a. 1. Calor o caluroso, cálido, pero que no llega al estado de caliente (hot, heated). 2. Cálido, que tiene cierto grado de calor; expuesto al calor; que no tiene invierno. 3. Ardiente, acalorado, vivo, activo, caliente, furioso, violento, celoso, conforme sea la cosa a que se aplica. 4. Conmovido, arrebatado, apasionado. 5. Muy unido, encariñado, afectuoso. 6. (Art.) Que tiene matices predominantes de rojo o amarillo. 7. Recién hecho; fresco (la pista de la caza). 8. Cercano al objeto buscado; se dice en los juegos de niños. 9. (Fam.) Molesto, fastidioso, peligroso. **A warm climate**, un clima cálido. **A warm friend**, un amigo cariñoso, abnegado. **A warm heart**, un corazón ardiente, generoso. **A warm temper**, un carácter vivo, ardiente. **Warm work**, tarea difícil, dura. **To be warm**, tener calor, y familiarmente, estar sudando. **It is warm**, hace calor. **To keep warm**, conservar caliente. **To get warm**, calentar, calentarse; comenzar a hacer calor; animarse. **To make warm**, calentar. **Lukewarm**, tibio. **Warm-blooded**, (a) de sangre caliente; se dice de los mamíferos y las aves; (b) entusiasmado, ardiente, apasionado. **Warm-hearted**, de corazón ardiente, afectuoso; simpático.

warm, va. 1. Calentar, comunicar el calor. 2. Calentar, avivar, encender, enfervorizar. 3. Simpatizar, entusiasmarse con **To warm over**, volver a calentar; calentar lo que estaba frío. **Everybody warmed with her**, todo el mundo simpatizó con ella. s. Calentamiento.

warming-pan [ˌwɔːmɪŋˈpæn] [uor-min-pan], s. Calentador.

warmly [ˈwɔːmlɪ] [uorm-li], adv. Con calor, ardientemente, con ardor, con eficacia, con empeño.

warmth [wɔːmθ] [uormz], s. 1. Calor moderado. 2. Celo, ardor, fervor, ardimiento, viveza. 3. Fantasía, entusiasmo. **Warmth of coloring**, (Pint.) color de fuego claro; color vivo.

warn [wɔːn] [uorn], va. 1. Precaver, avisar, caucionar (to call, notice, get in). 2. Advertir, aconsejar. 3. Avisar, anticipadamente, prevenir; notificar a.

warning [ˈwɔːnɪŋ] [uor-nin], s. 1. Amonestación, advertencia, aviso, caución; escarmiento; ejemplo terrorífico. 2. Notificación de dejar el servicio, o de salir de una casa o tienda alquilada. **To take warning**, estar atento, precaverse. **To give warning**, prevenir, advertir, avisar o hacer saber anticipadamente alguna cosa.

warp [wɔːp] [uorp], s. 1. Torcedura, alabeo, el estado de lo torcido, alabeado, retorcido o deformado; prevención del ánimo. 2. Urdiembre, urdimbre, el conjunto de hilos ya ordenados y dispuestos para el telar. 2. Espía, calabrote entalingado, jarcia que se usa para espiar una embarcación. 3. Capa o sedimento aluvial que el agua deposita sobre las tierras bajas. 4. Cierta medida longitudinal de soga o cordel. **Warp-beam**, enjullo, plegador, cilindro sobre el cual el tejedor va arrollando la tela. **Warp and woof**, trama y urdimbre.

warp, va. 1. Torcer, desviar, deformar como por encogimiento o por el calor. 2. Dar a algo una tendencia falsa, prevenir el ánimo; retorcer. 3. Urdir, formar de la urdimbre una madeja en el urdidor para pasarla al telar. 4. (Mar.) Remolcar; hacer mudar de posición a la embarcación. 5. Tergiversar. -vn. 1. Torcerse; alabearse (madera). 2. Desviarse, alejarse,

apartarse del camino recto. 3. (Hiland.) Urdir, estirar o preparar el hilo. 4. (Mar.) Ir a remolque, moverse a remolque, espiarse.

warrant [ˈwɒrənt] [uo-rant], va. 1. Garantir, garantizar la calidad o suficiencia de; asegurar, salir o constituirse fiador o garante. 2. Responder, poner a cubierto, defender, preservar de; sacar. **I warrant you**, (Fam.) yo se lo aseguro. 3. Autorizar, dar autoridad. 4. Justificar (to justify), ser fundamento o razón suficiente para (una creencia, conclusión, etc.). 5. Asegurar, afirmar, certificar. **I warrant it good**, se lo garantizo a Vd. como bueno. **Reason warrants it**, la razón lo justifica. **I warrant that he was here**, certifico que él estuvo aquí.

warrant, s. 1. (For.) Auto o decreto de prisión. 2. Cualquier cédula. oficio, escritura, etc., que confiere algún privilegio o gracia especial poder o autoridad; autorización, poder, documento justificativo; (Com.) certificado de depósito. 3. Autoridad o apoyo de lo que se dice; testimonio; sanción. 4. Justificación, apología, razón. **Special warrant**, se llama así al auto dado por un magistrado mandando a los oficiales de justicia que conduzcan presa a su presencia a la persona nombrada en él. **General warrant**, auto dado para prender a todas las personas implicadas en un delito. **Death-warrant**, la orden que se da al *sheriff*, para que haga ajusticiar a un reo. **Warrant-officers**, oficiales subalternos de mar. **Land-warrant**, cédula emitida por el gobierno declarando que el poseedor tiene título a la cantidad de terreno público en ella especificada.

warrantable [ˈwɒrəntəbl] [uo-ran-ta-bol], a. Que se puede abonar, garantizar, justificar o defender.

warrantably [ˈwɒrəntəblɪ] [uo-ran-ta-bli], adv. Justificadamente.

warranted [ˈwɒrəntɪd] [uo-ran-tid], a. Garantizado, justificado.

warrantee [ˈwɒrəntiː] [uo-ran-ti], s. (For.) Afianzado, el que recibe alguna garantía.

warranter [ˈwɒrəntəʳ] [uo-ran-taʳ], s. El que autoriza; garante, fiador, fianza.

warrantor [ˈwɒrəntəʳ] [uo-ran-tarʳ], s. (Der.) Garante, fiador; correlativo de *warrantee*.

warranty [ˈwɒrəntɪ] [uo-ran-ti], s. 1. (For.) Garantía, la acción de afianzar y asegurar lo estipulado en un contrato cualquiera; garantía del vendedor. **A warranty clause**, cláusula de evicción y saneamiento. 2. Seguridad. 3. Autoridad para ejecutar alguna cosa.

warren [ˈwɒrən] [uo-ren], s. 1. Conejera, conejar, vivar de conejos, soto de conejos o el sitio destinado para criar conejos. 2. Cercado para guardar la caza menuda; depósito para la pesca del pescado en los ríos. 3. Laberinto (maze, network).

warrior [ˈwɒrɪəʳ] [uo-rioʳ], s. Guerrero, soldado.

wart [wɔːt] [uort], s. 1. Verruga, excrecencia cutánea. 2. (Bot.) Verruga, excrecencia de la superficie de una planta. 3. Excrecencia en la cuartilla de los caballos. **He has warts on his fingers**, tiene verrugas en sus dedos.

warty [ˈwɔːtɪ] [uor-ti], a. Verrugoso, que tiene muchas verrugas; de la naturaleza de las verrugas.

wary [ˈweərɪ] [uea-ri], a. 1. Cauto, cauteloso, prudente, avisado, precavido contra engaños o peligro, circunspecto (cautious, careful, prudent, politic). 2. Astuto, artificioso, sagaz, sutil. **In this country you must be very wary**, en ese país debes ser prudente.

was [wɒz] [uos], pret, de verbo TO BE.

wash [wɒʃ] [uosh], va. 1. Lavar, limpiar con agua u otro fluido; blanquear la ropa sucia (to clean, sluice). 2. Bañar, regar o tocar el agua alguna cosa; cubrir con agua; también llevarse algo el agua. 3. Lavar, purificar, quitar algún defecto o mancha. 4. Recubrir de una capa delgada de metal. 5. Dar una mano ligera de color sobre una superficie. **Many people wash their cars on Sundays**, mucha gente lava su coche los domingos. -vn. 1. Lavarse. 2. Lavar ropa. 3. Gastarse por la acción del agua. 4. Moverse, como el agua, suavemente de aquí para allá. 5. Lamer; correr; chapalear (to flow). 6.

Llevarse. 7. Colar. **To wash one's face or hands,** lavarse la cara o las manos. **To wash away, off o out,** lavar, borrar, hacer desaparecer; quitar lavando. **To wash down,** separar una cosa de otra lavándolas; hacer bajar, tragar. **To wash over,** sumergir, inundar; dar de otro color o dar una mano de otro color en la pintura. **To wash a picture,** bañar una pintura o dar una mano de color transparente sobre otra.

wash, s. 1. Lavadura, lavación, loción, ablución; lavatorio, la acción de lavar; de aquí, el conjunto de ropa lavada de una vez. 2. Preparación o mezcla que se usa para dar una capa, bañar o salpicar; agua de tocador, cosmético; loción, preparación líquida para uso externo. 3. El romper del agua sobre la orilla; el ruido que hace el agua moviéndose. 4. Superficie bañada por el mar o un río; pantano. 5. Aluvión, depósito, materias depositadas por el agua. 6. Bazofia, lavazas. 7. Un licor que se extrae de la cebada germinada y fermentada para destilar. 8. Colada. 9. Enjuague. 10 Capa. 11. Remolino. **Wash-ball,** bola de jabón, jaboncillo de olor. **Wash-board,** 1. Tablilla de lavandera (con superficie corrugada); 2. Faja de madera en la parte baja de las paredes; 3. *(Mar.)* Falca, batemar. **Wash-bowl (wash-hand-basin),** jofaina, palangana. **Wash-house,** lavadero. **Wash-leather,** gamuza o imitación de ella. **Wash-off,** fugitivo, que se destiñe. **Wash-pot,** bacía, particularmente, vasija en que se da la última capa de estaño. **Wash-stand,** palanganero, lavabo, aguamanil. **Wash-tub,** cuba artesón de lavar. **Wash of an oar,** *(Mar.)* pala de remo.

washed-out ['wɒʃtaʊt] [uosht-aut], *a.* Agotado, gastado.

washed-up ['wɒʃtʌp] [uosht-ap], *a.* Acabado (defeated, finished, failed).

washer ['wɒʃəʳ] [uo-shaʳ], *s.* 1. Lavador, lavandero, lavandera, el o la que lava; máquina para lavar. 2. Volandera, círculo de hierro plano puesto en los ejes de las ruedas; disco de cuero u otro material que sirve para empaquetadura en una manguera, etc. 3. Arandela. **Automatic dish-washer,** lavadora,

washer-woman ['wɒʃəˌwʊmən] [uo-sha-vu-man], *s.* Lavandera.

washing ['wɒʃɪŋ] [uo-shin], *s.* Lavadura, loción, lavatorio; blanqueadura. **Washing-machine,** máquina para lavar. **Washing-soda,** sosa para blanquear, carbonato de sodio.

washout ['wɒʃaʊt] [uosh-aut], *s.* 1. Deslave, derrubio. 2. *(Fam.)* Fracaso, desilusión.

washy ['wɒʃɪ] [uo-shi], *a.* 1. Húmedo, mojado. 2. Débil, falto de solidez.

wasp [wɒsp] [uosp], *s.* Avispa.

waspish ['wɒspɪʃ] [uos-pish], *a.* 1. Enojadizo, caprichudo, de mal humor, áspero de genio, irascible (irascible, unpleasant in manner)). 2. Que tiene talle o cintura de avispa. **She is spiteful and waspish,** ella es rencorosa y irascible.

waspishly ['wɒspɪʃlɪ] [uos-pish-li], *adv.* Enojadamente, ásperamente, con mal rumor.

waspishness ['wɒspɪʃnɪs] [uos-pish-nes], *s.* Mal genio, mal humor, aspereza de genio, naturaleza irascible, irascibilidad.

wassail ['wɒseɪl] [uo-seil], *s.* 1. Bebida hecha con manzanas, azúcar y cerveza, muy usada antiguamente en Inglaterra. 2. Borrachera, reunión alegre en que se cometen excesos en la bebida; orgía. **Wassail-bowl,** taza, cubilete.

wassailer ['wɒseɪləʳ] [uo-sei-laʳ], *s.* Borrachón, gran bebedor.

waste [weɪst] [ueist], *va.* 1. Malgastar, disipar, destruir, echar a perder, desperdiciar (to miss, misspent). 2. Gastar, ir consumiendo alguna cosa; agotar, quitar las fuerzas, hacer peder el vigor (to consume, spend). 3. *(Ant.)* Desolar, arruinar, asolar, talar. *-vn.* Gastarse, irse consumiendo alguna cosa; usarse, alterarse, dañarse. **To waste away,** decaecer, ir a menos, perder poco a poco la salud, vigor, etc.; menguar, disminuirse, irse consumiendo poco a poco; echar a perder.

waste, *a.* 1. Desechado, inútil, sin importancia práctica, sin valor. 2. Desierto, inculto. 3. Desolado, arruinado. 4. Superfluo, sobrante. *-s.* 1. Despilfarro, gasto inútil, acción de malgastar. 2. Disminución de las fuerzas o vigor; decadencia. 3. Restos, despojos, desperdicios. 4. Baldío,

terreno inculto, desierto; de aquí, extensión, inmensidad. 5. Artefacto o aparato de desagüe o para remover los desperdicios. 6. Desperdicio; destrozo, asolamiento, destrucción, daño. **Waste-basket,** cesto para papeles y desechos. **Waste paper,** papel de desecho. **Waste-pipe,** tubo de desagüe, desaguadero.

waste-book ['weɪstbʊk] [ueist-buk], *s.* Borrador, libro de memoria.

wasteful ['weɪstfʊl] [ueist-ful], *a.* 1. Manirroto, gastador, pródigo, disipador. 2. Destructivo, dañoso, ruinoso.

wastefully ['weɪstfəlɪ] [ueist-fu-li], *adv.* Pródigamente.

wastefulness ['weɪstfəlnɪs] [ueist-ful-nes], *s.* Prodigalidad; gasto inútil.

waster ['weɪstəʳ] [ueis-taʳ], *s.* Disipador, gastador.

wasting ['weɪstɪŋ] [ueis-tin], *a.* Que usa, agota o consume. *-s.* Consumición, agotamiento; acción del verbo *waste,* en cualquier sentido; lo que se agota o consume.

wastrel ['weɪstrəl] [ueis-tral], *s.* 1. Desperdicios. 2. Terreno no cultivado, pastos comunes.

wasty ['weɪstɪ] [ueis-ti], *a.* 1. Desierto, inculto. 2. Desechado, sobrante, sin importancia práctica.

watch [wɒtʃ] [uoch], *s.* 1. Vela, la acción de velar; cuidado, vigilancia, observación vigilante. 2. Desvelo, vigilia, estado de vela, falta de sueño. 3. Centinela; guardia, sereno, vigilante. 4. Vela, velación, el período de tiempo durante el cual está de guardia un sereno; de aquí, cierta división de la noche. 5. *(Mar.)* Cuarto, servicio que hace cada una de las dos divisiones de la tripulación con sus oficiales, para velar por la seguridad de una nave; la duración de cada vela es de cuatro horas. 6. Reloj de pulsera, de bolsillo. 7. Vigilancia nocturna. **Watch and ward,** patrulla, ronda. **Watch-glass,** 1. Cristal de reloj. 2. *(Mar.)* Ampolleta de media hora. **Larboard watch,** *(Mar.)* guardia de babor. **Starboard watch,** *(Mar.)* Guardia de estribor. **Dog-watch,** *(Mar.)* segunda guardia. **Morning-watch,** *(Mar.)* guardia de la madrugada. **To set the watch,** *(Mar.)* rendir la guardia. **To spell the watch,** *(Mar.)* llamar a la guardia. 6. Muestra, reloj de faltriquera. **Repeating-watch,** reloj de repetición. **Lever watch,** reloj de escape. **Hunting-case watch,** saboneta (de doble caja). **Open-faced watch,** muestra (de una sola caja). **Open-faced watch,** muestra (de una sola caja). **Stop watch,** reloj de segundos muertos. **My watch is too fast, too slow,** mi reloj adelanta, atrasa. **To wind a watch,** dar cuerda a un reloj. **Watch-case,** caja de reloj, relojera. **Watch-guard,** cadena o cinta de reloj. **Watch-spring,** muelle de reloj. **Watch-stand,** porta-reloj. **Watch-tower,** atalaya, torre de observación; garita. **Watch-work,** el mecanismo de un reloj de bolsillo. **To be upon the watch,** estar alerta.

watch, *va. y vn.* 1. Velar, estar sin dormir. 2. Velar, hacer centinela o guardia. 3. Velar, observar o cuidar atentamente alguna cosa (to be careful of, guard, invigilate). 4. Guardar, custodiar. 5. Espiar, observar. 6. Mirar, observar (to look at). 7. Esperar (to wait for). **Please, watch my baby while I go shopping,** por favor, vigila mi bebé mientras voy de compras.

watcher ['wɒtʃəʳ] [uo-chaʳ], *s.* Velador, observador, espía.

watchful ['wɒtʃfʊl] [uoch-ful], *a.* Vigilante, cuidadoso (alert, cautious).

watchfulness ['wɒtʃfʊlnɪs] [uoch-ful-nes], *s.* Vigilancia, cuidado; desvelo, falta de sueño.

watch-house ['wɒtʃhaʊs] [uoch-jaus], *s.* El cuerpo de guardia de la policía.

watching ['wɒtʃɪŋ] [uo-chin], *s.* Vigilancia; desvelo, falta de sueño; vela, el acto de vigilar, velar, guardar o espiar.

watchmaker ['wɒtʃmeɪkəʳ] [uoch-mei-kaʳ], *s.* Relojero.

watchman ['wɒtʃmən] [uoch-man], *s.* Sereno, guarda, la persona destinada para decir por la noche en voz alta la hora que es, y para rondar, prevenir los robos y avisar en caso de incendio.

watchword ['wɒtʃwɜːd] [uoch-uerd], *s. (Mil.)* Contraseña, santo y seña, consigna que se da a un centinela.

water ['wɔːtəʳ] [uo-taʳ], *s.* 1. Agua (H2O). **Rain-water,** agua llovediza. **Fresh-water,** agua dulce. **Spring-water,**

agua de fuente o de manantial. **Holy water**, agua bendita. **Well-water o pump-water**, agua de pozo. **Running water**, agua viva o corriente. **Salt water**, agua del mar, agua salada. 2. Cualquier extensión determinada de agua; v. gr. un lago, un río, un mar. **To go by water**, ir por mar. **High water**, marea alta. **Low water**, marea baja. 3. Serosidad o humor de los animales; transpiración, lágrimas u orina. 4. Agua, preparación acuosa que tiene una substancia gaseosa o volátil en solución. **Ammonia water**. agua amoniacal. **Chlorine water**, agua de cloro. **Orange-flower water**, agua de azahar. 5. Aguas, los visos que hacen las piedras preciosas. 6. Viso ondeante de los tejidos. 7. *(Com.)* Acciones que se emiten sin aumento del capital pagado para representarlas. **Smooth water**, agua mansa, agua tranquila. **Still waters run deep**, *(Prov.)* del agua mansa líbreme Dios, que de la recia (o brava) me guardaré yo. **To swim under water**, nadar entre dos aguas. **Water**, se usa en inglés muy a menudo en composición para expresar lo que sirve para contener agua, y lo que está o crece en ella. etc. **Water-back**, sistema de tubos en una estufa para la circulación de agua caliente. **Water-bath**, baño de María. **Water-bird**, ave acuática. **Water-boatman, water-bug**, chinche de agua, insecto hemíptero que nada sobre su espalda. **Water-borne**, flotante, que flota o camina sobre el agua. **Water-brash**, pirosis, sensación picante que va del estómago a la boca. **Water-butt, water-cask**, vasija de agua, pipa. **Water-carriage**, (a) transporte por agua; (b) transporte del agua por medio de cañerías. **etc.** **Water-closet**, letrina a la inglesa; retrete excusado. **Water-colors** *(Pint.)* aguadas, colores líquidos de que se usa en la pintura al temple; acuarela. **Painting in water-colors**, pintura a la aguada o lo que se pinta con colores líquidos. **Water-course**, (a) corriente de agua; río, arroyo; (b) madre, lecho de un río o arroyo; (c) derecho de aguas. **Water-cure**, (a) hidroterapia, tratamiento de ciertas enfermedades por medio del agua; (b) establecimiento de hidroterapia. **Water-dog**, (a) perro de aguas; (b) *(Fam.)* marinero viejo. **Water-engine**, máquina hidráulica. **Water-gage, water-gauge**, indicador de nivel de agua. **Water-gilding**, loradura. **Water-gruel**, una especie de polenta hecha con harina de avena mondada y cocida en agua. **Water-hammer**, sacudimiento que hace el agua cuando se detiene su corriente de un modo repentino; también, martillo de agua (toy). **Water-ice**, sorbete; helado hecho con algún zumo de fruta sabrosa, azúcar y agua solamente. **Water-level**, nivel de agua; instrumento para hacer las nivelaciones. **Water-lily**, *(Bot.)* ninfea, nenúfar; cualquier planta del género Castalia. **Yellow water-lily**, nenúfar amarillo, lirio amarillo de agua. **Water-line**, *(Mar.)* línea de agua, línea de flotación. **Load-water-line**, *(Mar.)* línea de agua cargada. **Water-logged**, *(Mar.)* anegado en agua. **Water-mark**, (a) la señal que se hace para saber a donde llega el agua; (b) filigrana, marca translúcida hecha en el papel al tiempo de fabricarlo. **Water-mill**, aceña, molino de agua. **Water-mint**, *(Bot.)* hierbabuena acuática. **Water-mite**, cresa de agua, pequeño insecto acuática. de patas ciliadas que le permiten nadar. **Water-pail**, cubo. **Water-pot**, aguamanil; jarro para servir el agua; regadera. **Water-pitcher**, (a) aguamanil, cántaro para agua. (b) *(Bot.)* cualquier planta de la familia americana de las sarracenáceas. **Water-plantain**, alisma. **Water-power**, (a) fuerza motriz del agua aplicada a la maquinaria; (b) caída o descenso en una corriente, de la cual puede obtenerse fuerza motriz. **Water-proof**, *a.* Impermeable, a prueba de agua. - *va.* Hacer impermeable. -*s.* Material impermeable; capote u otra prenda de vestir hecha de ese material. **Water-trough**, abrevadero. **Water-tank**, aljibe, cisterna, receptáculo para el agua. **Water-tower**, (a) tubo de alimentación, el que sirve para la distribución del agua; (b) armazón de acero semejante a una torre para sostener una manguera con la cual se hace llegar el agua a lo alto de los edificios. **Water-wheel**, rueda hidráulica. **Water-ouzel**, cinclo de agua, pájaro. **Water-rail**, rascón, ave zancuda. **Water-rate**, costo del abono a las aguas de una ciudad. **Water-scorpion**, escorpión

de agua, nepa, insecto hemíptero. **Water-shed**, vertiente de una montaña; línea divisoria de las aguas. **Water-side**, borde u orilla de agua. **Water-soak**, *va.* meter, empapar en agua. **Water-spaniel**, perro fino de aguas. **Water-tight**, impermeable, que no deja pasar el agua. **Water-rat**, rata de agua. **Water-sail**, *(Mar.)* vela de agua. **Water-sapphire**, zafiro oriental. **Water-spring**, manantial. **Water-way**, *s.* (a) canal o corriente de agua como medio de comunicación; (b) *pl. (Mar.)* trancaniles, canalones. **Water-worn**, gastado, hecho liso por la acción del agua.

water, *va.* 1. Regar, humedecer, mojar, bañar. 2. Hacerse agua. 3. Llorar, lagrimear. **To water cattle**, abrevar, dar de beber al ganado. **To water ships**, *(Mar.)* hacer aguada. **To water wine**, aguar o bautizar el vino. -*vn.* Chorrear agua o humedad. **His mouth waters**, le da dentera, se le hace agua la boca.

water-cooled ['wɔːtəkuːld] [uo-ta-kuld], *a.* Enfriado por agua.

water-cress ['wɔːtəkres] [uo-ta-kres], *s. (Bot.)* Berro, planta crucífera comestible.

waterfall ['wɔːtəfɔːl] [uo-ta-fol], *s.* Cascada, caída de agua.

water-fowl ['wɔːtəfaʊl] [uo-ta-faul], *s. (Orn.)* Ave acuática.

water front ['wɔːtəfrʌnt] [uo-ta-front], *s.* Parte de la ciudad que da al mar, lago, etc.

water glass ['wɔːtəglɑːs] [uo-ta-glas], *s.* 1. Vaso para beber agua. 2. Nivel de agua. 3. Clepsidra.

water heater ['wɔːtəhiːtə'] [uo-ta-ji-ta'], *s.* Calentador de agua.

watering ['wɔːtərɪŋ] [uo-ta-rin], *s.* 1. Riego; acción del que riega, moja o abreva; irrigación. 2. *(Mar.)* Acción de hacer agua; aguada. 3. El hacer ondulaciones o visos ondeantes en algo, como adorno.

watering-place ['wɔːtərɪŋˌpleɪs] [uo-ta-rin-pleis], *s.* 1. Aguadero o abrevadero. 2. El pueblo o paraje, ordinariamente a la orilla del mar, a donde concurre mucha gente a tomar baños y divertirse. 3. *(Mar.)* El lugar donde se hace aguada.

watering-pot ['wɔːtərɪŋpɒt] [uo-ta-rin-pot], *s.* Regadera.

watermelon ['wɔːtəmelən] [uo-ta-me-lon], *s. (Bot.)* Sandía, planta y su fruto. *(S. Am.)* Patilla.

water meter ['wɔːtəˌmiːtə'] [uo-ta-mi-ta'], *s.* Contador de agua.

water ski ['wɔːtəskiː] [uo-ta-ski], *s.* Esquí acuático.

water softener ['wɔːtəsɒfnə'] [uo-ta-sof-na'], *s.* Suavizador o adelgazador de agua.

water-spout ['wɔːtəspaʊt] [uo-ta-spaut], *s.* Manga, bomba marina, torbellino de agua.

water tower ['wɔːtətaʊə'] [uo-ta-taua'], *s.* Depósito elevado de agua.

water wave ['wɔːtəweɪv] [uo-ta-ueiv], *s.* Ondulado al agua. Se aplica al cabello.

water-work ['wɔːtəwɜːk] [uo-ta-uek], *s.* 1. Cualquier máquina o artificio hidráulico, como cascadas, surtidores o chorros de agua que saltan, etc. 2. *pl.* Obras hidráulicas, sistema de máquinas, edificios y enseres para la distribución de las aguas.

watery ['wɔːtərɪ] [uo-ta-ri], *a.* 1. Acuoso, ácueo, aguanoso; húmedo, lleno de agua. 2. Claro, ralo o líquido como agua. 3. Insípido, evaporado. 4. Lloroso. **This soup is watery**, esta sopa está acuosa.

watt [wɒt] [uot], *s.* Vatio, cantidad de trabajo eléctrico equivalente a un julio por segundo; grado en que la fuerza electro-motriz es de un voltio, y la intensidad de la corriente un amperio.

wattage ['wɒtɪdʒ] [uo-tich], *s.* Potencia en vatios.

wattle ['wɒtl] [uo-tel], *s.* 1. Zarzo, el tejido de varas, cañas o mimbres. 2. Barbas de gallo, la excrecencia de carne roja que les cuelga a los gallos debajo del pico.

wattle, *va.* Enzarzar, poner zarzas o cubrir algo con ellas; entretejer, entrelazar; asegurar con mimbres.

wave [weɪv] [ueiv], *s.* 1. Ola, onda. 2. Aguas, visos, vetas o desigualdades que forman algunas piedras, cristales, etc. **Beating of the waves**, embate del agua o de las olas. **Shock of a wave**, golpe de mar. 3. *(Fís.)* Onda, undulación, alteración del equilibrio de un cuerpo o de un medio, que se propaga de uno a otro punto con movimiento continuo. **Soundwave,**

light-wave, onda del sonido, de la luz. 4. Undulación, movimiento semejante al de las ondas; movimiento de la mano, ademán. 5. Ola, lo que sobreviene a manera de oleaje, en gran volumen o con mucha fuerza; diluvio. 6. Apariencia ondulante en una tela. 7. Comba, curva que se halla en una superficie o canto ondulante. 8. Racha (rise, increase). 8. Ademán, seña. **Wave-offering**, ofrenda de las primicias entre los judíos. **The pain came in waves**, el dolor vino a rachas.

wave, *va. y vn.* 1. Tremolar, batir, hablando de banderas, gallardetes, etc. 2. Agitar alguna cosa de modo que forme ondas. 4. Ondear, hacer que una cosa tenga la figura o el movimiento de las ondas. 5. Fluctuar o vacilar entre dos cosas o pareceres opuestos. 6. Blandir, mover alguna cosa con un movimiento trémulo. 7. Hacer señas.

waved ['weɪvd] [ueivd], *a.* Ondeado.

wavelength ['weɪvleŋθ] [uei-lenz], *s.* *(Radio)* Longitud de onda.

waver ['weɪvəʳ] [uei-vaʳ], *vn.* 1. Ondear, ondearse. 2. Fluctuar, vacilar, balancear, dudar, estar suspenso, estar perplejo o indeciso(to doubt, hesitate, hover).

wavering ['weɪvərɪŋ] [uei-ve-rin], *a.* Ligero, inconstante. -*s.* Irresolución, incertidumbre, vacilación.

wavy ['weɪvɪ] [ueivi], *a.* Ondeado, undoso, que hace ondas o que se levanta a manera de ondas. **She has a wavy hair**, ella tiene el pelo ondeado.

wax [wæks], *s.* 1. Cera, substancia crasa que segregan las abejas. 2. Cera de los oídos. 3. Cera vegetal o mineral. 4. Lacre. **Wax-candle**, vela de cera; cirio, bujía. **Wax-taper**, blandón, hacha de cera. **Wax-tape**, cerilla. *(Amer.)* Cerillo. **Wax in large cakes**, cera en marquetas. **Wax-chandler**, cerero. **Sealing-wax**, lacre. **Ear-wax**, cera de los oídos. **Shoemaker's wax**, cerote de zapatero. **Maple-wax**, *(E.U.y el Canadá)* Substancia espesa que se obtiene cociendo la savia del arce sacarino. **Wax doll**, muñeca de cera. **Wax-end**, hilo encerado para coser calzado. Se escribe también *waxed end*. **Wax light**, vela de cera; cerilla. **Wax-like**, semejante a la cera. **Wax model(I)ing**, modelado en cera.

wax, *va.* Encerar con cera alguna cosa. -*vn.* 1. Crecer, aumentarse (to grow, increase). 2. Cundir; hacerse; ponerse, irse haciendo. **To wax warm**, acalorarse, encenderse en cólera. **This opinion is waxing stronger every day**, esta opinión se va haciendo más fuerte de día en día.

waxen ['wæksn] [uak-sen], *a.* De cera; que consta totalmente o en parte de cera; semejante a la cera: plástico.

wax paper ['wæksən] [uak-sen], *s.* Papel encerado.

waxwing ['wækswɪŋ] [uaks-uin], *s.* Pájaro con cresta y de plumaje pardo en su mayor parte, con los extremos de las plumas secundarias del ala guarnecidos de apéndice córneos parecidos a lacre encarnado o amarillo; picotera. Ampelis.

waxwork ['wækswɜːk] [uaks-uerk], *s.* Obra en cera; figura de cera. -*pl.* Colección de figuras de cera.

waxy ['wæksɪ] [uak-si], *a.* 1. Semejante a cera; plástico, blando, que cede. 2. De color de cera. 3. Hecho de cera o abundante en ella; frotado o pulido en cera.

way [weɪ] [uei], *s.* 1. Camino, vía, la tierra hollada por donde se transita; camino, senda, conducto, según sea la cosa de que se habla; pasaje, curso, canal; lugar para pasar; oportunidad para pasar, para ir o para venir (passageway). 2. Espacio recorrido; de aquí, espacio de terreno. 3. Curso o dirección; ruta, rota, derrota, camino de viaje (a route, direction). 4. Modo, medio o manera para hacer una cosa; expediente (a method, manner). 5. Uso, costumbre, hábito; máxima (habit). 6. Conducta o modo de obrar; sistema, línea de conducta; manera de portarse. 7. Medio, medida, acto. 8. Modo. punto o relación. **He erred in two ways**, erró de dos modos. 9. Paso de un lugar a otro; movimiento progresivo; adelantamiento. 10. *pl. (Mec.)* Maderos longitudinales de la basada para botar al agua un buque. 11. *(Fam.)* Estado o condición (de salud). 12. Estorbo, obstáculo. 13. Distancia (distance). **Am I in your way?**, ¿estorbo a Ud.?, ¿sirvo a Ud. de estorbo? **Over the way o Across the way**, a otro lado, en

el otro lado, en frente. **Every way**, por todas partes, de todos lados. **By the way** de paso, de camino, de pasada, por incidencia. **any way**, de cualquier modo, de cualquiera manera, como se quiera. **No way**, de ningún modo, de ninguna manera. **Crossway**, travesía. **Path-way**, senda, sendero. **Way in**, entrada. **Way through**, pasaje. **Way out**, salida. **We are a great way off**, estamos aún muy lejos o estamos muy distantes. **To go the same way**, llevar el mismo camino. **To make way**, atravesar, abrirse camino. **Make way!** ¡fuera, fuera! apartarse, dejen Vds. pasar. **To go out of the way**, extraviarse. **To keep out of the way**, esconderse, ocultarse, evitar el encontrarse con alguno. **To have one's way**, *(Fam.)* Salirse con la suya. **Use your own way**, hágalo Vd. como quiera o hágalo Vd. a su modo. **Go your ways**, anda, vete. **Ways and means**, medios y arbitrios. **To get under way**, *(Mar.)* levar, comenzar a navegar, hacerse a la vela. **To fetch way**, *(Mar.)* tener juego. **Ship's way**, *(Mar.)* andar del bajel. **The ship has head-way**, *(Mar.)* el navío lleva vía. **To have stern-way**, *(Mar.)* ir atrás. **Covered o covert way**, *(Fort.)* camino cubierto. **Cross way**, encrucijada. **Milky way**, vía láctea; camino de Santiago. **On the way**, en ruta, al pasar. **By way of**, por la vía de, pasando por. **By the way**, de camino, al pasar por; sea dicho de paso. **On the way to**, en camino de, con rumbo a. **Out of the way**, fuera del camino; escondido; poco ordinario, extraordinario, original. **To be out of the way**, estar fuera del camino, desviarse. **You are out of the way**, Ud. no está en el buen camino. **To be in the way**, estar en el camino o en la vía; incomodar, servir de estorbo. **To go the way of all things**, ir donde todo va. **To go the way of all the earth**, morir. **Right of way**, derecho de paso por la propiedad de otro; servidumbre de paso.

wayfarer ['weɪfɛərəʳ] [uei-fea-raʳ], *s.* Pasajero, viajador, viajante, caminante.

wayfaring ['weɪfɛərɪŋ] [uei-fea-rin], *a.* Que camina, que va de viaje o de camino.

waylay ['weɪleɪ] [uei-lei], *va.* Insidiar, poner asechanzas o celadas, acechar o asechar (to ambush).

waylayer ['weɪleɪəʳ] [uei-leiaʳ], *s.* Acechador, espía.

wayless ['weɪlɪs] [uei-les], *a.* Sin sendero, vereda ni vestigio, sin camino.

waymark ['weɪmɑːk] [uei-mark], *s.* Mojón, poste para señalar el camino.

way station ['weɪˌsteɪʃən] [uei-stei-shon], *s.* *(F.C.)* Estación intermedia.

way train ['weɪtreɪn] [uei-trein], *s.* *(F.C.)* Tren local.

way ward ['weɪwəd] [uei-uord], *a.* 1. Díscolo, indócil, cabezudo, porfiado; que se aparta de la conducta debida, desobediente (undisciplined, selfwilled, rebellious). 2. Que no tiene curso definido, vacilante.

waywardly ['weɪwədlɪ] [uei-uord-li], *adv.* Porfiadamente, con indocilidad, con perversidad; malamente.

waywardness ['weɪwədnɪs] [uei-uord-nes], *s.* Indocilidad, perversidad; capricho, petulancia; malignidad, ruindad.

we [wiː] [ui], *pron. prim. pers. pl.* de I. 1. Nosotros, nosotras. **We are all well**, todos estamos buenos. **We are right**, tenemos razón, hacemos bien en. 2. La gente en general, la especie humana; se expresa a menudo en español por el pronombre se. **We are told**, se nos dice, nos dicen. 3. El escritor u orador.

weak [wiːk] [uik], *a.* 1. Débil, endeble, flojo, flaco, feble, tanto en lo físico como en lo moral (dicky, faint, feeble, infirm). 2. Frágil, débil, sujeto a errar o pecar; falto de juicio o prudencia. 3. Deficiente en fuerza, estabilidad o eficacia (instrumento, estructura, parte); incapaz de sostener un ataque a viva fuerza; mal fortificado; sin recursos; no convincente; no apoyado en la razón, en la verdad; que no contiene bastantes principios activos, estimulantes, nutritivos; ligero. 4. Enfermizo, enclenque. 5. Imbécil. 6. Flojo de precio, cuyo precio va bajando. **The wheat market is weak**, el mercado de trigo está flojo o en baja. 7. *(Gram. ingl.) (Verbo)* regular;

que se conjuga añadiendo *ed, d, o t*, para formar el pretérito y el participio pasado; que forma el plural, añadiendo *s* o *es* al singular; *(adjetivo)* de comparación regular. **Weakhanded,** que tiene escasos ayudantes; también, que tiene las manos débiles. **Weak-headed,** débil o pobre de inteligencia. **Weak-kneed,** que tiene las rodillas débiles; *(Fig.)* falto de resolución, de energía. **Weak-minded,** débil de espíritu, pobre de inteligencia; simple, mentecato. **Weak side,** el flaco, la flaqueza, la debilidad, fragilidad o falta principal por donde una persona claudica, y también la pasión que la domina; el lado débil.

weaken ['wiːkən] [ui-ken], *va.* 1. Debilitar, enflaquecer, quitar o disminuir las fuerzas. 2. Disminuir, atenuar. *-vn.* Enflaquecer, hacerse menos fuerte.

weakling ['wiːklɪŋ] [ui-klin], *s.* Alfeñique, persona delicada de cuerpo y complexión.

weakly ['wiːklɪ] [ui-kli], *adv.* Débilmente, sin vigor, ni fuerzas; fríamente. *-a.* Enfermizo, achacoso, enclenque.

weakness ['wiːknɪs] [uik-nes], *s.* 1. Debilidad, falta de vigor y fuerzas, flaqueza, endeblez, flojedad. 2. Fragilidad, debilidad, considerada moralmente; el flaco o la parte flaca de una persona. 3. Imbecilidad, mentecatez.

weal [wiːl] [uil], *s.* 1. Felicidad, prosperidad, bien, bienestar (felicity, happiness). 2. Estado, república, interés público; hoy se usa sólo en ciertas locuciones.

weald [wiːld] [uild], *s.* Bosque. *V.* WOLD.

wealth [welθ] [uilz], *s.* 1. Riqueza, abundancia de dinero, bienes o cosas preciosas; caudal (riches). 2. Prosperidad; opulencia; gran abundancia.

wealthily ['welθɪlɪ] [uel-zi-li], *adv.* Ricamente, opulentemente.

wealthy ['welθɪ] [uel-zi], *a.* Rico, opulento (rich). **Wealthier,** más rico.

wean [wiːn] [uin], *va.* 1. Destetar, apartar del pecho de la madre. 2. Apartar de algún vicio o costumbre anterior; enajenar el afecto de. **The child is being weaned,** se está destetando al niño.

weapon ['wepən] [ue-pon], *s.* 1. Arma; todo género de instrumento destinado para atacar y ofender. 2. *pl. (Biol.)* Púas, espinas; aguijones, garras, etc,; todos los medios de defensa de los vegetales y animales. **Deadly weapon,** arma mortífera. **Cutting weapon,** arma de corte, arma blanca.

weaponed ['wepənd] [ue-pond], *a.* Armado, surtido de armas.

weaponless ['wepənlɪs] [ue-pon-les], *a.* Desarmado, que no lleva armas.

weaponry ['wepənrɪ] [ue-pon-ri], *s.* Armamentos, armas, arsenal.

wear [wɛəʳ] [ueaʳ], *va. (pret.* WORE. *pp.* WORN). 1. Usar, llevar o traer alguna cosa encima del cuerpo (to dress, carry). 2. Mostrar, llevar usualmente, de una manera determinada. 3. Mostrar, tener aspecto o apariencia de, exhibir (to display). 4. Gastar o consumir la cosa de que uno se sirve; consumir la cosa de que uno se sirve: consumir aniquilando o destruyendo lentamente, como lo hace el tiempo, el uso, etc.; disminuir por el roce. 5. Consumir gastando el tiempo. 6. Apurar, hacer perder la fuerza o paciencia; aburrir, enfadar. 7. Consentir (to approve, accept) *-vn.* 1. Gastarse, consumirse o destruirse lentamente una cosa. 2. Pasarse, correr el tiempo. **To wear away.** gastar o ir gastando, consumiendo o destruyendo; decaer; gastarse, consumirse. **To wear down,** gastar, consumir, disminuir por el roce. **To wear off,** usarse, gastarse; borrarse; pasarse, disiparse, desaparecer. **To wear on,** pasarse lentamente. **To wear one's heart on one's sleeve,** andar con la cara descubierta, llevar el corazón en la mano. **To wear out,** gastar, romper o romperse a fuerza de uso; cansar, fastidiar. **To wear out one's patience,** hacer perder la paciencia. **Worn to a thread, worn threadbare,** gastado hasta dejar ver la trama; enteramente gastado. **To wear a youthful form,** tener aspecto juvenil. **To wear a tall hat,** llevar sombrero de copa, o de copa alta. **Worn-out clothes,** vestidos usados. **To wear well,** durar largo tiempo, ser duradero, estar bueno para usarse.

wear, *va. y vn. (Mar.)* Virar; virar viento atrás. *(Por VEER).*

wear, *s.* 1. Uso, gasto, la acción y efecto de usar alguna cosa; acción de llevar, estado de lo llevado. 2. La cosa que se usa o gasta; moda, boga. **It is for my own wear,** es para mi propio uso. **Very little the worse for wear,** casi nuevo, casi sin usar. **Wear and tear,** desgaste, deterioro. **Silk for summer wear,** seda para verano.

wear *s. V.* WEIR.

wearable ['wɛərəbl] [uea-ra-bol], *a.* Que se puede llevar, usar o gastar.

wearer ['wɛərəʳ] [uea-raʳ], *s.* El que lleva, gasta o usa alguna cosa.

wearied ['wɛərɪəd] [uea-ried], *a.* Cansado, fatigado, enfadado, fastidiado.

weariness ['wɛərɪnɪs] [uea-ri-nes], *s.* 1. Lasitud, cansancio, fatiga. **2.** Enfado, fastidio.

wearing ['wɛərɪŋ] [uea-rin], *s.* 1. Acción o manera de llevar. 2. Desgaste, deterioro; pérdida (por el roce o por el tiempo). 3. Decaimiento, paso. *-a.* 1. Que se lleva. 2. Cansado, pesado (exhausting). **Wearing apparel,** vestidos, ropaje, ropa exterior.

wearisome ['wɛərɪsəm] [uea-ri-som], *a.* Tedioso, fastidioso, pesado, enfadoso; fatigante, cansado.

weary ['wɛərɪ] [uea-ri], *va.* Cansar, fatigar, aburrir, enfadar, molestar. *-vn.* Fatigarse, cansarse. **To weary out,** moler, cansar la paciencia, fatigar.

weary, *a.* 1. Cansado, abrumado, fatigado, rendido de cansancio (tired). 2. Aburrido, enfadado, fastidiado. 3. Enfadoso, tedioso, fastidioso. **He's a weary man,** es un hombre aburrido.

weasel ['wiːzl] [ui-sel], *s.* Comadreja, mamífero carnívoro del género Putorius.

weather ['weðəʳ] [ue-daʳ], *s.* 1. Tiempo, estado atmosférico en una época dada, o en general. 2. *(Fig.)* Vicisitudes de la suerte. 3. Temporal, tempestad; el conjunto o uno cualquiera de los fenómenos meteorológicos ordinarios, frío, calor. **How is the weather today?** ¿qué tiempo, hace hoy? **It is bad weather, fine weather,** hace mal tiempo, buen tiempo. **Weather Bureau,** oficina de Señales Meteorológicas (en el Ministerio de Agricultura de Washington). **Weather-board,** (a) tabla superpuesta; (b) lado del viento (de un buque). **Weather-boarding,** solapadura de tablas; *(Mar.)* falcas, cubichete. **Weather-gange,** barlovento o lof; cualquier ventaja lograda. **Weather-proof,** a prueba del tiempo. **Weather-prophet,** pronosticador de las mudanzas del tiempo. **Weather-signal,** señal meteorológica (bandera, etc.), que se emplea para indicar las variaciones del tiempo. **Weather-tight,** a prueba de aire, impenetrable al aire. **Weather-side,** *(Mar.)* costado de barlovento. **Weather-sheets,** *(Mar.)* escotas de barlovento. **Hard a weather,** meter todo a barlovento. **Stress of weather,** mal tiempo. *-a.* Al viento del lado del viento.

weather, *va.* 1. Aguantar (el temporal), resistir a, sufrir, superar; sobrevivir a (la adversidad). 2. Orear, airear, poner alguna cosa a que le dé el aire; secar. 3. *(Mar.)* Montar o ganar barlovento; doblar, pasar más allá. *-vn.* 1. Sufrir cambios resultantes de la exposición al aire. 2. Resistir los efectos de los cambios atmosféricos. **To weather out,** sufrir, superar. **The poor fellow weathers it out,** el pobre va tirando. **To weather a point,** salirse con algo o conseguir una cosa venciendo algún obstáculo.

weather-beaten ['weðəˌbiːtn] [ue-da-bi-ten], *a.* Curtido, acostumbrado a las inclemencias del aire; gastado, extenuado, fatigado (por el mal tiempo). **A weather-beaten o weatherdriven ship,** bajel trabajado por la tormenta.

weather-cock ['weðəkɒk] [ue-da-kok], *s.* 1. Gallo de campanario, la figura de gallo que sirve de remate a las veletas de las torres, o que forma por sí misma la veleta y señala la parte por donde viene el viento. 2. Veleta, persona inconstante, fácil o mudable. **Weather-eye,** observación de las variaciones del tiempo; se usa principalmente en la locución **to keep one's weather-eye open,** estar alerta, ser circunspecto. **Weather-glass,** una forma de barómetro. **Poor**

man's weather-glass, *(Bot.)* anagálida, hierba pajarera, cuyas flores no se abren en mal tiempo.

weathering ['weðərɪŋ] [ue-da-rin], *s. (Geol.)* Desgaste de las rocas por la acción atmosférica.

weatherly ['weðəlɪ] [ue-da-li], *a. (Mar.)* Que va de bolina, de barlovento.

weather-strip ['weðəstrɪp] [ue-da-strip], *s.* Burlete. *-va.* Acondicionar con burlete.

weathertile ['weðətaɪl] [ue-da-tail], *va.* Poner tejas en la extremidad de una tapia o pared para resguardarla del tiempo.

weather-vane ['weðəveɪn] [ue-da-vein], *s.* Veleta de torre, de campanario, etc.

weave [wi:v] [uiv], *va.* 1. Tejer; trenzar, cruzar una cosa con otra tejiéndolas (to knit, spin). 2. Unir, reunir. 3. Entrelazar, interponer; construir con elaboración. *-vn.* Tejer, trabajar en telar. **The old woman was weaving on her loom**, la anciana estaba tejiendo su telar.

weaver ['wi:vəʳ] [ui-vaʳ], *s.* 1. Tejedor, el artesano que teje telas, sean de seda o lana, etc. 2. *V. Weaver-bird.* 3. Araña tejedora. **Weaver-bird**, tejedor, páaro parecido a un pinzón, que construye nidos entrelazados.

weaving ['wi:vɪŋ] [ui-vin], *s.* Tejido, el arte y modo de tejer.

web [web] [ueb], *s.* 1. Tela, tejido, obra tejida. 2. Hoja o rollo de material, formados como una tela. 3. Trama, lazo; artificio engañoso, trampa. 4. Palmura, membrana que une los dedos de los palmípedos. 5. Tela de araña. 6. Barba o pelo de pluma. 7. Plancha (de metal) que une las partes de alguna cosa.

webbed [webd] [uebd], *a.* 1. Lo que está unido por medio de una telilla. 2. Palmípedo.

webbing ['webɪŋ] [ue-bin], *s.* 1. Cinta para cinchas. 2. Pretal.

web-footed ['web'fʊtɪd] [ueb-fu-tid], *a.* Palmeado. palmípedo.

wed [wed] [ued], *va.* 1. Casar; tomar por marido o por mujer. 2. Dar en casamiento. 3. Unirse para siempre a, o emprender una cosa con intención de no dejarla nunca. *-vn.* Casarse, contraer matrimonio.

wedded ['wedɪd] [ue-did], *pp.* Casado. **Wedded to his own opinion**, testarudo, encasquetado, casado con su opinión.

wedding ['wedɪŋ] [ue-din], *s.* 1. Boda, nupcias, casamiento. la celebración del matrimonio (a marriage ceremony). 2. Aniversario de boda. **Silver wedding**, las bodas de plata, el aniversario vigésimo quinto de la boda. **Golden wedding**, bodas de oro, el aniversario quincuagésimo de la boda. **Wedding dress**, traje nupcial o de boda. **Wedding ring**, anillo nupcial (de novio o novia). **She often talks her wedding day**, ella habla con frecuencia del día de su boda.

wedding cake ['wedɪŋkeɪk] [ue-din-keik], *s.* Pastel o torta de boda.

wedge [wedʒ] [uedch], *s.* 1. Cuña para partir leña o abrir otros cuerpos duros, y cualquier otro cuerpo que tiene su figura. 2. *(Geom.)* Prisma triangular.

wedge, *va.* 1. Acuñar, meter cuñas para rajar, fácilmente alguna cosa. 2. Apretar, abrir o fijar con cuñas.

wedlock ['wedlɒk] [ued-lok], *s.* Matrimonio, himeneo; poéticamente connubio.

Wednesday ['wenzdeɪ] [uens-dei], *s.* Miércoles, el cuarto día de la semana. **Ash-Wednesday**, miércoles de ceniza. **Wednesday morning**, el miércoles por la mañana.

wee [wi:] [ui], *a. (Fam. y esco.)* Pequeño, chico (small, tiny).

weed [wi:d] [uid], *s.* 1. Hierbajo, mala hierba, cualquiera hierba nociva o inútil; también toda planta herbácea que se halla fuera de su propio lugar. 2. Lo que crece en abundancia dañosa o inútil. 3. *(Fam.)* Tabaco. 4. Prenda (de vestir) o ropa de luto. **Sea-weed**, alga. **Window's-weeds**, el vestido y los velos de luto de una viuda.

weed, *va.* 1. Escardar, desarraigar o arrancar las hierbas nocivas o inútiles. 2. Escardar, apartar lo malo de lo bueno. 3. Librar de alguna cosa ofensiva o dañosa.

weeder ['wi:dəʳ] [ui-daʳ], *s.* 1. Escardador. 2. El que libra o separa de alguna cosa ofensiva o dañosa.

weedhook ['wi:dhʊk] [uid-juk], *s.* Escarda, azadilla con que se arrancan las hierbas nocivas.

weedless ['wi:dlɪs] [uid-les], *a.* Libre de malas hierbas o hierbajos.

weedy ['wi:dɪ] [ui-di], *a.* Lleno de malas hierbas, por escardar.

week [wi:k] [uik], *s.* 1. Semana, el espacio de siete días; *(Fam.)* ocho días. 2. Los seis días de trabajo. **So much a week**, tanto por semana o a la semana. **The next week**, la semana que viene. **This day week**, de hoy en ocho.

week-day ['wi:kdeɪ] [uik-dei], *s.* Feria, cualquiera de los días de la semana excepto el domingo; día de trabajo.

week end ['wi:k'end] [uik-end], Fin de semana.

weekly ['wi:klɪ] [ui-kli], *a.* Semanal, que sucede o se hace una vez a la semana; hebdomadario, de la semana. **Weekly paper**, semanario. *-s.* Periódico semanal. *-adv.* Semanalmente, por semana, en todas las semanas o en cada una de ellas.

weep [wi:p] [uip], *va. y vn.* (*pret. y pp.* WEPT). 1. Llorar, verter lágrimas, hacer duelo o sentimiento por alguna cosa. 2. Llorar, verter o derramar lágrimas por algún pesar o placer. 3. Llorar, lamentar, condolerse de las calamidades o infortunios. 4. Llorar, destilar, caer el líquido gota a gota: se dice de algunas plantas. 5. Estar pendiente, inclinarse hacia el suelo. **To weep for**, llorar de. **Weeping ash, weeping willow**, fresno llorón, sauce llorón.

weeper ['wi:pəʳ] [ui-paʳ], *s.* 1.Llorador, el que llora. 2. Llorón, el que llora mucho.

weeping ['wi:pɪŋ] [ui-pin], *s.* Lloro, lágrimas. **Weeping-grounds**, tierras pantanosas o muy húmedas.

weepingly ['wi:pɪŋlɪ] [ui-pin-li], *adv.* Llorosamente, con lágirmas, con lloro.

weet [wi:t] [uit], *vn.* Saber. *V.* WIT.

weever ['wi:vəʳ] [ui-vaʳ], *s.* Traquino, dragón marino; pez británico.

weevil ['wi:vl] [ui-vil], *s.* 1. Gorgojo, insecto coleóptero diminuto. 2. Cualquier insecto dañino para las mieses entrojadas. 3. Larva de una mosca perjudicial al trigo.

weft [weft] [ueft], *s.* 1. Trama, hebra que pasa de un lado a otro de la urdimbre. *V.* WOOF. 2. *(Des.) V.* WAIF. **Weft of hair**, trenza de cabello.

weigh [weɪ] [uei], *va.* 1. Pesar, averiguar el peso de una cosa por medio de algún instrumento. 2. Pesar, examinar o considerar con relación al valor, a la importancia o a las ventajas; poner en la misma balanza, apreciar. 3. Sobrecargar, agobiar, oprimir. 4. Levar anclas. *-vn.* 1. Pesar, tener o hacer tanto o cuanto, pesar una cosa. 2. Pesar, tener estimación y valor, ser digno de mucho aprecio, ser de importancia, ser estimado. 3. Pesar sobre, ser opresivo, estar a carga. 4. *(Mar.)* Levar anclas; hacerse a la vela. **To weigh down**, pesar más una cosa que otra, exceder en peso, sobrepujar; hundirse una cosa por su propio peso; sobrecarga; oprimir. **To out-weigh**, sobrepasar. **To weigh out**, pesar (en cantidades pequeñas). **To weigh anchor**, *(Mar.)* levar el ancla. **This reason ought to weigh with you**, esta razón debe ser de peso para Vd.

weighable ['weɪəbl] [uei-a-bol], *a.* Capaz de ser pesado o vendido al peso.

weigher ['weɪəʳ] [ueiaʳ], *s.* Pesador. **Public weigher**, almotacén, juez de pesos y medidas.

weighing ['weɪɪŋ] [uei-in], *s.* 1. Peso, acción de pesar. 2. Pesada, cantidad pesada de una sola vez. **Weighing-machine**, máquina para pesar.

weight [weɪt] [ueit], *va.* Cargar un peso o con un peso; atar un peso a. *-s.* 1. Peso, pesantez, la fuerza natural con que los cuerpos se mueven hacia abajo, procedente de la pesadez o gravedad. 2. Pesadez, gravedad, la calidad de todo cuerpo grave. 3. Pesa, trozo de metal de un peso dado, que se emplea para pesar. 4. Peso, la gravedad determinada de una cosa, y también el instrumento que sirve para examinarla; masa, masa pesada. 5. Peso, carga, gravamen. 6. Peso, entidad, sustancia, importancia. 7. Sistema graduado de pesas. **Overweight**, sobrepeso. **Gross weight**, peso bruto. **Net o neat weight**, peso neto. **Defect in weight**, desmedro. **Make-weight**, añadidura. **Stamped weight**, peso marcado, señalado o pasado por el contraste. **Hundred-weight**, quintal. **By-weight**, al peso. **To make weight**, completar, hacer el peso. **It is worth its weight in gold**, vale su peso en oro. **Standard weight**, peso legal, peso normal o modelo.

weightily ['weɪtɪlɪ] [uei-ti-li], *adv.* Pesadamente, con peso.

weightiness ['weɪtɪnɪs] [uei-ti-nes], *s.* 1. Ponderosidad, pesadez, gravedad. 2. Solidez, firmeza, fuerza. 3. Importancia, momento.

weightless ['weɪtlɪs] [ueit-les], *a.* Ingrávido.

weightlessness ['weɪtlɪsnɪs] [ueit-les-nes], *s.* Ingravidez.

weightlifting ['weɪtˌlɪftɪŋ] [ueit-lif-tin], *s.* Halterofilia.

weighty ['weɪtɪ] [uei-ti], *a.* 1. Ponderoso, pesado. 2. Grave, serio, importante, de consecuencia.

weir [wɪəʳ] [uiaʳ], *s.* 1. Paradera, compuerta de una acequia, molino, etc.; esclusa de canales; presa o parada de ríos. 2. Nasa, cañal, cerco de cañas para pescar en las presas de los ríos.

weird [wɪəd] [uiad], *a.* Sobrenatural o que se refiere a ello; que despierta sentimientos supersticiosos, no terrestre. **The Weird Sisters**, Las Parcas.

welcome ['welkəm] [uel-kom], *a.* 1. Bienvenido, bien llegado, recibido con agrado. 2. Agradable, que se recibe con placer. 3. Admitido al goce de; que puede servirse de alguna cosa. **A welcome present**, un regalo agradable. **You are welcome**, sea Vd. bienvenido. **You are welcome to it**, está al servicio de Vd.; a la disposición de Vd.; puede Vd. disponer de ello. *-inter.* ¡Bienvendio! ¡bien llegado! modo de saludar a un recién llegado. *-s.* 1. Bienvenida, buena acogida; saludo de bienvenida; el parabién que se da a otro por haber llegado con felicidad; feliz llegada o arribo. 2. El gasto o agrado con que se recibe a alguno, y el agasajo con que se le obsequia.

welcome, *va.* Dar la bienvenida a alguno.

welcomer ['welkəməʳ] [uel-ko-maʳ], *s.* El que acoge o da la bienvenida.

weld ['weld] [ueld], *s. (Bot.)* Gualda, planta de que se sirven los tintoreros para teñir de amarillo. V. WOAD.

weld, *va.* 1. Juntar o unir a golpe de martillo los pedazos de metal hechos ascua; soldar a martillo. 2. Unir en un todo homogéneo. *-s.* Soldadura a martillo en caliente.

welding ['weldɪŋ] [uel-din], *s.* Soldadura.

welfare ['welfɛəʳ] [uel-feaʳ], *s.* Bienestar. **Welfare work**, trabajo de beneficencia, obras caritativas.

welkin ['welkɪn] [uel-kin], *s. (Poét.)* Firmamento, cielo, el orbe diáfano que rodea la tierra.

well [wel] [uel], *va.* Verter, derramar, como de manantial. *-vn.* Manar, salir como de manantial; correr, finir.

well, *s.* 1. Pozo para sacar agua, gas natural, o petróleo. 2. Fuente, mananatial, nacimiento del agua. 3. Fuente, origen; lo que mana sin intermisión. 4. Cavidad, depresión o copa que se asemeja a un pozo; caja o pozo, el hueco que ocupa una escalera; vivar en una embarcación de pesca para conservar vivo el pescado; *(Mar.)* caja de bombas o sentina. **Well-borer, well-digger**, pocero. **Well-curb**, brocal (de pozo). **Well-hole**, hueco o caja de escalera; boca de pozo. **Well-spring**, manantial, fuente. **Well-sweep**, cigüeñal o cigoñal, pértiga que se usa para sacar agua. **Well-water**, agua de pozo. **Well-cleanser**, pocero, el que limpia los pozos. **Well of a fishing-boat**, *(Mar.)* Pozo de barco pescador. **Well of a ship**, *(Mar.)* arca de bomba.

well, *a.* 1. Feliz, dichoso; bein hecho o arreglado, agradable. 2. Conveniente, ventajoso, que tiene cuenta. 3. Bueno, sano. sin lesión o enfermedad alguna. 4. Que está en buen estado, que se ha repuesto de alguna desgracia o infortunio. 5. *(Ant.)* Valido, favorecido. *-adv.* bien, felizmente; favorablemente; suficientemente; convenientemente. **Well-nigh**, casi; poco más o menos. *-conj.* Pues: sea. **As well**, tan bien, lo mismo da. **As well as**, así como, también como, tanto como, lo mismo que. **Well is he**, dichoso aquél. **Well enough**, bastante bien. **Well and good**, enhorabuena, bien está. **Well, well!** ¡bien! ¡bien! como Vd. quiera. **Well then**, con que, pues bien. *Well* se usa muy frecuentemente en composición para expresar el buen estado de alguna cosa o la calidad digna de alabanza en los nombres a que se junta. **It is well for you**, afortunadamente para Vd. **All's well that ends well**, el fin corona la obra; hasta el fin nadie es dichoso. **All's well!** ¡centinela alerta! **To be well of**, tener medios de fortuna, hacer buenos negocios. **To be well to do**, estar desahogado, tener el riñón bien cubierto. **To like well**, gustar bastante. **Full well**, muy bien. **Well-accomplished**, completo, consumado; lleno de perfecciones; muy bien educado. **Well-accustomed**, muy hecho o muy acostumbrado, que tiene mucha experiencia en alguna cosa. **Well-acquainted**, muy conocido o íntimamente conocido, bien enterado. **Well-adapted**, bien adaptado o acomodado; muy a propósito para una cosa. **Well-advanced**, (a) muy adelantado; (b) lo que se propone con mucho fundamento. **Well-advised**, bien aconsejado. **Well-affected**, bien intencionado. **Well-appointed**, bien equipado. **Well-balanced**, bien equilibrado. **Well-behaved**, cortés, urbano, bien criado, atento; que tiene buena conducta. **Well-born**, bien nacido, que pertenece a buena familia. **Well-bred**, bien criado, bien educado, cortés, político. **Well-disposed**, caritativo, bien intencionado. **Well-doing**, benéfico. *-s.* Beneficencia, buenas acciones, buenas obras; prosperidad. **Well-favored**, hermoso, bien parecido, agradable a la vista. **Well-meaning**, bien inclinado, honrado, sincero, ingenuo; a menudo tiene una significación algo despreciativa. **Well-meant**, bien intencionado, hecho con buena intención. **Well-read**, que ha leído mucho, instruído, erudito. **Well-spent**, bien empleado, pasado honradamente. **Well-stricken**, muy avanzado en años. **Well-spoken**, que se expresa bien, bien dicho; urbano, de lenguaje y modales afables. **Well-stored**, bien provisto; copioso. **Well-tasted**, sabroso. **Well-timed**, oportuno, hecho a propósito. **Well-to-do**, que vive holgadamente, que tiene el riñón bien cubierto. **Well-turned**, (a) simétrico o primoroso (como el trabajo hecho a torno); (b) construido o ejecutado con gracia o maña. **Well-wisher**, amigo, partidario, la persona que tiene cariño o afecto a otra. **Well-worded**, bien dicho, bien expresado. **Well-worn**, (a) gastado, echado a perder por el uso; (b) llevado u ostentado decorosamente. **Well-wrought**, bien trabajado.

welladay ['welədeɪ] [ue-la-dei], *inter.* Hola; ay de mí.

well-aimed ['wel'eɪmd] [uel-eimd], *a.* Certero.

well-attended ['weləˈtendɪd] [uel-a-ten-did], *a.* Bien concurrido.

well-being ['welˌbiːɪŋ] [uel-biin], *s.* Felicidad, prosperidad, bienestar, comodidad.

well done ['wel'dʌn] [uel-dan], *inter.* ¡Ánimo! ¡a las mil maravillas! ¡bien va!

well-founded ['wel'faʊndɪd] [uel-faun-did], *a.* Bien fundado, justo.

well-grounded ['wel'graʊndɪd] [uel-faun-did], *a.* Bien fundado.

well-known ['wel'nəʊn] [uel-noun], *a.* Bien conocido, famoso.

well-off ['welɒf] [uel-of], *a.* Rico, adinerado, acomodado.

well-spring ['wel'sprɪŋ] [uel-sprin], *s.* Manantial, fuente.

well-suited ['wel'suːted] [uel-su-ted], *a.* Adecuado. **Well-suited to each other**, que congenian mutuamente.

Welsh [welʃ] [uelsh], *a.* Galo, del país de Gales; perteneciente a Gales. *-s.* 1. Los naturales de Gales. 2. Idioma del país de Gales; dialecto de la lengua címrica. **Welsh girl**, joven gala. **Welsh rabbit (o rarebit)**, tostada con queso; queso tostado o derretido que se sirve con pan tostado.

Welshman ['welʃmən] [uelsh-man], *s.* Galo, habitante o natural de Gales.

welt [welt] [uelt], *s.* 1. Ribete (de ropa); vira del zapato. 2. Costurón, señal que deja un latigazo. 3. *(Fam.)* El acto de azotar o de dar tundas.

welt, *va.* 1. Ribetear, echar ribetes. 2. Azotar cruelmente de surete que se formen costurones.

welter ['weltəʳ] [uel-taʳ], *vn.* 1. Introducirse en un fluido turbio. 2. Revolcarse en agua, cieno o lodo. 3. Hincharse o moverse las olas hacia adelante. *-s.* 1. Movimiento ondulante de las olas; de aquí, conmoción, agitación, tumulto. 2. Aquello en que algo o alguien se revuelca; cenagal, revolcadero.

welterweight ['weltəwert] [uel-ta-ueit], *s.* En el boxeo, peso welter, peso mediano ligero.

wen [wen] [uen], *s.* Lobanillo, lupia; excreencia. **Wen on the throat**, papera.

wench [wentʃ] [uench], *s.* 1. Moza, muchacha, una mujer joven de condición humilde; criada. 2. Mozuela; usado como término de desprecio. 3. *(Fam. E.U.)* Negra. 4. *(DEs.)* Cantonera, andorra.

wench, *vn.* Putañear.

wend [wen] [uen], *va.* Dirigir (su curso), andar. *-vn.* Ir, continuar su camino; avanzar, pasar.

went [went] [uent], *pret.* del verbo TO GO: *(pret.* desusado de *wend*). **I went home**, yo me fui a casa.

wentletrap ['wentltræp] [uen-tel-trap], *s.* Escalaria, concha de escalera, molusco gasterópodo.

wept [wept] [uept], *pret.* y *pp.* del verbo TO WEEP.

were [wɜːʳ] [ueʳ], *pret. pl.* del verbo TO BE, tanto subjuntivo como indicativo; en el subjuntivo es también singular. **You were**. Vd. era, estaba; Vd. fue, estuvo; Vds. eran, estaban; Vd. fue, estuvo; Vds. eran, estaban, fueron, estuvieron; vosotros erais, estabais, etc. **If I were**, si yo fuera o fuese, estuviera o estuviese. **As it were**, por decirlo así; como si fuese. **Even though he were to see it, he would not believe it**, aun cuando él lo viese no lo creería. **Were I asked my opinion**, si me preguntasen mi opinión. **There were**, había, hubo. **There were ten**, había diez.

west [west] [uest], *s.* Oeste, poniente, occidente. *-a.* Occidental, del oeste. *-adv.* A poniente o hacia el poniente; hacia el occidente. **West End**, barrio aristocrático de Londres, al oeste de Charing Cross. **West Indies**, las Indias occidentales, las Antillas. **West-Indian**, de las Antillas, de las Indias occidentales.

westerly ['westəlɪ] [ues-ter-li], *a.* Que se dirige a poniente; hacia el oeste. **In a westerly direction**, en dirección al oeste. **A westerly wind**, viento del oeste. *-adv.* Hacia el oeste u occidente.

western ['westən] [ues-tern], *a.* Occidental, que está en el occidente o hacia el poniente; al oeste, que viene del oeste, o es característico del oeste; también, menguante.

westernmost ['westənməʊst] [ues-tan-moust], *a.* Lo más el oeste, los más remoto hacia el oeste.

westward ['westwəd] [uest-uod], *adv.* A poniente, hacia occidente, hacia el oeste.

westward, *a.* Que tiende al oeste, que está al oeste.

wet [wet] [uet], *a.* Húmedo, mojado, humedecido, lluvioso. **Wet blanket**, aguafiestas. **Wet paint**, pintura fresca. *-s.* Humedad, agua, tiempo húmedo.

wet, *va.* Moar, humedecer.

wether ['wesdəʳ] [ue-daʳ], *s.* Carnero llano, el que está castrado.

wetness ['wetnɪs] [uet-nes], *s.* Humedad.

wet-nurse ['wetnɜːs] [uet-ners], *s.* Ama de leche, ama de cría, nodriza.

whack [wæk] [uak], *va. (Fam.)* Pegar, golpear, vapulear. *-vn.* 1. Golpear con ruido, dar una tunda, una zurra. 2. *(Ger.)* Ajustar cuentas; tener parte en, gozar con otros. *-s.* 1. Golpe ruidoso. 2. *(Ger.)* Parte, porción.

whacking ['wækɪŋ] [ua-kin], *a. (Fam.)* Grueso, desmesurado, enorme.

whale [weɪl] [ueil], *va. (Fam.)* Azotar; vapulear, vapular, dar una tunda.

whale, *vn.* Dedicarse a la pesca de la ballena.

whale, *s.* Ballena, mamífero cetáceo. **Whale-back**, embarcación de cubierta cerrada y redondeada, que se usa en aguas peligrosas.

whalebone ['weɪlbəʊn] [ueil-boun], *s.* Ballena o barba de ballena, tira que se saca de la mandíbula superior de dicho cetáceo.

whalefin ['weɪlfɪn] [ueil-fin], *s.* Aleta de ballena.

whale-oil ['weɪlɔɪl] [ueil-oil], *s.* Aceite o grasa de ballena.

whaler ['weɪləʳ] [uei-laʳ], *s.* Ballenero, pescador de ballenas; buque, ballenero, barco dedicado a la pesca de la ballena.

whaling ['weɪlɪŋ] [uei-lin], *s.* 1. El acto o la industria de pescar ballenas. 2. *(Fam.)* Tunda, zurra.

whang [wæŋ] [uan], *va. y vn. (Fam. o Prov.)* Golpear (con resonancia); dar tundas. *-s.* Tunda.

wharf [wɔːf] [uorf], *s. (pl.* WHARFS o WHARVES). Muelle, embarcadero o desembarcadero, construcción donde cargan y descargan los barcos cómodamente.

wharfage ['wɔːfɪdʒ] [uor-fich], *s.* Muellaje, un derecho que se cobra por el uso de un muelle; derecho de muelle.

what [wɒt] [uot], *pron.* 1. Que, qué cosa; cuál; el que, la que, lo que aquello que. 2. Cuanto. **What time?**, ¿cuándo? **What time**, cuando, al tiempo que, en el día que. **What a man!**, ¡qué hombre! **What man?**, ¿quién? **What though**, sin embargo que, a pesar de que, aun cuando; ¿qué importa que? **What else?**, ¿y qué más? **What of that?**, ¿qué importa eso? **What is that?**, ¿qué es eso? **For what?**, ¿por qué? ¿para qué? **What if he should come?** ¿y qué diría Vd. si viniese? **What more?**, ¿qué más? **What ho!**, ¡hola! *-adv.* En parte; tanto, sea. **What with hunger and what with weariness**, parte por hambre y parte por cansancio. **To know what's what**. *(Fam.)* comprender las cosas, estar en autos, estar al corriente. **What for**, *(Fest.)* qué clase de; (del alemán *was für*). **What for a dog have you?** ¿qué clase de perro tiene Ud.?

whatever [wɒt'evəʳ] [uot-e-vaʳ], *pron.* Cualquier o cualquiera cosa que, todo lo que, por cualquiera, sea lo o la que fuere, que sea.

what-not ['wɒtnɒt] [uot-not], *s.* 1. Rinconera, estante, pequeño mueble con anaqueles. 2. *(Fam.)* Lo que Vd. guste, cualquiera cosa.

wheal [wiːl] [uil], *s.* Raya, amoratada en la piel causada por un latigazo o por las ortigas.

wheat [wiːt] [uit], *s. (Bot.)* Trigo.

wheaten ['wiːtn] [ui-ten], *a.* Hecho de trigo.

wheedle ['wiːdl] [ui-del], *va.* Halagar, acariciar, persuadir con palabras halagüeñas, engaitar o engañar con lisonjas, popar o tratar con mucha blandura y regalo; sonsacar.

wheel [wiːl] [uil], *s.* 1. Rueda, máquina circular que da vueltas sobre un eje; en sentido figurado, fuerza motriz. **Spinning-wheel**, torno para hilar. **Wheel of the helm**, *(Mar.)* rueda del timón. 2. Instrumento o aparato que se asemeja a una rueda o que tiene una rueda como elemento distintivo, v. g. una bicicleta, un fuego artificial giratorio, una polea, etc. 3. Rueda, máquina con que se daba suplicio. **Balance-wheel**, volante. 4. *(Met.)* Revolución, vuelta, rotación; acción de rodar, de dar vueltas. **To break upon the wheel**, enrodar. **Wheel and axle**, cabria, aparato para levantar pesos. **Cog-wheel**, ruedad dentada. **Driving-wheel**, rueda motriz. **Fly-wheel**, volante. **Paddle-wheel**, rueda de paletas. **Potter's wheel**, rueda de alfarero. **Breast wheel**, rueda hidráulica de costado. **Catharine wheel**, (a) rosa, ventana de rosetón; (b) sol, rueda de fuegos artificiales; (c) rueda catalina. **Wheel-animalcule**, rotífero. **Wheel-barometer**, barómetro de cuadrante. **Wheel-horse**, caballo de varas (cuando va delante otro caballo). **Wheel-house**, carroza o garita de timonel.

wheel, *vn.* 1. Rodar, moverse por la tierra dando vuelts alrededor del eje o centro del cuerpo que se mueve. 2. Rodar, moverse alguna cosa con ruedas. 3. Rodar, divagar, andar de acá para allá o por muchas partes; girar, volar. 4. Rodar, suceder las cosas casualmente y como en el trascurso del tiempo. *-va.* 1. Rodar o hacer rodar, transportar, llevar sobre ruedas. 2. Volver, girar, dar vuelta o vueltas a alguna cosa. 3. Proveer de una rueda. 4. Formar o trabajar con rueda. **To wheel about**, rodar, divagar; dar vueltas, andar rodando o de acá para allá; no fijarse, cambiar muy fácilmente de opinión, de partido, etc.

wheelbarrow ['wiːlbærəʊ] [uil-ba-rou], *s.* Carretón de una rueda; la carretilla o caja con una rueda en que llevan los albañiles los materiales.

wheel base [ˈwiːlbeɪs] [uil-beis], *s.* Distancia entre ejes de vehículo.

wheel chair [ˈwiːltʃeəʳ] [uil-cheaʳ], *s.* Silla de ruedas.

wheeler [ˈwiːləʳ] [ui-laʳ], *s.* 1. El que hace ruedas; el que rueda o da vueltas. 2. Caballería uncida cerca de las ruedas. 3. Vapor de ruedas. **Stern-wheeler**, *V.* STERN. 4. Carretero.

wheeling [ˈwiːlɪŋ] [ui-lin], *s.* 1. Rodaje, transporte sobre ruedas; el acto o costumbre de usar una bicicleta. 2. Condición de los caminos en lo relativo al paso de vehículos de ruedas. 3. Movimiento de rotación.

wheelman [ˈwiːlmən] [uil-man], *s.* 1. Timonero, timonel, el que gobierna una embarcación. 2. *(Neol.)* El que usa una bicicleta, biciclista, ciclista.

wheelwright [ˈwiːlraɪt] [uil-rait], *s.* Carretero, el que hace carros, carretas o carruajes; el que hace juegos de ruedas para los carruajes.

wheelwork [ˈwiːlwɜːk] [uil-uerk], *s.* El conjunto de ruedas de una máquina.

wheeze [ˈwiːz] [uis], *vn.* Jadear, respirar con dificultad y fatiga; respirar haciendo mucho ruido.

whelk [welk] [uelk], *s.* 1. Concha univalva espiral. 2. Tumorcillo, grano.

whelp [welp] [uelp], *s.* 1. Cachorro, el perro de poco tiempo. y también la cría de otros animales carnívoros. **Bear whelp**, osezno. 2. Un muchacho u hombre muy joven, en este sentido se usa sólo por desprecio y para notar a un muchacho de atrevido y perverso.

whelp, *vn.* Parir: por lo común se entiende de la perra o la hembra de algunos otros animales carnívoros.

when [wen] [uen], *adv.* Cuando, al tiempo que, o mientras que; desde que; que, en que. **When?** ¿cuándo? ¿en qué tiempo? **Since when?** ¿desde cuándo, de cuando acá? **Even when**, aun cuando. **The moment when**, al momento en que. **When I learned this**, desde que o supe esto.

whence [wens] [uens], *adv.* De donde o desde donde, de que o quien; de qué causa; por eso es que; por consiguiente. **Whence it may be seen**, de aquí se ve, o resulta. **From whence** es un pleonasmo poco usado.

whenever [wenˈevəʳ] [uen-e-vaʳ], *adv.* Cuando quiera que, siempre que, en cualquier tiempo que sea, todas las veces que.

where [weəʳ] [ueaʳ], *adv.* Donde, en que lugar, en donde, por donde, adonde. **Anywhere**, en cualquier parte, sitio o paraje, donde Ud. quiera. **Everywhere**, en todas partes, por todas partes.

whereabout [ˈweərəbaʊt] [uea-ra-baut], *adv.* Hacia donde, hacia qué sitio, poco más o menos donde.

whereabouts [ˈweərəbaʊts] [uea-ra-bauts], *s.* Lugar cercano o aquel en que se halla una persona o cosa; situación aproximada, paradero.

whereas [weərˈæz] [uear-as], *conj.* Por cuanto, siendo así que, mientras que; cuando; por el contrario; pues que, ya que.

whereat [weərˈæt] [uear-at], *adv.* A lo cual.

whereby [weəˈbaɪ] [uea-bai], *adv.* Por lo cual, con lo cual, por donde, de que; por medio del cual: ¿por qué? ¿cómo?

wherefore [ˈweəfɔːʳ] [uea-foʳ], *adv.* Por lo que, porque, por el cual motivo; por eso, por consiguiente.

wherein [weərˈɪn] [uear-in], *adv.* Donde, en donde, en lo cual, en que.

whereinto [weərˈɪntʊ] [uear-in-tu], *adv.* En donde, dentro de lo que o dentro de lo cual, en lo cual, a lo que.

whereof [weərˈɒv] [uear-ov], *adv.* De lo cual, de que; ¿de qué?

whereon [weərˈɒn] [uear-on], *adv.* Sobre lo cual, sobre que.

wheresoever [ˌweəsəʊˈevəʳ] [uea-sou-e-vaʳ], *adv.* Donde quiera, en cualquier parte que, en cualquier sitio que sea.

whereto [ˌweəˈtuː] [uea-tu], *adv.* A lo que, a que.

whereupon [ˈweərəpɒn] [uea-ra-pon], *adv.* Sobre que; entonces, así que sucedió esto.

wherever [weərˈevəʳ] [uear-e-vaʳ], *adv.* Donde quiera que, por donde quiera que, en donde quiera.

wherewith [weəˈwɪθ] [uea-uiz], *adv.* Con que, con lo cual; ¿con qué? *-s.* Los medios o recursos necesarios; dinero necesario.

wherry [ˈwerɪ] [ue-ri], *s.* 1. Esquife, barca, barco. 2. *(Ingl.)* Barca de pescador con cubierta y dos velas.

wherry, *va.* Pasar en barco.

wherryman [ˈwerɪmən] [ue-ri-man], *s.* Barquero.

whet [wet] [uet], *va.* 1. Afilar, amolar. 2. Agriar, exasperar; en este último sentido se usa casi siempre con la preposición *on.* 3. Excitar el apetito o dar apetito.

whether [ˈweðəʳ] [ue-daʳ], *conj.* Si, sea, sea que, ora, ya. *-pron. (Ant.)* Cual, cual de los dos. **Whether you will or not**, que quieras, que no quieras.

whetstone [ˈwetstəʊn] [uet-stoun], *s.* Aguzadera, piedra de amolar o afilar.

whetter [ˈwetəʳ] [ue-taʳ], *s.* Amolador.

whew [hwjuː] [jiu], *inter.* ¡Ah! ¡caramba! ¡cáspita! expresa asombro; ¡ay! expresa congoja.

whey [weɪ] [uei], *s.* Suero, la parte acuosa de la leche separada de la parte grumosa de ella.

which [wɪtʃ] [uich], *pron. rel.* 1. Que, el cual, la cual, los cuales, las cuales, cual, cuyo. *Which* se usa sólo para hacer relación a las cosas o a los animales. aunque antiguamente también se usaba para las pesonas; interrogativamente se dice de personas y cosas. 2. Lo que representa una cláusula o frase. **He says his copy is better printed, which is true**, dice que su ejemplar está mejor impreso, lo que es cierto. **Which book do you prefer?**, ¿qué libro prefiere Ud.? **The canary which has a crest**, el canario que tiene cresta. **Both of which**, ambos. los dos. **All of which, all which**, todo esto. **In the progress of which**, en cuyo progreso. **Which will you have?**, ¿cuál quiere Vd.? **Which way?**, ¿por dónde? ¿por qué camino?

whichever [wɪtʃˈevəʳ] [uich-e-vaʳ], *pron.* Cualquiera.

whiff [wɪf] [uif], *s.* Vaharada, el efecto de arrojar el vaho, aliento o respiración; bocanada de humo, soplo de viento.

whiff, *va.* 1. Llevar por el aire, transportar con un soplo. 2. Echar bocanadas de humo o vaharadas. 3. Fumar (una pipa) echando bocanadas de humo. *-vn.* Lanzar o echar bocanadas.

whiffle [ˈwɪfl] [ui-fel], *va.* 1. Hacer bambolearse, hacer inclinar. 2. Hacer desaparecer una cosa a soplos; poner a un lado o desechar alguna cosa con desprecio. *-vn.* Divertirse en bagatelas o cosa insignificantes; moverse o agitarse con mucha volubilidad; ser inconstante o voluble.

whig [wɪg] [uig], *s.* Nombre de un partido político de Inglaterra que pide reformas liberales, liberal: de los Estados Unidos, (a) partidario de la revolución; (b) partido opuesto a *Democrat*, predecesor del actual partido republicano.

while [waɪl] [uail], *s.* Rato, espacio corto de tiempo; vez. **A while ago**, hace algún tiempo. **A little while**, un ratito. **A little while ago**, hace poco, ahora mismo, hace un rato, no hace mucho. **A while ago**, rato ha. **All this while**, en todo este tiempo o durante todo este tiempo. **A while after**, algo después o poco después. **For a while**, durante algún tiempo o por algún tiempo. **In the meanwhile**, en el intervalo, entre tanto. **Between whiles**, de cuando en cuando, a intervalos. **'Tis not worth while**, no merece o no vale la pena.

while, *adv.* Mientras, durante, entre tanto, en el interin. **While she sings, they converse**, mientras ella canta, ellos conversan.

while, *va.* Pasar, hacer pasar (el tiempo). **To while away one's time**, haraganear, pasar el tiempo; divertirse.

whim [wɪm] [uim], *s.* 1. Antojo, capricho, fantasía, genialidad, extravagancia. **To be full of whims**, ser lunático, tener rarezas, ser muy caprichoso o muy extravagante. 2. *(Mec.)* Cabria, trucha. **Whim-gin**, cabria, trucha.

whimper [ˈwɪmpəʳ] [uim-paʳ], *vn.* Sollozar, llorar sin gritar, gemir, quejarse; lloriquear, fingir que se llora, como lo hacen los niños. *-s.* Quejido, lloriqueo. *V.* WHINE.

whimsical [ˈwɪmzɪkəl] [uim-si-kal], *a.* 1. Caprichoso, caprichudo, fantástico, extravagante, ridículo. 2. Construído fantásticamente.

whimsicality [ˌwɪmzɪˈkælɪtɪ] [uim-si-ka-li-ti], *s.* La calidad de ser caprichoso o fantástico, extravagancia, ridiculez.

whimsically [ˈwɪmzɪkəlɪ] [uim-si-ka-li], *adv.* Caprichosamente, con extravagancia, de un modo raro.

whimsy [ˈwɪmzɪ] [uim-si], *s. V.* WHIM, en ambas acepciones.

whine [waɪn] [uain], *vn.* Llorar o lamentar sin ruido; quejarse, lamentarse; lloriquear (como hace un niño).

whine, *s.* Quejido, lamento; lloriqueo.

whining [ˈwaɪnɪŋ] [uai-nin], *s.* Quejas.

whinny [ˈwɪnɪ] [ui-ni], *vn.* Relinchar (especialmente en voz baja). -*s.* Relincho, voz del caballo o la yegua.

whinny, *a.* Abundante en hiniesta o tojo.

whip [wɪp] [uip], *va.* 1. Azotar, dar azotes; dar con vergas, flagelar. 2. Castigar a un niño, dándole azotes. 3. Efectuar con, o como con, golpes. 4. Asir, arrebatar, o coger con un movimiento rápido; se usa con preposición, v. gr. *away, in, off, on*, etc, 5. *(Fam. E.U:)* Exceder, sobresalir en una contienda; vencer. 6. Batir huevos, crema. 7. Hilvanar, filetear. 8. Dar varias vueltas con hilo a un pedazo de cuerda; envolver un cabo con cuerdecilla. 9. Izar con candeliza; levantar con precipitación. **To whip a horse**, dar latigazos a un caballo. **It was whipped with black**, estaba fileteado de negro. -*vn.* 1. Andar de prisa. 2. Echar repetidas veces el anzuelo en el agua. **To whip down**, bajar corriendo o bajar volando. **To whip off a thing**, despachar alguna cosa o negocio prontamente. **To whip out**, zafarse, escaparse; llevarse alguna cosa con precipitación. **To whip up**, agarrar, coger, tomar o asir algo de repente; subir corriendo o volando: *(Mar.)* izar con la candeliza, alzar levantar o subir con precipitación.

whip, *s.* 1. Azote: látigo, zurriago; fusta, *(Amer.)* fuete. **Horsewhip**, látigo. **Coachman's whip**, manopla. **Whip-money**, agujetas. 2. *(Mar.)* Palanquín de estay. **Whip and spur**, con la mayor prisa, a todo correr. **Stroke of a whip**, latigazo. **To crack a whip**, hacer chasquear un látigo. **Whip-cord**, (a) cordel de látigo. *(Mex.)* Pajuela: (b) cordel de cuerda de tripa. **Whip-hand**, la mano que tiene el látigo; mano derecha; *(Fig.)* ventaja. **To have the whip-hand of**, tener la ventaja sobre, tener vara alta. **Whip-lash**, punta de látigo.

whip-graft [ˈwɪpgræft] [uip-graft], *va.* Injertar a la inglesa. **Whip-grafting**, injerto inglés.

whipped [wɪpt] [uipt], *a.* Batido. **Whipped cream**, crema batida.

whippet [ˈwɪpɪt] [ui-pit], *s.* 1. Perro lebrero. 2. Cosa pequeña y veloz.

whipping [ˈwɪpɪŋ] [ui-pin], *s.* Acción de azotar, flagelación. **To give a whipping**, dar un latigazo, una mano de azotes. **Whipping-post**, la columna o poste a que atan a los reos para azotarlos.

whipsaw [ˈwɪpsɔː] [uip-so], *s.* Serrucho.

whipstaff [ˈwɪpstɑːf] [uip-staf], *s. (Mar.)* Pinzote del timón.

whipster [ˈwɪpstəʳ] [uip-staʳ], *s.* Hombre ligero y ágil.

whir [wɜːʳ] [ueʳ], *va. y vn.* Girar, dar vueltas o llevarse con estruendo, zumbar; moverse o volar con ruido, rehilar. -*s.* Ruido que hacen las aves al remontar el vuelo; zumbido, sonido de un giro muy rápido.

whiring [ˈwɜːrɪŋ] [ue-rin], *s.* Zumbido, de las alas o de ciertas máquinas.

whirl [wɜːl] [uerl], *va. y vn.* 1. Girar, dar vueltas alrededor o circularmente con mucha rapidez. 2. Hacer girar o dar vueltas en círculo. 3. Mover o moverse rápidamente.

whirl, *s.* Giro vuelta, rotación o movimiento circular muy rápido; cualquier cosa que se mueve circularmente con giros muy rápidos.

whirlbone [ˈwɜːlbəʊn] [uerl-boun], *s.* Rótula, choquezuela, el hueso de la rodilla.

whirligig [ˈwɜːlɡɪɡ] [uerl-guig], *s.* 1. Perinola. 2. Tío vivo. *V. Merry-go-round.* 3. Cualquier cosa que se mueve

circularmente con giros rápidos. 4. Girín, escarabajo de agua, insecto coleóptero de vivos colores metálicos.

whirlpool [ˈwɜːpuːl] [uerl-pul], *s.* Vórtice, remolino u olla de agua; agua que gira con violencia.

whirlwind [ˈwɜːlwɪnd] [uerl-uind], *s,* Torbellino, remolino, viento violento que se mueve circularmente. *(Fam.)* **To raise a whirlwind**, levantar una tremolina. **Sow the wind, and reap the whirlwind**, quien siembra vientos, recoge tempestades; o, haces mal, espera otro tal.

whirr [wɜːʳ] [ueʳ], *v. y s. V.* WHIR.

whish [wɪʃ] [uish], *s. (Fam.)* Sonido agudo semejante al que hace una varita cortando en el aire. *V.* SWISH. (Voz imitativa).

whisk [wɪsk] [uisk], *s.* 1. Escobilla, copillo. 2. Un movimiento pronto y violento. 3. Antiguamente una parte del vestido de mujer.

whisk, *va.* 1. Cepillar, limpiar con escobilla, quitar el polvo. 2. Arrastrar o mover rápidamente. -*vn.* 1. Hopear, menear la cola los animales. 2. Moverse con velocidad alguna cosa. **To whisk away** o **off**, quitar vivamente, hacer desaparecer, marcharse de prisa.

whisker [ˈwɪskəʳ] [uis-kaʳ], *s.* Patilla, barbas a uno y otro lado de la cara; bigotes del gato.

whiskey, whisky [ˈwɪskɪ] [uis-ki], *s.* Aguardiente de grano; güisqui, licor alcohólico que se obtiene destilando un compuesto amiláceo en estado de fermentación. *V.* USQUEBAUCH.

whisper [ˈwɪspəʳ] [uis-paʳ], *va. y vn.* 1. Cuchichear o cuchuchear, hablar al oído; murmurar. 2. Susurrar, hablar quedo; hablar muy bajo o bajito. 3. Apuntar, soplar o sugerir a otro en voz baja lo que debe decir, 4. Secretear.

whisper, *s.* Susurro, ruido sordo, cuchicheo, voz baja.

whisperer [ˈwɪspərəʳ] [uis-pa-raʳ], *s.* 1. El que habla bajo. 2 Cuchicheador, el amigo de cuchichear. 3. Susurrador, el que susurra quedo.

whispering [ˈwɪspərɪŋ] [uis-pa-rin], *s.* Cuchicheo; susurro; el acto de hablar quedo o bajito. **Whispering-gallery**, una galería o corredor en forma de bóveda, construido de tal modo que en toda su extensión se puede oír el más pequeño ruido hecho en un punto cualquiera del mismo.

whist [wɪst] [uist], *a.* Silencioso, mudo, callado, -*inter.* ¡Chitón! ¡calla! ¡punto en boca!. -*s.* Un juego de naipes parecido a la malilla, que se juega entre cuatro personas.

whistle [ˈwɪsl] [ui-sel], *va. y vn.* 1. Silbar, formar el silbo o silbido. 2. Chiflar, dar chiflidos. 3. Llamar a alguno dando silbidos. **To whistle down the wind**, hablar por demás, gastar saliva en balde. **To whistle for**, llamar dando silbidos; *(Fam.)* buscar en vano lo que se desea.

whistle, *s.* 1. Silbo, silbido. 2. Silbato, chiflato; pito. 3. Silbido del viento. 4. *(Ger.)* Pico, gaznate. **To pay (too) dear for one's whistle**, pagar demasiado cara una chuchería, una bagatela. **To wet one's whistle**, *(Ger.)* humedecerse el gaznate, beber. **Fog-whistle**, pito de alarma en tiempo de niebla, *V. Fog-horn.*

whistle stop [ˈwɪslstɒp] [ui-sel-stop], *s. (E.U.)* Pueblo pequeño.

whistler [ˈwɪsləʳ] [uis-laʳ], *s.* Silbador.

whistling [ˈwɪslɪŋ] [uis-lin], *s,* 1. Silbo, silbido, la acción de silbar. 2. Chiflido, la acción de chiflar. **Whistling-buoy**, boya de pito de alarma.

whit [wɪt] [uit], *s.* Ápice, jota, punto, la mínima parte de alguna cosa; algo, un poco. **Every whit**, de todo punto; enteramente. **Not a whit**, nada de eso.

white [waɪt] [uait], *a.* 1. Blanco; del color de la nieve; lo opuesto a negro. 2. Blanco, del color de la raza caucásica; rubio, blondo; también, pálido, descolorido. 3. Cano, hablando del pelo. 4. Puro, inmaculado, sin mancha; inocente. 5. Feliz, propicio. **Milk-white**, blanco como la leche, de un blanco lechoso. **To get white**, ponerse blanco. **To render white**, blanquear. **White with age**, encanecido por los años, por la edad. **White lie**, mentirilla. -*s.* 1. Blancura, color blanco, reunión de todos los colores del espectro solar. 2. Blanco, una señal fija y determinada para apuntar cuando se tira. 3. La clara del huevo. 4. La parte blanca de los ojos, la esclerótica. 5. Persona blanca. **Spanish white**, blanco de España, yeso mate. **Chinese white**, blanco de la China, óxido de zinc. **White ant**, hormiga blanca, termita. *V.* TERMITE. **White House**, La Casa Blanca, la residencia oficial del Presidente de los Estados Unidos. **While-lead**, albayalde, cal de plomo. **White leather**, baldés, piel curtida, con alumbre. **White-livered**, cobarde, doble, envidioso, maligno. **White meat**, manjar blanco: lacticinio, manjar compuesto con leche. **White wine**, vino blanco.

white, whiten [ˈwaɪtn] [uai-ten], *va.* Blanquear, poner blanca alguna cosa. *-vn.* Emblanquecerse.

white-collar [ˈwaɪtˌkɒləʳ] [uait-ko-laʳ], *a.* Oficinesco. **White-collar job**, trabajo de oficina. **White-collar worker**, oficinista.

white elephant [ˈwaɪtˈelɪfənt] [uait-e-li-fant], *s.* Elefante blanco, algo que cuesta mucho mantener y no presta utilidad alguna.

white feather [ˈwaɪtˈfeðəʳ] [uait-fe-daʳ], *s.* Pluma blanca, símbolo de cobardía.

whitefish [ˈwaɪtfɪʃ] [uait-fish], *s.* 1. Pez de los lagos septentrionales, parecido al salmón. 2. Albur, cadoce; merlán; y *V.* MENHADEN. 3. La ballena blanca.

white gold [ˈwaɪtgɒʊld] [uait-gould], *s.* Oro blanco.

whitener [ˈwaɪtnəʳ] [uait-naʳ], *s.* Blanqueador.

whiteness [ˈwaɪtnɪs] [uait-nes], *s.* 1. Blancura; palidez. 2. Pureza, candor.

whitening [ˈwaɪtnɪŋ] [uait-nin], *s.* Blanqueo, la acción y efecto de blanquear.

whites [ˈwaɪts] [uaits], *s.* 1. Flores blancas, leucorrea. 2. Flor de harina, la harina más blanca y más fina.

whitewash [ˈwaɪtwɒʃ] [uait-uosh], *s.* 1. Lechada, leche de cal, el blanqueo que se da a las paredes. 2. Blanquete, afeite con el cual se blanquea el rostro. 3. Informe en que se atribuye a uno virtudes que no tiene, o el acto de encubrir sus faltas.

whitewash, *va.* 1. Blanquear, enlucir con yeso blanco una pared. 2. Encalar o blanquear con cal; enjalbegar. 3. Tapar o encubrir las faltas o defectos. 4. *(Fam. Ingl.)* Poner a un deudor insolvente al abrigo de procedimientos ulteriores. 5. *(Fam. E.U.)* Vencer al partido opuesto en un juego, sin permitirle hacer tantos.

whitewasher [ˈwaɪtsɒʃəʳ] [uait-uo-shaʳ], *s.* Encalador, blanqueador.

whitewashing [ˈwaɪtwɒʃɪŋ] [uait-uo-shin], *s.* 1. Blanqueo, encaladura, enjalbegadura, jalbegue. 2. *V.* WHITEWASH, 3ª acep.

whither [ˈwɪðəʳ] [uai-tin], *adv.* ¿Adónde?, ¿a qué parte?; ¡hasta dónde?; donde quiera.

whiting [ˈwaɪtɪŋ] [uai-tin], *s.* 1. Merlán, pez gádido; albur, cadoce. 2. Blino plateado. 3. Blanco de España, yeso mate, tiza, carbonato de cal que se usa para pulimentar.

whitish [ˈwaɪtɪʃ] [uai-tish], *a.* Blanquizco, blanquecino, que tira a blanco.

whitishness [ˈwaɪtɪʃnɪs] [uai-tish-nes], *s.* Color blancuzco o color blanquecino.

whitlow [ˈwɪtləʊ] [uit-lou], *s.* Panadizo, panarizo.

whitsuntide [ˈwɪtsntaɪd] [uit-son-taid], *s.* Pentecostés, fiesta del Espíritu Santo. **Whitsunday**, día de Pentecostés.

whittle [ˈwɪtl] [ui-tel], *va.* 1. Cortar o formar con navaja. 2. Cercenar, ir disminuyendo poco a poco. 3. Aguzar, dar un corte agudo. *-vn.* Cortar un pedazo de madera con una navaja.

whittle, *s.* 1. Navajilla, navaja pequeña; cuchillito que se lleva a la cintura. 2. Una especie de manta lanuda usada antiguamente por las mujeres.

whiz [wiz] [uis], *vn.* Zumbar o silbar, producir un ruido agudo como el que hace una flecha o una bala que hiende el aire; moverse rápidamente con ese ruido. *-s.* Sonido entre zumbido y silbido. **Whizzing noise**, zumbido.

who [huː] [ju], *pron.* (interrogativo) ¿Quién? (relativo) Quien, que, la persona que. **Who is there?**, ¿quién está ahí?, ¿quién va? Este pronombre se usa sólo hablando de personas. **As who should say**, como si dijéramos, como quien dice.

whoa [wɒʊ] [uou], *inter.* ¡So! ¡cho o jo! (voz usada para hacer que se paren las bestias).

whoever [huːˈevəʳ] [hu-e-vaʳ], *pron.* Quienquiera que, cualquiera que.

whole [həʊl] [joul], *a.* 1. Todo, total, entero. 2. Sano, entero, libre de daño; en buena salud. *-s.* Total, el todo. **Upon the whole**, en el todo, en suma, en general.

wholehearted [ˈhəʊlˈhɑːtɪd] [joul-jar-tid], *a.* Cordial, de todo corazón, con entusiasmo.

wholeness [ˈhəʊlnɪs] [joul-nes], *s.* Todo, integridad, totalidad.

wholesale [ˈhəʊlseɪl] [joul-seil], *a.* Al mayoreo, al por mayor. *-s.* Mayoreo, venta al por mayor.

wholesaler [ˈhəʊlˌseɪləʳ] [joul-sei-laʳ], *s.* Mayorista.

wholesome [ˈhəʊlsəm] [joul-som], *a.* 1. Sano, saludable, que conduce a la salud. 2. Bienhechor, favorable a la virtud; moral.

wholesomely [ˈhəʊlsəmlɪ] [joul-som-li], *adv.* Saludablemente.

wholesomeness [ˈhəʊlsəmnɪs] [joul-som-nes], *s.* Salud, sanidad, salubridad, naturaleza sana.

whole-wheat [ˈhəʊlwiːt] [joul-wit], *a.* De trigo entero. **Whole-wheat bread**, pan de trigo entero.

wholly [ˈhəʊlɪ] [jou-li], *adv.* Cabalmente, totalmente, enteramente.

whom [huːm] [jum], *pron.* Acusativo de WHO. Quien, que, cual. **Whom have you seen?**, ¿a quién ha visto Vd.? **He whom you revere**, aquél a quien Vd. reverencia.

whoop [huːp] [jup], *s.* 1. Algarada, gritería; grito de agitación o de estímulo. 2. Grito de señal. 3. Inspiración ruidosa y convulsiva después de un ataque de tos. 4. Grito de buho o lechuza.

whoop, *vn.* 1. Huchear, chiflar, gritar, vocear. 2. Respirar ruidosa y convulsivamente, como después de un paroxismo de tos. *-va.* Insultar con gritos. **Whooping-cough**, tos ferina o convulsiva.

whop [wɒp] [uop], *va. (Vulg.)* Zurrar.

whopper [ˈwɒpəʳ] [uo-paʳ], *s. (Fam.)* 1. El que zurra. 2. Algo grande o notable, particularmente una gran mentira.

whopping [ˈwɒpɪŋ] [uo-pin], *a.* Muy grande, enorme.

whore [hɔːʳ] [joʳ], *vn.* 1. Putear. 2. En la Sagrada Escritura, dar culto a dioses falsos. *-va.* Putear, corromper por medio de la lascivia.

whore, *s.* Puta, prostituta.

whorish [ˈhɔːrɪʃ] [jo-rish], *a.* Lascivo, putesco.

whorl [wɜːl] [uerl], *s.* 1. Contrapeso de la rueca. 2. *(Bot.)* Verticilo, conjunto de hojas, flores u otros órganos en el torno de un tallo. 3. *(Zool.)* Espiral de una concha univalva.

whose [huːz] [jus], Genitivo de **WHO** y **WHICH**. Cuyo, de quien.

whosoever [ˌhuːsəʊˈevəʳ] [ju-sou-e-vaʳ], *pron.* Quienquiera, cualquiera.

why [waɪ] [uai], *adv.* y *conj.* Por qué. **Why so?** ¿Por qué así? **Why?** ¿Qué? *Why* se usa frecuentemente para dar énfasis al discurso, y en este caso deja de traducirse en castellano. **Why truly**, pero verdaderamente. *-inter.* A veces se representa por sí; p. ej.: **Why, I just saw it**, si lo acabo de ver. **Why, he must be crazy**, debe estar loco; otras veces por ¡y bien! ¡pero! ¡cómo! **Why ten!** ¡pero y qué! **Why, she is here!** ¡y bien, aquí está ella! **Why, man alive!** ¡cómo, hombre de Dios!

wick [wɪk] [uik], *s.* Torcida, mecha, pábilo.

wick, *s.* Aldea o pueblo: se hallan en voces compuestas; v. gr. *Berwick, Greenwick.*

wicked [ˈwɪkɪd] [ui-kid], *a.* 1. Malvado, perverso, inicuo. 2. Travieso, picaresco, juguetón.

wickedly [ˈwɪkɪdlɪ] [ui-kid-li], *adv.* Inicuamente, malamente, perversamente.

wickedness [ˈwɪkɪdnɪs] [ui-kid-nes], *s.* Maldad, iniquidad, perversidad, malignidad; vicio, pecado, impiedad, irreligión.

wicker [ˈwɪkəʳ] [ui-kaʳ], *a.* Mimbroso, tejido de mimbres. *-s.* 1. Mimbre, ramita flexible de sauce; mimbrera. 2. Cestería. **Wicker basket**, cesto de mimbres. **Wickerwork**, cestería, tejido o artículos hechos de mimbres.

wicket ['wɪkɪt] [ui-kit], *s.* Portillo, postigo, portezuela.

wide [waɪd] [uaid], *a.* 1. Ancho, vasto, dilatado. 2. Extenso, amplio. 3. Del ancho de, de ancho. **Five inches wide**, cinco pulgadas de ancho. 4. Remoto, apartado, lejano. 5. Que tiene amplitud intelectual, liberal, comprensivo. 6. Muy abierto, completamente desarrollado. **The wide world**, el ancho mundo. *-adv.* 1. Lejos, a gran distancia. 2. Anchamente. **Wide open**, abierto del todo o de par en par. **Far and wide**, a lo ancho y a lo largo; por todas partes, por todos lados, completamente. **Wide-awake**, bien, despierto, sobre sí, vigilante. *-s.* Sombrero bajo con alas levantadas. **Wide-gauge**, *V. Broad-gauge.* **To cut a wide swath**, hacer alarde, hacer ostentación de algo. **Wide-angle lens**, lente gran angular.

widely ['waɪdlɪ] [uaid-li], *adv.* 1. Lejos, a gran distancia. 2. Extensamente, muy, mucho, anchamente.

widen ['waɪdn] [uai-den], *va.* Ensanchar, extender, dilatar, aumentar en extensión. *-vn.* Ensancharse, dilatarse.

wideness ['waɪdnɪs] [uaid-nes], *s.* Anchura, extensión a lo ancho.

widespread ['waɪdspred] [uaid-spred], *a.* Diseminado, esparcido por todas partes.

widgeon ['wɪdʒən] [uid-chon], *s.* Mareca, especie de pato.

widow ['wɪdəʊ] [uidou], *s.* Viuda, la mujer a quien se le ha muerto el marido. **Widow-bird**, viuda. *V.* WHIDAHBIRD. **Widow-wail**, olivo enano, arbusto pequeño del género Cneorum. **Widow's weeds**, prendas de luto de una viuda. **Mourning-widow**, escabiosa, pianta herbácea.

widow, *va.* 1. Privar a una mujer de su marido. 2. Dotar con viudedad o dar una viudedad. 3. Privar de una cosa muy útil.

widower ['wɪdəʊəʳ] [ui-doua'], *s.* Viudo, hombre cuya mujer ha muerto.

widowhood ['wɪdəʊhʊd] [ui-dou-jud], *s.* Viudez, viudedad.

width ['wɪdθ] [uidz], *s.* Anchura.

wield [wiːld] [uild], *va.* 1. Manejar, empañar, usar con cabal efecto 2. Ejercer autoridad sobre, mandar. **To wield the sword**, manejar la espada, usarla con habillidad.

wieldy ['wiːldɪ] [uil-di], *a.* Manejable.

wife [waɪf] [uaif], *s.* (*pl.* WIVES). 1. Esposa, mujer casada o simplemente mujer, cuando se habla con relación al marido. 2. Ama de casa. 3. Se usa también provincialmente para designar a una mujer empleada en algún oficio humilde.

wifehood ['waɪfjʊd] [uaif-jud], *s.* Estado de mujer casada; carácter propio de una mujer casada, también, las esposas en general.

wifeless ['waɪdlɪs] [uaid-les], *a.* Que no tiene esposa, sin mujer.

wifely ['waɪflɪ] [uaif-li], *adv.* Como mujer casada, que conviene a una esposa, propio de casadas.

wig [wɪg] [uig], *s.* 1. Peluca o cabellera postiza. 2. Especie de torta. 3. (*Fest. Ingl.*) Juez. **Wig-maker**, peluquero, fabricante de pelucas.

wigged ['wɪgɪd] [ui-guid], *a.* Que lleva peluca.

wiggle ['wɪgl] [ui-guel]. *va. y vn.* (*Fam.*) Mover o moverse rápidamente de un lado a otro, torcerse, andar como un gusano.

wight [waɪt] [uait], *s.* Persona, criatura racional.

wigwag ['wɪgwæg] [uig-uag], *va. y vn.* 1. Menear, moverse hacia adelante y hacia atrás. 2. Hacer señales con banderas.

wigwam ['wɪgwæɪn] [uig-uam], *s.* 1. Choza o jacal de los Indios norteamericanos. 2. (*Fam. E.U:*) Gran edificio público que se usa para reuniones políticas, etc.

wild [waɪld] [uaild], *a.* 1. Silvestre, salvaje, que vive en los bosques, en los desiertos, no domesticado, bravo, feroz; que crece o se cría sin cultivo. **A wild boar**, jabalí. 2. Desierto, inhabitado, solitario, despoblado. 3. Turbulento, alborotado, tosco; aturdido, disparatado; atronado, alocado, extraño, descabellado. 4. Desenfrenado, libre, desarreglado, desordenado; extravagante, loco, insensato. **Wild-eyed**, de ojos huraños. 5. Impetuoso, violento; de tempestad, borrascoso. 6. Fogoso, vivamente descoso. 7. Lejano del curso debido, o del objeto propuesto o deseado. *-s.* Yermo, desierto, paraje despoblado. **Wild carrot**, zanahoria silvestre. **Wildcat**, atolondrado, irresponsable; se usa mucho

hablando de especulaciones o empresas quiméricas. Gato silvestre. **To run wild**, (a) volver (un jardín, etc.) al estado natural o primitivo, (b) desencadenarse. **To be wild in one's youth**, tener una juventud borrascosa. **Wild conceits**, disparates, desatinos, desvaríos.

wilderness ['waɪldənɪs] [uail-da-nes], *s.* 1. Desierto, yermo. 2. Tosquedad, selvatiquez, falta de cultura.

wildfire ['waɪldfaɪəʳ] [uaild-faia'], *s.* 1. Cualquier composición de materias combustibles que se enciende con facilidad y es muy difícil de apagarse, fuego griego. 2. Erisipela, sarpullido.

wild-goose [ˌwaɪldˈguːs] [uaild-gus], *s.* (*orn.*) Ganso silvestre; ganso del Canadá.

wild-goose-chase [ˌwaɪldˈguːstʃeɪs] [uaild-gus-cheis], *s.* Caza de gansos silvestres, (*Fig.*) empresa quimérica, insensata.

wilding ['waɪldɪŋ] [uail-din], *s.* Manzana silvestre, planta que crece silvestre; árbol frutal con sus propias raíces que crece por entre frutales injertos.

wildly ['waɪldlɪ] [uaild-li], *adv.* Sin cultivo, desatinadamente.

wildness ['waɪldnɪs] [uaild-nes], *s.* 1. La calidad de lo que está baldío o sin ningún cultivo. 2. Selvatiquez, tosquedad, rusticidad, falta de cultura, rudeza, brutalidad. 3. Estado salvaje, inculto, carácter salvaje, ferocidad, calidad de feroz. 4. Travesura o acción culpable por demasiada viveza. 5. Desvarío de la imaginación, locura.

wild-oat ['waɪldəʊt] [uaild-out], *s.* Avena loca o silvestre. **To sow one's wild-oats**, (*Fam.*) hacer de las suyas, correrla, pasar sus mocedades.

wile [waɪl] [uail], *va.* 1. Desviar, atraer con astucia, corromper, vendar a uno los ojos. 2. Divertirse, pasar un rato, por lo común con *away*. *V.* WHILE. *-s.* Dolo, fraude, engaño; astucia.

wilful ['wɪlfʊl] [uil-ful], *a.* 1. Porfiado, voluntarioso, testarudo, cabezudo, repropio, rehacio (se dice de las caballerías). 2. Voluntario, premeditado, lo que se ejecuta de intento o lo que se hace con toda intención.

wilfully ['wɪlfəlɪ] [uil-fu-li], *adv.* 1. Tercamente, obstinadamente. 2. Voluntariamente, con toda intención, de propósito o a propósito.

wilfulness ['wɪlfəlnɪs] [uil-ful-nes], *s.* Terquedad, obstinación; perversidad.

wiliness ['wɪlɪnɪs] [ui-li-nes], *s.* Fraude, engaño; maña.

will [wɪl] [uil], *s.* 1. Voluntad, facultad de querer; albedrío; discreción. 2. Acto de la voluntad, volición, elección o escogimiento. 3. Volición, decisión: entusiasmo práctico, energía de carácter. 4. Intención, resolución, designio. 5. Testamento, declaración de la última voluntad. 6. (*Ant.*) Gana, propensión, inclinación o deseo de alguna cosa. 7. (*Ant.*) Precepto, mandato. **At will**, a voluntad. **At one's will**, a su gusto. **Thy will be done**, hágase tu voluntad. **To make one's will**, hacer uno su testamento. **Ill-will**, mala voluntad, malquerer, tirria, odio. **Good-will**, cariño, buena voluntad, disposición o propensión favorable, buena intención. **Good-will of a house** o **shop**, la recomendación que da a sus parroquianos el que vende o traspasa una tienda o establecimiento, para que continúen favoreciendo al nuevo poseedor. **To have all things at will**, tenerlo todo a medida de su deseo. **Will-o'-the-wisp**, fuego fatuo, especie de meteoro.

will, *va. y vn.* 1. Querer, desear. 2. Resolver, mandar. 3. Rogar, suplicar. 4. Testar o hacer testamento. **I will have him do it**, quiero qué él lo haga. **Do as you will**, haga Vd. lo que quiera. **Will he, will he**, que quiera, que no quiera. *-Will*, signo verbal del futuro de indicativo inglés. (Véase la Introducción). En las oraciones afirmativas sirve para expresar resolución, promesa o amenaza de parte de quien habla en la primera persona, y para anunciar o mandar en las segundas y terceras. **I will punish you**, yo te castigaré, tengo voluntad de castigarte, estoy resuelto a castigarte o quiero castigarte. **You will receive the letter tomorrow**, recibirá Vd. la carta mañana, anuncio a Ud. que recibirá la carta mañana, o creo que recibirá Ud. mañana la carta. En las oraciones interrogativas se usa *will* en las segundas personas, para indagar la voluntad del sujeto a quien se dirige la pregunta, y en la tercera persona, para averiguar la voluntad de esta tercera persona. **Will you go to London?**, ¿irá Ud. a Londres? **Will your father give you leave?**, ¿le dará a Ud. licencia su padre?, ¿sabe Vd. si le dará licencia su padre?

willed [wɪld] [uild], *pret.* y *pp.* del verbo TO WILL. **Ill-willed**, maligno, el que tiene mala voluntad. **Self-willed**, obstinado, terco.

willing ['wɪlɪŋ] [ui-lin], *a.* 1. Inclinado, pronto, deseoso. 2. Complaciente. 3. Ofrecido o hecho de buena gana; franco, voluntario. **God willing**, mediante Dios, si Dios quiere. **To be willing**, querer, no tener repugnancia. **To be willing to**, querer, consentir en.

willingly ['wɪlɪŋlɪ] [ui-lin-li], *adv.* Voluntariamente, de buena gana, con gusto.

willingness ['wɪlɪŋnɪs] [ui-lin-nes], *s.* Buena voluntad, buena gana, gusto o buena disposición para hacer algo.

willow 1 ['wɪləʊ] [ui-lou], *s.* Sauce; cualquier árbol o arbusto del género Salix de las salicíenas. **Weeping willow**, *(Bot.)* sauce de Babilonia o de Judea, suace llorón. **Willow-plot**, saucedal, salceda. **Willow-herb**, hierba perenne de la familia de las onagráceas. (Epilobium angustifolium). Se llama también *Persian* o *French willow*, y crece en terrenos bajos. **Hairy willow-herb**, especie británica de Epilobium. **Willow-warbler, willow-wren**, o **chiffchaff**, curraquilla. Phylloscopus rufus. **Willow-oak**, roble americano de gran tamaño, con hojas semejantes a las del sauce.

willow 2, *s.* Diablo, máquina para limpiar el algodón, la lana, el lino, etc.

willowish ['wɪləʊɪʃ] [ui-louish], *a.* Que tiene color de sauce.

willy-nilly ['wɪlɪ'nɪlɪ] [ui-li-ni-li], *a.* y *adv.* Sin respeto a los deseos de otro, a fuerzas.

wilt 1 [wɪlt] [uilt], *va.* Marchitar, ajar, hacer decaer, volver mustio. *-vn.* 1. Marchitarse, secarse, perder su frescura una planta; *(Fig.)* perder la energía o vitalidad. 2. *(Ger.)* Amansarse; ponerse a salvo repentinamente después de verse vencido.

wilt, 2ª pers. *sing.* del presente de indicativo de WILL.

wily ['waɪlɪ] [uai-li], *a.* Astuto, falso, mañoso, cauteloso, insidioso.

wimble ['wɪmbl] [uim-bel], *s.* Berbiquí, especie de barrena.

wimple ['wɪmpl] [uim-pel], *s.* Toca: hoy griñón, toca de liezno o seda que se ponen las mojas y beatas en la cabeza y les rodea el rostro.

wimple, *va.* Tirar hacia abajo; cubrir con griñón.

win [wɪn] [uin], *va.* y *vn.* 1. Ganar, lograr o adquirir alguna cosa. 2. Ganar, conquistar. 3. Obtener, alcanzar. 4. Persuadir, atraer, arrastrar. 5. Llevarse, arrastrar tras sí. 6. Prevalecer, tener más poder o valor que otro.

wince [wɪns] [uins], *vn.* Retroceder, recular como a consecuencia de un dolor o de un golpe; echar pie atrás; de aquí, cocear, tirar coces; mostrarse terco al ser reprendido.

winch [wɪntʃ] [uinch], *s.* 1. Cigüeña de torno, manivela, manubrio en forma de codo que sirve para hacer girar el eje o árbol de una máquina. 2. Argana, argüe, molinete, aparato para subir cosas de mucho peso: cabria.

wind [wɪnd] [uind], *s.* 1. Viento, aire en movimiento; una corriente de aire. 2. Viento, aire. el que se mueve por algún artificio. 3. Resuello, aliento, respiración. 4. Flatulencia, flato, ventosidad, pedo. 5. Cualquier cosa muy ligera y de poco momento. 6. Viento, husmo, el olor que viene de alguna cosa; un secreto dejado escapar o descubierto. **To get wind of a plot**, husmear, descubrir una entruchada o intriga. 7. Viento, en náutica la dirección del viento o del aire movido en la atmósfera. **Wind-bound**, detenido por falta de viento. **Westerly wind**, viento de poniente. **Wind on the beam**, *(Mar.)* viento derrotero. **Wind aft**, *(Mar.)* viento en popa. **Wind on end or ahead**, *(Mar.)* viento por la proa. **Steady wind**, viento hecho. **Land-winds**, terrales. **Light winds**, *(Mar.)* ventolinos. **Trade-winds**, vientos alisios. **Southwest winds**, vendavales. **Quarter-wind**, *(Mar.)* viento al anca o a la cuadra. **The wind is very high**, hace mucho viento, o el viento es muy fuerte. **Between wind and water**, a flor del

agua. **Puff of wind**, soplo, ventolera. **Gale of wind**, temporal, ventarrón. **Gust of wind**, racha de viento, ráfaga, ventarrón. **In the wind's eye, in the teeth of the wind**, directamente opuesto a la dirección del viento. **To keep the wind**, *(Mar.)* Navegar de bolina, mantenerse ciñendo el viento. **To sail against wind and tide**, ir contra viento y marea. **Down the wind**, en decadencia, decayendo. **To take or to have or to get the wind**, dominar a alguno; ganar la superioridad; ganar por la mano, anticiparse. **Something is in the wind**, se trama algo.

wind, *va.* (*pret.* y *pp.* WOUND o WINDED). 1. Serpear o serpentear; girar o moverse alrededor, hacer pasar espiralmente alrededor de un eje fijo. 3. Dar cuerda a, renovar la marcha de, arrollando una cuerda, un resorte, etc. 4. *(Mar.)* Virar, mudar o cambiar el rumbo de un buque; manejar, dirigir, gobernar, ganar influencia sobre. 5. Perseguir, seguir las vueltas o los rodeos de. 6. Devanar, hacer ovillos; tejer. 7. *(Ingl.)* Alzar con árgano o molinete. -*vn.* 1. Moverse o estar dispuesto de una manera circular o en espiral; serpentear. 2. Rodear, ir por rodeos o circunloquios; de aquí, insinuarse, lograr un fin con astucia. 3. Tener forma torcida. 4. Enroscarse, retortijarse, volverse, cambiarse.

wind along, hacer eses, serpentear, seguir.

wind about, enrollarse alrededor de; dar vueltas a.

wind down, bajar dando vueltas, bajar serpenteando.

wind off, devanar; desarrollar, desenredar lo que está enredado o enmarañado; desembarazarse, libertarse, salir de algún enredo o laberinto.

wind up, concluir, acabar, finalizar. **To wind up a watch or clock**, dar cuerda al reloj. **To wind up thread**, devanar hilo, reducirlo a ovillos. **To wind a call**, *(Mar.)* Tocar el pito.

wind, *va.* 1. Ventear, tomar el viento por el olfato. 2. Agotar, gastar el aliento o respiración de; también, recobrar la respiración. 3. Dar aire, exponer al viento, orear.

wind, *va.* y *vn.* 1. Soplar, echar viento por la boca. 2. Tocar un instrumento de viento.

windage ['wɪndɪdʒ] [uin-dich], *s. (Art.)* Viento de un cañón.

wind-bound ['wɪnbaʊnd] [uind-baund], *a. (Mar.)* Detenido por vientos contrarios.

winded ['wɪndɪd] [uind-did], *a.* **Short-winded**, que respira dificultosamente. **Long-winded**, largo; enfadoso, enmarañado.

winder ['waɪndəʳ] [uain-daʳ], *s.* 1. Argadillo, devanador, devanadera. 2. *(Bot.)* Planta enredadera. V. TWINER. 3. Escalón de abanico.

windfall ['wɪndfɔːl] [uind-fol], *s.* 1. Fruta caída del árbol; fruta abatida por el viento. 2. Provecho, ganga, ventaja o ganancia inesperada.

windflower ['wɪndflaʊəʳ] [uind-flauaʳ], *s. (Bot.)* Anémone, anémona.

wind-gauge ['wɪndɡeɪdʒ] [uind-gueich], *s.* Anemómetro, instrumento que mide la fuerza y velocidad de los vientos.

windiness ['wɪndɪnɪs] [uin-di-nes], *s.* 1. Tiempo ventoso; calidad de ventoso. 2. Ventosidad, flatulencia o flato. 3. Hinchazón, vanidad, presunción.

winding ['wɪndɪŋ] [uin-din], *s.* 1. Vuelta, revuelta, giro, rodeo; recodo (de un camino). 2. El acto o la condición del que arrolla o envuelve. 3. Alabeo, comba, combadura. 4. *(Elec.)* Modo como se arrolla un alambre. **Windings and turnings**. las vueltas y revueltas o los rincones y recovecos que hacen tortuosa a una cosa. **Winding of the voice**, la inflexión de la voz. **Winding-sheet**, mortaja, la sábana, en que se envuelve el cadáver. **Winding-stair**, escalera de caracol u ojo. **Winding-tackle**, *(Mar.)* aparejo de estrelleras o candelizas de combés. **Winding up**, (a) acto de dar cuerda (watch, clock); (b) liquidación, conclusión; desenlace. -*a.* 1. Sinuoso, tortuoso, que serpea o serpentea, que se mueve haciendo vueltas o tornos como la serpiente. 2. Que se arrolla, que se enreda o envuelve.

windlass ['wɪndləs] [uind-las], *s.* 1. Argüe, árgana o árgano, máquina para levantar cosas de gran peso. 2. *(Mar.)* Cabrestante pequeño o molinete, instrumento que se usa a bordo de las embarcaciones pequeñas para sacar las anclas del fondo y otros objetos. 3. En las minas de Méjico, malacate.

windle ['wɪndl] [uin-del], *s*. 1. *(Prov.)* Devanadera o cualquier cosa que se usa para dar vueltas o envolver. 2. Medida desusada de 3.50 *bushels* o fanegas.

windmill ['wɪndmɪl] [uind-mil], *s*. Molino de viento.

window ['wɪndəʊ] [uin-dou], *s*. Ventana; vidriera. **Glass window**, **Window-glass**, vidrio de ventana o plano. **Window-shutter**, postigo de ventana; contraventana. **Bay window, bow window**, mirador, ventana saliente o cimbrada. **Dormer o garret window**, lumbrera, tragaluz de bohardilla o desván. **Round o rose window**, rosetón. **Show window**, escaparate de una tienda. **Window-blind**, contravidriera; también, celosía, transparente, persiana. **Window-frame**, bastidor o marco de ventana. **Window-shade**, persiana, transparente. **To look out of the window**, mirar por la ventana.

windpipe ['wɪndpaɪp] [uind-paip], *s*. Tráquea, traquearteria.

windrow ['wɪndrəʊ] [uin-drou], *s*. Línea de hierba segada; montón de maíz o de turba. *-va*. Arrastrar el heno en una hilera o línea.

wind-up ['waɪndʌp] [uaind-ap], *s*. 1. Acción final; fin, término. 2. *(Coloq.)* Broma (joke), chiste.

windward ['wɪndwəd] [uind-uord], *a*. Al viento, expuesto al viento. *-s*. Barlovento, lado de donde sopla el viento. *-adv*. A barlovento. **The Windward Islands**, las Islas de Barlovento. **A windward tide**, marea contraria al viento. **To lie to windward**, barloventear.

windy ['wɪndɪ] [uin-di], *a*. 1. Ventoso, tempestuoso, borrascoso. 2. Expuesto al viento, a barlovento. 3. Vano, dado al estilo hinchado o pomposo. 4. Flatulento. **It is windy**, hace viento. **On the windy side**, del lado del viento.

wine [waɪn] [uain], *s*. 1. Vino, el zumo de las uvas exprimido y fermentado. 2. El vino, el zumo de otros vegetales que se cuece y fermenta al modo del de las uvas. **Sorry wine**, zupia, purriela, vino malo. **Red wine**, vino tinto. **Currant wine**, vino de grosellas. **To season with wine**, envinar. **Wine-bibber**, borracho, odre. **Wine-cellar**, bodega, cueva donde se guardan los vinos. **Wine-cooler**, receptáculo para enfriar el vino. **Wine-fly**, mosca pequeña del género Piophila que se cría en el vino, la sidra, etc. **Wine-glass**, vaso para vino. **Wine-grower**, viñadero, viticultor. **Wine-measure**, medida líquida, medida para vino. **Wine-merchant**, mercader de vino. **Wine-palm**, palmera de la cual se obtiene vino. **Wine-press**, lagar. **Wine-skin**, odre, pellejo de vino. **Wine-taster**, catador de vinos. **Wine tasting**, cata de vinos. **Wine-vault**, candiotera, cueva para conservar el vino. **Wine-whey**, suero con vino.

wine (to), *va*. y *vn*. Convidar u obsequiar con vino; beber vino.

winery ['waɪnərɪ] [uai-na-ri], *s*. Establecimeinto para hacer vino; cuarto para afinar y conservar el vino, candiotera.

wing [wɪŋ] [uing], *s*. 1. Ala, la parte del cuerpo de las aves o murciélagos, y de ciertos insectos, de que se sirven para volar. 2. Lo que proporciona o comunica movimiento veloz. **Upon the wings of the wind**, en alas del viento. 3. Vuelo, la acción de volar. **To take wing**, volar. 4. *(Mil.)* Ala, la parte del ejército que cubre el centro. 5. Ala de un edificio, costado, flanco. 6. Cualquier lado, apéndice, parte, etc., semejante a un ala; apéndice foliáceo, uno de los dos pétalos de la corola papilionácea. 7. Guardabarros. 8. *(Polit.)* Ala. **Right wing, left wing**, ala derecha, ala izquierda. **On the wing**, al vuelo. **Wing-case, wing-cover, wing-sheath**, elitro, estuche que cubre las alas de los insectos. **To be upon the wing**, ir a salir, ir a marchar, estar para salir.

wing, *va*. 1. Llevar, transportar sobre las alas; ejecutar por medio de las alas. 2. Pasar, atravesar, recorrer (flying). 3. Dar o prestar alas a, impeler. 4. Proveer de alas, dar o poner alas. 5. Flanquear, poner flancos. 6. Herir en el ala o en alguna parte análoga; dañar, incapacitar, inhabilitar. *-vn*. Alear, volar, mover las alas.

wing chair ['wɪŋtʃɛəʳ] [uing-cheaʳ], *s*. Sillón con respaldo en forma de alas.

winged [wɪŋd] [uingd], *a*. 1. Alado, que tiene alas; que vuela. 2. Que vuela como con alas; elevado, en éxtasis. 3. Lleno o poblado de seres alados. **Broken-winged**, aliquebrado.

winger ['wɪŋgəʳ] [uin-gaʳ], *s. (Sport)* Ala, alero.

wingless ['wɪŋlɪs] [uing-les], *a*. Falto de alas, sin alas; áptero.

wingy ['wɪŋɪ] [uin-gui], *a*. Alado.

wink [wɪŋk] [uink], *vn*. 1. Cerrar los ojos y abrirlos rápidamente. 2. Guiñar; hacer señas guiñando; pestañear guiñando. 3. Pasar por alto, tolerar, disimular, dejar pasar una falta; en este sentido casi siempre lleva tras sí la partícula at. **A winking light**, una luz poco clara.

wink, *s*. 1. La acción de tener los ojos cerrados. 2. Pestañeo, el movimiento de cerrar y abrir los ojos guiñando. 3. Guiño, la acción de guiñar haciendo señas. 4. Ojeada, mirada pronta y ligera. **I did not sleep a wink all night**, no he cerrado los ojos en toda la noche, o no he podido pegar ojo en toda la noche. **Without further winks or nods**, sin más acá ni más allá. **To wink at a thing**, hacerse el desentendido; no hacer alto en una cosa. *(Fam.)* **Forty winks**, sueño de corta duración.

winker ['wɪŋkəʳ] [uin-kaʳ], *s*. 1. Guiñador, el que guiña; el que pestañea; el que tolera o disimula. 2. Anteojera (de caballo). 3. *(Fam.)* Pestaña. 4. El músculo con el cual se produce el pestañeo.

winkingly ['wɪŋkɪŋlɪ] [uin-kin-li], *adv*. 1. Por medio de guiñadas o guiñando. 2. Con los ojos medio abiertos o entreabiertos. 3. Con tolerancia, con indulgencia. **Winking at**, connivencia.

winkle ['wɪŋkl] [uin-kel], *s*. Caracol marino, uno cualquiera de varios grandes gasterópodos, particularmente del género Fulgur.

winner ['wɪnəʳ] [ui-naʳ], *s*. 1. Ganador, vencedor. 2. Tanto (goal) decisivo de la victoria.

winning ['wɪnɪŋ] [ui-nin], *s*. Ganancia, lucro. *-a*. 1. Atractivo, encantador (appealing), que lleva o arrastra tras sí; persuasivo, que gana la voluntad de otro. 2. Seguro del éxito, ganador (victorious). **Winning back**, desquite, el acto de desquitarse. **Winning side**, el partido que triunfa, gana o lleva la ventaja.

winning post ['wɪnɪŋpəʊst] [ui-nin-poust], *s*. Llegada, meta.

winnings ['wɪnɪŋz] [ui-nins], *s.pl*. Ganancias.

winnow ['wɪnəʊ] [ui-nou], *va*. 1. Aventar, aechar, separar la paja del grano. 2. Examinar, escudriñar. 3. Agitar, batir el aire (como con alas). 4. Soplar; dispersar soplando. *-vn*. Abalear, aechar el grano. **Winnowing-machine**, aventador, abaleador mecánico.

winsome ['wɪnsəm] [uin-som], *a*. Atractivo, que tiene apariencia o maneras atractivas o persuasivas, que gana el corazón, encantador (charming).

winter ['wɪntəʳ] [uin-taʳ], *s*. 1. Invierno, la estación fría del año. **A hard winter**, invierno crudo. **Winter clothes**, ropa de invierno. **Winter season**, invernada. **Winter's bark**, corteza magelánica. **Winter-berry**, apalachina, arbusto de la familia de las ilicineas, con bayas escarlata. **Winter-bloom**, V. WICH-HAZEL. **Winter-solstice**, solsticio hiemal. 2. Epoca triste o lúgubre. 3. *(Poét.)* Año.

winter, *va*. 1. Hacer invernar. 2. Alimentar o conservar durante el invierno. *-vn*. Invernar, pasar el invierno. **Winter-kill**, *(E.U.)* hacer perecer por la severidad del invierno.

wintergreen ['wɪntəgriːn] [uin-ta-grin], *s. (Bot.)* 1. Pirola. 2. Gualteria, planta de la familia de las ericáceas.

wintering ['wɪntərɪŋ] [uin-ta-rin], *s*. 1. Acción de invernar o pasar el invierno. 2. Forraje y abrigo para el ganado durante el invierno.

winterish ['wɪntərɪʃ] [uin-ta-rish], *a*. Algo semejante al invierno.

winterize ['wɪntəraɪz] [uin-ta-rais], *va*. Acondicionar para uso invernal.

winterless ['wɪntəlɪs] [uin-ta-les], *a*. Sin invierno frío; tropical.

wintery ['wɪntərɪ] [uin-ta-ri], *a*. Brumal, invernal o invernizo, lo perteneciente al invierno.

wintertime ['wɪntətaɪm] [uin-ta-taim], *s*. Invierno. **In the wintertime**, en invierno.

wintry ['wɪntrɪ] [uin-tri], *a*. Invernal, de invierno.

wipe

wipe [waɪp] [uaip], *va.* 1. Enjugar, frotar ligeramente; limpiar (clean) por medio de alguna cosa blanda y suave. 2. Quitar o separar frotando ligeramente; restregar, acepillar. 3. Aplicar la soldadura por medio de un pedazo de tela o cuero. **To wipe away**, quitar sacudiendo, estregando o limpiando con suavidad. **To wipe off**, borrar, cancelar (cancel); limpiar, lavar o quitar alguna cosa que ensuciaba o manchaba a otra. **To wipe out**, borrar, cancelar, hacer nulo; destruir, hacer desaparecer. **To wipe out of**, arrojar, defraudar.

wipe, *s.* 1. Limpión, limpiadura ligera. 2. *(Ger.)* Golpe de lado, revés, manotón. *V.* SWIPE.

wiper ['waɪpəʳ] [uai-paʳ], *s.* 1. Persona que enjuga o restriega. 2. Trapo, lienzo, útil, destinado a enjugar o usado para enjugar. 3. *(Mec.)* Leva, álabe, saliente fijado sobre un eje. 4. Limpiaparabrisas.

wire ['waɪəʳ] [uaiaʳ], *va.* 1. Proveer de alambre; atar o liar con hilo metálico. 2. Coger (caza) con un lazo de alambre. 3. *(Fam.)* Transmitir por telégrafo. *-vn. (Fam.)* Enviar un telegrama; telegrafiar. *-s.* 1. Alambre, el hilo tirado de un metal dúctil. 2. El telégrafo eléctrico como medio de comunicación. 3. Cuerda de un instrumento músico. 4. Hilo fino metálico, o juego de líneas finamente rayadas en el foco de un telescopio. 5. Varilla de cortina. **Iron-wire**, hilo o alambre de hierro. **Wires**, arillos para aretes. **Wire-plate**, hilera de tirar alambre. **Wire edge**, filbán (de una navaja nueva, tijera, etc.). **Wire fence**, alambrada. **Wire-gauge**, calibrador de alambre. **Wire-gauze**, gasa de alambre, tela metálica. **Wire-puller**, titiritero; intrigante. **Wire-pulling**, maquinaciones secretas, por bajo cuerda. **Wire-work**, enrejado, alambrado. **Wire-worm**, larva a modo de gusano de elátero.

wire cutters ['waɪəˌkʌtəz] [uaia-ka-tars], *s.* Cortaalambres, cizalla.

wireless ['waɪəlɪs] [uaia-lis], *s.* Abreviatura de **Wireless telegraph**, telegrafía inalámbrica. **Wireless telephony**, radiotelefonía, etc. *(Ingl.)* Radio-emisora. *-va.* y *vn.* Comunicarse por radiograma. **Wireless transmission**, transmisión por radio.

wire tapping ['waɪəˈtæpɪŋ] [uaia-ta-pin], *s.* Conexión telefónica clandestina para interceptar mensajes, escuchas telefónicas.

wiring ['waɪərɪŋ] [uaia-rin], *s.* 1. Alambrado. 2. Instalación de alambrado eléctrico.

wiry ['waɪərɪ] [uaia-ri], *a.* 1. Hecho de alambre; reducido a alambre; semejante a un alambre; tieso, tenso. 2. De mucha resistencia; flaco pero fuerte y nervioso. 3. Débil: se dice del pulso.

wis ['wɪz] [uis], *vn. (Des.)* Pensar, creer.

wisdom ['wɪzdəm] [uis-dom], *s.* 1. Sabiduría, cordura, prudencia, juicio, discreción; sentido común; buena conducta, buen modo de proceder. 2. Alto grado de conocimiento, erudición. 3. Dicho profundo. **Wisdom-tooth**, muela cordal o del juicio. **A man of wisdom**, hombre sabio, muy advertido, muy leído.

wise [waɪz] [uais], *a.* Sabio, docto, hábil; grave, cuerdo (sane), juicioso, prudente, discreto, advertido, sensato, erudito, sabido. **A wise man**, un sabio, un filósofo. *-s.* Modo, manera de ser, estar o hacer. Se usa en composición frecuentemente, como **otherwise**, de otro modo; **likewise**, también; **sidewise**, de lado; **in no wise**, de ningún modo, de ninguna manera, absolutamente. **Wise up**, espabilarse.

wiseacre ['waɪzˌeɪkəʳ] [uais-ei-kaʳ], *s.* Persona sabihonda, el que presume de sabio; de aquí, necio, tonto.

wisecrack ['waɪzkræk] [uais-krak], *s.* Observación ingeniosamente chistosa.

wisely ['waɪzlɪ] [uais-li], *adv.* Sabiamente, con prudencia, con discreción, con cordura, juiciosamente; con mucha habilidad.

wish [wɪʃ] [uish], *va.* 1. Desear, querer, apetecer lo que no se posee. 2. Pedir o suplicar para conseguir lo que se desea. 3. Anhelar, ansiar, desear con ansia o tener ansia o deseo vehemente

de conseguir alguna cosa. 4. Estar inclinado o dispuesto a hacer algo. **I wish you joy**, le doy a Ud. la enhorabuena o el parabién. *-inter.* **I wish!** ¡Ojalá! ¡Quiera el cielo!

wish, 1. Anhelo, ansia, deseo (desire); la cosa deseada. **To make a wish**, pedir un deseo. 2. Petición, demanda, expresión de un deseo. **Wish-bone**, hueso de la pechuga en las aves; hueso delgado ahorquillado formado por la unión de las clavículas, se le llama a veces **merry-thought**.

wisher ['wɪʃəʳ] [ui-shaʳ], *s.* Deseador. **Well-wisher**, el que desea el bien de alguna persona.

wishful ['wɪʃfʊl] [uish-ful], *a.* Deseoso, ansioso, anheloso; ávido (hungry). **Do you know for sure that they're leaving or is it just wishful thinking**? ¿sabes a ciencia cierta que se van o es simplemente lo que tú querrías?

wishfully ['wɪʃfʊlɪ] [uish-fu-li], *adv.* Ansiosamente, ardientemente, con anhelo.

wishing well ['wɪʃɪŋwel] [ui-shin-uel], *s.* Pozo de los deseos.

wishy-washy ['wɪʃɪwɒʃɪ] [ui-shi-uo-shi], *a. (Fam.)* Débil (weak), ligero, diluido (drink); de aquí, flojo, falto de fuerza.

wisp [wɪsp] [uisp], *va.* 1. Acepillar, limpiar con escobilla. 2. *V.* CRUMPLE. *-s.* 1. Manojito de heno, pajar larga u otra cosa. 2. Mechón, puñado de cabellos. 3. Escobilla pequeña. 4. Fuego fatuo. 5. Enfermedad que ataca los pies del ganado mayor.

wispy ['wɪspɪ] [uis-pi], *a.* Tenue, ralo.

wist [wɪst] [uist], *pret.* del verbo TO WIT. «**Moses wist not that his face shone**», «Moisés no sabía que su rostro estaba resplandeciente».

wisteria [wɪsˈtɪərɪə] [uis-tia-ria], *s. (Bot.)* Wistaria, vistaria.

wistful ['wɪstfʊl] [uist-ful], *a.* Nostálgico (nostalgic).

wistfully ['wɪstfəlɪ] [uist-fu-li], *adv.* Con añoranza o nostalgia.

wit [wɪt] [uit], *va.* y *vn.* *(pret.* WIST) *(Ant.)* Saber, recibir una noticia. **To wit**, a saber, es decir.

wit, *s.* 1. Inteligencia (intelligence), rasgo de ingenio, agudeza, dicho agudo, asociación de ideas que causa pasmo; sal. *V.* HUMOR. 2. Ingenio, el sujeto de mucha viveza de imaginación. 3. Entendimiento, ingenio; viveza de imaginación o fantasía; seso. 4. Juicio, discurso, prendas, conocimientos, luces. **Wits**, *pl.* Juicio, sentido, razón; industria. **The five wits**, los cinco sentidos; también, las facultades intelectuales. **Ready wit**, genio agudo. **Mother wit**, sentido común, entendimiento natural. **To be at one's wit's end**, estar, hallarse apurado, cortado; sin saber qué decir; perder la chaveta. **To be out of one's wits**, estar fuera de juicio o fuera de sí; no saber uno lo que se hace. **To live by his wits**, campar de golondro, vivir de gorra, o de expediente, vivir y campar a costa ajena, ser un estafador o un petardista. **To be thought a wit**, pasar por hombre de ingenio. **To have one's wits about one**, conservar uno su presencia de ánimo.

witch [wɪtʃ] [uich], *s.* 1. Bruja, hechicera. 2. Vejarrona, mujer fea.

witch, *va.* Encantar, maleficiar, hechizar, embrujar. *V.* TO BEWITCH.

witchcraft ['wɪtʃkrɑːft] [uich-kraft], *s.* 1. Brujería (sorcery), hechicería, sortilegio (spell), maleficio. 2. Encantamiento, poder mágico, fascinación.

witch hazel ['wɪtʃˌheɪzl] [uich-jei-sel], *s. (Bot.)* 1. Hamamelis de Virginia. 2. Loción de Hamamelis de Virginia.

witch-hunt ['wɪtʃhʌnt] [uich-jant], *s.* Persecución, campaña de desprestigio.

witching ['wɪtʃɪŋ] [ui-chin], *a.* Halagüeño, encantador, que fascina; mágico. **The witching hour**, la medianoche.

with [wɪθ] [uiz], *prep.* 1. Con preposición que se usa para explicar el medio, modo o instrumento con que se hace una cosa; juntamente con, en compañía de. 2. De; toma muchas veces este sentido con los verbos y participios, y con ciertos adjetivos; por ejemplo: **To fill with water**, llenar de agua. **Attended with**, acompañado de. **Congenial with**, que está en el carácter de. **Smitten with**, enamorado de. **Taken with**, encantado de. **With all my heart**, de todo corazón. 3. Por, contra, a, en, entre. **With all speed**, con la mayor prisas, lo más pronto posible. **He does not find fault with it**, nada tiene que decir. **I have nothing to do with you**, nada tengo que ver con Vd. **With your leave**, con permiso de Ud. **To struggle with adversity**, luchar contra la adversidad. **Angry with**, enfadado con. 4. En caso de, con respecto a, para con, concerniente. **Deal not harshly with me**, no sea Ud. duro para conmigo. **To go with**, (a) convenir, sentar bien; (b) acompañar; (c) tomar el partido de. 5. Así que, luego que, inmediatamente, después de. **With that** , así que dijo esto. **To have to do with**, tener que habérselas con. **Away with him!**, ¡quítenlo de mi presencia! ¡fuera con él! ¡que muera! **It is so with the rich**, así sucede entre los ricos. **I don't know what course to take with them**, no sé qué partido tomar para con (o respecto a) ellos.

with-. Prefijo que indica oposición; contra, re. **To withdraw**, retirar, remover. **To withhold**, retener. **To withstand**, oponerse a.

withal [wɪˈðɔːl] [ui-zol], *adv.* 1. Además, a más de esto; también. 2. Por otra parte. 3. Al mismo tiempo. 4. *(Ant.)* Con.

withdraw [wɪθˈdrɔː] [uiz-dro], *va. (pret.* WITHDREW, *pp.* WITHDRAWN). 1. Quitar, privar; distraer; también alejar, descaminar, remover. 2. Retirar (recall), apartar, separar. **She will withdraw her children from the school**, va a sacar a sus hijos del colegio. 3. Desdecir, retractar un aserto; retractarse. *-vn.* Retirarse, apartarse, separarse; irse, salir.

withdrawal [wɪθˈdrɔːəl] [uiz-droal], *s.* Retiro, retirada, el acto o hecho de retirar o de retirarse; Acción de retirar un proyecto de ley presentado a un cuerpo legislativo. **Withdrawal symptoms**, síndrome de abstinencia.

withdrew [wɪθˈdrjuː] [uiz-driu], *pret.* del verbo WITHDRAW.

withe [wɪð] [uid], *s.* 1. Mimbre. 2. Vencejo, atadero hecho de mimbres. **wither»[]»**, *va.* 1. Marchitar, ajar, deslucir, poner mustias o secas las plantas. 2. Hacer perder las carnes o la fuerza muscular; agotar. 3. Hacer perecer o consumirse; también, avergonzar, sonrojar. *-vn.* Marchitarse, secarse, perder su frescura natural.

wither-band [ˈwɪðəbænd] [ui-da-band], *s.* La barra de hierro que sujeta los fustes de la silla de montar.

withered [ˈwɪðəd] [ui-dard], *a.* Marchito, mustio, atrofiado.

withering [ˈwɪðərɪŋ] [ui-da-rin], *a.* 1. Abrasador (burning), agostador. 2. Fulminante.

withers [ˈwɪðəz] [ui-dars], *s. pl.* Cruz, la parte del cuerpo del caballo que está detrás del nacimiento del cuello.

withhold [wɪðˈhəʊld] [uiz-jould], *va. (pret.* y *pp.* WITHHELD). 1. Detener, impedir, retener, apartar, contener. 2. Negar, rehusar (refuse).

within [wɪˈðɪn] [uiz-in], *prep.* 1. Dentro, adentro, en lo interior de. 2. Dentro de, en el espacio de, a la distancia de. 2. Al alcance de. **Within hearing**, al alcance de la voz. 4. Debajo de. **Keep your expenses within your income**, mantenga Vd. sus gastos dentro de los límites de sus ingresos. 5. Por poco; a, casi a, cerca de. **Within a short distance**, a poca distancia. **To reckon within an inch**, calcular pulgada más o menos. **He was within a little of being killed**, por poco lo matan. **From within**, de adentro. **Within four months**, dentro de cuatro meses. **He is within**, está dentro. *-adv.* 1. Interiormente, en la parte interior, dentro; de aquí, en el corazón o en la mente. 2. En casa, en su casa, en la habitación.

without [wɪˈðaʊt] [uiz-aut], *prep.* 1. Sin, con falta de. **Do it without cheating**, hazlo sin hacer trampas. 2. Fuera de, afuera. **Without my reach**, fuera de mi alcance. 3. En lo exterior, por fuera. *-adv.* 1. Por afuera, por fuera, hacia fuera, de la parte de afuera. 2. Exteriormente, en lo exterior. *-conj.* Si no, sin que, a menos que, si no es que. **Without jesting**, bromas aparte. **Without day**, sin fecha. **To do o to go without**, privarse de, pasarse sin. **Without being reminded**, sin que alguien le llame la atención (a o hacia).

withstand [wɪðˈstænd] [uid-stand], *va. (pret.* y *pp.* WITHSTOOD). Resistir, hacer resistencia u oposición. oponerse a; soportar (endure).

witless [ˈwɪtlɪs] [uit-les], *a.* Necio, tonto (fool), falto de ingenio o entendimiento.

witling [ˈwɪtlɪŋ] [uit-lin], *s.* Truhán, chocarrero; el que afecta ingenio.

witness [ˈwɪtnɪs] [uit-nes], *s.* 1. Testigo, espectador. 2. Testimonio, atestación de un hecho; el o lo que da fe, prueba; testigo (ante un tribunal). **To be a witness of**, ser testigo de. **To bear witness to**, dar testimonio, atestiguar. **In witness where of**, en fe de lo cual. **Eye-witness**, testigo de vista, testigo ocular. **Earwitness**, testigo de oídas, o auricular. **With a witness**, *(Ant.)* efectivamente, con efecto.

witness, *va.* 1. Ver (see, observe) o saber por experiencia personal; ser espectador de o concurrir. 2. Atestiguar, testificar. 3. Firmar como testigo; establecer la autenticidad de un instrumento legal, autentificar (authenticate). 4. Exhibir alguna señal de; mostrar. *-vn.* Ser testigo de una cosa o presenciarla; servir de testigo.

witted [ˈwɪtɪd] [ui-tid], *a.* Ingenioso. **Quick-witted**, perspicaz, vivo de ingenio.

witticism [ˈwɪtɪsɪzəm] [ui-ti-si-sem], *s.* Dicho agudo, ocurrencia (funny remark), chiste, gracia, gracejo, chulada; frecuentemente se toma por chocarrería, bufonada o agudezas fuera de tiempo o poco delicadas.

wittily [ˈwɪtɪlɪ] [ui-ti-li], *adv.* Ingeniosamente (funnily), agudamente, con agudeza.

wittiness [ˈwɪtɪnɪs] [ui-ti-nes], *s.* Ingenio, sal, gracia, agudeza, chiste, ingenioso y fino, concepto agudo; viveza de ingenio.

wittingly [ˈwɪtɪŋlɪ] [ui-tin-li], *adv.* Conocidamente, adrede, de propósito.

witty [ˈwɪtɪ] [ui-ti], *a.* 1. Ingenioso, lleno de ingenio, gracia o invención, agudo, chistoso, gracioso. 2. *(Ant.)* Satírico, mordaz, picante. **A witty saying**, un chiste, una gracia o agudeza.

wive [waɪv] [uaiv], *vn.* Casarse, contraer matrimonio el hombre con la mujer. *-va.* 1. Casar, desposar, dar mujer. 2. (Poco us.) Tomar por mujer.

wives [waɪvz] [uaivs], *s. pl.* de WIFE. Mujeres casadas, esposas.

wizard [ˈwɪzəd] [ui-sard], *a.* Hechizero, mago, que encanta. -*s.* 1. Brujo (warlock), hechicero, encantador, adivino. 2. Jugador de manos, titiritero.

wizened [ˈwɪznd] [ui-send], *va.* y *vn.* Desecar, marchitar; desecarse, marchitarse; encogerse, estrecharse. *-a.* Encogido; marchito (withered), ajado, mustio, arrugado (wrinkled).

wo o woe [wəʊ] [uou], *s.* Dolor, pena (sorrow), angustia, pesar, aflicción; calamidad, infortunio, desastre, miseria. **A tale of woe**, un drama. **Woe to you**, pobre de ti, ay de ti. *-inter.* ¡Ay, infeliz! **Wo to the vanquished!** ¡ay de los vencidos! **Woe is me!** ¡desgraciado de mí! ¡pobre de mí! **Woe worth the day!** ¡mal haya el día en que!

woad [wəʊd] [uoud], *s.* 1. Hierba, pastel o glasto; hierba de la familia de las crucíferas. 2. Tinte azul extraído de las hojas de esta planta.

wobble [ˈwɒbl] [uo-bel], *vn.* V. WABBLE.

wobbly [ˈwɒblɪ] [uo-bli], *a.* Tembloroso, flojo, poco firme. **Your legs are wobbly**, te tiemblan las piernas.

woebegone [ˈwəʊbɪɡɒn] [uou-bi-gon], *a.* Abrumado de pesares o de desgracias, consumido por los infortunios, lleno de angustia, angustiado (distress).

woful, woeful [ˈwəʊfəl] [uou-ful], *a.* 1. Triste, afligido (sorrowful), angustiado. 2. Lastimero, doloroso; calamitoso, funesto, desastroso. 3. Ruin, bajo, despreciable.

wofully [ˈwəʊfəlɪ] [uou-fu-li], *adv.* Tristemente, ruinmente, miserablemente, funestamente, desastrosamente, dolorosamente.

wog [wɒɡ] [uog], *s.* Extranjero.

wold [wəʊld] [uould], *s.* Campiña, espacio o comarca de tierras altas ligeramente inclinadas o con pequeñas eminencias. V. DOWN.

wold, *s.* Gualda. V. WELD.

wolf [wʊlf] [vulf], *s.* *(pl.* WOLVES). 1. Lobo. **She-wolf**, loba. **Young wolf**, lobezno, lobato, cachorro de lobo. 2. Mamífero semejante a un lobo. 3. Toda persona o cosa voraz, cruel o rapaz. 4. *(Ento.)* La larva destructiva de varios escarabajos y mariposas nocturnas. 5. Una especie de úlcera cancerosa. *V.* LUPUS. **To cry wolf**, gritar «al lobo», dar falsa alarma (alusión a la fábula). **To have a wolf by the ears**, ver las orejas al lobo, hallarse en gran peligro. **To have a wolf in the stomach**, tener apetito voraz. **To keep the wolf from the door**, cerrar la puerta al hambre, mantener alejada la pobreza o la necesidad.

wolf-dog ['wʊlfdɒg] [vulf-dog], *s.* 1. Mastín, perro grande para cazar lobos. 2. Perro-lobo. **Wolf-fish**. lobo marino, pez grande con dientes sumamente fuertes.

wolfish ['wʊlfɪʃ] [vul-fish], *a.* Lobero, lo que es propio de lobos o pertenece a los lobos.

wolfram ['wʊlfrəm] [vul-fram], *s.* Wolframio o tungsteno.

wolverine ['wʊlvəri:n] [vul-va-rin], *s. (Zool.)* Especie de glotón norteamericano, carcayú.

woman ['wʊmən] [uo-man], *s. (pl.* WOMEN). 1. Mujer, criatura racional del sexo femenino. **A beautiful woman**, una hermosa mujer. **You're a lucky woman**, tienes suerte. 2. La porción femenina de la raza humana; las mujeres colectivamente. 3. Carácter mujeril, el conjunto de las propiedades peculiares a las mujeres. 4. Mujer, criada, sirvienta. **Woman of the town**, dama cortesana.

woman-hater ['wʊmənˌheɪtəʳ] [uo-man-jei-taʳ], *s.* Aborrecedor de las mujeres.

womanhood ['wʊmənhʊd] [uo-man-jud], *s.* El estado o la condición de mujer; el conjunto de las propiedades peculiarse a las mujeres.

womanish ['wʊmənɪʃ] [uo-ma-nish], *a.* Mujeril, femenino, que pertenece a la mujer; afeminado (effeminate), muelle, débil, pusilánime.

womanize ['wʊmənaɪz] [uo-ma-nais], *va.* 1. (Poco us.) Afeminar. 2. Andar detrás de las mujeres.

womanizer ['wʊmənaɪzəʳ] [uo-ma-nai-saʳ], *s.* Mujeriego, donjuán.

womankind ['wʊmənˈkaɪnd] [uo-man-kaind], *s.* El sexo femenino considerado como el conjunto o agregado de todas la mujeres; mujeres.

womanliness ['wʊmənlɪnɪs] [uo-man-li-nes], *s.* Naturaleza o carácter adecuado a la mujer o propio de ella.

womanly, womanlike ['wʊmənlɪ] [uo-man-li] ['wʊmənlaɪk] [uo-man-laik], *a.* Mujeril, mujeriego, de mujer, propio o perteneciente a las mujeres; femenino, que conviene a la mujer; no masculino ni pueril. *-adv.* Mujerilmente, a manera de mujer, como una mujer.

womb [wu:m] [vum], *s.* 1. Útero (uterus), matriz, madre, víscera en que se concibe y alimenta el feto; de aquí, el sitio donde una cosa es engendrada o dada a luz. 2. Cavidad que encierra algo; caverna, seno, entrañas.

wombat ['wɒmbæt] [vom-bat], *s.* Fascolomis, mamífero nocturno de los marsupiales de Australia.

women ['wɪmɪn] [ui-men], *s. pl.* de WOMAN.

won [wʌn] [uan], *pret. y pp.* del verbo WIN.

wonder ['wʌndəʳ] [uan-daʳ], *va.* Querer saber, tener curiosidad por saber, preguntarse; (con una cláusula como complemento). **I wonder why he came**, me pregunto por qué vino él. *-vn.* Admirarse, asombrarse, extrañar, mirar una cosa con admiración. **To wonder at**, extrañar, maravillarse de, quedar admirado o espantado.

wonder, *s.* 1. Admiración, el acto de admirar o admirarse. **We gazed in wonder at the scene**, contemplamos la escena maravillados. 2. Milagro (miracle), portento, pasmo, maravilla (marvel). **To do wonders**, hacer maravillas. **Wonder-worker**, fabricador de prodigios o milagros. **It is a wonder**, es un prodigio. **No wonder**, no hay que extrañar, no es mucho o no es gracia. *-a.* Milagroso.

wonderer ['wʌndərəʳ] [uan-da-raʳ], *s.* Admirador, el o la que se maravilla.

wonderful ['wʌndəfʊl] [uan-da-ful], *a.* Admirable, maravilloso, portentoso, pasmoso. **We had a wonderful time**, lo pasamos maravillosamente.

wonderfully ['wʌndəfəlɪ] [uan-da-fu-li], *adv.* Admirablemente, maravillosamente, prodigiosamente,

portentosamente; de una manera sorprendente, asombrosa o admirable. **Wonderfully well**, a maravilla, a las mil maravillas.

wonderfulness ['wʌndəfəlnɪs] [uan-da-ful-nes], *s.* Naturaleza maravillosa o sorprendente, rareza.

wondering ['wʌndərɪŋ] [uan-da-rin], *a. part. y pa.* Admirado, suspenso, que se maravilla de, que manifiesta sorpresa.

wonderland ['wʌndəlænd] [uan-da-land], *s.* País de las maravillas. **Alice in wonderland**, Alicia en el país de las maravillas.

wonderment ['wʌndəmənt] [uan-da-mant], *s.* 1. Sentimiento de admiración o sorpresa; embeleso. 2. Maravilla, cosa admirable, embeleso.

wonder-struck ['wʌndəstrʌk] [uan-da-strak], *a.* Atónito, pasmado, espantado, asombrado.

wondrous ['wʌndrəs] [uan-dros], *a.* Extraño, maravilloso, admirable, portentoso, pasmoso, asombroso (amazing).

wondrously ['wʌndrəslɪ] [uan-dros-li], *adv.* Pasmosamente, maravillosamente.

wonky ['wɒŋkɪ] [uon-ki], *a.* 1. (Coloq.) Poco firme (wobbly, unsteady). 2. Torcido (askew).

wont [wəʊnt] [uount], *a.* Acostumbrado, que usa o hace habitualmente. **To be wont**, *vn.* Soler, acostumbrar, tener costumbre de; estar ordinariamente en.

wont, *s.* Uso, costumbre, hábito (habit).

won't [wəʊnt] [uount], Abreviatura familiar de WILL NOT.

wonted ['wəʊntɪd] [uoun-tid], *a.* Acostumbrado, usual, habitual, ordinario.

wontedness ['wəʊntɪdnɪs] [uoun-tid-nes], *s.* (Poco us.) La costumbre o hábito de hacer alguna cosa, habituación.

woo [wu:] [vuu], *va.* 1. Cortejar, galantear, enamorar, requerir de amores; pretender a una mujer. 2. (Ant.) Instar, invitar con instancia. *-vn.* 1. Enamoricarse; emplearse en cortejar o galantear. 2. Solicitar, rogar encarecidamente.

wood [wʊd] [vud], *va.* 1. Proveer de madera. 2. Cubrir con bosques; convertir en selva. *-s.* 1. Bosque, selva, monte, cualquier paraje poblado de árboles; se usa a menudo en plural. 2. Madera, sustancia dura y sólida de un árbol o arbusto; madero, palo, leña, leño, según los casos en que se hable. 3. Algo hecho de madera. **Coppice-wood**, monte tallar. **Firewood**, leña. **Split-wood**, leña rajada o en astillas. **Cabinet-maker's wood**, madera de ebanistería. **Cord-wood**, leña hacinada de cuatro pies de largo que se vende por cuerdas. *V.* CORD. **Dye-wood**, madera de tinte. **Drift-wood**, madera de deriva o de flotación. **Sap-wood**, albura; (Carp.) sámago. **Small wood**, brusca, verdasca, leña menuda. **Warped wood**, madera alabeada. **Wood-acid**, ácido pirolenoso. *V.* **Wood-vinegar. Wood-anemone** (Bot.) anémona silvestre o de los bosques. **Wood-ant**, hormiga leonada. **Wood-carving**, (a) el arte, método o procedimiento de esculpir en madera; (b) talla en madera. **Wood-chopper**, leñador. **Wood-drink**, cocimiento o infusión de maderas medicinales. **Wood-hole**, leñera. **Wood-house**, leñera, el paraje donde se encierra la leña. **Wood-lark**, (Orn.) alondra, cogujada, calandria silvestre, un pájaro pequeño. **Wood-louse**, (Ent.) cucaracha, crustáceo isópodo; también, carcoma. **Wood-note**, música campestre. **Wood-nymphs**, *pl.* Dríades. **Wood-offering**, leña para holocausto. **Wood-pease**, guisante silvestre. **Wood-pigeon**, (Orn.) paloma torcaz o paloma zura. **Wood-pile**, pila de leña; hoguera. **Wood-screw**, tornillo para madera. **Wood-shed**, leñera, lugar destinado a guardar y hacinar la leña. **Wood-sorrel**, cualquiera especie de oxálida; (Bot.) acedera silvestre. **Wood-stack**, pila o montón de leña. **Wood-thrush**, tordo pardo, notable por la dulzura de su canto, que se halla en el este de los Estados Unidos. **Wood-vinegar**, vinagre de madera, ácido pirolenoso, un ácido acético impuro.

woodbine ['wʊdbaɪn] [wud-bain], *s.* (Bot.) 1. Madreselva de Europa. 2. Trepadora virginiana.

woodchuck ['wʊdtʃʌk] [wud-chak], *s.* Marmota grande de América.

woodcock [ˈwʊdkɒk] [wud-kok], *s*. Chocha, chochaperdiz o becada.

woodcraft [ˈwʊdkrɑːft] [wud-kraft], *s*. Conocimineto y práctica en lo concerniente a la vida en los bosques.

woodcut [ˈwʊdkʌt] [wud-kat], *s*. Grabado en madera.

wood cutter [ˈwʊdkʌtəʳ] [wud-ka-taʳ], *s*. 1. Leñador. 2. *(Fam.)* Grabador en madera.

wooded [ˈwʊdɪd] [wu-ded], *a*. Arbolado, plantado o cubierto de árboles; provisto de leña o de madera.

wooden [ˈwʊdn] [wu-den], *a*. 1. Hecho de palo o madera; grosero. 2. Semejante a un trozo de madera; rudo, torpe, sin espíritu, estúpido, mecánico. **Wooden bowl**, artesilla de panaderos. **Wooden-head, wooden-headed**, zote, zopenco, lerdo, estúpido, bolo. **Wooden leg**, pata de palo. **Wooden shoes**, zuecos. **Wooden spoon**, cuchara de palo.

woodiness [ˈwʊdɪnɪs] [wu-di-nes], *s*. Estado leñoso, calidad leñosa.

woodland [ˈwʊdlænd] [wud-land], *s*. Arbolado; la tierra plantada o cubierta de árboles. -*a*. Arbolado, cubierto de árboles; perteneciente a los árboles, a la leña o a la madera.

woodless [ˈwʊdlɪs] [wud-les], *a*. Falto de madero o selvas, sin bosques.

woodman [ˈwʊdmən] [wud-man], *s*. 1. Leñador. 2. Guardabosque: habitante de los bosques.

woodpecker [ˈwʊdpekəʳ] [wud-pe-kaʳ], *s*. Picamaderos, picaposte, pico, ave, **Ivory-billed woodpecker**, carpintero real.

woodruff [ˈwʊdrʌf] [wud-raf], *s*. *(Bot.)* Aspérula, planta herbácea de la familia de las rubiáceas.

woodsman [ˈwʊdzmən] [wuds-man], *s*. El que vive o trabaja en el bosque; guardabosque, leñador.

woodward [ˈwʊdwɔːd] [wud-uord], *s*. Guardabosque.

woodwork [ˈwʊdwɜːk] [wud-uek], *s*. Enmaderamiento, maderaje, maderamen, el conjunto de maderas para edificar o para otros usos.

woody [ˈwʊdɪ] [wu-di], *a*. 1. Leñoso; de la naturaleza de la madera. 2. Perteneciente o parecido a la madera. 3. Arbolado, abundante en madera; selvoso.

woof [wuːf] [wuf], *s*. 1. Trama, la hebra que pasa de un lado a otro de la urdimbre; conjunto de hilos cruzados. *V*. WEFT. 2. Textura, la disposición y orden de los hilos en una tela. 3. *(Coloq.)* Ladrido.

woofer [ˈwuːfəʳ] [wu-faʳ], *s*. Altavoz para sonidos graves.

wooing [ˈwuːɪŋ] [wuin], *s*. Galanteo, cortejo.

wooingly [ˈwuːɪŋlɪ] [wuin-li], *adv*. Agradablemente (nicely), dulcemente.

wool [wʊl] [wul], *s*. 1. Lana. 2. Pelo inferior de un animal cuya piel se utiliza en la peletería. 3. Cabello espeso y crespo, como el de un negro. 4. Algo que se parece a la lana; v. gr. la pelusa larga y blanda que cubre ciertas plantas e insectos. **All wool**, todo de lana, de lana pura. **Coarse wool**, lana burda o churla. **Fine carded wool**, estambre. **Fleece wool**, lana de vellón, toisón. **Cotton wool**, algodón en rama, lana de algodón. **Long-staple woool**, lana larga de cardar. **Short-staple wool**, tundizno, lana corta. **Mineral wool**, lana mineral, sustancia de aspecto parecido al de la lana, **Natural wool**, lana en bruto. **To dye in the wool**, teñir la lana antes de hilarla; de aquí, confirmar, establecer firmemente una opinión. **Wool-ball**, pelotón de lana, que a veces se encuentra en el estómago de un carnero. **Wool-bearing**, lanar. **Wool-comber**, cardador, cardadora de lana. **Wool-combing**, cardadura de lana. **Wool-grower**, criador de ganado lanar. **Woolpack**, (a) saca o fardo de lana; (b) cúmulo (cloud). **Wool-pated**, que tiene los cabellos encrespados. **Woolsack**, el asiento del canciller y de los jueces en la cámara de los pares. **Wool-sorter**, escogedor de lana. **Wool-sorter's disease**, especie de envenenamiento de la sangre por medio de la lana infectada; probablemente ántrax. **Wool-stapler**, comerciante en lanas. **Wool-winder**, vellonero.

wooled [wʊld] [wuld], *a*. Que tiene lana, con lana; forma a menudo palabras compuestas. **Fine-wooled**, con lana fina.

wool-gathering [ˈwʊlˌɡæðərɪŋ] [wul-ga-de-rin], *a*. Descarriado, divertido. -*s*. Ocupación trivial o sin objeto; distracción.

woolen, woollen [ˈwʊlən] [wu-lan], *a*. Hecho de lana; de lana (como mercadería). -*s*. Cualquier tela o tejido hecho de lana. **Woollen or woolen manufacturers**, manufactura de lana. **Woollen cloth**, paño de lana. **Woollen-draper**, pañero, comerciante en paños. **Woollen-dyer**, tintorero de lana.

woolly [ˈwʊlɪ] [wu-li], *a*. 1. Lanudo, lanoso, que consta de lana; cubierto, vestido de lana o semejante a la lana; coposo; (cabello) cresp, pasudo. 2. *(Bellas artes)* Falto de detalles, impreciso (unclear), vago y borroso. 3. *(Meteo.)* (Nube) que tiene la apariencia de la lana. 4. *(Bot.)* Lanoso, lanuginoso, que tiene una especie de lanilla o pelusa.

woolman [ˈwʊlmən] [wul-man], *s*. Lanero.

woozy [ˈwuːzɪ] [wu-si], *a*. *(Coloq.)* Atontado, grogui.

word [wɜːd] [wued], *s*. 1. Palabra (term), vocablo, voz, sonido o conjunto de sonidos articulados que expresan una idea. 2. Palabra, representación gráfica de estos sonidos. 3. Palabra, habla, voz, la facultad de hablar. 4. Conversación corta o breve, pocas palabras, observación breve; de aquí, dicho, sentencia, apotegma. 5. Palabra, promesa, oferta. 6. Aviso, recado, mensaje. 7. Escritura, la palabra de Dios. 8. Palabra, Verbo la segunda persona de la Santísima Trinidad. 9. Contraseña; señal, voz de mando, orden, mandato. 10. *pl* Palabras mayores, disputa, contienda verbal. **To keep one's word**, cumplir su palabra, tener palabra. **Take my word for it**, créame Vd.; puede Vd. creerme bajo palabra. **Wordsquare**, sopa de letras. **Words of course**, cumplimientos. **Soft words**, palabras dulces o melosas. **By word of mouth**, de boca, de viva voz. **By-word**, proverbio. **High words**, palabras mayores o dichos injuriosos. **Vain words**, palabras al aire. **To write to send word**, enviar a decir. **Big words**, disputa; palabras mayores.

word, *va*. 1. Expresar, explicar, enunciar, redactar, dictar (write). 2. Instar con palabras, afectar por medio de una palabra. **To word a letter**, dictar bien una carta.

word-book [ˈwɜːdbʊk] [ued-buk], *s*. Vocabulario, léxico.

wordiness [ˈwɜːdɪnɪs] [uer-di-nes], *s*. Verbosidad, prolijidad; expresión con abundancia de palabras.

wording [ˈwɜːdɪŋ] [uer-din], *s*. Dicción, estilo, manera de expresarse en palabras; fraseología; palabras usadas, expresión, términos, redacción.

wordless [ˈwɜːdlɪs] [uerd-les], *a*. Falto de palabras, mudo.

wordy [ˈwɜːdɪ] [uer-di], *a*. 1. Verbal, de la naturaleza de palabras o perteneciente a ellas. 2. Verboso, difuso, abundante en palabras, farragoso (involved).

wore [wɔːʳ] [uoʳ], *pret*. del verbo TO WEAR.

work [wɜːk] [uerk], *va*. 1. Trabajar, labrar, poner en obra; explotar (operate) (mine, priviledge, etc.); bordar, tallar (una piedra). 2. Fabricar, manufacturar; producir, hacer nacer (working); trabajar en; preparar por medio de algún procedimiento. 3. Trabajar, formar o componer con arreglo y esmero las obras de ingenio. 4. Obrar sobre, influir, impeler, excitar, regir por medio de esfuerzo; a veces implica corrupción o soborno. 5. Investigar o resolver (a problem). 6. Hacer trabajar, obrar, mover, funcionar, ir o poner en movimiento, emplear, servirse, usar de (as an instrument); mover nerviosamente (fingers); abrirse camino; hacer fermentar. 7. *(Mar.)* Maniobrar. 8. Causar, efectuar, poner por obra. -*vn*. 1. Trabajar, ocuparse en cualquier trabajo o ejercicio, estar empleado en algún negocio o tráfico. 2. Obrar, surtir efecto o hacer efecto alguna cosa. 3. Estar en movimiento o en acción; funcionar, ir, desempeñar. 4. Obrar u operar las medicinas. 5. Trabajar, darse pena para hacer algo, esforzarse para ejecutar alguna cosa. 6. Fermentar, ponerse un cuerpo en movimiento de fermentación. **To work oneself into favor**, insinuarse en la amistad de alguno, ganar su favor, **to work oneself off**, salir de un apuro a fuerza de trabajo o de fatigas, desembarazarse de un negocio complicado. **To work one's way**, abrirse camino para la ejecución o el logro de alguna cosa. **To work against**, trabajar contra; oponerse a. **To work at**, trabajar en, ocuparse en o de. **To work down**, hacer descender, descender, bajarse. **To work in**, trabajar en; insinuarse en, entrar poco a poco. **To work into**, entrar en, penetrar en. **To work out**, acabar alguna cosa a fuerza de trabajo; borrar o expiar, cuando se habla de faltas, culpas, etc.; lograr o conseguir un objeto a fuerza de fatigas, ejecutar, efectuar; agotar (a mine). **To work-round**, volverse lentamente y con esfuerzo. **To work through**, penetrar; atravesar a fuerza de trabajo, salir al otro lado. **To work up**, labrar, dar forma una cosa; servirse de; amasar; agotar, consumir; excitar, estimular (stimulate), inflamar; elevarse, subir con esfuerzo; levantar. **To work upon**, obrar sobre, trabajar en, estar ocupado en un trabajo manual; sublevar, excitar, mover a compasión. **To work to windward**, (Mar.) barloventear, navegar de bolina, ceñir el viento.

work, *s.* 1. Trabajo, ejercicio u obra de cualquier especie. **The building work is still going on**, todavía están en obras. 2. Fábrica, obra, tarea, lo que está por hacer, aquello en que se trabaja; costura, cosido; bordado, bordadura, dibujo hecho con al aguja. 3. Obra, trabajo, labor; producto del que trabaja manualmente o con la inteligencia; obra de un ingeniero; fortificación. 4. Fatiga. 5. Obra, toda suerte de acción moral. 6. Empleo (employment) u ocupación. 7. Fábrica, taller, establecimiento; en plural, por lo común. 8. *pl.* Rodaje, engranaje, motor, movimiento, maquinaria. **Needle-work**, labor de aguja. **Press-work**, triada, **Work-bag**, saco de labor. **Work-box**, caja de labor. **Work-days**, días útiles o de trabajo. **To set to work**, emplear, ocupar, dar empleo u ocupación. **To be at work**, estar haciendo alguna cosa; estar ocupado en hacer algo; estar trabajando. **To be hard at work**, estar muy afanado o muy ocupado en hacer algo. **Work-folk, work-folks, work-people**, obreros, operarios. **Work-room**, taller, pieza en que se trabaja.

working [ˈwɜːkɪŋ] [ue-kin], *s.* 1. Maniobra de navío, faena. **Working aloft**, (Mar.) maniobra alta. **Lubberly working**, maniobra basta. 2. Trabajo, obra, operación; agitación.

workable [ˈwɜːkəbl] [ue-ka-bol], *a.* 1. Que puede funcionar; que se puede hacer funcionar o trabajar (máquina). 2. Factible (feasible), practicable. 3. (Min.) Explotable. 4. Apto para el trabajo, capaz de trabajar. 5. Que puede ser influido o excitado.

workaday [ˈwɜːkədeɪ] [ue-ka-dei], *a.* 1. Relativo a un día de trabajo. 2. Afanoso, laborioso, prosaico (prosaic).

workaholic [ˌwɜːkəˈhɒlɪk] [ue-ka-jo-lik], *s.* (Coloq.) Trabajoadicto, fanático del trabajo.

work book [ˈwɜːkbʊk] [uek-buk], *s.* 1. Manual de trabajo. 2. Manual de estudios.

work day [ˈwɜːkdeɪ] [uek-dei], *s.* Día de trabajo.

worker [ˈwɜːkəʳ] [ue-kaʳ] *s.* 1. Trabajador, obrero; operario. **Office worker**, oficinista. 2. Abeja u hormiga obrera (con los órganos sexuales no desarrollados) que trabaja en comunidad.

work-fellow [ˈwɜːkfeləʊ] [uek-fe-lou], *s.* Compañero de trabajo, obrero.

workhouse [ˈwɜːkhaʊs] [uek-jaus], *s.* 1. Hospicio (hospice), casa de misericordia, la destinada para albergar a los pobres. 2. Obrador, taller. 3. Casa de corrección en que recogen a los vagos y ociosos para que trabajen.

working [ˈwɜːkɪŋ] [ue-kin], *a.* 1. Que trabaja; que funciona, que se mueve. 2. De trabajo, adaptado al uso de un obrero o operario; obrero. **All my working life**, toda mi vida activa. 3. Usado o puesto aparte para conducir un negocio; activo, productivo. **Working capital**, capital activo. **Working beam**, balancín. **Working class**, la clase obrera, operaria. **Working-drawing**, (Arq.) montea. **Working-man**, gañán, obrero u operario a jornal, jornalero. **Working parts**, piezas vivas, partes que funcionan.

workman [ˈwɜːkmən] [uek-man], *s.* Artífice, labrador.

workmanlike [ˈwɜːkmənlaɪk] [uek-man-laik], *a.* Eficiente (efficient), profesional.

workmanship [ˈwɜːkmənʃɪp] [uek-man-ship], *s.* 1. Manufactura, artificio, trabajo manual, hechura. 2. Habilidad o destreza del artífice. **A fine piece of workmanship**, una obra perfectamente ejecutada, una obra maestra.

works [ˈwɜːks] [ueks], *s. pl.* 1. Taller, fábrica (factory). 2. Movimiento (of a watch), mecanismo (mechanism). 3. Engranaje de una máquina. 4. Obras. **Road works**, obras viales.

workout [ˈwɜːkaʊt] [uek-aut], *s.* (Vul.) Prueba, ensayo.

workshop [ˈwɜːkʃɒp] [uek-shop], *s.* Taller, obrador.

work-woman [ˈwɜːkwʊmən] [uek-uo-man], *f.* Costurera, obrera.

world [wɜːld] [ueld], *s.* 1. Mundo, el conjunto de todos los cuerpos que componen el universo. 2. Mundo, el modo de vida, trato y relaciones de los hombres. **For all the world**, exactamente, cabalmente; rectamente. 3. Mundo, esfera o globo terrestre (earth). 4. (Met.) Gente, gentío, muchedumbre o concurso de muchas personas, infinidad. 5. Mundo; en la mística se toma por los hombres corrompidos o profanos. **World without end**, para siempre jamás; por los siglos de los siglos.

worldliness [ˈwɜːldlɪnɪs] [ueld-li-nes], *s.* Carácter mundano; profanidad, vanidad mundana; apego o afición desmedida a los halagos del mundo.

worldly [ˈwɜːldlɪ] [ueld-li], *a.* Mundano, terreno, que pertenece al mundo, humano, común. -*adv.* Profanamente, según el mundo.

worldwide [ˈwɜːldwaɪd] [ueld-uaid], *a.* Mundial, del mundo entero. -*adv.* Por todo el mundo. **They are famous worldwide**, son mundialmente famosos.

worm [wɜːm] [uem], *s.* 1. Gusano (maggot), animalillo invertebrado blando que se arrastra, como son las lombrices de tiera, las ascárides, etc.; lombriz que se cría en la tierra o se engendra en el cuerpo de los animales. 2. Larva rastrera de un insecto, oruga. 3. Polilla que se cría en la ropa; carcoma de la madera, coco, el gusanito que se cría en las legumbres y semillas; gorgojo, el que se cría en los granos; (Fig.) gusano roedor, remordimeinto, pesadumbre secreta. 4. Persona vil, despreciable; mortal débil comparable a un gusano. 5. (Mec.) Tornillo sin fin, rosca. 6. (Quím.) Serpentín. 7. Sacatrapos. **Still-worm**, serpentín de alambique. **Worm in the conscience**, gusano de la conciencia, el remordimiento. **Glow-worm**, gusano de luz, luciérnaga. **Silk-worm**, gusano de seda. **Vine-worm o wine-grub**, pulgón de las viñas. **Worm fence**, cercado en zigzag. **Worm-like**, vermicular, semejante a un gusano. (Med.) **Worms**, *pl.*, lombrices. **Worm-tea**, tisana vermífuga; infusión antihelmíntica. **Worm and wheel**, engranaje de tornillo sin fin.

worm, *vn.* Trabajar u obrar lentamente. -*va.* 1. Insinuarse, entrar en, como un gusano; arrastrar; arrastrarse como un gusano (wriggle). 2. Sacar, descargar por medio del sacatrapos; (Fig.) echar o suplantar por medios secretos. 3. Quitar a los perros la lita que se dice tienen debajo de la lengua, para que no rabien. 4. **To worm a cable**, (Mar.) embutir un cable.

worm-eaten [ˈwɜːmˌiːtn] [uem-i-ten], *a.* Carcomido, apolillado, roído, corroído o comido de gusanos, cocoso, dañado del coco.

worm gear [ˈwɜːmgɪəʳ] [uem-guiaʳ], *s.* (Mec.) Rueda para tornillo sin fin.

worm-holes [ˈwɜːmhəʊlz] [uem-jouls], *s. pl.* Carcoma.

wormwood [ˈwɜːmwʊd] [uem-wud], *s.* (Bot.) Ajenjo, planta amarga, perenne, del género artemisa.

wormy [ˈwɜːmɪ] [ue-mi], *a.* Agusanado, lleno de gusanos.

worn [wɜːn] [uern], *pp.* del verbo TO WEAR. **Worn out**, gastado, consumido por el uso; cansado, muy fatigado (exhausted). **The sails are worn out**, las velas son de media vida.

worried [ˈwʌrɪd] [ua-rid], *a.* Preocupado. **I'm worried about you**, estoy preocupado por ti.

worry [ˈwʌrɪ] [ua-ri], *va.* 1. Preocupar (trouble). **I don't want to worry you**, no quiero preocuparte. 2. Acosar (harass), perseguir, vejar, molestar, atormentar, jorobar. 3. Lacerar, desgarrar o matar mordiendo o sacudiendo. -*vn.* 1. Atormentarse, incomodarse, inquietarse. 2. Morder o lacerar, como los perros cuando riñen.

worry, *s.* Cuidado, ansia (anxiety), preocupación (trouble, problem), tormento, molestia. **Financial worries**, problemas económicos.

worrying ['wʌrɪɪŋ] [ua-riin], *a.* Inquietante, preocupante.

worse [wɜːs] [uers], *a.* comp. de BAD, ILL o EVIL. 1. Peor, más malo, más imperfecto, inferior. 2. Más enfermo, peor, más malo. 3. colocado en peor estación o situación. **You are wore than your word**, Vd. no cumple su palabra. *-adv.* Peor, de un modo más malo, más fuerte, más grandemente. **Worse and worse**, de mal en peor, peor que nunca; cada vez más malo (o peor); cada vez más fuerte. **To be worse**, valer menos, ser más malo; estar peor. **To be worse off**, estar menos bien, estar peor; ser menos feliz. **To become, to get, to grow worse**, emperorarse; ponerse peor, ir peor. **To make, to render worse**, empeorar. **So much the worse**, tanto peor. **For the worse**, en mal. **Worse than ever**, peor que nunca. **The cloak is but little the worse for use**, la capa está apenas usada. *-s.* Menoscabo, detrimento; lo peor. **He had the worse**, llevó la peor parte.

worsen [wɜːsn] [uer-sen], *va.* y *vn.* Hacer peor, empeorar; ponerse peor, empeorarse.

worship ['wɜːʃɪp] [uor-ship], *s.* 1. Culto, adoración. **Sun worship**, el culto al sol. 2. Respeto, deferencia u honor que se tributa a la virtud, al poder, etc. 3. Dignidad, eminencia, excelencia. 4. Un tratamiento que se da en Inglaterra a los magistrados y a algunos empleados municipales, y corresponde a señoría en castellano. **Your worship**, usía; vuestra señoría.

worship, *va.* Adorar, honrar, venerar o reverenciar con culto religioso; respetar. **He worships her**, la adora. *-vn.* Dar culto.

worshipful ['wɜːʃɪpfʊl] [uor-ship-ful], *a.* Venerable, honorable (honorable), respetable, digno de honra, respeto o veneración. Es también palabra de tratamiento. **The worshipful president**, el respetable presidente. **Worshipful master**, (entre los francmasones), El Venerable.

worshipper ['wɜːʃɪpəʳ] [uor-shi-paʳ], *s.* Adorador, el que da culto. **Worshipper of idols**, idólatra.

worshipping ['wɜːʃɪpɪŋ] [uor-shi-pin], *s.* Adoracón, culto; acción de adorar.

worst [wɜːst] [uerst], *a. superl.* de BAD, ILL o EVIL. 1. Pésimo, malísimo, lo más malo, lo peor. 2. Lo más enfermo, lo más malo. 3. Lo más fuerte, lo más grande. **He is the worst of men**, él es el más perverso de los hombres. *-adv.* Lo peor, lo más malo, lo más fuerte, lo menos. *-s.* Lo peor, lo más malo, el estado más desesperado o más calamitoso, la mayor miseria; inferioridad; mal andar. **I am at the worst**, me hallo en el estado más triste, no puedo estar peor. **This is racism at its worst**, esto es racismo de la peor especie.

worst, *va.* Vencer, rendir, sujetar, triunfar de.

worsted ['wɜːstɪd] [uers-tid], *pp.* del verbo WORST. Vencido.

worsted, *s.* 1. Estambre, la hebra de lana torcida. **Worsted stockings**, medias de estambre. 2. Material que no es algodón ni seda y se emplea en la manufactura de fleco o galón.

wort [wɜːt] [uet], *s.* 1. Planta, hierba, se usa en composición. 2. Legumbre del género de la col o berza; repollo. 3. La cerveza nueva que no ha fermentado y a veces también la que está fermentando. **Spleen-wort**, *(Bot.)* Hepática.

worth [wɜːθ] [uerz], *vn. (Ant.)* Suceder, sobrevenir. **Woe worth the day**, véase bajo el título Wo.

worth, *s.* 1. Mérito; consideración, importancia, entidad; de aquí, valor, precio. **To prove one's worth**, demostrar su valía. 2. Excelencia mental y moral. *-a.* 1. Digno, benemérito. 2. Que tiene mérito. 3. Que tiene dinero, rentas, etc. 4. Que vale; que tiene precio, de igual valor o precio que. **To be worth**, (a) tener, poseer, cuando se habla de personas. (b) valer, cuando se habla de cosas; valer la pena de, merecer, ser digno de. **He is worth a million**, posee un millón. **A place worth keeping**, una colocación o destino que vale la pena. **That is little worth**, eso no vale gran cosa. **He is**

worth his weight in gold, él vale su peso en oro. **To be worth while**, merecer o valer la pena de.

worthily ['wɜːðɪlɪ] [uer-zi-li], *adv.* Dignamente, honorablemente; convenientemente (conveniently), como corresponde; con justos motivos.

worthiness ['wɜːðɪnɪs] [uer-zi-nes], *s.* Dignidad, mérito (merit), excelencia, realce.

worthless ['wɜːθlɪs] [uerz-les], *a.* Indigno, falto de mérito; vil, bajo, de ningún valor.

worthlessness ['wɜːθlɪsnɪs] [uerz-les-nes] *s.* Indignidad, vileza; falta de mérito.

worthwhile ['wɜːθwaɪl] [uerz-uail], *a.* Que vale la pena. **The look on your face made it all worthwhile**, mereció la pena sólo por ver la cara que pusiste.

worthy ['wɜːθɪ] [uer-zi], *a.* Digno (estimable), benemérito, merecedor de recompensa u honor, acreedor a algún premio. **A point worthy of mention**, algo digno de mención. *-s.* Héroe, varón ilustre y grande; en este sentido se usa comúnmente en plural.

wot [wɒt] [uot], *vn.* 1ª y 3ª pers. sing. indic. pres. de TO WIT. Yo sé, él sabe.

would [wʊd] [wud], *pret.* del verbo WILL. Se usa también como verbo auxiliar en el condicional; expresa también la inclinación, el deseo, la súplica o la costumbre, y la acción determinada o resuelta. **I would have her do it**, yo querría que ella lo hiciese. **He would not do it**, no quiso hacerlo. **Do what he would**, por más que él hacía. **I would learn the reason if I could**, yo averiguaría la razón si pudiese. **I would do it**, yo lo haría. **Would to God!** ¡ojalá! ¡plegue a Dios!

would-be ['wʊdbiː] [wud-bi], *a.* Titulado, presumido, supuesto o fingido. **A would-be poet**, presumido de poeta. **A would-be star**, aspirante a estrella.

wound [waʊnd] [vaund], *pret.* y *pp.* del verbo TO WIND. **He has wound up the clock**, él ha dado cuerda al reloj.

wound, *s.* 1. Herida, llaga, solución de continuidad en la piel y carne de un animal o en la corteza o sustancia de un árbol o planta. 2. Ofensa, golpe, causa de pena o de pesar. **Incised wound**, herida incisa, cortadura, incisión. **Lacerated wound**, laceración. **Punctured wound**, herida penetrante, picadura. **To reopen old wounds**, abrir viejas heridas.

wound, *va.* 1. Herir, hacer una herida, llagar. 2. Herir, ofender, dañar, agraviar, causar algún mal físico o moral.

wounded ['waʊndɪd] [wun-did], *a.* Herido, dolido.

wounding ['waʊndɪŋ] [wun-din], *a.* Hiriente.

woundless ['waʊndlɪs] [wund-les], *a.* Sin herida, ileso (unhurt).

woundy ['waʊndlɪ] [wun-di], *a. (Prov. o des.)* Excesivo.

wove, woven [waʊv] [uouv] [waʊvn] [uou-ven], *pret.* y *pp.* del verbo TO WEAVE.

wow [waʊ] [uau], *interj. (Coloq.)* ¡Ah! *-vt.* Enloquecer, volver loco.

wrack [ræk] [rak], *s.* 1. Fuco, ova; vegetación y otros objetos que el agua arroja a la orilla. 2. Naufragio, ruina. 3. Despojos de naufragio. **To go to wrack**, decaer, arruinarse, ir en decadencia; correr a su perdición.

wrack, *s.* Montón de nubes; vapor flotante.

wraith [reɪθ] [reiz], *s.* Fantasma, espectro de una persona viva y que se suponía precursor de la muerte de dicha persona, aparición (apparition); aparecido, ánima en pena.

wrangle [ræŋgl] [ran-guel], *vn.* Pelotear, reñir, disputar (argue), contender.

wrangle, *s.* Pelotera, pendencia, riña, contienda, disputa (quarrel).

wrangler ['ræŋgləʳ] [ran-glaʳ], *s.* 1. Pendenciero, disputador, amigo de disputas; originalmente, argumentador, defensor de una tesis. 2. En la Universidad de Cambridge, Inglaterra, el alumno que obtiene el primer grado en los exámenes de matemáticas. 3. *(E.U.)* Vaquero, cowboy.

wrangling ['ræŋglɪŋ] [ran-glin], *s.* Disputa, quimera, zipizape, altercación.

wrap [ræp] [rap], *va. (pret.* y *pp.* WRAPPED o WRAPT). 1. Arrollar, rollar o revolver una cosa en sí misma. 2. Envolver, cubrir una cosa dando vueltas alrededor de ella con alguna otra, entrelazar (entwine). **To wrap up**, rollar, arrollar; envolver; arrebatar, asombrar, llenar de admiración; contener; comprender, dar fin a. **He is wrapped up in his son,** (*Fam.*) él está encantado con su hijo. **She is wrapped up in herself,** ella es muy presumida. **To wrap up a deal,** cerrar un trato.

wrap, *s.* Bata, abrigo, chal (shawl), prenda de vestir holgada, en plural, todas las prendas exteriores que se llevan además de la ropa ordinaria, como capas, bandas, etc. **Wrap-rascal,** abrigo ahuecado y por regla general de paño burdo.

wrapper ['ræpəʳ] [ra-paʳ], *s.* 1. El que arrolla o rolla; el que envuelve; el que arrebata. 2. Envoltvedero, envolvedor, cubierto, carpeta, papel. 3. Bata, peinador, ropaje holgado, flotante. 4. (*Fam.*) Elástica, cualquier cosa que sirve para envolver. **Wrapper** (hablando del tabaco), capa o envoltura.

wrapping ['ræpɪŋ] [ra-pin], *s.* Envoltura, forro. **Wrapping paper,** papel de envolver.

wrap-up ['ræpʌp] [rap-ap], *s.* Resumen.

wrath [rɒθ] [raz], *s.* Ira, furor, rabia (rage), cólera, indignación. **The grapes of wrath,** las uvas de la ira.

wrathful ['rɒθfʊl] [raz-ful], *a.* Furioso (furious), colérico, indignado, irritado.

wrathfully ['rɒθfəlɪ] [raz-fu-li], *adv.* Furiosamente, coléricamente, con indignación.

wreak [riː] [rik], *va.* 1. Vengar, tomar satisfacción del agravio recibido. 2. Ejecutar alguna resolución violenta. **To wreak one's anger,** descargar la cólera.

wreath [riːθ] [riz], *s.* 1. Cualquiera cosa en figura de rosca o sortija. 2. Corona, guirnalda; festón, trenza. 3. Banda circular o espiral. **Bridal wreath,** corona nupcial.

wreathe [riːð] [ridz], *va.* Ensortijar, enroscar, entrelazar, torcer, ceñir.

wreck [rek] [rek], *s.* 1. Naufragio, pérdida de un buque; ruina, destrucción. **The wreck of the Titanic,** el naufragio del Titanic. 2. Buque naufragado, barco perdido. 3. Destrozos de bajel, objetos arrojados a la costa después de un naufragio. 4. Fuco, ova.

wreck, *va.* y *vn.* 1. Naufragar, padecer naufragio; quebrarse o quebrantarse el buque, irse a pique. 2. Naufragar, perderse o salir mal de algún intento o negocio. 3. Hacer naufragar, causar naufragio. 4. Arruinar (ruin), perder a uno. **To go to wreck,** ir a su ruina, a su pérdida; perderse. **To suffer wreck,** naufragar. **Wrecking-car,** coche, carro de auxilio (ferrocarril); surtido de herramientas para despejar de obstáculos en una vía férrea.

wreckage ['rekɪdʒ] [re-kidch], *s.* 1. Acción de naufragar o el estado de náufrago. 2. Despojos de naufragio.

wrecker ['rekəʳ] [re-kaʳ], *s.* 1. Destructor. 2. Persona que roba los despojos de buques naufragados. 3. Persona o embarcación empleada para recobrar embarcaciones naufragadas o sus cargamentos. 4. Automóvil de auxilio.

wrecking ['rekɪŋ] [re-kin], *s.* Demolición, derribo.

wren [ren] [ren], *s.* Reyezuelo, troglodita, abadejo; pajarillo de plumaje variado y vistoso.

wrench [rentʃ] [rench], *va.* 1. Arrancar, tirar o sacar con violencia, arrebatar torciendo. 2. Torcer, volver en sentido contrario y apretando; apartar una cosa del uso o destino propios. 3. Dislocar (sprain), desencajar, forzar, sacar de quicio. **To wrench one's foot,** torcerse el pie.

wrench, *s.* 1. Arranque, tirón violento; torcedura, arrancamiento. 2. Dolor (emotional pain). **It was a terrible wrench leaving my family,** fue muy doloroso tener que separarme de mi familia. 3. Llave inglesa, llave para destornillar; palanca con ojo que sirve para dar vueltas a otras herramientas. **Monkey-wrench,** llave inglesa.

wrest [rest] [rest], *va.* 1. Arrancar, quitar a la fuerza o con violencia. 2. Apartar del sentido, carácter, destino o aplicación verdaderos, pervertir. **To wrest from,** arrebatar.

wrest, *s.* Violencia; controsión, torcimiento; dislocación; fuerza; acción de arrancar retorciendo, aplicación falsa, mal uso, perversión; artificio, dolo; un instrumento que se usaba para templar los de música.

wrestle [resl] [re-sel], *vn.* 1. Luchar (grapple), lidiar a brazo partido, esforzarse. 2. Disputar, altercar.

wrestler ['resləʳ] [res-laʳ], *s.* Atleta, luchador, el que lucha cuerpo a cuerpo.

wrestling ['reslɪŋ] [res-lin], *s.* Lucha. **Wrestling-place,** palestra.

wretch [retʃ] [rech], *s.* Un infeliz o un pobre infeliz (unfortunate person), un hombre muy miserable o muy necesitado; un desventurado o un hombre que sufre mucho por cualquier causa o tiene poca fortuna; ente vil, despreciable; miserable.

wretched ['retʃɪd] [re-chid], *a.* 1. Infeliz, desdichado, miserable, desgraciado, desventurado. 2. Calamitoso, lastimero (pitiable); lleno de aflicciones. 3. Vil, despreciable, perverso; mezquino. **To look wretched,** tener aspecto lastimoso.

wretchedly ['retʃɪdlɪ] [re-chid-li], *adv.* Infelizmente, miserablemente, con muchos trabajos, con mucha miseria; ruinmente, vilmente.

wretchedness ['retʃɪdnɪs] [re-chid-nes], *s.* 1. Infelicidad, desdicha, miseria, desgracia (misfortune), desventura. 2. Vileza, ruindad, bajeza. 3. Naturaleza miserable; pobreza; mala índole.

wriggle ['rɪgl] [ri-guel], *vn.* 1. Bullir, menearse o agitarse con un movimiento continuado e irregular. 2. Insinuarse en el ánimo de alguno. -*va.* Mover o agitar alguna cosa con un movimiento irregular y continuo. **To wriggle away,** escaparse alguna cosa a fuerza de moverse. **To wriggle into,** insinuarse en. **To wriggle off,** escaparse culebreando, retorciéndose. **To wriggle out of,** salir de, escaparse, deslizarse fuera.

wriggling ['rɪglɪŋ] [ri-glin], *s.* Enroscadura, torcedura, movimiento análogo al de una lombriz de tierra; rosca, vuelta u onda, hablando del movimiento de las culebras.

wriggly ['rɪglɪ] [ri-gli], *a.* Movedizo, escurridizo, que serpentea.

wright [raɪt] [rait], *s.* Artífice, artesano, obrero. **Wheelwright,** tornero, **Cartwright,** carretero. **Shipwright,** carpintero de ribera o de buque, el que trabaja en los astilleros.

wring [rɪŋ] [ring], *va.* (*pret.* y *pp.* WRUNG o WRINGED). 1. Torcer o dar vueltas a una cosa con violencia, comprimir torciendo. 2. Arrancar, quitar a la fuerza. 3. Estrujar, apretar con mucha fuerza. 4. Obligar a hacer o ejecutar alguna cosa por medios violentos o por fuerza. 5. Atormentar, aquejar. 6. Torcer, interpretar mal el sentido de algún escrito. 7. Forzar, encorvar, apartar de la posición normal (v. gr. un mástil).-*vn.* (*Des*) Acongojarse, padecer angustias y tormentos. **To wring one's hands,** retorcerse las manos. **Wrung from the poor,** arrancado a los pobres. **To wring off,** arrancar retorciendo. **To wring out,** exprimir, hacer salir. **To wring water out of a garment,** retorcer una prenda de vestir para exprimir el agua. **Wring-bolt,** perno de atraca, clavija de apretar, argolla.

wringer ['rɪŋɡəʳ] [rin-gaʳ], *s.* 1. Torcedor, torcedora, la persona que tuerce. 2. Exprimidor para la ropa.

wrinkle ['rɪŋkl] [rin-kel], *s.* 1. Arruga del rostro. 2. Arruga o doblez del paño. 3. Cualquier aspereza o desigualdad. 4. Enfoque (angle, aspect).

wrinkle, *va.* Arrugar, hacer arrugas; poner alguna cosa áspera o desigual. **To wrinkle one's brow,** fruncir o arrugar las cejas. **To wrinkle up,** arrugar, plegar.

wrinkled ['rɪŋkld] [rin-keld], *a.* Arrugado.

wrinkly ['rɪŋklɪ], [rin-kli], *a.* (*Coloq.*) Arrugado, lleno de arrugas.

wrist [rɪst] [rist], *s.* Muñeca, articulación de la mano con el brazo. **To slash one's wrists,** cortarse las venas.

wristband ['rɪstbænd] [rist-band], *s.* 1. Puño de camisa. 2. Pulsera (bracelet); correa (strap); muñequera (sweatband).

wristlet ['rɪstlɪt] [rist-let], *s.* Elástico (para retener un guante).

wrist watch ['rɪstwɒtʃ] [rist-uach], *s.* Reloj de pulsera.

writ [rɪt] [rit], *s.* 1. Escrito; escritura; orden. 2. (*For.*) Auto, mandamiento o mandato jurídico, citación; auto o decreto de prisión. **Holy writ,** la Sagrada Escritura. **To issue a writ,** dar una orden o un decreto.

write [raɪt] [rait], *va.* (*pret.* WROTE, *pp.* WRITTEN). 1. Escribir, formar of figurar letras; inscribir. 2. Trazar, inscribir letras que representan sonidos o ideas. 3. Escribir, componer, producir como escritor o autor. 4. Imprimir o grabar una cosa fuertemente en el ánimo, en el corazón, etc. -*vn.* 1. Escribir, trazar o inscribir letras sobre una superficie. 2. Escribir, tener correspondencia por medio de cartas. 3. Escribir, componer como escritor o autor.

write after, copiar, escribir según un modelo.

write back, contestar a la carta o esquela de otra persona.

write down, poner por escrito, redactar.

write out, escribir un relato completo de algo, escribir enteramente; copiar, trasladar, transcribir.

write over again, volver a escribir, poner en limpio. **To write in a hurry**, zurcir, hilvanar un discurso, un escrito, etc. **To write oneself**, calificarse, tomar algún título, calidad, honor, etc. **To write down a person**, publicar todo lo malo que se sabe de una persona; acabarla a escritos o publicaciones. **To write one**, continuar escribiendo, escribir sobre. **To write a good hand**, escribir bien, hacer buena letra, ser pendolista.

write up, a ensalzar, encomendar al favor de alguien escribiendo; realzar, exaltar por medio de la pluma. (b) describir completamente por escrito; poner al día o hasta la fecha (el libro mayor).

write-off [ˈraɪtɒf] [rait-of], *va.* 1. Cancelar (una cuenta, etc.) 2. Descontar por depreciación.

writer [ˈraɪtəʳ] [rai-taʳ], *s.* Escritor, autor (author); escribiente, amanuense. **The writer of this book**, el autor de este libro.

write-up [ˈraɪtʌp] [rait-ap]. *s.* Crítica, reseña, artículo (report), reportaje.

writhe [raɪð] [raidz], *va.* Torcer, poner torcida alguna cosa. -*vn.* Acongojarse, padecer agonía o angustias, torcerse, dar vueltas con dolor.

writing [ˈraɪtɪŋ] [rai-tin], *s.* 1. Escritura, acción de escribir. 2. Escritura (script), mano, caracteres escritos. 3. Lo que está escrito o expresado en letras, escritura, escrito, manuscrito, obra o composición por escrito. 4. Letra (handwriting). **To commit to writing**, poner por escrito. **In one's own writing**, de su puño y letra. **Writing-book**, cuaderno de escritura. **Writing-machine**, máquina para escribir. **Writing-desk**, escritorio, bufete, escribanía **Writing-master**, maestro de escritura. **Writing-paper**, papel para escribir. **The writings of Kant**, la obra de Kant.

written, *pp.* del verbo TO WRITE.

wrong [rɒŋ] [rong], *s.* 1. Injuria, injusticia (injustice), agravio, perjuicio, detrimento conocido, mal, daño, perjuicio. 2. Culpa, sinrazón. 3. Error, extravío, falsedad. **You are in the wrong**, Vd. no tiene razón. -*a.* 1. Injusto, que viola el derecho o la justicia; malo, no derecho ni digno. 2. Erróneo, inexacto, incorrecto, falso; irregular, equivocado, que no conviene. **I took the wrong glove**, cogí un guante en lugar de otro. **Wrong side**, envés, el revés, el lado malo. **Wrong side out (ward)**, al envés, al revés. **To be wrong**, ser malo; no ser justo, no tener razón. **To be very wrong**, tener mucha culpa. **That is wrong**, eso no es justo, eso es malo, no es eso. **Wrong measures**, medidas falsas, malas, -*adv.* Mal, sin razón, sin causa, injustamente, al revés, **Right or wrong**, a tuertas o a derechas, por fas o por nefas, a diestro o a siniestro; a trochemoche. **To be in the wrong**, no tener razón, estar equivocado. **To do wrong**, obrar o hacer mal; hacer daño, causar perjuicio.

wrong, *va.* 1. Hacer daño a, causar perjuicio, ofender. 2. Agraviar (offend), injuriar, hacer alguna injusticia.

wrong-doer [ˈrɒŋduːəʳ] [rong-duaʳ], *s.* El que es injusto con otro, el que injuria a otro; perverso.

wrongful [ˈrɒŋfʊl] [rong-ful], *a.* Injusto, inicuo (wicked), que hace u obra mal, supuesto, falso. **Wrongful arrest**, arresto ilegal.

wrongfully [ˈrɒŋfəlɪ] [rong-fu-li], *adv.* Injustamente, sin razón, sin motivo o causa, falsamente.

wrong-headed [ˈrɒŋˈhedɪd] [rong-je-did], *a.* Disparatado, el que tiene mala cabeza, desatinado, descabezado; terco, obstinado.

wrong-headedness [ˈrɒŋˈhednɪs] [rong-jed-nes], *s.* El estado o la disposición del que tiene sentimientos u opiniones extravagantes y las sostiene con tenacidad; terquedad, obstinación.

wrongly [ˈrɒŋlɪ] [ron-gli], *adv.* Injustamente; mal, fuera de tiempo o de propósito, equivocadamente (mistakenly).

wrongness [ˈrɒŋnɪs] [rong-nes], *s.* Calidad de injusto; injusticia, maldad (wickedness); falsedad, error, inexactitud.

wrote [rəʊt] [rout], pret. del verbo TO WRITE.

wroth [rɒθ] [roz], *a.* (*Ant.*) Encolerizado, airado, enojado.

wrought [rɔːt] [rot], *pret. y pp irreg.* del verbo TO WORK. (Hoy anticuado excepto en los sentidos de «forjado, labrado o efectuado»). -*a.* **Wrought iron**, hierro forjado o batido. **Wrought upon**, influido. **Wrought up to**, excitado, impelido.

wrung [ˈrʌŋ] [rang], *pret. y pp.* del verbo TO WRING. A **wrung mast**, (*Mar.*) palo que hace comba.

wry [raɪ] [rai], *a.* 1. Torcido, tuerto, no derecho, no recto; alejado, oblicuo. 2. Pervertido, alterado, mal interpretado. **To make a wry face**, torcer el gesto, poner mala cara. **Wryneck**, tortícolis, mal o dolor que no deja poner derecha la cabeza.

wryed [ˈraɪd] [raid], *a.* Lo que está sesgado, torcido.

wryly [ˈraɪlɪ] [rai-li], *adv.* Sesgadamente, oblicuamente, irónicamente.

wryneck [ˈraɪnek] [rai-nek], *s.* 1. (*Orn.*) Tortecuello, pico del género Iynx. 2. Tortícoli, dolor reumático del cuello.

wryness [ˈraɪnɪs] [rai-nes], *s.* Condición de lo que es torcido u oblicuo.

wych-elm [ˈwɪtʃˈelm] [uich-elm], *s.* Olmo escocés.

wych-hazel [ˈwɪtʃˈheɪzl] [uich-jei-sel], *s.* V. WICH-HAZEL.

wye [waɪ] [uai], *s.* La letra Y, o algo en forma de y.

X

x [eks] [eks], vigésima cuarta letra del alfabeto inglés, tiene dos sonidos, uno fuerte y otro suave. El primero equivale a cs en castellano; v. g. **excellence, execute, tax**; y el segundo a gz, pronunciando la z como en francés; v. g. **exalt, example, executor**. Ninguna palabra propiamente inglesa empieza con X; y en las derivadas del griego, que la tienen, como **Xenophon**, se les da el sonido de la z francesa. La X como número vale 10; y a causa de su forma en cruz, se usa como abreviatura de Christ; v. g. Xmas., por Christmas; Xpher. por Christopher. Lo mismo se hacía a veces en español.

xanthic [ˈzæntɪk] [san-tik], *a.* Xántico, amarillo o amarillento. **Xanthic acid**, ácido xántico, compuesto pesado y líquido (CHOS).

xanthin, xanthine [ˈzæntɪn] [san-tin], *s.* 1. Xantina, compuesto blanco cristalizable contenido en la sangre, la orina y en otras secreciones animales. 2. Xantina, materia colorante amarilla e insoluble de ciertas flores.

xanthous [ˈzæntəs] [san-zos], *a.* 1. Perteneciente al tipo amarillento o mogol de la raza humana. 2. Rubio, blondo, que tiene cabellos amarillentos.

xenium [ˈzenɪəm] [se-niom], *s.* (*pl.* XENIA). 1. Golosina, manjar delicado con que se obsequiaban mutuamente los antiguos en prenda de amistad. 2. Cuadro de caza, frutas o pescado, en una habitación destinada a huéspeds o amigos. 3. Presente o regalo que se da a un huésped o extranjero.

xenodochium [ˈzenədəkɪəm] [se-no-do-kiom], *s.* Mesón, posada, hospicio.

xenon [ˈzenɒn] [se-non], *s.* (*Quím.*) Xenón.

xenophobia [ˌzenɒˈfəʊbɪə] [se-no-fou-bia], *s.* Xenofobia.

xenophobic [ˌzenɒˈfəʊbɪk] [se-no-fou-bik], *a.* Xenófobo.

xerophyte [ˈzerəfaɪt] [se-ro-fait], *s.* Xerófila, planta de suelos secos.

xerosis [ˈzerəʊsɪs] [se-rou-sis], *s.* Xerodermia, condición de sequedad anormal de la piel o de las membranas mucosas.

xerox [ˈzerɒks] [se-roks], *vt.* Fotocopiar (photocopy), xerografiar.

xiphias ['zıfıəs] [si-fias], *s.* 1. Pez espada, xifia, jifia, pez de la familia de los escombéridos. 2. *(Astr.)* Jifia, dorada, una de las constelaciones del hemisferio austral.

xiphoid ['zıfɔıd] [si-foid], *a.* Xifoideo.

Xmas ['eksməs] [eks-mas], *s.* Navidad.

X-rated ['ek,reıtıd] [eks-rei-tid], *a.* Sólo para adultos, clasificado X.

X-rays ['ekreıs] [eks-reis], *s. pl.* Rayos X, rayos Roentgen. **X-ray picture**, radiografía. **X-ray specialist**, radiógrafo. -*vt.* Hacer o sacar una radiografía, radiografiar.

xylaloes ['zıləlɔʊz] [si-la-lous], *s.* Madera de aloe.

xylocopa ['zaılə'koʊpə] [sai-lo-kou-pa], *s.* Jilocopo, xilocopo, inssecto himenóptero.

xylograph ['zaıləgrɑːf] [sai-lo-graf], *s.* Grabado en madera, o estampa hecha de él.

xylographer [zaılə'græfəʳ] [sai-lo-gra-faʳ], *s.* Grabador en madera.

xylography [zaı'lɒgrəfı] [sai-lo-gra-fi], *s.* Xilografía, el arte de grabar o el grabado en madera.

xylophagous [zaılə'fægəs] [sai-lo-fa-gos], *a.* Xilófago, que come o roe la madera, como lo hacen varias larvas de insectos.

xylophone ['zaıləfəʊn] [sai-lo-foun], *s.* Xilórgano, xilófono, armónica de madera.

xyst ['zıst] [sist], *s.* 1. Xisto, sala o lugar cubierto destinado entre los antiguos a diversos ejercicios. 2. Paseo o terrado de jardín.

xyster ['zıstəʳ] [sis-taʳ], *s.* Raspadera, instrumento quirúrgico para raer y raspar los huesos.

Y

y [waı] [uai], se pronuncia como en castellano al principio de las voces. y en este caso se la considera en inglés como letra consonante. Cuando está al fin de las palabras se pronuncia como i castellana pronunciada rápidamente, y en este caso se la considera como vocal. También se halla la y en medio de algunas voces de derivación griega, como en **hydraulics**, la hidráulica; **hypothesis**, hipótesis, y entonces se pronuncia como el diptongo *ai* castellano.

yacht [jɒt] [yot], *s. (Mar.)* Yate (pleasure cruiser), embarcación de recreo; embarcación muy ligera, de vela o de vapor, destinada para recreo o regatas en ríos o lagos o en el mar. **Yacht club**, club náutico. **Yacht race, regata**. -*vn.* Viajar en yate; gobernar el yate. **They went yachting**. se fueron a navegar.

yachting ['jɒtıŋ] [yo-tin], *s.* Viaje en yate, navegación a vela; el acto o la ocupación de dirigir un yate o de navegar en él.

yachtsman ['jɒtzmən] [yots-man], *s.* 1. Propietario o timonel de un yate. 2. Regatista.

yack [jæk] [yak], *s. (Coloq.)* Cotorrear.

yak [jæk] [yak], *s.* Yak, rumiante bovino del Tíbet, especie intermedio entre el búfalo y el toro.

yam [jæk] [yak], *s.* Ñame, raíz comestible de varias especies de Dioscorea.

yank [jæŋk] [yank], *va. (Fam.)* Tomar, quitar o dislocar por medio de un tirón repentino; dar un tirón. -*vn. (Ingl.)* 1. Moverse rápidamente. 2. Farfullar, regañar. -*s. (Fam.)* Tirón repentino, estirón.

Yankee ['jæŋkiː] [yan-ki], *a.* Perteneciente a los yanquis o característico de ellos. -*s. (Fam.)* Yanqui, el natural o habitante de la Nueva Inglaterra; de aquí, ciudadano de los Estados del Norte y en general de todos los Estados Unidos, apodo que emplean principalmente los extranjeros. **Yankee doodle**, canción popular de los norteamericanos.

yap [jæp] [yap], *vn. (Prov.)* Ladrar como un perrito (bark). -*s.* Ladrido agudo.

yard [jɑːd] [yard], *va.* Acorralar, apriscar. -*s.* 1. Corral, patio de una casa u otro edificio; cercado; por extensión, espacio descubierto situado delante o alrededor de una casa. 2.

Parque, cercado de construcción. **Dock-yard**, arsenal, taller de la marina, astillero. **Lumber-yard**, leñera, depósito en maderas. 3. Yarda, medida inglesa. 4. *(Mar.)* Verga, nombre que se da a las piezas de madera que sirven para llevar las velas. **Yard-arms**, penoles de las vergas. **Lateen-yards**, vergas latinas. **Main-yard**, verga mayor. **Main-topsail-yard**, verga de gavia. **Sprit-sail-yard**, verga de cebadera. **Cross-jack-yard**, verga seca o verga de gata. **Square yards**, vergas redondas. **To brace the yards**, bracear las vergas. **To top the yards**, amantillar las vergas. **To top the yards a-port or a-starboard**, amantillar a babor o estribor. **To square the yards**, poner las vergas en cruz. 5. *(Vulg.)* Verga, miembro viril.

yardmaster [,jɑːd'mɑːstəʳ] [yard-mas-taʳ], *s.* Mayordomo, superintendente de un patio de ferrocarril.

yardstick ['jɑːdstık] [yard-stik], *s.* Vara graduada que sirve para medir una yarda.

yardwand ['jɑːdwænd] [yard-uand], *s.* La medida de una yarda o de una vara inglesa.

yare [jɛəʳ] [yeaʳ], *a. (Esco. o des.)* 1. Manejable, pronto a responder al timón; se dice de un bajel. 2. Pronto, ligero, diestro (skillful) o hábil para ejecutar algo.

yarn [jɑːn] [yarn], *s.* 1. Hilaza, hilo de lana; hilo de lino; porpularmente, cualquier hilo; hilado. 2. *(Fam.)* Historia, cuento largo y extravagante. **To spin a yarn**, hacer una hilaza; *(Fig.)* referir una historia larga, hablar sobremanera. **Cotton yarn**, hilo de torzal, hilaza de algodón. **hemp yarn**, hilaza o hilo de cáñamo. **Weaver's yarn**, hilaza. **Rope-yarn**, *(Mar.)* filástica. **Spunyarn**, *(Mar.)* meollar. **Tarred yarn**, hilo negro, encerado o alquitranado.

yarrow ['jærəʊ] [ya-rou], *s.* Milenrama, mil hojas, aquilea.

yashmak ['jɑːʃmək] [yash-mak], *s.* Velo que llevan algunas mujeres musulmanas.

yaw [jɔː] [yo], *s.* 1. *(Mar.)* Guiñar, mover la proa del buque apartándola hacia uno y otro lado, moviendo el timón. 2. Andar haciendo eses.

yawing ['jɔːıŋ] [yoin], *s. (Mar.)* Guiñada.

yawl [jɔːl] [yol], *s. (Mar.)* 1. Embarcación pequeña *(Amer. yola)*, con aparejo de balnadra y un mástil pequeño adicional en la popa. 2. Serení, especie de embarcación pequeña destinada al servicio de un navío. 3. Barca pescadora.

yawn [jɔːn] [yon], *vn.* 1. Bostezar, abrir ancha o involuntariamente la boca. 2. Quedarse con la boca abierta; por extensión, suspirar por, anhelar. 3. Abrirse del todo, como pronto para engolfar o recibir alguna cosa.

yawn, *s.* 1. Bostezo, la acción y efecto de bostezar. 2. Aburrimiento (bore). 3. Acción de abrirse del todo.

yawner ['jɔːnəʳ] [yo-naʳ], *s.* Bostezador, el que bosteza mucho.

yawning ['jɔːnıŋ] [yo-nin], *a.* Que bosteza, que está soñoliento, que se está cayendo de sueño. -*s.* Bostezo.

yaws [jɔːz] [yos], *s.* Erupción cutánea y contagiosa de los trópicos, caracterizada por pequeños tubérculos rojizos; **(yaw, sing.** uno de los tubérculos).

ye [jiː] [yi], *nom.pl.* de THOU. Vosotros, vos.

yea [jeı] [yei], *adv.* 1. Sí, ciertamente, verdaderamente (indeed, truly). 2. Y aun, y además, no solamente, y sino. **Yea or nay, sí o** no. -*s.* Sí, voto afirmativo. **The yeas and nays**, votos en pro y en contra; lista de los miembros de una asamble o junta, con la indicación de sus votos. *V.* YES.

yeah [jɛə] [yea], *interj. (Coloq.)* Sí.

yean [jiːn] [yin], *vn.* Parir la oveja.

yenaling ['jiːnəlıŋ] [yi-na-li], *s.* Cordero o cabrito mamantón.

year [jıəʳ] [yiaʳ], *s.* 1. Año, el espacio de doce meses, duración de una revolución de la tierra en su órbita alrededor del sol. 2. Año, el tiempo que emplea un planeta en recorrer su órbita; revolución. 3. Curso. **He was in my year at school**, estaba en el mismo curso que yo en el colegio. 4. Cosecha. 5. *pl.* Años, edad, época de la vida; edad avanzada, vejez. **Once a year**, una vez al año o cada año. **Every other year**, de dos en dos años o cada dos años. **New-year's day**, día de año nuevo. **New-year's gift**, aguinaldo. **Leap year**, año bisiesto. **A man in years**, un anciano, un hombre de edad o un hombre de mucha edad. **To grow in years**, envejecer. **Last year**, el año último, el año pasado. **Next year**, el año próximo, el año que viene. **By the year**, al año. **Of late years**, en estos últimos años. **Once a year**, una vez al año. **One year with another**, un año con otro. **To be in years**, ser viejo. **To wish a happy New-year**, desear feliz año nuevo.

yearling ['jɪəlɪŋ] [yia-lin], *s.* El animal que tiene un año. **Yearling bullock**, becerro añal.

yearly ['jɪəlɪ] [yia-li], *a.* Anual, que sucede o se hace cada año; que dura por un año. *-adv.* Anualmente, todos los años, cada año o una avez al año. **I do my tests twice yearly**, hago mis pruebas dos veces al año.

yearn [jɜːn] [yern], *vn.* Anhelar, desear vivamente, suspirar por; (con for); compadecerse, apiadarse, sentir interiormente un movimiento de piedad o compasión; (con over).

yearning ['jɜːnɪŋ] [yer-nin], *s.* Deseo ardiente acompañado de un sentimiento de ternura, de afecto; ternura, lástima, compasión.

yeast [jiːst] [yist], *s.* 1. Jiste, la espuma de la cerveza que fermenta y sirve para levadura; la espuma de un honguillo microscópico; fermento. 2. Espuma (de la mar agitada).

yelk [jelk] [yelk], *s.* (Dialecto) V. YOLK.

yell [jel] [yel], *va. y vn.* Dar alaridos (shout), gritar furiosamente, quejarse a gritos y con voces lastimeras. **To yell out**, gritar, decir algunas palabras a gritos.

yell, *s.* 1. Alarido, grito (shout) o quejido fuerte y lastimero. 2. Grito salvaje, grito feroz (como de guerra). 3. Grito formado con un conjunto de palabras acordadas de antemano; v. gr. el de los estudiantes de un colegio determinado.

yellow ['jeləʊ] [ye-lou], *a.* 1. Amarillo, que es del color del oro, del limón, del latón, etc. 2. Rubio, dorado (hair). **To grow yellow**, amarillear. *-s.* 1. Amarillo, color amarillo. **Chrome yellow**, amarillo de cromo, cromato de plomo. **King's yellow**, oropimente. **To become, to get, to grow** o **to turn yellow**, ponerse amarillo. **Yellow berries**, bayas persas, semillas del cambrón de que se hace uso en el tinte; pizacantas. **Yellow-boy**, *(Vulg.)* guinea u otra moneda de oro. **Yellow press**, prensa amarilla o sensacionalista. **Yellow-bird**, (a) acanta de América. (b) La silvia amarilla, «pájaro del estío». (c) Chamariz u oropéndola (**golden oriole**). **Yellow bunting**, *V.* yellow-hammer. **Yellow fever**, fiebre amarilla (fam. vómito negro). Se llama también **Yellow Jack**. **Yellow-hammer**, (a) verderol, emberiza. (b) *(E.U.)* Colapto, pico grande del género Colaptes. *V.* FLICKER. **Yellow-jacket**, avispa social del género Vespa, con rayas amarillas y cuya picadura es dolorosa. **Yellow spot**, (a) mácula pequeña en el fondo del ojo, el sitio de la visión más aguda en todos los vertebrados; (b) mariposa americana con una mancha amarilla en las alas posteriores. **Yellow-throat**, Curruca de Marilandia, de pecho y cuello amarillos. **Yellow wood**, fustete, cloreta, xantóxilo. **Yellow-lead**, albayalde calcinado.

yellowish ['jeləʊɪʃ] [ye-louish], *a.* Amarillento, que tira a amarillo o que amarillea.

yellowishness ['jeləʊɪʃnɪs], [ye-louish-nes], *s.* El color amarillento o que tira a amarillo.

yellowness ['jeləʊnɪs] [ye-lou-nes], *s.* Amarillez.

yelp [jelp] [yelp], *vn.* Latir, gañir, chillar el perro. *-s.* Gañido, chillido, grito agudo del perro lastimado o doliente.

yelping ['jelpɪŋ] [yel-pin], *s.* Gañido.

Yemen ['jemən] [ye-men], *s.* Yemen.

Yemeni ['jemənɪ] [ye-me-ni], *a.* Yemenita.

yen [jen] [yen], *s.* Unidad de la moneda japonesa. **To have a yen to**, tener unas ganas locas de.

yeoman ['jəʊmən] [you-man], *s. (pl.* YEOMEN). 1. Hacendado, el que tiene hacienda en tierras; labrador acomodado. 2. Nombre de ciertos guardias del rey de Inglaterra. 3. *(Mar.)* Pañolero; en la marina de los E.U., guardaalmacén, almacenero, guardián. **Gunner's yeoman**, pañolero de la Santa Bárbara. **Boatswain's yeoman**, pañolero del pañol de proa. **Yeoman of the Guard**, alabardero de la Casa Real.

yeomanry ['jəʊmənrɪ] [you-man-ri], *s.* 1. El conjunto o agregado de los hacendados de una provincia. 2. Uno de los cuerpos de guardias del rey de Inglaterra.

yerk [jɜːk] [yerk], *va. (Prov. o des.) V.* TO JERK.

yes [jes] [yes], *adv.* Sí, partícula afirmativa; sí tal; bien está; verdaderamente.

yes-man ['jesmən] [yes-man], *s.* Individuo servil, adulador que dice sí a todo.

yester ['jestər] [yes-taʳ], *a.* Pasado, último; que pertenece al día de ayer.

yesterday ['jestədeɪ] [yes-ta-dei], *s.* Ayer, el día de ayer. **Yesterday was a happy day**, ayer fue un día muy feliz. *-adv.* Ayer. **Yesterday morning**, ayer por la mañana.

yesternight ['jestənaɪt] [yes-ta-nait], *s.* Anoche o la noche pasada. *-adv.* Ayer por la tarde.

yet [jet] [yet], *conj.* Con todo, sin embargo (nevertheless); pero, empero. *-adv.* 1. Además, todavía, además de eso. 2. Aún, hasta ahora, hasta aquí; a lo menos. **As yet**, hasta ahora, hasta aquí. **Not yet**, todavía no, aún no.

yeti ['jetɪ] [ye-ti], *s.* Yeti.

yew ['juː] [yu], *s.* 1. *(Bot.)* Tejo, árbol parecido al abeto; cualquier árbol o arbusto del género Taxus. 2. Madera de este árbol; arco hecho de esta madera.

Yiddish ['jɪdɪʃ] [yi-dish], *s.* Yidish, yiddish.

yield [jiːld] [yild], *va.* 1. Producir utilidad o en retorno por el trabajo. **To yield six per cent**, producir seis por ciento. 2. Dar, dar de sí, ser origen natural de ofrecer. 3. Ceder, admitir, conceder, deferir, condescender; devolver, restituir. 4. Acordar, admitir como verdadero, reconocer. 5. Permitir, sufrir; conceder, otorgar. **To yield consent**, dar consentimiento, consentir. *-vn.* 1. Producir provecho por el trabajo, sacar utilidad. 2. Ceder; rendirse (surrender), sujetarse, someterse. 3. Asentir, convenir en lo que otro dice. **I yield to it**, consiento en ello. 4. Flaquear, ceder, hacer lugar, como bajo presión. **To yield one's right**, ceder su derecho. **To yield up**, ceder, entregar; devolver; abandonar; entregar (el alma). **To yield to the temptation**, ceder, sucumbir a la tentación. *-s.* 1. Rendición, acción de rendirse. 2. *(For.)* Rédito, rendimiento, renta, beneficio que rinde un capital.

yielding ['jiːldɪŋ] [yil-din], *a.* Fácil, complaciente (indulgent); flojo; que cede o se somete con facilidad; condescendiente.

yieldingly ['jiːldɪŋlɪ] [yil-din-li], *adv.* Libremente; flojamente.

yieldingness ['jiːldɪŋnɪs] [yil-din-nes], *s.* Facilidad en ceder o en condescender.

yippee [jiːpiː] [yi-pi], *interj. (Coloq.)* ¡Yupi!

yob [jɒb] [yob], *s.* Vándalo, gamberro (hooligan).

yodel ['jəʊdl] [you-del], *va. y vn.* Cantar modulando la voz rápidamente desde el tono natural al falsete, y viceversa. *-s.* Acción de tararear una canción o un estribillo sin pronunciar las palabras.

yoga ['jəʊɡə] [you-ga], *s.* Yoga.

yoghurt, yoghourt, yogurt ['jəʊɡər] [you-gaʳ], *s.* Yogur, yoghourt.

yoke [jəʊk] [youk], *s.* 1. Yugo, el instrumento con que se une un par de bueyes. 2. Yugo (burden), servidumbre, esclavitud. **To throw off the yoke**, sacudir el yugo. 3. Barra de timón; balancín, pedazo de madera escotado que llevan los aguadores al cuello. 4. *sing. y pl.* Yunta, cuando se habla de bueyes, y se usa también para expresar un par de otros animales. **Yoke of land**, yugada.

yoke, *va.* 1. Uncir, atar al yugo los bueyes. 2. Unir, juntar. 3. Sojuzgar (subjugate), sujetar, reducir a la esclavitud; retener, reprimir.

yoke-elm ['jəʊk͵elm] [youk-elm], *s. (Bot.)* Carpe, especie de olmo.

yokel ['jəʊkl] [you-kel], *s.* Pueblerino.

yolk [jəʊk] [youk], *s.* 1. Yema de huevo, amarillo. 2. Una exudación jabonosa en la lana de las ovejas y carneros.

yon, yonder [jɒn] [yon] ['jɒndər] [yon-daʳ], *a. y adv.* Allí, allá: dícese de lo que está a la vista aunque algo distante. **Yonder he is**, mírale allí.

yoo-hoo ['juːˈhuː] [yu-ju], *interj.* ¡Yuju!, ¡eh!

yore [jɔːʳ] [yoʳ], *s. (Ant. y poét.)* Tiempos pasados, otro tiempo. **Of yore**, hace mucho tiempo; antaño, antiguamente, en otro tiempo. **In days of yore**, en otros tiempos.

you [juː] [yu]. Pronombre personal de la segunda persona, correspondiente en castellano a te, a vosotros, a Ud. o a Uds. en el primer caso, y a tú o Ud., vosotros o Uds. en el segundo. **You** también se usa en inglés indefinidamente, y en este caso se debe traducir en castellano por el pronombre indefinido. **As you come near it, you see nothing**, al llegar cerca de ello, no se ve nada.

young [jʌŋ] [yang], *a.* 1. Joven, mozo, en la edad de la juventud; que está en la primera parte de su desarrollo. 2. No avanzado, nuevo. 3. Lleno de vigor o frescura. 4. Nuevo, novicio, inexperimentado. 5. *(Fam.)* Más joven que otro u otra del mismo nombre, título o especie. **A young child**, un niño. **A young man; a young girl, a young woman**, un joven; una joven. **A young face**, cara remozada. **A young plant**, planta tierna. -*s.* Hijuelos, las crías de los animales. **Young one**, hijuelo. **To grow young again**, rejuvenecer. **To look young**, tener la traza joven. **With young**, en cinta, preñada.

younger [jʌŋəʳ] [yan-gaʳ], *a.* Más joven. **Younger brother**, hermano menor. **To be the younger hand**, ser pie o el último que echa la carta en el juego.

youngish [jʌŋɪʃ] [yan-guish], *a.* Mozuelo, jovencillo, tierno.

youngling [jʌŋlɪŋ] [yan-glin], *s.* Pequeñuelo.

youngster [jʌŋstəʳ] [yangs-taʳ], *s.* Jovencito, chico, mozalbete (lad).

younker [jʌŋkəʳ] [yan-kaʳ], *s.* 1. Propietario campesino alemán. 2. *(Ant.)* Mozalbete, chico. 3. Señorito, joven.

your [joəʳ] [yuaʳ], *pron.* Vuestro; de usted, de ustedes. **Your brothers, your sisters**, vuestros hermanos, vuestras hermanas.

yours [joəz] [yuas], *pron.* El vuestro, la vuestra, los vuestros, las vuestras; lo de usted quqe le pertenece. **You have my pen, and I have yours**, Ud. tiene mi pluma y yo tengo la de Ud. **This penknife is yours**, este cortaplumas es de Ud. (el suyo). **I am yours**, estoy a la disposición de Ud. **Yours truly**, su seguro servidor (S.S.S.). **Yours very truly**, su afectísimo.

yourself [jəˈself] [ya-self], *pron.* Tú mismo, Ud. mismo. **Stop thinking about yourself**, deja de pensar en ti mismo o deje de pensar en sí mismo. **Yourselves**, *pl.* vosotros o Uds. mismos.

youth [juːθ] [yuz], *s.* 1. Juventud, mocedad, adolescencia, el período de la vida comprendida entre la niñez y la edad viril. **Youth club**, club de jóvenes. 2. Un joven; juventud, el agregado o conjunto de jóvenes.

youthful [juːθɔl] [yuz-ful], *a.* Juvenil, joven, fresco, vigoroso (energetic), juguetón.

youthfully [juːθɔlɪ] [yuz-fu-li], *adv.* De un modo juvenil, como muchacho.

youthfulness [juːθɔlnɪs] [yuz-ful-nes], *s.* Mocedad, juventud.

youth hostel [juːθhɒsl] [yuz-jo-sel], *s.* Albergue juvenil.

yowl [jaʊl] [yaul], *vn. (Fam. o Prov.)* Aullar, ladrar; dar alaridos, gritar. -*s.* Aullido, grito fuerte (de aviso o advertencia); alarido. *V.* HOWL y YELL.

yo-yo [jəʊjəʊ] [you-you], *s.* 1. Yo-yo. 2. *(Coloq.)* Subir y bajar a lo loco. **I was up and down like a yo-yo all morning**, me pasé toda la mañana de arriba para abajo.

yttria [ɪtrɪə] [i-tria], *s.* Itria, substancia blanca, terrosa, insoluble, óxido de itrio. (YO).

yttrium [ɪtrɪəm] [i-triom], *s. (Quím.)* Itrio, elemento metálico del grupo cerio; fue descubierto por medio de su espectro.

yucca [jʌkə] [ya-ka], *s. (Bot.)* Yuca, género de plantas de la familia de las liláceas; una planta de este género.

yuck [jʌk] [yak], *interj. (Coloq.)* ¡Puaj!

yucky [jʌkɪ] [ya-ki], *s. (Coloq.)* Asqueroso.

Yugoslavian [juːgəʊˈslaːvɪən] [yu-gous-la-vian], *a.* Yugoslavo.

yule [juːl] [yul], *s.* 1. Navidad, tiempo de la Navidad o pascua. 2. *(Culin.)* Tronco de Navidad.

yummy [jʌmɪ] [ya-mi], *a. (Coloq.)* Riquísimo. -*interj.* ¡Hmm!, ¡qué rico!

yum yum [jʌmjʌm] [yam-yam], *interj. (Coloq.)* Ñam ñam.

yunx [jʌŋks] [yanks], *s.* Género de pájaros cuyo tipo ese el torcecuello. *V.* WRYNECK, 1ª acep.

yuppie, yuppy [jʌpɪ] [ya-pi], *s. (Coloq.)* Yuppy.

Z

z [zed] [sed], vigésima sexta y última letra del alfabeto.

zaffer, zaffre [zəfəʳ] [sa-faʳ], *s. (Min.)* Zafre, azul que se saca del cobalto; mineral de cobalto calentado con sílice.

zaftig [zæftɪŋ] [saf-tin], *a.* Rellenita y curvilínea.

Zairean [zɑːˈiːərɪən] [sa-ia-rian], *a.* Zaireño.

Zambian [zæmbɪən] [sam-bian], *a.* Zambiano.

zambo [zæmbəʊ] [sam-bou], *s. V.* SAMBO.

zany [zeɪnɪ] [sei-ni], *s.* El gracioso de las comedias italianas; un bufón, un truhán; simplonazo. -*a. (Coloq.)* Chiflado, alocado (crazy).

Zanzibar [zænzɪbɑːʳ] [san-zi-baʳ], *s.* Zanzíbar.

zap [zæp] [sap], *vt.* 1. Liquidar (blast). 2. *(Inform.)* Eliminar, borrar.

zea [ziː] [si], *s. (Bot.)* Zea, género de altas plantas gramíneas. **Zea mays** es el maíz.

zeal [ziːl] [sil], *s.* Celo; fervor; ardor; amor o afición desmedida, devoción entusiasta. **In his zeal for reform**, en su afán reformista.

zealot [zələt] [se-lot], *s.* 1. Celador, entusiasta, el que es muy amante de la religión, de la patria, etc; partidario inmoderada, fanático (fanatic). 2. Miembro de un partido fanático judío, en casi continua sublevación contra los romanos.

zealotism [zelətɪzəm] [se-lo-ti-sem], *s.* Celo ciego, fanatismo (fanatism).

zealotry [zelətrɪ] [se-lo-tri], *s.* La conducta o disposición de una person celosa o fanática.

zealous [zeləs] [se-los], *a.* Celoso, el que cela, defiende o toma mucho empeño en alguna causa.

zealously [zeləslɪ] [se-los-li], *adv.* Apasionadamente (passionately), con pasión y celo; con ardor.

zealousness [zeləsnɪs] [se-los-nes], *s.* La propiedad de ser celoso; ardor, conato.

zebec [zebek] [se-bek], *s. V.* XEBEC.

zebra [zebrə] [ze-bra], *s.* Cebra, animal cuadrúpedo de África parecido al mulo, con listas transversales pardas o negras en toda la piel. **Zebra crossing**, paso de cebra o de peatones.

Zebu [zebuː] [se-bu], *s.* Zebú, cebú, buey de la India (Bos indicus) con giba en la cruz.

zed [zed] [sed], *s.* La letra z; zeda o zeta; casi siempre llamada zi en los Estados Unidos.

Zen [zen] [sen], *s. (Relig.)* Zen.

zenana [zenənə] [se-na-na], *s.* En la India las habitaciones de las mujeres, el harén indio.

zend [zend] [send], *s.* Zendo, idioma de la familia indoeuropea usado antiguamente en las provincias septentrionales de Persia.

zenith [zenɪθ] [se-niz], *s.* 1. Cenit o zenit, el punto que en la esfera celeste está perpendicularmente sobre nuestra cabeza, opuesto al nadir. 2. Punto culminate de la prosperidad, cumbre; colmo de la grandeza. **He is at the zenith of his popularity**, está en el cenit o apogeo de su popularidad.

zephyr [zefəʳ] [se-faʳ], *s.* 1. Céfiro, favonio, viento de la parte de poniente. 2. *(Poet.)* Céfiro, cualquier viento que sopla blanda y apaciblemente. 3. Hilaza floja de lana muy ligera de peso, para bordar.

zephyrus [zefɪrəs] [se-fi-ros], *s.* Céfiro, Favonio.

zeppelin [zeplɪn] [sep-li], *s.* Zepelín.

zero [zɪərəʊ] [si-rou], *s.* 1. Cero, el guarismo arábigo 0. 2. De aquí, la ausencia de cantidad, nada. 3. Punto en un pitipié o escala desde el cual se gradúa un termómetro, etc.; se mide generalmente en direcciones opuestas; de aquí, el punto más bajo. **As a leader he's a total zero**, como dirigente es un inútil. **Zero in on**, centrarse en, concentrar la atención sobre.

zero-rated ['zɪərəʊˌreɪtɪd] [si-rou-rei-tid], *a.* No sujeto a IVA.

zest [zest] [sest], *s.* 1. Excitación agradable del ánimo que acompaña el ejercicio mental o físico, entusiasmo (relish). 2. Sainete, el sabor que se da a alguna cosa, sabor, sazón (flavor). 3. (Poco us.) Luquete, cortecita de naranja que se echa en el vino para darle gusto. 4. (Poco us.) Bizna, la membranita que hay entre los cachos de la nuez. 5. *(Culin.)* Cáscara, peladura.

zeta ['zetə] [se-ta], *s.* Letra sexta del alfabeto griego.

Zeus [zjuːs] [sius], *s.* Nombre de la deidad suprema de los griegos, correspondiente al Júpiter de los romanos.

zigzag ['zɪgzæg] [sig-sag], *va.* y *vn.* Zigzaguear; ir en zigzags, hacer zigzags. *-a.* Que está en una línea interrumpida con irregularidades a uno y otro lado. *-s.* Zigzag, serie de líneas que forman ángulos entrantes y salientes.

zilch ['zɪltʃ] [silch], *s.* Nada de nada.

Zimbabwean [zɪmˈbɑːbwɪən] [sim-bauian], *a.* Zimbauense, de Zimbabue.

zinc [zɪŋk] [sink], *s.* Cinz, zinc, metal blanco azulado y fácil de fundir. **Zinc chloride**, cloruro de cinc. **Sulphate of zinc o white copperas**, sulfato de cinc o caparrosa blanca. **Zinc blende**, blenda, sulfuro de cinc nativo. **Zinc white**, blanco de cinc, óxido de cinc. *-va.* Plaquear, dar una capa de cinc.

zing [zɪŋ] [sing], *s. (Coloq.)* Silbido (hiss). *-vi.* Silbar. **To zing past.** pasar silbando.

zinnia ['zɪnɪə] [si-nia], *s. (Bot.)* Zinnia.

zion ['zaɪən] [saion], *s.* 1. Zión, colina de Jerusalén; de aquí, la antigua teocracia hebrea o la moderna Iglesia de Cristo. 2. Cielo.

Zionism ['zaɪənɪzəm] [saio-ni-sem], *s.* Sionismo.

Zionist ['zaɪənɪst] [saio-nist], *a.* Sionista.

zip [zɪp] [sip], *s.* 1. Garra, brío. 2. Silbido (hiss). *-vt.* Cerrar la cremallera.

zip gun ['zɪpgʌn] [sip-gan], *s.* Remachador de tipo de pistola; pistola o revólver de confección doméstica.

zipper ['zɪpəʳ] [si-paʳ], *s.* Cremallera, cierre relámpago.

zippy ['zɪpɪ] [si-pi], *a. (Coloq.)* Brioso (energetic), veloz.

zircon ['zɜːkən] [ser-kon], *s.* Circón, silicato adamantino de circonio de diversos colores. Se usa como piedra fina.

zirconium ['zɜːkənɪəm] [ser-ko-niom], *s.* Circonio, metal muy raro cuyas sales tienen uso limitado.

zit ['zɪt] [sit], *s. (Coloq.)* Grano.

zither ['zɪðəʳ] [si-daʳ], *s.* Cítara, instrumento músico de cuerda algo parecido a la guitarra, que se toca con púa.

zodiac ['zəʊdɪæk] [sou-diak], *s.* 1. Zodíaco, faja o zona imaginaria que se extiende unos ocho grados a uno y otro lado de la elíptica, y que contiene las doce constelaciones que el sol recorre aparentemente en los doce meses del año, así como los planetas mayores. 2. Circuito completo, círculo.

zodiacal [zəʊˈdaɪækəl] [sou-daia-kal], *a.* Zodiacal, que pertenece al zodíaco.

zoic [zɔɪk] [soik], *a.* 1. Zoico, concerniente al animal o a la vida animal. 2. En geología, que contiene fósiles; se dice de las rocas.

zombie, zombi ['zɒmbɪ] [som-bi], *s.* Zombie, zombi.

zonal ['zəʊnl] [sou-nal], *a.* Perteneciente a una zona o banda; marcado con bandas o zonas.

zone [zəʊn] [soun], *s.* 1. *(Geol.)* Zona (area), cualquiera de las cinco partes o bandas en que se considera dividida la superficie de la tierra de polo a polo. **Time zone**, zona horaria. 2. Banda circular, faja; raya o línea de color diferente. 3. Originalmente, y hoy en poesía, cinturón o cíngulo.

zoned ['zəʊnd] [sound], *a.* 1. Zonado, marcado con fajas coloreadas y concéntricas. 2. Que lleva un cinto o cíngulo.

zoneless ['zəʊnlɪs] [soun-les], *a.* Que no tiene cinto.

zonked ['zɒŋt] [sonkt], *a.* 1. Colocado (high on drugs). 2. Reventado, hecho polvo (exhausted).

zoo [zuː] [su], *s. (Fam.)* Jardín zoológico. *(Abrev. de* **zoological**.)

zoographer ['zuːɡrəfəʳ] [su-gra-faʳ], *s.* Zoógrafo, el que escribo o compone un tratado de zoografía.

zoographic [zuːˈgræfɪk] [su-gra-fik], *a.* Zoográfico, perteneciente o relativo a la zoografía.

zoolatry ['zuːlətrɪ] [su-la-tri], *s.* Zoolatría, descripción de la naturaleza y las propiedades de los animales.

zoolite ['zuːlaɪt] [su-lait], *s.* Zoolito, zoomorfito; los restos fósiles de un animal petrificado. Se escribe también Zoolith.

zoological [ˌzəʊəˈlɒdʒɪkəl] [su-lo-yi-kal], *a.* Zoológico, perteneciente a la zoología.

zoologist [zəʊˈɒlədʒɪst] [su-o-lo-yist], *s.* Zoólogo, el profesor de zoología.

zoology [zəʊˈɒlədʒɪ] [su-o-lo-yi], *s.* 1. Zoología, la ciencia que trata de los animales. 2. El reino animal o ejemplares locales de él, considerados biológicamente. 3. Zoología, tratado científico sobre los animales.

zoom [zuːm] [sum], *vn. (Aer.)* Subir bruscamente en ángulo máximo. **Zoom in**, hacer un zoom. *-s.* Zumbido. *(Cin., Fot.)* **Zoom lens**, teleobjetivo.

zoometry ['zuːmɪtrɪ] [su-mi-tri], *s.* Zoometría, medición de los animales.

zoophyte ['zəʊəˌfaɪt] [su-fait], *s.* Zoófito, animal invertebrado que se asemeja algo a la planta en su forma y crecimiento: v. gr. el coral y la esponja.

zootic ['zuːtɪk] [su-tik], *a.* Zoótico; se dice de un terreno que contiene cuerpos organizados.

zoroastrian [ˌzɒrəʊˈæstrɪən] [so-rou-as-trian], *a.* Zoroástrico, perteneciente a Zoroastro o a sus doctrinas.

zounds ['zaʊndz] [sounds], *inter.* ¡Voto al chápiro! ¡por vida de sanes! ¡válgame Dios! (Corrupción de **God's wounds**.)

zucchini [zuːˈkiːnɪ] [su-ki-ni], *s.* Calabacín, calabacita.

Zulu, zooloo ['zuːlʊ] [su-lu], *a.* Zulú, perteneciente a los zulúes o a su idioma. *-s.* Zulú, individuo de ciertas tribus negras que habitan el África austral; su dialecto o idioma.

zygote ['zaɪgəʊt] [zai-gout], *s.* Cigoto, cigota.

zyme ['zaɪm] [zaim], *s.* 1. Un fermento. 2. Germen de enfermedad; lo que se considera causa específica de una enfermedad cimótica o infecciosa.

zymic ['zaɪmɪk] [zai-mik], *a.* Címico, concerniente a la fermentación o producido por ella.

APÉNDICE

Lista Alfabética de los Nombres
de Países, Naciones, Provincias, Mares, Pueblos, Ríos, Montañas, Etc.

QUE NO SE ESCRIBEN DEL MISMO MODO EN INGLÉS QUE EN ESPAÑOL

CON el objeto de hacerla lo más corta posible, no han sido comprendidos en ella los que tienen una misma ortografía en ambas lenguas, y los que pueden ser traducidos fácilmente con sólo mudar su terminación extranjera en la castellana; para lo cual se deberán observar las reglas siguientes.

Los acabados en *burgh* y *borough* que no se hallen en la lista, se traducirán mudando solamente estas terminaciones en la castellana *burgo*, como *Augsburg*, Augsburgo; *Petersburg*, Petersburgo; *Hamburg*, Hamburgo; *Cobourg*, Coburgo; y *Peterborough*, Peterburgo, etc.

Hay muchos nombres geográficos universalmente conocidos que terminan en *e*, y se traducen con sólo cambiar la *e*, en *a*, como *Europe*, Europa; *Rome*, Roma, etc.

Los ingleses suelen designar algunos de los condados en que dividen la Gran Bretaña por medio de la terminación *shire* añadida al nombre del condado, distrito o provincia, como *Derbyshire*, que se traducirá El condado, distrito o provincia de Derby; *Yorkshire*, El condado de York, etc.

NOTA.-Los adjetivos derivados de los nombres propios se hallarán en sus respectivos lugares en el texto de este diccionario.

A

Aachen ['ɑːxən], o **Aix-la-Chapelle** ['eɪkslæʃəˈpel], Aquisgrán (Alemania).
Abyssinia [æbɪˈsɪnɪə], Abisinia, *V.* ETHIOPIA.
Achaea ['æki:ə], Acaya (región de la antigua Grecia).
Addis Ababa ['ædɪsˈæbəbə], Addis Abeba (Etiopía).
Admiralty Islands ['ædmərəltɪ aɪlənds], Islas del Almirantazgo.
Adrianople ['eɪdrɪənəpl], o **Edirne** [eˈdɜːn], Adrianópolis o Andrinópolis (Turquía).
Adriatic Sea [eɪdrɪˈætɪk siː], Mar Adriático.
Aegean Sea [iːˈdʒiːən siː], Mar Egeo.
Agincourt [əˈɡɪnkɔːt], Azincourt (Francia).
Aix-la Chapelle, *V.* AACHEN.
Aleutian Islands [əˈluːʃən aɪlənds], Islas Aleutianas.
Alexandria [ælɪɡˈzɑːndrɪə], Alejandría (Egipto).
Algeria [ælˈdʒɪərɪə], Argelia.
Algiers [ælˈdʒɪəz], Argel (ciudad de Argelia, África).
Alps [ælps], Alpes (montañas del S. de la Europa central).
Alsace-Lorraine ['ælsæsləˈreɪn], Alsacia-Lorena.
Amazon River ['æməzən rɪvəˈ], Río Amazonas.
Andalusia [ændəˈluːzɪə], Andalucía (España).
Antarctic Ocean [ænˈtɑːtɪk oʊʃən], Océano Antártico.
Antilles, Greater [ænˈtɪliːz ɡreɪtəˈ], Antillas Mayores.
Antilles, Lesser [ænˈtɪliːz lesəˈ], Antillas Menores.
Antioch ['æntɪɒk], Antioquía (Turquía).
Antwerp ['æntwɜːp], Amberes (Bélgica).
Apennines ['æpɪnaɪnz], Apeninos (montañas de Italia).
Appalachian Mountains [æpəˈleɪtʃɪən maʊntɪnz], Montes Apalaches.
Arabian Sea [əˈreɪbɪən siː], Mar Arábigo.
Archipelago [ɑːkɪˈpelɪɡəʊ], El Archipiélago Griego o del Mar Egeo.
Arctic Ocean ['ɑːktɪk oʊʃən], Océano Artico.
Ardeness Mountains [ɑːˈdənz maʊntɪnz], Sierra Ardenas.
Assisi [əˈsiːzɪ], Asís (Italia).
Assyria [əˈsɪrɪə], Asiria.
Athens ['æθɪnz], Atenas (Grecia).
Atlantic Ocean [ətˈlæntɪk oʊʃən], Océano Atlántico.
Attica ['ætɪkə], Atica (Grecia).
Austria-Hungary ['ɒstrɪə], Austria-Hungría.
Avignon ['ævɪnjɒ] Aviñón (Francia).

B

Babylon ['bæbɪlən], Babilonia.
Balearic Islands [bælɪˈærɪk aɪləndz], Islas Baleares.
Balkans ['bɔːlkəns], Balcanes.
Baltic Sea ['bɔːltɪk siː], Mar Báltico.
Barbary Coast ['bɑːbərɪ kəʊst], Berbería (África).
Basle [bɑːl], o **Basel** ['bɑːzəl], Basilea (Suiza).
Bavaria [bəˈveərɪə], Baviera (Alemania).
Bayonne [barˈjɒn], Bayona (Francia).
Beirut o Beyrouth [beɪˈruːt], Beirut (Líbano).
Belgian Congo ['beldʒən kɒŋɡəʊ], Congo Belga.
Belgium ['beldʒəm], Bélgica.
Belgrade [belˈɡreɪd], Belgrado (Yugoslavia).
Bengal [beŋˈɡɔːl], Bengala.
Berne o Bern [bɜːn], Berna (Suiza).
Bethlehem ['beθlɪhem], Belén (Jordania).
Beyrouth, *V.* BEIRUT.
Biscay ['bɪskeɪ], Vizcaya (España).
Black Forest ['blæk fɒrɪst], Selva Negra.
Black Sea ['blæk siː], Mar Negro.
Blue Mountains ['bluː maʊntɪnz], Montañas Azules.
Bologna [bəˈləʊnjə], Bolonia (Italia).
Bordeaux [bɔːˈdəʊ], Burdeos (Francia).
Bosphorus ['bɒsfərəs], Bósforo, Estrecho del.
Brazil [brəˈzɪl], Brasil.
Britain, Great ['brɪtən ɡreɪt], Gran Bretaña.
British Isles ['brɪtɪʃ aɪlz], Islas Británicas.
Bruges [bruːz], Brujas (Bélgica).
Brussels ['brʌslz], Bruselas (Bélgica).

Bucharest [ˌbuːkəˈrest], Bucarest (Rumania).
Burgundy [ˈbɜːgəndɪ], Borgoña.
Burma [ˈbɜːmə], Birmania.
Byzantium [baɪˈzæntɪəm], Bizancio (nombre antiguo de Constantinopla). *V.* ISTANBUL.

C

Calcutta [kælˈkʌtə], Calcuta (India).
Cambodia [kæmˈbəʊdɪə], Camboya (Indochina).
Canal Zone [kəˈnæl zəʊn], *V.* PANAMA CANAL ZONE.
Canary Islands [kəˈnærɪ aɪləndz], Islas Canarias.
Cantabrian Mountains [kænˈtæbrɪən maʊntɪnz], Cordillera Cantábrica.
Cape Breton Island [ˈkeɪpˌbretən aɪlənd], Isla Cabo Bretón (Nueva Escocia, Canadá).
Cape Horn [ˈkeɪpˈhɔːn], Cabo de Hornos.
Capetown [ˈkeɪptaʊn], Ciudad del Cabo (Unión Sudafricana).
Cap Haitian [ˈkæpˌheɪʃɪən], Cabo Haitiano.
Caribbean Sea [ˌkærɪˈbiːən siː], Mar Caribe o de las Antillas.
Carpathian Mountains [kɑːˈpeɪʃɪənz maʊntɪnz], Montes Cárpatos.
Carthage [ˈkɑːθɪdʒ], Cartago (antigua ciudad del África del Norte).
Cashmere o Kashmir [kæʃˈmɪəʳ], Cachemira (estado de la región del Himalaya).
Caspian Sea [ˈkæspɪənˌsiː], Mar Caspio.
Castile, New [kæsˈtiːl njuː], Castilla la Nueva (España).
Castile, Old [kæsˈtiːl əʊld] . Castilla la Vieja (España).
Catalonia [ˌkætəˈləʊnɪə], Cataluña (España).
Caucasus [ˈkɔːkəsəs], Cáucaso.
Cayenne [ˈkeɪen], Cayena (Guayana Francesa).
Central America [ˈsentrələˈmerɪkə], América Central.
Ceylon [sɪˈlɒn], Ceilán.
Champagne [ʃæmˈpeɪn], Champaña (Francia).
Cologne [kəˈləʊn], Colonia (Alemania).
Constantinople [ˌkɒnstæntɪˈnəʊpl], Constantinopla (Turquía). *V.* ISTANBUL.
Copenhagen [ˌkəʊpnˈheɪgən], Copenhague (Dinamarca).
Corinth [ˈkɒrɪnθ], Corinto (Grecia).
Corsica Córcega (Isla del Mediterráneo).
Crete o Krete [kriːt], Creta (Isla del Mediterráneo.)
Cyprus [ˈsaɪprəs], Chipre (Isla del Mediterráneo).
Czechoslovakia [ˈtʃekəʊsləˈvækɪə], Checoslovaquia.

D

Dalmatia [dælˈmeɪʃə], Dalmacia.
Damascus [dəˈmɑːskəs], Damasco (Siria).
Danube [ˈdænjuːb], Danubio (río de Europa).
Dardanelles [ˌdɑːdəˈnelz], Dardanelos (antiguamente Helesponto).
Dead Sea [ˈdedˈsiː], Mar Muerto.
Denmark [ˈdenmɑːk], Dinamarca.
Dordonge [dɔːˈdɒŋ], Dordoña (río de Francia).
Douro [ˈdəʊərəʊ], Duero (río de la Península Ibérica).
Dresden [ˈdrezdən], Dresde (Alemania).
Dunkirk [dʌnˈkɜːk], Dunquerque (Francia).

E

East Indies [ˈiːstˈɪndɪz], Indias Orientales.
Edinburgh [ˈedɪnbərə], Edimburgo (Escocia).
Edirne [eˈdɜːn], *V.* ADRIANOPLE.
Egypt [ˈiːdʒɪpt], Egipto.
Elba River [ˈelbə rɪvəʳ], Río Elba.

England [ˈɪŋglənd], Inglaterra.
English Channel [ˈɪŋglɪʃˈtʃænl], Canal de la Mancha.
Ephesus [ˈɪfɪsəs], Éfeso (antigua ciudad griega en Asia Menor).
Epirus [ˈɪpɪrəs], Epiro (Grecia).
Ethiopia [ˌiːθɪˈəʊpɪə], Etiopía (ant. Abisinia).
Euphrates [juːˈfreɪtiːz], Eufrates (río de Asia).

F

Falkland Islands [ˈfɔːlkləndˌaɪləndz], Islas Malvinas o Falkland.
Finland [ˈfɪnlənd], Finlandia.
Flanders [ˈflɑːndəz], Flandes.
Florence [ˈflɒrəns], Florencia (Italia).
France [frɑːns], Francia.
French Guiana [ˌfrentʃgaɪˈænə], Guayana Francesa.
Friendly Islands [ˈfrendlɪ aɪləndz], Islas de los Amigos o de la Amistad. *V.* TONGA.
Frisian Islands [ˈfriːʒən aɪləndz], Islas Frisias.

G

Galilee [ˈgælɪliː], Galilea.
Garonne [gəˈrɒn], Garona (río de Francia).
Gascony [ˈgæskənɪ], Gascuña (Francia).
Gaul [gɔːl], Galia.
Geneva [dʒɪˈniːvə], Ginebra (Suiza).
Genoa [ˈdʒenəʊə], Génova (Italia).
Germany [ˈdʒɜːmənɪ], Alemania.
Ghent [gent], Gante (Bélgica).
Gold Coast [ˈgəʊldˈkəʊst], Costa de Oro (África Occidental).
Good Hope, Cape of [ˈgʊdˌhəʊp keɪp ɒv], Cabo de Buena Esperanza.
Great Britain [ˈgreɪtˈbrɪtn], Gran Bretaña.
Great Lakes [ˈgreɪtˈleɪks], Grandes Lagos.
Greece [griːs], Grecia.
Greenland [ˈgriːnlənd], Groenlandia.

H

Hague, The [ˈheɪg], La Haya (Holanda).
Haiti Island [ˈheɪtɪ aɪlənd], Haití.
Hangchow [ˈhæŋkəʊ], Hangcheú (puerto marítimo de China).
Hankow [ˈhæŋkəʊ], Hankeú (ciudad de China).
Havana [həˈvænə], Habana (Cuba).
Havre, Le [ˈhævr leɪ], El Havre (puerto de Francia).
Hawaiian Islands [həˈwaɪjən aɪləndz], Islas Hawaii.
Hebrides [ˈhebrɪdiːz], Islas Hébridas.
Hellespont [ˈheləspɒnt], Helesponto. *V.* DARDANELLES.
Holland [ˈhɒlənd], Holanda.
Holy Land [ˈhəʊlɪˌlænd], Tierra Santa.
Hungary [ˈhʌŋgərɪ], Hungría.

I

Iberian Peninsula [aɪˈbɪərɪənpəˈnɪnsjʊlə], Península Ibérica.
Iceland [ˈaɪslənd], Islandia.
Indian Ocean [ˈɪndɪənˈəʊʃən], Océano Índico.
Indus [ˈɪndəs], Indo (río de la India y Pakistán).
Ionian Sea [aɪˌəʊnɪənˈsiː], Mar Jónico.
Iraq [ɪˈrɑːk], Irak.
Ireland [ˈaɪələnd], Irlanda.
Istanbul [ˈɪstænˈbuːl], Estambúl (ant. Constantinopla).
Italy [ˈɪtəlɪ], Italia.
Ivory Coast [ˈaɪvərɪˈkəʊst], Costa de Marfil.

J

Japan [dʒəˈpæn], Japón.
Jerusalem [dʒəˈruːsələm], Jerusalén.
Jordan [ˈdʒɔːdn], Jordania.

K

Kazakhstan [ˌkæzəkˈstɑːn], Kazajistán, Kazakistán.
Key West [ˈkiːˌwest], Cayo Hueso (Florida, E.U.A.).
Khartoum [kɑːˈtuːm], Jartum.
Korea [kəˈrɪə], Corea.
Kyoto [ˈkɪətə], Kioto (Japón).
Kyrgyzstan Kirguizia, Kirguizistán, Kirguizstán.

L

Lapland [ˈlæplænd], Laponia.
Latin America [ˈlætɪnəˈmerɪkə], América Latina o Iberoamérica.
Lausanne [ləʊˈzæn] Lausana (Suiza).
Lebanon [ˈlebənən], Líbano.
Leghorn [ˈlegˈhɔːn], Liorna (Italia).
Leningrad [ˈlenɪŋgræd], Leningrado (ant. San Petersburgo y Petrogrado).
Libya [ˈlɪbɪə], Libia.
Liége [liːdʒ], Lieja (Bélgica).
Lille [liːl], Lila (Francia).
Lisbon [ˈlɪzbən], Lisboa (Portugal).
Lithuania [ˌlɪθjʊˈeɪnɪə], Lituania.
London [ˈlʌndən], Londres (Inglaterra).
Lorraine [loˈreɪn], Lorena. V. ALSACE-LORRAINE.
Louisiana [luˌiːzɪˈænə], Luisiana (E.U.A.).
Louvain [ˈluːveɪn], Lovaina (Bélgica).
Low Countries [ˈlaʊˌkʌntriːz], Países Bajos. V. NETHERLANDS.
Lower California [ˈlaʊəˌkælɪˈfɔːnɪə], Baja California (México).
Lucerne o Luzern [luːˈsɜːn], Lucerna (Suiza).

M

Magellan, Strait of [məˈgelən streɪt ɒv], Estrecho de Magallanes.
Mainz [maɪnts], Maguncia (Alemania).
Majorca o Mallorca [məˈjɔːkə], Mallorca (isla del Mediterráneo).
Malay [məˈleɪ], Malaca, Malaya.
Maldive Islands [ˈmɔːldaɪvˌaɪləndz], Islas Maldivas.
Marrakesh [ˌmærəˈkeʃ], Marrakech.
Marseille o Marseilles [mɑːˈseɪlz], Marsella (Francia).
Martinique [ˌmɑːtɪˈniːk], Martinica.
Mauritius [məˈriːʃəs], o Ile de France [ˌiːldəˈfrɑːns], Mauricio.
Mediterranean Sea [ˌmedɪtəˈreɪnɪən], Mar Mediterráneo.
Meuse [mɜːz], Mosa (río de Francia y Bélgica).
Mexico [ˈmeksɪkəʊ], Méjico o México.
Minorca o Menorca [mɪˈnɔːkə], Menorca (isla del Mediterráneo).
Mississippi River [ˌmɪsɪˈsɪpɪ], Río Misisipí.
Missouri [mɪˈzʊərɪ], Misuri (estado y río de E. U.A.).

Moluccas [ˈmələkəs], o Spice Islands [luːˈsɜːn], Islas Molucas o de las Especias.
Morocco [məˈrɒkəʊ], Marruecos.
Moscow [ˈmɒskəʊ], Moscú (Rusia).
Moselle [məʊˈzel], Mosela (río de Francia y Alemania).

N

Naples [ˈneɪplz], Nápoles (Italia).
Near East [ˈnɪərˈiːst], Cercano Oriente.
Netherlands [ˈneðələndz], Países Bajos u Holanda.
Newfoundland [ˈnjuːfəndlənd], Terranova.
New Orleans [njuːˈɔːlɪəns], Nueva Orleans (Luisiana E.U.A.).
New South Wales [ˈnjuːsaʊθˈweɪlz], Nueva Gales del Sur.
New York [ˈnjuːˈjɔːk], Nueva York (E.U.A.).
New Zealand [njuːˈziːlənd], Nueva Zelanda.
Niagara Falls [naɪˈægrə fɔːlz], Cataratas del Niágara.
Nice [niːs], Niza (Francia).
Nile [naɪl], Nilo (río de África).
Nippon [ˈnaɪpn], Nipón. V. JAPAN.
Normandy [ˈnɔːməndɪ], Normandía (Francia).
North America [ˈnɔːθəˈmerɪkə], Norte América o América del Norte.
North Pole [ˌnɔːθˈpəʊl], Polo Norte.
Norway [ˈnɔːweɪ], Noruega.
Nova Scotia [ˈnəʊvəˈskəʊʃə], Nueva Escocia.

O

Odessa [ˈədesə], Odesa (puerto de la U.R.S.S.).
Olympus, Mount [əʊˈlɪmpəs], Monte Olimpo.
Ostend [ɒsˈtend], Ostende (Bélgica).

P

Pacific Ocean [pəˈsɪfɪkˈəʊʃən], Océano Pacífico.
Palestine [ˈpælɪstaɪn], Palestina.
Papal States [ˈpeɪpəlˌsteɪts], Estados Pontificios.
Parnassus, Mount [pɑːˈnæsəs], Parnaso (monte de Grecia).
Peloponnesus [ˌpeləpəˈniːsəs], Peloponeso (Grecia).
Pennsylvania [ˌpensɪlˈveɪnɪə], Pensilvania (E.U.A.).
Perugia [pəˈruːdʒɪə], Perusa (Italia).
Philadelphia [fɪləˈdelfɪə], Filadelfia (E.U.A.).
Philippines [ˈfɪlɪpiːnz], Filipinas.
Phoenicia [fɪˈnɪʃɪə], Fenicia.
Poland [ˈpəʊlənd], Polonia.
Pompeii [pɒmˈpeɪɪ], Pompeya (Italia).
Port-au-Prince [ˈpɔːtˌəˈprɜːns], Puerto Príncipe (Haití).
Port of Spain [ˈpɔːtəvsˌpeɪn], Puerto España (Trinidad).
Port Said [ˈpɔːtseɪd], Puerto Said (Egipto).
Prague [prɑːg], Praga (Checoslovaquia).
Pyrenees [ˌpɪrəˈniːz], Pirineos.

R

Rangoon [ræŋˈguːn], Rangún (Birmania).
Red Sea [ˈredˈsiː], Mar Rojo.
Rhine [raɪn], Rhin o Rin (río de Europa).
Rhodes [rəʊdz], Rodas (isla del Mar Egeo).
Rhone [rəʊn], Ródano (río de Europa).
Rocky Mountains [ˈrɒkɪˈmaʊntɪnz], Montañas Rocosas.
Rouen [ruːˈɑːŋ], Ruan (Francia).

Russia [ˈrʌʃə], Rusia. *V.* ant. UNION OF SOVIET
SOCIALIST REPUBLICS (U.S.S.R.).

S

Salonika [səˈlɒnɪkə], o **Thessalonike** [ˌtesəˈlɒnɪkə],
Salónica (Grecia).
Sardinia [sɑːˈdɪnɪə], o **Sardegna** [sɑːˈdeɪnə], Cerdeña (isla
del Mediterráneo).
Saudi Arabia [ˈsaʊdɪəˈreɪbɪə], Arabia Saudita.
Saxony [ˈsæksənɪ], Sajonia (ant. reino alemán).
Scandinavia [ˌskændɪˈneɪvɪə], Escandinavia.
Scheldt [ʃelt], Escalda (río de Bélgica).
Scotland [ˈskɒktlənd], Escocia.
Seine [seɪn], Sena (río de Francia).
Siam [saɪˈæm], *V.* THAILAND.
Sicily [ˈsɪsɪlɪ], Sicilia (isla del Mediterráneo).
Smyrna [ˈsmɜːnə], Esmirna (Turquía).
Society Islands [səˈsaɪətɪˌaɪləndz], Islas de la Sociedad.
South America [ˌsaʊθəˈmerɪkə], Sud América o América del
Sur.
Spain [speɪn], España.
Sparta [ˈspɑːtə], Esparta (ant. ciudad de Grecia).
Stockholm [ˈstɒkhəʊm], Estocolmo (Suecia).
Stromboli [ˈstrɒmbəlɪ], Estrómboli (volcán de Sicilia).
Surinam [sʊərɪˈnæm], Surinam.
Sweden [ˈswiːdn], Suecia.
Switzerland [ˈswiːtsələnd], Suiza.
Syracuse [ˈsaɪərəkjuːz], Siracusa.
Syria [ˈsɪrɪə], Siria.

T

Tajikistan [tɑːdʒɪkɪsˈtɑːn], Tayikistán.
Tangier [tænˈdʒɪəʳ], Tánger (Marruecos).
Taurus Mountains [ˈtɔːrəsˌmaʊntɪnz], Montañas Tauro
(Turquía).
Tehran o **Teheran** [tɛəˈrɑːn], Teherán (Irán).
Texas [ˈteksəs], Tejas (E.U.A.).
Thailand [ˈtaɪlænd], Thailandia o Siam.
Thames [teɪmz], Támesis (río de Inglaterra).
Thebes [θiːbz], Tebas (ant. ciudades de Grecia y de Egipto).
Thermopylae [θɜːˈmɒpɪliː], Termópilas (desfiladero de
Grecia).
Thessalonike, *V.* SALONIKA.
Thessaly [ˈθesəlɪ], Tesalia (Grecia).
Thrace [θreɪs], Tracia.
Tokyo [ˈtəʊkɪəʊ], Tokio (Japón).
Tonga [ˈtɒŋə], o **Friendly Islands**, Tonga o Islas de los
Amigos de la Amistad.

Toulon [tuːˈlɔːn], Tolón (Francia).
Toulouse [tuːˈluːz], Tolosa (Francia).
Trent [ˈtrent], Trento (Italia).
Troy [trɔɪ], Troya.
Tunis [ˈtjuːnɪs], Túnez.
Turkey [ˈtɜːkɪ], Turquía.
Tuscany [ˈtʌskənɪ], Toscana (Italia).
Tyre [ˈtaɪəʳ], Tiro (ant. puerto fenicio, actualmente puerto de
Líbano).
Tyrrhenian Sea [tɪˈriːnɪənˌsiː], Mar Tirreno.

U

Ukraine [juːˈkreɪn], Ucrania.
Union of South Africa [ˈjuːnɪənɒvˌsaʊθˈæfrɪkə], Unión
Sudafricana.
Union of Soviet Socialist Republics (ant. U.S.S.R.)
[ˈjuːnɪənɒvˌsəʊvɪətˈsəʊʃəlɪstrɪˈpʌblɪks], Unión de
Repúblicas Socialistas Soviéticas (abrev. URSS).
United Kingdom [juːˈnaɪtɪdˈkɪŋdɒm], Reino Unido.
United States of America [juːˈnaɪtɪdˈsteɪtsɒvəˈmerɪkə],
Estados Unidos de América.
Ural Mountains [ˈjuːərəlˌmaʊntɪnz], Montes Urales.

V

Vatican City [ˈvætɪkənˈsɪtɪ], Ciudad del Vaticano.
Venice [ˈvenɪs], Venecia (Italia).
Versailles [veəˈsaɪ], Versalles (Francia).
Vesuvius [vɪˈsuːvɪəs], Vesubio (monte y volcán de Italia).
Vienna [vɪˈenə], o **Wien** [ˈvɪen], Viena (Austria).
Virgin Islands [ˈvɜːdʒɪnˌaɪləndz], Islas Vírgenes.

W

Wales [weɪlz], Gales.
Warsaw [ˈwɔːsɔː], Varsovia (Polonia).
West Indies [ˈwestˈɪndiːz], Indias Occidentales.
Windward Islands [ˈwɪndwədˌaɪləndz], Islas de
Barlovento.

Y

Yellow River [ˈjeləʊˌrɪvəʳ], o **Hwang Ho**, Río Amarillo o
Hoang Ho.
Yellow Sea [ˈjeləʊˌsiː], **Hwang Hai**, Mar Amarillo.

Lista Alfabética
de los Nombre Propios de Personas

QUE SE USAN ABREVIADOS FAMILIARMENTE EN INGLÉS, CON SUS EQUIVALENTES EN CASTELLANO

De casi todos los equivalentes se pueden forman diminutivos o nombres familiares en castellano añadiéndoles una de estas terminaciones; *ito, ico, illo*. Dichos equivalentes pierden la letra final si es vocal, y mudan la *o* en *a* para los femeninos; y en los acabados en *co* o *ca* se convierten estas sílabas en *qu*; v.g. Francisco, *Francisquito*; Francisca, *Francisquita*; por esto sólo se insertan los que tienen un nombre irregular además del regular.

Alec [ælɪk] *por* **Alexander**, Alejandro.
Bab *por* **Barbara**. Bárbara, Barbarita.
Bart *por* **Bartholomew**, Bartolomé, Bartolo.
Bee, Becky [ˈ] *por* **Rebecca**, Rebeca.
Bel, Belle [ˈ] *por* **Isabella**, Isabel.
Ben *por* **Benjamin**, Benjamín.
Bert, Bertie [ˈ] *por* **Herbert** o **Albert**, Heberto o Alberto.
Bess, Beth, Betsy, Bessy, Betty, Lizzie *por* Elizabeth, Belita, Belica.
Biddy *por* **Bridget**, Brigida.
Bob, Rob *por* **Robert**, Roberto.
Bill, Billy *por* **William**, Guillermo.

Carrie *por* **Caroline**, Carolina.
Charley, Charlie *por* **Charles**, Carlos, Carlitos.
Cis *por* **Cecile**, Cecilia.
Clare [ˈ] *por* **Clara**.

Dan *por* **Daniel**, Daniel.
Davy *por* **David**, David.
Dick, Dicky *por* **Richard**, Ricardo.
Dol, Dotty *por* **Dorothy**, Dorotea.
Dorick [ˈ] *por* **Theodoric**, Teodoro.
Di [ˈ] *por* **Diana**, Diana.

Eddy *por* **Edward** o **Edwin**, **Edgar** o **Edmund**, Eduardo, Edmundo.
Effie [ˈ] *por* **Euphemia**, Eufemia.
Etta [ˈ] *por* **Henrietta**, Enriqueta.

Fan, Fanny *por* **Frances**, Francisca, Frasquita, Paquita, Panchita, Currita, Paca, Farruca.
Fred *por* **Frederick**, Federico.

Hal, Harry *por* **Henry**, Enrique.
Hatty, Hetty, Netty *por* **Henrietta**, Enriqueta.
Hodge [ˈ] *por* **Roger**, Rogerio.

Jack, Johnny *por* **John**, Juan.
Jeft *por* **Geoffrey** o **Jefferson**.
Jem, Jemmy *por* **James**, Santiago, Jaime, Jacobo.
Jerry *por* **Jeremiah, Jetorde**, Jeremías, Jerónimo.
Jennie, Jenny *por* **Jane**, Juana.
Joe, Josy *por* **Joseph**, José, Pepe, Pepito, Pepillo.
Josie [ˈ] *por* **Josephine**, Pepa, Pepita, Pepilla.
Kate, Kitty, Kit *por* **Catharine**, Catalina, Catujita.
Kit *por* **Christopher**, Cristóbal, Tobalito.

Larry, Laurie, Lawrie *por* **Lawrence**, Lorenzo.
Len *por* **Leonard**, Leonardo.
Letty *por* **Letitia**, Leticia.
Libby, Lib, Lizzie, Liz *por* **Elizabeth**, Isabel.
Lulu [ˈ] *por* **Lucy** y **Louisa**, Lucía y Luisa, Luisita.

Madge, Meg *por* **Margery**, Margarita.
Mat *por* **Matthew**, Mateo.
Mat, Matty *por* **Martha**, Marta, y **Mathilda**, Matilde.
Maud [ˈ] *por* **Mathilda**.
Mike [ˈ] *por* **Michael**, Miguel.
Mol, Molly *por* **Mary**, María, Marquita, Maruca, Maruja.

Nan, Nancy *por* **Ann**, Ana.
Ned, Neddy, Teddy *por* **Edward** o **Edwin**, Eduardo.
Nel, Nelly *por* **Ellen** y **Eleanor**, Elena y Leonor.
Netty *por* **Henrietta**, Enriqueta.
Nick *por* **Nicholas**, Nicolás.

Pam *por* **Pamela**, Pamela.
Patty *por* **Pat**, Patricia, Patricia.
Peg, Peggy *por* **Margaret**, Margarita.
Pen *por* **Penelope**, Penélope.
Phil *por* **Philip**, Felipe.
Prue [ˈ] *por* **Prudence**, Prudencia,

Reta, Rita [ˈ] *por* **Margaret**, Margarita.

Sal, Sally *por* **Sarah**, Sara.
Sam *por* **Samuel**, Samuel.
Sil *por* **Silvester**, Silvestre.
Sim *por* **Simon**, Simón, Simoncito.

Ted, Teddy, Theo *por* **Theodore**, Teodoro'
Tilda *por* **Mathilda**, Matilde.
Tim *por* **Timothy**, Timoteo.
Tom, Tommy *por* **Thomas**, Tomás.
Tony *por* **Anthony**, Antonio, Toño, Antoñito.
Tracy *por* **Theresa**, Teresa.

Val *por* **Valentine**, Valentín.
Vin *por* **Vincent**, Vicente.

Walt *por* **Walter**, Gualterio.
Will *por* **William**, Guillermo.

Zach [ˈ] *por* **Zachary**, Zacarías.

Lista Alfabética de las Abreviaturas

MÁS USUALES EN INGLÉS

A. Academy, America.
a. accepted, acre, adjective, aged, answer, at.
aA. ana (de cada cosa). *Med.*
A.B. *Artium baccalaureus* (Bachelor of Arts).
abbr. abbreviated, abbreviation.
abt. about (poco más o menos).
A. C. *Ante Christum* (antes de Jesucristo).
A. C., AC, a. c. Alternating current.
acct., a/c. account.
ACTH. Adrenocorticotrophic hormone.
A. D. *Anno domini* (año de Cristo).
ad., adv. advertisement.
ad fin. *ad finem* (al fin).
adj. adjective, adjectival.
ad lib. *ad libitum* (a voluntad).
adv. adverb.
AFL, A.F. of L. American Federation of Labor.
Ala. Alabama.
A. M. *Anno mundi* (año del mundo); *artium magister* (maestro en artes); *ante meridiem* (antes del mediodía).
non. Anonymous.
AP, A. P. Associated Press.
arith. arithmetic.
Ark. Arkansas.
A.-S., AS. Anglo-Saxon.
at. wt. atomie weight.
athl. athletics.
Atty. Attorney.
Av., ave. Avenue.
av., avdp. avoirdupois.
avg. average.
AWOL, A. W. O. L., a. w. o.l. absent without leave (mil.)

b. born (nacido).
B. Bay, British.
B. A. Bachelor of Arts; Buenos Aires.
bal. balance (saldo).
Balt., Balto. Baltimore.
Bart., Bt. Baronet.
bbl. barrel.
B. C. Before Christ; British Columbia.
B. D. Bachelor of Divinity.
bds. boards (pasta).
bet. between.
B/L, b. l. bill of lading.
bldg. building.
bot. botany, botanical.
b. p. bills payable.-**bp.** bishop.
Br. Breton, British.
Bros. brothers.
bu., bus. bushel, bushels.

C. Caesar, Caius, carbon, centigrade, Congress, conservative.

c. *caput*, cent, centime, centimeter. *centum.*
C. A. Central America.
Cal., Calif., California.
cap. capital (mayúscula); caput (capítulo).
Capt. captain.
Carp. carpentry.
cc,C. C. carbon copy; cashier's check; chief clerk.
C. C. C. Civilian Conservation Corps (organismo oficial de E. U. A.)
C. E. civil engineer.
cf. confer (cotéjese); calf binding.
C. f. & i. cost, freight, and insurance.
C. G. Consul-general; Captain general; Coast Guard.
cg. centigram(me).
ch. chapter; child, children.
chap. chapter.
Chas. Charles.
Ch. E. Chemical Engineer.
Chem. chemical, chemistry.
C. I. F., c. i. f. cost, insurance, and freight.
cir., circ. *circa* (hacia o alrededor).
civ. civil.
cl. cloth (pasta, de libros); centiliter.
c. l. carload.
cm. centimeter.-**cm²** square centimeter.-**cm³** cubic centimeter.
cml. commercial.
Co. Company, county, cobalt.
C. 0. Commanding officer (mil.)
C. 0. D. collect (o cash) on delivery.
Col. Colonel.
Col., Colo. Colorado.
coll., colloq. colloquial, colloquialism.
com., coml. commercial.
comp. comparative compare; compiled; composer, compound.
con. conclusion, contra.
Cong. Congregational; Congressional; Congress.
conj. conjunction, conjugation.
Conn. (oficial) Connecticut.
constr. construction.
cont. containing; contents; continent; continued.
co-op. cooperativa.
Cor. coroner.
cor. corpus, correction, correlative, correspondent; corner.
cp. compare (cotéjese, véase).
c. p. candlepower.
C.P.A., CPA Certified Public Accountant.
Cpl. Corporal.
C. R. Costa Rica.
Cr. credit; creditor.
cres. crescendo.
cs. cases (cajas).
C. S. Christian Science.
C. S. T. Central Standard Time.

Ct. Connecticut, Court, Count.
cu., cub. cubic.
cur. currency; current.
c w. o. cash with order.
cwt. hundredweight(s).
C. Z. Canal Zone.

d. daughter, day, dead, denarius (penique), died, dime, dollar.
D. A. District Attorney.
Dan. Daniel: Danish.
D. A. R. Daughters of the American Revolution (organización de E. U. A.).
D. C. *Da capo*, District of Columbia; District Court.
D. D. Doctor of Divinity.
D. D. S. Doctor of Dental Surgery.
Dec. December.
def. definition, defined.
deg. degree.
Del. Delaware.
Dem. Democrat, Democratic.
Den. Denmark.
Dep., Dept. Department; deponent, deputy.
der., deriv. derivation, derived.
dft. defendant; draft.
D. G. *Dei gracia* (por la gracia de Dios).
dial. dialect, dialectical.
diam. diameter.
diff. difference, different, differs.
dig. digest.
dim. diminuendo, diminutivo.
disc. discount; discovered.
dist. distance; district; distinguished.
div. divided; dividend; division; divorced.
D. L. O. Dead Letter Office.
DNA. Deoxyribosenucleic acid.
do. ditto (ídem, lo mismo).
dol., doll. $, dollar.
dom. domestic; dominion.
doz. dozen, dozens.
Dr. Debtor; doctor.
d. s. days after sight (giro bancario).
D. S. Doctor of Science.
DSC. Distinguished Service Cross.
D. S. T. Daylight Savings Time.
d. t. delirium tremens.
dup. duplicate.

E. East, eastern, earl, English.
ea. each.
eccl., eccles. ecelesiastic.
econ. economic; economy.
Ed. (Eds. *pl*.) editor (redactor).
ed., edit. edited, edition.
e. g., ex. gr. *exempli gratia* (por ejemplo).
elec., elect. electrical, electricity.
elev. elevation
enc., encl. enclosure.
E. N. E. East-northeast.
Eng. England, English.
eng. engin. engineering.
engr. engineer; engraved; engraving.
E. & O. E., e. & o. e. errors and omissions excepted.
Episc. Episcopal.
eq. equal, equivalent.
E. S. E. East-southeast.
esp. (espec.) especially.
Esq., Esqr. (pl. con s). Esquire.
est. established; estimate.
et al. *et alibi*. (y en otra parte); *et alii* (y otros).
etc., &c. et cetera.
ethnol. ethnology.

et seq. et sequentia (y lo que sigue).
ex. example; export.
Ex., Exod. Exodus.
exam. examination.
Exc. Excellency.
exc. except; excellent.
Exch. Exchange; exchequer.
excl., exclam. exclamation, exclamatory.
Exec., Exr. Executor.
exec. executive; executor.
Execx., Exrx., Exx. Executrix.
ex lib. ex libris (from the books of).
exp. export, exported; express.
ext. extension; externally; extra; extract.

F. Felix, fellow, fluorin (e); France, French, Friday.
F., Fah., Fahr. Fahrenheit.
f. farthing, fathom, feminine, florin, folio, foot, frane, forte (música).
fac. facsimile.
F. A. M. Free and Accepted Masons.
fam. familiar, family.
F. B. I. Federal Bureau of Investigation.
FCC. Federal Communications Commission.
fcp., fcap. foolscap.
Feb. February.
fed. federal, federated, federation.
fem. feminine.
ff. folios, following, fortissimo.
FHA. Federal Housing Administration.
fig. figurative(ly), figure.
fin. financiar.
Fin. Sec. Financial Secretary.
fl. florin; flourished.
Fla. Florida.
fl. oz. fluid ounce or ounces.
FM, F. M., f m. frequency modulation (radio).
fm. fathom; from.
fo., fol. folio.
f. o. b. free on board.
fok, fon. following.
F. P. fire-plug.
Fr. France, Francis, French, Friday.
fr. fragments, from.
fr., frequent, frequentative.
Fri. Friday.
frt. freight.
Ft. Fort.-ft. feet, foot.
furn furnished.
fut. future.
fwd. forward.

G., Ger., Germ. German, Germany.
g. genitive, gram(me), guide.
Ga. (Geo.) Georgia.
gal., gaU. (pl. gals.) gallon.
G. A. R. Grand Army of the Republic.
G. B. Great Britain.
G. B. & I. Great Britain and Ireland.
g. c. m. greatest common measure.
gen. gender, general(ly), genus.
Gen General, Genesis, Geneva.
gen., genit. genitive.
gent. gentleman.
geog. geographer, geographical, geography.
geol. geological, geologist.
geom. geometry, geometrical.
GHQ, G. H. Q. General Headquarters.
GI, G. I. General issue. (Aplícase al soldado de E. U. A. Véase el Vocab.)
gloss. glossary.

G. M. General Manager.
G. O. P. Grand Old Party (partido Político republicano de E. U. A.).
Gov. Government, governor.
Gov. Ptg. Off. Government Printing Office.
Govt. Government.
G. P. O. General Post Office.
Gr. Greece, Greek.
gr. grain, gram (me), great.
grad. graduate; graduated.
gram. grammar, grammatical.
gro. gross.
GS, G. S. General Staff; Girl Scout.
Gt. Br., Gt. Brit. Great Britain.
guar. guaranteed.

H. hydrogen.
h. Harbor, hardness, height, hour, hundred, husband.
h. c. l. high cost of living.
hd. head.
hdkf. handkerchief.
hdqrs. headquarters.
H. E. His Eminence, His Excellency; Hydraulic Engineer.
h. e. hic est. hoc est (esto es, eso es).
Heb., Hebr, Hebrews, Hebrew.
her. heraldie, heraldry.
hf. half.-**hf. cf.** half calf.
H. H. His Highness; His Holiness (el Papa).
hhd. hogshead.
H. I. Hawaiian Islands.
H. I. H. His (o Her) Imperial Highness.
H. I. M. His (o Her) Imperial Majesty.
hist. historian, history, historical.
H. M. His (o Her) Majesty.
Hon. Honorable, honorary.
hort., hortic. horticultura.
hosp. hospital.
h. p. horse Power; half pay.
HQ., H. Q., hq. h. q. headquarters.
hr. (Pi. hrs.) hour.
H. R. H. His (o Her) Royal Highness.
H. S. H. His (o Her) Serene Highness.
ht. height.
hyd. hydraulics, hydrostatics.

ICBM. Intercontinental ballistic missile.
IRBM. Intermediate range ballistic missile.
I. Idaho; Island.
i. intransitive; island.
Ia., Io. Iowa.
ib., ibid. ibidem (ibídem).
ich., ichth. Ichthyology.
id. idem (idem).
Ida. Idaho.
i.e. id est (esto es, es decir).
Ill. Illinois.
ill., illus. illustrated, illustration.
imp. imperial, imported, importer.
imp., imper. imperative.
imp., imperf., impf. imperfect (tense).
imp., impers. impersonal.
in. (pl. ins.) inch.
inc. inclosing; including; inclusive; income; incorporated; increase.
incog. incógnito.
Ind. India, Indian, Indiana.
ind., indic. indicative.
indef. indefinite.
inf. infinitive; information.
init. initial.
in loc. cit. In the place cited.

insep. inseparable.
insp. inspector; inspected.
inst. instant, institute.
int. interest, interjection, international.
interj. interjection.
internat. internacional.
intr., intrans, intransitive.
inv. invented, inventor, invoice.
I. O. U. I owe you.
IQ, I. Q. intelligence quotient.
i. q. idem quod (lo mismo que)
irreg. irregular.
Is., Isl. Island, islands, isles.
It., Ital. Italian, Italic, Itaiy,

J. Judge, Julius, Jupiter.
Jan. January.
Jap. Japan, Japanese.
Jas. James.
J. C. Jesus Christ; Julius Caesar; Justice Clerk.
Jno. John.
Jon., Jona. Jonathan.
Jos. Joseph.
Josh. Joshua.
J. P. Justice of the Peace.
jr., jun., junr. junior.
Judg. Judges.
Jul. Julian, Julius, July.
Jun. June, Junius.
Junc. Junction (empalme, f. c.).
juv. juvenile.

K. Kalium, potassium; King, Knight.
Kan., Kans., Kas. (oficial) Kansas.
K. C. Knight of Columbus.
Ken., Ky. (oficial) Kentucky.
K. G. Knight of the Garter.
kg. kilogram.
kilo., kilog. kilogram (me).
kilo., kilom., km. kilometer.
km. kilometer-**km2** square kilometer.
Knt., Kt. Knight.
kt. carat.
K. W. H., kw-h, kw-hr kilowatt-hour.
Ky. Kentucky.

L. Lucius, lady, lake, Latin, Liberal, libra, Lithium, London, Lord.
l. latitude, league, length, line, liter o litre.
La. Lanthanum, Louisiana.
Lat. Latin-lat. latitude.
lb. (lbs. pl.) libra, pound.
l. c. lower case, left center, letter of credit.
L. C. L., l. c. l. less than carload lot.
l. c. m. least common multiple.
leg, Legis. Legislature, legislative.
leg. legal; legislature.
Lev., Levit. Leviticus.
Lex. Lexicon.
L. G. Life Guards, Low Gerinan.
l. h. left hand.
Li. Lithium.
lib. liber (libro).
Lieut., Lt. Lieutenant.
lin. lineal, linear.
Linn. Linneus, Linnean.
liq. liquid, liquor.
lith., lithog. lithograph, lithography.
log. logarithm.
lon. long. longitude.
loq. loquitur (habla).

L. S. locus sigilli (lugar del sello).

-l. s. left side.

L. (o ?) **s. d.** Librae, solidi, denarii. Pounds, shillings, pence.

Lt. Lieutenant.

Ltd., ltd. limited.

M. Monday; Monsieur; thousand.

m. Married, masculine, meridiem (mediodía), meter, mile, minim, month, **moon.-m.2** square meter.-**m.2** cubic meter.

M. A. Magister artium, Master of Arts.

mach., machine. machinery, machinist.

mag. magazine; magnitude; magnetism.

Maj. Major.

man. manual (teclado).

Manit. Manitoba.

manuf. manufactures, manufacturer.

Mar., Mch. March.-**mar.** maritime.

marg. margin; marginal,

mas., masc. masculine.

Mass. Massachusetts.

math. mathematics.

Matt. Matthew.

max. maximum.

M. C. Master of Ceremonies; Medical Corps; Member of Congress (de E. U. A.)

mc, M. C. megacycle.

M. D. Medicinae doctor. Doctor of Medicine.

Md. Maryland.

Mdlle. Mademoiselle.

mdse. merchandise.

M. E. Methodist Episcopal, Mining Engineer, Mechanical Engineer. Middle English.

Me. Maine.

meas. measure.

mech. mechanic, mechanical.

med. medical, medicine; medieval.

Medit. Mediterranean.

meg. megacycle.

Mem. memorandum.

mem. member; memorándum; memoir.

mer. meridian.

Messrs., MM. Messieurs.

met. metaphor; metaphysics; metropolitan.

metal. metall. metallurgy.

Meth. Methodist.

Mex. Mexican, Mexico.

mf. mezzo forte (algo fuerte).

mfd. manufactures.

mfg. manufacturing.

Mg. Magnesium. -**mg.** milligram,

Mgr. Manager; Monsignor.

Mi. mile; mill.

Mich. Michigan, Michaelmas.

micros. microscopy.

mid. middle; midshipman.

mil., milit. military.

min., mineral. mineralogy.

min. minimum; mining; minor; minute; mineralogy.

Minn. Minnesota.

misc. miscellaneous, miscellany.

Miss. Mississippi; mission, missionary.

ml. milliliter, millilitre.

mm. millimeter.-m2 square millimeter.-m3 cubic millimiter.

Mme. (Mmes. pl.) Madam.

Mo. Missouri; molybdenum; Monday.

M. O., M. 0. money order.

mo. (pl. mos.), mth. month.

mod. moderato, modern.

Mon. Monday; Monsignor.

Mons. Monsieur.

Monsig. Monsignor.

Mont. Montana.

morn. morning.

M. P. Member of Parliament.

MP, M. P. military police.

M. P., M. P. melting point.

mph., m. p. h. miles per hour.

Mr. Mister, Master (Señor).

Mrs. Mistress (Señora).

MS. (pl. MSS.) manuscript.

m. s., M/S. months after sight (giro bancario).

m. s. l. mean sea level.

MST, M. S. T. Mountain Standard Time.

Mt. (Mts. pl.) Mount, mountain.

mus. music; museum.

myth. mythological, mythology.

N. North, Norse; nitrogen, Nero.

n. name, natus (nacido, da), neuter, nominative, noon, noun, number.

N. A. North America.

nat. national; native; natural.

NATO. North Atlantic Treaty Organization.

naut. nautical.

nav. naval, navigation.

N. B. New Brunswick, North Britain, North British; nota bene (nótese bien).

N. C. North Carolina; New Church.

n. d. no date (sin fecha).

N. Dak. North Dakota.

N. E. northeast, northeastern.

N. E., N. Eng. New England.

Neb., Nebr. (oficial). Nebraska.

Neth. Netherlands.

neut. neuter.

Nev. Nevada.

New Test. New Testament.

N. F. Newfoundland.

N. G. National Guard.

Ng. Norwegian. -**n. g.** no good.

N. H. New Hampshire.

N. J. New Jersey.

N. lat. North latitude.

N. M. N. Mex. New Mexico.

N. N. E. north-northeast.

N. N. W. north-northwest.

No. Number (nos. pl.); north.

N. 0. New Orleans; natural order.

nom., nomin. nominative.

non seq. non sequitur (no sigue).

Norw. Norway, Norwegian.

Nos. numbers.

Nov. November.

N. P. Notary Public.

N. S. Nova Scotia; New School (teol.); New Style.

n. s. not specified.

N. S. W. New South Wales.

N. T. New Testament; new translation.

nt. wt. net weight.

n. u. name unknown.

Num., Numb. Numbers (Biblia).

N. W. Northwest.

N. Y. New York.

N. Z., N. Zeal. New Zealand.

O. Ohio; oxygen.

ob. obit. (murió), obiter (de paso).

obj. object, objection, objective.

obs. observation, observatory, obsolete.

Oct. October.

O. K. All correct (oll korrect, visto bueno).

Okla. Oklahoma.

Old Test., O. T. Old Testament.

Ont. Ontario.
O. P., OP, op, O. P. out of print.
OP. opposite; opus (obra).
Opt. optative, optical, optician, opties, optional.
Or. Oregon, Oriental.
orch. orchestra.
ord. ordained, order, ordinance.
Ore. (oficial), Oreg. Oregon.
org. organic, organized.
orig. original, originally.
Oz. (Os. u oza. pl.). ounce.

p. page, part, participle, past, piano (suave), pint, pipe, pole, population.
P. Phosphorus.
p. a. participial adjective.
Pa. Pennsylvania.
Pal. Palestine.-**pal**. paleontology,.
P. and L. profit and loss.
par. paragraph, parallel, parish.
Part. participle.
Pass. passive.
Pat. patent, patented.
Path., pathol. pathology.
Paym't, Pay't. payment.
Pb. Plumbum (plomo).
P/C, p/c. petty cash; prices current.
pc. piece; price.
P. D., p. d. per diem (por día).
Pen., pen. Peninsula.
Penn. Pennsylvania.
per an., per ann. per annum (por año).
per ct. per cent.
perf. perfect,
perh. perhaps.
pers. person, personal(ly)
pert. pertaining.
Peruv. Peruvian.
pf. perfect, preferred.
PfC. Private, First Class. (Ejército de E. U. A.)
pfd. preferred.
Pg. Portugal. Portuguese.
Phar., Pharm. Pharmacy, pharmacopeia, pharmaceutical.
Ph. D. Doctor of Philosophy.
Phfl. Philosophy.
Phil., Phila. (oficial). Philadelphia.
phon. phonetics.
phot., photog. Photographic, photography.
Phys. Physician, physics.
Phys. Sci. Physical Science.
P.I. Philippine Islands.
pkg. (pkgs. pl.) package.
pl. place, plate, plural.
plf, plff, pltff. plainttiff.
plup., plupf. pluperfect.
plur. plural, plurality.
p.m. post meridiem (tarde); postmortem.
P. M. Postmaster, Post meridiem (tarde); Paymaster.
Pmkd. Postmarked.
p. n. P/N. promissory note.
P. O. Post Office.
poet. poetic, poetical.
polit. political; politics.
polit. econ. political economy.
P. O. D. Post Office Department.
pop. popular(ly), population.
pos., posit. positive.
pos., poss. possession, possessive.
pot. potential.
PP. pages, pianissimo.

P. P., p. p. parcel post; past participle; postpaid.
Ppd. postpaid, prepaid.
pr. pair, price, pronoun, proper, present.
P. R. Puerto Rico.
prec. preceding.
pref. preface, preference, prefix.
prep. preparation; preparatory; prepare; preposition.
Pres. President.
pret. preterit, past tense.
prin. principal(ly), principles.
print. printing.
priv. privative.
prob. Probably; problem.
Prof. Professor.
pron. pronoun, pronunciation.
prop. properly, proposition.
Prot. Protestant.
pro tem. pro tempore (provisionalmente).
Prov. Proverbs; Provençal, Provence, province, provincial.
prox. próximo (el mes que viene).
Prs. printers.-**prs**. pairs.
P. S. Postscript.
ps. pieces.
PST, P. S. T. Pacific Standard Time.
pt. part, payment, pint.
Pt. platinum, point, port.
P. T. A., PTA Parent-Teacher Association.
pta. peseta.
P. T. O. Please turn over.
pub. public, published, publisher.
Pub.Doc. Public Documents.
Pvt. Private (soldado raso de E. U. A.).
PW Prisoner of War.
pwt. pennyweight.
pxt. *pinxit* (lo pintó).

Q. Quebec, Queen, Quintus.
q. quasi, query, quintal.
Q., qu., ques. question.
q. e. *quod est* (lo cual es).
q e. d. *quod erat demostrandum* (lo que se trataba de demostrar).
q. e. f: *quod erat faciendum* (lo que se trataba de hacer).
q. l. *quantum libet* (tanto como se desee).-ql. quintal.
q. s. *quantum sufficit* (lo que baste); quarter-section.
qt. quantity, quart.-**qts**. quarts.
qu., **qy**- query.
Que. Quebec.
quot. quotation.
q. v. *quantum* vis (cuanto se quiera); *quod vide* (véase).

R. radical, railway, recipe, river; Republican.
r. rod rood, rupee.
Rad. radical.-**rad**. radix (raíz).
R. A. F., RAF Royal Air Force (Inglaterra).
R. C. Roman Catholic, Red Cross.
rept., rec't., rect. receipt.
Rd. radium.
R. D. Rural Delivery.
rec'd., recd. received.
ref. reference, referred, reformed, reformer.
reg. registry, regular.
Reg., Regt. Regent, regiment.
rel. relative(ly), religion, religious, relics.
rel. pron. relative pronoun.
rem. remark.
Rep. report, reporter, Representative.
Rep., Repub. Republic, Republican.
res. reserve; residence; resigned.
Rev. Revelation; revenue. Reverend (Revs. pl.), review.
Rev. Ver. Revised Version (de la Biblia).

R. F., r. f. radio frequency-: rapid fire.

r. h. relative humidity.

Rh. Rhodium.-**r. h.** right hand.

R. H. Royal Highness.

rhet. rhetoric, rhetorical.

R. I. Rhode Island.

R. I. P. requiescat in pace (descanse en paz).

rit., ritard. ritardando (el compás).

riv. river.

R. N. Registered Nurse; Royal Navy.

Robt. Robert.

Rom. Cath. Roman Catholic.

rpm, r.P.M. revolutions per minute.

R. R. Railroad.

R. S. Recording Secretary; Revised Statutes.-**r. s.** right side.

R. S. V. P. Répondez, s'il vous plaît. (Sírvase Ud. contestar.)

Rt. Hon. Right Honorable.

Rt. Rev. Right Reverend.

R. W., Rw., Ry. Railway.

S. Saxon, Servius, Sextus; scribe, sign, society, south, sulphur, Sunday.

s. second, section (ss. pl.), series, shilling, singular, substantive.

S. A. Salvation Army; South America; South Africa.

S., Sab. Sabbath.

Sa., Sat. Saturday.

s. a. secundum artem (según arte); sine anno (sin fecha).

S. Am. South America.

San., Sans., Skr., Skt. Sanskrit.

Sax. Saxon, Saxony.

S. C. South Carolina; Supreme Court.

s. c., s. caps., sm. caps. small capitals (versalitas).

sc. seene; scilicet (a saber).

Scot. Scotch, Scotland; Scottish.

sculp., sculpt. sculpsit (lo esculpió); sculptor, sculptural, sculpture.

s. d. sine die.

S. Dak. South Dakota.

S. E. southeast, southeastern.

Sec. Secretary.-**sec.** second.

Sen. Senate, senator.

sep. separate.

Sep., Sept. September.

Serg., Sergt. Sergeant.

s. g. specific gravity.

sh. shilling.

So. South.

Soc. Society, Sócrates.

sop. soprano.

Sp. Spain, Spanish; Spirit.

spec. special, specially.

sp. gr. specific gravity.

spt. seaport.

S. R. 0. standing room only.

sq. square: *sequentes-tia* (siguiente (s)).

Sr. Senior, sir, strontium.

S. S. Sunday School, Sabbath School; Steamship.

s. s. steamship.

S. S. E. south-southeast.

S. S. W. south-southwest.

s. t. short ton.

St. Saint; strait, street.

st. stanza, street, strophe.

ster., stg. sterling.

stge. storage.

stk. stock.

sts. streets.

sub. subject, substitute, suburb, suburban.

subj. subject, subjective, subjunctive.

suf., suff. suffix.

Sun., Sund. Sunday.

sup., super. superior, superfine.

Sup., Supp. Suplement.

Supt. Superintendent.

Surg., surg. Surgeon, surgery, surgical.

Surv. Surveying, surveyor.

S. W. southwest, southwestern

Sw. Sweden, Swedish.

Swit., Switz. Switzerland.

syn. synonym, synonymous.

synop. synopsis.

T. Territory, Testament, Tuesday.

t. tenor, ton, town, transitive.

T. B., Tb. t. b. tuberculosis, tubercular.

tbs., tbsp. tablespoon.

tech. technical, technically.

tech., technol. technology.

tel., teleg. telegram, telegraph.

temp. temperatura temporary.

Tenn. Tennessee.

Ter., Terr. Territory.

Test. Testament (Biblia).

Tex. Texan, Texas.

Th., Thu., Thur., Thurs. Thursday.

theat. theatrical.

theol. theologian, theological, theology.

Tho., Thos. Thomas.

T. O. Turn over.

topog topographical. topography.

tr. transpose, trill.

tr., trans. transitive, translation, translated, transaction, transportation.

transp. transportation.

trav. traveler, travels.

treas. treasurer, treasury.

trig., trigon. trigonometry

tsp. teaspoon.

TV television.

typ., typo., typog. typographer, typographic(al). typography.

U. Uranium.

U. C. upper case, (letra mayúscula).

U.H. P., u. h. f. ultra high frequency.

U. K. United Kingdom.

ult., ulto. último (el mes pasado).

UN, U. N. United Nations.

UNESCO United Nations Educational, Scientific, Cultural Organization.

Univ. Universalist, university.

UNRRA United Nations Relief and Rehabilitation Administration.

U. P. United Press.

U. S. United States.

U.S.A. United States of America, United States Army.

U. S. M. United States Mail, United States Marines.

U. S. N. United States Navy.

U. S. S. United States Seriate. United States Stemer.

U.S.S.R., USSR Union of Soviet Socialist Republics.

usu. usual, usually.

V. Vanadium, vector, venerable, vice, Victoria, violin, volunteers.

v. verse, versus (contra), village, vocative, volume.

v., vb. verb.

v., vid. Vide (Véase).

V. a. verb active, verbal adjective.

Va. Virginia.

val. value.

var. variant, variety.

Vat. Vatican.

Ven. Venerable.
Venez. Venezuela.
vet., **veter**. veterinary.
Vet. **Surg**. Veterinary surgeon.
v. i. verb intransitive.
Vice Pres. Vice-President.
v. imp. verb impersonal.
VIP, V. I. P. very important person (coll.).
v. irr. verb irregular.
viz. videlicet (a saber).
v. n. verb neuter.
voc. vocative.
vocab. vocabulary.
vol. volume (pl. vols.); volunteer.
vox pop. vox populi, voice of the people.
V. P. Vice-President.
V. S. Veterinary surgeon.
vs. versus (contra).
v.t. verb transitive.
vul., **vulg**. vulgar, vulgarly.
Vul., **Vulg**. Vulgate (Biblia)

w. week, wife.
W. Warden, Welsh, West, western, William, wolfram, Wednesday.
W., w. watt.
W. A. A. C. Women's Army Auxiliary Corps. (E. U. A.)
WAC Women's Army Corps (E. U. A.).
WAVES Women Accepted for Volunteer Emergency Service (Marina de E. U. A.)
We., **Wed**. Wednesday.
Wash. Washington (el estado).
w.c. water closet.
W. C. water closet; without charge.

W.D. War Department (E.U.A.).
wf. wrong font (imprenta).
wh. **whr**. watt-hour.
Whf. wharf.
W.I. West Indies.
w.i. when issued (stocks).
Wis. Wisc. Wisconsin.
Wk. week.
W. Ion. West longitude.
Wm. William.
W. N. W. west-northwest.
WP. Worship.
WPful. Worshipful.
WRENS, W. R. N. S. Women's Royal Naval Service (Gran Bretaña).
W. S. W. west-southwest.
wt. weight.
W. Va. West Virginia.
Wyo. Wyoming.

Xmas. Christmas.

y. yard, year.
Y.B., Yr. B. Yearbook.
yd. (pl. yds.) Yard (medida).
Y. M. C. A. Young Men's Christian Association.
yr. (P1 - yrs.) year, younger, your.
Y. W. C. A. Young Women's Christian Association.

Z. atomic number; zenith distance (astron.)
Z., z. zone.
Zn. Zinc.
Zool. Zoology, zoological.

Pesas y Medidas

(Weights and Measures)

LINEALES
(Linear)

Medidas de E.U.A. (U.S. Measures)			Medidas Métricas (Metric Measures)		
Mile	1.6093	kms.	Kilometer	0.62137	miles.
Naut. mile	1.853	kms.	Meter	39.37	inches.
Yard	0.9144	ms.	Decimeter	3.937	inches
Foot	0.3048	ms.	Centimeter	0.3937	inches
Inch	2.54	cms.	Milimeter	0.03937	inches

SURFACE
(Superficie)

Acre	0.4453	hectares.	Sq.kilometer	247.104	acres
Square mile	259	hectares.	Hectare	2.471	acres
Square yard	0.8361	sq. meters.	Square meter	1550	sq. inches.
Square foot	929.03	sq. cms.	Square decimeter	15.50	sq. inches
Square inch	6.4516	sq. cms.	Square centimeter	0.155	sq. inches

VOLUMEN
(Cubic)

Cubic inch	16.387	cu. cm.	Cubic meter	1.308	cu. yards.
Cubic foot	0.0283	cu ms.	Cubic decimeter	61.023	cu. inches.
Cubic yard	0.7646	cu ms	Cubic centimeter	0.0610	cu. inches

CAPACIDAD
(Capacity)

Liquid quart	0.9463	liters	Hectoliter	2.838	bushels
Dry quart	1.101	liters		or 26.418	gallons.
Gallon	3.785	liters	Liter	0.9081	dry qt.
Bushel	35.24	liters		or 1.0567	liq. qts.

PESAS
(Weights)

Ounce (avoirdupois)	28.35	grams.	Ton	2204.6	lbs.
Pound "	0.4536	kgs.	Kilogram	2.2046	lbs.
Long ton	1.0161	met. tons.	Gram	15.432	grains.
Short ton	0.9072	met. tons.	Centigram	0.1543	grains.
Grain	0.0648	grams.			

Monedas de América

y de la Península Ibérica

(Monetary Units of America and the Iberian Peninsula)

Country	Monetary Units
ARGENTINA	— Peso
BOLIVIA	— Boliviano
BRAZIL	— Real
CANADA	— Dollar
CHILE	— Peso
COLOMBIA	— Peso
COSTA RICA	— Colón
CUBA	— Peso
DOMINICAN REPUBLIC	— Peso
ECUADOR	— Sucre/ Dollar
EL SALVADOR	— Colón/ Dollar
GUATEMALA	— Quetzal/ Dollar
HAITI	— Gourde
HONDURAS	— Lempira
MEXICO	— Peso
NICARAGUA	— Córdoba
PANAMA	— Balboa/ Dollar
PARAGUAY	— Guaraní
PERU	— Nuevo Sol
PORTUGAL	— Euro
SPAIN	— Euro
UNITED STATES OF AMERICA	— Dollar
URUGUAY	— Nuevo Peso
VENEZUELA	— Bolívar